PEOPLE OF TODAY

Anno MMVIII

Editor
Daniel Sefton

Assistant Editors
Ellie Major
Laura Winter

Editorial Assistants
Benjamin Goode
Jonah Goodman

Chairman
Conrad Free

Copyright © Debrett's Limited 2007
ISBN 978 1 870520 95 9

Debrett's *People of Today 2008*
Published by Debrett's Limited
18–20 Hill Rise, Richmond, Surrey TW10 6UA
Tel: +44 (0) 20 8939 2250 Fax: +44 (0) 20 8939 2251
E-mail: people@debretts.co.uk Website: www.debretts.co.uk

Any omissions or errors will be corrected in a future edition

Database typesetting by Polestar Applied Solutions, Milton Keynes, Bedfordshire
Printed and bound by William Clowes Limited, Beccles, Suffolk

CONTENTS

FOREWORD

In June and July 2007, the heavens opened, and many parts of England were subject to the worst flooding in recorded history. The personal suffering was considerable; the insurance bills cataclysmic. Inevitably, debate raged between those inclined to blame the floods directly on accelerating climate change, and those who steadfastly refused to acknowledge that there was any direct cause-and-effect at all.

Self-respecting scientists are loathe to put their hands on their hearts and declare that any one particular flood, drought, hurricane, firestorm or heatwave is a direct consequence of the build up of CO_2 and other greenhouse gases in the atmosphere over the last two decades. There are now, however, very few scientists who believe there is no connection at all between the rising emissions of those gases and the countless extreme weather events the world is currently witnessing. Apart from a few die-hard deniers, the basic "truth" of climate change is no longer in dispute.

The title of Al Gore's Oscar-winning film, "An Inconvenient Truth", accurately captures what many feel about this development. Over the last couple of years climate change has placed itself bang in the middle of contemporary politics, cutting right across every aspiration politicians may have, and making the business of building a safer, more prosperous world for everyone a great deal more complicated. Indeed, it seems inevitable that the complex challenges of dealing with climate change will command more and more political space as the years go by.

Even just a few years ago, the majority of people would have seen such assertions as both politically contentious and scientifically "dodgy". Now I would expect that most of the 25,000 People of Today who populate these pages would find themselves in broad agreement.

That our generation seems to have leapt, in one fell swoop, from denial to despair is particularly disempowering for young people. If you subscribe to that uplifting aphorism that "we do not inherit the Earth from our parents, but borrow it from our children", then we've made a real mess of things and, what's more, now seem intent on stealing whatever reasons the people of tomorrow might still have to be hopeful.

So on what grounds can optimism still be justified? For the best part of fifteen years, I have been fortunate enough to work with a large number of people at senior level in many fields across government and business – through Forum for the Future, the UK Sustainable Development Commission and The Prince of Wales's Business and the Environment Programme. My overwhelming impression is that more and more of them are now determined to find more sustainable ways of doing their jobs.

The change of heart amongst business people is particularly encouraging. For many of them, sustainable development has been positioned in the wrong psychological box over all these years – the one labelled "regulation and red tape", "constraint on business", "increased costs" or "high risk". Only during the last few years have we seen the other box – labelled "opportunity", "innovation", "increased market share" and "stronger brands" – opening up in such a way as to provide wealth creators with an entirely different and far more positive proposition. This is critical: however necessary or desirable something may be, it is unlikely to obtain the necessary traction in today's world unless the business community can be persuaded and inspired to get behind it.

This gathering awareness is both extremely welcome and timely – in that there is still time to make a real difference. I am not one of those who believe it's all too late; the bad news about climate change does indeed go on getting worse, but allowing our civilization to collapse is not yet our destiny. As long as we get moving without further delay!

Jonathon Porritt is Founder Director of Forum for the Future (www.forumforthefuture.org) and Chairman of the UK Sustainable Development Commission (www.sd-commission.org.uk).

THE ROYAL FAMILY

For further details see Debrett's *Peerage & Baronetage*.
All references are to the 2008 edition unless otherwise stated.
Army units are listed in order of precedence.

HM THE QUEEN; Elizabeth Alexandra Mary Windsor; declared in Council 9 April 1952 that she and her children would be styled and known as the House and Family of Windsor and 8 Feb 1960 that her descendants other than those enjoying the style, title or attribute of HRH and the titular dignity of Prince or Princess and female descendants who marry and their descendants should bear the name Mountbatten-Windsor, though this declaration overridden when Lady Louise Windsor b 2003 (*see below*); proclaimed Queen 8 Feb 1952; style in the United Kingdom: Elizabeth II, by the Grace of God, of the United Kingdom of Great Britain and Northern Ireland, and of Her Other Realms and Territories, Queen, Head of the Commonwealth, Defender of the Faith; crowned Westminster Abbey 2 June 1953; celebrated: Silver Jubilee 1977, Golden Jubilee 2002; er da of HM King George VI (d 6 Feb 1952), and Lady Elizabeth Angela Marguerite Bowes-Lyon (HM Queen Elizabeth The Queen Mother; d 2002), da of 14 Earl of Strathmore and Kinghorne (*see Debrett's Peerage & Baronetage*); *b* 21 April 1926; *Educ* privately; *m* 20 Nov 1947, HRH The Prince Philip, Duke of Edinburgh, KG, KT, OM, GBE, AC, QSO, PC, *qv,* 3 s, 1 da (*see below*), who all by letters patent 22 Oct 1948 take style HRH and titular dignity of Prince/Princess; *Heir* eld s, Prince of Wales, *qv*; WWII as Subaltern then Jr Cdr ATS, LG 1947, Lord High Adm of the United Kingdom; Col-in-Chief (UK): Life Gds 1952–, Blues and Royals (Royal Horse Gds and 1 Dragoons) 1969–, Royal Scots Dragoon Gds (Carabiniers and Greys) 1971–, Queen's Royal Lancers 1993–, Royal Tank Regt 1953–, RE 1952–, Grenadier Gds (which HM inspected on her 16th birthday, it being her first official engagement) 1952–, Coldstream Gds 1952–, Scots Gds 1952–, Irish Gds 1952–, Welsh Gds 1952–, Royal Welch Fus 1953, The Royal Welsh 2006–, The Royal Regt of Scotland 2006–, The Duke of Lancasters Regt 2006–, Adj Gen's Corps 1992–,Royal Mercian and Lancastrian Yeo 1994–; Col-in-Chief (Commonwealth): Govr Gen's Horse Gds (Canada) 1953–, Canadian Forces Mil Engrs Branch 1977–, King's Own Calgary Regt 1953–, Royal 22e Regt (Canada) 1953–, Govr-Gen's Foot Gds (Canada) 1953–, Canadian Grenadier Gds 1953–, Le Régiment de la Chaudière (Canada) 1947–, Royal New Brunswick Regt 1956–, 48 Highlanders Canada 1947–, Argyll and Sutherland Highlanders Canada (Princess Louise's) 1950–, Royal Canadian Ordnance Corps 1958–, Calgary Highlanders 1981–, Royal Australian Engrs 1953–, Royal Australian Inf Corps 1953–, Royal Australian Army Ordnance Corps 1953–, Royal Australian Army Nursing Corps 1953–, Corps of Royal New Zealand Engrs 1953–, Royal New Zealand Inf Regt 1964–, Malawi Rifles 1964–; Affiliated Col-in-Chief Queen's Gurkha Engrs; Royal Col The Argll and Sutherland Highlanders 8th Battalion, Royal Regt of Scotland 2006–; Capt-Gen: RA 1952–, HAC 1952–, CCF 1953–, Royal Regt of Canadian Artillery 1952–, Royal Regt of Australian Artillery 1953–, Royal Regt of New Zealand Artillery 1953–, Royal New Zealand Armoured Corps 1953–; patron Royal Army Chaplains' Dept; Air Cdre-in-Chief: RAuxAF, RAF Regt, Air Reserve Canada, RAAF Reserve, Territorial Air Force (New Zealand); Cmdt-in-Chief RAF Coll Cranwell; Royal Hon Air Cdre: RAF Marham, 603 (City of Edinburgh) Sqdn RAuxAF; Sovereign of all British Orders of Knighthood, Order of Merit, Royal Order of Victoria and Albert, Order of Crown of India, Order of Companions of Honour, Order of Canada, Distinguished Service Order and Imperial Service Order; Sovereign Head of Order of Hosp of St John of Jerusalem, Order of Australia and Queen's Service Order of New Zealand; Freedom: City London, Edinburgh 1947; FRS 1947; racehorse owner (colours: purple body with gold braid, scarlet sleeves, black velvet cap with gold fringe), as which presented with Cartier Millennium Award 2000 honouring achievements as owner-breeder and patron of the Turf; major races won incl: King George VI Chase 1950 (Manicou), Coronation Cup 1954 (Aureole), King George VI & Queen Elizabeth Diamond Stakes 1954 (Aureole, champion 4–year old 1954), Sussex Stakes 1954 (Landau), Norfolk Stakes 1957 (Pall Mall), Oaks 1957 (Carozza), Yorkshire Oaks 1957 (Almeria), Two Thousand Guineas 1958 (Pall Mall, first win by a horse bred by HM), Coronation Stakes 1961 (Aiming High), Eclipse Stakes 1965 (Canisbay), Goodwood Cup 1965 (Apprentice), Goodwood Cup 1966 (Gaulois), One Thousand Guineas 1974 (Highclere, first filly also to win French Oaks), Oaks 1977 (Dunfermline), St Leger 1977 (Dunfermline); *Style*— HM The Queen; *Residences* Buckingham Palace, London SW1A 1AA; Windsor Castle, Berkshire SL4 1NJ; Palace of Holyroodhouse, Canongate, Edinburgh EH8 8DX; Balmoral Castle, Aberdeenshire AB35 5TB; Sandringham House, Norfolk PE35 6EN

EDINBURGH, HRH I DUKE OF (UK 1947); Philip Mountbatten; KG (1947), KT (1952), OM (1968), GBE (Mil 1953), AC (1988), QSO (1981), PC (1951, Canada 1957); also Baron Greenwich and Earl of Merioneth (UK 1947); naturalised British subject and adopted surname of Mountbatten (dropped f's name 'of Greece and Denmark', renouncing right of succession to those countries' crowns) 1947; granted title, style and attribute of HRH 19 Nov 1947; granted precedence next to HM The Queen except where otherwise provided by Act of Parliament (Royal Warrant 18 Sept 1952); granted style and titular dignity of Prince of United Kingdom 1957; only s of HRH Prince Andrew of Greece and Denmark, GCVO (d 1944), and HRH Princess (Victoria) Alice Elizabeth Julia Marie (d 1969), da of 1 Marquess of Milford Haven (*see Debrett's Peerage & Baronetage* descendant of Queen Victoria); *b* 10 June 1921; *Educ* Salem Sch Baden, Gordonstoun (head of sch, capt cricket and hockey), RNC Dartmouth (King's Dirk, prize as best cadet of his entry); *m* 20 Nov 1947, Princess Elizabeth (later HM The Queen, *qv*); 3 s, 1 da (*see below*); *Heir* (to peerages, but not titular dignity of Prince) eld s, Prince of Wales, *qv*; *Career* WWII: Midshipman 1940, as which served HMS Ramillies Indian Ocean 1940 and Valiant Mediterranean Fleet 1941 (despatches and Greek War Cross of Valour following Battle of Cape Matapan 1941, in which i/c Valiant's searchlight unit), Sub-Lt 1941, Lt July 1942, 1 Lt (2 i/c) HMS Wallace 1942 (participated Sicily landings 1943) then HMS Whelp 27 Destroyer Flotilla British Pacific Fleet Indian Ocean and Pacific, Instr Petty Offrs' Sch, attended RN Staff Coll Greenwich, 1 Lt HMS Chequers 1949 (Leader 1 Destroyer Flotilla Mediterranean Fleet), Lt-Cdr 1950, cmd HMS Magpie (frigate), Cdr 1952; 1939–45, Atlantic, Africa, Burma (with Pacific Rosette) and Italy Stars; War Medal 1939–45 (with oak leaf) and French Croix de Guerre (with palm); Personal ADC to HM King George VI 1948; Adm of the Fleet: RN, RAN, RNZN, Royal Canadian Sea Cadets; Capt-Gen RM; Field Marshal: United Kingdom 1953, Australian Mil Forces 1954, New Zealand Army 1977; Col-in-Chief (UK): Queen's Royal Hussars 2002–, The Rifles 2007–, Intelligence Corps 1977–, ACF 1953–; Col-in-Chief (Commonwealth): Royal Canadian Regt 1953–, Royal Hamilton LI (Wentworth Regt of Canada) 1978–, Cameron Highlanders Ottawa 1967–, Queen's Own Cameron Highlanders Canada 1967–, Seaforth Highlanders Canada 1967–, Royal Canadian Army Cadets 1953–, Royal Australian Corps Electrical and Mech Engrs 1959–, Australian Army Cadet Corps 1963–; Col Grenadier Gds 1975–; Royal Col Highlanders 4th Battalion, Royal Regiment of Scotland; Royal Hon Col: City of Edinburgh Univs OTC 1965–, Trinidad and Tobago Regt 1964–; Marshal: RAF, RAAF, RNZAF; Air Cdre-in-Chief: ATC, Royal Canadian Air Cadets; Royal Hon Air Cdre RAF Kinloss; Adm Royal Yacht Sqdn; chllr: Univ of Wales 1948–76, Univ of Edinburgh 1952–, Univ of Salford 1967–91, Univ of Cambridge 1976–; life govr KCL; pres: CCPR 1951–, BAAS 1952, FEI 1964–86 (hon pres 1986–); as pres FEI instrumental in founding Nations Cup Series, estab ctee to examine introduction of carriage driving (specifically four-in-hand driving) as FEI event 1969 (instituted 1970); competed in six World Championships: team Bronze medal 1978, 1982 and 1984, team Gold medal 1980, individual sixth place 1982; memb British team at three European Championships; fndr memb British Equestrian Centre, memb Horse Driving Trials Assoc, memb Equestrian Hall of Fame 2007; hon memb: BHS, USA Equestrian Assoc, Canadian Horse Cutting Assoc; past pres MCC (twice); pres emeritus WWF (first (fndr) pres 1961–82, int pres 1981–96); patron: Duke of Edinburgh's Award 1956– (chm of tstees 1956–2001), Industrial Soc, London Guildhall Univ; Grand Master Guild of Air Pilots and Air Navigators; Master Trinity House 1969– (Er Bro 1952–69); King George VI 1937 and Queen Elizabeth II 1953 Coronation Medals; Grand Master and First or Princ Knight Order of the British Empire 1953; FRS 1951; *Style*— HRH The Prince Philip, Duke of Edinburgh, KG, KT, OM, GBE, AC, QSO, PC

WALES, HRH The Prince of; Charles Philip Arthur George Windsor; KG (1958, invested and installed 1968), KT (1977), GCB and Great Master Order of the Bath (1975), OM (2002), AK (1981), CD (1982), QSO (1977); PC (1977); cr Prince of Walesand Earl of Chester 1958 (invested 1969); also Duke of Cornwall, Duke of Rothesay, Earl of Carrick, Baron of Renfrew, Lord of the Isles and Prince and Great Steward of Scotland; eld s and h of HM The Queen, *qv*, *b* 14 Nov 1948; *Educ* Gordonstoun, Geelong GS Australia, Trinity Coll Cambridge (MA, Polo half blue), UCW Aberystwyth; *m* 1, 29 July 1981 (m dis 1996), Lady Diana Frances Spencer (d 1997), 3 da of 8 Earl Spencer (*see Debrett's Peerage & Baronetage*); 2 s (*see below*); *m* 2, 9 April 2005, Mrs Camilla Rosemary Parker Bowles (Col 4th Battlion The Rifles 2006–; Cdre-in-Chief Naval Medical Services 2006–; for a list of her charities see http://www.princeofwales.gov.uk), da of late Maj Bruce Middleton Hope Shand, MC (*see Debrett's Peerage and Baronetage* Ashcombe, B), and formerly w of Brig Andrew Henry Parker Bowles, OBE (*see Debrett's Peerage & Baronetage* Macclesfield, E); *Heir* er s, HRH Prince William of Wales, *qv*; *Career* RN: served HMS Norfolk 1971–72, HMS Minerva 1972–73 and HMS Jupiter 1974, helicopter pilot trg RNAS Yeovilton 1974–75, pilot with 845 NAS aboard HM Hermes 1975, cmd HMS Bronington (minehunter) as Cdr 1976, Capt 1988, RearAdm 1998, Vice Adm 2002, Adm 2006, Cdre-in-Chief Plymouth 2006–; Gen 2006 (Lt-Gen 2002, Maj-Gen 1998); Col-in-Chief (UK): 1st Queen's Dragoon Gds 2003–, Royal Dragoon Gds 1992–, Parachute Regt 1977–, Royal Gurkha Rifles 1994–, Army Air Corps 1992–; Royal Col: The Black Watch 3rd Battalion 2006–, The Royal Regt of Scotland, 51st Highland 7th Battalion, The Royal Regt of Scotland 2006–, The Mercian Regt 2007–, Col-in-Chief (Commonwealth): Royal Canadian Dragoons 1985–, Lord Strathcona's Horse (Royal Canadians) 1977–, Royal Regt of Canada 1977–, Royal Winnipeg Rifles 1977–, Royal Australian Armoured Corps 1977–, 2 Bn Royal Pacific Islands Regt 1984–, Black Watch (Royal Highland Regt) Canada 2004–, Toronto Canada Regt 1977–, Air Reserve Gp Air Cmd Canada 1977–,Toronto Scottish Regt (Queen Elizabeth The Queen Mother's Own) 2005–; Dep Col-in-Chief Highlanders (Seaforth, Gordons and Camerons) 1994–; Personal ADC to HM The Queen 1973–; Col Welsh Gds 1975–; Royal Hon Col Queen's Own Yeo 2000–; RAF: Air Chief Marshal 2006 (Wing Cdr 1976, Gp Capt 1988, Air Vice Marshal 1998, Air Marshal 2002), Hon Air Cdre RAF Valley 1977–; Air Cdre-in-Chief RNZAF 1993–; for a list of his charities see http://www. princeofwales.gov.uk; hon bencher Gray's Inn 1975;

hon fell Trinity Coll Cambridge 1988; Coronation Medal 1953, Queen's Silver Jubilee Medal 1977, Queen's Golden Jubilee Medal 2002, New Zealand Commemoration Medal 1990; *Publications* The Old Man of Lochnagar (1980, illustrations Sir Hugh Casson, dramatised Aberdeen and London West End 1986, also TV production for Channel 4, DVD 1999), A Vision of Britain (1989); *Style—* HRH The Prince of Wales, KG, KT, GCB, OM, AK, CD, QSO, PC; *Residences* Clarence House, London SW1A 1BA; Highgrove House, Doughton, Tetbury, Gloucestershire GL8 8TN

WALES, HRH Prince William of; William Arthur Philip Louis Windsor; s and h of HRH The Prince of Wales, *qv*, *b* 21 June 1982; *Educ* Eton, Univ of St Andrews (MA), RMA Sandhurst; Queen's Golden Jubilee Medal 2002; Cdre-in-Chief, Scotland and Submarines 2006–; 2nd Lt, Blues and Royals 2006; pres: The Football Assoc 2006; patron: Centrepoint 2005, The Tusk Trust 2005, English Swimming Sch's Assoc 2007, Mountain Rescue 2007, Royal Marsden Hosp 2007; vice-patron: Welsh Rugby Union 2007–; *Style—* HRH The Prince William of Wales

WALES, HRH Prince Harry of; Henry Charles Albert David (Harry) Windsor; yr s of HRH The Prince of Wales, *qv*, *b* 15 Sept 1984; *Educ* Eton, RMA Sandhurst; Queen's Golden Jubilee Medal 2002; Cdre-in-Chief, Small Ships and Diving 2006; 2nd Lt, Blues and Royals 2006; patron: Sentebale 2006, Dolen Cymru 2007, MapAction 2007, WellChild 2007; *Style—* HRH The Prince Harry of Wales

YORK, HRH 1 Duke of (UK 1986); Andrew Albert Christian Edward Windsor; KG (2006), KCVO (2003, CVO 1979), CD (2001); also Baron Killyleagh and Earl of Inverness (UK 1986); 2 s of HM The Queen, *qv*, *b* 19 Feb 1960; *Educ* Gordonstoun, Lakefield Coll Sch Canada, RNC Dartmouth; *m* 23 July 1986 (m dis 1996), Sarah Margaret, da of Maj Ronald Ivor Ferguson (d 2003; *see Debrett's Peerage & Baronetage* Hampden, V), by his 1 w Susan Mary, da of FitzHerbert Wright (*see Debrett's Peerage & Baronetage* (1990 edn) Powerscourt, V), later Mrs Hector Barrantes (d 1998); 2 da (*see below*); *Career* RN: joined 1979 as Seaman Offr, helicopter pilot HMS Invincible S Atlantic Campaign 1982 (Campaign Medal 1982), Lt 1984, Lt Cdr 1992, cmd HMS Cottesmore (minehunter) 1993–94, Cdr 1998, left RN 2001, Hon Capt 2005; Adm Sea Cadet Corps 1992–; Cdre-in-Chief Fleet Air Arm 2006–; Col-in-Chief (UK): 9/12 Royal Lancers 2003–, Royal Irish Regt 1992–, Small Arms Sch Corps 2003–; Royal Col: Royal Highland Fus, 2nd Battalion, The Royal Regiment of Scotland 2006–, Yorkshire Regt 2006–; Col-in-Chief (Commonwealth): Canadian Airborne Regt 1991–, Queen's York Rangers (1 American Regt) 1997–, Royal Highland Fus of Canada 2003–, Princess Louise Fus 2005-, Royal New Zealand Army Logistic Regt 1997–; Hon Air Cdre RAF Lossiemouth 1996–; Personal ADC to HM The Queen 1984–; UK special rep Int Trade and Investment 2001-; Silver Jubilee Medal 1977, New Zealand Commemoration Medal 1990, Golden Jubilee Medal 2002; Cdre Royal Thames Yacht Club 1986–; pres: Royal Aero Club of GB 1982–; patron: Greenwich Hospital 1994–, Nat Maritime Museum 1995, English Nat Ballet 2001–, Tall Ships Youth Trust 2005–; *Books* Photographs (1985); *Style—* HRH The Duke of York, KCVO, CD; *Residence* Buckingham Palace, London SW1A 1AA

YORK, HRH Princess Beatrice of; Beatrice Elizabeth Mary Windsor; er da of HRH The Duke of York, *qv*, *b* 8 Aug 1988; *Educ* St George's Sch Ascot; *Style—* HRH Princess Beatrice of York

YORK, HRH Princess Eugenie of; Eugenie Victoria Helena Windsor; yr da of HRH The Duke of York, *qv*, *b* 23 March 1990; *Educ* St George's Sch Windsor, Marlborough; *Style—* HRH Princess Eugenie of York

WESSEX, HRH 1 Earl of (UK 1999); Edward Antony Richard Louis Windsor; KG (2006), KCVO (2003, CVO 1989); also Viscount Severn (UK 1999); 3 s of HM The Queen, *qv*, *b* 10 March 1964; *Educ* Gordonstoun, Jesus Coll Cambridge; er house tutor and jr master Wanganui Collegiate Sch New Zealand; *m* 19 June 1999, Sophie Helen (Col-in-Chief Queen Alexandra's Royal Army Nursing Corps 2003–; The Lincoln and Welland Regt 2004–; Royal Col 5th Batalion The Rifles 2007–; pres Girlguiding UK 2003–; Hon Fellow Royal Coll of Obstetricians and Gynaecologists 2006; DJStJ 2005–), da of Christopher Bourne Rhys-Jones (*see Debrett's Peerage & Baronetage* Molesworth, V); 1 da (*see below*); *Career* 2 Lt RM 1983 (resigned 1987); Cdre-in-Chief Royal Fleet Auxiliary 2006–; Col-in-Chief: Hastings and Prince Edward Regt 2002–, Saskatchewan Dragoons 2003–; Royal Col 2nd Battalion The Rifles 2007–; Royal Hon Col Royal Wessex Yeo 2003–; Personal ADC to HM The Queen 2004–; film/TV prodr as Edward Windsor, dir Ardent Productions 1993–2002; tstee: Duke of Edinburgh's Award Int Fndn 1987–, Duke of Edinburgh's Award 1988-; pres: Commonwealth Games Federation 1990-, Children's Film Unit 1992-; Silver Jubilee Medal 1977, Golden Jubilee Medal 2002, New Zealand Commemorative Medal 1990; *Style—* HRH The Earl of Wessex, KG, KCVO; *Residence* Bagshot Park, Bagshot, Surrey GU19 5PJ

WINDSOR, Lady Louise Alice Elizabeth Mary (MOUNTBATTEN-); only da of HRH The Earl of Wessex, *qv*, *b* 8 Nov 2003; *Style—* Lady Louise Windsor

HRH THE PRINCESS ROYAL; Anne Elizabeth Alice Louise Windsor; KG (1994), KT (2000), GCVO (1974), CD (1990), QSO (1990); declared Princess Royal 13 June 1987; only da of HM The Queen, *qv*, *b* 15 Aug 1950; *Educ* Benenden; *m* 1, 14 Nov 1973 (m dis 1992), Capt Mark Anthony Peter Phillips, CVO, ADC(P) (*see*

main text); 1s, 1 da (*see below*); *m* 2, 12 Dec 1992, Vice-Adm Timothy James Hamilton Laurence, CB, MVO, RN (*see main text*); *Career* equestrian, individual winner European Three-Day Event Burghley 1971 (Sportswoman of the Year Sports Writers' Assoc, Daily Express and World Sport (BOA jl), BBC Sports Personality of the Year), memb three-day event team Olympic Games Montreal 1976, fndr and course designer Gatcombe Park One-Day Event 1995; UK memb (one of two) IOC 1988–; Cdre-in-Chief Portsmouth 2006–; Col-in-Chief (UK): King's Royal Hussars 1992–, Royal Corps of Signals 1977–, Royal Logistic Corps 1993–, Royal Army Veterinary Corps 2003–; Col-in-Chief (Commonwealth): 8 Canadian Hussars (Princess Louise's) 1972–, Canadian Forces Communications and Electronics Branch 1977–, Grey and Simcoe Foresters (Royal Canadian Armoured Corps) 1972–, Royal Regina Rifle Regt 1982–, Canadian Forces Medical Branch, Royal Australian Corps Signals 1977–, Royal New Zealand Corps of Signals 1977–, Royal New Zealand Nursing Corps 1977–, Royal Newfoundland Regt; Affiliated Col-in-Chief: Queen's Gurkha Signals 1993–, Queen's Own Gurkha Signals 1993–; Col Blues and Royals (Royal Horse Gds and 1 Dragoons) 1998–; Royal Col: Scots Borderers 1st Battalion 2006–; 52nd Lowland 6th Battalion, The Royal Regt of Scotland 2006–; Royal Hon Col Univ of London OTC 1989–; Royal Hon Air Cdre: RAF Lyneham 1977–, London University Air Sqdn 993–; Cmdt-in-Chief First Aid Nursing Yeo (Princess Royal's Vol Corps) 1981–; Rear Adm and Chief Cmdt Women in the RN; sponsor: HMS Albion, HMS Talent; chllr Univ of London 1981–; Silver Jubilee Medal 1977, New Zealand Commemorative Medal 1990, Golden Jubilee Medal 2002; GCStJ; *Books* Riding Through My Life (1991); *Style—* HRH The Princess Royal, KG, LT, GCVO, QSO; *Residences* Buckingham Palace, London SW1A 1AA; Gatcombe Park, Minchinhampton, Gloucestershire GL6 9AT

PHILLIPS, Peter Mark Andrew; only s of HRH The Princess Royal, *qv*, *b* 15 Nov 1977; *Educ* Gordonstoun (head boy, memb Scottish Schs Rugby Team 1996), Univ of Exeter (BSc); *Career* events mangr (corporate hospitality) Jaguar Formula One Team 2001–02, account mangr Williams F1 2003–05, with Royal Bank of Scotland 2005; *Style—* Peter Phillips, Esq

PHILLIPS, Zara Anne Elizabeth; MBE (2006); only da of HRH The Princess Royal, *qv*, *b* 15 May 1981; *Educ* Gordonstoun, Univ of Exeter; *Career* qualified equine physiotherapist 2002; professional equestrian, sponsored by Cantor Index (spread betting firm) 2003–; achievements incl: Silver medal European Young Riders Championship 2002, second place Burgley Horse Trials 2003, winner Military Trophy Gatcombe Park One-Day Event 2004, third place Festival of British Eventing Gatcombe 2005, memb British team European Three-Day Event Championship 2005, European Eventing Champion 2005, World Eventing Champion 2006, Equestrian of the Year 2006, BBC Sports Personality of the Year 2006; pres Club 16–24 (Cheltenham young racegoers gp) 2000-05; memb Cheltenham Ladies Hockey Club; *Style—* Miss Zara Phillips; *Residence* The Bothy, Gatcombe Park, Minchinhampton, Gloucestershire GL6 9AT

LINLEY, Viscount; David Albert Charles Armstrong-Jones; only s of HRH The Princess Margaret (d 2002), and s and h of 1 Earl of Snowdon (*see main text*); *b* 3 Nov 1961; *Educ* Bedales, John Makepeace Sch of Woodcraft Beaminster; *m* 8 Oct 1993, Hon Serena Alleyne Stanhope, only da of Viscount Petersham (*see main text*); 1 s (Hon Charles Patrick Inigo *b* 1 July 1999), 1 da (Hon Margarita Elizabeth Rose Alleyne *b* 14 May 2002); *Career* furniture designer; chm: David Linley Furniture Ltd 1985–, David Linley Co 1998–; dir Christie Intl 2005–, chm Christie's UK 2006; *Books* Classical Furniture (1993, 2nd ed 1998), Extraordinary Furniture (1993), Design and Detail in the Home (2000); *Style—* Viscount Linley

CHATTO, Lady Sarah Frances Elizabeth; *née* Armstrong-Jones; only da of HRH The Princess Margaret (d 2002), and 1 Earl of Snowdon (*see main text*); *b* 1 May 1964; *Educ* Bedales, Camberwell Coll of Art, Royal Acad Sch; *m* 14 July 1994, Daniel Chatto, yr s of late Thomas Chatto; 2 s (Samuel David Benedict *b* 28 July 1996, Arthur Robert Nathaniel *b* 5 Feb 1999); *Style—* Lady Sarah Chatto

GLOUCESTER, HRH 2 Duke of (UK 1928); Richard Alexander Walter George Windsor; KG (1997), GCVO (1974); also Earl of Ulster and Baron Culloden (UK 1928); yr but only surviving s of HRH Prince Henry, 1 Duke of Gloucester (3 s of King George V; d 1974), and Princess Alice, Duchess of Gloucester (d 2004), da of 7 Duke of Buccleuch; *b* 26 Aug 1944; *Educ* Eton, Magdalene Coll Cambridge (MA, DipArch, including one year practical experience with Offices Devpt Gp Ministry Public Building and Works); *m* 8 July 1972, Birgitte Eva, GCVO, GCStJ (Col-in-Chief: Royal Army Dental Corps 1977–, Royal Australian Army Educational Corps 1977–, Royal New Zealand Army Educational Corps 1985–, Bermuda Regt 2003–; Dep Col-in-Chief Adj-Gen's Corps 1992–; Royal Col 7th Battalion The Rifles 2007–; sponsor: HMS Gloucester (guided missile destroyer), HMS Sandown (minesweeper), da of Asger Preben Wissing Henriksen, lawyer, of Odense, Denmark, by his 1 w Vivian, da of Waldemar Oswald van Deurs, whose surname Birgitte assumed; 1 s, 2 da (*see below*); *Heir* s, Earl of Ulster; *Career* architect in private practice 1969–72, corporate memb RIBA 1972–; Col-in-Chief: Royal Army Medical Corps 2003–, The Royal Anglian Regt 2006; Dep Col-in-Chief: Royal Logistic Corps 1993–; Royal Col 6th Battalion The Rifles 2007–; Royal Hon Col Royal Monmouthshire RE (Militia) 1977–; RAF: Hon Air Marshal 1996–, Royal Hon Air Cdre RAF Odiham, No 501 (County of Gloucester) Sqdn RAuxAF 1993–; pres: British-Nepal Soc, British Expertise, British Leprosy Relief Assoc, Cancer Research Campaign, Christ's Hosp, London Soc, National Assoc of Clubs for Young People,

Pevsner Memorial Tst, Public Monument and Sculpture Assoc, Royal Smithfield Club, St Bartholomew's Hosp, Soc of Architect-Artists, Victorian Soc; patron: American Friends of English Heritage, Architects Benevolent Soc, Assoc for Smoking and Health (ASH) 1974–, British Assoc of Friends of Museums 1976–, British Homeopathic Assoc, British Limbless Ex Service Assoc, British-Mexican Soc, British Museum, Canine Partners, Construction Industry Tst for Youth, Cncl for Educn in World Citizenship, Fenland Archaeological Tst, Friends of Gloucester and Peterborough Cathedrals, Habitat for Humanity GB, Inner London Probation Service, Islington and Hackney Housing Assoc, Japan Soc, League of Friends of Royal National Orthopaedic Hosp, London Chorus, Magdalene Australia Soc, NormandyVeterans Assoc, Oriental Ceramic Soc, Pestalozzi Children's Village Tst, Richard III Soc, Royal Acad of Schs, Royal Anthropological Inst, Severn Valley Railway, Soc of Antiquaries of London, Tramway Museum; fell Inst of Clerks of Works for GB Inc; FIStructE, FRIAS, FRSA, GCStJ (1975); Grand Cross Order of St Olav (Norway) 1973, Royal Order of the Northern Star (Sweden) 1975; *Style*— HRH The Duke of Gloucester, KG, GCVO; *Residence* Kensington Palace, London W8 4PU

ULSTER, EARL OF; Alexander Patrick Gregers Richard Windsor; only s and h of HRH 2 Duke of Gloucester, GCVO, *qv, b* 24 Oct 1974; *Educ* Eton, King's Coll London (BA), RMA Sandhurst; *m* 22 June 2002, Dr Claire Alexandra Booth, da of Robert Booth; 1 s *(see below)*; *Heir* s, Baron Culloden; *Career* King's Royal Hussars: joined 1998, Capt 2000, served Kosovo 2002; *Style*— Earl of Ulster

CULLODEN, BARON; Xan Richard Anders; only s and h of Earl of Ulster, *qv, b* 12 March 2007;

LEWIS, Lady Davina Elizabeth Alice Benedikte; *née* Windsor; er da of HRH 2 Duke of Gloucester, GCVO, *qv, b* 19 Nov 1977; *Educ* St George's Sch Ascot, Univ of the West of England Bristol; *m* 31 July 2004, Gary Lewis, eld s of Larry Lewis, of Gisborne, New Zealand, and Viki, *née* Smiler; *Style*— Lady Davina Lewis

WINDSOR, Lady Rose Victoria Birgitte Louise; yr da of HRH 2 Duke of Gloucester, GCVO, *qv, b* 1 March 1980; *Style*— Lady Rose Windsor

KENT, HRH 2 Duke of (UK 1934); Edward George Nicholas Paul Patrick Windsor; KG (1985), GCMG (1967), GCVO (1960); also Earl of St Andrews and Baron Downpatrick (UK 1934); er s of HRH 1 Duke of Kent, KG, KT, GCMG, GCVO, PC (4 s of King George V; k on active service 1942), and HRH Princess Marina, CI, GCVO, GBE (d 1968), yst da of HRH Prince Nicholas of Greece and Denmark (d 1938); *b* 9 Oct 1935; *Educ* Eton, Le Rosey Switzerland, RMA Sandhurst (Sir James Moncrieff Grierson languages prize, qualified French interpreter, Company Instr 1968–70); *m* 8 June 1961, Katharine Lucy Mary, GCVO, only da of Sir William Arthington Worsley, 4 Bt *(see Debrett's Peerage & Baronetage)*; 2 s, 1 da *(see below)*; *Heir* er s, Earl of St Andrews; *Career* Army: 2 Lt Royal Scots Greys 1955, Personal ADC to HM The Queen 1966–, GSO II E Cmd 1966–68, Cmd C Sqdn Royal Scots Greys 1970-71,GSO I, MOD 1972-76, ret as Lt-Col 1976, Maj-Gen 1983, Field Marshal 1993; Col-in-Chief: Royal Regt of Fus 1969–, Lorne Scots (Peel, Dufferin and Hamilton Regt) 1977–; Dep Col-in-Chief Scots Dragoon Gds 1993–, Col Scots Gds 1974–; Royal Col 1st Battalion The Rifles 2007–; Hon Air Chief Marshal RAF 1998, Royal Hon Air Cdre RAF Leuchars; Grand Master United Grand Lodge Freemasons of England, Grand Master Order of St Michael and St George; pres: Commonwealth War Graves Cmmn, RAF Benevolent Fund, RNLI, Stroke Assoc, All England Lawn Tennis and Croquet Club, UK Scout Assoc; pres-in-chief British Racing Drivers' Club; patron: Hanover Band, LPO, Opera North, S Bank Fndn, Trinity Coll of Music; chllr Univ of Surrey; visitor Cranfield Univ; hon degrees: Univ of Durham, Univ of Leeds, Univ of York; FRS 1990; King George VI and Queen Elizabeth Coronation Medal 1937, Silver Jubilee Medal 1977, Golden Jubilee Medal 2002; *Books* On Public View (1970), The Face of London (1975), Oxford and Cambridge (1980); *Style*— HRH The Duke of Kent, KG, GCMG, GCVO; *Residence* Wren House, Palace Green, London W8 4PY

ST ANDREWS, Earl of; George Philip Nicholas Windsor; er s and h of HRH 2 Duke of Kent, KG, GCMG, GCVO, *qv, b* 26 June 1962; *Educ* Eton, Downing Coll Cambridge; *m* 9 Jan 1988, Sylvana Palma, da of Maximilian Karl Tomaselli, and formerly w of John Paul Jones, whereupon he became excluded from succession to the throne through having married a Roman Catholic; 1 s (Edward Edmund Maximilian George, Lord Downpatrick b 2 Dec 1988, converted Roman Catholic 2003, hence excluded from succession to throne), 2 da (Lady Marina-Charlotte Alexandra Katharine Helen b 30 Sept 1992, Lady Amelia Sophia Theodora Mary Margaret b 24 Aug 1995); *Career* FCO 1987–88, Books and Manuscripts Dept Christie's 1996; trustee: GB-Sasakawa Fndn 1995–, SOS Children's Village UK 1999–, Golden Web Fndn 2003–; patron: Assoc for Int Cancer Research 1995–, Princess Margarita of Romania Trust 1997–; *Style*— Earl of St Andrews

WINDSOR, Lord Nicholas Charles Edward Jonathan; yr s of HRH 2 Duke of Kent, KG, GCMG, GCVO, *qv,* converted Roman Catholic 2001, hence excluded from succession to throne; *b* 25 July 1970; *Educ* Harrow; *m* 19 Oct 2006 (civil) and 4 Nov 2006 (religious), Paola, da of Don Louis Doimi de Frankopan, and Ingrid, née Detter; *Style*— Lord Nicholas Windsor

TAYLOR, Lady Helen Marina Lucy; *née* Windsor; only da of HRH 2 Duke of Kent, KG, GCMG, GCVO, *qv, b* 28 April 1964; *m* 18 July 1992, Timothy Verner (Tim)

Taylor, art dealer, eld s of Cdr Michael Verner Taylor, RN, of Stoke St Gregory, Somerset, and Mrs Colin Walkinshaw; 2 s (Columbus George Donald b 6 Aug 1994, Cassius Edward b 26 Dec 1996), 2 da (Eloise Olivia Katherine b 2 March 2003, Estella Olga Elizabeth b 21 Dec 2004); *Style*— Lady Helen Taylor

KENT, HRH Prince Michael of; Michael George Charles Franklin Windsor; GCVO (2003, KCVO 1992); yr bro of 2 Duke of Kent, *qv, b* 4 July 1942; *Educ* Eton, RMA Sandhurst (qualified Russian interpreter); *m* 30 June 1978, Baroness Marie-Christine Agnes Hedwig Ida, da of Baron Günther Hubertus von Reibnitz, by his w Countess Marianne Szapáry de Mura-szombath, Széchysziget et Szapár, and formerly w of Thomas Troubridge (*see Debrett's Peerage & Baronetage* Troubridge, Bt), whereupon he became excluded from succession to the throne through having married a Roman Catholic; 1 s, 1 da *(see below)*; *Career* Army: cmmnd 11 Hussars (Prince Albert's Own) 1963, MOD 1968–70, UN Force Cyprus 1971, Def Intelligence Service 1974–76, GSO Def 1974–76, Army Recruiting Directorate 1976–78, GSO Def Intelligence Staff 1978–81, ret as Maj 1981; Col-in-Chief Essex and Kent Scottish Regt Ontario 2002–; Hon Rear Adm RNR 2004 (Hon Cdre 1994); Cdre-in-Chief Maritime Reserves 2006–; liveryman Guild of Air Pilots and Air Navigators; Adm Royal Naval volunteer Reserve Yacht Club; memb HAC; Royal Hon Air Cdre RAF Benson 2002; hon mem Air Sqdn; fellow: Inst of Motor Industry, Royal Aeronautical Soc; pres: Dogs' and Cats' Home Battersea, Inst of Road Safety, Kennel Club, National Eye Research Centre, RAC Fndn, SSAFA Forces Help, Royal Patriotic Fund; Commonwealth pres RLSS; fndr patron Pan-European Genesis Initiative; patron: Battle of Britaim Memorial Tst, Brooklands Museum Tst, Chatham Historic Dockyard Volunteer Service, Children's Fire and Burns Tst, First Gear, Harefield Research Fndn, Museum of Army Flying, Russo-British C of C, World Monuments Fund (UK), Soc of Genealogists; dir Cantium Services; memb British team in international bobsleigh events (reserve Winter Olympics Sapporo 1972); memb team 1929 Bentley Special Millbrook 1992 (1,000-mile record for cars over 5,000 cc); Hon Dr Plekhanov Economics Acad Moscow; Coronation Medal 1953, UN Peacekeeping Medal 1971, Silver Jubilee Medal 1977, Golden Jubilee Medal 2002; KJStJ 2000; *Style*— HRH Prince Michael of Kent, GCVO; *Residence* Kensington Palace, London W8 4PU.

WINDSOR, Lord Frederick Michael George David Louis (Freddie); *b* 6 April 1979; *Educ* Eton (Oppidan scholar), Magdalen Coll Oxford; *Career* trainee barrister until 2004, with London film company Brass Hat Productions 2004, banker JPMorgan 2006–; *Style*— Lord Frederick Windsor

WINDSOR, Lady Gabriella Marina Alexandra Ophelia (Ella); *b* 23 April 1981; *Educ* Downe House Sch, Brown Univ RI; *Career* journalist, contrib Night & Day (Mail on Sunday colour supplement); *Style*— Lady Gabriella Windsor

HRH Princess Alexandra, The Hon Lady Ogilvy; Alexandra Helen Elizabeth Olga Christabel Ogilvy; KG (2003), GCVO (1960); sis of 2 Duke of Kent, *qv, b* 25 Dec 1936; *Educ* Heathfield Sch Ascot, finishing sch Parim 24 April 1963, Sir Angus James Bruce Ogilvy, KCVO, PC (d 2004), 2 s of 12 Earl of Airlie, KT, GCVO, MC *(see Debrett's Peerage & Baronetage)*; 1 s, 1 da *(see below)*; Col-in-Chief (Commonwealth): Queen Own Rifles 1960-, Canadian Scottish Regt (Princess Mary's) 1977–; Dep Col-in-Chief Queen's Royal Lancers 1993–; Royal Col 3rd Battalion The Rifles 2007–; Hon Royal Col Royal Yeo 2002–; Dep Royal Hon Col The King's Own Yorkshire Yeo 1996–, Hon Col North Irish Horse 1957–; pres: Royal Patriotic Fund Corp, Star and Garter Home for Disabled Sailors, Soldiers and Airmen; vice-pres British Red Cross Soc; patron Queen Alexandra's Royal Naval Nursing Service, Alexandra House; patron and Air Chief Cmdt Princess Mary's RAF Nursing Service; Hon Cmdt Women's Royal Australian Naval Service 1966–; Royal Hon Air Cdre RAF Cottesmore; Hon Dr: Univ of Hong Kong, Univ of Liverpool, Univ of Mauritius, Univ of Queensland; Hon DMus Univ of Lancaster; Hon FRCPS, Hon FRCA; King George VI and Queen Elizabeth Coronation Medal 1937, Coronation Medal 1953, Silver Jubilee Medal 1977, Golden Jubilee Medal 2003; *Style*— HRH Princess Alexandra, The Hon Lady Ogilvy, KG, GCVO; *Residence* Thatched House Lodge, Richmond Park, Surrey TW10 5HP

OGILVY, James Robert Bruce; *b* 29 Feb 1964; *Educ* Eton, Univ of St Andrews; *m* 30 July 1988, Julia, eld da of Charles Frederick Melville Rawlinson, of Arkesden, Essex; 1 da (Flora Alexandra b 15 Dec 1994), 1 s (Alexander Charles b 12 Nov 1996); *Career* publisher Luxury Briefing (magazine) 1996–; *Style*— James Ogilvy, Esq

MOWATT, Marina Victoria Alexandra; *b* 31 July 1966; *Educ* St Mary's Sch Wantage; *m* 2 Feb 1990 (m dis 1997) Paul Julian Mowatt; 1 da (Zenouska May b 26 May 1990), 1 s (Christian Alexander b 4 June 1993); *Style*— Mrs Marina Mowatt

See also the entries for the Duke of Fife, the Earl of Harewood, KBE, and the Countess Mountbatten of Burma in Debrett's People of Today

THE ORDER of SUCCESSION

PRINCE OF WALES

PRINCE WILLIAM

PRINCE HARRY

DUKE OF YORK

PRINCESS BEATRICE

PRINCESS EUGENIE

EARL OF WESSEX

LADY LOUISE WINDSOR

PRINCESS ROYAL

PETER PHILLIPS

ZARA PHILLIPS

VISCOUNT LINLEY

HON CHARLES ARMSTRONG-JONES

HON MARGARITA ARMSTRONG-JONES

LADY SARAH CHATTO

SAMUEL CHATTO

ARTHUR CHATTO

DUKE OF GLOUCESTER

EARL OF ULSTER

BARON CULLODEN

LADY DAVINA LEWIS

LADY ROSE WINDSOR

DUKE OF KENT

LADY MARINA-CHARLOTTE WINDSOR

LADY AMELIA WINDSOR

LADY HELEN TAYLOR

COLUMBUS TAYLOR

CASSIUS TAYLOR

ELOISE TAYLOR

ESTELLA TAYLOR

A Reader's Guide

The following notes should be borne in mind when reading an entry in Debrett's *People of Today*.

Surnames are listed by the initial letter; double-barrelled and hyphenated names, as well as those prefixed 'de' and 'von', are thus listed by their first part. 'Mac_____' and 'Mc_____' are listed together, as if they were all spelt 'Mac_____'.

Brackets around entrants' first forenames indicate names not used, while brackets around later forenames denote nicknames by which they are generally known. If clarification is needed, see the Style section towards the end of each entry.

It is standard genealogical practice to list sons first, followed by daughters. In recent times the editors have felt it appropriate to relax this rule and entries will predominantly list daughters first if an entrant's first-born child was female.

Careers generally begin by detailing the entrant's main professional career, including military service where applicable, in chronological order. This will typically be followed by involvement with other career-related organisations, then any charitable, public or other appointments. Honours, distinctions and awards are listed next, with the section concluding with memberships or fellowships of professional bodies. Because of the wide range of entrants' activities in Debrett's *People of Today*, there is necessarily considerable variation in the way career information is presented. With the exception of Armed Forces and Police Service related careers, job titles are largely styled lower case.

Clubs are generally in London unless otherwise stated. The word 'Club' is normally omitted from their names.

The entrant's style is the preferred way to address him or her in correspondence, in line with commonly accepted correct form and as agreed by the entrant. The styles given in Debrett's *People of Today* do not generally include professional qualifications or academic distinctions after an entrant's name, though it may be appropriate to do so in correspondence pertaining to the entrant's particular profession (see Debrett's *Correct Form* for further information).

Addresses and telephone numbers are given as required for writing or dialling from within the United Kingdom.

DISCLAIMER

Debrett's Limited makes every effort to check and update the extensive information contained in this publication. Any errors or omissions are unintentional, and no liability of any kind is accepted by the publisher or distributor in respect of them. Such errors or omissions should be drawn to the attention of Debrett's Limited for correction in future editions.

ABBREVIATIONS

A

AA	Automobile Association; Architectural Association; Anti-Aircraft
AAA	Amateur Athletic Association (now BAF)
AAAS	American Association for the Advancement of Science
AABC	Architect Accredited in Building Conservation
AAC	Army Air Corps
AACCA	Associate, Association of Certified and Corporate Accountants
AADipl	Diploma of the Architectural Association
A&AEE	Aeroplane and Armament Experimental Establishment
AAF	Auxiliary Air Force
AAFCE	Allied Air Forces Central Europe
AAG	Assistant Adjutant-General
AAGBI	Associate, Anaesthetists of Great Britain and Ireland
AAI	Associate, Chartered Auctioneers' and Estate Agents' Institute
AALPA	Association of Incorporated Auctioneers and Landed Property Agents
AAM	Association of Assistant Mistresses in Secondary Schools
AAPG	American Association of Petroleum Geologists
AA&QMG	Assistant Adjutant & Quartermaster-General
AASA	Associate, Australian Society of Accountants
AAT	Association of Accounting Technicians
AB	Bachelor of Arts (USA); Able-bodied Seaman
ABA	Associate of the British Archaeological Association; Antiquarian Booksellers' Association; Amateur Boxing Association
ABCC	Association of British Chambers of Commerce
ABI	Association of British Insurers
ABIA	Associate, Bankers' Institute of Australia; Association of British Introduction Agencies
ABIBA	Associate, British Institute of Brokers Association
ABIM	Associate, British Institute of Management (now ACMI)
ABIPP	Associate, British Institute of Professional Photographers
ABP	Associated British Ports (formerly BTDB)
ABPS	Associate, British Psychological Society
ABRC	Advisory Board for the Research Councils
ABSA	Association for Business Sponsorship of the Arts
ABTA	Association of British Travel Agents
AC	Companion of the Order of Australia
ACA	Associate, Institute of Chartered Accountants
Acad	Academy
ACARD	Advisory Council for Applied Research and Development
ACAS	Advisory, Conciliation and Arbitration Service
ACBSI	Associate, Chartered Building Societies Institute
ACC	Association of County Councils
ACCA	Associate, Chartered Association of Certified Accountants
ACCM	Advisory Council for the Church's Ministry
ACCS	Associate, Corporation of Secretaries
AcDipEd	Academic Diploma in Education
ACDS	Assistant Chief of Defence Staff
ACE	Association of Consulting Engineers
ACENVO	Association of Chief Executives of National Voluntary Organisations (now ACEVO)
ACEVO	Association of Chief Executives of Voluntary Organisations
ACF	Army Cadet Force
ACFA	Army Cadet Forces Association
ACG	Assistant Chaplain General
ACGI	Associate, City and Guilds of London Institute
ACGS	Assistant Chief of General Staff

ACIArb	Associate, Chartered Institute of Arbitrators
ACIB	Associate, Chartered Institute of Bankers
ACII	Associate, Chartered Insurance Institute
ACInstT	Associate, Chartered Institute of Taxation (formerly AInstT)
ACIOB	Associate, Chartered Institute of Building
ACIS	Associate, Institute of Chartered Secretaries (now ICSA)
ACMA	Associate, Institute of Cost and Management Accountants
ACMI	Associate, Chartered Management Institute
ACNS	Assistant Chief of Naval Staff
ACORD	Advisory Committee on Research and Development
ACOS	Assistant Chief of Staff
ACOST	Advisory Council on Science and Technology
ACP	Association of Clinical Pathologists; Associate, College of Preceptors
ACPO	Association of Chief Police Officers
ACPOS	Association of Chief Police Officers in Scotland
ACRE	Action with Rural Communities in England
ACS	American Chemical Society
ACSEA	Allied Command South East Asia
AcSS	Academician, Academy for the Learned Societies in the Social Sciences
ACT	Australian Capital Territory; Australian College of Theology; Association of Corporate Treasurers
actg	acting
ACTT	Association of Cinematograph, Television and Allied Technicians
ACVO	Assistant Chief Veterinary Officer
ACWA	Associate, Institute of Cost and Works Accountants
ADAS	Agricultural Development and Advisory Service (MAFF)
ADB	Associate of the Drama Board
ADC	Aide-de-Camp
AD Corps	Army Dental Corps
ADC(P)	Personal Aide-de-Camp to HM The Queen
Adj	Adjutant
Adj-Gen	Adjutant-General
Adm	Admiral
admin	administration; administrative; administrator
ADMS	Assistant Director of Medical Services
Admty	Admiralty
ADNI	Assistant Director of Naval Intelligence
ADOS	Assistant Director of Ordnance Service
ADP	Automatic Data Processing
ADPR	Assistant Director of Public Relations
ADS&T	Assistant Director of Supplies and Transport
Adv-Gen	Advocate-General
ADVS	Assistant Director of Veterinary Services
advsr	advisor
advsy	advisory
advtg	advertising
A&E	Accident and Emergency
AE	Air Efficiency Award
AEA	Air Efficiency Award; Atomic Energy Authority
AEAF	Allied Expeditionary Air Force
AEC	Army Educational Corps (now RAEC); Agricultural Executive Committee
AED	Air Efficiency Decoration
AEEU	Amalgamated Engineering and Electrical Union (now AMICUS)
AEF	Amalgamated Union of Engineering and Foundry Workers
AEM	Air Efficiency Medal
AER	Air Emergency Reserve
AERE	Atomic Energy Research Establishment
AEU	Amalgamated Engineering Union

AF	Air Force
AFAEP	Association of Fashion, Advertising and Editorial Photographers (now Association of Photographers)
AFAIM	Associate Fellow, Australian Institute of Management
AFB	Air Force Base (USA)
AFBPsS	Associate Fellow, British Psychological Society
AFC	Air Force Cross; Association Football Club
AFCENT	Allied Forces Central Europe
affrs	affairs
AFHQ	Allied Forces Headquarters
AFI	Associate, Faculty of Insurance; American Film Institute
AFIMA	Associate Fellow, Institute of Mathematics and its Applications
AFM	Air Force Medal
AFOM	Associate, Faculty of Occupational Medicine
AFRAeS	Associate Fellow, Royal Aeronautical Society
AFRC	Agricultural and Food Research Council (now BBSRC)
AFS	Auxiliary Fire Service
AFV	Armoured Fighting Vehicles
AFVPA	Advertising, Film and Video Producers' Association
AG	Attorney-General
Agent-Gen	Agent-General
AGI	Alliance Graphique Internationale
AGRA	Association of Genealogists and Researchers in Archives (formerly Association of Genealogists and Record Agents)
agric	agriculture; agricultural
AGSM	Associate, Guildhall School of Music and Drama
AHA	Area Health Authority
AHA(T)	Area Health Authority (Teaching)
AHQ	Army Headquarters
AHRB	Arts and Humanities Research Board (now AHRC)
AHRC	Arts and Humanities Research Council (formerly AHRB)
AHSM	Associate, Institute of Health Services Management
AIA	American Institute of Architects; Associate, Institute of Actuaries; Association of International Artists
AIAA	Associate, Institute of Administrative Accountants
AIAC	Associate, Institute of Company Accountants
AIAS	Associate Surveyor Member, Incorporated Association of Architects and Surveyors
AIB	Associate, Institute of Banking
AIBD	Associate, Institute of British Decorators
AICA	Associate Member, Commonwealth Institute of Accountants
AICE	Associate, Institute of Civil Engineers
AIChor	Associate, Institute of Choreography
AICS	Associate, Institute of Chartered Shipbuilders
AICTM	Associate, Imperial College of Tropical Medicine
AIEE	Associate, Institution of Electrical Engineers
AIF	Australian Imperial Forces
AIG	Adjutant-Inspector-General
AIIA	Associate, Institute of Industrial Administration
AIIMR	Associate, Institute of Investment Management and Research
AIL	Associate, Institute of Linguists
AIM	Associate, Institution of Metallurgists
AIMarE	Associate, Institute of Marine Engineers
AIMarEst	Associate, Institute of Marine Engineering, Science and Technology
AIMgt	Associate, Institute of Management (now ACMI)
AIMSW	Associate, Institute of Medical Social Workers
AINA	Associate, Institute of Naval Architects
AInstM	Associate Member, Institute of Marketing
AInstP	Associate, Institute of Physics
AInstT	Associate, Institute of Taxation (now ACInstT)
AInstTport	Associate, Institute of Transport
AIP	Association of Independent Producers
AIPM	Associate, Institute of Personnel Management
AIRC	Association of Independent Radio Contractors
Air Cdre	Air Commodore
AIRMIC	Associate, Insurance and Risk Managers in Industry and Commerce
AISVA	Associate, Incorporated Society of Valuers and Auctioneers
AK	Knight of the Order of Australia; Alaska
aka	also known as
AKC	Associate, King's College London
AL	Alabama
ALA	Associate, Library Association
ALAM	Associate, London Academy of Music and Dramatic Art
ALAS	Associate Member of Chartered Land Agents' Society
ALCD	Associate, London College of Divinity
ALCM	Associate, London College of Music
ALCS	Authors' Licensing and Collecting Society
ALFSEA	Allied Land Forces South East Asia
ALI	Argyll Light Infantry; Associate, Landscape Institute
ALIA	Associate, Life Insurance Association
ALL	Association of Language Learning
ALLC	Association for Literary and Linguistic Computing
Alta	Alberta
AM	Member of the Order of Australia; Albert Medal; Master of Arts (USA); Alpes Maritimes; Member, National Assembly for Wales; Member, London Assembly
AMA	Associate, Museum Association; Association of Metropolitan Authorities
ambass	ambassador
AMBIM	Associate, Member of the British Institute of Management
AMCT	Associate, Manchester College of Technology
AMEC	Association of Management Education for Clinicians
AMEI	Associate Member, Energy Institute
AMEME	Association of Mining, Electrical and Mechanical Engineers
AMF	Australian Military Forces
AMI	Association of Media Independents
AMICE	Associate Member, Institution of Civil Engineers
AMIChemE	Associate Member, Institution of Chemical Engineers
AMICUS	Amalgamated Engineering and Electrical Union (formerly AEEU)
AMIEE	Associate Member, Institution of Electrical Engineers
AMIEEIE	Associate Member, Institution of Electronic and Electrical Incorporated Engineers
AMIMechE	Associate Member, Institution of Mechanical Engineers
AMIMinE	Associate Member, Institution of Mining Engineers
AMIPE	Associate Member, Institution of Production Engineers
AMIStructE	Associate Member, Institution of Structural Engineers
AMP	Air Ministry Personnel; Advanced Management Programme
AMRAeS	Associate Member, Royal Aeronautical Society
AMRINA	Associate Member, Royal Institution of Naval Architects
AMS	Army Medical Service; Assistant Military Secretary
AMSI	Associate Member, Securities Institute
AMSO	Air Member for Supply and Organisation
AMTPI	Association of the Town Planning Institution
AnalaR	Analytical Reagents
ANU	Australian National University
AO	Air Officer; Officer of the Order of Australia
AOA	Air Officer in Charge of Administration
AOC	Air Officer Commanding
AOC-in-C	Air Officer Commanding-in-Chief
AOD	Army Ordnance Department
AOEng	Air Officer Engineering
AOM	Air Officer Maintenance
AOP	Association of Photographers
APA	American Psychiatric Association
APEX	Association of Professional, Executive, Clerical and Computer Staffs
APM	Assistant Provost Marshal
APP	Associate of Psychoanalytic Psychotherapy
appt	appointment
APR	Accredited Public Relations Practitioner
APRA	Association of Political Risks Analysts
APS	American Physical Society
APU	Anglia Polytechnic University
AQ	Administration and Quartering
AQH	Association of Quality Assurance in Healthcare
AQMG	Assistant Quartermaster-General
AR	Arkansas
A&R	Artistes and Repertoire
ARA	Associate, Royal Academy; Amateur Rowing Association
ARAD	Associate, Royal Academy of Dancing
ARAeS	Associate, Royal Aeronautical Society
ARAgS	Associate, Royal Agricultural Societies
ARAM	Associate, Royal Academy of Music
ARB	Architects' Registration Board (formerly ARCUK); Airworthiness Requirements Board
ARBA	Associate, Royal Society of British Artists
ARBS	Associate, Royal Society of British Sculptors
ARC	Agricultural Research Council
ARCA	Associate, Royal College of Art
ARCM	Associate, Royal College of Music
ARCO	Associate, Royal College of Organists
ARCS	Associate, Royal College of Science
ARCST	Associate, Royal College of Science and Technology
ARCUK	Architects' Registration Council of the UK (now ARB)
ARCVS	Associate, Royal College of Veterinary Surgeons
ARE	Associate, Royal Society of Painter-Etchers and Engravers
ARELS	Association of Recognised English Language Schools
ARIAS	Associate, Royal Incorporation of Architects in Scotland
ARIBA	Associate, Royal Institute of British Architects
ARIC	Associate, Royal Institute of Chemistry
ARICS	Associate, Royal Institution of Chartered Surveyors
ARINA	Associate, Royal Institution of Naval Architects

ARMCM	Associate, Royal Manchester College of Music
armd	armoured
ARP	Air Raid Precautions
ARPS	Associate, Royal Photographic Society
ARRC	Associate, Royal Red Cross
ARSA	Associate, Royal Scottish Academy
ARSM	Associate, Royal School of Mines
ARTC	Associate, Royal Technical College
ARWS	Associate, Royal Society of Painters in Water Colours
ASA	Associate Member, Society of Actuaries; Australian Society of Accountants; Army Sailing Association; Advertising Standards Authority
ASAA	Associate, Society of Incorporated Accountants and Auditors
ASC	Army Service Corps
ASCAP	American Society of Composers, Authors and Publishers
ASCL	Association of School and College Leaders (formerly SHA)
ASD	Armament Supply Department
ASEAN	Association of South East Asian Nations
ASFA	Associate, Institute of Shipping and Forwarding Agents
A&SH	Argyll and Sutherland Highlanders
ASIAD	Associate, Society of Industrial Artists and Designers
ASIP	Associate, Society of Investment Professionals
ASLIB	Association of Special Libraries and Information Bureaux
ASM	Association of Senior Members
ASME	American Society of Mechanical Engineers; Association for the Study of Medical Education
ASO	Air Staff Officer
assas	assassinated
ASSC	Accounting Standards Steering Committee
assoc	association; associate; associated
asst	assistant
Assur	Assurance
ASTD	Associate Member, Society of Typographic Designers
ASTMS	Association of Scientific, Technical and Managerial Staff (now MSF)
ASWE	Admiralty Surface Weapons Establishment
ATA	Air Transport Auxiliary
ATAF	Allied Tactical Air Force
ATC	Air Training Corps; Art Teachers' Certificate
ATCL	Associate, Trinity College of Music, London
ATD	Art Teachers' Diploma
ATI	Associate, Textile Institute
ATII	Associate Member, Institute of Taxation
ATO	Ammunitions Technical Officer
ATS	Auxiliary Territorial Service
AUEW	Amalgamated Union of Engineering Workers
Aust	Australian; Australia
AUT	Association of University Teachers
Authy	Authority
Aux	Auxiliary
Ave	Avenue
AVR	Army Volunteer Reserve
AWeldI	Associate of the Welding Institute
AWRE	Atomic Weapons Research Establishment
AZ	Arizona

B

b	born
BA	Bachelor of Arts; British Airways
BAAB	British Amateur Athletics Board
BAAL	British Association for Applied Linguistics
BAAS	British Association for the Advancement of Science
BAc	Bachelor in Acupuncture
BAC	Battersea Arts Centre; British Aircraft Corporation
BACB	British Association of Communicators in Business (formerly BAIE)
Bacc	Baccalauréate
BAcc	Bachelor of Accountancy
BADA	British Antique Dealers' Association
BAEM	British Association for Accident and Emergency Medicine
BAF	British Athletic Federation (formerly AAA)
BAFO	British Air Forces Occupation
BAFSEA	British Air Forces South East Asia
BAFTA	British Academy of Film and Television Arts
BAgric	Bachelor of Agriculture
BAI	Baccalarius in Arte Ingeniaria
BAIE	British Association of Industrial Editors (now BACB)
BALPA	British Airline Pilots' Association
BAO	Bachelor of Obstetrics
BAOL	British Association of Otolaryngologists
BAOMS	British Association of Oral and Maxillo-Facial Surgeons

BAOR	British Army of the Rhine
BARB	Broadcasters' Audience Research Board
BARC	British Automobile Racing Club
BArch	Bachelor of Architecture
BARR	British Association of Rheumatology Rehabilitation (now BSR)
barr	barrister
Bart's	St Bartholomew's Hospital
BAS	Bachelor in Agricultural Science
BASc	Bachelor of Applied Science
BASC	British Association of Shooting and Conservation
BASCA	British Academy of Songwriters, Composers and Authors
Batty	Battery
BBA	British Bankers' Association; Bachelor of Business Administration
BBC	British Broadcasting Corporation
BBFC	British Board of Film Classification
BBS	Bachelor of Business Studies
BBSRC	Biotechnology and Biological Sciences Research Council (formerly AFRC)
BC	British Columbia; Borough Council
BCC	British Council of Churches
BCE	Bachelor of Civil Engineering
BCh	Bachelor of Surgery
BChir	Bachelor of Surgery
BCL	Bachelor in Civil Law
BCom	Bachelor of Commerce
BComm	Bachelor of Commerce
BCS	British Computer Society; Bengal Civil Service
BCU	British Canoeing Union
BD	Bachelor in Divinity
Bd	Board
BDA	British Dental Association; Broadcasting Design Association
Bde	Brigade
BDMA	British Direct Marketing Association (now DMA)
BDS	Bachelor of Dental Surgery
BE	Bachelor of Engineering
BEA	British European Airways
BEAMA	Federation of British Electrotechnical and Allied Manufacturers Association
BEC	Business Education Council (now BTEC)
BEcon	Bachelor of Economics
BECTU	Broadcast Entertainment Cinematograph and Theatre Union
BEd	Bachelor of Education
Beds	Bedfordshire
BEE	Bachelor of Electrical Engineering
BEF	British Expeditionary Force
BEM	British Empire Medal
BEng	Bachelor of Engineering
BERA	British Educational Research Association
Berks	Berkshire
BESO	British Executive Services Overseas
BFBS	British Forces Broadcasting Service
BFI	British Film Institute
BFME	British Forces Middle East
BFPO	British Forces Post Office
BFSS	British Field Sports Society
BGGS	Brigadier-General, General Staff
BGS	Brigadier, General Staff
BHA	British Hoteliers' Association (formerly BHRCA)
BHRA	British Hydromechanics Research Association
BHRCA	British Hotel, Restaurant and Catering Association (now BHA)
BHS	British Horse Society
BIBA	British Insurance Brokers' Association
BICC	British Insulated Callender's Cables
BIEE	British Institute of Energy Economics
BIFU	Banking, Insurance and Finance Union
BIIBA	British Insurance and Investment Brokers' Association
BIID	British Institute of Interior Design
BIM	British Institute of Management
BIPP	British Institute of Professional Photographers
BIR	British Institute of Radiology
BJSM	British Joint Service Mission
BJur	Bachelor in Jurisprudence
BJuris	Bachelor in Jurisprudence
BL	Bachelor of Law; British Leyland
BLA	British Army of Liberation
bldg	building
BLESMA	British Limbless Ex-Servicemen's Association
BLitt	Bachelor of Letters
BM	Bachelor of Medicine (Oxford); Brigade Major
BMA	British Medical Association
BMedBiol	Bachelor of Medical Biology

BMedSci	Bachelor of Medical Science
BMet	Bachelor of Metallurgy
BMH	British Military Hospital
BMJ	British Medical Journal
BMus	Bachelor of Music
Bn	Battalion
BN	Bachelor of Nursing
BNA	British Neuroscience Association
BNAF	British North Africa Force
BNC	Brasenose College (Oxford)
BNES	British Nuclear Energy Society
BNF	British Nuclear Fuels
BNFL	British Nuclear Fuels Ltd
BNSC	British National Space Centre
BOA	British Olympic Association
BOAC	British Overseas Airways Corporation
BOAG	British Overseas Aid Group
BOT	Board of Trade
BOTB	British Overseas Trade Board
BP	British Petroleum
BPA	British Paediatric Association
BPG	Broadcasting Press Guild
BPharm	Bachelor of Pharmacy
BPhil	Bachelor of Philosophy
BPI	British Phonographic Industry
BPIF	British Printing Industries' Federation
BPMF	British Postgraduate Medical Federation
BPNA	British Paediatric Neurology Association
Br	British
BR	British Rail
BRCS	British Red Cross Society
BRDC	British Racing Drivers' Club
Brig	Brigadier
BRNC	Britannia Royal Naval College
bro	brother
BS	Bachelor of Surgery; Bachelor of Science (USA)
BSA	Building Societies Association
BSAC	British Screen Advisory Council; British Sub-Aqua Club
BSACI	British Society for Allergy and Clinical Immunology
BSc	Bachelor of Science
BSC	British Steel Corporation; British Society of Cinematographers
BSCC	British-Soviet Chamber of Commerce
BSDA	British Soft Drinks Association
BSI	British Standards Institution; British Society for Immunology
BSJ	Bachelor of Science in Journalism
BSME	British Society of Magazine Editors
BSocSc	Bachelor of Social Science
BSocSci	Bachelor of Social Science
BSR	British Society of Rheumatology (formerly BARR)
BSS	Bachelor of Social Sciences (USA)
Bt	Baronet
BT	British Telecom
BTA	British Troops in Austria; British Tourist Authority; British Theatre Association
Bt-Col	Brevet-Colonel
Btcy	Baronetcy
BTDB	British Transport Docks Board (now ABP)
BTEC	Business and Technicians Education Council (formerly BEC)
BTh	Bachelor of Theology
Btss	Baroness
Bucks	Buckinghamshire
BUPA	British United Provident Association
BV	Besloten Vennootschap (Netherlands)
BVA	British Veterinary Association
BVetMed	Bachelor of Veterinary Medicine
BVMS	Bachelor of Veterinary Medicine and Surgery
BVSc	Bachelor of Veterinary Science
BWI	British West Indies
BWM	British War Medal
BWS	Member, British Watercolour Society

C

c	children
C	Conservative
ca	circa
CA	Chartered Accountant; County Alderman; California
CAA	Civil Aviation Authority
CAABU	Council for the Advancement of Arab and British Understanding
CAB	Citizens Advice Bureau

CACA	Chartered Association of Certified Accountants
CAFOD	Catholic Agency for Overseas Development
Calif	California
Caltech	California Institute of Technology
CAM	Communications, Advertising and Marketing
Cambs	Cambridgeshire
CAMRA	Campaign for Real Ale
Cantab	of Cambridge
Capt	Captain
CARE	Cottage and Rural Enterprises
CAS	Chief of Air Staff
CB	Companion of the Order of the Bath
CBA	Council for British Archaeology
CBC	County Borough Council
CBE	Commander of the Order of the British Empire
CBI	Confederation of British Industry
CBIM	Companion, British Institute of Management (now CIMgt)
CBiol	Chartered Biologist
CBIREE	Companion, British Institute of Radio and Electronic Engineers
CBSO	City of Birmingham Symphony Orchestra
CC	County Council; Companion of the Order of Canada; Cricket Club
CCA	County Councils' Association
CCAB	Consultative Committee of Accounting Bodies
CCBE	Consultative Council of European Bars and Law Societies (Commission Consultative des Barreaux de la Communant Européenne)
CCBI	Council of Churches for Britain and Ireland
CCC	Corpus Christi College (Oxford and Cambridge); County Cricket Club
CCF	Combined Cadet Force
CCG(BE)	Control Commission, Germany (British Element)
CChem	Chartered Chemist
CCHMS	Central Committee for Hospital and Medical Services
CCIBS	Companion, Chartered Institute of Building Services
CCIPD	Companion, Chartered Institute of Personnel and Development
CCMI	Companion, Chartered Management Institute
CCncllr	County Councillor
CCO	Conservative Central Office
CCPR	Central Council of Physical Recreation
CCRA	Commander Corps of Royal Artillery
CCRE	Commander Corps of Royal Engineers
CCRSigs	Commander Corps of Royal Signals
CCS	Casualty Clearing Station
CCSC	Central Consultants and Specialists Committee
CD	Canadian Forces Decorations; Compact Disc
CDipAF	Certified Diploma in Accounting and Finance
CDir	Chartered Director
Cdr	Commander
Cdre	Commodore
CD-ROM	Compact Disc Read-Only Memory
CDS	Chief of Defence Staff
CE	Chief Engineer; Church of England
CEDEP	Centre Européen d'Education Permanente
CEDR	Centre for Dispute Resolution
CEFIC	Conseil Européen des Federations de l'Industrie Chimique
CEGB	Central Electricity Generating Board
CEI	Council of Engineering Institutions
CEng	Chartered Engineer
ceo	chief executive officer
CERI	Centre d'Etudes et de Recherches Internationales (Paris)
CERN	Conseil (now Organisation) Européenne pour la Recherche Nucléaire
Cert	Certificate
CertEd	Certificate of Education
CertTheol	Certificate of Theology
CF	Chaplain to the Forces
CFBOA	Companion Fellow, British Orthopaedic Association
CFM	Canadian Forces Medal
CFR	Commander, Order of the Federal Republic of Nigeria
CFS	Central Flying School
CFTC	Commonwealth Fund for Technical Co-operation
C&G	City and Guilds of London Institute (formerly CGLI)
CGA	Country Gentlemen's Association
CGC	Conspicuous Gallantry Cross
CGeog	Chartered Geographer
CGeol	Chartered Geologist
CGIA	City and Guilds of London Insignia Award
CGLI	City and Guilds of London Institute (now C&G)
CGS	Chief of the General Staff
CH	Companion of Honour

ChB	Bachelor of Surgery
CHB	Companion of Honour Barbados
CHC	Community Health Council
ChCh	Christ Church (Oxford)
chem	chemical
Chev	Chevalier
chllr	chancellor
chm	chairman
ChM	Mastery of Surgery
ChStJ	Chaplain of the Order of St John of Jerusalem
CI	Order of the Crown of India; Channel Islands
CIAgrE	Companion, Institute of Agricultural Engineers
CIArb	Chartered Institute of Arbitrators
CIBS	Chartered Institute of Building Services
CIBSE	Chartered Institution of Building Services Engineers
CIC	Construction Industry Council
CICAP	Criminal Injuries Compensation Appeal Panel
CICeram	Companion, Institute of Ceramics
CICHE	Committee for International Co-operation in Higher Education
CID	Criminal Investigation Department
CIE	Companion of the Order of the Indian Empire
CIEE	Companion, Institution of Electrical Engineers
CIGE	Companion, Institute of Gas Engineers
CIGRE	Conference Internationale des Grands Réseaux Electriques
CIGS	Chief of the Imperial General Staff
CIHM	Companion, Institute of Healthcare Management
CII	Chartered Insurance Institute
CILIP	Chartered Institute of Library and Information Professionals
CILT	Chartered Institute of Logistics and Transport (formerly CIT)
CIM	Chartered Institute of Marketing
CIMA	Chartered Institute of Management Accountants
CIMarE	Companion, Institute of Marine Engineers
CIMarEst	Companion, Institute of Marine Engineering, Science and Technology
CIMechE	Companion, Institution of Mechanical Engineers
CIMgt	Companion, Institute of Management (formerly CBIM)
C-in-C	Commander-in-Chief
CInstE	Companion, Institute of Energy
CInstSMM	Companion, Institute of Sales and Marketing Management
CIOB	Chartered Institute of Building
CIOJ	Chartered Institute of Journalists
CIPD	Companion, Institute of Personnel and Development (formerly CIPM)
CIPFA	Chartered Institute of Public Finance and Accountancy
CIPM	Companion, Institute of Personnel Management (now CIPD)
CIPR	Chartered Institute of Public Relations (formerly IPR)
CIRIA	Construction Industry Research and Information Association
CIT	Chartered Institute of Transport (now CILT)
CITP	Certified Information Technology Professional
CLA	Country Landowners' Association (now Country Land and Business Association)
CLit	Companion of Literature
CLP	Constituency Labour Party
CM	Member of the Order of Canada; Master of Surgery
CMA	Cost and Management Accountant (NZ)
CMath	Chartered Mathematician
CMC	Certified Management Consultant
cmd	commanded; command
cmdg	commanding
Cmdt	Commandant
CMF	Commonwealth Military Forces; Central Mediterranean Force
CMG	Companion of the Order of St Michael and St George
CMI	Chartered Management Institute
cmmn	commission
cmmnd	commissioned
cmmr	commissioner
CMO	Chief Medical Officer
CMP	Corps of Military Police
CMS	Church Missionary Society
CNAA	Council for National Academic Awards
Cncl	Council
cncllr	councillor
CND	Campaign for Nuclear Disarmament
CNRS	Centre Nationale de la Recherche Scientifique
CNS	Chief of Naval Staff
cnsllr	counsellor
CNZM	Companion of the New Zealand Order of Merit
CO	Commanding Officer; Colorado
Co	Company; County
COD	Communications and Operations Department (FO)
C of C	Chamber of Commerce

C of E	Church of England
COGS	Chief of General Staff
COHSE	Confederation of Health Service Employees
COI	Central Office of Information
Co L	Coalition Liberal
Col	Colonel
Coll	College
Comp	Comprehensive
Conf	Conference
Confedn	Confederation
Conn	Connecticut
Cons	Conservative
conslt	consultant
consltg	consulting
contrib	contributor; contributed; contribution
Co-op	Co-operative
Corp	Corporation; corporate
Corpl	Corporal
corr	correspondent
COS	Chief of Staff
COSIRA	Council for Smaller Industries in Rural Areas
cous	cousin
CP	Captain of a Parish (IOM)
CPA	Commonwealth Parliamentary Association; Chartered Patent Agent
CPC	Conservative Political Centre
CPE	Common Professional Examination (of the Law Society)
CPFA	Member/Associate, Chartered Institute of Public Finance and Accountancy
CPhys	Chartered Physicist
CPL	Chief, Personnel & Logistics
CPM	Colonial Police Medal
CPRE	Council for the Protection of Rural England
CPRS	Central Policy Review Staff
CPS	Crown Prosecution Service; Canadian Pacific Steamships
CPSA	Civil and Public Services Association
CPsychol	Chartered Psychologist
CPU	Commonwealth Press Union
CQSW	Certificate of Qualification in Social Work
cr	created
CRA	Commander Royal Artillery
CRAC	Careers Research and Advisory Council
CRAeS	Companion, Royal Aeronautical Society
CRASC	Commander, Royal Army Service Corps
CRC	Community Relations Commission
CRD	Conservative Research Department
CRE	Commanding Royal Engineers
CRMP	Corps of Royal Military Police
CRO	Commonwealth Relations Office
CS	Clerk to the Signet
CSA	Commonwealth Society of Artists; Chair, Schools Association
CSCE	Conference on Security and Co-operation in Europe
CSci	Chartered Scientist
CSD	Chartered Society of Designers
CSERB	Computer Systems and Electronics Requirements Board
CSI	Companion of the Order of the Star of India; Council for the Securities Industries
CSIR	Council for Scientific and Industrial Research
CSIRO	Commonwealth Scientific and Industrial Research Organisation
CSO	Chief Signal Officer; Chief Staff Officer; Chief Scientific Officer; Central Statistical Office
CSS	Council for Science and Society
CStat	Chartered Statistician (formerly FSS)
CSTI	Council of Science and Technology Institutes
CStJ	Commander of the Order of St John of Jerusalem
CSV	Community Service Volunteers
Ct	Court
CT	Connecticut
CTA	Chartered Tax Advisor
CTBI	Churches Together in Britain and Ireland
CTC	City Technology College
Ctee	Committee
CText	Chartered Textile Technologist
CUBC	Cambridge University Boat Club
CUF	Common University Fund
CUP	Cambridge University Press
CVCP	Committee of Vice-Chancellors and Principals of the UK
CVL	Central Veterinary Laboratory
CVO	Commander of the Royal Victorian Order
CWA	Crime Writers' Association
Cwlth	Commonwealth

D

d	died; death
D(Th)	Doctor of Theology
da	daughter
DA	Diploma in Anaesthetics; Diploma in Art
DAAG	Deputy Assistant-Adjutant-General
DAA&QMG	Deputy Assistant-Adjutant and Quartermaster-General
DACG	Deputy Assistant Chaplain-General
DACOS	Deputy Assistant Chief of Staff
D&AD	Designers & Art Directors' Association
DAD	Deputy Assistant Director
DADGMS	Deputy Assistant Director-General of Medical Services
DADMS	Deputy Assistant Director of Medical Services
DADOS	Deputy Assistant Director of Ordnance Services
DADR	Deputy Assistant Director of Remounts
DADST	Deputy Assistant Director of Supplies and Transport
DAG	Deputy Adjutant-General
DAMS	Deputy Assistant Military Secretary
DAPM	Deputy Assistant Provost Marshal
DAPS	Director of Army Postal Services
DA&QMG	Deputy Adjutant and Quartermaster-General
DAQMG	Deputy Assistant Quartermaster-General
DAvMed	Diploma in Aviation Medicine
DBA	Doctor of Business Administration; Design Business Association
DBE	Dame Commander of the Order of the British Empire
DBO	Diploma of British Orthoptics
DC	District Council; Doctor in Chiropractics; District of Columbia
DCA	Department for Constitutional Affairs
DCAe	Diploma of the College of Aeronautics
DCAS	Deputy Chief of Air Staff
DCB	Dame Commander of the Order of the Bath
DCDS	Deputy Chief of Defence Staff
DCGS	Deputy Chief of General Staff
DCH	Diploma in Child Health
DCL	Doctor of Civil Law
DCLI	Duke of Cornwall's Light Infantry
DCM	Distinguished Conduct Medal
DCMG	Dame Commander of the Order of St Michael and St George
DCMS	Deputy Commissioner Medical Services; Department for Culture, Media and Sport
DCom	Doctor of Communications
DCSO	Deputy Chief Scientific Officer
DCVO	Dame Commander Royal Victorian Order
DD	Doctor of Divinity
DDDS	Deputy Director of Dental Services
DDes	Doctor of Design
DDME	Deputy Director of Mechanical Engineering
DDMS	Deputy Director of Medical Services
DDO	Diploma in Dental Orthopaedics
DDOS	Deputy Director of Ordnance Services
DDPS	Deputy Director of Personal Services
DDR	Deputy Director of Remounts
DDS	Doctor of Dental Surgery; Director of Dental Services
DDSD	Deputy Director of Staff Duties
DDS&T	Deputy Director Supplies and Transport
DDVS	Deputy Director of Veterinary Services
DDWE&M	Deputy Director of Works, Electrical and Mechanical
DE	Doctor of Engineering (USA); Delaware
DEA	Department of Economic Affairs
decd	deceased
DEd	Doctor of Education
Def	Defence
DEFRA	Department for Environment, Food and Rural Affairs
DèsL	Docteur ès Lettres
delg	delegate
delgn	delegation
Dem	Democrat
DEM	Diploma in Education Management
DEME	Director of Electrical and Mechanical Engineering
DEng	Doctor of Engineering
dep	deputy
Dept	Department
Derbys	Derbyshire
DES	Department of Education and Science
DesRCA	Designer, Royal College of Art
DETR	Department of the Environment, Transport and the Regions
Devpt	Development
DFA	Doctor of Fine Arts
DFC	Distinguished Flying Cross

DFE	Department for Education
DfEE	Department for Education and Employment
DfES	Department for Education and Skills
DFFP	Diploma, Faculty of Family Planning and Reproductive Health
DFH	Diploma of the Faraday House
DFID	Department for International Development
DFM	Distinguished Flying Medal; Diploma in Forensic Medicine
DG	Director-General
DGAMS	Director-General of Army Medical Services
DGCStJ	Dame Grand Cross of the Order of St John of Jerusalem
DGDP	Diploma in General Dental Practice
DGMS	Director-General of Medical Services
DGS	Diploma in Graduate Studies
DGStJ	Dame of Grace of the Order of St John of Jerusalem
DH	Doctor of Humanities
DHA	District Health Authority
DHL	Doctor of Humane Letters; Doctor of Hebrew Literature
DHMSA	Diploma in the History of Medicine (Society of Apothecaries)
DHQ	District Headquarters
DHSS	Department of Health and Social Security
DHy	Doctor of Hygiene
DIC	Diploma of the Imperial College
DIH	Diploma in Industrial Health
Dio	Diocese
Dip	Diploma; Diplomatic
DipAD	Diploma in Art and Design
DipAg	Diploma in Agriculture
DipArch	Diploma in Architecture
DipAvMed	Diploma in Aviation Medicine
DipBA	Diploma in Business Administration
DipCAM	Diploma in Communications, Advertising and Marketing of the CAM Foundation
DipCD	Diploma in Civic Design
DipCThand M	Diploma in Christian Theology and Ministry
DipEd	Diploma in Education
DipEE	Diploma in Electrical Engineering
DipESL	Diploma in English as a Second Language
DipFM	Diploma in Forensic Medicine
DipHA	Diploma in Hospital Administration
DipHSM	Diploma in Health Services Management
DipLA	Diploma in Landscape Architecture
DiplArch	Diploma in Architecture
DipLD	Diploma in Landscape Design
DipLP	Diploma in Legal Practice
DipM	Diploma in Marketing
DipMRS	Diploma of the Market Research Society
DipN	Diploma in Nursing
DipOrthMed	Diploma in Orthopaedic Medicine
DipRAM	Diploma of the Royal Academy of Music
DipTh	Diploma in Theology
DipTP	Diploma in Town Planning
dir	director
dis	dissolved (marriage)
Dist	District
Div	Division
Divnl	Divisional
DJ	disc jockey
DJAG	Deputy Judge Advocate-General
DJStJ	Dame of Justice of the Order of St John of Jerusalem
DK	Most Esteemed Family Order of Brunei
DL	Deputy Lieutenant
DLC	Diploma Loughborough College
DLI	Durham Light Infantry
DLit	Doctor of Literature
DLitt	Doctor of Letters
DLO	Diploma in Laryngology and Otology/Otorhinolaryngology; Defence Logistics Organisation
DM	Doctor of Medicine
DMA	Direct Marketing Association (formerly BDMA); Diploma in Municipal Administration
DMD	Doctor in Dental Medicine
DME	Director of Mechanical Engineering
DMI	Director Military Intelligence
DMJ	Diploma in Medical Jurisprudence
DMO&I	Director Military Operations and Intelligence
DMRD	Diploma in Medical Radiological Diagnosis
DMRE	Diploma in Medical Radiology and Electrology
DMRT	Diploma in Medical Radiotherapy
DMS	Director of Medical Services; Diploma in Management Studies
DMSI	Director of Management and Support Intelligence
DMT	Director of Military Training

DMus	Doctor of Music
DNB	Dictionary of National Biography
DNI	Director of Naval Intelligence
DNO	Director of Naval Ordnance
DO	Divisional Officer; Diploma in Ophthalmology; Diploma in Osteopathy
DOAE	Defence Operational Analysis Establishment
DObstRCOG	Diploma Royal College of Obstetricians and Gynaecologists
DOC	District Officer Commanding
DOE	Department of Environment
DOI	Department of Industry
DOMS	Diploma in Ophthalmic Medicine
DOR	Director of Operational Requirements
DOrthRCS	Diploma in Orthodontics Royal College of Surgeons
DOS	Director of Ordnance Services
DPA	Diploma in Public Administration
DPCP	Department of Prices and Consumer Protection
DPH	Diploma in Public Health
DPhil	Doctor of Philosophy
DPL	Director of Pioneers and Labour
DPM	Diploma in Psychological Medicine
DPMO	Deputy Principal Medical Officer
DPP	Director of Public Prosecutions
DPR	Director of Public Relations
DPS	Director of Personal Services
DQMG	Deputy Quartermaster-General
Dr	Doctor
DRA	Defence Research Agency
DRC	Diploma of the Royal College of Science and Technology, Glasgow
DRCOG	Doctor, Royal College of Obstetricians and Gynaecologists
DRD	Diploma in Restorative Dentistry
Dr jur	Doctor of Laws
DrPA	Doctor of Public Administration (USA)
DRSAMD	Diploma of the Royal Scottish Academy of Music and Drama
DrScNat	Doctor of Natural Sciences
DRVO	Deputy Regional Veterinary Officer
DS	Directing Staff
DSA	Diploma in Social Administration
DSAC	Defence Scientist Advisory Committee
DSAO	Diplomatic Service Administration Office
DSC	Distinguished Service Cross
DSc	Doctor of Science
DSCHE	Diploma of the Scottish Council for Health Education
DSD	Director of Staff Duties
DSIR	Department of Scientific and Industrial Research
DSLitt	Doctor of Sacred Letters
DSM	Distinguished Service Medal (USA)
DSO	Companion of the Distinguished Service Order
DSocSc	Doctor of Social Sciences
dsp	*decessit sine prole* (died without issue)
DSP	Docteur en Sciences Politiques (Montreal)
DSS	Department of Social Security
DSSc	Doctor of Social Sciences
DSSS	Doctor of Science in Social Sciences
DS&T	Director of Supplies and Transport
DStJ	Dame of Grace of the Order of St John of Jerusalem
DTech	Doctor of Technology
DTh	Doctor of Theology
DTI	Department of Trade and Industry
DTLR	Department of Transport, Local Government and the Regions
DTM	Diploma in Tropical Medicine
DTM&H	Diploma in Tropical Medicine and Hygiene
DUniv	Doctor of the University
DUP	Democratic Unionist Party
DVFS	Director, Veterinary Field Services
DVM	Doctor of Veterinary Medicine
DVMS	Doctor of Veterinary Medicine and Surgery
DVO	Divisional Veterinary Officer
DVS	Director of Veterinary Services
DVSM	Diploma of Veterinary State Medicine
DWP	Department for Work and Pensions
DX	Document Exchange

E

E	East; Earl; England
EAMBES	European Alliance for Medical and Biological Engineering and Sciences
EASA	Ecclesiastical Architects and Surveyors' Association

EBRD	European Bank for Reconstruction and Development
EBU	European Broadcasting Union
EC	European Commission, European Community
ECB	England and Wales Cricket Board (formerly TCCB)
ECFMG	Educational Council for Foreign Medical Graduates
ECGD	Export Credit Guarantee Department
Econ	Economic
ed	editor; edited
ED	Efficiency Decoration; European Democratic (Group)
EDC	Economic Development Committee
EdD	Doctor of Education
EDG	European Democratic Group (UK Conservative Group, European Parliament)
edn	edition
Educn	Education
educnl	educational
EEA	European Economic Area
EEF	Engineering Employers' Federation
EETPU	Electrical, Electronic, Telecommunications and Plumbing Union (now AEEU)
EFTA	European Free Trade Association
EIU	Economist Intelligence Unit
eld	eldest
ELT	English Language Teaching
EMBL	European Molecular Biology Laboratory
EMBO	European Molecular Biology Organisation
EMEA	Europe, Middle East and Africa
EMS	Emergency Medical Service
EN (G)	Enrolled Nurse (General)
Eng	English; England
Engr	Engineer
Engrg	Engineering
ENO	English National Opera
ENSA	Entertainments National Services Association
ENT	Ear, Nose and Throat
ENWFC	England North West Film Commission
EP	European Parliament
EPLP	European Parliamentary Labour Party
EPP	European People's Party
EPSRC	Engineering and Physical Sciences Research Council (formerly SERC)
er	elder
ERA	Electrical Research Association
ERD	Emergency Reserve Decoration
Esq	Esquire
ESRC	Economic and Social Research Council
ESRO	European Space Research Organisation
estab	established; establishment
ESU	English Speaking Union
ETH	Eidgenössische Technische Hochschule
EU	European Union (formerly European Community)
EurGeol	European Geologist
Eur Ing	European Engineer
Euro	European
exec	executive
exhbn	exhibition
expdn	expedition
ext	extinct; extension

F

f	father
FA	Football Association
FAA	Fellow, Australian Academy of Science
FAAAS	Fellow, American Academy of Arts & Sciences
FAAO	Fellow, American Academy of Optometry
FAAP	Fellow, American Academy of Paediatrics
FAAV	Fellow, Central Association of Agricultural Valuers
FABRP	Fellow, Association of Business Recovery Professionals (formerly FSPI)
FACC	Fellow, American College of Cardiology
FACCA	Fellow, Association of Certified and Corporate Accountants
FACD	Fellow, American College of Dentistry
FACE	Fellow, Australian College of Education
FACM	Fellow, Association of Computing Machines
FACOG	Fellow, American College of Obstetricians and Gynaecologists
FACP	Fellow, American College of Physicians
FACS	Fellow, American College of Surgeons
FACT	Fellow, Association of Corporate Treasurers
FACVT	Fellow, American College of Veterinary Toxicology

FAE	Fellow, Academy of Experts (formerly FBAE)
FAES	Fellow, Audio Engineering Society
FAI	Fellow, Chartered Auctioneers' and Estate Agents' Institute; Fellow, Financial Accountants' Institute
FAIA	Fellow, American Institute of Architects
FAIE	Fellow, British Association of Industrial Editors (now FCB)
FAIM	Fellow, Australian Institute of Management
FAIP	Fellow, Australian Institute of Physics
FAIRE	Fellow, Australian Institute of Radio Engineers
FAM	Fellow, Academy of Marketing
FAMGP	Fellow, Association of Managers in General Practice
FAMS	Fellow, Ancient Monuments Society
FANY	First Aid Nursing Yeomanry
FANZCA	Fellow, Australian and New Zealand College of Anaesthetists
FAO	Food and Agriculture Organisation of the United Nations
FAPA	Fellow, American Psychiatric Association
FAPM	Fellow, Association of Project Managers
FAQMC	Fellow, Association of Quality Management Consultants
FARELF	Far East Land Forces
FAS	Fellow, Antiquarian Society
FASA	Fellow, Australian Society of Accountants
FASCE	Fellow, American Society of Civil Engineers
FASI	Fellow, Architects and Surveyors' Institute
FASME	Fellow, American Society of Mechanical Engineers
FBA	Fellow, British Academy
FBAA	Fellow, British Acupuncture Association; Fellow, British Archaeological Association
FBAE	Fellow, British Academy of Experts (now FAE)
FBAM	Fellow, British Academy of Management
FBCO	Fellow, British College of Opticians (now FCOptom)
FBCS	Fellow, British Computer Society
FBEC(S)	Fellow, Business Education Council (Scotland)
FBEng	Fellow, Association of Building Engineers
FBHI	Fellow, British Horological Institute
FBI	Federation of British Industries
FBIAC	Fellow, British Institute of Agricultural Consultants
FBIBA	Fellow, British Insurance Brokers' Association
FBID	Fellow, British Institute of Interior Design
FBIEE	Fellow, British Institute of Energy Economists
FBIM	Fellow, British Institute of Management (now FIMgt)
FBIPP	Fellow, British Institute of Professional Photographers
FBIS	Fellow, British Interplanetary Society
FBISA	Fellow, British Institute of Sports Administration
FBKSTS	Fellow, British Kinematograph, Sound and Television Society
FBOA	Fellow, British Optical Association; Fellow, British Orthopaedic Association
FBPsS	Fellow, British Psychological Society
FBSI	Fellow, Boot and Shoe Industry
FC	Football Club
FCA	Fellow, Institute of Chartered Accountants
FCAI	Fellow, Canadian Aeronautical Institute
FCAM	Fellow, Communications Advertising and Marketing Educational Foundation
FCAnaes	Fellow, College of Anaesthetists
FCB	Fellow, British Association of Communicators in Business (formerly FAIE)
FCBSI	Fellow, Chartered Building Societies Institute
FCCA	Fellow, Chartered Association of Certified Accountants
FCCS	Fellow, Corporation of Certified Secretaries
FCEC	Federation of Civil Engineering Contractors
FCEM	Fellow, College of Emergency Medicine
FCFA	Fellow, Cookery and Food Association
FCFI	Fellow, Clothing and Footwear Institute
FCGI	Fellow, City and Guilds of London Institute
FCIA	Fellow, Corporation of Insurance Agents
FCIArb	Fellow, Chartered Institute of Arbitrators
FCIB	Fellow, Corporation of Insurance Brokers; Fellow, Chartered Institute of Bankers
FCIBS	Fellow, Chartered Institution of Building Services; Fellow, Chartered Institute of Bankers of Scotland
FCIBSE	Fellow, Chartered Institution of Building Service Engineers
FCII	Fellow, Chartered Insurance Institute
FCILT	Fellow, Chartered Institute of Logistics and Transport (formerly FCIT)
FCIM	Fellow, Chartered Institute of Marketing (formerly FInstM)
FCInstT	Fellow, Chartered Institute of Taxation (formerly FInstT)
FCIOB	Fellow, Chartered Institute of Building
FCIPA	Fellow, Chartered Institute of Patent Agents (now CPA)
FCIPD	Fellow, Chartered Institute of Personnel and Development
FCIPR	Fellow, Chartered Institute of Public Relations
FCIPS	Fellow, Chartered Institute of Purchasing and Supply

FCIS	Fellow, Institute of Chartered Secretaries and Administrators
FCIT	Fellow, Chartered Institute of Transport (now FCILT)
FCIWEM	Fellow, Chartered Institution of Water and Environmental Management (formerly FIWEM)
FCIWM	Fellow, Chartered Institute of Waste Management
FCMA	Fellow, Institute of Cost and Management Accountants; Fellow, Communications Management Association
FCMC	Fellow grade Certified Management Consultant (Institute of Management Consultancy)
FCMI	Fellow, Chartered Management Institute (formerly FIMgt)
FCMSA	Fellow, College of Medicine of South Africa
FCO	Foreign & Commonwealth Office
FCOG	Fellow, College of Obstetrics and Gynaecology
FCollP	Ordinary Fellow, College of Preceptors
FConsE	Fellow, Association of Consulting Engineers
FCOphth	Fellow, College of Ophthalmology (now FRCOphth)
FCOptom	Fellow, College of Optometrists (formerly FBCO)
FCP	Academic Fellow, College of Preceptors
FCPA	Fellow, Australian Society of Certified Practising Accountants
FCPS	Fellow, College of Physicians and Surgeons
FCS	Fellow, Chemical Society; Federation of Conservative Students (now Conservative Collegiate Forum)
FCSD	Fellow, Chartered Society of Designers
FCT	Fellow, Institute of Corporate Treasurers
FCWA	Fellow, Institute of Cost and Works Accountants
FDI	Fédération Dentaire Internationale
FDR	Federalische Deutsche Republik
FDS	Fellow in Dental Surgery
FDSRCPS	Fellow in Dental Surgery, Royal College of Physicians and Surgeons
FDSRCS	Fellow in Dental Surgery, Royal College of Surgeons of England
FDSRCSE	Fellow in Dental Surgery, Royal College of Surgeons of Edinburgh
FDSRCSI	Fellow in Dental Surgery, Royal College of Surgeons in Ireland
FE	Further Education
FEAF	Far East Air Force
FEBU	Fellowship of European Boards of Urology
Fed	Federal
Fedn	Federation
FEFC	Further Education Funding Council
FEI	International Equestrian Federation; Fellow, Energy Institute
FEIS	Fellow, Educational Institute of Scotland
fell	fellow
FESC	Fellow, European Society of Cardiology
FFA	Fellow, Faculty of Actuaries (Scotland); Fellow, Institute of Financial Accountants
FFAEM	Fellow, Faculty of Accident & Emergency Medicine
FFARACS	Fellow, Faculty of Anaesthetists Royal Australasian College of Surgeons
FFARCS	Fellow, Faculty of Anaesthetists, Royal College of Surgeons (now FRCA)
FFARCSI	Fellow, Faculty of Anaesthetists Royal College of Surgeons of Ireland
FFAS	Fellow, Faculty of Architects and Surveyors
FFB	Fellow, Faculty of Building
FFCM	Fellow, Faculty of Community Medicine (now FFPH)
FFCS	Founding Fellow, Institute of Contemporary Scotland
FFDRCSI	Fellow, Faculty of Dentistry, Royal College of Surgeons in Ireland
FFFP	Fellow, Faculty of Family Planning (of the RCOG)
FFGDP	Fellow, Faculty of General Dental Practice
FFHom	Fellow, Faculty of Homeopathy
FFOHM	Fellow, Faculty of Occupational Health Medicine
FFOM	Fellow, Faculty of Occupational Medicine
FFPathRCPI	Fellow, Faculty of Pathology Royal College of Physicians of Ireland
FFPH	Fellow, Faculty of Public Health (formerly FFPHM)
FFPHM	Fellow, Faculty of Public Health Medicine (formerly FFCM, now FFPH)
FFPHMI	Fellow, Faculty of Public Health Medicine Royal College of Physicians of Ireland
FFPM	Fellow, Faculty of Pharmaceutical Medicine
FFR	Fellow, Faculty of Radiologists
FFRRCSI	Fellow, Faculty of Radiologists, Royal College of Surgeons in Ireland
FFY	Fife and Forfar Yeomanry
FGA	Fellow, Gemmological Association
FGCM	Fellow, Guild of Church Musicians
FGDP	Faculty of General Dental Practitioners
FGS	Fellow, Geological Society
FGSM	Fellow, Guildhall School of Music
FHCIMA	Fellow, Hotel Catering and Institutional Management Association
FHEA	Fellow, Higher Education Academy
FHG	Fellow in Heraldry and Genealogy

FHKCPath	Fellow, Hong Kong College of Pathologists
FHKIE	Fellow, Hong Kong Institute of Engineers
FHS	Fellow, Heraldry Society; Forces Help Society
FHSA	Family Health Services Authority
FHSM	Fellow, Institute of Health Services Management
FIA	Fellow, Institute of Actuaries; Fédération Internationale de l'Automobile
FIAA	Fellow, Institute of Administrative Accountants
FIAC	Fellow, Institute of Company Accountants
FIAcadE	Fellow, Irish Academy of Engineering
FIAeS	Fellow, Institute of Aeronautical Sciences
FIAgrE	Fellow, Institution of Agricultural Engineers
FIAgrM	Fellow, Institution of Agricultural Management
FIAL	Fellow, International Institute of Arts and Letters
FIAM	Fellow, International Academy of Management
FIAP	Fellow, Institute of Analysts and Programmers
FIArb	Fellow, Institute of Arbitration
FIAS	Fellow, Institute of Aeronautical Sciences (USA); Fellow, Incorporated Society of Architects
FIB	Fellow, Institute of Bankers (now FCIB)
FIBA	Fellow, Institute of Business Advisers (formerly FIBC)
FIBC	Fellow, Institute of Business Counsellors (now FIBA)
FIBF	Fellow, Institute of British Foundrymen
FIBiol	Fellow, Institute of Biology
FIBM	Fellow, Institute of Builders' Merchants
FIBMS	Fellow, Institute of Biomedical Science (formerly FIMLS)
FIBrew	Fellow, Institute of Brewing
FIBScot	Fellow, Institute of Bankers in Scotland
FICA	Fellow, Institute of Chartered Accountants in England and Wales (now FCA); Fellow, Independent Consultants' Association
FICAI	Fellow, Institute of Chartered Accountants in Ireland
FICAS	Fellow, Institute of Chartered Accountants in Scotland
FICD	Fellow, Institute of Civil Defence
FICE	Fellow, Institution of Civil Engineers
FICeram	Fellow, Institute of Ceramics
FICFor	Fellow, Institute of Chartered Foresters
FIChemE	Fellow, Institution of Chemical Engineers
FICM	Fellow, Institute of Credit Management
FICMA	Fellow, Institute of Cost and Management Accountants
FICorrST	Fellow, Institute of Corrosion Science and Technology
FICPD	Fellow, Institute of Continuing Professional Development
FICS	Fellow, Institute of Chartered Shipbrokers; Fellow, International College of Surgeons
FICSA	Fellow, Institute of Chartered Secretaries and Administrators
FIDE	Fédération Internationale des Échecs; Fellow, Institute of Design Engineers; Fédération Internationale pour le Droit Européen
FIDM	Fellow, Institute of Direct Marketing
FIDPM	Fellow, Institute of Data Processing Management
FIE	Fellow, Institution of Engineers
FIE(Aust)	Fellow, Institution of Engineers (Australia)
FIED	Fellow, Institution of Engineering Design
FIEE	Fellow, Institution of Electrical Engineers
FIEEE	Fellow, Institution of Electrical and Electronics Engineers (USA)
FIEI	Fellow, Institution of Engineers of Ireland
FIElecIE	Fellow, Institution of Electronic Incorporated Engineers
FIERE	Fellow, Institution of Electronics and Radio Engineers
FIEx	Fellow, Institute of Export
FIFF	Fellow, Institute of Freight Forwarders (now FIFP)
FIFireE	Fellow, Institute of Fire Engineers
FIFM	Fellow, Institute of Fisheries Management
FIFor	Fellow, Institute of Forestry
FIFP	Fellow, Institute of Freight Professionals
FIFST	Fellow, Institute of Food Science and Technology
FIGasE	Fellow, Institution of Gas Engineers
FIGD	Fellow, Institute of Grocery Distribution
FIGE	Fellow, Institute of Gas Engineers
FIGeol	Fellow, Institute of Geology
FIHE	Fellow, Institute of Health Education
FIHort	Fellow, Institute of Horticulture
FIHospE	Fellow, Institute of Hospital Engineering
FIHSM	Fellow, Institute of Health Service Managers
FIHT	Fellow, Institute of Highways and Transportation
FIHVE	Fellow, Institution of Heating and Ventilating Engineers
FIIA	Fellow, Institute of Internal Auditors
FIIB	Fellow, International Institute of Biotechnology
FIIE	Fellow, Institution of Incorporated Engineers
FIIM	Fellow, Institute of Industrial Managers
FIInfSc	Fellow, Institute of Information Scientists (now FCLIP)
FIInst	Fellow, Imperial Institute
FIL	Fellow, Institute of Linguists
FILA	Fellow, Institute of Landscape Architects
FILDM	Fellow, Institute of Logistics and Distribution Management
FilDr	Doctor of Philosophy
FILog	Fellow, Institute of Logistics
FILT	Fellow, Institute of Logistics and Transport
FIM	Fellow, Institute of Materials (formerly Institute of Metals)
FIMA	Fellow, Institute of Mathematics and its Applications
FIMarE	Fellow, Institute of Marine Engineers
FIMarEst	Fellow, Institute of Marine Engineering, Science and Technology
FIMBRA	Financial Intermediaries, Managers and Brokers Regulatory Association
FIMC	Fellow, Institute of Management Consultants
FIMechE	Fellow, Institution of Mechanical Engineers
FIMF	Fellow, Institute of Metal Finishing
FIMfgE	Fellow, Institution of Manufacturing Engineers
FIMFT	Fellow, Institute of Maxillo-Facial Technology
FIMgt	Fellow, Institute of Management
FIMH	Fellow, Institute of Material Handling; Fellow, Institute of Military History
FIMI	Fellow, Institute of Motor Industry
FIMinE	Fellow, Institute of Mining Engineers
FIMIT	Fellow, Institute of Musical Instrument Technology
FIMLS	Fellow, Institute of Medical and Laboratory Sciences (now FIBMS)
FIMM	Fellow, Institution of Mining and Metallurgy
FIMMM	Fellow, Institute of Materials, Minerals and Mining
FIMS	Fellow, Institute of Mathematical Statistics
FIMT	Fellow, Institute of the Motor Trade
FIMTA	Fellow, Institute of Municipal Treasurers and Accountants
fin	finance; financial
FInstAA	Fellow, Institute of Administrative Accountants
FInstAM	Fellow, Institute of Administrative Management
FInstCES	Fellow, Institution of Civil Engineering Surveyors
FInstCS	Fellow, Institute of Chartered Secretaries
FInstD	Fellow, Institute of Directors
FInstE	Fellow, Institute of Energy (formerly FInstF)
FInstF	Fellow, Institute of Fuel (now FInstE)
FInstFF	Fellow, Institute of Freight Forwarders
FInstGasE	Fellow, Institution of Gas Engineers
FInstGeol	Fellow, Institute of Geologists
FInstHE	Fellow, Institution of Highway Engineers
FInstLEx	Fellow, Institute of Legal Executives
FInstM	Fellow, Institute of Marketing (now FCIM)
FInstMC	Fellow, Institute of Measurement and Control
FInstMSM	Fellow, Institute of Marketing and Sales Management
FInstNDT	Fellow, Institute of Non-Destructive Testing
FInstP	Fellow, Institute of Physics
FInstPet	Fellow, Institute of Petroleum
FInstPS	Fellow, Institute of Purchasing and Supply (now FCIPS)
FInstSMM	Fellow, Institute of Sales and Marketing Management
FInstT	Fellow, Institute of Taxation (now FCInstT)
FInstTT	Fellow, Institute of Travel and Tourism
FINucE	Fellow, Institute of Nuclear Engineers
FIOA	Fellow, Institute of Acoustics
FIOB	Fellow, Institute of Building
FIOP	Fellow, Institute of Printing
FIOSc	Fellow, Institute of Optical Science
FIOSH	Fellow, Institute of Occupational Safety and Health
FIP	Fellow, Institute of Packaging; Fellow, Australian Institute of Petroleum
FIPA	Fellow, Institute of Public Administration; Fellow, Institute of Practitioners in Advertising; Fellow, Insolvency Practitioners' Association
FIPD	Fellow, Institute of Personnel and Development (now FCIPD)
FIPG	Fellow, Institute of Professional Goldsmiths
FIPHE	Fellow, Institution of Public Health Engineers
FIPI	Fellow, Institute of Professional Investigators
FIPlantE	Fellow, Institute of Plant Engineers
FIPM	Fellow, Institute of Personnel Management (now FCIPD)
FIPR	Fellow, Institute of Public Relations
FIProdE	Fellow, Institute of Production Engineers (now FIEE)
FIPS	Fellow, Institute of Purchasing and Supply
FIPSM	Fellow, Institute of Physical Sciences in Medicine
FIQ	Fellow, Institute of Quarrying
FIQA	Fellow, Institute of Quality Assurance
FIRE	Fellow, Institution of Radio Engineers
FIRI	Fellow, Institution of the Rubber Industry
FIRM	Fellow, Institute of Risk Management
FIRSE	Fellow, Institute of Railway Signalling Engineers
FIRTE	Fellow, Institute of Road Transport Engineers
FIS	Fellow, Institute of Stationers
FISA	Fédération Internationale des Sociétés d'Aviron

FISE	Fellow, Institute of Sanitary Engineers
FISITA	Fédération Internationale des Sociétés d'Ingénieurs des Techniques de l'Automobile
FISM	Fellow, Institute of Supervisory Managers
FISP	Fellow, Institute of Sales Promotion
FISTC	Fellow, Institute of Scientific and Technical Communicators
FISTD	Fellow, Imperial Society of Teachers of Dancing
FIStructE	Fellow, Institution of Structural Engineers
FISVA	Fellow, Incorporated Society of Valuers and Auctioneers
FITA	Fellow, International Archery Federation
FITD	Fellow, Institute of Training and Development (now FIPD)
FIWEM	Fellow, Institution of Water and Environmental Management (now FCIWEM)
FIWES	Fellow, Insititute of Water Engineers and Scientists
FIWSc	Fellow, Institute of Wood Science
FKC	Fellow, King's College London
FL	Florida
FLA	Fellow, Library Association (now FCLIP)
FLAS	Fellow, Land Agents Society
FLCM	Fellow, London College of Music
FLCOM	Fellow, London College of Osteopathic Medicine
FLI	Fellow, Landscape Institute
FLIA	Fellow, Life Insurance Association
FLS	Fellow, Linnean Society
Flt	Flight
Flt Lt	Flight Lieutenant
FMA	Fellow, Museums Association
FMedSci	Fellow, Academy of Medical Sciences
FMES	Fellow, Minerals Engineering Society
FMPA	Fellow, Master Photographers Association
FMS	Fellow, Institute of Management Services; Fellow of the Medical Society; Fellow, Manorial Society
FNAEA	Fellow, National Association of Estate Agents
Fndn	Foundation
fndr	founder
FNI	Fellow, Nautical Institute
FNIAB	Fellow, National Institute of Agricultural Botany
FO	Foreign Office
FODA	Fellow, Overseas Doctors' Association
FOR	Fellowship of Operational Research
FPA	Family Practitioners' Association
FPC	Family Practitioner Committee
FPCA	Fellow of Practising and Commercial Accountants
FPCS	Fellow, Property Consultants' Society
FPEA	Fellow, Physical Education Association
FPhS	Fellow, Philosophical Society of England
FPMI	Fellow, Pensions Management Institute
FPMS	Institution of Professionals, Managers and Specialists
FPRI	Fellow, Plastics and Rubber Institute
FPS	Fellow, Philological Society of Great Britain
FPWI	Fellow, Permanent Way Institution
FRACDS	Fellow, Royal Australian College of Dental Surgeons
FRACGP	Fellow, Royal Australian College of General Practitioners
FRACI	Fellow, Royal Australian Chemical Institute
FRACMA	Fellow, Royal Australian College of Medical Administrators
FRACO	Fellow, Royal Australian College of Ophthalmologists
FRACP	Fellow, Royal Australasian College of Physicians
FRACR	Fellow, Royal Australasian College of Radiologists
FRACS	Fellow, Royal Australasian College of Surgeons
FRAD	Fellow, Royal Academy of Dancing
FRAeS	Fellow, Royal Aeronautical Society
FRAgS	Fellow, Royal Agricultural Societies
FRAI	Fellow, Royal Anthropological Institute
FRAIA	Fellow, Royal Australian Institute of Architects
FRAIC	Fellow, Royal Architectural Institute of Canada
FRAM	Fellow, Royal Academy of Music
FRANZCP	Fellow, Royal Australian and New Zealand College of Psychiatrists
FRANZCR	Fellow, Royal Australian and New Zealand College of Radiologists
FRAS	Fellow, Royal Astronomical Society; Fellow, Royal Asiatic Society
FRASE	Fellow, Royal Agricultural Society of England
FRBS	Fellow, Royal Botanic Society; Fellow, Royal Society of British Sculptors
FRCA	Fellow, Royal College of Art; Fellow, Royal College of Anaesthetists (formerly FFARCS)
FRCD(C)	Fellow, Royal College of Dentists of Canada
FRCGP	Fellow, Royal College of General Practitioners
FRCM	Fellow, Royal College of Music
FRCN	Fellow, Royal College of Nursing
FRCO	Fellow, Royal College of Organists
FRCO(CHM)	Fellow, Royal College of Organists with Diploma in Choir Training

FRCOG	Fellow, Royal College of Obstetricians and Gynaecologists
FRCOphth	Fellow, Royal College of Ophthalmologists (formerly FCOphth)
FRCP	Fellow, Royal College of Physicians
FRCPA	Fellow, Royal College of Pathologists of Australia
FRCPath	Fellow, Royal College of Pathologists
FRCP(C)	Fellow, Royal College of Physicians of Canada
FRCPCH	Fellow, Royal College of Paediatrics and Child Health
FRCPE	Fellow, Royal College of Physicians of Edinburgh
FRCPEd	Fellow, Royal College of Physicians of Edinburgh
FRCPGlas	Fellow, Royal College of Physicians and Surgeons of Glasgow
FRCPI	Fellow, Royal College of Physicians in Ireland
FRCPS	Fellow, Royal College of Physicians and Surgeons of Glasgow
FRCPsych	Fellow, Royal College of Psychiatrists
FRCR	Fellow, Royal College of Radiologists
FRCS	Fellow, Royal College of Surgeons; Fellow, Royal Commonwealth Society (formerly Royal Empire Society)
FRCSEd	Fellow, Royal College of Surgeons Edinburgh
FRCSGlas	Fellow, Royal College of Physicians and Surgeons of Glasgow
FRCSI	Fellow, Royal College of Surgeons in Ireland
FRCVS	Fellow, Royal College of Veterinary Surgeons
FREconS	Fellow, Royal Economic Society
FREng	Fellow, Royal Academy of Engineering
FRES	Fellow, Royal Entomological Society
FRG	Federal Republic of Germany
FRGS	Fellow, Royal Geographical Society
FRHistS	Fellow, Royal Historical Society
FRHS	Fellow, Royal Horticultural Society
FRIA	Fellow, Royal Institute of Arbitrators
FRIAS	Fellow, Royal Incorporation of Architects in Scotland
FRIBA	Fellow, Royal Institute of British Architects
FRIC	Fellow, Royal Institute of Chemistry (now FRSC)
FRICS	Fellow, Royal Institute of Chartered Surveyors
FRIN	Fellow, Royal Institute of Navigation
FRINA	Fellow, Royal Institution of Naval Architects
FRIPH	Fellow, Royal Institute of Public Health
FRIPHH	Fellow, Royal Institute of Public Health and Hygiene
FRMetS	Fellow, Royal Meteorological Society
FRMS	Fellow, Royal Microscopical Society
FRNCM	Fellow, Royal Northern College of Music
FRNS	Fellow, Royal Numismatic Society
FRPharmS	Fellow, Royal Pharmaceutical Society
FRPI	Fellow, Institute of Rubber and Plastics Industry
FRPMS	Fellow, Royal Postgraduate Medical School
FRPS	Fellow, Royal Photographic Society
FRPSL	Fellow, Royal Philatelic Society, London
FRS	Fellow, Royal Society
FRSA	Fellow, Royal Society of Arts
FRSAIre	Fellow, Royal Society of Antiquaries of Ireland
FRSAMD	Fellow, Royal Scottish Academy of Music and Drama
FRSBS	Fellow, Royal Society of British Sculptors
FRSC	Fellow, Royal Society of Canada; Fellow, Royal Society of Chemistry
FRSCM	Fellow, Royal School of Church Music
FRSE	Fellow, Royal Society of Edinburgh
FRSGS	Fellow, Royal Scottish Geographical Society
FRSH	Fellow of the Royal Society of Health
FRSL	Fellow, Royal Society of Literature
FRSM	Fellow, Royal Society of Medicine
FRSNZ	Fellow, Royal Society of New Zealand
FRSS	Fellow, Royal Statistical Society
FRSSA	Fellow, Royal Scottish Society of Arts (Science and Technology)
FRSTM&H	Fellow, Royal Society of Tropical Medicine and Health
FRTPI	Fellow, Royal Town Planning Institute
FRTS	Fellow, Royal Television Society
FRVA	Fellow, Rating and Valuation Association
FRVC	Fellow, Royal Veterinary College
FRZS	Fellow, Royal Zoological Society
FSA	Fellow, Society of Antiquaries; Financial Services Authority (formerly SIB)
FSA Scot	Fellow, Society of Antiquaries of Scotland
FSAA	Fellow, Society of Incorporated Accountants and Auditors
FSAE	Fellow, Society of Arts Education
FSAI	Fellow, Society of Architectural Illustrators
FSALS	Fellow, Society of Advanced Legal Studies
FSCA	Fellow, Society of Company and Commercial Accountants
FScotvec	Fellow, Scottish Vocational Educational Council
FSDC	Fellow, Society of Dyers and Colourists
FSE	Fellow, Society of Engineers
FSF	Fellow, Institute of Shipping and Forwarding Agents
FSG	Fellow, Society of Genealogists
FSGD	Fellow, Society of Garden Designers

FSI	Fellow, Royal Institution of Chartered Surveyors (see also FRICS); Fellow, Securities Institute
FSIA	Fellow, Society of Industrial Artists
FSIAD	Fellow, Society of Industrial Artists and Designers (now FCSD)
FSLAET	Fellow, Society of Licensed Aircraft Engineers and Technologists
FSLGD	Fellow, Society for Landscape and Garden Designs
FSMPTE	Fellow, Society of Motion Pictures and Television Engineers (USA)
FSNAME	Fellow, American Society of Naval Architects and Marine Engineers
FSPI	Fellow, Society of Practitioners of Insolvency (now FABRP)
FSRP	Fellow, Society for Radiological Protection
FSS	Fellow, Royal Statistical Society (now CStat)
FSSP	Priestly Fraternity of St Peter
FSTD	Fellow, Society of Typographical Designers
FSUT	Fellow, Society for Underwater Technology
FSVA	Fellow, Incorporated Society of Valuers and Auctioneers
FT	Financial Times
FTC	Flying Training Command
FTCL	Fellow, Trinity College of Music, London
FTI	Fellow, Textile Institute
FTII	Fellow, Institute of Taxation
FTMA	Fellow, Telecommunications Managers' Association (now FCMA)
FTS	Fellow, Tourism Society
Fus	Fusiliers
FVI	Fellow, Valuers Institution
FWA	Fellow, World Academy of Arts and Sciences
FWCMD	Fellow, Welsh College of Music and Drama
FWeldI	Fellow, Welding Institute
FZS	Fellow, Zoological Society

G

g	great
Ga	Georgia
GA	Geologists' Association; Georgia
Gall	Gallery
GAPAN	Guild of Air Pilots and Air Navigators
GATT	General Agreement on Tariffs and Trade
GB	Great Britain
GBA	Governing Bodies Association
GBE	Knight/Dame Grand Cross of the Order of the British Empire
GBSM	Graduate, Birmingham and Midland Institute School of Music
GC	George Cross
GCB	Knight/Dame Grand Cross of the Order of the Bath
GCBS	General Council of British Shipping
GCGI	Graduate, City and Guilds of London Institute
GCH	Knight Grand Cross of the Hanoverian Order
GCHQ	Government Communications Headquarters
GCIE	Knight/Dame Grand Commander of the Order of the Indian Empire
GCLJ	Grand Cross of St Lazarus of Jerusalem
GCMG	Knight/Dame Grand Cross of the Order of St Michael and St George
GCON	Grand Cross of the Order of the Niger
GCSE	General Certificate in Secondary Education
GCSG	Knight Grand Cross of the Order of St Gregory the Great
GCSI	Knight Grand Commander of the Order of the Star of India
GCSJ	Knight Grand Cross of Justice of the Order of St John of Jerusalem
GCStJ	Bailiff/Dame Grand Cross of the Order of St John of Jerusalem
GCVO	Knight/Dame Grand Cross of the Royal Victorian Order
gda	granddaughter
GDBA	Guide Dogs for the Blind Association
GDC	General Dental Council
gdns	gardens
GDPA	General Dental Practitioners' Association
GDR	German Democratic Republic
Gds	Guards
GDST	Girls' Day School Trust (formerly GPDST)
Gen	General
Ger	Germany
gf	grandfather
ggda	great granddaughter (and so forth)
ggs	great grandson (and so forth)
GHQ	General Headquarters
GIFireE	Graduate, Institute of Fire Engineers
GIMechE	Graduate, Institution of Mechanical Engineers
GKT	Guy's, King's College and St Thomas' Hospitals Medical and Dental School (formerly UMDS)
GLA	Greater London Authority

GLAA	Greater London Arts Association (now GLAB)
GLAB	Greater London Arts Board (formerly GLAA)
GLC	Greater London Council
Glos	Gloucestershire
GLR	Greater London Radio
GM	George Medal; genetically modified
gm	grandmother
GMB	Great Master of the Bath; (Union for) General, Municipal, Boilermakers
GMBATU	General Municipal Boilermakers and Allied Trade Unions (now GMB)
GMC	General Medical Council
GME	General Ministerial Examination
GMIE	Grand Master of the Order of the Indian Empire
GMMG	Grand Master of the Order of St Michael and St George
GMSI	Grand Master of the Order of the Star of India
GMWU	General and Municipal Workers' Union (now GMB)
gn	great nephew; great niece
GO	Grand Officier (de la Légion d'Honneur)
GOC	General Officer Commanding
GOC-in-C	General Officer Commanding-in-Chief
govr	governor
Govt	Government
GP	General Practitioner; General Practice
gp	group
Gp Capt	Group Captain
GPDST	Girls' Public Day School Trust (now GDST)
GPMU	Graphical, Paper and Media Union
GPO	General Post Office
grad	graduate; graduated
GRCM	Graduate, Royal College of Music
GRSM	Graduate, Royal Schools of Music
GS	General Staff; Grammar School
gs	grandson
GSA	Girls' Schools Association
GSM	General Service Medal; Guildhall School of Music and Drama
GSO	General Staff Officer
Gt	Great
GTCL	Graduate, Trinity College of Music, London
Gtr	Greater
Guy's	Guy's Hospital
GWR	Great Western Railway

H

h	heir
ha	heir apparent
HA	Health Authority; Historical Association
HAA	Heavy Anti-Aircraft
HAC	Honourable Artillery Company
Hants	Hampshire
HBM	His/Her Britannic Majesty
hc	*honoris causa*
HCF	Hon Chaplain to the Forces
HCIMA	Hotel, Catering and Institutional Management Association
HCITB	Hotel and Catering Industry Training Board
HD	home defence; honourable discharge; (51st) Highland Division
HDE	Higher Diploma in Education
HDipEd	Higher Diploma in Education
HDip in Ed	Honorary Diploma in Education
HE	His/Her Excellency; Higher Education
HEFCE	Higher Education Funding Council of England
HEQC	Higher Education Quality Council
Herefords	Herefordshire
Herts	Hertfordshire
HESIN	Higher Education Support for Industry in the North
HFEA	Human Fertilisation and Embryology Authority
HG	Home Guard
HGTAC	Home Grown Timber Advisory Committee
HH	His/Her Highness; His Holiness
HHA	Historic Houses Association
HI	Hawaii
high cmmr	high commissioner
HIH	His/Her Imperial Highness
HIllH	His/Her Illustrious Highness
HIM	His/Her Imperial Majesty
Hist	Historical
HKIA	Member, Hong Kong Institute of Architects
Hldgs	Holdings
HLI	Highland Light Infantry

ind	independent
Inf	Infantry
info	information
INSEAD	Institut Européen d'Administration des Affaires
inspr	inspector
Inst	Institute
Instn	Institution
instr	instructor
Insur	Insurance
int	international
IOC	International Olympic Committee
IOD	Institute of Directors
IOM	Isle of Man
IOW	Isle of Wight
IPA	Institute of Practitioners in Advertising; Insolvency Practitioners' Association
IPC	International Publishing Corporation
IPCS	Institution of Professional Civil Servants
IPFA	Member/Associate, Chartered Institute of Public Finance and Accountancy
IPG	Independent Publishers' Guild; Industrial Painters' Group
IPHE	Institution of Public Health Engineers
IPI	Institute of Patentees and Inventors
IPM	Institute of Personnel Management
IPMS	Institute of Professionals, Managers and Specialists (formerly IPCS)
IPPA	Independent Programme Producers' Association
IPPF	International Planned Parenthood Federation
IPPR	Institute of Public Policy Research
IPR	Institute of Public Relations (now CIPR)
IPRA	International Public Relations Association
IProdE	Institute of Production Engineers
IPS	Indian Political Service
IPSA	International Political Science Association
IPT	Industry and Parliament Trust
IPU	Inter-Parliamentary Union
IQA	Institute of Quality Assurance
Ir	Irish
IRA	Irish Republican Army
IRC	Industrial Re-organisation Corporation
IRE	Indian Corps of Royal Engineers; Institute of Radio Engineers (USA)
IRN	Independent Radio News
IRRV	Institute of Revenues, Rating and Valuation
Is	Island(s)
ISBA	Incorporated Society of British Advertisers
ISC	Indian Staff Corps; Imperial Service College; Independent Schools' Council (formerly ISJC)
ISCO	Independent Schools Careers Organisation
ISE	Indian Service of Engineers
ISI	International Statistical Institute
ISID	International Society of Interior Design
ISIS	Independent Schools Information Service
ISJC	Independent Schools Joint Council (now ISC)
ISM	Imperial Service Medal; (Member/Associate) Incorporated Society of Musicians
ISO	Imperial Service Order; International Standards Organisation
ISOCARP	International Society of City and Regional Planning
ISP	Institute of Sales Promotion; International Study Programme
ISPP	International Society of Political Psychology
ISSC	International Social Science Council
IStructE	Institution of Structural Engineers
ISVA	Incorporated Society of Valuers and Auctioneers
IT	Information Technology
ITA	Independent Television Authority
ITC	Independent Television Commission
ITCA	Independent Television Companies Association
ITN	Independent Television News
ITU	International Telecommunications Union
ITV	Independent Television
ITVA	Independent Television Association
IUCN	International Union for the Conservation of Nature and Natural Resources
IUPAC	International Union of Pure and Applied Chemistry
IUPAP	International Union of Pure and Applied Physics
IUTAM	International Union of Theoretical and Applied Mechanics
IVF	In Vitro Fertilisation
IWEM	Institution of Water and Environmental Management
IWS	International Wool Secretariat
IY	Imperial Yeomanry
IYRU	International Yacht Racing Union

J

JACT	Joint Association of Classical Teachers
JAG	Judge Advocate General
JCD	Doctor of Canon Law (Juris Canonici Doctor)
JCR	Junior Common Room; Junior Combination Room (Cambridge)
JD	Doctor of Jurisprudence
JDipMA	Joint Diploma in Management Accounting Services
JETRO	Japan External Trade Organisation
Jl	Journal
JMB	Joint Matriculation Board
JMN	Johan Mangku Negara (Malaysia)
JP	Justice of the Peace
jr	junior
JSDC	Joint Services Defence College
jsdc	Qualified at Joint Service Defence College
JSM	Johan Seita Mahkota (Malaysia)
JSSC	Joint Services Staff College
jssc	Qualified at Joint Services Staff College
jt	joint
jtly	jointly

K

k	killed
ka	killed in action
KAR	King's African Rifles
KASG	Knightly Association of St George the Martyr
KBE	Knight Commander of the Order of the British Empire
KC	King's Counsel
KCB	Knight Commander of the Order of the Bath
KCH	King's College Hospital
KCHS	Knight Commander of the Order of the Holy Sepulchre
KCIE	Knight Commander of the Order of the Indian Empire
KCL	King's College London
KCMG	Knight Commander of the Order of St Michael and St George
KCS	King's College School
KCSG	Knight Commander of the Order of St Gregory the Great
KCSI	Knight Commander of the Order of the Star of India
KCVO	Knight Commander of the Royal Victorian Order
KDG	King's Dragoon Guards
KEH	King Edward's Horse (Regiment)
KEO	King Edward's Own
KG	Knight of the Order of the Garter
KGStJ	Knight of Grace of the Order of St John of Jerusalem
KGVO	King George V's Own
KHC	Honorary Chaplain to the King
KHDS	Honorary Dental Surgeon to the King
KHP	Honorary Physician to the King
KHS	Honorary Surgeon to the King; Knight of the Order of the Holy Sepulchre
K-i-H	Kaisar-i-Hind (Emperor of India, medal)
KJStJ	Knight of Justice of the Order of St John of Jerusalem
KM	Knight of Malta
KMN	Kesatria Mangku Negara (Malaysian decoration)
KORR	King's Own Royal Regiment
KOSB	King's Own Scottish Borderers
KOYLI	King's Own Yorkshire Light Infantry
KP	Knight of the Order of St Patrick
KPFSM	King's Police and Fire Service Medal
KPM	King's Police Medal
KRI	King's Royal Irish
KRRC	King's Royal Rifle Corps
KS	Kansas
KSG	Knight of the Order of St Gregory the Great
KSLI	King's Shropshire Light Infantry
KStJ	Knight of the Order of St John of Jerusalem
KT	Knight of the Order of the Thistle
kt	knighted (Knight Bachelor)
KY	Kentucky

L

L	Labour
LA	Los Angeles; Louisiana
La	Louisiana
LAA	Light Anti-Aircraft
Lab	Labour; Laboratory

Lab Co-op	Labour and Co-operative
LAC	Leading Aircraftsman
LACOTS	Local Authorities' Co-ordination of Trading Standards Committee
LACSAB	Local Authorities' Conditions of Service Advisory Board
LAH	Licentiate, Apothecaries Hall, Dublin
LAMDA	London Academy of Music and Dramatic Art
LAMSAC	Local Authorities' Management Services and Computer Committee
LAMTPI	Legal Association Member, Town Planning Institute (now LMRTPI)
Lancs	Lancashire
LAPADA	London and Provincial Antique Dealers' Association
LBC	London Broadcasting Company
LBIPP	Licentiate, British Institute of Professional Photographers
LCC	London County Council
LCDS	London Contemporary Dance Studio
LCDT	London Contemporary Dance Theatre
LCGI	Licentiate, City and Guilds of London Institute
LCh	Licentiate in Surgery
LCJ	Lord Chief Justice
LCP	Licentiate, College of Preceptors
LDDC	London Docklands Development Corporation
ldr	leader
LDS	Licentiate in Dental Surgery
LDSRCS	Licentiate in Dental Surgery, Royal College of Surgeons
LDV	Local Defence Volunteers
LEA	Local Education Authority
LEB	London Electricity Board
lectr	lecturer
Leics	Leicestershire
LEPRA	Leprosy Relief Association
LèsL	Licencié ès Lettres
LF	Land Forces
LG	Life Guards; Lady Companion of the Order of the Garter
LGSM	Licentiate, Guildhall School of Music and Drama
LH	Light Horse
LHD	Litterarum Humaniorum Doctor
LHSM	Licentiate, Institute of Health Services Management
LI	Light Infantry
Lib	Liberal
LIBC	Lloyd's Insurance Brokers' Committee
Lib Dem	Liberal Democrat
Lieut	Lieutenant
LIFFE	London International Financial Futures and Options Exchange
Lincs	Lincolnshire
LIOB	Licentiate, Institute of Building
lit	literature
LittD	Doctor of Letters (Cambridge and Dublin)
LLA	Lady Literate in Arts
LLB	Bachelor of Laws
LLC	Limited Liability Company
LLCM	Licentiate, London College of Music
LLD	Doctor of Laws
LLL	Licenciate in Laws
LLM	Master of Laws
LLP	Limited Liability Partnership
LM	Licentiate in Midwifery
LMA	League Managers' Association
LMBC	Lady Margaret Boat Club (St John's College, Cambridge)
LMCC	Licentiate of Medical Council of Canada
LMH	Lady Margaret Hall (Oxford)
LMRTPI	Legal Member, Royal Town Planning Institute
LMSSA	Licentiate in Medicine and Surgery, Society of Apothecaries
LNat&U	Liberal National and Unionist
LNER	London and North East Railway
LPh	Licentiate in Philosophy
LPO	London Philharmonic Orchestra
LPTB	London Passenger Transport Board
LRAM	Licentiate, Royal Academy of Music
LRCP	Licentiate, Royal College of Physicians
LRCPE	Licentiate, Royal College of Physicians of Edinburgh
LRCPI	Licentiate, Royal College of Physicians of Ireland
LRCS	Licentiate, Royal College of Surgeons of England; League of Red Cross Societies
LRCSE	Licentiate, Royal College of Surgeons of Edinburgh
LRCSI	Licentiate, Royal College of Surgeons in Ireland
LRFPS	Licentiate, Royal Faculty of Physicians and Surgeons (Glasgow)
LRIBA	Licentiate, Royal Institute of British Architects
LRPS	Licentiate, Royal Photographic Society
LRSC	Licentiate, Royal Society of Chemistry
LRT	London Regional Transport
LSA	Licentiate, Society of Apothecaries

LSC	Learning and Skills Council
LSCA	London Society of Chartered Accountants
LSE	London School of Economics
LSHTM	London School of Hygiene and Tropical Medicine
LSO	London Symphony Orchestra
Lt	Lieutenant
LTA	Lawn Tennis Association
LTC	Lawn Tennis Club; Low Temperature Carbonization
LTCL	Licentiate, Trinity College of Music, London
Lt-Col	Lieutenant-Colonel
Ltcy	Lieutenancy
Ltd	Limited
LTE	London Transport Executive (now LRT)
Lt-Gen	Lieutenant-General
LTh	Licentiate in Theology
LU	Liberal Unionist
LVO	Lieutenant of the Royal Victorian Order
LWT	London Weekend Television

M

m	married; marriage
M&A	Mergers and Acquisitions
MA	Master of Arts; Military Assistant; Massachusetts
MAAEM	Member, American Association of Electrodiagnostic Medicine
MAAF	Mediterranean Allied Air Forces
MAAT	Member, Association of Accounting Technicians
MABRP	Member, Association of Business Recovery Professionals
MACC	Member, American College of Cardiology
MACE	Member, Association of Conference Executives; Member, Association of Consulting Engineers
MACM	Member, Association of Computing Machines
MACP	Member, Association of Child Psychotherapists
MACS	Member, American Chemical Society
MAE	Member, Academy of Experts (formerly MBAE)
MAFF	Ministry of Agriculture, Fisheries and Food
MAI	Master of Engineering
MAIAA	Member, American Institute of Aeronautics and Astronautics
MAIE	Member, British Association of Industrial Editors (now MCB)
Maj	Major
Maj-Gen	Major-General
mangr	manager
MAP	Ministry of Aircraft Production
MAPM	Member, Association of Project Managers
MaPS	Member, Association of Planning Services
MArch	Master of Architecture
Marq	Marquess
MASAE	Member, American Society of Agricultural Engineers
MASCE	Member, American Society of Civil Engineers
MASME	Member, American Society of Mechanical Engineers
Mass	Massachusetts
MB	Bachelor of Medicine
MBA	Master of Business Administration
MBAC	Member, British Association of Chemists
MBAE	Member, British Academy of Experts (now MAE)
MBC	Metropolitan/Municipal Borough Council
MBCS	Member, British Computer Society
MBE	Member of the Order of the British Empire
MBEDA	Member, Bureau of European Design
MBFR	Mutual and Balanced Force Reductions
MBHI	Member, British Horological Institute
MBIM	Member, British Institute of Management (now MIMgt)
MBIPP	Member, British Institute of Professional Photography
MBISC	Member, British Institute of Sports Coaches
MBKS	Member, British Kinematograph Society
MBO	Management Buyout
MBOU	Member, British Ornithologists' Union
MBPsS	Member, British Psychological Society
MBSG	Member, British Society of Gastroenterology
MC	Military Cross
MCAM	Member, Institute of Communications, Advertising and Marketing
MCB	Master of Clinical Biochemistry; Member, British Association of Communicators in Business (formerly MAIE)
MCC	Marylebone Cricket Club; Metropolitan County Council
MCCI	Manchester Chamber of Commerce and Industry
MCD	Master of Civic Design
MCFA	Member, Cookery and Food Association
MCGI	Member, City and Guilds of London Institute
MChir	Master in Surgery
MChOrth	Master of Orthopaedic Surgery

MCIA	Member, Chartered Institute of Arbitrators
MCIArb	Member, Chartered Institute of Arbitrators
MCIB	Member, Chartered Institute of Banking
MCIBSE	Member, Chartered Institution of Building Services Engineers
MCIH	Member, Chartered Institute of Housing (formerly MIH)
MCII	Member, Chartered Insurance Institute
MCIJ	Member, Chartered Institute of Journalists
MCIM	Member, Chartered Institute of Marketing
MCIOB	Member, Chartered Institute of Building
MCIPD	Member, Chartered Institute of Personnel and Development
MCIPR	Member, Chartered Institute of Public Relations
MCIPS	Member, Chartered Institute of Purchasing and Supply
MCIT	Member, Chartered Institute of Transport
MCIWEM	Member, Chartered Institution of Water and Environmental Management (formerly MIWEM)
MCLIP	Member, Chartered Institute of Library and Information Professionals
MCMB	Molecular and Cellular Medicine Board
MCMI	Member, Chartered Institute of Management (formerly MIMgt)
MCom	Master of Commerce
MConsE	Member, Association of Consulting Engineers
MCOphth	Member, College of Ophthalmologists (formerly Faculty of Ophthalmologists, FacOph, and Ophthalmic Society of UK, OSUK)
MCP	Member of Colonial Parliament; Member, College of Preceptors
MCPath	Member, College of Pathologists
MCPCH	Member, College of Paediatrics and Child Health
MCPS	Member, College of Physicians and Surgeons
MCSD	Member, Chartered Society of Designers
MCSP	Member, Chartered Society of Physiotherapy
MCT	Member, Association of Corporate Treasurers
MD	Doctor of Medicine; Maryland
md	managing director
MDC	Metropolitan District Council
MDes	Master of Design
m dis	marriage dissolved
MDiv	Master of Divinity
MDS	Master of Dental Surgery
ME	Middle East; Maine
MEAF	Middle East Air Force
MEC	Member, Executive Council
MECAS	Middle East Centre for Arab Studies
mech	mechanical; mechanised
MECI	Member, Institute of Employment Consultants
MEd	Master of Education
Med	medical; medicine; Mediterranean
MEF	Mediterranean Expeditionary Force
MEI	Member, Energy Institute
MEIC	Member, Engineering Institute of Canada
MELF	Middle East Land Forces
memb	member
Meml	Memorial
MENCAP	Royal Society for Mentally Handicapped Children and Adults
MEP	Member of the European Parliament
MESC	Member, European Society of Cardiology
Met	Metropolitan
MFA	Master of Fine Arts (USA)
MFARCS	Member, Faculty of Anaesthetists, Royal College of Surgeons
MFB	Member, Faculty of Building
MFC	Mastership in Food Control
MFCM	Member, Faculty of Community Medicine (now MFPHM)
MFGDP	Member, Faculty of General Dental Practitioners
MFH	Master of Foxhounds
MFHom	Member, Faculty of Homeopathy
MFOM	Member, Faculty of Occupational Medicine
MFPH	Member, Faculty of Public Health (formerly MFPHM)
MFPHM	Member, Faculty of Public Health Medicine (now MFPH)
MFPHMI	Member, Faculty of Public Health Medicine Royal College of Physicians of Ireland
mfr	manufacturer
mfrg	manufacturing
MGC	Machine Gun Corps
MGDS RCS	Member in General Dental Surgery, Royal College of Surgeons
MGGS	Major-General General Staff
mgmnt	management
MGO	Master-General of the Ordnance
Mgr	Monsignor
MGRA	Major-General Royal Artillery
MH	Military Hospital
MHCIMA	Member, Hotel Catering and Institutional Management Association

MHK	Member of the House of Keys (IOM)
MHM	Masters in Health Management
MHR	Member of the House of Representatives (USA and Australia)
MHRA	Modern Humanities Research Association
MHSM	Member, Institute of Health Services Management
MI	Military Intelligence; Michigan
MIAA	Member, International Advertising Association
MIAeE	Member, Institute of Aeronautical Engineers
MIAM	Member, Institute of Administrative Management
MIBE	Member, Institution of British Engineers
MIBG	Member, Institute of British Geographers
MIBiol	Member, Institute of Biology
MICAS	Member, Institute of Chartered Accountants of Scotland
MICE	Member, Institution of Civil Engineers
MICEI	Member, Institution of Civil Engineers of Ireland
MICFM	Member, Institute of Charity Fundraising Managers
MIChemE	Member, Institution of Chemical Engineers
MICM	Member, Institute of Credit Management
MIConsE	Member, Institute of Consulting Engineers
Middx	Middlesex
MIDM	Member, Institute of Direct Marketing
MIDPM	Member, Institute of Data Processing Management
MIED	Member, Institution of Engineering Design
MIEE	Member, Institution of Electrical Engineers
MIEEE	Member, Institute of Electrical and Electronics Engineers (USA)
MIEI	Member, Institute of Engineering Inspection
MIEIE	Member, Institute of Electronic Incorporated Engineers
MIERE	Member, Institution of Electronic and Radio Engineers
MIES	Member, Institution of Engineers and Shipbuilders, Scotland
MIEx	Member, Institute of Export
MIFA	Member, Institute of Field Archaeologists
MIH	Member, Institute of Housing (now MCIH)
MIHE	Member, Institute of Health Education
MIHort	Member, Institute of Horticulture
MIHT	Member, Institute of Highways and Transportation
MIIA	Member, Institute of Internal Auditors
MIIExE	Member, Institute of Incorporated Executive Engineers
MIIM	Member, Institute of Industrial Managers
MIInfSc	Member, Institute of Information Sciences (now MCLIP)
MIL	Member, Institute of Linguists
Mil	Military
MILDM	Member, Institute of Logistics and Distribution Management
MILE	Member, Institution of Locomotive Engineers
MILog	Member, Institute of Logistics
MIM	Member, Institute of Materials (formerly Institute of Metals)
MIMarE	Member, Institute of Marine Engineers (now MIMarEst)
MIMarEst	Member, Institute of Marine Engineering, Science and Technology
MIMC	Member, Institute of Management Consultants
MIMCE	Member, Institute of Municipal and County Engineers
MIMechE	Member, Institution of Mechanical Engineers
MIMfgE	Member, Institution of Manufacturing Engineers
MIMgt	Member, Institute of Management
MIMI	Member, Institute of the Motor Industry
MIMinE	Member, Institution of Mining Engineers
MIMM	Member, Institution of Mining and Metallurgy
min	minister
MIngF	Member, Danish Engineers' Association
MInstB	Member, Institute of Bankers
MInstD	Member, Institute of Directors
MInstE	Member, Institute of Energy
MInstEnvSci	Member, Institute of Environmental Sciences
MInstF	Member, Institute of Fundraising
MInstGasE	Member, Institution of Gas Engineers
MInstHE	Member, Institution of Highway Engineers
MInstM	Member, Institute of Marketing
MInstMC	Member, Institute of Measurement and Control
MInstMet	Member, Institute of Metals
MInstP	Member, Institute of Physics
MInstPet	Member, Institute of Petroleum
MInstPS	Member, Institute of Purchasing and Supply (now MCIPS)
MInstR	Member, Institute of Refrigeration
MInstTT	Member, Institute of Travel and Tourism
MINucE	Member, Institution of Nuclear Engineers
Miny	Ministry
MIOB	Member, Institute of Building
MIOSH	Member, Institution of Occupational Safety and Health
MIPA	Member, Institution of Practitioners in Advertising; Member, Insolvency Practitioners' Association
MIPD	Member, Institute of Personnel and Development
MIPharmM	Member, Institute of Pharmacy Management
MIPHE	Member, Institute of Public Health Engineers

MIPlantE	Member, Institute of Plant Engineers
MIPM	Member, Institute of Personnel Management
MIPR	Member, Institute of Public Relations
MIProdE	Member, Institute of Production Engineers (now MIMfgE)
MIQ	Member, Institute of Quarrying
MIRA	Motor Industry Research Association
MIRE	Member, Institution of Royal Engineers
MIRS	Member, Investor Relations Society
MIS	Member, Institute of Statisticians
misc	miscellaneous
MISI	Member, Iron and Steel Institute
Miss	Mississippi
MIStructE	Member, Institution of Structural Engineers
MIT	Massachusetts Institute of Technology (USA)
MITD	Member, Institute of Training and Development (now MIPD)
MITI	Member, Institute of Translation and Interpreting
MIWEM	Member, Institution of Water and Environmental Management (now MCIWEM)
mktg	marketing
MLA	Member, Legislative Assembly (Northern Ireland); Modern Language Association; Master in Landscape Architecture
MLC	Member, Legislative Council
MLI	Member, Landscape Institute
MLIA	Member, Life Insurance Association
MLib	Master of Library Science
MLitt	Master of Letters
MLO	Military Liaison Officer
MLS	Master of Library Science
MM	Military Medal
MMC	Monopolies and Mergers Commission
MMet	Master of Metallurgy
MMIM	Member, Malaysian Institute of Management
MMin	Master of Ministry
MMRS	Member, Market Research Society
MMS	Master of Management Services; Member, Institute of Management Services
MMSA	Master of Midwifery, Society of Apothecaries
MMus	Master of Music
MN	Merchant Navy; Minnesota
MNECInst	Member, North East Coast Institution of Engineers and Shipbuilders
MNI	Member, Nautical Institute
MO	Medical Officer; Missouri
MOD	Ministry of Defence
MOH	Medical Officer of Health
MOI	Ministry of Information; Ministry of the Interior
MOMA	Museum of Modern Art
MOP	Ministry of Power
MOS	Ministry of Supply
MP	Member of Parliament
MPA	Master of Public Administration
MPBW	Ministry of Public Building Works
MPH	Master of Public Health
MPhil	Master of Philosophy
MPO	Management and Personnel Office
MPS	Member, Pharmaceutical Society of Great Britain
MR	Master of the Rolls
MRAC	Member, Royal Agricultural College
MRAD	Member, Royal Academy of Dancing
MRad	Master of Radiology
MRAeS	Member, Royal Aeronautical Society
MRAS	Member, Royal Asiatic Society
MRC	Medical Research Council
MRCGP	Member, Royal College of General Practitioners
MRCOG	Member, Royal College of Obstetricians and Gynaecologists
MRCP	Member, Royal College of Physicians
MRCPath	Member, Royal College of Pathologists
MRCPGlas	Member, Royal College of Physicians and Surgeons of Glasgow
MRCPI	Member, Royal College of Physicians of Ireland
MRCPsych	Member, Royal College of Psychiatrists
MRCR	Member, Royal College of Radiologists
MRCS	Member, Royal College of Surgeons
MRCVS	Member, Royal College of Veterinary Surgeons
MRI	Member, Royal Institution
MRIA	Member, Royal Irish Academy
MRIAI	Member, Royal Institute of the Architects of Ireland
MRIC	Member, Royal Institute of Chemistry
MRICS	Member, Royal Institution of Chartered Surveyors
MRIN	Member, Royal Institute of Navigation
MRINA	Member, Royal Institution of Naval Architects
MRIPHH	Member, Royal Institute of Public Health and Hygiene
MRO	Member, Register of Osteopaths
MRPharmS	Member, Royal Pharmaceutical Society
MRS	Market Research Society; Medical Research Society
MRSC	Member, Royal Society of Chemistry
MRSH	Member, Royal Society of Health
MRST	Member, Royal Society of Teachers
MRTPI	Member, Royal Town Planning Institute
MRUSI	Member, Royal United Service Institute for Defence Studies
MRVA	Member, Rating and Valuation Association
MS	Master of Surgery; Manuscript; Master of Science (USA); Mississippi
MSAE	Member, Society of Automotive Engineers (USA)
MSC	Manpower Services Commission
MSc	Master of Science
MScD	Master of Dental Science
MSCI	Member, Society of Chemical Industry
MScL	Member, Society of Construction Law
MSE	Member, Society of Engineers; Master of Science in Engineering (USA)
MSEE	Member, Society of Environmental Engineers
MSF	Manufacturing, Science and Finance Union (formerly ASTMS)
MSI	Member, Securities Institute (formerly member of the Stock Exchange)
MSIA	Member, Society of Industrial Artists
MSIAD	Member, Society of Industrial Artists and Designers
MSM	Meritorious Service Medal
MSocIS	Member, Societé des Ingenieurs et Scientifiques de France
MSocSci	Master of Social Sciences
MSP	Member of Scottish Parliament
MSPI	Member, Society of Practitioners of Insolvency
MSR	Member, Society of Radiographers
MSSCC	Member, Scottish Society of Contamination Control
MSST	Member, Society of Surveying Technicians
MSt	Master of Studies
MSTD	Member, Society of Typographic Designers
MT	Montana
MTAI	Member, Institute of Travel Agents
MTB	Motor Torpedo Boat
MTh	Master of Theology
MTPI	Member, Town Planning Institute
MUniv	Master of the University
MusB	Bachelor of Music
MusD	Doctor of Music (Cambridge)
MusM	Master of Music
MV	Motor Vessel
MVO	Member of the Royal Victorian Order
MVSc	Master of Veterinary Science
MW	Master of Wine
MWB	Metropolitan Water Board
MWeldI	Member, Welding Institute
MY	Motor Yacht

N

N	North; Nationalist
n	nephew; niece
NAAFI	Navy, Army, and Air Force Institutes
NABC	National Association of Boys' Clubs
NAC	National Agriculture Centre
NACF	National Art Collectors' Fund
NACRO	National Association for the Care and Resettlement of Offenders
NADFAS	National Association of Decorative and Fine Arts Societies
NAEB	National Association of Educational Broadcasters
NAG	Northern Army Group
NAHAT	National Association of Health Authorities and Trusts
NAHT	National Association of Head Teachers
NALGO	National and Local Government Officers' Association
NAMH	National Association for Mental Health
NAO	National Audit Office
NAPE	National Association of Primary Education
NAQA	National Association of Quality Assurance in Healthcare (now AQM)
NAS	Naval Air Squadron
NASDAQ	National Association of Securities Dealers Automated Quotations (USA)
NASUWT	National Association of Schoolmasters/Union of Women Teachers
nat	national
NATCS	National Air Traffic Control Services
NATFHE	National Association of Teachers in Further and Higher Education
Nat Lib	National Liberal
NATO	North Atlantic Treaty Organisation

NBL	National Book League
NBPI	National Board for Prices and Incomes
NC	Nautical College; North Carolina
NCA	National Cricket Association; National Certificate of Agriculture
NCB	National Coal Board
NCCI	National Committee for Commonwealth Immigrants
NCCL	National Council for Civil Liberties
NCLC	National Council of Labour Colleges
NCO	Non-Commissioned Officer
NCRI	National Cancer Research Institute (formerly UKCCCR)
NCTJ	National Council for the Training of Journalists
NCVCCO	National Council for Voluntary Child Care Organisations
NCVO	National Council for Voluntary Organisations
NCVQ	National Council for Vocational Qualifications
ND	Diploma in Naturopathy; North Dakota
NDA	National Diploma in Agriculture
NDC	National Defence College
NDD	National Diploma in Dairying; National Diploma in Design
NE	Nebraska
NEAC	New English Art Club
NEAF	Near East Air Force
NEC	National Executive Committee
NEDC	National Economic Development Council
NEDO	National Economic Development Office
NESTA	National Endowment for Science, Technology and the Arts
NERC	Natural Environment Research Council
NFER	National Foundation for Educational Research
NFS	National Fire Service
NFU	National Farmers' Union
NFWI	National Federation of Women's Institutes
NGO	Non-Governmental Organisation
NH	New Hampshire
NHS	National Health Service
NI	Northern Ireland
NICE	National Institute for Health and Clinical Excellence
NICS	Northern Ireland Civil Service
NID	Naval Intelligence Department
NIESR	National Institute of Economic and Social Research
NIH	National Institute of Health (USA)
NILP	Northern Ireland Labour Party
NJ	New Jersey
NLF	National Liberal Federation
NM	New Mexico
NMCU	National Meteorological Co-ordinating Unit Committee
NN	The Niadh Nask (Military Order of the Golden Chain)
Northants	Northamptonshire
Notts	Nottinghamshire
NP	Notary Public
NPQH	National Professional Qualification for Headship
NRA	National Rifle Association
NRDC	National Research Development Corporation
NRPB	National Radiological Protection Board
ns	Graduate of the Royal Naval Staff College, Greenwich
NS	Nova Scotia
NsgMD	Nursing Management Diploma
NSPCC	National Society for the Prevention of Cruelty to Children
NSW	New South Wales
NT	National Theatre
NTDA	National Trade Development Association
NTO	National Training Organisation
NUBE	National Union of Bank Employees (now BIFU)
NUGMW	National Union of General and Municipal Workers
NUI	National University of Ireland
NUJ	National Union of Journalists
NUM	National Union of Mineworkers
NUMAST	National Union of Marine, Aviation, and Shipping Transport Officers
NUPE	National Union of Public Employees
NUR	National Union of Railwaymen
NUS	National Union of Students
NUT	National Union of Teachers
NV	Naamloze Vennootschap (Netherlands); Nevada
NVQ	National Vocational Qualification
NWFP	North West Frontier Province
NY	New York
NYC	New York City
NYSE	New York Stock Exchange
NYU	New York University
NZ	New Zealand
NZEF	New Zealand Expeditionary Force

O

o	only
OA	Officier d'Académie
OAS	Organisation of American States
OB	Order of Barbados
OBE	Officer of the Order of the British Empire
OBStJ	Officer Brother of the Order of St John of Jerusalem
OC	Officer Commanding; Officer of the Order of Canada
OCF	Officiating Chaplain to the Forces
OCR	Oxford and Cambridge and RSA Examination Board
OCS	Officer Cadet School
OCTU	Officer Cadet Training Unit
ODA	Overseas Development Administration
ODI	Overseas Development Institute
ODM	Ministry of Overseas Development
ODPM	Office of the Deputy Prime Minister
OE	Order of Excellence (Guyana)
OECD	Organisation for Economic Co-operation and Development
OEEC	Organisation for European Economic Co-operation
OER	Officers' Emergency Reserve
offr	officer
OFMCap	Order of Friars Minor Capuchin (Franciscans)
OFMConv	Order of Friars Minor Conventual (Franciscans)
OFT	Office of Fair Trading
OGS	Order of the Good Shepherd
OH	Ohio
OIC	Officer in Charge
OJ	Order of Jamaica
OK	Oklahoma
OM	Order of Merit
O&M	Organisation and Method
OMC	Oxford Military College
ON	Order of the Nation (Jamaica)
ONC	Ordinary National Certificate
OND	Ordinary National Diploma
ONZ	Order of New Zealand
O&O	Oriental and Occidental Steamship Company
OP	Observation Post
OPB	Occupational Pensions Board
oppn	opposition
ops	operations
OR	Order of Roraima (Guyana); Oregon
Orch	Orchestra
Orgn	Organisation
ORS	Operational Research Society
ORT	Organisation for Rehabilitation by Training
OSB	Order of St Benedict (Benedictines)
OSC	Graduate of Overseas Staff College
OSCE	Organization for Security and Co-operation in Europe
OSNC	Orient Steam Navigation Company
OSRD	Office of Scientific Research and Development
OStJ	Officer of the Order of St John of Jerusalem
OTC	Officers' Training Corps
OUAC	Oxford University Athletics Club
OUBC	Oxford University Boat Club
OUCA	Oxford University Conservative Association
OUDS	Oxford University Dramatic Society
OUP	Oxford University Press
Oxon	Oxfordshire; of Oxford

P

PA	Personal Assistant; Pennsylvania
pa	per annum
Pa	Pennsylvania
pac	Passed final exam of advanced class Military College of Science
PACT	Producers' Alliance for Cinema and Television
Paiforce	Palestine and Iraq Force
PAO	Prince Albert's Own
Parl	Parliament
Parly	Parliamentary
PBWS	President, British Watercolour Society
PC	Privy Counsellor; Peace Commissioner (Ireland); Parish Council
PCC	Parochial Church Council; Press Complaints Commission
PCFC	Polytechnics and Colleges Funding Council
PCL	Polytechnic of Central London
PCT	Primary Care Trust
PDSA	People's Dispensary for Sick Animals

Abbreviations

Abbreviations

PDTC	Professional Dancers' Training Course Diploma
PE	Procurement Executive; Physical Education
PEI	Prince Edward Island
PEN	International Association of Poets, Playwrights, Editors, Essayists, and Novelists
PEng	Registered Professional Engineer (Canada); Member, Society of Professional Engineers
PEP	Political and Economic Planning
perm	permanent
PFA	Professional Footballers' Association
PFI	Private Finance Initiative
PGA	Professional Golfers' Association
PGCE	Postgraduate Certificate of Education
PHAB	Physically Handicapped and Able-Bodied
PhC	Pharmaceutical Chemist
PhD	Doctor of Philosophy
PhL	Licentiate of Philosophy
PIA	Personal Investment Authority
PIARC	Permanent International Association of Road Congresses
PID	Political Intelligence Department
PIRA	Paper Industries Research Association
PLA	Port of London Authority
plc	public limited company
PLP	Parliamentary Labour Party
PM	Prime Minister
PMD	Program for Management Development (USA)
PMG	Postmaster-General
PMN	Panglima Mangku Negara (Malaysia)
PMO	Principal Medical Officer
PNEU	Parents' National Educational Union
PNG	Papua New Guinea
PO	Pilot Officer; Post Office
POD	Personnel Operations Department
POEU	Post Office Engineering Union
Poly	Polytechnic
P&OSNCo	Peninsular and Oriental Steam Navigation Company
postgrad	postgraduate
POUNC	Post Office Users' National Council
POW	Prisoner of War
PPA	Periodical Publishers Association
PPARC	Particle Physics and Astronomy Research Council (formerly SERC)
PPE	Philosophy, Politics and Economics
PPL	Private Pilot's Licence
PPRA	Past President, Royal Academy
PPRIBA	Immediate Past President, Royal Institute of British Architects
PPRSA	Past President, Royal Scottish Academy
PPS	Parliamentary Private Secretary
PR	Public Relations
PRA	President, Royal Academy
PRC	People's Republic of China
PRCA	Public Relations Consultants Association
PRCS	President, Royal College of Surgeons
PRE	President, Royal Society of Painters, Etchers and Engravers
Preb	Prebendary
Prep	Preparatory
pres	president
prev	previously
PRI	Plastics and Rubber Institute (now part of Inst of Materials)
princ	principal
PRO	Public Relations Officer; Public Records Office
prodn	production
prodr	producer
prods	products
prof	professor
prog	programme
prop	proprietor
Prov	Provost; Provincial
PRS	President, Royal Society
PRWS	President, Royal Society of Painters in Water Colours
PS	Pastel Society
psa	Graduate of RAF Staff College
PSA	President, Society of Antiquaries; Property Services Agency
psc	Staff College Graduate
PSD	Petty Session Division
PSI	Policy Studies Institute
psm	Certificate of the Military School of Music
PSM	President, Society of Miniaturists
PSNC	Pacific Steam Navigation Company
PSO	Principal Staff Officer
PSPA	Professional Sports Photographers' Association

pt	part
PT	Physical Training
PTA	Parent-Teacher Association
PTE	Passenger Transport Executive
ptnr	partner
ptsc	passed Technical Staff College
pt/t	part time
Pty	Proprietary; Party
pub	public
pubns	publications
PWD	Public Works Department
PWO	Prince of Wales' Own
PWR	Pressurised Water Reactor
PYBT	Prince's Youth Business Trust

Q

QAIMNS	Queen Alexandra's Imperial Military Nursing Service
QALAS	Qualified Associate of Land Agents' Society
QARANC	Queen Alexandra's Royal Army Nursing Corps
QARNNS	Queen Alexandra's Royal Naval Nursing Service
QC	Queen's Counsel
QCB	Queen's Commendation for Bravery
QCVSA	Queen's Commendation for Valuable Service in the Air
QDR	Qualified Dispute Resolver
QFSM	Queen's Fire Service Medal for Distinguished Service
QGM	Queen's Gallantry Medal
QHC	Honorary Chaplain to The Queen
QHDS	Honorary Dental Surgeon to The Queen
QHNS	Honorary Nursing Sister to The Queen
QHP	Honorary Physician to The Queen
QHS	Honorary Surgeon to The Queen
Qld	Queensland
QMAAC	Queen Mary's Army Auxiliary Corps
QMC	Queen Mary College, London
QMG	Quartermaster-General
QO	Qualified Officer
QOH	Queen's Own Hussars
QPM	Queen's Police Medal
qqv	qua vide (which see, plural)
QRIH	Queen's Royal Irish Hussars
QS	Quarter Sessions
QSM	Queen's Service Medal (NZ)
QSO	Queen's Service Order (NZ)
qv	quod vide (which see)
QVRM	Queen's Volunteer Reserves Medal
QVRM	Queen's Volunteer Reserves Medal

R

(R)	Reserve
R&A	Royal and Ancient Club (St Andrews)
RA	Royal Artillery; Royal Academician
RAAF	Royal Australian Air Force
RAAMC	Royal Australian Army Medical Corps
RAC	Royal Armoured Corps; Royal Automobile Club; Royal Agricultural College
RACGP	Royal Australian College of General Practitioners
RAChD	Royal Army Chaplains' Department
RACI	Royal Australian Chemical Institute
RACP	Royal Australasian College of Physicians
RACS	Royal Australasian College of Surgeons
RADA	Royal Academy of Dramatic Art
RADC	Royal Army Dental Corps
RAE	Royal Australian Engineers; Royal Aircraft Establishment
RAEC	Royal Army Educational Corps
RAeS	Royal Aeronautical Society
RAF	Royal Air Force
RAF(H)	Royal Air Force Hospital
RAFA	Royal Air Force Association
RAFO	Reserve of Air Force Officers
RAFRO	Royal Air Force Reserve of Officers
RAFVR	Royal Air Force Volunteer Reserve
RAI	Royal Anthropological Institute
RAIA	Royal Australian Institute of Architects
RAIC	Royal Architectural Institute of Canada
RAM	(Member) Royal Academy of Music
RAMC	Royal Army Medical Corps
RAN	Royal Australian Navy

RSAMD	(Diploma of) Royal Scottish Academy of Music and Drama
RSBA	Royal Society of British Artists
RSBS	Royal Society of British Sculptors
RSC	Royal Shakespeare Company; Royal Society of Canada; Royal Society of Chemistry
RSCM	Royal Society of Church Music
RSCN	Registered Sick Children's Nurse
RSE	Royal Society of Edinburgh
RSF	Royal Scots Fusiliers
RSGS	Royal Scottish Geographical Society
RSL	Royal Society of Literature; Returned Services League (Australia)
RSM	Royal Society of Medicine; Royal Society of Music; Regimental Sergeant Major
RSMA	Royal Society of Marine Artists
RSME	Royal School of Military Engineers
RSNC	Royal Society for Nature Conservation
RSPB	Royal Society for the Protection of Birds
RSPCA	Royal Society for the Prevention of Cruelty to Animals
RSPP	Royal Society of Portrait Painters
RSRE	Royal Signals and Radar Establishment
RSS	Royal Statistical Society
RSSPCC	Royal Scottish Society for the Prevention of Cruelty to Children
RSW	(Member) Royal Scottish Society of Painters in Water Colours
Rt	Right
RTC	Royal Tank Corps
RTE	Radio Telefis Eireann
Rt Hon	Right Honourable
RTO	Railway Transport Officer
RTPI	Royal Town Planning Institute
RTR	Royal Tank Regiment
Rt Rev	Right Reverend
RTS	Royal Television Society
RUA	Royal Ulster Academy
RUC	Royal Ulster Constabulary
RUFC	Rugby Union Football Club
RUI	Royal University of Ireland
RUKBA	Royal United Kingdom Beneficent Association
RUR	Royal Ulster Regiment
RUSI	Royal United Services Institute for Defence Studies (formerly Royal United Services Institution)
RVC	Royal Veterinary College
RVO	Regional Veterinary Officer
RWAFF	Royal West African Frontier Force
RWAR	Royal West African Regiment
RWEA	(Member) Royal West of England Academy
RWF	Royal Welch Fusiliers
RWS	Royal Society of Painters in Water Colours
RYA	Royal Yachting Association
RYS	Royal Yacht Squadron
RZS	Royal Zoological Society

S

s	son
S	South; Scotland, Scottish (Peerages)
S4C	Sianel Pedwar Cymru (Channel 4 Wales)
SA	South Africa; South Australia; Société Anonyme; Sociedad Anónima
SAAF	South African Air Force
sac	Qualified at Small Arms Technical Long Course
SAC	Senior Aircraftsman; Scientific Advisory Committee
SACEUR	Supreme Allied Commander Europe
SACLANT	Supreme Allied Commander Atlantic
SACRO	Scottish Association for the Care and Resettlement of Offenders
SACSEA	Supreme Allied Commander, South East Asia
SADG	Société des Architectes Diplômés par le Gouvernement
Salop	Shropshire
SAS	Special Air Service
Sask	Saskatchewan
SASO	Senior Air Staff Officer
SAT	Senior Member Association of Accounting Technicians
SATRO	Science and Technology Regional Organisation
SBAC	Society of British Aircraft Constructors (now Society of British Aerospace Companies)
SBNO	Senior British Naval Officer
SBStJ	Serving Brother of the Order of St John of Jerusalem
SBTD	Society of British Theatre Designers
sc	Student at the Staff College
SC	Senior Counsel (Australia, Guyana, Ireland, South Africa); South

	Carolina
SCAR	Scientific Commission for Antarctic Research
ScD	Doctor of Science (Cambridge and Dublin)
SCF	Senior Chaplain to the Forces
SCGB	Ski Club of Great Britain
Sch	School
sci	science
SCI	Society of Chemical Industry
SCL	Student in Civil Law
SCM	State Certified Midwife
SCONUL	Standing Conference of National and University Libraries
Scot	Scotland; Scottish
SCR	Senior Common Room; Senior Combination Room (Cambridge)
SCUA	Scottish Conservative Unionist Association
SD	South Dakota
SDA	Scottish Diploma in Agriculture
SDLP	Social Democratic and Labour Party
SDP	Social Democratic Party
SEAC	South East Asia Command
SEATAG	South East Asia Trade Advisory Group
sec	secretary
Secdy	Secondary
sec-gen	secretary-general
Sen	Senator
SEN	State Enrolled Nurse
sep	separated
SERC	Science and Engineering Research Council (now EPSRC and PPARC)
SERT	Society of Electronic and Radio Technicians
Serv	Service
SFA	Securities and Futures Authority
SFInstE	Senior Fellow Institute of Energy
SFTA	Society of Film and Television Arts
SG	Solicitor-General
SGM	Sea Gallantry Medal
Sgt	Sergeant
SHA	Secondary Heads Association (now ASCL)
SHAEF	Supreme Headquarters, Allied Expeditionary Force
SHAPE	Supreme Headquarters, Allied Powers Europe
SHHD	Scottish Home and Health Department
SHMIS	The Society of Headmasters and Headmistresses of Independent Schools
SHO	Senior House Officer
SIAD	Society of Industrial Artists and Designers
SIB	Securities and Investments Board (now FSA)
SICOT	Société Internationale de Chirurgie Orthopédique et de Traumatologie
sis	sister
SJ	Society of Jesus (Jesuits)
SJD	Doctor of Juristic Science
SLAET	Society of Licensed Aircraft Engineers and Technologists
SLD	Social and Liberal Democrats
SLDP	Social, Liberal and Democratic Party
slr	solicitor
SM	Service Medal of the Order of Canada; Master of Science (USA); Member, Society of Miniaturists
SME	School of Military Engineering
SMIEEE	Senior Member, Institute of Electrical and Electronic Engineers (USA)
SMMT	Society of Motor Manufacturers and Traders
SMN	Seri Maharaja Mangku Negara (Malaysia)
SMO	Senior Medical Officer; Sovereign Military Order
SMOM	Sovereign Military Order of Malta
SNO	Senior Naval Officer
SNP	Scottish Nationalist Party
SNTS	Society for New Testament Studies
SO	Scottish Office; Staff Officer
SOAS	School of Oriental and African Studies
Soc	Society
SOE	Special Operations Executive
SOGAT	Society of Graphical and Allied Trades
SOLACE	Society of Local Authority Chief Executives
SOLT	Society of London Theatres (formerly SWET)
Som	Somerset
SOTS	Society for Old Testament Studies
Sov	Sovereign
sp	sine prole (without issue)
SPAB	Society for the Protection of Ancient Buildings
SPCK	Society for Promoting Christian Knowledge
SPG	Society for the Propagation of the Gospel
SPNM	Society for the Promotion of New Music

SPSO	Senior Personnel Staff Officer
SPTL	Society of Public Teaching of Law
SPUC	Society for the Protection of the Unborn Child
Sq	Square
Sqdn	Squadron
Sqdn Ldr	Squadron Leader
sr	senior
SR	Special Reserve; Southern Railway; Southern Region
SRC	Science Research Council
SRDE	Signals Research and Development Establishment
SRHE	Society for Research in Higher Education
SRN	State Registered Nurse
SRO	Supplementary Reserve of Officers
SRP	State Registered Physiotherapist
SRR	State Registered Radiographer
SSA	Society of Scottish Artists
SSAFA	Soldiers', Sailors', and Airmen's Families Association
SSC	Solicitor, Supreme Court (Scotland); Short Service Commission
SSEES	School of Slavonic and East European Studies
SSMLL	Society for the Study of Modern Languages and Literature
SSO	Senior Supply Officer
SSRC	Social Science Research Council
SSStJ	Serving Sister of the Order of St John of Jerusalem
STA	Society of Technical Analysts
Staffs	Staffordshire
STC	Senior Training Corps
STD	Doctor of Sacred Theology
STh	Scholar in Theology
STL	Licentiate of Sacred Theology
STM	Master of Sacred Theology
STSO	Senior Technical Staff Officer
Subalt	Subaltern
Subs	Submarines (RN)
subseq	subsequent; subsequently
subsid	subsidiary
suc	succeeded
SUNY	The State University of New York
sup	supérieure
supp	supplementary
Supt	Superintendent
surgn	surgeon
survg	surviving
SWA	Sports Writers' Association
SWB	South Wales Borderers
SWEB	South Western Electricity Board
SWET	Society of West End Theatres (now SOLT)

T

TA	Territorial Army
TAA	Territorial Army Association; Tropical Agriculture Association
TAF	Tactical Air Force
T&AFA	Territorial and Auxiliary Forces' Association
TANS	Territorial Army Nursing Service
TARO	Territorial Army Reserve of Officers
TAS	Torpedo and Anti-Submarine Course
Tas	Tasmania
T&AVR	Territorial and Army Volunteer Reserve
TAVRA	Territorial Auxiliary and Volunteer Reserve Association (now RFCA)
Tbnl	Tribunal
TC	Order of the Trinity Cross (Trinidad and Tobago)
TCCB	Test and County Cricket Board (now ECB)
TCD	Trinity College Dublin
TD	Territorial Officers' Decoration; Teachta Dala (member of the Dáil, Parliament of Ireland)
TEC	Training and Enterprise Council
tech	technical
technol	technology; technological
TEFL	Teaching English as a Foreign Language
TEM	Territorial Efficiency Medal
temp	temporary
temp	*tempore* (in the time of)
TEP	Member, Society of Trust and Estate Practitioners
TES	Times Educational Supplement
TF	Territorial Force
TfL	Transport for London
TGWU	Transport and General Workers' Union
ThD	Doctor of Theology
Theol	Theological

ThM	Master of Theology
ThSchol	Scholar of Theology
TLS	Times Literary Supplement
TMA	Theatre Managers' Association
TN	Tennessee
tport	transport
trans	translation; translated; translator
TRE	Telecommunications Research Establishment
treas	treasurer
Treasy	Treasury
trg	training
TRH	Their Royal Highnesses
TRIC	Television and Radio Industries' Club
Tst	Trust
tstee	trustee
TUC	Trades Union Congress
TV	Television
TVEI	Technical and Vocational Educational Initiative
TX	Texas

U

U	Unionist
UAE	United Arab Emirates
UAR	United Arab Republic
UAU	Universities' Athletic Union
UC	University College
UCAS	Universities and Colleges Admissions Service
UCATT	Union of Construction, Allied Trades and Technicians
UCCA	Universities' Central Council on Admissions
UCD	University College Dublin
UCE	University of Central England
UCH	University College Hospital (now UCHL)
UCHL	University College Hospital, London
UCL	University College London
UCLA	University of California at Los Angeles
UCNS	Universities' Council for Non-Academic Staff
UCNW	University College of North Wales
UCS	University College School
UCW	University College of Wales
UDC	Urban District Council
UDF	Union Defence Force; Ulster Defence Force
UDR	Ulster Defence Regiment
UDS	United Drapery Stores
UDUP	Ulster Democratic Unionist Party
UEA	University of East Anglia
UFAW	Universities' Federation of Animal Welfare
UFC	Universities' Funding Council
UFO	Unidentified Flying Object
UGC	University Grants Committee
UHS	University High School
UK	United Kingdom
UKAEA	United Kingdom Atomic Energy Authority
UKCC	United Kingdom Central Council for Nurses, Midwives and Health Visitors
UKCCCR	United Kingdom Co-ordinating Committee on Cancer Research (now NCRI)
UKIP	United Kingdom Independence Party
UKLF	United Kingdom Land Forces
UKMIS	UK Mission
UKREP	United Kingdom Permanent Representation to the European Union
UMDS	United Medical and Dental Schools of Guy's and St Thomas' Hospitals (now GKT)
UMIST	University of Manchester Institute of Science and Technology
UN	United Nations
UNA	United Nations Association
unc	uncle
UNCTAD	United Nations Conference on Trade and Development
undergrad	undergraduate
UNDP	United Nations Development Programme
UNESCO	United Nations Educational, Scientific and Cultural Organisation
UNFAO	United Nations Food and Agricultural Organisation (now FAO)
UNHCR	United Nations High Commissioner for Refugees
UNHQ	United Nations Headquarters
UNIC	United Nations Information Centre
UNICE	Union des Industries de la Communauté Européenne
UNICEF	United Nations International Children's Emergency Fund (now United Nations Children's Fund)
UNIDO	United Nations Industrial Development Organisation

UNIDROIT	Institut International pour l'Unification du Droit Privé
UNIPEDE	Union Internationale des Producteurs et Distributeurs d'Énergie Électrique
Univ	University
UNO	United Nations Organisation
UNRRA	United Nations Relief and Rehabilitation Administration
UP	Uttar Pradesh; United Provinces; United Presbyterian
UPNI	Unionist Party of Northern Ireland
URSI	Union Radio-Scientifique Internationale
US	United States
USA	United States of America
USAF	United States Air Force
USDAW	Union of Shop, Distributive, and Allied Workers
USM	Unlisted Securities Market
USMC	United States Military College
USN	United States Navy
USNR	United States Naval Reserve
USPG	United Society for the Propagation of the Gospel
USSR	Union of Soviet Socialist Republics
UT	Utah
UTC	University Training Corps
UU	Ulster Unionist
UWE	University of the West of England
UWIST	University of Wales Institute of Science and Technology

V

v	versus
V&A	Victoria and Albert (Museum)
VA	Lady of the Order of Victoria and Albert; Virginia
Va	Virginia
VAD	Voluntary Aid Detachment
VAT	Value Added Tax
VBF	Veterinary Benevolent Fund
VC	Victoria Cross
VCAS	Vice-Chief of the Air Staff
VCC	Vintage Car Club
VD	Volunteer Officers' Decoration (now VRD); Venereal Disease
VDC	Volunteer Defence Corps
Ven	Venerable
Very Rev	Very Reverend
vet	veterinary
VHF	Very High Frequency
Visc	Viscount
VM	Victory Medal
VMH	Victoria Medal of Honour (Royal Horticultural Society)
VO	Veterinary Officer
vol	volunteer; volume
VPRWS	Vice-President, Royal Society of Painters in Water Colours
VRD	Volunteer Reserve Officers Decoration
VSCC	Vintage Sports Car Club
VSO	Voluntary Service Overseas
VT	Vermont

W

w	wife
W	West
WA	Western Australia; Washington
WAAA	Women's Amateur Athletics Association
WAAF	Women's Auxiliary Air Force (later WRAF)
Warks	Warwickshire
WBA	World Boxing Association
WBC	World Boxing Council
WBO	World Boxing Organisation
WEA	Workers' Educational Association
WEU	Western European Union
WFTU	World Federation of Trade Unions
WHO	World Health Organisation
WI	West Indies; Wisconsin; Women's Institute
wid	widow
Wilts	Wiltshire
WIPO	World Intellectual Property Organisation
WIS	Wales Information Society
Wm	William
WNO	Welsh National Opera
WNSM	Welsh National School of Medicine
WO	War Office
Worcs	Worcestershire
WRAC	Women's Royal Army Corps
WRAF	Women's Royal Air Force (formerly WAAF)
WRNR	Women's Royal Naval Reserve
WRNS	Women's Royal Naval Service
WRVS	Women's Royal Voluntary Service (formerly WVS)
w/s	war substantive
WS	Writer to the Signet
WV	West Virginia
WVS	Women's Voluntary Service
WWF	World Wide Fund for Nature (formerly World Wildlife Fund)
WWI	First World War
WWII	Second World War
WY	Wyoming

Y

YCs	Young Conservatives
Yeo	Yeomanry
YHA	Youth Hostels Association
YMCA	Young Men's Christian Association
YOI	Young Offenders Institution
Yorks	Yorkshire
yr	younger
yst	youngest
YTS	Youth Training Scheme
YWCA	Young Women's Christian Association

Abbreviations

PEOPLE OF TODAY
BIOGRAPHICAL ENTRIES

A

A

à BRASSARD, Nigel Courtenay; s of Maj Herbert Forbes à Brassard, of Oxfordshire, and Elisabeth Kane, *née* McCue; *b* 7 June 1955; *Educ* Cheltenham Coll, KCL (BA); *m* 16 March 1996, Adèle, da of Dr and Mrs Herman Dexter Webster, of New Orleans, Louisiana; 2 s (Louis Forbes b 20 Dec 1996, William Claiborne b 5 Oct 1999), 1 da (Celeste Ninette b 22 Sept 2001); *Career* Samuel Montagu Co Ltd London 1977–86, seconded to Dominguez Barry Samuel Montagu Ltd Sydney 1984–85; md Dresdner Kleinwort Benson Ltd 1986–2001, dir Dresdner Kleinwort Benson Iberfomento SA, global head equity capital markets, head of M&A and head corp fin Dresdner Kleinwort Benson North America 2001–; md: Lenox Hill Investments Ltd, Market Town Asset Management Ltd; fndr and md British Polo Enterprises Ltd (promoter of British Polo Championship); *Publications* Modern Merchant Banking, SCP Guide for Issuers and Investors, A Glorious Victory - A Glorious Defeat, A Posthumous Life - Keats in Rome, Tommy Hitchcock - A Tribute; *Recreations* polo, cricket, opera, game shooting; *Clubs* Buck's, Pilgrims, Cirencester Park Polo, MCC, Sydney Cricket Ground, Winchester House, Krewe d'Etat, Shuttlecock; *Style*— Nigel à Brassard, Esq

AARONS, Elaine; da of Lionel Freedman, of Manchester, and Freda Freedman; *b* 7 February 1958, Manchester; *Educ* Manchester HS for Girls, KCL (LLB); *m* 28 June 1977, Dr Stephen Aarons; 2 da (Elizabeth Ruth b 12 Jan 1985, Abigail Rivka b 27 April 1991), 1 s (Robert Joshua b 24 April 1987); *Career* admitted slr 1982; slr specialising in employment law; asst slr Norton Rose 1980–89, ptnr Eversheds 1989–2006, princ Withers LLP 2006–; memb Editorial Bd Complinet HR; memb Mgmnt Ctee Employment Lawyers' Assoc 1992–2001 (sometime trg co-ordinator, chair Legislative and Policy Ctee and co sec), chair Employers Forum on Social Policy 1997–, vice-chair Employment Law Sub-Ctee London Law Soc 2003–; govr Hasmonean HS 2002–03, fndr N London Learning Prog for Girls 2003; *Publications* Tolleys Termination of Employment (gen ed); *Recreations* entertaining, charitable events; *Style*— Mrs Elaine Aarons

AARONSON, Graham Raphael; QC (1982); s of Jack Aaronson (d 1973), of London, and Dora, *née* Franks; *b* 31 December 1944; *Educ* City of London Sch, Trinity Hall Cambridge (MA); *m* 1 (m dis 1992); 2 s (Oran b 1968, Avi b 1974), 1 da (Orit b 1970); m 2, 12 May 1993, Pearl Isobel, da of Harold Rose, and Berta Rose (d 2001); 2 step s (Adam b 1976, Simon b 1986), 1 step da (Sara b 1978); *Career* called to the Bar Middle Temple 1966 (bencher 1991); md Worldwide Plastics Development Ltd 1973–77, fndr Standford Grange Rehabilitation Centre for Ex-Offenders, advsr on taxation Treasy Israel 1986–92; chm: Tax Law Review Ctee 1994–98, Revenue Bar Assoc 1995–98, Dietary Res Fndn 1989–91; *Style*— Graham Aaronson, Esq, QC; ✉ Pump Court Tax Chambers, 16 Bedford Row, London WC1R 4EB

AARONSON, Sir Michael John (Mike); kt (2006), CBE (2000); s of Edward John (Jack) Aaronson, of Wanborough, Wilts, and Marian, *née* Davies; *b* 8 September 1947; *Educ* Merchant Taylors' Sch Northwood, St John's Coll Oxford (Sir Thomas White scholar, Trevelyan scholar, MA); *m* 27 Aug 1988, Andrene Margaret Dundas, da of late John Sutherland; 1 da (Katherine Sara Dundas b 22 Feb 1989), 2 s (Benedict Lodwick MacGregor b 24 Aug 1991, Nathanael Aeron Sutherland b 10 Feb 1994); *Career* field co-ordinator Nigeria Save the Children Fund 1969–71; HM Dip Serv 1972–88: third, second and first sec Paris 1973–77, Lagos 1981–83, Rangoon 1987–88; DG Save the Children Fund 1995–2005 (overseas dir 1988–95), dir Oxford Policy Mgmnt Ltd 2006–; UK rep EC NGO Liaison Ctee 1994–2000, pres EC NGO Liaison Ctee 1998–2000; govr Westminster Fndn for Democracy 2001– (vice-chair 2006–), chair Centre for Humanitarian Dialogue Geneva 2001–; visiting fell Nuffield Coll Oxford 2004–, sr research assoc KCL 2006–; Civil Serv cmmr 2007–; chm Frimley Park Hosp NHS Fndn Tst 2006–; Freeman: City of London, Worshipful Co of Merchant Taylors; FRSA; *Recreations* sports, the performing arts; *Clubs* MCC; *Style*— Sir Mike Aaronson, CBE; ✉ Dingley Dell, Glaziers Lane, Normandy, Guildford, Surrey GU3 2EB (tel 01483 811655, fax 0870 052 0566, e-mail aaronson@ddell.demon.co.uk)

AARONSON, Robin Hugh; s of Edward John (Jack) Aaronson, of Wanborough, Wilts, and Marian, *née* Davies; *b* 7 July 1951; *Educ* Merchant Taylors', Balliol Coll Oxford (MA, OU Prize for Comparative Philology, pres Dramatic Soc), LSE (MSc, Eli Devons Prize for Economics), Metanoia Inst (BA); *m* 1 (m dis), Janet Charmian Christabel, da of Joseph Evans; m 2, Veronica Fay, da of Ronald Feltham; 1 s (Matthew John), 3 step c; *Career* admin trainee MOD 1974–80 (on secondment to LSE 1978–80), economic advsr HM Treasy 1980–86 (speechwriter to Chancellor of the Exchequer, advsr on economic effects of tax changes), sr economic advsr Monopolies and Mergers Cmmn 1986–89 (advsr on numerous investigations); PricewaterhouseCoopers (formerly Coopers & Lybrand before merger): joined as mangr 1989, ptnr responsible for competition policy advice servs 1993–98; dir: LECG Ltd 1998–, Akousis Counselling Ltd 2003–; visiting lectr on Euro competition policy Centre des Études Européennes Strasbourg 1994–97, specialist advsr House of Commons Trade and Industry Ctee 1991; memb Bd Countrywide Workshops Charitable Tst 1998–2001; memb PO Users Nat Cncl 1998–2000, memb Postal Services Cmmn 2000–; *Recreations* mountains, photography, gardening; *Clubs* Alpine; *Style*— Robin Aaronson, Esq; ✉ LECG Ltd, 5 Southampton Street, London WC2E 7HA (tel 020 7632 5000, fax 020 7632 5050, e-mail robin.aaronson@lecg.com)

ABBAY-BOWEN, David Ian Henry; s of Ivor Llewelyn Bowen, of Mumbles, Swansea, and Marjorie Abbay; *b* 8 June 1950; *Educ* Dynevor GS Swansea, Swansea Coll of Technol; *m* 16 Nov 1984, Elizabeth Mary; 1 s (James b 9 Dec 1984); *Career* presenter/prodr Swansea Sound 1974–80, journalist/presenter Hereward Radio 1980–83, prog controller Radio Aire 1983–84, gp head of music GWR Group plc 1984–90, md Bowen-Sklar Programming 1990–93, gp prog controller West Country Broadcasting (WCB) 1993–95, ceo: The Executive Network North America, Positive Health Systems 1996– (also currently md); md Hillcrest House Holdings Ltd; *Recreations* motorcycling, golf; *Style*— Dave Abbay-Bowen, Esq; ✉ Hillcrest House, Higher Lane, Langland, Mumbles SA3 4NS (e-mail dave@positivehealthsystems.com)

ABBESS, Lynne Margaret; da of Lawrence Peter Abbess (d 2003), and Margaret Thelma, *née* Scott (d 1986); *b* 1956, Kent; *Educ* Newstead Wood Sch for Girls, Kingston Univ (LLB), Coll of Law Guildford; *Career* admitted slr 1982; Hempsons Slrs: articled clerk 1980, ptnr 1985–; memb: Law Soc 1982, Assoc of Partnership of Practitioners (former hon sec), Ctee Primary Care Premises Forum; *Publications* The Law and General Practice: Partnership Agreements (contrib), Making Sense of Partnerships: When Partners Fall Out - Legal Remedies (contrib), A Practitioner's Guide to Partnership and LLP Law and Regulation (contrib), Primary Healthcare Premises: An Expert Guide (co-ed); regular columnist GP and Medeconomics; *Recreations* property renovation, interior design, skiing, travel; *Style*— Miss Lynne Abbess; ✉ Hempsons Solicitors, Hempsons House, 40 Villiers Street, London WC2N 6NJ (tel 020 7484 7534, fax 020 7484 7565, e-mail l.abbess@hempsons.co.uk)

ABBOTT, Diane Julie; MP; *b* 27 September 1953; *Educ* Harrow County Girls' GS, Newnham Coll Cambridge; *Children* 1 s (James Alexander Abbott-Thompson b 21 Oct 1991); *Career* successively: admin trainee Home Office, race relations offr NCCL, researcher Thames TV, reporter TV-am, equality offr ACTT, press and PR offr GLC, princ press offr Lambeth BC; MP (Lab) Hackney North and Stoke Newington 1987–; memb: Treasy Select Ctee 1989–97, Foreign Affrs Select Ctee 1997–2001; joined Lab Pty 1971, memb Lab Pty Nat Exec, sec Campaign Gp of Lab MPs 1992–; memb Westminster City Cncl 1982–86; *Style*— Ms Diane Abbott, MP; ✉ House of Commons, London SW1A 0AA (tel 020 7219 4426, fax 020 7219 4964)

ABBOTT, Laurie; *Educ* SW Tech Coll London; *Career* architect; Team 4 1964–71, Piano + Rogers 1971–77, dir Richard Rogers Partnership 1977–; *Projects* incl: Creek Vean Cornwall, Reliance Controls electronics factory Wilts, Pompidou Centre Paris, Coin Street, Whittington Avenue, Royal Acad exhibit 'London as it could be', London Royal Docks strategic plan, London Heathrow Airport Terminal 5, Lloyd's Bldg, offices for Daimler Benz in Berlin, housing in Berlin; conslt to Fiat with Ove Arup and Partners; *Style*— Laurie Abbott, Esq; ✉ Richard Rogers Partnership, Thames Wharf, Rainville Road, London W6 9HA

ABBOTT, Adm Sir Peter Charles; GBE (1999), KCB (1994); *b* 12 February 1942; *Educ* St Edward's Sch Oxford, Queens' Coll Cambridge (MA), RCDS; *m* 1965, Susan, *née* Grey; 3 da; *Career* articled clerk Blackburn Robson Coates and 2 Lt RMFVR 1963, resigned and joined RN as Sub Lt 1964; CO HMS Chawton 1972, on staff of Sr Naval Offr W Indies and promoted Cdr 1975, CO HMS Ambuscade 1976, 2 i/c HMS Bulwark and promoted Capt 1980, Chief of Defence Staff briefer during Falklands War 1982, CO HMS Ajax and First Frigate Sqdn 1983, RCDS 1985, Dir of Navy Plans 1985–89, promoted Rear Adm 1989, Flag Offr Second Flotilla 1989–91 in HM Ships Ark Royal, Cumberland, London, Argonaut and Cardiff, Asst Chief of Naval Staff 1991–93, promoted Vice Adm 1993, Dep Supreme Allied Cdr Atlantic 1993–95, promoted Adm 1995, C-in-C Fleet 1995–97, Vice Chief of Defence Staff 1997–2001; cmmr Cwlth War Graves 2001–; conslt: Bechtel 2003–, Close Bros 2003–; chm of tstees: Royal Naval Museum, Regular Forces Employment Agency Ltd; *Style*— Adm Sir Peter Abbott, GBE, KCB; ✉ Commonwealth War Graves, 2 Marlow Road, Maidenhead, Berkshire SL6 7DX

ABBOTT, Stephen (Steve); s of Wilfrid Lockley Abbott (d 2006), of Bradford, W Yorks, and Lily Templeton, *née* Limbert; *b* 28 July 1954; *Educ* Bradford GS, CCC Cambridge (MA); *m* 1992 (m dis 1998), Karen Lesley Lewis; 1 da (Francesca b 1986), 1 s (James Alexander b 1989); *Career* film and television producer; Price Waterhouse London 1976–79, Hand Made Films London 1979–81, Mayday Management Ltd 1981–, chm Prominent Features Ltd 1989– (md 1986–89), dir Prominent Television 1992– (exec prodr Himalaya 2004 and New Europe 2006 (both with Michael Palin)); dir Nat Film Tstee Co Ltd 2002–06; chair Screen Yorkshire 2002–, tstee Training and Performance Showcase 2001–06; ambass to City of Bradford 1997; memb: AMPAS, BAFTA, EFA (Euro Film Acad); Hon DLitt Univ of Bradford 1998; FCA 1990 (ACA 1979), FRSA 1999; *Films* exec prodr: A Fish Called Wanda 1988, Fierce Creatures 1995 (released 1997); prodr: American Friends 1990, Blame It On the Bellboy 1991, Brassed Off 1996; *Style*— Steve Abbott, Esq; ✉ Prominent Television Ltd, 34 Tavistock Street, London WC2E 7PB (tel 020 7497 1100, fax 020 7497 1133)

ABBOTT, Air Cdre Steven; CBE (2003); s of Norman Abbott, of Attleborough, Norfolk, and Doris Marguerite, *née* Davis (d 2004); *b* 5 February 1956, Geilenkirchen, Germany; *Educ* various grammar and serv schs, UEA (BA), Downing Coll Cambridge (MPhil); *m* 25 March 1989, Patricia, *née* Bunting; 1 s (James Edward b 27 Aug 1990), 1 da (Jennifer Katharine b 15 July 1992); *Career* cmd and staff appts MOD, Strike Cmd and RAF Germany 1977–2002 (incl mil asst to Cdr Br Forces Hong Kong 1990–92), Cdr Kabul Airfield (Operation Fingal Afghanistan) 2001–02, Station Cdr RAF Honington 2003–05, ACOS RAF Trg Gp 2005–; memb RIIA; QCVS 2000; *Recreations* field sports, military history, cricket, Cresta Run; *Clubs* RAF, St Moritz Tobogganing; *Style*— Air Cdre Steven Abbott, CBE

ABBOTT, Stuart; MBE (2004); *b* 3 June 1978, Cape Town, South Africa; *Educ* Western Province Prep Sch, Diocesan Coll Cape Province, Univ of Stellenbosch; *Career* rugby union player (centre); clubs: Western Stormers (South Africa), London Wasps RUFC 2001– (winners Parker Pen Challenge Cup 2003, Zurich Premiership 2003, Heineken Cup 2004); England: 8 caps, 2 tries, debut v Wales 2003, ranked no 1 team in world 2003, winners World Cup Aust 2003; also represented South Africa at Under 23 level (1 cap); *Recreations* playstation, DVDs, waterskiing; *Style*— Stuart Abbott, Esq, MBE; ✉ c/o Rugby Football Union, Rugby House, Rugby Road, Twickenham, Middlesex TW1 1DS

ABBOTT-WATT, Thorhilda Mary Vivia (Thorda); da of Samuel Abbott-Watt, and Elva Mary, *née* Clare Gibson; *b* 11 February 1955, London; *Educ* Stonar Sch, Atworth; *Partner* Reef Talbot Hogg; *Career* joined HM Dip Serv 1974, third sec FCO 1974–79, temporary duty tours Latin America and Far and Middle East 1979–80, vice-consul Paris 1981–84, third sec (Chancery) UK Representation to EU 1984–86, second sec FCO 1986–88, second sec Bonn 1988–81, first sec EU and Western Europe Depts FCO 1991–95, first sec and head Commercial Section Kiev 1995–98, first sec Belgrade 1998–99, first sec and head Visa Policy Section Jt Entry Clearance Unit 1999–2001, charge d'affaires Dushanbe 2001–02, ambass to Armenia 2003–06; life memb NACF, memb ICA, friend Royal Acad; *Recreations* riding, reading, theatre; *Style*— Miss Thorda Abbott-Watt; ✉ c/o Foreign and Commonwealth Office, King Charles Street, London SW1A 2AH

ABBS, Prof Peter Francis; s of Eric Charles Abbs (d 1987), and Mary Bertha, *née* Bullock (d 1994); *b* 22 February 1942; *Educ* Norwich Tech Coll, Univ of Bristol (BA), Univ of Sussex (PhD); *m* (m dis 2002) Barbara Ann, da of Jack Beazeley; 2 da (Annabel b 20 Oct 1964, Miranda b 22 July 1966), 1 s (Theodore b 29 March 1973); *Career* English teacher Bristol 1966–70, res asst Univ of Wales 1970–76; Univ of Sussex: reader in educn 1976–, prof of creative writing 1999–; has lectured widely in USA, Aust, India, Denmark, Ireland, Belgium and elsewhere; memb: Soc of Authors, Assoc of Univ Teachers; fndr memb New Metaphysical Art 1996; *Poetry* For Man and Islands, Songs of a New

Taliesin, Icons of Time, Personae, Angelic Imagination, Love After Sappho, Earth Songs, Selected Poems, Viva la Vida; *Non-Fiction* English For Diversity, Root and Blossom - The Philosophy, Practice and Politics of English Teaching, English Within the Arts, The Forms of Poetry, The Forms of Narrative, Autobiography in Education, Proposal for a New College (with Graham Carey), Reclamations - Essays on Culture, Mass-Culture and the Curriculum, A is for Aesthetic - Essays on Creative and Aesthetic Education, The Educational Imperative, The Polemics of Imagination - Selected Essays on Art, Culture and Society; ed: The Black Rainbow - Essays on the Present Breakdown of Culture, Living Powers - The Arts in Education, The Symbolic Order - A Contemporary Reader on the Arts Debate, Against the Flow - The Arts, Postmodern Culture and Education; *Recreations* swimming, walking, film, music; *Style*— Prof Peter Abbs; ✉ Graduate Research Centre in the Humanities, Arts Building B, University of Sussex, Falmer, Brighton BN1 9QN (tel 01273 872597, fax 01273 625972, e-mail p.f.abbs@sussex.ac.uk)

ABDELA, Lesley Julia; MBE (1990); da of Frederick Abdela (d 1985), and Henrietta, *née* Hardy (d 1959); *b* 17 November 1945; *Educ* Glendower London, Queen Anne's Caversham, Châtelard Sch Les Avants Switzerland, Queen's Coll Harley St, Hammersmith Coll of Art, London Sch of Printing; *m* 1972 (m dis); 1 s (Nicholas b 1973); *Career* int conslt on equal opportunities and trainer in democratic skills (primary clients EU, UNDP, Br Cncl, Harvard, DfID, FCO), feature writer, author, TV and radio bdcaster on politics; formerly advtg exec Royds London, researcher House of Commons and House of Lords 1976–77, Parly candidate (Lib) Herts E 1979, fndr All-Party 300 Gp for Women in Politics 1980, USA Leader Grant visiting Washington DC, LA and Seattle 1983, studied Third World by residence in the Gambia 1984–86, currently sr ptnr Eyecatcher Associates (journalism, copywriting, research, conference speakers) and sr ptnr Shevolution; conslt on women and politics in East and Central Europe Project Liberty Kennedy Sch of Government Harvard Univ 1992–98, political ed Cosmopolitan 1993–96, accredited journalist UN 4th World Conf on Women Beijing 1995, chief exec Project Parity 1996–, dep dir for democratisation for OSCE Mission in Kosovo 1999–2000; vice-pres Electoral Reform Soc 1995–; memb: Bd International Inst for Environment and Devpt 1992–96, Bd of Govrs Westminster Fndn for Democracy 1996–97, Bd of Govrs Br Cncl; experience of gender issues in post-conflict reconstruction and peace-building ops in Aceh, Iraq, Afghanistan, Sierra Leone and Kosovo, conducts bi-annual workshops on implementation of UN Security Cncl Resolution 1325 (mainstreaming gender into peace ops and civil military cooperation) Swedish Armed Forces Int Centre, ldr workshops for NATO sr civil servants on gender and culture in Afghanistan NATO HQ Brussels 2006 and 2007; govr Nottingham Trent Univ 1997–2000; winner EC's UK Woman of Europe Award (for servs to EU) 1995, listed fourth in New Statesman's Top 50 Heroes of Our Time 2006; FRGS, FRSA 1991; *Books* Women with X Appeal (1989), Breaking Through The Glass Ceilings (Met Authys Recruitment Agency guide, 1991), What Women Want, 1993–2000 (ed, 1993), DO IT! - Walk the Talk (1994); *Recreations* travel, painting; *Style*— Ms Lesley Abdela, MBE

ABDIN, Dr Hasan; *b* 1940, Sudan; *Educ* Univ of Khartoum (BA), Univ of Wisconsin USA (MA, PhD); *m* with 3 da, 2 s; *Career* lectr Univ of Khartoum 1970–77; state min in Presidency 1977–78, memb National Assembly 1978–80; assoc prof: Univ of Khartoum 1980–83, Univ of King Saud Saudi Arabia 1983–88; ambass to Algeria 1990–92, ambass to Iraq 1993–97; Miny of External Relations: DG Political Affairs 1997–98, under sec 1998–2000; ambass to the Ct of St James's 2000–; *Publications* Introduction to African History (in Arabic, 1974), Early Sudanese Nationalism 1919–1925 (1985); *Style*— HE Dr Hasan Abdin; ✉ Sudan Embassy, 2 Cleveland Row, St James's, London SW1A 1DD (tel 020 7839 8080, fax 020 7839 7560, e-mail hasabdin@hotmail.com)

ABDU'ALLAH, Faisal; *b* 5 August 1969, London; *Educ* Central St Martins Coll (BA), Massachusetts Coll of Art, RCA (MA); *Career* artist; Individual Artist Award London Arts Board 1995; *Solo Exhibitions* Censored, Nigger to Nubian (198 Gallery London) 1993, Revelations (Bonnington Gallery Nottingham and 198 Gallery London) 1995, Heads of State (Margaret Harvey Gallery Herts, Standpoint Gallery London and Middlesbrough Art Gallery) 1997–98, The Collection (The Agency Contemporary Art London) 2000, The Agency Contemporary Art London 2000, 2001, 2002 and 2004, Horniman Museum London 2001, Chisenhale Gallery London 2002; *Group Exhibitions* African Themes (V&A) 1993, Borderless Print (Rochdale Art Gallery) 1993, Presences (Photographers' Gallery London) 1993, Us An' Dem (Storey Inst Lancs and Art '94 London) 1994, Different Stories (Netherlands Photo Inst Rotterdam) 1994, Make Believe (RCA) 1995, The Impossible Science of Being (Photographers' Gallery London, Leeds Museum Gallery and Brighton Museum) 1996, Radical Images (Neue Galerie Austria and Szombatheley Art Gallery Hungary) 1996, The 90's: Family of Man (Forum de l'Art Contemporain Luxembourg) 1997–98, On the Bright Side of Life (NGBK Berlin) 1997–98, Transforming the Crown (Studio Museum Harlem NYC) 1997–98, Out of the Blue (MOMA Glasgow) 1997–99, In Visible Light (MOMA Oxford and tour) 1997–99, They don't know me but, (De la Warr Pavillion Brighton, Winchester Art Gallery and Pitshanger Manor London) 1998, LKW (OK Centre for Contemporary Art Linz) 1999, Basel Liste 99 1999, Holland Festival Rotterdam 1999, Missing Link (Kunstmuseum Bern) 1999, Hackney Empire Benefit Auction London 1999, film screening London 1999, Project X (S London Gallery) 1999, Cologne Artfair (The Agency Cologne) 1999 and 2000, Warningshots (Royal Armouries Leeds) 2000, Tirannicidi (Calcografia Nat Gallery Rome and Archivio de Stato Turin) 2000, LKW (Kunstverein Bregenz) 2000, Ecce Homo (Kunsthal Rotterdam) 2000, Aesthetic Terrorism (The Agency Contemporary Art London) 2001, ARCO Artfair Madrid 2001, Nat Maritime Museum London 2001, BIG Torino Biennial Turin 2002, Sharjah International Biennale (UAE) 2003, Aspex Gallery Portsmouth (with David Adjaye) 2003, Independence (South London Gallery) 2003, The Veil (touring exhbn, venues incl Stockholm and Modern Art Oxford) 2003–04, Britannia Works Athens 2004; *Style*— Faisal Abdu'Allah, Esq

ABDY, Sir Valentine Robert Duff; 6 Bt (UK 1850), of Albyns, Essex; s of Sir Robert Abdy, 5 Bt (d 1976), and Lady Diana, *née* Bridgeman (d 1967), da of 5 Earl of Bradford; *b* 11 September 1937; *Educ* Eton; *m* 1971 (m dis 1982), Mathilde, da of Etienne Coche de la Ferté; 1 s (Robert Etienne Eric b 22 Feb 1978); *Heir* s, Robert Abdy; *Career* set up (with Peter Wilson) Sotheby's first offices abroad in Paris and Munich; special advsr Int Fund for Promotion of Culture UNESCO, first rep Smithsonian Inst (Washington DC) in Europe 1983–2000, Nat Bd Smithsonian 1994–97; formerly: Conseil d'Administration Union National des Arts Décoratifs Paris, memb Comité Scientifique Conservatoire National des Arts et Métiers Paris; memb Comité d'Orientation Cité de l'Espace Toulouse; FRSA; Chevalier de l'Ordre des Arts et des Lettres (France) 1995; *Style*— Sir Valentine Abdy, Bt; ✉ 7 bis Allée de Villeneuve L'Etang, 92430 Marnes-la-Coquette, France; 2 New Square, Lincolns Inn, London WC2A 3RZ

ABEL, Prof Edward William; CBE (1997); s of Sydney John Abel (d 1952), of Kenfighill, and Donna Maria, *née* Grabham (d 1981); *b* 3 December 1931; *Educ* Bridgend GS Glamorgan, UC Cardiff (BSc), Northern Poly London (PhD); *m* 6 Aug 1960, Margaret Rosina, da of Glyndwr Vivian Edwards (d 1974), of Porthcawl; 1 s (Christopher b 23 Oct 1963), 1 da (Julia b 4 April 1967); *Career* Nat Serv 1953–55; research fell Imperial Coll London 1957–59, lectr and reader Univ of Bristol 1959–71, prof of inorganic chemistry Univ of Exeter 1972–95 (head of dept 1977–88, dep vice-chllr 1991–94), dep chm governing body Univ of Glamorgan 1999–2002; visiting prof: Univ of Br Columbia 1970, Japan 1971, Tech Univ of Braunschweig 1973, ANU Canberra 1990; int sec Int Confs on Organometallic Chemistry 1972–88; RSC: memb Cncl 1978–82, 1983–89 and 1990–2002, pres 1996–98, chm Local Affrs Bd 1983–87, chm Divnl Affairs Bd 1990–92, chm Scientific Affrs Bd 1992–95, chm Parly Ctee 1995–2003, memb Dalton Divnl Cncl 1977–83 and 1987–91 (sec and treas 1977–82, vice-pres 1989–91, pres 1987–89); Univ Grants Ctee: memb 1986–89, chm Physical Sci Sub Ctee 1986–89; Cncl for Nat Academic Awards: chm Physical Sci Ctee 1987–91, memb Academic Affairs Ctee 1987–91, memb Cncl 1991–93, chm Advsy Ctee on the Lab of the Govt Chemist 1998–2003; nat advsr for chemistry to Exec Univ Funding Cncl 1989–93, assessor to Research Ctee Poly and Coll Funding Cncl 1988–90; Main Gp Chemistry award RSC 1976, Tilden medal and lectr RSC 1981; Hon DUniv London Met Univ 1998, Hon DSc Univ of Exeter 2000, Hon DSc Univ of Glamorgan 2003; FRSC; *Books* Royal Society of Chemistry Specialist Periodical Reports on Organometallic Chemistry (Vols 1–25, jt ed, 1970–96), Comprehensive Organometallic Chemistry (9 Vols, exec ed, 1984), Comprehensive Organometallic Chemistry II (14 Vols, ed, 1995), Royal Society of Chemistry Tutorial Chemistry Texts (21 Vols, ed-in-chief, 2003); *Recreations* gardening; *Style*— Prof Edward Abel, CBE; ✉ 1A Rosebarn Avenue, Exeter, Devon EX4 6DY (tel 01392 270272)

ABEL SMITH, Caroline Bridget; OBE (1994); da of late Capt Howard Bennett Bartlam (d 1970), of Arkholme, Lancs, and Mary Isobel Bartlam (d 2002); *b* 26 September 1945; *Educ* Casterton Sch; *m* 1970, John Lawrence Abel Smith, s of late Maj Desmond Abel Smith; 2 s (Alexander Howard Lawrence b 19 March 1971, Oliver Desmond b 13 June 1974), 1 da (Helen Isobel Katherine b 18 Aug 1976); *Career* trained as med lab technician Lancaster and Guy's Hosps, subsequently personal asst in PR The Times and Sunday Times, lay memb GDC 1989–, non-exec dir S Bucks NHS Tst 1992–98; Cons Women's Nat Ctee: memb 1988–99, dep chm 1994–95, chm 1996–99; memb Cons Pty Nat Union Exec Ctee 1991–98, pres Cons Women's Nat Cncl 1999–2002, elected memb Cons Pty Bd of Mgmnt 1999–2003, chm Cons Party Conference 2002; tstee and memb Appeal Ctee Buckinghamshire Historic Churches Tst; *Recreations* gardening, fishing, tapestry work; *Style*— Mrs John Abel Smith, OBE; ✉ The Old Vicarage, Aston Abbotts, Aylesbury, Buckinghamshire HP22 4NB (tel 01296 681001, e-mail cbjlas@talk21.com)

ABEL SMITH, David Francis; s of Sir Alexander Abel Smith, KCVO, TD, JP (d 1980), of Quenington Old Rectory, Cirencester, Glos, and Elizabeth, *née* Morgan (d 1948); *b* 3 February 1940; *Educ* Gordonstoun, Stockton and Billingham Tech Coll; *m* 18 Nov 1982, Lucy Marie, da of Col Sir Bryce Muir Knox, KCVO, MC, TD (former Lord Lt of Ayr and Arran); 1 da (Eliza Violet Daria b 15 March 1991); *Career* exec dir The Delta Group plc 1974–82 (joined 1961), md Benjamin Priest Group plc 1983–91, chief exec Marling Industries plc 1992–97; exec chm Majorlift Hldgs Ltd 2003–, Zimbabwe Agricultural Tst 2006–; non-exec chm: Equitalk Ltd 1999–2006, VectorCommand Ltd 2000–03, Permali Gloucester Ltd 2001–, Brandauer Holdings Ltd 2001–05, Mosandam Ltd 2004–06; non-exec dir Metalwash Ltd 2000–04; chm The Cotswold Arcadians 1998–2001; collector, cmmr and promoter of contemporary applied arts incl glass, ceramics and furniture, co-fndr and tstee Quenington Sculpture Tst 1998–; memb Quenington Parish Cncl 1987–93; Freeman City of London, memb Worshipful Co of Fishmongers; *Recreations* country sports; *Clubs* Pratt's, The Pilgrims; *Style*— David Abel Smith, Esq; ✉ Quenington Old Rectory, Cirencester, Gloucestershire GL7 5BN (tel 01285 750358, fax 01285 750540, mobile 07785 315134, e-mail asquen@dircon.co.uk)

ABELL, (John) David; s of Leonard Abell, and Irene Craig, *née* Anderson; *b* 15 December 1942; *Educ* Univ of Leeds (BA), LSE (Dip Business Admin); *m* 1, 1967 (m dis), Anne Janette, *née* Priestley; 3 s; m 2, 1981 (m dis), Sandra Dawn, *née* Atkinson; 1 s, 1 da; m 3, 1988, Juliana, da of late Prof John Lister Illingworth Fennell, of Oxford; *Career* Ford Motor Co 1962–65, AEI 1965–67, various appts British Leyland 1968–72 and 1974–81 (incl md Trucks and Buses and dir), First National Finance Corp 1972–73, chm and chief exec Suter plc 1981–96, chm Jourdan plc 1997–; CIMgt; *Style*— J David Abell, Esq; ✉ The Old Rectory, Branston-by-Belvoir, Grantham, Lincolnshire NG32 1RU

ABELL, Prof Peter Malcolm; s of John Raymond Abell (d 1987), and Constance, *née* Moore (d 1998); *b* 18 August 1937; *Educ* Wakefield GS, Univ of Leeds (BSc, PhD); *m* (m dis); 3 s (Paul b 1963, Simon b 1968, Johnathon b 1988); *Career* dir of research Industrial Sociology Unit Imperial Coll London 1970–75; prof of sociology: Dept of Sociology Univ of Birmingham 1976–79, Univ of Surrey 1979–91; dir The Interdisciplinary Inst of Mgmnt London Sch of Economics and Political Science 1991–2003, visiting prof Copenhagen Business Sch 2003–; *Books* Model Building in Sociology (1972), Socio-Economic Potential of Producer Co-ops in Developing Countries (1987), The Syntax of Social Life (1988), Support Systems for Co-ops in Developing Countries (1988), Rational Choice (1991); *Recreations* walking, music; *Style*— Prof Peter Abell; ✉ 37 The Ridgeway, Radlett, Hertfordshire WD7 8PT; London School of Economics and Political Science, Houghton Street, London WC2A 2AE

ABERCONWAY, 4 Baron (1911 UK); (Henry) Charles McLaren; s of 3 Baron (d 2003); *b* 26 May 1948; *Educ* Eton, Sussex Univ (BA); *m* 1981, Sally Ann, yr da of Capt Charles Nugent Lentaigne, RN (d 1981), of Hawkley Place, Hawkley, Liss, Hants, and formerly w of Philip Charles Bidwell; 1 da (Hon Emily b 1982), 1 s (Hon Charles Stephen b 27 Dec 1984), 1 step s (Alex b 1975); *Heir* s, Hon Charles McLaren; *Style*— The Rt Hon the Lord Aberconway

ABERCORN, 5 Duke of (I 1868); Sir James Hamilton; 15 Bt (I 1660), KG (1999); also Lord Paisley (S 1578), Lord Abercorn (S 1603), Earl of Abercorn and Lord Paisley, Hamilton, Mountcastell, and Kilpatrick (S 1606), Baron of Strabane (I 1617), Baron Mountcastle and Viscount Strabane (I 1701), Viscount Hamilton (GB 1785), Marquess of Abercorn (GB 1790 - title in House of Lords), and Marquess of Hamilton (I 1868); s of 4 Duke of Abercorn (d 1979), and Lady Kathleen Mary, GCVO, *née* Crichton (d 1990), sis of 5 Earl of Erne; *b* 4 July 1934; *Educ* Eton, RAC Cirencester; *m* 1966, Alexandra Anastasia, da of Lt-Col Harold Pedro Phillips (d 1980), of Checkendon Court, Berks, also sis of Duchess of Westminster and gda through her m, Georgina, of late Sir Harold Wernher, 3 Bt, GCVO, TD, DL, by his w, late Lady Zia, CBE, *née* Countess Anastasia Mikhailovna (er da of HIH Grand Duke Mikhail Mikhailovitch of Russia, himself gs of Tsar Nicholas I); 2 s (James, Marquess of Hamilton b 1969, Lord Nicholas b 1979), 1 da (Lady Sophia b 1973); *Heir* s, Marquess of Hamilton; *Career* 2 Lt Grenadier Gds; MP (UU) Fermanagh and S Tyrone 1964–70; dir Local Enterprise Devpt Unit 1971–77; chm Laganside Devpt Corp 1989–96, dir Northern Bank Ltd 1970–97; pres: RUKBA 1979–, Building Socs Assoc 1986–92, NI Concrete Soc 1991–, NI Business in the Community 1992–; dir: NI Industrial Devpt Bd 1982–87, Inter Trade Ireland 1993–2003, Nat Gallery of Ireland 2003–; memb: Cncl of Europe 1968–70, Economic and Social Ctee EEC 1973–78; tstee: Winston Churchill Meml Tst 1991–2002, Omagh Fund 1998–2003; patron Royal Ulster Agric Soc 1990–95; High Sheriff Co Tyrone 1970, HM Lord-Lt Co Tyrone 1987–; Lord Steward of HM's Household 2001; Col Irish Gds 2000; Hon LLB Queen's Univ Belfast 1997; *Recreations* shooting; *Clubs* Brooks's; *Style*— His Grace the Duke of Abercorn; ✉ Barons Court, Omagh, Co Tyrone BT78 4EZ (tel 028 816 61470, e-mail duke.baronscourt@talk21.com); Barons Court Estate Office, Omagh, Co Tyrone BT78 4EZ (tel 028 8166 1683, fax 028 8166 2231)

ABERCROMBIE, Ian Ralph; QC (Scot 1994); s of Ralph Abercrombie (d 2002), of Edinburgh, and Jean Hamilton Brown Lithgow (d 1992); *b* 7 July 1955; *Educ* Milton HS Bulawayo, Univ of Edinburgh (LLB); *Career* admitted to Faculty of Advocates 1981; *Style*— Ian Abercrombie, Esq, QC; ✉ Tippermallo House, Methven, Perthshire PH1 3RH; c/o Advocates' Library, Parliament House, Edinburgh EH1 1RF (tel 0131 226 5071)

ABERCROMBIE, Prof Nicholas; s of Michael Abercrombie (d 1978), and Jane Abercrombie (d 1984); *b* 13 April 1944; *Educ* UCS, The Queen's Coll Oxford (BA), LSE (MSc), Lancaster Univ (PhD); *m* 1969, Brenda, da of Harry Patterson; 2 s (Robert b 1971, Joseph b 1974); *Career* hon research asst UCL 1968–70; Lancaster Univ: lectr in sociology 1970–83, sr lectr 1983–88, reader 1988–90, prof of sociology 1990–, dean of undergraduate studies 1992–95, pro-vice-chllr 1995–98, dep vice-chllr 1998–2004; memb British Sociological Soc 1968; FRSA 1999; *Books* incl: The Dominant Ideology Thesis (with S Hill and B Turner, 1980), The Penguin Dictionary of Sociology (with S Hill and B Turner, 1984, 4 edn 2000), Sovereign Individuals of Capitalism (with S Hill and B Turner, 1986), Contemporary British Society (jtly, 1988, 3 edn 2000), Television and Society (1996), Audiences (with B Longhurst, 1998), Sociology (2004); also author of numerous articles in learned jls; *Recreations* gardening, walking; *Style—* Prof Nicholas Abercrombie; ✉ 12 Mount Road, Lansdown, Bath BA1 5PW (tel 01225 471241, e-mail nick.abercrombie@btinternet.com)

ABERDARE, 5 Baron (UK 1873); Alastair John Lyndhurst Bruce; s of 4 Baron Aberdare, KBE, PC, DL (d 2005); *b* 2 May 1947; *Educ* Eton, ChCh Oxford; *m* 1971, Elizabeth Mary Culbert, da of John F Foulkes; 1 s, 1 da; *Career* IBM UK Ltd 1969–91; ptnr Bruce Naughton Wade Public Affairs Mgmnt Conslts 1991–99, dir ProbusBNW Ltd Corporate Reputation Conslts 1999–; *Books* The Musical Madhouse (2003); *Style—* The Rt Hon the Lord Aberdare; ✉ 16 Beverley Road, London SW13 0LX

ABERDEEN AND ORKNEY, Dean of; *see:* Stranraer-Mull, Very Rev Gerald

ABERDEEN AND TEMAIR, 7 Marquess of (UK 1916); Alexander George Gordon; DL (Aberdeenshire 1998); s of 6 Marquess of Aberdeen and Temair (d 2002); *b* 31 March 1955; *Educ* Harrow, Poly of Central London (Dip Bldg Econs); *m* 30 May 1981, Joanna Clodagh, da of late Maj Ian George Henry Houldsworth, of Forres, Moray; 3 s (George Ian Alastair, Earl of Haddo b 4 May 1983, Lord Sam Dudley b 25 Oct 1985, Lord Charles David b 8 June 1990), 1 da (Lady Anna Katharine b 2 Sept 1988); *Heir* s, Earl of Haddo; *Career* London & Edinburgh Trust plc 1986–94, chm Kellie Estates Ltd 1995–, dir Gordon Enterprise Tst Ltd 1998–2002, chm Gordon Land Ltd 2000–, chm Braiklay Estates Ltd 2006–; landowner (7,000 acres); ARICS 1979–96; *Recreations* sport, music, art; *Clubs* MCC, Royal Aberdeen Golf, Meldrum House Golf; *Style—* The Most Hon the Marquess of Aberdeen and Temair, DL; ✉ House of Formartine, Methlick, Ellon, Aberdeenshire AB41 7EQ; Estate Office, Mains of Haddo, Tarves, Aberdeenshire (tel 01651 851664)

ABERNETHY, Rt Hon Lord; (John) Alastair Cameron; PC (2005); s of William Philip Legerwood Cameron (d 1977), of Edinburgh, and Kathleen Milthorpe, *née* Parker (d 1966); *b* 1 February 1938; *Educ* Clergy Sch Khartoum, St Mary's Sch Melrose, Glenalmond Coll Perth, Pembroke Coll Oxford (MA); *m* 1968, Elspeth Mary Dunlop, da of James Bowie Miller (d 1994), of E Lothian; 3 s (Hamish b 1970, Neil b 1972, Iain b 1975); *Career* Nat Serv 2 Lt RASC Aldershot & Malta 1956–58; called to the Bar Inner Temple 1963, advocate 1966, advocate depute 1972–75, vice-dean Faculty of Advocates 1983–92; standing jr counsel to: Dept of Energy 1976–79, Scot Devpt Dept 1978–79; QC Scotland 1979; pres Pensions Appeal Tbnls for Scotland 1985–92 (legal chm 1979–85), chm Faculty Services Ltd 1983–89 (dir 1979–89); Lord of Session (Senator of the College of Justice) 1992–2007; Int Bar Assoc: chm Judges' Forum 1994–98 (vice-chm 1993–94), memb Cncl Section on Legal Practice 1998–2002, memb Cncl Human Rights Inst 1998–2000 and 2002–05; pres The Scottish Medico-Legal Soc 1996–2000; memb: Exec Ctee Soc for the Welfare and Teaching of the Blind (Edinburgh and SE Scotland) 1979–92; chm Arthur Smith Memorial Tst 1990–2001 (tstee 1975–2001); govr Sr Mary's Sch Melrose 1998– (vice-chm 2004–); hon fell Pembroke Coll Oxford 1993–; *Publications* Medical Negligence: An Introduction (1983), contrib to Reproductive Medicine and the Law (ed A A Templeton and D J Cusine, 1990); *Recreations* travel, Africana, nature conservation; *Style—* The Rt Hon Lord Abernethy; ✉ 4 Garscube Terrace, Edinburgh EH12 6BQ (tel 0131 337 3460, fax 0131 240 5711)

ABINGDON, Earl of ; *see:* Lindsey and Abingdon, Earl of

ABINGER, 9 Baron (UK 1835); James Harry Scarlett; s of 8 Baron (d 2002); *b* 28 May 1959; *Educ* Univ of Aberdeen (BSc), Univ of Cambridge (MPhil); *Family* 1 s (Hon Louis William Shelley b 1 Nov 2000); *Heir* Hon Louis Scarlett; *Career* author; FRGS, FLS; *Style—* The Rt Hon the Lord Abinger

ABLE, Graham George; s of George Jasper Able, and Irene Helen, *née* Gaff; *b* 28 July 1947; *Educ* Worksop Coll, Trinity Coll Cambridge (MA, PGCE), Univ of Durham (MA); *m* Mary Susan, da of John Sidney Thomas Munro; 1 s (Richard Graham Munro b 10 May 1973), 1 da (Lisa Maria b 17 June 1976); *Career* Sutton Valence Sch: teacher of chemistry 1969–83, cricket master 1971–76 and 1980–83, hockey master 1972–83, boarding housemaster 1976–83; second master Barnard Castle Sch 1983–88, headmaster Hampton Sch 1988–96, master Dulwich Coll 1997–; fndr memb Kent Schs Sports Cncl 1976–83; chm of Conf Ctee BSA Housemasters' and Headmistresses' Conf 1980 and 1981; HMC: memb 1988–, chm 2003, memb Sports Sub-Ctee 1989–91, memb Assisted Places Working Pty 1991–96, chm London Div 1993–94, chm Acad Policy Ctee 1998–2001 (memb 1995–2001); memb: Assisted Places Ctee ISJC 1991–96, Assoc for Science Educn 1968–88, SHA 1988–, Cncl Imperial Coll 1999–2006, Fin Ctee EDEXCEL 1998–2003, Ct of Imperial Coll London 1998–2006, Cncl of Roedean 2000–; pres Int Boys Schs Coalition 2006–; MInstD; FRSA 1994; *Recreations* cricket and golf, sailing, contract bridge, the theatre; *Clubs* East India & Public Schools (hon memb), MCC; *Style—* Graham Able, Esq; ✉ Elm Lawn, Dulwich Common, London SE21 7EW (tel 020 8693 0546); Dulwich College, London SE21 7LD (tel 020 8693 3601, fax 020 8693 6319, e-mail the.master@dulwich.org.uk)

ABLEMAN, Sheila; da of late Dennis Hutton-Fox, of Hove, E Sussex, and late Rosamund Alice Evelyn, *née* Tapsell; *b* 3 February 1949; *Educ* Cheam Co Sch for Girls, Epsom Art Sch, Cambridge Art Sch, Queen Mary Coll London (BA); *m* 1978, Paul Victor Ableman, novelist and playwright (d 2006); 1 s (Thomas Mark b 7 July 1981); *Career* designer's asst Weidenfeld & Nicolson Ltd 1970, editorial asst Victor Gollancz 1976–78; BBC Books: commissioning ed 1978–90, editorial dir 1990–99, literary agent 2000–; *Style—* Mrs Sheila Ableman; ✉ Lymehouse Studios, 38 Georgiana Street, London NW1 0EB

ABLETT, Timothy Andrew (Tim); s of Peter Edgar Ablett (d 1999), and Kathleen Vera Ablett (d 2000); *b* 14 October 1949; *Educ* Gravesend GS, Glyn GS, Kingston Poly; *m* 28 May 1977, Ann Millwood, *née* Hughes; 2 s (Justin Peter b 7 Nov 1978, Tarrant Paull b 28 Aug 1982), 1 da (Davinia Claire b 12 March 1980); *Career* chartered accountant; trainee rising to trg and audit ptnr John Baker, Sons & Bell 1968–83, gp fin controller Wigham Poland Hldgs Ltd 1983–86, gp fin dir The Legal Protection Gp Ltd 1986–90; Sun Alliance (now Royal & Sun Alliance): divnl mangr Broker Div Sun Alliance UK 1990–95, divnl mangr Personal Lines Sun Alliance Gen Insurance 1995–96, chief exec Bradford Pennine Insurance 1995–96, dir of personal insurances Broker Div Royal & Sun Alliance 1996–98, dir Healthcare and Assistance Royal & Sun Alliance Insurance Gp plc 1998–99; md Groupama Insurances 1999–2003, chief exec First Assist Gp Hldgs Ltd 2003–06 (non-exec dir 2006–, also non-exec dir First Assist Services Hldgs Ltd); chm Premier Occupational Health Co Ltd; non-exec dir: Int Assistance Gp SAS Paris 2004–06, Equity Insurance Brokers Ltd, Project Consltg Ptnrs Ltd, Marshall-James HR Ltd; memb Editorial Panel Insurance Times; chm Motor Ctee and memb Gen Insurers Mgmnt Ctee Assoc of Br Insurers 2001–03; chm of govrs Fallibroome HS Macclesfield 1992–98; Freeman City of London, Freeman Worshipful Co of Horners, Liveryman and memb Ct of Assts Worshipful Co of Insurers; memb Inst of Insurers; FCA 1974; *Recreations* avid hockey supporter (player, coach, umpire); *Clubs* RAC, Alderley Edge Hockey (vice-pres); *Style—* Tim Ablett, Esq; ✉ Benover House, Rectory Lane, Saltwood, Kent CT21 4QA (tel 01303 265460, fax 0870 131 6678, e-mail timablett@aol.com); First Assist Group Holdings Ltd, Marshall's Court, Marshall's Road, Sutton, Surrey SM1 4DU (e-mail tim.ablett@firstassist.co.uk)

ABOUD, Alan Kieran; s of Kibon M Aboud, and Mary, *née* Neylon; *b* 13 May 1966, Dublin; *Educ* Belvedere Coll Dublin, Nat Coll of Art and Design Dublin, St Martin's Sch of Art (BA); *m* 11 Sept 1993 (sep), Patricia Keating; 2 s (Victor Sylvester, Milo Van (twins) b 2 June 1995); *Career* designer; estab ABOUD SODANO with Sandro Sodano, *qv*, 1990 (currently creative dir); *Awards* Citation for Typographic Excellence NY Type Dirs' Club 1992, Silver Bell Award Irish Inst of Creative Advtg and Design 1994, Br D&AD Silver Award 1997 and 2002, Silver Cube Award NY Art Dirs' Club 2002, Gold Award Art Dirs' Club of Europe 2002; *Publications* Growing (1995), The End (2002); *Recreations* music, music video, film, armchair football supporter; *Style—* Alan K Aboud; ✉ ABOUD SODANO, Studio 26, Pall Mall Deposit, 124–128 Barlby Road, London W10 6BL (tel 020 8968 6142, fax 020 8968 6143, e-mail mail@aboud-sodano.com, website www.aboud-sodano.com)

ABRAHAM, Ann; *b* 25 August 1952; *Educ* Bedford Coll London (BA), City of London Poly (postgrad DMS); *Career* grad trainee (latterly estate mangr) London Borough of Tower Hamlets 1975–79, estate action mangr London Borough of Islington 1979–80; The Housing Corp: joined 1980, regnl dir 1986–89, ops dir 1989–90; chief exec Nat Assoc of Citizens Advice Bureaux 1991–97, legal servs ombudsman for England and Wales 1997–2002, UK Parly ombudsman and health serv ombudsman for England 2002–; chair British and Irish Ombudsman Assoc (BIOA) 2004–06 (memb Validation Ctee 2006–), memb Ctee on Standards in Public Life 2000–02; non-exec dir Benefits Agency 1997–2001; MCIH; *Recreations* family, friends, football and walking; *Style—* Ms Ann Abraham; ✉ Office of the Parliamentary and Health Service Ombudsman, Millbank Tower, Millbank, London SW1P 4QP (tel 020 7217 4211, e-mail privateoffice@ombudsman.gsi.gov.uk)

ABRAHAM, Neville Victor; CBE; s of Solomon Abraham (d 1991), and Sarah Raphael (d 1999); *b* 22 January 1937, Calcutta, India; *Educ* Brighton Coll, Univ of London, LSE (BSc); *m* Nicola Leach; *Career* sr princ Board of Trade and private sec to Min of State 1963–71; corporate policy advsr Whitehead Consulting Group 1971–76; fndr chm and md Amis du Vin Gp and Les Amis du Vin Ltd 1974–86; gp exec dir Kennedy Brookes plc 1984–86, dir Creative Business Communications plc 1986–91; fndr chm and chief exec: Groupe Chez Gérard Restaurants Ltd 1986–99, Groupe Chez Gérard plc 1994–2003 (exec chm 1999–2000 and 2002–03, non-exec chm 2000–02); non-exec chm Liberty Wines Ltd 2003–; visiting lectr at leading business schs 1974–83; jt exec chm BOC Covent Garden Festival 1991–99, chm London String Quartet Fndn 2000–06; vice-chm Restaurateurs Assoc of GB 1994–99; govr Brighton Coll 2006–; *Books* Big Business and Government: The New Disorder (1974); *Recreations* music, wine and food, sport; *Clubs* RAC, MCC, Home House; *Style—* Neville Abraham, CBE; ✉ 82 Addison Road, London W14 8ED

ABRAHAM, Prof Raymond John; s of Judah H Abraham (d 1989), and Elizabeth, *née* Harrop (d 2006); *b* 26 November 1933; *Educ* Magnus GS Newark, Univ of Birmingham (BSc, PhD, DSc); *m* 1, 16 Aug 1958 (m dis 1986), June Roslyn; 1 da (Susan Elizabeth b 8 Sept 1959), 2 s (David Joseph b 3 Sept 1962, Simon Douglas b 27 Oct 1969); m 2, 17 Sept 1988, Barbara Ann, da of Henry Broadbent (d 1982); *Career* postdoctoral fell NRC Canada 1957–59, sr fell Nat Physical Lab 1959–61, Univ of Liverpool 1961– (lectr, sr lectr, reader, prof 2001–, emeritus prof); visiting prof: Carnegie-Mellon Univ Pittsburgh 1966–67, Univ of Calif 1981–89; Ciba-Geigy fell Univ of Trondheim 1979; *Books* The Analysis of NMR Spectra (1971), Proton and Carbon 13 NMR Spectroscopy (with P Loftus, 1978), Introduction to NMR Spectroscopy (with J Fisher and P Loftus, 1988); *Recreations* golf, gardening, theatre; *Style—* Prof Raymond Abraham; ✉ 11 Lawns Avenue, Raby Mere, Wirral CH63 0NF; The Robert Robinson Laboratories, The Chemistry Department, The University of Liverpool, PO Box 147, Liverpool L69 3BX (tel 0151 794 3511, fax 0151 794 3588, e-mail abrahamr@liv.ac.uk)

ABRAHAM-WILLIAMS, Rev Gethin; s of late Lt-Col Alderman Emlyn Abraham-Williams, TD, DL, and late Anne Elizabeth Abraham-Williams; *Educ* Ardwyn GS Aberystwyth, UC of Wales Aberystwyth, Regent's Park Coll Oxford; *m* 1977, Denise Frances, *née* Harding; 1 s (Owain Huw), 1 da (Ellen Sian); *Career* asst min Queen's Road Baptist Church Coventry with Lenton's Lane Hawkesbury 1964–68, ordained 1965, min Chester Road Baptist Church Sutton Coldfield 1968–73, Westlake pastoral lectr Oxford 1973, min Sutton Baptist Church Surrey 1973–80, ecumenical offr and exec sec Milton Keynes Christian Cncl and Bishop of Oxford's ecumenical offr Milton Keynes 1980–90, gen sec ENFYS (Covenanted Churches in Wales) 1990–98, gen sec CYTÛN (Churches Together in Wales) 1998–2006 (memb Cncl 1995–); priory chaplain Order of St John of Jerusalem 2002–; memb: Consultative Ctee for Local Ecumenical Projects in Eng 1981–90 (moderator 1988–90), Bd for Ecumenical Affrs BCC 1987–90, Free Church Cncl 1991–96, Steering Ctee Cncl of Churches for Br and I 1992–, Ecumenical Advsy Gp Anglican Consultative Cncl 1997; Baptist Union of GB: accredited 1965, memb Cncl 1971–73 and 1993–95, memb Working Gp on Local Ecumenical Projects 1982–90, memb Worship and Doctrine Ctee 1993–95; memb local ecumenical ctee 2002; ed Baptist Ministers' Fellowship Jl 1998–2002; contrib: The Expository Times, Epworth Review, Baptist Times, Cristion; sometime presenter for radio stations incl: BBC World Serv, BBC Radio 4, BBC Radio Wales; *Books* Christian Baptism and Church Membership Vol II (ed, 1994), Letters to Friends (co-ed, 1996), Towards the Making of an Ecumenical Bishop in Wales (ed, 1997), Women, Church and Society in Wales (ed, 2004); *Videos* Perthyn i'n Gilydd (1994), People with Connections (1994), Mewn Amser (1998), Partners in Time (1998); *Recreations* radio, travel, theatre, books, eating out; *Style—* The Rev Gethin Abraham-Williams; ✉ 13 Millbrook Road, Dinas Powis, Vale of Glamorgan CF64 4BZ (tel 029 2051 5884)

ABRAHAMS, Col (Sidney) Anthony George; TD; s of Anthony Claude Walter Abrahams, of Goldsmith Building, Temple, London, and Laila, *née* Myking; *b* 30 October 1951; *Educ* Bedford Sch; *m* 6 Oct 1979, Kathryn Helen Anne, da of Humphrey John Patrick Chetwynd-Talbot, of South Warnborough, Hants; 2 da (Annika b 1983, Harriett b 1988), 1 s (Thomas b 1985); *Career* cmmnd 1976, Lt-Col 1994 rising to Col, Royal Green Jackets (V); admitted slr 1978; Wade-Gery and Brackenbury 1980–84, Alexander Farr and Son 1984–88, Pictons 1988 (head slr 2000), currently ptnr Heald Heffon; dep district judge Co Court 1989–; memb Law Soc; Freeman City of London 1985, Liveryman Worshipful Co of Glaziers and Painters of Glass 1985; *Recreations* TA, tennis, food and drink; *Clubs* Army and Navy; *Style—* Col Anthony Abrahams, TD; ✉ Woodfield, Honeydon Road, Colmworth, Bedfordshire MK44 2LZ (tel 01234 378996, e-mail abrahamsfamily@colmworth.demon.co.uk); Heald Heffron, Stewart House, 69–71 Bromham Road, Bedford MK40 2QD (tel 01234 360400, fax 01234 272419)

ABRAHAMS, Ivor; s of Harry Abrahams (d 1984), of Southport, and Rachel, *née* Kalisky (d 1983); *b* 10 January 1935; *Educ* Wigan GS, Southport Sch of Arts and Crafts, St Martin's Sch of Art, Camberwell Sch of Art (NDD); *m* 1, Victoria, da of Henry James Taylor; 1 s (Saul Benjamin b 27 March 1966 (decd)); m 2, Evelyne, da of Andre Horvais; 1 s (Etienne b 17 April 1973); *Career* artist, sculptor, photographer; teacher Royal Acad Schs 1999–; work incl: book illustrations and photographs, short films and videos; visiting lectr: Birmingham Coll of Art and Crafts 1960–63, Coventry Coll of Art and Crafts 1964–66, Goldsmiths' Coll of Art 1968–69, RCA 1980–81, Slade Sch UCL 1982, Winston Churchill fell 1990; RA 1991 (ARA 1989); *Solo Exhibitions* Arnolfini Gallery

Bristol 1971, Mappin Art Gallery Sheffield and Aberdeen Art Gallery 1972, Lijnbaan Centrum Rotterdam 1973, Kölnischer Kunstverein Cologne 1973, Ferens Art Gallery Kingston upon Hull 1979, Portsmouth City Art Gallery 1979, Middlesbrough Art Gallery 1979, Stoke-on-Trent City Museum 1979, St Enoch's Gallery Glasgow 1980, Warwick Arts Tst London 1982, Bolton Museum and Art Gallery 1984, Yorkshire Sculpture Park Wakefield 1984; *Group Exhibitions* 26 Young Sculptors (ICA London) 1961, Br Art Today (Palazzo Realle Milan) 1976, Silver Jubilee Exhibition (contemporary sculpture, Battersea Park) 1977, New Orleans Museum of Art 1978, Br Art Show 1980, Landscape Prints (Tate Gallery) 1981, Br Sculpture in the 20th Century 1951–80 (Whitechapel Art Gallery) 1982; public collections incl: Aberdeen Art Gallery and Museum, Arts Cncl of GB, Bibliothèque Nationale Paris, Br Cncl London, Metropolitan Museum New York, MOMA New York, Nat Gallery of Australia Canberra, Tate Gallery London, V&A, Buymans Museum Rotterdam, Denver Museum Colorado, Minneapolis Art Inst, Strasbourg Museum, Walker Art Gallery Liverpool, Wedgwood Museum Stoke-on-Trent, Wilhem Lembruke Museum Duisburg, Williams Coll Museum of Art Williamstown; *Commissions* Black Lion House London EC2, 24 Chancery Lane London EC1, Painshill Park Cobham, Kensington and Chelsea Town Hall; *Recreations* golf, photography, reading, collecting; *Clubs* Chelsea Arts; *Style*— Ivor Abrahams, Esq, RA; ✉ e-mail ieabrahams@onetel.com

ABRAHAMS, Mark Simon; s of Robert Abrahams; *b* 24 February 1955; *Educ* Wanstead Co HS, Trinity Coll Cambridge (MA); *m* 24 Aug 1991, Lucia Mary Caitriona; *Career* fin dir Coloroll Carpets/Edinburgh Crystal 1987–90, chief exec Fenner plc 1994– (gp fin dir 1990–94); non-exec chm: Darby Gp plc 1999–2003, Inditherm plc 2001–; memb Econ Affrs Ctee CBI; FCA 1979; *Recreations* travel, bridge, opera, fine wine; *Clubs* Oxford and Cambridge; *Style*— Mark Abrahams, Esq; ✉ Fenner plc, Hesslewood Country Office Park, Ferriby Road, Hessle HU13 0PW (tel 01482 626501, fax 01482 626502, e-mail mark.abrahams@fenner.com)

ABRAHAMS, Michael David; CBE 1994 (MBE 1988), DL (N Yorks 1994); s of Alexander Abrahams, and Anne, *née* Sokoloff; *b* 23 November 1937; *Educ* Shrewsbury, Worcester Coll Oxford; *m* 1967, Amanda, *née* Atha; 2 da (Emily, Victoria), 1 s (Rupert); *Career* cmmnd Royal Marines; md A W (Securities) Ltd 1968–73; dir: John Waddington plc 1984–2000, Drummond Group plc 1989–; chm Cavaghan and Gray Group plc (formerly Dalepak Foods plc) 1992–97 (dir 1987–97), non-exec chm Kingston Communications plc 1999–, non-exec chm Amteus plc; dep chm: York Trust plc 1985–88, John Crowther plc 1985–88, Prudential Corporation plc 1991–2000 (dir 1984–2000); non-exec dir Minorplanet Systems plc 1997–2004 (latterly non-exec chm); dir The Rank Fndn 1992–; pres British Carpet Manufacturers' Assoc 1979–80; chm: Ripon Improvement Tst 1994–, Nat Tst Regl Ctee for Yorks 1996–2002, The London Clinic 1996– (govr 1990–); dep chm Cncl Prince of Wales's Inst of Architecture 1991–99; High Sheriff N Yorks 1993–94; breeder of pedigree beef shorthorns; jt master and huntsman West of Yore Hunt 1970–81, jt master Bedale Hunt 1971–79; Hon Freeman City of Ripon 2002; Master Worshipful Co of Woolmen 1996; *Recreations* reading, architecture, shooting, sailing; *Clubs* Garrick, Pratt's; *Style*— Michael Abrahams, Esq, CBE, DL; ✉ Newfield, Mickley, Ripon, North Yorkshire HG4 3JH (tel 01765 635426, fax 01765 635461)

ABRAHAMS, Paul Richard; s of Anthony Claud Walter Abrahams, of London, and Laila, *née* Myking; *b* 20 April 1962; *Educ* Radley, Downing Coll Cambridge (BA, MA), Darwin Coll Cambridge (PhD, Fencing half blue); *m* 1997, Abby Deveney; 1 da (Sophie Eleanor Deveney Abrahams b 1997), 1 s (Matthew Paul Deveney Abrahams b 2000); *Career* FT: technol corr 1988–89, dep defence and aerospace corr 1989–91, chemicals and pharmaceuticals corr 1991–94, Lex columnist 1994–95, int cos ed 1995–97, bureau chief Tokyo 1997–2000, bureau chief Silicon Valley 2000–03; md Waggener Edstrom Ltd 2003–06, dir of communications Europe Nomura 2006–; *Publications* La Haute-Savoie contre elle-même: 1939–45 (2006); *Recreations* skiing, fencing; *Clubs* Garrick, Lansdowne, Ski Club of GB; *Style*— Paul Abrahams, Esq

ABRAM, Rev Paul Robert Carrington; MVO (2007); s of Rev Norman Abram (d 1985), and Madge Alice Abram (d 1994); *b* 21 July 1936; *Educ* Farnborough GS, King Alfred Sch Plön Holstein Germany, Hymers Coll Hull, Keble Coll Oxford (MA), Chichester Theol Coll; *m* 24 June 1961, Joanna Rose, da of Rev Lewis Victor Headley; 4 da (Felicity Shân b 26 Aug 1962, Kathryn Lucy Elaine b 29 May 1965, Rachel Alice Sophie b 27 Oct 1968, Emily Jane Patience b 23 March 1970); *Career* curate St Peter's Redcar Cleveland 1962–65; army chaplain 1965–89: sr chaplain 16 Para Bde 1974–76, Dortmund Garrison 1976–78, Shrivenham 1978–80, Hong Kong 1980–82, 2 Div 1982–83, Falklands 1983–84, Berlin 1984–86, NI 1986–87, Western Dist/Wales 1987–89; vicar of Salcombe Devon 1989–96; dep priest in ordinary 1996–; chaplain: HM Tower of London 1996–, Worshipful Co of Slrs 1996–, Worshipful Co of Builders' Merchants 1996–; also Missions to Seamen chaplain Pool of London, chaplain HMS President; FRGS 1960; *Recreations* sailing, maps, collecting books; *Clubs* Special Forces; *Style*— The Rev Paul Abram, MVO; ✉ 1 The Green, HM Tower of London, London EC3N 4AB (tel 020 7488 5689, fax 020 7702 2214, e-mail paul.jo@virgin.net)

ABRAM, Prof Richard Arthur; s of Richard Abram (d 1991), and Kathleen Lilian, *née* Radbourne (d 1989); *b* 25 March 1947, Southport, Lancs; *Educ* Chiswick Co GS for Boys, Univ of Manchester (BSc, Dip Advanced Studies in Science, PhD); *m* 29 Dec 1973, Jane, da of Dennis Cuppello (d 2004), of Ashton-under-Lyne, Lancs; 1 s (Edward John b 17 July 1976), 2 da (Anna Christabel b 6 Oct 1979, Francesca Clare b 12 July 1985); *Career* sr scientist rising to princ scientist Plessey Research (Caswell) Ltd 1972–78, conslt GEC-Marconi Materials Technol Ltd 1978–94; Univ of Durham: lectr in applied physics 1978–85, sr lectr in applied physics 1985–92, reader in physics 1992–95, prof of physics 1995–, head Dept of Physics 2003–; chm Semiconductor Physics Gp Inst of Physics 1999–2003 (memb Ctee 1987–91); memb: Electronic Materials Ctee SERC 1992–94, Physics Ctee SERC 1993–94, EPSRC Peer Review Coll 1995–, Advsy Bd Inst of Physics Jl of Physics: Condensed Matter 2000–03; author of numerous research papers in scientific jls; memb Senate Durham Univ 2003–; CEng, CPhys, FInstP, FHEA; *Style*— Prof Richard Abram; ✉ Department of Physics, University of Durham, Durham DH1 3LE (tel 0191 334 3637, fax 0191 334 3551, e-mail r.a.abram@durham.ac.uk)

ABRAMOVICH, Solomon; s of Dr Jacob Abramovich, MD (d 1977), and Bronia Maisel (d 1980); *b* 12 December 1946; *Educ* Sch of Music, Kaunas Med Sch (MSc, MB BS); *Children* 1 s (Alexander Jacob b 5 Jan 1992), 2 da (Natalia Bronia b 6 Jan 1996, Katerina Rachel b 31 July 2000); *Career* Radcliffe Infirmary Oxford 1974–75, Hammersmith Hosp London 1975, UCH 1976–78, King's Coll Hosp 1979, clinical fell Univ of Toronto 1983, St Bartholomew's and Nat Hosp for Neurology and Neurosurgery London 1982, conslt ENT surgn St Mary's Hosp London and Central Middlesex Hosp 1988; hon clinical sr lectr ICSTM 1989, hon conslt Royal London Hosp, hon conslt Charing Cross Hosp London, hon conslt to Gibraltar; memb: Int Barany Soc, Int Maniere's Soc; fndr memb: Standing Ctee Euro Acad of Otology, Cochlear Implant Gp; memb RSM (memb Cncl); FRCS (MRCS), LRCP; *Books* Electric Response Audiometry in Clinical Practice (1990), Clinical Surgery Textbook (contrib, 2001, revised edn 2004); *Recreations* tennis, skiing, playing the violin; *Clubs* Athenaeum; *Style*— Solomon Abramovich, Esq; ✉ 106 Harley Street, London W1G 6JE (tel 020 7935 0604, fax 020 7935 1022, e-mail solomon@abramovich.org.uk)

ABRAMS, Charles; s of Mozus Mischa Abrams (d 1987), of London, and Evelyn Joyce, *née* Spitzel (d 1996); *b* 2 November 1952; *Educ* St Paul's, Trinity Coll Cambridge (BA); *m* 30 Aug 1987, Georgia Gitelle Devora, da of James Leo Rosengarten, of London, and Naomi, *née* Alexander; 1 da (Alexandra Berina Amelia b 29 May 1990), 1 s (Boris Yoshua Avitzur b 27 July 1992); *Career* slr Linklaters & Paines 1976–85 (articled 1974), ptnr SJ Berwin & Co 1988– (slr 1985–88); special legal advsr to Opposition Treasy Team on the Fin Services and Markets Bill; FSA Ctee Assoc of Private Client Investment Mangrs and Stockbrokers; memb Fin Servs Gp CBI; memb Fin Servs Sub-Ctee City of London Law Soc; various pubns in jls and speaker at seminars on securities law; formerly: arbitrator Securities and Futures Authy Consumer Arbitration Scheme, special advsr on venture capital Investment Mgmnt Regulatory Orgn; memb: City Regulatory Panel CBI, Law Soc; *Books* Guide to Financial Services Regulation (jtly, 3 edn 1997), A Short Guide to the Financial Services and Markets Act 2000 (2000); contrib: Pension Fund Investment (1987), Bond Market Compliance (1992), Futures Trading Law and Regulation (1993), International Survey of Investment Adviser Regulation (2 edn 1999), Butterworths Financial Services Law Guide (chapter on market abuse with Tamasin Little, 2002); *Recreations* looking after my children, theatre; *Style*— Charles Abrams, Esq; ✉ SJ Berwin & Co, 222 Gray's Inn Road, London WC1X 8XF (tel 020 7533 2222, fax 020 7533 2000)

ABRAMSKY, Jennifer (Jenny); CBE (2001); da of Chimen Abramsky, and Miriam, *née* Nirenstein (d 1997); *b* 7 October 1946; *Educ* Holland Park Sch, UEA (BA); *m* Alasdair D MacDuff Liddell, CBE, *qv*; 1 s, 1 da; *Career* BBC: joined 1969 as progs ops asst, prodr The World At One 1973 (ed 1981), jt prodr special prog on Nixon 1974, ed PM 1978, prodr Radio 4's Budget progs 1979–86, ed Today Prog 1986–87, ed News and Current Affrs Radio 1987–93 (set up Radio 4 Gulf FM for duration of Gulf War), controller Radio 5 Live and head of Ceefax 1994–96, dir Continuous News 1996–98, dir BBC Radio 1998–2000, dir BBC Audio and Music 2000–; dep chair Digital Radio Devpt Bureau (DRDB) 2002–, memb Bd of Govrs BFI 2000–; special award for Radio 5 Live Sony Radio Awards 1995, UK Station of the Year Sony Radio Awards 1996; Woman of Distinction award (Jewish Care) 1990; appointed to ESRC 1992–96; News Int visiting prof of broadcast media Univ of Oxford 2002, hon prof Thames Valley Univ 1994; dir Rajar 1995–, chm Hampstead Theatre 2005 (dir 2003–05); fell Radio Acad 1998; *Recreations* theatre, music; *Style*— Ms Jenny Abramsky, CBE; ✉ Room 2811, Broadcasting House, Portland Place, London W1A 1AA (tel 020 7765 4561)

ABSE, Dr Dannie; s of Rudolf Abse (d 1964), of Cardiff, and Kate, *née* Shepherd (d 1981); *b* 22 September 1923; *Educ* St Illtyd's Coll Cardiff, Univ of Wales Cardiff, King's Coll London, Westminster Hosp London (MRCS, LRCP); *m* 4 Aug 1951, Joan (d 2005), da of John Mercer, of St Helens, Lancs; 2 da (Keren Danielle b 1953, Susanna Ruth b 1957), 1 s (Jesse David b 1958); *Career* RAF 1951–54 Sqdn Ldr i/c Chest Clinic Central Med Estab London 1954–82; poet, playwright and novelist; sr fell of humanities Princeton Univ 1973–74; pres: Poetry Soc 1979–92, Welsh Acad of Letters 1995; Hon DLitt: Univ of Wales 1990, Univ of Glamorgan 1997; fell The Welsh Acad 1991–95, hon fell Univ of Cardiff Med Sch 1999; FRSL 1983; *Poetry* After Every Thing Green (1948), Walking Under Water (1952), Tenants of the House (1957), Poems Golders Green (1962), A Small Desperation (1968), Funland and Other Poems (1973), Collected Poems (1977), Way Out in the Centre (1981), Ask the Bloody Horse (1986), White Coat, Purple Coat (1989), Remembrance of Crimes Past (1990), On The Evening Road (1994), Welsh Retrospective (1997), Arcadia, One Mile (1998), New and Collected Poems (2003); *Prose* A Strong Dose of Myself (1983), Journals from the Ant-Heap (1986), Intermittent Journals (1994); *Novels* Ash on a Young Man's Sleeve (1954), Some Corner of an English Field (1957), O Jones, O Jones (1970), There Was a Young Man from Cardiff (1991), The Strange Case of Dr Simmonds and Dr Glas (2002); *Autobiography* A Poet in the Family (1974), Goodbye, Twentieth Century (2001), The Presence (2006); *Plays* House of Cowards (1960), The Dogs of Pavlov (1969), Pythagoras (1976), Gone in January (1978); *Anthologies* ed: Mavericks (with Howard Sergeant, 1957), Modern European Verse (1964), Voices in the Gallery (with Joan Abse, 1986), The Music Lover's Literary Companion (with Joan Abse, 1988), The Hutchinson Book of Post-War British Poets (1989), 20th Century Anglo-Welsh Poetry (1997); *Style*— Dr Dannie Abse; ✉ Green Hollows, Craig-yr-Eos Road, Ogmore-by-Sea, Glamorgan, South Wales

ABULAFIA, Prof David Samuel Harvard; s of Leon Abulafia (d 1963), and Rachel, *née* Zafransky (d 1997); *b* 12 December 1949; *Educ* St Paul's, King's Coll Cambridge (BA), Gonville & Caius Coll Cambridge (MA, PhD, LittD); *m* 12 Dec 1979, Dr Anna Sapir Abulafia; 2 da (Bianca Susanna b 15 Nov 1984, Rosa Alexandra b 6 March 1987); *Career* fell Gonville & Caius Coll Cambridge 1974– (tutor for grad students 1984–91); Univ of Cambridge: lectr in history 1983–91 (asst lectr 1978–83), reader in Mediterranean history 1991–2000, prof of Mediterranean history 2000–, chm Faculty of History 2003–; Rome scholar Br Sch at Rome 1972–74; delivered guest lectures at Nat Gall of Art Washington, Bibliotheca Alexandrina Egypt and numerous univs (incl: Tokyo, Kyoto, Jerusalem, Tel Aviv, Aix, Naples, Pisa, Barcelona); memb Review Ctee Ben Gurion Univ of Negev 1999–2000, project co-ordinator EU Culture 2000 2000–03; govr Perse Sch Cambridge 2002–; memb Academia Europaea 2002–, FRHistS 1981; Commendatore dell'Ordine della Stella della Solidarietà Italiana 2003; *Books* incl: The Two Italies (1977), Italy, Sicily and the Mediterranean (1987), Frederick II (1988, 3 edn 2002), Spain and 1492 (1992), Church and City (jt ed, 1992), Commerce and Conquest in the Mediterranean (1993), A Mediterranean Emporium (1994), The French Descent into Renaissance Italy (ed, 1995), The Western Mediterranean Kingdoms (1997), En las costas del Mediterráneo occidental (jt ed, 1997), The New Cambridge Medieval History vol 5 (ed, 1999), Mediterranean Encounters (2000), Medieval Frontiers (jt ed, 2002), The Mediterranean in History (ed, 2003), Italy in the Central Middle Ages (ed, 2004), The Discovery of Mankind (2008); *Recreations* travel; *Style*— Prof David Abulafia; ✉ Gonville & Caius College, Cambridge CB2 1TA (tel 01223 332400, fax 01223 332456, e-mail dsa1000@hermes.cam.ac.uk)

ACHER, Gerald (Gerry); CBE (1999), LVO (2002); s of David Acher (d 1979), and Andrée Diana, *née* Laredo; *b* 30 April 1945; *Educ* KCS Wimbledon; *m* 18 July 1970, Joyce Kathleen, *née* White; 2 s (James David b 4 July 1973, Mark Gerald b 3 Jan 1976); *Career* articled clerk Bird Potter & Co 1961–66; KPMG (and predecessor firms): asst mangr 1967–73, mangr 1973–75, sr mangr 1975–80, ptnr 1980–, memb UK Bd 1987–2001, head Corp Fin 1990–93, UK head Audit and Accounting 1993–98, chm World-Wide Audit and Accounting Ctee 1995–98, chm Client Service Bd 1998–2001, sr ptnr London 1998–2001; non-exec dir: BPB plc 2002–, Camelot Group plc 2002– (interim chm 2004); chm London Mayoral Cmmn into an Int Convention Centre for London; memb: Cncl and chm Audit Faculty ICAEW 1995–2001, Bd London First Centre 1998–2001, Bd and dep chm London First 1999–, Advsy Ctee for Business and the Environment; govr and vice-chm Motability, tstee Motability 10th Anniversary Tst, chm of Govrs Milbourne Lodge Jr Sch; William Quilter Prize, Plender Prize for Auditing ICA 1966; memb Ct of Assts Worshipful Co of Chartered Accountants (Master 2003–04); FCA 1977 (ACA 1967), fell Securities Industries Assoc, FRSA (also tstee, memb Cncl and sr treas); *Recreations* mountain walking, rallying, classic and vintage cars, opera and music, gardening, watching rugby; *Clubs* Travellers; *Style*— Gerry Acher, Esq, CBE, LVO; ✉ Church Stile House, Church Street, Cobham, Surrey KT11 3EG (tel 01932 865224, e-mail achers@church-stile.fsnet.co.uk); 8 Salisbury Square, London EC4Y 8BB (tel 020 7311 8640, fax 020 7311 8718)

ACKFORD, Paul John; *b* 26 February 1958; *m* Suzie Mummé; *Career* former rugby union player (lock); clubs: Plymouth Albion, Rosslyn Park, Metropolitan Police, Harlequins; England: B debut 1979, full debut v Aust 1988, Five Nations debut v Scotland 1989, memb Grand Slam winning team 1991, memb World Cup runners-up team 1991, 22 caps; 3 test appearances Br Lions 1989; memb: RFU Ctee 1992–94, Surrey RFU Ctee 1992–94;

former police offr; currently rugby corr The Sunday Telegraph; *Recreations* cooking, entertaining, golf; *Style*— Paul Ackford, Esq; ✉ c/o The Sunday Telegraph, 1 Canada Square, Canary Wharf, London E14 5AR (tel 020 7538 5000)

ACKLAND, Joss (Sidney Edmond Jocelyn); CBE (2001); s of Maj Sidney Norman Ackland (d 1981), and Ruth, *née* Izod (d 1957); *b* 29 February 1928; *Educ* Dame Alice Owens Sch, Central Sch of Speech Training and Dramatic Art; *m* 18 Aug 1951, Rosemary Jean (d 2002), da of Capt Robert Hunter Kirkcaldy (d 1954); 5 da (Melanie b 1952, Antonia b 1956, Penelope b 1958, Samantha b 1962, Kirsty b 1963), 2 s (Paul b 1953 d 1982, Toby b 1966); *Career* actor; worked in theatre since 1945, tea planter Central Africa 1954–55, disc jockey in Cape Town 1955–57; memb: Drug Helpline, Amnesty International, Covent Garden Community Assoc; *Theatre* rep work incl: Stratford-on-Avon, Arts Theatre, Buxton, Croydon, The Embassy Coventry, Oxford, Pitlochry; Old Vic Theatre Co 1958–61, roles incl: Toby Belch, Caliban, Pistol, Lord Froth in The Double Dealer, Aegisthus in The Oresteia and Falstaff in Henry IV part 1, The Merry Wives of Windsor; artistic dir Mermaid Theatre 1961–63; roles incl: Galileo, Long John Silver, Bluntschli in Arms and the Man, Scrofulovsky in The Bedbug, Kirilov in the Possessed; dir Plough and the Stars; *West End* roles incl: Professor in The Professor, Gus in Hotel in Amsterdam, Come As You Are, Sam in The Collaborators, Mitch in A Streetcar Named Desire, Brassbound in Captain Brassbound's Conversion, Stewart in A Pack of Lies, Clarence Darrow in Never the Sinner, Weller Martin in The Gin Game; *Other* roles incl: Gaev in The Cherry Orchard (Chichester), Petruchio in The Taming of the Shrew, Sir in The Dresser (both nat tours), Eustace Perrin State in The Madras House, Romain Gary in Jean Seburg (both NT); Opening of the Barbican Theatre: Falstaff in Henry IV Parts 1 and 2, Captain Hook and Mr Darling in Peter Pan; most recently Alfred Ill in The Visit (Chichester) 1995, John Tarleton in Misalliance (Chichester) 1997, Captain Shotover in Heartbreak House (Chichester) 2000; *West End Musicals* incl: Squeezum in Lock Up Your Daughters, title role in Jorrocks, Fredrik in A Little Night Music, Peron in Evita, Captain Hook and Mr Darling in Peter Pan - The Musical, Honore L'Achailles in Gigi, The King in The King and I; *Television* numerous appearances incl: Kipling in the Kipling series, D'Artagnan in Twenty Years After, Barrett in The Barretts of Wimpole Street, C S Lewis in Shadowlands, Clarence Darrow in Never the Sinner, Terence Fielding in A Murder of Quality, Archie in Voices in the Garden, Alan Holly in First and Last, Bondarchuk in Citizen X, Henry VII in Henry VIII, Mustrum Ridcully in The Hogfather; mini-series incl: Heat of the Sun, Herman Goering in The Man Who Lived at The Ritz, Sir Burton in Queenie, Onassis in A Woman Named Jackie; *Radio* roles incl: God, Macbeth, Falstaff, Flashman, Kafka's Dog, Victor Hugo, Georges Simeon; *Film* incl: Seven Days to Noon, Forbush and the Penguins, The House that Dripped Blood, Villain, Crescendo, The Happiness Cage, England Made Me, Hitler - The Last Ten Days, The Black Windmill, The Little Prince, S-P-Y-S, Royal Flash, One of our Dinosaurs is Missing, Operation Daybreak, Silver Bears, Watership Down, Who is Killing the Great Chefs of Europe?, Saint Jack, The Apple, Rough Cut, Lady Jane, A Zed and Two Noughts, It Couldn't Happen Here, Don Masino in The Sicilian, The Colonel in To Kill a Priest, Sir Jock Delves Broughton in White Mischief, Arjen Rudd in Lethal Weapon 2, Russian Ambassador in The Hunt for Red October, The Man of Power in The Palermo Connection, Tre Colonne in Cronaca, The Object of Beauty, The Sheltering Desert, The Bridge, Georgino, Brando in Occhio Pinocchio, Hale in Nowhere to Run, Isaac in The Bible, Miracle on 34th Street, Stringer in Mad Dogs and Englishmen, Gerald Carmody in Daisies in December, King Francis in Till the End of Time, King Arthur in A Kid at the Court of King Arthur, Mighty Ducks 1 & 3, Matisse in Surviving Picasso, The Captain in Deadly Voyage, Lord Claire in Firelight, Swaffer in Amy Foster, Bennett in Hall of Mirrors, Lord Wyndham in Son of Sandokarn, Milk, Passion of Mind, Mumbo Jumbo, Defense Min Malinovsky in K19 the Widowmaker, Mr Quarre in The House on Turk Street, Evil Edmonds in I'll Be there, Randolph Caulffield in A Different Loyalty, Jack Straffen in Asylum, The Icon in Icon, Charlie in These Foolish Things; *Books* I Must Be in There Somewhere (autobiography, 1989); *Recreations* writing, painting, reading, 31 grandchildren, 3 great grandchildren; *Style*— Joss Ackland, Esq; ✉ c/o Harris Pearson, 64–66 Millman Street, London WC1N 3EF (tel 030 7430 9890, fax 020 7430 9229, website www.harrispearson.co.uk)

ACKLAND-SNOW, Brian Percy; s of Frank Whittlesey Ackland-Snow (d 1974), and Ivy Jesse Byway; *b* 31 March 1940; *Educ* Harrow Sch of Art; *m* 24 Sept 1960, Carol Avis, da of James Dunsby (d 1963); 1 s (Andrew b 1961), 1 da (Amanda b 1963 d 2007); *Career* prodn designer and art director; memb: BAFTA, AMPAS, ATAS; *Films* incl: Death on the Nile, McVicar, Superman III, Room with a View (BAFTA Award for Production Design, Academy Award for Art Direction), Maurice, Without a Clue, The Secret Garden, Scarlett (Emmy Award for Art Direction), Animal Farm, The Magnificent Ambersons; *Recreations* historical architecture, archaeology; *Style*— Brian Ackland-Snow, Esq

ACKROYD, Jane Victoria Macleod; da of late Sir John Robert Whyte Ackroyd, 2 Bt, and Jennifer Eileen Macleod, *née* Bishop; *b* 25 February 1957; *Educ* Godolphin & Latymer Sch, St Martin's Sch of Art (BA), Royal Coll of Art (MA); *m* (m dis 2001), David Robert Ewart Annesley; 1 s (William Harry Macleod b 31 August 1992); *Career* artist; exhibitions incl: The Albert Exhibition 1983, Anti-thesis (Angela Flowers Gallery) 1986, Anderson O'Day summer exhibition 1987 and 1988, The Royal Academy Summer Exhibition 1988, 1989, 1997, 1998, 2001 2002 and 2005; solo exhibitions incl: Kingsgate Workshops Gallery 1984, 1985, 1986, 1987 and 2002, Anderson O'Day Gallery 1988 and 1991, Provost's Garden Worcester Coll Oxford (major retrospective exhibition) 1997, Lynne Gould's 102 2004; work in public and private collections incl: The Arts Cncl of GB, The Contemporary Arts Soc, The Harlow Arts Tst; cmmn: Moonlight Ramble (Haymarket) 1992, Limehouse Narrow Street (Herring Gull) 1994; Pollock/Krasner Fndn Award USA 1995; Freeman: City of London 1980, Worshipful Co of Carpenters; *Recreations* walking, music; *Style*— Miss Jane Ackroyd; ✉ Kingsgate Workshops, 116 Kingsgate Road, London NW6 (tel 020 7328 7878, mobile 07931 543426, e-mail jane.ackroyd@blueyonder.co.uk, website www.janeackroyd.co.uk)

ACKROYD, Norman; CBE (2007); s of Albert Ackroyd (d 1976), of Leeds, and Clara Briggs (d 1979); *b* 26 March 1938; *Educ* Cockburn HS Leeds, Leeds Coll of Art, RCA; *m* 1, 1963 (m dis 1975), Sylvia, *née* Buckland; 2 da (Felicity b 1964, Justine b 1966); m 2, 1978, Penelope, da of Blair Hughes-Stanton; 1 da (Poppy b 1981), 1 s (Simeon b 1983); *Career* artist (painter and etcher); tutor in etching Central Sch of Arts London 1965–93; TV appearances: Artists in Print (BBC 2) 1981, Paul Sandby (Central) 1987, Prospects of Rivers (Channel 4) 1988; RE 1985, RA 1991 (ARA 1988); *Solo Exhibitions* incl: Anderson O'Day Gallery London 1980 and 1988, Associated American Artists Philadelphia 1981 and 1983, Mickelson Gallery Washington DC 1982, Yehudi Menuhin Sch Surrey 1983, Jersey Arts Centre Channel Islands 1984, Dolan/Maxwell Gallery Philadelphia 1985, 1987 and 1989, Dena Clough Gallery Halifax 1986, Nat Museum of Art Santiago Chile 1987, Royal Soc of Painter-Etchers and Engravers London 1988, Compass Gallery Glasgow 1990, Harewood House 1997; Work in public collections incl: The Br Museum, Tate Gallery, Albertina Museum Vienna, Arts Cncl GB, Boston Museum of Fine Arts, Br Cncl, Chicago Art Inst, Musée D'Art Historie Geneva, MOMA NY, National Galleries of Norway, Canada, Scotland and SA, Queensland Art Gallery Aust, Rijksmuseum, V&A; cmmnd murals for: Albany Hotel Glasgow 1974, Albany Hotel Birmingham 1977, Haringey Cncl 1982–83, Lloyds Bank 1990, British Airways 1991; *Awards* SE States Open exhibition 1969, Bradford International Biennale 1972 and 1982, Royal Soc of Painter-Etchers and Engravers 1984 and 1985, Frechen Triennale Germany 1986; *Recreations* cricket; *Clubs* Chelsea Arts, Arts; *Style*— Norman Ackroyd, Esq, CBE, RA

ACKROYD, Peter; CBE (2003); s of Graham Ackroyd, and Audrey, *née* Whiteside; *b* 5 October 1949; *Educ* Clare Coll Cambridge, Yale Univ; *Career* writer; The Spectator: lit ed 1971–77, managing ed 1977–81; chief book reviewer The Times 1986–; Somerset Maugham Prize 1984, The Guardian Fiction Award 1985, Whitbread Prize for Best Biography 1984/85; Hon DLitt: Univ of Exeter 1992, City Univ 1997, Univ of London 2001; FRSL; *Poetry* London Lickpenny (1973), Country Life (1978), The Diversions of Purley (1987); *Non-Fiction* Notes for a New Culture (1976), Ezra Pound and His World (1980), T S Eliot (1984), Dickens (1990), Introduction to Dickens (1991), Blake (1995), The Life of Thomas More (1998), London: The Biography (2000), The Collection (2001), Albion: The Origins of the English Imagination (2002), Chaucer (2004), Shakespeare: The Biography (2005), Thames: Sacred River (2007); *Novels* The Great Fire of London (1982), The Last Testament of Oscar Wilde (1983), Hawksmoor (1985), Chatterton (1987), First Light (1989), English Music (1992), The House of Doctor Dee (1993), Dan Leno and the Limehouse Golem (1994), Milton in America (1996), The Plato Papers (1999), The Clerkenwell Tales (2003), The Lambs of London (2004); *Style*— Peter Ackroyd, Esq, CBE, FRSL; ✉ c/o Sheil Land Associates, 43 Doughty Street, London WC1N 2LF (tel 020 7405 9351)

ACKROYD, Sir Timothy Robert Whyte; 3 Bt (UK 1956), of Dewsbury, W Riding of Yorks; s of Sir John Robert Whyte Ackroyd, 2 Bt (d 1995), and Jennifer Eileen MacLeod, *née* Bishop (d 1997); *b* 7 October 1958; *Educ* Bradfield, LAMDA; *Heir* bro, Andrew Ackroyd; *Career* actor; dir Martingale Productions 1985–, fndr Archview Film Prodns, dir LISA 1991–; conslt Hotspur Fim Prodns and 11th Duke of Northumberland; hon memb Theatre of Comedy 1984, fndr tstee and patron of charity Tusk Tst 1989, tstee: Marjorie & Dorothy Whyte Memorial Fund 1992, The Ackroyd Tst 1994, Ackroyd/Pullan Prodns 1994, Ackroyd & Co 2004; memb: Exec Ctee Earth 2000, Ctee Have-A-Go-Holidays; Freeman City of London, Liveryman Worshipful Co of Carpenters 1982; *Theatre* incl: Agamemnon (West End Theatre Critics' Award nomination Most Promising Newcomer) 1976, On Approval 1979, Much Ado About Nothing 1980, A Month in the Country 1981, Man and Superman 1982, A Sleep of Prisoners 1983, Pygmalion 1984, Another Country 1986, No Sex Please - We're British 1987, Black Coffee 1988, The Reluctant Debutante 1989, Jeffrey Bernard is Unwell 1989–91, Journey's End 1993, The Bad Soldier Smith 1995, Super-Beasts 1997, A Step Out of Time 1998, Jeffrey Bernard is Unwell 1999, The Rivals 2000, A Step Out of Time 2000 (USA 2001), Village Wooing 2002, You're Alright - How Am I 2002, Henry IV Part I 2003, Les Parents Terribles 2004, A Compassionate Satirist 2005 and 2006; *Films and Television* incl: Jack Be Nimble 1979, Martin Luther - Heretic 1983, Creator 1984 (Hollywood), Man and Superman 1985, That Has Such People In It 1987, Pied Piper 1989, Bullseye 1989, The Wildlands (Kenya) 1992, A Royal Scandal 1996, The Mummy's Curse 1998, The New Avengers 1998, Timewatch 2003; *Radio* Jakob Beer in Fugitive Pieces 1998, Life Story 2003; *Publications* Ackroyd's Ark (2004); *Recreations* rugby, literature, history, sumo wrestling; *Clubs* MCC, Garrick; *Style*— Sir Timothy Ackroyd, Bt

ACLAND, Lt-Col Sir (Christopher) Guy Dyke; 6 Bt (UK 1890), of St Mary Magdalen, Oxford; LVO (1999, MVO 1990), DL (Isle of Wight 2002); s of Sir Antony Acland, 5 Bt (d 1983), and Margaret, Lady Acland; *b* 24 March 1946; *Educ* Allhallows Sch, RMA Sandhurst; *m* 1971, Christine Mary Carden, da of late John William Brodie Waring; 2 s (Alexander b 1973, Hugh b 1976); *Heir* s, Alexander Acland; *Career* cmmnd RA 1966, served UK, Germany and Hong Kong, 2 i/c 1 RHA 1985–88, Equerry to HRH The Duke of Edinburgh 1988–90, Lt-Col 1990, SO1 Mgmnt Servs (Org 3) MOD 1990–92, cmd Southampton UOTC 1992–94, ret; Dep Master HM Household and Equerry to HM The Queen 1994–99, Extra Equerry to HM The Queen 1999–; administrator HSA Charitable Tst 2000–06; Vice Lord-Lt IOW 2006–; *Recreations* sailing, gardening; *Clubs* Royal Yacht Squadron, Royal Artillery Yacht; *Style*— Lt-Col Sir Guy Acland, Bt, LVO, DL

ACLAND, Sir John Dyke; 16 Bt (E 1678, with precedence from 1644), of Columb-John, Devon; eldest s of Sir Richard Thomas Dyke Acland, 15 Bt (d 1990), and Anne Stella, *née* Alford (d 1992); *b* 13 May 1939; *Educ* Clifton, Magdalene Coll Cambridge (MA), Univ of West Indies (MSc); *m* 1, 9 Sept 1961, Virginia, yr da of Roland Forge, of Barnoldby-le-Beck, Lincs; 2 s (Dominic Dyke b 1962, Piers Dyke b 1965), 1 da (Holly b 1972); m 2, 24 Aug 2001, Susan, 2 da of Herbert Hooper, of Bury St Edmunds, Suffolk; *Heir* s, Dominic Acland; *Style*— Sir John Acland, Bt; ✉ 26A Cambridge Place, Cambridge CB2 1NS

ACLAND, (Anne) Maureen; OBE (1988); da of Stanley Ryder Runton (d 1983), of Ilkley, W Yorks, and Kathleen Ryder Runton, CBE, *née* Carter (d 1974); *b* 3 October 1934; *Educ* privately in England and Paris; *m* 1956, Martin Edward Acland, JP, DL; 3 s (Michael Christopher Dyke b 1958, Richard Arthur Dyke b 1962, Peter Edward Dyke b 1964); *Career* FO 1954–56; memb Cncl St John Herts 1970–, memb London Choral Soc 1970–78 (memb Cncl 1973–78); Nat Gardens Scheme: co-organiser 1971–87, memb Nat Cncl 1978–2006, tstee 1989–2006; pres and tstee Herts Nursing Tst 1975–, vice-pres Queen's Nursing Inst 2003– (chm 1978–2002), vice-pres and exec Ctee Dist Nursing Assoc UK 1979–95, memb Grants Ctee Nation's Fund for Nurses 1980–, Cdr St John Ambulance Herts 1987–99 (co cmmr 1987–99), chm Florence Nightingale Fndn 1987–, assoc tstee Florence Nightingale Museum Tst 1988, tstee Anne Driver Tst 2005–; Order of St John: Dame of Justice, Chapter Gen 1987–99, memb Cncl 1993–99; Liveryman Worshipful Co of Musicians; FRSM 1990 (memb Cncl Open Section 1985–2004, treas 1990–93, vice-pres 1993–99), LRAM, FRSA, FRSM; *Recreations* life (country, family, wild), music, and the arts (creative, performing and spectator), music, gardening, tennis, designing and making; *Clubs* Seaview Yacht, Royal Over-Seas League; *Style*— Mrs Maureen Acland, OBE; ✉ Standon Green End, Ware, Hertfordshire SG11 1BN (tel 01920 438233, fax 01920 438527)

ACLAND HOOD GASS, *see:* Gass

ACLOQUE, Hon Mrs (Camilla Anne Bronwen); *née* Scott-Ellis; da of 9 Baron Howard de Walden and 5 Baron Seaford (d 1999), and his 1 w, Countess Irene Harrach (d 1975); *b* 1 April 1947; *Educ* Convent of the Sacred Heart Woldingham; *m* 1971, Guy, s of John Acloque (d 1971), of Reigate, Surrey; 1 s, 2 da (twins); *Career* co-heiress to Barony of Howard de Walden; *Style*— The Hon Mrs Acloque; ✉ Alderley Grange, Wotton-under-Edge, Gloucestershire GL12 7QT (tel 01453 842161)

ACTON, Prof the Hon Edward David Joseph LYON-DALBERG-; 4 s of 3 Baron Acton, CMG, MBE, TD (d 1989); *b* 4 February 1949; *Educ* Univ of York (BA), Univ of Cambridge (PhD); *m* 1972, Stella Marie, da of Henry Conroy (d 1990), of Bolton; 2 da; *Career* sr lectr in history Univ of Manchester 1988–91, prof of modern Euro history UEA 1991–, pro-vice-chllr UEA 2003–; FRHS; *Books* Alexander Herzen and the Role of the Intellectual Revolutionary (1979), Rethinking the Russian Revolution (1990), Russia: the Tsarist and Soviet Legacy (1995), Critical Companion to the Russian Revolution 1914–21 (co-ed, 1997), Nazism and Stalinism: A Suitable Case for Confusion? (1998), La Transición a la Politica de Masas (co-ed, 2001); *Recreations* tennis, bridge, racing; *Style*— Prof the Hon Edward Acton; ✉ 365 Unthank Road, Norwich NR4 7QG (tel 01603 505673); Vice-Chancellor's Office, University of East Anglia, Norwich NR4 7TJ (tel 01603 592793)

ACTON, 4 Baron (UK 1869); Sir Richard Gerald Lyon-Dalberg-Acton; 11 Bt (E 1644); also a Patrician of Naples (1802); patron of one living (but being a Roman Catholic cannot present); sits as Baron Acton of Bridgnorth (Life Peer UK 2000), of Aldenham in the County of Shropshire; eldest s of 3 Baron Acton, CMG, MBE, TD (d 1989), and Hon

Daphne, *née* Strutt (d 2003), da of 4 Baron Rayleigh; *b* 30 July 1941; *Educ* St George's Coll Salisbury Rhodesia, Trinity Coll Oxford (MA); *m* 1, 1965, Hilary Juliet Sarah (d 1973), 2 da of Dr Osmond Laurence Charles Cookson, of Perth, Western Australia; 1 s (Hon John Charles Ferdinand Harold b 19 Aug 1966); m 2, 1974 (m dis 1987), Judith Garfield, da of Hon Sir Garfield Todd, of Famone, Bulawayo (formerly PM of Southern Rhodesia); m 3, 1988, Patricia, o da of late M Morey Nassif, of Cedar Rapids, Iowa; *Heir* s, Hon John Acton; *Career* called to the Bar Inner Temple 1976; dir Coutts & Co 1971–74; sr law offr Zimbabwe Miny of Justice Legal and Parly Affairs 1981–85; memb: House of Lords Refreshment Ctee 1998–99, Select Ctee on the Constitution 2001–05, Jt Select Ctee Consolidation Bills 2002–05 and 2006–, Select Ctee on Delegated Policy and Regulatory Reform 2006–07; sponsor Br Defence Aid Fund for South Africa 1980–94; hon pres Assoc of American Study Abroad Progs UK 2006–; patron: Mind Jubilee Appeal 1996–, Mulberry Bush Sch 1998–, Apex Tst 2002– (vice-patron 1995–), Frank Longford Tst 2002–, Hansard Soc 2003–; tstee Old Creamery Theatre Co Iowa 1995–; memb: Ct Oxford Brookes Univ 1999–2004, State Historical Soc of Iowa Library Advsy Ctee 1999–; contrib to various anthologies and periodicals; hon citizen of Iowa; *Books* The Spectator Annual (contrib, 1993), To Go Free: A Treasury of Iowa's Legal Heritage (with Patricia Nassif Acton, Benjamin F Shambaugh Award 1996), A Brit Amoung the Hawkeyes (1998), Outside In: African-American History in Iowa 1838–2000 (contrib, 2001); *Style*— The Rt Hon the Lord Acton; ✉ House of Lords, London SW1A 0PW (e-mail actonr@parliament.uk); 152 Whitehall Court, London SW1A 2EL (tel and fax 020 7839 3077); 100 Red Oak Lane South East, Cedar Rapids, Iowa 52403, USA (tel and fax 00 1 319 362 6181, e-mail r.acton@prodigy.net)

ACTON DAVIS, Jonathan James; QC (1996); s of Michael James Acton Davis (d 1994), of London, and Elizabeth Margaret; *b* 15 January 1953; *m* Lindsay Alice Boswell, QC, *qv*; 1 s (Matthew James Acton Davis); *Career* called to the Bar Inner Temple 1977 (bencher 1995, master of house 1999–2005); asst recorder 1997–2000, recorder 2000–; memb Gen Cncl of the Bar 1993–98; chm Professional Conduct and Complaints Ctee 2001–02 (vice-chm 1999–2000), memb Legal Services Consultative Panel 2004–; *Recreations* cricket, walking, South West France; *Clubs* MCC, Garrick; *Style*— Jonathan Acton Davis, Esq, QC; ✉ Atkin Chambers, 1 Atkin Building, Gray's Inn, London WC1R 5AT (tel 020 7404 0102, fax 020 7405 7456, e-mail clerks@atkinchambers.law.co.uk)

ACTON-STOW, Derek; OBE (1979); s of Ivor Acton-Stow (d 1972), of East Dean, E Sussex, and Ada Beatrice, *née* Smith (d 1999); *b* 20 September 1929; *Educ* Epsom GS, Kingston Coll of Art; *m* 1, 1955 (m dis 1959), Julia Weightman; m 2, 1959, Gwyneth, da of David John Pugh (d 1965), of London; 3 da (Anna b 1959, Katherine b 1962, Harriet b 1968); *Career* architect; Powell and Moya 1953–62; sr ptnr: Derek Stow & Partners 1962–, Halpin Stow Partnership 1992–; awards incl: Civic Tst 1970, 1973, 1978 and 1986, Concrete Soc 1973, Euro Prize for Architecture 1974, RIBA 1978, Structural Steel 1978 and 1980; assoc Soc of Artist Architects; Freeman City of London 1984, Liveryman Worshipful Co of Chartered Architects 1989; FRIBA 1951; *Recreations* visual arts, music, literature; *Style*— Derek Acton-Stow, Esq, OBE; ✉ 6 Little Bornes, Alleyn Park, Dulwich, London SE21 8SE (tel and fax 020 8761 3831, e-mail stow@f2s.com)

ACWORTH, Ven Richard Foote; s of Oswald Roney Acworth, of Warminster, Wilts, and Jean Margaret, *née* Coupland; *b* 19 October 1936; *Educ* St John's Sch Leatherhead, Sidney Sussex Coll Cambridge (MA), Cuddesdon Theol Coll; *m* 22 Oct 1966, Margaret Caroline Marie, da of Edward Knight Jennings; 1 da (Rachel Margaret b 15 Aug 1967), 2 s (Thomas Richard b 28 Sept 1968, Edward Roney b 20 July 1971); *Career* Nat Serv RNVR 1956–58, Univ of Cambridge 1958–61, Cuddesdon Theol Coll Oxford 1961–63; ordained: deacon (St Paul's Cathedral) 1963, priest (Manchester Cathedral) 1964; asst curate: St Etheldreda's Fulham 1963, All Saints and Martyrs Langley Manchester 1964–66, St Mary's Bridgwater 1966–69; vicar St Mary the Virgin Yatton 1969–81, priest-in-charge St John's and St Mary's Taunton 1981–84, vicar St Mary Magdalene Taunton 1984–93, archdeacon of Wells 1993–2003 (archdeacon emeritus 2003–); memb Gen Synod C of E 1980–95 and 1998–2000; *Recreations* walking, gardening, ornithology, DIY; *Style*— The Ven Richard Acworth; ✉ Corvedale Cottage, Ganes Terrace, Croscombe, Wells BA5 3QJ (e-mail vendick@surefish.co.uk)

ADAIR, Gilbert; *b* 1944; *Career* writer and journalist; contrib to: The Sunday Times, Esquire, The Guardian, The Independent, The Independent on Sunday, Tatler, Harpers & Queen, The Evening Standard, The Daily Telegraph, Sight and Sound, TLS, The New Statesman, The Spectator, The Washington Post, The Boston Globe, Time Out, The Sunday Telegraph, The European; *Radio* Kaleidoscope, Reading Around, Meridian, Le Journal des Arts, Night Waves; *Films* The Territory 1981, The Dreamers 2003; *Books* fiction: Alice Through the Needle's Eye (1984), Peter Pan and the Only Children (1987), The Holy Innocents (1988), Love and Death on Long Island (1990), The Death of the Author (1992), The Key of the Tower (1997), A Closed Book (1999), The Dreamers (2003), Buenas Noches Buenos Aires (2004), Klimt (2006), The Act of Roger Murgatroyd (2006), A Mysterious Affair of Style (2007); poetry: The Rape of the Cock (1992); non-fiction: Hollywood's Vietnam (1981), Myths & Memories (1986), The Postmodernist Always Rings Twice (1992), Flickers (1995), Surfing the Zeitgeist (1997), The Real Tadzio (2001); translations: Orson Welles (André Bazin, 1974), Kubrick (Michel Ciment, 1983), John Boorman (Michel Ciment, 1986), Letters (François Truffaut, 1990), Wonder Tales (ed Marina Warner, 1994), A Void (Georges Perec, 1994); contribs: Anatomy of the Movies (1981), What's What in the 1980s (1982), Rediscovering French Film (1983), La Petite Voleuse (1989), The Time Out Film Guide (1989), Ariel at Bay (1990), New Writing (1992), Heroes and Villains (1994), Projections 8 (1998), Zazie in the Metro (2000); *Style*— Gilbert Adair, Esq

ADAM, *see also:* Forbes Adam

ADAM, Brian James; MSP; s of James Pirie Adam, and Isabella, *née* Geddes; *b* 10 June 1948; *Educ* Keith GS, Univ of Aberdeen (BSc, MSc); *m* 12 Dec 1975, Dorothy McKillip, *née* Mann; 4 s (Neil b 22 Nov 1976, James b 23 May 1978, David b 22 April 1982, Alan b 19 Feb 1986), 1 da (Sarah 25 Feb 1980); *Career* MSP (SNP): Scotland North East (regnl list) 1999–2003, Aberdeen North 2003–; *Style*— Brian Adam, Esq, MSP; ✉ c/o 825–7 Great Northern Road, Aberdeen AB24 2BR (tel 01224 789457, fax 01224 695377, mobile 07713 063634, e-mail brian.adam.msp@scottish.parliament.uk)

ADAM, Dr Gordon Johnston; s of John Craig Adam (d 1969), of Carlisle, and Deborah Armstrong, *née* Johnston (d 1978); *b* 28 March 1934; *Educ* Carlisle GS, Univ of Leeds (BSc, PhD); *m* 22 Dec 1973, Sarah Jane, da of John Lockhart Seely (d 1990), of Stakeford, Northumberland; 1 s ((John) Duncan b 11 May 1979); *Career* mining engr NCB 1959–79; cncllr Whitley Bay BC 1971–74; N Tyneside MBC: cncllr 1973–80, chm 1973–74, mayor 1974–75, dep ldr 1975–80; memb Northern Econ Planning Cncl 1974–79; Parly candidate (Lab) Tynemouth 1966, Berwick-upon-Tweed 1973 (by-election), Feb 1974 and 1992; MEP (Lab): Northumbria 1979–99, NE Region 2000–04; vice-chm European Parl Energy Research and Technol Ctee 1984–99; memb: Northern Arts Gen Cncl 1975–77, Whitley Bay Playhouse Theatre Tst 1975– (chm 1975–80), Northern Sinfonia Mgmnt Ctee 1978–80; chm Newcastle Free Festival 1992–99 (memb Bd 1989–99); memb Bd Northern Stage Co 1989–2001; chm Northumbria Energy Advice Centre 1993–, chm Northern Energy Initiative 1995–2002, life memb Parly Gp for Energy Studies, memb Bd S Tyneside Groundwork Tst 2004–; MIMMM (MIMinE 1953), FIE, CEng; *Style*— Dr Gordon Adam; ✉ East House Farm, Killingworth Village, Newcastle upon Tyne NE12 6BQ (tel 0191 216 0154, e-mail gordonjadam@aol.com)

ADAM, Ian Clark; s of George Adam (d 1976), of Dundee, and Natalie Jane Gibson, *née* Clark (d 1997); *b* 2 September 1943; *Educ* Harris Acad; *m* 25 Sept 1967, Betty Anne, da of Norman James McKie Crosbie; 1 da (Allison Jane b 26 July 1968), 1 s (Garry Clark b 19 Dec 1970); *Career* trainee accountant Henderson & Logie 1962–67; Price Waterhouse: audit sr and asst mangr (Rio de Janeiro) 1967–70, mangr Bristol 1970–76, ptnr Edinburgh 1976–86, sr ptnr Scotland 1986–95; fin dir Christian Salvesen plc 1995–98; non-exec dir: Fishers Holdings Ltd 1996–2004, Britannia Building Society 1998– (non-exec chm 2004–); memb Cncl Scottish Further and Higher Educn Funding Cncl; Old Master Co of Merchants of the City of Edinburgh; memb High Constable City of Edinburgh; MICAS 1967; *Recreations* reading, golf, shooting and travel; *Clubs* Royal Burgess Golfing Soc of Edinburgh, Royal & Ancient; *Style*— Ian C Adam, Esq; ✉ Gowanfield, 2 Cammo Road, Edinburgh EH4 8EB (tel 0131 339 6401)

ADAM, Robert; s of Robert Adam, and Jessie Adam; *b* 10 April 1948; *Educ* Univ of Westminster; *m* 1970, Sarah; 1 s, 1 da; *Career* architect; dir Robert Adam Architects (formerly Winchester Design) 2000– (co-fndr 1986); fndr and chm Popular Housing Group 1995–, chm INTBAU 2000–; RIBA: memb Planning and Urban Design Gp 1995–, chm Pres Special Working Party 1995, cncllr 1999–2005, hon sec 2001–03, tstee RIBA Tst 2003–; British Sch at Rome: chm Faculty of Fine Art 1993–97 (memb 1989), vice-chm Cncl 1997–99; memb: Architecture Club Ctee 1987–, Eng Heritage London Advsy Gp 1996–2002, DOE Good Practice Guidance on Design in the Planning System Project Sounding Bd 1997, design advsr Cmmn for Architecture and the Built Environment (CABE) 1999–2004; lectr incl tours in USA and Russia; Bro of the Art Worker's Guild 1982; tstee Maria Nobrega Charitable Tst 2003–; RIBA, FRSA 1988; *Projects* primary care centre and housing for the elderly Pulborough W Sussex; new country houses: Hants, Cambridge, Yorks, S Oxon, Glos, Wilts, Bucks, Dorset; restaurant and display buildings Nagano Prefecture Japan, roof garden Daimaru Dept Store Osaka Japan, new villages for the Duchy of Cornwall in Shepton Mallet and Midsomer Norton, new town centre Rocester Staffs, village extension Trowse nr Norwich, master plan St Andrews Hosp Northampton, master plan new dist Leith Scotland, new co HQ Dogmersfield Park, Humanities Library Univ of Oxford, new gallery Ashmolean Museum Oxford, Solar House W Sussex, Millennium Temple Private Estate Hants, alterations, repairs and additions to Heveningham Hall and Park Suffolk, new offices Piccadilly London; *Exhibitions* RIBA Heinz Gall 1990, Sculpture in the Garden Wimborne Dorset 1991, Ruskin, Tradition and Architecture (Peter Scott Gall Lancaster Univ) 1992, Visions of Europe Bologna 1992, The Eye of the Architect (RIBA) 1993, Contemporary British Architecture USA 1994, Models Trial Exhibition London 1996, Vision of Europe (Urban Renaissance) 1996, Royal Acad Summer Exhibition 1993, 1996 and 1997; *Work in Public Collections* V&A Contemporary Furniture Collection (Pembroke table for Alma Furniture Co), RIBA Drawings Collection Tower of the Orders; *Awards* commendation London Borough of Richmond-upon-Thames Conservation and Design Awards Scheme 1991, winner Copper Roofing Competition Copper Devpt Assoc 1995, Elmbridge BC Design/Conservation Award 1998, RIBA Southern Regn Nat Housebuilder Design Award, Best Partnership Devpt Commendation for Roman Ct Rocester 2000, Marsh Country Life Awards 2001; *Publications* Classical Architecture - A Complete Handbook, Buildings By Design; author of numerous articles for pubns incl nat newspapers, magazines and jls; contrib to numerous TV and radio progs; *Style*— Robert Adam, Esq; ✉ Robert Adam Architects, 9 Upper High Street, Winchester, Hampshire SO23 8UT (tel 01962 843843, e-mail admin@robertadamarchitects.com)

ADAMS, Prof Anthony Peter; s of Sqdn Ldr Henry William John Adams (d 1986), and Winifred Louise, *née* Brazenor (d 1989); *b* 17 October 1936; *Educ* Epsom Coll, Univ of London (MB BS, PhD); *m* 1, 30 Sept 1961 (m dis 1972), Martha Jill Vearncombe, da of Herbert William Davis (d 1985), of Yeovil, Somerset; 2 s (Christopher b 1963, Paul b 1965); m 2, 12 May 1973, Veronica Rosemary, da of Raymond Ashley John, of Maidenhead, Berks; 1 da (Jenny b 1975), 1 s (Adrian b 1979); *Career* conslt anaesthetist and clinical lectr Nuffield Dept of Anaesthetics Oxford 1968–79; KCL (formerly UMDS): prof of anaesthetics 1979–2001, chm Div of Anaesthetics 1984–89 and 1995–97, vice-chm Div of Anaesthetics 1989–95, vice-chm Div of Surgery and Anaesthesia 1997–2001, chm Dept of Anaesthetics 1998–2001; emeritus prof of anaesthetics Univ of London 2001–; hon conslt anaesthetist: Guy's Hosp 1979–2001, St Thomas' Hosp 1990–2001, The Maudsley Hosp 1992–95, King's Coll Hosp 1995–2001; emeritus hon conslt anaesthetist Guy's and St Thomas' Hosp NHS Tst 2001–, conslt emeritus to the Army 2001–; examiner: FFARCS 1974–86, RCVS 1986–93, Univ of the W Indies 1986–88, 1995, 1997–98, Univ of Wales 1988–93, Univ of Singapore 1988, Chinese Univ Hong Kong 1990, GMC 2001–06; visiting professorships incl: Univ of Texas 1983, Johns Hopkins Hosp Baltimore 1983, Yale Univ 1984, Univ of Zimbabwe 1985, Univ of W Ontario 1985; regnl advsr in anaesthetics SE Thames 1980–88, conslt SE Asia WHO 1982; Royal Coll of Anaesthetists: memb Cncl 1989–97, chm Educn Ctee 1990–93, chm Info Technol Ctee 1996–97, chm Standing Ctee on Dental Anaesthesia 1996–97, memb Examinations Ctee 1996–97 pres Section of Anaesthesia RSM 2001–02; memb: Exec Ctee Anaesthetic Res Soc 1983 (chm 1990–94), Safety Ctee Assoc of Anaesthetists GB and Ireland 1984–96 (chm 1987–89); sr Euro Acad of Anaesthesiology 1985–95 (academician 1981–, memb exec ctee 1997–2004); pres: SE Thames Soc of Anaesthetists 2000–01, Sutton and District Medical Soc 2006–07; assoc ed: Survey of Anesthesiology 1984–2001, Euro Jl of Anaesthesiology 1987–94 (chm Ed Bd 1997–2000, ed-in-chief 2000–03); memb: Editorial Bd Br Jl of Anaesthesia 1984–97, Jl of Anaesthesia (Japan) 1995–2001; memb: Shabbington Parish Cncl 1977–79, Bd of Govrs Sutton HS 1988–96 (chm 1991–96); FRCA, FFARCS, FANZCA, FFARACS, MRCS, LRCP; *Books* Principles and Practice of Blood - Gas Analysis (jtly, 2 edn 1982), Intensive Care (jtly, 1984), Emergency Anaesthesia (jtly, 1986), Recent Advances in Anaesthesia (jtly, 22 edn 2002), Anaesthesia, Analgesia and Intensive Care (jtly, 1991), Principles and Practice Series (jt series ed, 1994–2001); *Recreations* cinema, croquet, tennis, badger watching; *Clubs* Royal Soc of Med; *Style*— Prof Anthony Adams; ✉ e-mail anthonypadams@gmail.com

ADAMS, Aubrey John; s of John William Lane Adams (d 1999), and Nichole, *née* Stevenson (d 2000); *b* 16 October 1949; *Educ* Univ of Cambridge (MA); *m* 6 May 1972, Angela Mary, *née* Stevens; 3 da (Katie b 1975, Sara b 1978, Felicity b 1983); *Career* with Price Waterhouse (later Price Waterhouse Associates) 1970–78, fin dir Peachey Property Corp plc 1978–89; Savills plc: md 1990–2000, gp chief exec 2000–; non-exec dir Unitech Corporate Parks plc 2006–; tstee Wigmore Hall; *Recreations* golf, gardening, music; *Style*— Aubrey Adams, Esq; ✉ Vines Farm, Kidmore End, Reading, Berkshire RG4 9AP (tel 0118 972 2004); Savills plc, 20 Grosvenor Hill, London W1K 3HQ (tel 020 7409 9921, fax 020 7491 0505, e-mail aadams@savills.com)

ADAMS, Colin; CBE (1995), AFC (1973); s of Maj Ronald Adams, RAC and Chindits (ka Burma 1944), of Bury, W Sussex, and Margaret, *née* Carne (d 1987); *b* 1 April 1940; *Educ* Christ's Hosp, RAF Coll Cranwell; *m* Josephine (Jo) Adams, da of Herbert Colton; 2 da (Sophie b 1 Nov 1965, Pip b 23 April 1967), 1 s (Nick b 23 May 1969); *Career* cmmnd RAF 1961, served in various reconnaissance flying appts UK, Middle East, Far East, Malta and Cyprus, flying instr, RN Staff Coll 1974, memb Tornado Aircraft Project Team Munich 1977–81, dep dir RAF Personnel Mgmnt 1983–86, CO RAF Akrotiri Cyprus 1986–88, project dir RAF Estate Rationalisation 1989–90, Defence Attaché Br Embassy Paris 1990–95, ret RAF 1995 (Air Commodore); chief exec BCCB (British Consultants and Construction Bureau, formerly BCB) 1995–2004, dir Colin Adams Int Consultancy (CAIC) Ltd 2004– (conslt to Shadbolt and Co LLP, JLT Risk Solutions Ltd, Rotary Int

A

Gp Ltd and Chinese construction cos); memb: Sydney 2000 Olympics Task Force DTI 1995–98, London Chamber Int Cmmn 1996–2000, Worldaware Business Gp DfID 1996–2000, Br Trade Int Sectors and Projects Gp 1997–2000, Int Ctee CBI 1998–2003, UK Public/Private Sector Task Forces Kosovo 1999, Serbia 2001 and Iraq 2003, Trade Partners UK Business Advsy Panel 2001–04, memb Bd BOND 1998–2004, Cncl Union Jack Club 2002–; FIPD 1989; Hon Cdr Ordre National du Mérite (France) 1992, Humanitarian Gold Medal (France) 1993; *Books* The International Guide to Management Consultancy (contrib); *Recreations* offshore sailing, golf, skiing, fly fishing, visual arts, IT; *Clubs* RAF; *Style—* Colin Adams, CBE, AFC; ✉ mobile 07768 685982

ADAMS, Prof (Charles) David; s of Richard Adams, and Sylvia Mary, *née* Wolf; *b* 10 September 1954; *Educ* Rossall Sch, Univ of Liverpool (MCD), Univ of Cambridge (MA, PhD); *m* 11 March 1989, Judith; 1 s (Daniel Stuart b 10 Jan 1995), 1 da (Eleanor Mary b 10 Aug 1996); *Career* planning asst Leeds City Cncl 1978–83; research asst Univ of Reading 1983–84; lectr in urban planning and devpt Univ of Manchester 1984–93; Univ of Aberdeen: sr lectr in land economy 1993–95, reader in land economy 1995–97, prof of land economy 1997–2004; Ian Mactaggart prof of property and urban studies Univ of Glasgow 2004–; MRICS, FRTPI, FRSA; *Publications* Urban Planning and the Development Process (1994), Land for Industrial Development (with L Russell and C Taylor-Russell, 1994), Greenfields, Brownfields and Housing Development (with C Watkins, 2002), Planning, Public Policy and Property Markets (with C Watkins and M White, 2005); author of over 100 chapters, papers and articles on urban planning, land development and related subjects; *Recreations* walking, listening to classical music; *Style—* Prof David Adams

ADAMS, David Howard; s of Capt Bernard Adams, RA (d 1982), of Newcastle, and Eve, *née* Glass (d 1987); *b* 15 November 1943; *Educ* Manchester Grammar; *m* 22 June 1969, Zoe, da of Victor Joseph Dwek (d 1989), of Manchester; 2 da (Gisele b 1970, Zanine b 1975); *Career* chief exec Henry Cooke Lumsden plc (dir 1975–94), exec dir Private Client Gp Capel-Cure Myers Capital Management Ltd 1994–96, business coach (specialist in unlocking creativity), performance poet; currently md David H Adams Ltd; freelance chm Vistage International (UK) Ltd, non-exec chm Xchangeteam Ltd; past chm: Manchester Stock Exchange, Inst for Fiscal Studies NW, Gtr Manchester Arts Centre Ltd (Cornerhouse); pres London Soc of CAs 2003–04; dir Hampstead Theatre Ltd; memb: Professional Speaker's Assoc, Assoc for Coaching; past memb Mensa, FCA 1967, FSI 1992; *Recreations* skiing, computers, reading, theatre; *Style—* David H Adams, Esq; ✉ David H Adams Ltd, 6 Albion Street, Hyde Park, London W2 2AS (tel 07971 267157, fax 020 7402 0044, e-mail david@dhadams.co.uk, www.unlockingcreativity.com)

ADAMS, Prof David Keith; OBE (1997); s of Sidney Adams (d 1976), of Bredon, Worcs, and Dagmar Ruth Cawnpore, *née* Judge (d 1985); *b* 11 August 1931; *Educ* Abbey House and William Ferrer's GS Tewkesbury, Univ of Rennes, Clare Coll Cambridge (MA), Yale Univ (AM), Oriel and Nuffield Colls Oxford (MA, DPhil); *m* 1, 23 March 1961 (m dis 1981), Virginia Mary Hope, da of Walton White (d 1976), of Edinburgh; 3 s (Giles b 4 March 1963, Roderick b 25 Nov 1965, Thomas b 9 June 1967); m 2, 5 Sept 1992, Sarah Louise, da of Peter Shuttleworth, and Jennifer Shuttleworth, of Bishop's Sutton, Hants; *Career* Henry fellowship Yale 1954–55, tutor in modern history Univ of Oxford 1955–59, visiting lectr in American studies Univ of Manchester 1959–60, lectr in American studies UCNS 1961 (asst lectr in history 1957–60), ACLS fellowship George Washington Univ 1965–66; Keele Univ: sr lectr in American studies 1965–72, head Dept of American Studies 1965–93, prof 1972–97, prof emeritus and univ fell 1997–, hon pres David Bruce Centre for American Studies 2005– (dir 1969–96, chm 1997–2005); visiting sr scholar Clare Coll Cambridge 1970, visiting prof Univ of Tulsa 1981, visiting scholar Western Carolina Univ 1987, visiting prof Chester Coll 1999–2002; Canada-UK Colloquia: chm 1990–93, dep chm 1993–98, hon vice-pres 1998–; chm Br-American-Canadian Assocs London 1986–96; memb Advsy Ctee Roosevelt Study Centre Middelburg The Netherlands 1986–2000; memb: BAAS, EAAS, OAH, SHAFR; Hon DLitt Keele Univ 2000; *Books* America in the Twentieth Century (1967), An Atlas of North American Affairs (1969 and 1979), Franklin D Roosevelt and the New Deal (1979), British Documents on Foreign Affairs - North America 1919–1939 (ed 25 vols, 1986–95), American Literary Landscapes - The Fiction and the Fact (jt ed, 1988), Studies in US Politics (ed, 1989), Britain and Canada in the 1990s (ed, 1992), Environmental Issues (ed, 1993), Facing the Energy Challenge (ed, 1993), Reflections on American Exceptionalism (jt ed, 1994), Aspects of War in American History (jt ed, 1997), Religious and Secular Reform in America (jt ed, 1999), TransAtlantic Encounters: Public Uses and Misuses of History (jt ed, 2000), Before the Special Relationship (2002); *Recreations* books, travel; *Clubs* The Pilgrims; *Style—* Prof David Adams, OBE; ✉ David Bruce Centre for American Studies, Keele University, Keele, Staffordshire ST5 5BG

ADAMS, Gerard (Gerry); MP, MLA; s of Gerard Adams (d 2003); *b* 6 October 1948; *Educ* St Mary's GS Belfast; *m* 1971, Colette McArdle; 1 s; *Career* fndr memb Northern Ireland Civil Rights Assoc; interned by British Govt 1971, released for talks with Govt 1972, re-interned 1973; sentenced to 18 months imprisonment for attempted escape; released 1977; charged with IRA membership 1978, but charges unproven and released after seven months; elected to: Northern Ireland Assembly 1982, Stormont Assembly 1998; MP (Sinn Fèin) Belfast W 1983–92 and 1997–; pres Sinn Fèin 1983– (vice-pres 1978–83); *Books* Peace In Ireland, Politics of Irish Freedom, Pathway to Peace, Falls Memories, Cage 11, The Street and Other Stories, Free Ireland: Towards A Lasting Peace, Before the Dawn: An Autobiography, An Irish Voice: The Quest for Peace, An Irish Journal, Hope and History, The New Ireland: A Vision for the Future, An Irish Eye; *Style—* Gerry Adams, Esq, MP, MLA; ✉ 51–55 Bothár na bhFál, Beál Feirste BT12 4PD (tel 028 9022 3000)

ADAMS, Dr James Noel; *b* 24 September 1943; *Educ* North Sydney Boys' HS, Univ of Sydney (BA, Univ medal), BNC Oxford (DPhil); *m* 1, 22 March 1971 (m dis 2000), Geneviève Lucienne, *née* Baudon; 1 s (Nicholas James b 20 July 1976); m 2, 28 Sept 2001, Iveta, *née* Mednikarova; 1 da (Elena Rosemary b 16 Dec 2002); *Career* teaching fell Dept of Latin Univ of Sydney 1965–67, Rouse res fell in classics Christ's Coll Cambridge (MA on election) 1970–72; Univ of Manchester: lectr 1972–78, sr lectr 1978–82, reader 1982–93, prof of Latin 1993–95; prof of Latin Univ of Reading 1995–97, sr research fell All Souls Coll Oxford (MA on election) 1998–; visiting sr research fell St John's Coll Oxford 1994–95; memb Philological Soc 1972; FBA 1992, fell Australian Acad of the Humanities 2002; *Books* The Text and Language of a Vulgar Latin Chronicle (1976), The Vulgar Latin of the Letters of Claudius Terentianus (1977), The Latin Sexual Vocabulary (1982), Wackernagel's Law and the Placement of the Copula esse in Classical Latin (1994), Pelagonius and Latin Veterinary Terminology in the Roman Empire (1995), Bilingualism and the Latin Language (2003); *Recreations* cricket; *Style—* Dr J N Adams, FBA; ✉ All Souls College, Oxford OX1 4AL (tel 01865 279379)

ADAMS, Jennifer; LVO (1993); da of Arthur Roy Thomas Crisp, and Joyce Muriel, *née* Davey; *b* 1 February 1948; *Educ* City of London Sch for Girls, IPRA Staff Coll; *m* 21 Sept 1968, Terence William Adams; *Career* mangr Central Royal Parks 1983–97 (actg bailiff 1990–92), head of inner parks and commerce Royal Parks Agency 1997–2001, dir of open spaces Corp of London 2001–08; pres Inst of Horticulture 1996–98 (pres-elect 1994–96); Liveryman Worshipful Co of Gardners; assoc of honour RHS 1999; FILAM, Dip PRA, FIHort; *Style—* Mrs Jennifer Adams, LVO, FILAM, FIHort; ✉ Open Spaces Department, PO Box 270, Guildhall, London EC2P 2EJ (tel 020 7332 3033, fax 020 7332 3522, e-mail jennifer.adams@cityoflondon.gov.uk)

ADAMS, His Hon John Douglas Richard; s of Gordon Arthur Richard Adams (d in enemy hands 1944), and Marjorie Ethel, *née* Ongley (d 1983); *b* 19 March 1940; *Educ* Watford GS, Univ of Durham (LLB); *m* 12 April 1966, Anne Easton, da of Robert Easton Todd (d 1967); 2 da (Katharine b 1975, Caroline b 1978); *Career* called to the Bar Lincoln's Inn 1968, bencher Inner Temple 1997; lectr in law: Univ of Newcastle upon Tyne 1963–71, UCL 1971–78; also practised at the Revenue Bar until 1978; special cmmr of Income Tax 1978–82, Registrar of Civil Appeals 1982–98, recorder of the Crown Court 1992–98, circuit judge (SE Circuit) 1998–2002; hon lectr St Edmund Hall Oxford 1976–2008, visiting lectr Univ of Oxford 1995–2008; memb Bd of Tstees Hospice of St Francis Berkhamsted 2004–; *Books* International Taxation of Multinational Enterprises (with J Whalley, 1977), Chitty & Jacob's Queen's Bench Forms (ed, 1987), Atkin's Court Forms (ed, 1991), Supreme Court Practice (ed, 1999), Jordan's Civil Court Service (ed, 2003), Jordan's Emergency Remedies in the Family Courts (ed, 2005), Halsbury's Laws of England (4 edn, Vol 10 Courts); *Recreations* music, walking, dining; *Style—* His Hon John Adams; ✉ e-mail johndradams@btinternet.com

ADAMS, Prof John Norman; s of Vincent Smith Adams, of Lintz Green, Tyne & Wear, and Elsie, *née* Davison (d 1964); *b* 24 December 1939; *Educ* Royal GS Newcastle upon Tyne, Univ of Durham; *Career* slr in private practice 1965–71, lectr in law Univ of Sheffield 1971–79, called to the Bar Inner Temple 1984, prof of commercial law Univ of Kent 1987–94 (sr lectr in law 1979–87), prof of intellectual property Univ of Sheffield 1994–2005; visiting prof: Univ of Maryland 1974–75, Nat Law Centre Washington DC 1981, Université Paris X 1989–91; adjunct prof Notre Dame Law Sch Concannon Centre 1986–87 and 2000–; dir Intellectual Property Inst 1991–99; *Books* incl: A Bibliography of Eighteenth Century Legal Literature (1982), Franchising (1981, 5 edn 2005), Merchandising Intellectual Property (1987, 3 edn 2007), Understanding Contract Law (1987, 4 edn 2004), Commercial Hiring and Leasing (1989), Understanding Law (1992, 4 edn 2006), A Bibliography of Nineteenth Century Legal Literature (vol 1 1992, vol 2 1994, vol 3 1996), Key Issues in Contract (1995), Atiyah's Sale of Goods (ed 11 edn, 2005); *Recreations* music, walking; *Clubs* Savage, Lansdowne; *Style—* Prof John N Adams; ✉ 26 Priory Terrace, London NW6 4DH (tel 020 7328 8676); 49 Endcliffe Hall Avenue, Sheffield S10 3EL; Hogarth Chambers, 5 New Square, Lincoln's Inn London WC2A 3RJ (tel 020 7404 0404, fax 020 7404 0505, e-mail john@johnadams3.wanadoo.co.uk)

ADAMS, Prof Judith Elizabeth; da of late Percy Charles Lockyer, of Hale, Cheshire, and Barbara, *née* Bailey; *b* 16 May 1945; *Educ* Roedean, UCH London (MB BS); *m* 16 Sept 1972, Prof Peter Harold Adams, s of late Alfred Adams, of Penarth, Wales; 2 s (Charles Edward b 25 Dec 1978, James Lindsay b 26 Jan 1983); *Career* prof of diagnostic radiology Univ of Manchester 1993– (lectr 1976–79, sr lectr 1979–), hon conslt radiologist Royal Infirmary Manchester 1978–, dean Faculty of Clinical Radiology RCR 1993– (vice-pres RCR 1994–95), acad gp ldr Imaging Sci and Biomedical Engrg 1998–; clinical dir of radiology Central Manchester Healthcare Tst (CMHT) 1997–2000; chm Examining Bd pt 1 FRCR 1984–89 (examiner 1980–84); memb: Editorial Bd British Journal of Radiology 1984–89, Editorial Bd Skeletal Radiology 1987–95, Int Skeletal Soc 1987–; non-exec memb Manchester Health Authy 1995–98, chm Congress Ctee Radiology UK 1997 and 1998; hon sec Br Assoc Clinical Anatomists 1990–93; FRCR 1975, FRCP (MRCP) 1988; *Publications* author of scientific pubns on: quantitative computed tomography for bone mass measurement, imaging in metabolic bone disorders and endocrine diseases, effective use of radiological resources, bone mineral density in cystic fibrosis, growth hormone deficiency, coeliac disease and following childhood chemotherapy and radiotherapy; *Recreations* embroidery, flower arranging, sewing, swimming; *Style—* Prof Judith Adams

ADAMS, Prof Mac; *b* Brynmawr, S Wales; *Educ* Cardiff Coll of Art (NDD, ATD), Rutgers Univ (MFA); *Career* artist, sculptor and photographer; assoc prof SUNY; *Solo Exhibitions* incl: Farideh Cadot Gallery NY 1990, Gracie Mansion Gallery NY 1990, Sable/Castelli Gallery Toronto 1990, Yoshiaki Inoue Gallery Osaka 1992, John Gibson Gallery NY 1992, Jersey City Museum NJ 1993, Art Awareness Lexington NY 1993, Galerie Froment and Putman Paris 1994, Exposition Monographique (Mai de Reims) 1996, Stux gallery NY 1997, Todd Gallery London 1997, Silence of Shadows (touring exhbn UK) 1998–2000, Serge Aboukrat Gallery Paris 2000, One Hundred Eyes (Center Photgraphique D'Ile-de-France) 2001, G/B Agency Paris 2002–03 and 2007, Musees de Chateauroux 2004, Mens Rea (CEAAC Strasbourg) 2006; *Public Commissions* Sweptaway (N Princeton Developmental Center NJ), Serpent Bearer (Montclair State Coll NJ), New York Korean War Memorial (Battery Park NY) 1991, Meditation (Botanical Gardens Louis Pasteur Univ Strasbourg) 1996, Mustangs at Noon (Henry Gonzalez Convention Center San Antonio) 1998, Solar Pavilion (belvedere, Penarth Haven Park) 1999, Wings and Wheels (solar pavilion, Dept of Transportation Cherry Hill NJ) 2001, Apparitions (Castle Blois France) 2002, Wetlands (photo mosaics, Secausus Transfer Railway Station NJ) 2003, Life Force (aluminium sculpture, NJ Sch of Medicine and Dentistry Newark) 2005, The Falls (glass and stone mosaic, Richard Stockton Coll NJ) 2006, Glass Tapestry (window, Rutgers Univ Law Sch NJ) 2007; *Public Collections* incl: Musée National d'Art Modern Center Pompidou Paris, Musée Nicephore Niepce Chalon sur Saone, Getty Musuem of Art LA, Fonds Regnl d'Art Contemporain (FRAC) Basse-Normandie, Microsoft Corp, Maison Europeenne de la Photographie Paris, DG Bank Frankfurt, Welsh Nat Museum, Goldman Sachs Investment Co, Harvard Univ, Fonds Regnl d'Art Contemporain (FRAC) Limousin, Fonds Nat d'Art Contemporain (FNAC) Paris, Caisse des Depots Paris, Lhoist Collection Belgium, Museum of Fine Arts Houston, MOMA NY, LA County Museum, Brooklyn Museum, First Nat Bank of Chicago, La Jolla Museum of Contemporary Art CA, Guggenheim Museum NY, Jersey City Museum NJ, Jane Voorhees-Zimmerli Art Museum Rutgers Univ, New Jersey State Cncl for the Arts, Ludwig Museum Cologne, Hamilton Art Gallery Ontario, Univ of Iowa Museum, Georgia Museum of Art, Welsh Arts Cncl Cardiff, Commodities Corp of New Jersey, V&A, Chase Manhattan Bank NY, Musée de Toulon, Morton Neumann Family Collection Chicago; *Awards* Nat Endowment Fellowship for the arts 1976, 1980 and 1982, Berlin Deutscher Akademischer Austauschdienst Berliner Kunstlerprogram 1981, NY State Fellowship for the Arts 1988, Chllr's Research Award for Excellence in the Arts and Humanities NY State Univ 2002; *Style—* Prof Mac Adams; ✉ 18 Llewllyn Road, Montclair, NJ 07042, USA (tel and fax 00 1 973 746 2761, e-mail mbadams2@aol.com, website www.macadamsstudio.com)

ADAMS, Paul Michael; s of Michael Adams, of Budleigh Salterton, Devon, and Celia, *née* Pridham; *b* 21 March 1961, Beirut, Lebanon; *Educ* Sevenoaks Sch, Univ of York (BA); *m* 13 July 1996, Susanna Berry; 2 s (William b 24 Feb 1999, Felix b 8 April 2002); *Career* English teacher Br Cncl Yemen 1983–85; BBC: Arabic service World Service 1989, Jerusalem corr 1989–92, Belgrade corr 1993–95, reporter World TV 1995–97, Middle East corr 1997–2001, defence corr 2001–04, chief dip corr BBC News 24 2004–; winner Amnesty Int TV News Award 2001; MRUSI; *Books* The Battle for Iraq (contrib, 2003); *Recreations* walking, photography, birdwatching, cinema; *Style—* Paul Adams, Esq; ✉ Room 2505, BBC Television Centre, Wood Lane, London W12 7RJ (tel 020 8624 8547, fax 020 8743 7591, mobile 07714 226403, e-mail paul.adams@bbc.co.uk)

ADAMS, Paul Nicholas; s of Peter Charles Adams (d 2001), of Nantwich, Cheshire, and Joan, *née* Smith; *b* 12 March 1953; *Educ* Culford Sch Bury St Edmunds, Ealing Coll London (BA); *m* 26 Aug 1978, Gail Edwina, da of Emil Keith McCann; 1 s (Maximilian James b 8 April 1987), 2 da (Francesca Lindsay b 20 May 1989, Georgia Lucy b 25 Nov 1994); *Career* mktg dir Beecham Products Int 1983–86, European mktg vice-pres Pepsi Int 1986–91; British American Tobacco plc: regnl dir Asia-Pacific 1991–98, regnl dir

Europe 1999–2001, dep md 2001, md 2002–03, chief exec 2004–; non-exec dir Allied Domecq plc 2003–05; *Recreations* shooting, theatre, rugby; *Style*— Paul Adams, Esq; ✉ British American Tobacco plc, Globe House, 4 Temple Place, London WC2R 2PG (tel 020 7845 1000, fax 020 7845 2184)

ADAMS, Ralph Gange; s of Ralph Noel Adams (d 1988), and Catherine Anne, *née* Reid (d 1988); *b* 30 October 1955; *Educ* Trinity Coll Glenalmond, Univ of Dundee (LLB); *m* 3 Aug 1989, Kirstine Mary Park, da of Rev Keith Campbell (d 1994); 2 da (Catherine Christine Campbell b 27 May 1992, Mairi Kirstine Reid b 17 May 1999), 2 s (Angus Keith Gange b 5 May 1994, Gavin Graham McFarlane b 11 March 1996); *Career* Deloitte & Touche: indentured student 1976–79, qualified chartered accountant 1979, seconded to Melbourne 1980, seconded to Bank of Scotland 1984–85, ptnr (specialist in corp fin) 1986–, ptnr i/c Edinburgh office 1989–93, ptnr i/c Scotland and NI offices 1993–99, memb UK Bd of Ptnrs 1993–99, managing ptnr Global Fin Advsy Servs 1999–; Deloitte Touche Tohmatsu: managing ptnr global fin advsy services and corp fin 1999–, memb Global Mgmnt Ctee; MICAS 1979; *Recreations* golf; *Clubs* Prestwick Golf, Golf House (Elie); *Style*— Ralph Adams, Esq; ✉ Deloitte & Touche, Saltire Court, 20 Castle Terrace, Edinburgh EH1 0BR (tel 0131 221 0002, fax 0131 535 7301)

ADAMS, Richard George; s of Evelyn George Beadon Adams, and Lilian Rosa, *née* Button; *b* 9 May 1920; *Educ* Bradfield, Worcester Coll Oxford (MA); *m* 1949, (Barbara) Elizabeth Acland; 2 da (Juliet, Rosamond); *Career* author; Army Serv 1940–46; entered Civil Serv 1948, ret as asst sec DOE 1974; writer in residence: Univ of Florida 1975, Hollins Coll Virginia 1976; pres RSPCA 1980–82; Carnegie Medal 1972; FRSL 1975; *Books* Watership Down (1972, filmed 1978), Shardik (1974), Nature Through the Seasons (with Max Hooper, 1975), The Tyger Voyage (narrative poem, 1976), The Ship's Cat (narrative poem, 1977), The Plague Dogs (1977, filmed 1982), Nature Day and Night (with Max Hooper, 1978), The Iron Wolf (short stories, 1980), The Girl in a Swing (1980, filmed 1988), Voyage Through The Antarctic (travel book, 1982), Maia (1984), The Bureaucats (1985), Nature Diary (1985), The Legend of Te Tuna (narrative poem, 1986), Traveller (1988), The Day Gone By (autobiography, 1990), Tales from Watership Down (1996), The Outlandish Knight (2000), Daniel (2006); contrib to and ed: Occasional Poets anthology (1986); *Style*— Richard Adams, Esq, FRSL; ✉ 26 Church Street, Whitchurch, Hampshire, RG28 7AR

ADAMS, Prof Robert David; s of William Peter Adams (d 1973), and Marion Adams; *b* 13 April 1940; *Educ* Hanley HS, Imperial Coll London (BSc, ACGI, DSc), St John's Coll Cambridge (PhD); *m* 28 Sept 1963, Susan, da of John Felix Waite, GM, of Aston, Market Drayton; 1 da (Rosie b 11 April 1968), 1 s (Joss b 26 Sept 1970); *Career* Dept of Mech Engrg Univ of Bristol: successively lectr, reader and prof 1967–, head of dept 1994–98, grad dean 1998–2004; memb Adhesives Gp Inst of Materials; FIMechE, FInstP, FIMMM; *Books* Structural Adhesive Joints in Engineering (with William C Wake and John Comyn, 1997), over 200 papers in scientific and tech jls; *Recreations* rowing, gardening, wine; *Clubs* Rotary Club (Clifton; pres 1999–2000), MacInnes; *Style*— Prof Robert Adams; ✉ 63 Merton Court, Oxford OX2 6QZ (tel 01865 556227); epartment of Mechanical Engineering, University of Bristol, University Walk, Bristol BS8 1TR (tel 0117 928 7743, fax 0117 929 4423)

ADAMS, Robin William; s of late William Edward Leo Adams, of Edmonton, London, and Jennie Alfreda Adams; *b* 17 October 1944; *Educ* Huxley Sch Enfield, Enfield Tech Coll; *m* 1967, Pauline; 1 da (Julia b 1968), 1 s (John b 1972); *Career* dep press offr The Rank Organisation 1962–65, press offr Rank Audio Visual Ltd 1965–67, central press offr The Rank Organisation 1967–70, press and publicity mangr Guild Holdings Ltd 1970–72; dir: McLeish Associates Ltd 1972–79, GEA Public Relations Ltd 1979–2001, Robin Adams Ltd 2001–; former memb: Professional Practices Ctee, Cncl IPR; memb Nat Ctee on Editorial Independence 1997–; hon press offr Film '69, '71 and '73 (int conf and exhbn for film and TV industries); corp memb Br Kinematograph Sound and TV Soc, memb Int Bldg Press; ed Architectural Ironmongery Jl 1973–2004; FCIPR 1995 (MCIPR 1974); *Books* The After-Dinner Speaker's Handbook (ed, 1990–91); *Recreations* reading and writing; *Style*— Robin Adams, Esq; ✉ tel 020 8364 2389, fax 020 8360 5447, e-mail robin@adamsltd.fsnet.co.uk

ADAMS, His Hon (John) Roderick Seton; s of George G Adams (d 1980), of Edinburgh, and M Winifred, *née* Wilson (d 1990); *b* 29 February 1936; *Educ* Whitgift Sch, Trinity Coll Cambridge (MA); *m* 19 April 1965, (Pamela) Bridget, da of Rev David Edmund Rice, MC (d 1978), of Hexham; 3 s (Robert b 5 Jan 1966, James b 14 Aug 1967, John b 9 Oct 1973); *Career* 2 Lt Seaforth Highlanders 1955–56, Capt Parachute Regt 1960–65; called to the Bar Inner Temple 1962, in practice 1968–90, recorder Crown Ct 1980–90; circuit judge: SE Circuit 1990–96, NE Circuit 1996–2003; *Recreations* fishing, hill walking, growing old roses; *Style*— His Hon Roderick Adams; ✉ 8 Melville Road, Eskbank, Midlothian EH22 3BY (tel 0131 654 9274); Melness House, by Lairg, Sutherland IV27 4YR (tel 01847 601255)

ADAMS, Victoria; *see:* Beckham, Victoria

ADAMSON, (Ronald) Crawfurd; s of Ronald Adamson, of Edinburgh, and Janette Elizabeth Minna, *née* Bauermeister, of Edinburgh; *b* 24 March 1953; *Educ* Duncan of Jordanstone Coll of Art Dundee (Scottish Educn Dept travelling scholar, postgrad commendation), Elizabeth Greenshields Fndn Canada; *m* 1974, Mary Ann Elizabeth, da of Andrew Alexander Hansen Phimister; 1 s (Matthew Andrew b 1978), 1 da (Cassie Francesca b 1981); *Career* artist; gave up teaching to paint full time 1983; invited artist Salon d'Automne Paris 1993; works in numerous collections incl Met Museum of Art NYC; *Solo Exhibitions* incl: Cylinder Gallery London 1984 and 1985, Trinity Arts Centre Kent 1985, Scottish Gallery Edinburgh 1987, 1988 and 1989, Thumb Gallery London 1988, Scottish Gallery London 1989, Parnham House Dorset 1991, Jill George Gallery London 1991, 1993, 1995 and 1997, Château de la Muette Paris 1993, Art First London 1999, Schoeni Gallery Hong Kong 2001, Broderick Gallery Portland OR 2001, 2002, 2003 and 2004, Bohun Gallery Henley-on-Thames 2002, Broderick Gallery OR 2007; *Group Exhibitions* incl: Soc of Scottish Artists 1978 and 1979, Royal Scottish Acad 1979, Prix International d'Art Contemporain de Monte-Carlo 1984 and 1993, Contemporary Scottish Art (touring Japan, 1990), Scottish Art in the 20th Century (Royal W of England Acad Bristol) 1991; *Recreations* woodworking, music; *Style*— Crawfurd Adamson, Esq; ✉ 14 Sedlescombe Road South, St Leonards on Sea, East Sussex TN38 0TA

ADAMSON, Dr Donald; s of Donald Adamson (d 1982), of Lymm, Cheshire, and Hannah Mary, *née* Booth (d 1994); *b* 30 March 1939; *Educ* Manchester GS, Magdalen Coll Oxford (Heath Harrison travelling scholar, Zaharoff travelling scholar), Univ of Paris (MA, MLitt, DPhil); *m* 24 Sept 1966, Helen Freda, da of Frederick Percival Griffiths, TD (d 1970), of Mossley Hill, Liverpool; 2 s (Richard Henry Egerton b 17 Jan 1970, John Daniel b 21 April 1971); *Career* author and historian; recognised teacher Univ of London 1971–89 (chm Bd of Examiners 1983–86), visiting scholar Wolfson Coll Cambridge 1981 (visiting fell 1989–90, sr memb 1990); chm Bow Group Research Ctee Museums and Libraries Policy 1969–71, fndr and sec Bow Group Standing Ctee on the Arts 1975–80; judge Museum of the Year Awards 1979–83, memb Exec Ctee Nat Heritage 1980–92; JP: City of London 1983–92, Cornwall 1993; Lord of the Manor of Dodmore; Liveryman: Worshipful Co of Haberdashers 1976, Worshipful Co of Curriers 1991; FSA 1979, FRSL 1983, FCIL 1989, FRHistS 2007; Order of St John: OStJ 1985, CStJ 1992, KStJ 1998, dir of ceremonies Essex 1992, asst dir of ceremonies Order of St John Grand Priory 1995–99, Priory of England and the Islands 1999–2007 (dep dir 2007–08); Chevalier dans l'Ordre des Palmes Académiques (France) 1986, Chevalier du Tastevin 2005; *Books* The Genesis of Le Cousin Pons (1966), Dusty Heritage (1971), T S Eliot: A Memoir (ed, 1971), The House of Nell Gwyn (jtly, 1974), A Rescue Policy for Museums (1980), Balzac: Illusions Perdues (1981), Les Romantiques français devant la peinture espagnole (1989), Blaise Pascal: Mathematician, Physicist, and Thinker about God (1995, 2 edn 2001), Rides Round Britain, The Travel Journals of John Byng, 5th Viscount Torrington (ed, 1996), The Curriers' Company: A Modern History (2000); Balzac and the Tradition of the European Novel (online, 2001); translations of works by Balzac (1970 and 1976) and Maupassant (1993), numerous French literature, historical and political articles; *Recreations* swimming, travel, collecting, gastronomy; *Clubs* Reform, Beefsteak, City Livery; *Style*— Dr Donald Adamson; ✉ Dodmore House, The Street, Meopham, Kent DA13 0AJ; Topple Cottage, Polperro, Cornwall PL13 2RS (mobile 07747 733931 or 07890 824213, e-mail aimsworthy@tesco.net, website www.dodmore.co.uk)

ADAMSON, Hamish Christopher; OBE (1996); s of John Adamson (d 1985), of Perth, Scotland, and Denise, *née* Colman-Sadd; *b* 17 September 1935; *Educ* Stonyhurst, Lincoln Coll Oxford (MA); *Career* admitted slr 1961; Law Soc: asst sec 1966–81, sec Law Reform and Int Rels 1981–87, dir Int Div 1987–95; sec UK Delgn Cncl of Bars and Law Socs of Euro Community 1981–95, exec sec Cwlth Lawyers Assoc 1983–95, dir Franco-Br Lawyers Soc 1991–, chm Tstee Ctee Commonwealth Human Rights Initiative 1993–95, tstee Acad of Euro Law Trier 1995–2003; *Books* The Solicitors Act 1974 (1975), Butterworth's Free Movement of Lawyers (1992, 2 edn 1998); *Recreations* plants, books, travel; *Style*— Hamish Adamson, Esq, OBE; ✉ 133 Hartington Road, London SW8 2EY (tel 020 7720 4406, fax 020 7720 4406)

ADAMSON, Dr (Samuel) Ian Gamble; OBE (1998); s of John Gamble Sloan Adamson (d 1985), of Conlig, Co Down, and Jane Gamble Sloan, *née* Kerr; *b* 28 June 1944; *Educ* Bangor GS, Queen's Univ Belfast (MB, BCh, BAO), DCH RCSI, DCH RCPSGlas; *m* 1998, Kerry Christian, da of Douglas David Patrick Carson; *Career* doctor; registrar in paediatrics: Royal Belfast Hosp for Sick Children 1974–76, Ulster Hosp Dundonald 1976–77; specialist in community child health and travel med N and W Belfast HSS Tst 1981–2004; memb (UUP) Belfast City Cncl 1989–, Lord Mayor of Belfast 1996–97; MLA (UUP) Belfast E 1998–2003; pres Belfast Civic Tst 2001; chm Farset Youth and Community Devpt 1988–90; fndr chm: Somme Assoc 1989–, Ulster-Scots Language Soc 1992–2002 (vice-pres 2002–); fndr pres Ullans Acad 1992–, fndr rector Ulster-Scots Acad 1994 (chm 1994–2004); fndr memb: Cultural Traditions Gp NI CRC 1988, Ultach Tst 1990; memb: Ulster-Scots Agency 2003–, Ulster-Scots Acad Implementation Gp 2005–, Faculty of Community Health (MFCH); fndr memb Ulster Soc 1985–; FRIPH; holds Wisdom-Keeper status among Lakota (Sioux) nation; OStJ 1998; *Publications* The Cruthin (1974, 5 edn 1995), Bangor: light of the world (1979, 2 edn 1987), The Battle of Moira (1980), The Identity of Ulster (1982, 4 edn 1995), The Ulster People (1991), 1690: William and the Boyne (1995), Dalaradia: kingdom of the Cruthin (1998, 2 edn 2003); *Recreations* oil painting, theatre, travel; *Clubs* Ulster Reform Belfast, Clandeboye Golf; *Style*— Dr Ian Adamson, OBE; ✉ Members' Room, City Hall, Belfast BT1 5GS (tel and fax 028 9042 1005, e-mail nosmada-cruthin@utvinternet.com, website www.ianadamson.net)

ADAMSON, Dr James; CBE (1997, OBE 1970); s of Charles Adamson (d 1980), and Magdalene Adamson (d 1964); *b* 25 May 1941, Rosyth; *Educ* Kings Road Secdy Sch (Dux, Tech Cert), Royal Dockyards Tech Coll (ONC, HNC); *m* 24 Oct 1964, Ann May, da of George Gargett; 2 s (James b 10 May 1965, Joseph b 16 Oct 1966), 2 da (Rachel b 5 May 1970, Rebecca b 1 Jan 1978); *Career* civilian tech offr RN; various posts: Honeywell, AT&T, ITT, GEC; vice-chm NCR Financial Systems Ltd, fndr and chm amf INSIGHT 1998–; non-exec dir: East Bd Royal Bank of Scotland, First Banking Systems; memb Advsy Cncl Scottish Cncl for Devpt and Industry; hon pres Fife Soc for the Blind, tech advsr RNIB; hon fell Univ of Abertay Dundee, Hon Dr Heriot-Watt Univ, Hon Dr Univ of Dundee (also visiting prof); FRSA, FRSE; *Recreations* sailing, singing; *Style*— Dr James Adamson, CBE

ADAMSON, Martin Gardiner; s of Alan S Adamson (d 1981), and Janet J Adamson (d 1999); *b* 14 September 1939; *Educ* St Mary's Sch Melrose, Sedbergh; *m* 1964, Kathleen Jane, *née* Darby; 2 s (Alan b 1966, James b 1967), 1 da (Louise b 1970); *Career* trainee Graham, Smart & Annan Edinburgh 1957–62, managing ptnr Thomson McLintock & Co 1983–86 (ptnr 1967, staff ptnr 1970), various mgmnt roles, ptnr i/c risk mgmnt and memb Bd KPMG (following merger of Thomson McLintock and Peat Marwick Mitchell) 1983–96, non-exec chm Associated British Foods 2002– (Bd dir 1999); MICAS 1962; *Recreations* gardening, golf, reading, theatre; *Clubs* Caledonian, MCC, Royal Cinque Ports Golf, Wildernesse Golf; *Style*— Martin Adamson, Esq; ✉ Associated British Foods plc, Weston Centre, 10 Grosvenor Street, London W1K 4QY (tel 020 7399 6500, fax 020 7399 6580)

ADAMSON, Nicolas Clark; LVO (2002), OBE (1982); s of Joseph Clark Adamson (d 1986), and Prudence Mary, *née* Gleeson; *b* 5 September 1938, London; *Educ* St Edward's Sch Oxford, RAF Coll Cranwell; *m* 4 Sept 1971, Hilary Jane, *née* Edwards; 2 da (Sara b 23 March 1976, Catherine b 15 Feb 1978); *Career* cmmnd RAF 1959, served various fighter sqdns UK and ME 1960–65, Flt Lt 1962, Flying Instr 1965–67, ADC to CDS 1967–69; FCO: first sec 1969, Brussels (EC) 1972–75, Islamabad 1979–82, Paris 1986–90, counsellor 1990, ret 1993; private sec to HRH The Duke of Kent 1993–; MRAeS 1998; *Recreations* classical music, fine arts, walking tours; *Clubs* RAF, Athenaeum; *Style*— Nicolas Adamson, Esq, LVO, OBE; ✉ Office of The Duke of Kent, York House, St James's Palace, London SW1A 1BQ (tel 020 7930 4872, fax 020 7930 1223, e-mail nicolas.adamson@royal.gsx.gov.uk)

ADAMSON, Paul; *Educ* European Univ Inst Florence, Institut d'Etudes Politiques Grenoble, Kingston Univ; *Career* res aide to MEPs 1979; former head European affrs BSMG Worldwide (co-chair global public affrs practice), ceo Adamson BSMG Worldwide Brussels, chm WeberShandwick Adamson; currently chm and co-fndr The Centre Brussels; tstee Inst for Citizenship; fndr and publisher E! Sharp (European affrs magazine); sometime: chm EU Ctee Br C of C Brussels, memb Exec Ctee and Policy Gp EU Ctee American C of C; regular writer and speaker on European affrs; *Style*— Paul Adamson, Esq; ✉ The Centre, Avenue Marnix laan 22, B-1000 Brussels, Belgium

ADAMSON, Stewart Marr; s of Stewart Marr Adamson (d 1996), of Newcastle upon Tyne, and Josephine, *née* Mooney; *b* 9 August 1939; *Educ* ONC and HNC in Mechanical Engrg, Univ of Durham (BSc, Stephenson Medal for tech excellence in marine engrg); *m* Elaine, da of Michael Coakley (d 2003), of Sale, Cheshire; 1 da (Larissa Jane b 28 Oct 1991); *Career* indentured engrg apprentice and jig and tool designer Hawthorn Leslie (Engineers) Ltd 1954–61, Univ of Durham 1961–64, head Main Propulsion Research Gp Br Ship Research Assoc (BSRA) 1964–68, chief engrg designer and tech servs mangr Vosper Thornycroft Ltd 1968–74, tech mangr David Brown Vosper (Offshore) Ltd 1974–78, european mangr Lockheed Petroleum Services (UK) Ltd (part of the Lockheed Corp) 1978–81, md Kongsberg Engineering Ltd 1981–85, md Fuel Subsea Engineering Ltd 1985–97, md Eurozone Ventures Ltd 1997–2000; ind conslt Adamson Consulting 2000–02; Offshore Technology Conference Inc (OTC) USA: memb Prog Ctee 1978–94 (vice-chm 1994), prog chm 1995 (first non-American), memb Bd and dir 1995–2001 (first non-American); President's Award Soc of Underwater Technol 2002; FREng 1996; *Publications* incl: The Type 21 Frigate (RN Jl, 1970), Offshore LNG Terminal Review: Small Scale Gas Recovery Systems for Hostile Environments (OTC, 1978), Garoupa Subsea Production System (Offshore Europe Conf, 1979), Impact of Subsea Maintenance Activities on Floating Production Facilities in Deep Water (OTC, 1984), The Development of Diverless Subsea Production Systems (Brazil Oil and Gas Seminar, 1987), Application of Subsea Production Systems Offshore USSR (Neftegas Conf, 1987), Application of Subsea Production Systems to Deep Water in the US Gulf of Mexico (Houston, 1990); *Recreations* making classical guitars, lutes and balalaikas; *Style—* Stewart M Adamson, FREng

ADCOCK, Fleur; OBE (1996); da of Cyril John Adcock, and Irene, *née* Robinson; *b* 10 February 1934; *Educ* Wellington Girls' Coll NZ, Victoria Univ of Wellington (MA); *m* 1, 1952 (m dis 1958), Alistair Teariki Campbell; 2 s (Gregory Stuart b 1954, Andrew Robert Teariki b 1957); m 2, 1962 (m dis 1966), Barry Crump; *Career* poet; asst librarian: Univ of Otago 1959–61 (asst lectr 1958), Alexander Turnbull Library 1962, FCO 1963–79; freelance writer 1979–; Northern Arts Fellowship in Literature Univs of Newcastle upon Tyne and Durham 1979–81, Eastern Arts Fellowship UEA 1984, writer in residence Univ of Adelaide 1986; FRSL 1984; *Awards* Buckland Award 1967 and 1979, Jessie MacKay Award 1968 and 1972, Cholmondeley Award 1976, NZ Book Award 1984, Arts Cncl Bursaries 1982 and 1988, Queen's Gold Medal for Poetry 2006; *Books* The Eye of the Hurricane (1964), Tigers (1967), High Tide in the Garden (1971), The Scenic Route (1974), The Inner Harbour (1979), Below Loughrigg (1979), The Oxford Book of Contemporary NZ Poetry (1982), Selected Poems (1983), The Virgin and the Nightingale: medieval Latin poems (1983), Hotspur: a ballad for music (1986), The Incident Book (1986), The Faber Book of 20th Century Woman's Poetry (1987), Orient Express: poems by Grete Tartler (trans, 1989), Time Zones (1991), Letters from Darkness: poems by Daniela Crasnaru (trans, 1991), Hugh Primas and the Archpoet (ed and trans, 1994), The Oxford Book of Creatures (ed with Jacqueline Simms, 1995), Looking Back (1997), Poems 1960–2000 (2000); *Style—* Ms Fleur Adcock, OBE, FRSL; ✉ 14 Lincoln Road, London N2 9DL

ADDINGTON, 6 Baron (UK 1887); Dominic Bryce Hubbard; s of 5 Baron Addington (d 1982), and Alexandra Patricia, *née* Millar; *b* 24 August 1963; *Educ* Hewett Sch, Norwich City Coll, Univ of Aberdeen (MA); *m* 27 March 1999, Elizabeth Ann Morris; *Heir* bro, Hon Michael Hubbard; *Recreations* rugby football; *Clubs* National Liberal; *Style—* The Rt Hon the Lord Addington

ADDISON, 4 Viscount (UK 1945); William Matthew Wand Addison; also 4 Baron Addison (UK 1937); s of 3 Viscount Addison (d 1992), and Kathleen (d 2007), da of Rt Rev and Rt Hon John William Charles Wand, KCVO, DD, 110 Bishop of London; *b* 13 June 1945; *Educ* King's Sch Bruton, Essex Inst of Agric; *m* 1, 1970 (m dis), Joanna Mary, eldest da of late John Ivor Charles Dickinson; 2 da (Hon Sarah Louise b 1971, Hon Caroline Amy b 1979), 1 s (Hon Paul Wand b 1973); m 2, 1991, Lesley Ann, da of George Colin Mawer; *Heir* s, Hon Paul Addison; *Career* vice-pres: The Cncl for Nat Parks 1995–, Br Tst for Conservation Vols 1996–2006; chm AICOM 1998–2000, dir Commensus 2000–02, conslt Environmental Impact Assessment 2002–; memb Ctee on Jt Statutory Instruments 1993–2000, memb Parly Information Technol Ctee 1997–; memb All-Pty Motorcycle Gp, pres Motor Activities Trg Cncl 1997–; *Recreations* walking, sailing (yachtmaster offshore), flying (PPL); *Clubs* House of Lords Yacht, RAC; *Style—* The Rt Hon the Viscount Addison; ✉ Stallingborough, Cotterstock, Peterborough PE8 5HH

ADEBOWALE, Maria Seun; *Educ* Univ of Lancaster (BA), Huddersfield Poly (CPE), De Montfort Univ, SOAS (LLM); *Career* dir Environmental Law Fndn 1998–2001, fndr and dir Capacity Global 2001–; visiting fell School of Built Environment South Bank Univ 2001–02, research fell Centre for Sustainable Devpt Sch of Architecture and the Built Environment 2003–04; memb: Information and Communication Ctee ESRC 2004–, Science Funding Grants Panel Science Wise DTI 2004–; cmmr English Heritage 2003–, chair Waterwise 2005–, tstee Allavida 2006–; *Style—* Ms Maria Adebowale; ✉ Capacity Global, 16 Boone Street, London SE13 5SB (tel 020 852 8030)

ADEBOWALE, Dr Olutayo Omonitan (Tayo); *b* 28 August 1963, Huddersfield; *Educ* Manchester Met Univ (BSc), Univ of Manchester (PhD); *Career* project mangr UMIST Environmental 1989–93, sr environmental scientist Jacob Babtie Gp Ltd 1993–97, sr conslt Environmental Resources Management 1997–2002, environmental scientist Cirkadia 2003–; assoc lectr Open Univ 1988–2001, visiting lectr Water Framework Directive, writer and teacher Industrial Environmental Mgmnt module Liverpool John Moores Univ, non-exec forestry cmmr, non-exec memb Countryside Agency Bd (memb: Audit & Risk Ctee, Landscape Access & Recreation Task Gp, Natural England Steering Gp); nominee NW Business Environment Award 2005; memb: Inst of Leadership and Mgmnt, BAAS, Int Assoc of Water Quality, Chartered Inst of Water and Environmental Mgmnt (chair N Western and N Wales Branch 2004–05), chartered environmentalist, chartered water and environmental mangr; *Style—* Dr Tayo Adebowale; ✉ Cirkadia, PO Box 215, Manchester M13 1WX (tel 0161 248 6902)

ADEBOWALE, Baron (Life Peer UK 2001), of Thornes in the County of West Yorkshire; Victor Olufemi Adebowale; CBE (2000); s of E O Adebowale, and Grace Adebowale; *b* 21 July 1962; *Educ* Thornes House Wakefield; *Children* 1 s (Hon Adam b 1994), 1 da (Isabella b 2005); *Career* London Borough of Newham: private sector repairs admin 1983, estate offr 1983–84, sr estate mangr 1984–86; permanent property mangr Patchwork Community Housing Assoc 1986–88, regnl dir Ujima Housing Assoc 1988–90, dir Alcohol Recovery Project 1990–95; chief exec Centrepoint 1995–2001, ceo Turning Point 2001–; chair: IPPR Review of Social Housing 1999, Fabian Soc/Barrow Cadbury Tst Review of Life Chances and Poverty 2003–04, Advsy Panel on Race Impact Assessment ODPM; co-chair Black and Minority Ethnic Mental Health Steering Gp 2003–, chair Stop and Search Community Panel 2005; chair Mental Health Steering Gp Dept of Health 2002–; memb: New Deal Task Force, Policy Action Team 12 on Young People Social Exclusion Unit, Advsy Cncl Demos, Nat Employment Panel; tstee Nat Sch of Govt; patron: Nursing Cncl on Alcohol, The Tomorrow Fndn, Rich Mix Centre; memb Cncl Inst of Fiscal Studies 2002–; hon fell South Bank Univ, hon sr fell Health Servs Mgmnt Centre Univ of Birmingham, hon visiting prof Lincoln Univ; Hon PhD Univ of Central Eng, Hon PhD Univ of East London, Hon DLitt Lincoln Univ; *Publications* Alcohol Problems in the Community: Drinking Problems Among Black Communities (1996); *Recreations* kite flying, reading, writing poetry, music; *Style—* The Rt Hon the Lord Adebowale, CBE

ADER, His Hon Judge Peter Charles; s of Max Ader (d 1978), and Inge, *née* Nord; *b* 14 May 1950; *Educ* Highgate Sch, Univ of Southampton (LLB); *m* 30 June 1979, Margaret Judith, da of Ronald G Taylor (d 1999); 2 da (Caroline Sarah b 1985, Catherine Elizabeth b 1993), 1 s (David Max b 1989); *Career* called to the Bar Middle Temple 1973; in private practice (specialising in criminal law) 1974–99, circuit judge (SE Circuit) 1999–; memb Worshipful Co of Clockmakers; *Recreations* squash, tennis, skiing, golf, travel; *Clubs* Hampstead Golf; *Style—* His Hon Judge Ader; ✉ 3 Temple Gardens, Temple, London EC4Y 9AU (tel 020 7353 3102)

ADÈS, Prof (Josephine) Dawn; OBE (2002); da of A E Tylden-Pattenson, CSI (d 1955), and Ruth Breakwell, *née* Morton (d 1993); *b* 6 May 1943; *Educ* Guildford HS, Cheltenham Ladies' Coll, St Hilda's Coll Oxford (BA), Courtauld Inst of Art London (MA); *m* 9 July 1966, Timothy Adès; 3 s (Thomas b 1971, Harry b 1973, Robert b 1981); *Career* prof of history and theory of art Univ of Essex 1990– (lectr 1978–); dir: Burlington Magazine 1996–, AHRC Research Centre for Studies of Surrealism and its Legacies 2002–; tstee: Tate 1995–2005, Nat Gallery 1998–2005, Elephant Tst 2000–, Henry Moore Fndn 2003–; memb: Bd Canning House 2002–, Collections Cncl Tate 2005–; FBA 1995; *Exhibitions* curator: Art in Latin America: the modern era 1820–1980 (Hayward Gallery London) 1989, Dali's Optical Illusions (Wordsworth Atheneum Hartford CT) 2000, Undercover Surrealism (Hayward Gallery London) 2006; co-curator: Dada and Surrealism Reviewed (Arts Cncl of GB) 1978, Art and Power: Europe under the Dictators 1930–45 (Hayward Gallery London) 1995, Dali (Palazzo Grassi Venice and Phildelphia Museum of Art) 2004; *Books* Dada and Surrealism Reviewed (1978), Salvador Dalí (1982), Photomontage (1986), Art in Latin America (1989), André Masson (1994), Siron Franco (1995), Surrealist Art (1997), Marcel Duchamp (with Cox and Hopkins, 1999); *Style—* Prof Dawn Adès, OBE; ✉ Department of Art History and Theory, University of Essex, Colchester CO4 3SQ (tel 01206 873007, fax 01206 873003, mobile 07850 152055, e-mail ades@essex.ac.uk)

ADÈS, Prof Thomas Joseph Edmund; s of Timothy Raymond Ades, of London, and Prof Dawn Ades, *née* Tylden-Pattenson; *b* 1 March 1971; *Educ* Univ Coll Sch, Guildhall Sch of Music, King's Coll Cambridge, St John's Coll Cambridge; *Career* composer, pianist, conductor; composer-in-association Hallé Orch 1993–95, fell commoner in creative arts Trinity Coll Cambridge 1995–97, Benjamin Britten prof of music RAM 1997–, music dir Birmingham Contemporary Music Gp 1998–, artistic dir Aldeburgh Festival 1999–; subject of retrospective festival Barbican London 2007; several CD releases of performances and compositions; Editor's Choice Gramophone Award 1998, Munich Ernst von Siemens Prize for Young Composers 1999; Hon Dr Univ of Essex 2004; *Compositions* Five Eliot Landscapes 1990, O thou who didst with pitfall and gin (choral) 1990, Chamber Symphony 1990, Catch (chamber ensemble) 1991, Still Sorrowing (piano) 1991–92, Under Hamelin Hill (chamber organ) 1992, Fool's Rhymes (choral) 1992, ...but all shall be well (orchestral) 1993, Sonata da Casccia (chamber ensemble) 1993, Life Story (soprano and chamber ensemble) 1993, Living Toys (chamber ensemble) 1993 (Paris Int Rostrum of Composers 1994), Arcadiana (string quartet) 1994 (Elise L Stoeger Prize 1998, Salzburg Easter Festival Composition Prize 1999), The Origin of the Harp (chamber ensemble) 1994, Les baricades mistérieuses (chamber ensemble) 1994, Powder Her Face (chamber opera) 1995, Traced Overhead (piano) 1996, These Premises are Alarmed (orchestral) 1996, Asyla (orchestral) 1997 (Royal Philharmonic Society Prize 1997), Concerto Conciso (piano and chamber ensemble) 1997–98, America (mezzo-soprano, orchestra, and chorus) 1998–99, Piano Quintet 2000, Brahms (baritone and orchestra) 2001, The Tempest (opera) 2003–04, Concentric Paths (violin concerto) 2005, Three Studies from Couperin (chamber orchestra) 2006, Tevot 2007; *Recreations* reading; *Clubs* Black's; *Style—* Prof Thomas Adès; ✉ c/o Faber Music, 3 Queen Square, London WC1N 3AU

ADEY, John Fuller; s of Frank Douglas Adey (d 1978), and Doreen Adey (d 1998); *b* 12 May 1941; *Educ* Glyn Sch Epsom, St Edmund Hall Oxford (MA), Harvard Business Sch (MBA); *m* 25 Sept 1965, Marianne, da of George Hugh Banning; 2 da (Helen Doreen b 1 July 1971, Francesca Ruth b 26 May 1977), 2 s (Matthew Frank George b 19 May 1975, Michael Douglas John b 31 Dec 1984); *Career* manufacturing mangr then int mktg dir Raychem Ltd 1973–83; md: Courtaulds Chemicals and Plastics 1983–86, Baxter Healthcare 1986–93; chief exec National Blood Authority 1993–98; chm: Adams Healthcare Ltd 1999–2000, Medical Engrg Investments plc 2003–05; dir: API plc 1987–97, Seton Healthcare plc 1996–98; non-exec dir New Horizons 2005–; Swindon and Marlborough NHS Trust: non-exec dir 2002–06, dep chm 2003–06; gen cmmr Income Tax 1983–; chm: Aldbourne Nursing Home Ltd 2000–, Royal Merchant Navy Sch Fndn 2002– (tstee 1999–); chm of govrs John O'Gaunt Sch Hungerford 2001–; CEng 1970, MIMechE 1970, MIEE 1976, FInstD 1994; *Recreations* tennis, cycling; *Style—* John Adey, Esq

ADGEY, Prof (Agnes Anne) Jennifer; CBE (2002); da of Robert Henry Adgey (d 1973), of Newtownards, Co Down, and Sarah Jane, *née* Menown (d 1990); *b* 2 October 1941; *Educ* Regent House Sch Newtownards Co Down, Queen's Univ Belfast (MB, MD); *Career* res fell in cardiology Presbyterian Med Centre San Francisco 1967–68; Royal Victoria Hosp Belfast: jr house offr 1964–65, sr house offr and registrar 1965–67, sr registrar in cardiology 1968–71, conslt cardiologist 1971–, prof of cardiology 1991–; examiner and censor RCP London, expert Advsy Panel on Cardiovascular Diseases WHO, examiner RCP Ireland 1988; memb: Cncl Br Cardiac Soc 1995–, Cncl Med Defence Union 1995–; memb: Br Cardiac Soc 1973, Assoc of Physicians of GB and Ireland 1980, NY Acad of Sci 1983, Resuscitation Cncl UK 1987; fell American Coll of Cardiology 1975; MRCP 1967, FRCP 1978, FESC 1995; *Books* The Acute Coronary Attack (with J F Pantridge, J S Geddes and S W Webb, 1975), Developments in Cardiovascular Medicine (1982), Acute Phase of Ischemic Heart Disease and Myocardial Infarction (ed), numerous papers on cardiology; *Recreations* piano and classical music; *Style—* Prof Jennifer Adgey, CBE; ✉ Mossvale House, 71 Ballyskeagh Road, Lisburn, Co Antrim BT27 5TE (tel 028 9062 9773); Regional Medical Cardiology Centre, Royal Victoria Hospital, Belfast BT12 6BA (tel 028 9063 2171, fax 028 9031 2907)

ADIE, Kathryn (Kate); OBE (1993); d of Babe Dunnet, *née* Issitt, and adopted da of John Wilfrid Adie (d 1993), and Maud, *née* Fambely (d 1990); *b* 19 September 1945; *Educ* Sunderland Church HS, Univ of Newcastle upon Tyne (BA); *Career* technician and prodr BBC local radio 1969–76, reporter BBC TV South 1977–78; BBC TV News: reporter 1979–81, corr 1982, chief news corr 1989–2003; presenter From Our Own Correspondent (BBC Radio 4) 1998–; hon prof broadcasting and journalism Univ of Sunderland 1995; Hon MA: Univ of Bath 1987, Univ of Newcastle upon Tyne 1990; Hon DLitt: City Univ 1989, Loughborough Univ 1991, Univ of Sunderland 1993, Robert Gordon Univ 1996, Univ of Nottingham 1998, Nottingham Trent Univ 1998; Hon DUniv: Oxford Brookes 2002, Anglia Poly 1999; hon fell: Royal Holloway Univ of London 1996, Univ of Central Lancashire 2002, Univ of Cardiff 2004, York St John Univ 2006; visiting fell Bournemouth Univ 1998–; RTS: News Award 1981 and 1987, Judges' Award 1989; Monte Carlo Int TV News Award 1981 and 1990, BAFTA Richard Dimbleby Award 1989; Freedom of City of Sunderland, Hon Freeman City of London 1995, memb Worshipful Co of Glaziers 1996; *Publications* The Kindness of Strangers (memoirs 2002), Corsets to Camouflage: Women and War (2003), Nobodys Child : Who Are You When You Don't Know Your Past? (2005); *Style—* Ms Kate Adie, OBE; ✉ c/o PO Box 317, Brentford TW8 8WX

ADJAYE, David; OBE (2007); s of Affram Adjaye, and Cecilia Adjaye; *b* 22 September 1966, Dar-Es-Salaam, Tanzania; *Educ* South Bank Univ (BA), RCA (MA); *Career* architect; Chassay Architects 1988–90, David Chipperfield Architects 1991, Eduardo Souto de Moura Architects Portugal 1991, founding ptnr Adjaye & Russell 1994–2000, princ Adjaye/Associates 2000–; projects: Idea Store Chrisp Street London 2004, Nobel Peace Centre Oslo 2005, Idea Store Whitechapel London 2005, Rivington Place London 2007, Bernie Grant Centre London 2007, Stephen Lawrence Centre London 2007, Museum of Contemporary Art USA 2007; lectr: South Bank Univ 1993–98, RCA 1998–2002; delivered numerous talks and lectures worldwide; RIBA, ARB; *Exhibitions* Sumi (Kyoto Geidai Gallery Japan) 1993, Papers (Architecture Foundation London) 1995, Tasty (Selfridges London) 1997, Outside/In: London Architecture (Architeckturforum Innsbruck) 2000, Adjaye/Associates Recent Work (Hanover Univ) 2001, David Adjaye Making Public Buildings (Whitechapel Gall) 2006; *Awards* First Prize Housing British Gas Student Competition 1992, First Prize Bronze Medal RIBA 1993, Highly Commended Phoenix Meml Competition 1993, First Prize Lewes Ideas Competition 1993, Stirling Prize nomination 2006; *Style—* David Adjaye, Esq, OBE; ✉ Adjaye/Associates, 23–28 Penn Street, London N1 5DL (tel 020 7739 4969, fax 020 7739 3484, e-mail david@adjaye.com)

ADKINS, Richard David; QC (1995); s of Walter David Adkins, and Patricia, *née* Chimes; *b* 21 October 1954; *Educ* Leamington Coll for Boys, Hertford Coll Oxford (MA); *m* 1977, Jane Margaret, da of Derek and Ella Sparrow; 2 s, 1 da; *Career* admitted slr 1978; called to the Bar Middle Temple 1982; memb Ctee Chancery Bar Assoc 1991–93; *Publications* Encyclopaedia of Forms and Precedents (Vol 3, 1985), Company Receivers: A New Status? (1988), Gore-Browne on Companies (contrib 44 edn, 1992–); *Recreations* opera, skiing, tennis; *Clubs* Bromley Cricket; *Style*— Richard Adkins, Esq, QC; ✉ 3–4 South Square, Gray's Inn, London WC1R 5HP (tel 020 7696 9900, fax 020 7696 9911, e-mail richardadkins@southsquare.com)

ADLAM, Lance Edward Stott; s of Edward Douglas Stott Adlam (d 1991), of Cotleigh, Devon, and Margaret Elsie, *née* May-Arrindell (d 1996); *b* 3 April 1944; *Educ* Acton Central Sch, The Elms Secdy Sch Acton, Chiswick Poly, Thames Poly (formerly Hammersmith Coll of Art & Building), Poly of Central London; *m* 1 July 1967, Angela Marie, da of Vivian Egerton Saunders; 2 s (Mark Edward Vivian b 1970, Paul Andrew John b 1972); *Career* architect: Fitzroy Robinson & Partners 1960–71, Bucks Co Architects' Dept 1971–78, Architects' Dept Ind Coope Ltd 1978–80, Fitzroy Robinson Partnership 1980–83; ptnr T P Bennett Partnership (formerly T P Bennett & Son) 1989–93 (assoc 1983–89), princ Lance Adlam Architects 1993–; chm: Princes Risborough Chamber of Trade 1998–2005, Princes Risborough Town Forum 1999–; pres Risborough Area Business Gp 2005–; ARB 1974, RIBA 1974; *Recreations* railway modelling, railway history, philately, music, reading; *Clubs* Thame Badminton (chm 1988–96), chm Aylesbury and District Badminton Assoc 2005–, Princes Risborough Bowls (chm 2005–), Great Western Soc, Quainton Railway Soc (Chinnor and Princes Risborough Railway Assoc), N Gauge Soc, Buckinghamshire Family History Soc, Buckinghamshire Genealogical Soc; *Style*— Lance Adlam, Esq; ✉ 6 Salisbury Close, Princes Risborough, Buckinghamshire HP27 0JF (tel and fax 01844 345423, e-mail l.adlam@lance-adlam-architects.org.uk)

ADLARD, David Boyd; s of Clifford Boyd Adlard (d 1985), of Norwich, and Elsie Lawrence, *née* Fielder (d 1990); *b* 13 June 1944; *Educ* Gresham's, Univ of Sussex (BSc), Middlesex Poly (Dip Mgmnt Studies), Kilburn Poly (Catering Studies); *m* Aug 1984 (m dis 1999), Mary Ellen, da of Edward Patrick Healy, of North Worcester, Mass; 1 da (Lucy Elizabeth b Nov 1987), 1 s (Matthew John Boyd b Aug 1991); *Career* work study engr then prodn mangr Alcan Industries Ltd 1966–73, prodn mangr Cape Universal Building Products 1973–74; chef: various hotels and restaurants 1975–77, Connaught Hotel Mayfair 1978–81; chef tournant Le Talbooth Restaurant Dedham Colchester Essex 1981–82, pastry chef and asst to Maître D'Hotel Castle Restaurant Leicester Mass USA 1982, restaurant mangr The Terrace Restaurant Dedham Vale Hotel Dedham Colchester Essex 1982, opened Adlard's Restaurant Wymondham Norfolk 1983 (moved restaurant to 79 Upper St Giles St Norwich 1989); columnist Eastern Daily Press Monthly magazine; memb Br Acad of Culinary Arts 1988–; *Awards* (for Adlard's restaurant) Michelin one rosette 1987–92 and 1995–2005, nomination Glenfiddich Food & Drink Awards Regional Writer 2001, Outstanding Achievement Award Eastern Daily Press Food Awards 2005; *Recreations* wine, golf, searching for wild mushrooms and dining out; *Style*— David Adlard, Esq; ✉ Adlards Restaurant, 79 Upper St Giles Street, Norwich, Norfolk NR2 1AB (tel 01603 633522, home tel 01603 661988, e-mail info@adlards.co.uk, website www.adlards.co.uk)

ADLER, Prof Michael William; CBE (1999); s of late Gerhard Adler, and Hella, *née* Hildergard; *b* 12 June 1939; *Educ* Middlesex Hosp Med Sch (MB BS, MD); *m* 1 (m dis 1978), Susan Jean Burnett; m 2, 23 June 1979 (m dis 1994), Karen Hope Dunnell, da of Richard Henry Williamson (d 1984); 2 da (Zoe b 1980, Emma b 1982); m 3, 26 March 1994, Baroness Jay of Paddington, *qv*; *Career* house offr and registrar in med (Middx Hosp, Central Middx Hosp, Whittington Hosp) 1965–69, lectr St Thomas' Hosp Med Sch 1970–75, sr lectr Middx Hosp Med Sch 1975–79, prof of genito urinary med UCL Med Sch (formerly Middx Hosp Med Sch) 1979–; non-exec dir Camden and Islington Community Health Servs NHS Tst 1993, non-exec dir Health Devpt Agency 2000–; MRC memb: Res Advsy Gp on epidemiological studies of sexually transmitted diseases 1975–80, Working Pty to coordinate lab studies on the gonococcus 1979–83, Working Pty on AIDS 1981–87 (Sub-Ctee therapeutic studies 1985–87), Ctee epidemiological studies on AIDS 1985–94, Ctee on clinical studies of prototype vaccines against AIDS 1987; Jt Ctee of Higher Med Trg: memb Advsy Ctee on genito urinary med 1981–86, sec 1982–83, chm 1984–86; memb EC Working Gp on AIDS 1985–, chm RCP Ctee on Genito Urinary Med 1987–91 (memb 1981–91), advsr Parly All-Pty Ctee on AIDS 1987–, chm and tstee Nat AIDS Tst 1987–2000, dir AIDS Policy Unit 1988–89, memb Cncl Med Soc for Study of Venereal Diseases (pres 1997–99); DOH: memb Expert Advsy Gp AIDS 1984–92, memb Gp on health care workers 1987–91; memb: Exec Ctee Int Union against Venereal Diseases 1986–, BMA AIDS Working Pty 1986–, RCS Ctee on HIV Infection/AIDS 1991–, Cncl RCP 1999–; advsr in venereology WHO 1983–, memb Med Advsy Ctee Brook Advsy Centres 1984–94, memb Cncl Royal Inst of Public Health and Hygiene 1993–94, memb Governing Cncl Int AIDS Soc 1993–99; dir Terrence Higgins Tst 1982–88; fndr ed AIDS (monthly jl) 1986–94; memb Editorial Panel: Genitourinary Medicine, Current Opinion on Infectious Diseases; Evian Health Award 1990; FFPHM, FRCP; *Books* ABC of Sexually Transmitted Diseases (1984, 5 edn 2004), ABC of AIDS (1987, 5 edn 2001), Diseases in the Homosexual Male (ed, 1988); also articles on sexually transmitted diseases and AIDS in medical jls; *Recreations* yoga, theatre; *Style*— Prof Michael Adler, CBE; ✉ Academic Department of Sexually Transmitted Diseases, The Mortimer Market Centre, Mortimer Market, off Capper Street, London WC1E 6AU (tel 020 7380 9892, fax 020 7380 9669)

ADLINGTON, Jonathan Peter Nathaniel; s of Sidney Roy Adlington, JP (d 1982), of Mylor, Cornwall, and Patricia, *née* Moxon (d 1998); *b* 26 April 1949; *Educ* Downside, Univ of Liverpool (LLB); *m* 2 June 1973, Carolyn Patricia Lilian Marie, da of Brian B W Bromley, of Crowborough, E Sussex; 2 da (Emily b 3 May 1975, Tamsin b 19 Sept 1976), 1 s (Edward b 25 Dec 1983); *Career* admitted slr 1973; sr ptnr Trowers & Hamlins 2000– (articled clerk 1971–73, ptnr 1976–); memb Law Soc; *Recreations* sailing; *Clubs* RAC; *Style*— Jonathan Adlington, Esq; ✉ Trowers & Hamlins, Sceptre Court, 40 Tower Hill, London EC3N 4DX (tel 020 7423 8000, fax 020 7423 8001)

ADORNO-S, Jesus Antonio; s of Luciano Adorno Rolon (d 1958), of Santa Cruz, Bolivia, and Maria Sanabria Osorio (d 2002); *b* Santa Cruz, Bolivia; *Educ* Gaston Guillaux Coll Santa Cruz; *m* (m dis); 2 da (Diana Luz b 16 May 1985, Monica Maria b 4 March 1987); *Career* waiter: Fredericks Restaurant 1974–75, Jardin des Gourmet 1974–76, Inigo Jones 1977–81; head waiter rising to restaurant mangr Le Caprice 1981–, dir Caprice Holdings 1990–, dir Daphne's Restaurant 1992–; freelance journalist: The Telegraph, The Mail on Sunday, Orient Express Magazine; Fashion Restaurant of the Year 2000; supporter Anglo-Bolivian Soc; *Recreations* football, walking, snorkling, cricket; *Clubs* Destroyers (Bolivia), Tottenham Hotspur; *Style*— Jesus Adorno-S, Esq; ✉ Le Caprice, Arlington House, Arlington Street, London SW1A 1RT (tel 020 7629 2239, fax 020 7493 9040)

ADRIAN (aka WARNE), John Adrian Marie Edward Warne; s of Col John Edward Marie William Warne, REME (d 1971), and Agnes Amelia Diana, *née* Mills; *b* 29 January 1938; *Educ* Dulwich Coll, Salesian Coll Burwash; *Career* served RAF Cyprus 1955–58; singer and dancer 1959–72; theatre mangr 1972–87: Nat Youth Theatre, Stoll Moss Theatres London, St George's Shakespeare Theatre, Garrick Theatre London, Royal Cultural Theatre Amman Jordan, Theatre Royal Windsor; memb Soc for Theatre Res; sec Grand Order of Water Rats Charities Fund 1987–; Freeman City of London, memb Worshipful Co of Firefighters; *Recreations* historical research, swimming and cycling; *Clubs* East India & Public Schools, Green Room; *Style*— John Adrian, Esq; ✉ Grand Order of Water Rats Charities Fund, 328 Gray's Inn Road, London WC1X 8BZ (tel 020 7407 8007, e-mail charities@gowr.net)

ADRIANO, Dino B; s of Dante Adriano, and Yole Adriano; *b* 24 April 1943; *Educ* Highgate Coll, Strand GS; *m* 1966, Susan Rivett; 2 da; *Career* articled clerk George W Spencer & Co 1959–64; J Sainsbury plc: joined as accountant 1964, gen mangr Homebase 1981–86, area dir 1986–89, md Homebase 1989–93 (chm 1991–Sept 1996), main bd dir 1990–2000, chm Shaw's Supermarkets Inc 1994–96 (dep chm 1993–94), dir Giant Food Inc 1994–96, asst md 1995–96, dep chief exec 1996–97, chm and chief exec Sainsbury's Supermarkets Ltd 1997–2000 (dep chief exec 1996–March 1997), gp chief exec J Sainsbury plc 1998–2000; dir Laura Ashley plc 1996–98; tstee: Oxfam 1990–96 and 1998–2004 (vice-chm 2001–04, advsr 1996–98 and 2004–), WRVS 2001–; chair of govrs Thames Valley Univ 2004–; FCCA 1980 (ACCA 1965); *Style*— Dino Adriano, Esq

ADSETTS, Sir (William) Norman; kt (1999), OBE (1988); s of Ernest Norman Adsetts (d 1992), and Hilda Rachael, *née* Wheeler (d 1986); *b* 6 April 1931; *Educ* King Edward VII Sch Sheffield, The Queen's Coll Oxford (MA); *m* 20 Oct 1956, Eve, da of Eric Stefanuti (d 1985); 1 da (Helen Eve b 1957), 1 s (Philip Norman b 1959); *Career* Nat Serv flying offr Equipment Branch RAF 1950–52; appts in sales and mktg and product devpt Fibreglass Ltd 1955–66; chm: Sheffield Insulating Co Ltd 1985–89 (dir 1966, md 1970), Sheffield Insulations Gp plc 1989–96, Sheffield Partnerships Ltd 1988–93, South Yorkshire Supertram Tst Ltd 1993–98; non-exec dir Sheffield Theatres Ltd 1988–94, dep chm Sheffield Devpt Corp 1991–97 (memb Bd 1988–91); chm: Kelham Island Museum Ltd (renamed Sheffield Industrial Museums Tst in 1997) 1994–98, Sheffield Theatres Tst 1996–2005, Kelham Riverside Devpt Agency 1998–2001; vice-pres Assoc for the Conservation of Energy Ltd 1990– (chm 1985–90 and 1993–95); pres Sheffield C of C 1988–89; chm: CBI Yorkshire and Humberside 1989–91, Sheffield First for Investment 1999–2001, Bd of Govrs Sheffield Hallam Univ 1993–99; tstee: Hillsborough Disaster Appeal 1989–95, Research Autism 2006–; memb: Advsy Ctee on Business and the Environment 1991–93, Yorkshire and Humberside Arts Bd 1991–94, Bd Opera North Ltd 1991–94, Fin Bd RC Diocese of Hallam 1998–2004, Nat Cncl of Arts Cncl of England 2002–05; chm of govrs Mount St Mary's Coll 1999– (govr 1998–); *Recreations* reading, local history, grandchildren; *Style*— Sir Norman Adsetts, OBE; ✉ Churchfield House, Rotherham Road, Eckington, Sheffield S21 4FH (tel 01246 431008, fax 01246 431009)

ADSHEAD, John E; CBE (1997); *Educ* Univ of Exeter, Cranfield Sch of Mgmnt (MBA); *Career* Ford Motor Co 1968 (joined as trainee), Bank of America 1976 (latterly sr vice-pres HR, IT and admin EMEA), gp personnel and IT dir J Sainsbury plc 1989–2004; non-exec dir Barts and The London NHS Tst 2004– (currently vice-chm); *Style*— John Adshead, Esq, CBE

ADUGNA, HE Fisseha; *b* 27 September 1955, Fitche, Ethiopia; *Educ* Tafari Mekonnen HS Addis Ababa, Addis Ababa Univ (BA), Diplomatic Acad Vienna (MA); *m*; 2 c; *Career* Ethiopian diplomat; Miny of Foreign Affrs: third sec Policy, Planning and Research Dept 1980–84, promoted second sec 1984, desk offr Western European Countries 1984–86, cnsllr and head Neighbouring Countries Div 1986–91, actg head Africa Dept 1991–92; dep chief of mission (min cnsllr) Washington DC 1992–2000, chargé d'affaires London 2000–02, ambass to the Ct of St James's 2002–; attendee: Orgn of African Unity (OAU) Heads of States Summits, Inter-Governmental Authy of Devpt (IGAD) Meetings, US-Africa Ministerial Conf 1988, UN Gen Assembly 1990, World Bank Gp and IMF Annual Meeting 1999; *Style*— HE Mr Fisseha Adugna

AFRIYIE, Adam; MP; *b* 4 August 1965, Wimbledon, London; *Educ* Addey and Stanhope GS, Imperial Coll London (BSc); *m* Aug 2005, Tracy-Jane Newall; 1 s; *Career* founding dir Connect Support Services 1993–, former chm DeHallivand Info Services plc, chm Adfero; MP (Cons) Windsor 2005–; dir Policy Exchange, former govr Museum of London, chm Young Enterprise N Berks; *Style*— Adam Afriyie, Esq, MP; ✉ House of Commons, London SW1A 0AA

AFSHAR, Farhad; s of Aziz Afshar Yazdi, and Btoul, *née* Ameli; *b* 4 December 1941; *Educ* Lord Wandsworth Coll, London Hosp Med Coll (BSc, MB BS, MD); *m* 1, 23 Aug 1968 (m dis 1983), Lucille Anne, da of William E Goodfellow (d 1985); 3 s (Iain b 1970, Daniel b 1973, Brett b 1974), 1 da (Nina b 1977); *Career* fell in neurosurgery Ohio State Univ 1974–75, conslt neurosurgeon and sr lectr in neurosurgery London Hosp 1975–85, sr registrar in neurosurgery London Hosp and Bart's 1977, conslt neurosurgeon Bart's 1985–, also currently sr conslt neurosurgeon Royal London Hosp; author of numerous chapters and scientific papers on neurosurgery, examiner in surgery Univ of London; memb: Soc of Br Neurosurgeons, Congress of American Neurosurgeons, Euro and World Sterotaxic Surgns, World Pituitary Surgns; FRSM, LRCP, FRCS (MRCS); *Books* Stereotaxic Atlas of Human Brain Stem and Cerebellar Nuclei (1978); *Recreations* photography, natural history, walking; *Style*— Farhad Afshar, Esq; ✉ 145 Harley Street, London W1G 6BJ (tel 020 7935 7505, fax 020 7935 7245, e-mail faryafshar@hotmail.com); Department of Neurosurgery, St Bartholomew's Hospital, London EC1 7BE (tel 020 7601 8888); Senior Consultant Neurosurgeon, Royal London Hospital, London E1 1BB (tel 020 7377 7000)

AGA KHAN (IV), HH The; Prince Karim; KBE (2004), Hon CC (2004); s of late Prince Aly Khan, and Hon Joan, *née* Yarde-Buller (later Viscountess Camrose d 1997), da of 3 Baron Churston, MVO, OBE; gs of late Sir Sultan Mahomed Shah Aga Khan (III) (d 1957); *b* 13 December 1936; *Educ* Le Rosey Switzerland, Harvard Univ (BA); *m* 1, 1969 (m dis 1995), Sarah Frances (Sally), *née* Croker-Poole; 2 s (Prince Rahim b 1971, Prince Hussain b 1974), 1 da (Princess Zahra (Mrs Mark Boyden) b 1970); m 2, 1998 (m dis 2004), Princess Gabriele zu Leiningen; 1 s (Prince Aly Muhammad b 2000); *Career* Spiritual Leader and Imam of Ismaili Muslims 1975–, granted title HH by HM The Queen 1957, and HRH by late Shah of Iran 1959; philanthropist; fndr: Aga Kham Devpt Network; fndr and chm: Aga Khan Fndn Switzerland 1967 (branches/affiliates in Bangladesh, Canada, India, Kenya, Pakistan, Portugal, Tajikistan, Tanzania, Uganda, UK and USA), Aga Khan Award for Architecture 1977, Inst of Ismaili Studies London 1977, Aga Khan Fund for Econ Devpt 1984, Aga Khan Tst for Culture Switzerland 1988, Aga Khan Agency for Micro-finance 2005; fndr and chllr: Aga Khan Univ Pakistan 1983, Univ of Central Asia (by treaty with Kurgyzstan, Tajikistan and Kazakhstan) 2000; leading owner and breeder of race horses in France, Ireland and UK; winner Derby: 1981 (Shergar), 1986 (Shahrastani), 1988 (Kahyasi), 2000 (Sinndar); winner Irish Derby: 1981 (Shergar), 1986 (Shahrastani), 1988 (Kahayasi), 2000 (Sinndar), 2003 (Alamshar); winner Prix de L'Arc de Triomphe: 1982 (Akiyda), 2000 (Sinndar), 2003 (Dalakhani); winner Prix de Jockey Club: 1960 (Charlottesville), 1979 (Top Ville), 1984 (Darshaan), 1985 (Mouktar), 1987 (Natroun), 2003 (Dalakhani); winner Prix de Diane: 1993 (Shemaka), 1997 (vereva), 1998 (Zainta), 1999 (Daryaba); Dr of Laws (hc): Peshawar Univ Pakistan 1967, Sind Univ Pakistan 1970, McGill Univ Canada 1983, McMaster Univ Canada 1987, Univ of Wales 1993, Brown Univ USA 1996, Univ of Toronto Canada 2004; DLitt (hc) Univ of London 1989, Dr of Humane Letters (hc) American Univ of Beirut 2005; hon prof Univ of Osh Kyrgyzstan 2002; foreign hon memb American Acad of Arts and Sciences; Thomas Jefferson Meml Fndn Medal in Architecture 1984, American Inst of Architects Honor 1984, Medalla de Oro Consejo Superior de Colegios de Arquitectos Spain 1987, Huésped de Honor de Granada Spain 1991, Hon FRIBA 1991, Medaille d'Argent Académie d'Architecture France 1991, Gold Medal City of Granada 1998, Insignia of Honour Int Union of Architects France 2001; hon memb: American Inst of Architects 1992, Hadrian Awards World Monuments Fund; Vincent Scully Prize USA 2005; Commandeur Ordre du Mérite Mauritanien 1960; Grand-croix: Order of Prince Henry Portugal 1960, Ordre National de la Côte d'Ivoire 1965, Ordre National de la Haute-Volta 1965, Ordre Malgache 1966, Ordre du Croissant Vert des Comores 1966; Grand Cordon Order of the Tadj Iran 1967, Nishan-i-Imtiaz Pakistan 1970, Cavaliere di Gran Croce dell'Ordine al Merito della Repubblica Italy 1977, Grand Officier Ordre National du Lion Sénégal 1982,

Nishan-e-Pakistan 1983, Grand Cordon Ouissam-al Arch Morocco 1986, Cavaliere del Lavoro Italy 1988, Cdr de la Légion d'Honneur France 1990, Gran Cruz de la Orden del Merito Civil Spain 1991, Grand-croix Order of Merit Portugal 1998, Order of Friendship Tajikistan 1998; State Award of Peace and Progress Kazakhstan 2002; hon citizen Islamic Ummah of Timbuktu Mali 2003; Order of Bahrain (first class) 2003; *Recreations* yachting, skiing; *Clubs* Royal Yacht Squadron, Yacht Club Costa Smeralda (Sardinia, fndr and pres); *Style*— His Highness the Aga Khan; ✉ Aiglemont, 60270 Gouvieux, France

AGGISS, Prof Liz; da of James Henry Aggiss, of Terling, Essex (d 2004), and Marie Elizabeth, *née* Chamberlain (d 1975); *b* 28 May 1953; *Educ* Hornchurch GS, Madeley Coll, Nikolais/Louis Dance Theatre NY; *Career* choreographer, dancer, performer, film maker; artistic dir Divas Dance Theatre (in collaboration with Billy Cowie), prof of visual performance Univ of Brighton 2002– (subject ldr BA Hons Dance Visual Art 1993–2002), artistic dir SE Dance Agency 1997–98; contrib dance entries Fontana Dictionary of Modern Thought (1988); memb The Wild Wigglers (formed 1982, touring worldwide); work with Divas Dance Co (formed 1985, touring worldwide) incl: Torei en Veran Veta Arnold! 1986–87, Eleven Executions 1988, Dorothy and Klaus 1989–91, Die Orchidee im Plastik Karton 1989–91, Drool and Drivel They Care 1990–91, La Petite Soupe 1990–91, La Chanson Bien Douce 1991; solo performances incl: Grotesque Dancer 1986–89, Stations of the Angry 1989, Tell Tale Heart 1989, El Puñal Entra En El Corazón 1991, Vier Tänze (reconstructions from the 1920s and '30s by Hilde Holger) 1992, Falling Apart at the Seams (So it Seems) 1993, No Man's Land 1993, Absurditties 1994, Hi Jinx 1995, The Fetching Bride 1995, Divagate (cmmnd by Gardner Arts and Royal Festival Hall) 1997; cmmns incl: Dead Steps/Die Totenschritte (for Extemporary Dance Theatre) 1988–89, Banda Banda and La Soupe (for Carousel) 1989–90, Bird in A Ribcage (for Transitions Dance Co) 1994, Taped Up Sea of Heads Film for TVS 1997, The 38 Steps (for Intoto Dance Co), The Surgeon's Waltz (for Carousel) 2000, Rice Rain (for Carousel) 2001; *Awards* Colorado Coll scholarship to study with Hanya Holm 1980, Brighton Festival Special Award 1989, Brighton Festival Zap Award for Dance 1989, Brighton Festival BBC Radio Award 1990, Alliance and Leicester Award 1990 and 1992, Time Out/Dance Umbrella Award 1990, Arts Cncl and BBC2 Dance for Camera Award 1992 (Beethoven in Love) and 2000, Bonnie Bird Choreography Award 1994, BBC/Arts Cncl Dance for Camera 2000 (Motion Control), Arts Cncl Ind Dance Fellowship 2002, Capture 2002 (film award, Anarchic Varitations), Capture Award 2003 (The Men in the Wall), Czech Crystal Award Golden Prague Int TV Awards 2002, Special Jury Golden Award World Film Festival Houston 2003, Best Woman Film Mediawave Hungary 2003, Romanian Nat Office of Cinematography Prize 2003, Capture 2004 and New Art Gall Walsall Cmmn (Doppelgänger) 4Dance Channel 4 Cmmn (Break); *Publications* The Rough Guide to Reconstruction (animated magazine) 1999, Juggling not Struggling (Dance Theatre Jl Vol 15 No 4) 2000, Outsider Performance (animated magazine) 2001, Being There (animated magazine, 2003), Anarchic Dance (jtly with Billy Cowe and Ian Bramley, 2006); *Recreations* music, cinema; *Style*— Prof Liz Aggiss; ✉ 20 Montpelier Street, Brighton, East Sussex BN1 3DJ (website www.lizaggiss.com)

AGIS, Gaby; *b* 1960; *Career* independent choreographer 1983–; choreographer in residence Riverside Studios 1984–86, launched own co 1985; progs incl: Close Streams 1983, Crossing Under Upwards 1983, Surfacing 1984, Borders 1984, Shouting Out Loud 1984, Between Public Places 1985, Undine and the Still 1985, This Is, What, Where 1985, In Anticipation of Surrender 1986, Fow Fold 1986, Lying On the Warm Concrete 1986, Trail 1986, Kin 1987, Freefall 1988, Don't Trash My Altar/Don't Alter My Trash 1988, Mlada (LSO) 1989, Hess Is Dead (RSC) 1989, Dark Hours And Finer Moments 1989, Pale Shelter 1990, Cold Dark Matter 1991, The Family 1994, Beyond the Edges (AA) 1997, Silver for Boty (Union Chapel) 1998, Doctor Oxo's Experiment (ENO) 1998, touch Unsited (AA) 2000, Tamar's Revenge (RSC) 2004, Explicit Faith 2004; performance art venues incl: Tate Gallery Liverpool, Chisenhale Gallery, Whitechapel Art Gallery, Riverside Studios Gallery, MOMA Oxford, Cornerhouse Gallery Manchester; TV and film appearances incl: Hail the New Puritan 1985, Imaginary Women 1986, Freefall 1988, Dark Hours and Finer Moments 1994; awards incl Distinguished Visitors award of US Govt 1986; *Style*— Ms Gaby Agis; ✉ c/o Bolton & Quinn, 10 Pottery Lane, London W11 4LZ (tel 020 7221 5000, fax 020 7221 8100)

AGIUS, Marcus Ambrose Paul; s of Lt-Col Alfred Victor Louis Benedict Agius, MC, TD (d 1969), and Ena Eleanora, *née* Hueffer (d 2000); *b* 22 July 1946; *Educ* St George's Coll Weybridge, Trinity Hall Cambridge (MA), Harvard Business Sch (MBA); *m* 1971, Kate Juliette, da of Maj Edmund Leopold de Rothschild, TD, CBE, of Hants; 2 da (Marie-Louise Eleanor b 1977, Lara Sophie Elizabeth b 1980); *Career* Lazard: joined 1972, dir 1981–85, md 1985–90, vice-chm 1990–2001, chm 2001–06, dep chm Lazard LLC 2002–06; chm: BAA plc 2002–2006 (non-exec dir 1995–, dep chm 1998–2002), Barclays plc 2007– (non-exec dir 2006–); non-exec dir: Exbury Gardens Ltd 1977–, Exbury Gardens Retail Ltd 1998; sr ind dir BBC 2006–; chm Fndn and Friends of the Royal Botanic Gardens Kew 2004, tstee Royal Botanic Gardens Kew 2006–; *Recreations* gardening, shooting, skiing, sailing; *Clubs* White's, Swinley Forest; *Style*— Marcus Agius, Esq

AGNEW, Sir John Keith; 6 Bt (UK 1895), of Great Stanhope Street, Hanover Square, London; s of Sir (George) Keith Agnew, 5 Bt, TD (d 1994), and his w, *née* Baroness Anne Merete Louise Schaffalitzky de Muckadell; *b* 19 December 1950; *Heir* bro, George Agnew; *Style*— Sir John Agnew, Bt; ✉ The Estate Office, Rougham, Bury St Edmunds, Suffolk IP30 9LZ

AGNEW, Jonathan Geoffrey William; s of late Sir Geoffrey Agnew, and late Hon Doreen, da of 1 Baron Jessel, CB, CMG; *b* 30 July 1941; *Educ* Eton, Trinity Coll Cambridge (MA); *m* 1966 (m dis 1986), Hon Agneta Joanna Middleton (d 2002), yr da of Baron Campbell of Eskan (Life Peer, d 1994); 1 s (Caspar Jonathan William b 1967), 2 da (Lara Joanna b 1969, Katherine Agneta b 1971); m 2, 1990, Marie-Claire, er da of Bernard Dreesmann; 1 da (Clarissa Virginia b 1992), 1 s (George Jonathan Henry b 1999); *Career* The Economist 1964–65, World Bank 1965–67, Hill Samuel & Co 1967–73 (dir 1971), Morgan Stanley & Co 1973–82 (md 1977), J G W Agnew & Co 1983–86, gp chief exec Kleinwort Benson Group plc 1989–93 (joined 1987); chm: Henderson Geared Income and Growth Trust plc 1995–2003, Limit plc 1993–2000, Gerrard Gp plc 1998–2000, Nationwide Building Soc 2002–07 (non-exec dir 1997–2007, dep chm 1999–2002), Beazley Gp plc 2003– (non-exec dir 2002–), The Cayenne Tst plc 2006–, Leo Capital plc 2006–; dir: Thos Agnew and Sons Ltd 1969–, Rightmove plc 2006–; *Clubs* White's, Automobile (Paris); *Style*— Jonathan Agnew, Esq

AGNEW, Jonathan Philip; s of Philip Agnew, of Ketton, Lincs, and Margaret, *née* McConnell; *b* 4 April 1960; *Educ* Uppingham; *m* 1, 8 Oct 1983 (m dis 1994), Beverley Measures; 2 da (Jennifer Ann b 31 Oct 1985, Rebecca Louise b 18 Sept 1988); m 2, 4 May 1996, Emma Norris; *Career* former cricketer (bowler); joined Leics CCC 1978, took 101 wickets 1987 season, ret 1990; played for Eng 1984 and 1985 (3 tests, 3 one day ints); cricket corr Today 1990–91, BBC cricket corr 1991–; Radio Acad Best Sports Reporter Sony Radio Awards 1993; *Books* 8 Days a Week (1988), Over to You, Aggers (1997); *Recreations* golf, gardening; *Style*— Jonathan Agnew, Esq

AGNEW, (Morland Herbert) Julian; yr s of Sir Geoffrey William Gerald Agnew (d 1986), and Hon Doreen Maud Jessel, da of 1 Baron Jessel, CB, CMG; *b* 1943; *Educ* Eton, Trinity Coll Cambridge (scholar and sr scholar, MA); *m* 1, 1973 (m dis), Elizabeth Margaret, yst da of William B Mitchell, of Blanefield, Stirlingshire; 1 s (Thomas Julian Noel b 1975), 2 da (Amelia Elizabeth b 1979, Georgina Helen b 1982); m 2, 4 Sept 1993, Victoria, 2 da of Maj (Henry) Ronald Burn Callander, MC, and Penelope, Countess of Lindsay; 1 s (Benjamin Geoffrey David Callander b 6 Oct 1996); *Career* Agnew's: joined 1965, dir 1968, md 1987, chm 1992–; pres BADA 1979–81, chm Soc of London Art Dealers 1986–90, chm Friends of the Courtauld Inst 2002–05 (tstee 2006–), pres Evelyn Tst Cambridge; FRSA; *Recreations* grand opera, music, books, tennis, golf; *Style*— Julian Agnew, Esq; ✉ Thos Agnew & Sons Ltd, 43 Old Bond Street, London W1S 4BA (tel 020 7290 9250, fax 020 7629 4359, e-mail julianagnew@agnewsgallery.co.uk)

AGNEW OF LOCHNAW, Sir Crispin Hamlyn; 11 Bt (NS 1629), of Lochnaw, Wigtownshire; QC (Scot 1995); Chief of the Name of Agnew; s of Sir Fulque Melville Gerald Noel Agnew of Lochnaw, 10 Bt (d 1975), and Swanzie (d 2000), da of Maj Esme Nourse Erskine, CMG, MC (descended from the Earls of Buchan), late Consular Serv; *b* 13 May 1944; *Educ* Uppingham, RMA Sandhurst; *m* 27 Sept 1980, Susan Rachel Strang, da of late Jock Wykeham Strang Steel of Logie (2 s of Sir Samuel Strang Steel of Philiphaugh, 1 Bt, TD, DL, and Vere Mabel, 2 da of 1 Baron Cornwallis) and Lesley (da of Lt-Col Sir John Graham of Larbert, 3 Bt, VC, OBE, and Rachel, 5 da of Col Sir Alexander Sprot of Stravithie, 1 Bt, CMG); 3 da (Isabel Sevilla Wilhelmina b 1984, Emma Rachel Elizabeth b 1986, Roseanna Celia Nancy b 1989), 1 s (Mark Douglas Noel, younger of Lochnaw b 1991); *Heir* s, Mark Agnew of Lochnaw, yr; *Career* Maj RHF (ret 1981); admitted Faculty of Advocates 1982; Slains Pursuivant of Arms to the Lord High Constable of Scotland (The Earl of Erroll) 1978–81, Unicorn Pursuivant of Arms 1981–86, Rothesay Herald of Arms 1986–; dep social security and child support cmmr 2000–, pt/t chm Pensions Appeal Tbn 2002–; ldr of expeditions to: Greenland 1968, Patagonia 1972, Api Himal 1980; memb of expeditions to: Greenland 1966, Elephant Island, Antarctica 1970, Nuptse Himal 1975, Everest 1976; tstee John Muir Tst 1989–2005; *Books* The Licensing (Scotland) Act 1976 (co-author with Heather Baillie, 2 edn 1989, 5 edn 2002), Connell on the Agricultural Holdings (Scotland) Act (co-author with Donald Rennie, OBE, 7 edn, 1996), Agricultural Law in Scotland (1996), Variation & Discharge of Land Obligations (1999), Crofting Law (2000); *Recreations* yachting (yacht 'Pippa's Song'); *Style*— Sir Crispin Agnew of Lochnaw, Bt, QC; ✉ 6 Palmerston Road, Edinburgh EH9 1TN (tel 0131 668 3792, fax 0131 668 4357)

AGNEW-SOMERVILLE, Sir Quentin Charles Somerville; 2 Bt (UK 1957), of Clendry, Co Wigtown; s of Sir Peter Agnew, 1 Bt (d 1990), and his 1 w, Enid Frances (d 1982), da of Henry Boan, of Perth, WA; assumed by Royal Licence 1950 additional surname of Somerville after that of Agnew, and the arms of Somerville quarterly with those of Agnew, on succeeding to the Somerville estate of his maternal unc by m, 2 and last Baron Athlumney, who d 1929, leaving a widow, Margery, da of Henry Boan and sis of Enid, Sir Quentin's mother; *b* 8 March 1929; *Educ* RNC Dartmouth; *m* 1963, Hon (Margaret Irene) April Drummond, da of 15 Baron Strange (d 1982); 2 da (Amelia Rachel (Mrs Nicholas Hannaford) b 1965, Geraldine Margaret (Mrs William Osborne-Young) b 1967), 1 s (James Lockett Charles b 1970); *Heir* s, James Agnew-Somerville; *Career* Sub Lt RN to 1950, when invalided from serv; co dir; *Clubs* Brooks's, Kildare Street and University; *Style*— Sir Quentin Agnew-Somerville, Bt; ✉ Mount Auldyn House, Jurby Road, Ramsey, Isle of Man IM8 3PF (tel 01624 813724, fax 01624 816498)

AGUTTER, Jennifer Ann (Jenny); da of Derek Brodie Agutter, OBE, of London, and Catherine (Kit), *née* Lynam; *b* 20 December 1952; *Educ* Elmhurst Ballet Sch Camberley; *m* 4 Aug 1990, Johan Carl Sebastian Tham; 1 s (Jonathan Volrath Sebastian b 25 Dec 1990); *Career* actress; *Theatre* incl: School for Scandal 1972, Rooted 1973, The Ride Across Lake Constance, Arms and the Man 1973, The Tempest (NT) 1974, Spring Awakening (NT) 1974, The Unified Field LA 1987, Breaking the Code (Neil Simon Theatre, NY) 1987; RSC 1982–83, 1985 and 1995–96: Fontanelle in Lear, Regan in King Lear, Alice Arden in Arden of Faversham, Grace in the Body, Breaking the Silence 1985, Love's Labour's Lost 1995, English Places English Faces 1996, Mothers and Daughters 1996; Peter Pan (RNT) 1997, Equus 2007; *Television* incl: Long After Summer 1967, The Wild Duck 1971, The Snow Goose 1971, A Legacy 1971, A War of Children 1972, Amy 1980, Love's Labour's Lost 1984, Silas Marner 1985, Murder She Wrote 1986, The Equaliser 1988, Not a Penny More Not a Penny Less 1989, TECX 1990, Boon 1991, The Good Guys 1991, Love Hurts 1994, Heartbeat (ITV) 1994, The Buccaneers (BBC) 1995, September 1995, Alexis Sayle Show 1995, Connie in And The Beat Goes On (Channel 4) 1996, Heartbeat 1996, A Respectable Trade 1997, Bramwell 1998, The Railway Children (ITV) 2000, Spooks (BBC) 2002, Alan Clark Diaries (BBC) 2004, Poirot: After the Flood 2005, Diamond Geezer II 2006; *Radio* incl: Jamaica Inn (BBC) 1996, Silas Marner (USA) 2000, Lunch In Fairyland (BBC) 2002, My Love Must Wait (BBC) 2005; *Films* incl: East of Sudan (debut) 1964, Ballerina 1964, Gates of Paradise 1967, Star! 1968, I Start Counting, Walkabout 1969, The Railway Children 1970, Logan's Run 1975, The Eagle Has Landed 1976, The Man in the Iron Mask 1976, Equus 1976, Dominique 1977, China 9 Liberty 37 1978, Riddle of the Sands, Sweet William, The Survivor 1980, An American Werewolf in London 1981, Secret Places 1983, Dark Tower 1987, King of the Wind 1989, Child's Play II 1989, The Dark Man 1990, Freddie as Fro7 1992, Blue Juice 1995, The Parole Officer 2001, At Dawning 2001, The Lonely Troll 2003, Act of God 2006, Irina P 2006; *Awards* incl: Royal Variety Club Most Promising Artist 1971, Emmy Award Best Supporting Actress (for The Snow Goose) 1971, BAFTA Award Best Supporting Actress (for Equus) 1976; *Books* Snap (1984); *Style*— Miss Jenny Agutter

AGUTTER, Richard Devenish; JP; s of Anthony Tom Devenish Agutter (d 1960), and late Joan Hildegarde Sabina, *née* Machen (later Mrs Fleming); *b* 17 September 1941; *Educ* Marlborough; *m* 29 June 1968, Lesley Anne, da of late Kenneth Alfred Ballard, MC, and late Mrs Mildred Ballard; 3 s (Rupert William Devenish b 3 Nov 1972, Tom Alexander Devenish b 17 July 1975, Giles Edward Devenish b 6 April 1979); *Career* articled W T Walton & Sons 1960; KPMG (formerly KPMG Peat Marwick Mitchell): joined 1964, ptnr 1977–98, chm KPMG Int Corp Fin Network 1990–96, sr advsr 1998–2005; non-exec dir Braemar Seascope Group plc; vice-chllr Wine Guild of UK; Alderman City of London (Castle Baynard Ward) 1995–2005, Sheriff City of London 2000–01, Master Guild of Freemen of the City of London 2004–05; Liveryman Worshipful Co of Chartered Accountants, Hon Freeman: Worshipful Co of Lightmongers; memb Ct of Assts: Worshipful Co of Goldsmiths, Worshipful Co of Marketors, Worshipful Co of Tax Advsrs; FCA (ACA 1964), MSI, FRSA; *Recreations* sailing, gardening, wine; *Clubs* City Livery; *Style*— Richard Agutter, Esq; ✉ Leabridge Farmhouse, West Burton, Pulborough, West Sussex RH20 1HD (tel 01798 839169); Trelake, Pendrift, Blisland, Cornwall PL30 4JT (tel 01208 850224); Flat 19, Towerside, 146 Wapping High Street, London E1W 3PE (tel 020 7702 9113, mobile 07050 277988)

AHERN, Dermot; TD; s of Jeremiah Ahern, and Gertrude, *née* McGarrity; *b* 2 February 1955, Drogheda, Co Louth; *Educ* Marist Coll Dundalk, UCD (LLB); *m* 20 August 1980, Maeve, *née* Coleman; 2 da (Dearbhal b 20 Feb 1989, Aislinn b 4 May 1990); *Career* slr and politician; memb Louth CC 1979–91, TD (Fianna Fáil) Louth 1987–, Govt chief whip 1988–91, min of state Dept of Taoiseach and Dept of Defence 1991–92, chm Br-Irish Interparliamentary Body 1991–97 (co-chm 1993–95), min for social community and family affrs 1997–2002, min for communications marine and natural resources 2002–04, min for foreign affrs 2004–; memb Law Soc of Ireland; *Recreations* windsurfing, golf, skiing, swimming; *Style*— Dermot Ahern, Esq, TD; ✉ Iveagh House, 80 St Stephen's Green, Dublin 2, Ireland (tel 00 353 1 478 0822, fax 00 353 1 408 2400, e-mail minister@dfa.ie); 28 Francis Street, Dundalk, County Louth, Ireland (tel 00 353 42 933 9609, fax 00 353 42 932 9016)

AHERNE, Caroline Mary; *b* 24 December 1963, London; *Educ* The Hollies GS Didsbury, Liverpool Poly (BA); *Career* barmaid, chip shop worker, secretary, comedienne, writer, actress, dir, prodr, exec prodr and novelist; *Television* incl: It's A Mad World, World, World, World 1993, The Fast Show 1994, The Mrs Merton Show 1994, The Royle Family (dir) 1998–2000, Mrs Merton & Malcolm 1999, Dossa and Joe (writer and dir) 2002; *Style*— Ms Caroline Aherne; ✉ c/o Lucy Ansbro, Phil McIntyre Entertainment Ltd, 2nd Floor, 35 Soho Square, London W1V 5DG (tel 020 7439 2270, fax 020 7439 2280)

AHLÅS, (Lars) Peter Richard; *b* 22 September 1948; *Educ* Högre Allmana Laroverket å Kungsholmen Stockholm, Royal Swedish Naval Acad, London Sch of Foreign Trade (Dip Shipping & Marine Insur); *m* 1973, Sian Fiona, *née* Holford-Walker; 2 da; *Career* Lt Cdr Royal Swedish Navy 1969–71, Res 1971–; marine insurance broker; W K Webster 1971–73, gen mangr Liberian Insurance Agency 1973–74, broker Bland Payne 1974–78; dir: Jardine Glanvill Marine 1978–86, Gibbs Insurance Holdings Ltd 1986–, HSBC Shipping Services Ltd 2000–; HSBC Insurance Brokers Ltd (formerly Gibbs Hartley Cooper Ltd): chief exec Marine Cargo and Aviation Divs 1986–, chm global marine practice 2006–; memb IBRC; *Recreations* shooting, polo, riding; *Clubs* SOSS; *Style*— Peter Ahlås, Esq; ✉ HSBC Insurance Brokers Ltd, Bishops Court, 27–33 Artillery Lane, London E1 7LP (tel 020 7991 8888, fax 020 7661 2930, telex 8950791, e-mail peter.ahlas@hsbc.com)

AHMED, Ajaz Quoram Khowaj; s of Khowaj Ahmed, of Maidenhead, and Sughran Ahmed; *b* 1 May 1973, Taplow, Bucks; *Career* at Apple until 1995, co-fndr and chm AKQA Inc 1995–; reviewer MIT, mentor Said Business Sch Univ of Oxford 2003; memb Cncl ICA 2004–; Advertising Age Int and Forbes Media Innovator of the Year 1998; Hon Dr Oxford Brookes Univ 2002; FRSA 2005; *Style*— Ajaz Ahmed, Esq; ✉ AKQA Limited, 1 St John's Lane, London EC1M 4BL (website www.akqa.com)

AHMED, Prof Haroon; s of Mohammad Nizam Ahmed (d 1980), and Bilquis Jehan, *née* Abbasi (d 1988); *b* 2 March 1936; *Educ* St Patrick's Sch Karachi, Imperial Coll London (BSc), King's Coll Cambridge (PhD), Univ of Cambridge (ScD); *m* 4 July 1969, Evelyn Anne Travers, da of Alec Thorpe Goodrich; 2 da (Ayesha Fehmina b 12 March 1971, Rehana Sara b 17 Aug 1972), 1 s (Imran Saleem b 28 Nov 1982); *Career* GEC and Hirst Research Centre 1958–59; Univ of Cambridge: research studentship King's Coll 1959–62, Turner and Newall research fell 1962–63, univ demonstrator Dept of Engrg 1963–66, lectr in engrg 1966–84, reader in microelectronics Cavendish Lab 1984–92, prof of microelectronics Cavendish Lab 1992–2004 (now emeritus prof); CCC Cambridge: fell 1967–, warden of Leckhampton 1993–98, master 2000–06; non-exec dir Addenbrooke's NHS Tst 2002–05; pres Cambridge Philosophical Soc 2005; FREng 1990, FIEE, FInstP; *Books* Introduction to Physical Electronics (with A H Beck, 1968), Electronics for Engineers (with P J Spreadbury, 1973, 2 edn 1984); *Recreations* golf; *Style*— Prof Haroon Ahmed, ScD, FREng; ✉ Corpus Christi College, Cambridge CB2 1RH (e-mail ha10@cam.ac.uk)

AHMED, Muquim Uddin; s of Haji Mubarak Ahmed (d 1992), and Omar Jan (d 2002); *b* 1 September 1954, Dhaka, Bangladesh; *Educ* SE London Coll (HND); *m* 15 Oct 1976, Rashmi, *née* Bakshi; 1 s (Miraj b 16 Jan 1991), 1 da (Monique b 30 Aug 1993); *Career* early career with family business importing goods (incl electrical appliances, Bedford trucks and re-conditioned cars) into Bangladesh, fndr travel agency (largest UK operator for Bangladesh Airlines) 1977, fndr record business for Bangladeshi artists 1978, owner Naz cinema Brick Lane (importing Bangladeshi films, also distributing videos) 1980, fndr MILFA properties, owner Sylto Cash and Carry and Asian Foods Ltd, owner Cafe Naz Brick Lane (now part of restaurant chain) 1996, estab ready meals business 2006; md Notun Din newspaper; vice-chm Bethnal Green and Bow Cons Assoc; Bangladesh Br C of C: pres London region 1991–2001, chm 2001–05, dir 2006–; nominated Asian Jewel Awards 2005; *Recreations* gardening; *Style*— Muquim Ahmed, Esq; ✉ Asian Foods Limited, Caxton Street North, London E16 1JL (tel 020 7476 6969, fax 020 7476 8555, e-mail muquim@aol.com)

AHMED, Baron (Life Peer UK 1998), of Rotherham in the County of South Yorkshire; Nazir Ahmed; JP (Rotherham 1992); s of Haji Mohammed (d 1989), and Rashim Bibi; *b* 24 April 1957; *Educ* Spurley Hey Secdy Sch, Thomas Rotherham Coll, Sheffield Hallam Univ; *m* 1974, Sakina, da of Chaudhary Manga Khan; 1 da (Hon Maryam b 26 Nov 1977), 2 s (Hon Ahmar b 22 Feb 1979, Hon Babar b 1 Sept 1982); *Career* shop mangr 1978–82, petrol station mangr 1982–84, with marble mining indust 1984–87, business devpt mangr 1987–; cncllr Met Borough of Rotherham 1990–2000; chm South Yorks Met Lab Pty 1993–2000; vice-chm: South Yorks Euro-constituency, Policy Bd Housing and Environmental Health Bd Rotherham Met Borough Cncl, Ferham Advice Centre; fndr and convenor Nat Forum of Br Muslim Councillors; first Muslim male in the House of Lords; former chm All-Pty Libya Gp, co-chm Forced Marriage Working Gp, chm All Pty Interfaith Interreligions Gp, vic-chm All Pty Entrepreneurship Gp; interested in human rights conflict resolution; chm 7/7 Working Gp on Imams and Mosques; memb: Amnesty Int, Kashmir Policy Gp, Rotherham Racial Equality Cncl 1976–98, Standing Advsy Cncl of Religious Educn 1976–2000, USDAW; pres S Yorks Victim Support; JP 1992–2000; *Recreations* volleyball; *Style*— The Rt Hon Lord Ahmed; ✉ House of Lords, London SW1A 0PW (tel 020 7219 1396, e-mail ahmedn@parliament.uk)

AHRENDS, Peter; s of Steffen Bruno Ahrends, and Margarete Maria Sophie Ahrends; *b* 30 April 1933; *Educ* AA Sch of Architecture (AADipl); *m* 1954, Elizabeth Robertson; 2 da; *Career* architect; fndr ptnr and dir Ahrends Burton & Koralek 1961–; princ works incl buildings and devpt plans in areas such as educn, housing, health, govt, public tport, museums and retail; memb: Cncl AA 1965–67, Design Cncl 1988–93; chm UK Architects Against Apartheid 1988–93, chm Architect's Support Gp (South Africa); visiting prof of architecture Kingston Poly 1984–85, prof of architecture Bartlett Sch of Architecture and Planning UCL 1986–89; pt/t teaching posts, external examiner and workshops UK, Africa, HK and Canada; exhibitions of drawings and works incl: RIBA Heinz Gallery 1980, Douglas Hyde Gallery Dublin 1981, Alvar Aalto Museum Finland 1982, AA HQ Oslo 1983; RIBA 1959; *Publications* Monograph on Ahrends Burton & Koralek (1991), Collaborations: The Architecture of ABK (2002), and various pubns in the architectural press internationally; *Style*— Peter Ahrends, Esq; ✉ Ahrends Burton & Koralek, 7 Chalcot Road, London NW1 8LH (tel 020 7586 3311, fax 020 7722 5445, e-mail abk@abklondon.com, website www.abk.co.uk)

AICHROTH, Prof Paul Michael; s of Gerald Paul Aichroth, of Vancouver, Canada, and Elsie, *née* Webb; *b* 30 April 1936; *Educ* Alleyn's Sch Dulwich, KCL, Westminster Med Sch (MB BS, MS); *m* 17 June 1961, Angela, da of Frederick George Joslin, of Bournemouth, Dorset; 1 s (Mark Jonathan Paul); *Career* conslt orthopaedic surgn Chelsea and Westminster Hosp and Wellington Hosp 1971–; visiting prof Dept of Surgery Imperial Coll London 2002; author of various papers and theses on knee disorders; Hunterian prof RCS 1973, Robert Jones Gold medallist 1973, annual orator London Med Soc 1991–, orator Hunterian Soc 2000; pres Br Assoc for Surgery of the Knee 1992, hon memb Arthroscopy Assoc of N America 2004; memb: Br Orthopaedic Assoc, RSM, BMA 1963; Master of Surgery (Univ of London) 1972; FRCS 1965; *Books* Harris's Orthopaedics (contrib, 1975 and 1995), Operative Surgery (contrib, 1990), Insall Knee Surgery (contrib, 1992), Knee Surgery: Current Practice (1992), Interactive Knee (2000); *Recreations* boats, countryside, Mozart, claret; *Clubs* Athenaeum; *Style*— Prof Paul Aichroth; ✉ Frome Vauchurch House, Frome Vauchurch, Dorchester DT2 0DY (tel 01300 321793, e-mail paul.aichroth@btopenworld.com)

AIKENS, Hon Mr Justice; Sir Richard John Pearson; kt (1999); s of Maj Basil Aikens (d 1983), and Jean Eleanor, *née* Pearson; *b* 28 August 1948; *Educ* Norwich Sch, St John's Coll Cambridge (MA); *m* 3 March 1979, Penelope Anne Hartley, da of Hartley Baker (d 1961); 2 s (Christopher b 1979, Nicholas b 1981), 2 step da (Jessica b 1964, Anna b 1966); *Career* called to the Bar Middle Temple 1973 (bencher 1994); in practice 1974–99, a jr counsel to the Crown common law 1981–86, QC 1986, recorder of the Crown Court 1993–99, judge of the High Court of Justice (Queen's Bench Div) 1999–, presiding judge SE Circuit 2001–04, judge i/c Commercial Court 2005–06; memb Supreme Court Rules Ctee 1984–88; dir: Bar Mutual Indemnity Fund Ltd 1988–2000 (chm 1998–99), ENO 1995–2004, Temple Music Fndn 2003– (chm); govr Sedbergh Sch 1988–97; hon fell St John's Coll Cambridge 2005; *Books* Bullen and Leake on Pleadings and Practice (contributing ed, 13 edn 1991), Bills of Lading (jntly, 2006); *Recreations* music, the country, Le Pays Basque; *Clubs* Leander, Groucho; *Style*— The Hon Mr Justice Aikens; ✉ Royal Courts of Justice, Strand, London WC2 2LL

AIKIN, Olga Lindholm (Mrs J M Driver); CBE (1997); da of late Sidney Richard Daly, of Buckley, Clwyd, and Lilian May, *née* Lindholm (d 1966); *b* 10 September 1934; *Educ* Ilford Co HS for Girls, LSE (LLB), KCL, London Business Sch; *m* 1, 1959 (m dis 1979), Ronald Sidney Aikin; 1 da (Gillian); m 2, 1982, John Michael Driver; 1 step da (Katie); *Career* called to the Bar Gray's Inn 1956; lectr: KCL 1956–59, LSE 1959–70, London Business Sch 1971–90; dir gen Law Div Lion Int 1985–90, ptnr Aikin Driver Partnership 1988–; ed Law & Employment series Inst of Personnel Mgmnt; chm Bd of Mgmnt Nat Conciliation Service Qualitas Furnishing Standards Ltd 1992–94, memb Cncl ACAS 1982–95; *Books* Employment, Welfare and Safety at Work (1971), Legal Problems of Employment (1990), Contracts (1992); *Recreations* collecting cookery books and glass; *Style*— Mrs Olga Aikin, CBE; ✉ Aikin Driver Partnership, 22 St Lukes Road, London W11 1DP (tel 020 7727 9791)

AILESBURY, 8 Marquess of (UK 1821); Sir Michael Sydney Cedric Brudenell-Bruce; 14 Bt (E 1611); also Baron Brudenell (E 1628), Earl of Cardigan (E 1661), Baron Bruce (GB 1746), Earl of Ailesbury (GB 1776), and Earl Bruce and Viscount Savernake (both UK 1821); s of 7 Marquess of Ailesbury (d 1974); *b* 31 March 1926; *Educ* Eton; *m* 1, 1952 (m dis 1961), Edwina, da of late Lt-Col Sir Edward Wills, 4 Bt; 1 s, 2 da; m 2, 1963 (m dis 1974), Juliet, da of late Hilary Kingsford; 2 da; m 3, 1974 (m dis 1992), Caroline, da of late Cdr Owen Wethered, JP, DL, RN; *Heir* s, Earl of Cardigan; *Career* late Lt RHG (reserve); memb London Stock Exchange 1954–; *Style*— The Most Hon the Marquess of Ailesbury; ✉ Luton Lye, Savernake Forest, Marlborough, Wiltshire SN8 3HP (fax 01672 512370)

AILSA, 8 Marquess of (UK 1831); Archibald Angus Charles Kennedy; also Lord Kennedy (S 1452), Earl of Cassillis (S 1509), and Baron Ailsa (UK 1806); s of 7 Marquess of Ailsa, OBE, DL (d 1994), and Mary, *née* Burn; *b* 13 September 1956; *m* 1979 (m dis 1989), Dawn Leslie Anne, o da of David A Keen, of Paris; 2 da (Lady Rosemary Margaret b 1980, Lady Alicia-Jane Lesley b 1981); *Heir* bro, Lord David Kennedy; *Recreations* shooting, skiing, youth work; *Clubs* New (Edinburgh); *Style*— The Most Hon the Marquess of Ailsa; ✉ Cassillis House, Maybole, Ayrshire (tel 01292 56310)

AINGER, David William Dawson; TD (1969); s of Rev John Dawson Ainger (d 1987, Lt Cdr RN), of Weston Super Mare, and Frieda Emily, *née* Brand; *b* 10 March 1935; *Educ* Marlborough, Univ of Oxford (MA), Cornell Univ; *m* 25 July 1964, Elizabeth Ann, da of Albert William Lewis (d 1991), of London; 3 s (William b 1969, Luke b 1972, Ruairidh b 1980), 2 da (Katharine b 1966, Siobhan b 1976); *Career* Nat Serv 2 Lt RE 1953–55, AER and TA&VR RE and RCT 1955–69; called to the Bar Lincoln's Inn 1961 (bencher 1993), conveyancing counsel of the Supreme Court 1991–; visiting lectr in law Univ of Southampton 1961–71; *Style*— David Ainger, Esq, TD; ✉ 10 Old Square, Lincoln's Inn, London WC2A 3SU (tel 020 7242 5002, fax 020 7831 9188)

AINGER, Nicholas (Nick); MP; *b* 24 October 1949; *Educ* Netherthorpe GS Staveley Derbys; *m* Sally; 1 da; *Career* rigger Marine and Port Services Ltd Pembroke Dock, sr TGWU shop steward and branch sec 1978–92; MP (Lab): Pembroke 1992–97, Carmarthen W and S Pembrokeshire 1997–; PPS to Ron Davies, MP as Sec of State for Wales 1997–98, PPS to Alun Michael MP as Sec of State for Wales 1998–99, PPS to Paul Murphy MP 1999–2001; a Lord Cmmr to HM Treasy (Govt whip) 2001–05 Parly under sec of state Wales Office 2005–; Dyfed CC: cncllr 1981–93, served on various ctees; memb: Amnesty International, Dyfed Wildlife Tst, RSPB; *Style*— Nick Ainger, Esq, MP; ✉ House of Commons, London SW1A 0AA (tel 020 7219 4004, fax 020 7219 2690); constituency office: Ferry Lane Works, Ferry Lane, Pembroke Dock, Pembrokeshire, SA71 4RE (tel 01646 684404, fax 01646 686900)

AINLEY, His Hon Judge Nicholas John; s of Edgar Ainley, and Jean Olga, *née* Simister; *b* 18 March 1952; *m* 14 June 1980, Susan Elizabeth, *née* Waugh; 2 s (Thomas b 6 July 1981, Christopher b 26 Nov 1989), 1 da (Astrid b 28 Jan 1992); *Career* called to the Bar 1973; recorder 2000 (asst recorder 1996), circuit judge (SE Circuit) 2003–; *Recreations* family, travel, books; *Clubs* Sussex Yacht, Royal de Panne Sand Yacht; *Style*— His Hon Judge Ainley; ✉ c/o Croydon Court Centre, Altyre Road, Croydon CR9 5AB

AINSLEY, David Edwin; s of Edwin Ainsley (d 2004), of Bebington, Merseyside, and Gertrude Mary, *née* Fletcher (d 1978); *b* 13 September 1944; *Educ* Portsmouth GS, Sch of Architecture Univ of Liverpool (BArch), Columbia Pacific Univ (MA); *m* 1 (m dis 1984), Pauline Elisabeth, da of Aubrey Highton; 2 s (Sam b 21 Sept 1975, Christian b 24 May 1978); m 2, Beatrix Hinchliffe Parry, da of William Ellis, of Oxton, Merseyside; 2 step s (Nathan b 22 Dec 1971, Benjamin b 7 Feb 1976); *Career* ptnr Ainsley Gommon Architects; winner of twenty-five national and international design awards incl: Royal Town Planning Inst commendation, Housing Centre Tst Award, Liverpool Int Garden Festival Best Home Garden, twice winner of RIBA Community Enterprise Scheme Award, RIBA Housing Design Awards, three Civic Tst commendations, Welsh Nat Eisteddfod Architecture Prize; dir Denbighshire Foyer Ltd 1997–2000; memb: Cncl Liverpool Architectural Soc 1988–97 (pres 1993–94), Cncl Liverpool C of C and Industry 1993–95; vice-chair Liverpool Architecture and Design Tst 1997–2005; memb Stoke Urban Vision Design Review Panel 2005–, RIBA client design advsr 2007–; tstee Artsworks Wirral Arts Devpt Agency 1994–98, tstee LADT Trg 1999–2003; fndr memb and former chm Oxton Soc; co-fndr Tst for the Encouragement of Pastoralist Educn in Africa (TEPEA); memb Cncl Merseyside Civic Soc 1999–2002, memb Exec Ctee Hopes (Liverpool Hope Street Quarter Assoc) 2000–02, memb Bd Liverpool Habitat for Humanity 2005–; govr Christchurch C of E Primary Sch Birkenhead 1992–98 (chair Fin Ctee 1997–98); FCIOB, RIBA, FRSA; *Recreations* music (keyboard and saxophone), walking, cycling, gardening; *Style*— David Ainsley, Esq; ✉ 10 South Bank, Oxton, Birkenhead CH43 5UP (tel 0151 652 4064, e-mail david@ainsleyparry.fsnet.co.uk); Ainsley Gommon Architects, 1 Price Street, Hamilton Square, Birkenhead, Merseyside CH41 6JN (tel 0151 647 5511, fax 0151 666 2195, website www.ainsleygommonarchitects.co.uk)

AINSLEY, John Mark; s of John Alwyn Ainsley, of Maidenhead, and (Dorothy) Sylvia *née* Anderson; *b* 9 July 1963; *Educ* Nunnery Wood Secdy Modern Worcester, Worcester Royal GS, Magdalen Coll Oxford; *Career* tenor; lay clerk ChCh Oxford 1982–84; currently studies with Diane Forlano, professional debut singing Stravinsky's Mass (Royal Festival Hall under Simon Rattle) 1984, operatic debut in Scarlatti's Gli Equivoci nel Sembiante (Innsbruck Festival) 1988; former memb Deller Consort, former memb Gothic Voices, has sung with all major Baroque ensembles, also soloist in later repertoire; performed with numerous orchs incl: London Philharmonic, Royal Liverpool Philharmonic, BBC Symphony, City of Birmingham Symphony, English Chamber, Scottish Chamber, Bournemouth Symphony, London Classical Players, Berlin Philharmonic, Montreal Symphony; appeared at numerous international venues incl: Konzerthaus Vienna, Musikverein Vienna, Philarmonic Berlin, Gewandhaus Leipzig, Stuttgart Festival,

A

Göttingen Festival, others in New York, Boston, France, Holland and Switzerland; *Performances* operatic roles incl: Return of Ulysses (ENO) 1989, Fenton in Falstaff (Scottish Opera), Idamantes in Idomeneo (WNO under Sir Charles Mackerras and Munich), Don Ottavio in Don Giovanni (Lyon Opera and Aix en Provence Festival, Glyndebourne Festival and San Francisco), Ferrando in Cosi fan Tutte (Glyndebourne Festival, La Monnaie Brussels) 1992; concert performances incl world première of Tavener's We Shall See Him as He Is (Chester Festival, later BBC Proms) 1992, Bach Mass in B minor (with The English Concert under Trevor Pinnock, BBC Proms) 1997; *Recordings* incl: Handel's Nisi Dominus (with Choir of Westminster Abbey under Simon Preston, Deutsche Grammophon), Purcell's Odes (with English Concert under Trevor Pinnock, Deutsche Grammophon), Mozart's C Minor Mass and Handel's Acis and Galatea (with Acad of Ancient Music under Christopher Hogwood, Decca), Handel's Saul (under John Eliot Gardiner, Philips), Handel's Acis and Galatea and Joshua (under King, Hyperion), title role in Monteverdi's Orfeo (Decca), Mozart's Requiem (under Roger Norrington, EMI), Charlie in Brigadoon (EMI), Ottavio in Mozart's Don Giovanni (under Roger Norrington, EMI) Frederic in Gilbert and Sullivan's Pirates of Penzance (Mackerras/Telare), Mendelssohn's Elijah (under Herrewege, Harmonia Mundi), Berlioz's Les Troyens (under Dutoit, Decca), various works by Britten for EMI, Decca and Philips, Haydn's Die Schöpfung (under Brüggen, Philips), Purcell's Odes (under Trevor Pinnock, DG Archiv), Quilter Songs (with Malcolm Martineau on piano, Hyperion), Complete Schubert Edition (with Graham Johnson on piano, Hyperion), Stravinsky's Oedipus Rex (under Welser-Möst, EMI), Stravinsky's Pulcinella (under Bernard Haitink, Philips), Finzi's Dies Natalis/Intimations of Immortality (under Best, Hyperion), Vaughan Williams's Serenade to Music (under Roger Norrington, Decca); *Recreations* chocolate, early Flemish painting; *Style*— John Mark Ainsley, Esq; ✉ c/o Jane Balmer, Askonas Holt, Lonsdale Chambers, 27 Chancery Lane, London WC2A 1PF (tel 020 7400 1700)

AINSLIE, David Galbraith; s of Patrick David Lafone Ainslie (d 1999), and Agnes Ursula, *née* Galbraith; *b* 13 October 1947; *Educ* Wellington, Pembroke Coll Cambridge (MA); *m* 16 July 1993, Catherine Mary Ruth, *née* Green; 2 s (Jonathan David Alexander b 6 April 1996, Richard Hugh Campbell b 22 August 1998); *Career* admitted slr 1973; joined Dawson & Co 1969; ptnr: Lovell White & King 1981–83 (joined 1976), Towry Group (ind fin advsrs) 1983–2002, Pitmans, Slrs 2003–05, Horsey Lightly Fynn, Slrs 2006–; tstee Towry Law Charitable Tst 1997–; memb Bank of England Money Laundering Working Party 1994–96; memb: UK Falkland Islands Ctee 1973–, Exec Ctee Falkland Islands Assoc 1977–; tstee UK Falkland Islands Tst 1981–, tstee Berks Community Fndn 1999–2005 (vice-chm 2002–05); memb Law Soc 1971; Freeman City of London, Liveryman Worshipful Co of Haberdashers 1971; *Books* Practical Tax Planning with Precedents (contrib, 1987–2002); *Recreations* fishing, shooting; *Style*— David Ainslie, Esq; ✉ Watermeadow Lodge, Forge Hill, Hampstead Norreys, Thatcham, Berkshire RG18 0TE (tel 01635 201355); Towry Law Charitable Trust, c/o Horsey Lightly Fynn, Solicitors, 20 West Mills, Newbury Berkshire RG14 5HG (tel 01635 580858, e-mail dainslie@hlf.uk.com)

AINSWORTH, Sir Anthony Thomas Hugh; 5 Bt (UK 1916), of Ardanaiseig, Co Argyll; s of Sir (Thomas) David Ainsworth, 4 Bt (d 1999); *b* 30 March 1962; *Educ* Harrow; *Children* 1 da (Anna Alexandra b 6 April 2006); *Career* Lt Royal Hussars (PWO) 1982–85; dir Richard Glynn Consultants 2000–, dir IIC Partners 2002–06; *Style*— Sir Anthony Ainsworth, Bt; ✉ 2305 The Lakes, 123/96 Ratchadapisek Road, Klongtoey, Bangkok 10110, Thailand

AINSWORTH, (Mervyn) John; s of Gordon John Ainsworth (d 1974), and Eileen, *née* MacDonald; *b* 28 January 1947; *Educ* Stanfield HS Stoke-on-Trent, Goldsmiths Coll London (CertEd, DipEd); *m* Marta Christina, o da of Piotr Marmolak (d 1973); 2 s (Andrew Edward John b 5 Dec 1975, Peter Gordon John b 10 July 1983), 1 da (Stefanie Mary b 28 Sept 1978); *Career* asst clerk to the Governors and Bursar Dulwich Coll 1969–74, princ asst CEGB 1974–77, secretarial asst and mangr Secretariat Servs BTDB (now ABP) 1977–78; BPIF: sec 1978–84, fin dir 1983–84; sec gen Inst of Admin Mgmnt 1984–90, chief exec and sec Inst of Chartered Secretaries and Administrators 1990–; Freeman City of London, memb Ct of Assts Worshipful Co of Secs and Admins; Hon DBA Bournemouth Univ 1997, Hon DUniv Anglia Ruskin Univ 2006; FIMgt 1978, FCIS 1980, FInstAM 1983, hon fell Canadian Inst of Certified Admin Mangrs 1987, hon memb C&G 2006; *Recreations* golf, gardening, travel; *Style*— John Ainsworth, Esq; ✉ Institute of Chartered Secretaries and Administrators, 16 Park Crescent, London W1N 4AH (tel 020 7580 4741, fax 020 7323 1132, e-mail ceo@icsa.co.uk)

AINSWORTH, Mavis; OBE (1997); da of Reginald Frederick Davenport (d 1967), of Totley, Sheffield, and Wilhelmina, *née* Mynette (d 1997); *b* 6 September 1931; *Educ* Univ of London (BA, PGCE), Univ of Illinois (MA); *m* 8 Aug 1953, Stanley Ainsworth, step s of late Andrew Rutherford, of Heaton Chapel, Stockport; 2 s (Jonathan Grieve b 1960, Quentin Paul b 1961); *Career* head of English Dept Totley Thornbridge Coll of Educn Sheffield 1969–76; Sheffield Hallam Univ: head English Dept 1976–87, dean Faculty of Cultural Studies 1987–89, dir Sch of Cultural Studies 1989–96, hon fell 1996; reviewer for the Univs' Quality Assurance Agency 1998–2001; FRSA 1994; *Recreations* theatre, travel, visiting London; *Style*— Mrs Mavis Ainsworth, OBE; ✉ c/o School of Cultural Studies, Sheffield Hallam University, Psalter Lane, Sheffield S11 8UZ (tel 0114 253 2601, fax 0114 253 2603)

AINSWORTH, Peter; MP; s of Lt Cdr Michael Lionel Yeoward Ainsworth (d 1978), and Patricia Mary, *née* Bedford; *b* 16 November 1956; *Educ* Bradfield Coll, Lincoln Coll Oxford; *m* 1981, Claire, *née* Burnett; 1 s, 2 da; *Career* res asst to Sir John Stewart-Clark MEP 1979–81, investment analyst Laing & Cruickshank 1981–85, dir S G Warburg Securities 1989–92 (joined as investment analyst 1985); MP (Cons) Surrey E 1992–; memb Environment Select Ctee 1993–94, PPS to Jonathan Aitken as chief sec to the Treasy 1994–95, PPS to Virginia Bottomley as sec of state for Nat Heritage 1995–96, asst Govt whip 1996–97, oppn dep chief whip 1997–98, shadow sec of state Culture, Media and Sport 1998–2001, shadow sec of state for the environment, food and rural affrs 2001–02, chm Environmental Audit Ctee 2003–05, shadow sec of state for environment, food and rural affrs 2005–; cncllr London Borough of Wandsworth 1986–92 (sometime chm Cons Gp); memb Bow Gp 1983– (memb Cncl 1984–86); memb Bd Plantlife Int 2003–; chm Elgar Fndn 2005–; presenter Discord: Music and Dissent (Radio 4) 2000; *Recreations* family, music, gardening; *Clubs* MCC; *Style*— Peter Ainsworth, Esq, MP; ✉ House of Commons, London SW1A 0AA (tel 020 7219 5078)

AINSWORTH, Rt Hon Robert (Bob); PC (2005), MP; s of late Stanley Ainsworth, and Pearl Ainsworth; *b* 19 June 1952; *Educ* Foxford Comp Sch Coventry; *m* 22 June 1974, Gloria, *née* Sandall; 2 da; *Career* sheet metal worker Jaguar Cars Ltd Coventry 1971–91, MP (Lab) Coventry NE 1992–; oppn whip 1995–97, a Lord Cmmr of HM Treasy (Govt whip) 1997–2001; Parly under sec of state: DETR 2001, Home Office 2001–03; treas HM Household (Govt dep chief whip) 2003–; MSF (formerly TGWU): shop steward 1974–80, sr steward 1980–91, sec jt shop stewards 1980–91, branch pres 1983–87; Coventry City Cncl: cncllr 1984–92, dep ldr 1988–91, chm Fin Ctee 1989–92; *Recreations* walking, chess, reading, cycling; *Style*— The Rt Hon Bob Ainsworth, MP; ✉ House of Commons, London SW1A 0AA (tel 020 7219 4047, constituency tel 024 76226707, fax 024 76226707, e-mail ainsworthr@parliament.uk)

AINSWORTH, William Robert; OBE (1998); s of William Murray Ainsworth (d 1964), of Stockton-on-Tees, Co Durham, and Emma Laura Mary, *née* Easley (d 1981); *b* 24 June 1935; *Educ* Holy Trinity Sch Stockton-on-Tees, Stockton GS, Sch of Architecture Univ of Durham (BArch); *m* 7 Nov 1959, Sylvia Vivian, da of Norman Brown, of Buenos Aires, Argentina; 3 da (Graciela Glenn b 1960, Anita Susan b 1964, Lucia Emma b 1977); *Career* chartered architect, designer and urban planner; fndr ptnr Ainsworth Spark Assocs 1963– (completed over 3,500 projects throughout UK and Europe for local, nat and int companies); working tours of: S America, USA, and Europe; visiting studio tutor Sch of Architecture Newcastle upon Tyne 1961–63; external examiner: Sch of Architecture, Coll of Arts and Technol Newcastle upon Tyne; RIBA: chm Northern Region 1972–73, fndr chm Nat Ctee for Environmental Educn 1977, dir Bd of Servs Ltd London, memb and vice-pres Nat Cncl 1980–82; vice-pres and hon librarian Br Architectural Library 1987–90; bd govr Coll of Arts and Technol 1984–86, chm Bd of Govrs Newcastle Coll 1999–2000 (vice-chm 1996–99, memb Bd and govr 1991–); initiator of World Day of Architecture in UK 1989, chm Int Conf UIA/UNESCO (Art and Architecture) 1997; chm Sculpture Tst Northern Arts 1981– (fndr), memb Bd Arts Resources 1995–2000; fndr chm Northumberland and Durham Lord's Taverners; memb Union of Int Architects (UIA); FRIBA 1967, MCSD 1977, IOB 1980, FRSA 1985; *Recreations* cricket, golf, gardening (lifetime project building quarry garden), reading, painting (watercolours), music (guitar); *Clubs* Arts (London), Northumberland Golf, Durham CCC; *Style*— William Ainsworth, Esq, OBE; ✉ Ainsworth Spark Associates, Summerhill House, 9 Summerhill Terrace, Newcastle upon Tyne NE4 6EB (tel 0191 232 3434, fax 0191 261 0628, e-mail bill@ainsworthspark.com, website www.ainsworthspark.com)

AIRD, Sir (George) John; 4 Bt (UK 1901), of Hyde Park Terrace, Paddington, Co London; s of Col Sir John Renton Aird, 3 Bt, MVO, MC, JP, DL (d 1973), sometime extra equerry to King George VI and to HM The Queen, of Forest Lodge, Windsor Great Park, and Lady Priscilla, *née* Heathcote-Drummond-Willoughby (d 2002), yr da of 2 Earl of Ancaster; *b* 30 January 1940; *Educ* Eton, ChCh Oxford (MA), Harvard Univ (MBA); *m* 31 Aug 1968, Margaret Elizabeth, yr da of Sir John Harling Muir, 3 Bt, TD, DL; 2 da (Rebecca b 1970, Belinda Elizabeth b 1972), 1 s (James John b 1978); *Heir* s, James Aird; *Career* page of honour to HM The Queen 1955–57; engr Sir Alexander Gibb & Partners 1961–65, mangr John Laing & Co 1967–69, chm and md Sir John Aird & Co 1969–96; chm: Matcon Gp plc 1981–, Healthcare Devpt Services 1995–2006; Liveryman Worshipful Co of Drapers; MICE 1965; *Recreations* skiing, hunting, tennis; *Style*— Sir John Aird, Bt; ✉ Grange Farm, Evenlode, Moreton-in-Marsh, Gloucestershire GL56 0NT (tel 01608 650607, e-mail johnaird@aol.com)

AIREY, Clifford; s of Maj William Airey (d 1986), of Preston, Lancs, and Ellen, *née* Hogg (d 1974); *b* 16 January 1939; *Educ* Br Army Schs Overseas, Univ of Liverpool, Univ of Manchester; *m* 1, 23 Jan 1960 (m dis 1980), Maureen, *née* Fowler; 2 da (Dawn Elizabeth Airey, *qv*, b 1960, Rachel Louise b 1967), 1 s (Shawn James b 1965); m 2, 1982 (m dis), Gina Margarita, *née* Kingdon, 2 s (Sebastian Jon b 1983, Clifford Lloyd b 1985), 1 da (Dominique Ellen 1984); *Career* res ptnr Jubb & Partners consulting engrs 1964–73, sr ptnr Airey and Coles consulting engrs 1973–2001, ret; sr lectr Plymouth Poly 1967–70; past chm Inst of Structural Engrs, memb Plymouth Philatelic Soc; CEng, FIStructE, MConsE, FFB; *Recreations* fly fishing, sailing, shooting, stamp and coin collecting; *Style*— Clifford Airey, Esq; ✉ 148 Leatfield Drive, Plymouth, Devon PL6 5EY (tel 01752 219047)

AIREY, Dawn Elizabeth; da of Clifford Airey, *qv*, and Maureen Airey; *b* 1960; *Educ* Girton Coll Cambridge; *Career* controller then dir of prog planning Central Independent Television until 1992 (joined as mgmnt trainee 1985), controller of daytime and children's progs ITV Network Centre 1993–94, controller of arts and entertainment Channel Four Television 1994–96; Channel 5 Broadcasting: dir of progs 1996–2000, ceo 2000–02; British Sky Broadcasting: md Sky Networks 2003–07, md of channels and servs 2006–07; chief exec Iostar 2007, dir of global content ITV plc 2007–; exec chair Media Guardian Edinburgh Int TV Festival 2002–05, memb bd Int Acad of TV Arts 2002–; non-exec dir: Easyjet 2004–, Taylor Nelson Sofres plc 2007; FRTS 1998, FRSA 1998; *Style*— Ms Dawn Airey

AIRLIE, 13 Earl of (S 1639); Sir David George Coke Patrick Ogilvy; KT (1985), GCVO (1984), PC (1984), JP (Angus 1989), Royal Victorian Chain 1997; also Lord Ogilvy of Airlie (S 1491) and Lord Ogilvy of Alyth and Lintrathen (S 1639); s of 12 Earl of Airlie, KT, GCVO, MC (d 1968), and Lady Alexandra Coke (d 1984), da of 3 Earl of Leicester; *b* 17 May 1926; *Educ* Eton; *m* 1952, Virginia Fortune, DCVO (1995; vice-pres Women of the Year, tstee Tate Gallery 1980–94, chm of tstees Nat Gallery of Scotland 1997–2000, Lady of the Bedchamber to HM The Queen 1973–), da of John Barry Ryan (d 1966), of Newport, RI, and Margaret Dorothy (Nin) (d 1995), da of Otto Kahn, of NY; 3 da (Lady Doune (Lady Doune Wake) b 1953, Lady Jane (Lady Jane Nairac) b 1955, Lady Elizabeth (Lady Elizabeth Baring) b 1965), 3 s (David, Lord Ogilvy b 1958, Hon Bruce b 1959, Hon Patrick b 1971); *Heir* s, Lord Ogilvy; *Career* Lt Scots Gds 1944; Capt ADC to High Cmmr and C-in-C Austria 1947–48, Malaya 1948–49, resigned cmmn 1950; chief cmmr for Scotland Scout Assoc 1960–61 (treas 1962–86, hon pres 1988); Capt Gen and Gold Stick-in-Waiting Queen's Body Guard for Scotland (Royal Co of Archers) 2004– (Ensign 1975–85, Lt 1985–96, Capt 1996–2001, Pres 2001–04); chm: Westpool Investment Trust until 1982 (also resigned directorships), Ashdown Investment Trust Ltd 1968–82, Schroders plc 1977–84, General Accident Fire & Life Assurance Corporation 1987–97 (dir 1962, dep chm 1975–87); dir: J Henry Schroder Wagg & Co 1961–84 (chm 1973–77), Scottish & Newcastle Breweries 1969–83, Baring Stratton Investment Trust plc (formerly Stratton Investment Trust) 1986–92, Royal Bank of Scotland 1991–93; Lord Chamberlain of the Queen's Household 1984–97, Chllr Royal Victorian Order 1984–97, a permanent lord in waiting to HM The Queen 1998–; pres Nat Trust for Scotland 1997–2002, chm Historic Royal Palaces Trust 1998–2002, tstee Prince's Fndn 2003–06; govr Nuffield Hosps 1984–89, dep chm of tstees Royal Collection Trust 1993–97, first chllr Univ of Abertay Dundee 1994–; HM Lord-Lt Tayside Region District of Angus 1989–2001 (DL Angus 1964); Hon LLD Univ of Dundee 1990; KStJ 1995 (CStJ 1981); *Clubs* White's; *Style*— The Rt Hon the Earl of Airlie, KT, GCVO, PC; ✉ Cortachy Castle, Kirriemuir, Angus (tel 01575 570108)

AIRS, Graham John; s of George William Laurence Airs (d 1999), and Marjorie, *née* Lewis (d 1967); *b* 8 August 1953; *Educ* Newport GS Essex, Emmanuel Coll Cambridge (MA, LLB); *m* 4 April 1981, Stephanie Annette, da of William Henry Marshall; *Career* admitted slr 1978; Slaughter and May 1976–80; ptnr: Airs Dickinson 1980–84, Slaughter and May 1987– (rejoined as asst slr 1984–87); memb Law Soc; *Books* Tolley's Tax Planning (contrib); *Style*— Graham Airs, Esq; ✉ Slaughter and May, 1 Bunhill Row, London EC1Y 8YY (tel 020 7600 1200, direct line 020 7090 5050, fax 020 7090 5000, e-mail graham.airs@slaughtermay.com)

AITCHISON, Craigie John Ronald; CBE (1999); yr s of Rt Hon Lord Aitchison, PC, KC, LLD (Scottish Lord of Session, Lord Justice-Clerk and Lord Advocate Scotland under Ramsay MacDonald; noted for never losing a case involving an indictment on a capital charge when defending); *b* 13 January 1926; *Educ* Univ of Edinburgh, Middle Temple London, Slade Sch of Fine Art; *Career* painter; RA 1988 (ARA 1978); *Solo Exhibitions* Beaux Arts Gallery London 1959, 1960 and 1964, Marlborough Fine Arts (London) Ltd 1968, Compass Gallery Glasgow 1970, Basil Jacobs Gallery London 1971, Rutland Gallery London 1975, Scottish Arts Cncl 1975, M Knoedler & Co Ltd London 1977, Kettles Yard Gallery Cambridge 1979, Arts Cncl Retrospective Exhibition Serpentine Gallery London 1981, David Grob Fine Art London 1981, Artis Monte Carlo Monaco 1985, Albemarle Gallery London 1987, 1989, Thomas Gibson Fine Art 1993, Harewood House Leeds (retrospective 1954–94) 1994, Gallery of Modern Art Glasgow (retrospective) 1996,

Timothy Taylor Gallery London 1998 and 2004, Waddington Galleries London 1998, Galeria Ramis Barquet New York 2000, Waddington Galleries London 2001, Royal Acad of Arts (retrospective) 2003; has participated in many mixed exhibitions; *Work in Collections* Aberdeen Art Gallery and Museum, Arts Cncl of GB, Glasgow Art Gallery and Museum, Grundy Art Gallery Blackpool, Newcastle Region Art Gallery NSW Australia, Perth City Art Gallery and Museum, Rugby Borough Cncl Collection, Scottish Arts Cncl Edinburgh, Scottish Nat Gallery of Modern Art Edinburgh, Tate Gallery, Walker Art Gallery Liverpool; *Awards* British Cncl Italian Govt Scholarship 1955, Arts Cncl Purchase Award 1965, Edwin Austin Abbey Premier Scholarship 1970, Prizewinner John Moores Liverpool Exhibition 1974, Lorne Scholarship 1974–75, Arts Cncl Bursary 1976, First Johnson Wax Prize RA 1984, Korn Ferry Int Award RA 1989 and 1991, First Jerwood Fndn Painting Prize 1994; *Style*— Craigie Aitchison, Esq, CBE, RA; ✉ c/o Royal Academy of Arts, Burlington House, London W1V 0DS

AITCHISON, Prof Jean Margaret; da of John Frederick Aitchison (d 1997), of Debden Green, Essex, and Joan Eileen, *née* Chivers (d 1994); *b* 3 July 1938; *Educ* Wimbledon HS GPDST, Girton Coll Cambridge (MA), Radcliffe Coll Harvard (AM); *m* 3 July 2000, John Robert Ayto; *Career* asst lectr in Greek Bedford Coll London 1961–65, lectr, sr lectr and reader in linguistics LSE 1965–92, Rupert Murdoch prof of language and communication Univ of Oxford 1993–2003, professorial fell Worcester Coll Oxford 1993–2003 (emeritus 2003–); BBC Reith lectr 1996; *Books* Linguistics (1973, 6 edn 2003), The articulate mammal: An introduction to psycholinguistics (1976, 5 edn 2007), Language change: Progress or decay? (1981, 3 edn 2001), Words in the mind: An introduction to the mental lexicon (1987, 3 edn 2003), Introducing language and mind (1992, new edn 2003), Language Joyriding (1994), The seeds of speech: Language origin and evolution (1996, extended edn 2000), The language web: The power and problem of words (1997), New media language (ed jtly, 2003), The word weavers: Newshounds and wordsmiths (2007); *Recreations* gardening; *Style*— Prof Jean Aitchison; ✉ 45 Malvern Road, London E8 3LP (tel 020 7249 3734, e-mail jean.aitchison@worc.ox.ac.uk)

AITKEN, Alexander William; s of Alexander John Aitken (d 1979), of Edinburgh, and Freda, *née* Trueman, of Dunbar, East Lothian; *b* 9 May 1958; *Educ* RAF Changi GS Singapore, Leamington Coll for Boys, The Mountbatten Sch Romsey (played rugby and basketball to county level); *m* 9 May 1977, Caroline, da of Herbert Douglas Abbott; 2 s (Justin Richard b 1 April 1980, Alexander Joseph b 28 June 1983); *Career* deck hand Scot fishing trawler 1975, waiter Whitbread Wessex Potters Heron Motel Ampfield 1976, asst head waiter The Slipway Restaurant Lymington 1976, head waiter Grosvenor Hotel Stockbridge 1976, catering mangr Silhouette Casino 1976–77, restaurant mangr Le Chanteclere Restaurant Cadham Hants 1977–82, The Elizabethan Restaurant Winchester 1982–83, opened Le Poussin Restaurant 1983 (moving to Parkhill Hotel Lyndhurst 1999); featured in The Best of Europe series Discovery Channel TV; chef/cookery presenter: At Home with Maggie Philbin (Meridian TV), Southern Flavours (Meridian TV); memb: Master Chefs of GB 1986, Br Culinary Inst 1989; *Awards* three rosettes AA Restaurant Guide, one star Egon Ronay Guide, one star Michelin Guide, 4/5 Good Food Guide, Good Food Guide Hampshire Restaurant of the Year 1987 and 1992, Clover Award Ackerman Guide, Out of Town Restaurant of the Year The Times 1990–91, Daily Telegraph Restaurant of the Year 1996–97, AA Red Star Top 200 Hotels in GB& I; *Recreations* sailing, dressage, scuba diving, mushroom hunting; *Style*— Alexander Aitken, Esq; ✉ Le Poussin at Parkhill, Beaulieu Road, Lyndhurst, Hampshire SO43 7RB (tel 023 80 282944, fax 023 80 283268, website www.lepoussinatparkhill.co.uk)

AITKEN, Gillon Reid; s of James Aitken (d 1954), and Margaret Joane, *née* Simpson (d 1982); *Educ* Charterhouse, privately; *Career* with Stuart's Advtg Agency 1958–59, ed Chapman & Hall Ltd 1959–66, ed Hodder & Stoughton Ltd 1966–67, dir Anthony Sheil Assocs Ltd 1967–71, md Hamish Hamilton Ltd 1971–74, vice-pres Wallace, Aitken & Sheil Inc (NY) 1974–77; chm: Gillon Aitken Associates Ltd 1977–, Christy & Moore Ltd 1977–, Hughes Massie Ltd 1985–; *Books* The Captain's Daughter and Other Stories (by A S Pushkin, trans, 1962), The Complete Prose Tales of A S Pushkin (trans, 1966), One Day in the Life of Ivan Denisovich (by Aleksandr Solzhenitsyn, trans, 1970); *Recreations* crossword puzzles, ping-pong; *Clubs* Brooks's, Beefsteak; *Style*— Gillon Aitken, Esq; ✉ Garden Flat, 4 The Boltons, London SW10 9TB (tel and fax 020 7373 7438, mobile 07713 633899); Gillon Aitken Associates Ltd, 18–21 Cavaye Place, London SW10 9PG (tel 020 7373 8672, fax 020 7373 6002, e-mail gillon@gillonaitken.co.uk)

AITKEN, Brig Robert Hanbury Tenison; s of Capt Harry Aitken, MC (d 1997), and Anne, *née* Tenison; *b* 18 May 1956, Jamaica; *Educ* Eton, The Queen's Coll Oxford (choral bursar), RMA Sandhurst; *m* 11 April 1987, Joanna, da of Maj-Gen L A H Napier, CB, OBE, MC; 2 s (Freddie b 3 Aug 1994, James b 31 Aug 1996); *Career* Royal Regt of Wales: cmmnd 1977, Platoon Cdr 1977–80, Adj 1984–86, Co Cdr 1990–92, CO 1995–97; ADC to GOC Wales 1981, on secondment Bde of Gurkhas 1982–84, COS 54 Inf Bde 1988–90, instr Sch of Inf 1992–93; staff posts: HQ Land Command 1994–95, MOD 1997, HQ Adj-Gen 1997–2000; Cdr Br Forces Bosnia 2000–01, Cdr 160 (Wales) Bde 2001–03; Liveryman Welsh Livery Guild; OStJ 2003; *Recreations* field sports, singing; *Style*— Brig Robert Aitken; ✉ Regimental HQ, The Royal Regiment of Wales, Maindy Barracks, Cardiff CF14 3YE (tel 01874 613242)

AITKEN, Robin Peter; s of William Ferguson Kent Aitken, and Dorothy Fane Brown; *Educ* Prior Park Coll Bath, Univ of Bristol; *m* 1978, Sarah Anne Nagle; 2 da; *Career* reporter; trained West Midlands Press Ltd 1973–76; BBC: joined 1978, worked on successively Radio Brighton, BBC Scotland, BBC Radio News, Money Programme, BBC Breakfast, On The Record, Today Programme; *Recreations* walking, reading history, skiing, gardening, rugby; *Style*— Robin Aitken, Esq; ✉ Today Programme, BBC TV Centre, London W12 7RJ

AITKEN, William (Bill); JP, DL (Glasgow 1992), MSP; s of William Aitken (d 1977), and Nell (d 1978), of Glasgow; *b* 15 April 1947; *Educ* Allan Glen's Sch Glasgow, Glasgow Coll of Technol; *Career* insurance underwriter 1965–99; district ct judge 1985–; cncllr City of Glasgow 1976–99 (ldr of the oppn 1980–84 and 1992–95, convenor Licensing Ctee, vice-convenor Personnel Ctee 1977–80), bailie City of Glasgow 1980–84, 1988–92 and 1996–99, MSP (Cons) Glasgow 1999–; Scot Parl: Cons Parly justice spokesman, vice-convenor Justice 2 Ctee; chief whip Cons Pty 2003–, Parly Business Mangr 2003–; *Recreations* walking, foreign travel, reading, wining and dining with friends; *Style*— Bill Aitken, Esq, DL, MSP; ✉ The Scottish Parliament, Edinburgh EH99 1SP (tel 0131 348 5642, fax 0131 348 5655, mobile 07977 579262)

AITMAN, David Charles; s of Gabriel Aitman, and Irene Bertha, *née* Polack; *b* 11 April 1956; *Educ* Clifton, Univ of Sheffield (BA); *m* 26 March 1983, Marianne Lucille, da of Edward Atherton; 1 s (Marcus), 2 da (Lauren, Polly); *Career* admitted slr 1982; ptnr: Denton Hall (formerly Denton Hall Burgin & Warrens) 1988–2001, Freshfields Bruckhaus Deringer 2001– (departmental managing ptnr 2003–); memb Law Soc; LRAM; *Books* Butterworth's Encyclopaedia of Competition Law (chapter on intellectual property licensing, 1991), Practical Intellectual Property (chapter on competition law), Yearbook of Media Law (chapter on competition law), Bellamy & Child's European Community Law of Competition (chapter on telecommunications); *Recreations* tennis, wind surfing, music (performing and concert going); *Style*— David Aitman, Esq

AITTCHISEN, (Sir) Lance Walter; 4 Bt (UK 1938), of Lemmington, Co Northumberland; changed name by statutory declaration from Charles Walter de Lancey Aitchison 2004; s of Sir Stephen Charles de Lancey Aitchison, 3 Bt (d 1958), and Elizabeth Anne Milburn, *née* Reed (now Mrs Roland Antony Cookson); *b* 27 May 1951; *Educ* Gordonstoun; *m* 1984, Susan, yr da of late Edward Ellis, of Hest Bank, Lancs; 1 da (Tessa Charlotte b 1982), 1 s (Rory Edward de Lancey b 1986); *Heir* s, Rory Aitchison; *Career* late Lt 15/19 The King's Royal Hussars, RARO 1974–78; ARICS 1984; *Recreations* fishing; *Style*— Lance Aittchisen

AKENHEAD, Robert; QC (1989); s of Lt-Col Edmund Akenhead, TD (d 1990), and Angela Miriam, *née* Cullen; *b* 15 September 1949; *Educ* Rugby, Univ of Exeter (LLB); *m* 9 Dec 1972, Elizabeth Anne, da of Capt Frederick Hume Jackson, CMG, OBE, of Tonbridge, Kent; 1 s (Edmund b 1983), 3 da (Eleanor b 1978, Isobel b 1980, Rosalind b 1985); *Career* called to the Bar Inner Temple 1972 (bencher 1997), recorder of the Crown Court 1994– (asst recorder 1991); examiner Diocese of Canterbury 1991; *Books* Building Law Reports (jt ed), Site Investigation and the Law (with J Cottington, 1984); *Recreations* cricket, skiing, theatre; *Style*— Robert Akenhead, Esq, QC; ✉ 1 Atkin Building, Gray's Inn, London WC1R 5AT

AKERS-DOUGLAS, Francis Alexander Moreton (Frank); s of Anthony George Akers-Douglas (d 1991), and Dorothy Louise, *née* Gage; *b* 23 September 1948; *Educ* Eton, Brown Univ USA; *m* 1, 1974 (m dis 1997), Hon Julian Mary, eld da of 2 Baron Bruntisfield, *qv*; 2 s (Joseph Michael Aretas b 1979, James George b 1989); m 2, 1998, Lorna Farquharson; 1 s (Maxwell Alastair Edward b 1998), 1 da (Emma Claire b 2000); *Career* Binder Hamlyn: articled clerk 1967, ptnr 1978–97, head Private Client Servs 1980–97; ptnr Smith & Williamson 1997–; memb: Tax Faculty ICAEW, Soc of Trust and Estate Practitioners 1993; FCA 1971; *Books* Butterworths: Self Assessment and Simplification (1994), Corporal Haggis (1996); *Recreations* tennis, cricket, woodlands management; *Style*— Frank Akers-Douglas, Esq; ✉ Smith & Williamson, 15 Moorgate, London EC2R 6AY (tel 020 7131 4232, e-mail fad@smith-williamson.co.uk)

AKHTAR, Prof Muhammad; s of Muhammad Azeem Chaudhry; *b* 23 February 1933; *Educ* Punjab Univ Pakistan (MSc), Imperial Coll London (PhD, DIC); *m* 3 Aug 1963, Monika E, *née* Schurmann; 2 s (Marcus, Daniel); *Career* res scientist Res Inst for Med and Chemistry Cambridge USA 1959–63; Univ of Southampton: lectr 1963–, sr lectr then reader, prof of biochemistry 1973–98, head Dept of Biochemistry 1978–93, chm Sch of Biochemical and Physiological Sciences 1983–87, chm Inst of Biomolecular Sciences 1989–91, emeritus prof 1998–; distinguished nat prof and DG Sch of Biological Sciences Univ of the Punjab Lahore Pakistan 2002–; dir SERC Centre for Molecular Recognition 1990–94; author of articles in learned jls; founding fell Third World Acad of Sci 1984 (vice-pres 1998–, treas 1993–98, lectr 1996); memb: Royal Soc of Chemistry, American Chem Soc, Biochemical Soc; award of Sitara-I-Imtiaz by Govt of Pakistan 1981, Flintoff medal 1993; Hon DSc Univ of Karachi 2000; FRS (memb Cncl 1983–85); *Style*— Prof Muhammad Akhtar, FRS; ✉ Department of Biochemistry, The University of Southampton, Bassett Crescent East, Southampton SO16 7PX (tel 023 8059 4338)

AL-DUWAISAN, HE Khaled; Hon GCVO; *b* 15 August 1947; *Educ* Cairo Univ (BA), Univ of Kuwait (business admin dipl); *m*; 2 c; *Career* Kuwaiti diplomat; researcher Miny of Foreign Affairs 1970–71, diplomatic attaché 1971–72, third sec 1972–74, second sec 1974–76, joined Embassy of Kuwait in Washington DC 1975, first sec 1976–80, counsellor 1980–84, ambass extraordinary and plenipotentiary to the Netherlands 1984–90, appointed non-resident ambass to Romania 1988, ambass to the Ct of St James's 1993– (Doyen of Diplomatic Corps 2003); non-resident ambass: Denmark, Norway and Sweden 1994–95, Republic of Ireland 1995–; memb: Advsy Bd Centre of Near and ME Studies SOAS 1998–, Management of Public Sector Projects and facilities: an Executive Program for Kuwait Harvard Univ 2005–; co-ordinator with UN during creation of the demilitarised zone and with UN ctee for return of missing and stolen property 1992; Freeman City of London 2001; memb: IOD, RIIA; *Clubs* Queen's Tennis; *Style*— HE Mr Khaled Al-Duwaisan, GCVO; ✉ Embassy of the State of Kuwait, 2 Albert Gate, London SW1X 7JU (tel 020 7590 3400)

AL FAYED, Mohamed Abdel Moneim; *b* 27 January 1933, Alexandria, Egypt; *m*; 4 c; *Career* owner: L'Hotel Ritz Paris 1978–, House of Fraser 1985 (floated on London Stock Exchange 1994), Harrods 1985–, Turnball and Asser, Fulham FC 1997–; jt prodr Chariots of Fire 1980 (4 Academy Awards); fndr Liberty Publishing, relaunched Punch magazine 1996; La Grande Médaille de la Ville de Paris 1985, Plaque de Paris, Offr Légion d'Honneur (France) 1993 (Légion d'Honneur 1986), Commendatore Order of Merit (Italy) 1990; *Style*— Mr Mohamed Al Fayed; ✉ Harrods Limited, 87–135 Brompton Road, London SW1 7XL

AL-HASSANI, Prof Salim T S; *b* 23 July 1941; *Educ* Victoria Univ of Manchester (BSc, MSc, PhD); *Career* prof of high energy rate engrg UMIST (now Univ of Manchester); tech dir: Reverse Engrg Ltd UK, EROS project; chm Fndn for Science, Technol and Civilisation; conslt: BP, John Brown, MOBIL, HEREEMA, Br Gas, AMOCO, BUKOM; expert witness on explosion damage in process plants, aircraft and offshore facilities; MInstD, FInstPet; *Publications* author of over 200 scientific papers in int jls and books; *Style*— Prof T S Al-hassani; ✉ MACE, University of Manchester, PO Box 88, Sackville Street, Manchester M60 1QD (tel 0161 200 3850, fax 0161 200 3852, e-mail salim.al-hassani@manchester.ac.uk)

AL MUHAIRI, Dr Abdul Rahman; *b* 7 October 1964, UAE; *Educ* Univ of London (MSc, PhD), Univ of Hull (MBA); *m*; 3 c; *Career* registrar in nuclear medicine Hammersmith Hosp London 1994–96, registrar then specialist registrar in nuclear medicine St Bart's 1996–2000, hon conslt of nuclear medicine and sr lectr in nuclear medicine Dept of Nuclear Medicine London Univ 2002–; Cromwell Hosp London: sr physician in nuclear medicine 2002–, exec bd dir 2002–, co sec 2003–06, dep ceo 2003–05, acting ceo 2005–06, pres 2006–; pres Healthcare Investment Holdings UAE, vice-chm Injaz UAE, memb Bd Life Bridge Germany; co-author of many publications in medical jls; memb: Br Nuclear Medicine Soc, European Assoc of Nuclear Medicine, Soc of Nuclear Medicine USA, American Soc of Nuclear Cardiology, Br Nuclear Cardiology Soc; *Style*— Dr Abdul Al Muhairi; ✉ Cromwell Hospital, Cromwell Road, London SW5 0TU (tel 020 7460 5517, fax 020 7460 5833)

ALAGIAH, George Maxwell; *b* 22 November 1955, Sri Lanka; *Educ* St John's Coll Southsea, Univ of Durham; *m*; 2 s; *Career* South Magazine London 1981–89; BBC: joined 1989, foreign affrs corr 1989–94, Africa corr 1995–98, presenter BBC News 24 1998, presenter BBC TV News 1999–; BBC assignments incl news reports/documentaries on: trade in human organs India, street children Brazil, civil war in Liberia, famine and civil war in Somalia, persecution of Kurds in Iraq, effects on developing countries of GATT Agreement, ethnic conflict in Burundi, civil war in Afghanistan, genocide in Rwanda, Kosovo Crisis, East Timor, Asian tsunami; *Awards* Monte Carlo TV Festival and RTS awards for Somalia reports 1993, BAFTA commendation for Newsnight Kurdistan reports 1994, Amnesty International Press Awards Journalist of the Year 1994, Broadcasting Press Guild Journalist of the Year 1994, James Cameron Memorial Tst Award 1995, One World Broadcasting Tst TV News Premier Award 1995, Bayeux War Reporting Award 1996, Ethnic Minority Media Awards Media Personality of the Year 1998, Asian Film and TV Best TV Journalist 1999; *Books* A Passage to Africa (2001); *Style*— George Alagiah; ✉ BBC News, Room 2254, BBC Television Centre, Wood Lane, London W12 7RJ (tel 020 8624 9929, e-mail george.alagiah@bbc.co.uk)

ALAMBRITIS, Stephen; s of Andreas Alambritis, of Cyprus, and Christina, *née* Skardashi (d 1995); *b* 22 February 1957; *Educ* Elliott Sch Putney, Birmingham Poly (BA), LSE (MSc), City Poly (MA); *m* 11 Oct 1987, Athanasia, *née* Georgiou; 1 da (Maria b 20 Jan 1989), 1 s (Andreas b 14 Oct 1992); *Career* researcher Assoc of Ind Businesses 1984–88, head of public affairs Fedn of Small Businesses 1988–; memb: Rural Affrs Task Force DEFRA

A

2001–02, Better Regulation Task Force Cabinet Office 1998–2001, Consumer Advsy Panel DCA 2005–; cmmr Disability Rights Cmmn 2004–; chm Enterprise Insight Ltd; cncllr (Lab) Ravensbury Ward London Borough of Merton 2003–; memb: NUJ 1985, AMICUS 1999, CAMRA 1995; MCIPR 1990; *Recreations* FA referee grade I; *Style*— Stephen Alambritis, Esq; ✉ 10 Woodland Way, Morden, Surrey SM4 4DS (tel 020 8543 6003, e-mail stephen.alambritis@btinternet.com); Federation of Small Businesses, 2 Catherine Place, Westminster, London SW1E 6HF (tel 020 7592 8112, mobile 07788 422155, fax 020 7828 5919, e-mail stephen.alambritis@fsb.org.uk)

ALANBROOKE, 3 Viscount (UK 1946); Alan Victor Harold Brooke; s of 1 Viscount Alanbrooke, KG, GCB, OM, GCVO, DSO (d 1963), and his 2 w, Benita Blanche (d 1968), da of Sir Harold Pelly, 4 Bt, JP, and wid of Sir Thomas Lees, 2 Bt; suc half-bro, 2 Viscount, 1972; *b* 24 November 1932; *Educ* Harrow, Bristol Univ (BEd); *Heir* None; *Career* served Army 1952–72, Germany, Korea, Malaya, UK, Capt RA ret; qualified teacher 1975; lectr for MOD Princess Marina Coll Arborfield 1978–97; hon pres Salisbury and Dist Branch The 1940 Dunkirk Veterans 1970; The UK Veterans of King Leopold III: patron 1977–87, hon pres 1987–97; fell: Cheltenham & Gloucester Coll of HE 1993–98, Univ of Gloucestershire 1998–; pres Field Marshal Alanbrooke Shellhole, Memorable Order of Tin Hats (MOTHs) Doncaster 1995– (succeeded HM Queen Elizabeth the late as Nat Patron 2006–); patron Int Sch for Search and Explosives Engrs (ISSEE) 2000–; *Recreations* walking, enjoying post-Lloyd's poverty, rearranging the wreckage for remaining family, writing many letters, enjoying wonderful neighbours and friends, church wardening; *Style*— The Rt Hon the Viscount Alanbrooke

ALBARN, Damon; *b* 23 March 1968; *Career* singer; memb Blur 1990–, co-creator Gorillaz 2000–, memb The Good, the Bad and the Queen 2006–; singles with Blur incl: There's No Other Way, Girls & Boys, To The End, Parklife, End Of A Century, Country House (UK no 1, Aug 1995), The Universal, Stereotypes, Charmless Man, Beetlebum (UK no 1, Jan 1997), Song 2, On Your Own, MOR, Tender, Coffee & TV, No Distance Left to Run, Music Is My Radar; albums with Blur: Leisure (UK no 7, Gold), Modern Life Is Rubbish (UK no 15, Gold), Parklife (UK no 1, 4 x Platinum) 1994, The Great Escape (UK no 1, Triple Platinum) 1995, Live at the Budokan 1996, Blur (UK no 1, Platinum) 1997, 13 (UK no 1, Platinum), Bustin' + Dronin' (remixes) 1998, 13 1999, The Best of Blur 2000, Think Tank 2003; albums with Gorillaz: Gorillaz (UK no 3) 2001, G-Sides 2002, Laika Come Home 2002, Demon Days (UK no 1) 2005; other albums: Democrazy (solo album) 2003, The Good, the Bad and the Queen 2007; writer of original score for film 101 Reykjavik (with Einar Örn Benediktsson, 2000); *Soundtracks* Ravenous (with Michael Nyman); Ordinary Decent Criminal (composed original score, 1999); appeared in film Face 1997; *Videos* Starshaped (1993), Showtime (1995) No Distance Left To Run (2000, DVD); *Awards* Best Band, Best Album, Best Video and Best Single (all for Parklife) BRIT Awards 1995, jt winner Songwriter of the Year Ivor Novello Awards 1996, Mercury Music Prize nomination 1999, Best Dance Artist (Gorillaz) MTV Europe Awards, Best Song (Clint Eastwood - Gorillaz) MTV Europe Awards 2001, Best Group (Gorillaz) MTV Europe Awards 2005; *Style*— Damon Albarn

ALBEMARLE, 10 Earl of (E 1696); Rufus Arnold Alexis Keppel; also Baron Ashford and Viscount Bury (both E 1696); s of Viscount Bury (d 1968, eld s of 9 E of Albemarle, MC) and his 2 w, Marina, da of late Lt Cdr Count Serge Orloff-Davidoff, RNVR, and late Hon Elisabeth, *née* Scott-Ellis, 2 da of 8 Baron Howard de Walden; *b* 16 July 1965; *m* 2001, Sally Tadayon; 1 s (Augustus Sergei Darius, Viscount Bury b 8 Feb 2003); *Heir* s, Viscount Bury; *Career* designer; prop Rufus Albemarle Associates LLC USA; *Style*— The Rt Hon the Earl of Albemarle

ALBERGE, Dalya; da of Maurice Ernest Alberge, and Ella Alberge; *Educ* S Hampstead HS, Trinity Coll of Music London (GTCL), Keele Univ (MA); *Career* asst ed Brevet Publishing magazines 1981–83, freelance journalist 1983, asst ed Classical Music Magazine 1984–86, art market corr and arts writer The Independent 1986–94, arts corr The Times 1994–; memb Educn Advsy Bd Dulwich Picture Gallery 1991–, Arts Cncl adjudicator British Gas Working for Cities public art award 1992–93; judge UKIC Conservation Awards 2004; *Recreations* the arts; *Style*— Ms Dalya Alberge; ✉ The Times, 1 Pennington Street, London E98 1TF (tel 020 7782 5950, fax 020 7782 5959, e-mail dalya.alberge@thetimes.co.uk)

ALBERY, Ian Bronson; s of Sir Donald Arthur Rolleston Albery (d 1988), and Ruby Gilchrist, *née* MacGilchrist (d 1956); Ian Albery is the fifth generation in the theatre and both f (Sir Donald Albery) and gf (Sir Bronson Albery) as well as step ggf (Sir Charles Wyndham) were all knighted for servs to the theatre; *b* 21 September 1936; *Educ* Stowe, Lycée de Briançon France; *m* 1, 1966 (m dis 1985), Barbara Yu Ling, *née* Lee (d 1997); 2 s (Wyndham b 1968, Bronson b 1971); 1 da (Caitlin b 1985), by Jenny Beavan; *Career* Soc of W End Theatres (SOLT): exec 1965–89, pres 1977–79, vice-pres 1979–82; tstee Theatres Tst 1977–96; memb: Drama Panel Arts Cncl of GB 1974–76, Drama and Dance Panel Br Cncl 1978–88; dep chm London Festival Ballet Ltd/English National Ballet 1984–90, dir Ticketmaster Ltd 1985–92, md The Wyndham Theatres Ltd and associated companies 1978–87; prodr and md: Theatre of Comedy Co Ltd 1987–90, Wyndham Ltd 1987–2000; chief exec and prodr Sadler's Wells Tst Ltd 1994–2002, chief exec GSA Conservatoire 2002–; prodr or co-prodr of over 50 West End prodns; *Clubs* Garrick; *Style*— Ian B Albery, Esq; ✉ GSA Conservatoire, Millmead Terrace, Guildford GU2 4YT (tel 01483 560701, fax 01483 5335431, e-mail ceo@conservatoire.org)

ALBU, Sir George; 3 Bt (UK 1912), of Grosvenor Place, City of Westminster, and Richmond, Province of Natal, Repub of South Africa; s of Sir George Werner Albu, 2 Bt (d 1963); *b* 5 June 1944; *Educ* Michaelhouse South Africa, Cedara Agric Coll; *m* 23 April 1969, Joan Valerie, da of late Malcolm Millar, of Weybridge, Surrey; 2 da (Camilla Jane (Mrs Neilsen) b 22 Aug 1972, Victoria Mary b 14 Jan 1976); *Heir* none; *Career* trooper Imperial Light Horse Regt 1963, rifleman Commandos 1989; gen investor; *Recreations* horse racing (flat), motor racing; *Clubs* Victoria (Pietermaritzburg), Richmond Country (South Africa), Natal; *Style*— Sir George Albu, Bt; ✉ Glen Hamish, PO Box 62, Richmond 3780, Natal, South Africa (tel 00 27 3322 2587)

ALBUM, Edward Jonathan Corcos; s of Harry Album (d 1988), of London, and Matilda, *née* Corcos (d 1999); *b* 8 September 1936; *Educ* Emanuel Sch, ChCh Oxford (MA); *m* 14 July 1970, Elizabeth Ann, da of Lancelot Ezra, of London; 1 s (Richard b 1974), 1 da (Victoria b 1977); *Career* Capt Res TA 1962–70; slr; dir: Macsteel International UK Ltd, The London Metal & Ore Co Ltd, LMO Investments Ltd; chm: Sanderling Ltd, Settle & Carlisle Railway Tst; vice-pres Friends of the Settle-Carlisle Line; Liveryman Worshipful Co of Basketmakers, memb City of London Slrs' Co, memb Hon Artillery Co; FCIArb, FInstD, FCT; *Recreations* military history, ornithology, railway preservation; *Clubs* Sir Walter Scott (Edinburgh), Army and Navy, Oriental, AC Owners', AEC Soc; *Style*— Edward Album, Esq; ✉ 47 Lyndale Avenue, London NW2 2QB (tel 020 7431 2942, e-mail ejcalbum@miuk.co.uk); Sanderling House, High Street, Cley, Norfolk NR25 7RG (tel 01263 740810)

ALBURY, Simon Albert; s of Cyril Lyon Albury (d 1971), and Eileen Palmer, *née* Lloyd-Jones (d 1986); *b* 9 February 1944; *Educ* West House Sch Birmingham, Clifton, Univ of Nottingham (BA), Brandeis Univ, Univ of Sussex (MA); *m* 14 Jan 1989, Phillida Bartels-Ellis; 1 s (David Kwamena Bartels b 25 March 1989); *Career* info offr Govt Social Survey 1967, res assoc American Psychological Assoc project on Scientific Info Exchange in Psychology 1968, reporter World in Action Granada Television 1969, with BBC Current Affrs Gp 1969–73, BBC Open Univ 1973–74, sr prodr Granada Television (progs incl: World in Action, What the Papers Say, End of Empire, The Outrageous Millie Jackson) 1974–89, dir Campaign for Quality Television 1989–90; dir of public affrs: Meridian Broadcasting Ltd 1991–99 (dir of strategy 1991), MAI Broadcasting 1994–95 (dir of strategy 1990), MAI Media 1995–96, United Broadcasting and Entertainment 1996–99; chief exec RTS 2000–; presenter (as Sam Scott) gospel music show Hallelujah (Capital Radio) 1973–75; chair BSAC Ctee for Ethnic Minority Employment in Film 2000–, memb Bd Int Broadcasting Convention 2001–; tstee Meridian Broadcasting Charitable Tst 1993–99; chair Centre for Investigative Journalism 2005–, special advsr Nafsiyat The Intercultural Therapy Centre 2001– (non-exec dir 2000–01), memb Advsy Bd Elizabeth R Fund 2002–03; *Recreations* music and travel; *Style*— Simon Albury, Esq; ✉ The Royal Television Society, Kildare House, 3 Dorset Rise, London EC4Y 8EN (tel 020 7822 2815, e-mail simon@rts.org.uk)

ALDCROFT, Prof Derek Howard; s of Leslie Howard Aldcroft, and Freda, *née* Wallen; *b* 25 October 1936; *Educ* Univ of Manchester (BA, PhD); *Career* lectr in economic history Univ of Leicester and Univ of Glasgow 1960–71, reader Univ of Leicester 1971–73, prof of economic history Univ of Sidney 1973–76, prof of economic history Univ of Leicester 1976–94, research prof in economic history Manchester Met Univ 1994–2001 (visiting prof 2001–), fell Univ of Leicester 2002–; visiting prof Anglia Poly Univ 1993–1999; series ed Modern Economic and Social History; memb Economic History Soc; *Books* incl: From Versailles to Wall Street (1977), The European Economy 1914–90 (1993), Full Employment: The Elusive Goal (1984), The British Economy 1920–51 (1986), Economic Change in Eastern Europe since 1918 (with Steven Morewood, 1995), Studies in the Interwar European Economy (1997), Exchange Rate Regimes in the Twentieth Century (with Michael Oliver, 1998); Trade Unions and the Economy 1870–2000 (with Michael Oliver, 2000), The European Economy 1914–2000 (1993, 4 ed 2001), Europe's Third World: The European Periphery in the Interwar Years (2006); *Recreations* tennis, swimming, the Stock Exchange and gardening; *Style*— Prof Derek Aldcroft; ✉ 10 Linden Drive, Evington, Leicester LE5 6AH (tel 0116 273 5951); School of History, University of Leicester, Leicester LE1 7RH

ALDENHAM (AND HUNSDON OF HUNSDON), 6 (and 4) Baron (UK 1896 and 1923 respectively); Vicary Tyser Gibbs; s of 5 Baron Aldenham and 3 Baron Hunsdon of Hunsdon (d 1986); *b* 9 June 1948; *Educ* Eton, Oriel Coll Oxford, RAC Cirencester; *m* 16 May 1980, Josephine Nicola, er da of John Richmond Fell, of Farnham, Surrey; 1 da (Hon Jessica Juliet Mary b 1984), 3 s (Hon Humphrey William Fell b 31 Jan 1989, Hon Thomas Antony John b 13 Oct 1992, Hon Theodore Harry Charles b 14 July 2000); *Heir* s, Hon Humphrey Gibbs; *Career* dir: Hundred Oaks Co 1978–, Montclare Shipping Co 1986–; chm Herts & Middx CLA 1995–98, chm Watling Chase Community Forest 1997–99; Liveryman Worshipful Co of Merchant Taylors 1979; *Style*— The Rt Hon Lord Aldenham

ALDER, Samuel George (Sam); s of George Parker Alder (d 1981), of Douglas, IOM, and Brenda Margaret, *née* Moore (d 1980); *b* 28 January 1944; *Educ* King Williams Coll IOM, Grey Coll Durham (BA); *m* 6 Sept 1983, Helen Mary, da of Dr Algernon Ivor Boyd, OBE, of St Johns, Antigua; 1 da (Alison Margaret b 16 Feb 1989), 1 s (Samuel Moore Boyd b 6 Oct 1991); *Career* Whinney Murray & Co (chartered accountants) 1966–71; chm and md EG Gp of Cos 1977– (fin dir 1971–77), sr ptnr Alder Dodsworth & Co (CAs) 1984–, chm and owner The Clypse Estate Ltd 1988–; chm: Villiers Gp plc 1981–, Yeoman Security Gp plc 1986–91, London Musici Orch 1997–98, The Athol Media Co plc 1988–, 3FM Ltd 2004–; dir: Douglas Gas plc 1990–96, Sefton Gp plc 1997–; mangr: Roxy Music 1972–83, King Crimson 1972–85; hon treas: Fund Raising Ctee Music Therapy Charity 1975–81, Duke of Edinburgh's Award Int Project 1987, Duke of Edinburgh's Award Special Projects Gp 1988–92 (dep chm 1992–97), Appeal Ctee Museum of Garden History 1989–97; tstee: Bishop Barrow's Charity 1985–, British Record Industry Tst 1994–2007, The IOM Golden Jubilee Tst 2002–; memb Advsy Bd London Musici Orch 1998–; Nordoff-Robbins Music Therapy: sec and treas 1981–97, govr 1981–2007, tstee 1996–2007, chm Int Tst 1996–97, chm Bd of Govrs 1997–2007, dir Nordoff-Robbins Music Therapy in Scotland 1997–2007 (hon treas 2001–2007); chm Exec Ctee IOM Milk Mktg Assoc 2004– (prodr memb 1998–, vice-chm 2001), prodr memb IOM Agricultural Mktg Soc 1998–; exec chm IOM Arts Cncl 2006– (memb 2003–); hon sec and treas The Barrovian Soc 2004–(pres 2003–04); chm Bd of Govrs King William's Coll IOM 1997– (govr 1991–), jt dep chm Exec Ctee Assoc of Governing Bodies of Ind Schs 2007– (memb 2001–); FCA 1977 (ACA 1971); *Recreations* music, farming, history; *Clubs* RAC; *Style*— S G Alder, Esq; ✉ Alder Dodsworth & Co, 22 Athol Street, Douglas, Isle of Man IM1 1JA (tel 01624 622865, fax 01624 661410, e-mail sam.adco@manx.net)

ALDERDICE, David William; s of William Alderdice (d 1982), and Ella Alderdice (d 1973); *b* 21 May 1955; *Educ* Sullivan Upper Sch Holywood, Univ of Ulster (BA), UCL (MA); *m* 7 March 1984, Nel Veenstra; 2 da (Caitlin b 20 Aug 1991, Josephine b 7 April 1994); *Career* Br Cncl: asst dir Bangladesh 1994–97, dep dir Thailand 1997–99, dep dir Argentina 1999–2002, dir Netherlands 2002–06, dir Iraq 2006–; *Recreations* rugby, football; *Style*— David Alderdice, Esq

ALDERDICE, Baron (Life Peer UK 1996), of Knock in the City of Belfast; John Thomas Alderdice; s of Rev David Alderdice, of Ballymena, NI, and (Annie Margaret) Helena, *née* Shields; *b* 28 March 1955; *Educ* Ballymena Acad, Queen's Univ Belfast (MB BCh, BAO); *m* 30 July 1977, Dr Joan Margaret Hill, da of late James Hill, of Ballymena, NI; 2 s (Hon Stephen David b 6 Dec 1980, Hon Peter James b 7 Dec 1983), 1 da (Hon Joanna Margaret (Anna) b 7 March 1988); *Career* conslt psychiatrist in psychotherapy E Health and Social Servs Bd 1988–, hon sr lectr in psychotherapy Queen's Univ Belfast 1999 (hon lectr 1990–99), exec med dir South and East Belfast Health & Social Servs Tst 1994–97, visiting prof Dept of Psychiatry Univ of Virginia USA 2006–; dir NI Inst of Human Rels 1990–95; Alliance Pty of NI: memb Exec Ctee 1984–98, vice-chm 1987, ldr 1987–98; Parly candidate 1987 and 1992, Euro Parly candidate 1989; cncllr (Victoria Area) Belfast City Cncl 1989–97; leader Alliance Delgns: to Inter-Party and Intergovernmental talks on the future of NI 1991–98, to Forum for Peace and Reconciliation Dublin Castle 1994–96; Liberal Int (LI): vice-pres 1992–99, bureau memb 1996–, chair Human Rights Ctee 1999–2005, dep pres 2000–05, pres 2005–; treas Euro Lib Dem and Reform Party 1995–99 (vice-pres 1999–2003), elected memb NI Assembly 1998–2003 (Forum 1996–98), speaker NI Assembly 1998–2004; memb Ind Monitoring Cmmn 2003–; memb Cwlth Cmmn on Respect and Understanding 2006–07; hon memb: Peruvian Psychiatric Assoc 2000, Br Psychoanalytical Soc 2001; hon prof Faculty of Med Univ of San Marcos Peru 1999; John F Kennedy Profile in Courage Award 1998, W Averell Harriman Award for Democracy 1998, Medal of Honor Coll of Medicine of Peru 1999, Int Psychoanalytic Assoc Extraordinary Meritorious Service to Psychoanalysis Award 2005, World Fedn of Scientists Ettore Majorana Erice Prize 2005; Hon FRCPI 1997, Hon FRCPsych 2001 (MRCPsych 1983, FRCPsych 1997); Knight Cdr of the Order of Frances I (KCFO) 2002; *Recreations* reading, music, gastronomy; *Clubs* Ulster Reform (Belfast), National Liberal; *Style*— The Rt Hon Lord Alderdice; ✉ House of Lords, London SW1A 0PW (tel 020 7219 5050, e-mail alderdicej@parliament.uk)

ALDERMAN, Prof Geoffrey; s of Samuel Alderman (d 1987), of London, and Lily, *née* Landau (d 2006); *b* 10 February 1944; *Educ* Grocers' Company's Sch Hackney, Lincoln Coll Oxford (open exhibitioner, MA, DPhil, DLitt); *m* 9 Sept 1973, Marion Joan, yr da of Eliezer and Stella Freed; 1 da (Naomi Alicia b 1974), 1 s (Eliot Daniel b 1978); *Career* res asst Dept of History UCL 1968–69, temp lectr Dept of Political Theory and Govt UC Swansea 1969–70, postdoctoral res fell Univ of Reading 1970–72; Royal Holloway Coll London: lectr in politics 1972–84, reader in politics 1984–88, prof of politics and contemporary history 1988–94; Univ of London: chm Academic Cncl 1989–94, pro-vice-chllr for academic standards 1992–93, dean of arts 1992–94; Middlesex Univ: head of Academic Devpt and Quality Assurance Unit 1994–99, pro-vice-chllr 1996–99, emeritus prof 2002; vice-pres for international programs Touro Coll NYC 2000–02 (emeritus prof 2002), sr vice-pres American Intercontinental Univ London 2004–06 (vice-pres 2002–04); visiting prof: Univ of Northumbria at Newcastle 1993–96, Sheffield Hallam Univ 1994–97; sr assoc Oxford Centre for Hebrew and Jewish Studies 1996–99, professorial research assoc SOAS Univ of London 1996–98, visiting res fell Inst of Historical Research Univ of London 2007–08; govr Newham Coll 1998–99; tstee Huntleigh Fndn 1998–2003 (chm 1999–2000); memb Academic and Accreditation Advsy Ctee Global Alliance for Transnational Educn 2001–03; Loewenstein-Wiener fell American Jewish Archives Cincinnati Ohio; memb Exec: Cncl of Validating Univs 1997–2000, Soc for Research into Higher Educn 1997–2000; memb Cncl Jewish Historical Soc of England 1997–99; FRHistS 1971, FRSA 1991, MCQI 1995, MCMI 1998, FICPD 1999; *Books* incl: The Railway Interest (1973), The Jewish Community in British Politics (1983), Pressure Groups and Government in Great Britain (1984), Modern Britain (1986), London Jewry and London Politics (1989), Modern British Jewry (1992, 2 edn 1998); *Recreations* music, reading; *Clubs* Athenaeum; *Style*— Prof Geoffrey Alderman; ✉ e-mail geoffreyalderman@hotmail.com, website www.geoffreyalderman.com

ALDERSLADE, Prof Richard; s of Herbert Raymond Alderslade, and Edna F Alderslade; *b* 11 August 1947, Aldingbourne, Sussex; *Educ* Chichester HS for Boys, ChCh Oxford (MA, BM BCh), St George's Hosp Med Sch London; *m* 1, 1974 (m dis 1999), Elizabeth Rose; 2 s, 1 da (and 1 da decd); m 2, 1999, Angela Hendriksen; 1 step da; *Career* house physician Dorset Co Hosp Dorchester 1972–73, casualty offr St George's Hosp London 1974 (house surgn 1973–74), GP Kirklees and asst police surgn W Yorks 1974–76, clinical asst A/E Dewsbury Gen Hosp 1975–76, registrar in community med NW Thames RHA 1976–78 (hon sr registrar 1978–79), lectr in community med Middx Hosp Med Sch 1978–79; DHSS: MO 1979–82, SMO 1982–83, private sec to Chief MO 1984–85 (also med staff offr 1984); specialist in community med Hull HA 1985–88 (community unit gen mangr 1986–88), hon res fell Dept of Social Policy and Professional Studies Univ of Hull 1985–88, regnl dir of public health and regnl MO Trent RHA 1988–94 (exec memb 1990–94), special prof of health policy Nottingham Univ 1992–, prof of community care Univ of Sheffield 1994–95, regnl advsr co-ordination and humanitarian assistance WHO Regnl Office for Europe 1995–2001, seconded to DfID as co-ordinator High Level Gp for Romanian Children and advsr on child health, welfare and protection services to PM of Romania 2001–02, sr external rels offr WHO Office at UN NY 2002–06, currently chief exec Children's High Level Gp; adjunct assoc prof of public and health administration NYU Wagner; pt/t sec MRC Health Servs Res Ctee 1986–88; memb: Central Ctee for Community Med BMA 1977–79, BMA/DHSS Working Pty on Future of Community Health Doctors 1978–79, Microbiological Sub-Gp Nat Water Cncl 1980–81, MRC Standing Ctee on Use of Med Info for Res 1981–82, Educn Ctee of Faculty of Public Health Med 1989–95, Standing Med Advsy Ctee 1989–92; FFPHM 1987 (MFCM 1982), FRCP 1993; *Publications* various articles on public health; *Recreations* railway history, music, theatre; *Style*— Prof Richard Alderslade; ✉ Children's High Level Group, 45 Great Peter Street, London SW1P 3LT

ALDERSON, Prof Derek; s of late Frederick Alan Alderson, of Birtley, Co Durham, and Mary Annie, *née* Brown; *b* 18 January 1953; *Educ* Chester-le-Street GS, Univ of Newcastle upon Tyne (MB BS, MD); *m* 19 Oct 1975, Lyn Margaret, da of late Anthony Smith, of Pelton, Co Durham; 1 s (Kevin b 1979), 1 da (Helen b 1981); *Career* house offr Royal Victoria Infirmary Newcastle upon Tyne 1976–77, surgical registrar Newcastle AHA 1979–81, Wellcome surgical training fell 1981–83, sr registrar in surgery Northern RHA 1983–88, res fell Washington Univ St Louis USA 1985–86; Univ of Bristol: conslt sr lectr in surgery 1988–96, conslt surgn and chair of gastrointestinal surgery 1997–2005; conslt surgn and Barling prof of surgery Univ of Birmingham 2005–; memb: Soc Academic and Research Surgeons, Assoc of Surgns of GB and I, Br Assoc of Surgical Oncology, Br Soc of Gastroenterology, Pancreatic Soc of GB and I, past pres Assoc of Upper Gastrointestinal Surgns of GB and I; FRCS 1980; *Recreations* jogging, diving; *Style*— Prof Derek Alderson; ✉ University Department of Surgery, Room 29, 4th Floor, Queen Elizabeth Hospital, Birmingham B15 2TH (tel 0121 627 2276, fax 0121 472 1230, e-mail d.alderson@bham.ac.uk)

ALDERSON, John Cottingham; CBE (1981), QPM (1974); s of late Ernest Cottingham Alderson, and Elsie Lavinia Rose; *b* 28 May 1922; *Educ* Barnsley; *m* 1948, Irene Macmillan Stirling; 1 s; *Career* served WWII Warrant Offr Army Physical Training Corps N Africa and Italy; called to the Bar Middle Temple; Police Coll 1954, inspr 1955, dep chief constable Dorset 1964–66, dep asst cmmr (Training) 1968, Cmdt Police Coll 1970, asst cmmr (Personnel and Trg Div) 1973, chief constable Devon and Cornwall 1973–82; visiting prof Centre for Police Studies Univ of Strathclyde 1983–89; conslt on human rights to Cncl of Europe 1981–, dir of human rights Strasbourg; fell commoner CCC Cambridge 1982, fell Inst of Criminology Cambridge 1982, Gwilym Gibbon research fell Nuffield Coll Oxford 1982–83, Aust Cwlth fell Aust Govt 1987, hon research fell Centre for Police Studies Univ of Exeter 1987–93, research fell Inst for Police and Criminal Studies Univ of Portsmouth 1995–2000; Parly candidate (Lib) Teignbridge Devon 1983; Hon LLD Exeter 1979, Hon DLitt Bradford 1981; *Books* Encyclopaedia of Crime and Criminals (contrib, 1960), The Police We Deserve (with P J Stead, 1973), Policing Freedom (1979), Law and Disorder (1984), Human Rights and Police (1984), Principled Policing (1998); *Style*— John Alderson, Esq, CBE, QPM

ALDERSON, Matti; *b* 20 December 1951; *Educ* Bearsden Acad, Open Univ (BA); *Career* DG Advtg Standards Authy 1990–2000 (joined 1975), md FireHorses Ltd 2000–; sec Ctee of Advtg Practice 1990–99, vice-chm Euro Advtg Standards Alliance Brussels 1991–2000; cmmr PCC 2002– (memb Audit Ctee); chm Direct Mktg Authy 2007–; memb: Food Advsy Ctee MAFF 1997–2002, Doctors' and Dentists' Pay Review Body 1998–2001, Bd Better Regulation Task Force 1998–2004, Bd Removals Industry Ombudsman Scheme 2004–; patron Westminster Media Forum 2001–, memb Forum UK; FRSA 1993, FCAM 1993; *Recreations* design, reading, studying, driving; *Clubs* Commonwealth; *Style*— Mrs Matti Alderson; ✉ Raglan House, Windsor Road, Gerrards Cross, Buckinghamshire SL9 7ND (tel 01753 885445, e-mail matti@firehorses.com)

ALDINGTON, 2 Baron (UK 1962) Charles Harold Stuart Low; s of 1 Baron Aldington, KCMG, CBE, DSO, TD, PC, DL (d 2000), and Araminta, *née* MacMichael; bro of Hon (Priscilla) Jane Stephanie (Hon Lady Roberts, CVO, *qv*); *b* 22 June 1948; *Educ* Winchester, New Coll Oxford, INSEAD; *m* 16 Sept 1989, Regine, da of late Erwin von Csongrady-Schopf; 1 s (Hon Philip Toby Augustus b 1 Sept 1990), 2 da (Hon Louisa Charlotte Patience, Hon Marie-Therese Sophie Araminta (twins) b 8 July 1992); *Heir* s, Hon Philip Low; *Career* formerly with Citibank and Grindlays Bank; chm Deutsche Bank London 2002– (md Deutsche Bank AG London 1988–2002); dir GTT Duisburg 1986–87; chm: Euro Vocational Coll 1993–96, Centec 1995–96, Focus Central London 1996–99; memb Cncl German Br C of C 1994–; tstee: English Int 1979–86, Whitechapel Art Gallery Fndn 1992–96, Royal Acad Tst 2003–; memb Oxford Univ Ct of Benefactors 1990–, govr Ditchley Fndn 2006–; Liveryman Worshipful Co of Grocers; *Clubs* Brooks's, Hong Kong; *Style*— The Lord Aldington; ✉ Deutsche Bank AG London, 1 Great Winchester Street, London EC2N 2DB (tel 020 7545 7505, fax 020 7545 7844)

ALDISS, Brian Wilson; OBE (2005); s of Stanley Aldiss, and May, *née* Wilson; *b* 18 August 1925; *Educ* Framlingham Coll, West Buckland Sch; *m* 1, 1949 (m dis 1965); 1 s (Clive b 1955), 1 da (Wendy b 1959); m 2, 11 Dec 1965, Margaret Christie, da of John Manson (d 1997); 1 s (Tim b 1967), 1 da (Charlotte b 1969); *Career* author and critic; served RCS 1943–47, India, Assam, Burma, Sumatra, Singapore, Hong Kong; bookseller Oxford 1948–56, lit ed Oxford Mail 1956–71; pres Br Science Fiction Assoc 1960–64, ed SF Horizons 1964–70, chm Oxford Branch Conservation Soc 1968–69, vice-pres The Stapledon Soc 1975–, jt pres Euro SF Ctees 1976–79, pres World SF 1982–84 (fndr memb); Soc of Authors: memb Ctee of Mgmnt 1976–78, chm 1978, chm Cultural Exchanges Ctee 1979–; memb: Arts Cncl (Lit Panel) 1978–80, Cncl for Posterity 1990–97; vice-pres West Buckland Sch 1997–; Grand Master of Science Fiction 2000; prolific lectr, contrib articles to newspapers and jls; Observer Book Award for Science Fiction 1956, Ditmar Award for Best Contemporary Writer of Science Fiction 1969, James Blish Award for SF Criticism (only recipient) 1977, Pilgrim Award 1978, Award for Distinguished Scholarship Int Assoc for the Fantastic in the Arts (first recipient) 1986; Hon DLitt Univ of Reading 2000; FRSL 1990; Vision Award (Macedonia) 2001; *Books* novels incl: The Brightfount Diaries (1955), Non-Stop (1958), Greybeard (1964), Barefoot in the Head (1969), The Hand-Reared-Boy (1970), Soldier Erect (1971), Frankenstein Unbound (1973), The Malacia Tapestry (1976), A Rude Awakening (1978), Life in the West (1980), The Helliconia Trilogy (1982–85), Forgotten Life (1988), Dracula Unbound (1990), Remembrance Day (1993), Somewhere East of Life (1994), White Mars (with Roger Penrose) 1999, Super-State (2002), Affairs at Hampden Ferrers (2004), Jocasta (2005), Sanity and the Lady (2005), Walcot (2007); short stories collections incl: Space, Time and Nathaniel (1957), The Canopy of Time (1959), The Saliva Tree (1966), Intangibles Inc (1969), The Moment of Eclipse (1970), Last Orders (1977), Seasons in Flight (1984), Best Science Fiction Stories of Brian W Aldiss (1988), A Romance of the Equator (1989), A Tupolev Too Far (1993), The Secret of This Book (1995), Supertoys Last All Summer Long (2001), Cultural Breaks (2005); non-fiction incl: Cities and Stones (travel, 1966), The Shape of Further Things (1970), Billion Year Spree (1973), Trillion Year Spree (update, 1986), Bury My Heart at W H Smiths (1990), The Detached Retina (1995), Twinkling of an Eye (autobiography, 1998), When the Feast is Finished (1999); poetry incl: At the Caligula Hotel (1995), The Poems of Makhtumkuli (1996); *Recreations* amateur theatricals, limericks, painting; *Style*— Brian Aldiss, Esq, OBE, FRSL; ✉ Hambleden, 39 St Andrews Road, Old Headington, Oxford OX3 9DL (tel 01865 762464, fax 01865 744435, e-mail aldiss@dial.pipex.com, website www.brianwaldiss.com)

ALDOUS, Charles; QC (1985); s of Guy Travers Aldous (d 1981), of Suffolk, and Elizabeth Angela, *née* Paul; *b* 3 June 1943; *Educ* Harrow, UCL (LLB); *m* 17 May 1969, Hermione Sara, da of Montague George de Courcy-Ireland (d 1987), of Abington Pigotts Hall, Royston, Herts; 3 da (Hermione b 1971 (d 1972), Charlotte b 1973, Antonia b 1975), 1 s (Alastair b 1979); *Career* called to the Bar Inner Temple 1967, bencher Lincoln's Inn 1993, head of chambers; *Style*— Charles Aldous, QC; ✉ Maitland Chambers, Lincoln's Inn, London WC2A 3SZ (tel 020 7406 1200, fax 020 7406 1300, e-mail clerks@maitlandchambers.com)

ALDOUS, Hugh Graham Cazalet; s of Maj Hugh Francis Travers Aldous (d 1979), and Emily, *née* Watkinson; *b* 1 June 1944; *Educ* Scarborough HS, Univ of Leeds (BCom); *m* 25 Aug 1967, Christabel, da of Alan Marshall (d 1974); *Career* accountant; RSM Robson Rhodes: ptnr 1976, seconded to Dept of Tport 1976–79, head corp fin consultancy 1983–85, dep managing ptnr 1985–87, managing ptnr 1987–97; DTI: inspr into affairs of House of Fraser Holdings plc 1987–88, inspr into TransTec 2002–03; dir: Freightliner Ltd 1979–84, Sealink UK Ltd 1981–84, The Eastern European Tst plc (formerly First Russian Frontiers Trust) 1995–, Elderstreet Millennium Venture Capital Tst plc (formerly Gartmore Venture Capital Trust plc) 1995–, RSM International (chm) 1996–2001, Henderson TR Pacific Investment Tst plc 2003–, Octel Corp 2005–; memb: Br Waterways Bd 1983–86, Tech Directorate ICAEW 1995–98; chm CILNTEC 1994–97 (dir 1991–97), dep chm FOCUS 1996–98, memb Comp Cmmn 1998–2001; chm: Protocol Assoc BV 2000–02, Instèm Ltd 2001–04, Craegmoor Ltd 2001–; FCA 1979 (ACA 1970); *Recreations* walking, tennis, music; *Clubs* RAC; *Style*— Hugh Aldous, Esq; ✉ RSM Robson Rhodes, 30 Finsbury Square, London EC2P 2YU

ALDOUS, Lucette (Mrs Alan Alder); da of Charles Fellows Aldous (d 1983), of Sydney, Aust, and Marie, *née* Rutherford; *b* 26 September 1938; *Educ* Dux Randwick HS for Girls; *m* 17 June 1972, Alan Richard Alder, s of Richard Alder; 1 da (Floeur Lucette b 2 July 1977); *Career* ballet dancer; prima ballerina Ballet Rambert London England 1957–62; ballerina: London Festival Ballet 1962–66, Royal Ballet Covent Garden 1966–71; prima ballerina Australian Ballet 1972–76; sr adjudicator Nat Eisteddfods 1979–, head of classical dance Dance Dept WA Acad until 1999, guest teacher Australian Ballet, Royal New Zealand Ballet and W Australian Ballet Co 1988–, guest teacher Australian Ballet Sch and Co 2000–; memb: Dance Panel for Performing Arts Bd of Australian Cncl 1986–88, Advsy Cncl Care Australia, Exec Ctee WA Ballet Co, Australia Cncl for the Arts 1996–; hon memb Imperial Soc of Teachers of Dancing, London patron Cecchetti Soc of Australia Inc; American Biographical Inst Woman of the Year 1996; Hon DLitt Edith Cowan Univ 2000; *Style*— Ms Lucette Aldous; ✉ c/o Dance Department, Western Australian Academy of Performing Arts, 2 Bradford Street, Mount Lawley, Perth, WA 6050, Aust (tel 00 619 370 6442, fax 00 619 370 2910)

ALDOUS, Rt Hon Sir William; kt (1988), PC (1995); s of Guy Travers Aldous, QC (d 1981), and Elizabeth Angela, *née* Paul; *b* 17 March 1936; *Educ* Harrow, Trinity Coll Cambridge (MA); *m* 1960, Gillian Frances, da of John Gordon Henson, CBE; 1 s, 2 da; *Career* called to the Bar Inner Temple 1960; memb jr counsel DTI 1972–76; QC 1976; chm Performing Right Tbnl 1987–88; judge of the High Court of Justice (Chancery Div) 1988–95, a Lord Justice of Appeal 1995–2003; *Recreations* horses; *Style*— The Rt Hon Sir William Aldous

ALDRED, Adam David; s of Ian Alastair Scott, OBE (d 1982), and Brenda Marion Aldred, *née* Farthing; step s of Peter Norman Aldred, DFC, of Sydney, Aust; *b* 2 November 1962, Sydney, Aust; *Educ* Cranbrook Sch Sydney, Slrs' Admission Bd Sydney (Dip Law), Trinity Hall Cambridge (LLM); *m* 12 Jun 1993, Ruth Elizabeth, *née* Chatterton; 3 da (Sophie Elena b 30 Jul 1996, Emily Elizabeth b 18 Nov 1998, Lucy Eloise b 16 Sept 2006); *Career* admitted slr: NSW 1987, Eng & Wales 1991; admitted as slr advocate 2000; slr specialising in EU and competition law; Norton Rose 1989–93, Hammond Suddards Edge 1994–2001, Addleshaw Goddard 2002–; accredited mediator ADR Net 1999, memb Competition Law Forum Br Inst of Int and Comparative Law; memb Law Soc 1991; Competition/Regulatory Team of the Year The Lawyer Awards 2006; *Recreations* family, water skiing, snow skiing, horses; *Clubs* White Rose Water Ski; *Style*— Adam Aldred, Esq; ✉ Addleshaw Goddard LLP, Sovereign House, Sovereign Street, Leeds LS1 1HQ (tel 0113 209 2132, fax 0113 209 2060, e-mail adam.aldred@addleshawgoddard.com)

ALDRIDGE, (Michael) John; s of John Edward Aldridge (d 1991), of Derbys, and Margery, *née* Taft (d 1969); *b* 1 December 1942; *Educ* Beckett Sch Nottingham, Univ of Birmingham Med Sch (BSc, MB ChB); *m* 4 April 1970, Eva Robin, da of James Nicholson, of Harare, Zimbabwe; 4 s (James Hugh b 1971, Gregory b 1972, Stephen b 1974, Nicholas b 1978); *Career* RAMC Lt Col 202 Midland Gen Hosp (cmmnd Capt 1973), ret 1993; house offr Queen Elizabeth Hosp Birmingham 1968–69, then trained in gen and orthopaedic surgery, conslt orthopaedic surgn Coventry and Warwickshire Hosp Coventry 1977–, orthopaedic advsr to Br Amateur Gymnastics Assoc 1979–; team doctor: World Gymnastics Championship 1981, 1983, 1985, 1987 and 1989, Men's European Championship Gymnastics 1981, 1983, 1985, 1987, 1989 and 1990, Women's European Championship Gymnastics 1989, 1990 and 1992, Jr European Championships 1982, 1984,

1986, 1988 and 1991, Olympic Games Seoul 1988; HQ doctor: Cwlth Games Auckland 1990, Olympic Games Barcelona 1992, Olympic Games Atlanta 1996; memb Med Cmmn of Int Gymnastics Fedn 1990–; course writer for Nat Coaching Fndn, presented papers at int meetings on sports injuries; memb BMS, FBOA, FRCSEd 1973, fell Inst of Sports Med 1996, FRSM 1997; *Publications* Stress Injuries to Adolescent Gymnasts' Wrists (1988); contrib to orthopaedic jls on gymnastic injuries; *Style*— John Aldridge, Esq; ✉ South Lodge, 29 Westfield Road, Rugby, Warwickshire CV22 6AS (tel 01788 576583); Coventry and Warwickshire Hospital, Stoney Stanton Road, Coventry CV1 4FH (tel 024 7622 4055); 15 Palmerston Road, Coventry (tel 024 7667 8472)

ALDRIDGE, Simon Anthony; s of Maj Anthony Harvey Aldridge, TD (d 1994), of Elstead, Surrey, and Betty Angela *née* Harbord (d 1998); *b* 12 April 1942; *Educ* Marlborough, Grenoble Univ; *m* 23 Feb 1968, Jennifer Roberta Anne, da of Maj Denzil Robert Noble Clarke (d 1986), of Wokingham, Surrey; 1 da (Victoria Helmore Elizabeth b 1 May 1969); *Career* md Savory Milln 1986–89 (ptnr 1969–86), co chm SBC Stockbroking 1988–89; dir: Baring Securities Ltd 1989–93, Baring Securities (Europe) Ltd 1991–93, Baring Securities Bourse SA 1992–93; md BZW Securities Ltd 1993–98, pres BZW Bourse SA 1997–98, dir Credit Suisse First Boston 1998, dir int sales Fauchier Partners 1999–; dir: Northgate Pacific Fund Jersey 1982–, Paragon Capital Appreciation Fund 2003–; dep chm Croissance Britannia Paris 1987–; Ordre Nationale du Mérite (France) 1989; *Recreations* art, golf, shooting, tennis; *Clubs* Cercle de l'Union Interalliée (Paris), City of London, Garrick; *Style*— Simon Aldridge, Esq; ✉ 31 Cadogan Street, London SW3 2PP (tel 020 7589 3895)

ALDRIDGE, Trevor Martin; Hon QC (1992); s of Dr Sidney Aldridge (d 1972), and Isabel Rebecca, *née* Seelig (d 1960); *b* 22 December 1933; *Educ* Frensham Heights Sch, Sorbonne, St John's Coll Cambridge (MA); *m* 1966, Joanna van Dedem, da of Cyril van Dedem Edwards (d 1992), of Isle of Man; 1 da (Deborah b 1968), 1 s (Neil b 1969); *Career* admitted slr 1960; ptnr Bower Cotton & Bower 1962–84; law cmmr 1984–93; pres: Special Educnl Needs Tbnl (later Special Educnl Needs and Disability Tbnl) 1994–2003, Protection of Children Act Tbnl 2000–01; gen ed Property Law Bulletin 1980–84; pres Bd of Govrs Frensham Heights Sch 1996– (chm 1976–95); hon visiting prof City Univ 1994–95; hon life memb Law Soc 1995; *Books* Boundaries, Walls and Fences (1962, 9 edn 2004), Finding Your Facts (1963), Directory of Registers and Records (1963, consltg ed 5 edn 1993), Service Agreements (1964, 4 edn 1982), Aldridge's Residential Lettings (1965, 11 edn 1998), Betterment Levy (1967), Letting Business Premises (1971, 8 edn 2004), Your Home and the Law (1975, 2 edn 1979), Managing Business Property (jtly, 1978), Criminal Law Act 1977 (1978), Guide to Enquiries of Local Authorities (1978, 2 edn 1982), Guide to Enquiries Before Contract (1978), Guide to National Conditions of Sale (1979, 2 edn 1981), Leasehold Law (1980), Housing Act 1980, and as amended 1984 (2 edn 1984), Powers of Attorney (ed, 5 edn 1986 to 10 edn 2007), Guide to Law Society's Conditions of Sale (1981, 2 edn 1984), Questions of Law: Homes (1982), Law of Flats (1982, 3 edn 1994), Practical Conveyancing Precedents (1984), Practical Lease Precedents (1987), Companion to Standard Conditions of Sale (1990, 3 edn 2004), Companion to Property Information Forms (1990), First Registration (1991), Commonhold Law (2002); *Clubs* Oxford and Cambridge; *Style*— Trevor M Aldridge, Esq, QC

ALEKSANDER, Prof Igor; s of Branimir Aleksander (d 1972), and Maja, *née* Unger (d 1990); *b* 26 January 1937; *Educ* Marist Bros Coll Johannesburg, Univ of the Witwatersrand (BSc), Univ of London (PhD); *m* 23 March 1963 (m dis 1977), Myra Jeanette, *née* Kurland; *Career* section head Standard Telephone & Cable Co 1958–61, reader Univ of Kent 1968–74; prof and head: Electrical Engrg Dept Brunel Univ 1974–84, Kobler Unit Mgmnt IT Imperial Coll 1984–88; head Electrical Engrg Dept Imperial Coll London 1988–96, pro rector (external) Imperial Coll London 1997–2001, emeritus research investigator 2002–; FRSA 1983, FIEE 1988, FREng 1989, FCGI; *Books* Introduction To Logic Circuit Theory (1971), Microcircuit Learning Computers (1971), Automata Theory: An Engineering Approach (with F K Hanna 1978), The Human Machine (1978), Reinventing Man (with Piers Burnett 1984), Designing Intelligent Systems (1985), Decision and Intelligence (with Forraney and Ghalab 1986), Thinking Machines (with Piers Burnett 1987), An Introduction to Neural Computing (with H Morton 1989), Neurons and Symbols: The Stuff that Mind is Made of (with H Morton 1993), Impossible Minds: My Neurons my Consciousness (1996), How To Build a Mind (2000), The World in my Mind (2005); *Style*— Prof Igor Aleksander, FREng; ✉ Department of Electrical and Electronic Engineering, Imperial College of Science, Technolology and Medicine, Exhibition Road, London SW7 2BT (tel 020 7594 6176, fax 020 7594 6274, e-mail i.aleksander@imperial.ac.uk)

ALESBURY, Alun; s of George Alesbury (d 2007), and Eveline, *née* Richards, of Weybridge, Surrey; *b* 14 May 1949; *Educ* Univ of Cambridge, Univ of Seville; *m* 26 June 1976, Julia Rosemary, 6 da of Herbert Archibald Graham Butt (d 1971), of Sibford Gower, Oxon; 1 s (Rupert b 1980), 2 da (Lucy b 1982, Katie b 1990); *Career* called to the Bar Inner Temple 1974, legal corr The Architect 1976–80, memb Panel of Jr Treasy Counsel (Lands Tbnl) 1978–, memb Supplementary Panel Common Law (Planning) 1991–2000; memb: Parly Bar Mess, Br-Spanish Law Assoc, Admin Law Bar Assoc, Ecclesiastical Law Soc; fndr memb Planning and Environment Bar Assoc 1986 (hon sec 1986–88); appointed to hold inquiry into: Palmeira Avenue fire Hove 1992, Lake Windermere speed limit inquiry 1994–95, Canbury Gardens Kingston 1998–99, Chardon LL (GM seed licensing) 2000–02, several village green registration inquiries; memb South Downs Jt Ctee (formerly Sussex Downs Conservation Bd) 2001–; *Publications* incl: Highways (contrib 4 edn Halsburys Laws of England), articles on planning law; *Recreations* walking, travel, old buildings, skiing, sailing; *Style*— Alun Alesbury, Esq; ✉ 2–3 Gray's Inn Square, Gray's Inn, London WC1R 5JH (tel 020 7242 4986, fax 020 7405 1166, e-mail chambers@2-3graysinnsquare.co.uk)

ALESSI, Prof Dario Renato; *b* 23 December 1967, Strasbourg, France; *Educ* European Sch of Brussels II, Univ of Birmingham (BSc, PhD, Univ Undergraduate Prize, Science Faculty Scholarship, Perry Prize, Wellcome Trust Prize Studentship); *Career* MRC Protein Phosphorylation Unit Univ of Dundee: MRC postdoctoral trg fell 1991–94, MRC scientist 1994–96, princ investigator 1997; awarded career appt MRC 2000, hon reader Univ of Dundee 2001 (hon lectr 1997); advsr Biomedical Central Cancer, memb Scientific Advsy Bd Kinasource; memb Editorial Bd: Biochemical Jl, Jl of Cell Science; author of numerous articles in learned jls, delivered lectures and seminars worldwide incl R D Lawrence lecture Diabetes UK 2004; Colworth Medal Biochemical Soc 1999, Eppendorf Young European Investigator Award 2000, Morgagni Young Investigator Prize 2002, Pfizer Academic Award 2002, Makdougall Brisbane Prize Royal Soc of Edinburgh 2002, Philip Leverhulme Prize 2002, Fedn of European Biochemical Socs (FEBS) Anniversary Prize 2003, Gold Medal EMBO 2005, Francis Crick lectr Royal Soc 2006; memb: Biochemical Soc, EMBO 2005; FRSE 2002; *Style*— Prof Dario Alessi; ✉ MRC Protein Phosphorylation Unit, University of Dundee, MSI/WTB Complex, Dow Street, Dundee DD1 5EH (e-mail d.r.alessi@dundee.ac.uk)

ALEXANDER, Prof Alan; *b* 13 December 1943; *Educ* Univ of Glasgow (MA); *Career* res and educn offr Gen and Municipal Workers' Union 1965, asst prof Dept of Political Science Lakehead Univ 1969–71 (lectr 1966–69), lectr in politics Univ of Reading 1971–87; Strathclyde Business Sch Univ of Strathclyde: dir Scottish Local Authorities Mgmnt Centre and prof of mgmnt in local govt 1987–93, prof of local and public mgmnt 1993–2000 (emeritus prof 2000), head Dept of Human Resource Mgmnt 1993–96; scholar Rockefeller Fndn 1984, Fulbright visiting prof of politics Randolph-Macon Woman's Coll 1986; Parly candidate (Lab) Henley gen election 1974; chm: Developing Strathclyde Ltd (Glasgow Regeneration Fund) 1998–2001, West of Scotland Water Authy 1999–2002, Scottish Water 2002–; pres Instn of Water Offrs 2005–06; memb: Reading CBC 1972–74, Berks CC 1973–77, Bd Housing Corp 1977–80, Working Gp on internal mgmnt of local authorities Scottish Office 1992–93, Cmmn on Local Govt and the Scottish Parliament 1998–99, Accounts Cmmn for Scotland 2002–, ESRC 2003–; memb Editorial Bd Scottish Affairs 1991–; FRSE 2003; *Books* Local Government in Britain since Reorganisation (1982), The Politics of Local Government in the United Kingdom (1982), L'amministrazione locale in Gran Bretagna (1984), Borough Government and Politics: Reading 1835–1985 (1985), Managing the Fragmented Authority (1994); author of numerous articles in jls and contribs to books; *Style*— Prof Alan Alexander, FRSE

ALEXANDER, Anthony George Laurence; s of G W Alexander, of Beaconsfield; *b* 4 April 1938; *Educ* St Edward's Sch Oxford; *m* Frances, *née* Burdett; 1 s, 2 da; *Career* dir Hanson plc 1976–96 (UK chief operating offr 1986–96); non-exec dep chm Imperial Tobacco Group plc; *Recreations* golf; *Style*— Tony Alexander, Esq; ✉ Crafnant, Gregories Farm Lane, Beaconsfield, Buckinghamshire HP9 1HJ; 150 Brompton Road, London SW3 1HX (tel 020 7584 6817, fax 020 7589 6431)

ALEXANDER, Sir Charles Gundry; 2 Bt (UK 1945), of Sundridge Park, Co Kent; s of Sir Frank Alexander, 1 Bt, JP (d 1959), and Elsa, da of Sir Charles Collett, 1 Bt; *b* 5 May 1923; *Educ* Bishop's Stortford Coll, St John's Coll Cambridge (MA); *m* 1, 1944, Mary Neale, o da of late Stanley Robert Richardson, of Maple Lawn, Lyndhurst, Hants; 1 s (Richard b 1947), 1 da (Jennifer b 1949); m 2, 1979, Eileen Ann, da of Gordon Stewart, of Inveresk, Finchampstead; *Heir* s, Richard Alexander; *Career* served WWII Lt RN N Atlantic and Far East; chm Alexander Shipping Co 1959–87; chm Bd of Govrs Care Ltd 1975–86; memb Ct of Assts Worshipful Co of Merchant Taylors (Master 1981–82), Prime Warden Worshipful Co of Shipwrights 1983–84; AIMarE; *Clubs* RAC; *Style*— Sir Charles Alexander, Bt; ✉ Newland House, 68 Newland, Sherborne, Dorset DT9 3AQ (tel 01935 389758)

ALEXANDER, Danny; MP; *b* 15 May 1972; *Educ* Lochaber HS, Univ of Oxford; *m* 9 July 2005, Rebecca Louise; *Career* press offr Scottish Lib Dems 1993–95, dir of communications European Movement 1996–99, head of communications Br in Europe 1999–2004, head of communications Cairngorms Nat Park 2004–; MP (Lib Dem) Inverness, Nairn, Badenoch and Strathspey 2005–, shadow minister for Social Exclusion 2007–; *Style*— Danny Alexander, MP; ✉ House of Commons, London SW1A 0AA (tel 020 7219 2300, e-mail alexanderdg@parliament.uk)

ALEXANDER, Douglas; PC (2005), MP; *b* 1967, Glasgow; *Educ* Univ of Edinburgh (chair Univ Labour Club, MA, LLB, Dip Legal Practice), Univ of Pennysylvania (scholar.); *Career* slr; MP (Lab): Paisley S 1997–2005 (by-election), Paisley and Renfrewshire S 2005–; min of state for e-commerce and competitiveness 2001–02, min of state Cabinet Office 2002–03, min for the Cabinet Office and Chllr of the Duchy of Lancaster 2003–04, min of state for trade, investment and foreign affrs 2004–05, min of state for Europe FCO 2005–06, sec of state for tport 2006–07, sec of state for Scotland 2006–, sec of state Int Devpt 2007–; memb Lab Pty 1981–; *Style*— The Rt Hon Douglas Alexander, MP; ✉ House of Commons, London SW1A 0AA

ALEXANDER, Helen Anne; CBE (2004); da of Bernard Alexander (d 1990), and Tania von Benckendorff (d 2004); *b* 10 February 1957; *Educ* St Paul's Girls' Sch, Hertford Coll Oxford (2 half blues), INSEAD (MBA); *m* Feb 1985, Timothy Suter, s of Martin Edward Hayles Suter; 1 da, 2 s; *Career* Duckworth & Co 1978–79, Faber & Faber 1979–83, The Economist Newspaper Ltd 1985–93, md The Economist Intelligence Unit 1993–96; chief exec The Economist Group London 1997–; non-exec dir: Northern Foods plc 1994–2002, BT plc 1998–2002, Centrica plc 2003–; tstee Tate Gallery 2003–; hon fell Hertford Coll Oxford; *Style*— Ms Helen Alexander, CBE; ✉ The Economist Group, 25 St James's Street, London SW1A 1HG (tel 020 7830 7001, fax 020 7930 3092, e-mail helenalexander@economist.com)

ALEXANDER, His Hon Judge Ian Douglas Gavin; QC (1989); s of Dr Archibald Douglas Park Alexander (d 1968), of Lancing, W Sussex, and Dilys, *née* Edwards; *b* 10 April 1941; *Educ* Tonbridge, UCL (LLB); *m* 13 Dec 1969, Rosemary Kirkbridge, da of Kenneth Richards; 1 s (Justin b 6 June 1978), 1 da (Victoria b 26 Jan 1980); *Career* called to the Bar Lincoln's Inn 1964 (bencher); recorder Midland & Oxford Circuit 1982–2002, circuit judge (Midland Circuit) 2002–; pres Mental Health Review Tbnl 1999–; United Grand Lodge of England: Grand Registrar Craft 2001–06, Grand Registrar Chapter 2001–; *Recreations* field sports, skiing, sailing, gardening, freemasonry; *Clubs* Naval and Military; *Style*— His Hon Judge Alexander, QC; ✉ 5 Fountain Court, Steelhouse Lane, Birmingham B4 6DR (tel 0121 606 0500, fax 0121 606 1501, DX 16075 BIRMINGHAM)

ALEXANDER, John Bernard Alexei; s of B G Alexander, of Great Haseley, Oxon, and T Alexander, *née* Benckendorff; *b* 23 August 1941; *Educ* Westminster, Balliol Coll Oxford; *m* 1 July 1969, Jacquelyn, da of John Bray, of Sydney, Aust; 2 s (Nicolas b 1971, Christopher b 1974); m 2, 14 April 1981, Judy, da of Maj Patrick Chilton, of West Ashling, W Sussex; 1 da (Tania b 1982); *Career* merchant banker; dir Hill Samuel & Co Ltd 1973–83, md Edmond de Rothschild Ltd 1984–; dir: C A Sperati plc 1986–, Port of Bristol 1991–, Banque Privée Edmond de Rothschild Geneva 1994–, Sterling Insurance Group Ltd 1995–, La Compagnie Financière Edmond de Rothschild Banque Paris 1996–, LCF Holding Benjamin et Edmond de Rothschild SA 1996–; chm: CPRE Oxfordshire Buildings Preservation Trust Ltd 1995–, Assoc of Small Historic Towns and Villages of the UK (ASHTAV) 2004–; dep chm Rowland Hill Benevolent Fund; *Recreations* skiing, tennis, gardening; *Clubs* Brooks's; *Style*— John B A Alexander, Esq; ✉ Edmond de Rothschild Ltd, 5 Upper St Martin's Lane, London WC2H 9EA (tel 020 7845 5900, fax 020 7240 1815, e-mail j.alexander@lcfr.co.uk)

ALEXANDER, Dr John Huston (Ian); s of late John Alexander, of Bath, and late Agnes Margaret Crawford, *née* Huston; *b* 5 April 1941; *Educ* Campbell Coll Belfast, St Edmund Hall Oxford (BLitt, MA, DPhil); *m* 1970, Flora Munro, da of late Angus Ross, of Invergordon; 2 da (Ruth b 1971, Jane b 1974), 2 s (Mark b 1976, Patrick John b 1977); *Career* sessional lectr in English Univ of Saskatchewan Saskatoon Canada 1966–67, reader in English Univ of Aberdeen 1996–2001 (lectr in English 1968–84, sr lectr 1984–96); ed: The Scott Newsletter 1982–2001, Scottish Literary Journal 1991–95; gen ed Edinburgh Edn Waverley Novels 1984–; *Books* Two Studies in Romantic Reviewing (1976), The Lay of the Last Minstrel: Three Essays (1978), The Reception of Scott's Poetry by his Correspondents (1979), Marmion: Studies in Interpretation and Composition (1981), Scott and His Influence (ed with David Hewitt, 1983), Reading Wordsworth (1987), The Tavern Sages: Selections from the Noctes Ambrosianae (ed, 1992), Scott in Carnival (ed with David Hewitt, 1993), Walter Scott: Kenilworth - A Romance (ed, 1993), Walter Scott: The Bride of Lammermoor and A Legend of the Wars of Montrose (ed, 1995), Walter Scott: Tales of a Grandfather: The History of France (second series, ed with William Baker, 1996), Walter Scott: Anne of Geierstein (ed, 2000), Walter Scott: Quentin Durward (ed with G A M Wood, 2001), Walter Scott: Count Robert of Paris (ed, 2006), Walter Scott: Castle Dangerous (ed, 2006); *Recreations* music, walking; *Style*— Dr J H Alexander; ✉ 14 Holley Crescent, Headington, Oxford OX3 8AW (tel 01865 764524, e-mail geierstein@yahoo.co.uk)

ALEXANDER, Dr John Innis; s of William Bahudur Alexander (d 1984), of Surbiton, Surrey, and Winifred Edith, *née* Cottle (d 2001); *b* 17 March 1942; *Educ* KCS Wimbledon, UC and Med Sch London (MB BS, MRCS, LRCP); *m* 22 April 1978, Susan Diane, da of Philip Lionel Taylor, of Newport, Gwent; 1 da (Phyllida b 1980), 1 s (Christopher b 1982); *Career*

SHO in anaesthesia Norfolk and Norwich Hosp 1967–68, registrar in anaesthesia Royal Free Hosp London 1968–69, res fell in anaesthesia Scottish Home and Health Dept 1970–72, conslt in anaesthesia and pain mgmnt United Bristol Hosps 1974–2007 (sr registrar in anaesthesia 1969–74); examiner in pharmacology Royal Coll of Anaesthetists 1990–2002; chm: Bristol Research Ethics Ctee 1993–2001, South West Multicentre Research Ethics Ctee 2003–06; memb: Anaesthetic Res Soc 1970, Int Assoc for the Study of Pain 1975, Editorial Bd Frontiers of Pain 1990–92; FRCA 1969 (examiner 1991–2002); *Books* Postoperative Pain Control (1987); *Recreations* woodwork, swimming; *Style*— Dr John Alexander; ✉ Holly Tree House, 278 Church Road, Frampton Cotterell, Bristol BS36 2BH

ALEXANDER, Kenneth Alston; s of Brig-Gen Sir William Alexander, KBE, CB, CMG, DSO, MP (d 1954), and his 1 wife Beatrice Evelyn, *née* Ritchie (d 1928); *b* 21 November 1928; *Educ* Winchester, Trinity Coll Cambridge (BA); *m* 1957, Linda Mary, da of Edward Lefevre, of Cochin and Gargrave, N Yorks; 1 s, 3 da; *Career* Royal Tank Regt; chem merchant and manufacturer; dir Tennants Consolidated Ltd 1972–2003 (former chm and ceo, previously holding various directorships within the Tennant Group); *Recreations* shooting, music; *Clubs* RAC; *Style*— Kenneth Alexander, Esq; ✉ Tennants Consolidated Ltd, 69 Grosvenor Street, London W1K 3BP (tel 020 7493 5451)

ALEXANDER, Lesley-Anne; *m*; 1 s; *Career* various positions rising to dir of housing Housing Dept London Borough of Enfield 1992–98, dir of ops Peabody Tst 1998–2003, chief exec RNIB 2004–; tstee and memb Bd Waltham Forest Community-Based Housing Assoc 1998–2003; Br Judo Assoc: memb Bd 1990–2001, chm 1997–2001, currently chm London Region; fndr memb Willesden Judo Club; *Style*— Lesley-Anne Alexander; ✉ Royal National Institute of the Blind, 105 Judd Street, London WC1H 9NE (tel 020 7388 1266, fax 020 7388 2034)

ALEXANDER, Prof (Robert) McNeill; CBE (2000); s of Robert Priestley Alexander (d 1973), of Lisburn, Co Antrim, and Janet, *née* McNeill; *b* 7 July 1934; *Educ* Tonbridge, Trinity Hall Cambridge (MA, PhD), Univ of Wales (DSc); *m* 29 July 1961, Ann Elizabeth, da of Gordon Francis Coulton (d 1947), of Pentney, Norfolk; 1 da (Jane b 1962), 1 s (Gordon b 1964); *Career* sr lectr in zoology UCNW 1968–69 (asst lectr 1958–61, lectr 1961–68), prof of zoology Univ of Leeds 1969–99 (head Dept of Pure and Applied Zoology 1969–78 and 1983–87); visiting prof: Harvard Univ 1973, Duke Univ 1975, Univ of Nairobi 1976, 1977 and 1978, Univ of Basle 1986, St Francis Xavier Univ 1990, Univ of Calif Davis 1992; memb Biological Scis Ctee SRC 1974–77, sec Zoological Soc of London 1992–99 (vice-pres 1990–91, memb Cncl 1988–91); pres: Soc for Experimental Biology 1995–97 (vice-pres 1993–95), Int Soc for Vertebrate Morphology 1997–2001; ed Proceedings of the Royal Society (B) 1998–2004; hon memb Soc for Integrative and Comparative Biology (formerly American Soc of Zoologists) 1986, foreign hon memb American Acad of Arts and Sciences 2001; Scientific Medal Zoological Soc 1969, Linnean Medal Linnean Soc 1979, Muybridge Medal Int Soc for Biomechanics 1991, Borelli Award American Soc for Biomechanics 2003; Hon DSc Univ of Aberdeen 2002, Dr (hc) Wageningen Univ 2003; memb: Academia Europaea 1996, European Acad of Sciences 2004; FIBiol, FRS 1987, Hon FZS 2003; *Books* Functional Design in Fishes (1967), Animal Mechanics (1968), Size and Shape (1971), The Chordates (1975), The Invertebrates (1979), Optima for Animals (1982), Elastic Mechanisms in Animal Movement (1988), Dynamics of Dinosaurs and other Extinct Giants (1989), Animals (1990), The Human Machine (1992), Exploring Biomechanics (1992), Bones (1994), Energy for Animal Life (1999), Principles of Animal Locomotion (2003), Human Bones (2004), and other books and papers; *Recreations* history of biology and of tableware; *Style*— Prof McNeill Alexander, CBE, FRS; ✉ 14 Moor Park Mount, Leeds LS6 4BU (tel 0113 275 9218, e-mail r.m.alexander@leeds.ac.uk)

ALEXANDER, Rt Rev Mervyn Alban; s of William Paul Alexander (d 1968), of Salisbury, Wilts, and Grace Evelyn, *née* Newman (1973); *b* 29 June 1925; *Educ* Bishop Wordsworth Sch Salisbury, Prior Park Coll Bath, Gregorian Univ Rome (DD); *Career* curate Clifton Pro-Cathedral Bristol 1951–64, RC chaplain Univ of Bristol 1953–67, parish priest Our Lady of Lourdes Weston-super-Mare 1967–72, aux bishop of Clifton 1972–74, bishop of Clifton 1974–2001; *Style*— The Rt Rev Mervyn Alexander

ALEXANDER, Prof Michael Joseph; s of Joseph Brian Alexander, MBE, JP (d 1984), and Winifred, *née* Gaul (d 1985); *b* 21 May 1941; *Educ* Downside, Trinity Coll Oxford (MA); *m* 1, 1 Sept 1973, Eileen Mary (d 1986), da of Anthony Hamilton McCall; 2 da (Lucy b 1977, Flora b 1982), 1 s (Patrick b 1980); m 2, 11 July 1987, Mary Cecilia Sheahan; *Career* ed William Collins 1963, fell Princeton Graduate Sch 1965, lectr Univ of Calif 1966, ed André Deutsch 1967, lectr UEA 1968, reader Univ of Stirling 1985 (lectr 1969), Berry prof of Eng lit Univ of St Andrews 1985–2003 (hon prof 2003–); fell Eng Assoc; rep Scotland Round Britain Quiz (BBC); *Books* translations incl: The Earliest English Poems (1966, 3 edn 1991), Beowulf (1973, 2 edn 2001), Old English Riddles from the Exeter Book (1980, 2 edn 2007); other publications incl: Twelve Poems (1977), The Poetic Achievement of Ezra Pound (1979, new edn 1998), Macmillan Anthology of English Literature (jt ed, 1989), Beowulf (ed, 1995, 2 edn 2005), Sons of Ezra (jt ed, 1995), The Canterbury Tales: The First Fragment (ed, 1996), A History of English Literature (2000, 2 edn 2007), Medievalism: The Middle Ages in Modern England (2007); *Clubs* Athenaeum; *Style*— Prof Michael Alexander; ✉ 1 Lovers' Walk, Wells, Somerset BA5 2QL (tel 01749 672174); School of English, The University, St Andrews KY16 9AL (e-mail mja4@st-andrews.ac.uk)

ALEXANDER, Michael Richard; s of Pauline Alexander, *née* Parkinson; *b* 17 November 1947; *Educ* King George GS Southport, UMIST (BSc, MSc); *m* 1974, Clare, *née* Hollingsworth; 2 s (James Richard b 2 June 1977, Simon Elliot b 18 May 1981); *Career* British Gas (now Centrica plc following demerger): commercial mangr Exploration and Prodn 1991–93, dir CIS and Central Europe 1993, md British Gas Supply 1993–96, md British Gas Trading Ltd 1996–2002, exec dir Centrica plc 1996–2003, chief operating offr Centrica plc 2002–03; ceo British Energy plc 2003–05; non-exec dir: Energy Saving Tst 1994–2001, Associated British Foods 2002–, Costain plc 2007–; CEng, MIChemE, FIGasE, FIEE; *Recreations* squash, walking, dining; *Style*— Michael Alexander, Esq

ALEXANDER, Pamela Elizabeth (Pam); da of Reginald William Purchase Alexander (d 2007), and Marion Elizabeth, *née* Ross (d 2000); *b* 17 April 1954; *Educ* Lady Eleanor Holles Sch, Newnham Coll Cambridge (MA); *m* 8 Sept 1994, Dr Roger Booker, s of Thomas William Booker; 3 step s (Simon Henry b 1967, Oliver Henry b 1968, Benjamin b 1973), 1 step da (Joanna b 1970); *Career* Dept of the Environment 1975–94, dep chief exec (ops) The Housing Corporation 1995–97, mgmnt conslt Br Library 1997, chief exec English Heritage 1997–2001, advsr Cabinet Office 2001–02, chief exec South East of England Devpt Agency (SEEDA) 2004–; vice-pres First Div Assoc of Sr Civil Servants 1988–90; fndr memb Bd English Villages Housing Assoc 1987–92; associate New Economics Fndn 2002–; non-exec dir: The Housing Finance Corporation 2002–, Quintain E&D plc 2003, Brighton Dome and Festival Ltd 2006–; memb Ctee Joseph Rowntree Tst 1997–2006, chair Peabody Tst 2004– (govr 2000–); FRSA 1997, FRGS 1999, CGeog 2004; *Recreations* choral singing, tennis, walking, talking; *Style*— Ms Pam Alexander; ✉ SEEDA, Cross Lanes, Guildford GU1 1YA (e-mail pamalexander@seeda.co.uk)

ALEXANDER, Roger Michael; s of Hyman Isador Alexander, of London, and Anna, *née* Blumberg; *b* 29 June 1942; *Educ* Dulwich Coll, Law Soc Coll of Law; *m* 26 June 1966, Monica Anne, da of Freddie Freedman; 2 da (Jessica Louise b 6 June 1969, Lucy Katharine b 27 Feb 1971); *Career* admitted slr 1965; Lewis Silkin: ptnr 1965, lead ptnr 1989–98, head of Mktg Servs Law Gp 1990–92 and 1998–2005, sr ptnr 1998–2005, chm 2005–; non-exec dir: EDS Financial Services Div 1995–96, Walker Books Ltd 1999–, London String Quartet Fndn 2003–, Central Sch of Speech and Drama 2005; hon slr London Marriage Guidance Cncl 1988 (memb Exec Cncl 1986–90); memb Law Soc 1965; *Recreations* books, theatre, photography, gardening, travel; *Style*— Roger Alexander, Esq; ✉ Lewis Silkin, 12 Gough Square, London EC4A 3DW (tel 020 7074 8001, fax 020 7832 1700, e-mail roger.alexander@lewissilkin.com)

ALEXANDER, Wendy; MSP; da of Rev D Alexander, and Dr J Alexander; *b* 27 June 1963; *Educ* Park Mains HS, Pearson Coll Canada, Univ of Glasgow (MA), Univ of Warwick (MA Econ), INSEAD (MBA); *m* 2003, Prof Brian Ashcroft; 2 c; *Career* research offr Scottish Lab Pty 1988–92, mgmnt conslt Booz, Allen & Hamilton 1994–97, special advsr to Sec of State for Scotland 1997–98, MSP (Lab) Paisley N 1999–, min for Communities 1999–2000, min for Enterprise and Lifelong Learning 2000–01, min for Enterprise, Tport and Lifelong Learning 2001–02; *Publications* First Ladies of Medicine (1987), The World is Divided: Women's Work in Scotland (contrib,1990), The State and the Nations (contrib, 1996), The Ethnicity Reader (contrib, 1997), New Wealth for Old Nations (co-ed, 2005), Donald Dewar: Scotland's First First Minister (ed, 2005); ed LEDIS 1987–88; *Recreations* theatre, swimming, ornithology, Scotland's islands; *Style*— Ms Wendy Alexander, MSP; ✉ The Scottish Parliament, Edinburgh EH99 1SP (tel 0141 560 1025, fax 0141 560 1026, e-mail wendy.alexander.msp@scottish.parliament.uk)

ALEXANDER, William (Bill) (né Paterson); s of William Paterson, of Warton, Lancs, and Rosemary, *née* McCormack; *b* 23 February 1948; *Educ* St Lawrence Coll Ramsgate, Keele Univ (BA); *m* 1 June 1977, Juliet Linda, da of Michael Hedley Harmer, of Petworth, W Sussex; 2 da (Jessie b 1974, Lola b 1979); *Career* director; seasons with The Other Company, Bristol Old Vic and Royal Court 1972–78, hon assoc dir RSC 1991– (assoc dir RSC 1978–91), artistic dir Birmingham Rep Theatre 1992–2000; *Theatre* Bristol Old Vic incl: The Ride Across Lake Constance, Twelfth Night, Old Times, Butley, How the Other Half Loves; Royal Court incl: Sex and Kinship in a Savage Society 1976, Amy and the Price of Cotton 1977, Class Enemy 1978, Sugar and Spice 1979; RSC incl: Factory Birds 1977, Shout Across the River, The Hang of the Gaol, Captain Swing 1978, Men's Beano 1979, Bastard Angel 1980, Henry IV 1980 (tour), Accrington Pals 1981, Volpone 1983, Richard III 1984, The Merry Wives of Windsor 1985, A Midsummer Night's Dream 1986, Twelfth Night, The Merchant of Venice, Cymbeline 1987, Duchess of Malfi 1989, The Taming of the Shrew 1990 and 1992, Much Ado About Nothing 1991, The School of Night 1992, Titus Andronicus 2003, King Lear 2004; Birmingham Rep incl: Othello 1993, Volpone 1993, Old Times 1993, The Snowman 1993, Awake and Sing 1994, The Tempest 1994, The Servant 1995, Macbeth 1995, Way of the World 1995, Divine Right 1996, Dr Jekyll and Mr Hyde 1996, The Alchemist 1996, The Merchant of Venice 1997, The Snowman 1997, Frozen 1998, Hamlet 1998, The Four Alice Bakers 1999, Jumpers 1999, Nativity 1999, Quarantine 2000, Hamlet 2000, Twelfth Night 2000; other credits incl: Troilus and Cressida (Shakespeare Theatre Washington) 1992, The Importance of Being Earnest (Northampton) 2002, Mappa Mundi (RNT) 2002, Enemy of the People (Theatr Clwyd) 2002, Frozen (RNT) 2002, Henry IV parts 1 and 2 (Shakespeare Theatre Washington) 2004; *Style*— Bill Alexander, Esq; ✉ Rose Cottage, Tunley, Cirencester, Gloucestershire GL7 6LP

ALEXANDER, William John (Bill); CBE (2005); s of John Fryer Alexander, and Kathleen Mary, *née* Berry; *b* 15 February 1947, Corbridge, Northumberland; *m* Dorothy (Dee), *née* Full; 1 s (Paul b 6 Aug 1972), 1 da (Sarah b 6 April1976); *Career* British Coal Corp (formerly NCB): joined as graduate trainee 1970, area mech engr Scotland 1982–83, chief engr Scottish Region 1983–86, chief mech engr HQ 1986–87, head of engrg 1987–89; Thames Water Utilities Ltd: engrg dir 1989–91, tech dir 1991–92, md 1992–94; Thames Water plc: exec main bd dir (incl responsibility for construction of Thames Water London Ring Main) 1994–96, group md 1995–97, chief exec 1997–2005; non-exec chm: Xansa 2004–, Invesco Perpetual Income and Growth Investment Tst plc 2007–; non-exec dir CBI; former non-exec dir: RMC Gp plc, Laporte plc; former pres Inst of Mining Electrical and Mining Mechanical Engrs (IMEMME); chm Henley Music FestivalHon DSc: Univ of Reading 2002, Cranfield Univ 2003; CEng, FIMechE, FREng, Hon FIMMM, Hon FCIWEM; *Recreations* classic cars, tennis, golf; *Clubs* Mark's, Phyllis Court, Carnegie; *Style*— Bill Alexander, Esq, CBE, FREng; ✉ Xansa plc, 420 Thames Valley Park Drive, Thames Valley Park, Reading RG6 1PU

ALEXANDER OF TUNIS, Countess; Hon Davina Mary; *née* Woodhouse; LVO (1991); da of 4 Baron Terrington (d 1998); *b* 12 April 1955; *Educ* Hatherop Castle; *m* 1981, as his 2 w, 2 Earl Alexander of Tunis, *qv*; 2 da (Lady Rose b 1982, Lady Lucy b 1984); *Career* lady in waiting to HRH the late Princess Margaret, Countess of Snowdon 1975–79; extra lady in waiting 1979–2002; party co-ordinator Alexander Events 1998–; pres: SOS (stars orgn supporting action for people with cerebral palsy) 1992–95, Society of Stars (celebrity support for children and adults with cerebral palsy) 1996–99; memb Governing Cncl Friends of The Elderly 1986–2002; *Recreations* tennis, skiing, cooking; *Style*— The Rt Hon the Countess Alexander of Tunis, LVO; ✉ 28 Clonmel Road, London SW6 5BJ (tel 020 7731 0878, fax 020 7384 2113, e-mail alexevents@btinternet.com)

ALEXANDER OF TUNIS, 2 Earl (UK 1952); Shane William Desmond Alexander; also Viscount Alexander of Tunis (UK 1946) and Baron Rideau (UK 1952); s of Field Marshal 1 Earl Alexander of Tunis, KG, GCB, OM, GCMG, CSI, DSO, MC, PC (3 s of 4 Earl of Caledon), and Lady Margaret Bingham, GBE, JP (d 1977), da of 5 Earl of Lucan (gs of the Crimean War commander); *b* 30 June 1935; *Educ* Harrow, Ashbury Coll Ottawa; *m* 1, 1971 (m dis 1976), Hilary, da of John van Geest, of Lincs; m 2, 1981, Hon Davina Woodhouse, LVO (Countess Alexander of Tunis), *qv* former Lady-in-Waiting to HRH The Princess Margaret, da of 4 Baron Terrington (d 1998); 2 da (Lady Rose Margaret b 23 April 1982, Lady Lucy Caroline b 20 Sept 1984); *Heir* bro, Hon Brian Alexander, CMG; *Career* Lt Irish Gds (res); Lord in Waiting to HM The Queen 1974; patron Br-Tunisian Soc 1975–99, dir: International Hospitals Group 1981–, Kyrgoil Corp (Canada) 1995–, Marketform Ltd 1996–; pres Br-American Canadian Assocs 1988–94, chm and tstee Canada Meml Fndn 1990–; Liveryman Worshipful Co of Mercers 1965; Order of Republic of Tunisia 1996; *Recreations* tennis, skiing, music; *Clubs* MCC; *Style*— The Rt Hon Earl Alexander of Tunis; ✉ 28 Clonmel Road, London SW6 5BJ (tel 020 7736 2604)

ALFORD, Prof Bernard William Ernest; s of Ernest Edward Alford (d 1970), of Uffculme, Devon, and Winifred Daisy Alford (d 1966); *b* 17 October 1937; *Educ* Tiverton GS, LSE (BSc, PhD); *m* 18 Aug 1962, Valerie Sandra, da of Albert Thomas North (d 1963), of Cullompton, Devon; 1 da, 2 s; *Career* asst lectr in econ history LSE 1961–62; Univ of Bristol: lectr then reader in econ and social history 1962–82, head Dept of Historical Studies 1982–2001, prof of econ and social history 1982–2001, prof emeritus 2001–; numerous contribs to books and learned jls; treas Economic History Soc 1988–96 (memb Cncl 1979, chm Pubns Ctee 1983–88); memb: Lord Chllr's Advsy Ctee on The Public Records 1988–94, Advsy Cncl Inst of Contemporary Br History 1989–2000, Research Grants Bd ESRC 1989–93; AcSS 2001, FRHistS; *Books* A History of the Carpenters' Company (with T C Barker, 1968), Depression and Recovery? British Economic Growth, 1918–1939 (1972), W D and H O Wills and the Development of the UK Tobacco Industry 1783–1965 (1973 and 2005), British Economic Performance, 1945–1975 (1988 and 1995), Economic Planning in Britain 1943–1951 (with R Lowe and N Rollings, 1992), Britain in the World Economy since 1880 (1996); *Recreations* bridge, family life; *Style*— Prof Bernard Alford; ✉ The Bank House, High Street, Marshfield, Chippenham, Wiltshire SN14 8LT (tel 01225 891660); Department of Historical Studies, University of Bristol, 13–15 Woodland Road, Bristol BS8 1TB (tel 0117 331 7932, e-mail b.alford@bristol.ac.uk)

ALFORD, Richard Harding; CMG (2003), OBE (1988); s of Jack Harding Alford (d 1984), of London, and Gertrude Sylvia, *née* Buckland (d 1990); *b* 28 December 1943; *Educ* Dulwich Coll, Keble Coll Oxford (open Grove exhbn in modern history, BA, Dip History and Philosophy of Science); *m* Penelope Jane, da of James Wort (decd); 2 da (Harriet Jane b 18 April 1971, Jessica Louise b 21 March 1980), 1 s (Joseph William b 1 June 1973); *Career* VSO Aitchison Coll Lahore 1966–67; British Cncl: asst cultural attaché British Embassy Prague 1969–72, various posts (Middle East Dept, Policy Res Dept and Educn Contracts Dept) 1972–77; Project Planning Centre Univ of Bradford and Inst of Educn Univ of London 1977–78; British Cncl: asst rep New Delhi 1978–81, dir E Europe and N Asia Dept 1982–85, rep Poland 1985–89, dir Personnel 1989–93, regnl dir Central Europe 1993–96, dir Italy 1996–2003; sec Charles Wallace India Tst 2003–; govr: Centre for Int Briefing Farnham Castle 1992–96, British Inst of Florence 1996–2003, Atlantic Coll 2005–; chair Keats Shelley Meml House Rome 1999–2001; *Recreations* tennis, theatre; *Clubs* Friends of Dulwich Coll; *Style—* Richard Alford, Esq, CMG, OBE; ✉ c/o British Council, 10 Spring Gardens, London SW1A 2BN

ALFREDS, Michael Guy Alexander (Mike); s of John Mark Alfreds (d 1978), and Hylda, *née* Metz (d 1994); *b* 5 June 1934; *Educ* Bradfield, American Theater Wing NY, Carnegie-Mellon Inst Pittsburgh (BFA); *Career* theatre director; dir of prodns Summer Stock Kennebunkport Maine 1958–59; freelance dir 1963–70, Israeli theatre and TV 1970–75, 1983 1989 and 2001; assoc dir RNT 1985 and 1987–88; appts as artistic dir incl: Theatre West Tucson Arizona 1960, Cincinnati Playhouse-in-the-Park 1961–62, Khan Theatre Jerusalem 1972–75, Shared Experience 1975–87 (fndr), Cambridge Theatre Co 1991–95, Method & Madness 1995–99; teacher of acting and directing at various instns incl: LAMDA, Beijing Central Acad of Drama, Univ of Tel Aviv, Arts Cncl Wellington, Royal Shakespeare Co, Royal Court Theatre, Australian Int Workshop Festival, NIDA Sydney, Soros Fndn Ulaanbaatar, Mongolia, World Stages Festival Toronto, Graeae Theatre Co; author of several articles in professional jls and co-adaptor of Eugene Sue's The Wandering Jew (1987); memb: Arts Cncl Drama Panel 1981–85, Arts Cncl Drama Projects Sub Ctee 1982–85, Mgmnt Ctee The Actor's Centre 1988, Working Pty of Gulbenkian Fndn Enquiry Into Dir Trg (report A Better Direction) 1987–89; bd dir: Almeida Theatre 1982–89, Shared Experience 1975–97, David Glass Ensemble 1990–94, Unicorn Theatre for Children 2000–02; *Theatre* prodns at Shared Experience incl: Arabian Nights Trilogy 1975–77, Bleak House 1977–78, Science Fictions 1978–79, Cymbeline 1979–80, The Merchant of Venice, La Ronde, A Handful of Dust 1982, The Comedy Without A Title, Successful Strategies, False Confidences 1983, Marriage 1984, The Three Sisters, Too True To Be Good 1986, The Seagull 1991; Cambridge Theatre Co: Lady Windermere's Fan, The Country Wife 1991, The Revenger's Tragedy, The Game of Love and Change (and NT) 1992, The Hypochondriac, The Dearly Beloved, Les Enfants du Paradis 1993, A Handful of Dust, Uncle Silas, Emma 1994, What I Did in the Holidays 1995; prodns for Method & Madness incl: Jude the Obscure 1995, Private Lives, Flesh and Blood, Ghosts 1996, The Winter's Tale 1997, A Cherry Orchard 1998, Demons and Dybbuks, The Black Dahlia 1998, Buried Alive 1999; other prodns incl: Suitcase Packers (Cameri Theatre Tel Aviv 1983, Le Theatre des Nations 1984, Edinburgh Festival 1985), 1001 Nights (Theater der Stadt Heidelberg 1984, Nationale Scene Bergen 1986), The Cherry Orchard (RNT) 1985, The Wandering Jew (RNT) 1987, Countrymania (RNT) 1987, Blood Wedding (Tarragon Theatre Toronto and Banff Centre) 1988, A Streetcar Named Desire (Tianjin People's Art Theatre China) 1988, Ghosts (Beersheba Municipal Theatre Israel) 1989, The Miser (Oxford Stage Co) 1990, Trouble in Paradise (Talking Pictures) 1990, The Seagull (Oxford Stage Co) 1991, A Flea in her Ear (Theatr Clwyd and W Yorks Playhouse) 1993, Demons (Cameri Theatre Tel Aviv) 2000, Buried Alive (Hampstead Theatre) 2001, Cymbeline (Shakespeare's Gobe) 2001, A Midsummer Night's Dream (Shakespeare's Globe) 2002, The Comedy of Errors (Dartmouth Coll NH) 2002, Collateral Damage (Lamda), The Black Dahlia (Yale Rep Theatre) 2003, Twelfth Night (Rutgers Univ at Shakespeare's Globe), Pedro the Great Pretender (Rutgers Univ at Shakespeare's Globe) 2004, Troilus and Cressida (Rutgers Univ at Shakespeare's Globe) 2005, Much Ado About Nothing (RSC) 2006, The Winter's Tale (Rutgers Univ at Shakespeare's Globe) 2007; *Awards* Best Revival BTA Drama Awards for The Seagull 1982, Best Dir BTA Drama and Plays and Players Awards for The Cherry Orchard 1986, Israel Kinoor David Award for Best Dir and Best Prodn for Mandragola (Haifa Theatre) 1971 and Suitcase Packers (Cameri Theatre) 1984), Best Dir Regional Theatre Awards for Jude the Obscure, Private Lives and Flesh and Blood (Method & Madness) 1996; *Style—* Mike Alfreds; ✉ tel and fax 020 7724 8158, e-mail alfreds@london.com

ALI, Monica; *b* 1967, Dhaka, Bangladesh; *Educ* Wadham Coll Oxford; *m* Simon Torrance; 1 s, 1 da; *Career* novelist; formerly employed in publishing, design and branding; named in Granta Best of Young British Novelists list 2003; *Books* Brick Lane (2003, shortlisted Man Booker Prize for Fiction 2003, shortlisted Guardian First Book Award 2003, Debut Novel Award W H Smith People's Choice Awards 2004, Newcomer of the Year British Book Awards 2004), Alentejo Blue (2006); *Style—* Ms Monica Ali

ALIBHAI-BROWN, Yasmin; da of Kassam Damji (d 1970), and Jena Damji; *b* 10 December 1949; *Educ* Univ of Oxford (MPhil); *m* 1, 1972 (m dis 1990), Shiraz Alibhai; 1 s (Ari b 30 Jan 1978); m 2, 1990, Colin Brown; 1 da (Leila b 11 April 1993); *Career* journalist and broadcaster; contrib various newspapers incl: The Guardian, New Statesman, The Independent (columnist); research fell IPPR 1996–, sr fell Foreign Policy Centre; memb Home Office Race Forum, advsr on race matters; pres Inst of Family Therapy, vice-pres UN Assoc (UK), special ambass Samaritans; govr RSC, one woman show (RSC, UK and int tour); George Orwell Prize for Politicial Journalism 2002; hon degree Open Univ 1999, hon fell Liverpool John Moores Univ 2003; *Books* No Place Like Home, True Colours (1999), Who Do We Think We Are? (2000), After Multiculturalism (2000), Mixed Feelings (2001), Some of my Best Friends are... (2004); *Recreations* theatre, cookery; *Style—* Ms Yasmin Alibhai-Brown; ✉ The Foreign Policy Centre, Elizabeth House, 39 York Road, London SE1 7NQ (tel 020 7005 2764); The Independent, 191 Marsh Wall, London E14 9RS

ALIDAD, (né Alidad Mahloudji); s of Khalil Mahloudji, of London, and Farzaneh Mahloudji; *b* 18 July 1954; *Educ* Tehran, Switzerland, Mill Hill Sch London, UCL (BSc); *Career* interior designer; dir Islamic Dept Sotheby's London 1977–84, estab Alidad Ltd 1985; cmmns for restoration of Nat Tst houses (incl saloon and music room at Buscot House Oxon) and many private residences in the UK and abroad; launched furniture collection 2004, launched fabric collection (for Pierre Frey) 2005; exhibited Br Interior Design Exhbn 1988, 1989 and 1997 (Best Interior Designer The World of Interiors, House and Garden and Elle Decoration magazines 1997); articles and photographs published in numerous interior design magazines and books; memb: Br Interior Design Assoc (BIDA) 1992–, Int Interior Design Assoc (IIDA) 1999–; Best Product of the Year Award World of Interiors 2004; memb charity ctees incl Chicken Shed Theatre Co; *Clubs* Chelsea Arts; *Style—* Alidad; ✉ The Lighthouse, Gasworks, 2 Michael Road, London SW6 2AD (tel 020 7384 0121, fax 020 7384 0122, e-mail info@alidad.com, website www.alidad.com)

ALINEK, Ruth Susan; da of Dennis Alinek (d 1994), and Evelyn, *née* Fineman; *b* 27 February 1953, London; *Educ* Heriots Wood GS Stanmore, Univ of Warwick (BA, MA), Garnett Coll Roehampton (PGCE); *Partner* David Wilkins; *Career* teacher of English Oakham Sch 1975–77, second in English Dept Aldenham Sch 1978–82, head of drama Haberdashers' Aske's Sch for Girls Elstree 1982–85, head of sixth form and sr teacher Chelmsford Co HS for Girls 1986–92, dep head (curriculum) Westcliff HS for Girls 1992–95, headmistress Southend HS for Girls 1995–2003, headmistress Aylesbury HS 2003–; memb: SE Essex SHA, Essex Grammar Schs' Consortium; *Style—* Ms Ruth Alinek; ✉ Aylesbury High School, Walton Road, Aylesbury, Buckinghamshire HP21 7SX (tel 01296 415237, fax 01296 388200, e-mail secretary@ahs.bucks.sch.uk)

ALISON, Fiona; da of Harry Widdup (d 1976), of Weymouth, Dorset, and Nell Roberts (d 1968); *b* 7 March 1939; *Educ* Weymouth GS, Weymouth Coll, Univ of London (CertEd); *m* 30 June 1962, Peter Alison (d 1995), s of Youssof Alison; 1 s (Julian Piers b 16 June 1969), 1 da (Elizabeth Charlotte b 10 Jan 1973); *Career* int child photographer 1980–; works incl: children's portraiture 1980–84, children's fashion and advertising photography GB 1984–87, photographic assignments and lectures worldwide 1988–; exhibition of work at Glaziers' Hall London 1983, numerous appearances on radio and TV, first woman judge BP Chemicals World Photographic Competition 1990, tutor Fuji Film UK Sch of Photography Cyprus and GB 1991, judge 1997 Fuji Awards, judge Southampton Int 90th Exhibition 2003, selector Royal Photographic Soc Int Exhibition 2005; int speaker Nikon-PSS Master Photographer Seminar Singapore 2007; Afocier Agrupacio Foto-Cine Cardanyola-Ripollet Aqueducte 2004: 3 images retained for the Museum of Contemporary Photography; RPS Int Print Exhbn Bronze Medal 2004; FBIPP 1988 (LBIPP 1981, ABIPP 1982), FRSA 1982, FRPS 1992 (Fellowship and Associateship Applied Distinctions Panel, 1993), FMPA 1995 (first woman pres 2006–07); *Awards* Kodak Nat Portrait Award winner (first woman to win) 1980, 3M Nat Portfolio Award winner (first woman to win) 1983, BIPP Peter Grugeon Award (first woman to win) 1988, Salon International de la Photographie Mayet Prix du Public Gold Award 2004; *Recreations* reading, theatre; *Clubs* London Portrait Gp; *Style—* Mrs Fiona Alison; ✉ Normandy Cottage, 14 Avon Park, Ashley, Ringwood, Hampshire BH24 2AT (e-mail fiona@littlepics.freeserve.co.uk)

ALLAM, Roger William; s of Rev William Sydney Allam (d 1977), of London, and Kathleen, *née* Service (d 1995); *b* 26 October 1953; *Educ* Christ's Hosp, Univ of Manchester (BA); *Career* actor; fndr memb Monstrous Regiment Theatre Co; repertory work in Manchester, Birmingham and Glasgow; author of contribs on Mercutio and Duke Vincentio in Players of Shakespeare II and III; *Theatre* roles incl: Angelo in Measure for Measure, title role in Macbeth, Macheath in Threepenny Opera, Dr Rock in The Doctor and The Devils; RSC (joined RSC 1981 (assoc artist 1990)) roles incl: Richmore in Twin Rivals, Conrad in Our Friends in The North, Theseus and Oberon in A Midsummer Night's Dream, Mercutio in Romeo and Juliet, Victor in Today, Ford in The Party, The Officer in The Dream Play, Javert in Les Miserables, Adrian in The Archbishop's Ceiling, Clarence in Richard III, Pimm in Heresies, Brutus in Julius Caesar, Sir Toby Belch in Twelfth Night, Duke Vincentio in Measure for Measure, Benedick in Much Ado About Nothing, Trigorin in The Seagull, Dr Jekyll in The Strange Case of Dr Jekyll and Mr Hyde, Macbeth; RNT roles incl: Mirabell in The Way of the World, Ulysses in Troilus and Cressida (Clarence Derwent Award), Graves in Money (Olivier Award), Bassov in Summer Folk (Olivier nomination); RNT: Hitler in Albert Speer, Lophakin in The Cherry Orchard, Willy Brandt in Democracy (Olivier nomination); other roles incl: Oberon in The Fairy Queen (Aix-en-Provence Festival) 1989, Angelo in Una Pooka (London) 1992, Philip Madras in The Madras House (London) 1992, Stone in City of Angels (London) 1993 (Olivier nomination), Bernard Nightingale in Arcadia (London) 1994, John Worthing in The Importance of Being Earnest (Birmingham Rep and Old Vic) 1995, Serge in Art (London) 1997, Marc in Art (London) 1998, Captain Terri in Privates on Parade (London) 2001 (Olivier Award for Best Actor 2002), What the Night is For (London) 2002, Abanazar in Aladdin (Old Vic) 2004 and 2005, Ray in Blackbird (Edinburgh) 2005 and (London) 2006, Lambert le Roux in Pravda (Chichester) 2006, Bernard in Boeing Boeing (London) 2007; *Television* incl: Who Bombed Birmingham?, Summerchild in A Landing on the Sun, Between the Lines, Morse, Charlie in The Creatives, Peter Mannion in The Thick of It; *Radio* incl: Jean Valjean in Les Miserables, Svengali in Trilby, Laughter in the Dark (Sony Award), Gilbert Harding, Henry Gosse in Father and Son; *Film* incl: Stranded, The Roman Spring of Mrs Stone, A Cock and Bull Story, V for Vendetta, The Wind that Shakes the Barley, The Queen, Speed Racer; *Recreations* playing and listening to music, cooking, drinking red wine; *Style—* Roger Allam, Esq; ✉ c/o Claire Maroussas, ICM, Oxford House, 76 Oxford Street, London W1D 1BS (tel 020 7636 6565, fax 020 7323 9867)

ALLAN, *see also:* Havelock-Allan

ALLAN, Alexander Claud Stuart (Alex); s of Baron Allan of Kilmahew, DSO, OBE (Life Peer, d 1979), and Maureen Catherine Flower, *née* Stuart Clark; *b* 9 February 1951; *Educ* Harrow, Clare Coll Cambridge (MA), UCL (MSc); *m* 1978, Katie Christine, da of Keith Clemson (d 1988); *Career* admin trainee HM Customs and Excise 1973–76, various roles HM Treasy 1976–82, freelance computer conslt Sydny and Perth 1983–84, princ Reform of Local Govt Finance HM Treasy 1985–86, princ private sec to Chllr of the Exchequer 1986–89, under sec for international finance HM Treasy 1989–90, under sec for general expenditure policy HM Treasy 1990–92; princ private sec to the PM 1992–97, high cmmr to Australia 1997–99, e-envoy Cabinet Office 1999–2000, living in Western Aust 2001–04 (roles incl conslt Centre for Global Studies and memb Premier's Science Cncl, Senate Univ of Western Aust and ICT Industry Devpt Forum), perm sec DCA 2004–07, perm sec Min of Justice 2007–; *Recreations* Grateful Dead music, sailing, computers; *Clubs* Royal Ocean Racing; *Style—* Alex Allan, Esq; ✉ Ministry of Justice, Selborne House, 54–60 Victoria Street, London SW1E 6QW

ALLAN, Andrew Norman (Andy); *b* 26 September 1943; *m* 1; 2 da; m 2, Joanna, *née* Forrest; 2 s, 1 da; *Career* early career as presenter, prodr and editor with ABC and ITN, various positions rising to head of news Thames Television 1969–78, prog controller rising to md Tyne Tees Television 1978–84; Central Independent Television: dir of progs 1984–93, also md Central Broadcasting 1990–93, md Central Independent Television plc 1993–94; Carlton Television (following takeover of Central by Carlton Communications plc): chief exec 1994–95, dir of progs 1996–98; dir TV12 1999–; media conslt 1998–; chm: Birmingham Rep 2000–, Route 4 plc 2001; FRTS; *Style—* Andy Allan, Esq; ✉ Cheviot View, Hedley on the Hill, Stocksfield, Northumberland NE43 7SW (tel 01661 842185)

ALLAN, (Gordon) David; s of Joseph Allan (d 1981), of Banbury, Oxon, and Isobel Joyce, *née* Williams (d 1982); *b* 7 August 1940; *Educ* Bury GS; *m* 1972, Margaret Elizabeth, da of John Beresford Humphries; 2 s (Simon b 24 Oct 1978, Robin b 2 June 1981); *Career* country music disc jockey; gen factotum then asst stage mangr Manchester Library Theatre 1957–59, backstage jobs in various rep theatres incl Theatre Royal Windsor 1959–64, stage mgmnt in West End incl asst stage mangr for Barbra Streisand's Funny Girl 1964–67, disc jockey Radio 390 (pirate station) 1967–68, announcer/newsreader Anglia TV 1968–69; BBC TV and Radio: continuity announcer BBC2 1969–94, freelance country music broadcaster Radio 2 1969–, presenter/co-prodr TV coverage of annual Wembley Country Music Festival 1969–89; presenter: Sunday Early Show (Radio 2) 1988–92, internetcountryshow.com, Prime Time Radio 2004; continuity announcer: The History Channel; hon citizen Nashville Tennessee 1978; memb Country Music Assoc of America 1970; *Awards* Disc Jockey of the Year Br Country Music Assoc 1977, 1978 and 1979, Most Popular Euro Country Music Disc Jockey (poll taken in 5 countries by Br Jl Country Music Roundup) 1990, Favourite Presenter UK Country Radio Awards 2001, Int Broadcaster Country Music Assoc 2002; *Recreations* photography, swimming, lying in the (preferably Spanish) sun; *Style—* David Allan, Esq; ✉ Redmayne, Bull Lane, Gerrards Cross, Buckinghamshire SL9 8RF (tel and fax 01753 882541, e-mail daviallan@hotmail.com)

ALLAN, Prof Dennis Joseph; s of Joseph Sharp Allan (d 1963), and Annie Irene, *née* Parker (d 1975); *b* 10 May 1933; *Educ* Lawrence Sheriff Sch Rugby, Rugby Coll of Engrg (BSc(Eng) external); *m* Glenis Carole Elizabeth, *née* Lake; 2 da (Karen Grace b 1957, Melanie Jane b 1962); *Career* student/graduate apprentice BTH Co Ltd Rugby 1951–56, Nat Serv Tech Servs REME 1957–58, asst chief engr AEI Transformers Ltd Wythenshaw 1964–68 (devpt section ldr Rugby 1959–64); GEC Transformers Ltd Stafford: chief devpt engr 1968–78, quality mangr 1978–80, engrg mangr 1980–83; dir and tech mangr GEC Alsthom T & D Transformers Ltd Stafford 1983–97; engrg conslt 1997–; Royal Acad of Engrg chair in principles of engrg design UMIST 1991–; visiting prof in power distribution engrg Univ of Manchester 2002–; chm: Study Ctee 12 (Transformers) CIGRE 1986–94 (chm BNC 1994–), Power Div IEE 1990–91, TC14 (Transformers) IEC 1993–, Mgmnt Bd EAQA; FIEE 1971, FIMechE 1971, FIEEE 1992, FREng 1993; *Recreations* industrial archaeology, medieval architecture; *Style—* Prof Dennis Allan, FREng; ✉ Crosswinds, Battle Ridge, Hopton, Stafford ST18 0BG (tel 01785 42773, fax 01785 212642)

ALLAN, Geoffrey Robert John; s of Dr Robert Leitch Allan (d 1976), and Elsie Kathleen, *née* Stewart; *b* 25 March 1941; *Educ* Strathallan Sch, Univ of Glasgow (BDS Glas, Rugby blue), Univ of London (MSc); *m* 1, 1969; 2 s (Christopher Geoffrey b 4 Nov 1973, Nicholas Cochran Robert b 4 Jan 1975), 1 da (Kimberley Kathleen b 12 Nov 1977); m 2, 1984, Rosalind Mary, da of David Smith; 1 step s (Gavin David b 10 April 1973), 1 step da (Suzanne Mary b 27 Feb 1975); *Career* trainee rising to shift supt Clyde Paper Co 1960–64; house offr, SHO, registrar and sr registrar Glasgow Dental Hosp Canniesburn and Stobhill 1969–77, Eastman Dental Hosp London 1975, conslt in restorative dentistry Guy's Hosp London 1977–79, joined Glynn Setchell (now called Glynn, Setchell and Allan) 1979; examiner RCPS Glasgow 1985–; appointed to the new Restorative Dentistry Specialist List 1998 and to the Surgical Dentistry Specialist List 2000; memb: BDA, Int Coll of Dentists; FDS RCPS Glas, MRD RCPS Glas; *Books* BDA Booklet on Treatment of the Cleft Palate Patient; *Recreations* family, golf, skiing; *Clubs* Wildernesse, Royal Cinque Ports Golf; *Style—* Geoffrey Allan, Esq; ✉ Glynn, Setchell & Allan, 35 Devonshire Place, London W1N 1PE (tel 020 7935 3342, fax 020 7224 0558)

ALLAN, Prof James Wilson; *b* 5 May 1945; *Educ* Marlborough, St Edmund Hall Oxford (MA, DPhil); *m* 1970, Jennifer Robin, *née* Hawksworth; 2 s, 2 da; *Career* Dept of Eastern Art Ashmolean Museum: asst keeper 1966–88, sr asst keeper 1988–91, keeper 1991–2005, prof of eastern art 1996–, dir Inter-Faith Exhbn Serv 2005–06; fell St Cross Coll 1990–2005 (emeritus fell 2005–); pres Br Inst of Persian Studies 2002–06; *Publications* Medieval Middle Eastern Pottery (1971), Persian Metal Technology 700–1300 AD (1978), Islamic Metalwork: Nuhad Es-Said Collection (1982), Nishapur: Metalwork of the Early Islamic Period (1982), Metalwork of the Islamic World: the Aron Collection (1986), A Short Account of Early Muslim Architecture (1989), Persian Steel: The Tanavoli Collection (with B Gilmour, 2000), Metalwork Treasures from the Islamic Courts (2002); *Recreations* music, ornithology, walking, travel; *Style—* Prof James Allan

ALLAN, John; CBE (2005); *b* 20 August 1948; *Educ* Univ of Edinburgh (BSc); *Career* mktg trainee then brand mangr Lever Bros 1970–74, mktg appts Consumer Products Div Bristol-Myers 1974–77, various appts rising to mktg and buying dir Fine Fare 1977–85, main bd dir i/c business servs Europe and gp mktg dir BET plc 1985–94, chief exec Exel plc (formerly Ocean Group plc) 1994–2005, chief exec DHL Logisitics 2006–, memb Mgmnt Bd Deutsche Post World Net 2006–; non-exec dir: Hamleys plc 1996–2001, Wolseley plc 1999–2004, PHS plc 2001–05, Nat Grid plc 2005–, Samsonite 2007–; pres Freight Tport Assoc 2003–05, chm Freight Forwarding Int 2006–; chm Tport Policy Ctee CBI 1998–2001; memb: Pres's Ctee CBI 2001–, Int Advsy Ctee Econ Devpt Bd Singapore 2002–07, Univ of Edinburgh Campaign Bd; *Style—* John Allan, Esq, CBE; ✉ DHL Logistics, Ocean House, The Ring, Bracknell, Berkshire RG12 1AN (tel 01344 302000, fax 01344 744352, e-mail john.allan@dhl.com)

ALLAN, Sheriff John Douglas; OBE (2006); s of Robert Taylor Allan (d 2002), of Edinburgh, and Christina Helen Blythe Allan (d 1970); *b* 2 October 1941; *Educ* George Watson's Coll Edinburgh, Univ of Edinburgh (LLB), Napier Univ (Dip Mgmnt Studies); *m* 1966, Helen Elizabeth Jean, da of William Aiton (d 1959); 1 s (Graeme b 1967), 1 da (Anne b 1970); *Career* slr and Notary Public; slr 1963–67, dep procurator fiscal 1967–71, sr legal asst Crown Office 1971–76, asst procurator fiscal Glasgow 1976–77, sr asst procurator fiscal Glasgow 1978–79, asst slr Crown Office 1979–83, regnl procurator fiscal for Lothians & Borders 1983–88; Sheriff of S Strathclyde, Dumfries and Galloway at Lanark 1988–2000, Sheriff of Lothian and Borders at Edinburgh 2000–; chm Judicial Cmn of Gen Assembly of Church of Scotland 1998–2003; memb Bd Scottish Children's Reporter Administration 1995–2003 (dep chm 2002–03); Sheriffs' Assoc: pres 2000–02, vice-pres 1997–2000, sec 1991–97; regnl vice-pres Cwlth Magistrates and Judges Assoc 2003– (memb Cncl 2000–03), memb Judicial Appointments Bd for Scotland 2002–; *Recreations* youth work, church work, walking; *Style—* Sheriff J Douglas Allan, OBE; ✉ Minard, 80 Greenbank Crescent, Edinburgh EH10 5SW (tel 0131 447 2593); Sheriff Court, 27 Chambers Street, Edinburgh EH1 1LB (tel 0131 225 2525)

ALLAN, Richard Bellerby; *b* 2 August 1940; *Educ* Marlborough, Merton Coll Oxford (MA); *m* 17 Sept 1966, Diana Rosemary Cotton, QC, *qv*; 2 s (Jonathan Bellerby b 28 June 1972, Jeremy Richard b 7 Aug 1974), 1 da (Joanna Frances b 10 March 1977); *Career* KPMG (and predecessor firms): articled clerk 1962–65, qualified sr 1965–69, mangr 1969–77, ptnr 1977–96; non-exec dir: T&G Allan Ltd, Shelter Trading Ltd; Bodley fell Merton Coll Oxford; FRGS; *Style—* Richard Allan, Esq; ✉ 8 Northampton Park, London N1 2PJ (tel 020 7226 7440)

ALLAN, Prof Robert Norman; s of Dr Malcolm Allan (d 1994), and Kathleen Mary, *née* Tuck (d 1972); *b* 26 July 1941; *Educ* Ashby-de-la-Zouch Boys' GS, Univ of Birmingham (MB ChB, MD, PhD); *m* 8 July 1978, Ann-Marie Teresa, da of Bernard Sommereux; 2 da (Charlotte Louise b 16 May 1981, Sophie Marie b 25 March 1989); *Career* house physician: Queen Elizabeth Hosp Birmingham 1965 (house surgn Dept of Neuro-Surgery 1964), Children's Hosp Birmingham 1965; SHO Warwick Hosp 1966–67, Sheldon clinical res fell Dept of Pathology Warwick Hosp and Dept of Biochemistry Queen Elizabeth Hosp 1967–68, house physician Dept of Neurology Hammersmith Hosp London 1968, asst lectr Dept of Med Royal Post Grad Med Sch London 1968–69, med registrar The Gen Hosp Birmingham 1970–71, sr med registrar Nutritional and Intestinal Unit United Birmingham Hosps 1972–74 and 1975–76, US post-doctoral res fell Gastroenterology Unit Mayo Grad Sch of Med Rochester Minnesota 1974–75, hon prof of med, conslt physician (with an interest in gastroenterology) 1977–2006, dir of med educn Univ Hosp Birmingham NHS Tst (dep med dir 2002–06), dir of pubns and ed Clinical Medicine jl RCP 2006–, conslt advsr in gastroenterology to Royal Navy 2000–; Br Soc of Gastroenterology: past pres, chm Cncl 2002–03, ed GUT 1988–95, memb Educn and Sci Ctee 1980–86 and 1990–95, memb Clinical Servs Ctee 1993–97; chm: Endowment Research Fund Univ Hosp Birmingham NHS Tst 1993–2000, Ctee on Gastroenterology and Hepatology RCP 2002–03; regnl Royal Coll advsr RCP 1993–97; memb British Soc of Gastroenterology 1974; FRCP 1980; *Books* Inflammatory Bowel Diseases (1983, 3 edn 1996), Gastroenterology Textbook of Clinical Science and Practice (1984, 2 edn 1993), author of pubns on the epidemiology, incidence, prognosis and cancer risk in inflammatory bowel disease; *Recreations* opera, political biography, gardening; *Style—* Prof Robert Allan; ✉ 5 Carpenter Road, Edgbaston, Birmingham B15 2JT (tel 0121 454 1943, e-mail robertnallan@aol.com)

ALLAN, Robert William; s of William Bennett Allan (d 1986), of NY, USA, and Mona Teresa, Bradley, *née* Langford; *b* 4 May 1945; *Educ* Xaverian Coll Brighton; *m* 15 July 1979, Elizabeth (d 2000), da of John Jackson, of Newcastle; 2 da (Charlotte b 1979, Kirsty b 1982); *Career* admitted slr 1967; ptnr: Roney & Co 1971–73, Simons Muirhead & Allan 1973–86, Denton Wilde Sapte 1986–2003, Mayer Brown Rowe & Maw LLP 2003–; memb Law Soc; *Recreations* music, food, wine, skiing, clay pigeon shooting, travel; *Clubs* Groucho; *Style—* Robert W Allan, Esq; ✉ Mayer Brown Rowe & Maw LLP, 11 Pilgrim Street, London EC4V 6RW (tel 020 7782 8549, fax 020 7782 8155, e-mail rallan@mayerbrownrowe.com)

ALLAN, Stephen David; s of Gerry Allan, of London, and Sonja, *née* Geiringer; *b* 26 June 1963; *Educ* City of London Sch; *m* 21 March 1991, Hayley Sara, da of Jeffrey Frankel; *Career* mangr Fotofast 1981, trainee media exec Yershon Media 1981; The Media Business Group plc (floated 1995): media exec 1982, assoc dir 1986, bd dir holding co 1987, equity shareholder 1988, first dir of new business 1989–93, md 1993– (merged with Mediacom 1998); Mediacom: joint md 1998–2000, chief exec 2000–04, vice-chm 2004– (taken over by WPP 2005); ceo Group M 2006–; MIPA 1988; *Recreations* football, golf, shooting, travel; *Clubs* Coombe Hill Golf; *Style—* Stephen Allan, Esq; ✉ 124 Theobald's Road, London WC1X 8RX (tel 020 7158 5000, fax 020 7158 5003, e-mail stephen.allan@groupm.com)

ALLAN, Timothy Neil (Tim); s of Dr Tom and Helen Allan, of Godalming; *b* 5 March 1970; *Educ* Royal GS Guildford, Godalming Coll, Sorbonne Paris, Pembroke Coll Cambridge (BA), INSEAD (MBA); *Partner* Ms Carey Scott; *Career* restaurant reviewer Paupers' Paris 1989, researcher for Rt Hon Tony Blair, MP 1992–94 (as oppn spokesman on home affrs), prodr A Week in Politics Channel Four TV 1994, press offr to Rt Hon Tony Blair, MP 1994–98 (as ldr of Oppn 1994–97 and Prime Minister 1997–98), dir of corp communications BSkyB 1998–2001; fndr Portland 2001–; *Recreations* football, golf, New York, not reading newspapers, wine tasting; *Clubs* Soho House; *Style—* Tim Allan, Esq

ALLARDYCE, Sam; *b* 19 October 1954, Dudley; *Career* professional footballer and manager; clubs as player: Bolton Wanderers 1969–1980 (debut 1973, winners Second Division 1978), Sunderland 1980–81, Millwall 1981–83, Tampa Bay Rowdies (USA) 1983, Coventry City 1983–84, Huddersfield Town 1984–85, Bolton Wanderers 1985–86, Preston North End 1986–89; player-coach: West Bromwich Albion 1989–91, Preston North End 1992–93; mangr: Limerick (Ireland) 1993–94, Blackpool 1994–96, Notts County 1997–99 (winners Third Division 1998), Bolton Wanderers 1999–2007 (promoted to Premier League 2001), Newcastle United 2007–; *Style—* Mr Sam Allardyce

ALLASON, Julian Edward Thomas; s of Lt-Col James Harry Allason, OBE, FRSA; *Educ* Downside, Univ of Sussex, Aix-en-Provence Univ, St John's Coll Nottingham; *m* 1976 (m dis 1989), Jessica Marland, da of Richard Thomas Wingert, of Conn, USA; 2 s (James b 1980, Benjamin b 1984), 1 da (Chloe b 1982); m 2, 1999, Dr Sarah King; 2 s (Gabriel b 2000, Raphael b 2004); *Career* dir: Apricot Computers plc 1979–86, Sharp Technology Fund plc 1984–99; md The Blackthorn Gp 1989–; author; publisher Microcomputer Printout Magazine 1979–83; columnist: The Observer 1981–83, Daily Telegraph 1983–86; contrib ed Condé Nast magazines 1997–2002; contrib FT 1999–; JP Inner London 1973–78; memb Information Technol NEDC 1984–86; Knight SMOM 1985 (Cdr of Merit 1989), Knight Order of St Maurice and St Lazarus 1995 (Cdr 1998); *Books* The Pet Companion (1981), English Legal Heritage (co-ed, 1979), Prayers of the Order of Malta (1990), Counselling and Happiness (1997), Ringside Seat (ed, 2006); *Recreations* photography, messing about in boats; *Clubs* White's, Jet; *Style—* Julian Allason, Esq; ✉ PO Box 41, Wallingford, Oxfordshire OX10 6TD (fax 01491 641017)

ALLASON, Rupert William Simon; s of Lt-Col James Harry Allason, OBE, FRSA; *b* 8 November 1951; *Educ* Downside, Univ Hall Buckland, Univ of Lille, Univ of Grenoble; *m* 1979 (m dis 1996), Nicole Jane, da of M L Van Moppes (d 1963), of Bermuda; 1 s (Thomas b 1980), 1 da (Alexandra b 1987); *Career* author (pen name Nigel West); special constable 1975–82, BBC TV 1978–82, Euro ed Intelligence Quarterly 1985–; Parly candidate (Cons): Kettering 1979, Battersea 1983; MP (Cons) Torbay 1987–97; *Books* The Branch - A History of the Metropolitan Police Special Branch 1883–1983 (1983); as Nigel West: SPY! (with Richard Deacon, 1980), MI5 (1981), A Matter of Trust (1982), MI6 (1983), Unreliable Witness (1984), GARBO (with Juan Pujol, 1985), GCHQ (1986), Molehunt (1987), The Friends (1988), Games of Intelligence (1989), The Blue List (1989), Cuban Bluff (1990), Seven Spies (1991), Secret War (1992), The Faber Book of Espionage (ed, 1993), The Illegals (1993), The Faber Book of Treachery (1995), The Secret War for the Falklands (1997), Counterfeit Spies (1998), Crown Jewels (with Oleg Tsarev, 1998), Venona (1999), The Third Secret (2000), Mortal Crimes (2004), The Guy Liddell Diaries (2005), MASK (2005), The Historical Dictionary of British Intelligence (2005), At Her Majesty's Secret Service (2006), Historical Dictionary of Cold War Counter-Intelligence (2007); *Recreations* skiing, sailing; *Clubs* White's, Special Forces, Royal Yacht Sqdn; *Style—* Rupert Allason, Esq; ✉ 6 Burton Mews, London SW1W 9EP (tel 020 7352 1110)

ALLCOCK, Anthony (Tony); MBE; s of Ernest Stacey Allcock (d 1999), and Joan Winifred Allcock (d 1986); *b* 11 June 1955; *Educ* Norwich City Coll; *Career* bowls player; world outdoor champion 1980, 1984 and 1988, world outdoor singles champion 1992 and 1996, world indoor singles champion 1986, 1987 and 2002, world indoor pairs champion (with David Bryant, CBE) 1986, 1987, 1989, 1990, 1991, 1992 and 1996, world pairs champion (with David A Holt) 2003; Eng Bowls Capt 1998–; chief exec English Bowling Assoc 2003–; patron English Nat Assoc of Visually Handicapped Bowlers; *Books* Improve your Bowls (1988), Step by Step Guide to Bowls (1988), End to End - a year in bowls (1989), Bowl to Win (1994); *Recreations* countryside, opera, horses, antiques, showing and breeding dogs; *Clubs* Cheltenham Bowling, Cotswold and Mid Glos; *Style—* Tony Allcock, Esq, MBE; ✉ Holly Cottage, Church Lane, Ferring, West Sussex BN12 5HN

ALLCOCK, John Paul Major; s of John Gladding Major Allcock, CB (d 1986), and Eileen Winifred Arnold, *née* Baiss (d 2003); *b* 8 July 1941; *Educ* St Edward's Sch Oxford, KCL (BSc), Faculté Polytechnique de Mons Belgium (Maîtrise en Science Appliquée); *m* 7 Nov 1981 (m dis 1992), Caroline Anne, da of Arthur Frederick Lyle Rocke, of Olney, Maryland, USA; 2 da (Arabella Louise b 27 April 1983, Lucinda Anne b 20 Feb 1990), 1 s (Oliver John Llewelyn b 1 March 1985); *Career* chartered patent agent 1968, admitted slr 1977, ptnr specialising in intellectual property Bristows (formerly Bristows Cooke & Carpmael) 1981–2002 (conslt 2002–05); European patent attorney 1978, registered trade mark agent 1990; memb Law Soc; fell Chartered Inst of Patent Agents 1968, MIEE 1971, CEng 1971; *Recreations* sailing, walking and travelling; *Style—* John Allcock, Esq; ✉ e-mail jpallcock@aol.com

ALLDAY, John Philip; s of Philip Frederick Allday (d 1994), of Northwood, Middx, and Kathleen Mary Clifford Green (d 2003); *b* 8 September 1939; *Educ* Bradfield Coll; *m* 22 Aug 1992, Leonie Ann, da of (Leonard) Keith Robinson, CBE, DL (d 2003); 1 da (Susannah Mayne b 2 Sept 1969), 1 s (Andrew Charles Philip b 8 Oct 1971), 1 step s (Christopher Michael b 10 July 1975), 1 step da (Catherine Clara b 12 Nov 1977); *Career* Turquands Barton Mayhew & Co (formerly Barton Mayhew & Co): articled clerk 1958–63, accountant 1963–75, ptnr 1975–79; ptnr Ernst & Young (formerly Ernst & Whinney) 1979–99 (nat dir of valuation 1989–99); memb Worshipful Co of Needlemakers; FCA; *Recreations* golf, cricket, gardening, music; *Clubs* MCC, Burnham & Berrow Golf; *Style—* John Allday, Esq; ✉ The Old Farmhouse, Bullocks Lane, Kingston Seymour, North Somerset BS21 6XA (tel 01934 876528, fax 01934 835720)

ALLDIS, Christopher John; s of John Henry Alldis (d 1981), and Isabel Marjorie, *née* Carter (d 1999); *b* 16 May 1947; *Educ* Birkenhead Sch, Emmanuel Coll Cambridge (MA, LLB);

m 14 Sept 1985, Marcia Elizabeth, *née* Kidman; 2 da (Amy Elizabeth b 1987, Rebecca Isabel Amelia b 1989); *Career* called to the Bar Gray's Inn 1970; practising Northern Circuit, recorder of the Crown Court 1994–; *Recreations* gliding, light aviation, skiing, fishing; *Clubs* Naval and Military; *Style*— Christopher Alldis, Esq; ✉ Romsdal, 3 Prenton Lane, Birkenhead, Merseyside (tel 0151 608 1828); Oriel Chambers, Water Street, Liverpool (tel 0151 236 4321, fax 0151 236 3332, e-mail christopheralldis@compuserve.com)

ALLDRITT, Prof Keith; *b* 10 December 1935, Wolverhampton, W Midlands; *Educ* Wolverhampton GS, St Catharine's Coll Cambridge; *m* Joan Hardwick; 2 s (Mark, Benjamin), 1 da (Miranda); *Career* lektor Univ of Vienna 1957–58, asst prof Univ of Illinois 1958–63, prof Univ of Br Columbia 1963–2000; Master Teacher Award Univ of Br Columbia; memb Soc of Authors; FRSL 1977; *Books* The Good Pitman (1976), The Lover Next Door (1977), Elgar on the Journey to Hanley (1979), T S Eliot's Four Quartets (1987), The Greatest of Friends - Winston Churchill and Franklin Roosevelt 1941–45 (1995), The Poet as Spy (1997), W B Yeats: A Biography (1998), David Jones: Writer and Artist (2003); *Recreations* classical music, opera; *Style*— Prof Keith Alldritt; ✉ c/o David Higham Associates Ltd, 5–8 Lower John Street, Golden Square, London W1F 9HA (tel 020 7437 7888, fax 020 7437 1072)

ALLEN, Prof Adrian; s of Philip John Frances Allen (d 1979), of Bognor Regis, W Sussex, and Mary Isobel, *née* Parry (d 1985); *b* 27 January 1938; *Educ* ChCh Oxford (MA, DPhil); *m* 22 July 1960, Pauline Elizabeth; 3 da (Susan b 1961, Deborah b 1965, Katherine b 1967), 1 s (Adam b 1969); *Career* Univ of Newcastle upon Tyne: lectr 1967, reader 1976, prof of physiological biochemistry 1980–2003, emeritus prof 2003–; *Recreations* ornithology, hill walking; *Style*— Prof Adrian Allen; ✉ 46 Heddon Banks, Heddon on the Wall, Newcastle upon Tyne NE15 0BU (tel 01661 852664)

ALLEN, Benedict; *Educ* Bradfield Coll, UEA (BSc); *Career* author and explorer; TV presenter and filmmaker, pioneer of the filming of authentic expeditions for TV; walked and canoed (with indigenous help) 600 miles across NE Amazonia 1983, made first contact with threatened Obini people (Irian Jaya), first outsider to undergo secret sacred Niowra male initiation ceremony Papua New Guinea 1984–85, investigated apemen stories Sumatra 1987, first contact with threatened Yaifo people Papua New Guinea, crossed Central Range of Papua New Guinea and (by small craft with two companions) Torres Strait from New Guinea to Aust to live with Aboriginals in Gibson Desert 1988–89, crossed (often alone on foot) Amazon Basin at widest point (5600 km), walked entire length (1000 miles) of Skeleton Coast/Namib Desert Namibia 1996 (first to be allowed to make this journey), 5.5 month trek by horse and camel through Mongolia (incl 6 week lone crossing of the Gobi Desert) 1997, obtained point-of-view of indigenous people accused of murder of Col Fawcett 1998, researched and filmed Last of the Medicine Men (first major TV documentary series on practises of shamans and medicine men) 2000, journeyed (with dogteams with assistance of Chukchi people) 1000 miles through Siberia 2001; supporter: Survival Int, Save the Rhino, Orang Utan Fndn; FRAI 1985, FRGS 1985; *Television* Raiders of the Lost Lake 1995, Mombasa to the Mountains of the Moon 1996, The Skeleton Coast 1997, Edge of Blue Heaven 1998, The Bones of Colonel Fawcett 1998, Last of the Medicine Men 2000, Ice Dogs 2002, The Big Read: His Dark Materials 2003, Adventure for Boys: The Lost Worlds of Rider Haggard (2006); *Publications* Mad White Giant (1985), Into the Crocodile Nest (1987), Hunting the Gugu (1989), The Proving Grounds (1991), Through Jaguar Eyes (1994), More Great Railway Journeys (jtly, 1996), The Skeleton Coast (1997), Edge of Blue Heaven (1998), Last of the Medicine Men (2000), The Faber Book of Exploration (2002), Into the Abyss (2006); *Style*— Benedict Allen, Esq; ✉ 9 Redan Street, London W14 0AB (e-mail info@benedictallen.com)

ALLEN, Charles Lamb; CBE; *b* 4 January 1957; *Career* accountant British Steel 1974–79, dep audit mangr TM Gp Galaghers plc 1979–82; Grand Metropolitan plc: dir GrandMet International Services Ltd 1982–85, gp md Compass Vending and Grand Metropolitan Innovations Ltd 1986–87, md GIS Middle East Ltd 1987–88; md Compass Group plc (following buyout from GrandMet) 1988–91; chief exec Leisure Div Granada Gp plc 1991–92, chief exec Granada TV 1992–96 (chm 1996–), chm Granada Leisure and Services to Business Div 1994–2000, chief exec LWT (following takeover by Granada) 1994–96 (chm 1996–), chief operating offr Granada Gp plc 1995–96, chief exec Granada Gp plc 1996–2000, chm Forte plc (following takeover by Granada) 1996–, chm GMTV 1996–2000 (dep chm 1994–96), chm Yorkshire Tyne Tees Television 1997–, dep chm Granada Compass plc 2000–01, exec chm Granada plc 2000–04, chief exec ITV plc 2004–07, currently chm Grandmet Gp LLP and chief advsr Home Office; non-exec dir Tesco plc 1999–; Race for Opportunity 1997–2000; dir International Cncl; vice-pres RTS; dep chm Business in the Community 1997–; chm Br Hospitality Cncl 1998–2000, dir Br Hospitality Assoc 1998–2000, chm Manchester 2002 Commonwealth Games 2000–03, vice-chm London 2012 2003–; HRH The Prince of Wales Ambassador Award 1999; Hon DBA Manchester Metropolitan Univ 1999, Hon DLitt Univ of Salford 2002; fell Chartered Mgmnt Accountants (FCMA), FHCIMA, FRSA; *Recreations* theatre, swimming, travel; *Style*— Charles Allen, CBE

ALLEN, Dr Christopher Michael Colquhoun; s of Christopher Oswald Colquhoun Allen, of Kingsbridge, S Devon, and Barbara Louise, *née* Archer; *b* 1 December 1948; *Educ* Eastbourne Coll, Christ's Coll Cambridge (MA, MD), Guy's Hosp Med Sch; *m* 28 July 1973, Susan Valerie, da of Alan Douglas Belcher (d 1971), of Sheffield; 2 da (Kate b 1978, Joanna b Dec 1979), 1 s (Samuel b 1982); *Career* sr house offr: renal medicine St Thomas' Hosp 1976–77, Nat Hosp for Nervous Diseases 1977; hon sr registrar Dept of Neurology Guy's Hosp 1979–82 (house offr Med Professorial Unit 1973–74, med registrar 1977–79), neurology registrar Middx Hosp 1982–84, sr registrar in neurology Charing Cross Hosp 1984–86, conslt neurologist Addenbrooke's Hosp Cambridge 1986–, dean Sch of Clinical Med Univ of Cambridge 1996–2003; fell Wolfson Coll Cambridge 1996–; FRCP; *Books* The Management of Acute Stroke (1988), contrib (with Dr C Luek) Diseases of the Nervous System in Davidson's Textbook of Medicine (1999); *Recreations* listening to Mozart, writing book reviews, windsurfing, sailing; *Style*— Dr Christopher Allen; ✉ 232 Hills Road, Cambridge CB2 8QE (tel 01223 247694, fax 01223 414904, e-mail cmca100@cam.ac.uk); Department of Neurology, Addenbrooke's Hospital, Cambridge CB2 8QQ (tel 01223 216301, fax 01223 336941)

ALLEN, Fergus Hamilton; CB (1969); s of Charles Winckworth Allen (d 1971), of Dublin, and Marjorie Helen, *née* Budge (d 1986); *b* 3 September 1921; *Educ* Newtown Sch Waterford, Trinity Coll Dublin (MA, MAI, ScD); *m* 1947, Margaret Joan, da of Prof Michael J Gorman (d 1982), of Dublin; 2 da (Mary, Elizabeth); *Career* asst engr Sir Cyril Kirkpatrick and Partners 1943–48, Port of London Authy 1949–52, dir Hydraulics Res Station Dept of Scientific and Industrial Res (now SERC) 1958–65 (asst dir 1952–58), chief scientific offr Cabinet Office 1965–69, civil serv cmmr 1969–74, first civil serv cmmr Civil Serv Dept 1974–81; ICE: memb 1947–57, fell 1957–86, Telford Gold Medal 1958, memb Cncl 1962–67 and 1968–71; FRSL 2000; *Books* The Brown Parrots of Providencia (1993), Who Goes There? (1996), Mrs Power Looks Over the Bay (1999), Gas Light & Coke (2006); *Recreations* reading, gardening; *Clubs* Athenaeum; *Style*— Fergus Allen, Esq, CB; ✉ Dundrum, Wantage Road, Streatley, Reading, Berkshire RG8 9LB (tel 01491 873234, e-mail fergusallen@btinternet.com)

ALLEN, Gary James; CBE (1991), DL (1993); s of late Alfred Allen, of Sutton Coldfield, W Midlands, and late Alice Jane Allen; *b* 30 September 1944; *Educ* King Edward VI GS Birmingham, Univ of Liverpool (BCom); *m* 10 Sept 1966, Judith Anne, da of William Nattrass (d 1961); 3 s (Andrew b 1969, Anthony b 1971, James b 1979); *Career* md IMI Range Ltd 1973–77; IMI plc: dir 1978–2005, asst md 1985–86, chief exec 1986–2000, chm 2001–05; chm Eley Ltd 1981–85; non-exec dir: NV Bekaert SA Belgium 1987–, Marley plc 1989–97 (dep chm 1993–97), Birmingham European Airways 1989–91, London Stock Exchange 1994–, The Nat Exhibition Centre Ltd 1989–, Temple Bar Investment Tst plc 2001–; memb Cncl: Birmingham Chamber of Industry and Commerce 1983–98 (pres 1991–92, memb Bd 1994–96), Univ of Birmingham 1985–90 (hon life memb Ct 1984–), CBI 1986–99 (W Midlands Regnl Cncl 1983–89); Midland Businessman of the Year 1989; pres W Midlands Region Lord's Taverners 1994– (chm 1987–93, memb Cncl 1995–2001, tstee 1995–2001); memb Bd Birmingham Royal Ballet 1993–2003, pres Midlands Club Cricket Conf 1995–96, tstee Industry in Educn 1998–, chm Birmingham Children's Hosp Appeal 1995–2000; High Sheriff W Midlands 2002–03; Freeman Worshipful Co of Gunmakers; Hon DSc Univ of Birmingham 2003; FCMA 1985, CIMgt 1986, FRSA 1988; Order of Leopold II (Belgium) 2002; *Recreations* sport, reading, gardening, cooking; *Clubs* Lord's Taverners, RAC; *Style*— Gary J Allen, Esq, CBE, DL

ALLEN, Prof Sir Geoffrey; kt (1979); s of John James Allen, and Marjorie Allen, of Wingerworth, Derbys; *b* 29 October 1928; *Educ* Clay Cross Tupton Hall GS, Univ of Leeds (BSc, PhD); *m* 1973, Valerie Frances, da of Arthur Duckworth (d 1979); 1 da (Naomi); *Career* scientist; prof of chemical physics Univ of Manchester 1965–75, prof of chemical technol Imperial Coll London 1976–81; chm Sci Res Cncl 1977–81 (memb 1976); visiting fell Robinson Coll Cambridge 1980–; head res engrg Unilever 1981–90, dir Unilever plc and Unilever NV 1982–90, exec advsr Kobe Steel Ltd 1990–2000; pres: SCI 1990–92, Plastics and Rubber Inst 1990–91, Inst of Materials 1993–94; dir: Courtaulds plc (non-exec) 1987–93, Cambridge Quantum Fund 1990–94; chllr UEA 1994–2003; Hon MSc Univ of Manchester; Hon DUniv: Open Univ 1981, Univ of N London; Hon DSc: Univ of Durham 1984, UEA 1985, Univ of Bath 1985, Univ of Bradford 1985, Loughborough Univ 1985, Univ of Essex 1986, Keele Univ 1986, Univ of Leeds 1986, Cranfield Inst of Technol 1988, Surrey Univ 1989, Univ of Sheffield 1993; hon fell UMIST; CEng 1986, FRS 1976, Hon FIChemE 1989, Hon FCGI 1990, FREng 1993, Hon FIM 2002, FIC, FInstP, FRICS, FPRI; *Recreations* opera, walking, talking; *Style*— Prof Sir Geoffrey Allen, FRS, FREng; ✉ 18 Oxford House, 52 Parkside, London SW19 5NE (tel 020 8947 7459, fax 020 8879 1959)

ALLEN, Rev Canon Geoffrey Gordon; s of Walter Gordon Allen (d 1961), of Alton, Hampshire,and Joan Frances, *née* Aylward (d 1988); *b* 14 May 1939; *Educ* Alton Co Secdy Sch, KCL, Salisbury Theological Coll; *m* 1 Oct 1966, Geertruida Dina, da of Hendrik van Elswijk; 2 s (Hendrik Gordon Pieter b 14 June 1967, Johannes Geoffrey b 11 March 1971); *Career* ordained: deacon 1966, priest 1967; curate St Mary's Langley Bucks 1966–70; chaplain Missions to Seamen Tilbury Docks 1970–72, chaplain Schiedam Netherlands 1972–74 chaplain St Mary's Rotterdam 1978–83 (asst chaplain 1972–74), hon chaplain to HM Forces Antwerp 1974–78, chaplain Missions to Seamen Port of Rotterdam 1978–83, asst chaplain The Hague Voorschoten and Leiden 1983–93, canon Pro Cathedral Brussels Dio of Europe 1989–, chaplain East Netherlands Gp of Chaplaincies 1993–, archdeacon of NW Europe Dio of Europe 1993–2004; anglican rep Dutch Nat Cncl of Churches 1998–2004, pres Arnhem-Nijmegan Branch Royal Br Legion 1993–; chaplain Military and Hospital Order St Lazarus of Jerusalem 1982; *Recreations* bird watching, ornithology, nature ramblings, swimming, walking; *Clubs* Rotary (The Hague Metropolitan), Holterberg Past Rotarians, Penn; *Style*— Rev Canon Geoffrey Gordon Allen; ✉ Hans Brandts Buyslaan 22, 6952 BK Dieren, The Netherlands (tel 00 31 313 412 533, e-mail g.g.allen@zonnet.nl)

ALLEN, Graham William; MP; s of William Allen, and Edna, *née* Holt; *b* 11 January 1953; *Educ* Robert Shaw Primary, Forest Fields GS; *Career* warehouseman Nottingham 1971–72, Lab Pty res offr 1978–83, Local Govt offr GLC 1983–84, Trades Union nat co-ordinator Political Fund Ballots Campaign 1984–86, regnl res and educn offr GMBATU 1986–87, MP (Lab) Nottingham N 1987–; memb: Public Accounts Ctee 1988–90, Procedure Ctee, 1990 Fin Bill Ctee; chm PLP Treasy Ctee 1990–92; oppn frontbench spokesman on social security 1991–92, shadow min (democracy and the constitution) Home Office 1992–94, shadow min (media) Dept of Nat Heritage 1994–95, shadow min (buses, air and sea) Dept of Tport 1995–96, shadow min (health and safety) Dept of Environment 1996–97, a Lord Cmmr of HM Treasy (Govt whip) 1997–98, vice-chamberlain HM Household 1998–2001; *Publications* Reinventing Democracy (1995), The Last Prime Minister - Being Honest About the UK Presidency (2002); *Recreations* painting, golf, cooking, cricket, walking, democratising the UK; *Clubs* Basford Hall Miners' Welfare, Strelley Social, Dunkirk Cricket, Beechdale Community Assoc, Lords and Commons Cricket; *Style*— Graham W Allen, Esq, MP; ✉ House of Commons, London SW1A 0AA

ALLEN, Hugh Edward Keith; *b* 22 April 1934; *Educ* Oundle, Univ of Cambridge (MA), Royal Sch of Mines Imperial Coll London (BScEng); *m* 8 Aug 1959, Ann, *née* Barling; 5 c; *Career* Anglo/De Beers Gp: engr 1959–78, mangr Orapa Diamond Mine Botswana 1973–76; reader Imperial Coll London 1978–87, mining advsr RTZ Corporation plc 1987–90, dir RTZ Technical Services Ltd 1990–96, ptnr Allen Associates 1996–; Hon DSc 1997; ARSM, Hon FIMM (pres 1991–92), FREng 1993; *Style*— Hugh Allen, Esq, FREng; ✉ 12 Roxborough Park, Harrow on the Hill, Middlesex HA1 3BE (tel 020 8422 0300, fax 020 8426 4544, e-mail hugh_e_allen@compuserve.com)

ALLEN, Prof Dame Ingrid Victoria (Mrs Barnes Thompson); DBE (2001, CBE 1993), DL (1989); da of Rev Dr Robert Allen (d 1968), of Belfast, and Doris Victoria, *née* Shaw (d 1990); *b* 30 July 1932; *Educ* Ashleigh House Belfast, Cheltenham Ladies' Coll, Queen's Univ Belfast (MB BCh, BAO, MD, DSc); *m* 1, 30 May 1972, Alan Watson Barnes (d 1987), s of Sidney W Barnes (d 1992), of Martin Cross, Salisbury; m 2, 6 Sept 1996, Prof John Thompson; *Career* house offr Royal Victoria Hosp Belfast 1957–58; Queen's Univ Belfast: Musgrave res fell 1958–59, tutor in pathology 1959–61, Calvert res fell in multiple sclerosis 1961–64; sr registrar Pathology Dept Royal Victoria Hosp 1964–65; Queen's Univ Belfast and Royal Victoria Hosp: sr lectr and conslt in neuropathology 1966–78, reader and conslt in neuropathology 1978–79, prof of neuropathology, conslt and head Dept of Neuropathology 1979–97 (emeritus prof 1997); dir of R&D Health and Personal Social Services (HPSS) in NI 1997–2001; visiting prof Univ of Ulster; MRIA 1993, FRCPath 1965, FRCPI 1985, FRCPGlas 1987, FRCPE 1995, FMedSci 1998; *Books* Pathology of Multiple Sclerosis in McAlpine's Multiple Sclerosis (2 edn, 1980), Demyelinating Diseases in Greenfield's Neuropathology (5 edn, 1992); *Recreations* my local church, enjoying my island retreat in Donegal, Irish history, fashion, architecture; *Clubs* Athenaeum; *Style*— Prof Dame Ingrid V Allen, DBE, DL; ✉ 95 Malone Road, Belfast BT9 6SP (tel 028 9066 6662)

ALLEN, Isabel Clare; da of Very Rev John Edward Allen, *qv*, and Eleanor Allen; *b* 30 May 1968; *Educ* Univ of Manchester (BA), Univ of Westminster (RIBA pt I), South Bank Univ (DipArch, RIBA pt II, RIBA dissertation prize); *Career* journalist; ed Architects Jl 1999– (buildings ed 1996–99); memb Cncl AA; judge of various architectural awards incl RIBA Stirling Prize 2006; IBP Young Journalist of the Year 1997; *Publications* Structure as Design (2000); *Clubs* Architecture; *Style*— Ms Isabel Allen

ALLEN, James Hendricuss; QC (1995); *Educ* Morley GS, Univ of Nothumbria (BA); *Career* recorder of the Crown Court 1995–, dep judge of the High Court (Chancery Div and Queen's Bench Div) 2000–; asst parly cmmr for England 2000–; *Style*— James H Allen, Esq, QC; ✉ Barristers Chambers, 6 Park Square, Leeds LS1 2LW (tel 0113 245 9763, fax 0113 242 4395, e-mail chambers@no6.co.uk, website www.no6.co.uk)

ALLEN, Jeremy Roger; s of Guy Lancelot Allen (d 1990), and Joan Isobel Lingwood, *née* Wright (d 2005); *b* 5 July 1944, Bournemouth, Dorset; *Educ* Bedales, Coll of Law; *m* 24 Jan 1970, Margaret, *née* Gilbert; 2 s (Jonathan Guy b 5 March 1974, Nicholas William b 11 March 1982), 1 da (Charlotte Lucy b 16 March 1977); *Career* admitted slr 1970; articled Johnstone Sharp & Walker, with Raleigh Industries 1968–72, ptnr Hunt Dickins 1973–94 (asst slt 1972, managing ptnr 1987), co-fndr Poppleston Allen Licensing Slrs 1994; memb: Magistrates' Court Rule Ctee 1982–2002, Cncl Law Soc 1986–92 (chm Criminal Law Ctee 1987–91), Lord Chllr's Efficiency Cmmn 1987–89, Advsy Ctee on Licensing Act DCMS; legal dir: Bar Entertainment & Dance Assoc, Br Beer and Pub Assoc; memb Law Soc; companion Br Inst of Innkeeping; *Recreations* reading, theatre, running, watching sport; *Clubs* Nottingham and Notts United Servs; *Style—* Jeremy Allen, Esq; ✉ 10 Pelham Crescent, The Park, Nottingham NG7 1AW (tel 0115 947 3471); Poppleston Allen, 37 Stoney Street, The Lace Market, Nottingham NG1 1LS (tel 0115 953 8500, fax 0115 953 8501, e-mail jeremy@popall.co.uk)

ALLEN, Very Rev John Edward; s of Rev Canon Ronald Edward Taylor Allen, MC (d 1984), and Isabel Edith, *née* Otter-Barry (d 1994); *b* 9 June 1932; *Educ* Rugby, UC Oxford (MA), Fitzwilliam Coll Cambridge (MA), Westcott House Cambridge; *m* 1957, Eleanor, *née* Prynne; 1 s (Christopher), 3 da (Rebecca, Madeleine, Isabel, *qv*); *Career* chaplain Univ of Bristol 1971–79, vicar Chippenham 1979–82, provost Wakefield 1982–97 (provost emeritus 1997–); memb: Gen Synod C of E 1985–97, Bd of Social Responsibility C of E 1985–90, Bd of Mission 1991–96; vice-chm Partnership for World Mission 1987–96; vice-chm Wakefield HA 1991–97, chm Wakefield Med Research Ethics Ctee 1991–97, memb Multi-Centre Research Ethics Ctee Northern and Yorks Regn 1997–2001, chm Scarborough and NE Yorks Hosps NHS Tst 1997–2001; religious advsr Yorkshire Television 1994–96; govr Queen Elizabeth GS Wakefield 1982–98, chm of govrs Cathedral HS 1992–97; *Recreations* walking, fishing, people; *Style—* The Very Rev John Allen; ✉ The Glebe Barn, Sawdon, North Yorkshire YO13 9DY (tel 01723 859854, e-mail jeallen@globalnet.co.uk)

ALLEN, Prof John Edward; s of Thomas Edward Allen (d 1984), and Rose, *née* Boorman (d 1978); *b* 6 December 1928; *Educ* Univ of Liverpool (BEng, PhD, DEng), Univ of Cambridge (MA), Univ of Oxford (MA, DSc); *m* 16 July 1952, Margaret, da of Arthur Perrin (d 1965); *Career* res student then fell Electrical Engrg Dept Univ of Liverpool 1949–52, scientific offr then sr scientific offr AERE Harwell Controlled Thermonuclear Reaction Gp 1952–58, conslt and fndr memb Laboratorio Gas Ionizzati 1958–64, prof Univ of Rome 1958–64, asst dir of res Dept of Engrg Univ of Cambridge 1964–65, sr memb Churchill Coll Cambridge 1964–65, UC Oxford: reader then prof of engrg science, currently prof emeritus, fell 1965– (dean 1993–96, now emeritus fell); visiting prof in physics Imperial Coll London 2004–; chm: Plasma Physics Gp, Int Scientific Ctee Conf on Phenomene in Ionized Gases; memb Atomic and Molecular Physics Sub-Ctee Inst of Physics; memb various editorial bds, memb Plasma Panel Physics Ctee SERC; conslt: Ferranti, Oxford Plasma Technol, Solar Physics Corp, UKAEA; numerous publications in scientific jls on plasma physics, gas discharges and electrodynamics; IEE Achievement Medal for Science, Educn and Technol 1998, von Engel Prize Int Conf on Phenomena in Ionized Gases 2003, Inst of Physics Festschrift 2003, IEE Innovation Award 2005; fell American Physical Soc 1989; FInstP 1961, FIEE 1965; *Style—* Prof John Allen; ✉ University College, Oxford OX1 4BH (tel 01865 276602, fax 01865 276790, e-mail john.allen@univ.ox.ac.uk)

ALLEN, Prof John Walter; s of Walter Allen (d 1992), and B M Allen (d 1999); *b* 7 March 1928; *Educ* King Edward's HS Birmingham, Sidney Sussex Coll Cambridge (open major scholar, MA); *m* 1, Mavis Joan, *née* Williamson (d 1972); 1 s (Matthew John b 1962); m 2, 1981, Hania Renata, *née* Szawelska; *Career* Nat Serv RAF Educn Branch 1949–51; staff scientist Ericsson Telephones Beeston Nottingham 1951–56; research scientist Royal Naval Scientific Serv Electronics Research Lab 1956–64; visiting assoc prof Stanford Univ California 1964–66; Univ of St Andrews: Tullis Russell fell Dept of Physics 1968–72, reader in physics 1972–80, personal chair in solid state physics 1980–; memb American Physical Soc; FSA Scot, FRSE 1985; *Recreations* traditional dance, archaeology; *Style—* Prof John W Allen, FRSE; ✉ 2 Dempster Terrace, St Andrews, Fife KY16 9QQ (tel 01334 474163); Department of Physics and Astronomy, University of St Andrews, North Haugh, St Andrews, Fife KY16 9SS (tel 01334 463331, fax 01334 463104, e-mail jwa@st-andrews.ac.uk)

ALLEN, Dr Justin Norman Bertram; *b* 7 December 1945; *Educ* Northgate GS for Boys Ipswich, Guy's Hosp Med Sch (MB BS, LRCP MRCS, DObstRCOG, FRCGP 1986); *m* Sue; 3 c; *Career* pre-registration appts Guy's and Lewisham Hosps 1969–70, internship Pittsfield Massachusetts 1970–71, Ipswich Vocational Trg Scheme 1971–73, in gen practice 1973–2003 (sr ptnr 1980–92); RCGP: co-opted memb Cncl 1993–2005, memb Int Ctee 1993–2004, jt sec Jt Ctee on Postgraduate Training for Gen Practice 1993–2005, pres Euro Acad of Teachers in Gen Practice 2001–05; gp postgrad dean LNR Deanery 2001–06, hon prof of family medicine De Montfort Univ Leicester 2005–; author of various pubns in academic jls; *Style—* Prof Justin Allen; ✉ e-mail justinallen@btinternet.com

ALLEN, Keith Howell Charles; s of Edward Allen, and Mary Elizabeth, *née* John; *b* 2 September 1953; *Educ* Sir Anthony Browns Brentwood, Brune Park Comp Gosport; *Children* 1 da (Lily Rose b 2 May 1985), 1 s (Alfie b 11 Sept 1986); *Career* actor and writer; writer England World Cup Song (World in Motion) 1990 and Euro Cup Song (Englands Irie, with Black Grape) 1996, performed unofficial England World Cup Song (Vindaloo) 1998; *Theatre* acting credits incl: Street Trash (NT Studio), DC Barry Hooper in Murmuring Judges (RNT) 1993, Teddy in The Homecoming (RNT) 1997, The Room/Celebration (Almeida Theatre) 2000; as writer and performer: The Yob, The Bullshitters, Detectives on The Verge of a Nervous Breakdown, Whatever You Want, I Love Keith Allen; *Television* credits incl: Comic Strip Presents..., The Gatekeeper, Born to Run, Martin Chuzzlewit, Sharman, Dangerfield, A Very British Coup, The Life and Crimes of William Palmer, You Are Here, Roger Roger, Jack of Hearts, Bob Martin, Inspector Morse, Murder in Mind; *Films* incl: Shallow Grave, Trainspotting, Second Best, Loch Ness, Blue Juice, Scandal, Chicago Joe and the Showgirl, Kafka, Beyond Bedlam, Preaching to the Perverted, Mauvaise passe, Rancid Aluminium, My Wife is an Actress, Bear's Kiss; *Clubs* The Colony Room, Groucho; *Style—* Keith Allen, Esq

ALLEN, Kenton Paul Benbow; *b* 16 June 1967, Warks; *Educ* Grange Comp Stourbridge, King Edward VI Stourbridge; *m* Sept 1999, Imogen Edwards-Jones; 1 s (Zac Louis Kenton b July 1989), 1 da (Allegra Carmen Elizabeth b May 2005); *Career* prodr Granada TV 1995–2000, creative dir Shine Entertainment 2000–03, creative head of comedy BBC TV 2003–; columnist Broadcast magazine 2005–; Best Comedy (The Royle Family) BAFTA Awards 2000, Best Live Action Short (Six Shooter) Oscars 2006; memb: BAFTA, RTS; *Clubs* Soho House, Groucho; *Style—* Kenton Allen, Esq; ✉ Room 4020, BBC Television Centre, Wood Lane, London W12 7RJ (tel 07802 183583, e-mail kenton.allen@bbc.co.uk)

ALLEN, Leon R; *b* 21 April 1939; *Educ* Stanford Univ (BA); *Career* mktg mgmnt and general mgmnt Procter & Gamble Co 1961–79, vice-pres Clorox 1979–82; RJR Nabisco 1982–90: vice-pres Latin America Del Monte and Canada Dry 1982–86, regnl dir Northern Latin America Int Nabisco Brands 1986–88, pres and chief exec Del Monte Foods Europe 1988–90; chm and chief exec: Del Monte Foods Int Ltd 1990–93, Tetley Gp Ltd 1995–99; chm: Devro plc 1992–98, Braes Group Ltd 1999, Appleshaw Group Ltd; non-exec dir Abbey National plc 1998–2004; *Style—* Leon Allen; ✉ Appleshaw Group Ltd, Suite 21, Phoenix House, Caxton Close, East Portway Industrial Estate, Andover, Hampshire SP10 3FG (e-mail leon.allen@bigfoot.com)

ALLEN, Leonard; s of Joseph Allen (d 1956), of Bournemouth, and Henrietta Emily, *née* Fowle; *b* 30 November 1930; *m* 1, 1955 (m dis 1969), Diana, *née* Love; m 2, 27 April 1970, Theodora Jane, da of John Russell (d 1984), of Caversham, Reading; 1 da (Henrietta Sophie b 1972); *Career* public affairs advsr; Nat Serv RTR 1949–50; Cons Central Office: agent Reading 1959–64, political educn offr Eastern Area 1964–67 (dep area agent 1967–74), dep dir and head Local Govt Dept 1974–77; chief exec Fedn of Recruitment and Employment Servs 1977–93, dep chm Machinery Users' Assoc 1995–98, dep chm MUA Management Services Ltd 1995–98; sec gen Int Confedn of Temp Work Businesses 1990–93 (currently advsr); conslt T L Dallas (City) Ltd 1995–, corp affrs dir Stirling Recruitment Group Ltd 1996–; policy advsr CBI 1998–; vice-chm Southern Region UNs Assoc 1955–57, chm Recruitment Soc 1982–84, memb Governing Body SPCK 1977–80, vice-chm Bow Gp 1959–64, memb DOE Advsy Ctee on Women's Employment 1980–92; govr Battle Abbey Sch; Freeman: City of London 1978, Worshipful Co of Woolmen; memb NUJ, MIPR, FRSA; *Recreations* conversation, music, reading, art galleries, dining out and in; *Clubs* Athenaeum, IOD, Leander, West Norfolk Hunt Supporters'; *Style—* Leonard Allen, Esq; ✉ 1 Cottage Farm Mews, The Street, Marham, King's Lynn, Norfolk PE33 9JQ (tel 01760 338201, mobile 07913 332314, e-mail leoadvise@supanet.com)

ALLEN, Mary; *b* 22 August 1951; *Educ* Sch of St Helen and St Katherine, New Hall Cambridge (BA); *Career* actress BBC, West End and repertory 1973–76, agent London Management 1977–78, arts sponsorship mangr Mobil Oil Company Ltd 1978–81, asst dir Assoc for Business Sponsorship of The Arts 1982–83, training conslt 1986–90, arts mgmnt conslt 1983–90, dir Watermans Arts Centre 1990–92, sec-gen Arts Cncl of England 1994–97 (dep sec-gen 1992–94), chief exec Royal Opera House 1997–98; chm Breast Cancer Campaign 2002–06; chm Public Art Devpt Tst 1983–92, memb Art Panel and Ethnic Minority Arts Ctee and advsr to Percent for Art Steering Gp Arts Cncl 1986–90, memb Bd Cheek by Jowl 1989–92, tstee City of London Festival 2003–05; mentor IDDAS (Independent Direction Directors Advsy Serv); *Books* Sponsoring The Arts: New Business Strategies for the 1990s, A House Divided; *Style—* Ms Mary Allen

ALLEN, Peter; *b* 4 February 1946; *Career* journalist with various newspapers in England and Australia 1965–73, political corr then political ed LBC/IRN 1973–83, political ed Granada TV 1983–86, chief political corr ITN 1986–93, political ed and prog presenter LWT 1993–94; presenter: 5 Live Breakfast BBC Radio 5 Live 1994–98, Drive Time BBC Radio 5 Live 1998–; Best News Presentation Sony Awards 1996, Best Breakfast Prog Sony Awards 1998, Best Radio Prog TRIC 1998, Sony News Broadcaster of the Year 2002; *Recreations* golf, waiting for Spurs to be great again, bird-watching; *Style—* Peter Allen, Esq; ✉ BBC Radio 5 Live, Wood Lane, London W12 7RJ

ALLEN, Peter William; s of Alfred William Allen (d 1987), of Sittingbourne, Kent, and Myra Nora, *née* Rogers (d 1982); *b* 22 July 1938; *Educ* Borden GS, Sidney Sussex Coll Cambridge (MA); *m* 1965, Patricia Mary, da of Joseph Frederick Dunk, of Sheffield; 3 da (Samantha, Joanna, Annabel); *Career* RAF 1957–59; Coopers & Lybrand: joined 1963, qualified CA 1966, ptnr 1973, chm Int Personnel Ctee 1975–78, ptnr i/c London Office 1983, managing ptnr 1984–90, memb UK Mgmnt Ctee 1984–90, memb Int Exec Ctee 1988–90 and 1992–94, dep chm Coopers & Lybrand 1990–94 (memb Bd 1990–94), chm Mgmnt Consulting Servs UK 1990–94; non-exec dir: Charter plc 1994–2001, Schroder Ventures Group 1994–, The Post Office 1995–98; memb Governing Bd Lister Inst of Preventive Med 1998–2005; memb Bd BRCS 1999–2000; Freeman City of London 1988, Liveryman Worshipful Co of Glaziers and Painters of Glass 1989–2003; FCA 1969, CIMgt 1993–2003; *Recreations* golf, painting; *Clubs* Reform; *Style—* Peter W Allen, Esq; ✉ John O'Gaddesden's House, Little Gaddesden, Berkhamsted, Hertfordshire HP4 1PF (tel 01442 842148)

ALLEN, Prof Raymond William Kenneth (Ray); s of Raymond Kenneth Allen, of Bishopstoke, Hants, and Dee, *née* Powell; *b* 14 February 1948; *Educ* Portsmouth GS, UMIST (MSc), McGill Univ Montreal (PhD); *m* April 1978, Rosemarie; 3 da (Aemelia Catherine Payard b 1979, Hermione Sarah Payard b 1990, Beatrice Eleanor Payard b 1994), 1 s (Sebastian Alexander Payard b 1983); *Career* Harwell Res Laboratory: industry res fell 1975–95, head Environmental and Process Engrg Dept 1988–93, head Tech Area for Chemical and Process Engrg 1990–95, business devpt dir 1993–95; prof of chemical engrg Univ of Sheffield 1995– (head Dept of Chemical and Process Engrg 1995–2000), seconded DTI Innovation Unit 1995–98; visiting prof Dept of Chemical Engrg Univ of Newcastle upon Tyne 1989–93; tech ed Filtration and Separation Jl 1983–88; memb: Editorial Bd Jl of Separation Technol 1979–89, Chemicals Sector Foresight Panel 1996–99; memb Cncl Filtration Soc 1985–86 (chm 1985–86), chm Standing Conf of Chemical Engrg Profs 2000–06, pres Engrg Profs Cncl 2006–; FIChemE 1986 (memb Cncl 1990–92 and 2000–02), FREng 1993; *Recreations* practical politics, fireworks, almost any activity with my family; *Style—* Prof Ray Allen, FREng; ✉ Department of Chemical and Process Engineering, University of Sheffield, Mappin Street, Sheffield S1 3JD (tel 0114 222 7600, fax 0114 276 2154, e-mail r.w.k.allen@sheffield.ac.uk)

ALLEN, Robert Edward; s of Edward Allen (d 1964), of Liverpool, and Elsie Allen; *b* 2 September 1946; *Educ* Liverpool Collegiate Sch; *m* 1972, Ann-Marie; 1 da (Sophie Elizabeth b 1978), 1 s (Oliver Edward b 1982); *Career* NHS mgmnt trainee Liverpool 1965–69, asst hosp sec Winchester 1969–71, dep hosp sec Wolverhampton 1971–74, sector administrator Hull 1974–76, dist support servs mangr SE Kent Health Authy 1976–79, asst dist administrator S Nottingham Dist Health Authy 1979–82, dep dist administrator Nottingham Dist Health Authy 1982–85, gen mangr Seacroft and Killingbeck Hosps Leeds 1985–90, dist gen mangr Airedale Health Authy 1990–92, chief exec Airedale NHS Tst 1992–; MHSM (DipHSM); memb Inst of Health Services Mgmnt; *Recreations* family, squash, walking, swimming, cycling, running; *Style—* Robert E Allen, Esq

ALLEN, Robert Geoffrey Bruère (Robin); QC (1995); s of Rev Canon Ronald Edward Taylor Allen (d 1984), of Ludlow, Salop, and Isabel Edith Allen (d 1994); *b* 13 February 1951; *Educ* Rugby, UC Oxford (MA); *m* 3 Sept 1977, (Elizabeth) Gay, da of Dr Anthony James Moon, of Rickmansworth, Herts; 2 s; *Career* co-organiser Free Representation Unit 1973; called to the Bar Middle Temple 1974 (bencher 2004); in practice 1976–, employment law advsr to Legal Action Gp 1978–80, legal advsr to Local Govt Gp Inst of PR 1988–90, asst recorder 1997–2000, recorder 2000–, head Cloisters Barr's Chambers 2002–; expert advsr to EC on UK law affecting the most disadvantaged 1993; sec Lambeth Central Constituency Lab Party 1977; chm: London Youth Advsy Centre 1984–90, Bd of Govrs Eleanor Palmer Sch 1988–91, Brandon Centre 1991–93; Employment Law Bar Assoc: fndr ctee memb 1994–, vice-chm 1996, chm 1997–99; chm Bar Pro Bono Unit 2000–02 (vice-chm 1996–2000); memb Bar Cncl 1999–2001, chm Bar Conf 2002 (vice-chm 2001); memb Home Office Human Rights Task Force 1999–2001, special advsr to Disability Rights Cmmn 2002–; conslt: Age Concern 2004–, Age Europe 2004–; tstee London Bombing Relief Charitable Fund 2005–; *Television* The Great Ape Trial (Channel 4) 1995; *Books* How to Prepare a Case for an Industrial Tribunal (1987), Employment Law Manual (contrib, 1988), Civil Liberty (contrib, 1989), The Legal Framework and Social Consequences of Free Movement of Persons in the European Union (contrib, 1998), Women Work and Inequality, the Challenge of Equal Pay in a Deregulated Labour Market (contrib, 1999), Study Guide to Human Rights Act (ed, 2000), Bullen and Leake and Jacob's Precedents of Pleading (contrib, 2001), The Legal Regulation of the

Employment Relationship (contrib, 2001), Human Rights and Employment Law (2002, 2 edn 2007), A proposal for a Council Directive implementing the principle of equal treatment in respect of Age (2006), Equality Law in an Enlarged Europe (contrib, 2007); *Recreations* family life, fishing, fireworks; *Style*— Robin Allen, Esq, QC; ✉ Cloisters, 1 Pump Court, Temple, London EC4Y 7AA (tel 020 7827 4000, fax 020 7827 4100)

ALLEN, Simon John Nicholas; s of Adrian Allen, of Sheffield, and Sheila, *née* Moore; *b* 6 August 1959, Preston, Lancs; *Educ* Preston Catholic Coll, De La Salle Coll Sheffield, Leicester Poly (BA), Chester Law Sch; *m* 4 Aug 1987, Rosalind Ann, *née* Howe; 2 da (Gabrielle Julia b 22 Oct 1989, Susannah Fiona b 1 April 1998), 1 s (Sebastian Charles b 12 March 1992); *Career* slr; Brian Thompson & Partners 1985–89 (ptnr 1988–89); Russell Jones & Walker: slr 1989, ptnr 1990–, jt head Personal Injury Dept 2005–; memb: Law Soc (Personal Injury Panel assessor 2002), Sheffield Law Soc, Assoc of Trial Lawyers of America 1985, Assoc of Personal Injury Lawyers (APIL) 1986; *Publications* APIL Guide to Damages (2005), Kemp & Kemp: Personal Injury Law Practice and Procedure (2006), APIL Personal Injury Law Practice and Precedents (2006); writer Personal Injury Update section Law Soc Gazette; *Recreations* family, photography, studying Italian, supporting Sheffield United and Manchester United; *Style*— Simon Allen, Esq; ✉ Russell Jones & Walker, 7th Floor, Fountain Precinct, 1 Balm Green, Sheffield S1 2JA (tel 0114 276 6868, fax 0114 252 5600, e-mail s.j.allen@rjw.co.uk); 234 Millhouses Lane, Ecclesall, Sheffield S11 9JA (tel 0114 262 0782)

ALLEN, Brig Simon Richard Burton; s of William Richard Burton Allen (d 1990), and Anne Frederica, *née* Thwaites (d 1985); *b* 5 November 1952; *Educ* Rugby, RMA Sandhurst; *m* 3 Sept 1976, Ferlina Diana, da of late Sir William Lindsay; 2 da (Claire Diana b 16 Sept 1978, Camilla Anne 26 March 1982), 1 s (Richard William Burton b 28 Aug 1984); *Career* cmmnd Royal Scots Dragoon Gds 1972, student Staff Coll 1984; Cdr RAC Demonstration Sqdn Warminster 1987–88, instr Staff Coll 1990–93, Cdr Royal Scots Dragoon Gds 1993–95, COS HQ Dir Royal Armoured Corps 1995–99, memb RCDS 1999, Cdr 51 Highland Bde 1999–2002, COS Kosovo Force 2002–; pres The Regular Cmmns Bd 2003–; chm: Army Point to Point, Army Alpine Skiing; *Recreations* National Hunt racing, point to point racing, fishing; *Clubs* Cavalry and Guards'; *Style*— Brig Simon Allen; ✉ Regular Commissions Board (tel 01373 828141)

ALLEN, Steve James; s of James Arthur Allen (d 1998), of Manchester, and Doris, *née* Waters (d 1998); *b* 29 January 1953; *Educ* South Wythenshawe HS, Mid-Cheshire Coll of Art & Design; *Career* photographer; Wythenshawe Gen Hosp: trainee med photographer 1972–74, qualified med photographer 1974–76, head of dept med illustration 1976–83; company dir Photographic Images (Manchester) Ltd 1983–89, sr ptnr Steve Allen Photography 1989–; Qualified European Photographer (QEP); int judge and speaker at nat and int photographic events in UK, Ireland, Norway, Singapore, Indonesia, Cyprus, Malta, Tunisia and Belgium, contrib numerous articles in professional photographic magazines; FBIPP, FMPA; *Recreations* photography, travel, reading; *Style*— Steve Allen, Esq; ✉ Steve Allen Photography, Lindon House, The Green, Slingsby, North Yorkshire YO62 4AA (tel and fax 01653 628687, e-mail mail@steveallenphotography.com, website www.steveallenphotography.com)

ALLEN, Susan Jennifer (Susie); da of Henry Francis Metcalfe (d 1991), and Yolande, *née* Senior-Ellis (d 1999); *b* 12 May 1949; *Educ* Kingston Poly (BA), RCA (MA), Cite Int des Arts Paris (RCA travelling scholarship); *m* 1, 1969 (m dis 1985); m 2, 1990, Prof Paul Huxley, RA, *qv*; *Career* artist and curator; cmmnd to design sets and costumes IBIS Dance Co Theatre Royal Stratford East 1982; curator RCA Collection 1989–99 (Fine Art Devpt Office RCA 1994–99), dir Artwise Curators Ltd 1996–; pt/t and visiting lectr 1981–99: RCA, Wimbledon Sch of Art, Kingston Poly, Ruskin Sch of Drawing Univ of Oxford, Chelsea Coll of Art, Central/St Martin's Coll of Art, Edinburgh Coll of Art; contemporary art consltt: British Airways, NACF, CAS, Wedgwood, TI Group, Visa Int, Virgin Atlantic Airways, Absolut Vodka; recipient NACF Award for Outstanding Services to the Arts 1988–89; FRCA 1990, FRSA 2002; *Selected Exhibitions* New Contemporaries ICA 1978–79, Demarco Gallery Edinburgh 1979, Edinburgh City Art Gall 1980, Mulhouse Print Biennale France 1981, 35 printmakers RCA touring exhbn UK and France 1983–86, Raab Gallery 1987, Artist's Choice V&A 1987, RCA Anniversary exhbn Barbican Art Gall 1987, Homage to the Square Flaxman Gallery 1988, Galerie zur Alten Deutschen Schule Switzerland 1989, 1990, 1992, 1993 and 1995, Cabinet Paintings Gillian Jason Gallery London and touring 1991–92, Artistic Assocs Gillian Jason Gallery 1992, Gallery 7 Hong Kong 1995, Thinking Eye Gallery 7 Hong Kong 1996 (and curator); *Work in Public Collections* South London Art Gallery, Scottish Arts Cncl, British Cncl, Govt Art Collection, V&A; *Curator* British Art Britain in Vienna British Art Show for Contemporary Art Soc Vienna 1986, Exhbn Road Painters at the RCA 1988, 3 Ways British Cncl touring exhbn E Europe and Africa 1989–96, Absolut RCA 1995, An American Passion Contemporary Br Painting The Kasen/Summer Collection 1994–95, Absolut Secret 1995–98, Absolut Secret NY 1998, Decorative Forms Over the World - Edward Allington London and NY 1996–99; Artwise commissions incl: two wall drawings by Sol Le Witt, sculptures by Andy Goldsworthy, *qv*, David Nash and Janet Cardiff 1998–; Tribe Art cmmns by Julian Opie 2002 and Hussein Chalayan 2003; *Style*— Ms Susie Allen; ✉ 2 Dalling Road, Hammersmith, London W6 0JB (tel 020 8563 9495, fax 020 8563 9578, e-mail mail@artwisecurators.com)

ALLEN, Sir Thomas Boaz; kt (1999), CBE (1989); s of Thomas Boaz Allen (d 1987), of Seaham, Co Durham, and Florence, *née* Hemmings (d 1990); *b* 10 September 1944; *Educ* Robert Richardson GS Ryhope, Royal Coll of Music (ARCM); *m* 1, 30 March 1968 (m dis 1986), Margaret, da of George Holley (d 1980), of Seaham, Co Durham; 1 s (Stephen Boaz b 31 Jan 1970); m 2, 12 March 1988, Jeannie Gordon Lascelles, da of Norman Gordon Farquharson, of Southbroom, Natal, SA; *Career* opera singer; princ baritone: WNO 1969–72, ROH Covent Garden 1972–77; celebrated 25 seasons at Covent Garden 1996; guest appearances: Metropolitan Opera NY (debut) 1981, Bayerische Staatsoper München 1985, Wiener Staatsoper, Paris Opera, La Scala Milan (opened 1987/88 season as Don Giovanni), ENO, San Francisco Opera, Chicago Lyric Opera, LA, Glyndebourne, Aldeburgh and Salzburg Festivals, BBC Proms (with LPO under Sir Charlew Mackerras) 1997, Last Night of the Proms Royal Albert Hall 2004; dir Albert Herring RCM 2002; Prince Consort prof RCM, hon fell Jesus Coll Oxford 2001, kammersänger Bayerische Staatsoper 2003; Hon MA Univ of Newcastle upon Tyne 1984, Hon DMus Univ of Durham 1988, Hon RAM 1988; FRCM 1988; *Books* Foreign Parts: A Singer's Journal; *Recreations* golf, drawing and painting, ornithology, fishing; *Clubs* Garrick, Athenaeum; *Style*— Sir Thomas Allen, CBE; ✉ c/o Askonas Holt, Lonsdale Chambers, 27 Chancery Lane, London WC2A 1PF

ALLEN, Timothy James; s of John Edward Allen, of Uckfield, Kent, and Jean Dorothy Allen; *b* 26 May 1971; *Educ* Judd Sch Tonbridge, Univ of Leeds (BSc); *Career* photographer; environmental consltt Repub of Indonesia 1993–97, photographer Sunday Telegraph 1998–2000, photographer The Independent 2000–, chief photographer Independent on Sunday 2002–; exhbns incl: Trade (Exposure) 1999, Karen, Burma's Forgotten Tribe (Exposure) 2000, Daily Press (Visa Pour L'Image International Photojournalism Festival) 2002; corporate campaigns incl Barclays Bank and Sky TV; memb NUJ, memb Br Press Photographers Assoc; *Awards* Internationaler Preis für Jungen Bildjournalismus 1999, Fuji Film Features Photographer of the Year 2001, finalist Br Press Awards Photographer of the Year 2002 and 2003, Fuji Film Arts Photographer of the Year 2002 and 2003, Lord Mayor's Award for Business and Industry Photographer of the Year 2003, BG Gp Magazine Photographer of the Year 2005, Nikon Celebrity Photgrapher of the Year 2005, commended The Guardian Weekend Photograph Prize 2006, First Prize Business Industry and Technol Press Photographers of the Year Awards 2007 (shortlisted: Photo Essay, News, Entertainment and News Features 2006, Portrait, Photo Essay and Sports Feature 2007); *Recreations* woodland owner, kite surfer; *Style*— Timothy Allen, Esq; ✉ Axiom Photographic Agency, The Saga Building, 326 Kensal Road, London W10 5BZ (tel 020 8964 9970, fax 020 8964 8440, e-mail info@axiomphoto.co.uk and people@photojournal.co.uk)

ALLEN, William Anthony; s of Derek William Allen, and Margaret Winifred, *née* Jones; *b* 13 May 1949; *Educ* KCS Wimbledon, Balliol Coll Oxford (BA), LSE (MScEcon); *m* 29 July 1972, Rosemary Margaret, da of Richard Kelland Eminson; 1 s (Edmund James b 1979), 2 da (Rosalind Jane b 1976, Lucy Ruth b 1983); *Career* Bank of England: Econ Intelligence Dept 1972–77, Cashiers Dept 1977–78, secondment Bank for International Settlements Basle Switzerland 1978–80, Economics Div 1980–82, Gilt-Edged Div 1982–86, head of Money Market Ops Div 1986–90, head of Foreign Exchange Div 1990–94, dep dir (monetary analysis) 1994–98, dep dir (market operations)1999–2002, dir for Europe and dep dir (fin stability) 2002–03; econ advsr Brevan Howard Asset Mgmnt LLP 2004–, visiting sr fell Faculty of Fin Cass Business Sch City Univ 2004–, pt/t advsr to National Bank of Poland; *Recreations* gardening, jazz; *Style*— William Allen, Esq; ✉ Brevan Howard Asset Management LLP, Almack House, 28 King Street, London SW1Y 6XA (e-mail bill.allen@brevanhoward.com)

ALLEN, Maj-Gen William Maurice; CB (1983); s of William James Allen, and Elizabeth Jane Henrietta Allen; *b* 29 May 1931; *m* 1, 1956, Patricia Mary Fletcher (decd); 1 da (decd); m 2, 1998, Elizabeth Irving; *Career* cmmnd RASC 1950, RCT 1965, regtl and staff appts Korea, Cyprus, Germany and UK, Staff Coll Camberley 1961, Instr Staff Coll Camberley and RMCS Shrivenham 1968–70, RCDS 1976, Asst Cmdt RMA Sandhurst 1979–81, Dir-Gen Tport and Movements (Army) 1981–83, ret; dir of trg and educn Burroughs Machines Ltd 1983–85; dir European Management Information 1988–89; consltt: Mondial Defence Systems 1989–, Fortis Aviation Group; md: Fortis International Ltd 1990–93, Pulsar Aviation Ltd, Aviation Services Inc; memb Cncl: IAM 1982–85, NDTA 1983–; chm Milton Keynes IT Trg Centre 1983–85, assoc St George's House; Freeman City of London 1981, Hon Liveryman Worshipful Co of Carmen 1981; FCIT, FIMI, FILDM, FIMgt, MInstPet; *Recreations* vigneron du Languedoc, economics, gardening, ocean cruising, squash, keeping fit; *Clubs* Overseas, Bristol Channel Yacht; *Style*— Maj-Gen William Allen, CB; ✉ c/o Royal Bank of Scotland plc, Holts Farnborough Branch, Lawrie House, 31–37 Victoria Road, Farnborough, Hampshire GU14 7NR

ALLEN, Prof William Richard (Twink); CBE (2002); *b* 29 August 1940; *Educ* Auckland GS, Univ of Auckland (Med Intermediate Cert), Univ of Sydney (BVSc), Univ of Cambridge (PhD, ScD); *Career* with large animal veterinary practice Kaitaia NZ 1965–66, principal veterinary research offr TBA Equine Fertility Unit Animal Research Station Cambridge 1972–89 (post-doctoral sci 1970–71), dir TBA Equine Fertility Unit Mertoun Paddocks Newmarket 1989– (joined 1975), Jim Joel prof of equine reproduction Dept of Clinical Veterinary Med Univ of Cambridge 1995– (assoc lectr 1990–95), professorial fell Robinson Coll Cambridge 1996; hon professorial fell Univ Coll of Wales Aberystwyth 1980–85, adjunct prof Faculty of Veterinary Microbiology Cornell Univ NY 1984–, special prof Dept of Physiology and Environmental Sci Univ of Nottingham 1994–; Hon DSc: Jagellonian Univ Krakow 1990, Univ of Gent 2007; Hon FRAgS 1996, CBiol, FIBiol 1997, foreign memb Polish Acad of Sci 1999; *Style*— Prof Twink Allen, CBE; ✉ Thoroughbred Breeders' Association Equine Fertility Unit, Mertoun Paddocks, Woodditton Road, Newmarket, Suffolk CB8 9BH (tel 01638 662491, fax 01638 667207)

ALLEN-JONES, Charles Martin; s of Air Vice-Marshal John Ernest Allen-Jones, CBE (d 1999), of Dunmow, Essex, and Margaret Ena, *née* Rix (d 1974); *b* 7 August 1939; *Educ* Clifton; *m* 25 June 1966, Caroline, da of Keith Beale, OBE (d 1979), of Woodchurch, Kent; 1 s (Christof b 1968), 2 da (Nicola b 1970, Anna b 1972); *Career* articled to Clerk of the Justices Uxbridge Magistrates Ct 1958–60, articled to Vizard Oldham Crowder and Cash 1960–63; admitted slr 1963; Linklaters: joined 1964, ptnr 1968–2001, Hong Kong Office 1976–81, head Corporate Dept 1985–91, sr ptnr 1996–2001, co-chm Linklaters & Alliance 1998–2001; non-exec dir: Caledonia Investments plc 2001–, Hongkong Land Holdings Ltd 2001–; memb: City Taxation Ctee 1973–75, Hong Kong Banking Advsy Ctee 1978–80, Fin Reporting Cncl 2001–, Financial Reporting Review Panel 2005–; memb: Barbican Advsy Cncl 1997–2005, Cncl RCA 2004– (vice-chm 2007–), Ctee Hong Kong Assoc 2002–; tstee: Br Museum 2000–04, Asia House 2001– (chm 2005–06); *Recreations* gardening, tennis, travel, reading; *Clubs* Hong Kong, Athenaeum; *Style*— Charles Allen-Jones, Esq

ALLEN OF ABBEYDALE, Baron (Life Peer UK 1976), of the City of Sheffield; Sir Philip Allen; GCB (1970, KCB 1964, CB 1954); yr s of Arthur Allen (d 1962), of Sheffield, and Louie, *née* Tipper; *b* 8 July 1912; *Educ* King Edward VII Sch Sheffield, Queens' Coll Cambridge (MA); *m* 1938, Marjorie Brenda (d 2002), da of Thomas John Colton Coe (d 1944); *Career* sits as Independent in House of Lords; entered Home Office 1934, Offices of War Cabinet 1943–44, Cwlth fellowship in USA 1948–49, dep chm Prison Cmmn for England and Wales 1950–52, asst under sec of state Home Office 1952–55, dep sec Miny of Housing and Local Govt 1955–60, dep under sec of state Home Office 1960–62, second sec Treasy 1963–66, perm under sec of state Home Office 1966–72; chm: Occupational Pensions Bd 1973–78, Gaming Bd for GB 1977–85, Mencap 1982–88, Cncl Royal Holloway Univ of London 1985–92; memb: Security Cmmn 1973–91, Tbnl of Inquiry into Crown Agents 1978–82; chief counting offr EEC Referendum 1975; hon fell: Queens' Coll Cambridge, Royal Holloway Univ of London; *Style*— The Rt Hon the Lord Allen of Abbeydale, GCB; ✉ Holly Lodge, Englefield Green, Surrey TW20 0JP (tel 01784 432291)

ALLENBY, 3 Viscount (UK 1919); Michael Jaffray Hynman Allenby; s of 2 Viscount Allenby (d 1984), s of Capt Frederick Allenby, CBE, JP, RN; n of 1 Viscount Allenby, GCB, GCMG, GCVO, and his 1 w (Adelaide) Mary Lethbridge, *née* Champneys (d 1988); *b* 20 April 1931; *Educ* Eton; *m* 29 July 1965, Sara Margaret, o da of Lt-Col Peter Milner Wiggin; 1 s (Hon Henry Jaffray Hynman b 29 July 1968); *Heir* s, Hon Henry Allenby; *Career* cmmnd 2 Lt 11 Hussars (PAO) 1951, served Malaya 1953–56, ADC to Govr Cyprus 1957–58, Bde Maj 51 Bde Hong Kong 1967–70, Lt-Col Royal Hussars, CO Royal Yeo 1974–77, GSO1 Instr Nigerian Staff Coll Kaduna 1977–79; chm Quickrest Ltd 1987–91, vice-pres The International League for the Protection of Horses 1999– (chm 1997–99); dep speaker and dep chm ctee House of Lords 1993–; *Clubs* Naval and Military; *Style*— The Viscount Allenby; ✉ House of Lords, London SW1A 0PW

ALLENDALE, 4 Viscount (UK 1911) Wentworth Peter Ismay Beaumont; s of 3 Viscount (d 2002); *b* 13 November 1948; *Educ* Harrow; *m* 1975, Theresa Mary Magdalene, da of Frank More O'Ferrall (d 1977); 1 s, 3 da; *Career* landowner; *Recreations* shooting, skiing, horseracing; *Clubs* Jockey, Northern Counties, White's; *Style*— The Rt Hon the Viscount Allendale; ✉ Bywell Castle, Stocksfield-on-Tyne, Northumberland NE43 7AB (tel 01661 842450, office 01661 843296, fax 01661 842838, mobile 07703 367740); Flat 5G, Cliveden Place, London SW1W 8LA (tel 020 7881 0820)

ALLERTON, Air Vice-Marshal Richard Christopher; CB (1988), DL (Cornwall 1995); er s of Air Cdre Ord Denny Allerton, CB, CBE (d 1977), and Kathleen Mary, *née* Tucker (d 1993); *b* 7 December 1935; *Educ* Stone House Broadstairs, Stowe; *m* 14 March 1964, Marie Isabel Campbell, er da of Capt Sir Roderick Edward François McQuhae Mackenzie (11 Bt, cr 1703), CBE, DSC, RN (d 1986), and Lady Mackenzie (Marie Evelyn Campbell, *née* Parkinson) (d 1993); 2 s (James Roderick Ord b 1967, Christopher Edward Ord b 1970); *Career* Mil Serv RAF, cmmnd 1954; served 1955–78: RAF Hullavington, Oakington, Feltwell, Kinloss, HQ Coastal Cmd, RAF MB SAFI (Malta), HQ Maintenance Cmd, No 3

Sch TT Hereford, RAF Central Flying Sch Little Rissington, RAF Coll Cranwell, student RAF Staff Coll Bracknell, staff HQ RAF Germany, chief instructor S&S WG RAF Coll Cranwell, student Nat Def Coll Latimer, MOD Harrogate; dep dir RAF supply policy MOD 1978–80, station cdr RAF Stafford 1980–82, ADC to HM The Queen 1980–82, student RCDS 1983, air cdre supply and movements HQ Strike Cmd 1983–86, dir gen of supply RAF 1987–90, ret; chm Sharpe's of Aberdeen 1995; memb Cncl Order of St John for Cornwall; SBStJ 1997; *Recreations* shooting, fishing, cricket (pres RAF Cricket Assoc 1987–89, hon vice-pres 1990–); *Style*— Air Vice-Marshal Richard Allerton, CB, DL; ✉ c/o Lloyds Bank, 13 Broad Street, Launceston, Cornwall PL15 8AG

ALLEYNE, Rev Sir John Olpherts Campbell; 5 Bt (GB 1769), of Four Hills, Barbados; s of Capt Sir John Alleyne, 4 Bt, DSO, DSC, RN (d 1983), and Alice Violet Emily, *née* Campbell (d 1984); *b* 18 January 1928; *Educ* Eton, Jesus Coll Cambridge (MA); *m* 28 Sept 1968, Honor Emily Margaret, da of late William Albert Irwin, of Linkview Park, Upper Malone, Belfast; 1 da (Clare Emma Gila b 1969), 1 s (Richard Meynell b 23 June 1972); *Heir* s, Richard Alleyne; *Career* ordained: deacon 1955, priest 1956; curate Southampton 1955–58; chaplain: Coventry Cathedral 1958–62, Clare Coll Cambridge 1962–66, to Bishop of Bristol 1966–68; Toc H area sec SW England 1968–71, vicar of Speke 1971–73, rector 1973–75, rector of St Matthew's Weeke Dio of Winchester 1975–93; *Recreations* supporting asylum seekers, sailing, mountain walking, astronomy; *Style*— The Rev Sir John Alleyne, Bt; ✉ 2 Ash Grove, Guildford, Surrey GU2 8UT (tel 01483 573824, e-mail jocalleyne@hotmail.com)

ALLFORD, Simon; s of David Allford, CBE (d 1997), and M B Allford, *née* Roebuck; *b* 27 July 1961; *Educ* Hampstead Comp, Univ of Sheffield (BA(Arch)), UCL (DipArch); *Career* architect; with Nicholas Grimshaw & Partners 1983–85, Building Design Partnership 1986–89, princ Allford Hall Monaghan Morris Architects 1989–; tutor: Bartlett School of Architecture 1988–, Univ of Nottingham 1992–94; involvement with projects incl: The Poolhouse (RIBA Award 1996), The Broadgate Club (RIBA Award 1998), Walsall Bus Station, Essex Sch (RIBA Award 2000), Monsoon Building (Royal Fine Arts Cmmn Tst Building of the Year Award 2002), commercial offices, doctors' surgeries and numerous large scale housing projects for The Peabody Tst and others; columnist Architects' Jl 2004–; Architectural Assoc: memb Cncl 1996–, hon sec 2000–, hon treas 2003–, vice-pres 2005–; vice-pres of educn RIBA 2004–; CABE Design Review Ctee 2004–; RIBA 1988; *Recreations* travel, art, architecture and literature, following Sheffield Wednesday FC; *Clubs* The Bond, Architecture; *Style*— Simon Allford, Esq; ✉ Allford Hall Monaghan Morris, 5–23 Old Street, London EC1V 9HL (tel 020 7251 5261, fax 020 7251 5123)

ALLFREY, Peter Charles Scudamore; s of Lt-Gen Sir Charles Walter Allfrey, KBE, CB, DSO, MC, JP, DL (d 1964), and Geraldine Clara, *née* Lucas Scudamore (d 1982); *b* 13 January 1942; *Educ* Eton, Univ of Grenoble; *m* 19 Sept 1991, Delia Rose Anne, da of Lt-Col Hugh G E Dunsterville; 2 step s (William Robert Templer, Tristram James Templer), 1 step da (Sophie Anne Dalrymple); *Career* Whitbread & Co plc: joined 1967, dir Whitbread (London) Ltd 1972–73, overseas investment mangr Stowells of Chelsea 1973–75, Thresher & Co Ltd 1976–79, left Whitbread group 1982; with Grant Thornton Chartered Accountants 1983–90, own mgmnt consultancy firm 1991–; dir: Malcolm Innes Gallery Ltd 1973–2004 (merged with Tryon Gallery 2001), Mark Wilkinson Furniture Ltd 1985–2005, Royal Nat Hosp for Rheumatic Diseases 1990–98, Aventura Group of Companies 1996–; FCA 1965; *Recreations* country sports, pictures, music, food and drink; *Style*— Peter Allfrey, Esq; ✉ Dolphin Lodge, Rowdefield, Devizes, Wiltshire SN10 2JD (tel 01380 725991, office 01380 736474)

ALLIANCE, Baron (Life Peer UK 2004), of Manchester in the County of Greater Manchester; Sir David Alliance; kt (1989), CBE (1984); *b* 15 June 1932, Iran; *Educ* Etehad Sch Kashan; *m* (m dis); 2 s, 1 da; *Career* Coats Viyella: chief exec 1975–90, chm 1989–99, acquired Thomas Houghton 1956, Spirella 1968, Vantona 1975, Carrington Viyella 1983 and Coats Paton and Nottingham Manufacturing 1985; chm: N Brown Gp plc 1968–, Tootal Group 1991–99; hon fell: UMIST 1988, Shenkar Israel; Hon LLD: Victoria Univ of Manchester 1989, Univ of Liverpool 1996; Hon DSc Heriot-Watt Univ 1991; COMPTI 1984, CCMI (CBIM 1985), FRSA 1988, Hon FCGI 1991; *Recreations* art, Persian poetry and music, reading; *Style*— The Lord Alliance, CBE; ✉ House of Lords, London SW1A 0AA

ALLIES, Edgar Robin (Bob); s of Edgar Martyn Allies, of Reading, Berks, and Lilian Maud, *née* Smith; *b* 5 September 1953; *Educ* Reading Sch, Univ of Edinburgh (MA, DipArch); *m* 8 Nov 1991, Jill Anne, da of Cyril William Franklin; 1 s (Patrick), 1 da (Isabel); *Career* architect; co-fndr (with Graham Morrison, *qv*) Allies and Morrison 1983; architects to Royal Festival Hall 1994–98; projects incl: The Clove Bldg (RIBA Award 1991), Pierhead Liverpool, Sarum Hall Sch (RIBA Award 1996, Civic Tst Award 1996), Nunnery Square Sheffield (RIBA Award 1996), Rosalind Franklin Bldg Newnham Coll Cambridge (RIBA Award 1996), Br Embassy Dublin (RIBA Award 1997), Abbey Mills Pumping Station Stratford (RIBA Award 1997), Rutherford Info Servs Bldg Goldsmiths Coll London (RIBA Award 1998), Blackburn House London (RIBA Award 2000), Blackwell Cumbria (RIBA Award 2003, Civic Tst Award 2003), extension to Horniman Museum London (Civic Tst Award 2004, RIBA Award 2004), 85 Southwark St London (London Civic Tst Award 2004, RIBA London Bldg of the Year Award 2004, nat winner Corporate Workplace Bldg British Cncl for Offices Awards 2004), BBC Media Village White City (RIBA Award 2005), court and theatre Fitzwilliam Coll Cambridge (RIBA Award 2005), Br Cncl Lagos Nigeria (RIBA Int Award 2006), library and archive Girton Coll Cambridge (RIBA Award 2006); Allies and Morrison winner Architectural Practice of the Year The Bldg Awards 2004; exhibitions: New British Architecture (Japan) 1994, Retrospective (USA Schs of Architecture) 1996–98; lectr Univ of Cambridge 1984–88, George Simpson visiting prof Univ of Edinburgh 1995, visiting prof Univ of Bath 1996–99, Kea distinguished visiting prof Univ of Maryland 1999, external examiner Univ of Brighton 2001–; memb: Faculty of Fine Arts Br Sch at Rome 1997–2002, Cncl AA 2004–07, design panel commission for Architecture and the Built Environment 2005–; tstee Soc for the Promotion of New Music 2006–; Edinburgh Architectural Assoc Medal for Architecture 1977, Rome Scholar in Architecture 1981–82; RIBA 1978, FRSA; *Publications* Model Futures (ICA, 1983), Allies and Morrison (Univ of Michigan Architectural Papers, 1996); *Recreations* contemporary music; *Style*— Bob Allies, Esq; ✉ 12 Well Road, London NW3 1LH (tel 020 7443 9309); Allies and Morrison, 85 Southwark Street, London SE1 0HX (tel 020 7921 0100, fax 020 7921 0101, e-mail boballies@alliesandmorrison.co.uk)

ALLINGTON, Edward Thomas; s of Ralph Allington, of Troutbeck Bridge, Cumbria, and Evelyn Hewartson (d 1988); *b* 24 June 1951; *Educ* Lancaster Sch of Art, Central Sch of Art (DipAD), RCA (Herbert Read meml prize); *m* 1974 (sep 1981), Susan Jean Bradley (d 1984); partner, 1983, Julia Wood; 1 s (Harry Roland Allington Wood b 1991), 1 da (Thalia Evelyn Allington Wood b 1988); *Career* sculptor; *Solo Exhibitions* incl: 1B Kensington Church Walk London 1977, Spacex Gallery Exeter 1981, Exe Gallery Exeter 1982, Spectro Gallery Newcastle upon Tyne 1983, ICA London 1983–84, Lisson Gallery London 1984, Midland Gp Arts Centre Nottingham 1984, Gallery Schmela Düsseldorf 1984, Riverside Studios London 1985, Lisson Gallery 1985, Northern Centre for Contemporary Art Sunderland 1985–86, Abbot Hall Art Gallery Kendal 1986, Diane Brown Gallery NY 1986, Galerie 565 Aalst Belgium 1986, Galerie Adrien Maeght Paris 1986, Galerie Montenay-Delsol Paris 1986, Marlene Eleini Gallery London 1987, Diane Brown Gallery NY 1987, Fuji TV Gallery Tokyo 1988, Gallery Face Tokyo 1988, Lisson Gallery 1990, Galerie Faust Geneva 1990, Vaughan and Vaughan Minneapolis, Kohji Ogura Gallery Nagoya; *Group Exhibitions* incl: Summer Show (Serpentine Gallery London) 1976, Objects and Sculpture (Arnolfini Gallery Bristol) 1981, London/NY 1982, Lisson Gallery 1982, Teme Celeste (Museo Civico D'Arte Contemporanea Gibellina Sicily) 1983, Beelden/sculpture 1983 (Rotterdam Arts Cncl) 1983, The Sculpture Show (Hayward and Serpentine Galleries London) 1983, Metaphor and/or Symbol (Nat MOMA Tokyo and Nat Museum of Osaka) 1984–85, Space Invaders (Mackenzie Art Gall Regina and tour Canada) 1985, Time after Time (Diane Brown Gallery NY) 1986, Britain in Vienna 1986, British Art (Künstlerhaus Vienna) 1986, 3eme Ateliers Internationaux FRAC Pays de la Loire 1986, Prospect 86 (Kunstverein Frankfurt) 1986, Vessel (Serpentine Gallery) 1987, Inside/Outside (Museum van Hedendaagse Kunst Antwerp) 1987, Die Grosse Oper (Bonner Kunstverein Bonn and tour) 1987–88, Britannia 30 Ans de Sculpture (Musée des Beaux Arts Brussels) 1988, British Now Sculpture et Autre Dessins (Musée D'Art Contemporain de Montreal) 1988–89, 2000 Jahre Die Gegenwart der Vergangenheit (Bonner Kunstverein Bonn) 1989; *Major works* His Favourite Was David Smith But She Preferred Dame Barbara Hepworth 1975, Ideal Standard Forms 1980, The Fruit of Oblivion 1982, We Are Time 1985, Building With Missing Columns 1986, Seated in Darkness 1987, Victory Boxed 1987, Light Temple PAS Heizcraftwerk Saarbrucken 1989, Inverted Architrave 1990, set for prodn of Apollon La Nuit 1990; *Awards* prizewinner John Moores 16 Liverpool Exhbn 1989, Gregory fell in Sculpture Univ of Leeds; *Style*— Edward Allington, Esq; ✉ Lisson Gallery, 52–54 Bell Street, London NW1 5BU (tel 020 7724 2739, fax 020 7724 7124)

ALLINSON, Richard John McNeill; s of Deryck Edward Allinson, and Edith Allinson; *Educ* Tudor Grange GS Solihull, Solihull Sixth Form Coll, Lancaster Univ (BA); *Career* broadcaster; Capital Radio 1980–97, BFBS Radio 1985–, BBC World Serv 1986–87, VH1 TV 1994–98, BBC Radio 2 1997–; judge: Olivier Theatre Awards 1988–89, Ivor Novello Awards, Sony Radio Awards; chm Commercial Radio Convention; dir Magnum Opus Broadcasting Ltd; Gold Award Sony Radio Awards 1993 (for National Music Day), Gold Award Sony Radio Awards 1997 (for Radio 2 Late Show); memb Radio Acad; *Recreations* theatre, rediscovering my record collection, piano-playing, boating, cooking, tormenting the children...; *Style*— Richard Allinson; ✉ c/o Tanya Glenn (tel 07831 834074); c/o Bob Voice, International Artists

ALLISON, (Samuel) Austin; s of Dr Samuel Allison, of Stedham, W Sussex (d 2003), and Helen Burns Brighton, *née* Wilson (d 2000); *b* 30 June 1947; *Educ* Liverpool Coll, Wadham Coll Oxford (BA, BCL); *m* 5 June 1971, June, da of late Henry Edward Brassington, of Crofton, Kent; 2 s (Giles b 1973, Jonathan b 1975); *Career* called to the Bar Middle Temple 1969 (bencher 2003); private practice at the Bar 1970–87, head of gp compliance Standard Chartered Bank 1987–95, dir West Merchant Bank 1996–98, dir compliance and legal affairs Westdeutsche Landesbank 1999–2000; head of compliance and legal affairs TT International 2000–, ptnr TT International 2001–, dir TT International Funds plc; memb: Panel of Arbitrators City Disputes Panel, Gen Cncl of the Bar 1991–96; vice-pres Bar Assoc of Commerce Fin and Indust Ctee 1997– (chm 1995); accredited mediator Centre for Dispute Resolution, FCIArb, fell Indian Cncl of Arbitration, fell Indian Soc of Arbitrators; *Publications* Banking and the Financial Services Act (jtly, 1993), Banking and Financial Services Regulation (jtly, 1998, 2 edn 2003); *Recreations* the turf; *Style*— Austin Allison, Esq; ✉ 156 Kingston Lane, Teddington, Middlesex TW11 9HD; TT International, Level 13, Moor House, 120 London Wall, London EC2Y 5ET (tel 020 7509 1256, fax 020 7509 1281, e-mail allisona@ttint.com)

ALLISON, Prof David John; s of Denis Allison (d 1982), of Leeds, and Eileen, *née* O'Connell (d 1966); *b* 21 March 1941; *Educ* Prince Rupert Sch Germany, Wimbledon Coll, KCH London (BSc, MB BS, MD, DMRD); *m* 16 April 1966, Deirdre Mary, da of Patrick Flynn (d 1975), of New Malden, Surrey; 2 da (Catherine b 1967, Helen b 1969), 1 s (Richard b 1970); *Career* conslt and sr lectr Royal Post Grad Med Sch Univ of London 1975–83, dir of radiology Hammersmith Hosp and Imperial Coll Sch of Med at Hammersmith Hosp (Royal Post Grad Med School before merger) 1983–2001, currently emeritus prof of imaging Univ of London; author of numerous publications on cardiovascular and interventional radiology and physiology; memb Fleischner Soc 1979–; memb Cncl: Br Inst of Radiology 1985–88, RCR 1987–; Cardiovascular and Interventional Soc of Europe: memb Exec Ctee 1986–, pres 1990–95; memb: RCR 1973, Br Inst of Radiology 1973, BSG 1978, CIRSE 1980; MRCS, FRCP, FFR, FRCR; *Books* Diagnostic Radiology: An Anglo-American Textbook of Imaging Volumes 1, 2 and 3 (with R G Grainger, 1985, 2 edn 1991, 3 edn 1997), Acronyms and Synonyms in Medical Imaging (with N Strickland, 1996), The Encyclopaedia of Medical Imaging Vols 1–8 (with H Pettersson, 1998); *Recreations* gardening, food and wine (at others' expense); *Style*— Prof David Allison; ✉ Department of Imaging, Imperial College School of Medicine at Hammersmith Hospital, Du Cane Road, London W12 0HS (tel 020 8383 1023, fax 020 8743 5409)

ALLISON, Prof Robert John; s of Gordon Allison, and Elizabeth Anne, *née* Oman; *b* 4 February 1961; *Educ* Univ of Hull (BA), KCL (NERC funded research student, PhD); *Career* Addison Wheeler research fell Dept of Geography Univ of Durham 1986–89, lectr in engrg sedimentology UCL 1989–93; Univ of Durham: lectr in geography 1993–95, reader in geography 1995–99, prof of geography 1999–2006, chm Bd of Studies in Geography (head of dept) 2000–03, dean Faculty of Social Sciences and Health 2003–06; pro-vice-chllr and prof of geography Univ of Sussex 2006–; tutor EPSRC Grad Schs Trg Prog 1996–, course/prog dir ESRC/NERC Grad Research Sch 1999; scientist: Oman Wahiba Sands Research Project RGS (with IBG) 1986, Kimberley Research Project RGS (with IBG) 1988; geomorphology prog dir Jordan Badia R&D Prog RGS (with IBG) 1992–, memb Jordan Steering Ctee Badia R&D Prog 1998–2001; gen sec Int Assoc of Geomorphologists 1993–97, hon sec RGS (with IBG) 1998–2001 (memb Cncl Exec Ctee 1999–2001), chair Exec Ctee Br Geomorphological Research Gp 2006–07 (memb 1989–92, jr vice-chair 2004–05, vice-chair 2005–06); convenor, keynote speaker and plenary lectr at int confs and symposia; Jan De Ploey Prize Katholieke Universitat Leuven 1993, Charles Lyell Award BAAS 1995, Cuthbert Peek Award RGS (with IBG) 1997; *Publications* Landslides of the Dorset Coast (ed, 1990), The Coastal Landforms of West Dorset (ed, 1992), Landscape Sensitivity (jt ed, 1993), Applied Geomorphology: Theory and Practice (ed, 2002); also author of articles in refereed jls and other pubns; *Style*— Prof Robert J Allison; ✉ Sussex House, University of Sussex, Brighton BN1 9RH (tel 01273 678212, fax 0191 678254, e-mail r.j.allison@sussex.ac.uk)

ALLISON, Roderick Stuart; CB (1996); s of Stuart Frew Allison (d 1960), and Poppy, *née* Hodges (d 1974); *b* 28 November 1936; *Educ* Dumfries Acad, Manchester Grammar, Balliol Coll Oxford (MA); *m* 1968, Anne Allison; 1 s (Edward b 16 Nov 1972), 1 da (Carrie b 5 May 1974); *Career* Ministry of Labour: asst princ 1959–63, private sec to Perm Sec 1963–64, princ 1964–69, seconded to Civil Serv Dept 1969–71, grade 5 1971, grade 3 1977; Health and Safety Executive: dir Special Hazards 1989–92, dir Safety Policy 1992–94, chief exec Offshore Safety Div 1994–96, memb Exec 1995–96; head of UK Delgn and jt chm Channel Tunnel Safety Authority 1997–2003; memb Inter-Governmental Cmmn on Channel Tunnel 1997–2003; *Recreations* languages, art, theatre, music, reading; *Style*— Roderick Allison, Esq, CB; ✉ Channel Tunnel Safety Authority, 1 Kemble Street, London WC2B 4AN (tel 020 7282 2036)

ALLISON, Ronald William Paul; CVO (1978); s of Percy Allison, and Dorothy, *née* Doyle; *b* 26 January 1932; *Educ* Weymouth GS, Taunton's Sch Southampton; *m* 1, 1956, Maureen Angela Macdonald (d 1992); 2 da; m 2, 1993, Jennifer Loy Weider; 1 s (David William Helton b 28 Feb 1996); *Career* reporter and corr BBC 1957–73, press sec to HM The Queen 1973–78, md Ronald Allison & Assocs 1978–80; Thames TV: presenter 1978–, controller of sport and outside broadcasts 1980–85, dir corp affrs 1986–89; conslt freelance writer and broadcaster 1989–; chm: TV Barter International 1990–2004, Grand

Slam Sports Ltd 1992–96 (md 1993), FCL IT Specialists 1998–2004; dir of corp affrs: BAFTA 1993–98, The Sponsorship Group 1996–99; *Books* Look Back in Wonder (1968), The Queen (1973), Charles, Prince of our Time (1978), Britain in the Seventies (1980), The Royal Encyclopedia (ed, with Sarah Riddell, 1993), The Queen - Fifty Years: A Celebration (2001); *Clubs* RAC; *Style*— Ronald Allison, Esq, CVO

ALLISON, Shaun Michael; s of Lt Cdr Jorgen Leslie William Michael Allison (d 1983), of Beenham, Berks, and Honoria Brenda, *née* Magill; *b* 12 January 1944; *Educ* Rugby; *m* 14 Sept 1968, Lucy Howard Douglas, da of Lt-Col Charles Robert Douglas Gray, of Basingstoke, Hants; 2 s (Piers Michael Douglas b 1971, Charles Howard b 1977), 1 da (Sophie Louise b 1974); *Career* stockbroker 1965; ptnr Hoare Govett Ltd 1978–85, dir Hoare Govett Securities Ltd 1986–92, corp fin dir Panmure Gordon 1992–2000; *Recreations* skiing, shooting, sailing; *Clubs* City of London; *Style*— Shaun M Allison, Esq

ALLISON, Prof Wade William Magill; s of Lt Cdr (Jorgen Leslie William) Michael Allison, RN (d 1983), and Honoria Brenda, *née* Magill; *b* 23 April 1941; *Educ* Rugby, Trinity Coll Cambridge (MA), ChCh Oxford (MA, DPhil); *m* 1, 9 Sept 1967 (m dis 1988); 1 s (Thomas b 1977), 3 da (Emma b and d 1968, Harriet (Mrs James Cridland) b 1972, Rachel b 1974); m 2, 6 Dec 1988, Marilyn Frances (Kate), *née* Easterbrook; 2 step da (Helen Mary Foss b 1973, Frances Margaret Foss b 1974); *Career* Univ of Oxford: res offr Nuclear Physics Laboratory 1970–75, lectr Christ Church 1973–75 (res lectr 1966–71), univ lectr 1976–96, sr tutor Keble Coll 1985–89 (tutorial fell 1976–), assoc chm of physics 1990–92, prof of physics 1996–, sub warden Keble Coll 1999–; author of numerous papers and articles on elementary particle physics and experimental methods; fell Royal Cmmn for the Exhibition of 1851 1966–68; MRIN; *Recreations* sailing, motoring, navigation; *Clubs* Royal Cornwall Yacht; *Style*— Prof Wade Allison; ✉ Southfields, Ludgershall, Aylesbury, Buckinghamshire HP18 9PB (tel 01844 237602); Keble College, Oxford OX1 3PG; Nuclear Physics Laboratory, Oxford (tel 01865 272734, fax 01865 273418, e-mail w.allison@physics.oxford.ac.uk)

ALLISS, Peter; s of Percy Alliss (d 1975), of Sheffield, and Dorothy, *née* Rust (d 1973); *b* 28 February 1931; *Educ* Queen Elizabeth GS Wimborne, Crosby House Sch Winton; *m* 1, 1953 (m dis 1968), Joan; 1 s (Gary b 1954), 1 da (Carol b 1960); m 2, 1969, Jacqueline Anne, da of Col Geoffrey Bridgeman Grey, CB, CBE, TD, DL, of Birmingham; 2 da (Sara b 1972, Victoria b 1973 d 1982), 2 s (Simon b 1975, Henry b 1983); *Career* Nat Serv RAF Regt 1949–51; professional golfer 1946; played in 8 Ryder Cup matches and 10 Canada Cup (now World Cup) matches, winner of 21 maj events incl open championships of Spain, Portugal, Italy and Brazil; golf commentator/broadcaster and corr (for BBC and ABC) following retirement, also golf course designer; former pres: Br Greenkeepers' Assoc 1977–86, Ladies Professional Golfers' Assoc 1980–86; twice capt PGA 1962–87, pres Nat Assoc of Public Golf Courses; Hon Doc: Univ of Bournemouth, Univ of Humberside, Univ of St Andrews; *Books* Alliss in Wonderland (autobiography, 1964), Easier Golf (with Paul Trevillion, 1969), Bedside Golf (1980), Peter Alliss: An Autobiography (1981), Shell Book of Golf (1982), The Duke (1983), Play Golf with Peter Alliss (1983), The Who's Who of Golf (1983), The Open (with Michael Hobbs, 1984), Golfer's Logbook (1984), Lasting the Course (1984), More Bedside Golf (1984), Peter Alliss's Most Memorable Golf (1986), Yet More Bedside Golf (1986), Play Better Golf with Peter Alliss (1989), Peter Alliss's Best 100 Golfers (1989), The Best of Golf (with Bob Ferrier, 1989), A Golfer's Travels (1997), Peter Allis Golf Heroes (2002), My Life (autobiography, 2004); *Recreations* conversation (with wine!); *Clubs* Lansdowne, Motcombs, Ritz, Crockfords, R&A (hon memb), Wentworth (hon memb), Stoke Park (hon memb), Royal Cinque Ports (hon memb); *Style*— Peter Alliss, Esq; ✉ Peter Alliss Golf Designs, 44 Northlands, Potters Bar, Hertfordshire EN6 5DE (tel 01707 661539)

ALLISTER, James Hugh (Jim); QC, MEP; s of Robert Allister (d 1998), and Mary Jane, *née* McCrory (d 1996); *b* 2 April 1953, Crossgar, Co Down; *Educ* Regent House GS, Queen's Univ Belfast (LLB); *m* 14 July 1978, Ruth Elizabeth, *née* McCullagh; 1 da (Karen Jane b 7 Sept 1982), 2 s (Graeme Alexander James b 23 Aug 1984, Philip Robert Andrew b 11 Nov 1986); *Career* called to the Bar: NI 1976, Inner Bar NI 2001; practising barr 1976–80, asst to Dr Ian Paisley MEP in the European Parl 1980–82, memb NI Assembly 1982–86 (also chief whip DUP Gp), practising barr specialising in criminal def work 1987–2004, MEP (DUP until 2007, subsequently Ind) NI 2004–; memb Constitutional Affrs Ctee and Fisheries Ctee European Parl; author of various political pubns; *Style*— Jim Allister, Esq, MEP, QC; ✉ 139 Holywood Road, Belfast BT4 3BE (tel 02890 655011, fax 02980 654314, e-mail jallister@europarl.eu.int, website www.jimallister.org)

ALLNER, Andrew James; s of Cedric George Allner (d 2002), and Jennifer Jane, *née* Swallow; *b* 16 December 1953, Northwich, Cheshire; *Educ* Bedford Sch, Exeter Coll Oxford (BA); *m* 25 April 1981, Susan Isabel, *née* McCann; 1 da (Elizabeth Kate b 14 March 1990), 1 s (James Stephen b 28 Oct 1995); *Career* Pricewaterhouse 1975–92 (ptnr 1987–92), Guinness plc 1992–96; gp finance dir: Nycomed Amersham 1996–98, Dalgety plc (latterly PIC Int Gp plc) 1998–2000; ceo Enodis plc 2000–03, gp finance dir RHM plc 2004–07; non-exec dir: Moss Bross plc 2001–05, Marshalls plc 2003–; FCA (ACA 1978); *Recreations* sailing, skiing; *Clubs* Royal Thames Yacht, Roehampton; *Style*— Andrew Allner, Esq

ALLPORT, Denis Ivor; s of late A R Allport, and E M, *née* Mashman; *b* 20 November 1922; *Educ* Highgate Sch; *m* 1949, Diana, *née* Marler; 2 s, 1 da; *Career* served WWII Indian Army; Metal Box plc: dir 1973, md 1977–79, chief exec 1977–85, dep chm 1979, chm 1979–85; memb Nat Enterprise Bd 1980–83; dir: Beecham Gp 1981–88, Marley plc 1986–91; chm Castle Underwriting Agents Ltd 1989–94; govr Highgate Sch 1981–94, memb Neill Cmmn of Enquiry into Lloyd's 1986; CIMgt, FRSA; *Style*— Denis Allport, Esq; ✉ Petersham House, Peppard Common, Henley-on-Thames, Oxfordshire RG9 5JD (tel 01491 629526)

ALLSOP, Prof Richard Edward; OBE (1997); s of Edward James Allsop, of Mackworth, Derbys, and Grace Ada, *née* Tacey (d 1984); *b* 2 May 1940; *Educ* Bemrose Sch Derby, Queens' Coll Cambridge (MA), UCL (PhD, DSc); *m* 23 June 1990, Frances Elizabeth, da of Henry James Killick (d 1978); *Career* sci offr Road Research Laboratory 1964–66, research fell UCL 1967–69, lectr in tport studies UCL 1970–72, dir Tport Ops Research Gp Univ of Newcastle upon Tyne 1973–76, prof of tport studies UCL 1976–2005, emeritus prof UCL 2005–; visitor to Traffic Gp Tport and Road Res Laboratory 1987–92, external research advsr Dept for Tport 1993–; dir Parly Advsy Cncl for Tport Safety 1995–, memb Bd European Tport Safety Cncl 2005–; memb: Road Traffic Law Review 1985–88, Road Safety Advsy Panel 2000–, War on Want, Chiltern Soc; winner of Highways and Transportation Award 1997; visiting prof Univ of Karlsruhe 1977, visiting fell Univ of Osaka 1981, visiting Erskine fell Univ of Canterbury Christchurch 1997, visiting prof Univ of Natural Resources and Applied Life Sciences Vienna 2002, visiting prof Univ of Newcastle upon Tyne 2006–, adjunct prof Queensland Univ of Technol 2006–; hon prof: Technol Univ Cracow 2000, Moscow Automobile and Road Inst State Technol Univ 2001; fell UCL 2000; FCIT 1981, FIHT 1983, CEng, FICE 1990, FREng 1996, fell Tport Research Fndn 1998, FCILT (FILT 1999); *Publications* Transportation and Traffic Theory 2007 (jt ed, 2007); author of over 200 papers in learned jls and proceedings; *Recreations* photography, theatre, walking; *Style*— Prof Richard Allsop, OBE, FREng; ✉ Centre for Transport Studies, University College London, Gower Street, London WC1E 6BT (tel 020 7679 1555, fax 020 7679 1567, e-mail rea@transport.ucl.ac.uk)

ALLSOPP, Michael Edward Ranulph; s of Samuel Ranulph Allsopp, CBE (d 1975), of Stansted, Essex, and Hon Norah Hyacinthe, *née* Littleton (d 1997); *b* 9 October 1930; *Educ* Eton; *m* 1953, Patricia Ann, da of Geoffrey H Berners (d 1972), of Faringdon, Oxon; 4 da (Frances Jane Berners (Mrs David Woodd) b 1956, Carolyn Ann Berners b 1957, Davina Hyacinth Berners (Lady Powell), Jessica Elizabeth Berners (Hon Mrs Edward Leigh Pemberton) (twins) b 1960); *Career* Subaltern 7 QOH, Capt Royal Wilts Yeo (TA); chm: Allen Harvey & Ross Ltd 1968–79, London Discount Market Assoc 1974–76, Allied Dunbar & Co Ltd 1979–86, Granville Holdings plc 1987–99, Granville & Co Ltd 1987–99, Granville Bank 1987–99, St David's Investment Trust plc, Berners Allsopp Estate Management Co; *Recreations* foxhunting (Master Old Berks Hounds 1960–81); *Clubs* White's, Pratt's; *Style*— Michael Allsopp, Esq; ✉ Baccarat Little Coxwell, Faringdon, Oxfordshire SN7 7LW (tel 01367 240580, office 01367 240138)

ALLTHORPE-GUYTON, Marjorie; da of Maurice Jack Allthorpe-Guyton, of Norwich, and Edith Florence, *née* Clark (d 1972); *b* 29 July 1948; *Educ* Blyth GS Norwich, UEA (BA), Leverhulme scholarship, Courtauld Inst London; *m* 1, 12 Dec 1970 (m dis), Brian Collison; m 2, 27 Oct 1989 (m dis), John Mullis; 1 da (Elise Charlotte Allthorpe-Mullis b 30 Sept 1984), 1 s (Theodore Edmund Allthorpe-Mullis b 14 Feb 1991); m 3, 15 April 2000, Paul Dale; *Career* asst keeper Norwich Castle Museum 1969–79, researcher Norwich Sch of Art 1980–82, lectr Open Univ 1983, lectr London program Univ of Connecticut 1982–88, visiting lectr in theoretical studies Norwich Sch of Art 1985–88; co-selector Art Cncl British Art Show 1982–84; external assessor: BA and MA Fine Art Goldsmiths Coll London 1988–94, BA Fine Art Univ of Plymouth (formerly Poly SW) and Exeter Coll of Art 1989–93, Oxford Brookes Univ 1997–2000, City Univ London 2003–, Univ of Oxford; UK contrib ed Flash Art 1987–89, ed Artscribe 1991–92 (assoc ed 1989–91), conslt VIART 1993, dir of visual arts Arts Cncl of GB 1993–2006; author of several oeuvre catalogues, numerous articles for art jls and press, contrib to various exhbn catalogues; assoc: Museums Assoc 1975, Art Historians' Assoc 1979; memb exec Ctee Int Assoc of Art Critics 1996; Cncl Goldsmiths Coll London 1997–2006; Hon Dr Anglia Polytechnic Univ 2005; FRSA 1993, FRCA 1999, FRIBA 2003; *Recreations* family, art, cooking, film (especially European), yacht racing; *Clubs* Chelsea Arts, Blacks, Two Brydges; *Style*— Miss Marjorie Allthorpe-Guyton; ✉ 1 Thornhill Road, London N1 1HX (tel 020 7607 7903, fax 020 7607 7903, e-mail mallthorpeguyton@hotmail.com)

ALLUM, William Herbert; s of Herbert Edward Allum (d 1987), of Oxford, and Gladys Marion, *née* Bolton; *b* 9 February 1953; *Educ* St Edward's Sch Oxford, Univ of Birmingham (BSc, MB ChB, MD); *m* 23 April 1983, (Pamela) Anne, da of Joseph Anthony Collier (d 1995), of Stratford-upon-Avon; 3 s (Charles b 1985, Henry b 1987, James b 1990); *Career* house offr posts 1977–78, demonstrator in anatomy Univ of Southampton 1978–79, SHO in surgery Reading Hosps 1979–80; registrar in surgery: Central Birmingham 1980–82, Hereford Hosps 1982–83; lectr in surgery Univ of Birmingham 1985–88 (hon res fell 1983–85), sr lectr Univ of Leicester and hon conslt surgn Leicester Hosps 1988–90; conslt surgn: Bart's London 1991–93, Epsom Dist Gen Hosp 1993–2003, Royal Marsden Hosp 2001–; memb: Physiotherapists' Bd Cncl of Professions Supplimentary to Med, Specialist Advsy Ctee Jt Ctee on Higher Surgical Trg 2003–; hon sec Assoc of Upper Gastrointestinal Surgns; RCS: memb Ct of Examiners, regnl advsr; memb: Surgical Res Soc, Br Assoc of Surgical Oncology (nat ctee memb); FRCS 1982; *Books* Cancer of the Stomach - Clinical Cancer Monographs 1989 (co-author), Premalignancy and Early Cancer in General Surgery (co-author, 1996); *Recreations* golf, cricket; *Clubs* MCC, RAC, Walton Heath Golf; *Style*— William Allum, Esq; ✉ The Chestnuts, 21 Greville Park Road, Ashtead, Surrey KT21 2QU (tel 01372 813318); Royal Marsden Hospital, Downs Road, Sutton, Surrey SM2 5PT (tel 020 8661 3982)

ALLVEY, David Philip; s of Edgar Frederick Allvey, and Kathleen Beatrice, *née* Lamb; *b* 13 March 1945; *Educ* Lewes County GS, Univ of London; *m* 15 July 2000, Alison Cullen; 2 s from previous m (Mark James b 11 Dec 1979, Philip Duncan b 4 May 1982); *Career* various mgmnt positions in construction industry until 1972, articled clerk with accountancy firm, mangr International Tax Dept Price Waterhouse London until 1980; BAT Industries plc: joined as gp dep tax mangr 1980, fin dir gp cosmetic interests and fin advsr and taxation mangr British-American Tobacco Co Ltd 1984–86, head of Finance Dept BAT Industries 1986, gp fin dir 1989–98, dir various gp subsids incl Eagle Star and Allied Dunbar, memb Chief Exec's Ctee (formerly Chm's Policy Ctee) 1992–98; chief of corp operations Zurich Financial Services 1998–99; fin dir Barclays plc 1999–2001; non-exec dir McKechnie plc 1993–2000, Intertek 2000–, Costain 2001–, Resolution (formerly Britannic) 2002–, William Hill 2002–, My.Travel 2003–; memb UK Accounting Standards Bd 1993–2003, chm Fiscal Ctee Hundred Gp of Financial Dirs 1994–2001; FCA, ATII; *Recreations* golf; *Style*— David Allvey, Esq

ALLWEIS, His Hon Judge Martin Peter; s of Jack Allweis (d 1993), and Iris, *née* Mosco; *b* 22 December 1947; *Educ* Manchester Grammar, Sidney Sussex Coll Cambridge (BA); *m* 1 April 1984, Tracy Ruth, da of late Hyam Barr, and Bernice Barr; 2 c (Sophie May b 21 June 1990, Steven Charles b 8 Aug 1992); *Career* called to the Bar Inner Temple 1970; in practice 1970–94, recorder 1990–94, circuit judge (Northern Circuit) 1994–, designated family judge for Gtr Manchester 1996–2005; *Recreations* family, football (Manchester City FC), squash; *Style*— His Hon Judge Allweis; ✉ c/o Manchester County Court, Courts of Justice, Crown Square, Manchester M60 9DJ

ALMOND, Darren; *b* Wigan, 1971; *Educ* Winchester Sch of Art (BA); *Career* artist; winner Art & Innovation Prize 1996; *Solo Exhibitions* Crawford Art College Cork 1991, KN120 (Great Western Studios London) 1995, Jay Jopling/White Cube London 1997, Darren Almond (ICA London) 1997, Darren Almond (Galerie Max Hetzler Berlin) 1999, Darren Almond (The Renaissance Soc Chicago) 1999, Traction (Chisenhale Gallery London) 2000, Darren Almond (The Approach London) 2000, Darren Almond (Matthew Marks Gallery NY) 2000 and 2005, Night as a Day (Tate Britain) 2001, At Speed (Galerie Max Hetzler Berlin) 2002, A (Fourth Wall PADT London) 2002, Nightvision (Sommercontemporaryart Tel Aviv) 2003, 11 miles...from safety (White Cube London) 2003, If I Had You (Galerie Max Hetzler Berlin) 2004, Life Sentence (Lentos Museum of Modern Art Linz) 2004, Darren Almond (K21 Kuntstsammlung Nordhein-Westfalen Dusseldorf) 2005; *Group Exhibitions* incl: Southampton Quays Southampton 1992, Winchester Gallery Winchester 1993, A Small Shifting Sphere of Serious Culture (ICA London) 1996, Something Else (Exmouth Market London) 1996, Art & Innovation Prize (ICA London) 1996, Sensation (Royal Acad London) 1997, Delta (Musée d'Art Moderne de la Ville de Paris) 1998, View Four (Mary Boone Gallery NY) 1998, Hidden Desires and Images (Art Dynamics Tokyo) 1998, Art Crash (Arhus Kunstmuseum Denmark) 1999, Chronos and Kairos (Museum Fridericanum Kassel Germany) 1999, Seeing Time (San Francisco MOMA) 1999, Concrete Ashtray (Friedrich Petzel Gallery NY) 1999, Common People (Fondazione Sandretto Re Rebaundengo Turin) 1999, Diary (Cornerhouse Manchester) 2000, Out There (White Cube 2 London) 2000, Apocalypse (Royal Acad London) 2000, Geographies (Galerie Chantal Crousel Paris) 2000, Deliberate Living (Greene Naftali Gallery NY) 2001, Unreal Time Video (Fine Art Center The Korean Culture & Arts Fndn Seoul) 2001, Tracking (Kent & Vicki Logan Gallery Calif Coll of Arts and Crafts Oakland) 2001, Berlin Biennale 2001, Nature in Photography (Galerie Nachst St Stephan Vienna) 2001, Casino 2001 (SMAK and Bijlokenmuseum Ghent) 2001, 10th Anniversary Exhibition. 100 Drawings and Photographs (Matthew Marks Gallery NY) 2001, In the Freud Museum (Freud Museum London) 2002, Presentness is Grace - Experiencing the Suspended Moment (Spacex Gallery Exeter) 2002, The Rowan Collection. Contemporary British & Irish Art (Irish MOMA Dublin) 2002, Contextualize (Kunstverein Hamburg) 2002, The Hate U Give Little Infants Fucks Everyone (Smart Project Space Amsterdam) 2002, Video - Zone (1st International video-art biennal in Israel Tel Aviv) 2002, Melodrama (Centro José Guerrero and Palacio de los Condes de Gabia Granada) 2002, Video Acts (PS1 and Krammlich

Collection NY) 2002, Breathing the Water (Galerie Hauser & Wirth & Presenhubera Zurich) 2003, Edén (La Colección Jumex Mexico City) 2003, Witness (Barbican Art Gallery and Curve Gallery London) 2003, La Biennale di Venezia 2003, Hot Summer in the City (Sean Kelly Gallery NY) 2003, Skulptur Biennale Münsterland (Stadtmuseum Beckum) 2003, Melodrama (MARCO Vigo) 2003, Other Times: Br Contemporary Art (City Art Gall Prague) 2004, Open Secrets (Imperial War Museum London) 2004, Universal Experience (Museum of Contemporary Art Chicago) 2005, The Mind is a Horse Part II (Bloomberg Space London) 2005; *Work in Public Collections* Art Inst Chicago, La Coleccion Jumex Mexico, DaimlerChrysler Berlin, Government Art Collection London, Imperial War Museum London, Met Museum of Art NY, Paine Webber Art Collection NY; *Style*— Darren Almond, Esq

ALMOND, David William; s of George Sydney Almond (d 1999), of Lymington, Hants, and Madge Lilian, *née* Skegg (d 1993); *b* 24 October 1945; *Educ* Purley GS; *m* 6 June 1970, Elizabeth (Liz), da of Percy Thomas Bisby (d 1978), of Aldwick, W Sussex; 2 da (Amanda Jane b 25 Feb 1974, Juliette b 10 March 1977); *Career* CA; articles City of London 1962–67, ptnr Alliotts (formerly Evans Peirson) 1969–2002, chm Alliott Peirson Associates 1974–86; Alliott Gp: chm 1979–89, md and sec 1989–2002; md Blue Hole Consulting Ltd; dir: Accounting Firms Associates Inc 1982–92; chm: Croydon Soc of CAs 1979–80 (sec 1975–79), Storrington Rural Preservation Soc 1995–99; Freeman City of London 1976, memb Ct of Assts Worshipful Co of Coachmakers and Coach Harness Makers 1977 (Master 2001); FCA 1967; *Recreations* sailing, gardening, travel; *Style*— David Almond, Esq; ✉ Fryern Place, Storrington, West Sussex RH20 4HG (e-mail david@b-h-c.com)

ALMOND, Peter John; s of Herbert John Almond (d 1991), and Winifred Mary, *née* Munds; *b* 18 January 1946; *Educ* Woolverstone Hall Sch Ipswich Suffolk; *m* 27 Dec 1969, Anna, da of R Collinson, of Skirlaugh, Hull; 2 s (Nicholas b 28 Feb 1979, Jeffrey b 28 Dec 1981); *Career* trainee reporter Northern Echo Darlington 1964, apprentice journalist Yorkshire Evening Press York 1965–68 (NCTJ cert), info offr Br Army W Germany 1969; Cleveland Press Ohio USA: police reporter 1970–71, suburban reporter 1971–73, educn reporter 1973–78, labour reporter 1978–79, environment reporter 1979–80, Nieman fell in journalism Harvard Univ 1980–81, investigative reporter 1981–82; Washington Times Washington DC: State Dept corr 1982–83, Br, Euro and ME corr 1983–87, defence corr Washington 1987–90; defence corr Daily Telegraph 1990–95; currently freelance defence writer; pres Defence Correspondents' Assoc; *Books* Aviation: The Early Years (1998), A Century of Flight (2002); *Recreations* jogging, movies, reading, walking; *Style*— Peter Almond; ✉ 36 Heathside, Hinchley Wood, Esher, Surrey KT10 9TF (tel 020 8398 5178)

ALNER, Robert Henry; s of Henry Frederick George Alner (d 1975), and Daisy, *née* Coffin; *b* 21 November 1943; *Educ* Beaminster and Neatherbury GS; *m* 14 November 1970, Sally Elizabeth, da of Harold Coleman; 2 da (Jennifer Sally b 26 November 1973, Louise Elizabeth b 29 December 1975); *Career* national hunt jockey; 53 wins incl National Hunt Chase Cheltenham 1970; trainer; winners incl: Uncle Eli (Fulwell Handicap Chase 1994), Hops and Pops (Golden Eagle Novice Chase 1994), High Baron (Kestrel Handicap Hurdle 1994 and Wayward Lad Novice Chase 1994), Seven of Diamonds (Peregrine Handicap Chase 1995), Flyer's Nap (The Fulke Walwyn Kim Muir Chase Cheltenham 1995, Astec Buzz Shop National Hunt Chase Cheltenham 1997, John Hughes Grand National Trial Chase 1997), Harwell Lad (Whitbread Gold Cup 1997), Cool Dawn (Betterware Cup Ascot 1997 and Tote Gold Cup 1998), Super Tactics (Racing Post Chase 1998), Honeymount (The Fulke Walwyn Kim Muir Chase Cheltenham 2000), Kate's Charm (Cleeve Hurdle Cheltenham 2002), Sir Rembrandt (Chepstow Rehearsal Chase 2003), Kingscliff (Betfair Chase Haydock 2005); *Recreations* hunting, shooting, point-to-pointing (champion in 1992 and 212 wins); *Style*— Robert Alner, Esq; ✉ Robert Alner Racing, Locketts Farm, Droop, Blandford Forum, Dorset DT11 0EZ (tel and fax 01258 817271, e-mail robertalner@btopenworld.com)

ALPASS, John; *Career* Security Serv 1973–95, intelligence co-ordinator Cabinet Office 1996–99; head of fraud strategy DWP 2000–; *Style*— John Alpass, Esq; ✉ Department for Work and Pensions, The Adelphi, 1–11 John Adam Street, London WC2N 6HT

ALPTUNA, HE Dr Akin; s of H Kamil Alptuna, and Cahide Alptuna; *b* 23 May 1942, Turkey; *Educ* Ankara Univ (BA, PhD); *m* Esin; 2 s; *Career* Turkish diplomat; joined Miny of Foreign Affrs 1967, second and first sec Copenhagen 1972–75, first sec Nicosia 1975–77, head of section Int Economic Agreements Dept and memb Cabinet for min of Foreign Affrs 1977–79, cnsllr Perm Delgn of Turkey to EU Brussels 1979–81, consul Düsseldorf 1981–83, head Dept for Int Economic Orgns 1983–85, dep head of mission Turkish Perm Delgn to UN 1985–89, dep DG Multilateral Political Affrs 1989–93, DG EU Dept 1993–95, ambass to Finland 1995–97, ambass Perm Rep of Turkey to OECD 1997–2000, dep under sec for EU and Western Europe 1999–2003, ambass to the Ct of St James's 2003–; *Clubs* Travellers, Cavalry and Guards'; *Style*— HE Dr Akin Alptuna; ✉ Turkish Embassy, 43 Belgrave Square, London SW1X 8PA (tel 020 7393 0202, fax 020 7393 9213)

ALRED, David (Dave); MBE (2004); *b* 2 April 1948, London; *Educ* Loughborough Univ (PhD); *Career* rugby union coach; played for Bristol RUFC and Bath RUFC, also Minnesota Vikings (American football), Sheffield (rugby league), Blue Dragons (rugby league); coach: GB (rugby league) 1984, Bath RUFC 1990–92, St George Aust (rugby league) 1991–93, Bristol RUFC 1993–94, Newcastle RUFC, Aust 1993–94; asst (kicking) coach England 1998–2006 (winners Six Nations Championship 2000, 2001 and 2003 (Grand Slam 2003), winners World Cup Aust 2003), kicking coach Br and Irish Lions South Africa 1997, Aust 2001 and NZ 2005; awarded Mussabini medal; *Style*— Dave Alred, Esq, MBE; ✉ e-mail dave@davealred.com

ALSOP, Prof William Allen; OBE (1999); s of Francis John Alsop (d 1964), and Brenda Ethelwyn, *née* Hight (d 1998); *b* 12 December 1947; *Educ* Eaglehurst Coll Northampton, AA Sch of Architecture, Br Sch in Rome (Bernard Webb scholar); *m* 1972, Sheila Elizabeth, da of George Bean; 2 s (Oliver b 1977, Piers b 1984), 1 da (Nancy b 1980); *Career* architect; with: Maxwell Fry 1971, Cedric Price 1973–77, Roderick Ham 1977–79; in private practice Alsop Lyall and Störmer 1980–91, chm Alsop and Störmer 1991–2000, currently Alsop Architects; visiting prof Faculty of the Built Environment UCE (formerly Birmingham Poly) 1992–93, hon prof Bremen Acad for Art and Music, prof Vienna Tech Univ 1995–; memb Design Cncl 1994–1998; awards incl: Société Architectes Diplômes par le Gouvernement, William Van Allen Medal for Architects, RIBA Nat Award (for Cardiff Visitors' Centre) 1991, Le Gran Bleu Marseille 1997, RIBA Civic and Community Architecture Award 1997, RIBA Stirling Prize for Building of the Year (for Peckham Library) 2000; Hamburgische Architektenkammer 1992, Hon LLD Univ of Leicester 1996, Hon Dr Sch of Architecture Nottingham Trent Univ 2001, hon fell Sheffield Hallam Univ 2002, fell Ontario Coll of Art Toronto 2004; memb: Bundes Deutsches Architecten, AA 1968, RIBA 1977, Russian Acad of Art 1995; FRSA 1983, Hon FRSBS 1996, RA 2000; *Recreations* architecture, fishing; *Clubs* Chelsea Arts; *Style*— Prof William Alsop, OBE, RA; ✉ SMC Alsop, Parkgate Studio, 41 Parkgate Road, London SW11 4NP (tel 020 7978 7878, fax 020 7978 7879, e-mail info@alsoparchitects.com)

ALSTEAD, Brig (Francis) Allan Littlejohns; CBE (1984), DL (City of Edinburgh 1996); s of Prof Stanley Alstead, CBE (d 1992), of Dunblane, Perthshire, and his 1 w, Nora, *née* Sowden (d 1980); *b* 19 June 1935; *Educ* Glasgow Acad, RMA Sandhurst, UCW Aberystwyth (MPhil), Univ of Edinburgh (NATO res fell); *m* 4 April 1964, Joy Veronica, da of George Alexander Edwards (d 1991), of Carlisle, Cumbria; 2 s (Robert b 24 Dec 1965, Jonathan b 13 Nov 1968); *Career* cmmnd KOSB 1955, RN Staff Coll 1966, JSSC 1971, cmd 1 Bn KOSB 1974–76 (despatches 1976), MA to QMG 1976–79, ACOS Log Plans BAOR 1981–84, cmd 51 Highland Bde 1984–87; NATO reinforcement co-ordinator 1987–90; chief exec Scottish Sports Cncl 1990–99, chief exec SportScotland 1999–2000, Chef de Mission Scottish Cwlth Games Team Manchester 2002; md Alstead Consulting 2000–; chm Mercy Corps Europe 2001–, memb Bd Mercy Corps Int (USA) 2001–; non-exec dir JRG Ltd 1996–2007; memb Exec Scottish Cncl for Devpt and Industry 1995–2000 and 2002–; memb Queen's Body Guard for Scotland (Royal Co of Archers), Dep Hon Col City of Edinburgh Univs OTC 1990–99; regimental tstee KOSB; pres Edinburgh and Lothians SSAFA/Forces Help 2003–05 (pres Edinburgh and Midlothian 1991–98), memb Lowland Territorial and Volunteer Assoc 1995–; dir and tstee: Seagull Tst 1995–, Youth Sport Tst 1996–2000; tstee Cncl for the Advancement of Arts, Recreation and Education (CAARE) 2003–; govr: Moray House Coll Edinburgh 1991–96, Glasgow Acad 1995–2001; memb: Gen Cncl Erskine Hosp 2001–, Cncl Nat Playing Fields Assoc (NPFA) 2001–; FCMI (FIMgt 1984), FCIPD (FIPD 1986), FCILT 1989, FInstAM 1990, FInstD 1993, FBISA 2000; *Recreations* skiing, archery, walking, classical music; *Style*— Brig Allan Alstead, CBE, DL; ✉ 49 Moray Place, Edinburgh EH3 6BQ

ALSTON, John Alistair; CBE (1988), DL (Norfolk 1991); s of David Alston (d 1989), of Lavenham, Suffolk, and Bathia Mary Davidson (d 1987); *b* 24 May 1937; *Educ* Sherborne, RAC Cirencester; *Career* farmer; elected Norfolk CC 1973 (ldr 1981–87 and 1989–93, chm 1988); chm: Norwich HA 1994–96, E Norfolk Health Cmmn 1994–96, Norfolk HA 1996–2002; memb: Broads Authy 1988–95 (chm Broads Bill Steering Ctee), Regnl Ctee Nat Tst 1994–2000; tstee: Norwich City FC 1992–, Norfolk & Norwich Festival E Anglia Arts Fndn; chm: Norfolk & Norwich Millennium Ctee, Norfolk County Strategic Partnership 2002–; vice-chm Cncl UEA until 2002; High Sheriff Norfolk 2004–05; hon DCL UEA 2004; *Recreations* shooting, gardening, fishing; *Style*— J A Alston, Esq, CBE, DL; ✉ Besthorpe Hall, Norfolk NR17 2LJ (tel 01953 452138, fax 01953 450308)

ALSTON, Robert John; CMG (1987), QSO (2004), DL (Kent 2004); s of late Arthur William Alston (d 1993), and late Rita Alston; *b* 10 February 1938; *Educ* Ardingly, New Coll Oxford (BA); *m* 1969, Patricia Claire, *née* Essex; 1 da (Nadine b 1970), 1 s (Jeremy b 1972); *Career* Dip Serv: third sec Kabul 1963, Eastern Dept FO 1966, head Computer Study Team FCO 1969, first sec (economic) Paris 1971, first sec and head of Chancery Tehran 1974, Energy Science and Space Dept FCO 1977, head Jt Nuclear Unit FCO 1978, political cnsllr UK Delgn to NATO 1981, head Def Dept FCO 1984, ambass to Oman 1986–90, seconded Home Civil Serv 1990–92, asst under sec (public depts) FCO 1992–94, high cmmr to NZ and concurrently non-resident high cmmr to Independent State of Western Samoa and non-resident govr Pitcairn, Henderson, Ducie and Oeno Islands 1994–1998, ret; conslt to Archbishop of Canterbury on Anglican Communion Affairs 1999–2002; dir Romney Resource 2000, chm UK NZ Link Fndn 1999–2004, tstee Antarctic Heritage Tst 1998–, tstees rep Cwlth Inst 2002–; Kent ambass 1998–; govr Ardingly Coll 2003– (chm 2005–), chm of govrs Marsh Acad 2007; memb Ct of Assts Worshipful Co of World Traders 2003– (Jr Warden 2005, Sr Warden 2006); *Recreations* gardening, travel, music; *Style*— Robert J Alston, Esq, CMG, QSO, DL; ✉ 16 Carlisle Mansions, Carlisle Place, London SW1P 1HX (e-mail robert.alston@which.net)

ALSTON, Robin Carfrae; OBE; s of Wilfred Louis Alston (d 1993), and Margaret Louise, *née* Mackenzie (d 1975); *b* 29 January 1933; *Educ* Queen's Royal Coll Trinidad, Lodge Sch Barbados, Rugby, Univ of Br Columbia (BA), Univ of Oxford (MA), Univ of Toronto (MA), Univ of London (PhD); *Career* bibliographer; teaching fell UC Toronto 1956–58, lectr Univ of New Brunswick 1958–60, lectr in English literature Univ of Leeds 1964–76, hon res fell UCL 1987–, prof of library studies Univ of London 1990–98 (emeritus prof 1998–), dir Sch of Library, Archive and Info Studies UCL 1990–98; David Murray lectr Univ of Glasgow 1983, Cecil Oldman lectr Univ of Leeds 1988–89, Klein visiting prof Univ of Texas 1990; fndr chm and ed Scolar Press 1965–73 (md 1984–), fndr and md Janus Press 1973–80; conslt bibliographer to Br Library 1977– (memb Advsy Ctee 1975–77), ed-in-chief Eighteenth Century Short Title Catalogue 1978–90, editorial dir The Nineteenth Century 1985–; Bibliographical Soc: pres 1986–88, memb Cncl 1968–86, memb Pubns Ctee 1970–92, ed Occasional Papers 1984–92; memb: Organising Ctee 18th Century Short Title Catalogue 1976–80, Advsy Ctee MLA of America for the Wing Project 1978–, Advsy Panel Aust Res Grants Ctee 1983–, Ctee Br Book Trade Index 1984–92; external examiner Inst of Bibliography Univ of Leeds 1983–91, advsr New Univ of Barbados 2005–; fndr memb Cncl Ilkley Literature Festival 1973–, co-fndr Sir Frederic Madden Soc 1990 (ed Soc's occasional pubns); Samuel Pepys Gold Medal Ephemera Soc 1984, Smithsonian Instn Award 1985, Gold Medal Bibliographical Soc of London 1996; Hon DLitt Univ of London 2005; Hon FLA 1986, FSA 1988; *Publications* incl: Anglo-Saxon Composition for Beginners (1959), Materials for a History of the English Language (2 vols, 1960), An Introduction to Old English (1961, 1962), A Concise Introduction to Old English (1966), Alexander Gil's Logonomia Anglica 1619 (ed with B Danielsson, 1979), Cataloguing Rules for the Eighteenth Century Short Title Catalogue (1977), Bibliography, Machine Readable Cataloguing and the ESTC (with M J Jannetta, 1978), Eighteenth Century Subscription Lists (with F J G Robinson and C Wadham, 1983), The Eighteenth Century Short Title Catalogue: the British Library Collection (ed, 1983), The Nineteenth Century Subject Scope and Principles of Selection (1986), The Nineteenth Century - Cataloguing Rules (1986), Bibliography of the English Language 1500–1800 (22 vols, 1–18 published to date), The British Library: Past Present Future (1989), A Checklist of Women Writers 1801–1900 (1990), Handlist of Unpublished Finding Aids to the London Collections of the British Library (1991), The Journal of Sir Frederic Madden: abstract (1991), Books with Manuscript (1994), Order and Connexion: Studies in Bibliography and the History of the Book (1997); *Style*— Robin Alston, Esq, OBE, FSA; ✉ 67 Ocean City, St Philip, Barbados (e-mail r_alston@sunbeach.net)

ALTMAN, His Hon Judge John; s of Lionel Altman (d 1987), of Leeds, and Vita, *née* Levi (d 1969); *b* 21 June 1944; *Educ* Moorlands Sch Leeds, Bootham Sch York, Univ of Bristol (LLB); *m* 25 Feb 1968, Elizabeth, da of Ralph and Helen Brown; 2 da (Claire Rose b 11 Aug 1973, Vivien Simone b 10 April 1976); *Career* called to the Bar Middle Temple 1967; practised at the Bar in London and N Eastern Circuit, chm Industrial Tbnls 1986–91 (pt/t chm 1983–86), recorder 1989–91 (asst recorder 1985–89), circuit judge: NE Circuit 1991–2001, SE Circuit 2001–; designated family judge: Milton Keynes 2003–07, Luton 2004, Oxford 2005–07, London 2007; sr circuit judge 2007–; past chm W Yorks Family Mediation Service, past pres The Leeds Jewish Historical Soc; memb Hon Soc of Middle Temple; *Recreations* reading, music, theatre, photography, gardening; *Style*— His Hon Judge Altman

ALTMAN, Lionel Phillips; CBE (1979); s of late Arnold Altman, and late Catherine, *née* Phillips; *m* 1989, Diana; 1 s and 2 da by previous marriages; *Career* dir: Sears Holdings Motor Group 1963–73, C & W Holdings 1974–77; chm: Equity & General plc Gp of Cos 1978–91, Westminster Consultancy 1992–; chm and chief exec: Pre-Divisional Investments 1972–94, H P Information plc 1985–91; chm: United Technologists 1981–, European Cleaning Services Gp 1991–94, Hydro-Lock Europe Ltd 1992–96; dep chm Technology Transfers 1984–90; advsr Monopolies and Mergers Cmmn 1990–92, parly special advsr 1991–; pres Motor Agents Assoc 1975–77 (memb Nat Cncl 1965–), vice-pres and memb Cncl Inst of Motor Industry 1970–78; chm: Industry Taxation Panel 1975–82, Publicity Club of London 1961–63, Automotive VIP Club 1988–91, Retail Motor Industry Working Pty on SE Market 1988–93, Barbican Assoc 1995–98; memb: Cncl CBI 1977–89, CBI Industrial Policy Ctee 1979–86, Dun & Bradstreet Industry Panel 1982–86, Jt Consultative Ctee London Ct of Int Arbitration 1999–; dep chm Wallenberg Fndn 1997–; memb Exec Ctee Battle of Britain Monument 2004–; life vice-pres Devon Agricultural Assoc; govr Cripplegate Schools Fndn 1998–2000, govr Guildhall Sch of Music and

Drama 1999–, tstee Guildhall Sch Tst 1995–2000; Corp of London: chm Libraries Guildhall Art Galleries and Archives Ctee 2001–, dep chm Standards Ctee 2001–03, memb Finance Ctee 1997–2005, memb Policy and Res Ctee 2000–, memb Establishment Ctee 2002–04, dep chm Audit Ctee 2006–; Liveryman and former hon treas Worshipful Co of Coachmakers and Coach Harness Makers' Co, Burgess Guild Bro; Freeman: City of London 1973, City of Glasgow 1974; memb Ct of Common Cncl Corp of London 1996–; FIMI, FCIM, fndr MIPR 1948; *Style*— Lionel P Altman, Esq, CBE; ✉ 405 Gilbert House, Barbican, London EC2Y 8BD (fax 020 7638 3023)

ALTMANN, Dr Ros; *Educ* Henrietta Barnett Sch London, UCL (Hume-Lloyd scholar, BSc), Harvard Univ (Kennedy scholar), LSE (PhD); *Career* fund mangr Prudential Assurance 1981–84, head of int equities Chase Manhattan Bank 1984–89, dir Rothschild Asset Mgmnt 1989–91, dir NatWest Investment Mgmnt 1991–93, ind conslt on investment strategy, pensions and savings policy 1993–; conslt to HM Treasy on Myners Review of Institutional Investment April-Sept 2000, advsr on savings, pensions and retirement policy to 10 Downing St Policy Unit 2000–05, memb Lord Chllr's Strategic Investment Bd 2004–; author of numerous articles in newspapers, jls and industry magazines; govr and non-exec dir LSE 1989–, govr Pensions Policy Inst 2002–; tstee The Age Employment Network; MSI, MInstD; *Recreations* charity fundraising, swimming, table-tennis; *Style*— Dr Ros Altmann; ✉ e-mail ros@rosaltmann.com

ALTON, Her Hon Judge Caroline; da of George Frederick Alton, and Margaret, *née* Hodgson; *b* 31 July 1946, West Hartlepool; *Educ* West Hartlepool HS for Girls, KCL (LLB); *m* 1, 14 Dec 1974 (m dis 1987), Ian William Searle; m 2, 15 Nov 2003, David Charles Cooke; *Career* called to the Bar Gray's Inn 1968 (Mould and McKenzie scholar); barr 1968–81 (disbarred at own request), slr 1981–97; ptnr Pinsent & Co (now Pinsent Masons) 1981–92, circuit judge (Midland & Oxford Circuit, later Midland Circuit) 1992–, judge i/c Technol and Construction Court Birmingham 1997–2000, sr circuit judge and designated judge of Mercantile Court Birmingham 2000–; memb Gray's Inn 1964–92 and 2000–; *Recreations* gardening, reading, trying to paint; *Style*— Her Hon Judge Alton

ALTON, Roger; *Educ* Exeter Coll Oxford; *Career* Liverpool Post 1969–74; The Guardian: chief news sub ed 1976–81, dep sports ed 1981–85, arts ed 1985–90, ed Weekend Guardian 1990–93, features ed 1993–96, asst ed 1996–98; ed The Observer 1998–; Ed of the Year What the Papers Say Awards 2000, Ed of the Year GQ Men of the Year Awards 2005, Newspaper of the Year Br Press Awards 2007; *Recreations* skiing, climbing, films, sports; *Style*— Roger Alton, Esq; ✉ The Observer, 3–7 Herbal Hill, London EC1R 5EJ (tel 020 7278 2332, fax 020 7837 7817, e-mail editor@observer.co.uk)

ALTON OF LIVERPOOL, Baron (Life Peer UK 1997), of Mossley Hill in the County of Merseyside; David Patrick Alton; s of late Frederick Alton, of Bow, London, and Bridget, *née* Mulroe; *b* 15 March 1951; *Educ* Campion Sch, Christ Coll Liverpool, Univ of St Andrews; *m* 23 July 1988, Elizabeth, *née* Bell; 1 da (Hon Marianne b 1989), 3 s (Hon Padraig b 1990, Hon Philip b 1992, Hon James b 1997); *Career* teacher of children with special needs 1972–79; cncllr Liverpool City Cncl 1972–80 (dep ldr Cncl 1978–79, chm Housing Ctee 1978–79), nat pres Nat League of Young Liberals 1979; MP (Lib): Liverpool Edge Hill March 1979–83, Liverpool Mossley Hill 1983–97; chm Lib Pty Standing Ctee (Policy) 1980–81, memb Select Ctee on the Environment 1981–85, Lib chief whip 1985–87, Lib and Alliance spokesman on NI 1986–87; sits as Ind cross-bench peer in House of Lords; memb House of Commons Privileges Ctee 1994–96; chm: All-Pty Mersey Barrage Group 1990–97, All-Pty British-North Korea Gp; vice-chm: All-Pty Drug Abuse Group 1992–96, All-Pty Mental Health Gp 1995–97, All-Pty Tibet Gp; treas: All-Pty Pro-Life Gp 1996–, All-Pty Anti-Personnel Land Mines Gp 1996–99; sec All Pty Sudan Gp; prof of citizenship Liverpool John Moores Univ 1997–, visiting fell Univ of St Andrews; dir Banner Financial Servs; fndr Movement for Christian Democracy 1990; nat vice-pres Life; vice-pres: Liverpool YMCA, Assoc of Cncllrs; pres Liverpool Branch NSPCC; chm Merseyside Cncl for Voluntary Services 1997–2001; patron and co-fndr Jubilee Campaign and Jubilee Action 1986–; past chm Forget-me-Not Appeal; treas All-Pty friends of CAFOD; columnist: Catholic Pictorial 1982–95, The Universe 1989–, Liverpool Daily Post 1997–98; Knight Order of Constantine and St George 2002; *Books* What Kind of Country (1987), Whose Choice Anyway? (1988), Faith in Britain (1991), Signs of Contradiction (1996), Life After Death (1997), Citizen Virtues (1999), Pilgrim Ways (2001), Citizen 21 (ed, 2001), Passion and Pain (2003), Euthanasia: Heart of the Matter (2005), Abortion: Heart of the Matter (2005); *Style*— The Rt Hon Lord Alton of Liverpool; ✉ Jacob's Ladder, Lower Road, Knowle Green, Lancashire PR3 2YN (tel 01772 786551, website www.davidalton.com); House of Lords, London SW1A 0PW (tel 020 7219 3551, e-mail altond@parliament.uk); Liverpool John Moores University (tel 0151 231 3852, e-mail davidalton@mail.com)

ALTRICHTER, Petr; *b* 24 May 1951; *Educ* Ostrava Conservatory, Janacek Acad of Music Brno; *m* Barbora Altrichterova; 2 s; *Career* conductor Bohemia Chamber Philharmonie 1981–86 (princ conductor 1987–89); princ guest conductor State Philharmonic Brno 1984–87 (chief conductor 2002–); Prague Symphony Orch: princ guest conductor 1987–90, chief conductor 1990–91, princ conductor 2003–; chief conductor Südwestdeutsche Philharmonie Konstanz 1993–2004, conductor Royal Liverpool Philharmonic 1994 (princ conductor 1997–2001); orchs conducted incl: BBC Symphony Orch, Berlin Symphony Orch, Bruckner Orch Linz, Niederosterreichisches Tonkünstlerorchester Wien, Radio Symphony Orch Basel, Japan Symphony Orch, London Philharmonic Orch, SWF Symphony Orch, Philharmie Krakow, Orchestra Milano, Royal Scottish National Orch, The Symphony Orch Riga, Nürnberger Symphoniker, Symfony Orchester RTL Luxembourg; int tours incl: USA, Germany, Japan, Taiwan, Spain, Italy, Austria, France, Greece, Switzerland; festivals performed at incl: Edinburgh, Paris, Madrid, Seville, St Etienne, Palermo, Avignon, Zurich, Salzburg, Vienna, Prague, Chicago, Athens, Antwerp; *Style*— Petr Altrichter, Esq; ✉ c/o Sibylle Jackson, Hazard Chase, 25 City Road, Cambridge CB1 1DP (tel 01223 312400, fax 01233 460827, e-mail sibylle.jackson@hazardchase.co.uk)

ALTRINCHAM, 3 Baron (UK 1945) Anthony Ulick David Dundas Grigg; yr s of 1 Baron Altrincham, KCMG, KCVO, DSO, MC, PC (d 1955), suc bro, John Edward Poynder Grigg (2 Baron, who disclaimed Peerage for life 1963; d 2002); *b* 12 January 1934; *Educ* Eton, New Coll Oxford; *m* 1965, Eliane, da of the Marquis de Miramon; 2 s (Hon Sebastian b 1965, Hon Steven b 1969), 1 da (Hon Casilda b 1967); *Heir* s, Hon Sebastian Grigg; *Style*— The Rt Hon the Lord Altrincham; ✉ La Musclera, Tamariu 17212, Palafrugell, Girona, Spain (tel (34) 972 620 180, fax (34) 972 620 404)

ALTY, Prof James Lenton; s of William Graham Alty (d 1959), of Haslingden, Lancs, and Annie Alty (d 1989); *b* 21 August 1939; *Educ* King Edward VII Sch Lytham, Univ of Liverpool (BSc, PhD); *m* 16 Jan 1965, Mary Eleanor, da of Thomas Roberts (d 1986), of Llanerchymedd, Anglesey; 2 s (Gareth Thomas b 1965, Graham James b 1971), 2 da (Carys Ann b 1967, Sian Cathryn b 1968); *Career* account exec IBM (UK) Ltd 1971–72 (sr systems engr 1968–71), dir Computer Laboratory Univ of Liverpool 1972–82 (Oliver Lodge res fell 1962–64, Leverhulme res fell 1966–68), exec dir Turing Inst 1984–90, BT prof of computer sci Univ of Strathclyde 1989–90 (prof of computer sci 1982–89, dir Scot HCI Centre 1984–90); Loughborough Univ: prof of computer sci 1990–, head Computer Science Dept 1991–2000, dean Faculty of Science 2001–04, prof emeritus 2004–; prof of human computer interaction Middlesex Univ 2004–06; over 100 pubns in academic jls and conf proceedings; memb: Computer Bd for Univs and Res Cncls 1975–81, Cncl Br Computer Soc 1981–84 (fell 1982); FBCS 1986, FRSA 1987, FIEE 1993; *Books* Computing Skills and the User Interface (with M J Coombs, 1982), Human Computer Interaction (with G R S Weir, 1990), Industrial Applications of Artificial Intelligence (with Mikulich, 1991), People and Computer VIII (with Diaper and Guest, 1993), Expert Systems: Concepts and Examples (with M J Coombs, 1984); *Recreations* skiing, musical composition; *Clubs* National Liberal; *Style*— Prof James Alty; ✉ 168 Station Road, Cropston, Leicestershire; Loughborough University, Loughborough, Leicestershire LE11 3TU (tel 01509 222681, fax 01509 211586, e-mail j.l.alty@ntlworld.com)

ALVAREZ, Alfred (Al); s of Bertie Alvarez (d 1965), of London, and Katie, *née* Levy (d 1982); *b* 5 August 1929; *Educ* Oundle, CCC Oxford (MA); *m* 1, 1956 (m dis 1961), Ursula Barr; 1 s (Adam); m 2, 1966, Anne, da of Jack Gilmore Adams, of Toronto, Canada; 1 s (Luke b 1968), 1 da (Kate b 1971); *Career* poet and author; sr scholar CCC Oxford 1952–55 and Goldsmiths' Co 1952–55; Procter visiting fellowship Princeton 1953–54, visiting fell Rockefeller Fndn USA 1955–56 and 1958, lectr in creative writing and Gauss Seminarian Princeton 1957–58, D H Lawrence fellowship Univ of New Mexico 1958; visiting prof: Brandeis Univ 1960, New York State Univ Buffalo 1966; poetry critic and ed The Observer 1956–66; Vachel Lindsay Prize for Poetry 1961; Hon DLitt Univ of East London 1998; hon fell CCC Oxford 2001; *Books* The Shaping Spirit (1958), The School of Donne (1961), The New Poetry (ed and introduction, 1962), Under Pressure (1965), Beyond All This Fiddle (1968), Lost (poems, 1968), Penguin Modern Poets No18 (1970), Apparition (poems, 1971), The Savage God (1971), Beckett (1973), Hers (1974), Hunt (1978), Autumn to Autumn and Selected Poems (1978), Life After Marriage (1982), The Biggest Game in Town (1983), Offshore (1986), Feeding the Rat (1988), Rainforest (1988), Day of Atonement (1991), The Faber Book of Modern European Poetry (ed and introduction, 1992), Night (1995), Where Did it All Go Right? (1999), Poker: Bets, Bluffs and Bad Beats (2001), New and Selected Poems (2002), The Writer's Voice (2005), Risky Business: People, Pastimes, Poker and Books (2007); *Recreations* music, poker, cold water swimming; *Clubs* Climbers', Alpine, Beefsteak; *Style*— Al Alvarez, Esq; ✉ c/o Gillon Aitken Associates, 18–21 Cavaye Place, London SW10 9PG

ALVEY, John; CB (1980); s of George Clarence Vincent Alvey (d 1929), and Hilda Eveline, *née* Pellat (d 1955); *b* 19 June 1925; *Educ* Reeds Sch, Univ of London (BSc); *m* 1955, Celia Edmed, da of Dr Cecil Brittain Marson (d 1932); 3 s (David, Peter, Stephen); *Career* London Stock Exchange until 1943, RN 1943–46, RN Scientific Serv 1950, head of weapons projects Admty Surface Weapons Estab 1968–72, DG Electronics Radar PE MOD 1972–73, DG Airborne Electronic Systems PE MOD 1974–75, dir Admty Surface Weapons Estab 1976–77, dep controller R&D Estab and Res C and chief scientist (RAF) MOD 1977–80, md Devpt and Procurement and engr-in-chief British Telecom 1983–86 (sr dir Technol 1980–83), LSI Logic Ltd 1986–91; chm SIRA Ltd 1987–94; memb Cncl: Fellowship of Engrg 1985–92 (vice-pres 1989–92), Fndn for Sci and Technol 1986–90, City Univ 1985–93; Hon DSc City Univ 1984, Hon DTech CNAA 1991; fell Queen Mary & Westfield Coll London 1988; FIEE, FRSA, FREng 1984; *Recreations* skiing, walking, reading, travel; *Style*— John Alvey, Esq, CB, FREng; ✉ 9 Western Parade, Emsworth, Hampshire PO10 7HS

ALVINGHAM, 2 Baron (UK 1929); Robert Guy Eardley; CBE (1977, OBE 1972), DL (Oxfordshire 1996); s of 1 Baron Alvingham (d 1955), and Dorothea Gertrude Yerburgh (d 1927); *b* 16 December 1926; *Educ* Eton; *m* 1952, Beryl Elliot, da of William D Williams, of Hindhead; 1 s (Robert), 1 da (Susannah); *Heir* s, Hon Robert Yerburgh; *Career* formerly Coldstream Gds (joined 1945, cmmnd 1946), served Palestine, Tripoli, FARELF, S America, BAOR; Head Staff CDS 1972–74, RCDS 1975, dep dir Army Staff Duties 1975–78, Maj-Gen 1978, dir Army Quartering MOD 1978–81; patron Oxfordshire Co Royal British Legion; pres Royal Lancashire Agriculture Soc 1984, 1988 and 1989; *Style*— Maj-Gen The Rt Hon Lord Alvingham, CBE, DL; ✉ Bix Hall, Henley-on-Thames, Oxfordshire RG9 6BW

AMANN, Prof Ronald; s of George James Amann, of Newcastle upon Tyne, and Elizabeth Clementson, *née* Towell (d 1983); *b* 21 August 1943; *Educ* Heaton GS Newcastle upon Tyne, Univ of Birmingham (MSocSci, PhD); *m* 28 Aug 1965, Susan Frances, da of Leslie Peters, of S Porcupine, Ontario, Canada; 2 s (Edmund b 1968, Timothy Francis b 1970), 1 da (Jessica Louise b 1974); *Career* conslt OECD 1965–68; Univ of Birmingham: sr lectr (formerly asst lectr and lectr) 1968–83, dir Centre for Russian and E Euro Studies 1983–89, prof of comparative politics 1985–, dean Faculty of Commerce and Social Sci 1989–91, pro-vice-chllr 1991–94; chief exec and dep chm ESRC 1994–99, DG Centre for Management and Policy Studies Cabinet Office 1999–; former memb Cncl Sch of Slavonic and E Euro Studies Univ of London, specialist advsr and witness Foreign Affrs Ctee and Ctee on Sci and Technol House of Commons; chm Steering Ctee ESRC E-W Res Initiative, chm Centre for Res on Innovation and Competition (CRIC) Univ of Manchester, memb Nat Technol Foresight Steering Gp, memb Steering Ctee Centre for the Analysis of Risk and Regulation (CARR) LSE; *Books* Science Policy in the USSR (with Berry and Davies, 1969), The Technological Level of Soviet Industry (with Cooper and Davies), Industrial Innovation in the Soviet Union (with Cooper, 1982), Technical Progress and Soviet Economic Development (with Cooper); *Recreations* walking, modern jazz, cricket; *Clubs* Athenaeum; *Style*— Prof Ronald Amann; ✉ Centre for Management and Policy Studies, Cabinet Office, Admiralty Arch, The Mall, London SW1A 2WH

AMARATUNGA, Prof Gehan Anil Joseph; s of Carl Herman Joseph Amaratunga (d 1966), and Swarna Mallika, *née* Undugodage; *b* 6 April 1956; *Educ* Royal Coll Colombo Sri Lanka, Pelham Meml HS Westchester NY, UC Cardiff (BSc), Univ of Cambridge (PhD); *m* 19 Sept 1981, Praveen Dharshini, da of John Hitchcock; 1 s (Ravindran b 9 Oct 1985), 2 da (Minoli b 19 April 1989, Gitanjali b 1 July 1990); *Career* res fell Microelectronics Centre Univ of Southampton 1983–84, lectr Dept of Electronics and Computer Sci Univ of Southampton 1984–87; lectr Dept of Engrg Univ of Cambridge 1987–95; prof of electrical engrg Univ of Liverpool 1995–98; prof of engrg Univ of Cambridge 1998–, fell Churchill Coll Cambridge 1998– (and 1987–95); founding dir and chief technol offr Cambridge Semiconductor Ltd 2000–, co-fndr Ekecsys Ltd 2003; RAE Research Award (Univ of Cambridge) 1979–82, IEE Prize 1979, Royal Acad of Engrg Overseas Secondment Award (Stanford Univ) 1989; FREng 2004, FIEE 2004; *Publications* over 400 academic publications in jls and symposia proceedings incl: Transactions of the IEEE, Physical Review, Nature, Jl of Applied Physics; *Recreations* jazz, cinema, vintage sports cars, cricket, supporting Liverpool FC; *Style*— Prof Gehan Amaratunga; ✉ Department of Engineering, Electrical Engineering Division, 9 J J Thomson Avenue, Cambridge CB3 0DF (tel 01223 748320, fax 01223 748322, e-mail gaja1@cam.ac.uk)

AMBERG, Bill; s of M J Amberg, and J A Can; *Career* fashion designer; opened shops: London 1997, New York; Freeman: City of London, Worshipful Co of Makers of Playing Cards; *Recreations* family life; *Style*— Bill Amberg, Esq

AMBLER, Prof Richard Penry; s of Henry Reason Ambler, OBE (d 1970), and Anne Sarah Ellen, *née* Evans (d 1993); *b* 26 May 1933; *Educ* Haileybury, Pembroke Coll Cambridge (minor scholar, MA, PhD); *m* 1, 1957 (m dis), Ann Patricia, da of Leonard Waddington (d 1991); 2 da (Anne b 9 April 1962, Jane b 14 Sept 1964); m 2, 1994, Susan (d 2004), da of Stanley Hewlett (d 2003); *Career* 2 Lt Royal Signals 1953–55; Univ of Cambridge: res fell Pembroke Coll 1959–62, res MRC Laboratory of Molecular Biology 1962–65; Univ of Edinburgh: lectr 1965–73, sr lectr 1973–75, reader 1975–87, head Dept of Molecular Biology 1984–90, prof of protein chemistry 1987–, head Inst of Cell and Molecular Biology 1990–93; memb: Biochemical Soc 1958, Euro Molecular Biology Orgn 1985, Soc of Antiquaries of Scotland 1985; tstee Darwin Tst of Edinburgh 1984–94; *Recreations* railways and ancient history; *Clubs* New (Edinburgh); *Style*— Prof Richard Ambler

AMBRASEYS, Prof Nicholas; s of Neocles Amvrasis (d 1999), of Athens, and Cleopatra, *née* Yambani (d 1986); *b* 19 January 1929; *Educ* Nat Tech Univ of Athens, Imperial Coll London (DIC), Univ of London (PhD, DSc); *m* 25 Aug 1955, Xeni, da of Alexander Stavrou; *Career* lectr in civil engrg Imperial Coll London 1958–62, assoc prof of civil engrg Univ of Illinois 1963, prof of hydrodynamics Nat Tech Univ Athens 1964; Imperial Coll London: lectr in engrg seismology 1965–68, univ reader 1969–72, prof 1973–94, head Engrg Seismology Section 1969–94, sr res fell 1994–; chm Br Nat Ctee for Earthquake Engrg 1961–71, dir Int Assoc for Earthquake Engrg 1961–77, vice-pres Euro Assoc for Earthquake Engrg 1964–75, vice-chm UNESCO Int Advsy Ctee on Earthquake Risk 1979–81 (memb 1969–81); ldr UN/UNESCO earthquake reconnaissance missions to Pakistan, Iran, Turkey, Romania, Yugoslavia, Italy, Greece, Algeria, Nicaragua, E and Central Africa; chm Int Cmmn for Earthquake Protection of Historical Monuments 1977–81; hon memb Int Assoc of Earthquake Engrg 1993–, hon memb Euro Assoc of Earthquake Engrg, hon memb Earthquake Research Inst USA 2001; Decennial Award European Assoc for Earthquake Engrg 1975, Busk Medal RGS 1975, W Smith Medal Geological Soc of London 2002; Freedom City of Skopje 1999; memb Acad of Athens 2002; Dr (hc) Univ of Athens 1993, fell C&G 2000; FREng 1985, FICE, FGS, FRGS; *Books* The Seismicity of Egypt, Arabia and the Red Sea - A History of Persian Earthquakes (with C Melville, 1982 and 1994), The Seismicity of Turkey (with C Finkel, 1995), Seismicity of Central America (2000), Seismicity of Iceland (2000); *Recreations* historical geography, archaeology; *Style—* Prof Nicholas Ambraseys, FREng; ✉ 19 Bede House, Manor Fields, London SW15 3LT (tel 020 8788 4219); Department of Civil Engineering, Imperial College of Science and Technology, London SW7 2BU (fax 020 7225 2716, e-mail n.ambraseys@imperial.ac.uk)

AMBROSE, (Neil) Simon; s of Neil Trevor Ambrose (d 1952), and Margaret, *née* Donaldson; *b* 17 May 1950; *Educ* Campbell Coll Belfast, King's Coll Hosp Med Sch (MB BS, MS); *m* 11 Sept 1976, (Elizabeth) Jane, da of William John Arthur Cowley; 2 s (Benjamin Neil b 1981, Jeremy William b 1983), 1 da (Felicity Jane b 1986); *Career* lectr in surgery Univ of Birmingham 1983–88, conslt surgn and sr clinical lectr Univ of Leeds 1988–, surgical tutor Leeds Eastern Health Authy 1989–94, chm Leeds Eastern Dist Audit Ctee 1990–91; sec Assoc of Surgns in Trg 1985–87; chm: St James's Univ Hosp Tst Audit Ctee 1991–, Yorks Gastrointestinalo Tumour Gp 1989–93; memb: Yorks Regnl Audit Ctee 1991–, Yorks Regnl Cancer Orgn Policy Ctee 1993–, Regnl Higher Surgical Trg Ctee 1994–; FRCS 1979; *Recreations* travel, reading, swimming, golf, gardening, DIY; *Style—* Simon Ambrose, Esq; ✉ St James's University Hospital, Beckett Street, Leeds LS9 7TF (tel 0113 243 3144)

AMBROSE, Timothy Michael; s of Henry Ambrose, and Janet, *née* Millard; *b* 8 December 1949; *Educ* Dauntsey's Sch West Lavington, Univ of Southampton (BA, CertEd); *m* 21 Sept 1974, Hon Angela Francesca Hayward Blanch, 3 da of Rt Rev Baron Blanch, PC, DD (Life Peer, d 1994); 2 da (Bethany Beatrice Hayward b 24 July 1978, Emily Kate b 15 May 1981); *Career* res asst Univ of Oxford Inst of Archaeology and archivist Ashmolean Museum Library 1972–74, pubns asst DOE 1974–75, res asst in Euro archaeology Univ of Oxford 1975–77, asst keeper of archaeology Lincolnshire Museums 1977–82; Scottish Museums Cncl: dep dir 1982–86, dir 1986–94; sr res fell City Univ Dept of Arts Policy and Mgmnt 1994–96, head of practice Museum Resource Management (UK and int museum advsrs) 1994–99; chm Exec Bd ICOM UK 1992–98; assoc dir L & R Consulting 1996–99, dir Locum Destination Consulting 1999–2004, assoc dir Locum Consulting 2004–, princ Timothy Ambrose Consulting 2004–; hon sr res fell Dept of Arts Policy and Management City Univ 1996–; author of numerous reports, reviews and papers; FMA 1990 (AMA 1980), FSA 1993; *Books* New Museums - A Start-Up Guide (1987), Education in Museums, Museums in Education (1987), Working with Museums (1988), Presenting Scotland's Story (1989), Money, Money, Money and Museums (1991), Forward Planning - a Handbook (1991), Museum Basics (1993), Managing New Museums (1993), Museum Basics (2006); *Recreations* gardening; *Style—* Timothy M Ambrose, Esq, FSA; ✉ Friars Cottage, The Street, Kingston, Lewes, East Sussex BN7 3PD (tel 01273 478423, e-mail tambrose@locumconsulting.com)

AMERY, Shenda (KHAZAL-); da of William Charles Garrett, and Lily Herring; *b* 28 November 1937, London; *Educ* Shipwrights Sch, Rayleigh Tech Sch, Southend Municipal Coll (HNC); *m* 22 July 1961, Sheikh Nezam Khazal Kabi-al-Amery; 2 s (Roknedin b 22 March 1963, Saladin b 24 Feb 1966); *Career* sculptor; early career as chemist Physical Chemical Research Dept May & Baker 1954–59, lectr and asst chemist Tehran Univ 1959–61; first one-woman show Tehran 1970 (three subsequent one-woman shows); returned to UK 1979; numerous one-woman exhbns incl: RSBS, Dorman Museum Cleveland, The Orangery Holland Park, Loggia Gallery London, Biltmore Gallery Arizona, Osbourne Gallery London, Edith Grove Gallery; gp exhbns incl: Royal Acad, Paris Salon, Osborn Studio Gallery, Gagliardi Gallery; subjects of sculptures incl: Margaret Thatcher (now Baroness Thatcher), John Major (then PM), Cherie Blair, King Hussain and Queen Noor of Jordan, Betty Boothroyd, Mo Mowlam, David Blunkett, Clare Short, Anita Roddick; sculptures in Regent's Park (Ambika Fountain and Unseen Prey), painting of Tony Blair hanging in Chequers; Arts Cncl Award 1995–96; former memb Cncl RSBS, chm Ladies Ctee Help the Aged, memb Ladies Ctee European Atlantic Gp; ARBS; *Style—* Sheikha Shenda Amery; ✉ 25a Edith Grove, Chelsea, London SW10 0LB (tel 020 7352 1775, fax 020 7376 7738, website www.shendaamery.co.uk)

AMES, Ethan Ojai; s of Richard McCurdy Ames, of Santa Barbara, and Ann, *née* Jones (d 1992); *b* 16 June 1949; *Educ* Summerhill Sch, East Ham Tech Coll (LSIAD); *m* 11 Aug 1973 (m dis 1985), Julia Rosemary, *née* Stone; 1 da (Tacita Amelia Charlotte Inez Tora b 1 March 1974); partner, Robert William Thomas Chapman; *Career* graphic designer; sr lectr/course tutor East Ham Coll of Technol 1973–78, sr graphic designer Thames TV 1978–82, head of design and graphics TV-am 1982–88, prodn graphic designer Thames TV 1988–92; BBC TV: graphic design mangr News and Current Affrs 1992–94, head of Graphic Design 1994–97, creative dir Post Prodn and Graphic Design 1997–98; freelance conslt 1998–; dir of studies Ravensbourne Coll of Design & Communication 2001– (sr lectr 1999–2001); work published in D&AD, Modern Publicity, Print Magazine, Graphics World, Monotype Recorder, Changing Image, Television Graphics - From Pencil to Pixel; memb: D&AD 1978, RTS 1982, BDA 1993; FRSA; *Style—* Ethan Ames, Esq; ✉ 81 Queens Road, Twickenham TW1 4EU (tel 020 8892 6552, e-mail mail@ethanames.co.uk)

AMES, Gerald George Singleton; s of George Singleton Ames (d 1956), and Florence Christian, *née* Hart (d 1982); *b* 15 April 1927; *Educ* Wade Deacon GS, Manchester Sch of Architecture (DipArch); *m* 4 Feb 1950, Margaret, da of Frederick Atherton (d 1983), of Hillcrest, Cheshire; 2 s (Stephen b 1956, Mark b 1960); *Career* dir John Finlan Ltd 1956–70, md and deputy chm Finlan Group plc 1970–85, dir Finlan Group plc (company concerned in property design and development, export of building services and components, materials handling and merchanting) 1985–87, chm and md Sefton Group Ltd (property devpt, mgmnt and investment); dir: Sefton Land Ltd, Sefton Securities Ltd, Sefton Plard Ltd; ARIBA; *Recreations* sailing, music; *Clubs* Liverpool Artists'; *Style—* Gerald Ames, Esq; ✉ Sefton Group Ltd, Queen Insurance Buildings, 9 Queen Avenue, Liverpool L2 4TZ (tel 0151 227 1553, fax 0151 236 1046)

AMESS, David Anthony Andrew; MP; s of James Henry Valentine Amess (d 1986), and Maud Ethel, *née* Martin; *b* 26 March 1952; *Educ* St Bonaventures GS, Bournemouth Coll of Technol (BSc); *m* 1983, Julia Margaret Monica, da of Graham Harry Arnold, of Southend-on-Sea, Essex; 1 s, 4 da; *Career* teacher 1970–71, insurance underwriter Leslie & Godwin Agency 1974–76, sr conslt Accountancy Personnel 1976–80, ptnr Accountancy Aims Employment Agency 1981–87; chm: Accountancy Solutions 1987–90, Accountancy Aims Group 1990–96, 1912 Club 1996–; memb Cons Pty 1968–, Parly candidate (Cons) Forest Gate 1974 and 1978, GLC candidate Newham NW 1977, Parly candidate (Cons) Newham NW 1979; MP (Cons): Basildon 1983–97, Southend W 1997–; PPS at DHSS 1987 to: Edwina Currie, Michael Portillo, Lord Skelmersdale; PPS to Michael Portillo: as Min of State Dept of Tport 1988–90, at DOE 1990–92, as Chief Sec to the Treasy 1992–94, as Sec of State for Employment 1994–95, as Sec of State for Def 1995–97; dir Parly Broadcasting Unit 1997–99; memb Broadcasting Select Ctee 1995–97, memb Health Select Ctee 1998–; jt chm All-Pty: Scouts Gp, Fire Gp; vice-pres Lotteries Cncl 1998–; Chm's Panel 2001; Redbridge Cncl: elected 1982, vice-chm Housing Ctee 1981–85; *Publications* The Road to Basildon (1993), Conservatives Fight Back (1994); contrib to various magazines and pamphlets; *Recreations* reading, writing, sport, theatre, gardening, popular music; *Clubs* Carlton, Kingswood Squash and Racketball (Basildon), St Stephens; *Style—* David Amess, Esq, MP; ✉ House of Commons, London SW1A 0AA (tel 020 7219 6387, fax 020 7219 2245, e-mail amessd@parliament.uk)

AMEY, Julian Nigel Robert; s of Robert Amey, of Barton Seagrave, Northants, and Diana, *née* Coles; *b* 19 June 1949; *Educ* Wellingborough Sch, Magdalene Coll Cambridge (MA); *m* 16 Dec 1972, Ann Victoria, da of Thomas Frank Brenchley, CMG, of London, and Edith, *née* Helfand; 3 da (Joanna b 9 Sept 1981, Frances b 12 Oct 1984, Charlotte b 7 Jan 1990); *Career* dir of int sales and marketing Longman Group Ltd 1985–89, exec dir BBC English World Service 1989–94, seconded to DTI 1994–96, DG Canning House (Hispanic and Luso Brazilian Cncl) 1996–2001; chief exec: CIBSE 2001–06, Trinity Coll London 2006–; govr Bath Spa Univ; *Books* Spanish Business Dictionary (1979), Portuguese Business Dictionary (1981); *Recreations* cricket, travel; *Clubs* Hawks' (Cambridge), ESU, Rumford; *Style—* Julian Amey, Esq

AMHERST OF HACKNEY, 4 Baron (UK 1892); (William) Hugh Amherst Cecil; s of 3 Baron Amherst of Hackney, CBE (d 1980), and Margaret Eirene, *née* Clifton Brown; *b* 28 December 1940; *Educ* Eton; *m* 1965, Elisabeth, da of Hugh Humphery Merriman, DSO, MC, TD, DL (d 1983); 1 da (Hon Aurelia Margaret Amherst (Hon Mrs Stephenson) b 1966), 1 s (Hon (Hugh) William Amherst b 1968); *Heir* s, Hon William Cecil; *Career* dir: E A Gibson Shipbrokers Ltd 1975–90, Seascope Sale and Purchase Ltd 1994–97, Short Sea Europe plc 1995–2001, ret memb Baltic Exchange; memb Cncl RYA 1999–2002; younger bro Trinity House; patron: St-John-at-Hackney, St John of Jerusalem (S Hackney); *Recreations* sailing (yacht 'Hal'); *Clubs* Royal Yacht Sqdn (vice-cdre 1993–98, cdre 2001–05), Royal Ocean Racing, Royal Cruising, Royal Lymington; *Style—* The Rt Hon the Lord Amherst of Hackney; ✉ Hawthorn House, New Street, Lymington, Hampshire SO41 9BJ

AMIEL, Jonathan Michael (Jon); s of Barry Conrad Amiel (d 1978), of London, and Anita, *née* Barron; *b* 20 May 1948; *Educ* William Ellis Sch London, Univ of Cambridge (MA); *m* Tara, da of Lawrence Fuccella, and Sally Byrd; 4 s (Leo Barry, Jack Barry, Luke Barry, Max Barry); *Career* freelance director; admin Oxford & Cambridge Shakespeare Co 1970–73, literary mangr then assoc dir Hampstead Theatre Club 1973–76, asst then assoc dir Royal Shakespeare Co 1976–78, story ed BBC TV 1978–79; directed numerous prodns for BBC Play for Today 1980–85, incl: Preview, Lunch, A Sudden Wrench, Busted, Gates of Gold, Nobody's Property; other credits as dir incl: Tandoori Nights (series, Channel 4) 1985, Silent Twins (film) 1986, The Singing Detective (BBC) 1986, Queen of Hearts (feature film) 1988, Aunt Julia & The Scriptwriter (US title Tune In Tomorrow) 1990, Sommersby (with Richard Gere and Jodie Foster) 1993, Copycat (with Sigourney Weaver and Holly Hunter) 1995, The Man Who Knew Too Little (with Bill Murray) 1997, Entrapment (with Sean Connery and Catherine Zeta-Jones) 1999, The Core (with Aaron Ectchart, Hilary Swank and Stanley Tucci) 2002; winner numerous awards for The Singing Detective, several festival awards for Queen of Hearts and Tune In Tomorrow; *Style—* Jon Amiel, Esq; ✉ Steve Rabineau, William Morris Agency, 151 El Camino, Beverly Hills, CA 90210 (tel 001 310 859 4366, e-mail sr@wma.com)

AMIES, Timothy John; *b* 1 July 1938; *Educ* Oundle; *m* 6 Nov 1969, Clare Rosemary, *née* Crawfurd; 3 s (Tom b 1971, Edward b 1973, Harry b 1979), 2 da (Sarah b 1974, Alice b 1985); *Career* Queen's Own Cameron Highlanders 1956–58; Casselton Elliott 1959–64, Morgan Grenfell 1964–68, stockbroker Laurie Milbank & Co 1968–86, Chase Manhattan Bank 1986–90; dir: Chase Investment Bank Ltd 1987–90, HG Capital Tst 1991–, World Vision (UK) 1996–2002, Amies International Ltd 2000–; FCA, MSI; *Recreations* travel, gardening; *Clubs* City of London, IOD; *Style—* Timothy Amies, Esq; ✉ The Old Farm, Great Brickhill, Milton Keynes, Buckinghamshire MK17 9AH (tel 01525 261243); Ballachar, Loch Ruthven, Farr, Inverness (tel 01808 521258, e-mail tim@amiesinternational.com)

AMIN, Prof Ash; *Educ* Univ of Reading (PhD); *Career* Univ of Durham: prof of geography, head Dept of Geography 2002–05, exec dir Inst of Advanced Study 2006–; fell Swedish Collegium of Advanced Study in the Social Sciences 1999; visiting posts: Univ of Naples, Univ of Bologna, Univ of Copenhagen, Univ of Rotterdam; memb Research Priorities Bd ESRC 1997–2001, memb Cncl European Assoc for Evolutionary Political Economy until 2002; AcSS 2000, fell World Acad of Art and Science 2003; *Books* Technological Change, Industrial Restructuring and Regional Development (jt ed, 1986), Towards a New Europe? (jt ed, 1991), Post-Fordism: A Reader (ed, 1994), Globalisation, Institutions and Regional Development in Europe (jt ed, 1994), Behind the Myth of European Union (jt ed, 1995), Beyond Market and Hierarchy: Interactive Governance and Social Complexity (jt ed, 1997), Cities for the Many not the Few (jtly, 2000), Placing the Social Economy (jtly, 2002), Cities: Reimagining the Urban (jtly, 2002), Decentering the Nation: A Radical Approach to Regional Inequality (jtly, 2003), The Blackwell Cultural Economy Reader (jt ed, 2003), Architectures of Knowledge: Firms, Capabilities and Communities (jtly, 2004); *Style—* Prof Ash Amin; ✉ Department of Geography, Science Laboratories, South Road, Durham DH1 3LE

AMIN, Mohammed; s of Shadi Mehrban (d 1987), and Riaban Mehrban (d 1992); *b* 29 October 1950, Kalyanpur, Pakistan; *Educ* Central GS Manchester, Clare Coll Cambridge (BA), Univ of Leeds (CertEd); *m* 1978, Tahara; 2 s (Ibrahim b 1980, Ismail b 1982), 2 da (Scheherazade b 1985, Khadijah b 1988); *Career* teacher Counthill Sch Oldham 1973–74, trainee accountant Graham H Wood & Co 1974–77, tax sr then tax mangr Arthur Andersen 1977–84, sr tax mangr then tax ptnr John Fairhurst & Co 1984–87, ptnr Price Waterhouse (now PricewaterhouseCoopers LLP) 1990– (sr tax mangr 1987–90, currently memb UK Supervisory Bd); chm Manchester Branch Inst of Taxation 1985–87, memb Cncl Chartered Inst of Taxation 2003–, memb Technical Ctee ACT 2004–; fndr memb Muslim Jewish Forum of Gtr Manchester 2004–; memb Cncl Manchester and Dist Chess Assoc 1983– (pres 1981–83), finance dir Br Chess Fedn 1985–89; listed in: Asian Power 100 2005, Muslim Power 100 2007; assoc memb ACT 1995, FCA (ACA 1977), FCInstT 2000 (ATII 1978); *Publications* The Taxation of Equity Derivatives and Structured Products (contrib, 2002); Finance and Treasury Web Log: pwc.blogs.com/mohammed_amin; *Recreations* chess, go (Japanese board game), listening to classical and modern music, reading science fiction; *Style—* Mohammed Amin, Esq; ✉ PricewaterhouseCoopers LLP, 101 Barbirolli Square, Manchester M2 3PW (tel 0161 245 2000, fax 0161 245 2906, e-mail mohammed.amin@uk.pwc.com)

AMINI, Hossein; s of Iradj Amini and Vida Amini; *Educ* Bryanston, Wadham Coll Oxford (scholarship); *m* Alexandra; 2 da (Nina, Nieve); *Career* writer; *Film* incl: The Dying of the Light 1994 (TV film, BAFTA nomination Best Single Drama), Jude 1996 (Michael Powell Award for Best Br Film Edinburgh Film Festival, Best Film Dinard Film

Festival), The Wings of the Dove 1997 (Oscar nomination Best Adapted Screenplay 1998, nomination Best Adapted Screenplay Writer's Guild of America 1998, nomination Best Adapted Screenplay BAFTA Awards 1998) 1997, In a Lonely Place 1997, Four Feathers 2000, Shanghai 2000, Gangs of New York (draft for Martin Scorsese) 2001, Mila 18 2002; *Publications* Jude (1996), Wings of the Dove (1998); *Style—* Hossein Amini, Esq; ✉ c/o Curtis Brown, Haymarket House, 28–29 Haymarket, London SW1Y 4SP (tel 020 7396 6600, fax 020 7396 0110)

AMIS, Martin Louis; s of Sir Kingsley William Amis, CBE (d 1995), and his 1 w, Hilary Ann, *née* Bardwell; *b* 25 August 1949; *Educ* Exeter Coll Oxford (BA); *m* 1, (m dis 1996), Antonia; m 2, 1998, Isabel; *Career* writer; literary ed New Statesman 1977–79, special writer The Observer 1980–; tennis corr The New Yorker 1992–; FRSL 1983; *Books* The Rachel Papers (1973, Somerset Maugham Award 1974), Dead Babies (1975), Success (1978), Other People: A Mystery Story (1981), Money (1984), The Moronic Inferno and Other Visits to America (1986), Einstein's Monsters (1987), London Fields (1989), Time's Arrow (1991), The Information (1995), Night Train (1997), Heavy Water and Other Stories (short stories, 1998), Experience (2000, James Tait Black Memorial Prize), The War Against Cliché: Essays and Reviews 1971–2000 (2001), Koba the Dread: Laughter and the Twenty Million (2002), Yellow Dog (2003); *Style—* Martin Amis, Esq; ✉ c/o Wylie Agency, 17 Bedford Square, London WC1B 3JA (tel 020 7908 5900)

AMLOT, Roy Douglas; QC (1989); s of Air Cdre Douglas Lloyd Amlot, CBE, DFC, AFC (d 1979), of Portugal, and Ruby Luise, *née* Lawrence; *b* 22 September 1942; *Educ* Dulwich Coll; *m* 26 July 1969, Susan Margaret, da of Sir Henry McLorinan McDowell, KBE (d 2000), of Dulwich, London; 2 s (Thomas b 1971, Richard b 1978); *Career* called to the Bar Lincoln's Inn 1963 (bencher 1987, treas 2007); jr prosecuting counsel to the Crown (Central Criminal Court) 1977, sr prosecuting counsel to the Crown (Central Criminal Court) 1981, first sr prosecuting counsel to the Crown 1987, chm of the Bar 2001–02; chm Criminal Bar Assoc 1997–98; *Publications* Phipson on Evidence (ed 11 edn); *Recreations* skiing, windsurfing, music, squash; *Style—* Roy Amlot, Esq, QC; ✉ 6 King's Bench Walk, Temple, London EC4Y 7DR

AMORY, *see also:* Heathcoat-Amory

AMORY, Mark; s of Richard Heathcoat Amory (d 1957), and Hon Gaenor Scott-Ellis (d 2002); *b* 1 May 1941; *Educ* Eton, ChCh Oxford; *m* 20 Nov 1982, Charlotte Elizabeth, da of Evelyn Joll; 3 da (Evelyn b 18 July 1985, Olivia b 30 March 1988, Katharine b 21 June 1991); *Career* tutor to The Kabaka of Buganda 1962–63; journalist and writer; currently lit ed The Spectator; FRSL; Order of the Star of Ethiopia (second class); *Books* Lord Dunsany (1972), The Letters of Evelyn Waugh (ed, 1980), The Letters of Ann Fleming (ed, 1985), Lord Berners (1998); *Recreations* bridge, tennis, films, plays; *Style—* Mark Amory, Esq, FRSL; ✉ 20 Grafton Square, Clapham, London SW4 0DA; Hele Manor, Dulverton, Somerset TA22 9RN; c/o The Spectator, 22 Old Queen Street, London, SW1H 9HP (tel 020 7961 0200, fax 020 7961 0250)

AMOS, Gideon John; s of Francis John Clarke Amos, CBE (d 2003), and Geraldine Amos, MBE, *née* Sutton; *b* 16 January 1965, Liverpool; *Educ* Wells Cathedral Sch, Oxford Poly (BA), Oxford Brookes Univ (DipArch, DipUD, MA); *m* 6 May 1995, Caroline, da of David Ellis; *Career* dep pres Oxford Poly Students Union 1988–89, architectural asst R J Harrison Architects 1989–90, devpt designer WS Atkins 1994–97, dir Planning Aid for London 1997–2000 Town and Country Planning Assoc (TCPA): dir 2000–06, chief exec 2006–; memb Planning Advsy Gp Dept for Communities and Local Govt 2003–; cncllr Oxford City Cncl 1992–96 (ldr of the oppn 1995–96); memb Hackney Soc; RIBA 1994, MRTPI 2004, FRSA 2006; *Publications* Programme for Sustainable Communities (co-author, 2001), Connecting England: A Framework for Regional Development (ed, 2006); *Style—* Gideon Amos, Esq; ✉ Town and Country Planning Association, 17 Carlton House Terrace, London SW1Y 5AS (tel 020 7930 8903, fax 020 7930 3280, e-mail tcpa@tcpa.org.uk)

AMOS, Baroness (Life Peer UK 1997), of Brondesbury, in the London Borough of Brent; Valerie Amos; PC (2003); *b* 13 March 1954; *Educ* Univ of Warwick (BA), Univ of Birmingham (MA), UEA; *Career* Lambeth Borough Cncl 1981–82, women's advsr London Borough of Camden 1983–85, freelance organisational and mgmnt devpt conslt 1984–89, head of mgmnt servs London Borough of Hackney 1987–89 (head of trg and devpt 1985–87); chief exec Equal Opportunities Cmmn 1989–94, md Quality and Equality 1994–95, dir Amos Fraser Bernard 1995–98; a Baroness in Waiting (Govt whip) 1998–2001, Parly under-sec of state FCO 2001–03, sec of state for International Devpt 2003, ldr House of Lords and Lord Pres of the Cncl 2003–07; former non-exec dir UCLH; author and presenter numerous papers at nat and int confs; external examiner Univ of Liverpool 1991–97, hon prof Thames Valley Univ; former memb: Cncl Inst of Employment Studies, Cncl King's Fund; former dep chair Runnymede Tst; chair: Bd of Govrs RCN, AFIYA Tst (formerly); former dir Hampstead Theatre, former tstee Inst of Public Policy Research; Hon Dr jur Univ of Warwick, Hon Dr jur Univ of Staffordshire, Hon Dr jur Univ of Manchester; FRSA; *Style—* The Rt Hon Baroness Amos, PC; ✉ House of Lords, London SW1A 0PW

AMPHLETT, Philip Nicholas; s of Colin Bernard Amphlett, of Wootton Village, Oxon, and Hilda, *née* Price (d 1972); *b* 20 October 1948; *Educ* Winchester, Balliol Coll Oxford (BA); *m* 4 Aug 1969, Marjolein Erantha, da of Jan Cornelius de Vries (d 1952), of Eindhoven, Holland; 2 da (Jessica b 9 Jan 1970, Catherine b 14 Nov 1974), 1 s (Jan b 17 Aug 1972 d 2001); *Career* trainee mangr W H Brandts Sons and Co Ltd 1971–73, dir Henry Ansbacher and Co Ltd 1981–85 (joined 1973), sr vice-pres Bank Julius Baer and Co Ltd 1985–97, exec dir EFG Private Bank 1997–; *Recreations* sailing, swimming, tennis; *Style—* Philip Amphlett, Esq; ✉ Howletts, Great Hallingbury, Bishop's Stortford, Hertfordshire CM22 7TR (tel 01279 654563); Ballaminers Cottage, Little Petherick, Wadebridge, Cornwall PL27 7QT; EFG Private Bank Ltd, 12 Hay Hill, London W1X 8EE

AMPTHILL, 4 Baron (UK 1881); Geoffrey Denis Erskine Russell; CBE (1986), PC (1995); s of late 3 Baron Ampthill, CBE, by his 1 w, Christabel, da of Lt-Col John Hart, by his w, Blanche, 4 da of Capt David Erskine (2 s of Sir David Erskine, 1 Bt); suc 1973; *b* 15 October 1921; *Educ* Stowe; *m* 1, 1946 (m dis 1971), Susan Mary Sheila (d 2001), da of Hon Charles Winn (2 s of 2 Baron St Oswald, JP, DL) by his 1 w, Hon Olive Paget (da of 1 and last Baron Queenborough, GBE, JP); 2 s (and 1 s decd), 1 da; m 2, 1972 (m dis 1987), Elisabeth Anne-Marie, da of late Claude Mallon, of Paris, and of Mme Chavane; *Heir* s, Hon David Russell, *qv*; *Career* WWII Capt Irish Gds; gen mangr Fortnum & Mason 1947–51, chm New Providence Hotel Co Ltd 1952–58, md various theatre owning and producing cos 1953–71; dir: Dualvest 1980–87, United News & Media plc (formerly United Newspapers) 1981–96 (dep chm 1991–96), Express Newspapers plc 1985–98 (dep chm 1989–98); dep chm of ctees House of Lords 1981–92 (chm 1992–94), dep speaker 1983–; chm Select Ctee on: Channel Tunnel Bill 1987, Channel Tunnel Rail Link Bill 1996; chm London Helicopter Emergency Service 1991–98; dir Leeds Castle Fndn 1980–82; *Style—* The Rt Hon the Lord Ampthill, CBE, PC; ✉ 6 North Court, Great Peter Street, London SW1P 3LL (tel 020 7233 0133, fax 020 7233 0122)

AMWELL, 3 Baron (UK 1947), of Islington, Co London; Keith Norman Montague; s of 2 Baron Amwell (d 1990), and Kathleen Elizabeth, *née* Fountain; *b* 1 April 1943; *Educ* Ealing GS, Univ of Nottingham (BSc); *m* 1970, Mary, o da of Frank Palfreyman, of Potters Bar, Herts; 2 s (Hon Ian b 1973, Hon Christopher b 1977); *Heir* s, Hon Ian Montague; *Career* consulting civil engr Brian Colquhoun and Partners 1965–94; dir: Thorburn Colquhoun Ltd 1994–96, Construction Industry Research and Information Assoc (CIRIA) 1998–2005, Civil Engrg and Environmental Quality Awards (CEEQUAL) Ltd 2004–; CEng, CGeol, FICE, FGS, MIQA; *Recreations* walking, gardening, photography, badminton; *Style—* The Rt Hon Lord Amwell

AMYES, Prof Sebastian Giles Becket; s of Julian Charles Becket Amyes (d 1992), of London, and Katherine Anne Smith, *née* Allan (d 1999); *b* 6 May 1949; *Educ* Cranleigh Sch, UCL (BSc), Univ of Reading (MSc), Univ of London (PhD, DSc); *m* 17 April 1976 (m dis 2006), Dorothy Mary, da of William Thomas Gregory; 1 s (Rupert William Becket b 26 May 1978), 1 da (Alexandra Katherine Becket b 15 Nov 1979); *Career* teaching fell Sch of Pharmacy Univ of London 1974–77; Univ of Edinburgh: lectr 1977–88, reader 1988–92, prof of microbial chemotherapy 1992–, head Medical Microbiology Dept 1997–2001; author of 426 pubns; Annual Science award Royal Pharmaceutical Soc 1984, C L Oakley lectr Pathological Soc 1987; Dr (hc) Semmelweis Medical Univ 2004; FRCPath 1995 (MRCPath 1985), FIBiol 1988; *Recreations* fishing, foreign exploration, antique maps, opera; *Style—* Prof Sebastian Amyes; ✉ Centre for Infectious Diseases, College of Medicine and Veterinary Medicine, Chancellors Building, 49 Little France Crescent, Edinburgh EH16 4SB (tel 0131 242 6652, fax 0131 242 6611 e-mail s.g.b.amyes@ed.ac.uk)

ANCASTER, Earl of ; *see:* Willoughby de Eresby, Baroness

ANCRAM, Rt Hon Michael; *see:* Lothian, 13 Marquess of

ANDENAS, Dr Mads; s of Tonnes Andreas Madsson Andenas (d 1975), and Henny Marie Jenssen; *b* 27 July 1957; *Educ* Univ of Oslo, Univ of Oxford (MA, DPhil), Univ of Cambridge (PhD); *m* 1981 (m dis 1987), Kristin, da of Knut Utstein Kloster; *Career* admitted advokat Norway 1991; called to the Bar Middle Temple 1996, bencher Inner Temple 2003; hon dir of studies then sr research fell Inst of Advanced Legal Studies Univ of London 1993–, dir Centre of European Law KCL 1994–99 (lectr then sr lectr in law 1992–94, now visiting prof), dir Br Inst of Int and Comparative Law 1999–; sr teaching fell in EC law Inst of European and Comparative Law Univ of Oxford, fell Harris Manchester Coll Oxford 2000–, prof Univ of Leicester 2005–; gen ed: International and Comparative Law Quarterly, European Business Law Review; memb numerous editorial bds and author or ed of 40 books; visiting prof: QMC London, Univ Libre de Bruxelles 2002–03, Univ of Rome (La Sapienza) 2005–08, Univ of Paris I (Sorbonne) 2006; memb Worshipful Co of Pattenmakers; *Clubs* Athenaeum; *Style—* Dr Mads Andenas; ✉ The British Institute of International and Comparative Law, Charles Clore House, 17 Russell Square, London WC1B 5JP (tel 020 7862 5151, fax 020 7862 5152, e-mail m.andenas@biicl.org)

ANDERSON, Alexander Beveridge (Sandy); DL (1991); s of John Weir Anderson, of Methil, Fife, and Elizabeth Warrender, *née* Beveridge (d 1979); *b* 16 April 1944; *Educ* Buckhaven HS, Heriot-Watt Univ (BSc); *m* 1970, Mary Bell Scott, *née* Wemyss (d 2001); 3 s; *Career* general mangr ICI Teeside Operations 1989–94, dir of engrg ICI plc 1994–96, ops dir Tioxide Gp Ltd 1994–97, sr vice-pres of technology ICI plc 1997–2000, ret; dir: Teesside Development Co 1989–98, Teesside TEC 1991–94, Eutech Engineering Solutions Ltd 1994–2001; chm: Teesside Training Enterprise 1990–94, Teesside Tomorrow Ltd 1990–94; dir ICI Pakistan Ltd 1998–2000; chm Bd of Governors Univ of Teesside 2005–; FIChemE 1990, FREng 1997; *Recreations* golf, reading, music, theatre, gardening; *Style—* Sandy Anderson, Esq, DL, FREng; ✉ Carperby Lodge, 39 Abbey Road, Darlington, County Durham DL3 8LR (tel 01325 354386, fax 01325 360389, e-mail sandy_anderson@talk21.com)

ANDERSON, Dr Alun Mark; s of Peter Marchmont Anderson, of Denbigh, N Wales, and Jane Watkin James; *b* 27 May 1948; *Educ* Rhyl GS, Univ of Sussex (BSc), Univ of Edinburgh (PhD), Univ of Oxford (IBM res fell), Univ of Kyoto Japan (Royal Soc fell); *Career* Nature (Int Jl of Sci): news and views ed 1980–83, Tokyo bureau chief 1983–86, Washington bureau chief 1986–90; int ed Science 1991–92, ed-in-chief and publishing dir New Scientist 2000–05 (ed 1992–2000), sr conslt New Scientist 2005–; dir IPC Magazines 1997–98; memb: Royal Soc Ctee on the Public Understanding of Science 1997–2000, Royal Soc Faraday Prize Ctee 1999–, Br Cncl Science, Engrg and Environment Ctee 2001–, Cncl Royal Inst 2005–; tstee St Andrews Prize 1999–; Ed of the Year BSME 1993, 1995 and 1997, Eds' Ed of the Year 1997; memb Cncl Univ of Sussex 1998–2001; *Books* Science Technology In Japan (1984, 2 edn 1990); *Recreations* mountain walking, photography; *Style—* Dr Alun Anderson; ✉ New Scientist, Lacon House, 84 Theobald's Road, London WC1X 8NS (tel 020 7611 1204)

ANDERSON, Anthony John; QC (1982); s of A Fraser Anderson (d 1982), and Margaret Gray, *née* Spence (d 1986); *b* 12 September 1938; *Educ* Harrow, Magdalen Coll Oxford (MA); *m* 1970, Fenja Ragnhild, da of Havard Gunn, OBE; *Career* 2 Lt Gordon Highlanders 1957–59; called to the Bar Inner Temple 1964 (bencher 1992), recorder of the Crown Court 1995–99; chm of tbnls Securities and Futures Authy (formerly The Securities Assoc) 1988–; *Recreations* golf, fishing; *Clubs* Garrick, MCC; *Style—* Anthony Anderson, Esq, QC

ANDERSON, Brett; *b* 29 September 1967; *Career* singer; fndr memb Suede 1989–; singles: The Drowners 1992, Metal Mickey 1992, Animal Nitrate 1993, So Young 1993, Stay Together 1994, We are the Pigs 1994, The Wild Ones 1994, New Generation 1995, Trash 1996, Beautiful Ones 1996, Saturday Night 1997, Lazy 1997, Film Star 1997, Electricity 1999, She's in Fashion 1999, Everything Will Flow 1999, Can't Get Enough 1999, Positivity 2002; albums: Suede 1993 (UK no 1), Dog Man Star 1994, Coming Up 1996 (UK no 1), Sci-Fi Lullabies 1997 (compilation), Head Music 1999 (UK no 1), A New Morning 2002; memb The Tears 2004–; singles: Refugees 2005, Lovers 2005; album: Here Come The Tears 2005; Mercury Music Award 1993; *Style—* Brett Anderson, Esq; ✉ c/o Charlie Charlton, Incepta Enterprises, First Floor, 98 White Lion Street, London N1 9PF (tel 020 7278 8001)

ANDERSON, Clive Stuart; *Educ* Selwyn Coll Cambridge (MA, pres Cambridge Footlights); *Career* television presenter and barrister; called to the Bar Middle Temple 1976; host The Cabaret Upstairs (BBC Radio 4) 1986–88, chm Whose Line Is It Anyway? (Radio 4 1988, Channel 4 1988–98), host Clive Anderson Talks Back (Channel 4) 1989–95 presenter Notes and Queries (BBC2) 1991–93, presenter Great Railway Journeys of the World: Hong Kong to Outer Mongolia (BBC2) 1994, documentary series Our Man In... (BBC2) 1995–96 (author of book to accompany the series entitled Our Man In...), and Our Man In Heaven & Hell 1996; presenter: Clive Anderson All Talk (BBC 1) 1996–1999, Unreliable Evidence (BBC Radio 4) 1998–, If I Ruled the World (BBC2) 1998–99, Clive Anderson Now (BBC1) 2001, CA Bites the Ballot (Radio 2), The Real..... (Radio 5), Clive Anderson's Chat Room (BBC Radio 2) 2004–, Back in the Day (Channel 4) 2005; occasional presenter/guest numerous other progs; formerly scriptwriter: Weekending (BBC Radio 4), The Frankie Howerd Variety Show (Radio 2), Not the Nine O'Clock News (BBC2), Alas Smith & Jones (notably head-to-head dialogues, BBC2), Around Midnight (LWT), The World According to Smith & Jones (LWT); memb revue group An Evening Without (toured England, Scotland and Aust) 1979, numerous stand-up comedy appearances Comedy Store and other venues in early 1980s; author of various articles in The Times, The Observer and The Guardian, former regular columnist Sunday Correspondent, regular columnist Independent on Sunday; pres The Woodland Tst 2004–; *Awards* Comedy Presenter of the Year RTS Awards 1991, Top Channel 4 Presenter British Comedy Awards 1992; for Whose Line Is It Anyway?: Best Light Entertainment Prog RTS Awards 1990, Best International Comedy Series ACE Awards 1991, Best Light Entertainment Prog Br Academy Awards 1991 (also nominated 1990 and 1992), also nominated for Top Entertainment Series Br Comedy Awards 1991 and Best Popular Arts Prog International Emmy Awards 1991, TRIC Best ITV/Channel 4 TV Personality Award 1995; for The

Real...: Sony Gold Award 2004; *Style—* Clive Anderson, Esq; ✉ Curtis Brown, Haymarket House, 28–29 Haymarket, London SW1Y 4SP (tel 020 7393 4400, fax 020 7393 4401, e-mail cb@curtisbrown.co.uk)

ANDERSON, (Richard James) Colin; OBE (1997); s of Richard Henry Anderson (d 1979), and Roseina, *née* Blaney; *b* 11 May 1954; *Educ* Regent House GS, Univ of Ulster; *m* 18 May 1978, Hilary Ann, da of Wilson Somerville Smyth; 2 s (Kyle, Jeffrey), 1 da (Kelly); *Career* trainee Thomson Newspapers Orgn, fndr chm and princ shareholder AndersonSprattGroup Ltd; chm: Anderson Spratt Gp Holdings Ltd, Tibus Ltd, NI Film and TV Cmmn (Govt appt) 2001–; visiting prof Sch of Psychology and Communication Univ of Ulster; memb NI Tourist Bd (Govt appt) 1988–94, pres NI C of C and Industry 1996–97 and 1997–98, dir NI Quality Centre 1993–96, former memb Cncl NI Branch Inst of Mktg; rugby rep for: Ulster, Ards Rugby Club, CIYMS Rugby Club; Duke of Edinburgh's Gold Award (memb Ctee NI 1989–92); MInstD, FCIM; *Recreations* yachting, skiing, golf, rugby; *Clubs* Royal Ulster Yacht, Killyleagh Yacht; *Style—* RJC Anderson, OBE; ✉ Anderson Spratt Group Holdings Ltd, Anderson House, Holywood Road, Belfast BT4 2GU (tel 028 9080 2020, fax 028 9080 2021, e-mail canderson@andersonspratt.com)

ANDERSON, David; MP; *b* 2 December 1953; *Educ* Maltby GS, Durham Tech Coll, Doncaster Tech Coll, Univ of Durham; *Career* former miner (active in 1984–85 strike), former care worker and lay trade union official; MP (Lab) Blaydon 2005–; memb: NEC Bd Unison, Gen Cncl TUC; *Style—* David Anderson, Esq, MP; ✉ House of Commons, London SW1A 0AA

ANDERSON, Judge David Heywood; CMG (1982); *b* 14 September 1937; *Educ* Univ of Leeds (LLB), LSE (LLM); *Career* called to the Bar Gray's Inn 1963; FCO: asst legal advsr 1960–69, legal advsr British Embassy Bonn 1969–72, legal cnsllr 1972–79, legal advsr UK Mission to the UN New York 1979–82, legal cnsllr 1982–87, dep legal advsr 1987–89, second legal advsr 1989–96; judge Int Tbnl for the Law of the Sea 1996–2005; visiting prof Univ of Durham; memb UK Delgn to: Vienna Conf on the Law of Treaties 1968, UN Ctee on Peaceful Uses of the Seabed 1973, Third UN Conf on the Law of the Sea 1973–77, S Atlantic Fisheries Cmmn (Argentina and UK) 1991–96; ldr UK Delgn for: Preparatory Cmmn for the Int Sea Bed Authy and the Int Tribunal for the Law of the Sea 1990–94, Maritime Boundary Negotiations 1986–96, UN Conf on Straddling Fish Stocks and Highly Migratory Fish Stocks 1993–95; memb: Study Gp of the British Inst of Int and Comparative Law on Jt Devpt of Offshore Oil and Gas 1989, Ctee on Public Int Law British Inst of Int and Comparative Law 1992–, British Branch Int Law Assoc; *Style—* Judge David Anderson, CMG; ✉ e-mail d.h.anderson@btinternet.com

ANDERSON, David Munro; s of late Alexander Anderson, and late Jessica Hope, *née* Vincent-Innes; *b* 15 December 1937; *Educ* Strathallan Sch; *m* 1, Veronica Jane, da of late Reginald Eric Stevens; 2 s (Angus b 1 Oct 1967, Duncan b 10 Nov 1968), 1 da (Lucy b 29 Sept 1973); m 2, Ruth, da of late Lt-Col E Lewis-Bowen (late RAVC); *Career* cmmnd: The Black Watch 1956–59, The London Scottish 1963–68; chm: Allingham Anderson Roll Ross Ltd 1990–96, Anderson Finance Ltd 1996–, Anderson Quantrend Ltd 1996–; dir Malcolm Innes Gallery 1990–2000; churchwarden Holy Innocents Lamarsh, memb Lamarsh PCC, tstee Friends of Lamarsh Church; MSI; *Recreations* shooting, skiing, gundog training, the arts; *Clubs* Caledonian; *Style—* David Anderson, Esq; ✉ The Old Gardens, Kersey, Ipswich, Suffolk IP7 6ED

ANDERSON, David William Kinloch; QC (1999); s of Sir Eric Anderson, KT, FRSE, *qv*, of Eton, and Poppy, *née* Mason; *b* 5 July 1961; *Educ* New Coll Oxford (open scholarship, MA), Downing Coll Cambridge (BA); *m* 1989, Margaret Elizabeth, *née* Beeton; 2 da (Frances Elizabeth b 1993, Isobel Kinloch b 1995); *Career* lawyer Covington & Burling, Washington DC 1985–86; stagiaire Cabinet of Lord Cockfield EC 1987–88; barrister Brick Court Chambers 1988–, recorder 2004; memb: Cncl of Mgmnt Br Inst of Int and Comparative Law 2001–, Exec Ctee Lord Slynn of Hadley Euro Law Fndn 2002–, Governing Body Br Assoc for Central and Eastern Europe 2002–; KCL: visiting lectr 1989–95, visiting fell 1995–99, visiting prof of law 1999–; *Publications* References to the European Court (1995, 2 edn 2002), various articles in legal jls; *Recreations* sailing, hill walking, history; *Clubs* Athenaeum, Royal Harwich Yacht; *Style—* David Anderson, Esq, QC; ✉ Brick Court Chambers, 7–8 Essex Street, London WC2R 3LD (tel 020 7379 3550, fax 020 7379 3558)

ANDERSON, Dr Digby Carter; s of Donald Anderson (d 1975), and Elizabeth Nance Ethel Anderson (d 1986); *b* 25 May 1944; *Educ* St Lawrence Coll, Univ of Reading (BA), Brunel Univ (MPhil, PhD); *m* 1965, Judith, *née* Harris; *Career* lectr then sr lectr Luton Coll of HE 1965–77, research fell Univ of Nottingham 1977–80, assoc lectr Brunel Univ 1977–78, dir Social Affairs Unit 1980–2004; memb ESRC 1989–93; columnist: The Times 1984–88, The Spectator 1984–2000, Sunday Telegraph 1988–89, Sunday Times 1989–90, National Review 1991–99; ordained: deacon 1985, priest 1986; hon asst priest St Saviour's Luton 1986–; *Books* incl: Health Education in Practice (ed, 1979), The Ignorance of Social Intervention (ed, 1980), Evaluating Curriculum Proposals (1980), Breaking the Spell of the Welfare State (1981), The Kindness that Kills (ed, 1984), A Diet of Reason (ed, 1986), The Spectator Book of Imperative Cooking (1987), Drinking to your Health: the allegations and the evidence (1989), The Loss of Virtue: moral confusion and social disorder in Britain (ed, 1988), This Will Hurt: the restoration of civic order in America and Britain (ed, 1995), Gentility Recalled: mere manners and the making of social order (ed, 1996), Faking It: the sentimentalisation of modern society (jt ed, 1998), The Dictionary of Difficult Words (jt ed, 2000), Losing Friends (2001), All Oiks Now (2004), The English at Table (2006); author of numerous papers in learned jls incl: Sociology, Jl of Curriculum Studies, Social Policy Review, Economic Affairs; *Recreations* the seaside, dinner, nostalgia; *Clubs* National, Mount Pelerin Soc; *Style—* Dr Digby Anderson; ✉ 17 Hardwick Place, Woburn Sands, Buckinghamshire MK17 8QQ (tel 01908 584526)

ANDERSON, Douglas Hardinge; s of James Alasdair Anderson (d 1982), of Tullichewan, and Lady Flavia Joan Lucy Anderson, *née* Giffard (d 1998); *b* 8 August 1934; *Educ* Eton; *m* 1, 1962 (m dis), Mary Jenkins; 1 da (Lucy Elizabeth b 1962), 1 s (James Henry Wallace b 1964); m 2, 1974, Veronica, da of John Markes; 1 da (Sophie Esme b 1977); *Career* portrait painter and wildlife artist; trained with Pietro Annigoni in Florence; exhbns in Florence, Munich, RA London, Royal Hibernian Acad Ireland, Gothenburg, Stockholm, New York and others; paintings in private collections in Europe, USA, etc; cmmnd for portraits of HM The Queen, HM Queen Elizabeth The Queen Mother and HRH The Princess of Wales (for The Royal Marsden Hosp); memb RSPP 1957; *Recreations* painting, gardening, orchids and cooking; *Style—* Douglas Anderson, Esq; ✉ Luthy, Recess, Co Galway, Ireland (tel and fax 00 353 95 51076)

ANDERSON, Douglas Kinloch; OBE (1983); s of William James Kinloch Anderson, of Edinburgh, and Margaret, *née* Gowenlock Harper; *b* 19 February 1939; *Educ* George Watson's Coll Edinburgh, Univ of St Andrews (MA), Univ of Edinburgh; *m* 14 June 1962, Deirdre Anne, da of Leonard Walter Loryman (d 1985); 1 da (Claire Deirdre b 1964), 2 s (Peter Douglas b 1968, John William b 1972); *Career* Kinloch Anderson Ltd: dir 1962–72, md 1972–, chm 1980– (Queen's Award for Export Achievement 1979); chm Kinloch Anderson (Holdings) Ltd; dir: Fidelity Special Values plc, Martin Currie Portfolio Investment Tst plc, F&C Private Equity Tst plc; pres: Edinburgh Assoc of Royal Tradesmen 1986–88, Edinburgh C of C 1988–90, Royal Warrant Holders Assoc 1994–95; memb: Bd Scottish Tourist Bd 1986–92, Edinburgh Festival Cncl 1988–90, Scottish Ctee IOD; hon memb St Andrews Soc Washington DC 1985; Edinburgh Merchant Company: asst 1976–79, treas 1988–90, Master 1990–92; Leith High Constable, Freeman City of London; *Recreations* fishing, golf, travel, reading; *Clubs* New (Edinburgh), The Honourable Co of Edinburgh Golfers, Bruntsfield Golfing Soc, Caledonian; *Style—* Douglas Kinloch Anderson, Esq, OBE; ✉ Brockham Green, 36A Kings Road, Longniddry, East Lothian EH32 0NN; Kinloch Anderson Ltd, Commercial Street/Dock Street, Leith, Edinburgh EH6 6EY (tel 0131 555 1355, fax 0131 555 1392, e-mail douglaska@kinlochanderson.com)

ANDERSON, Eric George; s of Charles G Anderson (d 1984), of Alyth, Perthshire, and Margery Drysdale, *née* Taylor (d 1992); *b* 7 June 1940; *Educ* Dundee HS, Univ of St Andrews (MB ChB), Univ of Salford (MSc), Dip Sports Med (Jt Scottish Royal Colls); *m* 26 March 1966, Elizabeth Clare (Liz), da of Donald George Cracknell (d 1995), of Appin, Argyll; 1 s (Colin b 1967), 2 da (Fiona b 1969, Heather b 1973); *Career* sr registrar Robert Jones and Agnes Hunt Orthopaedic Hosp Oswestry and Birmingham Accident Hosp 1973–78, conslt orthopaedic surgn Western Infirmary and Gartnavel Gen Hosp Glasgow 1978–97, hon clinical sr lectr Univ of Glasgow 1978–97, clinical assoc Univ of Strathclyde 1979–2000, visiting lectr in surgery Glasgow Caledonian Univ 1994–; former: memb Surgical Faculty Coll of Podiatrists, hon med advsr Scot Amateur Swimming Assoc, pres Br Orthopaedic Foot Surgery Soc, dep ed Injury; sec-gen Int Fedn of Foot and Ankle Socs (fndr memb 1999), sec Euro Foot and Ankle Soc (emeritus memb 2001); memb Editorial Bd: Foot, Foot and Ankle Surgery; memb: Int Soc Prosthetics and Orthotics 1976, Br Orthopaedic Foot Surgery Soc 1981 (hon memb 2000); int memb American Orthopaedic Foot and Ankle Soc 1996; hon memb Société Française de Médecine et Chirurgie du Pied; Hon FChS, FRCSEd 1971, FRSM 1973, FBOA 1978, FRCSGlas 1981; *Books* contrib: Common Foot Disorders (1989), The Foot and its Disorders (1991), Airds Companion to Surgical Studies (1997), Atlas of Foot Surgery (1997); *Recreations* philately, modelling buses and tramways, music; *Style—* Eric Anderson, Esq; ✉ 102 Prestonfield, Milngavie, Glasgow G62 7PZ (tel 0141 956 3594, fax 0141 955 0324)

ANDERSON, Sir (William) Eric Kinloch; KT (2002); s of William James Kinloch Anderson, of Edinburgh; *b* 27 May 1936; *Educ* George Watson's Coll, Univ of St Andrews (MA), Balliol Coll Oxford (MLitt); *m* 1960, Anne Elizabeth (Poppy), da of William Mattock Mason (d 1988), of Yorks; 1 s (David b 1961), 1 da (Catherine b 1963); *Career* asst master: Fettes 1960–64 and 1966–70, Gordonstoun 1964–66; headmaster: Abingdon Sch 1970–75, Shrewsbury Sch 1975–80, Eton Coll 1980–94; rector Lincoln Coll Oxford 1994–2000, provost of Eton 2000–; tstee Nat Heritage Meml Fund 1996–2001 (chm 1998–2001), tstee Royal Collections 2000–06; chm Tstees of Cumberland Lodge 1998–; visitor Harris Manchester Coll Oxford 2001–, hon fell Balliol Coll Oxford 1989, Lincoln Coll Oxford 2000; Hon DLitt: Univ of St Andrews 1981, Univ of Hull 1994, Univ of Siena 1999; FRSE 1985; *Books* Journal of Sir Walter Scott (ed, 1972 and 1998), The Percy Letters Vol IX (ed, 1989); *Recreations* golf, fishing, theatre; *Style—* Sir Eric Anderson, KT, FRSE; ✉ Eton College, Windsor, Berkshire SL4 6DH (tel 01753 671234)

ANDERSON, Dr Gordon; *b* 22 May 1954; *Educ* Univ of Dundee (BArch), Univ of Aberdeen (PhD); *m* Catherine Ann, *née* MacInnes; *Career* architect; various architectural appts in private and public sector Western Isles 1981–96, princ Anderson Associates Stornoway 1996–; memb: Assoc of Planning Supervisors, Assoc of Project Managers; RIBA, FRIAS 2001 (past memb Cncl); *Recreations* fishing, gardening, reading, art; *Style—* Dr Gordon Anderson; ✉ Tigh-na-Beinne, 68 Leurbost, Lochs, Isle of Lewis HS2 9NS (tel 01851 860226); Anderson Associates, Chartered Architects, 20 North Beach, Stornoway, Isle of Lewis, Western Isles HS1 2XQ (tel 01851 701500, fax 01851 701515, website www.anderson-associates.info)

ANDERSON, Gordon Alexander; CBE (1999); s of Cecil Brown Anderson (d 1965), of Glasgow, and Janet Davidson, *née* Bell (d 1966); *b* 9 August 1931; *Educ* The High Sch of Glasgow; *m* 12 March 1958, Eirené Cochrane Howie, da of Richmond Douglas (d 1980), of Troon; 2 s (David b 1958, Colin b 1961), 1 da (Carolyn b 1967); *Career* Nat Serv RN (Sub Lt RNVR) 1955–57; CA 1955; Moores Carson & Watson Glasgow (which became McClelland Moores 1958, Arthur Young McClelland Moores 1968, Arthur Young 1985, Ernst & Young 1989): trainee 1949–55, sr asst 1957–58, ptnr 1958–90, memb Exec Ctee 1972–84, office managing ptnr Glasgow 1976–79, chm 1987–89, dep sr ptnr 1989–90; memb Cncl on Tribunals and its Scottish Ctee 1990–96; chm Bitmac Ltd 1990–96 (dir 1985–96), dir Douglas Firebrick Co Ltd 1960–70, chm TSB Bank Scotland plc 1994–99 (dir 1991–99), dir TSB Group plc (now Lloyds TSB Group) 1993–99; dir HS of Glasgow Ltd 1975–81 and 1990–2001 (chm Govrs 1992–2001), dir Merchants House of Glasgow 1996–2002, pres Glasgow HS Club 1978–79, memb Scot Milk Mktg Bd 1979–85; Inst of Chartered Accountants of Scot: memb Cncl 1980–84, vice-pres 1984–86, pres 1986–87; FCMA 1984; *Recreations* golf, gardening, opera; *Clubs* Western (Glasgow), Glasgow Golf, Buchanan Castle Golf; *Style—* Gordon A Anderson, Esq, CBE; ✉ 4 Manse Road Gardens, Bearsden, Glasgow G61 3PJ (tel and fax 0141 942 2803)

ANDERSON, Hamish; s of Dr James Anderson, of Plymouth, and Joan, *née* Caughey; *b* 12 July 1948; *Educ* Clifton, Kingston Poly (LLB), UCL (LLM); *m* 1, 1972 (m dis); 1 s (James b 1975), 1 da (Bryony b 1977); m 2, 2002, Amanda Jane Le Page; *Career* admitted slr 1973; pt/t lectr in law and res asst Kingston Poly 1969–71, licensed insolvency practitioner 1987–; ptnr: Bond Pearce 1977–96 (joined 1971), Norton Rose 1996–; memb Insolvency Practices Cncl, former vice-chm Jt Insolvency Examination Bd, former memb Cncl R3, former ed Recovery, memb Editorial Bd Insolvency Law & Practice, former publications offr Ctee J (creditor's rights) Int Bar Assoc; past pres Insolvency Lawyers' Assoc; memb: Law Soc (memb Insolvency Sub-Ctee), City of London Law Soc (chm Insolvency Ctee); visiting fell Kingston Univ; *Books* Administrators - Part II of the Insolvency Act 1986, Anderson's Notes on Insolvency Conveyancing, Agricultural Charges and Receivership, Commercial Aspects of Trusts and Fiduciary Obligations (contrib), Current Issues in Insolvency Law (contrib), Lightman and Moss: The Law of Receivers of Companies (contrib), Tolley's Insolvency Law (contrib), Banks and Remedies (contrib), Practitioner's Guide to Cross-Border Insolvencies (contrib), Cross-Border Security and Insolvency (contrib), Practitioner's Guide to the Role of Directors and their Duties and Responsibilities (contrib), Transaction Avoidance in Insolvencies (conslt ed); *Style—* Hamish Anderson, Esq; ✉ Norton Rose, 3 More London Riverside, London SE1 2AQ (tel 020 7283 6000, fax 020 7283 6500, e-mail hamish.anderson@nortonrose.com)

ANDERSON, James Michael; *b* 30 July 1982, Burnley, Lancs; *Career* cricketer; Lancashire CCC 2002–; England: 19 Test caps, 76 one day appearances, 3 Twenty20 appearances, Test debut v Zimbabwe Lord's 2003, one day debut v Aust Melbourne 2002, memb squad World Cup 2003; NBC Denis Compton Award 2002; ✉ England and Wales Cricket Board, Lord's Cricket Ground, St John's Wood Road, London NW8 8QZ

ANDERSON, Janet; MP; da of late Tom Anderson, and late Ethel, *née* Pearson; *b* 6 December 1949; *Educ* Kingsfeld Comp Sch Bristol, Poly of Central London (Dip Bilingual Business Studies), Univ of Nantes; *Children* 2 s (James, David), 1 da (Katie); *Career* sec The Scotsman and Sunday Times 1971–74; PA to: Rt Hon Barbara Castle MP, 1974–81, Jack Straw, *qv*, 1981–87; PLP campaign offr 1987–89, co-ordinator Lab Pty's Industry 2000 Campaign for Gordon Brown 1989–90, northern regnl organiser Shopping Hours Reform Cncl 1990–92; MP (Lab) Rossendale and Darwen 1992– (also contested 1987); PPS to Rt Hon Margaret Beckett MP, *qv*, 1992–93, oppn whip for Home & Legal Affrs 1995–96, shadow min for women 1996–97; vice-chamberlain HM's Household (Govt whip) 1997–98, Parly under sec Dept of Culture, Media and Sport 1998–2001; memb Select Ctee on Home Affrs 1994–95; PLP rep House of Commons Cmmn 1993–94, co-ordinator Home Affrs Campaigns 1994–95, sec Tribune Gp of Labour MPs 1994–96; memb Steering Ctee

Lab Women's Network, vice-pres Assoc of Dist Cncls, hon advsr Emily's List UK; memb: Blackburn & Darwen CND, Blackburn & Darwen Anti-Apartheid, Rossendale & Dist Amnesty Int, League Against Cruel Sports; visiting fell St Antony's Coll Oxford; FRSA; *Recreations* playing the piano, opera; *Style*— Ms Janet Anderson, MP; ✉ House of Commons, London SW1A 0AA (tel 020 7219 3000, fax 020 7219 2148, e-mail andersonj@parliament.uk)

ANDERSON, Prof John; s of John Anderson (d 1963), of Newcastle upon Tyne, and Norah, *née* French (d 1992); *Educ* Royal GS Newcastle upon Tyne, The Med Sch Kings Coll Durham (Philipson scholar, MB BS); *m* 12 May 1959, Mary, o da of Percival Bynon; 1 s (David Guy b 14 Aug 1960), 1 da (Deborah Jane b 13 Sept 1963); *Career* med registrar Royal Victoria Infirmary Newcastle upon Tyne 1962–64, research fell Univ of Virginia Charlottesville 1965–66; Univ of Newcastle upon Tyne: first asst in med 1967–68, sr lectr in med 1968–85, academic sub-dean Med Sch 1975–85, postgrad dean and dir Postgrad Inst for Med and Dentistry and prof of med educn 1985–98 (emeritus 1998–); hon conslt physician Royal Victoria Infirmary 1968–; memb: GMC 1980–2001, GDC 1986–99, Assoc for the Study of Med Educn (vice-pres); FRCP 1973 (MRCP 1961), FRCOG (ad eundem) 1983, FRCPGlas 1992; *Books* The Multiple Choice Question in Medicine (1976, 2 edn 1982); numerous chapters in books and papers in scientific jls on med, diabetes and med educn; *Recreations* listening to music, computing, watching cricket, reading (anything), walking; *Clubs* Yorkshire CCC, Durham CCC; *Style*— Prof John Anderson; ✉ 6 Wilson Gardens, Newcastle upon Tyne NE3 4JA (e-mail andersgos@jander.demon.co.uk)

ANDERSON, John Stewart; TD (and Bar); s of Percy Stewart Anderson (d 1960), and Mabel France, *née* Jones (d 1962); *b* 3 August 1935; *Educ* Shrewsbury, Univ of Manchester (BA), Univ of Salford (MSc); *m* 28 Sept 1963, Alice Beatrice, da of Arthur Shelmerdine (d 1996), of Holmes Chapel, Cheshire; 1 s (Guy Stewart b 1964); *Career* Nat Serv Canal Zone 1953–55 (GSM), 2 Lt RE 1954, Lt Suez Reserve 1956, Maj TA RE and RCT 1956–76; architect and planner in private and public offices 1962–74, dir of planning and architecture Lincoln City Cncl 1974–85, conslt architect and town planner (ptnr John Anderson Planning) specialising in urban design and conservation (UK and overseas) 1985–; chm Assoc of Conslt Planners 1999–2000, sec gen and vice-pres Cwlth Assoc of Planners 2000–06 (hon vice-pres 2006–); memb Cncl RTPI 1977–91 and 1993–95 (pres 1984), sr vice-pres Euro Cncl of Town Planners 1988–90, memb Leicester Diocesan Panel of Architects 1990–, memb Lincoln Panel of Architects 2005–; Freeman: City of London 1988, Co of Watermen and Lightermen 1989; ARIBA, FRTPI, FRSA; *Style*— John S Anderson, Esq, TD; ✉ The Old Stables, Harston, Grantham, Lincolnshire NG32 1PP (tel 01476 870424, fax 01476 870816, e-mail japlan@nascr.net)

ANDERSON, John Victor Ronald; OBE (1997), JP (1978), DL (1998); s of Ronald Anderson (d 1971), of Caer Rhun Hall, Conwy, and Muriel Dorothy, *née* Hilton (d 1985); *b* 10 April 1937; *Educ* Sidney Sussex Coll Cambridge (MA); *m* 1, 1961 (m dis 1982), Judith, *née* Lindsay; 2 s, 2 da; *m* 2, 1986, Rosemary, *née* Ditchburn; *Career* ptnr V R Anderson & Son (chartered accountants) 1962–90; Accountancy Tuition Centre: ptnr 1983–90, dir 1983–2000; chm North Wales Magistrates 1996–2002; memb Cncl ICAEW 1995–2003 (chm 2000–02); pres Liverpool Soc of Chartered Accountants 1989–90; Chartered Accountants Award for Outstanding Achievement 2001; called to the Bar 1972; ACA 1962; *Recreations* own gardens, music, wine; *Style*— John Anderson, Esq, OBE, DL; ✉ Caer Rhun Hall, Conwy, North Wales LL32 8HX (tel 01492 660707, fax 01492 660188, e-mail anderson.ffrwd@virgin.net)

ANDERSON, Keith David; s of Dr Redvers Edward Anderson (d 1947), of Luton, Beds, and Norah Mary Agnes, *née* Payne (d 1972); *b* 3 June 1939; *Educ* Alton Castle Sch, St Bernardine's Coll Buckingham; *m* 1, 27 July 1963 (m dis 1974), Sarah Jane, *née* Beddow; 1 s (Timothy Stuart b 26 Sept 1967), 1 da (Jane Ann b 24 May 1964); *m* 2, 21 March 1975, Susan Lesley, da of late Gordon Rodney Kent; 1 s (Stuart David b 20 July 1978); *Career* Nat Serv 1959–61, RAPC attached to RNF in 1 Gurkha Inf Bde; local govt offr Aylesbury 1954–64; BBC TV: mangr Alexandra Palace 1965–69, organiser Arts Dept 1970–74, prog planning mangr 1974–78, head prog planning resources 1978–82, gen mangr prog planning 1982–89, controller planning and prog servs 1989–92; md: Anderson Associates 1992–, Production Finance and Management Ltd (PFM) 1992–2000; dir: Stock Productions Ltd 2000–03, Windmill TV Productions Ltd 2000–04, Track Prodns Ltd 2000–06, Deleste Prodns Ltd 2000–; chm: Horsebridge Prodns Ltd 2001–, Highpoint Productions Ltd 2006–; advsr V Good Productions; FRTS 1991, MInstD; *Recreations* golf, squash; *Clubs* Groucho, Ellesborough Golf, Holmer Green Squash; *Style*— Keith Anderson, Esq

ANDERSON, Prof Malcolm; s of James Armstrong Anderson (d 1959), and Helen, *née* Potts (d 1985); *b* 13 May 1934; *Educ* Altrincham GS for Boys, UC Oxford; *m* 1, 1957 (m dis), Eileen Mary, *née* Callan; 2 s (Denis Ian Gervaise b 7 June 1958, Keith James b 18 Feb 1961), 1 da (Helen Catherine b 17 Oct 1963); *m* 2, 1991, Marie Jacqueline Larrieu; *Career* lectr in govt Univ of Manchester 1960–64, Rockefeller research fell Fondation Nationale des Sciences Politiques Paris 1964–65, prof of politics Univ of Warwick 1973–79 (sr lectr 1965–73); Univ of Edinburgh: prof of politics 1979–98, dean of Faculty and provost of Faculty Gp of Law and Social Sciences 1989–93, dir Int Social Sciences Inst 1994–98, emeritus prof 1998–; sr fell Centre for European Policy Studies Brussels 2000–02; temp teaching posts in Canada, USA and France; fell ESRC 1976–77, Nuffield fell 1986–87 and 1997–98; pres Euro Community Studies Assoc; hon prof Jean Monnet 2004; FRSE 1995, FRSA 1995; *Books* Government in France (1970), Conservative Politics in France (1974), Frontiers Regions in Western Europe (ed, 1983), Policing the World (1989), Policing the European Union (1995), Frontiers (1996), The Frontiers of Europe (ed, 1998), States and Nationalism (2000), Frontiers of the European Union (2001), Striking a Balance between Freedom, Security and Justice in an Enlarged European Union (2002); *Recreations* reading, walking; *Style*— Prof Malcolm Anderson, FRSE; ✉ 28 Rue Fondary, 75015 Paris, France (tel 00 33 1 45 77 26 73); Maison Asserquet, 6440–Lescun, France (tel 00 33 5 59 34 74 22, e-mail malcolma@club-internet.fr)

ANDERSON, Prof Malcolm; *Educ* Univ of Nottingham (BSc), Univ of Cambridge (PhD), Univ of Bristol (DSc); *Career* sr research hydrologist US Corps Engrs Waterways Experiment Station Vicksburg MS, sr research geotechnical engr Geotechnical Control Office Hong Kong, currently pro-vice-chllr (research) Univ of Bristol; Quarter Centenary visiting fell Emmanuel Coll Cambridge; fndr and ed-in-chief Hydrological Processes, fndr and jt series ed Advances in Hydrological Processes, memb Editorial Advsy Bd Water Science and Technol 1994–; memb Cncl NERC; technical advsr Poverty Reduction Fund St Lucia; author of eight co-edited research texts in hydrology and geotechnics; Gill Meml Award for Research in Geomorphology RGS, Senior Science Fellowship Nuffield Fndn, Trevithick Premium Triennial Award ICE; life fell Indian Assoc of Hydrologists; FICE, CEng; *Style*— Prof Malcolm Anderson; ✉ Senate House, University of Bristol, Tyndall Avenue, Bristol BS8 1TH

ANDERSON, Mark Andrew D'Arcy; s of Graham D'Arcy Anderson, of Inverness-shire, and Diana, *née* Hatch; *b* 10 July 1961, Dingwall, Ross and Cromarty; *Educ* Haileybury and ISC, RMA Sandhurst; *m* 26 Aug 1986, Lucy, *née* Page Ratcliff; 2 da (Holly Beatrice D'Arcy b 21 June 1993, Daisy Lucinda D'Arcy b 22 Sept 1995); *Career* HM Forces (Queen's Own Highlanders) 1982–89, resigned as Capt; Hamptons Int: joined 1990, appointed to Gp Ops Bd 1998, chief operating offr 2003, md residential agency 2004–; *Recreations* skiing, salmon fishing; *Clubs* Highland Brigade; *Style*— Mark Anderson, Esq; ✉ Hamptons International, 32 Grosvenor Square, London W1K 2HJ (tel 020 7758 8488)

ANDERSON, Prof Michael; OBE (1999); *b* 21 February 1942; *Educ* Queens' Coll Cambridge (MA, PhD); *Career* Univ of Edinburgh: reader Dept of Sociology 1975–79 (asst lectr 1967–68, lectr 1969–75), prof of economic history Dept of Economic and Social History 1979–2007 (head of dept 1979–85 and 1988–97), dean Faculty of Social Sciences 1985–89, vice-princ 1989–93 and 1997–2000, sr vice-princ 2000–07; memb ESRC 1990–94, chm Research Resources Bd 1992–94, memb Soc and Politics Research Devpt Gp ESRC (vice-chm 1991–92); memb: Scottish Records Advsy Cncl 1984–93, History of Medicine Ctee Wellcome Tst 1988–93, Br Library Bd 1994–2003 (dep chm 2000–03), Cncl of Br Acad 1995–98; curator Cncl RSE 1997–99; convener of funding cncls Research Support Libraries Programme 1998–2003; tstee Nat Library of Scotland 1999– (chm 2000–); FBA 1989, FRSE 1990; *Publications* Family Structure in Nineteenth Century Lancashire (1971), Sociology of the Family: Readings (ed with introductions, 2 edn 1979), Approaches to the History of the Western Family 1500–1914 (1981), Population Change in North-Western Europe 1750–1850 (1988), British Population History from the Black Death to the Present Day (ed and contrib 1996); *Style*— Prof Michael Anderson, OBE, FBA, FRSE; ✉ School of History and Classics, University of Edinburgh, Edinburgh EH8 9JY (tel 0131 650 3844, e-mail m.anderson@ed.ac.uk)

ANDERSON, Michael Arthur; JP (Chester 1979); s of Alexander William Anderson (d 1971), and Winifred Ann, *née* Pusill (d 1978); matriculation of Arms granted in 1980 by Lord Lyon, King of Arms, based on Arms granted in 1780 but in use prior to 1665; *b* 23 March 1928; *Educ* LSE (BSc); *m* 1954, Anne, da of Joseph Beynon (d 1965); 2 s (Michael d 1992, Richard), 2 da (Sarah, Deborah); *Career* fin dir Caribbean Printers Ltd Trinidad 1960–61, sr fin appts Ford Motor Co and Ford of Europe 1962–67, fin dir Manchester Guardian and Evening News Ltd 1968–69, gp fin dir Tillotson & Son Ltd 1970–71, sr fin appts BL 1972–75, fin dir Mersey Docks & Harbour Co 1975–84; dir: Liverpool Grain Storage & Transit Co Ltd 1979–89, Anderson & Co (Chartered Accountants) 1984–96, Small Firms Business Advisors Ltd 1989–96; business cnsllr to Govt Small Firms Serv 1985–91, business advsr 1994–; chm The Anderson Association 1993–2003; FCA, FCMA, FIBA; *Books* Anderson Families (1984); *Recreations* genealogy, astronomy, walking, opera, classical music; *Style*— Michael A Anderson, Esq; ✉ Kintrave, Wood Lane, Burton-in-Wirral, Cheshire CH64 5TB (tel 0151 336 4349)

ANDERSON, Prof Michael John; s of Ronald Arthur Anderson (d 1981), of Llantwit Major, and Dorothy Alma Anderson; *b* 4 June 1937; *Educ* Taunton Sch, Univ of Bristol (BA); *m* 29 Dec 1973, Alessandra Pierangela Lucia, da of dott Girolamo di Gregorio (d 1983), of Bisceglie, Italy; 2 da (Silvia b 1977, Marina b 1980); *Career* The Welch Regt 1956–58; mangr New Theatre Cardiff 1963–64, lectr in drama Univ of Bristol 1964–78; prof of drama: Univ Coll of North Wales Bangor 1978–90 (chm Standing Ctee of Univ Drama Depts 1979–82), Univ of Kent 1990–99 (prof emeritus 1999–); memb Welsh Arts Cncl 1985–90 (chm Drama Ctee), joint sec gen Int Fndn for Theatre Res 1989–98, memb Bd Centre for Performance Research Aberystwyth 2003–; FRSA; *Books* Classical Drama and its Influence (ed, 1965), Anger and Detachment: A Study of Osborne Arden and Pinter (1976), The Medieval European Stage 500–1550 (assoc ed, 2001); *Recreations* travel, films; *Clubs* Royal Commonwealth Soc, Circolo Unione Bisceglie (Italy); *Style*— Prof Michael Anderson; ✉ 59 King's Road, Cardiff CF11 9DB (tel 029 2039 7100, e-mail anderson@nunnery.u-net.com)

ANDERSON, Prof Olive Ruth; da of Donald Henry Frere Gee (d 1964), and Ruth Winifred, *née* Clackson (d 1950); *b* 27 March 1926; *Educ* King Edward VI GS Louth, St Hugh's Coll Oxford (MA, BLitt); *m* 10 July 1954, Matthew Smith (d 2006), s of Matthew Smith Anderson (d 1960), of Perth; 2 da (Rachel b 1955, Harriet b 1957); *Career* Dept of History Westfield Coll London: asst lectr 1949–56, lectr 1958–69, reader 1969–86, prof and head of dept 1986–89; Queen Mary & Westfield Coll London (now Queen Mary Univ of London): prof and dep head of dept 1989–91, emeritus prof and hon research fell 1991–, fell 1995–; James Ford special lectr Univ of Oxford 1992; memb Academic Cncl Univ of London 1989–91 (memb Exec Ctee 1990–91), tstee Theodora Bosanquet Tst 1995–98; Br Fedn of Women Graduates Charitable Fndn: memb Fin Ctee 1996–99, memb Grants Ctee 1998–2001; FRHistS 1968 (assoc 1953, cncllr 1986–90, vice-pres 1991–95, hon vice-pres 2001–); *Books* A Liberal State at War (1967), Suicide in Victorian and Edwardian England (1987); *Style*— Prof Olive Anderson; ✉ 45 Cholmeley Crescent, Highgate, London N6 5EX (tel 020 8340 0272); History Department, Queen Mary, University of London, Mile End Road, London E1 4NS (tel 020 7882 5016, fax 020 8980 8400)

ANDERSON, Prof Robert David; s of Robert David Anderson (d 1956), of London, and Gladys, *née* Clayton (d 1973); *b* 20 August 1927; *Educ* Harrow, Gonville & Caius Coll Cambridge (MA); *Career* dir of music Gordonstoun Sch 1958–62, extra mural lectr in Egyptology Univ of London 1966–77, assoc ed The Musical Times 1967–85, conductor Bart's Hosp Choral Soc 1965–90, visiting fell in music City Univ 1983–90; hon sec Egypt Exploration Soc 1971–82 (admin dir EES dig at Qasr Ibrim 1976–79); prof of history Univ of Rostov-on-Don 2002; music critic for The Times, radio and TV for BBC, co-ordinating ed Elgar Complete Edition 1984–2003; Freeman: City of London 1977, Worshipful Co of Musicians 1977; Hon DMus City Univ 1985, Hon DHist Russian State Univ for Humanities Moscow 2000, Medal of Honour Inst of Arts Warsaw 2000; FSA 1983; *Books* Catalogue of Egyptian Antiquities in the British Museum III, Musical Instruments (1976), Wagner (1980), Egypt in 1800 (jt ed, 1988), Elgar in Manuscript (1990), Elgar (1993), Elgar and Chivalry (2002), Baalbek (2006); *Recreations* modulating from music to Egyptology; *Style*— Prof Robert Anderson, FSA; ✉ 54 Hornton Street, London W8 4NT (tel 020 7937 5146)

ANDERSON, Dr Robert Geoffrey William; er s of late Herbert Patrick Anderson, and Kathleen Diana, *née* Burns; *b* 2 May 1944; *Educ* Univ of Oxford (BSc, MA, DPhil); *m* 1, 1973 (m dis 2003), Margaret Elizabeth Callis, da of John Austin Lea; 2 s (William b 1979, Edward b 1984); *m* 2, 2005, Jane Virginia Portal; *Career* asst keeper: Royal Scottish Museum 1970–75, Science Museum 1975–78; dep keeper Wellcome Museum of the History of Medicine 1978–80, keeper of chemistry Science Museum 1980–84 (sec Advsy Cncl 1978–80); dir: Royal Scottish Museum 1984–85 (formerly curator of the history of science), Nat Museums of Scotland 1985–92, British Museum 1992–2002; fell Inst for Advanced Study Princeton 2002–03, by-fell Churchill Coll Cambridge 2003–04, visiting fell CCC Cambridge 2004–05, fell Clare Hall Cambridge 2006–; memb Cncl: Soc for the History of Alchemy and Chemistry 1978– (chm 2006–), Gp for Scientific Technological and Medical Collections 1979–83, Br Soc for the History of Sci 1981–84 (pres 1988–90), Scottish Museums 1984–91, Museums Assoc 1988–92; memb Editorial Bd: Annals of Sci 1981–, Annali di Storia della Scienza 1986–2006, Journal of the History of Collections 1993–; sec Royal Scottish Soc of Arts 1973–75, pres Scientific Instrument Cmmn Int Union of the History and Philosophy of Sci 1982–97, memb Br Nat Ctee for the Hist of Sci 1985–89, memb Bd Chemical Heritage Fndn Philadelphia 2006–; tstee Boerhaave Museum Leiden 1994–99; Dexter Prize American Chemical Soc 1986; Hon DSc: Edinburgh 1995, Durham 1998; hon fell St John's Coll Oxford 2002; FRSC 1984, FSA 1986, FRSE 1990, Hon FSA Scot 1991; *Books* The Mariner's Astrolabe (1972), Edinburgh and Medicine (1976), The Early Years of the Edinburgh Medical School (1976), The Playfair Collection and the Teaching of Chemistry at the University of Edinburgh (1978), The History of Technology Vol VI (contrib, 1978), Science in India (1982), Science, Medicine and Dissent - Joseph Priestley 1733–1804 (ed, 1987), Joseph Black: A Bibliography (1992), Making Instruments Count (jt ed, 1993), The Great Court and the British Museum (2000); *Clubs* Athenaeum; *Style*— Dr R G W Anderson, FRSE, FSA

ANDERSON, Prof Robert Henry; s of Henry Anderson (d 1981), and Doris Amy, *née* Callear (d 1977); *b* 4 April 1942; *Educ* Wellington GS, Univ of Manchester (BSc, MB ChB, MD); *m* 9 July 1966, Christine, da of Keith Ibbotson, of Grantham, Lincs; 1 da (Elizabeth b 1970), 1 s (John b 1972); *Career* travelling fell MRC Univ of Amsterdam 1973, sr res fell Br Heart Fndn Brompton Hosp 1974, Joseph Levy prof of paediatric cardiac morphology Nat Heart and Lung Inst (formerly Cardiothoracic Inst): Imperial Coll Sch of Med Univ of London 1979–99 (reader 1977), Inst of Child Health UCL 1999–; visiting prof Univ of Pittsburgh 1984–, hon prof Univ of North Carolina 1984–, visiting prof Univ of Liverpool 1988–; Excerpta Medica Travel Award 1977, Br Heart Fndn Prize for Cardiovascular Res 1984; FRCPath 1986; *Publications* 610 articles, 250 chapters in books; 36 books incl: Cardiac Anatomy (1978), Cardiac Pathology (1983), Surgical Anatomy of the Heart (1985, 3 edn 2004), Paediatric Cardiology (2 volumes, 1987, 2 edn 2002); *Recreations* music, golf, wine; *Clubs* Roehampton, Saintsbury, Walton Heath Golf; *Style—* Prof Robert Anderson; ✉ Cardiac Unit, Institute of Child Health, University College, London WC1N 1EH (tel 020 7905 2295, fax 020 7905 2324, e-mail r.anderson@ich.ucl.ac.uk)

ANDERSON, Prof Sir Roy Malcolm; kt (2006); s of James Anderson, and Elizabeth, *née* Watson-Weatherburn; *b* 12 April 1947; *Educ* Duncombe Sch, Richard Hale Sch, Imperial Coll London (BSc, PhD, DIC); *m* 1, 16 Aug 1974 (m dis 1989), Mary Joan, da of Peter Mitchell; m 2, 21 July 1990, Claire, da of Rev Peter Baron; *Career* IBM research fell Univ of Oxford 1971–73, lectr Dept of Zoology KCL 1973–77; Dept of Biology Imperial Coll London: lectr 1977–80, reader 1980–82, prof 1982–93, head of dept 1984–93; dir Wellcome Centre for Parasite Infections 1989–93, dir Wellcome Tst Centre for the Epidemiology of Infectious Disease 1993–2000, Linacre prof of zoology and head of zoology Dept Univ of Oxford 1993–98, fell Merton Coll Oxford 1993–2000, prof of infectious disease epidemiology and head Dept of Infectious Disease Epidemiology Faculty of Med Imperial Coll London 2000–04, chief scientific advsr MOD 2004–; visiting prof Imperial Coll London 1993, Genentech distinguished prof Dept of Biostatistics Univ of Washington 1998; chm Sci Advsy Cncl DEFRA 2004–05; memb: NERC 1988–91, Cncl Zoological Soc 1988–90, Advsy Cncl on Science and Technol 1989–91, Cncl Royal Soc 1989–91, Cncl RPMS Hammersmith 1992–95, Cncl LSHTM 1993–, Spongiform Encephalopathy Advsy Ctee 1997–2004, Scientific Advsy Ctee Health Protection Agency 2004–, Cncl EPSRC 2004–, Cncl RUSI 2005–; govr The Wellcome Tst 1991–2000 (tstee 1991); author of over 450 scientific jls and books; Huxley Meml medal 1981, Zoological Scientific medal 1982, C A Wright Meml medal 1986, David Starr Jordan prize 1987, Chalmers medal 1988, Weldon prize 1989, John Grundy Lecture medal 1990, Frink medal for Br Zoologists 1993; Storer lectr Univ of Calif Davis 1994, Croonian lectr Royal Soc 1994, Joseph Smadel lectr Univ of N Carolina 1994, P H Thiel lectr Boerhaave Course on Travel Med Leiden 1995, Thomas Francis meml lectr Univ of Michigan 1995, Nuffield lectr RSM 2002; hon fell Linacre Coll Oxford 1993; Hon DSc: UEA 1997, Univ of Stirling 1998; fell Academia Europaea 1998, foreign memb Inst of Med Nat Acad of Sciences USA 1999; Hon MRCP 1991, Hon FRCPath 1999, FRS 1986, Hon FIA 2000, Hon FRSS 2002 (FRSS), Hon FRASE 2002, FIBiol, FMedSci, ARCS, Hon FRAgS 2002; *Books* Population Dynamics of Infectious Diseases (1982), Infectious Diseases of Humans: Dynamics and Control (jtly, 1990); *Recreations* croquet, hill walking, music, natural history; *Clubs* Athenaeum; *Style—* Prof Sir Roy Anderson, FRS

ANDERSON, Sarah Pia; da of Stewart Angus Anderson, and Eldina Pia Anderson; *b* 19 July 1952; *Educ* The Cedars Sch, Univ of Swansea (BA); *Career* theatre and television director; prof of dramatic art Univ of Calif Davis; memb: Dirs' Guild of GB, Dirs' Guild of America, Women in Film (UK), BAFTA LA; *Theatre* trained at Crucible Theatre Sheffield; prodns incl: Hello and Goodbye, What The Butler Saw, Ashes, The Caucasian Chalk Circle; prodns for Bush Theatre incl: Blisters, Gin Trap, First Blush Last Resort, The Estuary, These Men, The Nest; prodns for RSC incl: Indigo, Old Year's Eve, Across Oka, Mary and Lizzie; other prodns incl: Rosmersholm (NT, La Mama Theatre NY), Carthagians (Abbey and Hampstead), Mary Stuart and St Joan (Shakespeare Theatre Washington DC), The Winter's Tale (Santa Cruz Shakespeare Festival), Hedda Gabler (Roundabout Theatre NY); *Television* incl: Blisters, Stepping Out, Shaping Up, Pity in History, A Woman Calling (Samuel Beckett Award), Summers Awakening, This Is History Gran, The Bill (15 episodes), The Alleyn Mysteries, Dr Finlay (Scottish BAFTA for Best Series 1995), Prime Suspect (Emmy Award for Best Series 1993–94), The Profiler, ER, Nothing Sacred (Prism Award for Directing 1998, Peabody Award 1998), Plastic Man, Ally McBeal (Emmy Award for Best Series 2000), Dead Like Me, Huff (Emmy Award), Ugly Betty (Golden Globe Award for Best Series and Best Leading Actress), Big Love (nominated Golden Globe Award); *Recreations* photography, tennis, swimming, cycling; *Style—* Ms Sarah Pia Anderson

ANDERSON, Steve; *b* 9 May 1958; *m* 3 c; *Career* South Lancashire Newspapers 1974–78, Liverpool Daily Post and Echo 1978; researcher World in Action, news ed and prodr regnl magazine progs Granada TV Manchester 1978–84; BBC TV: BBC Network Features 1984–87, prodr and dir BBC Breakfast Time 1987, Newsnight 1987–92, prodr Election 92 and Election 97, sr prodr One O'Clock News and Six O'Clock News 1992–93, prodr and dir BBC News and Current Affrs Weekly Progs (progs incl Here and Now, Panorama) 1993–95, ed BBC Consumer Progs (progs incl Watchdog, Weekend Watchdog, Watchdog Healthcheck, Value for Money, Face Value, Computers Don't Bite) 1995–97; controller News, Current Affrs, Arts and Religion ITN Network Centre 1997–2004, currently creative dir Mentorn; *Style—* Steve Anderson, Esq

ANDERSON, Prof Thomas; s of Frederick Anderson (d 1992), and May, *née* Barrett (d 1987); *b* 24 July 1947; *Educ* Blaydon GS, Univ of Newcastle upon Tyne (BSc, PhD); *m* 3 Aug 1968, Patricia, da of Robert Ormston; 1 s (Iain b 1972), 1 da (Claire b 1975); *Career* Univ of Newcastle upon Tyne: dir Centre for Software Reliability 1982–, prof 1986–, head Computing Science Dept 1992–97, dean of science 1998–2004; MIEEE, FBCS; *Books* Fault Tolerance - Principles and Practice (with P A Lee, 2 edn 1990), also ed 22 other volumes 1979–2007; *Recreations* fell walking, singing; *Style—* Thomas Anderson, Esq; ✉ Centre for Software Reliability, University of Newcastle upon Tyne, Newcastle upon Tyne NE1 7RU (tel 0191 221 2222, fax 0191 222 7995, e-mail tom.anderson@newcastle.ac.uk)

ANDERSON, Victor Frederick; s of Tom Anderson, and Iris Anderson; *b* 7 February 1952; *Educ* Whitgift Sch, BNC Oxford (BA); *m* 1987, Joan Rawlinson; 1 s; *Career* lectr Paddington Coll of FE 1982–87, researcher New Economics Fndn 1987–92, researcher Plaid Cymru 1992–2000, memb London Assembly (Green) 2000–03; memb Bd London Devpt Agency 2000–, environment advsr to Mayor of London 2001–, memb London Sustainable Devpt Cmmn 2002–; *Publications* Alternative Economic Indicators (1991), Energy Efficiency Policies (1993), Greens and the New Politics (2001); *Style—* Victor Anderson, Esq

ANDERSON OF SWANSEA, Baron (Life Peer UK 2005), of Swansea in the County of West Glamorgan; Donald Anderson; PC; s of David Robert Anderson (d 1954), of Swansea, and Eva, *née* Mathias (d 1994); *b* 17 June 1939; *Educ* Swansea GS, UC Swansea (BA), Inns of Court Sch of Law; *m* 28 Sept 1963, Dr Dorothy Mary, da of Rev Frank L Trotman (d 1969), of Bolivia; 3 s (Hon Robert b 24 Dec 1964, Hon Huw b 17 Nov 1967, Hon Geraint b 20 Sept 1972); *Career* called to the Bar Inner Temple 1969; HM Foreign Serv 1960–64 (third sec Br Embassy Budapest 1963–64); lectr in politics UC Swansea 1964–66; MP (Lab): Monmouth 1966–70, Swansea E 1974–2005; PPS to: Min of Defence 1969–70, Attorney Gen 1974–79; chm Select Ctee on Welsh Affairs 1981–83; oppn spokesman: foreign affairs 1983–92, defence 1993–94, legal affairs 1995–96; chm Select Ctee on Foreign Affairs 1997–2005; memb Chairmen's Panel 1995–97; chm: Welsh Lab Gp 1977–78, Br Zimbabwe Gp, Parly Christian Fellowship 1990–93, chm Br German Parly Gp 1994–97, Br French Parly Gp 1997–2001, Br Norwegian Gp (jtly) 1997–2005, Br South African Gp 1997–99, UK Branch CPA 1997–2001; ldr UK delgn: to NATO Parly Assembly 1997–2001 (ldr Socialist Gp), to OSCE 1997; vice-chm and treas IPU 1986–90 (treas 1990–91 and 1993–95); cncllr Royal Borough of Kensington and Chelsea 1971–75; chm Nat Prayer Breakfast 1989, memb Bd World Vision of Britain 1991–94, pres The Boys' Brigade in Wales 1991–97; Freeman City and County of Swansea 2000; Parly fell St Antony's Coll Oxford 1999–2000; hon fell UC Swansea; Cdr's Cross Order of FRG for contrib to Br German Relations 1986; *Style—* The Rt Hon the Lord Anderson of Swansea

ANDRAE, Michael Anton; s of Emile Anton Andrae (d 1974), of London, and Minnie Jenette Isobel, *née* Nisbett (d 1984); *b* 20 September 1932; *Educ* Hornsey County GS, Enfield Tech Coll; *m* 12 March 1955, Laura, da of Alfred George Smith; 2 da (Vivienne Jane b 11 June 1960, Gillian Louise b 16 Oct 1963); *Career* Nat Serv RAF 1951–53; former mgmnt apprentice British Oxygen; PA to md Medico-Therapeutics Ltd 1956–58, PA to md rising to sales mangr then sales and mktg dir Heinke Ltd 1959–65, dir Heinke-Trelleborg Ltd 1959–65, mktg dir Gemma Group 1965–75, dir Mecco Marine Ltd (UK mktg and distribution co for Pirelli Milan inflatable craft) 1965–75, md and chief exec Hunt Instrumentation Ltd 1972–77; dir: Midar Systems Ltd 1975–87, Bond Instrumentation Gibraltar Ltd 1975–87, Bond Instrumentation (Singapore) PTE Ltd 1975–87 (and alternating chm); commercial dir and co sec Bond Instrumentation and Process Control Ltd 1975–87, mktg and business conslt and various non-exec directorships 1987–; memb Bd of Mgmnt Services Sound and Vision Corporation 1991–; Chartered Inst of Mktg: nat treas 1987–88, nat chm 1989–90, President's Award 1988; Freeman City of London 1989, Liveryman Worshipful Co of Marketors 1989; FInstD 1985, fell Mktg Inst of Singapore 1988, Hon FCIM 1990, FRSA 1990; *Recreations* fine art, shooting, fishing; *Style—* Michael Andrae, Esq; ✉ 54 Anne Cleves House, Queens Reach, Hampton Court, Surrey KT8 9DE

ANDRÉ, Martin; *b* 10 December 1960; *Educ* Yehudi Menuhin Sch, Univ of Cambridge; *m* Karin; 2 da (Sophie, Emily), 1 s (Ben); *Career* conductor; sometime resident conductor WNO, freelance conductor, music dir English Touring Opera 1993–96; performances with WNO incl: chamber version of Aida (professional debut), Falstaff, Jenufa, Ernani, Rigoletto, Madama Butterfly, Un Ballo in Maschera, Eugene Onegin, Il Barbiere de Siviglia; freelance prodns incl: The Merry Widow and La Clemenza di Tito (Scottish Opera), The Love for Three Oranges and John Buller Bakxai (world première, ENO), Madama Butterfly (Opera North), Le Nozze di Figaro, Mozart Die Entführung aus dem Serail (Opera 80), Janácek From the House of the Dead (N American première for Vancouver Opera), Ariadne (Vancouver Opera), La Traviata (Opera Zuid Maastricht and Vancouver Opera), L'amour des Trois Oranges (Lisbon, Stuttgart and New Israeli Opera), Carmen (US debut, Seattle Opera), Un Ballo in Maschera (Royal Opera House debut), Christoph Rilke's Song of Love and Death (UK première, Glyndebourne Touring Opera), Don Pasquale (New Israeli Opera), Cunning Little Vixen (Scottish Opera), La Traviata (Opera NI), Cav and Pag (Staastheater Stuttgart), Makropulos Case (Glyndebourne Touring Opera), Aida (Opera NI), Julietta (Opera Zuid Holland), Macbeth, Madam Butterfly (Staatsoper Cologne), The Magic Flute (Opera NI), world premières by James MacMillan and Craig Armstrong Edinburgh Int Festival, Cosi fan Tutte, Orpheus and Euridice, La Bohème, Werther, Rigoletto (all for English Touring Opera); also performances with English Chamber Orch, Royal Scottish National Orch, Scottish Chamber Orch, BBC Concert Orch, Ulster Orch, New London Sinfonia, London Soloists Chamber Orch, London Concert Orch, City of London Chamber Orch, New Queen's Hall Orch, Northern Sinfonia, Jerusalem Symphony Orch and Philharmonia, Limburges Symphonie Orkest, Collegium Musicum Bergen, Bergen Filharmoniske Orkester, Tromsø Symfoniorkester, Queensland Philharmonic Orch, Tasmanian Symphony Orch, Orquestra Nacional do Porto, Remix Contemporary Ensemble Portugal, Peking Symphony Orch Macau; *Recreations* has season ticket for Arsenal FC; *Style—* Martin André, Esq

ANDREAE, Sophie Clodagh Mary (Mrs D E Blain); da of Herman Kleinwort (Sonny) Andreae, and Clodagh Mary, *née* Alleyn; *b* 10 November 1954; *Educ* St Mary's Sch Ascot, Newnham Coll Cambridge; *m* 1984, Douglas Ellis Blain; 3 s, 1 da; *Career* chm SAVE Britain's Heritage 1984–88 (sec 1976–84), head London Div English Heritage (Historic Bldgs and Monument Cmmn for England) 1988–93, memb Royal Fine Art Cmmn 1996–99, memb Cmmn for Architecture and the Built Environment (CABE) 1999–2004, chm CABE Educn Fndn 2002–06; tstee Heritage of London Tst 1985–2003; memb: London Diocesan Advsy Ctee 1988–2001, Fabric Advsy Ctee St Paul's Cathedral 1991–, Exec Ctee Georgian Gp 1993–, Cncl London Historic Parks and Gardens Tst 1993–2002, CABE/English Heritage Urban Panel 2004–, Places of Worship Forum English Heritage 2005–; dir Action for Market Towns 1998–2003; vice-chm Patrimony Ctee RC Bishops' Conf 2002–, chm Friends of St Andrew's Church Presteigne Powys 1998–, pres Offa's Dyke Assoc 2003–; memb Cncl Nat Tst 2006–; tstee Greenwich Fndn for the Old Naval Coll 2007–; High Sheriff Powys 2002–03; *Publications* Preserving the Past: the rise of heritage in modern Britain (contrib, 1996); ed and contrib to numerous SAVE Britain's Heritage reports; *Style—* Miss Sophie Andreae; ✉ 23 Brompton Square, London SW3 2AD

ANDRESEN GUIMARÃES, HE Fernando; *m* Graca; *Career* Portuguese diplomat; early postings: Malawi, London, Rome, NY; consul-gen Luanda 1982–86, ambass to Iraq 1986–88, ambass to Algeria 1988–91, DG Foreign Aid Prog Foreign Miny 1991, pres Interministerial Cmmn on Macau 1992–95, ambass to USA 1995–99, perm rep to NATO and WEU 1999–2003, ambass to the Ct of St James's 2003–; *Style—* HE Senhor Fernando Andresen-Guimarães; ✉ Portugese Embassy, 11 Belgrave Square, London SW1X 8PP

ANDREW, Derek; MBE (2001); s of Harold Andrew, of Chadderton, Oldham, and Elisabeth, *née* Bogaard; *b* 14 October 1955, Oldham, Lancs; *Educ* Oldham Hulme GS, Univ of Newcastle upon Tyne (BA); *m* 6 June 1993, Rebecca, *née* Westwood; *Career* Marstons plc (formerly Wolverhampton and Dudley Breweries plc): joined 1980, managerial positions 1980–90, managed house ops controller 1990–91, md Cameron's Brewery Co 1991–97, main bd dir 1994–, gp sales dir 1997–2001, chm Cameron's Brewery Co 1997–2001, md Pathfinder Pubs 2001–; chm Pathfinder Local Heroes Fndn 2001–; chm Midland Counties Br Beer and Pub Assoc 2000–03; govr Hartlepool Coll of FE 1993–97; chm Teeside TEC Investors in People 1994–97; *Recreations* music, sport, theatre, cars, horses; *Style—* Derek Andrew, Esq, MBE; ✉ Marstons plc, Marstons House, Marstons Road, Wolverhampton WV1 4JT

ANDREW, Hugh; s of Hubert and Elizabeth Andrew; *Educ* Magdalen Coll Oxford; *Career* md: Birlinn Ltd 1992–, SEOL Ltd 1994–; dir Compass Independent Booksales Ltd 1998–; memb Lib Dems; FSA Scot; *Recreations* reading, music, travel, archaeology; *Style—* Hugh Andrew; ✉ West Newington House, 10 Newington Road, Edinburgh EH9 1QS (tel 0131 668 4371, fax 0131 668 4466, e-mail hugh@birlinn.co.uk)

ANDREW, Dr Kenneth; s of late Arthur James Andrew, of Benfleet, Essex, and late Emily Sarah, *née* Elderkin; *b* 21 December 1944; *Educ* Enfield Coll of Technol (ONC), Imperial Coll London (MSc, DIC), Univ of Wales (BEng), Int Mgmnt Centre (DPhil); *m* 21 July 1967, Elizabeth Honora (d 2002), da of late Dilwyn Thomas, of Pontypridd, S Wales; 2 s; *Career* apprentice draughtsman 1961–64, various posts including head of operational res, branch mgmnt City and West End London, head of mktg NatWest Bank plc 1969–84, gp markets dir Good Relations Group plc 1984–85, dir consumer mktg Europe The Chase

Manhattan Bank NA 1985–87, gp dir strategy and mktg National & Provincial Building Society 1987–90, independent business conslt 1990–91; dir: DBS Management plc 1993–99, Manitous 1991–96, St James International 1995–98; chm: St James Business Centres 1995–99, Sherwood International Gp plc 1997–2003, Assuresoft Ltd 1998–99, Recall Gp plc 2001–02; sr vice-pres, chm and md Aetna UK 1991–93; industrial prof of fin servs mgmnt IMCB; dir Mount Vernon Watford Hosp NHS Tst 1994–97; chm Membs' Cncl Link Network 2004–; Hon MPhil IMCB 1984; MIMgt, MBBA, MInstScB, FInstD, FRSA; *Books* The Bank Marketing Handbook (1986), The Financial Public Relations Handbook (1990), Bank Marketing in a Changing World (1991); *Recreations* swimming, reading, writing, travel; *Clubs* MCC, Carlton; *Style*— Dr Kenneth Andrew; ✉ mobile 07710 488282, e-mail kandrew@politics.fsbusiness.co.uk

ANDREW, Prof Malcolm Ross; s of John Malcolm Young Andrew, of Latchley, nr Gunnislake, Cornwall, and Mary Lilian, *née* Faulkner; *b* 27 January 1945; *Educ* The Perse Sch Cambridge, St Catharine's Coll Cambridge (BA, MA), Simon Fraser Univ BC Canada (MA), Univ of York (DPhil); *m* 17 Aug 1968, Lena Margareta, da of Gustaf Bernström, of Göteborg, Sweden; 1 s (Christopher b 1980 d 2003), 1 da (Elizabeth b 1982); *Career* asst English master Haileybury Coll 1973–74, lectr then sr lectr Sch of English and American Studies UEA 1974–85; Queen's Univ Belfast: prof of English 1985–2007, head of dept then dir Sch of English 1986–92, dean Faculty of Arts 1992–96, provost of humanities 1993–98, pro-vice-chllr 1998–2002; memb: Steering Ctee Cncl for Univ English 1989–92, English Panel Humanities Research Bd 1995–98, Humanities Research Bd British Acad 1997–98, Arts and Humanities Research Bd 1998–2000; founding fell Eng Assoc 1999; DLit Queen's Univ Belfast 1995; *Books* On the Properties of Things, Book VII (1975), Poems of the Pearl Manuscript (with R Waldron, 1978), The Gawain-Poet: An Annotated Bibliography (1979), Two Early Renaissance Bird Poems (1984), Critical Essays on Chaucer's Canterbury Tales (1991), Variorum Chaucer: General Prologue to the Canterbury Tales (1993), Geoffrey Chaucer, The Canterbury Tales (ed with A C Cawley, 1996), Geoffrey Chaucer: Comic and Bawdy Tales (ed with A C Cawley, 1997), Geoffrey Chaucer: Three Tales about Marriage (ed with A C Cawley, 1998), Geoffrey Chaucer: Three Tales of Love and Chivalry (ed with A C Cawley, 2000), The Palgrave Literary Dictionary of Chaucer (2006); *Recreations* literature, art, architecture, music; *Style*— Prof Malcolm Andrew; ✉ 39 Cranmore Gardens, Belfast BT9 6JL (tel 028 9066 7869); School of English, The Queen's University of Belfast, Belfast BT7 1NN (tel 028 9097 3317, fax 028 9031 4615, e-mail m.andrew@qub.ac.uk)

ANDREW, Nicholas Anthony Samuel; s of Samuel Ogden Lees Andrew (d 1966), of Hants, and Rosalind Molly Carlyon, *née* Evans (d 1984); *b* 20 December 1946; *Educ* Winchester, Queens' Coll Cambridge (MA); *m* 28 Nov 1981, Jeryl Christine, da of Col John George Harrison, OBE, TD, DL, of Devon; 2 da (Venetia b 1989, Olivia b 1992); *Career* chartered accountant; ptnr: Robson Rhodes 1986–90, Rawlinson & Hunter 1990–92; md: Robson Rhodes Financial Services Ltd 1986–90, Nicholas Andrew International Tax Consultancy and Nicholas Andrew Financial Planning 1992–; *Books* Yuppies and their Money (1987), Robson Rhodes Personal Financial Planning Manual (jtly, 2–6 edns), How to Make Yourself Wealthy in the 1990's; *Recreations* golf, music, travel; *Clubs* MCC, RAC, Automobile (Monaco); *Style*— Nicholas A S Andrew, Esq; ✉ 39–40 St James's Place, London SW1A 1NS

ANDREW, (Christopher) Robert (Rob); MBE (1995); *b* 18 February 1963; *Educ* Barnard Castle, Univ of Cambridge (BA, Rugby blue, Cricket blue); *m* 18 Aug 1989, Sara; 3 da (Emily b 5 July 1990, Beth b 29 March 1995, Iola b 6 June 2000); *Career* rugby union player (fly-half) and coach; amateur rugby player until 1995, professional player 1995–99, chartered surveyor until 1995 (latterly a dir Debenham Thorpe DTZ); clubs as player: Middlesbrough RUFC, Cambridge Univ 1981–84, Nottingham RFC 1984–87, Gordon RFC (Aust), Wasps FC 1987–91 and 1992–96, Toulouse 1991–92, Barbarians RFC; dir of rugby Newcastle RFC 1995–2006 (also player until 1999, promoted to First Division 1997, winners Tetley's Bitter Cup 2001 (finalists 1999) and Powergen Cup 2004), elite dir of rugby RFU 2006–; rep: North 1985 and 1987, London 1989, England B (debut 1988), Home Unions 1989 (capt v France); England: debut v Romania 1985, Five Nations debut v France 1985, memb World Cup squad (2 appearances) 1987, tour Aust & Fiji 1988 (3 test appearances), tour Romania 1989, memb Grand Slam winning team 1991, 1992 and 1995, memb runners-up team World Cup 1991, memb team semi-finalists World Cup 1995, tour to South Africa 1994, over 50 caps, ret; kicked 6 penalties and scored 21 points v Wales 1986, record holder for drop goals in internationals, highest individual scoring mark (30 points v Canada, equalling world record) 1994; memb Br Lions tour Aust (2 tests) 1989; cricket: first class Yorkshire CCC 2nd XI, Cambridge Univ CC (capt 1985); *Style*— Rob Andrew, Esq, MBE; ✉ c/o RFU, Rugby House, Rugby Road, Twickenham TW1 1DZ

ANDREWS, Anthony; *b* 12 January 1948; *Educ* Royal Masonic Sch; *m* Georgina, *née* Simpson; 1 s (Joshua), 2 da (Jessica, Amy-Samantha); *Career* actor and film producer; memb: Equity, Screen Actors Guild USA, BAFTA; *Theatre* incl: 40 Years On (Apollo), One of Us 1986, Coming Into Land (NT) 1987, Dragon Variation (Duke of York's), Time and the Conways, A Midsummer Night's Dream (The New Shakespeare Co), Romeo & Juliet (The New Shakespeare Co), Vertigo, Ghosts (Comedy Theatre London), Henry Higgins in My Fair Lady (Theatre Royal Drury Lane), A Woman in White (Palace Theatre) 2005, The Letter (Wyndhams Theatre) 2007; 2 seasons Chichester Festival Theatre; *Television* incl: Brideshead Revisited, Danger UXB, Much Ado About Nothing, Romeo and Juliet, Jewels, Bluegrass, The Law Lord, Columbo Goes To The Guillotine, The Fortunes of Nigel, The Beast with Two Backs, Suspicion, Z For Zachariah, Burning Bridges, A Superstition, The Woman He Loved, Dixon of Dock Green, The Judge's Wife, Alma Mater, AD, Sparkling Cyanide, The Scarlet Pimpernel, Ivanhoe, La Ronde, Upstairs Downstairs, David Copperfield, The Pallisers, Follyfoot, A Day Out, French Without Tears, The Country Wife, London Assurance, QBVII, As the Actress Said to the Bishop, Woodstock, Doomwatch, The Duchess of Duke Street, Hands of a Murderer (USA), The Strange Case of Dr Jekyll and Mr Hyde (USA), Ruth Rendell's Heartstones, Mothertime, Love in a Cold Climate, The Cambridge Spies, Miss Marple; *Film* incl: The Scarlet Pimpernel, Under the Volcano, The Holcroft Covenant, Second Victory, The Light Horseman, Hannah's War, A War of Children, Take Me High, Operation Daybreak, Mistress of Paradise, Lost in Siberia (also prodr), Haunted (also prodr); *Clubs* Garrick; *Style*— Anthony Andrews, Esq; ✉ c/o Simon Beresford, Dalzell & Beresford, 26 Astwood Mews, London SW7 4DE (tel 020 7341 9411, fax 020 7341 9412, website www.anthony-andrews.com)

ANDREWS, Anthony Peter Hamilton; s of Col Peter Edward Clinton Andrews, of Hants, and Margaret Jean Hamilton, *née* Cooke; *b* 23 December 1946; *Educ* King's Sch Worcester, Univ of St Andrews (Kitchener scholar, MA, PGCE); *m* 8 Sept 1973, Alison Margaret Dudley, da of (David) Dudley Morgan, of Essex; 2 da (Jocelyn Amanda Hamilton b 30 July 1977, Gail Louise Hamilton b 15 June 1980), 1 s (David Dudley Hamilton b 1 March 1983); *Career* Offr Royal Marines 1964–71 (scholar 1962); trainee land agent J T Sutherland & Co 1975–76; British Council: VSO support offr Nigeria 1976–78, Br Information Centre Belgrade 1979–82, asst dir Oman 1982–85, dir NE Brazil 1985–89, dir Scotland 1990–96, dir Br Cncl Russia and cultural cnsllr Br Embassy Moscow April 1996–Jan 2000, Br Cncl Germany Berlin March 2000–, chief exec The Scottish Countryside Alliance 2002–; *Recreations* river management, fly fishing, shooting, sailing, visual arts, music, Scotland's history and culture; *Clubs* New (Edinburgh); *Style*— Tony Andrews; ✉ Milton of Finavon House, By Forfar, Angus DD8 3PY (tel and fax (office) 01356 623232); c/o The Scottish Countryside Alliance, East Gate, Royal Highland Showground, Ingliston EH28 8NF

ANDREWS, Dr Christopher John Horner; s of Prof William Henry Horner Andrews (d 1978), and Dr Jean Romer, *née* Young; *b* 31 December 1946; *Educ* Royal GS High Wycombe, St George's Coll Jamaica, Univ of London (MB BS, PhD); *m* 21 Oct 1972, Victoria Catherine, da of Charles Samuel Weston (d 1987); 2 s (Jeremy Charles Horner b 1977, William Jonathan Horner b 1979); *Career* MO Br Antarctic Survey 1972–76, SHO in anaesthetics The London Hosp 1976–77, registrar Royal Devon and Exeter Hosp 1977–80, sr registrar Bristol Royal Infirmary 1980–84, conslt Plymouth HA 1984–2005; Plymouth Hosps NHS Tst: clincal dir (anaesthetics) 1992–95 and 2001–03, med dir 1996–99, clinical dir (renal med) 2003–05; ret 2005; dir Remote Health Care 1999–2005, tstee Diving Diseases Research Centre 1999–; memb: BMA 1972, Assoc of Anaesthetists 1977; FFARCS 1980, FRCPEd 2001; *Recreations* fell walking; *Style*— Dr Christopher Andrews; ✉ 21 Seymour Park, Mannamead, Plymouth PL3 5BQ (tel 01752 664830)

ANDREWS, Claire Marguerite; da of David Andrews, of Rugby, Warks, and Kathleen Andrews; *b* 25 October 1956, Newbold-on-Avon, Warks; *Educ* Rugby HS for Girls, Univ of Manchester (LLB); *m* 16 March 1991, Paul Boyle; 1 s (Patrick b 4 Sept 1988), 2 da (Marguerite b 2 Dec 1992, Eleanor b 25 Nov 1994); *Career* called to the Bar 1979; memb of chambers 2 Harcourt Buildings 1980–84, with Home Office 1984–86, memb Gough Square Chambers 1986– (head of chambers with William Hibbert 2006); asst boundary cmmr; legal memb Mental Health Review Tbnl 1995–; memb: London Common Law and Commercial Bar Assoc, Administrative Law Bar Assoc; FCIArb; *Publications* The Enforcement of Regulatory Offences; *Recreations* tennis, painting; *Style*— Miss Claire Andrews; ✉ 52 Scatterdells Lane, Chipperfield, Hertfordshire WD4 9EX (tel 01923 265157, fax 01923 291513); Gough Square Chambers, 6–7 Gough Square, London EC4A 3DE (tel 020 7353 0924, fax 020 7353 2221, e-mail claire.andrews@goughsq.co.uk)

ANDREWS, Rev Clive Francis; s of Francis Edward Andrews (d 1966), of New Malden, Surrey, and Iris Emily Amelia, *née* Barton (d 1991); *b* 14 February 1950; *Educ* King's Coll Sch Wimbledon, KCL (BD, AKC, Tinniswood Prize), St George's Coll Jerusalem (Goldsmiths' Scholar), St Augustine's Coll Canterbury (pres), Open Univ Business Sch, ICSA; *m* 20 Feb 1982 (m dis 1992), Diana Ruth, da of Harry John Scrivener (d 1982), of Burstow, Surrey; 2 da (Siobhan b 1983, Caroline b 1986); *Career* exec offr Home Office 1968–69, curate Clapham Parish Church 1973–75, curate i/c St Nicholas Kidbrooke 1975–78, diocesan youth advsr Southwark 1979–84, vicar St Augustine's Honor Oak 1984–89, project conslt Harris City Technol Coll 1989–90, admin dir City Technol Colls Tst 1990–95 (also co sec 1991–95), self-employed business conslt 1995–96, charities asst Worshipful Co of Weavers 1996–98, ceo Royal Masonic Trust for Girls and Boys 2005– (asst sec 1998–2005); memb: Surrey Cncl for Voluntary Youth Orgns 1979–84, London Youth Ctee 1981–83, London S Ctee The Prince's Tst 1984–89 (vice-chm 1986–89); chm: Lewisham Youth Ctee 1982–84, Bacon's Sch Bermondsey 1985–91 (govr 1981–91); dir The English Dance Consort 1986–91; Freeman City of London 2000; FRSA 2007; *Publications* A Handbook of Parish Youth Work (1984), An End of All Education? Moral and spiritual development in secondary schools (1994); author of articles in various pubns; *Recreations* building restoration, keyboard playing, walking, spending time with my daughters, painting; *Style*— The Rev Clive Andrews

ANDREWS, Prof David; *Educ* Stationers' Co Sch Hornsey, UCL (BSc, MSc, PhD); *Career* awarded RCNC cadetship 1965, Constructor Lieut RCNC 1971; MOD Ship Dept Bath: submarine and ship design 1971–80, TRIDENT submarine project 1984–86, chief constructor (head of amphibious gp) 1986–90; head of concept design (naval) 1990–93, dir frigates and mine counter measures then integrated project team leader Future Surface Combatant Defence Procurement Agency 1998–2000; UCL: lectr in naval architecture 1980–84, MOD prof of naval architecture 1993–98, prof of engrg design Dept of Mechanical Engrg 2000–; RINA: chair Individual Case Exemption Panel 1991–, memb Cncl 1992–, memb Exec Ctee 1993–99 and 2006–, chair Membership Ctee 1993–2000, chair Future Directions Ctee 2000–; chair Design Methodology Panel IMDC 1995–, UK memb Int Marine Design Conference 1995–, memb RAE 2008 Sub Panel Engrg 2005–; Freeman Worshipful Co of Engineers 2007; memb RCNC 1972; FRINA 1987, FRSA 1996, FREng 2000, FIMechE 2002; *Publications* Synthesis in Ship Design (PhD thesis, 1984), FE Analysis and Design of Thin Walled Ship Structures (book chapter, 1987), Technology, Shipbuilding and Future Combat Beyond 2020 (book chapter, 2001), Multi-Hull Vessels (book chapter, 2004); author of numerous papers on ship design to RINA, Royal Soc, conferences etc; *Recreations* painting and sketching, reading, cinema and theatre-going, re-exploring London; *Style*— Prof David Andrews; ✉ Department of Mechanical Engineering, University College London, Torrington Place, London WC1E 7JE (tel 020 7679 3874, fax 020 7388 0180, e-mail d_andrews@meng.ucl.ac.uk)

ANDREWS, Prof Edgar Harold; s of Richard Thomas Andrews (d 1968); *b* 16 December 1932; *Educ* Dartford GS, Univ of London (BSc, PhD, DSc); *m* 1961, Thelma Doris, da of Selby John Walker, of Watford, Herts; 1 da (Rachel b 1962), 1 s (Martyn b 1964); *Career* dean Faculty of Engrg Queen Mary Coll London 1971–74 (prof of materials 1968–98, emeritus 1998–); dir: QMC Industrial Research Ltd 1970–88, Denbyware Ltd 1971–81, Materials Technol Consultants Ltd 1974–, Evangelical Press 1975–2004, Fire and Materials Ltd 1985–88; ed Evangelical Times 1998–; recipient A A Griffith Silver Medal 1977; FIP, FIM, CEng, CPhys; *Books* Fracture in Polymers (1968), From Nothing to Nature (1978), God, Science and Evolution (1980), The Promise of the Spirit (1982), Christ and the Cosmos (1986), Free in Christ (1996), A Glorious High Throne (2003), Preaching Christ (2005); *Recreations* writing, music, church work; *Style*— Prof Edgar Andrews; ✉ 25 Russellcroft Road, Welwyn Garden City, Hertfordshire AL8 6QX (tel 01707 331680)

ANDREWS, Sir Ian Charles Franklin; kt (2007), CBE (1992), TD (1989); s of Peter Harry Andrews, and Nancy Gwladys, *née* Franklin; *b* 26 November 1953; *Educ* Solihull Sch, Univ of Bristol (BSc); *m* 1985, Moira Fraser McEwan; 2 s, 1 da; *Career* MOD: joined 1975, private sec to Second Perm Under Sec of State 1979–81, short serv vol cmmn 1981–82, princ 1982, NATO Def Coll 1984–85, asst private sec to Sec of State for Def 1986–88, head Def Lands 1988–90, Resources and Prog (Army) 1990–93, civil sec Br Forces Germany/BAOR 1993–95, md (facilities) DERA 1995–97, chief exec Def Estates 1998–2002, second perm under sec of state for def 2002–; Maj TA 1972–93; FRGS 1996; *Recreations* travel, skiing; *Style*— Sir Ian Andrews, CBE, TD; ✉ c/o Ministry of Defence, Whitehall, London SW1A 2HB

ANDREWS, Prof John A; CBE (2000), JP (1975, supplemental list 1992); s of Arthur George Andrews (d 1980), of Newport, Gwent, and Hilda May Andrews (d 1989); *b* 29 January 1935; *Educ* Newport HS, Wadham Coll Oxford (MA, BCL); *m* 2 April 1960, Elizabeth Ann Mary, da of Frederick Edward Wilkes (d 1939), of King's Heath, Birmingham; 2 da (Carolyn Elizabeth b 1963, Susan Rebecca b 1966); *Career* called to the Bar Gray's Inn 1960 (bencher 1991); asst lectr Univ of Manchester 1957–58, lectr Univ of Birmingham 1958–67; Univ of Wales Aberystwyth: head Dept of Law 1970–92, prof of law 1967–92, vice-princ 1985–88, hon prof of law 1992–2000, emeritus prof 2000–; chief exec Further and Higher Educn Funding Cncls for Wales 1992–2000; visiting prof Univs of: Thessaloniki 1974 and 1990, Cracow 1978, Maryland 1983; ed Legal Studies 1981–93; chm: Cncl of Validating Univs 1987–90, Police Promotions Examinations Bd 1987–2002, Wales Advsy Body for Local Authy Higher Educn Standing Working Gp 1990–92, Agricultural Wages Bd 1999–2003, Gen Teaching Cncl for Wales 2000–04; memb Police Skills and Standards Orgn 2001–04; law advsr to the Universities Funding Cncl 1989–93;

pres SPTL 1988–89; memb: Ct of Govrs Univ of Wales 1969–92 and 2000–04, Ct of Govrs Nat Library of Wales 1979–92, Police Trg Cncl 1987–2002 (acad advsr 1997–2002), Lord Chllr's Advsy Ctee on Legal Educn 1987–90, Welsh Economic Cncl 1994–96, SE Wales Economic Forum 1997–2000, Criminal Injuries Compensation Appeals Panel 2000–06, Cncl Univ of Cardiff 2000–, Police Accreditation and Licensing Bd 2002–06, Cncl Univ of Wales Coll of Med 2000–04, Policing Ctee Justice Sector Skills Cncl 2004–06, Actuarial Profession Disciplinary Panel 2004–, Ctee NCH Wales 2004–, Bd of Dirs Royal Welsh Coll of Music and Drama 2006–; govr: Univ of Glamorgan 2002– (vice-chm and pro-chllr 2005–), Llanishen HS 2005–; tstee: Hamlyn Tst 1969–2000, SPTL 1990–2005, AHRB 2001–05; hon fell Univ of Wales Coll Newport 2000; FRSA; *Books* Welsh Studies in Public Law (ed, 1970), Human Rights in Criminal Procedure (ed, 1982), The Welsh Language in the Courts (jtly, 1984), The International Protection of Human Rights (jtly, 1987), Criminal Evidence (jtly, 1987, 2 edn 1992), Criminal Evidence - Statutes and Materials (1990); *Recreations* walking, theatre, opera, food; *Clubs* Brynamlwg; *Style—* Prof John Andrews, CBE; ✉ 7 Maeshendre, Aberystwyth, Ceredigion SY23 3PR (tel 01970 623921); The Croft, 110 Mill Road, Lisvane, Cardiff CF14 0UG (tel 029 2075 3980); Department of Law, University of Wales, Aberystwyth SY23 3DY (tel 01970 622712, fax 01970 622729)

ANDREWS, John Malcolm; OBE (2003); s of Leslie Andrews (d 1980), and Gwen, *née* Eite (d 2004); *b* 11 June 1942; *Educ* Bromley GS; *m* Elizabeth Faith, da of Harry Crispin Smith; 2 s (Thomas Crispin b 2 Feb 1970, James Henry b 7 July 1972); *Career* Inland Revenue 1962–65; PricewaterhouseCoopers (formerly Coopers & Lybrand before merger): joined 1965, head of tax 1986–93, sr tax ptnr 1994–98; pres Chartered Inst of Taxation 1997–98 (memb Cncl 1992–, dep pres 1996–97), chm Low Incomes Tax Reform Gp 1998–; chm Music for Change 1997–; FTII 1967, FCA 1974; *Books* Taxation of Directors and Employees (1977, 4 edn, 1995); *Recreations* all sport; *Style—* John Andrews, Esq, OBE; ✉ Vicarage Farm, Postling, Kent CT21 4ET

ANDREWS, Leighton; AM; s of Thomas Leonard Andrews (d 1967), and Peggy, *née* Squires; *b* 11 August 1957, Cardiff; *Educ* Poole GS, Univ of Wales Bangor (BA), Univ of Sussex (MA); *m* 6 July 1996, Ann Beynon; 2 step c; *Career* vice-pres NUS 1980–81, parly offr Age Concern 1982–84, UK campaign dir UN Int Year of Shelter 1984–87, dir then md Sallingbury Casey 1988–91, dir then jt md Rowland Co 1991–93, head of public affrs BBC 1993–96, chm Political Context and Welsh Context 1996–99, dir then md Westminster Strategy 2000–02, md Smart Co 2001–02, lectr Univ of Cardiff Journalism Sch 2002–03, memb Nat Assembly for Wales (Lab) Rhondda 2003–; visiting prof: Univ of Westminster 1997–, Cardiff Univ 2004–; memb Editorial Bd Jl of Public Affrs; memb: Bevan Fndn, Inst of Welsh Affrs; supporter Homeless Int; MIPR; *Publications* Wales Says Yes (1999); author of various chapters in books and articles; *Recreations* watching Cardiff City FC, reading, cinema, cooking; *Clubs* Ferndale Rugby; *Style—* Leighton Andrews, Esq, AM; ✉ National Assembly for Wales, Cardiff Bay, Cardiff CF99 1NA (tel 029 2089 8784, e-mail leighton.andrews@wales.gov.uk)

ANDREWS, Prof Malcolm Yardley; s of Francis Yardley Andrews (d 1980), and Marguerite Joan, *née* West; *b* 1 September 1942, Talyllyn, Wales; *Educ* Lancing, Gonville & Caius Coll Cambridge (BA), London Institute of Education (PGCE), Birkbeck Coll London (PhD); *m* 1, 1967 (m dis 1973), Mildred, *née* Randolph; 1 s (Richard Randolph Yardley b 18 Feb 1971), 1 step da (Megan Jennifer Clarke b 5 Oct 1962); m 2, 1981, Kristin Avelda, *née* Wade; 2 s (Peter Nigel b 18 Dec 1982, Francis Hunter b 7 June 1984); *Career* lectr: Dept of English Univ of Guelph 1966–67, Dept of English Birkbeck Coll London 1969–70, Sch of English Univ of Kent 1971– (prof 1996–); pres Dickens Soc USA 2003–04, ed The Dickensian jl 1991–; memb AHRC Peer Review Coll 2004–; *Books* Dickens on England and the English (1979), The Search for the Picturesque: Landscape Aesthetics and Tourism in Britain, 1750–1800 (1989), Dickens and the Grown-up Child (1994), The Picturesque: Sources and Documents (ed, 3 vols, 1994), Landscape and Western Art (1999), Charles Dickens and His Performing Selves: Dickens and the Public Readings (2006); *Recreations* writing, reading, public readings of Dickens, Languedoc holidays and wines; *Style—* Prof Malcolm Andrews; ✉ School of English, Rutherford College, University of Kent, Canterbury, Kent CT2 7NX (tel 01227 823335, fax 01227 827001, e-mail m.y.andrews@kent.ac.uk)

ANDREWS, Mark Björnsen; s of Harry Field Andrews, of Reading, and Ruth Margaret, *née* Legge; *b* 12 July 1952; *Educ* Reading GS, Hertford Coll Oxford (BA); *Career* admitted slr 1976; Wilde Sapte (now Denton Wilde Sapte): ptnr 1979–, head of Insolvency Gp 1990–, sr ptnr 1996–2000, dep chm 2000–02; chm CBI Insolvency Panel; memb: Law Soc 1974, Assoc of Business Recovery Practioners 1991, City of London Slrs' Co 1994, Int Bar Assoc 1994, Int Insolvency Inst 2005; tstee Pimlico Opera and Grange Park Opera Endowment Fund; *Recreations* music, history, outdoor activities, ornithology; *Style—* Mark Andrews, Esq; ✉ Denton Wilde Sapte, Number 1 Fleet Place, London EC4M 7WS (tel 020 7246 7000, fax 020 7246 7777, e-mail markandrews@dentonwildesapte.com)

ANDREWS, Mark Canter; s of Peter J Andrews (d 1993), of Bristol, and Joyce, *née* Abbey; *b* 9 November 1954; *Educ* Bristol Cathedral Sch; *Career* trainee architect Moxley Jenner & Partners 1973–74; graphic designer: BBC Bristol 1974–76, ITV (ATV, HTV, Westward TV) 1976–78; prodr Freeman Mathews & Milne advtg agency 1978–80; Collett Dickenson Pearce & Partners: prodr 1980–86, bd dir/head of TV 1986–89, fndr chm Independent Image (subsid) 1989–92; fndr md Propaganda Films Europe (subsid of Polygram plc) 1992–95, md Rogue Films (subsid of Carlton plc) 1995–96, fndr md Tsunami Films Ltd 1996–2002, Manifesto Films 2002–, M-A-D-E Ltd (Mark Andrews Digital Emporium Ltd) 2004–; chm Pliatsky II Ctee 1994–95; former memb: ACTT, IPA; memb AFVPA 1992; *Recreations* skiing, wine, fly fishing, lunch, big hi-fi; *Clubs* Soho House; *Style—* Mark Andrews, Esq; ✉ 25 Battersea Church Road, London SW11 3LY (tel 020 7801 0025, e-mail info@m-a-d-e.net, website www.m-a-d-e.net)

ANDREWS, Peter John; QC (1991); s of Reginald Percy Andrews, of Sutton Coldfield, and Dora, *née* Carter; *b* 14 November 1946; *Educ* Bishop Veseys GS, Univ of Bristol (undergraduate scholar), Christ's Coll Cambridge; *m* 10 Sept 1976, (Hilary) Ann, da of Graham Chavasse (d 1978); 2 da (Emily Alice b 19 May 1979, Fleur Victoria b 17 May 1981); *Career* called to the Bar Lincoln's Inn 1970 (Hardwicke scholar; bencher 1999), barrister specialising in catastrophic personal injury and clinical negligence law, jr Midland & Oxford Circuit 1973–74, dir Birmingham Legal Advice Centre 1974–75, recorder of the Crown Court 1990– (asst recorder 1986–90), chm Fountain Court Chambers Ltd 1994–2004, head of chambers 199 Strand 1997–2000, dep High Court judge 1998–; memb Professional Conduct Ctee GMC 2001–, legal chm Mental Health Review Tbnl 2007–; *Books* Catastrophic Injuries: A Guide to Compensation (1997), Personal Injury Handbook (contrib, 2000), The Court of Protection (2001), Kemp & Kemp: The Quantum of Damages, Periodical Payments, Pension Loss Claims, Taxation and Personal Injury Damages, and Incapable Claimants - The Court of Protection (contrib, 2004), Kemp & Kemp: The Quantum of Damages (contributing ed, 2004); *Style—* Peter Andrews, Esq, QC; ✉ 7 Bedford Row, London WC1R 4BS (tel 020 7242 3555, fax 020 7242 2511, e-mail pandrews@7br.co.uk)

ANDREWS, Richard Edward; s of William Reginald Andrews (d 1983), and Agnes Ruby Whiffen (d 1994); *b* 15 August 1936; *Educ* Cambridgeshire HS, St Catharine's Coll Cambridge (scholar, MA, Figgis prize); *m* 20 Aug 1982, Stephanie Elizabeth, da of Percy Craig, of Motueka, NZ; 1 s, 1 da; *Career* Fly Offr RAF 1955–57; sr conslt PA 1965–72, personnel mangr BLMC 1972–74, personnel dir Franklin Mint USA 1974–78, business mangr Cassells 1979, gp personnel dir Dixons Gp plc 1980–95; dir Dixons Bradford CTC Tst 1988–; memb: Industry In Educn 1994–97, Industrial Tbnls 1995–98; FIPD, FRSA; *Publications* Selection and Assessment (1989), Ethics in Business (1995); various articles on pay and personnel mgmnt; *Recreations* playing bad golf, watching good rugby, surfing the net and sketching badly; *Clubs* Maungakiekie Golf, Achilles; *Style—* Richard Andrews, Esq; ✉ 18 Golf Road, Epsom, Auckland, New Zealand (tel 00 64 9 631 5562, e-mail re.andrews@xtra.co.nz)

ANG, Dr Swee Chai; da of P L Ang, of Singapore, and L H Ang, *née* Lee; *b* 26 October 1948; *Educ* Raffles GS, Univ of Singapore (MB BS, MSc); *m* 29 Jan 1977, Francis Khoo, *qv*, s of Anthony T E Khoo (d 1972), of Singapore; *Career* orthopaedic surgn HS of Beirut 1976–, surgn UN Gaza Strip 1988–89, conslt surgn WHO Gaza and W Bank 1989, sr conslt orthopaedic surgn Newham Gen Hosp London 1994–96, conslt orthopaedic surgn Royal London Hosp 1996–; fndr memb Br Charity Medical Aid for Palestinians; memb BMA; FBOA, FRCS; *Books* From Beirut to Jerusalem (1989), Manual of War Surgery (1994); *Recreations* music, poetry; *Style—* Dr Swee Ang; ✉ Medical Aid for Palestinians, 33A Islington Park Street, London N1 1QB (tel 020 7226 4114, fax 020 7226 0880)

ANGEL, Anthony Lionel (Tony); s of William Angel, of London N3, and Frances Beatrice, *née* Berman; *b* 3 December 1952; *Educ* Haberdashers' Aske's, Queens' Coll Cambridge (MA); *m* 2 Nov 1975, Ruth Frances Barbara, da of Ivan Frank Hartog, of Northwood, Middx; 2 s (Benjamin b 3 Dec 1978, Jonathan b 18 Sept 1982); *Career* admitted slr 1978; Linklaters: joined 1976, ptnr 1984–, head of tax 1994–98, managing ptnr 1998–2007; tstee Cystic Fibrosis Tst 1998– (hon treas 1998–2006); memb: Worshipful Co of Slrs, Law Soc; *Recreations* tennis, swimming, skiing; *Style—* Tony Angel, Esq; ✉ Linklaters, One Silk Street, London EC2Y 8HQ (tel 020 7456 5636, fax 020 7456 2000, e-mail tony.angel@linklaters.com)

ANGEL, Dr Heather; da of Stanley Paul Le Rougel (d 2002), and Hazel Marie, *née* Sherwood; *b* 21 July 1941; *Educ* 14 schs in England and NZ, Univ of Bristol (BSc, MSc); *m* 3 Oct 1964, Martin Vivian Angel, s of Thomas Huber Angel; 1 s (Giles Philip b 25 May 1977); *Career* marine biologist, professional wildlife photographer, author and lectr; special prof Dept of Life Science Univ of Nottingham 1994–; columnist Amateur Photographer 1990–97; television appearances (demonstrating photographic techniques): Me and My Camera 1981 and 1983, Gardeners' World 1983 and 1991, Nature 1984, Nocon on Photography 1988; pres RPS 1984–86; RPS Hood medal 1975, Medaille de Salverte (Société Française de Photographie) 1984, Louise Schmidt Laureate 1998; Hon DSc Univ of Bath 1986; Hon FRPS 1986 (FRPS 1972), FBIPP 1972; *Solo Exhibitions* Kodak Exhibition The Natural History of Britain and Ireland (Science Museum) 1981, Nature in Focus (Nat Hist Museum) 1987, The Art of Wildlife Photography (Nature in Art Gloucester) 1989, Natural Visions (Dimbola Lodge Isle of Wight, Gilbert White's House Selborne, The Yard Gallery Nottingham and Nature in Art Gloucester) 2000, Natural Visions (Edinburgh Botanic Garden, Aberystwyth Arts Centre, Gosport Gallery, Bradford Design Exchange, Lynn Museum Kings Lynn, Booth Museum Brighton, Oxford Univ Museum, Astley Hall Museum Chorley, Royal Botanic Gardens Kew, Somerset County Museum Taunton, New Walk Museum Leicester, Grosvenor Museum Chester, Bristol Museum and Art Gallery, Haslemere Educational Museum, Kuala Lumpur, Cairo and Beijing) 2001–04; *Books* Nature Photography: Its Art and Techniques (1972), Photographing Nature (5 vols, 1975), Life in The Oceans (1977), The Book of Nature Photography (1983), Camera in the Garden (1984), The Book of Close-up Photography (1986), A View from a Window (1988), Nature in Focus (1988), Landscape Photography (1989), Animal Photography (1991), Kew: A World of Plants (1993), Photographing the Natural World (1994), Outdoor Photography: 101 Tips and Hints (1997), Pandas (1998), How to Photograph Flowers (1998), How to Photograph Water (1999), Natural Visions (2000), Giant Pandas (2006), Puffin (2007), Macro through a Nikon Lens (2007); *Recreations* travelling to remote parts of the world to photograph wilderness areas and unusual aspects of animal behaviour; *Style—* Dr Heather Angel; fax 01252 727464, e-mail hangel@naturalvisions.co.uk, website www.naturalvisions.co.uk

ANGEL, Marie Louise; da of Francis John Angel (d 1968), of Australia, and Thelma Lilie, *née* Sandow (d 1974); *b* 30 July 1953; *Educ* Methodist Ladies' Coll Adelaide; *m* 1985, David Charles Freeman, s of Howard Freeman; 1 da (Catherine Elinor b 13 May 1989), 1 s (Lachlan John b 28 Feb 1993); *Career* soprano; with Opera Factory London 1982–; winner Gulbenkian prize 1977, Countess of Munster prize 1977, Kammersägerin 1997; *Performances* with Opera Factory incl: Pretty Polly 1983, Donna Anna in Don Giovanni 1990 and 1992, Countess Almaviva in Don Giovanni 1992 (later filmed for Channel 4), Fiordiligi in Cosi fan Tutte 1986 (later filmed for Channel 4), Hannah in Yan Tan Thethera 1992, title role in L'Incoronazione di Poppea 1992, Sarajevo 1994 (several acting roles incl Cassandra in Trojan Women), Dido in Dido & Aeneas London and Zürich 1995; others incl: Oracle of the Dead in The Mask of Orpheus (ENO) 1986, Donna Anna (Melbourne State Opera) 1990, cr role Morgan le Fay in Gawain (Royal Opera House Covent Garden) 1991, cr role Esmerelda in Rosa (Peter Greenaway and Louis Andriessen, Netherlands Opera) 1994 (filmed 1998), cr role Ingrid in Lovendier Esmée Holland Festival 1995, Kagel's Aud Deutchland (1997), Countess in Soldaten (ENO) 1996 and (Basel Theatre) 1998–99, Fortunata in Satyricon (with Herbert Wernicke and Basel Theatre) 1998, title role in Lustige Witwe (Herbert Wernicke and Basel Theatre) 1999, Ottavia in L'Incoronazione di Poppea (Basel Theatre) 2003–04; also appeared in Peter Greenaway's film Prospero's Books 1991, Facing Goya (throughout Spain) 2000–01, Kagel/Mozart Project (La Fenice, Venice) 2001, John Cage's Europera 5 2001–02; *Recordings* Gawain (Grammy of the Year 1997), Mask of Orpheus 1997, Prospero's Books, Rosa 1999, Facing Goya 2002 *Videos* Gawain, Rosa, Aus Deutchland, Cosi fan Tutte, Don Giovanni, The Marriage of Figaro, Seven Deadly Sins; *Recreations* gardening; *Style—* Ms Marie Angel; ✉ c/o Allied Artists' Agency, 42 Montpelier Square, London SW7 1JZ (tel 020 7589 6243)

ANGELINI, Prof Gianni Davide; s of Marzio Angelini, of Siena, Italy, and Erina Angelini; *b* 29 January 1953, Siena, Italy; *Educ* Instituto T Sarrocchi Siena (Dip Mech Engrg), Univ of Siena Sch of Med (Lode Prize, MD), Univ of Wales Coll of Med (MCh); *m* 5 July 1985, Rosalind, da of Arthur John, and Megan John; 3 s (Jonathan b 7 Dec 1986, Timothy b 5 April 1988, Simon b 27 Dec 1994); *Career* Univ Hosp of Siena 1979–80 (latterly SHO in cardiovascular surgery), registrar in cardiac surgery Italian Hosp London 1980, locum registrar in gen surgery Royal Masonic Hosp London 1980; SHO: in cardiothoracic surgery Llandough Hosp Cardiff 1981, in gen surgery Univ Hosp of Wales Cardiff 1981–82, in casualty/accident Royal Gwent Hosp Newport 1982–83; registrar then sr registrar in cardiothoracic surgery Univ Hosp of Wales Cardiff 1983–88, sr registrar in cardiothoracic surgery Thoraxcenter Erasmus Univ Rotterdam 1988–89, lectr and Br Heart Fndn intermediate research fell in cardiothoracic surgery Univ Hosp of Wales Cardiff 1989, sr lectr and conslt in cardiothoracic surgery Univ of Sheffield 1989–92; currently: Br Heart Fndn prof of cardiac surgery and head Div of Cardiac Surgery, Cardiology, Radiology and Anaesthetics Univ of Bristol, dir Bristol Heart Inst, assoc dir of cardiac surgery United Bristol Healthcare Tst (memb Med Research Ctee); visiting prof: Univ of the WI 1992, Queen Alia Med Centre Amman 1995, Univ of Buffalo 1996, Chinese Univ of Hong Kong 1997, European Hosp Paris 1997, Univ of Groningen 1997, Univ of Milan 1997 and 1999, Univ of Chieti 1998, St Luke's Hosp Thessaloniki 1999, Univ of Utrecht 2000, Hosp Univ Kebangsaan Malaysia 2001; regnl advsr to the Royal Colls NHS R&D Exec; expert assessor: Med Devices Directorate Dept of Health, Nat Inst for Clinical Excellence (NICE), Cardiosource; rep of profs of surgery Cardiothoracic SAC Jt Ctee of Higher Surgical Trg; memb Project Grant Ctee: Br Heart Fndn, EPSRC; memb:

Br Soc for Cardiovascular Res (past chm), Br Cardiac Soc (exec memb Cncl), Soc of Cardiothoracic Surgeons of GB and I (exec memb Cncl Cardiothoracic Section), Int Soc for Heart Research, European Soc of Cardiology (exec memb Pathogenesis of Atherosclerosis Gp, memb Study Gp on Advanced Heart Failure), European Soc for Cardiothoracic Surgery, Br Atherosclerosis Soc, American Assoc for Thoracic Surgery; Young Research Workers Prize Br Cardiac Soc 1986, Peter Allen Prize Soc of Cardiothoracic Surgns of GB and I 1988, First Research Prize European Soc for Vascular Surgery 1990, David Cooper Prize Soc of Cardiothoracic Surgns of GB and I 1991; Cavaliere al Merito della Repubblica Italiana; FRCSGlas 1986, fell European Bd of Thoracic and Cardiovascular Surgns (FETCS) 1998; *Recreations* jazz music, running; *Style*— Prof Gianni Angelini; ✉ Bristol Heart Institute, Bristol Royal Infirmary, Bristol BS2 8HW (tel 0117 928 3145, fax 0117 929 9737, e-mail g.d.angelini@bristol.ac.uk)

ANGELL, Prof Ian Oakley; s of Roy Oakley Angell, of Bargoed, Mid Glamorgan, and Eluned Angell (d 1972); *b* 8 July 1947; *Educ* Lewis Sch Pengam Mid Glamorgan, Univ of Wales (BSc), Univ of London (PhD); *m* 30 July 1971, Florence Mary, da of John Graham Davies, of Bargoed, Mid Glamorgan; *Career* Univ of London: lectr Royal Holloway Coll 1971–84, sr lectr UCL 1984–86, prof of info systems LSE 1986–; fndr memb Euro Orgn for East-West Co-operation, memb Steering Ctee of UNESCO Regnl Office for Sci and Tech for Europe (Venice), conslt global consequences of IT, strategic information systems and int and organisational information tech policies; *Books* incl: A Practical Introduction To Computer Graphics (1981), High Resolution Computer Graphics Using C (1990), Information Systems Management (1991), Advanced Graphics on VGA and XGA cards with Borland C++ (1992), The New Barbarian Manifesto (2000); *Recreations* opera, ballet, cats, computing; *Style*— Prof Ian Angell; ✉ London School of Economics and Political Science, Department of Information Systems, Houghton Street, London WC2A 2AE (tel 020 7955 7638, fax 020 7955 7385, e-mail i.angell@lse.ac.uk)

ANGEST, Henry; *Educ* Univ of Basel Switzerland (LLL); *Career* chm: Arbuthnot Banking Gp plc (also chief exec), Arbuthnot Latham & Co Ltd, Arbuthnot Securities Ltd, Secure Trust Bank plc; Jr Warden Guild of Int Bankers, memb London Investment Bankers Assoc (memb Chm's Ctee, chm Banking Ctee); *Recreations* dendrology; *Clubs* City of London, Carlton, City Swiss (chm); *Style*— Henry Angest, Esq; ✉ Arbuthnot Banking Group plc, 20 Ropemaker Street, London EC2Y 9AR (tel 020 7012 2400, fax 020 7012 2401)

ANGIER, Carole; da of Jussi Brainin, and Liesl, *née* Kelsen; *b* 30 October 1943, London; *Educ* McGill Univ Montreal (BA), Univ of Oxford (MA), Univ of Cambridge (MLitt); *Children* 1 s (Thomas Peter Stephen b 22 May 1970); *Career* lectr in literature and philosophy: Univ of Cambridge and Univ of Sussex 1975, external studies depts Univ of Oxford and Univ of Bristol 1975–80, Open Univ 1975–85; Univ of Warwick: fndr and teacher of the practice of biography 2003–04, Royal Literary Fund Advsy fell 2003–05 (fell 1999–2003), project fell (teaching creative writing to refugees and asylum seekers in Oxford) 2004; teacher of modern biography Birkbeck Coll Univ of London 2005–; mentor Arts Cncl Writers' Pool 2003–05; book reviewer The Spectator, New Statesman, The Independent, The Daily Telegraph, The Sunday Times and Literary Review 1975–; freelance journalist, articles in numerous publications incl: The Guardian, London Review of Books, London Magazine, Sight & Sound, Jewish Quarterly; wrote and presented Edgar Reitz for Omnibus (BBC2) 1991, wrote English subtitles for Edgar Reitz's Die Zweite Heimat 1991; Commonwealth Scholarship 1964–66, Canada Cncl Fellowship 1969–75; Writers Guild Non-Fiction Award 1991, Southern Arts Non-Fiction Award 1991, Winston Churchill Travelling Fellowship 1993, Arts Cncl Writers Award 1998; shortlisted Whitbread Biography Prize 1991; patron Nat Acad of Writing, vol worker Asylum Welcome Oxford (visitor to immigration detainees), message and tracing vol Red Cross, supporter Med Fndn for the Victims of Torture; memb: PEN, Writers in Oxford, Soc of Authors; FRSL 2002; *Books* Life of Margaret Hill (1978), Jean Rhys (1985), Jean Rhys: Life and Work (1990), The Double Bond: Primo Levi, A Biography (2002), The Story of my Life: Refugees Writing in Oxford (ed, 2005); *Recreations* walking, talking; *Style*— Carole Angier, FRSL; ✉ 13 High Street, Ascott-under-Wychwood, Oxfordshire OX7 6AW (tel 01993 830414), c/o Rogers, Coleridge & White Ltd, 20 Powis Mews, London W11 1JN (tel 020 7221 3717)

ANGIOLINI, Rt Hon Elish Frances; PC (2006), QC (2001), WS (2005); da of James McPhilomy (d 1981), and Mary McPhilomy; *b* 24 June 1960, Glasgow; *Educ* Notre Dame Sch Glasgow, Univ of Strathclyde (LLB, DipLP); *m* 14 Sept 1985, Domenico Angiolini; 2 s (Domenico b 16 Nov 1996, David b 4 April 2000); *Career* admitted slr 1985; early career as depute procurator fiscal Airdrie and with Mgmnt Servs Gp Crown Office, sr depute procurator fiscal then asst procurator fiscal Glasgow 1995–97, head of policy Crown Office 1997–2000, regnl procurator fiscal Grampian, Highlands and Islands 2000–01, slr gen for Scotland 2001–; Hon LLD Glasgow Caledonian Univ 2005; FRSA; *Style*— The Rt Hon Elish Angiolini, QC, WS; ✉ The Crown Office, 25 Chambers Street, Edinburgh EH1 1LA (tel 0131 247 2875, fax 0131 226 6910, e-mail solicitorgeneral@scotland-gsi.gov.uk)

ANGLESEY, 7 Marquess of (UK 1815); Sir George Charles Henry Victor Paget; 10 Bt (I 1730); also Lord Paget of Beaudesert (E 1552) and Earl of Uxbridge (GB 1784); s of 6 Marquess of Anglesey (d 1947), and Lady Marjorie Manners, da of 8 Duke of Rutland; *b* 8 October 1922; *Educ* Eton; *m* 16 Oct 1948, Elizabeth Shirley Vaughan, DBE, LVO (Marchioness of Anglesey, *qv*), da of Charles Langbridge Morgan, the writer; 2 s, 3 da; *Heir* s, Earl of Uxbridge; *Career* Maj RHG 1946; JP 1959–68 and 1983–89; dir Wales Nationwide Building Society 1973–89; pres Anglesey Cons Assoc 1949–83, chm Historic Bldgs Cncl for Wales 1977–92, tstee National Portrait Gallery 1979–90; memb: National Heritage Memorial Fund 1980–92, Royal Cmmn on Historical Manuscripts 1984–91; Vice Lord-Lt Anglesey 1960–83 (DL 1960), HM Lord-Lt Gwynedd 1983–89; Octavia Hill Medal 2002; Hon DLitt Univ of Wales 1984, hon prof UCW (Bangor) 1986; FSA, FRHistS, FRSL, Hon FRIBA; *Books* The Capel Letters (1955), One-Leg (1961), Sergeant Pearman's Memoirs (1968), Little Hodge (1971), A History of the British Cavalry 1816–1919 (Vol I 1973, Vol II 1975, Vol III 1982 (Templer Award), Vol IV 1986, Vol V 1994, Vol VI 1995, Vol VII 1996, Vol VIII 1997 (Cheney Gold Medal)); *Recreations* music, gardening; *Style*— The Most Hon the Marquess of Anglesey, FSA; ✉ Plâs Newydd, Llanfairpwll, Anglesey, Gwynedd (tel 01248 714330)

ANGLESEY, Marchioness of; (Elizabeth) Shirley Vaughan Paget; DBE (1982, CBE 1977), LVO (1993); da of late Charles Morgan (novelist), and Hilda Vaughan (novelist); *b* 4 December 1924; *Educ* Francis Holland Sch, St James' Sch West Malvern, Kent Place Sch USA; *m* 1948, 7 Marquess of Anglesey, *qv*; 2 s, 3 da; *Career* chm Nat Fedn of Women's Insts 1966–69, vice-chm Govt Working Pty on Methods of Sewage Disposal 1969–70, dep chm Prince of Wales Ctee 1970–80, chm Welsh Arts Cncl 1975–81, memb IBA 1976–81, chm Br Cncl Drama and Dance Advsy Ctee 1981–91, chm Broadcasting Complaints Cmmn 1987–91, memb and subsequently vice-chm Museums and Galleries Cmmn 1981–96, vice-pres City & Guilds 1998–; tstee: Pilgrim Tst 1982–2001, Theatres Tst 1992–95; hon fell UCNW Bangor 1990; Hon LLD Univ of Wales 1977, Hon FCGI 2002; *Style*— The Most Hon the Marchioness of Anglesey, DBE, LVO; ✉ Plâs Newydd, Llanfairpwll, Anglesey LL61 6DZ (tel 01248 714330)

ANGUS, Dr Rachel Jean; da of Prof Edward A Thompson, FBA (d 1994), and Dr Thelma Phelps; *b* 13 January 1951; *Educ* Nottingham HS for Girls, St Hugh's Coll Oxford (MA); *m* 28 Jan 1978, Peter D Angus, FRCS, s of Roland Angus; 1 s (Iain b 12 Jan 1980), 1 da (Miriam b 3 Nov 1981); *Career* conslt physician (elderly med) Huddersfield Royal Infirmary 1990–; elected memb GMC 1999; memb: BMA, Br Geriatric Soc, Med Women's Fedn; FRCPEd 1994, FRCP 1995; *Recreations* cycling, travel, embroidery; *Style*— Dr Rachel Angus; ✉ Huddersfield Royal Infirmary, Lindley, Huddersfield HD3 3EA (tel 01484 342000)

ANGUS, Robin John; s of Ian Gordon Angus (d 1994), of Forres, Moray, and Morag Ann (Sally), *née* Macdonald; *b* 15 September 1952; *Educ* Forres Acad, Univ of St Andrews (MA), Peterhouse Cambridge; *m* 20 Aug 1977, Lorna Christine, da of James Smith Campbell (d 1986), of Drumlemble, Argyll; *Career* investment mangr Baillie Gifford & Co 1977–81, investment tst analyst Wood Mackenzie & Co 1981–85, asst dir Wood Mackenzie & Co Ltd 1985–88; dir: Personal Assets Tst plc 1984–, Hill Samuel Securities Ltd 1985–88, NatWest Securities Ltd (incorporating Wood Mackenzie & Co Ltd) 1988–91 (dir Equities 1991–98), Charlotte Marketing Services Ltd 1991–94, The Edinburgh Agency Ltd 1991–, Ivory & Sime Trustlink Ltd 1994–98, Collective Assets Tst plc 1998–2005; advsr Centre for Fin Markets Research Univ of Edinburgh 1995–; memb Gen Synod Scottish Episcopal Church 1987–91; memb Monks of St Giles 2004–; Grand Makar Von Poser Soc of Scotland 1997–, Laureate Edinburgh Morayshire Soc 1996–; hon fell Faculty of Social Sciences Univ of Edinburgh 1999–; MSI 1993; Knight of St Sylvester 2001; *Books* Independence - The Option for Growth (1989), Haec Olim - Exploring the World of Investment Trusts 1981–1991 (1991), Capital - A Moral Instrument? (contrib, 1992), Dictionary of Scottish Church History and Theology (contrib, 1993), Personal Assets Trust Quarterlies: The 1990s and Beyond (2002); *Recreations* church work, politics (Scottish Nationalist), history, music, reading, writing verse; *Clubs* New (Edinburgh), Scottish Arts (Edinburgh), McSkate's (St Andrews); *Style*— Robin Angus, Esq; ✉ Personal Assets Trust plc, 10 Colme Street, Edinburgh EH3 6AA

ANHOLT, Catherine; da of Daniel Hogarty, and Diane, *née* Kelly; *Educ* Stroud Girls' HS, Falmouth Sch of Art (BA), RCA (MA); *m* Laurence Anholt , *qv*; 1 s (Tom), 2 da (Claire, Maddy); *Career* illustrator of children's books; involved with Bookstart (early years literacy campaign); *Books* Big Book of Families, What Makes me Happy?, Here Come the Babies, What I Like, Kids, The Twins, Two By Two, Bear and Baby, Come Back, Jack!, Baby's Things, First Words, Colours, Clothes, Can You Guess?, Chimp and Zee, Animals, Animals All Around, Look What I Can Do, Sun, Snow, Stars, Sky, One, Two, Three Count With Me, All About You, The Snow Fairy and the Spaceman, Tom's Rainbow Walk, When I Was A Baby, Aren't You Lucky!, Harry's Home, Billy and the Big New School, Good Days Bad Days, Going To Playgroup, Sophie and the New Baby, The New Puppy, Animal Friends, Bed Time, Busy Day, Play Time, A Kiss Like This, Little Copy Cub, Chimp and Zee and the Big Storm; *Awards* Right Start Toy and Book Award 1998 (three titles), overall winner Kid's Club Network Award 1999, Nestlé Smarties Gold Award 1999 and 2001, US CCBC Choices 2001 (two titles), Oppenheim Portfolio Gold Award (twice), The English Assoc 4–11 Awards (two titles); *Recreations* family life, cycling, fishing; *Style*— Mrs Catherine Anholt; ✉ website www.anholt.co.uk

ANHOLT, Laurence; s of Gerry Anholt, and Joan, *née* Pickford (d 2003); *Educ* Boxhill Sch, Epsom Sch of Art, Falmouth Sch of Art (BA), Royal Acad of Art (MA); *m* Catherine Anholt , *qv*; 1 s (Tom), 2 da (Claire, Maddy); *Career* carpenter, sch teacher, author and illustrator of children's books; involved with Bookstart (early years literacy campaign); *Books* author and illustrator: Camille and the Sunflowers, Degas and the Little Dancer, Picasso and the Girl With a Ponytail, Leonardo and the Flying Boy, The Forgotten Forest; illustrated by Catherine Anholt: Big Book of Families, What Makes me Happy?, Here Come the Babies, What I Like, Kids, The Twins, Two By Two, Bear and Baby, Come Back, Jack!, Baby's Things, First Words, Colours, Clothes, Can You Guess?, Chimp and Zee, Animals, Animals All Around, Look What I Can Do, Sun, Snow, Stars, Sky, One, Two, Three Count With Me, All About You, The Snow Fairy and the Spaceman, Tom's Rainbow Walk, When I Was A Baby, Aren't You Lucky!, Harry's Home, Billy and the Big New School, Good Days Bad Days, Going To Playgroup, Sophie and the New Baby, The New Puppy, Animal Friends, Bed Time, Busy Day, Play Time, A Kiss Like This, Little Copy Cub, Chimp and Zee and the Big Storm; Seriously Silly Stories (illustrated by Arthur Robins): Cinderboy, Daft Jack and the Beanstack, Rumply Crumply Stinky Pin, Billy Beast, The Emperor's Underwear, The Rather Small Turnip, The Fried Piper of Hamstring Town, Little Red Riding Wolf, Snow White and the Seven Aliens, Shampoozel, Eco Wolf and the Three Pig, Ghostyshocks and the Three Scares, Seriously Silly Stories - The Collection; The One and Only series (illustrated by Tony Ross): Harold the Hairiest Man, Ruby the Rudest Girl, Boris the Brainiest Baby, Polly the Most Poetic Person, Bruno the Bravest Man, Ben the Bendiest Boy, Tina the Tiniest Girl, Micky the Muckiest Boy; other books: The Superkid Handbook (illustrated by Martin Chatterton), Knee High Nigel (illustrated by Arthur Robins), The Magpie Song (illustrated by Dan Williams), Summerhouse (illustrated by Lynne Russell), I Like Me (illustrated by Adriano Gon), Stone Girl, Bone Girl (illustrated by Sheila Moxley); *Awards* Right Start Toy and Book Award 1998 (three titles), overall winner Kid's Club Network Award 1999, Nestlé Smarties Gold Award 1999 and 2001, US CCBC Choices 2001 (two titles), Oppenheim Portfolio Gold Award (twice), The English Assoc 4–11 Awards (two titles); *Recreations* a long soak in a warm book; *Style*— Laurence Anholt, Esq; ✉ e-mail info@anholt.co.uk, website www.anholt.co.uk

ANKARCRONA, Jan Gustaf Theodor Stensson; s of Sten Stensson Ankarcrona, RVO (d 1981), of Stockholm, Sweden, and Ebba, *née* Countess Mörner (d 1999); *b* 18 April 1940; *Educ* Östra Real Stockholm, Stockholm Sch of Econ (MBA), Univ of Calif Berkeley (MBA); *m* 1, 16 June 1968 (m dis 1978), E Margaretha Antonie, da of Erik von Eckermann (d 2004), of Ripsa, Sweden; 2 s (Johan b 1969, Edward b 1972); m 2, 6 March 1981, Sandra, da of E B Coxe (d 2007), of Hobe Sound, USA; 2 da (Aurore b 1983, Ariane b 1988); *Career* Royal Swedish Navy 1958–61, Lt-Cdr Royal Swedish Navy Reserve 1974; Stockholms Enskilda Bank Stockholm 1964–65, Gränges AB Stockholm 1966–69, American Express Securities SA Paris 1969–70, dep md Nordic Bank Ltd London 1971–83, md and chief exec Fennoscandia Bank Ltd London 1983–91, md Lexa UK Ltd London 1992–; chm China Devpt Capital GP Ltd; non-exec dir: Martin Currie Absolute Return Funds, Martin Currie Global Funds; OStJ Sweden; *Recreations* shooting, sailing, tennis, music, history; *Clubs* Brooks's, Hurlingham, Nya Sällskapet Stockholm; *Style*— Jan Ankarcrona, Esq; ✉ 29 Argyll Road, London W8 7DA (tel 020 7937 9438); Lexa UK Ltd, 14 Queen Anne's Gate, London SW1H 9AA (tel 020 7222 0400, fax 020 7222 0125, e-mail mail@janankarcrona.co.uk)

ANNALY, 6 Baron (UK 1863); Luke Richard White; o s of 5 Baron Annaly (d 1990), and his 1 w, Lady Marye Isabel Pepys (d 1958), da of 7 Earl of Cottenham; *b* 29 June 1954; *Educ* Eton, RMA Sandhurst, RAC Cirencester; *m* 1983, Caroline Nina, yr da of Col Robert Hugh Garnett, MBE, of Hope Bowdler Court, Salop; 3 da (Hon Lavinia Marye b 1987, Hon Iona Elizabeth b 1989, Hon Clementine Isabel b 2001), 1 s (Hon Luke Henry b 1990); *Heir* s, Hon Luke White; *Career* Lt Royal Hussars 1974–78, RAC Reserve 1978–86; govt whip and Lord-in-Waiting 1994–; jt master Bicester Hunt 1985–88; *Recreations* cricket, tennis, fox hunting, country pursuits; *Style*— The Rt Hon Lord Annaly

ANNANDALE AND HARTFELL, 11 Earl of (S, by Charter, 1662); Patrick Andrew Wentworth Hope Johnstone of Annandale and of that Ilk; DL (Dumfriesshire 1987); also Lord of Johnstone (S 1662), Hereditary Steward of Stewartry of Annandale, Hereditary Keeper of Castle of Lochmaben, and Chief of Clan Johnstone; s of Maj Percy Wentworth Hope Johnstone, TD, JP, RA (TA), *de jure* 10 Earl (d 1983), by his 2 w, Margaret Jane Hunter-Arundell (Dowager Countess of Annandale and Hartfell) (d 1998); claim to Earldom (which had been dormant since 1792) admitted by Ctee for Privileges of House of Lords, and a writ issued summoning him to Parl in the Upper House 1986; *b* 19 April 1941; *Educ* Stowe, RAC Cirencester; *m* 1969, Susan, o da of Col Walter John Macdonald Ross, CB, OBE, TD, JP, Lord-Lt of the Stewartry, of Netherhall, Castle Douglas, Kirkcudbrightshire; 1 s (David Patrick Wentworth, Lord Johnstone and Master of Annandale and Hartfell b 13 Oct 1971), 1 da (Lady Julia Clare b 1974); *Heir* s, Lord Johnstone; *Career* underwriting memb Lloyd's 1976–2004; memb: Solway River Purification Bd 1970–86, Scottish Valuation Advsy Cncl to Sec of State for Scotland 1984–86, Annan Fishery Bd 1983–, Standing Cncl of Scottish Chiefs, various ctees Dumfries CC 1970–75, Dumfries & Galloway Regnl Cncl 1974–86; chm: Royal Jubilee and Prince's Tst for Dumfries and Galloway 1984–88, Royal Scottish Forestry Soc 1981–84; dir: Bowerings Members Agency 1985–88, Murray Lawrence Members Agency 1988–92; co-dir: The Maclay Group, Raehills Farms Ltd, Skairfield Ltd; Vice Lord-Lt Dumfriesshire 1992; *Recreations* golf; *Clubs* Puffin's (Edinburgh); *Style*— The Rt Hon the Earl of Annandale and Hartfell, DL; ✉ Annandale Estates Office, St Anns, Lockerbie, Dumfriesshire DG11 1HQ

ANNESLEY, (Arthur) Noël Grove; s of Edmund Patrick Grove Annesley, OBE (d 1975), of Annes Grove, Castletownroche, Co Cork, and Ruth, *née* Rushforth (d 2007); *b* 28 December 1941; *Educ* Harrow, Worcester Coll Oxford (open scholarship, MA); *m* 7 Sept 1968, Caroline Susan, da of Thomas Henry Waldore Lumley; 2 s (Marcus Robert Grove b 27 March 1972, James Alexander Grove b 22 May 1974); *Career* Christie, Manson & Woods Ltd: joined 1964, fndr Dept of Prints, Drawings and Watercolours, auctioneer 1967–, dep chm 1985–91 (dir 1969–91); dep chm Christie's International plc 1992–98 (dir 1989–98), dep chm Christie's Fine Art Ltd 1998–2000, chm Christie's Education 2000–, chm Christie's International Fine Art Specialist Group 2000–03, hon chm Christie's Int (UK) Ltd 2004–; holds world record prices for Old Master drawings (Michelangelo and Leonardo da Vinci) and Br watercolours (J M W Turner); an authority on Old Master drawings with discoveries incl drawings by Michelangelo, Sebastiano del Piombo, Raphael and Rubens; tstee: Dulwich Picture Gallery (dep chm 2006–), Villiers David Fndn, Yehudi Menuhin Sch (chm Concert Hall Appeal Ctee until 2005), Michael Marks Charitable Tst 2006–, Advsy Panel Nat Heritage Meml Fund 2006; *Publications* The Touch of the Artist: Master Drawings from the Woodner Collection (contrib, 1995), The Expert versus the Object (contrib, 2004); contribs to Burlington Magazine and other specialist art jls; *Recreations* music (esp chamber), gardening, exploring classical sites, Ireland; *Clubs* Brooks's, Garrick, MCC; *Style*— Noël Annesley, Esq; ✉ Christie's, 8 King Street, St James's, London SW1Y 6QT (tel 020 7389 2241, fax 020 7389 2520, e-mail nannesley@christies.com)

ANNESLEY, 11 Earl (I 1789); Philip Harrison; also Baron Annesley (I 1758) and Viscount Glerawly (I 1766); s of 9 Earl Annesley (d 1979), bro of 10 Earl Annesley (d 2001); *b* 29 March 1927; *Educ* Strode's GS Egham, Army Tech Sch; *m* 1951, Florence Eileen (d 1995), da of late John Arthur Johnston, of Gillingham, Kent; *Heir* bro, Hon Michael Annesley; *Career* REME 1942–57: leading artisan 1948, armament artificer 1951–57; test and calibration engr Rediffusion Simulation Ltd 1957, system designer 1963, systems trg mangr Hughes Rediffusion Simulation Ltd 1989–91; *Style*— The Rt Hon the Earl Annesley

ANSARI, Dr Joseph Mohammad Ayub; s of Hakim Mohammad Yusuf Ansari (d 1971), and Hasina Khatoan, *née* Kidwai (d 1971); *b* 25 June 1938; *Educ* Shia Degree Coll Lucknow India (BSc), King Edward VII Med Coll Lahore Pakistan (MB BS); *m* 26 May 1972, Ruth, da of William Haughton Hill (d 1975), of Merseyside; 1 s (Arif b 20 Oct 1974), 1 da (Sarah b 16 Jan 1977); *Career* Dept of Psychiatry Univ of Liverpool: lectr 1971–75, sr lectr 1975–76, clinical lectr 1976–; conslt in psychological med 1976, med dir Regnl Alcohol Unit Liverpool 1976–, supervisor for Sr Registrar Training in Psychiatry Merseyside 1986–89; sec and treas NW Div RCPsych, treas Liverpool Psychiatric Soc (former pres); memb: Nat Cncl of Alcohol 1980–, World Psychiatric Assoc 1985–, BMA 1988–; author of several contribs on psycho-sexual problems and mental illness in leading medical jls; DPM 1970, MPsyMed 1975, FRCPsych 1985, FRSM 1997; *Recreations* photography, painting and reading; *Clubs* Rotary (Prescot Merseyside); *Style*— Dr Joseph Ansari; ✉ 31 Rodney Street, Liverpool L1 9EH (tel 0151 709 1978)

ANSBRO, David Anthony; s of David Thomas Ansbro (d 1963), and Kathleen Mary, *née* Mallett; *b* 3 April 1945; *Educ* Xaverian Coll Manchester, Univ of Leeds (LLB), Coll of Law, Univ of Birmingham (Advanced Mgmnt Course); *m* 1967, Veronica Mary, *née* Auton; 2 da (Lucy b 10 Aug 1968, Kate b 10 Sept 1970); *Career* admitted slr 1969, dep dir of admin W Yorks CC 1977–81 (asst dir of admin 1973–77), town clerk and chief exec York City Cncl 1981–85; chief exec: Kirklees Cncl 1985–87, Leeds City Cncl 1988–91; Eversheds: ptnr Leeds 1991, managing ptnr Leeds 1994–95, managing ptnr Leeds and Manchester 1995–2000, nat managing ptnr 2000–03, conslt 2003–06; memb Local Govt Cmmn for England 1992–95, dir Leeds TEC 1990–99; chm: Leeds Renaissance Partnership 2005, SFL Ltd 2005–; pro-chllr Univ of Leeds 2000–; dir and tstee Nat Centre for Early Music, tstee Henry Moore Fndn 2003–; awarded Papal Medal 1982; memb SOLACE 1981; *Recreations* golf, wine, sport of any kind (except synchronised swimming!), passionate supporter of Manchester City FC; *Clubs* Honley Cricket, Upper Wharfedale RUFC; *Style*— David Ansbro, Esq; ✉ The Green, Airton, Skipton, North Yorkshire BD23 4AH (tel 01729 830451, mobile 07721 868684, e-mail david.ansbro@btinternet.com)

ANSELL, His Hon Judge Anthony Ronald Louis; s of Samuel Ansell (d 1974), of London, and Joan Teresa, *née* Berman; *b* 9 September 1946; *Educ* Dulwich Coll, UCL (LLB); *m* 28 June 1970, Karen Judith (Kaye); 1 s (Simon b 1 Jan 1978), 1 da (Naomi b 4 May 1979); *Career* called to the Bar Gray's Inn 1968, in practice until 1979, slr 1980–95, circuit judge (SE Circuit) 1995–, judge of Employment Appeal Tbnl 2002–; memb Sentencing Advsy Panel 2005–; vice-pres United Synagogue 1992–97; *Books* Kalms Review - A Time for Change (co-author, 1992); *Recreations* opera, music, theatre, walking, swimming, gardening; *Style*— His Hon Judge Ansell; ✉ Wood Green Crown Court, Woodall House, Lordship Lane, London N22 5LF (tel 020 8881 1400)

ANSELL, Mark John; s of John Frederick Ansell, of Birmingham, and Irene Francis, *née* Spiers (d 1982); *b* 2 January 1952; *Educ* Waverley GS Birmingham; *m* 2 March 1974, Sheila Mary, da of Victor William Marston, of Sutton Coldfield; *Career* CA 1973; ptnr Joslyne Layton Bennett & Co Birmingham 1977 (later merging with Binder Hamlyn), managing ptnr BDO Binder Hamlyn 1988–94 (Birmingham office taken over by Touche Ross 1994), head of corp fin Touche Ross (now Deloitte & Touche) 1994–97; Aston Villa plc: fin dir 1997–2001, dep chief exec 2001–03; interim chief exec Marketing Birmingham 2004, currently prop Mark Ansell Consulting Ltd; dir: Chase Midland plc, Scout 7 Hldgs Ltd, De Montfort Fine Art Publishing, Whitewall Galleries Ltd, John Austin & Ptnrs; formerly: sr vice-pres Aston Villa FC, non-exec dir Good Hope Hosp NHS Tst, chm City of Birmingham Round Table, treas Birmingham Rotary Club; FCA 1977 (ACA 1973), BMA 1987; *Recreations* golf, tennis, football (watching Aston Villa FC); *Clubs* Walmley Golf, Four Oaks Tennis; *Style*— Mark Ansell, Esq

ANSELM, Marilyn; da of Henry Charlton (d 1961), and Mabel, *née* Draisey (d 1966); *b* 30 December 1944; *Educ* Homelands GS Derby, Derby Sch of Art, Central Sch of Art (DipAD); *m* 1968, Yoram Anselm, s of Isaac Anselm; 2 da (Aimie b 1969, Kate b 1972); *Career* fndr own retail business 1970, co-fndr/designer Bertie Shoes 1977, fndr/designer Hobbs clothing and shoe retailers 1980–2002 (international with 37 UK outlets); *Recreations* opera, theatre, literature, equestrian pursuits, skiing, gardening; *Style*— Marilyn Anselm

ANSON, Cdr (Norman) Alastair Bourne; OBE (1983); s of Sir (George) Wilfrid Anson, MBE, MC (d 1974), of Bristol, and Dinah Maud Lilian, *née* Bourne; *b* 14 October 1929; *Educ* Winchester; *m* 1, 23 Feb 1952 (m dis 1965), Collette Lavinia (d 2006), da of Lt-Col Richard Eldred Hindson (d 1964); 1 s (Richard b 11 Nov 1952), 1 da (Crispin b 4 Sept 1955); m 2, 27 Nov 1968, Lavinia Maude, da of Rear Adm Ion Tower, DSC (d 1941); *Career* RN 1947–82; CO HMS Carhampton Med 1956–58, Lt Cdr 2 i/c HMS Loch Lomond Persian Gulf 1959–61, Naval rep RMA Sandhurst 1961–63, CO HMS Keppel Arctic Fishery Sqdn 1963–65, CO HMS Londonderry Far E 1965–66, asst sec Chiefs of Staff Ctee 1967–69, 2 i/c HMS Fearless 1969–71, Cabinet Office 1972–75, NATO HQ Naples 1975–78, trg dir Sea Cadet Corps 1979–82, ret 1982; memb Panel Lord Chllr's Ind Inquiry Insprs responsible for inquiries on maj trunk road and motorway schemes 1982–98; chm Bishop Ho Ming Wah Assoc 2003–; St Martin-in-the-Fields: dir, churchwarden 1992–2000; Freeman City of London 1982, Liveryman Worshipful Co of Tin Plate Workers 1982; FIL 1959, FRGS 1983; *Recreations* music (organist), tennis, skiing, photography; *Clubs* City Livery, Hurlingham; *Style*— Cdr Alastair Anson, OBE; ✉ 38 Catherine Place, London SW1E 6HL (tel 020 7834 5991)

ANSON, Charles Vernon; CVO (1996, LVO 1983); s of Philip Vernon Anson (d 1998), of E Sussex, and Stella, *née* Parish; *b* 11 March 1944; *Educ* Lancing, Jesus Coll Cambridge (BA), Johns Hopkins Univ; *m* 1976 (m dis 2005), Clarissa Rosamund, da of Christopher John Denton, of Lavant, W Sussex; 1 da (Gemma b 1977), 1 s (Louis b 1979); *Career* HM Dip Serv 1966–87, third then second sec (commercial) Br Embassy Washington 1968–71, FCO 1971–74, asst private sec to Min of State 1974–76, second sec (commercial) Tehran 1976–79, seconded to Press Office 10 Downing Street 1979–81, first sec (info) Br Embassy Washington 1981–85, FO 1985–87; dir of PR Kleinwort Benson Ltd 1987–90, press sec to HM The Queen 1990–97, dir of corporate affrs Grand Metropolitan plc (now Diageo plc following merger with Guinness plc) 1997–1998, head of communications European Broadcasting Union 1998–2000, dir Corporate Communications Hilton Gp plc 2000–01, media advsr The Queen's Golden Jubilee Weekend Tst 2001–02, vice-chm Cubitt PR, assoc dir Siren PR, conslt The Company Agency 2002–; tstee: Elizabeth Finn Tst, Brogdale Horticultural Tst; *Clubs* Hurlingham; *Style*— Charles Anson, Esq, CVO; ✉ tel 020 7367 5100, e-mail ansoncharles@hotmail.com

ANSON, Vice Adm Sir Edward Rosebery; KCB (1984); s of Ross Rosebery Anson (d 1959), and Ethel Jane, *née* Green; *b* 11 May 1929; *Educ* Prince of Wales Sch Nairobi, BRNC Dartmouth; *m* 1960, Rosemary Anne, *née* Radcliffe; 1 s (Jonathan b 1965), 1 da (Mea); *Career* served Naval Air Sqdns 1952–64, graduated Empire Test Pilots Sch 1957, RN Test Pilot on Buccaneer Blackburn Aircraft Ltd 1959–61, CO 801 Sqdn 1962–64, CO HMS Eskimo 1964–66, Cdr (Air) RNAS Lossiemouth 1967–68, Cdr (Air) HMS Eagle 1969–70, CO InterService Hovercraft Unit 1971 (Capt 1971), Naval and Air Attaché Tokyo and Seoul 1972–74; cmd: HMS Juno and Capt 4 Frigate Sqdn 1974–76, HMS Ark Royal 1976–78 (last CO of the last traditional Br aircraft carrier); Flag Offr Naval Air Cmd 1979–82, Rear Adm 1980, Vice Adm 1982, COS to C-in-C Fleet 1982–84; Naval Weapons Div Br Aerospace 1984–86, pres and ceo Br Aerospace Inc Washington DC USA 1986–89, sr naval advsr Br Aerospace plc 1989–91, aerospace conslt IAD Aerospace Ltd Worthing 1991–93; memb Air League Cncl 1995; FRAeS 1982; *Recreations* golf, photography, walking; *Style*— Vice Adm Sir Edward Anson, KCB; ✉ The Haybarn, Kingstone, Ilminster, Somerset TA19 0NS (tel and fax 01460 55372)

ANSON, Lady Elizabeth; *see:* Shakerley, Lady Elizabeth Georgiana

ANSON, Rear Adm Sir Peter; 7 Bt (1831), of Birch Hall, Lancashire; CB (1974), DL (Surrey 1993); s of Sir Edward Reynell Anson, 6 Bt (d 1951), and Alison (d 1997), da of Hugh Pollock (gs of Sir George Pollock, 1 Bt, GCB, GCSI); *b* 31 July 1924; *Educ* RNC Dartmouth; *m* 16 April 1955, Dame Elizabeth Audrey Anson, DBE, JP, DL, da of Rear Adm Sir (Charles) Philip Clarke, KBE, CB, DSO (d 1966); 2 da (Louisa Frances b 1956, Sarah Elizabeth b 1966), 2 s (Philip Roland b 1957, Hugo William b 1962); *Heir* s, Philip Anson; *Career* RN: Cdr Naval Forces, Gulf 1970–71 (Cdre), asst chief of Def Staff (Signals) 1972–74 (Rear Adm), ret 1975; divnl mangr satellites Marconi Space and Defence Systems Ltd 1977 (asst mktg dir 1975), chm Matra Marconi Space UK Ltd 1985–91 (md 1984–85), chm IGG Component Technology Ltd 1992–97; High Sheriff Surrey 1993–94; CEng, FIEE; *Recreations* gardening, golf; *Style*— Rear Adm Sir Peter Anson, Bt, CB, DL; ✉ Rosefield, 81 Boundstone Road, Rowledge, Farnham, Surrey GU10 4AT (tel and fax 01252 792724, e-mail pandeanson@aol.com)

ANSTEE, Eric E; *b* 1 January 1951; *m*; 4 c; *Career* audit trainee Keens Shay Keens & Co 1969–74, audit sr to mangr Turquand Barton Mayhew 1974–76, joined Ernst & Young 1976, advsr DTI (secondment to Industrial Devpt Unit/MAFF) 1976–77, sr mangr Ernst & Young (Singapore) 1977–80, fin and business advsr (secondment) Cambridge Instrument Co Ltd 1980–83, commercial accountancy advsr (secondment) H M Treasy 1983–86, ptnr i/c co-ordinating work in Public Sector Ernst & Young 1986–88; Ernst & Young Mgmnt Consultants: ptnr, dir World-wide Privatisation Servs and dir UK Utilities Servs 1988–92, memb Mgmnt Bd 1992–93; gp fin dir Eastern Gp plc 1993–97, fin dir The Energy Gp plc 1997–98, gp fin dir Old Mutual plc 1998–99, chief exec Old Mutual Financial Servs (UK) plc 2000–01, managing ptnr Anstee Associates 2002–03, chief exec ICAEW 2003–06 (memb Senate 1996); non-exec chm Mansell plc 2002–03; non-exec dir: Severn Trent 1999–2003, SSL Int plc 2002–03, Insight Investments 2006–, ScreenFX plc 2007–, CCAB Ltd, Insight Investment Management Ltd; fndr bd memb Centre for the Study of Regulated Industries, memb UITF of Accounting Standards Bd 1997–2003; FCA 1979 (ACA 1974); *Recreations* golf, tennis, badminton, gardening; *Clubs* Athenaeum; *Style*— E E Anstee, Esq

ANSTEE, Prof John Howard; DL (Durham 2003); s of Stanley George Anstee (d 1978), of Milford Haven, and Anne May, *née* Griffiths (d 1992); *b* 25 April 1943; *Educ* Milford Haven GS, Univ of Nottingham (BSc, PhD); *m* 18 July 1966, Angela June, da of Emlyn Havard Young; 1 s (Quentin Mark b 7 Feb 1973); *Career* Univ of Durham: sr demonstrator in zoology 1968–71, lectr 1971–81, sr lectr 1981–96, dean Faculty of Science 1994–97 (dep dean 1991–94), prof of biological sciences 1996–2004 (emeritus 2004–), pro-vice-chllr 1997–2004, subwarden 2000–04; Nepark scientific dir Co Durham Devpt Co 2004–, dir of a number of cos; memb Cncl Durham Cathedral 2005– (chair Steering Ctee 2006–); hon sec Soc for Experimental Biology 1990–94 (memb 1972); author of numerous articles on insect physiology and biochemistry; FRES (memb Cncl 1991–94), FZS 1967; *Recreations* cricket, dinghy sailing and rugby; *Style*— Prof John H Anstee, DL; ✉ 35 Albert Street, Western Hill, Durham DH1 4RJ (tel and fax 0191 386 3073, e-mail johnanstee@btinternet.com)

ANSTEE, Dame Margaret Joan; DCMG (1994); da of Edward Curtis Anstee (d 1971), and Anne Adaliza, *née* Mills (d 1972); *b* 25 June 1926; *Educ* Chelmsford Co HS for Girls, Newnham Coll Cambridge (MA), Univ of London (BSc); *Career* lectr in Spanish Queen's Univ Belfast 1947–48, third sec FO 1948–52, admin offr UN Tech Assistance Bd Manila Philippines 1952–54, Spanish supervisor Univ of Cambridge 1955–56; UN Tech Assistance Bd: offr i/c Bogotá Colombia 1956–57, resident rep Uruguay 1957–59, dir Special Fund progs and UN Info Centre La Paz Bolivia 1960–65, resident rep UNDP Ethiopia 1965–67, liaison offr with UN Econ Cmmn for Africa 1965–67, sr econ advsr PM's UK 1967–68, sr asst to cmmr i/c of Study of Capacity of UN Devpt System 1968–69; resident rep UNDP: Morocco 1969–72, Chile and liaison offr with UN Econ Cmmn for Latin America 1972–74; dep to UN Under Sec-Gen i/c of UN relief operation to Bangladesh and dep co-ordinator of UN emergency assistance to Zambia 1973; UNDP NY: dep asst admin and dep regnl dir for Latin America 1974–76, dir Admins Unit for

Special Assignments 1976, asst dep admin 1976, asst admin and dir Bureau for Prog Policy and Evaluation 1977–78, asst Sec-Gen UN Dept of Tech Co-operation for Devpt 1978–87, special rep of Sec-Gen for co-ordination of int assistance following Mexico earthquake 1985–87, chm Advsy Gp on review of UN World Food Cncl 1985–86, special co-ordinator of UN Sec-Gen to ensure implementation of Gen Assembly resolution on fin and admin reform of the UN 1986–87; special rep of UN Sec-Gen for Bolivia 1982–92, rep UN Sec-Gen at Conf for the Adoption of a Convention Against Illicit Traffic in Narcotic Drugs and Psychotropic Substances 1988, sec-gen Eighth UN Congress on the Prevention of Crime and the Treatment of Offenders Havana 1990, special rep of the UN Sec-Gen for Peru 1990–92, Sec-Gen's co-ordinator for addressing the effects of the Chernobyl disaster 1991–92, Sec-Gen's personal rep to co-ordinate UN efforts to counter impact of burning oilfields in Kuwait and region 1991–92; DG UN office Vienna, under sec gen UN, head Centre for Social Devpt and Humanitarian Affrs 1987–92, co-ordinator of all UN drug control related activities 1987–91, under sec-gen and special rep of UN Sec-Gen for Angola and head UN Angolan Verification Mission (UNAVEM II) 1992–93, ind conslt and advsr to Pres and Govt of Bolivia 1993–1997 and 2002–, advsr to the UN Sec-Gen on peacekeeping, post-conflict peacebuilding and training troops for peacekeeping missions and to various govts 1994–; lectr and author; memb Bd of Tstees Help Age Int 1993–97, memb Advsy Cncl on UN Studies Yale Univ 1994–, memb Cncl of Advsrs Oxford Res Gp 1996–, chm Expert Advsy Gp to Lessons Learned Unit UN Dept Peacekeeping Operations 1996–2002, patron and memb Bd British-Angola Forum 1998–, memb Int Advsy Cncl UN Intellectual History Project 1999–; memb Jimmy Carter's Int Cncl for Conflict Prevention 2001–; vice-pres UK UN Assoc; subject of documentary 'Nine Lives' BBC4 2002; hon fell Newnham Coll Cambridge; Hon LLD: Univ of Essex 1994, Univ of Westminster 1996, Univ of Cambridge 2004; Hon DSc (Econ) Univ of London 1998; foreign honours: Commandeur Ouissam Alaouite (Morocco) 1972, Dama Gran Cruz Condor of the Andes (Bolivia) 1986, Das Grosse Goldene Ehrenzeichen am Bande (Austria) 1993, Reves Peace Prize William & Mary Coll USA 1993, Grand Offr Order of Bernardo O'Higgins 2006 (Chile); *Books* The Administration of International Development Aid (USA 1969), Gate of the Sun: a Prospect of Bolivia (1970, USA 1971), Africa and the World (ed with R K A Gardiner and C Patterson, 1970), Orphan of the Cold War: The Inside Story of the Collapse of the Angolan Peace Process 1992–93 (1996, UK, US and Portugal 1997), Never Learn to Type: A Woman at the United Nations (2003, 2 edn 2004); numerous articles and chapters in books on UN reform, peackeeping, economic and social development; *Recreations* writing, gardening, hill walking (preferably in the Andes), bird-watching, swimming; *Clubs* Oxford and Cambridge; *Style*— Dame Margaret J Anstee, DCMG; ✉ The Walled Garden Knill, Powys LD8 2PR (tel 01544 267411 or 01544 260331); c/o PNUD, Casilla 9072, La Paz, Bolivia (fax 00 519 2 2795820)

ANSTRUTHER, Harriet Joan Campbell; da of Sir Ian Fife Campbell Anstruther, 8 Bt, of Petworth, W Sussex, and Susan Margaret, *née* Paten; *b* 24 March 1967; *Educ* Queen's Coll London, City & Guilds Sch of Art, Byam-Shaw Sch of Fine Art; *m* 1, 19 July 1991 (m dis), Hamish Howard Anthony Summers, s of Anthony Gilbert Summers; 1 da (Celestia Nell Campbell b 23 Aug 1993); m 2, 27 July 2002, Henry Bourne, s of Prof Kenneth Bourne; *Career* textile, interior and fashion designer and design conslt, stylist and art dir; fndr Hufitts (T-shirt design/wholesale business) 1991–92, fndr Harriet Anstruther (accessories, men's and women's ready to wear and furnishing fabrics) 1991–97, over 340 stockists worldwide (Australia, Japan, Europe and America); jt fndr Selina Blow, Harriet Anstruther, Lulu Guinness (shop in Elizabeth St SW1) 1995–, fndr Harriet Anstruther Design Consultancy (incorporating all areas of design and styling incl china, fashion, textile, furnishing fabric, wallpaper, costume, set and interior design and illustrations, TV film design and consultation) 1996–; freelance writer, designer and stylist; *Recreations* painting, music and gardening; *Style*— Harriet Anstruther; ✉ e-mail hat@anstruther01.demon.co.uk

ANSTRUTHER-GOUGH-CALTHORPE, Sir Euan Hamilton; 3 Bt (UK 1929), of Elvetham Hall, Elvetham, Co Southampton; s of Niall Hamilton Anstruther-Gough-Calthorpe (d 1970), and Martha (who m 2, 1975, Sir Charles Nicholson, 3 Bt, *qv*), da of Stuart Warren Don; suc gf, Brig Sir Richard Anstruther-Gough-Calthorpe, 2 Bt, CBE (d 1985); *b* 22 June 1966; *Educ* Harrow, Univ of Reading, RAC Cirencester; *m* 8 June 2002, Anna Joan, da of Christopher Wysock Wright, of Horsted Keynes, W Sussex; 1 s (Barnaby Charles b 28 Oct 2005); *Career* property mangr; Freeman Worshipful Co of Armourers & Brasiers; *Clubs* Brooks's; *Style*— Sir Euan Calthorpe, Bt; ✉ Elvetham, Hartley Wintney, Hampshire RG27 8AW

ANTHONY, Barbara (pen name Antonia Barber); da of Derek Wilson, and (Edith Jessie) Julie, *née* Jeal; *Educ* Rye GS, UCL (BA); *m* 1956, Kenneth Charles Anthony (k 1981), s of late Charles Arthur Anthony; 2 s (Jonathan Charles b 1968, Nicholas James b 1972), 1 da (Gemma Thi-Phi-Yen b 1974); *Career* writer of children's books 1966–; supporter of: Friends of the Earth, Greenpeace, Amnesty Int, Ramblers ASP, Woodland Tst, Nat Tst; memb Soc of Authors; *Books* incl: The Ghosts (1969, filmed as The Amazing Mr Blunden 1971), The Ring in the Rough Stuff (1983), The Enchanter's Daughter (1987), The Mousehole Cat (1990), Catkin (1994), The Monkey and the Panda (1995), Tales from the Ballet (1996), Dancing Shoes (series, 1998–2000), Noah and the Ark (1998), Apollo and Daphne (1998), Hidden Tales from Eastern Europe (2002), The Frog Bride (2006); *Recreations* walking, reading, theatre, TV, gardening; *Style*— Mrs Barbara Anthony; ✉ Hornes Place Oast, Appledore, Ashford, Kent TN26 2BS; c/o David Higham Associates, 5–8 Lower John Street, Golden Square, London W1R 4HA (tel 020 7437 7888, fax 020 7437 1072)

ANTHONY, David Gwilym; s of Ernest Anthony (d 1990), and Megan Euron, *née* Davies (d 2004); *b* 10 February 1947; *Educ* Hull GS, St Catherine's Coll Oxford (MA); *m* 8 June 1974, (Ellen) Brigid, da of Air Vice-Marshal W J Crisham (d 1987); 1 s (Peter b 1979), 1 da (Jane b 1980); *Career* Barton Mayhew (now Ernst & Young) 1969–73, Dymo Business Systems Ltd 1973–75, Slater Walker Finance Ltd 1975–77, Forward Trust (Ireland) Ltd 1977–82, md Hitachi Capital (UK) plc 1982–, chm Hitachi Capital Vehicle Solutions Ltd 1991–; dir: Hitachi Capital Insurance Corp Ltd 1995–, Hitachi Capital Credit Mgmnt Ltd 2000–, Secure Tst Bank plc 2007–; FCA 1973, FRSA 2007; *Books* Words to Say (2002), Talking to Lord Newborough (2004); *Recreations* fell walking, skiing, poetry; *Style*— David G Anthony, Esq; ✉ Retreat, Church Lane, Stoke Poges, Buckinghamshire SL2 4NZ (tel 01753 530895); Hitachi Capital (UK) plc, Wallbrook Business Centre, Green Lane, Hounslow, Middlesex TW4 6NW (tel 020 8572 7554, fax 020 8577 9939, e-mail david.anthony@hitachicapital.co.uk, website www.davidgwilymanthony.co.uk)

ANTHONY, Rear Adm Derek James; MBE (1983); s of James Kenwood Anthony (decd), and Nora Evelyn, *née* Honnor; *b* 2 November 1947; *Educ* Eastbourne Coll, BRNC Dartmouth; *m* 1970, Denyse Irene Hopper Wright; 2 da; *Career* joined RN 1966; served HM Ships 1970–80: Opossum, Revenge, Andrew, Oxley, Oberon, Sovereign; CO HMS Onslaught 1981–82, exchange service USN 1982–84, jsdc 1985, CO HMS Warspite 1986–88, CO submarine cmd course 1988–90, head RN Seaman Officers Policy MOD 1990–91, CO HMS Cumberland 1991–93, dir Naval Service Conditions 1993–96, hcsc 1996, dep Flag Offr Submarines 1996–97, naval attaché, asst defence attaché Washington and UK Nat Liaison Rep to SACLANT 1997–2000, Flag Offr Scotland, Northern England and NI 2000–03; chm Assoc of Royal Naval Offrs, chm Royal Naval Benevolent Soc for Offrs, memb Ctee RN Club; clerk Worshipful Co of Shipwrights 2003–, memb Incorporation of Wrights of Glasgow; *Recreations* golf, gardening, tennis, history, music; *Clubs* Army and Navy, RN 1765 and 1785; *Style*— Rear Adm Derek Anthony, MBE; ✉ 36 Blackwood Close, West Byfleet, Surrey KT14 6PP (tel 01932 345153, e-mail dj.anthony@btinternet.com)

ANTHONY, Graham; s of Edward Herbert Claude Anthony (decd), and Hilda May, *née* Pohler (decd); *b* 26 March 1938; *Educ* Hamilton House Sch, Architectural Assoc (AA Dip Arch); *m* 1 (m dis), Sheila, *née* McGregor; 2 da (Lucinda Jane b 1964, Justine b 1966); m 2, Jacqueline Dorothy, *née* Miller (decd); 2 da (Lara Catherine b 1967, Alice b 1975); *Career* architect; Ahrends Burton Koralek 1966–72 and 1976–80, Wadley Anthony Architects 1972–76, Richard Rogers Partnership 1980–87, Graham Anthony Architects 1987–89; Sheppard Robson (architects, planners and interior designers) London: joined 1990, assoc 1996–97, design dir 1997–, ptnr 1998–2003, design conslt 2003–; projects incl: Central Plant facility for Glaxo Stevenage 1990–92, The Helicon EC2 for London and Manchester 1992–95 (RIBA Regnl Award for Architecture, Civic Tst Award commendation 1998), Motorola HQ Swindon 1996–98 (RIBA Regnl Award for Architecture, Structural Steel Design Award 1999, High Commendation Br Construction Industry Award), Pfizer HQ Walton Oaks 1997 (RIBA Nat Award for Architecture, Br Cncl of Offices Award, Art and Work Award), Arup HQ London 2001–03; *Recreations* watercolouring, music, weight training, running; *Style*— Graham Anthony, Esq; ✉ Sheppard Robson, 77 Parkway, London NW1 7PU (tel 020 7504 1700, fax 020 7504 1701, e-mail graham.anthony@sheppardrobson.com)

ANTHONY, His Hon Judge (Michael) Guy Anthony; s of Kenneth Anthony (d 1995), and June, *née* Gallifent; *b* 5 March 1950; *Educ* St Paul's, Magdalen Coll Oxford (MA); *m* 1974, Jane Rosemary, da of Peter Farrer, MC; 1 s (Christopher b 4 Nov 1986); *Career* barr 1972–98, asst recorder 1989–93, recorder 1993–98, circuit judge (SE Circuit) 1998–; memb Mental Health Review Tbnl 2002–; *Recreations* travel, reading, rugby and other sports, spending time with family; *Style*— His Hon Judge Anthony; ✉ Lewes Combined Court, The Law Courts, High Street, Lewes, East Sussex BN7 1YB (tel 01273 480400, fax 01273 485269)

ANTHONY, Prof Peter Paul; s of Dr Miklos Anthony (d 1989), and Maria, *née* Sedon (d 1966); *b* 22 June 1933; *Educ* Gymnasia of Eger and Jaszapati, Univ of Budapest Hungary, St Bartholomew's Hosp Med Coll London; *m* 27 May 1961, Mary, da of Norman Capstick (d 1983); 1 s (Stephen), 1 da (Nicola); *Career* sr lectr in pathology and conslt: Univ of East Africa 1969–71, Middx Hosp Med Sch Univ of London 1971–77; Exeter and Royal Devon and Exeter Hosps: conslt and sr lectr 1977, reader 1983, prof of clinical histopathology 1986; author of over 100 articles, reviews and chapters in books; memb Cncl: Int Acad of Pathology 1988–91 (also 1978–81), Assoc of Clinical Pathologists 1988–91 (also 1981–84), RCPath 1993–96 (also 1983–87 and 1989–92); memb ctees: WHO, BMA, SW RHA; pres Assoc of Clinical Pathologists 1992–93; FRCPath 1982 (MRCPath 1968); *Books* Recent Advances in Histopathology vols 10–17 (jtly, 1978–1994), Pathology of the Liver (jt ed, 1 edn 1978, 2 edn 1987, 3 edn 1994), Diagnostic Pitfalls in Histopathology and Cytopathology Practice 1998; *Recreations* sailing, walking, photography; *Clubs* Starcross Yacht, Exe Yacht; *Style*— Prof Peter Anthony; ✉ 2 St Leonards Place, Exeter EX2 4LZ; Royal Devon & Exeter Hospital (Wonford), Department of Pathology, Church Lane, Exeter, Devon EX2 5AD; Postgraduate Medical School, University of Exeter, Barrack Road, Exeter (tel 01392 402943, fax 01392 402946)

ANTONELLI, Count Pietro Hector Paolo Maria; s of Count Giacomo Antonelli (Cavalry Gen Italian Army; d 1963), and Countess Luisa Antonelli, *née* Piva (d 1954); of the same family as Cardinal Giacomo Antonelli, sec of State to Pope Pius IX, and of Count Pietro Antonelli, African explorer and diplomat; *b* 14 March 1924; *Educ* Univ of Rome (Degree in Philosophy); *m* 1 (m dis 1976), Countess Maria Benedetta Bossi Pucci; 3 da (Sibilla b 27 April 1947 d 2003, Santa b 12 Nov 1950, Serena b 18 Jan 1953); m 2, Monika Oppenheim, *née* Brucklmeier; *Career* official Banca Commerciale 1948–62; md: Caboto Spa 1962–72, Banca Provinciale di Depositi e Sconti 1971; mangr and subsequently dir Hambros Bank Ltd 1972–98; dir Piaggio & Co SpA 1994–96; chm: Nuova Holding Subalpina (NHS) SpA 1998–2000, S Paolo IMI Mgmnt Ltd 2000–; Grande Ufficiale Ordine al Merito della Repubblica Italiana 1991 (Commendatore 1983); *Recreations* yachting; *Clubs* Circolo della Caccia (Rome); *Style*— Count Pietro Antonelli

ANTONIADES, Reno Michael; s of Michael Antoniades, and Joy, *née* Post; *b* 27 July 1966, London; *Educ* Alleyn's Sch Dulwich (head boy), Univ of Leicester (LLB); *m* 6 Sep 1997, Julie Cunningham; 1 da (Madeleine Anastasia b 29 June 2003), 1 s (Noah Michael Laurence b 20 Nov 2005); *Career* slr; Herbert Smith 1989–93, Olswang 1993–94, Lee & Thompson 1994–; memb: Law Soc 1991, BAFTA; *Recreations* cinema, golf, football (season ticket holder Tottenham Hotspur FC); *Clubs* Edward Alleyn, Soho House; *Style*— Reno Antoniades, Esq; ✉ Lee & Thompson, Greengarden House, 15–22 St Christopher's Place, London W1U 1NL (tel 020 7935 4665, fax 020 7563 4949, e-mail renoantoniades@leeandthompson.com)

ANTONOWICZ, Anton; s of Marian Antonowicz, of Brixworth, and Eileen, *née* Kelly; *b* 29 December 1950; *Educ* St Ignatius Coll Enfield, Univ of Warwick (BA); *m* 1979, Nasrin, *née* Abdollahi (d 1998); 1 da (Anna-Yasmin b 28 July 1981), 1 s (Stefan b 30 March 1983); *Career* chief feature writer The Mirror (joined 1977); memb: NUJ, BAJ; life memb Newspaper Press Fund; *Awards* Cudlipp Award 1986, 1987 and 2003, Foreign Reporter of the Year British Press Awards 1998, Newspaper Reporter of the Year Amnesty Int 2002; *Recreations* walking, tennis; *Style*— Anton Antonowicz, Esq; ✉ The Mirror, 1 Canada Tower, London E14 5AP (tel 020 7293 3066, fax 020 7293 3834, e-mail a.antonowicz@mirror.co.uk)

ANTRIM, 9 Earl of (I 1785); Alexander Randal Mark McDonnell; also Viscount Dunluce; s of 8 Earl of Antrim, KBE (d 1977), and Angela Christina, da of Col Sir Mark Sykes; *b* 3 February 1935; *Educ* Downside, ChCh Oxford, Ruskin Sch of Art; *m* 1, 1963 (m dis 1974), Sarah Elizabeth Anne, 2 da of St John Bernard Vyvyan Harmsworth (d 1995); 2 da (Lady Flora Mary b 1963, Lady Alice Angela Jane (Lady Alice Gwinn) b 1964), 1 s (Randal Alexander St John, Viscount Dunluce b 1967); m 2, 1977, Elizabeth, da of Michael Moses Sacher; 1 da (Lady Rachel Frances b 1978); *Heir* s, Viscount Dunluce, *qv*; *Career* Tate Gallery: restorer 1965–75, keeper of conservation 1975–90, head of collection servs 1990–93, dir of collection servs 1994–95; memb: Exec Ctee City and Guilds of London Art Sch, Art Advsy Ctee Nat Museums and Galleries of Wales 1995–; chm Rathlin Island Tst 1990–93, chm Northern Salmon Co 1999–, former dir Ulster TV, dir Antrim Estates Co, memb High Cncl of the Clan Donald 2001–; Prime Warden Hon Co of Fishmongers 1995–96; FRSA; *Recreations* vintage cars; *Clubs* Beefsteak; *Style*— The Rt Hon the Earl of Antrim; ✉ Deer Park Cottage, Glenarm, Co Antrim BT44 0BQ

ANTROBUS, Sir Edward Philip; 8 Bt (UK 1815), of Antrobus, Cheshire; s of Sir Philip Coutts Antrobus, 7 Bt (d 1995), and Dorothy Margaret Mary, *née* Davis (d 1973); *b* 28 September 1938; *Educ* Univ of the Witwatersrand (BSc), Magdalene Coll Cambridge (MA); *m* 1, 7 Oct 1966, Janet Sarah Elizabeth (d 1990), da of Philip Walter Sceales, of Johannesburg, South Africa; 2 da (Barbara Joanna b 27 Jan 1968, Sarah Diana b 9 April 1970), 1 s (Francis Edward Sceales b 24 Oct 1972); m 2, 29 Nov 1996, Rozanne Penelope, da of Neville Simpson, of Durban, South Africa; *Heir* s, Francis Antrobus; *Career* landowner; *Recreations* golf, tennis; *Clubs* Johannesburg Country; *Style*— Sir Edward Antrobus, Bt

ANWAR, Tariq Rafiq; s of Rafiq Anwar (d 1976), of Chiswick, and Edith Fordham, *née* Reich (d 1994); *b* 21 September 1945; *Educ* Walpole GS, Sir John Cass Coll London; *m* 29 Sept 1966, Shirley Natalie, da of John Richard Hills (d 1990), of Hainault, Essex; 1 s (Dominic b 1967), 1 da (Gabrielle b 1970); *Career* film ed with BBC; films incl: Madness of King George, The Crucible, Wings of the Dove, Tea with Mussolini, American Beauty, Stage Beauty, The Good Shepherd; best ed BAFTA Awards: Caught on a Train, Oppenheimer, American Beauty; BAFTA nominations: Monocled Mutineer, Fortunes of War, Summer's Lease, Madness of King George; ACE (Cable) nomination for Tender is the Night; ACE (Editors Guild) nomination for American Beauty; Oscar nomination American Beauty; memb Motion Picture Editors Guild (MPEG); *Recreations* music, tennis; *Style—* Tariq Anwar, Esq; ✉ c/o Lynda Mamy, PFD, Drury House, 34–43 Russell Street, London WC2B 5HA (tel 020 7344 1000)

ANWAR, Yasmin Trina; da of Mohammed Shafique (d 2004) and Margaret Anwar (d 1998); *b* 3 April 1962; *Educ* Wadham Coll Oxford; *m* 26 May 1990, John Francis Fitzpatrick, s of late Jeremiah Fitzpatrick; 1 da (Maeve Margaret b 17 Nov 2000); *Career* local govt 1985–87, documentary researcher 1988–90, news prodr at BBC and European Business Channel 1990–91, series prodr 1991–94, exec prodr BBC 1994–96; Channel Four TV Corp: dep commissioning ed 1997, commissioning ed Multicultural Progs 1997–2003; chair GLA Cultural Strategy Gp for London; memb: RTS 1998–, RTS Cncl 1999–; project mangr Barts and the London NHS Tst; tstee Nat Endowment for Sci, Technol and the Arts (NESTA); *Recreations* travelling rough, the company of libertarians; *Style—* Ms Yasmin Anwar

ANWYL, Her Hon Judge Shirley Anne; QC (1979); da of James Ritchie (d 1991), of Johannesburg, South Africa, and Helen Sutherland, *née* Peters (d 2000); *b* 10 December 1940; *Educ* St Mary's Diocesan Sch Pretoria, Rhodes Univ (BA, LLB); *m* 23 May 1969, Robin Hamilton Corson Anwyl, s of Douglas Fraser Corson (d 1978); 2 s (Jonathan b 1973, James b 1975); *Career* called to South African Bar 1963 and Inner Temple 1966 (bencher 1985); recorder of the Crown Court 1981–95, circuit judge (SE Circuit) 1995–, resident judge Woolwich Crown Court 1999–2007; memb: Senate of Inns of Court and Bar 1978–81, Gen Cncl of the Bar 1987, Criminal Injuries Compensation Bd 1980–95, Mental Health Review Tbnl 1983–99; chm Barristers' Benevolent Assoc 1989–95; Liveryman Worshipful Co of Fruiterers 1996; FRSA; *Recreations* theatre, music, sailing; *Clubs* Guild of Freemen of the City of London; *Style—* Her Hon Judge Anwyl, QC; ✉ Snaresbrook Crown Court, 75 Hollybush Hill, London E11 1QW (tel 020 8530 0000, e-mail hhjudge.anwylqc@judiciary.gsi.gov.uk)

APICELLA, Lorenzo; *b* Ravello, Italy; *Educ* Univ of Nottingham, Canterbury Coll of Art, RCA; *Career* early career with Skidmore, Owings & Merrill, CZWG and Imagination; fndr Apicella Assocs 1989, currently ptnr Pentagram (joined 1998); external examiner: Univ of Birmingham, Oxford Brookes Univ; RIBA, FCSD, FRSA; *Style—* Lorenzo Apicella, Esq

APPIGNANESI, Dr Lisa; da of Aron Borenstein (d 1981), and Hena Lipszyc (d 2001); *b* 4 January 1946, Poland; *Educ* McGill Univ Montreal (BA, MA), Univ of Sussex (PhD); *Family* 1 s (Joshua Appignanesi b 5 May 1975); partner, Prof John Forrester; 1 da (Katrina Forrester b 1 March 1986); *Career* univ lectr 1971–80, fndr memb Writers and Readers Publishing 1976–89, dep dir ICA 1981–90, freelance writer 1990–; vice-pres English PEN 2004– (memb Prison Ctee 2003–), chair No Offence campaign; memb: Cncl ICA 1999–, Ctee on the Arts LSE 1999–2000, Mgmnt Ctee Soc of Authors 1996–99, Soc of Authors, PEN; judge Betty Trask Prize 1993, patron Writers in Exile; participant in numerous confs, int lectr and memb many panels; Chevalier de l'Ordre des Arts et des Lettres (France) 1988; *Television* exec prodr: No Place Quite Like It (BBC) 1987, Intruders at the Palace (BBC) 1988, The World of Gypsy Music (BBC) 1988, England's Henry Moore (Channel 4) 1991, Seductions (four short plays by Marina Warner, Jenny Diski, Geoff Dyer and Edmund White, Channel 4) 1991; series conslt Fin de Siècle (Channel 4) 1992, co-dir and author Rendez Vous à New York: Un portrait de Salman Rushdie (FR3) 1999; series ed Writers in Conversation (ICA video) 1993–90; *Radio* writer and presenter: Cabaret (BBC Radio 4) 1978, The Case of Sigmund Freud (BBC Radio 4) 2000; presenter: Nightwaves (BBC Radio 3) 2002–03, Freudian Slips (Radio 4) 2005; contrib to numerous progs incl Routes of English, Kaleidoscope, Woman's Hour, Start the Week; *Publications* fiction incl: Memory and Desire (1991), Dreams of Innocence (1994), A Good Woman (1996), The Things We Do for Love (1997), The Dead of Winter (1999), Sanctuary (2000), Paris Requiem (2002, new edn 2005), Kicking Fifty (2003), The Memory Man (2004); non-fiction incl: Dialogue of Generations (1974), Femininity and the Creative Imagination: James, Proust and Musil (1974), Cabaret: The First Hundred Years (1976, new edn 1986, revised and enlarged edn 2004), Simone de Beauvoir (1988, new edn 2005), Freud's Women (with John Forrester, 1992, new edn 2005), Losing the Dead (1999); edited volumes: Science and Beyond (with Stephen Rose, 1986), The Rushdie File (with Sara Maitland, 1989), Dismantling Truth (with Hilary Lawson, 1989), Ideas from France (1989), Postmodernism (1989), written and reviewed for newspapers incl: The Guardian, The Sunday Times, The Daily Telegraph, The Observer, The Independent; trans of pubns and books from French, Italian and German; *Style—* Dr Lisa Appignanesi; ✉ c/o Clare Alexander, Gillon Aitken Associates, 18–21 Cavaye Place, London SW10 9PT (tel 020 7373 8672, fax 020 7373 6002)

APPIO, Isabel Anne; da of Chief Gabriel Fenton Appio (d 1992), of Lagos, Nigeria, and Marguerite, *née* Lancaster-Cooper; *b* 30 June 1959; *Educ* Blackheath HS London, Central London Poly (BA); *Career* asst ed Caribbean Times newspaper 1981–83, asst music ed Time Out 1986–91, ed The Weekly Journal 1992–, chief editorial dir Voice Communications Group, dir Sugar Media; *Style—* Ms Isabel Appio; ✉ tel 020 7407 7747, fax 020 7407 6800, e-mail isabel@sugarmedia.co.uk

APPLEBY, His Hon Brian John; QC (1971); s of Ernest Joel Appleby; *b* 25 February 1930; *Educ* Uppingham, St John's Coll Cambridge; *m* 1, 1958, late Rosa Helena, *née* Flitterman; 1 s, 1 da; m 2, 1998, Lynda Jane, *née* Eaton; *Career* called to the Bar Middle Temple 1953 (bencher 1980); recorder of the Crown Court 1972–88, circuit judge (Midland & Oxford Circuit) 1988–2003 (dep circuit judge 2003–); dep chm Notts QS 1970–71; dist referee Notts Wages Conciliation Bd NCB 1980–88; memb Notts City Cncl 1955–58 and 1960–63; pres Court of Appeal: Falkland Is 1982, Indian Ocean Territories 1982, St Helena 1998–; *Style—* His Hon Brian Appleby, QC

APPLEBY, (Lesley) Elizabeth (Mrs Michael Collins); QC (1979); o da of Arthur Leslie Appleby, and Dorothy Evelyn, *née* Edwards; *b* 12 August 1942; *Educ* Dominican Convent Brewood, Wolverhampton Girls' HS, Univ of Manchester (LLB); *m* 6 Jan 1978, Michael Kenneth Collins, OBE, BSc, MICE; 1 s (Andrew b 23 Jan 1980), 1 da (Emma b 13 Feb 1984); *Career* called to the Bar Gray's Inn 1965, ad eundem Lincoln's Inn 1975; in practice Chancery Bar 1966–; memb of Senate of Inns of Court and Bar 1977–80 and 1981–82; bencher Lincoln's Inn 1986, recorder of the Crown Court 1989–, dep judge of the High Ct, jt head of chambers; chm Ethics & Integrity Ctee Cons Pty; *Recreations* gardening, swimming; *Style—* Miss Elizabeth Appleby, QC; ✉ 4/5 Gray's Inn Square, Gray's Inn, London WC1R 5AY (tel 020 7404 5252, fax 020 7242 7803)

APPLEBY, His Hon Judge John Montague; s of Montague Eric Appleby (d 1983), and Carmen Irene Appleby (d 1993); *b* 8 November 1945; *Educ* Dauntsey's Sch West Lavington, Univ of Nottingham (LLB, pres Univ Law Students' Soc, capt Univ and UAU hockey); *m* 30 May 1970, Barbara Joan, da of Arthur Plumb; 1 s (Luke Justin b 17 July 1976); *Career* admitted slr 1970, asst slr Leicester 1970–72; Truman Close Kendall & Appleby (formerly Trumans & Appleby): joined 1972, ptnr 1974–88, managing ptnr (following merger of Truman & Appleby and Close Kendall & Co) 1988–98, memb Mgmnt Bd Nelsons (following merger of Trumans and Nelsons) 1999–2003; recorder 1999–2003 (asst recorder 1993–99), circuit judge (Northern Circuit) 2003–; sec Notts Young Slrs Gp 1973 (Nat Ctee rep 1976–82), chm Nat Ctee Young Slrs Gp 1980–81; pres Notts Law Soc 1997 (vice-pres 1996); Law Soc: memb 1970–, memb Regnl Cncl (for Lincs and Notts) 1984, memb Cncl 1984–99, chm Family Law Ctee 1987–90, chm Cts and Legal Servs Ctee 1990–93, memb Remuneration & Practice Devpt Ctee 1986–89, dir Slrs Indemnity Fund 1987–90, memb Practice Devpt Ctee 1993–96, memb Civil Litigation Ctee 1993–99, memb Trg Ctee 1996–2001; *Books* Professional Management of a Solicitors Practice (contrib); *Recreations* golf, travel, wine, theatre; *Clubs* Notts Hockey Assoc (pres 1994–96), Nottingham Hockey (vice-pres), Nottingham CC (vice-pres), Bacchanalians Hockey, Hale Golf; *Style—* His Hon Judge John Appleby; ✉ Manchester Court Centre, Crown Square, Manchester M60 9DJ

APPLEBY, Keith David; s of Cornelius Appleby, of Amersham, Bucks, and Doreen Mary, *née* Briscoe; *b* 14 May 1953; *Educ* Bucks Coll of Higher Educn (BA), RCA (MA); *m* 1987, Margaret Ann, da of Anthony Lepps; 3 s (Frederick William b 25 March 1990, Noah Alexander b 21 April 1996, Joseph John b 22 October 1997); *Career* designer Habitat Designs Ltd 1978–81, sr designer Habitat-Mothercare plc 1981–84, assoc dir Storehouse plc 1984–88, mktg dir RSCG Conran Design 1993–96 (design dir 1988–93), design and mktg dir Dorma Gp Ltd 1998– (design dir 1996–98); *Style—* Keith Appleby, Esq

APPLEBY, Prof (James) Louis John; CBE (2006); s of James Appleby, of Livingston, W Lothian, and Doris, *née* Cooper; *b* 27 February 1955; *Educ* Bathgate Acad, Univ of Edinburgh (BSc, MB ChB, MD); *m* 26 Sept 1992, Juliet Elisabeth, *née* Haselden; 2 s (Matthew, Tom), 2 da (Michelle, Rebecca); *Career* trg Maudsley Hosp London 1983–86, lectr Inst of Psychiatry London 1986–91; Univ of Manchester: sr lectr 1991–96, prof of psychiatry 1996–; dir Nat Confidential Inquiry into Suicide and Homicide 1996–; Dept of Health: nat dir for mental health 2000–, chair Mental Health Task Force 2000–; ambass Samaritans; FRCP 1995 (MRCP 1983), FRCPsych 1997 (MRCPsych 1986); *Publications* A Medical Tour Through the Whole Island of Great Britain (1994); *Recreations* clarinet, family, astronomy, ornithology, Manchester United; *Style—* Prof Louis Appleby, CBE; ✉ The Department of Health, Richmond House, 79 Whitehall, London SW1A 2NS (e-mail louis.appleby@doh.gsi.gov.uk); University of Manchester, Oxford Road, Manchester M13 9PL

APPLEBY, Malcolm Arthur; s of James William Appleby (d 1976), of West Wickham, Kent, and Marjory, *née* Stokes (d 1991); *b* 6 January 1946; *Educ* Hawesdown Co Secdy Modern Sch for Boys, Beckenham Sch of Art, Ravensbourn Coll of Art and Design, Central Sch of Arts and Crafts, Sir John Cass Sch of Art, Royal Coll of Art; *Career* started career as engraver 1968, currently designer for silver and specialist gun engraver (developed gold fusing onto steel and created new silver engraving techniques); research into platinum engraving techniques for Ayrton Metals 1992 (resulting in a platinum and gold collection); fndr chm Br Art Postage Stamp Soc; memb: Br Art Medal Soc, Butterfly Conservation Soc, SPAB, Silver Soc, Steering Ctee Highland Perthshire Communities Land Tst 2001–02; life memb: Nat Tst Scotland, British Dragonfly Soc, John Muir Tst, Maclaren Soc; hon memb Grandtully & Strathtay WRI, life memb Orkney Small Boat Museum; former memb: Crathes Drumoak and Durris Community Cncl (chm 1992), Grandtully Hall Ctee; life memb Butterfly Conservation; winner First Inches Carr Craft Bursary 1997; Liveryman Worshipful Co of Goldsmiths 1991; Hon DLitt Heriot-Watt Univ; RSE; *Work* incl: engraving orb on Prince of Wales's Coronet, King George VI Diamond Stakes trophy 1978, 500th anniversary silver cup for London Assay Office, V&A seal, condiment set destined for 10 Downing St, major silver cmmn (cup and cover) for Royal Museum of Scotland 1990, former designer to Holland & Holland Gunmaker, silver centre piece for the new Scottish Parliament, gold millennium casket for Worshipful Co of Goldsmiths, pair of tazzas for the Soc of Writers to Her Majesty's Signet, bell push as a 100th birthday present to HM The Queen Mother from a member of her family, RSE Royal Medal 2000, 22 carat gold medal for Gannochy Tst Innovation Award of RSE, The Muckle Buckle of Braemar, Trafalgar Medal; *Collections* work in collections incl: Aberdeen Art Gallery Nat Museum of Scotland, Aland's Bay Maritime Museum, Nat Museum of Finland, South Aust Maritime Museum, Royal Armouries, V&A, Crafts Cncl, BR Museum, Contemporary Arts Soc, Goldsmiths' Co, Fitzwilliam Museum, Hunterian Museum, Perth Museum and Art Galleries, Ashmolean Museum; *Exhibitions* Br Cncl Crafts Exhibition to Japan, Sotheby's Contemporary Arts Exhibition to Japan, Chicago New Art Forms Exhibition (with the Scottish Gallery), one-man show Pier Arts Centre Stromness Orkney (prints and silver), major one-man show Aberdeen Art Gallery, Silversmiths Gallery Museet Pa Koldinghus Denmark, Inspirations (Goldsmiths Hall), Precious Statements (Goldsmiths Hall), Cutting Edge (Museums of Scotland); *Recreations* work, standing in the garden, cups of herbal tea with friends and neighbours, low cholesterol diet, still darning my very old but colourful pullover, kissing baby daughter and kissing her mother even harder; *Style—* Malcolm Appleby, Esq; ✉ Aultbeag, Grandtully, Perthshire PH15 2QU (tel 01887 840484)

APPLEGARTH, Adam John; *b* 3 August 1962; *Educ* Sedbergh, Univ of Durham (BA); *m* Patricia Catherine; 2 s (Gregory Richard, Benedict John); *Career* Northern Rock plc: joined 1983, head of planning 1989–93, general mangr 1993–96, exec dir 1996–, chief exec 2000–; non-exec dir Persimmon plc 2005–; govr Royal GS Newcastle upon Tyne; *Recreations* cricket, football, rugby; *Style—* Adam J Applegarth, Esq; ✉ Northern Rock plc, Northern Rock House, Gosforth, Newcastle upon Tyne NE3 4PL (tel 0191 279 4525, fax 0191 213 2203)

APPLETON, His Hon Judge John Fortnam; s of Lt-Col George Fortnam Appleton, OBE, TD, JP, DL, of Southport, Lancs (d 2006), and Patricia Margaret, *née* Dunlop (d 1990); *b* 8 April 1946; *Educ* Harrow, Univ of Bristol (LLB); *m* 1 July 1983, Maureen, da of Frederick Williams; 1 s (George Frederick Fortnam b 12 April 1984); *Career* Northern Circuit: barr, circuit jr 1970, recorder 1985–92, circuit judge 1992–; designated civil judge: Preston Gp 1999–2002, Lancs and Cumbria Gp 2002–; *Recreations* the countryside; *Style—* His Hon Judge Appleton; ✉ c/o Northern Circuit Office, 15 Quay Street, Manchester M60 9FD

APPLEYARD, Bryan Edward; s of Cyril John Snowdon Appleyard (d 1965), and Freda Bendelsen (d 1971); *b* 24 August 1951; *Educ* Bolton Sch, King's Coll Cambridge; *m* Christena Marie-Thérèse; 1 da (Charlotte Mary Freda b 26 June 1982); *Career* journalist; South London News Group 1972–75, United Newspapers City Office 1975–76, journalist The Times 1976– (financial news ed and dep arts ed 1981–84), freelance journalist and author 1985–; columnist: The Independent (The Bryan Appleyard Interview 1990–), The Times; weekly columnist The Sunday Times (Bryan Appleyard's Forum), also writer The Sunday Times Magazine; also contrib to: Vogue, Spectator, London Review of Books; TV critic The Tablet; British Press Awards: General Feature Writer of the Year 1986, commended Feature Writer of the Year 1992, Feature Writer of the Year 1996 and 2006; Brave New Worlds highly commended in the Br Med Assoc Med Books competition 1999; *Books* The Culture Club (1984), Richard Rogers - A Biography (1986), The Pleasures of Peace (1989), Understanding the Present - Science and the Soul of Modern Man (1992), The First Church of the New Millennium (1994), Brave New Worlds: Staying Human in the Genetic Future (1998), Aliens: Why They Are Here (2005), How to Live Forever or Die Trying: on the New Immortality (2007); *Recreations* writing; *Clubs* Groucho, The Academy; *Style—* Bryan Appleyard, Esq

APPLEYARD, Dr (William) James; s of Edward Rollo Appleyard (d 1937), and Maud Oliver, *née* Marshall (d 1979); *b* 25 October 1935; *Educ* Canford Sch, Exeter Coll Oxford, Guy's Hosp London, Univ of Louisville Sch of Med Kentucky (Alumnus award); *m* 1964, Elizabeth Anne, *née* Ward; 1 s (Richard James b 1966), 2 da (Lisa Jane b 1968, Suzanne Mary b 1970); *Career* SHO Hosp for Sick Children Gt Ormond St London 1967, Dyers'

Co research registrar St Thomas' Hosp London 1968, sr paediatric registrar Guy's Hosp London 1969–71, conslt paediatrician Kent and Canterbury Hosp 1971–98 (hon conslt paediatrician 1998–99); dean of clinical studies (UK) St George's Univ Sch of Med Grenada WI 1995–97 (prof of paediatrics 1983–95); dean of clinical sciences Kigezi Int Sch of Med (Uganda) 2000–04; BMA: chm Representative Body 1993–95, hon treas 1996–2002, vice-pres 2003–; pres World Med Assoc 2003–04 (memb Cncl 1994–2005, chm Ethical Ctee 1996–99), treas Br Paediatric Assoc 1983–88, memb GMC 1984–2003; memb: Kent AHA 1974–79, Supra Regnl Servs Advsy Ctee Dept of Health 1990–95, Expert Panel of Examiners Int Assoc of Medical Colls NY 2005– (also chair Ethics Ctee and memb Advsy Cncl); hon life memb Kent Postgraduate Medical Centre 1998– (hon treas 1999); patron Dyspraxia Tst; Liveryman Worshipful Soc of Apothecaries (memb Livery Ctee); Hon MD Univ of Kent 1999, Hon DHL Univ of St Georges, Grenada 2000; FRCP 1978, Hon FRCPCH 2002 (FRCPCH 1997); *Publications* articles in refereed based med jls on the newborn, disabled children, medical manpower and medical ethics; *Recreations* lawn tennis, photography; *Clubs* Athenaeum, Oddfellows; *Style—* Dr James Appleyard; ✉ Thimble Hall, Blean Common, Kent CT2 9JJ

APPLEYARD, Sir Leonard Vincent; KCMG (1994, CMG 1986); s of Thomas William Appleyard (d 1979), of Cawood, W Yorks, and Beatrix, *née* Golton (d 1982); *b* 2 September 1938; *Educ* Read Sch Drax, Queens' Coll Cambridge (MA); *m* 1, 3 May 1964 (m dis), Elizabeth Margaret, da of John Lees West, of Grasmere, Cumbria; 2 da (Caroline b 1965, Rebecca b 1967); m 2, 27 Aug 1994, Joan Jefferson; *Career* FO 1962, third sec Hong Kong 1964, second sec Peking 1966, second (later first) sec FO 1969; first sec: Delhi 1971, Moscow 1975, HM Treasy 1978; fin cnsllr Paris 1979–82, head of Econ Rels Dept FCO 1982–84, princ private sec 1984–86, ambass to Hungary 1986–89, dep sec Cabinet Office 1989–91, political dir FCO 1991–94, ambass to China 1994–97; vice-chm Barclays Capital 1998–2003 (special advsr 2005–); chm Farnham Castle 2003–, pro-chllr Bournemouth Univ 2003–; memb Cncl Winchester Cathedral 2000–; *Recreations* music, reading, golf; *Clubs* Brooks's; *Style—* Sir Leonard Appleyard, KCMG

APTED, Michael D; *b* 10 February 1941; *Educ* Univ of Cambridge (BA); *Career* film director; began as researcher Granada TV; credits as TV dir incl: Coronation Street, The Lovers (Best Comedy Series BAFTA), Folly Foot (Best Children's Series BAFTA), Another Sunday and Sweet FA, Kisses at Fifty (Best Dramatic Dir BAFTA), The Collection, Stronger than the Sun, P'Tang Yang Kipperbang, Crossroads, Socrates, Rome; film dir: Triple Echo 1972, Stardust 1975, The Squeeze 1977, Agatha 1979, Coal Miner's Daughter 1980 (nominated Directors' Guild of America award), Continental Divide 1981, Gorky Park 1983, Kipperbang 1983 (BAFTA nomination), First Born 1984, Bring on the Night 1985 (Grammy award), Critical Condition 1987, Gorillas in the Mist 1988, The Long Way Home 1989, Class Action 1990, Incident at Oglala 1992, Thunderheart 1992, Blink 1993, Moving the Mountain 1993, Nell 1994, Extreme Measures 1996, Inspirations 1997, Always Outnumbered 1998, James Bond - The World is not Enough 1999, Me and Isaac Newton 1999, Enigma 2001, Enough, 2002, Amazing Grace 2007; exec prodr: Bram Stoker's Dracula, Strapped, Criminal Justice; dir on-going documentary series revisiting gp of 14 people every 7 years (began with 7 Up 1963), 28 Up (BAFTA Award, Int Emmy and Int Documentary awards), 35 Up (BAFTA Award); *Style—* Michael Apted, Esq; ✉ Michael Apted Film Co, 1901 Avenue of the Stars, Suite 1245, Los Angeles, CA 90067–6013, USA

ARAD, Ron; *b* 1951, Tel Aviv, Israel; *Educ* Jerusalem Acad of Art, AA Sch of Architecture; *Career* architect and furniture/product designer; jt fndr with Caroline Thorman: One Off Ltd (design studio, workshops and showroom) London 1981–93, Ron Arad Associates (architecture and design practice) 1989–, Ron Arad Studio Como 1994–99; prof of product design Hochschule Vienna 1994–97, prof of product design RCA 1997–; projects incl: The New Tel Aviv Opera foyer architecture 1989–94, Maserati HQ showroom 2002–03, Y's (Yohji Yamamoto) store Roppongi Hills 2003, Upper World Hotel Battersea Power Station London 2003, Design Museum Holon 2004, 7th Floor Hotel Puerto America Madrid 2005, Hotel Duomo Rimini 2005, designs for Alessi, Kartell, Cassina, Fiam, Moroso, Flos, Driade, Magis, Vitra International and Swarovski; exhibition designs incl: Winning the Design of Sport Glasgow 1999, Louisiana MOMA 1996; architectural projects incl: Belgo Centraal London 1995, Belgo Noord London 1994, Adidas Sports Cafe France 1996, Amiga House (private residence) London 1997, Alan Journo (boutique) Milan 1999, Windwand Canary Wharf London 1999, The Big Blue Canary Wharf London 2000, Selfridges Technology Hall 2001; Art guest ed 1994 Int Design Yearbook and Designer of the Year 1994; work featured in design/architectural books and magazines worldwide, subject of various monographs; one-man exhbns incl: Powerhouse Museum Sydney 1997, Gallery Mourmans 1999, Before and After Now (V&A) 2000, Not Made by Hand Not Made in China (Gió Marconi Milan) 2000, Delight in Dedark (Gió Marconi Milan) 2001, Two Floors (Gió Marconi Milan) 2002, Permetre's la Ilisertat (Centre d'Art Santa Monica Barcelona) 2003, Ron Arad: A Retrospective Exhibition (Barry Friedman Ltd NY) 2005, Ron Arad: Architectural Installations (Phillips de Pury & Co NY) 2005, There is no solution because there is no problem (Barry Friedman Gallery NY) 2006, Blo-Glo (Milan) 2006, The Dogs barked (de Pury & Luxembourg Zurich) 2006–07, Bodyguards (Milan) 2007; work in many public collections incl: Musée des Arts Decoratifs Paris and Musée National d'Art Moderne/Centre Georges Pompidou Paris, Metropolitan Museum of Art NY, V&A and Design Museum London, Stedelijk Museum Amersterdam, Tel Aviv Museum, Powerhouse Museum Aust, Montreal Museum of Decorative Arts, Vitra Design Museum Weil am Rhein, Design Museum Osaka; Barcelona Primavera International Award for Design 2001, Jerusalem Prize for Arts and Letters Bezalel Acad of Arts and Design Israel 2006, FX Magazine Designer of the Year 2005, Visionary Award Museum of Arts & Design NY 2006; RDI 2002; *Style—* Ron Arad; ✉ Ron Arad Associates Ltd, 62 Chalk Farm Road, London NW1 8AN (tel 020 7284 4963, e-mail info@ronarad.com, website www.ronarad.com)

ARAYA, Dr Negusse; s of Araya Tewoldemedhin (d 1982), and Haregewoin Misgina; *b* 16 January 1950; *Educ* Gelawdeos Secdy Sch Ethiopia, Haile Selassie I Univ Ethiopia (Dip), Addis Ababa Univ (BA), Humboldt Univ of Berlin (MA, PhD); *m* 4 Jan 1974, Gebriela, *née* Woldemariam; 4 c (Yoseph b 4 Dec 1975, Winta b 7 Jan 1978, Biniam b 1 Nov 1979, Samuel b 6 March 1984); *Career* teacher and dir of jr and secdy schs 1972–82; Univ of Asmara: lectr, asst prof and head Educn Unit 1988–91, dean Faculty of Social Scis 1991–92, dir Educn Prog 1992–93; dir Br Cncl Eritrea 1994–, resident rep BESO 1995–; chair Bd of dirs Haben (Eritrean community devpt NGO) 2000–, memb Prog Planning and Research Ctee Family Reproductive Health Assoc of Eritrea; memb Univ Teachers Assoc of Eritrea 1983– (pres 1992–93); *Recreations* visiting historical places, hiking, reading; *Style—* Dr Negusse Araya; ✉ PO Box 9217, Asmara, Eritrea (tel 00 291 1 125777, fax 00 291 1 127230, e-mail negusse@cts.com.er); The British Council, Lorenzo Tazaz Street, PO Box 997, Asmara, Eritrea (tel 00 291 1 123415, fax 00 291 1 127230, e-mail negusse.araya@britishcouncil.org.er)

ARBOUR, Anthony Francis (Tony); JP (Richmond upon Thames 1975), AM; s of Charles Arbour, and Magdalen Arbour; *Educ* Surbiton Co GS, Kingston Coll of Tech (BSc), City Univ Business Sch (MBA); *Career* admitted Gray's Inn 1967; sr lectr 1968–2000: Kingston Coll of Technol, Kingston Poly, Kingston Univ Business Sch; visiting fell Kingston Univ 2000–07; memb London Borough of Richmond Cncl 1968– (ldr 2002–06), GLC (Cons) Surbiton 1983–86; GLA: memb London Assembly (Cons) South West 2000–, chm Planning Ctee 2000–03, chm Planning and Spatial Ctee 2005–; chm Hampton Wick United Charity 1978–; vice-chm Kingston & Richmond FHSA 1990–96; govr: Tiffin Sch 1990–94, Kingston Poly 1998–2000; memb Industrial Tbnl 1992–; *Recreations* book collecting, car booting, watching TV soap operas; *Clubs* Hounslow Cons; *Style—* Tony Arbour, AM; ✉ London Assembly, City Hall, Queens Walk, Southwark, London SE1 2AA (tel 020 7983 4361)

ARBUCKLE, Andrew David; s of John Arbuckle (d 1989), and Lydia, *née* Young (d 1986); *b* 12 April 1944, Perth; *Educ* Bell Baxter HS Cupar, Elmwood Coll Cupar (HND); *m* (m dis); 2 da (Lydia Margaret b 1971, Elizabeth Joy b 1974); *Career* farmer Logie Farm Newburgh 1972, farming ed Dundee Courier 1986–2005; cncllr Newburgh District Fife Cncl 1986–, MSP (Lib Dem) Mid-Scotland and Fife 2005–07; former memb Ct Univ of St Andrews; memb NFU Scotland; FRAgS 2000; *Recreations* sport (former Scottish pole vault champion), reading, music; *Clubs* Fife Athletic (former chm); *Style—* Andrew Arbuckle, Esq; ✉ Fliskmillan Cottage, Newburgh, Fife (tel and fax 01337 870209, e-mail cllr.andrew.arbuckle@fife.gov.uk)

ARBUTHNOT, James Norwich; PC (1998), MP; yr s of Sir John Sinclair-Wemyss Arbuthnot, 1 Bt, MBE, TD (d 1992), and (Margaret) Jean, *née* Duff; hp of bro, Sir William Reierson Arbuthnot, 2 Bt, *qv*; *b* 4 August 1952; *Educ* Eton, Trinity Coll Cambridge (MA); *m* 6 Sept 1984, Emma Louise, da of (John) Michael Broadbent, of S Glos; 1 s (Alexander Broadbent b 1986), 3 da (Katherine Rose Joste b 1989, Eleanor Sophie Duff b 1992, Alice Tempest Wemyss b 1998); *Career* called to the Bar Inner Temple 1975; practising barr 1977–92; cncllr Royal Borough of Kensington and Chelsea 1978–87; Parly candidate (Cons) Cynon Valley 1983 and May 1984; MP (Cons): Wanstead and Woodford 1987–97, Hants NE 1997–; PPS to Min of State for Armed Forces 1988–90, PPS to Sec of State DTI 1990–92, asst whip 1992–94, Parly under sec of state DSS 1994–95, min of state (def procurement) MOD 1995–97, oppn chief whip in the House of Commons 1997–2001, shadow sec of state for Trade 2003–05; memb Intelligence and Security Ctee 2001–05, chm House of Commons Defence Select Ctee 2005–; pres Cynon Valley Cons Assoc 1983–92; *Recreations* skiing, computers, guitar, cooking; *Style—* The Rt Hon James Arbuthnot, MP; ✉ House of Commons, London SW1A 0AA (tel 020 7219 3000)

ARBUTHNOT, Sir Keith Robert Charles; 8 Bt (UK 1823), of Edinburgh; s of Sir Hugh Arbuthnot, 7 Bt (d 1983), and his 1 w, Elizabeth Kathleen (d 1972); *b* 23 September 1951; *Educ* Wellington, Univ of Edinburgh (BSc); *m* 22 May 1982, Anne, yr da of Brig Peter Moore (d 1992), of Churchill, Oxon; 2 s (Robert Hugh Peter b 2 March 1986, Patrick William Martin b 13 July 1987), 1 da (Alice Elizabeth Mary b 22 March 1990); *Heir* s, Robert Arbuthnot; *Style—* Sir Keith Arbuthnot, Bt

ARBUTHNOT, Sir William Reierson; 2 Bt (UK 1964), of Kittybrewster, Aberdeen; s of Sir John Sinclair-Wemyss Arbuthnot, 1 Bt, MBE, TD (d 1992), and (Margaret) Jean, *née* Duff; *b* 2 September 1950; *Educ* Eton, Coll of Law; *Heir* bro, Rt Hon James Arbuthnot, MP, *qv*; *Career* Scottish American Investment Co 1969–70, Arbuthnot Latham Holdings Ltd 1970–76, Joynson-Hicks & Co (slrs) 1978–81; dep chm High Premium Gp 1994–, dir ALM Ltd 1997–; memb Lloyd's 1971–; memb Families Need Fathers; Liveryman Worshipful Co of Grocers; *Recreations* genealogy; *Style—* Sir William Arbuthnot, Bt; ✉ 37 Cathcart Road, London SW10 9JG (tel 020 7795 0707, fax 020 7823 3344, e-mail wra@arbuthnot.org)

ARBUTHNOTT, 16 Viscount of (S 1641); John Campbell Arbuthnott; KT (1996), CBE (1986), DSC (1945); also Lord Inverbervie (S 1641); s of 15 Viscount of Arbuthnott (d 1966), and Ursula, *née* Collingwood (d 1989); Lord Arbuthnott is the thirty third Laird of Arbuthnott and the twenty seventh in descent from Hugh de Swinton, who acquired the estate of Aberbothenoth, of which he is recorded as having been styled *thanus* and *dominus*, towards the end of the twelfth century, and who was gggggggggggs of Edulf Edulfing, 1 Lord of Bamburgh (d 912); *b* 26 October 1924; *Educ* Fettes, Gonville & Caius Coll Cambridge; *m* 1949, Mary Elizabeth Darley, er da of Cdr Christopher Oxley, DSC, RN (himself 2 s of Adm Charles Oxley, JP, and whose yst sis m 14 Viscount of Arbuthnott); 1 s, 1 da (*see* Hon Mrs Smith); *Heir* s, Master of Arbuthnott, *qv*; *Career* served RNVR Fleet Air Arm Far E & Pacific 1942–46; chartered surveyor and land agent; Agricultural Land Serv 1949–55, land agent Scottish Nature Conservancy 1955–67; dir: Aberdeen & Northern Marts 1973–91 (chm 1986–91), Scottish Widows' Fund and Life Assurance Soc 1978–94 (chm 1984–87), Scottish North Investment Trust 1979–85, Clydesdale Bank 1985–92, Britoil plc 1988–90, BP Scottish Advsy Bd 1990–96; pres: Br Assoc for Shooting and Conservation (formerly Wildfowlers Assoc of GB and Ireland) 1973–92, RZS Scotland 1976–96, Royal Scottish Geographical Soc 1982–85; dep chm Nature Conservancy Cncl 1980–85 (chm Scottish Advsy Ctee); memb: Ct Univ of Aberdeen 1978–84, Royal Cmmn on Historical Manuscripts 1987–94; pres Highland TAVRA 1984–89; Hon Air Cdre No 612 (County of Aberdeen) Sqdn RAuxAF 1998–; HM Lord High Cmmr to Gen Assembly of Church of Scotland 1986 and 1987; HM Lord-Lt Grampian Region (Kincardineshire) 1977–99; Bailiff Grand Cross and Prior of the Order of St John of Jerusalem in Scotland 1983–95; Liveryman Worshipful Co of Farmers; Hon LLD Univ of Aberdeen 1995; FRSE 1984, FRSA, FRICS; GCStJ; *Recreations* countryside activities, historical research; *Clubs* Army and Navy, New (Edinburgh); *Style—* The Rt Hon the Viscount of Arbuthnott, KT, CBE, DSC, FRSE; ✉ Arbuthnott House, by Laurencekirk, Kincardineshire AB30 1PA (tel 01561 361226)

ARBUTHNOTT, Master of; Hon John Keith Oxley; DL (Kincardineshire 2000); s and h of 16 Viscount of Arbuthnott, CBE, DSC, *qv*; *b* 18 July 1950; *Educ* Fettes, N Scotland Coll of Agric Aberdeen (HND, Dip Farm Business, Orgn and Mgmnt), Robert Gordon's Inst of Technol Aberdeen (Dip Mgmnt Studies); *m* 1974, Jill Mary, eld da of Capt Colin Farquharson, of Whitehouse, Aberdeenshire; 2 da (Clare Anne b 1974, Rachel Sarah b 1979), 1 s (Christopher Keith b 20 July 1977); *Career* owner/mangr Arbuthnott Estate; vice-convenor Scottish Landowners' Fedn 2002–05, chm Scottish Rural Property and Business Assoc 2005–; memb Grampian Health Bd 1993–97; *Style—* The Master of Arbuthnott; ✉ Kilternan, Arbuthnott, Laurencekirk, Kincardineshire AB30 1NA (e-mail keith@arbuthnott.co.uk)

ARBUTHNOTT, Prof Sir John Peebles; kt (1998); s of James Anderson Arbuthnott (d 1961), and Jean, *née* Kelly (d 1982); *b* 8 April 1939; *Educ* Hyndland Sr Secdy Sch, Univ of Glasgow (BSc, PhD), Trinity Coll Dublin (MA, ScD); *m* 2 July 1962, Elinor Rutherford, da of John Smillie (d 1986); 2 da (Anne b 6 March 1966, Alison b 11 Nov 1974), 1 s (Andrew b 10 Feb 1969); *Career* res fell Royal Soc 1968–72, sr lectr Dept of Microbiology Univ of Glasgow 1972–75 (asst lectr 1960–63, lectr 1963–67), bursar Trinity Coll Dublin 1983–86 (prof of microbiology 1976–88), prof of microbiology Univ of Nottingham 1988–91, princ and vice-chllr Univ of Strathclyde 1991–2000, sec and treas Carnegie Tst for the Univs of Scotland 2001–04; chm Jt Information Systems Ctee 1993–98, vice-chm CVCP 1997–99, convener Ctee of Scottish Higher Educn Princs 1994–96; author of many papers on bacterial toxins and microbial pathogenicity; memb Cncl Soc of Gen Microbiology 1981–86 (sr ed 1980–84, treas 1987–92), meetings sec Fedn of Euro Microbiology Socs 1986–90; chm: National Review of Allocation of Health Resources in Scotland 1997–99, Scottish Food Advsy Ctee 2000–02, Standing Ctee on Resource Allocation in NHS Scotland 2001–03, Gtr Glasgow NHS Health Bd 2002–, Cmmn on Boundary Changes and Voting Systems 2004–06; memb: Microbiological Safety of Food Ctee 1989–90, AFRC Animal Res Bd 1989–92, Public Health Laboratory Serv Bd 1991–97, DTI Multimedia Industry Advsy Gp 1994–96, Educn Counselling Serv Bd Br Cncl 1995–96, Glasgow Devpt Agency 1995–2000, Nat Ctee of Enquiry into Higher Educn 1996–97, Bd Food Standards Agency 2000–02; memb: Soc of Gen Microbiology 1968–2005, Glasgow Science Tst 1999–2001, Scottish Science Tst 1999–; hon degree: Poly Univ Lodz, Queens Univ Belfast, Univ of Glasgow, Univ of Aberdeen, Univ of

Strathclyde, Univ Techol Malaysia, Int Med Univ Kuala Lumpur, Glasgow Caledonian Univ, Queen Margaret UC; hon fell TCD 1992; MRIA 1985, FIBiol 1988, FRSE 1993, FIIB 1993, FRCPath 1995, Hon FRCPSGlas, FMedSci 1998; *Books* Isoelectric Focussing (jt ed, 1974), Determinants of Microbial Pathogenicity (jt ed, 1983), Foodborne Illness: a Lancet review (jtly, 1991), Fair Shares for All - Final Report (for the NHS in Scot, 2000); *Recreations* photography, bird watching; *Clubs* Western (Glasgow); *Style—* Prof Sir John Arbuthnott, FRSE; ✉ 9 Curlinghall, Largs KA30 8LB (tel 0141 334 8329, e-mail j.arbuthnott@btinternet.com)

ARCHARD, Dr Graham Eric; s of Eric Harry Archard, of Bournemouth, Dorset, and Irene Lilian Mary, *née* Etchell; *b* 31 March 1951, Winchester, Hampshire; *Educ* Canford Sch Wimborne, Univ of Leeds (BSc, MB ChB); *m* 24 Sept 1977, Honor, *née* Guy; 1 da (Elizabeth Honor b 5 Sept 1983), 1 s (Guy Graham Robin b 1 Aug 1985); *Career* princ in gen practice 1984–; jt chm S & E Dorset PCT 2003–, vice-chm RCGP 2005–; clinical governance lead NHS Alliance 2000–05; author of articles in professional jls; Jamieson Medal and Prize in practical anatomy 1978; memb: BMA, NHS Alliance; FRCGP; *Recreations* music (guitar and piano), walking, qualifications in wine tasting; *Clubs* Bournemouth & Poole Med Soc; *Style—* Dr Graham Archard; ✉ Willowmarsh, St Catherine's Hill Lane, Christchurch, Dorset BH23 2NL (tel 07768 910273); Stour Surgery, 49 Barrack Road, Christchurch, Dorset BH23 1PA (tel 01202 464500, fax 01202 464529, e-mail g.archard@doctors.org.uk)

ARCHDALE, Sir Edward Folmer; 3 Bt (UK 1928), of Riversdale, Co Fermanagh; DSC (1943); s of Vice Adm Sir Nicholas Archdale, 2 Bt, CBE (d 1955), and Gerda, da of Frederik Sievers, of Copenhagen; *b* 8 September 1921; *Educ* Copthorne Sch, RNC Dartmouth; *m* 24 July 1954 (m dis 1978), Elizabeth Ann Stewart, da of Maj-Gen Wilfrid Boyd Fellowes Lukis, CBE, RM (d 1969); 2 da (Annabel Frances b 1956 d 1996, Lucinda Grace b 1958), 1 s (Nicholas Edward b 1965); *Heir* s, Nicholas Archdale; *Career* RN: joined 1935, serv WWII (despatches), Capt (ret); def conslt, political economist; *Style—* Sir Edward Archdale, Bt, DSC; ✉ 16 Addison Crescent, London W14 8JR (tel 020 7602 7102)

ARCHDEACON, Antony; s of Maurice Ignatius Archdeacon (d 1973), of Ruislip, Middx, and Nora Margery May, *née* Ball; *b* 25 January 1925; *Educ* Oxford House Sch, Univ of Buckingham (LLB); *m* 1, 3 Dec 1956 (m dis 1965), Elizabeth, da of Samuel Percy Ball, of Great Horwood, Bucks; 1 s (Timothy b 1957); m 2, 24 Aug 1992, Ursula, da of Fritz Mentze, of Iserlohn, Germany; *Career* admitted slr 1950; dir: Skim Milk Supplies Ltd 1967–, Business Mortgages Trust plc 1969–86; chm Forum of St Albans plc 1985–2001; pres: Rotary Club Buckingham 1968, Northampton Anglo-German Club 1988–; town clerk Buckingham 1951–71; Freeman: City of London 1972, Worshipful Co of Feltmakers 1972; *Recreations* walking, languages; *Clubs* Carlton; *Style—* Antony Archdeacon, Esq; ✉ 14 Mallard Drive, Buckingham MK18 1GJ (tel and fax 01280 823640, e-mail aarchdeacon@btinternet.com)

ARCHER, Prof Brian Harrison; s of Arthur Cecil Arthur (d 1969), and Elizabeth, *née* Summerscales (d 2002); *b* 31 July 1934; *Educ* Liverpool Coll, Fitzwilliam House Cambridge (MA), Univ of London (BSc), Univ of Wales (PhD); *Career* cmmnd King's Regt Liverpool 1955, Maj TAVR 1955–65; schoolmaster Monmouth 1958–69, Inst of Economic Research UCNW 1969–77 (sr research offr, lectr, sr lectr, dir); Univ of Surrey: prof and head Dept of Mgmnt Studies 1978–91, pro-vice-chllr 1987–94, emeritus prof 1994–; conslt to: Cwlth Secretariat, UNDP, World Bank, WTO; author of numerous pubns in jls; ind memb devpt and mktg ctees BTA 1984–94; govr Charterhouse 1991–95; *Books* The Impact of Domestic Tourism (1973), Demand Forecasting in Tourism (1976), Tourism Multipliers: The State of the Art (1977); *Recreations* travel, watching cricket and rugby; *Style—* Prof Brian Archer; ✉ 3 The Cedars, Milford, Godalming, Surrey GU8 5DH (tel 01483 429932, e-mail brian@brianarcher.force9.co.uk)

ARCHER, Colin Robert Hill; s of Robin Hamlyn Hill Archer, and Cherrie Mary, *née* Gourlay; *b* 13 August 1949; *Educ* Stowe, Univ of Essex (BA); *m* 27 March 1976, (Mary) Jane, da of John Rutherford Blaikie; 1 da (Sarah b 11 March 1981), 1 s (Charles b 18 Aug 1983); *Career* articled clerk then asst mangr Thomson McLintoch 1971–77, mangr corp fin Kleinwort Benson 1977–85, divnl dir corp fin BHS plc 1985–86, gp fin controller Storehouse plc 1988–89 (gp co sec 1986–88), gp fin dir Swan Hill Group plc (formerly Higgs and Hill plc) 1989–; FCA; *Recreations* tennis, golf, skiing, reading; *Clubs* Hurlingham, Berkshire Golf; *Style—* Colin Archer, Esq

ARCHER, David Birdwood; s of Geoffrey Archer, of Renson Mill, N Devon, and Hon Sonia, *née* Birdwood; *b* 18 June 1959, Montreal, Canada; *Educ* Cheltenham Coll, LSE (LLB); *m* 25 Feb 1984, Gwenyth, *née* Highley; 2 s (Thomas b 3 Sept 1988, James b 28 July 1990), 1 da (Isabel b 28 Sept 1992); *Career* slr: Norton Rose 1982–88, Baker & MacKenzie Aust 1988–90, Clifford Chance 1990–92, Pitmans 1992– (md Pitmans Trustees Limited 1994–); memb Law Soc 1982; *Clubs* Brooks'; *Style—* David Archer, Esq; ✉ Pitmans, 47 Castle Street, Reading RG1 7SR (tel 0118 957 0303, fax 0118 957 0333, e-mail darcher@pitmans.com)

ARCHER, Geoffrey Wilson; s of Thomas Wilson Archer, of Salisbury, Wilts, and Dorothy Maude, *née* Monahan; *b* 21 May 1944; *Educ* Highgate Sch; *m* 17 Aug 1974, Eva Jenny Lucia, da of Gustaf Janson; 1 da (Alison Susanne b 24 July 1975), 1 s (James Alexander b 22 Dec 1977); *Career* author; researcher Southern Television 1964, reporter/prodr Anglia Television 1965–69, reporter/presenter Tyne-Tees Television 1969; ITN: news reporter 1969–79, defence/science corr 1979–83, defence/dip corr 1983–95; *Books* Sky Dancer (1987), Shadow Hunter (1989), Eagle Trap (1993), Scorpion Trail (1995), Java Spider (1997), Fire Hawk (1998), The Lucifer Network (2001), The Burma Legacy (2002), Dark Angel (2004); *Recreations* sailing, film and theatre; *Style—* Geoffrey Archer, Esq; ✉ c/o Century/Arrow Books, 20 Vauxhall Bridge Road, London SW1V 2SA (website www.geoffreyarcher.com)

ARCHER, Dr Gordon James; s of Sqdn Ldr Percival John Archer (d 2001), of Cleveleys, Lancs, and Doris Elizabeth Archer (d 1996); *b* 21 August 1942; *Educ* Kirkham GS, Univ of Manchester (MB ChB); *m* 21 Sept 1968, Barbara, da of Alwyn Johns (d 1996), of Penllergaer, W Glamorgan; 1 s (Gareth b 9 Oct 1974), 1 da (Joanne b 3 Sept 1976); *Career* med registrar Cardiff Royal Infirmary 1969–71, thoracic med registrar London Chest Hosp 1971–73, sr med registrar Leeds Gen Infirmary 1973–74, conslt physician with special interest chest diseases Stockport AHA 1974–, clinical teacher Univ of Manchester 1983–; chm Stockport Asthma Care Fund; past memb: Regnl Med Ctee Br Thoracic Soc, NW Regnl Assoc Physicians; past med dir Stockport Health Authy; pres Macclesfield Castle Rotary Club 1994–95; MRCP 1969, FRCP 1990; *Publications* numerous pubns in jls incl: Treatment of Pneumothorax by Simple Aspiration (1983), Results of Pneumothorax Aspiration (1985); *Recreations* golf; *Style—* Dr Gordon Archer; ✉ Ryley Mount Consulting Rooms, 432 Buxton Road, Great Moor, Stockport, Cheshire SK2 (tel 0161 483 9333)

ARCHER, Graham Robertson; CMG (1997); *b* 4 July 1939; *m* 1963, Pauline, *née* Cowan; 2 da (b 1965 and 1968); *Career* HM Dip Serv: entered 1962, Cwlth Rels Office FCO 1962–64, private sec to high cmmr New Delhi 1964–66, vice-consul Kuwait 1966–67, FCO 1967–70, second sec Washington 1970–72, FCO 1972–75, head of Chancery Wellington 1975–79, FCO 1979–81, scrutiny exercise 1981–82, head of Chancery Pretoria 1982–86, dep head of mission The Hague 1986–90, FCO 1990–95, high cmmr to Republic of Malta 1995–99; dep chm National Trust Regnl Ctee for the SE, memb Central Cncl Royal Over-Seas League; KStJ 1999; *Style—* Graham Archer, Esq, CMG; ✉ c/o Royal Over-Seas League, Park Place, St James's Street, London SW1A 1LR

ARCHER, Janet; *Educ* Welsh Coll of Music and Drama (Dip Theatre Studies), Rambert Sch, London Sch of Contemporary Dance; *Career* dancer, choreographer and dir; dancer Jumpers Dance Theatre 1981, freelance dir, choreographer and performer 1982–85 (credits incl: HTV, WNO, Nat Youth Theatre of Wales, Cardiff Univ, Sherman Theatre) 1982–85, dance ldr CATO Bridgend 1985–86, artistic dir Nexus Dance Co 1987–91, arts mangr Welwyn Hatfield Cncl 1989–91 (dance animateur 1986–89), artistic dir and ceo DanceCity Newcastle upon Tyne 1991–; memb Bd: Phoenix Dance Co (interim chm 2001), Dance UK, Dancers Career Devpt, Newcastle Arts Forum, Graingertown Arts Ctee; former memb Bd: Fndn for Community Dance, Diversions Dance Theatre, Nat Youth Dance Festival; judge Jerwood Award 2000; Cosmopolitan Young Dancer of the Year 1981, Digital Dance Award 1987, Northern Electric Arts Award 1992, British Gas Working for Cities Award 1993, Cosmoplitan Woman of the Year 1995; *Recreations* film, food, psychology, entertaining, books, spending time with my daughter; *Style—* Ms Janet Archer; ✉ Dance City, Temple Street, Newcastle upon Tyne NE1 4BR (e-mail janet.archer@dancecity.co.uk)

ARCHER, Prof John Stuart; CBE (2002); s of Stuart Leonard Gordon Archer; *b* 15 June 1943; *Educ* GS for Boys Chiswick, City Univ London (BSc), Imperial Coll London (PhD, DIC); *m* 30 Sept 1967, Lesley, da of Leslie Arthur Oaksford, of Yeovil, Somerset; 1 da (Louise b 19 Jan 1973), 1 s (Adam John b 21 Feb 1975); *Career* student trainee ICI 1961–64, res reservoir engr ESSO Resources Canada 1969–73, petroleum reservoir engr British Gas Corp 1973–74, mangr reservoir studies D&S Petroleum Conslts 1974–77, conslt ERC (Energy Resource Conslts) 1977–84 (fndr and dir Reservoir Studies 1977–80); Imperial Coll London: joined 1980, prof of petroleum engrg (former reader), head Dept of Mineral Resources Engrg 1986–94, dean Royal Sch of Mines 1989–91, pro-rector 1991–94, dep rector 1994–96; princ and vice-chllr Heriot-Watt Univ 1997–2006; former chm: Educn UK Partnership, Educn UK Scotland, Univs UK Res Policy Strategy Gp; pres IChemE 2005–06; UK memb Research Working Gp European Univs Assoc; memb Cncl EPSRC 2000–; memb Soc of Petroleum Engrg 1973; CEng 1974, FInstPet 1977, FREng 1992, FRSE 1998, FCGI, FIE, FRSA; *Books* Petroleum Engineering - Principles and Practice (1986); *Recreations* golf, skiing, walking, gardening, theatre; *Clubs* New (Edinburgh), Caledonian; *Style—* Prof John Archer, CBE, FRSE, FREng; ✉ Geroge Heriot Wing, Heriot-Watt University, Edinburgh EH14 4AS (tel 0131 451 3360)

ARCHER, Malcolm David; s of Gordon and Joan Archer, of Bolton-le-Sands, Lancs; *b* 29 April 1952; *Educ* King Edward VII Sch Lytham, RCM (RJ Pitcher scholar, ARCM), Jesus Coll Cambridge (organ scholar, MA, CertEd), FRCO; *m* 1994, Alison Jane, *née* Robinson; 1 s (Nathaniel Luke b 27 Dec 1997), 1 da (Tabitha Jane b 5 Nov 1999); *Career* asst dir of music Magdalen Coll Sch Oxford 1976–78, asst organist Norwich Cathedral 1978–83, organist and master of the choristers Bristol Cathedral 1983–90, head of chapel music Clifton Coll 1994–96, freelance composer, conductor and organist 1990–96, organist and master of the choristers Wells Cathedral 1996–2004, organist and dir of music St Paul's Cathedral 2004–; fndr and musical dir City of Bristol Choir 1991–99, musical dir Wells Cathedral Oratorio Soc; examiner Assoc Bd of Royal Schs of Music; memb: Cncl RCO 1996–, Cathedral Organists Assoc, Friends of Cathedral Music; Hon fell North and Midlands Sch of Music (Hon FNMSM), Hon FGCM; *Publications* Love Unknown (1992), Requiem (1993); over 150 published works; *Recreations* swimming, cooking, travel, painting, classic cars; *Clubs* Rolls Royce Enthusiasts; *Style—* Malcolm Archer, Esq; ✉ 5B Amen Court, London EC4M 7BU (tel 020 7248 6868)

ARCHER, Prof Margaret Scotford; da of Ronald Archer (d 1964), and Elise, *née* Scotford; *b* 20 January 1943; *Educ* Sheffield HS for Girls, LSE (BSc, PhD), Ecole Pratique des Hautes Etudes Paris; *m* 1 May 1973, (Gilbert) Andrew Jones, s of Kingsley Boardman (d 1975); 2 s (Kingsley b 1975, Marcus b 1979); *Career* lectr Univ of Reading 1966–73, prof Univ of Warwick 1979– (reader 1973–79); memb Br Sociological Assoc, pres Int Sociological Assoc; counsellor Pontifical Acad of Social Scis; *Books* Social Conflict and Educational Change in England and France 1789–1848 (with M Vaughan, 1971), Contemporary Europe, Class, Status and Power (ed with S Giner, 1971), Students, University and Society (ed, 1972), Contemporary Europe, Social Structures and Cultural Patterns (ed with S Giner, 1978), Social Origins of Educational Systems (1979), The Sociology of Educational Expansion (ed, 1982), Culture and Agency (1988), Realist Social Theory: the Morphogenetic Approach (1995), Rational Choice Theory: Resisting Colonization (ed with J Tritter, 2000), Being Human: the Problem of Agency (2000), Structure, Agency and the Internal Conversation (2003); *Recreations* equestrian; *Style—* Prof Margaret Archer; ✉ Department of Sociology, University of Warwick, Coventry, Warwickshire CV4 7AL (tel 024 7652 3499, fax 01869 37146, e-mail m.s.archer@warwick.ac.uk)

ARCHER OF SANDWELL, Baron (Life Peer UK 1992), of Sandwell in the County of West Midlands; Peter Kingsley Archer; PC (1977), QC (1971); s of Cyril Kinglsey Archer, MM (d 1974), and May, *née* Baker (d 1976); *b* 20 November 1926; *Educ* Wednesbury Boys' HS, Univ of London (external LLB), LSE (LLM), UCL (BA); *m* 7 Aug 1954, Margaret Irene, da of Sydney John Smith (d 1936), of London, Ontario, Canada; 1 s (Hon John Kingsley b 1962); *Career* called to the Bar Gray's Inn 1952 (bencher 1974); commenced practice 1953, recorder of the Crown Court 1982–98; MP (Lab): Rowley Regis and Tipton 1966–74, Warley W 1974–92; PPS to Attorney Gen 1967–70, Slr Gen 1974–79; chief oppn front bench spokesman on: legal affrs 1979–82, trade 1982–83; shadow NI sec 1983–87; front bench spokesman on foreign affairs House of Lords 1992–98; chm: Parly Gp for World Govt 1970–74, Br section Amnesty Int 1971–74, Cncl on Tribnls 1992–99, Enemy Property Claims Assessment Panel 1999–; chm Pre-Legislative Ctee on Freedom of Information Bill House of Lords 1999; memb: Delegated Powers and Regulation Select Ctee 1997–2000, Jt Ctee on Parly Privilege 1998–99, Intelligence and Security Ctee 1998–2006, Jt Ctee on House of Lords Reform 2002–05; vice-chm Anti-Slavery Soc 1970–74; pres: Fabian Soc 1993– (chm Exec Ctee 1980–81, memb 1974–86), Methodist Homes for the Aged 1993–, Soc of Labour Lawyers 1993– (chm 1971–74 and 1980–93), World Disarmament Campaign 1994–; ombudsman Mirror Group Newspapers 1989–92; fell UCL 1978; *Books* The Queen's Courts (1956), Social Welfare and the Citizen (ed, 1957), Communism and the Law (1963), Freedom at Stake (with Lord Reay, 1966), Human Rights (1969), Purpose in Socialism (jtly, 1973), The Role of the Law Officers (1978), More Law Reform Now (co-ed, 1984), From Chaos to Cosmos (2006); *Recreations* music, writing, talking; *Style—* The Rt Hon Lord Archer of Sandwell, PC, QC; ✉ Highcroft, Hill View Road, Wraysbury, Staines, Middlesex (tel 01784 483136)

ARCHER OF WESTON-SUPER-MARE, Baron (Life Peer UK 1992), of Mark in the County of Somerset; Jeffrey Howard Archer; s of William Archer (d 1956), and Lola, *née* Cook; *b* 15 April 1940; *Educ* Wellington Sch Somerset, BNC Oxford (Athletics blues 1963–65, Gymnastics blue 1965, Oxford 100 yds record 1966); *m* 11 July 1966, Dr Mary Doreen Archer, *qv*, da of Harold Weeden (d 1971); 2 s (Hon William Harold b 1972, Hon James Howard b 1974); *Career* politician and author; memb GLC Havering 1966–70, MP (C) Louth 1969–74; dep chm Cons Pty 1985–86; tstee RWS 1989–; pres: Somerset AAA 1973, Somerset Wyverns 1983–98, World Snooker Assoc 1997–99; FRSA 1973; *Books* Not a Penny More, Not a Penny Less (1975, televised 1990), Shall We Tell The President? (1977), Kane and Abel (1979, televised 1986), A Quiver Full of Arrows (1980), The Prodigal Daughter (1982), First Among Equals (1984, televised 1986), A Matter of Honour (1986), Beyond Reasonable Doubt (play, 1987), A Twist in The Tale (short stories, 1989), Exclusive (play, 1989), As the Crow Flies (1991), Honour Among Thieves (1993), Twelve Red Herrings (1994), The Fourth Estate (1996), Collected Short Stories (1997), The

Eleventh Commandment (1998), To Cut a Long … ort (2000), The Accused (play, 2000), A Prison Diary (vol I, Hell) (2002), … (2003), A Prison Diary (vol II, Purgatory) (2003), A Prison Diary (vol III, … Mallory: Walking Off the Map (screenplay, 2005), False Impression (200… ay 2006), The Gospel According to Judas by Benjamin Iscariot (with P… oney, 2007); *Recreations* theatre, auctioneering, watching Somerset pl… outh Working Men's; *Style*— The Rt Hon Lord Archer of Weston-su… enthouse, 93 Albert Embankment, London SE1 7TY

ARCHER OF WESTON-SUPER-MA… reen Archer; da of Harold Norman Weeden (d 1971), and Dore… December 1944; *Educ* Cheltenham Ladies' Coll, St Anne's C… Coll London (PhD); *m* 11 July 1966, Baron Archer of Westo… 2 s; *Career* jr res fell St Hilda's Coll Oxford 1968–71, temp… Coll Oxford 1971–72, res fell Royal Instn of Great Brit… wnham Coll Cambridge and lectr in chemistry Trinity… Univ of Hertfordshire 1993–2005; dir Fitzwilliam Mu… ergy Fndn 1999– (chm 1989–99), Solar Energy Soc… NHS Fndn Tst (formerly Addenbrooke's Hosp NHS… ce-chm 1999–2002); non-exec dir: Anglia Television… 1988–95, Cambridge and Newmarket FM Radio… 2, Cheltenham Ladies' Coll 1991–99; tstee Scie… ch Musicians 1989–; Melchett Medal Inst … mistry of Ireland 2007; Hon DSc Univ of … ooks Rupert Brooke and the Old Vicarage, … Photovoltaics (2000), Molecular to Global … hemistry at Cambridge (2005); *Recreations* … rcher; ✉ The Old Vicarage, Grantchester, … 01223 842882); Peninsula Heights, 93 Albert … 735 0077, fax 020 7582 2406)

… E5); s of Thomas Guy Arculus, and Mary, *née* … msgrove Sch, Oriel Coll Oxford (MA), London … e Murdoch, da of Howard Leslie Sleeman; 1 da … o 30 Jan 1978, Nicholas b 13 Nov 1979); *Career* … MAP plc: joined 1972, gen mangr magazines … exhbns 1981–84, gp dep md 1984–89, gp md … ews and Media plc 1997–98; chm: IPC Magazines …–2004 (non-exec dir 1996–2004), Earls Court and … nO2 2004– (non-exec dir 2003–); non-exec dir: Norcros … 997–, Guiton Gp plc 2000–02; chm: PPA 1990, Better … 02–; treas Fedn of Int Periodical Press 1992–94, dep pres CBI … Ctee 2003), memb Nat Consumer Cncl 1993–96; fell Industry and … ssoc of MBA 1972; Freeman City of London 1990, Liveryman … Stationers and Newspaper Makers 1992; Hon Dr Univ of Central …, MInstD 1993; *Recreations* cricket, hill walking, reading; *Clubs* Oxford and …, MCC, Thirty, Groucho; *Style*— Sir David Arculus

…Andrew Paul Russel; QC (1991); s of Sidney Russel Arden (d 2000), and Helen …e, *née* Prevezer (d 1991); *b* 20 April 1948; *Educ* Stowe, Univ Coll Sch, UCL (LLB); … 19 Sept 1991, Joanne, da of Joseph Leahy, of Cramlington, Northumberland, and Sheila Leahy; 1 da (Emma b 1992); *Career* called to the Bar Gray's Inn 1974; dir Small Heath Community Law Centre Birmingham 1976–78, established Arden Chambers 1993; visiting prof Sch of Environment and Devpt Sheffield Hallam Univ 2001; *Legal Publications* Manual of Housing Law (1978, 8 edn (jtly) 2007), Housing Act 1980 (1980), Homeless Persons: Part III, Housing Act 1985 (1982, 7 edn as Homelessness and Allocations, (jtly) 2007), Private Tenants Handbook (1985, 2 edn 1989), Public Tenants Handbook (1985, 2 edn 1989), Homeless Persons Handbook (1986, 2 edn 1988), Housing Act 1985 (1986), Quiet Enjoyment (jtly, 1980, 6 edn 2002), Housing Law (jtly, 1983, 2 edn 1994), Rent Acts & Regulations, Amended and Annotated (jtly, 1981), Housing & Building Control Act 1984 (jtly, 1984), Landlord & Tenant Act 1985 (jtly, 1986), Housing Associations Act 1985 (jtly, 1986), Housing Act 1988 (jtly, 1989), Local Government & Housing Act 1989 (jtly, 1990), Assured Tenancies (Vol 3 'The Rent Acts', jtly, 1989), Local Government Finance Law and Practice (jtly, 1994), Housing Act 1996 (jtly, 1996), Housing Grants, Construction and Regeneration Act 1996 (jtly, 1996), Local Government Constitutional and Administrative Law (jtly, 1999, 2 edn 2007); gen ed: Encyclopaedia of Housing Law (1978–), Housing Law Reports (1981–), Jl of Housing Law (1997–), Local Government Law Reports (1999–2001); *Fiction* The Motive Not The Deed (1975), No Certain Roof (1985), The Object Man (1986), The Programme (2001); also author series of 4 thrillers (written under pseudonym); *Recreations* Southern Comfort, Camels, Hill St Blues; *Clubs* Manzis Luncheon; *Style*— Andrew Arden, Esq, QC; ✉ Arden Chambers, 2 John Street, London WC1N 2ES (tel 020 7242 4244, fax 020 7242 3224, e-mail andrew.arden@ardenchambers.com)

ARDEN, John; s of C A Arden, and A E Layland; *b* 26 October 1930; *Educ* Sedbergh, King's Coll Cambridge, Edinburgh Coll of Art; *m* 1957, Margaretta Ruth D'Arcy; 4 s (and 1 decd); *Career* playwright and novelist; FRSL; *Plays* incl: The Life of Man (1956), The Waters of Babylon (1957), Live Like Pigs (1958), Sergeant Musgrave's Dance (1959), Soldier Soldier (for TV, 1960), Wet Fish (for TV, 1962), The Workhouse Donkey (1963), Ironhand (1963), Armstrong's Last Goodnight (1964), Left-Handed Liberty (1965), The True History of Squire Jonathan and his Unfortunate Treasure (1968); for radio: All Fall Down (1955), The Bagman (1970), Pearl (1978), To Put It Frankly (1979), Don Quixote (1980), Garland for a Hoar Head (1982), The Old Man Sleeps Alone (1982), Little Novels of Wilkie Collins (1998), Woe Alas, the Fatal Cashbox (1999), Wild Ride to Dublin (2003), Poor Tom, Thy Horn is Dry (2004); *with Margaretta D'Arcy* The Business of Good Government (1960), The Happy Haven (1960), Ars Longa Vita Brevis (1964), Friday's Hiding (1966), The Royal Pardon (1966), The Hero Rises Up (1968), Muggins is a Martyr (1968), Island of the Mighty (1972), The Ballygombeen Bequest (1972), Portrait of a Rebel (TV documentary, 1973), The Non-Stop Connolly Cycle (1975), Vandaleur's Folly (1978), The Little Gray Home in the West (1978), The Manchester Enthusiasts (for radio, 1984), Whose is the Kingdom? (radio, 1988), A Suburban Suicide (for radio, 1994); *Publications* To Present The Pretence (essays on theatre, 1978), Silence Among The Weapons (novel, 1982), Books of Bale (novel, 1988), Awkward Corners (essays, etc with Margaretta D'Arcy, 1988), Cogs Tyrannic (novel, 1991), Jack Juggler and the Emperor's Whore (novel, 1995), The Stealing Steps (short stories, 2003); *Recreations* antiquarianism, mythology; *Style*— John Arden, Esq; ✉ c/o Casarotto Marsh Ltd, National House, 4th Floor, 60–66 Wardour Street, London W1V 3HP (tel 020 7287 4450, fax 020 7287 9128)

ARDEN, The Rt Hon Lady Justice; Rt Hon Dame Mary Howarth; DBE (1993), PC (2000); da of Lt-Col Eric Cuthbert Arden (d 1973); *Educ* Girton Coll Cambridge (MA, LLM), Harvard Univ (LLM); *m* 26 May 1973, Sir Jonathan Hugh Mance (Baron Mance, PC (Life Peer), *qv*); 2 da, 1 s; *Career* called to the Bar 1971, QC 1986, asst recorder of Crown and Co Courts 1990–93, dep High Court judge 1990–93, attorney-gen Duchy of Lancaster 1991–93, judge of the High Court of Justice (Chancery Div) 1993–2000, ad hoc judge European Court of Human Rights 2000, Lady Justice of Appeal 2000–, judge i/c int judicial rels (for Eng and Wales) 2005–; bencher of Lincoln's Inn 1994–; chm: Law Cmmn 1996–99, Judges' Cncl Working Pty on Constitutional Reform 2004–06; chm CAB Royal Courts of Justice Charitable Tst 1994–97; inspector Rotaprint plc under sections 432 and 444 of the Companies Act 1985 1988–91; pres: Assoc of Women Barristers 1994–98, Trinity Hall Law Soc 1996, Holdsworth Club Faculty of Law Univ of Birmingham 1999–2000; ed-in-chief Chancery Guide 1995–2000; chair Papers Ctee Cwlth Law Confs 2004–05; memb: Law Soc's Company Law Ctee (ldr Insolvency Working Pty) 1976–, Insolvency Sub-Ctee Consumer and Commercial Law Ctee of Law Soc (previously Jt Working Pty of the Bar and the Law Soc on Insolvency) 1979–97, Financial Law Panel 1993–2000, Bd Inst of Advanced Legal Studies 1996–99, Advsy Cncl for Socio-Legal Studies Univ of Oxford 1996–99, Steering Gp Company Law Review Project DTI 1998–2001, Ed Bd Practical Law for Cos (PLC magazine) 1998–, Common Law/Common Bond Project 1999–2000, Corporate and Commercial Law Advsy Ctee Faculty of Law Univ of Cambridge 1999–; The Times Woman of Achievement Lifetime Award 1997; elector: Herchel Smith Professorship in Intellectual Property Law Univ of Cambridge 1993–94, Downing Professorship of Laws of England 1996–2000, Professorship of English Law Univ of Oxford 1997; hon memb: Soc of Public Teachers of Law 1993–, Soc Tst and Estate Practitioners (STEP) 1996–; academic tstee Kennedy Memorial Tst 1995–2005; hon fell Girton Coll Cambridge 1995–, hon fell Soc for Advanced Legal Studies 1997, memb Inst Advanced Legal Studies 1997–2000; Hon DUniv Essex 1997; Hon LLD: Univ of Liverpool 1998, Royal Holloway and Bedford New Coll London 1999, Univ of Warwick 1999, Univ of Nottingham 2002, Liverpool John Moores Univ 2006; *Publications* contrib to numerous legal reference works, author of numerous articles in legal jls; Buckley on the Companies Acts (jt gen ed, 2000); *Style*— The Rt Hon Lady Justice Arden, DBE, PC; ✉ c/o Royal Courts of Justice, Strand, London WC2A 2LL

ARESTIS, Prof Philip; *b* 24 October 1941, Famagusta, Cyprus; *Educ* Athens Grad Sch of Economics and Business Studies (BA), LSE (MSc), Univ of Surrey (PhD); *Career* pt/t lectr: Kingston Poly 1968–69, Univ of Surrey 1969–80; Thames Poly: lectr in economics 1969–71, sr lectr in economics 1971–77, princ lectr in economics and head Economics Div 1977–88, memb Faculty Bd 1978–81, dep head Sch of Social Sciences 1987–88; prof of economics and head Dept of Applied Economics (later Dept of Economics) NE London Poly (later Poly of East London then Univ of E London) 1988–97 (numerous ctee appts incl chair Research Degrees Ctee 1991–95), research prof of economics Univ of E London 1997–2000, prof of economics and dir of research South Bank Univ Business Sch 2000–02, dir of research Centre of Economic and Public Policy Dept of Land Economy Univ of Cambridge 2004–, sr research fell Wolfson Coll Cambridge 2004– (memb Cncl 2005–); hon research fell Dept of Economics UCL 1991, visiting research fell Univ of N London Business Sch 1998–2000, sr research fell Levy Economics Inst Bard Coll NY 1998–2002 (research prof of economics 2002), visiting prof Dept of Economics Candido Mendes Univ Rio de Janeiro 2000–02, visiting prof of economics Leeds Business Sch Univ of Leeds 2003, professorial research assc Dept of Finance and Mgmnt Studies SOAS 2003, visiting prof of economics Univ of Paris 2004–05; academic conslt Macmillan Publishing Ltd 1997–2002, external advsr to UK Govt Economic Serv 2005–; jt ed Thames Papers in Political Economy 1979–93, ed Br Review of Economic Issues 1982–88 (memb Editorial Bd 1979–88), fndr and jt commissioning ed Int Papers in Political Economy 1993–, assoc ed and memb Editorial Bd Review of Social Economy 1995–, co-ed Ekonomia (formerly Cyprus Jl of Economics) 1996– (memb Editorial Bd 1988–), memb Editorial Advsy Bd EAST-WEST: Jl of Economics and Business 1997–, memb Managing Bd Jl of Post Keynesian Economics 1998–, Eastern Economic Jl 1999, assoc ed Applied Economics 2001– (memb Editorial Bd 1996–), assoc ed and memb Editorial Bd Greek Economic Review 2003–, fndr Int Papers in Political Economy 2005–; memb Editorial Bd: Jl of Economic Issues 1988–91, Review of Political Economy 1988–93, Int Review of Applied Economics 1988–, Applied Economics Letters 1996–, Zagreb Int Review of Economics and Business 1997–; author of numerous pubns in learned jls; memb: Cncl Royal Economic Soc 1994–99, Bd Eastern Economics Assoc USA 2004; memb various CNAA ctees and panels (incl: Economics Bd 1983–87, Social Sciences Research Degrees Sub-Ctee 1984–88), memb various ESRC and ESRC-funded research gps; advsr on economics-related degrees, staff appts and research to numerous univs, colls and polys, memb Hong Kong Cncl for Academic Accreditation 1990; numerous lectures, organiser and chair of confs; govr: Bell Lane Sch Barnet 1985–87, Copthall Sch Barnet 1988–92; memb: Assoc for Poly Teachers in Economics 1971–93, Royal Economic Soc 1982–, Assoc for Evolutionary Economics 1982–, European Assoc for Evolutionary Economics 1988–93, Assoc for Social Economics 1995–, European Soc for the History of Economic Thought 1997–, Athens Inst for Educn and Research 2000–; *Books* Introducing Macroeconomic Modelling: An Econometric Study of the United Kingdom (1982), Post-Keynesian Economic Theory: A Challenge to Neo-Classical Economics (jt ed, 1985), Post-Keynesian Monetary Economics: New Approaches to Financial Modelling (1988), Contemporary Issues in Money and Banking: Essays in Honour of Stephen Frowen (1988), Theory and Policy in Political Economy: Essays in Pricing, Distribution and Growth (jtly, 1990), Business and the UK Cypriot Community (jtly, 1991), Biographical Dictionary of Dissenting Economists (jtly, 1992), Recent Developments in Post-Keynesian Economics (1992), The Post-Keynesian Approach to Economics: An Alternative Analysis of Economic Theory and Policy (1992), On Money, Method and Keynes: Selected Essays by Victoria Chick (jt ed, 1992), Biographical Dictionary of Dissenting Economists (jtly, 1992, 2 edn 2000), Money and Banking: Issues for the 21st Century, Essays in Honour of Stephen Frowen (1993), Handbook of Radical Political Economy (jtly, 1994), The Political Economy of Full Employment: Conservatism, Corporatism and Institutional Change (jtly, 1995), Finance, Development and Structural Change: Post-Keynesian Perspectives (jtly, 1995), Keynes, Money and Open Economies: Essays in Honour of Paul Davidson, Vol 1 (1996), Employment, Economic Growth and the Tyranny of the Market: Essays in Honour of Paul Davidson, Vol 2 (1996), Method, Theory and Policy in Keynes: Essays in Honour of Paul Davidson, Vol 3 (1998), Capital Controversy, Post Keynesian Economics and the History of Economic Theory: Essays in Honour of Geoff Harcourt, Vol 1 (jtly, 1997), Markets, Unemployment and Economic Policy: Essays in Honour of Geoff Harcourt, Vol 2 (jtly, 1997), Money, Pricing, Distribution and Economic Integration (1997), The Relevance of Keynesian Policies Today (1997), The Political Economy of Economic Policies (jtly, 1998), The Political Economy of Central Banking (jtly, 1998), Money and Macroeconomic Policies: Essays in Macroeconomics in Honour of Bernard Corry and Maurice Peston, Vol 1 (jtly, 1999), The History and Practice of Economics: Essays in Honour of Bernard Corry and Maurice Peston, Vol 2 (jtly, 1999), Regulation, Strategies and Economic Policies: Essays in Honour of Bernard Corry and Maurice Peston, Vol 3 (jtly, 1999), What Global Economic Crisis? (jtly, 2001), Money, Finance and Capitalist Development (jtly, 2001), Economics of the Third Way: Experience from Around the World (jtly, 2001), The Euro: Evolution and Prospects (jtly, 2001), Money, Macroeconomics and Keynes: Essays in Honour of Victoria Chick, Vol One (jtly, 2002), Methodology, Microeconomics and Keynes: Essays in Honour of Victoria Chick, Vol Two (jtly, 2002), Monetary Union in South America: Lessons from EMU (jtly, 2003), Globalization, Regionalism and Economic Policy (jtly, 2003), The Post-Bubble US Economy: Implications for Financial Markets and the Economy (jtly, 2004), The Rise of the Market: Critical Essays on the Political Economy of Neo-Liberalism (jtly, 2004), Neo-Liberal Economic Policy: Critical Essays (jtly, 2004), Re-examining Monetary and Fiscal Policies in the Twenty First Century (jtly, 2004), Financial Liberalization: Beyond Orthodox Concerns (jtly, 2005), The New Monetary Policy: Implications and Relevance (jtly, 2005), Financial Developments in National and International Markets (jtly, 2006), Alternative Perspectives on Economic Policies in the European Union (jtly, 2006); *Style*—

Philip Arestis, Esq; ✉ Cambridge Centre for Economic and Public Policy, Department of Land Economy, University of Cambridge, 19 Silver Street, Cambridge CB3 9EP (tel 01223 766971, fax 01223 337130, e-mail pa267@cam.ac.uk)

ARGENT, Denis John; s of Robert Argent (d 1983), and Ellen, *née* Newman (d 1992); *b* 28 August 1943; *Educ* Cardinal Vaughan Sch; *m* 30 July 1966, Marie Rose, da of John Barnard (d 1980); 3 s (Nicholas b 1968, Phillip b 1970, Christopher b 1973), 1 da (Marianne b 1981); *Career* mgmnt conslt Coopers & Lybrand 1972–79, chief accountant Cancer Research Fund 1979–84, co sec Cancer Research Fund Biotechnology Transfer 1984–87, dir of resources Royal Pharmaceutical Soc of GB 1987–2001, dir Waxwell Conslts 2001–; FCCA; *Recreations* rugby, squash, golf, badminton, choral singing, travel; *Clubs* MCC, East India, Harrow Rugby, Pinner Hill Golf, Pinner Rotary; *Style*— Denis Argent, Esq; ✉ 112 Waxwell Lane, Pinner, Middlesex (tel 020 8866 1526)

ARGENT, Douglas; *Career* BBC floor mangr, prodn mangr then dir and prodr; TV series incl: Till Death Us Do Part, Taxi, Feydeau Farces, The Liver Birds, Steptoe and Son, Fawlty Towers (BAFTA award 1979), Crimewriters; freelance 1980; TV series incl: The Cuckoo Waltz, The Schoolmistress, Astronauts, That Beryl Marsden, Union Castle, The Lady is a Tramp, It Takes a Worried Man, Lonelyhearts Kids, Flying Lady, Never the Twain, Anybody for Murder, Edge of Fear, EastEnders; dir corporate video ideas for: Shell Chemicals (UK) Ltd, Lloyds Bank Ltd, Mobil Oil, British Airways, Crown Paints, Guardian Royal Exchange, Trustee Savings Bank; memb: Dirs' Guild of GB, BAFTA (memb Cncl 1978–82, 1984–86 and 1990–91); *Style*— Douglas Argent, Esq; ✉ 21 Kingsbrook Drive, Hillfield, Solihull, West Midlands B91 3UU (tel 0121 705 3105)

ARGYLL, 13 Duke of (S 1701 and UK 1892); Sir Torquhil Ian Campbell; 15 Bt (NS 1627); also Lord Campbell (S 1445), Earl of Argyll (S 1457), Lord Lorne (S 1470), Marquess of Kintyre and Lorne, Earl of Campbell and Cowal, Viscount Lochow and Glenilla, and Lord Inveraray, Mull, Morvern and Tiry (all S 1701), Baron Sundridge (GB 1766), Baron Hamilton (GB 1776), Hereditary Master of HM's Household in Scotland, keeper of the Great Seal of Scotland, keeper of Dunoon, Carrick, Dunstaffnage and Tarbert Castles, Admiral of the Western Coasts and Isles, hereditary sheriff of Argyll, 27 Chief of Clan Campbell; only s of 12 Duke of Argyll (d 2001); *b* 29 May 1968; *Educ* Cargilfield Sch Edinburgh, Glenalmond Coll Perthshire, RAC Cirencester; *m* 8 June 2002, Eleanor Mary *née* Cadbury, da of Peter H G Cadbury; 2 s (Archie Frederick, Marquess of Lorne b 9 March 2004, Lord Rory James b 3 Feb 2006); *Heir* s, Marquess of Lorne; *Career* page of honour to HM The Queen 1981–83; asst land agent Buccleuch Estates Ltd Selkirk 1991–93; sales mangr Grosvenor House (Trust House Forte plc) 1994–96; marketing mangr Casella Far East Ltd Hong Kong 1996–2001, currently with Chivas Brothers (Pernod Ricard) London 2001–; Liveryman Worshipful Co of Distillers 2005; *Clubs* New (Edinburgh), White's; *Style*— His Grace the Duke of Argyll; ✉ Inveraray Castle, Argyll PA32 8XF

ARGYLL AND THE ISLES, Bishop of (RC) 1999–; Rt Rev Ian Murray; s of John Murray (d 1982), and Margaret, *née* Rodgers; *b* 15 December 1932; *Educ* Blairs Coll Aberdeen, Royal Scots Coll Valladolid Spain, Open Univ (BA); *Career* curate: Fife 1956–61, Edinburgh 1961–63; chaplain Univ of Stirling 1970–74, rector Scots Coll Spain 1987–94 (vice-rector 1963–70); parish priest: Cowdenbeath 1978–85, Edinburgh 1985–87, Galashiels 1994–96, Falkirk 1996–99; canon Archdiocese of St Andrew's and Edinburgh 1997; Prelate of Honour 1989; chm Scottish Catholic Int Aid Fund; Knight Cdr (with Star) Equestrian Order of the Holy Sepulchre 2000; *Style*— The Rt Rev the Bishop of Argyll and the Isles; ✉ Bishop's House, Corran Esplanade, Oban PA34 5AB (tel and fax 01631 571395)

ARIF QUADRI, Saleem; s of Dr S A Quadri, and Sayeedunisa Quadri; *b* 28 May 1949; *Educ* Birmingham Coll of Art, RCA (MA); *Career* artist; selected solo exhibitions: Art Heritage Gallery New Delhi 1984, Ipswich Museum 1986, Winchester Art Gallery 1987, Anderson O'Day Gallery London 1988, Laing Art Gallery Newcastle upon Tyne 1991, Birds of Breath (Midland Art Centre Birmingham) 1993, The Downstairs Art Gallery Burnley 1994, Arks Gallery London 1997, Open Studio London 1999, Drawing into Discovery New York 2000, Sensual Songs (Art Exchange Gallery Nottingham) 2003, Shrishti Art Gallery Hyderabad 2006; selected gp exhibitions: Serpentine Gallery Summer Show London 1981, Hayward Annual London and Edinburgh 1982, From Two Worlds (Whitechapel Gallery London and Fruitmarket Gallery Edinburgh) 1986, The Other Story (Hayward Gallery London and tours Wolverhampton Art Gallery and Cornerhouse Manchester) 1989–90, The Third World and Beyond (Art Int Confrontation of Contemporary Galleria Civica D'Arte Contemporánea Marsala Sicily) 1991, Cagnes-sur-Mer Int Exhibition (British Cncl) France; most important works: Itinerary 1972, Dante's Inferno (set of forty) 1980–81, Birds of Aspirations 1989, Birds of Breath 1991–93, Garden of Grace (The Central Library Birmingham) 1995–96, Essence of Oldham 1998, Landscape of Longing (Tate London) 1994–99, Sensual Songs of Sacred Space 2002–03, Invocations (manuscript book) 2002–06; selected collections: Govt Collection London, Ipswich Museum, Arts Cncl of GB, David Villiers Fndn Geneva, Birmingham Museum and City Art Gallery, Manchester City Art Gallery, Preston Museum & Art Gallery, Tate London; selected video and television: Believing People (Tyne Tees TV) 1991, Islam in Britain 1999 (FO); selected awards: prize winner Young Sculptor of the Year Sunday Telegraph Competition 1971, Italian Govt Bursary Florence 1982, Villers David Fndn travel award 1989; curator: Kanu Ghandi's Mahatma (touring exhbn) 1995–, Apna Arts (Galleries of Justice Nottingham) 2002–; *Publications* The Spirit of Tomorrow: interview with the artist in Indian Express (1985), Seed of Celebrations and Moment of Grace in Arts and the Islamic World (text by Dr Sarah Wilson, 1994), The Art of Saleem Arif (text by Sue Hubbard, 1994), Gardens of Grace (text by Mary Rose Beaumont, 1997), India is my Inspiration (website artist statement, 2003); *Recreations* collecting Indian contemporary folk art, photography, travelling; *Style*— Saleem Arif Quadri, Esq; ✉ 1 Boadicea Street, Islington, London N1 0UA (e-mail saleemaquadri@hotmail.com)

ARIS, Brian; *Career* portrait and feature photographer; charity work incl: Save the Children Fund, Prince's Trust, Band Aid, Nordoff Robbins Music Therapy; estab stock library (incl: official portraits of HM The Queen, actors, musicians, pop stars and industrialists); *Recreations* golf; *Style*— Brian Aris, Esq; ✉ Brian Aris Archive, Queens Hall Studios, Faversham, Kent ME13 8QE (tel 01795 597505, e-mail ba@brianarisonline.com, website www.brianarisonline.com)

ARKELL, James Rixon; TD, DL (Wiltshire 1996); s of Peter Arkell, and Anne, *née* Falcon; *b* 28 May 1951; *Educ* Milton Abbey; *m* 7 Sept 1974, Carolyn Jane, da of Charles Ralph Woosnam; 3 s (George b 9 Dec 1978, John b 17 April 1983, Alexander b 15 Aug 1985), 1 da (Emma 6 Feb 1976); *Career* Royal Wiltshire (Yeo) TA 1974, Sqdn-Ldr 1983, 2 i/c 1989, CO Royal Yeo Regt 1993–95; md Arkells Brewery Ltd Swindon; high sheriff of Wiltshire 2004–05; *Recreations* shooting, fishing, hunting, skiing; *Clubs* Cavalry; *Style*— James Arkell, Esq, TD, DL

ARKELL, Julian; OBE (1992); 2 s of William Joscelyn Arkell (d 1958), and Ruby Lilian, *née* Percival (d 1983); *b* 22 October 1934; *Educ* Bryanston, King's Coll Cambridge (MA); *m* 1, 5 Sept 1964 (m dis 1976); 2 da (Claire b 25 Aug 1966, Katie b 8 July 1968); *m* 2, 29 April 1983, Elaine; *Career* Shell-Mex and BP Ltd 1956–62, ptnr Robert Matthew Johnson-Marshall & Partners 1972–86 (partnership sec 1962–72), co sec RMJM 1968 1986–91, dir Applied Service Economics Centre Geneva 1991–; in practice as conslt t/a International Trade and Services Policy (clients have incl: British Invisibles, RMJM Gp, Carana Corp (for US Agency for Int Devpt (USAID)), EC, FCO, Geneva Assoc, Hill & Knowlton, HTSPE (for DfID), Commonwealth Business Cncl, Cwlth Secretariat, ICC, Int

Centre for Trade and Sustainab[...] (IDPM) Manchester, ITC, Maxwe[...] OECD, The Services Gp (TSG) In[...] Nations Inst for Trg and Research (TSD), Inst for Devpt Policy and Mgmnt Ctee RIBA 1974–92, Lotis Ctee BI[...]aterhouseCoopers, Islamic Devpt Bd, Commerce and Industry (LCCI) 1983[...]TAD, UNDP, DTI, UNICE, United Services World Forum Geneva 1992–; [...]Commerce, UPSI; memb: Fees Brussels 1990–94; chm: Euro Community [...]Panel London Chamber of Gp WTO Ctee UNICE 1994–95; Hon R[...]Consts Bureau 1992, Bd ✉ International Trade and Services Policy [...]Working Gp UNICE Spain (tel and fax 00 34 9 71 36 63 [...]1986–93, Servs www.arkell.info) [...]Esq, OBE; [...] Menorca, [...] website

ARKELL, Peter; OBE; s of Sir Noel Arkell, DL (d[...] 1988); *b* 24 January 1923; *m* Anne, da of Michael[...] 3 da (Jane, Alison, Rosalind); *Career* Mil Serv RAF[...] 161 Sqdn (Special Duty) Lysander, Tempsford [...] BURMA; Medal of Distinction USAFE; chm Arkell's[...] Worshipful Co of Brewers; Freeman City of London; [...] country pursuits; *Clubs* Special Forces, RAF, Leander[...] ✉ Whelford Mill, Fairford, Gloucestershire GL7 4DY

ARKWRIGHT, Johnnie; s of Pup Arkwright (d 1989), [...] Guilsborough, Northants; *b* 3 February 1953, Northampto[...] Cambridge; *m* 1999, Arabella, *née* Robb; 2 s (Jack (twin) b[...] 2001), 2 da (Lucy (twin) b 7 Sept 1989, Violet b 4 Nov 200[...] 1983–, Pembroke plc 1986–89, Bibendum Wine Ltd 1988–2[...] 1995–2004, Bowmans Leisure Ltd 2001–; dir Countryside Allia[...] Community Fund 2007–; High Sheriff Warks 2007–08; MRICS 19[...] sports, golf, tennis; *Clubs* White's, Annabel's; *Style*— Johnnie Arkw[...] House, Hatton, Warwick CV35 7LD (tel 01926 843411, fax 0[...] johnniearkwright@hattonworld.com)

ARKWRIGHT, Thomas James; s of Thomas Joseph Arkwright (d 1963), [...] and Mary Edna, *née* Ashurst (d 1995); *b* 22 March 1932; *Educ* Moun[...] Sheffield, Univ of Liverpool (LLB); *m* 27 Aug 1958, (Margaret) Muriel[...] Hague (d 1973), of Wigan, Lancs; 5 da (Louise b 1960, Julie b 1963, Clare[...] b 1968, Helen b 1971), 1 s (Paul b 1962); *Career* admitted slr 1955, Notary P[...] to Sir John B McKaig Liverpool 1950–55; ptnr Cyril Morris & Co (Cyril Morris[...] & Co from 1965) 1957–71, sr ptnr Cyril Morris Arkwright Bolton 1971–92, pra[...] Tom Arkwright & Co Notary Public 1996– (Tom Arkwright & Co Slrs [...] Sheffield Prize for highest slr's finals results (with first class hons), John Mackre[...] Daniel Reardon Prize, Enoch Harvey Prize, Timpron Martin Gold Medal Prize, [...] Bremner Gold Medal Prize, Vice-Chllr of the Duchy of Lancaster Prize; memb Jt Stan[...] Ctee Law Soc and HM Land Registry 1972–91; pres: Bolton Catholic Musical and Ch[...] Soc 1968–2003 (pres emeritus 2003–), Bolton C of C and Industry 1971–73, Bolton La[...] Soc 1972, Bolton West Cons Assoc 1973–76 and 1989–93 (sec 1961–66, tstee 1965–9[...] chm 1966–71, treas 1981–84, hon life vice-pres); hon slr Northern Mill Engine Soc 1968[...] (hon life memb 1997), dep pres Bolton Coronary Care 1970–2002, dep treas NW Cons [...] Pty 1972–73, chm NW C of C and Industry 1973, treas and mangr NW Catholic History[...] Soc 1987–90 (hon life memb 1990), memb Ctee Friends of Lancashire Archives 1992–99 [...] (hon sec 1992–95), memb Ctee Chorley Civic Soc 1995–2001 (treas 1996–2001), memb Bd [...] of Mgmnt Broughton Catholic Charitable Soc 1995– (pres 1975), chm Mount St Mary's [...] Coll Sheffield Centenary Further Educn Fund 1986–, govr Mount St Mary's Coll Sheffield [...] 1992–96, treas The Mount Assoc 1995–2005 (pres 1994–95); memb: Law Soc 1955, [...] Notaries Soc 1960; local history author; *Publications* Quarterly series: The Local Catholic [...] Gentry, The Trafford Family of Croston, The Church of St Bede Clayton Green, The [...] Blessed Roger Wrennall; *Recreations* historical studies and writing, genealogy, industrial [...] archaeology, canal walking, gardening and garden design; *Style*— Thomas Arkwright, [...] Esq; ✉ Ivy Cottage, Limbrick, Chorley, Lancashire PR6 9EE (business tel and fax 01257 [...] 233000, e-mail tom.arkwright2@virgin.net)

ARLIDGE, Anthony John; QC; s of John Maurice Arlidge, (d 1985) of Sidcup, and Doris [...] Lilian, *née* Whitecross (d 1984); *b* 18 February 1937; *Educ* Chislehurst and Sidcup GS, [...] Queen's Coll Cambridge; *m* 12 Aug 1964 (sep), Enid Beryl Townsend; 2 da (Catherine b [...] 24 May 1966, Victoria b 1 May 1971), 2 s (John b 5 Nov 1968, Mathew 10 Oct 1974); [...] *Career* barr; called to the Bar Middle Temple 1962, recorder of the Crown Court 1979–99, [...] QC 1981; treas Middle Temple 2002; *Publications* Contempt of Court (with Eady and [...] Smith), Fraud (with Parry), Shakespeare and the Prince of Love; *Recreations* sport, [...] theatre, gardening; *Style*— Anthony Arlidge, Esq, QC

ARLINGTON, Baroness (E 1672); Jennifer Jane Forwood; da of Maj-Gen Sir (Eustace) John [...] Blois Nelson, KCVO, CBE, DSO, MC (d 1993), and Lady (Margaret) Jane Nelson, *née* [...] Fitzroy (d 1995); suc on termination of abeyance 1999; *b* 7 May 1939, London; *Educ* [...] Downham Sch Hatfield Heath; *m* 8 Dec 1964, Rodney Simon Dudley Forwood (d 1995); [...] 2 s (Hon Patrick John Dudley b 23 April 1967, Hon James Roland Nelson b 16 March [...] 1969); *Heir* s, Hon Patrick Forwood; *Recreations* bridge, gardening, horse racing; *Clubs* [...] Sloane; *Style*— The Rt Hon the Baroness Arlington

ARMAGH, Archbishop of and Primate of All Ireland 2007–; Most Rev Alan Edwin Thomas [...] Harper; OBE (1996); s of Thomas Henry Harper (d 1987), and Maria Muriel, *née* Collins; [...] *b* 20 March 1944; *Educ* Queen Elizabeth's GS Tamworth, Univ of Leeds (BA), Univ of [...] Dublin (Divinity Testimonium); *m* 23 Sept 1967, Helen Louise, *née* McLean; 3 da [...] (Catherine Sarah b 1968, Emma Louise b 1976, Anne Frances b 1976), 1 s (Richard [...] Patrick Edwin b 1971); *Career* map curator and librarian Dept of Geography Univ of [...] Leeds 1965–66, sr inspr Historic Monuments NI 1966–74; ordained 1978; rector Moville [...] Gp of Parishes 1980–82, rector Christ Church Londonderry 1982–86, rector Malone [...] 1986–2002, archdeacon of Connor 1996–2002, bishop of Connor 2002–07; canon St [...] Patrick's Nat Cathedral 1990–2000; founding chm Ulster Historic Churches Tst, memb [...] Historic Monuments Cncl for NI 1980–96 (chm 1989–96); *Recreations* music, reading, [...] history, archaeology, gardening; *Clubs* Ulster Reform (Belfast); *Style*— The Most Rev the [...] Archbishop of Armagh, OBE; ✉ Church House, 46 Abbey Street, Armagh BT61 7DZ [...] (tel 028 3752 7144, e-mail archbishop@armagh.anglican.org); 5 Beresford Row, Armagh [...] BT61 9AU (tel 028 3752 2851)

ARMAGH, Archbishop of (RC), and Primate of All Ireland 1996–; Most Rev Sean Brady; [...] *b* 16 August 1939; *Educ* St Patrick's Coll Cavan, St Patrick's Coll Maynooth (BA, [...] HDipEd), Pontifical Irish Coll Rome, Lateran Univ Rome (STL, DCL); *Career* ordained [...] priest 1964; prof St Patrick's Coll Cavan 1967–80, vice-rector Irish Coll Rome 1980–87, [...] rector 1987–93, parish priest Castletara Co Cavan 1993–95, co-adjutor archbishop of [...] Armagh 1995–96; chm Irish Episcopal Conf and Standing Ctee 1996–, chm of Episcopal [...] Visitors to and tstees of St Patrick's Coll Maynooth 1996–2000; *Style*— The Most Rev [...] the Archbishop of Armagh; ✉ Ara Coeli, Armagh BT61 7QY (tel 028 3752 2045, fax [...] 028 3752 6182, e-mail admin@aracoeli.com)

ARMATRADING, Joan Anita Barbara; MBE (2001); da of Amos Ezekiel Armatrading, and [...] Beryl Madge, *née* Benjamin; *b* 9 December 1950; *Educ* Secdy Sch Birmingham, BA; [...] *Career* singer and songwriter; first album Whatever's For Us 1972 (with Pam Nestor), [...] stage debut Fairfield Hall Croydon 1972, first non-jazz act downstairs at Ronnie Scott's [...] 1973, first major hit Love and Affection 1976, first Gold album Joan Armatrading 1976 album Into the Blue debuted at number 1 on USA Billboard Blues Chart 2007; numerous silver, gold and platinum discs; concerts: Blackbush with Bob Dylan (before 100,000 plus audience) 1978, Prince's Tst 1982 and 1986, Amnesty Int (Giant Stadium) 1986, Amnesty Int (Secret Policeman's Ball) 1987, Nelson Mandela's 70th Birthday 1988, First King's Tst Swaziland 1989 and 1990; Ivor Novello Award for Best Contemporary Song Collection 1996; nominated: Grammy Best Female Vocal 1980 and 1983, Best Female Vocal UK 1976 and 1983, Best Female Artist Brit Awards 1995; voted one of the top 100 influential women in rock VH1; Key to Sydney 1983, guest of honour St Kitt's Independence Celebration 1983; wrote special tribute song for Nelson Mandela, performed LSE April 2000; pres Women of the Year UK 2005–; hon fell Liverpool John Moores Univ, hon fell Univ of Northampton, Hon Dr Univ of Birmingham, Hon DLitt Aston Univ Birmingham 2006; *Recreations* reading British comics, owner of two vintage cars; *Style*— Miss Joan Armatrading, MBE; ✉ website www.joanarmatrading.com

ARME, Prof Christopher; s of Cyril Boddington Arme, of Smalley, Derbys, and Monica Henriette, *née* Hawkins; *b* 10 August 1939; *Educ* Heanor GS, Univ of Leeds (BSc, PhD), Keele Univ (DSc); *Children* 3 s (Patrick b 16 May 1965, Mark b 19 April 1967, Peter b 12 Aug 1969); *Career* SRC/NATO res fell Univ of Leeds 1964–66, res fell Rice Univ Houston 1966–68, lectr/reader in zoology Queen's Univ Belfast 1968–76, princ lectr in biology and head of biology N Staffs Poly 1976–79, prof of zoology Keele Univ 1979–, secondment as dir of terrestrial and freshwater sciences NERC 1993–95, dean of natural sciences Keele Univ 1998–2001; Br Soc of Parasitology: memb, Silver Jubilee lectr 1987, pres 1990–92, hon memb 1992; memb: American Soc of Parasitology, Zoological Soc London, Linnean Soc, Inst of Biology (hon treas 1986–93); hon memb Czechoslovak Parasitological Soc 1990, hon memb All Russia Soc of Helminthologists 1992, hon treas Euro Fedn of Parasitologists 1992; K I Skryabin Medal 1995, Charter Award Inst of Biology 1995; Hon DSc Slovak Acad of Sciences 1995; *Publications* author of several books and over 100 scientific pubns incl Parasitology (ed with R S Phillips); *Style*— Prof Christopher Arme; ✉ School of Life Sciences, Keele University, Keele, Staffordshire ST5 5BG (tel 01782 583025, fax 01782 583516, e-mail c.arme@keele.ac.uk)

ARMES, Timothy Joseph Patrick; s of Harry Armes (d 1986), and Teresa, *née* O'Mahony; *b* 1 October 1953; *Educ* St Richard of Chichester Sch, Westminster Tech Coll (ONC), The City Univ; *m* 14 July 1989, Susan McKenzie, da of John Self (d 1996), of Oxted, Surrey; 1 da (Olivia Charlotte McKenzie b 31 March 1990), 1 s (Henry Timothy Alexander b 30 Nov 1991); *Career* advertising exec; J Walter Thompson 1976–78 (trainee buyer rising to media buyer), media gp head MWK & P 1978–83, media gp dir Young & Rubicam 1983–89, devpt dir The Media Shop 1990–92; MediaVest (formerly The Media Centre): media gp dir 1992–95, dir of press buying/bd dir 1995–98, gp account dir 1998–99, client services dir 1999–2001, mktg dir 2001–; memb Exec Ctee The Media Circle; tstee MB&B Gp Pension Scheme 2002–; parent rep to bd of tstees Royal Sch 2002–; *Recreations* cricket, horse racing, wine, collecting antiques, being a father, opera, theatre, cinema, restaurants, travel; *Clubs* RAC, MCC; *Style*— Timothy Armes, Esq; ✉ MediaVest Ltd, Pembroke Building, Kensington Village, Avonmore Road, London W14 8DG (tel 020 7751 1661, fax 020 7071 1016, e-mail lord.armes@mediavest.co.uk)

ARMFIELD, Diana Maxwell; da of (Joseph) Harold Armfield (d 1981), of Ty Newydd, Gwynedd, and Gertrude Mary, *née* Uttley (d 1983); *b* 11 June 1920; *Educ* Bedales, Slade Sch, Central Sch of Arts and Crafts; *m* 12 Feb 1949, (Andrew Harold) Bernard Dunstan, RA, *qv*, s of Dr Albert Ernest Dunstan (d 1960), of Cambridge; 3 s (Andrew Joseph b 1950, David James b 1952, Robert Maxwell b 1955); *Career* painter; cultural activities organiser Miny of Supply 1942–46; tutor: Textile Dept Central Sch Art 1949–50, Byam Shaw Art Sch 1959–90; visiting tutor various art schs 1959–91, reg exhibitor Royal Acad 1966–; memb Cncl Royal Acad 1991–92; exhibitor: Festival of Britain 1951, Tonic for the Nation (V&A), Diana Armfield's Choice (Albany Gallery Cardiff) 1991, Albany Gallery Cardiff 1995, Glyn-Y-Weddw Llanbedrog N Wales 1995; artist in residence: Perth W Aust 1985, Jackson Wyoming USA 1989; NEAC Centenary Sothebys' 1986; one man show: Browse & Darby London 1979–2006, Bala 1997, Gall Gérard Wassenaar Holland 1998, Art of the Garden (Lampeter Univ of Wales) 2000, Royal Cambrian Acad 2001, Albany Gallery Cardiff 2001 and 2006, Curwen & New Acad Gallery (etchings) 2005; perm collections: V&A (textiles), cmmns Reuters 1986–87, Contemporary Art Soc Wales 1987, Nat Tst 1988–89, HRH Prince of Wales 1989, Farringdon Tst, Yale Center for British Art, Govt Picture Collection, Br Museum, Royal Watercolour Soc, Lancaster Co Museum, Royal W England Acad, Royal Acad Diploma Collection, Mercury Asset Mgmnt; retrospective exhbn RA 1995; group exhibitions: Hollis Taggart Gallery Washington DC 1993, Barneys Greenwich Connecticut USA 1993 and 1995, Women Artists of Wales (Albany Gallery) 2002; guest artist S Wales Acad of Fine and Applied Art 2002; buyer for Contemporary Art Soc Wales 1990–91; memb: Cncl of the Protection of Rural Wales, Friends of the Earth; subject of book 'The Art of Diana Armfield' by Julian Halsby 1995; MCSD 1951, memb Royal Cambrian Acad (hon ret academician), memb NEAC 1970 (hon memb 2001), RWA 1975 (hon ret), RWS 1980, RA 1991 (ARA 1989); *Books* Painting In Oils (1982); *Recreations* musical appreciation, gardening; *Clubs* Arts; *Style*— Miss Diana Armfield, RA; ✉ 10 High Park Road, Kew, Richmond, Surrey TW9 4BH (tel and fax 020 8876 6633); Llwynhir, Parc, Bala, Gwynedd (tel 01678 540289)

ARMIGER, Paul Gower; s of Wing Cdr Brian Armiger, OBE, of Edinburgh, and Peggy Joyce, *née* Oldfield; *b* 25 August 1942; *Educ* Karachi GS India, Cranbrook Sydney Aust, Haileybury and ISC, Bloxham Sch; *m* 28 June 1964, Patricia Gillian, da of Sqdn Ldr Charles Clinch; 2 s (Andrew Gower b 9 April 1968, Steven Paul b 21 Feb 1971); *Career* photographer; staff photographer Montgomery Advertiser and Alabama Journal USA 1960–61, freelance photographer Washington DC (work for Time, Life, Newsweek, Washington Post, Nat Geographic) 1961–64, freelance photographer The Daily Telegraph London 1965, staff photographer The Daily Telegraph 1967–97 (semi retirement 1997); assignments covered for The Daily Telegraph incl: NI 1969–74, Darien Gap Expedition 1971; estab Paul Armiger Photography Flushing Cornwall 1997; hon memb Naval Air Cmd Sub Aqua Club, fndr memb Br Soc of Underwater Photographers 1969, memb Underwater Archaeological Expeditions Assoc Hollandia Colossus 1967–72; second class diver BSAC 1970, holder commercial diver's licence (Part IV Diver at work) 1980; *Recreations* scuba diving, photography, golf, model shipwright (18th century ship models); *Clubs* Press (Washington and London), Royal Over-Seas League, Flushing Sailing, Royal Cornwall Yacht; *Style*— Paul Armiger, Esq

ARMITAGE, Edward Phillip (Phil); s of Leslie Armitage, of Barnsley, and Alice Emily, *née* Dufton; *b* 20 January 1947; *Educ* Barnsley Holgate GS, Univ of Sussex (BSc, MSc, MA); *m* 24 Aug 1974, Elizabeth, da of Joseph Blackburn Sweeney; 1 s (Richard John b 27 Dec 1978), 1 da (Jennifer Elizabeth b 16 Oct 1980); *Career* Lt Cdr RD RNR; sr lectr in statistics Coventry Poly 1968–78, res fell in student assessment Open Univ 1978–85, dir educn and training ICAEW 1985–2002, Govt Statistical Service 2002–; *Recreations* music, bridge, fell walking; *Style*— Phil Armitage, Esq; ✉ West Ridge, Aspley Guise, Milton Keynes MK17 8DX (tel 01908 584473, e-mail lizandphil@amitage.uk.com)

ARMITAGE, Simon Robert; s of Peter Armitage, and Audrey May Armitage, of Huddersfield, W Yorks; *b* 26 May 1963; *Educ* Colne Valley HS, Portsmouth Poly (BA), Univ of Manchester (CQSW, MA); *Career* probation offr Greater Manchester Probation Serv, sr lectr Manchester Met Univ; ed Poetry Chatto & Windus; wrote lyrics for Feltham Sings (film) 2002; Eric Gregory Award, Forward Poetry Prize 1992, Sunday Times Young Writer of the Year 1993; for Feltham Sings: Ivor Novello Award, BAFTA; Hon DLitt: Univ of Huddersfield 1996, Univ of Portsmouth 1996; *Poetry Collections* Zoom! (1989, Poetry Book Soc Choice), Xanadu (1992), Kid (1992), Book of Matches (1993), The Dead Sea Poems (1995), CloudCuckooland (shortlisted Whitbread Poetry Award 1997), Killing Time (1999), Selected Poems (2001), The Universal Home Doctor (2002), Travelling Songs (2002), The Odyssey: A Retelling (2006), Tyrannosaurus Rex versus the Corduroy Kid (2006), Sir Gawain and the Green Knight (trans, 2007); *Prose* All Points North (1998), Little Green Man (2001), The White Stuff (2004); *Recreations* as expected; *Style*— Simon Armitage; ✉ c/o David Godwin Associates, 55 Monmouth Street, London WC2H 9DG (tel 020 7240 9992)

ARMITAGE, Dr (John) Vernon; s of Horace Armitage, and Evelyn, *née* Hauton; through his mother, Dr Armitage is 2 cous of Baron Richardson of Duntisbourne (Life Peer), *qv*; *b* 21 May 1932; *Educ* Rothwell GS, UCL (BSc, PhD), Cuddesdon Theol Coll; *m* 1963, Sarah Catherine Clay; 2 s (Jonathan Mark, Nicholas Richard); *Career* asst master: Pontefract HS 1956–58, Shrewsbury Sch 1958–59; lectr in maths Univ of Durham 1959–67, sr lectr in maths King's Coll London 1967–70, prof of mathematical educn Univ of Nottingham 1970–75 (special prof 1976–79); Univ of Durham: princ Coll of St Hild and St Bede 1975–97, dean of colls 1988–93, hon sr fell mathematical sciences 1997–; chm Mathematical Instruction Sub-Ctee Br Nat Ctee for Maths Royal Soc 1975–78; *Publications* A Companion to Advanced Mathematics (with H B Griffiths, 1969); papers on theory of numbers in professional jls; *Recreations* railways, cricket and most games; *Style*— Dr Vernon Armitage; ✉ 7 Potters Close, Potters Bank, Durham DH1 3UB (tel 0191 384 4028)

ARMITSTEAD, Claire Louise; da of Charles Henry Wilfrid Armitstead (d 1996), of Haywards Heath, W Sussex, and Gillian Louise, *née* Bartley (d 1987); *b* 2 December 1958; *Educ* Bedales, St Hilda's Coll Oxford (BA); *m* 17 Sept 1983, John Christopher Yandell, s of Canon Owen James Yandell; 1 s (Arthur James Armitstead b 7 Sept 1990), 1 da (Rosa Louise Armitstead b 11 June 1993); *Career* journalist; sub-ed and theatre critic: South Wales Argus Newport 1983–84 (trainee reporter The News 1980–83), Hampstead & Highgate Express 1984–89; theatre critic The Financial Times 1986–92; The Guardian: theatre critic 1992–96, arts ed 1995–99, literary ed 1999–; memb: NUJ 1980, Critics' Circle 1990, Int Assoc of Theatre Critics 1988; *Recreations* finding time to read novels and keep fit; *Style*— Ms Claire Armitstead; ✉ The Guardian, 119 Farringdon Road, London EC1R 3ER (tel 020 7278 2332, fax 020 7713 4366)

ARMOUR, Prof Sir James; kt (1995), CBE (1989); s of James Angus Armour (d 1948), and Margaret Brown, *née* Roy (d 1959); *b* 17 September 1929; *Educ* Marr Coll Troon, Univ of Glasgow (MRCVS, PhD, Golf blue); *m* 1, 1953, Irene (d 1988), da of Arthur Brunton Morris (d 1971); 2 da (Linda Margaret 17 June 1954, Fiona Marion 22 Sept 1957), 2 s (Donald George b 10 Dec 1955, Malcolm Craig 30 Sept 1961); m 2, 1992, Christine McTavish Strickland; *Career* research offr Colonial Vet Serv Nigeria 1953–60, vet researcher Cooper McDougall & Robertson 1960–63; Univ of Glasgow: research fell 1963–67, lectr in vet parasitology 1967–71, sr lectr 1971–73, reader 1973–76, prof 1976–95, vice-princ 1990–95; chm: Vet Products Ctee 1987–95, Governing Body Inst for Animal Health 1990–95, Glasgow Dental Hosp and Sch NHS Tst 1995–99; vice-pres RSE 1997–2000; chm Moredun Fndn for Animal Health and Welfare 2000–05, chm St Andrews Clinics for Children in Africa 2000–; RCVS: memb 1952, fell 1995, John Henry Steel Medal; BVA: memb 1952, Wooldridge Medal, Chiron Award; Bledisloe Award RASE, Pfizer Award for research World Assoc for Vet Parasitology, Bicentenary Medal RSE; Dr (hc) Univ of Utrecht 1981, DVMS (hc) Univ of Edinburgh 1995, Hon DUniv Glasgow 2001, Hon DUniv Stirling 2005; FRSE 1990; FMedSci 1998, Hon FIBiol 2001; *Books* Veterinary Parasitology (1988, 2 edn 1995); *Recreations* golf (Br Boys Champion 1947), watching football and rugby; *Clubs* Royal Troon, Turnberry Golf; *Style*— Prof Sir James Armour, CBE, FRSE, FMedSci; ✉ 4B Towans Court, Prestwick KA9 2AY (tel and fax 01292 470869)

ARMOUR, Robert Malcolm; OBE (2007), WS; *b* 25 September 1959, Edinburgh; *Educ* Edinburgh Univ (LLB, MBA); *m* 26 June 1987, Anne; *Career* admitted slr 1983, NP 1984; ptnr Wright Johnston & Mackenzie 1986–90, co sec Scottish Nuclear 1990–95 (dir of performance devpt 1993–95); British Energy Gp plc (formerly British Energy plc): co sec 1995–, dir of corp affrs 1997–2003, gen counsel 2000–; dir Nuclear Industries Assoc, memb Civil Nuclear Police Authy; memb Bd Scottish Cncl for Devpt and Industry; In House Lawyer of the Year The Lawyer Awards 2005; memb Law Soc of Scotland; *Recreations* golf; *Clubs* New (Edinburgh); *Style*— Mr Robert Armour, OBE; ✉ British Energy Group plc, Systems House, Alba Campus, Livingston EH54 7EG (e-mail robert.armour@british-energy.com)

ARMSON, (Frederick) Simon Arden; s of Frank Gerald Arden Armson (d 1982), and Margaret Fenella, *née* Newton (d 2002); *b* 11 September 1948; *Educ* Denstone Coll, Univ of London (MSc), Dip Clinical Psychotherapy, Dip NLP; *m* 8 Feb 1975, Marion Albinia, da of David Hamilton-Russell (d 1988), and Pauline, *née* Slade; 3 c (Meriel Albinia b 1979, Patrick David Arden b 1982, Katharine Geraldine b 1984); *Career* early trg in health serv mgmnt, various managerial and admin posts NHS 1970–84; pt/t lectr in NHS industrial rels Oxford Poly 1977–82; The Samaritans: asst gen sec 1984–89, gen sec 1989–90, chief exec 1990–2004; dir Samaritan Enterprises Ltd 1996–2004; chm: Telephone Helpline Gp 1992–96, BBC Radio Helpline Advsy Cncl 1995–98, CancerBacup Service Devpt Advsy Ctee 1998–2001; memb: Exec Ctee ACENVO 1992–94, Steering Ctee for Structure Review of Br Red Cross Soc 1995–96, Suicide Prevention Sub-Gp Dept of Health Wider Health Working Gp 1995–97, RCN Men's Health Forum 1995–97, Steering Gp BT Forum for Better Communications Res Project into effective communication in young people 1995–98, Advsy Ctee Inst for Volunteer Research 1996–2001; Mental Health Act cmmr 2002–, memb Bd Mental Health Act Cmmn 2004–, lay memb Mental Health Review Tribunal 2006–; tstee: ChildLine 1999–2006, Broadcasting Support Servs 2003–, Mental Health Media 2004–, Nat Nightline 2005–06 (hon assoc 2006), Maytree Respite Centre 2005–; hon memb Telephone Helplines Assoc 1999; chm Panel of Judges: Guardian Jerwood Award 1995–99, Guardian Charity Award 2000–04; memb: Ringel Award Ctee 2001–03, Int Assoc for Suicide Prevention (IASP) 2001–03 (chair Nat Dels, memb Exec Ctee, UK nat rep 1996–2003), Suicide Prevention Advsy Gp 2001–04, Ind Ctee for the Supervision of Standards of Telephone Info Servs (ICSTIS) 2001–07, Nat Inst for Clinical Excellence (NICE) 2003–04, Self-Harm Guidelines Devpt Gp; pres Mid-Thames branch CMI 2006–; memb UK Cncl for Psychotherapists (UKCP) 2003; FRSA 1993, CCMI (CIMgt 1995); *Publications* International Handbook of Suicide and Attempted Suicide (contrib, 2000), Every Family in the Land (contrib, 2004), Prevention and Treatment of Suicidal Behaviour (contrib, 2005), Relating to Self-harm and Suicide: Psychoanalytic Perspectives on Practice, Theory and Research (2007); *Recreations* sailing, skiing, walking, music, cycling (cross country); *Clubs* Reform; *Style*— Simon Armson, Esq; ✉ Broad Oak, Hurley, Maidenhead, Berkshire SL6 5LW (tel 01628 824322, e-mail armson@btinternet.com)

ARMSTRONG, Andrew Charles; s of Terence George Armstrong, of Linton, Cambs, and Marion, *née* Rigg; *b* 15 March 1959; *Educ* Newport GS Essex; *m* 4 July 1981, Jacqueline Mary, da of Anthony Rokeby Roberts, of Stansted, Essex; 2 s (Robert Charles b 1985, David Alexander b 1989); *Career* JPMorgan 1978–; *Recreations* flying, skiing; *Style*— A C Armstrong, Esq; ✉ JPMorgan, PO Box 127, JPMorgan House, Grenville Street, St Helier, Jersey (tel 01534 626335, fax 01534 768906)

ARMSTRONG, Very Rev Christopher; s of John Armstrong, and Susan Elizabeth Armstrong; *b* 18 December 1947; *Educ* Dunstable GS, Bede Coll Durham (CertEd), Kelham Theol Coll, Univ of Nottingham (BTh); *m* 3 Jan 1976, Geraldine; 1 da (Sarah b

2 June 1978), 2 s (Jonathan b 1 Feb 1980, Simon b 23 July 1985); *Career* teacher Brewers Hill Sch Dunstable 1969–72; asst curate All Saints Maidstone 1975–79, chaplain St Hild and St Bede Coll Durham 1979–85, domestic chaplain to Archbishop of York and Diocesan Dir of Ordinands 1985–91, incumbent Scarborough St Martin Dio of York 1991–2001, dean of Blackburn 2001–; selector: ACCM, Anglican Bd of Mission (ABM); memb General Synod 2003–05, memb House of Bishops Inspectorate 2003–; various chaplaincies to police, theatre and univ depts 1991–2001; chm Scarborough Christian Aid Ctee 1996–98, chm of govrs St Martin's Aided Deanery Jr Sch 1991–99, memb N Yorks LEA 1997–99, govr The Friends of the Anglican Centre Rome 1996–; *Recreations* sport, mountaineering, theatre, music, gardening, travel; *Style*— The Very Rev the Dean of Blackburn; ✉ The Deanery, Preston New Road, Blackburn, Lancashire BB2 6PS (e-mail armstrong@deanery2001.fsnet.co.uk); office tel 01254 503090, fax 01254 689666

ARMSTRONG, Lt-Col Sir Christopher John Edmund Stuart; 7 Bt (UK 1841), of Gallen Priory, King's Co; MBE (1979); s of Sir Andrew Clarence Francis Armstrong, 6 Bt, CMG (d 1997); *b* 15 January 1940; *Educ* Ampleforth, RMA; *m* 1972, Georgina Elizabeth Carey, 2 da of late Lt-Col W G Lewis, of Hayling Island; 3 s (Charles Andrew b 1973, James Hugo b 1974, Sam Edward b 1986), 1 da (Victoria Jane b 1980); *Heir* s, Charles Armstrong; *Career* Lt-Col RLC; *Style*— Lt-Col Sir Christopher Armstrong, Bt, MBE

ARMSTRONG, Christopher Paul (Kit); s of Robert Armstrong, of Preston, Lancs, and Pauline, *née* Moreland; *b* 19 October 1955; *Educ* Univ of Edinburgh (MB ChB, MD); *Children* 1 s (James Robert b 25 July 1986), 1 da (Charlotte Beth b 25 Dec 1988); *Career* trg in surgery various hosps (Edinburgh, Cape Town, Manchester, Bristol), consltsurgn Frenchay Hosp Bristol 1990–; specialist in laparoscopic surgery for gallstones, hiatus hernia and hernia; author of numerous pubns on the subject of surgery; FRCSEd 1982, FRCS 1984; *Style*— Kit Armstrong, Esq; ✉ Department of Surgery, Frenchay Hospital, Beckspool Road, Frenchay, Bristol BS16 1lE; Bupa Hospital, Bristol BS6 6UT

ARMSTRONG, Craig; s of John Armstrong, and Barbara, *née* MacKenzie; *b* 29 April 1959; *Educ* Royal Acad of Music London (Charles Lucas Prize, Harvey Lohr Scholarship); *m* Laura; 3 s (Niall, Stefano, Jack), 1 da (Angelina); *Career* composer and arranger; resident student composer London Contemporary Dance Theatre 1980, music and dance specialist Strathclyde Regnl Cncl 1982; cmmns incl: Arts Cncl 1985, Third Eye Centre 1988, Tron Theatre Co Glasgow 1988 and 1993, Scottish Chamber Orch 1989, RSC 1994, BT Ensemble 1999, Hebrides Ensemble 2000, Royal Scottish Nat Opera 2001; film scores incl: Romeo and Juliet 1996 (Anthony Asquith BAFTA Award 1996, Ivor Novello Award 1996), Orphans 1997, Plunkett & Macleane 1999, Best Laid Plans 1999, One Day in September 1999, The Bone Collector 1999 (ASCAP Award 1999), Moulin Rouge 2001 (World Soundtrack Award 2001, American Film Inst Award 2001, Australian IF Award 2001, Golden Globe 2002), Kiss Of The Dragon 2001 (Discovery of the Year Award 2001), The Quiet American 2002 (Ivor Novello Award 2002), The Magdalene Sisters 2003, Wimbledon 2004, Layer Cake 2004; sometime memb pop bands Hipsway, Texas and The Big Dish, worked with numerous artists incl Hole, Melanie C and Massive Attack; solo albums: The Space Between Us 1998, As If To Nothing 2002; GLAA Young Jazz Musician of the Year Award 1980; hon research fell Univ of Glasgow; FTCL, ARAM; *Style*— Craig Armstrong, Esq; ✉ Symphonic Ltd, 38 Park Terrace Lane, Glasgow G3 6BQ (tel 0141 331 2878, fax 0141 331 2906, e-mail symphonic.music@virgin.net)

ARMSTRONG, Prof David Millar; s of James Armstrong (d 1990), and Jean Alexandra, *née* Millar (d 1998); *b* 25 May 1941; *Educ* Workington GS, Univ of Oxford (BA, BSc), Australian Nat Univ (PhD); *m* 12 Aug 1964, Lucinda Russell, da of George Graham Kennedy (d 1955); 1 da (Katherine Anne b 1965), 1 s (James Graham b 1966); *Career* Univ of Bristol: lectr 1968–78, reader 1978–84, prof of physiology 1984–2004, head of dept 1990–95 and 2003–04, emeritus prof and sr research fell 2004–; memb: Neurosciences and Mental Health Bd MRC 1987–91, Trg Awards Ctee MRC 1989–93; memb: Marine Biological Assoc 1965, Physiological Soc 1968; *Recreations* walking, reading, social and medical historical research; *Style*— Prof David Armstrong; ✉ Department of Physiology, School of Medical Sciences, University of Bristol, University Walk, Bristol BS8 1TD (tel 0117 928 9101, fax 0117 928 8923, e-mail d.m.armstrong@bristol.ac.uk)

ARMSTRONG, Dr Ernest McAlpine (Mac); CB (2005); s of Ernest Armstrong (d 1988), and Mary Brownlie McLean, *née* McAlpine (d 1980); *b* 3 June 1945; *Educ* Hamilton Acad, Univ of Glasgow (BSc, MB, ChB); *m* 15 July 1970, Dr Katherine Mary Dickson, da of Dr William C Young; 2 s (Euan McAlpine b 1 March 1972, Neil William b 4 Feb 1976); *Career* jr house offr Glasgow 1970–71, lectr in pathology Univ of Glasgow 1971–74, princ in general practice Connel 1975–93, sec BMA 1993–2000, chief med offr Scottish Exec 2001–05; trainer in general practice 1980–90; FRCP (Glasgow), FRCPEd, FRCGP, FFPHM, FRCSEd; *Recreations* music, travelling, sailing; *Clubs* Caledonian; *Style*— Dr Mac Armstrong, CB

ARMSTRONG, Fiona Kathryn (Lady MacGregor of MacGregor); da of Robert Armstrong, of Cumbria, and Pauline, *née* Moreland; *b* 28 November 1956; *Educ* St Thomas Moore Sch Preston, Tuson Coll Preston, UCL; *m* 14 May 2005, Sir Malcolm MacGregor of MacGregor, Bt, *qv*; *Career* reporter Radio 210 Reading 1980–82, journalist BBC TV Manchester 1982–85, reporter Border TV Cumbria 1985–87, newscaster ITN 1987–92, presenter GMTV 1992–93, freelance 1993– (incl antiques, lifestyle, fishing and political progs for ITV and Sky); md Border Heritage TV Prodn Co; pres: NSPCC N Cumbria, Jigsaw Appeal; dir Clan Armstrong Tst; tstee: Second Chance Charity, Kingmore Tst; memb: Salmon and Trout Assoc, Tyburn Angling Soc; hon fell Univ of Central Lancs; *Books* 'F' is for Flyfishing (1993), The Commuter's Cookbook (1995), Let's Start Flyfishing (1999), Big Food for Wee Macs (2004); *Recreations* fishing, cooking; *Clubs* Reform; *Style*— Ms Fiona Armstrong; ✉ tel 01387 371780, e-mail fiona@borderheritage.co.uk; c/o Knight Ayton Management, 114 St Martin's Lane, London WC2N 4BE (tel 020 7836 5333, fax 020 7836 8333, e-mail info@knightayton.co.uk)

ARMSTRONG, Frank William; s of Frank Armstrong (d 1965), and Millicent Armstrong (d 1989); *b* 26 March 1931; *Educ* Stretford GS, Royal Tech Coll Salford, QMC London (MSc); *m* 1957, Diane Tranter, da of Stanley Varley, and Doreen Varley; 3 da (Catherine Mary b 6 Nov 1961, Jennifer Clare b 10 June 1963, Rachel Jane b 23 April 1967); *Career* engrg trg Massey-Harris Ltd Manchester 1947–51, QMCl London 1951–56, tech asst De Havilland Engine Co Edgware 1956–58, Admty Engrg Lab West Drayton 1958–59; Nat Gas Turbine Estab Pyestock: joined 1959, head of Noise Research 1971–75, head of Performance and Design Research 1975–78; Engine Div MOD (PE) London 1978–81, dep dir R&D Nat Gas Turbine Establishment 1981–83; Royal Aircraft Establishment Farnborough (later Royal Aerospace): head of Propulsion Dept 1983–87, dep dir (Aircraft) 1987–89, dir (Aerospace Vehicles) 1989–91; ind tech conslt 1991–; specialist areas incl: gas turbines for aircraft and non-aeronautical applications, heat engines and energy conversion systems, aerospace technol and design, mgmnt and orgn of research (incl int collaboration); contrib to learned society jls on aeronautical research, gas turbines and aircraft propulsion; winner Akroyd Stuart Prize Royal Aeronautical Soc 1975, jt winner George Taylor Prize Royal Aeronautical Soc 1997; FRAeS 1981, FIMechE 1981, FREng 1991; *Recreations* walking and mountaineering, aviation history, music; *Style*— Frank W Armstrong, Esq, FREng; ✉ 6 Corringway, Church Crookham, Fleet, Hampshire GU52 6AN (tel and fax 01252 616526, e-mail armstrongfleet@totalise.co.uk)

ARMSTRONG, Rt Hon Hilary Jane; MP; da of Rt Hon Ernest Armstrong (d 1996), and Hannah, *née* Lamb; *b* 30 November 1945; *Educ* Monkwearmouth Comp Sch Sunderland, West Ham Coll of Technol (BSc), Univ of Birmingham (Dip Social Work); *m* 17 Oct 1992, Paul Corrigan; *Career* VSO teacher Murray Girls' HS Kenya 1967–69, social worker Newcastle City Social Servs Dept 1970–73, community worker Southwick Neighbourhood Action Project Sunderland 1973–75, lectr in community and youth work Sunderland Poly 1975–86, sec/researcher to father Ernest Armstrong MP 1986–87, MP (Lab) Durham NW 1987–; oppn spokesman on educn 1988–93, PPS to John Smith, Leader of the Oppn 1992–94, Treasy Team 1994–95, shadow min for local govt 1995–97; min of state (local govt and housing 1997–99, English regions 1999–2001) DETR 1997–2001, Parly sec to the Treasy (Govt chief whip) 2001–06, min for the Cabinet Office and for social exclusion and Chllr of the Duchy of Lancaster 2006–07; memb Educn Select Ctee 1988, chm PLP Educn Ctee; memb Durham CC 1985–87; *Recreations* theatre, reading; *Style*— The Rt Hon Hilary Armstrong, MP; ✉ House of Commons, London SW1A 0AA; Constituency Office (tel 01388 767065)

ARMSTRONG, Prof Isobel Mair; da of Richard Aneurin Jones (d 1953), and Marjorie, *née* Jackson; *b* 25 March 1937; *Educ* Friends Sch Saffron Walden Essex, Univ of Leicester (BA, PhD); *m* 9 Aug 1961, (John) Michael Armstrong, s of Rev Charles Armstrong (d 1947); 2 s (Thomas b 5 Oct 1968, Stephen b 24 April 1975), 1 da (Ursula b 16 Aug 1971); *Career* post doctoral fell in English Westfield Coll London 1962–63, asst lectr then lectr in English UCL 1963–70, lectr then sr lectr in English Univ of Leicester 1970–79; prof of English: Univ of Southampton 1979–89, Birkbeck Coll London 1989–2002 (emeritus prof 2002–); Breadloaf Sch of English: visiting prof MA Prog Middlebury Coll Vermont, Robert Frost chair Sch of English 2002; visiting prof: Dept of English Princeton Univ, English Dept Harvard Univ, Hinkley prof English Dept Johns Hopkins Univ; gen ed British Council Writers and their Work (second series) 1990–2006; fndr ctee memb Ctee for Univ English, co-ed Women - A Cultural Review 1988, fndr ctee memb Br Assoc of Victorian Studies 2001; pres Br Assoc for Victorian Studies 2003–06 (memb 2000–); FBA 2003; *Books* incl: Every Man Will Shout (with R Mansfield, 1964), The Major Victorian Poets - Reconsiderations (1969), Victorian Scrutinies (1972), A Sudden Line (1976), Language as Living Form in Nineteenth Century Poetry (1982), Jane Austen - Mansfield Park (1988), Victorian Poetry: Poetry, Poetics and Politics (1993), Jane Austen - Sense and Sensibility (1994), Nineteenth Century Women Poets: An Oxford Anthology (co-ed, 1996), The Radical Aesthetic (2000); contrib to various other books incl: Victorian Poetry (1968), Critical Essays on George Eliot (1970), Augustan Worlds (1978), The Oxford Literary Review (1981), Women Reading Women's Writing (1987), Dickens and Other Victorians (1988), Textuality and Sexuality (1993), Women's Poetry of the Enlightenment and Women's Poetry Late Romantic to Late Victorian (with Virginia Blain, 1999), Transactions & Encounters (2002), Multimedia Histories (2006); contrib reviews to various jls incl: Times Literary Supplements 1986–, Victorian Studies, Jl of Victorian Culture, Textual Practice; *Recreations* travel, drawing, writing; *Style*— Prof Isobel Armstrong, FBA; ✉ 15 Furzedown Road, Highfield, Southampton SO17 1PN; School of English and Humanities, Birkbeck College, Malet Street, London WC1E 7HX (tel 020 7631 6000, fax 020 7631 6072, e-mail isobel.armstrong@logic-net.co.uk)

ARMSTRONG, Dr James Hodgson; OBE (1996); s of John James Armstrong (d 1958), of Carlisle, Cumbria, and Margaret Eleanor, *née* Hodgson (d 1959); *b* 11 May 1926; *Educ* Carlisle GS, Univ of Glasgow (BSc); *m* 18 March 1950, Marjorie, da of Allan Victor Cartner (d 1960); 1 da (Jane b 1951), 1 s (Hugh b 1954 d 1994); *Career* engr; Duff and Geddes consulting engrs Edinburgh 1946–49, Rendel Palmer and Tritton (Scotland, Tyneside and London) 1949–54, specialist geotechnical engr Soil Mechanics Ltd London 1954–60, Harris and Sutherland conslts 1960–63, ptnr Building Design Partnership London 1966–89 (joined 1963); visiting prof: Cooper Union Coll NY 1978–82, Kingston Univ (formerly Kingston Poly) 1983–2000, Queen's Univ Belfast 1988, Univ of Leeds 1987–93; external examiner: Univ of Herts 1985–88, Univ of Strathclyde 1989–94; past pres: IStructE 1990, Br Masonry Soc 1991; chm Bd of Tstees Euro Christian Industrial Movement 1978–, chm of tstees and chm Devpt Ctee Higher Educn Fndn 1996–2002, govr St James's Schools Kensington; dep chm Tstees Partnership Awards 1990–97, tstee Varanasi Educnl Tst 1989–, tstee Maryport Heritage Tst 1990–2000; chm Design Matters Gp Royal Acad of Engrg 1992–2002; memb several professional/educnl ctees; Hon DEng Kingston Univ 1993, hon fell Harris Manchester Coll Oxford 2002; FREng 1990, FICE 1951, FIStructE 1951, MConsE, FASCE, FInstD, FRSA; *Recreations* philosophy, reading, walking, photography; *Clubs* Reform; *Style*— Dr James Armstrong, OBE, FREng; ✉ 32 Langford Green, London SE5 8BX (tel 020 7733 6808, e-mail j.armstrong@langfordgreen.demon.co.uk)

ARMSTRONG, Rear Adm John Herbert Arthur James (Louis); CBE (2004); s of John William Armstrong (d 1999), of Frome, Somerset, and Marie Helen, *née* Clarke (d 1979); *b* 4 September 1946; *Educ* King's Sch Canterbury, BRNC Dartmouth, Magdalen Coll Oxford (MA); *m* 7 April 1973 (m dis 2006), Marjorie Anne (Darjie), *née* Corbett; 1 s (Mark b 21 Feb 1976), 1 da (Mandy b 10 June 1978); partner, Sibley Pyne; *Career* served Royal Navy 1964–98; serv at sea in HM Ships Fife, Intrepid, Zulu, Illustrious and HM Yacht Britannia (also various staff, legal and admin posts ashore) 1970–87; called to the Bar Middle Temple 1976; seconded to Cabinet Office (Overseas and Def Secretariat) 1987–89, dep dir Naval Operational Requirements MOD 1989–91, RCDS 1992, dir Naval Manpower Planning 1993, dir Corp Programming Naval Personnel 1994, cmdt RN Staff Coll Greenwich 1994–95, Sr Naval Directing Staff RCDS 1996–98, chief exec RICS 1998–; memb Cncl London Inst of City and Guilds 2005–, dir Inst of Leadership and Mgmnt 2006–; FRSA, FCMI; *Recreations* music (choral singing), the arts, tennis, skiing, parties; *Clubs* Reform; *Style*— Rear Adm Louis Armstrong, CBE; ✉ Royal Institution of Chartered Surveyors, 10–12 Great George Street, Parliament Square, London SW1P 3AD (tel 020 7334 3707, fax 020 7222 5074, e-mail chiefexec@rics.org)

ARMSTRONG, Karen Andersen; da of John Oliver Seymour Armstrong (d 1975), and Eileen Hastings, *née* McHale; *b* 14 November 1944; *Educ* Convent of the Holy Child Jesus Edgbaston Birmingham, St Anne's Coll Oxford (MA, MLitt, Violet Vaughan Morgan prize); *Career* writer and broadcaster; Soc of the Holy Child Jesus (RC teaching order of nuns) 1962–69, tutorial research fell Bedford Coll London 1973–76, head of English James Allen's Girls' Sch Dulwich 1976–82, freelance writer and broadcaster 1982–; winner Calamus Fndn Annual Award 1991; winner Muslim Public Affrs Cncl Media Award 1999; *Television* work incl: The First Christian (six part documentary on St Paul) 1984, Varieties of Religious Experience (interview series) 1984, Tongues of Fire (interview series) 1985; *Books* Through the Narrow Gate (1981), Beginning the World (1983), The First Christian (1983), Tongues of Fire (1985), The Gospel According to Woman (1986), Holy War - The Crusades and their Impact on Today's World (1988), Muhammed - A Western Attempt to Understand Islam (1991), A History of God (1993), The End of Silence - Women and Priesthood (1993), A History of Jerusalem: One City, Three Faiths (1996), In the Beginning - A New Interpretation of Genesis (1996), The Battle for God - Fundamentalism in Judaism, Christianity and Islam (2000), Islam: A Short History (2000), Buddha (2001), The Spiral Staircase: My Climb Out of Darkness (2004), A Short History of Myth (2005), The Great Transformation: The Beginning of Our Religious Traditions (2006); *Recreations* music, theatre, fiction, having dinner with friends; *Style*— Ms Karen Armstrong

ARMSTRONG, Prof Peter; s of Alexander Armstrong, of London, and Ada, *née* Lapidas (d 1963); *b* 31 August 1940; *Educ* Marylebone GS, Middx Hosp Med Sch (MB BS); *m* Carole Jennifer Armstrong; 2 s (Damon Oliver b 17 Oct 1971 d 1972, Jethro Karl b 22 Feb 1974), 1 da (Natasha Janine b 23 Nov 1972); *Career* house physician Middx Hosp 1963, house surgn Kettering General Hosp 1964; sr registrar in radiology: Middx Hosp 1965–68

A

(registrar 1964–65), Guy's Hosp 1968–70; conslt in radiology KCH 1970–77, prof and vice-chm Univ of Virginia Hosp 1981–89 (assoc prof 1977–81), prof of radiology and Mercer chair of diagnostic radiology Bart's 1989–2005; RCR: George Simon lectr 1993, warden clinical radiology 1994–98, pres 1998–2001; ed Clinical Radiology 1990–94; pres Euro Soc of Thoracic Imaging 1995–96; Robley Dunglison Prize Univ of Virginia Med Sch 1983 and 1984; memb: Br Inst of Radiology 1966, RSM 1984; FRCR 1968, FMedSci 1999, FRCP 2000; *Books* Diagnostic Imaging, Imaging of Diseases of the Chest, Diagnostic Radiology in Surgical Practise, Concise Textbook of Radiology; *Recreations* reading, theatre, art; *Clubs* Shadow's Radiology; *Style—* Prof Peter Armstrong; ✉ Academic Department of Radiology, St Bartholomew's Hospital, London EC1A 7BE (tel 020 7601 8864, fax 020 7601 8868, e-mail j.k.jessop@qmul.ac.uk)

ARMSTRONG, His Hon Judge Peter John Bowden; s of William David Armstrong, MBE (d 1966), of Durham, and Kathleen Mary, *née* Wood (d 1997); *b* 19 December 1951; *Educ* Durham Johnston Grammar Tech Sch, Trinity Coll Cambridge (MA); *m* 1976, Joanna, da of late Brian Charles Arthur Cox; 2 da (Charlotte Kate b 8 Feb 1979, Helen Joanna b 1 Oct 1980); *Career* called to the Bar Middle Temple 1974; barr NE Circuit 1976–2000, head Fountain Chambers Middlesbrough 1992–2000, recorder 1994–2000 (asst recorder 1990–94), circuit judge (NE Circuit) 2000–; *Recreations* golf, cricket, rugby, music; *Clubs* Eaglescliffe Golf, Durham CCC; *Style—* His Hon Judge Armstrong; ✉ Teesside Combined Court Centre, Russell Street, Middlesbrough TS1 2AE (tel 01642 340000, fax 01642 340002)

ARMSTRONG-DAMPIER, Philip Donald; s of Donald Armstrong-Dampier, and Audrey Armstrong-Dampier; *b* 21 February 1959, St Asaph, Denbighshire; *m* Lynn, *née* Hoptrough; 2 s (Guy Yohji, Max Oliver Xan); *Career* TV prodr; early career with 20th Century Fox and CBS News, prodr and dir TVS 1988–92, freelance prodr and dir then md Outpost Films, head ITN Factual 2003– (dep hd and exec prodr 2000–02); exec prodr of numerous documentaries and series for ITV, Channel 4, five, Discovery Channel, Nat Geographic and Travel Channel; exhbns: Oriel Theatr Clwyd, New Contemporaries ICA 1981, White Elephant Gallery Leeds; FRGS; *Recreations* swimming, travelling; *Clubs* Lansdowne; *Style—* Philip Armstrong-Dampier, Esq; ✉ ITN Factual, 16 Mortimer Street, London W1T 3JL (tel 020 7430 4782, e-mail philip.dampier@itn.co.uk)

ARMSTRONG OF ILMINSTER, Baron (Life Peer UK 1988), of Ashill in the County of Somerset; Sir Robert Temple Armstrong; GCB (1983, KCB 1978, CB 1974), CVO (1975); s of Sir Thomas (Henry Wait) Armstrong (d 1994), and Hester Muriel, *née* Draper (d 1982); *b* 30 March 1927; *Educ* Eton, ChCh Oxford; *m* 1953 (m dis 1985), Serena Mary Benedicta (d 1994), er da of Sir Roger James Ferguson Chance, 3 Bt, MC; 2 da (Hon Jane Orlanda b 1954, Hon Teresa Brigid b 1957); m 2, 1985, (Mary) Patricia, o da of Charles Cyril Carlow (d 1957); *Career* asst sec: Cabinet Office 1964–66, Treasury 1967–68; under sec Treasury 1968–70, princ private sec to PM 1970–75, dep under sec Home Office 1975–77, perm under sec 1977–79, sec of the Cabinet 1979–87, head Home Civil Service 1981–87; chm: Biotechnology Investments Ltd 1989–2000, Bristol and West Building Society 1993–97 (non-exec dir 1988–97), Forensic Investigative Associates (London) 1997–2003; non-exec dir: BAT Industries plc 1988–97, NM Rothschild and Sons Ltd 1988–97 (conslt 1997–2000), Rio Tinto plc (formerly RTZ Corporation plc) 1988–97 (non-exec dir CRA Ltd Dec 1995–97), Shell Transport and Trading plc 1988–97, Inchcape plc 1988–95, Lucas Industries plc 1989–92, Carlton Television Ltd 1991–95, IAMGOLD Corp Ltd (Canada) 1995–2003, Bank of Ireland 1997–2001, 3i Bioscience Investment Tst plc 2000–02; chm: bd of tstees V&A 1988–98, Hestercombe Gardens Tst Ltd 1996–2005, bd of govrs RNCM 2000–05, Leeds Castle Fndn 2001–07 (tstee 1987–2007); memb bd of dirs Royal Opera House 1988–93 (sec 1968–87); chllr Univ of Hull 1994–2006; Hon Liveryman Salters' Co 1983; fell Eton Coll 1979–94; hon student ChCh Oxford 1985, Rhodes tstee 1975–97, Hon FRAM 1985; hon bencher Inner Temple 1986; Hon LLD Univ of Hull 1994; *Recreations* music; *Clubs* Brooks's, Garrick; *Style—* The Rt Hon the Lord Armstrong of Ilminster, GCB, CVO; ✉ House of Lords, London SW1A 0PW

ARMYTAGE, Sir (John) Martin; 9 Bt (GB 1738), of Kirklees, Yorkshire; s of Capt Sir John Lionel Armytage, 8 Bt (d 1983), and Evelyn Mary Jessamine, *née* Fox; *b* 26 February 1933; *Educ* Eton, Worcester Coll Oxford; *Heir* cous, Capt David Armytage, CBE, RN; *Clubs* Naval and Military; *Style—* Sir Martin Armytage, Bt; ✉ Kirklees Park, Brighouse, Yorkshire; Halewell, Withington, Cheltenham, Gloucestershire GL54 4BN

ARNELL, Richard Anthony Sayer; s of Richard Sayer Arnell (d 1952), and Hélène Marie Ray Scherf (d 1942); *b* 15 September 1917; *Educ* The Hall Hampstead, Univ Coll Sch, Royal Coll of Music; *m* 1992, Joan Cynthia Nita Heycock; 3 da from prev m (Jessie, Claudine, Jennifer), 1 s from prev m; *Career* composer, conductor, poet and teacher; princ lectr Trinity Coll of Music 1981–87 (teacher of composition 1949–81), music conslt BBC N American Serv 1943–46, lectr Roy Ballet Sch 1958–59, ed The Composer 1961–64; vice-pres Composers' Guild of GB 1991 (chm 1965 and 1974–75); memb Br Acad of Composers and Songwriters (formerly Composers' Guild) 2000; chm: Young Musicians' Symphony Orch Soc 1973–75, Tadcaster Civic Soc - Music and Arts 1988–91, Saxmundham Music and Arts 1992– (pres 1995–); visiting lectr (Fulbright Exchange) Bowdoin Coll Maine 1967–68, visiting prof Hofstra Univ NY 1968–70, music dir and bd memb London Int Film Sch 1971–80, music dir Ram Filming Ltd 1980–91, dir Organic Sounds Ltd 1982–84, Composer of the Year 1966 (Music Teachers' Assoc award), Tadcaster Town Cncl Merit Award 1991; compositions include: 7 symphonies, 2 concertos for violin, concerto for harpsichord, 3 concertos for piano, 6 string quartets, 2 quintets, piano trio, piano works, songs, cantatas, organ works, music for string orchestra, wind ensembles, brass ensembles, song cycles, electronic music, music theatre; opera: Love in Transit, Moonflowers; puppet operetta: Petrified Princess; ballet scores: Punch and the Child for Ballet Soc NY 1947, Harlequin in April Sadler's Wells Theatre Ballet 1951, The Great Detective for Sadler's Wells Theatre Ballet 1953, The Angels for Royal Sadler's Wells Theatre Ballet 1957, Giselle (Adam) reorchestrated for Ballet Rambert 1965; film scores: The Land 1941, Opus 65 1961, The Third Secret 1963, The Visit 1964, The Man Outside 1966, Topsail Schooner 1966, Bequest for a Village 1969, Second Best 1972, Stained Glass 1973, Wires over the Border 1974, Black Panther 1977, Antagonist 1980, Dilemma 1981, Toulouse Lautrec 1984, Light of the World 1990; other works: Symphonic Portrait Lord Byron for Sir Thomas Beecham 1953, Landscapes and Figures for Sir Thomas Beecham 1956, Robert Flaherty Impression for Radio Éireann 1960, Musica Pacifica for Edward Benjamin 1963, Festival Flourish for Salvation Army 1965, 2nd piano concerto for RPO 1967, Overture Food of Love for Portland Symphony Orch 1968, My Lady Green Sleeves for Hofstra Univ 1968, Nocturne Prague 1968, I Think of All Soft Limbs for Canadian Broadcasting Corp 1971, Astronaut One 1973, Life Boat Voluntary for RNLI 1974, Call for LPO 1982, Ode to Beecham for RPO 1986, Xanadu for Harlow Choral Society 1992–93, Fanfare for a Lifeboat for RNLI 1994, Ode to Beecham for RPO 1998, Symphonic Statement 7 for President Mandela 2004; Hon FTCL; *Publications* Not Wanted on Voyage (poem, 2001); *Clubs* Savage; *Style—* Richard Arnell; ✉ c/o Jennifer Johnson, 34 Park Village East, London NW1 7PZ

ARNOLD, Bruce; OBE (2003); *b* 1936; *Educ* Kingham Hill Sch, TCD (MA), UCD (DLitt); *m*; 3 c; *Career* journalist 1960s: The Irish Times, The Irish Press, The Sunday Independent, Hibernia National Review; corr The Guardian 1962–68; Irish Independent: political commentator and parly corr 1972–86, London ed 1986–87, literary ed 1987–2000, chief critic 2000–; hon fell Trinity Coll Dublin 2001, FRSL 1994; *Novels* A Singer at the Wedding, The Song of the Nightingale, The Muted Swan, Running to Paradise; *Non-Fiction* A Concise History of Irish Art, Orpen: Mirror to an Age, What Kind of Country, Margaret Thatcher: A Study in Power, An Art Atlas of Britain and Ireland (1991), William Orpen (1991), The Scandal of Ulysses (1991, revised edn 2004), Mainie Jellett and the Modern Movement in Ireland (1991), Haughey: His Life and Unlucky Deeds (1993), Jack Yeats (1998), Swift: An Illustrated Life (1999), Jack Lynch: Hero in Crisis (2001), The Spire and Other Essays in Irish Culture (2003); *Clubs* Athenaeum; *Style—* Bruce Arnold, Esq, OBE, FRSL; ✉ c/o Jonathan Williams Literary Agency, Rosney Mews, Upper Glengeary Road, Co Dublin, Ireland (tel 00 353 1 280 3482)

ARNOLD, Dr David; s of Ernest Edward, (d 1984), and Teresa Eliza Mary, *née* Grimsdell (d 1996); *b* 18 June 1943; *Educ* St Ignatius Coll, Wandsworth Tech Coll (HNC), South Bank Poly, Univ of Bristol (MSc), Cranfield Inst (PhD); *m* 28 Sept 1963, Jean Selina, da of Charles Owen George Brodie; 2 da (Melanie b 8 March 1967, Louise b 14 Oct 1979), 1 s (Mark b 19 April 1969); *Career* trainee engr 1962, trainee Edward A Pearce and Partners Consulting Engrs 1962–66; Troup Bywaters and Anders Consulting Engrs: intermediate engr 1962–73, sr ptnr 1991–99 (ptnr 1973); CIBSE co-fndr Thermal Storage Gp (formerly chm, pres 1994–95); chm: Strategy 2000 Ctee, CLIMA 2000 Exec Ctee 1989–93, NES 1993–98; memb ASHRAE (Ed Bd ASHRAE Jl, Publishing Cncl 1993–97, dir 1996–99 and 2002–05); CEng, FCIBSE (memb 1969–, chm Meetings Ctee 1980–85, memb Cncl 1984–87), MIMechE 1970, FREng 1993; author of numerous tech papers; *Recreations* photography, cycling; *Clubs* Royal Photographic Soc, Sonning Working Men's; *Style—* Dr David Arnold, FREng; ✉ Troup, Bywaters and Anders, 11 Queen Victoria Street, Reading RG1 1SY (tel 0118 957 6840, fax 0118 957 6825, e-mail davidarnold@beeb.net)

ARNOLD, Prof David John; s of Mansel John Arnold (d 1996), and May, *née* Dominey (d 1995); *b* 1 October 1946, London; *Educ* Univ of Exeter (BA), Univ of Sussex (DPhil); *m* 1988, Juliet, *née* Miller; *Career* prof of the history of S Asia SOAS Univ of London; FBA 2004; *Books* The Problem of Nature: Environment, Culture and European Expansion (1996), Science, Technology and Medicine in Colonial India (2000), Gandhi (2001), The Age of Discovery 1400–1600 (2 edn, 2002), The Tropics and the Traveling Gaze: India, Landscape and Science 1800–1856 (2006); *Style—* Prof David J Arnold; ✉ Department of History, School of Oriental and African Studies, Thornhaugh Street, Russell Square, London WC1H 0XG

ARNOLD, David Philip James; s of Philip Arthur Arnold (d 1988), and Christine May, *née* Rowe; *b* 13 August 1955; *Educ* Merchant Taylors', Univ of Exeter; *m* 19 Aug 1978, Carol Alice, da of Arthur George Edward Williams (d 1973); 2 da (Kirsten b 7 Feb 1986, Lucy b 4 May 1993), 1 s (James b 7 July 1995); *Career* CA; ptnr Ernst & Young LLP 1988–; Freeman City of London 1976, Liveryman Worshipful Co of Fishmongers 1982; FCA 1979; *Style—* David Arnold, Esq; ✉ Ernst & Young LLP, 1 More London Place, London SE1 2AF (tel 020 7951 1913, fax 020 7951 9315, e-mail darnold@uk.ey.com)

ARNOLD, Graham; s of Charles Arnold (d 1971), of Brighton, E Sussex, and Mildred, *née* King (d 1963); *b* 24 May 1932; *Educ* Beckenham Sch of Art, RCA; *m* 1961, Ann, da of Prof Edmund Telfer; *Career* painter in residence Digswell House Herts 1960–63, sr lectr in fine art Kingston Poly 1963–72; visiting tutor in fine art: Westminster Sch 1961–65, Royal Acad Schs 1966–71; fndr memb The Brotherhood of Ruralists (with Ann Arnold, David Inshaw, Peter Blake, Jann Howarth, Graham Ovenden, and Annie Ovenden) 1975; work in public collections incl: Royal Acad of Arts, Bristol City Art Gallery, Contemporary Arts Soc, Univ of Liverpool Gallery, Nat Gallery of NZ, Br Museum, Southport Museum and Art Gallery; illustrations for numerous books incl: Round About a Great Estate, The Epic of Gilgamesh; RCA travelling scholarship to Italy 1958–60, Univ of London scholarship for painting 1973, Chichester Nat Art Exhibition prize for painting 1975; Royal Academician SW Acad of Fine and Applied Arts 2000; FRAS 2004; *Exhibitions* Royal Acad Summer Exhibition 1950, 1959 and 1976, Festival Gallery Bath 1977, The Fine Arts Soc Edinburgh 1977, Doncaster Museum and Art Gallery 1977, Southampton Univ Art Gallery 1977, Bodmin Fine Arts 1978, Southampton City Art Gallery 1978, Upottery Arts Festival 1978, Gainsborough's House Museum Sudbury 1979, Charleston Manor Festival 1979, Wren Library Trinity Coll Cambridge 1980, Bristol City Art Gallery 1980, Brotherhood of Ruralists touring exhibition supported by the Arts Cncl and the Eng Tourist Bd (Arnolfini Gallery Bristol, Birmingham City Art Gallery, Third Eye Centre Glasgow and Camden Arts Centre London) 1981, The Definitive Nude (Ruralist project shown at Tate Gallery as part of Peter Blake exhibition) 1983, Salute to Elgar (The David Paul Gallery Chichester) 1984, The Continuing Tradition (touring David Paul Gallery Chichester, Tunbridge Wells Art Gallery, Devizes Museum and Art Gallery, The Fine Art Soc Glasgow and Piccadilly Gallery London) 1985–86, The Secret Garden (touring) 1989, Alice (touring Bearnes Rainbow Torquay, Machynlleth, Plymouth Art Gallery, Christchurch Gallery Oxford and Piccadilly Gallery London) 1990, The Power of the Image (Berlin) 1996; solo exhibitions incl: Brighton Art Gallery (with Ann Arnold) 1971, Festival Gallery Bath 1976, George Gallery Bristol 1978, Brillig Art Centre Bath 1979, Festival Gallery Bath 1980, Bodmin Gallery 1981, The David Paul Gallery Chichester 1982, Piccadilly Gallery London 1983, 1986, 1988 (with Ann Arnold), 1991, 1993 and 1995, major retrospective MOMA Wales Machynlleth 1992, Royal Acad Summer Show (by special invitation) 2001, Silk Top Hat Gallery (Festival of English Song Ludlow) 2002, MOMA Wales 2002 and 2003, Three Decades - A Celebration (The Ruralists) (MOMA Machynleth) 2003, Leicester Galleries 2005, Wiltshire Heritage Museum 2006; *Recreations* beekeeping, music, poetry and writing, astronomy, being in deep countryside, gardening; *Clubs* Arts; *Style—* Graham Arnold, Esq; ✉ c/o Silk Top Hat Gallery, 4 Quality Square, Ludlow, Shropshire SY8 1AR

ARNOLD, Jacques Arnold; s of late Samuel Arnold, and Eugenie Arnold; *b* 27 August 1947; *Educ* sch in Brazil, LSE (BSc Econ); *m* 22 May 1976, Patricia Anne, da of late Dennis Maunder, of Windsor, Berks; 2 da (Hazel Jane b 1979, Philippa Rachel b 1981), 1 s (David Samuel b 1984); *Career* asst gp rep Midland Bank Brazil 1976–78, regnl dir Thomas Cook Gp 1978–84, asst trade fin dir Midland Bank 1984–85, dir American Express Europe Ltd 1985–87; Parly candidate (Cons) Coventry SE 1983, MP (Cons) Gravesham 1987–97, Parly candidate 2001; PPS to David Maclean as: min of state for the environment and countryside 1992–93, min of state Home Office 1993–95; memb: Educn, Science and Arts Select Ctee 1989–92, Treasy Select Ctee 1997; chm Cons Backbench Constitutional Affrs Ctee 1996–97 (vice-chm 1995–96); sec: Cons Backbench Foreign and Cwlth Affrs Ctee 1990–92 and 1995–97, Br-Latin American Parly Gp 1987–97; chm: Br-Brazil Parly Gp 1992–97, Br-Portuguese Parly Gp 1994–97; vice-chm Cons Backbench Pty Orgn Ctee 1995–97; advsr for: Latin America, GEC plc 1998–99, BAE Systems plc 1999–2004; patron Gravesham Cons Assoc 1997–; tstee Environment Fndn 1989–2003; chm Kent County Scout Cncl 1998–2000; co cncllr Oundle Northants 1981–85; Grand Official Order of the Southern Cross (Brazil) 1993; *Books* A History of Britain's Parliamentary Constituencies (2007), The Royal Houses of Europe (various editions); *Recreations* family life, gardening, genealogy; *Clubs* Carlton; *Style—* Jacques A Arnold, Esq; ✉ Fairlawn, 243 London Road, West Malling, Kent ME19 5AD (tel 01732 848573, office tel and fax 01732 848388)

ARNOLD, Jennette; AM; *Career* nurse 1973–81, health visitor 1981–86, pre-pregnancy project co-ordinator W Midlands Regnl HA 1986–87; RCN: industrial rels offr 1987–89, special advsr (on equalities) to Gen Sec 1989–91, sr offr NE Thames region 1991–94, sr advsr 1994–97; assoc Beacon Organisational Devpt and Trg Servs 1997–, dir JSA Consultancy 1997–; memb London Assembly GLA (Lab) London 2000–; London Assembly: memb Mayor's Advsy Cabinet, memb Health and Public Service Ctee, memb Econ and Social Devpt Ctee, memb EU Ctee of the Regions; chair London Health Cmmn

(LHC) 2004–, vice-chm London Cultural Consortium 2004; memb: Metropolitan Police Authy, Police Advsy Bd; memb Lab Pty Nat Policy Forum, memb Bd Lab Women's Network; memb London Regnl Cncl Arts Cncl, tstee Sadler's Wells Theatre Fndn; vice-chair Stephen Lawrence Charitable Tst, govr Coram Family Childcare Charity; *Style—* Mrs Jennette Arnold, AM; ✉ London Assembly, City Hall, Queens Walk, Southwark, London SE1 2AA (tel 020 7983 4349, fax 020 7983 5874, e-mail jennette.arnold@london.gov.uk)

ARNOLD, Prof John André; s of Capt André Eugene Arnold (d 1974), and May, *née* Vickers (d 1977); *b* 30 April 1944; *Educ* Haberdashers' Aske's, LSE (MSc); *Family* 2 da (Kate Lynne b 1976, Mandy Louise b 1978); m, 29 March 1997, Sylvia, *née* Bailey; *Career* teaching fell Mgmnt Studies LSE 1967–69, lectr in accounting Univ of Kent 1969–71; Univ of Manchester: lectr in accounting 1971–75, sr lectr 1975–77, prof of accounting 1977–86, KPMG Peat Marwick prof of accounting 1986–94, dean Faculty of Econ and Social Studies 1987–89, pro-vice-chllr 1990–94, dir Manchester Business Sch and KPMG prof of accounting and fin mgmnt 1994–2006; visiting prof Univ of Washington 1981–82; dir of research ICAEW 1987–94; non-exec dir PZ Cussons plc 2007–; pres Manchester Soc of CAs 1991–92 (vice-pres 1989–90, dep pres 1990–91), chm Pro Manchester 2007–08; Hon MA (Econ) Univ of Manchester; FCA 1967; *Books* Pricing and Output Decisions (1973), Topics in Management Accounting (1980), Accounting for Management Decisions (1983, 3 edn 1996), Management Accounting Research and Practice (1983), Financial Accounting (1985, 2 edn 1994), Management Accounting: British Case Studies (1987), Management Accounting: Expanding the Horizons (1987), Financial Reporting: The Way Forward (1990), The Future Shape of Financial Reports (1991); *Recreations* squash, tennis; *Clubs* Marple Cricket & Squash; *Style—* Prof John Arnold; ✉ Manchester Business School, Booth Street West, Manchester M15 6PB (tel 0161 275 7149, fax 0161 275 6585, e-mail john.arnold@mbs.ac.uk)

ARNOLD, Rt Rev John Stanley; s of (Stanley) Kenneth Arnold, and Mary, *née* Murray (d 2005); *b* 1953, Sheffield; *Educ* Ratcliffe Coll Leics, Trinity Coll Oxford (BA), Gregorian Univ Rome (BPhil, BTh); *Career* barr-at-law Cncl of Legal Educn 1975–76; Westminster Cathedral: hosp and cathedral chaplain 1985–88, cathedral sub-administrator 1988–93; parish priest Our Lady of Mount Carmel and St George Enfield 1993–2001, vicar gen and chllr Westminster RC Diocese 2001–06, moderator of the Curia 2005–, auxilary bishop of Westminster 2006– (titular bishop of Lindisfarne 2006–); *Publications* Quality of Mercy: A Re-evaluation of the Sacrament of Reconciliation (1993); *Style—* The Rt Rev John Arnold; ✉ Archbishop's House, Ambrosden Avenue, London SW1P 1QJ (tel 020 7931 6062, fax 020 7931 6058, e-mail johnarnold@rcdow.org.uk)

ARNOLD, Luqman; s of Claude Ian Morris Arnold (d 2003), and Muftiah, *née* Dutt; *b* 16 April 1950, Calcutta; *Educ* Oundle, Univ of London (BSc (Econs)); *m* 14 April 1988, Chumsri Sawangpanit; 1 s (Jocelyn Sivakorn b 31 March 1994); *Career* First National Bank in Dallas 1972–76, Manufacturers Hanover Corporation 1976–82, head of investment banking origination Credit Suisse First Boston 1982–92, research sabbatical 1992–93, memb Exec Ctee and Bd Banque Paribas 1993–96, chm Gp Exec Bd and pres UBS AG 1996–2001, chief exec Abbey National plc 2002–04, sr advsr to chm Grupo Santander 2004–06, chm Olivant Advsrs Ltd 2006–; chm Design Museum 2005–; memb: Bd Architecture Fndn 2005–, Devpt Cncl Univ of the Arts 2005–; *Recreations* horse riding, tennis, skiing; *Clubs* Hurlingham, Oriental, Tanglin; *Style—* Luqman Arnold, Esq; ✉ Olivant Advisers Limited, 2 Basil Street, London SW3 1AA (tel 020 7225 4100, fax 020 7225 4141, e-mail luqman.arnold@olivant.com)

ARNOLD, Malcolm; s of Colin William Arnold (d 1988), of Northwich, Cheshire, and Jane, *née* Powell; *b* 4 April 1940; *Educ* Verdin GS Winsford Cheshire, Loughborough Univ; *m* Madelyn, *née* Morrissey; 1 s (Andrew b 20 Jan 1966), 1 da (Helen b 27 Sept 1964); *Career* athletics coach; dir of coaching Uganda 1968–72, nat athletics coach Wales 1974–94, head of coaching and devpt British Athletic Federation 1994–97, exec dir Performance Athlete Services Ltd 1997–, head coach of track and field Univ of Bath 1998–99, performance mangr UK Athletics High Performance Centre Univ of Bath 1999–; coach to Olympic teams: Uganda 1968 and 1972, GB and NI 1980, 1984, 1988, 1992 and 2000; head coach GB and NI Olympic Team 1996; coach to: late John Akii-Bua (Olympic 400m hurdles champion 1972, world record holder 1972–76), Colin Jackson (world champion 1993 and 1999, world record holder 60m and 110m hurdles), Kay Morley (Cwlth 100m hurdles champion 1990), Mark McKoy (Olympic 110m hurdles Gold medal 1992), Jason Gardener (World 60m Champion (indoors) 2004), numerous Br int athletes; *Books* author of ten athletics books; *Recreations* rally driver of enthusiasm but no distinction; *Style—* Malcolm Arnold, Esq; ✉ Froxfield House, 139 The Street, Broughton Gifford, Melksham, Wiltshire SN12 8PH (e-mail malarnold@aol.com)

ARNOLD, Michael; s of Dr Alan George Arnold (d 1990), and Kathleen, *née* McGuirk (d 1947); *b* 16 September 1947; *Educ* Royal Wolverhampton Sch, Univ of Reading (BSc); *m* 8 April 1972, Pauline Ann, da of Berwyn Elvet Pritchard; 2 s (David Paul b 4 July 1975, Stuart Michael b 12 May 1978); *Career* actuarial trainee Prudential Assurance Co Ltd 1969–71; Hymans Robertson: joined as actuarial trainee 1971, ptnr 1974, sr ptnr 1995–2002; princ Milliman 2002–; Liveryman Worshipful Co of Actuaries 1985; FIA 1973; *Recreations* golf, travel; *Clubs* City Livery, Kingswood Golf, Walton Heath Golf; *Style—* Michael Arnold, Esq; ✉ Milliman, Finsbury Tower, 103–105 Bunhill Row, London EC1Y 8LZ (tel 020 7847 6100, fax 020 7847 6105)

ARNOLD, Michael John; s of Thomas Henry Arnold (d 1991), and Cecily May Arnold (d 1996); *b* 1 April 1935; *m* 21 Jan 1989, Jane, *née* Benson; *Career* Nat Serv Lt RA 1958–59; Hilton Sharpe & Clark 1951–57, qualified CA 1957, ptnr Arthur Young 1966–89 (joined 1960), chm AY Management Consultants 1973–83, nat dir Corporate Recovery and Insolvency 1975–89, sole practitioner (corp restructuring and recoveries) 1989–; dir: Roux Restaurants 1987–2000, Carlisle Group plc 1998–99, Jourdan 1998–2004, Behavioural Science Systems 2005–; chm: Prelude Technology Holdings 1991–96, Luminar plc 1994–2001, Brooke Industrial Holdings plc 2000–03; court appointed receiver NUM 1984–86; hon treas: Youth Clubs UK 1984–92, Racehorse Owners' Assoc 1991–99; tstee Volunteer Reading Help 2001–07 (hon treas 2001–06); memb Fin Ctee Br Horseracing Bd 1993–2000; FCA, FCMC, FIPA; *Recreations* horse racing, country; *Clubs* Turf; *Style—* Michael Arnold, Esq; ✉ Brockhill, Naunton, Cheltenham, Gloucestershire GL54 3BA (tel 01451 850191, fax 01451 850199)

ARNOLD, Richard David; QC (2000); s of late Francis Arnold, of London, and Ann, *née* Churchill; *b* 23 June 1961; *Educ* Highgate Sch, Magdalen Coll Oxford (MA), Westminster Univ (Dip Law); *m* 24 March 1990, Mary, da of Edwin Elford; 2 da (Judith Alice b 22 Oct 1996, Elizabeth Jean b 27 Oct 2000); *Career* barr; called to the Bar 1985; chm Ctee on Code of Practice for Promotion of Animal Medicines 2001–, appointed to hear trade mark appeals 2003–, dep High Court judge 2004–; *Publications* Computer Software and Legal Protection in the UK (jtly, 1992), Entertainment and Media Law Reports (ed, 1993–2004), Performers' Rights (2004); *Recreations* collecting contemporary British abstract paintings and ceramics, music, cinema, theatre, opera, cooking; *Clubs* MCC; *Style—* Richard Arnold, Esq, QC; ✉ 11 South Square, Gray's Inn, London WC1R 5EY (tel 020 7405 1222, fax 020 7242 4282, e-mail clerks@11southsquare.com)

ARNOLD, Sheila May; da of John Millar Arnold (d 1949), and Mabel, *née* Walker (d 1951); *b* 24 May 1930; *Educ* RCSI (LPCP, LPCS); *m* 4 April 1955, Thomas Matthew Maguire, s of Philip Francis Maguire (d 1932); 2 da (Ailsa Catherine b 1965, Kim Caroline b 1970); *Career* house surgn and physician Richmond Hosp Dublin 1954–55; sr house surgn: Kent and Sussex Hosp 1956, Derbys Royal Infirmary 1957, Newcastle Royal Infirmary 1959; personal physician and surgn to Pres Kwame Nkruma Ghana Med Serv investigating deafness in village children 1959–62, St Mary Abbots Hosp London 1963, sr registrar Guy's and Lewisham Hosps 1970–73, sr conslt ENT surgn Frimley Park Hosp 1973–; memb: Royal Soc of Med, Regnl Med Advsy Ctee Br Soc of Otolaryngologists; LRCP, LRCS 1954, DLO 1961, FRCS 1973; *Publications* The Vulnerability of the Chorda Tympani Nerve and Middle Ear Disease (paper, 1973); *Recreations* badminton, skiing, swimming, foreign travel, squash; *Style—* Miss Sheila Arnold; ✉ Robin Hill, 18 Murdoch Road, Wokingham, Berkshire RG40 2DE (tel 0118 978 7027); Frimley Park Hospital, Portsmouth Road, Frimley, Surrey GU16 5UJ (tel 01276 692777)

ARNOLD, Susan Hillary (Sue); da of Morny McHarg, and Marjorie James; *Educ* Elmhurst Ballet Sch Camberley, Trinity Coll Dublin (MA); *m* twice; 6 c; *Career* journalist: Lancashire Evening Telegraph Blackburn 1967–68, Evening Standard 1968–69, Tehran Jl 1969–70, The Observer 1970–; radio and audiobook reviewer The Observer and The Guardian 1970–, columnist The Independent 1998–; commended Magazine Writer Br Press awards 1982, Magazine Writer of the Year 1983; *Books* Little Princes (1981), Curiouser & Curiouser (1984), A Burmese Legacy (1996); *Recreations* housewifery; *Clubs* Chelsea Arts; *Style—* Ms Sue Arnold; ✉ c/o The Guardian, 119 Farringdon Road, London EC1R 3ER

ARNOLD, Tom; s of Arthur Arnold (d 1982), and Theresa, *née* Healy (d 1992); *b* 5 October 1948, Dublin; *Educ* Corduff National Sch, De La Salle Coll Skerries, Franciscan Coll Gormonston, UCD (BAgrSc), Catholic Univ Louvain (MBA), TCD (MSc); *m* 4 April 1986, Gillian Davidson; 1 s (Patrick b 19 Feb 1987), 1 da (Laura b 8 Feb 1989); *Career* EC 1973–83, sr economist Farm Advsy Serv (ACOT) Ireland 1983–88; Dept of Agriculture and Food: chief economist 1988–93, asst sec gen 1993–2001; ceo Concern Worldwide 2001–; chm Ctee of Agriculture OECD 1993–98, vol UN Millennium Project Hunger Task Force 2003–05, memb Advsy Bd UN Central Emergency Response Fund 2006–; FRSA 2006; *Style—* Tom Arnold, Esq; ✉ Concern Worldwide, Camden Street, Dublin 2, Ireland (tel 00 353 1 417 7775, e-mail tom.arnold@concern.net)

ARNOLD, Wallace; *see:* Brown, Craig Edward Moncrieff

ARNOLD-BAKER, Prof Charles; OBE (1966); s of Baron Albrecht von Blumenthal, and Alice Wilhelmine, *née* Hainsworth; *b* 25 June 1918; *Educ* Winchester, Magdalen Coll Oxford; *m* 1943, Edith, *née* Woods; 1 s, 1 da; *Career* served WWII Army Inf and War Office 1940–46; called to the Bar Inner Temple 1948; Admty Bar 1948–52, sec Nat Assoc of Local Cncls 1953–78, memb Royal Cmmn on Common Lands 1955–58; dep chm: Eastern Traffic Cmmrs 1978–90, E Midlands Traffic Cmmrs 1981–86; visiting prof City Univ 1983–93 (conslt lectr 1978–83); ed Road Law 1991–96; author and occasional broadcaster; King Haakon VII Freedom medal (Norway) 1946; *Books* Everyman's Dictionary of Dates (1954), Parish Administration (1958), New Law and Practice of Parish Administration (1966), The Five Thousand and the Power Tangle (1967), The Local Government Act 1972 (1973), Local Council Administration (1975, 6 edn 2002), The Local Government, Planning and Land Act 1980 (1981), Practical Law for Arts Administrators (1983, 2 edn 1992), The Five Thousand and the Living Constitution (1986), The Companion to British History (1996, 2 edn 2000), For He is an Englishman: Memoirs of a Prussian Nobleman (2007); *Recreations* travel; *Clubs* Oxford Union; *Style—* Prof Charles Arnold-Baker, OBE; ✉ Top Floor, Mitre Court Buildings, Temple, London EC4Y 7BX (tel 020 7353 3490)

ARNOT, Richard James; s of Thomas Arnot, of Newcastle upon Tyne, and Judith, *née* Richardson; *b* 7 December 1966; *Educ* LLB; *Career* admitted slr 1992; trainee slr Mincoffs, head of licensing Dickinson Dees, ptnr and head of licensing Mincoffs 2005–; author of numerous articles on licensing law; owner of property business in NE; memb Law Soc 1992; *Recreations* running; *Style—* Richard Arnot, Esq; ✉ Mincoffs, 5 Osborne Terrace, Newcastle upon Tyne NE2 1SQ (tel 0191 212 7703, fax 0191 281 8069, e-mail richard.arnot@mincoffs.co.uk)

ARNOTT, Sir Alexander John Maxwell; 6 Bt (UK) 1896, of Woodlands, St Anne, Shandon, Co Cork; s of Sir John Robert Alexander Arnott, 5 Bt (d 1981), and Ann Margaret, *née* Farrelly; *b* 18 September 1975; *Heir* bro, Andrew Arnott; *Style—* Sir Alexander Arnott, Bt

ARNOTT, Prof Eric John; s of Capt Sir Robert Arnott, 4 Bt (d 1967), of Ounavarra, Lucan, Co Dublin, Ireland, and Cynthia Anita Amelia, *née* James (d 1948); *b* 12 June 1929; *Educ* Harrow, Trinity Coll Dublin (BA, MB BCh, BAO, MA), Univ of London (DO); *m* 19 Nov 1960, Veronica Mary (d 2001), da of Capt Arvid Langué Querfeld von der Seedeck (d 1986), of Hartley Wintney, Hants; 2 s (Stephen John b 1962, Robert Lauriston John b 1971), 1 da (Tatiana Amelia b 1963); *Career* house offr Adelaide Hosp Dublin 1954–55, registrar Royal Victoria Eye and Ear Hosp Dublin 1956–57, resident offr (later sr resident offr) Moorfields Eye Hosp London 1959–61, sr registrar UCH 1962–65; conslt ophthalmologist: Royal Eye Hosp 1966–72, Charing Cross Hosp and Charing Cross Gp of Hosps London 1967–94; hon conslt ophthalmologist Royal Masonic Hosp London 1970–90, med dir Fyodorov Arnott Apple Int Eye Inst Gibraltar 1999–2000; conslt emeritus Cromwell Hosp London 1999–; reader Univ of London 1972–, hon visiting prof Devi Ahilya Univ Indore India 1998–; pres Int Assoc of Ocular Surgeons 1994, pres and fndr Euro Soc for Phaco and Laser Surgery, former examiner Br Orthoptic Cncl; pioneer of phacoemulsification in Europe 1968–75, designer intraocular lens implants 1976–1994, pioneer of excimer laser for correction of refractive disorders of the eye 1991–99; tstee MBMEU devpt of mobile eye surgery unit for Indian camps 1999–; fndr and chm Arnott Tst and Gtr London Treasure Hunt; guest of honour American Soc of Cataract and Refractive Surgery 2007; FRCS 1963, Hon FRCOphth 1988; *Books* Emergency Surgery (jtly, 1977), Cataract Extraction and Lens Implantation (jtly, 1983), Phacoemulsification (contrib, 1988), A New Beginning in Sight (2005), The Birth of Lens Implants (contrib, 2007); *Recreations* swimming, golf, sailing; *Clubs* Kildare St (Dublin), Garrick, RAC; *Style—* Prof Eric J Arnott; ✉ Trottsford Farm, Headley, Bordon, Hampshire GU35 8TF (tel 01420 472136, fax 01420 473477, e-mail arnottev@compuserve.com, website www.anewbeginninginsight.com)

ARNOTT, Ian Emslie; s of Henry Arnott (d 1967), of Galashiels, and Margaret Hume Paton Emslie (d 1961); *b* 7 May 1929; *Educ* Galashiels Acad, Edinburgh Coll of Art (DA (Edin), Dip TP (Edin)); *m* 17 Sept 1955, Mildred Stella; 1 da (Gillian Elisabeth b 1958); *Career* Flying Offr RAF 1955–57; architect; chm Campbell & Arnott Architects 1963–94 (conslt 1994–97), chm Saltire Soc; projects: Saltire Court Castle Terrace Edinburgh, Edinburgh Park, AEU HQ London; Gold Medal for Architecture Royal Scot Acad, five Civic Tst Awards, two Edinburgh Architectural Assoc Awards; RSA, RIBA, ARIAS; OStJ; *Recreations* walking, travel, music, reading, photography; *Clubs* New (Edinburgh); *Style—* Ian Arnott, Esq; ✉ The Rink, Gifford, East Lothian EH41 4JD (tel 01620 810278, fax 01620 810278, e-mail iana@therink.fsbusiness.co.uk)

ARNOTT, Prof Struther; CBE (1996); s of Charles McCann, and Christina Struthers Arnott; *b* 25 September 1934; *Educ* Hamilton Acad Lanarkshire, Univ of Glasgow (BSc, PhD); *m* Greta M, *née* Edwards; 2 s; *Career* King's Coll London: scientist MRC Biophysics Res Unit 1960–70, physics demonstrator 1960–67, dir of postgrad studies in biophysics 1967–70, fell 1997; Purdue Univ Indiana: prof of biology 1970–, head of biological sciences 1975–80, vice-pres (res) and dean Graduate Sch 1980–86; Univ of Oxford: sr visiting fell Jesus Coll 1980–81, Nuffield res fell Green Coll 1985–86; princ and vice-chllr Univ of St Andrews 1986–2000 (princ and vice-chllr emeritus 2000–); Haddow prof of biomolecular structure Chester Beatty Labs 2000–03, visiting prof and sr res fell Imperial Coll of Science, Technol and Med London 2002–; hon prof London Sch of Pharmacy 2000–; Guggenheim Meml Fndn fell 1985, Leverhulme Fellowship 2002 Hon ScD St

Andrews Laurinburg 1994, Hon DSc Purdue Univ Indiana 1998, Hon LLD Univ of St Andrews 1999; FKC 1997; FRS 1986, FRSE 1987; *Publications* papers in learned jls on structures of fibrous biopolymers, especially nucleic acids and polysaccharides, and the techniques for visualising them; *Recreations* birdwatching, botanising, talking; *Style—* Prof Struther Arnott, CBE, FRS; ✉ Number One Yorkshire, South Parade, Bawtry DN10 6JH (tel 07980 529386, e-mail no1yorkshire@onetel.com); Faculty of Medicine, Imperial College London, 376 Sir Alexander Fleming Building, Exhibition Road, London SW7 2AZ (tel 020 7594 3192, e-mail s.arnott@imperial.ac.uk)

ARRAN, 9 Earl of (I 1762); Sir Arthur Desmond Colquhoun Gore; 11 Bt (I 1662); also Viscount Sudley, Baron Saunders (both I 1758), and Baron Sudley (UK 1884); s of 8 Earl of Arran (d 1983), and Fiona, Countess of Arran; *b* 14 July 1938; *Educ* Eton, Balliol Coll Oxford; *m* 1974, Eleanor, er da of Bernard van Cutsem and Lady Margaret Fortescue, da of 5 Earl Fortescue; 2 da (Lady Laura Melissa b 1975, Lady Lucy Katherine b 1976); *Heir* kinsman, William Gore; *Career* Nat Serv Grenadier Gds; asst mangr Daily Mail 1972–73, md Clark Nelson 1973–74, asst gen mangr Daily and Sunday Express 1974; dir Waterstone & Co Ltd 1984–87; a lord-in-waiting (Govt whip) 1987–89 and July 1994–Jan 1995; spokesman for: Home Office, DES and DHSS 1987–89, Dept of the Environment 1988–89; Parly under sec of state: for the Armed Forces MOD 1989–92, Northern Ireland Office 1992–94, Dept of the Environment 1994; dep chief whip (House of Lords) 1994–95; Parly conslt to Inst of Waste Mgmnt 1995–2000; chm Children's Country Holidays Fund, chm Waste Industry Nat Trg Orgn (WINTO); non-exec dir: HMV (Thorn/EMI) 1995–98, South West Enterprise Ltd 1996–98, Bonhams 1997–2000; *Recreations* tennis, golf, gardening; *Clubs* Turf, Beefsteak, Pratt's, White's, Annabel's; *Style—* The Rt Hon the Earl of Arran; ✉ House of Lords, London SW1A 0PW

ARRAND, Ven Geoffrey William; s of Thomas Staniforth Arrand (d 1992), and Alica Ada, *née* Costello (d 1995); *b* 24 July 1944; *Educ* Scunthorpe GS, KCL (BD, AKC), St Boniface Coll Warminster; *m* 1, (m dis 1986), Mary Marshall; 2 da (Bridget Mary b 1972, Rebekah Kate b 1974), 1 s (Thomas William b 1976); m 2, 1 Oct 2005, Margaret Elizabeth Frost; *Career* curate: Washington Dio of Durham 1967–70, South Ormsby Gp Dio of Lincoln 1970–73; team vicar Great Grimsby Dio of Lincoln 1973–79, team rector Halesworth Dio of St Edmundsbury and Ipswich 1979–85, rector of Hadleigh, Layham and Shelley 1985–94, dean of Bocking 1985–94, rural dean of Hadleigh 1986–94, canon of St Edmundsbury 1992–, archdeacon of Suffolk 1994–; non-exec dir Ipswich Hosp NHS Tst; OStJ 1994; *Recreations* golf; *Style—* The Ven the Archdeacon of Suffolk; ✉ Glebe House, The Street, Ashfield-cum-Thorpe, Stowmarket, Suffolk IP14 6LX (tel 01728 685497, fax 01728 685969); Diocese of St Edmundsbury & Ipswich, Diocesan House, 13/15 Tower Street, Ipswich, Suffolk IP1 3BG (tel 01473 298500, fax 01473 298501/2, e-mail archdeacon.geoffrey@stedmundsbury.anglican.org)

ARRINDELL, Sir Clement Athelston; GCMG (1984), GCVO (1985), kt (1982), QC (1984); s of George Ernest Arrindell, and Hilda Iona Arrindell (d 1975); *b* 16 April 1931; *Educ* Bradley Private Sch, Basseterre Boys' Elementary, St Kitts-Nevis GS (Island scholar); *m* 1967, Evelyn Eugenia, da of Michael Cornelius O'Loughlin (d 1934), of Basseterre, St Kitts, and his w Dulcie (d 1972); *Career* treasy clerk Treasy Dept St Kitts 1951–54; called to the Bar Lincoln's Inn 1958; in practice 1958–66, dist magistrate 1966–72, chief magistrate 1972–78, judge W Indies Assoc States Supreme Court 1978–81; govr-gen St Kitts-Nevis 1983–95 (govr 1981–83), ret 1995; *Recreations* gardening, piano playing, classical music; *Style—* Sir Clement Arrindell, GCMG, GCVO, QC

ARROWSMITH, Anthony (Tony); s of late Arthur Arrowsmith and late Winifred, *née* McDonough; *b* 11 May 1945; *Educ* St Chad's Coll Wolverhampton, Matthew Boulton Coll (DipCAM); *m* 4 May 1968, Yvonne Mary da of late George Brannon; 1 s (Aidan b 1970), 2 da (Alexa b 1973, Sian b 1982); *Career* chm and chief exec Barkers Birmingham 1976–2002, chm Barkers Scot 1986–2002, chm and chief exec Barkers Communications 1989–2002, chm McCann-Erickson Birmingham 2002–03; dir: BNB Resources Gp 1984–2002, BNB Resources plc 1987–2002, The Penn Gp 2003–; chm St Dominic's Brewood Tst Ltd 2000–04; non-exec dir W Midlands Ambulance Serv NHS Tst 2006–; FIPA (memb Cncl 1996–2003); *Style—* Tony Arrowsmith, Esq; ✉ The Hollies, Histons Hill, Codsall, Staffordshire WV8 2ER

ARROWSMITH, Sue; *b* 1950; *Educ* Nottingham Fine Art, The Slade Sch of Art London; *Career* artist; *Solo Exhibitions* incl: Beside Myself (Matt's Gallery London) 1982, Ancient Mirrors: Fragile Traces (Serpentine Gallery London) 1985, Egg of Night (Ikon Gallery Birmingham) 1986, Anthony Reynolds Galley 1987, Qualities of Silence (Kettle's Yard Cambridge) 1987, Works on Paper (Lime Kiln Gallery London) 1996, Living on the Edge of Rain (Cabinet for Art Schiedam Holland) 1997, Sue Arrowsmith: Artworks (Dash Gallery London) 2002; *Group Exhibitions* incl: Young Contemporaries (RA) 1970, The Lisson Wall Show (Lisson Gallery) 1970, The British Avant-Garde (NY Cultural Centre) 1971, Art Systems (MOMA Buenos Aires) 1971, Experiment 4 (Midland Gp Nottingham) 1975, British Polaroid Exhibition (Spectro-Arts Newcastle and touring) 1982, Home and Abroad (Serpentine Gallery and touring) 1984, Between Identity/Politics (Gimpel Fils London and NYC) 1986, John Moores Exhbns 15 and 16 (Walker Art Gallery Liverpool) 1987 and 1989–90, Athena Art Awards (Barbican London) 1987, On a Plate (Serpentine Gallery) 1987, Artists in Dialogue (Kettle's Yard) 1987, Public Workshop (Riverside Studios London) 1987, Excavations (Galerie Hubert Winter Vienna and John Hansard Gallery Southampton) 1988, Polaroid work with Jan Hnizdo (V&A) 1989, Shocks to the System (Arts Cncl touring exhbn) 1991, Art for Amnesty (Bonham's London) 1991, invited artist RA Summer Show 1993 and various exhbns at Anthony Reynolds Gallery, The Int Monuments Tst Croatia Appeal (London) 1994, Faith, Hope, Love and Death (Kunsthalle Vienna) 1995–96, Comfort of Strangers: Medical Fndn Caring for Victims of Torture (Waterstones Gall London) 1999, Live in Your Head (Whitechapel Art Gall) 2000, Point of View (Richard Salmon Gall London) 2000, Live in Your Head (Museu do Chiado Lisbon Portugal) 2001, Sculpture in the Park (Mile End Park London) 2001; drawings featured in Lifeclass (HTV West) 2002; *Curator of Exhibitions* Photo(graphic) Vision (Winchester Gallery) 1983, Incidentally... (Winchester Gallery and Goldsmiths' Gallery London) 1986, Artists in Dialogue (Kettle's Yard) 1987; *Public Collections* incl: Arts Cncl of GB, V&A, Wolfson Coll Cambridge (artist/fell); *Awards* Arts Cncl of GB major award 1987, prizewinner John Moores Liverpool Exhbn 16 1990, London Arts Bd Award 1997; *Style—* Ms Sue Arrowsmith; ✉ 117 Devons Road, Bow, London E3 3QX

ARTHUR, Alan David; s of David Edward John Arthur, of Glamorgan, and Elizabeth Ann, *née* Howell; *b* 3 July 1949; *Educ* Bedwellty GS, UC of Wales Aberystwyth (BSc); *Career* chartered accountant; ptnr int practice Deloitte Haskins & Sells 1983–84 (previous posts in S Wales, W Yorks and Zambia), ptnr Booth & Co CAs 1986–89, former dir of corp fin WBS Corp Fin, currently chm and md Padarn Ltd; *Recreations* work, rugby, Rotary; *Clubs* Bradford, Bradford Blaize; *Style—* Alan Arthur, Esq; ✉ 76 Hallowes Park Road, Cullingworth, West Yorkshire BD13 5AR (tel 01535 273074); Padarn Ltd (tel 07877 269661, e-mail alan.arthur@hemscott.net)

ARTHUR, Christine; da of W J Arthur, of Hemel Hempstead, Herts, and R Arthur, *née* Campion; *b* 14 July 1966; *Educ* Parmiters Sch Watford, Univ of Birmingham (BA); *m* 1990, N J S Davies, s of Brian Davies; *Career* Rote PR 1988–92, assoc dir Haslimann Taylor 1992–93, md and main bd dir IAS Smarts (formerly Citigate Communications) Birmingham 1993–; author of various feature articles for nat, local and trade press; memb PRCA, MCIPR; *Recreations* tennis, foreign travel, piano, antiques; *Clubs* Moor Pool Tennis; *Style—* Ms Christine Arthur; ✉ IAS Smarts Ltd, 9 The Apex, 6 Embassy Drive, Edgbaston, Birmingham B15 1TP (tel 0121 456 3199, fax 0121 456 3192, e-mail christine.arthur@iassmarts.com)

ARTHUR, Sir Gavyn Farr; kt (2004); s of Maj the Hon (George) Leonard Arthur (d 1997), of Bath and London, and (Gladys) Raina, *née* Farr; *b* 13 September 1951; *Educ* Harrow, ChCh Oxford (MA); *Career* called to the Bar 1975, bencher Middle Temple 2001; recorder 2001–; memb W Circuit Ctee 1988–; chm Research Ctee on Child Care Proceedings 1987; memb Ct of Common Cncl Ward of Farringdon Without 1988–91; govr: St Bride's Inst Fndn 1989, City of London Sch for Girls 1991–, Christ's Hosp, Bridewell Royal Hosp, Cripplegate Fndn, City of London Freemen's Sch 1996–; Lord Mayor of London 2002; HM Lieutenancy City of London 2002–; Chief Magistrate City of London 2002–; Admiral of the Port of London 2002–, chancellor City Univ London 2002–; govr The Hon the Irish Soc 2004–, Vice-Adm of the Northern Waters 2004–; chm Arab Financial Forum 2004–, dir Halyk Bank; tstee Sir John Soane Museum; Alderman Ward of Cripplegate 1991; pres Cripplegate Ward Club, vice-pres Br Red Cross, vice-pres Inst of Export; memb Cook Soc; Sheriff City of London 1998; Freeman City of London 1979; Master Worshipful Co of Gardeners 2007–; memb Ct of Assts: Worshipful Co of Wax Chandlers, Guild of PR Practitioners; Hon DCL City Univ; Order of Honour Repub of Georgia 2003; KJStJ 2003 (OStJ 2000, KGStJ 2002); *Recreations* travel, writing; *Clubs* Brooks's, Pilgrims, Coningsby; *Style—* Sir Gavyn Arthur; ✉ 2 Harcourt Buildings, Temple, London EC4Y 9DB

ARTHUR, Lt-Col John Reginald; OBE (1985); s of Col Lionel Francis Arthur, DSO, OBE (d 1952), of Camberley, Surrey, and Muriel Irene, *née* Tilley (d 1995); *b* 25 June 1935; *Educ* Winchester; *m* 21 Dec 1965, Princess Valerie Isolde Mary de Mahe, da of Prince John Bryant Digby de Mahe, MBE; 1 da (Anneliese Mary b 8 March 1967), 2 s (Malcolm Ian Charles b 5 Sept 1969, John Benjamin George b 25 Nov 1971); *Career* RMA Sandhurst 1954–55, cmmnd Scots Gds 1955, Staff Coll Camberley 1966, Lt-Col 1976, ret 1984; co sec: Laurence Prust & Co Ltd 1986–89, Credit Commercial de France (UK) Ltd 1989–90, md The Wisley Golf Club plc 1991–98, club and golf conslt 1998–; *Recreations* golf, gardening, music; *Clubs* MCC, Berkshire Golf, Royal St George's Golf, Hon Co of Edinburgh Golfers; *Style—* Lt-Col John Arthur, OBE; ✉ Lantern House, Milll Road, Ridgewell, Halstead CO9 4SG (e-mail arthurjava@aol.com)

ARTHUR, Dr John Willins; s of Archibald Arthur (d 2003), and Mary Arthur (d 1998); *b* 12 July 1949; *Educ* Boroughmuir Sr Secdy, Univ of Toronto (BSc), Univ of Edinburgh (PhD); *m* 25 June 1976, Norma, *née* Cairney; 1 da (Sarah Elizabeth b 2 Sept 1980), 1 s (Andrew John b 20 Nov 1982); *Career* engr; research fell Univ of Edinburgh: Dept of Physics 1974–76, Wolfson Microelectronics Liaison Unit 1976–79; Racal-MESL (now Thales-MESL Ltd): joined 1979, dir Signal Processing 1990–92, dir Electronic Products 1992–96, tech dir 1996–2003; ind conslt 2003–; pt/t conslt: Adaptive Venture Managers 2000–02, Hearing Enhancement plc 2000–02; awards for Racal-MESL: Queen's Award for Technol (jtly) 1989, Millennium Product Award Design Cncl 2000; memb Industrial Advsy Bd: Napier Univ 2000–04 (industrial advsr 1994–95, external examiner 1997–2000), Univ of Edinburgh 2000–; Scot Optoelectronic Assoc: memb Cncl 1997–2001, memb Displays Subgroup Steering Ctee 1997–2001; memb Standing Ctee for Research and Secondment Schemes Royal Acad of Engrg 2003–07; hon research fell Sch of Engrg and Electronics Univ of Edinburgh 2006–; Oliver Lodge premium IEE 1997; CPhys 1976, CEng 1998, FIEE 1998, FRSE 2002, FREng 2002, FInstP 2002, SMIEEE 2003; *Style—* Dr John Arthur, FREng, FRSE; ✉ tel 0131 334 2992, e-mail john.arthur@tiscali.co.uk

ARTHUR, Sir Michael Anthony; KCMG (2004, CMG 1992); s of John Richard Arthur (d 1982), and Mary Deirdre, *née* Chaundy; *b* 28 August 1950; *Educ* Watford GS, Rugby, Balliol Coll Oxford (Nettleship music scholar, BA); *m* 1974, Plaxy Gillian Beatrice, *née* Corke; 2 da (Zoe Mary b 1978, Olivia Anne b 1980), 2 s (Julian J B b 1982, Guy Tristram b 1985); *Career* HM Dip Serv: joined FCO 1972, third sec UK Mission to UN NY 1972–73, UN Dept FCO 1973–74, second sec UK Perm Rep to EEC Brussels 1974–76, second sec Kinshasa 1976–78, FCO 1978–80, private sec to Lord Privy Seal (successively Sir Ian Gilmour, Humphrey Atkins, Lord Belstead, Lady Young) 1980–83, first sec Bonn 1983–88, head EC Dept (internal) FCO 1988–93, sr assoc memb St Antony's Coll Oxford spring/summer 1993, cnsllr and head of Chancery Paris 1993–97, dir of resources and princ fin offr FCO 1997–99, min Washington 1999–2001, DG (economics) EU FCO 2001–03, high cmmr to India 2003–07, ambass to Germany 2007–; Freeman City of Oxford 1971; *Recreations* music, travel, books; *Style—* Sir Michael Arthur, KCMG; ✉ c/o Foreign & Commonwealth Office, King Charles Street, London SW1A 2AH (e-mail michael.arthur@fco.gov.uk)

ARTHUR, Prof Michael James Paul; s of Reginald Alfred John Arthur (d 1989), and Patricia Margaret, *née* Marsh; *b* 3 August 1954, Purley, Surrey; *Educ* Burnt Mill Comp Sch Harlow, Univ of Southampton (BM, DM); *m* 17 March 1979, Elizabeth Susan, *née* McCaughey; 2 da (Rachel Susan b 11 Jan 1983, Sarah Elizabeth b 14 June 1985), 1 s (James William b 4 Oct 1987); *Career* SHO Nottingham 1978–80, med registrar Wessex rotation 1980–82; Univ of Southampton: lectr in med 1982–89, sr lectr in med 1989–92, prof of med 1992–2004, head Sch of Med 1998–2001, dean of med health and life sciences 2003–04; vice-chllr Univ of Leeds 2004–; Fogarty fell Univ of Calif San Francisco 1986–88, Fulbright distinguished scholar Mount Sinai Sch of Med NY 2002–; memb Cell and Molecular Panel Wellcome Tst 1998–2003 (chair 2003), chair Nat Steering Gp Nat Student Survey; pres Br Assoc Study of the Liver 2001–03, chair of tstees Br Liver Tst 2003–06; memb Bd Yorkshire Forward 2006–, chair Worldwide Univs Network 2007–; Research Prize American Liver Fndn 1987, Linacre Medal RCP 1994, Gold Medal Amity Univ Delhi 2006; FRCP 1993, FMedSci 1998, FRSA 2006; *Publications* Wright's Liver and Biliary Disease (jt ed, 3 edn, 1993), author of numerous pubns in scientific jls on cell and molecular pathogenesis of liver disease and liver fibrosis; *Recreations* sailing; *Clubs* Royal Southern Yacht; *Style—* Prof Michael Arthur; ✉ Vice-Chancellor's Office, University of Leeds, Leeds LS9 2JT (tel 0113 343 3000, e-mail m.j.p.arthur@adm.leeds.ac.uk)

ARTHUR, Lt-Gen Sir (John) Norman Stewart; KCB (1985), CVO (2007), JP; s of Col Evelyn Stewart Arthur (d 1963), of Montgomerie, Mauchline, Ayrshire, and Elizabeth, *née* Burnett-Stuart (d 1976); *b* 6 March 1931; *Educ* Eton, RMA Sandhurst; *m* 1960, Theresa Mary, da of Francis and Ursula Hopkinson, of Elmsted, Kent; 1 da (Camilla b 1962), 1 s (Simon b 1967), 1 s decd; *Career* cmmnd Royal Scots Greys 1951; CO Royal Scots Dragoon Gds 1972–74 (despatches 1974), cmd 7 Armd Bde 1976–77, GOC 3 Armd Division 1980–82, Dir Personal Servs (Army) MOD 1983–85, Col Cmdt Mil Provost Staff Corps 1983–88, GOC Scotland Govr Edinburgh Castle 1985–88, Col The Royal Scots Dragoon Gds (Carabiniers and Greys) 1985–92, Col 205 (Scot) Gen Hosp RAMC (V) 1988–93, Col Scottish Yeomanry 1992–97; Offr Queen's Body Guard for Scotland (Royal Co of Archers); memb Br Olympic Team (equestrian three-day event) 1960; vice-pres Riding for the Disabled Edinburgh and Borders 1988–94; chm: Army Benevolent Fund Scotland 1988–2000, Leonard Cheshire Services SW Scotland 1994–2000; pres Scottish Conservation Projects Tst 1989–94, pres Combined Cavalry Old Comrades Association 1995–2000, pres Reserve Forces and Cadets Assoc Lowlands 2000–06; humanitarian aid work Croatia and Bosnia 1992–; memb: Ctee AA 1990–98, Bd of Dirs Edinburgh Military Tattoo Co 1988–91; HM Lord-Lt Stewartry of Kirkcudbright 1996–2006 (DL 1989); *Recreations* country pursuits, reading, field sports; *Style—* Sir Norman Arthur, KCB, CVO; ✉ Newbarns, Colvend, by Dalbeattie, Kirkcudbrightshire DG5 4PY (tel 01556 630227, fax 01556 630409)

ARTHUR, Peter Alistair Kennedy; s of Jack Kennedy Arthur (d 1993), of Troon, Ayrshire, and Margaret Kerr, *née* Morisson; *b* 16 June 1956; *Educ* Loretto, Univ of Edinburgh (LLB); *m* 5 June 1982, Dorothy, da of William Erskine; 3 s (Michael Kennedy b 22 Aug 1984, Graeme Erskine b 4 March 1987, Duncan Robert b 26 Oct 1989); *Career* trainee then asst slr Murray Beith & Murray 1977–80; co sec: Noble & Co 1980–83, ESCO Oil Management Ltd 1983–87; Edinburgh Fund Managers plc: asst co sec and compliance offr 1987–89, co sec 1989–90, admin dir 1990–95, jt md 1995–97; chief legal counsel for Europe Templeton Investment Management 1997–99, dir ISIS Asset Management plc (formerly Friends Ivory & Sime plc) 1999; FCIS; *Recreations* golf, skiing, family; *Clubs* HCEG, Royal Troon, Royal Portrush; *Style*— Peter Arthur, Esq

ARTHUR, Sir Stephen John; 6 Bt (UK 1841), of Upper Canada; s of Hon Sir Basil Malcolm Arthur, 5 Bt, MP (d 1985), and Elizabeth Rita, da of late Alan Mervyn Wells; *b* 1 July 1953; *Educ* Timaru Boys' HS; *m* 1978 (m dis), Carolyn Margaret, da of Burnie Lawrence Diamond, of Cairns, Aust; 2 da (Amanda b 1975, Melanie b 1976), 1 s (Benjamin Nathan b 1979); *Heir* s, Benjamin Arthur; *Style*— Sir Stephen Arthur, Bt

ARTHUR, Terence Gordon (Terry); s of William Gordon Arthur (d 1971), of West Hartlepool, and Dorothy, *née* Baker; *b* 5 September 1940; *Educ* West Hartlepool GS, Univ of Manchester (BSc), Univ of Cambridge (Dip Statistics, Rugby blue); *m* 1, 15 May 1965 (m dis 1983), Valerie Ann Marie, da of Stephen Daniels; 2 da (Louise b 1966, Frances b 1968), 1 s (Richard b 1970); m 2, 25 Nov 1983, Mary Clare, *née* Austick; *Career* asst sec Equity & Law Life Assurance Soc 1967 (joined 1963), ptnr Duncan C Fraser & Co Actuaries 1969–76 (joined 1967), T G Arthur Hargrave Actuaries 1976–91 (fndr 1976) (merged with Bacon and Woodrow 1989); professional non-exec 1991–; dir: Financial Mathematics Ltd 1978, SVM Global Fund plc (formerly Warrants & Value Investment Tst plc) 1993–, WVT Dealing Ltd 1993–, Allianz Dresdner Second Endowment Policy Tst plc 1993–, TKM Gp Pensions Tst Ltd 1994–2006 (chm 1998–), Royal Mail Pensions Tstees Ltd (formerly Post Office Pensions Tstees Ltd) 1998–2004; former dir: Whittingdale Holdings Ltd, Whittingdale Ltd, Police Mutual Assurance Soc, Wesleyan Assurance Soc, Jupiter Extra Income Tst plc, Wiggins Teape Pensions Ltd, Scottish Provident Inst, AXA Rosenberg Investment Mgmnt; memb: Cncl Inst of Actuaries 1977–94 (treas 1985–86), Co of Actuaries; 2 caps England rugby football 1966; Freeman City of London; FIA 1966, FIS 1975, fell Inst of Pensions Mgmnt 1977; *Books* 95 per cent is Crap - A Plain Man's Guide to British Politics (1975); *Clubs* Royal Over-Seas League, Hawks' (Cambridge), Luffenham Heath Golf; *Style*— Terry Arthur, Esq; ✉ 17 Barnack Road, St Martin's Without, Stamford, Lincolnshire PE9 2NA (tel 01780 753525, fax 01780 579073)

ARTHURS, Prof Arnold Magowan; s of James Arthurs (d 1969), of Islandmagee, Antrim, and Mary, *née* Scott (d 1992); *b* 2 September 1934; *Educ* Royal Belfast Academical Instn, Queen's Univ Belfast (BSc), Jesus Coll Oxford (MA, DSc); *m* 6 July 1963, Elspeth Marie, da of Arthur John Lonsdale (d 1977), of Hornsea, E Yorks; 3 s (William b 1965, Henry b 1967, Jack b 1971); *Career* praelector in mathematics and fell The Queen's Coll Oxford 1962; Univ of York: reader 1964, prof of mathematics 1976–2001, prof emeritus 2001–; visiting prof Perugia Univ 2001–; hon treas Sydney Smith Assoc 2000–; *Books* Probability Theory (1965), Complementary Variational Principles (1970, 2nd edn 1980), Calculus of Variations (1975); *Recreations* music, visual and decorative arts; *Style*— Prof Arnold Arthurs; ✉ Department of Mathematics, University of York, Heslington, York YO10 5DD (tel 01904 433074, e-mail ama5@york.ac.uk)

ARUNDEL AND BRIGHTON, Bishop of (RC) 2001–; Rt Rev Kieran Thomas Conry; *b* 1 February 1951, Coventry, Warks; *Educ* Cotton Coll, Ven English Coll Rome, Gregorian Univ Rome (PhB, STB); *Career* ordained priest 1975; teacher Cotton Coll 1976–80, private sec to Archbishop Bruno Heim then to Archbishop Luigi Barbarito 1980–88; appointed monsignor 1984; priest Leek parish 1988, admin St Chad's Cathedral 1990, dir Catholic Media Office 1994–2001, priest St Austin's parish Stafford 2001; memb Nat Conf of Priests 1988–93 (vice-chm 1992–93), chm Birmingham City Centre Churches 1992–93, trainer of counsellors Catholic Marriage Care 1993–2000; *Style*— The Rt Rev the Bishop of Arundel and Brighton; ✉ High Oaks, Old Brighton Road, Pease Pottage, West Sussex RH11 9AJ

ASANTE-MENSAH, Evelyn Justina; OBE (2006); da of Kwaku Asante-Mensah (d 2004), of Ghana, and Beatrice Gyamfi, *née* Amoo-Mensah; *b* 11 October 1965, Ghana; *Educ* Nicholls Ardwick HS Manchester, South Manchester Coll, Manchester Met Univ (Dip Women's Studies, MA); *Partner* Yoni Ejo; 4 c (Leon Joseph b 23 June 1986, Sade Lydia b 4 May 1988, Esi b 3 June 2001, Afua b 31 Jan 2003); *Career* chief exec Black Health Agency 1992–; chair: Central Manchester PCT 2000–, Race for Health 2003–, Black and Minority Ethnic (BME) Advsy Gp NHS Appts Cmmn 2005–; cmmr Equal Opportunities Cmmn 2005–; strategic advsr Govt Office for the NW; memb ACEVO 2000–; Hon DLitt Manchester Met Univ 2002; FRSA 2003; *Recreations* reading, travel, gardening, time with family; *Style*— Ms Evelyn Asante-Mensah, OBE; ✉ Black Health Agency, 464 Chester Road, Old Trafford, Manchester M16 9HE (tel 0161 875 2062, fax 0845 450 3247, e-mail evelyn@blackhealthagency.org.uk)

ASBURY, Dr (Adrian) John; *b* 16 April 1948; *Educ* Sandbach GS, Univ of Birmingham (MB ChB), Univ of Sheffield (PhD, MD); *m*; 2 c; *Career* SHO E Birmingham Hosp 1972–73 (house appts 1971–72), registrar E Birmingham Hosp, E Birmingham Chest Branch Marston Green Maternity Hosp and Hollymoor Psychiatric Hosp 1973, lectr in anaesthesia Huggins Sch of Med Salisbury Southern Rhodesia 1974–75, registrar Dudley Road Hosp Birmingham, Birmingham and E Midlands Eye Hosp and ENT Hosp 1975–76; sr registar (Midland rotation): Queen Elizabeth Hosp, Birmingham Maternity Hosp, Gen Hosp, Birmingham Dental Hosp and Smethwick Centre for Neurology and Neurosurgery 1976–77, Stoke City Gen Hosp and N Staffs Royal Infirmary 1977, Dudley Rd Hosp Clinical Investigation Unit, Birmingham and E Midlands Eye Hosp and ENT Hosp 1977–78; lectr in anaesthesia Dept of Anaesthetics Univ of Sheffield 1978–84, reader in anaesthesia Univ of Glasgow 1995– (sr lectr 1984–95); hon conslt anaesthetist 1984–: Gtr Glasgow Health Bd, Western Infirmary Glasgow (head Dept of Anaesthetics 1994–96); Hartree Premium IEE jtly 1986 and 1993, Cybernetics Soc Prize Edinburgh jtly 1991; memb: BMA, Assoc of Anaesthetists, Anaesthetic Research Soc, Intensive Care Soc, IEE (assoc), Scottish Soc of Anaesthetists, Euro Acad of Anaesthesiology, Glasgow and W Soc of Anaesthetists, Northern Br Pain Assoc; FRCA; *Books* ABC of Computers (BMA, 1989), A Career and Study Guide to Anaesthesia (Glasgow Univ Press, 1989); contrib various book chapters and author of numerous articles in learned jls; *Recreations* local church and its activities, industrial history and its ramifications, recreational mathematics, long distance walking; *Style*— Dr A J Asbury; ✉ University Department of Anaesthesia, Gartnavel General Hospital, Glasgow G12 0YN (tel 0141 531 3716, fax 0141 531 3771, e-mail aj1p@clinmed.gla.ac.uk)

ASCOTT, Robert Henry Charles; s of late James Robert Ascott, of London, and Joan Daisy, *née* Le Feuvre; *b* 7 March 1943; *Educ* St Paul's, Trinity Coll Cambridge (MA), Admin Staff Coll Henley; *Career* pres EMI-Capitol de Mexico SA de CV 1975–79, md Emidata 1979–82, gp sr exec Intermed 1982–84, bursar Univ of Reading 1984–2001, dir Dresdner RCM Income Growth Investment Tst plc 1998–2006; *Recreations* coaching rowing, choral conducting, singing, organ playing, foreign languages; *Clubs* Leander; *Style*— Robert Ascott, Esq; ✉ 17 Staveley Court, Eastbourne, East Sussex BN20 7JS

ASH, Charles John; s of Leonard John Ash (d 1965), of Cirencester, Glos, and Mary Elizabeth, *née* Watson; *b* 26 November 1945; *Educ* Cirencester GS, Hatfield Poly (BSc); *m* 1976, Pamela Monica, da of late Cecil Jenkins; 1 da (Emily Clare b 1978); *Career* Hawker Siddeley Dynamics: jr design engr 1964, design engr 1966, sr design engr 1968–72; design engr Broomwade 1967, project leader Instron 1978–82, head of ops IDEO (formerly Moggridge Associates) 1982–2004, conslt 2004–, sr ptnr ICFBA 2005–; Br Design Award for cordless telephone 1990; Eur Ing 1996, MIMechE; *Style*— Charles Ash, MIMechE; ✉ 36 Flora Grove, St Albans, Hertfordshire AL1 5ET (tel 0845 330 9106, mobile 07855 750442, e-mail charlesash@icfba.biz)

ASH, Dr Daniel V; *b* 18 October 1943; *Educ* London Hosp Med Coll (MB BS, James Anderson Prize, Letheby Prize, Francis Hocking Prize); *m*; 2 c; *Career* house surgn London Hosp 1968–69 (house physician 1968), rotating registrar in gen med N Staffs Hosp Stoke-on-Trent 1971 (rotating SHO 1969–Dec 1970), lectr in internal med Makerere Univ Kampala Uganda 1972–73, registrar in radiotherapy Churchill Hosp Oxford 1973–76, sr registrar Royal Marsden Hosp 1976–77, lectr in radiotherapy Inst of Cancer Research Sutton Surrey 1977–79, conslt in radiotherapy and oncology Cookridge Hosp Leeds 1979–; Lewis Smith Prize in Clinical Med 1969, Ciba Anglo-French Exchange Bursary (Institut Gustave Roussy Paris) 1975, W B travelling fell Rotterdam Radiotherapy Inst 1978, BIR Melville Meml Award (Centre Leon Bernard Lyon) 1981, visiting prof Toronto Univ 1993, Royal Coll of Radiologists Cochrane Shanks travelling prof 1996, Jean Papillon Medal 1997, visiting prof Prince of Wales Univ Hosp Sydney Aust 1998; invited lectr at home and abroad; memb MRC Working Pty: on Radiation Sensitisers 1980–84, of Lung Cancer 1984–88; memb GMC Specialist Assessment Working Gp in Oncology 1995–97; memb Main Bd Euro Soc of Therapeutic Radiology and Oncology (ESTRO) 1989–92 (memb Scientific Ctee 1991–93); pres: Br Oncological Assoc 1994–97 (memb Main Bd 1986–89, chm Scientific Ctee 1986–87), Euro Curietherapy Go (GEC) 1995–98, RCR 2001–; dean Faculty of Clinical Oncology Royal Coll of Radiologists 1998– (registrar 1996–98, dean 1998–2000, pres 2001–04); advsy ed: Euro Jl of Cancer, Bulletin du Cancer; author of numerous articles in learned jls; FRCR 1976, FRCP 1992; *Style*— Dr Daniel V Ash; ✉ Cookridge Hospital, Hospital Lane, Cookridge, Leeds L16 6QB (tel 0113 392 4426)

ASH, Douglas Terence (Doug); s of Sydney Alexander Ash (d 1994), and Doreen Victoria, *née* Gornall; *b* 19 December 1947; *Educ* Wallington GS, Univ of Nottingham (BA), Harvard Business Sch (MBA); *m* 19 Aug 1972, Rhona Helen, da of Harold James Bennett (d 1978), former vice-pres Rotary Int; 3 da (Belinda 1975, Isobel b 1976, Amelia b 1981), 1 s (Laurence b 1981); *Career* formerly: exec dir Ocean Gp plc; chief exec: MSAS Cargo International, English First Division Rugby; dep chm Direct Wines Ltd, dir Refresh (UK) Ltd, dir Four Soft Ltd; *Recreations* Henley Rugby Football (pres); *Style*— Doug Ash, Esq; ✉ Direct Wines Ltd, New Aquitaine House, Theale, Berkshire RG7 4PL (tel 0118 903 0903, fax 0118 903 1208, e-mail dougash@directwines.co.uk)

ASH, Prof Sir Eric Albert; kt (1990), CBE (1982); s of Walter J Ash (d 1970), and Dorothea Cecily, *née* Schwarz (d 1974); *b* 31 January 1928; *Educ* UC Sch, Imperial Coll of Science & Technol London (BSc, DIC, PhD, DSc); *m* 30 May 1954, Clare Mosher, *née* Babb; 5 da (Gillian Carol (Mrs Barr) b 1958, Carolyn Dian b 1960, Lucy Amanda b 1962, Emily Jane, Jennifer Dian (twins) b 1966); *Career* res fell Stanford Univ California 1952–54, res engr Standard Telecom Labs 1954–63; Dept of Electronic and Electrical Engrg UCL: sr lectr 1963–65, reader 1965–67, prof 1967–85, Pender prof and head of dept 1980–85; rector Imperial Coll London 1985–93, prof Dept of Physics UCL 1993–97; treas and dep pres Royal Soc 1997–2002; chm Ocean Power Technology (OPT) Inc 2003–; non-exec dir: BT plc 1987–93, SLC 1994–2000; chm: Cncl Royal Inst 1995–97 (sec 1984–88), Sci Advsy Ctee BBC 1987–94; tstee: Sci Museum 1988–94, Wolfson Fndn 1988–; memb: Exec Bd Fellowship of Engrg (now Royal Acad of Engrg) 1981–84, ABRC 1989–93; Faraday Medal IEE 1980, Royal Medal Royal Soc 1986; hon doctorates: Aston Univ 1987, Univ of Leicester 1988, Univ of Edinburgh 1988, Institut National Polytechnique de Grenoble 1987, Poly Univ NY 1988, Univ of Sussex 1993, Univ of Glasgow 1994, Chinese Univ of Hong Kong 1994, Univ of Warwick 1998, City Univ of Hong Kong 1998, Univ of Surrey 2001, Nanyang Technol Univ Singapore 2002; hon fell: UCL 1985, Imperial Coll London 1995; FREng 1978, FRS 1977, FCGI, FIEE, FIEEE, FInstP, MInstD; *Recreations* reading, music, swimming, skiing; *Style*— Prof Sir Eric Ash, CBE, FRS, FREng; ✉ 11 Ripplevale Grove, London N1 1HS (tel 020 7607 4989, fax 020 7700 7446, e-mail eric_ash99@yahoo.co.uk)

ASHBOURNE, 4 Baron (UK 1885); (Edward) Barry Greynville Gibson; s of Vice Adm 3 Baron Ashbourne, CB, DSO, JP (d 1983), and Reta Frances Manning, *née* Hazeland (d 1996); *b* 28 January 1933; *Educ* Rugby; *m* 25 March 1967, Yvonne Georgina, da of late Mrs Flora Ham; 3 s (Hon Edward Charles d'Olier b 1967, Hon William Rodney Colles b 1970, Hon Patrick Mayne b 1977); *Heir* s, Hon Edward Gibson; *Career* RN 1951–72: Lt Cdr, cmd HMS Crofton 1963–64; RN Staff Coll 1965; stockbroker 1972–77, investment mktg 1979–88; pres: Harting and District Branch Chichester Cons Assoc, Hampshire Autistic Soc, Christian Broadcasting Cncl; vice-pres Cons Against a Federal Europe; patron: Christian Voice, Christian Deaf Link UK; *Recreations* sailing, gardening, fishing; *Style*— The Rt Hon the Lord Ashbourne; ✉ Colebrook Barn, East Harting Farm, Petersfield, Hampshire GU31 5LU

ASHBROOK, Kate Jessie; da of John Benjamin Ashbrook, of Denham Village, Bucks, and Margaret, *née* Balfour; *b* 1 February 1955; *Educ* High March Sch, Benenden, Univ of Exeter (BSc); *Career* sec Dartmoor Preservation Assoc 1981–84 (pres 1995–), gen sec Open Spaces Soc 1984– (memb Exec Ctee 1978–), ed Open Space 1984–; Ramblers' Assoc: memb Nat Exec Ctee 1982–, vice-chm 1993–95, chm 1995–98 and 2006–, chm Access Ctee 1997–, footpath sec and press offr Bucks and W Middx area 1986–, chm Central Rights of Way Ctee 1991–98; sec Countryside Link Gp 1989–92; memb: Gen Cncl CPRE 1984–95, Exec Ctee Cncl for Nat Parks 1983– (vice-chm 1998–2003, chm 2003), Bd Countryside Agency 1999–, Nat Parks Review Advsy Panel DEFRA 2002, Common Land Stakeholder Working Gp DEFRA 2002–03; chm Turville Sch Tst 1994–95; memb Inst of Public Rights of Way Mangrs 1999; won landmark Appeal Court ruling (R (Ashbrook) v E Sussex CC); *Books* Severnside - A Guide to Family Walks (contrib The Southern Quantocks, 1977), The Walks of SE England (contrib A Walk Round Denham, 1975), Common Place No More, Common Land in the 1980s (1983), Make for the Hills (1983), Our Common Right (1987); *Recreations* walking, campaigning for access to countryside, music; *Style*— Miss Kate Ashbrook; ✉ Telfer's Cottage, Turville, Henley-on-Thames, Oxfordshire RG9 6QL (tel 01491 638396); Open Spaces Society, 25A Bell Street, Henley-on-Thames, Oxfordshire RG9 2BA (tel 01491 573535)

ASHBROOK, 11 Viscount (I 1751); Michael Llowarch Warburton Flower; JP (Cheshire 1983), DL (Cheshire 1982); s 10 Viscount Ashbrook, KCVO, MBE (d 1995), and Elizabeth, *née* Egerton-Warburton (d 2002); *b* 9 December 1935; *Educ* Eton, Worcester Coll Oxford (MA); *m* 8 May 1971, Zoë Mary, da of Francis Henry Arnold Engleheart, of Stoke-by-Nayland, Suffolk (d 1963); 1 da (Hon Eleanor Filumena (Hon Mrs Hoare) b 1973), 2 s (Hon Rowland Francis Warburton b 1975, Hon Harry William Warburton b 1977); *Heir* s, Hon Rowland Flower; *Career* 2 Lt Grenadier Gds 1955; landowner; admitted slr 1963; ptnr: Farrer & Co 1966–76, March Pearson & Skelton 1986–91, Pannone March Pearson 1991–92, conslt Pannone & Partners 1992–96; chm Taxation Sub-Ctee CLA 1984–86, pres Cheshire Branch CLA 1990–99; Vice Lord-Lt Cheshire 1990–; *Recreations* gardening, shooting, the countryside; *Clubs* Brooks's; *Style*— The Rt Hon the Viscount Ashbrook, JP, DL; ✉ The Old Parsonage, Arley Green, Northwich, Cheshire CW9 6LZ (tel 01565 777277, fax 01565 777465)

ASHBURTON, 7 Baron (UK 1835) John Francis Harcourt Baring; KG (1994), KCVO (1990, CVO 1980), kt (1983), DL (1994); s of 6 Baron Ashburton, KG, KCVO, JP, DL (d 1991), and Hon Doris Mary Thérèse (d 1981), da of 1 Viscount Harcourt; *b* 2 November 1928; *Educ* Eton, Trinity Coll Oxford (MA); *m* 1, 1955 (m dis 1984), Hon Susan Mary Renwick, da of 1 Baron Renwick, KBE; 2 da (Hon Lucinda Mary Louise (Hon Mrs Michael Vaughan) b 1956, Hon Rose Theresa b 1961), 2 s (Hon Mark Francis Robert b 1958, Hon Alexander Nicholas John b 1964); m 2, 27 Oct 1987, Mrs Sarah Crewe, da of John George Spencer Churchill, and Mrs Angela Culme Seymour; *Career* chm: British Petroleum plc 1992–95 (non-exec dir 1982–92), Baring Bros & Co Ltd 1974–89 (md 1955–74), Barings plc 1985–89 (non-exec dir 1985–94), Baring Stratton Investment Trust plc 1986–98, Baring Fndn 1987–98 (memb Cncl 1971–98); dir: Trafford Park Estates Ltd 1964–77, Bank of England 1983–91, Jaguar plc 1989–91, Outwich Investment Tst 1965–86, Royal Insurance Co 1964–82 (dep chm 1975–82), Dunlop Holdings 1981–84; memb: Br Tport Docks Bd 1966–71, President's Ctee of CBI 1976–79; chm: Ctee on Fin for Industry (NEDC) 1980–86, Accepting Houses Ctee 1977–81; receiver-gen Duchy of Cornwall 1974–90, Lord Warden of the Stannaries and Keeper of the Privy Seal of the Duke of Cornwall 1990–94; pres Overseas Bankers' Club 1977–78, vice-pres Br Bankers' Assoc 1977–81, memb Exec Ctee NACF 1989–99, Rhodes tstee 1970–99 (chm 1987–99); tstee: Royal Jubilee Tsts 1979–95, Nat Gallery 1981–87, Univ of Southampton Devpt Tst 1986–96, Winchester Cathedral Tst 1989– (chm 1993–), The Police Fndn (hon treas) 1989–2001; fell Eton Coll 1982–97; hon fell: Hertford Coll Oxford 1976, Trinity Coll Oxford 1989; High Steward of Winchester Cathedral 1991–; *Clubs* Pratt's, Flyfishers', Beefsteak; *Style*— The Rt Hon Lord Ashburton, KG, KCVO, DL; ✉ Lake House, Northington, Alresford, Hampshire SO24 9TG (tel 01962 734293, fax 01962 735472)

ASHBY, Prof the Hon Michael Farries; CBE (1997); er s of Baron Ashby, FRS (Life Peer; d 1992), and Elizabeth Helen Margaret, *née* Farries; *b* 20 November 1935; *Educ* Campbell Coll Belfast, Queens' Coll Cambridge (MA, PhD); *m* 1962, Maureen, da of James Stewart, of White House, Montgomery, Powys; 2 s, 1 da; *Career* asst Univ of Göttingen 1962–65, asst prof Harvard Univ 1965–69, prof of metallurgy Harvard Univ 1969–73, prof of engineering materials Univ of Cambridge 1973–89, Royal Society research prof Dept of Engineering Univ of Cambridge 1989–; visiting prof RCA 2001–; ed Acta Metallurgica 1974–94; memb Akademie der Wissenschaften zu Göttingen 1980–; Hon MA Harvard 1969; FRS 1979, FREng 1993; *Books* Engineering Materials (parts 1 and 2), Deformation-Mechanism Maps, The Structure and Properties of Cellular Solids, Materials Selection in Mechanical Design, Metal Foams: A Design Guide, Materials and Design: The Art and Science of Material Selection in Product Design; *Recreations* music, design; *Style*— Prof the Hon Michael Ashby, CBE, FRS, FREng; ✉ 51 Maids Causeway, Cambridge CB5 8DE

ASHCOMBE, 4 Baron (UK 1892); Henry Edward Cubitt; s of 3 Baron Ashcombe (d 1962) by his 1 w, Sonia, da of Lt-Col Hon George Keppel, MVO, (3 s of 7 Earl of Albemarle); *b* 31 March 1924; *Educ* Eton; *m* 1, 12 Sept 1955 (m dis 1968), Ghislaine, o da of Cornelius Willem Dresselhuys, of Long Island and formerly w of late Maj Denis James Alexander (later 6 Earl of Caledon); m 2, 1973 (m dis 1979), Hon Virginia Carington, yr da of 6 Baron Carrington; m 3, 1979, Elizabeth, da of Dr Henry Davis Chipps, of Lexington, Kentucky, and widow of Geoffrey Mark Dent-Brocklehurst, of Sudeley Castle, Glos; *Heir* kinsman, Mark Cubitt; *Career* served WWII RAF; consul-gen for Monaco in London 1961–68, chm Cubitt Estates Ltd; *Clubs* White's; *Style*— The Rt Hon the Lord Ashcombe; ✉ Sudeley Castle, Winchcombe, Cheltenham, Gloucestershire GL54 5JD; Flat H, 14 Holland Park Road, London W14 8LZ

ASHCROFT, HE Andrew; *b* 28 May 1961; *m* Amanda; *Career* diplomat; FCO: entered 1980, head of section Fin Dept 1980–81, South Asian Dept 1981–82; third sec Muscat 1982–86, third later second sec Tel Aviv 1987–91, second sec Harare 1991, asst private sec Min of State's Office FCO 1991–95, first sec Harare 1996–99, head Caribbean Section Latin America and Caribbean Dept FCO 1999–2001, ambass to Dominican Repub 2001–06 (concurrently non-resident ambass to Haiti); *Style*— Andrew Ashcroft, Esq; ✉ c/o Foreign & Commonwealth Office, King Charles Street, London SW1A 2AH

ASHCROFT, Kenneth; s of James Martland Ashcroft (d 1969), of Preston, Lancs, and Mary Winifred, *née* Walker; *b* 22 March 1935; *Educ* Preston GS; *m* 1957, Patricia Maria, da of Henry Hothersall (d 1946), of Preston; 2 da (Jill (Mrs Campion) b 1961, Jayne (Mrs Bowtell) b 1963); *Career* formerly with Philips Holland and Ford of Europe; dir: Ideal Standard 1970–73, Comet 1973–75, Hepworth-Next 1975–82, Dixons Ltd 1983–85, Amstrad plc 1985–92; chm Betacom plc 1992–94; non-exec dir Trinity House (and chm Audit Ctee) 1994–2001; memb Advsy Gp to Employment Serv Bd 1993–98; treas Radio Soc of GB 1997–2004; FCA, FCMA; *Recreations* music, gardening, amateur radio (G3MSW); *Style*— Kenneth Ashcroft, Esq; ✉ Fendley Corner, Sauncey Wood, Harpenden, Hertfordshire AL5 5DW (tel 01582 715549, fax 01582 763390, e-mail ken@g3msw.demon.co.uk)

ASHCROFT, Baron (Life Peer UK 2000), of Chichester in the County of West Sussex; Sir Michael Anthony Ashcroft; KCMG (2000); s of Frederic Parker Ashcroft, and Mary Lavinia Long; *b* 4 March 1946; *Educ* King Edward VI GS Norwich, Royal GS High Wycombe, Mid-Essex Tech Coll Chelmsford; *m* 1, 1972 (m dis 1984) Wendy Mahoney; 2 s, 1 da; m 2, 1986, Susi Anstey; *Career* int businessman and entrepreneur; chm BB Hldgs 1987–; fndr and chm Crimestoppers Tst 1988–; former chm: Hawley Group, ADT Ltd, Copen Allman International plc; dir Tyco Int Ltd 1984–2002, varied business interests with investments and participation in public and private cos in UK, USA and Caribbean; Cons Pty: treas 1998–2001, dep chm 2005–; treas Int Democratic Union; ambass of Belize to UN 1998–2000; chm ADT Coll 1991–, chllr Anglia Ruskin Univ (formerly Anglia Poly Univ) 2001–; *Publications* Smell the Coffee: A Wake Up Call to the Conservative Party (2005), Dirty Politics, Dirty Times (2005), Victoria Cross Heroes (2006); *Recreations* researching the Victoria Cross, entertaining friends, trying something new, messing about in boats; *Style*— The Rt Hon the Lord Ashcroft, KCMG; ✉ House of Lords, London SW1A 0PW (website www.lordashcroft.com)

ASHCROFT, Richard; *Educ* Upholland HS Wigan; *m* Kate Radley; *Career* pop singer; lead singer of The Verve 1989–99, solo artist 2000–; *Albums* with The Verve incl: Verve (EP, 1992), Storm in Heaven (1993), No Come Down (1994), A Northern Soul (1995), Urban Hymns (1997); solo albums: Alone With Everybody (2000), Human Conditions (2002); *Singles* with The Verve incl: All in the Mind (1992), She's A Superstar (1992), Gravity Grave (1992), Blue (1993), Slide Away (1993), This is Music (1995), On Your Own (1995), History (1995), Bitter Sweet Symphony (1997), The Drugs Don't Work (1997), Lucky Man (1997); solo singles: A Song For Lovers (2000), Money To Burn (2000), C'mon People (2000); *Style*— Richard Ashcroft

ASHDOWN, David William; s of William Curtis Thomas, and Jean Vida Ashdown; *b* 11 December 1950; *Educ* Wandsworth Comp; *m* 12 Aug 1978, Carol, da of Andrew Allan Smith (d 1963); 2 s (Michael b 1974, Peter b 1979); 1 da (Elizabeth Rose b 22 Aug 1991); *Career* photographer: Keystone Press 1968–78, Daily Star 1978–86; chief sports photographer The Independent 1986–; FRPS; *Awards* Ilford Press Photographer of the Year 1974, runner-up Br Press Picture Awards 1979, Ilford Sports Picture of the Year 1985 and 1991, Nikon Press Sports Photographer of the Year 1987, Adidas Euro Sports Picture of the Year 1987, Sports Photographer of the Year 1987 and 1990, Euro Sports Photographer of the Year 1993, Photographer of the Year British Press Awards 1998; *Recreations* golf, old motorbikes; *Style*— David Ashdown, Esq; ✉ mobile 07710 613 969

ASHDOWN OF NORTON-SUB-HAMDON, Baron (Life Peer UK 2001), of Norton-sub-Hamdon in the County of Somerset; Sir Jeremy John Durham (Paddy) Ashdown; GCMG (2006), KBE (2000), PC (1989); s of John W R D Ashdown, and Lois A Ashdown; *b* 27 February 1941; *Educ* Bedford Sch, Language Sch Hong Kong (qualified first class Chinese interpreter); *m* 1961, Jane Courtenay; 1 s (Hon Simon), 1 da (Hon Kate); *Career* RM 1959–72, served Borneo, Persian Gulf and Belfast, cmd Special Boat Section (SBS) in the Far East; first sec (FO) Br Mission to UN Geneva 1971–76, with Westland Helicopters 1976–78, sr mangr Morlands Ltd 1978–81, youth offr Dorset CC 1981–83, MP (Lib until 1988, Lib Dem 1988–2001) Yeovil 1983–2001 (Parly candidate (Lib) 1976); ldr Lib Dems 1988–99; Lib/Alliance/Lib Dem spokesman: on trade and industry 1983–86, on educn and sci 1987–88, on NI 1989–90; unpaid non-exec dir Time Gp 1999–2002; Peace Implementation Cncl's High Rep for Bosnia 2002–06, EU special rep for Bosnia and Herzegovina 2002–06; *Clubs* National Liberal; *Style*— The Rt Hon the Lord Ashdown of Norton-sub-Hamdon, GCMG, KBE, PC

ASHE, Geoffrey Thomas Leslie; s of Arthur Ashe (d 1959), and Thelma Hoodless Ashe (d 1959); *b* 29 March 1923, Acton; *Educ* St Paul's, Univ of British Columbia (BA), Univ of Cambridge (MA); *m* 1, 1946, Dorothy Irene Train (d 1990); 4 s (Thomas b 1949, John b 1950, Michael b 1951, Brendan b 1958), 1 da (Sheila b 1953); m 2, 1998, Dr Patricia Chandler; *Career* admin asst Ford of Canada 1952–54, lectr in mgmnt studies The Polytechnic London 1956–62, co-fndr and sec Camelot Research Ctee 1965–74, full-time writer and lectr 1968–; visiting prof 1980–97: Univ of Southern Mississippi, Univ of Minnesota Duluth, Portland State Univ, Univ of Alabama Birmingham, Univ of New Mexico; memb: Medieval Acad of America, Int Arthurian Soc, Labour Party; FRSL 1963; *Publications* incl: King Arthur's Avalon: The Story of Glastonbury (1957, new edn 1992), From Caesar to Arthur (1960), Land to the West: St Brendan's Voyage to America (1962), The Land and the Book: Israel, the Perennial Nation (1965), Gandhi: A Study in Revolution (1968, new edn 2000), The Quest for Arthur's Britain (ed and contrib, 1 edn 1968), Camelot and the Vision of Albion (1971), The Quest for America (ed and contrib, 1971), Do What You Will: A History of Anti-Morality (1974, re-published as The Hell-Fire Clubs: A History of Anti-Morality 2000), The Finger and the Moon (novel, 1973, new edn 2004), The Virgin: Mary's Cult and the Re-Emergence of the Goddess (1976, new edn 1988), The Ancient Wisdom (1977), Miracles (1978), A Guidebook to Arthurian Britain (1980, re-published as A Traveller's Guide to Arthurian Britain 1997), A Certain Very Ancient Book: Traces of an Arthurian Source in Geoffrey of Monmouth's History (article in Speculum: The Journal of the Medieval Academy of America, 1981), Kings and Queens of Early Britain (1982, new edn 2000), Avalonian Quest (1982), The Discovery of King Arthur (1985, new edn 2003), The Arthurian Encyclopedia (ed and contrib, 1986), The Arthurian Handbook (collaborator, 1990), Mythology of the British Isles (1990, new edn 2002), King Arthur: The Dream of a Golden Age (1990), The New Arthurian Encyclopedia (ed and contrib, 1991), Dawn Behind the Dawn (1992), Atlantis: Lost Lands, Ancient Wisdom (1992), The Book of Prophecy: From Ancient Greece to the Millennium (1999, new edn 2002), The Encyclopedia of Prophecy (2001), Merlin (2002), Labyrinths and Mazes (2003), Merlin: The Prophet and his History (2006), The Offbeat Radicals (2007); author of numerous articles in periodicals; *Style*— Geoffrey Ashe, Esq; ✉ c/o Rogers, Coleridge & White Literary Agency, 20 Powis Mews, London W11 1JN (cara@rcwlitagency.com)

ASHE, (Thomas) Michael; QC (England and Wales 1994, Northern Ireland 1998); s of John Ashe (d 1977), and Nancy, *née* O'Connor (d 1992); *b* 10 March 1949; *Educ* Finchley Catholic GS, Inns of Court Sch of Law; *m* 23 April 1977, Helen Morag, da of Lt Col Kenneth Wheeler Nicholson (d 1963); *Career* Estate Duty Office Inland Revenue 1967–70; called to the Bar: Middle Temple 1971 (bencher 1998), Ireland 1975, NI 1993; with Schroders and Arbuthnot Latham (merchant banks) 1971–76; in practice at Bar 1978–; memb Board Soc of Advanced Legal Studies 1997–2003, auditor and notary Diocese of Brentwood 1997–, recorder of the Crown Court 2000, sr counsel Irish Republic 2000; Knight of the Holy Sepulchre 2000; *Books* Money (4 edn, Halsbury's Laws of England, 1980), Injunctions (4 edn (reprint), Halsbury's Laws of England, 1991), Insider Trading (2 edn, 1993), Insider Crime (1993), International Tracing of Assets (ed, 1997), Guide to Financial Services Regulation (1997), Moneylaundering (2000, 2 edn 2007); *Recreations* walking, railways, music; *Style*— Michael Ashe, Esq, QC; ✉ 9 Stone Buildings, Lincoln's Inn, London WC2A 3NN (tel 020 7404 5055, fax 020 7405 1551, e-mail masheqc@compuserve.com)

ASHE, Rosemary Elizabeth; da of late Philip Stephen Ashe, and Dorothy May, *née* Watts; *b* 28 March 1953; *Educ* Lowestoft GS, Royal Acad of Music, London Opera Centre; *Career* soprano; *Theatre* roles incl: Ruth in The Pirates of Penzance (UK and American tours), Madame Spritzer in 13 Rue De L'Amour (Northampton Theatre), Nunsense (Redgrave Theatre), Viv Nicholson in Spend, Spend, Spend! (West Yorkshire Playhouse), Miss Andrew in Mary Poppins (Prince Edward Theatre); *Opera* roles incl: The Queen of Night in The Magic Flute (Opera North), Marionette in The Cunning Widow (Wexford Festival), Fiakermilli in Arabella, Esmeralda in The Bartered Bride, Papagena in The Magic Flute, Venus in Orpheus in the Underworld (ENO), Lucy Lockitt in The Beggar's Opera and Despina in Cosi fan Tutte (dir Jonathan Miller for BBC TV), Musetta in La Bohhme (Opera Northern Ireland), Frasquita in Carmen (Earls Court prodn repeated in Japan), Violetta in La Traviata (Holland Park), Dinah in Trouble in Tahiti (Music Theatre Transparant Belgium); roles in musicals incl: Janet in The Rocky Horror Show, Maria in West Side Story, Hortense in The Boy Friend, Yum Yum in The Mikado, created the role of Carlotta in The Phantom of the Opera, Manon and Sari in Bitter Sweet (Sadler's Wells Opera), title role in La Belle Hilhne (New Sadler's Wells Opera), Cunegonde in Candide (Old Vic Theatre), Josephine in HMS Pinafore (City Center Opera NY), Julie in Showboat (RSC/Opera North), The Witch in Into the Woods (Wolsey Theatre Ipswich), Madame Thinardier in Les Misirables (Palace), Widow Corney in Oliver (Palladium); other performances incl: Masterpiece Theatre Anniversary Celebrations (New York Forbidden Broadway Company Los Angeles and Washington), The Killer Soprano (one-woman show), Annie in Annie Get Your Gun (Wolsey Theatre Ipswich), Hermia in A Midsummer Night's Dream (Barbados Festival), Lottie Grady in When We Are Married and Orinthia in The Applecart (both Wolsey Theatre Ipswich), Asphynxia in Salad Days (nat tour), Zou Zou in La Belle Vivette (ENO), Mrs Darling in Peter Pan (Theatre Royal Nottingham), Dottie Otley in Noises Off (Salisbury Playhouse), Felicia Gabriel in The Witches of Eastwick (Theatre Royal Drury Lane and Princess Theatre Melbourne, Olivier Award nomination); regular broadcaster on Friday Night is Music Night and Songs From The Shows (Radio 2); *Television* incl: The Music Game (Channel 4), Whale On (Channel 4), House of Eliot (BBC), An Audience With Ronnie Corbett (LWT); *Recordings* incl: The Phantom of the Opera, The Boyfriend, Bitter Sweet, Kismet, The Student Prince, The Song of Norway, Oliver, The Killer Soprano, The Witches of Eastwick, Serious Cabaret; *Style*— Ms Rosemary Ashe; ✉ c/o Hilary Gagan Associates, 187 Drury Lane, London WC2B 5QD (tel 020 7404 8794, fax 020 7430 1869, e-mail hilary@hgassoc.freeserve.co.uk, website www.rosemaryashe.com)

ASHENFORD, Marcus Frank; s of David Ashenford, of Minchinhampton, Glos, and Josephine, *née* Broomhall; *b* 5 December 1969; *Educ* Cheltenham Coll; *m* 24 Jan 1997, Kate, *née* Gregory; 1 da (Alicia b 5 Dec 1998); *Career* chef; worked at: Gloscat 1986–88, Calcot Manor Tetbury 1988–91 (1 Michelin Star), Waterside Inn Bray 1991–94 (3 Michelin Stars); head chef: Lovells Windrush Farm 1994–97 (1 Michelin Star, 1 Egon Ronay Star, Acorn Award, 3 AA Rosettes, 6/10 Good Food Guide), Chavignol Chipping Norton 1998–2001 (1 Michelin Star, 3 AA Rosettes, 7/10 Good Food Guide), Chavignol The Old Mill Shipston on Stour 2001–03 (1 Michelin Star, 7/10 Good Food Guide); chef and prop 5 North Street 2003– (1 Michelin Star 2004); *Recreations* golf; *Clubs* Bristol City FC; *Style*— Marcus Ashenford, Esq

ASHER, Bernard Harry; *Career* dir HSBC Holdings plc 1989–98, formerly exec dir investment banking HSBC Holdings plc, formerly chm HSBC Investment Banking plc (subsid); non-exec chm Lonrho Africa 1998–2004; non-exec dir: Rémy Cointreau SA 1992–2001, The China Fund Inc 1995–2000, Rangold Resources Ltd 1997–, Morgan Sindall plc 1998–, Seymour Pierce 2000–; vice-chm and sr ind dir Legal & General plc 2000–04 (non-exec dir 1998–2004), chm Lion Trust Asset Mgmnt plc 2004–; investment advsr and memb Advsy Panel RCP 1998–; tstee The Health Fndn 1998–, vice-chm of govrs LSE 1998–2004; *Style*— Bernard Asher, Esq

ASHER, Jane; da of Richard Alan John Asher (d 1969), and Margaret, *née* Eliot; *b* 5 April 1946; *Educ* North Bridge House, Miss Lambert's PNEU; *m* Gerald Anthony Scarfe, *qv*, s of Reginald Thomas Scarfe (d 1972); 1 da (Katie b 1974), 2 s (Alexander b 1981, Rory b 1983); *Career* actress and novelist; proprietor Jane Asher Party Cakes and Sugarcraft Shop Chelsea, designer Jane Asher range Debenhams, conslt Victoria Foods; contrib: TV and radio current affairs progs, newspaper and magazine articles; reg columns: Daily Telegraph, The Independent, The Express; patron numerous charities; pres: Nat Autistic Soc, Arthritis Care, Parkinson's Disease Soc; vice-pres: Nat Deaf Children's Soc, Child Accident Prevention Tst; memb BAFTA, assoc RADA; Hon LLD Univ of Bristol; FRSA; *Theatre* incl: Housemaster 1957, Muriel Webster in Will You Walk A Little Faster (Duke of York's) 1960, Wendy in Peter Pan (Scala) 1961; Bristol Old Vic 1965–72: Cleo, Great Expectations, The Happiest Days of Your Life, Sixty Thousand Nights, Romeo and Juliet, Measure For Measure; Eliza Doolittle in Pygmalion (Watford), Juliet in Romeo and Juliet, Julietta in Measure for Measure (both City Centre NY) 1967, Look Back in Anger (Royal Court) 1969, Celia in The Philanthropist (Mayfair and Broadway) 1970, Sally in Old Flames (Bristol Old Vic) 1974, Ann in Treats (Royal Court and Mayfair) 1975, Charlotte in Strawberry Fields, To Those Born Later (NT) 1976, Dr Scott in Whose Life Is It Anyway? (Mermaid and Savoy), Peter in Peter Pan 1979, Before The Party (also prodr, Queens Theatre) 1981, Ruth in Blithe Spirit (Vaudeville) 1986, Robot/Wife in Hence forward.... (Vaudeville) 1989, Lady Sneerwell in The School for Scandal (RNT) 1990, Diana in Making It Better (Hampstead & Criterion) 1992/93, Laura in The Shallow End (Royal Court) 1997, Barbara in Things we do for Love (Gielgud) 1998, House and Garden (Royal Nat Theatre) 2000, What the Butler Saw (Theatre Royal Bath and tour) 2001, Festen (Almeida and Lyric) 2004, The World's Biggest Diamond (Royal Court) 2006; *Television* incl: The Mill on The Floss, The Recruiting Officer, Hedda Gabler, Brideshead Revisited 1981, Love is Old Love is New, Voyage Round My Father, East Lynne, Bright Smiler, The Mistress 1986, Wish Me Luck 1987–89, Eats for Treats 1990, Closing Numbers 1993, The Choir 1995, Good Living 1997 & 1998, Crossroads 2003, Marple 2005, New Tricks 2005, A for Andromeda 2006, Holby City 2007; *Radio* incl: Crown House, Winter Journey (Sony Award); *Films* incl: Mandy 1951, Greengage Summer 1961, Alfie 1966, Deep End 1970, Henry VIII and His Six Wives 1970, Runners 1984, Dream Child 1985, Paris By Night 1988, Tirant lo Blanc 2005, Death at a Funeral 2007; *Books* Jane Asher's Party Cakes (1982), Jane Asher's Quick Party Cakes (1983), Jane Asher's Fancy Dress (1983), Silent Nights for You and Your Baby (1984), Easy Entertaining (1987), Moppy Is Happy (with G Scarfe, 1987), Moppy Is Angry (with G Scarfe, 1987), Keep Your Baby Safe (1988), Jane Asher's Children's Parties (1988), Calendar of Cakes (1989), Eats for Treats (1990), Jane Asher's Complete Book of Cake Decorating Ideas (1993), Time to Play (1995), The Longing (1996), 101 Things I wish I'd Known (1996), The Question (1998), The Best of Good Living (1998), Good Living at Christmas (1998), Tricks of the Trade (1999), Losing It (2002), Cakes for Fun (2005), Moppy is Sad, Moppy is Calm (with G Scarfe, 2005), Beautiful Baking (2007); *Recreations* Times crossword, reading, music; *Style*— Jane Asher; ✉ c/o PFD, Drury House, 34–43 Russell Street, London WC2B 5HA (tel 020 7344 1093, e-mail lking@pfd.co.uk); website www.jane-asher.co.uk

ASHER, Jeremy; s of Gerald Asher, of San Francisco, USA, and Judith Asher, of London; *b* 16 July 1958; *Educ* Winchester, LSE (BSc), Harvard Grad Sch of Business Admin (MBA); *m* 30 May 1985 (m dis), Barrie, *née* Gilbert; 3 s (Alexander b 16 April 1988, Hannibal b 12 Jan 1991, Tamerlane b 26 Feb 1994); *Career* conslt rising to mangr Mercer Management Consulting Washington DC 1980–84, co-head Global Oil Products, Trading & Processing Glencore AG 1985–89, md Beta Raffinerieges Wilhelmshaven mbH 1990–97 (memb Supervisory Bd), gp chief exec PA Consulting Gp 1998–2001, chm SkyVision Holdings Ltd 2002–04, chm Agile Energy Ltd 2005–; *Recreations* tennis, soccer; *Clubs* Queen's; *Style*— Jeremy Asher, Esq; ✉ Agile Energy Limited, Hirzel Court, St Peter Port, Guernsey GY1 2NL (tel 020 7792 2055, fax 0870 051 7708, e-mail jeremy.asher@agilenergy.co.uk)

ASHER, Michael John; s of Frederick William Asher (d 1992), of Stamford, Lincs, and Kathleen Frances Kew (d 1992); *b* 21 April 1953; *Educ* Stamford Sch, Univ of Leeds (BA), Leeds Poly (CertEd); *m* 1986, Mariantonietta, only da of Gen Pasquale Peru, of Rome, Italy, and Prof Italia Peru; 1 s (Burton Frederick Pascal b 1991), 1 da (Jade Isabelle b 2001); *Career* author and explorer; served 2 Bn Parachute Reg Europe, Malyasia, NI 1971–74 (awarded GSM NI 1972), 23 Special Air Serv Reg 1974–77, 2 Section Special Patrol Gp RUC Belfast 1978–79; vol teacher remote rural areas Sudan 1979–82, lived with Bedouin tribe (Kababish) Sudan 1982–85, conslt UNICEF 1985, made first west-east crossing of Sahara by camel (4,500 miles, with Mariantonietta Peru) 1986–87, project offr UNICEF Red Sea Hills Sudan 1988–89; travel incl: Papua New Guinea, Thar Desert of India/Pakistan 1989–90, journeys of Wilfred Thesiger and various expeditions 1990–94, crossing of Great Sand Sea Egypt by camel 1991, Jordan, Syria, Lebanon, Sinai, Palestine and Tibet 1994–; presenter: In Search of Lawrence (Channel 4) 1997, Death Deceit and the Nile (Channel 4) 2000, The Real Bravo Two Zero (Channel 4) 2002; dir Survivors (KTN) 2005; author of articles for: The Guardian, The Washington Post, Readers' Digest, Daily Telegraph, Geographical, World; dir Lost Oasis Expeditions - adventure camel treks in the Sahara; RGS Ness Award for exploration 1993, RSGS Mungo Park Medal for exploration 1996; FRGS 1984, FRSL 1996; *Books* In Search of the Forty Days Road (1984), A Desert Dies (1986), Impossible Journey (1988), Shoot to Kill - A Soldier's Journey Through Violence (1990), Thesiger - A Biography (1994), The Last of the Bedu - In Search of the Myth (1996), Sahara (with Kazoyoshi Nomachi, 1996), Phoenix Rising - The United Arab Emirates, Past, Present and Future (with Werner Forman, 1996), Lawrence: The Uncrowned King of Arabia (1998), The Eye of Ra (1999), Firebird (2000), Rare Earth (2002), The Real Bravo Two Zero (2002), Sandstorm (2003), Get Rommel (2004), Khartoum - The Ultimate Imperial Adventure (2005), The Great Saharan Railway (2006); *Recreations* travel, running; *Clubs* Geographical; *Style*— Michael Asher, Esq, FRSL; ✉ c/o David Higham Associates, 5–8 Lower John Street, Golden Square, London W1R 4HA (tel 020 7437 7888, fax 020 7437 1072, e-mail anthonygoff@davidhigham.co.uk); website www.lost-oasis.org

ASHER, Prof Ronald E; s of Ernest Asher, and Doris, *née* Hurst; *b* 23 July 1926; *Educ* King Edward VI GS Retford, UCL (BA, PhD), Univ of Edinburgh (DLitt); *m* 1960, Chin; 2 s (David b 1966, Michael b 1968); *Career* asst Dept of French UCL 1951–53, lectr in linguistics and Tamil SOAS Univ of London 1953–65; Univ of Edinburgh: sr lectr Dept of Linguistics 1965–70, reader 1970–77, prof of linguistics 1977–93, dean Faculty Arts 1986–89, memb Univ Ct 1989–92, vice-princ 1990–93, curator of patronage 1991–93, hon fell 1993–, dir Centre for Speech Technol Res 1994; visiting prof: of Tamil Univ of Chicago 1961–62, of linguistics Univ of Illinois 1967, of Tamil and Malayalam Michigan State Univ 1968, of linguistics Univ of Minnesota 1969, Collège de France Paris 1970, of linguistics and int communication Int Christian Univ Tokyo 1994–95, of 20th century Malayalam literature Mahatma Gandhi Univ Kottayam 1995–96; memb Gen Cncl of Tamil Sahitya Acad (Chennai India) 2000–; fell Kerala Sahitya Akademi (Kerala Acad of Letters) India 1983, Gold Medal of the Akademi for distinguished servs to Malayalam language and literature, hon fell Sahitya Akademi (Nat Acad of Letters) India 2007; FRAS 1964, FRSE 1991; *Books* A Tamil Prose Reader (1971), Aspects de la littérature en prose dans le sud de l'Inde (1972), Some Landmarks in the History of Tamil Prose (1973), Scavenger's Son (trans from Malayalam, 1975), Me Grandad 'ad an Elephant (trans from Malayalam, 1980), Towards a History of Phonetics (ed with E J A Henderson, 1981), Tamil (1982), Malayala bhasha-sahitya pathanangal (Malayalam - Studies on Malayalam Language and Literature) (1989), National Myths in Renaissance France (1993), Atlas of the World's Languages (jt ed, 1994), The Encyclopedia of Language and Linguistics (ed-in-chief, 1994), Concise History of the Language Sciences from the Sumerians to the Cognitivists (jt ed, 1995), Malayalam (1997), Basheer svatantryasamara kathakal (Malayalam - Basheer: Stories of the Freedom Struggle) (ed, 1998), Basheer, Malayalattinre sargavismayam (Malayalam - Critical Studies on the Novels and Stories of V M Basheer) (1999), Colloquial Tamil (with E Annamalai, 2002), What the Sufi said (trans from Malayalam, with N Gopalakrishnan, 2002), Wind Flowers: Contemporary Malayalam Short Fiction (with V Abdulla, 2004); *Style*— Prof R E Asher, FRSE; ✉ Linguistics and English Language, University of Edinburgh, Adam Ferguson Building, Edinburgh EH8 9LL (tel 0131 650 3484, e-mail r.e.asher@ed.ac.uk)

ASHKENAZY, Vladimir; s of David Ashkenazy (d 1997), of Gorky, and Evstolia Plotnova (d 1979); *b* 6 July 1937; *Educ* Moscow Central Sch of Music, Moscow Conservatory (second prize Chopin int piano competition 1955, first prize Brussels int piano competition 1956, first prize Tchaikovsky int piano competition 1962); *m* 25 Feb 1961, Thorunn Sofia, da of Johann Tryggvason, of Iceland; 2 s (Vladimir Stefan b 1961, Dimitri Thor b 1969), 3 da (Nadia Liza b 1963, Sonia Edda b 1974, Alexandra Inga b 1979); *Career* concert pianist and conductor; studied under Lev Oborin class Moscow Conservatory 1955, debut in the UK with London Symphony Orch 1963, debut solo recital London (Festival Hall) 1963; music dir: Royal Philharmonic Orch London 1987–95, Radio Symphony Orch (now Deutsches Sinfonie-Orchester) Berlin 1989–99, Czech Philharmonic Orch 1998–2003, NHK Symphony Orch Tokyo 2004–; Hon RAM 1972; Order of Falcon Iceland 1988; *Books* Beyond Frontiers (with Jasper Parrott, 1985); *Style*— Vladimir Ashkenazy, Esq

ASHLEY, Bernard John; s of Alfred Walter Ashley (d 1967), and Vera, *née* Powell (d 1978); *b* 2 April 1935; *Educ* Sir Joseph Williamson's Mathematical Sch Rochester, Trent Park Coll of Educn, Cambridge Inst of Educn (Advanced DipEd); *m* 1957, Iris Frances, da of Harold Edward Holbrook; 3 s (Christopher b 1 Jan 1961, David b 1 June 1963, Jonathan b 17 April 1965); *Career* writer; teacher in Kent until 1965; head teacher: Hertford Heath CP Sch 1965–71, Hartley Jr Sch Newham 1971–77, Charlton Manor Jr Sch London 1977–95; memb: Writers' Guild of GB, Bd of Directors Greenwich Theatre, BAFTA Children's Ctee; Hon DEd Univ of Greenwich, Hon DLitt Univ of Leicester; *Novels* The Trouble with Donovan Croft (1974, The Other Award 1975), Terry on the Fence (1975), All My Men (1977), A Kind of Wild Justice (1979), Break in the Sun (1981), Dodgem (1983), High Pavement Blues (1984), Janey (1985), Running Scared (1986), Bad Blood (1988), Johnnie's Blitz (1995), Tiger Without Teeth (1998), Little Soldier (1999), Revenge House (2002), Freedom Flight (2003), Ten Days to Zero (2005), Smokescreen (2006); *Short Story Collections* Clipper Street (1988), Seeing Off Uncle Jack (1991), Dockside School (1992), The Puffin Book of School Stories (1993), City Limits (1997); *Picture Books* Cleverstick (with Derek Brazell, 1992), I Forgot, said Troy (with Derek Brazell, 1996), A Present for Paul (with David Mitchell, 1996), Growing Good (with Anne Wilson, 1999), Double the Love (with Carol Thompson, 2002), The Bush (with Lynne Willey, 2003); *Television* BBC TV serials: Break In the Sun (1981), Running Scared (1986), The Country Boy (1989), Dodgem (1991, winner Best Children's Entertainment Prog, RTS 1992); Three Seven Eleven (Granada TV series), Justin and the Demon Drop Kick (Carlton for EBU); *Plays* The Old Woman who lived in a Cola Can (tour, 1988/89), The Secret of Theodore Brown (Unicorn Theatre London, 1990); *Recreations* theatre, concerts; *Style*— Bernard Ashley, Esq; ✉ 128 Heathwood Gardens, London SE7 8ER (tel 020 8854 5785, fax 020 8244 0131, website www.bashley.com)

ASHLEY, Cedric; CBE (1984); s of Ronald Bednall Ashley (d 1980), and Gladys Vera, *née* Fincher; *b* 11 November 1936; *Educ* King Edward's Sch Birmingham, Univ of Birmingham (BSc, PhD); *m* 1, 1960, Pamela Jane (decd), da of William Turner; 1 s (Paul); m 2, 1965 (m dis 1989), (Marjorie) Vivien, da of Arnold Joseph Gooch (d 1960); 1 da (Juliet b 1967), 1 s (William b 1971); m 3, 1991, Auriol Mary Keogh, da of John Kelly; *Career* with Rolls-Royce Ltd Derby 1955–60; lectr Univ of Birmingham 1965–73 (ICI research fell 1963), int tech dir Bostrom Div UOP Ltd 1973–77, dir Motor Industry Research Assoc 1977–87, md Lotus Engineering Ltd 1987–88, chm Cedric Ashley and Associates 1988–, chief exec British Internal Combustion Engine Research Inst 1989–91, md Steyr Power Technology Ltd 1992–; dir Euromotor 1992–2006, chm euromotor-autotrain LLP 2006–; chm: SEE 1970–72, RAC Tech Ctee 1980–87; memb: SMMT Tech Bds 1977–87, Bd Assoc of Independent Contract Research Orgns 1977–86 (pres 1982–84), Coventry and District Engrg Employers' Assoc 1978–85, Court Cranfield Inst of Technol 1977–87, Engine and Vehicles Ctee DTI 1980–88, Three Dimensional Design Bd CNAA 1981–87; tstee Sir Henry Royce Meml Fndn 2006–; Cementation Muffelite Award SEE 1968, Design Cncl Award 1974; Liveryman Worshipful Co of Carmen; FIMechE 1978 (chm Automobile Div 1990–91), FRSA 1983; *Recreations* walking, motoring; *Clubs* Thursday; *Style*— Cedric Ashley, Esq, CBE; ✉ 148 Clydesdale Tower, Holloway Head, Birmingham B1 1UH (tel 0121 622 7476, fax 0121 414 7151, e-mail c.ashley@bham.ac.uk)

ASHLEY, Prof Christopher Charles; s of Charles Arthur Ashley, and Esther Lillian Ashley; *b* 29 August 1941; *Educ* King George V GS Southport, Univ of Bristol (BSc, PhD), Univ of Oxford (MA, DSc); *m* 1967, Catherine Helen Brown; 1 s, 2 da; *Career* Fulbright travel scholar 1965–68, NIH post-doctoral fell Univ of Oregon 1965–68, MRC post-doctoral fell Univ of Bristol 1968–70, lectr in physiology Univ of Bristol 1970–76, visiting prof Univ of Bochum Germany 1976–77; Univ of Oxford: lectr 1976–, fell and med tutor CCC Oxford 1976– (Corange fell 1991), prof of physiology 1996–; adj prof of molecular and cellular pharmacology Univ of Miami Med Sch 1991–; external examiner: Univ of Dundee 1980–83, Univ of Liverpool 1988–90; memb: MRC Grants Ctee A 1988–92, Muscular Dystrophy Scientific Ctee 1993–, MRC Advsy Bd 1997–, MRC Coll of Experts 2005–; ed Cell Calcium 1980–90, co-founding ed J Muscle Research & Cell Motility 1980–, special advsr HEFCE Res Assessment Exercise 2001, contrib and ed of numerous reviews and chapters in learned jls; awarded: NIH Prog Grant (CoPI) 1986–90 and 1990–95, MRC Prog Grant (PI) 1990–95, Br Heart Fndn Prog Grant (CoPI) 1997–2003 and 2003–; EMBO Fellowship DESY Hamburg 1988 and 1990; memb: Biochemical Soc, Physiological Soc, American Physiological Soc (elected foreign memb), US Biophysical Soc; Hon MRCP 1998, FMedSci 2002; *Recreations* music, playing the piano, fell walking, natural history, collecting; *Style*— Prof Christopher Ashley; ✉ Corpus Christi College, Oxford OX1 4JF (tel 01865 272493, e-mail ash@herald.ox.ac.uk)

ASHLEY, (Hon) Jackie; da of Baron Ashley of Stoke (Life Peer), *qv*, and Pauline Kay, *née* Crispin (d 2003); *b* 10 September 1954; *Educ* Rosebery GS Epsom, St Anne's Coll Oxford (BA); *m* Aug 1987, Andrew Marr, *qv*, s of Donald Marr; 1 s (Harry Cameron b 5 July 1989), 2 da (Isabel Claire b 4 Oct 1991, Emily Catherine b 3 Nov 1994); *Career* news trainee BBC 1978–80, prodr Newsnight 1980–82, politics prodr C4 News 1982–86, presenter Their Lordships House and The Parliament Programme 1986–88, political corr

A

ITN 1988–98, political ed New Statesman 2000–02; currently: columnist and interviewer The Guardian, presenter The Week in Westminster (BBC Radio 4); *Recreations* running, swimming; *Style*— Ms Jackie Ashley

ASHLEY OF STOKE, Baron (Life Peer UK 1992), of Widnes in the County of Cheshire; Jack Ashley; CH (1975), PC (1979); s of John Ashley (d 1927), and Isabella, *née* Bridge; *b* 6 December 1922; *Educ* Ruskin Coll Oxford (scholarship), Gonville & Caius Coll Cambridge (scholarship, chm Cambridge Lab Club, pres Cambridge Union); *m* 1951, Pauline Kay (d 2003), da of Clarence Adley Crispin, of Liverpool; 3 da ((Hon) Jacqueline (Jackie) Ashley, *qv*, b 1954, Hon Jane Elizabeth (Hon Mrs Rosenbaum) b 1958, Hon Caroline (Hon Mrs Dewdney) b 1966); *Career* labourer and cranedriver 1936–46, cnclr Borough of Widnes 1945, shop steward convenor and memb Nat Exec Chem Workers' Union 1946; student 1946–51; BBC: radio prodr 1951–57, sr television prodr 1957–66, memb Gen Advsy Cncl 1967–69 and 1970–74; MP (Lab) Stoke-on-Trent S 1966–92; PPS to Sec of State for: Econ Affairs 1966–67, Health and Social Security 1974–76; memb Nat Exec Ctee of Lab Pty 1976–78; chllr Univ of Staffordshire 1993–2003; pres: Hearing and Speech Tst 1985–2001, Royal Nat Inst for the Deaf, Royal Coll of Speech & Language Therapists; *Books* Journey into Silence (1973), Acts of Defiance (1992); *Style*— The Rt Hon Lord Ashley of Stoke, CH, PC; ✉ House of Lords, London SW1A 0PW

ASHLEY-SMITH, Prof Jonathan; s of Ewart Trist Ashley-Smith (d 1972), of Sutton Valence, Kent, and Marian Tanfield, *née* Smith (d 2006); *b* 25 August 1946; *Educ* Sutton Valence, Univ of Bristol (BSc, PhD), Univ of Cambridge; *m* 19 Aug 1967, Diane Louise, *née* Wagland; 1 s (Joseph Daniel b 1975), 1 da (Zoë Elizabeth b 1985); *Career* V&A: scientific offr 1973–77, head of Conservation Dept 1977–2002, sr res fell in conservation studies 2002–04; visiting prof RCA 2000–; memb: Conservation Ctee Cncl for Care of Churches 1978–85, Crafts Cncl 1980–83 (memb Conservation Ctee 1978–83), Bd of Govrs London Coll of Furniture 1983–85, Bd Cultural Heritage National Training Organisation (formerly Museums Training Inst) 1997–2005; UK Inst for Conservation: memb 1974–, memb Exec Ctee 1978–84, vice-chm 1980–83, chm 1983–84; sec gen Int Inst for Conservation 2003–06; Plowden Medal winner 2000; hon fell RCA 1992, Leverhulme fell 1994–95; Fell Int Inst for Conservation (FIIC) 1985, FRSC 1987, CChem 1987, FMA 1988; *Books* Science for Conservators (scientific ed, Vols 1–3, 1984), Risk Assessment for Object Conservation (1999); author of articles in learned jls; *Recreations* legal combinations of driving fast, getting drunk, and heavy rock music; *Clubs* Anglesea; *Style*— Prof Jonathan Ashley-Smith; ✉ e-mail jonsmith@jonsmith.demon.co.uk

ASHMORE, Gillian Margaret; da of John Roger Oxenham, of Heytesbury, Wilts, and Joan, *née* Palmer; *b* 14 October 1949; *Educ* Walthamstow Hall Sevenoaks, Winchester Co HS for Girls, Newnham Coll Cambridge (BA); *m* 1971, Frederick Scott Ashmore, s of Prof Philip George Ashmore; 2 da (Beatrice b 1980, Olivia (Polly) b 1989), 2 s (Edward (Ned) b 1982, John b 1986); *Career* civil servant; various housing and tport positions 1971–85 (Housing Corp 1974), dep dir Enterprise & Deregulation Unit Dept of Employment (became unit of DTI 1987) 1986–89, head Central Fin Div Dept of Tport 1990–92, dir Privatisation and Internal Communication BR 1992–94, regnl dir Govt Office for the SE 1994–98; md Mulberry Consulting 1999–2007; chief exec Equal Opportunities Cmmn 2001–02, actg chief exec Rich Mix Cultural Fndn 2006–07; chm Kingston Victim Support 1998–2001, chair Refugee Housing Assoc 1999–2007, exec dir Fostering Network 2003; tstee: London Victim Support 1999–2001, Metropolitan Housing Partnership 1999–2007; recording clerk Religious Soc of Friends 2007–; govr Richmond Adult and Community Coll 2000–07; assoc Newnham Coll Cambridge 1998–; FRSA; *Recreations* friends, children, walking, swimming, novels; *Style*— Ms Gillian Ashmore; ✉ 47 Lower Teddington Road, Hampton Wick, Kingston upon Thames, Surrey KT1 4HQ (e-mail gillian@ashmores.me.uk)

ASHMORE, Prof Jonathan Felix; s of Eric Peter Ashmore (d 1997), of Fermoy, Co Cork, and Rosalie Sylvia, *née* Crutchley (d 1997); *b* 16 April 1948; *Educ* Westminster (Queen's scholar), Univ of Sussex (BSc), Imperial Coll London (PhD), UCL (MSc); *m* 1974, Sonia Elizabeth Newby, da of George Eric Newby, CBE, MC, FRSL (d 2006); 1 s (Joseph Prospero b 14 Nov 1974), 1 da (Lucia b 30 May 1979); *Career* visiting scientist ICTP Trieste 1971–72, Nuffield biological scholar 1972–74, research asst Dept of Biophysics UCL 1974–77, visiting research physiologist Dept of Ophthalmology Univ of Calif San Francisco 1977–80; Univ of Sussex: temp lectr 1980–82, MRC research assoc 1982–83; Univ of Bristol: lectr 1983–88, reader in physiology 1988–93, prof of biophysics 1993–96; Bernard Katz prof of biophysics UCL 1996–, dir UCL Ear Inst 2005; chief scientific advsr Defeating Deafness 2002–07; Fulbright scholar 1977–80, G L Brown prize lectr Physiological Soc 1992–93, chaire Blaise Pascal Institut Pasteur Paris 2007–; author of various research reports in learned jls; memb Physiological Soc 1980; FRS 1996, FMedSci 2001; *Recreations* reading, travel (virtual and actual); *Style*— Prof Jonathan Ashmore, FRS; ✉ Department of Physiology, University College London, Gower Street, London WC1E 6BT (tel 020 7679 2141, fax 020 7813 0530, e-mail j.ashmore@ucl.ac.uk, website www.inner-ear.org)

ASHTIANY, Saphié (Sue); da of Ali Asghar Nourredin Ashtiany (d 2004), and Amir Banou Faily (d 1993); *b* Iran; *Educ* Padworth Coll, Univ of Warwick (BA), Univ of Birmingham (MSocSci); *m* 1973, Prof Paul Lyndon Davies; 2 da (Megan b 1979, Tessa b 1981); *Career* ptnr: Cole & Cole Slrs (later Morgan Cole) 1989–2001, Nabarro Slrs 2001– (also head Employment Gp); memb Editorial Panel Butterworths Discrimination Law Compensation; vice-pres: Industrial Law Soc 1996–, Employment Lawyers Assoc (memb Policy Sub-Ctee); cmmr Equal Opportunities Cmmn 2000–, chair Oxfordshire Advsy Bd Common Purpose 2000–03, memb Diversity Panel London First; non-exec dir and vice-chair Oxfordshire Ambulance NHS Tst 1993–2003 (actg chair 2001–03), non-exec dir Channel 4 2003–; trustee City of Oxford Music Tst, memb Advsy Ctee Oxford Piano Festival; memb Ct Oxford Brookes Univ 2000–; hon fell Harris Manchester Coll Oxford 2003; fell Inst of Advanced Legal Studies 2000–03, FRSA 2004; *Publications* Britain's Migrant Workers (1976), Tolley's Employment Law (contributing ed, chapter on Race Discrimination), FT Law and Tax Employment Precedents and Company Documents (contributing ed); author of articles in specialist publications incl Lawyer Jl, Solicitors Jl, Employment Lawyers Assoc and Personnel Today; *Recreations* music, opera, dance, theatre; *Style*— Ms Sue Ashtiany; ✉ Nabarro, Lacon House, Theobald's Road, London WC1X 8RW (tel 020 7524 6572, fax 020 7524 6524, e-mail s.ashtiany@nabarro.com)

ASHTON, Andrew Keith Maxwell; s of Sqdn Ldr Hugh Alan Ashton, DFC (d 1989), and Joan Maxwell, *née* Mann (d 2004); *b* 18 September 1950; *Educ* Framlingham Coll, Wells Cathedral Sch, Trent Poly, Univ of London (LLB); *m* 20 April 1985, Dr Patricia Mary White, da of Norman Ernest White (d 1981); 1 s (Richard), 1 da (Catherine); *Career* admitted slr 1974; ptnr Herbert Mallam Gowers 1976–2007 (conslt 2007–); memb: Wallingford Rowing Club, Warborough and Shillingford Soc; memb Law Soc; *Recreations* watching children and their sporting endeavours, bar mgmnt, taming the garden, travel; *Clubs* Law Soc; *Style*— Andrew Ashton, Esq; ✉ Little Cranford, Moulsford, Oxfordshire OX10 9HU (tel 01491 651305); Herbert Mallam Gowers, 126 High Street, Oxford OX1 4DG (tel 01865 244661, fax 01865 241842, e-mail akma@hmg-law.co.uk)

ASHTON, Rt Rev Cyril Guy; *see:* Doncaster, Bishop of

ASHTON, David Julian; *b* 23 October 1948; *Educ* LSE (BSc); *m* April 1976, Marilyn Joy Ashton; 2 s (Richard b July 1977, Michael b March 1981); *Career* ptnr Arthur Andersen 1982–2002 (joined 1970), dir LECG Ltd 2002–; dep ldr London Borough of Harrow Cncl; MInstPet, FCA; fell Acad of Experts (FAE), FIArb; *Recreations* politics, skiing, walking; *Style*— David Ashton, Esq; ✉ LECG Ltd, The Davidson Building, 5 Southampton Street, London WC2E 7HA (tel 020 7632 5020, fax 020 7632 5050, e-mail dashton@lecg.com)

ASHTON, Prof John Richard; CBE (2000); s of Edward Ashton (d 1978), of Woolton, and Lena Irene Ashton, *née* Pettit; *b* 27 May 1947, Woolton, Liverpool; *Educ* Quarry Bank HS Liverpool, Univ of Newcastle upon Tyne Med Sch (Nuffield Fndn scholar in tropical med Fiji Islands, Charlton scholar in med, MB BS), LSHTM (MSc, Sir Allen Daley meml prize in social med); *m* 1, 1968 (m dis 2001), Pamela Doreen, *née* Scott; 3 s (Keir Edward, Matthew James, Nicholas John); *m* 2, 2003, Catherine Benedicte (Maggi) Morris; 1 s (Fabian Ché Jed), 2 step s (Alesaunder James Wystan, Dylan Carey Michael); *Career* house physician and house surgn Newcastle upon Tyne Univ Hosp Gp 1970–71, gen practice locum Great Yarmouth and Mid Wales 1971, SHO in gen med and geriatrics 1971–72, SHO and registrar psychiatry 1972–74, princ in gen practice Newcastle upon Tyne and Northumberland 1974–75, lectr in primary med care (mental health) Univ of Southampton and princ in gen practice Hants Family Practitioner Ctee 1975–76, postgrad student in social med LSHTM 1976–78, sr registrar in community med Hants and lectr in community med Univ of Southampton 1978–79, sr lectr Dept of Community Med LSHTM 1980–82, sr lectr Dept of Public Health Univ of Liverpool 1983–93 (personal chair in public health policy and strategy 1993), dir Liverpool Public Health Observatory 1990–93; regnl dir of public health and regnl med offr: Mersey RHA 1993–94, NW Regnl Office NHS Exec 1994–2002, Govt Office NW 2002–06; dir of public health Cumbria 2007–; external examiner Galway Coll, TCD, UCD and Cork Univ Coll; visiting prof Valencian Inst for Public Health Studies 1988, professorial fell Liverpool Sch of Tropical Med 1994, Oliver Tambo visiting prof Cape Town 1997, Wei Lun visiting prof Univ of Hong Kong 1998; visiting prof: Liverpool John Moores Univ 1998, Univ of Manchester 2001–, Univ of Central Lancs 2004, Univ of Lancaster 2006; Chadwick lectr Chartered Inst of Environmental Health Officers 1990, Chadwick lectr Univ of Manchester 1997, Milroy lectr RCP London 2000, Audrey Wise lectr Univ of Central Lancashire 2005; Kings Fund Scholar N America 1974, Premio Nenufar Award for contributions to int public health Galicia 1997, Alwyn Smith Medal Faculty of Public Health Med for lifelong contribs to public health 2002; inaugural coordinator Euro WHO Healthy Cities Project 1986–88; advsr to WHO on the devpt of educn progs the devpt of city-based public health strategies (Europe, Eastern Mediterranean, The Americas, SE Asia); gen rapporteur 44th World Health Assembly Tech Discussions on urban health Geneva 1991; jt ed Jl of Epidemiology and Community Health (with Prof Carlos Alvarez, Alicante) 1998; memb: Int Scientific Advsy Gp Inst of Public Health Valencia 1995, NW Regnl Assembly and NW RDA Health Partnership 1999–2001, Br Humanitarian Aid Delgn to Kosovo 1999; former memb Bd Faculty of Public Health Med and Exec RCP; fndr memb The Duncan Soc Liverpool 1997; cncllr Hampshire CC 1981–82 (memb Educn and Police Ctees), chm of tstees Carston Cultural Village Liverpool 2006, tstee Merseyside Fire Support Network 2007–, govr Royal Liverpool Children's NHS Tst 2007–; hon fell Liverpool John Moores Univ 2003; FFPHM 1986 (MFPHM 1979), MFFPRHC 1993, FRCPsych 1993 (MRCPsych 1975), FRCPEd 2003, FRCP 2004; *Books* Everyday Psychiatry (1980), Esmedune 2000 (A Healthy Liverpool) - Vision or Dream? (1986), The New Public Health - The Liverpool Experience (with H Seymour, 1988, Spanish edn 1990), Healthy Cities (ed, 1991), The Urban Health Crisis - Strategies for All in the Face of Rapid Urbanisation (ed, 1991), The Epidemiological Imagination - A Reader (ed, 1994), The Pool of Life - A Public Health Walk in Liverpool (with Maggi Morris, 1997), The Gift Relationship (ed with Ann Oakley); also author of numerous book chapters, papers and editorials in learned jls; *Recreations* family, small holding and poultry keeping, Skye and Ockie the Springers, walking and cycling, Liverpool FC, reading the papers; *Style*— John Ashton; ✉ 8 Church Road, Much Woolton, Liverpool LS2 5JF

ASHTON, Prof Rosemary Doreen; OBE (1999); *b* 11 April 1947; *Educ* Univ of Aberdeen (MA, Seafield medal, Senatus prize), Newnham Coll Cambridge (Lucy fell, PhD); *Family* 3 c; *Career* temp lectr in English Univ of Birmingham 1973–74; UCL: lectr in English 1974–86, reader in English 1986–91, prof of English 1991–, Quain prof of English language and literature 2002–; Deutscher Akademischer Austauschdienst (DAAD) Stipendium Univ of Heidelberg 1966–67, Literary Review Award for The German Idea 1980, DAAD Travel Scholarship 1983, British Acad Thank-Offering to Britain fell 1984–85, British Acad Research Readership 1988–90, visiting fell Beinecke Library Yale Univ 1989, Leverhulme Res Fellowship 1995; memb: Int Assoc of Univ Profs of English, Humanities Research Bd Br Acad; founding fell Eng Assoc 2000; FRSL 1999, FBA 2000, FRSA 2002; *Books* The German Idea: Four English Writers and the Reception of German Thought 1800–1860 (1980), George Eliot (1983), Little Germany: Exile and Asylum in Victorian England (1986), The Mill on the Floss: A Natural History (1990), G H Lewes: A Life (1991), The Life of Samuel Taylor Coleridge: A Critical Biography (1996), George Eliot: A Life (1996), Thomas and Jane Carlyle: Portrait of a Marriage (2002), 142 Strand: A Radical Address in Victorian London (2006); author of numerous edition introductions and articles and reviews in jls; *Style*— Prof Rosemary Ashton, OBE, FBA; ✉ University College London, Gower Street, London WC1E 6BT (tel 020 7679 3143, fax 020 7916 2054, e-mail r.ashton@ucl.ac.uk)

ASHTON, Ruth Mary (Mrs E F Henschel); OBE (1991); da of Leigh Perry Ashton, and Marion Lucy, *née* Tryon; *b* 27 March 1939; *Educ* Kenya HS for Girls, Clarendon Sch (lately Abergele), The London Hosp, Queen Mother's Hosp and High Coombe Midwife Teachers' Trg Coll (RN 1965, RM 1967, MTD 1970); *m* 7 April 1984, E Fred Henschel; *Career* staff midwife and midwifery sister Queen Mother's Hosp Glasgow 1967–69, nursing offr and midwifery tutor King's Coll Hosp London 1971–75; Royal Coll of Midwives: tutor 1975–79, professional offr 1979, gen sec 1980–94; non-exec dir Optimum NHS Tst 1995–99, non-exec dir Community Health South London NHS Tst 1999–2000, non-exec dir and vice-chair Bromley Primary Care NHS Tst 2001–07; chair NHS SE London Workforce Devpt Confedn 2002–06; temp prof March of Dimes LA 1982; memb and vice-pres Royal Coll of Midwives, treas Int Confedn of Midwives 1997–2002; ACIArb 1995; Offr Sister OStJ 1988; *Books* Your First Baby (ed and author, 1980), Report on Activities, Responsibilities and Independence of Midwives in the European Union (1996); *Recreations* gardening, travel; *Style*— Miss Ruth Ashton, OBE; ✉ tel and fax 020 8851 7403, e-mail ruhens@tiscali.co.uk

ASHTON, William Michael Allingham; MBE (1978); s of Eric Sandiford Ashton (d 1983), of Lytham St Annes, and Zilla Dorothea, *née* Miles (d 1944); *b* 6 December 1936; *Educ* Rossall Sch, St Peter's Coll Oxford (BA, DipEd); *m* 22 Oct 1966, Kay Carol, da of John Stallard Watkins (d 2000), of New Quay, Dyfed; 2 s (Grant b 1967, Miles b 1968), 1 da (Helen b 1983); *Career* Nat Serv RAF 1955–57; fndr and musical dir Nat Youth Jazz Orchestra (NYJO) 1965–; numerous appearances before royalty incl Royal Variety Performance 1978, toured many countries on behalf of Br Cncl (USA, USSR, Aust, Turkey); chm NYJO Ltd 1972–; composer of over 60 recorded songs; memb: Musicians' Union, Br Assoc of Jazz Musicians; owner Stanza Music; fell Leeds Coll of Music 1995; *Awards* for NYJO: Best Br Big Band Br Jazz Awards 1993, 1995, 1998 and 2002, Critics' Choice 1992, 1995 and 1997, BBC Radio 2 Award for Servs to Jazz 1995, Silver Jazz Medal Worshipful Co of Musicians 1996, All Party Parly Jazz Appreciation Gp Special Award 2007; *Recreations* reading, song writing, snorkelling; *Style*— William Ashton, Esq, MBE; ✉ 11 Victor Road, Harrow, Middlesex HA2 6PT (tel 020 8863 2717, fax 020 8863 8685, e-mail bill.ashton@virgin.net, website www.nyjo.org.uk)

ASHTON OF HYDE, 3 Baron (UK 1911); Thomas John Ashton; TD; s of 2 Baron Ashton of Hyde, JP, DL (d 1983), and Marjorie Nell, *née* Brooks (d 1993); *b* 19 November 1926; *Educ* Eton, New Coll Oxford (MA); *m* 18 May 1957, Pauline Trewlove, er da of Lt-Col Robert Henry Langton Brackenbury, OBE, of Long Compton, Shipston on Stour; 2 s, 2 da; *Heir* s, Hon Thomas Henry Ashton; *Career* formerly Lt 11 Hussars, Maj Royal Glos Hussars (TA); sr exec local dir Barclays Bank Manchester 1968–81, dir Barclays Bank plc and subsidiary cos 1969–87; Liveryman Worshipful Co of Goldsmiths; JP Oxon 1965–68; *Clubs* Boodle's; *Style*— The Rt Hon the Lord Ashton of Hyde, TD; ✉ Fir Farm, Upper Slaughter, Cheltenham, Gloucestershire GL54 2JR (tel 01451 830652)

ASHTON OF UPHOLLAND, Baroness (Life Peer UK 1999), of St Albans in the County of Hertfordshire; Catherine Margaret Ashton; PC (2006); da of late Harold Ashton, and late Clare Margaret Ashton; *b* 20 March 1956, Upholland, Lancs; *Educ* Upholland GS, Bedford Coll London (BSc); *m* 1988, Peter Jon Kellner, *qv*, s of late Michael Kellner; 1 s (Hon Robert Peter b 1989), 1 da (Hon Rebecca Clare b 1992), 2 step da (Tara b 1977, Katherine b 1979), 1 step s (Michael b 1981); *Career* administrative offr CND 1977–79, Coverdale Orgn 1979–81, Central Cncl for Educn and Trg in Social Work 1981–83, dir of community devpt and public affrs Business in the Community 1983–89, public policy advsr 1989–, dir Political Context 1996–98, seconded by London First to Home Office 1998–99; Parly under-sec of state: DfES 2001–04, DCA 2004–; ldr House of Lords and Lord Pres of the Cncl 2007–; chm Herts HA 1998–2001; advsr Lattice Fndn 2000–01, tstee Verulamium Museum, patron Grove Hospice St Albans, ambass Herts Guides; Min of the Year House Magazine 2005, Peer of the Year Channel 4 2005, Politician of the Year Stonewall 2006; *Clubs* Royal Cwlth Soc; *Style*— The Baroness Ashton of Upholland, PC; ✉ House of Lords, London SW1A 0PW (tel 020 7210 8708, fax 020 7210 8620, e-mail catherine.ashton@cabinet-office.x.gsi.gov.uk)

ASHTOWN, 7 Baron (I 1800); Sir Nigel Clive Cosby Trench; KCMG (1976, CMG 1966); s of Clive Newcome Trench (d 1964, s of Hon Cosby Godolphin Trench, 2 s of 2 Baron Ashtown), and Kathleen, da of Maj Ivar MacIvor, CIE; suc kinsman, 6 Baron Ashtown (d 1990); *b* 27 October 1916; *Educ* Eton, CCC Cambridge; *m* 1, 1 Dec 1939, Marcelle Catherine (d 1994), da of Johan Jacob Clotterbooke Patyn van Kloetinge, of Zeist, Holland; 1 s; m 2, 17 Dec 1997, Mary, Princess of Pless, da of Lt-Col Richard George Edward Minchin (d 1985); *Heir* s, Hon Roderick Trench; *Career* serv KRRC WWII (UK and NW Europe, despatches); Foreign Serv 1946, first sec 1948, first sec (commercial) Lima 1952, cnsllr Tokyo 1961, cnsllr Washington 1963, Cabinet Office 1967, ambass to Korea 1969–71, memb Civil Serv Selection Bd 1971–73, ambass to Portugal 1974–76, memb Police Fire and Prison Serv Selection Bds 1977–86; Order of Dip Serv Merit (Repub of Korea) 1984; *Style*— The Rt Hon Lord Ashtown, KCMG; ✉ 4 Kensington Court Gardens, Kensington Court Place, London W8 5QE

ASHURST, Prof John; *b* 14 March 1937; *Career* architect; asst architect in private practice with Scott Brownrigg and Turner and J Brian Cooper 1961–69, architect Directorate of Ancient Monuments and Historic Buildings DOE 1969–75, princ architect DAMHB (later English Heritage) 1975–90, heritage restoration conslt in private practice 1990–91; prof of heritage conservation Dept of Conservation Sciences Bournemouth Univ 1991–95 (also dir Historic Building and Site Servs), currently consultant in conservation of historic buildings and archaeological sites; sometime lectr: Inst of Advanced Architectural Studies Univ of York, Int Centre for the Study of the Preservation and the Restoration of Cultural Property (Rome), Architectural Assoc Sch of Architecture, Soc for the Protection of Ancient Buildings, Standing Joint Ctee on Natural Stones, Directorate of Ancient Monuments and Historic Buildings, Heriot-Watt Sch of Architecture, Univ of Edinburgh, Oxford Brookes Univ, Inst of Archaeology; research projects: Surface Treatments for Stone 1970–72, Desalination of Masonry Walls 1970–74, Biocide Performance 1970–75, Stone Consolidant Development 1972–81, Limestone Consolidation 1975–84, Plaster Consolidation 1984–87, Conservation of Clunch 1985–87, Smoke Deposited Insecticides 1970–90, Mortar Performance 1989–; *Books* Specification - Stone Masonry (with Francis Dimes, 1975), Stone in Building - Its Use and Potential Today (with Francis Dimes, 1977), Mortars, Plasters and Renders in Conservation (1983 and 1999), Practical Building Conservation (5 vols, with Nicola Ashurst, 1988), The Conservation of Building and Decorative Stone (2 vols, with Francis Dimes, 1990), Stone Cutter, Restoration Mason (with Keith Blades, 1991), The Conservation of Ruins (2005); also author of various tech papers; *Style*— Prof John Ashurst; ✉ Ingram Consultancy Ltd, Manor Farm House, Chicklade, Hindon, Salisbury, Wiltshire SP3 5SU (tel 01747 820170, fax 01787 820175, e-mail john@ingram-consultancy.co.uk)

ASHURST, Mark; *b* 10 May 1970, Bristol; *Educ* King Edward VI Sch Southampton, Itchen Sixth Form Coll Southampton, Ecole Nationale de la Musique Paris, Ecole Normale de la Musique Paris, UC Oxford (BA); *Career* writer and broadcaster; asst to Simon Hughes, MP, *qv*, 1992, copywriter Matla Tst (South African voter education gp) 1993–94 (also observer for Westminster Fndn for Democracy), political and media reporter Business Day South Africa 1994, conslt Strategic Planning Unit South African Broadcasting Corp 1995, South African corr FT 1995–98, business ed BBC Africa 1998–; prodr Fabulous (BBC Radio 5) 1993, presenter Crossing Continents (BBC Radio 4) 2002, contrib From Our Own Correspondent (BBC Radio 4); contrib: The Guardian, The Independent, Daily Telegraph, Newsweek, BBC Radio 5, BBC World, BBC News 24 TV; former columnist Independent Newspapers of South Africa; speechwriter Nelson Mandela's opening address to Union of African Radio and TV Broadcasters Congress Johannesburg 1995; one-man show Harare Int Festival of Arts Zimbabwe 2001; Zanzibar Int Film Festival 2002; *Style*— Mark Ashurst, Esq

ASHURST, (Kenneth William) Stewart; s of Kenneth Latham Ashurst, OBE, and Helen Ferguson, *née* Rae; *b* 19 May 1945; *Educ* Royal GS Newcastle upon Tyne, King Edward VI GS Lichfield, Exeter Coll Oxford (MA), Coll of Law Guildford, Univ of Birmingham (MSocSc); *m* 1984, Catherine Mary, da of George and Margaret Sample; 1 da (Olivia b 6 Jan 1985), 2 s (William b 5 June 1987, Edward b 19 June 1989); *Career* articled clerk Leicester County BC 1967–68, articled clerk then asst slr Newcastle upon Tyne County BC 1968–71, SSRC post graduate Univ of Birmingham 1971–72, asst slr Cumberland CC 1972–73, asst county clerk Cumbria CC 1973–79, county slr and dep county clerk Suffolk CC 1981–85 (dep county sec 1979–81), chief exec Essex CC 1994– (dep chief exec and clerk 1985–94); dir: Essex TEC 1995–2001, Year of Opera and Musical Theatre 1996–98; memb Senate Univ of Essex; other positions incl: clerk to Essex Police Authy 1995–2002, clerk to Essex Fire Authy, clerk to Essex Lieutenancy, sec Lord Chllr's Advsy Ctee, clerk to River Crouch Harbour Authy, sec Stansted Airport Consultative Ctee; nat chm Assoc of County Chief Execs 2003–04; local govt memb Cncl Law Soc of England and Wales 1989–97, memb Local Govt Gp Law Soc (former nat chm); FCMI, FRSA; *Recreations* wine tasting; *Style*— Stewart Ashurst, Esq; ✉ Essex County Council, County Hall, Duke Street, Chelmsford, Essex CM1 1LX (tel 01245 430015, fax 01245 256731)

ASHWORTH, Prof Andrew John; Hon QC (1997); s of Clifford Ashworth (d 1993), and Amy, *née* Ogden (d 2005); *b* 11 October 1947; *Educ* Rishworth Sch, LSE (LLB), New Coll Oxford (DCL), Univ of Manchester (PhD); *m* 1, 1971 (m dis), Gillian, *née* Frisby; 2 da (Susannah b 1974, Alison b 1976); m 2, Veronica, *née* Fellows; *Career* lectr then sr lectr in law Univ of Manchester 1970–78, fell and tutor in law Worcester Coll Oxford 1978–88, Edmund-Davies prof of criminal law and criminal justice KCL 1988–97, Vinerian prof of English law Univ of Oxford 1997–; ed Criminal Law Review 1975–99; bencher Inner Temple 1997; Hon LLD De Montfort Univ 1998, Hon JD Univ of Uppsala 2003; FBA 1993; *Books* Principles of Criminal Law (1991, 5 edn 2006), Sentencing and Criminal Justice (1992, 4 edn 2005), The Criminal Process (1994, 3 edn 2005), Human Rights, Serious Crime and Criminal Procedure (2002); *Recreations* travel, walking, bridge; *Style*— Prof Andrew Ashworth, QC, FBA; ✉ All Souls College, Oxford OX1 4AL (tel 01865 279379, fax 01865 279299)

ASHWORTH, Anne Mary Catherine; s of Peter Ashworth (d 1997), of Wimbledon, and Joan, *née* Kay (d 1975); *b* 13 June 1954; *Educ* Ursuline Convent Wimbledon, King's Coll London (BA); *m* 1985, Tom Maddocks; 1 s (George b 1990); *Career* journalist; Accountancy magazine 1980–82, Sunday Express 1982–86, Today 1986, Daily Mail 1986–87, personal fin ed and assoc city ed Mail on Sunday 1987–94, personal fin ed The Times 1994–; *Style*— Ms Anne Ashworth; ✉ The Times, 1 Pennington Street, London E98 1TA (tel 020 7782 5000)

ASHWORTH, Prof Graham William; CBE (1980), DL (Lancs 1991); s of Frederick William Ashworth (d 1978), and Ivy Alice, *née* Courtiour (d 1982); *b* 14 July 1935; *Educ* Devonport HS, Univ of Liverpool (BArch, MCD); *m* 2 April 1960, Gwyneth Mai, da of John Morgan Jones (d 1959); 3 da (Clare, Alyson, Kate); *Career* architect and planner: London CC 1959–62, Graeme Shankland Associates 1962–64; architect Civic Tst 1964–65, dir Northwest Civic Tst 1965–73 (chm Exec Ctee 1973–87); Univ of Salford: prof of urban environmental studies 1973–87, dir Environmental Inst 1978–87, dir Campaign to Promote Univ of Salford (CAMPUS) 1981–87, res prof of urban environmental studies 1987–2000, visiting prof of environmental law 2003–; DG Tidy Britain Group 1987–2000; chm: Inst of Environmental Sciences 1980–82, Ravenhead Renaissance Ltd 1988–2002, Going for Green 1994–2000, World of Glass 1998–2004; pres Fndn for Environmental Educn 1997–2004, vice-pres Environmental Campaigns (ENCAMS) 2004–05 (chm 2000–03); dir: Merseyside Devpt Corp 1981–92, Norweb 1985–88; ed Int Jl of Environmental Educn and Information 1981–2001; memb: NW Economic Planning Cncl 1968–79 (chm Sub-Gp), Skeffington Ctee on Public Participation in Planning 1969, NW Advsy Cncl of BBC 1970–75, Countryside Cmmn 1974–77; pres RTPI 1973–74; memb: Baptist Union Cncl 1975– (pres 2000–01), Cncl St George's House Windsor 1982–88; tstee Manchester Museum of Science and Industry 1988–91; assoc pastor Carey Baptist Church Preston 1977–86; RIBA 1962, FRSA 1968, FRTPI 1969, FIMgt 1986; *Books* An Encyclopaedia of Planning (1973), Britain in Bloom (1991), The Role of Local Government in Environmental Protection (1992); *Clubs* Athenaeum; *Style*— Prof Graham Ashworth, CBE, DL; ✉ Spring House, Preston New Road, Samlesbury, Preston, Lancashire PR5 0UP (tel 01254 812011, e-mail g_ashworth@btconnect.com)

ASHWORTH, Dr John Michael; s of Jack Ashworth (d 1975), and Mary Constance, *née* Ousman (d 1971); *b* 27 November 1938; *Educ* West Buckland Sch, Exeter Coll Oxford (BA, BSc, MA), Univ of Leicester (PhD), Univ of Oxford (DSc); *m* 1, 13 July 1963, Ann (d 1985), da of Peter Knight (d 1977); 3 da (Harriet b 23 Oct 1964, Sophia b 2 Dec 1968, Emily b 3 Aug 1970), 1 s (Matthew b 24 Sept 1971); m 2, 23 July 1988, Auriol Hazel Dawn Stevens; *Career* Dept of Biochemistry Univ of Leicester: research demonstrator 1961–63, lectr 1963–71, reader 1971–73; prof of biology Univ of Essex 1974–79, seconded to central policy review staff 1976–79, under sec Cabinet Office 1979–81, chief scientist CPRS 1979–81, vice-chllr Univ of Salford 1981–90, dir LSE 1990–96, chm Bd British Library 1996–2001; chm: Salford University Business Services Ltd and Business Enterprises Ltd 1981–90, Bd National Computer Centre Ltd 1983–92; dir: BR (London Mainland) 1987–92, Granada TV 1986–89, Granada Compass plc (formerly Granada Gp) 1990–2000, J Sainsbury plc 1993–97, Granada plc 2001–02; chm Barts and the London NHS Tst 2003–, dep chm Bd of Tstees Inst of Cancer Research; pres Cncl for the Assistance of Refugee Academics (CARA) 2004–; memb: Library and Info Servs Cncl 1980–84, Electronics Industry EDC (NEDO) 1983–86, Info Technol Econ Devpt Cncl 1983–86, Nat Accreditation Cncl for Cert Bodies BSI 1984–88, Advsy Cncl DEMOS; govr Ditchley Fndn; pres R&D Soc 1988; Colworth Medal Biochemical Soc 1972; FIBiol 1973, CIMgt 1984; *Books* The Slime Moulds (with J Dee, 1970), Cell Differentiation (1972); *Recreations* sailing; *Style*— Dr John Ashworth

ASHWORTH, Richard James; MEP; s of Maurice Ashworth, of Rye, E Sussex, and Eileen, *née* Simpson (d 1983); *b* 17 September 1947, Folkestone, Kent; *Educ* King's Sch Canterbury, Seale Hayne Coll Newton Abbott (NDA, CDA, CDFM); *m* 6 Oct 1973, Sally, *née* Poulton; 3 da (Phillipa b 21 Jan 1976, Sarah b 13 May 1977, Joanna b 20 June 1979); *Career* farmer E Sussex 1970–2001; chm United Milk plc 1995–2003; MEP (Cons) SE England 2004– (UK Parly candidate N Devon 1997, European Parly candidate 1999), chief whip Br Cons Delgn, memb European Budget Ctee; chm Plumpton Coll 1992–2000; *Recreations* sport, music, country pursuits; *Clubs* Farmers'; *Style*— Richard Ashworth, Esq, MEP; ✉ 4 Temeraire Heights, Hospital Hill, Folkestone, Kent CT20 3TL (tel 01303 237736, e-mail richardashworth@aol.com); 5 Hazelgrove Road, Haywards Heath, West Sussex RH16 3PH (tel 01444 474858, e-mail rashworth@europarl.eu.int, website www.richardashworth.com)

ASHWORTH, Thomas Leslie (Tom); s of William Leslie Ashworth (d 1982), and Katharine Elizabeth, *née* Cubbin (d 2003); *b* Upton, Cheshire; *Educ* Birkenhead Inst, QMC London (BSc), Univ of Liverpool (MSc); *m* 28 July 1979, Roslyn, *née* Williams; 2 da (Zoe Elizabeth b 17 June 1982, Stephanie Jane b 4 June 1985); *Career* mathematics teacher Birkenhead Sch 1973–83, sr teacher and head of mathematics Ripon GS 1983–88, dep head master Reading Sch 1988–89, head master Ermysted's GS Skipton 1998–; memb ASCL 1998; memb Skipton Mechanics Inst; *Recreations* rugby (RFU panel referee 1988–2000), philately, IT, travel; *Style*— Tom Ashworth, Esq; ✉ Ermysted's Grammar School, Gargrave Road, Skipton, North Yorkshire BD23 1PL (tel 01756 792186, fax 01756 793714, e-mail admin@ermysteds.n-yorks.sch.uk)

ASKEW, Adrian William; *b* 21 May 1948, Guildford, Surrey; *Educ* St Michael's Coll Hitchin; *m* Jean; 1 s (Nathan), 2 da (Claudine, Katherine); *Career* trade unionist; engrg fitter Borg Warner Ltd 1968–71, memb and shop steward AEU 1968–71, engr British Aircraft Corp 1971–74; APEX: memb Assoc of Professional, Exec Clerical and Computer Staff (jtly APEX/GMB) 1971–, sr rep and branch sec 1972–74, area organiser 1974–77; EMA: negotiating offr Engrs and Mangrs Assoc 1977–80, gen sec Shipbuilding and Engrg Gp 1980–87; Soc of Telecom Execs (now Connect): asst sec 1987–96, dep gen sec 1996–2002, gen sec 2003– (gen sec designate 2002–03); vice-pres Uni Europa Telecom 2007–; memb: Bd Shipbuilding Industry Trg Assoc 1982–87, Shipbuilding Negotiating Ctee Confedn of Shipbuilding and Engrg Unions 1984–87, EU Telecoms Social Dialogue Ctee 2002–, Bd e-Skills Sector Skills Cncl 2005–, Bd Union Modernisation Fund 2005–; memb Lab Pty 1972–; *Recreations* music, skiing; *Style*— Mr Adrian Askew; ✉ Connect, 30 St George's Road, Wimbledon, London SW19 4BD

ASKEW, Sir Bryan; kt (1989); s of John Pinkney Askew (d 1940), and Matilda Brown (d 2004); *b* 18 August 1930; *Educ* Wellfield GS Wingate, Fitzwilliam Coll Cambridge (MA); *m* 10 Aug 1955, Millicent Rose, da of Thomas Henry Holder (d 1966); 2 da (Penelope Jane b 1957, Melissa Clare b 1966); *Career* ICI Ltd 1952–59, Consett Iron Co Ltd (later part of Br Steel Corp) 1959–71, own consultancy 1971–74; Samuel Smith Old Brewery Tadcaster: joined 1974, personnel dir 1982–95; chm Advanced Digital Telecom Ltd 1997–99; chm Yorks RHA 1983–94; cncllr Consett UDC 1967–71; Parly candidate (Cons): Penistone 1964 and 1966, York 1970; memb: Duke of Edinburgh's Third Cwlth Study Conf Australia 1968, Ct Univ of Leeds 1985–2006 (memb Cncl 1988–2000), Working Gp on Young People and Alcohol Home Office Standing Conf on Crime Prevention 1987; chm Br Polio Fellowship 2003–; chm Burgage Holders of Alnmouth Common 2003–; Hon LLD Univ of Hull 1992; FRSA 1986 (chm Yorks Regn 1997–99), FRSM 1988; *Style*— Sir

Bryan Askew; ✉ 27 Golf Links Avenue, Tadcaster, North Yorkshire LS24 9HF (tel 01937 833216); Flat 1, The Manor House, Alnmouth, Northumberland NE66 2RJ (tel 01665 830047)

ASLAM, Nadeem; *b* Pakistan; *Career* writer; *Books* Season of the Rainbirds (1993, Betty Trask Award, Best First Novel Author's Club Award, shortlisted Best First Novel Whitbread Award, shortlisted John Llewelyn Rhys Memorial Prize, longlist Booker Prize), Maps for Lost Lovers (2006, Kiriyama Prize 2005, shortlisted IMPAC 2006); ✉ A. M. Heath & Co Ltd, 6 Warwick Court, London WC1R 5DJ

ASLET, Clive William; s of Kenneth Charles Aslet, and Monica, *née* Humphreys; *b* 15 February 1955; *Educ* KCS Wimbledon, Peterhouse Cambridge (MA); *m* 27 Sept 1980, Naomi Selma, da of Prof Sir Martin Roth; 2 s (William Kenneth Samuel b 26 May 1995, John Francis Independence b 4 July 1997, Charles Emmanuel Martin b 21 Dec 2000); *Career* Country Life: architectural writer 1977–84, architectural ed 1984–88, dep ed 1988–92, ed 1993–2006, ed-at-large 2006–; founding hon sec The Thirties Soc 1979–87; FRSA; *Books* The Last Country Houses (with Alan Powers, 1982), The National Trust Book of the English House (1985), Quinlan Terry, The Revival of Architecture (1986), The American Country House (1990), Countryblast (1991), Anyone for England? (1997), Inside The House of Lords (with Derry Moore, 1998), The Story of Greenwich (1999), Greenwich Millennium (2000), A Horse in the Country (2001), Landmarks of Britain (2005); *Recreations* challenging parking tickets; *Clubs* Garrick; *Style—* Clive Aslet, Esq; ✉ c/o Country Life, King's Reach Tower, Stamford Street, London SE1 9LS (tel 020 7261 6969, fax 020 7261 5139)

ASLETT, Judy Jane; da of Michael Eric Aslett, and Gillian, *née* Kenyon; *b* 1 October 1962; *Educ* Culford Sch, Univ of St Andrews, Central London Poly (BA); *m* 1991, John Stephen, s of Stephen Parkin; 1 da (Emily Claire b 16 June 1992); *Career* editorial trainee ITN 1986–87, prodr Independent TV News 1987–90, corr South Africa Channel 4 News 1991–95 (Sky News 1990–91), foreign ed Channel 4 News 1995–97, diplomatic ed Channel 5 1997–; *Style—* Ms Judy Aslett; ✉ Channel 5 Broadcasting Ltd, 22 Long Acre, London WC2E 9LY (tel 020 7550 5555, fax 020 7497 5222)

ASPDEN, Peter James; s of William James Aspden, and Aphrodite Aspden; *Educ* Latymer Upper Sch, St Edmund Hall Oxford, City Univ (Dip Journalism); *Career* journalist: Cambridge Evening News 1980–84, The Times Higher Education Supplement 1985–94, Financial Times 1994– (currently arts writer); *Recreations* watching Queens Park Rangers FC; *Style—* Peter Aspden, Esq; ✉ Financial Times, 1 Southwark Bridge, London SE1 9HL (tel 020 7873 3450, e-mail peter.aspden@ft.com)

ASPEL, Michael Terence; OBE (1993); s of Edward Aspel, and Violet Aspel; *b* 12 January 1933; *Educ* Emanuel Sch; *m* 1, 1957 (m dis), Dian; 2 s (Gregory (decd), Richard); m 2, 1962 (m dis), Ann; 1 s (Edward), 1 da (Jane (twin)); m 3, 1977, Elizabeth Power; 2 s (Patrick, Daniel); *Career* writer and broadcaster; Nat Serv KRRC and Para Regt TA 1951–53; radio actor 1954–57, BBC TV news reader 1960–68 (announcer 1957–60), freelance 1968–; daily show Capital Radio 1974–84; presenter: The Six O'Clock Show (LWT), Aspel & Company (LWT) 1984–93, This Is Your Life (Thames TV until 1994 thereafter BBC TV) 1988–2003, BAFTA Awards, Strange... But True? (LWT), Antiques Roadshow (BBC TV) 2000–; Independent Radio Personality Variety Club Award 1983, ITV Personality Variety Club Award 1988, elected to RTS Hall of Fame 1996; vice-pres Baby Life Support Systems (BLISS) 1981–, hon vice-pres Assoc for Spina Bifida and Hydrocephalus (ASBAH) 1985–, patron Plan International 1986–; hon fell Cardiff Univ 2002; *Books* Polly Wants a Zebra (autobiography, 1974), Hang On! (for children, 1982); *Recreations* theatre, cinema, eating, travel, water sports; *Clubs* Lord's Taverners, RYA; *Style—* Michael Aspel, Esq, OBE; ✉ c/o Christina Shepherd, 4th Floor, 45 Maddox Street, London W1S 2PE (tel 020 7495 7813, fax 020 7499 7535)

ASPINALL, Beverley Ann; da of David Thomas (d 1962), and Joyce Browning, *née* Ling; *b* 4 December 1958, Beds; *Educ* Univ of York (BA); *m* 15 June 2002, David Aspinall; 1 da (Eleanor Charlotte Bolton b 16 Jan 1989), 1 s (James Rhys Day Bolton b 19 Nov 1990); *Career* John Lewis Partnership: joined 1981, various roles in buying and selling, md John Lewis Peterborough 1995–97, md Peter Jones 1997–2005; md Fortnum & Mason 2005–; non-exec dir: V&A Enterprises, Univ of York Devpt Bd; MInstD; *Recreations* classical music, gardening; *Style—* Mrs Beverley Aspinall; ✉ Fortnum & Mason, 181 Piccadilly, London W1A 1ER (tel 020 7973 5610, e-mail beverley.aspinall@fortnumandmason.co.uk)

ASPINALL, Robin Michael; *b* 3 August 1949; *Educ* Cathedral Sch Bristol, Lancaster Univ (BA (Econ)), Univ of Manchester (MA (Econ)); *m*; 2 s; *Career* Barclays Bank plc 1966–69, univ 1969–73, mangr of forecasting Economic Models Ltd 1973–76, head of economics Imperial Group plc 1976–86, chief economist Schroder Securities Ltd 1986–89, dir of currency economics Security Pacific/Hoare Govett 1989–90, chief economist Schroders 1991–92, chief economist/strategist Panmure Gordon & Co 1992–96, chief economist Financial Mkts Europe National Australia Bank 1996–2000, co economist Teather & Greenwood Ltd 2000–02, currently with Rhombus Research Ltd; *Style—* Robin Aspinall, Esq

ASPINALL, Wilfred; *b* 14 September 1942; *Educ* Poynton Secdy Modern Sch, Stockport Coll for Further Educn; *m* 1973, Judith Mary (d 2005); 1 da (Isabel b 1980); *Career* memb European Econ and Social Consultative Assembly Brussels (MESC) 1986–98, princ Aspinall & Assocs and Aspinall Brussels Professionals in Europe 1990–; dir EU Public Affairs Eversheds 1998–2000, EU Policy and Strategy advsr Eversheds Fin Serv Forum 2000–, estab The Forum in the European Parliament for Construction (FOCOPE) 2003; with National Provincial Bank Ltd 1960–69, asst gen sec Nat Westminster Staff Assoc 1969–75, memb Banking Staff Cncl 1970–77, gen sec Confedn of Bank Staff Assoc 1975–79, treas and consIt Managerial Professional and Staff Liaison Gp 1978–79; exec dir and consIt Fedn of Managerial Professional and General Assocs (MPG) 1979–94, vice-pres Confédération Européen des Cadres 1979–94, established The Strategy Centre Brussels 2004; memb: Hammersmith Special HA 1982–90, North Herts Dist HA 1982–86, North West Thames RHA 1986–88; *Style—* Wilfred Aspinall, Esq; ✉ The Coach House, Shillington Road, Pirton, Hitchin, Hertfordshire SG5 3QJ (tel 01462 712316, e-mail wilfredaspinall@aol.com); 31 Rue Wiertz, 1050 Brussels, Belgium (tel 00 32 22 30 8510, e-mail wa@wilfredaspinall.eu)

ASPREY, William Rolls; s of John Rolls Asprey, of London, and Katrina Pauline Milnes Gaskell, *née* Culverwell; *b* 27 November 1965, London; *Educ* Monkton Combe Sr Sch, RMA Sandhurst; *m* 16 July 1994, Lucinda Jane, *née* Kinnell; 2 da (Emily Charlotte b 2 July 1996, Annabel Rachel b 16 Nov 1997), 1 s (Thomas John Rolls b 26 Sept 1999); *Career* Royal Green Jackets 3 Bn 1987–90; Asprey Bond Street 1990–99, William & Son 1999–; memb: Worshipful Co of Gunmakers, Worshipful Co of Goldsmiths; *Recreations* shooting, skiing, wine, food; *Clubs* Marks, George, Walbrook, Annabel's; *see:* Mark's, George, Walbrook, Annabel's *Style—* William Asprey, Esq; ✉ William & Son, 10 Mount Street, London W1K 2TY (tel 020 7493 8385, fax 020 7493 8386, e-mail william.asprey@williamandson.com)

ASQUITH, Viscount; Raymond Benedict Bartholomew Michael Asquith; OBE; s and h of 2 Earl of Oxford and Asquith, KCMG, *qv*; *b* 24 August 1952; *Educ* Ampleforth, Balliol Coll Oxford; *m* 1978, Clare, da of Francis Pollen (d 1987), and Thérèse, da of His Hon Sir Joseph Sheridan, and gda of late Arthur Pollen (gn of Sir Richard Pollen, 3 Bt) by his w Hon Daphne Baring, da of 3 Baron Revelstoke; 1 s (Hon Mark Julian b 13 May 1979), 4 da (Hon Magdalen Katharine b 1981, Hon Frances Sophia b 1984, Hon Celia Rose b 1989, Hon Isabel Anne b 1991); *Heir* s, Hon Mark Asquith; *Career* HM Dip Serv 1980–97: FCO 1980–83, first sec (Chancery) Moscow 1983–85, FCO 1985, on loan to Cabinet Office 1985–92, cnsllr (Political) Kiev 1992–97; dir: Dessna Co Ltd, WUVP Dnieper Fund; non-exec dir JKX Oil & Gas plc 1997–; *Style—* Viscount Asquith, OBE

ASSCHER, Prof Sir (Adolf) William; kt (1992); s of William Benjamin Asscher (d 1982), and Roosje, *née* van der Molen (d 1993); *b* 20 March 1931; *Educ* Maerlant Lyceum The Hague, London Hosp Med Coll (BSc, MB BS, MD); *m* 1, 1959, Corrie, *née* van Welt (d 1961); m 2, 3 Nov 1962, Jennifer (d 2006), da of Wynne Lloyd, CB (d 1973), of Cardiff; 2 da (Jane (Mrs Stephen Barrett) b 1963, Sophie (Mrs Philip Hughes) b 1965); *Career* Nat Serv 1949–51, cmmnd Lt RE; jr med appts London Hosp 1957–59, lectr in med London Hosp Med Coll 1959–64; WNSM Cardiff (later Univ of Wales Coll of Med): conslt physician and sr lectr in med 1964–70, reader in med 1970–76, prof of med 1976–80, prof and head Dept of Renal Med 1980–87; princ St George's Hosp Med Sch Univ of London 1988–96, hon conslt physician St George's Hosp 1988–96, chm Morriston Hosp NHS Tst 1996–99; RCP: regnl advsr 1973–77, cncllr 1977–80, pres Faculty of Pharmaceutical Med 1995–97; memb Medicines Cmmn DHSS 1981–84, chm Ctee on Review of Medicines DHSS 1984–87; chm: Ctee on Safety of Medicines Dept of Health 1987–93 (memb 1984–87), Med Benefit Risk Fndn 1993–96, UKCCCR 1997–2001, Bd of Sci and Educn BMA 1997–2001; memb SW Thames RHA 1988–90; non-exec dir: Wandsworth DHA 1988–93, St George's Healthcare Tst 1993–96, Vernalis plc 1996–2002; memb Welsh Arts Cncl 1985–88; BMA Gold Medal 2002; Liveryman Worshipful Soc of Apothecaries 1960; Hon DUniv Kingston 1996; hon fell: St George's Hosp Med Sch 1996, Queen Mary & Westfield Coll 1998; memb: Renal Assoc 1962 (sec 1972–77, pres 1986–89), Assoc of Physicians 1970, Med Res Soc 1957 (memb Cncl 1966); FRCP 1970 (MRCP 1959), FFPM 1993, FRSA 1995; *Books* Urinary Tract Infection (1973), The Challenge of Urinary Tract Infections (1981), Nephrology Illustrated (with D B Moffat and E Sanders, 1982), Nephro-Urology (with D B Moffat, 1983), Microbial Diseases in Nephrology (with W Brumfitt, 1986), Medicines and Risk-Benefit Decisions (with S R Walker, 1986), Clinical Atlas of the Kidney (with J D Williams, 1990); *Recreations* visual arts, watercolour painting; *Clubs* Cardiff and County, Welsh Livery, Radyr Lawn Tennis (chm 1972–78); *Style—* Prof Sir William Asscher; ✉ 10 The Paddock, Cowbridge, Vale of Glamorgan CF71 7EJ (tel and fax 01446 772407, e-mail william@asscher.freeserve.co.uk)

ASSHETON, Hon Nicholas; CVO (2002); s of 1 Baron Clitheroe, KCVO, PC (d 1984), and Sylvia, Lady Clitheroe (d 1991), da of 6 Baron Hotham; *b* 23 May 1934; *Educ* Eton, ChCh Oxford (MA); *m* 29 Feb 1960, Jacqueline Jill, da of Marshal of the RAF Sir Arthur Harris, 1 Bt, GCB, OBE, AFC (d 1984), of Goring-on-Thames, Oxon, by his 2 w; 2 da (Caroline b 1961, Mary Thérèse b 1967), 1 s (Thomas b 1963); *Career* formerly 2 Lt Life Gds, Lt Inns of Court Regt; memb The Stock Exchange (memb Cncl 1969–88); sr ptnr Montagu Loebl Stanley & Co 1978–87 (ptnr 1960); dep chm Coutts & Co 1993–99 (dir 1987–99); chm SG Hambros Bank 2000–07; treas Corp of the Church House 1988–2002, treas and extra equerry to Queen Elizabeth The Queen Mother 1998–2002, chief hon steward Westminster Abbey 2002–06; Liveryman Worshipful Co of Vintners; FSA (memb Cncl 1998–2001); *Clubs* Pratt's, White's, Beefsteak; *Style—* The Hon Nicholas Assheton, CVO; ✉ 15 Hammersmith Terrace, London W6 9TS (tel 020 8748 3464)

ASTAIRE, Edgar; s of Max Astaire; *b* 23 January 1930; *Educ* Harrow; *m* 1958 (m dis 1975); 3 s (Mark b 1959, Simon b 1961, Peter b 1963); *Career* stockbroker; chm: Jewish Meml Cncl, Br Technion Soc 1978–85; Master Worshipful Co of Pattenmakers 1982; *Clubs* MCC, Queen's, Chelsea Arts; *Style—* Edgar Astaire, Esq; ✉ 11 Lowndes Close, London SW1X 8BZ (tel 020 7235 5757, fax 020 7823 2249, e-mail edgar@edgarastaire.com)

ASTALL, (Amanda) Elisabeth (Lis); da of John W Iceton, of St Duen, Jersey, and Wendy, *née* Lambert; *b* 28 June 1960, St Helier, Jersey; *Educ* Jersey Ladies Coll St Helier, Université de Nice, LSE (BA); *m* 30 July 1988, Mark Astall; 1 da (Katie b 9 Nov 1989); *Career* Accenture (previously Arthur Andersen, then Andersen Consulting): joined as mgmnt info conslt 1984, ptnr 1994–, global head of human servs industry 1997–98, global head of strategy in govt 1999–2001, chm UK and Ireland Cncl 2002–06, UK md 2003–06, Europe, Africa and Latin America md for govt 2006–; memb: Nat Employment Panel 2003–, E-skills Bd for Technol 2003–06, Cncl for Industry and HE 2003–06; vice-patron Working Families 2004–; *Recreations* horse riding, sailing, skiing; *Style—* Mrs Lis Astall; ✉ Accenture, 20 Old Bailey, London EC4M 7AN (tel 020 7844 0667, e-mail lis.astall@accenture.com)

ASTBURY, Nicholas John (Nick); s of John Schonberg Astbury (d 1993), of Poole, Dorset, and Noel Hope, *née* Gunn; *b* 21 February 1949, Parkstone, Dorset; *Educ* Rugby, Guys Hosp Medical Sch (MB BS); *m* 27 June 1970, Susan Patricia, *née* Whall; 2 da (Victoria b 21 Dec 1974, Tessa b 26 Feb 1979), 2 s (Timothy b 17 Oct 1976, Jack b 22 July 1983); *Career* ophthalmologist; sr registrar KCH and Moorfields Eye Hosp 1981–83, conslt ophthalmic surgn Norfolk and Norwich Univ Hosp 1983–; pres Royal Coll of Ophthalmologists 2003–06 (vice-pres and chm Professional Standards Ctee 2000); conslt advsr Norfolk and Norwich Assoc of the Blind, conslt Int Centre for Eye Health Vision 2020 Links Prog; tstee Impact Fndn; memb: Royal Soc of Medicine, UK and I Soc of Cataract and Refractive Surgns; FRCS 1977 (MRCS 1972), FRCOphth 1989, FRCP 2005; *Publications* The Future of the NHS (contrib, 2006); author of papers in learned jls; *Recreations* running, sailing, horology, photography, making automata; *Style—* Nick Astbury, Esq; ✉ Rectory Farmhouse, The Street, Shotesham, Norwich NR15 1YL (tel 01508 550377, e-mail nick.astbury@virgin.net); Norfolk and Norwich University Hospital NHS Trust, Colney Lane, Norfolk NR4 7UY (tel 01603 288374, fax 01603 288261, e-mail nick.astbury@nnuh.nhs.uk)

ASTBURY, HE Nicholas Paul (Nick); s of Nigel Astbury, and Yvonne, *née* Harburn; *b* 13 August 1971, Buenos Aires, Argentina; *Educ* Hills Road Sixth Form Coll Cambridge, UCL (BA, MA); *Career* diplomat; entered HM Dip Serv 1994, desk offr EU Dept FCO 1994–95, second sec (Chancery) Colombo 1995–99, head of section EU Dept FCO 1999–2000, EU spokesman News Dept FCO 2001, private sec Parly Under Sec of State's Office FCO 2001–02, dep head of UK visas FCO 2002–04, dep head British Embassy Drugs Team Kabul 2005, ambass to Eritrea 2006–; *Style—* HE Mr Nick Astbury; ✉ c/o Foreign & Commonwealth Office (Asmara), King Charles Street, London SW1A 2AH

ASTILL, Sir Michael John; kt (1996); s of late Cyril Norman Astill, of Thurnby, Leics, and late Winifred, *née* Tuckley; *b* 31 January 1938; *Educ* Blackfriars Sch Laxton; *m* 1 June 1968, Jean Elizabeth, da of late Dr John Chisholm Hamilton Mackenzie; 1 da (Katherine b 11 July 1971), 3 s (Matthew, James (twins) b 28 Dec 1972, Mark b 11 Nov 1975); *Career* admitted slr 1962, called to the Bar Middle Temple 1972; recorder 1980–84, circuit judge (Midland & Oxford Circuit) 1984–96, judge of the High Court of Justice 1996–2004, presiding judge Midland & Oxford Circuit 1999–2002; pres Mental Health Tribunals 1986–96, chm Magisterial Ctee of the Judicial Studies Bd 1994–99; *Recreations* reading, music, gardening, sport; *Style—* Sir Michael Astill

ASTLEY, Dr Neil Philip; s of Philip Thomas Astley, of Adelaide, Aust, and Margaret Ivy Astley (d 1976); *b* 12 May 1953; *Educ* Price's Sch Fareham, Univ of Newcastle upon Tyne (BA); *Career* md and ed Bloodaxe Books Ltd (fndr 1978); Hon DLitt Univ of Newcastle upon Tyne 1996; *Awards* Eric Gregory Award 1982, Poetry Book Soc Recommendation 1988, Dorothy Tutin Award for Servs to Poetry 1989; *Books* Ten North-East Poets (ed, 1980), Darwin Survivor (1988), Poetry with an Edge (ed, 1988 and 1993), Tony Harrison (ed, 1991), Biting My Tongue (1995), New Blood (ed, 1999), The End of My Tether (2002), Staying Alive (ed, 2002), Pleased to See Me (ed, 2002), Do Not Go Gentle (ed, 2003), Being Alive (ed, 2004), The Sheep who Changed the World (2005), Passionfood (ed, 2005), Bloodaxe Poetry Introductions (ed, vols 1 and 2, 2006, vol 3, 2007), Soul Food (jt ed, 2007), Earth Shattering (ed, 2007); *Recreations* books, countryside, sheep, folklore; *Style—*

Dr Neil Astley; ✉ Bloodaxe Books Ltd, Highgreen, Tarset, Northumberland NE48 1RP (tel 01434 240500, fax 01434 240505, e-mail editor@bloodaxebooks.com)

ASTLEY-COOPER, Sir Alexander Paston; 7 Bt (UK 1821), of Gadebridge, Herts; s of Sir Patrick Graham Astley-Cooper, 6 Bt (d 2002); *b* 1 February 1943; *Educ* Kelly Coll Tavistock; *m* 1974, Minnie Margeret, da of Charles Harrison (d 1959); *Career* engineering consultant; *Recreations* cricket, badminton, rugby union, theatre, travel; *Clubs* Lions International; *Style*— Sir Alexander Astley-Cooper, Bt; ✉ Gadebridge, 8 Berkshire Close, Leigh-on-Sea, Essex SS9 4RJ (tel 01702 421920)

ASTON, Prof Peter George; s of Dr George William Aston (d 1980), and Dr Elizabeth Oliver Aston, *née* Smith (d 1979); *b* 5 October 1938; *Educ* Tettenhall Coll, Birmingham Sch of Music (GBSM), Univ of York (DPhil); *m* 13 Aug 1960, Elaine Veronica, da of Harold Neale (d 1942); 1 s (David b 1963); *Career* sr lectr in music Univ of York 1972–74 (lectr 1964–72); UEA: prof and head of music 1974–98, dean Sch of Fine Arts and Music 1981–84, professorial fell 1998–2001, emeritus prof 2001–; music dir: Tudor Consort 1959–65, Eng Baroque Ensemble 1967–70; conductor Aldeburgh Festival Singers 1975–88; princ guest conductor: Zephyr Point Church Music Festival Nevada 1991, 1993, 1995, 1997 and 1999, Sacramento Bach Festival Calif 1993–2001, Incontri Corali Int Choral Festival Alba 1997, Schola Cantorum Gedanensis Poland 1999; editorial advsr Pavane Publishing USA 2001–; gen ed UEA Recordings 1979–98, jt fndr and artistic dir Norwich Festival of Contemporary Church Music 1981–97; published compositions incl chamber music, church music, opera, choral and orch works; ed complete works of George Jeffreys and music by various Baroque composers; numerous recordings and contribs to int jls; hon patron: Great Yarmouth Musical Soc 1975–, Lowestoft Choral Soc 1986–; chm: Eastern Arts Assoc Music Panel 1975–81, Norfolk Assoc for the Advancement of Music 1990–93, Acad Bd Guild of Church Musicians 1996–, Ctee Norfolk and Norwich Area Royal School of Church Music 1998–2006; pres Norfolk Assoc for the Advancement of Music 1993–2000, Bury St Edmunds Bach Soc 2005–; chorus master Norfolk & Norwich Triennial Festival 1982–85, hon pres Trianon Music Gp 1984–96; hon fell Curwen Inst 1987; hon lay canon Norwich Cathedral 2002–; Hon RCM 1991, Hon FGCM 1995, Hon FRSCM 1999; FTCL, FCI, ARCM, FRSA 1980; *Books* George Jeffreys and the English Baroque (1970), Sound and Silence (jtly, 1970), The Music of York Minster (1972), The Collected Works of George Jeffreys (3 vols, 1977), Music Theory in Practice (jtly, 3 vols 1992–93); *Recreations* travel, bridge, chess, cricket; *Clubs* Athenaeum, Norfolk (Norwich); *Style*— Prof Peter Aston; ✉ University of East Anglia, Music Centre, School of Music, Norwich NR4 7TJ (tel 01603 592452, fax 01603 250454, telex 975197)

ASTOR, David Waldorf; CBE (1994), DL (Oxon 2007); s of Hon Michael Langhorne Astor (MP for Surrey East 1945–51, d 1980, 3 s of 2 Viscount Astor), and his 1 w, Barbara Mary (d 1980), da of Capt Ronald McNeill; n of Hon Sir John Astor (d 2000); *b* 9 August 1943; *Educ* Eton, Harvard Univ; *m* 19 Sept 1968, Clare Pamela, er da of Cdr Michael Beauchamp St John, DSC, RN; 2 s (Henry b 17 April 1969, Tom b 24 July 1972), 2 da (Joanna b 23 June 1970, Rose b 9 June 1979); *Career* short serv cmmn Royal Scots Greys 1962–65; farmer 1973–; dir: Jupiter Tarbutt Merlin 1985–91, Priory Investments Holdings 1990–2006; chm Classic FM 1986–91; chm: Cncl for the Protection of Rural England 1983–93, Southern Arts Bd 1998–2002, Action for Prisoners' Families 2003–, Turn2Us 2007–; Parly candidate (SDP) Plymouth Drake 1987; tstee: Glyndebourne Arts Tst 1995–2005, Elizabeth Finn Tst 2004–; FRSA 1988; *Recreations* books, sport; *Clubs* Brooks's, Beefsteak, MCC; *Style*— David Astor, Esq, CBE, DL; ✉ Bruern Grange, Milton-under-Wychwood, Chipping Norton, Oxfordshire OX7 6HA (tel 01993 830413, e-mail dastor@uk2.net)

ASTOR, 4 Viscount (UK 1917); William Waldorf Astor; also Baron Astor (UK 1916); only child of 3 Viscount Astor (d 1966), by his 1 w, Hon Sarah, *née* Norton, da of 6 Baron Grantley; *b* 27 December 1951; *Educ* Eton; *m* 1976, Annabel Lucy Veronica, da of Timothy Jones (himself s of Sir Roderick Jones, KBE, sometime chm of Reuters, and his w, better known as the writer Enid Bagnold). Annabel's mother was Pandora, *née* Clifford (niece of 11 and 12 Barons Clifford of Chudleigh and sis of Lady Norwich - *see* 2 Viscount Norwich); 1 da (Hon Flora Katherine b 7 June 1976), 2 s (Hon William Waldorf b 18 Jan 1979, Hon James Jacob b 4 March 1981); *Heir* s, Hon William Astor; *Career* a Lord in Waiting (Govt whip) 1990–93; Govt House of Lords spokesman: for DOE 1990–91, on home affrs 1991–92, on national heritage 1992–97; Parly under-sec of state: Dept of Social Security 1993–94, Dept of Nat Heritage 1994–95; oppn House of Lords spokesman: on home affrs 1997–, on transport 2001–; dir: Chorion plc, Urbium plc; *Clubs* White's; *Style*— The Rt Hon The Viscount Astor; ✉ Ginge Manor, Wantage, Oxfordshire OX12 8QT (tel 01235 833228)

ASTOR OF HEVER, 3 Baron (UK 1956); John Jacob Astor; DL; 3 Baron (UK 1956); s of 2 Baron Astor of Hever (d 1984), by his w, Lady Irene Violet Freesia Janet Augusta Haig (d 2001), da of FM 1 Earl Haig, KT, GCB, OM, GCVO, KCIE; *b* 16 June 1946; *Educ* Eton; *m* 1, 1970 (m dis 1990), Fiona Diana Lennox, da of Capt Roger Harvey, JP, DL, Scots Gds, and Diana (da of Sir Harry Mainwaring, 5 and last Bt, by his w Generis, eld da of Sir Richard Williams-Bulkeley, 12 Bt, KCB, VD, JP, and Lady Magdalen Yorke, da of 5 Earl of Hardwicke); 3 da (Hon Camilla Fiona b 1974, Hon Tania Jentie b 1978, Hon Violet Magdalene b 1980); m 2, 1990, Hon Elizabeth Constance, da of 2 Viscount Mackintosh of Halifax, OBE, BEM (d 1980), 1 s (Hon Charles Gavin John b 10 Nov 1990), 1 da (Hon Olivia Alexandra Elizabeth b 21 Aug 1992); *Heir* s, Hon Charles Astor; *Career* Lt LG 1966–70, served Malaysia, Hong Kong, NI; md SCI Astor Riviera 2001–; pres: Astor Enterprises Inc 1983–, Sevenoaks Westminster Patrons Club 1991–, Earl Haig Branch Royal Br Legion 1994–, Motorsport Industry Assoc 1995–, RoSPA 1996–99, Conservatives in Paris 2002–, Kent Branch Royal Br Legion 2003–; chm Cncl of St John Kent 1987–97; vice-chm: Thames Gateway Gp, Malaysia Parly Gp; sec: All-Pty Motor Gp 1997–, All-Pty Gp on Autism, All-Pty Gp on Shooting and Conservation; treas: British-S Africa Parly Gp, All-Pty Franco-Br Parly Relations Gp; memb oppn whip's office House of Lords 1998–; Social Sec 1998–01; oppn front bench spokesman: Health 1998–2003, Foreign and Commonwealth Affairs 2001–, Int Devpt 2001–, Defence 2003–; patron: Edenbridge Music and Arts Tst 1989–, Bridge Tst 1993–, Kent Youth Tst 1994–; govr Cobham Hall Sch 1992–96; tstee: Rochester Cathedral Tst 1988–, Canterbury Cathedral Tst 1992–, Astor of Hever Tst 1986–, Astor Fndn 1988–; Liveryman Worshipful Co of Goldsmiths; *Clubs* White's, Riviera Golf; *Style*— The Lord Astor of Hever, DL; ✉ House of Lords, London SW1A 0PW (tel 020 7219 5475, e-mail astorjj@parliament.uk)

ASTWOOD, Hon Sir James Rufus; kt (1982), KBE (1994), JP; s of late James Rufus Astwood, and Mabel Winifred Astwood; *b* 4 October 1923; *Educ* Berkeley Inst Bermuda, Univ of Toronto; *m* 1952, Gloria Preston Norton; 1 s, 2 da; *Career* called to the Bar Gray's Inn 1956; started practice at Jamaican Bar 1956; Jamaican Legal Serv 1957–74: dep clerk of courts Jamaica 1957–58, stipendiary magistrate and judge of Grand Court Cayman Islands 1958–59, clerk of courts Jamaica 1958–63, resident magistrate Jamaica 1963–74, puisne judge Jamaica 1971–73; sr magistrate Bermuda 1974–76, slr-gen Bermuda 1976–77, acting attorney-gen Bermuda 1976 and 1977, temp acting dep govr Bermuda during 1977, chief justice Bermuda 1977–93, justice of appeal Bermuda 1994–95, pres Court of Appeal Bermuda 1995–2003; Hon MA Gray's Inn 1985; *Style*— The Hon Sir James Astwood, KBE; ✉ The Pebble, 7 Astwood Walk, Warwick WK08, Bermuda (tel 00 441 236 1097, fax 00 441 236 8816); Appeal Court, Hamilton HM12, Bermuda (tel 00 441 292 1350)

ATALLA, Ash; s of Albert Atalla, and Adele Atalla; *b* 18 June 1972, Cairo, Egypt; *Educ* Univ of Bath (BSc); *Career* former stockbroker; joined BBC features, former commissioning ed BBC Comedy, comedy ed Talkback Productions until 2007, founder Roughcut Television 2007; prodr: The Way It Is... (BBC Radio 4) 1998, Yes Sir I Can Boogie (BBC Radio 4 and BBC2 pilot) 1999 and 2000, Up Late With Ralph Little (BBC Choice) 2001, Come Together with Ricky Gervais (Play UK) 2001, The Office (2 series and Christmas Special, BBC2) 2001–03; script ed Comedy Nation (series 1, BBC2) 1998, presenter Freak Out (Channel 4) 2000; author of Last Word column Independent on Sunday 2000, author of articles on disability, sport and television Time Out, contrib The Guardian (columnist 2005); *Awards* for The Office: South Bank Show Award for Best Television Comedy 2001, Broadcast Award for Best Comedy 2002, Br Comedy Award for Best New Television Comedy 2002, BAFTA for Best Situation Comedy 2002 and 2003; for The Office Christmas Specials: Golden Globe for Best Musical or Comedy Series 2004, BAFTA for Best Situation Comedy 2004; *Recreations* messing around; *Style*— Ash Atalla, Esq

ATAMAN, Kutlug; *b* 1961, Istanbul; *Educ* UCLA (BA, MFA); *Career* film maker and artist; Carnegie Prize 2004, shortlisted Turner Prize 2004; *Solo Exhibitions* incl: Lux Gallery London 2000, Tensta Konsthal Sweden 2001, Long Streams (Serpentine Gallery London and Copenhagen Contemporary Art Centre) 2002, Lehmann Maupin NY 2002, Women Who Wear Wigs (Istanbul Contemporary Arts Museum) 2002, A Rose Blooms in the Garden of Sorrows (BAWAG Fndn Vienna) 2002, Long Streams (Serpentine Gallery London and Nikolaj Copenhagen Contemporary Art Centre) 2002, Kuba (Artangel and Museum of Contemporary Art Sydney) 2005, De-Regulation With the Work of Kutlug Ataman (MuHKA, Belgium) 2006, Paradise (Orange County Museum of Art) 2007; *Group Exhibitions* incl: Istanbul Biennale 1997, Manifesta 2 Luxembourg 1998, 48th Venice Biennale 1999, Berlin Biennial 2001, Documenta 11 Kassel Germany 2002, Days Like These: Tate Triennial Exhibition of British Art (Tate Britain London) 2003, Witness (Barbican Art Gallery London) 2003, Testimonies: between Fiction and Reality (Nat Museum of Contemporary Art Athens) 2003, Istanbul Biennale 2003, Documentary Fictions (CaxiaForum Barcelona) 2004, Carnegie International Pittsburgh 2004, Without Boundary, Seventeen Ways of Looking (MOMA NY), Moscow Biennial 2007; *Style*— Kutlug Ataman; ✉ c/o Lehmann Maupin, 540 West 26 Street, NY, USA (tel 00 1 212 255 2923, fax 00 1 212 255 2924)

ATHA, Bernard Peter; CBE (2007, OBE 1991); s of Horace Michael Atha, of Leeds (d 1984), and Mary, *née* Quinlan (d 1951); *b* 27 August 1928; *Educ* Leeds Modern GS, Univ of Leeds (LLB), RAF Sch of Educn (DipEd); *Career* Nat Serv FO RAF 1950–52; called to the Bar Gray's Inn 1950; actor and variety artist, films and TV incl Kes and Coronation Street; princ lectr in business studies Huddersfield Tech Coll 1973–90; elected Leeds City Cncl 1957 (former chm Educn Social Servs Ctee, Cultural Servs Ctee and Watch Ctee), Lord Mayor of Leeds 2000–01; contested (Lab): Penrith and Border 1959, Pudsey 1964; chm Leeds Co op Soc 1971–96; pres English Fedn Disability Sport 1999–; chm: Yorks and Humberside Regnl Sports Cncl 1966–76, Nat Watersports Centre 1978–84, UK Sports Assoc for People with Mental Handicap 1980–, Leeds Leisure Servs Ctee 1988–90, Br Paralympic Assoc 1989–97, Int Sports Assoc for People with Mental Handicap 1993–, Disability Sports Devpt Tst; vice-chm: Sports Cncl 1976–80, EU Ctee on Sport for the Disabled 1997–99 (memb 1992–99); memb: Sports Aid Fndn, Sports Aid Tst, Int Paralympic Ctee 1993–98, Sports Eng Lottery Panel 1995–2002; vice-chm: W Leeds HA 1988–90, St James Univ Hosp NHS Tst 1993–98 (dir 1990–98), United Leeds Hosps Charitable Fndn (formerly United Leeds Teaching Hosps NHS Tst) 2001–; currently chm: Leeds Playhouse, Leeds Grand Theatre, Northern Ballet Theatre 1995–, City of Varieties, Red Ladder Theatre Co, Yorkshire Dance Centre Tst, Craft and Design Centre Leeds 1988–, Yorks Youth Dance 2006–; dir Opera North; pres Br and Int Festival of Festivals; memb: Royal Acad of Dance 1948, Arts Cncl 1979–82; chm Liz Dawn Cancer Appeal, vice-chm United Leeds Hosps Charitable Fndn; hon fell Leeds Coll of Music 2002; FRSA; *Recreations* the arts, sport, politics; *Style*— Bernard Atha, Esq, CBE; ✉ 25 Moseley Wood Croft, Leeds LS16 7JJ

ATHANAS, Christopher Nicholas (Chris); WS (1979); s of Nicholas Athanas (d 1947), and Elizabeth Christison, *née* Tasker (d 1972); *b* 26 August 1941, Aden; *Educ* Fettes, Univ of Aberdeen (MA, LLB); *m* 30 June 1963, Sheena Anne, *née* Stewart; 2 da (Gillian Elizabeth b 10 Oct 1964, Carol Anne b 11 Nov 1965), 1 s (Nicholas Murray b 14 Nov 1979); *Career* admitted slr Scotland 1966, NP 1969; slr specialising in corporate law and financial servs law; trainee then slr Paull & Williamsons 1964–68, ptnr Dundas & Wilson 1969–96 (slr 1968–69, memb Strategy Bd 1991–95), ptnr Tods Murray 1996–2006 (head Investment Funds and Financial Servs Gp 1997–2006), ret 2006; princ external legal advsr on oil-related deals Shetland Islands Cncl 1974–88; memb Law Soc of Scotland 1966; memb Soc of HM Writers to the Signet 1979; *Recreations* the arts, collecting, walking, golf, angling; *Clubs* Blairgowrie Golf, Royal Burgess Golfing Soc of Edinburgh, Royal Perth Golfing Soc and County and City, Square; *Style*— Chris Athanas, Esq, WS; ✉ tel 0131 447 4315

ATHANASOU, Prof Nicholas Anthony; s of Anthony James Athanasou (d 1964), and Angela, *née* Pappas (d 1974); *b* 26 April 1953; *Educ* Sydney HS, Univ of Sydney (MB BS, MD), Univ of London (PhD); *m* 27 April 1985, Linda Joan, da of Anthony Hulls, of Chislehurst, Kent; *Career* conslt pathologist Nuffield Orthopaedic Centre 1991–; Univ of Oxford: prof of orthopaedic pathology, fell Wadham Coll; MRCP 1981, FRCPath 1996 (MRCPath 1986); *Books* Hybrids (short stories, 1995), Atlas of Orthopaedic Pathology (1999), Pathological Basis of Orthopaedic and Rheumatic Disease (2001), The Greek Liar (novel, 2002); *Recreations* cricket, reading, writing; *Style*— Prof Nicholas Athanasou; ✉ Pathology Department, Nuffield Department of Orthopaedic Surgery, Nuffield Orthopaedic Centre, Headington, Oxford OX3 7LD (tel 01865 738136, e-mail nick.athanasou@ndos.ox.ac.uk)

ATHERTON, Candice Kathleen (Candy); da of late Denis Gordon Walles Atherton, and Pamela Ada Margaret, *née* Osborn; *b* 21 September 1955; *Educ* Convent of the Sacred Hearts Epsom, Midhurst GS, Poly of North London (BA); *m* 25 May 2002, Broderick Ross; *Career* successively: researcher for Jo Richardson, MP and Judith Hart, MP, probation offr, launched women's magazine Everywoman, press offr Lab Pty, with UNISON, journalist various nat broadsheet newspapers, MP (Lab) Falmouth and Camborne 1997–2005 (contested (Lab) Chesham and Amersham 1992), memb Educn and Employment Select Ctee 1997–2001, memb DEFRA Select Ctee 2003–05; dir Atherton Assocs Public Affrs 2007–; chair Rural Housing Advsy Gp 2007–, non-exec memb Bd Housing Corp 2005–; currently conslt Weber Shandwick Public Affrs; London Borough of Islington: cncllr 1986–92, mayor 1989–90, chm various ctees, former memb Islington HA; former chm Lab Pty's South and West Women's Ctee, memb Emily's List UK (former ed Emily News); pres Residential Boat Owners Assoc 2003; Freeman City of London 1990; *Recreations* birdwatching, canal boating, gardening, gliding; *Clubs* Falmouth Labour, House of Commons Yacht (Cdre); *Style*— Ms Candy Atherton; ✉ Pink Moors Cottage, Pink Moors, St Day, Cornwall TR16 5NL (e-mail candyatherton@btinternet.com)

ATHERTON, David; OBE; s of Robert Atherton, and Lavinia, *née* Burton; *b* 3 January 1944; *Educ* Univ of Cambridge (MA); *m* 5 Sept 1970, Ann Gianetta, da of Cdr J F Drake (d 1978), of Ware, Herts; 2 da (Elizabeth b 13 Feb 1974, Susan b 10 June 1977), 1 s (John b 14 May 1979); *Career* conductor and musical dir London Sinfonietta 1968–73 (fndr 1967) and 1989–91; Royal Opera House: repetiteur 1967–68, resident conductor 1968–80;

A

Royal Liverpool Philharmonic Orch: princ conductor and artistic advsr 1980–83, princ guest conductor 1983–86; musical dir and princ conductor San Diego Symphony Orch 1980–87, princ guest conductor BBC Symphony Orch 1985–89, musical dir and princ conductor Hong Kong Philharmonic Orch 1989–2000; artistic dir and conductor: London Stravinsky Festival 1979–82, Ravel/Varèse Festival 1983–84; artistic dir and fndr Californian Mainly Mozart Festival 1989–, princ guest conductor BBC Nat Orch of Wales 1994–97, Conductor Laureate Hong Kong Philharmonic Orch 2000–; co-fndr, pres and artistic dir Global Music Network 1998–; youngest conductor Henry Wood Promenade Concerts Royal Albert Hall and Royal Opera House 1968; Royal Festival Hall debut 1969; performances abroad incl: Europe, M East, Far East, Australasia, N America; major works conducted incl: Billy Budd (San Francisco Opera 1978, Met Opera NY 1985, ENO 1988 and 1991), Peter Grimes (Dallas Opera 1980, Met Opera 1985, 1997 and 1998, ENO 1991 and 1994), Stravinsky Le Rossignol and Ravel L'Enfant et les Sortileges (Royal Opera House 1987 and 1989), Berlioz Romeo and Juliet (Philharmonia Orch) 1989, The Love for Three Oranges (ENO) 1989, Wozzeck (Canadian Opera) 1990, Les Huguenots (Royal Opera House) 1991, Death in Venice (Metropolitan Opera) 1994, The Barber of Seville (Met Opera) 1995, Turandot (ENO) 1995, Midsummer Night's Dream (Met Opera 1996 and 2002, Glyndebourne 2001), Der Rosenkavalier (ENO) 1997, Salome (ENO) 1999, King Priam (RFH, with BBC Nat Orch of Wales) 1999, The Makropulos Case (Glyndebourne in NYC) 2001; awards incl: Composers' Guild of GB Conductor of the Year 1971, Edison Award 1973, Grand Prix du Disque 1977, Koussevitzky Award 1981, Int Record Critics' Award 1982, Prix Caecilia 1982; adapted and arranged Pandora by Roberto Gerhard for Royal Ballet 1975; *Books* The Complete Instrumental and Chamber Music of Arnold Schoenberg and Roberto Gerhard (ed, 1973), Pandora and Don Quixote Suites by Roberto Gerhard (ed, 1973), The Musical Companion (contrib, 1978), The New Grove Dictionary (1981); *Recreations* travel, computing, theatre; *Style*— David Atherton, Esq, OBE; ✉ c/o Askonas Holt, Lonsdale Chambers, 27 Chancery Lane, London WC2A 1PF

ATHERTON, Dr David John; s of Dr Desmond Joseph Atherton, of Coventry, and Hildegard, *née* Rowe, MBE; *b* 24 April 1949; *Educ* Ampleforth, Pembroke Coll Cambridge (MA, MB BChir); *m* 1971 (m dis); 3 s (James b 1976, Joseph b 1984, Jay b 1998); *Career* conslt in paediatric dermatology 1982–: Gt Ormond St Hosp for Children, St John's Inst of Dermatology; sr lectr in paediatric dermatology Inst of Child Health 1986–; FRCP; *Books* Eczema in Childhood (1994); *Recreations* tennis, gardening; *Style*— Dr David Atherton; ✉ Great Ormond Street Hospital for Children, London WC1N 3JH (tel 020 7405 9200, fax 020 7829 8643)

ATHERTON, Howard William; s of William Atherton (d 1989), of Sudbury, Suffolk, and Rose Charlotte Atherton (d 1984); *b* 12 August 1947; *Educ* Sudbury GS, London Film Sch; *m* 12 Aug 1972, Janet Ruth, da of Ronald William Simpson, of Lavenham, Suffolk; 2 da (Rebecca Louise b 1977, Charlotte Letitia Rose b 1985), 1 s (Oliver Luke b 1979); *Career* director of photography; memb: Br Soc of Cinematograpers, BAFTA, Acad of Motion Picture Arts and Sciences (AMPAS); *Film* incl: Helen, Runners 1983, Keep Off the Grass, Fatal Attraction 1986, The Boost 1987, Mermaids 1989, Indecent Proposal 1992, Bad Boys 1994, Gulliver's Travels 1995, Lolita 1995, Deep Rising 1996, Hanging Up 1999, Abduction Club 2000, Colour Me Kubrick 2004, Lassie 2005, And when did you last see your father 2006; *Style*— Howard Atherton, Esq; ✉ Clarence House, Clarence Drive, Englefield Green, Surrey TW20 0NL

ATHERTON, Kevin; s of William Edward Atherton, of Douglas, Isle of Man, and Elizabeth, *née* Clague; *b* 25 November 1950; *Educ* Douglas HS for Boys IOM, IOM Coll of Art, Leeds Poly (BA); *m* 1977, Victoria (d 2005), da of Francis Sidney Thomas Robinson; *Career* sculptor, artist and lectr in art; pt/t teacher 1978–86: Slade Sch of Fine Art, RCA, Norwich Sch of Art, Winchester Sch of Art, Maidstone Coll of Art, Chelsea Sch of Art, Fine Art Dept Middx Poly, Fine Art Dept South Glamorgan Inst of Higher Educ Cardiff; artist in residence London Borough of Richmond upon Thames 1989; Kingston Poly: Picker lectr in public art Fine Art Dept 1989, Stanley Picker lectr in video performance and public art 1990; lecture tour of Australia 1990; princ lectr in media Fine Art Dept Chelsea Sch of Art 1990–99 (project ldr research project into Virtual Reality as a Fine Art Medium); head Dept of Media Nat Coll of Art and Design Dublin 2000–; organiser and speaker Virtual Reality and the Gallery conf (Tate Gallery) 1995; specialist advsr CNAA 1985–; judge Arts Cncl Br Gas Awards 1990–91; awards incl ABSA Award for Best Cmmn in Any Media 1986; numerous exhbns in England and Europe incl: one-man exhbn Perth Inst of Contemporary Art 1990, Kevin Atherton, Three Decades, Three Works (mini retrospective, arthouse Dublin and Manx Museum Douglas IOM) 2001, In Two Minds - Past and Future Versions (video performance, Dundee Contemporary Arts) 2006, In Two Minds - Past Version (video performance, Tate Britain) 2006, In Two Minds - Past Version (video installation) and Time Embodied (Lewis Glucksman Gallery Cork) 2007; Virtual Reality Work selected for the 8th Biennial of the Moving Image Geneva 1999; *Work in Public Collections* Sheffield City Poly, Merseyside CC, Graves Art Gallery Sheffield; *Commissions* incl: A Body of Work (Tower Hamlets) 1982, Upon Reflection (Islington) 1985, Platforms Piece (BR Brixton) 1986, Cathedral (Forest of Dean, Glos) 1986, Iron Horses (BR) 1986–87, The Architect (Harlow New Town) 1990, Conversation Piece (Leicester CC) 1990, Art Within Reach (Hampshire Sculpture Tst) 1991, To The Top (New Civic Offices Twickenham) 1990, A Different Ball Game (Kingshill W Malling Kent) 1993, A Private View (Taff Viaduct Cardiff Bay) 1995, Virtual Reality Gallery Guide Museum of Contemporary Art Chicago 1997 and MOMA Stockholm 1998, Field of Vision (GlaxoSmithKline HQ Brentford) 2001, Handshake (HG Capital London) 2002, A Reflective Approach (Clarence Dock Leeds) 2007; *Recreations* the turf; *Style*— Kevin Atherton, Esq; ✉ 114 Belleview, Islandbridge, Dublin 8, Ireland (tel 00 353 1 6706855, e-mail kevinatherton@ncad.ie)

ATHERTON, Brig Maurice Alan; CBE (1981), JP (1982), DL (Kent 1984); s of Rev Harold Atherton (d 1975), of Sheffield, and Beatrice, *née* Shaw (d 1958); *b* 9 October 1926; *Educ* St John's Sch Leatherhead, Staff Coll Camberley; *m* 28 Aug 1954, Guendolene Mary (Wendi), da of Col James Bryan Upton, MBE, TD, JP, DL (d 1976), of Hotham, York; 1 da (Christine Wendy b 6 March 1965), 1 s (James Patrick b 7 Sept 1966); *Career* cmmnd E Yorks Regt 1946 (serv in Egypt, Sudan, Malaysia, Austria, Germany, UK), MA to CBF Hong Kong 1959–62, coll chief instr RMA Sandhurst 1964–67, CO 1 Green Howards 1967–69, GSO 1 NI 1969–70, def advsr Ghana 1971–73; cdr Dover Shorncliffe Garrison and Dep Constable Dover Castle 1976–81; magistrate Dover Bench Kent 1982–91; High Sheriff Kent 1983–84, Vice Lord-Lt Kent 2000–02; county pres: Royal Br Legion 1982–91, Men of the Trees 1985–95; chm Kent Ctee Army Benevolent Fund 1984–97; chm Christ Church UC Canterbury 1993–99; Hon DCL Univ of Kent 1996; *Recreations* shooting, gardening; *Clubs* Lansdowne; *Style*— Brig M A Atherton, CBE, JP, DL; ✉ Digges Place, Barham, Canterbury, Kent CT4 6PJ (tel 01227 831420, fax 01227 832311)

ATHERTON, Michael Andrew (Mike); OBE (1997); s of Alan Atherton, and Wendy, *née* Fletcher; *b* 23 March 1968; *Educ* Manchester Grammar, Downing Coll Cambridge (MA, Cricket blue and capt); *Career* professional cricketer; first class debut Cambridge Univ v Essex April 1987; Lancashire CCC: debut v Warwickshire July 1987, awarded county cap 1989, vice-capt 1992–2001, ret 2001; England: former English School's rep, capt Young England to Sri Lanka 1987 and Aust 1988, first team debut v Aust Aug 1989, first full tour Aust and NZ 1990–91, memb team touring India and Sri Lanka 1992–93, capt England July 1993–98 and 2001 (for two matches v Australia), capt team touring West Indies 1993–94, Aust 1994–95, South Africa 1995–96, Zimbabwe and NZ 1996–97 and West Indies 1998, memb winning team v South Africa 1998, memb squad Emirates Trophy 1998, memb team touring Aust 1998–99, memb team touring South Africa 1999–2000, memb team touring Pakistan and Sri Lanka 2000–01, highest test score 185 not out v South Africa 1995, 115 test matches, 54 one-day ints, ret 2001; currently cricket commentator Channel 4; Professional Cricketers' Assoc Young Cricketer of Year 1990, Cricket Writers' Young Cricketer of Year 1990, Wisden Cricketer of the Year 1991, Cornhill Player of the Year 1994; *Recreations* reading, golf, squash, rugby, football (Manchester United supporter), good food; *Style*— Mike Atherton, Esq, OBE

ATHERTON, Peter; s of Joseph Ignatius Atherton (d 1984), of Wrightington, and Winifred, *née* Marsh; *b* 8 November 1952; *Educ* Mount St Mary's Coll Derby, Univ of Birmingham (LLB), Coll of Law; *m* 17 Oct 1981, Jennifer Marie, da of Charles Birch, of Ontario, Canada; 1 da (Hilary Anne b 4 Jan 1984), 1 s (Timothy Peter b 4 Sept 1985); *Career* called to the Bar Gray's Inn 1975; jr Northern Circuit 1978–79, recorder of the Crown Court 1999–; chm Young Barrs Ctee Senate of Inns of Ct and Bar Cncl for England and Wales 1982–83; *Recreations* tennis, golf, theatre; *Style*— Peter Atherton, Esq; ✉ Deans Court Chambers, 24 St John's Street, Manchester M3 4DF (tel 0161 214 6000, e-mail atherton@deanscourt.co.uk)

ATHILL, Diana; da of Col L F I Athill (d 1968), and Alice Katharine, *née* Carr (d 1990); *b* 21 December 1917, London; *Educ* Runton Hill Sch Norfolk, Lady Margaret Hall Oxford (BA); *Career* author; ed Allan Wingate publishers 1946–50, editorial dir André Deutsch Ltd 1951–92; FRSL; *Books* Instead of a Letter (1963), Don't Look at Me Like That (1967), After a Funeral (1986), Make Believe (1993), Stet (2000), Yesterday Morning (2002); *Recreations* reading, writing, gardening; *Style*— Ms Diana Athill; ✉ c/o The Royal Society of Literature, Somerset House, Strand, London WC2R 1LA

ATHOLL, 11 Duke of (S 1703); John Murray; also Lord Murray of Tullibardine (S 1604), Earl of Tullibardine (S 1606), Earl of Atholl (S 1629), Marquess of Atholl (S 1676), Marquess of Tullibardine (S 1703), Earl of Strathtay and Strathardle (S 1703), Viscount of Balwhidder, Glenalmond and Glenlyon (S 1703), and Lord Murray, Balvenie, and Gask (S 1703); only s of George Murray (d 1940), and Joan, *née* Eastwood; suc kinsman, 10 Duke 1996; *b* 19 January 1929; *Educ* Univ of the Witwatersrand (BSc(Eng)); *m* 1956, Margaret Yvonne, only da of late Ronald Leonard Leach; 1 da (Lady Jennifer (Lady Jennifer Glodek) b 1958), 2 s (Bruce George Ronald Murray, Marquess of Tullibardine b 6 April 1960, Lord Craig John Murray b 1963); *Heir* s, Marquess of Tullibardine; *Style*— His Grace the Duke of Atholl; ✉ c/o The Estate Office, Blair Castle, Blair Atholl, Perthshire

ATIYAH, Sir Michael Francis; OM (1992), kt (1983); s of Edward Selim Atiyah (d 1964), and Jean, *née* Levens (d 1964); *b* 22 April 1929; *Educ* Victoria Coll Egypt, Manchester Grammar, Univ of Cambridge (MA, PhD); *m* 1955, Lily Jane Myles, da of John Cameron Brown (d 1970); 3 c; *Career* fell Trinity Coll Cambridge 1954–58 and 1997–, Savilian prof of geometry Univ of Oxford 1963–69, prof of mathematics Inst for Advanced Study Princeton USA 1969–72, Royal Soc res prof Mathematical Inst Univ of Oxford 1973–90, dir Isaac Newton Inst for Mathematical Scis Cambridge 1990–96; Master Trinity Coll Cambridge 1990–97, chllr Univ of Leicester 1996–2005, hon prof Univ of Edinburgh 1997–; pres: Royal Soc 1990–95, Royal Soc Edinburgh 2005–; Fields Medal 1966, Abel Prize 2004; Hon ScD Univ of Cambridge; FRS 1962, Hon FREng 1993; *Recreations* gardening; *Style*— Sir Michael Atiyah, OM, FRS; ✉ School of Mathematics, King's Buildings, Mayfield Road, Edinburgh EH9 3JZ (tel 0131 650 4883, fax 0131 650 6553, e-mail m.atiyah@ed.ac.uk)

ATKIN, Edward; s of David Atkin (d 1972), of London, and Klari, *née* Salpeter; *b* 30 August 1944, Bradford, Yorks; *Educ* Clifton Coll Bristol; *m* 1981, Celia; 1 s (Ross b 15 March 1982), 1 da (Lara b 11 Oct 1983); *Career* joined Cannon Rubber 1965 (suc f as md 1972); founded: Avent 1984, Avent America 1994, Cannon Avent Gp 1998 (sold Avent part of Gp 2005); currently md Cannon Auto; 5 Queen's Awards, Civic Tst Award, various awards for architecture; *Recreations* golf, sailing, the arts; *Clubs* Hampstead Golf; *Style*— Edward Atkin, Esq

ATKIN, Peter Richard (Pete); s of Cyril William Atkin, of Cambridge, and Elsie Rose Cowell (d 1980); *b* 22 August 1945; *Educ* Perse Sch Cambridge, St John's Coll Cambridge (BA); *m* 24 Nov 1973, Mary Louise, da of Lewis Lynch Lowance, of Manassas, VA; *Career* radio prodr; scriptwriter, critic, songwriter (with Clive James, *qv*) and recording artist of 6 albums 1970–75 (reissued See for Miles 1997 and 2001), former furniture maker and woodwork corr Vole magazine 1976–77; chief prodr BBC Radio Light Entertainment 1986–89 (prodr 1981, script ed 1983), head of network radio BBC South Bristol 1989–93, ind prodn co-ordinator BBC Radio 4 1993; ind radio prodr and conslt 1994–, script ed Hat Trick Productions 1994–2002; prodr: This Sceptred Isle (BBC Radio 4) 1995–99, This Sceptred Isle: Empire (BBC Radio 4) 2006 (Best New Radio Prog Voice of the Viewer and Listener Awards 2006); voice dir Thomas the Tank Engine and Bob the Builder (US versions) 2004–, voice actor Mr Crock in Wallace & Gromit: The Curse of the Were-Rabbit (film) 2006; Together Again At Last (with Clive James, UK tour) 2002, The Lakeside Sessions (double CD) 2002, Words and Music (with Clive James, UK, Australia and Hong Kong tour) 2003, Winter Spring (CD, new songs with Clive James) 2003, At It Again (with Clive James, UK tour) 2005, Midnight Voices: The Clive James and Pete Atkin Songbook, Vol 1 (CD) 2007; winner Best Non-Fiction Talkie of the Year Talkie Awards 1996; tstee St George's Music Tst Bristol; *Recreations* words, music, wood; *Style*— Pete Atkin, Esq; ✉ 19 Archfield Road, Bristol BS6 6BG (tel 0117 942 1582, e-mail pete@peteatkin.com, website www.peteatkin.com)

ATKIN, Ron; s of late Oscar Ridgeway, of Barrow-on-Soar, Leics, and late Agatha Victoria, *née* Hull; *b* 3 February 1938; *Educ* Loughborough Coll of Art, Royal Acad Schs (Cert); *m* 23 July 1960, Ann, da of Capt Arthur Charles Fawssett, DSO, RN (d 1961); 2 s (Francis Charles Edward b 1961, Richard Bernard b 1963); *Career* artist; RA summer exhibition 1960, 1970 and 1975, Royal Watercolour Soc Galleries Bond Street 1961, mixed exhibition Roland Browse and Delbanco Cork Street London and SA 1961 and 1964, Paintings and Sculpture from some Oxford Jr Common Rooms Leics Museum and Art Gallery 1962; one-man shows: Plymouth City Museum and Art Gallery 1976, Chenil Art Gallery King's Road London 1982; paintings in private collections: GB, Aust, USA, Canada, Germany, Zurich, Lucerne; paintings in public collections incl: Dartington Tst Devon, Devon CC Schs Museum Serv, Lincoln Coll Oxford, Plymouth City Museum and Art Gallery; shortlisted for a Gulbenkian Printmakers' Award 1984; featured in Dictionary of British Art Vol VI, 20th Century Painters, Dictionary of Artists in Britain since 1945; *Publications* Trilogy (2005); *Recreations* walking; *Style*— Ron Atkin; ✉ Wild Flower Studios, Abbots Bickington, Devon EX22 7LQ

ATKIN, Timothy John (Tim); s of Ronald George Atkin, and Brenda Irene, *née* Burton (d 1982); *b* 26 August 1961, Dartford, Kent; *Educ* St Dunstan's Coll London, Univ of Durham (BA), LSE (MSc); *Career* with Haymarket Publishing 1985–89; wine corr: The Guardian 1989–93, The Observer 1993–; ed Harpers Wine & Spirit Weekly 2000–03; Glenfiddich Wine Writer of the Year 1989, 1991, 1993, 2004 and 2006, Lanson Wine Writer of the Year 1999, 2002, 2003 and 2004; memb: Greenpeace, Amnesty Int; MW 2001; *Publications* Chardonnay (1991), Vin de Pays D'Oc (1992), Grapevine (with Anthony Rose, 1993, 1994, 1995, 1996 and 1997); *Recreations* reading, tennis, golf, cinema, folk guitar; *Clubs* Groucho, Coombe Hill Golf; *Style*— Tim Atkin, MW; ✉ c/o Lucas Alexander Whitley, 14 Vernon Street, London W14 0RJ (tel 020 7471 7900, fax 020 7471 7910, e-mail julian@lawagency.co.uk)

ATKINS, Prof Anthony George; s of Walter George Atkins (d 1975), and Emily Irene, *née* Aldridge (d 1996); *b* 10 October 1939; *Educ* Canton HS Cardiff, UC Cardiff (BSc), Trinity Coll Cambridge (PhD, ScD), Exeter Coll Oxford (MA); *m* 4 March 1971, Margaret Ann, da of Lt-Col Richard Risely Proud, CVO, OBE (d 1976); 2 s (Philip George b 1973, Richard James b 1976), 1 da (Margaret Ruth b 1980); *Career* US Steel Corpn 1965–67, BSC fell Univ of Oxford 1967–70, assoc prof in mechanical engrg Univ of Michigan 1970–75, research mangr Delta Metal 1975–81, prof of mechanical engrg Univ of Reading 1981–; memb CPRE; FIMMM (FIM 1986), FIMechE 1987, CEng, FREng 2002; *Books* Strength and Fracture of Engineering Solids (jtly, 1984, 2 ed 1996), A History of GWR Goods Wagons (jtly, 1986, 3 edn 1999), Manufacturing Engineering (jtly, 1987), Elastic and Plastic Fracture (jtly, 2 edn, 1988), GWR Goods Services (vol 1, jtly, 2000); *Recreations* music, skiing, woodwork; *Style*— Prof Tony Atkins, FREng; ☒ White House, Heads Lane, Inkpen Common, Hungerford, Berkshire RG17 9QS (tel 01488 668253); Department of Engineering, Box 225, University of Reading, Whiteknights, Reading RG6 6AY (tel 0118 931 8562, fax 0118 931 3327, e-mail a.g.atkins@reading.ac.uk)

ATKINS, Charlotte; MP; da of Ron Atkins; *m* Gus Brain; m; 1 da (Emma b 24 Oct 1986); *Career* MP (Lab) Staffordshire Moorlands 1997–; PPS to Rt Hon Baroness Symons of Vernham Dean, PC, *qv* 2001–02; asst govt whip 2002–04, Parly under sec Dept for Tport 2004–05; memb Select Ctee: on Educn and Employment 1997–2001, on Health 2005–; memb Lab Pty Backbench Ctees on: Agric 1997–2001, Educn and Employment 1997–2001, DETR 1997–2001, Educn and Skills 2001–, FCO, DTI; memb: Women's Ctee Lab Pty NEC 1992–98, Selection Ctee 1997–2000, PLP Ctee 1997–2000; London Borough of Wandsworth: cncllr 1982–86, chief whip 1983–84, dep leader of Lab Gp 1985–86; *Recreations* keeping fit, theatre; *Style*— Mrs Charlotte Atkins, MP; ☒ House of Commons, London SW1A 0AA (tel 020 7219 3591, e-mail atkinsc@parliament.uk); constituency (tel and fax 01782 777661)

ATKINS, Dame Eileen June; DBE (2001, CBE 1990); da of late Arthur Thomas Atkins, and Annie Ellen, *née* Elkins (d 1984); *b* 16 June 1934; *Educ* Latymer GS, Guildhall Sch of Music and Drama (AGSM); *m* 1, 1957 (m dis 1966), Julian Glover, *qv*; m 2, 1978, William B Shepherd; *Career* actress; hon memb GSM; *Theatre* incl: Twelfth Night, Richard III, The Tempest (Old Vic) 1962, The Killing of Sister George (Bristol Old Vic transfd Duke of York, Best Actress Standard Award) 1963, The Cocktail Party (Wyndham's transferred Haymarket) 1968, Vivat! Vivat! Regina! (Piccadilly, Variety Award) 1970, Suzanne Andler (Aldwych) 1973, As You Like It (Stratford) 1973, St Joan (Old Vic) 1977, Passion Play (Aldwych) 1981, Medea (Young Vic) 1986, Winter's Tale, Cymbeline (Olivier Award), Mountain Language (NT) 1988, A Room of One's Own (Hampstead, NY Critics' Special citation) 1989, Exclusive (Strand) 1989, Prin (NY) 1990, Hannah Jelkes in The Night of the Iguana (Critics' Circle Award) 1992, John Gabriel in Bork Man (NT) 1997, Agnes in A Delicate Balance (Haymarket Theatre Royal (Evening Standard Best Actress Award)) 1998, The Unexpected Man (RSC, The Pit and The Duchess) 1998, A Room of One's Own (Hampstead Theatre) 2001, Unexpected Man (Promenade Theatre NY) 2001, Honour (Cottesloe NT, Olivier Award), The Retreat from Moscow (Booth Theatre) 2003–04, The Birthday Party (The Duchess) 2005, Doubt (Walter Kerr Theatre NY) 2005–06, There Came a Gypsy Riding (Almeida) 2007; *Television* incl: The Duchess of Malfi, Sons and Lovers, Smiley's People, Nelly's Version, The Burston Rebellion, Breaking Up, The Vision, Mrs Pankhurst in In My Defence (series) 1990, A Room of One's Own 1990, Lost Language of Cranes 1992, The Maitlands 1993, A Dance to the Music of Time 1997, Talking Heads 1998, David Copperfield 1999, Madame Bovary 2000, Elizabeth and Bertie 2001, The Lives of Animals 2002, Waking the Dead 2006, Cranford 2007; *Film* incl: Equus 1974, The Dresser 1984, Let Him Have It 1990, Wolf 1993, Cold Comfort Farm 1995, Jack and Sarah 1995, The Avengers 1998, Women Talking Dirty 1999, Gosford Park 2001, The Hours 2002, What a Girl Wants 2003, Vanity Fair 2003, Ask the Dust 2004, Evening 2007; also co-creator of Upstairs Downstairs and The House of Eliott, writer/adaptor Mrs Dalloway (1998); *Style*— Dame Eileen Atkins, DBE; ☒ c/o ICM, Oxford House, 76 Oxford Street, London W1D 1BS (tel 020 7636 6565, fax 020 7323 0101)

ATKINS, Frances Elizabeth (Mrs Gerald Atkins); da of Thomas Colyer Venning, MBE (decd), of Ilkley, W Yorks, and Hilary Susan, *née* Harris; *b* 8 September 1950; *m* 1, 1976 (m dis 1984), George Alfred Carman, QC (d 2001); m 2, 1984, Gerald Atkins; *Career* chef and restaurateur; Atkins Restaurant: Great Missenden 1984–86, The Old Plow Inn Speen 1986–88, Farleyer House Aberfeldy 1988–92; chef prop Shaw's Restaurant 1993–96, prop The Yorke Arms 1996–; memb Bd of Scottish Chefs 1992; fell Master Chefs of GB 1993, César Country Inn of the Year 2000 Good Hotel Guide, Restaurant of the Year in Eng Which Good Food Guide 2001 (jtly), Chef of the Year Yorkshire Life Magazine 2002/03, Michelin Star 2003, AA Top 200 Hotels 2004, Top 25 Restaurants in the UK Egon Ronay Guide 2005/06; *Recreations* work, art appreciation, collecting furniture; *Style*— Mrs Gerald Atkins; ☒ Yew Bank House, Ramsgill-in-Nidderdale, Harrogate HG3 5RL

ATKINS, Paul; *Educ* Univ of Sussex (BEd), Univ of Reading (MSc), Brunel Univ (Dip Business Mgmnt), CIM; *Career* field dir and team ldr Christian Outreach Thailand 1979–81, head of physics Robert Haining Sch Mytchett 1981–84, head of science, mathematics and computer studies St Andrew's Sch Kenya 1984–86; Br Cncl: asst dir Lesotho 1987–90, dep dir Malawi 1990–93, dep dir int seminars London 1993–95, dir (designate) Sierra Leone 1995–96, dir int seminars London and Oxford 1996–99, dir NZ 1999–2004; gp mangr Int Investments Fndn for Research Sci and Technol 2004–07, gp mangr communications and audience/market devpt Creative New Zealand 2007–; co-chm for Br Cncl Hornby Tst 1996–97, chm Bd of Mgmnt Oxford Overseas Student Housing Assoc Ltd 1996–99, memb Mgmnt Bd Britain/NZ Link Fndn 1999–2004, chair Bd of Mgmnt Shakespeare's Globe Centre NZ 2004–, memb Bd of Tstees NZ String Quartet 2004–; memb: Woodland Tst, RSPB, Wildfowl and Wetland Tst; CPhys, MInstP, MCMI, memb Royal Soc of NZ; *Publications* Digital Developments in Higher Education - theory and practice (co-author, 2001); travel photographs in calendars; *Recreations* ornithology, conservation, photography, triathlon and multi-sport endurance events, squash, cycling; *Style*— Paul Atkins, Esq; ☒ Creative New Zealand, PO Box 3806, Wellington, New Zealand (tel 00 64 4 498 0723)

ATKINS, Prof Peter William; s of William Henry Atkins (d 1988), and Ellen Louise, *née* Edwards (d 1978); *b* 10 August 1940; *Educ* Dr Challoner's Amersham, Univ of Leicester (BSc, PhD), Univ of Oxford (MA), UCLA; *m* 1, 20 Aug 1964 (m dis 1983), Judith Ann Kearton; 1 da (Juliet b 1970); m 2, 30 March 1991 (m dis 2005), Baroness Greenfield, CBE (Life Peer), *qv*; *Career* Harkness fell 1964–65; Univ of Oxford: univ lectr in physical chemistry 1965–96, prof of chemistry 1996–, fell and tutor Lincoln Coll 1965– (actg rector 2007); visiting prof: China, France, Israel, Japan, New Zealand; Dreyfus lectr California 1980, Firth visiting prof Univ of Sheffield 1984, Nyholm lectr and medal 1999; chm Ctee on Chemistry Educn IUPAC 2002–05, memb Cncl Royal Inst 1999–2005; memb Ct Univ of Leicester 2001; hon prof Mendeleyev Univ Moscow 2006; Hon DSc Univ of Utrecht 1992, Hon DSc Univ of Leicester 2002; Meldola Medal 1969, Literaturpreis des Fonds der Chemischen Industrie 2003; hon assoc Rationalist Press Assoc 1993; FRSC 2002; *Books* The Structure of Inorganic Radicals (1967), Molecular Quantum Mechanics (1970, 4 edn 2005), Quanta: A Handbook of Concepts (1974, 2 edn 1991), Physical Chemistry (1978, 8 edn 2006), Solutions Manual for Physical Chemistry (1978, 7 edn 2002), The Creation (1981), Principles of Physical Chemistry (1982), Solutions Manual for MQM (1983, 4 edn 2005), The Second Law (1984), Molecules (1987, 2 edn 2003), Chemistry: Principles and Applications (1988), General Chemistry (1989, 2 edn 1992), Inorganic Chemistry (1990, 4 edn 2006), Atoms, Electrons and Change (1991), Elements of Physical Chemistry (1992, 4 edn 2005), Creation Revisited (1992), The Periodic Kingdom (1995), Concepts of Physical Chemistry (1995), Chemistry: Molecules, Matter and Change (1997, 4 edn 1999), Chemical Principles (1999, 3 edn 2004), Galileo's Finger (2003); *Recreations* art; *Clubs* Athenaeum; *Style*— Prof Peter Atkins; ☒ Lincoln College, Oxford OX1 3DR (tel 01865 279800, fax 01865 279802, e-mail peter.atkins@lincoln.ox.ac.uk)

ATKINS, Rt Hon Sir Robert James; kt (1997), PC (1995), MEP (Cons) NW England; s of late Reginald Alfred Atkins, of Great Missenden, Bucks, and Winifred Margaret Atkins; *b* 5 February 1946; *Educ* Highgate Sch; *m* 1969, Dulcie Mary, da of Frederick Moon Chaplin, of Bexley, London; 1 da (Victoria b 1976), 1 s (James b 1979); *Career* MP (Cons): Preston N 1979–1983, South Ribble 1983–97; former jt sec Cons Parly Def Ctee and vice-chm Aviation Ctee, nat pres Cons Trade Unionists 1984–87; PPS to: Norman Lamont as Min of State for Industry 1982–84, Lord Young of Graffham as Min Without Portfolio and Sec of State for Employment 1984–87; Parly under sec of state DTI 1987–89, min for roads and traffic Dept of Tport 1989–90, Parly under sec of state Dept of the Environment and min for sport 1990, Parly under sec of state Dept of Educn and Science and min for sport 1990–92, min of state Northern Ireland Office 1992–94, min of state Dept of Environment 1994–95; MEP (Cons) NW England 1999–, dep ldr Br Cons MEPs, Cons spokesman on parly petitions; *Recreations* cricket, Holmesiana, ecclesiology, wine; *Clubs* MCC, Carlton, Middlesex CCC, Lancashire CCC (vice-pres), Garstang CC (pres), Lord's Taverners; *Style*— The Rt Hon Sir Robert Atkins, MEP

ATKINS, Rosie; da of Robert Vernon William Atkins, and Agnes Dunn Atkins; *Educ* St Michael's Girls Sch Limpsfield; *Career* journalist; Sunday Times 1968–82, columnist Today 1983–90, ed Gardens Illustrated; gardening contrib various newspapers and magazines; Editor of the Year Br Soc of Magazine Editors 1996; curator Chelsea Physic Garden 2002–; bd memb: Thrive, Disabled Gardeners Assoc; *Recreations* gardening, travel, writing; *Clubs* Chelsea Arts; *Style*— Ms Rosie Atkins; ☒ Chelsea Physic Garden, 66 Royal Hospital Road, London SW3 4HS (tel 020 7352 5646)

ATKINSON, Sir Anthony Barnes (Tony); kt (2000); s of Norman Joseph Atkinson (d 1988), and Esther Muriel, *née* Stonehouse; *b* 4 September 1944; *Educ* Cranbrook Sch, Churchill Coll Cambridge (MA); *m* 11 Dec 1965, Judith Mary, da of Alexander Mandeville, of Swansea; 2 s (Richard b 1972, Charles b 1976), 1 da (Sarah b 1974); *Career* fell St John's Coll Cambridge 1967–71, prof of economics Univ of Essex 1971–76, prof Univ of London 1976–92 (Thomas Tooke prof of econ sci and statistics 1987–92), fell Churchill Coll and prof of political economy Univ of Cambridge 1992–94, warden Nuffield Coll Oxford 1994–2005; ed Jl of Public Economics 1971–97; pres: Econometric Soc 1988, Euro Econ Assoc 1989, Int Econ Assoc 1989–92, Royal Econ Soc 1995–98, Section F BAAS; vice-pres Br Acad 1988–90; memb: Royal Cmmn on Distribution of Income and Wealth 1978–79, Retail Prices Advsy Ctee 1984–90, Conseil D'Analyse Economique 1997–2001; UAP Sci prize 1986; Freeman City of London 1983, Liveryman Worshipful Co of Barbers 1985; Hon Dr Rer Pol Univ of Frankfurt 1987; Hon DSc Econ Univ of Lausanne 1988; Hon DUniv: Liège 1989, Athens 1991, Stirling 1992, Edinburgh 1994, École Normale Supérieur Paris 1995, Essex 1995, Bologna 1996, South Bank 1996, Louvain 1996, Nottingham 2000, London Met 2002, European Univ Inst 2004, Antwerp 2004, Gent 2004; hon memb American Econ Assoc 1985; FBA 1984; Chevalier de la Légion d'Honneur 2001; *Books* Poverty in Britain and the Reform of Social Security (1969), Unequal Shares (1972), The Tax Credit Scheme (1973), Economics of Inequality (1975), Distribution of Personal Wealth in Britain (with A J Harrison, 1978), Lectures on Public Economics (with J E Stiglitz, 1980), Social Justice and Public Policy (1982), Parents and Children (jtly, 1983), Unemployment Benefits and Unemployment Duration (with J Micklewright, 1986), Poverty and Social Security (1989), Economic Transformation in Eastern Europe and the Distribution of Income (with J Micklewright, 1992), Public Economics in Action (1995), Incomes and the Welfare State (1996), Three Lectures on Poverty in Europe (1998), The Economic Consequences of Rolling Back the Welfare State (1999), Social Indicators: The EU and Social Inclusion (with B Cantillon, E Marlier and B Nolan, 2002); *Recreations* sailing; *Style*— Sir Tony Atkinson; ☒ 93 Hamilton Road, Oxford OX2 7QA (tel 01865 813373, e-mail tony.atkinson@nuffield.ox.ac.uk)

ATKINSON, Prof Anthony Curtis; s of Harold Atkinson (d 1944), of Sidcup, Kent, and Iris Madge, *née* Ellison (d 1990); *b* 22 June 1937; *Educ* Christ's Hosp, Univ of Cambridge (MA), Imperial Coll London (PhD); *m* 1, 13 June 1972 (m dis 2000), Ruth Mary, da of Robert Mantle Rattenbury (d 1970), of Cambridge; 2 da (Alison b 1972, Rachel b 1975); m 2, 9 Aug 2000, Barbara Bogacka, da of Edmund Buchert, of Poznan, Poland; *Career* Shell Chemical Co 1960–64, American Cyanamid NJ USA 1965–67, prof of statistics Imperial Coll London 1983–89 (lectr 1969–78, reader 1978–83), prof of statistics LSE 1989–2002 (emeritus prof 2002–); MISI, FSS, fell American Statistical Assoc (FASA); *Books* A Celebration of Statistics (jtly, 1985), Plots, Transformations and Regression (1985), Optimum Experimental Designs (jtly, 1992), Robust Diagnostic Regression Analysis (jtly, 2000), Exploring Multivariate Data with the Forward Search (jtly, 2004), Optimum Experimental Designs, with SAS (jtly, 2007); *Recreations* music, architecture; *Style*— Prof Anthony Atkinson; ☒ Department of Statistics, London School of Economics and Political Science, Houghton Street, London WC2A 2AE (tel 020 7955 7646, fax 020 7955 7416, e-mail a.c.atkinson@lse.ac.uk)

ATKINSON, Rt Rev Dr David John; *see:* Thetford, Bishop of

ATKINSON, Dr Harry Hindmarsh; s of Harry Temple Atkinson (late Cmmr of Patents NZ, d 1961), and Constance Hindmarsh, *née* Shields (d 1973); gf, Sir Harry Atkinson (PM of NZ five times between 1873 and 1890, d 1892); *b* 5 August 1929; *Educ* Nelson Coll NZ, Canterbury UC NZ (BSc, MSc), Cornell Univ, Corpus Christi Coll and Cavendish Lab Cambridge (PhD); *m* 28 March 1958, Anne Judith, da of Thomas Kenneth Barrett (d 1964); 1 da (Katherine Hindmarsh b 1959), 2 s ((Harry) David b 1960, (John) Benedict b 1966); *Career* asst lectr in physics Canterbury UC 1952–53, res asst Cornell Univ 1954–55, sr res fell AERE Harwell UK 1958–61, head Gen Physics Gp Rutherford Lab UK 1961–69, staff chief sci advsr to UK Govt Cabinet Office UK 1969–72; UK Sci Res Cncl: head Astronomy Space and Radio Div 1972–78, under sec dir of astronomy space and nuclear physics 1979–83; under sec dir of sci UK SERC (incl responsibility for int affrs) 1983–88, under sec (special responsibilities) 1988–92; conslt 1992–; assessor Univ Grants Ctee 1986–89, UK memb EISCAT Cncl 1976–86, chm of Cncl Euro Space Agency 1984–87 (vice-chm 1981–84, UK delegate Cncl 1972–81); UK memb: South African Astronomical Observatory Ctee 1979–85, Anglo-Aust Telescope Bd 1979–88; chm Anglo-Dutch Astron Ctee 1981–88, UK delegate Summit Gp on High Energy Physics 1982–88, chm and memb Steering Ctee Inst Laue Langevin (ILL) Grenoble 1984–88, UK delegate to Cncl Synchrotron Radiation Facility 1986–88, memb Working Gp on Int Collaboration ACOST Cabinet Office 1989, memb NI Ctee Univ Funding Cncl 1989–93, coordinator UK Aust NZ Science Collaboration 1989–94, pt/t chief scientist Loss Prevention Cncl 1990–98, chm UK Govt Task Force on Hazardous Near Earth Objects (asteroids and comets) 2000, memb Euro Science Fndn Working Gp on Near Earth Objects 2001; conslt: Hong Kong Govt Univ Grants Ctee 1993–95, Univ of Oxford Cmmn on the Future of the Univ 1995–96; FRAS; *Clubs* Athenaeum; *Style*— Dr Harry Atkinson; ☒ Atkinson Associates, Bampton, Oxfordshire OX18 2JN

ATKINSON, Jane Elizabeth; da of William Gledhill (d 1969), and Ethel, *née* Stopps (d 1978); *b* 20 July 1947; *Educ* Kesteven and Sleaford HS for Girls; *m* 1, 1967 (m dis 1973), David Hayward; 1 s (Anthony b 1967); m 2, 1975, George Ronald Atkinson; 1 s (Nicholas b 1980), 1 da (Caroline b 1984); *Career* sec until 1975, asst account exec Planned Public

Relations International 1975–76, account exec Welbeck PR 1976–78, sr client conslt Bell Capper PR 1978–80, bd dir Eurocom PR 1980, jt md Granard Communications (after merger with Eurocom PR 1982) 1988, dep chm The Rowland Company (result of Granard merger with Kingsway PR) 1990–94, jt md Affinity Consulting Ltd (Countrywide Group) 1992–95, ptnr Atkinson Courage Communications 1995–97, dir Bell Pottinger Conslts (formerly Bell Pottinger Communications) 2000–02 (sr conslt 1997–2000), dir of global communications JCB 2002–03, dir Glenfern Communications Mgmnt Consultancy 2004–, dir Surprisecharter 2004–; media advsr to Diana, Princess of Wales Jan-July 1996 (resigned); past pres Women in Public Relations; memb Bd Forum UK, memb Bd of Govrs Eastbourne Coll, chm Eastbourne Coll Fndn; tstee Prostate Cancer Research Tst; FRSA; *Recreations* cooking, reading, walking, amateur dramatics, boating; *Style*— Mrs Jane Atkinson; ✉ 77 Sutton Court Road, London W4 3EG (tel 020 8994 7082)

ATKINSON, Prof John; s of John Jennings Atkinson (d 1974), and Cecil Priscilla, *née* Sully (d 1996); *b* 10 March 1942; *Educ* Norwich Sch, Imperial Coll London; *m* 17 July 1978, Josephine, da of John Thomas Kirby, of Brentford, Middx; 2 s (Robert b 1978, Nicholas b 1981); *Career* engr; Coffey & Ptnrs Brisbane 1967–69, Imperial Coll London 1969–73, Univ of Cambridge 1973–76, UC Cardiff 1976–80; currently prof of soil mechanics City Univ; CEng, CGeol, FICE, FGS; *Books* The Mechanics of Soils (1978), Foundations and Slopes (1981), The Mechanics of Soils and Foundations (1993); *Recreations* sailing, surfing, the countryside; *Clubs* Norfolk Punt; *Style*— Prof John Atkinson; ✉ Department of Civil Engineering, City University, Northampton Square, London EC1V 0HB (tel 020 7040 5060, e-mail j.h.atkinson@city.ac.uk)

ATKINSON, Kate; *b* York; *Educ* Univ of Dundee (MA); *Family* 2 da (Eve b 1975, Helen b 1984); *Career* writer; *Books* Behind the Scenes at the Museum (1995, Whitbread Book of the Year), Human Croquet (1997), Emotionally Weird (2000), Not the End of the World (2002), Case Histories (2004); *Plays* Abandonment (2000); *Style*— Ms Kate Atkinson; ✉ c/o Doubleday, Transworld Publishers, 61–63 Uxbridge Road, London

ATKINSON, Kenneth Neil; s of William Atkinson (d 1972), and Alice, *née* Reid (d 1990); *b* 4 April 1931; *Educ* Kingussie HS, Open Univ (BA); *Career* various appts Miny of Labour and Dept of Employment 1948–67, dep chief conciliation offr Dept of Employment 1968–72, dir youth trg MSC Trg Agency 1983–89 (dir indust trg bd relations 1975–78, dir Scotland 1979–82), md The Travel Training Co (Nat Trg Bd ABTA until 1994, of which dir) 1989–95; chm Prince's Tst Community Venture 1989–92; memb Cncl: CGLI 1991–98, Prince's Tst Volunteers 1993–94; ARCM 1961, FCIPD (FIPD 1986), FRSA 2003; *Recreations* tennis, choral singing, conducting (musical dir Ruislip Operatic Soc 1994–); *Clubs* RAC; *Style*— Kenneth N Atkinson, Esq; ✉ 14/7 St Margaret's Place, Edinburgh EH9 1AY (tel 0131 447 5975); 4 Morford Close, Ruislip HA4 8SW (tel 020 8866 2581)

ATKINSON, (Michael) Kent; s of Carl Kent Atkinson (d 1999), and Jill, *née* Gilbert (d 1980); *b* 19 May 1945; *Educ* Blundell's; *m* 17 Oct 1970, Eufemia Alexandra, da of Enrique Alarcón; 2 s (Carl Kent b 15 March 1972, Michael Alexander b 24 March 1976); *Career* Lloyds Bank plc (formerly Bank of London & South America): joined 1964, various appts in Colombia and Ecuador 1967–70, mangr Colon Free Zone Panama 1971–75, mangr Bahrain 1976, mangr Dubai 1976–80, general mangr Paraguay 1980–83, general mangr Latin American Southern Cone 1983–89, dep regnl exec dir S E Region 1989–91, regnl exec dir S E Region 1991–94, general mangr Retail Ops 1994; Lloyds TSB Gp plc (formerly Lloyds Bank plc): chief fin offr 1995–96, gp fin dir 1997–2003, currently main bd exec dir, dir Lloyds TSB Bank plc, dir Lloyds Bank Financial Services (Holdings) Ltd, dir Lloyds Bank Subsidiaries Limited, dir Three Copthall Avenue Ltd; non-exec dir: Coca-Cola HBC SA, Marconi plc 2002–, Marconi Gp 2002–, Cookson Gp plc 2003–, Standard Life 2005–; memb Hundred Gp of Fin Dirs 1995; *Recreations* tennis, golf, rugby union, soccer, personal computers, theatre, opera; *Clubs* Effingham Golf, Horsley Sports; *Style*— M Kent Atkinson, Esq

ATKINSON, Peter; MP; s of Maj Douglas Atkinson (ka 1945), and Amy Atkinson; *b* 19 January 1943; *Educ* Cheltenham Coll; *m* 7 April 1976, Brione, da of Cdr A T Darley; 2 da; *Career* journalist The Journal Newcastle 1968–72, various posts rising to news ed Evening Standard 1972–81; chm Southern Free Press Gp 1981–87, public affrs conslt 1983–92; MP (Cons) Hexham 1992–; PPS to: Rt Hon Sir Jeremy Hanley, KCMG, *qv*, 1994–96 (resigned), Sir Nicholas Bonsor, Bt, *qv*, 1995–96 (resigned), Rt Hon the Lord Parkinson, PC, *qv*, 1997–98; oppn whip 1999–2002 and 2003–05; memb: European Legislation Ctee 1992–97, Scottish Affrs Select Ctee 1992–2001, Deregulation Select Ctee 1995–97, Chms Panel 1997–99, 2002–03 and 2005–, Procedure Ctee 2003–05; sec Cons Agriculture Backbench Ctee 1992–94; cncllr: London Borough of Wandsworth 1978–82, Suffolk CC 1989–92; memb Wandsworth HA 1982–89, dir of public affrs Br Field Sports Soc 1983–92; *Recreations* shooting, gardening, racing; *Clubs* Albert Edward (Hexham), Northern Counties; *Style*— Peter Atkinson, Esq, MP; ✉ House of Commons, London SW1A 0AA

ATKINSON, Very Rev Peter Gordon; s of Thomas John Collins Atkinson (d 1986), of Maidstone, and Adèle Mary, *née* Cox (d 2000); *b* 26 August 1952; *Educ* Maidstone GS, St John's Coll Oxford (scholar, sr scholar, Denyer and Johnson student, Liddon student, MA), Westcott House Cambridge; *m* 1983, Lynne, da of Brian Wilcock; 2 s (James David b 1985, Leo Francis b 1992), 1 da (Elizabeth Grace b 1987); *Career* ordained: deacon 1979, priest 1980; asst curate Clapham Old Town Team Miny 1979–83, priest-in-charge St Mary's Tatsfield 1983–90, rector of Holy Trinity Bath 1990–91, princ Chichester Theol Coll 1991–94, rector of Lavant 1994–97, residentiary canon Chichester Cathedral 1991–2007 (Bursalis preb 1991–94, chllr 1994–2007), proctor in convocation 2000–05, dean of Worcester 2007–; *Publications* Friendship and the Body of Christ (2004); *Style*— The Very Rev the Dean of Worcester; ✉ The Deanery, 10 College Green, Worcester WR1 2LH (e-mail peteratkinson@worcestercathedral.org.uk)

ATKINSON, Dr Ronald James; s of Robert William Atkinson (d 1974), and Ellen, *née* Whiteside (d 1991); *b* 8 September 1945; *Educ* Bangor GS, Queen's Univ Belfast (MD); *m* 25 Oct 1974, (Sarah) Pamela, da of Robert Samuel Gawley (d 1990); 2 da (Claire b 1977, Sarah b 1981); *Career* fell Cancer Research Campaign 1976–78, sr lectr Queen's Univ Belfast 1980–2004 (acting head Oncology Dept 1993–96), conslt Belfast City Hosp 1980–; vice-chair NI REC 2 2004–, memb Bd NI Medical and Dental Postgrad Trg Agency 2005–; former sec British Gynaecological Cancer Soc; FRCS, FRCOG; *Recreations* gardening, travel; *Style*— Dr Ronald J Atkinson; ✉ 29A Carnreagh, Hillsborough, Co Down BT26 6LJ; Oncology, Bridgewater Suite, Belfast City Hospital, Lisburn Road, Belfast BT9 7AB (tel 028 9026 3697, fax 028 9026 3727, e-mail rja@doctors.net.uk)

ATKINSON, Rowan Sebastian; s of Eric Atkinson (d 1984), and Ella May Atkinson (d 1998); *b* 6 January 1955; *Educ* Durham Cathedral Choristers' Sch, St Bees' Cumbria, Univ of Newcastle upon Tyne (BSc), The Queen's Coll Oxford (MSc); *m* 1990, Sunetra Sastry; *Career* actor and writer; *Theatre* West End performances incl: One Man Show 1981 and 1986 (SWET Award for Comedy Performance of the Year), The Nerd 1984, Chekhov's The Sneeze 1988; one man show tours to Aust, Canada, USA, and Far East; *Television* for BBC incl: Not The Nine O'Clock News 1979–82, The Black Adder 1983, Blackadder II 1985, Blackadder the Third 1987, Blackadder Goes Forth 1989; other credits incl: Mr Bean (Tiger Aspect for ITV) 1990–95, The Thin Blue Line (Tiger Aspect for BBC) 1995 and 1996, Mr Bean (animated series) 2002–03; *Films* The Tall Guy 1989, The Appointments of Dennis Jennings 1989, The Witches 1990, Hot Shots - Part Deux 1993, Four Weddings and a Funeral 1994, The Lion King (voiceover) 1994, Bean - The Ultimate Disaster Movie 1997, Blackadder Back and Forth (Millennium Dome) 1999, Maybe Baby 2000, Rat Race 2001, Scooby Doo 2002, Johnny English 2003, Love Actually 2003, Keeping Mum 2006, Mr Bean's Holiday 2007; *Awards* BBC TV Personality of the Year 1980 and 1989, Br Acad Award 1980 and 1989; *Recreations* motor cars (regular columnist Car magazine 1992–94), motor sport; *Style*— Rowan Atkinson, Esq; ✉ c/o PBJ Management Ltd, 7 Soho Street, London W1D 3DQ (tel 020 7287 1112, fax 020 7287 1191, e-mail general@pbjmgt.co.uk)

ATKINSON, Prof Sue; CBE (2002); *b* 10 August 1946; *Educ* Merchant Taylors' Sch for Girls, UCNW (BSc), Univ of Cambridge (MA, MB BChir), Middx Hosp Med Sch London (LRCP); *Career* SHO Addenbrooke's Hosp Cambridge 1975–76, registrar (paediatrics) Southmead Hosp Bristol 1976, gen paediatrics and paediatric oncology Royal Hosp for Sick Children Bristol 1977, DCH 1977, res assoc Dept of Child Health Univ of Bristol/Avon AHA 1977–79, registrar then sr registrar in community med Avon AHA 1980 and 1982–85, res fell Nat Health and MRC Unit of Epidemiology and Preventative Med Univ of Western Australia 1980–81, GP 1981–82, conslt in public health med Bristol and Western HA 1985–87, sr lectr UMDS and conslt in public health Lewisham and N Southwark HA 1987, dir of public health and serv devpt Lewisham and N Southwark HA and sr lectr UMDS 1988–91, dir of public health SE London HA 1991–93 (actg chief exec 1993), dir of health strategy/regnl dir of public health Wessex then S and W RHA 1993–94, dir of public health/med dir S Thames RHA/RO 1994–98, dir of public health/med dir London RO 1999–, health advsr to Mayor and GLA 2000–, currently regnl dir of public health (London) Dept of Health, Dept of Health lead for London Olympics and Paralympics bid 2005–; special advsr to House of Commons Select Ctee in its examination of NHS Reforms and NHS Tsts 1991–92; Faculty of Public Health Med: memb Bd 1990–93, memb Exec Ctee 1990–93, examiner and visitor for SpR posts; memb Soc for Social Med 1983, chair Ct LSHTM 2001– (also memb Bd), visiting prof UCH London 2002–; memb Bd Patients Assoc 1999–2001; MRCS, FFPHM 1990 (MFPHM 1985); *Publications* author of numerous papers in professional jls; *Style*— Prof Sue Atkinson, CBE

ATKINSON, Terry; s of Reginald Atkinson (d 1951), of Rotherham, S Yorks, and Lily, *née* Hampshire; *b* 16 July 1939; *Educ* Wath-upon-Dearne GS, Barnsley Sch of Art, Slade Sch of Fine Art; *m*; 2 c; *Career* artist; fndr memb Art & Language 1966–74; Turner prize nominee 1985; author of numerous articles and essays; *Art & Language Group Exhibitions* incl: The British Avant-Garde (NY Cultural Centre) 1971, Dokumenta 5 (Museum Friedericianum Kassel) 1972, The New Art (Hayward Gallery) 1972; *Other Group Exhibitions* incl: Art for Society (Whitechapel Gallery) 1979, 5th Sydney Biennale 1984, Aperto Venice Biennale 1984, Turner Prize Nominee's Exhbn (Tate Gallery) 1985, State of the Art Exhbn (ICA) 1987, Innocence and Childhood (Manchester City Art Galleries) 1992, Mind the Gap (Gimpel Fils Gallery) 1992, Circumstantial Evidence (Univ of Brighton) 1996; *Solo Exhibitions* incl: Work 1977–83 (Whitechapel Art Gallery) 1983, Art for the Bunker (Gimpel Fils London) 1985, Mute 1 (Galleri Prag Copenhagen) 1988, Work (Stampa Basel) 1989, Greasers & Mutes (Galerie Sophia Ungers Cologne) 1990, Mute 3 - Work 1988–91 (Kunstsmuseum Sorø Denmark) 1992, Irish Mus of Modern Art Dublin 1992, Cornerhouse Manchester 1992, Ruses Mutes Monochromes & Bombers (Galerie Patricia Asbaeck Copenhagen) 1992, Bunker Entrance, outside site specific project Furka Pass Switzerland 1992, Fragments of a Career (Kunstwerk Berlin) 1994–95, Work 1974: in leaving Art & Language (Archivio Di Nuovo Scrittura Milan) 1995, Enola Gay Works (Galleria Inga-Pin Milan) 1995, Cultural Instrument 1993–98 (Real Gallery NY) 1999, Fragments of a Career 2 (Silkeborg Museum Denmark) 2000, EG + 1 NCW Work (Moller-Witt Gallery Denmark) 2000, Cultural Implement (Galerie M & R Fricke Düsseldorf) 2000, Conflict and Continuation (Leeds City Art Gallery) 2004; *Sculpture* with Sue Atkinson for: Mute 2 Exhbn (Orchard Gall Derry) 1988, A New Necessity (Gateshead Garden Festival) 1991, Sharjah Biennial 2005; *Style*— Terry Atkinson, Esq; ✉ 12 Milverton Crescent, Leamington Spa, Warwickshire CV32 5NG (tel and fax 01926 311894, e-mail rats@leamington1.wanadoo.co.uk)

ATLAY, Robert David; DL (Merseyside 2003); s of Robert Henry Atlay (d 1997), of Freshfield, Lancs, and Sarah, *née* Griffiths (d 2002); *b* 26 June 1936; *Educ* Wirral GS, Univ of Liverpool (MB ChB); *m* 11 Feb 1967, Jean, da of William Alfred Stephen Cole (d 1993), of Prenton, Merseyside; 2 da (Josephine b 8 May 1969, Victoria b 3 April 1973); *Career* conslt obstetrician and gynaecologist; formerly at: Mill Road Maternity Hosp 1970, Royal Liverpool Hosp 1978; clinical lectr in obstetrics and gynaecology and past chm Faculty of Med Univ of Liverpool, past med dir Liverpool Women's Hosp Obstetrics and Gynaecology NHS Tst; past chm Euro Ctee RCOG, past chm CME/CPD Ctee RCOG; examiner: RCOG, Royal Aust Coll of Obstetrics and Gynaecology, Univs of Liverpool, Cambridge, Manchester, Birmingham, Glasgow, London, the W Indies and Amman; hosp visitor Royal Women's Hosp Brisbane 1981; papers in specialist jls, contrib RCOG Yearbooks, Clinics in obstetrics and gynaecology 1989–2002; past pres Union Professionelle Internationale Obstetrics and Gynaecology; Sec of State appointee memb: Maternity Servs Advsy Ctee, Nat Transplant Panel, English Nat Bd Nursing Midwifery and Health Visiting; hon sec RCOG 1980–87 (memb Cncl 1973–95); govr Wirral GS 1993–2000, past pres Waterloo RUFC; High Sheriff Merseyside 2003–04; FRCOG; *Recreations* rugby union football, golf, skiing, traditional jazz; *Clubs* Waterloo Football, Formby Golf, Liverpool Artists (past pres), Gynaecological Travellers; *Style*— Robert Atlay, Esq, DL; ✉ 9 St Andrews Drive, Blundellsands, Liverpool L23 7UX; 35 Rodney Street, Liverpool, Merseyside L1 9EN (tel 0151 708 9528); Liverpool Women's Hospital, Crown Street, Liverpool L8 7SS (tel 0151 708 9988, fax 0151 702 4137)

ATTA, Hatem Riad; s of Riad Gorgi Atta (d 1995), of Egypt, and Jozephine Matta, *née* Ebrahim (d 1989); *b* 12 August 1951; *Educ* Private Mission Sch Egypt, DO London (MB BCh); *m* 26 June 1982, Janet Ann, da of Samuel John Saunders (d 1988); *Career* sr registrar in ophthalmology West Midlands RHA 1983–88, fell in ophthalmic ultrasonography Miami Sch of Med 1986–87, conslt ophthalmic surgn Aberdeen Royal Infirmary 1988–; hon sr lectr Univ of Aberdeen 1988; author of papers in scientific jls; memb: Oxford Congress, Int Soc of Ophthalmic Ultrasound; FRCSEd 1980, FRCOphth 1988; *Books* Techniques and Application of Diagnostic Ultrasound (1990), Ophthalmic Ultrasound - a practical guide (1996); *Recreations* racquet sports, golf, scuba diving; *Clubs* Aberdeen Petroleum, Royal Aberdeen Golf, Aberdeen Medical Golf Society; *Style*— Hatem Atta, Esq; ✉ Eye Department, Aberdeen Royal Infirmary, Foresterhill, Aberdeen (tel 01224 553217, fax 01224 861849)

ATTALLAH, Naim Ibrahim; s of Ibrahim Attallah, and Genevieve Attallah; *b* 1 May 1931; *Educ* Battersea Poly; *m* 1957, Maria, da of Joseph Nykolyn; 1 s; *Career* foreign exchange dealer 1957, fin conslt 1966, dir of companies 1969–; book publisher and prop: Quartet Books 1976–, The Women's Press 1977–, Robin Clark 1980–; magazine prop: The Literary Review 1981–2001, The Wire 1984–2000, The Oldie 1991–2001; articles in The Literary Review, princ interviewer The Oldie; Asprey plc: fin dir and jt md 1979–92, chief exec 1992–95; md Mappin & Webb 1990–95, md Watches of Switzerland 1992–95, exec dir Garrard 1990–95; prop The Academy Club 1989–97; parfumier: launched Parfums Namara 1985 with Avant l'Amour and Aprés l'Amour, Naïdor in 1986, l'Amour de Namara 1990; theatrical prodr: Happy End (co-presenter, Lyric) 1975, The Beastly Beatitudes of Balthazar B (presenter and prodr, Duke of York's) 1981, Trafford Tanzi (co-prodr, Mermaid) 1982; film prodr: The Slipper and the Rose (co-prodr with David Frost) 1974–75, Brimstone and Treacle (exec prodr) 1982; also produced and presented TV documentaries; Retail Personality of the Year UK Jewellery Awards 1993; Hon MA Univ of Surrey 1993; FRSA; *Books* Women (1987), Singular Encounters (1990), Of a

Certain Age (1992), More of a Certain Age (1993), Speaking for the Oldie (1994), A Timeless Passion (1995), Tara and Claire (1996), Asking Questions (1996), In Conversation with Naim Attallah (1998), A Woman a Week (1998), Insights (1999), Dialogues (2000), The Old Ladies of Nazareth (2004), The Boy In England (2005), In Touch with his Roots (2006), Fulfilment & Betrayal (2007); *Recreations* classical music, opera, theatre, cinema, photography; *Clubs* Arts, Beefsteak; *Style*— Naim Attallah, Esq; ✉ 25 Shepherd Market, London W1J 7PP (tel 020 7499 2901, fax 020 7499 2914, e-mail nattallah@aol.com)

ATTENBOROUGH, Sir David Frederick; OM (2005), CH (1996), kt (1985), CVO (1991), CBE (1974); s of Frederick Levi Attenborough (d 1973), and Mary, *née* Clegg (d 1961); bro of Baron Attenborough, CBE (Life Peer), *qv*; *b* 8 May 1926; *Educ* Wyggeston GS for Boys Leicester, Clare Coll Cambridge (hon fell 1980); *m* 1950, Jane Elizabeth Ebsworth Oriel (d 1997); 1 s, 1 da; *Career* naturalist, traveller, broadcaster and writer; served RN 1947–49; editorial asst in an educational publishing house 1949–52, prodr talks and documentary progs BBC 1952, controller TV BBC2 1965–68, dir of Programmes TV and memb Bd of Management BBC 1969–72; zoological and ethnographic filming expeditions to: Sierra Leone 1954, Br Guiana 1955, Indonesia 1956, New Guinea 1957, Paraguay and Argentina 1958, South West Pacific 1959, Madagascar 1960, Northern Territory Australia 1962, Zambesi 1964, Bali 1969, Central New Guinea 1971, Celebes 1973, Borneo 1973, Peru 1973, Columbia 1973, Mali 1974, Br Columbia 1974, Iran 1974, Solomon Islands 1974, Nigeria 1975; writer and presenter BBC series: Zoo Quest 1954–64, Tribal Eye 1976, Life on Earth 1979, The Living Planet 1984, The First Eden 1987, Lost Worlds Vanished Lives 1989, The Trials of Life 1990, The Private Life of Plants 1995, The Life of Birds 1998, The Blue Planet 2001, Life In The Undergrowth 2005, Planet Earth 2006; tstee: World Wildlife Fund UK 1965–69, 1972–82 and 1984–90, World Wildlife Fund Int 1979–86, Br Museum 1980–, Science Museum 1984–87, Royal Botanic Gardens Kew 1986–92, Learning Through Landscapes 1990–; memb Nature Conservancy Cncl 1973–82, corresponding memb American Museum of Natural History 1985, Huw Wheldon Meml Lecture RTS 1987; fell BAFTA 1980; awards: Special Award SFTA 1961, Silver Medal Zoological Soc of London 1966, Silver Medal RTS 1966, Desmond Davis Award SFTA 1970, Cherry Keaton Medal RGS 1972, Kalinga Prize UNESCO 1981, Washburn Award Boston Museum of Science 1983, Hopper Day Medal Acad of Natural Sciences Philadelphia 1983, Founder's Gold Medal RGS 1985, Int Emmy Award 1985, Encyclopaedia Britannica Award 1987, Livingstone Medal RSGS 1990; Hon Freeman City of Leicester 1990; hon fell: Manchester Poly 1976, UMIST 1980; Hon DLitt: Univ of Leicester 1970, City Univ 1972, Univ of London 1980, Univ of Birmingham 1982; Hon LLD: Univ of Bristol 1977, Univ of Glasgow 1980; Hon DSc: Univ of Liverpool 1974, Heriot-Watt Univ 1978, Univ of Sussex 1979, Univ of Bath 1981, Ulster Univ 1982, Univ of Durham 1982, Keele Univ 1986, Univ of Oxford 1988; Hon DUniv: Open Univ 1980, Univ of Essex 1987; Hon ScD Univ of Cambridge 1984; Cdr of the Golden Ark (Netherlands) 1983; Hon FRCP 1991, FRS 1983, Hon FRSE 2005; *Books* Zoo Quest to Guiana (1956), Zoo Quest for a Dragon (1957), Zoo Quest in Paraguay (1959), Quest in Paradise (1960), Zoo Quest to Madagascar (1961), Quest under Capricorn (1963), The Tribal Eye (1976), Life on Earth (1979), The Living Planet (1984), The First Eden (1987), The Trials of Life (1990), The Private Life of Plants (1995), The Life of Birds (1998), The Blue Planet (2001), Life on Air (2002), Life of Mammals (2002), Life In The Undergrowth (2005); *Recreations* tribal art, natural history; *Style*— Sir David Attenborough, OM, CH, CVO, CBE, FRS; ✉ 5 Park Road, Richmond, Surrey TW10 6NS

ATTENBOROUGH, Hon Michael John; s of Baron Attenborough, CBE (Life Peer), *qv*, and Sheila Beryl Grant, *née* Sim; *b* 13 February 1950; *Educ* Westminster, Univ of Sussex (BA, pres Univ Drama Soc); *m* 1, 10 July 1971 (m dis 1976), Jane Seymour, *qv*; m 2, 14 April 1984, Karen Esther, yr da of Sydney Victor Lewis (d 1990), of London; 2 s (Thomas Frederick Richard b 13 Oct 1986, William Grant Oliver b 26 June 1991); *Career* freelance theatre director; asst dir Gardner Centre Theatre 1972; assoc dir: Mercury Theatre Colchester 1972–74, Leeds Playhouse 1974–79, Young Vic Theatre 1979–80; artistic dir: Palace Theatre Watford 1980–84, Hampstead Theatre 1984–89, Turnstyle Group 1989–90; princ assoc dir RSC 1990–2002, artistic dir Almeida Theatre 2002–; freelance work as dir incl prodns for: Open Space Theatre, Red Ladder, Newcastle Playhouse, Citadel Theatre Edmonton, Abbey Theatre Dublin, Tricycle Theatre, Royal Court Theatre London and Nat Theatre; dir of over 100 plays to date; vice-chair Cncl RADA, dep chair Drama Panel Arts Cncl; former memb: Greater London Arts, Bubble Theatre Bd, Cncl Directors' Guild; currently dir Susan Smith Blackburn Prize; Time Out Theatre Award for Observe The Sons of Ulster Marching Towards The Somme 1986, nominated Best Dir London Theatre Critics Awards 1985, nominated Outstanding Achievement Award (as dir Hampstead Theatre) Olivier Awards 1986; Hon DLitt Univ of Sussex 2005; *Recreations* being with my family, football, music, theatre; *Style*— The Hon Michael Attenborough, DLitt; ✉ Almeida Theatre, Almeida Street, London N1 1TA (tel 020 7288 4900, fax 020 7288 4901)

ATTENBOROUGH, Neil Richard; RD (1980, and Bar 1989); s of John William Attenborough, and Eileen, *née* Ward; *b* 4 May 1940; *m* 1, 10 Sept 1968 (m dis 1980), Josephine; 2 s (Paul Alexander b 1971, Tristan Alistair b 1973); m 2, 10 June 1982, Jennifer Mary; 1 s (Thomas William b 1983); *Career* conslt oral and maxillo-facial surgn SW Surrey and NE Hants Dist Authys, dir Guildford Dental Trg and Treatment Centre; inventor and prodr Attenborough Sea Drogue; CO London Sailing Project, memb: RNSA, BDA, RSM; FDSRCS, FDSRCSEd; *Recreations* sailing, squash, cricket; *Style*— Neil Attenborough, Esq, RD; ✉ Mount Alvernia, Harvey Road, Guildford, Surrey GU1 3LX (tel 01483 538066 and 01483 455370)

ATTENBOROUGH, Baron (Life Peer UK 1993), of Richmond upon Thames in the London Borough of Richmond upon Thames; Sir Richard Samuel Attenborough; kt (1976), CBE (1967); s of Frederick Levi Attenborough (d 1973), and Mary, *née* Clegg (d 1961); bro of Sir David Attenborough, *qv*; *b* 29 August 1923; *Educ* Wyggeston GS for Boys Leicester, RADA (Leverhulme scholar, Bancroft Medal); *m* 22 January 1945, Sheila Beryl Grant, *née* Sim, JP (actress), da of Stuart Grant Sim (d 1975), of Hove, E Sussex; 1 s (Hon Michael John, *qv*, b 13 February 1950), 2 da (Hon Jane (Hon Mrs Holland) b 30 September 1955 d 2004, Hon Charlotte (Hon Mrs Sinclair) b 29 June 1959); *Career* actor, film producer and director; joined RAF 1943, flt sgt airgunner/cameraman, seconded RAF Film Unit 1944 (for Journey Together, 1944), demobbed 1946; formed: Beaver Films (with Bryan Forbes) 1959, Allied Film Makers 1960; memb: Cncl Br Actors' Equity Assoc 1949–73, Cinematograph Films Cncl 1967–73, Arts Cncl of GB 1970–73; chm: BAFTA 1969–70 (chm tstees 1970–, vice-pres 1971–94), RADA 1970– (memb Cncl 1963–), Capital Radio 1972–92 (life pres 1992), Help a London Child 1975–, UK Tstees Waterford-Kamhlaba Sch Swaziland 1976– (govr 1987–), Duke of York's Theatre 1979–92, BFI 1981–92, Goldcrest Films & TV 1982–87, Ctee of Inquiry into the Arts and Disabled People 1983–85, Channel 4 TV 1987–92 (dep chm 1980–86), Br Screen Advsy Cncl 1987–96 (hon pres 1996–), Euro Script Fund 1988–96 (hon pres 1996–); pres: Muscular Dystrophy Gp of GB 1971– (vice-pres 1962–71), The Gandhi Fndn 1983–, Brighton Festival 1984–95, Br Film Year 1984–86, The Actors' Charitable Tst 1988– (chm 1956–88), Combined Theatrical Appeals Cncl 1988– (chm 1964–88), Arts for Health 1989–, Gardner Centre for the Arts Univ of Sussex 1990– (patron 1969–90), Nat Film Sch 1997– (1970–81); tstee: King George V Fund for Actors and Actresses 1973–, Tate Gallery 1976–82 and 1994–96, Tate Fndn 1986–, Fndn for Sport and the Arts 1991–; dir: Chelsea FC 1969–82 (life vice-pres 1992–), Young Vic 1974–84; chllr Univ of Sussex 1998– (pro-chllr 1970–98), govr Motability 1977–; patron: Kingsley Hall Community Centre 1982–, RA Centre for Disability and the Arts Leicester 1990–; goodwill ambassador for UNICEF 1987–; Evening Standard Film Award for 40 Years Service to Br Cinema 1983, Award of Merit for Humanitarianism in Film Making Euro Film Awards 1988, Academy Award Sony Radio Awards 1992, Shakespeare Prize for Outstanding Contrib to Euro Culture 1992; Fleming Meml Lecture RTS 1989; Freeman City of Leicester 1990; Hon DLitt: Leicester 1970, Kent 1981, Sussex 1987, American Inst Univ of London 1994, Cape Town 2000; Hon DCL Newcastle 1974, Hon LLD Dickinson Pa 1983; fell: BAFTA 1983, BFI 1992, King's Coll London 1993; hon fell: Manchester Metropolitan Univ 1994, Univ of Wales Bangor 1997, Nat Film and Television Sch 2001; Martin Luther King Jr Peace Prize 1983, Padma Bhushan India 1983, Commandeur de l'Ordre des Arts et des Lettres (France) 1985, Chevalier Ordre de la Légion d'Honneur France 1988, Praemium Imperiale 1998; *Theatre* debut as Richard Miller in Ah Wilderness (Intimate Theatre Palmers Green) 1941, West End debut as Ralph Berger in Awake and Sing (Arts Theatre) 1942, The Little Foxes (Piccadilly) 1942, Brighton Rock (Garrick) 1943, The Way Back (Home of the Brave (Westminster)) 1949, To Dorothy a Son (Savoy 1950, Garrick 1951), Sweet Madness (Vaudeville) 1952, The Mousetrap (Ambassadors) 1952–54, Double Image (Savoy 1956–57, St James's 1957), The Rape of the Belt (Piccadilly) 1957–58; *Film* appearances incl: debut in In Which We Serve 1942, School for Secrets, The Man Within, Dancing with Crime, Brighton Rock 1947, London Belongs to Me, The Guinea Pig 1948, The Lost People, Boys in Brown, Morning Departure 1950, Hell is Sold Out, The Magic Box, Gift Horse, Father's Doing Fine, Eight O'Clock Walk, The Ship that Died of Shame, Private's Progress 1956, The Baby and the Battleship, Brothers in Law, The Scamp, Dunkirk 1958, The Man Upstairs, Sea of Sand, Danger Within, I'm All Right Jack 1959, Jet Storm, SOS Pacific, The Angry Silence (also co-prodr) 1960, The League of Gentlemen 1960, Only Two Can Play, All Night Long 1961, The Dock Brief, The Great Escape 1963, Séance On A Wet Afternoon (prodr, Best Actor San Sebastian Film Festival and Br Film Acad) 1964, The Third Secret, Guns At Batasi (Best Actor Br Film Acad) 1964, The Flight of The Phoenix 1966, The Sand Pebbles (Hollywood Golden Globe) 1967, Dr Doolittle (Hollywood Golden Globe) 1967, The Bliss of Mrs Blossom 1967, Only When I Larf 1968, The Last Grenade, A Severed Head, David Copperfield, Loot 1969, 10 Rillington Place 1970, And Then There Were None, Rosebud, Brannigan, Conduct Unbecoming 1974, The Chess Players 1977, The Human Factor 1979, Jurassic Park 1993, Miracle on 34th Street 1994, The Lost World 1997, Elizabeth 1998, Puckoon 2001; prodr: Whistle Down The Wind 1961, The L-Shaped Room 1962; prodr and dir: Oh! What A Lovely War (16 Int Awards incl Hollywood Golden Globe and BAFTA UN Award) 1969; dir: Young Winston (Hollywood Golden Globe) 1972, A Bridge Too Far (Evening News Best Drama Award) 1977, Magic 1978; prodr and dir: Gandhi (8 Oscars, 5 BAFTA Awards, 5 Hollywood Golden Globes, Dirs' Guild of America Award for Outstanding Directorial Achievement) 1980–81, A Chorus Line 1985, Cry Freedom (Berlinale Kamera and BFI Tech Achievement Award) 1987, Chaplin 1992, Shadowlands 1993 (BAFTA Alexander Korda Award for Outstanding Br Film of the Year), In Love and War 1997, Grey Owl 2000; *Books* In Search of Gandhi (1982), Richard Attenborough's Chorus Line (with Diana Carter, 1986), Cry Freedom A Pictorial Record (1987); *Recreations* collecting paintings and sculpture, listening to music, watching football; *Clubs* Garrick, Beefsteak; *Style*— The Rt Hon Lord Attenborough, CBE; ✉ Old Friars, Richmond, Surrey TW9 1NQ

ATTLEE, Air Vice-Marshal Donald Laurence; CB (1977), LVO (1964), DL (Devon 1991); s of Maj Laurence Gillespie Attlee (d 1968; bro of 1 Earl Attlee, PM of GB 1945–51), of Groombridge, E Sussex, and Letitia, *née* Rotton (d 1973); *b* 2 September 1922; *Educ* Haileybury; *m* 2 Feb 1952, Jane Hamilton, da of Capt Robert Murray Hamilton Young, RFC (d 1974), of Tichborne Grange, Hants; 1 s (Charles b 1955), 2 da (Carolyn (Mrs Kevin Moloney) b 1957, Jenny (Mrs Luke Ellis) b 1963); *Career* joined RAF 1942, Flying Instructor 1944–48, Staff Training Cmd 1949–52, 12 Sqdn 1952–54, Air Staff Air Miny 1954–55, RAF Staff Coll 1956, 59 Sqdn 1957–59, CO The Queen's Flight (Wing Cdr) 1960–63, HQ RAF Germany 1964–67, CO RAF Brize Norton 1968–70, IDC 1970, Policy Staff MOD 1971–72, dir of RAF Recruiting 1973–74, Air Cdre Intelligence 1974–75, Air Vice-Marshal 1975, AOA Trg Cmd Brampton 1975–77 (ret 1977); fruit farmer 1977–94; memb Mid Devon DC 1982–2003 (vice-chm 1987–89, chm 1989–91, ldr 2002–03, Hon Alderman 2003–), chm Mid Devon Business Club 1985–87, dir Mid Devon Enterprise Agency 1983–93; *Recreations* genealogy; *Clubs* RAF; *Style*— Air Vice-Marshal Donald Attlee, CB, LVO, DL; ✉ Wintergold, 31 Longmead, Hemyock, Devon EX15 3SG

ATTLEE, 3 Earl (UK 1955); John Richard Attlee; TD; also Viscount Prestwood (UK 1955); o s of 2 Earl Attlee (d 1991), and his 1 w, Anne Barbara, eldest da of James Henderson, CBE; gs of 1 Earl Attlee, KG, OM, CH, PC (d 1967, Lab PM 1945–51); *b* 3 October 1956; *Educ* Stowe; *Career* with engrg and automotive industries until 1993; international aid with British Direct Aid in Bosnia 1993–94, in-country dir British Direct Aid in Rwanda 1995–96; oppn whip and spokesman for Trade and Industry House of Lords; oppn spokesman House of Lords: Energy and Defence 1998, NI 1998–2001, Tport and Defence, Trade and Industry until 2005; pres Heavy Tport Assoc 1994–; TA Services Maj REME (V); *Style*— The Earl Attlee, TD; ✉ House of Lords, London SW1A 0PW (tel 020 7219 6071, fax 020 7219 5979, e-mail attleej@parliament.uk)

ATTWOOD, Brian Christopher; s of Raymond Attwood, and Eileen, *née* Power; *b* 29 February 1960, New Brighton, Wirral; *Educ* Watford Boys' GS, Univ of Stirling (BA), Centre for Journalism Cardiff (Dip Journalism); *m* 28 Sept 2002, Lisa, *née* Martland; 1 da (Eve Mary Chloe b 13 Sept 2001), 1 s (John Daniel b 19 April 2004); *Career* Chepstow Dist Reporter and News and Weekly Argus 1985, The Citizen Gloucester 1985–86, asst ed Stage and Television Today 1992–94 (reporter 1986–89, chief reporter 1989–92), ed The Stage 1994–; *Recreations* 20th century Irish history, entertainment, reading, the gym, family; *Style*— Brian Attwood, Esq; ✉ The Stage Newspaper Ltd, 47 Bermondsey Street, London SE1 3XT (tel 020 7403 1818)

ATTWOOD, Frank Albert; s of late Eric George Attwood, of Broadstairs, Kent, and Dorothy May, *née* Gifford; *b* 19 January 1943; *Educ* Simon Langton GS Canterbury, Leighton Park Sch Reading, Univ of Hull (BSc); *m* 10 July 1965, Pamela Ann Paget, da of late Samuel Kennedy Pickavor Hunter; 1 da (Rebecca b 1980); *Career* articled Sir Lawrence Robson 1965–68, CA 1968, chartered sec 1969, ptnr RSM Robson Rhodes LLP 1974–2004 (chm 1999–2004, conslt 2004–), ceo RSM International 1990–95, dir Medical Protection Soc 2004–; CCAB: former memb CAs Jt Int Cmmn, former memb Auditing Practices Ctee; ICAEW: former memb Insurance Sub-Ctee and Res Bd, jt auditor 1988–95; chm APC Lloyd's Working Pty 1982–90, dep chair Int Ethics Standards Bd for Accountants IFAC 2004–; chm Schoolmistresses and Governesses' Benevolent Inst, vice-chm Soc of Schoolmasters and Schoolmistresses, memb Bretton Woods Ctee; Freeman City of London 1989, Liveryman Worshipful Co of Scriveners 1989; FCA, FRSA, MAE; *Books* De Paula's Auditing (jtly, 1976, 1982, 1986), Auditing Standards From Discussion Drafts to Practice (jtly, 1978); *Recreations* rambling, gardening, travel, modern novels, weight-training, watching cricket; *Style*— Frank Attwood, Esq; ✉ RSM Robson Rhodes LLP, 30 Finsbury Square, London EC2P 2YU (tel 020 7184 4300, fax 020 7865 2450, e-mail frank.attwood@rsmi.co.uk)

ATTWOOLL, David; *b* 22 April 1949; *Educ* Lancing, Pembroke Coll Cambridge (open exhibitioner, MA); *m*; 3 c; *Career* publisher; Oxford University Press: joined 1970, editorial dir i/c gen books (trade hardbacks and paperbacks) Academic & Gen Div Oxford 1980–83, exec ed i/c reference books NY 1983–85, editorial dir Reference & Gen

Dept Arts & Reference Div Oxford 1985–89; Random Century: md Paperback Div 1989–90, md Reference Div 1990–92; md Helicon Publishing Ltd 1992–2002, dir Attwooll Associates Ltd 2002–; chair Liverpool Univ Press, non-exec dir Duncan Baird Publishing; *Style*— David Attwooll, Esq

ATWELL, Very Rev James Edgar; s of Joseph Norman Edgar Atwell (d 1965), of Rough Leaze Farm, Calne, Wilts, and Sybil Marion, *née* Burnett (d 1978); *b* 3 June 1946; *Educ* Dauntsey's Sch West Lavington, Exeter Coll Oxford (MA), The Divinity Sch Harvard Univ (ThM), Cuddesdon Theol Coll, Univ of Oxford (BD); *m* 1976, Lorna, da of Prof Geoffrey Goodwin (d 1995); 1 s (Luke Alexander Goodwin b 16 July 1978), 2 da (Elizabeth Anne Burnett b 8 Aug 1980, Mary Ellen Frances b 5 Nov 1982); *Career* ordained (Southwark Cathedral): deacon 1970, priest 1971; curate: of St John the Evangelist E Dulwich 1970–74, of Great St Mary's The Univ Church Cambridge 1974–77; chaplain of Jesus Coll Cambridge 1977–81, vicar of Towcester 1981–95 (rural dean 1983–91), dean of St Edmundsbury 1995–2005, dean of Winchester 2005–; *Publications* The Sources of the Old Testament (2004); *Recreations* driving a Land Rover, walking, the countryside, travelling, fairground organs; *Style*— Dean of St Edmundsbury; ✉ The Deanery, Winchester S023 9LS

AUBREY, David John; QC (1996); s of Raymond John Morgan Aubrey (d 1976), and Dorothy Mary, *née* Griffiths (d 1990); *b* 6 January 1950; *Educ* Cathays HS Cardiff, Univ of Wales Cardiff (LLB), Inns of Court Sch of Law; *m* 4 Oct 1980, Julia Catherine, da of Melville John Drew; 1 da (Elinor Mary b 24 June 1991); *Career* called to the Bar Middle Temple 1976 (bencher 2002); head of chambers Temple Chambers Cardiff and Newport; recorder of the Crown Court 1998–; treas Wales & Chester Circuit 1999–2003; legal memb Mental Health Review Tbnl; memb: Criminal Bar Assoc, Personal Injuries Bar Assoc, Wales Medico-Legal Soc, Bar Cncl; pres The Boys' Bde in Wales, memb Glamorgan CCC; memb Welsh Livery Guild; *Recreations* gardening, cricket, music, collecting (memb Boys' Bde Collectors' Club), genealogy (memb Soc of Genealogists); *Style*— David Aubrey, Esq, QC; ✉ 12 Clytha Park Road, Newport NP20 4PB (tel 01633 267403, fax 01633 253441); Temple Chambers, 32 Park Place, Cardiff, South Glamorgan CF1 3BA (tel 029 2039 7364, fax 029 2023 8423, e-mail david.aubrey1@virgin.net)

AUBREY, Juliet Emma; da of Roland Aubrey, of Llanelli, Dyfed, and Sylvia, *née* Sturgess, of Datchet, Berks; *Educ* Farnborough Hill Convent, Queen Anne's Sch Caversham, KCL (BA), Central Sch of Speech and Drama (Dip); *m* Steven James Dempster Ritchie; 2 da (Blythe, Lola-Blue); *Career* actress; *Theatre* incl: Anna Petrovna in Ivanov (RNT), Varvara in Summerfolk (RNT), Branwen in The Long Mirror (TheatrClwyd), Miranda in The Tempest (Oxford Stage Co), Pegeen in The Playboy of the Western World (King's Theatre), Irena in Three Sisters (Cry Havoc), Viola in Twelfth Night (Cry Havoc), Miss Nettles in Sammy's Magic Garden (Latchmere Theatre); *Television* incl: Madeleine in Ella and the Mothers, Elizabeth in Bertie and Elizabeth, Susan in The Mayor of Casterbridge, Esther in Cyclops, Annie in Extremely Dangerous, Sophia in The Unknown Soldier, Karen in Go Now, Dorothea in Middlemarch (BAFTA Award for Best Actress 1994, Broadcasting Press Guild Best Actress Award 1995), Sarah in The Moth, DI Chomsky in Supply and Demand, Isabella in Measure for Measure, Leah in Jacob, Kay in A Good Murder; *Radio* incl: Esther in Dirty Blonde, Marion in The Woman in White, Georgiana in Georgiana Duchess of Devonshire, Fanny Burney in Dear Little Burney, Portia in The Merchant of Venice, Desdemona in Othello, Eleanor in Chronicles of Barchester, Beatrice in Much Ado About Nothing; *Film* incl: Hannah in Jonah Who Lived in the Whale (Platea d'Oro Best Actress 1993), young Janet in Iris, Helen in Welcome to Sarajevo (official selection Cannes 1997), Martha in Time to Love, Madeleine in Food of Love (La Boule Best Actress 1997), Karen in Still Crazy (Golden Globe nomination 1999), Asya in The Lost Lover (Platea d'Oro Best Actress 2000), Lilian in For My Baby, Gloria in The Constant Gardener; *Style*— Ms Juliet Aubrey; ✉ c/o Jeremy Conway, Conway van Gelder Ltd, 18–21 Jermyn Street, London SW1Y 6HP

AUBREY-FLETCHER, Sir Henry Egerton; 8 Bt (GB 1782), of Clea Hall, Cumberland; o s of Sir John Henry Lancelot Aubrey-Fletcher, 7 Bt (d 1992), and Diana Mary Fynvola, *née* Egerton (d 1996); *b* 27 November 1945; *Educ* Eton; *m* 1976, (Sara) Roberta, da of late Maj Robert Buchanan, of Blackpark Cottage, Evanton, Ross-shire; 3 s (John Robert b 1977, Thomas Egerton b 1980, Harry Buchanan b 1982); *Heir* s, John Aubrey-Fletcher; *Career* co dir; High Sheriff Bucks 1995–96, HM Lord-Lt Bucks 2006– (DL 1997, Vice Lord-Lt 1997–2006); *Style*— Sir Henry Aubrey-Fletcher, Bt; ✉ Estate Office, Chilton, Aylesbury, Buckinghamshire HP18 9LR (tel 01844 265201, fax 01844 265203)

AUCKLAND, 10 Baron (I 1789 & GB 1793); Robert Ian Burnard Eden; s of 9 Baron Auckland (d 1997); *b* 25 July 1962; *Educ* Blundell's, Dublin City Univ (BBS); *m* 24 May 1986, Geraldine Caroll, of Dublin; 1 da (Hon Alanna Margaret b 2 Sept 1992); *Heir* unc, Hon Ronald Eden; *Style*— The Rt Hon the Lord Auckland; ✉ c/o Tudor Rose House, 30 Links Road, Ashtead, Surrey KT21 2HF

AUCOTT, John Adrian James; s of Arthur Aucott (d 1955), of Kingsbury, Staffs, and Beryl Joan, *née* Simmonds (d 1984); *b* 20 January 1946; *Educ* Coleshill GS; *m* 16 Sept 1969, Angela, da of Alan Baillie, of Rock, Cornwall; 2 da (Katherine Joanne (Kate) b 16 July 1971, Lucy Elizabeth (Lucie) b 6 March 1973); *Career* articled clerk Birmingham, admitted slr 1969; Edge & Ellison: ptnr 1974–97, sr ptnr 1990–95, conslt 1997; recorder of the Crown Court 1997–; chm Young Slrs Gp 1979–80 (memb 1975–80), pres Birmingham Law Soc 1992–93 (memb 1969–, memb Cncl 1978–2000); Law Society Services Ltd; dep registrar High Ct and Co Ct 1983–87; memb Law Soc 1969 (memb Cncl 1984–); *Books* contrib to various law pubns and to The Law of Meetings (1987); *Recreations* country sports, wine and gastronomy, family and friends; *Clubs* Little Aston Golf; *Style*— John Aucott

AUDLEY, Sir (George) Bernard; kt (1985); s of Charles Bernard Audley (d 1958), of Stoke-on-Trent, and Millicent Claudia, *née* Collier (d 1989); *b* 24 April 1924; *Educ* Wolstanton GS, Corpus Christi Coll Oxford (MA); *m* 17 June 1950, Barbara, da of Richard Arthur Heath (d 1964); 2 s (Maxwell Charles Audley, *qv*, b 1954, Robert James b 1956), 1 da (Sally Anne b 1959); *Career* Lt Kings Dragoon Gds 1943–46; asst gen mangr Hulton Press Ltd 1949–57, md TAM Ltd 1957–61, fndr and chm AGB Research plc 1962–89; chm: Pergamon AGB plc 1989–90, Caverswall Holdings 1990–, Arts Access 1986–98, Netherhall Tst 1962–2003; tstee St Brides Fleet St Worldwide Media Tst 1988–2005, memb Industry and Commerce Advsy Ctee William & Mary Tercentenary Tst 1985–89; vice-pres Periodical Publishers Assoc 1989– (pres 1985–89), visiting prof in business and mgmnt Middlesex Univ 1989–, govr Hong Kong Coll 1984–94; Freeman City of London 1978, Liveryman Worshipful Co of Gold and Silver Wyre Drawers 1975; FSS 1960, FRSA 1986; *Recreations* golf, reading, travel; *Clubs* Cavalry and Guards', MCC, Rye Golf; *Style*— Sir Bernard Audley; ✉ 56 River Court, Upper Ground, London SE1 9PE (tel 020 7928 6576)

AUDLEY, Maxwell Charles (Max); s of Sir (George) Bernard Audley, *qv*, of London, and Barbara, *née* Heath; *b* 27 April 1954, London; *Educ* Highgate Sch London, Univ of Bradford (BA), Univ of Bonn, Coll of Law; *m* 18 June 1983, Rosamund, *née* Shore; 3 da (Laura b 4 June 1984, Alice b 15 Feb 1989, Claudia b 21 Oct 1992), 1 s (Charles b 24 Oct 1986); *Career* admitted slr 1980; founding ptnr and head of corp Hobson Audley 1983–2003, ptnr and London head of corp Faegre & Benson LLP 2003–; Brennan's Wig & Pen Law Prize 1980; Freeman City of London 1984, Liveryman Worshipful Co of Broderers; memb Law Soc 1980; *Style*— Max Audley, Esq; ✉ Faegre & Benson LLP, 7 Pilgrim Street, London EC4V 6LB (tel 020 7450 4500, fax 020 7450 4545, e-mail maudley@faegre.com)

AUDLEY, Prof Robert John; s of Walter Audley (late Warrant Offr RE, d 1981), and Agnes Lilian, *née* Baker; *b* 15 December 1928; *Educ* Battersea GS, UCL (State scholar, BSc, PhD); *m* 1, 1952 (m dis 1977), Patricia Mary, *née* Bannister; 2 s (Matthew John b 1961, Thomas Giles b 1963 d 2006); m 2, 24 April 1990, (Vera) Elyashiv, da of Guttmann (d 1942); *Career* Nat Serv Sgt RE (mainly BAOR) 1947–49; Fulbright scholar and research asst Washington State Univ 1952–53; UCL: research scientist MRC Gp for the Experimental Investigation of Behaviour 1955–57, lectr in psychology 1957–64, reader in psychology 1964, prof of psychology 1965–, head Dept of Psychology 1979–93, dean Faculty of Sci 1985–88, vice-provost 1988–94, fell 1989, conslt and prof emeritus 1994–2000; visiting prof Columbia Univ NY 1962, visiting fell Inst for Advanced Study Princeton 1970, Miller visiting prof Univ of Calif Berkeley 1971; pres: Br Psychological Soc 1969 (hon librarian 1962–65), Experimental Psychology Soc 1975–76 (hon sec 1962–65); chm Jt Working Gp ESRC/HEFC Jt Information Systems Ctee 1990–; ed Br Jl of Mathematical and Statistical Psychology 1963–69, assoc ed Jl of Mathematical Psychology 1979–81; memb: MRC/RAF Flying Personnel Ctee 1965–75, Equipment Sub-Ctee UGC 1982–88, Computer Bd Universities and Res Cncl 1986–90; chm Psychology Sub-Ctee MRC/RN Personnel Res Ctee 1984–96; FBPsS 1972; *Recreations* crosswords, cooking; *Style*— Prof Robert Audley; ✉ 22 Keats Grove, London NW3 2RS (tel 020 7435 6655, e-mail rj.audley@btopenworld.com)

AUERBACH, Frank Helmuth; s of Max Auerbach (d 1942), of Berlin, and Charlotte Norah, *née* Borchardt (d 1942); *b* 29 April 1931, Berlin; *Educ* Bunce Ct Scht, Borough Poly Sch of Art, St Martin's Sch of Art, RCA; *m* 10 March 1958, Julia, da of James Wolstenholme (d 1981); 1 s (Jake b 1958); *Career* painter; public collections incl: Tate Gallery, Arts Cncl, Br Cncl, MOMA NY, Metropolitan Museum NY, Nat Gallery of Australia; one-man exhibitions incl: Beaux Arts Gallery 1956, 1959, 1961, 1962 and 1963, Marlborough Fine Art 1965, 1967, 1971, 1974, 1983, 1987, 1990, 1997 and 2004, Marlborough-Gerson NY 1969, Villiers Sydney 1972, Bergamini Milan 1973, Univ of Essex 1973, Municipal Gallery of Modern Art Dublin 1975, Marlborough Zürich 1976, Arts Cncl Retrospective (Hayward Gallery) 1978, Jacobson NY 1979, Marlborough NY 1982, 1994 and 1998, Anne Berthoud London 1983, Venice Biennale 1986 (Golden Lion Prize), Kunstverein Hamburg 1986, Museum Folkwang Essen 1986, Centro de Arte Reina Sofia Madrid 1987, Rijksmuseum Vincent van Gogh Amsterdam 1989, Yale Center for British Art 1991, National Gallery London 1995, RA London 2001, Marlborough Galeria Madrid 2002; numerous mixed exhibitions; ARCA 1955; *Style*— Frank Auerbach, Esq; ✉ c/o Marlborough Fine Art (London) Ltd, 6 Albemarle Street, London W1S 4BY (tel 020 7629 5161, fax 020 7629 6338)

AUGER, George Albert; s of Thomas Albert Auger (d 1977), and Lilian Daisy, *née* McDermott (d 1991); *b* 21 February 1938; *Educ* Finchley Co GS; *m* 8 Sept 1962, Pauline June; 2 da (Jacqueline Susan b 1965, Deborah Anne (Mrs Auld) b 1969); *Career* Nat Serv RAF 1957–59; sr insolvency ptnr BDO Stoy Hayward 1978–95; memb Cncl ACCA 1980–86 and 1994– (pres 2001–02), pres Insolvency Practitioners' Assoc 1981–82; chm govrs Channing Sch London; FCCA 1962, MIPA 1967 (sr moderator Jt Insolvency Exam Bd 1994–); *Books* Hooper's Voluntary Liquidation (1978); *Recreations* cricket, tennis, opera, porcelain; *Style*— George Auger, Esq; ✉ c/o ACCA, 29 Lincoln's Inn Fields, London WC2A 3EE

AUKIN, David; s of Charles Aukin (d 1981), and Regina, *née* Unger; *b* 12 February 1942; *Educ* St Paul's, St Edmund Hall Oxford (BA); *m* 20 June 1969, Nancy Jane, da of Herman Meckler, of London and New York; 2 s (Daniel b 1970, Jethro b 1976); *Career* admitted slr 1965; literary advsr Traverse Theatre Club 1970–73, admin Oxford Playhouse Co 1974–75; dir: Hampstead Theatre 1978–83 (admin 1975–78), Leicester Haymarket Theatre 1983–86; exec dir RNT 1986–90, head of drama Channel 4 TV 1990–97, co-fndr of HAL Films 1998, ceo Daybreak Pictures Ltd; *Recreations* golf; *Clubs* RAC; *Style*— David Aukin, Esq; ✉ 43 Whitfield Street, London W1T 4HA

AULD, Charles Cairns; s of James Auld (d 1975), of Newmilns, Ayrshire, and Janet, *née* Dunn (d 1971); *b* 29 June 1943; *Educ* George Watsons Coll Edinburgh, Univ of Edinburgh (MA); *m* July 1967, Margaret Jane (d 2005); 1 da (Caroline), 1 s (James); *Career* with Beecham 1971–80 (joining as brand mangr), md Spillers 1980–85, divnl md Nabisco 1985–87, md Intercraft 1987–91, chief exec General Healthcare Group plc (t/a BMI Healthcare) 1991–2004; dir Ind Healthcare Assoc 1995–2004; former chm: Mktg Soc, CAM Fndn; Freeman: City of London, Worshipful Co of Marketors; FMS, FCAM; *Recreations* cooking, France, sailing the Mediterranean (motor cruising), orchestral and choral music; *Clubs* Caledonian; *Style*— Charles Auld, Esq

AULD, Prof (Alan) Graeme; s of Alan Talbert Auld, and Alice Jolly, *née* Coull; *b* 14 August 1941; *Educ* Robert Gordon's Coll Aberdeen (Classical Dux, Mackenzie Shield), Univ of Aberdeen (MA, DLitt), Univ of Edinburgh (BD, PhD); *m* 23 Sept 1967, Dr Sylvia Joyce Auld, da of Maj Gen Stephen Lamplugh; 2 s (Alan Hamish b 20 Sept 1970, Fergus Stephen b 17 Feb 1973), 1 da (Caroline Mary b 28 April 1975); *Career* asst dir Br Sch of Archaeology Jerusalem 1969–72; Univ of Edinburgh: lectr 1972–85, sr lectr 1985–95, prof of Hebrew Bible 1995–, princ New Coll 2002–; pres Soc for Old Testament Study 2005; FRSE, FSA Scot; *Books* Joshua, Moses and the Land (1980), Amos (1986), Kings without Privilege (1994), Jerusalem I: From the Bronze Age to the Maccabees (with Margreet Steiner, 1996), Joshua Retold: Synoptic Perspectives (1998), Samuel at the Threshold (2004), Joshua: Jesus Son of Naué in Codex Vaticanus (2005); *Recreations* music, travel, walking; *Style*— Prof Graeme Auld; ✉ University of Edinburgh, New College, Mound Place, Edinburgh EH1 2LX (tel 0131 650 7992, fax 0131 650 7952, e-mail a.g.auld@ed.ac.uk)

AULD, Rt Hon Lord Justice; Rt Hon Sir Robin Ernest; kt (1988), PC (1995); s of late Ernest Auld; *b* 19 July 1937; *Educ* Brooklands Coll, KCL (LLB, PhD, FKC); *m* 1963 (m dis 2005), Catherine Eleanor Mary, elder da of late David Henry Pritchard; 1 s, 1 da; *Career* called to the Bar Gray's Inn 1959, QC 1975, recorder of the Crown Court 1977–87, bencher 1984, judge of the High Court of Justice (Queen's Bench Div) 1987–95, memb Judicial Studies Bd 1989–91 (chm Criminal Ctee 1989–91), presiding judge Western Circuit 1991–94, a Lord Justice of Appeal 1995–, sr presiding judge for Eng and Wales 1995–98, vice-chm Judicial Appts Cmmn 1996–; admitted New York State Bar 1984; memb Cmmn of Inquiry into Casino Gambling in the Bahamas 1967, chm William Tyndale Schs' Inquiry 1975–76, Dept of Trade inspr Ashbourne Investments Ltd 1975–79, legal assessor to Gen Med and Dental Cncls 1982–87, chm Home Office Ctee of Inquiry into Sunday Trading 1983–84, conducted Criminal Courts Review 1999–2001; sr research scholar Yale Law Sch 2001; Master Worshipful Co of Woolmen 1984–85; Hon LLD Univ of Herts 2002; *Clubs* Athenaeum, Yale (NYC); *Style*— The Rt Hon Lord Justice Auld; ✉ Royal Courts of Justice, Strand, London WC2A 2LL

AUMONIER, John Martin; s of Lt Cdr Timothy Peppercorn Aumonier (d 1983), of Billingshurst, W Sussex, and Maureen, *née* Leonard (d 1985); *b* 5 January 1952; *Educ* John Fisher Sch Purley Surrey, Ledsham Ct Hastings, St Mary's Coll Guildford; *m* 17 Feb 1979, Sally Wallace, da of Maj John Wallace Goodwyn Kay (d 1972), of Cranleigh, Surrey; 2 da (Jessica b 1985, Lucy b 1987); *Career* Advtg Dept London Evening News 1969–70, advtg exec Vogue 1970–72, media gp head Stewart & Jefferies Advertising 1972, sr exec Associated Independent Radio Services Ltd 1972–76, sales mangr Broadcast Marketing Services Ltd 1976–80; md: The Radio Business Ltd 1980–82, Radio Mercury plc 1982–92, Virgin Radio Ltd 1992–93, Talk Radio UK (third national independent station) 1993–95; chief exec Radio First plc; visiting examiner Crawley Coll of Technol;

Ordre des Chevaliers du Bellay; *Recreations* radio, wine, food, travel; *Style*— John Aumonier, Esq; ✉ tel 01798 817414, e-mail johnaumonier@btopenworld.com

AUSSIGNAC, Pascal; s of Camille Aussignac, of La Rochelle, France, and Simone, *née* Robert; *b* 30 June 1967; *Educ* Lyceé Hotelier de Talence Bordeaux; *Career* chef; commis de cuisine Les Trois Marches Versailles 1984–85, commis de cuisine Le Divellec Paris 1985, chef de partie Le Potager du Roy Versailles 1985–87, chef de partie Jacques Cagna Paris 1987, chef de partie tournant Carré des Feuillants Paris 1988, private cook to the head of staff of the French Air Force (Nat Serv) 1988–89, chef de partie Wing Song (luxury cruise ship) 1990, chef de partie tournant Guy Savoy Paris 1990–91, pastry chef Stohrer Paris 1991–92, premier maître d'hôtel L'Escargot Montorgueil Paris 1992, head chef and event organiser Yvan Paris and Yes Receptions Paris 1993–96, fndr, mangr and chef de cuisine Les Restanques Grimaud 1997–98, fndr and co-prop Club Gascon (restaurant), Cellar Gascon (wine bar) and Comptoir Gascon (delicatessen, bakery and caterers) London 1998–, fndr Le Cercle 2004–; supporter Leuka; *Recreations* gardening, archery, diving; *Style*— Pascal Aussignac, Esq; ✉ Club Gascon, 57 West Smithfield, London EC1A 9DS (tel 020 7796 0600, fax 020 7796 0601)

AUSTEN, David Lee; s of David Robert Austen, of Cambridge, and Joan Ellen, *née* Waters; *b* 11 April 1960; *Educ* Maidstone Coll of Art, RCA; *Partner* Mary Doyle; 1 da (Mia India b 19 Aug 1982), 1 s (Sam Joseph David b 21 Sept 1986); *Career* artist; solo exhibitions: Anthony Reynolds Gallery London 1986, 1988, 1991, 1992, 1994, 1995, 2000, 2001 and 2004, Serpentine Gallery 1987, Arnolfini Bristol 1988, Castle Museum and Art Gallery Nottingham 1989, Cirrus Los Angeles 1989, 1991, 1993 and 1994, Frith Street Gallery London 1990, Cornerhouse Manchester 1993, Mead Gallery Warwick Arts Centre 1997, Anthony Wilkinson London 1997, Inverleith House Edinburgh 1997, Galerie Holenbach Stuttgart 1997, Galerie Slewe Amsterdam 1998, Annandale Gallery Sydney 2001, Christchurch Mansion Ipswich 2001, Ingleby Gallery Edinburgh 2001, 2003 and 2006, Galleri Boumlou Bergen 2004, Peer London 2004, Milton Keynes Gallery 2007; gp exhibitions incl: Between Identity & Politics (Gimpel Fils London/NY) 1986, Works on Paper (Anthony Reynolds Gallery London) 1986, Object and Image: Aspects of British Art in the 1980s (City Museum and Art Gallery Stoke-on-Trent) 1988, Poiesis (Graeme Murray Gallery Edinburgh 1990 and Fruitmarket Gallery Edinburgh 1992), New Voices (Centre de Conférences Albert Borschette Brussels) 1992, Twelve Stars (Belfast, Edinburgh and London) 1992–93, MOMA Oxford 1996, Whitechapel London 1997, Kettles Yard Cambridge 2003, Anthony Reynolds Gallery 2007; *Style*— David Austen, Esq; ✉ c/o Anthony Reynolds Gallery, 60 Great Marlborough Street, London W1F 7BG (tel 020 7439 2201)

AUSTEN, Mark Edward; s of Capt George Ernest Austen (d 1987), of Ashtead, Surrey, and Eileen Gladys, *née* Thirkettle (d 1995); *b* 25 August 1949; *Educ* City of London Freemen's Sch, Harvard Business Sch (AMP); *m* 28 May 1977, Priscilla, da of Reginald Cyril Hart (d 1984), of Chiddingfold, Surrey; 1 s (Timothy b 1980), 1 da (Rachel b 1982); *Career* corp accounts trainee Reed International 1967–72, asst fin controller Henry Ansbacher 1972–75; PricewaterhouseCoopers Management Consultants (formerly Price Waterhouse before merger): conslt 1975–82, ptnr 1982–, ptnr in charge fin servs consltg UK 1985–90, Europe 1990–96 and worldwide 1996–2002, memb Global Consltg Mgmnt Bd 1996–2002, memb Global PwC Bd 2001–03; IBM Consulting Services 2003–04; dir: Smartstream Technologies 2004, Standard Bank plc 2005, Teminos AG 2006, Liverpool Victoria Friendly Soc 2006, IFB International 2006; chm and fndr: Fair Food Fndn 2006, What's On Your Plate? (WOYP) 2006; tstee Philharmonia Orch 2000; Freeman City of London; FCMA 1976; *Recreations* music, squash, food, wine; *Clubs* RAC, Colets; *Style*— Mark Austen, Esq; ✉ 18 Imber Park Road, Esher, Surrey KT10 8JB (e-mail mark.austen@gmail.com)

AUSTEN, HE Richard James; MBE (1996); *b* 25 May 1955; *Career* diplomat; with Inland Revenue 1972–77, entered HM Dip Serv 1981, posted Dar es Salaam 1983, third sec (consular) Ottawa 1987–90, second sec FCO 1990–93, dep high cmmr Banjul 1993–96, first sec FCO 1996–2001, dep high cmmr Port Louis 2001–03, ambass to Mongolia 2004–06, ambass to Panama 2006–; *Style*— HE Mr Richard Austen, MBE; ✉ c/o Foreign & Commonwealth Office (Panama City), King Charles Street, London SW1A 2AH

AUSTIN, Sir Anthony Leonard; 6 Bt (UK 1894), of Red Hill, Castleford, West Riding of York; s of Sir William Ronald Austin, 4 Bt (d 1989), and his 1 w, Dorothy Mary, *née* Bidwell (d 1957); suc bro, Sir Michael Trescawen Austin, 5 Bt (d 1995); *b* 30 September 1930; *Educ* Downside; *m* 1, 1956 (m dis 1966), Mary Annette, da of Richard Kelly, of Greenogue, Kilsallaghan, Co Dublin; 1 da (Caroline Dorothy b 1957), 2 s (Peter John b 1958, Nicholas Michael James b 1960); m 2, 1967, Aileen Morrison Hall, da of William Hall Stewart; 1 da (Rebecca Dorothy Mary b 1968); *Heir* s, Peter Austin; *Style*— Sir Anthony Austin, Bt; ✉ Stanbury Manor, Morwenstow, Bude, Cornwall EX23 9JQ

AUSTIN, Prof Brian; *b* 5 August 1951; *Educ* Mount Grace Comp Sch, Univ of Newcastle upon Tyne (BSc, PhD), Heriot-Watt Univ (DSc); *m* Dawn Amy, *née* Allen; 1 da (Aurelia Jean b 30 Sept 1987); *Career* res assoc Dept of Microbiology Univ of Maryland 1977–78 (postdoctoral fell 1975–77), sr scientific offr Fish Diseases Laboratory MAFF 1978–84; Dept of Biological Sciences Heriot-Watt Univ: lectr in aquatic microbiology 1984–89, reader 1989–92, head Div of Aquaculture 1990–93, prof 1992–, head of dept 1993–96; visiting prof: Central Univ of Venezuela 1985, 1992 and 1995, Univ of Kebangsaan 1989, Universidad del Zulia 1991; visiting scientist Ocean Univ of Qingdao 1990 and 1995 (guest prof 2000–); external examiner: Univ of Stirling 1982–83, Univ of Bombay 1984, Univ of Wales 1994, Univ of Rouen 1996, Robert Gordon Univ 1999, National Univ of Ireland 2000; non-exec dir Aquaculture Vaccines Ltd 1990–2002; memb: American Soc of Microbiology, Euro Assoc of Fish Pathologists, Soc of Applied Bacteriology, Soc for General Microbiology, UK Fedn of Culture Collections; author of numerous pubns and papers in learned jls; FRSA 1996, fell American Acad of Microbiology 1998, FHEA 2007; *Books* Modern Bacterial Taxonomy (with F G Priest, 1986, 2 edn 1993), Bacterial Fish Pathogens: disease in farmed and wild fish (with D A Austin, 1987, 4 edn 2007), Marine Microbiology (1988), Methods in Aquatic Bacteriology (ed, 1988), Methods for the Microbiological Examination of Fish and Shellfish (ed, 1989), Pathogens in the Environment (ed, 1991), The Genus *Aeromonas* (ed, 1996); *Recreations* gardening, literature, hiking, music, photography, theatre, travel, writing; *Style*— Prof Brian Austin; ✉ School of Life Sciences, John Muir Building, Heriot-Watt University, Riccarton, Edinburgh EH14 4AS (tel 0131 451 3452, fax 0131 451 3009, e-mail b.austin@hw.ac.uk)

AUSTIN, Prof Colin François Lloyd; s of Prof Lloyd James Austin (d 1994), of Cambridge, and Jeanne Françoise, *née* Guérin (d 1998); *b* 26 July 1941; *Educ* Lycée Lakanal Paris, Manchester Grammar, Jesus Coll Cambridge (MA), ChCh Oxford (DPhil), Freie Univ W Berlin; *m* 28 June 1967, Mishtu, da of Sreepada Mojumder (d 1963), of Calcutta; 1 da (Teesta b 21 Oct 1968), 1 s (Topun b 1 Aug 1971); *Career* Univ of Cambridge: fell Trinity Hall 1965–, asst lectr 1969–73, lectr 1973–88, reader 1988–98, prof of Greek 1998–; treas Cambridge Philological Soc 1971–; FBA 1983; *Books* Nova Fragmenta Euripidea (1968), Menandri Aspis et Samia (1969–70), Comicorum Graecorum Fragmenta in Papyris Reperta (1973), Poetae Comici Graeci 8 vols (1983–2001), Posidippi Pellaei Quae Supersunt Omnia (2002), Aristophanes Thesmophoriazusae (2004); *Recreations* cycling, philately, wine tasting; *Style*— Prof Colin Austin, FBA; ✉ 7 Park Terrace, Cambridge CB1 1JH (tel 01223 362732); Trinity Hall, Cambridge CB2 1TJ (fax 01223 332537)

AUSTIN, David Charles Henshaw; OBE (2007); s of Charles Frederick Austin (d 1980), of Broad Oak, Shrewsbury, and Lilian, *née* Kidson (d 1981); *b* 16 February 1926; *Educ* Shrewsbury; *m* 24 March 1956, Patricia Josephine, da of Leonard Dudley Braithwaite (d 1970); 1 da (Claire Rose 1957), 2 s (David Julian Charles b 1958, James b 1959); *Career* farmer 1943–70; professional rose breeder 1970– (non-professional 1946–70), fndr David Austin Roses 1970 (introduced 200 new English roses, distributed worldwide); memb Br Assoc of Rose Breeders; Hon DSc Univ of East London 1997; *Awards* Gold Veitch Memorial Medal RHS 1995, Royal Nat Rose Soc Award for Innovation in Rose Breeding 1995, Dean Hole Medal Royal Nat Rose Soc 2000, James Mason Award Royal Nat Rose Soc 2000, Victoria Medal of Honour RHS 2002, Lifetime Achievement Award Garden Centre Association 2004, The Queen Mother's Int Rose Award Nat Rose Soc 2007; *Books* The Heritage of the Rose (1988), Old Roses and English Roses (1992), Shrub Roses and Climbing Roses (1993), David Austin's English Roses (1993), The English Rose (1998), The English Roses (2005); *Recreations* reading and writing poetry, current affairs, swimming, looking at gardens and countryside, farming and walking with my Staffordshire Bull Terrier; *Style*— David Austin, Esq, OBE; ✉ David Austin Roses, Bowling Green Lane, Albrighton, Wolverhampton, West Midlands WV7 3HB (tel 01902 376300, fax 01902 372142, e-mail retail@davidaustinroses.com, website www.davidaustinroses.com)

AUSTIN, Ian; MP; *b* 6 March 1965; *Educ* Dudley Sch; *m* 3 c; *Career* cncllr Dudley Cncl 1991–95; former political advsr to Rt Hon Gordon Brown MP, memb Lab Pty W Midlands election campaign team 1997; MP (Lab) Dudley N 2005–; Parly prive sec to the PM 2007–; *Style*— Ian Austin, MP; ✉ Turner House, 157–185 Wrens Nest Road, Dudley, West Midlands DY1 3RU (tel 01384 342503); House of Commons, London SW1A 0AA (tel 020 7219 801)

AUSTIN, James Lucien Ashurst; s of Prof Lloyd James Austin, of Cambridge, and Jeanne, *née* Guérin; *b* 4 June 1940; *Educ* Lycée Lakanal Paris, Manchester Grammar, Jesus Coll Cambridge (MA), Courtauld Inst of Art London (postgrad degree); *m* 30 July 1969, Pauline Jeannette, da of Paul Aten; 2 s (Thomas b 18 Oct 1974, Benjamin b 7 June 1977), 1 da (Lucie b 27 May 1980); *Career* photographer; Courtauld Inst: asst Photographic Dept 1962–63, photographer to the Conway Library 1973–85; freelance photographer 1965–73 and 1985–2003; major cmmns incl: Emile Male: Religious Art in France (3 volumes published), The Buildings of England by Nikolaus Pevsner (over 15 volumes published), photography of Sainsbury Collection Univ of E Anglia, photographer to artist Ben Nicholson (4 exhibition catalogues published), inventory photography for Nat Trust and English Heritage, catalogue photography for Tate Gallery; photographs for facsimile edns of: Lambeth Palace Apocalypse, Bank of Eng Royal Charter, Commission and Subscriptions Book, Turner water colours for book on Turner at Petworth; FBIPP 1977 (assoc 1970); *Style*— James Austin, Esq; ✉ Pragelier, 24390 Tourtoirac, France

AUSTIN, John Eric; MP; s of late Stanley Austin, and late Ellen Austin; *b* 21 August 1944; *Educ* Glyn GS Epsom, Goldsmiths Coll London, Univ of Bristol; *m* 1965 (m dis 1997), Linda, *née* Walker; 2 s, 1 da; *Career* medical lab technician 1961–63; organiser and agent: Swindon CLP 1965–66, Greenwich CLP 1966–70; social worker London Borough of Bexley 1972–74, dir Bexley Cncl for Racial Equality 1974–92; MP (Lab): Woolwich 1992–97 (also contested 1987), Erith and Thamesmead 1997–; memb House of Commons Health Select Ctee 1994–2005, chair Socialist Campaign Gp of Lab MPs 1995–98, chair Br Slovenia, Syria, Ethiopia, Albania Overseas Territories All-Pty Parly Gps, chair Br Section Inter Parly Union 2001–04, co-chair Cncl for the Advancement of Arab British Understanding, jt chair UK Branch Parly Assoc for Euro-Arab Co-operation, sec Lebanon, Czech and Slovak and Hungary All-Pty Gps; memb: Exec Ctee Cwlth Parly Assoc (UK), Parly Assembly Cncl of Europe and WEU 2005–; London Borough of Greenwich: cncllr 1970–94, chm Social Services Ctee 1974–78, dep ldr 1981–82, ldr 1982–87, mayor 1987–89; chm: Greenwich MIND 1978–82, Assoc of Community Health Cncls for England and Wales 1981–83, London Boroughs Emergency Planning Info Ctee 1990–92, London Ecology Unit 1990–92; vice-chm: Assoc of London Authorities 1983–87 (environment spokesman 1989–92), London Strategic Policy Unit 1986–88, London Gp of Labour MPs; hon chair Br Caribbean Assoc; tstee: London Marathon Charitable Tst Ltd, Crossness Engines Tst; memb AMICUS/MSF; *Recreations* cooking, gardening, marathon running; *Style*— John Austin, Esq, MP; ✉ House of Commons, London SW1A 0AA (tel 020 7219 5195, fax 020 7219 2706)

AUSTIN, Wendy Elizabeth; da of Cecil William Stead Austin, of Londonderry and Belfast, and Irene Elizabeth Wilson, *née* Simpson; *b* 19 November 1951; *Educ* Victoria Coll Belfast, Queen's Univ Belfast; *m* 1, 1982 (m dis 1995), Peter Hutchinson; 1 s (Niall b 27 Sept 1983), 2 da (Kerry b 10 June 1985, Clare b 8 April 1988); m 2, 2003, Frank Hewitt; *Career* freelance broadcaster/presenter, conference moderator, awards MC; *Television* incl: Children in Need (BBC TV) 1980–, Inside Ulster (BBC NI TV) 1980–85, Breakfast Time (BBC NI TV) 1982–87, Open House (BBC NI TV) 1990–93, The DIY Show (BBC NI TV), Hillsborough Revisited 2007; *Radio* incl: Woman's Hour (from NI and London, BBC Radio) 1981–99, Good Arts Guide (BBC Radio Ulster) 1991, PM (BBC Radio 4) 1992–, Good Morning Ulster (BBC Radio Ulster) 1992–, The Exchange (BBC Radio 4), Breakfast Show (BBC Radio 5 Live); chm Arts and Business Ctee; patron Caring Breaks; Enniskillen Integrated Primary Sch; pres Spirit of Enniskillen Tst; Hon DLitt Univ of Ulster 2005; *Recreations* travel, music, walking; *Style*— Dr Wendy Austin; ✉ BBC, Broadcasting House, Belfast BT2 8HQ (tel 028 9269 8356, e-mail wendy.austin@bbc.co.uk, website www.wendyaustin.com)

AUSTIN-COOPER, Richard Arthur; o s of late Capt Adolphus Richard Cooper, SOE, Croix de Guerre, of Ditton, Kent, and Doris Rosina, *née* Wallen; see Burke's Irish Family Records under Cooper (of Killenure Castle, Co Tipperary, and Abbeville House, Co Dublin); assumed additional surname of Austin by Deed Poll 1963; *b* 21 February 1932; *Educ* Wellingborough GS, Tottenham GS; *m* 1, 1953 (m dis 1963), Sylvia Anne Shirley Berringer; m 2, 1963 (m dis 1974), Valerie Georgina, da of Henry Drage, of Tottenham, London; 1 da (Samantha b 1967), 1 s (Matthew b 1969); m 3, 1979 (m dis 1981), Mariola Danuta Sikorska; m 4, 1986, Rosemary Swaisland, *née* Gillespie; 1 step s (Richard Swaisland), 1 step da (Lucy Parkin, *née* Swaisland); *Career* served RA 1950–52 and TAVR in the RA, Intelligence Corps, 21 SAS Regt (Artists' Rifles), Essex ACF 1952–69 and the Hon Artillery Co 1978–79 (cmmnd 2 Lt TAVR 1968), OC ACF Canvey Island; with Barclays Bank 1948–60; head cashier: Bank of Baroda 1960–63, Lloyd's Bank 1963–69; dep head Stocks & Shares Dept Banque de Paris et des Pays Bas 1969–74, asst mangr Banking Div Brook St Bureau of Mayfair Ltd 1974–75, chief custodian and London registrar Canadian Imperial Bank of Commerce and registrar in London for Angostura Bitters Ltd 1975–78, HR Deutsche Bank AG London Branch 1978–85, sr mangr and head of personnel Deutsche Bank Capital Markets Ltd 1985–90, ptnr Charsby Associates recruitment conslts London 1989–91, ret; memb London Banks Personnel Mgmnt Gp 1989–90; fndr fell Inst of Heraldic and Genealogical Studies; memb Ct of Common Cncl City of London for Cripplegate Ward 1978–81; memb Bd of Mgmnt: Barbican YMCA, City of London Central Markets (Leadenhall Market, Billingsgate Market); memb: City of London TAVR Assoc, Coal Corn and Rates Ctee, Mgmnt Ctee Barbican Sch of Music and Drama (and mature student (tenor)), Irish Peers Assoc 1964–; govr: City of London Sch for Girls 1979–80, Lansbury Adult Educn Inst 1979–82, City of London Freemen's Sch 1980–81; life govr Sheriffs' and Recorders' Fund at the Old Bailey 1979–; represented the City of London Corp on the Gtr London Arts Cncl 1979–80, final tstee City of London Imperial Vols 1980–81; parish cncllr Wansford 1989–90, memb PCC Thurlby 1991–93; vice-pres Bourne Family History Soc 1993–2005; chm: Stamford Arthritis Care 1994–95, Eastbourne Branch Br Cardiac Patients Assoc 2003–07; vice-chm and tstee Friends of Eastbourne Hosps 2003–; pres Royal Artillery Assoc Eastbourne

2006–; govr American Coll in Oxford; prizes for: athletics (including winning Barclays Bank Cross-Country Championships), operatic singing (tenor), painting; Freeman City of London 1964; Hon LLD, Hon MA (USA); FHG 1965, FRSA 1974, FRSAIre 1980, FCIB 1987; *Books* Butterhill and Beyond (1991), The Beavers of Barnack (1995), The de Gidlow Family of Ince (1996), The Peisley Family of Clifton Hampden, Oxon (1996); *Recreations* genealogical research, tenor concerts, painting, sketching, judging art; *Clubs* SAS Regimental Assoc, Intelligence Corps Old Comrades Assoc, Artists' Rifles Assoc, Wellingborough GS Old Boys, Probus (Eastbourne), Motcombe Park Bowls (Eastbourne), Royal Artillery Assoc (Eastbourne); *Style—* Richard Austin-Cooper, Esq; ✉ 2 Lea House, 1 Mill Road, Eastbourne, East Sussex BN21 2LY (tel 01323 721933, e-mail r.austin-cooper@tiscali.co.uk)

AUTY, Helen Rees; da of Norman Auty (d 1980), of Little Common, E Sussex, and Eirwen Auty (d 1990); *b* 31 December 1939; *Educ* St Catherine's Sch Bramley, Univ of London (Dip History of Art); *Career* sec: The Distillers' Co 1958–60, RSA 1960–64, W D Scott & Co NZ 1964–65, The Northern Employers' Group Aust 1965; RSA: PA to chief exec 1966–70, head of design 1970–96 (i/c RSA annual Student Design Awards, RSA Art for Architecture and Young Designers into Industry scheme), design dir 1996–97, dir of external affrs 1997–99; memb Design Cncl 1990–98, dir Design for Transformation 1993–2003; acting sec Royal Designers for Industry Faculty Bd 1997–2000; govr: Falmouth Coll of the Arts 1989–97, Berkshire Coll of Art and Design 1990–96; govr Design Dimension Tst 1998–; Conf for Higher Educn in Art and Design (CHEAD) Medal for servs to art and design educn 1989, RSA Bicentenary Medal 1994; Freeman City of London 1998, Liveryman Worshipful Co of Pattenmakers 1998; Hon DDes De Montfort Univ 1996; Hon FRCA 1993, Hon RIBA 1999, Companion Faculty of Royal Designers for Industry 2000; *Recreations* country walks, garden history and gardening, art exhibitions, theatre, travelling, photography, second hand book shops, pottering; *Clubs* Chelsea Arts; *Style—* Ms Helen Auty; ✉ tel 020 8579 5997, e-mail helen@chesmor.fsnet.co.uk

AVEBURY, 4 Baron (UK 1900); Sir Eric Reginald Lubbock; 7 Bt (UK 1806); s of Hon Maurice Fox Pitt Lubbock (yst s of 1 Baron Avebury) and Hon Mary Stanley (eldest da of 5 Baron Stanley of Alderley and sis of the actress Pamela Stanley); suc cousin, 3 Baron 1971; *b* 29 September 1928; *Educ* Upper Canada Coll, Harrow, Balliol Coll Oxford (BA, Boxing blue); *m* 1, 1953 (m dis 1983), Kina Maria, da of Count Joseph O'Kelly de Gallagh (a yr s of the family whose head is a Count of the Holy Roman Empire by Imperial Letters Patent of 1767); 2 s (Hon Lyulph Ambrose Jonathan, Hon Maurice Patrick Guy), 1 da (Hon Ms Lubbock); m 2, 1985, Lindsay Jean, da of late Gordon Neil Stewart, and of late Pamela Hansford Johnson (Lady Snow), writer; 1 s (Hon John William Stewart); *Heir* s, Hon Lyulph Lubbock; *Career* Lt Welsh Gds 1949–51; engr with Rolls Royce 1951–56; mgmnt conslt: Production Engineering Ltd 1953–60, Charterhouse Group 1960; dir C L Projects Ltd 1966–, conslt Morgan-Grampian Ltd 1970–85; sits as Lib Dem in House of Lords; MP (Lib) Orpington 1962–70, Lib chief whip 1963–70, chm Br Parly Human Rights Gp 1976–97; Lib Dem frontbench spokesman on Africa House of Lords 2003–; pres: Data Processing Mgmnt Assoc 1972–75, Fluoridation Soc 1972–85, Conservation Soc 1973–82; memb: Cncl Inst of Race Relations 1972–74, Royal Cmmn on Standards of Conduct in Public Life 1974–76; pres: Kurdish Human Rights Project 1995–, TAPOL (Indonesian human rights orgn) 1997–, Angulimala Buddhist Prison Chaplaincy Orgn 1998–, Advsy Cncl for the Educn of Romanies and Travellers 2000–; co-fndr Parliamentarians for East Timor 1988, chm Peru Support Gp 2003–, chm Cameroon Campaign Gp 2003–; pres London Bach Soc and Steinitz Bach Players 1984–97; Liveryman Worshipful Co of Fishmongers; MIMechE, MBCS; *Recreations* listening to music, reading; *Style—* The Rt Hon the Lord Avebury; ✉ 26 Flodden Road, London SE5 9LH (e-mail ericavebury@gmail.com)

AVERILL, Michael Charles Edward; s of Charles Rochford Averill, of Harlaxton, Lincs, and Peggy Louise, *née* Cooke; *b* 14 May 1951, London; *Educ* Royal Sch of Mines Imperial Coll London (BSc), Cranfield Mgmnt Sch (MBA); *m* 15 March 1980, Janet Marjorie, *née* Phillips; 1 s (Thomas Rochford b 22 Dec 1981), 1 da (Lucy Jane b 21 Sept 1983); *Career* Henry Wiggin (Inco) Sales 1974–75, various positions (latterly bus devpt mangr) Plessey Co plc 1975–87, mktg dir Herga Electric Ltd 1987–89, md Environmental Servs Div Rechem/Shanks Gp 1989–94, gp chief exec Shanks Gp plc 1994–2007 (conslt 2007–08); non-exec dir TDG plc 2003–; dir Environmental Services Assoc, vice-pres European Federation of Waste Mgmnt and Environmental Servs Brussels, non-exec dir Waste and Resources Action Programme (WRAP); ARSM, FCIWM 2004; *Recreations* golf, gastronomy, motor sport; *Clubs* Home House; *Style—* Michael Averill, Esq; ✉ Shanks Group plc, Astor House, Station Road, Bourne End, Bucks SL8 5YP (tel 01628 554920, fax 01628 819267, e-mail michael.averill@shanks.co.uk)

AVERY, Dr Brice Johnson; s of William Johnson Avery, of Haultwick, Herts, and Margaret Norma, *née* Booth; *b* 31 December 1959; *Educ* Bishop's Stortford Coll, Univ of Reading (BSc), Univ of Southampton (BM BS), Univ of Edinburgh; *m* 10 Sept 1993, Tina Louise, da of Barry Stott; *Career* trained in psychology, med, psychiatry and psychoanalytic psychotherapy; child and family psychiatrist, adult psychotherapist, business conslt and writer; regular appearer on radio and TV in religious, psychological and science programmes; princ PsychoDynamics Business Consultants; PPL 1989 MRCPsych 1991, memb Soc of Authors 1994; *Books* Churches and How to Survive Them (1994), The Pastoral Encounter - Hidden Depths in Human Contact (1996), Principles of Psychotherapy (1996), The Plug at the Bottom of the Sea (1997), The Switch on the Back of the Moon (1998), Goodnight, Sleep Tight (contrib, 2000); *Style—* Dr Brice Avery; ✉ 4 Millerfield Place, Edinburgh EH9 1LW (tel 0131 662 0687, fax 0131 667 0252, e-mail briceavery@wacdrome.co.uk)

AVERY, Catherine Rosemary Reid (Kate); *b* 30 January 1960; *Educ* Cranfield Sch of Mgmnt (MBA); *m* 10 July 1999, Anthony Vine-Lott, *qv*; *Career* Barclays plc: joined 1978, project mangr then mktg mangr Barclaycard 1987–89, planning, research and budgeting mangr Personal Sector Mktg Dept 1989–91, md Barclays Stockbrokers Ltd 1995–96 (sales and mktg dir 1992–93, business planning dir 1993–95), md Barclays Bank Tst Co Ltd 1995–96; memb Conversion/Flotation Project Team Halifax plc 1996; Legal & General plc: gp mktg dir 1996, gp mktg and direct dir 1996–99, retail customer dir 1999–2001, gp dir partnerships and direct 2001–02, gp dir retail distribution 2002–06, gp exec dir wealth mgmnt 2006–, chair Gp Equality and Diversity Ctee; non-exec dir Kelda Gp plc 2005–; memb Distribution and Regulatory Ctee ABI 2004–; FSI, FCIM, ACIB; *Recreations* sailing, golf, gardening; *Style—* Mrs Kate Avery

AVERY, Dr Charles Henry Francis; s of Richard Francis Avery, of Richmond, Surrey, and Dorothea Cecilia, *née* Wharton; *b* 26 December 1940; *Educ* KCS Wimbledon, St John's Coll Cambridge (MA, PhD), Courtauld Inst of Art London (Academic Dip); *m* 11 June 1966, (Kathleen) Mary, da of Charles Gwynne Jones (d 1969); 3 da (Charlotte Frances, Susanna Mary, Victoria Jane (triplets) b 24 Feb 1970); *Career* dep keeper of sculpture V&A 1965–79, dir Sculpture Dept Christie's 1979–90, currently ind fine art conslt; Leverhulme research fell 1997–99; FSA 1985; Cavaliere Dell'ordine Al Merito della Repubblica Italiana 1979, Medal of Ministry of Culture Poland; *Books* Florentine Renaissance Sculpture (1970), Studies in European Sculpture (1981, 1987), Giambologna the Complete Sculpture (1987), Renaissance and Baroque Bronzes in the Frick Art Museum (1993), Donatello: An Introduction (1994), David Le Marchand (1674–1726), An Ingenious Man for Carving in Ivory (1996), Bernini, Genius of the Baroque (1997), Studies in Italian Sculpture (2001); *Recreations* writing, reading, tennis; *Clubs* Oxford and Cambridge, Beckenham Tennis; *Style—* Dr Charles Avery, FSA; ✉ Holly Tree House, 20 Southend Road, Beckenham, Kent BR3 1SD (tel 020 8650 9933, fax 020 8650 9950)

AVERY, Graham John Lloyd; s of Rev Edward Avery (d 1979), and Alice, *née* Lloyd; *b* 29 October 1943; *Educ* Kingswood Sch Bath, Balliol Coll Oxford (MA), Center for Int Affairs Harvard Univ; *m* 1, 1967, Susan Steele; 2 s (Matthew b 1974, John b 1976); m 2, 2002, Annalisa Cecchi; 1 s (Nicholas b 1993); *Career* MAFF: entered 1965, princ responsible for negotiations for entry to EC 1969–72, princ private sec to Fred Peart then John Silkin 1976; European Commission Brussels 1973–; memb cabinets of: Christopher Soames (vice-pres external rels) 1973–76, Roy Jenkins (pres) 1977–80, Finn Gundelach (cmmr for agric) 1981, Poul Dalsager (cmmr for agric) 1981, Frans Andriessen (vice-pres for agric) 1985–86; served in Directorate Gen for Agric 1981–84 and 1987–90, Directorate Gen for External Rels 1990–98, inspr gen 1998–2000, chief advsr Enlargement 2000–; author of articles in various econ and political jls; Freeman City of Indianapolis; *Style—* Graham Avery, Esq; ✉ European Commission, 1049 Brussels, Belgium (tel 00 32 2 299 2202)

AVERY, (Francis) John; s of Ronald Avery (d 1976), and Linda, *née* Jackson (d 1978); *b* 27 December 1941, Bath, Somerset; *Educ* Clifton Coll Bristol, Lincoln Coll Oxford (MA); *m* 23 Sept 1967, Sarah, *née* Midgley; 3 da (Frances Michelle b 11 Sept 1969, Katherine Joanna Ruth, Rosalind Christine Jane (twins) b 23 Nov 1975), 1 s (Richard Ronald b 6 Aug 1971); *Career* MW 1975; Averys of Bristol: joined 1966, dir 1967–75, md 1975–2003, dir 2003–; chief judge: NZ Nat Wine Show 1978 and 1981, Winpac (Wines of the Pacific Rim) Hong Kong 1989–; judge: Aust Nat Capital Wine Show Canberra 1982, 1986, 1989, 1990, 1998 and 2003, W Aust Wine Show 1985, Royal Melbourne Wine Show 1988 and 1989, Royal Hobart Wine Show 1990, 1996, 1999, 2001 and 2003; jt chm Japan Wine Challenge 2002–; wine advsr Worshipful Co of Grocers 1997–, memb Govt Hospitality Wine Advsy Ctee 1998–; chm: Int Wine and Food Soc 1996–2000, Inst of Masters of Wine 1999–2000; pres Anchor Soc, master Ancient Soc of St Stephen's Ringers 1994–95, memb Cncl St Monica Home for the Aged 1990–2003, memb Fundraising Ctee Bristol Theatre Royal; Liveryman Worshipful Co of Vintners 1964 (memb Ct of Assts 1998, Master 2004–05), memb Soc of Merchant Venturers 1980 (Master 1995–96); memb American Soc of Enologists 1964; *Recreations* skiing, yachting, cricket, watching horse racing and rugby; *Clubs* Garrick, MCC; *Style—* John Avery, Esq; ✉ Flat 2, The Grove, Wrington, Bristol BS40 5NS; Averys of Bristol, 4 High Street, Nailsea BS48 1BT

AVERY, Thomas Tilstone (Tom); s of Julian Avery, and Quenelda, *née* Kinsey; *b* 17 December 1975; *Educ* Harrow, Univ of Bristol (BSc); *Career* explorer; ldr Br Inca Mountains expdn to S American Andes 1997, ldr Br Silk Mountains expdn to Kyrgyzstan (incl 9 virgin summits up to 20,000 feet) 2000, youngest Briton to walk to S Pole (world record time for team travelling from the edge of Antartica to S Pole of 45 days 6 hours) 2002, ldr fastest group to walk to N Pole (Barclays Capital Ultimate North team, retracing Robert Peary's 1909 expedition; world record time of 36 days 22 hours 11 minutes) 2005, youngest Briton to walk to both N and S Pole; ldr and memb of numerous mountaineering expdns to Argentina, Chile, Morocco, Tanzania, NZ and the Himalayas; trainee accountant Arthur Andersen 1998–2000, dir Ski Verbier 2000–02; currently motivational speaker and writer; ambass: Prince's Tst, London 2012 Olympic Games bid; FRGS; *Publications* Pole Dance (2004); *Recreations* skiing, sailing, golf, cricket, mountaineering, foreign travel; *Clubs* MCC, Royal St George's Golf, Rye Golf; *Style—* Tom Avery, Esq; ✉ 26 Ranelagh House, Elystan Place, London SW3 3LD (tel 020 7589 1648, fax 020 7589 1615, e-mail info@tomavery.net)

AVERY JONES, John Francis; CBE (1987); s of Sir Francis Avery Jones, CBE (d 1998), and Dorothea Bessie, *née* Pfirter (d 1983); *b* 5 April 1940; *Educ* Rugby, Trinity Coll Cambridge (MA, PhD, LLM); *Career* admitted slr 1966, ptnr Bircham & Co 1970–85, sr ptnr Speechly Bircham 1985–2001; special cmmr of income tax 2002– (dep special cmmr 1991–2001), chm VAT and Duties Tbnls 2002– (pt/t chm 1991–2001); jt ed British Tax Review 1974–97, memb Editorial Bd Simon's Taxes 1977–2001, visiting prof of taxation LSE 1986–; pres Inst of Taxation 1980–82, chm Tax Law Review Ctee 1998–2005; memb: Keith Ctee 1980–84, Cncl Law Soc 1986–90, Cncl Inst of Fiscal Studies 1988–, Exec Ctee Int Fiscal Assoc 1988–94 (chm Br Branch 1989–91), Bd of Tstees Int Bureau of Fiscal Documentation 1989– (chm 1991–2002), Bd of Govrs Voluntary Hosp of St Bartholomew 1984–, Court of Govrs LSE 1995–; memb Ct of Assts Worshipful Co of Barbers (Master 1985–86), memb Ct of Assts City of London Solicitors' Co (Master 1997–98); memb Law Soc; Hon FTII; *Books* Encyclopedia of VAT (1972), Tax Havens and Measures Against Tax Avoidance and Evasion in the EEC (1974); *Recreations* music (particularly opera); *Clubs* Athenaeum; *Style—* John Avery Jones, Esq, CBE; ✉ The Finance and Tax Tribunals, 15/19 Bedford Avenue, London WC1B 3AS (tel 020 7612 9700, fax 020 7436 4151, e-mail john.averyjones@judiciary.gsi.gov.uk)

AVIS, Alice; da of Anthony Charles Avis (d 2004), of Ilkley, W Yorks, and Helen Lela Kyriacopoulou Avis; *b* 31 May 1962, Bradford, W Yorks; *Educ* Univ of Cambridge (MA), INSEAD (MBA); *m* 6 March 1999, Martyn Ward; 2 da (Daisy b 6 June 1999, Lola b 15 Aug 2001); *Career* account exec BMP 1984–86, conslt Bain & Co 1986–90, head of strategy Still Price Lintas 1991–92, md Cutler & Gross 1992–93, conslt 1993–94, dep md Hartstone plc 1994–95, global brand dir Diageo 1995–99, mktg dir Flutter.com 2000–01, mktg and e-commerce dir Marks & Spencer plc 2003–04, ceo Sanctuary Spa Holdings Ltd 2005–; *Style—* Ms Alice Avis

AWDRY, William Richard (Will); s of Richard Charles Visger Awdry, of Penn, Bucks, and Jocelyn Genesta St George, *née* Poole (d 1990); *b* 11 February 1961; *Educ* Marlborough, BNC Oxford (BA); *m* 5 Dec 1992, Clare Julia, *née* Marshall; *Career* advtg exec; account mgmnt trainee rising to exec McCormick Intermarco Farmer 1983–85; Bartle Bogle Hegarty: copywriter 1986–94, bd dir 1992–94, gp creative head 1993–94; copywriter, head of copy and bd dir The Leagas Delaney Partnership 1994–96, rejoined Bartle Bogle Hegarty 1996, subsequently with Partners BDDH, creative dir int accounts DDB London 2003–; *Recreations* music (percussion drummer on various infrequent occasions), practical as opposed to theoretical oenology; *Style—* Will Awdry, Esq

AWFORD, Ian Charles; s of Joseph Arthur Awford (decd), of Lyme Regis, Dorset, and Eva Rhoda, *née* McPherson (decd); *b* 15 April 1941; *Educ* Wellingborough Sch, Univ of Sheffield (LLB); *m* 1, 24 July 1965 (m dis 1983), Claire Sylvia, da of late Ralph Linklater, of Bexleyheath, Kent; 3 s (James b 16 Nov 1967, Giles b 13 Jan 1969, Guy b 27 Sept 1970); m 2, 2 Sept 1989, Leonora Maureen, da of late Robert James Wilson, of Sydney, Aust; 2 s (Alexander b 18 July 1991, Thomas b 26 April 1993), 1 da (Katherine Louise b 12 Dec 1995); *Career* admitted slr 1967, admitted slr Hong Kong 1988, admitted practitioner Supreme Court of Tasmania 1998, admitted slr Supreme Court of NSW 2002, CEDR accredited mediator 1998, IATA accredited arbitrator; ptnr with Barlow Lyde & Gilbert 1973–2001; Ebsworth and Ebsworth: ptnr 2002–06, special counsel 2006–; dir Int Court of Aviation and Space Arbitration; chm: Outer Space Ctee of the Int Bar Assoc 1985–90, Aerospace Law Ctee of the Asia Pacific Lawyers' Assoc 1987–90, Aerospace Law Ctee of the Inter Pacific Bar Assoc 1990–94; memb: Int Inst of Space Law of the Int Aeronautics Fedn, Int Soc of Air Safety Investigators, Air Law Gp Royal Aeronautical Soc, Air Law Working Gp Int C of C, American Bar Assoc, Int Assoc of Defence Counsel, Aviation Law Assoc of Aust and NZ, Euro Centre for Space Law, Euro Soc for Air Safety Investigators, Fedn of Insurance and Corp Counsel, Centre for Int Legal Studies; FRAeS 1987, FSALS 1998, FICPD 1998; *Books* Developments in Aviation Products Liability (1985), author of various pubns on outer space and aviation legal issues; *Recreations* skiing, art, music, theatre; *Style—* Ian Awford, Esq; ✉ 1 Fitzwilliam Road, Vancluse, Sydney, NSW, Australia (e-mail ian.awford@bigpond.com); Ebsworth and

Ebsworth, Level 21, Deutsche Bank Building, 126 Phillip Street, Sydney, NSW 2000, Australia (tel 00 61 29 234 2484, fax 00 61 29 235 3606, e-mail iawford@ebsworth.com.au)

AWTY, Ted; s of Frank Awty (d 1983), and Louisa Awty (d 2003); *b* 23 May 1951; *Educ* Biddulph GS, Imperial Coll London (BSc); *m* 1, 17 August 1974 (m dis 2006), Jeanette, da of late Samuel Reeves; 2 s (Richard b 28 July 1977, Philip b 1 May 1983), 1 da (Julia b 21 April 1979); m 2, 29 July 2006, June, da of Thomas Taylor; *Career* KPMG: joined 1972, ptnr 1985, head of audit and dir KPMG Audit plc 1998–2002, chm Client Serv Bd 2002–05, memb Bd 2002–05; memb Central Finance Bd Methodist Church; FCA 1978 (ACA 1975); FRSA; *Recreations* motorboating, walking, cinema, theatre, travel; *Style*— Ted Awty, Esq; ✉ KPMG, 8 Salisbury Square, London EC4Y 8BB (tel 020 7311 8328, fax 020 7311 1623, e-mail ted.awty@kpmg.co.uk)

AXE, Royden (Roy); s of Bernard Axe (d 1969), of Scarbrough, N Yorks, and Ruth Ann, *née* Fillingham (d 1992); *b* 17 June 1937; *Educ* Scarborough HS, Coventry Tech Coll; *m* 1961, Brenda Patricia, da of Charles Edgar Tomes; 1 da (Victoria Jane b 25 Dec 1961), 1 s (Christopher Royden b 13 March 1964); *Career* designer; Rootes Motors: joined as body engr/stylist, chief stylist until 1969; design dir Chrysler Europe (following t/o of Rootes) 1969–75, design dir Chrysler Corp USA 1975–82, design dir Austin Rover then Rover Group 1982–92, md Design Research Associates Ltd 1992–99, design conslt 1999–; Liveryman Worshipful Co of Coach Makers and Coach Harness Makers; Hon DUniv Univ of Central England; fell Coventry Univ; *Designs* for Rootes/Chrysler incl: Sunbeam Rapier, Hillman/Chrysler Avenger, Simca 1301, Chrysler 180, Chrysler/Talbot Sunbeam and Alpine, Chrysler Voyager (USA); for Rover incl: 200/400, 800, MG EX-E and Rover CCV concept cars; various others incl Bentley Java 1994, numerous VIP aircraft interiors; *Recreations* travel, design, reading, writing, family, all things related to classic cars; *Style*— Roy Axe, Esq; ✉ e-mail royaxe@aol.com

AXFORD, Dr David Norman; s of Norman Axford (d 1961), and Joy Alicia (d 1970); *b* 14 June 1934; *Educ* Merchant Taylors', Plymouth Coll, St John's Coll Cambridge (MA, PhD), Univ of Southampton (MSc), UNiv of Oxford (Dip); *m* 1, 26 May 1962 (m dis 1979), Elizabeth Anne Moynihan, da of Ralph J Stiles (d 1973); 2 da (Katy b 1964, Sophie b 1966), 1 s (John b 1968); m 2, 8 March 1980, Diana Rosemary Joan, da of Leslie George Bufton (d 1970); 3 step s (Simon b 1959, Timothy b 1961, Jeremy b 1963), 1 step da (Nicola b 1968); *Career* Nat Serv RAF 1958–60, PO 1958, Flying Offr 1959; Meteorological Office: Forecasting and Res 1960–68, Meteorological Res Flight and Radiosondes 1968–76, asst dir Operational Instrumentation 1976–80, asst dir Telecommunications 1980–82, dep dir Observational Servs (grade 5) 1982–84, dir of Servs and dep to DG of Meteorological Office (under sec grade 3) 1984–89; dep sec gen World Meteorological Orgn 1989–95, ret; independent conslt in int meteorology 1995–; conslt to Earthwatch Europe 1996–99; pres N Atlantic Observing Stations Bd 1983–86, chm Ctee of Operational Systems Evaluation 1986–89, vice-pres RMS 1989–91 (memb Cncl and hon gen sec 1983–88, chm Accreditation Bd 1999–2004), vice-pres and treas European Meteorological Soc (EMS) 2002–06 (memb Cncl 2002–06, chm Accreditation Ctee 2002–06); tstee Thames Valley Hospice Windsor 1996–98, tstee Stanford in the Vale Public Purpose Charity 2000– (chm 2000–02, clerk/corr 2002–), memb Exec Ctee Br Assoc of Former UN Civil Servants (BAFUNCS) 1996– (vice-chm 1998–99, chm 1999–2004, vice-pres 2004–), chm Stanford in the Vale Local History Soc 2004–; L G Groves Mem Prize for Meteorology 1970; FRMetS 1962, CEng 1975, FIEE 1982, CMet 1994; *Recreations* swimming, reading, good food and wine, garden, music, family and local history; *Style*— Dr David Axford; ✉ Honey End, 14 Ock Meadow, Stanford in the Vale, Oxfordshire SN7 8LN (tel 01367 718480)

AYAZ, Dr Iftikhar Ahmad; OBE (1998); s of Mukhtar Ahmad Ayaz (d 1969), of Tanzania, and Saleha Ayaz (d 1990); *b* 18 January 1936; *Educ* Univ of Newcastle upon Tyne (BEd), Univ of London (Dip Comparative Educn, DipTEFL, MA), Int Univ Fndn USA (PhD); *m* 6 Dec 1959, Amatul Basit, da of Maulana Abul Ata; 5 da (Rafi b 1962, Bushra b 1963, Quddus b 1969, Farzana b 1978, Sadiya b 1981), 1 s (Intisar b 1964); *Career* Dept of Educn Tanzania 1960–1978, positions incl: teacher, dist educn offr, nat inspr of schs, chm Teacher Educn Panel, head Dept of Educn; sr curriculum advsr Inst of Educn Univ of Dar es Salaam Tanzania 1978–81, publications offr Centre on Integrated Rural Devpt for Africa Arusha Tanzania 1981–85, educn advsr and conslt Cwlth Secretariat 1985–92, UNESCO co-ordinator and mangr Education For Life prog 1992–95, UN Human Rights Cmmn Workshop on Minority Gp Rights 1997–; hon consul for Tuvalu in the UK 1995–; int confs attended incl: Co-operation with Reference to Teaching of Foreign Languages London 1979, UNESCO Sub-Regnl Seminar on Nat Languages in Africa 1979, Consultation on Integrated Nat Action for Rural Children (sponsored by WHO) Nepal 1982, Peace Educn NZ 1987, Educn for All Aust 1990, UNESCO Gen Cncl (head Tuvalu delgn) 26 session 1991, 27 session 1993 and 28 session 1995, World Conf against Racism, Racial Discrimination, Xenophobia and Related Intolerance Durban SA 2001, World Peace Summit South Korea 2003, Poverty Alleviation in SE Asia Conference New Delhi 2004; ed Rural FOCUS and TEAM 1982–1990; broadcaster educn programmes for teachers: Tanzania 1979–81, Tuvalu 1985–88; co-ordinator Language Support for Immigrant Workers 1989; nat pres Ahmadiyya Muslims UK 1997–2001; hon chm RSPCA Tanga 1957–60, hon chm Overseas Students Union Newcastle upon Tyne 1973–75, hon fndr and sec-gen Tanzania Cwlth Soc 1979–84, hon sec East Africa Cwlth Soc for the Prevention of Disablement 1983–84, res advsr American Biographical Inst (ABI) 2007; estab Iftikhar Ayaz Award Fndn for services to humanity by ABI 2007; memb Cwlth Assoc; Alfred Nobel Medal 1991, Hind Ratan and Hind Ratan Gold Medal (India, for services to community and humanity) 2002, Nav Ratan and Nav Ratan Gold Medal (India) 2003, Fedn for World Peace USA Ambassador for Peace Award, Man of the Year 2004, Outstanding Professional Award 2004, NRI Welfare Gold Medal 2004, Int Peace Prize USA, Diplomate Cambridge Blue Book 2005, Glory of India 2005, Genius Laureate of England 2005, Gem of India 2006, Omex India Award of Honour 2006, NRI Extraordinaire 2006; ABI USA: Great Mind of the 21st Century 2004, one of 500 World's Greatest Geniuses 2006; Senator World Nations Congress; dep govr ABIRA; DEd (emeritus) Int Univ Fndn USA; int educn fell Cwlth Inst London 1976–77, Cwlth fellowship for Higher Educn; *Publications* numerous pubns on: educn theory, philosophy and sociology, linguistics, literature, curriculum devpt, HR devpt, culture in educn, peace educn, educn in small states; *Style*— Dr Iftikhar Ayaz, OBE; ✉ Tuvalu House, 230 Worple Road, London SW20 8RH (tel and fax 020 8879 0985, e-mail tuvaluconsulate@netscape.net)

AYCKBOURN, Sir Alan; kt (1997), CBE (1987); s of Horace Ayckbourn, and Irene Maude, *née* Worley; *b* 12 April 1939; *Educ* Haileybury; *m* 1, 1959 (m dis 1997), Christine Helen, *née* Roland; 2 s (Steven, Philip); m 2, 1997, Heather Elizabeth, *née* Stoney; *Career* playwright and theatre director; worked in rep as stage mangr/actor Edinburgh, Worthing, Leatherhead, Oxford and with late Stephen Joseph's Theatre-in-the-Round Scarborough (currently artistic dir Stephen Joseph Theatre), fndr memb Victoria Theatre Stoke-on-Trent 1962, BBC Radio drama prodr Leeds 1964–70, co dir NT 1986–87, Cameron Mackintosh visiting prof of contemporary theatre Univ of Oxford 1992 (concurrently fell St Catherine's Coll Oxford); Lloyd's Private Banking Playwright of the Year Award 1998, Sunday Times Award for Literary Excellence 2001; Hon DLitt: Univ of Hull 1981, Keele Univ 1987, Univ of Leeds 1987, Univ of Bradford 1994, Univ of Cardiff 1995, Univ of Manchester 2003; Hon DUniv: York 1992, Open Univ 1998; FRSL; *London Productions* Mr Whatnot (Arts) 1964, Relatively Speaking (Duke of York's) 1967 and (Greenwich) 1986 (televised 1969 and 1989), How the Other Half Loves (Lyric) 1970 and (Duke of York's) 1988, Time and Time Again (Comedy) 1972 (televised 1976), Absurd Person Singular (Criterion) 1973 (Evening Standard Drama Award Best Comedy 1975, televised 1985), The Norman Conquests (trilogy, Globe) 1974 (Evening Standard Drama Award Best Play, Variety Club of GB Award, Plays and Players Award, televised 1977), Jeeves (musical with Andrew Lloyd Webber, Her Majesty's) 1975, Absent Friends (Garrick) 1975 (televised 1985), Confusions (Apollo) 1976, Bedroom Farce (NT) 1977 (televised 1980), Just Between Ourselves (Queen's) 1977 (televised 1978, Evening Standard Drama Award Best Play), Ten Times Table (Globe) 1978, Joking Apart (Globe) 1979 (Plays and Players Award), Sisterly Feelings (NT) 1980, Taking Steps (Lyric) 1980, Suburban Strains (musical with Paul Todd, Round House) 1981, Season's Greetings (Apollo) 1982 (televised 1986), Way Upstream (NT) 1982 (televised 1987), Making Tracks (musical with Paul Todd, Greenwich) 1983, Intimate Exchanges (Ambassadors) 1984 (French films Smoking/NoSmoking 1994) A Chorus of Disapproval 1985 (also dir, Evening Standard Drama Award Best Comedy, Olivier Award Best Comedy, Drama Award Best Comedy 1985, transferred Lyric 1986, film 1989), Woman in Mind (Vaudeville) 1986 (also dir), A Small Family Business (NT) 1987 (also dir, Evening Standard Drama Award Best Play), Henceforward... (Vaudeville) 1988 (also dir, Evening Standard Drama Award Best Comedy 1989), Man of the Moment (Globe) 1990 (also dir, Evening Standard Drama Award Best Comedy 1990), Invisible Friends (for children, NT) 1991 (also dir), The Revengers' Comedies (Strand) 1991 (also dir, televised 1999), Mr A's Amazing Maze Plays (for children, NT) 1993 (also dir), Time of my Life (Vaudeville) 1993 (also dir), Wildest Dreams (RSC) 1993 (also dir), Communicating Doors (Gielgud and Savoy) 1995 (also dir, Olivier Award nomination for Best Comedy 1996, Writers' Guild Award for Best West End Play 1996), Things We Do For Love (Savoy, Gielgud and Duchess) 1998 (also dir), adaptation of Ostrovsky's The Forest (RNT) 1999, Comic Potential (Lyric) 1999 (also dir), House & Garden (RNT (Olivier/Lyttleton)) 2000 (also dir), Damsels in Distress (trilogy (GamePlan, FlatSpin, RolePlay), Duchess) 2002 (also dir); *Scarborough Productions* Body Language 1990, This Is Where We Came In (for children) 1990, Callisto 5 (for children) 1990, My Very Own Story (for children) 1991, Dreams From A Summer House (a comedy with music by John Pattison) 1992, Haunting Julia 1994, The Musical Jigsaw Play (for children, with music by John Pattison) 1994, By Jeeves 1996 (music by Andrew Lloyd Webber; transferred to Duke of York's, Lyric Theatres (Br Regnl Theatre Awards 1996 Best Musical)), The Champion of Paribanou (for children) 1996, The Boy Who Fell Into A Book (for children) 1998, Callisto #7 1999, Whenever (children's play with music by Denis King) 2000, Snake in the Grass 2002, The Jollies (for children) 2002, Orvin - Champion of Champions (with music by Denis King) 2003, Sugar Daddies 2003, My Sister Sadie 2003, Drowning on Dry Land 2004, Private Fears in Public Places 2004, Miss Yesterday 2004, Improbable Fiction 2005; *Plays directed for National Theatre* Tons of Money 1986, A View from the Bridge 1987, A Small Family Business 1987, 'Tis Pity She's a Whore 1988; *Books* The Norman Conquests (1975), Three Plays (Absurd Person Singular, Absent Friends, Bedroom Farce, 1977), Joking Apart and Other Plays (Just Between Ourselves, Ten Times Table, 1979), Sisterly Feelings and Taking Steps (1981), A Chorus of Disapproval (1986), Woman in Mind (1986), A Small Family Business (1987), Henceforward.... (1988), Mr A's Amazing Maze Plays (1989), Man of the Moment (1990), Invisible Friends (1991), The Revengers' Comedies (1991), Time of My Life (1993), Wildest Dreams (1993), Communicating Doors (1995), Things We Do For Love (1998), The Boy Who Fell into a Book (2000), Comic Potential (1999), House & Garden (2000), Whenever (2002), The Crafty Art of Playmaking (2002), Damsels in Distress (2002), The Jollies (2002), Orvin - Champion of Champions (2003), My Sister Sadie (2003), Snake in the Grass (2004), Plays 3 (2005), Drowning on Dry Land (2006), Improbable Fiction (2007); *Style*— Sir Alan Ayckbourn, CBE; ✉ c/o Casarotto Ramsay & Assoc Ltd, Waverley House, 7–12 Noel Street, London W1F 8GQ (tel 020 7287 4450, fax 020 7287 9128); website www.alanayckbourn.net

AYERS, Kenneth Edwin; *b* 1 April 1938; *Educ* Sherrardswood Sch Welwyn Garden City; *m* 1, 1960 (m dis), Anne Elizabeth, *née* Zoller; 2 da; m 2, 1977, Vivienne Susan Mary, *née* Connolly (decd); 1 step s, 1 step da; m 3, 2006, remarried Anne Elizabeth McQueen Johnston; *Career* actuarial clerk Standard Life Assurance Co 1955–59, ptnr's asst Chase, Henderson & Tennant 1959–62, salesman and analyst Quilter & Co 1962–65, inspr then asst actuary Standard Life Assurance Co 1965–70; Laurie, Millbank & Co: gilt salesman 1970–72, gilt ptnr 1972–84, second sr ptnr and sr gilt ptnr 1984–86; Chase Manhattan Securities: head of sterling fixed interest 1986, gilts business mangr 1987, business devpt mangr bond distribution 1988; Frank Russell Int: client exec 1988–91, dep md 1991–93, md ME region 1993–96, PR 1996–2000, conslt 2000–; advsr Allenbridge Gp plc 1996–; Nat Assoc of Pensions Funds (former chm Investment Cncl); former chm FTSE Actuaries Bond Index Ctee; author of numerous articles on pension fund investment; govr: Museum of London, Bridewell Royal Hosp, Christ's Hosp; chm Speed Events Ctee RAC Motor Sports Assoc 1998– (memb 1990–95 and 1996–); former vice-pres London District St John Ambulance; Order of St John (chm Investment Ctee 1999–2005); memb Common Cncl Ward of Bassishaw (chm Standards Ctee 2001–04, chm Community and Children's Servs Ctee); Sheriff City of London 1995–96, fndr memb Worshipful Co of Actuaries 1979 (memb Ct of Assts 1986, Master 1991–92); FIA, FSS, FPMI; KStJ, Commandeur Ordre Nationale du Mérite (France); *Recreations* motorsport (Br sprint champion 1982); *Clubs* City Livery, Royal Soc of St George, Coleman St Ward, Bassishaw Ward, Cripplegate Ward, Guild of Freemen; *Style*— Kenneth Ayers, Esq; ✉ 8 The Postern, Barbican, London EC2Y 8BJ

AYERS, Prof Michael Richard; s of Dick Ayers, and Sybil Kerr, *née* Rutherglen; *Educ* Battersea GS, St John's Coll Cambridge (BA, PhD); *Career* jr res fell St John's Coll Cambridge 1963–65; Univ of Oxford: fell and tutor in philosophy Wadham Coll 1965–2002 (emeritus fell 2002–), CUF lectr in philosophy 1965–94, reader 1994–96, prof of philosophy 1996–2002; visiting lectr Univ of Calif Berkeley 1964–65 (visiting prof 1979), visiting prof Univ of Oregon 1970–71, Exxon Fndn lectr Johns Hopkins Univ 1983, visiting fell Res Sch of Social Sciences ANU 1993, Gustav Berman lectr and Ida Beam distinguished visiting prof Univ of Iowa 1995, D C Williams lectr for 2000–01 Univ of Maryland 2001, Gabriel Nuchelmans meml lectr Univ of Leiden 2003; chm Editorial Bd Clarendon Edition of Locke's Works 1992– (memb 1984–); memb Academia Europaea 2006; FBA 2001; *Books* Refutation of Determination (1968), Locke: Epistemology and Ontology (2 vols, 1991), The Cambridge History of 17th-century Philosophy (ed with D Garber, 1998); *Recreations* natural history and conservation, walking, gardening; *Style*— Prof Michael Ayers; ✉ Wadham College, Oxford OX1 3PN (tel 01865 277900)

AYKROYD, Sir James Alexander Frederic; 3 Bt (UK 1929), of Birstwith Hall, Harrogate, Co York; s of Bertram Aykroyd (d 1983), and his 1 w, Margot, *née* Graham-Brown; suc his uncle Sir Cecil William Aykroyd, 2 Bt (d 1993); *b* 6 September 1943; *Educ* Eton, Univ of Aix-en-Provence, Univ of Madrid; *m* 1973, Jennifer, da of late Frederick William Marshall, of Porthcawl, Glamorgan; 2 da (Gemma Jane b 1976, Victoria Louise b 1977); *Heir* half-bro, Toby Aykroyd; *Style*— Sir James Aykroyd, Bt; ✉ Birstwith Hall, Harrogate, North Yorkshire HG3 2JW

AYKROYD, Sir William Miles; 3 Bt (UK 1920), of Lightcliffe, W Riding, Co of York, MC (1944); s of Sir Alfred Hammond Aykroyd, 2 Bt (d 1965), and Sylvia, *née* Walker (d 1992); *b* 24 August 1923; *Educ* Charterhouse; *Heir* cous, Michael Aykroyd; *Career* Lt 5 Royal Inniskilling Dragoon Gds 1943–47; dir Hardy Amies 1950–69; *Clubs* Boodle's; *Style*— Sir William Aykroyd, Bt, MC; ✉ Buckland Newton Place, Dorchester, Dorset (tel 01300 345259)

A

AYLEN, Leo William; s of Rt Rev Bishop Charles Arthur William Aylen (Bishop of Zululand, d 1972), and Elisabeth Margaret Anna, *née* Hills (d 1975); bro of Walter Aylen, QC, *qv*; *b* KwaZulu, South Africa; *Educ* New Coll Oxford (MA), Univ of Bristol (PhD); *Career* writer, actor, director; poetry incl: Discontinued Design (1969), I, Odysseus (1971), Sunflower (1976), Return to Zululand (1980), Red Alert: this is a god warning (1981), Jumping-Shoes (1983), Dancing the Impossible: New and Selected Poems (1997); for children: The Apples of Youth (opera 1980), Rhymoceros (poems 1989); contrib to over 100 anthologies incl: The Sun Dancing, What Makes Your Toenails Twinkle, Toughie Toffee, The Songmakers, Never Say Boo to a Ghost, Spaceways, Open the Door, The Methuen Book of Theatre Verse, 100 Major Modern Poets, 100 Favourite Animal Poems, Criminal Records, Big World Little World, A Glass of New Made Wine, The Moonlit Stream, One River Many Creeks; other pubns incl: Greek Tragedy and the Modern World (1964), Greece for Everyone (1976), The Greek Theater (1985); screenwriting incl Gods and Generals (2003); writer/director films for TV incl: 1065 and All that, Dynamo: a life of Michael Faraday, Who'll Buy a Bubble, Celluloid Love, 'Steel be my Sister', Six Bites of the Cherry (series), The Drinking Party (nominated for BAFTA award), The Death of Socrates, Soul of a Nation (documentary), Chaos & Pattern (series of documentaries on cutting-edge scientific experments); radio plays and features incl: The Birds, An Unconquered God, Le Far West, Woman's Brief Season, Zulu Dreamtime, Dancing Bach, Poetry in Action (3 series); theatre works incl: Down the Arches (lyrics), No Trams to Lime Street (adaption of Alun Owen's play), Antigone (dir of own trans); subject of 3 CBS programmes devoted to his work as poet/actor; Royal Literary Fund fell writer in residence Univ of Bath 2001–03; formerly: Hooker Distinguished visiting prof McMaster Univ Ontario, poet in residence Fairleigh Dickinson Univ New Jersey; awarded C Day Lewis Fellowship; prizewinner: Arvon Int Poetry Competition 1992 (commended 1998), Peterloo Poetry Competition 1996 and 2003, Bridport Poetry Competition 2002; memb: Poetry Soc of GB, Writers' Guild of GB, Writers' Guild of America, BECTU, Br Actors' Equity, BAFTA, Soc of Authors, Int PEN; *Recreations* church organ playing, distance running, mountains; *Clubs* BAFTA; *Style*— Leo Aylen; ✉ e-mail leo@leoaylen.demon.co.uk, website www.leoaylen.com

AYLEN, Walter Stafford; QC (1983); s of Rt Rev Bishop Charles Arthur William Aylen (d 1972), and Elisabeth Margaret Anna, *née* Hills (d 1975); bro of Leo Aylen, *qv*; *b* 21 May 1937; *Educ* Winchester, New Coll Oxford (scholar, sr scholar, MA, BCL); *m* 1967, Peggy Elizabeth Lainé Woodford, *qv*, da of Ronald Curtis Woodford; 3 da (Alison b 1968, Frances b 1970, Imogen b 1974); *Career* Nat Serv cmmnd 2 Lt 1 Bn KRRC 1956–57; called to the Bar Middle Temple 1962 (Harmsworth entrance exhibitioner and scholar, bencher 1991); recorder of the Crown Court 1985–2003 (asst recorder 1982), head of chambers 1991–2000, dep judge of the High Court 1993–2005; memb Gen Cncl of the Bar 1994–96, chm BSITC 1994 (vice-chm Fin Ctee 1995–96); ADR Chambers 2000–, memb ADR Int Panel 2001–; FRSA 1989, MCIArb 1999; *Recreations* music (especially lieder and opera), theatre, literature; *Style*— Walter Aylen, Esq, QC; ✉ 24 Fairmount Road, London SW2 2BL (tel 020 8671 7301); Hardwicke Building, New Square, Lincoln's Inn, London WC2A 3SB (tel 020 7242 2523, fax 020 7691 1234, e-mail walter.aylen@hardwicke.co.uk); 15 New Bridge Street, London EC4V 6AU (tel 020 7842 1900, fax 020 7842 1901)

AYLESFORD, 11 Earl of (GB 1714); Charles Ian Finch-Knightley; JP (Warks 1948); also Baron Guernsey (GB 1702); s of 10 Earl of Aylesford (d 1958); *b* 2 November 1918; *Educ* Oundle; *m* 1946, Margaret Rosemary (d 1989), da of Maj Austin Tyer, MVO, TD; 1 s, 2 da; *Heir* s, Lord Guernsey; *Career* served WWII Capt Black Watch; Vice-Lt Warks 1964–74, HM Lord-Lt W Midlands 1974–94; former regnl dir Lloyds Bank Birmingham & W Midlands Bd (resigned 1989); memb Water Space Amenity Cmmn 1973–83; patron Warks Boy Scouts Assoc 1974– (co cmmr 1949–74); pres: Warks CCC 1980–99, TAVRA 1982; Hon LLD Univ of Birmingham 1989; KStJ 1974; *Recreations* shooting, fishing, archery, nature conservation, preservation of wildlife; *Clubs* Flyfishers'; *Style*— The Rt Hon the Earl of Aylesford; ✉ Packington Old Hall, Coventry CV7 7HG (tel 01676 523273, office 01676 522020, office fax 01676 523399)

AYLETT, Philip John; s of late Leonard Charles Aylett, of Knutsford, Cheshire, and Mair Marguerite Aylett; *b* 7 December 1951; *Educ* Wilmslow GS, Mansfield Coll Oxford (MA), Univ of Manchester (MPhil); *m* 1978, Anne Maria, da Alexander Rowles; 1 s (Christopher b 1983), 1 da (Sophie b 1987); *Career* various posts Nat Tst Tatton Park 1976–79, communications offr Univ of Manchester 1979–84, press offr Central Office of Information NW Region 1984–86; sr press offr: Dept of the Environment 1986–88, DTI 1988–89, Prime Minister's Office 1989–91; chief press offr Dept of Health 1991–93, press offr (Europe) FCO 1993–95, head of information ODA (later Dept for Int Devpt) 1995–98, head of news Dept of Health 1998–99, press sec Neill Ctee 1999–2001, clerk Public Admin Ctee House of Commons 2001–05; Office of the Parly and Health Serv Ombudsman: dir of strategy and communications 2005–07, dir of policy, info and communication 2007–; chm Standards Ctee Herts CC; FRSA; *Publications* several articles on the history of lawyers in 18th century England; *Recreations* reading about history and politics, listening to music, watching football; *Style*— Philip Aylett, Esq; ✉ Office of Parliamentary and Health Service Ombudsman, Millbank Tower, Millbank, London SW1P 4QP (tel 020 7217 4225, e-mail philip.aylett@ombudsman.org.uk)

AYLING, Robert John; *b* 3 August 1946; *Educ* KCS Wimbledon; *m* 1972, Julia, *née* Crallan; 2 s, 1 da; *Career* admitted slr 1968; Elborne Mitchell & Co: joined 1969, ptnr 1971; DTI (formerly Dept of Trade): legal advsr 1974–79, asst slr and head of Aviation Law Branch 1979, UK delg UN Cmmn for International Trade Law 1979–83, under sec (legal) 1983–85; British Airways plc: legal dir 1985–91, co sec 1987–91, human resources dir 1988–91, mktg and ops dir 1991–93, gp md 1993–96, chief exec 1996–2000; non-exec chm Holidaybreak plc 2003–, chm Sanctuary Group plc 2006–; non-exec dir: Royal & Sun Alliance Insurance Gp plc 1993–2004, Business in the Community 1995–2000, BTA 1996–99, New Millennium Experience Co 1996–2000, Qantas Airways Ltd 1996–2000, Dyson Ltd 2001–; govr KCS Wimbledon 1995–2006; Hon LLD Brunel Univ 1996; *Clubs* Brooks's; *Style*— Robert Ayling, Esq

AYLMER, 14 Baron (I 1718); Sir (Anthony) Julian Aylmer; 17 Bt (I 1662), of Balrath; o s of 13 Baron Aylmer (d 2006); *b* 10 December 1951; *Educ* Westminster, Trinity Hall Cambridge; *m* 5 May 1990, Belinda Rosemary, o da of Maj Peter Parker (gs of 6 Earl of Macclesfield), of The Hays, Ramsden, Oxford; 1 s (Hon Michael Henry b 21 March 1991), 1 da (Hon Rosemary Sofia b 11 Dec 1993); *Heir* s, Hon Michael Aylmer; *Career* admitted slr 1976, ptnr Reynolds Porter Chamberlain 1982–; *Clubs* Brooks's; *Style*— The Lord Aylmer; ✉ 16 Edgarley Terrace, London SW6 6QF; Reynolds Porter Chamberlain LLP, Tower Bridge House, St Katharine's Way, London E1W 1AA (tel 020 3060 6000, fax 020 3060 7000)

AYLMER, Sir Richard John; 16 Bt (I 1622), of Donadea, Co Kildare; s of Sir Fenton Gerald Aylmer, 15 Bt (d 1987), and Rosalind Boultbee, *née* Bell (d 1991); *b* 23 April 1937; *m* 16 June 1962, Lise, da of Paul Emile Demers, of Montreal, Canada; 1 da (Geneviève b 16 March 1963), 1 s (Fenton Paul b 31 Oct 1965); *Heir* s, Fenton Aylmer; *Career* writer; *Style*— Sir Richard Aylmer, Bt

AYLOTT, Robert Alexander William; s of Rueben David Aylott (d 1978), of Hants, and Colleen Joy, *née* Horne; *b* 21 December 1948; *Educ* Charterhouse, Harrison Road; *m* 24 Oct 1970 (m dis 1999), Heather Jean, da of Philip Foot; 1 s (James Alexander Robert b 17 Dec 1973), 1 da (Michelle Heather b 28 Oct 1976); m 2, 23 March 2000 (m dis 2007), Denise Crawley; *Career* photo-journalist; darkroom asst: Sport & General Photo Agency Fleet Street 1964–65, Fox Photos London 1966–67; press photographer: Keystone Press Agency Fleet Street 1967–69, Daily Sketch 1969–70, Daily Mail 1970–75; photographer National Enquirer USA 1975–78; proprietor Front Page Press (Newspaper and Publishers) Hants 1978–87, photographer Express Newspapers 1987–95; features editor Amateur Photographer Magazine 2001; work exhibited at: World Press Photographers of the Year 1969, ICA Gallery 1972, first Press Exhibition (Photographers' Gallery London) 1972; contrib various books incl: Photography Year Books 1973–89, Eye Witness and Headline Photography (by Harold Evans), Chronicles of the 20th Century, Slip-Up, Naked Eye Astronomy (by Patrick Moore); awards incl: News Photographer of the Year 1968, Colour Sequence of the Year 1971, Nikon Picture of the Year 1972, World Press Photos Portrait Section 1977; fell Inst of Inc Photographers 1973, FRPS 1973; *Publications* Local History Publications: Fareham Two Views (1981), Unofficial Guide to Fareham (1982), Isle of Wight - Two Views (1982), Gosport - Two Views (1982), The Story of Porchester Castle (1983); *Recreations* painting, writing, photographic history; *Clubs* Press; *Style*— Robert Aylott, Esq; ✉ tel 07802 777373

AYLWARD, Adrian John Francis; s of John James Aylward (d 1978), and Cynthia, *née* Minch (d 1966); *b* 12 November 1957; *Educ* Worth Sch Sussex, Exeter Coll Oxford (BA), King's Coll London (PGCE); *m* Aug 1990, Caroline Lesley, da of John Cramer; 2 da (Molly b Aug 1991, Freya b Aug 1996), 1 s (Joseph b Dec 1994); *Career* headmaster; former investment banker 1981–86, with Royal Sovereign Gp plc (latterly chief exec) 1986–91, dir Emess plc 1990–91, housemaster/head of religious studies Downside Sch 1992–96, headmaster Stonyhurst Coll 1996–; memb Irish Assoc, KM; *Recreations* fishing, philosophy, sport, travel; *Clubs* Brooks's; *Style*— Adrian Aylward, Esq; ✉ Stonyhurst College, Stonyhurst, Lancashire BB7 9PZ (tel 01254 826345, fax 01254 826013)

AYLWARD, Prof Mansel; CB (2002); s of John Aylward (d 1991), and Cora Doreen, *née* Evans (d 2003); *b* 29 November 1942, Merthyr Tydfil; *Educ* Cyfarthfa Castle GS Merthyr Tydfil, Jesus Coll Oxford (BSc, Price open entrance scholar), London Hosp Med Coll Univ of London (MB BS, Buxton Prize, George Riddoch Prize); *m* 17 Aug 1963, Angela Bridget, *née* Besley; 1 s (Simon Mansel b 19 Jan 1965), 1 da (Rebecca Bridget b 24 July 1968); *Career* demonstrator in physiology London Hosp Med Coll 1963–66, house offr London Hosp 1967–68, MRC res fell (surgery) Experimental Surgery Dept London Hosp 1968–69, lectr in surgery London Hosp Med Coll 1969, GP Merthyr Tydfil and S Brecnockshire 1969–73, clinical asst minor surgery St Tydfil's Hosp Merthyr Tydfil 1970–76, research physician Singleton Hosp Swansea and Merthyr and Cynon Valleys 1973–76, chm and md Simbec Research Ltd Wales 1974–84 (BBC Company of the Year Award 1979, European Small Business Award 1980), pres Simbec Research (USA) Inc 1980–84, dir of clinical research Lyonaisse Industrielle Pharmaceutique France 1982–84, regnl med offr DHSS Cardiff 1985–88, SMO DSS London 1988–90, med sec Attendance Allowance Bd London 1990–91, princ med offr and dir of med policy Benefits Agency London 1991–95, CMO, med dir and chief scientist Dept for Work and Pensions (formerly DSS) 1995–2005, hon prof Univ of Wales Coll of Med 2002–, dir Unum Centre for Psychosocial and Disability Research Sch of Psychology and prof Cardiff Univ 2004–, chm Wales Centre for Health Welsh Assembly Govt Cardiff 2005–, chm Royal Mail Attendance Acad 2006–; dir Women's Health Concern London 1976–86; chief med advsr Veterans Agency MOD 2001–05, med advsr States of Jersey, conslt Social Security Admin USA; visiting prof Harvard Univ; non-exec dir: Elision Gp Ltd, Health Claims Bureau Ltd, AGIRX Ltd; memn Industrial Injuries Advsy Cncl 2005–memb Health Honours Ctee; vice-pres Shaw Tst 2006–; patron Vocational Rehabilitation Assoc; Expert Agrée Medicine Interne France 1982; FRSM 1981 (academic dean and hon treas), FFPM 1991, fell Assurance Med Soc 1997, FRCP 2001, DDAM 2001, FFOM 2003, hon memb Irish Soc of Occupational Med 2004, memb Soc of Occupational Med 2006; *Publications* Management of the Menopause and Post-menopausal Years (1975), The Disability Handbook (jt ed, 1991, 2 edn 1998), Back Pain, Incapacity for Work and Social Security Benefits: An international review and analysis (jtly, 2005), The Scientific and Conceptual Basis of Incapacity Benefits (jtly, 2005), The Power of Belief (jt ed, 2006); book chapters and papers; *Recreations* military history, travel, theatre, grandchildren, dining, reading everything, politics; *Clubs* Athenaeum; *Style*— Prof Mansel Aylward, CB; ✉ Cefn Cottage, Cefn Coed-y-Cymer, Merthyr Tydfil CF48 2PH (tel 01685 722324, fax 01685 375009); Unum Provident Centre for Psychosocial and Disability Research, Cardiff University, 51a Park Place, Cardiff CF10 3AT (tel 029 2087 9311, fax 029 2087 0196, e-mail aylwardm@cardiff.ac.uk)

AYLWIN, John Morris; s of Walter Edgar Aylwin (d 1978), of Worcs, and Rosamund, *née* Byng-Morris (d 1978); *b* 23 July 1942; *Educ* Uppingham, Emmanuel Coll Cambridge (MA), Coll of Law Guildford; *m* 4 July 1970, Angela, da of Conningsby Deryck Phillips (d 1995); 2 s (Michael Deryck Morris b 22 April 1972, Christopher John b 16 May 1974); *Career* Richards Butler solicitors: articled clerk 1965–67, asst slr 1967–72, ptnr 1972–2001, exec ptnr 1984–91, head of Environmental Law Gp 1991–2001, conslt 2001–03; memb Law Soc 1965, MInstD 1999; *Recreations* tennis, golf, rugby, gardening, theatre; *Clubs* Richmond FC, Dorking RFC, Rusper Golf; *Style*— J M Aylwin, Esq; ✉ Fair Ridge, Parkgate Road, Newdigate, Surrey RH5 5DX

AYRE, Richard; *b* 1949; *Educ* Univ of Durham; *Career* BBC 1972–2000: news trainee working on Today prog Radio 4, Radio Solent and Belfast 1972–74, regnl journalist Belfast 1974, reporter Belfast 1975–76, dep news ed NI 1976–79, dep news ed Intake TV News rising to home news ed TV News 1979–82, six month fellowship in broadcast journalism Univ of Chicago 1984–85, ed Special Projects TV News 1985–87, chief asst to Dep Dir News and Current Affrs then to Dir News and Current Affrs 1987–88, head of editorial devpt News and Current Affrs 1988–89, head of BBC Westminster 1990–93, controller Editorial Policy 1993–96, dep chief exec BBC News 1996–; conslt in mgmnt and media ethics 2000–, Civil Service cmmr 2005–06; chm Asian and Afro-Caribbean Reporters' Tst 1997–2000, tstee and int bd memb Article 19 - The Global Campaign for Freedom of Expression 1999–2005 (chm 2002–05), memb Bd Food Standards Agency 2000–07, freedom of info adjudicator Law Soc 2001–, bd memb for Eng Ofcom Content Bd 2006–; govr Teachers' TV 2006–; *Style*— Richard Ayre, Esq; ✉ The Old Dairy, Burgh Hall, Burgh Parva, Melton Constable, Norfolk NR24 2PU (e-mail richardayre@whats2hide.com)

AYRES, Gillian; OBE (1986); da of Stephen Ayres (d 1969), of Barnes, London, and Florence Olive, *née* Beresford Brown (d 1968); *b* 3 February 1930; *Educ* St Paul's Girls' Sch, Camberwell Sch of Art; *m* (m dis); 2 s (James, Sam); *Career* artist; teacher 1959–81 (Corham 1959–65, St Martin's 1966–78, head BA Painting Dept Winchester Sch of Art 1978–81); one-woman exhibitions incl: Knoedler Gallery London 1966–88, retrospective Serpentine Gallery 1983, Knoedler Gallery NY 1985, Fischer Fine Art 1990, RA 1997; sole Br rep in Indian Triennale Delhi 1991; works in public collections incl: Tate Gallery, MOMA NY, V&A; maj Arts Cncl bursary 1979; Br Cncl prizewinner Tokyo Biennale 1963, John Moores 2nd prize 1982, Charles Woolaston Award RA 1989, Critics' Prize RA 1990, Indian Triennale Gold Medal 1991; Hon DLit London 1994, hon fell Univ of the Arts London 2005; sr fell RCA 1996; ARA 1982, RA 1991; *Style*— Miss Gillian Ayres, OBE; ✉ c/o Alan Cristea Gallery, 31 Cork Street, London W1S 3NU (tel 020 7439 1866)

AYRES, Prof Jonathan Geoffrey (Jon); *b* 14 February 1950; *Educ* Woodhouse GS Finchley, Guy's Hosp (BSc, MB BS, MD); m; 1 s, 1 da; *Career* Guy's Hosp: house offr 1974–75, SHO 1976–78, res registrar 1979–81, registrar 1978–79 and 1981–82; SHO Brompton Hosp 1977–78, sr registrar E Birmingham Hosp 1982–84, conslt physician in respiratory and gen med Birmingham Heartlands Hosp 1984–2002, prof of respiratory med Univ of

Birmingham 2000–02, prof of respiratory med Univ of Warwick 1996–2000, prof of environmental and occupational med Univ of Aberdeen, hon conslt physician Aberdeen Royal Infirmary; author of numerous scientific pubns on severe asthma and health effects of air pollution; chm: Ctee on Medical Effects of Air Pollution Dept of Health 2001– (memb 1992–2001), Advsy Ctee on Pesticides DEFRA 2006–; memb: Br Thoracic Soc, American Thoracic Soc 1986, Int Epidemiology Assoc 1986, European Respiratory Soc 1988, Expert Panel on Air Quality Standards (DOE) 1994–, Soc of Occupational Medicine; FRCP 1989, FRCP(Edin) 2003, FFOM 2005; *Recreations* sketching in pencil and watercolours, singing; *Style*— Prof Jon Ayres; ✉ Department of Environmental and Occupational Medicine, University of Aberdeen, Foresterhill Road, Aberdeen AB25 2ZP (tel 01224 558188, e-mail j.g.ayres@abdn.ac.uk)

AYRES, Pam (Mrs Dudley Russell); MBE (2004); da of Stanley William Ayres (d 1981), of Stanford in the Vale, Oxon, and Phyllis Evelyn, *née* Loder (d 2001); *b* 14 March 1947; *Educ* Faringdon Secdy Modern Sch; *m* 1982, Dudley Russell, s of late Joe Russell; 2 s (William Stanley b 12 Dec 1982, James Joseph b 20 July 1984); *Career* poet, writer and entertainer 1974–; presenter: The Pam Ayres Radio Show (BBC Radio 2) 1996–99, Pam Ayres Open Road (BBC Radio 2) 2000–01, Ayres on the Air (BBC Radio 4) 2004 and 2006; *Books* incl Pam Ayres: Surgically Enhanced (2006); *Style*— Ms Pam Ayres, MBE; ✉ PO Box 64, Cirencester, Gloucestershire GL7 5YD (tel 01285 644622, fax 01285 642291)

AYRES, Rosalind Mary (Mrs Martin Jarvis); da of Sam Johnson (d 1986), of Westbury, Wilts, and Daisy, *née* Hydon (d 1987); *b* 7 December 1946; *Educ* George Dixon GS for Girls Birmingham, Loughborough Coll of Educn (Dip Educn); *m* 23 Nov 1974, Martin Jarvis, Esq, OBE, *qv*, s of Denys Jarvis, of Sanderstead, Surrey; *Career* actress, dir and prodr; *Theatre* incl: Hamlet, The Three Sisters, Uncle Vanya, The Perfect Party (Greenwich), Dracula (Shaftesbury), I Claudius (Queens's), A Dolls House (Thorndike), Exchange (Vaudeville), Just Between Ourselves (Greenwich), Now You Know (Hampstead); for LA Theatre Works: Make and Break, Exchange, Private Lives, The Third Man, The Norman Conquests, Thank You Jeeves (dir), The Doctor's Dilemma (dir), Another Time (dir); *Radio* A Room With A View, The Circle, Alphabetical Order, Modern Gal (dir), Black Pearls (dir), Spies (dir), On the Waterfront (dir), Glengarry Glen Ross (dir); for NPR USA: The Doctor's Dilemma, Thank You Jeeves, Another Time, Cakewalk (Audie Award), Ten by Maugham (Audie Award), The Cherry Orchard, The Lion in Winter (dir), Orson's Shadow (dir), Breaking the Code (dir), Betrayal (dir); *Television* incl: The Mill, The House of Bernarda Alba, Juliet Bravo, The Bounder (series), Father's Day (series), Hindle Wakes, The Good Guys, Casualty, The Cinder Path (mini-series), A Face to Die For (mini-series, US), Heartbeat, Chicago Hope (US), Profiler (US), Just Shoot Me (series, US), Trevor's World of Sport; *Film* incl: The Lovers, Tales from Beyond the Grave, Mr Smith, Cry Wolf, That'll be the Day, Stardust, The Slipper and the Rose, Emily's Ghost, Black Beauty, Titanic, Gods and Monsters, Beautiful People, Christmas in the Clouds; *Recreations* interior design, illustration; *Style*— Ms Rosalind Ayres; ✉ c/o Lou Coulson, 37 Berwick Street, London W1V 3RF (tel 020 7734 9633, fax 020 7439 7569); c/o Badgley Connor, 9229 Sunset Boulevard, Suite 311, Los Angeles, CA 90069 USA (tel 00 1 310 278 9313)

AYRES-BENNETT, Prof Wendy Margaret; da of Charles Ernest Banks (d 2004), and Olive Margaret, *née* Heath (d 1996); *b* 18 February 1958, Farnborough, Hants; *Educ* Nonsuch HS for Girls Cheam, Girton Coll Cambridge (BA), Univ of Oxford (PhD); *m* 22 Sept 1983, Andrew Bennett; 2 s (Matthew James b 15 Dec 1985, Luke Richard b 24 June 1990); *Career* Julia Mann research fell St Hilda's Coll Oxford 1982–83; successively asst lectr, lectr, reader then prof Univ of Cambridge 1983– (head Dept of French 2001–05); fell Queens' Coll Cambridge 1987–2001, fell New Hall Cambridge 2001–; memb: Editorial Bd Legenda 1995–2005, Advsy Editorial Bd Jl of French Language Studies 2003–; pres Soc for French Studies 2000–02 (vice-pres 1999–2000 and 2002–03); Prix d'Académie 1987; *Books* Vaugelas and the Development of the French Language (1987), A History of the French Language Through Texts (1996), Les Remarques de l'Académie Française sur le Quinte-Curce de Vaugelas (with P Caron, 1996), Problems and Perspectives: Studies in the Modern French Language (with J Carruthers, 2000), Sociolinguistic Variation in Seventeenth-Century France (2004); *Recreations* music; *Style*— Prof Wendy Ayres-Bennett; ✉ Department of French, University of Cambridge, Sidgwick Avenue, Cambridge CB3 9DA (tel 01223 335009, fax 01223 335062, e-mail wmb1001@cam.ac.uk)

AYRTON, Pete; s of Alfred Ayrton (d 1988), and Kyra Gerard, *née* Diment (d 1971); *b* 17 July 1943; *Educ* Stowe Sch, ChCh Oxford (BA), Bedford Coll London (MPhil); *m* 30 June 1995, Sarah Martin; 1 da (Carla b 19 Feb 1986), 1 s (Oscar b 31 Dec 1988); *Career* translator for various publishers 1967–72, ed Pluto Press 1972–86, fndr Serpent's Tail 1986–; memb PEN; Sunday Times Small Publisher of the Year 1988; *Recreations* sampling N London gastropubs, listening to Chet Baker; *Style*— Pete Ayrton, Esq

AZAGURY-PARTRIDGE, Solange; da of Albert and Esther Azagury; *Career* jewellery designer; asst Butler & Wilson, asst Gordon Watson art dealer; set up own business 1990, opened London shop 1995–, numerous jewellery and interior design commissions; creative dir Boucheron 2002–04, designed collection for H&M Christmas 2005; nominated Designer of the Year Design Museum 2003; *Exhibitions* Design Museum 2003, Musée des Arts Decoratifs du Louvre Paris 2004; *Style*— Mrs Solange Azagury-Partridge; ✉ 187 Westbourne Grove, London W11 2SB (tel and fax 020 7792 0197, e-mail info@solange.info)

AZIM-KHAN, Rafi; s of Tariq Azim-Khan, and Adeline Azim-Khan; *b* London; *Educ* Cranbrook Coll, Queen Mary Coll Univ of London (LLB), Coll of Law London; *m* Rebecca, *née* Bentley-Taylor; 1 da (Amélie Sophia Farah b 27 March 2005); *Career* admitted slr 1993; slr: Lewis Silkin 1993–95, Cameron McKenna 1995–97, Theodore Goddard 1997–2000; ptnr and head of e-business and mktg law McDermott, Will & Emery LLP 2000–03, ptnr and head of mktg law and e-commerce Wragge & Co LLP 2003–; memb Law Soc; *Publications* Regulation of the Internet (2001), E-Business: A Practical Guide (conslt ed, 2002), International Sales Promotion (2003), E-Commerce Cradle to Grave (2003), Encyclopaedia of E-Commerce Law (2005), Ad Law (co-author, 2005); *Recreations* motor racing, travel, football, tennis, music; *Clubs* P1; *Style*— Rafi Azim-Khan, Esq; ✉ Wragge & Co LLP, 3 Waterhouse Square, 142 Holborn, London EC1N 2SW (tel 0870 903 1000, e-mail rafiazimkhan@wragge.com)

AZIS, Jonathan Giles Ashley; s of Osman Azis, and Irene Elizabeth Winifred May, *née* Dean; *b* 14 April 1957; *Educ* Millfield, Pembroke Coll Oxford (MA); *m* 18 Aug 1984, Emily Susanna, da of Michael Fenwick Briggs, of Bath, and Isabel Colegate; 2 da (Matilda Winifred Katherine b 18 Dec 1986, Constance Irene Isabel b 28 Nov 1988), 1 s (Arthur Jonathan Osman b 25 March 1993); *Career* Barretts (slrs) 1979–82 and 1984–87, Walker Martineau (slrs) 1982–84, Nabarro Nathanson 1987, Kingston Smith (CAs) 1987–90, Beazer plc 1990–92; dir: Hanson plc 1997–98 (joined 1992, co sec 1995–97), Hanson Capital Ltd 1999–, Hanson Transport Gp 1999–2007; chief of staff Lord Hanson 1998–2004; chm Isotron plc 2003–07 (non-exec dir 2002), non-exec dir Victrex plc 2003–, finance dir Hanson Westhouse 2006–; tstee: Prostate Cancer Charity 1998–2006, Lord Hanson Fndn 1999–; memb Cncl Royal Albert Hall 2005–; memb Law Soc; FRSA; *Recreations* books, music, ironing; *Clubs* Brooks's, Lansdowne; *Style*— Jonathan Azis, Esq; ✉ Westwood Manor, Bradford on Avon, Wiltshire BA15 2AF (tel 01225 863374, fax 01225 867316, e-mail jonathan@azis.co.uk)

AZIZ, Khalid; LVO (1997), DL (Hants 1998); s of Ahmad Aziz (d 1978), of London, and Sheila Frances, *née* Light; *b* 9 August 1953; *Educ* Westminster City Sch, Aitcheson Coll Lahore; *m* 1, 27 March 1974 (m dis), Barbara Elizabeth, da of Harry Etchells, of Sherburn in Elmet, N Yorks; 2 da (Nadira b 1977, Fleur b 1981); m 2, 16 June 1994, Kim Kemp, da of Muriel Haslam, of Bassett, Hants; *Career* broadcaster, journalist and dir; prodr/presenter: BBC Radio and TV 1970–81, TVS 1981–91; presenter: On Course (Channel 4) 1988–89, The Small Business Programme (BBC2/Channel 4) 1990, Starnet Business Programme 1990; TV Journalist of the Year 1987–88; chm: The Aziz Corporation (specialists in spoken communication) 1983–, The Safe Partnership 1997–2002, The Dever Soc 2000–03 (pres 2006–), Accipitor Ltd 2005–; visiting professorial fell Sch of Mgmnt Univ of Southampton 2004–, hon prof Univ of Winchester 2006–; chm: Communication Ctee RAC Cirencester 1991–94, The Wessex Children's Hospice Tst 1992–97 and 1999–, Prince's Tst Hants 1977–97, S Counties Bd Prince's Youth Business Tst 1977–97; memb Advsy Ctee Office for Nat Statistics 1996–98; tstee: Winchester Med Tst, Winchester Med Fndn 1995–, Memorial Gates Tst 2000–; vice-pres Pestalozzi Int Children's Village; FRSA 2000; *Books* author of 11 books incl: The Barclays Guide to Small Business Computing (1990), Presenting to Win (2000); Managing in a Crisis (2004); monthly column in Management Today; *Recreations* aviation, fishing, shooting, computers; *Clubs* Naval and Military; *Style*— Khalid Aziz, Esq, LVO, DL; ✉ No 1, Aziz Court, Parkhill, Winchester, Hampshire SO21 3QX (tel 01962 774766, e-mail khalid@azizcorp.com, website www.azizcorp.com)

AZIZ, Mohammed Abdul; s of Moinul Islam, of Bangladesh, and Sundora Khatun; *b* 28 February 1971, Bangladesh; *Educ* St Paul's Way Sch Bow, Christ Church Coll Univ of Kent at Canterbury, UCL (LLB, LLM, PGCLE), Inns of Ct Sch of Law London; *m* 31 Oct 1998, Zayneb Duaa Izzidien; 1 s (Ihsan Karim b 30 Nov 2002), 1 da (Iman Sakinah b 30 Sept 2004); *Career* called to the Bar Gray's Inn 1997; home-sch liaison offr London Borough of Tower Hamlets 1992–94, co-ordinator religious studies prog Tower Hamlets Coll 1994–97, co-ordinator legal studies prog Islamic Fndn 1995–97, successively racial harrassment project offr, housing lawyer and princ racial harrassment policy offr London Borough of Tower Hamlets 1997–2000, founding ceo Forum Against Islamophobia and Racism 2000–02, founding ceo Br Muslim Research Centre 2002–04, co-dir FaithWise Ltd 2004–; cmmr: Cmmn for Racial Equality 2004–, Equal Opportunites Cmmn 2005–; memb: Nat Exec Ctee Young Muslim Orgn 1991–94, Nat Exec Ctee Fedn of Students Islamic Socs 1994–96, Nat Exec Ctee Assoc of Muslim Social Scientists 1998–2002 (sec 2000–02), Nat Exec Ctee Assoc of Muslim Lawyers 1998–2001, Nat Police-Community Consultative Panel Met Police Serv/ACPO 2001–02, Community Cohesion Faith Practitioners Panel Home Office 2002–03, Equality and Diversity Forum 2002–, Faith Princs' Chief Advsrs Gp 2002–, Panel of Advsrs on Interface with Faith Communities Home Office 2003–04, Mgmnt Ctee UK Race & Europe Network 2003–, Bd European Network Against Racism (ENAR) 2004–, Task Force then Steering Gp Cmmn for Equality and Human Rights DTI 2003–, Advsy Gp on Social Housing ODPM 2004–, Ind Advsy Gp London Criminal Justice Bd 2004–06, Cncl Liberty 2004–, Govt's Review of Treasy Counsel Appts 2004–, Reference Gp Govt's Review of Equalities 2005–, Honours Ctee (state and community, voluntary and local servs) 2005–; chair Security Working Gp Preventing Extremism Taskforce Home Office 2005–06; tstee: E London Mosque and London Muslim Centre 1992–, Book Fndn 2000–; *Recreations* swimming, gardening, reading; *Style*— Mohammed Aziz, Esq; ✉ FaithWise, 35 Glengall Grove, Docklands, London E14 3NE (tel 020 7093 4300, fax 020 7093 4700, e-mail maziz@faithwise.co.uk)

AZIZ, Suhail Ibne; s of Azizur Rahnan (d 1971), of Bangladesh, and Lutfunnessa Khatoon; *b* 3 October 1937; *Educ* RNC Dartmouth, Univ of London (MSc Econ); *m* 1960, Elizabeth Ann, da of Alfred Pyne, of Dartmouth; 2 da (Lisa, Rebecca); *Career* served Pakistan Navy 1954–61, served as RAF Offr 1968–70; personnel mangr Lever Bros Pakistan Ltd 1963–66, industrial rels offr London 1970–73, labour rels exec Ford Motor Co UK 1973–74, personnel offr Pedigree Petfoods 1974–78, dir Gen Servs Divs Cmmn for Racial Equality 1978–81, PA Int Mgmnt Conslts 1981–83, head Econ and Employment Div and dep dir London Borough of Lewisham 1984–89, mgmnt conslt Fullemploy Consultancy 1989–90, chm and md The Brettonwood Partnership Ltd 1990–; exec memb Nottingham Community Relations Cncl 1975–78; memb: Race Relations Bd Conciliation Ctee 1971–74, Gulbenkian Fndn 1976–82, Home Sec's Standing Advsy Cncl 1977–78, Dept of Employment Min's Employment Advsy Gp 1977–78, Advsy Ctee BBC 1977–82, Employers Panel Industrial Tbnls 1978–96, Bd of Tstees Brixton Neighbourhood Community Assoc 1979–82, Cncl Inst of Mgmnt Conslts 1988–91, 1991–93 and 1995–98, Exec Ctee Common Purpose 1991–94, Isle of Dogs Community Tst 1991–92, Res Advsy Ctee Queen Mary & Westfield Coll London 1987–95, Steering Ctee Devpt Policy Forum DFID 1998–99; chm: Third World Specialist Gp Inst of Mgmnt Conslts 1984–91, Developing Countries Gp 1991–95, Lambeth Healthcare NHS Trust 1997–99, Community Health South London NHS Tst 1999–2000; fndr chm E London Bangladeshi Enterprise Agency 1985, advsr Minority Business Devpt Unit City of London Poly 1986, tstee and dir East End Tourism Tst 1991–93; cmmr Cwlth Scholarship Cmmn 1996–, selected tstee SE London Community Fndn 1996–, tstee Community Devpt Fndn (Home Office) 1999–, govr London Guildhall Univ 1995–2002, govr Lambeth Coll 2000–, chair Gtr London Probation Bd (Home Office) 2001–; CRE bursary to USA to study minority econ devpt initiatives 1986, led preparation of Bangladeshi community response to House of Commons Select Ctee report Bangladeshis in Britain and assisted organisations in the preparation of implementation plans 1986; FCMI, FCMC; *Recreations* travel, reading political economy; *Clubs* Sudan (Khartoum), RAF; *Style*— Suhail Aziz, Esq; ✉ The Brettonwood Partnership, 126 St Julian's Farm Road, West Norwood, London SE27 0RR (tel 020 8766 6118, fax 020 8766 0212)

AZWAI, HE Mohamed Abu AlQassim Azwai; *m* Amena; *Career* Libyan diplomat; ambass to the Ct of St James's 2001–; *Style*— HE Mr Mohammed Azwai; ✉ The People's Bureau of the Great Socialist People's Libyan Arab Jamahiriya, 15 Knightsbridge, London SW1X 7LY

B

B

BABBIDGE, Adrian Vaughan; JP (1983); s of William Henry Vaughan Babbidge (d 2000), of Cwmbran, Gwent, and Violet, *née* Jenkins (d 1990); *b* 10 July 1949; *Educ* Jones' West Monmouth Sch Pontypool, UC Cardiff (BA), Univ of Leicester (postgrad museum studies cert, MA); *m* 24 Jan 2004, Rosemary Ewles; *Career* asst curator Thurrock Local History Museum Grays 1971–74, museum curator Borough of Torfaen Pontypool 1974–78, dir and sec Torfaen Museum Trust Pontypool 1978–89, dir E Midlands Museums Serv Nottingham 1989–2002 (sec 1992–2002), museum and heritage conslt co-fndr Egeria Heritage Consultancy 2002–; dir: Gwent Area Broadcasting Ltd 1981–89 (co sec 1981–85), Cardiff Broadcasting Co plc 1985–89, Museum Enterprises Ltd 1991–, Midlands Arts Marketing Ltd 1992–95 (vice-chair), Investors in People 1995–99, E Midlands Regnl Recognition Panel; memb Exec Ctee E Midlands Tourist Bd 1989–92; hon lectr Inst of Archaeology UCL; external examiner (heritage studies) Nottingham Trent Univ 1995–99, Arts & Humanities Peer Review Coll 2006–; tstee Glamorgan-Gwent Archaeological Trust 1985–89; memb Cncl Royal Archaeological Inst 2003–07; FMA 1982 (hon treas 1988–91, memb Ethics Ctee 1995–99), FRSA; *Recreations* pondering, cinema, discovering Italy, learning about the law; *Style*— Adrian Babbidge, Esq; ✉ 105 Greenway Avenue, London E17 3QL (tel and fax 020 8926 0442, e-mail adrian.babbidge@babbidge.net)

BACH, John Theodore; s of late Dr Francis Bach, and Matine, *née* Thompson; *b* 18 February 1936; *Educ* Rugby, New Coll Oxford (MA); *m* 15 April 1967, Hilary Rose, da of late Gp Capt T E H Birley, OBE; 2 da (Emily b 1968, Susannah b 1973), 1 s (Alexander b 1969); *Career* slr; ptnr Stephenson Harwood 1966–96, conslt 1996–99; Moorfields Eye Hosp: govr, later dir, vice-chm and actg chm 1976–2001, special tstee 2001–; tstee Gurkha Welfare Tst 1995–; Master Worshipful Co of Barbers 2002–03; *Clubs* City Univ, Huntercombe and Rye Golf; *Style*— John T Bach; ✉ 2 Elsworthy Terrace, London NW3 3DR (tel and fax 020 7483 3166)

BACK, Neil Antony; MBE (2004); *b* 16 January 1969, Coventry; *Educ* The Woodlands Sch Coventry; *Career* rugby union coach and former player; clubs: Barkers' Butts, Nottingham RFC until 1990, Leicester Tigers RFC 1990–2005 (338 appearances, 125 tries, sometime capt, winners 4 successive English league titles 1999–2002, winners Heineken Cup 2001 and 2002); England: 66 caps (4 as capt), 16 tries, 1 drop goal, debut v Scotland 1994, winners Six Nations Championship 2000, 2001 and 2003 (Grand Slam 2003), memb squad World Cup 1995 (4th place), 1999 and 2003 (champions), ranked no 1 team in the world 2003, ret 2004; memb Br Lions touring squad South Africa 1997, Aust 2001 and NZ 2005; RFU Player of the Year 1998, Players' Player of the Year Professional Players Assoc 1999, Premiership top try scorer 1999 (16 tries); tech (defence) coach Leicester Tigers 2005–; *Recreations* golf, tennis, squash; *Style*— Neil Back, Esq, MBE

BACK, Prof Paul Adrian Auchmuty; CBE (1994); s of Arthur William Back, QC (d 1960), of Grahamstown, South Africa, and Mary Helen Margaret, *née* Carter; *b* 30 May 1930; *Educ* St Andrew's Coll Grahamstown, Rhodes Univ (BSc), Univ of Cape Town (BSc), Trinity Coll Oxford (Rhodes scholar, PhD, Desborough Medal for servs to rowing, Hack Trophy for flying Univ Air Squadron); *m* 1965, Jacqueline Sarah, da of Walter Hide; 3 s (Jonathan Paul b 1966, Rupert James b 1968, Nicholas Hugo b 1976); *Career* Sir Alexander Gibb & Partners: joined 1955, assoc 1967–70, ptnr 1970–89, co dir and chief tech dir 1989–95; visiting prof of design Univ of Oxford 1992–1998; worked on Kariba Hydro-Electric Power Station and Dam 1955–60, worked on several hydro-electric projects incl Samanalawewa and Victoria Dam and Hydro-Electric Projects in Sri Lanka and Kariba North Hydro-Electric Power Station Zambia 1970–, advsr to World Bank on Tarbela Dam 1976–, memb Bd of Advsrs Nat Irrigation Admin of the Philippines Magat Dam 1977–, chm Advsy Panel Shaqikou Hydro-Electric Project China 1984–, chm Panel of Enquiry Kantalai Tank failure Sri Lanka 1986, chm Lesotho Highlands Conslts Review Panel for the Katse Dam 1987–, project dir for design and supervision of construction Cardiff Bay Barrage Wales 1989–, chm Advsy Panel on Dam Safety Latvia 1996–, Advsy Panel on Design of Nam Theun 2 Hydro Project in Laos 2000–; chief guest speaker Sri Lanka Assoc for the Advancement of Sci 1989, lectr (Dams in Difficulties) Br Assoc for Advancement of Science 1995; memb Cncl ICE 1989; memb Adjudicating Panel for MacRobert Award for Innovation in Industry Royal Acad of Engrg; Construction News Award of the Year for Victoria Dam Project Sri Lanka (ptnr i/c) 1985; memb Assoc of Consulting Engrs 1971, FICE 1971 (MICE 1961), FREng 1981; *Books* Seismic Design Study of a Double Curvative Arch Dam (jtly, 1969), P K Le Roux Dam - Spillway Design and Energy Dissipators (jtly, 1973), Hydro-Electric Power Generation and Pumped Storage Schemes Utilising the Sea (1978), Aseismic Design of Arch Dams (jtly, 1980), The Influence of Geology on the Design of Victoria Dam Sri Lanka (jtly, 1982), Automatic Flood Routing at Victoria Dam Sri Lanka, Darwinism and the Rise of Degenerate Science (2003); *Recreations* sailing, skiing; *Clubs* RAF London; *Style*— Prof Paul Back, CBE, FREng; ✉ Parsonage Farm, How Lane, White Waltham, Berkshire SL6 3JP (tel 0118 934 3973, fax 0118 934 3190, e-mail paul2back@aol.com)

BACKHOUSE, David John; s of Joseph Helme Backhouse (d 1989), and Jessie, *née* Chivers (d 2006); *b* 5 May 1941; *Educ* Lord Weymouth Sch Warminster, W of England Coll of Art; *m* 19 July 1975, Sarah, da of Philip Gerald Barber, CBE (d 1988); 2 da (Roma b 1977, Rosalind b 1984), 1 s (Theodore b 1980); *Career* sculptor; many public sculptures in UK incl: The Animals in War Meml monument Park Lane London 2004, bronzes in collections worldwide; one man exhibitions in: London, NY, Washington DC; RWA, FRBS, FRSA; *Recreations* garden design, walking, cycling; *Style*— David Backhouse, Esq; ✉ Lullington Studio, Lullington, Frome, Somerset BA11 2PW (tel 01373 831318, e-mail db@backhousesculptures.com); La Chapelle Pommier, 24340 Mareuil, Dordogne, France

BACKHOUSE, James Anderson; s of John Anderson Backhouse (d 1998), and Anne-Heather, *née* Bolton; *b* 22 June 1967, Blackburn, Lancs; *Educ* Queen Elizabeth's GS Blackburn, Staffs Poly (LLB), Chester Coll of Law; *m* 28 May 1999, Wendy Louise, *née* Campbell; 1 da (Katie Louise b 22 Aug 2004); *Career* admitted slr 1992; slr specialising in regulatory tport law; slr Vaudreys Slrs 1993 (articled clerk 1990–92), Backhouse Jones Slrs (family firm, formerly Backhouses Slrs) 1994–; memb Law Soc 1992; author of numerous articles for professional pubns on road tport regulations incl Croners, Commercial Motor and Route One; *Recreations* shooting, sailing, horse riding, cycling; *Clubs* RAC, Dist and Union (Blackburn, pres); ✉ Backhouse Jones Solicitors, The Printworks, Hey Road, Clitheroe, Lancashire BB7 9WD (tel 01254 828300, fax 01254 828301, e-mail james@backhouses.co.uk)

BACKHOUSE, Richard; s of T A Backhouse, of Polgooth, Cornwall, and Mrs R H Joel, *née* Mitchell; *b* 18 February 1968, Paignton, Devon; *Educ* Marlborough, Selwyn Coll Cambridge (MA); *m* 1993, Deborah; *Career* teacher Oundle Sch 1990–96; Bradfield Coll: head of economics and politics 1996–99, dir of pastoral and extra-curricular activities 1998–2000, housemaster 2000–05; princ Monkton Combe Sch 2005–; *Recreations* rowing, skiing, reading, supporting Southampton FC; *Style*— Richard Backhouse, Esq; ✉ Monkton Combe School, Monkton Combe, Bath BA2 7HG (tel 01225 721102, e-mail principal@monkton.org.uk)

BACKUS, Rear Adm Alexander Kirkwood (Sandy); CB (2003), OBE (1989); s of Jake Kirkwood Backus (d 1989), of Tobermory, Isle of Mull, and Jean, *née* Stobie; *b* 1 April 1948; *Educ* Sevenoaks Sch, BRNC Dartmouth, JSDC Greenwich; *m* Dec 1971, Margaret Joan Pocock; 2 s (Robert Ian Kirkwood b 1973, Alastair James Kirkwood b 1978), 1 da (Janet Elizabeth b 1976); *Career* joined RN 1966; served HMS Fiskerton and HMS Intrepid 1967, Correspondence Offr HMS Eastbourne 1970, Lieut 1971, Anti-Submarine Warfare Offr HMS Cavalier 1971, Navigating Offr HMS Bacchante 1972, served HMS Blake 1974, Princ Warfare Offr (A) HMS Arrow 1975, Advanced Warfare Offr HMS Dryad, Advanced Warfare Offr (A) Staff of Capt 4 Frigate Sqdn HMS Cleopatra 1978, Lieut Cdr 1979, Exec Offr HMS Torquay 1980, staff appt BRNC Dartmouth, Cdr 1983, CO HMS Arethusa 1984, Br Rep Standing Naval Force Atlantic 1985, Dep Sr Naval Offr and Queen's Harbour Master Falkland Islands, Directorate of Defence Programmes MOD 1986, Cdr Sea Training Portland 1988, Capt 1990, CO Capt 6 Frigate Sqdn HMS Hermione 1990, asst dir Directorate of Naval Ops MOD 1992, Cdre 1995, Cdre Br Forces Falkland Islands 1995–96, ACOS (Policy) to C-in-C Fleet, Rear Adm 1999, Flag Offr Sea Trg 1999–2001, Flag Offr Surface Flotilla 2001–02, COS (Warfare) 2002–03, ret; chm Devon Rural Skills Tst; patron: RSPB, RNLI; *Recreations* ornithology, photography, country sports, walking, tennis, skiing, rural skills; *Clubs* Western Isles Yacht, Royal Naval Argyll; *Style*— Rear Adm Sandy Backus, CB, OBE

BACON, Prof Jean Margaret; da of Samuel Goodram (d 1994), and Annie, *née* Lee; *b* 21 November 1942, Sheffield; *Educ* Royal Holloway Univ of London (BSc), Hatfield Poly (MSc, PhD, CNAA); *m* 1, 20 Dec 1964, Michael Bacon; 1 s (Thomas David b 3 March 1976); m 2, 30 Aug 2003, Ken Moody; *Career* Nat Physical Lab 1963, GEC Hirst Research Centre Wembley 1964, lectr Watford Coll of Technol 1968, sr and princ lectr Hatfield Poly 1973, successively lectr, reader and prof Univ of Cambridge Computer Lab 1985– (dir of studies in computer science 1997–), fell Jesus Coll Cambridge 1997–; visiting scientist: MIT 1994, ETH Zurich 1995, Victoria Univ Wellington NZ 2002, Tech Univ Darmstadt 2002; IEEE Computer Soc: Golden Core Award 2001, Distinguished Serv Award 2005; memb Assoc for Computing Machinery 1980, sr memb IEEE Computer Soc 1998, CEng 1998, FBCS 2000 (MBCS 1987); *Publications* Concurrent Systems (1993, 3 edn 2003), Operating Systems (co-author, 2003); numerous papers for jls and conferences; *Recreations* painting, wildlife, walking; *Style*— Prof Jean Bacon; ✉ University of Cambridge Computer Laboratory, J J Thomson Avenue, Cambridge CB3 0FD (tel 01223 334604, fax 01223 334678, e-mail jean.bacon@cl.cam.ac.uk)

BACON, Sir Nicholas Hickman Ponsonby; 14 and 15 Bt (E 1611 and 1627), of Redgrave, Suffolk, and of Mildenhall, Suffolk, respectively; DL (Norfolk 1998); Premier Baronet of England; s of Sir Edmund Bacon, 13 and 14 Bt, KG, KBE, TD, JP, by his w Priscilla, da of Col Sir Charles Ponsonby, 1 Bt, TD, and Hon Winifred Gibbs (da of 1 Baron Hunsdon), Sir Nicholas is 12 in descent from Rt Hon Sir Nicholas Bacon, Lord Keeper of the Great Seal under Elizabeth I 1558–78 (in which latter year he d), His eld s was cr a Bt 1611 and this eld son's 3 s cr a Bt in 1627, Lord Keeper Bacon's 5 s by a second m (but yr s by this w, Anne, da of Sir Anthony Cooke, sometime tutor to Edward VI) was Lord High Chllr and was cr Baron Verulam 1618 and Viscount St Albans 1621 both ext 1626; *b* 17 May 1953; *Educ* Eton, Univ of Dundee (MA); *m* 1981, Susan Henrietta, da of Raymond Dinnis, of Delaware Farm, Edenbridge; 4 s (Henry Hickman b 1984, Edmund b 1986, Nathaniel b 1989, Thomas Castell b 1992); *Heir* s, Henry Bacon; *Career* called to the Bar Gray's Inn 1978; page of honour to HM The Queen 1966–69; Liveryman Worshipful Co of Grocers; *Clubs* Pratt's; *Style*— Sir Nicholas Bacon, Bt, DL; ✉ Raveningham Hall, Norwich NR14 6NS (tel 01508 548206)

BACON, Richard Michael; MP; s of Michael Bacon, and Mrs Sheila Campbell; step s of Prof John Campbell, OBE, *qv*; *b* 3 December 1962; *Educ* King's Sch Worcester, LSE (BSc), Goethe Institut Berlin; *m* 28 Jan 2006, Victoria Louise, da of Stephen Panton and Elizabeth Panton, of Market Drayton, Shropshire; *Career* investment banker Barclays de Zoete Wedd 1986–89, financial journalist Euromoney Pubns 1993–94, dep dir Mgmnt Consultancies Assoc 1994–96, assoc ptnr Brunswick PR 1996–99, fndr English Word Factory 1999; MP (Cons) S Norfolk 2001– (Parly candidate Vauxhall (Cons) 1997); memb Public Accounts Select Ctee 2001–, European Scrutiny Select Ctee 2003–; held various posts in Cons Pty since 1978, co-fndr Cons Pty's Geneva project; *Recreations* playing the bongos; *Clubs* Ronnie Scott's; *Style*— Richard Bacon, Esq, MP; ✉ House of Commons, London SW1A 0AA (tel 020 7219 3000, fax 020 7219 1784); Constituency Office tel 01379 643728

BACON, Stephen Francis Theodore; s of Frank David Bacon (d 1982), of Prestbury, Cheshire, and Cecilia Nancy, *née* Purseglove (d 2003); *b* 3 September 1945, Oldham, Lancs; *Educ* Perse Sch Cambridge, KCL (LLB, AKC), Inns of Court Sch of Law; *m* 1; 1 s (Nicholas Giles b 24 Sept 1977), 1 da (Hannah France b 15 March 1980); m 2, 28 July 2001, Felicity Clare, *née* Quant; 1 da (Clio Francesca Grace b 25 Oct 2002); *Career* called to the Bar Gray's Inn 1969; practising barr Northern Circuit 1969–80, dep Northern legal mangr Daily Express 1980–87, head of legal Express Newspapers 1989– (legal advsr 1987–89); chm Bar Assoc for Commerce, Finance and Industry (BACFI) 1998 and 2006–07, memb Bar Cncl 1998–; regular contrib to legal jls; *Recreations* cricket, gardening, horse racing; *Style*— Stephen Bacon, Esq; ✉ Express Newspapers, Northern & Shell Building, 10 Lower Thames Street, London EC3R 6EN (tel 020 8612 7784, fax 0871 434 7967, e-mail stephen.bacon@express.co.uk)

BACON, Timothy Roger; s of Christopher Henry Bacon (d 1956), and Diana Sybil, *née* Richmond Brown (d 1995); *b* 4 December 1947; *Educ* Eton, Univ of Bristol (BSc); *m* 14 Sept 1985, Marylyn Rowan Ogilvie, da of William Arthur Grant; 2 da (Rosalind Sarah b 12 Jan 1987, Laura Charlotte b 11 July 1988); *Career* Brown Shipley & Co Ltd 1970–92 (dir 1988–92), md Colville Estate Ltd 1993– (dir 1976–), Columbus Asset Management Ltd 1992–2004; memb Cncl of St Dunstan's; memb Inst of Bankers; *Recreations* opera, theatre, travel; *Clubs* City University, Pratt's; *Style*— Timothy Bacon, Esq; ✉ Ramsden Farm, Stone, Tenterden, Kent TN30 7JB (tel 01797 270300)

BADAWI, Zeinab Mohammed-Khair; da of Mohammed-Khair El Badawi, of Southgate, London, and Asia Mohammed, *née* Malik; *b* 3 October 1959; *Educ* Hornsey Sch for Girls, St Hilda's Coll Oxford (BA), Univ of London (MA); *Partner* David Crook; 1 s (Joseph Badawi-Crook b 1994), 2 da (Sophia Badawi-Crook b 1996, Hannah Badawi-Crook b 1998); *Career* presenter and journalist in current affairs and documentaries Yorkshire TV 1982–86, current affairs reporter BBC TV 1987–88, former newscaster and journalist ITN (Channel Four News), broadcaster on BBC World Service, BBC Live political programmer; vice-pres United Nations Int Assoc, chair Article 19 Int Organisation for Freedom of Speech; advsr Foreign Policy Centre; memb: Hansard Cmmn into Scrutiny Role of Parliament, Panel 2000; *Recreations* yoga, opera, reading, languages; *Style*— Miss Zeinab Badawi

BADDELEY, Prof Alan David; CBE (1999); *b* 23 March 1934; *Educ* Cockburn HS Leeds, UCL (BA), Princeton Univ (MA), Univ of Cambridge (PhD); *m* 1964, Hilary Ann White; 3 s; *Career* memb scientific staff MRC Applied Psychology Unit Cambridge 1958–67, lectr then reader Univ of Sussex 1967–72, prof of psychology Univ of Stirling 1972–74, dir MRC Applied Psychology Unit Cambridge 1974–96, sr res fell Churchill Coll Cambridge 1987–95; prof of psychology Univ of Bristol 1995–; hon prof of cognitive psychology Univ of Cambridge 1991–95; memb: ESRC Psychology Ctee 1979–81; chm MRC Neurosciences Bd 1987–89 (memb 1981–85); memb Editorial Bds: Applied Cognitive Psychology (special editorial advsr), Cognition and Emotion, Consciousness and Cognition, Essays in Cognitive Psychology, European Jl of Cognitive Psychology, Learning and Individual Differences, Learning and Memory, Neuropsychological Rehabilitation; President's Award British Psychological Soc 1982 (Myers lectr 1980); pres: Experimental Psychology Soc 1984–86 (Bartlett lectr 1988), Euro Soc for Cognitive Psychology 1986–90; hon foreign memb American Acad of Arts and Scis 1996; Distinguished Scientific Contribution Award American Psychological Assoc 2001, Aristotle Prize 2001; Hon DPhil Umeå Univ Sweden 1991; Hon DUniv: Stirling 1996, Essex 1999, Plymouth 2001; Hon FBPsS 1995, FRS 1993, FAcMed Sci 1998; *Books* The Psychology of Memory (1976), Your Memory: A User's Guide (1982, 2 edn 1993), Working Memory (1986), Human Memory: Theory and Practice (1990), Working Memory and Language (with S Gathercole, 1993); jt ed: Attention and Performance IX (1981), Research Directions in Cognitive Science: A European Perspective - Vol 1: Cognitive Psychology (1989), Human Factors in Hazardous Situations (1990), Attention: Selection, Awareness and Control - A Tribute to Donald Broadbent (1993), Handbook of Mermory Disorders (1995, 2 edn 2002), Essentials of Human Memory (1999), Episodic Memory (2002); *Style*— Professor Alan Baddeley, CBE, FRS; ✉ Department of Psychology, University of York, Heslington, York YO10 5DD (tel 01904 432882, fax 01904 433181, e-mail ab50@york.ac.uk)

BADDELEY, Sir John Wolsey Beresford; 4 Bt (UK 1922), of Lakefield, Parish of St Mary Stoke Newington, Co London; s of Sir John Beresford Baddeley, 3 Bt (d 1979), and Nancy Winifred, *née* Wolsey; *b* 27 January 1938; *Educ* Bradfield Coll Berks; *m* 1, 1962 (m dis 1992), Sara Rosalind, da of late Colin Crofts, of Scarborough; 3 da (Sara Alexandra (Mrs Andrew Turner) b 1964, Anna Victoria (Mrs Brian A Chambers) b 1965, Emma Elisabeth b 1972); m 2, 1998, Carol Quinlan, *née* Greenham; *Heir* kinsman, Paul Allan Baddeley; *Career* FCA (ACA 1961); *Recreations* inland waterways, destructive gardening; *Style*— Sir John Baddeley, Bt; ✉ Springwood, Sandgate Lane, Storrington, West Sussex (tel 01903 743054)

BADDELEY, Julie Margaret; da of Stuart Frank Weston, and Margaret Rose, *née* Burrows, of Cambridge; *Educ* St Felix Sch Southwold, Somerville Coll Oxford (MA); *m* 1972 (m dis 1995), Philip Stirling Baddeley; 1 s (John Philip b 13 Dec 1977), 1 da (Sarah Margaret b 28 April 1979); *Career* exec dir Woolwich plc 1998–2000; ptnr Andersen Consulting 1992–96; md: Baddeley Associates Ltd 1982–87, Sema Gp Consulting 1987–91; dir Chrysalis VCT plc; non-exec dir: Yorkshire Building Soc, BOC Gp plc 2001–05, Computerland UK plc 2005–, Greggs plc 2005–; memb Audit Cmmn 1999–2003; non-exec dir: DWP Pensions Directorate 2000–06, Dept of Health 2005–; assoc fell Templeton Coll Oxford; Freeman City of London, Freeman Worshipful Co of Information Technologists 1990; CIMgt 2000; *Books* Understanding Industry (1979); *Recreations* music; *Style*— Ms Julie Baddeley; ✉ 29 De Vere Gardens, London W8 5AW (e-mail changefdn@aol.com)

BADDELEY, Stephen John; s of William Baddeley, and Barbara Isabel; *b* 28 March 1961; *Educ* Chelsea Coll London (BSc); *m* 16 June 1984 (m dis 1997), Deirdre Ilene, *née* Sharman; 1 s (James Scott William b 25 Jan 1991), 1 da (Selene Sharman b 16 April 1993); partner Kirsten Irene Gwerder; 1 s (Karl Thomas Stephen b 13 Aug 2001), 1 da (Astrid-Marie Rose b 12 Sept 2005); *Career* former badminton player; Eng nat singles champion 1981, 1985 and 1987, Eng nat men's doubles champion 1985, 1987 and 1989; Euro singles champion 1990; Cwlth Games: Gold medal team event 1982, 1986 and 1990, Gold medal singles 1986; winner men's singles: Indian Open 1985, Scottish Open 1986; represented Europe v Asia 1983, 1984 and 1986; 143 caps for Eng; hon memb Badminton Writers' Assoc, memb and chair Eng Badminton Players' Assoc 1989–90, chm World Badminton Players' Fedn 1989–90, ret as player 1990; dir of coaching and devpt Scottish Badminton Union 1990–92, mangr Br Olympic Badminton Team 1990–92, coach Nat Centre de Badminton Lausanne (asst nat Swiss coach) 1992–96, dir of tournament World Badminton Championships Lausanne 1995, dir Elite Play and Nat Coaching Policy Badminton Assoc of England Ltd 1996–99, chief exec Badminton Assoc of England 1998–2004, dir of sport Sport England 2004– (interim chief exec 2005–); *Books* Badminton In Action (1988), Go and Play Badminton (1992); *Recreations* jogging; *Style*— Stephen Baddeley, Esq; ✉ Sport England, 3rd Floor, Victoria House, Bloomsbury Square, London WC1B 4SE

BADDIEL, David Lionel; s of Dr Colin B Baddiel, and Sarah Fabian-Baddiel; *b* 28 May 1964; *Educ* Haberdashers' Aske's, King's Coll Cambridge (MA), UCL; *Partner* Morwenna Banks; 1 da (Dolly Banks-Baddiel b 31 Aug 2001), 1 s (Ezra b 9 Nov 2004); *Career* comedian and writer; writer and performer The Mary Whitehouse Experience (BBC Radio 1) 1988–90 (Sony Radio Award 1989), actor The Announcement (film) 2002; World Cup corr Evening Standard 2002, columnist The Guardian, The Times and FHM, occasional writer The Observer, The Times, The Independent, Daily Telegraph, Sunday Times, The Mirror and Esquire; judge Booker Prize 2002; writer and singer (with Frank Skinner, *qv*, and Lightning Seeds): Three Lions (official song for Euro '96, UK no 1 (twice), Germany no 17, NME Brat Award 1996), Three Lions '98 (UK no 1); supporter Holocaust Educnl Tst; *Television* The Mary Whitehouse Experience (BBC2) 1990–92 (Radio Times Best Newcomer Award 1991), Stab in the Dark (Channel 4) 1992–93, Newman and Baddiel In Pieces (BBC2) 1993, Fantasy Football League (BBC2) 1994–96, Fantasy World Cup (ITV) 1998, Baddiel and Skinner Unplanned (ITV) 2000–, Baddiel's Syndrome (Sky TV) 2001; *Videos* From The Mary Whitehouse Experience 1991, History Today 1992, Newman and Baddiel at Wembley Arena 1993, Fantasy Football League Unseen 1996, The Too Much Information Tour 1997, Baddiel and Skinner Unplanned Live in the West End 2001; *Publications* The Mary Whitehouse Experience Encyclopedia (1992), The Fantasy Football League Diary (1995); novels: Time For Bed (1996), Whatever Love Means (1999), The Secret Purposes (2004); *Recreations* football, tennis; *Clubs* Soho House, Camden Road; *Style*— David Baddiel, Esq; ✉ c/o Avalon Management Group Ltd, 4A Exmoor Street, London W10 6BD (tel 020 7598 7321, fax 020 7598 7300)

BADEN HELLARD, Ronald; s of Ernest Baden Hellard (d 1975), of Longfield, Kent, and Alice May, *née* Banks (d 1980); *b* 30 January 1927; *Educ* Liskeard GS, The Poly Sch of Architecture (Univ of Westminster) (DipArch), Loughborough Tech Coll (now Loughborough Univ); *m* 16 Dec 1950, Kay Peggy, *née* Fiddes (d 1998); 2 da (Sally b 1953, Diana Jacqueline b 1956); *Career* WWII Duke of Cornwall's LI 1944–48, Capt GHQ MELF 1947–48; fndr ptnr: Polycon Group 1952–, Polycon Building Industry Consultants 1955–; chm TQM/Polycon 1988–, chief exec Polycon 3A's Ltd 1994–; architect of various industrial and commercial bldgs incl Oxford Air Trg Sch at Kidlington; first chm Mgmnt Ctee RIBA 1956–64, developed a number of mgmnt techniques which are now standard mgmnt practice in construction industry; pres S London Soc of Architects 1967–69; Br Inst of Mgmnt: chm SE London Branch 1969–72, chm SE Region 1972–76, memb Nat Cncl 1971–77; dep chm Greenwich Water Front Devpt Partnership 2000–01; memb Cncl CIArb 1970–84 (actg sec 1973); Freeman City of London 1981, Liveryman Worshipful Co of Arbitrators 1981; FCIArb 1952, FRIBA 1955, FIMgt 1966, FAQMCI 1992; *Books* Management in Architectural Practice (1964), Metric Management Action Plan (1971), Training for Change (1972), Construction Quality Coordinators Guide (1987), Managing Construction Conflict (1988), Management Auditing in Construction (1992), Total Quality in Construction Projects (1993), Project Partnering: Principle and Practice (1995); *Recreations* tennis, travel, grandson Toby; *Style*— Ronald Baden Hellard, Esq; ✉ 97 Vanbrugh Park, Blackheath, London SE3 7AL (tel 020 8853 2006); Polycon Group (tel 020 8293 9533, fax 020 8293 6073, e-mail ronbadenhellard@aol.com)

BADEN-POWELL, 3 Baron (UK 1929); Sir Robert Crause Baden-Powell; 3 Bt (UK 1922); s of 2 Baron Baden-Powell (d 1962); *b* 15 October 1936; *Educ* Bryanston; *m* 1963, Patience, da of Maj Douglas Batty (d 1982); *Heir* bro, Hon Michael Baden-Powell; *Career* dir Bolton Building Soc 1972–88, md Fieldguard Ltd 1984–; vice-pres: World Scout Fndn 1978–88, Scout Assoc 1982– (chief scouts cmmr 1965–82); memb Cncl Scout Assoc 1965– (memb Ctee 1972–78), pres W Yorks Scout Cncl 1972–88; chm: Quarter Horse Racing UK 1985–88, Br Quarter Horse Assoc 1989–90 (memb Cncl 1984–90); vice-pres The Camping and Caravanning Club 2001– (pres 1992–2001); Liveryman Worshipful Co of Mercers; *Recreations* breeding racing Quarter Horses; *Style*— Lord Baden-Powell; ✉ Weston Farmhouse, The Street, Albury, Surrey GU5 9AY

BADENOCH, (Ian) James Forster; QC (1989); s of Sir John Badenoch (d 1996), and Anne Newnham, *née* Forster; *b* 24 July 1945; *Educ* Rugby, Magdalen Coll Oxford (Demy, MA); *m* Marie-Thérèse Victoria, da of Martin Hammond Cabourn Smith; 1 da (Isabel Grace b 1 Jan 1980), 2 s (William James Cabourn b 30 Jan 1982, Rory Martin Cabourn b 3 Nov 1984); *Career* called to the Bar Lincoln's Inn 1968 (bencher 2000), admitted to Hong Kong Bar (ad eundem); memb Inner Temple, recorder of the Crown Court 1987–, dep judge of the High Court 1994–; a pres Mental Health Review Tbnl 2000–, chm The Expert Witness Inst 2004–; memb: RSM, Harveian Soc of London, Medico-Legal Soc; MCIArb; *Books* Medical Negligence (contrib, Butterworths 1990, 2 edn 1994, 3 edn 2000), Urology and the Law (2006); *Recreations* fossil hunting, wildlife photography, the study of herons; *Style*— James Badenoch, Esq, QC; ✉ 1 Crown Office Row, Temple, London EC4Y 7HH (tel 020 7797 7500, fax 020 7797 7550)

BADGER, Prof Anthony John (Tony); s of Kenneth Badger (d 1979), of Bristol, and Iris Gwendoline, *née* Summerill; *b* 6 March 1947; *Educ* Cotham GS, Sidney Sussex Coll Cambridge (MA), Univ of Hull (PhD); *m* 28 June 1979, Ruth Catherine, da of Ronald Davis; 2 s (Nicholas, Christopher (twins) b 22 Aug 1981); *Career* Dept of History Univ of Newcastle upon Tyne: lectr 1971–81, sr lectr 1981–91, head of dept 1988–91, prof 1991; Univ of Cambridge: Paul Mellon prof of American history 1992–, fell Sidney Sussex Coll Cambridge 1992–2002 (vice-master 2000–02, hon fell 2003–), master Clare Coll 2003–; Hon DLitt Univ of Hull 1999; *Books* Prosperity Road: The New Deal, North Carolina and Tobacco (1980), North Carolina and The New Deal (1981), The New Deal: The Depression Years 1933–1940 (1989), The Making of Martin Luther King and The Civil Rights Movement (ed with Brian Ward, 1996), Southern Landscapes (ed with Walter Edgar and Jan Nordby Gretland, 1997), Contesting Democracy: Substance and Structure in American Political History (ed with Byron Shafer, 2001); *Recreations* walking, supporting Bristol Rovers FC; *Style*— Prof Tony Badger; ✉ The Master's Lodge, Clare College, Cambridge CB2 1TL (tel 01223 333241, e-mail ajb1001@cam.ac.uk)

BADRAWY, Dr Galal Akasha; s of Akasha Badrawy (d 1985), of Cairo, and Sanya Ahmed; *b* 4 June 1946; *m* 1974, Sylvia Anne, da of Edward Hatcher; 1 s (Adam b 1977), 1 da (Sarah b 1980); *Career* house surgn Mansoura Univ Hosp Egypt 1970–71, house physician Dar El Saha Hosp Beirut Lebanon 1971; SHO: Accident Emergency and Orthopaedics Princess Margaret Hosp Swindon 1972, Geriatric Med Stratton St Margaret's Hosp Swindon 1972–73, Orthopaedic Surgery Co Hosp York 1973–74; registrar: Naburn and Bootham Park Hosps York 1974–78 (SHO 1974), Child and Adolescent Psychiatry Southfield and Fairfield Units York 1978–79, York and Community Psychiatry St Andrew Day Hosp 1979–80; conslt psychiatrist and head Psychiatry Dept Abdulla Fouad Hosp Dammam Saudi Arabia, clinical asst Maudsley and The Bethlem Royal Hosp/Inst of Psychiatry 1982, registrar in psychiatry Horsham and Crawley Gen Hosp 1982–83; med dir Priory Psychiatric Clinic Lister Hosp 1984–89; locum conslt psychiatrist: Yorkshire RHA (with duties at St Mary's Hosp, Scarborough and Clifton Hosp, Scarborough Dist Hosp) 1983, Trent RHA (with duties at Rauceby Hosp Lincolnshire, Boston Gen Hosp, Skegness Gen Hosp) 1982–85, Ashford Gen Hosp Middx 1985–86; locum conslt: St Thomas' Hosp (based at Tooting, duties at Bec Hosp and Day Hosp Putney) 1986–87, Psychiatric Unit Basingstoke Hosp 1987, Abraham Cowley Unit St Peter's Hosp Chertsey 1987–88; locum conslt psychiatrist Wexham Park Hosp Slough 1988–90; in private practice Harley St 1983–, conslt psychiatrist Charter Nightingale Hosp Lisson Grove 1989– (med dir Arab Unit 1987–89), conslt psychiatrist The Ridgewood Centre, conslt psychiatrist Cardinal Clinic Windsor; subject of interviews by Harpers & Queen, several Arabic newspapers and by BBC Arabic stations; hon memb American Psychiatric Assoc; memb BMA; MRCPsych, FRSM; *Recreations* golf; *Clubs* Wentworth, Les Ambassadeurs; *Style*— Dr Galal Badrawy; ✉ 130 Harley Street, London W1N 1DH (tel 020 7935 6875, mobile 07973 111426)

BAGGALLAY, Roger; s of Merrik Baggallay (d 1988), and Valerie, *née* Thomas (d 1996); *b* 23 September 1954, Canterbury, Kent; *Educ* Marlborough (scholar), New Coll Oxford (MA); *m* 11 Sept 1982, Elizabeth Margaret, *née* Morcom; 2 s (Merrik David b 24 Oct 1984, Alexander Richard b 24 Aug 1987); *Career* admitted slr: England and Wales 1978, Hong Kong 1982; slr with Coward Chance London and Hong Kong 1978–87 (trainee slr 1976–78), ptnr Clifford Chance 1987– (also head Finance, Corporate and Regulatory Litigation Gp, chm Int Litigation Gp); chm Kimpton Parish Church Restoration Tst; memb Law Soc; *Publications* Aircraft Liens and Detention Rights (conslt ed Eng and Wales chapter, 1998), Butterworths International Litigation Handbook (conslt ed, 1999); *Recreations* music, sport, gardening; *Style*— Roger Baggallay, Esq; ✉ Clifford Chance LLP, 10 Upper Bank Street, London E14 5JJ

BAGGE, (Alfred) James Stephen; 2 s of Sir John Alfred Picton Bagge, 6 Bt, ED, DL (d 1990); *b* 7 December 1952; *Educ* Eton; *m* 10 Oct 1981, Victoria I, er da of Michael A Lyndon Skeggs, of Ross-shire; 1 da (Edwina Rose b 1985); *Career* Capt Blues and Royals, ADC to Govr S Australia 1975–77; barr 1979–93; ptnr Norton Rose Slrs; memb Hon Soc of Lincoln's Inn 1975–93, memb Law Soc; *Clubs* Boodle's; *Style*— James Bagge, Esq; ✉ Norton Rose, Kempson House, Camomile Street, London EC3A 7AN (tel 020 7283 6000, fax 020 7283 6500)

B

BAGGE, Sir (John) Jeremy Picton; 7 Bt (UK 1867), of Stradsett Hall, Norfolk; DL (Norfolk 1996); s of Sir John Alfred Picton Bagge, 6 Bt, ED, DL (d 1990), and Elizabeth Helena (Lena), *née* Davies (d 1996); *b* 21 June 1945; *Educ* Eton; *m* 1979, Sarah Margaret Phipps, da of late Maj James Shelley Phipps Armstrong, Agent-Gen for Ontario; 2 s (Alfred James John b 1 July 1980, Albert Daniel Bracewell b 1 April 1985), 1 da (Alexandra Mary Pleasance b 26 Dec 1982); *Heir* s, Alfred Bagge; *Career* farmer; fin advsr to HIH The Crown Prince of Ethiopia 1969–70; cncllr King's Lynn and West Norfolk Borough 1981–95 (chm Planning 1991–94, Hon Alderman 1995); chm: West Norfolk Enterprise Agency 1985–94, Norfolk Rural Devpt Cmmn 1989–99, Cambridge Rural Devpt Cmmn 1995–99, Norfolk Shaping the Future Agric Ctee 1998–2000, Norfolk Rural Strategy Ctee 1998–2002; memb: Norfolk Ctee CLA 1986–2006 (chm 1993–95), CLA Exec 1997–2002; High Sheriff Norfolk 2003–04; memb Bishop's Cncl (Ely Diocese) 1994–2005; dir and tstee Tapping House Hospice 1999–; Freeman: City of London, Worshipful Co of Haberdashers; FCA 1968; *Recreations* shooting, stalking, skiing, water skiing; *Clubs* Boodle's, Air Squadron, Allsorts; *Style*— Sir Jeremy Bagge, Bt, DL; ✉ Stradsett Hall, Stradsett, King's Lynn, Norfolk PE33 9HA (tel 01366 347562); Stradsett Estate Office, Stradsett, King's Lynn PE33 9HA (tel 01366 347642, fax 01366 347846)

BAGGE, Richard Anthony; s of Gordon Roy Bagge (d 1980), and Barbara Joan, *née* Sympson; *b* 5 August 1949; *m* 1, 15 June 1974; 2 s (Jonathan Richard, Jeremy Edward); m 2, 31 August 1991, Kirsty Jane, da of Iain Somerled Macdonald (d 2004); 1 s (Rupert Richard Somerled), 1 da (Phoebe Elizabeth May); *Career* Barclays Bank 1966–70, Northcote & Co 1970–75, dir INVESCO 1975–92, dir White Square Communications 1993, dir Newton Investment Management 1994–; *Recreations* sailing, gardening, antiques, music, theatre; *Style*— Richard Bagge, Esq; ✉ Regency Cottage, Bletchingley, Surrey; Bennet House, Modbury, Devon

BAGNALL, Air Chief Marshal Sir Anthony John Crowther; GBE (2003, OBE 1982), KCB (1998, CB 1994); *Educ* Stretford GS, RAF Coll Cranwell; *m* Pamela; 3 c; *Career* cmmnd RAF 1967, sqdn pilot then weapons instr (Lightnings) 1967–75, promoted Sqdn Ldr 1975, flt cdr 1975–78, attended RAF Staff Coll 1978, staff duties MOD 1978–80, promoted Wing Cdr 1980, Wing Cdr Air Defence HQ Strike Cmd 1980–83, CO 43 Sqdn then CO 23 Sqdn (Phantoms) Falkland Is 1983–85, promoted Gp Capt 1985, Dir of Air Staff Briefing and Co-ordination 1985–87, CO RAF Leuchars 1988–99, promoted Air Cdre 1990, RCDS 1990, Dir of Air Force Staff Duties MOD 1991–92, promoted Air Vice Marshal 1992, Asst Chief of Air Staff 1992–94, AOC No 11 Gp 1994–96, promoted Air Marshal 1996, Dep C-in-C Allied Forces Central Europe 1996–1998, Air Member for Personnel 1998–2000, promoted Air Chief Marshal 2000, C-in-C STC 2000–01, Vice Chief of Defence Staff 2001; FRAeS; *Recreations* fell walking, golf, bridge; *Style*— Air Chief Marshal Sir Anthony Bagnall, GBE, KCB, FRAeS; ✉ c/o Lloyds Bank plc, 55 King Street, Manchester M60 2ES

BAGNALL, John Keith; s of Alfred Studley Bagnall (d 1992), of Otley, W Yorks, and Margaret, *née* Kirkham (d 1983); *b* 30 December 1941; *Educ* Oundle; *m* 10 Oct 1964, Valerie, da of Leslie Moxon (d 1985); 1 da (Caroline b 1966), 1 s (Stephen b 1968); *Career* Alfred Bagnall & Sons Ltd: dir 1962, gp md 1972–2004, chm 2004; treas Keighley and Dist Trg Assoc 1966–70; memb Standing Ctee: Safety Health and Welfare 1976–79, Fin 1976–98, Econ and Public Affrs Gp 1983–93; pres: Nat Fedn Painting and Decorating Contractors 1979–80, Fedn of Bldg Specialist Contractors 1983–84; chm Bldg Employers' Confedn 1992–93 (memb Nat Cncl 1978–85, vice-pres 1986–90, dep chm 1991–92); memb: Construction Industry Jt Taxation Ctee 1990–2003, Good Practice of Construction Industry Bd 1996–99; FCA 1965, FIMgt 1972; *Recreations* chess, travel, golf; *Style*—John Bagnall, Esq; ✉ Shackleton House Farm, North Walk, Harden, West Yorkshire BD16 1RY; Alfred Bagnall & Sons Ltd, 6 Manor Lane, Shipley, West Yorkshire BD18 3RD (tel 01274 714800, fax 01274 530171)

BAGOT, 10 Baron (GB 1780); Sir (Charles Hugh) Shaun Bagot; 15 Bt (E 1627); s of 9 Baron (d 2001); *b* 23 February 1944; *Educ* Abbotsholme; *m* 16 July 1986, Mrs Sally Ann Stone, da of D G Blunden, of Farnham, Surrey; 1 da (Hon Grace Lorina Kitty b 17 Aug 1993); *Heir* kinsman, Richard Bagot; *Style*— The Rt Hon The Lord Bagot; ✉ Ty'n-y-Mynydd, Carnguwch, Llithfaen, Gwynedd LL53 6PD

BAGRI, Hon Apurv; s of The Lord Bagri, CBE (Life Peer), *qv*, of London, and Usha, *née* Maheshwary; *b* 11 November 1959, Mumbai, India; *Educ* Cass Business Sch London; *m* 26 Feb 1982, Alka, *née* Rakyan; 2 da (Aditi b 29 Dec 1985, Amisha b 22 Sept 1988); *Career* md Metdist Gp; past chm Int Wrought Copper Cncl, memb Bd Dubai Financial Servs Authy; dep chm Governing Body London Business Sch (chm Asia Bd), visiting prof Cass Business Sch, memb Governing Cncl City Univ, memb Corporation UC Sch; memb Advsy and Mgmnt Bds of the Royal Parks, tstee Royal Parks Fndn, cmmr Crown Estate Paving Cmmn; memb Bd Indo-Br Partnership; dep chm TiE Inc, chm TiE-UK; memb NSPCC Stop Organised Abuse Bd, tstee Asia House; Hon DSc City Univ; *Style*— The Hon Apurv Bagri, Esq; ✉ Metdist Limited, 80 Cannon Street, London EC4N 6EJ (tel 020 7280 0000, fax 020 7606 6650)

BAGRI, Baron (Life Peer UK 1997), of Regent's Park in the City of Westminster; Raj Kumar; CBE (1995); s of Sohan Lal Bagri; *Career* fndr and chm Metdist Gp 1970 (hon pres 2003–06), chm The London Metal Exchange Ltd 1993–2002 (dir 1983–2002, vice-chm 1990–93); memb Advsy Ctee Prince's Youth Business Tst, memb Governing Body SOAS Univ of London, memb Ct City Univ; chm of trustees Rajiv Gandhi (UK) Fndn, tstee Sangam, chm Bagri Fndn; DSc (hc) City Univ 1999, DSc (hc) Univ of Nottingham 2000; Hon fell London Business Sch 2004; *Recreations* fine art, classical music, antiques; *Clubs* MCC; *Style*— The Rt Hon the Lord Bagri, CBE; ✉ Metdist Group, 80 Cannon Street, London EC4N 6EJ (tel 020 7280 0000, fax 020 7606 6650, e-mail vmanning@metdist.com)

BAGULEY, Maurice Grant; s of Capt William Albert Baguley (d 1947), of Hounslow, Middx, and Phyllis Amy, née Laverne (d 1987); *b* 2 May 1926; *Educ* Spring Grove GS, Acton Tech Coll, Brighton Poly, City Univ (MSc); *m* 1, 20 Nov 1948, Ivy Ethel (d 1983), da of Reginald Arthur Coomber (d 1952), of Ashford, Middx; 1 da (Claire Susan b 1953); m 2, 19 Nov 1983, Julie Elizabeth, *née* Barker, wid of Alec John Shickle; *Career* structural draughtsman The Square Grip Co Ltd 1945–46, jr engr J H Coombs and Partners 1946–47, design engr Peter Lind & Co Ltd 1947–48, sr design engr Woodall Duckham 1948–53, ptnr Malcolm Glover and Partners 1953–62, fndr Maurice Baguley and Partners 1962, ret 1973; practised as Maurice Baguley Consultants; structural and civil engrg bldg control conslt (ret 2001): BAA, City of Westminster, Royal Borough of Kensington and Chelsea, Boroughs of Hammersmith and Fulham, Wandsworth, Hackney, Newham, Croydon and Tandbridge; IStructE awards: Wallace Premium 1950, Husband Prize 1953, Andrews Prize 1953; FICE 1973, FIStructE 1953, FFB 1982; MASCE 1974, FRSA 1994; *Recreations* sailing, cruising, pianoforte; *Clubs* RYA, Naval; *Style*— Maurice Baguley, Esq; ✉ The Barn, Ivy Mill Lane, Godstone, Surrey RH9 8NF (tel 01883 724500, fax 01883 744719, e-mail mbcons@aol.com)

BAHL, Kamlesh; CBE (1997); da of Swinder Nath Bahl (d 1978), and Leela Wati, *née* Madan; *b* 28 May 1956; *Educ* Minchenden Sch Southgate, Univ of Birmingham (LLB); *m* 1986, Dr Nitin Nanji Lakhani; *Career* slr: GLC 1978–81, BSC 1981–84, Texaco Ltd 1984–87; Data Logic Ltd: legal and commercial mangr 1987–89, co sec and mangr Legal Servs 1989–93, legal conslt 1993–; chairwoman Equal Opportunities Cmmn 1993–98; Law Soc: memb Cncl 1990–2000 and 2002–, dep vice-pres 1998–99, chair Commerce and Industry Gp 1988–89, vice-pres 1999–2000; non-exec memb: Barnet HA 1989–90, Parkside HA 1990–93; memb: Ethnic Minorities Advsy Ctee 1991–94, Judicial Studies Bd 1991–93, Justice Sub-Ctee on Judiciary 1991–92, Cncl of Justice 1993–95, Cncl of Nat Assoc of HAs and Tsts 1993–94, EC Advsy Ctee on Equal Opportunities for Women and Men 1993–98 (vice-chair 1997–98), Cncl of Justice 1993–95; non-exec memb London Transport Bd 1999–2003; independent memb No 1 Diplomatic Service Appeal Bd of Foreign and Cwlth Office 1993–; EC Rep EC Consultative Cmmn on Racism & Xenophobia 1994–97; patron UN Year for Tolerance 1995; tstee Refuge 1998–; memb Cncl Scouts Assoc 1996–99; non-exec dir Univ of Westminster 1997, memb Cncl Open Univ 1999; FIPD 1997; *Books* Managing Legal Practice in Business (ed, 1989); *Recreations* swimming, singing, travelling, theatre; *Style*— Kamlesh Bahl, CBE

BAIER, Frederick John Watt; s of Francis Clair Wolfgang Baier, of Birkenhead, and Violet, *née* Wood; *b* 15 April 1949, Kingston-upon-Hull; *Educ* Bootham Sch York, Hull GS Kingston upon Hull, Canterbury Coll of Art, Birmingham Coll of Art (DipAD Furniture), RCA (MA, fell); *m* 1988, Lucy Elizabeth Strachan, the sculptor, da of David Rankin Strachan (d 1979); 2 da (Billie Anna b 26 Jan 1989, Rebecca b 4 Feb 1990); *Career* furniture designer; in partnership with Barry Joseph Leister and Keith Clarke in Empire Workshops (architectural reclamation, interior schemes and prototype furniture) 1977–79; teaching: pt/t at Brighton Poly 1979–82, Wendell Castle Sch USA 1986–88, pt/t at RCA and Wiltshire Studio 1989–; numerous exhbns worldwide; consultancy work incl: Design Cncl, Crafts Cncl, A B K Architects, Terry Farrell, *qv*, David Davies, also regnl arts assocs, interior designers, manufacturers and educnl instns; collections and cmmns incl: V&A Museum, Birmingham Museum and Art Gallery, Southern Arts, Crafts Cncl Gallery, Shipley Art Gallery, Templeton Coll Oxford, City of Leeds Museums, Carnegie Museum of Art Pittsburgh PA, Chiltern Sculpture Trail, Contemporary Art Soc, Kesler Lincoln's Inn, Lotherton Hall, US Ambass to Denmark, Steam Museum of GWR; FRCA; *Books* Fred Baier Furniture in Studio, Vision and Reality; *Style*— Frederick Baier, Esq; ✉ 45 High Street, Pewsey, Wiltshire SN9 5AF (tel 01672 562974, fax 01672 563043, e-mail fredbaier@btopenworld.com); 5A High Street, Pewsey, Wiltshire SN9 5AE (e-mail fred@fredbaier.com, website www.fredbaier.com)

BAILEY, Adrian Edward; MP; s of Edward Arthur Bailey (d 1996), and Sylvia Alice Iles, *née* Bayliss; *b* 11 December 1945; *Educ* Cheltenham GS, Univ of Exeter (BA), Loughborough Coll of Librarianship (Dip Librarianship); *m* 3 April 1989, Jill Patricia, da of late William Hunscott; 1 step s (Daniel b 19 July 1983); *Career* librarian Cheshire County Cncl 1971–82, nat organiser Co-operative Pty 1982–2000, MP (Lab/Co-op) West Bromwich W 2000– (by-election); memb Labour Pty 1962–, memb Co-operative Pty 1974–; supporter and contrib: Action Aid, Friends of the Animals, Redwings Horse and Donkey Sanctuary; *Recreations* season ticket holder Cheltenham Town FC, dog walking, swimming; *Style*— Adrian Bailey, Esq, MP; ✉ House of Commons, London SW1A 0AA (tel 020 7219 6060)

BAILEY, Anthony Cowper; s of Cowper Goldsmith Bailey, and Phyllis Bailey; *b* 5 January 1933; *Educ* Price's Sch Fareham, Churcher's Coll Petersfield, Merton Coll Oxford (MA); *m* 1957, Margot, *née* Speight; 4 da; *Career* Nat Serv 2 Lt 3 Bn Gold Coast Regt W Africa 1951–52; staff writer The New Yorker 1956–92; author of poems, short stories, essays, reportage, memoirs, fiction and biographies; speaker and visiting lectr at various univs; visiting fell Yale Center for Br Art 2002; US Overseas Press Club Award for Best Magazine Reporting from Abroad 1973, Lowell Thomas Award for Best Travel Book 1994; chm Burney Street Garden Project Greenwich 1981–90; memb Bd of Govrs Greenwich Theatre 1985–89; vice-pres The Turner Soc 1999–; hon Citizen Oakwood Ohio 1982; fell commoner Magdalene Coll Cambridge 1992; *Books* author of 22 books incl: Acts of Union (1980), America, Lost and Found (1980), Major André (1987), Standing in the Sun - A Life of JMW Turner (1997), A View of Delft - Vermeer Then and Now (2001, shortlisted Whitbread Biography Prize), John Constable: A Kingdom of his Own (2006); work in various anthologies and trans into Dutch, German, Italian, Spanish, Hungarian and Japanese; *Style*— Mr Anthony Bailey; ✉ c/o Donadio & Olson, 121 West 27 Street, New York, NY 10001–6207 USA (tel 00 1 212 691 8077, fax 00 1 212 633 2837)

BAILEY, Anthony John James; *b* 13 January 1970, London; *Educ* Douay Martyrs Sch Ickenham, Univ of Veliko Turnovo Bulgaria (Dip), Univ of Sofia Bulgaria (Dip), Budapest Univ of Economics (Dip), Univ of London (BA); *Career* special projects exec Burson-Marsteller UK then account dir then sr account dir Burson-Marsteller Int 1991–95, prog mangr mgmnt communications IBM EMEA 1995–96, sr cnsllr Manning, Selvage and Lee Ltd UK 1996, chm Eligo Int Ltd 1997–, special counsel to HRH Prince Khalid Al-Faisal 1998–, chm Painting and Patronage Saudi Arabia/UK 1999–, special advsr Bd of Tstees Arab Thought Fndn Lebanon 2002–05; sr policy advsr Bd of Dirs Foreign Policy Centre 2006–; patron All Pty Parly Pro-Life Gp 2002–, memb London Challenge Ministerial Advsy Gp DfES 2003–, memb Ministerial task Force for Gifted and Talented Educn DfES 2007–; dir Maimonides Fndn 2002–, dir Forthspring Inter-Community Centre Belfast 2003–, memb Advsy Bd Three Faiths Forum UK 2003–, tstee Path to Peace in the Balkans Fndn 2003–, bd dir and tstee United Church Learning Tst 2004–, memb Advsy Cncl Fndn of Reconciliation in the ME UK 2006–, dep pres Venice Fndn Switzerland; memb Ctee Passage Homeless Centre; dep sec-gen and vice pres Gold Mercury Award 2002–; govr Douay Martys Sch Ickenham 2005–; offr Br-Saudi Soc 2002–, tstee: Br-Moroccan Soc 2004–07, Moroccan-Br Soc in Rabat 2004–; memb: RIIA, Royal Soc of Asian Affrs, Loriner's Co, Lab Finance and Industry Gp, Soho House, Assoc of Papal Knights (in both GB and I), Catholic Union of GB, European Movement, Br-Italian Soc, Anglo-Portugese Soc, Br-Syrian Soc, Br-Lebanese Soc, Br-Nepal Soc, Anglo-Yemen Soc, Bahrain Soc, CAABU, High Cncl for Foreign Direct Investment of Portugal 2006–; fndn govr RC Archdiocese of Westminster 2005–, memb Friends of Westminster Cathedral, chm St George's Chapel Appeal Westminster Cathedral; govr: Sheffield Park Acad 2006–, Sheffield Springs Acad 2006–; ambass-at-large Repub of The Gambia; Medal of Merit and Co-operation Luso-Arab Inst for Co-operation 2006; Freeman City of London 2004; MIPRA 1996, MCIPR 1997, FRSA 2004; Knight Cdr with Star Constantinian Order of St George (Grand Magistral Delegate for Inter-Church and Inter-Faith Relations 2006–), Knight Cdr Royal Order of St Francis I (Royal House of Bourbon Two Sicilies) 2001, First Class Syrian Order of Outstanding Merit 2004, Knight Cdr Royal Order of Al-Alaoui (Morocco) 2004, Knight Cdr Pontifical Order of Pope Saint Sylvester (Holy See/Vatican City) 2004, Grand Cross Nat Order of Juan Mora Fernandez (Costa Rica) 2004, Grand Offr Order of Manuel Amador Guerrero (Panama) 2004, Knight Cdr Nat Order of the Cedar (Lebanon) 2004, First Class Order of 22 May Unification (Yemen) 2004, Knight Cdr with Star Order of Infante Dom Henrique (Portugal) 2005, First Class Order of the Madara Horseman (Bulgaria) 2007, Knight Cdr Equestrian Order of the Holy Sepulchre (Holy See/Vatican City) 2007; *Clubs* Travellers; *Style*— Anthony Bailey, Esq, KCSS; ✉ Eligo International Limited, 12 Queens Gate Gardens, London SW7 5LY (tel 020 7591 0619, fax 020 7225 5279, e-mail abailey@eligo.net)

BAILEY, Charles Cooper; JP (N Yorks 1994); s of Gordon Nuttall Bailey, TD, FRCS (d 1990), and Isabel Ray, *née* Zossenheim, changed by Deed Poll to Leslie 1913 (d 1988); *b* 22 November 1947; *Educ* Harrow, RAC Cirencester (Dip Rural Estate Mgmnt); *m* 1, 20 Sept 1975 (m dis 2001), Camilla Margaret, da of John Kenneth Henderson (d 1990); 1 s ((Richard) Max Cooper b 3 Sept 1979, k in car crash 23 Oct 1998), 1 da (Zara Marcina b 8 May 1982); m 2, 26 June 2004, Elisabeth Susan (Libs) Going, er da of James Christy Brownlow; *Career* asst land agent Smiths Gore York 1971, asst Agricultural & Country Dept Savills 1972–77, ptnr John German Ralph Pay 1977–85 (land agents), dir and regnl md Hamptons Holdings plc until 1991 (previously ptnr Hampton & Sons), sr ptnr Charles C Bailey, FRICS, MRAC (chartered surveyors and land agents) 1991–; chm Harrogate Civic Soc 1995–97, memb Ripon Diocesan Bd for Social Responsibility 1994–97, memb

Goldsborough & Flaxby PC 1995–2001, currently memb Harrogate Stray Defense Ctee; pt/t lay memb NHS Independent Reviews 1995–2004, memb Health Care Cmmn 2005–06; vice-pres Kirkby Malzeard Playing Fields Assoc; MRAC 1971, FRICS 1981 (ARICS 1974); *Recreations* shooting, fishing, pictures, groundsman; *Style*— Charles C Bailey, Esq, JP, FRICS, MRAC; ✉ Highbank Cottage, Mickley, Ripon, North Yorkshire HG4 3JE (tel 01765 635555, fax 01765 635554, e-mail ccb@charlesbailey.co.uk)

BAILEY, Christopher; s of Douglas Bailey, and Eliana Bailey; *b* 11 May 1971, Halifax, W Yorks; *Educ* Univ of Westminster (BA), RCA (Bill Gibb scholarship, MA); *Career* womenswear designer Donna Karan 1994–96, sr womenswear designer Gucci 1996–2001, creative dir Burberry 2001–; Hon FRCA 2003; *Style*— Christopher Bailey, Esq; ✉ Burberry, 18–22 Haymarket, London SW1Y 4DQ (tel 020 7968 0466, fax 020 7980 2906)

BAILEY, David; CBE (2001); s of William Bailey, and Agnes, *née* Green; *b* 2 January 1938; *m* 1, 1960, Rosemary Bramble; m 2, 1967 (m dis), Catherine Deneuve, the film actress; m 3, 1975 (m dis 1985), Marie Helvin; m 4, 1986, Catherine Dyer; 2 s, 1 da; *Career* photographer; photographer for Vogue (British, American, Italian and French) 1959–, dir of commercials (over 500) 1966–, dir and prodr of TV documentaries 1968– (subjects include Beaton, Warhol, Visconti, Catherine Bailey (The Lady is a Tramp) and Models Close Up), also feature film The Intruder; memb Arts Cncl 1983–; FRPS, FSIAD, FRSA, FCSD; *Exhibitions* Nat Portrait Gallery 1971, V&A Museum (one man retrospective) 1983, Int Centre of Photography NY 1984, Photographs from the Sudan for Live Aid (ICA and tour) 1985, Bailey Now! (Royal Photographic Soc, Bath) 1989, Hamiltons Gallery London 1989 and 1992–, Fahey Klein Gallery LA 1990, Camerawork Berlin and Carla Sozzni Milan 1997, A Gallery (New Orleans), Birth of the Cool (touring exhbn, Barbican Art Gallery) 1999, Nat Museum of Photography Film and Television Bradford 1999–2000, Modern Museet Stockholm 2000; *Awards* for commercials incl: The Golden Lion (Cannes), The Cleo (USA), American TV Award, D&AD Gold (London), D&AD Presidents Award, EMMY Award (USA); *Books* Box of Pin-Ups (1964), Goodbye Baby and Amen (1969), Warhol (1974), Beady Minces (1974), Papua New Guinea (1975), Mixed Moments (1976), Trouble and Strife (1980), David Bailey's London NW1 (1982), Black and White Memories (1983), Nudes 1981–84 (1984), Imagine (1985), If We Shadows (1991), The Lady is a Tramp (1995), David Bailey's Rock and Roll Heroes (1997), Models Close Up (1998), Archive One (1999); *Recreations* photography, aviculture, travel, painting; *Style*— David Bailey, Esq, CBE

BAILEY, Dennis; s of Leonard Charles Bailey, and Ethel Louise, *née* Funnell; *b* 20 January 1931; *Educ* West Tarring Secdy Modern Sch Worthing, W Sussex Sch of Art Worthing, RCA (ARCA, RCA travelling scholar); *m* 20 July 1985, Nicola Anne, da of John Roberts; 1 da (Catherine Anne b 6 May 1984), 1 s (Peter John Leonard b 23 Dec 1990); *Career* graphic designer and illustrator; asst ed Graphics Zürich 1956; art ed: Olympus Press Paris 1962–63, Town magazine London 1964–66; ptnr Bailey and Kenny 1988–; lectr in graphic design Chelsea Sch of Art London 1970–81; *Catalogues and Graphics for Exhibitions* incl: Pompeii AD 79 (Royal Acad) 1977, Dada and Surrealism Reviewed 1978, Picasso's Picassos 1981, Le Corbusier 1987 (Arts Cncl of GB, Hayward Gallery); other work incl: House Styles, Royal Soc of Arts, design of business print for NM Rothschilds, design of British Med Jl 1996, New Statesman 1996; RDI 1980; *Style*— Dennis Bailey, Esq; ✉ Bailey and Kenny, 7 Coppergate House, 16 Brune Street, London E1 7NJ (tel 020 7721 7705, fax 020 7721 7763)

BAILEY, Sir Derrick Thomas Louis; 3 Bt (UK 1919), of Cradock, Province of Cape of Good Hope, Union of South Africa; DFC; s of late Sir Abe Bailey, 1 Bt, KCMG; suc half-bro, Sir John Milner Bailey, 2 Bt (d 1946); *b* 15 August 1918; *Educ* Winchester, ChCh Oxford; *m* 1, 1946 (m dis), Katharine Nancy, da of Robin Stormonth Darling (d 1956), of Kelso, Scotland; 4 s (John Richard b 1947, Thomas Noel b 1948, William Abe b 1950, Patrick James b 1959), 1 da (Patricia Rosemary (Mrs Collins) b 1951); m 2, 1980 (m dis 1990), Mrs Jean Roscoe; *Heir* s, John Bailey; *Career* Capt South African Air Force, formerly 2 Lt South African Irish; farmer; *Recreations* sports, games; *Clubs* Rand (Johannesburg); *Style*— Sir Derrick Bailey, Bt, DFC; ✉ Bluestones, Alderney, Channel Islands

BAILEY, His Hon Judge Edward Henry; s of Geoffrey Henry Bailey (d 1985), of London, and Ninette, *née* Adereth (d 1991); *b* 24 May 1949; *Educ* King's Sch Canterbury, Gonville & Caius Coll Cambridge (MA, LLB); *m* 30 July 1983, Claire Dorothy Ann, *née* From; 2 da (Cecilia Jane b 21 Oct 1985, Francesca Ann b 11 July 1993); *Career* called to the Bar Middle Temple 1970; circuit judge (SE Circuit) 2000–; lectr Inns of Court Sch of Law 1970–72; *Style*— His Hon Judge Bailey

BAILEY, George Henry Selborne; s of Dr Alison George Selborne Bailey (d 1997), of High Wycombe, Bucks, and Christine, *née* Delfosse (d 1982); *b* 13 August 1953; *Educ* Radley, Downing Coll Cambridge (BA); *m* 8 Nov 1986, Allison Gail; 2 s (Henry George Selborne b 15 Jan 1989, Matthew John Selborne b 15 March 1991); *Career* md Sotheby's (dir 1979–); ARICS 1978; *Clubs* Leander; *Style*— George Bailey, Esq; ✉ Sotheby's, 34–35 New Bond Street, London W1A 2AA (tel 020 7293 5000)

BAILEY, Glenda Adrianne; da of John Ernest Bailey, and Constance, *née* Groome; *b* 16 November 1958; *Educ* Noel Baker Sch Derby, Kingston Univ (BA); *Career* fashion forecasting Design Direction 1983–84, prodr dummy magazine for IPC 1985; ed: Honey magazine 1986, Folio magazine 1987, marie claire magazine (UK) 1988–96, marie claire magazine (US) 1996–2001; ed-in-chief Harper's Bazaar 2001–; Hon MA 1995, Hon Dr Univ of Derby 2001 *Awards* Women's Magazine Ed of the Year BSME 1989, Best Magazine award PPA 1991, Consumer Magazine of the Year Media Week Press Awards and PPA 1991, Magazine of the Year Media Week Awards 1992, Editor's Editor of the Year and Women's Magazine Editor of the Year BSME 1992, Consumer Magazine of the Year PPA 1993, Consumer Magazine of the Year IPC Annual Editorial Awards 1993, Best International Magazine and Best International Consumer Magazine IDP International Press Awards 1994, Editor of the Year Adweek 2001; *Style*— Miss Glenda Bailey; ✉ c/o Harper's Bazaar, 1700 Broadway, 37th Floor, New York, NY 10019, USA (tel 001 212 903 5000, fax 001 212 262 7101)

BAILEY, Harold William; s of Harold Wilfred Bailey, and Winifred, *née* Pollard; *Educ* John Ruskin GS Croydon; *m* 2001, Susan Alice, *née* Miller; *Career* Thomson McLintock & Co 1953–62; Associated British Foods plc: joined 1962, fin dir 1978–97, dep chm 1997–99, chm 2000–; MICAS 1959; *Recreations* sailing, diving, reading, gardening; *Clubs* RAC; *Style*— Harold Bailey, Esq; ✉ Associated British Foods plc, Weston Centre, Bowater House, 68 Knightsbridge, London SW1X 7LQ (tel 020 7589 6363, fax 020 7584 8560)

BAILEY, Rt Rev Jonathan Sansbury; KCVO (2005); s of Walter Eric Bailey (d 1994), of Port Erin, IOM, and Audrey Sansbury, *née* Keenan; *b* 24 February 1940; *Educ* Quarry Bank HS Liverpool, Trinity Coll Cambridge (MA); *m* 1965, Susan Mary, da of Maurice James Bennett-Jones (d 1980); 3 s (Mark, Colin, Howard); *Career* curate: Sutton Lancs 1965–68, Warrington 1968–71; warden Marrick Priory 1971–76, vicar Wetherby Yorks 1976–82, archdeacon of Southend 1982–92, Bishop's offr for industty and commerce Dio of Chelmsford 1982–92, suffragan bishop of Dunwich 1992–95, bishop of Derby 1995–2005; Clerk of the Closet to HM The Queen 1996–2005; chair Churches' Main Ctee 2002–05; memb: House of Lords 1999–2005, Glos Police Authy 2007; Hon DUniv Derby 2006; *Recreations* carpentry, music, theatre; *Style*— The Rt Rev Jonathan S Bailey, KCVO; ✉ 28 Burleigh Way, Wickwar, Wotton-under-Edge GL12 8LR (tel 01454 294112, e-mail jonathan.s.bailey@gmail.com)

BAILEY, Kim Charles; s of Kenneth Bailey (d 1996), and Bridgett Ann, *née* Courage (d 1987); *b* 25 May 1953; *Educ* Radley; *Family* 1 s (Harry), 1 da (Pandora); m, 3 March 2001, Clare Wills; 1 s (Archie); *Career* racehorse trainer 1979–; major races won: Seagram Grand National (Mr Frisk), Whitbread Gold Cup (twice, Mr Frisk and Docklands Express), SGB Chase (Man O Magic), Bollinger Chase (twice, Man O Magic and Kings Fountain), Golden Spurs Chase (Man O Magic), H & T Walker Chase (twice, Man O Magic and Kings Fountain), Scottish Champion Hurdle (Positive), BIC Razor Hurdle (Carnival Air), Anthony Mildway & Peter Cazalet Meml Handicap Chase (twice, Mr Frisk and Shifting Gold), Crown Paints Hurdle (Positive), Cheltenham Tote Gold Cup (Master Oats), Cheltenham Champion Hurdle (Alderbrook), Scottish Champion Hurdle (Alderbrook); *Recreations* shooting, cricket, tennis, fishing; *Style*— Kim Bailey, Esq; ✉ website www.kimbaileyracing.com

BAILEY, Laura Emily; *Educ* Wheatley Park Comp, Univ of Southampton; *Career* int model 1995–, appeared in select ind films; journalist for various pubns incl: Daily Telegraph, Glamour, Marieclaire, Harpers & Queen, Condé Nast Online; memb Equity 2002; patron: Fashion Acts, Tibet Fndn, Comic Relief; *Recreations* film and theatre, yoga, literature, travel; *Clubs* Soho House, Electric House, Harry's Social; *Style*— Ms Laura Bailey

BAILEY, (Robert) Malcolm; s of Brian Bailey, of Holmfirth, W Yorks, and Annie, *née* Hinchliffe; *b* 19 December 1950; *Educ* Holme Valley GS, Imperial Coll London (BSc); *m* 26 Aug 1972, Anne Elizabeth, da of late Thomas Edward Dawson; 2 da (Hannah Victoria, Ruth Mary), 1 s (Thomas Matthew); *Career* PricewaterhouseCoopers (formerly Price Waterhouse before merger): joined 1972, qualified CA 1975, ptnr 1984–, nat dir of human resources Nat Exec 1993–95, vice-chm World Petroleum Industry Gp 1995–97, sr client ptnr 1997–, global compliance offr 2006–; ARCS, FCA 1980; *Style*— Malcolm Bailey, Esq; ✉ PricewaterhouseCoopers, 1 Embankment Place, London WC2N 6RH (tel 020 7583 5000, fax 020 7804 2655)

BAILEY, (Christian) Martin; s of Dr Leslie Bailey, of Harpenden, Herts, and Marie Elisabeth, *née* Phillips; *b* 4 August 1949; *Educ* Aldwickbury Sch Harpenden, St Albans Sch, Royal Free Hosp Sch of Med (BSc, MB BS); *m* 24 April 1971, Dr Jane Nicola Rotha Bailey, da of John Stewart Barnfield; 1 s (Simon John Martin b 7 Aug 1975), 1 da (Laura Jane Susanna b 7 June 1978); *Career* past appts: Royal Free Hosp London (house surgn, house physician, SHO), SHO in otolaryngology Royal Nat Throat Nose & Ear Hosp London, SHO in gen surgery Royal Northern Hosp London, registrar then sr registrar in otolaryngology Royal Nat Throat Nose & Ear Hosp, sr registrar in otolaryngology Sussex Throat & Ear Hosp Brighton; TWJ Fndn clinical and research fell in otology and neuro-otology Univ of Michigan; conslt otolaryngologist: Great Ormond Street Hospital for Children London 1982–, Royal Nat Throat Nose & Ear Hosp London 1982–97 (hon conslt 1997–); hon conslt otolaryngologist: St Luke's Hosp for the Clergy London 1984–, King Edward VII's Hosp Sister Agnes 1999–2001; hon sr lectr: Inst of Laryngology & Otology London 1982–, Inst of Child Health 1985–; memb: BMA 1973, RSM 1976 (pres Section of Laryngology and Rhinology 2005–06), Br Assoc of Otorhinolaryngologists - Head and Neck Surgns 1982, Br Assoc for Paediatric Otorhinolaryngology 1990 (pres 2002–04); FRCS; *Books* Ear Nose & Throat Nursing (jtly, 1986), Scott-Brown's Otolaryngology (contrib, 1987 and 1997), Recent Advances in Otolaryngology (contrib, 1995), Practical Pediatric Otolaryngology (contrib, 1999), author of papers on various aspects of otology and paediatric otolaryngology; *Recreations* fell walking, computers, cars; *Style*— Martin Bailey, Esq; ✉ 7 Heathgate, Hampstead Garden Suburb, London NW11 7AR (tel 020 8455 8628, fax 020 8381 4292); 55 Harley Street, London W1G 8QR (tel 020 7580 2426, fax 020 7436 1645)

BAILEY, Norman Stanley; CBE (1977); s of Stanley Bailey (d 1986), and Agnes, *née* Gale; *b* 23 March 1933; *Educ* East Barnet GS, Rhodes Univ Grahamstown (BMus), Vienna State Acad (Dip Opera, Lieder, Oratorio); *m* 1, 21 Dec 1957 (m dis 1983), Doreen, da of late Leonard Simpson, of Kenya; 2 s (Brian Emeric b 1960, Richard Alan b 1967), 1 da (Catherine Noorah (Mrs Bailey) b 1961); m 2, 25 July 1985, Kristine, da of Roman Anthony Ciesinski, of Delaware, USA; *Career* operatic and concert baritone; princ baritone Sadler's Wells Opera 1967–71; prof of music RCM 1990–; regular engagements at world major opera houses and festivals incl: La Scala Milan, Royal Opera House Covent Garden, Bayreuth Wagner Festival, Vienna State Opera, Met Opera NY, Paris Opera, Edinburgh Festival, Hamburg State Opera, English Nat Opera; Schigolch in Berg's Lulu (BBC Proms) 1996; BBC TV performances: Falstaff, La Traviata, The Flying Dutchman, Macbeth; recordings incl: The Ring (Goodall), Meistersinger and Der Fliegende Holländer (Solti), Walküre (Klemperer); Hon DMus Rhodes Univ 1986; Hon RAM 1981; *Recreations* memb Baha'i world community, chess, notaphily, golf, microcomputing, indoor rowing (memb Concept2 16 Million Meter Club, winner North American Rowing Challenge 2004); *Style*— Norman Bailey, Esq, CBE

BAILEY, Paul; s of Arthur Oswald Bailey (d 1948), and Helen Maud, *née* Burgess (d 1984); *b* 16 February 1937; *Educ* Sir Walter St John's Sch London, Central Sch of Speech and Drama; *Career* freelance writer and radio broadcaster; actor 1956–64, writer in residence Univ of Newcastle upon Tyne and Univ of Durham 1972–73, visiting lectr in English literature North Dakota State Univ 1976–79; frequent radio broadcaster (mainly Radio 3), writer and presenter progs on Karen Blixen, Henry Green, I B Singer and Primo Levi; winner: Somerset Maugham award 1968, E M Forster award 1973, George Orwell meml prize 1977; FRSL 1982–84; *Books* At The Jerusalem (1967), Trespasses (1970), A Distant Likeness (1973), Peter Smart's Confessions (1977), Old Soldiers (1980), An English Madam (1982), Gabriel's Lament (1986), An Immaculate Mistake (autobiography, 1990), Sugar Cane (1993), Oxford Book of London (ed, 1995), First Love (ed 1997), Kitty and Virgil (1998), The Stately Homo: A Celebration of the Life of Quentin Crisp (ed, 2000), Three Queer Lives: Fred Barnes, Naomi Jacob and Arthur Marshall (2001), Uncle Rudolf (2002); *Recreations* visiting churches, opera, watching tennis; *Style*— Paul Bailey, Esq; ✉ 79 Davisville Road, London W12 9SH (tel 020 8749 2279, tel and fax 020 8248 2127)

BAILEY, Prof Richard Nigel; OBE (2007); s of William Bailey (d 2003), of Spilsby, Lincs, and Hilda Bailey (d 1959); *b* 21 May 1936; *Educ* Spilsby GS, Univ of Durham (MA, PhD); *m* 3 Sept 1960, Mary Isabel, da of Norman Carmichael (d 1984), of Morpeth, Northumberland; 1 s (Nigel), 1 da (Alison); *Career* lectr in English UCNW 1960–66; Univ of Newcastle upon Tyne: lectr in English 1966–74, sr lectr 1974–80, prof of Anglo Saxon civilisation 1980–98 (emeritus prof 1998–), dean Faculty of Arts 1985–88, pro-vice-chllr 1988–93 and 1995–98; vice-pres CBA 1998–2000; memb English Regnl Ctee Heritage Lottery Fund 1999–2001, chm NE Regnl Ctee Heritage Lottery Fund 2001–; ed Archaelogia Aeliana 1997–; lay canon Newcastle Cathedral 2002–06; FSA 1975; *Books* Viking-Age Sculpture (1980), Corpus of Anglo-Saxon Sculpture: Cumbria (1988), Dowsing and Church Archaeology (1988), England's Earliest Sculptors (1995); *Recreations* hill walking, visiting churches and country houses; *Style*— Prof Richard Bailey, OBE, FSA; ✉ 22 Ridgely Drive, Ponteland, Newcastle upon Tyne NE20 9BL (tel 01661 823128)

BAILEY, Ronald William; CMG (1961); s of William Staveley Bailey (d 1956), of Southampton, and May Eveline Bailey, *née* Cudlipp (d 1958); *b* 14 June 1917; *Educ* King Edward VI Sch Southampton, Trinity Hall Cambridge (Wootton Isaacson scholar); *m* 1946, Joan Hassall, *née* Gray (d 2001); 1 s, 1 da; *Career* HM Dip Serv: Beirut 1939–41, Alexandria 1941–45, Cairo 1945–48, FO 1948–49, first sec Beirut 1949–52, cnsllr Washington 1955–57 (first sec 1952–55), Khartoum 1957–60, chargé d'affaires Taiz 1960–62, consul-gen Gothenburg 1963–65, min Baghdad 1965–67, ambass Bolivia 1967–71, ambass Morocco 1971–75, ret; memb Cncl Anglo-Arab Assoc 1978–85; hon pres Br-Moroccan Soc 1989–99; hon vice-pres Soc for the Protection of Animals Abroad 1989–2001 (vice-pres 1975–87, pres 1987–89); chm Black Down Ctee Nat Tst 1982–87 (memb 1977–87); town cncllr Haslemere 1976–79; *Books* Records of Oman 1867–1960 (12 vols, 1988–92); *Recreations* walking, photography; *Clubs* Oriental; *Style*— Ronald Bailey, Esq, CMG; ✉ 3 Strand Court, Topsham, Exeter EX3 0AZ (tel 01392 879538)

BAILEY, Dr (Theodore Robert) Simon; s of Herbert Wheatcroft Bailey (d 1989), of Shepshed, Leics, and Norah Violet, *née* Roberts; *b* 20 December 1943; *Educ* King Edward VII GS Coalville, UCL (BSc), UCH Med Sch (MB BS, FRCGP, DRCOG); *m* 26 July 1975, Elizabeth Frances, da of John Harper, OBE (d 2006), of Aldergate, Lancs; 2 s (Jonathan b 1978, Timothy b 1981); *Career* GP 1973–, RMO Newmarket Races, clinical teacher Faculty of Med Univ of Cambridge; Freeman City of London 1996, Liveryman Worshipful Soc of Apothecaries 2001 (Yeoman 1995); *Recreations* music, classic cars, fine art; *Style*— Dr Simon Bailey; ✉ Lincoln Lodge, Newmarket, Suffolk CB8 7AB (tel 01638 663792, e-mail yeliabs@doctors.org.uk); Orchard Surgery, Newmarket, Suffolk CB8 8NU (tel 01638 663 322, fax 01638 56192)

BAILEY, Sir Stanley Ernest; kt (1986), CBE (1980), QPM (1975), DL (Tyne & Wear 1986); s of John William Bailey (d 1962), of London, and Florence Mary, *née* Hibberd (d 1945); *b* 30 September 1926; *Educ* Lyulph Stanley Sch London; *m* 1, 27 March 1954, Marguerita Dorothea (Rita) (d 1997), da of George Whitbread (d 1963), of London; m 2, 4 June 1998, Maureen Shinwell, da of William Connor; *Career* Met Police to Supt 1947–66, asst Chief Constable Staffs Police 1966–70, dir Police Res Home Office 1970–72, dep Chief Constable Staffs 1973–75, Chief Constable Northumbria Police 1975–91, police cdr designate No 2 Home Def Region until 1991; memb Assoc of Chief Police Offrs (ACPO) England Wales and N Ireland (vice-pres 1984–85, pres 1985–86), chm Ctee first Int Police Exhibition and Conf (IPEC) London 1987, dir and vice-chm Crime Concern 1988–94, dir Northumbria Coalition Against Crime 1988–91; police advsr Assoc of Metropolitan Authorities and memb Chernobyl Task Force Ctee 1987–91; chm (until 1991): ACPO Standing Ctee on Intruder Alarms, ACPO Sub-Ctee on Crime Prevention, chm BSI Tech Ctee on Security Systems 1976–91; former memb: CBI Business and Crime Prevention Working Gp and Business Crime Prevention Sub-Gp, Br Vehicle Retailers Leasing Assoc Steering Gp on Crime Prevention, Nat Approval Cncl for Security Systems; vice-pres Police Mutual Assurance Soc 1986–94, life memb Int Assoc of Chiefs of Police (memb Exec Ctee 1986), chm Advsy Ctee on Int Policy IACP 1985–89 (dir European World Regnl Office, observer on Private Security Ctee and memb Membership Ctee IACP); graduate of Nat Exec Inst FBI Acad Washington; ACPO rep at INTERPOL 1986–88; govr Int Inst of Security, observer Eighth UN Conf on Crime Prevention Havana 1990, fndr and chm First Conf Sr Police at UN Conf 1990; conslt on policing, crime prevention and security 1991–; conslt: Reay Security Ltd 1998–, Security Auditors Ltd 1993–99; vice-pres Ex-Police in Commerce and Industry (EPIC) 1992–98 (pres 1998–2005), pres Security Services Assoc (SSA; now Security Systems and Alarms Inspection Bd (SSAIB)) 1992–, tstee Suzy Lamplugh Tst 1991–93, patron Assoc of Security Conslts (ASC); fndr and jt chm Newcastle Univ/Northumbria Police Centre for Res into Crime, Community and Policing 1989–91; memb Editorial Bd Professional Security; ABIS Ken Bolton award for outstanding contribution to security and crime prevention 1990; lectr on crime prevention, policing and security: USA, Pacific, Far East and Europe; hon fell Int Inst Security; Freeman City of London 1988; CCMI (CIMgt) 1987; OStJ 1981; *Publications* Community Policing and Crime Prevention in America and England (with Robert C Wadman, 1993); author of articles in various police journals on specialist subjects incl management and research; *Recreations* gardening, travel; *Style*— Sir Stanley Bailey, CBE, QPM, DL; ✉ 26 Highbridge, Gosforth, Newcastle upon Tyne NE3 2HA (tel and fax 0191 284 1668, e-mail sirsebailey@supanet.com)

BAILEY, Sylvia (Sly); da of Thomas Lewis Grice, and Sylvia, *née* Bantick; *b* 24 January 1962; *Educ* St Saviour's and St Olave's GS for Girls; *m* 5 June 1998, Peter Bailey; *Career* IPC Magazines: joined 1989, advtg sales dir 1990–97, bd dir 1994–2002, md IPC tx 1997–99, chief exec IPC Media 1999–2002; chief exec Trinity Mirror 2003–; non-exec dir: Press Assoc 2003–, EMI 2004–07; pres Newstraid Benevolent Soc 2003–, memb Women in Advtg and Communications London (WACL); Marcus Morris Award PPA 2002; *Recreations* family; *Style*— Mrs Sly Bailey; ✉ Trinity Mirror, 1 Canada Square, Canary Wharf, London E14 5AP (tel 020 7293 2203, fax 020 7293 3225, e-mail sly.bailey@trinitymirror.com)

BAILEY, Terence Michael; s of Thomas Sturman Bailey, and Margaret Hilda, *née* Wright; *b* 22 October 1946; *Educ* Kettering GS, Lanchester Poly Coventry (BA); *m* 1, 21 Oct 1972 (m dis), Penelope Ann, da of Geoffrey Lever Butler; 1 s (Tobin b 1976); m 2, 20 July 1985, Susan Jane, da of Frederick Peter Runacres; 3 s (Tim b 1986, Christopher b 1987, David b 1990); *Career* slr to Corby Devpt Corp 1972–73, ptnr Toller Hales & Collcutt (Northants) 1973–98 (conslt 1998–2000), sole practitioner 2001–, sr ptnr Terence Bailey Slrs 2002–; chm Corby Industrial Gp (for promotion of industry in Corby area) 1991–94, Office Supervision of Solicitors Law Soc 1999–2001; tstee Lakelands Hospice Corby 2002–06; *Recreations* skiing, motor-cycling, gardening, keep-fit, reading; *Clubs* Northants Law Soc, Kettering Golf, RHS; *Style*— Terence M Bailey, Esq; ✉ Yew Tree Farm House, Little Oakley, Corby, Northamptonshire NN18 8HA (tel 01536 742233); Horsemarket, Kettering, Northamptonshire NN16 0DG (tel 01536 485888)

BAILEY, Timothy Guy; s of William John Joseph Bailey, and Maureen Ann, *née* Neenan; *b* 9 September 1964; *Educ* English Martyrs Sch Hartlepool, Univ of Newcastle upon Tyne (BA, BArch); *m* 16 Jan 1999, Ruth Martina, da of Frank Connorton; *Career* Browne Smith Baker: joined 1990, assoc 1993–97, ptnr 1997–2000; princ xsite architecture 2000–; chair Northern Architecture 1997–2006; dir Northern Stage Ltd 1998– (chm 2004–); RIBA: memb 1992–, chm Northumbria Branch 1994–96, chm Northern Region 1997–99, memb Cncl 1997–99; FRSA; *Recreations* reading, cooking; *Style*— Timothy Bailey, Esq; ✉ xsite architecture, Foundry Lane Studios, Foundry Lane, Newcastle upon Tyne NE6 1LH (tel 0191 287 2161, fax 0191 287 2166, website ww.xsitearchitecture.co.uk)

BAILHACHE, Sir Philip Martin; kt (1996); s of Sqdn Ldr Lester Vivian Bailhache, RAF (d 2005), and Nanette Ross, *née* Ferguson (d 1997); *b* 28 February 1946; *Educ* Charterhouse, Pembroke Coll Oxford (MA); *m* 1, 1967 (m dis 1982); 2 s (Robert b 1968, John b 1974), 2 da (Rebecca b 1969, Catherine b 1972); m 2, 1984, Linda, da of Martin Geoffrey Le Vavasseur dit Durell; 1 da (Alice b 1988), 1 s (Edward b 1990); *Career* called to the Bar Middle Temple 1968 (bencher 2003), called to the Jersey Bar 1969; advocate Jersey 1969–74 (dep for Grouville 1972–74), slr-gen Jersey 1975–86, attorney-gen Jersey 1986–93, QC 1989, bailiff of Jersey 1995– (dep bailiff 1994–95), pres Jersey Court of Appeal 1995–; ed Jersey Law Review 1997–; chm Jersey Arts Cncl 1987–89; hon fell Pembroke Coll Oxford 1995; *Recreations* music, the arts, gardening, wine; *Clubs* Reform, United (Jersey); *Style*— Sir Philip Bailhache; ✉ L'Anquetinerie, Grouville, Jersey (tel 01534 852533); Bailiff's Chambers, Royal Court House, St Helier, Jersey (tel 01534 502100, fax 01534 502198)

BAILIE, Roy E; OBE; *Educ* Harvard Business Sch; *Career* currently chm W&G Baird Holdings Ltd (dir 1982–); dir: W&G Baird Ltd 1977–, Graphic Plates Ltd 1977–, MSO Clelland Ltd 1984–, Biddles Ltd 1989–, Blackstaff Press Ltd 1995–, The Thanet Press Ltd 1995–, CDS Ltd 2000–; chm CBI (NI) 1992–94; non-exec dir: NI Cncl for HE 1985–90, Industrial Devpt Bd for NI 1990–95, Tacade 1990–99 (memb Advsy Cncl on Alcohol & Drug Educn), NI Tourist Bd 1996–2002 (chm), Ulster TV 1997–, Bank of England 1998–2003, Re-Solv (Soc for the Prevention of Solvent and Volatile Substance Abuse) 2001–, Bristol & West 2006–; memb Ct: Bank of England 1998, Bank of Ireland 1999; memb Exec Bd BPIF (vice-chm 1997–99, pres 1999–2001); *Recreations* sailing, golf, walking; *Style*— Roy Bailie, OBE; ✉ W&G Baird Holdings Ltd, Greystone Road, Antrim BT41 2RS (tel 028 9446 6107, fax 028 9446 6266, e-mail roy.bailie@thebairdgroup.co.uk)

BAILLIE, Andrew Bruce; QC; s of Edward Oswald Baillie (d 1974), and (Molly Eva Lavers) Renée, *née* Andrews (d 1985); *b* 17 May 1948; *Educ* KCS Wimbledon, Université De Besancon, Univ of Kent (BA); *m* 11 Sept 1976, Mary Lou Meech (d 1988), da of Stanley Harold Palmer (d 1988), of Portsmouth, Hants; 2 da (Emma b 1979, Victoria b 1981), 1 s (Oliver b 1984); *Career* called to the Bar Inner Temple 1970, recorder of the Crown Court 1989–; memb Criminal Bar Assoc; *Recreations* numerous, from rugby football to flower arranging; *Style*— Andrew Baillie, Esq, QC; ✉ 9 Gough Square, London EC4 (tel 020 7832 0500, e-mail abaillie@9goughsq.co.uk)

BAILLIE, Iain Cameron; s of David Brown Baillie (d 1976), and Agnes Wiseman, *née* Thomson (d 1992); *b* 14 July 1931; *Educ* Glasgow HS, Univ of Glasgow (BSc), Fordham Law Sch NY (JD); *m* 1959, Joan Mary Christine, da of Dr Allan Miller (d 1967), and Dr Margaret Miller (d 1971), of Rickmansworth, Herts; 1 s (Gordon); *Career* retired; formerly int lawyer; sr Euro ptnr Ladas & Parry (of NY, Chicago, LA, London, and Munich); admitted NY Bar and Fed Cts incl Supreme Ct (USA); dir MRC Collaborative Centre 1993–99; author of numerous articles and frequent lectr on business law; fell: Inst of Int Licensing Practitioners, Inst of Trade Marks, Inst of Patent Agents; FRSA; *Books* Practical Management of Intellectual Property (1986), Licensing - A Practical Guide for the Businessman (1987); *Recreations* law, walking, model making; *Clubs* Caledonian; *Style*— Iain Baillie, Esq; ✉ Town Mill, 191 High Street, Old Amersham, Buckinghamshire HP7 0EQ (tel 01494 723520, fax 01494 723521, e-mail baillie@talkgas.tv)

BAILLIE, Jackie; MSP; *b* 15 January 1964; *Career* Strathkelvin DC 1990–96, community devpt mangr East Dunbartonshire Cncl 1996–99, chair Scottish Labour Pty 1997–98; MSP (Lab) Dumbarton 1999–; min for social justice until 2001; memb Scottish Lab Pty Exec Ctee 1990–99; memb Bd of Volunteer Devpt Scotland; *Style*— Ms Jackie Baillie, MSP; ✉ Dumbarton Constituency Office, 125 College Street, Dumbarton G82 1NH (tel 01389 734214, fax 01389 761498, e-mail jackie.baillie.msp@scottish.parliament.uk)

BAILLIE, Prof John; s of Arthur Baillie (d 1979), of Glasgow, and Agnes Baillie (d 1981); *b* 7 October 1944; *Educ* Whitehill Sr Secdy Sch; *m* 3 June 1973, Annette, da of James Alexander; 1 da (Nicola b 13 Oct 1975), 1 s (Kenneth b 22 Feb 1979); *Career* CA 1967; ptnr: KPMG 1978–93, Scott-Moncrieff 1993–2001; author of various tech and professional papers to professional jls; ICAS: memb various ctees 1978–, convenor Research Ctee 1995–99; Johnstone Smith chair of accountancy Univ of Glasgow 1983–88, visiting prof of accountancy: Heriot-Watt Univ 1988–95, Univ of Glasgow 1998–; memb Reporting Panel Competition Cmmn 2002–, memb Accounts Cmmn 2003–, bd memb Audit Scotland 2004–; Hon MA Univ of Glasgow 1983; *Books* Systems of Profit Measurement (1985), Consolidated Accounts and The Seventh Directive (1985); *Recreations* keeping fit, reading, golf, music, hill walking; *Clubs* Western (Glasgow); *Style*— Prof John Baillie; ✉ The Glen, Glencairn Road, Kilmacolm, Renfrewshire PA13 4PJ (tel 01505 873254)

BAILLIE, Robin Alexander MacDonald; *b* 20 August 1933; *Educ* Larkhall Acad; *m* 7 Feb 1959, Dr Elizabeth Susan Baillie, da of John Ordish; 1 s (Jonathan Michael b 20 Oct 1962), 1 da (Caroline Elizabeth b 2 March 1971); *Career* Nat Serv Sub Lt RNVR 1952–54; divnl dir Grindlays Bank plc 1973 (bank offr Kenya, Uganda and India 1955–66), chief exec Exporters Refinance Corporation Ltd 1972 (joined 1966), md Wallace Brothers Group 1976–77 (joined 1973); Standard Chartered Group: md Standard Chartered Merchant Bank 1977–85, md MAIBL plc 1983, exec dir 1983–87, non-exec dir 1987–94; chm Burson-Marsteller Ltd 1987–92, chm Henderson Horizon Fund; sr ind dir Liberty International plc until 2004; non-exec dir: Henderson Global Investors (Holdings) plc 1992–2005, City Merchants High Yield Trust plc, Gartmore Smaller Companies Trust plc, Gartmore Irish Growth Fund plc, INVESCO Asia Trust plc; FCIBS, FRSA, FInstD; *Recreations* the opera, Victorian watercolours, Indian art; *Style*— Robin Baillie, Esq; ✉ Gartmore Investment Limited, 8 Fenchurch Place, London EC3M 4PH

BAILLIE, William James Laidlaw; CBE (1998); s of James Leitch Baillie (d 1987), of Edinburgh, and Helen Swan Laidlaw (d 1949), of Edinburgh; *b* 1923, Edinburgh; *Educ* Edinburgh Coll of Art (Andrew Grant scholar, DA), Moray House Coll of Educn Edinburgh; *m* 1961, Helen Gillon; 2 da (Wendy Louise Anne b 1964, Lucinda Elyse Jillian b 1965), 1 s (Jonathan William James b 1970); *Career* artist; served RCS 1942–47; teacher Edinburgh schs 1951–60; Edinburgh Coll of Art: lectr 1960, sec Staff Assoc 1961–66, sr lectr 1968, dep head Sch of Drawing and Painting 1974–77, academic staff memb Bd of Govrs 1974–77 and 1986, ret from teaching 1988; resident tutor Nat Gall of Canada Summer Sch 1955, visitor Harvard Univ 1958; EIS Award Royal Scot Acad 1980, Cargill Award Royal Glasgow Inst of the Fine Arts 1984, May Marshall Brown Award Royal Scot Soc of Painters in Water Colours 1989, Sir William Gillies Award Royal Scot Soc of Painters in Water Colours 1992; Hon DLitt Heriot-Watt Univ 1997; pres: Royal Scot Soc of Painters in Water Colours 1974–88 (memb 1963–), Royal Scot Acad 1990–98 (treas 1980); memb: Soc of Scottish Artists 1953 (hon memb 1994), Royal Glasgow Inst of the Fine Arts 1986; hon memb: Royal Acad of Arts 1991, Royal W of Eng Acad 1991, Royal Hibernian Acad 1991, Br Watercolour Soc 1992, Royal Ulster Acad 1994; RSA 1979 (ARSA 1968), Hon FRSBS 1992; *Solo Exhibitions* incl: Saltire Soc Festival Exhbn (Edinburgh) 1961, Silver Coin Gall Harrogate 1964, Douglas and Foulis Gall Edinburgh 1965, Calouste Gulbenkian Gall Newcastle 1966, Loomshop Gall Lower Largo 1971, 1973, 1977 and 1980, Heal's Gall London 1974, retrospective (Kircaldy Art Gall Fife) 1977, Peter Potter Gall Haddington 1978, ESU Gall Edinburgh 1981 and 1983, Macaulay Gall Stenton 1982 and 1985, Scottish Gall Edinburgh 1982 and 1986, Gallery 10 London 1983, 1985 and 1987, Lamp of Lothian Festival Exhbn (Haddington) 1984, Salisbury Theatre Festival Exhbn 1988, Kingfisher Gall Festival Exhbn (Edinburgh) 1989 and 1997, Thackeray Gall London 1992 and 1994; *Group Exhibitions* incl: Arts Cncl touring exhbn 1953 and 1962, Contemporary Scottish Art Reading 1964, Univ of Edinburgh Festival Exhbn 1966, Marjorie Parr Gall London 1967, Edinburgh Festival Exhbn (Coll of Art Edinburgh) 1971, Scottish Contemporary Drawings and Paintings 1973, ESU Gall Edinburgh 1973, Drawings and Paintings from Fife Collections (Kirkcaldy Art Gall Fife) 1975, Dumfries and Galloway Festival Exhbn 1980, Castle Douglas Art Gall 1980, Artist and Teacher Exhbn (Fine Art Soc Edinburgh and Glasgow) 1980, Contemporary Art from Scotland (touring exhbn) 1981, Bath Festival Contemporary Art Fair 1983, Barbican Int Arts Fair London 1984, Knightsbridge Gall Wichita 1985, Ten Scottish Painters (Royal Acad of Arts London) 1986, Solomon Gall London 1986, Artists Abroad (Royal Acad of Arts London) 1986, Wichita Art Museum 1987, Scottish Arts Club Edinburgh 1988, UK Presidents Exhbn Arundel 1988, Edinburgh Sch (Kingfisher Gall Edinburgh) 1988, Anniversary Exhbn (Kingfisher Gall Edinburgh) 1988, 25th Anniversary Exhbn (Loomshop Gall Lower Largo) 1989, Sheila Harrison Fine Art London 1989, Thackeray Gall London 1989, State of the Art (Fine Art Soc Edinburgh and Glasgow) 1989, Scottish Contemporary Paintings (Arts Club London) 1989, Summer Exhbn (Open Eye Gall Edinburgh) 1989, Scottish Water-Colours (Scottish Gall Edinburgh) 1989, 20th Century British Paintings (Fosse Gall Cheltenham) 1989, RGI Mayfest Exhbn (Glasgow Art Club) 1990, RGI Exhbn (Macaulay Gall Stenton) 1990, Works on Paper (Thackeray Gall London) 1990, Spring Exhbn (Loomshop Gall Lower Largo) 1990, Mistral Gall London 1990, Images of the Orient (Kingfisher Gall Edinburgh) 1990, Scottish Artists (Lynne Stern Assocs London) 1991, Summer Exhbn (Thackeray Gall London) 1991, Spring Exhbn (Loomshop Gall Lower Largo) 1991, Scottish Art 20th Century (Royal West of England Acad Bristol) 1991, Contemporary Scottsh Art (Hilton Hotel Hong Kong) 1994,

B

Richmond Hill Gall London 1994, Frames Gall Perth 1998, Albemarle Gall London 1999, Millennium Exhbn - Eight Academicians (Scottish show, Albemarle Gall London) 2000, 6 Royal Scottish Academicians (Albemarle Gall London) 2001, Scottish Paintings (New Acad Galls London) 2001, Colours Gall Edinburgh 2001; *Work in Collections* incl: Aberdeen Art Gall, Univ of Aberdeen, Carnegie Tst Dunfermline, City Art Centre Edinburgh, Dumbarton Educn Ctee, Edinburgh Coll of Art, Educnl Inst of Scot, ESU Edinburgh, Robert Fleming Hldgs London, Fox Linton Assocs London, Fife Educn Authy, General Accident HQ Perth, Glasgow Art Gall, Guinness plc London, Heriot-Watt Univ Edinburgh, Hunterian Collection Univ of Glasgow, Kirkcaldy Art Gall, Lothian Region Schs Collection, Lycium Investment Corp London, Mexican Embassy London, Miny of the Environment, Montagh Lobbl Stanley London, Nuffield Fndn, Reuters Ltd London, Royal Bank of Scot, Royal Edinburgh Hosp, Royal Scot Acad, Scot Arts Cncl, Scottish Equitable Assurance Edinburgh, Scot Nat Gall of Modern Art, Unilever London, Wichita Art Assoc KS; work in various private collections in Aust, Canada, Germany, Greece, Sweden, UK and USA; *Recreations* the arts, music, travel; *Clubs* Scottish Arts (Edinburgh), New (Edinburgh); *Style*— William J L Baillie, Esq, CBE, PPRSA; ✉ c/o Albemarle Gallery, 49 Albemarle Street, London W1S 4JR

BAILLIEU, 3 Baron (UK 1953); James William Latham Baillieu; er s of 2 Baron Baillieu (d 1973), and his 1 w, Anne Bayliss, da of Leslie William Page; *b* 16 November 1950; *Educ* Radley, Monash Univ Melbourne (BEc); *m* 1, 1974 (m dis 1985), Cornelia, da of late William Ladd; 1 s (Hon Robert Latham b 2 Feb 1979); m 2, 1986 (m dis 1995), Clare, da of Peter Stephenson; *Heir* s, Hon Robert Baillieu; *Career* 2 Lt Coldstream Gds 1970–73; Banque Nationale de Paris (Melbourne) 1978–80, asst dir Rothschild Australia Ltd 1980–88, dir Manufacturers Hanover Australia Ltd 1988–90, dir Standard Chartered Asia Ltd 1990–92, asst dir Credit Lyonnais Asia Ltd 1992–94, asst dir Nomura Int (Hong Kong) Ltd 1995, gen dir Regent European Securities 1995–96, dir CentreInvest Gp Moscow 1996–99, dir Anthony Baillieu and Assocs (Hong Kong) Ltd 1992–, md Bank NIKoil 2000–; *Clubs* Boodle's, Australian (Melbourne), Hong Kong (Hong Kong); *Style*— The Rt Hon the Lord Baillieu

BAIN, Chris; s of Derek Bain, of Borden, Kent, and Mary, *née* Hill (d 1995); *b* 27 November 1953, London; *Educ* Univ of Leicester (BA), Middlesex Univ (MBA), Open Univ (MSC); *Career* head of campaigns Oxfam 1992–96, head of progs VSO 1996–2003, chief exec CAFOD 2003–; dir Disasters Emergency Ctee 2003–, chair British Overseas Aid Gp; *Recreations* long distance pilgrimages, ale and whisky appreciation; *Style*— Chris Bain, Esq; ✉ CAFOD, Romero Close, Stockwell Road, London SW9 9TY (tel 020 7326 5500, e-mail cdb@cafod.org.uk)

BAIN, Prof Sir George Sayers; kt (2001); s of George Alexander Bain (d 2006), of Winnipeg, Canada, and Margaret Ioleen, *née* Bamford (d 1988); *b* 24 February 1939; *Educ* Winnipeg State Sch System, Univ of Manitoba (BA, MA), Univ of Oxford (DPhil); *m* 1, 24 Aug 1962 (m dis 1987), Carol Lynne Ogden, da of Herbert Fyffe White (d 1986); 1 da (Katherine Anne b 1967), 1 s (David Thomas b 1969); m 2, 28 Dec 1988, (Frances) Gwynneth Rigby, *née* Vickers; *Career* Royal Canadian Navy Reserve, Midshipman 1957–60, Sub Lt 1960, Lt 1963, ret 1963; lectr in economics Univ of Manitoba 1962–63, res fell in industrial rels Nuffield Coll Oxford 1966–69, Frank Thomas prof of industrial rels UMIST 1969–70; Univ of Warwick: dir Industrial Rels Res Unit of SSRC 1974–81 (dep dir 1970–74), titular prof 1974–79, Pressed Steel Fisher prof of industrial rels 1979–89, chm Sch of Industrial and Business Studies 1983–89; princ London Business Sch 1989–97, pres and vice-chllr Queen's Univ Belfast 1998–2004 (currently prof emeritus); distinguished visiting prof Univ of Manitoba 1985, Cecil H and Ida Green visiting prof Univ of British Columbia 1987; memb res staff Royal Cmmn on Trade Unions and Employers' Assoc (The Donovan Cmmn) 1966–67, consIt to Nat Bd for Prices and Incomes 1967–69; chm: Cncl Univ Mgmnt Schs 1987–90 (exec memb 1984–90), Food Sector Working Gp NEDO 1991–92, Cmmn on Public Policy and Br Business Inst Public Policy Research 1995–97, Low Pay Cmmn 1997–2002, NI Meml Fund 1998–2002, Conf of Univ Rectors in Ireland 2000–01, Work and Parents Task Force DTI 2001, Pensions Policy Inst 2002–04, Ind Review of Fire Service ODPM 2002, ACU 2002–03, NI Legal Servs Review Gp 2005–06, NI Ind Strategic Review of Educn 2006; memb: Exec Br Univs Industrial Rels Assoc 1971–80 (sec 1971–74), Mechanical Engrg Econ Devpt Ctee NEDO 1974–76 (consIt to NEDO 1982–85), Ctee of Inquiry on Industrial Democracy (Bullock Ctee) 1975–76, Cncl ESRC 1986–91, Cncl Nat Forum for Mgmnt Educn and Devpt 1987–90, Cncl Fndn for Mgmnt Educn 1991–97, American Assembly of Collegiate Schs of Business 1992–94, Int Cncl American Mgmnt Assoc 1993–96, Bd Fndn for Canadian Studies in the UK 1993–2001 and 2004–06, Sr Salaries Review Body 1993–96, Bd of Co-operation Ireland 1994–97, Cncl BESO 1995–97, Bd of Dirs Grad Mgmnt Admission Cncl 1996–97, GB Bd of Co-operation Ireland 1998–2004, Educn Honours Ctee 2005–; dir: Blackwell Publishers Ltd 1990–97, The Economist Group 1992–2001, Canada Life Gp (UK) Ltd 1994–, Canada Life Assurance Company 1996–2003, Electra Private Equity plc 1998–, Bombardier Aerospace Short Brothers plc 1998–2007, NI Science Park Fndn 1999–2004, Canada Life Capital Corp 2003–, Iain More Assocs 2004–, Entertainment One 2007–; advsr on Royal Mail to Sec of State for Trade and Industry 2005–; tstee: European Fndn for Mgmnt Devpt 1990–96 (memb Exec Ctee 1991–96, exec vice-pres 1991–95), Navam at Armagh 1999–2003, Scotch-Irish Tst 1999–, Cncl for Advancement and Support of Educn (CASE) 2004–, CASE Europe 2004–07; patron Somme Assoc 2004–; pres Involvement and Participation Assoc 2002–06; arbitrator/mediator for ACAS 1970–92; fell London Business Sch 1999, hon fell Nuffield Coll Oxford 2002; Hon DBA De Montfort Univ 1994; Hon LLD: NUI 1998, Univ of Guelph Canada 1999, UC of Cape Breton 1999, Univ of Manitoba 2003, Univ of Warwick 2003, Queen's Univ Canada 2004, Queen's Univ Belfast 2005; Hon DLitt: Univ of Ulster 2002, Univ of New Brunswick 2003; Hon DSc Cranfield Univ 2005; FRSA 1987, AcSS 2000, CCMI (CIMgt 1991), FBAM 1994; *Books* Trade Union Growth and Recognition (1967), The Growth of White-Collar Unionism (1970), The Reform of Collective Bargaining at Plant and Company Levels (1971), Social Stratification and Trade Unionism (1973), Union Growth and the Business Cycle (1976), A Bibliography of British Industrial Relations (1979 and 1985), Profiles of Union Growth (1980), Industrial Relations in Britain (ed 1983); *Recreations* genealogy, family history, Western riding, piano playing; *Clubs* Reform; *Style*— Prof Sir George Bain; ✉ c/o The Queen's University of Belfast, University Road, Belfast BT7 1NN

BAIN, Dr Neville Clifford; s of Charles Alexander Bain (d 1990), of St Kilda, Dunedin, NZ, and, Gertrude Mae, *née* Howe (d 1986); *b* 14 July 1940; *Educ* King's HS Dunedin, Univ of Otago (MCom, LLD); *m* 18 Sept 1987, Anne Patricia; from previous m, 1 da (Susan Mary b 1963), 1 s (Peter John b 1965), 1 step da (Kristina Knights b 1979); *Career* trainee inspr Inland Revenue NZ 1957–59, mangr Anderson & Co Chartered Accountants NZ 1960–62, various mgmnt posts Cadbury Schweppes plc 1963–90 (latterly gp fin dir and dep chief exec), gp chief exec Coats Viyella plc 1990–97 (resigned), chm Consignia plc (formerly The Post Office) 1998–2001 (resigned), chm Hogg Robinson plc 1997–2006; chm IOD 2006– (memb Cncl and chm of Audit and Risk Ctee 1993); professional dir and consIt; dir Biocon Ltd (India), dir United Breweries Ltd (India) 2003–05, non-exec dir Scottish & Newcastle plc 1997–2007, chm Nutrinnovator 2003–06, dir Provexis Ltd 2005–; formerly dir: Cadbury Schweppes Overseas Ltd, Cadbury Schweppes Australia, Cadbury Schweppes South Africa, Cadbury India Ltd, Amalgamated Beverages GB, Reading Scientific Services Ltd, Itnet Ltd; tstee Nat Centre for Soc Research 2002–06, memb Ctee Mgmnt Charter Initiative, memb Cncl for Excellence in Mgmnt and Leadership 1999–2001; tstee Otago Univ Tst 1987–; CMA, FCIS 1962, FCA 1989 (ACA 1959), FInstD 1993, FRSM 1995; *Books* Successful Management (1995), Winning Ways Through Corporate Governance (with Professor David Band, 1996), The People Advantage (with Bill Mabey, 1999); *Recreations* music, sport, writing; *Style*— Dr Neville C Bain

BAIN, Dr Peter George; s of George Bain, and Hélène Marie Josephine; *b* 1957; *Educ* Worth Sch, The Queen's Coll Oxford (MA), Bart's Med Coll (MB BS, Christopher Frears Prize in Neurology), Univ of London (MD); *m* Jane Francesca; 1 da, 2 s; *Career* house physician Professorial Med Unit Bart's 1982–83, house surgn Royal Berks Hosp 1983, SHO (med) rotation Guy's 1983–84, SHO (A&E) St Mary's and St Charles Hosps 1985, SHO (neurology) SE Thames Regnl Neurological and Neurosurgical Centre Brook Hosp 1985–86 and 1987, med Registrar Southmead Hosp Bristol 1986–87, neurology registrar Guy's 1987–89, visiting academic in neuropathology Dept of Neuropathology Inst of Psychiatry London 1989, tutor and demonstrator in physiology Dept of Physiology Univ of Bristol 1989–90, res registrar in neurology MRC Human Movement and Balance Unit Inst of Neurology London 1990–92, hon clinical asst in neurology Nat Hosp for Neurology and Neurosurgery London 1990–92, neurology registrar Radcliffe Infirmary Oxford 1992–94, neurology lectr and hon sr registrar Academic Unit of Neurosciences Charing Cross and Westminster Med Sch 1994–95, locum consIt neurologist Central Middx Hosp London 1995, consIt and sr lectr in neurology Imperial Coll Sch of Med London and W Middx Univ Hosp Tst 1995–99; Imperial Coll Sch of Med London: sr lectr in neurology 1999–2002, reader in neurology 2002–; GMC specialist register (neurology) 1996; clinical examiner Univ of London: MB BS med finals, MD thesis; Int Tremor Fndn: memb Advsy Panel ITF Tremor Investigation Gp (TRIG), fndr memb and hon sec Br Tremor Res Gp; tstee Nat Tremor Fndn; memb: Movement Disorder Soc, Br Soc of Rehabilitation Med, Assoc of Br Neurologists; memb Int Congress Ctees Kiel 1997 and 2001; Int Congress lectr: Keil Germany 1997 and 2000, Barcelona 2000, Copenhagen 2000, London 2001, Kyoto 2006; memb Editorial Bd: Current Medical Literature: Neurology 1996–, Continuous Professional Development: Neurology 1998–2002, Movement Disorders Jl 1999–; Duke Elder Nat Prize for Ophthalmology Inst of Ophthalmology London 1982; MRSM, FRCP 1998 (MRCP 1985); *Publications* Assessing Tremor Severity: a clinical handbook (jtly, 1993), Current Issues in Essential Tremor (jt monograph, 1999), Essential Tremor: The Facts (jtly, 2006); author of approx 200 editorials, reviews, papers for jls, letters, chapters, newsletters and conference work; *Recreations* surfing, rowing and sculling, karate, ju-jitsu, chess, zen koans, rock climbing; *Clubs* London Rowing, Anglo-Japanese Karate Club Dojo, Worth Old Boys' Golf; *Style*— Dr Peter Bain; ✉ Department of Neuroscience, Imperial College, Charing Cross Campus, Fulham Palace Road, London W6 8RF (tel 020 8846 1182)

BAINBRIDGE, Dame Beryl; DBE (2000); da of Richard Bainbridge, and Winifred Baines; *b* 21 November 1934; *Educ* Merchant Taylors' Sch Liverpool, Arts Educnl Schs Tring; *m* 1954 (m dis), Austin Davies; 1 s, 2 da; *Career* actress and writer; columnist Evening Standard 1987–93; Author of the Year Br Book Awards 1998 and 1999, James Tait Black Meml Prize British Book Awards 1999, David Cohen Prize (jtly) 2003; Hon LittD Univ of Liverpool 1986; fell Hunterian Soc; FRSL 1978; *Books* A Weekend with Claud (1967, revised edn 1981), Another Part of the Wood (1968, revised edn 1979), Harriet Said.... (1972), The Dressmaker (1973 shortlisted Booker Prize, film 1989), The Bottle Factory Outing (1974, Guardian Fiction Award, shortlisted Booker Prize), Sweet William (1975, film 1980), A Quiet Life (1976), Injury Time (1977, Whitbread Award), Young Adolf (1978), Winter Garden (1980), English Journey (1984, TV series), Watson's Apology (1984), Mum and Mr Armitage (1985), Forever England (1986, TV series 1986), Filthy Lucre (1986), An Awfully Big Adventure (1989, theatre adaptation Liverpool Playhouse 1992, film 1995, shortlisted Booker Prize), The Birthday Boys (1991), Something Happened Yesterday (1993, articles from Evening Standard), Collected Stories (1994), Every Man For Himself (1996, Whitbread Award for Best Novel, Eurasian Cwlth Prize, shortlisted Booker Prize), Master Georgie (1998, shortlisted Booker Prize Award, winner W H Smith Literary Award 1999), According to Queeney (2001); *Plays* Tiptoe Through the Tulips (1976), The Warrior's Return (1977), It's a Lovely Day Tomorrow (1977), Journal of Bridget Hitler (1981), Somewhere More Central (TV 1981), Evensong (TV 1986); *Recreations* painting, sleeping; *Style*— Dame Beryl Bainbridge, DBE, FRSL; ✉ 42 Albert Street, London NW1 (tel 020 7387 3113)

BAINBRIDGE, Guy Lawrence Tarn; s of David Tarn Bainbridge (d 1966), and Margaret, *née* Frost; *b* 13 September 1960, Darlington, Co Durham; *Educ* Oundle, St Johns Coll Cambridge (MA); *m* 21 Sept 1991, Katherine, *née* Godber; 2 s (Oliver b 24 Dec 1993, Charlie 22 Oct 1998), 1 da (Emily b 7 Nov 1995); *Career* KPMG (formerly Peat Marwick Mitchell & Co) 1982– (memb UK Bd 2005–); ACA 1985; *Recreations* tennis, golf, skiing; *Style*— Guy Bainbridge, Esq; ✉ KPMG, Saltire Court, 20 Castle Terrace, Edinburgh EH1 2EG (tel 0131 527 6731, e-mail guy.bainbridge@kpmg.co.uk)

BAINBRIDGE, John Philip; s of Philip James Bainbridge (d 2005), of Mottingham, London, and Joan Winifred, *née* Walker; *b* 28 August 1946; *Educ* Chislehurst and Sidcup GS; *m* 2 May 1970, Marilynne Ailsa, da of Stanley Joseph Kesler (d 1985), of Cranleigh, Surrey; 2 s (Daniel John b 1979, James Ashley b 1981); *Career* Blakemore, Elgar and Co 1964–73, Schroders 1973–2003; memb Cranleigh Parish Cncl; memb Ct of Assts Worshipful Co of Fuellers; FCA; *Recreations* reading, golf, wine, beekeeping, gardening; *Style*— John Bainbridge, Esq; ✉ Baltic House, The Common, Cranleigh, Surrey GU6 8SL (tel 01483 275949)

BAINBRIDGE, Prof Simon; *b* 30 August 1952; *Educ* RCM; *Career* studied under John Lambert and Gunther Schuller (Tanglewood 1973 and 1974); Forman fell in composition Univ of Edinburgh 1976–78, US/UK Bicentennial Fellowship 1978–79, sometime Nat Theatre, composer in res Southern Arts 1983–85, head of composition Royal Acad of Music 1999–, prof Univ of London 2001–; FRCM 1997, Hon RAM 2001; *Compositions* incl: Spirogyra (Aldeburgh Festival, 1971), Viola Concerto (cmmnd by Walter Trampler, 1978), Fantasia for Double Orch (1983–84), Double Concerto (cmmnd by Cheltenham Festival for Nicholas Daniel and Joy Farrell, 1990), Toccata (for orch, 1992), Ad Ora Incerta - Four Orchestral Songs from Primo Levi (1993), Clarinet Quintet (for Joy Farrall and Kreutzer String Quartet, 1993), For Miles (solo trumpet, 1994), Landscape and Memory (horn concerto for Michael Thompson and London Sinfonietta, 1995), Four Primo Levi Settings (cmmnd by Cheltenham Festival for Nash Ensemble and Susan Bickley, 1996), Éicha (Oxford Contemporary Music Festival, 1997); *Recordings* Fantasia for Double Orch, Viola Concerto, Concertante in Moto Perpetuo, Four Primo Levi Settings, Ad Ora Incerta; *Awards* Gemini Prize 1988, Univ of Louisville Grawemeyer Award for Music Composition (for Ad Ora Incerta) 1997; *Style*— Prof Simon Bainbridge, Esq

BAINES, Alan Leonard; s of Leonard Baines (d 1989), of Thorpe, Derbys, and Edna, *née* Hackston (d 1985); *b* 7 May 1948; *Educ* Chadderton GS Lancashire; *m* 1982, Carole, da of Colin Johnson; *Career* articled clerk Joseph Crossley & Sons Manchester, accountant Price Waterhouse 1970–74, Stoy Hayward (now BDO Stoy Hayward) 1975–2001 (ptnr 1976), ptnr Grant Thornton 2002–04, independent 2004–; specialist advsr on problems of corp strategies and growing businesses; FCA; *Recreations* the British coast and countryside, music, theatre; *Style*— Alan Baines, Esq

BAINES, Garron John; s of Roy Hubert Baines, of Tadgells, Housham Tye, Harlow, Essex, and Jillian Ann, *née* Wheeley; *b* 25 August 1952; *Educ* Oundle; *m* 6 July 1974, Irene Joyce, da of Richard Rennie Williams, of 19 Broadstone Ave, Port Glasgow, Renfrewshire, Scotland; 2 da (Laura Lockhart b 1 Nov 1978, Fiona Suzanne b 8 June 1982); *Career* former newspaper journalist E Midland Allied Press; ITN: joined as writer 1977, head Channel Four News until 1995 (news ed from launch 1982, dep ed 1989), ed international news progs 1995, head of prog devpt 1997–98, md ITN New Media 1998–2001; ptnr and managing princ Media and Entertainment Div IBM Business Consulting Services 2001; tstee NCH; *Recreations* talking, walking, sailing; *Style*— Garron Baines, Esq

BAINES, Rt Rev Nicholas; *see:* Croydon, Bishop of

BAINES, Paul Martin; s of Cyril Baines, of Pershore, Worcs, and Marion, *née* Guy; *b* 28 January 1956, Gidea Park, Essex; *Educ* Brentwood Sch, Trinity Hall Cambridge (MA); *m* 16 June 1984, Rosemary, *née* Hanson; 2 s (Mark b 8 Oct 1986, Luke b 5 Dec 1988), 1 da (Lydia b 20 Aug 1990); *Career* admitted slr 1980; Freshfields 1978–80, Antony Gibbs & Sons Ltd 1980–84; Charterhouse: joined 1984, md 1989, head of corporate finance and chief exec 1996–2000; Hawkpoint Partners Ltd: md 2000–03, chief exec 2003–; dir Parayhouse Sch Ltd 2001–05, dir Collins Stewart plc 2006–; *Recreations* mountain walking, tennis, bridge; *Style*— Paul Baines, Esq; ✉ Hawkpoint Partners Limited, 4 Great St Helen's, London EC3A 6HA (tel 020 7665 4568, e-mail paul.baines@hawkpoint.com)

BAINES, Stephen Philip; s of Charles Philip Baines (d 1986), and Edna, *née* Millard; *b* 16 January 1947; *Educ* Neath GS, Avery Hill Coll of Educn London (CertEd), Univ of Oregon USA (BSc, MSc); *m* 14 Sept 1985, (Emilie) Micheline; 1 da (Katherine Sian b 27 April 1986), 1 s (David Alexander b 3 Oct 1988); *Career* physical educn teacher: Wandsworth Comp Sch 1969–71, Pendle Hill HS Sydney Aust (also sportsmaster) 1971–73; exec dir Canadian Rugby Union Ottawa 1975–81, md Pro-Motion International Toronto 1981–83, dir of mktg Nat Assoc of Boys' Clubs London 1983–86; chief exec: The Hockey Assoc 1986–97, English Hockey Assoc 1997–98; ceo International Rugby Board 1998–; spoken at numerous conferences worldwide, author of various articles for magazines; memb: Henley Royal Regatta Stewards Enclosure; fell Br Inst of Sports Administration; MIMgt, FCIM; *Recreations* international sport, rugby, photography, travel, golf; *Clubs* London Welsh RFC, Neath RFC, International Sportsman's, East India, St Stephen's Green; *Style*— Stephen Baines, Esq; ✉ IRB, Huguenot House, 35–38 St Stephen's Green, Dublin 2, Ireland (tel 00 3531 662 5444, fax 00 3531 676 9334)

BAINSFAIR, Paul; s of Leslie John Bainsfair, and Doris, *née* Cressey; *m* Sophie; 2 s (Bruno, Teddy), 1 da (Phoebe); *Career* advtg exec JWT, joined Saatchi & Saatchi 1975 rising to md 1987; fndr Bainsfair Sharkey Trott 1990, sold to GGT plc 1997; chm TBWA UK Gp Ltd (part of Omnicom), pres (Europe) TBWA Worldwide 2004–; MIPA; *Recreations* golf, shooting, skiing; *Clubs* Salisbury and S Wiltshire Golf, Soho House, The Union, Harry's Bar, Mark's; *Style*— Paul Bainsfair, Esq; ✉ TBWA, 76–80 Whitfield Street, London W1T 4EZ (tel 020 7573 6666, fax 020 7573 7119, mobile 0468 333666, e-mail paul.bainsfair@tbwa-europe.com)

BAIRD, Sir James Andrew Gardiner; 11 Bt (NS 1695), of Saughton Hall, Edinburghshire; s of Sir James Richard Gardiner Baird, 10 Bt, MC (d 1997), and Mabel Ann (Gay) Tempest, *née* Gill; *b* 2 May 1946; *Educ* Eton; *m* 1984 (m dis), Jean Margaret, da of Brig Sir Ian Liddell Jardine, 4 Bt, OBE, MC (d 1982), of Coombe Place, Meonstoke, Southampton; 1 s (Alexander b 28 May 1986); *Heir* s, Alexander Baird; *Recreations* shooting, fishing, photography; *Clubs* Boodle's; *Style*— Sir James Baird, Bt

BAIRD, Air Marshal Sir John Alexander; KBE (1999), DL (Cambs 1998); s of late Dr D A Baird, of Aberdeen, and late Isobel, *née* McLeod; *b* 25 July 1937; *Educ* Merchiston Castle Sch Edinburgh, Univ of Edinburgh Med Sch (MB, ChB); *m* 8 Oct 1963, Mary Barron, *née* Clews; *Career* cmmnd RAF 1963; jr MO: RAF Coningsby 1963–64, RAF Tengah 1964–67; SMO RAF Church Fenton 1968–70, Flt Surgn Br Defence Staff Washington 1970–73; SMO: RAF Valley (Flt MO 1974) 1973–76, RAF Lossiemouth 1976–78, RAF Coll Cranwell 1978–80; Cmd Flt MO HQ Strike Cmd 1980–83, conslt in occupational med 1983, MOD 1983–87, Gp Capt 1984, CO RAF Hosp Ely 1987–88, Air Cdre 1988, PMO RAF Germany 1988–91, Air Vice Marshal 1991, PMO HQ Strike Cmd 1991–94, DG Med Servs (RAF) HQ Personnel and Trg Cmd 1994–97, Air Marshal 1997, Surgn Gen Armed Forces 1997–2000; QHP 1991–2000; patron Children and Families of the Far East Prisoners of War, chm St John Cncl for Cambridgeshire 2001–07; Richard Fox-Linton Meml Prize 1982; memb Int Acad of Aviation and Space Med; fell Aerospace Med Assoc, fell Assoc of Medical Secretaries, Practice Managers, Administrators and Receptionists (FAMS), FRSM, FRCPE, FRCSE, FFOM, FRAeS, DAvMed; CStJ 1997; *Recreations* bird watching, wildlife conservation, sport (particularly cricket), music, travel, photography; *Clubs* RAF; *Style*— Air Marshal Sir John Baird, KBE, DL; ✉ Braeburn, Barway, Ely, Cambridgeshire CB7 5UB (tel and fax 01353 624968, e-mail sirjbaird@btinternet.com)

BAIRD, HE Nicholas Graham Faraday (Nick); s of Colin Baird, of Reigate, Surrey, and Elizabeth, *née* Powell; *b* 15 May 1962, Redhill, Surrey; *Educ* Dulwich Coll, Emmanuel Coll Cambridge (MA); *m* 17 Aug 1985, Caroline Jane, *née* Ivett; 1 s (Dominic b 22 March 1989), 2 da (Eleanor b 14 Dec 1990, Antonia b 17 April 1992); *Career* diplomat; joined FCO 1983, third sec Kuwait 1986–89, first sec UK Rep to the EU Brussels 1989–93, private sec to Parly Under-Sec of State FCO 1993–95, head EU Intergovernmental Conf Unit FCO 1995–97, dep head of mission Muscat 1997–98, cnsllr UK Rep to the EU Brussels 1998–2002, head EU Dept (Internal) FCO 2002–03, seconded as sr policy dir Immigration and Nationality Directorate Home Office 2003–06, ambass to Repub of Turkey 2006–; *Recreations* reading, travel, jogging, tennis, music; *Style*— HE Mr Nick Baird; ✉ c/o FCO (Ankara), King Charles Street, London SW1A 2AH (tel 00 90 312 455 3201, fax 00 90 312 455 3320, e-mail nick.baird@fco.gov.uk)

BAIRD, Roger Neale; s of John Allan Baird (d 1992), of Edinburgh, and Margaret Edith, *née* Shand (d 1994), of London; *b* 24 December 1941; *Educ* Daniel Stewarts Coll Edinburgh, Univ of Edinburgh (BSc, MB ChB, ChM); *m* 12 Oct 1968, Affra Mary, da of Douglas Varcoe-Cocks (d 1964); 1 da (Susan b 1970), 1 s (Richard b 1972); *Career* SHO and registrar Royal Infirmary Edinburgh 1969–73 (house surgn 1966–67), res scholar in clinical surgery 1967–69, lectr and sr lectr Univ of Bristol 1973–81, Fulbright scholar Harvard Med Sch 1975–76, conslt surgn Royal Infirmary Bristol 1977–2006; med dir United Bristol Healthcare Tst 1996–99, chm Litfield House Medical Centre Ltd 1996–2000; charitable tstee: European Soc for Vascular Surgery 1987–2003, United Bristol Hosps 1997–99; pres: British Medico-Chirurgical Soc 1994–95, Vascular Surgical Soc of GB and Ireland 2000–01, Cncl Bristol Clifton and W of England Zoological Soc 2000–05, Surgical Club of SW England 2003; hon memb: Australian and NZ Chapter Int Soc for Cardiovascular Surgery 1997, American Soc for Vascular Surgery 2002, European Soc for Vacular Surgery 2002; corresponding memb Vascular Soc of SA 1997; High Sheriff City of Bristol 2005–06; FRCS, FRCSEd; *Books* Diagnosis and Monitoring in Arterial Surgery (1980), Human Disease for Dental Students (1981); *Recreations* golf, skiing, travel; *Clubs* Army and Navy, Clifton; *Style*— Roger Baird, Esq; ✉ 23 Old Sneed Park, Stoke Bishop, Bristol BS9 1RG (tel 0117 968 5523); Litfield House, Clifton Down, Bristol BS8 3LS (tel 0117 973123, fax 0117 9733303, e-mail rogerbaird@litfieldhouse.co.uk)

BAIRD, Shiona; MSP; *b* 14 September 1946, Hereford; *Educ* Hereford HS, Mary Erskine Sch Edinburgh, Univ of Edinburgh (BSc); *m*; 5 c; *Career* social worker West Lothian, farmer JS Baird & Sons 1976– (now ptnr), MSP (Green) NE Scotland 2003–; ldr Green Party (also party spokesperson on enterprise), memb Enterprise and Culture Ctee, subst memb Communities Ctee; dir and co sec Tayside Fndn for Conservation of Resources; *Style*— Ms Shiona Baird, MSP; ✉ 29 Exchange Street, Dundee DD1 3DJ (tel 01382 227195, fax 01382 227195); The Scottish Parliament, Edinburgh EH99 1SP (tel 0131 348 66363, e-mail shiona.baird.msp@scottish.parliament.uk, website www.shionabairdmsp.org)

BAIRD, Vera; QC (2000), MP; da of Jack Thomas, and Alice, *née* Marsland; *b* 13 February 1951, Oldham, Lancs; *Educ* Chadderton GS for Girls Oldham, Newcastle Poly (LLB), Open Univ (BA), London Guilhall Univ (MA); *m* 1, 1972 (m dis 1978), David John Taylor-Gooby; *m* 2, 1978, Robert Brian Baird (d 1979); 2 step s; *Career* called to the Bar Gray's Inn 1975 (bencher); barr in the chambers of: W Steer QC 1975, Lord Gifford QC 1984, Michael Mansfield QC 1986–; advocacy trainer Gray's Inn 1998–, human rights law trainer Criminal Bar Assoc/Bar Cncl Trg Faculty 1999–2002, visiting law fell St Hilda's Coll Oxford 1999; MP (Lab) Redcar 2001– (Parly candidate Berwick 1983); Parly under sec of state DCA 2006–; memb Parly Jt Select Ctee on Human Rights 2001–03; chm: All-Pty Parly Gp on Burma, All-Pty Parly Gp on Domestic Violence, ROSA (APPG Survivors Sex Abuse), All Party Gp on Equalities; vice-chair: Assoc Parly Gp on Sex Equality, PLP Departmental Ctee on Legal and Constitutional Affrs; sec All Party Gp for the Br Cncl; memb All-Pty Parly Gp on: Civil Liberties, Steel Industry, Fishing Industry, Regeneration, Int Devpt; memb Standing Ctee: Proceeds of Crime Bill 2001–02, Export Control Bill 2001, Sex Offences Bill 2003, Criminal Justice Bill 2003, Police Reform Bill 2003, Housing Bill 2004, Pension Bill 2004; memb: PLP Women's Gp, PLP Departmental Ctee on Home Affrs, PLP Departmental Ctee on Regional Affrs; memb: Jt Ctee Draft Corruption Bill 2003, Jt Ctee Draft Child Contact Bill 2005; ed Justice for All Soc of Lab Lawyers until 2002; chair: Advsy Ctee Liberty Research Project into Deaths in Custody, ISTC Gp of MPs, Cmmn on Women in the Criminal Justice System (based at the Fawcett Soc); memb: Ctee on Child Witnesses and Child Defendants Criminal Bar Assoc 1999, Steering Ctee Lab Women's Network, Lab Pty Nat Policy Forum, Work and Pensions Select Ctee; vice-pres Assoc of Women Barrs 2000–, vice-chair Soc for Lab Lawyers, vice-chair Fawcett Soc 1998–2001, chair-elect Lab Criminal Justice Forum, fndr Gender and Criminal Justice Forum; memb: TGWU 1982–, Criminal Bar Assoc, Cncl of Justice, Fabian Soc, Co-operative Pty, Cwlth Parly Union; nat patron Rape Crisis Fndn, nat patron Drug Rape Tst, northern patron Jubilee 2000; hon fell St Hilda's Coll Oxford; *Publications* The Judiciary (co-author, 1992), Response to Runciman (co-author, 1993), Negotiated Justice (co-author, 1993), Economical with the Proof (co-author, 1993), Rape in Court (1998), The Human Rights Act 1998 (2000), Defending Battered Women Who Kill (2002); author Archbold Practical Research Papers (on Harrassment, Perverting the Course of Justice and the Criminal Cases Review Commission) 1996–; regular book reviewer and occasional contrib of articles on general law topics and cases for legal periodicals incl Criminal Law Review, Legal Action, and Medicine, Science and the Law; *Style*— Mrs Vera Baird, QC, MP; ✉ House of Commons, London SW1A 0AA

BAIRD-SMITH, Robin Jameson; s of John Helenus Baird-Smith (d 1977), and Jean Marjorie Guthrie, *née* Priestman, OBE (d 1993); *b* 21 July 1946; *Educ* Winchester, Royal Acad of Music, Trinity Coll Cambridge (BA); *m* 17 Jan 1976, Sarah Mary-Ann (d 1994), da of Charles Stevens Hedley, MC (d 1976); 2 s (Max John b 1978, Archibald Victor b 1979 d 1994), 1 da (Leonora Frances b 1981); *Career* publisher; Darton Longman and Todd Ltd: ed 1968–71, editorial dir 1971–78; Collins Publishers: ed 1978–81, editorial dir 1981–85; Constable Publishers: editorial dir 1985–95, publishing dir 1992–95, jt md 1992–95; publisher and md Gerald Duckworth and Company Ltd 1995–99, publishing dir Continuum International Publishing Gp 1999–; dir Isis Medical Media Ltd (Oxford) 1997–99, dir The Tablet 1999–, tstee The Tablet Tst 2004–; opera critic Mail on Sunday Newspaper 1989–90; chm Guild of Catholic Writers 1984–85, memb Analytical Psychology Club 1985–; *Books* Living Water (1988), Winter's Tales Vols 2 - 11 (1986–95), God of the Impossible (1989); *Recreations* music, travel, gardening, reading; *Clubs* Travellers; *Style*— Robin Baird-Smith, Esq; ✉ 8 Lawn Road, London NW3 2XS (tel 020 7722 0716, e-mail rbairdsmith@continuumbooks.com)

BAKER, *see also:* Sherston-Baker

BAKER, Prof Alan; s of late Barnet, and Bessie, Baker; *b* 19 August 1939; *Educ* Stratford GS, UCL (BSc), Trinity Coll Cambridge (MA, PhD); *Career* Trinity Coll Cambridge: fell 1964–, res fell 1964–68, dir of studies in Mathematics 1968–74; prof of pure mathematics Univ of Cambridge 1974–2006 (prof emeritus 2006–); visiting prof Stanford Univ 1974 and other US univs, Royal Soc Kan Tong Po prof Univ of Hong Kong 1988, guest prof ETH Zürich 1989; MSRI Univ of Calif Berkeley 1993; Fields medal Int Congress of Mathematicians Nice 1970, Adams prize Univ of Cambridge 1972; Docteur (hc) Université Louis Pasteur Strasbourg 1998; fell UCL 1979, hon fell Indian Nat Science Acad 1980; memb Academia Europaea 1998, hon memb Hungarian Acad of Sciences 2001; FRS 1973; *Publications* Transcendental Number Theory (1975), A Concise Introduction to the Theory of Numbers (1984), New Advances in Transcendence Theory (ed, 1988); numerous papers in scientific jls; *Style*— Professor Alan Baker, FRS; ✉ Department of Pure Mathematics and Mathematical Statistics, Centre for Mathematical Sciences, Wilberforce Road, Cambridge CB3 0WB (tel 01223 337999); Trinity College, Cambridge CB2 1TQ (tel 01223 338400, e-mail a.baker@pmms.cam.ac.uk)

BAKER, Christopher James; s of James Alfred Baker, and Alice Marjorie Baker, *née* Yeomans (d 1991); *b* 5 November 1951; *Educ* Dulwich Coll, Christ's Coll Cambridge (MA); *m* 27 March 1978, Anne Elizabeth Sylvia, da of Francis George James Morris (d 1996), of Stockton-on-Tees; 2 s (James b 1981, Francis b 1985), 2 da (Amy b 1983, Hannah b 1988); *Career* principal HM Treasy 1973–80, banker Morgan Grenfell & Co Ltd 1981–83, dir Hill Samuel Bank Ltd 1987–89 (joined 1983), corp fin ptnr Coopers & Lybrand 1990–93, corp strategy dir The Littlewoods Organisation plc 1993–2000; non-exec chm Convergent Communications plc 2002–03 (dir 1998–); non-exec dep chm: Jacques Vert plc 2003– (dir 1999–), Blooms of Bressingham Holdings plc 2003–07 (dir 2001–); non-exec dir: Park Group plc 2001–, AI Claims Solutions plc 2002–, Teacher Training Agency (now Training and Devpt Agency for Schs) 2002–; chair Business Liverpool Ltd 2004–; *Recreations* walking, classic cars, theatre, photography; *Style*— Christopher J Baker, Esq; ✉ Woodlands, 18 Carrwood Road, Wilmslow, Cheshire SK9 5DL (tel 01625 529663, fax 01625 528349, e-mail christopherbaker@btconnect.com)

BAKER, David Leon; s of late Jack Charles Baker, of London, and Joan, *née* Grannard; *b* 14 May 1950; *Educ* St Marylebone GS London; *m* 23 June 1974, Helen Amanda (Mandy), da of Gerald Stone, and Joyce Stone, of London; *Career* Edward Erdman & Co, Erdman Lewis International Ltd (now Colliers CRE) 1968–2003, md and jt chief exec Motcomb Estates 2003–06, currently md DLB Estates Ltd; dep res Brokerage Ctee Int Real Estate Fedn, fndr memb Steering Ctee Office Agents Soc; memb Ctee of Mgmnt Br Cncl for Offices, exec and govr Chartered Surveyors Trg Tst; tstee: Rheumatology Discretionary Fund UCL Charity, Critical Care; hon surveyor Thames Valley Univ 1992; Freeman City of London 1990; hon fell UCL 2003; fell Property Conslts Soc, int affiliate Soc of Industrial and Office Realtors (SIOR), FPCS, FFB, MLandInst; *Recreations* theatre, cinema, the history of London architecture, tropical fish, watching most sport; *Style*— David L Baker, Esq; ✉ DLB Estates Ltd, St Georges House, 15 Hanover Square, London W1S 1HS (tel 020 7935 4330, fax 020 7935 7314, mobile 07768 500148, e-mail davidbaker@mobilemail.vodafone.net)

BAKER, Prof (Leonard Graham) Derek; s of Leonard Baker, and late Phoebe Caroline Baker; *b* 21 April 1931; *Educ* Christ's Hosp (open scholar), Oriel Coll Oxford (open major scholar, MA, BLitt); *m* 1970, Jean Dorothy Johnston; 1 s, 1 da; *Career* Capt Royal Signals 1950–52; Bishop Fraser res scholar Oriel Coll Oxford 1955–56, tutor Univ of Oxford (Oriel, Merton, Pembroke, Univ and New Colls) 1955–56, dir of history The Leys Sch Cambridge 1956–66, supervisor in history Univ of Cambridge 1957–59, lectr in medieval history Univ of Edinburgh 1966–79, headmaster Christ's Hosp 1979–85; Univ of N Texas: visiting prof of history 1986–94, asst dir Advanced Academic Programs 1990–94;

Gladstone travelling scholarship 1956, schoolmaster fell Merton Coll Oxford 1966, Goldsmiths' Co scholarship 1966; dir/asst dir three Int Colloquia in Ecclesiastical History 1969–81, dir and organiser various confs Univ of N Texas, dir Assoc for Gen Educn International 1991–; visiting prof in history Univ of Houston 1992–, dir and ed Academia Publishing and Media 1992–; examiner: Oxford and Cambridge Examination Bd 1959, Cambridge Local Examination Bd 1960–65, Scottish Schs Examination Bd 1971–76, Univ of Glasgow 1973–77, Univ of Nottingham 1976; pres: Texas Medieval Assoc 1991–93, Mid-America Medieval Assoc 1991–92; memb: Br Nat Ctee of Historians 1977–81, Ctee Inst for Advanced Studies in the Humanities Univ of Edinburgh 1976–77, Methodist Archives Advsy Ctee 1976–77, Central Bureau Cmmn Internationale d'Histoire Ecclesiastique Comparée 1977–81 (sec then pres Br Sub-Cmmn 1969–81), Exec Bd (and monograph ed) Haskins Soc 1990–, Exec and Editorial Bds Rocky Mountain Medieval and Renaissance Assoc 1990–94; associate Manuscript Research Group Corpus Christi Coll Cambridge 1991–; given numerous lectures and papers, author/ed of numerous articles and other publications on medieval and ecclesiastical history; FRHistS 1969; *Books* Portraits and Documents (Vol I 1967, 2 edn 1993, Vol II 1969, 2 edn 1993), Partnership in Excellence (1974), Studies in Church History (ed 7–17, 1970–80), SCH Subsidia (Vols 1–3, 1978–80), Women of Power 1 (1993), Feminea Medievalia (1993), Cistercian Foundation Documents (1999); *Recreations* singing, climbing, pot-holing, camping, good company; *Clubs* Leander, Nat Lib; *Style*— Prof Derek Baker; ✉ New House, The Street, Nutbourne, West Sussex RH20 2HE (tel and fax 01798 813033)

BAKER, Dr (John) Harry Edmund; s of late Joseph Elmer Grieff Baker, and Mary Irene Elizabeth, *née* Bolton; *b* 8 January 1949; *Educ* Epsom Coll, Middx Hosp Med Sch London (MA, BSc, MB, LLM); *Career* Maj RAMC TA, specialist pool HQ AMS, Br Army Trauma Life Support Team, chief med advsr ACFA/CCFA, lately DADMS (TA) HQ W Mid Dist; lectr Univ of Nottingham Med Sch 1976–77, registrar Nat Hosp for Nervous Diseases 1977–80, sr registrar Nat Spinal Injuries Centre Stoke Mandeville 1980–83, Midland Spinal Injury Centre Oswestry 1983–85, conslt in spinal injuries and rehabilitation med S Glamorgan Health and Welsh Health Common Servs Authy 1985–, consIt advsr in rehabilitation Dept of Social Security War Pensions Office; author of pubns in med jls on immediate care and emergency handling of spinal cord injury, mgmnt of spinal injuries at accident sites, accident and disaster med; former dep chm Med Exec St John Ambulance Bde, past chm Professional Panel St John Aero Med Servs, vice-chm Wales and memb Exec Bd (UK) Br Assoc of Socs of Immediate Care, memb Med Bd of St John Ambulance (Priory for Wales); memb Cncl: Int Soc of Aeromedical Servs, Int Med Soc of Paraplegia, World Assoc of Emergency and Disaster Med; consIt advsr to Conjoint Ctee of the Voluntary Aid Socs; advsr and lectr in mgmnt of spinal cord injury to: Fire Servs, NHS Trg Directorate, Ambulance Serv, Med Equestrian Assoc, various equestrian bodies, RAC, MSA, various other motor sports orgns, Mountain Rescue Team, RLSS; pt/t med memb Med Appeals Tbnls, memb Provincial Tbnl for Incapacitated Clerics Church in Wales; fell NY Acad of Science (USA) 1988, FRCP; CStJ 1988; *Books* Management of Mass Casualties (jtly, 1980), ABC of Major Trauma (1994); *Style*— Dr Harry Baker; ✉ 56 Bridge Street, Llandaff, Cardiff CF5 2EN (tel 029 2057 8091); 5 Bridge Road, Llandaff, Cardiff CF5 2PT (tel 029 2055 4167, business 029 2055 3030, fax 029 2055 3034, e-mail milfield@aol.com)

BAKER, Dr Harvey; s of Isaac Baker (d 1971), and Rose, *née* Rifkin (d 1982); *b* 19 August 1930; *Educ* Univ of Leeds (MB ChB, MD); *m* 6 June 1960, Adrienne Dawn, da of Leonard Lever, of London; 1 s (Laurence b 1961), 2 da (Caroline b 1962, Marion b 1967); *Career* Capt RAMC served KAR Kenya 1955–57; consIt physician The London Hosp 1968–90, consIt dermatologist 1968–2005; pres: St John's Hosp Dermatological Soc 1973, Br Assoc of Dermatologists 1990–91; FRCP; *Books* Concise Text Book of Dermatology (1979), Clinical Dermatology (1989); *Recreations* music, literature; *Style*— Dr Harvey Baker; ✉ 16 Sheldon Avenue, Highgate, London N6 4JT (tel 020 8340 5970)

BAKER, Dame Janet Abbott; CH (1994), DBE (1976, CBE 1970); da of Robert Abbott Baker and May, *née* Pollard; *b* 21 August 1933; *Educ* The Coll for Girls York; *m* 1957, James Keith Shelley; *Career* singer; memb Munster Tst, tstee Fndn for Sport and the Arts 1991–, chllr Univ of York 1991–2004, patron Leeds Int Pianoforte Competition 1999–; Hon DMus: Univ of Birmingham 1968, Univ of Leicester 1974, Univ of London 1974, Univ of Hull 1975, Univ of Oxford 1975, Univ of Leeds 1980, Lancaster Univ 1983, Univ of York 1984; Hon MusD Univ of Cambridge 1984, Hon DLitt Univ of Bradford 1983, Hon LLD Univ of Aberdeen 1980; hon fell: St Anne's Coll Oxford 1975, Downing Coll Cambridge 1985; Daily Mail Kathleen Ferrier Award 1956, Queen's Prize RCM 1959, Hamburg Shakespeare Prize 1971, Copenhagen Sonning Prize 1979, Gold Medal Royal Philharmonic Soc 1990; Commandeur de l'Ordre des Arts et des Lettres (France); Hon Freeman City of York 2005; FRSA 1979; *Books* Full Circle (autobiography, 1982); *Recreations* reading, walking; *Style*— Dame Janet Baker, CH, DBE

BAKER, Jeffrey; s of Peter Baker, of Norton-on-Tees, Cleveland, and Barbara Baker; *b* 22 October 1967; *Educ* Blakeston Comp Stockton-on-Tees; *m* Gosia; 1 da (Jessika b 23 Nov 2004); by previous relationship, 1 s (Jack Bosco b 12 Oct 1994), 1 da (Jasmine b 31 Aug 1996); *Career* chef; commis chef de partie Greenhouse Mayfair, chef de partie Rue St Jacques London, chef de partie Waltons London, estagé Restaurant Riesbachli Zurich, estagé Chateau Montreuil France, sous chef Bishopstrow House Relais & Chateau Wilts, sous chef Sud Ouest Knightsbridge, sous chef Stephen Bull Restaurant London, head chef Brasserie Forty Four Ltd Leeds 1992–2005, head chef Pool Court at 42 1994–2005 (Michelin Star 1996), currently prop and chef J Bakers Bistro Moderne; *Recreations* eating out, following Middlesbrough FC; *Style*— Jeffrey Baker, Esq; ✉ J Bakers Bistro Moderne, 7 Fossgate, York YO1 9TA (tel 01904 622688, website www.jbakers.co.uk)

BAKER, Jeremy Russell; QC (1999); *b* 9 February 1958; *Career* called to the Bar Middle Temple 1979; *Style*— Jeremy Baker, Esq, QC; ✉ Paradise Chambers, 26 Paradise Square, Sheffield, South Yorkshire S1 2DE

BAKER, Prof Sir John Hamilton; kt (2003), Hon QC (1996); s of Kenneth Lee Vincent Baker, QPM, of Hintlesham, Suffolk, and Marjorie, *née* Bagshaw; *b* 10 April 1944; *Educ* King Edward VI GS Chelmsford, UCL (LLB, PhD), Univ of Cambridge (MA, LLD); *m* 1, 20 April 1968 (m dis 1997), Veronica Margaret, da of Rev William Stephen Lloyd, TD (d 1971); 2 da (Alys b 1973, Anstice b 1978); m 2, 13 Dec 2002, Fiona Rosalind Holdsworth, *née* Cantlay (d 2005); *Career* called to the Bar Inner Temple 1966 (hon bencher 1988); lectr in law UCL 1967–71 (asst lectr 1965–67, fell 1990); Univ of Cambridge: fell St Catharine's Coll 1971– (pres 2004–07), librarian Squire Law Library 1971–73, lectr in law 1973–83, jr proctor 1980–81, reader in English legal history 1983–88, prof of English legal history 1988–98, Downing prof of the laws of England 1998–, chm Faculty of Law 1990–92; lectr in legal history Inns of Court Sch of Law 1973–78; visiting prof: Euro Univ Inst Florence 1979, Harvard Law Sch 1982, Yale Law Sch 1987, NY Univ Sch of Law 1988–; literary dir Selden Soc 1992– (jt literary dir 1981–91); Ames prize Harvard 1985; Hon LLD Univ of Chicago 1992; hon foreign memb American Acad of Arts and Sciences 2001; FRHistS 1980, FBA 1984; *Books* Introduction to English Legal History (1971, 4 edn 2002), English Legal Manuscripts (vol 1 1975, vol 2 1978), The Reports of Sir John Spelman (1977–78), Manual of Law French (1979, 2 edn 1990), The Order of Serjeants at Law (1984), English Legal Manuscripts in the USA (1985, 1990), The Legal Profession and the Common Law (1986), Sources of English Legal History: Private Law to 1750 (with S F C Milsom, 1986), The Notebook of Sir John Port (1986), Readings and Moots in the Inns of Court, Part II: Moots (with S E Thorne, 1990), Reports from the Lost Notebooks of Sir James Dyer (1994), Catalogue of English Legal Manuscripts in Cambridge University Library (1996), Spelman's Reading on Quo Warranto (1997), Monuments of Endlesse Labours: English Canonists and their Work (1998), Caryll's Reports (1999), The Common Law Tradition (2000), The Law's Two Bodies (2001), Readers and Readings (2001), Year Books 12–14 Henry VIII (2002), Oxford History of the Laws of England, Vol VI (2003), Reports from the Time of Henry VIII (2004); *Style*— Prof Sir John Baker, QC, FBA; ✉ St Catharine's College, Cambridge CB2 1RL (tel 01223 338317, fax 01223 338340)

BAKER, John W; *Educ* Univ of Oxford (BA); *Career* various appts in transport policy & finance then urban regeneration & housing rising to dep chief exec The Housing Corporation until 1979; Central Electricity Generating Bd: joined as co sec 1979, bd memb 1980, corp md (incl responsibility for privatisation) until 1990; National Power plc (following privatisation): chief exec 1990–95, non-exec chm 1995–97; dep chm Celltech Gp plc; non-exec dir: Royal & Sun Alliance Insurance Group plc 1995–, A & A EIC 1999–, Maersk Co 1996–; memb Business Cncl A P Moller Group, chm English Nat Opera; *Style*— John Baker, Esq

BAKER, Jonathan Leslie; QC (2001); s of Leslie Joseph Baker (d 1994), and Esther Frances Isobel, *née* Walter (d 2003); *b* 6 August 1955; *Educ* St Albans Sch, St John's Coll Cambridge (open scholar, MA); *m* 1980, Helen Mary, da of Russell Sharrock; 1 s (James Jonathan b 26 Oct 1984), 1 da (Clare Rachel b 20 Nov 1987); *Career* called to the Bar Middle Temple 1978; memb Harcourt Chambers 1979– (head of Chambers 2004–), asst recorder 1998–2000, recorder 2000–, dep judge of the High Court 2003–; memb Ctee Family Law Bar Assoc 2005–; chm Oxfordshire Relate 1997–; govr Magdalen Coll Sch Oxford 2005–; *Publications* Contact: The New Deal (jtly, 2006); *Recreations* music, history, family life; *Style*— Jonathan Baker, Esq, QC; ✉ Harcourt Chambers, 2 Harcourt Buildings, Temple, London EC4Y 9DB (tel 020 7353 6961)

BAKER, (Norman) Keith; s of Norman Baker (d 1985), of Bedford, and Lilian Hopper, *née* Robson (d 1994); *b* 25 April 1945; *Educ* Doncaster GS, Bedford Modern Sch; *m* 1973, Elizabeth Rhoda, da of John Avery Stonehouse; 2 da (Amelia Elizabeth b 1978, Alice Harriet Clarissa b 1981); *Career* Coopers & Lybrand: Bedford 1964–70, London 1970–73, mangr 1972, expert witness 1973, sr mangr Hong Kong 1973–75, sr mangr Bedford 1976–87; Mazars Chartered Accountants (formerly Neville Russell): joined 1987, ptnr 1988–, regnl standards ptnr for Chilterns region; FCA 1975 (ACA 1970); *Recreations* golf, crosswords; *Clubs* Bedford; *Style*— Keith Baker, Esq; ✉ Mazars Chartered Accountants, Sovereign Court, Witan Gate, Central Milton Keynes MK9 2JB (tel 01908 664466, fax 01908 690567, e-mail keith.baker@mazars.co.uk)

BAKER, Mark Alexander Wyndham; CBE (1998); s of Lt Cdr Alexander Arthur Wyndham Baker (d 1969), and Renée Gavrelle Stenson, *née* Macnaghten; *b* 19 June 1940; *Educ* Prince Edward Sch Salisbury Rhodesia, UC of Rhodesia and Nyasaland (BA), ChCh Oxford (Rhodes scholar, MA); *m* 30 July 1964, Meriel, da of late Capt Edward Hugh Frederick Chetwynd-Talbot, MBE, of Milton Lilbourne, Wilts; 1 s (Alexander b 1968), 1 da (Miranda b 1970); *Career* UKAEA: various admin appts 1964–76, sec AERE Harwell 1976–78 (gen sec 1978–81), dir of personnel and admin Northern Div 1981–84, authy personnel offr 1984–86, authy sec 1986–89; exec dir of corp affairs and personnel Nuclear Electric plc 1989–95, chm Magnox Electric plc 1996–98; chair Electricity Pensions Ltd 1997–; pres Inst of Energy 1998–99; non-exec dir Pension Protection Fund 2004–, memb Sr Salaries Review Body 2004–; dep chair: Police Negotiating Bd 2000–05, Police Advsy Bd 2001–05; memb Bd of Tstees Save the Children 1998–2004, memb Advsy Ctee Environmental Change Inst Univ of Oxford 1999–2004; FInstE 1997; *Recreations* golf, walking, gardening, words; *Clubs* Oxford and Cambridge, Antrobus Dining (Cheshire), Old Fogeys Golfing Soc; *Style*— Mark Baker, Esq, CBE; ✉ The Old School, Fyfield, Abingdon, Oxfordshire OX13 5LR (tel 01865 390724, fax 01865 390162, e-mail markwbaker@aol.com)

BAKER, Mary Geraldine; MBE (1995); da of George Wheeler, and Emily Wheeler; *b* 27 October 1936; *Educ* Bromley HS, Univ of Leeds (BA), Inst of Almoners; *m* 1960, Robert William John Baker; 3 s; *Career* almoner St Thomas' Hosp 1959–61, housewife and mother 1961–75, social worker 1975–82, princ med social worker Frimley Park Hosp 1982–83; Parkinsons Disease Soc of UK: nat welfare dir 1984–91 and 1992, actg chief exec 1991–92, dir of welfare devpt 1994, nat and int devpt consIt 1995–99, chief exec 1999–2001, ret; pres: European Parkinson's Disease Assoc 1992–, European Fedn of Neurological Assocs 2000–; vice-pres European Brain Cncl 2002–; chm WHO Ctee of Non-Govermental Organisations Concerned with the Prevention and Treatment of Neurological Disorders 1998–; memb: Advsy Gp on Rehabilitation Dept of Health 1992–94, Editorial Bd BMJ 2000–; World Fedn of Neurology: memb Med Educn Research Gp 1998–, PR and WHO Liaison Ctee 2002–; Paul Harris fell Rotary Fndn 1997; Hon Dr Univ of Surrey 2003; hon fell Coll of Speech and Language Therapists 1992; AIMSW; *Publications* Speech Therapy in Practice (with B McCall, 1988), Care of the Elderly (with P Smith, 1990), The Role of the Social Worker in the Management of Parkinson's Disease (1991); contrib to learned jls incl BMJ; *Recreations* music, theatre, reading, bridge, caravanning; *Clubs* Soroptomists', RSM; *Style*— Mrs Mary Baker, MBE; ✉ Kailua, Maybourne Rise, Mayford, Woking, Surrey GU22 0SH (tel 01483 763626)

BAKER, Dr Maureen; CBE (2004); da of William Murphy (d 1994), and Helen, *née* Nolan; *b* 20 September 1958, Motherwell; *Educ* Holy Cross HS Hamilton, Univ of Dundee (MB, ChB), Univ of Nottingham (DM); *m* 1984, Peter Lindsay Baker; 2 da (Carolyn Marie b 1988, Elena Louise b 1991); *Career* princ GP Lincoln 1985–2000, associate advsr in gen practice Univ of Nottingham 1992–, med advsr NHS Direct 2001–02, special clinical advsr Nat Patient Safety Agency 2002–07, nat clinical lead for safety NHS Connecting for Health 2007–; hon sec RCGP 1999–; author of numerous articles, chapters and books; MRCGP 1985; *Recreations* family, cinema; *Style*— Dr Maureen Baker, CBE; ✉ Royal College of General Practitioners, 14 Princes Gate, Hyde Park, London SW7 1PU

BAKER, His Hon Judge Michael Findlay; QC (1990); s of Rt Hon Sir George Baker, PC (d 1984), and Jessie Raphael, *née* Findlay (d 1983); *b* 26 May 1943; *Educ* Haileybury and ISC, BNC Oxford (BA); *m* 1973, Sarah Hartley Overton; 2 da (Helen Mary Hartley b 1976, Hannah Elizabeth Findlay b 1979); *Career* called to the Bar Inner Temple 1966, recorder of the Crown Court 1991–95, circuit judge (SE Circuit) 1995–, resident judge St Albans Crown Court 2000–; liaison judge Herts 1997–2001, memb Herts Probation Bd (formerly Probation Ctee) 1997–, chm Herts Area Criminal Justice Strategy Ctee (formerly Herts and Beds Area Criminal Justice Liaison Ctee) 1998–2003; sec Nat Reference Tribunals for the Coal-Mining Industry 1973–95; *Recreations* mountaineering; *Clubs* Alpine, Climbers'; *Style*— His Hon Judge Michael Baker, QC; ✉ St Albans Crown Court, 4 Bricket Road, St Albans, Hertfordshire AL1 3HY (tel 01727 753220)

BAKER, Prof Michael John; TD (1971); s of John Overend Baker (d 1960), of York, and Constance Dorothy, *née* Smith (d 1979); *b* 5 November 1935; *Educ* Worksop Coll, Gosforth & Harvey GS, Univ of Durham (BA), Univ of London (BSc), Harvard Univ (Cert ITP, DBA); *m* 1959, Sheila, da of Miles Bell (d 1964), of Carlisle; 1 s (John), 2 da (Fiona, Anne); *Career* served in TA 1953–55, 2 Lt RA 1956–57, Lt 624 LAA Regt RA (TA) 1958–61, Capt City of London RF 1961–64, Capt PWO 1965–67; salesman Richard Thomas & Baldwins (Sales) Ltd 1958–64, asst lectr Medway Coll of Technol 1964–66, lectr Hull Coll of Technol 1966–68, Fndn for Mgmnt Educn fell Harvard Business Sch 1968–71 (res assoc 1969–71); Univ of Strathclyde: prof of mktg 1971–99, dean Strathclyde Business Sch 1978–84, dep princ 1984–91, emeritus prof 1999–; visiting prof: City Univ 1978–2002, Univ of Surrey 1995–2003, Glasgow Caledonian Univ 2001–05, Univ of Nottingham 2001–; hon prof Univ of Wales Aberystwyth 1999; chm: Westburn Publishers Ltd 1982–,

Scottish Mktg Projects Ltd 1986–2005, SGBS Ltd 1990–97; dir: Stoddard Sekers Int plc 1983–97, Scottish Tport Gp 1987–90, ARIS plc 1989–94; Secretary of State for Scotland's Nominee Scottish Hosps Endowment Res Tst 1984–96; memb: Chief Scientist's Ctee SHHD 1985–96, SCOTBEC 1973–85 (chm 1983–85), UGC Business and Mgmnt Sub-Ctee 1985–89; dean Coll of Mktg 1994–2001, pres Acad of Mktg 1986–2005, chm Inst of Mktg 1987; fndr ed Jl of Marketing Management 1985; Hon LLD, Hon DUniv; FRSE, FCIM, FCAM, FRSA, FScotvec, FSQA, FAM, FEMAC; *Books* Marketing - An Introductory Text (1971, 7 edn 2006), Marketing New Industrial Products (1975), Marketing - Theory & Practice (1976, 3 edn 1995), Innovation - Technology, Policy & Diffusion (1979), Market Development (1983), Macmillan Dictionary of Marketing and Advertising (1984, 3 edn 1998), Marketing Management and Strategy (1985, 4 edn 2007), Organisational Buying Behaviour (1986), The Marketing Book (1987, 5 edn 2002), The Role of Design in International Competitiveness (1989), Marketing and Competitive Success (1989), Research for Marketing (1991), Companion Encyclopedia of Marketing (1995), Marketing Manual (1998), Product Strategy and Management (1998, 2 edn 2007), Marketing: Managerial Foundations (1999), The IEBM Encyclopedia of Marketing (1999), Marketing Theory (2000), Marketing: Critical Perspectives (5 vols, 2001), Business and Management Research (2003); *Recreations* travel, gardening, walking, sailing ('Mary Rose of Morar'); *Clubs* Royal Over-Seas League, RSMYC; *Style*— Prof Michael Baker, TD, FRSE; ✉ Westburn, Helensburgh, Strathclyde G84 8NH (tel 01436 674686, e-mail mjb@westburn.co.uk); University of Strathclyde, Glasgow G4 0RQ (tel 0141 552 4400)

BAKER, Michael Verdun; s of Albert Ernest Thomas Baker, of Frinton-on-Sea, Essex, and Eva Louisa Florence, *née* Phillips; *b* 30 July 1942; *Educ* Caterham Sch; *m* 21 Sept 1963, Rita Ann, da of Walter James Marks (d 1998), of Ilford, Essex; 2 da (Carolyn b 1967, Louise b 1970); *Career* insurance official Alliance Assurance Co Ltd 1959–63, O & M systems analyst Plessey Co 1963–66, sr conslt Coopers & Lybrand 1967–72; The Stock Exchange: talisman project dir 1972–78, settlement dir 1978–82, admin dir 1982–84, divnl dir settlement servs 1984–87, exec dir markets 1987–90, chief exec Assoc of Private Client Investment Mangrs and Stockbrokers 1990–94, chm Consort Securities Systems Ltd 1994–96, mgmnt conslt 1994–; *Recreations* running, photography, travel, golf, record collecting; *Style*— Michael Baker, Esq; ✉ 10 Maclarens, Wickham Bishops, Witham, Essex CM8 3XE (tel 01621 892158)

BAKER, Norman; MP; *Career* MP (Lib Dem) Lewes 1997–; Lib Dem shadow sec of state for environment, food and rural affrs until 2006; Inquisitor of the Year Zurich/Spectator Parly Awards 2001, Oppn Politician of the Year Channel 4 Awards 2002; *Style*— Norman Baker, MP; ✉ House of Commons, London SW1A 0AA (tel 020 7219 2864, e-mail bakern@parliament.uk)

BAKER, His Hon Paul Vivian; QC (1972); s of Vivian Cyril Baker (d 1976), and Maud Lydia, *née* Jiggins (d 1979); *b* 27 March 1923; *Educ* City of London Sch, UC Oxford (MA, BCL); *m* 2 Jan 1957, Stella Paterson, da of William Eadie (d 1942); 1 s (Ian David b 1958), 1 da (Alison Joyce b 1960); *Career* Flt Lt RAF 1941–46; called to the Bar Lincoln's Inn 1950, practised at Chancery Bar 1951–83, bencher Lincoln's Inn 1979, circuit judge (SE Circuit) 1983–96; chm Incorporated Cncl of Law Reporting 1992–2001; ed Law Quarterly Review 1971–87 (asst ed 1960–70); Freeman City of London 1946; *Books* Snell's Principles of Equity (jt ed 24–29 edn, 1954–90), Vol 6 (1914–65) of the Records of Lincoln's Inn (ed, 2001); *Recreations* music, walking, reading; *Clubs* Athenaeum, Authors; *Style*— His Hon Paul Baker, QC; ✉ 9 Old Square, Lincoln's Inn, London WC2A 3SR (tel 020 7242 2633)

BAKER, Richard Douglas James; OBE (1976), RD (1979); s of Albert Baker (d 1974), and Jane Isobel, *née* Baxter; *b* 15 June 1925; *Educ* Kilburn GS, Peterhouse Cambridge (MA); *m* 1961, Margaret Celia, da of Thomas Herbert Martin; 2 s (Andrew b 1962, James b 1964); *Career* broadcaster and author; served WWII RN 1943–46; actor 1948–49, teacher 1949–50; BBC 1950–95; announcer BBC Third Programme 1950–53, newsreader BBC TV 1954–82; TV commentaries on state and musical events incl: Last Night of the Proms, New Year Concert from Vienna 1960–95, Festival of Remembrance 1990–99; presenter: Omnibus (BBC 1) 1983, Start the Week (Radio 4) 1970–87; BBC progs incl: These You Have Loved (Radio 4) 1972–77, Baker's Dozen 1977–87, Music in Mind (Radio 4) 1987–88, Melodies For You (Radio 2) 1988–95 and 1999–2003, Richard Baker Compares Notes (Radio 4) 1988–95, Mainly for Pleasure and In Tune (Radio 3) 1988–95, Music for Awhile (World Service) 1990–91, Evening Concert (Classic FM) 1995–97, Sound Stories (Radio 3) 1998–99, Friday Night is Music Night (Radio 2) 1998–2005, Your 100 Best Tunes (Radio 2) 2003–07; one man theatre show Music In My Life; other theatre incl: Grand Tour to Melody, The Best of British (narrator), Mr Gilbert and Mr Sullivan (scriptwriter and Sullivan), Viva Verdi! (scriptwriter and narrator); host P&O Classical Music Cruises 1985–; memb Broadcasting Standards Cncl 1989–94, govr Nat Youth Orch of GB 1985–2000, tstee D'Oyly Carte Opera Co 1985–97; TV Newscaster of the Year Radio Industries Club 1972, 1974 and 1979, BBC Radio Personality of the Year Variety Club of GB 1984, Man of the Year 1990, Gold Award Sony Radio Awards 1996; Freeman City of London, memb Worshipful Co of Plaisterers; Hon LLD: Univ of Strathclyde 1979, Univ of Aberdeen 1982; Hon FLCM 1974, Hon RAM 1988; *Books* incl: Here is the News (1964), The Terror of Tobermory (1972), The Magic of Music (1975), Dry Ginger (1977), Richard Baker's Music Guide (1979), Mozart (1982, 2 edn 1991), Richard Baker's London (1990), Mozart (1991), Richard Baker's Companion to Music (1993), Schubert (1997); *Recreations* gardening, theatre; *Style*— Richard Baker, Esq, OBE, RD; ✉ c/o Stephannie Williams Artists, 16 Swanfold, Wilmcote, Stratford-upon-Avon CV37 9XH (tel 01789 266272, fax 01789 266467)

BAKER, Richard James; MSP; s of Rev James Baker, and Rev Anne Baker, *née* Brown; *b* 29 May 1974, Edinburgh; *Educ* St Bees Sch Cumbria, Univ of Aberdeen (MA); *m* 16 Oct 2004, Dr Claire Baker, MSP, *née* Brennan; 1 da (Catherine b 23 Dec 2005); *Career* pres NUS Scotland 1998–2000, Scottish press offr Help the Aged 2000–02, MSP (Lab) NE Scotland 2003–; memb Amicus; memb Church in Soc Ctee Scottish Episcopal Church; *Recreations* choral singing, football, reading; *Style*— Richard Baker, Esq, MSP; ✉ c/o Scottish Parliament Office, 68 Rosemount Place, Aberdeen AB25 2XJ (tel 01224 641171, fax 01224 641104, e-mail richard.baker.msp@scottish.parliament.uk)

BAKER, Robert James; s of John Edward Baker (d 1990), and Margaret Elsie Mary, *née* Palmer (d 2003); *b* 9 December 1947; *Educ* UEA (BA); *m* 15 June 1973, Beverley Joan, da of Paul Archdale Langford (d 1976); 2 da (Hannah Alice b 1979, Amy Margaret b 1981); *Career* dir: Hobsons Publishing plc 1982–99, Harmsworth Publishing 1994–99, Harmsworth Information Publishing 1996–99; md: Hobsons Academic Relations 1996–, Communication Resources Ltd 1996–; dir: Educational Communications 2000–02, Care Choices Ltd 2000–; *Recreations* art, antique collecting, racing; *Clubs* Reform; *Style*— Robert Baker, Esq; ✉ Porters Farm, Over, Cambridge CB4 5NB (tel 01954 230761); Communication Resources Ltd, Church Street Barns, Great Shelford, Cambridge CB2 5EL (tel 01223 844128 or 01223 847871, fax 01223 277175, e-mail rob.bakerinfo@books.co.uk)

BAKER, Prof Robin Richard Sebastian; OBE (2004); s of Walter Richard Baker (d 1975), and Victoria Rebecca, *née* Martin (d 1988); *b* 31 December 1942; *Educ* RCA (maj travelling scholar, Fulbright scholar, MA), Univ of Calif, Thames Poly; *m* 1, 1966 (m dis 1970), Teresa Osborne-Saul; m 2, 1971 (m dis 1975), Tamar Avital; m 3, 1981 (m dis 1990), Angela Mary Piers Dumas; m 4, 1991, Katherine Knowles; *Career* designer; designer with: Joseph Ezcherick Associates San Francisco 1964–65, Russell Hodgeson & Leigh (architects) 1965–66; fndr own design practice (maj exhibitions cmmns from Arts Cncl of GB, Br Airports Authy and Nat Tst) 1966–79, princ lectr (with responsibility for computer studies) Chelsea Sch of Art 1982–83, computer advsr Art & Design Inspectorate ILEA 1984–86, specialist advsr in computing Ctee for Arts & Design CNAA 1985–88, visitor in computing Art and Design Inspectorate and Poly of Hong Kong 1985, prof and dir of computing RCA 1987–94, dir Ravensbourne Coll of Design and Communication 1994–; design computing conslt to: Conran Fndn's Museum of Design 1987–, Comshare Ltd 1987–88, Arthur Young 1988–89, Burtons Ltd 1988–89, Marks & Spencer 1990–94, Centro Portugues 1992–93, National Tst 1994–97, Design Cncl 1996–; author of numerous articles in design technology jls; *Books* Designing the Future (1995); *Style*— Prof Robin Baker, OBE; ✉ Ravensbourne College of Design and Communication, Walden Road, Chislehurst, Kent BR7 5SN (tel 020 8289 4900)

BAKER, Dr Robin William; CMG (2005); s of William John David Baker (d 1971), and Brenda Olive, *née* Hodges (d 1978); *b* 4 October 1953; *Educ* Bishop Wordsworth's Sch, SSEES Univ of London (BA), UEA (scholar, PhD); *m* 1974 (m dis 1997), Miriam Joy, da of Bernard Frederick Turpin (d 1968); 2 s (Simeon Scott b 12 Nov 1979, Joel William b 3 Feb 1983); partner, 2005–, Margaret Meyer; *Career* exec offr MOD 1976–80, doctoral research UEA 1981–84; British Council: trainee 1984–85, asst rep South Africa 1985–89, head of recruitment London 1989–90, asst dir Hungary 1990–93, dir Thessaloniki 1994–96, dep dir Russia 1996–99, dir West and South Europe 1999, dir Europe 1999–2002, dep DG 2002–2005; pro-vice-chllr Univ of Kent 2005–; hon visiting fell SSEES Univ of London 1994–96, sr hon visiting fell Inst for Balkan Studies Greece 1995–; memb: Société Finno-Ougrienne 1982, Inst Romance Studies Advsy Bd 1999–2002, SSEES Advsy Bd 1999–, Br Inst in Paris Governing Bd 1999–2002, Cncl for Assisting Refugee Academics 2002–, Royal Soc Int Policy Ctee 2003–05, Cncl Univ of Kent 2003–; fell UCL 2004; FRSA 1998; *Books* The Development of the Komi Case System (1985); *Recreations* opera, walking, jazz; *Clubs* Travellers, Ronnie Scott's; *Style*— Dr Robin Baker, CMG; ✉ University of Kent, Registry, Canterbury, Kent CT2 7NZ

BAKER, Roger; s of William Ernest Baker (d 1982), and Norah Margaret, *née* Kay; *b* 15 November 1958, Bolsover, Derbys; *Educ* Shirebrook Comp Sch Mansfield, Univ of Manchester (MA), Univ of Derby (MBA); *m* 15 May 1999, Patricia Anne, *née* O'Callaghan; 2 da (Katie b 8 March 1989, Sophie b 1 June 1994); *Career* Chief Supt Derbys Constabulary 1999–2001 (joined 1977), Asst Chief Constable Staffs Police 2001–03, Dep Chief Constable N Yorks Police 2003–05, Chief Constable Essex Police 2005–; memb ACPO 2001; *Recreations* equestrian pursuits, golf, walking the dogs; *Style*— Roger Baker, Esq; ✉ PO Box 2, Essex Police Headquarters, Springfield, Chelmsford, Essex CM2 6DA (tel 01245 452110, fax 01245 452123, e-mail chief.constable@essex.pnn.police.uk)

BAKER, Roy Horace Ward; s of Horace John Baker (d 1964), of London, and Florence Amelia, *née* Ward (d 1971); *b* 19 December 1916; *Educ* Lycée Corneille Rouen, City of London Sch; *m* 1, 1940 (m dis 1944), Muriel Constance, da of late Evelyn Edward Bradford; m 2, 1948 (m dis 1987), Joan Sylvia Davies, da of Alfred William Robert Dixon; 1 s (Nicholas Roy b 18 Aug 1950); *Career* director; army serv 1940–46 (cmmnd Bedfordshire and Hertfordshire Regt 1941, Army Kinematograph serv 1943); prodn runner to asst dir Gainsborough Studios Islington 1934–40; *Television* over 100 series incl: The Avengers, Danger UXB, Minder, Irish RM, Flame Trees of Thika, The Good Guys; *Films* over 30 feature films incl: The October Man 1946, Morning Departure 1949, Don't Bother to Knock (in Hollywood, 1952–53), Night Without Sleep (in Hollywood), Inferno (in Hollywood), Tiger in the Smoke 1956, The One That Got Away 1957, A Night to Remember 1958, The Singer Not the Song 1960, Two Left Feet 1962, Quatermass and the Pit 1967, The Anniversary 1967, Asylum 1972; *Awards* incl: NY Critics Circle Best Ten 1959, Golden Globe 1959 (for A Night to Remember), Christopher (for direction), Paris Convention du Cinema Fantastique Grand Prix (for Asylum) 1972; *Publications* The Director's Cut (2000), On the Line (2001); *Recreations* woodwork; *Clubs* Athenaeum; *Style*— Roy Baker, Esq; ✉ 2 St Albans Grove, London W8 5PN (tel 020 7937 3964, e-mail roy.baker7@btopenworld.com)

BAKER, Sam; *Educ* Univ of Birmingham; *Career* journalist; successively practicals asst, dep practicals ed and features writer Chat 1989–92, sr features writer Take a Break 1992–93, dep ed New Woman 1995–96 (features ed 1993–95); ed: Just Seventeen 1996 (relaunched magazine as J-17), Minx 1997–98, Company 1998–2003, Cosmopolitan 2004–06, Red 2006–; *Books* Fashion Victim (2005), This Year's Model (2008); *Style*— Ms Sam Baker; ✉ Red, Hachette Filipacchi UK Ltd, 64 North Row, London W1K 7LL

BAKER, Rt Hon Lord Justice; Rt Hon Sir (Thomas) Scott Gillespie; kt (1988), PC (2002); s of Rt Hon Sir George Gillespie Baker, OBE (d 1984), and Jessie McCall, *née* Findlay (d 1983); *b* 10 December 1937; *Educ* Haileybury, BNC Oxford; *m* 1973, Margaret Joy Strange; 2 s, 1 da; *Career* called to the Bar Middle Temple 1961 (bencher 1985, treas 2004); recorder of the Crown Court 1976–88, QC 1978, Family Div liaison judge (Wales & Chester Circuit) 1990–92, presiding judge Wales & Chester Circuit 1991–95, judge of the High Court of Justice (Queen's Bench Div) 1993–2002 (Family Div 1988–92), lead judge Administrative Court 2000–02, a Lord Justice of Appeal 2002–; memb: Senate Inns of Court 1977–84, Bar Cncl 1988, Govt Ctee of Inquiry into Human Fertilisation (Warnock Ctee) 1982–84, Chorleywood UDC 1965–68; vice-chm Parole Bd 2000–2002; dep chm Appeals Ctee Cricket Cncl 1986–88, govr Caldicott Sch 1991–2005 (chm 1996–2003); hon fell BNC Oxford 2003; *Recreations* golf, fishing; *Clubs* MCC, Denham Golf; *Style*— The Rt Hon Lord Justice Baker; ✉ Royal Courts of Justice, Strand, London WC2A 2LL

BAKER, Timothy (Tim); s of Maurice Baker, and Mary Baker; *b* 9 May 1953; *Educ* Abingdon Sch, Univ of York (BA), Univ of Leeds (MA); *Career* theatre dir; actor and teacher Action Projects in Educn 1976–78, actor Cardiff Laboratory Theatre 1977–80, dir Spectacle Theatre 1978–80 (writer in residence 1980–81), co memb and musician Theatr Bara Caws 1981–83, musical dir Cwmni Hwyl a Fflag 1982, artistic dir Theatre W Glamorgan 1982–97, assoc dir Clwyd Theatr Cymru (Nat Theatre of Wales) 1997–; assoc RNT 2000–, assoc dir Frec a Frec Theatre Co Barcelona; visiting lectr and dir Welsh Coll of Music and Drama, visiting dir Setagaya People's Theatre Tokyo; memb Dir's Guild of GB 1998; *Productions* for Spectacle Theatre: Do You Mind, Trouble; for Theatre W Glamorgan incl: When the Wind Blows (Welsh language version), Shirley Valentine (Welsh language version), Rape of the Fair Country, Combrogos (also writer), Sothach a Sglyfach; for Clwyd Theatr Cymru incl: Rape of the Fair Country (part 1 The Alexander Cordell Trilogy, Prodn of the Year Liverpool Daily Post 1997), Blue Remembered Hills, Art, Of Mice and Men, Hosts of Rebecca (part 2 The Alexander Cordell Trilogy), Song of the Earth (part 3 The Alexander Cordell Trilogy), Hard Times, Accidental Death of an Anarchist, To Kill a Mockingbird (Best Prodn Liverpool Daily Post 2001, Best Dir Liverpool Daily Post 2001, Best Prodn Wales Theatre Awards 2002), A View from the Bridge (Best Rgnl Prodn Liverpool Daily Post 2003); for Clwyd Theatr Cymru as writer incl: Flora's War, The Secret, Word for Word; for Frec a Frec Theatre Barcelona: Voler es Poder, FDV, Gabia; other prodns incl: Silas Marner (Theatr Clwyd), Canterbury Tales (Mappa Mundi Theatre), Threepenny Opera (RNT); *Recreations* music (guitar and piano); *Style*— Timothy Baker, Esq; ✉ 29 Hendy Road, Mold, Flintshire CH7 1QS (tel 01352 758857, website www.tim-baker.com)

BAKER OF DORKING, Baron (Life Peer UK 1997), of Iford in the County of East Sussex; Kenneth Wilfred Baker; CH (1992), PC (1984); s of late Wilfred M Baker, OBE, of Twickenham, Middx, and Mrs Baker, *née* Harries; *b* 3 November 1934; *Educ* St Paul's, Magdalen Coll Oxford; *m* 1963, Mary Elizabeth, da of William Gray Muir, of Edinburgh; 1 s, 2 da; *Career* Nat Serv Lt Gunners N Africa 1953–55, artillery instr to Libyan Army; industrial conslt; memb Twickenham BC 1960–62; contested (Cons): Poplar 1964, Acton 1966; MP (Cons): Acton 1968–70, St Marylebone 1970–83, Mole Valley 1983–97; Parly sec CSD 1972–74, PPS to Ldr of Oppn 1974–75, min of state for industry (special responsibility for IT) 1981–84, min for local govt DOE 1984–85, sec of state for the environment 1985–86, sec of state for educn and science 1986–89, chm of the Cons Party and Chllr of the Duchy of Lancaster 1989–90, home sec 1990–92; memb: Public Accounts Ctee 1969–70, Exec 1922 Ctee 1975–81; chm Information Ctee House of Lords 2002–; chm Hansard Soc 1978–81, sec gen UN Conf of Parliamentarians on World Population and Devpt 1978; chm: The Belmont Press (London) Ltd 1999–, Business Serve plc 2000–06, Northern Edge Ltd 2000–05, Monstermob Ltd 2001–06, Teather & Greenwood 2004–; dir: Hanson plc 1992–2005, Videotron Corporation Ltd 1992–97, Wavetek Corporation 1992–98, Bell Cablemedia plc 1994–97, Millennium Chemicals Inc 1996–, Stanley Leisure plc 2001–; advsr: Lehman Bros Europe, Cross Border Enterprises LLC; pres Royal London Soc for the Blind 2000–; vice-chm Cartoon Museum; tstee Booker Prize Fndn; *Books* I Have No Gun But I Can Spit (ed, 1980), London Lines (ed, 1982), The Faber Book of English History in Verse (ed, 1988), Unauthorised Versions: Poems and Their Parodies (ed, 1990), The Faber Anthology of Conservatism (ed, 1993), The Turbulent Years: my life in politics (1993), The Prime Ministers - An Irreverent Political History in Cartoons (1995), Kings and Queens - An Irreverent History of the British Monarchy (1996), The Faber Book of War Poetry (1996), A Children's English History in Verse (2000), The Faber Book of Landscape Poetry (2000), George VI: A Life in Caricature (2005); *Recreations* collecting books and caricatures; *Clubs* Athenaeum, Garrick; *Style*— The Rt Hon Lord Baker of Dorking, CH, PC; ✉ House of Lords, London SW1A 0PW (tel 020 7219 3000)

BAKER WILBRAHAM, Randle; s and h of Sir Richard Baker Wilbraham, 8 Bt, DL, *qv*; *b* 28 May 1963; *Educ* Harrow; *m* 17 May 1997, Amanda, da of Robert Glossop, of Hants; 1 s (Rafe George William b 27 Oct 1999), 2 da (Eve Allerley b 31 Dec 2001, Willa Katharine b 26 April 2004); *Career* London Fire Bde 1983–89; Fine Art Course The Study Centre 1989–90, London-Cape Town Motorcycle Expedition 1990–91, Trans America Combi Expedition 1992, Leith's Cookery Sch 1992, London Coll of Printing 1994–95, fndr Rode Bindery London 1996–; Staffs Fire and Rescue Serv 2002–; *Recreations* astronomy; *Style*— Randle Baker Wilbraham, Esq; ✉ Rode Hall, Scholar Green, Cheshire ST7 3QP (tel 01270 873237); Rode Bindery, Moss Cottage, Lunts Moss, Scholar Green, Cheshire ST7 3QJ (tel 01270 874101)

BAKER WILBRAHAM, Sir Richard; 8 Bt (GB 1776); DL; s of Sir Randle John Baker Wilbraham, 7 Bt, JP, DL (d 1980); *b* 5 February 1934; *Educ* Harrow; *m* 2 March 1962, Anne Christine Peto, da of late Charles Peto Bennett, OBE, of Jersey; 1 s, 3 da; *Heir* s, Randle Baker Wilbraham, *qv*; *Career* Lt Welsh Gds 1952–54; dir: J Henry Schroder Wagg & Co 1969–89 (joined 1954), Westpool Investment Trust plc 1974–92, Brixton Estate plc 1985–2001 (dep chm), Charles Barker plc 1986–89, Really Useful Group plc 1985–90, Severn Trent plc 1989–94, Bibby Line Group Ltd 1989–97 (chm 1992–97), Majedie Investments plc 1989–2001, Grosvenor Estate Holdings 1989–99 (dep chm); Christie Hosp NHS Tst 1990–96; tstee Grosvenor Estate 1981–99; govr: Harrow Sch 1982–92, King's Sch Macclesfield 1986–2006, Nuffield Hosps 1990–2001, Manchester Metropolitan Univ 1998–2001; church cmmr 1994–2001; High Sheriff Cheshire 1991–92; Upper Bailiff Worshipful Co of Weavers 1994–95; *Recreations* field sports; *Clubs* Brooks's; *Style*— Sir Richard Baker Wilbraham, Bt, DL; ✉ Rode Hall, Scholar Green, Cheshire ST7 3QP (tel 01270 882961)

BAKEWELL, Joan Dawson; CBE (1999); da of John Rowlands, and Rose, *née* Bland; *b* 16 April 1933; *Educ* Stockport HS for Girls, Newnham Coll Cambridge (BA); *m* 1, 1955 (m dis 1972), Michael Bakewell, 1 s, 1 da; m 2, 1975 (m dis 2001), Jack Emery (theatre and TV prodr); *Career* broadcaster and writer 1964–; TV critic The Times 1978–81, arts corr BBC 1981–87, columnist Sunday Times 1987–91; chm BFI 1999–2002 (vice-chm 1996–99); memb Cncl Aldeburgh Productions 1987–99; hon pres Soc of Arts Publicists 1988–92, memb Cncl Members of the Tate Gallery, memb Bd RNT 1997–2003; assoc fell Newnham Coll Cambridge 1990–91 (assoc 1984–87); FRCA; *Television* BBC incl: Meeting Point 1964, The Second Sex 1964, Late Night Line Up 1965–72, The Youthful Eye 1968, Moviemakers at the National Film Theatre 1971, Film '72 and Film '73, For the Sake of Appearance 1973, Where is Your God? 1973, Who Cares? 1973, The Affirmative Way (series) 1973, What's it all About? (2 series) 1974, Time Running Out (series) 1974, The Brontë Business 1974, The Shakespeare Business 1976, Generation to Generation (series) 1976, My Day with the Children 1977, The Moving Line 1979, Arts UK: OK? 1980, Arts corr 1982–87, The Heart of the Matter 1988–2000, My Generation 2000, One Foot in the Past 2000, Taboo 2001; ITV incl: Sunday Break 1962, Home at 4.30 1964, Thank You Ron (writer and prodr) 1974, Fairest Fortune 1974, Edinburgh Festival Report 1974, Reports Action (4 series) 1976–78; also Memento (Channel 4) 1993; *Radio* Away from it All 1978–79, PM 1979–81, Artist of the Week (Radio 3) 1998–2000, The Brains Tst (Radio 3) 1998–2000, Belief (Radio 3) 2001–; radio plays: There and Back, Parish Magazine (3 episodes), Brought to Book (2005); *Books* The New Priesthood: British Television Today (with Nicholas Garnham, 1970), A Fine and Private Place (with John Drummond, 1977), The Complete Traveller (1977), The Heart of Heart of the Matter (1996), The Centre of the Bed (2003), Belief (2005), The View from Here (2006); *Recreations* cinema, theatre, travel, talk; *Style*— Ms Joan Bakewell, CBE; ✉ c/o Knight Ayton Management, 114 St Martin's Lane, London WC2N 4BE (tel 020 7836 5333, fax 020 7836 8333)

BALCHIN, Sir Robert George Alexander; kt (1993), DL (2001); s of Leonard George Balchin (d 1968), and Elizabeth, *née* Skelton (d 1997); the Balchin family settled in Surrey c 1190, Sir Roger de Balchen owning lands in both Normandy and Surrey, Adm Sir John Balchin (1669–1744) was Adm of the White and Governor of Greenwich RN Hosp; *b* 31 July 1942; *Educ* Bec Sch, Univ of London, Univ of Hull; *m* 1970, Jennifer, OStJ, da of Bernard Kevin Kinlay (d 1975), of Cape Town; 2 s (Alexander b 1975 d 1996, Thomas (twin) b 1975); *Career* teacher 1964–69, res Inst of Educn Univ of Hull 1969–71, headmaster Hill Sch Westerham 1972–80 (chm 1980–2000); chm: Grant-Maintained Schs Centre (formerly Fndn) 1989–99, Blacker Publishing Ltd 1989–, Choice in Educn 1989–94, Centre for Educn Mgmnt (now CEFM) 1995–; DG St John Ambulance 1984–90 (asst DG 1982–84); fndr chm: Balchin Family Soc 1993–; chm: St John Nat Schools Project 1990–95, Educn Cmmn 2003–; memb: Surrey CC 1981–85 (memb Educn and Social Servs Ctees), Funding Agency for Schs 1994–97; pres: English Schools Orch 1997–, League of Mercy 1999–; patron: Nat Centre for Volunteering 1999–2004, Gateway Project for Homeless 2000–; dep patron Nat Assoc for Gifted Children 1998–; memb Ct Univ of Leeds 1995–2001, memb Cncl Goldsmiths Coll London 1997–2005 (dep chm 1999–2005), pro-chllr Brunel Univ 2006–; chm Ct of Govrs Mill Hill Sch 2004–; Hon Col Humberside and S Yorks ACF 2004–; Imperial Soc of Knights Bachelor: memb Cncl 1995–, Knight Registrar 1998–2006, Knight Princ 2006–; Liveryman: Worshipful Co of Goldsmiths 1987 (Freeman 1981), Worshipful Co of Broderers 2004; Hon DPhil Northland Open Univ Canada 1985, Hon DLitt Univ of Hull 2006; Hon FCP 1987 (FCP 1971), Hon FHS 1987, Hon MCGI 1983, Hon FCGI 1997–; KStJ 1984, Cdr's Cross (Pro Merito Melitensi SMOM) 1987, Cdr Order of Polonia Restituta 1990; *Books* Emergency Aid in Schools (1984), Choosing a State School (jtly, 1989), Emergency Aid at Work (jtly, 1990); author of numerous articles on educn and politics; *Recreations* restoration of elderly house; *Clubs* Athenaeum, Beefsteak; *Style*— Sir Robert Balchin, DL; ✉ New Place, Lingfield, Surrey RH7 6EF (tel 01342 834543, fax 01342 835122); 88 Marsham Court, Westminster, London SW1P 4LA

BALDERSTON, Bernard; *b* Tynemouth, Northumberland; *Educ* Keele Univ; *Career* Procter & Gamble: joined 1968, assoc dir UK and Irish media 1999–, currently chm P&G Pension Fund Tstees; former chm Radio TV and Screen Advtg Ctee ISBA, former advsr Radio Advertising Bureau; dir Audit Bureau of Circulations; memb: Exec Ctee and TV Action Gp Ctee ISBA, Advisory Ctee on Advertising (ACA) 2005–; regular speaker at industry conferences; *Recreations* Newcastle United FC; *Style*— Bernard Balderston, Esq; ✉ Procter & Gamble, Cobalt 12, Silver Fox Way, Colbalt Business Park, Newcastle upon Tyne NE27 0QW

BALDING, Andrew M A; s of Ian Anthony Balding, LVO, *qv*, and Lady Emma Balding, *née* Hastings-Bass; bro of Clare Balding, *qv*; nephew of Toby Balding and 16 Earl of Huntingdon, LVO, *qv*; *b* 29 December 1972, London; *Educ* Radley, RAC Cirencester (BSc); *m* 15 July 2005, Anna Lisa, *née* Williams; *Career* horse trainer; amateur jockey with 20 winners 1992–97, asst trainer to Mrs J R Ramsden 1996–98, asst trainer to Mr I A Balding 1999–2003, trainer Park House Stables Kingsclere 2003– (notable wins: Vodafone Oaks, Canadian Int, Dubai Sheema Classic, Hong Kong Vase, Wonder Where SHRS, Imperial Cup, Kingwell Hurdle); IRB Int Trainer of the Year 2005; *Recreations* Southampton FC; *Clubs* Turf; *Style*— Andrew Balding, Esq; ✉ Park House Stables, Kingsclere, Newbury, Berkshire RG20 5PY (tel 01635 298210, fax 01635 298305, e-mail admin@kingsclere.com)

BALDING, Clare Victoria; da of Ian Balding, LVO, *qv*, and Lady Emma Balding; sis of Andrew Balding, *qv*; niece of Toby Balding and 16 Earl of Huntingdon, LVO, *qqv*; *b* 29 January 1971; *Educ* Downe House, Sorbonne, Univ of Cambridge (pres Cambridge Union); *Career* freelance broadcaster and journalist; TV work incl: horseracing presenter 1998–, co-presenter Sports Personality of the Century 1999 and 2000, presenter Grandstand, Sunday Grandstand, Winter Olympics, Olympic Games Sydney (Best Sports Prog BAFTA Awards) and Sydney Paralympics, Olympic Games Athens and Athens Paralympics, Crufts, presenter Housecall in the Country BBC1; radio work incl: sports presenter BBC Radio 1993–, Wimbledon BBC Radio 5 Live 1994–, presenter sports bulletins BBC Radio 1 and Radio 5 Live 1995–97, reporter and commentator Olympic Games Atlanta Radio 5 Live 1996, presenter Breakfast with Balding Sportsweek BBC Radio 5 Live 1997–2000 (interviews incl: Alex Ferguson, Jamie Redknapp, Mike Atherton, Angus Fraser, Frank Bruno, Jeffrey Archer, Tim Rice, Steve Davies, Frankie Dettori, Nigel Mansell, Ian Botham), presenter Ramblings BBC Radio 4, presenter Winter Olympics Turin 2006, presenter Cwlth Games Melbourne 2006, presenter Badminton and Burghley Horse Trials BBC, presenter Race Country; former contrib: Sunday Telegraph, Sporting Life, Racing Post; columnist: Evening Standard 1998–2003, The Observer 2004–07; Horserace Writers and Photographers Assoc (HWPA) Racing Journalist of the Year 2003, RTS Sports Presenter of the Year 2003, Sir Peter O'Sullevan Broadcaster of the Year 2004; leading amateur flat jockey 1989 and 1990, champion lady rider 1990; *Recreations* riding, tennis, skiing, theatre, cinema, travel, golf; *Style*— Miss Clare Balding; ✉ c/o Anna Lisa Balding, Park House Stables, Kingsclere, nr Newbury, Berkshire RG20 5PY (tel 01635 297645, fax 01635 297307, e-mail clarebalding@tiscali.co.uk)

BALDING, Gerald Barnard (Toby); s of Capt Gerald Matthews Balding (d 1957), of Weyhill, nr Andover, Hants, and Eleanor, *née* Hoagland (d 1987); bro of Ian Balding, LVO, *qv*; *b* 23 September 1936; *Educ* Marlborough; *m* 21 Jan 1960, Carolyn Anne (d 2004), da of Anthony Lister Barclay; 1 s (Gerald Barclay b 9 Jan 1961), 2 da (Serena Anne (Mrs J A Geake) b 1 Aug 1962, Camilla (Mrs T G Bridgewater) b 17 Oct 1963); *Career* Nat Serv HM Lifeguards 1955–57; point-to-point jockey 1954–57, racehorse trainer 1957–; trained ca 2000 winners on flat and over jumps incl: Grand National (twice), Topham Trophy (twice), Eider Chase (four times), Portland Handicap, Coronation Hurdle, Whitbread Trial Chase, Mildmay of Flete Chase (twice), Irish Sweeps Hurdle, John Porter Stakes, Stewards Cup, Cheltenham Gold Cup, Ayr Gold Cup, Tote Gold Trophy, Glen Int Gold Cup, Waterford Crystal Champion Hurdle (twice), Martell Aintree Hurdle (five times), Nat Hunt Chase (twice), Prix d'Arenberg France, Breeders Cup Chase USA (twice); horses trained incl: Highland Wedding, Little Polveir, Grandpa's Legacy, Caduval, Dozo, New World, Official, Tudor Legend, Belgrano, Reality, Bybrook, Decent Fellow, Green Ruby, Via Delta, Lucky Vane, Lonach, Sheer Gold, Far Bridge, So True, Neblin, Kildimo, Beech Road, Boraceva, Morley Street, Forest Sun, Palace Street, Regal Scintilla, Cool Ground; jt chm Nat Trainers Fedn, memb Cncl Racehorse Owners Assoc; world record for Nat Hunt prize money won on one day Aintree 8 April 1989, Morley Street voted Nat Hunt Horse of the Year UK and USA 1990 (first horse to win both awards); former jr rugby rep Dorset and Wilts; *Recreations* tennis, reading, eating, pretty girls (not necessarily in that order!); *Style*— Toby Balding, Esq; ✉ Kimpton Down Stables, Kimpton, Andover, Hampshire SP11 8PQ (tel 01264 772278, fax 01264 771221, e-mail serena@baldingstraining.co.uk, website www.tobybalding.co.uk)

BALDING, Ian Anthony; LVO (1992); s of Capt Gerald Matthews Balding (d 1957), of Weyhill, Hants, and Eleanor, *née* Hoagland (d 1987); bro of Toby Balding, *qv*; *b* 7 November 1938; *Educ* Marlborough, Millfield, Christ's Coll Cambridge (Rugby blue); *m* 25 Aug 1969, Lady Emma Alice Mary, da of late Peter Hastings-Bass, sis of 16 Earl of Huntingdon, LVO, *qv*; 1 da (Clare Victoria Balding, *qv*, b 29 Jan 1971), 1 s (Andrew Matthews Balding, *qv*, b 29 Dec 1972); *Career* racehorse trainer 1964–2002; notable horses trained incl: Glint of Gold, Mrs Penny, Mill Reef, Forest Flower, Diamond Shoal, Selkirk, Crystal Spirit, Lochsong; trained for: HM Queen Elizabeth The Queen Mother (won Imperial Cup with Insular), HM The Queen 1964–99, Paul Mellon KBE 1964–99; maj races won in UK and Ireland incl: Derby, King George VI & Queen Elizabeth Stakes, Eclipse Stakes, Dewhurst Stakes (4 times), Imperial Cup (nat hunt), 1000 Guineas (Ireland), Nat Stakes (Ireland, twice), Queen Elizabeth II Stakes (1991); races won abroad incl: Italian Derby, Prix de l'Arc de Triomphe, Prix Ganay, Prix de Diane, Prix Vermeille, Prix de l'Abbaye de Long Champ (3 times), Grosser Preis von Baden (twice), Preis von Europa (3 times); second leading flat trainer in first full year 1965, leading trainer 1971, leading int trainer 3 times; amateur nat hunt jockey winning over 70 races 1954–64 (incl Nat Hunt Chase Cheltenham), winning jockey various hunter chase and point to point races 1964–92; rugby: Bath 1956–66, Dorset & Wiltshire 1956–66, Cambridge Univ 1959–62, various appearances Southern Cos, Newbury RFC 1966–80; boxing Cambridge Univ, cricket Crusaders; *Recreations* jt master Berks and Bucks Drag Hunt, skiing, squash, tennis, golf; *Style*— Ian Balding, Esq, LVO; ✉ Park House, Kingsclere, Newbury, Berkshire RG20 5PY (tel 01635 298274/298210, fax 01635 298305, e-mail admin@kingsclere.com)

BALDOCK, Brian Ford; CBE (1997); s of Ernest John Baldock (d 1997), and Florence, *née* Ford (d 1983); *b* 10 June 1934; *Educ* Clapham Coll London; *m* 1 (m dis 1966), Mary Lillian, *née* Bartolo; 2 s (Simon b 1958, Nicholas b 1961); m 2, 30 Nov 1968, Carole Anthea, da of F R Mason (d 1978); 1 s (Alexander b 1970); *Career* Lt Royal W Kent Regt 1952–53, Corps of Royal Mil Police 1953–55; mgmnt trainee Procter & Gamble Ltd 1956–61, assoc dir Ted Bates Inc 1961–63, mktg mangr Rank Organisation 1963–66, dir Smith & Nephew 1966–75, vice-pres Revlon Inc (EMEA) 1975–78, md Imperial Leisure & Retail 1978–86; Guinness plc: dir 1986–96, gp md 1989–96, dep chm 1992–96; non-exec chm: Portman Gp 1989–96, Sygen International plc 1992–2005, Wellington Investments Ltd 1997–2002, Marks and Spencer plc 1999–2000 (non-exec dir 1996–2004), First Artist Corp plc 2001–03; non-exec dir Cornhill Insurance plc 1996–2002; chm MENCAP 1998–; Freeman: City of London 1988, Worshipful Co of Brewers 1988; FInstM 1976, fell Mktg Soc 1988, FRSA 1987, CIMgt 1992; *Recreations* theatre, music, travel; *Clubs* MCC, Garrick, Lord's Taverners (memb Cncl, chm 1992–95), Mark's; *Style*— Brian Baldock, Esq, CBE

BALDOCK, (Richard) Stephen; s of John Allan Baldock (d 1989), and Marjorie Procter, *née* Taylor; *b* 19 November 1944; *Educ* St Paul's, King's Coll Cambridge (John Stewart of Rannoch scholarship, MA), King's Coll London; *m* 5 July 1969, Dr Janet Elizabeth Cottrell, MA, MB, BChir, MRCGP; 3 da (Sarah Ruth b 5 April 1975, Emma Stephanie b 6 Aug

1978, Rachel Elizabeth b 17 June 1980), 1 s (Andrew James b 23 July 1976); *Career* St Paul's Sch: asst master 1970–77, housemaster 1977–84, surmaster 1984–92, high master 1992–2004; memb Cncl and educnl advsr Overseas Missionary Fellowship 1989–; govr: Durston House Prep Sch 1992–2004, The Hall Sch Hampstead 1993–2004, Orley Farm Sch 1996–2005, Monkton Combe Sch 2003–; tstee: Combined Tsts Scholarship Tst 2004–, The Ind Schs Christian Alliance (TISCA); memb: Tyndale Fellowship for Biblical Res, JACT; *Recreations* sport, travel, computers, music; *Clubs* MCC, Naval; *Style—* Stephen Baldock, Esq; ✉ c/o Old Pauline Club, St Paul's School, Lonsdale Road, London SW13 9JT

BALDRY, Antony Brian (Tony); MP; eldest s of Peter Edward Baldry, and Oina, *née* Paterson; *b* 10 July 1950; *Educ* Leighton Park Sch Reading, Univ of Sussex (BA, LLB); *m* 1, 1979 (m dis 1996), Catherine Elizabeth, 2 da of Capt James Weir, RN (ret), of Chagford, Devon; 1 s, 1 da; m 2, 2001, Pippa Isbell, da of Lt-Col R Payne; *Career* barr and publisher; called to the Bar Lincoln's Inn 1975; currently jt head of chambers 1 Essex Court Temple; dir: New Opportunity Press 1975–90, Newpoint Publishing Group 1983–90; PA to Mrs Thatcher in Oct 1974 election, in ldr of oppn's office Mar-Oct 1975, memb Carlton Club Political Ctee, MP (Cons) Banbury 1983– (Parly candidate (Cons) Thurrock 1979); chm Parly Select Ctee on Int Devpt 2001–05; memb Parly Select Ctee: on Employment 1983–85, on Trade and Industry 1997–2000, on Standards and Privileges 2001; PPS to: Min of State for Foreign and Cwlth Affrs 1985–87, Lord Privy Seal and Ldr of the House 1987–89, Sec of State for Energy 1989–90; Parly under sec of state: Dept of Energy 1990, DOE 1990–94, FCO 1994–95; min of state MAFF 1995–97, chm Parly Mainstream Gp 1997–2000; Robert Schuman Silver medal (Stiftung FVS Hamburg) for contribs to Euro politics 1978; chm: 3DM Gp Ltd, Angel Gate Property Ltd, Battlebridge Capital plc, Black Rock Oil and Gas plc; non-exec chm: Carbon Registry Services, Red Eagle Resources plc, SPDG Ltd; non-exec dir: Invicta Africa Ltd, Transense Technologies plc, Symphony Global Ltd; exec ptnr Diamond Film Partnership; memb Cncl: ODI, Chatham House; govr Cwlth Inst 1997–2005; advsr Shrimati Pushpa Wati Loomba Meml Tst, tstee Dr L V Singhvi Fndn; visiting fell St Antony's Coll Oxford 1998–99; Liveryman: Worshipful Co of Merchant Taylors, Worshipful Co of Stationers & Newspaper Makers; FCIOB, FCIPD, FCIArb, FInstD, FIMgt, FASI, FRSA; *Recreations* walking, beagling; *Clubs* Carlton, Farmers, Brass Monkey, United and Cecil (chm); *Style—* Tony Baldry, Esq, MP; ✉ House of Commons, London SW1A 0AA (tel 020 7219 4476, e-mail baldryt@parliament.uk)

BALDWIN, Clarissa Mary; OBE (2004); da of Rev Basil Alderson Watson, OBE, RN (d 2004), of Greenwich, and Janet Isabel, *née* Roderick; *b* 9 February 1949; *Educ* St Agnes & St Michael's Sch, Dartmouth Coll; *m* 18 March 1977, Roger Douglas Baldwin, s of Douglas Baldwin; 1 s (James Douglas Alderson b 18 Dec 1980); *Career* fashion model 1968–70, positions with Cambridge Evening News and Evening Standard, chief exec Dogs Trust 1986– (author slogan: A dog is for life....not just for Christmas); chm: Assoc of Dogs and Cats Homes, Greyhound Forum, Int Greyhound Forum, Pet Advtg Advsy Gp, Welfare Ctee Pet Plan Charitable Tst; tstee Hearing Dogs for the Deaf, memb Bd Pet Advsy Ctee, advsy dir World Soc for the Protection of Animals, tstee SNIP Int; *Recreations* tennis, theatre, ballet; *Style—* Mrs Clarissa Baldwin, OBE; ✉ Dogs Trust, 17 Wakley Street, London EC1V 7RQ (tel 020 7837 0006, fax 020 7833 2701, mobile 078 3113 5849, e-mail clarissa.baldwin@dogstrust.org.uk)

BALDWIN, Prof Sir Jack Edward; kt (1997); *b* 8 August 1938; *Educ* Brighton GS, Lewes GS, Imperial Coll London (BSc, PhD); *Career* lectr Imperial Coll of Science and Technol London 1966–67 (asst lectr 1963–66), assoc prof of chemistry Pennsylvania State Univ 1969–70 (asst prof of chemistry 1967–69), prof of chemistry MIT 1971–78 (assoc prof of chemistry 1970–71), Daniell prof of chemistry King's Coll London 1972; Univ of Oxford 1978–: Waynflete prof of chemistry, fell Magdalen Coll Oxford, head Dyson Perrins Laboratory; memb BBSRC 1994–; author of numerous articles and papers in academic jls; corresponding memb Academia Scientiarum Gottingensis Göttingen 1988; Corday Morgan Medal and Prize Chemical Soc 1975, Medal and Prize for Synthetic Organic Chemistry RSC 1980, Paul Karrer Medal and Prize Univ of Zürich 1984, Medal and Prize for Natural Product Chemistry RSC 1984, Hugo Muller Medal RSC 1987, Max Tischler Award Harvard Univ 1987, Dr Paul Janssen Prize for Creativity in Organic Synthesis Belgium 1988, Davy Medal Royal Soc 1994; hon foreign memb American Acad of Arts and Sciences 1994; Hon DSc: Univ of Warwick 1988, Univ of Strathclyde 1989; FRS 1978; *Style—* Prof Sir Jack Baldwin, FRS; ✉ Chemistry Research Laboratory, University of Oxford, Mansfield Road, Oxford OX1 3TA (tel 01865 275671)

BALDWIN, Jan; da of late Joseph John Baldwin, and Catherine Agnes, *née* Freeman; *b* 12 December 1946; *Educ* Chipping Norton GS, Bicester GS, Royal Coll of Art (MA); *m* 10 Dec 1988, Prof Henry Philip Wynn, s of Arthur Wynn; 2 step s (Hamish, Robin); *Career* therapy radiographer NY 1967–74, freelance photographer 1981–; memb AFAEP; *Recreations* film, theatre, travelling; *Style—* Ms Jan Baldwin; ✉ 11 Gibraltar Walk, London E2 7LH (tel 020 7729 2664, fax 020 7729 3861, e-mail studio@janbaldwin.co.uk)

BALDWIN, Prof John Evan; s of Evan Baldwin (d 1976), and Mary, *née* Wild (d 1983); *b* 6 December 1931; *Educ* Merchant Taylors', Queens' Coll Cambridge (Clerk Maxwell scholar, BA, MA, PhD); *m* 20 Sept 1969, Joyce, da of Alexander Thomas Cox (d 1979); *Career* Univ of Cambridge: res fell later fell Queens' Coll Cambridge 1956–74 and 1989–99 (life fell 1999), demonstrator in physics 1957–62, asst dir of res 1962–81, reader 1981–89, dir Mullard Radio Astronomy Observatory 1987–96, prof of radioastronomy 1989–99 (emeritus prof 1999–); memb SERC Ctees and Bds 1971–97, memb Int Astronomical Union 1961–; Guthrie Medal and Prize Inst of Physics 1997, Hopkins Prize Cambridge Phil Soc 1997, Jackson-Gwilt Medal and Gift RAS 2001; FRAS 1957, FRS 1991; *Recreations* mountain walking, gardening; *Style—* Prof John Baldwin, FRS; ✉ Cavendish Laboratory, Madingley Road, Cambridge CB3 0HE (tel 01223 337299, fax 01223 354599, e-mail jeb@mrao.cam.ac.uk)

BALDWIN, Dr John Paul; QC (1991); s of Frank Baldwin (d 2002), and Marjorie Baldwin (d 1966); *b* 15 August 1947; *Educ* Nelson GS, Univ of Leeds (BSc), St John's Coll Oxford (DPhil); *m* 19 Sept 1981, Julie, da of Merle Gowan, of N Adelaide, Aust; 2 da (Melissa Jay b 20 Sept 1982, Sarah Elizabeth b 21 March 1985); *Career* res fell Univ of Oxford 1972–75, barrister 1977, bencher Gray's Inn 2000, recorder 2004; *Books* Patent Law of Europe and UK (jt ed, 1983), numerous scientific publications; *Recreations* tennis, gardening; *Clubs* Queen's, Harbour, Campden Hill Lawn Tennis; *Style—* Mr John Baldwin, QC; ✉ 8 New Square, Lincoln's Inn, London WC2A 3QP (tel 020 7405 4321, fax 020 7405 9955, pager 0459 115439)

BALDWIN, Mark Phillip; s of Ronald William Baldwin (d 2006), of Australia, and Rose Thersa Evans (d 1969); *b* 16 January 1954; *Educ* St Kentigerns Coll NZ, Pakuranga Coll NZ, Suva GS Fiji, Elam Sch of Fine Arts, Univ of Auckland NZ; *Career* choreographer; dancer with: Limbs Dance Co NZ, NZ Ballet, Australian Dance Theatre, Rambert Dance Co 1982–92; major roles incl: Glen Etley's Pierot Lunaire, Richard Alston's Sonda Lake; fndr The Mark Baldwin Dance Co 1993–2001; choreographer Rambert Dance Co 1992–94, choreographer in res Sadlers Wells 1994–, res artist The Place 1995–96, choreographer in res Scottish Ballet 1996–, artistic dir Rambert Dance Co 2002–; with Rambert Dance Co: Island to Island 1991, Gone 1992, Spirit 1994, Banter Banter 1994, Constant Speed 2005; Scottish Ballet: Hyden Pieces 1995, A Fond Kiss 1996, More Poulenc 1996; other works choreographed incl: Labyrinth by Hans Werner Henze's (for Staatsoper Berlin) 1997, The Legend of Joseph by Richard Strauss 1998, The Demon by Paul Hindemith 1998, Towards Poetry (for the Royal Ballet) 1999, Ihi Frenzy (for Royal NZ Ballet) 2001, Dance Umbrella (Mark Baldwin Dance Co) 1995–98, The Bird Sings with its Fingers 2001; dance films: Echo 1996, Pointe Blank 2000, Frankenstein 2002; *Awards incl:* Time Out Dance Award, Special Judges' Prize for dance film Video Danse Grand Prix 1996, South Bank Show Award 2001, Theatrical Mgmnt Assoc (TMA) Award for Achievement in Dance 2006; *Recreations* music, modern art, painting, film, theatre; *Style—* Mark Baldwin, Esq

BALDWIN, Michael; s of Harold Jesse Baldwin (d 1990), of Meopham, Kent, and Elizabeth Amy Crittenden (d 1968); *b* 1930, Gravesend, Kent; *Educ* Gravesend GS for Boys, St Edmund Hall Oxford (open scholar); *m* 1, 1954 (m dis 1979), Jean Margaret Bruce; 2 s (Matthew James b 1959, Adam Richard b 1961); m 2, 1987, Gillian Beale; 1 s (Joel St John b 1988); *Career* author; Nat Serv Rifle Bde, Educn Corps and Airborne Forces 1949–50, cmmnd RA 1950, 415 Coast Regt RA (TA) 1950–55, 263 Light Regt RA (TA) 1955–60; lectr St Paul's Coll Cheltenham 1955–56, asst master St Clement Danes GS 1956–59, successively lectr, sr lectr, princ lectr, head of English and Drama Dept Whitelands Coll Putney 1959–78, head of English and drama elect Roehampton Inst 1978; Arvon Fndn: vice-chm 1972–90, chm Lumb Bank 1978–88; Rediffusion Prize 1970, honourable mention Japan Awards 1970, Cholmondeley Prize for Poetry 1983; FRSL 1984; *Publications* poetry: Death on a Live Wire (1962), How Chas Egget Lost his Way in a Creation Myth (1967), Hob (1972), The Buried God (1973), Snook (1980), King Horn (1983); autobiography: Grandad with Snails (1960), In Step with a Goat (1962); fiction: A World of Men (1962), Miraclejack (1963), Sebastian and Other Voices (short stories, 1966), The Great Cham (1967), Underneath and Other Situations (short stories, 1968), There's a War On (1970), The Cellar (1972), The Gamecock (1980), Exit Wounds (1988), Holofernes (1989), Ratgame (1991), The Rape of Oc (1993), The First Mrs Wordsworth (1996), Dark Lady (1998); pedagogic: Poems by Children, 1950–1961 (1962), Billy the Kid (anthology, 1963), The Way to Write Poetry (1982), The River and the Downs (topography, 1983), The Way to Write Short Stories (1986); *Recreations* hill walking on British mountains, motoring in Europe; *Clubs* Athenaeum, Colony Room; *Style—* Michael Baldwin; ✉ c/o Charles Walker, PFD, Drury House, 34–43 Russell Street, London WC2B 5HA (tel 020 7344 1000, fax 020 7836 9539)

BALDWIN, Nicholas Peter (Nick); s of Desmond Stanley Frederick Baldwin, of Guildford, and Beatrix Marie, *née* Walker; *b* 17 December 1952; *Educ* City Univ (BSc), Birkbeck Coll London (MSc); *Partner* Adrienne Plunkett; 1 da (Lauren b 1 Nov 1987), 1 s (Patrick b 15 Aug 1991); *Career* student apprentice Met Water Bd 1971–74, various positions Thames Water Authy 1974–80, various positions CEGB 1980–89; PowerGen: econ studies mangr 1989–90, business planning mangr 1990–92, head of strategic planning 1992–94, dir of strategy 1994–95, dir of generation 1995–96, md UK electricity prodn 1996–98, exec dir UK operations 1998–2001, chief exec 2001–02; ind dir DTI Energy Gp 2002–; non-exec dir: Nuclear Decommissioning Authy 2004–, Forensic Science Serv 2004–, Scottish & Southern Energy plc 2006–; advsr: Climate Change Capital 2003–, Towerbrook Capital Ptnrs 2004–; chm Worcester Community Housing 2002–; CEng 1979, MInstE 1982, FIMechE 1996 (MIMechE 1979), FRSA 1998; *Recreations* walking, cycling, jazz; *Clubs* Worcester CC; *Style—* Nick Baldwin, Esq

BALDWIN, Maj-Gen Peter Alan Charles; CBE (1994); s of Alec Baldwin, and Anne, *née* Dance; *b* 19 February 1927; *Educ* King Edward VI GS Chelmsford; *m* 1, 1953, Judith Elizabeth Mace; m 2, 1982, Gail J Roberts; *Career* enlisted 1942, cmmnd Royal Signals 1947, served WWII, Korean War and Borneo Ops (despatches 1967), Cdr 13 Signal Regt BAOR 1969–71, sec for studies NATO Def Coll 1971–74, Cdr 2 Signal Gp 1974–76, ACOS Jt Exercises Div AFCENT 1976–77, Maj-Gen CSO HQ BAOR 1977–79; dir of radio IBA 1987–90 (dep dir 1979–87), chief exec Radio Authy 1991–95, ret; chm The Eyeless Tst; tstee D'Oyly Carté Opera Co; fell Radio Acad 1992, FRSA 1993; *Recreations* cricket, theatre, music; *Clubs* Army and Navy, MCC; *Style—* Maj-Gen Peter Baldwin, CBE; ✉ c/o Lloyds Bank plc, 7 Pall Mall, London SW1Y 5NA

BALDWIN OF BEWDLEY, 4 Earl (UK 1937); Edward Alfred Alexander Baldwin; also Viscount Corvedale (UK 1937); s of 3 Earl (d 1976, 2 s of 1 Earl, otherwise Stanley Baldwin, thrice PM and 1 cous of Rudyard Kipling); *b* 3 January 1938; *Educ* Eton, Trinity Coll Cambridge (MA, PGCE); *m* 1970, Sarah MacMurray (d 2001), da of Evan James, of Upwood Park, Abingdon, Oxon (and sis of Countess of Selborne); 3 s (Benedict Alexander Stanley, Viscount Corvedale b 1973, Hon James Conrad b 1976, Hon Mark Thomas Maitland b 1980); *Heir* s, Viscount Corvedale; *Career* school teacher 1970–77, LEA educn offr 1978–87; sits as elected Peer in House of Lords; former memb Research Cncl for Complementary Med, chm Br Acupuncture Accreditation Bd 1990–98; jt chm Parly Gp for Integrated and Complementary Med 1992–2002, memb House of Lords Select Ctee Inquiry into Complementary and Alternative Med 1999–2000; *Recreations* mountains, tennis; *Clubs* MCC; *Style—* The Rt Hon The Earl Baldwin of Bewdley; ✉ Manor Farm House, Godstow Road, Upper Wolvercote, Oxfordshire OX2 8AJ (tel and fax 01865 552683)

BALE, Christian Morgan; *b* 30 January 1974, Pembrokeshire, Wales; *m* Sibi Blazic; 1 da; *Career* actor; hon memb bd of directors Ark Tst, memb bd of directors UKFilmLA; *Television* incl Heart of the Country 1986, Anastasia: The Mystery of Anna 1986, Treasure Island 1990, A Murder of Quality 1991, Mary, Mother of Jesus 1999; *Films* incl: Empire of the Sun 1987, Mio min Mio 1987, Henry V 1989, Newsies 1992, Swing Kids 1993, Little Women 1994, Prince of Jutland 1994, Pocahontas 1995, The Secret Agent 1996, The Portrait of a Lady 1996, Metroland 1997, Velvet Goldmine 1998, All the Little Animals 1998, A Midsummer Night's Dream 1999, American Psycho 2000, Shaft 2000, Captain Corelli's Mandolin 2001, Equilibrium 2001, Reign of Fire 2001, Laurel Canyon 2002, The Machinist 2004, Batman Begins 2005, The New World 2006, The Prestige 2006; *Awards* Best Juvenile Actor Nat Bd of Review 1988, nominated Best Actor London Films Critics Circle 2001, nominated Best Actor Online Film Critics Soc 2001; *Style—* Christian Bale, Esq

BALE, Stephen William; s of Dennis Alfred Amer Bale (d 1981), of Cardiff, and Ida, *née* George (d 1994); *b* 3 May 1952; *Educ* UC Cardiff (BA); *m* 14 July 1974, Fleur Elizabeth, da of late Richard John Gregory; 1 s (Owen John b 29 June 1980), 1 da (Lara Claire b 25 March 1985); *Career* Neath Guardian 1973–78 (NCTJ Proficiency Cert 1975), South Wales Evening Post Swansea 1978–80, South Wales Argus Newport 1980–83, Western Mail Cardiff 1983–86, rugby union corr The Independent 1988–96 (joined 1986), rugby corr Daily Express 1996–; memb: Welsh Rugby Writers' Assoc (chm 1996–97), Sports Writers' Assoc of GB, Rugby Union Writers' Club (chm 1998–2000); *Style—* Stephen Bale, Esq; ✉ 1 Orchard Barns, Broughton Lane, Shoreditch, Taunton, Somerset TA3 7BH (tel and fax 01823 325567, e-mail steve.bale@express.co.uk); Daily Express, Northern and Shell House, 10 Lower Thames Street, London EC3R 6EN (tel mobile 07768 446160)

BALEN, Malcolm; s of Henry Balen, and Elswyth Honor Balen; *b* 9 February 1956; *Educ* Peterhouse Cambridge (BA); *Career* news trainee BBC 1978, regnl journalist Manchester 1980–82, sr prog ed Channel Four News ITN 1989–94 (joined ITN 1982), ed BBC Nine O'Clock News 1994–97, exec ed BBC TV and Radio News Bulletins 1997–2000, head of news ITV London 2000–03, sr editorial advsr BBC News 2003–; occasional lectr Cncl of Europe 2000–; BAFTA award 1991 (for Channel 4 coverage of resignation of Margaret Thatcher 1990); *Books* Kenneth Clarke (1994), A Very English Deceit (2002); *Style—* Malcolm Balen, Esq

BALEN, Paul; s of Henry Balen (d 2004), and Elswyth Balen; *b* 25 February 1952, London; *Educ* Nottingham HS, Peterhouse Cambridge (BA, pres Law Soc); *m* 5 April 1981, Helen; 3 c (Robin b 14 July 1984, Rosalyn b 17 Jan 1986, Bryony b 21 Dec 1990); *Career* admitted slr 1977; slr specialising in medical and product liability; ptnr Freeth Cartwright 1980– (joined as articled clerk); sr fell Coll of Personal Injury Law 2000; memb Editorial Bd Health Care Risk Bulletin; nat sec and memb Exec Ctee Assoc of Personal Injury Lawyers 1998–2000, pres Nottinghamshire Law Soc 2005–06 (sec 1983–88), referral slr Action for Victims of Medical Accidents, memb External Reference Gp for Children's Servs Nat Patient Agency; memb: Law Soc (assessor Clinical Negligence Specialist Panel, memb Personal Injury Specialist Panel), pres elect Notts Medico-Legal Soc, Assoc of Midlands Mediators, American Assoc for Justice, Australian Plaintiffs Lawyers Assoc, Pan Europe Orgn of Personal Injury Lawyers, Inquest; Nottingham Roosevelt scholar 1977, currently chm of tstees Nottingham Roosevelt Scholarship Fund; govr Nottingham HS, past pres Old Nottinghamians Soc; ADR accredited mediator; *Publications* Multi Party Actions (jtly, 1995); contrib of several chapters to books and author of numerous articles; *Style*— Paul Balen, Esq; ✉ Freeth Cartwright LLP, Express Buildings, 29 Upper Parliament Street, Nottingham NG1 2AQ (tel 0115 936 9388, fax 0115 859 9623, e-mail paul.balen@freethcartwright.co.uk)

BALFOUR, Andrew Gordon; s of (James) Campbell Balfour, and Patricia, *née* Thurston-Moon; *b* 26 April 1957; *Educ* Nailsea Sch, Univ of Manchester (LLB); *m* 20 Aug 1983, Anne, *née* Dick; 1 da (Melanie b 23 Jan 1988), 2 s (James b 25 Feb 1990, Christopher b 25 March 1992); *Career* admitted slr 1981; Slaughter and May: joined 1979, ptnr 1988–, NY office 1991–93, head of financing practice 2004–; memb Law Soc 1981; Hon FACT; *Style*— Andrew Balfour, Esq; ✉ Slaughter and May, One Bunhill Row, London EC1Y 8YY (tel 020 7090 3029, e-mail andrew.balfour@slaughterandmay.com)

BALFOUR, Hon Charles George Yule; s of Eustace Arthur Goschen Balfour (d 2000), and (Dorothy Melicent) Anne, *née* Yule; bro of Earl of Balfour, *qv*; raised to the rank of an Earl's son 2004; *b* 23 April 1951; *Educ* Eton; *m* 1, 18 Sept 1978 (m dis 1985), Audrey Margaret, da of H P Hoare (d 1983), of Stourhead, Wilts; m 2, 1987, Svea Maria, da of Ernst-Friedrich Reichsgraf von Goess, of Carinthia, Austria; 1 da (Eleanor Cecilly Isabelle b 4 April 1989), 1 s (George Eustace Charles b 8 Dec 1990); *Career* Hoare Govett 1971–73, Hill Samuel 1973–76, Dillon Read 1976–79, exec dir Banque Paribas London 1979–91, dir Cragnotti and Partners Capital Investment (UK) Ltd 1991–92, md Nasdaq International 1993–2004, sr vice-pres The Nasdaq Stock Market Inc 1993–2003, Fleming Family Ptnrs 2004–, chm Continental Petroleum Ltd 2005–; dir: Bound Oak Properties Ltd 2005–, Wharf Land Investments Ltd 2006–; memb Supervisory Bd MCC Global NV 2006–; memb Queen's Body Guard for Scotland (Royal Co of Archers); *Recreations* gardening, shooting, fishing, bee-keeping; *Clubs* White's, Puffins; *Style*— The Hon Charles Balfour; ✉ 15 Oakley Street, London SW3;

BALFOUR, Christopher Roxburgh; s of Archibald Roxburgh Balfour (d 1958), and Lilian, *née* Cooper (d 1989); strong links with S America 1850–1960 via Balfour Williamson & Co; *b* 24 August 1941; *Educ* Ampleforth, The Queen's Coll Oxford (BA); *Career* merchant banker Hambros Bank Ltd 1968–95; dir: Hambros Bank Ltd 1984–98, Dunhill Holdings plc (non-exec) 1991–93, Vendôme plc and Vendôme SA (non-exec) 1993–98, Evans of Leeds plc (non-exec) 1994–99; exec dir Christie's International plc 1995–98, chm Christie's Manson & Woods Ltd Europe 1996–2001, dir Christie's Fine Art Ltd 1998–2001, dir Christie's International Europe Ltd 2000–, dir Christie's International UK Ltd 2000–; *Recreations* horses, tennis, shooting, bridge, skiing; *Clubs* Pratt's, Brooks's, White's, Beefsteak; *Style*— Christopher R Balfour, Esq; ✉ 35 Kelso Place, London W8 5QP (tel 020 7937 7178)

BALFOUR, Cdr Colin James; DL (Hants 1973); s of Maj Melville Balfour, MC (d 1962), of Durley, Hants, and Margaret (Daisy) Mary, *née* Lascelles (d 1972); *b* 12 June 1924; *Educ* Eton; *m* 27 Aug 1949, Prudence Elisabeth, JP, da of Adm Sir Ragnar Colvin, KBE, CB (d 1954), of Curdridge, Hants; 1 s (James b 1951), 1 da (Belinda (Mrs Hextall) b 1953); *Career* RN 1942, serv HMS Nelson Med 1943, D Day and N Russian Convoys 1944–45, HMS Cossack Korean War 1950–52, RN Staff Coll 1955, 1 Lt HM Yacht Britannia 1956–57, Cdr 1957, Cmd HMS Finisterre 1960–62, resigned 1965; CLA: chm Hants Branch 1980–81 (pres 1987–94), chm Legal and Parly Sub-Ctee and memb Nat Exec Ctee 1982–87; pres Hants Fedn of Young Farmers' Clubs 1982; liaison offr Hants Duke of Edinburgh's Award Scheme 1966–76, memb Hants Local Valuation Panel 1971–81 (chm 1977–), govr and vice-chm Lankhills Special Sch Winchester 1975–80, chm of govrs Durley C of E Primary Sch 1980–95; High Sheriff Hants 1972; Vice Lord-Lt Hants 1996–99; Freeman City of London, Liveryman Worshipful Co of Farmers 1983; *Recreations* shooting, small woodland mgmnt; *Clubs* Brooks's, Pratt's; *Style*— Cdr Colin Balfour, DL, RN; ✉ Wintershill Farmhouse, Durley, Hampshire SO32 2AH

BALFOUR, Doug John; s of Gwyn Balfour, of Bury St Edmunds, and Joy Balfour, of London; *b* 12 June 1958; *Educ* Univ of Southampton (MSc), Cranfield Sch of Mgmnt (MBA); *m* 1984, Anne Mary, da of Robin Watson; 1 da (Alexandra b 1988), 2 s (Jonathan b 1990, Ryan b 1993); *Career* sr exploration geologist De Beers (Kalahari desert) 1980–83, Lucas Industries (sr mgmnt conslt, materials mangr, sales and mktg mangr) 1984–89, support mangr Youth With A Mission Amsterdam 1989–92, relief dir MEDAIR Relief Agency (following Liberian Civil War) 1991–92, commercial mangr Lucas Engineering & Systems Ltd (internal mgmnt consultancy Lucas Gp) 1992–95, gen dir Tearfund (charity) 1995–2004, exec dir Integral (charity alliance) 2004–05, int dir Geneva Global Inc (research co) 2006–; *Recreations* travelling, history; *Style*— Doug Balfour; ✉ Geneva Global, 1550 Liberty Ridge Drive, Suite 330, Wayne, PA 19087, USA (tel 00 1 610 254 0000, e-mail dbalfour@genevaglobal.com)

BALFOUR, Dr (Elizabeth) Jean; CBE (1981), JP (Fife 1963); da of late Maj-Gen Sir James Syme Drew, KBE, CB, DSO, MC (d 1955), and late Victoria Maxwell of Munches; *b* 4 November 1927; *Educ* Univ of Edinburgh (BSc); *m* 1950, John Charles Balfour, OBE, MC, JP, DL; 3 s; *Career* dir A J Bowen & Co Ltd, ptnr Balbirnie Home Farms and Balbirnie Dairy Farm; dir: Chieftain Industries 1983–85, Scot Dairy Trade Fedn 1983–86, Scot Agric Colls 1987–89, Loch Duart Ltd 1999– (chm 1999–2006), Scottish Quality Salmon 2005–06; pres Royal Scot Forestry Soc 1969–71, chm Countryside Cmmn for Scot 1972–83, A New Look at the Northern Ireland Countryside (report to govt) 1984, hon vice-pres Scot YHA 1983–, vice-pres E Scot Coll of Agric 1982–88 (govr 1958–88); memb: Fife CC 1958–70, Nature Conservancy Cncl 1973–80, Scot Economic Cncl 1978–83, Ct Univ of St Andrews 1983–87; vice-chm Scottish Wildlife Tst 1969–72 (hon vice-pres 1983–), memb Cncl Inst of Chartered Foresters 1984–87, chm Regnl Advsy Ctee Forestry Cmmn (E Scot) 1963–84 and (Mid Scot) 1987–2000, memb Ctee of Enquiry on Handling of Geographical Info 1987–89, memb RSE Foot and Mouth Enquiry 2001–02; chm: Seafish Industry Authy 1987–90, W Sutherland Fisheries Tst 1996–99; dep chm Women's Sci Ctee Office of Sci and Technol (Cabinet Office) 1993–94; pres Scottish Arctic Club 1998–2001; memb: Forth River Purification Bd 1992–96, Scottish Office Task Force Trout Protection Orders 1998–; govr Duncan of Jordanstone Coll of Art 1992–94, tstee Royal Botanic Garden Edinburgh 1992–96, memb Cncl Scottish Landowners' Fedn 1992, chm Mid Scotland Branch and memb Cncl Timber Growers Assoc 2000–02; Order of the Falcon (Iceland) 1994; awarded Inst of Chartered Foresters Medal for services to Br forestry 1996; Hon DSc Univ of St Andrews 1977, Hon DUniv Stirling 1991; FRSA 1981, FRSE 1980, FICFor, FIBiol 1988, FRZS Scot 1983; *Recreations* hill walking, fishing, painting, exploring arctic vegetation, shooting; *Clubs* Farmers', New Edinburgh; *Style*— Dr Jean Balfour, CBE, FRSE; ✉ Kirkforthar House, Markinch, Glenrothes, Fife (tel 01592 752233, fax 01592 610314); Scourie, by Lairg, Sutherland; Kirkforthar House, Markinch, Glenrothes, Fife KY7 6LS

BALFOUR, John Manning; s of James Richard Balfour, and Eunice Barbara, *née* Manning; *b* 2 October 1952; *Educ* Fettes, Worcester Coll Oxford (MA); *Career* ptnr: Frere Cholmeley Bischoff 1986–97 (slr 1979), Beaumont and Son 1997–2005, Clyde & Co 2005–; *Books* Air Law (contrib ed, 1988–96), European Community Air Law (1995); *Recreations* swimming, reading; *Clubs* Lansdowne; *Style*— John Balfour, Esq; ✉ Clyde & Co, 51 Eastcheap, London EC3M 1JP (tel 020 7623 1244, fax 020 7623 5427)

BALFOUR, Michael William (Mike); s of Alexander Balfour (d 1999), and Winifred, *née* Kerr; *b* 3 May 1949, London; *Educ* Brockenhurst GS; *m* 30 Sept 1978, Margaret; 1 da (Sarah b 28 March 1981), 1 s (James b 12 July 1983); *Career* dir Mannai Investment Co 1985–92; Fitness First Holdings Ltd: co-fndr 1992, ceo 1992–2004, opened first gym in Bournemouth 1993, co floated 1996, MBO 2003, dep chm 2004–; dir: Fitness Industry Assoc, Skills Active; Entrepreneur of the Year PLC Awards 1999, Nat Entrepreneur of the Year Award (leisure category) Ernst & Young 2000, Entrepreneur of the Year Int Health, Racquet and Sportsclub Assoc (IHRSA) 2001; Hon DBA Bournemouth Univ 2004; FCA 1972; *Recreations* golf, sailing; *Style*— Dr Mike Balfour; ✉ Fitness First, 58 Fleets Lane, Poole, Dorset BH15 3BT

BALFOUR, Neil Roxburgh; s of Archibald Roxburgh Balfour, and Lilian Helen, *née* Cooper (d 1989); *b* 12 August 1944; *Educ* Ampleforth, UC Oxford (BA); *m* 1, 23 Sept 1969 (m dis 1978), HRH Princess Elizabeth of Yugoslavia; 1 s (Nicholas b 6 June 1970); m 2, 4 Nov 1978, Serena Mary Churchill, da of Edwin F Russell, and Lady Sarah Churchill; 1 da (Lily b 29 Nov 1979), 1 s (Alastair b 20 Aug 1981), 2 step da (Morgan b 19 June 1973, Lucinda b 14 Aug 1975); 1 other s (Kamil b 5 July 1995); *Career* called to the Bar Middle Temple 1968; Baring Bros & Co 1968–74, European Banking Co Ltd 1974–83 (exec dir 1980–83); chm: York Tst Ltd 1983–86, York Tst Gp plc 1986–91, York Mount Gp plc 1986–89, Yorkshire General Unit Tst 1985–88, Mermaid Overseas Ltd 1991–, Copernicus Finance Ltd 1995–2005, KP Capital 2006–; dir Mostostal Warszawa SA 1999– (ceo 2000–02); MEP (Cons) N Yorks 1979–84; *Books* Paul of Yugoslavia: Britain's Maligned Friend (with Sally Mackay, 1980); *Recreations* bridge, golf, fishing and shooting; *Clubs* Pratt's, Turf, White's, Royal St George's (Sandwich), Sunningdale; *Style*— Neil Balfour, Esq; ✉ 55 Warwick Square, London SW1V 2AJ (tel 020 7834 5114, fax 020 7834 5116, e-mail neilbalfour@aol.com)

BALFOUR, (George) Patrick; s of David Mathers Balfour, CBE (d 2001), and Mary Elisabeth, *née* Beddall (d 1988); gs of George Balfour, MP; *b* 17 September 1941; *Educ* Shrewsbury, Pembroke Coll Cambridge (MA); *m* 18 March 1978, Lesley Ann, da of John Denis Johnston, of Scotland; 3 s (James David Johnston b 1980, Matthew Alexander Patrick b 1982, Hugo Charles Beddall b 1989); *Career* slr; ptnr Slaughter and May 1973–2001; non-exec dir Interserve plc 2003–; dir Slrs Benevolent Assoc; memb Law Soc; *Recreations* theatre, opera, golf, country pursuits; *Style*— Patrick Balfour, Esq

BALFOUR, Robert Roxburgh; DL (Tweedale 1999); s of Alastair Norman Balfour (d 1996), and Elizabeth Eugenie, *née* Cowell (d 1997); *b* 29 June 1947; *Educ* Tabley House, Grenoble Univ (Dip), Madrid Univ (Dip); *m* 31 Jan 1973, (Camilla) Rose, da of Michael George Thomas Webster, of Hants; 1 s (Rupert Alastair b 23 April 1976), 2 da (Camilla Louise b 11 May 1979, Lara Selina b 1 June 1983); *Career* md Bell Lawrie White Financial Services Ltd 1984–93; dir: Bell Lawrie White & Co 1987–, Stocktrade 1998–; chm Personal Equity Plan Managers Assoc 1995–98; PEP & ISA Managers Assoc: chm 1998–2000, non-exec dir 2000–02; memb: Red Deer Cmmn 1984–92, Firearms Consultative Ctee 1989–90, Queen's Body Guard for Scotland (Royal Co of Archers) 1977–; IBRC 1980–97; FInstD 1985; *Recreations* shooting, photography; *Style*— Robert Balfour, Esq, DL; ✉ Wester Dawyck, Stobo, Peeblesshire EH45 9JU (tel 01721 760226, fax 01721 760330); 10 Murrayfield Avenue, Edinburgh EH12 6AX (tel 0131 337 6403); Stocktrade, 81 George Street, Edinburgh EH2 3EZ (tel 0131 240 0445, fax 0131 240 0424)

BALFOUR, 5 Earl of (UK 1922); Roderick Francis Arthur Balfour; s of Eustace Arthur Goschen Balfour (d 2000), and Anne, *née* Yule; suc kinsman, 4 Earl 2003; *b* 9 December 1948; *Educ* Eton, London Business Sch (Sr Exec Program); *m* 14 July 1971, Lady Tessa Fitzalan Howard, da of 17 Duke of Norfolk (d 2002); 4 da (Willa (Mrs George Franks) b 1973, Kinvara b 1975, Maria b 1977, Candida b 1984); *Career* ptnr Grieveson Grant and Co Stockbrokers 1972–81, investment dir Jessel Toynbee and Co 1981–83, dir UK investment Union Discount Co of London plc 1983–90, founder dir Winterflood Securities 1988–90, dir Rothschild Tst Corp 1990–; memb City of London Ctee STEP; Freeman City of London 1977, Liveryman Worshipful Co of Clothworkers 1986; *Recreations* gardening, music, painting, tennis, cricket, skiing, water skiing; *Clubs* White's, Walbrook, Eton Ramblers, Old Etonian Racquets and Tennis, Arundel Castle CC, Lord's Taverners; *Style*— The Rt Hon the Earl of Balfour; ✉ NM Rothschild & Sons Ltd, New Court, St Swithin's Lane, London EC4P 4DU (tel 020 7280 5000, fax 020 7929 5239)

BALFOUR OF BURLEIGH, Lady; (Dr Janet Morgan); da of Frank Morgan, and Sheila, *née* Sadler; *b* 5 December 1945; *Educ* Newbury Co Girls GS, St Hugh's Coll Oxford (MA), Nuffield Coll Oxford (DPhil), Univ of Sussex (MA), Harvard Univ (Kennedy Meml scholar); *m* 1993, 8 Lord Balfour of Burleigh, *qv*; *Career* res fell Wolfson Coll Oxford and res offr Univ of Essex 1971–72, res fell Nuffield Coll Oxford 1972–74, lectr in politics Exeter Coll Oxford 1974–76, dir of studies St Hugh's Coll Oxford 1975–76 and lectr in politics 1976–78, visiting fell All Souls Coll Oxford 1983; memb Central Policy Review Staff Cabinet Office 1978–81, dir Satellite Television Ltd 1981–83, special advsr to Dir-Gen BBC 1983–86, advsr to Bd Granada Group plc 1986–89, vice-pres Videotext Industry Assoc 1985–91; dir Hulton Deutsch Collection 1988–89; non-exec dir: Cable & Wireless plc 1988–, WH Smith Group plc 1989–95, Midlands Electricity plc 1990–96, Pitney Bowes plc 1991–92, Scottish American Investment Tst plc 1991–, Scottish Life plc 1995–2001, Scottish Oriental Smaller Companies Tst plc 1995–, Nuclear Liabilities Fund (formerly Nuclear Generation Decommissioning Fund Ltd) 1996– (chm 2004–), NMT Gp plc 1997–2004, BPB plc 2000–05, Stagecoach plc 2000–, Close Enterprise VCT 2007–; chm: Dorothy Burns Charity, Readiscovery (Scotland's Nat Book Campaign) 1994–96, Scottish Cultural Resources Access Network, Scottish Museum of the Year Award, Cable & Wireless Flexible Resource Ltd; tstee: American Sch in London 1985–88, Fairground Heritage Tst 1987–91, Cyclotron Tst 1988–89, Carnegie Endowment for the Univs of Scotland 1994–, Nat Library of Scotland 2002–, Trusthouse Charitable Fndn 2006–; memb: Lord Chllr's Advsy Cncl on Public Records 1982–86, Editorial Bd Political Quarterly, Bd Br Cncl 1989–99, Ancient Monuments Bd for Scotland 1990–97, Scottish Hosp Endowments Research Tst 1992–2000; Hon LLB Univ of Strathclyde, Hon DLit Napier Univ; FSA Scot, FRSE; *Books* The House of Lords and the Labour Government 1964–70 (1975), Reinforcing Parliament (1976), The Diaries of a Cabinet Minister 1964–70 by Richard Crossman 3 Vols (ed, 1975, 1976, 1977), Backbench Diaries 1951–63 by Richard Crossman (ed, 1980), The Future of Broadcasting (ed with Richard Hoggart, 1982), Agatha Christie: A Biography (1984), Edwina Mountbatten: A Life of her Own (1991), The Secrets of rue St Roch (2004); *Recreations* music of Handel, sea-bathing, ice skating out of doors, gardens, pruning; *Style*— Lady Balfour of Burleigh, professionally known as Dr Janet Morgan

BALFOUR OF BURLEIGH, Jennifer, Lady; Jennifer Ellis; da of E S Manasseh (d 1962), of London, and Phyllis Annette, *née* Barnard (d 1970); *b* 27 October 1930; *Educ* St Paul's Girls' Sch, Lady Margaret Hall Oxford; *m* 1, 12 Dec 1951 (m dis 1968), John Edward Jocelyn Brittain-Catlin (d 1987), s of Sir George Edward Gordon Catlin (d 1979), and his 1 w, Vera Brittain; 3 s (Daniel b 1953, Timothy b 1961, William b 1966); m 2, 30 Oct 1971 (m dis 1993), 8 Lord Balfour of Burleigh, *qv*; 2 da (Hon Victoria b 1973, Hon Ishbel b 1976); *Career* PR exec: Butter Information Cncl 1953–55, Patrick Dolan & Assoc

1955–56; sr PR exec Erwin Wasey Ruthrauff & Ryan 1956–61; conslt PR advsr to various companies incl Acrilan, Hoover, Vono, Carnation Milk, Littlewoods Stores, Scottish Crafts Centre 1961–71; dir Jamaica Street Ltd property developers 1980–97, mangr London & Scottish Property Services 1985–; dir: Scottish Opera 1990–96, ECAT Ltd (Edinburgh Contemporary Arts Tst) 1989–97, Boxcar Films plc (non-exec) 1994–97; chm Deal Summer Music Festival 1999–2002; memb Bd Link Housing Assoc 1974–97 (former chm Central Region Ctee), life pres Ochil View Housing Assoc (founding chm 1988–93); memb: Visiting Ctee HM Instn Glenochil 1980–85, CAB Alloa 1988–92, Exec Ctee Clackmannan Social & Liberal Democrats until 1993, Cncl National Tst for Scotland 1991–96 (memb Fin Ctee 1995–97), Bd The Grassmarket Project 1994–2001 (patron 2001–), Bd Children's Music Fndn Scotland 1994–97; writer of numerous booklets, pamphlets, newspaper and magazine articles; *Recreations* music, theatre; *Style*— Jennifer, Lady Balfour of Burleigh; ✉ 23 Callis Court Road, Broadstairs, Kent CT10 3AG

BALFOUR OF BURLEIGH, 8 (*de facto* and 12 but for the Attainder) Lord (S 1607); Robert Bruce; er s of 7 Lord Balfour of Burleigh (11 but for the Attainder, d 1967); *b* 6 January 1927; *Educ* Westminster; *m* 1, 30 Oct 1971 (m dis 1993), Jennifer, Lady Balfour of Burleigh, *qv*, da of E S Manasseh (d 1962), and former w of John Edward Jocelyn Brittain-Catlin; 2 da (Hon Victoria (Hon Mrs Bruce-Winkler) b 7 May 1973, Hon Ishbel b 28 Sept 1976); m 2, 29 Aug 1993, Dr Janet P Morgan, *qv*, da of Frank Morgan; *Heir* (hp) da, Hon Victoria Bruce-Winkler; *Career* served: 2 Herefords Bn Home Gd 1944–45, RN 1945–48; foreman and supt English Electric Co Ltd Stafford and Liverpool 1952–57; gen mangr: English Electric Co India Ltd 1957–64, English Electric Netherton Works 1964–66, D Napier & Son Ltd 1966–68; dir: Bank of Scotland 1968–91 (dep govr 1977–91), Scottish Investment Trust plc 1971–97, Tarmac plc 1981–90, William Lawson Distillers Ltd 1984–97, UAPT Infolink plc 1991–94; chm: Scottish Arts Cncl 1971–80, Viking Oil Ltd 1971–80, Fedn of Scottish Bank Employers 1977–86, Nat Book League Scotland 1981–86, Edinburgh Book Festival 1982–87 (dir 1982–97), The Turing Inst 1983–92, United Artists (Communications) Scotland Ltd (formerly Cablevision (Scotland) plc) 1983–96, Capella Nova 1988–, Advsy Bd Robert Gordon Univ Heritage Inst 1989–2002, Canongate Press plc 1991–93; memb: Forestry Cmmn 1971–74, Cncl ABSA 1976–94 (chm Scot Ctee 1990–94), BR (Scottish) Bd 1982–93; treas: Royal Scottish Corp 1967–2005, Royal Soc of Edinburgh 1989–94; tstee: John Muir Tst 1989–96, Bletchley Park Tst 1999–; Vice Lord-Lt Clackmannan 1996–2001; chllr Univ of Stirling 1988–98; Hon DUniv Stirling 1988, Hon DLitt Robert Gordon Univ 1995; CEng, FIEE, Hon FRIAS 1982, FRSE 1986; *Recreations* music, climbing, woodwork; *Style*— The Rt Hon the Lord Balfour of Burleigh, CEng, FIEE, FRSE; ✉ Brucefield, Clackmannan FK10 3QF (tel 01259 730228)

BALFOUR OF INCHRYE, 2 Baron (UK 1945); Ian Balfour; s of 1 Baron Balfour of Inchrye, MC, PC (d 1988), and his 1 w Diana Blanche (d 1982), da of Sir Robert Grenville Harvey, 2 Bt; *b* 21 December 1924; *Educ* Eton, Magdalen Coll Oxford (MA); *m* 28 Nov 1953, Josephine Maria Jane, o da of Morogh Wyndham Percy Bernard; 1 da (Roxane (Hon Mrs Laird Craig)); *Heir* none; *Career* business conslt, composer and gem historian; compositions include 9 operas, 6 symphonies, concertos for viola (3), violoncello (2), violin and violoncello, clarinet, orchestral, vocal and instrumental works; performances: Two Pieces for Strings - Haifa 1976, In Memoriam II for Oboe, Strings, Harp and Percussion - Dublin 1982, Suite No 1 for Cello Solo - Edinburgh and London 1986, Oxford Memories for small orchestra - Oxford and London 1996, Millenium Suprise for orchestra - Oxford, Eszterhaza, Hanover, Leipzig, Moscow and Prague 2000; *Books* Famous Diamonds (1987, 4 edn 2000); *Recreations* reading, walking, watching cricket and association football; *Clubs* Garrick; *Style*— The Rt Hon Lord Balfour of Inchrye; ✉ House of Lords, London SW1A 0PW

BALL, Anthony George (Tony); MBE (1986); s of Harry Clifford Ball, of Bridgwater, Somerset, and Mary Irene Ball; *b* 14 November 1934; *Educ* Bridgwater GS, Bromsgrove Coll of FE; *m* 1, 1957 (m dis 1997), Ruth, da of Ivor Parry Davies (d 1976), of Mountain Ash, S Wales; 2 s (Kevin, Michael, *qv*), 1 da (Katherine); m 2, 2000, Jan Kennedy; *Career* indentured engrg apprentice Austin Motor Co 1951, responsible for launch of Mini 1959, UK sales mangr Austin Motor Co 1962–66, sales and mktg exec BMC 1966–67, chm Barlow Rand UK Motor Group 1967–78 (md Barlow Rand Ford South Africa 1971–73 and Barlow Rand Euro Ops 1973–78); dir: British Leyland Cars, British Leyland International, Rover Gp, Austin Morris, Jaguar Cars, Jaguar Rover Triumph Inc (USA) and BL overseas subsids; chm Nuffield Press 1978–80, chm and md British Leyland Europe and Overseas 1979–82, world sales chief BL Cars 1979–81 (responsible for BL Buy British campaign and launch of Austin Metro 1980); chief exec Henlys plc 1981–83; chm Tony Ball Associates plc (mktg, product launch and event production agency) 1983–; dep chm: Lumley Insurance Ltd 1983–95, Lumley Warranty Services Ltd 1983–95; dir: Customer Concern Ltd 1986–92, Jetmaster Int 1989–97, Billy Marsh Associates Ltd (theatre agency) 1992–, Royal Carlton Hotel Blackpool 1998– (Blackpool's Hotel of the Year 2002–03 and 2003–04); mktg advsr to: Sec of State for Agric 1982, Sec of State for Energy 1983–87, Sec of State for Wales 1987–91; responsible for producing UK dealer launch of Vauxhall Astra for General Motors; launches and special events for: Br Motor Corp (BMC), Rover, Land Rover, Jaguar, MG, Mercedes-Benz, Fiat, Bedford Trucks, Mazda, Proton, Lada, Leyland DAF, LDV, Daihatsu, Optare Buses, AWD, GM Europe, Pioneer Electronics UK, Gillette Europe; responsible for prodn and promotion of SMMT Br International Motor Show; mktg advsr to relaunch of London Zoo; creator and producer: Rugby World Cup opening and closing ceremonies 1991 (England) and 1999 (Wales), Lloyds Private Banking Playwright of the Year Award 1995–, opening and closing ceremonies at Wembley Stadium of European Football Championships Euro '96, FA Cup Finals 1996–2000, RFU 125th Anniversary Twickenham 1996 and 6 Nations Championships 1996–, Scottish Motor Show 1997, 1999 and 2001, special events Ferodo Centenary 1997, opening ceremony 6 Nations Rugby Championship for RFU Francais at Stade de France Paris 1998, opening ceremony Cricket World Cup 1999; responsible for production of British Motor Industry Centenary Year 1996 for SMMT; advance planning advsr Cwlth Games ceremonies 2002; contrib FA presentation for England's bid to host World Cup 2006; broadcaster, writer, lectr and after-dinner speaker, Meml Lecture Univ of Birmingham 1982, various TV and radio documentaries, prodr ITV documentary The Birth of Rugby 1991, panellist BBC Any Questions; pres Austin Ex-Apprentices Assoc 2006–, vice-chm Fellowship of the Motor Industry 2007–; patron Wordsworth Tst 2005–; winner Benedictine Awards Business After Dinner Speaker of the Year 1992–93; Freeman City of London 1980; govr Bromsgrove Coll of FE 1982–90; Liveryman: Worshipful Co of Coach Makers and Coach Harness Makers 1980, Worshipful Co of Carmen 1983; hon memb City & Guilds of London 1982, Prince Philip Medal for Mktg Achievement and Servs to Br Motor Industry 1984; FIMI 1980, FCIM 1981, FCGI 1999; *Books* Metro - The Book of the Car (contrib), A Marketing Study of the Welsh Craft Industry (Govt report, 1988), Tales Out of School - Early Misdeeds of the Famous (contrib), Making Better Business Presentations (contrib), Men and Motors of The Austin (contrib); *Recreations* military history, theatre, after-dinner speaking, sharing good humour; *Clubs* Lord's Taverners; *Style*— Tony Ball, Esq, MBE; ✉ 76A Grove End Road, St John's Wood, London NW8 9ND (tel 020 7449 6930); Silverhowe, Red Bank Road, Grasmere, Cumbria LA22 9PX (website www.tonyball.co.uk)

BALL, Christopher Charles; s of Reginald Charles Ball, of Essex, and Amelia Ellen, *née* Garner; *b* 25 December 1945; *Educ* Harold Hill GS; *m* 17 July 1971, Frances Jean, da of Philip Elliott, of Barry Island, Wales; 1 s (Ian b 1987); *Career* dir: Linton Nominees Ltd 1986, Richardson Glover and Case Nominees Ltd 1986, Capel-Cure Myers Unit Trust Management Ltd 1990, National Investment Group 1990; chm Ridgefield Unit Trust Administration Ltd; MSI; *Recreations* golf, reading; *Style*— Christopher Ball, Esq; ✉ 147 Western Road, Leigh-on-Sea, Essex (tel 01702 711032); The Registry, Royal Mint Court, London EC3N 4EY (tel 020 7488 4000, fax 020 7481 3798, telex 9419251)

BALL, Sir Christopher John Elinger; kt (1988); er s of late Laurence Elinger Ball, OBE, and Christine Florence Mary, *née* Howe; *b* 22 April 1935; *Educ* St George's Sch Harpenden, Merton Coll Oxford (MA); *m* 1958, Wendy Ruth, da of late Cecil Frederick Colyer; 3 s (David, Peter, Richard), 3 da (Helen, Diana, Yasmin); *Career* 2 Lt Para Regt 1955–56; lectr in English language Merton Coll Oxford 1960–61, lectr in comparative linguistics SOAS Univ of London 1961–64; Lincoln Coll Oxford: fell and tutor of English language 1964–79, sr tutor 1971–72, bursar 1972–79, hon fell 1981; Keble Coll Oxford: warden 1980–88, hon fell 1989; hon fell Merton Coll Oxford 1987; chm Bd of Nat Advsy Body for Public Sector Higher Educn in England 1982–88, sec Linguistics Assoc of GB 1964–67, pres Oxford Assoc of Univ Teachers 1968–71, publications sec Philological Soc 1969–75, chm Univ of Oxford English Bd 1977–79, founding fell Kellogg Forum for Continuing Educn Univ of Oxford 1988–89, chm Educn-Industry (Industry Matters) RSA 1988–90, RSA fell in continuing educn 1989–92, RSA dir of learning 1992–97; memb: Jt Standing Ctee for Linguistics 1979–82, Conf of Colls Fees Ctee 1979–85, Gen Bd of the Faculties 1979–82, Hebdomadal Cncl 1985–89, CNAA 1982–88 (chm English Studies Bd 1973–80, chm Linguistics Bd 1977–82), BTEC 1984–90, IT Skills Shortages Ctee (Butcher Ctee) 1984–85, CBI IT Skills Agency 1985–88, CBI Trg Task Force 1988–89, CBI Educn and Trg Affrs Ctee 1989–97; chm: Strategic Educn Fora for Kent, Oxfordshire 1992–97, and Greater Peterborough 1992–95, Educn Policy Ctee RSA Exams Bd 1993–96; memb Cncl and Exec Templeton Coll Oxford 1981–92; govr: St George's Sch Harpenden 1985–89, Centre for Medieval and Renaissance Studies Oxford 1987–90; chm: Higher Educn Info Servs Tst 1987–90, Manchester Poly 1989–91 (hon fell 1988), Nat Inst for Careers Educn and Counselling 1989–92, Pegasus 1989–92, Brathay Hall Tst 1990–91 (hon fell 2003); visiting prof of higher educn Leeds Poly 1989–92, pres Assoc of Colls for Further and Higher Educn 1987–90, SEAL 2000–05; educnl conslt to Price Waterhouse 1989–92; founding chm: Nat Advsy Cncl for Careers and Educnl Guidance (NACCEG) 1994–96, The Talent Fndn 1999–2004 (patron 2004); chm The Global Univ Alliance 2000–05; chm Nat Campaign for Learning 1995–97 (patron 1998–), vice-chm Jigsaw 1998–2004; chllr Univ of Derby 1995–2003; jt founding ed (with late Angus Cameron) Toronto Dictionary of Old English 1970, memb Editorial Bd Oxford Review of Education 1984–95; hon fell Poly of Central London 1990, hon fell North East Wales Inst 1996; Hon DLitt CNAA 1989, hon fell Auckland Inst of Tech 1992 (Millennium fell 2000), Hon DUniv North London, Hon DEd Univ of Greenwich 1994, Hon DUniv Open Univ 2002, Hon DUniv Derby 2003; FRSA 1987; *Publications* Fitness for Purpose (1985), Aim Higher (1989), Higher Education into the 1990s (jt ed with Heather Eggins, 1989), More Means Different (1990), Learning Pays (1991), Sharks and Splashes!: The Future of Education and Employment (1991), Profitable Learning (1992), Start Right (1994); various contribs to philological, linguistic and educnl jls; *Style*— Sir Christopher Ball; ✉ 45 Richmond Road, Oxford OX1 2JJ (tel and fax 01865 310800)

BALL, David Martin James; s of Rev Thomas William Ball, of Perth, W Aust, and late Anne, *née* Rice; *b* 29 September 1943; *Educ* Annadale GS, Lisburn Tech Coll, Belfast Coll of Arts and Tech (Dip Civil Engrg); *m* 1, 1969 (m dis 1985); 2 da (Heidi b 5 Oct 1974, Joanna b 14 Aug 1977); m 2, 1986, Jacqueline Bernadette Margaret Mary, da of Maj Fredrick Jocelyn Clarke, of Weybridge, Surrey; 1 da (Victoria b 20 Nov 1989); *Career* civil engr Middle Level Cmmrs March Cambridge 1963–66, gen mangr A L Curtis (ONX) Ltd Chatteris Cambridge 1966–70, chm and md David Ball Gp plc Cambridge 1970–, dir and chm David Ball Ireland Ltd Cork Ireland 1982–; chm: Cambridge Philharmonic Soc 1986, Q 103 FM (local commercial radio) 1988, Cambridge Structures Ltd 1995–, David Ball Middle East Ltd 1998–, Concrete Bridge Devpt Gp 2007–; regnl chm East Anglia Energy Managers Gps 1990; dir: Cambridge and District C of C Industry 1997– (pres 1981–83), Business Link Central and South Cambs, CAMBSTEC Trg and Enterprise Cncl 1997–, Gtr Cambridge Partnership Ltd 2005–; memb Cncl Midland Examining Gp, vice-chm and co fndr Cambridge Enterprise Agency; chm: Cambridge Work Relations Gp, Working Pty Durability of Concrete Structures in Use by the Public; chm PCC, memb Synod, dir Ely Diocesan Bd of Fin Ltd 1991–, lay minister Diocese of St Edmundsbury and Ipswich and Ely 1994–, chm Mildenhall Team Miny Diocese of St Edmundsbury and Ipswich 1997; tstee Pye Fndn, patron Wintercomfort for the Homeless; memb Concrete Soc (dir and memb Cncl 2006–), FCMI 1981, fell Inst of Refractory Engrs 1981, FRSA 1985; *Recreations* gardening, tennis, walking; *Clubs* Lansdowne; *Style*— David Ball, Esq; ✉ Freckenham House, Freckenham, Suffolk IP28 8HX (tel 01638 720975, e-mail dmjball@lineone.net); David Ball Group plc, Huntingdon Road, Bar Hill, Cambridge CB23 8HN (tel 01954 780687, fax 01954 782912, mobile 07801 416191, e-mail chairman@davidballgroup.com)

BALL, Geoffrey Arthur (Geoff); s of late Henry Arthur Ball, of Bristol, and late Phyllis Edna, *née* Webber; *b* 4 August 1943; *Educ* Cotham GS Bristol; *m* 1968, Mary Elizabeth, da of late S George Richards, of Bristol; 3 s (Nicholas b 1971, Nathan b 1972, Thomas b 1975), 1 da (Esther b 1977); *Career* exec chm CALA Group Ltd, non-exec chm McCarthy & Stone; dir The Scottish Mortgage Investment Tst plc; pres Housebuilders Fedn in Eng and Wales 2001–03; chm Edinburgh Business Assembly; Clydesdale Bank Young Business Personality of the Year 1983; FCA; *Recreations* golf, music; *Clubs* New (Edinburgh), MCC, Hon Co of Edinburgh Golfers; *Style*— Geoff Ball, Esq; ✉ 26 Hermitage Drive, Edinburgh EH10 6BY (tel 0131 447 7909); CALA Group Ltd, Adam House, 5 Mid New Cultins, Edinburgh EH11 4DU (tel 0131 535 5200, fax 0131 535 5255)

BALL, Prof Sir John Macleod; kt (2006); *b* 19 May 1948; *Educ* Mill Hill Sch, St John's Coll Cambridge (open exhibitioner, BA), Univ of Sussex (DPhil); *Career* SRC postdoctoral res fell Brown Univ RI 1972–74; Heriot-Watt Univ: joined Dept of Mathematics 1972, lectr in mathematics 1974–78, reader in mathematics 1978–82, prof of applied analysis 1982–96; Sedleian prof of natural philosophy Mathematical Inst Univ of Oxford 1996–; visiting prof Dept of Mathematics Univ of Calif Berkeley 1979–80, sr fell SERC 1980–85, visiting prof Laboratoire d'Analyse Numérique Université Pierre et Marie Curie Paris 1987–88 and 1994, Ordway visiting prof Univ of Minnesota 1990, visiting prof Inst for Advanced Study Princeton 1993–94 and 2002–03, visiting prof Université Montpellier II 2003; pres: London Mathematical Soc 1996–98, Int Mathematical Union 2003–; delg OUP 1998–; memb EPSRC 1994–99, chair Scientific Steering Ctee Isaac Newton Inst 2006–; memb editorial bds various mathematical and scientific jls and book series, author of numerous mathematical and scientific pubns; Whittaker Prize Edinburgh Mathematical Soc 1981, jr Whitehead Prize London Mathematical Soc 1982, Keith Prize RSE 1990, Naylor Prize London Mathematical Soc 1995, von Karman Prize 1999, Royal Medal RSE 2006; foreign memb: French Acad of Sciences 2000, Istituto Lombardo 2005; Hon DSc: EPF Lausanne, Heriot-Watt Univ 1998, Univ of Sussex 2000, Montpellier II Univ 2003, Univ of Edinburgh 2004; FRSE 1980, FRS 1989; *Recreations* chess, music, travel; *Style*— Prof Sir John Ball, FRS, FRSE; ✉ Mathematical Institute, 24–29 St Giles', Oxford OX1 3LB (tel 01865 273577, fax 01865 273586)

BALL, Jonathan Macartney; MBE (1992); s of Christopher Edward Ball (d 1978), and Dorothy Ethel, *née* Macartney; *b* 4 June 1947; *Educ* Truro Sch, AA (AADipl); *m* 29 June 1974, Victoria Mary Ogilvie, da of Dr Anthony Blood (d 2005), of Bude, Cornwall; 2 da (Jemima Veryan b 1976, Morwenna Victoria b 1979); *Career* co-fndr (with Tim Smit) The Eden Project Cornwall, fndr The Great Atlantic Way Cornwall; chartered architect; princ

The Jonathan Ball Practice Bude 1974–2001 (8 nat and 7 regnl design awards 1980–2000), fndr ptnr Triangle Estates; occasional after dinner and conference speaker, assessor for architecture awards; tstee Br Architectural Library 1988–95; RIBA: memb Cncl 1981–99, chm Parly Liaison Ctee 1981–87, vice-pres 1983–85 and 1991–93, hon sec 1988–91 and 1993–95; memb Editorial Bd: RIBA Handbook of Architectural Practice and Management, The Millennium Book for Cornwall; RNLI 1966–: choir master Bude Lifeboat singers 1967–93, crew memb Bude Lifeboat (dep launching authy 1993–2003, sr helmsman 1996–95), co-sponsor RNLI Beach Lifeguard Prog, memb RNLI Cncl 2007–; Surf Life Saving Assoc of GB (SLSGB): Bude Surf Life Saving Club 1959–, pres 2000–, chm Rescue 2010 GB bid for World Life Saving Championships 2006–; SLSGB Long Service Award 1984, RNLI Lifeboat Crew Long Service Award 1989, Queen's Jubilee Medal 2002; Master Worshipful Co of Chartered Architects 2007–08 (Liveryman 1986, memb Ct of Assts 1991–), Freeman City of London 1987; Bard of the Cornish Gorseth 2002 (bardic name Tregarthen); Queen's Golden Jubilee Medal 2002; ACIArb 1978, FRSA 1985; *Recreations* enjoying Cornwall and the Isles of Scilly; *Clubs* Athenaeum; *Style—* Jonathan Ball, Esq, MBE; ✉ Tregarthens, Diddies Road, Stratton, Bude, Cornwall EX23 9DW (tel 01288 352198); Rescue 2010 GB Bid Office, 5 Belle Vue, Bude, Cornwall EX23 8JJ (tel 01288 353898, fax 01288 359961, e-mail jonathan@greatatlanticway.com and info@rescue2010.co.uk)

BALL, Michael Ashley; s of Anthony George (Tony) Ball, MBE, *qv*, of Bidford-on-Avon, Warks, and Ruth Parry Davies; *b* 27 June 1962; *Educ* Plymouth Coll, Farnham Sixth Form Coll, Guildford Sch of Acting; *Career* actor and singer; *Theatre* Surrey Youth Theatre 1980–81: The Boyfriend (1980), Under Milk Wood (1981); drama sch 1981–84, first professional role Judas/John the Baptist in Godspell 1984, first starring role Frederick in The Pirates of Penzance (Manchester Opera House) 1985, West End debut cr role of Marius in original prodn of Les Miserables (Barbican and Palace) 1985; other credits incl: Raoul in Phantom of the Opera (Her Majesty's) 1987, cr role of Alex in Aspects of Love (Prince of Wales 1989, Broadway debut 1990), Giorgio in Passion (Queen's) 1996, Alone Together (Donmar Warehouse) 2001, Caractacus Potts in Chitty Chitty Bang Bang (Palladium) 2002–03; numerous nat and int concert tours; *Television* incl: Coronation Street, Late Expectations, Save the Children Christmas Spectacular, Top of the Pops, Royal Variety Performance, GB rep Eurovision Song Contest 1992, two series of Michael Ball 1993 and 1994; Michael Ball in Concert (video) 1997, hosted National Lottery Live Show July 1997, An Evening with Michael Ball 1998, Lord Lloyd Webber's 50th Birthday 1998; *Recordings* incl: Les Miserables (original London cast album 1986, int cast album 1987), Rage of the Heart 1987, London cast album Aspects of Love 1989, Michael Ball 1992, West Side Story 1993, Always 1993, One Careful Owner 1994, The Best of Michael Ball 1994, Michael Ball - The Musicals 1996, Michael Ball - The Movies 1998, Christmas 1999, Live at the Royal Albert Hall 1999, This Time it's Personal 2000, Centre Stage 2001, A Love Story 2003, Love Changes Everything: The Essential Michael Ball 2004; *Films* Henry Purcell in England My England; *Awards* Most Promising Artiste Award Variety Club of GB 1989, The Variety Club Best Recording Artiste 1998, Theatregoers Club of GB Most Popular Musical Actor 1999; *Recreations* music, theatre, keeping fit, contemplating country life; *Style—* Michael Ball, Esq

BALL, Sir Richard Bentley; 5 Bt (UK 1911), of Merrion Square, City of Dublin, and Killybegs, Co Donegal; s of Sir Charles Irwin Ball, 4 Bt (d 2002); *b* 29 January 1953; *Educ* Dragon Sch Oxford, Sherborne, Univ of Leicester; *m* 31 Aug 1991, Beverley Ann, da of late Bertram Joffre Wright; 1 da (Anna Frances b 20 Feb 1996); *Career* CA; Peat Marwick Mitchell 1975–82, International Computers Ltd 1982–99, interim fin mangr 2000–02, fin mangr Interserve Investments 2003, fin controller McAlpine Project Investments 2004–05, interim fin mangr Antler Homes 2006; ACA; *Recreations* hockey, travel; *Style—* Sir Richard Ball, Bt; ✉ Evenshade, Sandown Road, Esher, Surrey KT10 9TT (tel 01372 464293)

BALL, Simon Peter; s of Peter Ball, of Bexleyheath, Kent, and Maureen, *née* Bishop; *b* 2 May 1960, London; *Educ* Chislehurst and Sidcup GS, UCL; *m* 30 May 1992, Sandra Marie; 2 da (Hannah b 12 May 1993, Katie b 3 Jan 1995); *Career* CA 1984, qualified with Price Waterhouse & Co; with Kleinwort Benson Ltd (then Dresdner Kleinwort Benson) 1985–98 (latterly finance dir then chief operating offr), gp finance dir Robert Fleming Hldgs Ltd 1998–2000 (also md Chase Manhattan International Ltd after 2000), DG of finance Dept for Constitutional Affrs 2003–05, finance dir 3i Gp plc 2005–; non-exec dir Cable & Wireless plc 2006–; *Style—* Mr Simon Ball; ✉ 3i Group plc, 16 Palace Street, London SW1E 5JD

BALL, Zoë; *b* 23 November 1970; *Educ* Holy Cross Sch Chalfont St Peter; *m* 1999, Norman Cook (aka Fatboy Slim); 1 s (Woody b 2000); *Career* runner Granada TV; researcher: BSkyB, Action Time; researcher and asst prodr Big Breakfast (Channel 4 TV Corp); TV presenter of progs incl: The Ozone (BBC TV, winner of Best Music Show Smash Hit Awards), The Big Breakfast 1996, Live & Kicking 1996–99 (BBC TV), The Priory 1999, Strictly Dance Fever (BBC) 2005 (contestant Strictly Come Dancing (BBC) 2005), Extinct (ITV) 2006, Soapstar Superstar (ITV) 2007, Grease is the Word (ITV) 2007; radio presenter: Breakfast Show BBC Radio 1 1997–2000, XFM 2002–04; *Style—* Ms Zoë Ball

BALLAMY, Iain Mark; s of Mark Donald Ballamy, and Sylvia, *née* Thompson; *b* 20 February 1964; *Educ* Merton Tech Coll (City & Guilds, Musical Instrument Technol); *Partner* Alison Lorna Duffell; *Career* jazz saxophonist and composer; with Balloon Man 1983–93, Loose Tubes (fndr memb, 1984–90), Billy Jenkins V.O.G. 1985–, Bill Bruford's Earthworks (1986–92), Human Chain and Delightful Precipice (both with Django Bates, *qv*, 1992–), ACME (leader, 1996–), Food 1998–; fndr and co dir Feral Records with Dave McKean; performed with numerous artists and bands incl: Hermeto Pascoal, George Coleman, Dewey Redman, Mike Gibbs, Gil Evans, Sankalpam (Indian dance gp), The Hungry Ants; performances in films incl: Legend, My Son the Fanatic, Joseph Losey - The Man with Four Names, Absolute Beginners, The Last Days of General Patten; numerous performances on radio and TV incl: The Tube, Bergerac, Right to Reply, Wogan, Signal to Noise (by Neil Gaiman, *qv*, and Dave McKean, BBC Radio 4); performed at numerous venues incl: Ronnie Scotts, Knitting Factory, FEZ and Bottom Line (all NY), New Morning (Paris), Royal Festival Hall, Royal Albert Hall, Barbican and most int jazz festivals; played Steve the prat in Out There (Simon Black's musical theatre prodn, 1995–96); Br Cncl concerts in Columbia, India, Lithuania, Senegal, Bosnia; memb: MU (Musicians' Union), PRS (Performing Rights Soc), MCPS (Mechanical Copyright Protection Soc), PAMRA (Performing Artists Media Rights Assoc); *Compositions* incl: Estuary English Apollo Saxophone Quartet 1995, Mirror Signal Manoeuvre Apollo Saxophone Quartet, ACME with Birmingham Jazz 1996, Oblique with Birmingham Jazz 1997, Four and a half minutes late (solo harpsichord, Jane Chapman, 1998), Walpurgis Night (duet for piano and tenor sax, Joanna MacGregor, 1998), cmmn work: Food Cheltenham Jazz Festival 1999, Bath Int Festival 2000; *Recordings* 45 CD appearances incl: Pepper Street Interludes (album), Food (album), ACME (album), All Men Amen (album), Balloon Man (album, 1989), Organic and GM Food (album, 2001); *Awards* Best Soloist John Dankworth Cup 1985, Best Ensemble BT British Jazz 1995, Special Award for Innovation BBC Jazz Awards 2001; *Recreations* black glass and early stoneware, metal detecting; *Style—* Iain Ballamy, Esq; ✉ website www.ballamy.com

BALLANCE, Chris Howard; MSP; s of Howard Marshall Ballance, and Gwyneth Olive Shrimpton; *b* 7 July 1952; *Educ* Alderman Newton's Sch Leicester, Reigate GS, Univ of St Andrews; *m* Alis; 1 s (Calum b 8 April 2006); *Career* theatre writer 1990–; plays incl: Water of Life 1989, Made from Girders 1991, Viva La Diva 2001; MSP (Green) South of Scotland 2003–; Edinburgh Fringe First Award 1989; memb: Equity 1991, Scottish Soc of Playwrights 1991, Writers' Guild of GB 1997; *Style—* Chris Ballance, Esq, MSP; ✉ The Scottish Parliament, Edinburgh EH99 1SP (tel 0131 348 6363, fax 0131 348 6375, e-mail chris.ballance.msp@scottish.parliament.uk)

BALLANTYNE, Prof Colin Kerr; s of Robert Morrison Ballantyne (d 1991), and Isabella Sturrock, *née* Kerr (d 1970); *b* 7 June 1951; *Educ* Hutchesons' GS Glasgow, Univ of Glasgow (MA), McMaster Univ (MSc), Univ of Edinburgh (PhD), Univ of St Andrews (DSc); *m* 1996, Rebecca Josephine, da of Graham Trengove; 1 s (Hamish Trengove b 16 July 1998), 1 da (Kate Iona b 19 June 2000); *Career* teaching asst McMaster Univ 1973–75, demonstrator Univ of Edinburgh 1977–79; Univ of St Andrews: lectr in geography 1980–89, sr lectr 1989–94, prof of physical geography 1994–, head Sch of Geography and Geosciences 1998–2001; Gordon Warwick Award Br Geomorphological Research Gp 1987, President's Medal Royal Scottish Geographical Soc 1991, Newbigin Prize Royal Scottish Geographical Soc 1992, Scottish Science Award Saltire Soc 1996, Wiley Award Br Geomorphological Research Gp 1999; FRSE 1996, FRSA 1996; *Books* The Quaternary of the Isle of Skye (1991), The Periglaciation of Great Britain (1994); *Recreations* mountaineering, skiing, music, modern history, travel; *Style—* Prof Colin Ballantyne, FRSE; ✉ Birchwood, Blebo Craigs, Fife KY15 5UF; School of Geography and Geosciences, University of St Andrews, St Andrews, Fife KY16 9AL (tel 01334 463907, fax 01334 463949, e-mail ckb@st-and.ac.uk)

BALLARD, Beatrice Rosalind; da of James Graham Ballard, of Shepperton, Middx, and Mary, *née* Matthews (d 1964); *b* 29 May 1959; *Educ* St David's Sch Ashford Middx, UEA (BA), City Univ of London (Journalism Dip); *Career* reporter New Statesman 1981, writer and researcher Radio Times 1981–82, asst prodr and dir John Craven's Newsround BBC TV 1983–85, prodr special progs LWT 1986–88; series prodr: Saturday Night Clive, Fame in the Twentieth Century, Clive James Postcards from Miami, New York and Paris, Clive James Meets Ronald Reagan BBC TV 1988; exec prodr Entertainment BBC TV 1994–97, currently creative head Entertainment BBC TV; exec prodr incl: Any Dream Will Do, How Do You Solve a Problem Like Maria?, The Two Ronnies Sketchbook, Parkinson, One Night with Robbie Williams, Elton John at The Royal Opera House, Aunties All Time Greats BBC TV 60th Anniversary, Ruby Wax Meets Madonna, Carrie Fisher on Hollywood, Br Acad Awards, BAFTA Tribute to Billy Connolly, exec prodr Entertainment BBC TV; series prodr: Saturday Night Clive, Fame in the Twentieth Century, Clive James Postcards From Miami, NY and Paris, Clive James Meets Ronald Reagan BBC TV; prodr special progs LWT; asst prodr and dir John Craven's Newsround (BBC); memb Cncl BAFTA, chm Television Ctee; *Recreations* reading, cinema, travel, eating out; *Style—* Ms Beatrice Ballard; ✉ 225 Westbourne Grove, London W11 2SE (e-mail beaballard@tiscali.co.uk)

BALLARD, (Richard) Graham John; s of Alfred John Ballard (d 1979), of Worcs, and Ada Mary Ballard (d 1981); *b* 17 January 1927; *Educ* Prince Henry's GS Evesham, Wadham Coll Oxford (MA), Univ of Cambridge (MA); *m* 10 July 1954, Domini Gabrielle, da of Dr Alfred Johannes Wright (d 1942), of Bucks; 2 s (Sebastian John b 1961, Toby Graham Dominic b 1963); *Career* chm and md Liebigs Rhodesia Ltd 1973–78, md Brooke Bond Kenya 1978–83, dir Tea Board of Kenya 1978–83, chm British Business Assoc Kenya 1982–83; fell commoner Christ's Coll Cambridge 1994– (bursar and fell 1983–94); administrator American Friends of Cambridge Univ 1996–2000; *Recreations* opera, chamber music, reading, bridge; *Style—* Graham Ballard, Esq; ✉ 23 Bentley Road, Cambridge CB2 8AW (tel 01223 323547)

BALLARD, Jackie; da of late Alexander Mackenzie, and Daisy, *née* Macdonald; *b* 4 January 1953; *Educ* Monmouth Sch for Girls, LSE (BSc), Yeovil Coll (FE Teacher's Cert); *m* 1975 (m dis 1989), Derek John Ballard; 1 da (Chris b 23 March 1979); *Career* formerly social worker London Borough of Waltham Forest then lectr in computing, psychology, communications and business studies, cncl support offr Assoc of Lib Dem Cncllrs 1993–97, MP (Lib Dem) Taunton 1997–2001 (Parly candidate 1992, memb Lib Dem Parly local govt team 1997–99, Lib Dem Parly spokesperson on women's issues 1997–99, dep home affrs spokesperson 1997–2001); DG RSPCA 2002–; computer mangr Paddy Ashdown's gen election team 1987, memb Lib Dems' Fed Policy Ctee 1990–95 and Fed Exec Ctee 1997–99; cncllr: South Somerset DC 1987–91 (dep ldr 1988–90, ldr 1990–91), Somerset CC 1993–97 (dep ldr 1993–95); *Recreations* swimming, celtic rock music, gardening, reading; *Style—* Jackie Ballard; ✉ RSPCA, Wilberforce Way, Southwater, Horsham, West Sussex RH13 9RS (tel 0870 010 1181, fax 0870 753 0048)

BALLARD, James Graham; s of late James Ballard, and Edna Ballard, *née* Johnstone; *b* 15 November 1930, Shanghai, China; *Educ* Leys Sch Cambridge, King's Coll Cambridge, Univ of London; *m* 1954, Helen Mary Matthews (d 1964); 1 s, 2 da; *Career* novelist; formerly copywriter and pilot RAF; *Books* The Drowned World (1962), The Four-Dimensional Nightmare (1963, reissued as The Voices of Time 1984), The Terminal Beach (1964), The Drought (1965), The Crystal World (1966), The Day of Forever (1967), The Disaster Area (1967), The Overloaded Man (1967), The Atrocity Exhibition (1970), Crash (1973, film adaptation 1996), Vermilion Sands (1973), Concrete Island (1974), High-Rise (1975), Low-Flying Aircraft and Other Stories (1976), The Unlimited Dream Company (1979), Chronopolis (1979), Hello America (1981), Myths of the Near Future (1982), Empire of the Sun (1984, winner Guardian Fiction Prize, jt winner James Tait Black Meml Prize for Fiction, film adaptation 1987), The Venus Hunters (1986), The Day of Creation (1987), Running Wild (1988), War Fever (1990), The Kindness of Women (1991), Rushing to Paradise (1994), A User's Guide to the Millennium (1996), Cocaine Nights (1996), Super-Cannes (2000, winner Best Book Eurasia Region Cwlth Writers' Prize), Complete Short Stories (2001), Millennium People (2003), Kingdom Come (2006); *Style—* J G Ballard, Esq; ✉ c/o Margaret Hanbury Literary Agency, 27 Walcot Square, London SE11 4UB

BALLARD, Mark; MSP; *b* 27 June 1971, Leeds; *Educ* Lawnswood Comp Sch Leeds, Univ of Edinburgh (MA); *m* 2002, Heather Stacey; *Career* various positions European Youth Forest Action 1994–98, ed Reforesting Scotland jl 1998–2001, environmental communications consultancy co 2002–03, MSP (Green) Lothian 2003–; Scottish Green Pty: spokesperson on int devpt 1999–2000, convenor Nat Cncl 2000–02, nat sec 2002–03; Lord Rector of Univ of Edinburgh 2006–; *Recreations* Indian cooking, cycling; *Style—* Mark Ballard, MSP; ✉ The Scottish Parliament, Edinburgh EH99 1SP

BALLARD, Richard Michael; s of Michael Agar Ballard, and Junella, *née* Ashton (d 1960); *b* 3 August 1953; *Educ* St Edmund's Coll Ware, Queens' Coll Cambridge (MA); *m* 28 Feb 1981, Penelope Ann, da of Dilwyn John Davies, DFC (d 1988), of Glamorgan; 3 s (Hayden b 1984, Thomas b 1985, James b 1992), 1 da (Sophie b 1987); *Career* admitted slr 1978; ptnr Freshfields 1984–; memb Law Soc; *Recreations* country pursuits; *Clubs* Oriental; *Style—* Richard Ballard, Esq; ✉ Freshfields Bruckhaus Deringer, 65 Fleet Street, London EC4Y 1HS (tel 020 7936 4000, fax 020 7832 7001)

BALLIN, Robert Andrew; s of Harold Ballin (d 1976), and Mollie Ballin, *née* Dunn (d 1989); *b* 8 July 1943; *Educ* Highgate Sch, City of London Coll; *m* 27 Nov 1975, Serena Mary Ann, da of Richard Goode, OBE (d 1966); 1 s (Edward b 1980), 2 da (Annabel b 1981, Chloe b 1985); *Career* Shell-Mex and BP 1962–67, SH Benson 1967–69, Gallagher-Smail/Doyle Dane Bernbach 1969–73; Foote Cone & Belding: joined 1973, int dir Impact-FCB Belgium 1975–77, dir 1977–98, dep chm 1988–98; currently mktg and communications conslt; memb Epsom Race Ctee 1994–; *Recreations* music, theatre, sport; *Clubs* White's, RAC, MCC; *Style—* Robert Ballin, Esq; ✉ 18 Sprimont Place, London SW3 3HU (tel 020 7581 5457)

B

BALLS, Alastair Gordon; CB (1995); s of Rev Ernest George Balls, of Stevenson, Ayrshire, and Elspeth Russell, *née* McMillan; *b* 18 March 1944; *Educ* Hamilton Acad, Univ of St Andrews (MA), Univ of Manchester (MA); *m* 26 Nov 1977, Beryl May, da of John Nichol, of Harlow, Essex; 1 s (Thomas b 1979), 1 da (Helen b 1982); *Career* asst sec Treasy Govt of Tanzania 1966–68, economist Dept of Tport UK Govt 1969–73, sec Cairncross Ctee on Channel Tunnel 1974–75, sr econ advsr HM Treasy 1976–79, under sec DOE 1983–87 (asst sec 1979–83), chief exec Tyne & Wear Urban Devpt Corp 1987–98; chm: NewcastleGateshead Initiative 2004–07, Northern Rock Fndn 2006–, The Int Centre for Life Newcastle upon Tyne (millennium project) 2007– (chief exec 1997–2007); non-exec dir Northumbrian Water Ltd 2002–; memb ITC 1998–2003, memb HE Funding Cncl for England (HEFCE) 2006–; CIMgt 1988; *Recreations* fishing, sailing, camping; *Clubs* Royal Northumberland Yacht, Wylam Angling; *Style*— Alastair Balls, Esq, CB; ✉ c/o The International Centre for Life Trust, Times Square, Scotswood Road, Newcastle upon Tyne NE1 4EP (e-mail alastair.balls@life.org.uk)

BALLS, Rt Hon Edward; PC (2007), MP; *b* 25 February 1967; *Educ* Nottingham HS, Keble Coll Oxford, Harvard Univ (Kennedy Scholar); *m* 10 Jan 1998, Yvette Cooper, MP, *qv*; 2 da (Meriel Eliza b 1 June 1999, Madelyn Beth b 26 July 2004), 1 s (Joel b 25 Aug 2001); *Career* teaching fell Dept of Economics Harvard Univ and research asst National Bureau of Economic Research USA until 1990, economics leader writer Financial Times 1990–94 (Young Financial Journalist of the Year Wincott Fndn 1992), economics columnist The Guardian 1994–97, economic advsr to Gordon Brown, MP 1994–99 (as shadow Chancellor of the Exchequer until 1997, then Chancellor of the Exchequer), chief economic advsr to HM Treasy 1999–2004, sr research fell Smith Inst 2004–05; MP (Lab) Normanton 2005–; economic sec to HM Treasy 2006–07, sec of state for Children, Schs and Families 2007–; ed European Economic Policy 1994–97, princ ed World Bank Devpt Report 1995; sec Economic Policy Cmmn Lab Pty until 1997; memb Cncl Royal Economic Soc; Hon Dr of Laws Univ of Nottingham 2003; *Publications* Reforming Britain's Economic and Financial Policy (with Gus O'Donnell, 2002), Microeconomic Reform in Britain (with Gus O'Donnell and Joe Grice, 2004); *Style*— The Rt Hon Edward Balls, MP; ✉ House of Commons, London SW1A 0AA

BALLYEDMOND, Baron (Life Peer UK 2004), of Mourne in the County of Down; Edward Enda Haughey; OBE (1987), JP (1986); s of Edward Haughey (d 1943), of Dundalk, Co Louth; *b* 5 January 1944; *Educ* Christian Brothers Sch Dundalk; *m* 1972, Mary Gordon, da of Alfred William Young (d 1977), of Donaghmore, Co Down; 1 da (Hon Caroline Philippa b 1975), 2 s (Hon Edward Gordon Shannon b 1979, Hon James Quinton Stewart b 1981); *Career* dir: Norbrook Laboratories Ltd 1969– (chm 1980–), Shorts Brothers plc 1989–; chm: Norbrook Holdings BV 1980–, Ballyedmond Farms Ltd 1991–, Haughey Airports 2000–, Haughey Air 2000–; dir Advsy Bd Bank of Ireland 1987–; appointed to Irish Senate 1994; memb: Forum for Peace and Reconciliation 1996–, Oireachtas Ctee for Foreign Affrs 1997–, British-Irish Inter-Policy Body 1997–, Inst of British-Irish Studies 2000–; hon consul for Chile in NI 1992; vice-pres RCVS Tst, tstee Dublin City Univ 1995–; Hon DBA, Hon LLD Nat Univ of Ireland 1997, hon fell Royal Vet Coll London; Hon FRCSI 1998, Hon ARCVS, FInstD, FIAM, FIMgt; Order of Bernardo O'Higgins (Chile) 1995; *Clubs* Savage, Reform (Belfast), Kildare St and Univ (Dublin); *Style*— The Rt Hon the Lord Ballyedmond, OBE

BALMER, Colin Victor; CB (2001); s of Peter Lionel Balmer (d 1982), and Adelaide Currie, *née* Hamilton; *b* 22 August 1946; *Educ* Liverpool Inst HS; *Children* 2 s (Thomas Montrésor b 29 June 1979, William John b 24 April 1987), 1 da (Lucy Caroline b 27 March 1981); *Career* clerical offr War Office 1963–68; MOD: exec offr 1968–70, asst princ 1970–72, asst private sec to Min of State 1972–73, private sec to Under Sec of State (RAF) 1973, princ civil advsr GOC NI 1973–77; Cabinet Office 1977–80; MOD: private sec to Min of State (Def Procurement) 1980–82, first sec UK Delgn NATO 1982–84, asst sec 1984–90, Min (Defence Matériel) Br Embassy Washington 1990–92, asst under sec of state (Mgmnt Strategy) 1992–94, asst under sec of state (Fin Mgmnt) 1994–96, dep under sec of state (Resources, Progs and Fin) 1996–98, princ fin offr 1998–2000, fin dir 2000–03; md Cabinet Office 2003–06; non-exec dir QinetiQ Group plc; *Recreations* golf, tennis, bridge, rock and roll music, playing guitar (badly); *Style*— Colin Balmer, Esq, CB; ✉ tel 07876 791002, e-mail colinbalmer@tiscali.co.uk

BALMFORD, Prof David Ernest Hall; OBE (1993); s of Edgar Balmford (d 1986), and Edna Hinchliffe (d 1974); *b* 3 April 1932; *Educ* Huddersfield Coll, Univ of Durham (BSc); *m* 1, 22 Feb 1958, Irene Mary (d 2002), da of Joseph Reece Williams; 1 da (Julia Dawn b 13 July 1967), 1 s (Richard Anthony Hall b 30 Dec 1968); *m* 2, 5 Dec 2005, Kathryn Anne Leach; *Career* chief dynamicist Fairey Aviation 1959–64 (stressman 1953–59); Westland Helicopters Ltd: chief dynamicist 1964–69, head Tech Dept 1971–77 (dep head 1969–71), dep chief engr (research) 1977–80, head of advanced engrg 1980–89, chief scientist 1989–94 (ret); conslt 1994–; visiting industrial prof Univ of Bristol 1991–; visiting lectr Imperial Coll of Science, Technology and Medicine 1996–99; chm Res Ctee Soc of British Aerospace Companies 1989–93, dep chm Cncl Aircraft Research Assoc 1993–95; FRAeS 1993, FREng 1994; *Awards* (with Westland Helicopters Ltd) MacRobert Award (jtly) for innovative technical design of Lynx helicopter 1975, Design Cncl Award (jtly) for design of Westland 30 helicopter 1983; *Books* Bramwell's Helicopter Dynamics (co-author, 2 edn 2001); *Recreations* recreational flying (PPL), fell walking; *Style*— Prof David Balmford, OBE, FREng; ✉ Fordhay Farm, East Chinnock, Yeovil, Somerset BA22 9EE (tel 01935 863286)

BALNIEL, Lord; Anthony Robert Lindsay; s and h of 29 Earl of Crawford and (12 of) Balcarres, PC, *qv*; *b* 24 November 1958; *Educ* Eton, Univ of Edinburgh; *m* 12 Aug 1989, Nicola A, yst da of Antony Bicket, of Derwas, Dolwen, N Wales; 2 s (Alexander Thomas, Master of Lindsay b 1991, Hon James Antony b 10 Nov 1992), 2 da (Hon Katherine Ruth Vere b 4 Sept 1996, Hon Isabel Rosemary b 1 May 2001); *Heir* s, Master of Lindsay; *Career* md J O Hambro Investment Management Ltd 2004– (dir 1987–); *Clubs* New (Edinburgh); *Style*— Lord Balniel; ✉ Balcarres, Colinsburgh, Fife; 6 Pembridge Place, London W2 4XB

BALSHAW, Iain; MBE (2004); *b* 18 April 1979, Blackburn, Lancs; *Educ* Stonyhurst; *Career* rugby union player (full back); with Bath RUFC 1997–2004, with Leeds Tykes 2004–; England: 24 caps, debut v Argentina 2000, winners Six Nations Championship 2001, ranked no 1 team in world 2003, winners World Cup Aust 2003; memb British and Irish Lions touring squad Aust 2001 (3 caps) and NZ 2005 (selected but missed tour following injury); *Recreations* golf; *Style*— Iain Balshaw, Esq, MBE; ✉ c/o Rugby Football Union, Rugby House, Rugby Road, Twickenham, Middlesex TW1 1DS

BALSTON, His Hon Antony Francis; s of Cdr Edward Francis Balston, DSO, RN (d 1999), and Diana Beatrice Louise, *née* Ferrers (d 1993); *b* 18 January 1939; *Educ* Downside, Christ's Coll Cambridge (MA); *m* 1966, Anne Marie Judith, da of Gerald Ball (d 1971); 2 s (James b 1967, Andrew b 1969), 1 da (Alexandra b 1972); *Career* RN 1957–59; admitted slr 1966, ptnr Herington Willings & Penry Davey (Hastings) 1966–85; recorder of the Crown Court 1980–85, hon recorder Hastings 1984–2005, circuit judge (SE Circuit) 1985–2005; *Recreations* gardening; *Clubs* Farmers'; *Style*— His Hon Antony Balston; ✉ e-mail abalston@cix.compulink.co.uk

BAMBER, David James; s of late Ernest Bamber, of Walkden, Salford, and late Hilda, *née* Wolfendale; *b* 19 September 1954; *Educ* Walkden Co Secdy Modern Sch, Farnworth GS, Univ of Bristol, RADA; *m* July 1982, Julia Swift (the actress), da of David Swift; 2 s (Theo Elia b 27 Dec 1991, Ethan b 17 Dec 1998); *Career* actor; RADA William Peel Prize, Carol Brahams Musical Comedy Prize, Bancroft Gold Medal; *Theatre* for NT incl: Oresteia 1981, Charlie in The Strangeness of Others 1988, John Littlewit in Bartholomew Fair 1988, Horatio in Hamlet 1989, Streaky Bacon in Racing Demon 1990–91, Mole in Wind in the Willows 1990–91; others incl: Joseph and His Amazing Technicolor Dreamcoat (Palace Theatre Westcliff) 1979, Outskirts (RSC Warehouse) 1981, Masterclass (Leicester Haymarket, Old Vic, Wyndhams) 1983–84, Kissing God (Hampstead) 1984, Amadeus 1986, Three Birds Alighting on a Field (Royal Court) 1991, Hikatier in Schippel (Greenwich Theatre & Edinburgh Festival), Martin Mirkheim in Search and Destroy (Theatre Upstairs), Guy in My Night with Reg (Theatre Upstairs and Criterion (winner Olivier Award for Best Actor 1995)) 1994, The Cocktail Party (Edinburgh Festival) 1997, Black Comedy and The Real Inspector Hound (Comedy Theatre), On the Razzle (Chichester Festival Theatre); RNT: Pandarus in Troilus and Cressida, Antonio in Merchant of Venice, Honk!, The Glee Club (Bush Theatre and Duchess Theatre) 2002, Where There's a Will (dir by Sir Peter Hall, CBE, *qv*, The Lisbon Traviatam Otherwise Engaged (Criterion); *Television* incl: Call Me Mister (BBC) 1986, Cockles (BBC) 1983, Buddha of Suburbia (BBC) 1993, Stalag Luft (YTV) 1993, Wycliffe, Pride and Prejudice, Chalk, Neville's Island, My Dads a Boring Nerd, My Night with Reg, The Railway Children, Casualty, Lush in Daniel Deronda (BBC), Midsomer Murders, Rome (HBO); *Films* incl: Privates on Parade 1982, High Hopes 1988, Gangs of New York, Miss Potter; *Recreations* listening to music, playing the piano, trying to keep fit usually at a gym, being married to Julia; *Style*— David Bamber, Esq; ✉ c/o Ken McReedie Ltd, 91 Regent Street, London W1B 4EL (020 7439 1456)

BAMBER, Roger; s of Frederick William Bamber (d 1987), of Leicester, and Vera Lilian, *née* Stephenson; *b* 31 August 1944; *Educ* Beaumont Leys Secdy Modern Leicester, Leicester Coll of Art; *m* 1, 1970 (m dis 1973), Joan Bergquist; m 2, 2004, Shan Lancaster; *Career* news photographer; Fleetway Publications 1963–64, Leicester Coll of Art 1964–65, Daily Mail 1965–69, The Sun 1969–88, The Observer 1988–89, The Guardian 1989–; Hon MA Univ of Brighton 2005; FRPS; *Exhibitions* Royal Photographic Soc 1992, Brighton Museum and Art Gallery 1993, Tom Blau Gallery London 1994, Month of the Image Dieppe 1995, Worthing Museum and Art Gallery 1996; *Awards* Br News Photographer of the Year 1973, Photographer of the Year and News Photographer of the Year (Br Press Awards) 1983, Nikon Features Photographer of the Year 1991, Kodak Features Photographer of the Year 1991, Ilford Press Photographer of the Year 1992 (runner up 1991), UK Picture Editors' Guild Award for features photography 1996, UK Picture Editors' Guild Award (business and indust category) 1997 and 1999 (two awards), Nikon Arts and Entertainment Photographer of the Year 1997 (runner up 1996), Features Award UK Picture Editors Guild 2001, Business and Industry Award UK Picture Editors Award 2004; *Style*— Roger Bamber, Esq; ✉ c/o The Guardian, 119 Farringdon Road, London EC1R 3ER (tel 020 7278 2332 and 01273 723689, mobile 078 6038 1255, e-mail pix@rogerbamber.co.uk, www.rogerbamber.co.uk)

BAMBRIDGE, Ron; *b* 6 November 1953; *m* 15 Feb 1986, Rose Angela, *née* Nielsen; 1 da (Daisy b 10 Nov 1988); *Career* asst photographer Photographic Dept Foote Cone & Belding (advtg agency) 1973–77, freelance photographer 1977–; specialist in still life photography until 1985, landscape, people and special panoramic photography since 1985; work for various clients incl: BA, ICI, London Transport, Rothschilds, British Gas, National Power, British Airports Authy, Welsh Devpt Agency, Seacontainers, Peugeot; work included in English Landscape in Danger (exhbn and auction cmmnd by CPRE) 1987; cmmn Royal Mail London Landmark stamps 1996; memb Assoc of Photographers (formerly AFAEP); *Awards* incl: highly commended Advtg People Category Ilford Awards 1984, AFAEP Gold Award (for landscape series) 1986, AFAEP Merit Award (for people series) 1988, Best Photography Award (Nat Business Calendar Awards) 1988, AFAEP Merit Award (for landscape) 1993, AFAEP Bronze Award (Best of Book in Contact Photographers) 1993, London Photographic Awards (winner still life series, environmental series and environmental colour) 1997, Silver and Merit Awards (for landscape) XV Assoc of Photographers Awards 1998, Personal Portraits Series XVI Assoc of Photographers Awards 1999, Cmmnd Structure Category Assoc of Photographers Awards 2000; *Books* 100 Years of Brooklands, Motorsport and Aviation (2007); *Style*— Ron Bambridge, Esq; ✉ e-mail ronbambridge@btinternet.com, website www.ronbambridge.com

BAMFORD, Sir Anthony Paul; kt (1990), DL (Staffs 1989); s of Joseph Cyril Bamford, CBE (d 2001); *b* 23 October 1945; *Educ* Ampleforth Coll, Grenoble Univ; *m* 1974, Carole Gray Whitt; 2 s, 1 da; *Career* joined JCB 1964, chm and md J C Bamford Group 1975–; dir Tarmac plc 1987–95; memb: President's Ctee CBI 1986–88, Design Cncl 1987–89; pres: Staffs Agric Soc 1987–88, Burton on Trent Cons Assoc 1987–90; High Sheriff of Staffs 1985–86; Hon MEng Birmingham 1987, Hon DUniv Keele 1988, Hon DSc Cranfield 1994, Hon DBA Robert Gordon Univ Aberdeen 1996, Hon DTech Univ of Staffordshire 1998, Hon DTech Loughborough Univ 2002; Young Exporter of the Year 1972, Young Businessman of the Year 1979, Top Exporter of the Year 1995, Entrepreneurial Award Br American Business Inc (BABI) 2003; Hon FCGI 1993, Hon FCSD 1994, fell Inst of Agricultural Engrgs 2003; Chevalier de l'Ordre National du Mérite (France) 1989, Commendatore al merito della Repubblica Italiana 1995; *Recreations* farming and gardening; *Clubs* Pratt's, White's, British Racing Drivers'; *Style*— Sir Anthony Bamford, DL; ✉ c/o J C Bamford Excavators Ltd, Rocester, Staffordshire ST14 5JP

BAMFORD, Colin; s of Firth Bamford (d 1986), of Blackburn, Lancs, and Edna, *née* Cockshutt; *b* 28 August 1950; *Educ* Queen Elizabeth's GS Blackburn, Trinity Hall Cambridge (scholar, MA); *m* 31 Jan 1975, Nirmala Rajah Bamford, da of Hon Mr Justice A P Rajah, of Singapore; 2 s (Rowan Firth Rajah b 13 March 1980, Daniel Chelva Rajah b 26 July 1986), 1 da (Roxanne Vijaya Rajah b 6 May 1990); *Career* Herbert Oppenheimer Nathan and Vandyk: articled clerk 1972–74, asst slr 1974–77, ptnr 1977–88; ptnr Richards Butler 1988–97, chief exec Financial Law Panel 1993–2002; called to the Bar (Middle Temple) 2002; dep chm Advsy Ctee Centre for Fin Regulation Cass Business Sch City Univ, memb Advsy Bd Centre for Corporate Law Studies Inst of Advanced Legal Studies Univ of London, memb Sub-Ctee on Int Fin Law Reform Int Bar Assoc; hon fell Soc for Advanced Legal Studies (memb Advsy Cmmn); FRSA; *Style*— Colin Bamford, Esq; ✉ 3–4 South Square, Gray's Inn, London WC1R 5HP (tel 020 7696 9900, fax 020 7696 9911, e-mail colinbamford@southsquare.com)

BAMFORD, Dr (Samuel Arnold) David; s of Samuel Arnold Brooks Bamford (d 2007), and Elsie, *née* Carew (d 1995); *b* 29 May 1946, Manchester; *Educ* Univ of Bristol (BSc), Univ of Birmingham (PhD); *m* 17 Jan 2004, Wendy Sheila, *née* Campbell; 2 da (Helen Elizabeth Brooks Hillard b 14 July 1976, Nicole Jennifer Bestford b 30 June 1984), 1 s (Matthew Bamford-Bowes b 2 Sept 1978); *Career* BP plc: joined 1980, chief geophysicist 1990–95, gen mangr W Africa 1995–98, gen mangr Norway 1998–99, head/vice-pres exploration 1999–2003; chm New Eyes Exploration Ltd 2005–; non-exec dir: Tullow Oil plc 2004–, Paras Ltd 2004–; FGS 1987; *Style*— Dr David Bamford

BAMFORD, David John; s of Samuel John Bamford, of Wellingborough, Northants, and Joan Sullivan, *née* Greenwood; *b* 28 June 1955; *Educ* Wellingborough GS, Univ of Aberdeen (MA), SOAS Univ of London (MSc); *m* 1, 19 July 1979 (m dis); 2 s (Thomas Rosh b 1981, Oliver Samuel b 1993); m 2, 4 Sept 2004, Maria Cecilia Caprari, da of Pasquale Caprari, of Collevecchio, Italy; *Career* BBC: political researcher Monitoring Serv 1980–83, journalist World Serv News 1983–, Ankara corr 1986–87, N Africa corr 1988–89, Nigeria corr 1991–93, W Africa corr 1994–97, sr broadcast journalist 1997–2000, N Africa corr 2001–02, Washington reporter 2003–04, Africa ed 2005–; contrib 1986–: The Guardian, Middle East Int, Middle East Economic Digest, Daily Telegraph, The

Economist; *Style*— David Bamford, Esq; ✉ BBC World Service News, PO Box 76, Bush House, Strand, London (tel 020 7240 3456, e-mail david.bamford@bbc.co.uk)

BAMJI, Dr Andrew Nariman; s of Dr Nariman Sorabji Bamji (d 1978), of Highgate, London, and Dr Joan Elizabeth Bamji, *née* Jermyn; *b* 14 August 1950; *Educ* Highgate Sch, Middx Hosp Med Sch London (MB BS); *m* 10 June 1978, Elizabeth Mary, da of Raymond William Millard, of Wembdon, Somerset; 1 da (Alexandra b 1981), 1 s (Nicholas b 1985); *Career* conslt in rheumatology and rehabilitation: SE Thames RHA Brook Gen Hosp 1983–89, Queen Mary's Hosp Sidcup 1983– (dir Elmstead Rehabilitation Unit 1985–, clinical tutor and dir of med educn 1990–95, assoc med dir Clinical Support Care Gp 1998–2002, curator Gillies Archives 1989–), Chelsfield Park Hosp Kent 1987–; chm: Jt Care Planning Gp for the Younger Disabled Bexley HA 1990–92, SE Thames Region Specialty Sub-Ctee in Rheumatology 1992–97, Clinical Affairs Ctee Br Soc for Rheumatology 1998–2001; pres Br Soc for Rheumatology 2006–; memb: BMA, London Topographical Soc, Western Front Assoc, Royal Photographic Soc, Osler Club; FRCP 1989; *Books* Atlas of Clinical Rheumatology (jt ed, 1986), Queen Mary's Hospital: A Commemoration 1974–94 (1994); *Recreations* antiques, gardening, pianola; *Style*— Dr Andrew Bamji; ✉ Torphins, 14 Burntwood Road, Sevenoaks, Kent TN13 1PT (e-mail andrewbamji@lineone.net); Queen Mary's Hospital, Frognal Avenue, Sidcup, Kent DA14 6LT (tel 020 8308 3070, fax 020 8308 3285, website www.sidcuprheum.org.uk); Chelsfield Park Hospital, Bucks Cross Road, Chelsfield, Kent BR6 7RG (tel 01689 877855, fax 01689 837439)

BANATVALA, Prof Jangu Edal; CBE (1999); s of Dr Edal Banatvala (d 1981), and Ratti, *née* Shroff (d 2004); *b* 7 January 1934; *Educ* Forest Sch, Gonville & Caius Coll Cambridge (MA), London Hosp Med Coll (MD (Sir Lionel Whitby Medal), DCH, DPH); *m* 15 Aug 1959, Roshan, da of Jamshed Mugaseth (d 1950); 3 s (Nicholas b 1961, Jonathan b 1963, Christopher b 1967), 1 da (Emma-Jane b 1968 d 1998); *Career* research fell Univ of Cambridge 1961–64, Fulbright scholar and post doctoral fell Yale Sch of Med 1964–65; St Thomas' Hosp Med Sch (now Guy's, King's College and St Thomas' Sch of Med): sr lectr 1965–71, reader in clinical virology 1971–75, prof 1975–99, emeritus prof 1999–; chm W Lambeth Dist Mgmnt Team and Med Advsy Ctee St Thomas' Hosp 1983–84; vice-pres: RCPath 1987–90 (registrar 1985–87, memb Cncl 1993–96), Cncl and Cases Ctee Med Def Union 1987–2004; pres European Assoc Against Virus Disease 1981–83; chm: Sub-Ctee on Measles Mumps and Rubella (CDVIP) MRC 1985–95, Dept of Health Advsy Gp on Hepatitis 1990–98, Sub Panel in Pathology Univ of London 1992–98; dir of Appeals Acad of Med Sciences 2000–02; memb: Jt Ctee on Vaccination and Immunisation 1986–95, Bd Dir CPA (UK) Ltd 1997–2001, Public Health Lab Serv Bd 1995–2001; examiner in pathology for MB: Univ of London, Univ of Cambridge, Univ of W Indies, Univ of Riyadh; examiner in virology RCPath; examiner higher degrees: Univ of London, Univ of Cambridge, Univ of Birmingham, Hong Kong Univ; elected memb Univ of London Senate 1987; hon conslt microbiologist to the Army 1992–97; govr: Forest Sch, Mill Hill Sch; Freeman City of London 1987, Liveryman Worshipful Soc of Apothecaries; memb: Soc of Gen Microbiology 1970, BMA 1970, Royal Soc of Tropical Med and Hygiene 1983; FRCP, FRCPath, FMedSci; *Books* Current Problems in Clinical Virology (1971), Principles and Practice of Clinical Virology (jtly, 1987, 5 edn 2004), Viral Infections of the Heart (1993), Rubella Viruses (2007); *Recreations* watching sports in which one no longer performs (rowing, cricket), playing tennis, exercising retrievers (infrequently), music, good conversation in good restaurants; *Clubs* Athenaeum, Leander, MCC, Hawks' (Cambridge (hon)); *Style*— Prof Jangu Banatvala, CBE; ✉ Little Acre, Church End, Henham, Bishop's Stortford, Hertfordshire CM22 6AN (tel 01279 850386, e-mail jangu@btinternet.com)

BANBURY, Martin John; s of Raymond Francis Banbury, of Fareham, Hants, and Molly Louise Banbury; *b* 30 March 1957; *Educ* Chelsea Coll London (BSc); *m* 1 (m dis 1992), Sarah, da of Peter Andrew Campbell; 2 da (Amber Sarah Edna, Emma Lucie); m 2, Carol, da of Colin White; 2 da (Jasmine, Rosie Kate), 1 s (Daniel Ray); *Career* mktg exec; Mktg Dept Procter & Gamble 1979–82, Cussons 1982–84, Britvic 1984–85; jt chm Connect One plc 1985–1999; dir Sold Ltd 1990–, chm The Mission Marketing Group Ltd 2003–; memb: Inst of Sales Promotion, Sales Promotion Conslts Assoc; FInstD; *Recreations* flying, sailing; *Style*— Martin Banbury, Esq; ✉ Rookery Farm, Coles Oak Lane, Dedham, Essex CO7 6DN

BANBURY, (Nigel Graham Cedric) Peregrine; s of Ralph Cecil Banbury (d 1951), of London, and Florence Leslie St Clair Keith; *b* 23 May 1948; *Educ* Gordonstoun; *m* 1, 17 Nov 1973, Rosemary Henrietta Dorothy, da of Capt Anthony Henry Heber Villiers, of Woodchester, Glos; m 2, 28 Sept 1978, Susan Margaret, da of Lt-Col Joseph Patrick Feeny (d 1970), of Estoril, Portugal; 2 s (Alexander b 1981, Ralph b 1987); m 3, 7 July 1992, Mrs Carol A Whistler, da of John Groves, CB, and former w of Laurence Whistler, CBE; *Career* Coutts & Co 1967–70, stockbroker 1971–81, Robert Fleming 1981–86, dir EBC Amro Asset Management Ltd 1986–87; Coutts & Co: head Asset Mgmnt 1987–96, ptnr Private Banking 1996–2000, client gp head 2000–, dir Coutts & Co Investment Management Ltd 1996–2000; dir: Exeter Preferred Capital Investment Trust (latterly Exeter Selective Assets Tst) 1992–2005 (chm 2005), Schroder Income Growth Trust 1995–, Securities Inst 1995–2001, dir City Merchants Investment Tst 2005–06; non-exec dir: Henderson Global Property Cos Ltd 2006–, Bankers Benevolent Fund 2006–; Freeman City of London; FSI; *Recreations* shooting, skiing, photography; *Clubs* Athenaeum, Pratt's; *Style*— Peregrine Banbury, Esq; ✉ Coutts & Co, 440 Strand, London WC2R 0QS (tel 020 7753 1000, fax 020 7649 4600, e-mail peregrine.banbury@coutts.com)

BANBURY OF SOUTHAM, 3 Baron (UK 1924); Sir Charles William Banbury; 3 Bt (UK 1902); s of 2 Baron Banbury, DL (d 1981), and Hilda, *née* Carr (m dis 1958; she m 2, Maj Robert O G Gardner, MC (d 1987), and 3, Richard Frederick Norman); *b* 29 July 1953; *Educ* Eton; *m* 1, 1984 (m dis 1986), Lucinda, er da of John Frederick Trehearne; m 2, 1989, Inger Marianne Norton, *née* Wiegert; 3 da (Hon Charlotte Rosa b 15 April 1990, Hon Poppy Isobel b 13 Nov 1991, Hon Nina Carolyn b 18 Nov 1997); *Style*— The Rt Hon the Lord Banbury of Southam; ✉ The Mill, Fossebridge, Cheltenham, Gloucestershire GL54 3JN

BANCE, Prof Alan Frederick; s of Frederick Bance, and Agnes Mary, *née* Wilson; *b* 7 March 1939; *Educ* Hackney Downs Sch (aka Grocers' Co Sch), UCL (BA), Univ of Cambridge (PhD); *m* 30 Aug 1964, Sandra, da of John Davis, of Hove, W Sussex; 2 da (Georgia b 1972, Miriam b 1976); *Career* lectr Univ of Strathclyde 1965–67, sr lectr Univ of St Andrews 1981 (lectr 1967–81); prof of German: Keele Univ 1981–84, Univ of Southampton 1984–2003 (emeritus prof 2003–); pres Conf of Univ Teachers of German in GB and Ireland 1994–96 (vice-pres 1993–94); memb: Res Selectivity Exercise UFC-HEFCE Res Assessment Panel for German Studies 1992 and 1996, Ctee Univ Cncl for Modern Languages 1994–97, selection panel for postgraduate awards Br Acad/AHRB 1996–99; ed Germanic Section Modern Language Review 1988–94; hon life memb Modern Humanities Res Assoc 1995; *Books* The German Novel 1945–60 (1980), Theodor Fontane: The Major Novels (1982), Weimar Germany: Writers and Politics (ed, 1982), Ödön von Horváth 50 Years On (ed with I Huish, 1988), Theodor Fontane: The London Symposium (ed with H Chambers and C Jolles, 1995), The Cultural Legacy of the British Occupation in Germany (ed, 1997), Millenial Essays on Film and Other German Studies (ed with D Berghahn, 2002), Sigmund Freud, Wild Analysis (trans, 2002), Brigitte Hamann, Winifred Wagner: A Life at the Heart of Hitler's Bayreuth (trans, 2005), Blitzkrieg in their Own Words: First-Hand Accounts from German Soldiers 1939–40 (trans, 2005), Cioma Schoenhaus: The Forger (trans, 2006), Hildegard Hammerschmidt-Hummel: The True Face of William Shakespeare (trans, 2006), Hildegard Hammerschmidt-Hummel: The Life and Times of William Shakespeare (trans, 2007), Lorenz Schroeter: Skylarks and Scuttlebutts (trans, 2007); *Recreations* keeping fit, gardening, foreign travel, theatre; *Style*— Prof Alan Bance; ✉ German Studies, Modern Languages, University of Southampton, Highfield, Southampton SO17 1BJ (tel 023 8055 4819, fax 023 8059 3288, telex 47661, e-mail a.f.bance@soton.ac.uk)

BANCEWICZ, John; s of Dr Anthony Bancewicz (d 1997), of Airdrie, Lanarkshire, and Helen, *née* Ulinskas (d 1950); *b* 26 March 1945; *Educ* St Aloysius Coll Glasgow, Univ of Glasgow (BSc, MB ChB), Univ of Manchester (ChM); *m* 5 Jan 1972, Margaret Kathleen, da of Dr Charles Douglas Anderson, MC (d 1998); 1 s (Peter b 1973), 1 da (Ruth b 1976); *Career* res fell Harvard Med Sch 1974–75, lectr in surgery Univ of Glasgow 1976–79, reader in surgery and conslt surgn Univ of Manchester 1988–2005 (sr lectr 1979–88), ret; Salford Royal Hosps NHS Tst: clinical dir in general surgery 1994–96, med dir for surgical specialities 1996–2000; dir Hope Hosp Total Quality Mgmnt Prog 1989–92, chm Salford Dist Med Audit Ctee 1990–93, memb Cncl Int Soc for Diseases of the Esophagus 1989–2001, memb Cncl Br Soc of Gastroenterology 1991–94; examiner in surgery RCPSGlas 1988–2003; memb: MRC Working Party on Oesophageal Cancer 1991–97, MRC Working Party on Gastric Cancer 1993–97, Surgical Gastroenterology Gp Assoc of Surgns of GB and Ireland 1993–97, Cncl Assoc of Upper Gastrointestinal Surgns of GB and Ireland 1996–2000 (chm Educn and Research Ctee); chm: Upper Gastrointestinal Specialty Working Gp NHS Clinical Terms Project 1992–95, Surgical Section Br Soc of Gastroenterology 1994–97, NW Deanery Surgical Trg Ctee 1996–2002 (vice-chm 1993–96), MRC Working Party on Upper GI Cancer 1997–99, UKCCCR and NCRI Upper GI Cancer Gp 1999–2003; pres Surgical Section Manchester Med Soc 1999–2000; memb: Educn Ctee Assoc of Surgeons of GB and Ireland 1997–2000, Cncl, Editorial Ctee and Editorial Bd Br Jl of Surgery 1995–2003, Cncl RCPSGlas 2002–, Steering Gp Nat Cancer Research Network 2003–05, MRC Independent Data Monitoring Ctee 2005–; hon memb Romanian Soc of Surgery 1993, hon memb Senate Univ of Sibiu Romania; FRCSGlas 1973; *Recreations* sailing, hill walking; *Style*— John Bancewicz, Esq; ✉ Old Bank House, Lower Granco Street, Dunning, Perthshire PH2 0SQ (tel 01764 684361)

BANCROFT, Craig John; s of John Haworth Bancroft (d 2001), of Portugal, and Susan, *née* Livsey; *b* 15 July 1961, Blackburn; *Educ* Denstone Coll; *m* 17 June 1990, Helen Elizabeth, *née* Grimshaw; 2 s (Christopher John b 20 Feb 1992, James Joseph b 31 March 1995); *Career* mgmnt trainee Trust House Forte 1979–83, gen mangr Northcote Manor 1983–86, md Northcote Manor 1986–, co dir Sandshow Ltd 1989–, md Ribble Valley Inns 2004–; Caterer and Hotelkeeper Acorn Award 1986; *Recreations* country sports, rugby, wine; *Clubs* Acad of Food and Wine Serv, Guild of Sommeliers; *Style*— Craig Bancroft, Esq; ✉ 17 Gleneagle Drive, Brockhall Village, Brockhall, Old Langho, Lancashire BB6 9BF (tel 01254 240555, fax 01254 245443, e-mail craigbancroft@northcotemanor.com)

BAND, Adm Sir Jonathon; KCB (2002); *b* 2 February 1950; *Educ* Brambletye Sch, Haileybury, Univ of Exeter (BA); *m* 1979, Sarah; 2 da; *Career* RN: joined 1967, HMS Soberton 1979–81, Fleet HQ 1981–83, HMS Phoebe 1983–85, MOD 1986–89, HMS Norfolk 1989–91, MOD 1991–95, HMS Illustrious 1995–97, Rear Adm 1997, Asst Chief of Naval Staff MOD 1997–99, Vice Adm 2000, head Defence Trg Review 2000–01, Dep C-in-C FLEET 2001–02, C-in-C E Atlantic 2002–03, C-in-C FLEET 2002–05, Cdr Allied Maritime Component Cmd Northwood 2002–05, First Sea Lord and Chief of Naval Staff 2006–; yr bro Trinity House; *Recreations* family dominated, tennis, boating, golf; *Clubs* Royal Albert Yacht (pres), Royal Naval (pres); *Style*— Adm Sir Jonathon Band, KCB, ADC

BANERJEE, Prof Arup Kumar; OBE (1996), JP; s of Ansumali Banerjee (d 1984), and Maya, *née* Chatterjee (d 2002); *b* 28 November 1935; *Educ* Univ of Calcutta Med Coll (MB BS); *m* 23 March 1959, Dr Aleya Banerjee, da of late Nakuleswar Banerjee; 3 s (Arpan b 14 Feb 1960, Anjan b 12 Sept 1962, Avijit b 2 Dec 1969); *Career* various jr hosp appts in India and UK 1958–67, sr registrar in med Southend Gen Hosp 1967–68, lectr in med Univ of Malaya Med Sch Kuala Lumpur 1968–71, sr registrar in elderly med Portsmouth and Southampton Univ Hosps 1971–73, conslt physician in elderly med Bolton Gen Hosp (now Royal Bolton Hosp) 1973–99 (med dir Bolton Hosp Tst 1994–98), hon clinical lectr in geriatric med Univ of Manchester 1975–, pt/t dir of Elderly Services and conslt physician in the elderly Univ of S Manchester 1998–2000, pt/t clinical dir of Elderly Services Wigan and Leigh NHS Tst 1999–2003; prof of health studies Univ of Bolton 2003–; conslt to Nat Health Advsy Serv, regnl specialist advsr in geriatric med RCP 1997–2002; memb NW RHA 1987–94 (vice-chm 1992–94); pres: Br Geriatrics Soc 1996–98, Manchester Med Soc 2002–03 (pres Med Section 1997–98), Over-50s Federation Bolton; county dir Research Into Aging N-W; memb: Geriatrics Ctee RCP London, Panel of Experts for Nat Registered Homes Tbnl; author of various pubns on med topics; memb: Br Geriatrics Soc, BMA (memb Med Specialities Ctee 1986–94, memb CCSC 1986–94); FRCPGlas 1979 (MRCPGlas 1965), FRCPEd 1980 (MRCPEd 1967), FRCP 1982 (MRCP 1967), FRCPI 1997; *Books* Haematological Aspects of Systematic Disease (contrib, 1976), The Principles and Practice of Geriatric Medicine (contrib, 1985, 1991 and 1998), A Guide to the Care of the Elderly (1995); *Recreations* travel, music, literature; *Style*— Prof Arup Banerjee, OBE; ✉ 2 Pilling Field, Egerton, Bolton BL7 9UG (tel 01204 305482, e-mail arup@banerjeel.freeserve.co.uk)

BANGOR, Bishop of 2004–; Rt Rev (Phillip) Anthony Crockett; s of Arthur George Crockett, and Mary, *née* Smith; *Educ* Pontypridd GS, KCL (BA, BD) St Michael's Coll Llandaff (Dip Pastoral Studies), Univ of Wales Cardiff (MA); *Career* curate Aberdare 1971–74, curate Whitchurch 1974–78, vicar of Llanafan Y Trawsgoed 1978–86, rector of Dowlais 1986–91, sec Bd of Ministry of the Church in Wales 1991–99, vicar of Cynwyl Elfed 1999–2004, archdeacon of Carmarthen 1999–2004; Winston Churchill Travelling Fell 1983; *Recreations* hill walking, fly fishing, reading; *Style*— The Rt Rev the Bishop of Bangor; ✉ Tŷ'r Esgob, Upper Garth Road, Bangor LL57 2SS (tel 01248 362895, fax 01248 372454, e-mail bishop.bangor@churchinwales.org.uk)

BANGOR, Rt Hon Viscountess; *see:* Bradford, Sarah Mary Malet

BANGOR, 8 Viscount (I 1781); William Maxwell David Ward; also Baron Bangor (I 1770); s of 7 Viscount Bangor (d 1993), and his 3 w, Leila Mary, *née* Heaton (d 1959); *b* 9 August 1948; *Educ* UCL; *m* 1976, Sarah Bradford, *qv*, da of Brig Hilary Anthony Hayes, DSO, OBE, and formerly wife of Anthony Bradford; *Heir* half-bro, Hon Nicholas Ward; *Career* antiquarian bookseller; patron Bangor FC; *Recreations* history, music, antiquity, Bolton Wanderers; *Style*— The Rt Hon the Viscount Bangor; ✉ 31 Britannia Road, London SW6 2HJ

BANHAM, Belinda Joan; CBE (1977), JP; da of Col Charles Harold Unwin (d 1939), of Chelsea, and Winifred Unwin, *née* Woodman Wilson (d 1922); *Educ* privately, West Bank Sch Bideford, Univ of London (BSc, Dip Social Studies), Soc of Apothecaries (Dip Philosophy of Med, SRN); *m* 1939, Terence Middlecott Banham (d 1995), s of Rev Vivian Greaves Banham, MC (d 1973); 2 s (Sir John Banham, *qv*, Simon), 2 da (Susan, Joanna); *Career* work in health servs 1937–; chm: Cornwall & Isles of Scilly HMC 1967–74 (memb 1964–77), Cornwall & Isles of Scilly AHA 1974–77, Kensington Chelsea & Westminster FPC 1979–85 (memb 1977–79), Paddington & N Kensington DHA 1981–86; memb: SW Regnl Hosp Bd 1965–74, MRC 1979–87, Lambeth Southwark & Lewisham FPC 1987–90; Lambeth Southwark and Lewisham Family Health Authy: non-exec dir 1990–, vice-chm 1990–93, chm 1993–97; vice-chm Lambeth Southwark and Lewisham Health Cmmn 1993–97; memb Delegacy King's Coll Sch of Med and Dentistry 1996–98, tstee Gen Practitioners' Counselling and Advsy Tst 1996–, convenor lay chair 'new' complaints procedure NHS Exec London region 1999–; memb MRC 1979–87; marriage guidance cnsllr 1960–72; vice-chm: Disabled Living Fndn 1983–90, Wytham Hall 1990–93 (tstee

1985–95); pres Friends of St Mary's Hosp 1993–98, vice-pres AFASIC 1989–; *Publications* Partnership in Action (jtly, 1990), Snapshots in time: Some experiences in health care 1936–1991 (1991), General Practice in the NHS or football round The Mulberry Bush 1918–1995 (1995); *Recreations* gardening, plant biology, theatre, medical ethics; *Style*— Mrs Belinda Banham, CBE; ✉ 60 Fairmantle Street, Truro, Cornwall TR1 2EG

BANHAM, Sir John Michael Middlecott; kt (1992), DL (1999); s of Terence Middlecott Banham, FRCS (d 1995), and Belinda Joan Banham, CBE, *qv*; *b* 22 August 1940; *Educ* Charterhouse, Queens' Coll Cambridge (MA); *m* 30 Oct 1965, Frances Barbara Molyneux, da of Cdr Richard Molyneux Favell, DSC, RN (d 1995), of St Buryan, Cornwall; 1 s (Mark Richard Middlecott b 1968), 2 da (Serena Frances Tamsin b 1970, Morwenna Bridget Favell b 1972); *Career* temp asst princ HM Dip Serv 1962–64, mktg exec J Walter Thompson 1964–65, mktg dir Wallcoverings Div Reed International 1965–69; McKinsey & Co Inc: assoc 1969–75, princ 1975–80, dir 1980–83; first controller Audit Cmmn for Local Authorities 1983–87; DG CBI 1987–92; chm: Westcountry Television 1991–97, Local Govt Cmmn for England 1992–95, Labatt Breweries of Europe 1992–95, ECI Ventures (venture capital mangrs) 1992–2005, Tarmac plc 1994–2000, Kingfisher plc 1996–2001 (non-exec dir 1995), Whitbread plc 2000–05 (non-exec dir 1999), Geest plc 2002–05, Cyclacel Ltd 2002–06, Johnson Matthey plc 2006–, Spacelabs Healthcare Inc 2006–; dir: National Westminster Bank plc 1992–98, National Power plc 1992–98, Merchants Trust plc 1992–, Amvescap plc 1998–; managing tstee Nuffield Fndn 1988–97, hon treas Cancer Research Campaign 1991–2002; hon fell Queens' Coll Cambridge 1989; Hon LLD Univ of Bath 1987, Hon DSc Loughborough Univ 1989, Hon LLD Univ of Exeter 1993, Hon LLD Univ of Strathclyde 1995; Hon FCGI; *Books* Anatomy of Change (1994); author of numerous reports on mgmnt, health and local authy servs; *Recreations* gardening, cliff walking, sailing, ground clearing; *Clubs* Travellers; *Style*— Sir John Banham; ✉ Penberth, St Buryan, Cornwall TR19 6HJ

BANKS, Charles Augustus; *b* 20 December 1940; *Educ* Brown Univ RI (BA), Univ of N Carolina; *m* Marie Ann Sullivan; 2 s (Charles Augustus IV, Douglas Lawrence), 1 da (Patricia Lyn (Mrs Scott Russell)); *Career* Lt US Navy 1962–64 (Reserves 1964–69); plant mangr Minerals Recovery Corp 1964–65, mortgage banker Cameron-Brown 1965–67; Ferguson Enterprises Inc: Peebles Supply Div 1967–69, Lenz Supply Div 1969–70, vice-pres and gen mangr Alexandria VA office 1970–77, pres and gen mangr Herndon VA office 1977–81, dir 1977–, regnl mangr 1981–87, sr exec vice-pres 1987–89, pres and chief ops offr 1989–93, pres and ceo 1993–2001, chm 2001–; Wolseley plc: dir 1992–2006, gp md 2001–06; non-exec dir Bunzl plc 2002–; memb: Nat Assoc of Wholesaler-Distributors (also chm), Southern Wholesaler Assoc (past chm and pres), American Supply Assoc (former memb Bd), Exec Ctee Nat Assoc of Plumbing-Heating-Cooling Contractors Educnl Fndn (past memb Bd); chm Bd of Sponsors William & Mary Sch of Business Williamsburg VA; dir: Hampton Roads Acad Newport News VA, Diabetes Inst Fndn, Virginia Living Museum; Hon Dr Christopher Newport Univ Newport News VA 2001; *Style*— Charles A Banks, III; ✉ Wolseley plc, Parkview 1220, Arlington Business Park, Theale, Berkshire RG7 4GA

BANKS, (Arthur) David; s of Arthur Banks (d 1988), of Warrington, Cheshire, and Helen, *née* Renton (d 1997); *b* 13 February 1948; *Educ* Boteler GS Warrington; *m* Gemma, da of Francis Xavier Newton; 1 da (Natasha Kate b 12 Dec 1978), 1 s (Timothy James b 28 Sept 1982); *Career* jr reporter Warrington Guardian 1965–68, reporter/sub ed Newcastle Journal 1968–71, sub ed Daily Express 1971–72, asst night ed Daily Mirror 1972–79, asst managing ed New York Post 1979–81, night ed/asst ed The Sun 1981–86, dep managing ed New York Daily News 1986–87, dep ed The Australian 1987–89, ed Daily Telegraph Mirror Sydney 1989–92, ed Daily Mirror 1992–94; Mirror Group Newspapers Ltd: editorial dir 1994–96, new media advsr 1996–97; conslt ed Sunday Mirror 1997–98, dir of info Mirror Group 1998–99; presenter Breakfast Show Talk Radio 1999–2000; currently nat affrs corr and columnist Press Gazette; broadcaster: LBC BBC Radio Live TV, Channel 4; pres London Press Club Cncl 1995–2000; *Recreations* dining, dieting; *Style*— David Banks, Esq

BANKS, Gordon Raymond; MP; s of William Banks (d 1968), and Patricia Marion, *née* MacKnight (d 1983); *b* 14 June 1955, Acomb, Northumberland; *Educ* Lornshill Acad, Glasgow Coll of Building and Printing, Univ of Stirling (BA); *m* 1981, Lynda, *née* Nicol; 1 da (Victoria Patricia Elizabeth b 1984), 1 s (Dominic Alexander William b 1986); *Career* Barratt: chief buyer Edinburgh 1976–84, chief buyer Falkirk 1984–86; md Cartmore Building Supply Co Ltd 1986–; MP (Lab) Ochil & Perthshire S 2005–; memb TGWU; memb Coeliac Soc; *Recreations* songwriting, guitar, football, motorsport; *Style*— Gordon Banks, Esq, MP; ✉ House of Commons, London SW1A 0AA (e-mail banksgr@parliament.uk); Constituency Office, 49–51 High Street, Alloa, Clackmannanshire FK10 1JF (tel 01259 721536, fax 01259 216761, e-mail ochilsp@btinternet.com)

BANKS, (Ernest) John; s of Ernest Frederick Banks (d 1995), and Marian Blanche, *née* Nuttall (d 1991); *b* 2 July 1945; *m* Rosemary Murray Banks; 1 da (Charlotte Frederique Marianne b 3 May 1983); *Career* formerly: gp chm and ceo Young and Rubicam Gp Advertising Agency, chm and managing ptnr Banks Hoggins O'Shea (formerly The Banks Partnership); gp chm and chief exec FCB London (formerly Banks Hoggins O'Shea) 1998–; hon sec IPA; FIPA; *Recreations* tennis, fishing, golf, shooting; *Clubs* Buck's, MCC, St Moritz Toboggan; *Style*— John Banks, Esq; ✉ Product of the Year Ltd, 93 Newman Street, London, W1T 3DT (tel 020 7580 8197)

BANKS, (William) Lawrence; CBE (1998), DL (Co Hereford 2006); s of Richard Alford Banks, CBE (d 1997), and Lilian Jean, *née* Walker (d 1973); *b* 7 June 1938; *Educ* Rugby, ChCh Oxford (MA); *m* 1963, Elizabeth Christina, da of Capt Leslie Swain Saunders, DSO, RN (d 1988), of Northants; 2 s (Richard b 1965, Edward b 1967); *Career* merchant banker; with Robert Fleming 1961–98, dep chm Robert Fleming Holdings Ltd 1996–98; chm: Caledonian Publishing 1993–96, Kington Connected Community Co Ltd 1993–2007, William Cook Holdings Ltd 1997–2002, Ambrian Ptnrs Ltd 2002–; dir: Roper Industries Inc 1994–, Blavod Extreme Spirits plc 2001–, Ambrian Capital plc 2001–07; cmmr 1851 Exhbn 1996–2006 (chm Fin Ctee); non-exec dir Nat Blood Authy 1994–2000, chm Cncl Royal Postgrad Med Sch Hammersmith 1990–97 (former treas); hon treas: RHS 1981–92 (vice-pres 1993–, Victoria Medal of Honour), Imperial Coll London 1999–2001; chm Int Dendrology Soc 1998–2003, chm Herefordshire Community Fndn, pres Herefordshire Branch CPRE; tstee: Chevening Estate 1998–2005 (chm Fin and GP Ctee), Hereford Mappa Mundi Tst, Hereford Cathedral Perpetual Tst, Lister Inst 1998–2006, Banks Archive Project; *Recreations* gardening, fishing, shooting, theatre; *Clubs* MCC, Pratt's, Flyfishers', Boodle's; *Style*— Lawrence Banks, Esq, CBE, DL; ✉ Ridgebourne, Kington, Herefordshire (tel 01544 230160, fax 01544 232031, e-mail banks@hergest.co.uk)

BANKS, Roderick Charles I'Anson; s of Charles I'Anson Banks (d 1991), and Suzanne Mary Gwendoline, *née* Hall; *b* 5 December 1951; *Educ* Westminster, UCL (LLB); *m* 11 Aug 1979, Susan Elizabeth Lavington, da of His Hon Albert William Clark (d 1998), of Worthing, W Sussex; 2 s (Oliver b 1982, Frederick b 1986); *Career* called to the Bar Lincoln's Inn 1974; head of chambers; legal author; accredited CEDR mediator; conslt to Law Cmmn: Partnership Law Review 1998–2003, Limited Partnership Law Review 2001–03; fndr memb Assoc of Partnership Practitioners; memb CLA; hon assoc BVA; *Books* Lindley on Partnership (co-ed, 14 edn 1979, 15 edn 1984), Lindley & Banks on Partnership (ed, 16 edn 1990, 17 edn 1995, 18 edn 2002, supplement 2005), Encyclopedia of Professional Partnerships (ed, 1987), Halsbury's Laws of England: Partnership Vol (conslt ed, 4 edn reissue 1994); *Recreations* reluctant gardener, TV/video addict; *Style*— Roderick I'Anson Banks, Esq; ✉ 48 Bedford Row, London WC1R 4LR (tel 020 7430 2005, fax 020 7831 1510)

BANN, Prof Stephen; CBE (2004); s of late Harry Bann, OBE, and Edna, *née* Pailin; *b* 1 August 1942; *Educ* Winchester (scholar), King's Coll Cambridge (major scholar, state studentship, MA, PhD); *Career* University of Kent at Canterbury: lectr in history 1967–75, sr lectr 1975–80, reader in modern cultural studies 1980–88, chair Bd of Studies in history and theory of art 1983–95, prof of modern cultural studies 1988–2000, dir Centre for Modern Cultural Studies 1990–2000, dir of grad studies Faculty of Humanities 1993–95; prof of history of art Univ of Bristol 2000–; sr fell Dumbarton Oaks Research Library Washington DC 2002–, Mellon sr fell Canadian Centre for Architecture Montreal 2003, Edmond J Safra Visiting Prof Nat Gall of Art Washington DC 2005; chm Research Ctee Arts and Humanities Research Bd 1998–2000; pres Comité International d'Histoire de l'Art (CIHA) 2000–04; memb: Art Panel Arts Cncl of GB 1975–78, Art Panel South-East Arts 1976–79 and 1982–88, Int Assoc of Art Critics (AICA) 1984–, Cncl Friends of Canterbury Cathedral 1990–2000, Humanities Research Bd 1997–98, Leverhulme Research Awards Advsy Ctee 1998–2005, Museums and Galleries Ctee AHRC 2004–08, Mgmnt Bd Inst for Garden and Landscape History 2006–; FBA 1998; *Books* Experimental Painting (1970), The Tradition of Constructivism (ed, 1974), The Clothing of Clio (1984), The True Vine (1989), The Inventions of History (1990), Under the Sign (1994), Romanticism and the Rise of History (1995), Paul Delaroche: History Painted (1997), Parallel Lines: Printmakers, Painters and Photographers in 19th Century France (2001, R H Gapper Prize for French Studies 2002), Jannis Kounellis (2003), The Reception of Walter Pater in Europe (ed, 2004), Ways around Modernism (2007); *Recreations* travel, collecting; *Clubs* Savile; *Style*— Prof Stephen Bann, CBE, FBA; ✉ Department of History of Art, University of Bristol, Bristol BS8 1UU (tel 0117 954 6050)

BANNER, Fiona; *b* 1966, Merseyside; *Educ* Kingston Poly (BA), Goldsmiths Coll London (MA); *Career* artist; *Solo Exhibitions* Pushing Back the Edge of the Envelope (City Racing London) 1994, Viewing Room (Luhring Augustine Gallery NY) 1995, Only the Lonely (Frith Street Gallery London) 1997, The Nam - 1000 page all text flick book (London) 1997, LOVE DOUBLE (Galerie Barbara Thumm Berlin) 1998, 130 PE (Brian Butler LA) 1998, Art Now (Tate Gallery London) 1998, STOP (Frith Street Gallery London) 1999, THE NAM and Related Material (Printed Matter NY) 1999, Don't Look Back (Brooke Alexander NY) 1999, ASTERISK (Gesellschaft für Aktuelle Kunst Bremen) 1999, Statements (Basel Art Fair) 1999, Murray/Guy (NY) 1999, 1301PE (Santa Monica) 2000, Soixante-Neuf (Charles H Scott Gallery Emily Carr Inst Vancouver) 2000, Rainbow (Hayward Gallery London) 2001, FIONA BANNER - ARSEWOMAN (Galerie Barbara Thumm Berlin and Murray Guy NY) 2001, (Wanker) (Frith Street Gallery London) 2002, My Plinth is your Lap (Dundee Contemporary Arts and Neuer Aachener Kunstverein) 2002, 130 IPE (Brian Butler LA) 2003; *Group Exhibitions* Art Unlimited (Arts Cncl Collection UK tour) 1994, Institute of Cultural Anxiety (ICA London) 1994, Laure Genillard Gallery London 1994, The Event (152c Brick Lane London) 1994, The Antidote (191 Gallery London) 1994, Drawings (Laure Genillard Gallery London) 1994, New Contemporaries (Camden Arts Centre UK tour) 1994, SuperStore Boutique (Sarah Staton London) 1994 (Sarah Staton San Francisco 1995), Perfect Speed (USF Contemporary Art Museum Tampa) 1995, General Release: Young British Artists (Scuola di St Pasquale Venice Biennale) 1995, Four Projects (Frith Street Gallery London) 1995, Moby Dick (Arsenali Medicei Pisa) 1995 (John Hansard Gallery Southampton 1996), Backpacker (4th Festival of Art and Culture Chiang Mai) 1996, Found Footage (Klemems Gasser & Tanja Grunert Cologne) 1996, Young British Artists (Roslyn Oxley Gallery Sydney) 1996, Mais do que ver (Moagens Harmonia Festival of Contemporary Art Oporto) 1996, into the void (Ikon Gallery Birmingham) 1996, Spellbound: Art and Film (Hayward Gallery London) 1996, MacDonald Stewart Art Center Toronto 1996, Die Arbeit des Zeichnens (Gesellschaft für Aktuelle Kunst Bremen) 1997, Légende (Centre Regional D'Art Contemporain Sète) 1997, Gasser & Grunert Cologne 1997, The Nam - 1000 page all text flick book (Galerie Barbara Thumm Berlin) 1997, The Mule (single issue national newspaper with internet access) 1997, 20/20 (Kingsgate Gallery London) 1997, Oktober (Norwich Gallery) 1997, Need for Speed (Grazer Kunstverein) 1997, City Gallery Wellington 1997, Art Gallery of South Australia Adelaide 1997, An Exhibition of Art from Britain (Museum of Contemporary Art Sydney) 1997, Whisper & Streak (Galerie Barbara Thumm Berlin) 1997, MUUten (Museum of Photography Helsinki) 1997, Blueprint (De Appel Amsterdam) 1997, Ground Control (Beaconsfield London) 1997, Urban Legends - London (Staatliche Kunsthalle Baden-Baden) 1997, The Tarantino Syndrome (Künstlerhaus Bethanien Berlin) 1998, Slipstream (Centre for Contemporary Arts Glasgow) 1998, Wrapped (Vestsjoelands Kunstmuseum) 1998, In the Beginning (Murray Guy NY) 1998, 5th Avenue Project (Saks NY) 1998, Disrupting the Scene (Cambridge Dark Room) 1998, Narrative Urge (Uppsala Konstmuseum) 1998, Super Freaks - Post Pop and the New Generation: Part 1 (GreeneNaftali NY) 1998, Point Break (project for Tate Magazine) 1998, 100 Drawings (PS1 NY) 1999, Let's get Lost (St Martin's Sch of Art London) 1999, To Be Continued (The New Art Gallery Walsall) 1999, True Stories (Fiona Banner, Sophie Calle, Joseph Grigely) (Barbara Gross Galerie Munich) 1999, Babel (Ikon Gallery Birmingham) 1999, Story (AC Project Room NY) 1999, From Memory (Platform London) 1999, 0 TO 60 IN 10 YEARS (Frith Street Gallery London) 1999, Afterall launch (Wallace Collection London) 1999, Cinema Cinema (Van Abbe Museum Eindhoven) 1999, To Infinity and Beyond: Editions for the Year 2000 (Brooke Alexander NY) 2000, The Living End (Boulder Museum of Contemporary Art) 2000, Murray Guy NY 2000, Summer Show (Frith Street Gallery London) 2000, Customized: Hot Rods, Low Riders and American Car Culture (ICA Boston) 2000, Eine Munition unter Anderen (Frankfurter Kunstverein) 2000, Ever get the feeling you've been...Cheated (A22 Projects London) 2000, All You Need is Love (Laznia Center of Contemporary Art Gdansk) 2000, CAB London 2001, A Pause for Breath (Frith Street Gallery London) 2001, American Tableaux (Walker Art Center Minneapolis) 2001, Total Object, Complete with Missing Parts (Tramway 2 Glasgow) 2001, Tatoo Show (Modern Art London) 2001, Dévoler (Institut d'art contemporain Villeurbanne) 2001, The Multiple Store (The New Art Centre Sculpture Park and Gallery Roche Court) 2001, Berlin Biennale 2001, Fiona Banner, Munro Galloway, Corey McCorkle (Murray Guy NY) 2001, Nothing: Exploring Invisibilities (Northern Gallery of Contemporary Art Sunderland, Rooseum Malmo and CAC Vilnius) 2001, definition (Murray Guy NY) 2001, Drawings (Frith Street Gallery London) 2001, Superman in Bed, Contemporary Art and Photography (The Collection Gaby and Wilhelm Schürmann Museum am Ostwald Dortmund) 2001, Featherweight (Susan Hobbs Gallery Toronto) 2001, City Racing (ICA London) 2001, The Green Room (Percy Miller Gallery London) 2001 and 2002, Remix: Contemporary Art and Pop (Tate Liverpool) 2002, Here, There and Elsewhere; Dialogues on Location and Mobility (London Print Studio Gallery) 2002, Turner Prize exhbn (Tate Britain London) 2002; *Work in Public Collections* incl: Contemporary Art at Penguin London, Contemporary Arts Soc London, FSA London, Met Museum of Art NY, Neuberger & Berman NY, Philadelphia Museum, Sammlung Ringier Zurich, The Arts Cncl of England, Br Cncl London, Tate Gallery London, Van Abbe Museum Eindhoven, Walker Art Gallery Minneapolis, Worcester Museum MA, MOMA NYC; *Style*— Ms Fiona Banner; ✉ c/o Karon Hepburn, Frith Street Gallery, 59–60 Frith Street, London W1D 3JJ

BANNER, Norman Leslie; s of Frank Leslie Banner (d 1986), of Warrington, and Clarice, *née* Rutter (d 1986); *b* 6 November 1947; *Educ* Lymm GS, Manchester Poly (BA); *m* 1, 1972 (m dis 1981), Andrea, *née* Atkinson; m 2, 1995, Louise, *née* Astley; 2 s (Mark

William Astley b 22 Jan 1998, Edward James Astley b 20 June 2003); *Career* Robert Davies & Co slrs Warrington: articled clerk 1971, admitted slr 1973, ptnr 1978–95; ptnr Ridgway Greenall Warrington 1995–2003; sr ptnr Davies Ridgway Warrington 2003–; chm: Warrington Ctee for the Disabled 1978–91, Warrington Crossroads Care Attendant Scheme 1980–99, Birchwood Project (Warrington) Ltd 1984–, Warrington Hosp NHS Tst 1993–2001, N Cheshire Hosps Tst 2001–04; non-exec dir Mersey RHA 1991–93; pres Assoc of Crossroads Care Attendant Schemes 1992–96 (chm 1983–92); dir Warrington Festival Tst 1982–93; memb Law Soc 1973, Rotary of Warrington 1984–2002 (past pres); *Clubs* Warrington; *Style*— Norman Banner, Esq; ✉ 12 Melton Avenue, Walton, Warrington, Cheshire (tel 01925 268186)

BANNERMAN, Sir David Gordon; 15 Bt (NS 1682), of Elsick, Kincardineshire; OBE (1976); yr s of Sir Donald Arthur Gordon Bannerman, 13 Bt (d 16 Sept 1989), and Barbara Charlotte, *née* Cameron; suc bro Sir Alexander Patrick Bannerman, 14 Bt (d 21 Nov 1989); *b* 18 August 1935; *Educ* Gordonstoun, New Coll Oxford (MA), UCL (MSc); *m* 25 June 1960, Mary Prudence, er da of Rev Philip Frank Ardagh-Walter, Vicar of Woolton Hill, Hants; 4 da (Clare Naomi (Mrs Michael O'Neill) b 1961, Margot Charlotte b 1962, Arabella Rose b 1965, Clodagh Isobel Rose b 1975); *Career* 2 Lt Queen's Own Cameron Highlanders 1954–56, HMOCS (Tanganyka) 1960–63, MOD 1963–97; chm Gordonstoun Assoc 1997–2000; *Recreations* painting, ornithology, architecture; *Style*— Sir David Bannerman, Bt, OBE; ✉ Drummond's, 49 Charing Cross, London SW1A 2DX

BANNISTER, Brian; s of Norman Bannister, and Sarah Ann, *née* Jolly; *b* 31 December 1933; *Educ* King Edward VII Sch Lytham St Annes, Birmingham Sch of Architecture (DipArch); *m* 1, 5 April 1961 (m dis 1973), Pauline Mary (d 2000), da of Jack Miller (d 1987), of Preston, Lancs; 1 da (Karen b 23 July 1962), 1 s (Dominic b 3 Feb 1964 d 1981); m 2, 25 May 1973, Avril, da of James Wigley Allen (d 1987); 1 s (Richard Allen b 8 July 1975), 1 da (Katie Louise b 10 Feb 1979); *Career* Nat Serv 1958–59; architect Lancs CC 1956–58 and 1960; John H D Madin & Partners: sr architect 1960–64, assoc 1964–68; assoc i/c Watkins Grey Woodgate International (Birmingham Office) 1968–70; ptnr: Burman Goodhall & Partners 1970–72, Brian Bannister & Associates 1972–85, Brian Bannister Partnership 1985–93; dir Brian Bannister Projects Ltd 1996–2006; dir and co sec BMW Properties Ltd 1986–93; dir: Co-ordinated Project Management Ltd 1971–92, Tweedale Planning and Design Group Ltd (trading as Bloomer Tweedale) 1993–94, Bloomer Tweedale Ltd (trading as Alex Gordon Tweedale) 1994–96; conslt FBDA Ltd 2006–; sub ed Architecture West Midlands 1970–75, memb Ctee Birmingham Architectural Assoc 1972–84 (vice-pres 1980–82, pres 1982–84), memb Ctee W Midlands Div Faculty of Building 1991–; ARIBA 1958, FIMgt 1980; *Recreations* golf, sailing; *Clubs* Edgbaston Golf; *Style*— Brian Bannister, Esq; ✉ 10 Strutt Close, Edgbaston, Birmingham B15 3PW (tel 0121 455 7431); FBDA Limited, the Old telephone Exchange, Gipsy Lane, Balsell Common, Coventry CV7 (tel 01676 535530, fax 01676 535537, e-mail brian@fbda.co.uk)

BANNISTER, (Richard) Matthew; s of Richard Neville Bannister, of Sheffield, and Olga Margaret, *née* Bennett; *b* 16 March 1957; *Educ* King Edward VII Sch Sheffield, Univ of Nottingham (LLB); *m* 1, 23 June 1984, Amanda Gerrard Walker; 1 da (Jessica b 3 Dec 1984); m 2, 14 Jan 1989, Shelagh Margaret Macleod; 1 s (Joseph b 1 May 1990); m 3, 19 May 2007, Katherine Jane Hood; *Career* presenter and reporter BBC Radio Nottingham 1978–81, presenter and prodr Capital Radio 1981–83, presenter Radio One Newsbeat 1983–85, head of news Capital Radio 1987–88 (asst head of news 1985–87); BBC: rejoined as managing ed Greater London Radio 1988–91, chief asst to BBC's Dir of Corporate Affrs 1991–92, project co-ordinator BBC Charter Renewal 1992–93, controller Radio One 1993–98, dir BBC Radio 1996–98, chief exec BBC Prodn 1998–99, dir Marketing and Communication BBC 1999–2000, currently presenter BBC Radio 4 and BBC Radio Five Live; fell Radio Acad 1997; *Recreations* theatre, rock music, collecting P G Wodehouse first editions; *Style*— Matthew Bannister, Esq

BANNISTER, Sir Roger Gilbert; kt (1975), CBE (1955); s of late Ralph Bannister and Alice Bannister, of Harrow; *b* 23 March 1929; *Educ* Univ Coll Sch London, Exeter and Merton Colls Oxford (MA, MSc, BM BCh, DM), St Mary's Hosp Med Sch London; *m* 1955, Moyra, da of Per Jacobsson (chm IMF), of Sweden; 2 s, 2 da; *Career* Athletics: winner Oxford v Cambridge Mile 1947–50, pres OUAC 1948, capt Oxford and Cambridge Combined American Team 1949, finalist Olympic Games Helsinki 1952, Br mile champion 1951, 1953 and 1954, first man to run 4 minute mile 1954, Br Empire Mile title and record 1954, Euro 1500m title and record 1954; Medicine: jr med specialist RAMC 1958, Radcliffe travelling fell from Oxford Univ at Harvard 1962–63; hon conslt physician Nat Hosp for Nervous Diseases London (formerly conslt physician 1963–90); hon conslt neurologist: St Mary's Hosp London (formerly conslt neurologist 1963–85), Oxford Regnl and Dist Health Authy 1985–93; Master of Pembroke Coll Oxford 1985–93; chm Govt Working Pty on Univ Sports Scholarships 1996–97; memb: Cncl King George's Jubilee Tst 1961–67, Miny of Health Advsy Ctee on Drug Dependence 1967–70; chm: Sports Cncl 1971–74, Med Ctee St Mary's Hosp 1983–85; pres: Nat Fitness Panel NABC 1956–59, Sussex Assoc of Youth Clubs 1972–79, Int Cncl for Sport and Physical Recreation 1976–83, Alzheimer's Disease Soc 1982–84; tstee Leeds Castle Fndn 1981–2005, ed Leeds Castle Med Conf Health Challenge Beyond Year 2000; govr: Atlantic Coll 1985–92, Sherborne Sch 1989–93; Liveryman Worshipful Soc of Apothecaries; hon fell: UMIST 1974, Exeter Coll Oxford 1979, Merton Coll Oxford 1986, Harris Manchester Coll Oxford 2006; Hon LLD Univ of Liverpool 1972, Hon DLitt Univ of Sheffield 1978; Hon Dr: Jyvaskyla Univ Finland 1983, Univ of Bath 1984, Imperial Coll London 1984, Grinnell USA 1984, Univ of Rochester NY 1985, Univ of Pavia Italy 1986, Williams Coll USA 1987, Victoria Univ Canada 1994, Univ of Wales Cardiff 1995, Loughborough Univ 1996, UEA 1997, Cranfield Univ 2002, RCS(Ed) 2002; FRCP; *Books* First Four Minutes (1955, 50th anniversary edn 2004), Brain and Bannister's Clinical Neurology (ed, 3–7 edn 1966–92), Autonomic Failure (1983, 5 edn (with Christopher Mathias, *qv*) 2007), Collingwood and British Idealism Studies (contrib, 2005); author of numerous papers on neurology and disorders of the autonomic nervous system; *Clubs* Athenaeum, Vincent's (Oxford); *Style*— Sir Roger Bannister, CBE; ✉ 21 Bardwell Road, Oxford OX2 6SU (tel 01865 511413)

BANNOCK, Graham Bertram; s of Eric Burton Bannock (d 1977), and Winifred, *née* Sargent (d 1972); *b* 10 July 1932; *Educ* Crewkerne Sch, LSE (Bsc); *m* 26 Feb 1971, Françoise Marcelle, *née* Vranckx; 1 s (Laurent Graham b 1972); *Career* Sgt RASC 1950–52; market analyst Ford Motor Co 1955–56; asst mangr: market res Richard Thomas & Baldwins Ltd 1957–58, Rover Co 1958–60; sr admin OECD Paris 1960–62; chief of econ and market res Rover Co 1962–67; mangr Advanced Progs Ford of Europe Inc 1968–69, dir Res Ctee of Inquiry on Small Firms 1970–71; md: Econ Advsy Gp Ltd 1971–81, Economist Intelligence Unit Ltd 1981–84, fndr Bannock Consulting Ltd (formerly Graham Bannock & Partners Ltd) 1985, exec dir Central Banking Publications Ltd 1990–; *Books* Business Economics and Statistics (with A J Merrett, 1962), The Juggernauts (1971), The Penguin Dictionary of Economics (with R E Baxter and Evan Davis, 1972), How to Survive the Slump (1975), Smaller Business in Britain and Germany (1976), The Economics of Small Firms (1981), Going Public (1987), The Economist International Dictionary of Finance (1989, revised 2003), Governments and Small Business (with Sir Alan Peacock, 1989), Taxation in the European Community (1990), Small Business Policy in Europe (with Horst Albach, 1991), Corporate Takeovers and the Public Interest (with Sir Alan Peacock, 1991), Small Business Statistics (with Michael Daly, 1994), The New Penguin Dictionary of Business (co-author, 2002); *Recreations* karate, the arts; *Clubs* RAC; *Style*— Graham Bannock, Esq

BANSKI, Norman Alexander Fyfe Ritchie; s of Richard Carol Stanislaw Bański, Lt 9 Polish Lancers (d 1970), of Kincardineshire, and late Marion Alexandra Watt Fyfe (later Mrs George A Ritchie); *b* 3 August 1955; *Educ* Laurencekirk Secdy Sch, Mackie Acad Stonehaven, Univ of Aberdeen (LLB); *m* 4 July 1997, Laura Ann Patricia, da of James George Emile Milton; 2 step da (Julia Dorothy Patricia Wardle, Alice Veronica Wardle); *Career* slr and NP; sr ptnr Banski & Co, registrar births deaths and marriages (ret), cemetery clerk (ret), census offr (S Kincardine) 1981 and 1991; tstee various local charitable tsts, dir Howe O'The Mearns Developments Ltd, sec and dir Caledonian Railway (Brechin) Ltd, chair Kincardine and Mearns Area Partnership; sec: Villages in Control, Mearns Area Project, Mearns Challenge Project; memb Laurencekirk and Dist Business Club, vice-chair Mearns Community Cncl; hon vice-pres: Laurencekirk and Dist Angling Assoc, PM Lodge St Laurence 136; past princ Chapter Haran 8; memb: Law Soc of Scotland, Nat Tst for Scotland, Scottish Rural Property and Business Assoc, Montrose Air Station Heritage Soc, WWF, Esk Dist Fishery Bd 1991–2001, Laurencekirk Business Club; treas Kincardine and Deeside Faculty of Slrs; *Recreations* golf, preserved railways, philately, rugby; *Clubs* Laurencekirk and Dist Angling Assoc, Laurencekirk and District Business, F P Rugby, Lodge St Laurence 136, Chapter Haran 8, Auchenblae Golf; *Style*— Norman Banski, Esq; ✉ Banski & Co, Royal Banks Buildings, Laurencekirk AB30 1AF

BANSZKY, Caroline Janet; da of Harold Arthur Armstrong While (d 1982), of East Molesey, Surrey, and Janet Bell Symington, *née* Clark; *b* 24 July 1953; *Educ* Wycombe Abbey, Univ of Exeter (BA); *m* 31 March 1984 (m dis 1995), Baron Nicholas Laszlo Banszky von Ambroz, s of Baron Dr Laszlo Banszky von Ambroz; 2 da (Genevra b 15 April 1985, Antonella b 1 Aug 1987); *Career* formerly articled clerk rising to audit asst mangr KPMG Peat Marwick McLintock; N M Rothschild & Sons Ltd: Corp Fin Div 1981–84, Fin Div 1984–97, chief fin offr 1988–89, exec dir 1989–, fin dir 1995–97; dep chief exec SVB Syndicates Ltd 1997–98, chief operating offr SVB Holdings plc 1998–2001, md The Law Debenture Corp plc 2002–; Liveryman Worshipful Co of Farriers 1978, Liveryman Worshipful Co of Tinplate Workers alias Wireworkers' Co 1998; FCA 1991 (ACA 1978); *Recreations* children, walking, riding, skiing; *Style*— Caroline Banszky; ✉ The Law Debenture Corporation plc, Fifth Floor, 100 Wood Street, London EC2V 7EX (tel 020 7696 5902, fax 020 7696 5243, e-mail caroline.banszky@lawdeb.co.uk)

BANTON, Prof Michael Parker; CMG (2001), JP (Bristol 1966); s of Francis Clive Banton (d 1985), of Maids' Moreton, Bucks, and Kathleen Blanche, *née* Parkes (d 1945); *b* 8 September 1926; *Educ* King Edward's Sch Birmingham, LSE (BScEcon), Univ of Edinburgh (PhD, DSc); *m* 23 July 1952, (Rut) Marianne, da of Lars Robert Jacobson (d 1954), of Lulea, Sweden; 2 s (Sven Christopher b 1953, Nicholas b 1956 d 1994), 2 da (Ragnhild b 1955, Dagmar b 1959); *Career* served RN 1944–47 (Sub-Lt RNVR); reader in social anthropology Univ of Edinburgh 1962–65 (lectr 1955–62); Univ of Bristol: prof of sociology 1965–92, emeritus prof 1992–, pro-vice-chllr 1985–88; visiting prof: MIT 1962–63, Wayne State Univ Detroit 1971, Univ of Delaware 1976, ANU 1981, Duke Univ 1982; ed Sociology 1966–69; memb Royal Cmmn on: Civil Disorders in Bermuda 1978, Criminal Procedure 1978–81; memb: UK Nat Cmmn for UNESCO 1963–66 and 1980–85, UN Ctee for Elimination of Racial Discrimination 1986–2001 (chm 1996–98); pres Royal Anthropological Inst 1987–89; Dr (hc) Stockholm 2000; FRSA 1981; *Books* The Coloured Quarter (1955), West African City (1957), White and Coloured (1959), The Policeman in the Community (1964), Roles (1965), Race Relations (1967), Racial Minorities (1972), Police-Community Relations (1973), The Idea of Race (1977), Racial and Ethnic Competition (1983), Promoting Racial Harmony (1985), Investigating Robbery (1985), Racial Theories (1987, 2 edn 1998), Racial Consciousness (1988), Discrimination (1994), International Action Against Racial Discrimination (1996), Ethnic and Racial Consciousness (1997), The International Politics of Race (2002); *Style*— Prof Michael Banton, CMG; ✉ Fairways, Luxted Road, Downe, Orpington, Kent BR6 7JT (tel 01959 576828, e-mail michael@banton.demon.co.uk)

BANVILLE, John; *Educ* Christian Brothers' Schs, St Peter's Coll Wexford; *m* Janet Dunham; 2 s (Colm, Douglas); *Career* novelist and journalist 1969–; *Awards* incl: Allied Irish Banks Fiction Prize, American-Irish Fndn Award, James Tait Black Meml Prize, Guardian Prize for fiction, Guinness Peat Aviation Award, Premio Ennio Flaiano 1991, Premio Nonino 2003; *Books* Long Lankin (short stories, 1970), Nightspawn (1971), Birchwood, Doctor Copernicus, Kepler, The Newton Letter, Mefisto, The Book of Evidence (shortlisted Booker Prize 1989), Ghosts (1993), Athena (1995), The Untouchable (shortlisted Whitbread Novel of the Year Award 1997), Eclipse (2000), Shroud (2002), Prague Pictures: Portraits of a City (non-fiction, 2003), The Sea (2005, Man Booker Prize 2005), Christine Falls (as Benjamin Black, 2006); *Style*— John Banville, Esq; ✉ c/o Ed Victor Limited, 6 Bayley Street, Bedford Square, London WC1B 3HE

BARAŃSKI, Prof Zygmunt Guido; s of Henryk Barański (d 1984), and Sonia, *née* Mariotti; *b* 13 April 1951; *Educ* St Bede's Coll Manchester, Univ of Hull (BA); *m* 7 April 1979, Margaret, *née* Watt; 1 da (Anna Matilde b 22 Oct 1986), 1 s (Edward Marek b 23 Sept 1989); *Career* lectr in Italian Univ of Aberdeen 1976–79; Univ of Reading: lectr in Italian studies 1979–89, sr lectr in Italian studies 1989–92, prof of Italian studies 1992–2002; Serena prof of Italian Univ of Cambridge 2002–, fell New Hall Cambridge 2002–; visiting prof: McGill Univ 1988 and 1997, Univ of Virginia Charlottesville 1991, Univ of Connecticut 1993, Yale Univ 1995, Univ of Notre Dame 1996,1998 and 2004, Univ of Bari 2001, Univ of Calif Berkeley 2002; Fondazione Il Campiello Medal for Italian literature 1990, Gold Medal of the City of Florence for Dante studies 1999, Valle dei Trulli Prize for literary criticism 2001; life memb Società Dantesca Italiana Florence 1997; Commendatore dell'Ordine della Stella della Solidarietà Italiana 2005; *Books* Libri Poetarum in Quattuor Species Dividuntur: Essays on Dante and Genre (1995), Luce Nuova, Sole Nuovo: Saggi sul Rinnovamento Culturale in Dante (1996), Pasolini Old and New (1999), Dante e i Segni (2000), Chiosar con Altro Testo: Leggere Dante nel Trecento (2001); *Recreations* following Manchester United FC, music, cycling; *Style*— Prof Zygmunt Barański; ✉ New Hall, Huntingdon Road, Cambridge CB3 0DF (tel 01223 762263 or 01223 335038, fax 01223 335062, e-mail zgb20@cam.ac.uk)

BARBENEL, Prof Joseph Cyril; s of Tobias and Sarah Barbenel; *b* 2 January 1937; *Educ* Hackney Down GS (Grocers' Co), Univ of London (BDS, prize in anatomy and dental anatomy), Univ of St Andrews (Nuffield fell, BSc, physics medal), Univ of Strathclyde (MSc, PhD, MRC Award for the further education in medical sciences); *m* 6 Aug 1964, Lesley Mary Hyde, *née* Jowett BDS LDS RCS(Eng); 1 da (Rachel b 14 July 1966), 2 s (David b 31 March 1968, Daniel b 2 Feb 1970); *Career* house surgn London Hosp 1960; Nat Serv Lt RADC Malaya 1960–61 (Capt 1961–62); gen dental practice NHS London 1962–63; student Univ of St Andrews 1963–66; student Bioengineering Unit Univ of Strathclyde 1966–67; lectr Dept of Dental Prosthetics Dental Sch and Hosp Univ of Dundee 1967–69; Bioengineering Unit Univ of Strathclyde: sr lectr 1970–73, head Tissue Mechanics Div 1973–82, reader 1982–85, personal prof 1985–89, prof 1989–2002, head of dept 1992–98; Univ of Strathclyde: vice-dean Faculty of Engrg 1997–2002, emeritus prof 2003–; visiting prof: Chongqinq Univ China 1986–, Univ of Technology Vienna 1987–; pres: Biological Engrg Soc 1988–90, Tissue Viability Soc 1989–92; President's Medal Soc of Cosmetic Scientists 1994, Lifetime Achievement Award EPUAP 2002; FRSE 1986, FIBiol 1987, FInstP 1988, FIPSM 1988, FRSM 1989, FEAMBES 2007 (founding fell); *Books* Progress in Bioengineering (co-ed, 1989), Blood Flow in the Brain (co-ed, 1989),

B

Blood Flow in Artificial Organs and Cardiovascular Prostheses (co-ed, 1989); *Recreations* work, music, theatre, cinema, reading, travel; *Style*— Prof Joseph Barbenel, FRSE; ✉ 151 Maxwell Drive, Glasgow G41 5AE (tel 0141 427 0765); University of Strathclyde, Department of Electronic and Electrical Engineering, Royal College Building, George Street, Glasgow G1 1XW (tel 0141 548 3221, fax 0141 552 2950, e-mail j.c.barbenel@strath.ac.uk)

BARBER, Dr Anthony Douglas; s of Douglas Robert Barber (d 2002), of Southwold, Suffolk, and Jean, *née* Arnold; *b* 9 October 1946; *Educ* Ashlyns Sch Berkhamsted, Univ of Nottingham (BSc, PhD); *m* 4 July 1970, Margaret Rose, da of Evalds Liepnieks (d 2005), and Elizabeth, *née* Salamon (d 1999); 1 s (Jeremy Janis b 19 Aug 1973), 1 da (Julia Zahra b 13 Oct 1976); *Career* research fell ETH-Zürich 1972–74, various positions as separations specialist Shell Research and Development 1974–82, research advsr Shell UK Exploration & Production 1982–84, head offshore research Koninklijke/Shell Exploratie en Produktie Laboratorium Rijswijk 1984–88, mangr equipment engrg Koninklijke/Shell Laboratorium Amsterdam 1988–96, dir engrg IChemE 1997, res mgmnt conslt 1997–; special prof in chemical engrg Univ of Nottingham 1992–2001, memb Cncl Univ of Nottingham 2002–; Moulton Medal IChemE 1974; CEng 1979, FIChemE 1986, MIMgt 1986, FREng 1996; *Publications* author of various papers on educn, foaming and offshore equipment incl: A Model for a Cellular Foam (1974), Foaming in Crude Distillation Units (1979), Some New Offshore Techniques (1988); *Recreations* genealogy, motor cruising; *Clubs* Royal Norfolk and Suffolk Yacht, Norfolk Broads Yacht; *Style*— Dr Anthony Barber, FREng; ✉ Redwood, Charles Close, Wroxham, Norwich NR12 8TT (tel 01603 784433, fax 01603 784434, e-mail adbarber@netcomuk.co.uk)

BARBER, Antonia; *see:* Anthony, Barbara

BARBER, Brendan Paul; s of John Barber (d 1996), of Southport, Merseyside, and Agnes Barber (d 2006); *b* 3 April 1951; *Educ* St Mary's Coll Crosby, City Univ (BSc, pres Students' Union); *m* 1981, Mary, *née* Gray; 2 da (Amy b 1985, Sarah b 1988); *Career* researcher Ceramic, Glass & Mineral Products ITB 1974–75; TUC: joined 1975, researcher Orgn Dept 1975–79, head Press and Information Dept 1979–87, head Orgn Dept 1987–93, dep gen sec 1993–2003, gen sec 2003–; memb Cncl ACAS 1995–2004, memb Sport England 1999–2002; dir Ct Bank of England 2003–; teacher VSO Ghana 1969–70; *Recreations* football (Everton FC and Barnet FC), golf, theatre, cinema; *Clubs* Muswell Hill Golf, Everton Supporters London Area; *Style*— Brendan Barber, Esq; ✉ Trades Union Congress, Congress House, Great Russell Street, London WC1B 3LS (tel 020 7467 1231, e-mail bbarber@tuc.org.uk)

BARBER, Daniel Mark; s of David Barber, and Gillian Barber; *b* 21 September 1964; *Educ* JFS Comp Sch, St Martin's Sch of Art (BA); *m* 6 June 1992, Sandra, da of Lèo Rogg; 1 s (Moses b 1996); *Career* designer/dir Lambie Nairn & Co 1988–93; creator of title sequence for BBC Nine O'Clock News and station identities for BBC1, BBC2, Carlton TV and various Euro TV stations; Rose Hackney Barber Productions (formerly Rose Hackney): commercials dir 1993–2005, ptnr 1995–2005; co-fndr Knucklehead 2005–; creator of TV and cinema commercials for clients incl BMW, Sony, Orange, Ford, Adidas, Daewoo, Shell, Saab, and The RAF; recipient of numerous awards/honours from industry bodies incl BAFTA, D&AD, BTA, RTS, Clio and Creative Circle; subject of profile articles in many industry magazines in Europe and America, work published in major design and advtg pubns; memb D&AD; *Recreations* cinema, tennis, shopping, driving, dieting, travel; *Style*— Daniel Barber; ✉ Knucklehead, Unit 22–23, Archer Street Studios, 10–11 Archer Street, London W1D 7AZ

BARBER, Sir (Thomas) David; 3 Bt (UK 1960), of Greasley, Co Nottingham; s of Sir William Francis Barber, 2 Bt, TD (d 1995), and his 1 w, Diana Constance, *née* Lloyd (d 1984); *b* 18 November 1937; *Educ* Eton, Trinity Coll Cambridge (MA); *m* 1, 1972 (m dis 1975), Amanda Mary, da of Frank Rabone, and wid of Maj Michael Healing, Gren Gds; 1 s (Thomas Edward b 14 March 1973); m 2, 1978, Jeannine Mary, former w of John Richard Boyle, by whom she had 3 s, and da of Capt Timothy John Gurney; 1 da (Sarah Emily b 19 June 1981), 1 s (William Samuel Timothy b 23 Sept 1982); *Heir* s, Thomas Barber; *Career* 2 Lt RA 1957–58; *Style*— Sir David Barber, Bt; ✉ Windrush House, Inkpen, Hungerford, Berkshire RG17 9QY (tel 01488 668 419)

BARBER, Prof David John; s of George William Barber (d 1981), and Amelia Sarah, *née* Harris (d 1973); *b* 14 February 1935; *Educ* Wanstead HS London, Univ of Bristol (BSc, PhD); *m* 1, 26 July 1958 (m dis 1974), Vivien Joan, da of Leslie George Hayward (d 1969); 2 s (Douglas b 1961, Peter b 1961 d 1979), 2 da (Rosalind b 1964, Alison b 1966); m 2, 17 Oct 1975, Jill Elizabeth Edith, da of Francis Joseph Sanderson, of Great Holland, Essex; 1 s (Alastair b 1978); *Career* investigator Alcan International 1959–62, gp leader Nat Bureau of Standards USA 1963–65 (scientist 1962–63); Univ of Essex: lectr 1965–74, sr lectr 1974–78, prof of physics 1979–96 (emeritus prof 1998–), pro-vice-chllr 1981–85; prof Dept of Physics Univ of Science and Technol Hong Kong 1989–96; visiting prof: Sch of Industrial and Manufacturing Science Cranfield Univ 1996–2002, Sch of Chemical and Life Sciences Univ of Greenwich 1997–, Wolfson Centre for Materials Processing Brunel Univ 2006–; visiting scholar: Univ of Calif 1970–71, 1980, 1989, 1991 and 1995, Pennsylvania State Univ 1979–80, SUNY Stonybrook 1989; vice-pres Mineralogical Soc (GB) 1987–88 (memb Cncl 1985–88); CPhys, FInstP, CEng, FIMMM; *Books* Introduction to the Properties of Condensed Matter (with R Loudon, 1989), Deformation Processes in Minerals, Ceramics and Rocks (ed with P G Meredith, 1990); *Recreations* sailing, gardening, carpentry; *Clubs* Royal Harwich Yacht, Walton and Frinton Yacht; *Style*— Prof David Barber; ✉ Physics Centre, University of Essex, Colchester, Essex CO4 3SQ; Twin Ridges, The Street, Tendring, Clacton-on-Sea, Essex CO16 9AR (tel 01255 830633, e-mail barbd@essex.ac.uk)

BARBER, David Stewart; s of Jack Barber (d 1961), of Manchester, and Margaret, *née* Hall (d 1960); *b* 21 September 1931; *Educ* Bacup and Rawtenstall GS; *m* 25 Jan 1965, Hazel Valerie, da of Francis Smith (d 1968), of Whitstable, Kent; 1 s (Nicholas b 1968), 1 da (Suzanna b 1971); *Career* 2 Lt Lancs Fus 1950–52; trainee and subsequently mangr Imperial Tobacco Co (John Player & Sons) 1952–57, PA Mgmnt Conslts (various appts) 1958–69, divnl chief exec Bovis Ltd 1969–71, chm and chief exec Halma plc 1972–95 (chm 1995–2003); *Recreations* tennis, golf; *Style*— David Barber, Esq; ✉ Halma plc, Misbourne Court, Rectory Way, Amersham, Buckinghamshire HP7 0DE (tel 01494 721111, fax 01494 728032)

BARBER, Donald Christopher (Chris); OBE; s of Donald Barber, CBE (d 1957), of West Byfleet, Surrey, and Henrietta Mary Evelyn Barber, JP; *b* 17 April 1930; *Educ* King Alfred Sch, St Paul's, Guildhall Sch of Music; *m* Kate; 1 s (Christopher Julian), 1 da (Caroline Mary) from previous m, 1 step da (Catherine); *Career* jazz musician and band ldr; instruments played: trombone, trumpet, baritone horn, double bass; formed first (amateur) band 1949, first professional band formed 1952 (led by Ken Colyer 1953–54); ldr: Chris Barber's Jazz Band 1954–68, Chris Barber's Jazz and Blues Band 1968–2001, The Big Chris Barber Band 2001–; over 200 LPs and CDs, extensive tours 1954–2003 (Europe, USA, Aust, NZ, Japan, ME, Canada), played approximately 12500 performances 1954–2003; hon citizen New Orleans; *Recreations* collecting Jazz and Blues records and antiques, motor racing (competitor 1957–63), snooker; *Style*— Chris Barber, Esq, OBE; ✉ Chris Barber Office, Entec Ltd, 517 Yeading Lane, Northolt, Middlesex UB5 6LN (tel 020 8842 4044, fax 020 8342 3310, e-mail cbarber@intonet.co.uk, website www.chrisbarber.net)

BARBER, Edmund Patrick Harty; s of Maj Leslie Bernard Michael Barber (d 1983), of Marley Common, Surrey, and Ellen, *née* Harty (d 2004); *b* 25 August 1946; *Educ* Glenstal Abbey Sch Co Limerick, UCD; *m* 20 Dec 1969, Elizabeth Marguerite, da of Eric Fowler Sherriff, of Tewin, Herts; 1 s (Samuel), 2 da (Catherine, Lucy); *Career* CA 1973– (specialising in int tax work and acquisition and disposal); dir: IAF Gp plc, MEON Capital plc, Rigidized Metals Ltd, Courtyard Leisure plc, Fluorocarbon Holdings Ltd; Freeman City of London, memb Worshipful Co of Chartered Accountants; FCA 1973; *Recreations* squash, golf; *Clubs* Leander, Reform, MCC, The Thunderers; *Style*— Edmund Barber, Esq; ✉ 1 Harmer Green Lane, Digswell, Welwyn, Hertfordshire (tel 01438 716088, fax 01438 840841); Flat 2, 25 Maiden Lane, Covent Garden, London WC2E 7NR (tel 020 7379 0422, fax 020 7379 6141); Barber & Co Chartered Accountants, Durham House, Durham House Street, London WC2N 6HG (tel 020 7839 8411, fax 020 7839 8403, e-mail edmund@barberco.net)

BARBER, Edward Simon Dominic; s of Simon Barber, of London, and Penelope, *née* Baldock (d 1974); *b* 6 April 1969; *Educ* Leeds Poly (BA), RCA (MA); *Partner* Suzy Hoodless; *Career* designer; fndr (with Jay Osgerby, *qv*) BarberOsgerby 1996–, founding dir and co-owner (with Jay Osgerby) Universal Design Studio Ltd 2001–; clients incl: Magis, Flos, Bute, Authentics, Venini, Isokon, Coca Cola, Levi's, Swarovski, Stella McCartney, Cappellini; commissioned to design furniture for De La Warr Pavilion Bexhill on Sea, RIBA, Portsmouth Cathedral; exhibited at: Sotheby's London, MoMA NY, Int Furniture Fair NY, Haute Definition Paris, Musée de la Mode et du Textil Paris, Design Museum London, Crafts Cncl London, Design Miami/Basel; work in permanent collections V&A London and Met Museum of Art NY; public lectures: 6th Int Congress of Architecture and Design Mexico City, ICFF NY, Tokyo Design Fair, Basel, Design Museum London; MCSD 2003, FRSA 2005, RDI 2007; *Awards* incl: Best New Designer ICFF NY 1998, shortlisted for Compasso d'Oro 2004, Jerwood Prize for Applied Arts 2004, winner Furniture Designer of the Year Blueprint Mgazine 2005, Best Furniture Design Award Design Week 2003 and 2004, Best Product Red Dot Awards 2006; *Style*— Edward Barber, Esq; ✉ 35 Charlotte Road, London EC2A 3PG (tel 020 7033 3884, fax 020 7033 3882)

BARBER, Frances Jennifer; da of S W Brookes, of Wolverhampton, and Gladys, *née* Simpson (d 1991); *b* 13 May 1958; *Educ* Municipal GS Wolverhampton, Univ of Bangor, Univ of Cardiff; *Career* actress; memb: Dr Barnardos, Terrence Higgins Tst, Cancer Research, The Labour Party; prodn bd memb BFI 1995–; *Theatre* incl: Ooh La La for Hull Truck (Plays and Players Award Most Promising Newcomer nomination 1980), Riff Raff Rules, Space Ache (Tricycle Theatre), La Guerra, Desperado Corner, Madam Louise (Glasgow Citizen's and Venice Festival), The Treat (ICA), The Mission (Soho Poly), Hard Feelings (Oxford Playhouse and Bush Theatre), Summer and Smoke (Leicester Haymarket), Viola in Twelfth Night, Lady Macbeth in Macbeth (Exchange Manchester), Eliza Doolittle in Pygmalion, Maxine Faulk in The Night of the Iguana (RNT), My Heart's A Suitcase (Royal Court), Over a Barrel (Palace Theatre Watford), Imagine Drowning (Hampstead), Insignificance (Donmar); for RSC credits incl: Camille (Olivier Award for Most Promising Newcomer 1985), Ophelia in Hamlet, Jacquetta in Love's Labour's Lost, Dolores in The Dead Donkey, Uncle Vanya (Regional Theatre Award for Best Supporting Actress, Olivier Award nomination Best Supporting Actress); *Television* incl: Home Sweet Home, A Flame to the Phoenix, Those Glory Days, Reilly Ace of Spies, Hard Feelings, Clem, Twelfth Night, Duck, Annie Besant, Behaving Badly, The Grasscutter, The Nightmare Years, The Storey Teller - The Greek Myths, Do Not Disturb, The Orchid House, Hancock, Inspector Morse, The Leaving of Liverpool, A Statement of Affairs, Inspector Alleyn, Spitting Image - Thatcherworld, Return to Blood River, In the Cold Light of Day, Dirty Old Town, Circle of Deceit, Rules of Engagement, Space Precinct, Rhodes, It Might be You, Royal Scandal, Real Women (3 part, BBC), Just In Time (Channel Four), Tea (MTV), Dalziel & Pascoe (BBC), The Ice House (BBC), Plastic Man, Love in a Cold Climate (BBC); *Films* incl: Rosie in Sammy and Rosie Get Laid, Megan in We Think the World of You, Leonie Orton in Prick up your Ears, A Zed and Two Noughts, Castaway, The Missionary, Acceptable Levels, White City, The Soul of the Machine, Young Soul Rebels, Secret Friends, The Lake, Soft Top, Hard Shoulder, The Fish Tale, Scarborough Ahoy! (Best Foreign Student American Academy Award), Three Steps to Heaven, Photographing Fairie, Still Crazy, Mauvaise passe, Esther Kahn, Shiner; also three french speaking films: Chambre a Part, Giorgino, Germaine et Benjamin; *Recreations* swimming, reading, walking the dog, poetry; *Style*— Ms Frances Barber

BARBER, Gerald William Priestman; LVO (1995); s of Alan Theodore Barber, of Ludgrove Sch, Wokingham (d 1987), and Dorothy, *née* Shaw (d 2004); *b* 3 October 1942, Windsor; *Educ* Eton, St Edmund Hall Oxford (MA); *m* 6 April 1968, Janet Delia, *née* Snell; 1 s (Simon William Theodore b 26 Feb 1970), 2 da (Lucy Melville b 14 April 1972, Alexandra Jane b 24 Oct 1974); *Career* teacher: Papplewick Sch Ascot 1962, Mowden Sch Hove 1965–66, Ludgrove Sch Wokingham 1966– (headmaster 1973–); memb IAPS 1973–; govr St George's Sch Ascot; hon sec Wokingham Dist AGC; *Recreations* cricket, golf, gardening; *Clubs* MCC, Free Foresters Cricket, Vincent's (Oxford), Eton Fives Assoc, Berkshire Golf (capt 2006–07); *Style*— Gerald Barber, Esq, LVO; ✉ Ludgrove School, Ludgrove, Wokingham, Berkshire RG40 3AB (tel 0118 978 9881, fax 0118 979 2973, e-mail jdb@ludgrove.berks.sch.uk)

BARBER, Prof James; *b* 16 July 1940; *Educ* UC Swansea (tech state scholar, BSc), UEA (Nuffield biological fell, MSc, PhD); *m* 1 s (b 1971), 1 da (b 1972); *Career* Unilever Biochemical Soc European fell Biophysics Dept Univ of Leiden 1967; Imperial Coll London: lectr Dept of Botany 1968–74, reader in plant physiology 1974–79, prof of plant physiology 1979–90, dean Royal Coll of Science 1989–91, head Dept of Biochemistry 1989–99, dir Centre for Photomolecular Science 1990–, Ernst Chain prof of biochemistry 1990–; Selby lectr of the Aust Acad of Sci 1996; Miller visiting prof Univ of Calif Berkeley 1989 and 2001, Burrough-Wellcome prof Univ of Calif 2000; memb Cncl Weizmann Inst Fndn London 1991–2001 (memb Cncl 2001–); memb editorial bds of numerous scientific jls; memb Academia Europaea 1989; Flintoff Medal RSC 2002, Novartis Medal and Prize Biochemical Soc 2005, Italgas Prize for energy and the environment 2005, Wheland Medal and Prize Univ of Chicago 2007; Hon Dr Univ of Stockholm 1992; CChem, FRSC, FRS 2005; *Books* Topics in Photosynthesis Vol 1–12 (series ed, 1976–92), Techniques and New Developments in Photosynthesis Research (ed with R Malkin), Trends in Photosynthesis Research (ed with H Medrano and M G Guerrero), Advances in Molecular Biology Vol 11 (ed), Frontiers in Molecular Biology (ed with B Andersson); published over 400 papers; *Recreations* sailing, gardening, carpentry; *Style*— Prof James Barber; ✉ Division of Molecular Bioscience, Faculty of Natural Sciences, Wolfson Laboratories, Imperial College London, Exhibition Road, London SW7 2AZ (tel 020 7594 5266, fax 020 7594 5267, e-mail j.barber@imperial.ac.uk)

BARBER, Prof James Peden; s of John Barber (d 1973), and Carrie Barber (d 1967); *b* 6 November 1931; *Educ* Liverpool Inst HS, Pembroke Coll Cambridge, The Queen's Coll Oxford (MA, PhD); *m* 3 Sept 1955, (Margaret) June Barber, da of Henry James McCormac, of Ainsdale, Lancs; 3 s (Michael James b 1958, Andrew John b 1959, Mark Henry b 1965), 1 da (Anne Elizabeth b 1965); *Career* Nat Serv PO RAF 1950–52; Colonial Serv Uganda: dist offr 1956–61, asst sec to PM and clerk to cabinet 1961–63; lectr Univ of NSW 1963–65, lectr in govt Univ of Exeter 1965–69 (seconded to UC Rhodesia 1965–67), prof of political sci Open Univ 1969–80; Univ of Durham: master Hatfield Coll 1980–96, pro-vice-chllr 1987–92, sub warden 1990–92, prof of politics 1992–96; advsr to House of Commons Select Ctee on Foreign Affrs 1990–91; JP Bedford 1977–80; memb RIIA 1968; pres: Durham Univ Soc of Fellows 1988, Durham Univ Hockey Club 1981–96, Bd Cambridge Univ Centre of Int Studies 1996–; fell South African Inst of Int Affairs 1996–;

Uganda Independence Medal; *Books* Rhodesia: The Road to Rebellion (1967), Imperial Frontier (1968), South Africa's Foreign Policy (1973), European Community: Vision and Reality (1974), The Nature of Foreign Policy (1975), Who Makes British Foreign Policy? (1977), The West and South Africa (1982), The Uneasy Relationship: Britain and South Africa (1983), South Africa: The Search for Status and Security (1990), The Prime Minister since 1945 (1991), The New South Africa (1994), South Africa in the Twentieth Century (1999), Mandela's World (2004); *Recreations* golf, walking, choral singing; *Clubs* Menzies Cambs Golf; *Style—* Prof James Barber; ✉ 14 North Terrace, Midsummer Common, Cambridge CB5 8DJ (tel and fax 01223 313453, e-mail jpbarber2001@yahoo.co.uk)

BARBER, Prof Karin Judith; *b* Gothenburg, Sweden; *Educ* Univ of Cambridge (BA, Eileen Alexander Prize), UCL (Dip Social Anthropology), Univ of Ife Nigeria (PhD); *Partner* Dr Paulo Fernando de Moraes Farias; *Career* teacher St Mary's Teacher Trg Coll Bukedea Uganda 1967–68, lectr Dept of African Languages and Literatures Univ of Ife Nigeria 1977–84, princ instr in Yorùbá language Dept of Linguistics/African Studies Center UCLA 1982, pt/t instr in Yorùbá language City Literature Inst London 1984–85; Centre of West African Studies Univ of Birmingham: lectr 1985–93, sr lectr 1993–97, reader in African cultural anthropology 1997–99, dir 1998–2001, prof of African cultural anthropology 1999–; Northwestern Univ Evanston: preceptor Inst for Advanced Study and Research in the African Humanities 1993–94, Melville J Herskovits chair in African Studies (visiting appt) 1999; Scholar for a Day Univ of Pennsylvania 2000, British Acad Research Readership 2001–03; pres African Studies Assoc of the UK (ASAUK) 2000–02 (memb Cncl 1987–90, vice-pres 1998–2000); FBA 2003; *Publications* Yorùbá Dùn ún So: A Beginner's Course in Yorùbá (part 1, 1984), Discourse and its Disguises: The Interpretation of African Oral Texts (ed with P F de Moraes Farias, 1989), Self-assertion and Brokerage: Early Cultural Nationalism in West Africa (ed with P F de Moraes Farias, 1990), I Could Speak Until Tomorrow: Oriki, Women and the Past in a Yorùbá Town (1991, Amaury Talbot Prize 1992), Yorùbá Popular Theatre: Three Plays by the Oyin Adéjobi Company (with Báyo Ògúndijo, 1994), West African Popular Theatre (with John Collins and Alain Ricard, 1997), Readings in African Popular Culture (ed, 1997), Yorùbá Wuyi (with Akin Oyetade, 1999), The Generation of Plays: Yorùbá Popular Life in Theater (2000, Herskovits Award 2001), Africa's Hidden Histories: Everyday Literacy and Making the Self (ed, 2006), The Anthropology of Texts, Persons and Publics: Oral and Written Cultures in Africa and Beyond (2007); author of numerous research articles and contribs to books and jls; *Style—* Prof Karin Barber; ✉ Centre of West African Studies, University of Birmingham, Edgbaston, Birmingham B15 2TT (tel 0121 414 5125, e-mail k.j.barber@bham.ac.uk)

BARBER, (Franklin) Lionel; s of Frank Douglas Barber, and Joan, *née* Nolan; *b* 18 January 1955, London; *Educ* Dulwich Coll, St Edmund Hall Oxford (BA); *m* 13 Dec 1986, Victoria Greenwood; 1 da (Francesca b 5 May 1988), 1 s (Dashiell b 8 Aug 1990); *Career* reporter The Scotsman 1978–81, business corr Sunday Times 1981–85; FT: Washington corr then bureau chief Brussels 1985–98, news ed 1998–2000, ed Continental Europe edn 2000–02, managing ed US 2002–05, ed 2005–; memb Knight-Bagehot Advsy Ctee Columbia Univ Journalism Sch 2002–05; Laurence Stern fell Washington Post 1985, Woodrow Wilson Fndn fell and lectr Davidson Coll 1991, visiting scholar Inst of Governmental Studies Univ of Calif Berkeley 1992, Eliot-Winant fell and lectr Harvard Univ, George Washington Univ, Univ of Maryland, Univ of Pittsburgh and Stanford Univ 1994, visiting fell European Univ Inst Florence 1996; Br Press Awards: Young Journalist of the Year 1981, nominated Foreign Corr of the Year 1998; included in Le Nouvel Observateur's 101 most influential Europeans 1998; *Publications* The DeLorean Tapes (co-author, 1984), The Price of Truth: The story of Reuters' millions (co-author, 1985), Not with Honour: The inside story of the Westland scandal (co-author, 1986), Britain and the New Europe (1998); contrib: The Scottish Government Year Book (1981), Defense Beat: The dilemmas of defense coverage (1991), The Birth of the Euro (1998), Europe in the New Century (2001), Les Etats aujourd'hui, choc et changement (2004), My Idea of the Land of Ideas: How the world sees Germany (2006); author of articles for pubns incl: Washington Post, New Republic, San Francisco Examiner, Europe magazine; *Recreations* sport, opera; *Style—* Lionel Barber, Esq; ✉ Financial Times, One Southwark Bridge, London SE1 9HL (tel 020 7873 3000, fax 020 7873 3924, e-mail lionel.barber@ft.com)

BARBER, Lynn; da of Richard Barber, of Ebbesborne Wake, Wilts, and Beryl Barber; *b* 22 May 1944; *Educ* The Lady Eleanor Holles Sch, St Anne's Coll Oxford (BA); *m* 1971, David Maurice Cloudesley Cardiff (d 2003), s of Maj Maurice Cardiff, CBE, of Little Haseley, Oxford; 2 da (Rose b 1975, Theodora b 1978); *Career* asst ed Penthouse magazine 1967–72, staff writer Sunday Express Magazine 1984–89, feature writer Independent on Sunday 1990–93, contributing ed Vanity Fair 1992; columnist Sunday Times 1993, currently feature writer The Observer; Br Press Awards: Magazine Writer of the Year 1986 and 1987 (commended 1992), Feature Writer of the Year 1990, Interviewer of the Year 1997 and 2002; What the Papers Say Award Interviewer of the Year 1990; *Books* How to Improve Your Man in Bed (1973), The Single Woman's Sex Book (1975), The Heyday of Natural History (1980), Mostly Men (1991), Demon Barber (1998); *Recreations* gossip; *Style—* Ms Lynn Barber; ✉ e-mail lynnbaba@aol.com

BARBER, Nicholas Charles Faithorn; CBE (2004); s of Bertram Harold Barber (d 1982), and Nancy Lorraine, *née* Belsham (d 1984); *b* 7 September 1940; *Educ* Shrewsbury, Wadham Coll Oxford (MA), Columbia Univ NY (MBA); *m* 8 Jan 1966, Sheena Macrae, da of Donald Graham (d 1984); 2 s (James Henry b 1969, George Belsham b 1974), 1 da (Fenella Macrae b 1972); *Career* lectr Marlboro Coll Vermont 1963–64; Ocean Group plc (latterly Exel plc) 1964–94: dir 1980–94, gp md 1986–87, gp chief exec 1987–94; chm: Innovative Electronics Co 1996–99, Orion Publishing Group Ltd 1997–98, Bolero Int Ltd 1998–, Kappa IT Ventures (GP) Ltd 1999–; dir: Costain Group plc 1990–93, Royal Insurance Holdings plc 1991–96 (dep chm 1994–96), Barings plc 1994–95, Bank of Ireland Financial Services UK plc 1994–2003 (dep chm 2001–03), Albright & Wilson plc 1995–99, Royal & Sun Alliance Insurance Group plc 1996–2003, Fidelity Japanese Values plc 2000–, The Maersk Co 2004–; chm: Huron Univ USA in London Ltd 1998–, Ashmolean Museum Oxford 2003–; tstee: Nat Museums and Galleries Merseyside 1986–94, British Museum 1993–2003 (chm British Museum Friends 1992–2003, chm British Museum Co 1996–2003), Country Houses Fndn 2004–; govr: NIESR 1991– (memb Exec Ctee 2001–), London Business Sch 1993–2001; dir Liverpool Playhouse 1982–87; vice-pres Liverpool Sch of Tropical Med 1988–; memb: Cncl Univ of Liverpool 1985–88, Advsy Ctee Tate Gallery Liverpool 1988–92, Cncl Industrial Soc 1993–99, Int Advsy Cncl Asia House 1996–; govr Shrewsbury Sch 1983–2003 (dep chm 1997–2003), tstee Shrewsbury Sch Fndn 1990–2006; Hon Dr Marlboro Coll VT 2005; FRSA 1994; *Recreations* cricket, mountain walking, woodland gardening, museums, reading; *Clubs* Brooks's, Denham Golf, MCC; *Style—* Nicholas Barber, Esq, CBE; ✉ 6 Lytton Court, 14 Barter Street, London WC1A 2AH

BARBER, Pamela; da of Harold Nunwick (d 1982), and Muriel, *née* Deighton (d 1996); *b* 8 May 1947; *Educ* Belle Vue Girls' GS Bradford, NW Poly London (BA), Univ of Leeds (PGCE); *m* 1995, Paul Barker; *Career* teacher Belle Vue Girls' Comp Bradford 1969–80 (promoted head of geography and head of sixth form), dep head Crossley Porter Sch Halifax 1980–85, dep head Crossley Heath Sch Halifax 1985–87, headteacher Lancaster Girls' GS 1987–, boarding headteacher Admty Interview Bd RN 1992–2005; Lancaster Univ: memb Court 1987–, memb Cncl 1989–95; non-exec dir Lancaster AHA 1990–93; *Recreations* foreign travel, horse riding, fell walking, gardening; *Style—* Mrs Pamela Barber; ✉ Lancaster Girls' Grammar School, Regent Street, Lancaster LA1 1SF (tel 01524 32010, fax 01524 846220, e-mail lggs@lggs.lancs.sch.uk)

BARBER, Ralph Gordon; s of John Leslie Barber, and Margaretta Primrose, *née* Sanders (d 2003); *b* 2 January 1951; *m* Elizabeth Anne Barber; *Career* co sec: The Hongkong and Shanghai Banking Corporation 1986–92, HSBC Holdings plc 1990–, HSBC Bank plc 1994–96; FCIS, FRSA; *Clubs* The Hong Kong Golf; *Style—* Ralph Barber, Esq; ✉ HSBC Holdings plc, 8 Canada Square, London E14 5HQ (tel 020 7991 0588, fax 020 7991 4639)

BARBER, Dr Richard William; s of Dr Geoffrey Osborn Barber (d 1988), of Dunmow, Essex, and Daphne, *née* Drew (d 1982); *b* 30 October 1941; *Educ* Felsted, Marlborough (sr scholarship), CCC Cambridge (MA, PhD, Trevelyan scholarship); *m* 1970, Helen Rosemary, *née* Tolson; 1 s (Humphrey Thomas b 1974), 1 da (Elaine Mary b 1976); *Career* publisher and author; fndr md Boydell Press (now Boydell & Brewer Ltd) 1969–; founding dir Univ of Rochester Press NY 1989; FRSL 1970, FRHistS 1976, FSA 1978; *Books* Arthur of Albion (1961), Henry Plantagenet (1963), The Knight and Chivalry (1970, Somerset Maugham Award, new edn 1996), The Figure of Arthur (1974), Edward Prince of Wales and Aquitaine (1976), Companion Guide to Southwest France (1977, new edn 1998), A Companion to World Mythology (1979), The Arthurian Legends (1979), King Arthur (1986), Tournaments (with Juliet Barker, 1989), Pilgrimages (1991), The Holy Grail (2004); ed for Folio Soc: Aubrey's Brief Lives (1975), Life and Campaigns of the Black Prince (1979), The Pastons (1981), Fuller's Worthies (1987), The Worlds of John Aubrey (1988), Bestiary (1992), British Myths and Legends (1998), Legends of King Arthur (2000), Edward III's Round Table at Windsor (jtly, 2007), Legends of the Grail (2007); *Recreations* sailing, gardening, travel, music; *Style—* Dr Richard Barber, FSA, FRSL; ✉ Boydell & Brewer Ltd, PO Box 9, Suffolk IP12 3DF

BARBER, Stephen David; s of Dr Frederick Barber (d 2000), and Edith Renate Wolfenstein (d 1987); *b* 15 March 1952; *Educ* Univ Coll Sch, LSE (BScEcon); *m* 1 April 1978, Suzanne Jane, da of Graham Hugh Presland (d 1986); 1 da (Claire Louise b 1982), 1 s (Andrew Charles b 1985); *Career* ptnr Price Waterhouse 1985–98 (joined 1973), finance dir Mirror Gp plc 1998–99, ptnr Ernst & Young 2000–05, chief operating offr Whitehead Mann Gp Ltd 2006–; non-exec dir Next plc 2007–; FCA; *Recreations* family, skiing, running, tennis, films; *Style—* Steve Barber, Esq; ✉ Sunbury, Fitzroy Park, London N6 6HX (tel 020 8348 5772, fax 020 8340 1366, e-mail steve@barber.uk.com)

BARBER, His Hon Judge Trevor Wing; s of Robert Barber, and Margaret Barber; *b* 10 June 1943; *Educ* Worksop Coll, King's Coll Newcastle upon Tyne (LLB); *m* 1967, Judith Penelope, *née* Downey; 1 s, 1 da; *Career* called to the Bar Inner Temple 1967; in practice Sheffield 1967–92, circuit judge (NE Circuit) 1992–; *Recreations* gardening, golf, reading; *Style—* His Hon Judge Barber; ✉ Lord Chancellor's Office, House of Lords, London SW1A 0PW

BARBER OF TEWKESBURY, Baron (Life Peer UK 1992), of Gotherington in the County of Gloucestershire; Sir Derek Coates Barber; kt (1984); s of Thomas Smith-Barber (d 1967), and Elsie Agnes, *née* Coates (d 1967); descendant of John Coats whose three sons due to a disagreement swore not to bear his name 1870, instead they adopted Coates, Cotts and Coutts; *b* 17 June 1918; *Educ* RAC Cirencester; *m* 1 (m dis 1981); m 2, 1983, Rosemary Jennifer Brougham, da of Lt Cdr Randolph Brougham Pearson, RN (ka 1946); *Career* farmer and land conslt; fndr memb Farming & Wildlife Advsy Gp 1969, environment conslt Humberts Chartered Surveyors 1972–93, chm BBC's Central Agric Advsy Ctee 1974–80, conslt Humberts Landplan 1974–89, chm Countryside Cmmn 1981–91, chm Booker plc Countryside Advsy Bd 1990–96; pres: Glos Naturalists Soc 1982–2005, RSPB 1990–91 (chm 1976–81, vice-pres 1982–98), Royal Agric Soc of England 1991–92, The Hawk and Owl Tst 1992–96, Br Pig Assoc 1995–97; vice-pres Ornithology Soc of Middle East 1987–97, patron Lancs Heritage Tst 1990–, tstee Farming and Wildlife Tst 1984–91; chm New Nat Forest Advsy Bd 1991–95, dep chm The Groundwork Fndn 1985–91; memb: Bd Centre for Econ and Environmental Devpt 1983–99, Advsy Ctee Centre for Agric Strategy 1985–88, Cncl Br Tst for Ornithology 1987–89, Cncl Rare Breeds Survival Tst 1987–93 (pres 1991–95 and 1997–99); John Haygarth Gold Medal in Agric 1939, Bledisloe Gold Medal for Distinguished Servs to UK Agric 1969, RSPB Gold Medal for Servs to Wildlife Conservation 1983, Massey-Ferguson Agric Award 1989, RASE Gold Medal for Distinguished Service to Agric 1991; Queen's Silver Jubilee Medal 1977; Hon DSc Univ of Bradford 1986; Hon FRASE 1986; *Books* Farming for Profits (with Keith Dexter, 1961), Farming in Britain Today (with Frances and J G S Donaldson, 1969), Farming and Wildlife: a Study in Compromise (1971), A History of Humberts (1980); *Recreations* birds, farming; *Clubs* Farmers'; *Style—* The Rt Hon Lord Barber of Tewkesbury; ✉ House of Lords, London SW1A 0PW

BARBIERI, Margaret Elizabeth; da of Ettore Barbieri, and Lea Barbieri; *b* 2 March 1947; *Educ* Durban, Royal Ballet Sr Sch; *m* 1982, Iain Webb, soloist with the Royal Ballet; 1 s (Jason Alexander b July 1987); *Career* Sadler's Wells Royal Ballet: joined 1965, princ 1970, sr princ 1974–90; guest artist with Birmingham Royal Ballet 1990 and 1991; prodr, freelance teacher and coach 1990–, dir Classical Graduates Course London Studio Centre, artistic dir Images of Dance Co 1990–, govr Royal Ballet 1992–2000; since 1990 has staged: Ashton's Façade, De Valois' Rake's Progress, Cranko's Pineapple Poll, Markova's Les Sylphides, Petipa's Raymonda Act III and Kingdom of the Shades Act from La Bayadère, Swan Lake Act II, Paquita Act II, La Corsaire Act III, Ashton's Façade (K Ballet Co Japan 2003, Oregon Ballet Theatre 2004), Nureyev's Raymonda Act III (K Ballet Co Japan 2003); appeared with Royal Ballet throughout Europe and in Canada, USA, South America, Australia, New Zealand, China, Japan, Yugoslavia, India, Egypt, Israel and elsewhere; made guest appearances in USA, Germany, South Africa, France, Norway and Czechoslovakia; *Performances* with Royal Ballet incl: Giselle (first performance in the role at Covent Garden 1968), Sleeping Beauty (first performance Leeds 1969), Swan Lake (first performance Frankfurt 1977), Romeo and Juliet (first performance Covent Garden 1979), Papillon, The Taming of the Shrew, Coppélia, Les Sylphides, Raymonda Act III, Le Spectre de la Rose, La Vivandière, Petrushka, Ashton's La Fille Mal Gardée, Two Pigeons, The Dream, Façade, Wedding Bouquet and Rendezvous, Cranko's Lady and the Fool, Card Game and Pineapple Poll, MacMillan's The Invitation and Solitaire, Elite Syncopation, Summer in The Four Seasons, de Valois' Checkmate and The Rake's Progress, van Manen's Grosse Fugue and Tilt, Tudor's The Lilac Garden, Howard's Fête Étrange, Layton's Grand Tour, Hynd's Summer Garden, both Killar's and Rodrigues' Cinderella; created roles in ballets incl: Tudor's Knight Errant, Drew's From Waking Sleep, Sacred Circles and The Sword, Cauley's Ante-Room, Layton's Oscar Wilde, Thorpe's Game Piano, Killar's The Entertainers, Hynd's Charlotte Brontë, Wright's Summertide, Bintley's Metamorphosis and Flowers of the Forest, Corder's The Wand of Youth; *Recreations* classical music, theatre, gardening; *Style—* Miss Margaret Barbieri; ✉ c/o London Studio Centre, 42–50 York Way, London N1 9AB

BARBOUR, James Jack; OBE (1992); s of Thomas Jack Barbour (d 1985), and Flora Jean Barbour (d 1999); *b* 16 January 1953; *Educ* Madras Coll, Univ of Strathclyde (BA); *Partner* Julie Barnes; *Career* grad mgmnt trainee NHS Scotland 1977–79, admin Gtr Glasgow Health Bd 1979–83, unit admin Gt Ormond St Hosps 1983–86, gen mangr Royal Manchester Children's Hosp 1986–87, gen mangr Acute Servs Grampian Health Bd 1987–92; chief exec: Aberdeen Royal Hosps NHS Tst 1992–94, Central Manchester Healthcare NHS Tst 1994–98, Sheffield HA 1998–2001, Lothian NHS Bd 2001–; hon prof: Queen Margaret Univ Edinburgh 2002–; burgess City of Aberdeen; EEC exchange scholarship W Germany 1981, alumnus London Business Sch 1989; memb RSA; founding fell Inst of Contemporary Scot 2001; *Recreations* sport, keeping fit; *Clubs* Royal Northern

(Aberdeen); *Style*— James Barbour, Esq, OBE; ✉ Lothian NHS Board, Deaconess House, 148 Pleasance, Edinburgh EH8 9RS (tel 0131 536 9001)

BARCLAY, Sir Colville Herbert Sanford; 14 Bt (NS 1668), of Pierston, Ayrshire; s of late Rt Hon Sir Colville Adrian de Rune Barclay, KCMG, 3 s of 11 Bt; suc unc, Sir Robert Cecil de Belzim Barclay, 13 Bt, 1930; *b* 7 May 1913; *Educ* Eton, Trinity Coll Oxford (MA); *m* 1949, Rosamond Grant Renton, da of late Dr Walter Armstrong Elliott; 3 s (Robert Colraine b 1950, Alistair James Elliott b 1952, Colville Edwin Ward b 1956); *Heir* s, Robert Barclay; *Career* third sec HM Dip Serv 1937–41; enlisted Navy 1941, Sub-Lt RNVR 1942, Lt 1943, Lt Cdr 1945, demobbed 1946; painter; exhibitor: Royal Acad, RBA, London Gp, Bradford City Gallery, Brighton Gallery; chm Royal London Homoeopathic Hosp 1970–74 (vice-chm 1961–65); plant-hunting expeditions to Crete, Turkey, Cyprus, Réunion, Mauritius and Nepal 1966–81; *Books* Crete: Checklist of Vascular Plants (1986); *Recreations* gardening; *Style*— Sir Colville Barclay, Bt; ✉ 23 High Street, Broughton, Stockbridge, Hampshire SO20 8AE (tel 01794 301650)

BARCLAY, Sir David Rowat; kt (2000); s of Frederick Hugh Barclay (d 1947), and Beatrice Cecilia, *née* Taylor (d 1989); er twin bro of Sir Frederick Barclay, *qv*; *b* 27 October 1934, Hammersmith, London; *Career* real estate agent and prop Hillgate Estate Agents (later became Barclays Hotels) in 1960s and 1970s (hotels owned since incl Londonderry, Lowndes, Grosvenor, Charing Cross and Great Western); jt prop (with bro, Frederick): Howard Hotel 1975–2000, Ellerman Gp 1983–, Gotaas-Larsen 1988–97, The European newspaper 1992–98, Automotive Financial Gp 1994–, Ritz Hotel 1995–, Scotsman Publications (pubns incl The Scotsman, Scotland on Sunday and Edinburgh Evening News) 1995–2006, The Business newspaper 1998–, Sears (bought with Philip Green) 1999–2000, Littlewoods 2002–, March UK (former GUS Gp catalogue business) 2003–, Telegraph Gp (pubns incl Daily Telegraph, Sunday Telegraph and The Spectator) 2004–, Hotel Mirabeau Monte Carlo; also investor in: Trigen Holdings, MonsterMob, SmartServ Online, Birdstep Technology; co-fndr and tstee The David and Frederick Barclay Fndn (formerly The Barclay Fndn) 1990–; co-owner Brecqhou (an island off Sark, CI) 1993–; Hon Dr Univ of Glasgow 1998; Offr Order of St Charles (Monaco) 2000; *Style*— Sir David Barclay; ✉ Le Montaigne, 7 avenue de Grande Bretagne, Monte Carlo 98000, Monaco

BARCLAY, Sir Frederick Hugh; kt (2000); s of Frederick Hugh Barclay (d 1947), and Beatrice Cecilia, *née* Taylor (d 1989); yr twin bro of Sir David Barclay, *qv*; *Career* real estate agent with bro David's co Hillgate Estate Agents (later became Barclays Hotels) in 1960s (appointed dir 1968, hotels co-owned since incl Londonderry, Lowndes, Grosvenor, Charing Cross and Great Western); jt prop (with bro, David): Howard Hotel 1975–2000, Ellerman Gp 1983–, Gotaas-Larsen 1988–97, The European newspaper 1992–98, Automotive Financial Gp 1994–, Ritz Hotel 1995–, Scotsman Publications (pubns incl The Scotsman, Scotland on Sunday and Edinburgh Evening News) 1995–2006, The Business newspaper 1998–, Sears (bought with Philip Green) 1999–2000, Littlewoods 2002–, March UK (former GUS Gp catalogue business) 2003–, Telegraph Gp (pubns incl Daily Telegraph, Sunday Telegraph and The Spectator) 2004–, Hotel Mirabeau Monte Carlo; also investor in: Trigen Holdings, MonsterMob, SmartServ Online, Birdstep Technology; co-fndr and tstee The David and Frederick Barclay Fndn (formerly The Barclay Fndn) 1990–; co-owner Brecqhou (an island off Sark, CI) 1993–; Hon Dr Univ of Glasgow 1998; Offr Order of St Charles (Monaco) 2000; *Style*— Sir Frederick Barclay; ✉ Le Montaigne, 7 avenue de Grande Bretagne, Monte Carlo 98000, Monaco

BARCLAY, Humphrey; s of John Barclay, and Patricia Slade; cous of Julian Slade; *b* 24 March 1941, Dorking, Surrey; *Educ* Harrow (head of sch), Trinity Coll Cambridge (BA); *Career* TV prodr; dir Cambridge Circus (Cambridge Footlights Revue starring John Cleese, *qv*, Graham Chapman, Tim Brooke-Taylor, *qv*, and Bill Oddie) West End, NZ and Broadway 1963; joined BBC Radio 1963 (prodr first 50 episodes I'm Sorry, I'll Read That Again), Rediffusion TV 1967–68 (invented Do Not Adjust Your Set (winner Prix Jeunesse 1968) starring Eric Idle, Terry Jones, Terry Gilliam and Michael Palin, Esq, CBE, *qqv*), LWT 1968–83 (head of comedy 1977–83), jtly estab ind prodn co Humphrey Barclay Prodns 1983, controller of comedy LWT 1996–99, head of comedy devpt Granada Media Int 1999–2000, devpt exec (comedy) Celador Prodns 2002–; assoc Limehouse Prodns 1983, sometime script ed Video Arts; progs produced for LWT incl: We Have Ways of Making You Laugh, The Complete and Utter History of Britain, No! No! No!, Doctor in the House, Hark at Barker (pairing Ronnie Barker, Esq, OBE and David Jason, Esq, OBE, *qv*), Six Dates with Barker, No - Honestly, Yes - Honestly, Pig in the Middle, The Pink Medicine Show, Two's Company, A Fine Romance, Bless Me Father, Now and Then, Agony (starring Maureen Lipman, CBE, *qv*, Best Situation Comedy Banff TV Festival), The Strange Case of the End of the World as We Know It, Metal Mickey, End of Part One (nominated Int Emmy Award), Whoops Apocalypse (Most Original Prog Award RTS), Maggie and Her, The Glums, Stanley Baxter's Christmas Box, Holding the Fort, The Top Secret Life of Edgar Briggs, Luck Feller, Mixed Blessings, Canned Laughter, Peter Cook and Co (Gold medal NY Film and TV Festival), No Problem!, Hale and Pace, Faith in the Future, Saturday Live, Blind Men, The People vs Jerry Sadowitz, Duck Patrol, Can We Still Be Friends?, Bostock's Cup, Jack and the Beanstalk, Cinderella, Spaced; progs produced for Humphrey Barclay Prodns: Party at the Palace, Relative Strangers (nominated Int Emmy Award, Silver Medal NY Film and TV Festival), Hot Metal, Thompson, Behaving Badly, Look Back in Anger, Surgical Spirit, Up The Garden Path, Conjugal Rites, What You Looking At?, Desmond's (Team Award and Silver Medal RTS, Br Comedy Best Sitcom Award), That's Love; progs produced for Limehouse Prodns: Short Vehicle, Up For Grabs, Celebration, Dream Stuffing; developed for Granada Media Int: Living Off Larry, Whetfish, Sit Down Shut Up; juror: BAFTA, Montreux Int Festival, RTS, Race in the Media Awards, Olivier Awards; ran comedy writing workshops in Johannesburg, Cape Town and Accra; adopted in the Ghanaian Royal family of Asona 2000, given the name Kwadwo Ameyaw Gyearbuor Yiadom I and appointed Nkosuohene (devpt chief) Kwahu Tafo 2001, fndr and chair Friends of Tafo 2002–; Freeman City of London, Liveryman Worshipful Co of Fishmongers; *Recreations* watercolour painting, theatre, travelling; *Clubs* Garrick; *Style*— Humphrey Barclay, Esq; ✉ website www.friendsoftafo.org

BARCLAY, James Christopher; OBE (2006); s of Theodore David Barclay (d 1981), and Anne Millard, *née* Bennett (d 1996); *b* 7 July 1945; *Educ* Harrow; *m* 1974, Rolleen Anne, da of Lt-Col Walter Arthur Hastings Forbes (d 1987); 2 c; *Career* served 15/19 King's Royal Hussars 1964–67; former bill broker; chm and jt md Cater Allen Ltd (bankers) 1981–98, chm Cater Allen Holdings plc 1985–98 (dep chm 1981–85); non-exec chm LTP Trade plc 2001–; dir: M&G Equity Investment Trust plc 1996– (chm 1998–), Abbey National Treasury Services plc 1997–98, Abbey National Offshore Holdings Ltd 1998–2001, Thos Agnew & Sons Ltd 1998–, New Fulcrum Investment Trust plc 1999–2005, UK Debt Management Office 2000–05, Rathbone Bros plc 2003–; chm Liontrust Knowledge Economy Tst plc 2001–03; chm London Discount Market Assoc 1988–90; *Recreations* fishing, shooting, sailing; *Clubs* Pratt's, Boodle's; *Style*— James Barclay, Esq, OBE; ✉ Rivers Hall, Waldringfield, Woodbridge, Suffolk IP12 4QX

BARCLAY, Prof John Martyn Gurney; s of Dr Oliver Rainsford Barclay, of Leicester, and Dorothy, *née* Knott (d 1963); *b* 31 July 1958; *Educ* UCS London, Queens' Coll Cambridge (scholar, MA, PhD); *m* 22 Aug 1981, Diana Jane, da of Sir John Knox; 2 s (Robert James b 14 July 1986, David Timothy b 3 Sept 1988), 1 da (Frances Elizabeth b 14 May 1991); *Career* res student Univ of Cambridge 1981–84; Univ of Glasgow: lectr 1984–96, sr lectr 1996–2000, prof of New Testament and Christian origins Dept of Theology and Religion Studies 2000–03; Lightfoot prof of divinity Univ of Durham 2003–; memb: Studiorum Novi Testamenti Societas 1990, Soc of Biblical Literature 1993; *Books* Obeying the Truth (1988), Jews in the Mediterranean Diaspora (1996), Colossians and Philemon (1998), Flavius Josephus, Translation and Commentary - Vol 10: Against Apion (2006); *Recreations* music, cycling, walking; *Style*— Prof John Barclay; ✉ Department of Theology and Religion, University of Durham DH1 3RS (tel 0191 334 3951, fax 0191 334 3941, e-mail john.barclay@durham.ac.uk)

BARCLAY, Jonathan Robert; DL (Norfolk); s of Robert Charles Sanford Barclay (d 2001), and Camilla, *née* Boughey (d 1997); *b* 9 March 1947, Denham, Bucks; *Educ* Eton, UEA (BA); *m* 28 June 1969, Clare Amabel, *née* Yorke; 1 da (Emily Rose b 2 July 1976), 1 s (Timothy Robert b 23 Dec 1984); *Career* admitted slr 1971; slr Withers London 1971–73; Mills & Reeve: slr 1974–76, ptnr 1976–2007, managing ptnr 1987–91, sr ptnr 1995–2007; chm Britten Sinfonia Ltd, chm Norwich Theatre Royal Ltd, dir The Forum Tst Ltd, dir Barratt & Cooke Ltd, dir R G Carter Hldgs Ltd; memb Law Soc; *Recreations* classical music, theatre, France, golf, skiing; *Clubs* Boodle's, Royal W Norfolk Golf, Aldeburgh Golf; *Style*— Jonathan Barclay, Esq; ✉ Hill House, Wacton, Norfolk NR15 2UE (e-mail jrbarclay@talktalk.net); Mills & Reeve, 1 St James Court, Whitefriars, Norwich NR3 1RU (tel 01603 693211, fax 01603 664670, e-mail jonathan.barclay@mills-reeve.com)

BARCLAY, Prof Leslie William (Les); OBE (1994); s of William Henry Barclay (d 1961), and Dorothy Ellen Jarvis (d 1998); *b* 26 September 1933; *m* 1960, Janet Elizabeth, da of late Cecil Clifford Allen; 2 s (Andrew Leslie b 1963, Philip Jeremy b 1967), 2 da (Susan Elizabeth b 1964, Mary Catherine b 1970); *Career* E K Cole Ltd: apprentice 1950–55, devpt engr 1955–56; undertook Antarctic Expedition Royal Soc Int Geophysical Year 1956–59, with Radio Research Station Slough 1959–60, with Marconi Research Labs 1960–77, various appointments rising to dep dir UK Radiocommunications Agency DTI 1977–94, conslt Radio Regulation and Spectrum Mgmnt Barclay Assoc Ltd 1994–; memb Ind Expert Gp on the Safety of Mobile Phones (Stewart report) 2000, vice-chm Mgmnt Ctee for the Mobile Telecommunications and Health Research Prog, chm DTI Measurement Advsy Ctee 2005–06; visiting prof: Lancaster Univ, Univ of Surrey; Polar Medal 1961, Int Telecommunication Union Silver Medal 1993; FIEE 1966, FREng 1998; *Publications* Ionospheric Physics in Royal Society International Geophysical Antarctic Expedition Halley Bay (1962), Propagation of Radio Waves (2003); *Recreations* hill walking, English folk dancing, amateur radio (call sign G3HTF); *Clubs* Athenaeum; *Style*— Prof Les Barclay, OBE, FREng; ✉ Barclay Associates Ltd, 12 St Stephen's Road, Cold Norton, Chelmsford CM3 6JE (tel 01621 828576, e-mail lesbarclay@iee.org)

BARCLAY, Brig Neil; OBE (2001), DL (Shropshire 1986); s of Eric Lionel Barclay (d 1974), of Chelmsford, Essex, and Muriel Clare, *née* Copeland (d 1975); *b* 18 April 1917; *Educ* private; *m* 27 Sept 1941, Mary Emma (Mollie) (d 2002), da of David Scott-Shurmer (d 1964), of Bicknacre, Essex; 1 s (John Allardice b 7 Aug 1944), 3 da (Jane Allardice b 13 Jan 1947, Mary Allardice b 23 Sept 1954 d 1991, Emma Allardice b 4 Nov 1957); *Career* RHA TA 1933–39, RA and Airborne RA 1939–51; served: Gibraltar, Malta, W Africa, NW Europe (Airborne Landings), India; transferred RAOC 1951; served: Libya, Persia and Gulf States, Iraq, Egypt, Germany, E Africa, SA, S Arabia; Lt-Col 1958, Col 1964, Brig 1968, ret 1972; writer and journalist 1933–39; sr princ planning inspr DOE 1972–89; St John Ambulance Shropshire: cmmr/cdr 1973–90, vice-pres Cncl 1998–2000; caseworker and memb Ctee SSAFA/Forces Help 1974–; vice-pres and princ fund raiser ABF Shropshire 1993–; pres: ACF League Branch 1972–, Worcester Yeomanry Old Comrades Assoc 1995–, Loyal Newport Volunteers 1995–, RA Assoc Branch; FASMC 1962, FIMgt 1968, FCIArb 1973; KStJ 1987; *Recreations* good companions, gardening; *Clubs* Army and Navy, Muthaiga (Nairobi); *Style*— Brig Neil Barclay, OBE, DL; ✉ Strinebrook House, The Hincks, Newport, Shropshire TF10 9HT (tel 01952 604204)

BARCLAY, Prof (Alan) Neil; s of Frank Rodney Barclay, of Dorchester, Dorset, and Betty Cowie, *née* Watson (d 1987); *b* 12 March 1950, Wantage, Oxon; *Educ* Univ of Oxford (BA, DPhil); *m* 10 July 1975, Ella, *née* Quinn; 2 s (Mark Robert b 23 April 1977, Luke Stuart b 3 Jan 1984), 1 da (Alison Tanum b 18 Dec 1979); *Career* post doctoral research fell Univ of Goteborg Sweden 1976–78; Univ of Oxford: MRC scientific staff MRC Cellular Immunology Unit 1978–99, prof of molecular immunology 1998–, MRC external scientist 1999–; fndr and chm Everest Biotech Ltd 1999–; hon memb Scandinavian Soc for Immunology 1993; memb: Biochemical Soc 1978, Br Soc for Immunology 1985, American Soc of Immunologists 2000; *Publications* The Leucocyte Antigens Factsbook (1992 and 1997); author of 120 pubns in scientific jls; *Recreations* running, music, writing children's stories (unpublished); *Style*— Prof Neil Barclay; ✉ Sir William Dunn School of Pathology, University of Oxford, South Parks Road, Oxford OX1 3RE (tel 01865 275598, fax 01865 275591, e-mail neil.barclay@path.ox.ac.uk)

BARCLAY, Patrick; s of Patricia Barclay (d 1978), and Guy Deghy (d 1992); *b* 15 August 1947; *Educ* Dundee HS; *Children* 1 da (Jennifer b 29 Nov 1968), 1 s (Duncan b 9 Nov 1972); *Career* journalist; trainee Evening Telegraph Dundee 1963–64; sub-ed: Evening Express Aberdeen 1965, Scottish Daily Mail 1966, The Sun 1966–67; football reporter and columnist The Guardian 1976–86 (sub-ed 1967–76); football corr: Today 1986, The Independent 1986–90, The Observer 1990–96; football columnist The Sunday Telegraph 1996–; Sports Journalist of the Year British Sports Journalism Awards 1993; *Style*— Patrick Barclay, Esq; ✉ e-mail patrick.barclay@telegraph.co.uk

BARCLAY, His Hon Judge Paul Robert; s of John Alexander Barclay (d 1994), and Mabel Elizabeth, *née* McMullen; *b* 12 December 1948; *Educ* Nottingham HS, St John's Coll Cambridge (MA); *m* 29 July 1972, Sarah Louise, da of Philip Arthur Jones, and Lois Mary Jones (d 1999); 4 c (Alice b 2 June 1975, Luke b 7 April 1977, Anna b 23 July 1979, Sam b 18 Feb 1982); *Career* barrister Albion Chambers Bristol 1972–98, recorder 1996–98 (asst recorder 1992–96), circuit judge (Western Circuit) 1998–; *Recreations* real village cricket; *Style*— His Hon Judge Barclay; ✉ c/o Bristol County Court, Small Street, Bristol BS1 1DA (tel 0117 929 4414)

BARDEN-STYLIANOU, Stephen; s of Eugene Stylianou (d 1983), and Constantia Stylianou, of East London, South Africa; *b* 26 June 1950; *Educ* Paul Roos Gymnasium Stellenbosch, Centre for Applied Social Science Univ of Natal, Harvard Business Sch (PMD), Oxford Sch of Coaching and Mentoring; *m* 1, Aug 1970; 1 c (Sascha b 27 July 1972); m 2, Feb 1979; 2 c (Rishad b 1 Sept 1980, Nuria b 11 Feb 1983), m 3, May 2003, Sibylle, da of Hans Fürchtenicht; *Career* radio and TV broadcaster South Africa 1970–81, prodr London Broadcasting Co 1981–82; TV-AM: journalist 1982–87, managing ed 1988–92, exec dir news 1988–92; gen mangr BSkyB 1992, md and ceo News Datacom Ltd and News Digital Systems Ltd 1992–95; dir 1995–99: Sigma Squared Ltd, Worldpipe Ltd, Millennium New Media Ltd; chief exec Axel Springer TV GmbH 1998–2000, md Axel Springer TV Productions GmbH 1999–2000, ceo Quadriga Worldwide 2000–01, executive coach-mentor 2001–; CIPD: memb Coaching and Mentoring Faculty, memb Working Gp on Advanced Coaching Practictioner Standards; memb Assoc for Coaching; *Clubs* Harvard Club of London; *Style*— Stephen Barden, Esq; ✉ 47 Carlyle Court, Chelsea Harbour, London SW10 0UQ (tel 020 7352 1503, e-mail stephen@stephenbarden.co.uk)

BARDHAN, Dr Karna Dev; OBE (2002); s of Maj-Gen Pramatha Nath Bardhan (d 1966), of Pune, India, and Anima, *née* Chaudhuri; *b* 16 August 1940; *Educ* Christian Med Coll of Vellore Univ of Madras (MB BS), Univ of Oxford (Rhodes scholar, DPhil); *m* 15 Dec 1972, Dr Gouri Bardhan, da of Maj-Gen P Ram Kumar, of Bangalore, India; 1 s (Satyajeet b 11 Nov 1977), 1 da (Suchitra Kaveri b 30 Sept 1980); *Career* house physician Oxford and Hammersmith Hosp London 1968–69, registrar Royal Hosp Sheffield 1969–70, conslt physician Dist Gen Hosp Rotherham 1973–, hon lectr in gastroenterology Sheffield Univ 1973– (lectr in med 1970–72); memb: Br Soc of Gastroenterology, Assoc of Physicians of GB and Ireland, American Gastroenterological Assoc, American Coll of Gastroenterology, American Coll of Physicians; FRCP, FACP; *Books* Perspectives in Duodenal Ulcer (1980), Topics in Peptic Ulcer Disease (ed, 1987), Non-Responders in Gastroenterology (ed 1991); *Recreations* photography; *Style*— Dr K D Bardhan, OBE; ✉ District General Hospital, Moorgate Road, Rotherham S60 2UD (tel 01709 820000, fax 01709 824168)

BARFIELD, Julia Barbara; MBE (2000); da of Arnold Robert Barfield, and Iolanthe Mary Barfield; *b* 15 November 1952; *Educ* Godolphin & Latymer Sch, AA Sch of Architecture; *m* 17 July 1981, David Joseph Marks, MBE, RIBA, *qv*; 1 s, 2 da; *Career* architect; Tetra Ltd 1978–79, Richard Rogers Partnership 1979–81, Foster Associates 1981–88, Marks Barfield Architects 1989–, London Eye Co (formerly Millennium Wheel Co) 1994–2006, Spiral Cafe Lightbox Brighton i360; subject of and contrib to TV and radio progs incl: The Biggest Wheel in the World (BBC2) 1999, The Millennium Wheel (Discovery) 2000, Wheel (Channel 4) 2000 and 2001, Women in Architecture (Channel 4) 2001; delivered numerous lectures at instns worldwide; assessor: Civic Tst Awards, RIBA Awards; memb Lambeth Democracy Cmmn 2000–01; memb: Cncl AA, Design Review Panel CABE, Thames Gateway Panel; memb ARCUK, RIBA; *Exhibitions* Tower Power Architecture Fndn, Royal Acad of Arts (annually) 1997–2001 and 2003–06, Sustainable London, RIBA, Materials Gallery Sci Museum (permanent exhbn); *Awards* Special Commendation Prince Philip Designers Prize 2000, American Inst of Architects Design Award 2000, Corus Construction Award 2000, Dupont Benedictus Award for Innovation 2000, London First Millennium Award 2000, People's Choice Award London Tourism Awards 2000, Tourism for Tomorrow Award 2000, Leisure Property Forum Award 2000, RIBA Award 2000, 2004 and 2006, RICS Award 2000, Walpole Award 2001, Euro Award for Steel Structures 2001, Silver and Gold D&AD Awards 2001, Design Week Special Award 2001, Blueprint Award 2001, Pride of Britain Award for Innovation 2001, Architectural Practice of the Year 2001, Queens Award for Enterprise 2003, CoolBrands (annually) 2003–06, Places and Genius overall winner BDI Awards 2005, Civic Tst Award 2006; *Recreations* family, travel, the Arts; *Style*— Ms Julia Barfield, MBE, RIBA; ✉ Marks Barfield Architects, 50 Bromells Road, London SW4 0BG (tel 020 7501 0180, e-mail jbarfield@marksbarfield.com)

BARHAM, His Hon Judge (Geoffrey) Simon; s of Denis Patrick Barham (d 1978) and Pleasance, *née* Brooke (d 2004); *b* 23 December 1945; *Educ* Malvern Coll, Christ's Coll Cambridge (MA); *m* 18 Sept 1976, Sarah, da of Rev Godfrey Seebold; 1 da (Lucy b 1979), 1 s (Thomas b 1980); *Career* called to the Bar Lincoln's Inn 1968; recorder of the Crown Court 1987–93, circuit judge (SE Circuit) 1993–; *Clubs* Norfolk; *Style*— His Hon Judge Barham; ✉ Norwich Combined Court Centre, Bishopgate, Norwich NR3 1UR

BARI, Dr Muhammad Abdul; MBE (2003); s of M Manikuddin (d 1999), and Karima Un Nessa (d 1969); *b* 2 October 1953, Bangladesh; *Educ* Univ of Chittagong Bangladesh (BSc, MSc), KCL (PhD, PGCE), Open Univ (Cert); *m* 10 Oct 1981; 4 c; *Career* offr Bangladesh Air Force 1978–82, physics researcher Royal Holloway Coll 1987–90, science teacher Haringey 1991–96, specialist teacher Tower Hamlets 1997–; memb: Muslim Cncl of Britain, Islamic Forum Europe, East London Mosque, London Muslim Centre, Muslim Aid, LOCOG (London Organising Ctee Olympic Games 2012); FRSA 2005; *Books* Building Muslim Families (2002), A Guide to Parenting (2003), Race, Religion and Muslim Identity in Britain (2005); *Recreations* reading, gardening, community work; *Style*— Dr Muhammad Abdul Bari, MBE, FRSA; ✉ 85 Harford Street, London E1 4PY (tel 020 7364 6452)

BARING, Sir John Francis; 3 Bt (UK 1911), of Nubia House, Northwood, Isle of Wight; s of Capt Raymond Alexander Baring (d 1967), and Margaret Fleetwood, OBE, JP, DL, *née* Cambell-Preston (who m 2, 6 Earl of Malmesbury and d 1994); suc unc Sir Charles Christian Baring, 2 Bt (d 1990); *b* 21 May 1947; *m* 1971 (m dis 2005), Elizabeth Anne, yr da of late Robert David Henle Pillitz, of Buenos Aires, Argentina; 2 s (Julian Alexander David b 1975, James Francis b 1984), 1 da (Andrea Hermione b 1977); *Heir* s, Julian Baring; *Career* Citibank NA 1971–72, Chemical Bank 1972–84, Kidder Peabody & Co 1984–89, GPA Group Ltd 1989, Hackman Baring & Co 1991–97, HB Communications Acquisition Corp (now Source Media Inc) 1993–95, Coopers & Lybrand Securities LLC (now PricewaterhouseCoopers Securities LLC) 1997–99, Mercator Capital LLC 1999–2004, Camphile Village USA Inc 2007–; *Recreations* fishing, gardening; *Style*— Sir John Baring, Bt; ✉ 328 Arcadia Drive, Ancramdale, NY 12503

BARING, Louise Olivia; da of Aubrey George Adeane Baring (d 1987), and Marina, *née* Bessel; *b* 28 July 1957; *Educ* Queen's Gate Sch; *m* 5 Feb 1997, Eric Franck, s of Louis Franck (d 1988), and Evelyn, *née* Aeby; *Career* journalist; letters arts and home affrs writer Britain section The Economist 1983–89, commissioning ed You magazine The Mail on Sunday 1989–90, asst features ed The Independent on Sunday 1990–93, feature writer Condé Nast Publications 1994– (contrib ed 1997–2005), arts contrib Daily Telegraph 2005–; *Books* Martine Franck (2007); *Style*— Ms Louise Baring; ✉ 7 Victoria Square, London SW1W 0QY (tel 020 7630 5972, e-mail lbaring@zoo.co.uk)

BARING, Nicholas Hugo; CBE (2003); s of Francis Anthony Baring (ka 1940), and Lady Rose Gwendolen Louisa McDonnell DCVO (d 1993); *Educ* Eton, Magdalene Coll Cambridge; *m* 1972, Elizabeth Diana, *née* Crawfurd; 3 s; *Career* late Lt Coldstream Gds; md Baring Brothers 1963–68, Barings plc 1968–89; dir Northern & Employers Assurance Co 1966, dir Commercial Union (following merger) 1968–98 (chm 1990–98); chm The Baring Fndn 1998–; chm Bd of Tstees Nat Gallery 1992–96; tstee Fitzwilliam Museum Tst 1997–; memb Cncl Nat Tst 1978–2002; *Style*— N H Baring, Esq, CBE; ✉ The Baring Foundation, 60 London Wall, London EC2M 5TQ (tel 020 7767 1136)

BARING, Hon Mrs (Susan Mary); OBE (1984), JP (Hants 1965); da of 1 Baron Renwick, KBE (d 1973); *b* 5 June 1930; *m* 1955 (m dis 1984), Hon John Francis Harcourt Baring, now 7 Baron Ashburton; 2 s, 2 da; m 2, 1997, Andre Newburg; *Career* chm Br Inst of Human Rights 1989–2004, memb Parole Bd for England and Wales 1971–74 and 1979–83, chm Hampshire Probation Ctee 1978–82, vice-chm Central Cncl of Probation Ctees 1979–82, vice-chm Inner London Probation Ctee 1999–2001 (chm 1996–99); tstee: Howard League for Penal Reform 1978–, Liberty 2004–; prospective Parly candidate: (Alliance) Reading East 1987, (Lib Dem) East Hampshire 1992; pres Hampshire Assoc of Youth Clubs 1977–79; devpt offr Richmond Fellowship 1984–86; memb Cncl KCL 1979–94, vice-chm Delegacy King's Coll Med Sch 1989–95, memb Wellbeing Cncl 1993–95; chm Nat Birthday Tst 1989–93, memb London Action Tst 1992–2004; memb Bd Almeida Theatre 1993–2003, tstee Children's Music Workshop 2001–; *Recreations* gardening, reading, music, family; *Style*— The Hon Mrs Baring, OBE; ✉ 18 Cleveland Square, London W2 6DG (tel 020 7706 1806, fax 020 7706 1805, e-mail suebaring@aol.com)

BARKER, Hon Adam Campbell; s of William Alan Barker, of Sandwich, Kent (d 1988), and Rt Hon Baroness Trumpington, DCVO, PC (Life Peer), *qv*; *b* 31 August 1955; *Educ* King's Sch Canterbury, Queens' Coll Cambridge (MA); *m* 1985, Elizabeth Mary, da of Eric Marsden, OBE (d 1996); 1 da (Virginia Giverny b 1987), 1 s (Christopher Adam b 1989); *Career* solicitor and attorney; barr 12 King's Bench Walk 1978–80; assoc Webster & Sheffield NY 1980–90, ptnr Sedgwick Detert Moran & Arnold (NY and London) 1990–; *Recreations* golf, tennis, horse racing (steward: Lingfield Park Racecourse 1992–, Windsor 2007–), bridge; *Clubs* Turf, Royal St George's (Sandwich), Hurlingham, Pilgrims; *Style*— The Hon Adam Barker; ✉ October Cottage, Town Croft, Hartfield, East Sussex TN7 4AD (tel 01892 770014); Sedgwick Detert Moran & Arnold, 120 Cannon Street, London EC4N 6LR (tel 020 7929 1829)

BARKER, Ann Botsford Callender; da of Frederick Botsford Callender (d 1975), and Louise Esther, *née* Fitzgerald (d 1975); *b* 5 August 1946; *Educ* The Westridge Sch for Girls Pasadena, Mount Holyoke Coll (BA, Phi Beta Kappa, Mary Lyon scholar), Harvard Univ (graduate prize fell, Woodrow Wilson fell, MA, PhD); *m* 1974, Godfrey Raymond Barker, s of H Lindsey Barker; 1 s (Frederick George Lindsey b 1983); *Career* historian; teaching fell Harvard Univ 1970–74, lectr Univ of Maryland 1983–89, memb Parole Bd 1993–, memb Police Complaints Authy 2001–, visiting fell Oxford Univ Centre for Criminological Res 2001–; chm Parole Bd/Assoc of Chief Offrs of Probation Liaison Ctee 1994–2000, vice-chm Central London Police Consultative Ctee 1984–88; JP 1997–2001; vice-chm Mayfair and Soho Conservatives 1979–89, memb Bd Nat Retreat Assoc 1984–86; govr: Soho Parish Sch 1980–89, Liddon Tst 1983–2001 (chm 2001–); memb: Grosvenor Chapel Ctee 1979–93, Circles of Support and Accountability 2000–; assoc All Saints Sisters of the Poor 1988–; *Books* Godly Mayfair (1981), The Debate on Indian Self-Rule 1780–1890 (1987), Paths Through Pain (1999); *Recreations* Bargello needlework; *Clubs* Univ Women's; *Style*— Mrs Ann Barker; ✉ 26 Charles Street, Berkeley Square, London W1J 5DT (tel 020 7409 2124, fax 020 7499 6058, e-mail abcbarker@aol.com); Police Complaints Authority, 10 Great George Street, London SW1P 3AE (tel 020 7273 6422)

BARKER, Anthony; QC (1985); s of late Robert Herbert Barker, of Barlaston, Stoke-on-Trent, Staffs, and Ellen Doreen; *b* 10 January 1944; *Educ* Newcastle-under-Lyme HS, Clare Coll Cambridge (BA); *family* 2 da; m 3, 2005, Vivienne Kate Veale; *Career* called to the Bar Middle Temple 1966, bencher 1997; asst recorder 1981, recorder of the Crown Court 1985–, head of chambers 1995–2002; fell Int Soc of Barristers 1999; *Recreations* gardening, music, walking; *Style*— Anthony Barker, Esq, QC; ✉ Hilderstone House, Hilderstone, Stone, Staffordshire ST15 8SF (tel 01889 505331); 5 Fountain Court, Steelhouse Lane, Birmingham B4 6DR (tel 0121 606 0500)

BARKER, (Brian) Ashley; OBE (1975); s of George Henry Barker (d 1980), of Aley Green, Beds, and Evelyn Dorothy, *née* Chandler (d 1994); *b* 26 May 1927; *Educ* Luton GS, AA London (AADipl); *m* 1, 27 Feb 1960 (m dis 1973); 2 s (James b 1961, David b 1964), 2 da (Rhiannon b 1963, Charlotte b 1967); m 2, 29 May 1973, (Sheila) Ann Margaret, da of Lt-Col George Broadhurst (d 1954), of Cheltenham, Glos; *Career* architect and conslt on historic bldgs; Surveyor of Historic Bldgs GLC (head of div) 1970–86, head London Div Historic Bldgs and Monuments Cmmn for England 1986–88; chm Culverin Holdings Ltd 1988–91; pres Assoc for Studies in the Conservation of Historic Bldgs 2004 (chm 1970–89); memb: London Diocesan Advsy Ctee for the Care of Churches 1978–95, Faculty Jurisdiction Cmmn 1980–84, Cathedrals Advsy Cmmn for England 1986–91, Canterbury Cathedral Fabric Advsy Ctee 1987– (chm 1992–2004), Bd Heritage of London Tst Ltd 1988–97, St Paul's Cathedral Fabric Advsy Ctee 1990–, Bd Taylor Warren Developments Ltd 1994–2004; tstee: Florence Tst 1988–93, Civic Tst 1989–2000; pres Surveyors' Club 1984–85; Freeman City of London 1972, Liveryman Worshipful Co of Chartered Architects 1988 (Master 1993–94); Queen's Silver Jubilee Medal 1977; FSA 1966, FRIBA 1967 (assoc 1949); *Recreations* music, visual arts; *Clubs* Athenaeum; *Style*— Ashley Barker, Esq, OBE, FSA; ✉ 3 South Parade, Penzance, Cornwall TR18 4DJ (tel 01736 361745)

BARKER, His Hon Judge Brian John; QC (1990); s of William Ernest Barker (d 1996); and Irene Gillow; *b* 15 January 1945; *Educ* Strode's Sch Egham, Univ of Birmingham (LLB), Univ of Kansas (MA); *m* 1977, Anne Judith (Hon Mrs Justice Rafferty, DBE), *qv*, 3 da (Camilla 11 April 1980, Edwina 6 Oct 1983, Felicity 7 June 1985); *Career* called to the Bar Gray's Inn 1969; recorder 1985, sr circuit judge 2000–, Common Serjeant of London Central Criminal Court 2005–; memb Senate and Bar Cncl 1976–79, pres Mental Health Review Tbnls 1993, chm Criminal Bar Assoc 1998–2000 (vice-chm 1998); govr Strode's Coll Egham; treas Sir John Cass Fndn 2005–07; Freeman City of London, Common Serjeant City of London 2005, memb Court of Assts Worshipful Co of Coopers, Liveryman Worshipful Co of Cutlers; *Recreations* golf, sheep rearing; *Clubs* Rye Golf, City Livery; *Style*— His Hon Judge Barker, QC; ✉ Central Criminal Court, Old Bailey, London EC4M 7EH

BARKER, Bridget Caroline; da of Michael John Barker, of Wilmslow, Cheshire, and Brenda, *née* Sawdon (d 1987); *b* 7 March 1958; *Educ* Haberdashers' Monmouth Sch for Girls, Univ of Southampton (LLB); *m* Simon Herrtage; 1 da (Alexandra); *Career* admitted slr 1983; Macfarlanes: joined 1981, ptnr 1988, currently head investment funds and fin services; Skadden Arps Slate Meagher & Flom NY 1986–87; memb: Law Soc, Int Bar Soc, Assoc of Women Slrs, City of London Slrs Co; *Recreations* tennis, travel, gardening; *Style*— Ms Bridget Barker

BARKER, Clive; s of Leonard Barker, of Liverpool, and Joan Ruby Revill; *b* 5 October 1952; *Educ* Quarry Bank GS Liverpool, Univ of Liverpool (BA); *Career* playwright, screenwriter, painter, producer, film and theatre director; *Theatre* plays incl Incarnations: Colossus, The History of the Devil, Frankenstein in Love and Forms of Heaven: Crazyface, Subtle Bodies, Paradise Street; *Films* incl: Hellraiser (dir/writer) 1987, Hellraiser II: Hellbound (exec prodr/story) 1988, Nightbreed (dir/writer) 1990, Hellraiser III: Hell on Earth (exec prodr/story) 1992, Candyman (exec prodr/story) 1992, Candyman: Farewell to the Flesh (exec prodr/story) 1995, Lord of Illusions (dir/writer/co-prodr) 1995, Hellraiser IV: Bloodline (exec prodr/story) 1996; *Exhibitions and Art Publications* incl: Clive Barker Illustrator, vol I (text by Fred Burke, 1990), Frontier Tales (LACE LA, 1990), Los Angeles Art Fare (1993), Clive Barker Illustrator vol II (text by Fred Burke, 1993), One Person Show (Bess Cutler Gallery NY, 1993–94), One Person Show (Laguna Art Museum/Gallery, 1995), One Flesh (La Luz de Jesus Gallery 1997), The Weird and The Wicked (La Luz de Jesus Gallery, 1998); *Books* Books of Blood Vols I-III (1984), Vols IV-VI (1985), The Damnation Game (1986), The Hellbound Heart (1986), Weaveworld (1987), The Great and Secret Show (1989), Imajica (1991), The Thief of Always (1992), Everville (1994), Sacrament (1996), Galilee (1998), The Essential Clive Barker (1999), Coldheart Canyon: A Hollywood Ghost Story (2001), Tortured Souls (2001), Abarat (2002), Abarat: Days of Magic, Nights of War (2004); biographies incl: Pandemonium (ed Michael Brown, 1991), Shadows in Eden (ed Steven Jones, 1992); *Style*— Clive Barker, Esq

BARKER, David Edward; s of Edward Reginald Barker, of Radlett, Herts, and Frances Barker, *née* Solly; *b* 28 May 1946; *Educ* Bushey Sch, Watford Art Coll; *m* 9 Oct 1971, Jennifer Ann, da of Ernest Farnham (d 1960), of Morden, Surrey; 1 da (Cassia Eve b 1978), 1 s (Leo Farnham b 1979); *Career* art dir Leo Burnett Ltd London 1966–68, creative gp head J Walter Thompson London and NY 1970–75 (art dir 1968–70); creative dir: Rupert Chetwynd 1975–79, Benton & Bowles London 1979–80, Geers Gross 1980–84; fndr and creative dir Humphreys Bull & Barker 1984–86, fndr and exec creative dir KHBB 1986–90, dir The Reject Shop plc 1990–94, founding ptnr chm and creative dir Mountain View 1998 (formerly Barker and Ralston 1991–98), fndr Ebou Consulting 2003, marketing dir Votiva 2007; memb Ernest and Julio Gallo Global Strategy Bd 2003; *Recreations* motor racing, photography, music; *Clubs* BARC, BRSCC, FOC; *Style*— David Barker, Esq; ✉ Ebou Ltd, High Point, Aldenham, Hertfordshire WD25 8BP (tel 01923 839979, fax 01923 856635)

BARKER, Dennis Malcolm; s of George Walter Barker (d 1970), of Oulton Broad, Suffolk, and Gertrude Edith, *née* Seeley (d 1979); *b* 21 June 1929; *Educ* Royal GS High Wycombe, Lowestoft GS; *m* Sarah Katherine, *née* Alwyn; 1 da (Eleanor Lucy); *Career* journalist and author; Suffolk Chronicle and Mercury 1947–48, East Anglian Daily Times 1948–58, Express and Star Wolverhampton 1958–63 (property ed, theatre and radio critic, columnist), The Guardian 1963– (Midlands corr, then in London, feature writer, columnist, media corr, People profile columnist, obituarist); regular broadcaster BBC Radio Stop The Week programme 1974–77; chm: Home Counties DC 1956–57, Suffolk branch NUJ 1958 (sec 1953–58); memb: Soc of Authors, Broadcasting Press Guild; life memb: NUJ, Writers' Guild of GB; *Books* non-fiction: The People of the Forces Trilogy (Soldiering On 1981, Ruling The Waves 1986, Guarding The Skies 1989), One Man's Estate (1983), Parian Ware (1985), Fresh Start (1990), The Craft of the Media Interview (1998), How To Deal With The Media - A Practical Guide (2000), Seize the Day (contrib, 2001), The Guardian Book of Obituaries (contrib, 2003), Oxford Dictionary of National Biography (contrib, 2004), Tricks Journalists Play (2007); novels: Candidate of Promise (1969), The Scandalisers (1974), Winston Three Three Three (1987), Games with The General (2007); *Recreations* painting, sailing, music, cinema; *Style—* Dennis Barker, Esq; ✉ 67 Speldhurst Road, London W4 1BY (tel 020 8994 5380); The Guardian, 119 Farringdon Road, London EC1R 3ER (tel 020 7278 2332)

BARKER, Prof Eileen Vartan; OBE (2000); da of Calman MacLennan (d 1943), and Mary Helen Muir (d 1972); *b* 21 April 1938; *Educ* Cheltenham Ladies' Coll, Webber Douglas Sch of Singing & Dramatic Art (gold medal), LSE (BSc, PhD); *m* 1958, Peter Johnson Barker, MBE; 2 da (Judith Katherine b 1961 d 2005, Rachel Anna MacLennan b 1963); *Career* LSE: on staff 1970–, dean of undergraduate studies 1982–86, prof of sociology (with special reference to the study of religion) 1992–2003 (now emeritus); fndr and chm Info Network Focus on Religious Movements (INFORM) 1988–; Leverhulme Emeritus Fellowship 2004–07; Hobhouse Meml Prize 1970, SSSR Distinguished Book Award 1985, Martin Marty Award for the Promotion of the Understanding of Religion 2000; pres: Soc for the Scientific Study of Religion 1991–93, London Soc for the Study of Religion 1994–96, Assoc for the Sociology of Religion 2001–02; FBA 1998; *Books* New Religious Movements: A Perspective for Understanding Society (ed, 1982); Of Gods and Men (ed 1983), The Making of a Moonie: Brainwashing or Choice? (1984), LSE on Freedom (ed, 1985), New Religious Movements: A Practical Introduction (1989), Secularization, Rationalism, and Sectarianism (co-ed, 1993), Twenty Years On: Changes in New Religious Movements (co-ed, 1995), New Religions and New Religiosity (co-ed, 1998); *Style—* Prof Eileen Barker, OBE, FBA; ✉ London School of Economics and Political Science, Houghton Street, London WC2A 2AE (tel 020 7955 7289, fax 020 8902 2048, e-mail e.barker@lse.ac.uk)

BARKER, Godfrey Raymond; s of Harold Lindsey Barker (d 1973), and Alys, *née* Singleton (d 1988); *b* 14 April 1945; *Educ* Dulwich Coll, Univ of Cambridge, Univ of Oxford and Cornell Univ (MA, DPhil); *m* 1974 (m dis 2004), Ann, da of Frederick Botsford Callender, of Pasadena, CA; 1 s (Frederick George Lindsey b 28 Oct 1983); *Career* Cons Res Dept 1966–67, second sec UN Dept FO 1972; The Daily Telegraph: joined 1972, parly sketchwriter and leader writer 1981–89, arts ed 1986, arts and political columnist 1989–97; arts columnist Evening Standard 1997–2000; articles in The Times, Daily Telegraph, Die Welt, Sunday Times, The Wall Street Journal, Forbes, The Economist, The Field, Art and Auction, Art Review and Artnews 2000–; lectr in history of the art market Sotheby's 2002–; broadcaster arts progs BBC; *Books* Visions of Europe (with Margaret Thatcher and others, 1993), Sovereign Britain (with Norman Lamont, 1995); *Recreations* campaigning for the National Heritage, opera, lieder, cricket; *Clubs* Beefsteak, Athenaeum; *Style—* Godfrey Barker, Esq; ✉ 26 Charles Street, Berkeley Square, London W1J 5DT (tel 020 7499 8516)

BARKER, Prof Graeme William Walter; s of Reginald Walter Barker (d 1987), and Kathleen, *née* Walton (d 1981); *b* 23 October 1946; *Educ* Alleyn's Sch Dulwich, St John's Coll Cambridge (Henry Arthur Thomas open scholar, BA, MA, PhD), Br Sch at Rome (Rome scholar in classical studies); *m* 3 Jan 1976 (m dis 1991), Sarah Miranda Buchanan; 1 da (Rachel Jessica b 14 Feb 1980), 1 s (Lewis William b 26 May 1983 d 2005); *Career* sr lectr in prehistoric archaeology Univ of Sheffield 1981–84 (lectr 1972–81), dir British Sch in Rome 1984–88; Univ of Leicester: prof and head Sch of Archaeological Studies 1988–2000, grad dean 2000–03, pro-vice-chllr 2003–04; Disney prof of archaeology and dir McDonald Inst for Archaeological Research Univ of Cambridge 2004–; chm Soc for Libyan Studies 1988–94; memb Ed Bds: CUP, Manuals in Archaeology, Jl of Mediterranean Archaeology, The Holocene, Antiquity; major field projects incl: Biferno Valley Survey 1974–80, UNESCO Libyan Valleys Survey 1979–89, Tuscania Survey 1986–91, Wadi Faynan Landscape Survey 1996–2000, Niah Cave Project 2000–; FSA 1979, FBA 1999; *Books* Landscape and Society: Prehistoric Central Italy (1981), Archaeology and Italian Society (co-ed with R Hodges, 1981), Prehistoric Farming in Europe (1985), Beyond Domestication in Prehistoric Europe (co-ed with C Gamble, 1985), Cyrenaica in Antiquity (co-ed with J Lloyd and J Reynolds, 1985), Roman Landscapes (co-ed with J Lloyd, 1991), A Mediterranean Valley: Landscape Archaeology and Annales History in the Biferno Valley (1995), The Biferno Valley Survey: the Archaeological and Geomorphological Record (1995), Farming the Desert: the UNESCO Libyan Valleys Archaeological Survey (with D Gilbertson, B Jones and D Mattingly, vol 1 1996, vol 2 1997), The Etruscans (with T Rasmussen, 1998), Companion Encyclopedia of Archaeology (ed, 1999), The Archaeology of Drylands: Living at the Margin (co-ed with D Gilbertson, 2000), The Archaeology of Mediterranean Landscapes (gen ed with D Mattingly, 5 vols, 2000), The Human Use of Caves in Peninsular and Island Southeast Asia (ed with D Gilbertson, 2005), The Agricultural Revolution in Prehistory: Why did foragers become farmers? 92006); *Recreations* walking, skiing, sailing; *Style—* Prof Graeme Barker, FBA; ✉ The Merchant's House, Pigg Lane, Norwich NR3 1RR (tel 01603 283736); McDonald Institute for Archeological Research, University of Cambridge, Downing Street, Cambridge CB2 3ER (tel 01223 333538, fax 01223 333536)

BARKER, Graham Harold; TD (1985); s of Harold George Barker (d 1962), and Dorothy, *née* Speechley (d 1986); *b* 11 January 1949; *Educ* Cambridge GS, KCL, St George's Hosp Med Sch London (MB BS, AKC); *m* 23 Sept 1978, Esther Louise, da of John Owen Farrow, of Norwich; 1 s (Douglas Graham b 23 June 1982), 1 da (Louise Elizabeth b 9 Jan 1987); *Career* Surgn 217 (L) Gen Hosp RAMC (V) 1973–91, Capt 1974, Maj 1980; lectr Inst of Cancer Res London 1977–79, registrar Queen Charlotte's and Chelsea Hosps London 1980, sr registrar in gynaecology and obstetrics Middx Hosp and UCH 1981–87, sr lectr in Obstetrics and Gynaecology St George's Hosp London 1987–2002, currently conslt gynaecologist and obstetrician Portland Hosp for Women London, Parkside Hosp London and London Bridge Hosp London; memb: Br Soc for Colposcopy and Cervical Pathology, Br Gynaecological Cancer Soc, Chelsea Clinical Soc; Astor fell Harvard Univ Hosps 1984; Freeman City of London, Liveryman Worshipful Soc of Apothecaries 1980; MD 1991; FRCSEd 1979, FRCOG 1993 (MRCOG 1978), FRSM; *Books* Family Health And Medicine Guide (1979), Your Search For Fertility (1981), Chemotherapy of Gynaecological Malignancies (1983), The New Fertility (1986), Your Smear Test - A Guide To Screening, Colposcopy And The Prevention Of Cervical Cancer (1987), Overcoming Infertility (1990); founding ed Obstetrics and Gynaecology Today; *Recreations* classic cars, trumpet, piano; *Style—* Graham Barker, Esq, TD; ✉ 12 Wolsey Close, Kingston upon Thames, Surrey KT2 7ER (tel 020 8942 2614); The Chimes, 11 The Suttons, Cambersands, Rye, East Sussex (e-mail grahambarker@colposcopy.org.uk, website www.colposcopy.org.uk)

BARKER, Greg; MP; *b* 1967, Sussex; *Educ* Steyning GS, Lancing Coll, Univ of London; *Career* early career with Centre for Policy Studies then smaller companies analyst Gerrard Vivian Gray and corporate fin dir Int Pacific Securites, assoc ptnr Brunswick Gp Ltd 1997–98, head int investor rels Siberian Oil Co 1998–2000, dir Bartlett Scott Edgar 1998–2001, MP (Cons) Bexhill and Battle 2001–; memb Environmental Audit Select Ctee 2001–, oppn whip 2003–; *Style—* Greg Barker, Esq, MP; ✉ House of Commons, London SW1A 0AA

BARKER, John Alfred; OBE (2006); s of Alfred Barker (d 1990), of Holborn, London, and Miriam Alice, *née* Kerley (d 1993); *b* 2 December 1929; *Educ* Neale's Mathematical Sch, City of London Coll; *m* 22 Sept 1962, Margaret Coutts (d 1999), da of Thomas Coutts Smith (d 1948), of Stonehouse, Lanark; *Career* Intelligence Corps TA & AVR 1959–69; Stock Exchange 1950–64, Inner London Probation Serv 1965–90, memb Local Review Ctee HMP Wandsworth 1986–90; common councilman City of London Corp: Cripplegate Without 1981–96, Cripplegate Within 1996– (dep 1993–); past master Cripplegate Ward Club; chm: Port Health and Environmental Services Ctee 2002–05, Barbican Centre Ctee 2006–; dep chm City Lands and Bridge House Estates Ctee 2007–08; memb: Bd of Mgmnt Barbican YMCA 1986–2005 (chm 1990–2005), Ct City Univ 2001–, Bd of Mgmnt City YMCA London 2005–, London Local Authy Arts Forum 2006–; govr: Bridewell Royal Hosp 1982–, City of London Sch for Girls 1982–, King Edward's Sch Witley 1989–, Christ's Hosp 1991–; tstee: Soc for Relief of Homeless Poor 1982–, Neale's Educnl Fndn 1983–, Charity of John Land 1983–, Mitchell City of London Charity and Educnl Fndn 1991–, St Luke's Parochial Tst 1995–, City Bridge Tst 1999–, London Rivers Assoc 2004, Thames21 Ltd 2004–; Freeman: City of London 1970, Worshipful Co of Basketmakers 1973; FRGS 1979, FZS 1980, FInstD 1984, MCMI (MIMgt 1985), FRSA 1992; *Recreations* travel, hill and mountain walking, club man; *Clubs* Reform, Guildhall, City Livery, Royal Over-Seas League, Rotary (London), City Pickwick; *Style—* John Barker, Esq, OBE; ✉ 319 Willoughby House, Barbican, London EC2Y 8BL (tel 020 7628 5381)

BARKER, John Edgar; s of Edgar Barker (d 1975), and Hilda, *née* Hitchinson (d 1992); *b* 23 September 1931; *Educ* Christ's Hosp, Royal Coll of Music London, Salzburg Mozarteum (Lovro von Matačič); *Career* conductor; has worked with Br opera cos incl: Glyndebourne Festival (memb music staff), Sadler's Wells (chorus master, conductor), ENO (head of Music Staff, conductor), The Royal Opera (former head Music Staff and head Music Dept); at Covent Garden has conducted: Le Nozze di Figaro, Don Giovanni, Troilus and Cressida, Peter Grimes, Madam Butterfly, Tosca, Turandot, Lucia di Lammermoor, Il Trovatore, La Bohème, La Cenerentola; conductor Royal Ballet 1988–89: Sleeping Beauty, Romeo and Juliet; repertoire at Sadler's Wells and ENO incl: Mozart, Rossini, Saint-Saëns, Verdi, Offenbach, Johann Strauss, Humperdinck, Stravinsky, Wagner (incl the Ring Cycle), Williamson's The Violins of St Jacques and Lucky Peter's Journey (world premiere); conducted: Carmen in Seoul, concert with Baltsa and Carreras in Tokyo on 1986 Far East Tour, two concerts with Domingo Royal Opera House 1988; conducted orchs incl: London Philharmonia, Boston Symphony, Radio Éireann Symphony, Bournemouth Symphony, Orquestra Sinfonica Mexico City, Iceland Symphony Orch 1992; ARCM, GRSM; *Style—* John Barker, Esq

BARKER, Prof John Reginald; s of Thomas Reginald Barker (d 1965), of Bamford, Derbys, and Marjorie, *née* Cutler (d 1979); *b* 11 November 1942; *Educ* New Mills GS, Univ of Edinburgh (BSc), Univ of Durham (MSc), Univ of Warwick (PhD); *m* 11 Aug 1966, Elizabeth Carol, da of George Patrick Maguire; 1 da (Emma Jane b 26 Aug 1970), 2 s (Tom Alexander Patrick b 31 July 1972, John Luke Patrick b 17 March 1974); *Career* SRC res student Dept of Applied Physics Univ of Durham 1966–67, jr res assoc Dept of Physics Univ of Warwick 1967–69, pt/t physics teacher Henry VIII GS Coventry 1968, pt/t lectr Canley Coll of FE; Univ of Warwick: SRC postdoctoral res fell Dept of Physics 1969–70, lectr 1970–84, sr lectr 1984–85; prof of electronics Dept of Electronics and Electrical Engrg Univ of Glasgow 1985–; co-dir: NATO Advanced Study Inst 1979 and 1990, NATO Advanced Res Inst 1982; dir 7th Int Workshop on Computational Electronics 2000; distinguished science lectr Yale Univ 1992; visiting prof: N Texas State Univ 1978, Colorado State Univ 1978–79 (affiliate prof 1979–83); visiting scientist: IBM T J Watson Res Centre NY 1978, NORDITA Neils Bohr Inst Copenhagen 1980, Bell Telephone Laboratories 1980–81, Electronics and Devices Laboratory US Army 1981; former memb of numerous SERC Ctees, presenter Venture series (Central) 1982, various appearances on Tomorrow's World and other science progs; FRSE 1990, FBIS 1992, FRAS 1999; *Publications* Physics of Non-Linear Transport in Semiconductors (1979), Physics of Granular Electronic Systems (1991); also author of over 240 scientific publications; *Recreations* hill walking, reading, cooking, astronomy, Volvo driving; *Style—* Prof John Barker, FRSE; ✉ 45 Hughenden Gardens, Glasgow G12 9YH (tel 0141 338 6026); Nanoelectronics Research Centre, Department of Electronics and Electrical Engineering, University of Glasgow, Glasgow G12 8QQ (tel 0141 330 5221, fax 0141 330 6010, e-mail jbarker@elec.gla.ac.uk)

BARKER, Jonathan David; s of Thomas William Barker, and Dorothy Joan Barker; *b* 17 July 1949; *Educ* Victoria Boys' Sch Watford, Cassio Coll of Futher Educn Watford, Birkbeck Coll London (BA, Frank Newton Prize for English), Poly of N London (Dip Librarianship and Info Science); *m* 23 July 1983, Deirdre Mary, da of Cornelius Joseph Shanahan; *Career* arboriculturalist Whippendell Woods Watford 1969–70, library asst Kensington Central Reference Library 1970–72, poetry librarian Arts Cncl Poetry Library 1973–88, asst sec Poetry Book Soc Ltd 1973–83, dep dir of literature Br Cncl 1988–2006, sr literature conslt Br Cncl 2007–; adjudicator numerous poetry competitions (incl: Arts Cncl Raymond Williams Prize for Publishing 1992 and 1993, Whitbread Book Awards 2002); MCLIP (ALA 1985); *Publications* Arts Council Poetry Library Short-Title Catalogue (6 edn 1981), Selected Poems of W H Davies (ed, 1985, new edn 1992), Poetry Book Society Anthology (ed, 1986), The Art of Edward Thomas (ed, 1987), Thirty Years of The Poetry Book Society - 1956–1986 (ed, 1988), Norman Cameron Collected Poems and Selected Translations (jt ed, 1990), A Select Bibliography of Poetry in Britain and Ireland (1995); contrib various critical articles to reference books and jls; *Recreations* music, gardening, travelling, book collecting; *Style—* Jonathan Barker, Esq; ✉ Literature Department, British Council, 10 Spring Gardens, London SW1A 2BN (tel 020 7389 3165, fax 020 7389 3175)

BARKER, Katharine Mary (Kate); CBE (2006); *b* 29 November 1957; *Educ* Stoke-on-Trent Sixth Form Coll, St Hilda's Coll Oxford; *m* 1982, Peter Donovan; 2 s (b 1988, b 1990); *Career* investment analyst Post Office Pension Fund 1979–81, res offr NIESR 1981–85, chief Euro economist Ford of Europe 1985–94, chief econ advsr CBI 1994–2001, non-exec dir Yorkshire Building Society 1999–2001, memb Monetary Policy Ctee Bank of England 2001–; commissioned by Govt to conduct ind review of UK Housing Supply 2003, ind review of Land Use Planning 2006; memb: HM Treasy independent panel of economic forecasting advsrs 1996–97, Bd of Tstees Anglia Ruskin Univ 1999–, Bd Housing Corporation 2004–; chair FA Fin Advsy Ctee 2003–; *Recreations* bell ringing; *Style—* Ms Kate Barker, CBE

BARKER, Prof Kenneth; CBE (1994); s of Thomas William Barker, and Lillian Barker; *b* 26 June 1934; *Educ* Royal Coll of Music (GRSM, ARCM), King's Coll London (BMus), Univ of Sussex (MA); *m* 1958, Jean Ivy Pearl; 1 s, 1 da; *Career* sch master 1958–62, lectr and univ teacher 1962–75, princ Gipsy Hill Coll 1975, pro-dir Kingston Poly 1975–86, dir Leicester Poly 1987–92 (dep dir 1986–87), chief exec and vice-chllr De Montfort Univ 1992–99, vice-chllr Thames Valley Univ 1999–2004; Liveryman Worshipful Co of Framework Knitters; Hon DSc, Hon DUniv, HonDEd; FRSA, FTCL, FLCM, CIMgt; *Recreations* music, theatre, watching rugby; *Clubs* Athenaeum, Reform, IOD; *Style—* Prof Kenneth Barker, CBE; ✉ Bramshott, Church Road, Long Ditton, Surbiton KT6 5HH (tel 020 8398 4700)

BARKER, Nicolas John; OBE (2002); s of Sir Ernest Barker (d 1960), and Olivia Stuart, *née* Horner (d 1976); *b* 6 December 1932; *Educ* Westminster, New Coll Oxford (MA); *m* 11

Aug 1962, Joanna Mary Nyda Sophia, da of Col Henry Edward Mariano Cotton, OBE (d 1988); 2 s (Christian b 1964, Cosmo b 1973), 3 da (Emma b 1963, Olivia b 1963, Cecilia b 1969); *Career* with Bailliere Tindall & Cox and Rupert Hart-Davis 1959, asst keeper Nat Portrait Gallery 1964, with Macmillan & Co Ltd 1965, with OUP 1971, dep keeper British Library 1976–92, libraries advsr to Nat Tst 1992–2000; William Andrews Clark visiting prof UCLA 1986–87, Sandars reader in bibliography Univ of Cambridge 1999–2000; pres: Amici Thomae Mori 1978–89, Double Crown Club 1980–81, Bibliographical Soc 1981–85; chm: Laurence Sterne Tst 1984–, London Library 1994– (memb Ctee 1971–), Library Ctee RHS 1996–; ed The Book Collector 1965–; memb: Publication Bd of Dirs RNIB 1969–92, Appeals Advsy Ctee BBC and ITV 1977–86, Arts Panel Nat Tst 1979–92; tstee The Pilgrim Tst 1977–; Panizzi Lectures Br Museum 2001, Rosenbach Lectures Univ of PA 2002; Hon DUniv York 1994; FBA 1998; *Books* The Publications of the Roxburghe Club (1962), The Printer and the Poet (1970), Stanley Morison (1972), Essays and Papers of ANL Munby (ed, 1977), The Early Life of James McBey - An Autobiography 1883–1911 (ed, 1977), Bibliotheca Lindesiana (1977), The Oxford University Press and the Spread of Learning 1478–1978 (1978), A Sequel to an Enquiry (with John Collins, 1983), Aldus Manutius and the Development of Greek Script and Type (1985), The Butterfly Books (1987), Two East Anglian Picture Books (1988), Treasures of the British Library (compiler, 1989), S Morison: Early Italian Writing-Books (ed, 1990), Medieval Pageant (with A Wagner and A Payne, 1993), Hortus Eystettensis: The Bishop's Garden and Besler's Magnificent Book (1994), The Great Book of Thomas Trevilian (2000), Form and Meaning in the History of the Book (2002); *Clubs* Garrick, Beefsteak; *Style*— Nicolas Barker, Esq, OBE, FBA; ✉ 22 Clarendon Road, London W11 3AB (tel 020 7727 4340)

BARKER, Patricia Margaret (Pat); CBE (2000); da of Moira Drake; *b* 8 May 1943; *Educ* Grangefield GS, LSE (BSc); *m* 29 Jan 1978, David Faubert Barker, s of Faubert Barker (d 1980); 1 s (John b 1970), 1 da (Annabel b 1974); *Career* novelist; jt winner Fawcett Prize 1983, elected one of twenty Best of British Young Novelists 1983, Guardian Fiction Prize 1993, Special Award Northern Electric Arts Awards 1993, Booksellers' Association Author of the Year Award 1996, Die Welt Literatur-Preis 2000; Hon MLitt Univ of Teesside 1993; Hon DLitt: Napier Univ 1996, Univ of Hertfordshire 1998, Univ of Durham 1998, Univ of London 2002, Univ of Leicester 2006; Hon Dr Open Univ 1997; memb: Soc of Authors 1983, PEN 1989; FRSL 1995; *Books* Union Street (1982, filmed as Stanley and Iris 1990 starring Robert de Niro and Jane Fonda), Blow Your House Down (1984), The Century's Daughter (1986, re-titled Liza's England 1996), The Man Who Wasn't There (1989), Regeneration (1991, filmed 1997, starring Jonathan Pryce, James Wilby and Jonny Lee Miller), The Eye in the Door (1993), The Ghost Road (1995, winner Booker Prize 1995), Another World (1998), Border Crossing (2001), Double Vision (2003), Life Class (2007); *Recreations* swimming, walking, reading; *Style*— Mrs Patricia Barker, CBE, FRSL; ✉ c/o Gillon Aitken Associates, 18–21 Cavaye Place, London SW10 9PT (tel 020 7373 8672)

BARKER, Paul; s of Donald Barker (d 1981), and Marion, *née* Ashworth (d 1989); *b* 24 August 1935; *Educ* Hebden Bridge GS, Calder HS, BNC Oxford (MA); *m* 1960, Sally, da of James Huddleston (d 1965); 3 s (Nicholas b 1961, Tom b 1966, Daniel b 1973), 1 da (Kate b 1963); *Career* writer and broadcaster; Nat Serv cmmnd Intelligence Corps 1953–55; lectr École Normale Supérieure Paris 1958–59; editorial staff: The Times 1959–63, Economist 1964–65; ed New Society 1968–86 (staff writer 1964, dep ed 1965–68), social policy ed Sunday Telegraph 1986–88, assoc ed The Independent Magazine 1988–90, social and political columnist Sunday Times 1990–91, social commentary London Evening Standard 1992– (townscape and arts columnist 1987–92), townscape columnist New Statesman 1996–99; contrib essays and articles in many newspapers and magazines incl TLS and Prospect; visiting fell Centre for the Analysis of Social Policy Univ of Bath 1986–2000, Leverhulme research fell 1993–95, fell Built Environment 2000–02; BPG Award (jtly) for Outstanding Radio Programme (My Country, Right or Wrong) 1988; jt dir: The Fiction Magazine 1982–87, Pennine Heritage 1978–86; Inst of Community Studies: fell 1992–95, sr fell 1995–2000, sr research fell 2000–05, chm 2000–01 (tstee 1991–2001); sr research fell The Young Fndn 2005–; memb UK Advsy Ctee Harkness Fellowships 1995–97; FRSA 1990; *Books* Youth in New Society (contrib, 1966), Your Sunday Paper (contrib, 1967), A Sociological Portrait (ed, 1972), One for Sorrow, Two for Joy (ed and contrib, 1972), The Social Sciences Today (ed, 1975), Arts in Society (ed and contrib, 1977, revised edn 2006), The Other Britain (ed and contrib, 1982), Founders of the Welfare State (ed, 1985), Britain in the Eighties (contrib, 1989), Towards A New Landscape (contrib, 1993), Young at Eighty (contrib, 1995), Gulliver and Beyond (ed and contrib, 1996), Living as Equals (ed and contrib, 1996), A Critic Writes (jt ed, 1997), Town and Country (contrib, 1998), Non-Plan (contrib, 2000), The Meaning of the Jubilee (contrib, 2002), From Black Economy to Moment of Truth (contrib, 2004), William Turner: An English Expressionist (contrib, 2005), Porcupines in Winter (contrib, 2006), The Rise and Rise of Meritocracy (contrib, 2008); *Recreations* architecture; *Style*— Paul Barker, Esq; ✉ 15 Dartmouth Park Avenue, London NW5 1JL (tel 020 7485 8861)

BARKER, Peter William; CBE (1988), DL (1990); s of William Henry George Barker, and Mabel Irene Barker; *b* 24 August 1928; *Educ* Royal Liberty Sch Romford, Dorking Co HS, South London Poly; *m* 1961, Mary Rose Hainsworth, MBE, JP, DL; 1 da (Clare (Mrs Justin Williams) b 1962), 1 s (Timothy Charles b 1964); *Career* J H Fenner & Co 1953–67, jt md Fenner International 1967–71, chief exec J H Fenner (Holdings) 1971–82, chm Fenner plc 1982–93; pro-chllr Univ of Hull 1993–2002 (pro-chllr emeritus 2002–); non-exec dir Neepsend plc 1984–93; memb: Yorks and Humberside Regnl Cncl CBI 1981–94 (chm 1991–93), Nat Cncl CBI 1985–94, Yorks and Humberside Regnl Industrial Devpt Bd 1981–95 (chm 1992–95); High Sheriff Humberside 1993–94; Hon DSc (Econ) Univ of Hull 1992; CIMgt, FInstD, FCIM, FRSA; *Recreations* sailing, skiing, tennis, music; *Clubs* Royal Thames Yacht, Royal Yorks Yacht; *Style*— Peter W Barker, Esq, CBE, DL; ✉ Swanland Rise, West Ella, Hull, East Yorkshire HU10 7SF

BARKER, Sebastian Smart; s of George Barker (d 1991), and Elizabeth Smart (d 1986); *b* 16 April 1945, Moreton-in-Marsh, Glos; *Educ* King's Sch Canterbury, CCC Oxford (MA), UEA (MA); *Family* 3 da (Chloë Therese Katherine b 7 Oct 1972, Miranda Rose Korrina Faith b 5 Jan 1975, Xanthi Raffaella b 14 Nov 1988), 1 s (Daniel Stathis b 6 Jan 1987); m 3, 7 Nov 1998, Hilary Susan, da of P Godfrey Davies; *Career* furniture restorer, carpenter and fireman 1971–76, cataloguer of modern first edns Sotheby's 1976–77, self-employed writer 1977–79, writer in residence South Hill Park Arts Centre Bracknell Berks 1980–83, writer in residence Stamford Arts Centre Lincs 1984–85, self-employed writer 1985–, chm The Poetry Soc 1988–92, fndr dir English Coll Fndn Prague 1991–; ed The London Magazine 2002–; participant at numerous festivals, conferences and univ seminars; dir and co-dir of literary festivals incl: Bracknell 1980–82, Epsom Surrey 1984, first Royal Berkshire Poetry Festival 1985; executor: Literature Panel Brighton Festival 1989–91, English PEN 1990–92, Friedrich Nietzsche Soc of GB 1991–94; judge: Dylan Thomas Award for Poetry (with Nigel Jenkins) 1989, Shell Young Poet of the Year (with Fleur Adcock, *qv*) 1989, BP Speak-a-Poem Competition (with Betty Mulcahy) 1990, Bournemouth Int Poetry Competition 1991, London Writing Competition (with Peter Reading) 1992, VS Pritchett Meml Prize RSL 2003–; Hawthornden fell 1990; FRSL 1997; *Awards* Arts Cncl Award for Poetry 1976, Ingram Merrill Fndn Award 1988, Soc of Authors Award 1990, Royal Literary Fund Award 1993; *Publications* poetry incl: Poems (1974), The Dragon and the Lion (1976), On the Rocks (1977), Epistles (1980), A Fire in the Rain (1982), A Nuclear Epiphany (1984), Boom (1985), O Mother Heal Your Son (1986), Lines for My Newborn Son (1987), The Dream of Intelligence (1992, Book of the Year The Independent 1992, Book of the Year The Spectator 1992), Guarding the Border: Selected Poems (1992), The Hand in the Well (1996), Damnatio Memoriae: Erased from Memory (2004), The Matter of Europe (2005), The Erotics of God (2005, Book of the Year The Tablet 2005), Sebastian Barker reading from his Poems (2006); Who is Eddie Linden (documentary novel, 1979, stage adaptation by William Tanner 1995); as ed: Aquarius, 10 (1978), Poetry London/Apple Magazine (1979), Poems by the Children and People of Bracknell (1980), A Zoo to Brood Upon (1981), Other People's Lives (1982), Pacing the Cage (1985), A Royal Audience (1985), Portraits of Poets (1986, Book of the Year The Observer 1986), Young Poets of a New Bulgaria (1990); *Recreations* exploring Wales, the south of France and Greece; *Clubs* Colony Room; *Style*— Sebastian Barker, Esq

BARKER, Timothy Gwynne; s of Lt-Col (Frank Richard) Peter Barker (d 1974), and Hon Olwen Gwynne, *née* Philipps (d 1998); *b* 8 April 1940; *Educ* Eton, Jesus Coll Cambridge (MA), McGill Univ Montreal; *m* 14 July 1964, Philippa Rachel Mary, da of Brig Mervyn Christopher Thursby-Pelham, OBE; 1 da (Camilla b 1968), 1 s (Christopher b 1970); *Career* vice-chm Kleinwort Benson Group plc 1993–98 (dir 1988–98), chm Kleinwort Benson Private Bank 1997–2004, vice-chm Dresdner Kleinwort Benson 1998–2000, chm Robert Walters plc 2000–07; non-exec dir: Electrocomponents plc 2000–, Drax Gp Ltd 2004–; DG: City Panel on Takeovers and Mergers 1984–85, Cncl for the Securities Indust 1984–85; memb Professional Oversight Bd for Accountancy; Liveryman Worshipful Co of Grocers; *Style*— Timothy Barker, Esq; ✉ c/o Anthem Corporate Finance, 20 Berkeley Square, London W1J 6EQ (tel 020 7514 5110)

BARKER, William D Milton (Bill); s of James Dalbert Barker, and Christina Celestria Barker; *Educ* South London Coll; *Career* advtg exec Rogets of London 1981, advtg exec Dorlands (formerly Ted Bates) 1982, J Walter Thompson 1983–98 (television dir 1996–98), fndr and managing ptnr MindShare 1998, assoc dir Pravda 2005–; *Recreations* skiing (both water and snow), windsurfing, kite boarding, riding and cycling; *Clubs* Hertfordshire Golf and County; *Style*— Bill Barker, Esq

BARKSHIRE, Robert Renny St John (John); CBE (1990), TD (1970), JP (Lewes 1980), DL (E Sussex 1986); s of Robert Hugh Barkshire, CBE; *b* 31 August 1935; *Educ* Bedford Sch; *m* 1, 1960 (m dis 1990), Margaret Robinson; 2 s (Charles b 1963, William b 1965), 1 da (Sarah b 1969); m 2, 1990, Audrey Witham; *Career* Nat Serv 2 Lt Duke of Wellington's Regt 1953–55, TA HAC 1955–74 (CO 1970–72, Regt Col 1972–74); banker; Cater Ryder & Co 1955–72 (jt md 1963–72); chm: Mercantile House Holdings plc 1972–87, Alexanders Laing & Cruickshank Holdings Ltd 1984–88, Int Commodities Clearing House 1986–90, Household Mortgage Group 1993–94 (non-exec dir 1985–94), Chaco Investments Ltd 1994–2001; non-exec dir: Extel Group 1979–87 (dep chm 1986–87), Savills plc 1988–95, Ctee on Market in Single Properties 1985–99, Sun Life and Provincial Holding plc 1988–99, TR Property Investment Trust plc 1993–2002; memb Advsy Bd: IMM Div of Chicago Mercantile Exchange 1981–84, Bank Julius Baer & Co Ltd London 1988–91; dir LIFFE 1982–91 (chm 1982–85); chm: FFWP 1980, LIFFE Steering Ctee 1981; gen cmmr for Income Tax City of London 1981–; chm: Eastborne Hosp NHS Ts 1993–, Nat Meml Arboretum 2003–; govr: Eastbourne Coll 1980–92 (dep chm 1983–92), Roedean Sch 1984–89, Burwash CE Primary Sch 2000– (chm 2002–); chm Bedford Sch 1984–89, cmmr Duke of York's Royal Mil Sch Dover 1986–95, memb Ct and Cncl Univ of Sussex 1997–99, memb Bd of Corp Salisbury Coll 2001–02, treas Sussex Historic Churches Tst 2003–; chm: Reserve Forces Assoc 1983–87, Sussex TA Ctee 1983–85, SE TAVR Assoc 1985–91, City of London TAVRA 1989–91, E Sussex Branch Magistrates Assoc 1986–91, E Sussex Magistrates Courts Ctee 1993–97, Sussex Shadow Magistrates Courts Ctee 2000–02, Sussex Magistrates Courts Ctee 2001–02, Royal Br Legion Trg Co 1999–2001; Hon Col 6/7 Queen's Regt 1986–91, vice-chm TA Sport Bd 1983–95 (memb 1979–95), co-opted memb Nat Cncl Royal Br Legion 1993–2005 (tstee 2005–); fin advsr: Victory Servs Club 1981–95, Royal Signals, Royal Engrs Funds, Army Sport Control Bd, Army Central Fund, Army Common Investment Fund 2002–05, TA Sport Bd; dir Offrs' Pensions Society Investment Co 1982–95, tstee Duke of Wellington's Regt 1989–2006, tstee SSAFA Forces Help 1997–, exec tstee Army Benevolent Fund 1999–, pres E Sussex Army Benevolent Fund 1999–, tstee Yorks Regt 2006–; Freeman City of London 1973, Liveryman Worshipful Co of Farmers 1981; ACIB; *Publications* Burwash: Domesday to Millennium (2000); *Recreations* sailing, shooting; *Clubs* City of London, Cavalry and Guards', MCC, Royal Fowey Yacht; *Style*— John Barkshire, Esq, CBE, TD, DL; ✉ Denes House, High Street, Burwash, East Sussex TN19 7EH (tel 01435 882646)

BARLEY, Dr Victor Laurence; s of George Alec Barley (d 1995), of Harrogate, N Yorks, and Evelyn Mary Barley (d 1971); *b* 16 June 1941; *Educ* Stamford Sch, Univ of Cambridge (MA, MB BChir), Univ of Oxford (MA, DPhil); *m* 1, 25 Jan 1969 (m dis 1989), Janet, da of Dr Stanley Devidson Purcell, of Clevedon, Avon; 1 s (Peter b 3 Dec 1969), 3 da (Elizabeth, Madeline (twins) b 6 Jan 1972, Christine b 16 July 1981); m 2, 3 Dec 1999, Anthea, da of Mr Sydney Sherlock Jones, of Cardiff; *Career* conslt clinical oncologist Bristol 1978–2003, clinical dir Bristol Oncology Centre 1988–96, Macmillan lead clinician Avon & Somerset Cancer Services 1997–99, clinical speciality advsr Nat Patient Safety Agency 2002–; chm Hosp Med Ctee United Bristol Healthcare NHS Tst 1997–99; memb Br Inst of Radiology; FRCSEd, FRCR; *Recreations* music; *Style*— Dr Victor Barley; ✉ North Archway Cottage, Barrow Court Lane, Barrow Gurney, Bristol BS48 3RP (tel 01275 463006, e-mail victor.barley@npsa.nhs.uk)

BARLING, Gerald Edward; QC (1991); *b* 18 September 1949; *Educ* St Mary's Coll Blackburn, New Coll Oxford (Peel fndn scholar, Thwaites travelling scholar (USA), Burnett open exhibitioner, MA), Inns of Court Sch of Law (Harmsworth entrance exhibitioner, Astbury law scholar); *m* Myriam Frances, *née* Ponsford; 3 da (Sophie, Bryony, Isobel); *Career* called to the Bar Middle Temple 1972 (bencher 2001); in practice: Manchester 1973–81, London 1981–; recorder of the Crown Court 1993– (asst recorder 1989–93), actg deemster IOM Court of Appeal 1999–, dep High Court judge 2007–; memb: Bar Cncl Working Pty on Restrictive Practices 1988–90, Ctee Bar Euro Gp 1988–; chm: Western Euro Sub-Ctee Bar Cncl 1991–92, Bar Euro Gp 1994–96; lectr in law New Coll Oxford 1972–77, tutor in law UCL 1972–73; *Publications* Butterworths European Court Practice (contrib, 1991), Butterworths European Law Service (conslt ed), Practitioners' Handbook of EC Law (joint ed, 1998); author of numerous professional papers on aspects of EC law; *Style*— Gerald Barling, Esq, QC; ✉ Brick Court Chambers, 7–8 Essex Street, London WC2R 3LD (tel 020 7379 3550, fax 020 7379 3558)

BARLOW, Celia; MP; *b* 28 September 1955, Cardiff; *Educ* Univ of Cambridge (MA), UC Cardiff (Dip Journalism), Central St Martins (MA); *m* Sam Jaffa; 3 c; *Career* joined Lab Pty 1971; former journalist and news prodr for the BBC, sometime BBC reporter House of Commons; lectr in video prodn Chichester Coll; Parly candidate (Lab) Chichester 2001, MP (Lab) Hove 2005–; *Style*— Ms Celia Barlow, MP; ✉ House of Commons, London SW1A 0AA

BARLOW, Sir Christopher Hilaro; 7 Bt (UK 1803), of Fort William, Bengal; s of Sir Richard Barlow, 6 Bt, AFC (d 1946), and Rosamund Sylvia, *née* Anderton; *b* 1 December 1929; *Educ* Eton, McGill Univ Montreal (BArch); *m* 1, 1952, Jacqueline Claire de Marigny (d 2002), da of John Edmund Audley (d 1980), of Chester; 2 da (Persephone Claire (Mrs Robert E Booth) b 1953, Caroline Claire (Mrs James C Jordan) b 1960), 1 s (Crispian John Edmund Audley b 1958) and 1 s decd; m 2, 2003, Mrs Jeane Gage, da of Douglas Hibbert Stevens (d 1993), of Hamilton; *Heir* s, Crispian Barlow; *Career* architect; former pres Newfoundland Architects' Assoc; *Clubs* The Tamahac; *Style*— Sir Christopher Barlow, Bt; ✉ 40 St James Place, Hamilton, Ontario L8P 2N4, Canada (tel 905 522 1928)

BARLOW, Prof David Hearnshaw; s of Archibald Edward Barlow, of Clydebank, and Annie Wilson, *née* Hamilton; *b* 26 December 1949; *Educ* Clydebank HS, Univ of Glasgow (BSc, MB ChB, MD), Univ of Oxford (MA); *m* Norma Christie, da of John Campbell Woodrow; 1 s (Neil John b 13 Oct 1975), 1 da (Catriona Charlotte Anne b 11 Feb 1986); *Career* various med trg positions Glasgow 1975–77, MRC trg fell 1977–78, Hall tutorial fell Univ of Glasgow 1979–81, sr registrar Queen Mother's Hosp 1981–84; Univ of Oxford: clinical reader in obstetrics and gynaecology 1984–90, fell Green Coll 1985–90 (hon sr assoc memb 1990–), Nuffield prof of obstetrics and gynaecology and head of dept 1990–2004, fell Oriel Coll 1990–2004, memb Bd Med Sciences Div 2000–04; exec dean of med Univ of Glasgow 2005– (also memb Sr Mgmnt Gp), memb Greater Glasgow Health Bd 2005– (chm Clinical Governance Ctee 2005–); chm: Dept of Health Advsy Gp on Osteoporosis 1993–95, Oxford Anglia Region NHS Exec Clinical Research and Devpt Ctee 1996–98, Wellbeing Scientific Advsy Ctee 1998–2000, SE Region NHS Exec Scientific Advsy Ctee 1998–2003, Br Menopause Soc 1999–2001 (treas 1995–99, memb Cncl 1991–2002), SE Region NHS R&D Project Grants Ctee 2001 (memb 1998–2001), Oxford Hosps NHS R&D Consortium 2001– (memb 1998–), Nat Inst of Clinical Excellence (NICE) Infertility Working Gp 2002–03, Nat Osteoporosis Soc 2002–04 (memb Cncl 1995–, dep chm 2000–02), Nat Stem Cell Bank Clinical Liaison Ctee 2003–; memb Cncl RCOG 1996–2002, memb Human Fertilisation and Embryology Authy 1998–; tstee: tstee Nat Endometriosis Soc 1996–2000, Oxford Hosps Charitable Tst Funds 2003–04; ed-in-chief Human Reproduction 2000–; FRCOG 1993 (MRCOG 1980), FMedSci 1999 (fndr fell), MRCP (without examination) 2004; *Recreations* music (listening and playing the viola), painting; *Style*— Prof David Barlow

BARLOW, Prof Frank; CBE (1989); s of Percy Hawthorn Barlow (d 1964), and Margaret Julia, *née* Wilkinson (d 1968); *b* 19 April 1911, Wolstanton, Staffs; *Educ* Newcastle HS, St John's Coll Oxford (open scholar, Bryce student, sr student, MA, BLitt, DPhil); *m* 1936, Moira Stella Brigid, *née* Garvey; 2 s (John Francis b 1947, Michael Edward b 1949); *Career* Fereday fell St John's Coll Oxford 1935–38, asst lectr UCL 1936–40, Nat Serv 1941–46 (cmmnd Intelligence Corps, demobbed as Maj); Univ of Exeter: lectr 1946, reader 1949, prof of history and head of dept 1953–76, dep vice-chllr 1961–63; public orator 1974–76; Hon DLitt Univ of Exeter 1981, hon fell St John's Coll Oxford 2001; FRHistS 1948, FBA 1970, FRSL 1971; *Publications* The Letters of Arnulf of Lisieux (1939), Durham Annals and Documents of the Thirteenth Century (1945), Durham Jurisdictional Peculiars (1950), The Feudal Kingdom of England (1955), The Life of King Edward Who Rests at Westminster (ed and trans, 1962), The English Church 1000–1066 (1963), William I and the Norman Conquest (1965), Edward the Confessor (1970), Winchester in the Early Middle Ages (with Martin Biddle, Olaf von Feilitzen and DJ Keene, 1976), The English Church 1066–1154 (1979), The Norman Conquest and Beyond (selected papers, 1983), William Rufus (1983), Thomas Becket (1986), Introduction to Devonshire Domesday Book (1991), English Episcopal Acta xi-xii (Exeter 1046–1257) (1996), Carmen de Hastingae Proelio (ed and trans, 1999), The Godwins (2002); *Recreations* gardening; *Style*— Prof Frank Barlow, CBE; ✉ Middle Court Hall, Kenton, Exeter EX6 8NA (tel 01626 890438)

BARLOW, George Francis; OBE (1998); s of late George Barlow, of Worcester Park, Surrey, and late Agnes Barlow; *b* 26 May 1939; *Educ* Wimbledon Coll, Hammersmith Sch of Art & Building, PCL; *m* 1969, Judith Alice, da of late Alice and late Alan (Tony) Newton; 2 da (Rachel b 1970, Jacqueline b 1974), 1 s (Daniel b 1972); *Career* chartered surveyor Building Design Partnership 1962–67, devpt surveyor GLC 1967–70, housing devpt offr London Borough of Camden 1970–76, dir/sec Metropolitan Housing Tst 1976–87, chief exec Peabody Tst 1987–99, ret; chm: London Housing Assoc Cncl 1978–82, Prince's Tst/BITC Homelessness Gp 1994–98, RICS Housing Policy Panel 1996–99, London Devpt Agency 2000–03; memb: Cncl Nat Fedn of Housing Assocs 1985–89, Housing Ctee RICS 1986–91, Ctee Community Self Build Agency 1989–93, Ctee Broomleigh Housing Assoc 1989–95, Bd E London Partnership 1994–99, Bd London Devpt Partnership; govr Univ of East London 1996–2000; sr assoc King's Fund 1999–2004; Hon DLitt: Univ of Westminster 2000, London South Bank Univ 2004; FRICS 1987 (ARICS 1968); *Recreations* theatre, gardening, travelling; *Style*— George Barlow, OBE

BARLOW, Gillian Claire Bernadette Judson (Dilly); da of Leonard Alfred Barlow (d 1996), of Horley, Surrey, and Sarah Elizabeth, *née* Judson (d 1979); *b* 6 May 1952; *Educ* St Anne's Coll Sanderstead Surrey, Univ of Manchester (BA); *Career* TV/radio presenter; newsreader and presentation announcer BBC Radio 4 1978–84; voice over and commentary artiste; *Recreations* looking after Dr John the famous cat, boating; *Clubs* The Academy; *Style*— Ms Dilly Barlow

BARLOW, James Mellodew; s of Capt Cecil Barlow (d 1988), of Oldham, Lancs, and Florence Patricia, *née* Mellodew (d 1997); *b* 23 December 1943; *Educ* Mill Hill Sch, Univ of Nottingham (LLB); *Career* admitted slr 1967; ptnr Clifford Chance LLP (formerly Coward Chance) 1980–; hon sec Cumberland LTC 1976–82 and 2004–; memb Worshipful Co of Slrs 1980; memb Law Soc 1967, ATII 1968; *Recreations* real tennis, tennis, skiing, fell walking, bridge; *Clubs* Old Millhillians, RAC; *Style*— James Barlow, Esq; ✉ 11 Edmunds Walk, London N2 0HU (tel 020 8883 6972); Clifford Chance LLP, 10 Upper Bank Street, London E14 5JJ (tel 020 7006 1000, fax 020 7006 5555, e-mail james.barlow@cliffordchance.com)

BARLOW, Sir John Kemp; 3 Bt (UK 1907), of Bradwall Hall, Sandbach, Co Chester; s of Sir John Denman Barlow, 2 Bt (d 1986), and Hon Diana Helen Kemp, yr da of 1 Baron Rochdale; *b* 22 April 1934; *Educ* Winchester, Trinity Coll Cambridge (MA); *m* 1962 (m dis 1998), Susan, da of Col Sir Andrew Horsbrugh-Porter, 3 Bt, DSO; 4 s ((John) William Marshal b 1964, (Thomas) David Bradwall b (Jan) 1966, (Andrew) Michael Kemp b (Dec) 1966, Charles James Bulkeley b 1970); m 2, Pauline Margaret, *née* Bancroft; *Heir* s, William Barlow; *Career* dir Majedie Investments plc (chm 1979–2000); chm Rubber Growers' Assoc 1974–75, steward Jockey Club 1988–90; High Sheriff Cheshire 1979; *Recreations* hunting, shooting, steeplechasing; *Clubs* Brooks's, Jockey, City of London; *Style*— Sir John K Barlow, Bt; ✉ Brindley, Nantwich, Cheshire CW5 8HX

BARLOW, Prof Martin Thomas; s of Andrew Dalmahoy Barlow (d 2006), and Yvonne Rosalind Barlow; *b* 16 June 1953, London; *Educ* St Paul's, Trinity Coll Cambridge (entrance scholar, BA), Univ of Cambridge (Dip), Univ of Wales (PhD); *m* 6 Aug 1994, Colleen, *née* McLaughlin; *Career* research fell Univ of Liverpool 1978–80, fell Trinity Coll Cambridge 1979–92, Statistical Lab Univ of Cambridge 1981–85, Royal Soc univ research fell Univ of Cambridge 1985–92, prof Univ of BC 1992–; author of papers in learned jls; winner Rollo Davidson Prize Univ of Cambridge 1984; FRSC, FRS 2005; *Style*— Prof Martin Barlow; ✉ Department of Mathematics, University of British Columbia, Vancouver, British Columbia, Canada V6T 1Z2 (tel 001 604 822 6377)

BARLOW, Stephen William; s of George William Barlow, of Witham, Essex, and Irene Catherine, *née* Moretti; *b* 30 June 1954; *Educ* Canterbury Cathedral Choir Sch, King's Sch Canterbury, Trinity Coll Cambridge (organ scholar, MA); *m* Oct 1986, Joanna, da of Maj James Lumley; *Career* assoc conductor Glyndebourne Festival Opera 1980–81, resident conductor ENO 1980–83; music dir: Opera 80 1987–90, Queensland Philharmonic Orch 1996–99; artistic dir Opera Northern Ireland 1996–99; conducting debut The Rake's Progress Glyndebourne Touring Opera 1977; opera cos conducted incl: Scottish Opera, Dublin Grand Opera, Opera North, Royal Opera House, Vancouver Opera, Netherlands Opera, San Francisco Opera, Florida Grand Opera, Victoria State Opera Melbourne, Opera New Zealand; orchs conducted incl: LPO, LSO, CBSO, LMP, RTE, ECO, BBC Scottish Symphony Orch, Orch of the Age of Enlightenment, Bournemouth Symphony Orch, Scottish Chamber Orch, Symphony Orch of Bilbao, City of London Sinfonia, Adelaide Symphony Orch, Canberra Symphony Orch, Melbourne Symphony Orch, Sydney Symphony Orch, New Zealand Symphony Orch, Detroit Symphony Orch, Belgrade Philharmonic Orch, Tafelmusik (Toronto); FRCO, FGSM 1986; *Recordings* incl: Joseph James' Requiem (Philharmonia), Graham Koehne Ballets (QPO), Peter and the Wolf (ENP), own composition Rainbow Bear (ENP); *Recreations* composition, wine, theatre, being at home; *Style*— Stephen Barlow, Esq; ✉ c/o Peter Hall, Musichall, Vicarage Way, Ringmer, East Sussex BN8 5LA (tel 01273 814240, fax 01273 813637)

BARLOW, Sir (George) William; kt (1977); s of Albert Edward Barlow, and Annice Barlow; *b* 8 June 1924; *Educ* Manchester Grammar, Univ of Manchester (BSc); *m* 1948, Elaine Mary Atherton, da of William Adamson; 1 s, 1 da; *Career* served RNVR 1944–47; various appts English Electric Co Ltd (Spain 1952–55, Canada 1958–62); md: English Electric Domestic Appliance Co Ltd 1965–67, English Electric Computers Ltd 1967–68; chm: Ransome Hoffman Pollard 1971–77 (gp chief exec 1969–77), PO 1977–80 (organised separation of PO and British Telecom 1980), Ericsson Ltd 1981–94, BICC plc 1984–91 (dir 1980–), Thorn EMI plc 1980–86, Vodafone plc 1988–98, Chemring Group plc 1994–97, Parsons Brinckerhoff 1997–2003; chm: Design Cncl 1980–86, Nationalised Industries Chairmen's Gp 1980, Engrg Cncl 1988–91; pres: BEAMA 1986–87, ORGALIME 1990–92, Royal Acad of Engrg 1991–96, Assoc of Lancastrians in London 1992; Master Worshipful Co of Engrs 1986–87; hon fell UMIST 1978; Hon DSc: Cranfield Inst of Technol 1979, Univ of Bath 1986, Aston Univ 1988, City Univ 1990; Hon DTech: Liverpool Poly (now Liverpool John Moores Univ) 1988, Loughborough Univ 1993; Hon DEng UMIST 1996; Hon FICE 1991, Hon FIMechE 1993, CEng, FREng 1979, FIMechE, FIEE, FCGI; *Recreations* golf; *Clubs* Brooks's, Huntercombe; *Style*— Sir William Barlow, FREng; ✉ 4 Parkside, Henley-on-Thames, Oxfordshire RG9 1TX (tel 01491 411101, fax 01491 410013)

BARLTROP, Prof Donald; s of Albert Edward Barltrop (d 1976), and Mabel, *née* Redding (d 1984); *b* 26 June 1933; *Educ* Southall GS, Univ of London (BSc, MB BS, MD); *m* 1 Aug 1959, Mair Angharad, da of Rev Richard Evan Edwards (d 1971), of Swansea; 2 s (Andrew b 1965, Richard b 1968), 1 da (Elen b 1970); *Career* Capt RAMC 1959–61; Fulbright scholar Harvard Univ 1963–64, Wellcome sr res fell in clinical sci 1968–74; reader in paediatrics: St Mary's Hosp 1975–78, Westminster Hosp 1978–82; prof of child health: Westminster Hosps Univ of London 1982–93, West London Hosp 1984–93, Univ of London 1984–98, Charing Cross Hosp 1984–98, Chelsea and Westminster Hosp 1993–98; emeritus prof Imperial Coll Sch of Med Univ of London 1998–; emeritus conslt paediatrician Chelsea and Westminster Hosp 1998–; adjunct prof of community health Tufts Univ 1984–98; examiner: RCP, Univs of London, Leicester, Manchester, Cape Town, Hong Kong, Al-Fateh Tripoli, and Wales; memb: Lead and Health Ctee DHSS, Working Pty on Composition of Infant Foods Ctee DHSS, Steering Ctee on Chemical Aspects of Food Surveillance MAFF; chm Westminster Children Res Tst; med advsr: Bliss, Buttle Tst, Inst of Sports Med; Freeman City of London 1977, past Master Worshipful Co of Barbers 1995, memb Lord Mayor and Sheriffs' Ctee 1995, memb Incorporation of Barbers of Glasgow, Burgess City of Glasgow; FRCP, FRCPCH; *Books* Mineral Metabolism in Paediatrics (jtly, 1969), Children in Health and Disease (jtly, 1977), Paediatric Therapeutics (jtly, 1991); *Recreations* offshore sailing; *Clubs* Naval, RNVR Yacht; *Style*— Prof Donald Barltrop; ✉ 7 Grove Road, Northwood, Middlesex HA6 2AP (tel and fax 01923 826461)

BARNABY, Dr (Charles) Frank; s of Charles Hector Barnaby (d 1932), and Lilian, *née* Sainsbury; *b* 27 September 1927; *Educ* Andover GS, Univ of London (BSc, MSc, PhD); *m* 19 Dec 1972, Wendy Elizabeth, da of Francis Arthur Field, of Adelaide, Aust; 1 da (Sophie b 1975), 1 s (Benjamin b 1976); *Career* physicist: AWRE Aldermaston 1951–57, UCL 1957–67; exec sec Pugwash Conf on Sci and World Affrs 1967–71, dir Stockholm Int Peace Res Inst 1971–81, guest prof Free Univ of Amsterdam 1981–85, conslt Oxford Res Gp 1995–, ed Int Jl of Human Rights 1997–; Hon Doctorate: Free Univ of Amsterdam, Univ of Southampton; *Books* Man and the Atom (1972), Nuclear Energy (1975), Prospects for Peace (1975), Verification Technologies (1986), Future Warfare (1986), Star Wars (1987), The Automated Battlefield (1987), The Gaia Peace Atlas (1989), The Invisible Bomb (1989), The Role and Control of Force in the 1990's (1992), How Nuclear Weapons Spread (1993), Instruments of Terror (1997), How To Build a Nuclear Bomb and Other Weapons of Mass Destruction (2003); *Recreations* astronomy, bird watching; *Style*— Dr Frank Barnaby; ✉ Brandreth, Station Road, Chilbolton, Stockbridge, Hampshire SO20 6AW (tel 01264 860423, fax 01264 860868, e-mail frank.barnaby@btinternet.com)

BARNARD, 11 Baron (E 1698); Harry John Neville Vane; TD (1960); patron of twelve livings; s of 10 Baron Barnard, CMG, OBE, MC, TD, JP (d 1964), and Sylvia Mary, *née* Straker (d 1993); *b* 21 September 1923; *Educ* Eton, Univ of Durham Business Sch (MSc); *m* 8 Oct 1952 (m dis 1992), Lady Davina Mary Cecil, DStJ, da of 6 Marquess of Exeter (d 1981); 1 s, 4 da; *Heir* s, Hon Henry Vane; *Career* Flying Offr RAFVR 1942–46, Northumberland Hussars 1948–66, Lt-Col Cmdg 1964–66, pres N of England TAVRA 1974–77 (vice-pres 1970 and 1977–88), Hon Col 7 (Durham) Bn LI 1979–89; landowner, farmer; cncllr Durham 1952–61, memb Durham Co Agric Exec Ctee 1953–72 (chm 1970–72), pres Durham Co Branch CLA 1965–89 (memb CLA Cncl 1950–80), memb N Regnl Panel MAFF 1972–76; dir Teesdale Mercury Ltd 1983– (chm); pres: Farmway Ltd 1965–2003, Teesdale & Weardale Search & Rescue 1969–2003, Durham Co St John Cncl 1971–88, Durham Co Scout Assoc 1972–88, Durham and Cleveland Co Branch Royal Br Legion 1973–92, Durham Wildlife Tst 1984–95; vice-pres Game Conservancy Tst 1997–; vice-chm Cncl BRCS 1987–93 (memb Cncl 1982–85), patron Durham Co Branch BRCS 1993–99 (pres 1969–87), jt patron County Durham and Teesside BRCS 1999–, hon vice-pres BRCS 1999–; patron Durham Co Royal Br Legion 2001–; HM Lord-Lt and Custos Rotulorum Co Durham 1970–88 (Vice-Lt 1969–70, DL 1956); JP Durham 1961; Sr Grand Warden United Grand Lodge of England 1970–71, Provincial Grand Master for Durham 1969–98; BRCS Queen's Badge of Honour 1991; KStJ 1971; *Clubs* Brooks's, Durham County, Northern Counties (Newcastle); *Style*— The Rt Hon the Lord Barnard, TD; ✉ Raby Castle, PO Box 50, Staindrop, Darlington, Co Durham DL2 3AY (tel 01833 660751)

BARNARD, Prof John Michael; s of John Claude Southard Barnard (d 1976), and Dora Grace, *née* Epps; *b* 13 February 1936; *Educ* King Alfred's GS Wantage, Wadham Coll Oxford (MA, BLitt); *m* 1 (m dis); 2 da (Josie b 1963, Clio b 1965), 1 s (Jason b 1966); m 2, 1991, Prof Hermione Lee, *qv*; *Career* Nat Serv sr radar technician RAF 1954–56; res asst Dept of English Yale Univ USA 1961–64, visiting lectr English Dept Univ of Calif Santa Barbara USA 1964–65; Sch of English Univ of Leeds: lectr then sr lectr 1965–78, prof 1978–2001; foreign expert Miny of Educn and Science Netherlands 1992–93; gen ed Longman Annotated English Poets 1977–, gen ed The Cambridge History of the Book in Britain 2001–; Br Acad Warton lectr 1989, McKenzie Lecture Univ of Oxford 2004; vice-pres Bibliographical Soc 1998– (memb Cncl 1990–94); memb Mid Wharfedale Parish Cncl 1974–84; fell English Assoc 1990; *Books* Congreve's The Way of the World (ed, 1972), Pope: The Critical Heritage (ed, 1973, reprinted 1995), John Keats: The Complete Poems (ed, 1973, 3 edn 1988), Etherege's The Man of Mode (ed, 1979, reprinted in Five Restoration Comedies, 1984), John Keats (1987), John Keats: Selected Poems (ed, 1988), The Early Seventeenth-Century Book Trade and John Foster's Inventory of 1616 (with Maureen Bell, 1994), Folio Society John Keats: The Complete Poems (ed, 2001), The Cambridge History of the Book in Britain, Volume IV 1557–1695 (gen ed with D F McKenzie (assisted by Maureen Bell), 2002), John Keats: Selected Poems (ed, 2007); also of many articles on late 17th Century English literature, the Romantics, book history and bibliography in several various learned jls; *Recreations* travel, walking; *Clubs*

Johnson; *Style*— Prof John Barnard; ✉ 13 Hill Top Road, Oxford OX4 1PB (tel 01865 725577); School of English, University of Leeds, Leeds LS2 9JT

BARNARD, John Vianney; s of Arthur James Barnard, and Mary Agnes Isabella, *née* Loomes; *b* 25 February 1944; *Educ* City of Norwich GS, Norwich City Coll (I Eng AMI Prod E), Open Univ, RSA CLAIT; *m* 1970, Jacqueline, *née* Greig; 2 s (James, Benjamin), 1 da (Joanna); *Career* furniture designer; prod mangr: Lawrence Scott Electromotors 1964–69, Duncan Tucker 1969–70, United Glass 1970–71; prop: The Design Workshop 1971–, John Barnard Furniture Ltd 2003–; cmmns incl: Norfolk CC (incl wedding present for HRH the Prince of Wales and Lady Diana Spencer), UEA, SS Peter and Paul Church Wakefield, Reedham Church Norfolk (Craftsmanship Award Norfolk Assoc of Architects), Norwich City Cncl, Worshipful Co of Info Technologists, Victory project (Nelson's Flagship, Mike Hicks Cup for Merit Norfolk Furniture Makers), Arpana Tst; pres Norfolk Furniture Makers Assoc (fndr memb 1972); memb: Norfolk Contemporary Crafts Soc (past chair), Norfolk Contemporary Arts Soc, Furniture Liaison Panel Norwich City Coll, Fedn of Small Businesses (FSB, past chm Policy Ctee); Freeman City of London 1998, Liveryman Worshipful Co of Furniture Makers 1998; MCSD 1997, MIEE; *Recreations* design, reading, travel, squash, creativity; *Style*— John Barnard, Esq; ✉ The Design Workshop, The Granary, Trowse Bridge, Bracondale, Norwich NR1 2EG (tel 01603 623959, fax 01603 761805); 60 St Giles Street, Norwich NR2 1LW (tel 01603 766944)

BARNARD, Sir Joseph Brian; kt (1986), JP (1973), DL (N Yorks 1988); s of Joseph Ernest Barnard (d 1942), and Elizabeth Loudon Barnard (d 1980); *b* 22 January 1928; *Educ* Sedbergh; *m* 21 Jan 1959, Suzanne Hamilton, da of Clifford Bray, of Ilkley, W Yorks; 3 s (Nicholas, Simon (twins) b 1960, Marcus b 1966); *Career* cmmnd KRRC 1946–48; dir: Joseph Constantine Steamship Line Ltd 1952–66, Teesside Warehousing Co Ltd 1966–98, NE Electricity Bd 1987–90, Indeck Energy Services (UK) Ltd 1991–2004, Financial Consultancy Centre 1999–2004; chm: E Harlsey Parish Cncl 1973–99, Northallerton Petty Sessional Div 1981–93, Govrs Ingleby Arncliffe C of E Primary Sch 1981–91, NE Electricity Consultative Cncl 1987–90, Indeck Energy Services (UK) Ltd 1991–, Worldwide Cargo Control Studies Ltd 1992–93, International Business Group 1993–98; pres: Yorks area Cons Trade Unionists, Yorks Magistrates Ct Ctee 1981–93; patron St Oswald's E Harlsey; chm: Yorks Area Cons 1983–88, Nat Union of Cons and Unionist Assocs 1990–91 (vice-chm 1988–90); hon life vice-pres Yorks Area Cons Clubs Advsy Ctee 1997–, hon life vice-pres Yorks Cons Advsy Ctee 1997–; pres Int Jousting Assoc 1995–; *Recreations* walking, shooting, gardening; *Clubs* Carlton; *Style*— Sir Joseph Barnard, DL; ✉ Harlsey Hall, Northallerton, North Yorkshire DL6 2BL (tel and fax 01609 882203)

BARNARD, Michael John; s of Cecil William Barnard, and Gladys Irene Mary, *née* Hedges; *b* 4 May 1944; *Educ* Licensed Victuallers Sch Slough; *m* 1 (m dis 1979), Jennifer, da of Charles Tyrrill; 1 s (Matthew b 15 Sept 1971); m 2, Charlotte Susan, da of Sir Kenneth Berrill; m 3, Jayne Ann, da of Brian Jenkinson; *Career* journalist and publisher: Kent Web Offset Group 1962–66, Westminster Press 1966–67 and 1968–71; managing ed First Features Ltd 1967–68, prodn dir Macmillan Magazines 1971–79, chm and md Macmillan Production Ltd 1979–2007; dir: Macmillan Publishers Ltd 1982–2007, Macmillan Ltd 1985–2007, Macmillan Publishers Group Administration Ltd 1988–2007; chm: Macmillan Distribution Ltd 1988–95 and 1997–2007, Macmillan Information Systems Ltd 1988–95; non-exec dir: Periodical Publishers' Association Ltd 1988–91, Gill & Macmillan Ltd 1990–94 and 1996–2002; chm New Media Investments Ltd 1994–2007; chm Bd of Tstees Printing Industries' Research Assoc 1995–2005; visiting prof London Inst (now Univ of the Arts London) 1998; Liveryman Worshipful Co of Stationers and Newspapermakers 1995 (Freeman 1993); MCB 1988, FRSA 1991, MILog 1993, FIOP 1999; *Books* Magazine and Journal Production (1986), Introduction to Print Buying (1987), Inside Magazines (1989), Introduction to Printing Processes (1990), The Print and Production Manual (1998), Transparent Imprint (2006); *Recreations* music, gardening, reading; *Clubs* Naval and Military; *Style*— Michael Barnard, Esq; ✉ Macmillan Ltd, Houndmills, Basingstoke, Hampshire RG21 6XS (tel 01256 329242, fax 01256 331248)

BARNARD, Robert; s of Leslie Barnard (d 1969), and Vera Doris, *née* Nethercoat (d 1998); *b* 23 November 1936; *Educ* Colchester Royal GS, Balliol Coll Oxford, Univ of Bergen Norway (DPhil); *m* 1963, Mary Louise Tabor, da of Geoffrey Tabor, of Armidale, Aust; *Career* author; lectr in English lit Univ of New England Armidale NSW 1961–66, lectr and sr lectr Univ of Bergen Norway 1966–76, prof of English lit Univ of Tromsø Norway 1976–83; memb: Soc of Authors, Crime Writers' Assoc (memb Ctee 1988–91); chm Brontë Soc 1996–99 and 2002– (memb Cncl and vice-chm 1991–95); Diamond Dagger for lifetime achievement in crime fiction 2003; *Books* incl: Death of An Old Goat (1974), Unruly Son (1978), Mother's Boys (1981), Sheer Torture (1981), A Corpse in a Gilded Cage (1984), A Short History of English Literature (1984), Out of the Blackout (1985), The Skeleton in the Grass (1987), City of Strangers (1990), Dead, Mr Mozart (as Bernard Bastable, 1995), A Scandal in Belgravia (1991), Masters of the House (1994), Unholy Dying (2000), Emily Brontë (2000), Cry from the Dark (2003); *Recreations* walking, opera, Edwin Drood; *Style*— Robert Barnard, Esq; ✉ Hazeldene, Houghley Lane, Leeds LS13 2DT (tel and fax 0113 263 8955); c/o Gregory & Company, 3 Barb Mews, London W6 7PA (tel 020 7610 4676, fax 020 7610 4686)

BARNARD, Stephen Geoffrey; s of Geoffrey Thomas Barnard, and Diana Pixie, *née* Rivron; *b* 4 May 1950; *Educ* Gresham's, Univ of Southampton (LLB); *m* 4 Oct 1980, Jane Elizabeth Lisa, da of Dr Oliver Vivian Maxim, of Gretton, Northants; *Career* admitted slr 1974; traveller 1974–75; Herbert Smith: joined 1976, NY 1980–82, ptnr 1983–; *Recreations* golf, bridge, walking, birds, skiing, reading, trying to paint, music, talking, wine; *Style*— Stephen Barnard, Esq; ✉ Herbert Smith, Exchange House, Primrose Street, London EC2A 2HS (tel 020 7374 8000, fax 020 7374 0888)

BARNES, Adrian Francis Patrick; CVO (1996), DL (Greater London 2002); s of Francis Walter Ibbetson Barnes (d 2000), and Heather Katherine, *née* Tamplin; *b* 25 January 1943; *Educ* St Paul's, City of London Poly (MA); *m* 31 May 1980, Sally Eve, da of Dr James Lawson Whatley (d 1986); 1 s (William b 1982), 1 da (Sophie b 1983); *Career* called to the Bar Gray's Inn 1973; Slr's Dept DTI 1975–82, dep remembrancer Corp of London 1982, City Remembrancer 1986–2003; doyen Gray's Inn Seniors in Hall 1992–2000, bencher 2000–; govr Music Therapy Charity 1995– (chm 1997–2003); Wimbledon Civic Forum: fndr memb, memb Exec Ctee 1999–2003, chm gen meetings on constitution 1999–2001, chm Educn Forum 2000–03; chm Exec Ctee Wimbledon Guild 2004– (memb 2003–, chm Centenary Ctee, Counselling Ctee and Mgmnt Ctee 2004–); Freeman City of London 1982, Liveryman Worshipful Co of Merchant Taylors 1989, Freeman Guild of Arts Scholars, Dealers and Collectors 2007–; *Recreations* music, cricket, biography, circuit training, chess, City lore, rowing; *Clubs* Garrick, Guildhall, MCC, Cannons; *Style*— Adrian Barnes, Esq, CVO, DL; ✉ 18 Clare Court, London SW19 4RZ

BARNES, Carol Lesley; da of Leslie Harry Barnes, of London, and Alexandra Barnes; *b* 13 September 1944; *Educ* St Martin in the Fields HS, Univ of Sheffield (BA), Univ of Birmingham (CertEd); *m* 30 July 1981 (sep), Nigel Thomson, s of Hugh Thomson, of Brighton; 1 da (Clare b 14 July 1979 d 14 March 2004), 1 s (James b 26 May 1982); *Career* presenter LBC Radio 1973–74, reporter World at One BBC Radio 4 1974–75, reporter and newscaster ITN 1975–99, presenter Meridian TV 1999–2000, presenter ITN News Channel 2000–05; TV and Radio Industries Newscaster of the Year 1994; *Recreations* exercise, golf, good food and wine, diving, skiing; *Style*— Ms Carol Barnes; ✉ c/o Knight Ayton Management, 114 St Martin's Lane, London WC2N 4BE (tel 020 7836 5333)

BARNES, Christian William; s of Oswald Edward Barnes (d 2002), of Great Houghton Hall, Northants, and Gillian, *née* Ralph; *b* 20 June 1959; *Educ* Uppingham, Univ of Durham (BA); *m* 1987, Melanie Joy, da of Kenneth Roy Eades (d 1996); 3 s (Elliot James Royston b 6 Feb 1991, Hamish William b 25 June 1993, Lewis Gabriel b 1 Jan 1996); *Career* advertisement sales mangr Dominion Press Ltd 1981–82, asst account mangr then account dir Leo Burnett Ltd 1982–87, fndr ptnr and co dir BV Gp plc 1987–2001, fndr ptnr and co dir The Blackbox Partnership Ltd 2001–; *Recreations* music, theatre, travel; *Style*— Christian Barnes, Esq; ✉ The Blackbox Partnership Ltd, Unit 302, 190 St John Street, London EC1V 4JY (e-mail christian@blackboxpartnership.com)

BARNES, Christopher John Andrew (Chris); CB; s of Eric Vernon Barnes (d 1988), and Joan Mary, *née* Benge; *b* 11 October 1944; *Educ* City of London Sch, LSE (BSc Econ); *m* 1, 1978 (m dis 1990), Carolyn Elizabeth Douglas Johnston; 2 s (Andrew Peter b 13 July 1978, Timothy Richard b 13 Nov 1980); m 2, 1990, Susan Elizabeth Bridle; 2 s (Nicholas James b 6 Jan 1991, Edward Christopher b 19 Nov 1993); *Career* civil servant; MAFF: exec offr 1962–67, asst princ 1967–69, private sec to Parly Sec 1969–71, princ 1971–80, asst sec 1980, chief regnl offr 1980–83, head Personnel Div 1983–88, head Res Policy Div 1988–90, Near Market R&D Review 1988–89, under sec Arable Crops, Horticulture and Alcoholic Drinks 1990–95, dir of Establishments 1995–96, ret; chm: Assured Produce Ltd 1999–2000, Assured Food Standards Ltd 2000–03; sr conslt Andersons 1996–98, dir Andersons Chamberlain Recruitment Ltd 1998; dir: Drew Associates Ltd 1996–99, The Hartington Group Ltd 2003–; md Currency Connect (UK) Ltd 2004–; a chair Civil Service Selection Bd 1995–97; non-exec dir Booker Food Services 1987–90; chm Bucks HA 1999–2000, memb Mgmnt Ctee Civil Serv Healthcare 1992–99 (vice-chm 1997–99); FRSA, FIHort; *Recreations* off-road vehicles, country living, France; *Clubs* Farmers'; *Style*— Chris Barnes, CB, FRSA, FIHort

BARNES, Colin Angus; CBE (2001); s of Maurice Angus Barnes (d 1991), and Dorothy Edith, *née* Hubbard (1981); *b* 6 July 1933; *Educ* Bradfield Coll; *m* 20 Oct 1962, Brenda Agnes, da of Robert Burnett Loughborough; 1 s (David Angus b 15 Aug 1963), 2 da (Nicola Elizabeth b 11 June 1965, Susannah Dorothy b 17 Dec 1971); *Career* Nat Serv RAF 1952–54, Pilot Offr 1954; BOAC: cadet pilot and trainee navigator 1955–56, flight navigator and second offr 1956, flight navigator Argonauts and Yorks 1956–57, co-pilot and navigator Britannia 102s 1957, first offr 1958, co-pilot and navigator Boeing 707s 1962–71, sr first offr 1963, check first offr (navigation) Boeing 707 and Bd of Trade authorised examiner (Flight Navigator's Licence) 1968, captain 1971, flight superintendent (technical) Boeing 707 1973; British Airways (following merger of BOAC and BEA): flight superintendent (technical) DC10 1974, dep flight mangr (technical) DC10 1977, asst chief pilot 747/Concorde/DC10 1978, chief pilot 1981, dir of flight crew 1986–91, chm subsid British Caledonian Flight Training Ltd 1989–90 (non-exec dir 1988–91), ret 1991; non-exec dir British Airways plc 1991–2001, chm BA Safety Review Ctee 1991–2001; Flight Safety Fndn: govr and memb Exec Ctee 1991–2000, govr emeritus 2001–; The Air League: memb Cncl 1993–2002, memb Exec Ctee 1994–2002; Freeman City of London 1997, Liveryman Guild of Air Pilots and Air Navigators 1997; FRAeS 1997; *Recreations* gardening, tennis; *Clubs* RAF; *Style*— Colin Barnes, Esq, CBE; ✉ Sandilands, Glebe Lane, Rushmoor, Farnham, Surrey GU10 2EW (tel and fax 01252 792115)

BARNES, Geoffrey Frederick; s of Frederick Albert Barnes, of Hertford, and Iris Alice Maud, *née* Neslen (d 2002); *b* 14 April 1945; *Educ* Down Lane Central Sch; *m* 1, 29 Sept 1969 (m dis 1987), Sheila Emily Birtwhistle; 1 da (Alison Marguerite b 10 March 1974), 1 s (Andrew Geoffrey b 22 Jan 1976); m 2, 19 June 2004, Birgithe Edwards; *Career* joined Ogden Parsons (merged with Harmood Banner 1970 then with Deloitte Haskins Sells 1973) 1963, seconded to HM Treasy 1977–79; Casson Beckman (merged with Baker Tilly 1997): joined 1979, exec chm 1990–97, ceo and pres Baker Tilly International 2000–; memn Int Advsy Bd ICAEW (memb Cncl 2003–04); FCCA, FCA; *Recreations* golf, walking, climbing, reading particularly the history of the American Civil War; *Clubs* Lord's Taverners, Brocket Hall Golf; *Style*— Geoff Barnes, Esq; ✉ Baker Tilly International, 2 Bloomsbury Street, London WC1B 3ST (tel 020 7314 3571, fax 020 7314 6876, e-mail geoff.barnes@bakertilly.co.uk)

BARNES, Harold (Harry); s of late Joseph Barnes, of Easington Colliery, Co Durham, and late Betsy, *née* Gray; *b* 22 July 1936; *Educ* Ruskin Coll Oxford, Univ of Hull (BA); *m* 14 Sept 1963, Elizabeth Ann, da of Richard Stephenson (d 1983); 1 s (Stephen b 1968), 1 da (Joanne b 1972); *Career* Nat Serv RAF 1954–56; railway clerk 1952–54 and 1956–62; lectr Univ of Sheffield 1966–87 (dir mature matriculation courses 1984–87); variety of positions NE Derbys Constituency Lab Pty 1970–87, MP (Lab) Derbyshire NE 1987–2005; memb Cncl of Nat Admin Cncl of Independent Lab Pubns 1977–80 and 1982–85; memb ctee stage: Local Govt Fin Act 1988, Employment Act 1989, Football Spectator Act 1989, Educn (Student Loans) Act 1990, NI (Emergency Provisions) Act 1990–91, Tport and Works Act 1992, Further and Higher Educn Act 1992, Civil Rights (Disabled Persons) Bill 1995, Community Care (Direct Payments) Act 1996, Pollution and Control Act 1999, Special Educn and Disability Act 2001, Fin Act 2001, Justice (NI) Act 2002, Enterprise Act 2002, Land Registration Act 2003; memb: Select Ctees Euro Legislation 1989–97, Members Interests 1990–92, Standing Ctee (A) on Euro Legislation 1991–97, Select Ctee on NI 1997–2004, memb Br-Irish Inter-Parly Body 1997–2005 (assoc memb 1992–97); vice-chm: Lab Back-Bench Ctee on NI 1989–93 and 1997–2005, E Midlands Gp Labour MPs 1990–95; chm: Lab Back-Bench Ctee on Environmental Protection 1993–97, All-Pty UK-Malta Gp 1993–2005; vice-pres Labour Friends of Iraq 2006– (jt pres 2004–06); *Clubs* Dronfield Contact; *Style*— H Barnes, Esq; ✉ website threescoreyearsandten.blogspot.com

BARNES, Prof Howard Anthony; OBE (1997); s of Elijah Barnes (d 1958), of Ystrad Mynach, Glamorgan, and Doris Mabel, *née* Liddy (d 1978); *b* 8 April 1944; *Educ* Bargoed GS, UC Wales Aberystwyth (BSc, PhD, DSc); *m* 1967, Pauline Sandra, *née* Brind; 3 s (Timothy b 7 March 1969, Andrew b 25 Sept 1971, Stephen b 3 Jan 1973); *Career* Unilever Research Port Sunlight Lab: scientist 1970–78, sr scientist 1978–2000, princ scientist 2000–04; research prof Univ of Wales Aberystwyth 2004–; pres Br Soc of Rheology 1994–96 (chm of Founding Ctee of European Soc of Rheology 1996); chm: Applied Rheology Subject Gp Inst of Chem Engrg, European Federation of Chem Engrg; memb: Soft Solids Initiative EPSRC 1997– (chm 1994–97), Engrg and Physical Sciences Ctee BBSRC, Engrg Sciences Panel EC; external examiner: Univ of Wales Aberystwyth, Univ of Bangalore, Univ of Bradford, Univ of Bristol, Univ of Cambridge, Univ of Cardiff, Univ of Glamorgan, Univ of Leeds, Univ of Swansea, UCL, Univ of Birmingham, Univ of London, Univ Coll Dublin; memb Christian Brethren (lay preacher); Royal Soc of Chemistry Solids Processing Award 1984, Hanson Medal 1993, Br Soc of Rheology Annual Award 2001; FIChemE, FIM, FREng; *Books* Dispersion Rheology (1980), An Introduction to Rheology (with J Hutton & K Walters, 1989), A Handbook of Elementary Rheology (2000), Viscosity (2002); *Style*— Prof Howard Barnes, OBE, FREng; ✉ Institute of Mathematical & Physical Sciences, University of Wales, Aberystwyth SY23 3BZ (tel 01970 622802, e-mail hab@aber.ac.uk)

BARNES, Jack Henry; s of James Barnes (d 1944), and Joan Ivy, *née* Sears; *b* 11 December 1943; *Educ* Hatfield Sch, Univ of Sussex (BA), LSE (MSc); *m* 1966, Nicola, *née* Pearse; 2 da (Sarah b 1969, Rachel b 1970); *Career* univ and private sector res conslt 1968–78; Dept of Health: Chief Scientist's Office 1978–83, Social Servs Inspectorate 1983–88, Res Mgmnt Div 1988–91, Primary Care Div NHS Exec 1991–95, head Int and Indust Div 1995–99; dir of res Nat Asthma Campaign 2000–; *Style*— Jack Barnes, Esq; ✉ National

Asthma Campaign, Providence House, Providence Place, London N1 0NT (tel 020 7226 2260)

BARNES, Jeremy (Jerry); s of John Woodley Barnes, of Cornwall, and Elizabeth Ann, *née* Polkinghorne; *b* 11 February 1961; *Educ* Truro Sch, KCL (BA); *m* 8 August 1987 (m dis 2005), Susan Elizabeth, da of William Alexander Peet (d 2003); 2 s (Matthew Robert b 1 March 1990, Henry Alexander b 6 Sept 1992); *Career* trainee accountant Saffery Champness 1982–86, fin accountant S G Warburg 1986–87; Saffery Champness: rejoined 1987, ptnr 1990–, sr ptnr Bristol Office from its opening 1998–; FCA 1997 (ACA 1986); *Recreations* rugby, shooting and fishing; *Clubs* Farmers', Clifton (Bristol); *Style*— Jerry Barnes, Esq; ✉ Saffery Champness, Beaufort House, 2 Beaufort Road, Clifton, Bristol BS8 2AE (tel 0117 915 1617, mobile 07831 308143, e-mail jerry.barnes@saffery.com)

BARNES, Prof Jonathan; s of Albert Leonard Barnes (d 1992), and Kathleen Mabel, *née* Scoltock (d 1997); *b* 26 December 1942; *Educ* City of London Sch, Balliol Coll Oxford; *m* Jennifer Mary, da of Ormond Postgate; 2 da (Catherine, Camilla); *Career* Univ of Oxford: fell Oriel Coll 1968–78, lectr in philosophy 1968, fell Balliol Coll 1978–94, prof of ancient philosophy 1989–94; prof of ancient philosophy: Univ of Geneva 1994–2002, Univ of Paris IV-Sorbonne 2002–06; visiting appointments at: Univ of Chicago, Inst for Advanced Study Princeton, Univ of Massachusetts Amherst, Univ of Texas Austin, Wissenschaftskolleg zu Berlin, Univ of Edmonton, Univ of Zürich, Istituto Italiano per gli Studi Filosofici Naples, École Normale Supérieure de Paris, Scuola Normale di Pisa; Condorcet Medal 1996; FBA 1987, Hon FAAAS 1999; *Books* The Ontological Argument (1972), Aristotle's Posterior Analytics (1975), The Presocratic Philosophers (1979), Aristotle (1982), Early Greek Philosophy (1987), The Toils of Scepticism (1990), Logic and the Imperial Stoa (1997), Porphyry: Introduction (2003), Truth, etc (2006); *Style*— Prof Jonathan Barnes, FBA; ✉ Les Charmilles, L'Auvergne, 36200 Ceaulmont, France

BARNES, Dr (Nicholas) Martin Limer; s of Geoffrey Lambe Barnes (d 1984), and Emily *née* Dicken (d 1976); *b* 18 January 1939; *Educ* King Edward's Sch Birmingham, Imperial Coll London (BScEng), UMIST (PhD); *m* 23 Feb 1963, Diana Marion, da of Barrie Campbell (d 1968); 1 da (Kate b 1964), 1 s (Matthew b 1966); *Career* res fell Univ of Manchester 1968–71, ptnr Martin Barnes and Partners 1971–85, ptnr Coopers and Lybrand Associates mgmnt conslt 1985–96; exec dir The Major Projects Assoc 1997–2006; visiting prof Univ of Birmingham 1998–2003, assoc fell Templeton Coll Oxford 2001–; Churchill Fellowship 1971; ACIArb, ACGI, MBCS, CCMI, FREng, FICE, FCIOB, FAPM (chm 1986–91, pres 2003–), FInstCES (pres 1978–86); *Books* Measurement in Contract Control (1977), The CESMM2 Handbook (1986), Engineering Management: Financial Control (ed, 1990), The CESMM3 Handbook (1992); *Recreations* railway and canal history, victorian paintings; *Style*— Dr Martin Barnes, FREng; ✉ Cornbrash House, Kirtlington, Oxfordshire OX5 3HF (tel 01869 350828, e-mail cornbrash@aol.com)

BARNES, Melvyn Peter Keith; OBE (1990); s of Harry Barnes (ka N Africa 1942), and Doris, *née* Milton (d 1997); *b* 26 September 1942; *Educ* Chatham House Sch Ramsgate, NW London Poly (Library Assoc Dip), private study (Dip Municipal Admin); *m* 18 Sept 1965, Judith Anne, *née* Leicester; 2 s (Jeremy b 1970, Timothy b 1972); *Career* public library posts in Kent, Herts and Manchester 1958–68, dep Borough librarian Newcastle-under-Lyme 1968–72, chief librarian Ipswich 1972–74, Borough librarian and arts offr Royal Borough of Kensington & Chelsea 1974–80, city librarian Westminster 1980–84, Guildhall librarian and dir of libraries and art galleries Corp of London 1984–2002; Library Assoc: assoc 1965, memb Cncl 1974–98, pres 1995 (vice-pres 1991–93); memb Library and Information Servs Cncl (England) 1984–89, pres Int Assoc of Met City Libraries 1989–92; Freeman City of London 1984, Liveryman Clockmakers' Co 1990–2002 (hon librarian), Hon Freeman Worshipful Co of Gardeners 1995; FIMgt 1980, FRSA 1983; *Books* Youth Library Work (1968 and 1976), Best Detective Fiction (1975), Murder in Print (1986), Dick Francis (1986), Root and Branch: A History of the Worshipful Co of Gardeners (1994); *Publications* numerous contribs to librarianship and crime fiction jls and reference books; *Recreations* reading, writing, theatre, history of the movies and stage musicals, amateur operatics; *Style*— Melvyn Barnes, Esq, OBE; ✉ e-mail melvyn.barnes@oldnewton.com

BARNES, Prof Michael Patrick; s of Capt William Edward Clement Barnes (d 1999), of Broadwey, Dorset, and Gladys Constance, *née* Hooper; *b* 28 June 1940; *Educ* High Canons Sch, Wynstones Sch Gloucester, Freie Waldorfschule Stuttgart, UCL (BA, MA, Rosa Morrison prize), Nansenskolen Lillehammer, Univ of Oslo; *m* 8 Aug 1970, Kirsten Heiberg, da of Trygve Ole Mathias Røer (d 1980); 3 da (Catherine b 1971, Anne Helen b 1973, Kirsten Emily b 1980), 1 s (William Michael b 1978); *Career* Dept of Scandinavian Studies UCL: asst lectr 1964–67, lectr 1967–75, reader 1975–83, prof of Scandinavian philology 1983–94, prof of Scandinavian studies 1994–2005; Viking Soc for Northern Research: memb 1963–, ed Saga Book 1970–83, jt hon sec 1983–2006; ed NOWELE 1989–; memb: AUT 1964–, Royal Gustavus Adolphus Acad Uppsala 1984 (corresponding memb 1977–84), Norwegian Acad of Science and Letters 1997; Hon Dr Univ of Uppsala 2002; Knight Icelandic Order of the Falcon 1992; *Books* Old Scandinavian Texts (1968), Draumkvæde: an edition and study (1974), The Runic Inscriptions of Maeshowe, Orkney (1994), The Runic Inscriptions of Viking Age Dublin (jtly, 1997), The Norn Language of Orkney and Shetland (1998), A New Introduction to Old Norse I: Grammar (1999), Faroese Language Studies (2001), Introduction to Scandinavian Phonetics: Danish, Norwegian and Swedish (jtly, 2005), The Scandinavian Runic Inscriptions of Britain (jtly, 2006); *Recreations* badminton, drinking real ale, walking disused railways; *Style*— Prof Michael Barnes; ✉ 93 Longland Drive, Totteridge, London N20 8HN (tel 020 8445 4697, e-mail michael@runes.demon.co.uk); Department of Scandinavian Studies, University College London, Gower Street, London WC1E 6BT (tel 020 7679 7176/7, fax 020 7679 7750, e-mail m.barnes@ucl.ac.uk)

BARNES, (David) Michael William; QC (1981); s of David Charles Barnes (d 1954), and Florence Maud, *née* Matthews (d 1967); *b* 16 July 1943; *Educ* Monmouth, Wadham Coll Oxford (BA); *m* 5 Sept 1970, Susan Dorothy, da of William Turner; 3 s (Andrew b 1972, Edmund b 1974, Peter b 1979); *Career* called to the Bar Middle Temple 1965 (bencher 1989); recorder of the Crown Court 1984–; hon res fell LMH Oxford 1979; chm Hinckley Point 'C' Public Inquiry 1988; visiting fell Univ of Auckland NZ 1996; *Publications* Leasehold Reform Act 1967 (1967), Hill and Redman's Law of Landlord and Tenant (ed 15–18 edns, 1970–88), Hill and Redman's Guide to Rent Review (2001); *Recreations* crime fiction, walking; *Clubs* Beefsteak; *Style*— Michael Barnes, Esq, QC; ✉ Wilberforce Chambers, 8 New Square, Lincoln's Inn, London WC2A 3QP (tel 020 7306 0102, fax 020 7306 0095)

BARNES, Prof Neil Christopher; s of Douglas Barnes (d 1988), and June, *née* Deacon; *b* 24 June 1954; *Educ* Vyners GS Ickenham, Trinity Hall Cambridge (MA), Westminster Med Sch (MB BS); *m* 1983, Mari; 3 s (Christopher b 20 July 1985, Andrew b 25 Dec 1987, Oliver b 14 Feb 1995); *Career* research fell KCH until 1987, sr registrar London Chest Hosp 1987–88, conslt Royal London Hosp and London Chest Hosp 1988–, prof of respiratory medicine Queen Mary Univ of London 2002–, jt dir of R&D Barts and the London NHS Tst and Barts and the London Med Coll 2005–; assoc ed Thorax 1990–2002; author of more than 90 peer-reviewed pubns and 70 invited articles on the subject of asthma and other lung disorders; memb: Br Thoracic Soc (chair Pharmacology Section UK Asthma Guidelines), BMA; work with: Nat Asthma Campaign, Br Lung Fndn; FRCP 1995; *Recreations* skiing, reading; *Style*— Prof Neil Barnes; ✉ Department of Respiratory Medicine, London Chest Hospital, Bonner Road, London E2 9JX (tel 020 8983 2406, fax 020 8983 2279, e-mail neil.barnes@bartsandthelondon.nhs.uk)

BARNES, Prof Peter John; s of John Barnes (d 1989), and Eileen, *née* Thurman (d 1998); *b* 29 October 1946; *Educ* Leamington Coll, St Catharine's Coll Cambridge (scholar, MA, numerous prizes), Worcester Coll Oxford (BM BCh, DM, DSc); *m* 1976, Olivia Mary, *née* Harvard-Watts; 3 s (Adam b 2 Jan 1978, Toby b 20 Feb 1981, Julian b 14 Nov 1988); *Career* med registrar UCH London 1975–78, MRC research fell Royal Postgrad Med Sch 1978–81, MRC travelling fell Cardiovascular Res Inst San Francisco 1981–82, sr registrar Hammersmith Hosp 1979–82, sr lectr/conslt physician Royal Postgrad Med Sch and Hammersmith Hosp London 1982–85, prof of clinical pharmacology Cardiothoracic Inst London 1985–87; currently: prof of thoracic med, dir Dept of Thoracic Med and head of respiratory med Imperial Coll Sch of Med, hon conslt physician Royal Brompton Hosp London; author of numerous invited review papers and chapters, ed over 30 books on asthma, lung pharmacology and related topics; ed Respiratory Res, former ed Pulmonary Pharmacology; assoc ed: American Jl of Respiratory Critical Care Med, Br Jl of Clinical Pharmacology, Jl of Applied Physiology; memberships incl: Physiological Soc, Br Pharmacology Soc, Br Thoracic Soc (memb Cncl), MRS; FRCP 1988, FMedSci 1999, FRS 2007; *Recreations* travel, gardening; *Style*— Prof Peter Barnes; ✉ Department of Thoracic Medicine, National Heart and Lung Institute, Dovehouse Street, London SW3 6LY (tel 020 7351 8174, fax 020 7351 5675, e-mail p.j.barnes@imperial.ac.uk)

BARNES, Richard Michael; AM; s of John William Barnes (d 1977), and Kate (Kitty), *née* Harper; *b* 1 December 1947; *Educ* Trinity HS Northampton, Wolverhampton Grammar Tech Sch (head boy), Univ of Wales Inst of Sci and Technol (BSc); *Career* ldr London Borough of Hillingdon 1991–1993 and 1998–2000 (ldr Cons Gp 1991–2000); GLA: memb London Assembly (Cons) Ealing and Hillingdon 2000–, chair 7 July Review Ctee, memb Health Ctee, memb Audit Panel Ctee; memb Met Police Authy; dep chair Hillingdon HA 1998–2002, non-exec dir NW London SHA 2006–; patron: Hillingdon AIDS Response Tst, Hillingdon Life Scis, Sullivan Tst for Deaf Children; tstee NW London Community Tst 2002–; fndn advsr The Book Tst; Freeman City of London; FRSA 2007; *Recreations* field sports, opera, music, literature, chelonia; *Style*— Councillor Richard Barnes, AM; ✉ Greater London Assembly, City Hall, Queens Walk, Southwark, London SE1 2AA (tel 020 7983 4414, fax 020 7983 4419, e-mail richard.barnes@london.gov.uk, website www.richard.barnes.info)

BARNES, Prof Robert Harrison; s of Robert H Barnes (d 1985), and Edna, *née* Farrier (d 2002); *b* 11 October 1944; *Educ* Reed Coll USA (BA), Univ of Oxford (BLitt, DPhil); *m* 29 June 1968, Ruth, *née* Weinlich; 1 da (Ina Florence b 11 Sept 1974), 1 s (Jan Lawrence b 14 Feb 1979); *Career* visiting asst prof Univ of Southern Calif 1972–74, lectr Univ of Edinburgh 1974–77, lectr Univ of Oxford 1978–96, faculty fell St Antony's Coll Oxford 1987–, prof of social anthropology Univ of Oxford 1996–; memb: Royal Anthropological Soc 1969, Assoc of SE Asianists UK 1977, Assoc of Social Anthropologists of the Cwlth 1980; *Books* Kédang: A Study of the Collective Thought of an Eastern Indonesian People (1974), Sea Hunters of Indonesia (1996); *Recreations* walking; *Style*— Prof R H Barnes; ✉ Institute of Social and Cultural Anthropology, 51 Banbury Road, Oxford OX2 6PE (tel 01865 274676, fax 01865 274630, e-mail robert.barnes@anthro.ox.ac.uk); St Antony's College, Woodstock Road, Oxford OX2 6PF (tel 01865 284701)

BARNES, Rosemary Susan (Rosie); da of Alan Allen, of Nottingham, and Kathleen, *née* Brown; *b* 16 May 1946; *Educ* Bilborough GS, Univ of Birmingham (BSocSci); *m* 1967, Graham Barnes; 2 s (Danny b 1973, Joseph b 1985), 1 da (Daisy b 1975); *Career* mgmnt trainee Unilever Research Bureau Ltd 1967–69, mktg exec Yardley of London Ltd 1969–72, primary teacher 1972, freelance researcher 1973–87, MP (SDP 1987–90, Social Democrat 1990–92) Greenwich 1987–92; non-exec dir Portman Building Society 1997–2002; dir Birthright (now WellBeing) 1992–96, chief exec Cystic Fibrosis Trust 1996–; *Style*— Mrs Rosie Barnes; ✉ Cystic Fibrosis Trust, 11 London Road, Bromley, Kent BR1 1BY (tel 020 8464 7211, fax 020 8313 0472, e-mail rbarnes@cftrust.org.uk)

BARNES, Simon Seton; s of Edward Walter Taylor Barnes (d 2001), of Chelsea, London, and Joan Constance Barnes (d 1985); *b* 26 January 1958; *Educ* Shiplake Coll, INSEAD (Advanced Mgmnt Prog); *m* 19 Aug 1983, Wendy Clare; 2 s (Oliver b 13 June 1986, Edward b 19 Jan 1988), 1 da (Phoebe b 9 July 1990); *Career* Alexander Howden Reinsurance Brokers Ltd: joined as trainee 1976, dir 1983, md 1986–90, chief exec 1990–95; md and chief operating offr Alexander Howden Non-Marine 1995–97, md Aon Group Ltd Non-Marine Reinsurance 1997–2001 (resigned), ptnr Jardine Lloyd Thompson Risk Solutions Ltd 2001–; *Recreations* golf, rugby, tennis; *Style*— Simon Barnes, Esq; ✉ JLT Re, One America Square, London EC3N 2JL (tel 020 7466 1300, fax 020 7466 1470, e-mail simon.barnes@jltre.com)

BARNES, Timothy Paul; QC (1986); s of late Arthur Morley Barnes, of Seal, Kent, and Valerie Enid Mary, *née* Wilks; *b* 23 April 1944; *Educ* Bradfield, Christ's Coll Cambridge (MA); *m* Aug 1969, Patricia Margaret, da of Leslie Ralph Gale (d 1974); 1 s (Christopher b 1973), 3 da (Olivia b 1975, Jessica b 1978, Natasha b 1986); *Career* called to the Bar Gray's Inn 1968 (bencher); asst recorder 1983–87, recorder of the Crown Court 1987–, memb Midland & Oxford Circuit; chm Greenwich Soc 1999–; *Recreations* hockey, gardening, music; *Clubs* MCC; *Style*— Timothy P Barnes, Esq, QC; ✉ 7 Bedford Row, London WC1R 4BU (tel 020 7242 3555)

BARNES JONES, HE Deborah Elizabeth Vavasseur; da of late Edward Henry Barnes, and Barbara Lucia, *née* Cobb; *b* 6 October 1956; *Educ* Benenden, Univ of Bristol (BA); *m* 7 June 1986, F Richard Jones; 2 da (Hilary, Jennifer (twins) b 1991); *Career* diplomat; second sec Moscow 1983–85, Cabinet Office 1985–86, first sec Tel Aviv 1988–92, head of section Hong Kong Dept 1992–94, personnel mangr 1994–96, dep head of mission Montevideo 1996–99, ambass to Georgia 2001–04, govr Monserrat 2004–07; MIPD 1996; *Recreations* choral singing; *Clubs* Royal Over-Seas League; *Style*— HE Mrs Deborah Barnes Jones; ✉ e-mail deborah.barnes_jones@fco.gov.uk

BARNETT, Prof Anthony Howard (Tony); s of Geoffrey Barnett, and Beulah, *née* Statman; *b* 29 May 1951; *Educ* Roundhay GS Leeds, KCH London (BSc, MB BS, MD); *m* 11 Nov 1975, Catherine Elizabeth Mary, da of John O'Donnell (d 1977); 3 s (James John, Jonathan Andrew, Robert David), 3 da (Clare Joanne, Sarah Suzanne, Anna Lucy); *Career* sr fell MRC 1979–81, sr registrar in med diabetes and endocrinology Christchurch NZ and Southampton 1981–83; Univ of Birmingham: sr lectr and conslt physician 1983, reader in med 1989, prof of med 1992–; sec NZ Diabetes Assoc 1981–82; memb: Assoc of Physicians of GB and Ireland, Br Diabetic Assoc, Euro Assoc for the Study of Diabetes; ed med educn jls: Hypertension Management, Modern Diabetes Management, Obesity in Practice, Practical Cardiovascular Risk Mgmnt; author of research papers in Nature, Nature Genetics and other learned jls; FRCP 1989 (MRCP 1978); *Books* Immunogenetics of Insulin Dependent Diabetes (1987), Hypertension and Diabetes (1990, 3 edn 2000), Lipids, Diabetes and Vascular Disease (1992, 2 edn 1997), Shared Care in Diabetes (1998), Insulin Made Easy (2001, 2 edn 2004), Clinical Management of Hypertension in Diabetes (2002), Diabetes Annual (2002), Current Diabetes (2003), Diabetes and the Heart (2004), Obesity and Diabetes (2004), Diabetes and Cardiovascular Disease (2004), Diabetes, Obesity and Cardiovascular Disease (2005), Diabetes and Renal Disease (2005), Applying the Evidence: Clinical Trials in Diabetes (2005), Diabetes: Best Practice and Research Compendium (2006), Patient Compliance in Diabetes (2007); *Recreations* reading, sport and family; *Style*— Prof Tony Barnett; ✉ Birmingham Heartlands Hospital, Undergraduate Centre, Birmingham B9 5SS (tel 0121 424 3587, fax 0121 424 0593, e-mail anthony.barnett@heartofengland.nhs.uk)

BARNETT, Anthony Peter John; *b* 10 September 1941; *Educ* Univ of Essex (MA), Univ of Sussex; *Career* writer and publisher; editorial dir Allardyce, Barnett, Publishers 1981–, ed Fable Bulletin - Violin Improvisation Studies 1993–, prodr AB Fable Recording 2002–; visiting scholar Meiji Univ Japan 2002; *Poetry and Prose* incl: Poem About Music (1974), Blood Flow (1975), Fear and Misadventure/Mud Settles (1977), A White Mess (1981), North North, I Said, No, Wait a Minute, South, Oh, I Don't Know (148 Political Poems) (1985), The Resting Bell (collected, 1987), Little Stars and Straw Breasts (1993), The Poetry of Anthony Barnett - Essays, Interview and Letters (1993), Carp and Rubato (1995), Anti-Beauty (1999), Lisa Lisa (2000); collaborations with artists: Forest Poems Forest Drawings (with David Nash, 1987), Would You Tread on a Quadruped? An Animal Alphabet of Questionable Rhymes (with Natalie Cohen, 1992), Etiquette in the City (with Yolski, 2001), Miscanthus: Selected and New Poems (2005); covered in anthologies incl: A Various Art (1987 and 1990), Poets On Writing - Britain, 1970–1991 (1992), Other: British and Irish Poetry since 1970 (1999); collected poetry to 1999 included in Chadwyck-Healey Twentieth-Century English Poetry online database; translations from Italian, French, Norwegian, Swedish and Japanese; *Music Books* Desert Sands: The Recordings and Performances of Stuff Smith, An Annotated Discography and Biographical Source Book (1995), Up Jumped the Devil (1998), Black Gypsy: The Recordings of Eddie South, An Annotated Discography and Itinerary (1999), Listening for Henry Crowder (2007); contrib: New Grove Dictionary of Jazz, New Grove Dictionary of Music and Musicians; *Recreations* music, mountains; *Style—* Mr Anthony Barnett; ✉ Allardyce, Barnett, Publishers, 14 Mount Street, Lewes, East Sussex BN7 1HL (website www.abar.net)

BARNETT, Bernard; s of Samuel Hyman Barnett (d 1978), and Anne, *née* Silver (d 1964); *b* 24 April 1942; *Educ* Torquay GS; *m* (m dis); 2 s (Danny b 10 June 1963, Guy b 3 April 1967), 1 da (Claire b 9 Aug 1965); *Career* reporter: Mid-Devon Advertiser 1960–63, Evening Tribune Nuneaton 1964; ed Mid-Devon Advertiser 1964–68, prodn ed rising to dep ed Campaign magazine 1968–72, exec ed Design magazine 1972; ed: Adweek 1973–75, Parents 1975–78; managing ed Psychology Today 1975–78; ed: Campaign 1978–84, Autocar 1984; ed/publisher Review 1985–86, ed Creative Review 1986, gp communications dir Abbott Mead Vickers advtg 1987–89, gp communications dir Ogilvy & Mather advtg 1989–91, editorial dir Campaign 1991–94, exec vice-pres and dir of corp affrs Young & Rubicam Europe 1994–; *Recreations* music, books, cars, cricket; *Style—* Bernard Barnett, Esq; ✉ Young & Rubicam Ltd, Greater London House, Hampstead Road, London NW1 7QP (tel 020 7387 9366)

BARNETT, His Hon Christopher John Anthony; QC (1983); s of Richard Adrian Barnett (d 1991), of Battle, E Sussex, and Phyllis, *née* Cartwright (d 1947); *b* 18 May 1936; *Educ* Repton, Coll of Law London; *m* 31 Oct 1959, Sylvia Marieliese (Marlies), da of George Lyn Ashby Pritt (d 1983), and Sylvia Marguerite, *née* Castleden (d 1993); 2 s (Peter b 1962, Marcus b 1970), 1 da (Susannah b 1965); *Career* Nat Serv with Kenya Regt and Kenya Govt, Dist Offr (Kikuyu Gd) 1954–56; Kenya Govt Serv 1956–60; dist offr HM Overseas Civil Serv in Kenya 1960–62; called to the Bar Gray's Inn 1965, recorder of the Crown Court 1982–88, jt head of chambers 4 Paper Buildings Temple 1983–88, circuit judge (SE Circuit) 1988–2003 (dep circuit judge 2003–), dep High Court judge (Queens Bench Div) 1991–97, designated family judge Suffolk 1991–2003; chm SE Circuit Area Liaison Ctee 1985–88, memb Ctee Cncl of Circuit Judges 1992–2003; pres Mental Health Review Tbnl Restricted Patients Panel 2002–, chm Bar Disciplinary Tbnl 2006–; memb: Ct Univ of Essex 1983–, Wine Ctee SE Circuit 1984–88; chm Suffolk Community Alcohol Services 1993–95; patron Relate West Suffolk 1998–; pres Old Reptonian Soc 2002; *Recreations* cricket, tennis, walking, travel, gardening under instruction; *Clubs* Kenya Kongonis Cricket; *Style—* His Hon Christopher Barnett, QC; ✉ c/o Judicial Secretariat, 2nd Floor, Rose Court, 2 Southwark Bridge, London SE1 9HS

BARNETT, Dr Correlli Douglas; CBE (1997); s of D A Barnett; *b* 28 June 1927; *Educ* Trinity Sch Croydon, Exeter Coll Oxford (MA); *m* 1950, Ruth Murby; 2 da; *Career* writer and historian; Intelligence Corps 1945–48; N Thames Gas Bd 1952–57, public rels 1957–63; Churchill Coll Cambridge: fell 1977–, keeper of the Churchill Archives Centre 1977–95; lectr in def studies Univ of Cambridge 1980–83; memb: Cncl RUSI 1973–85, Ctee London Library 1977–79 and 1982–84; chm Lit Panel and memb Exec Ctee E Arts Assoc 1972–78, pres E Anglian Writers 1969–88; historical conslt/writer to BBC TV series: The Great War 1963–64 (Screenwriters' Guild Award 1964), The Lost Peace 1965–66, The Commanders 1972–73; Chesney Gold medal RUSI 1991; hon pres Western Front Assoc 1998–, Hon DSc Cranfield Univ 1993; FRHistS, FRSL, FRSA, Hon FCGI 2003; *Books* The Hump Organisation (1957), The Channel Tunnel (with Humphrey Slater, 1958), The Desert Generals (1960, 2 edn 1983), The Swordbearers (1963), Britain and Her Army (1970, RSL award 1971), The Collapse of British Power (1972), Marlborough (1974), Bonaparte (1978), The Great War (1979), The Audit of War (1986), Hitler's Generals (ed, 1989), Engage the Enemy More Closely: The Royal Navy in the Second World War (1991, Yorkshire Post Book of the Year 1991), The Lost Victory: British Dreams, British Realities 1945–1950 (1996), The Verdict of Peace: Britain Between her Yesterday and the Future (2001); contrib to: The Promise of Greatness (1968), Governing Elites (1969), Decisive Battles of the Twentieth Century (1976), The War Lords (1976), The Economic System in the UK (1985), Education for Capability (1986); *Clubs* Beefsteak, Reeds (Norwich); *Style—* Dr Correlli Barnett, CBE, FRSL; ✉ Catbridge House, East Carleton, Norwich NR14 8JX (tel and fax 01508 570410)

BARNETT, Prof David Braham; CBE (2007); s of Joseph Barnett (d 1998), and Jeanne Barnett (d 1995); *b* 17 July 1944; *Educ* Sheffield Univ Med Sch (MB, Hon ChB, MD); *Career* Merck Int travelling fell 1975–76, sr lectr Univ of Leicester 1976–84, prof of clinical pharmacology Univ of Leicester and hon conslt physician Leicester Royal Infirmary 1984–; non-exec dir Leicester Royal Infirmary NHS Tst 1993–2000, chm Specialist Advsy Ctee for Gen (Internal) Med RCP 1995–99, chm Appraisals Ctee Nat Inst for Clinical Excellence 1999; FRCP 1981; *Publications* over 150 res publications in the fields of molecular pharmacology and gen cardiovascular clinical pharmacology with special interest in ischaemic heart disease; *Recreations* golf, reading, theatre; *Style—* Professor David Barnett, CBE; ✉ Department of Cardiovascular Sciences, Clinical Pharmacology Group, Level 4, Robert Kilpatrick Clinical Sciences Building, Leicester Royal Infirmary, Leicester LE2 7LX (tel 0116 252 3126, fax 0116 252 3108, e-mail dbb1@le.ac.uk)

BARNETT, Brig Garry Charles; OBE (1983); s of Peter William Barnett (d 1994), and Hon Vera Kate, *née* Churchman, da of Baron Woodbridge; *b* 18 May 1939; *Educ* Eton, RMA Sandhurst; *m* 13 Sept 1969, Margaret Jennifer, da of Thomas Moffatt Banks; 2 s (Robert b 29 March 1971, David b 2 Dec 1972), 1 da (Joanna b 29 Sept 1976); *Career* CO 1 Bn The Black Watch 1980–83, Cdr 20 Armd Bde Germany 1983–85, Cdr Br Military Advsy and Trg Team Zimbabwe 1991–93, Col The Black Watch 1992–2003; Freeman City of London, Liveryman Worshipful Co of Ironmongers; *Recreations* country pursuits; *Clubs* Army and Navy; *Style—* Brig G C Barnett, OBE; ✉ Campsie Hill, Guildtown, Perth PH2 6DP (tel 01821 640325, fax 01821 640785, e-mail campsie@globalnet.co.uk)

BARNETT, Baron (Life Peer UK 1983), of Heywood and Royton in Greater Manchester; Joel Barnett; PC (1975), JP (Lancs 1960); s of Louis Barnett (d 1964), of Manchester, and Ettie Barnett (d 1956); *b* 14 October 1923; *Educ* Derby Street Jewish Sch, Manchester Central HS; *m* 11 Sept 1949, Lilian Stella, da of Abraham Goldstone (d 1965); 1 da (Hon Erica Hazel b 7 Aug 1951); *Career* served WWII RASC and Br Mil Govt Germany; sr ptnr J C Allen & Co Manchester 1954–74; Parly candidate (Lab) Runcorn 1959, MP (Lab) Lancs Heywood and Royton 1964–83; chm Lab Party Econ and Financial Gp 1967–70; memb: Public Accounts Ctee 1966–71, Public Expenditure Ctee 1971–74, Select Ctee on Civil List 1972, Select Ctee on Tax Credits 1973; chief sec Treasury 1974–79 (oppn spokesman Treasury 1970–74), Cabinet memb 1977–79, chm Commons Select Ctee Public Accounts 1979–83; oppn spokesman (Lords) Treasury 1983–86; memb Hallé Soc of Manchester 1982–90; hon visiting fell Univ of Strathclyde 1980–, tstee V&A 1983–97, vice-pres Assoc of Metropolitan Authorities 1983–86; vice-chm BBC 1986–93; chm Hansard Soc for Parly Govt 1984–90; dir various public and private cos; chm Birkbeck Coll Appeal 1993–96; tstee Open Univ Fndn 1995–; Hon LLD Univ of Strathclyde 1983; hon fell Birkbeck Coll London; FCCA; *Books* Inside the Treasury (1982); *Recreations* hiking, reading, music, theatre; *Style—* The Rt Hon the Lord Barnett, PC; ✉ 7 Hillingdon Road, Whitefield, Manchester M45 7QQ (tel 0161 766 3634); 92 Millbank Court, 24 John Islip Street, London SW1 (tel 020 7828 3620)

BARNETT, Jonathan Ian; s of Louis and Frances Barnett; *Educ* St Marylebone GS; *m* Nava, 3 s (James, Joshua, Edward); *Career* sports agent; with: Curzon House Casino 1970–78, Coral Leisure 1978–82; self-employed conslt 1982–91, dir Stellar Promotions & Management 1991–; prodr Come On You Reds by Manchester United (single, highest chart position no 1); memb Bd of various charities; represented England schoolboys at swimming and rugby; *Recreations* collecting watches, wine and art; *Style—* Jonathan Barnett, Esq; ✉ Stellar Group Ltd, 16 Stanhope Place, London W2 2HH (tel 020 7298 0080, fax 020 7298 0099, e-mail jonathan.barnett@stellargroup.co.uk)

BARNETT, His Hon Judge Kevin Edward; s of Arthur Barnett (d 1987), of Solihull, W Midlands, and Winifred, *née* Jones; *b* 2 January 1948; *Educ* Wellesbourne Sch, Tudor Grange GS, City of Birmingham Coll (LLB, London); *m* 6 May 1972, Patricia Margaret, da of Dr Charles Hanby Smith; 1 da (Elizabeth Clare b 6 Aug 1981); *Career* called to the Bar Gray's Inn 1971; in practice Wales & Chester Circuit, recorder 1994–96 (asst recorder 1991), head of chambers 1995–96, circuit judge (Wales & Chester Circuit) 1996–; *Recreations* photography, painting, cooking; *Clubs* Lansdowne; *Style—* His Hon Judge Kevin Barnett; ✉ c/o Wales and Chester Circuit Office, Churchill House, Churchill Way, Cardiff CF1 4HH

BARNETT, Rosemary; da of Leslie Wilson Barnett (d 1976), of Kingston Hill, Surrey, and Ella, *née* Renwick; *b* 12 August 1940; *Educ* Kingston Sch of Art, Royal Acad Schs (Landseer Prize, Edward Stott Scholarship and Silver Medal); *m* 1963, Nigel John Burfield Holmes; 2 s (Mark Burfield b 1968, Robert Burfield b 1970), 2 da (Sasha Renwick b 1971, Tanya Renwick b 1973); *Career* sculptor; princ Sir Henry Doulton Sch of Sculpture, dir and fndr Frink Sch of Figurative Sculpture 1996–2005, curator Jerwood Sculpture Park at Witley Court 1999–2003, fndr Glasshouse Studios Staffs Moorlands 2006; dir Ceramic and Allied Trade Union (CATU) Commemorative Project 2000–05; Br Inst Award 1959; memb Bd Lichfield Int Music Festival 1993–98, memb Lichfield Cathedral Artreach 2002–04; memb Soc for the Study of Normal Psychology 1970–; FRBS 1998 (memb RBS 1966, memb Cncl 1992–95); *Recreations* walking, gardening; *Clubs* Reynolds (memb Cncl 1989–91); *Style—* Ms Rosemary Barnett; ✉ 25 Brookfield's Road, Ipstones, Staffordshire ST10 2LY

BARNETT, His Hon Judge William Evans; QC (1984); s of Alec Barnett (d 1981), of Penarth, S Glam, and Esmé Georgiana, *née* Leon (d 1989); *b* 10 March 1937; *Educ* Repton, Keble Coll Oxford (MA); *m* 24 July 1976, Lucinda Jane Gilbert, JP, da of Richard William Gilbert (d 1980), of Addington, Surrey; 2 s (Nicholas b 1978, James b 1980); *Career* Nat Serv RCS 1956–58; called to the Bar Inner Temple 1962; joined Midland & Oxford Circuit 1963, recorder Crown Court 1981–94, circuit judge (SE Circuit) 1994–; memb: Personal Injuries Litigation Procedure Working Pty 1976–78, Panel of Arbitrators Motor Insurers' Bureau 1987–94; judicial memb Mental Health Review Tbnl 1993–2004; memb Ctee Whitgift Sch 1996–2002, govr Whitgift Fndn (incl Whitgift, Trinity and Old Palace Schs) 2004–; *Recreations* golf, photography, gardening, DIY; *Clubs* RAC, Croydon Medico-Legal Soc; *Style—* His Hon Judge William Barnett, QC; ✉ Croydon Combined Court Centre, Altyre Road, Croydon, Surrey (tel 020 8410 4700)

BARNEVIK, Percy Nils; s of Einar Barnevik (d 1993), and Anna Barnevik (d 1989); *b* 13 February 1941; *Educ* Sch of Economics Gothenburg (MBA), Stanford Univ; *m* Anna; 2 s, 1 da; *Career* Johnson-Gp Sweden 1966–69; Sandvik AB Sweden: mangr mgmnt info systems 1969–74, pres (USA) 1975–79, exec vice-pres (Sweden) 1979, chm 1983–2002; chm Skansa AB Sweden 1992–97 (memb bd 1986–92), pres and ceo ASEA AB Sweden 1980–87; ABB Ltd Switzerland: pres and ceo 1988–96, chm and ceo 1996, chm 1997–2002; chm: Investor AB Sweden 1997–2002 (memb Bd 1986–), Astra Zeneca plc 1999–2004; memb Bd: duPont USA 1991–98, General Motors USA 1996–; memb: Acad of Engrg Sci Sweden and Finland, Business Cncl of American CEOs, Int Advsy Cncl Fed of Korean Industries, Int Investment Cncl advising SA Govt, WEF/CII India Advsy Cncl; memb Advsy Cncl: Foreign Relations USA, Wharton Sch of Business Admin Philadelphia, Humboldt Univ Berlin, Centre for Euro Reform UK; awards incl: World Trade Hall of Fame LA 1993, Int Mgmnt survey Europe's Top CEO 1994, Euro Leadership Award Stanford Univ 1997, World Trade Global Exec of the Decade 1998, Polish Business Oscar 1999, Appeal of Conscience Award 1999; Hon DUniv: Linköping, Gothenburg, Babson Coll MA, Cranfield, UMIST, Manchester; hon fell London Business Sch; foreign hon memb American Academy of Arts and Sciences; Hon FREng; Cdr Cross of the Star of the Medal of Merit of the Repub of Poland 1998; *Recreations* sailing, jogging, cross country; *Style—* Dr Percy Barnevik

BARNEWALL, Sir Reginald Robert; 13 Bt (I 1623), of Crickstown Castle, Co Meath; s of Sir Reginald John Barnewall, 12 Bt (d 1961); *b* 1 October 1924; *Educ* Xavier Coll Melbourne; *m* 1, 1946, Elsie Muriel (d 1962), da of Thomas Matthews Frederick, of Brisbane, Queensland; 3 da; m 2, 1962, Maureen Ellen, da of William Daly, of S Caulfield, Victoria; 1 s (Peter Joseph); *Heir* s, Peter Barnewall; *Career* wool grower, cattle breeder, orchardist; served Royal Australian Engineers Aust Imp Force WWII, cmd B Sqn Victorian Mounted Rifles Royal Australian Armoured Corps 1952–56; md Southern Airlines Ltd of Melbourne 1953–58, fndr and ops mangr Polynesian Airlines W Samoa 1958–62, md Orchid Beach (Fraser Island) Pty Ltd 1962–71, dir and vice-chm J Roy Stevens Pty Ltd (printers and publishers) 1962–75, dir Island Airways Pty Ltd Qld 1964–68, operator and owner Coastal-Air Co Qld 1971–76; *Clubs* United Service (Brisbane), Royal Automobile Club of Queensland, Returned Services League of Australia (Surfers' Paradise); *Style—* Sir Reginald Barnewall, Bt; ✉ Innisfree House, Normandie Court, Mount Tamborine, Queensland 4272, Australia

BARNICOAT, Thomas Humphry (Tom); s of John Barnicoat, and Jane Wright; *b* 21 October 1952; *Educ* Lycée Français de Londres, St John's Coll Oxford; *m* 1980, Katrina Chalmers; 3 da (Rebecca Jane b 29 Sept 1981, Laura Veronica b 22 Oct 1983, Phoebe Emmeline b 2 July 1991), 1 dog (Tug b 7 March 2000); *Career* BBC: grad trainee 1977, scriptwriter TV news 1979, prodr and dir TV current affrs 1981–86; prodr Crown Television 1986, dir of public affrs Sotheby's 1986–87, prodr Business Television 1987–89; Endemol UK plc (Broadcast Communications plc until 2000): dir of corp devpt 1990–93, dep chief exec 1993–95, chief exec 1995–2004; chief operating offr Endemol Group 2005–07; memb Scotch Malt Whisky Soc; *Clubs* Reform, Hurlingham; *Style—* Tom Barnicoat, Esq; ✉ >e-mail< tbarnicoat@mac.com

BARNSLEY, Victoria (The Hon Mrs Nicholas Howard); da of late T E Barnsley, OBE, and Margaret Gwyneth, *née* Llewellin; *b* 4 March 1954; *Educ* UCL (BA), Univ of York (MA); *m* Feb 1992, Hon Nicholas Paul Geoffrey Howard, 2 s of Baron Howard of Henderskelfe (d 1984); 1 da (Blanche Mary b 5 Oct 1994); *Career* fndr and publisher Fourth Estate Publishers 1984–2000, chief exec Harper Collins Publishers 2000–; dir Tate Enterprises Ltd; tstee: Tate Gallery 1998–2007, Nat Gallery 2005–07, Tate Fndn 2007–; hon fell UCL

2005; *Style*— Ms Victoria Barnsley; ✉ Harper Collins Publishers, 77–85 Fulham Palace Road, Hammersmith, London W6 8JB (tel 020 8307 4874, fax 020 8307 4249)

BARON, Hon Mrs Justice; Dame Florence Jacqueline; DBE (2003); *Educ* St Hugh's Coll, Oxford; *Career* called to the Bar (Middle Temple) 1976; QC 1995, head of chambers Queen Elizabeth Building until 2003, recorder 1999–2003, judge of the High Court of Justice (Family Div) 2003–; *Style*— The Hon Mrs Justice Baron

BARON, Frank; *b* 5 May 1947; *Educ* Tulse Hill Sch; *m* 1983, Lorna Margaret, da of Brian Dearnaley; 2 s (Christopher b 1983, Alexander b 1987); *Career* asst photographer Keystone Press Agency 1963–67, photographer Daily Sketch 1967–72, fndr and photographer Sporting Pictures 1972–85, sports photographer The Guardian 1985–; winner Sports Picture of the Year 1974, winner News Photographer of the Year 1999; fndr memb Professional Sports Photographers' Assoc, fndr Int Tennis Photographers' Assoc; *Recreations* tennis; *Clubs* Telford Lawn Tennis; *Style*— Frank Baron, Esq; ✉ 12 Ederline Avenue, Norbury, London SW16 (tel 020 8679 3056); The Guardian, 119 Farringdon Road, London EC1 (tel 020 7278 2332)

BARON, Dr (Jeremy) Hugh; s of Dr Edward Baron (d 1964), and Lilian Hannah (Dolly) Baron (d 1984); *b* 25 April 1931; *Educ* UCS Hampstead, The Queen's Coll Oxford (MA, DM), Middx Hosp Med Sch London; *m* 1, 8 Sept 1960, Wendy, da of Dr Samuel Barnet Dimson; 1 s (Richard b 1964), 1 da (Susannah b 1968); m 2, 31 Dec 1990, Carla Lord; *Career* Capt RAMC Royal Herbert Hosp Woolwich, BMH Singapore and Malaya, jr specialist med and offr i/c Med Div BMH Kuala Lumpur Malaya 1956–58; house physician, registrar, lectr, sr registrar Middx Hosp and Med Sch London 1954–67, Leverhulme research scholar 1961, MRC Eli Lilly travelling fell and fell in gastroenterology Mount Sinai Hosp NYC 1961–62, conslt physician Prince of Wales and St Ann's Hosps Tottenham 1968–71, sr lectr and hon conslt Depts of Surgery and Med Royal Postgrad Med Sch and Hammersmith Hosp London 1968–96, conslt physician and gastroenterologist St Charles Hosp London 1971–94, conslt physician and gastroenterologist St Mary's Hosp and hon clinical sr lectr St Mary's Hosp Med Sch Imperial Coll of Sci Technol and Med London 1988–96, co-dir Parkside Helicobacter Study Gp 1988–96, examiner Universities of Bristol, Cambridge, Cardiff, Glasgow, Leeds, London and Newcastle; sub dean St Mary's Hosp Med Sch 1983–87, hon sr lectr Faculty of Med Imperial Coll of Med 1996–, hon professorial lectr Mount Sinai Sch of Med NYC 1996–; Hunterian prof RCS 1993–94, Goodall lectr RCPSGlas 1994, Fitzpatrick lectr RCP 1994, Burki lectr CPSP 1995, Sydenham lectr Soc of Apothecaries 1996, Melrose lectr Gastroenterology Club RCPSGlas 2000, Harveian lectr Harveian Soc London 2001, Boas lectr German Soc Gastroenterology 2001; RSM: pres Clinical Section 1980–81, sr hon ed 1984–90, chm European Ctee 1991–93, vice-pres 1991–93; memb: Paddington & North Kensington HA 1982–86, Cncl RCP 1993–96, Governing Body Br Postgrad Med Fedn 1993–96; archivist Br Soc of Gastroenterology 1981–97, chm St Charles Hosp Beautification Ctee 1983–93, chm Med Writers' Gp The Soc of Authors 1985–87, chm Hammersmith Hosp Arts Ctee 1996–2000 (vice-chm 1988–96), pres Br Soc of Gastroenterology 1988–89, chm Mgmnt Ctee Br Health Care Arts Centre 1989–93; sec Prout Club 1972–96 (pres 1996–97), Br sec Euro Gastro Club 1982–96; Gold Medal Sociedad Argentina de Gastroenterologia 1973, Koster Prize Danish Gastroenterologists 1981, Siurala Prize Finnish Gastroenterological Assoc 1988, Boas Medal German Soc Gastroenterology 2001; hon memb: Société National Français de Gastroentérologie 1981, Br Soc of Gastroenterology 1996, Euro Gastro Club 1996, Harveian Soc of London 2001; Liveryman Worshipful Soc of Apothecaries 1972; memb BMA, RSM; FRCP, FRCPGlas, FRCS; *Books* Carbenoxolone Sodium (1970), Clinical Tests of Gastric Secretion (1978), Foregut (1981), Cimetidine in the 80s (1981), Vagotomy in Modern Surgical Practice (1982), St Charles Hospital Works of Art (1984, 2 edn 1993), History of The British Society of Gastroenterology, 1937–1987 (1987), Theoretical Surgery (co-ed, 1986–94), Art at the Hammersmith Hospitals and Medical Schools (1996), The Prout Club (1996, 2 edn 2007), Twenty-four Notable Mount Sinai Physicians and Scientists (2001), ABC of the Upper Gastrointestinal Tract (2002), Gastroenterology and Hepatology at the Mount Sinai Hospital 1852–2000 (2002), The Anglo-American Biomedical Antecedents of Nazi Crimes (2007); *Recreations* looking, beautifying hospitals; *Clubs* Oxford and Cambridge; *Style*— Dr J H Baron, DM, FRCP, FRCPG, FRCS; ✉ Thomas Hunt Gastroenterology Unit, St Mary's Hospital, London W2 1NY (tel 020 7725 1208, fax 020 7725 1138); Henry Janowitz Gastroenterology Division, Box 1069, Mount Sinai School of Medicine, New York 10029–6574, USA (tel 212 241 6749, fax 212 348 7428)

BARON, John Charles; MP; s of Raymond Arthur Ernest Baron, and Kathleen Ruby Baron; *b* 21 June 1959; *Educ* Wadham Sch Crewkerne, Queen's Coll Taunton, Jesus Coll Cambridge; *m* 29 Aug 1992, Thalia Anne Mayson, da of Barrie Laird; 2 da (Poppy b 11 Nov 1994, Leone b 10 July 1998); *Career* Capt RRF 1984–88; dir Henderson Private Investors 1988–99, dir Rothschild Asset Mgmnt 1999–2001; MP (Cons) Billericay 2001–; dir JT Investments Ltd; MSI; *Recreations* tennis, walking, cycling, family; *Style*— John Baron, Esq, MP; ✉ House of Commons, London SW1A 0AA (tel 020 7219 8138)

BARON, Dr Peter Kurt; *b* 8 September 1940; *Career* jr lectr Technical Univ Munich 1967–71, served German Govt Min of Agric, Food and Forestry Bonn 1971–93, exec dir Int Sugar Org 1994–; chm UN Sugar Conf Geneva (leading to present Int Sugar Agreement) 1992; *Style*— Dr Peter Baron; ✉ International Sugar Organisation, 1 Canada Square, London E14 5AA (tel 020 7513 1144, fax 020 7513 1146. e-mail exdir@isosugar.org)

BARON, Dr (Ora) Wendy; OBE (1992); da of Dr Samuel Barnet Dimson, of London, and Gladys Felicia, *née* Sieve; *b* 20 March 1937; *Educ* St Paul's Girls' Sch, Courtauld Inst of Art (postgrad studentship, BA, PhD); *m* 1, 1960, Dr Jeremy Hugh Baron, s of Edward Baron; 1 s (Richard b 1964), 1 da (Susannah b 1968); m 2, 1990, David Joseph Wyatt, s of Frederick Wyatt; *Career* Leverhulme Tst Fund fellowship 1972–74; dir Govt Art Collection 1978–97; tstee: Public Art Cmmns Agency 1990–99, Contemporary Art Soc 1997–2000, Arts Research Ltd 1998–2004, Nat Art Collections Fund 1998–; chm 20/21 Br Art Fair 2005–07; FRSA 1993, FSA 2007; *Books* Sickert (1973), Miss Ethel Sands and Her Circle (1977), The Camden Town Group (1979), Sickert Paintings (jt ed, 1992), Perfect Moderns (2000), Sickert: Paintings and Drawings (2006); *Style*— Dr Wendy Baron, OBE

BARON-COHEN, Prof Simon; *b* 15 August 1958; *Educ* New Coll Oxford (BA), UCL (MRC studentship, PhD), Inst of Psychiatry Univ of London (Univ of London scholarship, MPhil); *Career* lectr Dept of Psychology UCL 1987–88 (jt with Dept of Psychiatry St Mary's Hosp Med Sch London), sr lectr in developmental psychology Depts of Psychology and Child Psychiatry Inst of Psychiatry Univ of London 1991–94 (New Blood lectr 1988–91); Depts of Experimental Psychology and Psychiatry Univ of Cambridge: lectr in psychopathology 1994–99, reader in developmental psychopathology 1999–2001, prof of developmental psychopathology 2001–; fell Trinity Coll Cambridge 1995–, dir Cambridge Autism Research Centre (ARC) 1997–; conslt clinical psychologist Developmental Psychiatry Section NHS Lifespan Healthcare Tst Cambridge 1999–, dir CLASS (Cambridge Lifespan Asperger Syndrome Services) 1999–; Br Psychological Soc Spearman Medal 1990, American Psychological Assoc (Div 7) McCandless Award 1990, Br Psychological Soc (Clinical Psychology Section) May Davison Award 1993, BAAS Joseph Lister lectr 1998, nominated BAFTA Award Best DVD in off-line learning 2001; FBPsS 1996; *Publications* Autism: The Facts (jtly, 1993), Understanding Other Minds: Perspectives from Autism (jt ed, 1993), Mindblindness: An Essay on Autism and Theory of Mind (1995), Synaesthesia: Classic and Contemporary Readings (jt ed, 1997), The Maladapted Mind: Essays in Evolutionary Psychopathology (ed, 1997), Tourette Syndrome: The Facts (jtly, 1998), Teaching Children with Autism to Mind-read (jtly, 1999), Understanding Other Minds: Perspectives from Developmental Cognitive Neuroscience (jt ed, 2000), Mindreading: The Interactive Guide to Emotions (DVD-ROM, 2002), The Essential Difference: Men, Women and the Extreme Male Brain (2003), The Exact Mind (jt ed, 2003), Prenatal Testosterone in Mind (jtly, 2003); *Style*— Prof Simon Baron-Cohen; ✉ Autism Research Centre, Departments of Experimental Psychology and Psychiatry, University of Cambridge, Douglas House, 18B Trumpington Road, Cambridge CB2 2AH (tel 01223 746057, fax 01223 746033, e-mail s.baron-cohen@psychol.cam.ac.uk)

BARR, Alison Harvey; da of George Kidd Barr, and Muriel Margaret, *née* Harvey; *Educ* Uddingston GS Glasgow, Univ of Glasgow (MA); *Career* ed Routledge 1990–92 (assoc ed 1988–90), ed Scripture Union 1993–97, sr ed SPCK 1998– (ed 1997); *Books* Christmas According to St Luke: A Cantata (1983), Time for Christmas: Six Songs for Children (1985); *Recreations* music, walking; *Style*— Ms Alison Barr; ✉ SPCK, 36 Causton Street, London SW1P 4ST (tel 020 7592 3958, fax 020 7592 3939, e-mail abarr@spck.org.uk)

BARR, Derek Julian; s of Peter Joachim Barr (d 1993), of London, and Ingrid Gerda, *née* Dannenbaum; *b* 16 September 1945; *Educ* St Paul's, Imperial Coll London (BSc, ACGI); *m* 1, 19 Dec 1970 (m dis 1993), Zoe Maxine, da of Wing Cdr Jack Leon Elson-Rees (d 1962); 2 da (Katrina b 1972, Annabelle b 1974), 2 s (James b 1976, Nicholas b 1981); m 2, 10 May 1996, Susan Rose, da of Dr Denis Woodeson (d 1981), and Phyllis Woodeson; *Career* chemical engr (expert in industrial drying and process technol); md Barr & Murphy 1974–96 (founded firm with father 1962, awarded Queen's Award for Export Achievement 1976, co sold to GEA AG 1996), int starch industry co-ordinator and memb Gp Steering Ctee GEA AG 1996–2002; chm: 4 Future Holdings Ltd 2003–, InterResolve Ltd 2004–, Heliswirl Technologies Ltd 2004–; CEDR registered mediator 2001 (accredited mediator 1999); FIChemE 1987; *Recreations* skiing, sailing, tennis, music; *Clubs* IOD, Riverside; *Style*— Derek Barr, Esq; ✉ 43 Corfton Road, London W5 2HR (tel 020 8998 9531, e-mail derekjbarr@aol.com); InterResolve Limited, Tower 42, 25 Old Broad Street, London EC2N 1HN (website www.inter-resolve.com)

BARR, Felicity Jane; da of Alan Marshall Barr, and Mary Elizabeth, *née* Snell; *Educ* Chiltern Edge Sch, Henley Coll; *Career* reporter, newsreader and presenter 2TenFM radio station Reading 1990–95, sports reporter and presenter Meridian TV 1996–99 (also presenter A406), news and sports presenter and reporter London Tonight, presenter Goals Extra 1999–2001, sports corr and presenter ITV News 2001–06 (ITN's first female sports corr), London co-anchor Al Jazeera Int 2006–; *Recreations* theatre, ice skating, skiing, eating; *Clubs* Cats Protection; *Style*— Ms Felicity Barr

BARR, Ian; *b* 29 April 1950; *Educ* Salford Univ (BSc, pres Students' Union); *m*; *Career* grad recruitment offr rising to personnel mangr BL plc 1976–82, manpower resourcing mangr Watney Mann and Truman Brewers Ltd 1983, co-owner and dir Berry Wilson Associates Ltd 1983–86, gp personnel dir Chloride Gp plc 1987–89, HR dir NFC plc 1989–95, gp human resources dir Scholl plc 1995–98, co-fndr and jt md Ionann Management Consultants Ltd 1998–99, md Astar Managment Consultants Ltd 1999–; non-exec dir RTITBS Ltd 1991–95; memb CBI Equal Opportunities Panel 1992–95, memb CBI Equality Forum 2001–, cmmr Cmmn for Racial Equality 2002–06, chm Employment Tbnls System Steering Bd 2006–, fndr memb Leadership Gp Race for Opportunity Campaign; tstee and treas Windsor Fellowship 2000–; *Style*— Ian Barr, Esq; ✉ Astar Management Consultants Ltd, 6 Granary Buildings, Millow, Bedfordshire SG18 8RH (tel 01767 310800, fax 01767 310808, e-mail ianbarr@astarltd.co.uk)

BARR, Sheriff Kenneth Glen; o s of late Rev Gavin Barr, and Catherine McLellan, *née* McGhie (d 2000); *b* 20 January 1941; *Educ* Ardrossan Acad, Royal HS, Univ of Edinburgh (MA, LLB); *m* 1970, Susanne Crichton Keir (d 1996); *Career* admitted Faculty of Advocates 1964, sheriff of S Strathclyde Dumfries and Galloway 1976–; *Style*— Sheriff Kenneth Barr; ✉ Sheriff Court House, Dumfries DG1 2AN

BARRACLOUGH, Rachael Querida Maria; da of Dr Michael Barraclough, and Jenny, *née* Isard; *b* 16 January 1968; *Educ* Camden Sch for Girls, Univ of Bristol (BA); *Career* fndr Book Aid (charity sending books to Russia, collected over 2 million books) 1991–92; opening co-ordinator Eurotunnel; politics researcher Rory Bremner Who Else 1994–97, fndr Modern Ground contemporary design co 1998–, curator Sotheby's Contemporary Decorative Arts 1999–, co-fndr and creative dir LOSA 2001–; *Recreations* dancing, being a hostess, cooking, collecting contemporary decorative arts; *Style*— Miss Rachael Barraclough; ✉ Modern Ground, 56 Ferry Street, London E14 3DT (e-mail moderngound@hotmail.com)

BARRACLOUGH, Robert James; s of late Charles Brayshaw Barraclough, of Woosehill, Berks, and Winifred Elizabeth Gibson, *née* Moulton; *b* 17 April 1942; *Educ* Bootham Sch York; *m* 8 Sept 1973, Jillian Mary, da of late Frederick George Fennell, RN; 4 s (Paul Anthony b 9 March 1974, Nicholas Charles b 5 Aug 1975, Timothy Nigel b 31 May 1977, Tristan Toby William b 15 Aug 1978); *Career* ptnr Robson Rhodes Chartered Accountants Bradford 1971–90 (gen client serv ptnr, ptnr in charge of audit practice W Yorks), estab Litigation Support Unit in N England Haines Watts Bradford 1990–97, forensic servs ptnr Kidsons Impey Leeds 1997–99, estab Robert Barraclough & Company (forensic accountancy practice) 1999–2007; financially qualified memb Appeal Tbnls 2002–; lay assessor to Special Commissioners when dealing with appeals against assesments made by the Assets Recovery Agency 2004–; hon treas Bradford C of C 1988–95, memb Cncl Leeds C of C 1997–99; memb: Yorks Numismatic Soc (pres 1975), Acad of Experts 1989 (memb Cncl 1993–99); FCA 1965; *Recreations* theatre, fell walking, numismatics; *Clubs* Bradford; *Style*— Robert Barraclough, Esq; ✉ The Ballroom, Hawkswick, Skipton, North Yorkshire BD23 5QA (tel 01756 770361, e-mail info@robertbarraclough.co.uk)

BARRAN, Sir John Napoleon Ruthven; 4 Bt (UK 1895), of Chapel Allerton Hall, Chapel Allerton, West Riding of Co York, and of Queen's Gate, St Mary Abbots, Kensington, Co London; s of Sir John Leighton Barran, 3 Bt (d 1974), and Hon Alison (d 1973), da of 9 Lord Ruthven of Freeland, CB, CMG, DSO; n of Sir David Barran, former chm of the Midland Bank and former chm Shell; *b* 14 February 1934; *Educ* Winchester, UCL (BA 1994); *m* 1965, Jane Margaret, da of Sir Stanley George Hooker, CBE (d 1984), and his 1 w Hon Margaret Bradbury, da of 1 Baron Bradbury; 1 s (John Ruthven b 1971), 1 da (Susannah Margaret b 1981); *Heir* s, John Barran; *Career* Lt 5 Royal Inniskillen Dragoon Gds 1952–54; asst account exec: Dorland Advertising Ltd 1956–58, Masius & Fergusson Advertising Ltd 1958–61; account exec Ogilvy Benson & Mather (NY) Inc 1961–63, Overseas TV News Serv COI 1964, first sec (info) Br High Cmmn Ottawa 1964–67; COI: Home Documentary Film Section 1967–72, Overseas TV and Film News Servs 1972–75, TV Commercials and Fillers Unit 1975–78, head Viewdata Unit 1978–85, head Info Technol Unit 1985–87; memb Cncl Assoc of Lloyd's Members 1990–93; *Recreations* shooting, fishing, cricket (pres East Bergholt Cricket Club), gardening, entertaining; *Style*— Sir John Barran, Bt; ✉ 17 St Leonard's Terrace, London SW3 4QG (tel 020 7730 2801); The Hermitage, East Bergholt, Suffolk (tel 01206 298236); Middle Rigg Farm, Sawley, North Yorkshire (tel 01766 20207)

BARRATT, Jeffery Vernon Courtney Lewis; s of Arnold Douglas Courtney Lewis, and Edith Joyce, *née* Terry; *b* 31 October 1950; *Educ* Scots Coll Wellington NZ, Univ of Adelaide (LLB), Univ of Sydney (LLB, LLM); *Career* articled clerk Giovanell and Burges 1971–73, slr Stephen Jaques and Stephen 1973–75; Norton Rose: ptnr 1979– (estab Bahrain Office 1979–82, trg ptnr 1987–91), head SE Asian Project Fin Gp Hong Kong 1993–95, head of Project Finance Worldwide 1995–, chm Partnership Ctee 1997–2002, global head of banking 2002–06, memb Exec Ctee 2002–06, sr banking ptnr 2006–; memb: Editorial Bd

Butterworths Jl of Int Banking and Fin Law, Banking Law Sub-Ctee Law Soc 1991–93; author of numerous articles on selling loan assets, sterling commercial paper, securitisation and project fin in learned jls; memb: London Legal Educn Ctee 1987–91, Int Financial Services London (IFSL, formerly Br Invisibles) 1999–, Law Soc, IBA, Summer Sch Faculty QMC; *Recreations* cricket, squash, skiing, tennis, opera; *Clubs* Hampstead Cricket (capt 1987), Blackheath CC (Surrey, chm 2002–), RAC, MCC; *Style*— Jeffery Barratt, Esq; ✉ Norton Rose, Kempson House, Camomile Street, London EC3A 7AN (tel 020 7283 6000, fax 020 7283 6500, telex 883652, website www.nortonrose.com)

BARRATT, Sir Lawrence Arthur (Lawrie); kt (1982); *b* 14 November 1927; *m* 1, 1951 (m dis 1984); 2 s; m 2, 1984, Mary Sheila Brierley; *Career* Barratt Developments plc: fndr 1958, gp chm until 1988, life pres 1989–91, re-appointed chm 1991–97, re-appointed life pres 1997; FCIS; *Recreations* golf, shooting, sailing; *Style*— Sir Lawrie Barratt; ✉ Barratt Developments plc, Wingrove House, Ponteland Road, Newcastle upon Tyne NE5 3DP (tel 0191 286 6811)

BARRATT, Oliver William; MBE (1993); s of Lt-Col Roger Barratt, MBE (d 2004), of Cowmire Hall, Kendal, and Diana Norah, *née* While (d 1992); *b* 7 July 1941; *Educ* Radley, Edinburgh and E of Scotland Coll of Agric (SDA); *m* 5 April 1997, Mrs Victoria C Patterson, *née* Stanley; *Career* sec: Cockburn Assoc (The Edinburgh Civic Tst) 1971–92, Cockburn Conservation Tst 1978–92; dir: Lowwood Products Co Ltd 1997–, Crichton Tst 1997–2007; vice-pres Architectural Heritage Soc of Scotland 2002–07; chm Westmorland Damson Assoc 2005–; vice-pres Lakeland Housing Tst 2007–; tstee: Scottish Historic Bldgs Tst, Cockburn Conservation Tst; churchwarden St Anthony's Cartmel Fell 1994–; Hon FRIAS 1992; *Recreations* the hills, canals, travel, most of the arts; *Clubs* New (Edinburgh); *Style*— Oliver Barratt, Esq, MBE; ✉ Cowmire Hall, Crosthwaite, Kendal, Cumbria LA8 8JJ (tel 01539 568200, e-mail cowmire.hall@ecosse.net); 1 London Street, Edinburgh EH3 6LZ (tel 0131 556 5107)

BARRATT, Peter William; s of Robert Leslie Barratt (d 1974), of Jersey, CI, and Winifred Irene, *née* Kirton (d 2007); *b* 7 May 1934; *Educ* De La Salle Coll Salford, Prior Park Coll Bath; *m* 1, 1960 (m dis 1983), Shirley, da of Charles Littler (d 1955), of Swinton, Lancs; 1 s (Nigel b 1962), 2 da (Elizabeth b 1964, Jacqueline b 1966); m 2, 1990, Pamela Rose, da of Jonah Shapiro; *Career* articled clerk EA Radford Edwards Manchester 1952–59; Ashworth Sons Barratt (stockbrokers): joined 1959, ptnr 1961, sr ptnr 1968–88, dir FPG Securities Ltd (acquired Ashworth Sons & Barratt 1988) 1988; dir: Allied Provincial Securities Ltd 1989–95, Greig Middleton & Co Ltd 1995–2000; divnl dir Gerrard Ltd 2000–04; memb: Broughton Park RFC 1952–72 (IXV), Lancs RFC 1966–70 (England trial 1969); FSI (memb Stock Exchange 1961), FCA; *Recreations* theatre, antiques, reading, gardening, history; *Clubs* Broughton Park RFC, Lancs RFC, Sale RFC, Henty Soc; *Style*— Peter Barratt, Esq; ✉ Sandy Acre, 11 The Paddocks, Whitegate, Cheshire CW8 2DD

BARRATT, His Hon Judge Robin Alexander; QC (1989); s of Harold Robert Mathew Barratt (d 1974), and Phylis Lily Barratt (d 1968); *b* 24 April 1945; *Educ* Charterhouse, Worcester Coll Oxford (MA); *m* 1 April 1972 (m dis 1999), Gillian Anne, da of Peter Ellis; 1 s (Richard), 3 da (Sarah, Caroline, Joanna); *Career* called to the Bar Middle Temple 1970; Western Circuit 1971, recorder of the Crown Court 1993–98, circuit judge (SE Circuit) 1998–; lectr in law Kingston Poly 1968–71; cncllr London Borough of Merton 1978–86; *Recreations* music, fell walking, reading; *Style*— His Hon Judge Barratt, QC; ✉ Chichester Combined Court Centre, 41 Southgate, Chichester PO19 1SX (tel 01243 520700, fax 01243 533756)

BARRELL, Dr Anthony Charles; CB (1994); s of William Frederick Barrell (d 1973), and Ruth Eleanor, *née* Painter (d 1992); *b* 4 June 1933; *Educ* Friars Sch Bangor, Kingston GS, Univ of Birmingham, Imperial Coll London; *m* 26 Jan 1963, Jean, da of Francis Henry Hawkes, and Clarice Jean Silke, of Budleigh Salterton, Devon; 1 s (Andrew Mark b 1966), 1 da (Samantha Ruth b 1968); *Career* chemist Miny of Supply (later War Dept) 1959–64, commissioning engr African Explosives and Chem Industries 1964–65, shift mangr MOD 1965–66; HM Factory Inspectorate 1966–78, head Major Hazards Assessment Unit 1978–84, dir of technol Health and Safety Exec 1984–90, dir Hazardous Installations Policy 1990; chief exec: North Sea Safety Dept of Energy 1990–91, North Sea Safety Health and Safety Exec 1991–94; dir: BAA plc 1994–2001, Lloyd's Register 1998–; special advsr Nat Air Traffic Services Ltd 2000–; memb Cncl: IChemE 1989–94 (pres 1993–94), Royal Acad of Engrg 1994–97; Hon DEng Univ of Birmingham 1995; FIChemE 1984, Eur Ing 1988, FREng 1990 (CEng 1974); *Recreations* family, golf, travel; *Clubs* Royal Dart Yacht (cdr 2000–03), Churston Golf (chm 2004–06); *Style*— Dr Anthony Barrell, CB, FREng; ✉ Lloyd's Register, 71 Fenchurch Street, London EC3M 4BS (tel 020 7423 2402

BARRELL, Prof John; s of John Ellis Barrell, CBE (d 1982), and Beatrice Mary Barrell (d 1988); *b* 3 February 1943; *Educ* Dulwich Coll, Trinity Coll Cambridge (open exhbn, scholar, MA), Univ of Essex (PhD); *m* 1, 1965 (m dis 1975), Audrey Jones; 2 s ((John) Matthew b 1965, Joseph Ezra David b 1967); m 2, 1975 (m dis 1978), Jania Miller; m 3, 1992, Prof Harriet Guest; 1 da (Helena Frances b 1992); *Career* asst master Raine's Fndn GS London 1964–65, lectr Dept of Literature Univ of Essex 1968–72; coll lectr Newnham Coll Cambridge 1972–84, lectr Univ of Cambridge 1972–85 (fell King's Coll), prof of English Univ of Sussex 1986–93, prof of English Univ of York 1993– (hon res fell 1992–93); American Soc for Eighteenth-Century Studies fellowship Houghton Library Harvard 1993, Schaffner visiting prof Univ of Chicago 2002, visiting fell Inst of Advanced Study Univ of Indiana 2002; Leverhulme res award 1990, Br Acad readership 1991–93, Leverhulme major res fell 2002–04; James Clifford Prize American Soc for Eighteenth-Century Studies 1986; memb Editorial Bd History Workshop Jl 1989–94, assoc ed Trent Editions 1998–, advsy ed Nineteenth-Century Contexts 1993–, editorial advsr Cambridge Studies in Romanticism 1989–; memb Editorial Bd: Rural History 1988–, Literature in History 1991–, Textual Practice 1995–, Visual Culture in Britain 1998–; fell English Assoc 2001; FBA 2001; *Books* The Idea of Landscape and the Sense of Place 1730–1840: An Approach to the Poetry of John Clare (1972), Samuel Taylor Coleridge: On the Constitution of the Church and State According to the Idea of Each (ed, 1972), The Penguin Book of Pastoral Verse (ed with John Bull, 1974), The Dark Side of the Landscape: the Rural Poor in English Painting 1730–1840 (1980), English Literature in History 1730–1780 (1983), The Political Theory of Painting from Reynolds to Hazlitt: The Body of the Public (1986), Poetry, Language and Politics (1988), The Infection of Thomas De Quincey: A Psychopathology of Imperialism (1991), The Birth of Pandora and the Division of Knowledge (1992), Painting and the Politics of Culture: New Essays on British Art 1700–1850 (ed, 1992), Imagining the King's Death: Figurative Treason, Fantasies of Regicide 1793–1796 (2000), Exhibition Extraordinary!! Radical Broadsides of the Mid 1790s (ed, 2001), The Spirit of Despotism (2006), Trials for Treason and Sedition 1792–1794 (ed with Jon Mee, 8 vols, 2006–07); *Recreations* gardening, book collection, playing cricket, swimming; *Style*— Prof John Barrell; ✉ Centre for Eighteenth Century Studies, University of York, King's Manor, York YO1 7EP (tel 01904 434981, e-mail eng118@york.ac.uk)

BARRELL, Prof Raymond John; s of Herbert Harry Barrell (d 1981), of London, and Eva, *née* Parr (d 1996); *b* 25 May 1950; *Educ* Ambrose Fleming Sch Enfield, LSE (BSc, MSc); *Partner* Ursula van Almsick; 1 step s (Dominic van Almsick b 9 April 1992); *Career* lectr: Univ of Stirling until 1979, Brunel Univ until 1984; econ advsr HM Treasy 1984–87, sr res fell NIESR 1990– (sr res offr 1988–90); visiting prof of economics Imperial Coll London 1997–2004, pt/t prof Euro Univ Inst Florence 1998–99; memb Editorial Bd: Jl of Common Market Studies, Economic Modelling; *Publications* incl: Economic Convergence and Monetary Union (ed, 1992), Macroeconomic Policy Coordination in Europe: the ERM and Monetary Union (ed with J Whitley, 1992), The UK Labour Market (ed, 1994), Modern Budgeting in the Public Sector (ed with F Hubert, 1999), Investment, Innovation and the Diffusion of Technology in Europe (ed with N Pain, 1999), Productivity, Innovation and Economic Performance (ed with G Mason and M O'Mahony, 2000); reg contrib to NIESR Review; *Recreations* skiing, mountaineering; *Style*— Prof Raymond Barrell; ✉ National Institute of Economic and Social Research, 2 Dean Trench Street, London SW1P 3HE (tel 020 7222 7665, e-mail r.barrell@niesr.ac.uk)

BARRETT, *see also:* Scott-Barrett

BARRETT, Prof Ann; da of R D Brown, of Suffolk; *b* 27 February 1943; *Educ* Queen Elizabeth's Girls' GS Barnet, Bart's Hosp Med Sch (LRCP, MRCS, MB BS, MD); *m*; 3 c; *Career* sr house offr in general med Whipps Cross Hosp 1969–70 (house surgn and physician 1968–69), sr house offr in radiotherapy Bart's 1969–70, registrar in radiotherapy UCH and Middx Hosp 1971–72, sr registrar Dept of Radiotherapy Middx Hosp and Mount Vernon Hosp 1972–74, seconded to Fndn Curie and Institut Gustav-Roussy 1974, locum conslt radiotherapist Westminster Hosp 1975–76 (lectr in oncology 1974–75), chef de clinique Hôpital Tenon and Institut Gustav-Roussy 1976–77; Royal Marsden Hosp: sr lectr and hon conslt Inst of Cancer Res 1977–83, conslt in radiotherapy and oncology 1983–86; dir Beatson Oncology Centre Western Infirmary Glasgow 1986–91, prof of radiation oncology Univ of Glasgow 1986–2002, registrar RCR 2000–02, prof of oncology UEA 2002–, dean Faculty of Oncology RCR 2002–04; pres: Scottish Radiological Soc 1995–97, Euro Soc for Therapeutic Radiotherapy and Oncology 1997–99; FRCR 1974, FRCPGlas 1989, FRCP 1990, FMedSci; *Publications* author of 3 books and over 150 medical pubns; *Style*— Prof Ann Barrett; ✉ School of Medicine, Health Policy and Practice, University of East Anglia, Norwich NR4 7TJ

BARRETT, Prof Anthony Gerard Martin; s of Claude Edward Valentine Barrett, and Margaret Teresa, *née* Bannon; *b* 2 March 1952; *Educ* Imperial Coll of Sci and Technol London (BSc, PhD, DIC, Hofmann Prize, Edmund White Prize for Organic Chem, Frank Hatton Prize, RSA Silver Medal); *m* 15 Aug 1983, Jennifer Mary, da of Charles Madge; 1 s (Edward Michael b 14 Nov 1980), 1 da (Roxanne Eloise b 30 Oct 1982); *Career* Imperial Coll of Sci and Technol: lectr 1975–82, sr lectr 1982–83, dir Wolfson Centre for Organic Chem in Med Sci 1993–, Glaxo prof of organic chem 1993–, Sir Derek Barton prof of synthetic chem 1999–; prof of chem: Northwestern Univ 1983–90, Colorado State Univ 1990–93; conslt: W R Grace & Co 1981–90, Pfizer Central Research 1982–84, G D Searle & Co (now Pfizer) 1983–, B F Goodrich 1986–88, Amoco Technol 1987–91, Parke Davis (now Pfizer) 1992–, Roche Products Ltd 1993–2002, Quest International 1994, AECI 1994–2000, Celltech 1995–98, Unilever 1996–2003, Ligand Pharmaceuticals Inc 1996–98, Jouveinal (now Pfizer) 1997–, Eastman Chemical Co 1998–, Cooper Conslt Inc 1998–2000; chm Scientific Advsy Bd Diversomer Technologies 1996–97, dir of science and non-exec dir ChemMedICa (now Argenta Discovery Ltd) 1998–; memb: Scientific Advsy Bd Myco Pharmaceuticals 1993–96, Exec Scientific Advsy bd ChemGenics Pharmaceuticals Inc 1996–97, Scientific Advsy Bd NSC Technologies 1996–99, Bd of Scientific Advisors in Medicinal Chem Rhône-Poulenc Rorer Recherche-Développement 1996–98, Sci Advsy Bd New Chemical Entities Inc 1998–2000, NIH Medicinal Chemical A Study Section 1986–89, Chemicals Panel Technol Foresight Prog Office of Sci and Technol 1994. Perkin Div Cncl RSC 1996–98; RSC Meldola Medal 1980, Imperial Coll Armstrong Medal 1981, RSC Harrison Medal 1982, ACS Arthur C Cope Scholar Award 1986, RSC Corday-Morgan Medal 1986, Camille and Henry Dreyfus Teacher-Scholar Award 1987, Japan Soc for the Promotion of Sci Fellowship 1989, RSC Award in Synthetic Organic Chem sponsored by CIBA Specialty Chemicals 1997, Glaxo Wellcome Award for Innovative Chem 2000, RSC Award in Natural Products Chem 2001, Royal Soc Wolfson Research Merit Award 2002, RSC Pedler Lectr 2004, RSC Simonsen Lectr; MACS, MRSC, FRS 1999, FMedSci 2003; *Publications* author of over 320 scientific papers and articles; *Style*— Prof Anthony Barrett, FRS, FMedSci; ✉ Department of Chemistry, Imperial College London, London SW7 2AZ (tel 020 7594 5766, fax 020 7594 5805, e-mail agmb@ic.ac.uk)

BARRETT, John; MP; *b* 11 February 1954; *Educ* Forrester HS Edinburgh, Telford Coll, Napier Poly; *Career* cncllr (Lib Dem) Edinburgh CC 1995–2001; MP (Lib Dem) Edinburgh W 2001–; memb Scottish Lib Dem Pty Exec 2001–, Lib Dem spokesperson on int devpt 2002–05, memb Select Ctee Int Devpt 2002–05, sec All-Pty Microfinance/Microcredit Gp 2002–05, sec All-Pty Zimbabwe Gp 2003–05; vice-pres Scottish Lib Club, chair Edinburgh W Local Devpt Ctee 2000–01; memb: Advsy Bd Edinburgh Int Film Festival, Greenpeace, Amnesty Int; *Style*— John Barrett, Esq, MP; ✉ House of Commons, London SW1A 0AA

BARRETT, Rev John Charles Allanson; s of Leonard Wilfred Allanson Barrett, of King's Lynn, Norfolk, and Marjorie Joyce, *née* Hares; *b* 8 June 1943; *Educ* Culford Sch, Univ of Newcastle upon Tyne (BA), Fitzwilliam Coll and Wesley House Cambridge (MA); *m* 1967, Sally Elisabeth, da of William Mason Hatley; 1 s (James William Allanson b 16 March 1970), 1 da (Rachel Claire b 24 May 1972); *Career* chaplain and lectr in divinity Westminster Coll Oxford 1968–69, asst tutor Wesley Coll Bristol 1969–71, ordained Methodist min 1970, min Werrington Methodist Church Stoke on Trent and actg head of religious studies Birches HS Hanley 1971–73, chaplain and head of religious studies Kingswood Sch Bath 1973–83; headmaster: Kent Coll Pembury 1983–90, The Leys Sch Cambridge 1990–2004; memb HMC Ctee 1997–99; princ ACS (Int) Singapore; World Methodist Cncl: pres 2005– (vice-pres 2001–05), chm Exec Ctee 2005– (memb 1981–, vice-chm 2001–05), chm Educn Ctee 1991–2001, chm Prog Ctee 1991–96, memb Presidium 1996–, chm Br Ctee 1999–2004 (sec 1986–97); tstee Bloxham Project 2002– (memb Steering Ctee 1986–93); Hon DD Florida Southern Coll; FRSA; *Books* What is a Christian School? (1981), Family Worship in Theory and Practice (1982), A New Collection of Prayers (1983), Methodist Education in Britain (1989), Education - The Gift of Hope (contrib), Serving God with Heart and Mind (contrib); sections on Methodism in Encyclopaedia Britannica Year Books 1988–99; *Clubs* Tanglin, Singapore, Rotary; *Style*— The Rev John Barrett

BARRETT, John Edward; MBE (2007); s of Alfred Edward Barrett, and Margaret Helen, *née* Walker; *b* 17 April 1931; *Educ* UCS Hampstead, St John's Coll Cambridge (MA); *m* 1967, (Florence) Angela Margaret, *née* Mortimer; 1 s, 1 da; *Career* former tennis player, tennis promoter and sports conslt; currently journalist, broadcaster and author; Nat Serv RAF 1950–52; Dunlop Slazenger International Ltd (formerly Slazengers Ltd): mgmnt trainee 1957–59, asst home sales mangr 1959–65, asst mangr Tournament Dept 1965–74, mangr Tournament Dept 1974–75, tournament dir 1975, dir 1978–81, conslt 1981–94; tennis player: Middx jr doubles champion 1947 and 1948, nat schs singles and doubles champion 1949, rep Cambridge Univ v Oxford Univ 1952–54 (capt 1954), rep Oxford and Cambridge Univs v Harvard and Yale Univs (Prentice Cup) 1952 and 1954, RAF champion 1950 and 1951, nat indoor doubles champion (with D Black) 1953, competed at Wimbledon 1950–70, GB rep Davis Cup 1956–57 (non-playing capt 1959–62), ranked nationally 1952–70 (highest position 5); tennis admin: dir LTA Training Squad (Barrett Boys) 1965–68, qualified LTA coach 1969 (memb Trg Ctee), fndr and dir BP Int Tennis Fellowship 1968–80, fndr BP Cup (int under 21 team event) 1973–80, fndr and organiser Pepsi-Cola Jr Int Series 1975–79, memb All England Lawn Tennis Club 1955– (memb Ctee 1989–2004, vice-pres 2004), fndr bd memb Assoc of Tennis Professionals 1972–73, pres Int Lawn Tennis Club of GB 2004– (memb 1953–, memb Ctee 1957–, chm 1983–94); tennis commentator: BBC TV 1971–2006, Channel 9 Aust 1981–86, Channel 10 Aust 1987, Channel 7 Aust 1988–, various cable networks USA 1977–, Hong Kong Championships for ATV and TVB 1981–97, Canadian Open for CTV 1989–97; lawn tennis corr Financial Times 1963– (crossword contrib 1986–), editorial conslt and contrib LTA's magazine Serve and Volley (renamed ACE 1996) 1988–97; *Books* World of Tennis (fndr ed and contrib, annually 1969–2001), Tennis and Racket Games (1975), Play Tennis With Rosewall (1975), 100 Wimbledon Championships: a celebration (1986), From Where I Sit (with Dan Maskell, 1988), Oh, I Say! (with Dan Maskell, 1989), Wimbledon: The Official History of the Championships (2001); *Recreations* music, theatre, reading; *Clubs* All England Lawn Tennis, Queen's, International Lawn Tennis Club of GB; *Style*— John Barrett, Esq, MBE; ✉ All England Lawn Tennis Club, Church Road, Wimbledon, London SW19 5AE (e-mail jbcourtier@aol.com)

BARRETT, Rev Prof (Charles) Kingsley; s of Rev Fred Barrett (d 1957), and Clara, *née* Seed (d 1941); *b* 4 May 1917; *Educ* Shebbear, Pembroke Coll Cambridge (MA, BD, DD); *m* 1944, Margaret, da of Percy Leathley Heap (d 1952), of Calverley, W Yorks; 1 s (Martin), 1 da (Penelope); *Career* asst tutor Wesley Coll Headingley 1942, Methodist min Darlington 1943, prof of divinity Univ of Durham 1958–82 (lectr in theology 1945–58), visiting lectureships and professorships in Europe, Aust, NZ and USA; contrib to learned jls and symposia; pres Studiorum Novi Testamenti Societas 1973–74, vice-pres Br and Foreign Bible Soc; hon memb Soc of Biblical Literature USA, memb Royal Norwegian Soc of Scis and Letters 1991; Hon DD: Hull 1970, Aberdeen 1972; Hon DrTheol Hamburg 1981; Burkitt Medal for Biblical Studies 1966, Forschungspreis of the Von Humboldt-Stiftung 1988; hon fell Pembroke Coll Cambridge 1995; FBA 1961; *Books* incl: The Holy Spirit and The Gospel Tradition (1947), Gospel According to St John (1955, 2 edn 1978), The Epistle to the Romans (1967, 2 edn 1991), Jesus and the Gospel Tradition (1967), The First Epistle to the Corinthians (1968, 2 edn 1971), The Second Epistle to the Corinthians (1973), The Gospel of John and Judaism (1975), Essays on Paul (1982), Essays on John (1982), Freedom and Obligation (1985), Church, Ministry and Sacraments in the New Testament (1985), Paul (Outstanding Christian Thinkers series, 1994), The Acts of the Apostles (The International Critical Commentary series, Vol I 1994, Vol II 1998), Jesus and the Word, And Other Essays (1996), The Acts of the Apostles: A Shorter Commentary (2002), On Paul: Essays on his Life, Work and Influence in the Early Church (2003); *Style*— The Rev Prof C K Barrett, FBA

BARRETT, Lorraine; AM; *Career* former nurse; former memb Vale of Glamorgan Cncl, PA to Rt Hon Alun Michael MP 1987–99, memb Nat Assembly for Wales (Lab Co-op) Cardiff South & Penarth 1999–; *Recreations* cinema, walking, reading (thrillers/horror); *Style*— Lorraine Barrett, AM; ✉ National Assembly for Wales, Cardiff Bay, Cardiff CF99 1NA (tel 029 2089 8376, e-mail lorraine.barrett@wales.gov.uk)

BARRETT, Patrick William Austin; s of William Barrett, of Bletchingly, Surrey, and Sylvia, *née* Austin; *b* 16 March 1970; *Educ* St Bede's Redhill, Lancaster Univ (BA), Journalists Trg Centre Mitcham (NVQ); *m* 15 May 1999, Rosamunde, da of Dr Brian Snowdon; 1 s (Samuel Christopher Snowdon Barrett, b 20 July 2001); *Career* reporter then dep news ed Supermarketing Magazine 1994–96, reporter then dep news ed Marketing Magazine 1996–98, news ed then ed Media Week 1998–2002, freelance media journalist The Guardian 2002–04, dir The Media Foundry 2004–; *Recreations* mountain hiking, guitar, travel, film; *Style*— Patrick Barrett, Esq; ✉ The Media Foundry, Kent House, 14–17 Market Place, London W1W 8BY

BARRETT, Prof Spencer Charles Hilton; *Educ* Univ of Reading (BSc), Univ of Calif Berkeley (PhD); *Career* weed biologist Cwlth Devpt Corp Swaziland Irrigation Scheme 1969–70, aquatic weed conslt Int Research Inst Jari Lower Amazon Brazil 1974, prof Univ of Toronto 1986– (tenure granted 1982); visiting research scientist Genetic Resources Prog Div of Plant Industry CSIRO Canberra 1983–84, research assoc Dept of Botany Royal Ontario Museum 1992–, visiting prof Dept of Botany Univ of Hong Kong 1994, visiting Mellon scholar Rancho Santa Ana Botanic Garden Calif 1997, distinguished guest prof Wuhan Univ 2001–03, adjunct prof Xishuangbanna Tropical Botanical Garden Chinese Acad of Sciences Menglun 2004–06; memb: Ctee on the Scientific Basis for Predicting the Invasive Potential of Non-indigenous Plants and Plant Pests in the USA Nat Acad of Sciences and Nat Research Cncl USA 1999–2001, Expert Panel on the Future of Food Biotechnology Royal Soc of Canada 2000–01; ed Proceedings of the Royal Soc Series B, memb Editorial Bd Trends in Ecology and Evolution; E W Steacie Meml Fellowship Natural Sciences and Engrg Research Cncl of Canada 1988–90, Outstanding Teaching Award Faculty of Arts and Sciences Univ of Toronto 1992–93, Canada Research Chair 2001, Merit Award Botanical Soc of America 2003, Lawson Medal Canadian Botanical Assoc 2006, Premier's Discovery Award in Life Sciences Medicine 2007; FRSC 1998, FRS 2004; *Style*— Prof Spencer Barrett; ✉ Department of Ecology & Evolutionary Biology, University of Toronto, 25 Willocks Street, Toronto, Ontario, M5S 3B2, Canada

BARRETT, (Nicholas) Vincent John; s of Sidney Gordon Barrett, of East Hyde, Herts, and Francine Constance Alice, *née* Collins; *b* 9 June 1956; *Educ* Haileybury and ISC, Guy's Hosp (BDS), Univ of Texas San Antonio (MS), M D Anderson Cancer Hosp (Cert Maxillofacial Prosthodontics); *m* (m dis); 3 s (James Frederick b 12 Nov 1993, Daniel John b 26 July 1995, Peter Nicholas b 16 Nov 1998), 1 da (Naomi Francine b 28 July 2003); *Career* Guy's Hosp: house surgn Dept of Oral and Maxillofacial Surgery 1980, house offr Dept of Prosthetic Dentistry 1980–81; assoc in gen dental practice Feb-June 1981, dental practice London 1985–; appts also held: Westminster Hosp 1985–90, King's Coll Dental Sch 1986–87, Guy's Hosp Dental Sch 1986–97; Newland Pedley travelling scholar 1981, American Dental Soc award 1981; memb: American Coll of Prosthodontics, M D Anderson Cancer Hosp Assocs, American Dental Soc of London, American Dental Soc of Europe, BDA, Br Soc for the Study of Prosthetic Dentistry; *Books* Colour Atlas of Occlusion and Malocclusion (jtly, 1991); *Recreations* tennis; *Style*— Vincent Barrett, Esq; ✉ 38 Devonshire Street, London W1G 6QB (tel 020 7935 8621, fax 020 7224 5370, e-mail vincent_brrtt@yahoo.co.uk)

BARRETT-LENNARD, Rev Sir Hugh Dacre; 6 Bt (UK 1801), of Belhus, Essex; s of Sir Fiennes Cecil Arthur Barrett-Lennard (d 1963), gggs of 1 Bt; suc kinsman, Sir (Thomas) Richard Fiennes Barrett-Lennard, 5 Bt, OBE, 1977; *b* 27 June 1917; *Educ* Radley, Pontifical Beda Coll Rome; *Heir* cous, Richard Barrett-Lennard; *Career* served WWII NW Europe (despatches), enlisted London Scottish 1940, cmmnd 2 Lt 1940, Capt Essex Regt 1945; entered Congregation of the Oratory 1946, ordained priest Rome 1950; *Style*— The Rev Sir Hugh Barrett-Lennard, Bt; ✉ The Oratory, South Kensington, London SW7 SW7 2RP (tel 020 7589 4811)

BARRETTO, Dr John Harold; s of Harold James Barretto (d 1974), and Winifred Annie Alexander (d 1990); *b* 6 November 1941; *Educ* Newells Sch Horsham Surrey, KCS Wimbledon, St Bartholomew's Hosp Univ of London (MB BS, MRCS, LRCP); *m* 31 July 1964, Jeanette, da of Reginald Owens, of Phoenix, Arizona; 2 s (Mark b 15 July 1965, Dominic b 6 June 1975), 1 da (Roxane b 10 June 1968); *Career* house surgn and house physician Canadian Red Cross Meml Hosp Taplow 1965; SHO: gynaecology St Bartholomew's Hosp 1966, accident and neuro-surgery Radcliffe Infirmary Oxford 1967; in gen private practice 1968–; FRSM; *Recreations* shooting, tennis, squash, skiing; *Clubs* Hurlingham; *Style*— Dr John Barretto; ✉ 134 Harley Street, London W1N 1AH (tel 020 7487 2859)

BARRIE, Carol Hazel; da of Harry Batson, of Rowley Regis, W Midlands, and Prudence, *née* Crompton; *b* 23 December 1945; *Educ* Rowley Regis GS; *m* 30 Sept 1967, Robert Barrie, s of Robert Barrie; *Career* CA; with Charlton & Co (now part of Deloitte & Touche) Birmingham 1964–72 (articled clerk 1964–70); Peat Marwick Mitchell & Co (now KPMG): joined 1972, chm Nat Tax Gp for Partnerships 1988–95, head of tax Midlands Region 1995–97; Robson Rhodes: head of tax Midlands Region 1998–2001, nat head of private client servs 2001–04; tax ptnr Bentley Jennison 2004–; lectr for a variety of Professional Bodies, past memb Inst of Bankers' Approved Panel of Speakers, regular radio broadcasts for local radio, contrib to newspapers and technical jls; non-exec memb N Birmingham HA 1988–96; FCA 1971; *Recreations* reading, embroidery, theatre, classical music; *Style*— Mrs Carol Barrie; ✉ 7 Carnoustie Close, Sutton Coldfield, West Midlands B75 6UW (tel 0121 378 2465, mobile 07836 761455)

BARRIE, Christopher (Chris); s of Alexander Barrie, and Anne, *née* Pitt; *b* 7 November 1958; *Educ* St Dunstan's Coll Catford, Univ of Exeter (BA); *m* 7 April 1990, Elspeth Jane, da of Dr Craig Sinclair; 3 s (Thomas Alexander Sinclair b 9 Nov 1993, Gabriel Henry Sinclair, William Felix Sinclair (twins) b 3 May 1996); *Career* editorial asst Municipal Group London 1983–85, asst ed Autotrade (Morgan-Grampian publishers) 1985–86; The Engineer: asst ed 1986–89, news ed 1989–91, ed 1991–94; freelance journalist with The Guardian, Evening Standard and BBC 1994–95, fin writer The Guardian 1995–2000, columnist Evening Standard 1995–2000; dir Citigate Dewe Rogerson 2000–; Industrial Magazine Journalist of the Year 1990 (Industrial Journalism Awards), Business Journalist Award British Press Awards 1997; *Recreations* hill walking, reading; *Style*— Chris Barrie, Esq; ✉ 3 London Wall Buildings, London Wall, London EC2M 5SY (tel 020 7638 9571, fax 020 7282 8189)

BARRIE, (Charles) David Ogilvy; s of Alexander Ogilvy Barrie (d 1969), and Patricia Mary, *née* Tucker; *b* 9 November 1953; *Educ* Bryanston, BNC Oxford (MA); *m* 1978, Mary Emily, da of Rt Hon Sir Ralph Gibson, PC (d 2003); 2 da (Eleanor Ann Ogilvy b 11 Feb 1983, Miranda Jane Ogilvy b 30 June 1985); *Career* HM Diplomatic Serv: FCO 1975–76, Dublin 1976–80, seconded to Cabinet Office 1980–81, first sec and later asst head of dept FCO 1981–87; transferred to Home Civil Serv Cabinet Office 1988–92 (resigned); exec dir Japan Festival 1989, 1991 and 1992, dir The Art Fund (formerly Nat Art Collections Fund) 1992–; dir Guild of St George 1992–2004 (companion 1991); memb Bd Museums, Libraries and Archives Cncl 2000–06, memb Acceptance in Lieu Panel 2000–06; tstee: Civitella Ranieri Fndn 1995–99, Ruskin Fndn 1996–, Butterfly Conservation 2003–, Campaign for Museums 2004–; Good Guide to Britain Heritage Man of the Year 1999; *Books* Modern Painters (ed, by John Ruskin, 1987, 2 edn 2000); *Recreations* sailing, drawing, scuba diving; *Clubs* Royal Cruising, Arts, Emsworth Sailing; *Style*— David Barrie, Esq; ✉ The Art Fund, Millais House, 7 Cromwell Place, South Kensington, London SW7 2JN (tel 020 7225 4800, fax 020 7225 4848, e-mail dbarrie@artfund.org)

BARRIE, Dr Herbert; *b* 9 October 1927; *Educ* Wallington Co GS, UCL and Med Sch London (MB BS, MD); *m* 1963, Dr Dinah Barrie; 1 s (Michael), 1 da (Caroline); *Career* registrar Hosp for Sick Children Gt Ormond St 1955–57, research fell Harvard Univ Children's Med Center 1957, sr registrar and sr lectr Dept of Paediatrics St Thomas' Hosp 1959–65; conslt paediatrician: Moor House Sch for Speech Disorders 1968–74, Ashtead Hosp Surrey 1986–, New Victoria Hosp Kingston 1992–, Charing Cross Hosp (paediatrician 1966–84, physician in charge 1984–86); examiner Univ of London and RCP; former memb Vaccine Damage Tbnl; hon memb Br Assoc for Perinatal Medicine; FRCP 1972, FRCPCH; *Recreations* tennis, writing; *Style*— Dr Herbert Barrie; ✉ 3 Burghley Avenue, New Malden, Surrey KT3 4SW (tel 020 8942 2836)

BARRIE, Jane Elizabeth; OBE (2004); da of William Pearson, of Somerset, and Bessie, *née* Knowles; *b* 11 September 1946; *Educ* Bishop Fox GS for Girls, Imperial Coll of Sci and Technol London (BSc); *m* 12 Dec 1970, Dr William Robert Ian Barrie, s of Dr Robert Barrie, of Somerset; *Career* stockbroker; regnl dir NatWest Stockbrokers 1990–93; chm: Taunton Deane and W Somerset Div Avon and Somerset Constabulary Crime Prevention Panel 1987–91, Somerset Trg and Enterprise Cncl 1999–2001, Somerset Learning and Skills Cncl 2001–; non-exec dir Taunton and Somerset NHS Tst 1991–94, chm Somerset HA 1994–2002, chm Dorset and Somerset SHA 2002–06, chm Somerset Primary Care Tst 2006–; pres Soroptimist Int of GB and I 1990–91; memb Bd: Fairplay South West 2001–, Connexions Somerset 2002–07, NHS Commercial Advsy Bd 2003–; pres Care Focus Somerset 2006–; patron St Margaret's (Somerset) Hospice 2005–; chm of govrs: Bishop Fox's Sch Taunton 1984–2002, Taunton Sch 2001–; FSI (memb Stock Exchange 1973), ARCS, FRSA; *Recreations* sailing, bridge, wine appreciation; *Clubs* Royal Dart Yacht; *Style*— Mrs Jane E Barrie, OBE; ✉ Hollydene, Kingston St Mary, Taunton, Somerset TA2 8HW (tel 01823 451388, e-mail jbarrie@btinternet.com)

BARRIE, (Thomas) Scott; s of William Barrie, and Helen McBain, *née* Scott; *Educ* Auchmuty HS Glenrothes, Univ of Edinburgh (MA), Univ of Stirling (CQSW); *Career* Fife Regnl Cncl: social worker 1986–89, sr social worker 1989–91, team mangr 1991–97, princ offr (childcare) 1997–99; MSP (Lab) Dunfermline West 1999–2007; memb: Lab Pty 1979–, Unison (formerly NUPE) 1986–; former memb Dunfermline District Cncl (convenor Leisure and Recreation Ctee); *Recreations* sport, hill walking, travel, supporter of Dunfermline Athletic FC; *Style*— Scott Barrie, Esq

BARRINGTON-CARVER, John; *b* 8 December 1941; *Educ* BRNC Dartmouth; *m* 2 Jan 1965, Judith Rosemary, da of Douglas Arthur Garrett (d 1981); 1 da (Nicola Wynn Louise b 30 Sept 1965); *Career* RN: Seaman Offr, seagoing appts 1962–68, seconded RN Trg Team Kenya as Cmdg Offr KNS Chui 1966, ret at own request 1968; metals analyst and commodity and fin futures broker 1968–85; dir Streets Financial Communications 1985, dir and sr conslt Ogilvy Adams & Rinehart 1988–91, princ Public Relations and Marketing 1991–, ptnr HOWZAT media LLP; MCIPR; *Recreations* shooting, sailing, polo, antique restoration; *Clubs* Special Forces, Guards Polo, Cowdray Park Polo, City Naval; *Style*— John Barrington-Carver, Esq; ✉ 10 Paultons Square, Chelsea, London SW3 5AP (tel 020 7351 3409, e-mail johnbc@btconnect.com)

BARRISON, Dr Ian Graeme; s of Joseph Barrison (d 1991), and Zelda, *née* Sherr; *b* 16 July 1950, Salford, Lancs; *Educ* Manchester Grammar, Medical Sch of St Bartholomew's Hosp Univ of London (BSc, MB BS); *m* 27 May 1974, Penelope, *née* Norbrook; 1 da (Anna b 25 May 1977), 1 s (Ben b 24 Oct 1979); *Career* registrar West Middx Hosp 1977, registrar and tstees research fell Charing Cross Hosp 1978–81, sr registrar St Mary's Hosp, Central Middx Hosp, West Middx Hosp 1981–88, conslt physician and gastroenterologist St Albans City and Hemel Hempstead Hosps 1988–; chair Specialist Trg Ctee on Gen Internal Med London (North) Deanery 2003–; censor RCP 2005–; chm Clinical Servs and Standards Ctee Br Soc of Gastroenterology 2006–, sec Specialist Advsy Ctee in Acute and Internal Medicine 2007–, memb European Bd of Gastroenterology 2007–; Brackenbury Prize BMA 1980; FRCP 1993 (MRCP 1977); contrib to med jls incl Br Jl of Haematology and Br Med Jl; *Recreations* cricket, walking, antiquarian books; *Style*— Dr Ian Barrison; ✉ Department of Gastroenterology, Hemel Hempstead Hospital, Hillfield Road, Hemel Hempstead, Herts HP2 4AD (tel 01442 287041, fax 01442 287082, e-mail ian.barrison@whht.nhs.uk)

BARRIT, Desmond; s of Samuel Islwyn Brown (d 1998), and Gwyneth, *née* West (d 1970); *b* 19 October 1944; *Educ* Garw GS; *Career* actor; pres Friends of Theatre, vice-pres Friends of RSC; assoc actor RSC; ambass for Prince's Tst; organiser of charity events incl: Samaritans, The Lighthouse, Children in Need, Children North East, Richard Haines Charitable Tst; *Theatre* Brogard in Scarlet Pimpernel (Chichester and Her Majesty's); Cliton in The Liar (Old Vic), Then Again (Lyric Hammersmith), Birdboot and Harold in The Real Inspector Hound and Black Comedy (Comedy Theatre), Eddie Carbonne in A View from the Bridge (Greenwich Theatre), Monsieur Henri in Euridice (Whitehall Theatre), Bertozzo in Accidental Death of an Anarchist (Donmar Warehouse), Shylock in The Merchant of Venice (Chichester Festival Theatre), Sorin in The Seagull (Chichester Festival Theatre), Midsummer Night's Dream (Broadway); RNT incl: Archille Blond in The Magistrate, chauffeur in Jacobowsky, Charlie in 3 Men on a Horse (also at

Vaudeville), Toad in Wind in the Willows, Brazen in The Recruiting Officer, Cotrone in The Mountain Giants, Pseudolus in A Funny Thing Happened on the Way to the Forum, Dick Cheney in Stuff Happens, The History Boys (also Broadway); RSC incl: Trinculo in Tempest, Gloucester in King Lear, Porter/Ross in Macbeth, Tom Errand in Constant Couple, Banjo in The Man Who Came to Dinner 1990–91, Antipholus in Comedy of Errors, Bottom in A Midsummer Night's Dream, Malvolio in Twelfth Night, Falstaff in Henry IV Parts 1 and 2 (nomination Olivier Award for Best Actor in a Supporting Role 2002), Comedy of Errors (dir, Chicago), Toby Belch in Twelfth Night, Sir Joseph Porter in HMS Pinafore; *Television* incl: Boon, The Bill, Homer and his Pigeons, Poirot, True Tilda, Le Show, Dalziel and Pascoe, Oliver Twist, Madame Bovary, Midsomer Murders; *Film* incl: Lassiter, Rebecca's Daughters, A Midsummer Night's Dream, All for Love, Alice Through the Looking Glass, Christmas Carol, Northanger Abbey; *Concerts* My Fair Lady (LA), 3 Musketeers (6 concerts, Denmark); *Awards* Clarence Derwent Award for Trinculo, Olivier Award for Best Comedy Performance in Comedy of Errors 1988; for A Midsummer Night's Dream: Helen Hayes Award for Best Actor, Critics' Circle Award nomination, Fany Award nomination; *Recreations* antiques, cooking, travel; *Style*— Desmond Barrit, Esq; ✉ c/o Lou Coulson, 37 Berwick Street, London W1F 8RS (tel 020 7734 9633)

BARRON, Brian Munro; MBE (2007); s of Albert Barron (d 1986), and Norah, *née* Morgan; *b* 28 April 1940; *Educ* Bristol GS; *m* Jan 1974, Angela Lee Barron; 1 da (Fleur b 1982); *Career* jr reporter Western Daily Press Bristol 1956–59, Evening World Bristol 1960–61, Daily Mirror 1962, BBC External Servs 1965; BBC Radio: Aden corr 1967, Cairo corr 1968, SE Asia corr (Singapore) 1969–71; reporter BBC TV London 1972; BBC TV: Far East corr (Hong Kong) 1973, Africa corr (Nairobi) 1977–81, Ireland corr 1982, Washington corr 1983–86, Asia Bureau chief (TV and Radio) 1987–94, New York corr 1994, Rome corr 2000, NY corr 2004–07; Journalist of the Year UK (RTS) 1980, Int Reporting Award (RTS) 1985; *Recreations* cinema, opera, theatre, swimming, post-war British/Irish art; *Clubs* Oriental, Travellers; *Style*— Brian Barron, Esq, MBE; ✉ 98 Riverside Drive, Apartment 7A, New York, NY 10024, USA (e-mail brian.barron@bbc.co.uk)

BARRON, Sir Donald James; kt (1972), DL (N Yorks 1971); s of Albert Gibson Barron, of Edinburgh, and Elizabeth, *née* Macdonald; *b* 17 March 1921; *Educ* George Heriot's Sch Edinburgh, Univ of Edinburgh; *m* 1956, Gillian Mary, da of John Saville, of York; 3 s, 2 da; *Career* CA (Scot); Rowntree Mackintosh Ltd: joined 1952, dir 1961, vice-chm 1965, chm 1966–81; Midland Bank plc: dir 1972, vice-chm 1981–82, chm 1982–87; chm: CLCB 1983–85, Ctee of London and Scottish Bankers 1985–87; dir: Investors in Industry Group plc (subsequently 3i Group) 1980–91, Canada Life Assurance Co of GB Ltd 1980–96 (chm 1991–94), Canada Life Unit Tst Managers Ltd 1980–96, Canada Life Assurance Co Toronto 1980–96, Clydesdale Bank 1986–87; memb Bd of Banking Supervision 1987–89; tstee Joseph Rowntree Fndn 1966–73 and 1975–96 (chm 1981–96); memb: Cncl CBI 1966–81 (chm CBI Educn Fndn 1981–85), SSRC 1971–72, UGC 1972–81, Cncl BIM 1978–80, Cncl Policy Studies Inst 1978–85, Cncl Inst of Chartered Accountants of Scotland 1980–81, NEDC 1983–85; govr London Business Sch 1982–88, a pro-chllr Univ of York 1982–94 (treas 1966–72), chm York Millennium Bridge Tst 1997–2001; Hon Dr: Loughborough Univ 1982, Heriot-Watt Univ 1983, CNAA 1983, Univ of Edinburgh 1984, Univ of Nottingham 1985, Univ of York 1986; *Recreations* golf, tennis, gardening; *Clubs* Athenaeum; *Style*— Sir Donald Barron, DL; ✉ Greenfield, Sim Balk Lane, Bishopthorpe, York YO23 2QH (tel 01904 705675, fax 01904 700183)

BARRON, Iann Marchant; CBE (1994); s of William A Barron (d 1974), and Lilian E Barron (d 1969); *b* 16 June 1936; *Educ* UC Sch, Christ's Coll Cambridge (MA); *m* 1962 (m dis 1989), Jacqueline Rosemary, da of Arthur W Almond (d 1978); 2 da (Clare b 1963, Sian b 1969) 2 s (Marc b 1965, Simon b 1967); another s (Marchant b 1996); *Career* Elliott Automation 1961–65; md: Computer Technology Ltd 1965–72, Microcomputer Analysis Ltd 1973–78, Inmos Ltd 1981–88; chief strategic offr Inmos International plc 1984–89 (dir 1978–89); chm Division Gp plc 1989–99; visiting prof Westfield Coll London 1976–78, visiting industrial prof Univ of Bristol 1985–; visiting fell: QMC London 1976, Sci Policy Res Unit Univ of Sussex 1977–78; memb Cncl UC Sch 1983–2002; tstee The Exploratory 1990–98 (exec tstee 1992–97), dir Bristol 2000 1995–2000; RW Mitchell Medal 1983, J J Thompson Medal IEE 1986, IEE Achievement Medal for Computing and Control 1996; Hon DSc: Bristol Poly 1988, Univ of Hull 1989; hon fell Bristol Poly 1986, distinguished fell Br Computer Soc 1986; FBCS 1971, FIEE 1994; *Publications* The Future with Microelectronics (with Ray Curnow, 1977), technical papers; *Style*— Iann M Barron, Esq, CBE; ✉ Barrow Court, Barrow Gurney, Bristol BS48 3RP

BARRON, Prof John Penrose; s of George Barron (d 1984), and Minnie Leslie, *née* Marks (d 1994); *b* 27 April 1934; *Educ* Clifton, Balliol Coll Oxford (Thomas Whitcombe Greene prize, scholar, Barclay Head prize, MA, DPhil); *m* 1 Sept 1962, Caroline Mary, da of late William David Hogarth, OBE; 2 da (Catherine Alice Penrose b 25 Nov 1970, Helen Mary Hogarth b 19 July 1973); *Career* lectr in Latin Bedford Coll London 1961–64 (asst lectr 1958–61), reader in archaeology and numismatics UCL 1967–71 (lectr in archaeology 1964–67), prof of Greek language and literature KCL 1971–91 (head Dept of Classics 1972–84, visiting prof Centre for Hellenic Studies 2003–); Univ of London: dean Faculty of Arts 1976–80, public orator 1978–81 and 1986–88, dir Inst of Classical Studies 1984–91, dean Insts for Advanced Study 1989–91, pro-vice-chllr 1987–89, distinguished sr fell Sch of Advanced Study 2004–; master St Peter's Coll Oxford 1991–2003 (hon fell 2003); Univ of Oxford: chm Conf of Colls 1993–95, chm Admissions Ctee 1997–2000, jt chm Oxford and Cambridge Schs Exams Bd 1993–96; visiting memb Inst for Advanced Study Princeton 1973, Blegen distinguished visiting prof Vassar Coll Poughkeepsie NY 1981, T B L Webster visiting prof Stanford Univ CA 1986; memb UFC 1989–93; Crown rep and vice-chm SOAS 1993–99; pres Clifton Coll 1999– (govr 1996–); pres Soc for the Promotion of Hellenic Studies 1990–93 (tstee 1970–2000, hon sec 1981–90); tstee: Prince of Wales's Inst of Architecture 1990–96, Lambeth Palace Library 1997–; FKC 1988, FSA 1967 (vice-pres 2004–07); memb Academia Europaea 1990; *Books* Greek Sculpture (1965, revised edn 1981), Silver Coins of Samos (1966); *Recreations* travel, gardens; *Clubs* Athenaeum; *Style*— Prof John Barron, FSA; ✉ 9 Boundary Road, London NW8 0HE (tel 020 7722 6033)

BARRON, John Raymond (Christopher); s of Arthur William John Barron (d 1981), and Enid Caroline, *née* Brooks; *b* 17 November 1949; *Educ* Cheltenham GS, Central Sch of Speech and Drama, Univ of Wales (BA); *m* 29 Sept 1984, Julia, *née* Tompsett; *Career* stage mangr Glyndebourne, '69 Theatre Co, Wexford and Batignano Festivals 1967–74, gen mangr Watford Palace Theatre 1978–81, gen mangr Buxton Festival and Opera House 1981–84, gen mangr and assoc dir Edinburgh Int Festival 1984–92, dir Manchester City of Drama 1992–94, chief exec and artistic dir Brighton Festival and Dome 1995–2000, chief exec Scottish Ballet/Scottish Opera 2000–05, chief exec Birmingham Royal Ballet 2005–; bd dir: Dance Umbrella, Musica Nel Chiostro, Belfast Festival at Queen's, Nat Opera Studio; chm SE Dance Agency 1996–2000 (also fndr); Manchester Evening News Horniman Award for outstanding services to theatre 1994; *Recreations* hill walking, cabinet making; *Style*— Christopher Barron, Esq

BARRON, Rt Hon Kevin John; PC (2001), MP; s of Richard Barron and Edna Barron; *b* 26 October 1946; *Educ* Ruskin Coll; *m* 1969; 1 s, 2 da; *Career* NCB 1962–83 (NUM exec for Maltby Colliery), pres Rotherham and District TUC; MP (Lab) Rother Valley 1983–; shadow min for: energy 1988–92, employment 1992–93, health 1995–96, public health 1996–97; PPS to Neil Kinnock 1985–88 as Leader of the Opposition; memb: Energy Select Ctee 1983–85, Environment Select Ctee 1992–93, Intelligence and Security Ctee 1997–; chair: Yorkshire Gp of Lab MPs 1987–, PLP Health Ctee 1997–, All-Pty Gp on Pharmaceutical Industry 1997–, All-Pty Gp on Smoking & Health 1997–, Food Standards Agency Ctee; vice-pres Royal Soc of Health 2007–; lay memb GMC 1999–; *Style*— The Rt Hon Kevin Barron, MP; ✉ House of Commons, London SW1A 0AA (tel 020 7219 6306, fax 020 7219 5952, barronk@parliament.uk, website www.rothervalley.org.uk)

BARRON, Prof Laurence David; s of Gerald Landon Barron, of Southampton, and Stella, *née* Gertz; *b* 12 February 1944; *Educ* King Edward VI GS, Northern Poly (BSc), Lincoln Coll Oxford (DPhil); *m* 10 Aug 1969, Sharon Aviva, da of Denis Harris Wolf; 1 da (Susannah Mira b 23 Sept 1971), 1 s (Daniel Morris 17 May 1973); *Career* Ramsay meml fell Univ of Cambridge 1974–75 (research asst 1969–74); Univ of Glasgow: lectr 1975–80, reader 1980–84, prof of chemistry 1984–99, Gardiner prof of chemistry 1999–; G M J Schmidt meml lectr Weizmann Inst of Sci Israel 1984, F L Conover meml lectr Vanderbilt Univ USA 1987, visiting Miller research prof Univ of Calif Berkeley 1995, sr fell EPSRC 1995–2000; Corday-Morgan Medal and Prize Chemical Soc 1979, Sir Harold Thompson Award for Spectroscopy 1993; memb: RSC, APS, ACS; FInstP, FRSC, FRSE 1992, FRS 2005; *Books* Molecular Light Scattering and Optical Activity (2004); *Recreations* music, walking, watercolour painting, radio controlled model aircraft; *Style*— Prof Laurence Barron, FRS, FRSE; ✉ Chemistry Department, The University, Glasgow G12 8QQ (tel 0141 330 5168, fax 0141 330 4888)

BARRON, Steve; *Career* film and video dir/prodr; chm Limelight (London) Ltd 1996–; early career experience as camera asst on films incl Superman 1 and 2, A Bridge Too Far (dir Richard Attenborough, *qv*) and Duellists (dir Ridley Scott), concurrently experimented in early music video (The Jam and Sham 69) 1977, conceived and directed multi award winning promo Billy Jean (Michael Jackson) 1982, other promos incl Take on Me (A-HA, over 40 awards) 1985 and Money for Nothing (Dire Straits, MTV Video of Year) 1986, subsequently dir of various commercials incl Motorcycle Chains (D&AD Award) and others in UK and USA for clients incl Pepsi, Coca-Cola, Ford and Renault, dir Electric Dreams (first feature film, Best Dir Madrid Film Festival and Best Film Award Avoriaz Fantastique Film Festival) 1984, dir Hans my Hedgehog (Emmy Award), Fearnot and Sapsorrow (Storyteller episodes for NBC TV) 1987, dir Teenage Mutant Ninja Turtles (highest grossing ind film, CBS TV Award for Best Family Entertainment Film of Year) 1990, subsequently dir of music promos Calling Elvis (Dire Straits, Grammy nomination) 1991, Unforgettable (Natalie Cole, Billboard Best Dir Award) 1991 and Let's Get Rocked (Def Leppard, MTV nomination) 1992, dir feature film Coneheads 1993, exec prodr The Specialist (feature with Sylvester Stallone and Sharon Stone) 1994, exec prodr ReBoot (animated TV show, ABC TV 1994, UK 1995), exec prodr While You Were Sleeping 1995; dir: The Adventures of Pinocchio 1996, Merlin (NBC) 1998 (nominated for 15 Emmys and 4 Golden Globes), Arabian Nights (ABC) 1999 (5 Emmy nominations), Rat, Mike Bassett: England Manager 2001, Dreamkeeper 2003; *Style*— Steve Barron, Esq; ✉ c/o Mike Simpson, William Morris Agency (tel 001 310 859 4000)

BARROS D'SA, Prof Abilio Anacleto Joseph (Leo); s of Inaçio Francisco Purificação Saúde D'Sa (d 1978), of London, and Maria Eslinda Inês, *née* Barros (d 1998); *b* 28 April 1933; *Educ* Westminster Coll (Arbour E Day Award), Coll of Law London, Hon Soc of the Inner Temple (Inns of Court Sch of Law), Univ of Manchester (Arch, Kendal exhbn, PhD Law), PNL (DipArch), UCL (MSc), UCL Law Teachers Trg, Univ of Leicester (LLM), Univ of Middx (MA), King's Coll and Inst of Advanced Legal Studies Univ of London (postdoctoral), Wolfson Coll Cambridge (MSt), Kenwar MS National Prize, MKG Prize; *m* 12 Sept 1969, Erika, da of Friedrich Völkl, of Fürth, Bavaria; *Career* formerly asst architectural practices incl: WS Atkins, Farmer & Dark 1957–67; dir Professional Design Servs; md Greathead Ltd 1967–76; DOE architect, PSA design team ldr, superintending offr, conslt liaison and project mangr 1976–79, innovator of audit systems 1979, focal point for Conservation of Central London Bldgs of Special and Historical Interest 1982–87, PSA liaison Parliamentary House Jl and Ironbridge Museum 1983, conslt liaison Party Wall Awards 1984, area auditor and reviewer 1985, head of bldg advsy section, PSA rep on HSE and BSI Agŕment Cert Ctees, HQ advsr Cardington Consultative Ctee on govt contracts 1985–87, visiting lectr PhD law supervisor and examiner Univ of London, Univ of Oxford and Univ of Cambridge 1987– (visiting prof 1991 and 2000–), seconded from PSA to assist chm of DOE/DTI ministerial review on professional liability 1987–88, promotion bd panellist for sr professionals, acad advsr to postgrads, UCL law res postgrad 1989–91, HQ princ lectr in law and advsr on negotiation and pursuit of negligence claims for MOD and Civil Dept projects in UK regns home and abroad incl Gibraltar 1989–95, first govt appointed head of PSA Directorate Specialist Legal Services 1991 (md post privatisation 1995–), asst dir PSA Projects Bd 1992–95, law research into reform concurrent tortfeasors in solidum liability 1991–96, assoc dir head of TBV Legal Claims 1992–95, referee professional jls, Human Rights 2000 conf 1996, res into Latham-Egan reforms 1998–2001; sr ptnr: Leo Barros D'Sa Associates 1995–2003, Erika Barros D'Sa Ferneyhough Brown 2003–; jt chm Ethics and Transparency 2002–07; distinction award for res into Euro Court of Justice Acquired Rights Directive infractions and ambiguities 1992; memb: RIBA, Judicial Div Int Assoc of the American Bar Assoc, IPMS 1976–, CIArb 1976–97, Soc of Construction Law 1990–, Socio-Legal Studies Assoc 1996–, IOD, Soc Public Teachers of Law, Acad of Construction Adjudicators, Assoc of Univ Teachers, Euro Assoc of Psychology and Law, Int Soc of Criminologists, UK Assoc Legal & Social Philosophy, American Psychology-Law Soc, American Soc of Criminology, Amnesty Int, Legal Action Gp, Justice 1999, Bd CIDU 2003–; fndr memb The Adjudication Soc 2000–; Freeman City of London 1988, memb Worshipful Co of Chartered Architects; FRSA, FFB, FIMgt; *Publications* books incl: Professional Liability and Construction (1987 edn), PSA Tech Digests (co-author, 1988), Tech Feedback (PSA ed, 1988–89), Bishop Report (contrib Analysis 2 chapters, 1989); author and presenter of numerous papers on professional negligence and employment law, corporate crime, recidivism, femicide and other criminological issues; *Recreations* chess, opera, cine-soc, literature, scribbling, doodling, Tyrolean walks; *Clubs* Oxford and Cambridge, Royal Over-Seas League; *Style*— Prof Leo Barros D'Sa; ✉ 52 Elm Park Road, Winchmore Hill, London N21 2HS (tel 020 8360 0074, fax 020 8360 8700); Erika Barros D'Sa Ferneyhough Brown (tel 020 8245 9840); Wolfson College, University of Cambridge CB3 9BB

BARROS D'SA, Alban Avelino John; s of Inaçio Francisco Purificação Saude D'Sa (d 1978), of London, and Maria Eslinda Inez, *née* Barros (d 1998); *b* 25 October 1937; *Educ* Teacher Training Coll Nairobi Kenya, West Ham Coll London, Univ of Bristol (MB ChB, LRCP, MRCS, FRCSEdin, FRCS Eng, Leonard Pritchard Tibbits Prize in surgery, Barrett Roue Prize in ENT and ophthalmology, Henry Clarke Prize in obstetrics and gynaecology, Brocklehurst Prize); *m* 22 July 1972, Gwenda Anne, da of Richard Arthur Davies (d 2002), of Coventry; 1 da (Sonia Helen b 4 Sept 1974), 1 s (Ian James b 30 April 1976); *Career* house surgn and physician Bristol Royal Infirmary 1967–68, memb staff Faculty of Anatomy Univ of Bristol 1968–69, SHO in surgery (renal transplantion, orthopaedic, general, traumatic and cardio-thoracic surgery) Bristol Royal Infirmary, Southmead and Frenchay Hosps 1969–71, registrar in surgery and urology Musgrove Park Hosp Taunton 1971–74, Pfizer res fell (also tutor in surgery and hon sr registrar) Royal Postgrad Med Sch and Hammersmith Hosp 1974–75, sr registrar in gen and vascular surgery Univ Hosp of Wales Cardiff and Singleton Hosp Swansea; conslt surgn: Univ Hosps, Coventry and Warks NHS Tst 1979–2002, Nuffield Hosp Leamington Spa, BMI Meriden Hosp Coventry; clinical teacher Dept of Surgery Leicester Warwick Med Sch 2001–02, clinical dir of surgery St Cross Hosp Rugby 1990–93, surgical tutor RCS England 1987–93; examiner in gen surgery for FRCS and MRCS RCS Edinburgh 1990–, tutor in laparoscopic surgery for RCS England 1995–, convenor of laparoscopic surgery courses for Minimally Access Therapy Trg Unit RCS England 1996–, external conslt assessor to Health Serv Ombudsman 1999–, examiner in surgery Univ of Leicester 2002–, examiner in surgery Univ of Warwick 2002–, examiner in Intercollegiate MRCS in surgery 2004–; visiting lectr in laparoscopic surgery Goa Med Sch Univ of Goa 1995, invited guest lectr on complications of laparoscopic surgery XXth Annual Conf Delhi State Chapter Assoc of Surgns of India 2002; memb Ct Univ of Bristol 1969–97; sr memb: Br Soc of Gastroenterology, Midland Gastroenterology Assoc, Midland Surgical Soc; fndr memb Assoc of Endoscopic Surgns of GB and Ireland, sr fell Assoc of Surgns GB and Ireland; memb: Rugby and Dist Med Soc, Warks Medico-legal Soc, BMA; FRCS (ad eundem) 1997, RCS(Eng), quincentenary fell RCSEd 2005; *Books* Rhoads Textbook of Surgery (contrib chapter 5 edn, 1977); author of numerous pubns in med jls on oesophageal, gastric, pancreatic, vascular and thyroid surgery; *Recreations* travel, golf, piano; *Style—* Alban Barros D'Sa, Esq; ✉ 40 Nightingale Lane, Westwood Gardens, Coventry CV5 6AY (tel and fax 024 7667 5181, e-mail albangwenda@coventrybarrosdsa.freeserve.co.uk); 5 Davenport Road, Coventry CV5 6QA; Central Surgery, Corporation Street, Rugby (tel 024 7667 7838, 024 7667 2997, fax 024 7671 3822, mobile 079 9058 7505); Nuffield Hospital, Lemington Spa; BMI Meriden Hospital Walsgrave Site, Coventry

BARROTT, Michael Anthony Cooper; s of Brian Robert James Barrott (d 1963), and Betty Doreen, *née* Berryman (d 1998); *b* 9 December 1954; *Educ* Reading Sch, St John's Coll Oxford (scholar, MA), Open Univ (MBA); *m* 29 May 1982, Elizabeth Jelisaveta, da of Stojan Stosic (d 1994); 1 s (William b 12 Aug 1996); *Career* Price Waterhouse 1976–87, Scandinavian Bank plc 1987–90 (div dir 1989–90), fin dir Mortgage Trust Ltd 1990–95, chief exec Strategy, Finance & Governance 1995–; hon vice-pres Thames Valley Housing Assoc 2005– (non-exec dir 1992–2004, chm 1998–2004); memb Nat Cncl Nat Housing Fedn 1999–2004; FCA 1990 (ACA 1979); *Recreations* music, skiing, golf, history, restoring Georgian houses; *Clubs* IOD; *Style—* Michael Barrott, Esq; ✉ Strategy, Finance & Governance, 126 Kennington Road, London SE11 6RE (tel 020 7582 2453, e-mail michael.barrott@btinternet.com)

BARROW, Andrew James; s of Gerald Ernest Barrow, MBE, of Gustard Wood, Herts, and Angela Eileen, *née* Frank; *b* 17 May 1954; *Educ* King's Sch Canterbury, Univ of Nottingham (LLB); *m* 16 April 1983, Helen Elizabeth, da of Brian Carter; 3 s (Charles Andrew b 24 May 1984, Frederick Nicholas b 26 May 1986, Joshua Barnaby b 9 April 1993), 1 da (Clementine Elizabeth b 17 March 1988); *Career* slr; Travers Smith Braithwaite: articled clerk 1976–78, asst slr 1978–83, ptnr 1983–; memb City of London Slrs' Co; memb: Law Soc, Int Bar Assoc, Inter-Pacific Bar Assoc; *Recreations* family, golf, powerboating, motorbikes; *Clubs* City of London, Royal Wimbledon, Royal County Down; *Style—* Andrew Barrow, Esq; ✉ 10 Snow Hill, London EC1A 2AL (tel 020 7248 9133, fax 020 7236 3728, mobile 07831 386119, e-mail andrew.barrow@traverssmith.com)

BARROW, Colin; CBE (2004); s of Reginald Barrow (d 1981), of Gosport, Hants, and Margaret, *née* Jones (d 1994); *b* 18 June 1952; *Educ* Dulwich Coll, Clare Coll Cambridge (MA); *m* 25 June 1994 (sep 2005), Angelica, da of Hermann Bortis; 2 s (Simon b 26 Feb 1997, James b 29 Nov 1998); partner, Ana Smaldon; *Career* commercial mangr John Brown Gp 1974–83, md Funds Div E D & F Man Gp 1983–96, chm Sabre Fund Mgmnt Gp 1996–2005, chm Alpha Strategic plc 2005–; chm IDeA 2000–04; chm Nat Autistic Soc 2005– (treas 2004); dir: Rambert Dance Co 1997–2003, Policy Exchange 2002–05; memb: Suffolk CC 1997–2002, Westminster City Cncl 2002– (dep ldr 2005–); *Recreations* inexpert skier, scuba diver, bridge player; *Style—* Colin Barrow, Esq, CBE; ✉ 8 Barton Street, Westminster, London SW1P 3NE (tel 020 7222 2223, fax 020 7222 3025, e-mail mail@cbarrow.com)

BARROW, Geoffrey Paul; *b* 9 December 1971; *Career* fndr memb (with Beth Gibbons , *qv*) Portishead 1991– (sold over 8 million albums); also prodr for several artists inc McKay: Tell Him (single, 2003), McKay (album, 2003); various press, PRS, ASCAP and IFPI awards; *Albums* Dummy (1994, Mercury Music Prize 1995), Portishead (1997), PNYC (live album, 1998); *Singles* Numb (ep, 1994), Sour Times (1994), Glory Box (1995), Cowboys (1997), All Mine (1997), Only You (1998), Over (1998); *Films* To Kill A Dead Man (short film, 1994), PNYC (DVD, 2000); *Style—* Geoffrey Barrow, Esq

BARROW, Dame Jocelyn; DBE (1992, OBE 1972); *b* 15 April 1929; *Educ* Univ of London (BA); *m* Henderson Downer; *Career* dep chm Broadcasting Standards Cncl (and chm of its Complaints Ctee) 1985–92; govr: BBC 1981–88, Farnham Castle (centre for training Third World workers), Cwlth Inst (and chair of its Educn Ctee), Cwlth of Learning; gen sec Campaign Against Racial Discrimination 1964–69, vice-chm International Human Rights Year Ctee 1968, memb Community Relations Cmmn 1968–72, national vice-pres Nat Union of Townswomen's Guilds 1978–80 and 1987–, memb EC Econ and Social Ctee 1990–, devpt dir Focus Consultancy Ltd 1996–; fndr (now pres) Community Housing Assoc Camden, vice-chm E London Housing Assoc; govr and patron Goldsmiths Coll London (memb Equal Opportunities Ctee), patron Caribbean Centre (and its Caribbean Int Studies network); former sr lectr in educn Furzedown Teachers Coll, seconded to Inst of Educn Univ of London; chair Mayor's Cmmn on African & Asian Heritage 2003–05; Hon DLitt Univ of E London 1992; FRSA; *Style—* Dame Jocelyn Barrow, DBE

BARROW, John Anthony; s of Jack Farmer Barrow, and Nancy Elwyn Jones; *b* 11 July 1948; *Educ* C of E Boys' GS Brisbane, Queensland Inst of Technol, Royal Aust Inst of Architecture (Silver Medallist); *m* 1988, Frances Thomson; 1 da (Kit Elizabeth b 20 May 1982), 1 s (Adam Jack Sansom b 21 Aug 1988); *Career* architect; ptnr Marshall Haines Barrow 1979–87; dir: Lister Drew Haines Barrow 1987–1991, WS Atkins Architects 1991–93, Marshall Haines Barrow Ltd 1994–2000; sr princ HOK Sport Ltd 2001–; current and recent projects incl: Palasport speed skating arena Turin 2006 Winter Olympic Games, masterplanning, overlay and venue planning London 2012 Olympic Games, Glasgow 2014 Cwlth Games bid, O2 Arena Greenwich, stadium Milton Keynes, NI nat stadium, Point Arena Dublin, Formula 1 racetrack redevelopment Silverstone, Formula 1 autodrome Dubai, Olympique Lyonnais stadium France, Benfica stadium Lisbon, Algarve stadium Faro, Odyssey Arena Belfast; RIBA 1976; *Recreations* motor sports, antique car restoration, golf; *Clubs* RAC; *Style—* John Barrow, Esq; ✉ The Carriage House, Peper Harow, Godalming, Surrey GU8 6BG; HOK Sport, 14 Deodar Road, London SW15 2NU (tel 020 8874 7666, fax 020 8874 7470)

BARROW, Prof John David; s of Walter Henry Barrow (d 1979), of London, and Lois Miriam, *née* Tucker (d 1998); *b* 29 November 1952; *Educ* Ealing GS, Van Mildert Coll Durham (BSc), Magdalen Coll Oxford (DPhil); *m* 13 Sept 1975, Elizabeth Mary, da of James William East (d 1978), of London; 2 s (David Lloyd b 1978, Roger James b 1981), 1 da (Louise Elizabeth b 1984); *Career* jr res lectr ChCh Oxford 1977–80; Univ of Sussex: lectr 1981–89, prof of astronomy 1989–99, dir Astronomy Centre 1995–99; currently prof of mathematical sciences Univ of Cambridge (dir Millennium Math Project 1999–), fell Clare Hall Cambridge 1999– (vice-pres 2004–07); Gordon Godfrey visiting prof Univ of NSW 1999, 2000 and 2003, concurrent prof Univ of Nanjing 2005–, Gresham prof of astronomy 2003–07; Lindemann fell English Speaking Union Cwlth 1977–78, Miller fell Univ of Calif Berkley 1980–81, Nuffield fell 1986–87, Gifford lectr Univ of Glasgow 1988, Scott meml lectr Leuven 1989, Collingwood meml lectr Univ of Durham 1990, Sigma-Tau-Laterza lectures Milan Univ 1991, Leverhulme fell Royal Soc 1992, George Darwin lecture RAS 1992, Kelvin lecture 1999, Flamsteed lecture 2000, Tyndall lecture 2001, Darwin lecture 2001, Whitrow lecture RAS 2002, Brasher lecture 2002, Newton Lecture 2004, Hubert James lecture 2004, Von Weizsäker lectures 2004, McCrea lecture 2004, Wood lecture 2005, Hamilton lecture 2005, Knight lecture Monkton Coll Bath 2006, Borderlands lecture Univ of Durham 2007, Boyle lecture St Mary-le-Bow London 2007, Roscoe lecture John Moore Univ Liverpool 2007, Gunnar and Gunnel Källén lecture Lund 2007; Samuel Locker Award 1989, Templeton Award 1995, Kelvin Medal 1999, Premi Ubu Theatre Prize 2002, Italgas Prize 2004, Lacchini Medal 2005, Queen's Anniversary Prize 2006, Templeton Prize 2006; external examiner Open Univ; PPARC sr fell 1994–99, memb Cncl RAS 1999–, memb various ctees SERC; Hon DSc: Univ of Herts 1999, Univ of Szczecin 2007, Univ of Durham 2008; memb: Int Astronomical Union, ISSR; FRS, FRAS, FInstP, FRSA; *Books* The Left Hand of Creation (1983), The Anthropic Cosmological Principle (1986), L'Homme et Le Cosmos (1984), The World Within the World (1988), Theories of Everything (1991), Perché il mondo è matematico? (1992), Pi in the Sky (1992), The Origin of the Universe (1994), The Artful Universe (1995), Impossibility (1998), Between Inner Space and Outer Space (1999), The Universe That Discovered Itself (2000), The Book of Nothing (2000), The Constants of Nature (2002), The Infinite Book (2005), The Artful Universe Expanded (2005), New Theories of Everything (2007); *Recreations* athletics, books, theatre (play Infinities performed in Milan and Valencia 2002–03); *Style—* Prof John D Barrow, FRS; ✉ DAMTP, University of Cambridge, Wilberforce Road, Cambridge CB3 0WA (tel 01223 766696, fax 01223 765900, e-mail j.d.barrow@damtp.cam.ac.uk)

BARROW, Julian Gurney; s of G Erskine Barrow (d 1979), and Margaret Armine MacInnes (d 1977); *b* 28 August 1939; *Educ* Harrow; *m* 1971, Serena Catherine Lucy, da of Maj John Harington (d 1983); 2 da; *Career* landscape and portrait painter; pres Chelsea Art Soc 1990–; *Recreations* painting, travel; *Style—* Julian Barrow, Esq; ✉ 33 Tite Street, London SW3 4JP (tel 020 7352 4337, fax 020 7352 6757)

BARROW, Capt Sir Richard John Uniacke; 6 Bt (UK 1835), of Ulverstone, Lancs; s of Maj Sir Wilfrid John Wilson Croker Barrow, 5 Bt (d 1960); *b* 2 August 1933; *Educ* Beaumont; *m* 1961 (m dis 1974), (Alison) Kate, da of late Capt Russell Grenfell, RN; 1 s (Anthony John Grenfell b 1962), 2 da (Nony Mary Louise (Mrs Simon Kerr-Smiley) b 1963, Frances Teresa Catherine b 1971); *Heir* s, Anthony Barrow; *Career* served Irish Gds 1952–60; with Int Computers and Tabulators Ltd until 1973; *Style—* Capt Sir Richard Barrow, Bt

BARROW, Robert; s of Frederick Barrow, of Congleton, and Hannah, *née* Carless; *b* 27 December 1949; *Educ* Sandbach Sch, Univ of Warwick, Staffs Univ (BSc); *m* 14 Oct 1972, Pamela, da of Kenneth Stuart Snelgrove; 1 da (Alethea Mary Fiona b 20 June 1980); *Career* mgmnt staff Computing Div British Railways Bd 1972–77, conslt ICL Ltd 1977–82, co-fndr and chief exec JSB Software Technologies plc 1982–2000, chm Surf Control plc 2000–03, non-exec dir Quester & FIS 2000–; nominated for Duke of Edinburgh's special designers prize 1989; MBCS 1976, CEng 1990; *Style—* Robert Barrow, Esq

BARROW, Simon Hoare; s of G Erskine Barrow (d 1979), of IOM, and Margaret Armine MacInnes (d 1977); *b* 4 November 1937; *Educ* Harrow, ChCh Oxford, Hill Sch Pennsylvania (ESU exchange); *m* 1, 1964 (m dis 1977), Caroline Peto Bennett; 1 s (Thomas), 3 da (Sasha, Emmeline, Rebecca); m 2, 1983, Sheena Margaret, da of Maj-Gen Sir John Anderson, KBE; 2 da (Kate, Florence); *Career* 2 Lt Scots Gds 1956–58; brand mgmnt for Corn Products and Colgate-Palmolive 1967–78, dir Charles Barker Gp (now BNB Resources plc) 1978–92; chief exec: Ayer Barker 1978–86, Barkers Human Resources 1987–92; chm: People in Business mgmnt communication conslts 1992–, The Recruitment Soc 1992–98, Human Resource Interest Group Market Research Soc 1995–2000; memb Advsy Cncl European Movement 1992–; advsr to City Disputes Panel 1995–; columnist: Haymarket's Human Resources 2000–01, Acquisition Monthly 2002; memb Judging Panel Britain's Top Employers (with The Guardian) 2004–05; FRGS; *Books* The Employer Brand: Bringing the best of brand management to people at work (2005); *Recreations* sailing, tennis; *Clubs* Brooks's; *Style—* Simon Barrow, Esq; ✉ 16 Chelsea Embankment, London SW3 4LA (tel 020 7352 7531); Cowton House, Sudbourne, Suffolk IP12 2HB (tel 01394 450737); People in Business, 12 Great Newport Street, London WC2H 7JD (tel 020 7632 5910, e-mail simon@pib.co.uk)

BARRY, Prof (David) Andrew; s of Ernest Julian Barry, of Cornubia, Queensland, and Ann Elizabeth, *née* Hooper; *b* 19 April 1958; *Educ* Univ of Queensland (BA), Griffith Univ (BSc, PhD, DSc), Royal Melbourne Inst of Technol (BAppSci); *m* 16 May 1986, Suellen Jill de Waard; 1 da (Caitlin Ellen b 7 March 1992), 2 s (Julian Andrew b 1 July 1996, Richard John Barry b 28 Nov 2000); *Career* res assoc Centre for Environmental and Hazardous Materials Studies Virginia Poly Inst and State Univ 1985–86, postgraduate res soil scientist Dept of Soil and Environmental Sci Univ of Calif 1986–88; Univ of Western Australia: lectr in subsurface hydrology Centre for Water Res 1989–91, sr lectr and hydrology gp ldr Dept of Environmental Engrg 1991–93, assoc prof Dept of Environmental Engrg 1994–98 (hon fell 1998–99); Univ of Edinburgh: chair Environmental Engrg Sch of Civil and Environmental Engrg 1998–2005, head of sch 2000–05, dir Contaminated Land Assessment and Remediation Res Centre 1998–2005; prof École Polytechnique Fédérale de Lausanne (EPFL) 2005–; visiting assoc prof Dept of Environmental Sci and Engrg Univ of North Carolina 1994, visiting scientist Dept of Civil and Environmental Engrg MIT 1996; co-ed Advances in Water Resources, memb Editorial Bd Jl of Hydrology; memb: American Geophysical Union, Australian Assoc for Engrg Educn, Euro Geophysical Soc, Modelling and Simulation Soc of Australia and NZ, Int Soc of Soil Sci, Engrg and Physical Res Cncl Peer Review Coll, Inst for Learning and Teaching in Higher Educn; CMath, FIMA, FICE; *Publications* author of 7 book chapters, over 135 articles in learned and professional jls and over 35 conf papers; *Recreations* swimming, walking; *Style—* Prof D Andrew Barry

BARRY, Prof Brian Michael; *b* 1936; *Educ* The Queen's Coll Oxford (Southampton exhibitioner, MA, DPhil); *m*; *Career* Lloyd-Muirhead research fell Dept of Philosophy Univ of Birmingham 1960–61, asst lectr Dept of Moral and Political Philosophy Keele Univ 1962–63, lectr Dept of Politics Univ of Southampton 1963–65, tutorial fell UC Oxford 1965–66, official fell Nuffield Coll Oxford 1966–69 and 1972–75 (sr tutor 1968–69), prof of govt Univ of Essex 1969–72 (dean of social studies 1970–72), prof of political science Univ of Br Columbia 1975–77; Univ of Chicago: prof of political science and philosophy and memb Ctee on Public Policy 1977–81, distinguished serv prof 1981–82, dir of grad placement 1981–82; Caltech: prof of philosophy 1982–83, Edie and Lew Wasserman prof of philosophy 1983–86; prof (A3) in Dept of Social and Political Science Euro Univ Inst Florence 1986–87, prof of political science LSE 1987–88 (emeritus prof 1998–), convenor LSE 1992–94, Lieber prof of political philosophy Columbia Univ 1998–; visiting assoc prof of political science Univ of Pittsburgh 1967, John Hinckley prof dept of political science Johns Hopkins Univ Baltimore 1974, Olmsted visiting prof Yale Univ 1995, Tanner lectr Harvard Univ 1980; fndr ed The British Jl of Political Science 1971–72, section ed Political Theory 1973–75; Ethics - An International Jl of Social, Political and Legal Philosophy: ed 1979–82, manuscript ed 1982–86, assoc ed 1986–90; memb Editorial Bds of 13 jls; lifetime achievement in political studies award Political Studies Assoc 2000, Johan Skytte prize in political science 2001; Rockefeller fell in legal and political philosophy and fell Harvard Coll 1961–62, fell Center for Advanced Study in the Behavioral Sciences Stanford Univ 1976–77, visiting fell Dept of Politics Australian Nat Univ 1977, Rockefeller Fndn Humanities fell 1979–80, American Cncl of Learned Socs fell 1980, Leverhulme sr res fell (admin by Br Acad) 1991–92; Hon DSc Univ of Southampton 1989; FAAAS 1976, FBA 1988; *Books* Political Argument (1965, revised edn 1990), Sociologists, Economists and Democracy (1970), The Liberal Theory of Justice (1973), Power and Political Theory - Some European Perspectives (ed, 1976), Obligations to Future Generations (ed with Richard Sikora, 1978), Rational Man and Irrational Society? An Introduction and Source Book (ed with Russell Hardin, 1982), Theories of Justice (vol I of A Treatise on Social Justice, 1989), Democracy, Power and Justice - Essays in Political Theory (1989), Does Society Exist? The Case for Socialism (Fabian Soc tract, 1989), Democracy and Power - Essays in Political Theory 1 (1991), Liberty and Justice - Essays in Political Theory 2 (1991), Free Movement - Ethical Issues in the Transnational Migration of People and of Money (ed with Robert Goodin, 1992), Justice as Impartiality (vol II of A Treatise on Social Justice, 1995), Culture and Equality (2001), Why Social Justice Matters (2005); author of numerous articles in various jls; *Style*— Prof Brian Barry, FBA

BARRY, Prof Brian William; s of William Paul Barry (d 1982), and Jean, *née* Manson (d 1959); *b* 20 April 1939; *Educ* Univ of Manchester (BSc, DSc), Univ of London (PhD); *m* 26 March 1966, Betty Barry, da of John Hugh Boothby, of Portsmouth; 1 s (Simon John b 1967); *Career* community and industrial pharmacist 1960–62, asst lectr and lectr Univ of London 1962–67, sr lectr and reader Portsmouth Poly (now Univ of Portsmouth) 1967–77, prof Univ of Bradford 1977– (dean of Natural and Applied Sciences 1991–94); FRSC 1976; fell: Royal Pharmaceutical Soc 1982, American Assoc of Pharmaceutical Scientists 1990; *Books* Dermatological Formulations: Percutaneous Absorption (1983); author of numerous research papers and book chapters; *Recreations* swimming, walking, golf; *Style*— Prof Brian Barry; ✉ School of Pharmacy, University of Bradford, Bradford BD7 1DP (tel 01274 234760, e-mail b.w.barry@bradford.ac.uk)

BARRY, Dr David Walter; *b* 19 July 1943, Nashua, New Hampshire; *Educ* Yale Univ (BA), Sorbonne, Yale Univ Sch of Med (MD); *m*; 2 c; *Career* research assoc Rockefeller Fndn Yale Arbovirus Research Unit 1967–69, med resident Yale-New Haven Hosp 1969–72 (med intern 1969–70), cmmnd offr (sr surgn) US Public Health Serv 1972–77; Bureau of Biologics Food and Drug Administration: staff assoc Viral Pathogenesis Branch Div of Virology 1972–73, dir Gen Virology Branch Div of Virology 1973–77, actg dep dir Div of Virology 1973–77, dir Influenza Vaccine Task Force 1976–77; Burroughs Wellcome Co: head Dept of Clinical Investigation Med Div 1978–85 (head Anti-Infectives Section 1977–78), head Dept of Virology Wellcome Research Laboratories 1983–89, dir Div of Clinical Investigation 1985–86, vice-pres research Wellcome Research Laboratories 1986–89, memb Bd of Dirs Burroughs Wellcome Fund 1986–94, memb Bd of Dirs Burroughs Wellcome Co 1989–94, vice-pres of research, devpt and med affrs Wellcome Research Laboratories 1989–94, memb Bd of Dirs Family Health International 1990–, gp dir research devpt and med Wellcome Research Laboratories The Wellcome Foundation Ltd (Wellcome plc) 1994–95 (memb Bd of Dirs 1989–94), chm and ceo Triangle Pharmaceuticals 1995–; chm Intracompany Collaboration on AIDS Drug Devpt 1997–; visiting fell in infectious diseases Univ of Maryland Baltimore 1975–76, adjunct prof of med Duke Univ Sch of Med 1977–, Elisha Atkins visiting prof of med Yale Univ 1988; memb: AIDS Task Force and AIDS Program Advsy Ctee US Nat Insts of Health 1986, AIDS Task Force Pharmaceutical Mfrs' Assoc 1990, various other US anti-AIDS bodies and confs, Industry Liaison Panel Inst of Med 1992, Dean's Advsy Cncl Yale Med Sch, Research in Human Subjects Ctee Bureau of Biologists FDA, Med and Scientific Section Pharmaceutical Mfrs' Assoc, Scientific Affrs Ctee Nat Pharmaceutical Cncl, N Carolina Med Soc, N Carolina Industrial (Vaccine) Cmmn, American Soc for Virology, American Soc for Microbiology, American Fedn for Clinical Research, American Assoc for the Advancement of Science, American Med Assoc; memb Editorial Bd: AIDS Research and Human Retroviruses, AIDS Patient Care, Jl of Infectious Diseases (also ad hoc reviewer); Wellcome Scientist Lecture 1981, Peter A Leermakers Symposium Wesleyan Univ 1986, Harold Brun Soc Lecture San Francisco 1987; jt holder of numerous pharmaceutical patents, author of approx 100 papers in med jls; *Style*— Dr David Barry; ✉ Triangle Pharmaceuticals Inc., 4 University Place, 4611 University Drive, Durham, NC 27707, USA (tel 001 919 493 5980, fax 001 919 493 5925)

BARRY, Sir (Lawrence) Edward Anthony Tress; 5 Bt (UK 1899), of St Leonard's Hill, Clewer, Berks, and Keiss Castle, Wick, Caithness-shire; Baron de Barry of Portugal (1876), Lord of the Manors of Ockwells and Lillibrooke, Berks; s of Maj Sir Rupert Rodney Francis Tress Barry, 4 Bt, MBE (d 1977); *b* 1 November 1939; *Educ* Haileybury; *m* 1, 1968, Fenella, da of Mrs Hilda Hoult, of Knutsford, Cheshire; 1 s (William Rupert Philip Tress b 13 Dec 1973), 1 da (Alexandra Diana Frances Louise b 1977); *m* 2, 1992, Elizabeth Jill, da of G Bradley, of Fishtoft, Boston; *Heir* s, William Barry; *Career* former Capt Grenadier Gds; *Style*— Sir Edward Barry, Bt; ✉ Swinstead Cottage, High Street, Swinstead, Grantham NG33 4PA

BARRY, Helen; da of Bernard Barry (d 2001), and Patricia Barry (d 1986); *b* 18 August 1961, Liverpool; *Educ* Convent of Mercy GS Liverpool, Victoria Univ of Manchester (LLB), Chester Coll of Law; *Children* 1 da (Rachel b 3 Feb 1997); *Career* admitted slr 1986; articles Maxwell Cooke & Co 1984–86, Aneurin, Rees & Davis 1986–87, Anthony Landes Slrs 1987–88, equity ptnr Yaffe, Jackson Ostrin 1988–96, head of clinical negligence and equity ptnr Edwards, Abrams, Doherty 1996–; memb Specialist Clinical Negligence Panel Law Soc, memb Negligence Panel Action Against Medical Accidents; memb: Encephalitis Soc, Assoc of Personal Injury Lawyers (also sr litigator), Law Soc; *Recreations* theatre, swimming, reading; *Style*— Miss Helen Barry; ✉ EAD Solicitors, 127–131 Picton Road, Wavertree, Liverpool L15 4LG (tel 0151 735 1000, fax 0151 734 4339, e-mail helen.barry@eadsolicitors.co.uk)

BARRY, His Hon James Edward; s of James Douglas Barry (d 1971), of Southgate, Glamorgan, and Margaret Agnes, *née* Thornton; *b* 27 May 1938; *Educ* Merchant Taylors' Crosby, Brasenose Coll Oxford (MA); *m* 11 June 1963, (Ann) Pauline; 3 s (Matthew b 28 Sept 1967, David b 23 Jan 1972, William b 23 Dec 1976); *Career* Nat Serv RASC and Intelligence Corps 1957–59; called to the Bar Inner Temple 1963; practised NE circuit 1963–85, pt/t chm Industrial Tbnls 1983–85, stipendiary magistrate S Yorks 1985–94, recorder of the Crown Court 1985–94, circuit judge (NE Circuit) 1994–2006; *Recreations* reading, home life; *Style*— His Hon James Barry

BARRY, Joan Margaret; da of Stephen James Barry, and Katherine Margaret, *née* Robson; *b* London; *Educ* Univ of York (BA), Central Inst of Hindi New Delhi (Dip Hindi), Univ of Glasgow; *Career* prodn asst BBC: schs radio1981–82, radio news and current affrs 1982–83, current affrs magazine progs 1984, religious broadcasting 1985; British Cncl: prog organiser London 1988–90, asst dir Glasgow 1990–94, European liaison offr Brussels 1994–97, public affrs mangr Scotland 1997–2002, dir Norway 2002–03, dir Albania 2003–; *Style*— Ms Joan Barry

BARRY, Michael; *see:* Bukht, Michael John

BARRY, Sebastian; s of Francis Barry, and Joan O'Hara; *b* 5 July 1955, Dublin; *Educ* Catholic Univ Sch, TCD; *m* Alison; 3 c (Merlin, Coral, Tobias); *Career* playwright and novelist; writer in assoc Abbey Theatre 1989, writer fell TCD 1996, Heimbold visiting chair in Irish studies Villanova Univ PA 2006; *Plays* Boss Grady's Boys (1988, BBC/Stewart Parker Award), The Steward of Christendom (1995, Christopher-Ewart Biggs Memorial Prize, American Ireland Fund Literary Prize, Best New Play London's Critics' Circle, Best Fringe Play Writer's Guild, Playwright of the Year Award), Our Lady of Sligo (1998, Peggy Ramsay Play Award), Hinterland (2002), Whistling Psyche (2004); *Novels* Elsewhere: The Adventures of Belemus (children's book, 1985), The Whereabouts of Eneas McNulty (1998), Annie Dunne (2002), A Long Long Way (2005, Kerry Group Irish Fiction Award, shortlisted Man Booker Prize); *Poetry* The Water Colourist (1983), Fanny Hawke Goes to the Mainland Forever (1989), The Pinkening Boy

(2004); *Recreations* building, fly fishing; *Style*— Sebastian Barry, Esq; ✉ c/o A P Watt Ltd, 20 John Street, London WC1N 2DR

BARRY-WALSH, Paul Frederick; s of Michael Henry Barry-Walsh (d 1993), and Hazel Lillian, *née* Kerr (d 1999); *b* 18 August 1955, London; *Educ* Rossall Sch Fleetwood (scholar), Univ of Liverpool; *m* 18 May 1984, Jane, *née* McIlvenny; 1 da (Olivia b 6 Aug 1985), 1 s (Edward b 11 May 1988); *Career* joined IBM 1977, fndr and ceo SafetyNet 1986–2000, fndr and chm NetStore 1996– (ceo 2001–04); chm Frederick's Fndn 2001–; runner-up IT Entrepreneur of the Year 2002; FRSA 2002; *Recreations* golf, skiing, motor sport, cycling; *Clubs* Queen Wood Golf, Wentworth; *Style*— Paul Barry-Walsh, Esq; ✉ Kingsmoor, Titlarks Hill, Sunningdale, Berkshire SL5 0JB (tel 01344 620915, fax 01344 291567, e-mail pbw@netstore.net); Frederick's House, 39 Guildford Road, Lightwater, Surrey GU18 5SA (tel 01276 472722, fax 01276 472005)

BARSTOW, Dame Josephine Clare; DBE (1995, CBE 1985); da of Harold Barstow, of Sussex, and Clara Edith, *née* Shaw; *b* 27 September 1940; *Educ* Univ of Birmingham (BA), London Opera Centre; *m* 1, 1964 (m dis 1967), Terry Hands, *qv*, *m* 2, 1969, Ande Anderson (d 1996); *Career* soprano; debut with Opera for All 1964, studied at London Opera Centre 1965–66, Opera for All 1966, Glyndebourne Chorus 1967; contract principal: Sadler's Wells 1967–68, WNO 1968–70; freelance 1971–; US debut as Lady Macbeth in Miami 1977; has appeared with ENO, SNO, WNO, Glyndebourne, Opera North; has appeared at numerous international venues incl: Covent Garden, Vienna Staatsoper, Aix-en-Provence Festival, Bayreuth Festival, Salzburg, Munich, Zurich, Toulouse, San Francisco, Met Opera NY, Houston, Chicago, Adelaide, Bolshoi Moscow, Riga and Tbilisi; Hon DMus: Univ of Birmingham, Kingston Univ 1999, Sheffield Hallam Univ 1999, Univ of Hull 2000; *Roles* with WNO incl: Violetta in La Traviata, Fiordiligi in Cosi fan Tutte, Amelia in Simon Boccanegra, Elisabeth de Valois in Don Carlos 1973, Jenufa 1975, Ellen Orford in Peter Grimes 1978 and 1983, Tatyana in Eugene Onegin 1980, title role in Tosca 1985, Amelia in Un Ballo in Maschera 1986; at Covent Garden incl: Alice Ford in Falstaff 1975, title role in Salome 1982, Santuzza in Cavalleria Rusticana 1982, Ellen Orford in Peter Grimes 1988, Attila 1990, Fidelio 1993; with Glyndebourne Festival Opera incl: Lady Macbeth in Macbeth (for TV) 1972, Elektra in Idomeneo 1974, Leonore in Fidelio 1981; with ENO incl: various in The Tales of Hoffman, Emilia Marty in The Makropulos Case, Natasha in War and Peace, Violetta in La Traviata, Octavian and The Marschallin in Der Rosenkavalier 1975 and 1984, title role in Salome 1975, Elisabeth in Don Carlos 1976 and 1986, Tosca 1976 and 1987, Leonora in La Forza del Destino 1978 and 1992, title role in Aida 1979, Leonore in Fidelio 1980, Senta in Der Fliegende Holländer 1982, Mimi in La Boheme 1982, Sieglinde in Die Walküre 1983, Donna Anna in Don Giovanni 1986, Lady Macbeth of Mtsensk 1987 and 1991; appearances in world première performances incl: Denise in Tippett's The Knot Garden 1970, Marguerite in Crosse's The Story of Vasco 1974, Gayle in Tippett's The Ice Break 1977, Benigna in Penderecki's Die Schwarze Maske (Salzburg) 1986; other performances incl: Gudrun in Götterdämmerung (Bayreuth) 1983, title role in Katya Kabanova, Elizabeth I in Britten's Gloriana (Opera North Leeds and Covent Garden) 1994, Kostelnicka in Jenufa (Opera North) 1995, Medea and Marie in Wozzeck (Opera North) 1996, Aida (Opera North) 1997, Mother Marie in Carmelites (ENO) 1999, Kostelnicka (Antwerp) 1999, Alice (Opera North) 2000, Kabanicha (Amsterdam and ROH) 2000, Countess in Queen of Spades (ROH) 2001, Lady Billows (Opera North) 2002; *Films* Owen Wingrave 2001; *Recordings* incl: Un Ballo in Maschera, Kiss me Kate, Albert Herring, Gloriana: A Film, Jenufa, The Knot Garden, Wozzeck; *Recreations* breeding Arabian horses (stud farm in Devon); *Style*— Dame Josephine Barstow, DBE; ✉ c/o Musichall, Vicarage Way, Ringmer, East Sussex BN8 5LA

BARSTOW, Stan; s of Wilfred Barstow (d 1958), and Elsie, *née* Gosnay (d 1990); *b* 28 June 1928; *Educ* Ossett GS; *m* 1951, Constance Mary, da of Arnold Kershaw (d 1935); 1 s (Neil), 1 da (Gillian); *Career* draughtsman engrg indust 1944–62; novelist, short story-writer, script writer for TV; winner Best Br Dramatisation Writers' Guild of GB 1974; hon fell Bretton Coll, Hon MA Open Univ; FRSL; *Books* A Kind of Loving (1960), The Desperadoes (1961), Ask Me Tomorrow (1962), Joby (1964), The Watchers on the Shore (1966), A Raging Calm (1968), A Season with Eros (1971), The Right True End (1976), A Brother's Tale (1980), The Glad Eye (1984), Just You Wait and See (1986), B-Movie (1987), Give Us This Day (1989), Next of Kin (1991), In My Own Good Time (2001); *Plays* Ask Me Tomorrow (with Alfred Bradley, 1966), Listen for the Trains Love (1970), A Kind of Loving (with Alfred Bradley, 1970), Stringer's Last Stand (with Alfred Bradley, 1972), An Enemy of the People (1978); *Television* dramatisations: A Raging Calm (1974), South Riding (1974, RTS Writer's Award 1975), Joby (1975), The Cost of Loving (1977), Travellers (1978), A Kind of Loving (1982), A Brother's Tale (1983), The Man Who Cried (1993), A Small Country (with Diana Griffiths, 2006); scripts Joby (1977), The Human Element (1984), Albert's Part (1984); *Style*— Stan Barstow, Esq; ✉ c/o The Agency, 24 Pottery Lane, London W11 4LZ (tel 020 7727 1346)

BARTLAM, Thomas Hugh; s of Howard Bennett Bartlam (d 1970), and Mary Isobel Bartlam, *née* Lambert (d 2002), of Arkholme, Lancs; *b* 4 December 1947; *Educ* Repton, Selwyn Coll Cambridge (MA); *m* 4 June 1977, Elizabeth Gabriel, da of Andrew David Arthur Balfour, of Shalford, Surrey; 2 s (Edward b 1979, Henry b 1985), 1 da (Harriet b 1981); *Career* merchant banker; dir: Charterhouse Bank 1984–89, Charterhouse Venture Capital Fund, Charterhouse Buy-Out Fund, Charterhouse Business Expansion Fund; md Intermediate Capital Group plc 1989–2005 (non-exec dir 2005–); non-exec chm Pantheon International Participations plc; non-exec dir: Numis Corporation plc, F&C UK Select Tst plc; tstee Leonard Cheshire Fndn; FCA; *Recreations* opera, gardening, farming; *Clubs* Boodle's, MCC, City of London; *Style*— Thomas H Bartlam, Esq; ✉ Intermediate Capital Group plc, 20 Old Broad Street, London EC2N 1DP (tel 020 7628 9898)

BARTLE, Ronald David; s of Rev George Clement Bartle (d 1993), of Surrey, and Winifred Marie Bartle; *b* 14 April 1929; *Educ* St John's Sch Leatherhead, Jesus Coll Cambridge (MA); *m* 1981, Hisako (d 2004), da of Shigeo Yagi (d 1983), of Japan; 1 da (Elizabeth b 1965), 1 s (Nicholas b 1967) (both by former m); *Career* Nat Service 1947–49, RAEC 1948, army athletic colours 1954; called to the Bar Lincoln's Inn, practised in leading criminal chambers 1956–72; dep circuit judge 1974–78; Parly candidate 1958 and 1959; met stipendiary magistrate 1972–1999, dep chief magistrate 1992; chm Inner London Juvenile Courts 1973–79; memb: Home Office Advsy Cncl on Drug Abuse 1987–, Home Office Ctee on Magistrates' Courts Procedure 1989–; patron The Pathway-to-Recovery Tst; govr: RNLI, Corp of the Sons of the Clergy; memb: City of London Deanery Synod, Friends of City of London Churches; church warden; Freeman City of London 1976, elected Steward of Worshipful Co of Basket Makers 1987 (memb Court of Assts 1997, Under Warden 2002, Prime Warden 2005); *Books* Introduction to Shipping Law (1958), The Police Officer in Court (1984), Crime and the New Magistrate (1985), The Law and the Lawless (1987), Bow Street Beak (1999, placed in Royal Library by direction of HM The Queen), The Police Witness (2002); *Recreations* reading, walking, travel, relaxing at home; *Clubs* Garrick, City Livery, City Pickwick; *Style*— Ronald D Bartle, Esq

BARTLETT, Adrian; s of Alan Baskerville Bartlett (d 1981), and Marjorie Jesse, *née* Launder; *b* 31 March 1939; *Educ* Bedales, Camberwell Sch of Art, Univ of Durham; *m* 17 July 1962, Victoria Anne Bartlett, *qv*, *née* Howitt; 2 da (Zoë b 27 March 1965, Eve b 9 Feb 1967); *Career* artist; head of printmaking Morley Coll 1963–99; visiting lectr Univ of Oxford; UK rep Florence Biennale 1976; finalist Hunting/Observer Prize 1992; pres London Gp 1993 (memb 1979); *Solo Exhibitions* incl: British Cncl Athens 1985, Oxford Gallery 1987, Blenheim Gallery 1988, Tsikalioti Museum Greece 1989, Morley Gallery 1996, Walk

Gallery 1999, Piers Feetham Gallery 2007; *Group Exhibitions* numerous RA Summer Exhbns, 6th Int Art Fair London 1991; *Public Collections* Ashmolean Museum Oxford, British Museum, British Cncl, Berlin Graphothek, Dept for Educn, Herbert Art Gallery Coventry, McNay Inst Texas, Oldham City Art Gallery, St Thomas' Hosp, Surrey Educn Authy; *Books* Drawing and Painting the Landscape (1982), British Art in the Eighties (1983); *Clubs* Chelsea Arts; *Style*— Adrian Bartlett, Esq; ✉ 132 Kennington Park Road, London SE11 4DJ (tel 020 7735 0272, fax 020 7735 2989)

BARTLETT, Andrew Vincent Bramwell; QC (1993); *Educ* Whitgift Sch, Jesus Coll Oxford (BA); *Career* called to the Bar Middle Temple 1974 (bencher); recorder; pt/t chm: Financial Services and Markets Tbnl, Pensions Regulator Tbnl; pt/t dep chm Information Tbnl, dep head Crown Office Chambers; chartered arbitrator; vice-chm Technol and Construction Bar Assoc (TECBAR); FCIArb; *Style*— Andrew Bartlett, Esq, QC; ✉ Crown Office Chambers, 2 Crown Office Row, Temple, London EC4Y 7HJ (tel 020 7797 8100, fax 020 7797 8101)

BARTLETT, Anthony David (Tony); s of Clifford Sydney McDonald Bartlett, of Church Stretton, Salop, and late Sylvia Patricia, *née* Samson; *b* 21 February 1951; *Educ* Stamford Sch; *m* 1; 1 da (Melissa b 1982), 1 s (Joshua b 1984); m 2, 19 Aug 1993, Alison McNeill Kerr, da of late William Kerr; *Career* CA; Neville Russell & Co (now Mazars Neville Russell) 1971–74, ptnr Coopers & Lybrand 1984–95 (joined 1975), md Beeson Gregory 2002 (dir and head of corp fin 1995–2002); Arden Partners plc: chm of corp fin 2003–06, CEO 2006–; *Recreations* golf, fishing, sailing, theatre; *Clubs* Royal Mid Surrey Golf, RAC, Royal Dornoch Golf, Royal Cape Team; *Style*— Tony Bartlett, Esq; ✉ Skelbo House, Dornoch IV25 3QE (tel 07802 302401, e-mail bartletts@btinternet.com)

BARTLETT, Christopher John (Chris); s of Donald Leonard Bartlett, and Kathleen Doris, *née* Potts; *Educ* Mount Grace Secdy Sch Potters Bar, Middlesex Univ (BA); *Career* served Royal Hong Kong Police Force 1976–79 and 1983–85, joined HM Prison Serv 1985; various posts: Bullwood Hall, Canterbury, Blundeston, Prison Serv HQ, Swaleside; govr-in-charge HMP Blantyre House 2000–05, govr HMP Elmley 2006–; *Recreations* cookery, computers, music; *Style*— Chris Bartlett, Esq; ✉ HMP Elmley, Church Road, Eastchurch, Sheerness, Kent ME12 4DZ

BARTLETT, George Robert; QC (1986); s of Cdr Howard Volins Bartlett, RN (d 1988), of Putney, London, and Angela Margaret, *née* Webster (d 2004); *b* 22 October 1944; *Educ* Tonbridge, Trinity Coll Oxford (MA); *m* 6 May 1972, Dr Clare Virginia, da of Gordon Chalmers Fortin (d 1995), of Castle Hedingham, Essex; 3 s (William b 1973, Frederick b 1979, Charles b 1982); *Career* called to the Bar Middle Temple 1966 (bencher 1995); recorder of the Crown Court 1990–2000, dep judge of the High Court 1994–; asst parly boundary cmmr 1992–98, pres Lands Tbnl 1998–; *Books* Ryde on Rating (ed); *Style*— George R Bartlett, Esq, QC

BARTLETT, James Michael Gilbert; s of Maj Michael George Bartlett, TD (d 2002), and Elizabeth Marjorie, *née* Grieve (d 1997); *b* 21 March 1947; *Educ* Bromsgrove Sch; *m* 20 Sept 1975, (Patricia) Anne, da of Ronald Dean Cranfield (d 1976); 1 da (Catherine Anne b 1978), 1 s ((James) Michael Ronald b 1981); *Career* princ Bartlett & Co Chartered Accountants 1983–89, sr ptnr Bartlett Hall Chartered Accountants 1989–96, managing ptnr Bartlett Kershaw Trott Chartered Accountants 1996–; dir: BKT Consltg Ltd, Tax Mangr Ltd; formerly: chm Winchcombe Deanery Synod, memb Glos Diocesan Synod, dir Glos Diocesan Bd of Fin; treas Glos Branch Cncl for Preservation of Rural England 1987–93, vice-chm UK Nat Cadet Class Assoc 1996–97 (treas 1992–96); Freeman City of London 1979, Liveryman Worshipful Co of Builders Merchants; FCA 1971, FIMgt 1988; *Recreations* sailing; *Clubs* Royal Ocean Racing, Royal Northumberland Yacht, South Cerney Sailing (Cdre 1991–94), Mylor Yacht; *Style*— James Bartlett, Esq; ✉ Cleeve House, West Approach Drive, Cheltenham, Gloucestershire GL52 3AD (tel 01242 575000); Bartlett Kershaw Trott, 4 Pullman Court, Great Western Road, Gloucester GL1 3ND (tel 01452 527000, fax 01452 304585)

BARTLETT, Jeanne Elizabeth; da of Peter Anthony Bartlett, of Northam, E Sussex, and Joan, *née* Proctor; *b* 5 January 1962; *Educ* Alleyne's GS Uttoxeter, UCW Aberystwyth (LLB); *Career* admitted slr 1987 (admitted slr Hong Kong 1991); articled clerk then asst slr Slaughter and May 1984–89, sr asst slr Linklaters & Paines 1990–93, vice-pres in securitisation Bankers Tst 1993–95, gen counsel (capital markets) Bank of America 1996–99, co-managing ptnr Orrick, Herrington & Sutcliffe 2000–01, head of capital markets and securitisation DLA 2001–07; regular contrib of articles on capital markets and securitisation to fin jls incl International Securitisation Report and Euromoney; *Recreations* art, literature, tennis, travel; *Style*— Ms Jeanne Bartlett; ✉ tel and fax 020 7349 9339, e-mail jeanne.bartlett@btinternet.com

BARTLETT, Neil; OBE (2000); *b* 23 August 1958; *Educ* Magdalen Coll Oxford; *Partner* James Gardiner; *Career* performer, director, translator and writer; artistic dir Lyric Theatre Hammersmith 1994–2004; prodns incl: The Picture of Dorian Gray 1994, Splendid's 1995, The Letter 1995, Romeo and Juliet 1995, Mrs Warren's Profession 1996, Sarrasine 1996, A Christmas Carol 1996, Then Again 1997, Cause Célèbre 1998, Seven Sonnets of Michaelangelo 1998, Cinderella 1998, The Dispute 1999, The Servant 2001, The Prince of Homburg 2002, The Island of Slaves 2002, A Christmas Carol 2002, Pericles 2003, Oliver Twist 2004 and 2007, Don Juan 2004, Dido, Queen of Carthage 2005, The Rake's Progress 2006, The Maids 2007, The Pianist 2007, Twelfth Night 2007; fndr memb Gloria; *Stage Plays* incl: A Vision of Love Revealed in Sleep (1989), Sarrasine (1990), A Judgement in Stone (1992), Night After Night (1993), The Picture of Dorian Gray (1994), Lady into Fox (1996), The Seven Sacraments of Nicolas Poussin (1997), In Extremis (2000), A Christmas Carol (2002), Oliver Twist (2004), Solo Voices (2005), Great Expectations (2007); *Translations* The Misanthrope (Molière), The School for Wives (Molière), Bérénice (Racine), The Game of Love and Chance (Marivaux), The Dispute (Marivaux), Splendid's (Genet), The Threesome (Labiche), The Prince of Homburg (Kleist), The Island of Slaves (Marivaux), Camille (Dumas), La Casa Azul (Faucher), Don Juan (Molière), The Maids (Genet); *Films and Television* That's What Friends Are For (1988), Where is Love? (1988), That's How Strong My Love Is (1989), Pedagogue (with Stuart Marshall, 1988), Now That It's Morning (1992); *Biography* Who Was that Man - A Present for Mr Oscar Wilde (1988); *Novels* Ready To Catch Him Should He Fall (1990), Mr Clive & Mr Page (1996), Skin Lane (2007); *Style*— Neil Bartlett, Esq, OBE; ✉ c/o The Agency, 24 Pottery Lane, London W11 4LZ (tel 020 7727 1346, fax 020 7727 9037, e-mail lschmidt@theagency.co.uk, website www.neil-bartlett.com)

BARTLETT, Victoria Anne; da of Edgar Howitt; *b* 25 March 1940; *Educ* Camberwell Sch of Art, Univ of Reading; *m* 17 July 1962, Adrian Bartlett, *qv*; 2 da (Zoë b 27 March 1965, Eve b 9 Feb 1967); *Career* artist; visiting lectr: Morley Coll London 1975–99, Ruskin Sch of Drawing and Fine Art Univ of Oxford 1980–94, Goldsmiths Coll London 1982–2002; work in various public and private collections in UK and abroad; *Solo Exhibitions* The Egg & The Eye Gallery LA 1974, Van Doren Gallery San Francisco 1975, Morley Gallery London 1976, Edward Totah Gallery London 1981, Camden Arts Centre 1981, Galerie Simoncini Luxembourg 1985, Benjamin Rhodes Gallery London 1987 and 1991, Peralta Pictures 1994, Piers Feetham Gallery 2007; *Group Exhibitions* incl: RA Summer Exhbn 1973, 1979, 1989 and 1993, Flowers Gallery London 1977, The London Group Open and membs exhbns 1978–2007, Galerie Etienne de Causans Paris 1980, Central Museum of Textiles Lódz 1986, Ikon Gallery Birmingham touring exhbn 1987 and 1988, Browse and Darby London 1994–2005, Chicago International Art Fair 1995; *Style*— Ms Victoria Bartlett; ✉ 132 Kennington Park Road, London SE11 4DJ

BARTLETT, Warwick Winston; s of Leslie Winston Bartlett (d 1994), and Elizabeth Mary, *née* Kensett; *b* 13 March 1947, Paignton, Devon; *Educ* Tividale Comp Sch; *Partner* Jennifer Haynes; 1 s (Richard Leslie), 1 da (Sarah Jane); *Career* dir Bartletts Investments Ltd 1966–84, chm Cashline Ltd 1984–, chm Racing Data plc 1993–98, lead ptnr Global Betting & Gaming Conslts 1999–, dir Satellite Information Services Ltd 2005; chm: British Betting Office Assoc 1992–2002, Assoc of Br Bookmakers 2002–; memb Horserace Betting Levy Bd 2002–07 (chm Bookmakers Ctee 2002–07); memb Cons Pty; *Publications* The Global Gambling Report, The Smoking Ban: Casinos and Bingo; *Recreations* swimming, reading, music; *Style*— Warwick Bartlett, Esq; ✉ Global Betting & Gaming Consultants Limited, 23B St Michaels Street, West Bromwich, West Midlands, B70 8TH

BARTLEY, Luella Dayrell; da of Michael Francis Dayrell Bartley, of Salcombe, Devon, and Pamela Higgins, of Shipston on Stour, Warks; *b* 4 May 1973, Stratford-upon-Avon; *Educ* Trinity Sch Leamington Spa, St Martins Sch of Art (BA); *Partner* David Sims; 1 s (Kip Dustin b 25 June 2003), 1 da (Stevie Willow Frances b 9 April 2005); *Career* fashion designer; journalist: Evening Standard newspaper 1993–96, Evening Standard magazine 1996–97, Vogue UK 1997–99; prop Luella Bartley Ltd 1999–; Luella (own label): debut London Fashion Week 2000, regular exhibitor at seasonal shows worldwide, numerous stockists worldwide incl Harvey Nichols and Saks Fifth Avenue; created collection for New Look 2002; Elle Designer of the Year 2001; *Style*— Miss Luella Bartley; ✉ Luella Bartley Limited, Rochelle School, Arnold Circus, London E2 7ES (tel 020 7739 7566, fax 020 7739 9172)

BARTOLO, David Charles Craig; s of Albert Edward Bartolo (d 1993), of Malta, and (Evelyne Valerie) Jean, *née* Callie; *b* 21 July 1949; *Educ* Queen Elizabeth GS Carmarthen, St Mary's Hosp Med Sch Univ of London (MB BS, MS); *Children* 2 da (Victoria b 1979, Rebecca b 1980), 1 s (James b 1985); *Career* sr registrar SW RHA 1982–86, sr registrar St Mark's Hosp London 1985, hon conslt surgn Bristol Royal Infirmary 1987–90, conslt sr lectr Univ of Bristol 1987–90, conslt surgn Royal Infirmary of Edinburgh Lothian Health Bd 1990–; Hunterian prof RCS 1984–85, Moynihan travelling fell Assoc of Surgns of GB and Ireland 1987, jt winner Patey Prize SRS 1988, jt winner New England surgical prize American Soc of Colon and Rectal Surgns 1988; past memb Cncl Assoc of Coloproctology UK and Ireland, past memb Cncl Surgical Res Soc, memb Br Soc of Gastroenterology; hon life fell South African Assoc of Gastroenterology 1997, hon memb Section of Colon and rectal Surgery Royal Australasian Coll of Surgeons 2001, hon memb Chilean Assoc of Coloproctology 2001; FRCS 1976; *Style*— David Bartolo, Esq; ✉ 7 Campbell Road, Edinburgh EH12 6DT (e-mail dccb2107@aol.com); Western General Hospital, Edinburgh EH4 2XU (tel 0131 537 2344)

BARTON, Prof (Barbara) Anne; da of Oscar Charles Roesen (d 1955), of New York, and Blanche Godfrey Williams (d 1968); *b* 9 May 1933; *Educ* Bryn Mawr Coll (BA), Univ of Cambridge (PhD); *m* 1, 1957 (m dis 1968), William Harvey Righter; m 2, 1969, John Bernard Adie Barton, s of late Sir Harold Montagu Barton, of London; *Career* Girton Coll Cambridge: Rosalind Lady Carlisle res fell 1960–62, official fell in English 1962–72, dir of studies in English 1963–72; Hildred Carlile prof of English and head of dept Bedford Coll London 1972–74, fell and tutor in English New Coll Oxford 1974–84, Grace II prof of English Univ of Cambridge 1984–2000, fell Trinity Coll Cambridge 1986–; memb Editorial Bd: Shakespeare Survey 1972–98, Studies in English Literature 1976–, Shakespeare Quarterly 1981–2004, Romanticism 1995–; hon fell: Shakespeare Inst Univ of Birmingham 1982, New Coll Oxford 1989, Academia Europaea 1995; FBA 1991; *Books* Shakespeare and the Idea of the Play (1962), Introductions to the Comedies, The Riverside Shakespeare (1974), Ben Jonson, Dramatist (1984), The Names of Comedy (1990), Byron: Don Juan (1992), Essays, Mainly Shakespearean (1994); *Recreations* travel, opera, fine arts; *Style*— Prof Anne Barton, FBA; ✉ Trinity College, Cambridge CB2 1TQ (tel 01223 338466, e-mail ab10004@hermes.cam.ac.uk)

BARTON, Glenys; da of Alexander James Barton, and Gertrude Elizabeth, *née* Farmer; *b* 24 January 1944, Stoke-on-Trent; *Educ* RCA (MA); *m* Martin Hunt; 1 s (Felix b 1982); *Career* artist; pt/t lectr: Portsmouth Poly 1971–74, Camberwell Sch of Arts and Crafts 1971–87; studio and sculptures features in film Enduring Love 2003; *Solo Exhibitions* Museum of Decorative Art Copenhagen 1973, Sculpture and Drawings (Angela Flowers Gallery) 1974, Galerie Het Kapelhuis 1976, Germeenttelijk Museum Het Princessehof 1976), Sculpture and Reliefs (Angela Flowers Gallery) 1981 and 1983, Glenys Barton at Wedgwood (Crafts Cncl Gallery) 1977, Heads: Sculpture and Drawings (Angela Flowers Gallery) 1986, Artists and Green Warriors (Flowers East) 1990, Northern Centre for Contemporary Art 1991, New Sculpture (Flowers East) 1993, Portraits (Angela Flowers Gallery) 1994, New Sculpture (Flowers East at London Fields) 1996, Glenys Barton Portraits (Nat Portrait Gallery) 1997, Dreaming Edge (Manchester City Art Gallery and Stoke-on-Trent) 1997 and 1998, In Profile (Flowers West Gallery Santa Monica CA) 2000, Children of Silence and Slow Time (Flowers Central) 2003, Enduring Love (Flowers East London) 2004, Flowers NY 2007; *Group Exhibitions* Images of Man (ICA) 1980, Sculptures in Clay (Yorkshire Sculpture Park) 1980, Nudes (Angela Flowers Gallery) 1980–81, Art into the Eighties (Walker Art Gallery and The Fruitmarket) 1981, A Taste of British Art Today (Contemporary Art Soc Brussels) 1982, South Bank Show (Arts Cncl) 1982, Small Is Beautiful - Part 3 (Angela Flowers Gallery) 1983, Black and White (Angela Flowers Gallery) 1985, Small Is Beautiful - Part 4 (Angela Flowers Gallery) 1985, Sixteen Years Sixteen Artists (Angela Flowers Gallery) 1986, Multiplemedia (Nicholson Gallery) 1986, Sixteen Artists - Process and Product (Turnpike Gallery) 1987, Contemporary Portraits (Flowers East) 1988 and 1990, Figure 11 Naked (Aberystwyth Arts Centre and tour) 1988, The Face (Arkansas Arts Center) 1988, Out of Clay (Manchester City Art Gallery) 1988, Small Is Beautiful - Part 6 (Flowers East) 1988, Angela Flowers Gallery 1990 (Barbican Centre) 1989, Badge Art 11 (Flowers East) 1989, Colours of the Earth (Arts Cncl tour) 1990, Small Is Beautiful - Part 8 The Figure (Flowers East) 1990, Angela Flowers Gallery 1991 (Flowers East) 1991, Nudes (Watermans Arts Centre) 1991, Artist's Choice (Flowers East) 1992, Small Is Beautiful - Part 10 Animals (Flowers East) 1992, Portrait of the Artist's Mother Done From Memory (Flowers East) 1992, Decouvertes (Grand Palais Paris) 1993, The Portrait Now (National Portrait Gallery) 1993, The Contemporary Print Show (Barbican) 1995, Contemporary Sculpture (Collyer Bristow) 1995, The Twenty Fifth Anniversary Exhibition (Flowers East) 1995, Flowers at Koplin (Koplin Gallery LA) 1995, Methods and Materials of Sculpture (Nat Portrait Gallery) 1995, Angela Flowers Gallery (Ireland) 1996, Hot off the Press (Carlisle and tour) 1996, Gwenda Jay Gallery (Chicago) 1997, British Figurative Art Part Two Sculpture Flowers East, Angela Flowers Gallery 30th Anniversary Exhibition (Flowers East London and Flowers West Santa Monica CA) 2000, Flowers One (Flowers Central) 2000, Small is Beautiful - Self Portraits (Nat Portrait Gallery) 2000, Royal Acad Summer Exhbn 2000, 2001 and 2002, Mirror Mirror (Nat Portrait Gallery) 2001, Glenys Barton and Carole Hodgson - Multiples and Monoprints (Flowers Graphics) 2001, Small is Beautiful - Still Life (Flowers East) 2001, Mirror Mirror (Nat Portrait Gallery) 2001, Aboutface (Croydon Clocktower) 2002, Small is Beautiful - Voyage (Flowers East) 2002, Stirling Stuff (Gallery Pangolin Chalford) 2002 (also at Royal Acad and Sigurjon Olafsson Sculpture Museum Reykjavik 2003), Thinking Big (Guggenheim Venice) 2002, Relative Values (PM Gallery and House London) 2003, Small is Beautiful XXII (Flowers Central) 2004, Sculptures and Drawings (Flowers East) 2005, 35th Anniversary Exhbn (Flowers East London) 2005, Five Figurative Sculptors (Flowers Central, Francis Burrows Fine Art, Arts Creative Chesterfield) 2005, Discerning Eye (Mall Galleries London) 2005 and 2006, Small is

Beautiful (Flowers Central) 2005, Sculpture in Paradise (Chichester Cathedral) 2006–07, New Works by Gallery Sculptors (Flowers Central) 2006, Heads (Flowers East and Catmose Gallery Rutland) 2006; *Work in Public Collections* incl: Birmingham Museum and Art Gallery, Contemporary Art Soc, Crafts Cncl, Leeds Museum and Art Gallery, National Gallery of Victoria, Princessehoff Museum, Royal Scottish Museum, Manchester Museum and Art Gallery, Stockholm Museum, Pennsylvania State Univ MOMA, V&A, National Portrait Gallery, Scottish National Portrait Gallery; *Projects* Landmark East (East of Eng Devpt Agency competition) 2004, Somewhere We Meet (wall sculpture) for Hextable Dance 2006 (shortlisted Rowse Kent Public Art Awards); *Style—* Ms Glenys Barton; ✉ c/o Flowers East, 82 Kingsland Road, London E2 8DP

BARTON, Rev Prof John; s of Bernard Arthur Barton, and Gwendolyn Harriet Barton; *b* 17 June 1948; *Educ* Latymer Upper Sch, Keble Coll Oxford (MA, DPhil, DLitt); *m* 16 July 1973, Mary, da of Alfred Burn; 1 da (Katherine Rachel b 26 June 1975); *Career* ordained priest C of E 1973; Univ of Oxford: jr res fell Merton Coll 1973–74, jr chaplain Merton Coll 1973–76, univ lectr in theology 1974–89, reader in Biblical studies 1989–91, Oriel & Laing prof of the interpretation of Holy Scripture 1991–, fell St Cross Coll 1974–91 (emeritus fell 1991–), fell Oriel Coll 1991–; canon theologian Winchester Cathedral 1991–2003; Bampton lectr Oxford 1988, Hulsean lectr Cambridge 1990; Hon Dr Theol Univ of Bonn 1998; *Books* Amos's Oracles Against the Nations (1980), Reading the Old Testament - Method in Biblical Study (1984), Oracles of God - Perceptions of Ancient Prophecy in Israel after the Exile (1986), People of the Book? The Authority of the Bible in Christianity (Bampton lectures, 1988), Love Unknown - Meditations on the Death and Resurrection of Jesus (1990), What is the Bible? (1991), Isaiah 1–39 (1995), The Spirit and the Letter: Studies in the Biblical Canon (1997), Making the Christian Bible (1997), Ethics and the Old Testament (1998), The Cambridge Companion to Biblical Interpretation (1998), The Oxford Bible Commentary (jt ed, 2001), The Biblical World (2002), Understanding Old Testament Ethics (2003), The Original Story: God, Israel and the World (2004), Living Belief: Being Christian, Being Human (2005), The Nature of Biblical Criticism (2007), The Old Testament: Canon, Literature, Theology (2007); *Style—* The Rev Prof John Barton; ✉ Oriel College, Oxford OX1 4EW (tel 01865 276537)

BARTON, Jonathan Edmund (Jon); s of Edmund Barton (d 1985), and Marjorie, *née* Pitt-Watson; *b* 7 September 1950; *Educ* King James's GS Huddersfield, The Lakes Comp Sch Windermere, Emmanuel Coll Cambridge (MA), Dept of Educn Univ of Oxford (CertEd); *m* 1972, Margaret, *née* Course; 2 da (Sarah b 1975, Hannah b 1985), 1 s (Joseph b 1977); *Career* schoolteacher 1971–78, head of languages International School Moshi Tanzania 1978–80; freelance local radio reporter 1980–81, prodr Radio Derby 1981–84 (progs incl Barbed Wireless); BBC TV: prodr of current affrs (progs incl Sixty Minutes, The Money Programme, Breakfast Time) 1985, sometime asst ed Six O'Clock News, asst ed then dep ed and acting ed Newsnight 1988–94, ed One O'Clock News and Six O'Clock News 1994–96; ed Today Radio 4 BBC Radio 1996–98, exec ed of current affrs BBC TV 1998–2000; Reuters fell Green Coll Oxford 2000, conslt Trinity Communications Brunswick Gp 2000–01, head of media Christian Aid 2001–02, dir of communications Nat Tst 2002–, fndr Clarify Communications 2004; *Recreations* music, literature, mountains, politics, cross-country running, making things work, cycling, canoeing; *Style—* Jon Barton, Esq; ✉ 38B Brook Street, Watlington, Oxfordshire OX9 5JH (tel 01491 612519, e-mail jon.barton@clarifycommunications.co.uk)

BARTON, (Malcolm) Peter Speight; DL (Gtr London); s of Michael Hugh Barton (d 1996), and Diana Blanche, *née* Taylor; *b* 26 March 1937; *Educ* St Edward's Sch Oxford, Magdalen Coll Oxford (MA); *m* 7 Sept 1963, Julia Margaret, da of Hon James Louis Lindsay (d 1997); 1 da (Fenella (Mrs Nicholas Clements) b 1965), 2 s (Henry (Harry) b 1967, Christopher b 1970); *Career* Nat Serv 2 Lt Oxford and Bucks LI (later 1 Greenjackets) 1955–56, Capt London Rifle Bde Rangers TA 1960–63; admitted slr 1964; ptnr Travers Smith Braithwaite 1967–86; md corp fin Lehman Bros 1986–95; dir: Robert Fleming & Co Ltd 1995–99, Lambert Fenchurch Group plc 1998–99, Alliance & Leicester plc 1998–2007 (dep chm 2000–07), F&C US Smaller Companies plc 1998–, The Guinness Tst Gp 1999– (chm 2007–), Bramdean Alternatives Ltd 2007–; chm Howard de Walden Estates Ltd 1998–; chm of tstees Alliance & Leicester Pension Fund 2007–; advsr Armstrong Bonham Carter LLP; tstee dir Br Inst of Int and Comparative Law, tstee Leonard Ingrams Fndn; memb: Audit and Scrutiny Ctee Univ of Oxford, Gloucester Diocesan Finance Ctee, Law Soc, Int Bar Assoc, The Pilgrims (hon sec); MSI (memb Stock Exchange 1986); High Sheriff Gtr London 2000–01; *Recreations* walking, shooting, skiing; *Clubs* Brooks's, City of London, City Law, Rifle Brigade; *Style—* Peter Barton, Esq, DL; ✉ Sydenhams, Bisley, Gloucestershire GL6 7BU (tel 01452 770837, fax 01452 770584)

BARTON, Stephen James; s of Thomas James Barton (d 1996), of Birkenhead, Merseyside, and Vera Margaret, *née* Francis (d 1983); *b* 4 May 1947; *Educ* Birkenhead Sch, Jesus Coll Cambridge (MA), Coll of Law; *m* 20 April 1974, Catherine Monica Lloyd (d 1998), da of Arthur Frederick Buttery (d 1986); 2 da (Tamsin b 1975, Claire b 1977); m 2, 5 Feb 2005, Maureen Frances Langham *née* Welsh; *Career* admitted slr 1971; Herbert Smith Slrs: articled 1969, asst slr 1971–78, ptnr 1978–97, conslt 1997–2002; Jesus Coll Cambridge: fell commoner in law 1996–99, fell 1999–2007 (emeritus fell 2007–), sr bursar 1999–2007; sec Cambridge Univ Bursars' Ctee 2005–06; govr Netherhall Sch and Sixth Form Centre 2000–02, tstee Arthur Rank Hospice Charity 2003–07 (treas 2005–07); *Books* Butterworths Co Law Serv (contributing ed, 1985–2005), Buckley on the Companies Acts (contrib, 2000–05), Butterworths Company Law Guide (contrib, 2002); *Recreations* photography, gardening, walking, reading; *Style—* Stephen Barton, Esq; ✉ 16 Latham Road, Cambridge CB2 2EQ

BARTON-BRECK, Julie; da of Verdun Breck, of Scotland, and Jilly, *née* Harding (d 2000); *b* 15 December 1965, London; *Educ* Newstead Wood GS for Girls, Orpington Coll of FE; *m* 30 Aug 2000, Andrew Barton; *Career* practicals asst Woman 1993–95, assoc ed Prima 1995–99; ed: Safeway Magazine 1999–2002 (Magazine of the Year Award Assoc of Publishing Agencies 2001), Family Circle 2002–04, Essentials 2004–; memb BSME 1999–; *Recreations* cooking, interior design, travel; *Style—* Julie Barton-Breck; ✉ IPC Southbank, Blue Fin Building, 110 Southwark Street, London SE1 0SU (tel 020 3418 7210, e-mail julie_barton-breck@ipcmedia.com)

BARTTELOT, Col Sir Brian Walter de Stopham; 5 Bt (UK 1875), of Stopham, Sussex, OBE (1983), DL (W Sussex 1988); s of Brig Sir Walter de Stopham Barttelot, 4 Bt, DSO (ka 1944), and Sara Patricia (d 1998), da of late Lt-Col Herbert Valentine Ravenscroft, JP, of The Abbey, Storrington, W Sussex; *b* 17 July 1941; *Educ* Eton, Sandhurst, Staff Coll Camberley; *m* 1969, Hon Fiona Barttelot, MBE, DL, DStJ, *née* Weld-Forester; 4 da (Isabel Emily (Mrs Luke Sanders) b 1971, Sophie Rosalind (Mrs Nigel Weller) b 1973, Ursulina May b 1978, Emma Amelia b 1981); *Heir* bro, Robin Barttelot; *Career* cmmnd Coldstream Gds 1961, temp equerry to HM The Queen 1970–71, Camberley Staff Coll 1974, GSO2 Army Staff Duties Directorate MOD 1975–76, 2 i/c 2 Bn Coldstream Gds 1977–78, Mil Sec to Maj-Gen cmdg London Dist and Household Div 1978–81, GSO1 MOD 1981–82, CO 1 Bn Coldstream Gds 1982–85, GSO1 HQ BAOR 1985–86, Regimental Lt-Col cmdg Coldstream Gds 1987–92, Col Foot Gds 1989–92, ret; High Sheriff W Sussex 1997, HM Vice Lord-Lt W Sussex 1994–; dir Parham Park Ltd 1993–; Hon Col Sussex Army Cadet Force 1996–2007; pres: W Sussex Scouts 1993–, S of England Agric Soc 2000–02; memb HM Body Guard of the Hon Corps of Gentlemen at Arms 1993–; chm Exec Ctee Standing Cncl of the Baronetage 1996–2001; Liveryman Worshipful Co of Gunmakers 1980; *Clubs* Cavalry and Guards', Pratt's, Farmers'; *Style—* Col Sir Brian Barttelot, Bt, OBE, DL; ✉ Stopham Park, Pulborough, West Sussex RH20 1DY (office tel 01798 865861, fax 01798 865018)

BARWICK, Brian; *Educ* Univ of Liverpool; *m* 2 c; *Career* BBC: joined sports dept as asst prodr 1979, prodr and ed numerous programmes incl Match of the Day, Football Focus and Sportsnight, overseer major sporting events incl football 1990 and 1994 World Cups, Barcelona, Atlanta and Albertville Olympic Games, Commenwealth Games, Euro and World Athletics Championships, responsible for Sports Review of the Year, head of production 1995, head of TV sport until 1998; controller of sport ITV 1998–2005, dir of progs ITV2 1998–2001, chief exec The FA 2005–; *Style—* Brian Barwick, Esq

BARYLSKI, Patricia Ann; da of Theodore Barylski, and Teresa Sporcic Barylski; *Educ* Univ of Illinois (Phi Beta Kappa academic honours, BA), SOAS Univ of London (MA); *m* Geoffrey Newman, OBE; *Career* Business International Geneva 1977–81, Time-Life Books 1981–82; freelance publishing and teaching 1982–87: British Museum, Cncl of Europe, SOAS External Services, SOAS Intermediate Certificate Course; dep ed The Dictionary of Art 1987–94, series ed Art & Ideas Phaidon Press 1994–2002, managing ed teaching and learning materials City & Guilds 2002–; awarded: Fulbright grant to India 1965–66, SOAS External Studies Fellowship 1981–82; memb: Friends of British Library, Friends of British Museum, Royal Asiatic Soc, Soc for S Asian Studies; *Books* The Hindu World (1982), India, Pakistan and Bangladesh: A Handbook for Teachers (1982), Hinduism (1984); *Style—* Ms Patricia Barylski; ✉ City & Guilds, 1 Giltspur Street, London EC1A 9DD (tel 020 7294 8191, e-mail pat.barylski@cityandguilds.com)

BASING, Nicholas Andrew (Nick); s of Dennis Basing, of Bognor Regis, and Jane Elizabeth Basing; *b* 14 January 1962, Rustington; *Educ* Bedford Coll (BA), Univ of Middlesex (MBA), London Business Sch, Harvard Business Sch (AMP); *m* 4 April 1998, Samantha Jane, *née* Slumbers; 1 s (Max George), 1 da (Ella Grace); *Career* with Goodwood Gp 1992–93, with First Leisure 1993–95, with Rank plc 1995–99, with Unilever 2000–02, ceo Paramount Gp 2002–; memb Ctee London Club Harvard Business Sch, memb Young Presidents Organisation; *Recreations* tennis, ballet, autobiographies; *Clubs* All England Lawn Tennis and Croquet, Queen's; *Style—* Nick Basing, Esq; ✉ Paramount Restaurants, 8–10 Grosvenor Gardens, London SW1W 0DH (tel 020 7881 8777, fax 020 7881 8895, mobile 07720 557520, e-mail nick.basing@paramountrestaurants.co.uk)

BASINGSTOKE, Bishop of 2002–; Rt Rev Trevor Willmott; *b* 29 March 1950; *Educ* Plymouth Coll for Boys, St Peter's Coll Oxford (MA), Univ of Thessaloniki (Philip Usher scholar), Fitzwilliam Coll Cambridge (DipTh), Westcott House Cambridge, Dept of Continuing Educn Virginia Theological Seminary; *m* 1973, Margaret; 1 da (Elizabeth); *Career* ordained: deacon 1974, priest 1975; asst curate St George's Norton 1974–77 (actg ecumenical offr Dio of St Albans 1976–77), asst chaplain of Oslo with Trondheim 1978–79, chaplain of Naples with Capri, Bari and Sorrento and officiating chaplain to HM and American Armed Forces serving in Southern Europe 1979–83, rector of Ecton and warden Peterborough Diocesan Retreat House 1983–89, diocesan dir of ordinands and of post-ordination trg 1986–97, sec Diocesan Bd for the Devpt of Miny 1989–97, canon residentiary and precentor Peterborough Cathedral 1989–97, archdeacon of Durham and canon treas Durham Cathedral 1997–2002; memb Gen Synod C of E 2000–; sr selector Advsy Bd of Miny, chm Bd of Mgmnt Edward King Inst for Miny Devpt, chm Durham Diocesan Bd for Mission and Unity; govr Queen's Fndn Birmingham; *Recreations* travel, cooking, gardening, wine, sport (as spectator), music, opera, reading; *Clubs* Nikaean; *Style—* The Rt Rev the Bishop of Basingstoke; ✉ Bishopswood End, 40 Kingswood Rise, Four Marks, Alton, Hampshire GU34 5BD (tel 01420 562925, fax 01420 561251, e-mail trevor.willmott@dial.pipex.com)

BASKETT, Dr Peter John Firth; s of Sir Ronald Gilbert Baskett, OBE (d 1972), and Joan Shirley Staples, *née* Firth (d 1982); *b* 26 July 1934; *Educ* Belfast Royal Acad, Campbell Coll Belfast, Queens' Coll Cambridge (BA, MB BCh), Queen's Univ Belfast (MB BCh, BAO); *Career* TA RAMC (V) 1982–: Capt 1982–84, Maj 1984–87, Lt-Col 1988–92, Col 1992–95, Hon Col 1996–2004; hon civilian conslt in resuscitation to the Army and RN, conslt emeritus to the Army 1984; conslt anaesthetist Royal Infirmary and conslt anaesthetist Frenchay Hosp Bristol 1966–99, sr clinical lectr Univ of Bristol 1966–99, conslt anaesthetist emeritus Royal Infirmary Bristol 1996–, conslt emeritus Frenchay Hosp Bristol 1999–; author of numerous chapters and articles in books and med jls; hon sec Assoc of Anaesthetists 1978–80, hon sec RSM Anaesthesia 1980–82, fndr memb Resuscitation Cncl UK 1983–, chm Br Assoc for Immediate Care 1984–86, memb Bd Faculty of Anaesthetists 1984–88, vice-pres Assoc of Anaesthetists 1985–88, chm Monospecialist Ctee Union of Euro Med Specialists 1985–88 (UK rep 1982–89), academician Euro Acad of Anaesthesiology 1985–, memb Cncl Royal Coll of Anaesthetists 1984–96, fndr memb European Resuscitation Cncl (chm 1988–94); pres: Euro Section World Fedn of Socs of Anaesthesiology 1986–90 (hon sec 1982–86), World Assoc for Emergency and Disaster Med 1989–93 (hon sec 1979–89), Assoc of Anaesthetists 1990–92, Int Trauma and Critical Care Soc 1995–98, United Servs Section RSM 1997–99; author of over 180 papers relating to anaesthesia and resuscitation in scientific jls; ed-in-chief Resuscitation 1997–; Liveryman Worshipful Soc of Apothecaries 1990 (memb 1986); hon memb: Aust Soc of Anaesthetists, Ugandan Soc of Anaesthetists, Romanian Soc for Emergency and Disaster Med, Slovenian Soc for Emergency Med, Polish Resuscitation Cncl, Croatian Med Assoc, Assoc of Anaesthetists 1998, Br Assoc for Immediate Care 2001, Resuscitation Cncl (UK) 2001, European Resuscitation Cncl 2002, Italian Resuscitation Cncl 2005, Slovenian Medical Assoc 2005; FFARCS 1963, Dip IMC, FRCA 1992, FRCP 1999 (MRCP 1994), FFAEM 1999; *Books* Immediate Care (with Dr J Zorab, 1976), Pre Hospital Immediate Care (1981), Medicine for Disasters (with Dr R Weller, 1988), Cardiopulmonary Resuscitation (1989), Resuscitation Handbook (1989, 2 edn 1993), Practical Procedures in Anaesthesia and Critical Care (1994), A Pocket Book of the European Resuscitation Guidelines for Resuscitation (jt ed, 2006); *Style—* Dr Peter Baskett; ✉ Stanton Court, Stanton St Quintin, Chippenham, Wiltshire SN14 6DQ (tel 01666 837210, fax 01666 837775)

BASS, Dr John Charles; CBE (1988); *b* 29 July 1929; *Educ* Farnham GS, Univ of Southampton (BSc), KCL (MSc), Univ of Sheffield (PhD); *m* June 1954, Jean Edith Bass; 2 s (Stephen Michael John b 6 May 1958, David Nicholas John b 26 June 1960); *Career* AEI Research Laboratory Aldermaston Court 1954–63, researcher Univ of Sheffield Staff 1963–66, corp dir of research and memb Bd Plessey until 1990 (joined Plessey Research Caswell 1966), chm Phoenix VLSI Ltd 1990–; non-exec dir Argyll Consultancies plc 1990–98; hon prof of engrg Univ of Warwick 1982–; memb various governmental and EU scientific and engrg ctees 1980–; author of numerous publications on electronic materials and devices; FIEE 1975, FREng 1982; *Recreations* gardening, natural philosophy; *Style—* Dr John Bass, CBE, FREng; ✉ 10 Thorburn Road, Weston Favell, Northampton NN3 3DA

BASS, Dr Neville M; s of Arthur Bass, of Manchester; *b* 8 June 1938; *Educ* Manchester Grammar, Univ of Manchester, Turner Dental Sch (LDS, BDS), Eastman Dental Inst (DipOrth, FDSRCS); *m* 6 Jan 1968, Mona; 2 s (Alexander b 1970, Anthony b 1973); *Career* house surgn Manchester Dental Hosp 1960–61, Eastman Dental Hosp London 1961–62 (registrar Orthodontic and Paedodontic Depts 1962–63), gen dental practice 1964–65, conslt orthodontist USAF London 1965–69, private orthodontic practice 1969–, postgrad teaching staff Royal Dental Hosp London 1972–76, postgrad orthodontic teaching staff Royal London Hosp Med Coll Dental Sch 1989–; memb Tweed Orthodontic Fndn USA; Angle Soc of Europe: memb 1974–, sec 1978–81, memb Scientific Ctee 1988–94, chm 1994, pres 2000–02; certification Br Orthodontic Cert Bd 1984 (memb Mgmnt Ctee

1985–98); pres Br Orthodontic Soc 2000; *Recreations* sculpting, golf, skiing, reading, jazz and classical music, wind surfing, sailing; *Style*— Dr Neville Bass; ✉ 4 Queen Anne Street, London W1G 9LQ (tel 020 7580 8780)

BASS, Stephen Michael John; s of John Charles Bass, of Weston Favell, Northants, and Jean Edith Angel, *née* Stark; *b* 6 May 1958; *Educ* Northampton Sch for Boys, Oriel Coll Oxford (MA), Univ of Manchester (BLD), St Cross Coll Oxford (Osmaston scholarship, MSc); *m* 4 Sept 1982 Christine Anne, da of Lt-Col Kenneth Sydney Gittens; 2 da (Maria Hannah Danai b 7 Jan 1989, Sophie Anne Rose b 13 April 1991); *Career* World Conservation Union 1984–89: social forestry advsr to Aga Khan Fndn Pakistan, res advsr to Nat Conservation Strategies (Nepal and Zambia), set up seven-country prog in Southern Africa; Warren Weaver Fellowship Rockefeller Fndn 1989–90 developing grant progs in forestry and biodiversity; Int Inst for Environment and Devpt: dir of forestry and land use 1990–, dir of progs responsible for 25-country prog of research and training 1999–2003; chief environment advsr Dept for Int Devpt 2003–, sr fell Int Inst for Environment and Devpt; assoc researcher Euro Forest Inst Finland; affiliated assoc Island Resources Fndn USA; memb Cmmn on Econ and Social Policy World Conservation Union; Coopers Hill War Meml Prize 1984, Queen's Award for Forestry (for services to int forest initiatives) 2001; MIBiol 1986; *Books* co-author of several books incl: Plantation Politics (1992), Strategies for National Sustainable Development (1994), The Forest Certification Handbook (1995), The Sustainable Forestry Handbook (1999), Policy That Works for Forests and People (1999), Sustainable Development Strategies (2002), Reducing Poverty and Sustaining the Environment (2005); author of numerous articles; *Recreations* jazz (play drums), drawing, gardening, kitsch ephemera; *Style*— Stephen Bass, Esq; ✉ International Institute for Environment and Development, 3 Endsleigh Street, London WC1H 0DD (tel 020 7388 2117, e-mail stephen.bass@iied.org)

BASSAM OF BRIGHTON, Baron (Life Peer UK 1997), of Brighton in the County of East Sussex; John Steven (Steve) Bassam; s of late Sydney Steven and Enid Bassam, of Colchester, Essex; *b* 11 June 1953; *Educ* Clacton Secdy Sch, NE Essex Tech Coll, Univ of Sussex (BA), Univ of Kent (MA); *Partner* Jill; 2 s (Thomas Harry b 1988, Gregory John b Sept 1994, d Oct 1994), 2 da (Lauren Stephanie b 1990, Ellen Rose b 1995); *Career* social worker E Sussex CC 1976–77, legal advsr N Lewisham Law Centre 1979–83; policy advsr: London Borough of Camden 1983–84, GLC Policy Ctee 1984–86, London Strategic Policy Unit 1986–87; asst sec Police Fire Environmental Health and Consumer Affairs AMA 1988–97, head of environment health and consumer affairs Local Govt Assoc 1997–98; occasional journalist for local govt publications; memb (Lab) Brighton BC 1983–97 (ldr 1987–97), memb Brighton and Hove Unitary Cncl 1996–99 (ldr 1996–); min Home Office 1999–2001; Lord in Waiting (Govt whip) 2001–; patron Brighton Festival; memb: Labour Pty, Co-op Pty, Fabian Soc; hon fell Univ of Sussex, fell Brighton Coll; *Recreations* cricket, football fan (Brighton & Hove Albion); *Clubs* Preston Village CC; *Style*— The Rt Hon the Lord Bassam of Brighton; ✉ House of Lords, London SW1A 0PW

BASSET, Gerard Francis Claude; s of Pierre Rene Basset (d 1976), and Marguerite, *née* Conorton; *b* 7 March 1957; *Educ* Lycee Albert Camus Firminy France, Ecole Hoteliere de Dardilly Lyon France; *m* Nina, *née* Howe; 1 s (Romané); *Career* sommelier; commis de cuisine Frantel Hotel Marseille 1981–83, head waiter The Crown Hotel Lyndhurst Hants 1984–85 (chef de rang 1983–84), head waiter Morel's Haslemere 1985–86, Manley's Storrington W Sussex 1986–87, head waiter The Crown Hotel Lyndhurst 1987–88, chef sommelier Chewton Glen Hotel New Milton Hants 1988–94; co-fndr and dir Hotel du Vin Hotel Gp 1994–2004, co-prop Hotel du Vin & Bistro Winchester 1994–2004, gp hotels in Tunbridge Wells, Bristol and Birmingham; prop Busketts Lawn Hotel Hants 2007–; dir GB Wine Consultancy Ltd; fell Acad of Food and Wine Service (tech dir 1997), vice-chm Ct of Master Sommeliers; memb: Commendeur of French Gastronomy 1988, 3 Ceps St Bris 1989, Acad of Wine Service 1989, Cava and Penedes Inst 1993, Verre Galant (Cognac Camus) 1993, Coll du Cognac 1993, Cognac Inst 1994, Sommeliers Club of GB 1994, Acad of Culinary Arts 1995, Inst Masters of Wine 1998; assoc memb UK Bartenders Guild; *Awards* Best Sommelier for french wines and spirits in UK 1988 and 1992, Wine Waiter of the Year 1989 and 1992, winner Southern Sommelier Competition 1989, Calvet Cup of Acad of Wine Service (for overall outstanding achievement in wine knowledge and service) 1989, 1990 and 1992, Bronze Medal Best Sommelier in Euro Competition Reims 1990 and 1992, Champagne Travel Bursary 1990, winner Ruinart UK Selection for Euro 1990, winner Int Sommelier Competition Paris 1992, Silver Medal World Championship Rio de Janeiro 1992, Courvoisier Best of the Best Sommelier 1992, Marques de Caceres Food & Wine Person of the Year 1993, Rame d'Honneur (for servs given to wine) 1993, winner Euro Trophee Ruinart Reims 1996; for Hotel du Vin: Egon Ronay Cellnet Guide Newcomer of the Year 1996, Catey Award Newcomer of the Year 1996, Caesar Good Hotel Guide Best Hotel with Wine Theme 1998; *Books* The Wine Experience (2000); *Recreations* chess, ice-skating; *Style*— Gerard Basset, Esq

BASSETT, Douglas Anthony; s of Hugh Bassett, and Annie Jane Bassett; *b* 11 August 1927; *Educ* Llanelli GS for Boys, UCW Aberystwyth (BSc, PhD); *m* 1954, Elizabeth Menna, da of Gwylim Roberts; 3 da (Sarah, Sian, Rhian); *Career* lectr Dept of Geology Univ of Glasgow 1954–59, dir Nat Museum of Wales 1977–85 (keeper Dept of Geology 1959–77); chm: Ctee for Wales Water Resources Bd 1968–73, Royal Soc Ctee on History of Geology 1972–82, Advsy Ctee for Wales Nature Conservancy Cncl 1973–85; The Assoc of Teachers of Geology: fndr chm 1967, pres 1969, ed 1969–74; fndr memb and dir Nat Welsh-American Fndn 1980–87 and 1990– (vice-pres 1996–98); memb: Ordnance Survey Review Ctee 1978–80, Ctee for Wales Br Cncl 1983–90; ed Manual of Curatorship Museums Assoc 1983–; Silver Medal Czechoslovak Soc for Int Relations 1985, Aberconway Medal Instn of Geologists 1985; hon professorial fell Univ of Wales Coll of Cardiff 1977–97, hon res fell Nat Museum of Wales 1986–; Liveryman Welsh Livery Guild 2004; Officier de l'Ordre des Arts et des Lettres (France) 1984; *Books* Bibliography and Index of Geology and Allied Sciences for Wales and the Welsh Borders 1897–1958 (1961), A Source-book of Geological Geomorphological and Soil Maps for Wales and the Welsh Borders (1800–1966) (1967), Wales in Miniature (1993); contribs to various geological, museum, educational and historical jls and biographical dictionaries; *Recreations* bibliography, chronology; *Style*— Douglas A Bassett; ✉ 4 Romilly Road, Canton, Cardiff CF5 1FH (tel 029 20227823)

BASSEY, Dame Shirley; DBE (2000); *b* 1937, Cardiff; *Career* singer; early career as worker in local factory, perfomer Al Read Christmas Show (Adelphi Theatre London) 1955, performer Such Is Life 1956, live show NY and Las Vegas 1962, released numerous hit singles 1960s-; theme tunes for James Bond films Goldfinger 1964, Diamonds are Forever 1971 and Moonraker 1979; *Albums* incl: The Fabulous 1959, Shirley Bassey 1961, Shirley 1962, Lets Face the Music 1965, Shirley Bassey at the Pigalle 1965, Shirley Stops The Shows 1966, I've Got a Song For You 1967, And We Were Lovers 1968, This Is My Life 1969, Does Anybody Miss Me? 1970, Something 1970, Live at Talk of the Town 1970, Shirley Bassey Is Really Something 1971, Something Else 1972, I Capricorn 1972, And I Love You So 1973, Live at Carnegie Hall 1973, Never, Never, Never 1974, Nobody Does It Like Me 1974, Shirley Means Bassey 1975, Good, Bad But Beautiful 1976, Love, Life and Feelings 1978, Magic Is You 1982, All by Myself 1985, Sassy Bassey 1989, La Mujer 1991, New York, New York 1991, Keep the Music Playing 1995, Sings the Songs of Andrew Lloyd Webber 1998, Birthday Concert 1998, 'S Wonderful, Nobody Does It Like Me 1998, Let Me Sing and I'm Happy 1998, Sings the Movies 1998, Power of Love 1999, Something 2002, That's What Friends Are For 2003, Old Friends and Lovers 2003, Thank You for the Years 2003; *Style*— Dame Shirley Bassey, DBE

BASSI, Avinash; *b* 16 April 1960, India; *m* 19 Aug 1980, Nina; 2 da (Tina b 30 Oct 1982, Natasha b 29 Jan 1986), 1 s (Rahul b 26 Feb 1992); *Career* entrepreneur; market trader 1978, prop Talk of the Town (8 shops) 1982–88, estab distribution centre 1983, fndr and owner Duke Clothing Co and Bassi Fashions Ltd 2000–, prop Rockford; memb Nottingham C of C; London Thames Today magazine Best Co of the Year 2003; runner-up Asian Jewels Awards 2006; *Style*— Avinash Bassi, Esq

BASSI, (Paramjit) Paul Singh; s of Santokh Singh Bassi, of Birmingham, and Avtar Kaur, *née* Chaudri; *b* 21 March 1962, Birmingham; *Educ* Harlington Comp Sch Hayes, Sandwell Coll; *m* Priya Paula, *née* Narang; 2 da (Terri Kaur b 6 July 1988, Nikita Kaur b 1 Sept 1991), 1 s (Bobby Singh b 11 June 1990); *Career* fndr chm Bond Wolfe 1985–, regnl chm Coutts Bank 2000– (memb Executive Steering Bd 2006–), non-exec chm Corporatewear plc 2004–, md Real Estate Investors plc, vice-chm Bigwood Chartered Surveyors 2006, chm midlands Kaupthing Singer Freidlander 2007, chief exec Real Estate Investors plc 2007; dir Birmingham Hippodrome, West Midlands ambass, vice-pres C of C; Entrepreneur of the Year Asian Jewel Awards 2003, Lifetime Achievement Award Lloyds TSB 2005; *Recreations* tennis, racquetball, keep-fit; *Style*— Paul Bassi, Esq

BASU, Himansu Kumar; s of Sudhangsu Kumar Basu (d 1992), and Rajlaxmi, *née* Ghosh (d 1950); *b* 10 April 1934; *Educ* Gopalpur Acad and Calcutta Med Coll Univ of Calcutta (MB BS), Univ of Liverpool (PhD); *m* Lynda Ann, da of late Ronald Sanders, of Rochester, Kent; 1 da (Maya Louise b 1979), 1 s (Christopher Kumar b 1984); *Career* lectr in obstetrics and gynaecology Univ of Liverpool 1965–72, conslt obstetrician and gynaecologist Dartford and Gravesham NHS Tst 1972–98, med dir Multicare Int London 1998–2000; SE Gynaecological Soc: sec 1976–82, vice-pres 1984–86, treas 1987–91, pres 1991–96; RCOG: memb Cncl 1977–83, 1988–91 and 1993–99, memb Fin and Exec Ctee 1980–83 and 1998–99, memb Examination Ctee 1981–84; Overseas Doctors Training offr 1996–1999, convenor MRCOG courses 1999–2002; Section of Obstetrics and Gynaecology RSM: memb Cncl 1979–88 and 1994–, hon sec 1983–84, vice-pres 1985–88, pres 1995–96; chm Osprey's Gynaecological Soc 1981–84; examiner for MB ChB, DRCOG, MRCOG and FRCS; Ethel Boyce fell Univ of Liverpool 1967, William Blair Bell lectr RCOG 1969, Catherine Bishop Harman prize BMA 1969, Eden fell RCOG 1970; memb: Br Fertility Soc, Br Soc of Gynaecological Endoscopy, American Assoc of Gynaecological Laparoscopists (int advsr 1998–2001); chm Int Fellowship of Rotarian Physicians 1999–, district govr Kent and E Sussex Rotary Int 2004–05; FRCSEd, FRCOG; *Recreations* travel, photography, radio broadcasting; *Clubs* Royal Over-Seas League; *Style*— Mr Himansu Basu; ✉ Glengarry, Woodlands Lane, Shorne, Gravesend, Kent DA12 3HH (tel and fax 01474 822294, e-mail hbasu@aol.com)

BATCHELOR, Andrew Goolden Grant; s of Lt-Col Hugh Thomas Nicolas Batchelor (d 1976), and Margaret Irene, *née* Grant; *b* 28 August 1951; *Educ* Whitchurch HS, St Mary's Hosp Med Sch Univ of London (BSc, MB BS); *m* 3 Nov 1973, Rosemary Marion, da of Horace William Gibson, of Melksham, Wilts; 1 s (Thomas b 18 April 1980), 1 da (Elizabeth b 6 Oct 1982); *Career* surgical res King Edward VII Hosp Paget Bermuda 1978–79, sr house offr in gen surgery St Mary's Hosp London 1979–80, registrar in gen surgery Queen Elizabeth II Hosp Welwyn Gdn City 1980–81, sr house offr in plastic surgery Wexham Park Hosp Slough 1981–82, registrar in plastic surgery Nottingham City 1982–84, sr registrar W of Scotland Regnl Plastic Surgery Unit 1984–86, sr clinical lectr in surgery Univ of Leeds 1986–; conslt plastic surgn: St James's Hosp Gen Infirmary Leeds 1986–, S York Dist Hosp 1988– (clinical dir plastic surgery 1993–); memb Cncl British Assoc of Plastic Surgns 1993– (memb 1986); memb: Br Microsurgical Soc 1982, Br Soc of Head and Neck Oncologists 1986, Br Assoc of Aesthetic Plastic Surgns 1988; FRCS, FRCS (Plastic Surgns); *Books* contrib: Essential Surgical Practice (1988), Tissue Expansion (1989), Excision and Reconstruction in Head and Neck Cancer (1993); *Recreations* sailing, shooting; *Style*— Andrew Batchelor, Esq; ✉ Field House, 10 Sicklinghall Road, Wetherby, West Yorkshire LS22 6AA (tel 01937 583654); Department of Plastic Surgery, St James's University Hospital, Beckett Street, Leeds LS8 1DF (tel 0113 243 3144)

BATCHELOR, Prof Bruce Godfrey; s of Ernest Walter Batchelor (d 1982), of Rugby, Warks, and Ingrid Maud, *née* Wells; *b* 15 May 1943; *Educ* Lawrence Sheriff Sch Rugby, Univ of Southampton (BSc, PhD), Univ of Wales (DSc); *m* 21 Aug 1968, Eleanor Gray (JP 1983), da of Percy William Pawley (d 1993), of Cardiff; 2 c (Helen b 1969, David b 1972); *Career* engr Plessey Co Ltd 1968–70, lectr Univ of Southampton 1971–80, prof Univ of Wales Cardiff 1980–; conslt: Br Robotic Systems Ltd, 3M Co USA, Vision Dynamics Ltd, Spectral Fusion Technologies Ltd; visiting prof Dublin City Univ 1993–2002; author of over 220 tech articles; chm 15 int confs; CEng 1972, FRSA 1983, FIEE 1993 (memb 1972), fell SPIE 1994 (memb 1983), FBCS 1994, fell SME 1995 (sr memb 1994), CITP 2004; *Books* Practical Approach Pattern Classification (1975), Pattern Recognition, Ideas In Practice (ed, 1978), Automated Visual Inspection (ed, 1985), Intelligent Image Processing in Prolog (1991), Interactive Image Processing for Machine Vision (1993), Industrial Machine Vision Systems (ed, 1994), Intelligent Vision Systems for Industry (1997), Intelligent Machine Vision: Techniques, Implementation and Applications (2001), Machine Vision for the Inspection of Natural Products (jt ed, 2003); *Recreations* Presbyterian Church, walking, swimming, digital photography, antique silver; *Style*— Prof Bruce Batchelor; ✉ Cardiff School of Computer Science, Cardiff University, PO Box 916, Cardiff CF24 3XF (tel 029 2087 4390, fax 029 2087 4598, e-mail bruce.batchelor@cs.cf.ac.uk, website bruce.cs.cf.ac.uk/bruce/index.html)

BATCHELOR, Paul Anthony; s of Joseph John Batchelor (d 1963), of Little Chart, Ashford, and Irene Margaret, *née* Shoobridge; *b* 4 July 1946; *Educ* Ashford GS, St John's Coll Cambridge (coll scholar, MA, Dip Devpt Econs, Philip Lake Prize, Hughes and Wright Prizes, Larmor Award, David Richards travelling scholar); *m* 5 July 1969, Janet, da of Jack Rowden King; 1 da (Emma Jane b 16 May 1972), 1 s (Jonathan Mark b 12 Feb 1976); *Career* vol teacher Miny of Educn Zambia 1965, supervisor of studies in geography St John's Coll Cambridge 1968–69, govt economist Swaziland 1969–72, acting chief economist Office of the President & Cabinet Malawi 1973–74 (sr economist 1972–73); PricewaterhouseCoopers (formerly Coopers & Lybrand before merger): joined as econ conslt 1974, ptnr 1982–2004, chm Int Mgmnt Consulting Servs Exec 1989–95, ptnr i/c Mgmnt Consulting Servs Europe 1990–94, exec ptnr i/c Coopers & Lybrand Europe 1994–98, memb Global Mgmnt Team 1998–2004, global geography ldr 2002–04 (dep 1998–2002); dir: PricewaterhouseCoopers Development Associates Ltd 2004–06, EBE Ltd 2004–, Langham Partnership UKI 2005–; chm: Oxford Policy Mgmnt Ltd 2006–, Crown Agents for Overseas Govts and Admins 2007–; memb Int Advsy Cncl Transparency Int, memb Int Steering Gp AIESEC 2003–; churchwarden St Nicholas Sevenoaks 2001–07; Liveryman Worshipful Co of Mgmnt Conslts 1994; FIMC 1980; *Recreations* classical music, gardening, golf, mountain walking; *Clubs* Hever Golf; *Style*— Paul Batchelor, Esq; ✉ 3 Burntwood Grove, Sevenoaks, Kent TN13 1PZ; Les Chalets de la Beune 1, La Beunaz, St Paul en Chablais 74500, France; Oxford Policy Management Ltd, 6 St Aldates Courtyard, Oxford OX1 1BN (tel 01865 207300, e-mail pauljanetbatchelor@yahoo.co.uk)

BATE, Anthony; s of Hubert George Cookson Bate (d 1986), and Cecile Marjorie, *née* Canadine (d 1973); *b* 31 August 1927; *Educ* King Edward VI Sch Stourbridge, Central Sch of Speech & Drama (Gold medal); *m* 22 May 1954, Diana Fay, da of Kenneth Alfred Charles Cawes Watson (d 1939), of Seaview, IOW; 2 s (Gavin Watson b 25 Feb 1961, Mark Hewitt b 23 Sept 1963); *Career* Nat Serv RNVR 1945–47; actor, entered professional theatre 1953; memb BAFTA 1985; *Theatre* incl: first West End appearance Inherit the

Wind (St Martin's) 1960, Treasure Island (Mermaid) 1960, Happy Family (Hampstead) 1966, Much Ado About Nothing and Silence (RSC Aldwych) 1969, Find Your Way Home (Open Space Theatre) 1970, Eden End (tour) 1972, Economic Necessity (Haymarket Leicester) 1973, Getting Away with Murder (Comedy) 1976, Shadow Box (Cambridge) 1979, The Old Jest (tour) 1980, A Flea in her Ear (Plymouth Theatre Co) 1980, Little Lies (Wyndhams) 1983, Master Class (tour) 1984, The Deep Blue Sea (Theatre Royal Haymarket) 1988, Relative Values (Chichester Festival Theatre and Savoy) 1993–94; *Television* first TV appearance 1955; numerous appearances incl: James in Pinter's The Collection, Rogojin in The Idiot, MacDuff in Macbeth, Javert in Les Misérables, title role in Grady (a trilogy), T H Huxley in Darwin's Bulldog, Nikolai in Fathers and Sons, Creon in King Oedipus, Victor Hugo in Ego Hugo, Harry Paynter in Intimate Strangers, The Dutch Train Hijack 1976, Dr Dorn in The Seagull 1977, Kim Philby in Philby Burgess and Maclean 1977 (nominated Best Actor Monte Carlo Festival 1978), An Englishman's Castle 1978, title role in The Trial of Uri Urlov 1978, Tinker Tailor Soldier Spy 1978, Crime and Punishment 1979, 'Tis Pity She's a Whore 1979, The Human Crocodile 1980, Smiley's People 1981, A Woman Called Golda (with Ingrid Bergman) 1981, J A D Ingres in Artists and Models 1983, War and Remembrance 1986, Game Set and Match 1987, Countdown to War 1989, Medics 1991 and 1992, Prime Suspect 1994, Rebecca 1996, A Touch of Frost 1996, Bodyguards 1996, Silent Witness 1997, Midsomer Murders 2000; *Film* incl: The Set Up 1961, Stopover Forever 1963, Act of Murder 1964, Davey Jones' Locker 1964, Ghost Story 1973, Bismark 1975, Give My Regards to Broad Street 1982, Exploits at West Poley 1985, Eminent Domaine 1990, A Flight of Fancy 2002, Nowhere in Africa 2003 (Oscar for Best Film in a Foreign Language); *Recreations* listening to music, painting; *Clubs* Garrick; *Style*— Anthony Bate, Esq; ✉ c/o Ken McReddie Associates Ltd, 36–40 Glasshouse Street, London W1B 5DL (tel 020 7439 1456, fax 020 7734 6530)

BATE, David Christopher; QC (1994); s of Robert Leslie Bate (d 1954), of Mill Hill, London, and Brenda Mabel, *née* Price; *b* 2 May 1945; *Educ* Hendon Co GS, Univ of Manchester (LLB); *m* 1; 3 s (Tristan David Leslie b 1 June 1976, Simeon James Jonathan b 13 Nov 1978, Diccon Mark Julian b 30 March 1983), 1 da (Wendy Jeanne Alison b 3 Feb 1981); m 2, 20 Oct 2003, Fiona Adele, da of Samuel Graham; *Career* called to the Bar Gray's Inn 1969, VSO 1969–71, crown counsel Protectorate British Solomon Islands 1971, asst recorder 1989, recorder of the Crown Court 1992–; memb Criminal Bar Assoc; *Recreations* trying to sing in tune, the Seven Deadly Sins, swimming; *Style*— David Bate, Esq, QC; ✉ Hollis Whiteman Chambers, Queen Elizabeth Building, Temple, London EC4Y 9BS (tel 020 7583 5766, fax 020 7353 0339)

BATE, Jennifer Lucy; da of Horace Alfred Bate, and Dorothy Marjorie, *née* Hunt; *b* 11 November 1944; *Educ* Tollington GS, Univ of Bristol (BA); *Career* asst organist St James Muswell Hill 1955–78; superintendent Shaw Library LSE 1966–69; full time musician 1969–, int organist performing in over 40 countries including most major festivals and BBC Promenade concerts, specialist in eighteenth century Eng organ music, appeared frequently with Dolmetsch Ensemble at Haslemere Festival of Early Music, interpreter of romantic and modern music; world authy on works of the composer Olivier Messiaen, soloist at Br Première of Messiaen's Livre du Saint Sacrement at Westminster Cathedral, opened a series on the complete organ works of Messiaen on Radio France in the presence of the composer; designer (with Mander Organs) portable pipe organ and (with Wyvern Organs) a new type of digital electronic organ; collaborator with many contemporary composers; teacher: Master Classes, lectures and talks (for all ages in 5 languages); works written for her incl: Paraphrase on 'Salve Regina' (by Flor Peeters), Blue Rose Variations (by Peter Dickinson), Fenestra (by William Mathias); memb: Royal Soc of Musicians, Royal Philharmonic Soc, Br Music Soc (vice-pres), Incorporated Soc of Musicians; Hon Dr Brunel Univ 2007; FRCO, LRAM (organ performer), ARCM (organ performer); FRSA 2002; *Awards* GLAA Young Musician 1972, Personnalité de l'Année (France) 1990; Silver plaque for services to music: Alassio (Italy), Garbagna (Italy) and hon citizenship for servs to music 1996; *Recordings* over 30 incl: From Stanley to Wesley (6 Vols, winner Retailers' Assoc Award for Early Music 1991), Liszt & Schumann, Elgar and his English Contemporaries, complete organ works of Franck and Messiaen (awarded Grand Prix du Disque for Livre du Saint Sacrement), Organ Music by Samuel Wesley, The Wesleys and their Contemporaries, The Complete Organ Works of Felix Mendelsshon; *Music Published* Introduction and Variations on an Old French Carol, Four Reflections, Hommage to 1685, Toccata on a Theme of Martin Shaw, Canone Inglese, Lament: Variations on a Gregorian Theme, Grove's Dictionary of Music and Musicians (contrib); *Recreations* gardening, cooking, philately; *Style*— Miss Jennifer Bate; ✉ 35 Collingwood Avenue, Muswell Hill, London N10 3EH (tel 020 8883 3811, fax 020 8444 3695, e-mail jenniferbate@classical-artists.com, website www.classical-artists.com/jbate)

BATE, Prof (Andrew) Jonathan; CBE (2006); s of Ronald Montagu Bate (d 1978), and Sylvia Helen, *née* Tait (d 2003); *b* 26 June 1958; *Educ* Sevenoaks Sch, St Catharine's Coll Cambridge (T R Henn English scholar, Charles Oldham Shakespeare scholar, MA, PhD); *m* 1, 1984 (m dis 1995), Hilary Lorna, da of Prof Maxwell Gaskin; m 2, 1996, Paula Jayne, da of Timothy Byrne; 2 s (Thomas Montague b 1998, Harry Sebastian b 2006), 1 da (Elinor Clare b 2000); *Career* Harkness fell Harvard Univ 1980–81; research fell St Catharine's Coll Cambridge 1983–85, fell Trinity Hall and lectr Girton Coll Cambridge 1985–90; King Alfred prof of English literature Univ of Liverpool 1991–2003, prof of Shakespeare and Renaissance literature Univ of Warwick 2003–; Br Acad research reader 1994–96, Leverhulme personal research prof 1999–2004; hon fell St Catharine's Coll Cambridge 2000; memb Bd Royal Shakepeare Co 2003– (govr 2002–); FBA 1999, FRSL 2004; *Books* Shakespeare and the English Romantic Imagination (1986), Lamb's Essays (ed, 1987), Shakespearean Constitutions (1989), Romantic Ecology (1991), The Romantics on Shakespeare (ed, 1992), Shakespeare and Ovid (1993), The Arden Shakespeare: Titus Andronicus (ed, 1995), Shakespeare: An Illustrated Stage History (ed, 1996), The Genius of Shakespeare (1997), The Cure for Love (1998), The Song of the Earth (2000), John Clare: A Biography (2003, NAMI Book Award USA, Hawthornden Prize for Literature, James Tait Black Meml Prize for Biography), I Am: The Selected Poetry of John Clare (ed, 2004), The RSC Shakespeare: Complete Works (ed, 2007); *Recreations* gardening, tennis, walking, music; *Style*— Prof Jonathan Bate, CBE; ✉ Department of English, University of Warwick, Coventry CV4 7AL (e-mail bate@bardbiz.com)

BATE, Kenneth James (Ken); s of Maj Ernest James Bate, MBE, of Dudley, W Midlands, and Mary Joyce Adelaine, *née* Morgan (d 1970); *b* 20 June 1943; *Educ* Oldswinford Hosp Sch Stourbridge, Aston Univ (BSc, DipArch); *m* 26 Sept 1968, Susan Kay (d 1982); 2 s (Simon b 1972, Matthew b 1975); *Career* princ architect Wolverhampton Borough Cncl 1975–79, regnl architect Tarmac Construction Ltd 1979–84, ptnr Quest International Group Practice 1984–90, dir Tweedale Planning and Design Group Ltd and md Bloomer Tweedale Project Management Services Ltd 1991–93, own practice Kenneth J Bate Chartered Architect and Project Managers 1993–; memb: Assoc of Project Managers 1993; RIBA 1976; *Recreations* sailing; *Style*— Kenneth J Bate, Esq; ✉ Mount Pleasant, Hilton, Bridgnorth, Shropshire WV15 5PD (tel and fax 01746 716627)

BATELY, Prof Janet Margaret; CBE (2000); da of Alfred William Bately, TD (d 1985), and Dorothy Maud, *née* Willis (d 1988); *b* 3 April 1932; *Educ* Somerville Coll Oxford (Dip Comparative Philology, MA); *m* 20 Aug 1964, Leslie John (d 2006), s of John Summers (d 1965), of Bromley, Kent; 1 s (Michael b 23 Aug 1966); *Career* Birkbeck Coll London: asst lectr 1955–58, lectr 1958–69, reader in English 1970–76; KCL: prof of English language and medieval lit 1977–95, head Dept of English 1980–95, Sir Israel Gollancz research prof 1995–97, prof emeritus 1997–; memb: Cncl Early English Text Soc 1980–, Advsy Ctee Int Soc of Anglo-Saxonists 1985–90, Exec Ctee Fontes Anglo-Saxonici (formerly Sources of Anglo-Saxon Literature) 1985–, Exec Ctee Sources of Anglo-Saxon Lit and Culture 1987–, Humanities Res Bd 1994–95, Hon Advsy Devpt Bd Booktrust 2003–; govr: Cranleigh Sch 1982–88, KCS Wimbledon 1991–94, Notting Hill and Ealing High Sch 1998–2002; gen ed KCL Medieval Studies 1987–2000; hon fell Somerville Coll Oxford 1997; FKC 1986, FBA 1990, FRSA 2000; *Books* incl: The Old English Orosius (1980), The Anglo Saxon Chronicle - MS.A (1986), The Tanner Bede (1992), The Anglo-Saxon Chronicle - Texts and Textual Relationships (1991), Anonymous Old English Homilies: A Preliminary Bibliography of Source Studies (1993), A Palaeographer's View (ed with M Brown and J Roberts, 1993), Ohthere's Voyages: A Late 9th Century Account of Voyages Along the Coasts of Norway and its Cultural Context (co-ed, 2006); *Recreations* music, gardening; *Style*— Prof Janet Bately, CBE, FBA, FRSA; ✉ 86 Cawdor Crescent, London W7 2DD (tel 020 8567 0486, e-mail janet_bately@yahoo.com)

BATEMAN, Derek; s of Thomas Bateman, of Ellesmere Port, Cheshie, and Millicent, *née* Blackburn; *b* 8 February 1949; *Educ* Stanney Secdy Modern Tech Sch; *m* 5 Aug 1978, Jenny, da of Samuel Howarth (d 1986), of Gateshead, Tyne & Wear; 4 step s (Hilton b 1960, Sean b 1965, Wayne b 1967, Craig b 1971), 1 step da (Jaqualine b 1962); *Career* machinist and fitter Vauxhall Motors 1970–82 (engr 1965–70); borough cncllr Ellesmere Port and Neston 1974–78; Cheshire CC: memb 1977–, dep ldr 1985–91 and 1992–93, chm Environment Servs Ctee, ldr of Cncl 1997–2001, leader of Oppn 2001–; chm 1981–93: Manchester Ship Canal Steering Ctee, Nat Public Tport Forum, int authy Getting The Best From The Channel Tunnel representing all local govt assocs; Assoc of CCs: vice-chm Planning and Tport Ctee 1986–88, chm Public Tport Sub-Ctee 1987–88, Lab ldr Environment Ctee 1989–93 (chm 1993–); chm Local Govt Assoc: IT & Strategy Task Gp June-Oct 1997, Environment and Regeneration Bd 1997–99, Integrated Transport Task Gp, Environment and Regeneration Exec 2002– (Labour ldr 1993–, vice-chair 1993–2002); chief whip Lab gp Local Govt Assoc 2005– (dep whip 2003–05) conslt in politics 1993–95; chm The Public Tport Consortium 1987–; NW Regnl Assoc of Local Authorities: chm Transportation Working Pty 1992–94 (vice-chm 1995–98), chm Local Agenda 21 Steering Gp 1995–96, vice-chm and Labour ldr E & R Exec 1999–; chm NW Regnl Assembly 2000–01 (vice-chm 1999–2000); memb Cheshire Police Authy 1997–, memb Cheshire Combined Fire Authy 1997–b; *Recreations* Lab Pty; *Style*— Derek Bateman, Esq; ✉ 168 Cambridge Road, Ellesmere Port, Cheshire (tel 0151 355 6575, fax 0151 356 4912, e-mail derek.bateman@ntlworld.com); County Hall, Chester (tel 01244 602114, fax 01244 348645, e-mail derek.bateman@cheshire.gov.uk)

BATEMAN, Derek Walls; s of David Charteris Graham Bateman, of Selkirk, and Mary Ann, *née* Walls; *b* 10 May 1951; *Educ* Selkirk HS, Edinburgh Coll of Commerce; *m* 1, 11 Nov 1972, Alison, *née* Edgar (d 2001); 2 da (Eilidh b 24 March 1975, Lucy b 11 Nov 1978); m 2, June 2004, Judith Mackay; *Career* trainee journalist Scotsman Publications 1968–71; reporter: Edinburgh Evening News 1971–73, Glasgow Herald 1973–86; reporter and presenter BBC TV (Scotland) 1986–88, political ed Scotland on Sunday 1988–91, ed Bateman Associates (freelance journalism) 1991–97; presenter Good Morning Scotland (BBC Scotland); finalist Young Journalist of the Year Edinburgh Evening News 1973, runner-up Reporter of the Year Glasgow Herald 1986, USIA journalism participant 1991; memb: Selkirk Merchant Co, NUJ 1968; *Books* Unfriendly Games (with Derek Douglas, 1986); *Style*— Derek Bateman, Esq; ✉ 22 Lansdowne Crescent, Glasgow G20 6NG

BATEMAN, Prof Ian J; *b* 14 September 1961, Birmingham; *Educ* Univ of Birmingham (BSocSci), Univ of Manchester (MA), Univ of Nottingham (PhD); *m* Fiona; 1 s (Ben), 2 da (Freya, Natasha); *Career* lectr in economics and agric economics Dept of Economics Univ of Exeter 1987–89, economist The Boots Co plc 1989; Sch of Environmental Sciences UEA: lectr 1989–96, appointed reader 1996, currently prof; sr research fell Centre for Social and Economic Research on the Global Environment (CSERGE) UEA/UCL 1991–; visiting fell Dept of Environmental Studies Univ of the Aegean Lesvos; memb UK Nat Forum for Environmental Economics; exec ed Environmental and Resource Economics, memb Editorial Bd Int Jl of Agricultural Resources, Governance and Ecology; *Books* incl: Environmental Economics: An Elementary Introduction (jtly, 1994), Valuing Environmental Preferences: Theory and Practice of the Contingent Valuation Method in the US, EU and Developing Countries (jt ed, 1999), Environmental Risk Planning and Management (jt ed, 2001), Waste Management and Planning (jt ed, 2001), Economics of Coastal and Water Resources: Valuing Environmental Functions (jt ed, 2001), Water Resources and Coastal Management (jt ed, 2001), Urban Planning and Management (jt ed, 2001), Environmental Ethics and Philosophy (jt ed, 2002), Economic Valuation with Stated Preference Techniques: A Manual (jtly, 2002), Applied Environmental Economics: A GIS Approach to Cost-Benefit Analysis (jtly, 2003), Environmental Decision Making and Risk Management: Selected Essays (jt ed, 2004); *Style*— Prof Ian J Bateman; ✉ School of Environmental Sciences, University of East Anglia, Norwich NR4 7TJ

BATEMAN, Dr Nigel Turner; s of Sir Geoffrey Hirst Bateman (d 1998), and Margaret, *née* Turner; *b* 3 April 1943; *Educ* Marlborough, UC Oxford, St Thomas' Hosp (BM BCh); *m* 10 Dec 1966, Susannah Christian, da of Cdr A Denis Bulman, of The Old Manse, Midlem, by Selkirk, Scotland; 4 s (Thomas Andrew b 1969, Patrick Edward b 1971, Colin David b 1972, Michael Geoffrey b 1981); *Career* War Memorial scholarship Univ Coll Oxford 1962, assoc prof of preventive med Univ of Wisconsin 1978–79; conslt physician: St Thomas' Hosp 1980–93, Guy's and St Thomas' Hosp Tst 1993–; GKT: hon sr lectr 1992–, asst clinical dean 1993–2000; site dean St Thomas' Hosp 2000–05; censor RCP 2000–02; Freeman City of London 1985, Liveryman Worshipful Soc of Apothecaries 1985; FRCP 1985, FRCPGlas 1999, FRCPEd 2001; *Books* Respiratory Disorders (with I R Cameron, 1983); *Recreations* tennis, golf, fishing, hill walking; *Style*— Dr Nigel Bateman; ✉ St Thomas' Hospital, London SE1 7EH (tel 020 7188 5826, fax 020 7188 1290)

BATEMAN, Paul Terence; s of Nelson John Bateman (d 1983), and Frances Ellen, *née* Johnston (d 2003); *b* 28 April 1946; *Educ* Westcliff HS for Boys, Univ of Leicester (BSc); *m* 18 Jan 1969, Moira; 2 s (Michael b 1973, Timothy b 1977); *Career* Save and Prosper Group Ltd: graduate in secretarial dept 1967–68, asst to gp actuary 1968–73, mktg mangr 1973–75, gp mktg mangr 1975–80, gp mktg and devpt mangr 1980–81, exec dir mktg and devpt 1981–88, chief exec 1988–95; exec dir Robert Fleming Holdings Ltd (parent co of Save & Prosper) 1988–, exec chm Robert Fleming Asset Management (subsequently merged with Chase Manhattan) 1995–2000, global head Chase Fleming Asset Management (subsequently merged with JPMorgan) 2000, global head (outside America) JPMorgan Fleming Asset Management 2000–02, global ceo JPMorgan Fleming Asset Management 2002–07, chm JPMorgan Asset Mgmnt 2007–; dir: Lautro Ltd 1988–94, Personal Investment Authy 1993–94; chm Bd of Govrs Westcliff HS for Boys 1988–95; *Recreations* yachting, squash, golf, skiing; *Clubs* Royal Burnham Yacht; *Style*— Paul Bateman, Esq; ✉ 95 Thorpe Bay Gardens, Thorpe Bay, Essex SS1 3NW (tel 01702 587152, e-mail paul.bateman@dial.pipex.com); JPMorgan Asset Management, Finsbury Dials, 20 Finsbury Street, London EC2Y 9AQ (tel 020 7742 8475, fax 020 7751 8024)

BATES, Prof Colin Arthur; s of Ralph Mehew Bates (d 1965), and Annie Kathleen, *née* Cooper (d 1993); *b* 7 May 1935; *Educ* City of Norwich Sch, Univ of Nottingham (BSc, PhD); *m* 29 July 1961, Margaret, da of Edmund Green, of Nottingham; 1 da (Karen Nicola b 1965), 2 s (Julian Michael b 1967, Richard Daniel b 1971); *Career* sr research asst Stanford Univ 1961; Univ of Nottingham: demonstrator 1958, research assoc 1959, lectr in physics 1962, sr lectr in physics 1970, reader in theoretical physics 1974, prof 1984, prof and head of dept 1987–2000, dean of science 1996–2000, emeritus prof 2000–; author of various scientific articles; CPhys, FInstP; *Recreations* aquarist, sport, garden; *Style*— Prof Colin Bates; ✉ 26 Lime Grove Avenue, Beeston, Nottingham NG9 4AR (tel 0115 925 5568); School of Physics and Astronomy, University of Nottingham, University Park, Nottingham NG7 2RD (tel 0115 846 8241, fax 0115 951 5187, e-mail colin.bates@nottingham.ac.uk)

BATES, Prof David Richard; s of Jack Bates (d 1977), of Nuneaton, Warks, and Violet Anne Bates (d 1996); *b* 30 April 1945; *Educ* King Edward VI GS Nuneaton, Univ of Exeter (BA, PhD); *m* 4 Sept 1971, Helen Mary, *née* Fryer; 1 s (Jonathan Edward b 19 Nov 1975), 1 da (Rachel Emily b 23 Aug 1977); *Career* research asst Documents Section Imperial War Museum 1969–71 (head of section 1971); UC Cardiff (later Univ of Wales Cardiff): fell Univ of Wales Dept of History 1971–73, lectr 1973–87, memb Senate 1980–83 and 1986–92, sr lectr 1987–90, reader 1991–94, head of history and Welsh history 1988–92, memb Faculty of Arts (memb Bd); Univ of Glasgow: Edwards prof of medieval history 1994–2003, head Dept of Medieval History 1995–97, head Sch of History and Archaeology 1995–97, dir Centre for Medieval and Renaissance Studies 1996–98, head Dept of History 1997–2001, memb Senate; dir Inst of Historical Research Univ of London 2003–; A level examiner 1973–84 and 1986, examiner (admin grade admissions) Civil Service 1978–84; external examiner: Univ of Nottingham 1991–94, Queen's Univ Belfast 1992–96, Univ of Sheffield 1995, Univ of St Andrews 1996 and 2000–01, Univ of Cambridge 1997, Univ de Caen-Basse Normandie 1998, KCL 1998–2003, Univ of Birmingham 2001; DLitt assessor Univ of Reading 2002; Wolfson fellowship 1983, Huntington Library fell Henry E Huntington Library Pasadena 1984, professeur invité Ecole Nationale des Chartes Paris 1999, Br Acad Marc Fitch research reader 2001–03, visiting fell commoner Trinity Coll Cambridge 2002–03, directeur d'etudes invité Ecole Pratique des Hautes Etudes Paris 2003; delivered numerous lectures and conferences and symposia worldwide; vice-pres RHS 2003–06; memb: Postgrad Studentship Panel (History) AHRB/Br Acad 1996–99, Monitoring Bd The Acta of Henry II AHRB project 1996–, Benchmark Standards Working Gp in History Quality Assurance Agency (QAA) 1998–2000, Monitoring Bd Norman Pipe Rolls Leverhulme Tst research project 2001–03, Habilitation Panel Univ de Paris I (Panthéon-Sorbonne) 2002; gen ed The Medieval World (Longman/Pearson series) 1987–2001, academic reviewer QAA Trials in History 1998–88; memb Editorial Bd: Annales de Normandie, Facsimile of Domesday Book project Alecto Historical Editions; pres Cardiff Medieval Soc 1987–90, memb Cncl Royal Historical Soc 1995–99; Dr (hc) Univ of Caen 2000; centenary fell Historical Assoc 2006; FRHistS 1985, FSA 1993, FFCS 2001; *Books* Normandy before 1066 (1982), A Bibliography of Domesday Book (1986), William the Conqueror (1989, reissued 2001), Bishop Remigius of Lincoln 1067–1092 (1992), England and Normandy in the Middle Ages (jt ed, 1994), Conflict and Coexistence: Nationalism and Democracy in Modern Europe (jt ed, 1997), Regesta Regum Anglo-Normannorum: The Acta of William I, 1066–1087 (1998), Reordering the Past and Negotiating the Present in Stenton's First Century (2000), Domesday Book (jt ed, 2001), Writing Medieval Biography 750–1250: Essays in honour of Frank Barlow (jt ed, 2006); also author of numerous articles in learned jls; *Recreations* walking, music, reading, watching sport; *Style*— Prof David Bates; ✉ Institute of Historical Research, Senate House, Malet Street, London WC1E 7HU (tel 020 7862 8756, fax 020 7862 8811, e-mail david.bates@sas.ac.uk)

BATES, Django Leon; s of Ralf Bates, of West Norwood, London, and Frances Sinker, *née* Roseveare; *b* 2 October 1960; *Educ* Ilea Centre for Young Musicians, Morley Coll; *Children* 2 da (Lulu Holiday b 7 May 1989, Amélie Waterhouse b 13 Feb 2003), 1 s (Archy Woodrow 29 Oct 1992); *Career* jazz keyboard player and composer; band leader: Human Chain (originally Humans) 1980–, Delightful Precipice 1991–, Stormchaser 2005–; resident composer: Copenhagen 1996, Harrogate Int Festival 1997; prof in Rhythmic Music Rhythmic Music Conservatory (RMC) Copenhagen 2005–; performed in numerous countries incl: Japan, China, USA, India; artistic dir Fuse Festival Leeds 2004; assoc in music London Coll of Music, Hon RAM 2000, fell Leeds Coll of Music (FLCM) 2005; *Compositions* incl: What it's like to be alive (piano concerto for Joanna MacGregor) 1996, Out There (music theatre prodn) 1993, Jazz from Hell (orchestration) 2003, Umpteenth Violin Concerto 2004, commissions for Köln WDR Orch, London Sinfonietta; *Recordings* incl: Music for the third policeman 1990, Summer Fruits (and unrest) 1993, Autumn Fires (and green shoots) 1994, Winter Truce (and homes blaze) 1995, Good Evening...here is the news 1996, Like Life 1998, Quiet Nights 1998, You Live and Learn...(apparently) 2004; *Awards* Young Professional Musician of the Year Wavendon All Music 1987, Best UK Composer Wire Magazine 1987 and 1990, Best Band Wire Magazine 1989 (for Loose Tubes), Bobby Jaspar Prize French Academie du Jazz 1994, Danish Jazzpar Prize 1997; *Publications* Delightful Precipice (newsletter); *Recreations* beer, reading; *Style*— Django Bates, Esq; ✉ c/o Jeremy Farnell, 21 St Johns Church Road, London E9 6EJ (tel 020 8985 8754, e-mail management@djangobates.co.uk)

BATES, Prof (Alexander) John; *b* 18 August 1950, Buxton, Derbys; *Educ* Univ of Nottingham (BSc), Harvard Grad Sch of Business Admin (Baker scholar, MBA); *Career* devpt chemist Co-operative Wholesale Soc 1972, area sales mangr Eli Lilly & Co 1972–74, gen sales mangr Baird & Tatlock Zambia 1974–77, gp mktg mangr International Paint plc 1979–83, fndr, chm and md Datapaq Ltd 1984–92, fndr and dir Cambridge Mgmnt Gp 1984–, fndr and md Newmarket DataSystems Ltd 1993–97, exec dir Fndn for Entrepreneurial Mgmnt 1998–2005, fndr and non-exec dir Sussex Place Ventures Ltd 1998–, non-exec chm Multimedia Mapping Ltd (Multimap.com) 1998–, non-exec chm London Technology Network Ltd 2001–, non-exec dir and prog dir Centre for Creative Business Ltd 2004–; instr Harvard Grad Sch of Business Admin 1983–84, teaching fell London Business Sch 1984–2002; visiting lectr: Templeton Coll Oxford 1985–93, Institut Theseus (France Telecom) 1990–94, Cable & Wireless Coll 1994–96; visiting prof Univ of the Arts London 2002–, adjunct prof London Business Sch 2002–; chm London Region Judging Panel Ernst & Young Entrepreneur of the Year Award 2000–04, memb Invention and Innovation Awards Ctee NESTA 2002–06; *Style*— Prof John Bates, Esq; ✉ London Business School, Regent's Park, London NW1 4SA (tel 020 7000 8166, e-mail jbates@london.edu)

BATES, Sir Malcolm Rowland; kt (1998); s of late Rowland Bates; *b* 23 September 1934; *Educ* Portsmouth GS, Univ of Warwick (MSc), Harvard Grad Sch of Business Admin; *m* 1960, Lynda, da of late Maurice Price; 3 da; *Career* jt md Wm Brandt's & Sons 1972–75; GEC plc: joined 1976, main bd dir 1980–97, dep md 1985–97; chm: HHG plc (incl Pearl Assurance, London Life, NPI) 1996–2005, Premier Farnell plc 1997–2005; non-exec dir: Industrial Devpt Advsy Bd 1992–97, BICC plc 1997–99, Wavetek Corporation USA 1997–99, Grass Valley Group Inc USA 1999–2002, New Theatre Royal Portsmouth 1999–2001; special advsr to Paymaster General HM Treasy 1997–99; chm: Business in the Arts 1996–99, London Transport 1999–2003; govr and dep chm Univ of Westminster 1995–2002; Hon DLitt Univ of Westminster 2002; FCIS, FRAeS, CCMI; *Recreations* classical music, reading; *Style*— Sir Malcolm Bates; ✉ Mulberry Close, Croft Road, Goring-on-Thames, Oxfordshire RG8 9ES (tel 01491 872214, fax 01491 875934)

BATES, Matthew Oldham; s of David Oldham Bates, and Gillian, *née* Miles; *Educ* Downside, Univ of Reading (BA), Coll of Law London; *Career* articled clerk Boodle Hatfield Slrs 1989–91, asst to literary agent Sheil Land Associates 1992–95, literary agent The Sayle Agency 1995–; *Style*— Matthew Bates, Esq; ✉ Sayle Screen Ltd, 11 Jubilee Place, London SW3 3TE (tel 020 7823 3883, fax 020 7823 3363)

BATES, Michael; s of John Bates, and Ruth Bates; *b* 26 May 1961; *Educ* Heathfield Sr HS Gateshead, Gateshead Coll, Wadham Coll Oxford (MBA); *m* 25 June 1983, Carole, *née* Whitfield; 2 s; *Career* jr ptnr J M Bates & Co 1979–83, inspr Clerical Medical Investment Group 1983–86, conslt Hogg Robinson (benefit conslts) 1986–88, investment advsr Joseph Nelson (fund mangrs) 1988–91, asst dir Godwins Ltd (pensions conslts and actuaries) 1991–; MP (Cons) Langbaurgh 1992–97 (Parly candidate (Cons): Tyne Bridge 1987, Langbaurgh (by-election) 1991); PPS to: Rt Hon Nicholas Scott, MBE, MP as min of state DSS 1992–93, Rt Hon Sir John Wheeler, MP as min of state NI Office 1994: asst Govt whip 1994–95, Lord Cmmr HM's Treasy (sr Govt whip) 1995–96, Paymaster-Gen 1996–97, NE Sponsor Min 1996–97; Shell fell Industry and Parl Tst 1997–; dir of consultancy and research Oxford Analytica Inc 1998–2006 (sr advsr 2006–); dir: Financial Standards Foundation (Bermuda) Ltd 2001–03, estandardsforum Inc (NY) 2001–, Congregational & General plc 2001–, Walton Bates Assocs 2006–; memb: RIIA 1998–, Caux Roundtable 2001– (tstee 2006–), European Ideas Network 2002–, Business Advsy Forum Saïd Business Sch Univ of Oxford; chm Northern Area Young Conservatives 1985–87, memb YC Nat Advsy Ctee 1984–89; memb SCR Wadham Coll Oxford 1998; *Style*— Michael Bates, Esq; ✉ 42 Old Dryburn Way, Durham DH1 5SE (tel 0191 3740766, e-mail mb@waltonbates.com)

BATES, Michael Charles (Mike); OBE (1994); s of late Stanley Herbert Bates, of Sandy, Beds, and Winifred, *née* Watkinson; *b* 9 April 1948; *Educ* Stratton GS Biggleswade; *m* 29 May 1971, Janice Kwan Foh Yin, da of late Kwan Fui Kong, MBE; 1 da (Antonia b 14 March 1977), 1 s (Christopher b 23 Dec 1978); *Career* entered HM Dip Serv 1966, attaché New Delhi 1971–74, third sec Moscow 1974–77, FCO 1977–79, second later first sec Singapore 1979–83, first sec Brussels 1983–87, press offr PM's Office 1987–89, head of Parly Rels Unit FCO 1989–91, dep head of mission Riga 1991–92, chargé d'affaires Bratislava 1993–94, ambass to the Slovak Republic 1994–95, dep head of news FCO 1995–96, dep high cmmr Bombay 1996–2001, consul-gen Atlanta 2001–05; *Recreations* music, reading, travel; *Style*— Mike Bates, Esq, OBE; ✉ 15 Cedars Gardens, Brighton BN1 6YD

BATES, Mick; AM; *b* 24 September 1947; *Educ* Loughborough Coll Sch, Worcester Coll of Educn (Cert Ed), Open Univ (BA); *m* Buddug; 1 s (Daniel), 1 da (Ruth); *Career* teacher: Humphrey Perkins Jr HS Barrow in Soar 1970, Belvidere Secdy Sch Shrewsbury 1975, The Grove Sch Market Drayton (head of gen sci) 1975–77; farmer 1977–; chm: Llanfair Caereinion Branch NFU 1983–85, County Livestock Ctee 1988–91, NFU Co Public Affairs Ctee 1990–, NFU Co 1991, Llanfair Town Forum 1995–; produced and presented Radio Maldyn farming prog 1994–95; Lib Dem Pty: memb 1980, Llanfair Caereinion branch sec 1988, election sub-agent 1992, co cncllr for Dyffryn Banw 1994–95, memb Nat Assembly for Wales (Lib Dem) Montgomeryshire 1999–, chair Legislation Ctee Nat Assembly for Wales, chair and fndr memb Nat Assembly Sustainable Energy Gp (NASEG); memb: Educn and Learning Ctee, Econ Devpt Ctee; govr: Caereinion HS, Caereinion Primary Sch; *Recreations* farming, painting, poetry, Bob Dylan; *Style*— Mick Bates, Esq, AM; ✉ National Assembly for Wales, Cardiff Bay, Cardiff CF99 1NA (tel 029 2089 8340, fax 029 2089 8341)

BATES, Sir Richard Dawson Hoult; 3 Bt (UK 1937), of Magherabuoy, Co Londonderry; s of Sir Dawson Bates, 2 Bt, MC (d 1998), and Mary Murray, da of late Lt-Col Joseph Murray Hoult, RA; *b* 12 May 1956; *Educ* Winchester, Univ of Durham; *Style*— Sir Richard Bates, Bt

BATESON, Lynne; *b* 16 August 1952; *Educ* Univ of London (external BSc); *Career* gen reporter Pudsey News 1973–77, feature writer Yorkshire Evening Post 1978–81; city writer: United Newspapers 1981–84, Thomson Regnl Newspapers 1984–86; personal fin writer Daily Express 1986–87, features ed Money Magazine 1987–88; Sunday Express: personal fin ed 1988–94, fin ed 1994–95, asst ed 1995–96; dep gp managing ed Express Newspapers 1996–97, freelance journalist 1997–, columnist Sunday Express (Battling Bateson consumer column) 2001, ldr writer and features writer Daily Express and Sunday Express 2002–07 (also Daily Express), freelance writer and journalist 2007–; special commendation Bradford & Bingley's Personal Fin Journalist of the Year Award 1990, Br Insurance and Investment Brokers' Assoc Consumer Journalist of the Year (tabloid) 1993, Best General Insurance National Newspaper Writer 1999; *Recreations* mystery, history, and the psychic world, Wagner, Puccini, Debussy and soul, experiencing the USA, Oriental food, hot baths; *Style*— Ms Lynne Bateson; ✉ e-mail lynne.bateson@googlemail.com

BATESON, Prof Sir (Paul) Patrick Gordon; kt (2003); s of Capt Richard Gordon Bateson (d 1956), and Solvi Helene, *née* Berg (d 1987); *b* 31 March 1938; *Educ* Westminster, King's Coll Cambridge (BA, PhD, ScD); *m* 20 July 1963, Dusha, da of Kenneth Matthews, of Halesworth, Suffolk; 2 da (Melissa b 1968, Anna b 1972); *Career* Harkness fell Stanford Univ Med Center California 1963–65; Univ of Cambridge: sr asst in res Sub-Dept of Animal Behaviour 1965–69, lectr in zoology 1969–78, dir Sub-Dept of Animal Behaviour 1976–88, reader in animal behaviour 1978–84, prof of ethology 1984–2005, provost King's Coll 1988–2003 (professorial fell 1984–88); pres: Assoc for the Study of Animal Behaviour 1977–80, Cncl Zoological Soc of London 1989–92; tstee Inst for Public Policy Studies 1988–95, biological sec and vice-pres Royal Soc 1998–2003; memb Museum & Galleries Cmmn 1995–2000; foreign memb American Philosophical Soc 2006; Scientific Medal Zoological Soc of London 1976, Assoc for the Study of Animal Behaviour Medal 2001; Hon Dr Univ of St Andrews 2001; hon fell: Queen Mary Univ of London 2001, Zoological Soc of London 2002 (pres 2004–); FRS 1983; *Books* Growing Points of Ethology (ed with R A Hinde, 1976), Perspectives in Ethology Vols 1–9 (ed with P H Klopfer, 1972–91), Mate Choice (ed, 1983), Defended to Death (with G Prins & Others, 1984), Measuring Behaviour (with P Martin, 1986, 2 edn 1993), The Domestic Cat: The Biology of its Behaviour (ed with D Turner, 1988, 2 edn 2000), The Development and Integration of Behaviour (ed, 1991), The Behavioural and Physiological Effects of Culling Red Deer (1997), Design for a Life: How Behaviour Develops (with P Martin, 1999); *Style*— Prof Sir Patrick Bateson, FRS; ✉ The Old Rectory, Rectory Street, Halesworth, Suffolk IP19 8BL (tel 01986 873182)

BATEY, Prof Peter William James; s of Rev George Thomas Batey (d 1994), and Ruth, *née* Garstang (d 1998); *b* 17 August 1948; *Educ* Bury GS, Univ of Sheffield (BSc), Univ of Liverpool (MCD, PhD); *m* 1975, Joyce, da of Reginald Dover (d 1989); 1 da (Rachel Alexandra b 1979), 1 s (James Richard b 1981); *Career* planning offr Lancs CC 1969–73, sr planning offr Gtr Manchester CC 1973–75; Univ of Liverpool: lectr 1975–84, sr lectr 1984–87, reader 1987–89, Lever prof of town and regnl planning 1989–, head Dept of Civic Design 1989–97, dean Faculty of Social and Environmental Studies 1997–2003; Fulbright sr research scholar regnl sci program Univ of Illinois at Urbana-Champaign 1981–82; chm Conf of Heads of Planning Schs 1990–96; co-ed Town Planning Review 1992–; chm Bd of Mgmnt Merseyside Social Inclusion Observatory, memb NW Economic Forecasting Panel; dir Mersey Estuary Management Plan Study 1992–96, chm Mersey Basin Campaign, memb Bd Mersey Waterfront Regnl Park; world pres Regnl Sci Assoc Int 1997–98; govr Merchant Taylors Schs Crosby 1997–; Silver Jubilee Medal Hungarian Economic Assoc 1985, Kingfisher Award Mersey Basin Campaign 1996; foreign memb Russian Acad of Architecture and Construction Sciences 1994; FRGS 1969, FSS 1978, FRSA 1988, FRTPI 1988 (MRTPI 1975), AcSS 2000, CGeog 2003, fell Regnl Science Assoc Int 2006; *Publications* contrib to various planning jls and pubns incl: Town Planning Review, Jl of Regnl Sci, Economic Systems Research, Jl of Geographical Systems, Socio-Economic Planning Sciences, Regnl Studies; *Recreations* hill walking, travelling;

Style— Prof Peter Batey; ✉ 11 Blundell Road, Hightown, Liverpool L38 9EE; Department of Civic Design, University of Liverpool, Liverpool L69 7ZQ (tel 0151 794 3811, fax 0151 794 3125, e-mail pwjbatey@liv.ac.uk)

BATH, 7 Marquess of (GB 1789); Sir Alexander George Thynn (*sic*, reverted to this spelling); 10 Bt (E 1641); also Viscount Weymouth and Baron Thynne of Warminster (E 1682); s of 6 Marquess of Bath, ED (d 1992), and his 1 w, Hon Daphne Winifred Louise (Hon Mrs Fielding) (d 1997), da of 4 Baron Vivian; *b* 6 May 1932; *Educ* Eton, ChCh Oxford (MA); *m* 1969, Anna (Anna Gael, former actress, currently journalist and novelist), da of Laszlo Izsak Gyarmathy (d 2004), originally of Budapest but latterly of Los Angeles; 1 da (Lady Lenka Abigail b 1969), 1 s (Ceawlin Henry Laszlo, Viscount Weymouth b 1974); *Heir* s, Viscount Weymouth; *Career* late Lt Life Gds & Royal Wilts Yeo; contested: Westbury (Feb 1974) and Wells (1979) in Wessex Regionalist Pty's interest, Wessex (Euro elections 1979) Wessex Regionalist and European Fed Pty; on Lib Dem benches House of Lords 1993–99; painter; opened perm exhibition of murals in private apartments of Longleat 1973; dir Longleat Enterprises (incl Cheddar Caves) 1964–: planted first of the mazes within 'the Labyrinths of Longleat' 1975, Center Parcs Village Longleat Forest opened 1994; *Books* (as Alexander Thynne before 1976, Thynn thereafter); The Carry Cot (1972), Lord Weymouth's Murals (1974), A Regionalist Manifesto (1975), The King is Dead (1976), Pillars of the Establishment (1980), The New World Order of Alexander Thynn (2000); Strictly Private to Public Exposure (autobiography, 4 vols): The Early Years (2002), Top Hat and Tails (2003), Two Bites of the Apple (2003), A Degree of Instability: The Oxford Years (2005); *Record* I Play the Host (1974, singing own compositions); *Style*— The Most Hon the Marquess of Bath; ✉ Longleat, Warminster, Wiltshire BA12 7NN (home tel 01985 844300, fax 01985 844888, business tel 01985 844400, fax 01985 844885)

BATH AND WELLS, Bishop of 2001–; Rt Rev Peter Bryan Price; s of Rev Capt Alec H Price (d 1983), late RA, and Phyllis E M, *née* Bryan (d 1983); *b* 17 May 1944; *Educ* Glastonbury Sch Morden, Redland Coll Bristol (CertEd), Oak Hill Theol Coll London (Dip Patoral Studies), Heythrop Coll London (Research Studies); *m* Edith Margaret, da of Samuel Munro Burns; 4 s (David b 6 Aug 1968, Patrick b 26 Feb 1970, Neil b 5 Nov 1971, John-Daniel b 13 Sept 1982); *Career* asst teacher Ashton Park Sch 1966–70, sr tutor Lindley Lodge Young People's Centre 1970, head of religious studies Cordeaux Sch Louth 1970–72, student Oakhill Coll 1972–74, community chaplain Crookhorn and curate Christchurch Portsdown 1974–78, chaplain Scargill Community 1978–80, vicar of St Mary Magdalene Addiscombe 1980–88, chair Diocese of Southwark Bd of Mission 1987–92 (Bishop's advsr on church devpt 1980–86), chllr and residientiary canon Southwark Cathedral 1988–91, gen sec United Soc for the Propagation of the Gospel 1992–97, bishop of Kingston 1997–2001, chair Southwark Diocesan Bd of Educn 1998–2004; chair Manna Soc 1998–; memb: SPCK Governing Body 1996–99, Core Team New Way of Being Church 1998–; visitor Wadham Coll Oxford 2002–; *Books* Church as Kingdom (1987), Seeds of the Word (1996), Living Faith in the World (1998), Interactive Learning for Churches (1998), To Each Their Place (1998), Mark (2000), Jesus Manifesto (2000), Undersong (2002), Playing the Blue Note (2002), Changing Communities (2003); *Recreations* painting, walking, gardening, reading, conversation; *Style*— The Rt Rev the Bishop of Bath and Wells; ✉ The Palace, Wells, Somerset BA5 2PD

BATHER, John Knollys; s of Herbert Fiennes Bather (d 1944), of Lichfield, Staffs, and Christina Millar, *née* Brown (d 1984); *b* 5 May 1934; *Educ* Shrewsbury, Nat Foundry Coll; *m* 14 June 1960, Elizabeth Barbara, da of Wilmot Dixon Longstaff; 2 da (Rachel Elizabeth (Mrs Anselmi) b 28 Nov 1961, Camilla Mary (Mrs Wylie) b 18 Jan 1964), 1 s (Richard Herbert b 14 Sept 1967); *Career* Chamberlin & Hill plc: md 1976–94, dep chm 1994–2005; HM Lord-Lt Derbys; Liveryman Worshipful Co of Founders; OStJ; *Recreations* gardening, travel, shooting; *Clubs* Boodle's; *Style*— John Bather, Esq; ✉ Longford Grange, Longford, Ashbourne, Derbyshire DE6 3AH (tel 01335 330429)

BATHO, Sir Peter Ghislain; 3 Bt (UK 1928), of Frinton, Essex; s of Sir Maurice Benjamin Batho, 2 Bt (d 1990), and Antoinette Marie, da of Baron Paul d'Udekem d'Acoz, of Ghent, Belgium; *b* 9 December 1939; *Educ* Ampleforth, Writtle Farm Inst; *m* 29 Oct 1966, Lucille Mary, da of late Wilfrid Francis Williamson, of The White House, Saxmundham, Suffolk; 3 s (Rupert Sebastian Ghislain b 1967, Alexander Francis Ghislain b 1970, Hugh Charles Ghislain b 1973); *Heir* s, Rupert Batho; *Career* career in agriculture; cncllr Suffolk CC 1989–93; *Style*— Sir Peter Batho, Bt; ✉ Park Farm, Saxmundham, Suffolk IP17 1DQ

BATHURST, 8 Earl (GB 1772); Henry Allen John Bathurst; also Baron Bathurst (GB 1711) and Baron Apsley (GB 1771); s of Lt-Col Lord Apsley, DSO, MC, TD, MP (k on active serv 1942) and late Lady Apsley, CBE; suc gf (7 Earl) 1943; *b* 1 May 1927; *Educ* Eton, ChCh Oxford, Ridley Coll Canada; *m* 1, 1959 (m dis 1976), Judith Mary (d 2001), da of late Amos Christopher Nelson, of Cirencester, Glos; 2 s, 1 da; *m* 2, 1978, Gloria Wesley, da of Harold Edward Clarry, of Vancouver, Canada, and wid of David Rutherston; *Heir* s, Lord Apsley; *Career* Lt 10 Royal Hussars 1946–48, Royal Glos Hussars 1948–59, Capt TA; master VWH (Earl Bathurst's) Hounds 1950–64, jt master VWH Hounds 1964–66; hon sec Agric Ctee (Cons) House of Lords 1957, a Lord-in-Waiting 1957–61, jt Parly under sec of state Home Office 1961–62; govr Royal Agric Coll until 2003, pres Glos Branch CPRE until 1989, chllr Primrose League 1959–61; memb: Cncl CLA 1965 (chm Glos Branch CLA 1968–71), Cncl Timber Growers' Orgn 1966–77; DL Glos 1960–2003; pres: Royal Forestry Soc 1976–78, Inst of Sales & Mktg Mgmnt 1981–92, Assoc of Professional Foresters 1983–86 and 1995–98; dir Forestor Group 1986–92; *Clubs* White's, Cavalry and Guards'; *Style*— The Rt Hon the Earl Bathurst

BATISTE, Spencer Lee; s of late Samuel Batiste, and late Lottie Batiste; *b* 5 June 1945; *Educ* Carmel Coll, Sorbonne, Univ of Cambridge; *m* 1969, Susan Elizabeth, da of late Ronald William Atkin; 1 s, 1 da; *Career* slr in private practice 1970–2000; Euro Parly candidate (Cons) Sheffield, Chesterfield and NE Derbyshire 1979, MP (Cons) Elmet 1983–97; PPS to min of state for: Indust and Info Technol 1985–87, Def Procurement 1987–89; PPS to Sir Leon Brittan as Vice-Pres of EC Cmmn 1989–97; memb Select Ctees: on Energy 1985, on Sci and Technol 1992–97, on Info 1992–97; vice-chm: Cons Space Ctee 1986–97 (sec 1983–85), Cons Trade and Indust Ctee 1989–97, Small Business Bureau 1983–92; pres Cons Trades Unionists 1987–90 (chm Yorks Area 1984–87), chm Cons Academic Liaison Prog 1988–97; adjudicator Immigration Appellate Authy 1997–2002, vice-pres Immigration Appeal Tbnl 2002–05, sr immigration judge 2005–; law clerk to the Guardians of the Standard of Wrought Plate within the Town of Sheffield 1973–2000; memb: Cncl Univ of Sheffield 1982–92, British Hallmarking Cncl 1988–2000; *Recreations* gardening, reading, photography; *Style*— Spencer Batiste, Esq; ✉ Immigration Appeal Tribunal, Field House, 15 Breams Buildings, Chancery Lane, London EC4A 1DZ

BATSON, Brendon Martin; MBE (2001); *Career* professional footballer (over 400 Football League appearances): Arsenal FC 1969–74, Cambridge United FC 1974–78, West Bromwich Albion FC 1978–84; dep chief exec PFA 1984–2002 (PFA rep to Kick It Out professional football anti-racism campaign), md West Bromwich Albion FC 2002–03, appointed head of internal review of the FA's disciplinary procedure 2003, memb Bd Football Licensing Authy 2007–; *Recreations* golf, swimming, reading, theatre; *Style*— Brendon Batson, Esq, MBE; ✉ The Football Association, 25 Soho Square, London W1D 4FA (tel 020 7745 4545, fax 020 7287 1808)

BATTEN, Dr John Randolph; MBE (1996); s of John Alexandre Curtis Batten, of Eastbourne, E Sussex, and Isabel Nona Batten; *b* 29 July 1947; *Educ* Keswick Hall Norwich (CertEd), Western Carolina Univ (MA), Univ of Alabama (PhD); *m* 30 July 1983, Ruth Neri Villanueva; 2 da (Ligaya Isabelle b 1984, Marikit Rose b 1986); *Career* teacher Alperton HS 1969–70, teacher, head of Dept then dean of students Priory Sch Kingston Jamaica 1971–77, founding dir Priory Adult Coll of Educn (PACE) Kingston Jamaica 1973–77, chm Educn and Culture Gp Int Inst of Rural Reconstruction (IIRR) 1978–82, dir of int trg IIRR Philippines 1982–85, dep dir trg CARE Int 1986–89, country dir ActionAid Kenya 1989–95, chief exec ActionAid (UK) 1995–98, DG AMREF 1998–2001, int educn and devpt conslt 2002–; chm Resource Alliance; memb Bd: Assoc for Better Land Husbandry (ABLH) 2001–, Poverty Eradication Network (PEN) 2002–; memb ACENVO 1995, MInstD 1997; *Recreations* golf, tennis, music, theatre; *Style*— Dr John Batten; ✉ c/o UNEP, PO Box 47074, Nairobi, Kenya (tel 00 254 2 522235, e-mail jrbatten@africaonline.co.ke)

BATTEN, Stephen Duval; QC (1989); s of Brig Stephen Alexander Holgate Batten, CBE (d 1957), and Alice Joan, *née* Royden, MBE (d 1990); *b* 2 April 1945; *Educ* Uppingham, Pembroke Coll Oxford (BA); *m* 5 June 1976, Valerie Jean, da of George Ronald Trim (d 1982); 1 s (Henry b 1978), 1 da (Sarah b 1980); *Career* called to the Bar Middle Temple 1968 (bencher), recorder of Crown Court 1988–; *Recreations* golf, gardening, and the pursuit of private peace; *Style*— Stephen Batten, Esq, QC; ✉ 3 Raymond Buildings, Gray's Inn, London WC1R 5BH (tel 020 7400 6400, fax 020 7242 4221)

BATTERSBY, Prof Sir Alan Rushton; kt (1992); s of William Battersby (d 1967), and Hilda, *née* Rushton (d 1972); *b* 4 March 1925; *Educ* Leigh GS, Univ of Manchester (BSc, MSc), Univ of St Andrews (PhD), Univ of Bristol (DSc), Univ of Cambridge (ScD); *m* 18 June 1949, Margaret Ruth (d 1997), da of Thomas Hart (d 1965); 2 s (Martin b 29 July 1953, Stephen b 24 April 1956); *Career* asst lectr in chemistry Univ of St Andrews 1948–53, Cwlth Fund fell at Rockefeller Inst NY 1950–51 and Univ of Illinois 1951–52, lectr in chemistry Univ of Bristol 1954–62; second chair of organic chemistry Univ of Liverpool 1962, elected to chair of organic chemistry Univ of Cambridge 1969–92 (elected to 1702 chair 1988), hon fell St Catharine's Coll Cambridge; memb Cncl Royal Soc 1973–75, pres Bürgenstock Conf 1976, chm Exec Cncl Novartis Fndn 1983–90 (tstee 1992–2000); Chemical Soc: Corday-Morgan Medal 1959, Tilden Medal and lectr 1963, Hugo Müller Medal and lectr 1972, Flintoff Medal 1975, Award in Natural Product Chemistry 1978, Longstaff Medal 1984, Robert Robinson lectr and Medal 1986; Royal Soc: Paul Karrer Medal and lectr Zürich Univ 1977, Davy Medal 1977, Royal Medal 1984, Copley Medal 2000; Roger Adams Award in Organic Chemistry ACS 1983, Havinga Medal Holland 1984, Antoni Feltrinelli Int Prize for Chemistry Rome 1986, Varro Tyler lectr and Award Purdue 1987, Adolf Windaus Medal Göttingen 1987, Wolf Prize Israel 1989, Arun Guthikonda Meml Award Univ of Columbia 1991, August Wilhelm von Hofmann Meml Medal Gesellschaft Deutscher Chemiker 1992, Tetrahedron Prize 1995, Hans-Herloff Inhoffen Medal Braunschweig Germany 1997, Robert A Welch Award for Chemistry 2000, Robert B Woodward Award for Porphyrin Chemistry 2004; Hon DSc: Rockefeller Univ NY 1977, Univ of Sheffield 1986, Heriot-Watt Univ 1987, Univ of Bristol 1994, Univ of Liverpool 1996; Hon LLD Univ of St Andrews 1977; FRS 1966; memb: Deutsche Akademie der Naturforscher Leopoldina (Germany) 1967, Soc Royal de Chimie (Belgium) 1987; hon memb American Acad of Arts and Sci (USA) 1988, foreign fell Nat Acad of Scis India 1990, memb Academia Europaea 1990, foreign fell Indian Nat Sci Acad 1993; *Recreations* music, camping, hiking, sailing, gardening, fly fishing; *Style*— Prof Sir Alan Battersby, FRS; ✉ 20 Barrow Road, Cambridge CB2 8AS (tel 01223 363799); University Chemical Laboratory, Lensfield Road, Cambridge CB2 1EW (tel 01223 336400, fax 01223 336362)

BATTIE, David Anthony; s of Donald Charles Battie (d 1988), and Peggy Joan Battie; *b* 22 October 1942; *Educ* King James I Sch; *m* 1 Jan 1972, Sarah, da of Philip James Francis (d 1987); 2 da (Henrietta Victoria b 17 Aug 1977, Eleanor Harriet b 4 June 1980); *Career* dir Sotheby's 1976–99; expert BBC TV Antiques Roadshow 1977–, lectures, writes and broadcasts widely; FRSA; *Books* Price Guide to 19th Century British Pottery (1975), Sotheby's Encyclopedia of Porcelain (ed, 1990), Sotheby's Encyclopedia of Glass (co-ed, 1991), Readers' Digest Treasures in Your Home (conslt ed, 1992), Understanding 19th Century British Porcelain (1994); *Recreations* book binding; *Style*— David Battie, Esq; ✉ tel 01342 715244, e-mail battie@wildgoose.fsbusiness.co.uk

BATTISCOMBE, Christopher Charles Richard; CMG (1992), JP (2001); s of Lt-Col Christopher Robert Battiscombe (d 1989), and Karin Sigrid, *née* Timberg (d 1983); *b* 27 April 1940; *Educ* Wellington, New Coll Oxford (BA); *m* 1972, Brigid Melita Theresa, da of Peter Northcote Lunn; 1 da (Antonia b 1975), 1 s (Max b 1977); *Career* HM Dip Serv: MECAS 1963, second sec FO (later FCO) 1963, third sec Kuwait 1965, asst private sec to Chllr of Duchy of Lancaster 1969, UK delg OECD Paris 1971, first sec UK mission to UN New York 1974, asst head Eastern Euro and Soviet Dept FCO 1978, cnsllr (commercial) Cairo 1981, cnsllr (commercial) Paris 1984, cnsllr FCO 1986–90, ambass to Algeria 1990–94, asst under sec (public depts) FCO 1994–97, ambass to Jordan 1997–2000; DG Soc of London Art Dealers 2001–, sec Br Art Market Fedn 2001–; chm Anglo Jordanian Soc 2001–; *Recreations* golf, tennis, skiing; *Clubs* Kandahar, Temple; *Style*— Christopher Battiscombe, Esq, CMG

BATTLE, Rt Hon John Dominic; PC (2002), MP; s of John Battle, and Audrey, *née* Rathbone (d 1982); *b* 26 April 1951; *Educ* Upholland Coll, Univ of Leeds (BA); *m* 12 April 1977, Mary Geraldine, da of Jerry Meenan; 1 s (Joseph b 1978), 2 da (Anna b 1981, Clare b 1982); *Career* trg for RC priesthood 1969–73, res Univ of Leeds 1973–79, res offr to Derek Enright MEP 1979–83, nat co-ordinator Church Action on Poverty 1983–87, MP (Lab) Leeds W 1987–; House of Commons: shadow min of housing 1992–94, shadow min of sci and technol 1994–95, shadow energy min 1995–97, min of state (industry, energy, sci and technol) DTI 1997–99, min of state FCO 1999–2001, memb Int Devpt Select Ctee 2001–; cncllr Leeds CC 1980–87 (chm Housing Ctee 1983–85); *Recreations* walking, poetry; *Style*— The Rt Hon John Battle, MP; ✉ House of Commons, London SW1A 0AA (tel 020 7219 4201, e-mail battlej@parliament.uk)

BATTY, Andrew James; s of Francis Leslie Batty (d 1971), and Pamela, *née* Ball (d 2005); *b* 12 April 1956; *Educ* Roundhay GS, Jacob Kramer Coll Leeds; *m* 24 Oct 1992, Rachel Jane, *née* Sharman; 2 s (James Mark b 1995, Joseph Andrew b 1999), 1 da (Kathryn Ellen b 1997); *Career* copywriter Charles Walls Advertising 1975–79, creative dir Severn Advertising 1979–81, dir MCS Robertson Scott Yorks 1981–82, chm and md Creative Marketing Services 1982–; chm: Publicity Assoc of Bradford, Yorks Advertising and Communications Training, Nat CAM Graduates Assoc; MSIAD 1978, MIMgt 1984, FInstSMM 1987, Registered Marketer 1996, Chartered Marketer 1998, FCIM 1998 (MInstM 1981, chm Leeds Branch), MInstD 1999, FIPA 2001, FCAM 2003 (MCAM 1979), FIDM 2004 (MIDM 1996); *Publications* East Keswick Millennium Book (compiler, 2000); *Recreations* voluntary activities in advertising training, local history, cncllr East Keswick PC; *Style*— Andrew Batty, Esq; ✉ Larks Rise, Keswick Grange, East Keswick, West Yorkshire LS17 9BX (tel 01937 574692); Creative Marketing Services, Hollinthorpe Hall, Swillington Lane, Leeds LS26 8BZ (tel 0870 381 6222, fax 0870 381 6333, e-mail andrew.batty@cmsadvertising.co.uk)

BATTY, Prof (John) Michael; CBE (2004); s of Jack Batty (d 1970), of Cheltenham, Glos, and Nell, *née* Marsden (d 1995); *b* 11 January 1945; *Educ* Quarry Bank HS Liverpool, Univ of Manchester (BA, Clifford Holliday Prize), Univ of Wales (PhD); *m* 4 Jan 1969, Susan Elizabeth, da of Horace Howell; 1 s (Daniel Jack b 28 Sept 1976); *Career* asst lectr Dept of Town and Country Planning Univ of Manchester 1966–69, res asst Urban Systems Res Unit Dept of Geography Univ of Reading 1969–72, lectr in geography Univ of Reading 1972–74 and 1975–76 (reader 1976–79), asst prof (visiting) Dept of Civil Engrg Univ of Waterloo Ontario 1974–75 (adjunct prof of civil engrg 1976, 1977 and 1978);

Univ of Wales Cardiff: prof of city and regnl planning 1979–90, dean Sch of Environmental Design 1983–86, head of dept 1985–89; dir Nat Center for Geographic Information and Analysis (NCGIA) and prof of geography SUNY Buffalo 1990–95, dir Centre for Advanced Spatial Analysis (CASA) and prof of spatial analysis and planning UCL 1995–2004, Bartlett prof of planning UCL 2004–; chm: Planning Ctee SSRC 1980–82, ESRC-JISc Census Advsy Gp 2001–; vice-chm Environment and Planning Ctee ESRC 1982–84; memb: Br Section Regnl Sci Assoc 1975–79 (chm 1979–81), Res Bd RTPI 1979–85, Res Bd SSRC 1980–82, Jt Tport Ctee SERC and ESRC 1982–85, S Wales Branch Exec Ctee RTPI 1986–90, Computer Bd Univs and Res Cncls 1988–90, Ctee on Scientific Computing NERC 1988–90, Policy Bd SW Univs Regnl Computing Centre (SWURCC) 1988–90, Scientific Computing Advsy Panel SERC 1989–90, Int Advsy Ctee Nat Lab of Resources and Environmental Info Systems Chinese Acad of Sciences Beijing 1992–, Advsy Panel on Public Sector Information 2003–; Wesley Dougill Prize 1992, Back Award RGS 1999; AcSS 2001; FRSA 1982, FRTPI 1983 (MRTPI 1971), FCLIT 1990 (MCLIT 1984), FBA 2001; *Books* Urban Modelling (1976), Microcomputer Graphics (1987), Fractal Cities (1994), Cities and Complexity (2005); *Recreations* Indian Food, discovering America, China, reading, travel; *Style—* Prof Michael Batty, CBE; ✉ 9 White Horse House, 1 Little Britain, London EC1A 7BX (tel 020 7600 8186); University College London, Centre for Advanced Spatial Analysis, 1–19 Torrington Place, London WC1E 6BT (tel 020 7679 1781, fax 020 7813 2843, e-mail m.batty@ucl.ac.uk)

BATTY, His Hon Judge Paul Daniel; QC (1995); s of Vincent Batty (d 1973), of Seaham Harbour, and Catherine, *née* Kane; *b* 13 June 1953; *Educ* St Aidan's GS, Univ of Newcastle upon Tyne (LLB); *m* 30 Sept 1986, Angela Jane; 1 da (Sarah Georgina b 2 Nov 1987); *Career* called to the Bar Lincoln's Inn 1974 (bencher 2003); mess jr Newcastle Bar 1980–83, jr North Eastern Circuit 1984, recorder of the Crown Court 1994–2003 (asst recorder 1989–94), circuit judge (Northern Circuit) 2003–; *Recreations* swimming, boating, angling; *Clubs* Tynedale Rugby; *Style—* His Hon Judge Batty, QC; ✉ Carlisle Crown Court, Earl Street, Carlisle, Cumbria CA1 1DJ (tel 01228 520619)

BATTY, Peter Wright; s of Ernest Faulkner Batty (d 1986), of Surrey, and Gladys Victoria, *née* Wright (d 1979); *b* 18 June 1931; *Educ* Bede GS Sunderland, The Queen's Coll Oxford (MA); *m* 1959, Anne Elizabeth (d 2000), da of Edmund Stringer, of Devon; 2 s (David, Richard), 1 da (Charlotte); *Career* feature writer Financial Times 1954–56, freelance journalist USA 1956–58, prodr BBC TV 1958–64, memb original Tonight team (ed 1963–64); other BBC prodns incl: The Quiet Revolution, The Big Freeze, The Katanga Affair, Sons of the Navvy Man; exec prodr and assoc head of Factual Programming ATV 1964–68; prodns include: The Fall and Rise of the House of Krupp (Grand Prix for Documentary Venice Film Festival 1965, Silver Dove Leipzig Film Festival 1965), The Road to Suez, The Suez Affair, Vietnam Fly-in, Battle for the Desert; chief exec Peter Batty Productions 1970–; programmes directed, produced and scripted for BBC TV, ITV and Channel 4 incl: The Plutocrats, The Aristocrats, Battle for Cassino, Battle for the Bulge, Birth of the Bomb, Farouk Last of the Pharaohs, Operation Barbarossa, Superspy, Spy Extraordinary, Sunderland's Pride and Passion, A Rothschild and his Red Gold, Search for the Super, The World of Television, Battle for Warsaw, The Story of Wine, The Rise and Rise of Laura Ashley, The Gospel According to St Michael, Battle for Dien Bien Phu, Nuclear Nightmares, A Turn Up In a Million, Il Poverello, Swindle!, The Algerian War, Fonteyn and Nureyev: The Perfect Partnership, The Divided Union, A Time for Remembrance, Swastika Over British Soil; contrib 6 episodes (incl pilot prog) to The World at War series; life memb Kingston Soc; *Books* The House of Krupp (1966), The Divided Union (1987), La Guerre d'Algerie (1989); *Recreations* walking, reading, listening to music; *Clubs* Garrick; *Style—* Peter Batty, Esq; ✉ Claremont House, Renfrew Road, Kingston upon Thames, Surrey KT2 7NT (tel 020 8942 6304, e-mail peter@wbatty.freeserve.co.uk)

BATTY, Dr Vincent Bernard; s of Henry Joseph Batty, of London, and Ena Violet, *née* Cavenagh; *b* 8 June 1951; *Educ* St Aloysius Coll Highgate, Middx Hosp Med Sch (BSc, MB BS, DMRD, MSc, FRCR); *m* 21 Feb 1987, Dr Wilma Westensee, da of Rolf Westensee, of Grahamstown, South Africa; 1 s (Adam b 1980), 2 da (Louise b 1980, Anke b 1989); *Career* house physician Watford Gen Hosp 1977, house and casualty surgn Middx Hosp 1978, GP Hythe Hants 1979, conslt in radiology and nuclear med Southampton Gen Hosp 1984– (registrar in radiology 1979, sr registrar in radiology 1982), sr registrar in ultrasound and nuclear med Royal Marsden Hosp 1984, currently dir of nuclear med Southampton Univ Hosps; memb: Br Inst of Radiology, Br Nuclear Med Soc, Br Soc of Head and Neck Radiology, European Assoc of Musculo-Skeletal Radiology; memb Worshipful Soc of Apothecaries; FRCR; *Publications* Nuclear Medicine In Oncology (ed, 1986); author of papers on general and musculo-skeletal radiology and on nuclear med; *Recreations* general aviation, gardening, music, photography; *Style—* Dr Vincent Batty; ✉ Denny Cottage, Denny Lodge, Lyndhurst, Hampshire SO43 7FZ; Department of Nuclear Medicine, Southampton General Hospital, Tremona Road, Southampton SO16 6YD (tel 023 8079 6201, fax 023 8079 6927, e-mail vince.batty@suht.swest.nhs.uk)

BATY, Robert John (Bob); OBE (2002); s of Robert George Baty (d 1986), and Sarah, *née* Hall; *b* 1 June 1944, Timperley, Cheshire; *Educ* Calday Grange GS West Kirby Wirral, Liverpool Coll of Building; *m* Oct 1975, Patricia, *née* Fagan; 2 da (Claire Louise, Philippa Jane); *Career* NW Water: princ/resident engr 1974–83, dist mangr 1983–85, regnl mangr 1985–88; SW Water: engrg and scientific dir 1988–96, chief exec 1996–2006; non-exec dir Royal Devon & Exeter NHS Fndn Tst; Herbert Lapworth Medal IWEM 1981, Gold Medal for Environmental Work ICE 1995; CEng 1970, FCIWEM 1981, ACIArb 1981, FIWO 1990, CCMI 1990, FICE 1992, FREng 2000; *Recreations* sport (especially rugby), recreational flying, car restoration; *Style—* Bob Baty, Esq, OBE; ✉ Nanparah Lodge, Higher Broad Oak Road, West Hill, Ottery St Mary, Devon EX11 1XJ (tel and fax 01404 812327, e-mail rjbaty@tiscali.co.uk)

BAUCKHAM, Prof Richard John; s of John Robert Bauckham (d 1980), and Stephania Lilian, *née* Wells (d 1998); *b* 22 September 1946; *Educ* Enfield GS, Clare Coll Cambridge (MA, PhD); *Career* fell St John's Coll Cambridge 1972–75, lectr in theology Univ of Leeds 1976–77, reader in the history of Christian thought Univ of Manchester 1987–92 (lectr 1977–87), prof of New Testament studies St Mary's Coll Univ of St Andrews 1992–2007, Bishop Wardlaw prof Univ of St Andrews 2000–07; memb: Tyndale Fellowship for Biblical and Theological Research 1974, Soc for New Testament Studies 1979 (memb Ctee 1996–2002), Soc for the Study of Theology 1980, Assoc pour l'Etude de la Litterature Apocryphe Chrétienne 1986; gen ed Society of New Testament Studies Monograph Series 1996–2002, also author of numerous articles in books and theological jls; FBA 1998, FRSE 2002; *Books* Tudor Apocalypse: Sixteenth-century apocalypticism, millenarianism and the English Reformation (1978), Jude, 2 Peter (1983), Moltmann: Messianic Theology in the Making (1987), The Bible in Politics: How to read the Bible politically (1989), Word Biblical Themes: Jude, 2 Peter (1990), Jude and the Relatives of Jesus in the Early Church (1990), The Theology of the Book of Revelation (1993), The Climax of Prophecy: Studies on the Book of Revelation (1993), The Theology of Jürgen Moltmann (1995), The Fate of the Dead: Studies on the Jewish and Christian Apocalypses (1998), God Crucified: Monotheism and Christology in the New Testament (1998), James: Wisdom of James, Disciple of Jesus the Sage (1999), Hope Against Hope: Christian Eschatology in Contemporary Context (with Trevor Hart, 1999), Gospel Women (2002), God and the Crisis of Freedom, Bible and Mission (2003), Jesus and the Eyewitnesses (2006); *Recreations* gardening, walking, novels, poetry; *Style—* Prof Richard Bauckham, FBA, FRSE; ✉ St Mary's College, University of St Andrews, St Andrews, Fife KY16 9JU (tel 01334 462830, fax 01334 462852, e-mail rjb@st-andrews.ac.uk)

BAUDINO, Dr Catherine Anne; da of Jean Rene Baudino, and Anne-Marie, *née* Camus; *b* 26 October 1952; *Educ* Lycee Français de Londres, UCL (BA, PhD); *m* May 1994, Alastair Ian Alexander Garrow; *Career* dir Institutional Investor 1980–87; chief exec: Maxwell Satellite Communications Ltd 1987–89, Baudino Enterprises Ltd 1989–; non-exec dir VideoLink Business Communications Ltd 1992–94; cncllr to the French C of C 1991–95, pres The Franco-Br Construction Indust Gp 1992–94, business devpt dir The NASDAQ Stock Market 1994–95; md: BRIDGE Telecom Ltd 1999–2002, ID-360 Ltd 2002–; *Recreations* opera, theatre, wine and food; *Style—* Dr Catherine A Baudino; ✉ cab@baudino.net

BAUER, Eran Nicodemus; s of Dr Jacob Bauer (d 1961), and Gitta, *née* Gaal; *b* 25 February 1954; *Educ* King's GS Grantham; *m* 27 Aug 1994 (m dis 2001), Penelope Jane, da of Terence Griffiths, of Pudsey, W Yorks; 2 da (Florence Eloise and Charlotte Amelia (twins) b 10 April 1995), 1 s (Max Jacob b 14 Nov 1996); *Career* Parachute Regt 16 Ind Co (V) 1973–78; dir: Universal Cleaning Services (historic bldgs restoration conslt), Civil Defence Supply 1980–; chm PGI Br Standards Ctee PH/3/12 Police Protective Equipment; co-designer, patentee and inventor of military and police special ops equipment, patented first interlocking riot shield, introduced new side-handled batons and trg to UK police, chemical warfare civil def advsr to Saudi Arabian Govt during Gulf War, contrib pubns on police technol, security conslt to UK Govt depts, tech advsr to TV and films; dir Business Link Lincolnshire and Rutland 2001–, dir Mercian Matrix Enterprises 2001–; National DTI & ISI Interforum e-Commerce Award 1999; chm Weirfield Wildlife Hosp 2000–, memb RUSI for Def Studies, MRAeS; Chevalier Knight Order of the Temple of Jerusalem Grand Priory of Knights Templar in England and Wales 2005 (preceptor East of England 2006–, Knight Commander 2007); *Recreations* architecture, architectural drawing and rendering, flying, sports sponsorship, writing; *Clubs* Special Forces; *Style—* Eran Bauer, Esq; ✉ Civil Defence Supply, Ashby Hall, Ashby de la Launde, Lincoln LN4 3JG (e-mail bauer@civil-defence.org)

BAUER, Willy Benedikt (né Gegen-Bauer); s of Willy Gegen-Bauer (d 1990), of Stuttgart, Germany, and Maria, Elizabeth, *née* Schuhbauer (d 1965); *b* 8 November 1937; *Educ* GS and HS Biberachy, Hotel Sch Heidelburg (Dip); *Career* hotelier; mgmnt trg Hotel Rad Biberach Germany 1957–60; hotel trg: Lausanne and Geneva Switzerland 1961–62, Grand Hotel Eastbourne 1962–63, Grand Metropolitan Hotel London 1963–65; banqueting mgmnt trg Hilton International London 1965; various mgmnt positions Trust Houses 1965–69; gen mangr Trust House Forte: Red Lion Colchester 1969–71, Cairn Hotel Harrogate 1971–72, St George's Hotel Liverpool 1972–75, Hyde Park Hotel 1975–80; exec dir and gen mangr Grosvenor House Park Lane 1980–81, gen mangr The Savoy London 1982–83, md The Savoy Management Ltd (The Savoy, The Lygon Arms, Wiltons, St Quintous Restaurants) 1983–89, chief exec The Wentworth Group 1989–; dir: The Westbury Hotels (London and NY), Molton Brown; chm A B Hotels; memb The Walpole Ctee; European Hotelier of the Year 1985, Hotel of the Year Award 1988; Freeman City of London 1987; memb: Master Innholders 1987, Chaîne des Rotisseurs, Reunion des Gastronomes, Savoy Gastronomes (pres 2000), Univ of Surrey Food & Wine Soc 1986, RAGB 1990, IoD; hon memb Acad of Culinary Arts; FHCIMA 1987, FRSA 1993; *Recreations* music, theatre, sport, gardening, architecture, design, antiques; *Clubs* The Duke's 100–1990, Wentworth, Home House, RAC, Groucho (hon memb); *Style—* Willy B G Bauer, Esq, FHCIMA; ✉ A B Hotels, 50–60 Great Cumberland Place, London W1H 8DD

BAUGHAN, Bryan Frederick William; s of Frederick William Baughan, and Ethel Dorothy Janet, *née* Wilson; *b* 1 January 1941; *Educ* Shooters Hill GS London, City of London Coll (Stock Exchange Dip); *m* 3 Dec 1966, Josephine Mary, da of Capt Dennis Coppock; 1 da (Kathryn Mary b 27 Oct 1973), 1 s (Michael 12 Nov 1977); *Career* schoolmaster 1962–66; Govett Sons & Co (merged to become Hoare Govett Ltd (Stockbrokers) 1970): joined 1966, ptnr 1977, md Hoare Govett Financial Servs Gp Ltd 1982–88, dep chm until 1988; fndr and md City Merchants Investment Mgmnt Ltd (renamed Invesco Private Portfolio Mgmnt Ltd, now Atlantic Wealth Mgmnt Ltd) 1988–2004, global ptnr Amvescap plc 1994–2004, sr advsr to chief exec Singer & Friedlander Investment Mgmnt Ltd 2004–06, investment dir Ingenious Asset Mgmnt 2007–; chm of govrs Sutton Valence Sch, govr Emanuel Sch London, tstee United Westminster Schs Fndn; memb Gen Synod C of E 1980–85; pres Rotary Club Maidstone Riverside 1997–98; Freeman City of London; Liveryman: Worshipful Co of Cooks, Guild of Educators; FSI; *Recreations* good food, wine and conversation, golf, cricket, rugby football, opera, gardens; *Clubs* Naval and Military (In and Out), City of London, MCC; *Style—* Bryan Baughan, Esq; ✉ Ingenious Asset Management, 15 Golden Square, London W1F 9JG

BAUGHAN, Julian James; QC (1990); s of Prof Edward Christopher Baughan, CBE (d 1995), and Jacqueline Baughan (d 1986); bro of Michael C Baughan, *qv*; *b* 8 February 1944; *Educ* Eton, Balliol Coll Oxford (scholar, BA); *Career* called to the Bar Inner Temple 1967 (Profumo scholar, Philip Teichman scholar, maj scholar); prosecuting counsel DTI 1983–90, recorder of the Crown Court 1985–; *Style—* Julian Baughan, Esq, QC; ✉ 13 Kings Bench Walk, Temple, London EC4Y 7EN (tel 020 7353 7204)

BAUGHAN, Michael Christopher; s of Prof Edward Christopher Baughan, CBE (d 1995), and Jacqueline Fors, *née* Hodge (d 1986); bro of Julian Baughan, QC, *qv*; *b* 25 April 1942; *Educ* Westminster; *m* 1975, Moira Elizabeth, da of Percy Reginald Levy, MBE; 2 s (James b 1977, Nicholas b 1979); *Career* N M Rothschild & Sons 1959–66; Lazard Brothers & Co Ltd: joined 1966, dir 1979–86, md 1986–99, dir 2000–02, sr advsr 2002–03; non-exec dir Scapa Group plc 1994–2006; memb: Bd of Govrs Westminster Sch 1980–, Slrs Disciplinary Tbnl 1990–; *Clubs* Brooks's, Garrick; *Style—* Michael C Baughan, Esq

BAUM, Louis Clarence; s of Rudolf Josef Baum (d 1984), and Heather, *née* Shulman; *b* 15 March 1948; *Educ* SA Coll Sch, Univ of Cape Town (BA); *m* 1971 (m dis 1982), Stephanie, *née* Goodman; 1 s (Simon b 1979); *Career* author of children's books; journalist Cape Times 1969–74; The Bookseller: journalist 1976–79, ed 1980–99, ed rights report 1999–; *Books* JuJu and the Pirate (1983), I Want to see the Moon (1984), After Dark (1984), Are We Nearly There? (1986), Joey's Coming Home Today (1989), Tea with Bea (2006); *Recreations* writing; *Clubs* The Groucho (dir 1984–98); *Style—* Louis Baum, Esq

BAUM, Prof Michael; s of Isidor Baum (d 1980), and Mary, *née* Rosenberg (d 1974); *b* 31 May 1937; *Educ* George Dixon's GS Birmingham, Univ of Birmingham Med Sch (MB ChB, ChM); *m* 12 Sept 1965, Judith, da of Reuben Marcus, of Newcastle upon Tyne; 1 s (Richard b 20 Sept 1966), 2 da (Katie b 19 April 1969, Suzanne b 22 March 1973); *Career* lectr in surgery King's Coll London 1969–72, sr lectr in surgery (later reader) Welsh Nat Sch of Med 1972–79, prof of surgery King's Coll Sch of Med and Dentistry 1980–90, hon dir Cancer Res Campaign Clinical Trials Centre 1980–97, prof of surgery Inst of Cancer Res Royal Marsden Hosp 1990–95, visiting prof UCL 1995–97, prof of surgery UCL 1997–2000, emeritus prof of surgery and visiting prof Med Humanities 2000–; ed-in-chief Int Jl of Surgery 2004–; memb: UK Coordinating Ctee for Cancer Res 1989–2000 (past chm Breast Cancer Sub Ctee), Advsy Ctee on Breast Cancer Screening Dept of Health 1987–95, Int Advsy Bd of the Lancet; chm SE Thames Regnl Cancer Orgn 1988–90, vice-pres Euro Society of Mastology 1991–97, pres Br Oncological Assoc 1996–98, pres Euro Breast Cancer Conf 2002, chm Med Advsy Ctee Assoc Victims of Med Accidents (AVMA) 2001–05; past chm: Br Breast Gp, Higher Degrees Ctee Univ of London (vice-chm Bd of Studies in Surgery), Inst of Med Humanities; Skinner Medal Royal Coll of Radiologists 1990; Hon Dr of Med Univ of Gothenburg 1986; Int Master Surgn Int

Coll of Surgns 1994; FRCS 1965, FRSA 1998, Hon FRCR 1998; *Books* Breast Cancer The Facts (1984, 3 edn 1994), Fast Facts Breast Cancer (3 edn 2005); *Recreations* painting, sculpture, theatre, literature, philosophy, food, wine, walking; *Clubs* RSM, Athenaeum; *Style*— Prof Michael Baum; ✉ The Portland Hospital, Great Portland Street, London W1W 5QN (tel 020 7390 8447, fax 020 7390 8448, e-mail michael@mbaum.freeserve.co.uk)

BAUMAN, Irena; da of Zygmunt Bauman, and Janina, *née* Levinson; *b* 19 December 1955; *Educ* Poland, Israel, Lawnswood HS Leeds, Univ of Liverpool Sch of Architecture (BA, BArch); *m* 30 April 1983, Maurice Patrick Lyons; 1 s (Alexander b 26 July 1985), 1 da (Hannah b 21 March 1989); *Career* architect; estab: Bauman Pickles Assocs 1989, Bauman Lyons Architects 1992; projects incl: regeneration of the South Promenade Bridlington (commendation Nat Civic Tst Awards 1999, RIBA Award for Architecture 2000, RICS Pro Yorks Award for Tourism 2001), office conversion 31 The Calls Leeds (Leeds Architecture Award 1999), conversion of agriculture barns for Yorkshire Sculpture Park, Host Media Centre Leeds (Leeds Architecture Commendation 2001, commendation Civic Tst 2002, shortlisted RIBA Award 2002), bus shelters Bradford (shortlisted White Rose Award 2002, shortlisted Int Transport Award 2002, BBDA Award 2002, shortlisted RIBA Award 2003); cmmr CABE, advsr Architecture and Built Environment Panel Arts Cncl, memb Leeds Architecture and Design Initiative; delivers lectures throughout UK, external examiner Sheffield Sch of Architecture 2002–; featured in several books and jls on contemporary Br architecture; Corus Colourcoat Sustainable Devpt Award 2002, runner-up Eurocity Awards 2002, winner Designs on Democracy 2003; RIBA 1981, ARB 1981; *Exhibitions* incl: Imminent & Eminent Practices (Site Gallery Leeds) 1997, Interventions (Site Gallery Leeds) 1998, Quality in Urban Spaces (Design Centre Barnsley) 1999, New Architects 2 (Architecture Fndn) 2001, Designs on Democracy (RIBA Gallery) 2003, Do IT Better (RIBA Gallery) 2003; *Style*— Ms Irena Bauman; ✉ Bauman Lyons Architects Ltd, Regent House, 15 Hawthorn Road, Leeds, West Yorkshire LS7 4PH (tel 0113 294 4200, fax 0113 294 1234, e-mail irena@baumanlyons.co.uk)

BAUME, Jonathan Edward; s of George Frederick Baume (d 1998), and Mary Louisa, *née* Hardwick (d 1990); *b* 14 July 1953; *Educ* Queen Elizabeth GS Wakefield, Keble Coll Oxford (MA); *Career* with Oxfordshire CC 1974–77, Dept of Employment Gp 1977–87, TUC 1987–89 (memb Gen Cncl 2001–); FDA (formerly Assoc of First Division Civil Servants): asst gen sec 1989–94, dep gen sec 1994–97, gen sec 1997–; memb: Ministerial Advsy Gp on Openness in the Public Sector 1998–99, Ministerial Advsy Gp on Implementation of the Freedom of Information Act 2001–, Age Advsy Gp DTI 2004–; memb: CPRE, Nat Tst; FRSA; *Recreations* yoga, jazz, world music, rambling; *Clubs* Athenaeum; *Style*— Jonathan Baume, Esq; ✉ FDA, 8 Leake Street, London SE1 7NN (tel 020 7401 5555, fax 020 7401 5550, e-mail jonathan@fda.org.uk)

BAVIDGE, Elizabeth Mary (Liz); OBE (1997), JP (1979); da of Walter Robert Ashton (d 1972), and Mary Newton, *née* Donaldson (d 1986); *b* 24 August 1945; *Educ* Carlisle and Co HS for Girls, Univ of Newcastle upon Tyne (BA); *m* 1972, Nigel Patrick Bavidge, s of Dr Kenneth George Scott Bavidge (d 1972); 2 c (Gabrielle Mary b 1972, Fintan Nicholas Ashton b 1975); *Career* graduate trainee Shell-Mex and BP Ltd 1967–72, pt/t lectr in English language and literature Percival Whitley Coll 1980–87, asst princ Airedale and Wharfedale Coll Leeds 1992 (lectr in flexible learning opportunities 1987–92); nat pres Nat Cncl of Women 1990–92 (nat vice-pres 1988–90), co-chair Women's Nat Cmmn 1995–97, cmmr Cmmn on Women and the Criminal Justice System 2003–; dir: EM Associates (orgn devpt conslts), Women Returners' Network 1998–99; chair: Yorks and The Humber Fair Play Consortium 2002–, Fair Play Partnership, Yorkshire Youth and Music; memb Bd Together Women project Home Office 2005–; Hon Freeman Borough of Calderdale 2000; FRSA (memb Working Gp on Early Educn); *Books* Let's Talk to God (1980); *Recreations* playing the piano, making bread, speaking French, eating; *Style*— Mrs Liz Bavidge, OBE; ✉ 22 Savile Park, Halifax, West Yorkshire HX1 3EW (tel 01422 353955, fax 01422 330586, e-mail lizbavidge@aol.com)

BAWDEN, Nina Mary (Mrs Austen Kark); CBE (1995); da of Cdr Charles Mabey (d 1976), and Ellaline Ursula May, *née* Cushing (d 1986); *b* 19 January 1925; *Educ* Ilford County HS for Girls, Somerville Coll Oxford (MA); *m* 1 Oct 1946 (m dis 1954), Henry Walton Bawden, s of Victor Bawden; 2 s (Robert Humphrey Felix b 1951, Nicholas Charles b 1948 d 1982); m 2, 5 Aug 1954, Austen Steven Kark (d 2002), s of Maj Norman Benjamin Kark; 1 da (Perdita Emily Helena b 1957); *Career* novelist; pres Soc of Women Writers & Journalists; JP Surrey 1969–76; memb: Video Appeals Ctee, PEN, Soc of Authors; FRSL, hon fell Somerville Coll Oxford; *Books* Devil by the Sea (1955), Just Like a Lady (1960), In Honour Bound (1961), Tortoise by Candlelight (1963), Under the Skin (1964), A Little Love, A Little Learning (1965), A Woman of My Age (1967), The Grain of Truth (1969), The Birds on the Trees (1970), Anna Apparent (1972), George Beneath a Paper Moon (1974), Afternoon of a Good Woman (1976, Yorkshire Post Novel of the Year), Familiar Passions (1979), Walking Naked (1981), The Ice House (1983), Circles of Deceit (1987, shortlisted Booker Prize 1987), Family Money (1991), A Nice Change (1997); *Autobiography* In My Own Time (1994), Dear Austen (2005); *For Children* The Secret Passage, On The Run, The Witch's Daughter, The White Horse Gang, A Handful of Thieves, Squib, Carrie's War (Phoenix Award 1994), The Peppermint Pig (Guardian Prize for Children's Literature), The Finding, Keeping Henry, The Outside Child, Humbug (1992), The Real Plato Jones (1994, WH Short List - Mind Boggling Read, Young Telegraph Shortlist), Granny the Pag (shortlisted Carnegie Medal, 1996), Off the Road (1998), Ruffian on the Stair (2001), Dear Austen (2005); *Recreations* food, films, theatre, travel, politics, garden croquet; *Clubs* Groucho, Oriental; *Style*— Miss Nina Bawden, CBE, FRSL; ✉ 22 Noel Road, London N1 8HA (tel 020 7226 2839); 19 Kapodistriou, Nauplion, Greece (tel 00 30 7520 24771)

BAWTREE, David Kenneth; CB (1993), DL (Hampshire 1997); s of Kenneth Alfred Bawtree (d 1948), and Dorothy Constance Allen (d 1970); *b* 1 October 1937; *Educ* Christ's Hosp, Royal Naval Engrg Coll (BSc(Eng)); *m* 1961, Ann Cummins; 1 da (b 1963), 1 s (b 1968); *Career* RN 1955–93; served HM Ships Maidstone, Jutland, Diamond, Defender, Rothsay, Bristol and also MOD 1965–76; Staff: C-in-C Fleet 1979, of DG Weapons 1981; Dep Dir Naval Analysis 1983, RCDS 1985, Dep Dir Op Requirements (Navy) 1986, Dir Naval Engrg Trg 1987, FO Portsmouth 1990–93, ret as Rear Adm 1993; civil emergencies advsr Home Office 1993–97 (advsr 1998–), chm Portsmouth Hosps NHS Tst 1996–2001 (dir Portsmouth Healthcare NHS Tst 1993–96); chm: St Mary's Music Fndn 1990–2001 (pres 2001–), Hampshire Fndn for Young Musicians 1994–2002, Flagship Portsmouth 2000–05, Future Sailing Ship Project for the 21st Century (FSP21) 2001–; dir Visor Consultants 1998–, project mangr (Marine Div) MMI Research 2001–07; ed advsr Hampshire Life Magazine 1998–2002; conslt to Bishop of London 1998–2007; pres Portsmouth Model Boats Display Team 1993–; former chm Portsmouth News Snowball Appeal; past pres: Royal Naval & Royal Albert Yacht Club, Portsmouth Naval Home Club, RN & RM Children's Home, Royal Naval Squash Racquets Assoc; past memb: Victory Technical Advsy Ctee, Mary Rose Tst, Portsmouth Naval Base Heritage Tst; tstee Royal Naval Museum, chm of tstees HMS Warrior 1860 1997–; govr Penhale Infant Sch 1991–2002, chm of govrs Portsmouth GS 1993–; almoner Christ's Hosp 1998–2003; Liveryman Worshipful Co of Engrs (Master 2007); CEng 1971, FIMechE 1985, FIEE 1985, FRSA 2006; *Recreations* fives (winner UK Masters 2003, 2004, 2005, 2006 and 2007), squash, organs and their music, making miniature furniture; *Style*— David Bawtree, Esq, CB, DL, CEng, FIEE, FIMechE, FRSA; ✉ 49 Grant Road, Portsmouth, Hampshire PO6 1DU (tel and fax 023 9237 3679, e-mail david@bawtree.org)

BAX, Andrew; *Educ* Tonbridge; *Career* md Radcliffe Medical Press Ltd 1987–; *Style*— Andrew Bax, Esq; ✉ Radcliffe Medical Press Ltd, 18 Marcham Road, Abingdon, Oxfordshire OX14 1AA (tel 01235 528820)

BAXANDALL, Prof Michael David Kighley; s of David Kighley Baxandall (d 1993), and Sarah Isobel Mary, *née* Thomas (d 1990); *b* 18 August 1933; *Educ* Manchester Grammar, Downing Coll Cambridge (MA), Univ of Pavia, Univ of Munich, Warburg Inst Univ of London (jr fell); *m* 1963, Katharina Dorothea, da of late Sir Francis Simon; 1 da (Sarah Lucy b 1963), 1 s (Thomas David Franz b 1968); *Career* asst keeper Dept of Architecture and Sculpture V&A 1961–65; Warburg Inst Univ of London: lectr in renaissance studies 1965–72, reader in history of the classical tradition 1973–80, prof of history of the classical tradition 1981–88; prof of history of art Univ of Calif Berkeley 1986–96; Slade prof of fine art Univ of Oxford 1974–75, A D White prof-at-large Cornell Univ 1982–88, fell Wissenschaftskolleg Berlin 1992–93; hon fell Warburg Inst Univ of London 1988, Aby M Warburg prize City of Hamburg 1988, fell MacArthur Fndn 1988–93; FAAAS 1990, FBA 1982; *Books* Giotto and the Orators (1971), Painting and Experience in Fifteenth-Century Italy (1972), The Limewood Sculptors of Renaissance Germany (1980), Patterns of Intention (1985), Tiepolo and the Pictorial Intelligence (with Svetlana Alpers, 1994), Shadows and Enlightenment (1995), Words for Pictures (2003); *Style*— Prof Michael Baxandall, FBA

BAXENDALE, Helen; *Career* actress; *Theatre* After Miss Julie (Donmar Warehouse) 2004; *Television* Cardiac Arrest 1994, Dangerfield 1994, In Suspicious Circumstances 1994, Friends 1998–99, An Unsuitable Job for a Woman 1998, Cold Feet 1998–2003, Tales From The Mad House 2000, Adrian Mole - The Cappuccino Years 2001; *Films* The Marshall 1993, Truth or Dare 1996, Crossing the Floor 1996, Bolse Vita 1996, Macbeth 1997, The Investigator 1997, Respect 1998, Ordinary Decent Criminal 1999, Dead by Monday 2001, Flyfishing 2002, Skagerrak 2003; *Style*— Ms Helen Baxendale

BAXENDALE, Presiley Lamorna; QC (1992); da of Geoffrey Arthur Baxendale, and Elizabeth, *née* Stevenson (decd); *b* 31 January 1951; *Educ* St Mary's Sch Wantage, St Anne's Coll Oxford (BA); *m* 1978, Richard Kieran Fitzgerald; 1 da (Felicity b 3 Dec 1981), 1 s (Charles b 9 April 1986); *Career* called to the Bar Lincoln's Inn 1974, jr counsel to Crown 1991; memb: ICSSTIS 1986–90, Cncl Justice 1994–2003 (vice-chm Exec Ctee 1994–96); counsel to Scott Inquiry 1992–95; memb Ct of Govrs LSE 1988–; memb Administrative Law Bar Assoc; *Clubs* CWIL; *Style*— Miss Presiley Baxendale, QC; ✉ Blackstone Chambers, Temple, London EC4Y 9BW

BAXI, Vibhaker Kishore; s of Kishore Jayantilal Baxi (d 1967), and Indira Kishore Baxi; *b* 25 December 1947; *Educ* Brooklands Co Tech Coll, Univ of Surrey Guildford (BSc), Brunel Univ (PGCE), Manchester Business Sch (MBA); *m* 12 Nov 1978, Hina, da of Indulal Vaikunthrai Vaidya (d 2007) and Devi Indulal Vaidya, of India; 1 da (Dr Mamta Baxi b 1982); *Career* fin inst account offr Citibank Dubai 1975–76, asst treas Citibank NA Dubai 1976–78; treas: Citibank NA Bahrain 1979–80, Chemical Bank Hong Kong 1981–85; head and md Money Market & Securities Trading Chemical Bank London 1985–89, sr risk mangr (interest rates) Hongkong & Shanghai Banking Corp London 1989–92, jt md James Capel Gilts Ltd (HSBC subsid) 1991–92, global mangr money markets HSBC/Midland Global Markets 1992–94; chm and md Navras Records Ltd 1992–, risk mgmnt conslt and investment mangr 1994–, trading advsr Emeritus Fund SA (formerly Opus Fund SA) 1995–, advsr/mangr Amas Hinduja AAA Bond Fund Banque Amas SA 1996–98; MInstD; *Recreations* travel, music, current affairs, reading, fine wines, sports, fine art; *Clubs* Middlesex CCC; *Style*— Vibhaker Baxi, Esq; ✉ 22 Sherwood Road, London NW4 1AD (tel 020 8203 2553, fax 020 8203 2542, e-mail vibhaker.baxi@navrasrecords.com)

BAXTER, Alain; s of Ian Baxter, and Sue, *née* Dickson; *b* 26 December 1973, Edinburgh; *Educ* Kingussie HS, Inverness Tech Coll; *Career* professional skier; memb Br Alpine Ski Team 1991–, Br jr champion, Scot and Br champion, ranked 11 in world in slalom 2000–01 (highest ever position for a Br alpine racer), World Cup fourth place 2000–01, winner Bronze medal slalom Winter Olympic Games Salt Lake City 2002 (first ever Briton to win a medal in alpine skiing, forced to return medal to IOC following positive drugs test but later cleared of wrong-doing), seven times Br slalom champion; Pery Medal Ski Club of GB 2002, third place Johnnie Walker Keep Walking Forward Awards 2002; *Recreations* ice hockey, tennis, golf, shinty, motorbiking; *Clubs* Perth Panthers (ice hockey), Kincraig Shinty, Cairngorm Ski; *Style*— Alain Baxter, Esq; ✉ website www.alainbaxter.co.uk

BAXTER, Canon Dr Christina Ann; CBE (2005); da of Leslie John David Baxter, Sevenoaks, Kent, and Madge Adeline, *née* Law; *b* 8 March 1947; *Educ* Walthamstow Hall Sch Sevenoaks, Univ of Durham (BA), Univ of Bristol (CertEd), Univ of Durham (PhD); *Career* head of religious educn John Leggott Sixth Form Coll Scunthorpe 1973–76 (asst teacher 1969–73), pt/t tutor St John's Coll Durham and univ research student 1976–79; St John's Coll Nottingham: lectr in Christian doctrine 1979–, dean 1988–97, princ 1997–; guest prof of theol Princeton Theol Seminary 1990, Warfield lectr Princeton 1996; chm House of Laity Gen Synod C of E 1995– (vice-chm 1990–95); memb Archbishops' Cncl C of E 1999–; *Recreations* swimming, gardening, all things creative; *Style*— Canon Dr Christina Baxter, CBE; ✉ St John's College, Chilwell Lane, Bramcote, Nottingham NG9 3DS (tel 0115 925 1114, fax 0115 943 6438, e-mail principal@stjohns-nottm.ac.uk)

BAXTER, (Charles) Duncan; s of James Leslie Baxter, of Kingston upon Thames, and Doris, *née* Watson; *b* 20 February 1953, Malton, Yorks; *Educ* Trinty Coll Oxford (scholar, MA); *m* July 1977, Neredah, *née* Coupland; 2 s (Alexander b 13 April 1981, Sebastian b 11 Nov 1983); *Career* asst master Gresham's 1975–84, head of Eng and drama and academic dir Wycliffe Coll Stonehouse 1984–91, headmaster Kingston GS 1991–; FRSA, HMC 1991; *Publications* various articles on the poetry of John Milton 1988–, articles on educn in nat press 1992–; *Recreations* choral music, church architecture, hill walking, cricket, writing; *Clubs* East India; *Style*— Duncan Baxter, Esq; ✉ Kingston Grammar School, 70 London Road, Kingston upon Thames, Surrey KT2 6PY (tel 020 8546 5875, e-mail head@kingston-grammar.surrey.sch.uk)

BAXTER, Glen; s of Charles Bertie Baxter (d 1993), and Florence Mary, *née* Wood (d 1988); *b* 4 March 1944; *Educ* Cockburn HS Leeds, Leeds Coll of Art (NDD); *m* Carole Agis; 1 da (Zoë b 1975), 1 s (Harry b 1978); *Career* artist; pt/t lectr Goldsmiths Coll London 1974–87; exhibitions: Gotham Book Mart Gallery NY 1974, 1976 and 1979, ICA London 1981, MOMA Oxford 1981, Nigel Greenwood 1981, 1983, 1987 and 1990, Galleria Del Cavallino Venice 1984, Royal Festival Hall 1984, Holly Solomon Gallery NY 1985 and 1988, Sydney Biennale 1986, Fuller Goldeen San Francisco 1986, Saouma Gallery Paris 1987, 1989 and 1993, Musée de L'Abbaye Sainte-Croix Les Sables D'Olonne 1987, MUHKA Antwerp 1988, DC Art Sydney 1990, Adelaide Festival 1992, Michael Nagy Gallery Sydney 1992 and 1996, Anthony Wilkinson Fine Art London 1994 and 1996, Ginza Art Space Tokyo 1994, Artothèque de Caen France 1995, Le Salon d'Art Brussels 1996, Galerie de la Châtre Paris 1997, 2001 and 2004–05, Modernism Gallery San Francisco 1997, 1998, 2002 and 2006, Galerie de la Châtre Paris 1998, Angoulême France and Chatou Paris 1999, Palais de Congrès Paris 1999, Château Châlus 1999, Chris Beetles Gallery London 1999, La Louvière 1999, St Malo 2000, Lombard Freid Gallery NY 2001, Galerie Daniel Blau Munich 2001, Wetering Galerie Amsterdam 2004, Flowers Central London 2004 and 2006, Flowers Gallery NY 2005, Martine & Thibault de la Châthe Paris 2006; Glen Baxter Tableware launched by Richard Dennis Kensington London 1999;

Glen Baxter Tapestry Commande Publique manufactured in Limousin and exhibited at Château Chalus Chabrol; *Books* The Impending Gleam (1981), Atlas (1982), His Life (1983), Jodhpurs in the Quantocks (1987), Charles Malarkey and the Belly Button Machine (with William and Bren Kennedy), Welcome to the Weird World of Glen Baxter (1989), The Billiard Table Murders - A Gladys Babbington Morton Mystery (1990), Glen Baxter Returns to Normal (1992), The Collected Blurtings of Baxter (1993), The Wonder Book of Sex (1995), Glen Baxter's Gourmet Guide (1997), Blizzards of Tweed (1999), Podium (album of woodblock prints, 1999), The Unhinged World of Glen Baxter (2001), Trundling Grunts (2002), Loomings over the Suet (2004), Haro sur le Suif (2005), Speech with Humans (jtly, 2007); *Recreations* croquet, marquetry and stump work; *Clubs* Chelsea Arts, Groucho, Ale and Quail; *Style*— Glen Baxter, Esq; ✉ website www.glenbaxter.com

BAXTER, Margaret Eleanor (Maggie); da of Charles Frank Alexander Baxter, of Shaftesbury, Dorset, and Eleanor Frances Mary, *née* Bloomer; *b* 7 July 1947; *Educ* Godolphin Sch, Open Univ (BA); *m* 1 (m dis); m 2, George Sean Baine, s of Roney Baine (d 1988), of Belfast; 1 s (Alex b 13 May 1981), 1 da (Holly b 30 Jan 1985), 2 step s (Jack b 10 Feb 1972, Kieran b 25 May 1974); *Career* project dir Action Res Centre 1972–75, dir Dame Colet House Settlement Stepney 1975–80, vol orgns offr London Borough of Camden 1982–89, advsr Baring Fndn 1989–91; Comic Relief/Charity Projects: grants dir (UK) 1991–94, grants dir (UK & Africa) 1994–, grants dir and dep chief exec 1997–99, acting chief exec (secondment) Diana Princess of Wales Fund 1997–98, exec dir WOMANKIND Worldwide 1999–2007; ind conslt 2007–; tstee: Tst for London, City Parochial Fndn, Hilden Charitable Fund 1997, Women at Rosk 2003, Green Belt Movement Fndn 2005; tstee and chair Dance United 2001, assoc memb Oxfam 2001–06; ex-govr Beckford Sch (former chm); *Recreations* family, theatre, cinema, tennis; *Style*— Ms Maggie Baxter; ✉ 40 Hillfield Road, London NW6 1PZ (tel 020 7794 2636)

BAXTER, Prof Murdoch Scott; s of John Sawyer Napier Baxter (d 1977), and Margaret Hastie, *née* Murdoch; *b* 12 March 1944; *Educ* Hutchesons' Boys' GS, Univ of Glasgow (BSc, PhD); *m* 3 Aug 1968, Janice, da of James Henderson (d 1990), of Shawlands, Glasgow; *Career* visiting res fell (Apollo 11 Lunar Res) NY State Univ 1969–70, sabbatical res conslt IAEA International Laboratory of Marine Radioactivity Monaco (radioactive waste disposal) 1981–82; Univ of Glasgow: lectr in environmental radiochemistry Dept of Chemistry 1970–85, prof 1985–95, dir Scottish Univ Res and Reactor Centre 1985–90; dir IAEA Marine Environment Laboratory Monaco 1990–97; environmental conslt 1997–; advsr to Inst of Nuclear Technol (ITN) Portugal 2000–03; memb: Challenger Soc, Scottish Assoc for Marine Science, various IAEA expert gps, Editorial Bd Journal of Radioanalytical and Nuclear Chemistry 1985–2000; hon invited memb Int Union of Radioecology (memb advsy panel) 1999–; Fell Int Union of Eco-Ethics 1999–; CChem, FRSC 1984, FRSE 1989; Chevalier Order of St Charles 1997; *Publications* fndr ed Journal of Environmental Radioactivity, series ed Radioactivity in the Environment 1999–; author of more than 180 res papers in scientific lit; *Recreations* sports, walking, good food; *Clubs* Queens Park FC, Balvicar Golf, Scotch Malt Whisky Soc; *Style*— Prof Murdoch Baxter, FRSE; ✉ Ampfield House, Clachan Seil, By Oban, Argyll PA34 4TL (tel and fax 01852 300351, e-mail baxter@isleofseil.demon.co.uk)

BAYFIELD, Rabbi Anthony Michael (Tony); s of Ronald David Bayfield, of Redbridge, Essex, and Sheila Queenie, *née* Mann; *b* 4 July 1946; *Educ* Royal Liberty Sch Gidea Park, Magdalene Coll Cambridge (MA), Leo Baeck Coll London (Rabbinic ordination); *m* 3 Aug 1969, Linda Gavinia, da of Hyman Rose (d 1976); 2 da (Lucy b 1972, Miriam b 1979), 1 s (Daniel b 1975); *Career* rabbi NW Surrey Synagogue 1972–82; chief exec Reform Synagogues of Great Britain and The Reform Movement 1994–; lectr Leo Baeck Coll 1973–; dir: The Sternberg Centre for Judaism 1983–, Manor House Tst 1983–, Centre for Jewish Education Tst 1986–; cnsllr Spelthorne MGC 1973–82; chm: Assembly of Rabbis Reform Synagogues of GB 1980–81, Cncl of Reform and Lib Rabbis 1983–85; pres Cncl of Christians and Jews 2004–, vice-pres World Union for Progressive Judaism 1999–; tstee Michael Goulston Educnl Fndn; fndr ed Manna (quarterly jl) 1983–; *Books* Prejudice (1974), Churban - The Murder of the Jews of Europe (1982), Dialogue with a Difference (ed with Marcus Braybrooke, 1992), Sinai, Law and Responsible Autonomy: Reform Judaism and the Halakhic Tradition (1993), He Kissed Him and They Wept (ed with Brichto and Fisher, 2002); *Recreations* family, reading, walking, watching cricket and football; *Style*— Rabbi Tony Bayfield; ✉ The Sternberg Centre for Judaism, The Manor House, 80 East End Road, Finchley, London N3 2SY (tel 020 8349 5645, fax 020 8349 5699, e-mail tony.bayfield@reformjudaism.org.uk)

BAYLEY, Hugh; MP; s of Michael Bayley, and Pauline Bayley; *b* 9 January 1952; *Educ* Haileybury, Univ of Bristol (BSc), Univ of York (BPhil); *m* 1984, Fenella, *née* Jeffers; 1 s, 1 da; *Career* nat offr NALGO 1977–82 (dist offr 1975–77), gen sec International Broadcasting Tst 1982–86, res fell in health economics Univ of York 1987–92 (lectr in social policy 1986–87); MP (Lab): York 1992–97 (also contested 1987), City of York 1997–; PPS to sec of state for Health 1997–99, Parly under sec of state DSS 1999–2001; memb House of Commons Select Ctees: Health 1992–97, Int Devpt 2001–; memb NATO Parly Assembly 1997–99 and 2001– (rapporteur Ctee on Economics and Security); chair: Westminster Fndn for Democracy 2006–, Commonwealth Parly Assoc UK Branch, Africa All-Pty Parly Gp; vice-chair Parly Network on the World Bank; cncllr London Borough of Camden 1980–86 (chm Lab Gp 1982–85); sometime freelance TV prodr; memb York DHA 1988–90; memb BECTU; *Publications* The Nation's Health (1995); *Style*— Hugh Bayley, Esq, MP; ✉ 59 Holgate Road, York YO24 4AA; House of Commons, London SW1A 0AA

BAYLEY, Prof Peter James; s of late John Henry Bayley, of Portreath, Cornwall, and Margaret, *née* Burness; *b* 20 November 1944; *Educ* Redruth GS, Emmanuel Coll Cambridge (MA, PhD), Ecole Normale Supérieure Paris; *Career* Univ of Cambridge: fell Emmanuel Coll 1969–71, fell Gonville & Caius Coll 1971–, lectr in French 1978–85, Drapers prof of French 1985–, chm Sch of Arts and Humanities 2001–03; hon sr res fell Inst of Romance Studies Univ of London 1990; vice-pres Assoc of Univ Profs of French 1989–97; pres Soc for French Studies 1990–92; Chevalier du Tastevin (Burgundy) 1997, Commandeur des Palmes Académiques (France) 2006 (Officier 1988); *Books* French Pulpit Oratory 1598–1650 (1980), The Equilibrium of Wit: essays for Odette de Mourgues (ed with D Coleman, 1982), Selected Sermons of the French Baroque (1983), Présences du Moyen Âge et de la Renaissance en France Classique (2003); contrib: Critique et création littéraires en France (ed Fumaroli, 1977), Bossuet: la Prédication au XVIIe siècle (ed Collinet and Goyet, 1980), Catholicism in Early Modern History: a guide to research (ed O'Malley, 1988), Convergences: rhetoric and poetic in seventeenth-century France (ed Rubin and McKinley, 1989), Dictionnaire des littératures (ed Didier, 1994), Oxford Companion to Literature in French (ed France, 1995); contrib: Cambridge Review, Dix-Septième Siècle, French Studies, Modern Language Review, Seventeenth-Century French Studies, Acts of the North American Soc for Seventeenth-Century French Literature; *Recreations* Spain, wine and food, gardening; *Style*— Prof Peter Bayley; ✉ Gonville & Caius College, Cambridge CB2 1TA (tel 01223 332439, e-mail pb47@cam.ac.uk)

BAYLEY, Stephen Paul; s of late Donald Sydney Stainer Bayley, of Staffs, and late Anne, *née* Wood; *b* 13 October 1951; *Educ* Quarry Bank Sch Liverpool, Univ of Manchester (BA), Univ of Liverpool (MA); *m* 29 Sept 1981, Flo, da of Richard Ernest Fothergill, of London; 1 s (Bruno b 3 June 1985), 1 da (Coco b 9 March 1987); *Career* history and theory of art lectr: Open Univ 1974–76, Univ of Kent 1976–80; chief exec Design Museum 1981–90, dir Boilerhouse Project 1981–86; princ Eye-Q Ltd 1990–; creative dir New Millennium Experience 1997–98; commissioning ed: GQ 1991–97, Esquire 1997–, Management Today 1999–, Waitrose Food Illustrated 2004–, Car magazine; former memb Design Policy Ctee LRT, govr History of Advertising Tst 1985–96; Columnist of the Year PPA 1995; hon fell Univ of Wales Inst 2007; Chevalier de l'Ordre des Arts et des Lettres (France) 1989; *Books* In Good Shape (1979), Albert Memorial (1981), Harley Earl (1983), Conran Directory of Design (1985), Sex, Drink and Fast Cars (1986), Commerce and Culture (1989), Taste: The Secret Meaning of Things (1991), The Beefeater Two-Day Guide to London (1993), The Paris Style Guide (1994), The Lucky Strike Packet (1998), Labour Camp (1998), General Knowledge (2000), Sex (2001), The Dictionary of Idiocy (2003), Life's a Pitch (2007), Intelligence Made Visible (2007); *Recreations* words, pictures, food, drink, travel, sport; *Clubs* Hurlingham; *Style*— Stephen Bayley

BAYLEY, Trevor John; OBE (2007); *b* 22 September 1951; *Educ* Newcastle-under-Lyme HS; *m*; 5 c; *Career* articled clerk Alex G Duncan & Co 1970–74, PA to ptnr L George Fetzer & Co 1974–76, gp accountant Alfred Clough Ltd 1976–79; Britannia Building Society: fin accountant 1979–85, chief accountant 1985, dep gen mangr 1986, gen mangr (fin) 1987–88, fin dir 1988–94, gp fin dir 1994–98, corp devpt dir 1998–2000; also dir various subsid companies; fin dir and dep ceo Nat Savings and Investment 2001–06 (acting ceo 2006), dir Saffron Building Soc 2007–, dir A B Publishing Ltd 2007–; FCA (ACA 1974); *Recreations* clay pigeon shooting, sport, music; *Style*— Trevor Bayley, Esq, OBE; ✉ Woodside, Clay Lake, Endon, Stoke-on-Trent, Staffordshire, ST9 9DD

BAYLIS, Prof Peter H; s of Derek Howard Baylis (d 1995), and Lore Bertha, *née* Ahrens; *b* 9 August 1943; *Educ* Wallington GS, Univ of Bristol (BSc, MB ChB), Univ of Birmingham (Fulbright-Hays scholar, MD); *m* 1968, Susan Mary Baylis; 1 s (Mark Richard b 2 June 1973), 2 da (Katherine Louise b 6 May 1975, Vanessa Ruth 23 April 1983); *Career* registrar and research fell Professorial Unit Birmingham 1974–77, clinical research fell in endocrinology Indiana Univ Sch of Med Indianapolis 1977–78, lectr in med Univ of Birmingham 1978–80; conslt physician Royal Victoria Infirmary 1980–; Med Sch Univ of Newcastle upon Tyne: sr lectr in med and endocrinology 1980–90, prof of experimental med 1990–2005, dean of med 1997–2005, provost Faculty of Med Sci 2002–05; non-exec dir Newcastle Hosps NHS Tst 2003–; major research projects incl successful devpt of laboratory ways to measure small peptides, vasopressin and oxytocin with application to resolve clinical problems; memb Assoc of Physicians of GB and I 1984; FRCP 1983, FMedSci 1998; *Books* Endocrinology (contrib, 2001), Oxford Textbook of Med (contrib, 2003); *Recreations* theatre, music, gardening, road running (jogging now); *Style*— Prof Peter H Baylis; ✉ The Medical School, University of Newcastle upon Tyne, Framlington Place, Newcastle upon Tyne NE2 4HH (tel 0191 222 7003, fax 0191 222 6621, e-mail dean-of-medicine@ncl.ac.uk)

BAYLIS, Trevor Graham; OBE (1997); s of late Cecil Archibald Walter Baylis, and late Gladys Jane Baylis; *b* 13 May 1937; *Career* inventor; *early career* GB swimmer (aged 15) 1952, staff Soil Mechanics Lab Southall 1953–57 (pt/t day release to study mech and structural engrg at local tech coll), Nat Serv PT instr 1957–61 (rep Army and Imperial Services at swimming), salesman Purley Pools 1961, turned professional swimmer, stuntman and entertainer (incl performances as underwater escape artiste in Berlin circus), fndr Shotline Displays (aquatic display co) and Shotline Steel Swimming Pools (pool mfrs); *latter career* inventor: Orange Aids (for the disabled) 1985, wind up radio 1991 (manufactured as the Freeplay Radio from 1997); chm Trevor Baylis Brands plc; recipient: BBC Design for Best Product and Best Design 1996, Presidential Gold Medal IMechE 1998, Walpole Medal of Excellence 2001, Export Times Exporter of the Year Award, Rotary Club Paul Harris Fellowship; numerous appearances on TV incl: Tomorrow's World, QED, This is Your Life; visting prof Univ of Buckinghamshire; lectr and demonstrator British Council Africa and Australia 1998; vice-pres: European Women of Achievement Awards, Techknowlogy; after dinner speaker; hon memb: CBI, Radio Soc; patron: Heathrow Special Needs Farm (formerly Spelthorne Farm Project for the Handicapped), POPAN (Prevention of Professional Abuse Network), Motor Sport Endeavour; DTech (hc): Nottingham Trent Univ, Southampton Inst; Hon MSc: UEA, Univ of Teesside; Hon DUniv Open Univ, Hon Dr Middx Univ, Hon MBA Univ of Luton, Hon Degree Brunel Univ, Hon DUniv Oxford Brookes Univ, Hon DSci Heriot Watt Univ 2003, Hon DEng Leeds Met Univ 2005; hon res fell Sch of Journalism Univ of Wales Cardiff, hon fell Univ of Wolverhampton, hon fell Univ of Wales Inst; *Publications* Clock This (1999); *Style*— Trevor Baylis, Esq, OBE; ✉ Haven Studio, Eel Pie Island, Twickenham, Middlesex TW1 3DY (tel 020 8891 1151, fax 020 8891 0673, e-mail trevor@trevorbaylis.com)

BAYLISS, Dr Christopher Richard Butler; s of Sir Richard Bayliss, KCVO (d 2006), and Margaret Joan Hardman, *née* Lawson (d 1994); *b* 10 October 1945; *Educ* Rugby, Clare Coll Cambridge (MA, MB BChir); *m* 20 May 1978, (Felicity) Nicola, da of Ivor Adye (d 1972); 2 da (Clare Alexandra b 1982, Lucy Margaret b 1988), 1 s (Timothy Richard b 1985); *Career* sr registrar X-ray Dept Royal Postgrad Med Sch Hammersmith Hosp London 1976–79, conslt med diagnostic imaging Royal Devon and Exeter Hosp 1979–; chm: Radiology Sub-Ctee BMA 1993–99, SW Regnl Conslts and Specialists Ctee 1994–99, Clinical and Medical Directors Sub-Ctee BMA 1996–2000; memb Central Conslts and Specialists Ctee; FRCR; *Recreations* skiing, golf; *Clubs* East Devon Golf (Budleigh Salterton), St Endoc Golf (Cornwall); *Style*— Dr Christopher Bayliss; ✉ Royal Devon & Exeter Hospital, Exeter, Devon EX2 5DW (tel 01392 402325)

BAYLISS, Eur Ing David; OBE (1991); s of Herbert Bayliss (d 1968), of Blackpool, and Annie Ester, *née* Roper (d 1988); *b* 9 July 1938; *Educ* Arnold Sch Blackpool, UMIST (BSc Tech), Univ of Manchester (DipTP); *m* 25 Aug 1961, Dorothy Christine, da of Eric Algernon Carey Crohill; 2 s (Mark Andrew b 22 Dec 1963, Jason Peter b 14 Feb 1966), 1 da (Ruth Abigail b 12 Aug 1968); *Career* asst planning offr Manchester City Cncl 1963–66 (grad engr 1961–63), res offr GLC 1966–68, princ sci offr Centre for Environmental Studies 1968–69, asst divnl engr rising to chief tport planner GLC 1969–84, dir of planning London Transport 1984–99, dir Halcrow Consulting 1999–; visiting prof ICL 2000–; chm Regnl Studies Assoc 1978–81; pres: Br Parking Assoc 1987–89, Tport Studies Assoc 1989–90; vice-pres UITP 1997–99; chm Rees Jeffreys Road Fund 2004–; memb Bd Blackpool Urban Regeneration Cp 2005–; Freeman City of London 1993; CEng 1968, FICE 1980 (MICE 1978), fell Inst of Transportation Engrs 1984 (memb 1977), FIHT 1972 (MIHT 1972), FCIT 1977–2006; Eur Ing 1992, FREng 1993, FRSA 1994–2006; *Recreations* writing, travel, wine; *Clubs* RAC; *Style*— Eur Ing David Bayliss, OBE, FREng; ✉ 37 Ledborough Lane, Beaconsfield, Buckinghamshire HP9 2DB (tel 01494 673313, e-mail david.bayliss5@btinternet.com); Halcrow Consulting, Vineyard House, 44 Brook Green, London W6 7BY (tel 020 7348 3024, fax 020 7603 5783, e-mail baylissd@halcrow.com)

BAYLISS, Jeremy David Bagot; s of Edmund Bayliss (d 1990), of Guernsey, and Marjorie Clare Thompson (d 1983); *b* 27 March 1937; *Educ* Harrow, Sidney Sussex Coll Cambridge (MA); *m* 1962, Hon Mary Selina, 3 da of 2 Viscount Bridgeman, KBE, CB, DSO, MC (d 1982); 3 s (Jonathan Andrew Bagot b 2 Jan 1964, Richard Charles b 11 Dec 1965, Patrick Thomas Clive b 6 March 1968); *Career* Nat Serv 2 Lt Coldstream Gds 1956–57; Gerald Eve 1960–97: ptnr 1967, jt sr ptnr 1988, sr ptnr 1990–97; chm Gerald Eve Financial Services Ltd 1989–96; RICS: memb Gen Cncl 1987–, pres Planning and Devpt Div 1989–90, pres 1996–97; chief exec Royal Botanic Gardens Kew Fndn 1997–2002; Hon Co Organiser (Berks) NGS 2001–07; govr Bearwood Coll 2000– (chm 2003), tstee The Royal Merchant Navy Sch Fndn 2003–07, tstee Soc for Horticulture Therapy (Thrive) 2004–; FRICS 1971 (ARICS 1962); *Recreations* gardening, country pursuits, reading; *Clubs*

Boodle's; *Style*— Jeremy Bayliss, Esq; ✉ Loddon Lower Farm, Swallowfield, Berks RG7 1JE (tel 0118 988 3218, e-mail jeremy@baylissnet.com)

BAZALGETTE, Peter Lytton; s of Paul Bazalgette(d 1999), and Diana, *née* Coffin (d 1995); *b* 22 May 1953; *Educ* Dulwich Coll, Fitzwilliam Coll Cambridge (MA, pres Cambridge Union); *m* 1985, Hilary Jane, *née* Newiss; 1 da (b 1986), 1 s (b 1990); *Career* BBC News trainee 1977; TV formats created: Ready Steady Cook (BBC2), Can't Cook Won't Cook (BBC1), Changing Rooms (BBC2), Ground Force (BBC1); formats sold to 30 countries; UK prodr Big Brother (Channel 4); md Bazal Productions 1987–98, chm Endemol UK plc 2002–, chief creative offr Endemol 2004–, chief creative offr Endemol Gp 2005–; non-exec dir: Victoria Real, Zeppotron, Channel 4 2001–04, YouGov.com 2005–; dep chm Nat Film and TV Sch 2002–; Ind Prodr of the Year Broadcast Prodn Awards 1997, McTaggart lectr Edinburgh Int TV Festival 1998, Hat Trick Pioneer Award Indies 1998, Indie-vidual Award for Outstanding Personal Contribution to the Ind Sector 2000, RTS Weldon Lecture 2001, Judges' Award RTS 2003; chm Crossness Engines Tst, co-chm Br Acad of Gastronomes 1993–, tstee ENO 2004–; fell BAFTA 2000, FRTS; *Books* BBC Food Check (jtly, 1989), The Food Revolution (jtly, 1991), You Don't Have to Diet (jtly, 1993), The Big Food and Drink Book (jtly, 1994), Billion Dollar Game (2005); *Recreations* gluttony, cricket; *Clubs* Beefsteak, Hurlingham, BBC Mishits Cricket; *Style*— Peter Bazalgette, Esq; ✉ Shepherds Building Central, Charecroft Way, Shepherds Bush, London W14 0EE (tel 0870 333 1700, fax 0870 333 1800, e-mail peter.bazalgette@endemoluk.com)

BEACHAM, Stephanie; *b* 28 February 1947; *Educ* Convent of the Sacred Heart Whetstone, QEGGS, RADA, Mime Sch Paris; *m* 2 da (Phoebe b 1974, Chloe b 1977); *Career* actress; spokesperson American Speech Language and Hearing Assoc; *Theatre* incl: Tea Party and The Basement (Duchess) 1969, London Cuckolds (Royal Court) 1977, Venice Preserved (NT) 1985, The Rover (RSC) 1988, An Ideal Husband (Broadway and Australia) 1997, Funny About Love 1999, A Busy Day (Lyric Theatre) 2000, Nobody's Perfect 2001, Elizabeth Rex 2002; *Television* incl: Tenko 1982, Connie 1984, The Colbys and Dynasty (ABC USA) 1985–87 and 1988–89, Sister Kate (NBC USA) 1989; other credits incl: The Picnic (BBC), The Silent Preacher (BBC), All The World's A Stage (BBC), French and Saunders (series II), To Be The Best, Riders (Anglia), Seaquest (Amblin/NBC), Dorothea Grant in No Bananas (BBC), Bad Girls (ITV); *Films* incl: The Games, Tam Lyn, The Nightcomers, The Wolves of Willoughby Chase, The Lilac Bus, Foreign Affairs, Unconditional Love, Would I Lie to You, Love and Other Disasters; *Style*— Ms Stephanie Beacham

BEAL, Clifford Franklin; s of Clifford F Beal, and Lorraine F Beal; *b* 3 May 1958; *Educ* East Providence HS RI (Pell Medal in US History), Univ of Vermont (BA), Univ of Sussex (MA); *m* 1984, Anke C Middelmann; 2 da (Hannah L b 1990, Emma K b 1995), 1 s (Samuel J b 1998); *Career* asst ed Jl of Defence and Diplomacy 1984–86, public info offr American Inst of Aeronautics and Astronautics Washington DC 1986–89, managing ed Defense World 1989–90, freelance defence and aerospace journalist 1990–91, aerospace ed rising to ed-in-chief Jane's International Defense Review 1991–98, ed-in-chief Jane's Defence Weekly 1998–2003, dir The Strix Consultancy Ltd 2003–; guest lectr Ashridge Mgmnt Coll and Univ of Cardiff; broadcast commentator on defence issues; shortlisted BT Technol Journalist of the Year 1996 and 1997, shortlisted RAeS Journalist Awards 1998, BSME Ed of the Year 2000; *Publications* Quelch's Gold (2007); numerous articles in publications incl: Jane's Defence Weekly, Jane's IDR, Sunday Times, Military History Quarterly, New Scientist, Focus, Frontiers, World Monitor, International Herald Tribune; *Recreations* fencing, motorcycling, museums and galleries; *Clubs* Hurst House; *Style*— Clifford Beal, Esq; ✉ The Strix Consultancy Ltd, 7–10 Adam Street, The Strand, London WC2N 6AA (tel 020 7871 2634, e-mail clifford.beal@thestrixgroup.com or rapier@bealnet.co.uk)

BEAL, Dr Peter George; s of William George Beal, and Marjorie Ena, *née* Owen; *b* 16 April 1944, Coventry, Warks; *Educ* King Henry VIII GS Coventry, Univ of Leeds (BA, PhD); *m* 1, 1974 (m dis 1980), Gwyneth Morgan; *m* 2, 1982 (m dis 1994), Sally Josephine Taylor; 1 step s; *m* 3, 1998, Grace Janette Ioppolo; *Career* research ed Bowker Publishing and Mansell Publishing Ltd 1974–79; Sotheby's London: English manuscript expert 1980–2005, dir in Dept of Printed Books and Manuscripts 1996–2005 (dep dir 1990–96); J P R Lyell reader in bibliography Univ of Oxford 1995–96, visiting prof English Dept Univ of Reading 2000–02, sr research fell Inst of English Studies Univ of London 2002–, building on-line Catalogue of English Literary Manuscripts 1450–1700 (CELM) 2005–; memb Editorial Bd: English Literary Renaissance 2001–, Renaissance English Text Soc 2002–; advsr and conslt to various presses and projects incl OUP, Scolar Press, CUP and the Oxford DNB; numerous invited lectures in the UK, USA and Canada; memb: Cncl Br Acad 2000–01, Mgmnt Ctee Centre for Editing Lives and Letters QMC London 2001–07; FBA 1993, FSA 2007; *Publications* incl: Index of English Literary Manuscripts (Vol I Parts 1 and 2, 1980, Vol II Part 1 1987, Vol II Part 2 1993), English Verse Miscellanies of the Seventeenth Century (gen ed, 5 vols 1990), In Praise of Scribes: Manuscripts and their Makers in Seventeenth-Century England (1998), Parnassus Biceps 1656 (ed, 1990); co-fndr and co-ed English Manuscript Studies 1100–1700 (Vol 1 1989, Vol 2 1990, Vol 3 1992, Vol 4 1993, Vol 5 1995, Vol 6 1997, Vol 7 1998, Vol 8 2000, Vol 9 2000, Vol 10 2002, Vol 11 2002, Vol 12 2005, Vol 13 2007), Queen Elizabeth I and the Culture of Writing (co-ed, 2007); author of numerous articles in learned jls; *Style*— Dr Peter Beal, FBA, FSA; ✉ Institute of English Studies, Senate House, Malet Street, London WC1E 7HU (tel 020 7664 4864, e-mail peter.beal@sas.ac.uk)

BEALBY, Walter; s of Harry Bealby, of Nottingham, and Heulwen, *née* Morris; *b* 8 January 1953; *Educ* Henry Mellish GS Nottingham, Univ of Bristol (BA); *m* 22 Nov 1980, Finnula Leonora Patricia, da of Daniel O'Leary, of Abingdon, Oxon; 1 s (Thomas Henry b 21 Jan 1985), 1 da (Polly Megan b 5 July 1988); *Career* called to the Bar Middle Temple 1976; Blackstone scholarship 1977; *Recreations* motor cycling, opera; *Style*— Walter Bealby, Esq; ✉ 5 Fountain Court, Steelhouse Lane, Birmingham B4 6DR (tel 0121 606 0500, fax 0121 606 1501)

BEALE, Claire Elizabeth; da of Brian Beale, of Tamworth, Staffs, and Valerie, *née* Bingham; *b* 26 November 1966, Staffs; *Educ* Wilnecote HS, Univ of Manchester (BA); *Partner* Martin Loat; 1 s (Emerson b 28 Oct 2001), 1 da (Cordelia b 21 Dec 2005); *Career* media ed Marketing Magazine 1992; Campaign: media ed 1995, dep ed 2000, ed 2004–; memb Women in Advtg and Communications London (WACL); *Recreations* film, literature, walking; *Style*— Miss Claire Beale; ✉ Campaign, Haymarket Business Publications Ltd, 174 Hammersmith Road, London W6 7JP (tel 020 8267 4683, e-mail claire.beale@haymarket.com)

BEALE, Prof Hugh Gurney; Hon QC (2002); s of Charles Beale, TD (d 1989), and Anne Freeland, *née* Gurney-Dixon (d 1953); *b* 4 May 1948; *Educ* The Leys Sch Cambridge, Exeter Coll Oxford (BA); *m* 18 July 1970, Jane Wilson, da of Nathan Cox (d 1980), of Clarkton, N Carolina; 2 s (Ned b 1977, Thomas b 1979), 1 da (Martha b 1981); *Career* lectr Univ of Connecticut 1969–71, called to the Bar Lincoln's Inn 1971 (hon bencher 1999–), lectr UCW Aberystwyth 1971–73, reader Univ of Bristol 1986–87 (lectr 1973–86), prof of law Univ of Warwick 1987–; law cmmr 2000–07; memb Commission for Euro Contract Law 1987–99; FBA 2004; *Books* Remedies for Breach of Contract (1980), Contract Cases and Materials (with W D Bishop and M P Furmston, 1985, 1990, 1995, 2001 and 2007), Principles of European Contract Law, Part 1 and Part 2 (1995 and 1999), Chitty on Contracts (29 edn 2004), Casebooks on the Common Law of Europe: Contract (with A Hartkamp, H Kötz and D Tallow, 2002); *Recreations* fishing, music, walking;

Style— Prof Hugh Beale, QC; ✉ School of Law, University of Warwick, Coventry CV4 7AL (e-mail hugh.beale@virgin.net)

BEALE, Nicholas Clive Lansdowne; s of Prof Evelyn Martin Lansdowne Beale, FRS (d 1985), and Violette Elizabeth Anne, *née* Lewis; *b* 22 February 1955; *Educ* Winchester (scholar), Trinity Coll Cambridge (scholar, MA); *m* 16 July 1977, Christine Anne, da of Peter McPoland, of Bedford; 1 s (Rupert Christopher Lansdowne b 1977), 2 da (Rebecca Merryn Elizabeth b 1980, Rose Theodora Elizabeth b 1991); *Career* social philosopher and mgmnt conslt; md Beale Electronic Systems 1977–85, vice-chm Beale International Technology 1985–88, conslt McKinsey & Co 1988–89; chm: Beale Holdings 1988–95, Sciteb 1989–; dir: First Film Fndn 1991–95, Sector Dialogue Process 1992–; author of Sciteb/Sunday Times Poll of R&D Effectiveness, Intellectual Assets (in Professional Investor), Oil and Troubled Waters (2005) and various technical articles and speeches at int confs on computer communications and R&D mgmnt; co-author polkinghorne.net; Oblate Alton Abbey 1994–; Freeman City of London 1996, Liveryman Worshipful Co of Information Technologists 1997 (dep chm Ethical & Spiritual Devpt Panel); FRSA 1991; *Books* R&D Short-Termism? (1991), Engineering Consensus (ed), Good Disclosure Practice Code (ed), Industry/City Dialogue Guide (published with IoD, LIBA and IIMR), The Star Course (with Bishop Geoffrey Rowell), City Science and Technology Dialogue (with Sir Brian Jenkins, 1995), Addressing IMT in NHS Organisations (co-author), Cybernauts Awake! (co-author, 1999), Rational Values in the New Economy (ed and co-author), Constructive Engagement (2005); *Recreations* piano, music, running marathons, sailing; *Clubs* Royal Inst, IOD, Royal Inst of Philosophy, City Livery, Soc of Authors, London Corinthian Sailing, Shoreham Sailing, Serpentine Running; *Style*— Nicholas Beale, Esq; ✉ Sciteb, 1 Hay Hill, Berkeley Square, London W1J 6DH (tel 020 7381 1481, fax 020 7499 9253, e-mail nicholas.beale@sciteb.com)

BEALE, Lt-Gen Sir Peter John; KBE (1992); s of Basil Hewett Beale (d 1987), of Romford, Essex, and Eileen Beryl, *née* Heffer; *b* 18 March 1934; *Educ* St Paul's Cathedral Choir Sch, Felsted, Gonville & Caius Coll Cambridge (BA), Westminster Hosp (MB BChir, DTM&H); *m* 1, 22 Aug 1959, Julia Mary (d 2000), da of John Clifton Winter; 4 s (Simon Russell b 12 Jan 1961, Timothy John, Andrew Mark (twins) b 17 Jan 1962, Matthew James Robert b 25 Jan 1974), 2 da (Katie Louise b 28 June 1964, Lucy Ann b 10 Dec 1967 d 1971); *m* 2, 2 Dec 2001, Mary Elisabeth, da of Charles James Stanley Lucas; *Career* RMO 34 LAA Regt RA 1960–63, trainee and specialist physician 1963–71, conslt physician 1971–, cmd Med 2 Div 1981–83, Col AMD 3 1983–84, cmd Med 1 Br Corps 1984–87, cmd Med UKLF 1987–90, Surgn-Gen and DG Army Med Servs 1991–94; chief med advsr British Red Cross 1994–2000; govr Yehudi Menuhin Sch; pres: Tidworth Golf Club 1989–2003, Army Offrs Golf Soc 2001–05; author of various articles in med jls on mil med matters, jt author First Aid Manual; QHP 1988–94; memb: BMA, RIPHH, RSTM&H; FRCP, FFCM, FFOM; *Recreations* golf, squash, tennis, music (conducting and singing); *Style*— Lt-Gen Sir Peter Beale, KBE; ✉ The Old Bakery, Avebury, Marlborough, Wiltshire SN8 1RF

BEALES, Prof Derek Edward Dawson; s of Edward Beales (d 1984), and Dorothy Kathleen, *née* Dawson (d 1993); *b* 12 June 1931; *Educ* Bishop's Stortford Coll, Sidney Sussex Coll Cambridge (MA, PhD, LittD); *m* 14 Aug 1964, Sara Jean (Sally), da of Francis Harris Ledbury (d 1971); 1 da (Christina Margaret (Kitty) b 1965), 1 s (Richard Derek b 1967); *Career* Nat Serv Sgt RA 1949–50; Univ of Cambridge: asst lectr 1962–65, lectr 1965–80, prof of modern history 1980–97 (emeritus 1997–), chm Bd of History 1979–81; Sidney Sussex Coll Cambridge: res fell 1955–58, fell 1958–, vice-master 1973–75; visiting lectr Harvard Univ 1965, visiting prof Central European Univ Budapest 1995–97; fndr's meml lectr St Deiniol's Library Hawarden 1990, Stenton lectr Univ of Reading 1992, Birkbeck lectr Trinity Coll Cambridge 1993; chm Editorial Bd Historical Jl 1990–97 (ed 1971–75), chm Mgmnt Ctee Centre of Int Studies 1993–95; memb: Univ Library Syndicate Cambridge 1981–89, Gen Bd of the Faculties 1987–89, Standing Ctee for Humanities Euro Science Fndn 1994–99; Leverhulme emeritus fell 2000; author articles in learned jls; Paolucci/Bagehot Book Award Intercollegiate Studies Inst Wilmington DE 2004; FRHistS (memb Cncl 1984–88), FBA (memb 1989); *Books* England and Italy 1859–60 (1961), From Castlereagh to Gladstone (1969), The Risorgimento and the Unification of Italy (1971, new edn with E F Biagini 2002), History and Biography (1981), History Society and the Churches (ed with Geoffrey Best, 1985), Joseph II - in the Shadow of Maria Theresa 1741–80 (1987), Mozart and the Habsburgs (1993), Sidney Sussex College Cambridge: Historical Essays in Commemoration of the Quatercentary (ed with H B Nisbet, 1996), Prosperity and Plunder: European Catholic Monasteries in the Age of Revolution, 1650–1815 (2003), Enlightenment and Reform in Eighteenth-Century Europe (2005), Joseph II: Against the World 1780–1790 (2008); *Recreations* music, walking, bridge; *Clubs* Athenaeum; *Style*— Prof Derek Beales, FBA; ✉ Sidney Sussex College, Cambridge CB2 3HU (tel 01223 338833, e-mail derek@beales.ws)

BEAMISH, David Richard; s of Richard Ludlow Beamish, of Woodford Green, Essex, and Heather Margaret Ensor, *née* Lock (d 2001); *b* 20 August 1952; *Educ* Marlborough, St John's Coll Cambridge (MA, LLM); *m* 30 Sept 1989, Dr (Fiona) Philippa Tudor, *qv*, da of (James) Brian Tudor; 1 da (Amelia May Tudor b 31 May 1994); *Career* House of Lords: clerk 1974, sr clerk 1979, seconded to Cabinet Office as private sec to Leader of the House of Lords and Govt Chief Whip 1983–86, chief clerk 1987–93, princ clerk 1993, clerk of the jls 1993–95, clerk of ctees and clerk of the overseas office 1995–2002, clerk of the jls 2002–05, reading clerk 2003–07, clerk asst 2007–; winner Mastermind BBC TV 1988; *Publications* The House of Lords at Work (jt ed with Donald Shell, 1993); *Style*— David Beamish, Esq; ✉ Clerk Assistant, House of Lords, London SW1A 0PW (tel 020 7219 3000, e-mail beamishdr@parliament.uk)

BEAMISH, Sally; da of William Anthony Alten Beamish, of Sussex, and Ursula Mary, *née* Snow; *b* 26 August 1956; *Educ* Camden Sch for Girls, Trinity Coll of Music (jr), RNCM; *m* 1988, Robert Irvine; s of Joseph Irvine; 2 s (Laurence George b 3 Jan 1989, Thomas Stuart b 2 June 1990), 1 da (Stephanie Rose b 1 Oct 1995); *Career* composer; studied under Anthony Gilbert and Sir Lennox Berkeley; viola: Raphael Ensemble, London Sinfonietta, Lontano; artistic dir and co-fndr Chamber Group of Scotland 1991–; co-host composers' course: Scottish Chamber Orch Hoy (with Sir Peter Maxwell Davies) 1994 & 1995, St Magnus Composers' Course (with Alasdair Nicholson) 2007; composer in residence Swedish and Scottish Chamber Orchs 1998–2002; appearances on: BBC Radio 3, BBC TV, Scottish TV, Channel 4; works incl: Symphony no 1 1992, Tam Lin for oboe and orch 1993, Concerto for violin and orch 1994, Concerto no 1 for Viola and Orchestra (premiered BBC Proms) 1995, Concerto River for cello and orchestra 1997, Symphony No 2 1998, recordings 971, 1161, 1171, 1511 (BIS label), BBC Proms cmmn Knotgrass Elegy 2001, Viola Concerto no 2 2001 various film and TV scores; opera: Monster 2002; stage musical: Shenachie 2006; Arts Cncl Composer's Bursary 1989, Paul Hamlyn Award 1993, Scottish Arts Cncl Bursary 1999, Creative Scotland Award 2000; Hon Doctorate Univ of Glasgow 2001; memb: Performing Rights Soc, APC, RSM, MCPS; *Recreations* painting, writing; *Style*— Dr Sally Beamish; ✉ c/o Norsk Musikforlag (e-mail lisbet.froy@musikforlaget.no)

BEAN, Dr Charles Richard; s of Charles Ernest Bean, of Wilmslow, Cheshire, and Mary, *née* Welsh; *b* 16 September 1953; *Educ* Brentwood Sch, Emmanuel Coll Cambridge (MA), MIT (PhD); *Partner* Elizabeth Nan Callender; *Career* HM Treasy: economic asst 1975–79, economic advsr 1981–82; LSE: lectr 1982–86, reader 1986–90, prof 1990–2000; chief economist and exec dir Bank of England 2000– (memb Monetary Policy Ctee); advsr: HM Treasy 1992–2000, Treasy Select Ctee House of Commons 1997–2000; author of numerous pubns in learned jls; *Recreations* cricket, opera; *Style*— Dr Charles Bean; ✉ Bank of England, Threadneedle Street, London EC2R 8AH (tel 020 7601 4999, fax 020 7601 4112)

BEAN, Hon Mr Justice; Sir David Michael Bean; kt (2004); s of George Joseph Bean (d 1973), and Zdenka, *née* White; *b* 25 March 1954; *Educ* St Paul's, Trinity Hall Cambridge; *m* 2004, Dr Ruth Thompson; *Career* called to the Bar Middle Temple 1976 (bencher 2001); recorder of the Crown Court 1996–2004, QC 1997, judge of the High Court of Justice (Queen's Bench Div) 2004–, presiding judge South Eastern Circuit 2007–; chm Gen Cncl of the Bar 2002; chm Employment Law Bar Assoc 1999–2001, chm Immigration Servs Tbnl 2001–04; memb: GMC 2003–04, Civil Justice Cncl 2003–05; *Publications* Enforcement of Injunctions and Undertakings (with His Hon Judge Fricker, QC 1991), Law Reform for All (ed, 1996), Injunctions (9th edn 2007); *Recreations* opera, hill walking, books; *Style*— The Hon Mr Justice Bean

BEAN, Sean; *Career* actor; *Theatre* Romeo in Romeo and Juliet (RSC Stratford/Barbican), Spencer in Fair Maid of the West (RSC Stratford/Mermaid), Starvling in A Midsummer Night's Dream, Who Knew Mackenzie & Gone (Royal Court), Lederer in Deathwatch (Young Vic Studio), Last Days of Mankind (Citizens' Theatre Glasgow); *Television* BBC incl: Mellors in Lady Chatterley's Lover 1993, Fools Gold, Clarissa, Prince, Tell Me That You Love Me, Wedded, Small Zones, My Kingdom For A Horse; Central incl: title role in Sharpe's: Rifles, Gold, Company, Eagle, Enemy, Honour, Battle, Sword, Regiment, Seige, Mission, Revenge (separate progs 1993–96); Channel 4 incl: The Loser, The Border Country; other credits incl: A Woman's Guide to Adultery (ITV) 1993, Inspector Morse (Thames), Troubles (LWT), 15 Streets (World Wide/Tyne Tees), War Requiem (Anglo-Int Films), Winter Flight (Enigma), Samson & Delilah (Flamingo Films), The True Bride (TVS Films), Fenton in Scarlett, Esav in Jacob, Neal Byrne in Extremely Dangerous, Robert Aske in Henry VIII 2003; *Radio* title role in The True Story of Martin Guerre (Radio 4) 1992; *Audio* Sharpe's Devil; *Film* Sean Miller in Patriot Games, Rannucio in Caravaggio 1986, Carver Doone in Lorna Doone, Tadgh in The Field 1990, Brendan in Stormy Monday (Channel 4) 1987, Windprints 1989, Black Beauty, Shopping, Jimmy Muir in When Saturday Comes 1995, 006 in Goldeneye 1995, Spence in Ronin 1998, Jason Locke in Essex Boys 1999, Partridge in Equilibrium 2000, Koster in Don't Say a Word 2000, Paul in Tom and Thomas 2001, Boromir in Lord of the Rings: The Fellowship of the Ring 2001, The Two Towers 2002 and The Return of the King 2003, The Big Empty 2003, Odysseus in Troy 2004, National Treasure 2005; *Style*— Sean Bean, Esq; ✉ c/o ICM Ltd, Oxford House, 76 Oxford Street, London W1N 0AX (tel 020 7636 6565, fax 020 7323 0101)

BEANEY, Linda Margaret; da of Kenneth Ashley Beaney, of Gidea Park, Essex, and Kathleen Margaret, *née* Stainforth; *b* 1 December 1952; *Educ* Coborn Sch for Girls London; *Career* trainee property sales negotiator Edward Erdman & Co Mayfair London 1969; Hampton & Sons: joined 1976, ptnr 1981, md London 1989–91; dir Hornchurch Theatre Trust Ltd 1985–90, dir P H Gillingham Investments 1986–2000, jt chief exec Hamptons Residential Developments 1989–91, sr ptnr Beaney Pearce 1992–; memb Devpt Cncl The Globe Theatre 1998–; Freeman City of London 1984; memb Land Inst 1988, FInstD 1991, FNAEA 1992; *Recreations* theatre, tennis and golf; *Clubs* Queen's; *Style*— Ms Linda Beaney; ✉ Beaney Pearce, 14 Culford Gardens, Sloane Square, London SW3 2ST (tel 020 7590 9500, fax 020 7589 1171, e-mail lbeaney@beaneypearce.co.uk)

BEAR, Carolyn Ann; da of Richard E L Salter (d 1983), and Marjorie, *née* Rix; *b* 10 April 1944; *Educ* Univ of Newcastle upon Tyne (BA); *m* 1968, Peter Julian Bear, s of late Leslie W Bear, CBE; 2 da (Claudia b 1970, Leonora b 1974); *Career* writer (for children and teenagers); also multimedia and film scriptwriter; vol BESO; *Books* as Chloë Rayban: Under Different Stars (1988), Wild Child (1991), Virtual Sexual Reality (1994, shortlisted for Guardian Children's Fiction Prize 1995, feature film 1999), Love in Cyberia (1996, shortlisted for Guardian Children's Fiction Prize 1996, shortlisted for Carnegie Medal 1996), Models Series (1997), Models Move On (1998), Back 2 Back (1999), Terminal Chic (2000), Drama Queen (2004), Wrong Number (2004), My Life Starring Mum (2006), Hollywood Bliss: My life so far (2007); as Carolyn Bear: The Last Loneliest Dodo (1974), No Time for Dinosaurs (1975), Johnny Tomorrow (1978), The Tangled Spell (1986), Scrapman (1996); *Recreations* painting, collage, drawing; *Clubs* Hurlingham; *Style*— Mrs Carolyn Bear; ✉ c/o Laura Cecil (Literary Agent), 17 Alwyne Villas, London N1 2HG

BEARD, Prof (Winifred) Mary; da of Roy Whitbread Beard (d 1978), and Joyce Emily, *née* Taylor (d 1995); *b* 1 January 1955, Much Wenlock, Salop; *Educ* Newnham Coll Cambridge (MA), Univ of Cambridge (PhD); *m* 1985, Robin Sinclair Cormack; 1 da (Zoe Troy b 27 Oct 1985), 1 s (Raphael Christian b 24 July 1987); *Career* lectr in classics KCL 1979–83; Univ of Cambridge: fell Newnham Coll 1984–, lectr in classics 1984–99, reader in classics 1999–2004, prof of classics 2004–; classics ed TLS 1992–; chair Faculty of Archaeology, History and Letters British Sch at Rome 2002–06 (memb 1994–98); *Publications* Rome in the Late Republic (jtly 1985, 2 edn 1999), The Good Working Mother's Guide (1989), Pagan Priests (co-ed, 1990), Classics: A Very Short Introduction (jtly, 1995, 2 edn 1999), Religions of Rome I (co-author, 1998), Religions of Rome II: A Sourcebook (co-author, 1998), The Invention of Jane Harrison (2000), Classical Art: From Greece to Rome (jtly, 2001), The Parthenon (2002), The Colosseum (jtly, 2004); numerous scholarly articles, reviews and journalism; *Style*— Prof Mary Beard; ✉ Newnham College, Cambridge CB3 9DF (tel 01223 335162, fax 01223 335409, e-mail mb127@cam.ac.uk)

BEARD, Michael (Mike); s of Joseph Beard (d 1995), of Stockport, Cheshire, and Harriet Louvain, *née* Holmes (d 1990); *b* 18 August 1942; *Educ* St Bede's Coll Manchester; *m* 1966, Jennifer, da of John Robert Marr; 1 da (Katherine Louise b 1979); *Career* political organiser Cons Pty 1960–73, PRO then mangr British Leyland 1973–77, mktg servs mangr The Pilkington Gp 1977–79, dir of public affrs, advtg and promotion The Perkins Engines Gp 1979–83, md Burson-Marsteller Singapore 1983–84, head of PR The Wiggins Teape Gp 1984–86; dir of corp communications: Delta plc 1987–88, Taylor Woodrow plc 1989–95; dir of communication Lucas Varity (formerly Lucas Industries plc) 1995–96; dir of mktg Valpak Ltd 1996–99, dir of corp affrs Wastelink Gp Ltd (formerly Wastepack Gp Ltd) 1999–2004, corporate affrs conslt 2005–; pres IPR 1994 (treas 1992); FCIPR (FIPR 1991, MIPR 1979); *Publications* Running a Public Relations Department (1997, 2 edn 2001); *Recreations* sport, current affairs, travel, rock music; *Clubs* RAC; *Style*— Mike Beard, Esq; ✉ mobile 07785 381831, e-mail mikebeard4@hotmail.com

BEARD, (Christopher) Nigel; s of Albert Leonard Beard (d 1958), and Irene, *née* Bowes (d 1968); *b* 10 October 1936; *Educ* Castleford GS, UCL (BSc); *m* 1969, Jennifer Anne, da of Thomas Beckerleg Cotton, of Guildford, Surrey; 1 s (Daniel b 1971), 1 da (Jessica b 1973); *Career* supt land ops and reinforcement policy studies Def Operational Analysis Estab 1968–73, chief planner strategy GLC 1973–74, dir London Docklands Devpt Orgn 1974–79, sr mangr New Business Devpt ICI Millbank 1979–92, gp mangr R&D Planning ZENECA 1992–97; Parly candidate (Lab): Woking 1979, Portsmouth North 1983, Erith and Crayford 1992; MP (Lab) Bexleyheath and Crayford 1997–2005; memb: House of Commons Select Ctee on Science and Technol 1997–2000, Ecclesiastical Ctee (Jt Ctee of the Commons and Lords) 1997–2005, Treasy Select Ctee 2000–05, House of Commons Chairmen's Panel 2001–05; chm All-Pty Gp on Fin Services and Markets 2003–05; memb: SW Thames RHA 1978–86, Royal Marsden Cancer Hosp and Inst of Cancer Research 1981–90, Nat Constitutional Ctee Lab Party 1995–98; FRSA; *Recreations* reading, theatre, talking; *Clubs* Athenaeum, Royal Inst; *Style*— Nigel Beard, Esq; ✉ Lanquhart, The Ridgway, Pyrford, Woking, Surrey GU22 8PW (tel 01932 348630)

BEARDMORE, Prof John Alec; s of George Edward Beardmore, of Burton on Trent, and Anne Jean, *née* Warrington; *b* 1 May 1930; *Educ* Burton on Trent GS, Birmingham Central Tech Coll, Univ of Sheffield (BSc, PhD); *m* 26 Dec 1956, Anne Patricia, da of Frederick William Wallace (d 1951); 1 da (Virginia b 1957), 3 s (James b 1960, Hugo b 1963, Charles b 1965); *Career* radar operator RAF 1948–49; res demonstrator Univ of Sheffield 1954–56, Cwlth Fund fell (Harkness) Columbia Univ NY 1956–58, visiting asst prof of plant breeding Cornell Univ 1958, lectr in genetics Univ of Sheffield 1958–61, prof of genetics and dir Genetics Inst Univ of Groningen The Netherlands 1961–66, sr fell Nat Sci Fndn Pennsylvania State Univ 1966; Univ of Wales Swansea: prof of genetics 1966–97, head of dept 1966–87, dean of sci 1974–76, vice-princ 1977–80, dir Inst of Marine Studies 1983–87, head Sch of Bio Sci 1988–95, professorial fell 1997–2000, prof emeritus 2000–; chm Univ of Wales Validation Bd 1994–97; hon sec Inst of Biology 1980–85 (vice-pres 1985–87), vice-pres Galton Inst 2005–; memb: NERC Aquatic Life Sci Ctee 1982–87 (chm 1984–87), Br Nat Ctee for Biology 1983–87, Cncl Linnean Soc 1989–93; chm: CSTI Bd 1984–85, UK Heads of Biological Scis 1992–94; manager DFID Fish Genetics Research Prog 1990–2001; chm Fishgen Ltd; treas Gower Soc 2005–; Univ of Helsinki medal 1980; FIBiol, FRSA, FAAS, FRSM; *Books* Marine Organisms: Genetics Ecology and Evolution (co ed with B Battaglia, 1977), Artemia: Basic and Applied Biology (co-ed with Th J Abatzopoulos, JS Clegg and P Sorgeloos, 2002); *Recreations* bridge, golf, hill walking; *Style*— Prof John A Beardmore; ✉ 153 Derwen Fawr Road, Swansea SA2 8ED (tel 01792 206232); School of Medicine, Swansea University, Swansea SA2 8PP (tel 01792 295388, fax 01792 206232, e-mail j.a.beardmore@swansea.ac.uk)

BEARSTED, 5 Viscount (UK 1925); Sir Nicholas Alan Samuel; 5 Bt (UK 1903); er s of 4 Viscount Bearsted, MC, TD (d 1996), and his 2 w, Hon Elizabeth Adelaide (d 1983), da of Baron Cohen, PC (Life Peer, d 1973); *b* 22 January 1950; *Educ* Eton, New Coll Oxford (BA); *m* 1975, Caroline Jane, da of Dr David Sacks; 4 da (Hon Eugenie Sharon b 1977, Hon Natalie Naomi b 1979, Hon Zöe Elizabeth b 1982, Hon Juliet Samantha b 1986), 1 s (Hon Harry Richard b 23 May 1988); *Heir* s, Hon Harry Samuel; *Career* chm Insignia Solutions plc, non-exec dir Mayborn Gp plc 1981–; memb Cncl UCL; *Style*— The Rt Hon the Viscount Bearsted

BEASHEL, His Hon Judge John Francis; s of Nicholas Beashel (d 1983), of Bradford-on-Avon, Wilts, and Margaret Rita Beashel, JP, *née* McGurk (d 2005); *Educ* Trowbridge Commercial Inst, Coll of Law; *m* 1966, Kay, *née* Dunning; 3 s (Mark Nicholas b 12 March 1968, Simon John b 26 Oct 1969, Jeremy Peter b 29 Sept 1973), 1 da (Caroline Natasha b 11 July 1985); *Career* called to the Bar: Gray's Inn 1970, NSW 1989; dep clerk to the Justices Ipswich 1970–73, practising barr 3 Paper Buildings Temple London and Annexe Bournemouth 1973–93, recorder 1989– (asst recorder 1983–89), circuit judge Western Circuit 1993–, liaison judge for Dorset 1994–2006, resident judge Dorchester Crown Court 1995–2006; pres Dorset Branch Magistrates' Assoc 1998–2006; *Recreations* golf, travel, reading, walking; *Style*— His Hon Judge Beashel; ✉ Courts of Justice, Deansleigh Road, Bournemouth, Dorset BH7 7DS (tel 01202 502800)

BEASLEY-MURRAY, Caroline Wynne; da of Arthur Maelor Griffiths (d 2001), and Mavis Gwyneth, *née* Baker (d 2001); *b* 25 January 1946, Porthcawl, Glamorganshire; *Educ* Grove Park Girls' GS Wrexham, Girton Coll Cambridge (BA), Univ of Manchester (PGCE), Manchester Poly (CPE), Inns of Court Sch of Law; *m* 26 Aug 1967, Rev Dr Paul Beasley-Murray, *qv*; 3 s (Jonathan Paul b 6 Aug 1969, Timothy Mark b 19 Nov 1971, Benjamin James b 6 March 1976), 1 da (Susannah Caroline Louise b 21 Sept 1973); *Career* called to the Bar Inner Temple; barr: 5 Pump Court 1990–93, Tindal Chambers Chelmsford 1993–97, Fenners Chambers Cambridge 1997–2000; HM coroner for Essex 2000–; pres Mental Health Review Tbnls 1996–; JP: Trafford Bench 1980–86, Croydon Bench 1986–92; history mistress Bury GS for Girls 1968–69, home tutor Trafford Educn Authy 1980–86; memb: Coroners' Soc of England and Wales, Magistrates' Assoc, Br Acad of Forensic Sci; *Recreations* theatre, concerts, family, friends, church, entertaining, travel, tapestry work; *Clubs* Cambridge Soc; *Style*— Mrs Caroline Beasley-Murray; ✉ The Old Manse, 3 Roxwell Road, Chelmsford, Essex CM1 2LY (tel 01245 347016, fax 01245 267203, e-mail cbeasleymurray@btclick.com); PO Box 11, County Hall, Chelmsford CM1 1LX (tel 01245 438011, fax 01245 437142, e-mail caroline.beasley-murray@essexcc.gov.uk)

BEASLEY-MURRAY, Rev Dr Paul; s of Rev Dr George Raymond Beasley-Murray (d 2000), of Hove, E Sussex, and Ruth, *née* Weston; *b* 14 March 1944; *Educ* Trinity Sch of John Whitgift Croydon, Jesus Coll Cambridge (MA), Univ of Zurich, Univ of Manchester (PhD), N Baptist Coll, Int Baptist Theol Seminary Switzerland; *m* 26 Aug 1967, Caroline Wynne Beasley-Murray, *qv*; 3 s (Jonathan Paul b 6 Aug 1969, Timothy Mark b 19 Nov 1971, Benjamin James b 6 March 1976), 1 da (Susannah Caroline Louise b 21 Sept 1973); *Career* prof of New Testament Nat Univ of Zaïre at Kisangani (in assoc with Baptist Missionary Soc) 1970–72, pastor Altrincham Baptist Church 1973–86, princ Spurgeon's Coll London 1986–92, sr min Central Baptist Church Victoria Rd South Chelmsford 1993–; chm Ministry Today (formerly Richard Baxter Inst for Ministry); ed Ministry Today 1994–; memb Studiorum Novi Testamenti Societas; *Books* Turning the Tide (with Alan Wilkinson, 1980), Pastors Under Pressure (1989), Dynamic Leadership (1990), Mission to the World (ed, 1991), Faith and Festivity (1991), Radical Believers (1992), Anyone For Ordination? (ed, 1993), Prayers For All Peoples (co-ed, 1993), A Call to Excellence (1995), Happy Ever After? (1996), Radical Leaders (1997), Power for God's Sake (1998), The Message of the Resurrection (2000), Fearless for Truth (2002), Building for the Future (2003), Joy to the World (2005), Transform Your Church (2005), A Loved One Dies (2005); *Recreations* music, cooking, parties; *Clubs* Rotary; *Style*— The Rev Dr Paul Beasley-Murray; ✉ The Old Manse, 3 Roxwell Road, Chelmsford, Essex CM1 2LY (tel 01245 352996, fax 01245 267203, e-mail pbeasleymurray@btclick.com)

BEATON, Alistair; *Educ* Univ of Edinburgh, Univ of Bochum, Univ of Moscow; *Career* writer; *Theatre* with Ned Sherrin, *qv*, (book and lyrics): The Metropolitan Mikado, The Rateplayers' Iolanthe (Olivier Award), Small Expectations; other credits incl: The Nose (Nottingham Playhouse, Berlin, Bucharest), Die Fledermaus (English version for D'Oyly Carte Co), La Vie Parisienne (adaptation), Feelgood (Garrick Theatre, Evening Standard Theatre Award Best Comedy, What'sOnTheatre.com Award Best New Comedy, nominated Olivier Award Best New Comedy), Follow My Leader (Birmingham Rep, Hampstead Theatre); *Television* Not the Nine O'clock News (BBC), It'll be all Over in Half an Hour (with Jonathan Dimbleby, *qv*), A Question of Fact (BBC 2), Spitting Image (ITV), Minder (ITV), The Way, The Truth, The Video (Channel 4), Incident on the Line (Channel 4), Dunrulin' (BBC), Downwardly Mobile (co-author, ITV), Russian Language and People (BBC), Children of Icarus (ZDF), Mit Fünfzig Küssen Männer Anders (Regina Ziegler Filmproduktion), script conslt NDF Entertainment; *Radio* writer: Something Appealing, Something Appalling, Week Ending; writer/presenter: The World Tonight, Dome Alone; presenter Fourth Column; contrib: The News Huddlines, The Jason Explanation, Loose Ends; devised/presenter: Little England, Big World, The Beaton Generation; guested on: Quote Unquote, The News Quiz; *Books* The Thatcher Papers (with Andy Hamilton), Drop the Dead Donkey, The Little Book of Complete Bollocks, The Little Book of New Labour Bollocks, The Little Book of Mangement Bollocks, A Planet for the President; *Style*— Alistair Beaton, Esq; ✉ c/o Berlin Associates, 14 Floral Street, London WC2 9DH (tel 020 7632 5282)

BEATSON, Hon Mr Justice; Sir Jack Beatson; kt (2003); s of John James Beatson (d 1961), and Miriam, *née* White (d 1991); *b* 3 November 1948; *Educ* Whittinghame Coll Brighton, BNC Oxford (MA, BCL), Univ of Oxford (DCL), Univ of Cambridge (LLD); *m* 1973,

Charlotte, da of Lt-Col John Aylmer Christie-Miller, CBE, of Bourton-on-the-Hill, Glos; 1 s (Samuel J b 1976 d 2004), 1 da (Hannah A b 1979); *Career* called to the Bar Inner Temple 1972 (hon bencher 1993, bencher 2003); law cmmr England and Wales 1989–94, recorder 1994, QC 1998, judge of the High Court of Justice (Queen's Bench Div) 2003–; law lectr Univ of Bristol 1972–73, fell and tutor Merton Coll Oxford 1973–94 (hon fell 1995–); Univ of Cambridge: Rouse Ball prof of English law 1993–2003, fell St John's Coll 1994–2003 (hon fell 2005–), dir Centre for Public Law 1997–2001, chm Faculty of Law 2001–2003; visiting prof: Osgoode Hall Law Sch Toronto 1979, Univ of Virginia 1980 and 1983; memb Editorial Bd Law Quarterly Review; memb Civil Ctee Judicial Studies Bd 1994–98; memb Competition Cmmn 1996–2001; *Books* Administrative Law - Cases and Materials (jtly 1983, 2 edn 1989), The Use and Abuse of Unjust Enrichment (1991), Chitty on Contracts (jt ed, 1982–94), Good Faith and Fault in Contract Law (jt ed, 1995), European Public Law (jt ed, 1997), Anson's Law of Contract, (27 edn, 1998, 28 edn 2002), Human Rights: The 1998 Act and the European Convention (jtly, 1999), Unjustified Enrichment: Cases and Materials (jt ed, 2003), Jurists Uprooted: German-Speaking Émigré Lawyers in Twentieth Century Britain (jt ed, 2004); *Recreations* relaxing; *Style*— The Hon Mr Justice Beatson; ✉ Royal Courts of Justice, Strand, London WC2A 2LL

BEATTIE, Dr Alistair Duncan; s of Alexander Nicoll Beattie (d 1965), of Paisley, and Elizabeth McCrorie, *née* Nisbet (d 1961); *b* 4 April 1942; *Educ* Paisley GS, Univ of Glasgow (MB ChB, MD); *m* 29 Oct 1966, Gillian Margaret, da of Dr James Thomson McCutcheon (d 1964); 2 da (Charlotte b 23 May 1968, Deirdre b 25 May 1972), 3 s (Duncan b 16 Feb 1970, Douglas b 30 April 1975, Neil b 26 Aug 1979); *Career* res fell Scottish Home and Health Dept 1969–73, lectr materia medica Univ of Glasgow 1973–76, res fell MRC Royal Free Hosp 1974–75, conslt physician S Gen Hosp Glasgow 1976–2002, pt/t conslt advsr MOD 2002–; vice-pres (med) RCPSGlas 1999–2001; chm Med and Dental Def Union of Scotland; FRCPGlas 1983, FRCP 1985 (MRCP 1973), FFPM 1989, FRCPEd 1997; *Books* Emergencies in Medicine (jt ed, 1984), Diagnostic Tests in Gastroenterology (1989); *Recreations* golf, music; *Clubs* Douglas Park Golf; *Style*— Dr Alistair Beattie; ✉ Flat 3/2, 47 Novar Drive, Glasgow G12 9UB (tel 0141 334 0101)

BEATTIE, Basil; *b* 1935; *Educ* Royal Acad Schs; *Career* artist, lectr and reader; lectr Goldsmiths Coll London until 1998; *Solo Exhibitions* Greenwich Theatre Gallery London 1968, Mayfair Gallery London 1971, Consort Gallery London 1973, Hoya Gallery London 1974, New 57 Gallery Edinburgh 1978, Newcastle Poly 1979, Goldsmiths' Gallery London 1982, Minories Gallery Colchester 1982, Bede Gallery Jarrow 1984, Gray's Art Gallery Hartlepool 1986, Curwen Gallery London 1987 and 1990, Drawing on the Interior (installation at The Eagle Gallery London) 1991, Castlefield Gallery Manchester 1993, MAAK Gallery London 1993, Todd Gallery London 1994, 1995 and 1996, Ikon Gallery 1994, Newtown Gall Johannesburg 1994, Angel Row Gallery Nottingham 1995, Path Gallery Aalst Belgium 1996, Reg Vardy Gallery Sunderland 1997, Renate Bender Gallery Munich 1997, Todd Gallery London 1998, Storey Gallery Lancaster 2000, Works on Paper 1980–90 (Curwen Gallery London) 2001, That Irresistible Climb (paintings and prints, Advanced Graphics Gallery London) 2001, Above and Below (Sadler's Wells London) 2002, Making a Year (studio show) 2005; *Group Exhibitions* incl: John Moores Exhbn 4 (Liverpool) 1965, Large Paintings (Hayward Gallery) 1970, London Now in Berlin (Germany) 1970, Four Painters (MOMA Oxford) 1971, British Painting (Hayward Gallery) 1974, Hayward Annual (Hayward Gallery) 1980, Hayward Annual - British Drawing (Hayward Gallery) 1982, European Painting (Trier Germany) 1984, British Art Show (Arts Cncl travelling exhbn) 1984, John Moores Exhbn 15 (Liverpool) 1987, Presence of Painting (Mappin Gallery Sheffield) 1988, Three British Painters (Northern Centre for Contemporary Art Sunderland) 1988, John Moores Exhbn 16 (Liverpool) 1989, The Abstract Connection (Flowers East Gallery London) 1989, John Moores Exhbn 17 (Liverpool) 1991, Painting and Sculpture at the MAAK Gallery 1992, (Pomeroy Purdy Gallery London) 1992, Moving into View (Royal Festival Hall London) 1993, Summer Exhibition (Royal Academy London) 1993, (Morgan Stanley Bank) 1994, Painters and Prints (Curwen Gallery London) 1994, Lead and Follow (Bede Gallery Jarrow and Atlantis Gallery London) 1994, Summer Exhibition (Royal Academy London) 1994, Paintmarks (Kettles Yard Cambridge) 1994, British Abstract Art Part 1 (Flowers East Gallery London) 1994, Monotypes (Art Space Gallery London) 1995, Green on Red Gallery Dublin 1995, Ace! Arts Cncl Collection (travelling exhbn) 1996–97, Yellow (Todd Gallery London) 1997, John Moores Exhbn 20 (Liverpool) 1997, Jerwood Painting Prize Exhbn 1998, Four Artists (Eagle Gallery London) 1999, Thinking Aloud (Camden Art Centre London) 1999, Open Studio (Brooklyn New York) 1999, Summer Exhibition (Royal Academy London) 1999, Works on paper (West Beth Gallery NY) 1999, Regrouping (The Nunnery London) 1999, British Airways Terminal (JFK Airport NY) 2000, London Contemporary Art Fair 2000, 5 Br Abstract Painters (Flowers West Gallery LA) 2000, Contemporary Art Fair Islington 2001, Master Class (Alain de Gailiard Gallery Paris) 2001, Retrospective I (Eagle Gallery London) 2001, Master Class (Stephen Lacey Gallery London) 2001, Tradition and Innovation (York City Art Gallery) 2001, Monoprints (Art Space Gallery London) 2001, Jerwood Prize Shortlist Exhbn (Jerwood Gallery London) 2001, Royal Acad Summer Exhbn London 2001, Br Abstract Painting (Flowers East Gallery London) 2001, Made in Hartlepool (Art Gallery Hartlepool) 2001, Three Painters (Sarah Myerscough Gallery London) 2001, Drawing (ecArt London) 2001, Contemporary Art Fair (Islington London) 2002, Square Root (Sarah Myerscough Gallery London) 2002, Contemporary Drawing Exhibition (Prospect Gallery London) 2002, Drawings (Sarah Myerscough Gallery London) 2002, Summer Exhibition (RA London) 2002, Prospects (National Contemporary Drawing Exhbn London) 2003, Art 2003 (Advanced Graphics Contemporary Art Fair London) 2003, Contemporary Art Soc London 2003, Summer Exhbn (Royal Acad) 2003; *Collections* incl: Tate Gallery, Arts Cncl Collection London, Contemporary Arts Soc, Saatchi Collection, Govt Art Collection, Birmingham Museum and Art Gall, BUPA Collection London, Natwest Gp Collection London, The Creasy Collection of Contemporary Art and other public and private collections in the UK and overseas; *Commissions* incl: mural for Manors Station Newcastle Metro for Northern Arts; *Awards* major Arts Cncl Award 1976, Athena Awards winner 1986, John Moores second prize winner 1989, Nordstern Print Prize 1999; *Style*— Basil Beattie, Esq; ✉ c/o Emma Hill Fine Art, Eagle Gallery, 159 Farringdon Road, London EC1R 3AL (tel 020 7833 2674, e-mail emmahilleagle@aol.com)

BEATTIE, Jennifer Jane Belissa (Mrs Geoffrey Luckyn-Malone); da of Maj Ian Dunbar Beattie (d 1987), of Brighton, E Sussex, and Belissa Mary Hunter Graves, *née* Stanley; *b* 20 July 1947; *Educ* Queen Anne's Sch Caversham; *m* 11 July 1992, Maj William Geoffrey Luckyn-Malone, late Argyll and Sutherland Highlanders; *Career* slr; ptnr: Blacket Gill & Langhams 1973–77 (joined 1972), Blacket Gill & Swain 1977–85, Beattie & Co 1985–2005; conslt Wedlake Bell 2005–; Women's Nat Cancer Control Campaign: dep chm 1983–86, vice-pres 1986–92, dir 1992–2001; memb Law Soc 1972; *Recreations* skiing, tennis, reading, dog walking; *Clubs* Naval and Military; *Style*— Mrs Geoffrey Luckyn-Malone; ✉ 41 Great Percy Street, London WC1X 9RA (tel 020 7278 5203); Miss Jennifer Beattie, Wedlake Bell, 52 Bedford Row, London WC1R 4LR (tel 020 7395 3051, fax 020 7406 1601, e-mail jbeattie@wedlakebell.com)

BEATTIE, Trevor Stephen; s of John Vincent Beattie (d 1980), and Ada Alice, *née* Page; *b* 24 December 1958; *Educ* Moseley Art Sch Birmingham (BA), Wolverhampton Poly; *Career* copywriter Allen Brady & Marsh advtg agency 1981–83, dep creative dir Ayer Barker 1983–87, gp head Boase Massimi Pollitt 1987–90; creative dir TBWA (formerly TBWA Holmes Knight Ritchie) 1993–97 (joined 1990), creative dir BDDP GGT (merger of BST-BDDP and GGT Advertising) 1997–98; TBWA GGT Simons Palmer (following merger of TBWA International and BDDP Worldwide): creative dir 1998–2005, chairman 2001–2005; co-fndr Beattie McGuinness Bungay (BMB) 2005–; media columnist The Guardian 1997–, prodr Immodesty Blaize and Walter's Burlesque (Arts Theatre West End) 2005; *Recreations* film making, flying, tourism; *Style*— Trevor Beattie, Esq

BEATY, Prof Robert Thompson (Bob); OBE (2003); s of Laurence Beaty, of Ayrshire, and Elizabeth Todd, *née* Beattie; *b* 13 October 1943; *Educ* Hamilton Acad, Univ of Glasgow (Hoover scholar, BSc); *m* Anne Veronica, da of George Gray Gillies (d 1990); 2 s (Kenneth Robert b 23 Dec 1968, Steven Gillies b 5 Oct 1971); *Career* trainee then test engr Hoover Cambuslang 1966–68; IBM: quality engr Greenock Plant 1968–69, Uithoorn Devpt Lab Holland 1969–71, World Trade HQ White Plains NY 1973–74, second level mgmnt 1974 (mgmnt 1971), functional mangr quality assurance 1976–78, mangr PCB Business Unit 1978–80, various sr mgmnt positions 1980–87, asst plant mangr 1987–89, dir of ops European HQ Paris 1989–92, dir technol prod ops 1992, dir of manufacturing ops and location exec 1993, dir IBM Greenock 1994–96; chief exec Scottish Electronics Forum (SEF) 1996–97; md: RTB Professional Services 1996–98, GlenCon Ltd 1998–2006; non-exec dir: Semple Cochrane plc 1996–99, Turnkey Holdings Ltd 1996–2002, Calluna plc 1996–2003, MetFab Engrg Ltd 1998–99; visiting prof of product design Univ of Glasgow 1996–; dir: Renfrewshire Enterprise Co 1994–2003 (chm 1999–2003), Greenock Tall Ships 1999 Ltd 1996–98, Eng Educn Scheme Scotland 1997–; memb Bd: Engrg Educn Scheme for Scotland (EESS) 1999–, Scottish Inst for Enterprise 2002–05; memb Ct Univ of Paisley 1999– (vice-chair 2002–05, chair 2005–), memb Mgmnt Ctee James Watt Coll 2000– (vice-chair 2003–), Scottish Industrial Devpt Advsy Bd (SIDAB) 2003–; FIEE 1985, FIProdE 1987, FREng 1989; *Recreations* golf, jogging, hill walking, cycling, car restoration, DIY; *Style*— Prof R T Beaty, OBE, FREng; ✉ Glenside, 89 Newton Street, Greenock, Renfrewshire PA16 8SG (tel 01475 722027, mobile 07961 068614, e-mail bob.beaty@btopenworld.com)

BEAUCHAMP, *see also:* Proctor-Beauchamp

BEAUCHAMP, Brig Vernon John; s of Herbert George Beauchamp (d 1952), of Waterlooville, Hants, and Vera Helena, *née* Daly; *b* 19 September 1943; *Educ* Portsmouth GS; *m* 27 Nov 1971, Annemarie, da of Evert Teunis Van Den Born (d 1982), of Renkum, Holland; 2 s (Mark b 9 Dec 1972, Dominic b 16 Oct 1975); *Career* cmmnd Royal Warwickshire Fusiliers 1963, transferred 2 KEO Gurkha Rifles 1969, served in Germany, UK, Borneo, Hong Kong, Brunei, Nepal, Malaysia, Army Staff Coll 1976, Brigade Maj 20 Armoured Brigade 1977–79, Nat Defence Coll 1981, Cmdt 2 Bn 2 Gurkha Rifles 1981–84, sr staff appts MOD and HQ BAOR 1984–87, Cdr 48 Gurkha Infantry Brigade 1987–89, RCDS 1990, Cmdt Sch of Infantry; chief exec Royal Hospital for Neuro-disability 1992–2000, currently chief exec Nat Autistic Soc; *Recreations* golf, running; *Clubs* Fadeaways; *Style*— Brig Vernon Beauchamp; ✉ National Autistic Society, 393 City Road, London EC1V 1NG (tel 020 7833 2299, fax 020 7833 9666, e-mail vbeauchamp@nas.org.uk)

BEAUCLERK-DEWAR, Peter de Vere; RD (1980, bar 1990), JP (Inner London 1983); s of James Dewar, MBE, GM, AE (d 1983), and Hermione de Vere (d 1969), yr da and co-heir of Maj Aubrey Nelthorpe Beauclerk, of Little Grimsby Hall, Lincs (d 1916, heir-in-line to Dukedom of St Albans); recognised by Lord Lyon King of Arms 1965 in additional surname and arms of Beauclerk; *b* 19 February 1943; *Educ* Ampleforth; *m* 4 Feb 1967, Sarah Ann Sweet Verge, elder da of Maj Lionel John Verge Rudder, DCLI, of Clevedon, Somerset; 1 s (James William Aubrey de Vere b 30 Sept 1970), 3 da (Alexandra Hermione Sarah b 1 Aug 1972, Emma Diana Peta (Mme Amaury Amblard-Ladurantie) b 6 Sept 1973, Philippa Caroline Frances b 8 Aug 1982); *Career* Lt Cdr RNR 1977 (cmmnd London Div 1966), Intelligence Branch 1979–92, ret 1992; genealogist; Falkland Pursuivant Extraordinary 1975, 1982, 1984, 1986, 1987, 1991, 1994, 1996, 1997, 1999, 2001, 2003 and 2006; usher: (Silver Stick) Silver Jubilee Thanksgiving Serv 1977, (Liaison) HM Queen Elizabeth The Queen Mother's 80th Birthday Thanksgiving Serv 1980; heraldry conslt to Christie's Fine Art Auctioneers 1979–, chm Assoc of Genealogists and Record Agents 1982–83, vice-pres Royal Stuart Soc 1995 (hon treas 1985–94), tstee Inst of Heraldic and Genealogical Studies 1992– (hon treas 1979–94); chief accountant Archdiocese of Westminster 1982–85; dir: Mgmnt Search International Ltd 1985–87, Five Arrows Gp 1986–87, Clifton Nurseries (Holdings) Ltd 1986–88, Room Twelve Ltd 1987–88; underwriting memb Lloyd's 1987–97; princ and fndr Peter Dewar Associates 1988–, sr conslt Sanders and Sidney plc 1990–99; court chm Family Proceedings Court (Inner London) 1991–, chm Inner London Magistrates' Assoc 2000–04 (vice-chm 1994–95), dep chm East Central Petty Sessional Div 1994–2000; govr: More House Sch SW1 1986–95 (dep chm 1991–95), Good Shepherd Sch W12 (vice-chm) 1993–2003; hon treas Br Red Cross Queen Mother's Meml Fund 2002–06, chm and tstee Oregon Historical Soc (UK) 2003–; chm London Membs' Centre Nat Tst for Scotland 2005–; NADFAS lectr 1998–; memb Queen's Body Guard for Scotland (Royal Co of Archers) 1981–; Queen's Golden Jubilee Medal 2002; Liveryman Worshipful Co of Haberdashers 1968; FSA Scot 1968, FFA 1979, FMAAT 1982, Hon FHG 1982, FCMI (FIMgt 1988); Knight of Honour and Devotion SMOM 1971 (Dir of Ceremonies Br Assoc 1989–95), Knight of Justice Sacred Mil Order of Constantine St George 1981, OStJ 1987, Cdr of Merit with Swords 'Pro Merito Melitensi' 1989; *Books* The House of Nell Gwyn 1670–1974 (co-author), The House of Dewar 1296–1991, The Family History Record Book (1991), Burke's Landed Gentry (ed, 2001), Right Royal Bastards (co-author, 2006), contributor to many pubns; *Clubs* Puffin's, New (Edinburgh); *Style*— Peter Beauclerk-Dewar, Esq, RD, JP; ✉ 22 Faroe Road, Brook Green, London W14 0EP (tel 020 7371 1365, office and fax 020 7610 4163, mobile 078 6061 4817, e-mail peterdewar@btinternet.com)

BEAUFORT, 11 Duke of (E 1682); David Robert Somerset; also Baron Herbert of Raglan, Chepstow and Gower (E 1506), Earl of Worcester (E 1513), Marquess of Worcester (E 1642) and hereditary keeper of Raglan Castle; s of Henry Somerset, DSO (d 1965; ggs of 8 Duke), and Bettine (d 1978), yr da of Maj Charles Malcolm (bro of Sir James Malcolm, 9 Bt); suc kinsman, 10 Duke of Beaufort, KG, GCVO, PC, 1984; *b* 23 February 1928; *Educ* Eton; *m* 1950, Lady Caroline Jane Thynne (d 1995), da of 6 Marquess of Bath (d 1992); 3 s, 1 da; m 2, 2 June 2000, Miranda Elisabeth, da of Brig Michael Frederick Morley, MBE (decd); *Heir* s, Marquess of Worcester; *Career* late Lt Coldstream Gds; chm Marlborough Fine Art 1977–; pres Br Horse Soc 1988–90; *Clubs* White's; *Style*— His Grace the Duke of Beaufort; ✉ Badminton House, South Gloucestershire GL9 1DB

BEAUMAN, Christopher Bentley; s of Wing Cdr Eric Bentley Beauman (d 1989), of London, and Katharine Burgoyne, *née* Jones (d 1998); *b* 12 October 1944; *Educ* Winchester, Trinity Coll Cambridge, Johns Hopkins Sch of Advanced Int Studies and Columbia Univ (Harkness fell); *m* 1, 1966 (m dis 1976), Sally, *née* Kinsey-Miles; *m* 2, 1976, Nicola Beauman, *qv*, da of Dr Francis Mann (d 1991), of London; 1 s, 1 da, 3 step c; *Career* corp fin exec Hill Samuel 1968–72; dir: Guinness Mahon 1973–76, FMC Ltd 1975–81; advsr to chm: BSC 1976–81, Central Policy Review Staff 1981–83, Morgan Grenfell Group 1983–91 (planning dir 1989–91); sr advsr European Bank for Reconstruction and Development 1995– (sr banker 1991–95); memb: Governing Body Br Assoc for Central and Eastern Europe 1996–, English Heritage Commemorative Plaques Panel 1998–, BBC World Service Tst 1999–; hon fell Centre for Russian and East Euro Studies Univ of Birmingham 1997–; *Publications* incl: Privatizzazione E Nuove Strategie D'Impresa: Il Caso Della British Steel (2000); *Recreations* family, London, climate change; *Style*— Christopher Beauman, Esq; ✉ 35 Christchurch Hill, London NW3 (tel 020 7435 1975)

BEAUMAN, Nicola Catherine; da of Dr F A Mann, CBE (d 1991), and Lore, *née* Ehrlich (d 1980); *b* 20 June 1944; *Educ* St Paul's Girls' Sch, Newnham Coll Cambridge; *m* 1, 1965

(m dis 1976), Nicholas Lacey, s of John Lacey; 2 s (Josh b 1968, William b 1973), 1 da (Olivia b 1970); m 2, 1976, Christopher Beauman, *qv*, s of Wing Cdr Eric Bentley Beauman (d 1989); 1 da (Francesca b 1977), 1 s (Ned b 1985); *Career* freelance reviewer, ed and journalist 1967–; freelance writer; fndr Persephone Books 1998; chm Friends of Heath Library 1991–, assoc Newnham Coll Cambridge; winner Women in Publishing Pandora Award 2002; *Books* A Very Great Profession: The Women's Novel 1914–39 (1983), Cynthia Asquith: A Life (1987), Morgan: A Life of E M Forster (1993); *Recreations* urban conservation, walking on Hampstead Heath, rediscovering twentieth century women writers; *Style*— Mrs Nicola Beauman; ✉ 35 Christchurch Hill, London NW3 1LA (tel 020 7435 1975); Persephone Books, 59 Lamb's Conduit Street, London WC1N 3NB (tel 020 7242 9292, fax 020 7242 9272, e-mail nicola@persephonebooks.co.uk)

BEAUMONT, Sir George Howland Francis; 12 Bt (E 1661), of Stoughton Grange, Leicestershire; s of Sir George Arthur Hamilton Beaumont, 11 Bt (d 1933); *b* 24 September 1924; *Educ* Stowe; *m* 1, 1949 (m annulled 1951), Barbara, da of William Singleton; m 2, 1963 (m dis 1985), Henrietta Anne, da of late Dr Arthur Weymouth; 2 da (Georgina Brienne Arabella (Mrs Patrick Beaumont-Fay), Francesca Renée Henrietta (Mrs John Beaumont-Clarke) (twins) b 1967); *Heir* none; *Career* formerly warrant offr Australian Army; Coldstream Gds, Lt 60 Rifles WW II; *Clubs* Lansdowne; *Style*— Sir George Beaumont, Bt; ✉ Stretton House, Stretton-on-Fosse, Moreton-in-Marsh, Gloucestershire GL56 9SB (tel 01608 662845)

BEAUMONT, Prof John Richard; s of Jim Beaumont, of Leeds, and Betty Marie, *née* Jarratt; *b* 24 June 1957; *Educ* Temple Moor Leeds, Univ of Durham (BA); *m* 1, 21 July 1979 (m dis), Margret, da of Prof R Payne; 2 da (Judith Alison b 23 Nov 1980, Claire Marie b 27 Aug 1982); m 2, 19 June 1987 (m dis), Jeanne Ann, da of A Magro; *Career* res asst Univ of Leeds 1978–80, lectr Keele Univ 1980–83, sr conslt Coopers & Lybrand London and NYC 1983–85, jt md Pinpoint Analysis Ltd 1985–87, ICL prof Univ of Stirling 1987–90, prof of mgmnt Univ of Bath 1990–92, md StrataTech Ltd 1993, dir of strategy and business devpt Energis Communications Ltd 1993–99, md Planet Online Ltd 1998–; dir Metro Holdings Ltd 1998–; non-exec dir: Office for Nat Statistics 1996–99, European Telecommunications and Technology Ltd 1999–, Sci-warehouse Ltd 2000–; memb Cncl Economic and Social Res Cncl 1989–93; hon prof: Queen's Univ Belfast 1990–93, City Univ 1994–; FRGS 1985, MIMgt 1987, FRSA 1989; *Publications* Future Cities (1982), Projects in Geography (1983), Introduction to Market Analysis (1992), Information Resources Management (1992), Managing Our Environment (1993); *Recreations* writing, sport, food, wine and travel; *Clubs* Athenaeum; *Style*— Prof John Beaumont; ✉ Planet Online Ltd, The White House, Melbourne Street, Leeds LS2 7PS (tel 0113 207 6090)

BEAUMONT, John Richard; s of Stanley Beaumont (d 1992), of Denmead, Hampshire, and Winifred Louise, *née* Williams (d 1984); *b* 22 June 1947; *Educ* Wolverhampton GS, Merton Coll Oxford (MA); *m* 18 Oct 1986, Susan Margaret, da of Ivan Stanley Blowers, of Oulton Broad, Suffolk; 2 da (Anna Jane b 1988, Rosemary Clare b 1990), 1 s (Andrew James b 1994), 1 step s (Christopher Jones b 1983); *Career* schoolmaster Buckingham Coll Harrow 1969–71; Shelter National Campaign for the Homeless Ltd: regnl organiser W Midlands 1971–73, nat projects dir 1973–74; legal offr: Alnwick DC Northumberland 1974, Thurrock Borough Cncl 1974–75; called to the Bar Inner Temple 1976, memb Northern Circuit, full-time chm Industrial Tribunals 1994– (pt/t chm 1992), regnl chm Employment Tbnls (North West Region) 1999–, formerly pt/t legal advsr Assoc Newspapers plc; former memb Mgmnt Ctees of: Bradford Housing and Renewal Experiment (SHARE), North Islington Housing Rights Project; govr and vice-chm Knutsford HS 2000–; *Recreations* walking, reading history and Victorian literature, picnics; *Style*— John Beaumont, Esq; ✉ Regional Office of Employment Tribunals, Alexandra House, 14–22 The Parsonage, Manchester (tel 0161 833 6162)

BEAUMONT, Martin Dudley; s of Patrick Beaumont, DL, of Donadea Lodge, Clwyd, and Lindesay, *née* Howard; *b* 6 August 1949; *Educ* Stowe, Magdalene Coll Cambridge (MA); *m* 12 June 1976, Andrea Evelyn, *née* Wilberforce; 3 da (Alice b 11 July 1980, Jessica b 22 Dec 1981, Flora b 4 Oct 1989); *Career* ptnr KPMG (formerly Thomson McLintock) 1983–87 (dir 1980–83), gp fin dir Egmont Publishing Group 1987–90; chief exec Children's Best Sellers Ltd 1989–90; United Cooperatives: fin controller and sec 1990–92, chief exec 1992–2002; dir Cooperative Bank plc 1996–2000 (dep chair 2000–07), gp chief exec The Cooperative Gp 2002–07, dep chair Cooperative Fin Servs Ltd 2002–07, dir Cooperative Insurance Soc 2002–07; dep chm NW Business Leadership Team 2006–; FCA 1977, FIGD 2002; *Recreations* family, fishing, tennis; *Style*— Martin Beaumont, Esq

BEAUMONT, Mary Rose; da of Charles Edward Wauchope (d 1969), and Elaine Margaret, *née* Armstrong-Jones (d 1965); *b* 6 June 1932; *Educ* Prior's Field Godalming, Courtauld Inst Univ of London (BA); *m* 1955, Timothy Wentworth Beaumont (Baron Beaumont of Whitley, *qv*), s of Michael Wentworth Beaumont; 2 s (Hon Hubert Wentworth b 1956, Hon Alaric Charles Blackett b 1958 d 1980), 2 da (Hon Atalanta Armstrong b 1961, Hon Ariadne Grace b 1963); *Career* fndr Centre for the Study of Modern Art at ICA 1972; teacher at art schs and polys, lectr at Tate Gallery and National Gallery, lectr at Modern Art Studies Christie's Educn 1990–2001, lectr in humanities City & Guilds of London Art Sch 1996–; writer and art critic for newspapers and periodicals incl: FT, Sunday Telegraph, Art International, Arts Review, Art and Design; author of numerous catalogue introductions for individual artists; exhbn curator: for Br Cncl in E Europe and Far East 1983–87, The Human Touch (Fischer Fine Art) 1986, The Dark Side of The Moon (Benjamin Rhodes Gallery) 1990, Three Scottish Artists (Pamela Auchincloss Gallery NY) 1990; Picker Fellowship at Kingston Poly; exec and memb Cncl Contemporary Arts Soc 1980–90, memb Advsy Ctee Govt Art Collection 1994–2000; memb AICA; *Publications* Jean Macalpine: Intervals in Light (1998), Carole Hodgson (1999), George Kyriacou (1999), Jock McFadyen (contrib, 2000), New European Artists (contrib, 2001); *Recreations* listening to opera and reading novels; *Clubs* Chelsea Arts; *Style*— Ms Mary Rose Beaumont; ✉ 40 Elms Road, London SW4 9EX (tel and fax 020 7498 8664)

BEAUMONT, His Hon Judge Peter John Luther; QC (1986); s of S P L Beaumont, OBE, of Melbourne, Aust, and D V Beaumont, *née* McMeekan; *b* 10 January 1944; *Educ* Peterhouse Sch Rhodesia, Univ of Rhodesia (BSc(Econ)); *m* Ann, *née* Jarratt; 1 da (Kate b 21 Dec 1971), 1 s (James b 23 May 1975); *Career* called to the Bar Lincoln's Inn 1967 (bencher 2001); barr SE Circuit 1967–89, recorder of the Crown Court 1986–89, circuit judge (SE Circuit) 1989–, sr circuit judge Central Criminal Court 1995–; judicial memb Parole Bd 1992–97, memb Criminal Ctee Judicial Studies Bd 2000–03, memb Sentencing Guidlines Cncl 2004–; govr Felsted Sch 1989–2002 (chm 1993–98); Common Serjeant of London 2001, Recorder of London 2004, HM Lt City of London; memb Ct of Assts Worshipful Co of Loriners, Hon Liveryman Worshipful Co of Cutlers, Hon Liveryman Worshipful Co of Curriers; *Recreations* tennis, golf, gardening; *Clubs* Travellers; *Style*— His Hon Judge Beaumont, QC; ✉ Central Criminal Court, Old Bailey, London EC4M 7EH (tel 020 7248 3277)

BEAUMONT, Hon Richard Blackett; CVO (1995); 2 s of 2 Viscount Allendale, KG, CB, CBE, MC (d 1956); *b* 13 August 1926; *Educ* Eton; *m* 1971, Lavinia Mary (sometime Governess to HRH The Prince Edward), da of late Lt-Col Arnold Keppel (gggs of Rt Rev Hon Frederick Keppel, sometime Bishop of Exeter and 4 s of 2 Earl of Albemarle); *Career* joined RNVR 1944, Sub Lt 1946; PA to Sir Walter Monckton Hyderabad 1947–48, joined James Purdey and Sons 1949 (dir 1952), ADC to Sir Donald MacGillivray Malaya 1954–55, pres James Purdey and Sons 1996– (chm 1971–95); memb Ct of Assts Gunmakers' Co (Master 1969 and 1985); *Books* Purdey's, The Guns and the Family (1984); *Recreations* shooting, travel; *Clubs* White's, Turf, Pratt's; *Style*— The Hon Richard Beaumont, CVO; ✉ Flat 1, 13–16 Embankment Gardens, London SW3 4LW (tel 020 7376 7164)

BEAUMONT, Rupert Roger Seymour; s of Robert Beaumont, and Peggy Mary Stubbs, *née* Bassett (d 1988); *b* 27 February 1944; *Educ* Wellington, Univ of Grenoble; *m* 24 Feb 1968, Susie Diane, da of Noel Sampson James Wishart; 1 s (James b 1971), 1 da (Juliet b 1972); *Career* articled clerk Beaumont & Son 1962–68, admitted slr 1968, with Appleton Rice and Perrin NY 1968–69, ptnr Slaughter and May 1974–2001 (joined 1969, Hong Kong office 1976–81); author various articles for learned jls; memb: Law Soc 1973, Fin Reporting Review Panel 2002–; hon fell ACT; *Recreations* tennis, fishing, golf; *Clubs* Cavalry and Guards; *Style*— Rupert Beaumont, Esq

BEAUMONT, William Blackledge (Bill); OBE (1982); s of Ronald Walton Beaumont, of Croston, Lancs, and Joyce, *née* Blackledge; *b* 9 March 1952; *Educ* Ellesmere Coll; *m* 1977, Hilary Jane, da of Kenneth Seed, of Preston, Lancs; 2 s (Daniel b 1982, Samuel b 1985); *Career* rugby player and administrator; England nat team: 34 caps, capt 1977–82 (21 matches), winners Grand Slam 1980; capt: Br and Irish Lions tour to South Africa 1980, Barbarians, Lancashire; ret from rugby 1982; currently chm RFU Nat Playing Ctee and Br and Irish Lions Ctee, RFU rep to the Int Rugby Bd 1999–, tour mangr Br and Irish Lions tour to NZ 2005; dir: J Blackledge and Son Ltd 1981, Red Rose Radio 1981, Chorley and District Bldg Soc 1983; BBC sports analyst: Grandstand, Rugby Special; team capt A Question of Sport BBC1 until 1996; *Books* Thanks to Rugby (autobiography, 1982), Bill Beaumont: The Autobiography (2003); *Recreations* golf, boating; *Clubs* E India, Royal Lytham Golf, Fylde RUFC; *Style*— Bill Beaumont, Esq, OBE

BEAUMONT OF WHITLEY, Baron (Life Peer UK 1967), of Child's Hill in Greater London; Timothy Wentworth Beaumont; o s of late Maj Michael Wentworth Beaumont, TD (d 1958, gs of 1 Baron Allendale) by 1 w, Hon Faith Muriel, *née* Pease (d 1935), da of 1 Baron Gainford; *b* 22 November 1928; *Educ* Eton, Gordonstoun, ChCh Oxford, Westcott House Cambridge; *m* 13 June 1955, Mary Rose Beaumont, *qv*, yr da of Lt-Col Charles Edward Wauchope, MC (d 1969); 2 s (Hon Hubert Wentworth b 1956, Hon Alaric Charles Blackett b 1958, d 1980), 2 da (Hon Atalanta Armstrong b 1961, Hon Ariadne Grace b 1963); *Career* vicar of Christ Church Kowloon Hong Kong 1957–59 (resigned Holy Orders 1979, resumed 1984); proprietor various periodicals incl Time and Tide, Prism and New Christian 1960–70; pres Lib Pty 1969–70 (head of orgn 1965–66), delg to Parly Assembly Cncl of Europe and Western Euro Union 1974–77; chm Studio Vista Books 1963–68; dir Green Alliance 1977–79; memb: Nat Exec Church Action on Poverty (CAP) 1982–86 and 1991–94, Lib Dem Federal Policy Ctee 1992–95; Lib spokesman House of Lords on educn, arts and the environment 1967–85, Lib Dem spokesman House of Lords Conservation and the Countryside 1993–, treas All-Pty Family Farms Gp 1998–99, Green Pty spokesman on Agric 2000–; vice-pres Green Lib Dems 1997–99 (memb Exec Cncl 1993–97), memb Green Pty 1999– (memb Policy Ctee 2000–); vicar of St Luke's and St Philip's (The Barn Church) Kew 1986–91, co-organiser Southwark Diocese Spiritual Directors Course 1994–96; *Books* Where Shall I Place My Cross? (1987), The End of the Yellowbrick Road (1997); *Recreations* gardening, reading, listening to individuals; *Style*— The Rev the Rt Hon Lord Beaumont of Whitley; ✉ 40 Elms Road, London SW4 9EX (e-mail beaumontt@parliament.uk)

BEAVEN, Richard James; s of John Edwin Beaven, of Bath, Avon, and Patricia Anne Merrifield, of Exeter, Devon; *b* 5 May 1966; *Educ* Hele's Sch Exeter, Exeter Coll, Bristol Poly (HND Business Studies); *m* Marie-Regine Elisabeth, da of Jacques Astic; 1 da (Martha Beaven b 15 Dec 1997); *Career* media planner/buyer Geers Gross Advertising 1988–89, media mangr StarCom (formerly Leo Burnett Advertising) 1989–93, gp media dir Saatchi & Saatchi Advertising 1993–95, jt exec media dir/bd dir Leo Burnett Advertising 1996 (gp media dir 1995–96), former exec vice-pres and md MediaVest NY, ceo North America Initiative 2006–; *Recreations* photography, Chelsea FC, hill walking (first completed 3 Peaks Challenge in 1992); *Style*— Richard Beaven, Esq

BEAVER, Wendy Margaret; da of John Anthony Beaver, of Southport, and Beryl Mary, *née* Gillett; *b* 22 February 1960; *Educ* Southport HS for Girls, Univ of Sheffield (BSc); *m* Brendan Gibney; 2 s (Mark James b 13 Dec 1991, Matthew David b 23 Dec 1993); *Career* trainee Royal Life 1980–83; actuary and conslt: The Wyatt Company 1983–88, Towers Perrin 1988–92; chief actuary Govt Actuary's Dept 1992–99; Euro ptnr Mercer Human Resource Consulting 1999–; former chm Pensions Bd Inst and Faculty of Actuaries; FIA 1988; *Recreations* children, keep fit; *Clubs* Gallio, Actuaries'; *Style*— Ms W M Beaver; ✉ Mercer Human Resource Consulting, Tower Place, London EC3R 5BU (tel 020 7178 7185, fax 020 7178 7185)

BEAVERBROOK, 3 Baron (UK 1917); Sir Maxwell William Humphrey Aitken; 3 Bt (UK 1916); s of Sir Max Aitken, 2 Bt, DSO, DFC (d 1985; suc as 2 Baron Beaverbrook 1964, which he disclaimed for life 1964) by his 3 w, Violet (*see* Lady Aitken); *b* 29 December 1951; *Educ* Charterhouse, Pembroke Coll Cambridge; *m* 1974, Susan Angela (Susie), da of Francis More O'Ferrall and Angela (niece of Sir George Mather-Jackson, 5 Bt, and da of Sir Anthony Mather-Jackson 6 Bt, JP, DL, by his w, Evelyn, da of Lt-Col Sir Henry Stephenson, 1 Bt, DSO); 2 s (Hon Maxwell Francis b 1977, Hon Alexander Rory b 1978), 2 da (Hon Charlotte 1982, Hon Sophia b 1985); *Heir* s, Hon Maxwell Aitken; *Career* dir Ventech Ltd 1983–86, chm and pres Ventech Healthcare Corporation Inc 1988–92 (chm 1986); govt whip House of Lords 1986–88; treas: Cons Party 1990–92 (dep treas 1988–90), European Democratic Union 1990–92; chm Highway One Corporation Ltd 1996–99, chm Cheeky Moon Entertainment plc 2006–, dir British Racing Drivers Club Ltd 2006–; tstee Beaverbrook Fndn 1974– (chm 1985–); memb Cncl Homeopathic Tst 1989–92, chm Nat Assoc of Boys' Clubs 1989–92; European Grand Touring Car Champion 1998, Harmsworth Trophy 2004; chm British Powerboat Racing Club 2004–; Air Cdre RAuxAF 2004–; churchwarden St James Denchworth 1988–2006; *Clubs* White's, Royal Yacht Squadron, Br Racing Drivers; *Style*— The Rt Hon the Lord Beaverbrook

BEAZLEY, Thomas Alan George; QC (2001); s of late Derek Beazley, of Newport, and Rosemary Beazley; *b* 2 March 1951; *Educ* Emmanuel Coll Cambridge (BA, LLB); *m* 1980, Ingrid, da of late Ian Marrable; 2 da (Kim b 8 Sept 1980, Beatrice 14 Jan 1984); *Career* called to the Bar Middle Temple 1979; *Publications* Holding the Balance - Effective Enforcement, Procedural Fairness and Human Rights in Regulating Financial Services and Markets in the 21st Century (ed Ferran and Goodheart, 2001); articles on private international law and financial services; *Style*— Thomas Beazley, Esq, QC; ✉ Blackstone Chambers, Temple, London EC4Y 8BW (tel 020 7583 1770, e-mail thomasbeazley@blackstonechambers.com)

BEBE, Dawn; *b* 17 April 1966; *Educ* Dip Journalism; *Career* feature writer: South Wales Echo, Just 17; ed: Big!, Bliss, New Woman; publishing dir Red 1999–2000, publishing dir New Woman 1999–2000, md Emap Elan Women's Media 2000–02, md Emap Elan 2002–; memb Ctee BSME; winner: Magazine of the Year PPA Awards 1998, Most Improved Publication EMAP Awards 1998; *Style*— Miss Dawn Bebe; ✉ Emap Elan, 4th Floor, Endeavour House, 189 Shaftesbury Avenue, Covent Garden, London WC2 (tel 020 7437 9011, e-mail dawn.bebe@ecm.emap.com)

BECHER, Sir John William Michael (WRIXON-); 6 Bt (UK 1831), of Ballygiblin, Cork; s of late Sir William Wrixon-Becher, 5 Bt, MC, by his 1 w, later Countess of Glasgow (d 1984); *b* 29 September 1950; *Educ* Harrow, Neuchâtel Univ Switzerland; *Career* Lloyd's underwriter G N Rouse 1971–74, Lloyd's Brokers 1974–87, dir Wise Speke Financial Services 1987–93, fin conslt HSBC Gibbs Ltd 1993–99, ptnr Ford Reynolds and Associates Ltd 2000–05, princ Becher Ford Reynolds 2006–; dir: Old Street Productions

Ltd 2001–03, Wind Energy Ltd 2003–05; CII Fin Planning Certs; memb Personal Finance Soc; *Recreations* shooting, fishing, golf; *Clubs* White's, MCC, I Zingari, Swinley Forest, Annabel's; *Style—* Sir John Wrixon-Becher, Bt

BECHTLER, Hildegard Maria; da of Richard Bechtler (d 1973), and Klara, *née* Simon (d 1993); *b* 14 November 1951; *Educ* Camberwell Sch of Art, Central St Martins Sch of Art and Design; *m* Nov 1984, Bill Paterson, *qv*; 1 s (Jack b 10 April 1985), 1 da (Anna b 28 Sept 1989); *Career* set, costume and production designer; memb London Inst (LIMA) 2001; FRSA 2001; *Theatre and Opera* numerous credits incl: Electra (RSC) 1989, King Lear (RNT and world tour) 1990, La Wally (Bregenz Festival and Amsterdam Muziktheater) 1990, Electra (Riverside Studios and Bobigny Paris) 1991, Heddar Gabler (Abbey Dublin and Playhouse London) 1991, Peter Grimes (ENO and Munich Staatsoper) 1991, Don Carlos (Opera North) 1992, Wozzeck (Opera North) 1992, Coriolanus (Salzburg Festival) 1993, Lohengrin (ENO) 1993, Footfalls (Garrick) 1994, Don Giovanni (Glyndebourne) 1994–95, St Pancras Project 1995, Richard II (RNT) 1995, Simon Boccanegra (Munich Staatsoper) 1995, The Changing Room (Royal Court Classic Season and Duke of York's) 1996, The Doll's House (Odean Theatre de l'Europe Paris) 1997, Paul Bunyan (ROH)1997, Boris Godunov (ENO) 1998, Dialogue Des Carmélites (Seito Kinen Festival Japan and Palais Garnier Paris Opéra) 1998–99, The Merchant of Venice (RNT) 1999, Kátya Kabanova (Opera North) 1999, Der Ring Der Nibelungen, Rheingold (Scottish Opera and Edinburgh Festival) 2000 (also Walküre 2001, Siegfried 2002, Götterdämmerung 2003, The Ring Cycle 2003), War and Peace (ENO) 2000 and 2001, Blasted (by Sarah Kane, Royal Court Theatre) 2001, Lady Macbeth of Mjinsk (Sydney Opera) 2002, Terrorism (Royal Court Theatre Upstairs) 2003, The Masterbuilder (Albery Theatre) 2003, Blood (Royal Court Theatre) 2003, The Goat (Almeida and Apollo Theatre) 2004, The Sweetest Swing in Baseball (Royal Court Theatre) 2004, Iphigenia at Aulis (RNT) 2004, Primo (RNT) 2004, Forty Winks (Royal Court Theatre) 2004, By the Bog of Cats (Wyndham's Theatre) 2004, Dialogue des Carmélites (Bastille Paris Opera) 2004, My Name is Rachel Corrie (Royal Court Theatre Upstairs) 2005, La Cenerentola (Glyndebourne Festival Opera) 2005, Primo (Musicbox Theatre Broadway NY) 2005, Richard II (Old Vic Theatre) 2005, The Crucible (RSC) 2006, Dido and Aeneas (La Scala Milan) 2006, My Name is Rachel Corrie (Playhouse London and Minetta Lane Theatre NY) 2006, Exiles (NT) 2006, Krapp's Last Tape (Royal Court) 2006, Thérèse Racquin (NT) 2006, The Crucible (Apollo Theatre) 2006, The Seagull (Royal Court) 2007, The Lady from Dubuque (Haymarket) 2007, The Jewish Wife (Young Vic) 2007, The Hothouse (Nat Theatre) 2007, All About My Mother (Old Vic) 2007, Kátá Kabanova (Opera North) 2007, Madame Butterfly (Opera North) 2007; *Television and Film* numerous credits incl: Coming up Roses (feature) 1985, Hedda Gabler (BBC) 1993, The Waste Land (BBC) 1995, Richard II (BBC) 1996, The Merchant of Venice (RNT 1999) 2000, Krapp's Last Tape (BBC 4) 2007, Primo (HBO/BBC) 2007; *Awards* Olivier Award for Best Prodn (for Hedda Gabler) 1991, French Critics' Best Foreign Prodns Award (for Richard II) 1996, Olivier Award for Best Prodn (for Paul Bunyan) 1997, Evening Standard Award for Outstanding Achievement in Opera 1997, Japanese Critics Award for Best Production of the Year (for Dialogue Des Carmélites) 1999, Barclays TMA Award for Outstanding Achievement in Opera (for Walküre and Siegfried) 2002, South Bank Award for Best Opera Production (for The Ring Cycle) 2004, moniated Best Designer Evening Standard Awards (for Iphigenia at Aulis) 2004, Olivier Award for Best Revival (for The Crucible) 2007; *Style—* Ms Hildegard Bechtler; ✉ Cruickshank Cazenove Limited, 97 Old South Lambeth Road, London SW8 1XU (tel 020 7735 2933, fax 020 7582 6405, e-mail office@cruickshankcazenove.com)

BECK, Andrew; s of James Albert Beck (d 1997), and Kathleen May, *née* Ellis (d 2001); *b* 9 April 1958, Leeds; *Educ* Temple Moor HS Leeds, Huddersfield Poly (BA); *m* 19 July 1980, Diane Lesley, *née* Clough; 1 da (Samantha Victoria b 26 June 1984), 1 s (Richard Andrew b 13 June 1989); *Career* Walker Morris: slr 1989–96, ptnr 1996–; memb: Assoc of Northern Mediators, Property Litigation Assoc, Law Soc; *Style—* Andrew Beck, Esq; ✉ Walker Morris, Kings Court, Leeds LS1 2HL (tel 0113 283 2520, fax 0113 245 9412, e-mail ayb@walkermorris.co.uk)

BECK, Charles Theodore Heathfield; s of Richard Theodore Beck, and Margaret Beryl, *née* Page; *b* 3 April 1954; *Educ* Winchester, Jesus Coll Cambridge (MA); *m* 19 Sept 1992, Nathakan Piyawannahong, da of Wan Saklor; 1 s; *Career* Bank of England 1975–79; J M Finn & Co stockbrokers: joined 1979, ptnr 1984, fin ptnr 1988–91 and 1993–98, compliance and systems partner 1998–, compliance and systems dir 2006–; Freeman City of London 1980, Liveryman Worshipful Co of Broderers 1981; FSI, ASIP; *Recreations* fencing, Japanese fencing, archaeology; *Style—* Charles Beck, Esq; ✉ J M Finn & Co, 4 Coleman Street, London EC2R 5TA (tel 020 7600 1660, fax 020 7600 1661, e-mail charles.beck@jmfinn.com)

BECK, Clive; s of Sir Edgar Charles Beck, CBE (d 2000), and his 1 wife, Mary Agnes, *née* Sorapure (d 2000); *b* 12 April 1937; *Educ* Ampleforth; *m* 28 April 1960, Philippa Mary, da of Dr Philip Flood (d 1968), of Wimbledon; 3 da (Nicola b 17 Feb 1961, Emma b 19 Dec 1967, Sarah b 16 July 1971), 3 s (David b 28 July 1962, Andrew b 22 Sept 1964, Simon b 30 Dec 1965); *Career* 2 Lt The Life Guards 1955–57; John Mowlem & Co 1957, joined SGB Gp plc 1967 (dir 1968, chm 1985), rejoined John Mowlem & Co plc as dep chm and jt md; chm London Management Ltd; Freeman of City of London 1960, Liveryman Worshipful Co of Plaisterers; *Recreations* golf, travel; *Clubs* Royal Wimbledon Golf, Swinley Forest Golf; *Style—* Clive Beck, Esq; ✉ 8 Atherton Drive, Wimbledon, London SW19 5LB (tel 020 8946 5076)

BECK, David Clive; s of Clive Beck, and Philippa, *née* Flood; *b* 28 July 1962; *Educ* Ampleforth, Univ of Kent at Canterbury (BA); *m* 18 July 1992, Katherine, *née* Millar; 2 da, 1 s; *Career* Bell Pottinger Financial Ltd (formerly Lowe Bell Financial): joined 1986, dir 1992–2002, dep md 1995–97, md 1997–2002; dir of communications Marconi Corp plc 2002–06; *Recreations* golf, fishing, tennis; *Clubs* Swinley Forest Golf; *Style—* David Beck, Esq; ✉ 69 Burbage Road, London SE24 9HB

BECK, Dr Michael Hawley; s of William Hawley Beck, of Crewe, Cheshire, and June Aldersey, *née* Davenport; *b* 20 October 1948; *Educ* Sandbach Sch, Univ of Liverpool (MB ChB); *m* 18 March 1978, Gerralynn (Lynn), da of John Harrop (d 1986), of Worsley, Manchester; 2 s (Jamie b 1979, Robin b 1981); *Career* SHO: Clatterbridge Hosp Wirral 1972–74, neurosurgery Walton Hosp 1974; registrar in med Trafford HA 1976–77, registrar and sr registrar in dermatology Salford HA 1977–81 (SHO (gen med) 1974–76), conslt dermatologist Salford and Bolton NHS Tsts 1981–, dir Contact Dermatitis Investigation Unit Hope Hosp Salford 1981–; Univ of Manchester: hon assoc lectr in dermatology 1981–92, hon clinical lectr in dermatology and occupational health 1992–; dermatological advsr to the Ileostomy Assoc of UK and Ireland 1982–2001; chm NW Regnl Sub-Ctee on Dermatology 1985–88; memb: Ctee Br Contact Dermatitis Gp 1981– (chm 1992–95), Med Advsy Panel Nat Eczema Soc 1991–96, Steering Gp Epi-Derm 1994–, Scientific Ctee Jadassohn Centenary Congress 1996, Scientific Ctee Int Symposium on Contact Dermatitis (ISCD) Seoul 2003; memb Cncl: Euro Contact Dermatitis Soc 1992–95, N of England Dermatological Soc 1993–95, Manchester Med Soc 1995–98; memb Editorial Bd: Exogenous Dermatology 2001–06, Jl of Dermatological Treatment, Contact Dermatitis; author of various articles in med jls and books relating to clinical dermatology and contact dermatitis; Schering-Plough orator Clinical Assts Meeting Manchester 2002, Prosser White orator Br Assoc of Dermatologists meeting Brighton 2003; memb: Euro Contact Dermatitis Soc, American Contact Dermatitis Soc, Br Assoc of Dermatologists; FRCP 1991 (MRCP 1977); *Recreations* genealogy, Bolton Wanderers FC; *Clubs* Dowling, Lion of Vienna; *Style—* Dr Michael Beck; ✉ 57 Chorley New Road, Bolton BL1 4QR (01204 523270)

BECK, Paul William; *b* 19 June 1962, Northallerton, Yorks; *Educ* Nunthorpe GS York, Univ of Newcastle (HND); *m* 15 June 1996, Rachael, *née* Young; 1 da (Olivia b 12 March 1997), 1 s (James b 18 April 1999); *Career* Dunn & Bradstreet 1983–86, fndr PBA 1986–2001, fndr and chief exec LBM 1996–2006, fndr Bek Helicopters 2005–; managed and ran Andrew Flintoff Benefit Year 2006; *Recreations* owner of 30 racehorses, Lancs CCC (sponsor); *Style—* Paul Beck, Esq; ✉ Wrenshot House, Wrenshot Lane, Cheshire WA16 6PG

BECK-COULTER, (Eva Maria) Barbara; da of Wilhelm Beck (d 1979), of Hameln/Weser, Germany, and Clara Herta Edith Ursula Kothe (d 1989); *b* 14 October 1941; *Educ* Victoria-Luise Gymnasium Hameln, Munich Univ, Univ of London (BSc); *m* 1971, Ian Coulter, s of William Coulter; 2 s (William Angus b 29 Sept 1974, Benjamin Ian b 19 June 1976), 1 da (Catherine Barbara b 10 Sept 1978); *Career* The Economist: researcher 1965–69, writer on business affairs 1969–74, ed Euro Community Section 1974–78, Euro ed 1978–81, asst ed 1980–81, surveys ed 1995–; sec gen Anglo-German Fndn for the Study of Industrial Soc 1981–91, ed International Management Magazine (part of Reed Elsevier) 1991–94, head of public affairs (Europe) Andersen Consulting 1994; memb Cncl RIIA 1984–90 (memb Exec Ctee 1989–90), memb Academic Cncl Wilton Park (FCO Conf Centre) 1984–91, memb Steering Ctee Königswinter Conf 1982–91, memb Int Cncl Sci Centre Berlin (Social Sci Res) 1990–94, memb Cncl Federal Tst 1993–94; broadcaster, writer and lectr on current affairs in English and German; FRSA 1990; *Recreations* family, classical music, horse riding, food; *Clubs* Reform (chm 1992–93, tstee 1995–); *Style—* Mrs Barbara Beck-Coulter; ✉ c/o The Economist, 25 St James's Street, London SW1A 1HG (tel 020 7830 7168, fax 020 7839 2968, e-mail barbarabeck@economist.com)

BECKET, Michael Ivan H; *b* 11 September 1938; *Educ* Wynyard Sch Ascot, Sloane Sch Chelsea, Open Univ; *Career* Nat Serv 1957–59; lathe operator Elliot Bros (London) Ltd 1956–57, exhibition organiser Shell International Petroleum 1959–61, journalist Electrical & Radio Trading 1961, market res Young & Rubicam 1962; civil serv 1962–68 (Bd of Trade, Nat Bd for Prices and Incomes, Nat Econ Devpt Office); Daily Telegraph 1968–2003, freelance writer and journalist 2003–; *Books* Computer by the Tail (1972), Economic Alphabet (1976, 2 edn 1981), Bluff Your Way in Finance (1990), Office Warfare: An Executive Survival Guide (1993), An A-Z of Finance (1999), Stakeholder Pensions (2001), How the Stock Market Works (2002, 2 edn 2004), Starting Your Own Business (2003); *Style—* Michael Ivan H Becket, Esq; ✉ 9 Kensington Park Gardens, London W11 3HB (tel 020 7727 6941)

BECKETT, Maj-Gen Edwin Horace Alexander; CB (1988), MBE (1974); s of William Alexander Beckett (d 1986), of Sheffield, and Doris, *née* Whitham (d 1989); *b* 16 May 1937; *Educ* Henry Fanshawe Sch, RMA Sandhurst; *m* 1963, Micaela Elizabeth Benedicta, yr da of Col Sir Edward St Lo Malet, 8 Bt, OBE (d 1990); 1 da (Diana b 1964), 3 s (Simon b 1965, Alexander b 1979, Thomas b 1980); *Career* cmmnd West Yorks Regt 1957; regtl serv: Aden (despatches 1968), Gibraltar, Germany, NI; DAA and QMG 11 Armd Bde 1972–74, CO 1 PWO 1976–78 (despatches 1977), GSO1 (DS) Staff Coll 1979, Cmdt Jr Div Staff Coll 1980, Cdr UKMF and 6 Field Force 1981, Cdr UKMF 1 Inf Bde and Tidworth Garrison 1982; dir: Concepts MOD 1983–84, Army Plans and Progs MOD 1984–85; COS HQ BAOR 1985–88, head of Br Def Staff and def attaché Washington DC 1988–91; Col Cmdt King's Div 1988–93, Col PWO 1996–2001; dir of corp affrs International Distillers and Vintners Ltd 1991–96; fndr chm Br Producers and Brand Owners Group 1993–95, chm British Brands Group 1995–97 (pres 1998–2000), dir Southern Africa Business Assoc 1995–96; chm Calvert Tst Exmoor 1992–2000, fndr chm Exmoor Tst 1999–, dir Calvert Tst 1999–2003, vice-chm Directory of Social Change 2004–; *Recreations* fishing, golf; *Clubs* Army and Navy, Woodroffe's, Pilgrims; *Style—* Maj-Gen Edwin Beckett, CB, MBE

BECKETT, Frances Mary (Fran); OBE (2006); da of Josephine Godwin, *née* Beckett; *b* 20 November 1951; *Educ* CSQW, Cert in Biblical Studies, MSc Vol Sector Orgn; *Career* trainee mental welfare offr Somerset CC 1969–71, professional social work trg Trent Poly Nottingham 1971–73, rejoined Somerset CC as social worker 1973–75, religious educn studies ANCC Herts 1975–77, student counselling 1977–81, community worker and advice centre mangr 1981–86; Shaftesbury Society: social work advsr 1986–90, community care coordinator 1990–92, urban action dir 1992–95, chief exec 1995–2002; chief exec Church Urban Fund 2002–; chair: ACEVO 2002–05, Home Office Voluntary and Community Sector Advsy Gp 2003–06, Restore (Peckham) 2004–, XLP/Soul in the City 2005–07, Rebuilding Community Tst 2005–, Vol and Community Sector Cabinet Office Advsy Gp 2006–; memb Bd and dir FBRN 2005–, memb Bd NCVO 2005–07; memb: Cncl of Reference at Pioneer Tst, Social Workers Christian Fellowship, Links Int; FRSA 2002; *Books* Called to Action (1989), Love in Action (1993), Rebuild (2001); also author of various articles in religious and professional jls; *Recreations* local church involvement, jazz, cinema, theatre; *Style—* Ms Fran Beckett, OBE; ✉ Church Urban Fund, Church House, Great Smith Street, London SW1P 3AZ (tel 020 7898 1647, fax 020 7898 1601, e-mail fran.beckett@cuf.org.uk)

BECKETT, Keith Austin; s of Frank Austin James Beckett (d 1967), and Evelyn Amelia (d 1999), *née* Clarke; *b* 20 April 1934; *Educ* Lowestoft GS, Univ of Leicester (BSc London); *m* 1; 2 s (Douglas Keith b 1959, Stephen John b 1962); m 2, 1982, Mary Catherine Sharpe; *Career* Nat Serv Flying Offr RAF Signals Branch 1957–59; process engr Matthew Hall 1957–62; ICI: process design mangr Agric Div 1962–67, engrg conslt Central Mgmnt Servs 1967–69, process engrg mangr Organics Div 1969–74; dir Tech Div Burmah Oil 1974–76, dir and gen mangr Burmah Petrocarbon 1976–81, dir of project mgmnt Building Design Partnership 1981–82, gp chief engr Pilkington plc 1982–92, dir (Europe) Pilkington plc 1991–97, vice-pres engrg Pilkington plc 1994–97; co-inventor (with Prof S P S Andrew, FRS) patented process for producing methanol at low pressure; Senator Eng Cncl 1998; memb Ct of Govrs UMIST 1998–05, memb Cncl UMIST 2001–05, dir UMIST Ventures Ltd 2002–05; FIChemE 1972 (MIChemE 1964), FREng 1992; *Books* Plant Layout (jtly, 1969); *Recreations* golf, music, travel, antiques, theatre; *Style—* Keith Beckett, Esq, FREng

BECKETT, Rt Hon Margaret Mary; PC (1993), MP; da of Cyril Jackson, and Winifred Jackson; *b* 15 January 1943, Ashton-under-Lyne, Lancs; *Educ* Notre Dame HS, Manchester Coll of Sci and Technol, John Dalton Poly; *m* 1979, Leo Beckett; *Career* formerly: engrg apprentice (metallurgy) AEI Manchester, experimental offr Univ of Manchester; researcher (industrial policy) Lab Pty HQ 1970–74; MP (Lab, TGWU supported): Lincoln Oct 1974–79 (also contested Feb 1974), Derby South 1983–; PPS to min of Overseas Devpt 1974–75 (political advsr 1974), asst Govt whip 1975–76, min DES 1976–79; princ researcher Granada TV 1979–83; oppn front bench spokesman on social security 1984–89, shadow chief sec to the Treasy 1989–92, dep ldr of the opposition 1992–94 (ldr May-July 1994), shadow ldr of the House of Commons and Lab campaign co-ordinator 1992–94, candidate Lab Pty leadership and dep leadership elections 1994, shadow sec of state for health 1994–95, shadow sec of state for trade and industry 1995–97, Pres Bd of Trade (sec of state for Trade and Industry) 1997–98, Pres of the Cncl and Ldr of the House of Commons 1998–2001, sec of state for environment, food and rural affrs 2001–06, sec of state FCO 2006–07; memb: TGWU 1964–, Lab Pty NEC 1980–81, 1985–86 and 1988–98, Fabian Soc, NUJ, Anti-Apartheid Movement, BECTU, Socialist Educn Ctee, Derby Co-op Pty, Socialist Environment and Resources Assoc, Amnesty Int; memb Cncl St George's Coll Windsor 1976–82; hon pres Lab Friends of India; *Publications* Renewing the NHS (1995), Vision for Growth - A New Industrial Strategy for Britain (1996);

Recreations cooking, reading, caravanning; *Style*— The Rt Hon Margaret Beckett, MP; ✉ House of Commons, London SW1A 0AA

BECKETT, Martin; s of Vernon Beckett, of New Milton, Hants, and Dorothy Evelyn, *née* Heywood (d 1993); *b* 5 May 1954; *Educ* Ludlow GS, Manchester Poly; *Partner* Janet Ibbotson; *Career* photographer; formerly asst to many photographers incl David Swan, Alan Dunn and Chris Holland; Silver Award 1989 and Merit Award 1995 Assoc of Photographers; work exhibited in exhbns throughout Europe and featured in Art Dirs' Awards NY; chm Assoc of Photographers 1994–95 (vice-chm 1993–94), pres Pyramide Europe 2001–; ed Image Magazine, Fuji Times columnist Br Jl of Photography and Amateur Photographer; *Recreations* cuisine; *Style*— Martin Beckett, Esq; ✉ c/o Alex Vaughan, 59 Lambeth Walk, London SE11 6DX (tel 020 7735 6623, website www.martinbeckett.co.uk)

BECKETT, Sir Richard Gervase; 3 Bt (UK 1921), of Kirkdale Manor, Nawton, N Riding of Yorkshire, QC (1988); s of Sir Martyn Beckett, 2 Bt, MC (d 2001); *b* 27 March 1944; *Educ* Eton; *m* 1976, Elizabeth Ann, da of Maj (Charles) Hugo Waterhouse; 3 da (Willa Marjorie b 1977, Molly Rachel b 1979, Catherine Rose b 1983), 1 s (Walter Gervase b 1987); *Heir* s, Walter Beckett; *Career* called to the Bar Middle Temple 1965; *Recreations* walking; *Clubs* Pratt's, Portland; *Style*— Sir Richard Beckett, Bt, QC; ✉ Flat 2, 51 Lennox Gardens, London SW1X 0DF (tel 020 7589 5001)

BECKFORD, Prof James Arthur (Jim); *b* 1 December 1942; *Educ* Univ of Reading (BA, PhD, DLitt); *m*; 1 s, 2 da (twins); *Career* lectr in sociology Univ of Reading 1966–73, lectr rising to sr lectr in sociology Univ of Durham 1973–88, prof of sociology Loyola Univ of Chicago 1988–89, prof of sociology Univ of Warwick 1989–; visiting assoc prof Carleton Univ Ottawa 1974, visiting scholar Tsukuba Univ 1978, Fulbright sr visiting fell Univ of Calif Berkeley and Grad Theological Union Berkeley 1982–83; directeur d'études invité: Ecole des Hautes Etudes en Sciences Sociales Paris 2001, Ecole Pratique des Hautes Etudes Paris 2004; pres: Assoc for the Sociology of Religion 1988–89 (memb Cncl 1985–89 and 2003–), Int Soc for the Sociology of Religion 1999–2003 (vice-pres 1995–99, chair Editorial Ctee 2003–); vice-pres Int Sociological Assoc 1994–98 (chair Pubns Ctee 1994–98), memb Exec Ctee Conférence Internationale de la Sociologie des Religions 1982–86, memb Conseil Scientifique Observatoire des Religions Switzerland 1999–, govr Information Network Focus on Religious Movements (INFORM) 1991– (actg chm 1993–94); ed Current Sociology 1980–87, editorial assoc History of Sociology 1984–; assoc ed: Sociological Analysis 1983–86, International Sociology 1984–90 and 1998–2004, Review of Religious Research 1991–; memb Editorial Bd: Sage Studies in Int Sociology 1980–87, Religion 1989–99, Identity and Culture 1993–, Jl of Contemporary Religion 1994–2004, Encyclopedia of Politics and Religion 1996–99, Arxius 1996–, British Jl of Sociology 1998–, New Critical Thinking in Religious Studies 1999–, Religion-Staat-Gesellschaft 1999–; memb Comité de Rédaction Social Compass 1983–, memb Council of Reference Implicit Religion 1998–, memb Steering Ctee Dictionnaire des Faits religieux 2004–; fell Soc for the Scientific Study of Religion, FBA 2004; *Publications* incl: The Trumpet of Prophecy: A Sociological Study of Jehovah's Witnesses (1975), Religious Organization: A Trend Report and Bibliography (1975), Cult Controversies: Societal Responses to New Religious Movements (1985), Religion and Advanced Industrial Society (1989), The Changing Face of Religion (ed with T Luckmann, 1989), Secularization, Rationalism and Sectarianism (ed with E Barker and K Dobbelaere, 1993), Religion in Prison: Equal Rites in a Multi-Faith Society (with S Gilliat, 1998), Social Theory and Religion (2003), Challenging Religion: Essays in Honour of Eileen Barker (ed with J T Richardson, 2003), Muslims in Prison: Challenge and Change in Britain and France (with D Joly and F Khostokhavar, 2005), Theorising Religion: Classical and Contemporary Debates (ed with John Walliss, 2006), The Sage Handbook of the Sociology of Religion (ed with N J Demerath III, 2007); also author of numerous articles, book chapters and reports; *Style*— Prof Jim Beckford; ✉ Department of Sociology, University of Warwick, Coventry CV4 7AL

BECKHAM, David Robert Joseph; OBE (2003); s of Ted Beckham, of Chingford, London, and Sandra Beckham; *b* 2 May 1975, Leytonstone, London; *Educ* Chingford HS; *m* 4 July 1999, Victoria Adams, *qv*; 3 s (Brooklyn Joseph b 4 March 1999, Romeo James b 1 Sept 2002, Cruz b 20 Feb 2005); *Career* professional footballer; clubs: Manchester United FC until 2003 (first team debut Coca-Cola Cup v Brighton & Hove Albion 1992, League debut v Leeds United 1995, over 300 appearances, 64 goals, Premier League champions 1996, 1997, 1999, 2000, 2001 and 2003, winners FA Cup 1996 and 1999 (runners-up 1995), winners Charity Shield 1996 and 1997, winners European Champions League 1999), Real Madrid 2003–07, LA Galaxy 2007–; England: 97 full caps and 17 goals, capt 2000–06, debut v Moldova 1996, memb squad World Cup 1998, 2002 and 2006, memb squad European Championships 2000 and 2004; Young Player of the Year 1996/97, Sky Football Personality of the Year 1997, runner-up FIFA World Footballer of the Year 1999 and 2001, BBC Sports Personality of the Year 2001 (runner-up 1999); *Books* My World (2000), My Side (2003); *Recreations* family, dining and winetasting; *Style*— David Beckham, Esq, OBE

BECKHAM, Victoria, *née* Adams; da of Tony and Jackie Adams, of Goff's Oak, Herts; *b* 17 April 1974; *m* 4 July 1999, David Beckham, OBE, *qv*; 3 s (Brooklyn Joseph b 4 March 1999, Romeo James b 1 Sept 2002, Cruz b 20 Feb 2005); *Career* pop singer; fndr memb (with Emma Bunton, Melanie Brown (Mel B), Melanie Chisholm (Mel C) and formerly Geri Halliwell) The Spice Girls 1993; signed to Virgin Records 1995–; *Albums* (in excess of 40m albums sold worldwide): Spice 1996 (UK no 1), Spiceworld 1997 (UK no 1, platinum UK, double platinum US, no 1 in Holland, Norway, Denmark, New Zealand, Finland and Austria), Forever 2000; solo album Victoria Beckham 2001; *Singles* from album Spice Girls incl: Wannabe 1996 (debut single, UK no 1, first all-girl group to attain position since the Supremes 1964, 4m copies sold worldwide, no 1 in 31 territories incl American Billboard (first UK act to attain position on debut single) 1997), Say You'll Be There 1996 (UK no 1), 2 Become 1 1996 (UK Christmas no 1), Mama/Who Do You Think You Are (double A-side) 1997 (UK no 1, thus first ever band to go to no 1 in the UK with first 4 singles); from album Spiceworld: Spice Up Your Life 1997 (UK no 1), Too Much 1997 (UK Christmas no 1), Stop 1998 (UK no 2), Viva Forever 1998 (UK no 1); from album Forever: Holler/Let Love Lead The Way (double A-side) 2000 (UK no 1), Goodbye 1998 (UK Christmas no 1); solo singles: Out Of Your Mind (with Dane Bowers and Truesteppers) 2000 (UK no 2), Not Such an Innocent Girl 2001, A Mind of its Own 2002, Let Your Head Go/This Groove 2003; *Performances* incl: The Prince's Tst Gala Manchester 1997, Royal Variety Performance 1997 and 1998, Spiceworld world tour 1998; *Film* Spiceworld The Movie 1997; *Awards* Best Video (for Say You'll Be There) and Best Single (for Wannabe) Brit Awards 1997, two Ivor Novello song writing awards 1997, Best Br Band Smash Hits Show 1997, three American Music Awards 1998, Special Award for International Sales Brit Awards 1998, Outstanding Contribution to Music Brit Awards 2000; *Books* Learning to Fly (2001); *Style*— Victoria Beckham; ✉ c/o 19 Entertainment Ltd, Unit 33 Ransomes Dock, 35–37 Parkgate Road, London SW11 4NP (tel 020 7801 1919, fax 020 7801 1920)

BECKINGHAM, HE Peter; *b* 16 March 1949; *Educ* Chigwell Sch, Selwyn Coll Cambridge; *m* 1975, Jill Mary, *née* Trotman; 2 da; *Career* Decca Record Co 1970–74, Br Overseas Trade Bd 1974–79, entered HM Dip Serv 1979, consul (info) NY 1979–83; FCO: News Dept 1984, Science, Energy and Nuclear Dept 1984–86, East African Dept 1986–88; first sec Stockholm 1988–92, first sec and head Political Section Canberra 1992–96, dir Jt Export Promotion Directorate FCO 1996–99, consul-gen and DG (trade and investment) Sydney 1999–2004, ambass to the Philippines 2005–; *Recreations* golf, tennis, music; *Style*— HE Mr Peter Beckingham; ✉ c/o Foreign & Commonwealth Office (Manila), King Charles Street, London SW1A 2AH

BECKINSALE, Kate; da of Richard Beckinsale (d 1979), and Judy Loe; *b* 26 July 1973, London; *Educ* Godolphin & Latymer Sch; *m* 9 May 2004, Len Wiseman; 1 da by previous relationship (Lily Sheen b 1999); *Career* actress; *Theatre* The Seagull (nat tour), Sweetheart (Royal Court), Closer (NT Studio); *Television* incl: One Against the Wind 1991, Rachel's Dream 1992, Anna Lee 1993, Cold Comfort Farm 1995, Emma 1997, Alice Through the Looking Glass 1999; *Films* incl: Much Ado About Nothing 1993, The Prince of Jutland 1994, Uncovered 1994, Haunted 1995, Shooting Fish 1997, The Last Days of Disco 1998, Brokedown Palace 1999, The Golden Bowl 2000, Pearl Harbour 2001, Serendipity 2001, Laurel Canyon 2002, Underworld 2003, Tiptoes 2003, Van Helsing 2004, The Aviator 2005; *Style*— Kate Beckinsale; ✉ c/o ICM, Oxford House, 76 Oxford Street, London W1B 1DS

BECKLAKE, Dr (Ernest) John Stephen; s of Ernest Becklake, of Weare Gifford, Devon, and Evelyn Beatrice, *née* Stevens; *b* 24 June 1943; *Educ* Bideford GS, Univ of Exeter (BSc, PhD, Rugby colours); *m* 21 Aug 1965, Susan Elizabeth, da of Norman Buckle; 2 s (Peter Julian b 23 Nov 1972, Robin Edward b 22 April 1977); *Career* sr scientist EMI Electronics Wells 1967–69, postdoctoral fell Univ of Victoria BC 1969–70, sr engr Marconi Space and Def Systems Frimley 1970–72; Science Museum London: asst keeper (curator of space technol collection) 1972–80, head of engrg 1980–90, head of technol (dir of curatorial activities of all technol collections) 1990–94, sr res fell in astronautics 1994–, managing ed DERA History Project 1995–99; dir of numerous exhbn projects at Science Museum incl: Exploration 1977, Telecommunications 1982, Exploration of Space 1986, Robotics Japan 1991; conslt rocket history Aerospace Museum Gosford 1997–, head of astronautics Observatory Science Centre 1997–; memb and tstee Int Acad of Astronautics 1989–; FRAeS 1996; *Books* incl: Man and the Moon (1980), The Population Explosion (1990), Pollution (1991); author of over twenty papers on history of rocketry and spaceflight; *Recreations* sport (particularly rugby and golf), gardening, reading; *Clubs* Puttenham Golf, Farnborough RFC; *Style*— Dr John Becklake; ✉ Science Museum, Exhibition Road, London SW7 2DD

BECKWITH, Peter Michael; OBE (2007); s of Col Harold Andrew Beckwith (d 1966), of Hong Kong, and Agnes Camilla McMichael, *née* Duncan (d 1980); *b* 20 January 1945; *Educ* Harrow, Emmanuel Coll Cambridge (MA); *m* 19 Oct 1968, Paula, da of late Robin Stuart Bateman, of Cliftonville, Kent; 2 da (Tamara Jane b 1970, Clare Tamsin b 1972); *Career* admitted slr 1970; chm: London & Edinburgh Trust plc 1992, PMB Holdings Ltd 1992–, Aspria Holdings BV 2000–; Hon LLD Univ of Cambridge; *Recreations* association football, tennis, skiing, theatre, opera, gardening, dogs; *Clubs* Riverside Racquets (chm 1989–95), Old Harrovian AFC, Chelsea FC, Downhill Only (Wengen), Harbour (London and Milano), Austria Haus, Vail USA, The World of Residensea; *Style*— Peter Beckwith, Esq, OBE; ✉ PMB Holdings Ltd, Hill Place House, 55A High Street, Wimbledon, London SW19 5BA (tel 020 8944 1288, fax 020 8944 1054)

BEDDARD, His Hon Nicholas Elliot; s of Terence Elliot Beddard (d 1966), of London, and Ursula Mary Hamilton Howard, *née* Gurney-Richards, BEM (d 1985); *b* 26 April 1934; *Educ* Eton; *m* 25 April 1964, Gillian Elisabeth Vaughan, da of Llewelyn Vaughan Bevan (d 1987), of Cambridge; 2 s (James b 1966, Benedict b 1968), 1 da (Emily b 1974); *Career* Royal Sussex Regt 1952–54, cmmnd 1953, TA 1955–64; mgmnt trainee United Africa Co 1955–58, asst public policy exec RAC 1958–68; called to the Bar Inner Temple 1967; practised SE Circuit 1968–86, recorder of the Crown Court 1986, circuit judge (SE Circuit) 1986–2003 (dep circuit judge 2003–05); memb Cncl HM Circuit Judges 1986; undergrad Essex Univ 2005–; fndr memb Barnsbury Singers; Freeman City of London, Liveryman Worshipful Co of Skinners 1957; *Recreations* choral singing, skiing, golf; *Clubs* Lansdowne, Aldeburgh Golf; *Style*— His Hon Nicholas Beddard; ✉ Farrar's Building, Temple, London EC4Y 7BD (tel 020 7583 9241)

BEDDINGTON, Prof John; CMG (2004); s of Henry John Beddington, and Mildred, *née* Weale; *Educ* Monmouth, LSE (BSc, MSc), Univ of Edinburgh (PhD); *Career* lectr in population biology Univ of York 1970–80, sr fell Int Inst of Environmental Devpt 1980–83; Imperial Coll London: lectr rising to reader 1984–91, prof 1991–, dir Centre for Environmental Technol 1994–98, dir T H Huxley Sch 1998–2001, head Dept of Environmental Sci and Technol 2001–04; chm People's Tst for Endangered Species, chm Marine Educn and Conservation Tst, chm Science Advsy Cncl DEFRA 2005–; memb NERC 2000–06; City of Heidelberg Prize for Environmental Excellence 1997; FRS 2001; *Publications* various articles in learned jls and professional literature; *Recreations* hill walking, bird watching, amateur astronomy, paintings and sculpture; *Clubs* Travellers; *Style*— Prof John Beddington, CMG, FRS; ✉ Imperial College of Science, Technology and Medicine, Prince Consort Road, London SW7 2PB (tel 020 7594 9270, fax 020 7594 6403, e-mail j.beddington@imperial.ac.uk)

BEDDOES, Edward William; OBE (1996); s of James Ronald Beddoes (d 1989), of Bristol, and Elizabeth Phyllis, *née* Owen (d 2002); *b* 3 May 1937; *Educ* Llanelli Boys' GS, Preston Rd GS London, Borough Poly (HNC Electrical Engrg); *m* 1, Sept 1963, Yvonne; 1 da (Louise Caroline b July 1965); m 2 (m dis 2003), Dec 1972, Jane Priscilla; 1 da (Sarah Jane b Jan 1973), 2 s (Thomas James b Oct 1977, Jonathan Edward b June 1985); *Career* trainee MOD (Air) 1953–55 and 1957–59 (Nat Serv RAF 1955–57), R&D gp ldr Radio Systems Elliott Bros London Ltd (taken over by GEC) 1959–69, Racal Research/Redac 1970–76, chief engr rising to tech mangr Racal Communications Security 1976–82, tech dir Vodafone Ltd 1986–97 (tech mangr 1982–86), ceo and md Dolphin Telecom plc 1997–2000, dep chm Aerial Facilities 2000–, chm AXEON Ltd 2000–, non-exec dir Mac Ltd 2000–; CEng, FIEE 1985 (MIEE 1965), FREng 1995; *Recreations* music, antiques; *Style*— Edward Beddoes, Esq, OBE, CEng, FREng, FIEE

BEDDOW, Anthony John; s of Walter Matthew Beddow, of Kingswinford, W Midlands, and Mabel, *née* Tennant; *b* 28 November 1947; *Educ* Brierley Hill GS, Bournemouth Coll of Technol (BScEcon); *m* 11 Nov 1972, Susan Dorothy, da of Phillip Francis Gilbey Jarrold; 1 da (Louise Anne b 19 Dec 1973); *Career* nat trainee 1969–71, dep hosp sec Queen Elizabeth Hosp Birmingham 1971–74, actg personnel mangr United Birmingham Hosps 1974–75, sector admin Kidderminster Gen Hosp 1975–78, asst dist admin N Devon Health Dist 1978–82; chief exec: W Glamorgan HA 1991–96 (dist planning offr 1982–91), Morriston Hosp NHS Tst 1996–97; chm Swansea Neath Port Talbot Disability Information Advice Line; sr fell Welsh Inst for Health and Social Care Univ of Glamorgan 1997–; Nuffield travelling fellowship to NZ 1991; chm Gower Folk Festival Ctee; MHSM 1977; *Recreations* folk music, theatre; *Clubs* Swansea Rotary; *Style*— Anthony Beddow, Esq; ✉ University of Glamorgan, Glyntaff Campus, Pontypridd, Mid Glamorgan CF37 1DL (tel 01443 483070, fax 01443 483079, e-mail ajbeddow@glam.ac.uk)

BEDELIAN, Haro Moushegh; OBE (1986); s of Moushegh Haroutune Bedelian (d 1974), and Annig, *née* Nigogosian (d 2000); *b* 6 March 1943; *Educ* English Sch Nicosia Cyprus, St Catharine's Coll Cambridge (MA); *m* 1970, Yvonne Mildred, da of Stephen Gregory Arratoon (d 1993); 1 s (Stepan b 1973), 2 da (Lisa b 1975, Claire b 1978); *Career* dir Balfour Beatty Ltd 1988–98; chief exec: Transmanche Link (TML) 1993–97, Connect 1997–98; pres Export Gp for Constructional Industries (EGCI) 1995–98, visiting prof of civil engrg Univ of Portsmouth 1993–, ind conslt 1998–; vice-pres ICE 2001–04 (memb Cncl 1987–90); memb Cncl: Fedn of Civil Engrg Contractors 1989–93, Royal Acad of Engrg 1991–94; FREng 1989; *Recreations* tennis, golf; *Clubs* RAC; *Style*— Haro Bedelian,

OBE, FREng; ✉ Bryn Stoke, 30 Downs Way, Tadworth, Surrey KT20 5DZ (tel 01737 813261, fax 01737 814294, e-mail hbedelian@aol.com)

BEDELL-PEARCE, Keith Leonard; s of Leonard Bedell-Pearce, of Sanderstead, Surrey, and Irene, *née* Bedell; *b* 11 March 1946; *Educ* Trinity Sch of John Whitgift, Univ of Exeter (LLB), Univ of Warwick Grad Business Sch (MSc); *m* 2 Oct 1971, Gaynor Mary, da of Frederick Charles Pemberthy Trevelyan, of Exeter, Devon; 2 da (Olivia b 1976, Harriet b 1988), 1 s (Jack b 1980); *Career* systems analyst: Plessey 1969–70, Wiggins Teape 1970–72; Prudential Assurance Co Ltd: computer projects mangr 1972–75, Legal Dept 1975, slr 1978, gen mangr field operations 1986 (additional responsibility for mktg 1987), dir 1988–2001; chief exec and dir Prudential Financial Services Ltd 1991–95; dir: Prudential Portfolio Managers Ltd 1985, Prudential Unit Trust Managers Ltd 1986, various Prudential subsid cos, Staple Nominees Ltd 1991–, Prudential plc 1992–2001 (md UK Div 1995–96, dir Int Devpt 1996–2001), e-Commerce 2000–01; chm: Prudential Corporation Australia Ltd 1996–98, Prudential Europe 1999–2001, Norwich & Peterborough Building Soc 2001–; dir F&C Asset Mgmnt plc 2002–; chm: The Student Loans Co Ltd 2001–, Directgov 2004–, 4D Data Centres Ltd 2007–; Warwick Business Sch: memb Bd 1995–, hon prof 2001–; chm Croydon HS for Girls Scholarship Tst 2003–; memb Royal Soc Investment Advsy Ctee 2006–; memb Law Soc, fell Mktg Soc; *Books* Checklists for Data Processing Contracts (1978), Computers and Information Technology (1979, 2 edn 1982); *Recreations* shooting, modern British art; *Style*— Keith Bedell-Pearce, Esq; ✉ Norwich and Peterborough Building Society, Lynch Wood, Peterborough PE2 6WZ (tel 020 8660 0819, fax 020 8660 2099, e-mail kbp3@btinternet.com)

BEDFORD, Alan Frederick; s of Frederick Thomas Bedford (d 1967), of London, and Muriel Evelyn, *née* Sampson (d 1996); *b* 14 May 1947; *Educ* Strand GS, Westminster Med Sch (MB BS, MChOrth); *m* 11 Dec 1971, Janine Wendy, da of Kenneth Charles Smithson, of Thurston, Suffolk; 2 s (Mark b 1981, Nicholas b 1985), 1 da (Anna b 1984 d 1984); *Career* conslt in traumatic and orthopaedic surgery to West Suffolk Hosp 1982–2007; memb: Br Orthopaedic Assoc, BMA; FRCS; *Recreations* wine, photography, horticulture; *Clubs* Nibblers, Busted, West Suffolk Headway (former vice-pres), Rotary (pres); *Style*— Alan Bedford, Esq; ✉ Hydene Cottage, Hawkedon, Bury St Edmunds, Suffolk IP29 4NP (tel 01284 789483); Bury St Edmunds Nuffield Hospital, St Mary's Square, Bury St Edmunds, Suffolk (tel 01284 701371)

BEDFORD, 15 Duke of (E 1694); Andrew Ian Henry Russell; s of 14 Duke (d 2003); *b* 30 March 1962; *Educ* Harrow, Harvard Univ (BA); *m* 16 Oct 2000, Louise Rona, da of late Donald Ian Crammond, of Champignolles, France, and The Dowager Lady Delves Broughton; 1 da (Lady Alexandra Louisa Clare b 9 July 2001), 1 s (Marquess of Tavistock b 7 June 2005); *Heir* s, Marquess of Tavistock; *Career* dir: Tattersalls Ltd, Woburn Enterprises Ltd; *Recreations* country sports; *Clubs* Jockey, A D (Boston), Brook (NY); *Style*— His Grace the Duke of Bedford; ✉ Woburn Abbey, Woburn, Bedfordshire MK17 9WA (tel 01525 290333, fax 01525 290191, e-mail bedford@woburnabbey.co.uk)

BEDFORD, Anthony Peter; s of Philip Derek Bedford (d 1962), and Jean Rachel, *née* Whyman; *b* 30 September 1951; *Educ* King's Sch Canterbury, St Catherine's Coll Oxford (MA), Univ of London (MPhil); *m* 1, 14 March 1974, Anita Susan (d 1992), da of Charles Hamilton-Matthews, of Cornwall; 1 s (Tobias b 1974), 1 da (Anouska b 1977); m 2, 16 Jan 2003, Sandra Anne, da of Raymond Osborne Goodrich, of Essex; *Career* chartered clinical psychologist; head of Psychology Dept St Andrew's Hosp Northampton 1974–84; dir: Psychiatric and Psychological Consultant Services Ltd 1981–, PPCS Properties Ltd 1988–; dir of psychological servs AMI Psychiatric Div 1984–87; dir: Centre for Occupational Res 1984–94, The Rehabilitation Group 1989–92; AFBPsS; *Recreations* riding, aviation; *Style*— Anthony P Bedford, Esq; ✉ Flat 1, 14 Devonshire Place, London W1G 6HX (e-mail info@ppsltd.co.uk)

BEDFORD, Prof Peter George Courtney; *b* 2 June 1943; *Educ* King James's GS, RVC London (BVetMed, PhD); *Career* RVC London: Wellcome clinical fell Dept of Surgery 1971–91, Guide Dogs for the Blind Assoc prof of canine med and surgery 1992–2002, head Dept of Small Animal Med and Surgery 1996–2002, chair of veterinary ophthalmology 2002–03, prof emeritus veterinary ophthalmology 2003–; visiting prof in veterinary ophthalmology Univ of Illinois 1991; author of over 200 pubns; William Hunting award BVA 1983; BSAVA: Simon award 1977, Bourgelat award 1986, Blaine award 1995; David Cole fellowship Br Glaucoma Gp 1988; RCVS fndn diplomate in veterinary ophthalmology 1982, diplomate French Veterinary Ophthalmology Coll 1990, diplomate Euro Coll of Veterinary Ophthalmologists 1993; RCVS recognised specialist in ophthalmology 1992; pres: BSAVA 1982–83, Euro Soc for Veterinary Ophthalmology 1987–91, World Small Animal Veterinary Assoc 1994–96; memb Exec Bd Euro Coll of Veterinary Ophthalmologists; FRCVS 1977; *Recreations* sailing; *Style*— Prof Peter Bedford; ✉ Royal Veterinary College, Hawkshead Lane, Hatfield, Hertfordshire AL9 7TA (tel 01707 666229, fax 01707 666369, e-mail pbedford@rvc.ac.uk)

BEDFORD, Peter Wyatt; s of David Edwin Wyatt Bedford (d 1979), of Hants, and Ruth Lakin, *née* Jackson (d 1993); *b* 9 March 1935; *Educ* Spyway Sch Langton Matravers, Marlborough; *m* 1959, Valerie Clare, da of John Walton Collins (d 1989), of IOW; 4 s (Rupert b 1960, Julian b 1962, Mark b 1963, Hugo b 1970); *Career* dep chm Hampshire Youth Options; Master Worshipful Co of Haberdashers 1995–96; *Recreations* golf, shooting, horse racing; *Clubs* Naval and Military, Swinley Forest, Marlburian (pres 1998–99); *Style*— Peter Bedford, Esq; ✉ Swallick Farmhouse, Winslade, Basingstoke, Hampshire RG25 2NG (tel 01256 322408, fax 01256 322286)

BEDFORD, Bishop of 2003–; Rt Rev Richard Neil Inwood; s of Cyril Edward Inwood, and Frances Sylvia, *née* Burbridge; *b* 4 March 1946; *Educ* Burton-on-Trent GS, UC Oxford (MA, BSc), Univ of Nottingham (BA), St John's Coll Nottingham (Dip Pastoral Studies); *m* 27 Dec 1969, Elizabeth Joan, da of Robert Abram; 3 da (Hilary Rachel b 11 Aug 1976, Ruth Elizabeth b 1 Jan 1978, Alison Mary Joy b 9 Nov 1980); *Career* teacher Mvara Secdy Sch Uganda 1969, R&D chemist ICI Dyestuffs Div 1970–71, trg for Anglican miny St John's Coll Nottingham 1971–74, asst curate Christ Church Fulwood Sheffield 1974–78, dir of pastoring All Souls Langham Place London 1978–81, vicar St Luke's Bath 1981–89, hon chaplain Dorothy House Fndn Bath 1984–89, rector Yeovil with Kingston Pitney 1989–95, prebendary Wells Cathedral 1990–95, church cmmr 1991–95, archdeacon of Halifax 1995–2003; central chaplain to the Mothers' Union 2004–; chm Cncl St John's Coll Nottingham 1998–2002; tstee: Simeon's Tstees, Hyndman Tst 1984–2002; *Books* Biblical Perspectives on Counselling (1980), The Church (contrib, 1987); *Recreations* fell walking, music, family, essential gardening, films; *Style*— The Rt Rev the Bishop of Bedford

BEDFORD, (John Leslie) William; s of late Walter Bedford, and Florence Winifred, *née* Sarjeant, of Humberston, Lincs; *b* 9 December 1943; *Educ* Univ of Sheffield (BA, Moore Smith prize, Gibbons prize, PhD); *m* 13 Jan 1978, Fiona Mary, da of Rev Frederick William Hartland White, MBE, QHC; 1 da (Rachael Mary b 27 Jan 1987), 1 s (Thomas William b 3 Feb 1989); *Career* writer and poet; claims and new business broker with various Lloyds brokers 1963–71, founding ed Enigma 1966–67, postgrad tutor Univ of Sheffield 1977–79, ed Delta 1978–79, lectr Middlesex Poly 1980–81, tutor Open Univ 1981–82, contrib to Agenda (also occasional ed 1980, 1988 and 1989), Catholic Herald, Daily Telegraph, Encounter, Essays in Criticism, Harpers, The Independent, London Review of Books, London Magazine, The Nation (NY), Poetry Review, Poetry Salzburg Review, Punch, The Southern Review, Temenos Review, The Tribune, Washington Times and others 1978–; Arts Cncl Major Bursary 1978, runner-up Guardian Fiction Prize 1990, Soc of Authors Award 1993, Yorkshire and Humberside Arts Award 1993, Yorkshire Arts Award 2000, Royal Literary Fund Award 2007; *Books* Annual Bibliography of English Language and Literature (contrib, 1974, 1975 and 1976); *Poetry* Whatever There is of Light (1975), The Hollow Landscapes (1977), Journeys (1988), Imaginary Republics (1993), The Redlit Boys (2000); *Anthologies* incl: New Poetry (1975), Ten English Poets (1976), Go and open the door (1987), God gives nuts to those who have no teeth (1990), Wild and Wonderful (2002); *Fiction* Happiland (1990), Golden Gallopers (1991), All Shook Up (1992), Nightworld (1992), Catwalking (1993), The Lost Mariner (1995), Jacob's Ladder (1996), The Freedom Tree (1997), The Joy Riders (1998), Esme's Owl (1999), The Stowaway (2001), Great Expectations: a retelling (2002), Whitemen (2003), Nicholas Nickleby: a dramatisation (2004), Theseus and the Minotaur: a retelling (2004), The Glow-worm Who Lost Her Glow (2004), The Coral Island: a retelling (2004); *Drama* The Man Who Invented Words (BBC Radio Sheffield 1979), The Piano Player (BBC Radio 4, 2003); *Recreations* music, walking; *Style*— William Bedford, Esq; ✉ c/o Rogers Coleridge & White Ltd, 20 Powis Mews, London W11 1JN (tel 020 7221 3717)

BEDI, Prof Raman; s of Satya-Paul Bedi, and Raj, *née* Kaur; *b* 20 May 1953; *Educ* Headlands Sch, Univ of Bristol (BDS, DDS, DSc), Trinity Coll Bristol (DipTh), Univ of Manchester (MSc); *m* 1986, Kathryn Jane, *née* Walter; 3 s; *Career* lectr in paediatric dentistry: Univ of Manchester 1979–82, Univ of Hong Kong 1983–86, Univ of Edinburgh 1988–91; sr lectr in paediatric dentistry Univ of Birmingham 1991–96, prof and head Dept of Transcultural Oral Health Eastman Dental Inst UCL 1996–2002, chief dental offr for England Dept of Health 2002–05; co-dir WHO Collaborating Centre for Disability, Culture and Oral Health 1998–; non-exec dir Dental Defence Agency 2002–; memb Bd HE Funding Cncl Wider Participation 2003–, memb Bd HE Funding Cncl Leadership Fndn 200–; memb Gen Synod C of E 1995–; FDSRCSE 1982, FDSRCS 2002, FFPH 2003; *Publications* Betel-quid and Tobacco Chewing among the Bangladeshi Community in the United Kingdom: Usage and Health Issues (ed with P Jones, 1995), Embracing Goodwill: Establishing Healthy Alliances with Black Organisations (with P Jones, 1996), Dentist, Patients and Ethnic Minorities Towards the New Millennium (jt ed, 1996), Best Practice in Primary Healthcare: Oral Healthcare Delivery in a Multi-Ethnic Society (with P A Lowe, 1997), The Root Cause: Oral Healthcare in Disadvantaged Communities (with J Sardo Infirri, 1999); contribs to scientific jls; *Recreations* chess, tennis, travelling; *Clubs* Athenaeum; *Style*— Prof Raman Bedi

BEDINGFELD, Sir Edmund George Felix (PASTON-); 9 Bt (E 1661), of Oxburgh, Norfolk; co-heir to Barony of Grandison (abeyant since *temp* Edward III); s of Sir Henry Edward (Paston-)Bedingfeld, 8 Bt (d 1941), and Sybil, *née* Lyne-Stephens (d 1985 aged 101); *b* 2 June 1915; *Educ* Oratory Sch, New Coll Oxford; *m* 1, 1942 (m dis 1953), Joan Lynette (d 1965), da of Edgar G Rees, of Llwyneithin, Llanelly; 1 s, 1 da; m 2, 1957, Agnes Kathleen Susan Anne Danos (d 1974), da of late Miklos Gluck, of Budapest, Hungary; m 3, 1975, Mrs Peggy Hannaford-Hill (d 1991), of Fort Victoria, Rhodesia (now Zimbabwe); m 4, 15 Feb 1992, Mrs Sheila Riddell, eld da of late John Douglas, of Edinburgh; *Heir* s, Henry (Paston-)Bedingfeld, *qv*; *Career* Maj Welsh Gds, served WW2 (wounded, despatches), Palestine 1945–46; under sec (Agriculture and Forestry) RICS 1964–69, md Handley Walker (Europe) Ltd 1969–80; Freeman City of London 1988, Liveryman Worshipful Co of Bowyers; *Recreations* ornithology, heraldry, painting, fly fishing; *Clubs* Naval and Military; *Style*— Sir Edmund Bedingfeld, Bt; ✉ The Old Stables, Livermere Road, Great Barton, Bury St Edmunds, Suffolk (tel 01284 878160); Oxburgh Hall, Kings Lynn, Norfolk PE33 9PS

BEDINGFELD, Henry Edgar (PASTON-); s and h of Sir Edmund Bedingfeld, 9 Bt, *qv*, and his 1 w, Joan Lynette, *née* Rees (d 1965); *b* 7 December 1943; *Educ* Ampleforth; *m* 7 Sept 1968, Mary Kathleen, da of Brig Robert Denis Ambrose, CIE, OBE, MC (d 1974); 2 da (Katherine Mary b 4 Oct 1969, Charlotte Alexandra b 6 May 1971), 2 s (Richard Edmund Ambrose b 8 Feb 1975, Thomas Henry b 6 Sept 1976); *Career* chartered surveyor 1968; Rouge Croix Pursuivant of Arms 1983–93, York Herald of Arms 1993–; sec Standing Cncl of the Baronetage 1984–88; pres Norfolk Heraldry Soc 2006– (fndr chm 1975–80, vice-pres 1980–2006); vice-pres: Cambridge Univ Heraldic and Genealogical Soc, Suffolk Family History Soc, Norfolk Record Soc (also memb Cncl); memb Cncl Royal Soc of St George; rep of the Duke of Norfolk 1994–97, Cmmn d'Information et de Liaison des Associations Nobles d'Europe 1997–; delg of the Assoc of Armigerous Families of GB to the Cmmn; Freeman City of London 1985, Liveryman Worshipful Co of Scriveners (memb Ct of Assts 2003–), Liveryman Worshipful Co of Bowyers; Knight of Sov Mil Order of Malta 1975 (genealogist Br Assoc 1995–2000); *Books* Oxburgh Hall - The First 500 years (1982), Heraldry (jtly, 1993); *Recreations* redecorating; *Clubs* Boodle's; *Style*— Henry Bedingfeld, Esq, York Herald; ✉ Oxburgh Hall, Norfolk PE33 9PS (tel 01366 328269); The College of Arms, Queen Victoria Street, London EC4V 4BT (tel 020 7236 6420, e-mail yorkherald@btconnect.com)

BEECH, Brian Philip; s of Geoffrey Ewart Beech, of Salford, Greater Manchester, and Hilda, *née* Povah (d 1965); *b* 7 September 1954; *Educ* Worsley Wardley GS, Eccles Sixth Form Coll, Univ of Warwick (BA), Edge Hill Teacher Trg Coll Ormskirk; *m* 14 Nov 1994, Rebecca Elizabeth, da of Ernest Want; 1 s (Isaac Louie b 18 Aug 1997); *Career* teacher of English and drama Deane Sch Bolton 1977–79, head of promotional devpt Piccadilly Radio 1983–86 (successively researcher, sports prodr, features presenter and prodr then sr prodr 1979–83), account dir Greenwood Tighe Public Relations 1986–88, estab Piccadilly First Ltd (Piccadilly Radio) 1988–89; Greenwood Tighe Public Relations: md Manchester Office 1990–93, md i/c NW, Leeds and Edinburgh Offices 1993–96; jt md Communique Public Relations Manchester 1996–; Sony Award for Best Educnl Prog, PRCA Award for Outstanding Consultancy Practice; memb NW Ctee IPR; MPA; *Recreations* Manchester United, squash, golf; *Clubs* Mere Golf and Country; *Style*— Brian Beech, Esq

BEECH, Sydney John; s of Sydney Beech, of Stoke-on-Trent, Staffs, and Ruth, *née* Baskeyfield; *b* 6 February 1945; *Educ* Hanley HS, Univ of Sheffield (BA); *m* 6 Sept 1969, Jean Ann, da of Bertram Gibson, of Gillow Heath, Staffs; *Career* grad trainee Peat Marwick Mitchell & Co 1966–69, lectr in accounting taxation and quantitative techniques 1969–72; Lyon Griffiths: PA to ptnr 1972–74, ptnr 1974–86, sr ptnr 1986–2003, conslt 2003–; gp fin dir Fayrefield Gp Ltd; dir: Fayrefield Foods Ltd, Fayrefield Foodtec Ltd, Fayrefield Food Products Ltd, Fayrefield Foodtec A/S, Dairy Solutions Ltd, Fayrefield Int BV; CTA, FCA; *Recreations* golf, weightlifting, music; *Clubs* Reaseheath Golf; *Style*— S J Beech, Esq; ✉ 8 Woodland Avenue, Nantwich, Cheshire CW5 6JE; Fayrefield Foods Ltd, Englesea House, Barthomley Road, Crewe, Cheshire CW1 5UF (tel 01270 589311, fax 01270 582269)

BEECHAM, Alan; *b* 12 June 1935; *Educ* Boston GS, Open Univ (BA); *m* (m dis); 2 s (Jonathan b 1967, Christopher b 1969); *Career* Nat Serv Royal Lincolnshire Regt Malaya 1955–57; journalist 1951–62; newspapers: Lincolnshire Standard Series, Southern Times, Southern Journal, Surrey Comet, News Chronicle, Daily Express; external news serv BBC 1961–62; radio news and current affrs BBC 1962–89: chief sub ed 1967–69, duty ed 1969–70, sr duty ed 1970–78, asst ed radio news 1978–87, news output ed 1987–89; for radio: general election, Euro election, referenda, budget, local and by-election news progs, Falklands War coverage, Royal Weddings 1964–89; created modern BBC internal news agency and news serv between London and local radio; writer and journalist; film historian and lectr 2000–; Jack Cardiff in Conversation with Alan Beecham CD released 2004; FRSA (Silver Medal, advanced English); *Recreations* media, theatre, cinema, writing, Italy and France;

Clubs The Arts, RSA; *Style*— Alan Beecham, Esq; ✉ 7 Thalia Close, Greenwich, London SE10 9NA (tel 020 8858 7887)

BEECHAM, Sir Jeremy Hugh; kt (1994), DL (Tyne & Wear 1995); s of Laurence Beecham (d 1975), of Newcastle upon Tyne, and Florence, *née* Fishkin (d 1986); *b* 17 November 1944; *Educ* Royal GS Newcastle upon Tyne, UC Oxford (MA); *m* 7 July 1968, Brenda Elizabeth, da of Dr Sidney Woolf; 1 da (Sara b 1972), 1 s (Richard b 1973); *Career* admitted slr 1968; ptnr Beecham Peacock 1968–2002 (conslt 2002–); memb Lab Pty: NEC Local & Regnl Govt Sub-Ctee 1971–83, Jt Policy Ctee 1992–, Domestic and Int Policy Ctee 1992–98, NEC 1998– (vice-chm 2004–05, chm 2005–06), dir N Devpt Co Ltd 1986–91; memb: Theatre Royal Tst 1985–, Cncl Neighbourhood Energy Assoc 1987–89, President's Ctee Business in the Community 1988–; Newcastle upon Tyne City Cncl: cncllr 1967–, chm Social Serv Ctee 1973–77, chm Policy and Resources Ctee 1977–94, leader 1977–94, chm Fin Ctee 1979–84, Devpt Ctee 1995–97; AMA: dep chm 1984–86, vice-chm 1986–91, chm 1991–; cmmr English Heritage 1983–87; Parly candidate (Lab) Tynemouth 1970; vice-chm Northern Regnl Cncls Assoc 1985–91, vice-chm Local Govt Assoc 2004– (chm 1995–2004), memb Cncl Common Purpose 1989–; memb NHS Modernisation Bd 2000–; memb Int Advsy Bd Harold Hartog Sch of Govt Tel Aviv Univ 2006–, memb Exec New israel Fund 2007–; pres: Age Concern Newcastle 1995–, BURA 1996–, Newcastle Choral Soc 1997–; tstee Tyneside Cinema 1999–; Hon Freeman Newcastle upon Tyne 1995; hon fell Newcastle upon Tyne Poly 1989, Hon DCL Univ of Newcastle upon Tyne 1992; *Recreations* reading (esp novels and history), music; *Style*— Sir Jeremy Beecham, DL; ✉ 39 The Drive, Gosforth, Newcastle upon Tyne NE3 4AJ (tel 01912 851 888); 7 Collingwood Street, Newcastle upon Tyne NE1 1JE (tel 01912 323 048);

BEECHAM, Sir John Stratford Roland; 4 Bt (UK 1914), of Ewanville, Huyton, Co Palatine of Lancaster; s of Sir Adrian Beecham, 3 Bt (d 1982), and gs of Sir Thomas Beecham, 2 Bt, the conductor; *b* 21 April 1940; *Educ* Winchester, The Queen's Coll Oxford; *Heir* bro, Robert Beecham; *Recreations* walking; *Style*— Sir John Beecham, Bt; ✉ Shalom, Station Road, Shipston on Stour, Warwickshire CV36 4BT

BEECHEY, Prof (Ronald) Brian; s of Albert Ernest Beechey, of Heckmondwike, W Yorks, and Edna Beechey; *b* 24 April 1931; *Educ* Whitcliffe Mount GS Cleckheaton, Univ of Leeds (BSc, PhD); *Career* Scientific Staff MRC 1956–58, lectr Univ of Southampton 1958–63, princ scientist Shell Research Ltd 1963–83, currently prof emeritus Univ of Wales Aberystwyth; visiting prof: Physiological Lab Univ of Liverpool, Hannah Research Inst Ayr; hon meetings sec The Biochemical Soc 2001–07, treas Int Union of Biochemistry and Molecular Biology (IUBMB) 2001–06; author of articles in scientific jls; tstee Liverpool Hyperactivity and Attention Disorder Fndn 2007–; memb: Biochemical Soc, RSC, American Soc of Biochemistry and Molecular Biology; FRSC 1970; *Recreations* hill walking, squash; *Style*— Prof Brian Beechey; ✉ Department of Physiology, The University of Liverpool, Liverpool L69 3BX (tel 0151 794 5328, fax 0151 794 5337/0151 625 9021, e-mail rbeechey@liv.ac.uk)

BEECROFT, (Paul) Adrian Barlow; s of Thomas Ford Beecroft (d 1989), of E Yorks, and Jean Margaret, *née* Barlow; *b* 20 May 1947; *Educ* Hymers Coll Hull, The Queen's Coll Oxford (Hastings exhibitioner, MA), Harvard Business Sch (Harkness fell, Baker scholar, MBA); *m* 13 May 1972, Jacqueline Ann, *née* Watson; 2 da (Claire Damaris Watson Beecroft b 14 June 1977, Imogen May Watson Beecroft b 8 Feb 1991), 1 s (James Nicholas Watson Beecroft b 4 March 1980); *Career* account exec ICL 1968–73, project exec Ocean Transport and Trading 1973–74, vice-pres Boston Consulting Group 1976–84, sr managing ptnr Apax Partners Worldwide LLP 1984–; non-exec dir various cos incl: Alkane plc until 2003, Healthcare at Home Ltd; chm Br Venture Capital Assoc 1991–92; memb Chllr's Ct of Benefactors Univ of Oxford, sponsor Beecroft Inst for Particle Astrophysics and Cosmology Univ of Oxford; MRI, MSI 1992, FInstP; *Recreations* cricket, physics, steam railways, classic cars, travel; *Clubs* MCC, CCC, Incogniti CC; *Style*— Adrian Beecroft, Esq; ✉ Apax Partners, 15 Portland Place, London W1B 1PT (tel 020 7872 6330, fax 020 7636 6475, e-mail adrian.beecroft@apax.com)

BEEDHAM, Trevor; *Educ* Univ of London (BDS, MB BS); *m* Anne; 2 s, 1 da; *Career* Barts and the London NHS Tst: conslt obstetrician and gynaecologist 1981–, clinical dir Women and Children's Directorate 2003–, dep medical dir 2006–; assoc dean Queen Mary Sch of Med and Dentistry 2006–; examiner: MB BS London, MRCOG; GMC medical sch visitor 2001–; RCOG: NE Thames regnl advsr 1991–94, careers offr 1994–98, chm CME Ctee 1998–2001; memb: United Examining Bd Ctee 1993–2003, Part 1 Panel PLAB GMC 2001–; Freeman City of London 1984, Asst Worshipful Soc of Apothecaries 1996; FRSM, MIBiol 1979, FRCOG 1989 (MRCOG 1977); *Books and Publications* Treatment and Prognosis in Obstetrics and Gynaecology (1988), The Examination of Women (2001), Consultant Appraisal (2002), The Examination of Women (2007); *Recreations* swimming; *Style*— Trevor Beedham, Esq; ✉ John Harrison House, The Royal London Hospital, Whitechapel, London E1 1BB (tel 020 7377 7000, e-mail trevor.beedham@bartsandthelondon.nhs.uk)

BEER, Prof Dame Gillian Patricia Kempster; DBE (1998); da of Owen Thomas, and Ruth Winifred Bell, *née* Burley; *b* 27 January 1935; *Educ* Bruton Sch for Girls, St Anne's Coll Oxford (Charles Oldham scholar, MA, BLitt), Univ of Cambridge (LittD); *m* 7 July 1962, Prof John Bernard Beer, FBA, *qv*, s of Jack Beer; 3 s (Daniel b 1965, Rufus b 1968, Zachary b 1971); *Career* asst lectr Bedford Coll London 1959–62, pt/t lectr Univ of Liverpool 1962–64; Univ of Cambridge: fell Girton Coll 1965–94, asst lectr 1966–71, lectr then reader in literature and narrative 1971–89, Grace I prof of English 1989–94, pres Clare Hall 1994–2001, King Edward VII prof 1994–2002; vice-pres Br Acad 1994–96 (res reader 1987–89); chair Poetry Book Soc 1993–96, pres Br Assoc of Comparative Literature 2003–; memb: Cwlth Scholarship Cmmn 1987–94, Bd of Tstees of British Museum 1992–2002, Lab Party; Gold medallist MIT 2001; Hon LittD: Univ of Liverpool 1996, Anglia Poly Univ 1998, Univ of Leicester 1999, Univ of London 2001, Université de Paris Sorbonne 2001, Univ of Oxford 2005, Queen's Univ Belfast 2005; hon fell: Clare Hall Cambridge, St Anne's Coll Oxford, Girton Coll Cambridge, Univ of Wales Cardiff; hon foreign memb American Acad of Arts and Scis; FBA, FRSA, FRSL 2006; *Books* Meredith: A Change of Masks (1970), The Romance (1970), Darwin's Plots (1983 and 2000), George Eliot (1986), Arguing with the Past (1989), Forging the Missing Link (1992), Open Fields (1996), Virginia Woolf: the Common Ground (1996); *Recreations* music, travel, conversation; *Style*— Prof Dame Gillian Beer, DBE, FBA; ✉ Clare Hall, Herschel Road, Cambridge CB3 9AL (tel 01223 332360, fax 01223 332333, e-mail gpb1000@cam.ac.uk)

BEER, Prof John Bernard; s of late John Bateman Beer, and late Eva, *née* Chilton; *b* 31 March 1926; *Educ* Watford GS, St John's Coll Cambridge (MA, PhD, LittD); *m* 7 July 1962, Prof Dame Gillian Beer, DBE, FBA, *qv*, *née* Thomas; 3 s (Daniel, Rufus, Zachary); *Career* RAF 1946–48; lectr Univ of Manchester 1958–64; Univ of Cambridge: res fell St John's Coll 1955–58, fell Peterhouse 1964–93 (emeritus fell 1993), univ lectr 1964–78, reader 1978–87, prof of English literature 1987–93 (emeritus prof 1993), Leverhulme emeritus fell 1995–96, Stanton lectureship in philosophy of religion 2006–; pres Charles Lamb Soc 1989–2002; FBA 1994; *Books* Coleridge the Visionary (1959), The Achievement of E M Forster (1962), Coleridge's Poems (ed, 1963 and 1993), Milton Lost and Regained (1964), Blake's Humanism (1968, electronic version 2006), Blake's Visionary Universe (1969), Coleridge's Variety: Bicentenary Studies (ed, 1974), Coleridge's Poetic Intelligence (1977), Wordsworth and the Human Heart (1978), Wordsworth in Time (1979), E M Forster - A Human Exploration (ed with G K Das, 1979), A Passage to India - Essays in Interpretation (ed, 1985), Coleridge's Writings (general ed, 1990–), Aids to Reflection - Collected Coleridge (ed, 1993), Romantic Influences: Contemporary - Victorian - Modern (1993), Against Finality (1993), Questioning Romanticism (ed, 1995), Selected Poems of A H Clough (ed, 1998), Providence and Love: Studies in Wordsworth, Channing, Myers, George Eliot and Ruskin (1998), Coleridge's Writings on Religion and Psychology (ed, 2002), Romantic Consciousness: Blake to Mary Shelley (2003), Post-Romantic Consciousness: Dickens to Plath (2003), William Blake: A Literary Life (2005); *Recreations* walking in town and country, listening to music; *Clubs* Royal Over-Seas League; *Style*— Prof John Beer, FBA; ✉ Peterhouse, Cambridge CB2 1RD (tel 01223 356384, fax 01223 337578)

BEER, Ven John Stuart; s of John Gilbert Beer (d 2005), of Harrogate, N Yorks, and May Naomi, *née* Scott (d 1981); *b* 15 March 1944; *Educ* Roundhay Sch Leeds, Pembroke Coll Oxford (MA), Westcott House Cambridge, Fitzwilliam Coll Cambridge (MA); *m* 1970, Susan, da of Gordon Spencer (d 2000), and Jessie Spencer (d 1999); 2 s (Benjamin b 1973, Tobias b 1976), 1 da (Ophelia b 1979); *Career* advtg and fin Rowntree & Co Ltd York 1965–69; curate St John the Baptist Knaresborough 1971–74, fell and chaplain Fitzwilliam Coll and New Hall Cambridge 1974–80 (bye fell Fitzwilliam Coll 2001–), rector of Toft with Hardwick, Caldecote and Childerley 1980–87, dir of ordinands and of post-ordination trg Dio of Ely and vicar of Grantchester 1987–97; archdeacon of: Huntingdon 1997–2003, Huntingdon and Wisbech 2003–04, Ely 2004–06, Cambridge 2006–; memb Ethics Ctee Dunn Research Inst 1987–98; *Publications* Who is Jesus?; also contrib various theol jls; *Recreations* tennis, golf, cricket, good wine, music; *Style*— The Ven the Archdeacon of Cambridge; ✉ 1A Summerfield, Cambridge CB3 9HE (tel 01223 350424, fax 01223 360929)

BEESLEY, Mark; s of Nigel Patrick Beesley, of Steyning, West Sussex, and Mary Josephine; *b* 14 May 1961; *Educ* Univ of Essex (MA), Univ of Sussex (MSc); *m* 14 April 1990, Jan, *née* Collins; 1 da (Natasha b 14 Sept 1990), 1 s (Gregory b 1 Dec 1993); *Career* researcher Univ of Sussex 1984–87; opera singer; bass: studied under Elisabeth Abercrombie and Dennis Wicks, sung with various regnl opera cos incl City of Birmingham Touring, Opera 80 and Opera North 1987–89, princ bass Royal Opera 1989–96, freelance 1996–, princ bass ENO 1998–; *Roles* incl: Colline in La Bohème, Timur in Turandot, Sprecher in Die Zauberflöte, Ancient Hebrew in Samson and Delilah, Lodovico in Othello, Angelotti in Tosca, Sam in A Masked Ball; other roles incl: Fiesco in Simon Boccanegra with WNO, Pistol in Falstaff, Colline in La Bohème and Daland in The Flying Dutchman all with the ENO; int appearances incl: Midsummer Nights Dream at Aix-en-Provence, Peter Grimes at Palermo, First Nazarine in Salome at the Théâtre du Châtelet, Traviata at the Royal Opera Baden-Baden; *Recordings* incl: Pietro in Simon Boccanegra and Lodovico in Otello under Sir Georg Solti, First Nazarine in Salome under Sir Edward Downes, L'Incoronazione di Poppea under Richard Hickox, Pulcinella under Robert Craft, title role in Mendelsohn's Paulus; *Style*— Mark Beesley, Esq; ✉ c/o Athole Still International, Foresters Hall, 25–27 Westow Street, London SE19 3RY (tel 020 8771 5271, fax 020 8771 8172); website www.markbeesley.com

BEESLEY, Peter Frederick Barton; s of Ronald Fitzgerald Barton Beesley, and Mary Kurczyn, *née* Parker; *b* 30 April 1943; *Educ* King's Sch Worcester, Univ of Exeter (LLB), Coll of Law Guildford; *m* 1974, Elizabeth Jane, *née* Grahame; 1 s, 2 da; *Career* articled clerk and asst slr Windeatt & Windeatt 1965–68; Lee Bolton & Lee: asst slr 1968–69, ptnr 1969–, sr ptnr 2000–; jt registrar: Dio of St Albans 1969–78, Dio of Ely 1978–, Dio of Hereford 1983–; registrar: Faculty Office of the Archbishop of Canterbury 1981–, Dio of Guildford 1981–, Woodard Corp 1987–; pres City of Westminster Law Soc 1991–92; sec: Ecclesiastical Law Assoc 1978–98 (vice-chm 1998–2000, chm 2000–02), Ecclesiastical Law Soc 1987–; legal advsr Nat Soc (C of E) for Promoting Religious Educn 1975–, memb Legal Advice Cmmn Gen Synod of C of E 1992–; tstee Arbory Tst 2000–, Bishopsland Educational Tst 2002; govr: Hampstead Parochial Sch 1983–2003 (chm of govrs 1986–95), Sarum Hall Sch 1997–; chm Glaziers' Tst 2000–03 (memb 1996–, vice-chm 1998–2000); Master Worshipful Co Glaziers and Painters of Glass 2005 (Liveryman 1981, memb Ct of Assts 1995–); *Books* Encyclopaedia of Forms and Precedents (jt contrib vol 13 Ecclesiastical Law, 1987), Anglican Marriage in England and Wales, a Guide to the Law for Clergy (1992); *Clubs* Athenaeum, St Stephen's, MCC; *Style*— Peter Beesley, Esq; ✉ Lee Bolton & Lee, 1 The Sanctuary, Westminster, London SW1P 3JT (tel 020 7222 5381, fax 020 7799 2781)

BEESON, Andrew Nigel Wendover; s of Capt Nigel Wendover Beeson (d 1944), and Anne Margaret, *née* Sutherland; *b* 30 March 1944; *Educ* Eton; *m* 1, 1971 (m dis 1983), Susan Roberta Caroline, da of Guy Standish Gerard (d 1981); 1 da (Susanna Caroline b 27 June 1973), 1 s (James Gerard b 26 March 1976) m 2, 17 July 1986, Carrie Joy, da of Norman Joseph Martin (decd); 1 da (Christabel Alexandra Robina Martin b 4 Sept 1989); *Career* stockbroker; ptnr Capel-Cure-Carden 1972–85; dir: ANZ Merchant Bank 1985–87, ANZ McCaughan 1987–89; chm Evolution Gp plc 2001–02, dep chm Beeson Gregory Ltd 2001 (chief exec 1989–2001); non-exec dir: Woolworths Gp plc 2001–, IP2 IPO 2000–04, Nelson Bakewell 2003–, Schroders 2004–, Datawind Gp plc 2007–; *Recreations* real tennis, rackets, shooting, collecting; *Clubs* White's, Pratt's, MCC, Swinley; *Style*— Andrew N W Beeson, Esq; ✉ 21 Warwick Square, London SW1V 2AB (tel 020 7834 2903, e-mail andrew@thebeesons.com)

BEESON, Headley Thomas; s of Thomas Benjamin Beeson (d 1942), and Elizabeth, *née* Brezovits (d 2000); *b* 20 August 1942; *Educ* Clark's GS Surbiton; *m* 7 Sept 1968, Lesley Ann, da of Roland Conrad Wontner (d 1993); 1 s (Miles b 1973), 1 da (Caroline b 1975); *Career* Fenn & Crosthwaite stockbrokers 1962–67, investment mgmnt and mktg Barclays Bank Group 1967–81; dir: N M Schroder Unit Trust Managers Ltd 1981–88, Schroder Investment Management Ltd 1988–99, Brewin Dolphin Securities Ltd 1999–2001, Independent Investment Reviews Ltd 2001–06, founding dir Beeson Maisey Ltd 2006–; ASIP 1972; *Recreations* rowing, motor sports; *Style*— Headley Beeson, Esq; ✉ Courtlands, 14 The Ridings, Cobham, Surrey KT11 2PU; Beeson Maisey Limited, 18 Ellesmere Place, Walton on Thames KT12 5AE (tel 01932 242253, e-mail headleybeeson@beesonmaisey.co.uk, website www.beesonmaisey.co.uk)

BEESTON, Kevin Stanley; s of Denis Beeston (d 2002), and Patricia, *née* Hurle; *b* 18 September 1962, Ipswich, Suffolk; *Educ* Gorleston GS Great Yarmouth; *m* 12 April 1991, Jayne Anne, *née* Knowles; 2 s (Oliver b 9 April 1992, Lloyd b 25 Nov 1993), 1 da (Kathryn b 29 Sept 1995); *Career* Serco Gp plc: joined 1985, finance mangr Serco Services Ltd 1986–88, finance dir Serco Education Ltd 1988–89, finance dir then commercial dir Serco Space Ltd 1990–92, finance dir then md International Aeradio Ltd 1992–94, dir Serco Ltd 1992–94, chm and chief exec Serco International Ltd 1994–95, gp finance dir 1996–99, gp chief exec 1999–2002, gp exec chm 2002–07, non-exec chm 2007–; non-exec dir IMI plc 2005–; chm Public Services Strategy Bd and memb President's Ctee CBI; non-exec chm Partnerships in Care Ltd 2007–; dir Ipswich Town Football Club plc 2003–; FCMA 1990; *Recreations* soccer and rugby (spectating); *Style*— Kevin Beeston, Esq; ✉ Serco Group plc, Palm Court, 4 Heron Square, Richmond, Surrey TW9 1EW (tel 020 8334 4331, fax 020 8334 4301, e-mail kevin.beeston@serco.com)

BEETON, David Christopher; CBE (1998); s of Ernest Walter Beeton, and Ethel Louise, *née* Lemon; *b* 25 August 1939; *Educ* Ipswich Sch, King's Coll London (LLB); *m* 6 July 1968, Elizabeth Brenda; 2 s (Thomas b 1970, Samuel b 1972); *Career* admitted slr 1966; chief exec Bath City Cncl 1973–85, sec The Nat Tst 1985–89, chief exec Historic Royal Palaces 1989–1999, DG Br Casino Assoc 2000–; *Recreations* classical music, historic buildings, cooking; *Style*— David Beeton, Esq, CBE

BEEVERS, Prof (David) Gareth; s of Rev Charles Edward Beevers, CBE (d 1973), sometime rector of The Lophams, Norfolk, and Mabel, *née* Charlton (d 1991); *b* 4 June 1942; *Educ*

Dulwich Coll, The London Hosp Med Coll (MB BS, MD); *Career* clinical scientist MRC Blood Pressure Unit Western Infirmary Glasgow 1972–77, prof of med Univ of Birmingham 1977–, hon conslt physician City Hosp Birmingham 1977–; ed-in-chief Jl of Human Hypertension, past pres Br Hypertension Soc; memb: BMA, Int Soc of Hypertension, Euro Soc of Hypertension, Int Soc for the Study of Hypertension in Pregnancy, American Soc for Hypertension; FRCP 1981 (MRCP); *Books* Hypertension in Practice (with G A MacGregor, 1987, 3 edn 1999); *Recreations* collecting medical postage stamps and old toy soldiers; *Style*— Prof D G Beevers; ✉ Department of Medicine, City Hospital, Birmingham B18 7QH (tel 0121 554 3801)

BEEVOR, Antony James; s of John Grosvenor Beevor (d 1986), and Carinthia Jane, *née* Waterfield; *b* 14 December 1946, London; *Educ* Winchester, RMA Sandhurst; *m* 1 Feb 1986, Artemis Cooper, *qv*, da of 2 Viscount Norwich, CVO, *qv*; 1 da (Eleanor Allegra Lucy), 1 s (Adam John Cosmo); *Career* historian; Lt 11 Hussars (PAO) 1967, served BAOR and UK 1967–70; freelance journalist 1970, various mktg and advtg positions 1971–75, first novel published 1975, occasional journalist and literary critic; Lees-Knowles lectr Univ of Cambridge 2002–03, visiting prof Birbeck Coll London 2003–; participant Armed Forces into the 21st Century seminars KCL 1993–95, memb Exec Cncl French Theatre Season London 1996–97, tstee London Library 2002–04, chm Soc of Authors 2003–06 (memb Cncl 2002–); judge Shiva Naipaul Meml Prize 2000, judge Br Acad Book Prize 2004–05, judge David Cohen Prize 2005, memb Steering Ctee Samuel Johnson Prize 2004–; DLitt Univ of Kent 2004; FRSL 1999; Chevalier de l'Ordre des Arts et des Lettres (France) 1997; *Publications* four novels; The Spanish Civil War (1982), Inside the British Army (1990), Crete: The Battle and the Resistance (1991, Runciman Prize), Paris After the Liberation (with Artemis Cooper, 1994), Stalingrad (1998, Samuel Johnson Prize, Wolfson History Prize, Hawthornden Prize), Berlin: The Downfall (2002, Longman-History Today Award), The Mystery of Olga Chekhova (2004), A Writer at War: Vasily Grossman with the Red Army 1941–1945 (2005), The Battle for Spain: The Spanish Civil War 1936–1939 (2006); *Recreations* reading, gardening; *Clubs* Brooks's; *Style*— Antony Beevor, Esq; ✉ c/o Andrew Nurnberg Associates, 45–47 Clerkenwell Green, London EC1R 0QX (website antonybeevor.com)

BEEVOR, Antony Romer; s of Miles Beevor (d 1994), of Welwyn, Herts, and Sybil, *née* Gilliat (d 1991); *b* 18 May 1940; *Educ* Winchester, New Coll Oxford; *m* 1970, Cecilia, da of John Hopton (d 1969); 1 s, 1 da; *Career* slr Ashurst Morris Crisp 1962–72, Hambros Bank Ltd 1972–98 (exec dir 1982, on secondment DG Panel on Takeovers and Mergers 1987–89), dir Hambros plc 1990–98, md SG Hambros (a div of Société Générale) 1998–2000, chm Fairbridge 1999–, dep chm Panel on Takeovers and Mergers 1999–; non-exec dir: Rugby plc 1993–2000, Gerrard Gp plc 1995–2000, Croda International plc 1996–2005 (chm 2002–05), Helical Bar plc 2000–, Nestor Healthcare Gp plc 2000–03 (chm 2002–03); *Style*— Antony Beevor, Esq

BEEVOR, Sir Thomas Agnew; 7 Bt (GB 1784); s of Cdr Sir Thomas Lubbock Beevor, 6 Bt, RN (d 1943), and Edith Margaret, *née* Agnew (d 1985, having m 2, 1944, Rear Adm Robert Alexander Currie, CB, DSC); *b* 6 January 1929; *Educ* Eton, Magdalene Coll Cambridge; *m* 1, 1957 (m dis 1965), Barbara Clare, yst da of Capt Robert Lionel Brooke Cunliffe, CBE, RN (ret); 2 da (Bridget Anastasia (Mrs Matthew Porteous) b 1958, Juliana Clare (Mrs Roderick Marrs) b 1960), 1 s (Thomas Hugh Cunliffe b 1962); m 2, 1966 (m dis 1975), Carola, da of His Hon Judge Jesse Basil Herbert, MC, QC; m 3, 1976, Mrs Sally Elisabeth Bouwens, da of Edward Madoc, of Thetford, Norfolk; *Heir* s, Thomas Beevor; *Style*— Sir Thomas Beevor, Bt; ✉ Hargham Hall, Hargham, Norwich, Norfolk NR16 2JW

BEGBIE, David John; s of Donald Begbie, of Edinburgh, and Gwendoline Mary, *née* Potter; *b* 30 April 1955; *Educ* Hereson Co Secdy Sch for Boys, Thanet Tech Coll, Winchester Sch of Art, Gloucestershire Coll of Art and Design (BA), Slade Sch of Fine Art (HDFA); *m* 1, 1980 (m dis 1994), Katherine Frances, da of Maj Michael Everitt; 1 da (Rosalind Ruth b 1987); m 2, 2007, Eva Angela, da of Richard Selker; 1 da from a previous relationship (Danya Long b 1987); *Career* sculptor; ARBS; *Solo Exhibitions* Brompton Gallery London 1984, 1985 and 1986, Forum Zürich 1986, Navy Pier Chicago 1986, Savacou Fine Art Toronto 1986, Salama-Caro Gallery 1987, 1989, 1990 and 1991, ICAF Olympia 1987, Crucifix (Winchester Cathedral) 1988, Henley Festival 1988, Wates City Tower 1990, Gallery Differentiate London 1992–2001, Catto Gallery London 1993, Fire Station Gallery Sydney 1994, Emporio Armani London 1994, Joel Kessler Fine Art Miami Beach 1994–95, Magidson Fine Art Aspen Colorado USA 1995, Posner Fine Art Santa Monica USA 1995, Artopia New York 1996, Hannah Peschar Gallery and Sculpture Garden Surrey 1996, Festival of Erotica Olympia 1997, Inauguration Of Stirling Square London 1999, Gallery Different 2001–05, Plus One Plus Two Galleries London 2002, Platform for Art Gloucester Road London 2002, Galerie Bernd Duerr Munich 2002, Buschelm Mowatt Fine Art Vancouver 2002, Gallery Different London 2002–07, Camino Real Gallery Boca Raton FL 2003, Magidson Fine Art Aspen CO 2003, Spectrum Commonwealth Institute London 2003, Plus One Plus Two Gallery London 2003, Henley Festival 2003, Number Nine the Gallery Birmingham 2003, Hotel Linde Innsbruck 2004, Herman Miller London 2004, The Catto Gallery London 2005, Number Nine The Gallery Birmingham 2006, Form Olympia London 2007, Van Loon En Simons Vught Holland 2007, Il Ponte Contemporanga Rome 2007, Buschuen Mowatt Gallery Vancouver 2007; *Group Exhibitions* incl: Tristan (MOMA, Mallorca) 1986, Mandelzoom (CANINO, Italy) 1986, The Rachael Papers (Serpentine Gallery) 1987, Australian Fashion: The Contemporary Art (V&A) 1989, Philip Samuels Fine Art St Louis 1992, The Inventive Spirit (Autodrome, Brussels) 1992, Charles Whitchurch Gallery California 1993, Arij Gasiunasen Fine Art Palm Beach 1993, 1994, 1995 and 1996, The Olympian Art Exhbn (Centre Point) 1993, Masks Exhbn (West Soho Gallery) 1993, Joel Kessler Fine Art (Int Art Fair, Miami) 1994 and 1995, Bruce R Lewin Gallery NY 1994 and 1995, SeaJapan Exhbn Yokohama 1994, Olympian Arts Charity Auction (Fine Art Soc Galleries) 1994, The Inaugural Grosvenor Place Fine Arts Exhbn Sydney 1994, The Meridian Gallery Melbourne 1994, Gallerie Pierre Nouvion Monte Carlo 1994 and 1995, FIAC Crane Kalman Gallery Paris 1994, 1995 and 1996, Magidson Fine Art Aspen Colorado USA 1994–2007, Midsummer Art Fair Galleries Tower Bridge London 1995, Weiss Sori Fine Art Coral Gables Florida USA 1995, Miriam Shiel Fine Art Toronto Canada 1995, Jorge Sori Fine Art (Int Art Fair) Miami 1996, The Tresors Int Fine Art & Antiques Fair Singapore 1996 and 1997, The National Gallery of Ontario Toronto 1996, Solomon & Solomon Fine Art Chicago 1997 and 1998, Buschlen Mowlatt Fine Art Vancouver 1997–2007, The Glasgow Art Fair 1997 and 1998, Washington DC Int Fine Art & Antique Fair 1997, The Museum Annex Hong Kong 1997, Arthaus Jeremy Hunt Fine Art London 1998, Well Hung Gallery London 1998, Art98 London, The Galleries (Art for Offices) London 1998–2007, Palm Beach Int Art and Design Fair USA 1998 and 2005, Galerij Pantheon Belgium 1998, Marijke Raaijmakers Galerie Holland 1998 and 1999, PAN RAI Art Fair Amsterdam Holland 1998, Lamont Gallery London 1999, ART99 and ART 2000 London, Bankside Browser Tate Gallery London 1999, Hannah Peschar Sculpture Garden Surrey 1999–2003, Sausmarez Manor Heritage Tst Sculpture Trail Guernsey 1999–2007, KUNSTRAI Amsterdam 1999, Galerie Meissner Hamburg Germany 1999, Marijke Raaijmakers Galerie Holland, Pan Rai Amsterdam 1999, Big Time Sponsorship Showcase London 1999, Hengelo The Netherlands, Number Nine The Gallery 1999–2003, Birmingham England 1999–2007, Lloyds Building London 1999, The Kiss London 1999, 2000, 2001 and 2002, Four Galleries Event Tower Bridge Piazza London 1999, 2000, 2002, 2004 and 2005, Solomon & Solomon Fine Art Las Vegas USA 2000–05, Imagination Gallery, London Imperial Cancer Research 2000, Denise Salvestro Fine Art, Salmon Galleries Sydney Australia 2000, Core Arts Barings Bank London 2000, Vertigo Gallery Art 2001, Hyatt Carlton Tower London, Artparks International Belvoir Castle Leics 2001 and 2002, Art Parks International Druidstone Kent 2001 and 2002, Atlantic Gallery Plymouth 2001–02, Galerie Bernd Duerr 2001–05, Kunst Messe Munich Gallery 2001–03, Magidson Fine Art NY 2002–05, ArtLondon Plus One Plus Two Galleries 2002, Bloxham Galleries London 2002, Plus One Plus Two Galleries London 2002–03, MIPIM Cannes France 2002 and 2003, Vertigo Gallery 2002, Artparks International Sausmarez Manor Guernsey, Garden House and Newnham Paddox 2003–07, Somerville Gallery Plymouth 2003–07, Kiss (Spectrum Fine Art) 2004, Rebecca Hossack Gallery 2004–05, Etienne van Loon Netherlands 2004–05, Il Ponte Contemporanea Rome 2005–07, The Calto Gallery London 2005, Wagner Art Gallery 2004–05, Sculpture in the Garden Univ of Leicester 2004, Inside Annual (Royal Soc of Br Sculptors) 2005, Art Fortnight London (Galleries of Butler's Wharf) 2005, Den Haag Art Fair (Etienne Van Loon) 2005, SZ Art Gp Las Vegas 2005–07, Plateaux Gallery London Art Fair 2006, McHardy Coombs Sculpture Gallery 2006, Woolff Gallery London 2006–07, Albemarle Gallery London 2006–07, Van Loon En Simons Vught Holland 2007, Il Ponte Contemporanea Miart 2007, Woolff Gallery AAR NY 2007; *Work in Collections* Galleria Nationali de Arte Moderna Rome, National Gallery Canberra Australia, Museum Beelden aan Zee Holland, National Gallery of Canada, Citibank London, The Shrine of Walsingham Norfolk Crucifix 1988, Southwark Bridge Office Devpt 1989, City Place House London 1991, Hyatt Carlton London 1993 and 1997, Natural History Museum Primates Gallery London 1993, Cannons City Gym 1994, Royal Caribbean Cruise Lines 1996, The Hyatt Hamburg 1998, Labroke Sporting Casino London 1999, The Jam House Birmingham 1999, 60 Queen Victoria Street London, Faith Zone Millennium Dome London, St Mary the Less Chilbolton Hants, Fleet Place House, Holborn Viaduct London, Bedes World Jarrow Tyne & Wear, Ten Covent Garden London, The Lowry Hotel Manchester, Milan Bar JD Wetherspoon London, Hotel Linde Innsbruck, Radisson SAS Hotel Stansted, The Jame House Edinburgh A Angel 2005, San Domenico House Hotel Nuuda Nuudi Tunuud 2006, Radisson Edwardian Hotel London Genus Series Venis and Venus 2007; *Awards* Gane Travel Scholarship 1979, Elizabeth Greenshields Award 1980; *Recreations* gym, swimming; *Clubs* Soho House; *Style*— David Begbie, ARBS; ✉ c/o Karina Phillips, Gallery Different, Silver House, 289c Rotherhithe Street, London SE16 5EY (tel 0207 231 9672, e-mail different@davidbegbie.com, website www.davidbegbie.com)

BEGBIE, Hannah; da of Nigel Begbie, and Jenifer Begbie; *b* 22 December 1976, London; *Educ* City of London Sch for Girls, Univ of Cambridge (BA); *Partner* Tom Edge; *Career* with Outline Productions 1999–2000, agent representing comedians and writers for film and TV PFD 2003– (joined 2000); memb BAFTA; *Recreations* playing the piano, keeping fit; *Style*— Miss Hannah Begbie; ✉ PFD, Drury House, 34–43 Russell Street, London WC2B 5HA (tel 020 7344 1017, e-mail hbegbie@pfd.co.uk)

BEGENT, Prof Richard Henry John; s of Harry Begent (d 2003), of Devon, and Doris, *née* Burton; *b* 14 February 1945; *Educ* Haileybury and ISC, St Bartholomew's Hosp Med Sch London (MB BS, MD); *m* Dr Nicola Begent; 3 c; *Career* Ronald Raven prof of clinical oncology and head Dept of Oncology Royal Free and UC Med Sch UCL, head Cancer Research Campaign Targeting and Imaging Gp; author of pubns on med oncology and antibody targeting of cancer; FRCP, FRCR, FMedSci; *Style*— Prof Richard Begent; ✉ Department of Oncology, Royal Free and University College Medical School, Royal Free Campus, Rowland Hill Street, London NW3 2PF (tel 020 7472 6151, fax 020 7794 3341, e-mail r.begent@ucl.ac.uk)

BEGG, Dr Alan Robert; s of Robert William Begg (d 2001), and Sheena Margaret, *née* Boyd; *b* 27 June 1954; *Educ* Kelvinside Acad Glasgow, St John's Coll Cambridge (MA, PhD, pres Grad Common Room); *m* 5 August 1978, Sara Margaret, *née* Stewart; 2 s (Jonathan Peter b 8 May 1983, Henry Stewart b 15 Sept 1986); *Career* engineer; research scientist TI Research Labs 1979–81, project ldr BP Research Centre 1985–88 (sr research scientist 1981–85), head of mgmnt team BP Metal Composites 1988–93, md T&N Technology 1993–98, vice-pres of technol Technol Federal-Mogul 1998–2000, tech dir Morgan Crucible 2001–04, chief exec Automotive Acad 2004–07, gp sr vice-pres of technol devpt and quality SKF 2007–; chm Tstee Bd T&N Pensions 1999–2000; memb: Advsy Bd Materials Dept Univ of Nottingham 1994–98, IRC Steering Ctee Materials Dept Univ of Birmingham 1994–98, External Advsy Ctee Materials Dept Univ of Cambridge 1996–, Advsy Ctee Materials Dept Univ of Oxford 1997–, External Advsy Ctee Materials Dept Univ of Leeds 2001–, Industrial Advsy Bd Materials Dept Imperial Coll London 2003–, Technology Strategy Bd DTI 2004–; DSAC: memb Materials Ctee 1989–94, memb Aerospace Technol Bd 1992–93, chm Technol Bd 2004–07; Technol Foresight Office of Sci and Technol: memb Materials Panel 1994–96 and 2000– (vice-chm 1997–98), chm EPSRC Foresight Challenge 1996, memb Steering Gp Foresight Vehicle 1996–98, chm Engine and Powertrain Foresight Vehicle 1997–98, fndr and chm Materials Media Advsy Gp 1997–98; Inst of Materials, Minerals and Mining: memb Editorial Panel 1988–93, memb MMC Ctee 1991–93, memb Cncl 1998–2002, chm Materials Strategy Cmmn 1999– (memb 1997–98); memb: Engrg Ctee Soc of Motor Manufacturers 1994–98, R&D Ctee European Automotive Component Prodrs Assoc (CLEPA) 1995–98, Cncl TWI 1995–98, Industrial Liaison Serv MIT 1999–2000 and 2002–, Materials Centre Advsy Bd Nat Physical Lab 2002–; CEng 1981, FIM 1992, FREng 2002; *Style*— Dr Alan Begg; ✉ Claremont House, Grovehurst Park, Stoneleigh Abbey, Kenilworth, Warwickshire CV8 2XR (tel and fax 024 7684 9300, e-mail alanrbegg@hotmail.com)

BEGG, Anne; MP; da of David Begg, and Margaret Catherine, *née* Ross; *b* 6 December 1955; *Educ* Brechin HS, Univ of Aberdeen (MA), Aberdeen Coll of Educn (Secdy Teaching Cert); *Career* teacher of English and history Webster's HS Kirriemuir 1978–88, princ teacher of English Arbroath Acad 1991–97 (asst princ teacher of English 1988–91), MP (Lab) Aberdeen S 1997–; memb Work and Pensions Select Ctee, memb House of Commons Chm's Panel 2002–; memb: Educn Inst of Scotland, Gen Teaching Cncl for Scotland; pres Blue Badge Network; patron: Scottish Motor Neurone Disease Assoc, Angus Special Playscheme, Nat Fedn of Shopmobility; Disabled Scot of the Year 1988; *Recreations* reading, theatre, cinema, public speaking; *Style*— Miss Anne Begg, MP; ✉ House of Commons, London SW1A 0AA (tel 020 7219 2140)

BEGG, Prof David Knox Houston; s of Robert William Begg, of Glasgow, and Sheena Margaret, *née* Boyd; *b* 25 June 1950; *Educ* Kelvinside Acad Glasgow, Univ of Cambridge, Univ of Oxford (MPhil), MIT (PhD); *Career* Lloyd's fell in econs Worcester Coll Oxford 1977–86, visiting prof Princeton Univ 1979, research dir Centre Econ Forecasting London Business Sch 1981–83, research fell Centre Econ Policy Research 1983–, founding managing ed of Economic Policy 1984–2000, advsr econ policy research Bank of England 1986, prof of economics Birkbeck Coll London 1987–2003 (actg vice-master 1997), princ Tanaka Business Sch Imperial Coll London 2003–; chair Begg Cmmn on the UK and the Euro 2003; non-exec dir Trace Gp 2006–; memb: Academic Panel HM Treasy 1981–95, Research Awards Advsy Ctee Leverhulme Tst 1987–93; specialist advsr: Treasy and Civil Serv Ctee House of Commons 1983, House of Lords Euro Communities Ctee 1988–89, Commission of the Euro Cmmn 1989–90, Federal Govt of Czechoslovakia 1990–91, IMF 1995–97; FRSE 2004, FCGI 2006; *Books* The Rational Expectations Revolution in Macroeconomics (1982), Economics (with S Fischer and R Dornbusch, 1984, 9 edn 2008), Foundations of Economics (with S Fischer and R Dornbusch 2001, 3 edn 2007), Monitoring European Integration: The Impact of Eastern Europe (1990),

Monitoring European Integration: The Making of Monetary Union (1991), Monitoring European Integration: The Economics of EC Enlargement (1992), Monitoring European Integration: Making Sense of Subsidiarity (1993), EMU: Getting the End Game Right (1997); *Recreations* gardening, sport, food; *Style*— Prof David Begg, FRSE; ✉ Tanaka Business School, Imperial College, Exhibition Road, London SW7 (tel 020 7594 9100, e-mail d.begg@imperial.ac.uk)

BEGG, Prof Hugh MacKemmie; s of Hugh Alexander Begg (d 1978), of Glasgow, and Margaret Neil, *née* MacKemmie (d 1994); *b* 25 October 1941; *Educ* HS of Glasgow, Univ of St Andrews, Univ of British Columbia, Univ of Dundee; *m* 20 July 1968, Jane Elizabeth, da of Charles Wilfred Harrison (d 1995), of Salt Spring Island, BC; 2 da (Mary Margaret b 26 April 1970, Susan Morven b 28 Sept 1973); *Career* asst lectr Univ of St Andrews 1966–67, res fell Tayside Study 1967–69, lectr Univ of Dundee 1969–76, asst dir Tayside Regnl Cncl 1976–79, head Sch of Town and Regnl Planning Univ of Dundee 1981–93 (sr lectr 1979–81), visiting prof of economic devpt Univ of Abertay Dundee 2000–; conslt UN Devpt Project 1986–2003, conslt economist and chartered town planner in private practice 1993–; pt/t reporter Scottish Exec Inquiry Reporters Unit 1994–; external complaints adjudicator Scottish Enterprise 1997–2002, convener RTPI Scotland 1991, convenor Standards Cmmn for Scotland 2002–03; memb Local Govt Boundary Cmmn for Scotland 1999–; FRTPI 1989; *Recreations* hill walking, puppy walking guide dogs, rugby; *Clubs* Monifieth and Dist Rotary, Bonnetmaker Craft of Dundee; *Style*— Prof Hugh M Begg; ✉ 4 Esplanade, Broughty Ferry, Dundee DD5 2EL (tel and fax 01382 779642, e-mail hughbegg@blueyonder.co.uk)

BEGGS, Roy; MLA; s of Roy J Beggs , *qv*, and Elizabeth Wilhemina Beggs; *b* 3 July 1962; *Educ* Larne GS, Queen's Univ Belfast (BEng); *m* 1989, Sandra Maureen, *née* Gillespie; 2 s, 1 da; *Career* former prodn mangr and technical mangr; MLA (UUP) E Antrim 1998–; NI Assembly: memb Employment and Learning Ctee 1999–2002, memb Public Accounts Ctee 1999–2003, memb Ctee of the Centre 2000–03, vice-chm Fin and Personnel Ctee 2002–03; memb Carrickfergus BC 2001– (vice-chair Devpt Services Ctee); vice-chair: Carrickfergus Local Strategic Partnership, Community Safety Partnership; memb: Carrickfergus Town Centre Regeneration Ctee, Carrickfergus District Policing Partnership Bd 2001–04; UUP: memb Ulster Unionist Cncllrs Assoc, hon sec Ulster Young Unionist Cncl 1986–87, hon sec Larne Div 1991–98, hon sec E Antrim Ulster Unionist Assoc 1992–2002; offr 1 Raloo Boys' Bde; memb Ctee Raloo Presbyterian Church 1999–, govr Glynn Primary Sch; supporter Cancer Research Campaign; *Recreations* cycling, walking; *Clubs* Larne RFC; *Style*— Roy Beggs, Esq, MLA; ✉ East Antrim UUP Advice Centre, 32C North Street, Carrickfergus, Co Antrim BT38 7AQ (tel 028 9336 2995, fax 028 9336 8048, e-mail roy.beggs@btopenworld.com, website www.roy-beggs.co.uk); Northern Ireland Assembly, Parliament Buildings, Stormont, Belfast BT4 3XX (tel 028 9052 1546, fax 028 9052 1556)

BEGGS, Roy J; *b* 20 February 1936, Belfast; *Educ* Ballyclare HS, Stranmillis Training Coll; *m* Wilma; 2 s (1 of whom Roy Beggs, MLA, *qv*), 2 da; *Career* teacher/vice-princ Larne HS 1957–82; MP (UUP) Antrim E 1983–2005; memb House of Commons Public Accounts Cmmn 1984–, memb NI Affrs Select Ctee 1997–; chief whip UUP 2000–; memb Larne BC 1973–, Mayor of Larne 1978–83; elected to NI Assembly at Stormont 1982, chm Economic Devpt Ctee 1982–84; memb NE Educn and Library Bd 1973–, pres Assoc Educn and Library Bds NI 1984–85; memb NI Drainage Cncl 2006–; dir Larne Economic Devpt Co; farmer and landowner; vice-pres Gleno Valley Young Farmers' Club; memb Ulster Farmers' Union; *Recreations* fishing, agriculture; *Style*— Alderman Roy Beggs; ✉ 171 Carrickfergus Road, Larne, Co Antrim BT40 3JZ (tel 028 2827 8976, fax 028 2827 8976)

BEGLEY, Kim Sean Robert; s of William Begley (d 1989), of Birkenhead, and Elizabeth, *née* Cooke; *b* 23 June 1952; *Educ* Rock Ferry HS Birkenhead, Wimbledon Sch of Art, Guildhall Sch of Music and Drama, National Opera Studio; *m* 20 Oct 1986, Elizabeth Mary, da of Charles Collier; 2 s (Edward Charles William b 29 Jan 1988, William George b 17 May 1991); *Career* tenor; princ tenor Royal Opera House Covent Garden 1983–89, has also performed with numerous other opera cos and all major Br orchs; former actor, with Liverpool Playhouse and Watermill Theatre Newbury (also West End and tours of England and Canada), with RSC in Stratford and London 1977–78; fndr Broomhill Tst; *Performances* over thirty roles with Royal Opera incl: Lysander in A Midsummer Night's Dream, Achilles in King Priam, Prince in Zemlinsky's Florentine Tragedy, Cassio in Otello, Froh in Das Rheingold, Walther von der Vogelweide in Tannhäuser, Tichon in Katya Kabanova; others incl: Don Ottavio in Don Giovanni (Glyndebourne Touring Opera 1986, Opera Northern Ireland 1988, ENO 1991), Boris in Katya Kabanova (Glyndebourne Touring Opera 1989, Glyndebourne Festival Opera 1990), Graf Elemer in Arabella (Glyndebourne Festival) 1989, High Priest in Idomeneo (Glyndebourne Festival) 1991, Pellegrin in Tippett's New Year (Glyndebourne Festival and Touring) 1991, Laca in Jenufa (Glyndebourne Festival and Touring) 1992, Tanzmeister in Ariadne auf Naxos (Frankfurt Opera), title role in Lohengrin (Frankfurt Opera), Alfred in Die Fledermaus (Frankfurt Opera), Nadir in The Pearl Fishers (Scottish Opera), Prince Shuisky in Boris Godunov (Opera North), Fritz in Der Ferne Klang (Opera North), Satavyan in Savitri (Rome Opera), Vaudemont in Yolanta (Opera North), Dr Caius in Falstaff (Salzburg Easter Festival) 1993, Narraboth in Salome (Salzburg Summer Festival) 1993, Grigori in Boris Godunov (under Edo de Wart, Geneva) 1993, Male Chorus in Rape of Lucretia (ENO) 1993, Golitsin in Khovanshchina (ENO) 1994, Albert Gregor in The Makropulos Case (WNO 1994, Glyndebourne 1995 and 1997, Chicago Lyric Opera 1995/96), Jimmy Mahoney in the Rise and Fall of the City of Mahagonny (Opéra de la Bastille Paris) 1995, Skuratov in From the House of the Dead (Opéra de Nice) 1995, Loge in Das Rheingold (under James Conlon, Cologne) 1995, Florestan in Leonore (Salzburg and BBC Proms under John Eliot Gardiner) 1996, Regista in Un re in Ascolta (Chicago Lyric Opera) 1996, Loge in Das Rheingold (La Scala under Riccardo Muti) 1996, Novagerio in Palastrina (Royal Opera Covent Garden) 1997, Tambour Major Wozzeck (La Scala under Giuseppi Sinopli) 1997, Max in Der Freischutz (Deutsches Staatsoper Berlin under Zubin Mehta) 1997; concert engagements incl: Don Basilio in The Marriage of Figaro (with LPO under Sir Georg Solti in London, Paris, Frankfurt and Cologne), Alfred in Die Fledermaus (with RPO under Andre Previn), Dream of Gerontius (with the Philharmonia under Vernon Handley), Tippett's New Year (with LPO), Beethoven Ninth Symphony and Haydn Nelson Mass (with BBC Symphony Orch), Verdi Requiem (with Bournemouth Symphony Orch), Beethoven Ninth (with Cleveland Symphony Orch under Dohnányi), Janácek Glagolitic Mass (with London Philharmonic), Tambour Major in Wozzeck (with Cleveland Orch under Dohnányi, Carnegie Hall NY) 1995, Mahler 8th Symphony (with Cleveland Orch under Dohnányi) 1995, Mahler 8th Symphony (with LPO under Andrew Davis at BBC Proms) 1995, Britten War Requiem (Zürich Opera) 1995, Mahler 8th Symphony (with Halle Orchestra under Kent Nagano) 1996, Bruckner's Te Deum (Salzburg Festival under Claudio Abbado) 1997, title role in Stravinsky's Oedipus Rex (Cleveland Orchestra under Christoph von Dohnányi) 1997, Captain Vere in Billy Budd (Bastille) 1998, Max in Der Freischültz (La Scala) 1998, Jimmy Mahoney in Mahagonny (Chicago) 1998, Parsifal (ENO) 1998; *Recordings* audio incl: Turandot, Der Rosenkavalier, Falstaff (under Solti, Decca), Das Rheingold (under Dohnányi, Decca), Salome (under Dohnányi, Decca), Florestan in Leonore (under John Eliot Gardiner, Deutsche Grammophon) 1996; video incl: Norma (with Dame John Sutherland and Richard Bonynge), La Traviata (with Carlo Rizzi); *Style*— Kim Begley, Esq; ✉ c/o IMG Artists Europe, Lovell House, 616 Chiswick High Road, London W4 5RX (tel 020 8233 5800, fax 020 8233 5801)

BEHAN, Prof Peter Oliver; s of Patrick Behan (d 1985), and Mary Ellen, *née* Ryan; *b* 8 July 1935; *Educ* Christian Brothers Schs Authy, Univ of Leeds (MB ChB, MD), Nat Univ of Ireland (DSc); *m* 23 Aug 1968, Dr Wilhelmina Behan, da of Dr William Hughes (d 1981); 1 da (Charlotte b 1969), 2 s (Miles b 1973, Edmund b 1977); *Career* demonstrator in pathology Univ of Cambridge, res fell in psychiatry and special res fell neurology Harvard Univ, special res fell in neurology Univ of Oxford, asst prof of neurology Univ of Boston; Univ of Glasgow: lectr, sr lectr, reader, prof of neurology; med patron Scot Motor Neurone Disease Assoc; memb: Neuroimmunology Res Gp World Fedn of Neurology, Rodin Acad for Dyslexia Res; pres Ramsay Soc; Pattison Medal for Research, Dutch Int Award for Study of Fatigue States 1994; FRCP, FRCPG, FRCPI, FACP, FLS, fell American Neurological Assoc, hon fell Norwegian Neurological Assoc; *Books* Clinical Neuroimmunology (with S Curie, 1978), Clinical Neuroimmunology (with W Behan and J Aarli, 1987); *Recreations* salmon fishing, gardening; *Clubs* Savile, Flyfishers'; *Style*— Prof Peter Behan; ✉ 17 South Erskine Park, Bearsden, Glasgow G61 4NA (tel 0141 942 5113); Department of Neurology, Institute of Neurological Sciences, Southern General Hospital, Glasgow G51 4TF (tel 0141 201 2509, e-mail osslv@clinmed.gla.ac.uk)

BEHAR, His Hon Judge Richard Victor Montague Edward; s of Edward Behar, and Eilleen, *née* Evans; *b* 14 February 1941; *Educ* Stowe, St John's Coll Oxford (MA); *m* 1982, Iwona Krystyna, *née* Grabowska; 2 s, 1 da; *Career* called to the Bar Middle Temple; in private practice 1967–2000; asst recorder 1991, recorder 1995, circuit judge (SE Circuit) 2000–; pt/t immigration and asylum adjudicator 1998–2000; *Recreations* foreign languages and travel, cinema, theatre, reading; *Clubs* Oxford and Cambridge, Hurlingham; *Style*— His Hon Judge Behar; ✉ Judicial Secretariat for the London and South East Region, 3rd Floor, New Cavendish House, 18 Maltravers Street, London WC2R 3EU

BEHARRELL, Steven Roderic; s of late Douglas Wells Beharrell, TD, and Pamela, *née* Pearman Smith; *b* 22 December 1944; *Educ* Uppingham; *m* 1, 10 June 1967, Julia Elizabeth (d 1994), da of Canon William Wilson Powell, DL; 2 da (Victoria Jane b 5 Aug 1971, Rebecca Clare b 9 Oct 1973); m 2, 1 Sept 1995, Mary Rebecca Mortimer; 1 da (Natasha Mortimer b 7 Sept 1997); *Career* admitted slr 1969; ptnr Denton Hall Burgin & Warrens 1973–90, fndr ptnr Beharrell Thompson & Co 1990–93, ptnr Coudert Brothers 1993–2004 (chm 2001–03, of counsel 2004–05), sr counsel LeBoeuf Lamb Greene & MacRae 2005–; Freeman Worshipful Co of Drapers; memb Law Soc; *Style*— Steven Beharrell, Esq; ✉ LeBoeuf, Lamb, Greene & MacRae LLP, 1 Minster Court, Mincing Lane, London EC3R 7YL (tel 020 7459 5090, fax 020 7459 5099, e-mail steven.beharrell@llgm.com)

BEHRENS, John Stephen; JP (1970); s of Edgar Charles Behrens, CBE, JP (d 1975), of Ilkley, W Yorks, and Winifred Wrigley, *née* Luckhurst (d 1976); *b* 9 July 1927; *Educ* Rugby; *m* 1964, Kathleen Shirley, da of Richard Alfred Leicester Billson, JP (d 1949), and Kathleen Dalrymple Crawford, *née* Crooks (d 1975); 2 s (Charles, James), 1 da (Philippa); *Career* Nat Serv Rifle Bde 1945, cmmnd 1946, served 2 KRRC N Africa and Palestine, completed serv at Rifle Bde Depot Winchester 1948; dir Sir Jacob Behrens and Sons Ltd and subsidiary cos; chm: Francis Willey (British Wools 1935) Ltd and subsidiary cos, Craig Charity for Children, Bradford Tradesmen's Homes and assoc charities, Fred Towler Charity Tst; pres: Country Wool Merchants' Assoc 1971–99, Bradford Club 1990, Friends of Bradford Art Galleries and Museums 1996–98; High Sheriff W Yorks 1996–97; *Recreations* bonfires; *Clubs* Royal Greenjackets, Bradford; *Style*— John Behrens, Esq; ✉ Park Green, Littlethorpe, Ripon, North Yorkshire HG4 3LX (tel 01765 677262); Ravenscliffe Mills, Calverley, Pudsey, West Yorkshire LS28 5RY (tel 01274 612541)

BEITH, Rt Hon Alan James; PC (1992), MP; o s of James Beith (d 1962), of Poynton, Cheshire, and Joan Beith (d 1998); *b* 20 April 1943; *Educ* King's Sch Macclesfield, Balliol Coll and Nuffield Coll Oxford; *m* 1, 1965, Barbara Jean Ward (d 1998); 1 s (d 2000), 1 da; m 2, 2001, Baroness Maddock (Life Peer), *qv*; *Career* lectr Dept of Politics Univ of Newcastle upon Tyne 1966–73; MP (Lib, now Lib Dem) Berwick-upon-Tweed 1973– (also contested 1970), Lib chief whip 1976–85, Lib dep ldr and foreign affrs spokesman 1985–87, Treasy spokesman Lib Democrats 1988–94, home affairs spokesman Lib Democrats 1994–97, Lib Dem spokesman on home and legal affairs 1997–2001, dep ldr of Liberal Democrats 1992–2003, memb Intelligence and Security Ctee 1994–, chm Constitutional Affrs Ctee (formerly Lord Chllr's Dept Select Ctee) 2003–; memb House of Commons Cmmn 1979–97; chm Historic Chapels Tst 2002– (tstee 1993–); Hon DCL Univ of Newcastle upon Tyne 1998; *Recreations* walking, music; *Clubs* Nat Liberal, Athenaeum; *Style*— The Rt Hon Alan Beith, MP; ✉ House of Commons, London SW1A 0AA (tel 020 7219 3540, fax 020 7219 5890, e-mail cheesemang@parliament.uk)

BEITH, Ian Mark; s of Sir John Greville Stanley Beith, KCMG, of Winchester, Hants, and Diana, *née* Gilmour (d 1987); *b* 2 December 1950; *Educ* Univ of Cambridge (MA), Harvard Univ; *m* 18 Oct 1975, Mary Jane, da of late Harry Selwyn Spicer Few; 2 s (Mark b 9 Jan 1983, Nick b 29 Jan 1985); *Career* Citibank: Energy Dept UK Corp Bank 1972–75, Metals and Mining Dept NY 1975–80, team head Oil and Mining Dept London 1980–82, dir Euro Training Centre London 1982–84, head N Euro Shipping Gp 1984–86, head of UK corp banking 1986–88; Charterhouse Bank Ltd: dir of mktg debt related servs 1988, md and head of debt servs 1988–99; head Fin Dept Berwin Leighton until 1999; exec chm INSYS Ltd 2001–05; *Recreations* shooting, films, theatre; *Style*— Ian Beith, Esq; ✉ 26 Sutherland Street, London SW1V 4LA (tel 020 7834 4111)

BELBEN, Rosalind Loveday; da of Capt G D Belben, DSO, DSC, AM, RN (d 1944), and Joyce Belben (d 1972); *b* 1 February 1941, Dorset; *Educ* Stover, Henley Lodge; *Career* author; DAAD Berliner Künstlerprogramm fell 1987, FRSL 1999; *Books* The Limit (1974), Dreaming of Dead People (1979), Is Beauty Good (1989), Choosing Spectacles (1995), Hound Music (2001); *Style*— Miss Rosalind Belben; ✉ c/o Anthony Sheil, Gillon Aitken Associates Ltd, 18–21 Cavaye Place, London SW10 9PT (tel 020 7373 8672, e-mail reception@gillonaitken.co.uk)

BELCHAMBERS, Anthony Murray; s of Lyonel Eustace Belchambers (d 1981), of Ashburton, Devon, and Dorothy Joan, *née* Wylie; *b* 14 April 1947; *Educ* Christ Coll Brecon; *m* Joanna Anthonia Vestbirk; *Career* called to the Bar Inner Temple; in practice Western Circuit 1972–75; lawyer: DTI 1975–82, Dir of Public Prosecutions 1982–84, Treasy 1984–86; co sec and gen counsel Assoc of Futures Brokers and Dealers 1986–89, gen counsel Jt Exchanges Ctee 1989–93, chief exec The Futures and Options Assoc 1993–; memb Ct Guild of Int Bankers, memb various City ctees concerning financial services; memb Advsy Bd Capital Club; *Publications* incl: Soviet Financial Services: The Need for Technical Assistance and Training (1991), Poems from the Square Mile (1992), The British Derivatives Markets Handbook (1993); *Recreations* tennis, riding, bridge; *Clubs* HAC; *Style*— Anthony Belchambers, Esq; ✉ The Futures and Options Association, 2nd Floor, 36–38 Botolph Lane, London EC3R 8DE

BELCHER, Anthony Dennis (Tony); s of Dennis Frederick Belcher, of Chertsey, Surrey, and Kathleen Patricia, *née* Backhouse; *b* 26 February 1957; *Educ* Salesian Coll Chertsey, Poly of the South Bank (BSc); *m* 16 May 1981, Andrea Margaret, da of Victor Ernest Whatley; 2 s (Nicholas Anthony b 8 July 1983, Shaun Anthony b 21 Feb 1987), 1 da (Justine Emma b 22 Oct 1991); *Career* Mellersh & Harding: trainee surveyor 1975, salaried ptnr 1985, equity ptnr 1990–; FRICS 1981, DipArb 1994, FCIArb, MAPM, FBEng; *Recreations* skiing, badminton, squash, flying, restoration of French house, golf, travel; *Clubs* English Setter Assoc; *Style*— Tony Belcher, Esq; ✉ Mellersh & Harding, 6 Duke Street, St James's, London SW1Y 6BN (tel 020 7499 0866, fax 020 7522 8503, mobile 07780 740 501, e-mail abelcher@mellersh.co.uk)

B

BELCHER, Her Hon Judge Penelope Mary (Penny); da of Arthur John Lucas, of Painswick, Glos, and Margaret Elizabeth, *née* Attwood; *b* 27 August 1957, Beaconsfield, Bucks; *Educ* King Edward VI HS for Girls Birmingham, St Hugh's Coll Oxford (MA); *m* 13 April 1985, Simon James Belcher; 1 s (Timothy James b 24 Dec 1987), 1 da (Fiona Jane b 18 July 1991); *Career* called to the Bar Middle Temple 1980, admitted State Bar of California 1988, admitted slr 1993; practising barr and memb of chambers 4 Paper Buildings 1980–90, attorney Irvine & Cooper Palo Alto 1988–89; slr: Eversheds 1993–99 (ptnr 1995), Hammonds 2000–06 (asst dir for advocacy); recorder 2003–06, circuit judge 2006–; memb Law Soc 1993; *Recreations* sailing, racket sports, flute playing, classical music, theatre, reading; *Style*— Her Hon Judge Belcher; ✉ Leeds Combined Court Centre, The Court House, 1 Oxford Row, Leeds LS1 3BG (tel 0113 306 2800, e-mail hhjudgepenelope.belcher@judiciary.gsi.gov.uk)

BELHAVEN AND STENTON, 13 Lord (S 1647); Robert Anthony Carmichael Hamilton; s of 12 Lord Belhaven and Stenton (d 1961), and Heather Mildred Carmichael, *née* Bell (d 1992); *b* 27 February 1927; *Educ* Eton; *m* 1, 1952 (m dis 1973), (Elizabeth) Ann, da of late Col Arthur Henry Moseley, DSO, of NSW; 1 s, 1 da; m 2, 1973 (m dis 1986), Rosemary (d 1992), da of Sir Herbert Williams, 1 Bt, MP (d 1954), sis of Sir Robin Williams, 2 Bt, *qv*, and formerly w of Sir Ian Mactaggart, 3 Bt; 1 adopted da; m 3, 1986, Malgorzata Maria, da of Tadeusz Hruzik-Mazurkiewicz, Advocate, of Krakow, Poland; 1 da; *Heir* s, Master of Belhaven; *Career* Army 1945–48, cmmnd Cameronians 1947; farmer 1950–72, hotelier 1972–80; sat as Cons in House of Lords until 1999; Commander Cross of Order of Merit of the Republic of Poland 1995; *Recreations* writing children's stories; *Clubs* Carlton; *Style*— The Rt Hon the Lord Belhaven and Stenton; ✉ 710 Howard House, Dolphin Square, London SW1V 3PQ

BELL, Alan Scott; *b* 8 May 1942, Sunderland; *Educ* Ashville Coll, Selwyn Coll Cambridge (MA), Univ of Oxford (MA); *m* 1966, Olivia, da of late Prof J E Butt, FBA; 1 s, 1 da; *Career* asst registrar Royal Cmmn on Historical Manuscripts 1963–66, asst keeper Nat Library of Scotland 1966–81, visiting fell All Souls Coll Oxford 1980, librarian Rhodes House Library Univ of Oxford 1981–93, librarian The London Library 1993–2001; advsy ed Oxford DNB 1993–; chm Marc Fitch Fund 2001–; FSA 1995; *Books* Sydney Smith (1980), Leslie Stephen's Mausoleum Book (ed, 1976), Lord Cockburn (ed, 1979), Henry Cockburn: Selected Letters (2005); *Clubs* Brooks's, New (Edinburgh); *Style*— Alan Bell, Esq, FSA; ✉ 38 Danube Street, Edinburgh EH4 1NT

BELL, Maj Alexander Fulton; s of Harry Bell, OBE (d 1984), of Viewpark, St Andrews, Fife, and Sophia McDonald, *née* Fulton (d 1991); *b* 20 January 1937; *Educ* Shrewsbury, RMA Sandhurst, Dundee Coll of Technol and Commerce; *m* 1, 4 Jan 1969, Sophia Lilian Elizabeth Morgan (d 1971), da of Cdr Donald Hugh Elles, RN, of N Tullich, Inveraray, Argyll; 2 s (Harry b 7 Dec 1969, Thomas b 25 Feb 1971); m 2, 23 April 1984, Alison Mary, da of John Cole Compton, MBE, of Ward of Turin, Forfar, Angus; *Career* cmmnd Argyll and Sutherland Highlanders 1957, Capt HM The Queen's Gd Balmoral 1963, Adj 1 Bn Singapore/Borneo 1964–65, served Cyprus, BAOR, Borneo, Berlin; ADC to GOC 51 Highland Div 1966, ret 1969; Maj 1/51 Highland Vols TAVR 1972–74, Home Serv Force 1982–83; sales exec Assoc of Br Maltsters 1969; ABM (parent Dalgety plc): sales mangr 1971, dir of sales 1973–87; dir of mktg Pauls Malt (parent Harrisons and Crossfield plc) 1987–89, dir of sales J P Simpson & Co (Alnwick) Ltd 1989–98 (non-exec dir 1998–2000); dir Airborne Initiative Scotland Ltd 1998–2004; chm and pres Inst of Mktg (Tayside branch) 1975–77, memb Advsy Cncl Dundee Coll of Commerce 1976–78, govr Ardvreck Sch Crieff 1982–86; MInstM 1972, MCIM 1989; *Recreations* golf, fishing, shooting, skiing, walking; *Clubs* Royal & Ancient, Hon Co of Edinburgh Golfers, MCC, Highland Bde; *Style*— Maj Alexander Bell; ✉ Drumclune, By Forfar, Angus DD8 3TS (tel 01575 572074, fax 01575 573477)

BELL, Sheriff Andrew Montgomery; s of James Montgomery Bell (d 1953), of Edinburgh, and Mary, *née* Cavaye (d 1975); *b* 21 February 1940; *Educ* The Royal HS, Univ of Edinburgh (BL); *m* 3 May 1969, Ann Margaret, da of William Robinson (d 1956), of Darlington, Durham; 1 s (James b 1972), 1 da (Lucy b 1970); *Career* slr 1961–74; Sheriff of: S Strathclyde, Dumfries and Galloway at Hamilton 1979–84, Glasgow and Strathkelvin at Glasgow 1984–90, Lothian and Borders 1990–; memb Faculty of Advocates 1975; *Recreations* reading, listening to music; *Clubs* New (Edinburgh); *Style*— Sheriff Andrew Bell

BELL, Anne Margaret; *see:* Jobson, Anne Margaret

BELL, Dr Catherine; CB (2003); da of late Frank Douglas Howe, and Phyllis, née Walsh; *Educ* Balshaw's GS, Girton Coll Cambridge (BA), Univ of Kent (PhD); *m* 1993, Richard John Weber; 1 s; *Career* DTI: joined 1975, princ 1981–84, asst sec 1984–89, under sec 1989–91, head Competition Policy Div 1991–93, maternity leave 1993–94, on secondment to Cabinet Office as resident chm Civil Serv Selection Bd 1994–95, head DTI Central Policy Unit 1995–97, head inter-departmental review of utilities regulation 1997–99, head competition policy DTI 1998–99, DG Corporate and Consumer Affrs then Competition and Markets Gp 1999–2002, DG Services Gp 2002–05, actg permanent sec 2005; non-exec dir: Swiss Re (UK) 1999–, CAA 2006–, United Utilities plc 2007–; *Style*— Dr Catherine Bell, CB

BELL, Christopher; s of Shirley Aurelia, *née* Copping; *b* 18 November 1957; *Educ* Mexborough GS, Wolverhampton Poly (BA); *m*; 2 da; *Career* commercial trainee 1980–82, mktg mangr Ind Coope & Allsopp 1982–87, mktg, planning and co-ordination mangr Ind Coope Burton Brewery 1987–1988, mktg dir Allied Beer Brands 1988–89, mktg and buying dir Victoria Wine Co 1989–91; Hilton Gp plc: md Ladbroke Racing 1995–2000 (mktg dir 1991–93, dep md 1993–95), chief exec Ladbrokes Worldwide 2000–, exec dir Hilton Gp plc 2000–; non-exec dir Game Gp plc 2003–, dir Satellite Information Services; chm Betting Office Licensees Assoc 1998–, vice-chm Assoc of British Bookmakers; memb: Bookmakers Ctee, Horserace Betting Levy Bd, Horserace and Betting Ctee, Animal Health Tst, Princess Royal Industry Ctee; memb Fundraising Bd NSPCC; *Recreations* travel, wine, food, flying, reading; *Clubs* Mark's; *Style*— Christopher Bell, Esq; ✉ Ladbroke Worldwide, Imperial House, Imperial Drive, Rayners Lane, Harrow, Middlesex HA2 7JW (tel 020 8868 8899, fax 020 8866 1980)

BELL, Christopher Charles; s of London Bell (d 1986), and Dorothea Anne, *née* Preston (d 1989); *b* 31 December 1945; *Educ* Marlborough, Pembroke Coll Cambridge (BA); *m* 1, 1969 (m dis 1976), Caroline Robey; 1 da (Clarissa b 11 June 1973), 1 s (Edward b 5 Feb 1975); m 2, 1977 (m dis 2000), Dinah, da of Col John Erskine Nicholson; 2 da (Rowena b 3 April 1981, Octavia b 9 Dec 1982); *Career* slr; articled clerk Crossman Block & Keith 1969–71; Travers Smith Braithwaite: asst slr 1971, ptnr 1975–2006, sr ptnr 2000–06; *Style*— Christopher Bell, Esq

BELL, Sir David Charles Maurice; kt (2004); s of R M Bell (d 1992), and M F Bell (d 1973); *b* 30 September 1946; *Educ* Worth Sch, Trinity Hall Cambridge (BA), Univ of Pennsylvania (MA); *m* 30 Dec 1972, Primrose Frances, da of E S Moran (d 1973); 1 da (Emma Theodora b 1975), 2 s (Charles Alexander b 1977, Thomas George b 1981); *Career* Oxford Mail and Times 1970–72; Financial Times: news ed, int ed 1978–80, asst ed features 1980–85, managing ed 1985–89, advertisement and mktg dir 1989–93, chief exec 1993–96, chm 1996–; dir: Pearson plc (parent co of FT) 1996–, Vitec plc 1997–2007, Zen Research plc 2000–02; chm: Islington SDP 1981–86, Sadlers Wells 1995–, IWPR 1996–, Int Youth Fndn 1998–2007 (memb Bd 1996–), Windmill Partnership 1999–, Crisis 2002–, Millennium Bridge Tst; memb: UK Cncl INSEAD, Devpt Bd RNT; tstee Common Purpose 1994–, chm Common Purpose Europe 1996–; Civil Serv cmmr 2001–07; dir Ambache Chamber Orch 1987– (patron 1999–); *Recreations* theatre, cycling, family, Victorian social history, Italy, Arsenal FC; *Style*— Sir David Bell; ✉ 35 Belitha Villas, London N1 1PE (tel 020 7609 4000); Financial Times, No 1 Southwark Bridge, London SE1 9HL; Pearson plc, 80 Strand, London WC2R 0RL (e-mail david.bell@pearson.com)

BELL, David Mackintosh; s of David L Bell (d 1974), of Ayr, and Kathleen, *née* McBurnie (d 1985); *b* 2 August 1939; *Educ* Ayr Acad, Univ of Glasgow (MA), Jordanhill Coll of Educn; *m* 1, 1963 (m dis 1996), Ann Adair; 1 s (Michael David b 25 Nov 1969), 1 da (Suzanne Louise b 10 June 1976); m 2, 1996, Dominique van Hille; 1 s (Thomas Dominic b 29 July 1995); *Career* HM Dip Serv: joined Cwlth Relations Office 1960, Karachi 1961–63, Enugu Nigeria 1963–65, second sec Havana 1966–68, Olympic attaché Mexico City 1968, FCO 1969–71, Budapest 1971–74, first sec FCO 1974–77, commercial consul NYC 1977–81, FCO 1981–86, press sec Bonn 1986–90, cnsllr/consul-gen Lille 1990–95, DG Br Export Promotion in Switzerland and consul-gen Zürich 1995–; *Recreations* golf, reading; *Style*— David M Bell, Esq

BELL, Prof (Geoffrey) Duncan; s of Sqdn Ldr Robert Charles Bell (d 2002), of Gosforth, Newcastle upon Tyne, and Phyllis Pearl Hunter Codling (d 1992); *b* 19 June 1945; *Educ* Royal GS Newcastle upon Tyne, St Bartholomew's Hosp Med Coll, Univ of London (MB BS, LRCP, MSc, MD); *m* 21 June 1969, Joanna Victoria, da of Capt Joseph Henry Patterson (d 1981); 2 s (Jonathan b 8 March 1970 d 1994, Robert b 13 Oct 1977), 2 da (Anne Hélène b 30 Oct 1973 d 1975, Karen b 7 May 1980); *Career* lectr in med St Bartholomew's Hosp Med Sch 1973–76, sr lectr in therapeutics Univ of Nottingham 1976–83, conslt gastroenterologist Ipswich Hosp 1983–97, conslt gastroenterologist and prof of gastroenterology Sunderland Royal Hosp 1997–2002, hon conslt gastroenterologist Norfolk and Norwich Univ Hosp 2002–, dir Regnl Endoscopy Trg Centre Norwich 2004–; hon prof Sch of Computing Sciences UEA 2002–, visiting prof Sch of Computing and Technol Sunderland Univ 2002–, visiting prof Sch of Electrical, Electronic and Computer Engrg Univ of Newcastle upon Tyne 2003–; developer (with BT) of virtual reality remote endoscopy; memb Assoc of Physicians 1979, chm working party on endoscopic safety and monitoring Br Soc of Gastroenterology, fndr memb Suffolk Branch Br Digestive Fndn, Hunterian prof RCS 1990; MRCS, FRCP 1985 (MRCP), FRCPEd 1998; *Recreations* canoeing, boxing, rowing; *Style*— Prof Duncan Bell; ✉ Fishers Cottage, Falkenham, Ipswich IP10 0QY (tel 01394 448251, e-mail gdb@cmp.uea.ac.uk)

BELL, (Edward) Eddie; s of Edward and Jean Bell; *b* 2 August 1949; *Educ* Airdrie HS, Cert Business Studies; *m* 1969, Junette, da of Malcolm Bannatyne; 2 da (Catherine b 22 Oct 1969, Joanne b 24 May 1973), 1 s (Edward b 19 June 1984); *Career* Hodder & Stoughton 1970–85 (latterly dep md), md Collins Gen Div 1985–89 (dep md Fontana William Collins 1985), fndr Harper Paperbacks USA 1989–90; HarperCollins UK: dep chief exec and publisher 1990–91, chief exec and publisher 1991–92, exec chm and publisher 1992–2000; dir beCogent 2000–, chm Those Who Can Ltd 2001–, non-exec chm OAG Worldwide Ltd 2001–, ptnr Bell Lomax Literary & Sport Agency 2002–; *Recreations* reading, golf, supporting Arsenal, opera, collecting old books; *Clubs* RAC, Annabel's, Autowink (Epsom), The Savage, Addington Golf; *Style*— Eddie Bell, Esq

BELL, Eileen Helen Marie; da of Joseph and Mary Neeson; *b* 15 August 1943; *Educ* Dominican Coll Belfast, Univ of Ulster (BA); *m* 1968, Derek Bell; *Career* Alliance Pty: gen sec 1986–90, chair 1997–99, pres 2000–01, dep ldr 2001–, memb Pty Strategy Ctee, spokesperson Equality and Community Relations, former spokesperson Educn and Women's Issues; cncllr (representing Bangor W) N Down BC 1993–2000; memb: Policy and Resources Ctee, Leisure Tourism and Community Devpt Ctee (chair sub-ctees: Community Rels, Leisure Centres), Planning and Econ Devpt Ctee, Environmental and Tech Amenities Ctee, Corp Strategy Ctee, Health Ctee, Advsy Bd on Grant Applications for vol bodies; MLA (Alliance) N Down 1998–2007; presiding offr (speaker) NI Assembly 2006–07; memb: Assembly Cmmn, Educn Ctee, Ctee for the Central Dept; delg: Brooke-Mayhew Talks 1991–92, Dublin Forum for Peace and Reconciliation 1994–96 (memb: Fundamental Rights Ctee, Co-ordinating Ctee), NI Forum for Political Dialogue 1996 (memb Educn Ctee), Castle Building Talks (Good Friday Agreement) 1996–98; memb: N Down District Partnership 1996–2000, NI Probation Bd 1997–2003, NI Assoc for Care and Resettlement of Offenders; former memb: SE Educn and Library Bd, Local Govt Staff Cmmn; participated in Local Govt Research Consortium Univ of Warwick; *Recreations* reading, theatre, music; *Style*— Mrs Eileen Bell; ✉ 27 Maryville Road, Bangor BT20 3RH (tel 028 9145 2321, fax 028 9145 5995)

BELL, Eric Gairdner; OBE (2003); s of Richard Bell (d 1965), and Barrie, *née* Price (decd); *b* 23 April 1944; *Educ* Methodist Coll Belfast; *m* 3 Aug 1968, Eileen Marie, da of Maj George Roy; 2 s (Richard b 18 May 1972, Christopher b 27 May 1973); *Career* articled to Oughton Boyd McMillan & Co CAs (now part of KPMG), auditor then audit mangr Cooper Brothers (now PricewaterhouseCoopers); BDO Binder Hamlyn: joined as mangr 1971, ptnr 1973, insolvency practitioner, regnl managing ptnr 1986–94, sr ptnr Belfast Office Grant Thornton (following merger) 1994–; chm NI Div IOD 2000–02; FCA Ireland 1969; *Recreations* watching rugby at all levels, developing youth in sport and enterprise; *Clubs* Belfast Harlequins Rugby Football, Belvoir Park Golf; *Style*— Eric Bell, Esq, OBE; ✉ Grant Thornton, Water's Edge, Clarendon Dock, Belfast BT1 3BH (tel 028 9031 5500)

BELL, Dr Gary Thomas; s of Thomas George Bell, of Brisbane, Aust, and Constance Beth *née* Goodman; *b* 1 October 1953; *Educ* Brisbane GS, Univ of Qld (BA, MB BS); *m* 5 Oct 1991 Marcia Rosalind, da of Desmond Laurence Hall; 2 da (Ghillian Naomi Cavell b 24 Dec 1992, Elizabeth Richenda Cavell b 10 Aug 1999), 1 s (Christian Thomas Cavell b 24 Nov 1995); *Career* lectr and hon sr registrar Middx Hosp and UCH 1985–89, sr lectr and hon conslt Bart's 1989–93, conslt psychiatrist Royal Nat Orthopaedic Hosp Stanmore 1994–97, conslt psychiatrist Cancer Treament Centre Mount Vernon Hosp Northwood 1997–; visiting conslt psychiatrist: Cardinal Clinic Windsor 1992–, Thames Valley Nuffield Hosp Wexham 1997–, Capio Nightingale Hosp 2003–, The London Clinic 2007–, Wellington Hosp 2007–, Hosp of St John and St Elizabeth 2007–; staff conslt psychiatrist and clinical tutor Priory Hosp Roehampton 2004–05, medical dir Cwlth Healthcare 2005–; examiner: RCPsych 1998–2005, United Examining Bd 1998–2005; various chapters and original articles on med educn and liaison psychiatry; Historic Houses Assoc: memb Nat Exec Ctee, hon treas Thames and Chiltern region 1996–2005; chm Windsor Golden Jubilee Parade Ctee 2001–02, corporate companion Coll of St George Windsor Castle 2006–, lay steward St George's Chapel Windsor Castle 2007–; Liveryman Worshipful Soc of Apothecaries 1992 (memb Ct of Assts 2001); FRCPsych 2000 (MRCPsych 1985); CStJ 2004 (OStJ 1999, memb Cncl 1997–, chm Cncl Order of St John Berks 1999–); *Recreations* opera, oenology, period garden restoration; *Style*— Dr Gary Bell, FRCPsych; ✉ Hall Place, Beaconsfield, Buckinghamshire HP9 1NB (tel 01494 674700, fax 01494 676710)

BELL, Ian Ronald; MBE (2006); *b* 11 April 1982, Coventry; *Educ* Princethorpe Coll; *Career* cricketer; Warwickshire CCC 1999– (winners Benson and Hedges Cup 2002 and County Championship 2004); England: 30 Test caps, 54 one day appearances, 2 Twenty20 appearances, Test debut v WI The Oval 2004, one day debut v Zimbabwe Harare 2004, memb Ashes-winning team 2005, memb squad World Cup WI 2007; NBC Denis Compton Award 1999, 2000 and 2001, Professional Cricketers Assoc Young Player of the Year 2004, ICC Emerging Player of the Year 2006; columnist The Guardian; *Style*— Mr Ian Bell, MBE; ✉ c/o England and Wales Cricket Board, Lord's Cricket Ground, St Johns Wood Road, London NW8 8QZ

BELL, Prof John Irving; *b* 1 July 1952; *Educ* Ridley Coll Canada, Univ of Alberta (Province of Alberta scholar, BMedSci), Magdalen Coll Oxford (Rhodes scholar, Cwlth scholar, BA, BM BCh, DM, Radcliffe Infirmary prize in surgery, Spray prize in clinical biochemistry);

Career house offr John Radcliffe Hosp Oxford (Nuffield Dept of Clinical Med and Regnl Paediatric Surgery Serv) 1979–80; SHO: to Dept of Clinical Cardiology Hammersmith Hosp London 1980–81, to Renal Unit Guy's Hosp London 1981, in neurology Nat Hosp for Neurological Diseases Queen Square London 1981–82; res fell Nuffield Dept of Clinical Med Univ of Oxford 1982, clinical fell Dept of Med and postdoctoral fell Dept of Med Microbiology Stanford Univ 1982–87, Wellcome sr clinical fell and hon conslt physician Nuffield Dept of Clinical Med and Surgery John Radcliffe Hosp Oxford 1987–89; regius prof of med Univ of Oxford 2001– (univ lectr 1989–92, Nuffield prof of clinical med 1992–2001), emeritus fell Magdalen Coll Oxford, student CCC Oxford, memb Cncl Univ of Oxford; fndr Wellcome Tst Centre for Human Genetics; pres and memb Cncl Acad of Med Scis; memb Bd UK Biobank Ltd; tstee: Rhodes Tst, Nuffield Med Tst, Ewelme Almshouse Charity; FRCP 1992; *Style*— Prof John Bell; ✉ Office of the Regius Professor of Medicine, John Radcliffe Hospital, Headington, Oxford OX3 9DU

BELL, Sir John Lowthian; 5 Bt (UK 1885), of Rounton Grange, Co York; s of Sir Hugh Francis Bell, 4 Bt (d 1970), and his 2 w, Mary, *née* Howson (d 2000); *b* 14 June 1960; *Educ* Glenalmond, RAC Cirencester; *m* 22 June 1985, Venetia Mary Frances, 2 da of J A Perry, of Taunton, Somerset; 1 s (John Hugh b 1988), 1 da (Sophia Amelia Bridget b 10 April 1990); *Heir* s, John Bell; *Career* farmer; *Recreations* fishing, shooting; *Style*— Sir John Bell, Bt; ✉ Arncliffe Hall, Ingleby Cross, Northallerton, North Yorkshire (tel 01609 882202)

BELL, Joshua; *b* 1967, Indiana; *Career* violinist; studied with Josef Gingold, int debut with the Philadelphia Orch under Riccardo Muti 1981; appeared with orchs incl: London Philharmonic, Royal Philharmonic, BBC Symphony, The Philharmonia, Chicago Symphony, Boston Symphony, Cleveland Orch, NY Philharmonic, LA Philharmonic, Orchestre de la Suisse Romande, Orchestre Philharmonique, Acad of St Martin in the Fields, Czech Philharmonic, City of Birmingham Symphony, Berlin Philharmonic, Santa Cecilia Rome; worked with conductors incl: Vladimir Ashkenazy, Paavo Berglund, Riccardo Chailly, Charles Dutoit, John Eliot Gardiner, James Levine, Andrew Litton, Seiji Otawa, André Previn, Esa-Pekka Salonen, Leonard Slatkin, Yuri Temirkanov, Michael Tilson Thomas, Lorin Maazel, Sir Neville Marriner, Roger Norrington; gave premiere of Nicholas Maw violin concerto written specially for him 1993; regular guest at summer festivals incl: Salzburg, Tanglewood, Mostly Mozart, Edinburgh, BBC Proms, Ravinia; *Recordings* Mendelssohn and Bruch violin concertos, Tchaikovsky Violin Concerto and Wieniawski D Minor Violin Concerto, Lalo Symphonie Espagnole and Saint-Saëns Violin Concerto No 3, two recital and chamber music albums of French repertoire, Poeme (album of virtuoso classics, with RPO under Andrew Litton), Mozart Concertos Nos 3 and 5 (with Eng Chamber Orch under Peter Maag), Prokofiev Violin Concertos (with Montreal Symphony Orch under Charles Dutoit), Prokofiev Recital Disc (with Olli Mustonen), Kreisler Pieces (with Paul Coker), Brahms and Schumann Concertos (with Cleveland Orch under Dohnányi), Walton & Barber Concerti (with Baltimore Symphony under Zinman); formerly under exclusive contract to Decca, currently with Sony, new recordings with Sony: Goldmark/Sibelius Concertos, Nicholas Maw Concerto (Mercury Music Prize 2000, Grammy Award 2001), Gershwin Porgy and Bess Fantasy, Short Trip Home, The Red Violin (Music Soundtrack, Academy Award), Beethoven Conceto, Mendelssohn Concerto, Bernstein Serenade, West Side Story Suite, Romance of the Violin; *Recreations* chess, computers, golf, tennis, baseball; *Style*— Joshua Bell, Esq; ✉ c/o Kathryn Enticott, IMG Artists Europe, Lovell House, 616 Chiswick High Road, London W4 5RX (tel 020 8233 5800, fax 020 8233 5801, e-mail cthompson@imgworld.com, website www.joshuabell.com)

BELL, Karen Patricia; da of Roger Guyton, of Sawston, Cambs, and Audrey, *née* Melia; *Educ* Anglia Poly Univ, Middx Poly; *m* Chris Minett; 2 s (Oliver b 12 Dec 1985, Matthew b 27 Oct 1988); *Career* Cambs HA: unit personnel mangr Priority Servs Unit 1983–86, actg dist personnel mangr 1986–87; dir of personnel Cambridge City Cncl 1987–92, exec dir HR Lifespan Healthcare Cambs NHS Tst 1992–99, chief exec Huntingdon PCT 1999–; DFID int conslt in health servs South Africa, Namibia and Malawi; pres elect Nat Assoc of Health Serv HR Mgmnt (chair Anglia and Oxford branch); FIPD 1992 (MIPD 1978); *Recreations* sailing, reading, theatre, cinema; *Clubs* Greens; *Style*— Mrs Karen Bell; ✉ Huntingdonshire Primary Care Trust, The Priory, Priory Road, St Ives, Cambridgeshire PE27 5BB (tel 01480 308200, fax 01480 308234, e-mail karen.bell@hunts-pct.nhs.uk)

BELL, Kevin; s of Ronald Bell, of Durham, and Sylvia, *née* Hampton; *b* 24 September 1957; *Educ* Washington GS, Univ of Reading (BA); *Career* public affrs/PR conslt; advsr to MPs and PA to Cons Pty candidates 1979, 1983, 1987, 1992 and 1997 gen elections; account exec K H Publicity 1979–80, dir Michael Forsyth Associates 1980–84; The Grayling Company: dir 1984–86 and 1990–94, md 1991–93; Westminster Strategy: dir 1986–94, dep md 1990–93, md 1993–94; dir: St James's Corporate Communications 1991–94, Pagette Communications 1991–94; md Lowe Bell Political 1994–, md and vice-chm GPC 2000–, md Fleishman-Hillard UK, dep chm Bell PottingerPublic Affairs (formerly Lowe Bell Consultants) 1994–99; tstee IEA; *Recreations* keeping fit, gardening, opera, eating and drinking well, teasing my friends; *Clubs* Paris Gym, Reform; *Style*— Kevin Bell, Esq; ✉ GPC, 40 Longacre, London WC2E 9LG (tel 020 7395 7171, fax 020 7395 7194, e-mail kevin.bell@gpcinternational.com)

BELL, Laurence Bonamy Simon; s of Denys Le Merchant Bell, and Susan Hart Collier, *née* Abbott; *b* 22 October 1965, St John's Wood, London; *Educ* St Alban's Secdy Sch Ipswich; *partner* Jacqueline Marie Rice; *Career* buyer Tower Records 1988–90, A&R Fire Records 1990–93, fndr and md Domino Recording Co 1993–; *Style*— Laurence Bell, Esq; ✉ Domino Recording Co Ltd, Unit 3, Delta Business Park, Smugglers Way, London SW18 1EG (tel 020 8875 1390, fax 020 8875 1391)

BELL, (Caithleen) Maeve; OBE (1999); da of John McKeown (d 1968), of Armagh, and Olive Kathleen, *née* Sadd (d 1983); *b* 25 April 1944; *Educ* St Louis GS Kilkeel, The Queen's Univ Belfast; *m* Adrian Kennedy Bell; *Career* research offr The Queen's Univ Belfast 1968–77, sr educn and info offr Equal Opportunities Commission for NI 1977–83, dir Autographics Software (NI) Ltd 1983–85, dir Gen Consumer Council for NI 1985–2003; vice-chm Sports Cncl for NI 1979–81 (memb 1975–85); memb: Higher Educn Review Gp 1979–82, Broadcasting Cncl for NI 1981–85, Standing Advsy Cmmn on Human Rights 1984–86, NI Legal Servs Cmmn 2003–06; non-exec dir: Phoenix Natural Gas Co 2004–07, Odyssey Tst Co 2004–; *Clubs* Irish Cruising; *Style*— Mrs Maeve Bell, OBE; ✉ 1 The Drive, Richmond Park, Belfast BT9 5EG

BELL, Marian Patricia; CBE (2005); da of (Joseph) Denis Milburn Bell (d 1997), and Wilhelmina Maxwell, *née* Miller; *b* 28 October 1957; *Educ* Hertford Coll Oxford (BA), Birkbeck Coll London (MSc); *m* 1988, Richard Adkin; 2 da; *Career* London Enterprise Agency 1980–82, economist Royal Bank of Scotland 1982–89, economic advsr HM Treasury 1989–91, Royal Bank of Scotland 1991–2000 (latterly head of research, treasury and capital markets), conslt Alpha Economics 2000–02, memb Monetary Policy Ctee Bank of England 2002–05; dep chair Forum for Global Health Protection; govr: Contemporary Dance Tst, The Place; FRSA; *Recreations* contemporary dance, art; *Style*— Ms Marian Bell, CBE

BELL, Martin; OBE (1992); s of Adrian Bell (d 1980), and Marjorie, *née* Gibson (d 1991); *b* 31 August 1938; *Educ* The Leys Sch Cambridge, King's Coll Cambridge; *m* 1, 1971, Nelly, *née* Gourdon; 2 da (Melissa b 1972, Catherine b 1974); m 2, 1985 (m dis 1993), Rebecca, *née* Sobel; m 3, 1998, Fiona, *née* Goddard; *Career* BBC: news asst BBC Norwich 1962–64, gen reporter BBC London and overseas 1964–76, dip corr 1976–77, chief N American corr 1977–89, Berlin corr BBC TV News 1989–93, Vienna corr 1993–94, foreign affrs corr (based London) 1994–97; reported from 70 countries, covered wars in Vietnam, Middle East 1967 and 1973, Angola, Rhodesia, Biafra, El Salvador, Gulf 1991, Nicaragua, Croatia and Bosnia (wounded 1992); memb Panel 2000; RTS Reporter of the Year 1976 and 1992, TRIC Newscaster of the Year 1995, IPR President's Medal 1996; MP (Ind) Tatton 1997–2001; UNICEF special rep for humanitarian emergencies 2001, ambass for UN Children's Fund 2004–; Hon Dr Univ of Derby 1996, hon degree UEA 1997; *Books* In Harm's Way (1995), An Accidental MP (2001), Through Gates of Fire (2003); *Style*— Martin Bell, Esq, OBE; ✉ 71 Denman Drive, London NW11 6RA

BELL, (William) Michael; s of William Bell (d 1993), and Hilda, *née* Taylor (d 1984); *b* 16 September 1944; *Educ* Berwick-upon-Tweed GS; *m* 4 Oct 1969, Helen Robina, da of William John Brown (d 1978), of Wooler, Northumberland; 3 da (Alison b 1971, Sarah b 1974, Lesley b 1977); *Career* CA; Thornton Baker & Co 1967–70; Wheeler & Co (now Wheelers) Wisbech: joined 1970, ptnr 1972–2006, sr ptnr 1991–2006, ret; memb Wisbech Rotary 1982–94 (hon asst sec 1985–87, hon sec 1987–90), clerk and govr St Peter's Junior Sch Wisbech 1971–91, memb St Peter and St Paul PCC 1972–85 (hon treas 1972–85); FCA, MAE 1996; *Recreations* golf; *Clubs* Sutton Bridge Golf (capt 1989–90, hon treas 1983–94), Kings Lynn Golf (hon treas 2000–, capt 2003); *Style*— Michael Bell, Esq; ✉ Apple Acre, Park Lane, Leverington, Wisbech, Cambridgeshire PE13 5EH (tel 01945 870736, e-mail wmbell.t21@btinternet.com)

BELL, Michael Jaffray de Hauteville; s of Capt C L de Hauteville Bell, DSC, RD, RNR (d 1972); *b* 7 April 1941; *Educ* Charterhouse; *m* 1965, Christine Mary, *née* Morgan; 1 s, 4 da; *Career* conslt ptnr Watson Wyatt (formerly R Watson and Sons) 1993–98 (ptnr 1967–93), chm Century Life plc; non-exec dir Lombard International Assurance SA; FIA 1964, ASA, FPMI; *Style*— Michael Bell, Esq

BELL, Michael John Vincent; CB (1992); s of Christopher Richard Vincent, OBE (d 2006), and Violet Irene Edith Lorna (Jane) Bell, MBE (d 1989); *b* 9 September 1941; *Educ* Winchester, Magdalen Coll Oxford; *m* 3 Sept 1983, Mary, da of John William Shippen (d 1957); 1 s (John b 1985), 2 da (Julia b 1987, Jane b 1989); *Career* res assoc Inst for Strategic Studies 1964–65, asst princ MOD 1965, asst private sec to Sec of State for Def 1968–69, princ MOD 1969, private sec to Perm Under Sec MOD 1973–75, asst sec MOD 1975, on loan to HM Treasy 1977–79, asst under sec MOD 1982, asst sec gen def planning and policy NATO 1986–88, dep under sec of state (Fin) MOD 1988–92, dep under sec of state (Defence Procurement) 1992–95 (post re-titled dep chief of def procurement (Support) 1995–96), on secondment as project dir European Consolidation BAE Systems plc (formerly British Aerospace plc) 1996–99, gp head of strategic analysis BAE Systems plc 1999–2003, conslt export controls BAE Systems plc; *Recreations* military history; *Style*— Michael Bell, Esq, CB; ✉ BAE Systems, Farnborough, Hampshire GU14 6YU (tel 01252 384607, e-mail michael.j.bell@baesystems.com)

BELL, Nicholas Julian; s of Malcom Graham Bell, and Rose Ellen Bell; *b* 15 January 1961; *Educ* Lancing (1st XI football colours, 1st XI cricket colours); *m* 1991, Angela Joanne, *née* Herbert; 2 da (Tiffany b 1993, Elly-May b 1996), 1 s (Charles b 2000); *Career* writer Abbot Mead Vickers 1987–95; Leo Burnett: writer 1995–97, dep exec creative dir 1998–99, exec creative dir 1999–2003; exec creative dir J Walter Thompson (latterly JWT) 2003–07; memb Bd of Dirs Br TV Advt Awards, judge D&AD Awards 2005–; MIPA; *Awards* Cannes Advertising Festival Grand Prix, 4 Cannes Gold Lions, 2 Design and Art Direction Silver Awards, 10 Campaign Press Silver Awards, 2 NY Clio Gold Awards, US Andy Award of Excellence; *Recreations* football (1st XI Lancing Old Boys FC 1982–97, Arthurian League Premier Div champions 6 times, Arthur Dunn cup winner 4 times incl league and cup double 1983–1985), cricket; *Style*— Nicholas Bell, Esq

BELL, Dr Patrick Michael; s of Benjamin Jonathan Bell (d 1982), and Jane, *née* McIllveen; *b* 9 March 1953; *Educ* Friends' Sch Lisburn, Queen's Univ Belfast (MB BCh, BAO, MD); *m* 28 June 1979, (Dorothy Lavina) Patricia, da of Canon Leslie Walker, of Ballylesson, Co Down; 2 da (Jane b 1980, Katie b 1982), 1 s (Jonathan b 1987); *Career* DHSS res fell Royal Victoria Hosp and Belfast City Hosp 1981–82, sr registrar Royal Victoria Hosp 1982–84, Mayo Fndn fell in endocrinology (as Fulbright scholar) Mayo Clinic USA 1984–85, sr registrar Belfast City Hosp 1985–86, conslt physician Royal Victoria Hosp 1986–, hon prof Queen's Univ Belfast 2002–; Central Exec Ctee Alliance Pty of NI 1987–94, chm NI Ctee Br Diabetic Assoc 1992–98; numerous articles in learned jls on glucose metabolism; memb Assoc of Physicians of GB and Ireland 1994; FRCPGlas 1988, FRCPEd 1992, FRCPI 1992 (MRCPI 1989), FRCP 1995; *Books* Multiple Choice Questions in Medicine (1981); *Style*— Prof Patrick Bell; ✉ 14 Clonevin Park, Lisburn, Co Antrim BT28 3BL (tel 028 9267 4703); East Wing Office, Royal Victoria Hospital, Grosvenor Road, Belfast BT12 6BA (tel 028 9063 3423)

BELL, Prof Sir Peter Frank; kt (2002); s of late Frank Bell, of Sheffield, S Yorks, and late Ruby, *née* Corks; *b* 12 June 1938; *Educ* Marcliffe Secdy Sch Sheffield, High Storrs GS Sheffield, Univ of Sheffield (MB ChB, MD); *m* 26 Aug 1961, Anne, da of Oliver Jennings (d 1981), of Dewsbury, W Yorks; 2 da (Jane Marie b 1962, Louise b 1963), 1 s (Mark b 1967); *Career* registrar in surgery Sheffield Health Bd 1963–65, Sir Henry Wellcome travelling fell Wellcome Fndn Denver Coll 1968–69, sr lectr in surgery Univ of Glasgow 1969–74 (lectr 1963–68), fndn prof of surgery Univ of Leicester 1974–2003; formerly memb: Cell Bd MRC, Transplant Mgmnt Ctee DHSS, Advsy Panel Br Cwlth Fellowship, Bd of Govrs De Montfort Univ; past ed Euro Jl of Vascular Surgery, past cncl memb and hon treas British Jl of Surgery Society Ltd; currently pres Int Soc for Vascular Surgery; past pres: Vascular Society of GB & Ireland, Leicester Med Soc; vice-pres Cncl RCS (chm Research Bd); memb: Int Transplantation Soc (past sec), Surgical Research Soc (past hon sec and pres), American Soc of Transplant Surgns, Br Soc of Immunology and Transplantation (past Ctee memb), Royal Med Chirurgical Soc of Glasgow, Vascular Surgical Soc (past Ctee memb and chm Vascular Advsy Ctee), Collegium Internationale Chirurgiae, Br Transplantation Soc, European Soc for Vascular Surgery (past pres), Soc for Academic Surgns (past chm), Acad of Med Sciences; treas Euro Surgical Assoc; pres Hope Fndn Charity for Cancer Research, chm Circulation Fndn Charity for Vascular Research; FRCS 1965 (past memb Surgical Advsy Ctee), FRCSGlas 1969; *Books* Operative Arterial Surgery (1983), Surgical Aspects of Haemodialysis (1985), Vascular Surgery (ed and contrib, 1985), Arterial Surgery of the Lower Limb (1991), Surgical Management of Vascular Disease (ed jtly and contrib, 1991), Minimal Access Therapy for Vascular Disease (ed and contrib, 2002); author of numerous articles in academic jls; *Recreations* painting, gardening, woodwork; *Style*— Prof Sir Peter Bell; ✉ 22 Powys Avenue, Oadby, Leicester LE2 2DP (tel 0116 270 9579, fax 0116 210 7361, e-mail peterrfbell@ntlworld.com)

BELL, Quentin Ross; s of Ross Bell, and Violet Martha, *née* Douglas; *b* 24 June 1944; *Educ* Presentation Coll Reading; *m* Hilary Sian, da of Vernon Jones; 2 da (Verity Ross, Henrietta Ross); *Career* various appts: Reading Standard, Thomson Newspapers, Haymarket Publishing; chm The Quentin Bell Organisation plc 1973–98; non-exec dir Katalyst Ventures 1999–2007; memb Superbrands Cncl 1996–; bd dir Eng Nat Ballet 2000–06; chm PRCA 1994–96; PR Professional of the Year PR Week Awards 1995; MInstD, FCIM, FIPR; *Books* The PR Business: an insider's guide to real life public relations, Win that Pitch!; *Recreations* appearing as 'Uncle Quentin - Grumpy Old Git' on Riviera Radio, collecting art, clocks, watches, parrots, cars, wine and compliments; *Clubs* RAC; *Style*— Quentin Bell, Esq; ✉ 3 Queensberry Place, London SW7 2DL (tel 020 7589 5198, e-mail quentin@monaco.mc, website www.quentin-bell.com)

BELL, Rachel Anne; da of Stuart Bell (d 1997), and Sylvia, *née* Walker; *b* 25 February 1968; *Educ* Sandy Upper Sch; *m* 2 March 2000, Peter Hayward, s of Norman Hayward; 1 da (Isobel Stuart b 17 Aug 2000); *Career* with Hyatt Hotels 1985–89, account exec rising to account dir Freishman Hillard Int 1989–97, fndr and chm Shine Communications 1998– (winner of numerous industry awards); Media Boss of the Year 2000; memb: Consultancy Mgmnt Standard (CMS), PRCA, Mktg Soc; MIPR; *Style*— Ms Rachel Bell; ✉ Shine Communications, 101 Goswell Road, London EC1V 7ER (tel 020 7553 3333, fax 020 7553 3330, e-mail rachel@shinecom.com)

BELL, Richard; s of John Reed Bell (d 2003), and Audrey Holt Bell; *b* 4 March 1966; *Educ* Bury GS, Univ of Birmingham (BComm); *m* Vicky; 2 da (Charlotte, Beatrix); *Career* head of transaction servs UK regions Deloitte; ACA 1990; *Recreations* football, golf, skiing, music; *Style*— Richard Bell, Esq; ✉ Deloitte & Touche LLP, PO Box 500, 2 Hardman Street, Manchester M60 2AT

BELL, (John) Robin Sinclair; MBE (1999), WS; s of Ian Cardean Bell, OBE, MC (d 1967), and Cecile, *née* Rutherford (d 1980); *b* 28 February 1933; *Educ* Edinburgh Acad, Loretto, Worcester Coll Oxford (BA), Univ of Edinburgh (LLB); *m* 27 April 1963, Patricia, da of Edward Upton, of Whitby, N Yorks; 4 s (Charles b 1965 d 1969, Patrick b 1967, Peter b 1970, Jonathan b 1972); *Career* Nat Serv cmmnd Royal Scots Berlin 1951–53, Capt TA 1953–63; slr and WS; Coward Chance slrs 1961–62, sr ptnr Tods Murray WS Edinburgh 1987–94 (ptnr 1963); non-exec dir: Edinburgh Financial Trust plc 1983–87, Upton and Southern Holdings plc 1984–93, Citizens Advice Scotland 1997–99; Law Soc of Scotland: memb Cncl 1975–78, memb Co Law Ctee 1975–94; memb Co Law Ctee of Cncl Bars & Law Socs of EU 1976–94, memb East of Scotland Water Authy 1995–2002, Scottish Charities Nominee 1995–2001; *Recreations* game fishing, making and restoring furniture; *Clubs* New (Edinburgh), The Royal Scots (Edinburgh); *Style*— Robin Bell, Esq, MBE, WS; ✉ 29 Saxe Coburg Place, Edinburgh EH3 5BP (tel 0131 315 2299)

BELL, Sir Rodger; kt (1993); s of John Thornton Bell (d 1974), and Edith Bell (d 1994); *b* 13 September 1939; *Educ* Moulsham Sch, Brentwood Sch, BNC Oxford; *m* 27 Sept 1969, (Sylvia) Claire, da of William Eden Tatton Brown, CB (d 1997); 1 s (Benjamin b 1970), 3 da (Natasha b 1972, Lucinda b 1975, Sophie b 1982); *Career* called to the Bar Middle Temple 1963; recorder of the Crown Ct 1980, QC 1982, bencher Middle Temple 1989, legal memb Mental Health Review Tbnl 1983–93, memb Parole Bd 1990–93, chm NHS Tbnl 1991–93, judge Employment Appeal Tbnl 1994–2003; judge of the High Court of Justice (Queen's Bench Div) 1993–2006, presiding judge SE Circuit 2001–05; *Style*— Sir Rodger Bell

BELL, Sir Stuart; kt (2004), MP; s of Ernest and Margaret Rose Bell; *Educ* Hookergate GS Durham; *m* 1, 1960, Margaret, da of Mary Bruce; 1 s, 1 da; m 2, Margaret, da of Mary Allan; 1 s; *Career* called to the Bar Gray's Inn, sometime journalist; joined Lab Pty 1964; MP (Lab) Middlesbrough 1983– (Parly candidate (Lab) Hexham 1979); PPS to Rt Hon Roy Hattersley 1982–84, oppn front bench spokesman on NI 1984–87, oppn front bench spokesman on trade and industry 1992–97; chm House of Commons Cmmn 1999–, chm Fin and Services Select Ctee 1999–, chm Franco-Br Parly Relations Ctee 2005–; 2nd Church Estates cmmr 1997–; cncllr Newcastle City Cncl 1980–83; legal advsr Trade Unions for Lab Victory N Region, fndr memb Br-Irish Parly Body 1990, vice-chm Br Gp Inter-Parly Union 1992–, memb Police and Criminal Evidence Bill Ctee 1986 and Children's Bill Ctee 1989; memb: Soc of Labour Lawyers, Fabian Soc, Co-operative Soc, Gen and Municipal Boilermakers and Allied Trades Union; Freeman City of London 2003; Chevalier Legion d'Honneur (France) 2006; *Publications* Paris 69, Days That Used To Be, When Salem Came to the Boro, How to Abolish the Lords (Fabian tract), The Principles of US Customs Valuation (legal pubn), Annotation of the Children Act (legal pubn, 1989), Raising the Standard - The Case for First Past the Post (1998), Tony Really Loves Me (2000), Pathway to the Euro (2002), Binkie's Revolution (2002), The Honoured Society (2003), Lara's Theme (2004), Softly in the Dusk (2004); *Recreations* short story and novel writing; *Style*— Sir Stuart Bell, MP; ✉ House of Commons, London SW1A 0AA

BELL, Baron (Life Peer UK 1998), of Belgravia in the City of Westminster; Sir Timothy John Leigh (Tim) Bell; kt (1990); s of Arthur Leigh Bell (d 1963), of SA, and Greta Mary, *née* Findlay; *b* 18 October 1941; *Educ* Queen Elizabeth's GS Barnet; *m* 11 July 1988, Virginia Wallis, da of Dr John Wallis Hornbrook, of Sydney, Aust; 1 da (Hon Daisy Alicia Wallis b 1988), 1 s (Hon Harry Leigh b 22 April 1991); *Career* ABC TV 1959–61, Colman Prentis & Varley 1961–63, Hobson Bates 1963–66, Geers Gross 1966–70, chm and md Saatchi & Saatchi Compton 1975–85 (md 1970–75), gp chief exec Lowe Howard-Spink Campbell Ewald 1985–87, dep chm Lowe Howard-Spink & Bell 1987–89; currently chm Chime Communications plc; special advsr to chm NCB 1984–86; former dir Centre for Policy Studies; memb: PR Ctee Gtr London Fund for the Blind 1979–86, Public Affrs Ctee WWF 1985–88, Indust Ctee Save the Children Fund; pres Charity Projects 1993– (chm 1984–93); memb: Cncl Royal Opera House 1982–85, S Bank Bd 1985–86; govr BFI 1983–86; FIPA; *Recreations* golf, politics; *Clubs* RAC, Royal Prince Edward Yacht (Sydney); *Style*— The Rt Hon the Lord Bell; ✉ Chime Communications plc, 14 Curzon Street, London W1J 5HN (tel 020 7495 4044, fax 020 7491 9860)

BELL BURNELL, Prof Dame (Susan) Jocelyn; DBE (2007, CBE 1999); da of George Philip Bell (d 1982), of Solitude, Lurgan, NI, and Margaret Allison Bell, MBE, JP, *née* Kennedy; *b* 15 July 1943; *Educ* The Mount Sch York, Univ of Glasgow (BSc), New Hall Cambridge (PhD); *m* 21 Dec 1968 (m dis 1989), Martin Burnell, s of Arnold Burnell, of London; 1 s (Gavin b 1973); *Career* Univ of Southampton: SRC fell 1968–70, jr teaching fell 1970–73; Mullard Space Sci Laboratory UCL: pt/t grad programmer 1974–76, pt/t assoc research fell 1976–82; Royal Observatory Edinburgh: pt/t sr research fell 1982–86, astronomer i/c Visitor Centre 1985–86, pt/t sr sci offr and head of James Clerk Maxwell Telescope Section 1986–89, pt/t grade 7 and head of James Clerk Maxwell Telescope Section 1989–91; prof of physics Open Univ 1991–2001 (tutor, conslt, guest lectr 1973–88), dean of sci Univ of Bath 2001–2004, professorial fell Mansfield Coll Oxford 2004–; visiting prof: Princeton Univ 1999–2000, Univ of Oxford 2004–; ed The Observatory 1973–76; pres RAS 2002–04 (memb Cncl 1978–81 and 1992–97, vice-pres 1995–97), memb various bds, ctees and panels PPARC and SERC 1978– (incl: vice-chm Astronomy I Ctee 1983–84, chair Public Understanding of Sci Advsy Panel 2001–05, chair Advanced LIGO Oversight Ctee 2003–), chair EC Physics TMR-TTR Panel 1996–98 (vice-chair 1995); hon fell: Univ of Edinburgh 1988–91, New Hall Cambridge 1996–; hon assoc Nat Cncl of Women 1995–; hon memb Sigma Pi Sigma 2000–, memb Bd Edinburgh Int Sci Festival 1991–96, foreign memb Onsala Observatory Bd Sweden 1996–2002, memb Scientific Ctee for Physics Int Solvay Insts 2004–; Michelson medal Franklin Inst Philadelphia 1973, J Robert Oppenheimer meml prize Center for Theoretical Studies Miami 1978, Beatrice Tinsley prize American Astronomical Soc (first recipient) 1987, Herschel medal RAS London 1989, Edinburgh Medal (City of Edinburgh and Science Festival) 1999, Magellanic Premium (American Philosophical Soc) 2000; memb: Br Cncl of Churches Assembly 1978–90, Scottish Churches Cncl 1982–90 (Exec Ctee 1984–88), Open Univ Cncl 1997–99; tstee Nat Maritime Museum Greenwich 2000–; Hon DSc: Heriot-Watt Univ 1993, Univ of Warwick 1995, Univ of Newcastle upon Tyne 1995, Univ of Cambridge 1996, Univ of Glasgow 1997, Univ of Sussex 1997, Univ of St Andrews 1999, Univ of London 1999, Haverford Coll (USA) 2000, Univ of Leeds 2000, Williams Coll (USA) 2000, Univ of Portsmouth 2002, Queen's Univ Belfast 2002, Univ of Edinburgh 2003, Univ of Keele 2005; Hon DUniv York 1994; memb: Int Astronomical Union 1979, American Astronomical Soc 1992; foreign assoc US Nat Acad of Sciences 2005; FRAS 1969, FInstP 1992, FRSA 1999, FRS 2003 (memb Cncl 2004–06), FRSE 2004; *Recreations* swimming, learning languages, knitting and sewing, Quaker activities; *Style*— Prof Dame Jocelyn Bell Burnell, DBE

BELLAMY, Andrew James; *b* 19 September 1949; *Educ* Spalding GS, Univ of Wales Coll of Cardiff (BSc(Econ)), DipHSM; *m* Nicola; 1 da (Jane), 2 s (Ian, Richard); *Career* nat admin trainee SE Metropolitan Regnl Health Bd 1971–73, dep hosp sec Birkenhead Hosp Mgmnt Ctee/Wirral AHA 1973–75, princ admin Planning and Resources Sefton AHA 1975, sector admin Liverpool AHA 1975–79; asst dist admin: E Cumbria HA 1979–83, S Tees HA 1983–85; W Glamorgan HA: unit gen mangr 1985–90, asst gen mangr 1990–92 (secondment to Welsh Office 1991–92), unit gen mangr E Unit 1992–95; chief exec Glan-y-Môr NHS Tst 1995–99, dir Swansea NHS Tst 1999–2006; *Recreations* watching sport, golf, theatre, foreign travel; *Style*— Andrew Bellamy, Esq; ✉ tel 01792 234132, e-mail bellamy864@btinternet.com

BELLAMY, Sir Christopher William; kt (2000); s of Dr William Albert Bellamy, TD (d 1960), of Waddesdon, Bucks, and Vyvienne Hilda, *née* Meyrick (d 2001); *b* 25 April 1946; *Educ* Tonbridge, BNC Oxford; *m* Deirdre Patricia, da of Alexander Turner (d 1961); 1 s (Edward Alexander William), 2 da (Charlotte Elizabeth, Alexandra Anne); *Career* called to the Bar Middle Temple 1968, bencher 1994; in practice specialising in EC, public law and related matters 1970–92; QC 1986; asst recorder Crown Ct 1989–92, judge of the Ct of First Instance of European Communities 1992–99, pres Competition Cmmn Appeal Tribunals 1999–2003, pres Competition Appeal Tribunal 2003–07, dep High Ct judge 2000–, judge of Employment Appeal Tbnl 2000–07, recorder Crown Ct 2001–07, sr conslt Linklaters 2007–; pres: Assoc of European Competition Law Judges 2002–06, UK Assoc of European Law 2003–; memb Cncl of Mgmnt Br Inst of Int and Corp Law 2002–06; govr Ravensbourne Coll of Design and Communication 1988–92; Liveryman Worshipful Co of Broderers; fell Inst of Advanced Legal Studies; *Books* Common Market Law of Competition (with G Child, 1 edn 1973 and 6 edn (as European Community Law of Competition), 2008, ed P Roth and V Rose); *Recreations* history, walking, family life; *Clubs* Athenaeum, Garrick; *Style*— Sir Christopher Bellamy, QC; ✉ Linklaters, 1 Silk Street, London EC2Y 8HQ (tel 020 7456 3457)

BELLAMY, Prof David James; OBE (1994); s of Thomas James Bellamy (d 1988), and Winifred May, *née* Green (d 1979); *b* 18 January 1933; *Educ* Sutton County GS, Chelsea Coll of Sci and Technol (BSc), Bedford Coll London (PhD); *m* 3 Jan 1959, (Shirley) Rosemary, da of Frederick Herbert Froy (d 1959); 2 s (Rufus b 8 June 1966, Eoghain b 9 May 1975), 3 da (Henrietta b 14 Feb 1970, Brighid b 7 March 1972, Hannah b 24 June 1978); *Career* Univ of Durham: lectr in botany 1960–68, sr lectr in botany 1968–82, hon prof of adult educn 1982–; Univ of Nottingham: special prof of botany 1987–99, special prof of geography 2000–; visiting prof of natural heritage studies Massey Univ NZ 1989; dir: Botanical Enterprises Ltd, (fndr) Natural Heritage Conservation Fndn NZ, Conservation Fndn London; memb various professional ctees, recipient of many awards incl UNEP Global 500 1990; memb Cncl Zoological Soc of London 2003; Parly candidate (Referendum Party) Huntingdon 1997; hon prof Univ of Central Queensland 1998–; Hon DUniv Open Univ, Hon DSc CNAA; Hon FLS, FIBiol, FRGS, fell Inst of Environmental Sci, FRIN; Order of the Golden Ark (Netherlands) 1988, Commemoration medal (NZ) 1990, Busk medal RGS 2001; *Television* for BBC incl: Life in Our Sea 1970, Bellamy on Botany 1973, Bellamy's Britain 1975, Bellamy's Europe 1977, Up a Gum Tree 1980, Backyard Safari 1981, The Great Seasons 1982, Bellamy's New World 1983, You Can't See The Wood 1984, Seaside Safari 1985, Bellamy Rides Again 1992, Blooming Bellamy 1993; for ITV incl: Botanic Man 1979, The End of the Rainbow Show 1986, Bellamy's Bugle 1986, Turning the Tide 1986, Bellamy's Birds Eye View 1988, Don't Ask Me, It's Life, It's More Life, The Gene Machine, Swallow, Bellamy on Top of the World, Paradise Ploughed, The Owl and the Woodsman, England's Lost Wilderness 1991, England's Last Wilderness 1992, Routes of Wisdom 1993; other television incl: Moa's Ark (TVNZ) 1990, Westwatch 1996, A Welsh Herbal 1998, Buzz of Biodiversity 1999, Salt Solutions 1999, Can of Worms 2006; *Books* Bellamy on Botany (1972), Peatlands (jtly, 1973), Bellamy's Britain (1974), Life Giving Sea (1975), Green Worlds (jtly, 1975), The World of Plants (1975), It's Life (1976), Bellamy's Europe (1976), Botanic Action (1978), Botanic Man (1978), Half of Paradise (1979), Forces of Life (1979), Bellamy's Backyard Safari (1981), The Great Seasons (jtly, 1981), Il Libro Verde (1981), Discovering the Countryside (1982 and 1983), The Mouse Book (jtly, 1983), Bellamy's New World (1983), The Queen's Hidden Garden (jtly, 1984), Bellamy's Ireland (1986), Turning the Tide (jtly, 1986), Bellamy's Changing Countryside (1987), England's Last Wilderness (jtly, 1989), England's Lost Wilderness (jtly, 1990), Wetlands (jtly, 1990), Wilderness Britain (jtly, 1990), How Green are You (jtly, 1991), Tomorrow's Earth (jtly, 1991), World Medicine: Plants Patients and People (jtly, 1992), Blooming Bellamy (1993), Trees of the World (jtly, 1993), Poo You and the Potoroo's Loo (1997), Jolly Green Giant (autobiography, 2002), The Glorious Trees of Britain (jtly, 2002), A Natural Life (autobiography, 2003), The Bellamy Herbal (2003), Conflicts in the Countryside (2005); *Clubs* Farmers; *Style*— Prof David Bellamy; ✉ Mill House, Bedburn, Bishop Auckland, Durham DL13 3NN

BELLAMY, Stephen Howard George Thompson; QC (1996); s of George Bellamy (d 1976), and Clarice, *née* Thompson (d 1997); *b* 27 September 1950; *Educ* The GS Heckmondwike, Trinity Hall Cambridge (MA); *m* 15 Oct 1988, Rita James; 1 da (Nina Claudia Carla b 6 Nov 1991); *Career* called to the Bar Lincoln's Inn 1974 (bencher 2006); in practice SE Circuit, specialist in family law, recorder of the Crown Court 2000– (asst recorder 1997–2000), dep judge of the High Court 2000–; asst boundary cmmr 2000–; memb Ctee Family Law Bar Assoc 1989–96, memb Gen Cncl of the Bar 1993–96, chm Bar Cncl Scholarship Tst 2000–; memb Br Inst of Int and Comparative Law; fell Inst of Advanced Legal Studies; *Recreations* music, opera, gardening, tennis, skiing; *Style*— Stephen Bellamy, Esq, QC; ✉ 1 King's Bench Walk, Temple, London EC4Y 7DB (tel 020 7936 1500, fax 020 7936 1590, e-mail sbellamyqc@lkbw.co.uk)

BELLANY, Prof Ian; s of James Bellany (d 1984), of Sheffield and Bristol, and Jemima, *née* Emlay; *b* 21 February 1941; *Educ* Preston Lodge, Prestonpans, Firth Park Sheffield, Balliol Coll Oxford (state scholar, MA, DPhil); *m* 7 Aug 1965, Wendy Ivey, da of Glyndwr Thomas (d 1978), of Gilwern, Abergavenny; 1 s (Alastair b 1968), 1 da (Alison b 1971); *Career* asst princ FCO 1965–68, res fell ANU 1968–70; Lancaster Univ: lectr in politics 1970–74, sr lectr 1974–79, prof of politics 1979–2006, dir of the Centre for the Study of Arms Control and Int Security 1979–90, emeritus prof 2006–; founding ed Arms Control; external examiner in: Int Rels LSE 1985–88 and 1999–2002, Int Studies Univ of Birmingham 1989–92, Int Rels Univ of Aberdeen 1996–99; First Prize Trench Gascoigne Essay 2002, Leverhulme res fell 2003–04; *Books* Australia in the Nuclear Age (1972), Anti-Ballistic Missile Defence in the 1980s (ed 1983), The Verification of Arms Control Agreements (ed 1983), The Nuclear Non Proliferation Treaty (ed 1985), New Conventional Weapons and Western Defence (ed 1987), A Basis for Arms Control (1991), Reviewing Britain's Defence (1994), The Environment in World Politics (1997), Curbing the Spread of Nuclear Weapons (2005), Terrorism and Weapons of Mass Destruction (ed, 2007); *Recreations* broadcasting, carpentry and computing; *Style*— Prof Ian Bellany; ✉ Lancaster University, Bailrigg, Lancaster LA1 4YL (tel 01524 65201, e-mail i.bellany@lancaster.ac.uk)

BELLANY, Dr John; CBE (1994); s of Richard Weatherhead Bellany (d 1985), of Port Seton, E Lothian, and Agnes Craig Maltman Bellany; *b* 18 June 1942; *Educ* Cockenzie Sch, Preston Lodge Prestonpans, Edinburgh Coll of Art (DA), RCA (MA); *m* 1, 1964 (m dis 1974), Helen Margaret, da of late Harold Percy, of Golspie, Sutherland; 2 s (Jonathan b

22 Dec 1965, Paul b 21 Aug 1968), 1 da (Anya b 30 Sept 1970); m 2, 1980, Juliet Gray, *née* Lister (d 1985); m 3, 1986, his first wife Helen Margaret; *Career* lectr in fine art Winchester Sch of Art 1969–73, head Faculty of Painting Croydon Coll of Art 1973–78, visiting lectr in painting RCA 1975–84, lectr in fine art Goldsmiths Coll London 1978–84; artist in residence Victorian Coll of the Arts Melbourne 1983, fell commoner Trinity Hall Cambridge 1988; subject of: Bellany - Life, Death and Resurrection (film), A Day With John Bellany (book); Major Arts Cncl Award 1981, jt first prize Athena Int Award 1985, Korn Ferry Int Award Royal Acad of Arts 1993; elected sr fell RCA; Hon Dr: Univ of Edinburgh, Heriot-Watt Univ; Hon RSA 1987, RA 1991 (elected ARA 1986); *Exhibitions* major solo exhbns: Drian Gallery London 1970, 1971, 1972, 1973 and 1974, Aberdeen City Art Gallery 1975, Acme Gallery London 1977 and 1980, Scottish Arts Cncl Gallery 1978, 3rd Eye Centre Glasgow 1979, Southampton Art Gallery, Rosa Esman Gallery NY 1982, 1983 and 1984, Beaux Arts Gallery Bath 1989 and 1990, Fischer Fine Art London 1986, 1987, 1989 and 1991, Scot Nat Gallery of Modern Art 1986 and 1989, Raab Gallery Berlin 1989, Fitzwilliam Museum Cambridge 1991, Terry Dintenfass Gallery NY 1995, Gallerio Kin Mexico 1997, Beaux Arts Gallery London 1997, 1998, 1999 and 2003, Solomon Gallery Dublin 1999 and 2002, Irish Gallery of Modern Art Dublin 2000, Flowers West LA 2002, Open Eye Gallery Edinburgh 2002; Arts Cncl touring exhibition 1983: Ikon Gallery Birmingham, Walker Art Gallery Liverpool, Graves Art Gallery Sheffield; Arts Cncl touring exhibition 1984: Christine Abrahams Gallery Melbourne, Düsseldorf Gallery Perth, Roslyn Oxley Gallery Sydney, Nat Portrait Gallery 1986, Galerie Kirkhaar Amsterdam; one man exhibition (Beaux-Arts Gallery London) 2000, one man exhibition (Solomon Gallery Dublin) 2000; retrospective exhbns: Scot Nat Gallery of Modern Art 1986, Serpentine Gallery London, RCA Gallery 1987, Kunsthalle Hamburg 1989, Roslyn Oxley Gallery Sydney, Butler Gallery Kilkenny Castle, Hendrix Gallery Dublin, 3rd Eye Centre Glasgow (prints) 1988, Ruth Siegel Gallery NY 1988 and 1990, The Renaissance of John Bellany (Nat Gallery of Modern Art) 1988, Fisher Fine Art London 1988 and 1991, Raab Gallery Berlin 1990, Fitzwilliam Museum Cambridge 1991, A Long Night's Journey into Day: The Art of John Bellany (Kelvingrove Art Gallery and Museum, Glasgow) 1992, Berkeley Square Gallery London 1993, Recent Acquisitions: John Bellany (Nat Gallery of Modern Art Dublin) 2000; 60th birthday exhbn: Scottish Gallery of Modern Art, Beaux Arts Gallery London, Solomon Gallery Dublin, Flowers East LA, Open Eye Gallery Edinburgh, Ricci Museum Barga Italy; major gp exhbns: British Romantic Painting (Madrid), El Greco - Mystery and Illumination (Nat Gallery), Every Picture tells a Story (Br Cncl touring exhibition Singapore and Hong Kong), Eros in Albion (House of Messaccio Italy), Scottish Art since 1990 (Nat Gallery of Scotland and Barbican London), Scotland Creates 1990, The Great British Art Show 1990, Bellany and MacTaggart the Elder (Edinburgh Art Centre Festival Exhibition) 2000, Sea Change: John Bellany and Sir William MacTaggart (Edinburgh City Art Centre) 2000, Bourne Fine Art Festival exhibition 2000, John Bellany at Sixty (Scottish Nat Gallery of Modern Art) 2002, John Bellany in Italy (Ricci Fndn Tuscany) 2002; *Work in Public Collections* Aberdeen Art Gallery, Arts Cncl of GB, Br Cncl, Br Govt Collection Whitehall, Contemporary Arts Soc, Hatton Art Gallery, Kelvingrove Art Gallery, Leeds Art Gallery, Leicester Art Gallery, Middlesbrough Art Gallery, Nat Gallery of Poland Warsaw, Nat Library of Congress Washington DC, MOMA NY, Met Museum NY, Nat Portrait Gallery, Nat Gallery of Modern Art Scotland, Gulbenkian Museum Lisbon, J F Kennedy Library Boston, V&A, Br Museum, Tate; *Clubs* Chelsea Arts, Scottish Arts (Edinburgh); *Style*— Dr John Bellany, CBE, RA; ✉ The Clockhouse, Shortgrove Hall, Saffron Walden, Essex CB11 3TX (website www.bellany.com); 19 Great Stuart Street, Edinburgh EH3 7TP; c/o Berkley Square Gallery, 23A Bruton Street, London W1X 7DA (tel 020 7493 7939); represented by Beaux Arts Gallery, Cork Street, London W1S 3NA (tel 020 7437 5799)

BELLAS, Moira Aileen; da of Norman Spencer Bellas, of Worthing, and Catherine Winifred, *née* Whysall (d 1986); *b* 21 March 1950; *Educ* Woodfield Secdy Modern Sch Hounslow; *m* Dec 1974, Clive Alan Banks; 1 da (Kelly May b May 1987); *Career* jr clerk Pye Records 1965–67, press office asst Paragon Publicity 1967–68, press offr EMI Records 1968–70, press offr Three's Company (PR co) 1970–71; WEA Records (formerly Kinney Records): sec/PA 1971–73, press offr 1973–86, dir Artistic Devpt and Mktg 1986–92, md 1992–2000; co-founder MBC (PR co) 2000–, clients include: Madonna, REM, Mick Hucknall, Depeche Mode, Christina Aguilera, Charlotte Church, Pretenders and Melanie C; winner Leslie Perrin Publicity Award, Woman of the Year Women of the Year Awards (music industry) 2001; *Style*— Ms Moira Bellas; ✉ MBC, Wellington Building, 28–32 Wellington Road, London NW8 9SP (tel 020 7483 9205, e-mail moirabellas@mbcmanagment.com)

BELLENGER, Rt Rev Dom (Dominic) Aidan; s of Gerald Bellenger, of London, and Kathleen Patricia, *née* O'Donnell; *b* 21 July 1950; *Educ* Finchley GS, Jesus Coll Cambridge (Lightfoot scholar, MA, PhD), Angelicum Univ Rome; *Career* asst master St Mary's Sch Cambridge 1975–78; Downside Abbey: Benedictine monk 1982, priest 1988, prior 2001–06, abbot 2006–; Downside Sch: asst master 1978–82, housemaster 1989–91, head master 1991–95, govr 1999–; delg English Benedictine Congregation Gen Chapter 2001–; pt/t lectr: Univ of Bristol 1996–, Bath Spa UC 1997–, Univ of Birmingham 1998–2000, UC Worcester 1999–2000; assoc lectr Open Univ 1997–2004; memb: Ctee Ecclesiastical History Soc 1982–85, Ctee English Benedictine Historical Cmmn 1987–, Cncl Catholic Record Soc 1990–99 and 2005–, Cncl Somerset Record Soc 1998–; tstee: Catholic Family History Soc 1990–99, Friends of Somerset Churches 1996–; pres English Catholic History Assoc 1991–; govr: Moor Park Sch Ludlow 1991–99, St Anthony's Leweston 1991–93, St Mary's Sch Shaftesbury 1992–96, Moreton Hall Sch 1994–2000, St Joseph's Malvern 1997–2000, St Gregory's Bath 2001–05; English corr Revue d'Histoire de l'Eglise de France 1982–85, ed South Western Catholic History 1982–; Leverhulme Research Award 1986, first York Minster lectr 2001, visiting scholar Sarum Coll 2004–; FRHistS, FRSA, FSA; chaplain Knights of Malta 2004–; *Books* English and Welsh Priests 1558–1800 (1984), The French Exiled Clergy (1986), Opening the Scrolls (ed, 1987), Les Archives du Nord, Calendar of 20 H (jt ed, 1987), St Cuthbert (1987), Letters of Bede Jarrett (jt ed, 1989), Fathers in Faith (ed, 1991), The Great Return (ed, 1994), Downside, A Pictorial History (ed, 1998), Princes of the Church: The English Cardinals (2001), William Bernard Ullathorne (2001), Medieval Worlds (2003), The Mitre and the Crown: The Archbishops of Canterbury (2005), Medieval Religion (2006); author of articles in jls, newspapers and periodicals; *Recreations* books, church architecture, travel, the visual arts, writing; *Clubs* Stratton-on-the-Fosse CC (pres 1991–95); *Style*— The Rt Rev Dom Aidan Bellenger, FSA; ✉ Downside Abbey, Stratton-on-the-Fosse, Bath BA3 4RJ (tel 01761 235119, fax 01761 235105, e-mail admin@downside.co.uk)

BELLEW, 7 Baron (I 1848); Sir James Bryan Bellew; 13 Bt (I 1688); s of 6 Baron Bellew, MC; suc f 1981; *b* 5 January 1920; *m* 1, 1942, Mary Elizabeth (d 1978), er da of Rev Edward Hill, of West Malling; 2 s, 1 da; m 2, 1978, Gwendoline (d 2002), da of Charles Redmond Clayton-Daubeny, of Bridgwater, Somerset, and of Bihar, India, and formerly w of Maj P Hall; *Heir* s, Hon Bryan Bellew; *Career* late Capt Irish Gds, served WW II; *Style*— The Rt Hon the Lord Bellew

BELLEW, Patrick John; s of James Kevin Bellew (d 1972), and Judith Anne Bellew, *née* Peekston; *b* 12 June 1959, Osmotherley, N Yorks; *Educ* Stonyhurst Coll, Univ of Bath; *m* 8 Feb 1985, Lois Jane, *née* Clay; 2 da (Zoe Diana b 17 Dec 1986, Freya Judith b 23 Dec 1992), 1 s (Ruaraidh Alexander James b 12 May 1988); *Career* with Buro Happold Bath 1981–97, dir Synergy Consltg Engrs 1987–90; projects incl: Greenpeace UK HQ, Llangollen Eisteddfod Festival Structure; princ Atelier Ten Consltg Engrs 1990–, also dir Atelier Ten NY LLC and L'Atelier; projects incl: Charities Aid Fndn HQ West Malling, sustainable primary sch Notley Green, The Earth Centre, Sculpture Sch and BioMed Lab Yale Univ, Alpine House and Jodrell Lab Kew Gardens, Baltic Centre for Contemporary Arts Gateshead, Federation Sq Melbourne, Virginia Museum of Fine Art, Grand Rapids Art Museum, The Ashmolean Museum Oxford, Ruth Deech Building St Anne's Coll Oxford, The Esplanade Theatre Singapore, Gardens by the Bay Singapore; visiting lectr and tutor: Bartlett Sch of Architecture UCL 1991–93, Sch of Construction Univ of Reading 1991–2004, Grad Sch of Architecture Yale Univ 2001–05; govr Building Centre Tst 1996–, memb Design Review Ctee Cmmn for Architecture and the Built Environment (CABE) 1999–2003, founding memb UK Green Building Cncl 2006; FRSA 1997, Hon FRIBA 2000, FEI 2001 (memb 1987), FCIBSE 2001 (MCIBSE 1985), FREng 2004; *Recreations* guitar, music, reading; *Style*— Patrick Bellew, Esq; ✉ Atelier Ten, 19 Perseverance Works, 38 Kingsland Road, London E2 8DD (tel 020 7749 5952, fax 020 7729 5388, e-mail pb@atelierten.com)

BELLI, Dr Anna-Maria; da of Bartolomeo Antonio Luigi Belli, of Cwmgyn, Swansea, West Glam, and Carmen, *née* Lombardelli; *b* 5 August 1957; *Educ* Glanmôr Sch for Girls, Univ of London, Middx Hosp Med Sch (MB BS); *Career* sr registrar in radiology St George's Hosp 1985–87 (registrar 1982–85); sr lectr and hon conslt in radiodiagnosis: Univ of Sheffield 1987–90, Royal Postgrad Med Sch Hammersmith Hosp 1990–92; currently conslt St George's Hosp London; memb Cncl BSIR 1993; fell CIRSE 1994, FRCR 1985; *Books* An Imaging Atlas of Human Anatomy (contrib 1 edn, 1992), Vascular Diseases in the Limbs (contrib 1 edn, 1993), Practical Interventional Radiology of the Peripheral Vascular System (contrib and ed, 1993); *Style*— Dr Anna-Maria Belli; ✉ Department of Radiology, St George's Hospital, Blackshaw Road, London SW17 0QT (tel 020 8725 1481, fax 020 8725 2936)

BELLI, Lorella; *Educ* Univ of Venice (MA); *Career* literary agent; early career in publishing then agent Laurence Pollinger Ltd, estab Lorella Belli Literary Agency (LBLA) 2002; *Style*— Ms Lorella Belli; ✉ Lorella Belli Literary Agency, 54 Hartford House, 35 Tavistock Crescent, Notting Hill, London W11 1AY (tel 020 7727 8547, fax 0870 787 4194, e-mail info@lorellabelliaganecy.com, website www.lorellabelliaganecy.com)

BELLINGER, Christopher Henry; s of Clifford Bellinger (d 1992), of Cardiff, and Margaret Joy, *née* Boddington; *b* 20 February 1943; *Educ* Abingdon Sch; *m* 24 June 1972, Diana Penelope Margaret, da of Maj Frank Albert Bowater (d 1982), of London; *Career* BBC TV: Film Dept Wales 1964–70, TV presentation 1971–78, prodr Multi-Coloured Swap Shop, ed Saturday Superstore 1982, ed Going Live! 1986–93, ed Live and Kicking 1993–98; head of Children's Entertainment BBC Production 1998–2003, ed Xchange 2003–04, exec prodr ITV 2004–06, freelance exec prodr 2006–; *Style*— Christopher Bellinger, Esq; ✉ e-mail christopher.bellinger@virgin.net

BELLINGHAM, Prof Alastair John; CBE (1997); s of Stanley Herbert Bellingham (d 1997), and Sybil Mary, *née* Milne (d 1996); *b* 27 March 1938; *Educ* Tiffin Boys' Sch Kingston upon Thames, UCH Med Sch London; *m* 1, 24 May 1963, (Valerie) Jill (d 1997), da of Kenneth Morford (d 1971); 3 s (James b 24 April 1964, Richard b 14 April 1969, Paul b 5 Feb 1973); m 2, 20 Dec 2002, Julia, da of Harold de Quetteville Willott (d 1991), and Joan Marie Willott; *Career* Mackenzie-Mackinnon Streatfield fell RCP 1968–69, res fell Univ of Washington USA 1969–70, sr lectr in haematology UCH Med Sch London 1971–74; prof of haematology: Univ of Liverpool 1974–84, King's Coll London 1984–97; transition dir Merseyside and North Wales Blood Centre NBA 1996–98, chm of Confidentiality and Security Advsy Gp Dept of Health 1996–2001; pres Br Soc for Haematology 1991–92 (sec 1984–87), vice-pres Euro African Div Int Soc of Haematology 1992–97, chm Haematology Ctee RCP 1992, chm NHS Information Authority 1999–2005, chm Kennett and N Wiltshire PCT 2005–06; memb Cncl RCPath 1987–90; FRCP (London) 1976, FRCPath 1986 (vice-pres 1990–93, pres 1993–96), FRCPGlas 1995, Hon FCPath HK 1995, FRCPE 1996, FFPathRCPI 1996; *Publications* author of papers on red cell genetic disorders and red cell function, incl enzymopathies and sickle cell disease; *Recreations* photography, oenology, viticulture; *Clubs* Savage; *Style*— Prof Alastair Bellingham, CBE; ✉ Broadstones, The Street, Teffont Magna, Salisbury, Wiltshire SP3 5QP (tel 01722 716267, e-mail savage@teffont.freeserve.co.uk)

BELLINGHAM, Sir Anthony Edward Norman; 8 Bt (GB 1796), of Castle Bellingham, Co Louth; s of Sir Roger Bellingham, 6 Bt (d 1973); suc bro, Sir Noel Bellingham, 7 Bt, 1999; *b* 24 March 1947; *Educ* Rossall; *m* 1, 1990 (m dis 1998), Denise Marie, da of Henry Calvin Moity, of New Orleans, USA; 1 s (William Alexander Noel Henry b Aug 1991); m 2, 1998 (m dis 2001), Namphon Buchar; *Heir* s, William Bellingham; *Career* recruitment conslt; *Style*— Sir Anthony Bellingham, Bt

BELLINGHAM, Henry Campbell; MP; s of (Arthur) Henry Bellingham (d 1959), and June Marion, *née* Cloudesley Smith; *b* 29 March 1955; *Educ* Eton, Magdalene Coll Cambridge, Cncl of Legal Educn; *Career* called to the Bar Middle Temple 1978; MP (Cons) Norfolk NW 1983–97 and 2001–; vice-chm Cons Backbench Smaller Business Ctee 1987–90 (jt sec 1983–87), vice-chm Cons Backbench NI Ctee 1987–90 (jt sec 1983–87), memb Environment Select Ctee 1987–90, chm Cons Cncl on Eastern Europe 1989–93, PPS to Rt Hon Malcolm Rifkind 1990–97, memb British-Irish Parly Body 1992–97 and 2001–, memb NI Affrs Select Ctee 2001–02, memb DTI Select Ctee 2002–03, shadow min for trade and industry and for small businesses 2002–05, oppn whip 2005–; non-exec dir of several private cos and 3 plcs 1997–2001; *Clubs* White's; *Style*— Henry Bellingham, Esq, MP; ✉ House of Commons, London SW1A 0AA

BELLINGHAM, Kate; da of Roger Bellingham, of Pocklington, E Yorks, and Barbara, *née* Stapleton; *b* 7 July 1963; *Educ* Mount Sch York, The Queen's Coll Oxford (BA), Univ of Hertfordshire (MSc); *m* 10 June 1995; 2 c; *Career* science and technology broadcaster; computer programmer CAP Alderley Edge 1984–87, trainee electronic engr BBC Radio (London) 1987–90; presenter: BBC/IEE Faraday lecture tour 1988–89, Techno (BBC Schs TV) 1989, Tomorrow's World (BBC TV) 1990–94, The Acid Test (BBC Radio 5 Live) 1994–97, Showcase (BBC Schs TV) 1995–97, The Big Bang (ITV) 1996–97, Open Saturday (BBC) 1998, Science for Today (Channel 4) 1998, Troubleshooting (BBC TV) 1999, Testing Times (BBC Radio 4) 1999, Engineering Your Environment (BBC TV) 2002; pres Young Engineers 1997– (media advisor 1995–97); memb: EPSRC Coll, Pubns Advsy Bd IEE; BBC Engrg qualification 1990; Hon DTec Staffordshire Univ 1997; memb Women's Engrg Soc, MIEE; *Recreations* music, crosswords, choral singing, crosswords, school classroom helper; *Style*— Ms Kate Bellingham; ✉ c/o Dave Winslett, 6 Kenwood Ridge, Kenley, Surrey CR8 5JW (tel 020 8668 0531, fax 020 8668 9216, e-mail info@davewinslett.com)

BELLIS, Michael John; s of Herbert Henry Bellis (d 1976), of Sherborne, Dorset, and Marjorie Dudley, *née* Charlton (d 2006); *b* 28 April 1937; *Educ* Bancroft's Sch Woodford Green, Coll of Law; *Career* Nat Serv RCS 1956–58; admitted slr 1968, cmmr for oaths 1973; Edward Oliver and Bellis: sr ptnr 1975–90, conslt 1991–96; conslt Lucas Baron Jacobs 1997–2000; md Heritage Heirlooms (UK) Ltd 1990–2003; chm Med Serv Ctee FPC London Boroughs of Redbridge and Waltham Forest 1978–89, lay serv ctee memb Norfolk Family Health Serv Authy 1991–96, memb Mgmnt Ctee The Intaglio Fndn Norwich 1996–98, chm Discipline Panel Norfolk HA 1996–2002, chm Norfolk Dental Contracts Disputes Panel 2006–; former vice-pres W Essex Law Soc; hon slr and hon memb Rotary Club Ilford (former pres), Rotary Int Paul Harris fell; tstee, fundraising chm and memb Exec Ctee Redbridge Community Tst 1992–95, tstee London NE Community Fndn 1996–97; memb Law Soc 1968; Freeman City of London, Liveryman Worshipful Co of Bakers (memb Ct of Assts 1994, Master 2004–05, Dep Master 2005–06); *Recreations* collecting rare books, travel, growing and eating asparagus; *Clubs* Norfolk (Norwich), Law Society; *Style*— Michael John Bellis, Esq; ✉ Baron Art, 17 Chapel Yard, Albert Street, Holt, Norfolk NR25 6HG (tel 01263 713430, fax 01263 711670, e-mail baronbellis@aol.com)

BELLOS, Prof David Michael; s of Nathaniel Bellos, of London, and Katharine Mabel, *née* Shapiro; *b* 25 June 1945; *Educ* Westcliff HS, Univ of Oxford (MA, DPhil); *m* 1, 31 Dec 1966 (m dis 1985), Ilona, da of Sandor Roth (d 1945); 1 s (Alexander b 1969), 2 da (Amanda b 1971, Olivia b 1974); m 2, 1 July 1989 (m dis 1995), Susan Esther Currie, da of Prof A C Lendrum; m 3, 25 June 1996, Pascale Voilley, da of Jean Voilley; *Career* fell Magdalen Coll Oxford 1969, lectr in French Univ of Edinburgh 1972, prof of French Univ of Southampton 1982, prof and head Dept of French Studies Univ of Manchester 1985–96, prof of French and comparative literature Princeton Univ 1997–; Chevalier de l'Ordre des Palmes Académiques France 1988, Prix Goncourt de la biographie France 1994; *Books* Balzac Criticism in France, 1850–1900 (1976), Georges Perec - Life A User's Manual (trans, 1987), Georges Perec - A Life in Words (1993), Ismail Kadare - The Pyramid (trans, 1996), Jacques Tati - His Life and Art (1999); *Recreations* cycling; *Style*— Prof David Bellos; ✉ Department of French and Italian, Princeton University, Princeton, NJ 08544–5264, USA (tel 00 1 609 258 4500, fax 00 1 609 258 4535, e-mail dbellos@princeton.edu)

BELMAHI, (HE) Mohammed; *b* 18 August 1948, Rabat, Morocco; *Educ* Moulay Youssef HS Rabat, Nat Sch of Architecture Toulouse, Grad Sch of Public Admin NYU, Harvard Univ, Inst for Int Devpt, London Business Sch; *m* (sep); 1 c; *Career* Moroccan diplomat; staff memb and conslt UN Centre for Housing, Bldg and Planning NY 1974–76, conslt Grad Sch of Social Work Columbia Univ NY 1976; head Urban Planning Div Miny of Housing and Land Use Planning 1977, dir of nat land use planning Miny of Housing and Land Use Planning 1978–79, memb task force for state owned enterprise reform PM's Office 1979–82, dir of tourism Miny of Tourism 1982–87, DG Moroccan Nat Tourist Office (ONMT) 1987–88, gen mangr (tourism and real estate sector) and advsr to chm and ceo ONA Gp Casablanca 1988–96 (also memb Exec Ctee and md Casablanca World Trade Centre), ambass to India and Nepal 1996–99, ambass to the Ct of St James's 1999–; rep of Moroccan govt at experts gp meetings; responsible for creation of Moroccan Pavilion Disney World EPCOT Centre Florida 1982–84, memb Organising Ctee for Promotion of Moroccan Pavilion Seville World Expo 1992; memb Bd Moroccan American Cmmn for Educn and Cultural Exchange (Fulbright Cmmn) 1992–96; memb Bureau Int Union of Urbanists 1984, memb Steering Ctee Euro-Mediterranean Conf of Tourism Ministers 1993–96; prof of urban and regnl planning and admin orgn Nat Inst of Statistics and Applied Economics (INSEA) Rabat 1978–81, conslt for estab Inst of Strategic Studies Al Alkhawayn Univ Ifrane 1994; World Trade Centres Assoc NY (WTCA): bd dir WTCA Hldgs Ltd 1994, bd dir and chm Ctee on Trade Policy and Facilitation 1994–96, rep Exec Secretariat ME and N Africa Econ Summit Casablanca 1994 and Amman 1995; bd dir: Royal Air Maroc 1982–93, Hospitality Hldg Co 1988–96, Moussafir Hotels Co 1988–96, Societe Africaine de Tourisme 1988–96, Full Service Trade Card Ltd 1995–99; memb Admin Cmmn Ribat Al Fath Assoc 1988–, memb Delhi Rotary Club 1997–98, pres Br-Moroccan Soc 1999–; Indira Gandhi Meml Award 1997–98; freeman City of London 2006; Offr Order of Merit (Portugal) 1990, Knight Cdr Royal Order of Francis I (KCFO) 2003; *Publications* Slums and Squatter Settlements in Urban Areas of the Third World (1975), Global Review of Human Settlements (1976), Les Relations Etat-Entreprises Publiques (1981), Ambassadors and Envoys of the Kingdom of Morocco to the United Kingdom 1588–2000 (2001), Islam and Secularism (2004), The Other in the Making of National Identity: The Case of Britain and Morocco (2006); also author of various articles; *Recreations* golf, swimming, travel, portrait drawing, art history; *Clubs* Travellers, Athenaeum, Dar Es Salam Golf (Rabat); *Style*— Ambassador Mohammed Belmahi, KCFO; ✉ Embassy of the Kingdom of Morocco, 49 Queen's Gate Gardens, London SW7 5NE (e-mail mbelmahi@hotmail.com)

BELMORE, 8 Earl (I 1797); John Armar Lowry Corry; also Baron Belmore (I 1781) and Viscount Belmore (I 1789); s of 7 Earl Belmore, JP, DL (d 1960), and Gloria Anthea Harker (d 2005); *b* 4 September 1951; *Educ* Lancing; *m* 1984, Lady Mary Jane Meade, 2 da of 6 Earl of Clanwilliam (d 1989); 2 s (John Armar Galbraith, Viscount Corry b 1985, Hon Montagu Gilford George b 1989), 1 da (Lady Martha Catherine b 27 May 1992); *Heir* s, Viscount Corry; *Career* farmer; memb: Advsy Bd Public Record Office NI 1996–2006, Bd of Govrs and Guardians Nat Gallery of Ireland 1998–2003; *Recreations* art; *Style*— The Rt Hon the Earl of Belmore; ✉ The Garden House, Castle Coole, Enniskillen BT74 6JY (tel 028 6632 2463)

BELOFF, Hon Michael Jacob; QC (1981); er s of Baron Beloff, FBA (Life Peer, d 1999); *b* 19 April 1942; *Educ* Eton (King's scholar), Univ of Oxford (MA); *m* 1969, Judith Mary Arkinstall; 1 s, 1 da; *Career* called to the Bar Gray's Inn 1967 (bencher 1988, treas-elect 2008); former lectr Trinity Coll Oxford; recorder of the Crown Court 1985–95, dep judge of the High Court 1989–96, jt head of chambers 1993–2000, judge of the Court of Appeal of Guernsey and Jersey 1995–, sr ordinary appeal judge 2005–; chm ICC Code of Conduct Cmmn 2002–, dep chm Information Cmmn 2000, memb Court of Arbitration for Sport 1996–, ethics cmmr London 2012; pres Trinity Coll Oxford 1996–2006; emeritus chm Admin Law Bar Assoc; steward RAC 1998–; Hon DLitt Fairleigh Dickinson Univ NJ; FRSA, FICPD; *Clubs* Reform, Vincent's (Oxford), Achilles; *Style*— The Hon Michael Beloff, QC; ✉ Blackstone Chambers, Blackstone House, Temple, London EC4Y 9BW (tel 020 7583 1770, fax 020 7822 7350)

BELPER, 5 Baron (UK 1856); Richard Henry Strutt; s of 4 Baron Belper; *b* 24 October 1941; *Educ* Harrow; *m* 1, 1966 (m dis 1979), Jennifer Vivian, *née* Winser; 1 s (Hon Michael Henry b 1969), 1 da (Hon Henrietta Lavinia b 1970); m 2, 1980, Mrs Judith Mary de Jonge, da of James Twynam; *Heir* s, Hon Michael Strutt; *Style*— The Lord Belper

BELSHAW, Prof Deryke Gerald Rosten; s of Leonard Gerald Belshaw (d 1987), of Ash Vale, Hants, and Phyllis Guiver, *née* Rosten (d 2003); *b* 9 September 1932; *Educ* Hampton GS, Selwyn Coll Cambridge (MA), Hertford Coll Oxford (Dip Agric Econ); *m* 15 Aug 1959, Audrey Gladys, da of John Newell, MBE, VMH (d 1984), of Ringwood, Hants; 1 s (Jeremy b 1960), 2 da (Sarah b 1962, Anna b 1963); *Career* Nat Serv RA seconded to RWAFF Nigeria, gunner 1954, 2 Lt 1955, Lt 1956; res offr Sch of Agric Univ of Cambridge 1958–60, sr lectr then reader in agric economics Makerere Coll Univ of E Africa 1964–70 (lectr 1960–64); UEA: sr lectr then reader in agric economics 1970–85, dean 1981–84, prof of rural devpt 1985–97, prof emeritus 1997–; ODA economic advsr Govt of Kenya 1970–72, UNDP and FAO regnl devpt advsr Govt of Tanzania 1974–77 and 1980–82, FAO food strategy advsr Govt of Ethiopia (on secondment from Overseas Development Group Ltd UEA) 1986–89, IBRD UNDP visiting prof of economics Makerere Univ Uganda 1992–94, conslt UN Regnl Devpt Centre (Sri Lanka, Kenya, Zimbabwe, Malawi) 1993–99; dir Belshaw Consulting and Research Ltd 1999–, dir Christians Against Poverty in Tropical Africa and Asia Ltd (CAPITAA) 1999–; pres Agric Econ Soc 2001–04; memb: Advsy Bd Oxford Devpt Studies, Advsy Bd Concordis Int Cambridge 1999–; dean of devpt studies Oxford Centre for Mission Studies 1999–2005 (fell 1992–), dir Inst for Devpt Res Oxford 2001–; visiting scholar Wolfson Coll Oxford 1998–2000; awarded Jerusalem Tst research grant for post-disaster recovery projects in Ethiopia and Uganda 2005; *Books* Towards a Food and Nutrition Strategy for Ethiopia (1989), Regional Development Policy Analysis (1996), Faith in Development: The World Bank and the Church in Africa Partnership (2001), Renewing Development in Sub-Saharan Africa (2002); *Recreations* vinous evaluation; *Style*— Prof Deryke Belshaw; ✉ Institute for Development Research, PO Box 70, Oxford OX2 6HB (tel 01865 556071, fax 01865 510823, e-mail dbelshaw@ocms.ac.uk or rogerbelshaw@aol.com)

BELSHAW, Kenneth John Thomas; s of John Everton Belshaw (d 2002), and Lilian Elizabeth, *née* Stewart (d 2001); *b* 14 May 1952; *Educ* Orangefield Sch for Boys Belfast; *m* 24 Nov 1979, Iris Elizabeth, da of Sydney Miller McKeown (d 1998), of Stewartstown, Co Tyrone, NI; 3 da (Maeve Elizabeth b 1983, Barbara Ruth and Jennifer Mary (twins) b 1 Aug 1992), 1 s (Stephen John Doran b 1987); *Career* recruitment consIt; md: Grafton Recruitment Ltd (Ireland's largest employment agency), Grafton Recruitment UK Ltd 1982–; Queen's Award for Enterprise 2002 and 2006, Gratias Agit Award (for significant contribution to promotion of the Czech Republic) Czech Govt 2006; *Recreations* fine wines, reading; *Clubs* Kildare St and Univ (Dublin), Holywood Golf, Castletown Golf (IOM); *Style*— Kenneth Belshaw, Esq; ✉ Grafton Recruitment, 35–37 Queens Square, Belfast BT1 3FG (tel 028 9024 2824, fax 028 9024 2897)

BELTRAMI, Joseph; s of Egidio Beltrami (d 1971), and Isabel, *née* Battison; *b* 15 May 1932; *Educ* St Aloysius Coll Glasgow, Univ of Glasgow (BL); *m* 18 Jan 1958, Brigid, da of Edward Fallon; 3 s (Edwin Joseph b 23 Sept 1962, Adrian Joseph b 8 Nov 1964, Jason Joseph b 23 Sept 1967); *Career* Intelligence Corps 1954–56: attached to Br Mil Delgn to Euro Def Community at Br Embassy Paris, Detachment Cdr Field security SW Dist Taunton; admitted slr 1956, ptnr Beltrami & Co (slr in cases of only two Royal pardons in Scotland this century: Maurice Swanson 1975, Patrick Meehan 1976), advocate; instructed in more than 350 murder trials; memb Scottish Law Soc; formerly: pres Bothwell Bowling Club, mangr and coach Bothwell AFC; *Books* The Defender (1980), Glasgow - A Celebration (contrib, 1984), Tales of the Suspected (1988), A Deadly Innocence (1989), A Scottish Childhood (contrib, 1998); *Style*— Joseph Beltrami, Esq; ✉ 12 Valance Tower, Regents Gate, Bothwell G71 (tel 01698 817841); Beltrami & Co, 93 West Nile Street, Glasgow G1 2FH (tel 0141 221 0981)

BEMROSE, (William) Alan Wright; s of Col William Lloyd Bemrose, OBE (Mil), TD, Croix de Guerre (d 1980), and Lucy Mabel Lewis (d 1982); *b* 13 June 1929; *Educ* Repton; *m* 1, 21 July 1952 (m dis 1984), (Elizabeth) Anne; 1 da (Sarah b 15 July 1959); m 2, 31 Aug 1985, Elizabeth (Nibby), da of Reginald William Melling, of Downderry, Cornwall; *Career* served Sherwood Foresters (Notts & Derby); fndr chm Derbyshire Historic Tst 1974–, memb Historic Bldgs Cncl for England 1979–84, princ conslt bldgs at risk Historic Bldgs and Monuments Cmmn (memb Advsy Ctees Bldgs and Areas 1984–93), chief exec Bldgs at Risk Tst 1992–; tstee Chatsworth House Tst 1982–2004, tstee Stringer Lawrance Meml Tst 1995–; Derbyshire CC: memb 1964, alderman 1967, chm of fin 1967–74, ldr 1968–74, vice-chm 1977–79; govr Sir John Port's Charity (Repton Sch) 1965–2004, memb Repton Fndn 1997–2000 (chm 1997–2000, memb Audit Ctee 2003–); fndr chm Derbys Churches and Chapels Tst 1997; Freeman and Liveryman Worshipful Co of Stationers and Newspaper Makers 1952 (memb Ct of Assts 1979–87, currently emeritus memb Ct of Assts); FRSA 1985; *Recreations* hunting, equestrian sports; *Style*— Alan Bemrose, Esq; ✉ 41B New Road, Blakeney, Holt, Norfolk NR25 7PA (tel 01263 741103, fax 01629 826390, e-mail bart@dhbt.clara.net)

BEN-DAVID, Zadok; s of Moshe Ben-David, of Israel, and Hana Ben-David; *b* 1949, Bathan, Yemen; *Educ* Bezalel Acad of Art and Design Israel, Univ of Reading, St Martin's Sch of Art; *Career* asst to N H Azaz 1974, sculpture teacher St Martin's Sch of Art 1977–82, teacher Ravensbourne Coll of Art and Design 1982–85, visiting artist Stoke-on-Trent Museum 1987; sculptor; public cmmns: Runcorn Shopping City 1977, Tel-Hai Museum Israel 1983, Harlow Essex 1984, Villa Nova de Cerviera Portugal 1986, Forest of Dean Sculpture Project Glos 1988, Tel Aviv Promenade Israel 1989, Keren Karev Jerusalem 1990, ORS Building Tel Aviv 1990, Heaven and Earth (public sculpture) Tel Aviv 1995; solo exhibitions incl: AIR Gallery London 1980, Woodlands Art Gallery London 1982, 121 Gallery Antwerp 1984, Benjamin Rhodes Gallery London 1985, 1987, 1990 and 1992, Art and Project Amsterdam 1986, Albert Totah Gallery NY 1987, Newcastle Poly Gallery 1988, Luba Bilu Gallery Melbourne 1989, Collins Gallery Glasgow 1990, Annandale Gallery Sydney 1991, Albrecht Gallery Munich Germany 1991, Galerie im Happacher Esslingen 1993, Ecke Galerie Augsburg, Castlefield Gallery Manchester 1994, Jason Rhodes Gallery London 1995, Evolution and Theory (Israel, Germany, Australia) 1997, (USA and Holland) 1998, (Germany and Singapore) 1999, (Germany) 2000 and (Portugal) 2003, Refusalon (San Francisco Art Inst USA) 2000, Leuchter & Peltzer Dusseldorf 2000, Magica Realta (Place Arte Conteporanea Torino) 2001 and (Galleria Civica d'arte Moderna e Conteporanea Aosta) 2003, Esplanade Culture Centre Singapore 2003, Magica Realta Innerscapes (Annandale Galleries Sydney) 2004, Innerscapes (Cass Sculpture Fndn London) 2004, 1918 Artspace Shanghai 2006, Janet Oh Gallery Seoul 2006, Guangdong Art Museum Guangzhou 2007, Oroom Fndn Sch Korea 2007, Blackfield (Hales Gallery London) 2007; gp exhibitions incl: Atlantis Gallery London 1983, 80 Years of Sculpture (Israel Museum Jerusalem) 1984, Who's Afraid of Red Yellow & Blue? (Arnolfini Gallery Bristol) 1985, From Two Worlds (Whitechapel Art Gallery) 1986, IV Int Biennale Portugal 1986, Ek'ymose Art Contemporain Bordeaux 1987, Fresh Paint (Israel Museum Jerusalem) 1987, Museum of Israeli Art Ramat Gan Israel 1987, Israeli Artists (Brooklyn Museum NY) 1988, Galerie Albrecht Munich (with Joel Fisher and Franz Bernhard) 1989, Gimmel Gallery Jerusalem 1990, Kunst Europa Germany 1991, Places and Mainstream (Museum Hara Tokyo) 1991, The New Metaphysics (Ivan Dougherty Gallery Sydney) 1992, Nat Museum of Contemporary Art Seoul 1992, A Collaboration of Music and Art (with Peter Gabriel, Land Mark Tower Yokahama Japan) 1993, Anti Patos (Israel Museum Jerusalem) 1993, Locus (Fisher Gallery Los Angeles) 1993, Public Art (Annadale Gallery Sydney Australia) 1994, VIII Bienal Portugal 1995, 100 Park Lane London 1996, IX International Bienal Portugual 1997, Fantasia (Herzliya Museum Israel) 1997, Eight by Eight (Chichester) 1997, BUPA House London 1998, MOMA Croatia 1998, British Figurative Art Part 2 - Sculpture (Flowers East Gallery London) 1998, Israeli Sculpture 1948–1998 (Israel) 1998, The Shape of the Century (Salisbury Cathedral and Canary Wharf London) 1999, ANIMAL (Musee Bourdelle Paris) 1999, BRONZE (Holland Park London) 2000, Looking ahead - vision of Israel (ICA San Jose) 2000, L'Homme qui Marche (Palais Royal Paris) 2000, Narcisse Blesse (Passage de Retz Paris) 2000, Den Haag Sculpture 2000 and 2001, Tempo (Kunst im Schloss Untergroningen) 2001, Galerie en Lijstenmakerij The Hague 2001, The Train Ride (video installation, Herzliya Museum of Art Israel) 2001 and (Ambrosino Gallery Miamai) 2002, Blue (Place arte Conteporanea Cavgnolo) 2002, Sculptura Internazionale a la Mandria (Torino) 2002, Salto Naturale (Kunst im Schloss Untergroningen) 2002, Paper art Bienale (Leopold-Hoesch Museum Duren) 2002, Thinking Big (Peggy Guggenheim collection Venice) 2002, About Face (Croydon Clock Tower) 2002, Landscape (Pump Gallery Battersea) 2003, Science Fiction (Singapore Museum of Art) 2003, Telltale (Ewha Art Centre Seoul) 2005, Fatamorgana (Haifa Museum of Contemporary Art) 2006, Sequences & Repetition (Brunel Arts Centre Brunel Univ and Jerwood Space London) 2007, Rummage: Sculptors' Drawings (Winchester Gallery Univ of Southampton) 2007, Animal (Kunst im Schloss Untergroningen) 2007, Sculptuur Biennale The Hague 2007, XIV Biennale de Cerveira (Municipal Museum Caminha) 2007; various collections in: UK, Europe, Israel, USA, Aust; jointly represented Israel Venice Biennale 1988 (with Moti Mizrachi); *Style*— Zadok Ben-David, Esq; ✉ 65 Warwick Avenue, London W9 2PP (tel 020 7266 0536, fax 020 7266 3892); Studio tel 020 7328 6857, website www.zadokbendavid.com

BENAUD, Richard (Richie); OBE (1961); *b* 6 October 1930; *Educ* Parramatta HS; *m* Daphne; *Career* cricket commentator; former cricketer, capt Aust 1958–63 (without losing a series), toured England 1953, 1956 and 1961, first test cricketer to score 2,000 runs and take 200

wickets, also scored 10,000 runs and took 500 first class wickets; commentator: BBC 1960–99, Channel 4 1999–2005 and Nine Network (Aust) 1977–; int sports conslt; *Books* Way of Cricket (1960), Tale of Two Tests (1962), Spin Me a Spinner (1963), The New Champions (1965), Willow Patterns (1972), Benaud on Reflection (1984), The Appeal of Cricket (1995), Anything But...An Autobiography (1998), My Spin on Cricket (2005); *Recreations* golf; *Style*— Richie Benaud, Esq, OBE; ✉ 19–178 Beach Street, Coogee, NSW 2034, Australia

BENBOW, Michael; s of Arthur Benbow, of Cowbridge, Mid Glamorgan, and Sylvia, *née* Bailey; *b* 22 February 1957; *Educ* Trinity Secdy Modern Sch Bradford-on-Avon, Trowbridge Tech Coll, Salisbury Coll of Art, Cardiff Coll of Art (Dip Industrial Design Engrg); *m* 19 Sept 1981, Christine, da of Peter Collier; 1 da (Annette b 14 Oct 1994); *Career* design consultant; staff designer Gnome Photographic Products Ltd 1978–80, design mangr Bissell Appliances Ltd 1980–88, sr designer and business devpt mangr Ogle Design Ltd 1988–90, business devpt mangr Grey Matter Design Consultants plc 1990, design conslt 1990–; to date cmmnd to design attractive products for high volume manufacture; injection moulded plastics expertise; projects incl electronic consumer products, nursery equipment and housewares; first prize industrial design Eisteddfod Festival 1978; SIAD: working pty leader Diploma Members' Gp 1983, memb Product Gp 1986–90; corp MCSD 1985, CSD membership assessor (product) 1996–; appointed LEA govr Staples Rd Jr Sch 1999; press offr Loughton Residents Assoc 2002; govr Roding Valley HS 2006–; *Recreations* lawn tennis, squash; *Clubs* Woodford Wells; *Style*— Michael Benbow, Esq; ✉ 28 Brook Road, Loughton, Essex IG10 1BP

BENDALL, Dr (Michael) John; s of Edward Lewis Bendall (d 1987), of Risca, Gwent, and Edna May, *née* Williams (d 1983); *b* 7 June 1943; *Educ* Pontwaun GS Risca, Univ of London (BSc, MB BS), Univ of Nottingham (DM); *m* 4 Jan 1969, Patricia, da of Herbert Wyndham Jenkins (d 1980), of Newport, Gwent; 2 da (Megan b 1973, Elinor b 1983), 2 s (David b 1975, Thomas b 1977); *Career* conslt physician in geriatric med Colchester 1974–78, sr lectr and conslt physician in health care of the elderly Nottingham 1978–94, clinical dir of Health Care of the Elderly Queen's Med Centre Nottingham 1991–96 (conslt physician 1994–); memb: Br Geriatrics Soc, BMA; FRCP 1986; *Recreations* music, theatre, reading, photography, golf; *Style*— Dr John Bendall; ✉ Directorate of Health Care of the Elderly, Queen's Medical Centre, Nottingham NG7 2UH (tel 0115 924 9924)

BENDER, Sir Brian Geoffrey; KCB (2003), CB (1998); s of Arnold Eric Bender, of Leatherhead, Surrey, and Deborah, *née* Swift; *b* 25 February 1949; *Educ* Greenford GS, Imperial Coll London (BSc, PhD); *m* 1974, Penelope Gay, *née* Clark; 1 da (Laura Ann b 1979), 1 s (Russell Paul b 1983); *Career* DTI: admin trainee 1973–77, private sec to Sec of State for Trade (The Rt Hon Edmund Dell) 1976–77, first sec (Trade Policy) Office of UK Perm Rep to the EC 1977–82, princ Minerals and Metals Div 1982–84, cnsllr (Indust and Energy) Office of UK Perm Rep to the EC 1985–89, asst sec Mgmnt Servs and Manpower Div 1989–90, under sec and dep head of European Secretariat Cabinet Office 1990–93, head of Regnl Devpt Div DTI 1993–94, dep sec and head Euro Secretariat Cabinet Office 1994–98, head of public service delivery Cabinet Office 1998–99, perm sec: Cabinet Office 1999–2000, MAFF 2000–01, DEFRA 2001–05, DTI 2005–; *Style*— Sir Brian Bender, KCB, CB

BENDRE, Rajiv Ratnakar; OBE (2004); s of Ratnakar Bendre, of Poona, India, and Nalini Bendre (d 1995); *b* 9 November 1955, Bombay, India; *Educ* Cathedral Sch Bombay, Stowe, Keble Coll Oxford; *m* 1984, Katherine, *née* Staniforth; 2 da (Rebecca b 1988, Radhika b 1990); *Career* Price Waterhouse 1979–83, First Chicago 1984–85; Br Cncl: London 1985, Baghdad 1986–88, Amman 1989–91, Nigeria 1991–2000, Sierra Leone 2000–05, Baghdad 2005–06, Zimbabwe 2006–; annual public lecture series in Sierra Leone; memb ICAEW; *Recreations* dogs, reading; *Clubs* Royal Over-Seas League; *Style*— Rajiv Bendre, Esq, OBE; ✉ British Council, 10 Spring Gardens, London SW1A 2BN (tel 07906 308621, e-mail bendrerajiv@yahoo.co.uk); British Council, Corner House, Samora Machel Avenue, Harare, Zimbabwe

BENFIELD, James Richard; *b* 22 April 1949; *Educ* Leamington Coll for Boys, Univ of Birmingham (BA); *m* 1969, Penelope Jane Skew; *Career* Marks & Spencer plc: mgmnt trainee 1970–73, merchandiser various food buying depts from 1973 then mgmnt and exec divnl positions rising to divnl dir 1986–93, buying gp dir 1993–99, dir of mktg, ops and M&S Direct 1999–2000; chm Confetti Network Ltd 2000–, chief exec Christie Tyler Furniture; *Recreations* ballet, theatre, scuba diving, football; *Style*— James Benfield, Esq

BENGER, Patrick; s of Harold Albert Benger (d 1978), of Worcester, and Mildred Nancy, *née* Freeman (d 1988); *b* 29 September 1939; *Educ* Farnborough GS, RAE Tech Coll; *m* 20 Oct 1966, Frances Ann, *née* Finch; 1 da (Georgina Anne (Mrs Andrew Morgan) b 1968); *Career* asst experimental offr RAE Farnborough, seconded as tech offr E African Meteorological Dept Tanganyika 1962–64; conslt meteorologist to offshore industry: Middle East 1965–71, N Sea and Europe 1972–88; mgmnt systems conslt 1988–; md Seaplace Ltd 1985–90, dir Chaucer Gp Ltd 1991–; servs co-ordinator: UK-Continent Gas Interconnector Project 1994–98, Karachaganak Project Devpt 1999–2000, Interconnector (UK) Ltd 2001–; scientific advsr Hampshire Co Emergency Planning Orgn; author of papers and articles on technical aspects of offshore and onshore energy projects; *Recreations* antique collecting; *Style*— Patrick Benger, Esq; ✉ Cold Ash House, Liphook, Hampshire GU30 7SZ

BENINGTON, Prof Ian Crawford; OBE (1997); s of George Crawford Benington (d 1980), of Tunbridge Wells, Kent, and Edith, *née* Green; *b* 24 February 1938; *Educ* Dalriada Sch Ballymoney Co Antrim, Queen's Univ Belfast (BDS); *m* 10 July 1967, Eileen Agnes, da of Thomas Irwin (d 1988), of Belfast; 1 s (David b 28 May 1974), 1 da (Fiona b 3 April 1973); *Career* served Army Cadet Force N Irish Horse 1950–58; dental staff Queen's Univ Belfast 1961–62, sr registrar Eastman Dental Hosp and Inst of Dental Surgery London 1965–72, conslt Glasgow Dental Hosp and Sch 1972–78, dir Sch of Clinical Dentistry Royal Victoria Hosp Belfast 1989–98 (sr lectr and conslt 1978–83, prof of dental prosthetics and head of Dept of Restorative Dentistry 1985–90); chm Specialist Advsy Ctee for Higher Trg in Restorative Dentistry RCS, memb Eastern Health and Social Servs Bd in NI, memb Central Dental Advsy Ctee of Jt Ctee for Higher Trg in Dentistry; chm: Dental Alumni Assoc Queen's Univ of Belfast 1992–, Dental Technicians' Educn and Trg Advsy Bd Educn Ctee; pres: British Soc for the Study of Prosthetic Dentistry 1995–96, British Prosthodontic Conference 1998–; memb: Bd Faculty of Dental Surgery RCS England 1994, Intercollegiate Membership Bd in Restorative Dentistry RCSEng 1999; assessor Appeals Panels General Dental Cncl 1999; FDSRCS, FFDRCSI; memb: BDA, RSM, Gen Dental Cncl; *Recreations* music, hill walking; *Clubs* East India, Stephen's Green (Dublin); *Style*— Prof Ian Benington, OBE; ✉ 20 Killynure Road West, Carryduff, Belfast BT8 8EA (tel 028 90813696); Department of Restorative Dentistry, School of Dentistry, Royal Victoria Hospital, Grosvenor Road, Belfast BT12 6BA (tel 028 9089 4726, fax 028 9043 8861, e-mail i.benington@qub.ac.uk)

BENJAMIN, George; s of William Benjamin, and Susan, *née* Bendon; *b* 31 January 1960; *Educ* Westminster, Paris Conservatoire, King's Coll Cambridge, IRCAM Paris; *Career* composer, conductor, pianist; prof of composition Royal Coll of Music 1985–2001, Henry Purcell prof of musical composition KCL 2002–; princ works incl: Ringed by the Flat Horizon 1980, A Mind of Winter for soprano and orch 1981, At First Light (cmmnd by London Sinfonietta) 1982, Antara for computerised keyboards and ensemble (cmmnd for 10 anniversary of Pompidou Centre Paris) 1987, Upon Silence for mezzo-soprano and 5 viols (written for Fretwork) 1990, Sudden Time (written for London Philharmonic Orch) 1989–93, Three Inventions for Chamber Orch (cmmnd for 75 Salzburg Festival) 1993–95, Sometime Voices for baritone, chorus and orch (cmmnd for the opening of the Bridgewater Hall Manchester) 1996, Viola Viola (cmmnd by Tokyo Opera City) 1997, Palimpsests for orch (cmmd by LSO) 2002, Shadowlines for piano 2001, Dance Figures for orch (premièred by Chicago Symphony Orch) 2004, Into the Little Hill (Paris Opera) 2006; conductor of major int orchs and ensembles incl: Concertgebouw, Berlin Philharmonic, Cleveland, LSO, Ensemble Modern, London Sinfonietta; conducted Pelléas et Mélisande (operatic debut, La Monnaie Brussels) 1999; artistic dir Meltdown Festival South Bank 1993; dir Tanglewood Festival of Contemporary Music 2000; artistic conslt Sounding the Century (BBC Radio 3) 1996–99; By George (LSO, Barbican) 2002–03; retrosepctives: Brussels 2003, Berlin 2004–05, Strasbourg 2005, Madrid 2005, Paris 2006; awards incl: Lili Boulanger Award (Boston) 1985, Koussevitzky Int Record Award 1987, Grand Prix du Disque (Paris) 1987, Gramophone Contemporary Music Award 1990, Edison Award (Amsterdam) 1998, Schönberg Prize Berlin 2002, RPS Awards 2003 and 2004; FRCM 1994, Hon RAM 2003; Chevalier de l'Ordre des Arts et des Lettres (France) 1996, memb Bavarian Acad of Arts 2000; *Style*— George Benjamin, Esq; ✉ c/o Faber Music, 3 Queen Square, London WC1N 3AU (tel 020 7833 7900, fax 020 7833 7939)

BENJAMIN, Prof Irving Stuart; s of Isidore Benjamin (d 1969), of Manchester, and Elsie, *née* Dennerley (d 1971); *b* 22 June 1946; *Educ* Hutchesons' Boys' GS, Univ of Glasgow (BSc, MB ChB, MD); *m* Barbara Anne, da of Paul Anthony Breton (d 1994); 1 s (Matthew Stuart b 2 Aug 1972), 2 da (Lucie Katherine b 26 Oct 1973, Frances Joanna b 7 March 1977); *Career* Hall tutorial res fell Univ Dept of Surgery Glasgow 1972–73, Scottish Home and Health Dept res fell 1973–74, lectr in surgery Glasgow Royal Infirmary 1975–79, visiting fell and jr conslt surgn Groote Schuur and Univ of Cape Town 1978–79, Wellcome Tst then CRC research fell and lectr in surgery 1980–83, sr lectr in surgery and hon conslt surgn Royal Postgrad Med Sch and Hammersmith Hosp (concurrently fell in transplantation surgery for one year Nuffield Dept of Surgery Oxford) 1983–90, reader in surgery Royal Postgrad Med Sch 1990, prof of surgery and head Academic Dept of Surgery King's Coll Sch of Med and Dentistry 1990–; memb: Br Soc of Gastroenterology (memb Cncl 1990–93), Surgical Research Soc, RSM, Pancreatic Soc of GB and I, Br Assoc for the Study of the Liver, Br Transplantation Soc, Assoc of Surgns of GB and I, Soc for Minimally Invasive Surgery, Christian Med Fellowship, Amnesty Int, Int Hepatopancreatobiliary Surgery Assoc (formerly treas UK Chapter and memb Scientific Ctee World Assoc fo HPB Surgery), Br Assoc of Surgical Oncology; FRCSGlas 1976, FRCS 1991; *Publications* author of numerous pubns in med and scientific jls on the subject of hepatic and biliary surgery and research in these fields; *Recreations* church activities, sailing, music (playing the guitar), photography, personal computing; *Style*— Prof Irving Benjamin; ✉ Academic Department of Surgery, King's College School of Medicine and Dentistry, Denmark Hill, London SE5 9RS (tel 020 7346 3017, fax 020 7346 3438, e-mail irving.benjamin@kcl.ac.uk)

BENJAMIN, John Circus; s of Bernard Benjamin, and Doris, *née* Mindel; *b* 15 January 1955; *Educ* John Lyon Sch Middx; *m* 27 June 1986, Patricia Adele Ruane, da of Sqdn Ldr Michael Joseph Francis Burgess, of Hale, Cheshire; *Career* ind jewellery conslt; broadcaster, author and lectr on history of jewellery; formerly int dir of Jewellery Phillips Auctioneers 1990–99; admitted memb Worshipful Co of Goldsmiths 2000; FGA 1975, DGA 1976; *Books* Starting to Collect Antique Jewellery, The Jewellery and Silver of H G Murphy (co-author); *Style*— John Benjamin, Esq; ✉ PO Box 7, Aylesbury, Buckinghamshire HP22 5WB (tel 01296 615522, fax 01296 615577, e-mail johncbenjamin@btopenworld.com)

BENJAMIN, Leanne; OBE (2005); *b* 1964, Australia; *Educ* Royal Ballet Upper Sch (Adeline Genée Gold Medal, Prix de Lausanne); *Children* 1 s (b 2003); *Career* ballet dancer; Birmingham Royal Ballet (formerly Sadler's Wells Royal Ballet): joined 1983, soloist 1985–87, princ 1987–88; princ dancer English Nat Ballet (formerly London Festival Ballet) 1988–90, Deutsche Oper Ballet Berlin 1990–92, princ Royal Ballet 1993– (first soloist 1992–93); *Roles* princ roles with Birmingham Royal Ballet: Swan Lake, Giselle, La Fille mal Gardée, The Sleeping Beauty, Balanchine's Tchaikovsky Pas de Deux, Kenneth MacMillan's Las Hermanas, Quartet, Concerto and Elite Syncopations, Hans Van Manen's Five Tangos, cr role of Greta in Metamorphosis, cr role of Gerda in The Snow Queen, Flowers of the Forest; English Nat Ballet: Juliet and Livia in Rome and Juliet, lead in The Nutcracker, Olga in Onegin, Sphinx, Third Movement in Symphony in C, Swannhilda in Coppélia, lead girl in Études, Symphony in Three Movements, Odette/Odile in Swan Lake; Deutsche Oper Ballet incl: A Folktale, Apollo, First and Fourth Movement Symphony in C, Carmen, Giselle, Who Cares?, Twilight, Paquita, Pas de Trois, Different Drummer, Cinderella, Brunhilda in The Ring; Royal Ballet incl: Odette/Odile in Swan Lake (debut) 1993, title role in Romeo and Juliet, Manon, Anastasia, Irina in Winter Dreams, Girl in The Invitation, First Sister in My Brothers, My Sisters, Danses Concertantes, La Fin du Jour, Requiem, Triad, Herman Schmerman, Caught Dance, Sugar Plum Fairy in The Nutcracker, Thaïs pas de deux, Voices of Spring, Rhapsody, title role in Cinderella, Ballet Imperial, Marie in Different Drummer, Macmillan's Concerto, Swanhilda in Coppélia, title role in The Firebird, title role in Dance Variations, Triad, Song of the Earth, The Leaves are Fading, Beyond Bach, Polyphonia, Spectre de la Rose, Girl in Blue in Les Biches, Stravinsky Violin Concerto, Mr Worldy Wise, Amores, Two Part Invention, When We Stop talking 1998, Purple Girl in Masquerade 1999, Qualia 2003, Spring Rites 2004, Tanglewood 2005, Despite 2006, Queen of the Earth in Homage to The Queen 2006, Danse à grande vitesse 2006, The Girl in The Children of Adam 2007; guest appearances: Peter Wright's Mirrors Walkers pas de deux in honour of Sir Frederick Ashton Royal Opera House 1988, Madrid 1989, Le Corsaire pas de deux with Peter Schaufuss Saville 1990, Swan Lake (Dresden Ballet) 1991, Kirov Theatre 1991, Spain 1991; gala appearances: World Festival Tokyo 1985, pas de deux from La Fille mal Gardée with Australian Ballet Bicentennial celebrations 1988, CRUSAID charity gala 1991, Tchaikovsky Gala Royal Opera House 1994; *Television* appearances incl: The Snow Queen (Birmingham Royal Ballet), BBC Masterclass, BBC documentary about David Bintley and making of Metamorphosis, Swan Lake (English Nat Ballet); with Royal Ballet: The Judas Tree, Symphony in C, The Nutcracker, The Dream, Don Quixote, Gloria 1999, Coppélia 2000, The Firebird 2001, Voices of Spring 2004; *Style*— Ms Leanne Benjamin, OBE; ✉ c/o The Royal Ballet, Royal Opera House, Covent Garden, London WC2E 9DD

BENJAMIN, Prof Ralph; CB (1980); s of Charles Benjamin (d 1944), and Claire, *née* Stern (d 1944); *b* 17 November 1922; *Educ* Ludwig Georg's Gymnasium Darmstadt, Rosenberg Coll St Gallen, St Oswald's Coll Ellesmere, Imperial Coll London (BSc, ACGI, PhD, DSc); *m* 1951, Kathleen Ruth, *née* Bull; 2 s (John b 28 June 1956 d 1987, Michael b 30 Dec 1959); *Career* joined RN Scientific Serv 1944, head of research and dep chief scientist Admiralty Surface Weapons Estab 1960–64, dir Admiralty Underwater Weapons Estab (and dir MOD HQ) 1964–71, dir of sci and technol GCHQ 1971–82, head communications techniques and networks Supreme HQ Allied Powers in Europe Tech Centre 1982–87; visiting prof: Imperial Coll London 1988–2002, UCL 1988–, Open Univ 1991–96, Cranfield Univ 1992–96, Univ of Bristol 1993–; formerly: chm IEE Bristol Area, chm IEE Western Centre, memb IEE Cncl, memb IEE Electronics Div Bd; IEE Marconi Premium 1965, Heinrich Hertz Premium 1980 and 1984, Clark Maxwell Premium 1996, IET Award for Innovation in Electronics 2006; memb Ct Brunel Univ 1996–2002; Judo black belt, RN Diving Offrs Cert, first ascent North Face Cima di Moro; Hon DEng Univ of Bristol 2000; FIEE 1976, FCGI 1981, FREng 1983 (CEng 1962), FRSA 1984; *Books* Modulation, Resolution and Signal Processing (1966), Five Lives in One (autobiography, 1996);

numerous articles in learned jls; *Recreations* hill walking, watersports, work; *Clubs* Athenaeum; *Style*— Prof Ralph Benjamin, CB, FREng; ✉ 13 Bellhouse Walk, Rockwell Park, Bristol BS11 0UE (tel and fax 0117 982 1333. e-mail drbenjamin@aol.com)

BENJAMIN, Victor Woolf; s of Harry Benjamin, and Dorothy, *née* Cooper; *b* 2 March 1935; *Educ* Malvern Coll; *Family* 2 s (Daniel John, Harry), 2 da (Lucy Ann, Ruth Miranda); m 1990, Judith Powell; 1 step s (Alexander); *Career* slr 1957–96, ptnr then conslt Berwin Leighton Paisner; dep chm: Lex Service plc 1974–2001, Tesco plc 1981–96; chm: Tesco Pension Tstees Ltd 1986–2004, Beazer Homes plc 1994–2001, Wincanton plc 2001–05; dep chm English Partnerships 2000–04; dir: Gartmore plc until 1996, Richard Ellis 1997–2001, Liberty plc 1998–2001; tstee: Nat Maritime Museum 1996–2006, St Bartholomew's and Royal London Special Tstees 2000–; *Recreations* sailing, skiing, opera; *Clubs* Savile; *Style*— Victor W Benjamin, Esq; ✉ e-mail victor.benjamin@btinternet.com

BENN, Rt Hon Anthony Neil Wedgwood (Tony); PC (1964); s of 1 Viscount Stansgate, DSO, DFC, PC (d 1960), and Margaret Eadie, *née* Holmes (d 1991); suc as 2 Viscount 1960, but made it known that he did not wish to claim the Viscountcy; disclaimed his peerage for life 31 July 1963, having unsuccessfully attempted to renounce his right of succession 1955 and 1960; *b* 3 April 1925; *Educ* Westminster, New Coll Oxford; *m* 1949, Caroline Middleton (d 2000), da of James Milton De Camp (d 2000), of Cincinnati, USA; 3 s, 1 da; *Career* WW RAFVR 1943–45, RNVR 1945–46; joined Lab Pty 1943, memb Nat Exec Ctee Lab Pty 1959–60 and 1962–94 (chm 1971–72), chm Lab Home Policy Ctee 1974–82, candidate for Lab Pty leadership 1976 and 1988 (for dep leadership 1971 and 1981), memb Labour-TUC Liaison Ctee until 1982; MP (Lab): Bristol SE 1950–60 and 1963–83, Chesterfield 1984–2001; postmaster-gen 1964–66; min of: technol 1966–70, power 1969; oppn spokesman on trade and indust 1970–74; sec of state for industry and min for post and telecommunications 1974–75, sec of state for energy 1975–79; visiting prof of govt LSE 2001–03; pres EEC Council of Energy Mins 1977, pres Socialist Campaign Gp 1990–; Freeman City of Bristol 2003; ten honorary doctorates; hon fell New Coll Oxford 2006; *Publications* The Privy Council as a Second Chamber (1957), The Regeneration of Britain (1964), The New Politics (1970), Speeches (1974), Arguments for Socialism (1979), Arguments for Democracy (1981), Writings on the Wall - A Radical and Socialist Anthology 1215–1984 (ed 1984), Fighting Back - Speaking Out for Socialism in the Eighties (1988); Out of the Wilderness - Diaries 1963–67 (1987), Office Without Power - Diaries 1968–72, Against the Tide - Diaries 1973–76, Conflicts of Interest - Diaries 1977–80, A Future for Socialism (1991), The End of an Era - Diaries 1980–90 (1992), Common Sense (with Andrew Hood, 1993), Years of Hope - Diaries 1940–62 (1994), Benn Diaries 1940–90 (1995), Free At Last: Diaries 1991–2001 (2002), Free Radical (essays, 2003), Dare to be a Daniel (memoir, 2004); Speaking Up in Parliament (video, 1993), The Benn Tapes (Vol 1, 1994, Vol II, 1995), New Labour in Focus (video, 1999), An Audience With Tony Benn (video, 2003), Westminster behind Closed Doors (video, 1995); *Style*— The Rt Hon Tony Benn

BENN, Hilary James Wedgwood; PC (2003), MP; s of Rt Hon Tony Benn (disclaimed Viscountcy of Stansgate for life 1963); *b* 26 November 1953; *Educ* Holland Park Sch, Univ of Sussex; *m* 1, Rosalind Retey (d 1979); m 2, Sally Clark; 3 s, 1 da; *Career* Labour memb Ealing Cncl 1979–99, chair of educn and dep leader of Ealing Cncl 1986–90; chm Acton Labour Party, former head of Policy and Communications MSF; special advsr to sec of state for Educn and Employment 1997–99; MP (Lab) Leeds Central 1999–; Parly under-sec of state: Dept for Int Devpt 2001–02, Home Office 2002–03; min of state Dept for Int Devpt June-Oct 2003, sec of state Int Devpt 2003–07, sec of state for environment, food and rural affrs 2007–; *Style*— The Rt Hon Hilary Benn, Esq, MP; ✉ House of Commons, London SW1A 0AA

BENN, Sir (James) Jonathan; 4 Bt (UK 1914), of The Old Knoll, Metropolitan Borough of Lewisham; s of Sir John Andrews Benn, 3 Bt (d 1984), and Hon Lady (Ursula Helen Alers) Benn (d 2006), da of 1 Baron Hankey; bro of Timothy Benn, *qv*; *b* 27 July 1933; *Educ* Harrow, Clare Coll Cambridge (MA); *m* 2 July 1960, Jennifer Mary, eldest da of Dr Wilfred Vivian Howells, OBE (d 1987), of The Ferns, Clun, Shropshire; 1 s (Robert Ernest (Robin) b 1963), 1 da (Juliet Clare (Mrs Simon Erridge) b 1966); *Heir* s, Robin Benn; *Career* dir Reedpack Ltd 1988–90, chm and chief exec Reed Paper and Bd (UK) Ltd 1978–90, chm J & J Maybank Ltd 1988–90, dir The Broomhill Tst 1991–96, chm SCA Pension Tstees Ltd 1988–98; pres Br Paper and Board Industries Fedn 1985–87; Liveryman Worshipful Co of Stationers & Newspaper Makers; *Style*— Sir Jonathan Benn, Bt; ✉ Fielden Lodge, Tonbridge Road, Ightham, Sevenoaks, Kent TN15 9AN

BENN, Timothy John; s of Sir John Andrews Benn, 3 Bt (d 1984), and Hon Ursula Lady Benn, *née* Hankey (d 2006); bro of Sir Jonathan Benn, 4 Bt, *qv*; *b* 27 October 1936; *Educ* Harrow, Clare Coll Cambridge (MA), Princeton, Harvard Business Sch USA; *m* 1982, Christina Grace Townsend; *Career* served HM Forces 2 Lt Scots Gds 1956–57; Benn Brothers Ltd: memb Bd 1961–82, md 1972–82, dep chm 1976–81; chm Benn Brothers plc 1981–82; Ernest Benn: memb Bd 1967–82, md 1973–82, chm and md 1974–82; chm: Timothy Benn Publishing 1983–97, Bouverie Publishing Co 1983–97, Buckley Press 1984–97, Henry Greenwood and Co 1987–97, Dalesman Publishing Co 1989–, Countryman Publishing Co 2000–04, Huveaux plc 2001–06; prop Creel Press 1990–; pres Tonbridge Civic Soc 1982–87; Liveryman Worshipful Co of Stationers & Newspaper Makers; FCIM; *Books* The (Almost) Compleat Angler (1985); *Recreations* gardening, toymaking, flyfishing; *Style*— Timothy Benn, Esq; ✉ 4 Smith Square, Westminster, London SW1P 3HS

BENN, Rt Rev Wallace Parke; *see*: Lewes, Bishop of

BENNET, George Charters; s of George Charters Bennet (d 1968), and Euphemia, *née* Igoe; *b* 8 August 1946; *Educ* Holy Cross Acad, Univ of Edinburgh Med Sch (BSc, MB ChB); *m* 17 June 1978, (Kathryn) Louise, da of Dr Bernard Gwillam Spilbury; 3 s (George b 1979, Simon b 1982, Matthew b 1987); *Career* former med appts London, Oxford, Southampton and Toronto; currently: conslt surgn Royal Hosp for Sick Children Glasgow, hon clinical sr lectr Univ of Glasgow, hon conslt to the Army Children's Orthopaedic Surgery and Trauma, memb Bd Medical and Dental Defence Union of Scotland; past pres Br Soc for Childrens's Orthopaedic Surgery; FRCS, FBOA; *Books* Paediatric Hip Disorders (1987); chapters and research papers on children's orthopaedic surgery; *Recreations* game fishing, golf; *Style*— George C Bennet, Esq; ✉ Tamarack House, Moor Road, Strathblane, Stirlingshire G63 9HA (tel 01360 771249, e-mail georgecbennet@aol.com); Royal Hospital For Sick Children, Yorkhill, Glasgow G3 85J (tel and fax 0141 201 0275)

BENNETT, Alan; *b* 9 May 1934; *Educ* Leeds Modern Sch, Exeter Coll Oxford (MA); *Career* dramatist and actor; tstee Nat Gallery 1993–98; Hon DLitt Univ of Leeds 1990; hon fell Exeter Coll Oxford 1987; hon fell Royal Acad; Freeman City of Leeds 2006; *Theatre* incl: Beyond the Fringe (Royal Lyceum Edinburgh 1960, Fortune London 1961, NYC 1962); Forty Years On (Apollo) 1968, Getting On (Queen's) 1971, Habeas Corpus (Lyric) 1973, The Old Country (Queen's) 1977, Enjoy (Vaudeville) 1980, Kafka's Dick (Royal Court) 1986, Single Spies (NT, double bill of A Question of Attribution (BPG TV & Radio Writer's Award 1992)), An Englishman Abroad (also dir, NT) 1988, Wind in the Willows (adaptation, RNT) 1990, The Madness of George III (RNT) 1991–93, The Lady in the Van 1999, The History Boys (RNT) 2004; *Television* incl: On the Margin (series) 1966, A Day Out 1972, Sunset Across the Bay 1975, A Little Outing, A Visit from Miss Prothero 1977, Doris and Doreen 1978, The Old Crowd 1978, Me! I'm Afraid of Virginia Woolf 1978, All Day on the Sands 1979, Afternoon Off 1979, One Fine Day 1979, Intensive Care, Say Something Happened, Our Winnie, Marks, A Woman of No Importance, Rolling Home, An Englishman Abroad 1983, The Insurance Man 1986, Talking Heads (series) 1988 (Hawthornden Prize), 102 Boulevard Haussmann 1991, A Question of Attribution 1992, Talking Heads II 1998; TV documentaries: Dinner at Noon 1988, Portrait or Bust 1994, The Abbey 1995, Heavenly Stories 1997, Telling Tales 2000; *Films* A Private Function 1984, Prick Up Your Ears 1987, The Madness of King George (Evening Standard Award for Best Screenplay) 1995, The History Boys 2006; *Books* Beyond the Fringe (with Peter Cook, Jonathan Miller and Dudley Moore, 1962), Forty Years On (1969), Getting On (1972), Habeas Corpus (1973), The Old Country (1978), Enjoy (1980), Office Suite (1981), Objects of Affection (1982), A Private Function (1984), The Writer in Disguise (1985), Prick Up Your Ears (screenplay, 1987), Two Kafka Plays (1987), Talking Heads (1988, Hawthornden Prize), Single Spies (1989), The Lady in the Van (1990), The Wind in the Willows (adaptation, 1991), The Madness of George III (1991), Writing Home (1994, Bowater Book of the Year British Book Awards 1995), The Clothes They Stood Up In (1998), The Complete Talking Heads (1998), Father! Father! Burning Bright (2000), Telling Tales (2000), The Laying on of Hands (2001), The History Boys (2004), Untold Stories (2005), The Uncommon Reader (2007); *Style*— Alan Bennett, Esq; ✉ c/o PFD, Drury House, 34–43 Russell Street, London WC2B 5HA (tel 020 7344 1000)

BENNETT, Andrew John; CMG (1998); s of Leonard Charles Bennett (d 1994), and Edna Mary, *née* Harding (d 1984); *b* 25 April 1942; *Educ* St Edward's Sch Oxford, UCNW Bangor (BSc), Univ of W Indies Trinidad, Univ of Reading (MSc), Univ of Cranfield (DSc); *m* 1996, Yin Yin May, *née* Yonemo; 1 da; *Career* Lt 6/7 Bn Royal Welch Fus TA 1961–66; VSO Kenya 1965–66, agric res offr Govt of St Vincent W Indies 1967–69, maize agronomist Govt Republic of Malawi 1971–74, chief research offr (agric) Regnl Miny of Agric Southern Sudan 1976–80; DfID (formerly ODA): agric advsr 1980–83, nat resources advsr SE Asia Devpt Div Bangkok 1983–85, head Br Devpt Div in the Pacific Fiji 1985–87, chief nat research advsr 1987–2002, strategic dir Physical and Natural Environment 1998–99, dir Rural Livelihoods and Environment 1999–2002; exec dir Syngenta Fndn for Sustainable Agric 2002–; memb: Cncl RASE 1988–2004, Cncl ODI 2003–, Tropical Agric Assoc (pres 2003); dir Doyle Fndn 2002–; chair of tstees Centre of Int Forestry Research 2002–; dir Eynesbury Estates Ltd 1989–; FRSA 2000; *Recreations* walking, gardening; *Style*— Andrew Bennett, Esq, CMG

BENNETT, Dr Anna Teresa Natalie; da of Sydney Bennett (d 1974), and Ardene Hilton, of Devon; *b* 20 May 1959; *Educ* Lycée Français de Londres, Inst of Archaeology Univ of London (BSc), Inst of Archaeology UCL (PhD, Br Acad scholar); *m* 1991, Kevin Warren Conru; 2 s (Maximilian b 1996, Theodore b 1998); *Career* asst conservator English Heritage London 1978–79, antiquities conservator J Paul Getty Museum Los Angeles 1982–84, post-doctoral res fell Univ of London 1988–89, commercial art conservation and analytical practice at Univ of London 1989– (clients incl Nat Tst, English Heritage, Cncl for the Care of Churches, numerous museums and commercial and private orgns); project admin for conservation of Uppark contents on behalf of Nat Tst; conservation advsr Apulum Project in Romania, organiser of seminars on disaster mgmnt in the field of cultural heritage, author of numerous papers and lectrs on archaeology and conservation (incl The Sevso Treasure 1994); dir Centre for the scientific investigation of works of art Univ of London; current projects incl: weathering stone sculptures in SE Asia; television presenter BBC2 series on architectural history 2001–; hon fell Univ of London 1989–; registered with The Conservation Unit; memb: Int Inst for Conservation of Works of Art (IIC), Int Cncl of Museums (ICOM); FRS 2001; *Style*— Dr Anna Bennett; ✉ Conservation and Technical Services Ltd, PO Box 26157, London SW8 1FT (tel 00 32 479 658 110, e-mail atnbennett@analyzeark.com)

BENNETT, Clive Ronald Reath; CBE (2007); s of Ron Bennett, of Mayals, Swansea, and Betty Bennett; *b* 20 December 1947; *Educ* Hatfield Poly (BSc(Eng)); *m* 1970, Pauline, *née* Weeks; 2 da (Rochelle Clair (Mrs Elwood) b 1 Aug 1973, Leah Colette (Mrs Page) b 13 Dec 1976); *Career* held various sr exec positions: Rank Xerox, Polycell Products, Sara Lee Household & Personal Care; gp ops and business excellence dir Norton Healthcare 1995–2000, chief exec Driver and Vehicle Licensing Agency 2000–; CEng; MILT, MIEE, MInstD; *Style*— Clive Bennett, Esq, CBE; ✉ Driver and Vehicle Licensing Agency, Longview Road, Morriston, Swansea SA6 7JL (tel 01792 782363, fax 01792 783003, e-mail clive.bennett@dvla.gsi.gov.uk)

BENNETT, David Anthony; s of late Albert Henry Bennett, of Solihull, W Midlands, and Doris May, *née* Ward; *b* 4 October 1948; *Educ* Harold Malley GS Solihull, Univ of Portsmouth, Johns Hopkins Univ, Sch of Advanced Int Studies (scholar, BSc Econ, Dip Int Affrs); *Career* stagiaire and admin Euro Cmmn 1973–74, Econ Planning Div Br Gas 1976–84, dir public affairs Eurofi 1984–87, md Powerhouse Europe 1987–92, chm and md Beaumark Ltd 1993–2001, dir Citigate Public Affairs 2001–04, head City of London Office to EU Instns 2004–06, chief exec Assoc of Private Client Investment Managers and Stockbrokers (APCIMS) 2007–; dep chm Europe Analytica Ltd 1999–, chm Nat Assoc of Mutual Guarantee Socs 1993–2002; dir: Euro Assoc of Mutual Guarantee Schemes 1997–2002, Assoc of Professional Political Consultants 1997–2001; conslt speaker for Euro Cmmn, alternate memb Econ and Social Ctee of Euro Communities 1982–84 (expert 1990–91); sec Labour Econ Fin and Taxation Assoc (LEFTA) 1979–81; Parly candidate (SDP/Alliance) 1983 and 1987, Euro Parly candidate 1984, chm Lib Democrats Euro Gp 1991–97; MCIPR; *Books* The European Economy in 1975 (1975); *Recreations* tennis, skiing, walking, travel, theatre; *Clubs* Reform, Capital; *Style*— David Bennett, Esq; ✉ 20 Regent's Bridge Gardens, London SW8 1JR (tel 020 7735 0241); APCIMS, 114 Middlesex Street, London E1 7JH (tel 020 7247 7080)

BENNETT, David Jonathan; s of Peter Bennett, and Brenda, *née* Ashwood; *b* 26 March 1962; *Educ* KCS Wimbledon, Queens' Coll Cambridge; *m* 7 Dec 1991, Susan Elizabeth, da of George Moss; 2 s (Sam b 17 Oct 1994, Rory b 23 Sept 1996); *Career* fin dir Cheltenham & Gloucester plc 1995–96, dir of risk mgmnt Nat Bank of NZ 1996–98, chief exec Countrywide Bank 1998; Alliance & Leicester plc: gp treas 1999–2000, gp exec dir 2000–01, gp fin dir 2001–07, gp chief exec 2007–; non-exec dir easyJet 2005–; memb: Assoc of Corp Treasurers, Guild of Int Bankers; *Recreations* watching Gloucester RFC, hiking; *Style*— David Bennett, Esq; ✉ Alliance & Leicester plc, Carlton Park, Leicester (tel 0116 200 2000)

BENNETT, Dr David William; s of William Edwin Bennett, of Halesowen, W Midlands, and Irene Joan, *née* Davis; *b* 3 August 1955, Wolverhampton, Staffs; *Educ* Halesowen GS, Univ of Birmingham (BSc, SWJ Smith Prize), Trinity Coll Oxford (DPhil), London Business Sch (Cert in Corporate Finance); *partner* Valerie Carol Bennett; *Career* mangr Shell Research Ltd 1979–82, mangr Shell Int Petroleum Co 1982–86, dir McKinsey & Co Inc 1986–2004 (latterly sr ptnr), head PM's Policy Directorate and PM's Strategy Unit 2005–07; contrib research papers to Nuclear Physics 1977–1980; *Recreations* motor sports; *Style*— Dr David Bennett; ✉ 10 Downing St, Whitehall, London SW1A 2AA (tel 020 7930 4433)

BENNETT, His Hon Judge Dudley Paul; s of late Patrick James Bennett, of Bognor Regis, W Sussex, and Mary, *née* Edmondson; *b* 4 August 1948; *Educ* Bradfield Coll, Univ of London (LLB); *Children* 2 da (Olivia Mary b 4 Feb 1988, Emma-Jayne b 5 Oct 1989); *Career* called to the Bar Inner Temple 1972; recorder of the Crown Court 1988–93, circuit judge (Midland & Oxford Circuit) 1993–; *Recreations* gardening, travel; *Style*— His Hon Judge Bennett; ✉ Nottingham Crown Court, Canal Street, Nottingham NG1 7EJ

B

BENNETT, Guy Patrick de Courcy; s of Patrick John de Courcy Bennett (d 2001), of Thames Ditton, and Pamela Mary Ray, *née* Kirchner (d 2003); *b* 27 October 1958; *Educ* Wimbledon Coll, Univ of Manchester (BSc); *m* 5 Nov 1988, Monica Beatrice, da of Alfred Cecil Francis Brodermann (d 1974); 3 da (Emily b 1990, Olivia b 1991, Beatrice b 1994); *Career* investment analyst Equity & Law Life 1980–83; dir: Marketable Securities Div CIN Management 1984–96, EFM Japan Trust 1992–97, Genesis Malaysia Maju Fund 1992–96, Taiwan Capital Fund 1994–96; sr portfolio mangr Goldman Sachs Asset Management 1996–2001, Batterymarch 2001–; *Recreations* golf, tennis, squash; *Style*— Guy Bennett, Esq

BENNETT, Hon Mr Justice; Sir Hugh Peter Derwyn Bennett; kt (1995), DL (W Sussex 2003); s of Peter Ward Bennett, OBE (d 1996), and Priscilla Ann, *née* Troughton (d 1998); *b* 8 September 1943; *Educ* Haileybury and ISC, Churchill Coll Cambridge (MA); *m* 6 Dec 1969, Elizabeth, da of James Whittington Landon, DFC; 3 da (Ursula Ann (Lady Cholmeley) b 29 Jan 1971, Henrietta Mary (Mrs S R Hillier) b 1 July 1973, Rosamond Elizabeth (Mrs W Ashworth) b 13 Sept 1976), 1 s (Vivian Hugh James b 16 Nov 1974); *Career* called to the Bar Inner Temple 1966 (bencher 1993); QC 1988, recorder of the Crown Court 1990–95 (asst recorder 1987), dep judge of the High Court of Justice (Family and Queen's Bench Div) 1993–95, judge of the High Court of Justice (Family Div) 1995–, presiding judge NE Circuit 1999–2002, nominated judge of the Administrative Court 2004–; memb Supreme Court Rule Ctee 1988–92; chm Sussex Assoc for the Rehabilitation of Offenders (SARO) 1998–2004; hon legal advsr Sussex Co Playing Fields Assoc 1988–95, pt/t chm Horserace Betting Levy Appeal Tbnl 1989–95; govr Lancing Coll 1981–95, fell SE Div Woodard Corp 1987–99; *Recreations* cricket, tennis, shooting and fishing; *Clubs* MCC, Sussex, Pilgrims; *Style*— The Hon Mr Justice Bennett, DL; ✉ The Royal Courts of Justice, Strand, London WC2A 2LL

BENNETT, Jana; OBE; *b* USA; *Educ* Bognor Comprehensive, Univ of Oxford (BA), LSE (MSc); *m*; 2 c; *Career* co-ed Millennium (int relations jl) 1976–77; BBC TV: news trainee then current affrs prodr 1978–87, series prodr then ed Antenna 1987–90, ed Horizon 1990–94, head Science Dept 1994–97, dir of programmes and dep chief exec BBC Prodn 1997–1999; sr vice-pres and gen mangr of The Learning Channel USA 1999–2002, dir of television BBC 2002– (responsible for BBC One, Two, Three, Four, interactive television, UKTV and BBC America channel content); worked on: Nationwide, The Money Programme, Newsnight, Panorama; cmmns incl: Inside Chernobyl Sarcophagus, Red Star in Orbit, Assault on the Male, Emerging Viruses, Iceman, Fermat's Last Theorem; created/launched: Animal Hospital, Trust Me I'm a Doctor, Trouble at the Top, Earth Story, The Human Body, Walking with Dinosaurs, The Planets, Blood on the Carpet; memb: BAFTA, RTS, Women in TV and Radio; tstee Natural History Museum London 1998–2003, govr RSC; memb Cncl of Govrs LSE; *Awards* Golden Nymph Award for The Private Wars of Colonel North Monte Carlo 1988, Emmy for Inside Chernobyl Sarcophagus, Prix Italia and BAFTA Award for Fermat's Last Theorem; *Books* The Disappeared: Argentina's Dirty War (with John Simpson, 1986); *Recreations* mountaineering, kids, travel; *Style*— Ms Jana Bennett, OBE

BENNETT, Jeremy John Nelson; s of Denis Pengelley Bennett, and Jill, *née* Nelson; *b* 1 December 1939; *Educ* Haileybury, Clare Coll Cambridge (open scholar, MA), Univ of Copenhagen (Churchill fell); *m* 1963, Tine, *née* Langkilde; 3 s; *Career* with Br Cncl 1963–65; BBC: with European Service 1966–68, prodr and dir BBC TV Documentaries 1968–89, prodr Richard Dimbleby Lecture 1983–87, exec prodr Contemporary History Unit 1989–92; freelance prodr 1993–95, dir and exec prodr 3BM Television Ltd 1995–2004 (md and chm 1995–2001); assoc fell Cultural Policy Studies Univ of Warwick 2003–; TV prodns incl: The Saboteurs of Telemark 1973, Margrethe Queen of Denmark 1974, Hussein the Survivor King 1977, Alphabet - The Story of Writing 1980 (Silver Award New York Film and TV Festival, The Times Newcomer Award), Italians 1984, Juan Carlos - King of All the Spaniards 1986, Cry Hungary 1986 (Blue Ribbon Award American Film Festival), Monty - In Love and War 1987 (Blue Ribbon Award American Film Festival), Churchill 1992, The Cuban Missile Crisis 1992 (Emmy Award), Chairman Mao - The Last Emperor 1993, Hiroshima 1995, What Did You Do In The War, Auntie? 1995, The Suez Crisis 1996, Auntie - The Inside Story of the BBC 1997, The Berlin Airlift 1998, The Illuminator 2003; chm: Camberwell Society 1979–85 (pres 2007–), Southwark Environment Tst 1983–95, Groundwork Southwark and Lambeth (previously Groundwork Southwark) 1995–; memb Bd: Cross River Partnership 1995–2006, Groundwork Nat Fedn 1999–, Bd Southwark Alliance 2006–; Southwark Civic Award 2003, Cross of Merit, Order of Vitez (Hungary) 1987; *Books* British Broadcasting and the Danish Resistance Movement 1940–45 (1966), The Master-Builders (2004); *Recreations* fishing, walking in Powys, urban environment; *Style*— Jeremy Bennett, Esq; ✉ 30 Grove Lane, Camberwell, London SE5 8ST (tel 020 7703 9971)

BENNETT, Dr John Roderick; s of William Henry Bennett (d 1966), and Janet Elizabeth, *née* Earl (d 1990); *b* 15 September 1934; *Educ* Wallasey GS, Univ of Liverpool (MB ChB, MD); *m* 1963, Helen, da of Rt Rev Clifford Martin (d 1977); 2 s (Paul b 3 Aug 1964, Mark b 17 Dec 1965), 1 da (Sarah b 10 Aug 1969); *Career* conslt physician Hull Royal Infirmary 1969–97, hon prof of clinical med Univ of Hull 1994–97; memb GMC 1978–99; pres CORE (Digestive Disorders Fndn) 2005–, treas Royal Med Benevolent Fund 2002–; FRCP 1976 (vice-pres 1995–96, treas 1996–2003); *Books* Therapeutic Endoscopy and Radiology of the Gut (1980, 2 edn 1988), Practical Gastroenterology (1986); *Recreations* sailing, walking, gardening, music, literature; *Clubs* Athenaeum; *Style*— Dr John Bennett; ✉ Kingspring House, Vicarage Lane, Long Compton, Warwickshire CV36 5LH (tel 01608 684081)

BENNETT, Lilian Margery; OBE (1993); da of Maurice Sydney Barnett (d 1981), of London, and Sophia Levy (d 1975); *b* 22 August 1922; *Educ* West Ham Secdy Sch; *m* 2 Nov 1952, Ronald Bennett, s of Alec Bennett (d 1974), of London; 1 s (Jonathan b 1954); *Career* dir: Thermo-Plastics Ltd 1957–68, Manpower plc 1968–98 (chm 1990–1998), Girlpower Ltd 1968–98, Overdrive plc 1968–98, BTI Ltd 1996–2000, Irene Taylor Tst 1996–; memb The Parole Board 1984–87; FRSA; *Recreations* reading, music, community work; *Style*— Mrs Lilian Bennett, OBE; ✉ 87 Church Road, London SW19 5AL

BENNETT, Linda Kristin; OBE (2007); da of Peter Bennett, of London, and Hafdis, *née* Herbertsdottir; *b* 8 September 1962; *Educ* Haberdashers' Aske's Sch for Girls, Univ of Reading (BSc); *m* 29 July 2000, Philip W Harley, s of late Christopher Harley; 1 da (Isabel Kristin b 29 Jan 2001); *Career* shoe design asst Robert Clegerie France 1986, opened first L K Bennett shop Wimbledon Village 1990 (currently 35 shops incl flagship store Brook Street London and Rue de Grenelle Paris); Hon LLD Univ of Reading, hon fell Univ of the Arts London; *Awards* winner Consumer Product category Nat Ernst & Young Entrpreneur of the Year Awards 2002, winner Smaller Multiple category Drapers Record Awards 2002, Best Combined Clothing and Footwear Retailer UK Footwear Awards 2002, Best Women's Footwear Retailer UK Footwear Awards 2003, Veuve Clicquot Business Woman of the Year 2004 (finalist 1999); *Recreations* architectural history, British 20th century art, walking, travel, cinema; *Style*— Ms Linda Bennett, OBE; ✉ L K Bennett, 3 Cavendish Square, London W1G 0LB (tel 020 7637 6700, fax 020 7637 6701, e-mail linda.bennett@lkbennett.com)

BENNETT, Prof Michael David; OBE (1996); s of Stanley Roland Bennett, and Marion, *née* Woods; *b* 6 October 1943; *Educ* Gravesend Boys' GS, UC Wales Aberystwyth (BSc, PhD); *m* 28 Aug 1971, Anita Lucy, da of Harry Ring, of Northfleet, Kent; 2 da (Michelle b 1976, Danielle b 1977), 1 s (Nathan b 1980); *Career* res scientist (cytogeneticist) Plant Breeding Inst Cambridge 1968–87, BP Venture res fell 1986–92; Royal Botanic Gardens Kew: keeper of Jodrell Laboratory 1987–2006, hon research fell 2006–; fell Univ of Wales Aberystwyth 1999–; pres British Israel Bible Truth Fellowship 1987–; chm Annals of Botany Co 2004–; FLS 1988; *Recreations* gardening, reading, bible study; *Style*— Prof Michael Bennett, OBE; ✉ Jodrell Laboratory, Royal Botanic Gardens, Kew, Richmond, Surrey TW9 3AB (tel 020 8332 5322, fax 020 8332 5310, e-mail m.bennett@kew.org)

BENNETT, Neil Edward Francis; s of Dr (Albert) Edward Bennett, of Liston, Long Melford, Suffolk, and Jean Louise, *née* Dickinson; *b* 15 May 1965; *Educ* Westminster, UCL (BA), City Univ London (Postgrad Dip Journalism); *m* 19 Sept 1992, Carole, da of William Kenyon, of Allestree, Derby; 2 da (Violet Xanthe b 30 Oct 1995, Clementine Elizabeth b 13 March 1998); *Career* feature writer Investors' Chronicle 1987–89; The Times 1989–95: City reporter 1989–90, banking corr 1990–93, ed Tempus column 1993, dep ed Business News until 1995, City ed Sunday Telegraph 1995–2002, chief exec Gavin Anderson & Co UK 2002–; financial columnist: jagnotes-euro.com 1999–2000, Hemscott.net 2001–02; Wincott Jr Financial Journalist of the Year 1992, Business Journalist of the Year British Press Awards 1998 and 1999; *Recreations* antiquarian book collecting, long-distance running; *Clubs* East India; *Style*— Neil Bennett, Esq; ✉ Gavin Anderson & Company, 85 Strand, London WC2R 0DW (tel 020 7554 1400, fax 020 7554 1499)

BENNETT, Dr Peter John; s of Thomas Ronald Bennett (d 1992), and Ivy, *née* Wakelam; *b* 13 September 1952, Wolverhampton; *Educ* High Arcal GS Dudley, SOAS (BA, PhD); *Career* fieldworker among Vaishnavas of the Pushti Marg tradition in Ujjain India 1977–78, pt/t teacher and youth worker 1978–83, asst govr HM Young Offenders Instn Everthorpe 1983–88, head Hull Special Unit for dangerous and disruptive prisoners 1988–90, staff offr HM Prison Service HQ 1990–92, head of inmate activities HM Young Offenders Instn Moorland 1992–93, govr HMP Nottingham 1993–98, ops mangr Prison Serv Contracts and Competitions Gp 1998–2000, govr HMP Wellingborough 2000–02, govr HMP Springhill and HMP Grendon Therapeutic Community Prison Bucks 2002–; involved with Newbridge charity, tstee Koestler Tst 2006; FRAI 1985; *Books* The Path of Grace: Social Organization and Temple Worship in a Vaishnava Sect (1993); *Recreations* running, poetry, South Asian cultures and religions; *Style*— Dr Peter Bennett; ✉ HMP Grendon, Grendon Underwood, Bucks HP18 0TL (tel 01296 443005, e-mail peter.bennett02@hmps.gsi.gov.uk)

BENNETT, Dr Peter Norman; s of Norman Bennett (d 1989), and Elizabeth Jane, *née* Ogston (d 1997); *b* 25 November 1939; *Educ* Nairn Acad, Univ of Aberdeen (MB ChB, MD); *m* 31 Aug 1963, Jennifer Mary, da of Eric Arthur Brocklehurst, of Hull, Yorks; 2 s (Michael John b 1965, Neil Robert b 1968), 1 da (Sally-Ann Elizabeth b 1972); *Career* lectr in med Univ of Aberdeen 1967–71, Wellcome res fell UCH London 1971–73, lectr Royal Postgrad Med Sch 1973–76, conslt physician in clinical pharmacology and dir Clinical Pharmacology Unit Royal United Hosp Bath 1976–2004 (hon conslt physician 2004–); School of Postgrad Med Univ of Bath: sr lectr in clinical pharmacology 1976–90, dir Centre for Med Studies 1978–89, assoc dean 1989, reader in clinical pharmacology 1990–2004 (hon reader 2004–); memb Br Pharmacological Soc (treas Clinical Section 1982–87), chm WHO (Euro) Working Gp on Drugs and Breast Feeding 1983–90, memb Bd Euro Ethical Review Ctee 1990– (co-chm 1997); FRCP 1981, FRCPGlas 1981, FRCPEd 1999; *Books* Clinical Pharmacology (with D R Laurence, 5 edn 1980, 6 edn 1987, 7 edn 1992; with D R Lawrence and M J Brown, 8 edn 1997; with M J Brown, 9 edn 2003, 10 edn 2007), Multiple Choice Questions on Clinical Pharmacology (with D R Laurence and F Stokes, 1 edn 1983, 2 edn 1988), Drugs and Human Lactation (ed, 1988, 2 edn 1996), Ethical Responsibilities in European Drug Research (ed, 1991), Good Clinical Practice and Ethics in European Drug Research (ed, 1994), Self Assessment in Clinical Pharmacology (with D R Lawrence and M J Brown, 1999); *Recreations* fly fishing, theatre; *Clubs* RSM; *Style*— Dr Peter Bennett; ✉ Denmede, Southstoke Road, Combe Down, Bath BA2 5SL (tel 01225 832371, fax 01225 837278, e-mail p.n.bennett@bath.ac.uk)

BENNETT, Dr Philip Anthony; s of George Joseph Bennett (d 1997), of Brigg, and Rita, *née* Skelton (d 1984); *b* 1 September 1947; *Educ* Univ of York (PhD); *m* 1, 20 Sept 1969 (m dis 1996), Kathryn Margaret, da of Sidney French (d 1977); 2 s (Lance Andrew b 3 Jan 1972, Robin Michael b 3 Jan 1980); m 2, 1 Sept 2000, Eleanor Kathleen, da of Wilfred Allen Dolan (d 1975); *Career* apprenticeship Richard Thomas & Baldwin (later part of British Steel) 1963–69, sr engrg positions British Steel 1969–81, chm CSE International Ltd 1984–2008, chm York Software Engineering Ltd 1995–2006, dir of technol Cross London Rail Ltd 2007–; prof of safety critical systems Dept of Computer Science Univ of York 1993–2006; chm The Hazards Forum 1993–99; scouting 1977–91 (Cmmr); Freeman City of London 1990, Liveryman Worshipful Co of Engrs 1991 (memb Ct of Assts 1998–); FIEE 1989, FREng 1991 (CEng 1989), FICE 1995; *Books* Software Engineers Reference Book (contrib, 1991), Safety Aspects of Computer Control (ed, 1992); *Recreations* fly fishing, travel, reading; *Clubs* Athenaeum; *Style*— Dr P A Bennett, CEng, FREng; ✉ The Old Manor House, 2 Riverside, Scotter, Lincolnshire DN21 3UG (tel 01724 764745, e-mail pabennett@iee.org)

BENNETT, His Hon Raymond Clayton Watson; s of Harold Watson (Church Army Capt, d 1941), and Doris Helena, *née* Edwards (d 1988); *b* 20 June 1939; *Educ* Glasgow Acad, Bury GS, Univ of Manchester (LLB); *m* 24 April 1965, Elaine Margaret, da of William Haworth, of Clitheroe; 1 s (John b 1966), 1 da (Jane b 1969); *Career* slr Blackburn 1964–72; called to the Bar Middle Temple 1972; recorder of the Crown Court 1988–89 (asst recorder 1985–88), circuit judge (Northern Circuit) 1989–2004 (dep circuit judge 2004–), hon recorder Burnley 1998–2004; memb Hon Soc of Middle Temple; *Recreations* tennis, golf; *Style*— His Hon Raymond Bennett

BENNETT, Prof Richard Mark; s of Edward Bennett (d 1991), and Barbara, *née* Lack; *b* 4 June 1957, Chiswick; *Educ* St Paul's, Univ of Reading (BSc, PhD), Univ of Oxford (MSc); *m* 20 March 1981, Fiona, *née* Horne; 2 da (Alice b 20 June 1992, Constance b 2 June 1995); *Career* research fell, lectr, sr lectr then prof of agric economics Univ of Reading 1985–; memb Cncl and tstee Universities Fedn for Animal Welfare 1998–, tstee Humane Slaughter Assoc 1998–, memb Farm Animal Welfare Cncl 2005–, memb England Implementation Gp Animal Health and Welfare Strategy for GB 2005–; *Recreations* keen tennis player; *Style*— Prof Richard Bennett; ✉ Department of Agricultural and Food Economics, University of Reading, 4 Earley Gate, PO Box 237, Reading RG6 6AR (tel 0118 378 6478, fax 0118 935 6467, e-mail r.m.bennett@rdg.ac.uk)

BENNETT, Sir Richard Rodney; kt (1998), CBE (1977); s of H Rodney and Joan Esther Bennett; *b* 29 March 1936; *Educ* Leighton Park Sch Reading, Royal Acad of Music; *Career* composer; memb Gen Cncl Performing Right Soc 1975–, vice-pres London Coll of Music 1983–; author of various music articles in magazines and jls; *Works* operas: The Mines of Sulphur 1965 and A Penny for a Song 1968 (both cmmnd by Sadler's Wells), All The King's Men (children's opera) 1969, Victory 1970 (cmmnd by Royal Opera Covent Garden); music for films incl: Indiscreet, The Devil's Disciple, Only Two Can Play, The Wrong Arm of the Law, Heavens Above, Billy Liar, One Way Pendulum, The Nanny, Far from the Madding Crowd, Billion Dollar Brain, The Buttercup Chain, Figures in a Landscape, Lady Caroline Lamb, Voices, Murder on the Orient Express (SFTA award, Academy Award nomination, Performing Right Soc Ivor Novello award), Permission to Kill, Equus (BAFTA nomination), The Brinks Job, Yanks (BAFTA nomination), Return of the Soldier; music for TV incl: The Christians, L P Hartley Trilogy, The Ebony Tower, Tender is the Night, The Charmer, Poor Little Rich Girl, The Hiding Place, The Story of Anne Frank; other works incl: Guitar Concerto 1970, Spells (choral work) 1975, various chamber, orchestral and educational music works; *Recreations* cinema, modern jazz;

Style— Sir Richard Rodney Bennett, CBE; ✉ c/o Chester Music and Novello & Co Ltd, 8–9 Frith Street, London W1D 3JB (tel 020 7434 0066, fax 020 7287 6329)

BENNETT, Prof Robert John; s of Thomas Edward Bennett, of Southampton, and Kathleen Elizabeth, *née* Robson; *b* 23 March 1948; *Educ* Taunton's Sch Southampton, St Catharine's Coll Cambridge (MA, PhD); *m* 5 Sept 1971, Elizabeth Anne, da of William Allen, of Ormskirk, Lancs; 2 s (Phillip Stewart Edward b 1982, Richard John Charles b 1986); *Career* lectr UCL 1973–78, visiting prof Univ of Calif Berkeley 1978, lectr Univ of Cambridge 1978–85 (fell, tutor and dir of studies Fitzwilliam Coll 1978–85); LSE: prof of geography 1985–96, Leverhulme prof 1996–2000; prof of geography Univ of Cambridge 1996–, fell St Catharine's Coll Cambridge 1996–; gen ed Government and Policy 1982–; memb: Govt and Law Ctee ESRC 1982–87, Cncl Inst of Br Geographers 1985–87 (treas 1990–94); chm Election Studies Advsy Ctee ESRC 1987–88; conslt to House of Commons: Employment Ctee 1988–89, Scottish Affrs Ctee 1994–95, Educn and Employment Ctee 1997–2000; memb: Cncl Royal Geographic Soc 1995–2001 (vice-pres 1993–95 and 1998–2001), Research Awards Advsy Ctee Levenhulme Tst 2001–; chm: Postgraduate Review Ctee Br Acad 2000–01, Research Ctee Br Acad 2001–; memb IOD; FRGS 1982, FBA 1991; *Books* incl: Environmental Systems - Philosophy, Analysis and Control (with R J Chorley, 1978), Local Business Taxes in Britain and Germany (with G Krebs, 1988), Enterprise and Human Resource Development: local capacity building (with A McCoshan, 1993), Local and Regional Economic Development (with D Payne, 2000); *Recreations* genealogy, the family; *Style—* Prof Robert Bennett, FBA; ✉ Department of Geography, University of Cambridge, Downing Place, Cambridge CB2 3EN

BENNETT, Eur Ing Robert Michael; s of Frederick William Bennett (d 1980), of Friern Barnet, London, and Doris Annie, *née* Mallandaine (d 1990); *b* 29 November 1944; *Educ* Woodhouse GS Finchley, Northampton Coll of Advanced Technol (first and second year Dip Tech), Enfield Tech Coll (HND, IEE part III); *m* 1969, Norma, *née* Baldwin; 1 s (Simon Michael b 1971); *Career* apprenticeship trg Eastern Electricity Bd Wood Green 1963–68; design/contracts engr Christy Electrical Ltd Chelmsford 1969–72, electrical design engr Posford Pavry & Partners London (civil structural & building servs consltg engrs) 1972–73, sr electrical engr James R Briggs & Associates Hampstead (building servs consltg engrs) 1973–76, electrical assoc Donald Smith, Seymour & Rooley London 1981–86 (exec sr electrical engr 1976–81); electrical engrg ptnr: Building Design Partnership London 1986–91, Frederic J Whyte & Partners 1991–93; regnl/business devpt dir YRM Engineers 1994–96, business devpt mangr Donald Smith, Seymour & Rooley (now DSSR) London 1997–; chm South Bucks Area IEE 1984–85; memb Soc of Light and Lighting (MSLL); DipEE 1968, CEng 1978, FCIBSE 1985, FIEE 1987, Eur Ing 1988; *Books* Electricity and Buildings (jt author, 1984), CIBSE Applications Manual AM8 - Private and Standby Generation of Electricity (jtly, 1992); *Recreations* golf, theatre-going; *Clubs* Hazlemere Golf (Bucks), Beaconsfield 41; *Style—* Eur Ing Robert Bennett; ✉ DSSR, Craven House, 40 Uxbridge Road, London W5 2TZ (tel 020 8567 5621, fax 020 8579 5649, e-mail r.bennett@dssr.co.uk)

BENNETT, Sir Ronald Wilfrid Murdoch; 3 Bt (UK 1929), of Kirklington, Co Nottingham; o s of Sir (Charles) Wilfrid Bennett, 2 Bt, TD (d 1952), and Marion Agnes, OBE (d 1985), da of James Somervell, of Sorn Castle, Ayrshire; *b* 25 March 1930; *Educ* Wellington, Trinity Coll Oxford; *m* 1, 1953, Audrey Rose-Marie Patricia, o d of Maj A L J H Aubépin; 2 da (Anne-Marie Julia (Mrs Stephen Hickman) b 1954, Georgina Marion b 1956); m 2, 1968, Anne, da of late Leslie George Tooker; m 3; *Heir* kinsman, Mark Bennett; *Style—* Sir Ronald Bennett, Bt

BENNETT-JONES, Peter; s of Dr N Bennett-Jones, of Rhosneigr, Anglesey, and Ruth H Bennett-Jones; *b* 11 March 1955; *Educ* Winchester, Magdalene Coll Cambridge (MA); *m* 29 June 1990, Alison, *née* Watts; 2 s (Ludovic Robin Devereux b 1991, Albert George (Bertie) b 1994), 1 da (Matilda Emma b 1992); *Career* dir OCSC Ltd 1977–79, freelance prodn mangr 1979–81 (projects incl Bubble Theatre UK, Chung Ying Theatre Hong Kong, course dir City Univ London), dir Pola Jones Associates 1982–, md Talkback Productions 1983–86, md Corporate Communication Group Ltd 1986–88; chm: Tiger Television 1988–, PBJ Management 1988– (clients incl Rowan Atkinson, Lenny Henry, Barry Humphries, Harry Enfield, Eddie Izzard, Armando Iannucci, Reeves and Mortimer, Howard Goodall and Chris Morris), Tiger Aspect Productions 1993–; dir TEAM plc 1993–98; Tiger Aspect prodns incl: Mr Bean (ITV, winner numerous awards incl Int Emmy and Golden Rose of Montreux), The Vicar of Dibley (BBC1), Harry Enfield and Chums (BBC1), Murphy's Law (BBC1), Teachers (C4), The Catherine Tate Show (BBC2), Billy Elliot (Universal), Blackadder Back and Forth (NMEC and BSkyB), Our House (winner Olivier Award for Best New Musical 2003); dir Oxford Playhouse 2000–; chair of tstees Comic Relief 1997–; *Recreations* numerous; *Clubs* Oxford and Cambridge, Groucho; *Style—* Peter Bennett-Jones, Esq; ✉ Tiger Aspect Productions/PBJ Management, 7 Soho Street, London W1D 3DQ (tel 020 7434 6700, fax 020 7287 1191, car 077 7030 6065, e-mail pbj@tigeraspect.co.uk)

BENNETTS, Rt Rev Colin James; *see:* Coventry, Bishop of

BENNETTS, Denise Mary Margaret; da of James Smith, of Edinburgh, and Agnes Smith; *b* 26 January 1953, Edinburgh; *Educ* Heriot Watt Univ (BArch, DipArch), Edinburgh Coll of Art; *m* 23 Aug 1974, Robert (Rab) Bennetts; 1 s (Julian b 15 March 1984), 1 da (Louise b 31 Dec 1989); *Career* architect Casson Conder Partnership 1978–88, fndr and dir Bennetts Assocs 1987–; maj projects incl: Sophos HQ, Wessex Water Ops Centre, Basinghall Avenue, John Menzies, Powergen HQ, World Business Centre Heathrow; awards assessor Civic Tst 1997–, award assessor RIBA 2005, sometime examiner; RIBA 1978; *Style—* Ms Denise Bennetts; ✉ Bennetts Associates Architects, 1 Rawstorne Place, London EC1V 7NL (tel 020 7520 3300, fax 020 7520 3333, e-mail denise.bennetts@bennettsassociates.com)

BENNETTS, Rab; OBE (2003); s of Frank Vivian Bennetts, of Edinburgh, and Frances Bennetts; *b* 14 April 1953; *Educ* Heriot-Watt Univ (BArch), Edinburgh Coll of Art (DipArch); *m* 23 Aug 1974, Denise Margaret Mary, da of James Smith; 1 s (Julian b 15 March 1984), 1 da (Louise b 31 Dec 1989); *Career* architect; with Arup Assocs 1977–87; fndr ptnr Bennetts Assocs 1987–, maj projects incl Powergen HQ, John Menzies bldg Edinburgh, Heathrow Vistors' Centre, Gateway Centre Loch Lomond, Wessex Water Ops Centre, Hampstead Theatre, Brighton & Hove Central Library and Royal Shakespeare Theatre; special advsr to Govt on environmental sustainability and architecture; memb Competition Ctee RIBA; sometime lectr; author of numerous articles and pubns; dir Sadler's Wells Theatre; RIBA, FRSA; *Style—* Rab Bennetts, Esq, OBE; ✉ Bennetts Associates, 1 Rawstorne Place, London EC1V 7NL

BENNEWITH, Anthony John (Tony); s of Frank Bennewith, of Catford, and Elsie, *née* Poll; *b* 14 January 1946; *Educ* Catford Secdy Boys' Sch; *m* 8 June 1968, Babs, da of Jack Connolly; 4 da (Christine b 9 Jan 1971, Ruth b 4 June 1972, Heather b 8 Sept 1974, Antonia b 12 May 1988), 1 s (Graham b 15 Jan 1979); *Career* articled clerk 1962–67, internal audit Castrol Oil 1968–69; mangr Griffin Stone Mosscrop 1969–72; Neville Russell (latterly Mazars Neville Russell): mangr London 1972–73, ptnr Guildford 1974–86; own practice 1986–; memb Cncl ICAEW 1996–; deacon Godalming Baptist Church, treas Guildford Hospice, treas Guildford Sch of Acting, govr Rodborough Technol Coll; FCA 1978 (ACA 1968), FRSA 2005, FFA 2006; *Recreations* opera, walking, skiing, philately; *Clubs* County; *Style—* Tony Bennewith, Esq; ✉ Elmfield, Tuesley Lane, Godalming, Surrey GU7 1SJ (tel 01483 415107); A J Bennewith & Co, Hitherbury House, 97 Portsmouth Road, Guildford, Surrey GU2 4YF (tel 01483 539777, fax 01483 576235, mobile 07808 093806, e-mail tony@bennewith.co.uk)

BENNEY, (Adrian) Gerald Sallis; CBE (1995); s of Ernest Alfred Sallis Benney, and Aileen Mary, *née* Ward; *b* 21 April 1930; *Educ* Brighton GS, Brighton Coll of Art (Nat Dip), Royal Coll of Art (DesRCA); *m* 4 May 1957, Janet, da of Harold Neville Edwards; 3 s (Paul b 1959, Jonathan b 1961, Simon b 1966), 1 da (Genevieve b 1962); *Career* REME 1949–51; designer and maker of domestic and liturgical silver; started workshop in London in 1955, conslt designer to Viners Ltd 1957–59; holder of Royal Warrants to: HM The Queen 1974–, HRH The Duke of Edinburgh 1975–, HM the late Queen Elizabeth The Queen Mother 1975–, HRH The Prince of Wales 1980–; memb: Govt Craft Advsy Ctee 1972–77, Advsy Ctee UK Atomic Energy Ceramics Centre 1979–83; metalwork design advsr to Indian Govt 1977–78, chm Govt of India Hallmarking Survey 1981, memb Br Hallmarking Cncl 1983–88, export advsr and conslt designer to Royal Selangor Pewter Co Kuala Lumpur 1986–; commenced Reading Civic Plate 1960; major retrospective exhbn Goldsmiths Hall 2005; Freeman: City of London 1957, Borough of Reading 1984; Liveryman Worshipful Co of Goldsmiths 1964; Hon MA Univ of Leicester 1963; Hon FRCA, RDI 1971, FRSA 1971; *Recreations* landscape gardening, painting; *Style—* Gerald Benney, Esq, CBE, RDI; ✉ The Old Rectory, Cholderton, Salisbury, Wiltshire SP4 0DW (tel 01980 629614, fax 01980 629461); 73 Walton Street, London SW3 2HT (tel 020 7589 7002/3, e-mail gerald@gjbenney.com)

BENNINGTON, Prof Geoffrey Peter; s of Jonathan Bennington, of Embsay, N Yorkshire, and Lilian, *née* Lowther; *b* 24 July 1956; *Educ* Chesterfield Sch, St Catherine's Coll Oxford (jr and sr Heath Harrison travelling scholar, MA, DPhil); m 1, 1987 (m dis 1991), Rachel, *née* Bowlby; 1 step s (Louis Collard b 8 July 1986), 1 da (Alice b 15 Aug 1992); *Career* Laming fell Queen's Coll Oxford 1980–82, former prof of French Univ of Sussex (lectr 1983–89, sr lectr 1989–92), dir Centre for Modern French Thought Univ of Sussex 1997; currently Asa Griggs Candler prof of modern French thought Emory Univ; *Books* Sententiousness and the Novel (1985), Lyotard: Writing the Event (1988), Jacques Derrida (1991), Dudding: des noms de Rousseau (1991), Legislations (1994), Interrupting Derrida (2000), Frontiéres Kantiennes (2000); *Recreations* chess, computing, cricket, music (violin); *Style—* Prof Geoffrey Bennington; ✉ e-mail gbennin@emory.edu

BENNION, Francis Alan Roscoe; s of Thomas Roscoe Bennion (d 1968), of Hove, E Sussex, and Ellen Norah, *née* Robinson (d 1986); *b* 2 January 1923; *Educ* John Lyon's Sch Harrow, Univ of St Andrews, Balliol Coll Oxford (Gibbs law scholar, MA); *m* 1, 28 July 1951 (m dis 1975), Barbara Elizabeth, da of Harry Arnold Braendle (d 1964), of Little Hadham, Herts; 3 da (Sarah, Carola, Venetia); m 2, 2 Nov 1977, Mary Anne, wid of William Field, da of Patrick Lynch (d 1962), of Limerick; *Career* WWII Flt Lt Pilot RAFVR 221 Sqdn, Coastal Cmd 1941–46; called to the Bar Middle Temple (Harmsworth scholar) 1951; in practice 1951–53 and 1985–94, now full-time writer; lectr and tutor in law St Edmund Hall Oxford 1951–53, Parly counsel 1953–65 and 1973–75, sec-gen RICS 1965–68, research assoc Oxford Univ Centre for Socio-Legal Studies 1984–; constitutional advsr: Pakistan 1956, Ghana 1959–61, Jamaica 1969–71; govr Coll of Estate Mgmnt 1965–68, co-fndr and first chm Professional Assoc of Teachers 1968–72, fndr and first chm World of Property Housing Tst (now Sanctuary Housing Assoc) 1968–72 (vice-pres 1986–); fndr: Statute Law Soc 1968 (chm 1978–79), Freedom Under Law 1971, Dicey Tst 1973, Towards One World 1979, Statute Law Tst 1991; co-fndr Areopagitica Educnl Tst 1979; chm Oxford City FC 1988–89; *Books* Constitutional Law of Ghana (1962), Professional Ethics (1969), Tangling With The Law (1970), Consumer Credit Control (1976–2001), Consumer Credit Act Manual (1978, 3 edn 1986), Statute Law (1980, 3 edn 1990), Statutory Interpretation (1984, 5 edn 2007), Victorian Railway Days (1989), The Sex Code: Morals for Moderns (1991), Understanding Common Law Legislation (2001), The Blight of Blairism (2002), Sexual Ethics and Criminal Law (2003), Poemotions: Bennion Undraped (collected poems, 2003), Briefing on the Sexual Offences Act 2003 (2003); *Recreations* maintaining my website (with the help of my webmaster); *Clubs* MCC; *Style—* Francis Bennion, Esq; ✉ 29 Pegasus Road, Oxford OX4 6DS (tel 01865 775164, e-mail fbennion@aol.com, website www.francisbennion.com)

BENNISON, Richard; s of Douglas Bennison (d 2000), and Vera, *née* Weaver; *b* 17 April 1958, Windsor, Berks; *Educ* Maidenhead GS; *partner* Francesca Short; 1 s (Timothy b 11 April 1986), 2 da (Clare (twin) b 11 April 1986, Lucy b 9 Sept 1990); *Career* KPMG: trainee chartered accountant 1977, pntr 1991, head of financial servs audit 1997, head Financial Servs Advsy Practice 2003, head of UK audit and memb Bd 2006; govr Motability; ICAEW1981; *Recreations* skiing, sailing, walking; *Style—* Richard Bennison, Esq; ✉ KPMG, 8 Salisbury Square, London EC4Y 8BB (tel 020 7311 8934, fax 020 7311 1623, e-mail richard.bennison@kpmg.co.uk)

BENSON, Sir Christopher John; DL; s of late Charles Woodburn Benson and Catherine Clara, *née* Bishton; *b* 20 July 1933; *Educ* Worcester Cathedral Kings Sch, The Incorporated Thames Nautical Training Coll HMS Worcester; *m* 1960, Margaret Josephine (Jo) (Lady Benson, OBE, JP, DL), da of Ernest Jefferis Bundy; 2 s; *Career* Sub Lt RNVR; chartered surveyor and agricultural auctioneer Worcs, Herefords, Wilts, Dorset and Hants 1953–64; dir Arndale Developments Ltd 1965–69; fndr chm: Dolphin Developments 1969–71, Dolphin Property Ltd 1969–72, Dolphin Farms Ltd 1973; MEPC plc: dir 1974–93, md 1976–88, chm 1988–93; Royal & Sun Alliance Insurance Group plc (formerly Sun Alliance Group plc): dir 1988–98, dep chm 1992–93 and 1997–98, chm 1993–97; chm: LDDC 1984–88, Reedpack Ltd 1989–90, The Boots Co plc 1990–94, The Housing Corp 1990–94, Costain plc 1993–96, Albright and Wilson 1995–99, Bradford Particle Design plc 1999–2002, Cross London Rail Links Ltd (Crossrail) 2001–04; dep chm Thorn Lighting Group plc 1994–98; dir: House of Fraser plc 1982–86, Royal Opera House Covent Garden Ltd 1984–92, Eredene Capital Ltd 2006–; pres Br Property Fedn 1981–83, pres London C of C 2000–02, hon vice-pres Nat Fedn of Housing Assocs 1994–; chm: Civic Tst 1985–90, Property Advsy Gp to Dept of the Environment 1988–90, Steering Ctee British Red Cross Soc 1994–95, Funding Agency for Schools 1994–97, Coram Family 2005–, Stratford (E London) Renaissance Partnership; memb: Cncl Marlborough Coll 1982–90, Advsy Bd RA 1987–90; lay memb The Take Over Panel 1994–2003; tstee: Metropolitan Police Museum 1986–, Royal Flying Doctor Serv of Australia Friends in the UK 2005–; pres Nat Deaf Children's Soc 1994–; vice-pres: Royal Soc of Arts 1992–97, Macmillan Cancer Relief 1992–; patron Changing Faces 1993–; lay govr Royal London Hosp Med Coll 1993–95, govr Inns of Court Sch of Law 1996–2001 (princ 2000); lay canon Salisbury Cathedral 2000–; Past Master Co of Watermen and Lightermen; Liveryman: Guild of Air Pilots and Air Navigators, Worshipful Co of Gold and Silver Wyre Drawers, Worshipful Co of Chartered Surveyors; hon bencher Middle Temple 1984; hon fell Wolfson Coll Cambridge 1990; Hon DSc: City Univ 2000, Univ of Bradford 2001; FRICS, FRSA 1987, Hon FRCPath 1992, Hon FCIOB 1992; *Recreations* farming, aviation, opera, swimming (Worcs co diving champion 1949); *Clubs* Garrick, City Livery, Naval, RAC, Australian (Sydney); *Style—* Sir Christopher Benson; ✉ Pauls Dene House, Castle Road, Salisbury SP1 3RY; Flat 2, 50 South Audley Street, London W1K 2QE (e-mail sircjbenson@btconnect.com)

BENSON, David Holford; s of Lt-Col Sir Reginald (Rex) Lindsay Benson, DSO, MVO, MC (d 1968), of Singleton, W Sussex, and Leslie, *née* Foster (d 1981); *b* 26 February 1938; *Educ* Eton, Madrid; *m* 1964, Lady Elizabeth Mary, *née* Charteris, da of 12 Earl of Wemyss and (8 of) March, KT, JP; 1 s, 2 da; *Career* merchant banker; with Shell International 1957–63; Kleinwort Benson Group plc (latterly Dresdner Kleinwort Wasserstein): joined 1963, vice-chm 1989–92, non-exec dir 1992–98; sr advsr Fleming Family & Partners 2001–, chm Charter European Tst plc 1992–2003; non-exec dir: BG plc 1988–2004, Wemyss and March Estate Co, Daniel Thwaites plc 1998–2006, Murray

Int Investment Tst plc, The Rouse Co (NYSE listed co) until 2004, Dover Corporation (NYSE listed co); chm Charities Official Investment Fund (COIF) 1985–2005; chm of tstees Edward James Fndn (tstee 1995–), tstee The Phoenix Tst 1996–2001; *Recreations* painting; *Clubs* White's, ESU; *Style*— David Benson, Esq; ✉ Fleming Family & Partners, Ely House, 37 Dover Street, London W1S 4NJ

BENSON, Glenwyn; *Educ* Univ of Cambridge, Havard Univ, Charles Univ Prague, Stanford Univ (exec prog); *m* 1 s, 1 da; *Career* early work on The London Programme and documentary features rising to dep ed Weekend World LWT; BBC: ed On the Record, ed Panorama 1992–94, cmmr Adult Educn 1994–97, head of Science 1997–2000, controller Specialist Factual 2000–01, jt dir Factual and Learning 2001–03, memb Exec Ctee 2001–, controller Factual TV 2003–; *Style*— Mrs Glenwyn Benson; ✉ Room 6045, BBC Television Centre, Wood Lane, London W12 7RJ

BENSON, (John) Graham; s of Marshall Benson, of Stanmore, Middx, and Beatrice, *née* Stein; *b* 29 April 1946; *Educ* Central Foundation Boys' GS London; *m* 13 May 1978, Christine Margaret, *née* Fox; 1 da (Fay Cecily b 1 Nov 1983); *Career* stage mangr in theatre 1965–68, TV prodn mangr and assoc prodr Drama Plays Dept BBC 1968–76; prodr: Premiere Films, BBC and other TV drama 1976–78; Fox for Euston Films 1979; Euro prodn exec The Robert Stigwood Group 1980–82, freelance/independent prodr 1982–86, md Consolidated Productions 1986, controller of drama for TVS and dir Telso Communications 1987–92, chm and chief exec Blue Heaven Productions Ltd (prodrs of The Ruth Rendell Mysteries) 1992–; dir: Clivia Ltd (film financiers) 1998–2001, PrimeEnt plc 2001–02; dir corporate and creative strategy LAMU Entertainment Gp London and Bombay 2006–; freelance prodr many films incl: Thank You Comrades (BBC1) 1978, A Hole in Babylon (BBC1) 1978, Outside Edge (LWT) 1982, Red Monarch (theatrical feature, Channel 4) 1982, Meantime (Central/Channel 4) 1983, Charlie (Central) 1983, Honest Decent and True (BBC2) 1984, Coast to Coast (BBC1) 1984; chm: BAFTA 1985–87 (memb Cncl 1980–93), PACT 1996–98 (memb Cncl 1991–2005), TV12 IOW 1998–2002, Media Circus Gp plc 1999–2001, Headwater Cross Media plc 2000–01, Screen South 2002–, Bunbury Gp Ltd 2003–07, Trinorth Ltd 2004–, Directors' Cut Ltd 2006–07; memb: American Advisory Gp DTI 1996–2003, Markets Gp Br Trade Int 1998–2001, Marshall Aid Commemoration Cmmn 1998–2004 (chm ARM Ctee 2004–), UKTI Creative Export Gp 2000–; exec conslt Sunday Times Oxford Literary Festival 2005–, UK advsr Banff World TV Festival 1996–2003 and 2006–07; Hon DLitt Southampton Solent Univ 2003; FRSA 1987, FRTS 2000; *Recreations* food, drink, literature, jazz, opera, cricket, travel, walking; *Clubs* Savile, Surrey CCC, Ventnor CC, Ventnor Yacht; *Style*— Graham Benson, Esq; ✉ mobile 07786 448854, e-mail fcgbenson@aol.com

BENSON, John Trevor; QC (2001); s of Trevor Benson (d 1985), and Ruth, *née* Oliver (d 2004); *b* 22 January 1955, Oxford; *Educ* Helsby County GS, Univ of Liverpool (LLB); *m* Sheila, *née* Riordan; 3 c (Kate b 17 Jan 1988, Jack, Lily (twins) b 22 Nov 1991); *Career* barr; recorder 1998–, head of chambers Atlantic Chambers 2006– (also practising from Chambers of Lord Gifford QC); *Recreations* Liverpool FC, Italy, wine; *Style*— John Benson, Esq, QC; ✉ Ashburnham, 7 Knowsley Road, Cressington Park, Liverpool L19 0PF (tel 0151 494 1322, e-mail johntbenson@hotmail.com); Atlantic Chambers, 4–6 Cook Street, Liverpool L2 9QU (tel 0151 236 4421, fax 0151 236 1559, e-mail johnbenson@atlanticchambers.co.uk); 1 Mitre Court Buildings, Temple, London EC4Y 7BS (tel 020 7452 8400)

BENSON, Hon Michael D'Arcy; yr s of Baron Benson, GBE (Life Peer; d 1995), and Anne Virginia, *née* Macleod; *b* 23 May 1943; *Educ* Eton; *m* 1969, Rachel Candia Woods; 2 da (Catherine Rachel b 1971, Harriet Anne b 1974), 1 s (Charles D'Arcy b 1976); *Career* memb Research Dept L Messel & Co (Stockbrokers) 1965–67 (clerk on dealing floor 1963–65); Lazard Brothers & Co Ltd: joined 1967, dir Lazard Securities Ltd 1978 (head Private Client Dept and admin dir 1980), dir Lazard Brothers 1980–85, jt md Lazard Securities Ltd 1980, dir Lazard Securities (Jersey) Ltd 1981–85, dir Lazard Bros & Co (Jersey) Ltd 1981–85, dir Lazard Securities (Hong Kong) Ltd 1984–85, dir Lazard Bros & Co (Guernsey) Ltd 1984–85; md Scimitar Asset Management Ltd (London) 1985–92; dir: Standard Chartered Merchant Bank Ltd 1985, Gracechurch Nominees Ltd 1985–92, Scimitar Asset Management (CI) Ltd 1986, Scimitar Global Asset Management Ltd 1986–92, Scimitar Asset Management Asia Ltd 1986–92, Scimitar Worldwide Selection Fund Ltd 1986–92, Scimitar Asset Management (Singapore) Ltd 1988–92; chm: Scimitar Asset Management Ltd 1985–91, Scimitar Unit Trust Managers Ltd 1989–92; dir: Chartered Financial Holdings Ltd 1990, Capital House Investment Management 1992–93, Capital House Asia 1992–93, Capital House (Singapore) Ltd 1992–93; chief exec: Asia Pacific Region Invesco Group 1994–96, Invesco Global Asset Management 1996–2001; vice-chm Amvescap plc 2001–05 (dir 1994–); currently non-exec chm Ashmore Gp plc; non-exec dir: Morse plc 2007–, Invesco Japan Discovery Tst plc; dir: Border Asset Mgmnt Ltd, Badanloch Estates Ltd; *Style*— The Hon Michael Benson; ✉ Grange Farm, Westow, York YO60 7NJ (tel 01653 658296)

BENSON, Neil; s of Eric Benson (d 2000), and Vera, *née* Mower (d 1976); *b* 22 October 1954; *Educ* City GS Sheffield; *m* Joan Philippa; 2 s (Joseph Samuel b 29 Oct 1992, Rory Christopher b 15 March 1994), 1 da (Meredith Hope b 12 May 1995); *Career* The Star Sheffield 1974–79 (trainee reporter, sr reporter, news desk asst, news sub ed), Daily Express Manchester 1979–85 (features sub ed, sr news sub ed), Telegraph & Argus Bradford 1985–88 (features ed, asst ed), dep ed Chronicle & Echo Northampton Jan-June 1989, dep ed Telegraph & Argus Bradford 1989–91, ed and dir Coventry Evening Telegraph 1991–93, ed Newcastle Evening Chronicle 1993–96, new business devpt dir Newcastle Chronicle & Journal Ltd 1998–99 (exec ed daily newspapers 1996–98), md Gazette Media Co 1999–2001, editorial dir Trinity Mirror Regionals 2001–; chm Guild of Eds Northern Region 1996–97, chm Hold the Front Page, memb Bd Soc of Eds (vice-pres 2002–03, pres 2003–04); *Recreations* road running, supporting Leeds RLFC and Newcastle United; *Style*— Neil Benson, Esq; ✉ Trinity Mirror plc, Kingsfield Court, Chester Business Park, Chester CH4 9RE (e-mail neil.benson@trinitymirror.com)

BENSON, His Hon Judge Peter Charles; s of Robert Benson (d 1970), of Baildon, W Yorks, and Dorothy, *née* Cartman; *b* 16 June 1949; *Educ* Bradford GS, Univ of Birmingham (BSocSc); *Career* called to the Bar Middle Temple 1975, in practice NE Circuit 1975–, junior of NE Circuit 1979–80, recorder of the Crown Court 1995–2001 (asst recorder 1991–95), circuit judge 2001–; memb Parole Bd 2003–; *Recreations* golf, reading, conversation; *Clubs* Ilkley Golf, Ilkley Bowling, Ganton Golf, Bradford, East India; *Style*— His Hon Judge Peter Benson; ✉ Bradford Crown Court, Exchange Square, Bradford BD1 1JA

BENSON, Hon Peter Macleod; LVO (2001); er s of Baron Benson, GBE (Life Peer; d 1995), and Anne Virginia, *née* Macleod (d 1998); *b* 1940; *Educ* Eton, Univ of Edinburgh (MA); *m* 1, 1970 (m dis 1987), Hermione Jane Boulton; 2 da (Candida Jane b 1972, Hermione Emily b 1980), 1 s (Edward Henry b 1975); m 2, 3 Aug 1989 (m dis 2003), Señora Maria de los Angeles Martin, da of Don Victoriano Martinez Latasa; *Career* CA; ptnr PricewaterhouseCoopers (formerly Coopers & Lybrand before merger) 1971–2000; chm Sense Worldwide Gp 2003–; dir: Pixology plc 2003–, UK Biobank Ltd 2004–, Spectrum Interactive plc 2005–; memb Bd of Mgmnt RNT 1991–2003 (chm RNT Fndn 2003–), dir English Nat Ballet Sch 1996–, dir Chichester Festival Theatre 2002–; tstee Edward James Fndn 2002–; *Recreations* shooting, golf, theatre; *Clubs* Brooks's, Hurlingham, MCC, Tandridge Golf; *Style*— The Hon Peter M Benson, LVO; ✉ 2 King's Quay, Chelsea Harbour, London SW10 0UX

BENSON, Richard Anthony; QC (1995); s of Douglas Arthur Benson (d 1983), and Muriel Alice, *née* Fairfield (d 1984); *b* 20 February 1946; *Educ* Wrekin Coll, Inns of Court Sch of Law; *m* 1, 15 Sept 1967 (m dis 1996), Katherine Anne, da of Tom Anderson Smith, of Highfield, Glos; 1 s (Jake Alexander Fairfield b 22 Feb 1970), 2 da (Amy Rebecca b 26 April 1972, Chloe Kate b 25 Aug 1981); m 2, 29 May 2000 (m dis 2004), Sarah, da of Roger and Jenette Gaunt, of Montpon-Menesterol, France; 3 s (Max Jean-Luc b 1 Feb 1997, Oscar Morgan b 12 Jan 1999, Archie Richard b 6 Dec 2001), 1 da (Elysia Naomi b 23 Nov 2000); m 3, 23 Sept 2006, Dr Alison Jane Simmons, da of Michael and Barbara Simmons, of Roxburghshire, Scotland; *Career* called to the Bar Inner Temple 1974; in practice Midland & Oxford Circuit, asst recorder 1990, recorder 1995–; *Recreations* flying, offshore cruising, drama, after dinner speaking; *Clubs* British Airways Flying, Bar Yacht, HTC; *Style*— Richard Benson, Esq, QC; ✉ Citadel Chambers, 190 Corporation Street, Birmingham B4 6QD (tel 012 123850, e-mail rabqc@btopenworld.com)

BENSON, His Hon Judge Richard Stuart Alistair; *b* 23 November 1943; *Educ* Univ of Nottingham (BA); *Career* called to the Bar Gray's Inn 1968; in practice Midland & Oxford Circuit 1968–93, recorder 1991–93, circuit judge (Midland & Oxford Circuit) 1993–; *Style*— His Hon Judge Benson

BENSON, Prof Roger Smith; s of Joseph Benson, and Hilda Benson; *Educ* Haslingden GS, Univ of Swansea, UMIST (MSc, PhD); *m* Kathlyn; 2 s (Richard, Martyn), 1 da (Louise); *Career* works control engr ICI Nylon Works Ardeer 1971–78, control mangr Engrg Dept ICI 1978–83, new venture mangr ICI 1983–86, electrical mangr ICI Gp Control 1986–90, engrg technol mangr ICI Engrg 1990–91, chief engr Int Engrg Technol 1991–93, with Innovation Unit DTI 1993–95, chief engr ICI Mfrg Technol 1995–99, dir EUTECH Engrg Servs 1999–2001, technol dir ABB 2001–; visiting prof: Interdisciplinary Res Centre for Process Systems Engrg ICSTM London 1993, Dept of Chem Engrg Univ of Newcastle upon Tyne 1995–, Dept of Engrg Univ of Teesside 1996–; delivered numerous lectures and keynote addresses at confs worldwide; chm Centre for Process Analytics and Control Techol (CPACT) Foresight Centre 1998–, memb UK Mfrg Foresight Gp 1997–99, memb EPSRC User Gp 2000–; DTI judge Britain's Best Factory Award 1993–; finalist Prince of Wales Award for Industrial Innovation and Prodn 1984; memb Fédération Européenne d'Associations Nationales d'Ingénieurs (FEANI) 1991; CEng 1982, FIChemE 1982, FIEE 1991, FREng 1999; *Publications* Bench Marking in the Process Industries (jtly, 1999); also author of reports and papers; *Recreations* skiing, golf, mountain walking; *Style*— Prof Roger Benson, FREng; ✉ 8 Church Garth, Great Smeaton, Northallerton, North Yorkshire DL6 2HW (tel 01609 881366, e-mail rogersbenson@btclick.com); ABB, Belasis Hall Technology Park, PO Box 99, Teesside TS23 4YS (tel 01642 372379, fax 01642 372111, mobile 07860 907441, e-mail roger.benson@gb.abb.com)

BENSON, Stephen John; *b* 5 November 1955; *Educ* Bishop Vesey GS Sutton Coldfield, Univ of Manchester, Chester Coll of Law; *m* Gillian; 2 da (Helen Louise b 25 Sept 1988, Emma Clare b 3 Aug 1990), 1 s (Nicholas Edward b 6 Oct 1995); *Career* slr; sr ptnr Cobbetts LLP 2005– (former head Property Practice Area); memb Cncl CBI NW, membBd Br American Business Cncl (chm NW Eng); memb Law Soc; MInstD; FRSA; *Recreations* keeping fit, outdoor pursuits, motor cars, contemporary art; *Clubs* Mere Golf and Country; *Style*— Stephen Benson, Esq; ✉ Cobbetts LLP, 58 Mosley Street, Manchester M2 3HZ (tel 0845 165 5232, fax 0845 166 6704, e-mail stephen.benson@cobbetts.com)

BENT, Dr Margaret Hilda; da of late Horace Bassington, and Miriam, *née* Simpson; *b* 23 December 1940; *Educ* Haberdashers' Aske's, Girton Coll Cambridge (organ scholar, MusB, MA, PhD); *Career* sr lectr Goldsmiths Coll London 1974–75 (lectr 1972–74), prof Brandeis Univ 1976–81 (visiting prof 1975–76, chm Dept of Music 1978–79 and 1980–81), prof Princeton Univ 1981–92 (chm Dept of Music 1986–90), sr res fell All Souls Coll Oxford 1992–; Fowler Hamilton visiting res fell Christ Church Coll Oxford 1990–91, Guggenheim fell 1983–84, Dent medal Int Musicological Soc 1979; author of numerous pubns and articles on late-medieval music; hon memb American Acad of Arts and Sciences 1994, memb American Musicological Soc (pres 1984–86, corresponding memb 1995–), invited memb Academia Europea 1995; Hon DMus Univ of Glasgow 1997, Hon DFA Notre Dame Univ 2002; FBA 1993, FRHistS 1995, FSA 2002; *Style*— Dr Margaret Bent, FBA; ✉ All Souls College, Oxford OX1 4AL (tel 01865 279379, fax 01865 279299)

BENTALL, (Leonard) Edward; DL (Greater London 1999); s of (Leonard Edward) Rowan Bentall, DL (d 1993), and his 1 w, Adelia Elizabeth, *née* Hawes (d 1986); ggs of Frank Bentall, Fndr of Bentalls (d 1923); *b* 26 May 1939; *Educ* Stowe; *m* 1964, Wendy Ann, *née* Daniel; 3 da; *Career* articled clerk Dixon Wilson Tubbs & Gillett 1958–64, CA 1964; Bentalls PLC: joined 1965, merchandise controller 1968, merchandise dir Household and Furnishing Gp 1972, merchandise dir 1974, jt md 1977, md 1978, chm and md 1982, chm and chief exec 1990, chm 1992–2001; non-exec dir: Associated Independent Stores Ltd 1979–82, Kingston Hosp Tst 1990–98, Radio Riverside Ltd 1996–99; pres Textile Benevolent Assoc 1991–95; vice-pres Surrey PGA; govr: Brooklands Tech Coll 1981–90 (vice-chm Governing Body and chm Fin Ctee 1989–90), Kingston Coll of FE, Kingston GS 1992–2002; chm Bd Shooting Star Tst Children's Hospice Appeal 2000–03; tstee and memb Exec Ctee Kingston and Dist Steadfast Sea Cadet Corps (chm 1993–), tstee The Spirit of Normandy Tst 2000; steward Nat Greyhound Racing Club 1998–; FInstD; *Clubs* MCC, Surrey CCC, Saints and Sinners, Naval; *Style*— Edward Bentall, Esq; ✉ Runnymede, Sandpit Hall Road, Chobham, Surrey GU24 8AN (tel 01276 858256, fax 01276 855813, e-mail lebentall@aol.com)

BENTATA, (Morris) David Albert; s of Robert Victor Bentata (d 1961), of Didsbury, Manchester, and Joyce Ethel, *née* Weinberg; *b* 21 July 1938; *Educ* Blundell's, ChCh Oxford (MA); *m* 20 Feb 1964 (m dis 1991), Alison Jessica, da of Christopher Henley Boyle Gilroy, of Boundstone, Surrey; 1 da (Victoria b 10 Feb 1966), 1 s (Robert b 5 Nov 1968); *Partner* Linda Joan Smith; *Career* Nat Serv: enlisted N Staffs Regt 1957, OCS Eaton Hall and Mons 1957–58, cmmnd 2 Lt Intelligence Corps 1958, serv BAOR 1958–59, cmmnd Lt Intelligence Corps (TA) 1959, RARO 1963; md M Bentata & Son Ltd 1962–67, fndr int mangr Hill Samuel & Co Ltd 1969–72 (investment analyst 1968–69), int investment mangr Charterhouse Japhet Ltd 1972–79, dir Charterhouse Investment Management Ltd 1986–88 (int dir 1979–86), md Charterhouse Portfolio Managers Ltd 1986–88, fndr chm Bentata Associates Ltd 1988–; dir: Pegasus Financial Holdings Ltd 1989–92, INVESCO Perpetual European Investment Trust plc (formerly Murray European Investment Trust plc and European Project Investment Trust plc) 1990– (dep chm 2004–), Liberty Funds Europe (formerly Newport Capital Ltd) 1991–2003, Marcher Diagnostics plc 1996–98, DLSN Ltd 1997, Optimay Corporation Inc 1997–98, Camlab Ltd 1998–2005 (chm 2000–02), Lexicon Data Ltd 2004–, Lemdex Ltd 2006; chm: Sage Partners Ltd 1991–95, MMS Petroleum Services Ltd (formerly Gandalf Explorers International Ltd) 1996–98 (fndr fin dir 1989), Marine & Mercantile Securities plc 1996– (dir 1994–), VI Group plc 1998–99, Knowledge Mgmnt Software plc 1999–2001, Popkin Software & Systems Inc 2000–01, K M Ventures plc 2000–01, Composite Metal Technologies plc 2006; dep chm Composite Metal Technology Ltd 2002– (dir 1998–); elected Lloyd's underwriter 1976; vice-chm and chm Stoke d'Abernon Residents' Assoc 1969–77, memb Ctee Oxshott Cons Assoc 1969–72, vice-pres Oxford Univ Rifle Club 2002; memb The Sherlock Holmes Soc of London (memb Cncl 1992); Freeman City of London 1984, Liveryman Worshipful Co of Feltmakers 1983 (Steward 1989–91, memb Ct of Assts 1993, Fourth Warden 1998, Third Warden 1999, Renter Warden 2000, Upper Warden 2001, Master 2002), Liveryman Worshipful Co of Gunmakers 2004; ASIP 1969 (formerly AIIMR), FInstD 1988, FRGS 1988, FRSA 1995; *Recreations* full-bore rifle shooting, travel, dancing the minuet (Covent Garden Minuet Co); *Clubs* City of London, Athenaeum; *Style*— David Bentata, Esq

B

BENTHALL, Jonathan Charles Mackenzie; s of Sir (Arthur) Paul Benthall, KBE (d 1992), and Mary Lucy, *née* Pringle (d 1988); *b* 12 September 1941; *Educ* Eton (King's scholar), King's Coll Cambridge (MA); *m* 23 Oct 1975, Hon Zamira, da of Baron Menuhin, OM, KBE (Life Peer, d 1999); 2 s (Dominic b 1976, William b 1981), 1 step s (Lin b 1964); *Career* sec ICA 1971–73, dir RAI 1974–2000; ed Anthropology Today 1985–2000 (RAIN 1974–84), hon research fell Dept of Anthropology UCL 1994–; advsr on Islamic charities to Swiss Federal Dept of Foreign Affrs 2005–; chair Int NGO Trg & Research Centre 1998–2003; tstee Alliance of Religions & Conservation 1997–2004; Save the Children Fund: former memb UK Child Care Ctee, memb Cncl, memb Overseas Advsy Ctee, memb Assembly 1990–98; Anthropology in Media Award American Anthropological Assoc 1993, Patron's Medal RAI 2001; memb Assoc of Social Anthropologists 1983; Chevalier de l'Ordre des Arts et des Lettres (France) 1973; *Books* Science and Technology in Art Today (1972), The Body Electric - Patterns of Western Industrial Culture (1976), Disasters, Relief and the Media (1993), The Best of Anthropology Today (ed, 2002), The Charitable Crescent: Politics of Aid in the Muslim World (jtly, 2003); *Recreations* listening to music, swimming, mountain walking, books, writing light verse; *Clubs* Athenaeum; *Style—* Mr Jonathan Benthall; ✉ Downingbury Farmhouse, Pembury, Tunbridge Wells, Kent TN2 4AD

BENTHAM, Howard Lownds; QC (1996); s of William Foster Bentham (d 1982), and Elsie, *née* Lownds (d 1982); *b* 26 February 1948; *Educ* Malvern Coll, Univ of Liverpool (LLB); *m* Elizabeth, da of Robert Pickering Owen; 1 s (Robert b 29 Dec 1982); *Career* called to the Bar Gray's Inn 1970; recorder 1996– (asst recorder 1985); *Recreations* watching wildlife, rebuilding, driving, racing Lotus cars; *Style—* Howard Bentham, Esq, QC; ✉ Peel Court Chambers, 45 Hardman Street, Manchester M3 3PL (tel 0161 832 3791)

BENTINCK, Timothy; *see:* Portland, 12 Earl of

BENTLEY, Alexander Rufus; s of William Herbert Bentley, of London, and Carole-Ann Butler-Howe; *b* 2 February 1966; *Educ* Woolverstone Hall Sch Ipswich, Westminster Hotel Sch (Dip Professional Cooking); *Career* chef; Connaught Hotel London (under Michel Bourdin) 1986–89, Capital Hotel London (under Philip Britten, *qv*) 1989–91, St James Restaurant Johannesburg Sun and Towers 1991–93, Villa del Palazzo Palace Hotel Sun City (under Gaetano Ascione) 1993–94, Bill Bentley's London 1993–97, Monsieur Max Hampton 1997–2004 (Best French Restaurant London Carlton Awards 1999, one Michelin Star 1999, Gault Millau 2000, 7 out of 10 Good Food Guide 2003, 3 AA Rosettes 2003), Petersham Hotel Richmond 2004–; *Style—* Alexander Bentley, Esq; ✉ The Petersham, Nightingale Lane, Richmond, Surrey TW10 6UZ

BENTLEY, Rt Rev David Edward Bentley; s of William Edward Bentley (d 1980), of Gorleston, Norfolk, and Florence Maud Marion, *née* Dalgleish (d 1978); *b* 7 August 1935; *Educ* Great Yarmouth GS, Univ of Leeds (BA), Westcott House Cambridge; *m* 5 Sept 1962, Clarice May, da of Reginald Lahmers (d 1964), of KirkBride, Isle of Man; 2 da (Katharine (Mrs Martin Gorick) b 1963, Rachel (Mrs Michael Harrison) b 1964), 2 s (Simon b 1964, Matthew b 1966); *Career* Nat Serv 1956–58, 2 Lt 5 Regt RHA; curate: St Ambrose Bristol 1960–62, Holy Trinity with St Mary Guildford 1962–66; rector: All Saints, Headley 1966–73, Esher 1973–86; rural dean Emly 1977–82; hon canon Guildford Cathedral 1980–86, chm Diocesan Cncl of Social Responsibility 1980–86, bishop of Lynn 1986–93, bishop of Gloucester 1993–2003, hon asst bishop Dio of Lichfield 2003–; chm: ACCM Candidates Ctee 1987–91, ABM Recruitment and Selection Ctee 1991–93, ABM Ministry Development and Deployment Ctee 1993–98, Deployment, Remuneration and Conditions of Service Ctee 1999–2002, Church of England Pensions Bd 2002–06; warden All Hallows Convent Ditchingham 1990–93; took seat in House of Lords 1998; Hon PhD Univ of Glos 2002; *Recreations* music, theatre, sport, walking; *Clubs* MCC, Warwickshire CCC; *Style—* The Rt Rev David Bentley; ✉ 19 Gable Croft, Lichfield, Staffordshire WS14 9RY (tel 01543 419376)

BENTLEY, His Hon Judge David Ronald; QC (1984); s of Edgar Norman Bentley (d 1982), and Hilda, *née* Thirlwall (d 1959); *b* 24 February 1942; *Educ* King Edward VII Sch Sheffield, UCL (LLB, LLM), Univ of Sheffield (PhD); *m* 1978, Christine Elizabeth, da of Alec Stewart (d 1978); 2 s (Thomas b 1985, David b 1989); *Career* called to the Bar Gray's Inn 1969 (Macaskie scholar); recorder of the Crown Court 1985–88, circuit judge (NE Circuit) 1988–, designated civil judge for S Yorks 1999–; *Publications* Select Cases from the Twelve Judges Notebooks (1997), English Criminal Justice in the Nineteenth Century (1998), Victorian Men of Law (2000), The Sheffield Hanged (2002), The Sheffield Murders (2004); *Recreations* legal history, watching Sheffield United FC; *Style—* His Hon Judge David Bentley, QC; ✉ c/o North Eastern Circuit Office, West Riding House, Albion Street, Leeds LS1 5AA

BENTLEY, Prof George; s of George Bentley (d 1964), and Doris, *née* Blagden; *b* 19 January 1936; *Educ* Rotherham GS, Univ of Sheffield (MB ChB, ChM, DSc); *m* 4 June 1960, Ann Gillian, da of Herbert Hutchings (d 1953); 1 da (Sarah b 2 Dec 1962), 2 s (Paul b 3 March 1964, Stephen b 2 March 1966); *Career* lectr in anatomy Univ of Birmingham 1961–62, surgical registrar Sheffield Royal Infirmary 1963–65, orthopaedic registrar Orthopaedic Hosp Oswestry 1965–67, sr orthopaedic registrar Nuffield Orthopaedic Centre Oxford 1967–69, instr in orthopaedics Univ of Pittsburgh USA 1969–70, Univ of Oxford 1970–76 (lectr, sr lectr, clinical reader in orthopaedics); prof of orthopaedics: Univ of Liverpool 1976–82, Univ of London 1982–, Inst of Orthopaedics; hon conslt orthopaedic surgn Royal Nat Orthopaedic Hosp 1982–, dir Inst of Orthopaedics UC and Middx Sch of Med 1992–2000; pres: Br Orthopaedic Assoc 1991–92 (vice-pres 1990–91), RCS 2004– (memb Cncl RCS 1992–, vice-pres 2001–03), EFORT (Euro Fedn of Nat Associations of Orthopaedics and Traumatology) 2004–05 (vice-pres 2002–03); memb d'honaire French Soc for Orthopaedics and Traumatology 1999; FRCS 1968, FMedSci 1999, FRCSEd 2000; *Books* Mercer's Orthopaedic Surgery (jt ed, 1983, new edn 1996), Rob and Smith Operative Surgery - Orthopaedics Vols I and II (conslt ed, 1991); *Recreations* music, tennis, golf, horology; *Style—* Prof George Bentley; ✉ 19 High Street, Emberton, Buckinghamshire MK46 5JB (tel 01234 714956); University Department of Orthopaedics, Institute of Orthopaedics, Royal National Orthopaedic Hospital, Stanmore, Middlesex HA7 4LP (tel 020 8909 5532, fax 020 8954 3036)

BENTLEY, Keven Arthur; s of Royden Eccles Bentley (d 1992), of London, and Kaye, *née* Crichton Young; *b* 16 June 1958, Bangkok, Thailand; *Educ* Bradfield Coll Reading; *m* 1, 1987 (m dis 1992), Nicola Jane Rivière; m 2, 1992, Katherine Anne, *née* Palmer; 4 da (Kinvara b 24 Nov 1992, Olivia b 26 Aug 1994, Cordelia b 10 Oct 1995, Athena b 11 Mar 1998), 1 s (Edward b 22 Nov 2004); *Career* Lloyds broker C E Heath & Co 1979–84, Lloyds broker and dir Byas Mosley & Co 1984–96, fndr and chm Lonsdale Insurance Brokers 1996–; fndr and tstee Ackroyd Tst 1995–; Freeman City of London, Liveryman Worshipful Co of Carpenters 1998; memb Inst Registered Insurance Brokers; *Recreations* tennis, having children and gardening; *Clubs* City of London Club, Hurlingham; *Style—* Keven Bentley, Esq; ✉ 3 Whaddon House, Williams Mews, London SW1X 9HG (tel 07768 195068, fax 020 7816 0029); Lonsdale Insurance Brokers, 7 Birchin Lane, London EC3V 9BW (tel 020 7816 0028, e-mail keven.bentley@lonsdaleib.com)

BENTLEY, Phillip (Phil); s of Alan William Bentley, of Leeds, and Betty Bentley; *b* 14 January 1959, Bradford, W Yorks; *Educ* Woodhouse Grove Sch Bradford, Univ of Oxford (MA), INSEAD (MBA); *m* 25 June 1988, Mhairi McEwan, *qv*; 1 s, 1 da; *Career* finance and accountancy with BP 1980–95 (UK, China, US and Egypt), gp treas Grand Metropolitan 1995–97, gp treas and dir of risk mgmnt Diageo 1997–99, finance dir Guinness-UDV 1999–2000; Centrica plc: gp finance dir 2000–, md Europe 2004–; non-exec dir Kingfisher plc 2002–; MCT, fell Chartered Inst of Mgmnt Accountants; *Recreations* rugby, golf, wine, riding, skiing; *Style—* Phil Bentley, Esq; ✉ Centrica plc, Millstream, Maidenhead Road, Windsor SL4 5GD (tel 01753 494343)

BENTLEY, Rosemary (Rose); da of Donald Bruce Cameron (d 1987), of London, and Ruth Margaret, *née* Watson; *b* 16 February 1961; *Educ* Lady Margaret GS, Wadham Coll Oxford (MA); *m* 27 March 1999, Adam Bentley; 1 da (Leonora b 1993); *Career* news reporter and feature writer City of London Recorder 1982–84, PR conslt Communications Arc Ltd (subsid of General Advertising Ltd) 1984–85; Chambers Cox PR Ltd: sr PR conslt 1985–86, account dir 1986–89, dir 1989–93, md 1993–; memb Br Guild of Beer Writers 2001; Daily Express Young Sportswriter of the Year 1978; Freeman City of London 2000, Liveryman Worshipful Co of Tin Plate Workers alias Wireworkers 2000; MIPR, MInstD; *Recreations* theatre, cinema, music, drama, short story writing, cookery (finalist BBC Masterchef 1992), wine, literature, travel; *Style—* Ms Rose Bentley; ✉ Chambers Cox PR Ltd, 192–198 Vauxhall Bridge Road, London SW1V 1DX (tel 020 7592 3100)

BENTLEY, Tom; s of Richard Bentley, and Penelope, *née* Cheetham; *b* 7 July 1973, London; *Educ* Raine's Fndn Sch London, Haverstock Sch, Wadham Coll Oxford (BA); *m* 12 Feb 2000, Kylie Kilgour; 2 da (Esther b 5 Dec 2000, Iris b 24 Sept 2004); *Career* researcher Demos 1995–98, special advsr to Rt Hon David Blunkett, MP (as Sec of State for Educn and Employment) 1998–99, dir Demos 1999–2006, exec dir policy and cabinet Victorian Premier's Dept Aust 2006–, assoc dir Aust and NZ Sch of Govt 2006–; tstee: NESTA 2003–06, Community Action Network 1999–2006, Eidos Inst 2006, State Library of Victoria 2006–, Per Capita think tank 2007–; *Publications* Learning beyond the Classroom (1998), The Adaptive State (2003), Everyday Democracy (2005); *Style—* Tom Bentley, Esq; ✉ c/o Department of Premier and Cabinet, 1 Treasury Place, Melbourne, VIC 3000, Australia (tel +61 9651 5111, e-mail t.bentley@anzsog.edu.au)

BENTLIFF, Georgina Mary; da of D G R Bentliff, and A B Bentliff; *b* 1960; *Educ* James Allen's GS London, Clare Coll Cambridge (MA), Birkbeck Coll London (BSc); *m* Sept 1997, Teige O'Donovan; 2 da (Eleanor b March 1998, Isabella b July 2002), 1 s (Murrough b Jan 2000); *Career* publisher medical books and journals Churchill Livingstone 1986–92, manager medical books publishing Saunders UK 1992–94, dir of medical and health science publishing Hodder Arnold 1994–2004, md Hammersmith Press Limited 2004–, strategic devpt mangr Copyright Licensing Agency; Freeman City of London, memb Worshipful Co of Merchant Taylors; memb RSM; *Recreations* collecting books on Mexican history, especially pre-Colombian; *Style—* Ms Georgina Bentliff; ✉ Hammersmith Press Limited, 496 Fulham Palace Road, London SW6 6JD (tel 020 7736 9132, fax 020 7348 7521, website www.hammersmithpress.co.uk)

BENTON, Joseph Edward (Joe); JP, MP; s of Thomas Benton, and Agnes Benton; *b* 28 September 1933; *Educ* St Monica's Secdy Sch, Bootle Tech Coll; *m* Doris; 4 da; *Career* apprentice fitter 1949, Nat Serv RAF 1955; sometime personnel mangr Pacific Steam Navigation Co, with Girobank 1982–90; MP (Lab) Bootle 1990–; memb: Select Ctee on Energy 1991–92, House of Commons Privileges Ctee 1997–, Educn Sub-Ctee 1997–, Speaker's Panel of Chm 1997–, Br-Irish, Br-Spanish and Br-IOM All-Pty Gps; sometime NW regional Lab whip; cncllr Derby Ward Sefton Borough Cncl 1970–90 (ldr Lab Gp 1985–90), chm Bd of Govrs Hugh Baird Coll of Technol; memb Inst of Linguists, affiliate memb Inst of Personnel Mgmnt; *Recreations* reading, listening to classical music, squash, swimming; *Style—* Joe Benton, Esq, MP; ✉ House of Commons, London SW1A 0AA

BENTOVIM, Dr Arnon; s of Zvi Harry Bentovim (d 1989), and Gladys Rachel, *née* Carengold (d 1985); *b* 24 July 1936; *Educ* St Thomas' Hosp London (MB BS, DPM); *m* 1, 2 April 1958 (m dis 1987), Cecily Anne; 1 da (Ayalah b 1970); m 2, 1989, Marianne; *Career* psychoanalyst, family and child psychiatrist; registrar Maudsley Hosp 1962–66, sr registrar and conslt child psychiatrist Hosps for Sick Children Gt Ormond St 1966–94, hon sr lectr Inst of Child Health 1966–; conslt Tavistock Clinic 1975–94, conslt specialist advsr to House of Commons Select Ctee 1978–79, conslt Huntercombe Manor Hosp 1994–98; fndr: CIBA Fndn Study Gp, Trg Advsy Gp for the Sexual Abuse of Children, first sexual treatment prog in UK at Hosps for Sick Children 1981–94; pubns on: child psychiatry, family therapy, aspects of child abuse; fndr memb: Assoc for Family Therapy, Br Assoc for the Prevention of Child Abuse and Neglect, Inst of Family Therapy; pres Relate 1997, pres Int Family Therapy Assoc 2003–; chm Faithful Fndn, tstee Michael Sieff Fndn 1994; FRCPsych 1966; *Books* Family Therapy, Complimentary Frameworks of Theory and Practice (1984–89), Child Sexual Abuse within the Family - Assessment & Treatment (ed, 1988), Trauma Organised Systems - Physical & Sexual Abuse in the Family (1996), The Family Assessment: Assessment of Family Competance, Strengths and Difficulties (2001), Assessing Support Needs for Adopted Children and Their Families (2006); *Recreations* music (particularly jazz), theatre, opera, travel; *Style—* Dr Arnon Bentovim; ✉ London Child & Family Consultation Service, Pinero House, 115A Harley Street, London W1G 6AR (tel 020 7224 2800, e-mail drbentovim@lcfcs.co.uk)

BENYON, Richard; MP; *Educ* Bradfield Coll, RAC Cirencester (Dip Real Estate Mgmnt); *Career* cmmnd Royal Green Jackets 1980–85; chartered surveyor 1987–, farmer 1990–; cncllr (Cons) Newbury DC 1991–95; Parly candidate (Cons) 1997 and 2001, MP (Cons) Newbury 2005–; *Style—* Richard Benyon, Esq, MP; ✉ House of Commons, London SW1A 0AA (e-mail benyonr@parliament.uk, website www.richardbenyon.com)

BENYON, Thomas Yates; s of Capt Thomas Yates Benyon (d 1958, s of Capt Thomas Yates Benyon (d 1893) and Hon Christina Philippa Agnes, OBE, da of 11 Baron North, JP), and his 2 wife, Joan Ida Walters (d 1982); *b* 13 August 1942; *Educ* Wellington Sch, RMA Sandhurst, Wycliffe Hall Oxford (dip Bible and Theology); *m* 1968, (Olivia) Jane, da of Humphrey Scott Plummer by his w, Hon Pamela, *née* Balfour, da of 2 Baron Kinross, KC; 2 s, 2 da; *Career* former Lt Scots Gds, served Kenya, Muscat; MP (Cons) Abingdon 1979–83; dir Bucks Purchasing Authy; chm: Assoc of Lloyd's Membs 1982–86, Milton Keynes HA 1990–94; chm Guild of Shareholders; fndr Zane - Zimbabwe, a National Emergency; *Publications* London Insurance Insider, Guild Investor, As Easy as ABC (study on electoral reform); *Recreations* music; *Clubs* Pratt's; *Style—* Thomas Benyon, Esq

BENYON, Sir William Richard; kt (1994), DL (1970); s of Vice Adm Richard Benyon, CB, CBE (d 1968, 2 s of Sir John Shelley, 9 Bt, JP, DL, a distant cous of the Shelley Bts who produced the poet, and Marion, da of Richard Benyon), and Eve (d 1995), twin da of Rt Rev Lord William Cecil, sometime Bishop of Exeter (2 s of 3 Marquess of Salisbury); the Adm changed his name to Benyon by Deed Poll on inheriting the Benyon estates of his cous Sir Henry Benyon, Bt; *b* 17 January 1930; *Educ* BRNC Dartmouth; *m* 1957, Elizabeth Ann, da of Vice Adm Ronald Hallifax, CB, CBE (d 1943), of Shedfield, Hants; 2 s (Richard, Edward); 3 da (Catherine, Mary, Susannah); *Career* served RN 1947–56; Courtaulds Ltd 1957–67; MP (Cons): Buckingham 1970–83, Milton Keynes 1983–92; PPS to Paul Channon as Min for Housing 1972–74, oppn whip 1974–77, memb Exec 1922 Ctee 1982–89; JP Berks 1962–77; chm: Peabody Tst 1992–98, Ernest Cook Tst 1992–; hon degree: Open Univ, Univ of Reading; Vice Lord-Lt Berks 1994–2005, High Sheriff Berks 1995; *Clubs* Boodle's, Pratt's, Beefsteak; *Style—* Sir William Benyon, DL; ✉ Englefield House, Englefield, Reading, Berkshire RG7 5EN (tel 0118 930 2221, fax 0118 930 3226, e-mail benyon@englefield.co.uk)

BENZIE, Alan Athol Emslie; s of Athol Emslie Benzie (d 1976), of Aberdeen, and Helen Margaret, *née* Ritchie (d 1980); *b* 5 May 1947; *Educ* Lindisfarne Coll N Wales; *m* 3 June 1971, Penny Jane, da of Albert Victor Maynard; 1 da (Annie b 13 April 1973), 2 s (Toby b 11 Aug 1976, Ollie b 22 Sept 1984); *Career* articled clerk Thornton Baker 1964–69;

B

Peat Marwick Mitchell: Manchester, Johannesburg and London 1969–75; KPMG 1975–: ptnr 1977, head NW region corp fin 1984–95, managing ptnr Manchester 1989–95, UK gen ptnr 1995–, sr regnl ptnr 1996–97, chm Northern Business Area 1997–, memb UK Bd 1999–; chm: Corp Appeals Ctee Christies, K Ventures; memb Educational Leadership Team Business in the Community; FCA (ACA 1970); *Recreations* fishing, shooting, golf, gardening; *Clubs* Wilmslow Golf, Birdsgrove Fly Fishing; *Style*— Alan Benzie, Esq; ✉ KPMG, St James' Square, Manchester M2 6DS (tel 0161 838 4000)

BERCOW, John Simon; MP; s of late Charles Bercow, and of Brenda Bercow; *b* 19 January 1963; *Educ* Finchley Manorhill Sch, Univ of Essex (BA); *m*; 2 s (Oliver b Dec 2003, Freddie b Nov 2005); *Career* credit analyst Hambros Bank 1987–88, public affrs conslt Rowland Sallingbury Casey 1988–95 (board dir 1994–95); special advsr to: chief sec to the Treasy 1995, sec of state for Nat Heritage 1995–96; MP (Cons) Buckingham 1997– (Parly candidate Motherwell S 1987 and Bristol S 1992); oppn spokesman educn and employment 1999–2000, shadow Home Office min 2000–01, shadow chief sec to the Treasy 2001–02, shadow min for work and pensions 2002, shadow sec of state for int devpt 2003–04; cncllr Lambeth BC 1986–90 (dep leader Cons oppn gp 1987–89), nat chm Cons students 1986–87; *Recreations* tennis, reading, cinema, music; *Style*— John Bercow, Esq, MP; ✉ House of Commons, London SW1A 0AA (tel 020 7219 6346)

BERDAL, Prof Mats; s of Eivind and Ester Berdal, of Oslo, Norway; *b* 5 October 1965; *Educ* LSE (BSc), St Antony's Coll Oxford (DPhil); *m* Dr Dominique Jacquin-Berdal (d 2006), da of Paul Jacquin; 1 da (Ingrid b 29 Sept 2001); *Career* res assoc IISS 1992–97 (res fell 1994–97), res fell St Antony's Coll Oxford 1997–2000, dir of studies IISS 2000–03, prof Dept of War Studies Sch of Social Sci and Public Policy KCL 2003–; *Publications* Whither UN Peacekeeping? (1993), Disarmament and Demobilisation after Civil Wars (1996), The New Interventionism 1991–1994: The United Nations Experience in Cambodia, former Yugoslavia and Somalia (jt contrib, 1996), Boutros Ghali's Ambiguous Legacy (published in Survival (vol 41, no 3) 1999), Greed and Grievance: Economic Agendas in Civil Wars (co-ed with David Malone, 2000); *Style*— Prof Mats Berdal; ✉ Department of War Studies, School of Social Science and Public Policy, King's College London, Strand, London WC2R 2LS

BERESFORD, Elisabeth; MBE (1998); da of J D Beresford (the novelist), and Beatrice, *née* Roskams; *b* Paris; *Educ* St Mary's Hall Brighton, Brighton & Hove HS; *m*; 1 da (b 1951), 1 s (b 1956); *Career* author; formerly: shorthand typist CCO, ghost writer, reporter/interviewer Today and Woman's Hour (BBC Radio 4); creator: The Wombles (books and BBC TV series) 1973, The Adventures of Dawdle (ITV series) 1996; numerous other children's books published; Tokyo video award (for film Rosebud), Puffin award (for selling a million copies); dir Craigie Robertson Ltd; chm Aurignoco Ltd Media Services; fndr The Alderney Youth Tst 1982; *Recreations* gardening, entertaining, filming; *Style*— Ms Elisabeth Beresford, MBE; ✉ c/o Juvenilia, Avington, Winchester, Hampshire SO21 1DB (tel 01962 78656)

BERESFORD, Marcus de la Poer; CBE (2003); s of late Anthony de la Poer Beresford, TD, of Harrow-on-the-Hill, Middx, and Mary, *née* Canning; *b* 15 May 1942; *Educ* Harrow, St John's Coll Cambridge (MA); *m* 25 Sept 1965, Jean, da of late H T Kitchener, of Shepreth, Cambs; 2 s (Thomas, William); *Career* Smiths Industries 1960–83 (operating gp md 1979–83), dir and gen mangr Lucas Electronics & Systems 1983–85, md Siemens Plessey Controls Ltd 1985–92, dir Siemens plc 1991–92, dir GKN plc and md GKN Industrial Servs 1992–2001, chief exec GKN plc 2001–02; chm Ricardo plc 2003–; non-exec dir: Spirent plc (formerly Bowthorpe plc) 1999–2006, Cobham plc 2004–; Freeman City of London 1963, Liveryman Worshipful Co of Skinners; FIEE; *Recreations* golf; *Style*— Marcus Beresford, Esq, CBE

BERESFORD, Sir (Alexander) Paul; kt (1990), MP; *b* 6 April 1946; *Educ* Waimea Coll Richmond NZ, Univ of Otago NZ; *m* Julie Haynes; 3 s, 1 da; *Career* dental surgeon; London Borough of Wandsworth: cncllr 1978–94, former chm various ctees, ldr 1983–92; MP (Cons): Croydon Central 1992–97, Mole Valley 1997–; House of Commons: Parly under-sec of state Dept of Environment 1994–97, memb Procedure Select Ctee 1997–2001, memb Tport Local Govt and the Regions Select Ctee 2001– (memb Urban Select Sub-Ctee 2001–), chair All-Pty Gp for SE Tranport Integration; *Recreations* DIY, reading; *Style*— Sir Paul Beresford, MP; ✉ House of Commons, London SW1A 0AA (tel 020 7219 3000)

BERESFORD, Dr Richard Charles; s of Eric Beresford, of Whichford, Warks, and Barbara, *née* Gatenby (d 1989); *b* 25 February 1958; *Educ* Uppingham, Courtauld Inst of Art (BA, PhD), London Business Sch (MBA); *Career* research asst rising to curator of paintings pre 1800 The Wallace Collection 1982–94, curator Dulwich Picture Gallery 1995–97, sr curator (European Art, pre 1900) Art Gallery of New South Wales 1997–; *Publications* A Dance to the Music of Time by Nicolas Poussin (1995), Dulwich Picture Gallery Complete Illustrated Catalogue (1998), The James Fairfax Collection of Old Master Paintings, Drawings and Prints (2003); *Style*— Dr Richard Beresford; ✉ Art Gallery of New South Wales, Art Gallery Road, Sydney 2000, NSW, Australia (tel 00 61 29 225 1700, fax 00 61 29 225 1874, e-mail richardb@ag.nsw.gov.au)

BERESFORD-PEIRSE, Sir Henry Grant de la Poer; 6 Bt (UK 1814), of Bagnall, Waterford; s of Sir Henry Campbell Beresford-Peirse, 5 Bt, CB (d 1972), and Margaret, *née* Grant (d 1995); *b* 7 February 1933; *Educ* Eton, Ontario Agric Coll; *m* 1966, Jadranka, da of Ivan Njerš, of Zagreb; 2 s; *Heir* s, Henry Beresford-Peirse; *Career* investment mgmnt; *Recreations* tennis, golf, country homes in Yorkshire and Portugal; *Style*— Sir Henry Beresford-Peirse, Bt; ✉ Bedale Manor, Bedale, North Yorkshire DL8 1EP (tel 01677 422811); 34 Cadogan Square, London SW1X 0JL (tel 020 7589 1134)

BERG, Adrian; s of Charles Berg, and Sarah, *née* Sorby; *b* 12 March 1929; *Educ* Charterhouse, Gonville & Caius Coll Cambridge (MA), Trinity Coll Dublin (HDipEd), St Martin's Sch of Art, Chelsea Sch of Art (NDD), RCA; *Career* Nat Serv 1947–49; artist; work in permanent collections incl: Arts Cncl of GB, Br Cncl, Br Museum, Euro Parl, Govt Art Collection, Hiroshima City Museum of Contemporary Art, Tate Gallery, Tokyo Metropolitan Art Museum, V&A; RA 1992, Hon FRCA 1994; *Solo Exhibitions* incl: five at Arthur Tooth & Sons Ltd 1964–75, three at Waddington Galleries 1978–83, Waddington Galleries Montreal and Toronto 1979, Hokin Gallery Inc Chicago 1979, Paintings 1955–1980 (Rochdale Art Gallery) 1980, seven at The Piccadilly Gallery 1985–2002, Paintings 1977–1986 (Serpentine Gallery London and Walker Art Gallery Liverpool) 1986, watercolours 1999 (Royal Acad); Adrian Berg: A Sense of Place (Barbican and touring) 1993–94; *Style*— Adrian Berg, Esq, RA; ✉ c/o The Royal Academy of Arts, Burlington House, Piccadilly, London W1J 0BD (tel 020 7300 8000)

BERG, Geraldine Marion (Jodi); JP (Bromley 1989); da of late Jack Rosenberg, of London, and Hilda, *née* Davis; *b* 20 June 1950; *Educ* Copthall Co GS London, Univ of Manchester (LLB); *m* 21 Nov 1971, Steven Berg, s of Samuel Beg; 1 da (Corinne b 20 March 1975), 1 s (Andrew b 22 April 1979); *Career* admitted slr 1974; chair Ravensbourne NHS Tst 1993–98, SE London Probation Serv 1999–2001; ind complaints reviewer: HM Land Registry, Charity Cmmn, Housing Corp, National Archives; Audit Cmmn, NI Land Registers, Youth Justice Agency; past tstee Minerva Educnl Tst and Community Care Enterprises, past govr Newstead Wood Sch; memb Law Soc 1974, assoc memb Br and Irish Ombudsman Assoc 1998; FCIArb 1999, FRSA 2002; *Recreations* enjoying (too rare) time with family and friends, travel, theatre; *Style*— Mrs Jodi Berg; ✉ New Premier House, 150 Southampton Row, London WC1B 5AL (tel 020 7278 6251)

BERG, Robert Vivian Nathaniel; s of Bernard Berg (d 1975), of London, and Zena Berg; *b* 4 June 1947; *Educ* St Paul's, Magdalen Coll Oxford; *m* 1989, Gillian Margaret, da of John Thorn; *Career* KPMG: CA 1973, ptnr 1981–, memb bd 1989–; *Recreations* architecture, art; *Clubs* Athenaeum; *Style*— Robert Berg, Esq

BERGENDAHL, (Carl) Anders; s of Carl Johan Bergendahl (d 1995), of Djursholm, Sweden, and Ingrid Bergendahl (d 1964); *b* 20 March 1952; *Educ* Djursholm's Samskola, Stockholm Sch of Econs; *m* 18 March 1984, Maria, da of Stephen Heineman (d 1967); 2 s (David b 11 Sept 1985, Alexander b 18 June 1987); *Career* assoc Merrill Lynch 1977–, md Merrill Lynch & Co 1985–96, co-head Global Debt Capital Markets Merrill Lynch & Co Inc 1996–99, ceo Benelux & Nordic Regions, head of investment banking Switzerland 1999; pres Minna-James-Heineman Stifung 1993; memb Bd of Dirs: Heineman Medical Research Inc 1992, Heineman Fndn for Research, Educational, Charitable and Scientific Purposes Inc 1994; *Recreations* sailing, tennis, squash, skiing; *Clubs* Sallskapet, RAC; *Style*— Anders Bergendahl, Esq; ✉ Merrill Lynch International Ltd, Merrill Lynch Financial Centre, 2 King Edward Street, London EC1A 1HQ (tel 020 7995 2800, fax 020 7995 0901)

BERGER, Herbert; s of Herbert Berger, and Hedwig; *b* 19 April 1953; *Educ* Catering Coll Salzburg; *m* 16 Feb 1989, Jane, *née* Crawford; 1 da (Annie b 2 April 1990); *Career* apprentice Grand Hotel Zell/See Austria 1968–71, seasonal work various hotels Switzerland 1971–75, chef de partie then sous chef Fredericks Restaurant 1975–76, head chef Le Connoisseur Restaurant London (Michelin Star) 1977–79, various positions rising to sous chef Connaught Hotel 1980–85, premier sous chef Claridges Hotel 1985–86, head chef Mirabelle Restaurant Curzon Street 1986–88, owner Keats Restaurant Hampstead (Michelin Red M within 6 months of opening) 1988–91, ptnr Berger & Sawyer Restaurant Ltd 1988–91, ptnr Restaurant Partnership 1991–, exec chef Café Royal 1992–97, head chef, gen mangr and shareholder 1 Lombard St Restaurant 1997– (Michelin Star 2000–); subject of various magazine articles; guest appearances: Ascot Racecourse, The Good Food Show (BBC), The Restaurant Show, Telegraph House & Garden Food Show, Masterchef, Nat Museums & Galleries of Wales, Nat Gallery Washington DC, Trimbach Food and Wine Masterclass, Marco Polo Cruise Liner, The Big Breakfast, After Five Dilly Dines Out; guest chef: The Restaurauteurs Dinner, Assoc Culinaire de France Dinner, SOS Charity Dinner, Fundraising Acad Dinners; memb: Académie Culinaire de France UK 1986–, Euro Togue 1995, Assoc Culinaire de France, Club des Amis Connaught Hotel, Reunion des Gastronomes, Maitrisse Escoffier 2003; *Awards* mention d'honneur Prix Pierre Taittinger 1983, AA 3 Rosettes, Egon Ronay Star, Michelin Star (Grill Room Café Royal), Eros Award 1995, Mumm Stars of Gastronomy, Best New Restaurant Carlton Awards; *Recreations* travel, gastronomic tours, eating out, music, the arts, skiing; *Clubs* The Tabasco; *Style*— Herbert Berger, Esq; ✉ tel 020 7226 5367; 1 Lombard Street Restaurant, London EC3V 9AA (tel 020 7929 6611)

BERGIN, Prof Joseph; s of late Cornelius Bergin, and late Brigid, *née* Phelan; *b* 11 February 1948; *Educ* Rockwell Coll Co Tipperary Eire, UCD (BA, MA), Peterhouse Cambridge (PhD); *m* 1978, Sylvia Papazian; 1 s (Edward b 1981), 1 da (Olivia b 1985); *Career* lectr in history Maynooth Coll Eire 1976–78; Univ of Manchester: lectr in history 1978–88, sr lectr 1988–92, reader 1992–96, prof 1996–; winner Prix Richelieu 1995; LittD Univ of Manchester 2004; FRHistS 1988, FBA 1996; *Books* Cardinal Richelieu: Power and the Pursuit of Wealth (1985), The Rise of Richelieu (1991), The Making of the French Episcopate 1589–1661 (1996), Crown, Church and Episcopate under Louis XIV (2004); *Recreations* sports, book hunting; *Style*— Prof Joseph Bergin, FBA; ✉ Department of History, University of Manchester, Oxford Road, Manchester M13 9PL (tel 0161 275 3084, e-mail j.bergin@man.ac.uk)

BERGONZI, Prof Bernard; s of Carlo Bergonzi (d 1969), and Louisa, *née* Lloyd (d 1980); *b* 13 April 1929; *Educ* SE London Tech Coll, Wadham Coll Oxford (MA, BLitt); *m* 1, 1960, Gabriel, da of Bernard Wall (d 1984); *m* 2, 1988, Anne, *née* Samson, da of Cecil Britton; 1 s (Benet b 1961), 2 da (Clarissa b 1963, Lucy b 1965); *Career* in commercial employment 1945–55, asst lectr rising to lectr in English Univ of Manchester 1959–66; Univ of Warwick: sr lectr in English 1966, head English Dept 1971–74 and 1985–86, prof 1971–92 (emeritus prof 1992–), pro-vice-chllr 1979–82; visiting lectr Brandeis Univ 1964–65; visiting prof: Stanford Univ 1982, Univ of Louisville 1988, Nene Coll Northampton 1994–2000; visiting fell New Coll Oxford 1987; tstee Chatback; FRSL 1984; *Books* Descartes and the Animals (poetry, 1954), The Early H G Wells (1961), Heroes' Twilight (1965), An English Sequence (poetry, 1966), The Situation of the Novel (1970), Anthony Powell (1971), T S Eliot (1972), The Turn of a Century (1973), Gerard Manley Hopkins (1977), Reading the Thirties (1978), Years (poetry, 1979), The Roman Persuasion (novel, 1981), The Myth of Modernism and Twentieth Century Literature (1986), Exploding English (1990), Wartime and Aftermath (1993), David Lodge (1995), War Poets and Other Subjects (1999), A Victorian Wanderer (2003), A Study in Greene (2006); *Style*— Prof Bernard Bergonzi, FRSL; ✉ 19 St Mary's Crescent, Leamington Spa CV31 1JL (tel 01926 883115)

BERINGER, Guy; *b* 12 August 1955; *Educ* Campbell Coll Belfast, St Catharine's Coll Cambridge (MA); *m* 1979, Margaret Catherine, *née* Powell; 3 da; *Career* Allen & Overy: asst 1980–85, ptnr 1985–2000, sr ptnr 2000–; memb Law Soc; *Style*— Guy Beringer, Esq; ✉ Allen & Overy, One New Change, London EC4M 9QQ (tel 020 7330 3000, fax 020 7330 9999)

BERKELEY, Andrew Wilson Atkins; s of Andrew Berkeley, JP (d 1952), of Cookstown, Co Tyrone, and Mabel Berkeley; *b* 15 July 1936; *Educ* Rainey Sch Co Derry, Queen's Univ Belfast (BSc), Harvard Business Sch (AMP), KCL (MSc); *m* 30 Nov 1968, Carolyn Blyth Hinshaw Ross, of Milngavie, Glasgow; 2 da (Kirsten b 16 Nov 1972, Iona b 27 April 1978); *Career* int commercial lawyer and chartered arbitrator; called to the Bar Gray's Inn 1965; Legal Dept ICI Ltd 1966–78, dir ICI Petroleum Ltd 1978–81, sec The British Nat Oil Corp 1981–84, dir of legal corp affrs STC plc 1984–87, gp gen counsel and sec Laporte plc 1987–92; currently conslt ICC (UK) and int commercial arbitrator; vice-pres The Int Arbitration Club; FCIArb; *Recreations* kernel hacking; *Clubs* Athenaeum; *Style*— Andrew Berkeley, Esq; ✉ 49 Arden Road, London N3 3AD (tel 020 8343 4050, fax 020 8343 1762, e-mail aberkeley@attglobal.net)

BERKELEY, 18 Baron (E 1421); Anthony FitzHardinge Gueterbock; OBE (1989); sits as Baron Geuterbock (Life Peer UK 2000), of Cranford, London Borough of Hillingdon; o s of Brig Ernest Adolphus Leopold Gueterbock, late RE (d 1984), and Hon Cynthia Ella Foley (d 1991); suc aunt Mary Lallé Foley Berkeley, Baroness Berkeley (d 1992); *b* 20 September 1939; *Educ* Eton, Trinity Coll Cambridge (MA); *m* 1, 10 July 1965 (m dis 1998), Diana Christine, er da of Eric William John Townsend, MRCS, LRCP; 2 s (Hon Thomas FitzHardinge b 1969, Hon Robert William b 1970), 1 da (Hon Philippa Louise b 1975); m 2, 8 May 1999, Julia, o da of Michael Clarke; *Heir* s, Hon Thomas Gueterbock; *Career* engrg, construction and planning Sir Alexander Gibb and Partners 1961–67, construction, planning and business devpt George Wimpey plc 1967–85, public affrs mangr Eurotunnel plc 1985–95; chm: The Piggyback Consortium 1993–99, Rail Freight Group 1996–; advsr ADtranz 1995–2001; Lab whip and spokesman on tport House of Lords 1996–97, memb European Select Ctee 1998–99; Hon DSc Univ of Brighton 1996; CEng, MICE, FRSA, FCIT; *Recreations* sailing, skiing; *Style*— The Rt Hon the Lord Berkeley, OBE; ✉ House of Lords, London SW1A 0PW

BERKELEY, (Robert) John Grantley; TD (1967), JP (Glos 1960), DL (Glos 1982, Hereford and Worcester 1983); s of Capt Robert George Wilmot Berkeley (d 1969, himself 13 in descent from Hon Thomas Berkeley (4 s of 1 Baron Berkeley cr 1421, gs of 4 Baron Berkeley cr 1295, and descended in direct male line from Eadnoth the Staller, pre-Conquest Anglo-Saxon nobleman at Court of King Edward the Confessor) by his 2 w Isabel, da and co-heir of Thomas Mowbray, 1 Duke of Norfolk and Hon Myrtle, da of 14 Baron

Dormer; *b* 24 July 1931; *Educ* The Oratory, Magdalen Coll Oxford; *m* 25 Jan 1967, Georgina Bridget, eld da of Maj Andrew Charles Stirling Home Drummond Moray (d 1971), of Easter Ross, Comrie, Perthshire; 2 s (Robert Charles b 1968, Henry John Mowbray b 1969); *Career* Maj Queen's Own Warks Yeo 1963; jt master Berkeley Hunt 1960–84; High Sheriff: Worcs 1967, Glos 1982–83; *Clubs* Cavalry and Guards'; *Style—* R J Berkeley, Esq, TD, DL; ✉ Berkeley Castle, Gloucestershire (tel 01453 810 202); Spetchley Park, Worcestershire (tel 01905 345224)

BERKELEY, Michael Fitzhardinge; s of Sir Lennox Randal Francis Berkeley, CBE (d 1989), of 8 Warwick Ave, London, and Elizabeth Freda, *née* Bernstein; *b* 29 May 1948; *Educ* Westminster Cathedral Choir Sch, The Oratory, Royal Acad of Music (ARAM), postgrad work with Sir Richard Rodney Bennett, CBE, *qv*; *m* 19 Nov 1979, Deborah Jane, da of Guy Coltman Rogers (d 1976), of Stanage Park, Knighton, Powys; 1 da (Jessica Rose b 28 June 1986); *Career* composer and broadcaster; phlebotomist St Bartholomew's Hosp 1969–71, announcer BBC Radio 3 1974–79, regular broadcaster on music and the arts BBC radio and TV 1974–; music panel advsr Arts Cncl of GB 1986–90, artistic dir Cheltenham Int Festival of Music 1995–2004; memb: Central Music Advsy Ctee BBC 1986–89, Gen Advsy Cncl BBC 1990–95, Bd of Dirs ROH 1996–2003 (chm Opera Bd 1998–99); co-artistic dir Spitalfields Festival 1995–97; assoc composer Scottish Chamber Orch 1979, composer-in-assoc BBC Nat Orch of Wales and Welsh Coll of Music and Drama 2001–; visiting prof Univ of Huddersfield 1991–94; govr National Youth Orch of GB 1994–96, chm Bd of Govrs Royal Ballet 2003–; tstee Britten-Pears Fndn 1997–; compositions incl: Meditations (Guinness prize for composition) 1977, Primavera 1979, Uprising 1980, Wessex Graves 1981, Or Shall We Die? (oratorio) 1982, Music from Chaucer 1983, Fierce Tears 1984, Pas de Deux 1985, Songs of Awakening Love 1986, Organ Concerto 1987, The Red Macula 1989, Gethsemane Fragment 1990, Clarinet Concerto 1991, Baa Baa Black Sheep (opera) 1993, Viola Concerto 1994, Magnetic Field 1995, Winter Fragments 1996, Torque and Velocity 1997, Secret Garden 1997, The Garden of Earthly Delights 1998, Tristessa (orchestra) 2003, Jane Eyre (opera) 2000, Concerto for Orchestra 2005; FRAM 1996, fell Royal Welsh Coll of Music and Drama (FRWCMD) 2003, FRNCM 2004; *Publications* The Music Pack (1994); author of various articles in The Observer, The Guardian, The Listener, The Sunday Telegraph and Vogue; *Recreations* looking at paintings, reading, walking, hill farming in Mid Wales; *Style—* Michael Berkeley, Esq; ✉ c/o Oxford University Press, 70 Baker Street, London W1U 7DN (tel 020 7616 5900)

BERKOFF, Steven; *b* 3 August 1937; *Career* writer, actor and dir; fndr London Theatre Group 1968 (first professional prodn In The Penal Colony); *Theatre* adapted/dir/toured: The Trial, Metamorphosis, Agamemnon, Salome, The Fall of the House of Usher; dir/toured: Hamlet, Macbeth, own one man show (GB, USA, Aust); dir: Coriolanus (NY, Aust, UK and world tour also title role), Kvetch, Richard II (NY); Shakespeare's Villains (West End and world tour), Messiah (Edinburgh and Old Vic), The Secret Love Life of Ophelia, Sip and Shiver ((LA), Richard II (Ludlow Festival); *Television* appearances incl: Sins, War and Remembrance, Michaelangelo - Season of Giants; TV prodns incl: West (Channel Four) 1984, Metamorphosis (BBC 2) 1989, Harry's Christmas, Silent Night (Channel Four) 1991, Tell Tale Heart (Channel Four) 1991; *Radio* title role in Macbeth (Radio 4) 1995, the MC in Cabaret (musical debut, Radio 2) 1996, An Actor's Tale (Radio 4) 1997; *Film* appearances incl: A Clockwork Orange, Barry Lyndon, The Passenger, McVicar, Outlands, Octopussy, Beverly Hills Cop, Rambo, Underworld, Revolution, Under the Cherry Moon, Absolute Beginners, Prisoner of Rio, The Krays, Fair Game, Decadence, Flynn, Another 9 1/2 Weeks, Legionnaire, Rancid Aluminium, The Henchman; *Publications* original plays: East (first original play presented at Edinburgh Festival 1975), Decadence (1982), Greek (1982), West (1985), Harry's Christmas (1985), Lunch (1985), Sink The Belgrano! (1987), Massage (1987), Kvetch (1987), Acapulco (1987), Sturm und Drang, Brighton Beach Scumbags, Ritual in Blood, Messiah, The Secret Love Life of Ophelia (2001); other publications incl: The Trial (play adaptation, 1978), Gross Intrusion (1979), America (poetry and prose, 1988), A Prisoner in Rio (film journal, 1989), I am Hamlet (prodn diary, 1989), Coriolanus in Deutschland (1992), The Theatre of Steven Berkoff (photographic history), Meditations on Metamorphosis (1995), Free Association (autobiography, 1996), Graft: Tales of An Actor (1998), Shopping in the Santa Monica Mall (2002), Tough Acts! (2003); *Style—* Steven Berkoff, Esq

BERKSHIRE, Archdeacon of; *see:* Russell, Ven Norman Atkinson

BERLIAND, Richard David Antony; s of David Berliand, and Jill, *née* Puckle; *b* 7 October 1962, Oxshott, Surrey; *Educ* Eton, Downing Coll Cambridge (MA); *m* 19 Sept 1987, Lucilla; 1 s, 2 da; *Career* commodities broker Pacol Ltd 1984–87, investment banker JP Morgan 1987– (currently md); dir: JP Morgan Securities Ltd, JP Morgan Futures Inc, Liffe Administration & Management 1997–2005 (vice-chm 2002–05), London Clearing House Ltd 1999–2003; dir: Futures Industry Assoc USA 2001– (chm 2005–), National Futures Assoc 2003–04; govr Brambletye Sch Tst 1999–; memb HAC; Liveryman Worshipful Co of Haberdashers; *Recreations* aviation, golf, family; *Style—* Richard Berliand, Esq; ✉ JP Morgan Securities Ltd, 125 London Wall, London EC2Y 5AJ

BERLIN, Barry; *Educ* Brunel Univ (BSc); *Career* called to the Bar Gray's Inn 1981; currently memb St Philips Chambers; provincial Treasy counsel 1995–, memb Attorney Gen's A List (Crime) 2003, recorder Midland Circuit; hon lectr Univ of Birmingham; *Recreations* current affairs, British history, theatre, football, cricket; *Style—* Barry Berlin, Esq; ✉ St Philips Chambers, 55 Temple Row, Birmingham B2 5LS

BERMAN, Prof Edward David (ED); MBE (1979); s of Jack Berman, of America, and Ida, *née* Webber; *b* 8 March 1941; *Educ* Harvard Univ (BA), Exeter Coll Oxford (Rhodes scholar); *Career* playwright, theatre director and producer, actor and educationalist; theatre direction credits incl: Dirty Linen (premieres London and Broadway) 1976, The Dogg's Troupe Hamlet 1976 (filmed same year), The Irish Hebrew Lesson 1976, Samson and Delilah 1978, Dogg's Hamlet, Cahoot's Macbeth 1979; prodr of various plays for adults and for children 1967–95, artistic dir of annual public art projects 1968–95; ed: 2 anthologies of plays 1976–78, various community arts and action handbooks; maker of educnl films: The Head 1971, Two Wheeler 1972, Farm in the City 1977, Marx for Beginners cartoon (co-prodr) 1978; fndr chief exec, artistic dir and tstee Inter-Action Tst 1968–; Labrys Tst 1969–; clinical prof of social enterprise 2005–; dir and fndr various companies/gps/tsts concerning constructive leisure incl: Prof Dogg's Troupe for Children 1968–, Inter-Action Advsy Serv 1970, Infilms 1970, The Almost Free Theatre 1971, Inprint Publishing Unit 1972, City Farm 1 1972, Alternative Educn Project 1973–84, Ambiance Inter-Action Inc 1976, City Farm Movement 1976, Talacre Centre Ltd 1977, Weekend Arts Coll 1979; co-fndr: Inter-Action Housing Tst Ltd 1970, Community Design Centre (NUBS) 1974, Sport-Space 1976, Beginners Books Ltd 1978, London and Commonwealth Youth Ensemble 1981; chm: Save Piccadilly Campaign 1971–80, Talacre Action Gp 1972, Nat Assoc of Arts Centres 1975–79; dir Islington Bus Co 1974–76; fndr and co-dir: Int Inst for Social Enterprise 1980, Social Property Developments Ltd; fndr and tstee: Inter-Action Social Enterprise Tst Ltd, Social Enterprise Fndn of Inter-Action 1984; fndr and dir: Network Inter-Action, Youth-Tech, Learning Domes; special advsr on inner city matters to Sec of State for the Environment 1982–83; Cdre Ships-in-the-City 1988; *Publications* Prof R L Dogg's Zoo's Who I and II (1975), Selecting Business Software (1984), Make a Real Job of It, Breaks for Young Bands (1985), How to Set Up a Small Business (1987), Healthy Learning Songs and Activities (1989), New Game Songs and Activities (1989), Early Learning Maths Songs and Activities (1991), The Democracy Handbook (2000); *Style—* Prof ED Berman, MBE; ✉ 55 Anchorage Point, 42 Cuba Street, Isle of Dogs, London E14 8NF (tel 020 7515 4449, e-mail edbiaction@aol.com)

BERMAN, Sir Franklin Delow; KCMG (1994, CMG 1987); s of Joshua Zelic Berman, of Cape Town, and Gertrude, *née* Levin; *b* 23 December 1939; *Educ* Rondebosch Boys' HS, Univ of Cape Town (BA, BSc), Wadham and Nuffield Colls Oxford (MA); *m* 24 July 1964, Christine Mary, da of Edward Francis Lawler (d 1978); 2 s (Jonathan b 1966, Stefan b 1968), 3 da (Katharine b 1972, Judith b 1972, Victoria b 1972); *Career* called to the Bar Middle Temple 1966 (hon bencher 1997); joined HM Dip Serv 1965, asst legal advsr FCO 1965–71, legal advsr Br Mil Govt Berlin 1971–72, legal advsr Br Embassy Bonn 1972–74, legal cnsllr FCO 1974–82, cnsllr UK Mission UN NY 1982–85, legal advsr FCO 1991–99 (dep legal advsr 1988–91); judge ad hoc Int Court of Justice 2003–05; J C Smith visiting fell Univ of Nottingham 1993; chm: Dip Serv Assoc 1979–82, Appeals Bd Int Oil Pollution Compensation Fund 1985–2004, Austrian Nat Fund for Compensation of Victims of Nazi Persecution 2001–, Diplomatic Serv Appeals Bd 2002–06; memb: Bd Inst of Advanced Legal Studies Univ of London 1991–99, Governing Cncl Br Inst of Int and Comp Law 1992–2005, Cncl Br Branch Int Law Assoc 1992–, Appeals Bd Western EU 1994–96 and 2002–05, Editorial Bd Br Yearbook of Int Law 1994–, Advsy Cncl Centre for Euro and Comparative Law Univ of Oxford 1995–, Advsy Cncl Univ of Oxford Law Fndn 1998–2004; tstee: Edward Fry Memorial Library 1991–99, The Whittuck Tst 1992–, Greenwich Fndn Royal Naval Coll 1997–2005, UNiv of Cape Town Tst 1999–, Australian SAS Resources Tst 2005–, Br Inst of Int and Comp Law 2007–; visiting prof of international law Univ of Oxford and Univ of Cape Town; hon QC 1992; hon fell: Wadham Coll 1995 (prof fell 2000), Soc of Advanced Legal Studies 1997–; Grand Decoration of Honour in Gold with Star (Austria) 2007; *Recreations* reading, walking, choral singing, gardening; *Style—* Sir Franklin Berman, KCMG, QC; ✉ Essex Court Chambers, 24 Lincoln's Inn Fields, London WC2A 3EG (tel 020 7813 8000, fax 020 7813 8080, e-mail fberman@essexcourt.net)

BERNARD, Sir Dallas Edmund; 2 Bt (UK 1954), of Snakemoor, Co Southampton; s of Sir Dallas Gerald Mercer Bernard, 1 Bt (d 1975); *b* 14 December 1926; *Educ* Eton, CCC Oxford (MA); *m* 1, 1959 (m dis 1979), Sheila Mary, er da of late Arthur Gordon Robey; 3 da (Juliet Mary b 1961 d 1998, Alicia Elizabeth (Mrs William Micklethwait) b 1964, Sarah Jane (Mrs Matthew Boulton) b 1968); m 2, 1979 (m dis 2003), Mrs Monica J Montford, da of late James Edward Hudson; 1 da (Olivia Louise b 1981); m 3, 2003, Senora Graciela Scorza (formerly Senora de Jauregui), da of Francisco Scorza Fúster (d 2005), and Celmira Leguizamon O'Higgins (d 1987); *Heir* none; *Career* dir: Morgan Grenfell and Co Ltd 1964–77, Morgan Grenfell Holdings Ltd 1970–79, Italian International Bank plc 1978–89; memb Monopolies and Mergers Cmmn 1973–79; chm: Nat and Foreign Securities Trust Ltd 1981–86, Thames Trust Ltd 1983–86, DVB Ltd 2006–; dir: Dreyfus Intercontinental Investment Fund NV 1970–91, Dreyfus Dollar International Fund NV 1982–91; int fin conslt 1986–; memb Cncl GPDST 1988–93; *Clubs* Army and Navy; *Style—* Sir Dallas Bernard, Bt; ✉ Rycote Farm Cottage, Rycote Farm, Thame, Oxfordshire OX9 2PF

BERNAYS, Richard Oliver; s of Robert Hamilton Bernays, MP (MP for Bristol North 1931–45, ka 1945), and Nancy, *née* Britton (d 1987); *b* 22 February 1943; *Educ* Eton, Trinity Coll Oxford (MA); *m* 1, 12 Feb 1972 (m dis 1993), Karen Forney, of New Castle, PA; 3 da (Lucy b 1975, Mary b 1977 d 1993, Amy b 1979); m 2, 22 Feb 1996, Rosamund Horwood-Smart, QC, *qv*; *Career* vice-chm Mercury Asset Management plc, dir Mercury Fund Managers Ltd 1971–92; chief exec: Hill Samuel Investment Management Group 1992–96, Old Mutual International, Capel-Cure Sharp 1998–2001; chm: Gartmore Global Tst 2002–, Throgmorton Tst 2005–, Hermes Pensions Management 2005–; dir: Singer & Friedlander Gp 2003–05, WNS Gp 2006–; chm Cncl Cheltenham Ladies' Coll 1999–2004; *Recreations* golf, fishing, gardening, music; *Clubs* Brooks's, Flyfishers', Swinley Forest; *Style—* Richard Bernays, Esq; ✉ 82 Elgin Crescent, London W11 2JL

BERNBAUM, Prof Gerald; s of Benjamin Bernbaum (d 1967), of London, and Rebecca; *b* 25 March 1936; *Educ* Hackney Downs GS for Boys, LSE (BSc(Econ)), London Inst of Educn (PGCE); *m* 1959 (m dis 1987), Pamela Valerie, *née* Cohen; 2 s (Kevin Barry b 1962, Anthony David b 1965); *Career* asst master Mitcham County GS for Boys 1958–62; head of dept Rutherford Sch 1962–64; Univ of Leicester: lectr in educn 1964–70, sr lectr 1970–74, prof of educn 1974–93, dir Sch of Educn 1976–85, pro-vice-chllr 1985–87, exec pro-vice-chllr and registrar 1987–93; vice-chllr and chief exec South Bank Univ 1993–2001, ret; conslt OECD 1970–75; chm Bar Vocational Course Bd Gen Cncl of the Bar 2002–05; chm of govrs Morley Coll 2004–05; FRSA 1984; *Books* Social Change and the Schools 1918–44 (1967), Knowledge Ideology and Education (1977), Schooling in Decline (1978); *Recreations* professional sport, music, reading, walking in London, public affairs; *Style—* Prof Gerald Bernbaum; ✉ e-mail gb.pp@virgin.net

BERNERS, Baroness (E 1455; 16 holder of Barony); Pamela Vivien Kirkham; er da of Vera Ruby, Baroness Berners (15 holder of the Barony; d 1992), and Harold Williams, JP (d 1971); suc on termination of abeyance 1995; *b* 30 September 1929; *m* 1952, Michael Joseph Sperry Kirkham; 2 s (Hon Rupert William Tyrwhitt b 1953, Hon Robin Raymond Tyrwhitt b 1958), 1 da (Hon Caroline Rosemary Tyrwhitt (Hon Mrs Gordon) b 1956); *Heir* s, Hon Rupert Kirkham; *Style—* The Rt Hon Baroness Berners; ✉ Ashwellthorpe, 103 Charlton Lane, Cheltenham, Gloucestershire GL53 9EE

BERNEY, Sir Julian Reedham Stuart; 11 Bt (E 1620), of Parkehall in Reedham, Norfolk; s of Lt John Berney (ka Korea 1952), and Hon Jean Davina Stuart (d 2003, who m 2, Percy William Jesson; and 3, Michael D Ritchie), da of 1 Viscount Stuart of Findhorn, CH, MVO, MC, PC; suc gf 1975; *b* 26 September 1952; *Educ* Wellington, N E London Poly; *m* 1976, Sheena Mary, da of Ralph Day, of Maldon, Essex; 2 s (William Reedham John b 1980, Hugo Ralph b 1987), 1 da (Jessica Mary b 1982); *Heir* s, William Berney; *Career* chartered surveyor; Freeman Worshipful Co of Fishmongers; FRICS; *Recreations* sailing, travel, reading, photography; *Clubs* Royal Yacht Sqdn, Royal Ocean Racing, Royal Cruising; *Style—* Sir Julian Berney, Bt; ✉ Reeds House, 40 London Road, Maldon, Essex CM9 6HE (tel 01621 853420)

BERNS, Richard Michael; s of Leonard Berns (d 1978), and Elizabeth Grace, *née* Turner (d 2005); *b* 16 August 1947; *Educ* Dulwich Coll; *m* 16 Dec 1972, Roberta, da of Robert Dunlop Fleming (d 1978), of Perth, Scotland; 1 s (Ashley b 1969), 1 da (Antonia b 1974); *Career* slr; sr ptnr Piper Smith Watton LLP; memb Law Soc; *Recreations* sailing, skiing, tennis, scuba, motorcycling; *Style—* Richard M Berns, Esq; ✉ Leigh Hill House, Leigh Hill Road, Cobham, Surrey KT11 2HS (tel 01932 862284); Piper Smith Watton LLP, 31 Warwick Square, London SW1V 2AF (tel 020 7828 8000, fax 020 7828 8008, e-mail richard.berns@pswlaw.co.uk)

BERNSTEIN, David Alan; s of Henry Bernstein (d 2001), and Anne Bernstein (d 1998); *b* 22 May 1943; *Educ* Christ's Coll Finchley; *m* Gillian; 4 s (Lawrence, Peter, Richard, Nicholas); *Career* chartered accountant Bright Grahame Murray (subsequently jt sr ptnr) 1968–88, jt md Pentland Group plc 1988–94, non-exec chm Blacks Leisure Gp plc 1995–; chm: Manchester City FC 1998–2003, Adams Childrenswear Ltd 2000–05, Frank Thomas Ltd 2003–; non-exec dir French Connection Gp plc 1995–2001, Ted Baker plc 2003–, Wembley Nat Stadium Ltd 2003–, Carluccio's 2005–; chm Chandos Tennis Club; FCA 1996; *Recreations* sport (especially golf, running), theatre, opera, politics; *Style—* David Bernstein, Esq; ✉ 48 Fitzalan Road, Finchley, London N3 3PE (tel 020 8346 2345, fax 020 8343 0625)

BERNSTEIN, Dr Robert Michael; s of Dr Fred Julian Bernstein (d 1986), and Dr Emilie Ellen Bernstein, *née* Guthmann (d 1995); *b* 31 December 1947; *Educ* Highgate Sch, King's Coll Cambridge (MA, MD, BChir), UCH Med Sch; *m* 29 Sept 1978, Frances Jane Northcroft, da of Dr Christopher Tibbits Brown, of Wareham, Dorset; 3 s (Jonathan b 1979, Nicholas b 1983, Jeremy b 1993), 3 da (Laura b 1981, Alice b 1986, Clare b 1991); *Career* sr registrar Royal Postgrad Med Sch Hammersmith Hosp 1981–85, visiting scientist Cold Spring Harbor Laboratory USA 1983–84, conslt rheumatologist and clinical lectr Univ of Manchester and Manchester Royal Infirmary 1985–; late memb Res Advsy Panel Lupus UK; late memb Specialty Advsy Ctee in Rheumatology, former chm Fibromyalgia Assoc UK; late members' columnist RCP, late memb Editorial Bd Clinical and Experimental Immunology; late memb Nat Ctee Lupus UK, late bd memb Br Assoc for Performing Arts Med; late memb Cncl Reform Synagogues of GB; FRCP 1990 (MRCP 1975); *Recreations* mountains, music; *Style*— Dr Robert Bernstein; ✉ 23 Anson Road, Manchester M14 5BZ (tel 0161 248 2048, fax 0161 248 2049)

BERNSTEIN OF CRAIGWEIL, Baron (Life Peer UK 2000), of Craigweil in the County of West Sussex; Alexander Bernstein; s of late Cecil Bernstein, of London; *b* 15 March 1936; *Educ* Stowe, St John's Coll Cambridge; *m* 1, 1962 (m dis 1993), Vanessa Anne, da of Alwyn Mills, of London; 1 s (Hon Matthew b 1963), 1 da (Hon Kate Elizabeth b 1964); m 2, 1995, Angela Mary, da of Muriel Beveridge, of London, and former w of (Hon) Sir Nicholas Serota; *Career* dir Granada Group plc 1964–96 (chm 1979–96), jt md Granada Television Ltd 1971–75, md Granada Television Rental Ltd 1977–86; dir Waddington Galleries 1966–; chm: Royal Exchange Theatre 1983–95 (dep chm 1980–83), Old Vic Theatre Tst 1998–2001; tstee: Civic Tst for the NW 1964–86, Granada Fndn 1968–, Theatres Tst 1996–99, Trusthouse Charitable Fndn 1998–; memb Nat Theatre Devpt Cncl 1996–98; memb Ct: Univ of Salford 1976–87, Univ of Manchester 1983–98; Hon DLitt Univ of Salford 1987, Hon LLD Univ of Manchester 1996; *Style*— The Rt Hon the Lord Bernstein of Craigweil

BERRIDGE, Elizabeth; da of H S Berridge (d 1932), and Phyllis Cecilia, *née* Drew (d 1979); *b* 3 December 1919, London; *Educ* Clapham HS, Clapham Secdy Sch; *m* Oct 1940, Reginald Moore (d 1990); 1 s (Lawrence Gaunt b 1941), 1 da (Karen Veronica b 1944); *Career* author; ed Peter Owen Publishers 1951, reviewer for BBC and various magazines, fiction reviewer Daily Telegraph 1965–85; former Arvon tutor; judge: Silver Pen Award PEN, David Higham Award for First Novel, Katherine Mansfield Short Story Award, Dylan Thomas Short Story Award; memb: PEN 1970, Soc of Authors 2001; tstee Chase Charity; FRSL 1997; *Publications* novels: The Story of Stanley Brent, (novella, 1945), The House of Defence (1945), Be Clean Be Tidy (1949, published in USA as It Won't Be Flowers 1949), Upon Several Occasions (1953, serialised on radio), Rose Under Glass (1961, reprinted 1985), Across the Common (1964, Best Novel of the Year Yorkshire Post 1964, serialised on BBC radio 1970 and 1994, reprinted 1997, audio book 1997), Sing Me Who You Are (1967, reprinted 1985), People at Play (1982), Touch and Go (1995, reprinted 1998, audio book 1998, adapted for BBC Radio 4 2000); short stories: Selected Stories (1947, reissued as Tell It To A Stranger 2000), Family Matters (1980), Flying Solo (2004); for children: That Surprising Summer (1972), Run For Home (1981); The Barretts at Hope End (non-fiction, 1974); contrib stories to numerous literary collections and magazines; *Recreations* travel, gardening, reading, exhibitions of 19th Century art, Victorian literature; *Style*— Ms Elizabeth Berridge; ✉ c/o David Higham, 5–8 Lower John Street, Golden Square, London W1R 4HA (tel 020 7437 7888)

BERRIDGE, Prof Sir Michael John; kt (1998); s of George Kirton Berridge and Stella Elaine, *née* Hards; *b* 22 October 1938; *Educ* UC of Rhodesia and Nyasaland (BSc), Univ of Cambridge (PhD); *m* 5 March 1965, Susan Graham, *née* Winter; 1 da (Rozanne b 4 June 1967), 1 s (Paul b 19 March 1969); *Career* post doctoral fell Univ of Virginia 1965–66, res assoc Case Western Res Univ 1967 (post doctoral fell 1966–69); Univ of Cambridge: sr scientific offr Unit of Invertebrate Chemistry and Physiology 1969, chief sci offr Unit of Insect Neurophysiology and Pharmacology 1987–90; Agric Food Res Cncl Laboratory of Molecular Signalling 1990–94, The Babraham Inst Laboratory of Molecular Signalling 1994–2003 (emeritus Babraham fell 2003–); hon prof of cell signalling Univ of Cambridge 1994–; fell Trinity Coll Cambridge 1972; awards incl: Feldberg Prize 1984, The King Faisal Int Prize in Sci 1986, Louis Jeantet Prize in Med 1986, William Bate Hardy Prize (Cambridge Philosophical Soc) 1987, Abraham White Scientific Achievement Award (George Washington Univ Sch of Med) 1987, Gairdner Fndn Int Award 1988, Baly Medal (RCP) 1989, Albert Lasker Basic Med Res Award 1989, Heineken Prize Royal Netherlands Acad of Arts and Sciences 1994, The Wolf Fndn Prize in Med 1995, Shaw Prize in Med 2005; foreign assoc Nat Acad of Science Washington DC 1999, foreign hon memb American Acad of Arts and Science 1999, memb American Philosophical Soc 2007; FRS 1984 (Royal Medal); *Recreations* golf, gardening; *Style*— Prof Sir Michael Berridge, FRS; ✉ Laboratory of Molecular Signalling, Babraham Institute, Babraham, Cambridge CB22 3AT (tel 01223 496621, fax 01223 496033, e-mail michael.berridge@bbsrc.ac.uk)

BERRIGAN, Frances (Mrs Berrigan-Taplin); *b* 1943; *Educ* Santa Maria Ladies' Coll WA, Univ of Western Aust (BA, DipEd); *m*; 2 c; *Career* television prodr/dir; teacher Aust 1964–65, prodr educnl progs Australian Broadcasting Cmmn 1965–66, researcher children's and higher educn progs BBC TV 1969–70, prodr educn and community progs BBC Radio London 1970–72, freelance broadcaster and journalist Paris 1973–75 (features contrib BBC Radio 4 progs incl The World Tonight, World at One and Today, contrib TES and THES, media conslt and writer for UNESCO), research fell Middx Poly 1976–77, lectr in media research methods Open Univ 1976–78, prodr/dir and co-ordinating ed BBC Open Univ Prodn Centre 1979–84; Cicada Films: joined 1984 (after producing Nature in Focus series), md and prodr/dir 1987–, latterly md and sole proprietor; Cicada prodns incl: Blue Eye of Siberia (for Channel 4 Fragile Earth strand, NY Film Festival Silver Medal, Channel 4 entry in Prix D'Italia), Birds as Prey (for Fragile Earth), Unnatural Disasters, China: An Environment in Crisis, Making the Grade (for BBC Forty Minutes strand) and Soviet co-prodns Philby and The Krogers, Cutting Edge (Channel 4), The Club (Channel 4, finalist BAFTA Awards, 1995), Hidden Scrolls of Herculaneum (Channel 4), To the Ends of the Earth (Channel 4), In Search of Eden (Channel 4), The Volcano that Blew a World Away (Channel 4), Veerapan - The Last Bandit (Channel 4), various other wildlife and environmental films for Channel 4, BBC and others; *Style*— Ms Frances Berrigan; ✉ Cicada Films, 1 Marylands Road, London W9 2DU (tel 020 7266 4646, fax 020 7289 2599, e-mail cicada@cicadafilms.com)

BERRILL, Geoffrey William; s of William George Berrill (d 1969), of Cheam, Surrey, and Ada Alice, *née* Martin (d 2002); *b* 4 June 1948; *Educ* Uppingham; *m* 10 June 1972, Karen Peta, da of Peter Frank (d 1974), of Tadworth, Surrey; 2 da (Victoria b 6 April 1977, Charlotte b 3 Oct 1979); *Career* dir: Alexander Howden Insurance Brokers Ltd 1980–83, Alexander Howden Ltd 1983–85, Halford Shead & Co Ltd 1984–86, HSBC Insurance Brokers Ltd (formerly Hartley Cooper Associates Ltd) 1986–2001, liaison dir HSBC Private Bank 2001–; Freeman City of London 1969, Liveryman Worshipful Co of Glass Sellers 1969 (apprentice 1962); *Recreations* hill walking, gardening; *Clubs* Oriental; *Style*— Geoffrey Berrill, Esq; ✉ Rook Hall, Kelvedon, Essex CO5 9DB; HSBC Private Bank, 78 St James's Street, London SW1A 1JB (tel 020 7860 5063, fax 020 7860 5002, e-mail geoffrey.w.berrill@hsbcpb.com)

BERRY, Amanda; da of Thomas Berry, and Anita, *née* Booth; *Educ* York Coll of Art, Newcastle Poly; *Career* co-dir Duncan Heath Assoc (now ICM) 1982–88, res light entertainment and current affairs LWT 1989–90, prodr and devpt exec Scottish Television Enterprises 1990–98, dir of devpt and events BAFTA 1998–2000, chief exec BAFTA 2000–; Woman of the Year 1999, Media Boss of the Year 1999; *Recreations* cinema, travel, football, art, opera, music; *Clubs* Groucho, Soho House; *Style*— Ms Amanda Berry; ✉ The British Academy of Film & Television Arts, 195 Piccadilly, London W1J 9LN (tel 020 7734 0022, e-mail amandab@bafta.org)

BERRY, Andrew John; s of John Frederick Berry of Littlebourne, Kent, and Avril Jean, *née* Leicester; *b* 16 April 1958; *Educ* Hurstpierpoint Coll, King's Sch Canterbury; *m* 24 April 1982 (m dis 1998), Gail Louise, da of Peter Newmark (decd); 1 s (Alexander Andrew John b 15 Feb 1987), 1 da (Georgia Louise b 19 June 1988); *Career* vice-pres Merrill Lynch 1985–88, dir Chase Manhattan Bank 1988–1991, md Fimat Int Banque 1992–2000, chm Bawag-Refclear (Worldwide Gp) 2000–03, md ICAP plc 2004–; Freeman Worshipful Co of Horners; *Recreations* shooting, gardening, driving; *Style*— Andrew Berry, Esq; ✉ Little Fishfolds, Mayes Green, Ockley, Surrey RH5 5PN (tel 01306 621231, fax 01306 621271); ICAP plc, 2 Broadgate, London EC2 7UR (tel 020 7000 5768, fax 020 7000 5688, mobile 07740 082838)

BERRY, Anthony Charles; QC (1994); s of Geoffrey Vernon Berry (d 1983), and Audrey Millicent, *née* Farrar (d 2001); *b* 4 October 1950; *Educ* Downside, Lincoln Coll Oxford (BA); *m* Susan Carmen, da of Derek Traversi, CBE; 3 s (Edward Paul b 8 Jan 1983, James Andrew b 15 Aug 1985, Richard John b 15 Aug 1985), 1 da (Tessa Jane b 17 March 1990); *Career* called to the Bar 1976; sec Criminal Bar Assoc 1991–93, memb Bar Cncl 1994–97; *Recreations* golf, tennis; *Style*— Anthony Berry, Esq, QC; ✉ 9 Bedford Row, London WC1R 4AZ (tel 020 7489 2727, fax 020 7489 2928)

BERRY, Brig Anthony Edward; OBE (1982); s of Edward Joseph Berry, and Jean, *née* Larkin; *b* 4 December 1938; *Educ* RMA Sandhurst; *m* 3 Dec 1966, Sally, da of Lt-Col John Cairnes (ka 1943), of Dublin; 1 s (Nicholas Anthony b 1968), 1 da (Suzanna Claire b 1972); *Career* cmmnd KRRC 1958, 2 KEO Gurkha Rifles 1962–65, Staff Coll 1970, CO 4 Bn Royal Green Jackets 1977–79, asst defence attaché Washington 1986–88, defence advsr Br High Cmmn Islamabad 1989–92; dir Macmillan Cancer Relief 1993–2007; tstee and memb Cncl (Pakistan) Royal Cmmn Ex-Services League; Freeman City of London; KStJ 1993 (Dir of Ceremonies 1994–); *Recreations* fishing; *Clubs* Army and Navy, Pratt's; *Style*— Brig Anthony Berry, OBE; ✉ c/o Army and Navy Club, Pall Mall, London SW1Y 5JN

BERRY, Prof Christopher Jon (Chris); s of Joseph Berry (d 1988), and Audrey, *née* Barnes (d 1989); *b* 19 June 1946, St Helens, Lancs; *Educ* Upholland GS, Univ of Nottingham (BA), LSE (PhD); *m* 3 Aug 1968, Christine Emma, *née* Claxton; 2 s (Craig Adrian b 11 Nov 1976, Paul Duncan b 20 May 1979); *Career* Univ of Glasgow: successively asst lectr, lectr, sr lectr and reader Dept of Politics 1970–95, prof of political theory 1995–, head Dept of Politics 1998–2002, head Grad Sch and assoc dean Faculty of Law, Business and Social Sciences 2005–; visiting prof: Univ of Pittsburgh 1973–74, Coll of William and Mary Williamsburg USA 1980–81; FRSA 2001, FRSE 2005; *Publications* Hume, Hegel and Human Nature (1982), Human Nature (1986), The Idea of Democratic Community (1989), The Idea of Luxury: A Conceptual and Historical Investigation (1994), Social Theory of the Scottish Enlightenment (1997); over 50 academic articles and book chapters; *Recreations* contemporary fiction, hill walking; *Style*— Prof Chris Berry; ✉ Department of Politics, Adam Smith Building, University of Glasgow, Glasgow G12 8RT (tel 0141 330 5064, e-mail c.berry@lbss.gla.ac.uk)

BERRY, Graham; *Career* former: divnl chief accountant Trusthouse Forte, co sec Scottish Cncl for Educnl Technol; fin dir Univ of Stirling 1986–89 (fndr Stirling Mgmnt Centre); Scottish Arts Cncl: dir of fin 1989–96, dep dir 1996–2001, acting dir 2001–02, chief exec 2002–; MICAS; *Recreations* climbing, photography; *Style*— Graham Berry, Esq; ✉ Scottish Arts Council, 12 Manor Place, Edinburgh EH3 7DD (tel 0131 226 6051, fax 0131 225 9833, e-mail graham.berry@scottisharts.org.uk)

BERRY, Jack; s of Harry Berry (d 1989), and Nancy, *née* Potter (d 1953); *b* 7 October 1937; *Educ* Leeds and Boston Spa Secdy Modern Sch; *m* 30 Oct 1962, Josephine Mary Thames; 2 s (Alan Warwick b 30 May 1963, Martin Stratford b 13 April 1965); *Career* racehorse trainer; apprentice flat race jockey, nat hunt jockey for 16 years (first winner 1954); set record for a northern trainer with 143 flat winners in a season 1991, record holder for fastest 50 and fastest 100 flat winners in 1991, leading northern trainer 1991–95; tstee: Injured Jockey's Fund, Br European Breeders' Fund (BEBF); *Books* It's Tougher at the Bottom (1991), A Year in Red Shirts (1993), One To Go (2000); *Style*— Jack Berry, Esq, MBE; ✉ Well Close House, Hunton, Bedale, North Yorkshire DL8 1QN (tel 01677 450025)

BERRY, Jamie Alistair Jagoe; s of Raymond Berry, of Stonor, Oxon, and Phyllis, *née* Pegg; *b* 22 December 1955; *Educ* Harrow; *m* 2, 25 June 1992, Oonagh Mary Dode Patricia, da of U Alen-Buckley; 1 da (Venetia Marina Patricia b 22 April 1993), 1 s (George Michael Jagoe b 3 Aug 1995), 3 step c (Orlaith, Cian, Sorcha); *Career* GT Management plc 1973–81, md Berry Asset Management plc 1981–, dir T&G AIM VCT plc 2001–, chm Invesco Perpetual UK Smaller Companies Investment Tst; FIMBRA (memb Cncl 1984–87); *Recreations* sailing, shooting; *Clubs* City of London, Royal Thames Yacht, Sea View Yacht; *Style*— Jamie Berry, Esq; ✉ The Chambers, Chelsea Harbour, London SW10 0XF (tel 020 7376 3476)

BERRY, John Richard; s of Richard William Berry, of Cooden, E Sussex, and Margaret, *née* Hilliard; *b* 5 August 1948; *Educ* Berkhamsted Sch, Univ of Glasgow; *m* Anne Sarah, *née* Ronchetti; 1 s (Paul Mark), 1 da (Rachel Kathryn); *Career* Abbey National: joined 1969, trainee St Albans, various asst mangr appointments, branch mangr Putney and Ludgate Circus, nat sales mangr 1979–82, regnl dir London NE 1982–84, regnl dir Kent and S London 1984–87, regnl dir Central London 1987–88, field ops dir 1988–90, mktg dir 1990–93, European dir 1993–97, dir of corp sales 1997–98, dir of sales 1998–, md retail 2002–03 (dep md 2002), dir Transformation 2003; dir: Quickheart, South Essex Homes; int retail banking conslt 2004–; memb: Marketing Soc, Cncl Building Socs Inst; FIB, MIMgt; *Recreations* family, travel, gardening, vintage cars, politics, sport as spectator; *Style*— John R. Berry, Esq; ✉ John Berry Associates Ltd (tel 01442 863799, mobile 07785 330043)

BERRY, Norman Stevenson McLean; s of James Stevenson Berry, of Glasgow, and Mary Jane, *née* Oliver; *b* 23 January 1933; *Educ* Shawlands Acad Glasgow, Univ of Glasgow (BSc), Univ of Strathclyde (BSc); *m* 20 Oct 1965, Sheila Margaret, da of John Allan McMillan, DSO (d 1967), of Glasgow; 1 da (Ruth Margaret b 1966), 2 s (David John b 1969, Andrew James b 1970); *Career* student then asst engr Hugh Fraser & Partners 1952–57, Public Works Dept Eastern Nigeria 1957–61 (exec engr Roads Dept 1957, zone engr for Rural Water Supplies Programme 1958–61), water and sewerage engr Public Works Dept Solomon Is 1967–71; Babtie Shaw & Morton: asst engr water supply 1961–67, projects engr 1967, assoc 1975, ptnr 1977 (responsible for the Kielder Transfer Works incl 30km of hard rock tunnelling), md Water Div, dir Babtie Group 1993, sr conslt Babtie Group 1994–2000; memb Ct and Business Ctee Univ of Glasgow; treas Findlay Meml Church Glasgowm Bethany Christian Tst; treas: 1451 Assoc Univ of Glasgow, Maryhill Integration Network; FICE; >i<Awards>r< Telford Medal for paper on Kielder Transfer Works ICE 1983, Telford Premium for paper on Kielder Experimental Tunnel Final Results ICE 1984, Inst Medal for paper on Large Diameter Flexible Steel Pipes for the Transfer Works of the Kielder Water Scheme IWEM 1986; *Style*— Norman Berry, Esq; ✉ 2 Fintry Gardens, Bearsden, Glasgow G61 4RJ (tel 0141 942 0637)

BERRY, Peter Fremantle; CMG (1998); s of Dr John Berry, CBE, DL, FRSE (d 2002), of Newport-on-Tay, Fife, and Hon Bride Faith Louisa, *née* Fremantle (d 2003); bro of William Berry, WS, *qv*; *b* 17 May 1944, St Andrews; *Educ* Eton, Lincoln Coll Oxford (MA); *m* 1972, Paola, da of Giovanni Padovani (d 1951); 2 da (Sara b 1974, Anna b 1977), 1 s (Richard b 1979); *Career* mgmnt appts Harrisons & Crosfield plc SE Asia 1967–73, dir Anglo-Indonesian Corp plc 1974–82; dir assocs and subsids notably: Anglo-Asian Investments Ltd, Ampat Sumatra Rubber Estate Ltd, Central Province Ceylon Tea Holdings Ltd, Colman & Co (Agric) Ltd, Walker Sons & Co Ltd; Crown Agents For Overseas Governments and Administrations Ltd: dir Asia and Pacific (res Singapore) 1982–84, dir Middle East, Asia and Pacific 1984, md and Crown Agent 1988, dir various subsids and assocs, exec chm 1998–2002, chm 2002–07; pres The Crown Agents Fndn 2003–; dir: Thomas Tapling & Co Ltd 1987– (chm 2006–), Anglo-Eastern Plantations plc 1990–93, The Scottish Eastern Investment Tst 1994–99, Henderson T R Pacific Investment Tst plc 1994–, Keir Group plc 1997–2007, Martin Currie Capital Return Tst plc 1999–2000, Martin Currie Portfolio Investment Tst plc 1999– (chm 2000–); advsr on int and econ devpt Corp of London 2003–; memb: Indonesia Assoc 1974–93 (chm 1986–89), Cncl Malaysia, Singapore and Brunei Assoc 1982–87, Whitehall Export Promotion Ctee 1992–98, Transparency Int (Berlin) Int Cncl 1993–, CBI Int Ctee 1997–2002, Br Trade Int Business Advsy Gp 1998–2003, UK Trade and Investment Int Sectors Advsy Panel 2003–04; pres Transparency Int (UK) 2003–, dir UK-Japan 21st Century Gp 2000–03, dep chm Charities Aid Fndn 2004– (tstee 2000–, chm Int Ctee 2000–), dir Charity Bank 2003–, dir and tstee Scottish Crop Research Inst 2007–; FRSA; *Recreations* international development, wildlife, country pursuits, Italy; *Clubs* RAC; *Style—* Peter Berry, Esq, CMG; ✉ Crown Agents, St Nicholas House, Sutton, Surrey SM1 1EL (tel 020 8643 3311, fax 020 8643 6518)

BERRY, Prof Robert James (Sam); s of Albert Edward James Berry (d 1952), and Nellie, *née* Hodgson (d 1956); *b* 26 October 1934; *Educ* Shrewsbury, Gonville & Caius Coll Cambridge (MA), UCL (PhD, DSc); *m* 13 June 1958, Anne Caroline, da of Charles Rushton Elliott; 1 s (Andrew b 11 July 1963), 2 da (Alison (Mrs Glyn Jarvis) (twin) b 11 July 1963, Susan b 26 June 1965); *Career* lectr, reader then prof Royal Free Hosp Sch of Med 1962–78; UCL: prof of genetics 1978–2000, emeritus prof 2000–, Leverhulme emeritus fell 2001–04; pres: Linnean Soc 1982–85, British Ecological Soc 1987–89, Euro Ecological Fedn 1990–92, Christians in Science 1992–95, Mammal Soc 1995–97 (treas 1981–87); tstee Nat Museums and Galleries on Merseyside 1986–94, vice-pres Zoological Soc of London 1988–90, memb Human Fertilization and Embryology Authy 1990–96; govr: Monkton Combe Sch 1979–92, Walthamstow Hall 2001–05; memb: Gen Synod C of E 1970–90, Cncl NERC 1981–87; Gifford lectr Univ of Glasgow 1997–98, Hooker lectr Linnean Soc 2008; Marsh Award for Ecology 2001, Templeton UK Award 1996 for sustained advocacy of the Christian faith in the world of science; FIBiol 1974, FRSE 1981; *Publications* Teach Yourself Genetics (1965, 3 edn 1977), Adam and the Ape (1975), Inheritance and Natural History (1977), Natural History of Shetland (jtly, 1980), Neo Darwinism (1982), Free to be Different (jtly, 1984), Natural History of Orkney (1985), God and Evolution (1988), God and the Biologist (1996), Science, Life and Christian Belief (jtly, 1998), Orkney Nature (2000), God's Book of Works (2003); ed: Biology of the House Mouse (1981), Evolution in the Galapagos (1984), Encyclopaedia of Animal Evolution (1986), Nature, Natural History and Ecology (1987); Evolution, Ecology and Environmental Stress (1989), Real Science, Real Faith (1991 and 1995), Genes in Ecology (jtly, 1992), Environmental Dilemmas (1992), Care of Creation (2000), Environmental Stewardship (2006), When Enough is Enough (2007); *Recreations* walking, resting, rejoicing; *Style—* Prof Sam Berry, FRSE; ✉ Quarfseter, Sackville Close, Sevenoaks, Kent TN13 3QD; Department of Biology, University College London, Gower Street, London WC1E 6BT (e-mail rjberry@ucl.ac.uk)

BERRY, Roger Leslie; MP; s of Sydney Berry, and Mary Joyce Berry; *b* 4 July 1948; *Educ* Huddersfield New Coll, Univ of Bristol (BSc), Univ of Sussex (DPhil); *m* 1996, Alison Delyth; *Career* temp lectr in economics Sch of African and Asian Studies and assoc fell Inst of Devpt Studies Univ of Sussex 1973–74; lectr in economics: Univ of Papua New Guinea 1974–78, Univ of Bristol 1978–92; Avon CC: cncllr 1981–92, chm Fin and Admin Ctee 1983–86, dep ldr 1985–86, ldr Lab Gp 1986–92; Parly candidate (Lab) Weston-super-Mare 1983, European Parly candidate Bristol 1984, MP (Lab) Kingswood 1992– (also contested 1987); sec All-Pty Disability Gp 1995–, memb Select Ctee on Trade and Industry 1995–, chair Quadripartite Ctee on Strategic Export Controls 2001–; dir Tribune Publications Ltd 1997–2003; vice-pres Mobilise Orgn 1997–; tstee Snowdon Awards Scheme 1997–2003; memb Amicus; *Publications* contrib to learned jls; newspaper articles and pamphlets; *Recreations* travel, food, gardening, reading; *Clubs* Kingswood Labour; *Style—* Roger Berry, MP; ✉ House of Commons, London SW1A 0AA; constituency office (tel 0117 956 1837, fax 0117 970 1363, e-mail berryr@parliament.uk)

BERRY, (Anthony) Scyld Ivens; s of Prof Francis Berry, of Winchester, Hants, and Nancy Melloney, *née* Graham (d 1967); *b* 28 April 1954; *Educ* Westbourne Sch Sheffield, Ampleforth, Christ's Coll Cambridge (MA); *m* 2 April 1984, Sunita, da of Brig M K Ghosh; 2 s (Sceaf b 17 April 1993, Raefel b 10 Jan 1997), 1 da (Freya b 3 July 1991); *Career* cricket corr: The Observer 1978–89, Sunday Correspondent 1989–90, Independent on Sunday 1991–93, Sunday Telegraph 1993–; ed Wisden Cricketers' Almanack 2008; *Books* Cricket Wallah (1982), Train to Julia Creek (1984), The Observer on Cricket (ed, 1988), Cricket Odyssey (1988); *Recreations* village cricket; *Clubs* Hinton Charterhouse CC; *Style—* Scyld Berry, Esq; ✉ The Daily Telegraph, 111 Buckingham Palace Road, London SW1W 0DT

BERRY, (Roger) Simon; QC (1990); s of Kingsland Jutsum Berry, of Bristol, and Kathleen Margaret, *née* Parker; *b* 9 September 1948; *Educ* St Brendan's Coll Bristol, Univ of Manchester (LLB); *m* 1974, Jennifer Jane, da of Jonas Birtwistle Hall; 3 s (Richard James b 27 Nov 1979, Nicholas Peter b 25 June 1981, William Patrick b 17 Aug 1986); *Career* admitted slr 1973, ptnr Stanley Wasbrough (now Veale Wasbrough) 1975–77; called to the Bar Middle Temple 1977 (ad eundum Lincoln's Inn), (bencher of Lincoln's Inn 1996), recorder 2000, dep High Ct judge 2001–; memb: Middle Temple, Lincoln's Inn, Western Circuit, Chancery Bar Assoc, Ctee Chancery Bar Assoc 1984 and 1985, Professional Negligence Bar Assoc, Property Bar Assoc, Bar Cncl 1996–99; memb Theatre Panel of Judges for the Olivier awards 2000; *Recreations* family, the performing arts, cycling, skiing, keeping fit; *Clubs* Ski Club of GB, Riverside; *Style—* Mr Simon Berry, QC; ✉ 9 Old Square, Lincoln's Inn, London WC2A 3SR (tel 020 7405 4682, fax 020 7831 7107)

BERRY, William; DL, WS; s of Dr John Berry, CBE, DL, FRSE (d 2002), of Tayfield, Fife, and Hon Bride Faith Louisa, *née* Fremantle (d 2003); bro of Peter Fremantle Berry, CMG, *qv*; *b* 26 September 1939; *Educ* Eton, Univ of St Andrews (MA), Univ of Edinburgh (LLB); *m* 1973, Elizabeth, da of Sir Edward Warner, KCMG, OBE (d 2002), of Blockley, Glos; 2 s (John b 1976, Robert b 1978); *Career* Murray Beith Murray WS Edinburgh: ptnr 1967–2000, sr ptnr 1991–2000, chm 2000–04; dir Dawnfresh Holdings Ltd; former dir: Scottish American Investment Co, Fleming Continental European Investment Trust, Alliance Trust, Second Alliance Trust, Scottish Life Assurance Co (chm 1993–99), Inchcape Family Investments Ltd (chm 2000–03); memb Queen's Body Guard for Scotland (Royal Co of Archers); dep chm Edinburgh Int Festival 1985–89; chm: New Town Concerts Soc Edinburgh, Edinburgh Family Service Unit, Scottish Fiddle Soc; mangr New Club; tstee Royal Botanic Garden Edinburgh 1986–94, Hopetoun House Preservation Tst; memb: Cockburn Assoc, Edinburgh Civic Tst, Scottish Ctee Marie Curie Tst, Patrons Exec Ctee National Museums of Scotland, Exec Ctee Thistle Fndn; sr govr Univ of St Andrews 2002–07; FRSA; *Recreations* music, shooting, forestry, urban and rural conservation; *Clubs* New (Edinburgh); *Style—* William Berry, Esq, DL, WS; ✉ Tayfield, Newport-on-Tay, Fife DD6 8HA

BERRY OTTAWAY, Peter; s of Cecil Berry Ottaway (d 1986), of Sutton St Nicholas, Hereford, and Myfanwy, *née* Thomas (d 1999); *b* 17 February 1942; *Educ* Steyning GS, Univ of London (BSc), UC of Rhodesia and Nyasaland; *m* 21 Dec 1963 (m dis 2006), Andrea, da of Richard Sampson, ED, of Palm Springs, CA; 2 s (Gareth b 10 July 1965 (decd), Charles b 9 Oct 1986), 2 da (Samantha b 30 April 1969, Georgina b 17 Jan 1981); *Career* cmmnd Trg Branch RAFVR 1968–95 (Sqdn Ldr); res scientist Zambian Govt WHO 1963–65; res mgmnt: Unilever Ltd 1965–67, General Foods Ltd 1967–74; int consultancy in food technol, food science and nutrition 1974–81, dir of science and technol (Europe) Shaklee Corporation Calif 1981, md Berry Ottaway & Associates Ltd, dir Mercia Testing Laboratories Ltd, consulting scientist 1987–; memb Duke of Edinburgh's Award Ctee Herefordshire 1978–99, memb Ctee Sports Nutrition Fndn 1986–99; CSci, CBiol, FRSH 1974, MIBiol 1978, FIFST 1981, FRIPH; *Books* Food for Sport (1985), Nutrition in Sport (ed with Dr D H Shrimpton, 1986), Preservatives in Food (1988), Nutritional Enhancement of Food (jtly, 1989), The Technology of Vitamins in Food (ed, 1992), The Harmonisation of European Union Food Legislation (1995), The Sanyati Survival Expedition (1996), The Addition of Micronutrients to Foods (ed, 1997), Food Labelling (jtly, 1999), Forever Aircrew (ed, 1999), Prebiotics - New Developments in Functional Foods (jtly, 2000), Functional Foods (jtly, 2000), European Food Law (jtly, 2001), Gum and Stabilisers for the Food Industry (contrib, 2002), The Nutrition Handbook for Food Processors (contrib, 2002), International Review of Food Science and Technology (ed, 2002–06), Natural Antimicrobials for the Minimal Processing of Foods (contrib, 2003), Functional Foods, Ageing and Degenerative Disease (contrib, 2004), Regulation of Functional Foods and Nutraceuticals (contrib, 2005), Long-Chain Omega-3 Specialty Oils (contrib, 2007); assoc ed and contrib Encyclopaedia of Food Science and Nutrition (2003); *Recreations* light aviation, hill walking, art; *Clubs* RAF; *Style—* Peter Berry Ottaway, Esq; ✉ Kivernoll Cottage, Kivernoll, Much Dewchurch, Herefordshire HR2 8DS

BERTHOUD, Prof Jacques Alexandre; s of Rev Alexandre Léon Berthoud (d 1962), of Neuchatel, Switzerland, and Madeleine, *née* Bourquin (d 1989); *b* 1 March 1935; *Educ* Coll de Genève Switzerland, Maritzburg Coll Natal, Univ of the Witwatersrand (BA); *m* 1958, Astrid Irene, da of Maj Eugene Titlestad, of Qudeni, Zululand; 1 s (Tristan Alexandre b 1964), 2 da (Dr Mireille Christine Berthoud b 1958, Josephine Madeleine (Mrs Berthoud-Dubreuil) b 1960); *Career* lectr Dept of Eng Univ of Natal Pietermaritzburg 1961–67, lectr then sr lectr Dept of Eng Univ of Southampton 1967–80; Univ of York: prof Dept of English and Related Lit 1980–2002, head of dept 1980–97, dep vice-chllr 1987–90, currently emeritus prof; visiting fell Trinity Coll Cambridge 1990–91; nat chm Br Section Amnesty Int 1978–80, pres Int Assoc of Univ Profs of Eng 1987; memb: Cncl Joseph Conrad Soc, Laurence Sterne Tst; *Books* Uys Krige (jtly, 1966), Joseph Conrad (1978), Joseph Conrad: au coeur de de l'oeuvre (1992); *Style—* Prof Jacques Berthoud; ✉ 30 New Walk Terrace, Fishergate, York YO10 4BG (tel 01904 629212)

BERTIE, HMEH Prince and Grand Master of the Sovereign Military Hospitaller Order of St John of Jerusalem, of Rhodes and of Malta; Frà Andrew Willoughby Ninian; er s of Lt Cdr the Hon James Willoughby Bertie, RN (d 1966; yst s of 7 Earl of Abingdon), and Lady Jean Crichton-Stuart (d 1995), yr da of late 4 Marquess of Bute, KT; bro of (Charles) Peregrine Albemarle Bertie, *qv*; *b* 15 May 1929; *Educ* Ampleforth, ChCh Oxford (MA), SOAS Univ of London; *Career* Lt Scots Guards 1948–50; with City Press 1954–57, Ethicon 1957–59, Worth Sch 1960–83; elected Prince and Grand Master of the Sovereign Military Hospitaller Order of St John of Jerusalem, of Rhodes and of Malta 1988; *Recreations* reading, gardening, judo, fencing; *Clubs* Turf, RAC, Caccia (Rome), Scacchi (Rome), Casino (Malta); *Style—* His Most Eminent Highness the Prince and Grand Master of the Sovereign Military Hospitaller Order of St John of Jerusalem, of Rhodes and of Malta; ✉ Via Condotti 68, 00187 Rome, Italy (tel 00 39 06 675 811, fax 00 39 06 679 7202)

BERTIE, (Charles) Peregrine Albemarle; s of Lt Cdr the Hon James Willoughby Bertie, RN (d 1966, yst s of 7 Earl of Abingdon), and Lady Jean Crichton-Stuart (d 1995), yr da of 4 Marquess of Bute, KT; bro of the Prince and Grand Master SMOM (Andrew Willoughby Ninian Bertie), *qv*; *b* 2 January 1932; *Educ* Ampleforth; *m* 20 April 1960, Susan Griselda Ann Lyon, da of Maj John Lycett Wills (d 1999); 1 s (David Montagu Albemarle b 12 Feb 1963), 1 da (Caroline Georgina Rose (Mrs Andrew Carrington) b 16 March 1965); *Career* Capt Scots Gds 1950–54 and 1956–57, memb London Stock Exchange 1958–91; High Sheriff Berks 1986–87; pres The British Assoc SMOM 1995–2001; memb Queen's Body Guard for Scotland (Royal Co of Archers); Liveryman Worshipful Co of Armourers and Brasiers; Freeman City of London; Knight Cdr Order of St Gregory the Great, Grand Cross of Merit with Swords Order Pro Merito Melitensi, KStJ, Bailiff Grand Cross of Honour and Devotion in Obedience SMOM, Knight Grand Cross of Justice Constantinian Order of St George; *Clubs* Turf, White's, Pratt's, Puffin's; *Style—* Peregrine Bertie, Esq; ✉ Frilsham Manor, Hermitage, Newbury, Berkshire RG18 9UZ (tel 01635 201291)

BERTRAM, Dr Brian Colin Ricardo; s of Dr George Colin Lawder Bertram (d 2001), of Graffham, W Sussex, and Dr Cicely Kate Ricardo Bertram (d 1999); *b* 14 April 1944; *Educ* Perse Sch Cambridge, St John's Coll Cambridge (BA, PhD, TH Huxley Award Certificate of Commendation); *m* 3 May 1975, Katharine Jean, da of Francis Blaise Gillie, CBE (d 1981); 2 da (Joanna Mary Ricardo b 1981, Felicity Kate Ricardo b 1983), 1 s (Nicholas Blaise Ricardo (twin) b 1983); *Career* res fell Serengeti Res Inst Tanzania 1969–73, sr res fell King's Coll Cambridge 1976–79, curator of mammals Zoological Soc of London 1980–87, DG The Wildfowl & Wetlands Tst 1987–92; freelance zoological advsr 1993–99; co-ordinator overseas conservation prog Federation of Zoological Gardens 1994–96, special projects co-ordinator Bristol Zoo Gardens 1995–2003, zoological conslt Wildscreen Bristol (now Wildwalk @t Bristol) 1997–2000; vice-pres World Pheasant Assoc 1990–98, memb Cncl Zoological Soc of London 1993–97, 1999–2002 and 2004–07; FIBiol 1979; *Books* Pride of Lions (1978), The Ostrich Communal Nesting System (1992), Lions (1998); *Recreations* family, animals, garden, friends; *Clubs* Zoological; *Style—* Dr Brian Bertram; ✉ Fieldhead, Amberley, Stroud, Gloucestershire GL5 5AG (tel 01453 872796, e-mail bbertram@btopenworld.com)

BERTRAM, Robert David Darney; WS (1969); s of David Noble Stewart Bertram (d 1981), of Edinburgh, and Angela Jean Weston, *née* Devlin; *b* 6 October 1941; *Educ* Edinburgh Acad, Oriel Coll Oxford (MA), Univ of Edinburgh (LLB); *m* 23 Sept 1967, Patricia John, da of John Laithwaite, formerly of Prescot, Lancashire; 2 s (Andrew b 1972, Nicholas b 1975); *Career* ptnr Dundas and Wilson CS Edinburgh 1969–92, ptnr Corp Dept Shepherd & Wedderburn WS 1992–98; non-exec dir The Weir Group plc 1982–2000; memb: Tech Ctee Inst of Taxation 1986, Scottish Review Panel on Reform of Law on Security over Moveables 1986, Audit Advsy Bd Scottish Parliament Corp 2002, DTI Review of Co Law 1998–2001, Insolvency Practices Cncl 2001; assessor Univ of Edinburgh Court 2000–03; examiner Law Soc Scotland; memb: VAT Tbnl, Scottish Law Cmmn 1978–86, Competition Cmmn 1998–; tstee David Hume Inst 1998; CTA 1970; *Recreations* book collecting, jazz, browsing; *Clubs* Scottish Arts, Royal Over-Seas League; *Style—* R D Bertram, Esq, WS

BERTRAM, (Charles) William; s of Lt-Col Richard Bertram (d 1995), and Elizabeth Florence Oriana, *née* Bedwell (d 1991); *Educ* Sherborne, Architectural Assoc (AADipl); *m* 16 Nov 1963, Victoria Harriette, da of Reginald Addington Ingle, of Priston, nr Bath; 2 da (Clare Victoria Harriette b 1965, Josephine Alice b 1967), 1 s (Robert William b 1970); *Career* fndr architectural practice William Bertram and Fell of Bath (conslt architects to Abbotsbury 1972) 1969 (conslt 1995–), fndr William Bertram Consulting Architect 1996; personal architect to HRH the Prince of Wales at Highgrove Glos 1987–98, conslt to Eastern Region Duchy of Cornwall 1989–, architectural advsr to RNLI; converted Royal

Crescent Hotel into 5 star hotel, converted Cliveden into hotel 1986–89, designer of Cavendish Lodge Bath, redesigned Sir Winston Churchill's grave at Bladon 1998, restoration of Dinmore Manor and Gardens 2000–04, reordering of Parnham House 2003; received: UK Cncl Euro Architectural Heritage Year Award 1975, Civic Tst Award for conservation of Abbotsbury Village Dorset, Civic Tst award for Dower House Bath 1986, Bath Conservation Area Advsy Ctee Environmental Award 1987, award for environmental design St Ann's Place and Environs; tstee Bath Preservation Tst 1966–68, listed in Architects Registration Cncl of UK; memb Br Soc of Architects, RIBA; *Books* The Origins of Queen Square Bath (1962), An Appreciation of Abbotsbury (1973); *Recreations* tennis, walking, garden design, sketching; *Style*— William Bertram, Esq; ✉ The Studio, Woodrising, Loves Hill, Timsbury, Bath BA2 0EU (tel 01761 471100, fax 01761 479102)

BERTRAM-BROWN, Harvey; s of Dennis H Brown, of London, and Sandra M, *née* Finklestein; *b* 9 January 1966; *Educ* Haberdashers' Aske's, St Martin's Sch of Art, Ravensbourne Coll of Art & Design (BA), RCA (MA); *Career* fndr memb The New Renaissance 1991– (multi media co formerly specialising in fashion and accessory design, display, styling and art direction, currently directing TV commercials and music promos through The Pink Film Co); exhbns incl: Fouts and Fowler Gallery London 1991, Liberty London 1991, Premiere Classe Paris 1991, The World of The New RenaisCAnce (Royal Festival Hall and Parco Gallery Tokyo) 1992, Crafts in Performance (Crafts Cncl touring exhbn) 1993, In the Swim (Bremerhaven Germany) 1993; window design for Liberty and Harvey Nichols London; commercial and music promos incl: PowerGen 'Weathergens', Gordon's Gin, Diamond White Cider, George Michael, Elton John, LeAnn Rimes; *Style*— Harvey Bertram-Brown, Esq; ✉ The New Renaissance, c/o The Pink Film Company, 8–18 Smiths Court, off Great Windmill Street, London W1V 7PF (tel 020 7287 5502, fax 020 7287 5503, website www.thenewrenaissance.co.uk)

BESAG, Prof Julian E; s of Emil Besag (d 1987), and Irene, *née* Fuidge; *b* 26 March 1945, Loughborough, Leics; *Educ* Loughborough GS, Churchill Coll Cambridge, Univ of Birmingham (BSc); *m* 28 July 1966 (m dis 2003), Valerie; 1 s (David Haydn b 3 March 1972), 1 da (Charlotte b 15 Feb 1980); *Career* research asst Dept of Biomathematics Univ of Oxford 1968–70, lectr Dept of Computational and Statistical Science Univ of Liverpool 1970–75, reader Dept of Mathematical Sciences Univ of Durham 1975–86; prof: Dept of Mathematical Sciences Univ of Durham 1986–89, Dept of Statistics Univ of Washington Seattle 1989–90 and 1991–2007, Sch of Mathematics Univ of Newcastle upon Tyne 1990–91; visiting lectr Princeton Univ 1975, visiting prof Sch of Med Univ of Newcastle upon Tyne 1988–89, currently visiting prof Univ of Bath; author of numerous articles and discussion papers; Guy Medal Royal Statistical Soc 1983; memb: Royal Statistical Soc 1968, Int Statistical Inst 1983, Inst of Mathematical Statistics 1991; FRS 2004; *Recreations* sailing; *Clubs* Northwest Riggers Yacht, Washington Yacht; *Style*— Prof Julian Besag; ✉ Department of Statistics, Box 354322, University of Washington, Seattle, WA 98185, USA (tel 00 1 206 543 3871, fax 00 1 206 685 7419, e-mail julian@stat.washington.edu)

BESANT, Prof Colin Bowden; s of William Henry Besant (d 1949), of Plymouth, and Sarah Grace, *née* White (d 1975); *b* 4 April 1936; *Educ* Plymouth Coll, Plymouth Coll of Technol (BSc), Imperial Coll London (DIC, PhD); *m* (m dis); 1 da (Christine Tanzi b 23 March 1963), 1 s (Simon Bowden b 2 Jan 1968); *Career* scientific offr UKAEA 1960–64; Imperial Coll London: lectr 1964–75, reader in mechanical engrg 1975–89, prof of computer-aided manufacture 1989–2000; chm Turbo Power Systems Inc; HNC prizes IMechE and IEE; FREng 1988, FIMechE, FIEE, FINucE, FRSA; *Books* Computer-Aided Design and Manufacture (1986), Parallel Processing and Artificial Intelligence (1989); *Recreations* music, cricket; *Style*— Prof Colin Besant, FREng; ✉ Department of Mechanical Engineering, Imperial College, Exhibition Road, London SW7 2BX (tel 020 8564 4460, e-mail c.besant@ic.ac.uk)

BESLEY, Crispian George; s of Christopher Besley (d 2004), of Wimbledon, London, and Pamela Geraldine Margaret Edgeworth, *née* David; *b* 21 November 1958; *Educ* Wellington Coll; *m* 1, 1988 (m dis 1992), Elizabeth, da of Thomas Bridger; m 2, 1994, Sarah (Sally) Helen Catherine, da of Stanley Morris; 2 s (Hugo Alexander Edgeworth b 14 Nov 1996, Charlie George b 25 Jan 1999); *Career* formerly dir Prudential Bache Securities Japan 1986–87; dir Smith New Court Int 1987–95, main bd dir Schroder Securities 1996–2000, dir Schroder Japan 1996–2000, dir Credit Suisse First Boston (Europe) 2000–06, md Credit Suisse 2007–; *Recreations* amateur racing driver, skiing, Cresta run, all motorsports, classic cars; *Clubs* City Univ, Lansdowne, Annabel's, St Moritz Toboggan; *Style*— Crispian Besley, Esq; ✉ c/o Credit Suisse, One Cabot Square, London E14 4QS (tel 020 7888 8888, e-mail crispian.besley@credit-suisse.com)

BESLEY, Prof Timothy John; s of John Besley, of Oxford, and June, *née* Turton; *b* 14 September 1960; *Educ* Univ of Oxford (BA, MPhil, DPhil); *m* Aug 1993, Gillian, *née* Paull; 2 s (Thomas Arthur b 31 July 1995, Oliver John b 21 Oct 1997); *Career* fell All Souls Coll Oxford 1984–89, asst prof Princeton Univ 1989–95, prof of economics LSE 1995–2002, prof of economics and political science LSE 2002–; memb Cncl Econometric Soc 2002–, memb Monetary Policy Ctee Bank of England 2006–; co-ed American Economic Review 1998–2005, author of numerous contribs to scholarly jls; Richard Musgrave Prize 1999, Yrjö Jahnsson Prize 2005; fell Econometric Soc 2000, FBA 2001; *Recreations* squash, playing violin, watching cricket; *Style*— Prof Timothy Besley; ✉ London School of Economics and Political Science, Houghton Street, London WC2A 2AE (tel 020 7955 6702, e-mail t.besley@lse.ac.uk)

BESSBOROUGH, Madeleine, Countess of; Lady Madeleine Lola Margaret Ponsonby; da of Maj-Gen Laurence Douglas Grand, CB, CIE, CBE (d 1975), of Delaford Manor, Iver, Bucks, and Irene, *née* Mathew (d 1971); *b* 8 November 1935; *Educ* St Mary's Sch St Leonards-on-Sea, Priors Field Godalming; *m* 1963, as his 3 w, 11 Earl of Bessborough (d 2002); 2 s (Hon Matthew Douglas Longfield b 1965, Hon Charles Arthur Longfield b 1967); *Career* fndr The New Art Centre London 1957–, held over 200 exhbns of British and Euro art, group shows incl St Ives 1946–56 and British Sculpture of the 1950s and 1960s, Roche Court Sculpture Garden opened as addition to gallery 1986–; patron Salisbury Hospice 1999–; memb Cncl RCA 1963–72 (hon fell 1973), memb judging panel for various int art awards; FRSA; *Recreations* gardening; *Style*— Madeleine, Countess of Bessborough; ✉ New Art Centre, Sculpture Park, Roche Court, East Winterslow, Salisbury, Wiltshire SP5 1BG (tel 01980 862244, fax 01980 862447, e-mail nac@globalnet.co.uk)

BESSBOROUGH, 12 Earl of (I 1739); Myles Fitzhugh Longfield Ponsonby; also Baron Bessborough (I 1721), Viscount Duncannon (I 1723), Baron Ponsonby of Sysonby (GB 1749), and Baron Duncannon (GB 1834); s of 11 Earl of Bessborough (d 2002); *b* 16 February 1941; *Educ* Harrow, Trinity Coll Cambridge (MA); *m* 1972, Alison Marjorie, 3 da of William Storey, OBE; 2 s (Frederick Arthur William, Viscount Duncannon b 9 Aug 1974, Hon Henry Shakerley b 1977), 1 da (Lady Chloë Patricia b 1975); *Heir* s, Viscount Duncannon; *Career* banker; FCA; *Clubs* White's, Pratt's; *Style*— The Rt Hon the Earl of Bessborough; ✉ Broadreed, Stansted Park, Rowlands Castle, Hampshire PO9 6DZ

BESSELL, Dr Eric Michael; s of William Henry Bessell, and Doris Mabel, *née* Willson (d 1992); *b* 17 December 1946; *Educ* Radcliffe Sch Wolverton, Univ of Bristol (BSc), Inst of Cancer Research London (PhD), St Mary's Hosp Med Sch London (MB BS); *m* 31 July 1971, Deborah Jane; 1 da (Laura Elizabeth b 29 Dec 1976), 1 s (Andrew Thomas b 29 Sept 1979); *Career* registrar in clinical oncology Royal Postgrad Med Sch Hammersmith Hosp London 1980–83, sr registrar in clinical oncology Royal Marsden Hosp London 1983–85, conslt in clinical oncology Nottingham HA 1985–, clinical dir Dept of Clinical Oncology Nottingham 1986–96 and 2003–; chm Nottingham Div BMA 1990; examiner RCR 1994–2000, memb Lymphoma Clincal Studies Gp Nat Cancer Research Inst 2003–05; author of numerous papers on malignant lymphomas in learned jls; FRCR 1984, FRCP 1993 (MRCP); *Recreations* mountain walking, piano playing, opera; *Style*— Dr Eric Bessell; ✉ Department of Clinical Oncology, Nottingham City Hospital NHS Trust, Hucknall Road, Nottingham NG5 1PB (tel 0115 962 7986, fax 0115 840 2636, e-mail eric.bessell@nuh.nhs.uk)

BESSER, Prof (Gordon) Michael; *b* 22 January 1936; *Educ* St Bartholomew's Med Coll London (BSc, MB BS, MD, DSc); *Career* house offr posts Bart's, Hammersmith and Brompton Hosps 1961–63, lectr in med Bart's 1966–68 (jr lectr in therapeutics 1963–66), NIH postdoctoral fell Dept of Endocrinology Vanderbilt Univ Sch of Med Nashville TN 1968–69; Bart's: sr lectr in med and hon conslt physician Med Professorial Unit 1970–74, prof of endocrinology (Univ of London) and hon conslt physician 1974–92, dir Med Directorate 1990–92, chief exec Bart's NHS Gp 1992–95, prof of med 1992–2001, hon conslt physician and prof of med emeritus 2001–; hon conslt endocrinologist Maltese Govt 1989–2003, civilian endocrinologist RN 1989–2003; RCP: second censor 1992–93, sr censor and sr vice-pres 1995–97; review ed Clinical Endocrinology and Metabolism 1975–79; numerous int lectureships and professorships; Goulstonian lectr RCP 1974, Lumlean lectr RCP 1993, Simms lectr RCP 1999, Jubilee lectr Soc for Endocrinology 2001; Sommer meml lectr Portland OR 1977, Soc for Endocrinology Medal 1978, Chinese Acad of Med Sciences Medal 1982, Clinical Endocrinology Prize 1986, Serbian Acad of Science Medal 1987; Hon MD Univ of Turin 1985; European Neuroendocrine Assoc Medal 1999; memb/fell: Soc for Endocrinology 1969, Endocrine Soc USA 1971, Assoc of Physicians 1972, Euro Thyroid Assoc 1974, Thyroid Club 1975, Ovarian Club 1975, Physiological Soc 1978–82; William Julius Mickle fell for the advancement of med science Univ of London 1976, scientific fell RZS 1978–92, hon fell Queen Mary Univ of London 2005; hon memb: Assoc of American Physicians 1985, RSA 1994; FRCP 1973, FMedSci 1998 (memb Cncl 2001–04), Hon FRSM 2007; *Books* incl: Clinical Endocrinology: An Illustrated Text (jtly, 1 edn 1986, 3 edn 2002), Clinical Diabetes (jtly, 1988), Fundamentals of Clinical Endocrinology (jtly, 4 edn 1989), Atlas of Endocrine Imaging (jtly, 1993), Barts Endocrine Protocols (jtly, 1995); numerous published papers in learned jls; *Recreations* early Chinese ceramics, opera, ballet, theatre; *Clubs* Garrick; *Style*— Prof Michael Besser; ✉ London Clinic Centre for Endocrinology and Diabetes, 145 Harley Street, London W1G 6BJ (tel 020 7616 7790, fax 020 7616 7791, e-mail endo@thelondonclinic.co.uk)

BESSEY, Peter John Harvey; s of Cyril Leonard Bessey, of Twickenham, Middx, and Catherine Elizabeth, *née* Drury; *b* 17 May 1944; *Educ* Gunnersbury GS, Ealing Sch of Art, Central Sch of Art & Design (RSA bursary, industrial and furniture design DipAD); *Children* 1 s (Matthew John Harvey b 1991); *Career* res and analytical chemistry BP Sunbury 1961–66; assoc: Keith Townend Associates 1970–78, Satherley Design Associates 1978–85; sr product engr PA Design (later Brand New Product Development Ltd) 1985–89, fndr ptnr Hothouse Product Development Partners 1989–; projects incl: Xenotron XVC3 Graphic Workstation/Terminal 1985 (COID Design Award), Esselte Meto System 2500 retail anti-theft system 1989–90 and System 2600 1994, Gerry Baby Products Co nursery monitor 1994, Kimberley-Clark Handy Pack wipes dispenser 1995 (DBA Design Effectiveness Finalist 1996), Kimberley-Clark Roll Control wipes dispenser 1997 (DBA Design Effectiveness Award 1998, Millennium Product Selection 1998), ERA Security Products Codemaster digital door lock 1997, Klippan Prima and Futura Child Safety Seats 1999 (Mother and Baby Gold Awards 2000); PUR Ultimate Water Filtration Pitcher 2001 (PRW Plastics Industry Award Finalist 2002), Spinlock Bullseye BE Range 2002 (MAME Award Commendation 2002), Burgopak CD/DVD Cases 2002–03, Elekta Synergy Radiotherapy Machine 2003 (DBA Design Effectiveness Award 2003), Quin Systems SRV400 Motion Controller Range 2003, Elekta Oncology KVS X-Ray Imaging System 2004; fndr memb SIAD Alternative Design Gp 1974, chm CSD Product Gp 1986–88, CSD rep Cncl Camberwell Sch of Art 1987–89, visiting tutor Central St Martin's Sch of Art 1988–95, memb IT Task Gp DBA 1996–98; hon res fell London Inst Central St Martin's Sch of Art 2000–; FCSD (1985, MSIAD 1977), FRSA 2005; *Publications* contrib Rapid Prototyping Casebook 2001; *Recreations* dinghy racing, board sailing, photography, archaeology, travel; *Clubs* Upper Thames Sailing; *Style*— Peter Bessey, Esq; ✉ Hothouse Product Development Partners, Unit 1, College Fields Business Centre, Prince George's Road, London SW19 2PT (tel 020 8687 2093, fax 020 8646 1822, e-mail peter.b@hothouse-design.com)

BEST, Andrew Roger Riddell; s of John Riddell Best (d 1992), and Stella Mary, *née* Whitley (d 2003); *Educ* Charterhouse, Worcester Coll Oxford (MA); *m* 1984, Virginia, da of Angus Lloyd; 1 da (Amanda b 1987), 3 s (James b 1989, John b 1991, Angus b 1995); *Career* Union Bank of Switzerland (UBS) 1986–88, NatWest Markets 1988–92, Shandwick Consultants 1992–99 (dir), managing ptnr Shared Value Ltd 2000–; memb Investor Rels Soc; *Style*— Andrew Best, Esq; ✉ Shared Value Ltd, 30 St James Square, London SW1Y 4JH (tel 020 7321 5020, fax 020 7321 5010, e-mail abest@sharedvalue.net)

BEST, Gary Martin; s of Charles William Best, of South Shields, and Doreen, *née* Wright; *b* 6 October 1951; *Educ* South Shields Grammar Tech Sch, Exeter Coll Oxford (MA), Oxford Dept of Educn (PGCE); *m* 9 Aug 1975, Frances Elizabeth, da of Edward Albert Rolling, of Redruth; 1 da (Claire Frances b 1981); *Career* asst history teacher King Edward's Sch Bath 1974–80, head of Sixth Form Newcastle under Lyme Sch 1983–87 (head of history 1980–83), headmaster Kingswood Sch 1987–; Methodist local preacher; *Books* Seventeenth-Century Europe (1980), Wesley and Kingswood (1988), Continuity and Change (1998), John Wesley (2003), Charles Wesley (2007); *Recreations* painting, music, reading, walking; *Style*— Gary Best, Esq; ✉ Summerfield, College Road, Bath BA1 5SD (tel 01225 317907); Kingswood School, Bath BA1 5RG (tel 01225 734200, e-mail hmsecretary@kingswood.bath.sch.uk)

BEST, Dr Geoffrey Francis Andrew; s of Frederick Ebenezer Best (d 1940), and Catherine Sarah Vanderbrook, *née* Bultz; *Educ* St Paul's Sch, Trinity Coll Cambridge (BA, PhD), Harvard Univ (Joseph Hodges Choate fell); *m* 9 July 1955, (Gwenllyan) Marigold, da of Reginald Davies, CMG; 2 s (Simon Geoffrey b 1956, Edward Hugh b 1958), 1 da (Rosamund Margaret b 1961); *Career* 2 Lt RAEC 1946–47; asst lectr Univ of Cambridge 1956–61; Univ of Edinburgh: lectr 1961–66, Sir Richard Lodge prof of history 1966–73; Univ of Sussex: prof of history 1974–85, dean Sch of European Studies 1980–82; visitor and research fell LSE 1982–88; sr assoc memb St Antony's Coll Oxford 1988–2004; visiting fell: All Souls Coll Oxford 1969–70, Woodrow Wilson Center Washington DC 1978–79, Aust Nat Univ 1984; BRCS: chm Principles and Law Ctee 1980–84, hon conslt on humanitarian law 1985–91; jt winner ICRC triennial Paul Reuter Prize 1997, Churchill Centre Emery Reves Award 2002; FBA 2003; *Books* incl: Temporal Pillars (1964), Shaftsbury (1964), Mid-Victorian Britain (1971), Humanity in Warfare (1980), Honour Among Men and Nations (1982), War and Society in Revolutionary Europe (1982), The Permanent Revolution (1988), War and Law since 1945 (1994), Churchill: A Study in Greatness (2001), Churchill and War (2005); *Style*— Dr Geoffrey Best, FBA; ✉ 19 Buckingham Street, Oxford OX1 4LH (tel 01865 722793)

BEST, Dr Keith Howard; OBE (1983); s of Herbert Henry Best (d 1958), of Sheffield, and Margaret, *née* Appleyard (d 1925); *b* 16 January 1923; *Educ* High Storrs GS, Univ of Sheffield (BEng); *m* 5 April 1947, Maire Raymonde (d 2000), da of George Ernest Lissenden (d 1965); 1 da (Sarah b 1947), 2 s (Jonathan b 1949, Clive b 1952); *Career* served WWII 1942–46, parachute sqdns RE France and Germany, Lt 1944, Palestine

1945, Capt; Husband and Co: asst engr Sheffield 1947–54, princ engr Ceylon 1954–57, ptnr London 1957–70; Bullen and Partners: ptnr Croydon 1970–81, ptnr Durham 1981–88, sr ptnr 1988–89, conslt 1989–; memb Cncl IStructE 1968–71, pres Br Section Société des Ingénieurs et Scientifiques de France 1976, memb EDC (civil engrg) 1978–84; chm: Maritime Engrg Gp ICE 1981–84, Assoc of Consulting Engrs 1987–88, North region Engrg Cncl 1988–90; Freeman City of London, Liveryman Worshipful Co of Engrs 1985–2002; Hon DEng 1997; FICE 1958, FIStructE 1957, FREng 1983; *Books* Best Endeavours (1992), Best Mate (2005); *Clubs* Army and Navy; *Style*— Dr Keith Best, OBE, FREng; ✉ 7 Chessingham Gardens, York YO24 1XE (tel 01904 701744)

BEST, Keith Lander; TD; s of Peter Edwin Wilson Best (d 1984), of Hurstpierpoint, W Sussex, and Margaret Louisa, *née* Ambrose (d 1991); *b* 10 June 1949; *Educ* Brighton Coll, Keble Coll Oxford (MA); *m* 28 July 1990, Elizabeth Margaret Gibson; 2 da (Phoebe b 22 Oct 1991, Ophelia b 2 Aug 1993); *Career* Maj 289 Parachute Battery RHA (V) and Commando Forces, served on HMS Bulwark 1976, naval gunfire liaison offr; called to the Bar Inner Temple 1971, barr in Old Steine Brighton 1971–87; borough cncllr Brighton 1976–80, MP (Cons) Anglesey Ynys Môn 1979–87 (PPS to Sec of State for Wales 1981–84); direct mail conslt Nat Children's Home 1987, dir Prisoners Abroad 1989–93, chief exec Immigration Advsy Serv 1993–; chm: Assoc of Regulated Immigration Advsrs 2003–, Electoral Reform Soc, Cons Action for Electoral Reform, World Federalist Movement, Assoc of World Federalists, Electronic Immigration Network Charity; tstee Odyssey Tst; pres The Holyhead Festival Ltd; Freeman City of London, Liveryman Worshipful Co of Loriners; FRSA; *Books* Write Your Own Will (1978), The Right Way to Prove a Will (1980); *Recreations* walking, skiing, photography, being useful; *Clubs* New Cavendish; *Style*— Keith Best, Esq, TD; ✉ 15 St Stephen's Terrace, London SW8 1DJ (tel 020 7735 7699); 7 Alderley Terrace, Holyhead, Anglesey, Gwynedd LL65 1NL (tel 01407 762972); Immigration Advisory Service, 190 Great Dover Street, London SE1 4YB (tel 020 7967 1221, mobile 07785 323200, e-mail keithbest@hotmail.com)

BEST, Dr Michael Howard; s of Benjamin Frederick Best (d 1989), of Sidcup, Kent, and Betty Noreen, *née* Crawley (d 1970); *b* 6 August 1948; *Educ* Chislehurst and Sidcup GS, Univ of Newcastle upon Tyne (MB BS); *m* 4 July 1981, Dr Sylvia Renée Martina, da of Hermann Rolf Pabst (d 2000); *Career* house physician Dryburn Hosp Durham and house surgeon in paediatrics Newcastle Gen Hosp 1973–74, registrar Dept of Psychological Med Royal Victoria Infirmary Newcastle upon Tyne 1974–77, sr registrar Bethlem Royal and Maudsley Hosps London 1977–82; clinical lectr in mental health Univ of Bristol 1982–86; conslt psychiatrist: Bristol Royal Hosp for Children and Downend Child Guidance Clinic Bristol 1982–86, Charter Nightingale Hosp London 1987–98, Hayes Grove Priory Hosp 1998–2000, Godden Green Clinic Sevenoaks 2000–04, London Child and Family Consultation Service 2004–07; in private practice 1987–; MRCPsych 1977; *Recreations* swimming, fell walking, antiquarian medical books, history of spa medicine; *Style*— Dr Michael H Best; ✉ 10 Harley Street, London W1G 9PF (tel 020 7467 8554)

BEST, Baron (Life Peer UK 2001), of Godmanstone in the County of Dorset; Richard Stuart Best; OBE (1988); s of Walter Stuart Best, JP, DL (d 1984), and Frances Mary, *née* Chignell (d 1967); *b* 22 June 1945; *Educ* Shrewsbury, Univ of Nottingham (BA); *m* 1, 1970 (m dis 1976), Ima Akpan; 1 s (Peter b 1971), 1 da (Lucy b 1974); m 2, 1978, Belinda Janie Tremayne, da of Geoffrey Eustace Stemp, DFC, of Lamberhurst, Kent; 1 da (Jessica b 1981), 1 s (William b 1985); *Career* dir: Br Churches Housing Tst 1970–73, Nat Fedn of Housing Assocs 1973–88, Joseph Rowntree Fndn 1988–2006; sec Duke of Edinburgh's Inquiry into Br Housing 1984–91, cmmr Rural Devpt Cmmn 1989–98; chm: RDC Social Advsy Panel 1990–98, UK Nat Cncl UN City Summit 1995–96, Hull Partnership Liaison Bd 2003–04, The Giving Forum 2005–, House of Lords Audit Ctee 2005–, Hanover Housing Assoc 2006–; pres Local Govt Assoc 2005–, vice-pres Town and Country Planning Assoc 2007–; memb: Social Policy Ctee of C of E Bd for Social Responsibility 1986–91, BBC/IBA Central Appeals Advsy Ctee 1988–91, Exec Ctee Assoc Charitable Fndns 1989–92, Community Advsy Panel IBM UK Ltd 1990–93, Cncl for Charitable Support 1995–2005, NCVO Advsy Cncl 2001–; advsr: Environment Ctee House of Commons 1993, Min of Housing's Sounding Bd 1999–2001, DTI Foresight Built Environment Panel 1999–2001, Min of Local Govt's Sounding Bd 2001–05; tstee: RSA 2006–, Tree Cncl 2006–, Zimbabwe Phoenix Tst 2007–; pres Continuing Care Conf 2003–; Hon Dr: Univ of Sheffield, Univ of York; hon life memb Chartered Inst of Housing; Hon FRIBA 2001, CCMI 2006; *Clubs* Travellers; *Style*— The Rt Hon the Lord Best, OBE; ✉ House of Lords, London SW1A 0PW

BEST-SHAW, Sir John Michael Robert; 10 Bt (E 1665), of Eltham, Kent; s of Cdr Sir John Best-Shaw, 9 Bt, RN (d 1984), and Elizabeth Mary Theodora, eld da of late Sir Robert Heywood Hughes, 12 Bt of East Bergholt; *b* 28 September 1924; *Educ* Lancing, Hertford Coll Oxford (MA), Univ of London (PGCE); *m* 1960, Jane Gordon, 2 da of Alexander Gordon Guthrie, of Hampton Court House, Farningham, Kent; 1 da (Lucy Ann b 1961), 2 s (Thomas Joshua b 1965, Samuel Stevenson b 1971), and 1 c decd; *Heir* s, Thomas Best-Shaw; *Career* late Capt Queen's Own Royal W Kent Regt, served WWII NW Europe; with Fedn Malaya Police 1950–58, church work 1959–71, teaching 1972–82; Liveryman Worshipful Co of Vintners; *Recreations* bridge, writing; *Clubs* Commonwealth; *Style*— Sir John Best-Shaw, Bt; ✉ Belmont, 104 High Street, West Malling, Maidstone, Kent ME19 6NE (tel 01732 843823)

BESTERMAN, Tristram Paul; s of Prof Edwin Melville Mack Besterman, of Stony Hill, Jamaica, and Audrey, *née* Heald; *b* 19 September 1949; *Educ* Stowe (music scholar), Univ of Cambridge (MA); *m* 1977, Peregrine Mary Louise, da of Gilbert Garceau; 2 s (Julius b 12 July 1979, Hugo b 9 Oct 1980), 1 da (Anna b 21 April 1983); *Career* BBC Radio 1971–73, res and design Geological & Mining Mus Sydney 1974, jackaroo on cattle station Queensland 1974, educn offr Sheffield City Mus 1974–78, dep curator and keeper of geology Warwickshire Museums 1978–85, city curator Plymouth City Museums & Art Gall 1985–93, dir Manchester Museum 1994–2006; convenor Ethics Ctee UK Museums Assoc 1995–2001; memb: Coll Collections Advsy Bd UCL 1997–, Bd Sainsbury Centre for Visual Arts UEA 1998–, Ministerial Working Gp on Human Remains 2001–03; numerous articles in scientific and museological jls; FGS 1979, FMA 1985 (AMA 1979), FRSA 2001; *Recreations* music, cellist in chamber orchestras and quartets; *Style*— Tristram Besterman, Esq

BESWICK, David; s of Donald Beswick, of Shenstone, Staffs, and Eileen, *née* Thomas; *b* 18 February 1963, Liverpool; *Educ* John Wilmot Sch Sutton Coldfield, Univ of Newcastle upon Tyne (LLB), Coll of Law Chester; *m* 15 July 1989, Sally, *née* Webb; 2 da (Lois, Kirsty (twins) b 17 March 1998); *Career* admitted slr 1987; Eversheds 1985–2002, Hammonds 2002–; memb Employment Lawyers Assoc; memb Birmingham Forward; *Recreations* badminton, gym, theatre; *Style*— David Beswick, Esq; ✉ Hammonds, Rutland House, 148 Edmund Street, Birmingham B3 2JR (tel 0870 839 3536, fax 0870 460 2806, e-mail david.beswick@hammonds.com)

BESWICK, David John; JP (2006); s of David Beswick (d 1991), and Winifred Anne, *née* Davies (d 1985); *b* 30 November 1944; *Educ* Longton HS for Boys Stoke-on-Trent, Birmingham Coll of Food and Drink (Nat Dip Hotel Keeping); *m* 1 April 1967, Pauline Ann, da of Arthur John Bayliss (d 1980), and Dorothy Louise, *née*; Mitchell (d 1956); 2 da (Allison Jane b 7 Aug 1968, Amanda Louise b 8 March 1971); *Career* mgmnt trainee Grosvenor House Park Lane 1963–65, asst mangr Grosvenor House Sheffield 1967, gen mangr Gulf Hotel Bahrain 1967–74, mangr Sheraton Heathrow Hotel 1974–76, gen mangr Holiday Inns Inc Lagos Tel Aviv and Bermuda 1976–82, dir and gen mangr Broughton Park Hotel Preston 1982–88; gen mangr: Whitbread Hotel Co Dalmahoy Edinburgh 1989, St Pierre Chepstow, Redwood Lodge Hotel Bristol 1994–95, Marriott Hotel Cardiff 1988–98; dir and gen mangr Marriott Goodwood Park 1998–2005, ret; Master Innholder 1989–, Freeman City of London 1989; FIH 1975, MInstD 1992; *Recreations* golf, cricket, gardening, study of wine; *Clubs* Rotary; *Style*— David Beswick, Esq, JP; ✉ e-mail bezzie@ukonline.co.uk

BESWICK, Rev Esme Christiana; MBE (2001); da of Nathan Coleman (d 1973), of Jamaica, and Ambroline Coleman (d 1980); *b* 9 April 1938; *Educ* Wyma Nursing HS Kingston Jamaica, West Ham Coll, Central Bible Inst (DipTh), Univ of London (extra mural studies); *m* 2 Nov 1962, Herbert George Beswick; 2 s (Derick Paul b 14 Feb 1964, Mark Anthony b 21 July 1965), 2 da (Michelle Marcia b 15 Oct 1969, Sharon Deborah b 24 May 1971); *Career* student nurse Queen Mary Hosp Sidcup and St Leonard's Hosp Bromley 1961–63; ordained Pentecostal Church Jamaica 1961; pastor of The New Testament Assembly Brixton 1975, hosp chaplain Whipps Cross Hosp 1986–91, gen sec Jt Cncl for Anglo Caribbean Churches 1989, fndr Jt Cncl of Anglo Caribbean Churches Bible Sch; pres Churches Together in England, pres elect Christian and Muslim Forum; memb: British Cncl of Churches 1980–89, Cncl of Churches for Britain and Ireland 1989–, Inner City Religious Cncl; current pres: Jt Cncl for Anglo Caribbean Churches, Christian and Muslim Forum, Esme Beswick Educn Fndn Tst; currently ecumenical borough dean of Lambeth; patron: Christian Cncl on Aging, Race Equality in Employment Programme (REEP); *Recreations* reading, swimming, cricket; *Style*— The Rev Esme Beswick, MBE; ✉ c/o The Joint Council for Anglo Caribbean Churches, 141 Railton Road, London SE24 0LT (tel 020 7737 6542)

BETHEL, Martin; QC (1983); s of Rev Ralph Arnold Bethel (d 1946), and Enid Ambery, *née* Smith (d 1996); *b* 12 March 1943; *Educ* Kingswood Sch Bath, Fitzwilliam Coll Cambridge (MA, LLM); *m* 14 Sept 1974, Kathryn Jane, da of Isaac Allan Denby, of Riddlesden, W Yorks; 1 da (Sarah b 1976), 2 s (Thomas b 1980, William b 1981); *Career* called to the Bar Inner Temple 1965; recorder of the Crown Court (NE Circuit) 1979–, dep judge of the High Ct 1995–; memb: Criminal Injuries Compensation Bd 1999–2000, Criminal Injuries Compensation Appeals Panel 2000–; pres Runswick Bay Rescue Boat 2001–04; *Recreations* sailing, skiing; *Style*— Martin Bethel, Esq, QC; ✉ St Pauls Chambers, Park Square, Leeds LS1 2ND (tel 0113 245 5866)

BETHEL, Dr Robert George Hankin; s of Horace Hankin Bethel (d 1961), of London and Eastbourne, and Eileen Maude (Mollie), *née* Motyer (d 1996); *b* 7 June 1948; *Educ* Eastbourne GS, Pembroke Coll Cambridge (BA, MA, MB BChir), St Mary's Hosp Med Sch; *Career* med practitioner; house physician Queen Elizabeth II Hosp London 1972, house surgn Nottingham Gen Hosp 1973, SHO Northwick Park Hosp and Clinical Res Centre Harrow 1974, registrar W Middx Univ Hosp 1974–76, gen med practitioner Englefield Green and Old Windsor 1976–2005, sr ptnr Runnymede Med Practice 1997–2006; course tutor Open Univ 1979–80, hosp practitioner in geriatrics 1980–91, pt/t rheumatologist Heatherwood Hosp Ascot 1976–92, trainer for GP (Oxford region) 1984–2005, assoc teacher Imperial Coll of Sci, Technol and Med (formerly St Mary's Hosp Med Sch) 1989–2004; med memb Ind Tbnl Serv (Disability) 1991–99, med offr Brunel Univ 1993–98; author of various scientific papers in med jls with particular interest in rheumatological and gen practice topics; advsy ed Horizons 1988–91; performance assessor and PLAB examiner GMC 2002–; memb Exec Ctee E Berks BMA 1977–93 (divnl sec 1983–85), SW Thames Faculty Bd memb RCGP 1983–92, vice-pres Section of Gen Practice RSM 1995–97 (hon sec 1993–95); The Cambridge Soc: memb Cncl 1991–, vice-pres Surrey Branch 1995– (sec 1982–85, chm 1988–95); wandsman St Paul's Cathedral 1988–, vice-chm Old Windsor Day Centre 1989–94; memb Soc of Genealogists; Freeman City of London 1977, memb Guild of Freemen City of London 1979, memb Ct of Assts Worshipful Soc of Apothecaries 1998– (Freeman 1977, Liveryman 1981); fell Med Soc of London 1995; FRSM 1975, MRCGP 1979, FRSH 1989; *Recreations* genealogy, books, gardening; *Clubs* Oxford and Cambridge, Osler; *Style*— Dr Robert Bethel; ✉ Newton Court Medical Centre, Burfield Road, Old Windsor, Berkshire SL4 2QF (tel 01753 863642, fax 01753 832180)

BETHELL, (Charles) Andrew Richard; s of Maj-Gen Drew Bethell (d 1988), and Pamela, *née* Woosnam; *b* 17 November 1947; *Educ* Sherborne, Univ of Toronto (BA), Univ of Oxford (PGCE); *Partner* Claire Widgery; 3 c (Katherine b 26 June 1980, Matthew b 2 April 1983, Benjamin b 25 Nov 1988); *Career* teacher of English and media studies 1971–87, founded independent TV prodn co Double Exposure Ltd 1987, currently md Double Exposure Ltd; credits incl: Culloden (BBC 2), The House (BBC 2, winner of Best Factual Series BAFTA Awards 1997, winner of Best Arts Series Emmy 1997), Pleasure Beach (BBC 2); RTS Award for Outstanding Contribution to Educnl TV; *Style*— Andrew Bethell; ✉ 113 Bouverie Road, London N16 0AD (tel 020 8800 1047); Double Exposure Ltd, 63 Clerkenwell Road, London EC1 5PS (tel 020 7490 2499, fax 020 7490 2556)

BETHELL, Dr Hugh James Newton; MBE (1995); s of Brig Richard Brian Wyndham Bethell, DSO (d 1990), and Jackomina Alice, *née* Barton (d 1979); *b* 31 March 1942; *Educ* Tonbridge, St John's Coll Cambridge (BA), Guy's Hosp (MB BChir, DObstRCOG, MD); *m* 1, 1968, Astrid Jill, *née* Short (d 1979); 2 da (Katharine Emma b 25 Dec 1969, Christina Louise b 12 April 1973); m 2, 1984, Lesley, *née* Harris; *Career* cardiac registrar Charing Cross Hosp 1969–72, dermatology registrar Guy's Hosp 1972–74, princ in gen practice 1974–2002; dir Basingstoke and Alton Cardiac Rehabilitation Unit 1976–2002; chm Advsy Ctee on Coronary Rehabilitation to the Coronary Prevention Gp 1987–, founding pres British Assoc for Cardiac Rehabilitation, memb Br Cardiac Soc; fndr chm Alton Joggers; FRCGP 1991 (MRCGP), FRCP 1995 (MRCP); *Publications* Exercise Based Cardiac Rehabilitation (1996); author of numerous scientific papers, review articles, and book chapters; *Recreations* running, cinema; *Clubs* Hawks' (Cambridge); *Style*— Dr Hugh Bethell, MBE; ✉ Timbers, Boyneswood Road, Medstead, Alton, Hampshire GU34 5DY (tel 01420 563932, e-mail hugh@boyneswood.fsnet.co.uk)

BETHELL, Prof Leslie Michael; s of Stanley Bethell (d 1969), and Bessie, *née* Stoddart (d 2005); *b* 12 February 1937; *Educ* Cockburn HS Leeds, UCL (BA, PhD); *m* 1961 (m dis 1983); 2 s (Ben b 1966, Daniel b 1967); *Career* lectr in history: Univ of Bristol 1961–66, UCL 1966–74 (reader 1974–86); Univ of London: prof of Latin American history 1986–92, dir Inst of Latin American Studies 1987–92; Univ of Oxford: professorial fell St Antony's Coll 1997–2007 (research fell 1993–97), dir Centre for Brazilian Studies 1997–; visiting prof: Instituto Universitario de Pesquisas do Rio de Janeiro 1979, Univ of Calif San Diego 1985, Univ of Chicago 1992–93; fell Wilson Center Washington DC 1986 and 1996–97; chm Bloomsbury Theatre 1977–86; author of numerous articles and chapters on Latin American history, Brazilian history and politics, Britain and Latin America and the US and Latin America; ed Jl of Latin American Studies 1987–89; Grand Official Order of the Southern Cross (Brazil) 1999 (Cdr 1994); *Books* The Abolition of the Brazilian Slave Trade (1970), Latin America Between the Second World War and the Cold War 1944–48 (with Ian Roxborough, 1992), A Guerra do Paraguai (jtly, 1995); ed: The Cambridge History of Latin America - Colonial Latin America (vols I & II 1984), From Independence to c 1870 (vol III 1985), From c 1870 to 1930 (vols IV & V 1986), Mexico, Central America and the Caribbean since 1930 (vol VII 1990), Spanish South America since 1930 (vol VIII 1991), Latin America since 1930: Economy, Society and Politics (vol VI parts 1 and 2, 1994), Latin America since 1930: Ideas, Culture and Society (vol X 1995), Bibliographical Essays (vol XI 1995), Brasil: o fardo do passado, o promessa do futuro (ed, 2002), Brazil by British and Irish Authors (2003); *Style*— Prof Leslie Bethell; ✉ Centre for Brazilian Studies, 92 Woodstock Road, Oxford OX2 7ND (tel 01865 284460, fax 01865 284461, e-mail leslie.bethell@brazil.ox.ac.uk)

BETT, Sir Michael; kt (1995), CBE (1990); s of Arthur Bett, OBE, and Nina, *née* Daniells; *b* 18 January 1935; *Educ* Aldenham, Pembroke Coll Cambridge (MA); *m* 3 Oct 1959, Christine Angela Bett, JP, da of Maj Horace Reid, JP; 1 s (Timothy Mark b 1961), 2 da (Sally Maria b 1963, Lucy Ann b 1965); *Career* dir Industrial Rels Engrg Employers' Fedn 1970–72; personnel dir: GEC 1972–77, BBC 1977–81; British Telecom: main bd dir 1981–96 (non-exec 1993–96), personnel dir 1981–85, md Local Communications Servs Div 1985–87, md UK Communications 1987–88, md BT UK 1988–91, dep chm BT plc 1991–94; chm: Cellnet 1991–99, Pace Micro Techology plc 1999–2006, Compel plc; First Civil Service Cmmr 1995–2000; chm Pensions Investments Accreditation Bd 2000–06; non-exec dir: Eyretel plc 1996–2003, Ordnance Survey; memb: Pay Bd 1973–74, May Ctee of Inquiry into UK Prison Serv 1978–79, Ctee of Inquiry into Water Dispute 1983, Griffiths Inquiry into NHS Mgmnt 1983, Armed Forces Pay Review Body 1983–87, Manpower Servs Cmmn 1985–89; chm: Nurses Pay Review Body 1990–95, The Save the Children Fund 1993–98, TEC Nat Cncl 1994–95, Social Security Advsy Ctee 1993–94, Armed Forces Ind Review on Manpower 1994–95, Pensions Protection and Investment Accreditation Bd 2000–; memb Cncl Cranfield Inst of Technol 1982–87, chllr Aston Univ 2004– (pro-chllr 1993–2003); pres Chartered Inst of Personnel and Devpt 1993–98; chm: Nat Security Inspectorate, Royal Hosp for Neuro-disability, One World Broadcasting Tst, Ind Review of Higher Educn Pay and Conditions 1997–99; former vice-pres Royal TV Soc, former Hon Col 81 Sqdn (V) RCS; Hon DBA Liverpool John Moores Univ, Hon DSc Aston Univ; CIMgt, CCIPD; *Style*— Sir Michael Bett, CBE; ⊠ Colets Well, The Green, Otford, Kent TN14 5PD

BETTINSON, John Richard; OBE (2003); s of Harold Richard Bettinson, MC (d 1986), of Edgbaston, and Barbara, *née* Keene (d 1984); *b* 27 June 1932; *Educ* Haileybury, Univ of Birmingham (LLB); *m* 1 Nov 1958, (Margaret) Angela, da of Richard Good (d 1955), of Edgbaston; 1 s (Richard b 1961), 1 da (Hayley b 1963); *Career* Lt 3 Carabiniers 1955–57; admitted slr 1955; chm: Victoria Carpet Holdings plc (now Victoria plc) 1986–95, National Windscreens Ltd 1991–96, Birmingham Research Park Ltd 1987–2007; dep chm Concentric plc 1978–98, dir Warwickshire Care Services Ltd 1990–2005; chm: Birmingham AHA 1973–82, NAHAT 1976–79, Age Concern England 1989–92, Birmingham Heartlands Hosp NHS Tst 1991–94, Assay Office Birmingham 1988–2000; gen cmmr for income tax 1970–2007, pres Midland Rent Assessment Panel 1985–2003; dep pro-chllr Univ of Birmingham 1994–2001; Freeman Worshipful Co of Goldsmiths, memb Ct of Assts Worshipful Co of Glaziers & Painters of Glass; Hon LLD Univ of Birmingham; *Recreations* theatre, bricklaying, reading; *Clubs* Cavalry and Guards'; *Style*— John Bettinson, Esq, OBE; ⊠ Tetstill Mill, Neen Sollars, Shropshire DY14 9AH (tel 01299 270718)

BETTISON, Sir Norman George; kt (2006), QPM (2000); s of George Bettison (d 1995), and Betty, *née* Heathcote; *b* 3 January 1956; *Educ* Univ of Oxford (MA), Sheffield Business Sch (MBA); *Career* police offr S Yorks Police 1972–93, Asst Chief Constable W Yorks Police 1993–98, Chief Constable Merseyside Police 1998–2004, chief exec Centrex 2004–; chm United Tsts on Merseyside, memb Bd Royal Liverpool Philharmonic; *Recreations* tennis, classic cars, theatre, music; *Clubs* Athenaeum (Liverpool), Artists (Liverpool); *Style*— Sir Norman Bettison, QPM; ⊠ Centrex, Bramshill, Hook, Hampshire RG27 0JW

BETTISON, Paul David; s of Kenneth Henry David Bettison (d 2005), of Worcester Park, Surrey, and Ona Patricia, *née* Ratcliffe; *b* 18 April 1953; *Educ* Tiffin Boys' Sch Kingston upon Thames; *m* 15 May 1976, Jean Margaret, da of Kenneth Charles Bradshaw (d 2004), of Ewell, Surrey; 2 da (Clare Louise b 1983, Emily Margaret b 1985); *Career* memb mgmnt Rockwell Graphic Systems Ltd 1978–87; md: Graphic Systems International Ltd 1987–2003, Caxton House (UK) Ltd 2001–03; dir: Factistel Ltd 1988–2003, Tolerans Ingol (UK) Ltd 1990–93, Topefa Limited 1990–95, Pizza De Action Ltd 1995–2003, Pizza Cake Ltd 1995–2003, Tolerans Ingol Ltd 1999–2002, The Code Corporation (UK) Ltd 2001–03, Localis Research Ltd 2001–, Caxton International Ltd 2002–03, Bettison Associates Ltd 2003–; memb (Cons) Sandhurst Town Cncl 1991– (dep mayor 1992–93, mayor 1993–95), memb Bracknell Forest BC 1992– (chm Health and Safety Ctee 1993–95, vice-chm Personnel Ctee 1993–95, ldr Cons Gp 1996–, ldr Cncl 1997–, chm Strategy and Policy Ctee 1997–2001, chm Fin and Property Ctee 1997–2000, chm Electoral Review Ctee 1997–2001, chm Town Centre Ctee 1997–); chm: Local Govt Assoc Housing Exec 2000–02, Rural Cmmn 2002–04, Local Govt Assoc Environment Bd 2006–; e-govt champion 2003–; memb: Local Govt Assoc Cons Gp Exec 1999–2003 and 2005– (Gp Whip 2000–03), Bd Cons Cncllr's Assoc 2000–, Directgov 2004–, Local Govt Assoc Exec 2006–; cmmr Cmmn on Local Governance 2001–04; Cons nat local govt spokesman on ICT issues 2000–; memb Ct and Cncl Univ of Reading 1999–; govr: New Scotland Hill Primary Sch 1991–, Uplands County Primary Sch 1992–; CInstSMM 1996 (FInstSMM 1979); *Recreations* politics, flying light aircraft, travel, cars, wine; *Style*— Paul Bettison, Esq; ⊠ Longdown House, Mickle Hill, Little Sandhurst, Berkshire GU47 8QL (tel 01344 352041, fax 01344 352059, mobile 07836 287050, e-mail paul.bettison@bracknell-forest.gov.uk)

BETTON, David John William; s of John Clifford Betton (d 1993), of Taunton, Somerset, and Evelyn Naomi, *née* Byatt; *b* 30 December 1947; *Educ* Dulwich Coll, Emmanuel Coll Cambridge (MA); *m* 1, 6 Jan 1970 (m dis 1975), Christine Judith Patey, da of Very Rev Edward Patey, Dean of Liverpool, Merseyside; *m* 2, 5 Sept 1980 (m dis 1994), Nicola Mary Mallen, da of John McGregor Carter (d 1983); 1 s (Jack David McGregor), 3 da (Victoria Christine Naomi, Polly Nicola, Nancy Evelyn Mary); *m* 3, 19 Jan 1996, Baroness Gillian van Overstraeten, da of Rylance John Taylor; *Career* called to the Bar 1972; sr legal advsr HM Customs and Excise 1976–86, nat dir of VAT Clark Whitehill CAs 1986–91, senior VAT conslt KPMG 1991–; Freeman City of London, Liveryman Worshipful Co of Plumbers; *Recreations* cricket, theatre, walking; *Clubs* MCC; *Style*— David Betton, Esq; ⊠ KPMG, PO Box 486, 1 Puddle Dock, Blackfriars, London EC4V 3PD (tel 020 7311 1519, fax 020 7311 4088)

BETTON, Keith Findlay; s of Peter Joseph George Betton (d 1997), of Hampton, Middx, and Betty Patricia, *née* Findlay; *b* 29 June 1960; *Educ* Thames Valley GS, Richmond upon Thames Coll, N London Poly (HNC Business Studies); *m* 1990, Esther, da of Kenneth Hargreaves (d 1993), of Halifax, W Yorks; *Career* public affairs div Shell International and Shell UK Ltd 1978–85 (ed Shellstrand and asst ed Shell Times); exhibition mangr British Telecom National Networks 1985–86; account mangr Biss Lancaster Public Relations 1986–89; Association of British Travel Agents (ABTA): public affairs mangr 1989–91, head of corp affairs 1991–2006; md Keith Betton Consulting 2007–; ldr RSPB of Richmond and Twickenham Memb Gp 1979–85, regnl rep Br Tst for Ornithology Gtr London 1981–93 (memb Cncl 1987–91), vice-pres London Natural History Soc 1984– (pres 1982–84), memb Cncl London Wildlife Tst 1982–85, memb Cncl Surrey Wildlife Tst 1987–92, asst recorder Hampshire Ornithological Soc 1995–, memb Cncl RSPB 2004–; MCIPR 1989; *Publications* ABTA - The First Fifty Years (ed, 2000); *Recreations* bird watching anywhere in the world, recording natural history sounds, watching rugby league, wildlife photography, family history; *Clubs* British Ornithologists (memb Ctee 1985–86), African Bird (vice-chm 2000–06), Ornithological Soc of the ME (chm 2002–); *Style*— Keith Betton, Esq; ⊠ 8 Dukes Close, Folly Hill, Farnham, Surrey GU9 0DR (tel 01252 724068, e-mail keith@keithbetton.com)

BETTS, Charles Valentine; CB (1998); s of Harold Blair Betts, of South Harting, W Sussex, and Mary Ellis, *née* France (d 1990); *b* 10 January 1942; *Educ* Seaford Coll Worthing, Lysses Sch Fareham, Ryde Sch Isle of Wight, Merchant Taylors' Crosby, St Catharine's Coll Cambridge (MA, capt of boats), RNC Greenwich (Cert Naval Architecture), UCL

(MPhil); *m* 20 April 1965, Rev Patricia Joyce Betts (ordained priest 1997), er da of William Gordon Bennett, of Great Crosby, Liverpool; 2 s (Christopher Jeremy b 3 April 1968, Richard Anthony b 25 March 1970); *Career* postgrad trg for RCNC: RNEC Manadon Plymouth 1963–64, RNC Greenwich 1964–66; asst constructor FE Fleet 1966–67, constructor MOD Foxhill Bath 1971 (asst constructor 1967–70), seconded as lectr in naval architecture UCL 1971–74, constructor HM Dockyard Portsmouth 1974–77; chief constructor: MOD Foxhill Bath 1979–83 (constructor 1977–79), MOD London 1983–85; seconded as prof of naval architecture UCL 1985–89; MOD Foxhill Bath: dir Surface Ships B 1989–92, DG Surface Ships 1992–94, DG Submarines 1994–98; dep controller RN 1994–98, head RCNC 1992–98; ret from MOD 1998; non-exec dir: BMT Group 1999–2001, BMT Reliability Conslts Ltd 2000–01, British Maritime Technology Ltd 2001–05, BMT Gp Ltd 2005–; tstee and vice-chm The Coverdale Tst (formerly Alpha International Ministries) 1996–2004; vice-pres RINA 2003– (memb Cncl 1985–2002 and 2003–), memb Nat Historic Ships Ctee 2000–06; CEng 1968, FRINA 1981 (MRINA 1968), FREng 1991, FRSA 1992; *Books* The Marine Technology Reference Book (contrib, 1990); *Recreations* sailing, music, Christian activities; *Clubs* RNSA; *Style*— Charles Betts, Esq, CB, FREng; ⊠ c/o BMT Group Limited, Goodrich House, 1 Waldegrave Road, Teddington, Middlesex TW11 8LZ

BETTS, Clive James Charles; MP; s of Harold Betts (d 1992), of Sheffield, and Nellie, *née* Ellis (d 1991); *b* 13 January 1950; *Educ* King Edward VII Sch Sheffield, Pembroke Coll Cambridge (BA); *Career* economist TUC 1971–72; local govt offr: Derbyshire 1973–74, South Yorks 1974–86, Rotherham 1986–91; Parly candidate: Sheffield Hallam 1974, Louth 1979; MP (Lab) Sheffield Attercliffe 1992–; former chm Treasy Departmental Ctee Lab Pty, former memb Treasy Select Ctee, memb Lab Ldr's Campaign Team with responsibility for Environment and Local Govt, appointed Lab Pty oppn whip 1996–97, asst govt whip 1997–98, a Lord Cmmr (Govt whip) 1998–2001, memb Select Ctee Office of the dep PM 2001–; Lab Pty Sheffield City Cncl: cncllr (Lab) 1976–92, chm Housing Ctee 1980–86, chm Fin Ctee 1986–88, dep ldr 1986–87, ldr 1987–92; vice-pres Assoc of Met Authorities 1988–91 (chm Housing Ctee 1985–89); pres: Organising Ctee XVI Universiade 1990–91, SE Sheffield CAB; patron: Br Deaf Sports Cncl, Mosborough Township Youth Project; former patron Nat Assoc for Therapeutic Educn, former vice-pres Energy from Waste Assoc; memb Lab Pty 1969–; *Recreations* Sheffield Wednesday FC, squash, cricket, walking, real ale; *Style*— Clive Betts, Esq, MP; ⊠ Newlands, High Lane, Ridgeway, Sheffield S12 3XF; Barkers Pool House, Burgess Street, Sheffield S1 2HF (tel 0114 273 4444, fax 0114 273 9666); House of Commons, London SW1A 0AA (tel 020 7219 3588/5114, e-mail bettsc@parliament.uk)

BETTS, Thomas Matthew (Tom); s of Christopher Betts, of Charlbury, Oxon, and Ann, *née* Blyton; *b* 21 November 1964; *Educ* Warwick Sch, UCL (LLB), Coll of Law London; *m* 1, 1991 (m dis 1997), Janet Morrison; 1 s (Jack Alexander b 4 Feb 1993), 1 da (Katherine Alice b 15 Oct 1994); *m* 2, 1998, Karen, da of John Meek; 2 da (Eva Tallulah b 9 Jan 1998, Ruby Rose b 2 Sept 1999); *Career* legal asst United International Pictures 1987–88, articled clerk Denton Hall 1988–90, slr entertainment and media dept Denton Hall 1990–91, legal advsr Central Productions Ltd 1991–93; controller of commissioning and network business affairs Carlton TV 1994–97, commercial dir Carlton TV 1997–2001; dir HTV Gp Ltd 2000–01, dir Gaming Insight plc; chm: Digital 3 & 4 Ltd 1999–2001, ITV2 Ltd 2000–01; dir of business devpt Granada Media 2002–; memb Law Soc 1990; *Recreations* football, cinema, modern British literature, my four children; *Clubs* Bentham, Tottenham Hotspur FC; *Style*— Tom Betts, Esq; ⊠ Granada Media, London Television Centre, Upper Ground, London SE1 9LT

BETTS, Torben Anthony; s of Martin Frankland Betts, and Jennifer Ann Betts; *b* 10 February 1968; *Educ* Stamford Sch, Univ of Liverpool (BA); *m* 1997, Victoria, *née* Witcomb; 2 s (Stanley b 24 Sept 2001, Leo b 14 May 2005); *Career* dramatist; writer in residence Stephen Joseph Theatre Scarborough 1999; *Plays* incl: A Listening Heaven (1997), Spurning Comfort (1998), Incarcerator (1999), Mummies and Daddies (1999), Five Visions of the Faithful (2000), Clockwatching (2000), The Biggleswades (2001), The Last Days of Desire (2001), Silence and Violence (2002), The Optimist (2002), The Lunatic Queen (2003), The Trough (2003), The Unconquered (2004), The Error of Their Ways (2004), Glorious (2004), The Misfortune of Martha McLeod (2005), The Swing of Things (2006), The Company Man (2006); *Publications* Plays One, Plays Two, Plays Three, The Lunatic Queen, The Unconquered; *Style*— Torben Betts, Esq; ⊠ c/o Cathy King, ICM, Oxford House, 76 Oxford Street, London W1D 1BS

BETZ, Charles John Paul; s of Col Francis Betz (d 1949), of Calif, and Martha Abusdal Flannery (d 1988); *b* 8 September 1946; *Educ* American Grad Sch of Int Management (MBA), Stanford Univ (Cert), Calif State Univ (BS), Univ of Uppsala (Cert); *m* 6 Dec 1969, Birgitta, da of Erik Gideon Thorell, of Solleron, Sweden; 2 da (Anika Ingrid b 1975, Martina Mary b 1980), 2 s (Christian Michael b 1977, Clark Paul Erik b 1982); *Career* dir customer serv Transworld Airlines NY 1970–72, regnl vice-pres Bank of America London 1979–86 (various appts San Francisco 1973–76, vice-pres NY 1976–79), md Carré Orban and Ptnrs 1986–91, European Bank for Reconstruction and Devpt 1991–92, chm Int Acad for Educn and Devpt 1993–; md: Bridge Information Systems/Bridge Int Brokering 1995–97, Saracen Partners 1997–2002; chm and organizer Champion Polo Benefit; *Recreations* polo; *Clubs* Buck's, Pilgrims, Ham Polo, West Wycombe Park; *Style*— Charles Betz, Esq; ⊠ Atkins Farm, Great Missenden, Buckinghamshire (tel 01494 863762); 2809 Raccoon Trail, Pebble Beach, California, USA (tel 00 1 831 372 2429)

BEVAN, see also: Evans-Bevan

BEVAN, Anthony Richard Van (Tony); s of Adrian Van Cruiskerken Bevan, of Harbury, Warks, and Margaret Betty, *née* Pemberton; *b* 22 July 1951; *Educ* Bradford Sch of Art, Goldsmiths Coll of Art and Design London, Slade Sch of Fine Art London; *Partner* Glenys Johnson; 1 da (Rosa Elizabeth Donna Johnson Glen Bevan b 25 Jan 1991); *Career* artist; *Solo Exhibitions* incl: Matt's Gallery London 1981, 1982, 1986 and 1996, Tony Bevan Portraits and Emblems (Galeria Akumulatory 2 Poznan Poland) 1983, The Honest Portrait (Nat Portrait Gallery London) 1985, Tony Bevan - Paintings 1980–87 (ICA London touring Orchard Gallery Derry, Kettles Yard Cambridge and Cartwright Hall Bradford) 1987–88, Tony Bevan Neue Bilder (Kunsthalle Kiel Germany) 1988, Tony Bevan (Staatsgalerie Moderner Kunst Haus der Kunst Munich Germany) 1989, Tony Bevan (Kunstverein Lingen Germany) 1990, Tony Bevan Whitechapel Art Gallery 1993, Tony Bevan Paintings from the 80's and 90's (Cottbus Germany) 1997, Tony Bevan (Abbot Hall Art Gallery Kendal) 1999, Tony Bevan (Milton Keynes Gallery) 2003, Tony Bevan - Works From Deptford (Abbot Hall Art Gallery Kendal) 2003; RA 2007; *Style*— Tony Bevan, Esq; ⊠ c/o Galerie Wittenbrink, Jahnstrasse 18, München 5, Germany (tel 00 4989 260 5580, fax 00 4989 260 5868); c/o Robert Miller Gallery, 524 West 26th Street, New York, NY 1001, USA (tel 001 212 366 4774, fax 001 212 366 4454); c/o Matts Gallery, 42–44 Copperfield Road, London E3 4RR (tel 020 8983 1771, fax 020 8983 1435); c/o Michael Hue-Williams Fine Art Ltd, 21 Cork Street, London W1X 1HB (tel 020 7434 1318, fax 020 7434 1321)

BEVAN, His Hon Judge John Penry Vaughan; QC (1997); s of Llewelyn Vaughan Bevan (d 1987), and Hilda Molly, *née* Yates; *b* 7 September 1947; *Educ* Radley, Magdalene Coll Cambridge (BA); *m* 1, 1971 (m dis 1976), Dinah, *née* Nicholson; 2 da (Amelia b 1972, Lucinda b 1975); *m* 2, 1978, Veronica, *née* Aliaga-Kelly; 1 s (Henry b 1981), 1 da (Charlotte b 1985); *Career* called to the Bar Middle Temple 1970 (bencher 2001); recorder of the Crown Court 1987–2004 (asst recorder 1983–87), sr prosecuting counsel to the Crown at Central Criminal Court 1991–97, circuit judge (South Eastern Circuit) 2004–; *Recreations* sailing, tennis; *Clubs* Leander, Aldeburgh Yacht, Orford Sailing; *Style*— His Hon Judge Bevan, QC

BEVAN, (Edward) Julian; QC (1991); s of Capt Geoffrey Bevan (d 1994), and Barbara, *née* Locke (d 1991); *b* 23 October 1940; *Educ* Eton; *m* 17 Sept 1966, Bronwen Mary, da of Brig James Windsor Lewis, DSO, MC; 2 s (David, Dickon), 2 da (Anna, Henrietta); *Career* called to the Bar Gray's Inn 1962 (bencher 1989); standing counsel Inland Revenue 1973–77, first sr treasy counsel Central Criminal Court 1989 (jr treasy counsel 1977–84, sr treasy counsel 1984); *Clubs* Garrick; *Style*— Julian Bevan, Esq, QC; ✉ Cloth Fair Chambers, London EC1A 7JQ (tel 020 7583 5766)

BEVAN, Nicholas V; s of David Bevan (d 1986), of Bledington, Oxon, and Hilary, *née* Pakington; *b* 21 February 1942; *Educ* Shrewsbury, Balliol Coll Oxford (BA, Rowing blue), St John's Coll Cambridge (CertEd); *m* Aug 1978, Annabel, da of John O'Connor; 2 s (Edward, Oliver), 2 da (Kate, Emily); *Career* served King's Shropshire Light Inf 1963–69; asst master and jr form master Westminster Sch 1970–72; Shrewsbury Sch: pt/t teacher and campaign dir Friends of Shrewsbury Sch 1972–73, asst master 1973–79, housemaster 1980–88; exchange teacher and rowing coach Brighton GS Melbourne Aust 1979, headmaster Shiplake Coll 1988–2004; memb HMC 1998; memb: SHMIS (chm 1997), Nat Schs Regatta; govr: Moreton Hall Sch, Seaford Coll, St Piran's Sch; tstee: Balliol Soc Educnl Tst, Balliol Coll Boat Club; chm Kitchin Soc; JP Oxford; *Recreations* walking, travel, art, music and theatre, cartography, map collecting; *Clubs* Leander, Sabrina (pres); *Style*— Nicholas V Bevan, Esq; ✉ Mill Cottage, North Aston, Bicester OX25 6HZ (tel 01869 345153, e-mail nick@millcottageoxon.plus.com)

BEVAN, Sir Nicolas; kt (2001), CB (1991); s of Dr Roger Bevan (d 1973), formerly Lt-Col RAMC (despatches), and Diana Mary, *née* Freeman (d 1982); *b* 8 March 1942; *Educ* Westminster (Queen's scholar), CCC Oxford (Open scholar, MA); *m* 11 Dec 1982, (Helen) Christine, da of Norman Athol Berry, of Rhyl; *Career* MOD: asst princ 1964–69, princ 1969–76, private sec to Chief of Air Staff 1970–73, seconded to Cabinet Office 1973–75, asst sec 1976–84, RCDS 1981, asst under sec of state 1985–93, seconded to Cabinet Office 1992–93; Speaker's sec 1993–2003; *Style*— Sir Nicolas Bevan, CB

BEVAN, Tim; CBE (2005); *b* 1957; *Educ* Sidcot Sch; *m* (m dis), Joely Richardson; 1 da (Daisy b 1992); partner, Amy Gadney; 1 da (Nell b 2001), 1 s (Jago b 2003); *Career* film prodr; Working Title Films: co-fndr (with Sarah Radclyffe, *qv*) 1984, co-chm (with Eric Fellner, *qv*) 1992–, launched Working Title 2 (with Eric Fellner); films produced by Working Title: My Beautiful Laundrette 1985, Caravaggio 1985, Personal Services 1986, Wish You Were Here 1986 Sammy and Rosie Get Laid 1987, A World Apart 1987, Paperhouse 1987, For Queen and Country 1987, The Tall Guy 1988, Diamond Skulls 1988, Chicago Joe and the Showgirl 1989, Fools of Fortune 1989, Dakota Road 1990, Drop Dead Fred 1990, Rubin and Ed 1990, Edward II 1991, Robin Hood 1991, London Kills Me 1991, Bob Roberts 1992, Map of the Human Heart 1993, The Young Americans 1993, Romeo is Bleeding 1993, Posse 1993, The Hudsucker Proxy 1994, Four Weddings and a Funeral 1994, The Eye the Sky 1994, Panther 1995, French Kiss 1995, Moonlight and Valentino 1995, Loch Ness 1995, Dead Man Walking 1995, Fargo 1996, Matchmaker 1996, Bean 1997, The Borrowers 1997, The Big Lebowski 1998, What Rats Won't Do 1998, Elizabeth 1998, The Hi-Lo Country 1998, Plunkett & Macleane 1999, Notting Hill 1999, Oh Brother, Where Art Thou? 2000, Billy Elliot 2000, The Man Who Cried 2000, High Fidelity 2000, Captain Corelli's Mandolin 2001, Bridget Jones's Diary 2001, The Man Who Wasn't There 2001, Long Time Dead 2002, My Little Eye 2002, 40 Days and 40 Nights 2002, Ali G Inda House 2002, About a Boy 2002, The Guru 2002, Johnny English 2003, Ned Kelly 2003, Love Actually 2003, The Calcium Kid 2003, The Shape of Things 2003, Thirteen 2003, Shaun of the Dead 2004, Gettin' Square 2004, Thunderbirds 2004, Wimbledon 2004, Bridget Jones: The Edge of Reason 2004, The Interpreter 2005, Pride and Prejudice 2005, Nanny McPhee 2005; govr Nat Film and TV Sch; 4 Oscars, 20 BAFTA Awards, GQ Entrepreneur of the Year 2003, Michael Balcon Award for outstanding contribution to Br cinema 2004, Alexander Walker Film Award 2005; *Style*— Tim Bevan, Esq, CBE; ✉ Working Title Films, Oxford House, 76 Oxford Street, London W1D 1BS (tel 020 7307 3000)

BEVERIDGE, Crawford William; CBE (1995); s of William Wilson Beveridge, and Catherine Crawford Beveridge; *b* 3 November 1945; *Educ* Univ of Edinburgh (BSc), Univ of Bradford (MSc); *Career* various appts Hewlett Packard 1968–77, Digital Equipment Corp 1977–81, vice-pres corp resources Sun Microsystems 1985–90, chief exec Scottish Enterprise 1991–2000, exec vice-pres and chief HR offr Sun Microsystems Inc 2000–; non-exec dir: Memec Inc 2002–, Autodesk, Scottish Equity Partners; *Style*— Crawford W Beveridge, Esq, CBE

BEVERIDGE, David J; *Educ* Washington and Jefferson Coll (BA), Univ of Texas at Austin (JD); *m* Diane; 1 s (Michael), 1 da (Josephine); *Career* admitted to the NY Bar; slr specialising in int capital markets and banking and finance; ptnr Shearman & Sterling LLP (London office Capital Markets Gp 1998–); *Style*— David J Beveridge, Esq; ✉ Shearman & Sterling LLP, Broadgate West, 9 Appold Street, London EC2A 2AP (tel 020 7655 5005, fax 020 7655 5500, e-mail dbeveridge@shearman.com)

BEVERIDGE, John Caldwell; QC (1979); s of Prof William Ian Beardmore Beveridge, of Canberra, and Patricia Dorothy Nina, *née* Thomson (d 1996); *b* 26 September 1937; *Educ* Jesus Coll Cambridge (MA, LLB); *m* 1, 2 Aug 1973 (m dis 1988), Frances Ann Clunes Grant Martineau, da of Dr John Sutherland, of Edinburgh; m 2, 7 July 1989 (m dis 2003), Lilian Moira, da of John Weston Adamson (d 1977), of Oldstead Hall, N Yorks; m 3, 22 April 2005, Rebecca Rosemary Amara, da of Peter Boulos-Hanna, of Earls Barton, Northants; *Career* barr; recorder of the Crown Court (Western Circuit) 1975–95, bencher Inner Temple 1987; QC NSW Australia 1980; tstee Dogs Tst 1998, vice-pres Manchester Dogs Home 1999; chm St James's Conservation Tst 1999; Freeman City of London 1965, Liveryman Worshipful Co of Goldsmiths; *Recreations* wine, art; *Clubs* Beefsteak, Pratt's, Turf, Brook (NY); *Style*— John Beveridge, Esq, QC; ✉ 9 St James's Chambers, Ryder Street, London SW1Y 6QA (tel 020 7930 1118, fax 020 7930 1119)

BEVERLEY, Bishop of 2000–; Rt Rev Martyn William Jarrett; s of Frederick William Cyril Jarrett (d 2002), of Bristol, and Ivy Ruth, *née* Marsh (d 1989); *b* 25 October 1944; *Educ* Cotham GS, KCL (BD, AKC), Univ of Hull (MPhil); *m* 1968, Betty Mabel, da of Herbert Frank Wallis; 2 da (Mary Ruth b 1970, Judith Miriam b 1973); *Career* asst curate: St George E Bristol 1968–70, Swindon New Town 1970–74; vicar: St Joseph the Worker Northolt W End 1976–81 (priest-in-charge 1974–76), St Andrew Uxbridge 1981–85; sr selection sec ACCM 1989–91 (selection sec 1985–88), vicar Our Lady and All Saints Chesterfield 1991–94, bishop of Burnley 1994–2000; provincial episcopal visitor for the Province of York 2000–; *Recreations* psephology, biographies, bird watching; *Style*— The Rt Rev the Bishop of Beverley; ✉ 3 North Lane, Roundhay, Leeds LS8 2QJ (tel 0113 265 4280, fax 0113 265 4281, e-mail bishop-of-beverley@3-north-lane.fsnet.co.uk)

BEVERLEY, Michael; DL; s of George Kenneth Beverley (d 1977), and Emily, *née* Wood; *b* 28 June 1947; *Educ* Univ of Leeds (BA); *m* 28 March 1970, Jennifer Anne, da of Leslie Farrar (d 1974); 1 da (Rachel b 12 Nov 1972), 1 s (James Leslie b 1974 d 1997); *Career* Arthur Andersen: ptnr 1985, regnl office (North of England) managing ptnr 1994–98, UK regnl managing ptnr 1998–2001, ret; dir: Minorplanet Inc 2001–2004, Telemedcare Ltd 2004; chm: Yorkshire Ventures Ltd 2004, One Medical Ltd 2004; memb Industrial Devpt Bd DTI 2000–, Advsy Bd Univ of Leeds Business Sch 2001–; chm Opera North 1998; govr Leeds Metropolitan Univ 1991–98; FCA 1981 (ACA 1976), FRSA; *Recreations* opera, keeping fit, shooting, farming, skiing, watching football; *Clubs* Leeds United (vice-pres); *Style*— Michael Beverley, Esq, DL; ✉ 65 The Panoramic, 152 Grosvenor Road, London SW1V 3JL

BEVERLEY, Nigel; s of Jack Beverley, of Salhouse, Norfolk, and Amelia, *née* Hartley; *b* 22 June 1952; *Educ* High Storrs GS Sheffield, Univ of Nottingham (BSc); *m* Mary Elizabeth; 1 da (Katherine b 7 Dec 1983), 1 s (James b 25 May 1987); *Career* nat mgmnt trainee NE Thames RHA 1973–75, asst sector admin UCH 1975–77, sector admin Hammersmith Hosp 1977–80, asst dist admin Havering Dist Barking and Havering AHA 1980–82, unit gen mangr Colchester Gen Hosp 1985–88 (unit admin 1982–85), dist gen mangr Southend HA 1988–90, chief exec Southend Healthcare NHS Tst 1990–91, head Reforms Gp and head NHS Tst Unit NHS Mgmnt Exec 1991–92, tst unit dir NHS Exec (N Thames) 1992–96, chief exec Wellhouse NHS Tst 1996–98, chief exec North Essex Health Authority 1998, actg chief exec Cambridge City PCT 2006; currently business dept dir Atos Origin Medical Services; bd dir: Synovia Ltd, Get Well UK; MHSM (DipHSM), MInstD; *Recreations* squash, golf, skiing; *Style*— Nigel Beverley, Esq

BEVINGTON, Her Hon Judge Christian Veronica; da of late Michael Falkner Bevington, and late Dulcie Marian, *née* Gratton; *b* 1 November 1939; *Educ* St James's West Malvern, LSE (LLB); *m* 1961 (m dis 1973), David Levitt, OBE; 1 s (Aldhun), 2 da (Alison, Evelyn); *Career* called to the Bar: Inner Temple 1961 (bencher 1994), Lincoln's Inn (ad eundem) 1971; co-fndr charitable housing tst, co sec and housing mangr Circle 33 Housing Tst 1966–76; returned to full-time practice at the Bar 1980, head of chambers 1981–98, recorder 1994–98, circuit judge (SE Circuit) 1998–; chm Independent Inquiry for City and Co of Cardiff 1997; *Publications* The Bevington Report (1997); *Recreations* music, travel; *Style*— Her Hon Judge Bevington

BEVIS, Prof Michael John; s of Bernard John Bevis (d 2002), of Jersey, and Kathleen Mary Balston; *b* 25 April 1940; *Educ* De La Salle Coll Jersey, Univ of London (BSc, PhD); *m* 23 May 1964, Diana, da of Edgar Holloway (d 1976); 2 da (Katie Ann b 30 April 1965, Sarah Jane b 11 March 1972), 1 s (Andrew John b 12 Jan 1968); *Career* lectr rising to reader Dept of Metallurgy and Materials Sci Univ of Liverpool 1965–77; Brunel Univ: joined 1977, prof and head Dept of Non-Metallic Materials 1977–84, prof and head Dept of Materials Technol 1984–87, research prof and dir Wolfson Centre 1987–94, conslt dir Wolfson Centre 1994–2007; author of over 200 sci papers; UK ed Int Materials Review 1999–2007; vice-pres Inst of Materials 1992–95; awarded A A Griffith Silver Medal Inst of Metals 1988, Swinburne Gold Medal Plastics and Rubber Inst 1990; Freeman Worshipful Co of Horners 2000; FInstP 1971, FIMMM 1977, FPRI 1980, FREng 1986; *Style*— Prof Michael Bevis, FREng; ✉ The Stables, 11 Kiln Croft, Skelsmergh, Kendal LA9 6NE (tel 01539 720293)

BEVITT, Paul Antony; s of Geoffrey Bevitt, of Horsforth, W Yorks, and Betty, *née* Ibbotson; *b* 5 May 1951; *Educ* Ropewalk Secdy Modern, Wakefield Art Coll; *m* 30 July 1983, Diane, da of David Owen Fowles; 2 s (Christopher b 9 May 1984, Samuel b 30 July 1987); *Career* photographer's asst London 1969–74, Toronto Canada 1974–75, freelance photographer specialising in studio advtg London 1975–; *Awards* D&AD Silver 1986, Campaign Poster Silver 1987 and Gold 1988, Creative Circle Silver 1990, USA Art Dirs' Club Merit 1990, Ilford B&W Award 1990, 2 Campaign Poster Silvers 1990, USA Advtg Annual Award 1992, Assoc of Photographers Merit 1994; memb: Assoc of Photographers, D&AD; *Recreations* tennis, music, cinema, swimming, football; *Clubs* Highgate Lawn Tennis; *Style*— Paul Bevitt; ✉ 6E The Courtyard, 44 Gloucester Avenue, Primrose Hill, London NW1 8JD (tel 020 7586 8500, e-mail paul@paulbevitt.co.uk)

BEWES, Michael Keith; s of Rev Canon Thomas Francis Cecil Bewes (d 1993), and (Nellie) Sylvia Cohu, *née* De Berry; bro of Rev Prebendary Richard Thomas Bewes, OBE, *qv*; *b* 4 March 1936; *Educ* Marlborough, Emmanuel Coll Cambridge (MA); *m* 10 Oct 1964, (Patricia) Anrōs, *née* Neill; 3 s (Jonathan b 1965, Nicholas b 1967, Anthony b 1971), 1 da (Rebecca b 1973); *Career* Nat Serv 2 Lt RA 1954–56; BR 1959–66, Royal Exchange Assurance 1966–68, Guardian Royal Exchange plc 1968–96, chm The Willis Partnership 1996–; Chartered Insurance Inst: treas 1985–87, dep pres 1987–88, pres 1988–89; chm Insurance Industry Trg Cncl 1982–88; memb Governing Cncl Business in the Community 1983–96; chm of govrs Coll of Insurance 1992–99, pres Insurance Benevolent Fund 1995–96; chm Cncl Scripture Union 1988–94, tstee Dio of Central Tanganyika; govr Stowe Sch 1971–2005, dir Allied Schs; Freeman City of London 1990, Master Worshipful Co of Insurers 2003–04; FCIPD (FIPD 1983), FRSA 1989; *Recreations* fly fishing, heraldic painting, photography, music, Napoleon commemorative medals, various sports - lawn tennis and hockey; *Clubs* RAC, National, Hawks' (Cambridge); *Style*— Michael Bewes, Esq; ✉ Clifton House, Church Lane, Lexden, Colchester, Essex CO3 4AE (tel 01206 542710, fax 01206 574724, e-mail michael@bewes.com); The Willis Partnership, Alexandra House, 55A Catherine Place, Westminster, London SW1E 6DY (tel 020 7821 6543, fax 020 7630 6818, e-mail michaelbewes@willis-partnership.co.uk)

BEWES, Rev Prebendary Richard Thomas; OBE (2005); s of Rev Canon Thomas Francis Cecil Bewes (d 1993), and (Nellie) Sylvia Cohu, *née* De Berry; bro of Michael Keith Bewes, *qv*; *b* 1 December 1934; *Educ* Marlborough, Emmanuel Coll Cambridge (MA), Ridley Hall Theol Coll Cambridge; *m* 18 April 1964, Elisabeth Ingrid, da of Lionel Jaques; 2 s (Timothy b 1966, Stephen b 1971), 1 da (Wendy b 1968); *Career* vicar: St Peter's Harold Wood 1965–74, Emmanuel Northwood 1974–83; rector All Souls Langham Place London 1983–2004, prebendary St Paul's Cathedral 1988–; chm: C of E Evangelical Cncl 1992–2001, Anglican Evangelical Assembly 1992–2001; memb Guild of Br Songwriters 1975; Freedom of the City of Charlotte NC 1984; *Books* God in Ward 12 (1973), Advantage Mr Christian (1975), Talking About Prayer (1979, revised edn 2000), The Pocket Handbook of Christian Truth (1981), John Wesley's England (1981, revised edn 2003), The Church Reaches Out (1981), The Church Overcomes (1983), On The Way (1984), Quest For Life (1985), Quest For Truth (1985), The Church Marches On (1986), When God Surprises (1986), The Resurrection (1989), A New Beginning (1989), Does God Reign? (1995), Speaking in Public - Effectively (1998), Great Quotes of the 20th Century (1999, revised edn (as Words that Circled the World) 2002), The Lamb Wins (2000), The Bible Truth Treasury (2000), The Stone That Became a Mountain (2001), The Top 100 Questions (2002), Beginning the Christian Life (2004), 150 Pocket Bible Thoughts (2004); *Recreations* tennis, photography, broadcasting, reading, writing; *Style*— The Rev Prebendary Richard Bewes, OBE; ✉ The Liskeard Trust, Victoria House, Victoria Road, Buckhurst Hill, Essex IG9 5EX (e-mail richard.bewes@talk21.com, website www.richardbewes.com)

BEWICK, Tom; *b* 4 February 1971, Coventry; *Educ* Univ of Bath (BSc, MSc (jtly with Ljubljana Univ)); *Career* policy advsr TEC Nat Cncl 1994–96, policy advsr (educn and employment) Lab Party 1997–99, dir NTO Nat Cncl 1999–2001, ministerial advsr DfES 2001–03, dir LSC Thames Gateway 2003–04, chief exec Creative and Cultural Skills 2004–; co-fndr Centre for Social Inclusion 1996; non-exec dir TLMH Ltd 2005–2007; FRSA 1999, MInstD 2006; *Publications* Learning and Earning in the 21st Century (1996); *Recreations* travel, cricket, reading, social history; *Clubs* England Cricket Supporters; *Style*— Tom Bewick, Esq; ✉ Creative and Cultural Skills, Lafone House, Weston Street, London SE1 3HN (tel 020 7015 1800, e-mail tom.bewick@ccskills.org.uk)

BEYER, HE John Charles; *b* 29 April 1950; *m* 1972, Letty Marindin, *née* Minns; 1 s (Timothy), 1 da (Eleanor); *Career* academic and diplomat; Asia researcher Amnesty International 1981–82, Chinese language teacher Univ of Westminster 1982–84, dep dir Sino-British Trade Cncl 1984–98, dir China-Britain Trade Gp 1991–98; entered HM Dip Serv 1999, head of section EU Dept FCO 1999–2001, dep head of mission Luxembourg 2002–05, ambass to Moldova 2006–; *Style*— HE Mr John Beyer; ✉ c/o Foreign & Commonwealth Office (Chisinau), King Charles Street, London SW1A 2AH

BEYFUS, Drusilla Norman (Mrs Milton Shulman); da of late Norman Beyfus, and late Florence Noël Barker; *Educ* RN Sch, Channing Sch; *m* 1956, Milton Shulman (d 2004); 1 s (Jason), 2 da (Alexandra Shulman, *qv*, Nicola (The Most Hon the Marchioness of Normanby)); *Career* assoc ed Queen Magazine 1958–63, home ed The Observer 1963–64, assoc ed Daily Telegraph colour supplement 1964–70, ed Brides Magazine 1971–79, assoc ed British Vogue Magazine Condé Nast 1979–86, ed Harrods Magazine 1987–88, columnist Daily Mail magazine 1988–89, contributing ed Telegraph Magazine 1990–, weekly columnist You magazine (Mail on Sunday) 1994–2001; visiting tutor Central St Martin's Coll of Art 1989–; author and broadcaster; Hon MA London Inst 2002; *Books* Lady Behave (co-author), The English Marriage, The Bride's Book, The Art of Giving, Modern Manners (1992); The Done Thing: Courtship, Parties (1992), Business, Sex (1993), The You Guide to Modern Dilemmas (1996); *Style*— Miss Drusilla Beyfus; ✉ 51G Eaton Square, London SW1W 9BE (tel 020 7235 7162, fax 020 7823 1366)

BEYNON, David William Stephen; s of William Henry Beynon (d 1983), and Eileen Beynon (d 1992); *b* 14 March 1934; *Educ* King Edward VII Sch Sheffield, Trinity Hall Cambridge (MA); *m* 23 Sept 1961, Joyce Noreen, da of George Trevor Richards, of Wallasey, Cheshire; 1 da (Jane b 1962), 2 s (Stephen b 1965, Daniel b 1971); *Career* Nat Serv RA 1952–54; ICI: joined 1954, commercial appts Petrochemicals Div 1954–77, head Policy Gps Dept London 1977–79, dep chm Plastics Div 1979–81, gp dir Petrochemicals and Plastics Div 1981–87, dir ICI Chemicals & Polymers Ltd 1987–90, dir ICI Resources Ltd 1987–90, chm ICI Europe 1990–92; dir Holliday Chemical Holdings plc 1992–98; pres: Br Plastics Fedn 1987–88 (memb Cncl 1980–89), Assoc of Euro Plastics Mfrs (APME) 1990–92 (memb Cncl 1987–92); memb: Ctee Euro Petrochem Assoc (EPCA) 1985–91, Cncl Assoc of Euro Petrochem Mfrs (APPE) 1988–91; visiting prof Univ of Herts 1993–; dir Apex Charitable Trust Ltd 1993–; capt Great Ayton CC 1971–76; chm: Welwyn Garden City CC 1980–86 and 1993–98, chm Digswell Park Sports Assoc 1993–; pres Herts Co Cricket Assoc 2003– (memb Bd 1993–); Freeman City of London 1984, Master Worshipful Co of Horners 2002 (Liveryman 1984); *Recreations* family, cricket, golf; *Clubs* Forty, Hanbury Manor Golf, MCC; *Style*— David Beynon, Esq; ✉ 1 Downfield Court, Hanbury Drive, Thundridge, Ware, Hertfordshire SG12 0SB (tel and fax 01920 484614, e-mail beynondavid@hotmail.com)

BHAN, Dr Girdari Lal; s of Arjun Nath Bhan (d 1955), and Laxmi Bhan; *b* 25 December 1943; *Educ* Med Coll Srinagar India (MB BS); *m* 31 Aug 1968, Supriya, da of Varkie Cherian; 2 da (Archana b 7 Oct 1969, Kanchan b 25 Nov 1975); *Career* sr house offr: med East Birmingham Hosp 1974–75, neurology Midland Centre for Neurosurgery and Neurology 1976; registrar med East Birmingham Hosp 1977–79, sr registrar North West RHA 1980–81, conslt physician Royal Oldham Hosp 1982–; memb: BMA, BGS; MRCP, FRCPI, FRCP (London); *Recreations* classical music, gardening; *Style*— Dr Girdari Bhan

BHARUCHA, Dr Chitra; da of late George Gnanadickam, of Madras, India, and Mangalam, *née* Ramaiya; *b* 6 April 1945, Madurai, India; *Educ* Ewart Sch Madras, Christian Med Coll Vellore India (MB BS); *m* 18 Jan 1967, Hoshang Bharucha, s of Kaikusru Bharucha, of Bombay, India; 2 da (Anita b 3 June 1972, Tara b 8 Jan 1974); *Career* dep chief exec NI Blood Transfusion Serv 1981–2000, conslt haematologist Belfast City Hosp 1981–2000; non-exec dir UK Transplant Servs Authy 2000–01; chm: Advsy Ctee for Transfusion Transmitted Infections UK Blood Transfusion Serv 1998–2000, Advsy Ctee on Animal Feeding Stuffs Food Standards Agency 2002–; vice-chm NI Cncl for Postgrad Med Educn 1999–2000; memb: Expert Advsy Panel for Blood Products WHO 1988–2000, Advsy Ctee for Selection of Blood Donors UK Blood Transfusion Serv 1995–98, Lab Servs Advsy Ctee DHSS NI 1995–2000, Scientific Ctee European Sch of Blood Transfusion 1996–2000, Blood Safety Advsy Ctee NI 1998–2000, Standing Advsy Ctee for Pathology NI 1998–2000, Ptnrs Cncl NICE 1999–2000, Cncl RCPath 1996–99 (chm NI Affrs Ctee 1998–2000), Cncl Int Soc of Blood Transfusion 1996–2000; memb GMC 1999–2003 (assoc memb 2004–); pres Med Women's Fedn 1994–95; memb: Broadcasting Cncl BBC NI 1996–99, ITC 2001–03, Cncl Advtg Standards Authy 2004–, BBC Tst 2006– (vice-chm 2006–, actg chm 2006–07), Review Body for Judicial Complaints 2006–; govr Methodist Coll Belfast 1990–93, memb Exec Ctee Assoc of Governing Bodies of Vol Grammar Schs 1990–95; memb: Cncl Leprosy Mission for NI 1994–2003, NI Advsy Forum Sargent Cancer Care for Children 2000–03; FRCPath, FRSA 2002; *Recreations* opera, concerts, hill walking, experimental cookery; *Clubs* Reform, London and Ulster Reform; *Style*— Dr Chitra Bharucha

BHATIA, Vineet; s of Ved Prakash Bhatia, of Mumbai, India, and Sheila Bhatia; *b* 9 December 1967; *Educ* Inst of Hotel Mgmnt, Catering Technol and Applied Nutrition Bombay (Dip Hotel Mgmnt and Catering Technol), Univ of Bombay (BA), Alliance Française New Delhi (Cert), Oberoi Sch of Hotel Mgmnt New Delhi (Dip Food Prodn), Westminster Coll (Dip); *m* 18 June 1997, Rashima, da of Capt Brij Dev Madhok; 2 c (Varaul b 27 June 1998, Ronit b 24 Jan 2000); *Career* chef; exec chef Star of India London 1993–98, chef patron Vineet Bhatia Indian Restaurant London 1998–99, chef and patron Zaika and Bar Zaika Bazaar London 1999–2004, chef and patron Rasoi Restaurant 2004–; conslt: Tantra LA, Safran Le Touessrok Hotel Mauritius, BA (first class and business class in-flight food), Indego Grosvenor House Hotel Dubai, Indus Moscow, Rasoi by Vineet St Géran Mauritius; fell Guild of Master Craftsmen 1996; *Awards* Cert of Ingenuity Assoc of Italian Chefs 1994, Evening Standard Eros Award 1995, 1996 and 1997, 3 AA Rosettes 1999, 2000, 2001, 2002, 2003 and 2005, Indian Restaurant of the Year Moët & Chandon London Awards 2000 (nominee Best Chef and Best Newcomer), Restaurant Personality of the Year Best in Britain Awards 2001, Restaurateur's Restaurant of the Year 2001, Most Innovative Chef Cobra Awards 2001, Michelin Star 2001–06 (first Indian chef to be awarded a Michelin Star for 102 years), nominee Best Kitchen Tatler Restaurant Awards 2003; Best Indian Restaurant: The Times 1997 and 2000/01, Hardens 2000/01, Zagat 2000/01, Good Food Guide 2000/01, Best in Britain Awards 2001, Restaurant Magazines Restaurateur Awards 2002, Best Newcomer Tatler Restaurant Awards 2005, Best Indian Restaurant Tio Pepe ITV Carlton Restaurant Awards 2005; *Recreations* travelling, writing; *Style*— Vineet Bhatia, Esq; ✉ Rasoi Restaurant, 10 Lincoln Street, London SW3 2TS (website www.rasoirestaurant.co.uk)

BHATTACHARYYA, Baron (Life Peer UK 2004), of Moseley in the County of West Midlands; Sir (Sushantha) Kumar Bhattacharyya; kt (2003), CBE (1997); s of late Sudir Bhattacharyya, of Calcutta, India, and late Hemanalini, *née* Chakraborty; *b* 6 June 1940, Dacca, India; *Educ* IIT Kharagpur (BTech), Univ of Birmingham (MSc, PhD); *m* 1981, Brigid Carmel, da of Charles Rabbitt; 3 da (Anita b 16 April 1984, Tina b 9 March 1986, Malini b 17 Feb 1988); *Career* various positions in prodn and industrial mgmnt Lucas Industries Ltd 1961–67, head of mfrg systems Univ of Birmingham 1967–80, prof of mfrg Univ of Warwick 1980–, dir Warwick Mfrg Gp; non-exec dir Technol Rover Group 1986–92; tstee: IPPR, Coventry 2020; memb: Nat Consumer Cncl Agency 1990–93, Cncl for Science and Technol 1993–2003, W Midlands Devpt Agency 1999–2004; advsr to various int cos and govts on matters of competitive industrial policy; Mensforth Int Gold Medal IEE 1998, Sir Robert Lawrence Award ILT 1999; hon prof: Hong Kong Poly Univ 1992, Univ of Technol Malaysia 1993, Min of Machinery Beijing 1994; hon dean Harbin Inst of Technol 2003; Hon DSc: Univ of Surrey 1992, Univ of Technol Malaysia 1993, Univ of Birmingham 2004; Hon Dr Hong Kong Poly Univ 2003; MIMechE, FIEE 1975, FREng 1991, FILT 1996, CCMI 1996; Padma Bhusan (India) 2002; *Recreations* family, flying, cricket; *Clubs* Athenaeum; *Style*— The Rt Hon the Lord Bhattacharyya, CBE; ✉ International Manufacturing Centre, University of Warwick, Coventry CV4 7AL (tel 024 7652 3155, fax 024 7652 4027, mobile 07798 906166, e-mail s.k.bhattacharyya@warwick.ac.uk)

BHATTACHARYYA, Mukti Nath; DL (Gtr Manchester 2003); s of Manju Gopal Bhattacharyya (d 1981), of Calcutta, and Santilata Mukherjee (d 1936), of Calcutta; *b* 22 January 1935; *Educ* Univ of Calcutta (MB BS, Dip Gynaecology and Obstetrics), FRCOG London 1983 (MRCOG 1964); *m* 18 Oct 1969, Brenda Kathleen, da of L Evans (d 1996); 2 s (Neil b 27 Nov 1972, Robin b 10 Dec 1973); *Career* Int R G Kar Med Coll Calcutta 1959–61; Teaching Hosp Calcutta: res in surgery, med, obstetrics and gynaecology 1959–62; registrar in obstetrics and gynaecology Wisbech Hosp 1963–64, sr house offr obstetrics and gynaecology Huddersfield Hosp 1964, registrar in obstetrics and gynaecology Stockport 1965–67, registrar in diagnostic radiology Manchester 1967–70, conslt in genito-urinary med Royal Infirmary Sheffield 1973–79 (sr registrar in venereology 1971–73), conslt physician Manchester Royal Infirmary 1979–97, hon lectr Univ of Manchester 1979–97; memb and chm Manchester BMA 1987–90 (sec 1984–87); govr William Hulme's GS Manchester 1993–; memb: Manchester Med Soc, Cncl Manchester Literary and Philosophical Soc 2001–, Gen Assembly Univ of Manchester 2004– (memb Ct 1997–2004); SBStJ (memb Cncl Order of St John Gtr Manchester 1996–); *Publications* incl numerous papers in professional med jls; *Recreations* astronomy, music, sports, travel; *Clubs* Manchester Rotary; *Style*— Mukti Bhattacharyya, Esq, DL; ✉ 56 Green Pastures, Heaton Mersey, Stockport SK4 3RA (tel 0161 432 3832, fax 0161 432 3832, e-mail mukti.n.bhattacharyya@man.ac.uk)

BHOGAL, Amar; *Educ* Duke of Gloucester Sch Nairobi, Univ of Manchester; *m*; 2 s (twins), 1 da; *Career* Costain Gp: grad trainee, seconded to Int Div, responsible for design and construction methods Thames Barrier Project 1975, head Engrg Dept, chief engr 1986–93; supervising engr ICE Training Scheme, examiner ICE Professional Reviews; ICE: dir of engrg 1993–95, dep sec tech affrs 1995–2001, acting chief exec and sec 2001–02, dir of engrg knowledge and dep DG 2002–05; CEng, FICE; *Recreations* cooking, current affairs, football, DIY; *Style*— Amar Bhogal, Esq; ✉ Institute of Civil Engineers, One Great George Street, London SW1P 3AA

BHOGAL, Rev Dr Inderjit; OBE (2005); s of Gian Singh Bhogal (d 1984), of India, and Rajinder Kaur, *née* Mudhar; *b* 17 January 1953; *Educ* Dudley Tech Coll, Cliff Coll, Univ of Manchester (BA), Westminster Coll Oxford (MA); *m* 1 Nov 1986, Kathryn Anne, da of Henry Robinson (decd); 2 c (Liamarjit b 8 Aug 1989, Anjuli b 14 Jan 1991); *Career* labourer Dudley Brass Foundry 1974–75; min Wolverhampton 1979–84, min Wolverhampton and co-ordinator Wolverhampton Inter Faith Gp 1984–87, min Sheffield W chaplaincy in higher educn Sheffield 1987–94, dir of studies Urban Theology Unit and min in Sheffield Inner City Ecumenical Mission 1994–97, dir Urban Theology Unit Sheffield 1997–2004, theological conslt Christian Aid 2004–05, dir Yorks and Humber Faiths Forum 2005–; pres Methodist Conf 2000–01; convener Br Black Theology Forum Sheffield; memb Editorial Bd Black Theology in Britain Jl, fndr memb Sheffield Homeless and Rootless Gp, fndr City of Sanctuary Sheffield; Hon DUniv: Oxford Brookes 2001, Sheffield Hallam 2002; *Publications* A Table for All (2000), Theology on the Hoof (2001), Unlocking the Doors (2002), Pluralism and Mission in Today's World (2007); author of various articles on theology; *Recreations* walking, cooking, photography; *Style*— Rev Dr Inderjit S Bhogal, OBE; ✉ Yorkshire and Humber Faiths Forum, Suite E12, Joseph's Well, Hanover Walk, Leeds LS3 1AB (tel 0113 245 6444)

BHOPAL, Prof Rajinder Singh (Raj); CBE (2001); s of Jhanda S Bhopal, and Bhagwanti K Bhopal; *b* 10 April 1953; *Educ* Shawlands Acad Glasgow, Univ of Edinburgh (BSc, MB ChB, MD), Univ of Glasgow (MPH, MacKinlay prize 1985); *m*; 4 c; *Career* surgical/house offr 1978–79, med house offr 1979, SHO in accident and emergency 1979–80, trainee GP 1980–81, SHO in general med 1981–82, SHO in infectious and tropical diseases 1982, sr registrar in community med 1985 (registrar 1983–85), lectr and hon sr registrar in community med Univ of Glasgow 1985–88; Univ of Newcastle upon Tyne: sr lectr 1988–91, hon conslt in public health med 1988–99, prof of epidemiology and public health 1991–99, head Dept of Epidemiology and Public Health 1991–98; Bruce and John Usher chair of public health Univ of Edinburgh 1999–, head Div of Community Health Sci 2000–03; visiting prof Dept of Epidemiology Sch of Public Health Univ of North Carolina 1996–97; hon conslt in public health medicine Lothian Health Bd 1999–; non-exec dir Newcastle HA 1992–94, vice-chm and non-exec dir Newcastle and N Tyneside HA 1994–96, non-exec dir Health Educn Authy England 1996–99; visiting worker MRC Med Sociology Unit Glasgow 1986–94, memb Advsy Bd Int Respiratory Infection Taskforce Schering Plough 1993–96; assoc ed Jl of Public Health Med 1989–90, memb Editorial Bd Jl of Epidemiology and Community Health 1993–98; memb: MRC Health Services Research and Public Health Bd 1999–2003, GMC 1978–, MRC Advsy Bd 1997–99, MRC Cross Bd Gp 2000–02, Sci Ctee Biobank UK 2003–04, Steering Ctee Nat Resource Centre for Ethnic Minority Health Scot (chair 2002–); Soc of Public Health: Maddison Research Prize 1992, J T Neech Prize 1994; Royal Soc for the Promotion of Health JW Starkey Silver Medal 2000; author of numerous pubns, papers and book chapters on the health and health care of ethnic minorities, infectious diseases and environmental health, epidemiology and public health; Hon DSc Queen Margeret Univ Coll 2005; MRCP 1982, FRCPEd 2000, FFPHM 1995 (Littlejohn Gairdner prize 1986, MFPHM 1987); *Books* Concepts of Epidemiology (2002, winner Public Health Category BMA Book Awards 2003), The Epidemic of Coronary Heart Disease in South Asian Populations (ed with K C R Patel, 2003), Public Health: Past, Present and Future (ed with J Last, 2004), Ethnicity, Race and Health in Multicultural Societies (2007); *Recreations* chess, hill climbing, photography, travel, golf, cycling and walking; *Style*— Prof Raj Bhopal, CBE; ✉ Division of Community Health Sciences, Public Health Sciences, University of Edinburgh, Medical School, Teviot Place, Edinburgh EH8 9AG (tel 0131 650 3216, fax 0131 650 6909, e-mail raj.bhopal@ed.ac.uk)

BHUGRA, Prof Dinesh Kumar; s of Makhan Lal Bhugra (d 1989), and Shanta, *née* Chugh; *b* 8 July 1952; *Educ* MB BS, MSc, MPhil, MA, PhD; *Career* SHO (orthopaedics) Cork 1979–80, SHO (med) Northampton 1980, SHO then registrar (psychiatry) Leicester 1981–86, sr registrar (psychiatry) Maudsley Hosp 1986–89, researcher/lectr in psychiatry MRC Social and Community Psychiatry Unit 1989–92; Inst of Psychiatry London: sr lectr in psychiatry 1992–2000, reader in cultural psychiatry 2001–02, prof of mental health and cultural diversity 2002–; RCPsych: chm Faculty of Gen and Community Psychiatry 1997–2001, dean 2003– (sub-dean 2001–03), convenor working parties on homelessness and mental health 1992 and 1996 and on caring for a community 1995; pres Section of Psychiatry Steering Gp RSM, memb Steering Gp King's Fund on Mental Health; FRCPsych; *Books* SAQs in Psychiatry (1990), Case Presentations in Psychiatry (1992), Principles of Social Psychiatry (1993), Management for Psychiatrists (1992, 2 edn 1995), Religion and Psychiatry (1996), Homelessness and Mental Health (1996), Troublesome Disguises (1997), Ethnicity: An Agenda for Mental Health (1999), Mental Health of Ethnic Minorities: an annotated bibliography (1999), Cultural Psychiatry: a practical guide (2000), Psychiatry in Multicultural Britain (2001), Colonialism and Psychiatry (2001), Culture and Self-Harm (2004), Handbook of Psychiatry (2005), Culture and Mental Health (2007), Work Place Based Assessments in Psychaitry (2007); *Recreations* reading, theatre, cinema; *Style*— Prof Dinesh Bhugra; ✉ HSPRD, PO 25 Institute of Psychiatry, King's College London, De Crespigny Park, London SE5 8AF (tel 020 7848 0047, fax 020 7848 0333)

BICHAN, Dr (Herbert) Roy; *b* 5 November 1941; *Educ* Univ of Aberdeen (BSc), Univ of Leeds (PhD); *m* Fiona Keay; 2 da (Inga Jane b 16 Feb 1967, Susan Elizabeth b 1 Aug 1971), 1 s (Michael Roy b 8 May 1969); *Career* chm: The Robertson Group plc 1988–91, Force Petroleum Ltd 1998–2004, The Welsh Distillery Co Ltd 1999–2005; formerly dep chm Simon-Robertson, dir HSBC Enterprise Fund for Wales 1998–, dir and chm Clinical Diagnostic Chemicals Ltd 2000–; memb Cncl CBI 1991– (chm Wales 1993–95), chm Welsh Industrial Devpt Advsy Bd, dep chm Welsh Development Agency 1993–95, gp chm KMC Int 2004–; Adrian fell Univ of Leicester 1988–90; vice-chm of govrs Llandrillo Coll 2003–; FIMM (pres 1988–89), FREng 1989; *Recreations* golf; *Style—* Dr Roy Bichan, FREng

BICHARD, Sir Michael George; KCB (1999); s of George Bichard (d 1981), and Nora, *née* Reeves (d 1971); *b* 31 January 1947; *Educ* King Edward VI GS Southampton, Univ of Manchester (LLB), Univ of Birmingham (MSocSci); *m* Christine; 1 s (Philip Michael), 2 da (Charlotte Emma Christine, Emma-Louise Christine); *Career* articled clerk, slr then sr slr Reading BC 1969–73, county liaison officer Berkshire CC 1973–77, head of Chief Exec's Office Lambeth BC 1977–80; chief exec: Brent BC 1980–86, Glos CC 1986–90, Benefits Agency 1990–95; perm sec: Dept of Employment 1995, Dept for Education and Employment 1995–2001; rector Univ of the Arts London (formerly London Inst) 2001–; chair Legal Services Cmmn 2005–; chair Rathbone Trg Ltd 2001–; non-exec dir Reed Executive plc 2002–, non-exec chm RSE Consulting 2003–; govr: The Henley Coll 2002–04, Henley Mgmnt Coll 2002–; dir River and Rowing Museum Fndn 2002–; chair Bd of Dirs ARTIS 2003–, memb Cncl Dyslexia Inst 2003–; chair Ind Inquiry into Soham Case 2004; Hon Dr: Leeds Metropolitan Univ, Univ of Birmingham, Middx Univ, Southampton Inst 2002; FIPD, FRSA, CIMgt; *Recreations* food, wine, music, walking, Manchester United; *Style—* Sir Michael Bichard, KCB

BICK, David Robert; s of Roy Leslie Samuel Bick, and Vera Grace, *née* Collis; *b* 9 April 1957; *Educ* Glyn GS Epsom, Univ of Essex; *m* 21 July 1984, Susan Christine, da of Joseph Esmond Stobbs (d 1979); 2 s (Charles b 1991, Henry b 1994), 2 da (Antonia b 1987, Harriet b 1989); *Career* PA to David Atkinson MP 1979–80; exec: KH Publicity Ltd 1980–81, Shandwick Consits Ltd 1981–83; account dir Good Relations City Ltd 1984–85, dir and jt fndr Lombard Communications plc 1985–93; dir: Buchanan Communications Ltd 1993–95, Financial Dynamics Feb 1995–98, fndr Holborn PR 1998–; cncllr London Borough of Lambeth 1980–86 (chm Amenity Servs 1982); *Recreations* English cricket, football, sleep; *Style—* David R Bick, Esq

BICKERS, Patricia Evelyn; da of Norman Sefton Reece Bickers, and N Evelyn, *née* Hill; *b* 26 December 1950; *Educ* Sch of Saints Helen & Katharine Abingdon, Univ of Sussex (BA); *Career* lectr in art history: Harrow Sch of Art 1978–89 (lectr 1974–78), Univ of Westminster (formerly Poly of Central London) 1989–; external assessor: Glasgow Sch of Art 1997–, St Martin's Sch of Art 2000–03; Art Monthly: assoc ed 1989–91, dep ed 1991–92, ed 1992–; co-selector BT New Contemporaries 1993–94, judge Turner Prize Tate Britain 2001; TV and radio broadcaster: Kaleidoscope (BBC Radio 4) 1994–, World at One, Today Prog, BBC 24, Newsnight; buyer Contemporary Arts Soc 2003–04; memb Mgmnt Ctee Matt's Gallery 1992–2003, tstee Serpentine Gallery 1995–; memb: Assoc of Art Historians 1978, Int Assoc of Art Critics 1999; FRSA 2002 (memb Cncl 2004); *Books* The Brit Pack: Contemporary British Art, the view from abroad (1995), Talking Art: Art Monthly Interviews Since 1976 (2007); *Clubs* Lansdowne; *Style—* Miss Patricia Bickers; ✉ Art Monthly, 4th Floor, 28 Charing Cross Road, London WC2H 0DB (tel 020 7240 0389, fax 020 7497 0726, e-mail editorial@artmonthly.co.uk)

BICKFORD, (James) David Prydeaux; CB (1995); s of William Alfred John Prydeaux Bickford, of London, and Muriel Adelyn, *née* Smythe (d 1973); *b* 28 July 1940; *Educ* Downside; *m* 24 April 1965, Carolyn Jane, da of Maj William Arthur Richard Sumner (d 1943); 3 s (Nicholas b 1966, James b 1967, Peter John b 1972); *Career* slr of the Supreme Ct 1963, in practice with J J Newcombe & Co Devon 1963–69, crown counsel and legal advsr to Turks and Caicos Island Govt 1969–71, asst legal advsr then counsellor to the FCO 1971–87, legal advsr Br Military Govt Berlin 1979–82, under sec of state and legal advsr to the Security and Intelligence Agencies 1987–95, visiting prof of law Cleveland-Marshall Coll of Law Cleveland State Univ USA 1995–96, currently chm Bickford Associates; memb Panel of Legal Experts Int Telecommunications Satellite Orgn, chm Assembly Maritime Satellite Orgn 1985–87; Judge Ben C Green lectr in nat security law Case Western Univ Ohio USA; hon memb Nat Security Ctee American Bar Assoc; memb Law Soc; *Publications* Land Dealings Simplified in the Turks and Caicos Islands (1971), The Face of Tomorrow (novel, 2004); articles, lectures and web contributions on intelligence and organised crime; *Recreations* the family, fishing, sailing; *Style—* David Bickford, Esq, CB; ✉ c/o National Westminster Bank, Torrington, Devon

BICKHAM, Edward Sidney Côver; s of Eric Edward Bickham (d 1987), of Ringwood, Hants, and Frances Agnes, *née* Potter (d 2000), of Reading, Berks; *b* 10 August 1956; *Educ* Brockenhurst GS, St John's Coll Oxford (MA); *m* 1997, Elizabeth, *née* Ballard; 2 s (Rupert Francis Côver, Lysander Edmund Oliver); *Career* asst to Chairman Macmillan Publishers Ltd 1977–80, European desk offr Cons Research Dept 1980–83, special advsr to sec of state for NI 1983–85, special advsr to Home Sec 1985–88, exec dir Corp Communications British Satellite Broadcasting 1988–90, special advsr to Foreign Sec 1991–93, md corp and public affrs Hill & Knowlton (UK) Ltd 1993–2000 (dep chm and dir of strategy 1999–2000), exec vice-pres external affrs Anglo American plc 2000–; chair Int Investment Panel CBI 2005–, memb Int Advsy Gp Extractive Industries Transparency Initiative 2005–06 (memb Bd 2006–08); contested (Cons) Vauxhall ILEA seat 1986, dep chm Cons Gp for Europe 2003–06; Robert Schuman Silver Medal for Servs to European Unity 1983; MIPR 1995, FRSA 2001; *Publications* various pamphlets incl Raising Kane? Preserving Diversity in Media Ownership (1990); *Recreations* cinema, theatre, tennis, current affrs; *Style—* Edward Bickham, Esq; ✉ c/o Anglo American plc, 20 Carlton House Terrace, London SW1Y 5AN (tel 020 7968 8547, fax 020 7968 8637); 109 Black Lion Lane, London W6

BICKMORE, Peter Christopher; s of Lt-Col Lawrence Hyde Neild Bickmore, OBE (d 1997), of Kensington, London, and Anne Windsor Lewis, *née* Drummond (d 1985); *b* 4 April 1943; *Educ* Charterhouse; *m* 22 July 1975, Isabel Margaret, da of Maj-Gen Lord Michael Fitzalan Howard, KCVO, MC, of Fovant, Wilts; 2 s (Andrew Ralph b 1979, Rupert Nicholas b 1985), 1 da (Fiona Clare b 1981); *Career* Lt short serv cmmn Life Gds 1962–68; md: Pegasus Insurance Services Ltd 1979–89, BBA Insurance Services Ltd 1989–96, British Bloodstock Agency plc 1992–95; bloodstock insurance consIt Alexander Forbes Risk Servs Ltd 1999–2004, chm Bloodlines Thoroughbred Insurance Agency Ltd 2004–; sports consIt to Stuart Canvas Products 1995–; memb Insurance Brokers' Registration Cncl 1986; Freeman City of London 1964, Liveryman Worshipful Co of Skinners 1969; High Sheriff Oxfordshire 2006–07; *Recreations* tennis, golf, shooting; *Clubs* White's, Pratt's; *Style—* Peter Bickmore, Esq; ✉ PO Box 24, Watlington, Oxfordshire OX49 5YX (tel 01491 614100, fax 01491 613452, mobile 07860 964545, e-mail peter@pbickmore.fsnet.co.uk)

BICKNELL, Julian; s of Wing Cdr Nigel Bicknell, DSO, DFC (d 1990), and Sarah Greenaway, *née* Leith; *b* 23 February 1945; *Educ* Winchester, King's Coll Cambridge (MA, DipArch); *m* 18 Nov 1967, Treld, da of Arthur K O Pelkey (d 1979), of West Hartford, CT; 1 s (Titus P b 1971), 1 da (Poppaea E b 1982); *Career* architect and teacher; asst later ptnr Edward Cullinan 1966–72; tutor and dir of Project Office RCA 1973–80: The Old Gaol Abingdon (RIBA Award 1976), The Garden Hall and Library, Castle Howard (Carpenters' Award 1984); staff architect Arup Assocs 1981–84 (reconstruction of Bedford Sch); in private practice 1984–; projects incl: Henbury Rotonda, Upton Viva, Nagara Country Club Japan, High Corner, The Georgian Club Tokyo, Shakespeare Country Park Maruyama Japan, Forbes House, Jubilee Sun Dial for Palace of Westminster, Hunterian Museum RCS, Royal Crest House Takasaki, Carden Hall; external examiner Leeds Metropolitan Univ Sch of Architecture 1990–94, memb Advsy and Academic Bd and tutor Prince of Wales Inst of Architecture 1991–98; RIBA 1971, memb AA 1987, FRSA 1988, elected to Art Workers' Guild 1995; *Books* The Design for Need Papers (1979), Hiroshige in Tokyo (1994), Julian Bicknell: Designs and Buildings 1980–2000 (2000); *Recreations* architecture, music, the countryside; *Style—* Julian Bicknell, Esq; ✉ The Annexe Studio, 32A Larkfield Road, Richmond, Surrey TW9 2PF (tel 020 3274 1070, fax 020 3274 1080, e-mail info@julianbicknell.co.uk)

BIDDER, His Hon Judge Neil; QC (1998); s of Glyn Turner Bidder (d 1997), and Constance Mabel Longman; *b* 22 July 1953; *Educ* Ogmore GS, Queens' Coll Cambridge (MA), Dalhousie Univ Canada (LLM); *m* 1978, Madeleine, da of Dewi Thomas; 2 s (Rhys Michael b 13 October 1982, Patrick Thomas b 8 November 1985); *Career* called to the Bar 1976, recorder 1994–2004 (asst recorder 1991–94), circuit judge (Wales and Chester Region) 2004–; asst boundary cmmr; fndr chm Welsh Personal Injury Lawyers Assoc; memb: Lincoln's Inn, Personal Injury Bar Assoc; *Recreations* choral singing, gardening, sport; *Style—* His Hon Judge Bidder, QC

BIDDISS, Prof Michael Denis; s of Daniel Biddiss (d 1984), of Orpington, and Eileen Louisa, *née* Jones (d 1984); *b* 15 April 1942; *Educ* St Joseph's Acad Blackheath, Queens' Coll Cambridge (MA, PhD), Centre des Hautes Études Européennes Univ of Strasbourg; *m* 8 April 1967, Ruth Margaret, da of late Dr Frederick Fox Cartwright, of Swallowfield, Berks; 4 da (Clare b 1969, Kate b 1972, Sarah b 1974, Beth b 1977); *Career* fell and dir of studies in history and social and political sciences Downing Coll Cambridge 1966–73, lectr and reader in history Univ of Leicester 1973–79; Univ of Reading: prof of history 1979–2004, dean Faculty of Letters and Social Science 1982–85, emeritus prof 2004–; visiting professorships: Univ of Victoria BC 1973, Univ of Cape Town 1976 and 1978, Monash Univ 1989, Nanjing Univ 1997; chm History at the Univs Defence Gp 1984–87; memb Cncl: Historical Association 1985– (pres 1991–94, fell 2006–), Royal Historical Soc 1988–92 (jt vice-pres 1995–99); chm Bd of Dirs Government and Opposition Ltd 1996–2003; hon fell Faculty of History of Med Worshipful Soc of Apothecaries 1986– (pres 1994–98, Osler medal 1989, Locke medal 1996, Sydenham medal 2001); FRHistS 1974; *Books* Father of Racist Ideology (1970), Gobineau - Selected Political Writings (ed, 1970), Disease and History (jtly, 1972, new edn 2000), The Age of the Masses - Ideas and Society in Europe since 1870 (1977), Images of Race (ed, 1979), Thatcherism - Personality and Politics (jt ed, 1987), The Nuremberg Trial and the Third Reich (1992), The Uses and Abuses of Antiquity (jt ed, 1999), The Humanities in the New Millennium (jt ed, 2000); *Recreations* cricket, mountain walking, music and opera; *Style—* Prof Michael Biddiss; ✉ c/o School of History, University of Reading, Whiteknights, Reading RG6 6AA (e-mail m.d.biddiss@reading.ac.uk)

BIDDLE, Donald Frank; s of Kenneth Barrington Biddle, of Poole, Dorset, and Judy Hill, *née* Downie (d 1964); *b* 6 March 1933; *Educ* Uppingham; *m* 3 Oct 1963, Anne Muriel, da of Maj Charles Deane Cowper; 2 s (Justin b 1968, Mark b 1971), 2 da (Georgina, Anne-Marie (twins) b 1973); *Career* chartered accountant; 2 Lt RA Germany 1956–57, HAC 1957–63; Price Waterhouse 1957–62, ptnr Smith and Williamson 1962–93, gen cmmr of taxation 1970–87 and 1989–; tstee: English Language Servs Int (Int House) 1963–99, Ada Lewis Housing Tst 1967–82 (chm 1978–80), Samuel Lewis Housing Tst 1978–94, Southern Housing Gp 1993–94, Titsey Fndn, Bembridge Harbour Tst 2005–; sec Int Dragon Assoc 1982–89; memb Olympic Yachting Ctee 1964–74; Yr Bro Trinity House; FCA; OStJ (treas Cncl Order of St John of Jerusalem Dorset 1993–2003); *Recreations* yachting, wine; *Clubs* Carlton, Royal Yacht Sqdn; *Style—* Donald F Biddle, Esq; ✉ Vernon House, St Helens, Isle of Wight PO33 1XY (tel 01983 875593, fax 01983 875561)

BIDDLE, Prof Martin; OBE (1997); s of Reginald Samuel Biddle (d 1971), and Gwladys Florence, *née* Baker (d 1986); *b* 4 June 1937; *Educ* Merchant Taylors', Pembroke Coll Cambridge (MA), Univ of Oxford (MA); *m* 1, 9 Sept 1961 (m dis 1966), Hannelore Bäcker; 2 da (Joanna b 1962, Barbara b 1965); m 2, 19 Nov 1966, Birthe, da of Landsretssagfører Axel Th Kjølbye (d 1972), of Sønderborg, Denmark; 2 da (Signe b 1969, Solvej b 1971); *Career* 2 Lt 4 RTR 1956, Ind Sqdn RTR Berlin 1956–57; asst inspr of ancient monuments Miny of Public Bldg and Works 1961–63, lectr in medieval archaeology Univ of Exeter 1963–67, visiting fell All Souls Coll Oxford 1967–68, dir Winchester Research Unit 1968–, dir Univ Museum and prof of anthropology and history of art Univ of Pennsylvania 1977–81, lectr of the house ChCh Oxford 1983–86, Astor sr research fell in medieval archaeology and tutor in archaeology Hertford Coll Oxford 1989–2002, prof of medieval archaeology Univ of Oxford 1997–2002, emeritus prof Hertford Coll Oxford 2002–, Leverhulme Emeritus Fell 2005–06; author of numerous books and articles; excavations with: Sir Mortimer Wheeler St Albans and Stanwick 1949 and 1952, Dame Kathleen Kenyon Jericho 1957–58; fieldwork: Nonsuch Palace 1959–60, Winchester 1961–71, St Albans 1978, 1982–84, 1991, 1994–95, 2003 and 2006 (with Birthe Kjølbye-Biddle), Repton 1974–88 and 1993 (with Birthe Kjølbye-Biddle), Holy Sepulchre Jerusalem 1989–93 and 1998 (with Birthe Kjølbye-Biddle), Qasr Ibrim Nubia Egypt 1989–90, 1992, 1995, 2000 (with Birthe Kjølbye-Biddle); ptnr Biddle & Biddle archaeological consIts, clients incl: Canterbury Cathedral, St Albans Abbey and Cathedral Church, Eurotunnel, British Telecom, etc; chm: Rescue The Trust for Br Archaeology 1971–75, Winchester in Europe (Nat Referendum 1975); served Cons Pty Ctees in: Winchester 1973–77, Oxford 1982–97; cmmr Royal Cmmn on the Historical Monuments of England 1984–95; pres Soc for Medieval Archaeology 1995–98, vice-pres Soc of Antiquaries 2006–; Hon Knight of the Hon Soc of Knights of the Round Table 1971; Freeman: City of London 1963, Worshipful Co of Merchant Taylors 1963; Univ of Pennsylvania: Hon MA 1977, Hon Phi Beta Kappa 1978; Hon DLitt King Alfred's Coll/Univ of Southampton 2003; FSA 1964, FRHistS 1970, FBA 1985; *Books* Future of London's Past (1973), Winchester in the Early Middle Ages (ed, 1976), Object and Economy in Medieval Winchester (1990), Das Grab Christi (1998), The Tomb of Christ (1999), King Arthur's Round Table (2000), The Church of the Holy Sepulchre (2000), Henry VIII's Artillery Fort at Camber Castle (2001), Nonsuch Palace: The Material Culture of a Restoration Household (2005); *Recreations* travel, especially Hellenic, Middle East and S Asia, reading; *Clubs* Athenaeum; *Style—* Prof Martin Biddle, OBE, FBA; ✉ Hertford College, Oxford OX1 3BW (tel 01865 279400, e-mail martin.biddle@hertford.ox.ac.uk); research office (tel and fax 01865 559017)

BIDDLE, Neville Leslie; s of Walter Alan Biddle, of Nannerch, N Wales, and Beryl Mary, *née* Meadows; *b* 24 April 1951; *Educ* Wrekin Coll, UCW Aberystwyth (BSc(Econ)); *m* 2 Oct 1976, Sheila Ruth, da of Parimal Kumar Sen (d 1972); 4 da (Caroline b 22 Nov 1980, Josephine b 27 July 1982, Rebecca b 2 June 1986, Charlotte b 15 July 1991); *Career* called to the Bar Gray's Inn 1974; elected to Northern Circuit 1975, currently in practice Liverpool, asst recorder 1995–2000, recorder 2000–; memb Criminal Bar Assoc; non-exec dir R S Clare & Co Liverpool; *Style—* Neville Biddle, Esq; ✉ Chambers of Stephen Riordan, QC, 25–27 Castle Street, Liverpool L2 4TA (tel 0151 227 5661)

BIDDULPH, Sir Ian D'Olier; 11 Bt (E 1664); s of Sir Stuart Royden Biddulph, 10 Bt (d 1986), and Muriel Margaret, *née* Harkness (d 1995); *b* 28 February 1940; *Educ* Slade Sch Warwick Queensland; *m* 1967, Margaret Eleanor, o da of late John Gablonski, of Oxley, Brisbane; 1 s (Paul William b 1967), 2 da (Julie Denise b 1969, Roslyn Mary b 1971); *Heir* s, Paul Biddulph; *Career* grazier, ret; *Style*— Sir Ian Biddulph, Bt; ✉ 17 Kendall Street, Oxley, Queensland 4075, Australia

BIDDULPH, 5 Baron (UK 1903); (Anthony) Nicholas Colin Maitland Biddulph; er s of 4 Baron Biddulph (d 1988), and Lady Mary Maitland, da of Viscount Maitland, s of 15 Earl of Lauderdale; *b* 8 April 1959; *Educ* Cheltenham, RAC Cirencester; *m* 28 Aug 1993, Hon Sian Diana Gibson-Watt (m dis 2001), yr da of Baron Gibson-Watt, MC, PC (d 2002); 2 s (Hon Robert Julian Watt b 1994, Hon David Michael William b 1997); *Heir* s, Hon Robert Maitland Biddulph; *Career* interior designer, farmer and sporting mangr; Liveryman Worshipful Co of Armourers and Brasiers; *Recreations* shooting, fishing, racing, skiing, painting; *Clubs* Raffles, Cavalry and Guards, White's; *Style*— The Rt Hon Lord Biddulph; ✉ Makerstoun, Kelso, Roxburghshire TD5 7PA (tel 01573 460234); 8 Orbel Street, London SW11 3NZ (tel 020 7228 9865)

BIDE, Sir Austin Ernest; kt (1980); o s of Ernest Arthur Bide (d 1918), and Eliza, *née* Young (d 1976); *b* 11 September 1915; *Educ* Acton County Sch, Birkbeck Coll and Chelsea Poly Univ of London (BSc); *m* 1941, Irene, da of Ernest Auckland Ward (d 1953); 3 da; *Career* Maj 21 Army Gp Germany (CIOS); Dept of Govt Chemist until 1940; Glaxo Laboratories Ltd: Res Dept 1940, subsequently head Chem Investigation and Devpt Dept, PA to dep md Glaxo Laboratories Ltd 1946, head of patents and trademarks, first factory mangr Montrose 1951, dep sec Glaxo Laboratories Ltd 1954–59, sec 1959–65; dir Glaxo Group 1963–71; Glaxo Holdings plc: dep chm 1971–73, chief exec 1973–80, chm 1973–85, hon pres 1985–95; non-exec dir J Lyons & Co Ltd 1977–78, non-exec chm BL 1982–86 (non-exec dir 1977–82); former chm: CGEA (UK) Ltd, Onyx UK Ltd, Onyx Aurora Ltd, Comatech UK Ltd, Tyseley Waste Disposal Ltd; former admin Compagnie des Transports et Services Publiques France; dir Oxford Consultancy Ltd 1988–; CBI: chm Res and Technol Ctee 1977–86, memb Cncl 1976–85, memb Cos Ctee 1974–80, memb Pres Ctee 1983–86, memb Univs Polys and Industry Ctee 1984–85, memb Industrial Performance Steering Gp 1985; chm: Nat Appeal Ctee Salisbury Cathedral 1986–92 (memb Confraternity of Benefactors 1992–), Nat AIDS Tst 1987–91, Ct Shippers' Cncl (now Freight Transport Assoc) 1989–, World Humanity Action Tst 1993–, The Adam Smith Research Institute Ltd; memb: Cncl Imperial Soc for Knights Bachelor 1980–97, Advsy Ctee on Industry to the Vice-Chllrs and Princs of Univs of UK 1984–87, Cncl Inst of Manpower Studies 1985–, body to review the affrs of the Univ Grants Ctee 1985 (report published 1987); chm Visiting Ctee Open Univ 1982–89, tstee Br Motor Industry Heritage Tst 1983–86; memb MRC 1987–90 (chm Investments and Pensions Sub-Ctee, memb AIDS Sub-Ctee); former vice-pres Inst of Industrial Managers; Br Inst of Mgmnt: memb Cncl 1976–88, memb Cos Ctee 1974–84, chm Fin Ctee and dir BIM Fndn 1977–79; vice-pres Inst of Mgmnt (merger of Inst of Industrial Managers and Br Inst of Mgmnt) 1993–; winner: BIM Gold medal (for outstanding achievements in mgmnt of Glaxo Group 1982), Duncan Davies medal Research and Devpt Soc 1990; hon fell: Inst for Biotechnology Studies 1985 (memb Bd and fell Membership Ctee 1987–89), St Catherine's Coll Oxford 1987; Hon DSc: Queen's Univ Belfast, CNAA; Hon DUniv Open Univ 1991; CIMgt, FRSC, CChem, CIEx, Hon FIChemE 1983, FInstD 1989; *Publications* Biotechnology - A Report of a Joint Working Party (1980); *Clubs* Hurlingham, 1900; *Style*— Sir Austin Bide

BIDWELL, Sir Hugh Charles Philip; GBE (1989); s of late Edward Bidwell, and late Elizabeth Bidwell; *b* 1 November 1934; *Educ* Stonyhurst; *m* 1, 1962, Jenifer Celia Webb (d 2001); 2 s (one of whom James Richard Philip, *qv*), 1 da; m 2, Priscilla Pode, *née* Hunter; *Career* Nat Serv 1953–55, cmmnd E Surrey Regt, seconded to 1 Bn KAR Nyasaland; dir Viota Foods Ltd 1962–70 (joined 1957), dir Robertson Foods plc 1968–70; chm: Pearce Duff & Co Ltd 1970–84, Gill & Duffus Foods 1984–85, British Invisibles 1991–94, ITE Group plc (formerly International Trade & Exhibitions J/V) 1996–2003; non-exec dir: Argyll Group plc 1990–95, Rothschild Asset Management Ltd 1992–97, Fleming Geared Income & Assets Investment Trust plc 1993–97, Alpha Airports Group plc 1994–2003; non-exec chm: Riggs AP Bank Ltd 1989–92, Julius Group Ltd (formerly Octavian Group Ltd) 1993–97; memb: Exec Ctee Food Manufacturers' Fedn 1973–86, Cncl London C of C and Indust 1976–85, Food from Britain Cncl 1983–89 (chm Export Bd 1983–86); pres Br Food Export Cncl 1980–87, dep pres Food and Drink Fedn 1985 and 1986; memb: Euro Trade Ctee 1989–91, Chamber of Commerce 1989–92, China-Britain Trade Gp 1989–94, BOTB 1992–94; Lord Mayor of London 1989–90, Alderman Billingsgate Ward 1979–96, Sheriff City of London 1986–87, memb Worshipful Co of Grocers (Master 1984–85), Hon Liveryman Worshipful Co of Marketors; *Recreations* golf, fishing, tennis, cricket, shooting; *Clubs* City of London, MCC, Denham Golf, Royal St George's, Royal & Ancient, White's; *Style*— Sir Hugh Bidwell, GBE

BIDWELL, James Richard Philip; s of Sir Hugh Bidwell, GBE, *qv*, and Jenifer Celia, *née* Webb (d 2001); *b* 19 January 1965, London; *Educ* Eton, Univ of Bristol (BA); *m* 28 Jan 1995, Rebecca, *née* Mathiesen; 3 da (Lili Sarah b 29 April 1997, Willow Anna b 10 Oct 1999, Sage Jenifer b 8 June 2006); *Career* grad trainee Lowe Howard-Spink Advtg 1989–92, mktg mangr Walt Disney Attractions 1992–97, mktg dir Europe eToys Inc 1999–2001, mktg dir Selfridges plc 2001–05, ceo Visit London 2005–; memb: Mktg Soc 1994, Mktg Gp of GB 2001; Liveryman Worshipful Co of Grocers; *Recreations* skiing, mountain biking, flyfishing; *Clubs* Frensham Flyfishers, Home House; *Style*— James Bidwell, Esq; ✉ Visit London, 2 More London Riverside, London SE1 2RR (tel 020 7234 5801, e-mail jbidwell@visitlondon.com)

BIDWELL, Dr Robin O'Neill; CBE (1999); s of Philip John Bidwell (d 1993), and Ellen O'Neill, *née* Gibbons (d 1995); *b* 15 September 1944, Simla, India; *Educ* Charterhouse, ChCh Oxford (MA), Bradford Mgmnt Centre (PhD); *m* 1, 1970; 1 da (Charlotte b 1972), 1 s (Matthew b 1974); m 2, 1995, Veronica Rosemary Lucia, *née* Verey; *Career* ERL (now ERM): joined 1973, dir 1974–, md 1977–93, exec chm 1993–; non-exec memb Ofgem 2003–; advsr Int Business Ldrs Forum 1993–; tstee Heritage Tst 1987–96; memb: Exec Ctee Green Alliance 1995–, Sustainability Challenge Fndn Netherlands 1993–2003, NERC 1996–2002, UK Roundtable of Sustainable Devpt 1998–2000, Advsy Ctee on Business and the Environment 1999–2003; *Recreations* reshaping landscapes, skiing, reading; *Style*— Dr Robin Bidwell, CBE; ✉ Woodchester Park House, Nympsfield, Gloucester GL10 3UN; ERM, 8 Cavendish Square, London W1G 0ER (tel 020 7465 7331, fax 020 7465 7300, e-mail robin.bidwell@erm.com)

BIELCKUS, Colin David; s of Louis Reginald Bielckus, of Thornhill, Southampton, and Lorna Elizabeth Mary Bielckus; *b* 17 June 1956; *Educ* King Edward VI Sch Southampton, UEA (BSc); *m* 11 Oct 1981, Lorraine, da of Reginald Alexander, of Southampton; 1 da (Penelope Louise b 18 May 1995); *Career* chartered accountant; audit mangr Alliott Wingham (formerly Alliott Millar) Fareham 1985–90, audit ptnr Alliott Wingham Fareham 1990–2002, prop Avenue Business Services 2002–, pres and chm Central Southern England Div Nat Deposit Friendly Soc 2002– (chm 1990–2002), non-exec dir Nat Deposit Friendly Soc 2003–, chm Audit Ctee 2003–, finance dir Davis World Travel Ltd 2006–; memb Rotary Club of Fareham Meon 2000–; chm Community and Vocational Serv Ctee 2002–03 (chm entertainments 2003–04, vice-pres 2005–06, pres 2006–07); *Recreations* music, railways, collecting books, collecting beermats, collecting cacti and other succulent plants; *Style*— Colin Bielckus, Esq; ✉ 72 The Avenue, Fareham, Hampshire PO14 1PB (tel 01329 284728); Avenue Business Services, 72 The Avenue, Fareham, Hampshire PO14 1PB (tel 01329 238523, fax 01329 238523, e-mail cb@avenue-bs.com)

BIENZ, Dr Mariann; da of Jürg Bienz, and Lilly Bienz-Gubler; *b* 21 December 1953; *Educ* Gymnasium Winterthur Switzerland, Univ of Zürich (Dip Zoology, PhD); *m* 25 May 1996, Dr Hugh Pelham, FRS, *qv*; 1 da (Maya Joanne b 24 July 1990), 1 s (Benjamin Peter b 23 May 1993); *Career* postdoctoral research MRC Lab of Molecular Biology Cambridge 1981–86, asst prof Univ of Zürich 1986–90 (assoc prof 1990), sr staff scientist MRC Lab of Molecular Biology Cambridge 1991–; author of articles on cell and molecular biology in int jls; memb EMBO 1989–; Friedrich Miescher Prize 1990; FRS 2003, FMedSci 2006; *Recreations* music, mountain walking; *Style*— Dr Mariann Bienz; ✉ MRC Laboratory of Molecular Biology, Hills Road, Cambridge CB2 2QH (tel 01223 402055, fax 01223 412142)

BIGGAR, Allan Ramsay; s of Allan Ramsay Biggar, and Betty, *née* Tyson, of Galashiels, Scotland; *b* 27 January 1963; *Educ* Queen Elizabeth HS Hexham; *m* 11 May 2002, Bridget Susan, *née* Lucking; 1 da (Isobel Gillian Seddon b 27 May 1988), 2 s (Charles Arthur John Seddon b 18 Sept 1992, Jack Ramsay Biggar b 25 July 2002); *Career* Liberal Pty: vice-chm National League of Young Liberals 1980–83, memb Nat Exec 1981–84; area agent E Anglia 1984–87; Burson-Marsteller: md ME 1994–97, chm Public Affairs Europe 1997–2000, pres and chief exec UK 2000–04, jt chief exec Europe 2001–04, memb Worldwide Exec Bd 2001–05, global chm Corp and Fin Practice 2004–05, chm UK 2004–05; chm: I-SYT Ltd 2001–05, Brand Faith Ltd 2005–; chair International Insights Ltd 2005–, ceo All About Brands plc 2006–, non-exec chm Open Soho Ltd 2007–; non-exec dir: Corp Television Networks 2001–05, Smartcells Ltd 2005–, BrandSolutions Ltd 2007–; chm Business Advsy Gp UMIST Corp Communications MSc course 2002–, co-fndr European Communications Acad Univ of Brussels; previous owner/dir various PR and publishing ventures, reg writer on current affairs and political issues; *Publications* Effective Politics (1983); *Recreations* travel, antiques, cooking; *Clubs* RAC, National Liberal; *Style*— Allan R Biggar, Esq; ✉ Bluebell House, Newlands Drive, Maidenhead, Berkshire SL6 4LL (tel 01628 770481, e-mail allanrbiggar@hotmail.com); All About Brands plc, 77 St Martin's Lane, Covent Garden, London WC2N 4AA (tel 020 7379 3004, e-mail allan@aabplc.com)

BIGGLESTONE, John George; s of John Bigglestone (d 1992), and Lillian Bigglestone (d 1978); *b* 10 August 1934; *Educ* Bablake Sch Coventry, Coventry Coll of Art, Wolverhampton Poly; holder City & Guilds Full Technol Cert (photography), BIPP Final Cert and Cert in Educn (FE); *m* 22 Dec 1984, Annette Vivian, da of Kenneth Bull, and Audrey Bull, of Devizes, Wilts; *Career* professional photographer (prop Wharf Studios Devizes), journalist and lectr; sr lectr in photography: Salisbury Coll of Art 1966–93, Guildford Coll 1993–98; dir of studies, princ and sr tutor PPTutor-Online (online learning, professional photography) 1999–; formerly nat examiner photographic courses City & Guilds of London Inst and Further Educn Funding Cncl (FEFC) inspr; contrib to photographic magazines; photographic clients incl many leading industrial and advtg cos; sponsored seminar presenter to professional photographers and colls; full memb Assoc of Photographers; *Recreations* learning; *Style*— John Bigglestone, Esq; ✉ The Wharf Studio, Couch Lane, Devizes, Wiltshire SN10 1EB (tel 01380 720599, e-mail upstarts@phototutor-online.com, website www.thewharfstudio.com, www.pptutor-online.com)

BIGGS, John; AM; s of Robert Edmund Biggs (d 1974), and Mary Jeanette, *née* Phillips; *b* 19 November 1957; *Educ* Queen Elizabeth's Boys Sch Barnet, Univ of Bristol (BSc), Univ of London (Dip Com Sci), Univ of Westminster (Dip Law, LPC); *m* 1993, Christine Ann, da of Brian Sibley; 1 da (Helen b 3 Nov 1990); *Career* lab technician 1981–83, systems analyst 1984–90, oppn and Cncl ldr 1991–95, dir and vice-chm Tower Hamlets Housing Action Tst 1996–2004, dir Socialist Health Assoc (affiliate of Lab Pty) 1998–2000; GLA: memb London Assembly (Lab) City & East 2000–, lead memb Lab Gp on Budget, Social Inclusion and Major Infrastructure Projects, memb Met Police Authy 2000–03, memb London Fire and Emergency Planning Authy 2003–04; vice-chair London Devpt Agency 2004–, dep chm London Thames Gateway Urban Devpt Corp 2004–, dir Leaside Regeneration Ltd; *Recreations* reading, walking, politics; *Style*— John Biggs, Esq, AM; ✉ 7 Louisa Gardens, Stepney Green, London E1 4NG (tel and fax 020 7790 9710, mobile 07974 918322); London Assembly, City Hall, Queens Walk, Southwark, London SE1 2AA (tel 020 7983 4350, fax 020 7983 4418, e-mail john.biggs@london.gov.uk)

BIGGS, Lewis; s of Ian Biggs, of Culachy, Fort Augustus, Inverness-shire, and Penelope, *née* Torr; *b* 22 April 1952; *Educ* Wellington, New Coll Oxford (scholar, BA), Courtauld Inst Univ of London (MA); *m* 1983 (m dis 2002), Ann, da of Michael Compton; 1 da (Alison b 1987), 1 s (Nicholas b 1989); *Career* gallery co-ordinator Arnolfini Bristol 1979–84, exhibition offr Fine Art Dept Br Cncl 1984–87, curator of exhibitions Tate Gallery Liverpool 1987–90 (dir 1990–2000), chief exec Liverpool Biennial of Contemporary Art 2000– (dir 1998–2000); visiting prof Sch of Art and Design Liverpool John Moores Univ 2001–04; dir: Oriel Mostyn Llandudno 1991–97, Art Transpennine Ltd 1996–2002, NW Arts Bd 1998–2002, Culture Campus Ltd 2006–, Another Place Ltd 2006–; tstee: Liverpool Architecture and Design Tst 1997–99, Liverpool Biennial Tst 1998–2000; memb: Visual Arts Advsy Ctee Br Cncl 1992–2002, Fabric Advsy Ctee Liverpool Cathedral 1995–98, Visual Arts Panel Arts Cncl of England 1996–99; assoc fell Univ of Liverpool 1992–95; hon fell Liverpool John Moores Univ 1998; memb ICOM 1983–, CIMAM; FRSA; *Publications* Tate Modern Artists (series ed, 2000–); *Style*— Lewis Biggs, Esq; ✉ Liverpool Biennial, PO Box 1200, Liverpool L69 1XB (tel 0151 709 7444, fax 0151 709 7377, e-mail lewis@biennial.com)

BIGGS, Michael Nicholas; s of Eric Peter Biggs, and Hilda May, *née* Daldry; *b* 14 August 1952; *Educ* Alleynes GS Stevenage, Worcester Coll Oxford (MA); *m* Lynn (m dis); 2 s (Edmund Christopher Perrin b March 1986, Henry Michael Edward b Aug 1988); *Career* mgmnt trainee William & Glyns Bank 1974–75; Arthur Andersen & Co: audit asst rising to top sr 1975–80, top sr rising to jr mangr (Canada) 1980–83, audit mangr 1983–84; Hongkong & Shanghai Banking Corp: mangr (fin) 1984–86, mangr (services div) 1986–88; gp fin controller Morgan Grenfell Gp plc 1987–91; CGNU plc (Norwich Union prior to merger with CGU in 2000): gp fin controller 1991–94, gp dir (int) 1995–97, gp fin dir (Norwich) 1997–2000, dir UK General 2000–01, gp fin dir Aviva plc (formerly CGNU plc) 2001–03, chief fin offr Resolution Life Gp 2005–07, chief exec Resolution plc 2007–; ACA 1979; *Recreations* cricket, gardening, Saxon history, opera; *Style*— Michael Biggs, Esq

BIGGS, Prof Norman Linstead; s of Joseph John Biggs (d 1965), and Dorothy Linstead (d 1982); *b* 2 January 1941; *Educ* Harrow Co GS, Selwyn Coll Cambridge (MA), Univ of London (DSc); *m* 1, 1968 (m dis 1975), Rita Elizabeth, *née* Kelly; m 2, 20 March 1975, Christine Mary, da of Eric Richard Farmer, of Bromley, Kent; 1 da (Juliet b 1980); *Career* lectr Univ of Southampton 1963–70, reader in pure mathematics Royal Holloway Coll London 1976–88 (lectr 1970–76); LSE: prof of mathematics 1988–2006 (emeritus prof 2006–), govr 1995–99, dir Centre for Discrete and Applicable Mathematics 1995–2006, vice-chm Appts Ctee 1993–96; London Mathematical Soc: memb Cncl 1979–85 and 1999–2006, librarian 1999–2002, gen sec 2002–06, chm Computer Science Ctee 1985–89; chm Royal Soc Mathematical Instruction Ctee 1991–94; memb Br Numismatic Soc (memb Cncl 2001–03); *Books* Finite Groups of Automorphisms (1971), Algebraic Graph Theory (1974, 2 edn 1993), Graph Theory 1736–1936 (jtly, 1976), Interaction Models (1977), Permutation Groups and Combinatorial Structures (jtly, 1979), Introduction to Computing With Pascal (1989), Computational Learning Theory (jtly, 1992), English Weights (1993), Mathematics for Economics and Finance (jtly, 1996), Antique Weights (1998), Discrete Mathematics (2 edn 2002); *Recreations* metrology and numismatics; *Style*— Prof Norman Biggs; ✉ London School of Economics and Political Science, Houghton Street, London WC2A 2AE (tel 020 7955 7640, fax 020 7955 6877, e-mail n.l.biggs@lse.ac.uk)

BIGGS, Prof Peter Martin; CBE (1987); s of (George) Ronald Biggs (d 1985), and Cécile Agnes, *née* Player (d 1981); *b* 13 August 1926; *Educ* Bedales, Cambridge Sch Mass, RVC London (BSc), Univ of Bristol (PhD), Univ of London (DSc); *m* 9 Sept 1950, Alison Janet, da of late Malcolm Christian Molteno; 1 da (Alison (Mrs Stanley) b 27 May 1955), 2 s (Andrew b 20 May 1957, John b 15 Nov 1963); *Career* RAF: univ short course Queen's Univ 1944–45, air crew undertraining, remustered Corp, demobbed 1948; lectr in veterinary clinical pathology Univ of Bristol 1955–59 (res asst 1953–55); Houghton Poultry Res Station: head Leukosis Experimental Unit 1959–73, dep dir 1971–73, dir 1974–86; visiting prof RVC London 1982–, dir AFRC Inst for Animal Health 1986–88, Andrew D White prof-at-large Cornell Univ 1988–94; pres Inst of Biology 1990–92, vice-pres BVA 1996–98; chm: Robert Fraser Gordon Meml Tst 1982–, Scientific Advsy Ctee Animal Health Tst 1987–, The Houghton Tst 1992–, Br Egg Mktg Bd Res and Educn Tst 1993–; vice-chm Cncl RVC London 2000–; memb: Vet Prods Ctee, Meds Cmmn 1973–98, Advsy Ctee on Dangerous Pathogens 1988–91; Hon DVM Maximilian Univ Munich Germany, Hon DUniv Liège Belgium, Wolf Fndn Prize in Agric 1989; FRCVS, FRCPath, FMedSci, FIBiol, CBiol, FRS; *Recreations* music, natural history, gardening, photography; *Clubs* Athenaeum, Farmers'; *Style*— Prof Peter Biggs, CBE, FRS; ✉ Willows, London Road, St Ives, Cambridgeshire PE27 5ES (tel and fax 01480 463471)

BIGSBY, Prof Christopher William Edgar; s of Maj Edgar Edward Leo Bigsby (d 1968), and Ivy May, *née* Hopkins; *b* 27 June 1941; *Educ* Sutton GS, Univ of Sheffield (BA, MA), Univ of Nottingham (PhD); *m* 9 Oct 1965, Pamela Joan, da of Stephen Joseph Lovelady; 2 s (Gareth Christopher b 1968, Ewan James b 1976), 2 da (Kirsten Rebecca b 1972, Bella Juliet Natasha b 1974); *Career* prof of American studies UEA; writer and broadcaster; TV with Malcolm Bradbury: The After Dinner Game 1975, Stones 1976; BBC radio: Patterson 1983 (with Malcolm Bradbury), Fictions 1984, Long Day's Journey 1988, Kaleidoscope, Third Ear, Meridian; FRSL, FRSA; *Books* Confrontation and Commitment (1967), Albee (1969), Three Negro Plays (ed, 1969), The Black American Writer (2 vols, 1971), Dada and Surrealism (1972), Edward Albee (ed, 1975), Superculture (ed, 1975), Approaches to Popular Culture (ed, 1976), Tom Stoppard (1980), The Second Black Renaissance (1980), Contemporary English Drama (ed, 1981), A Critical Introduction to 20th Century American Drama (3 vols, 1982, 1984 and 1985), Joe Orton (1982), The Radical Imagination and the Liberal Tradition (ed, 1982), David Mamet (1985), Cultural Change in the United States since World War II (ed, 1986), Plays by Susan Glaspell (1987), File on Miller (1987), Arthur Miller and Company (1990), Modern American Drama 1945–1990 (1992), Nineteenth Century American Short Stories (ed, 1995), The Portable Arthur Miller (ed, 1995), The Cambridge Companion to Arthur Miller (ed, 1997), The Cambridge History of American Theatre (3 vols, ed with Don B Wilmeth, 1998, 1999, 2000), Jack London: The Call of the Wild and Other Stories (ed, 1998), Contemporary American Playwrights (1999), Edgar Allen Poe: The Pit and the Pendulum and Other Stories (ed, 1999), Modern American Drama 1945–2000 (2000), Writers in Conversation (2 vols, ed, 2000–01), The Cambridge Companion to David Mamet (ed, 2004), Arthur Miller: A Critical Study (2004), Remembering Arthur Miller (ed, 2005), A New Introduction to American Studies (ed, 2005), Remembering and Imagining the Holocaust: The Chain of Memory (2006), The Cambridge Companion to Modern American Culture (ed, 2006), Neil La Bute (2007), The Cambridge Companions to August Wilson (ed, 2007); *Novels* Hester (1994), Pearl (1995), Still Lives (1996), Beautiful Dreamer (2002), One Hundred Days: One Hundred Nights (2007); *Recreations* so far undiscovered; *Style*— Prof Christopher Bigsby; ✉ 3 Church Farm, Colney, Norwich NR4 7TX, (tel 01603 456048); School of English and American Studies, University of East Anglia, Norwich NR4 7TJ (tel 01603 456161)

BILES, John Anthony; TD; s of Kenneth Robert William Biles, of Pinner, Middx, and Sheila Colville, *née* Stones; *b* 29 June 1947, Norwich; *Educ* John Lyon Sch Harrow, Univ of Exeter (BSc); *m* 11 Sep 1976, Francoise Marie Doris, *née* Phillips; 2 da (Caroline Sarah Louise b 26 May 1979, Nicola Clare Victoria b 12 March 1982); *Career* Price Waterhouse & Co 1968–76, EMI Ltd 1976–78, AFA-Minerva (EMI) Ltd 1978–81, fin dir of various subsids Racal Electronics plc 1981–91; gp fin dir: Chubb Security plc 1991–97, FKI plc 1998–2004, dir: Armorgroup Int plc 2004–, Chapelthorpe plc 2005–07, Charter plc 2005–, Viridian plc 2005–, Hermes Pension Management Ltd 2005–, Sutton and E Surrey Water plc 2006–; memb HAC; FCA 1971; *Recreations* gardening, walking, travel, shooting, antiques; *Style*— John Biles, Esq

BILES, Dr Michael Edwin; s of Ronald James Biles (d 1993), of Winchester, Hants, and Rhoda Jessie, *née* Knight; *b* 9 December 1951; *Educ* Peter Symonds' GS Winchester (head boy, Hockey colours), Kingston Univ (BA), Univ of Southampton (PhD), Inns of Court Sch of Law; *m* 15 July 1978, Tina Margaret, da of Roy Bernard Phillips; 2 s (Mark Edwin b 7 June 1982, Craig Alexander b 15 Feb 1986), 1 da (Sally Kim Christina b 4 Nov 1993); *Career* called to the Bar Middle Temple 1983; head Sch of Law Southampton Inst 2001–; housing ombudsman; MCIArb 1999, Hon MCIH; *Publications* author of numerous papers and articles in legal jls; *Recreations* hockey, cycling, gardening, DIY, reading, listening to music, spending time with family and friends; *Clubs* Winchester Hockey; *Style*— Dr Michael Biles; ✉ 81 Aldwych, London WC2B 4HN (tel 020 7421 3800, fax 020 7831 1942, e-mail ombudsman@housing-ombudsman.org.uk)

BILIMORIA, Baron (Life Peer 2006), of Chelsea in the Royal Borough of Kensington and Chelsea; Karan Faridoon Bilimoria; CBE (2004), DL (Hounslow); *b* 26 November 1961; *Educ* Hebron Sch Ooty India, Indian Inst of Mgmnt and Commerce Osmania Univ (BCom), London Met Univ (Dip), Sidney Sussex Coll Cambridge (MA, Polo half blue, vice-pres Cambridge Union), Cranfield Univ Sch of Mgmnt; *m* Heather, *née* Walker; 2 s (Kai, Josh), 2 da (Zara, Lily); *Career* Ernst & Young 1982–87, consulting accountant Cresvale Ltd 1988, sales and mktg dir European Accounting Focus magazine 1989, fndr and chief exec Cobra Beer Ltd 1989–, fndr General Bilimoria Wines 1999, fndr and chm Cobrabyte Technologies 2000–; non-exec dir Brakes 2005–; memb: Nat Employment Panel Dept for Work and Pensions (chm Small and Medium Size Enterprise Bd), Neighbourhood Renewal Private Sector Panel ODPM, New Deal Taskforce DfEE 1999–2001, Tyson Taskforce on the Recruitment and Devpt of Non-Exec Dirs 2003; UK co-chm Indo-British Partnership UKTI, vice-chm Asian Business Assoc London C of C and Industry, memb Bd The Indus Entrepreneurs (TiE), fndr pres UK Zoroastrian C of C, chm Young Presidents' Orgn London; memb: Cncl RSA 2004–, London Business Sch Fndn for Entrepreneurial Mgmnt, Cranfield Mgmnt Assoc, CBI; visiting entrepreneur Centre for Entrepreneurial Learning Univ of Cambridge; founding patron Oxford Entrepreneurs, nat champion Nat Cncl for Grad Entrepreneurship; patron Thare Mache Starfish Initiative, patron Rethink, vice-patron Meml Gates Tst (chm Ctee), chm Advsy Bd Shrimati Pushpa Wati Loomba Meml Tst; hon pres Training for Life; champion Roko Cancer Appeal; memb Cncl Royal Soc of Arts 2004–; chllr Thames Valley Univ, govr Ditchley Fndn; hon life fell Royal Soc for the Encouragement of Arts, Manufactures and Commerce; FCA 2002 (ACA 1987), FRSA, FInstD; *Awards* Non-Resident Indian Millennium Honour India 2001, Outstanding Achievement Award Execs Assoc of GB 2002, Asian of the Year 2002, London Entrepreneur of the Year 2003, Entrepreneur of the Year Asian Achievers Awards 2003, Business of the Year (Cobra Beer Ltd) Asian Business Awards 2003, Entrepreneur of the Year London C of C and Industry 2003, Excellence Award Non-Resident Indian Inst 2003, Entrepreneur of the Year Nat Business Awards (London and SE) 2004, Pride of India Award Non-Resident Indian Inst 2004, Outstanding Achievement Award ICAEW 2005; Monde Selection awards for Cobra Beer Ltd: Gold Medal 2001, 2002 and 2003, Int High Quality Trophy 2003, two grand Gold Medals and four Gold Medals 2004; *Recreations* reading, current affairs, travel, art, music, theatre, tennis, riding, golf, scuba diving, sailing; *Clubs* Carlton, Guards Polo, Delhi Gymkhana, Secunderabad, Hawks' (Cambridge), Royal Cwlth Soc, Univ Pitt (Cambridge), Delhi Golf, FRIMA Golf (Dehra Dun), Kelvingrove (Cape Town); *Style*— The Lord Bilimoria, CBE, DL; ✉ Cobra Beer Ltd, Alexander House, 14–16 Peterborough Road, London SW6 3BN (tel 020 7731 6200, fax 020 7731 6201, e-mail kfbilimoria@cobrabeer.com)

BILK, Bernard Stanley (Acker); MBE (2001); *b* 28 January 1929; *m* Jean; 1 s (Pete), 1 da (Jenny); *Career* jazz musician, composer and bandleader; clarinettist with Ken Colyer's Band London, fndr Bristol Paramount Jazz Band 1951; singles incl: Somerset, Stranger on the Shore 1961 (first no 1 simultaneously in UK and America), Aria 1976; CDs incl: The One For Me, Sheer Magic, Evergreen (platinum), Chalumeau, Three in the Morning & At Sundown (with Humphrey Lyttelton), Giants of Jazz (with Kenny Ball), Chris & Acker (with Chris Barber), Clarinet Moods, Love Songs of the Nineties, Classic Themes (with strings), As Time Goes By; tours incl: Australia, New Zealand, Far East, Middle East, South Africa, Scandinavia, Poland, Hungary, America, Canada, New Orleans with Kenny Colyer Trust Band, Ireland, Europe (with Papa Bue, Monty Sunshine, Dutch Swing etc); select concerts with The Three Bs (Paramount Jazz Band, Kenny Ball and Chris Barber); Hon Degree in Music Univ of Bristol 2005; *Style*— Mr Acker Bilk, MBE; ✉ c/o Acker's Agency, 53 Cambridge Mansions, Cambridge Road, London SW11 4RX (tel 020 7978 5885, fax 020 7978 5882, e-mail pamela@ackersmusicagency.co.uk, website www.ackersmusicagency.co.uk)

BILL, Simon Jonathan Robert; *b* 1958, Kingston; *Educ* St Martins Sch of Art, RCA; *Career* artist; *Solo Exhibitions* From Hell (Cabinet Gallery London) 1992, I've Got Demons in My Stomach (Cabinet Gallery London) 1994, Blind Idiot God (Bloom Gallery Amsterdam) 1996, Simon Bill (Crown Gallery Brussels) 1997, 1500 to the Present Day (Crown Gallery Brussels) 1998, Corn Hole (Modern Art London) 1999, Bio Pop (Modern Art London) 2001, (The Cornerhouse Manchester) 2002; *Group Exhibitions* incl: Pet Show (Union Street London) 1993, Pop Maudite (Cabinet Gallery London) 1993, Unfair 93 (Koln Germany) 1993, MPD multiple personality disorder (Cabinet Gallery London) 1993, Please Don't Hurt Me (Gallerie Snoie Rotterdam) 1994, Painter's Opinion (Bloom Gallery Amsterdam) 1995, Please Don't Hurt Me (Cabinet Gallery London) 1995, White Hysteria (Contemporary Art Center Adelaide) 1996, The Death of the Death of Painting (NY) 1995, Yerselfesteem (Words and Pictures London) 1996, Popocultural (S London Gallery London) 1996, Popocultural II (Southampton City Art Gallery) 1997, Dissolution (Laurent De Laye Gallery London) 1997, Multislot (London) 1997, There's Something Odd about Painting (Konig Gallery Vienna) 1998, Show Me the Money (Dukes Mews London) 1998, Exit Art (NY) 1999, Papermake (Modern Art London) 1999, Animal Magic (Kunsthaus Karstruhe Germany) 1999, Abstract Art (Delfina Gallery London) 2000, Beck's Futures 2 (ICA London) 2001, Tattoo Show (Modern Art London) 2001; *Publications* Kindred Spirits (1991), "Gavin, What's Your Work About?" (1993), Some Things Which Fell to Earth (1994), Rabbit Droppings (essay, 1996), Essay on Gary Hume (1996); *Recreations* gardening, collecting antique edged weapons; *Style*— Simon Bill, Esq; ✉ 22 Tyers Estate, Bermondsey Street, London SE1 3JG (tel 020 7967 9037)

BILLINGHAM, Baroness (Life Peer UK 2000), of Banbury in the County of Oxfordshire; Angela Theodora; da of Theodore Vincent Case (d 1941), and Eva, *née* Saxby (d 1964); *b* 31 July 1939; *Educ* Aylesbury GS, Univ of London, Dept of Educn Oxford; *m* 1962, Anthony Peter Billingham (d 1992), s of late Cyril Billingham; 2 da (Zoë Ann b 31 Dec 1964, Caroline Lucy b 12 July 1967); *Career* numerous teaching posts most recently at Banbury Sch, former examiner for an examinations bd; cncllr: Banbury BC 1970–74, Cherwell DC 1974–84, Oxfordshire CC 1993–94; mayor of Banbury 1976; magistrate 1976–; contested gen election (Lab) Banbury 1992, MEP (Lab) Northants and Blaby 1994–99; chief whip Party of European Socialists (PES); memb: Economic and Monetary Affairs Ctee, European Select Ctee (Sub-Ctee D); substitute memb Agric and Rural Devpt Sec Sports Inter Gp, departmental liaison peer Dept for Culture, Media and Sport; chair Urban Regeneration Co Catalyst Corby; patron Supporters Direct; *sporting achievements* tournament and county tennis player for 25 years and currently capt Oxfordshire co tennis tea chairm, co hockey and badminton player; *Recreations* tennis, gardening, cinema, bridge; *Style*— The Rt Hon the Baroness Billingham; ✉ 6 Crediton Hill, London NW6 1HP (tel 020 7431 5570); House of Lords, London SW1A 0PW

BILLINGHAM, Prof John; s of Charles Noel Billingham, of Dudley, W Midlands, and Florence May, *née* Dennison; *b* 10 October 1939; *Educ* Dudley GS, Univ of Birmingham (BSc), Univ of Warwick (PhD); *m* 1962, Heather Doreen, da of Frederick Homer; 2 da (Jane Elizabeth b 1963, Carolyn Leslie 1966), 1 s (David John b 1973); *Career* Gillette Res Lab 1962–65, BSA Res Labs 1965–67, Fulmer Res Labs 1970–73; Cranfield Univ 1973–: dir Marine Technol Centre 1981–84, head Marine Technol Dept 1984–98, prof 1984–, head Sch of Industrial and Mfrg Sci 1998–; David Partridge Marine Technol Award 1994; FIM, FSUT, FREng 2000; *Publications* Steel - A Versatile Material in Marine Environments, Performance of High Strength Steels in Offshore Structures; *Recreations* golf, gardening, music; *Clubs* St Neots Golf; *Style*— Prof John Billingham; ✉ Cranfield University, Cranfield, Bedfordshire MK43 0AL (tel 01234 754074, fax 01234 754035)

BILLINGHAM, Richard; *b* 1970, Birmingham; *Educ* Univ of Sunderland (BA); *Career* photographer; artist in residence Irish MOMA 2001 (artists' work prog), Sargeant fellowship Br Sch at Rome 2002, Prince of Wales bursary for the Arts Athens 2003, Wonders of the Black Country Jubilee Arts West Midlands 2003, Art Sway residency New Forest Hampshire 2003, artist in residence VIVID Birmingham 2004; multimedia work incl Fishtank (film) 1998; patron Project Ethiopia; *Solo Exhibitions* Anthony Reynolds Gallery London 1996 and 1998, Nat Museum of Film and Photography Bradford 1996, Portfolio Gallery Edinburgh 1996, Luhring Augustine NY 1997, Regen Projects LA 1997, Galerie Jennifer Flay Paris 1997, Galeria Massimo De Carlo Milan 1997, Galerie Monika Reitz Frankfurt am Main 1999, Galerie Mot & Van de Boogaard Brussels 1999, Br Sch at Rome 1999, Contemporary Art Museum Nuoro 2000, Ikon Gallery Birmingham 2000 (and tour), Douglas Hyde Gallery Dublin, Nikolaj Contemporary Art Centre Copenhagen, Brno House of Arts Czech republic, Hasselblad Centre Gothenburg, Kunsthalle Willhelmshaven, New Pictures (Anthony Reynolds Gallery London) 2003, Trafo House of Contemporary Arts Budapest 2003, Sint Lukas Brussels 2004, New Forest (Art Sawy Galleries Hampshire) 2004, Black Country (New Art Gallery Walsall, La Fabrica Madrid, Galleria Marabini Bologna, Galway Arts Festival, Anthony Reynolds Gallery London) 2005, Zoo (Compton Verney Warks) 2006, Zoo (La Fabrica Madrid, Wolverhampton Art Gallery Wolverhampton, Anthony Reynolds Gallery London, Glynn Vivian Gallery Swansea) 2007, Constable (Town Hall Galleries Ipswich) 2007; *Books* Ray's A Laugh (1996), Richard Billingham (catalogue, 2000), Black Country, Richard Billingham (2004), Zoo, Richard Billingham (2007); *Clubs* Colony Room; *Style*— Richard Billingham, Esq; ✉ c/o Anthony Reynolds, 60 Great Marlborough Street, London W1F 2BA (tel 020 7439 2201, fax 020 7439 1869, e-mail info@anthonyreynolds.com)

BILLINGTON, Guy; s of Reginald Arthur Billington (d 1960), of 1 Arterberry Rd, London, and Constance May, *née* Riches; *b* 12 November 1946; *Educ* KCS Wimbledon, St John's Coll Cambridge (MA); *m* 5 July 1966, Christine Ellen, da of Rev Frederick Charles Bonner, of Upton upon Severn, Worcs; 2 da (Nicole b 13 Dec 1966, Suzanne b 21 Jan 1971); *Career* articled clerk Lovell White & King 1969–72, ptnr McKenna & Co 1977–97 (asst slr 1972–77), ptnr CMS Cameron McKenna 1997–2007; memb City of London Slrs' Co; memb

Law Soc; *Recreations* rugby, music; *Clubs* Rosslyn Park Football, Harlequins RFC; *Style—* Guy Billington, Esq; ✉ 16 Belvedere Grove, London SW19 7RL (tel 020 8946 4889); CMS Cameron McKenna, Mitre House, 160 Aldersgate Street, London EC1A 4DD (tel 020 7367 3000, fax 020 7367 2000, e-mail guy.billington@cms-cmck.com)

BILLINGTON, (Edward) John; CBE (1996), RD, DL; s of Edward Billington, and Nesta, *née* Boxwell; *b* 21 December 1934; *Educ* Uppingham; *m* 5 Dec 1964, Fenella, da of Dr Hamilton-Turner; 2 s (Edward b 1966, Richard b 1970), 1 da (Suzetta b 1968); *Career* RNR 1953–86; commodity broker; chm Edward Billington & Son Ltd; memb: NW Bd DTI 1988–96, Cncl Univ of Liverpool 1986–97; chm Mersey Partnership 1991–92, tstee: Nat Museums and Galleries on Merseyside 1986–96, Liverpool Sch of Tropical Med; dir Royal Liverpool Philharmonic Orch, dir Park Foods plc; High Sheriff Merseyside 1990–91; CIMgt; *Style—* John Billington, Esq, CBE, RD, DL; ✉ Edward Billington & Son Ltd, Cunard Building, Liverpool L3 1EL (tel 0151 236 5371)

BILLINGTON, Kevin; s of Richard Billington (d 1987), and Margaret, *née* Hennessy; *b* 12 June 1934; *Educ* Bryanston, Queens' Coll Cambridge; *m* 13 Dec 1967, Lady Rachel Billington, *qv*; 2 s (Nathaniel b 1970, Caspar b 1979), 2 da (Catherine Rose b 1973, Chloe b 1975); *Career* theatre/television/film director and producer; teacher British Centre in Sweden 1957–58, Economist Intelligence Unit London 1958–59, BBC Radio prodr Leeds 1959–60, BBC TV prodr Manchester 1960–61, prodr BBC Tonight 1961–64, documentary prodr BBC and ATV 1964–67, freelance dir 1968–2002; co-owner Billington-Scott 1979–86, manager and owner Court House Films 1982–88; memb Cncl IPPA 1982–84, memb Fulbright Panel 1993–95; BAFTA: memb Cncl 1983, vice-chm 1986–89, chm 1989–91, dep chm 1991–94; *Theatre* credits incl: Find Your Way Home (world premiere, Open Space Theatre) 1971, Me (world premiere, Citizen's Theatre Glasgow) 1972, The Birthday Party (first London revival, Shaw Theatre) 1974, Bloody Neighbours (world premiere, NT at ICA) 1975, Emigres (world premiere, NT at The Old Vic) 1976, The Caretaker (London revival, Shaw Theatre) 1976, The Homecoming (first London revival, Garrick and Jerusalem Festival) 1979, The Deliberate Death of a Polish Priest (Almeida) 1985, The Lover, A Slight Ache (both Vienna English Theatre and The Young Vic) 1987, The Breadwinner (nat tour) 1989, Veteran's Day (Haymarket) 1989, Quartermaine's Terms (nat tour) 1992, Old Times (Gate Theatre Dublin) 1993, Our Country's Good (MacOwen Theatre) 2000, Victory (MacOwen Theatre) 2001, Wild Honey (MacOwen Theatre) 2002; *Television and Film* documentaries 1964–67 incl: The English Cardinal, Twilight of Empire, Madison Avenue, All the Queen's Men, Matador (numerous awards incl: Encyclopaedia Britannica Prize, Screenwriters' Guild Awards, RTS Award, BAFTA Awards); other credits incl: Interlude (Columbia) 1968, The Rise and Rise of Michael Rimmer (Warner Bros) 1970, The Light at the Edge of the World (Nat General) 1971, And No One Could Save Her (ABC) 1972, Voices (Hemdale) 1973, Once Upon a Time is Now (NBC) 1977, Henry VIII (BBC/Time-Life) 1979, Echoes of the Sixties (NBC) 1979, The Jail Diary of Albie Sachs (BBC) 1980, The Good Soldier (Granada) 1981, Outside Edge (LWT) 1981, Shakespeare's Sonnets (Court House Films prodn for Channel Four) 1983, Reflections (Film on Four) 1984, Heartland (BBC Wales) 1989, Smith and Jones in Small Doses 1989, A Time to Dance (BBC Scotland) 1992, Handling Complaints and Managing Complaints (both Video Arts) 1994, I Wasn't Prepared for That (Video Arts) 1996, Balance Sheet Barrier (CD-Rom Video Arts) 1996, Loving Attitudes (screenplay) 2000, Bodily Harm (screenplay) 2001; *Recreations* swimming, football (QPR FC); *Clubs* Garrick; *Style—* Kevin Billington, Esq; ✉ c/o Judy Daish Associates, 2 St Charles Place, London W10 6EG (tel 020 8964 8811, fax 020 8964 8966)

BILLINGTON, Lady Rachel Mary; *née* Pakenham; da of 7 Earl of Longford, KG, PC (d 2001), and Elizabeth, Countess of Longford, CBE (d 2002); *b* 11 May 1942; *Educ* Univ of London; *m* 16 Dec 1967, Kevin Billington, *qv*; 2 s (Nathaniel b 1970, Caspar b 1979), 2 da (Catherine Rose b 1973, Chloe b 1976); *Career* author of 17 novels and 8 children's books; pres English PEN 1997–2000, memb Soc of Authors; *Novels* incl: A Women's Age, Occasion of Sin, Loving Attitudes, Theo and Matilda, Bodily Harm, Magic and Fate, Perfect Happiness, Tiger Sky, A Woman's Life, Far-Out! (for children), The Space Between, One Summer, There's More to Life (for children); *Non-Fiction* incl: The Family Year, The Great Umbilical - Mother Daughter Mother, the Unbreakable Bond, The Life of Jesus (for children), The Life of St Francis (for children); *Style—* Lady Rachel Billington; ✉ The Court House, Poyntington, Sherborne, Dorset DT9 4LF

BILLINGTON, Sandra; *b* 10 September 1943; *Educ* Bolton Sch for Girls, Lucy Cavendish Coll Cambridge (Quiller-Couch Prize, MA), Univ of Cambridge (Winchester Reading Prize, PhD); *Career* actress BBC Radio Manchester 1955–59, Guildhall Sch of Music and Drama 1960–62, RADA (scholar) 1965–67, actress theatre/film 1967–72; Univ of Glasgow Dept of Theatre, Film and TV Studies: lectr in Renaissance studies 1979–92, reader in medieval and Renaissance theatre 1992–2003; memb Traditional Cosmology Soc; awarded Katharine Briggs Prize for Folklore 1984, jt winner Michaelis-Jena Ratcliff Prize for Folklore 1991; FRSE 1997; *Publications* A Social History of the Fool (1984), Mock Kings in Medieval Society and Renaissance Drama (1991), The Concept of the Goddess (ed with Miranda Green, 1996), Midsummer: a cultural subtext from Chrétien de Troyes to Jean Michel (2000), Between Worlds (2005), The Land of Dreams (2007); *Recreations* gardening; *Style—* Dr Sandra Billington, FRSE; ✉ 3/1, 4 Doune Quadrant, Glasgow G20 6DL (e-mail sbillington@onetel.com)

BILLIS, Dr David; s of Harry Billis (d 1982), of London, and Anne, *née* Jacobson (d 1967); *b* 10 April 1934; *Educ* Hackney Downs GS, LSE (BSc(Econ), PhD); *m* 1957, Jacqueline Nahoma, *née* Ludwig; 2 s (Neeve Joseph b 1960, Tal b 1962); *Career* latterly i/c fin and cost accounts Kibbutz Zikkim 1957–66; fndr and dir Programme of Research and Training into Voluntary Action (PORTVAC) Brunel Univ, reader in social serv orgn and fndr dir Centre for Voluntary Orgn LSE (currently emeritus reader), visiting prof Imperial Coll Sch of Mgmnt 1998–2001; co-fndr NonProfit Management and Leadership; memb Assoc for Research on Non Profit Organisations and Voluntary Action 1985–; American Assoc for Research on Nonprofit Organizations and Voluntary Action (ARNOVA) Distinguished Lifetime Achievement Award 1995; *Books* incl: Welfare Bureaucracies (1984), Organisational Design (with R W Rowbottom, 1987), Organising Public and Voluntary Agencies (1993), Voluntary Agencies (with M Harris, 1996); *Recreations* gardening, walking, yoga; *Style—* Dr David Billis; ✉ 19 Cranbourne Road, London N10 2BT (e-mail worklevels@blueyonder.co.uk)

BILLS, David James; CBE (2001); s of Nigel Carey Bills (d 1994), and Susan, *née* Thompson, of Hobart, Tasmania; *b* 9 February 1948; *Educ* Hobart Matriculation Coll Tasmania, Australian Nat Univ (BSc), BC Inst of Tech (Dip), MIT USA (sr Mgmnt Programme); *m* Michele, da of Gilbert Ellis; 2 da (Jessica b Feb 1977, Amy b July 1985), 1 s (Thomas b Sept 1978); *Career* research scientist CSIRO Australia 1970–73, Dept of Agriculture Australia 1976, forest mangr Associated Pulp and Paper Mills Australia 1983, gen mangr North Forest Products, currently DG, dep chm and accounting offr Forestry Commission; vice-pres AFDI Australia 1983–86, pres Nat Assoc of Forest Industries Australia 1993–95, warden Hobart Marine Bd; author various scientific articles; memb Inst of Foresters in Australia (MIFA) 1970; *Recreations* tennis, music, skiing, sailing, classic cars; *Clubs* Edinburgh Sports; *Style—* David Bills, Esq, CBE; ✉ Forestry Commission, 231 Corstorphine Road, Edinburgh EH12 7AT (tel 0131 334 0363, fax 0131 334 1903)

BILSTON, Baron (Life Peer UK 2005), of Bilston in the County of West Midlands; Dennis Turner; s of Thomas Herbert Turner (d 1981), and Mary Elizabeth, *née* Peasley (d 1974); *b* 26 August 1942; *Educ* Stonefield Secdy Sch Bilston, Bilston Coll of Further Educn; *m* 19 June 1976, Patricia Mary, da of Joseph Henry Narroway (d 1984), of Bilston; 1 s (Hon Brendon Robert b 1977), 1 da (Hon Jenny Mary b 1980); *Career* chm: Springvale Co-op Ltd Bilston, Springvale Enterprises Ltd Bilston; dep ldr Wolverhampton MDC 1979–86 (sometime chm Social Servs, Housing Further Educn and Econ Devpt Ctees), cncllr W Midlands CC 1975–86; MP (Lab/Co-op) Wolverhampton SE 1987–2005; Lab whip for Health, Educn and Defence W Midlands 1987–97, PPS to Clare Short as Sec of State Int Devpt 1999–2003; chm House of Commons Catering Ctee 1997–2005, memb Exec Ctee Br Branch Cwlth Parly Assoc, memb Exec Ctee Inter-Parly Union, chm All Pty Parly FE Colls Gp, chm W Midlands Parly Gp of Labour MPs; vice-pres Local Govt Assoc; pres: Bilston Community Assoc, Bradley Community Assoc; sec and tstee Bradley and Dist Sr Citizens' Centre; Hon DLitt Univ of Wolverhampton 2006, Freeman City of Wolverhampton 2007; *Recreations* compereing, beer tasting, all card games; *Clubs* New Springvale Sports & Social (Bilston); *Style—* The Rt Hon the Lord Bilston; ✉ Ambleside, King Street, Bradley, Bilston, West Midlands (tel 01902 491822); Springvale House, Millfields Road, Bilston, West Midlands (tel 01902 492364)

BINDER, Alan Naismith; OBE (1974); s of Frederick John Binder (d 1961), and Kathleen Mary, *née* Darker (d 1967); *b* 4 August 1931; *Educ* Bedford Sch, Magdalen Coll Oxford (MA); *m* 1958, Gillian Patricia, da of George Francis Wilson, of Sussex; 2 da (Jennifer b 1959, Stephanie b 1960), 1 s (Jonathan b 1962); *Career* dir Shell International Petroleum Co Ltd 1984, pres Shell International Trading Co 1987–91; chm: United Communications Ltd 1991–99, Expro International Group 1992–99; dir: The Housing Finance Corporation 1993–2001, RJB Mining plc 1995–2000; *Recreations* tennis, skiing, reading, music; *Clubs* Carlton, Leander, MCC, Mosimann's; *Style—* Alan Binder, Esq, OBE; ✉ Old Place, Speldhurst, Kent TN3 0PA (tel 01892 863227, fax 01892 861478, e-mail alan.binder@tiscali.co.uk)

BINDING, Paul; s of Leonard Hubert Binding (d 1972), of Devon, and Muriel Hope, *née* Middleton (d 1965); *b* 7 January 1943; *Educ* Berkhamsted Sch, New Coll Oxford (open scholar, BA, BLitt); *Career* lectr in Eng literature Umeå Sweden 1970–72, a managing ed Oxford Univ Press 1974–77, dep literary and arts ed New Statesman 1979–81, writer in residence (Arts Cncl fellowship) St John's Sch Epping 1984, Eudora Welty visiting prof of Southern studies Millsaps Coll Jackson Mississippi 1985–86, lectr in Eng literature Univ of Macerata Italy 1987–89; lectr on works of Lorca, American Southern literature, animal issues, Scandinavian cultures, and other literary and cultural matters in US, UK, Sweden, Norway and Netherlands; contribs literary reviews to various pubns and articles on animal rights and Scandinavian matters to Independent on Sunday, Independent, Times Literary Supplement, Guardian etc, author of various introductions to works published by Virago Modern Classics and Gay Modern Classics; sr assoc memb St Antony's Coll Oxford 1999–2001; Br delg t Ibsen Centenary Conf Oslo 2006; juror Vondel Prize for best translation from Dutch 2007; memb: League Against Cruel Sports, Animal Aid, WWF (adopter of rhinocerus and orang-utan), Green Party, Br Union Against Vivisection, Fox Project, Movement for Compassionate Living, PEN; awarded prize by Sveriges Författarfond for promotion of Swedish literature; *Books* Separate Country (1979, revised edn 1988), Harmonica's Bridegroom (novel, 1984), Lorca - The Gay Imagination (1985), Dreams and Speculations (poems, with John Horder, 1986), Kingfisher Weather (novel, 1989), St Martin's Ride (autobiographical novel, 1990, J R Ackerley prize), Eudora Welty: Portrait of a Writer (1994), An Endless Quiet Valley: A Reappraisal of John Masefield (1998), Babel Guide to Scandinavian and Baltic Fiction (1999), My Cousin the Writer (novel, 2002), Imagined Corners: Exploring the World's First Atlas (2003), Tom, Dick and Harry (poems, 2003), With Vine-Leaves in His Hair: The Role of the Artist in Ibsen's Plays; *Recreations* listening to music, exploring Britain and Scandinavia, the Shropshire countryside, herbs and houseplants, the company of animals, Hollyoaks; *Style—* Paul Binding, Esq; ✉ The House, Bull Street, Bishop's Castle, Shropshire (tel 01588 638117, e-mail paulbinding@yahoo.co.uk)

BINDMAN, Sir Geoffrey Lionel; kt (2007); s of Dr Gerald Bindman (d 1974), and Lena Bindman (d 1989); *b* 3 January 1933; *Educ* Royal GS Newcastle upon Tyne, Oriel Coll Oxford; *m* 1961, Lynn Janice; 2 s, 1 da; *Career* slr; conslt Bindman & Partners London (formerly sr ptnr); chm Legal Action Gp 1976–78, legal advsr Cmmn for Racial Equality 1977–83, pres Discrimination Law Assoc 1999–, chm Soc of Labour Lawyers 1999–2001, chm Br Inst of Human Rights 2005–; hon visiting prof of law UCL 1990–, hon visiting fell in civil legal process Univ of Kent 1991–, hon visiting prof of law London South Bank Univ 2003–; tstee Wordsworth Tst 1993–; Gazette Centenary Award for Human Rights Achievement Law Soc 2003; Hon LLD: De Montfort Univ 2000, Kingston Univ 2006; hon fell Soc of Advanced Legal Studies 1998–; *Books* Race and Law (co-author, 1972), South Africa: Human Rights and the Rule of Law (ed, 1988); *Recreations* book collecting, music, walking; *Clubs* Law Soc, Commonwealth; *Style—* Sir Geoffrey Bindman; ✉ 275 Gray's Inn Road, London WC1X 8QB (tel 020 7833 4433, fax 020 7837 9792, e-mail g.bindman@ucl.ac.uk)

BINFIELD, Prof (John) Clyde Goodfellow; OBE (1991); s of Edward John Binfield, DSC (d 1976), and Margaret Florence, *née* Goodfellow (d 1976); *b* 5 December 1940; *Educ* Dover GS, Emmanuel Coll Cambridge (minor scholar, exhibitioner, Bachelor scholar, MA, PhD); *m* 1969, Noreen Helen, da of late William George Maycock; 2 da (Emma Victoria (Mrs James Stone) b 1970, Anna Alexandra b 1972); *Career* Univ of Sheffield: asst lectr in modern history 1964–67, lectr 1967–74, sr lectr 1974–84, reader 1984–98, head Dept of History 1988–91, assoc prof 1999–2004, emeritus prof 2004–; memb Exec Ctee World Alliance of YMCAs 1981–91 (chm of two ctees), chm Nat Cncl of YMCAs 1992–97 (vice-chm 1982–90), vice-pres YMCA England 1999–; pres: Ecclesiastical History Soc 1990–91, Chapels Soc 1992–98, Friends of Dr Williams's Library 1993–, United Reformed Church History Soc 2002–; chm Voluntary Action Sheffield 1990–93; govr: Stocksbridge Coll of Further Educn 1975–88, Northern Coll Manchester 1976–2005 (memb Educn Ctee, pres Bd of Govrs 2000–05), Silcoates Sch Wakefield 1977– (vice-chm 1982–83, chm of govrs 1983–93), Dunford (YMCA) Coll Sussex 1981–87, Loxley Tertiary Coll 1988–90; memb Cncl: YMCA George Williams Coll 1991–2001, Governing Bodies Assoc (GBA) 2000–03; tstee: Yorkshire Historic Churches Tst 1993–, South Yorkshire Historic Buildings Tst 1994– (chm 2004–06), Firth's Homes 1995–, Dr Williams's Library 2005–, Historic Chapels Tst 2006–; chm Fabric Advsy Ctee Wakefield Cathedral 2006–, memb Cncl Friends of Sheffield Cathedral 2006–; FRHistS 1983 (memb Cncl 1997–2002), FSA 1987; *Publications* George Williams and the YMCA: A Study in Victorian Social Attitudes (1973), So Down to Prayers: Studies in English Nonconformity 1780–1920 (1977), Pastors and People: The Biography of a Baptist Church: Queen's Road Coventry (1984), This Has Been Tomorrow: The World Alliance of YMCAs since 1955 (1991), The Contexting of a Chapel Architect: James Cubitt 1836–1912 (2001); ed of various books and jls and author of numerous articles, book chapters and reviews; *Recreations* travel, architecture, opera; *Clubs* Royal Over-Seas League; *Style—* Prof Clyde Binfield, OBE; ✉ 604 Royal Plaza, Westfield Terrace, Sheffield S1 4GG (tel 0114 272 2554)

BINGHAM, Charlotte; *see:* Brady, Hon Mrs (C M T)

BINGHAM, Lord; George Charles Bingham; s of 7 Earl of Lucan (decd), and Countess of Lucan; *b* 21 September 1967; *Educ* Eton, Trinity Hall Cambridge; *Career* investment banker; formerly with Kleinwort Benson Ltd then head of UK and European structured fin Dresdner Kleinwort Benson, currently dir of research Bailey Coates Asset Mgmnt; *Clubs* Turf, White's, Pratt's; *Style—* Lord Bingham

BINGHAM, Dr James Stewart; TD (1982); s of Dr William Bingham, of Cultra, Co Down, and Norah Mary, *née* Beckett; *b* 31 July 1945; *Educ* Campbell Coll Belfast, Queen's Univ Belfast (MB BCh, BAO); *m* 21 Sept 1974, Elizabeth Eleanor, da of Charles Arnold Stewart;

1 s (Stewart Mark b 20 Jan 1983); *Career* Univ Offrs' Trg Corp 1963–69, 253 (NI) Field Ambulance and 217 (L) Gen Hosp RAMC 1969–83, resigned as Lt-Col; house physician and surgn The Royal Victoria Hosp Belfast 1969–70; training posts in obstetrics and gynaecology in Belfast, Salisbury (Rhodesia) and Vancouver (Canada) 1970–75; The Middlesex Hosp London: sr registrar in genitourinary med 1975–77, conslt 1977–92, dir of serv 1983–91; conslt in genitourinary med Guy's and St Thomas' Hosps London 1992– (clinical dir 1997–2000); hon conslt in genitourinary med to Br Army 2000–; Med Soc for Study of Venereal Diseases: hon treas 1986–93, pres 1993–95, hon life fell 2007; chm Assoc for Genitourinary Med 1999–2001; pres Int Union Against Sexually Transmitted Infections 2001–03 (hon treas 1995–99), hon treas Br HIV Assoc 1996–2000, memb Specialist Advsy Ctee in Genitourinary Med 1988–95 and 2003– (chm 1993–95); UK rep Dermatovenereology Monospecialty Ctee Union of European Monospecialties 2003– (treas 2004–); memb Bd of Examiners for Dip Genitourinary Med: Soc of Apothecaries of London 1982– (convenor of examiners 1992–95), Univ of Liverpool 1996–98; memb Bd of Examiners for Dip HIV Med Univ of Liverpool 2003–; external examiner for MSc in Sexually Transmitted Infection UCL; memb: Genitourinary Sub-Ctee CCSC BMA 1986–92 (rep Sub-Ctee on CCSC 1989–91), Dermatology and Venereology Sub-Ctee CCSC BMA 1992–2007 (chm 1998–2000); Specialist Advsy Ctee in Genitourinary Med RCP 1988–95 (sec 1990–93, chm 1993–95); memb Editorial Bd: International Journal of STD and AIDS 1990– (ed Continuing Med Educn 1995–2000, asst ed 2003–), Genitourinary Med 1993–95; memb: BMA, RSM, Br Assoc for Sexual Health and HIV, Soc for the Study of Sexually Transmitted Diseases in Ireland, Euro Acad of Dermatology and Venereology; FRCOG, FRCP, FRCPE; *Books* Sexually Transmitted Diseases (1984, 2 edn 1990); *CD-ROMs* co-author Sexually Transmitted Infections and Genital Dermatoses - diagnosis and therapy (1998); *Recreations* British military history with particular emphasis on the Anglo-Irish contrib, reading military and political biographies, gardening; *Clubs* Army and Navy, City Volunteer Officers'; *Style—* Dr James Bingham, TD; ✉ Lydia Department, St Thomas' Hospital, Lambeth Palace Road, London SE1 7EH (tel 020 7188 2660, fax 020 7188 7706, e-mail james.bingham@gstt.nhs.uk)

BINGHAM, Judith Caroline; da of Jack Bingham (d 1993), and Peggy, *née* MacGowan (d 1997); *b* 21 June 1952; *Educ* High Storrs GS for Girls Sheffield, Royal Acad of Music; *m* 1985, Andrew Petrow; *Career* composer; studied under Hans Keller; singer BBC Singers 1983–95; works incl: The Divine Image 1976, Cocaine Lil 1977, A Hymn Before Sunrise in the Vale of Chamouni 1982, Into the Wilderness 1982, Cradle Song of the Blessed Virgin 1983, Scenes from Nature 1983, Just Before Dawn 1985, Brazil 1985, A Cold Spell 1987, Christmas Past, Christmas Present 1988, Chartres 1988, Dove Cottage by Moonlight 1989, I Have a Secret to Tell 1990, Unpredictable but Providential 1991, Four Minute Mile 1991, The Stars Above: The Earth Below 1991, The Uttermost 1992–93, Irish Tenebrae 1992, The Ghost of Combermere Abbey 1993, O Magnum Mysterium 1994, Santa Casa 1994, Beyond Redemption 1994–95, Evening Canticles 1995, Epiphany 1995, Salt in the Blood 1995 (premiered BBC Proms 1995), The Red Hot Nail (educn project for LSO, 1995), The Temple At Karnak 1996, The Mysteries of Adad 1996, No Discord 1996, The Waning Moon 1997, Gleams of a Remoter World 1997, Below the Surface Stream 1997, Chapman's Pool 1997, Passagio 1998, Missa Brevis 1998, The Clouded Heaven 1998, Shelley Dreams 1998, Unheimlich 1998, Vorarlberg 1998, Walzerspiele 1999, The Cathedral of Trees 1999, Water Lilies 1999, The Shooting Star 1999, Otherworld 2000, Starry Snowy Night 2000, Annunciation 2000, The Shepherd's Gift 2000, The Necklace of Light 2000, St Bride, Assisted by Angels 2000, These are OUR Footsteps 2000, 50 Shades of Green 2001, The Shadow Side of Joy Finzi 2001, The Island of Patmos 2001, First Light 2001, Der Spuk 2001, Bright Spirit 2001, My Father's Arms 2002, Ave Verum Corpus 2002, Enter GHOST 2002, Aquileia 2002, Uppon First Sight of New-England 2002, Incarnation with Shepherds Dancing 2002, Missa Brevis 2003, The Road to Emmaeus 2003, Ancient Sunlight 2003, The Moon over Westminster Cathedral 2003, The Christmas Truce 2003, Bach's Tomb, O Clap Your Hands 2003, The Ivory Tree 2004, The Secret Garden 2004, The Yearning Strong 2004, Limehouse Nocturne 2004, Lo in the Silent Night 2004, Our Faith is a Light 2004, Margaret Forsaken 2004, Down and Out 2004, Touch'd by Heavenly Fire 2004, In Nomine 2004, Hidden City 2006; BBC Young Composer 1977, Barlow Prize for Choral Music 2004, British Composer Award for Liturgical Music and for Choral Music 2004; ARAM; *Recreations* reading, friends, art; *Style—* Miss Judith Bingham

BINGHAM, Prof Nicholas Hugh; s of Robert Llewelyn Bingham (d 1972), of Dolgellau, and Blanche Louise, *née* Corbitt; *b* 19 March 1945; *Educ* Tadcaster GS, Trinity Coll Oxford (MA), Churchill Coll Cambridge (PhD, ScD); *m* 13 Sept 1980, Cecilie Ann, da of Ralph William Gabriel (d 1973), of Leigh-on-Sea; 2 s (James b 1982, Thomas b 1993), 1 da (Ruth b 1985); *Career* Univ of London: lectr then reader Westfield Coll 1969–84, reader 1984–85, prof of mathematics Royal Holloway and Bedford New Coll 1985–95, prof of statistics Birkbeck Coll 1995–99; prof of statistics Brunel Univ 2000–03, prof of probability Univ of Sheffield 2003–06, prof of math Imperial Coll London 2006–; ed book reviews 1981–90; memb London Mathematical Soc, Inst of Mathematical Statistics; RSS; *Books* Regular Variation (1987), Risk-Neutral Valuation (1998); *Recreations* running, gardening; *Style—* Prof Nicholas Bingham; ✉ 13 Woodside Grange Road, London N12 8SJ (tel 020 8445 5779); Department of Probability and Statistics, University of Sheffield, Sheffield S3 7RH (tel 0114 222 3714, e-mail nick.bingham@btinternet.com)

BINGHAM OF CORNHILL, Baron (Life Peer UK 1996); Sir Thomas Henry Bingham; KG (2005), kt (1980), PC (1986); s of Dr Thomas Henry Bingham, of Reigate, Surrey, and Catherine, *née* Watterson; *b* 13 October 1933; *Educ* Sedbergh, Balliol Coll Oxford; *m* 1963, Elizabeth Patricia, o da of Peter Noel Loxley (d 1945); 1 da (Catherine Elizabeth b 1965), 2 s (Thomas Henry b 1967, Christopher Toby b 1969); *Career* called to the Bar 1959, jr counsel Dept of Employment 1968–72, QC 1972, judge of the High Court of Justice (Queen's Bench Div) 1980–86, Lord Justice of Appeal 1986–92, Master of the Rolls 1992–96, Lord Chief Justice of England and Wales 1996–2000, Sr Lord of Appeal in Ordinary 2000–; ldr of investigations into: Supply of Petroleum and Petroleum Prods to Rhodesia 1977–78, Bank of Credit and Commerce International (BCCI) 1991–92; high steward Univ of Oxford 2001; fell: KCL 1992, Queen Mary & Westfield Coll London 1993, UCL 1997; visitor: Balliol Coll Oxford 1986 (also hon fell), Royal Postgrad Med Sch 1989, London Business Sch 1992, Darwin Coll Cambridge 1996, Templeton Coll Oxford 1996, UC Oxford; hon fell: American Coll of Trial Lawyers, UCL 1997, Coll of Estate Mgmnt 1997, Nuffield Coll Oxford 1998; hon bencher Inn of Court of NI 1993; Hon LLD: Univ of Birmingham 1993, Univ of Wales 1998, Univ of London 1999, Univ of Glamorgan 1999, Dickinson Sch of Law 2000, City Univ 2005; Hon DCL Oxford 1994, Hon DUniv Essex 1997; Hon FBA 2003; *Publications* The Business of Judging (2000); *Style—* The Rt Hon Lord Bingham of Cornhill, KG, PC; ✉ Law Lords' Office, House of Lords, London SW1A 0PW

BINGLEY, Lt-Col Robert Noel Charles; s of Col Robert Albert Glanville Bingley, DSO, OBE, MVO (d 1977), and Sybil Gladys Williamson, *née* Duff (d 2004); *b* 28 December 1936; *Educ* Abberley Hall Malvern, Charterhouse; *m* 23 Nov 1962, Elizabeth Anne, da of Col Thomas Charles Stanley Haywood, OBE, JP, DL, of Gunthorpe, Rutland; 1 da (Claire b 1963), 2 s (Piers b 1967, Alexander b 1971); *Career* Troop Ldr 11 Hussars (PAO) 1957, Staff Capt HQ 17 Div Malaya Dist 1965, Staff Coll Pakistan 1969, GSO 2 MOD 1970, 2 i/c Royal Hussars 1972, NDC 1974, instr Australia Army Staff Coll 1976, CO Royal Yeo 1977; antique dealer 1978–; memb Cancer Relief MacMillan Fund; High Sheriff Rutland 2000; *Recreations* shooting, fishing; *Style—* Lt-Col Robert Bingley; ✉ Wing House, Oakham, Rutland (tel 057 285 314); Coul Cottage, Scatwell, Marybank by Muir-of-Ord, Ross-shire; Robert Bingley Antiques, Church Street, Wing, Oakham, Rutland (tel 01572 737725, fax 01572 737284)

BINLEY, Brian; MP; *b* 1942; *Educ* Finedon Mulso Secdy Modern; *m* Jacquie; 2 s (James b 1970, Matthew b 1984); *Career* fndr and chm BCC Marketing Services 1988–, co-fndr Beechwood House Publishing Co Ltd 1993; joined Cons Pty 1959, cncllr (Cons) Northamptonshire CC 1997– (finance spokesman, chm Finance and Resources Security Ctee 2001–05, finance portfolio holder 2005–), MP (Cons) Northampton S 2005–; FRSA; *Style—* Brian Binley, Esq, MP; ✉ House of Commons, London SW1A 0AA; Constituency Office tel 01604 633414, e-mail brian.binley@brianbinley.com, website www.brianbinley.com

BINNEY, Prof James Jeffrey; s of Harry Augustus Roy Binney (d 1999), and Barbara, *née* Poole (d 1975); *b* 12 April 1950; *Educ* Univ of Cambridge (BA), Univ of Oxford (DPhil); *m* 1993, Lucy Elliot, da of A D Buckingham; 1 da (Carola Barbara b 1995), 1 s (Peter Amyand Jeffrey b 1998); *Career* Univ of Oxford: fell Magdalen Coll 1975–79, fell and tutor in physics Merton Coll 1981–, univ lectr 1981–90, ad hominem reader in theoretical physics 1990–96, prof of physics 1996–; Princeton Univ: Lindemann fell 1976, visiting asst prof in astrophysical sciences 1979–98, sometime visiting fell; Fairchild distinguished scholar Caltech 1983, visitor Inst of Advanced Study; IAU: pres Cmmn 33 1994–97, pres Div VII 1994–97, currently memb Organizing Ctee Cmmn 28; memb: Theory Panel SERC 1986–88, Theoretical Research Panel PPARC 1997–99, Jt Infrastructure Bd PPARC 1999–2000; Maxwell Prize and Medal Inst of Physics 1986, Brouwer Award American Astronomical Soc 2003; memb American Astronomical Soc 1976; FRAS 1973, FRS 2000, FInstP 2000; *Books* Galactic Astronomy (jtly, 1981), Galactic Dynamics (jtly, 1988), Pick for Humans (jtly, 1990), The Theory of Critical Phenomena (jtly, 1992), Galactic Astronomy (jtly, 1998); *Recreations* wood, metal and stone work, walking; *Style—* Prof James Binney; ✉ Department of Theoretical Physics, University of Oxford, 1 Keble Road, Oxford OX1 3NP (tel 01865 273979, fax 01865 273947, e-mail binney@thphys.ox.ac.uk)

BINNEY, Marcus Hugh Crofton; CBE (2006, OBE 1983); s of late Lt Col Francis Crofton Simms, MC, and Sonia (d 1985), da of Rear Adm Sir William Marcus Charles Beresford-Whyte, KCB, CMG (she m 2, 1955, as his 2 wife, Sir George Binney, DSO, who d 1972); *b* 21 September 1944; *Educ* Eton, Magdalene Coll Cambridge (BA); *m* 1, 1966 (m dis 1976), Hon Sara Anne Vanneck (d 1979), da of 6 Baron Huntingfield; m 2, 1981, Anne Carolyn, da of Dr Thomas Henry Hills of Merstham, Surrey; 2 s (Francis Charles Thomas b 1982, Christopher George Crofton b 1985); *Career* writer; Country Life: architectural writer 1968–77, architectural ed 1977–84, ed 1984–86; ed Landscape 1987, freelance architecture corr The Times 1991–; sec UK Ctee Int Cncl on Monuments and Sites 1972–81, dir Railway Heritage Tst 1984–; pres: Save Britain's Heritage 1984– (chm 1975–84), Save Europe's Heritage 1995–; co-organiser: The Destruction of the Country House (exhibition V&A) 1974, Change and Decay: The Future of our Churches (V&A) 1977; FSA, Hon FRIBA; *Books* Change and Decay: The Future of our Churches (with Peter Burman, 1977), Chapels and Churches: Who Cares? (with Peter Burman, 1977), Preservation Pays (with Max Hanna, 1978), Railway Architecture (ed jtly, 1979), Our Past Before Us (ed jtly, 1981), The Country House: To Be or Not to Be (with Kit Martin, 1982), Preserve and Prosper (with Max Hanna, 1983), Sir Robert Taylor (1984), Our Vanishing Heritage (1984), Country Manors of Portugal (1987), Chateaux of the Loire (1992), Glyndbourne: Building a Vision (with R Runciman, 1992), The Chateaux of France (1994), Architecture of Rail (1995), Town Houses (1998), Airport Builders (1999), The Ritz Hotel, London (1999, centenary edn 2006), The London Sketch Book (with Graham Byfield, 2001), The Women who Lived for Danger (2002), Great Houses of Europe (2003), Secret War Heroes (2005), Save Britain's Heritage: 30 Years of Campaigning (2005); contrib: Satanic Mills (1979), Elysian Gardens (1979), Lost Houses of Scotland (1980), Taking the Plunge (1982), SAVE Gibraltar's Heritage (1982), Vanishing Houses of England (1983), Time Gentlemen Please (1983), Great Railway Stations of Europe (1984); *Style—* Marcus Binney, Esq, CBE; ✉ Domaine des Vaux, St Lawrence, Jersey JE3 1JG, CI (tel 01534 864424)

BINNIE, Ann; da of late Jeffery Wyatt, of Brackley, Northants, and late Doreen Eugenie, *née* Manly; *b* 10 March 1953; *Educ* Brentwood Co HS for Girls, Univ of Bradford (BSc, MSc); *m* 8 Sept 1973, David John Binnie, s of late Harold F Binnie; 1 da (Isla Jane b 28 Sept 1987), 1 s (Jamie Joe b 24 July 1990); *Career* staff: Br Inst of Mgmnt 1975–77, Rex Stewart Group 1977–79, W S Crawford 1979–80; various positions rising to bd planning dir DMB&B (formerly DMM) 1980–87, bd planning dir/head of planning KHBB 1987–90, planning conslt 1990–92, bd planning dir/head of planning Arc Advertising 1992–94; planning conslt to ad hoc clients and retained by: Group X (for Royal Mail and Budgens), Arc Advertising (for BBC Network Radio) 1994–; fndr: Ann Binnie Brand Planning 1996 (planning conslt to clients incl: ARCOM, Ogilvy, The Communications Unit, The Children's Society, Landor, JWTSC), Mongrel Worlds Ltd, Grey Advertising, Enneagram Facilitators 1998 (conslt to clients incl: Young & Rubicam, Henley Centre, Grey Advertising), Amethist 2000 (mktg conslt to clients incl: Pedigree Masterfoods, AT Cross, Norwich Union, JWTSC, Landor), Brand Architects 2000 (brand strategy and design conslt to clients incl: Tradelink, Hummingbird Bakery); certified teacher of Enneagram in Narrative Tradition with Helen Palmer; memb Judging Panel DBA Effectiveness Awards 1990 and 1992; memb: MRS, Mktg Soc; FRSA; *Recreations* reading, theatre, life drawing, yoga, enjoying my children; *Style—* Mrs Ann Binnie; ✉ Amethist, 34 Bloomfield Road, Harpenden, Hertfordshire AL5 4DB (mobile 07778 675987, e-mail annbinnie@helloworld.com)

BINNIE, Christopher Jon Anthony; s of Lt Cdr William Anthony Charles Binnie (d 1947), of Minehead, Somerset, and Barbara Kathleen, *née* Goddard-Jackson; *b* 20 June 1938; *Educ* Stowe, Univ of Cambridge (MA), Imperial Coll London (Dip); *m* 14 Sept 1968, Deryn, da of Lt Col Ian Harry Keith Chauvel; 2 s (Anthony b 25 Feb 1974, Jeremy b 20 Dec 1975); *Career* graduate engr Binnie & Partners 1963–64, project engr NCB 1964–66, civil engr GEO Wimpey 1967–68, resident engr Durban Reservoir Murray & Roberts 1968–69; Binnie & Partners: sr engr (water resources) Malaysia 1969–71, project engr Marchlyn Dam 1972–78; dir Water Unit W S Atkins Consultants 1984–95 (chief engr Water Dept 1978–84), dir W S Atkins plc (formerly W S Atkins Group Ltd) 1994–97, dir SE Asia (resident Singapore) 1997–98; dep chm Binnie Black & Veatch 1998–2001; ind conslt on water 2001–; CIWEM: fndr chm Expert Panel on Water Resources 1991–94, chm Int Ctee 1992–97, pres 1995–96; memb Cncl: British Water Industries Group 1984–92, Fndn for Water Research Cncl 1989–95; visiting prof of design Kingston Univ 1995–; dir BCCB 1998–2002; Freeman City of London 1991, Liveryman Worshipful Co of Water Conservators 2000 (memb Ct of Assts 1989–94); memb: British Dams Soc 1974, British Geotechnical Soc 1979, Assoc of Consulting Engrs 1986; memb Senate Engrg Cncl 2001–02; Hon DEng Univ of Bradford 1997; FICE 1976, FCIWEM 1976, FREng 1994; *Publications* Water Supplies in the UK in the 1990's and Beyond (1991), Basic Water Treatment TTL (2002), and 37 others; *Recreations* sailing, riding; *Clubs* Royal Thames Yacht; *Style—* Christopher Binnie, FREng; ✉ Brockwell Farm, Wootton Courtney, Minehead, Somerset (tel 01643 841212, fax 01643 841233)

BINNIE, Prof Colin David; s of Horace David Binnie, of Leigh-on-Sea, Essex, and Doris Amy, *née* Read (d 1966); *Educ* Felsted, Univ of Cambridge (MD, MA, BCh), Guy's Hosp Med Sch; *m* 1, 31 Oct 1964, (Florence) Margaret, da of George Shields (d 1980); 1 da (Caroline b 1965), 1 s (Nicholas b 1968); m 2, 11 April 2006, Alexandra Vivien MacKay, widow of Geoffery Eldin-Taylor; *Career* physician i/c Dept of Clinical Neurophysiology Bart's and Southend Hosp 1972–76, head of clinical neurophysiology serv Inst Voor Epilepsie Bestrjding Heemstede Netherlands 1976–86, conslt clinical neurophysiologist Bethlem Royal Hosp and Maudsley Hosp 1986–, clinical dir of neurosciences 1991–95, prof of clinical neurophysiology GKT 1995–2003, emeritus prof of clinical neuroscience GKT 2003–; visiting prof of physiology UCL; pres British Soc for Clinical Neurophysiology, chm Neurosurgical Cmmn of International League against Epilepsy; memb: Int League Against Epilepsy, chm Electroencephalography and Clinical Neurophysiology Educnl Bd, Electrophysiological Tech Assoc, RSM 1965, Assoc Br Clinical Neurophysiologists 1970, Br Assoc for Neuropsychiatry 1988, Assoc of British Neurologists; MRCS, FRCPGlas, FRCP; *Publications* A Manual of Electroencephalographic Technology (1982), Biorhythms and Epilepsy (1986), Clinical Neurophysiology (vol 1 2003, vol 2 2005), numerous pubns on Electroencephalography and Epilepsy; *Recreations* opera, languages; *Style*— Prof Colin Binnie; ✉ Department of Clinical Neurophysiology, King's College Hospital, Denmark Hill, London SE5 9RS (tel 020 7346 4342, fax 020 7346 3725, e-mail colin.binnie@kcl.ac.uk)

BINNS, Malcolm; s of Douglas Priestley Binns (d 1988), of Keighley, W Yorks, and May, *née* Walker; *b* 29 January 1936; *Educ* Bradford GS, RCM; *Career* prof RCM 1961–65; concert pianist: London debut 1959, debut Promenade Concerts 1960, regular performances at Proms 1962–, Royal Festival Hall debut 1961, has appeared in London Philharmonic seasons 1962–; soloist with all major Br orchs, over 30 recordings, first complete recording of Beethoven Piano Sonatas on original instruments, played Far E and toured with Scot Nat Orch and Limbourg Orch 1987–88; ARCM; *Recreations* gardening; *Style*— Malcolm Binns, Esq; ✉ c/o Michael Harrold Artist Management, 13 Clinton Road, Leatherhead, Surrey KT22 8NU (tel 01372 375728)

BINT, Dr Adrian John; s of Arthur Herbert Bint, of Birmingham, and Lily, *née* Naylor; *b* 3 April 1948; *Educ* Moseley GS Birmingham, Univ of Birmingham (MB ChB); *m* 12 June 1971, Marilyn Joyce, da of Charles Bourne Wathes, of Kingsbury, Staffs; 1 s (Alastair Halford b 1974), 1 da (Nicola Sarah b 1975); *Career* conslt microbiologist Royal Victoria Infirmary Newcastle 1979–2007 (clinical dir for lab servs 2003–07), ret; meetings sec Br Soc for Antimicrobial Chemotherapy 1980–83; chm Clinical Servs Ctee Assoc of Med Microbiologists 1994–98, Northern Regional Cncl of RCP 2001–04, Microbiology Coll Advsy Training Team RCP 2001–04; memb: Cncl Assoc of Clinical Pathologists 1983–86, Editorial Bd Jl of Clinical Pathology 1988–93; ed Jl of Antimicrobial Chemotherapy 1994–96 and 2000–04; memb Expert Witness Inst 1998–; FRCPath 1989 (MRCPath 1977); *Recreations* fell walking, badminton; *Style*— Dr Adrian Bint

BINTLEY, David Julian; CBE (2001); s of David Bintley, of Honley, W Yorks, and Glenys, *née* Ellinthorpe; *b* 17 September 1957; *Educ* Holme Valley GS, Royal Ballet Upper Sch; *m* 12 Dec 1981, Jennifer Catherine Ursula, da of Bernard Mills, of San Diego, CA; 2 s (Michael b 21 March 1985, Gabriel b 7 Sept 1995); *Career* Sadler's Wells Royal Ballet 1976–86: debut The Outsider 1978, resident choreographer and princ dancer 1983–86; resident choreographer and princ dancer Royal Ballet 1986–93, freelance 1993–95, artistic dir Birmingham Royal Ballet 1995–; other works incl: Galanteries 1986, Allegri Diversi 1987, Hobson's Choice 1989, Edward II 1995, Carmina Burana 1995; Evening Standard Award for Choros and Consort Lessons 1983, Olivier Award for performance in Petrushka (title role) 1984, Manchester Evening News Award for Still Life at the Penguin Café 1988; Hon DUniv Univ of Central England 1999, Hon DLett Univ of Birmingham 2001; *Style*— David Bintley, Esq, CBE; ✉ Birmingham Royal Ballet, Hippodrome Theatre, Thorp Street, Birmingham B5 4AU (tel 0121 622 2555, fax 0121 689 3070, e-mail davidbintley@brb.org.uk)

BION, Dr Julian Fleetwood; s of Dr Wilfred Ruprecht Bion, DSO (d 1979), and Francesca, *née* Purnell; *b* 30 July 1952; *Educ* Harrow, Charing Cross Hosp, Univ of London (MB BS); *m* 15 June 1985, Nitaya, da of Sanit Tangchurat (d 1979), of Bangkok, Thailand; 2 c (Alexander, Victoria (twins) b 14 April 1992); *Career* previous appts in anaesthesia, gen med and cardiology, sr anaesthetist Red Cross surgical team Thai-Cambodian border 1983; Univ of Birmingham: sr lectr in intensive care 1989–97, reader in intensive care med 1997–; former memb Editorial Bds: British Jl of Hosp Med, Clinical Intensive Care, Intensive Care Med, Intensive and Critical Care Nursing; author of numerous publications on aspects of intensive care med, audit, infection-prevention, outcome prediction and scoring systems; BUPA Med Fndn Dr of the Year award 1985; pres European Soc of Intensive Care Med (memb Cncl) 2004–06; memb: Intensive Care Soc UK (memb Cncl 1993–99), Assoc of Anaesthetists, BMA, Intercollegiate Bd for Trg in Intensive Care Med (chair competency-based trg working gp) 1998–2004; advsr Commonwealth Scholarships Cmmn; FFARCS 1982, FRCA 1988, MD 1991, FRCP 1996 (MRCP 1980); *Style*— Dr Julian Bion; ✉ University of Birmingham, N5, Queen Elizabeth Hospital, Birmingham B15 2TH (tel 0121 627 2060, fax 0121 627 2062)

BIRCH, Clive Francis William; MBE (2001); s of Raymond William Birch, CBE (d 1980), and (Olive Edith Charlton) Valerie, *née* Fry (d 2000); *b* 22 December 1931; *Educ* Uppingham; *m* 1, 1957 (m dis 1961), Gillian May, *née* Coulson; m 2, 1961 (m dis 1978), Penelope Helen, *née* Harman; 1 s (James b 1962), 1 da (Emma b 1964), 1 adopted s (Richard b 1957), 1 adopted da (Cally b 1959); m 3, 16 April 1983, Carolyn Rose, da of Thomas Desborough (d 1978); 1 step da (Katie b 1970), 1 step s (Jamie b 1974); *Career* Nat Serv radar RAF 1950–52; office jr Stretford Telegraph 1952, reporter Stockport Express 1952, dist reporter Kent and Sussex Courier 1953, chief reporter Herts Newspapers 1954, ed Bucks Examiner 1956, press offr Frigidaire Div General Motors Ltd 1958, product devpt Metro-Cammell Weyman Ltd 1959, gp advertisement mangr Modern Transport Publishing Co Ltd 1965, mangr Electrical Press Ltd 1966; dir: Birch Bros Ltd 1966–, Illustrated Newspapers Ltd 1969; ed Illustrated London News 1970, dir Northwood Publications Ltd 1971, md designate Textile Trade Pubns Ltd 1972, publishing dir Mercury House Ltd 1973, fndr chm Barracuda Books Ltd 1974–92, dir Quotes Ltd 1985–97, princ Radmore Birch Associates 1991–, dir TLC Pharmacies Ltd 1995–98, fndr Baron Books 1997–, publishing conslt Boltneck Publications Ltd 2005–06, publishing dir Boltneck Publications Ltd and Medavia Publishing 2006–; fndr chm Buckingham and Dist Chamber of Trade Commerce and Indust 1983; pres Buckingham Heritage Tst 1997–2001 (founder chm 1985), tstee Camberwell Housing Soc 2002–; hon life memb: Chiltern Car Club 1956, Inst of the Royal Corps of Tport 1985; govr Royal Latin Sch Buckingham 1989–93, former memb Cncl Chesham Round Table; memb Carmen's Awards Ctee 1969– (chm 1999–), fndr chm Carmen's Charity Ball 1985, chm Carmen's Media and Mktg Ctee 1994–2007, hon ed 2002–; chm RSA Carmen Lectures 1991–; chm Past Masters 2004–, sr past master 2005–; RCA: fndr Carmen Research Fellowship 2001, visiting lectr 2002–, visiting tutor 2003–, memb Ct 2007–; Freeman City of London 1960; Worshipful Co of Carmen: Freeman and Liveryman 1960: memb Ct of Assts 1966–, Master 1984–85, Dep Master 1988–89; FRSA 1980, FSA 1981; Chevalier Confrèrie des Chevaliers du Trou Normand 1991; *Books* incl: The Book of Chesham (1974, 4 edn 1997), The Book of Aylesbury (1975, 3 edn 1993), The Freedom-History and Guilds of the City of London (jtly, 1982), Buckingham in Camera (1987), Chiltern Thames in Camera (1990), Yesterday's Town: Amersham (jtly, 1991), Old Milton Keynes in Camera (1992), On the Move - The Road Haulage Association 1945–94 (jtly, 1995), Wish You Were Here: Buckingham (1997), Wish You Were Here: Chesham (1997), Carr & Carman (1999), Royal College of Art Vehicle Design (ed, 2006 and 2007), A Decent Man (novel, 2006), Moving Forward (assoc author, 2006); *Style*— Clive Birch, MBE, FSA; ✉ Radmore Birch Associates, King's Cote, Valley Road, Finmere, Buckingham MK18 4AL (tel 01280 848847, fax 01280 847874, e-mail clive.birch@booksbybaron.co.uk or clive.birch@medavia.co.uk)

BIRCH, Prof David; s of late James William Birch, and late Hilda Mary, *née* Gibbons; *b* 19 December 1949, Southport, Lancs; *Educ* Victoria Univ of Manchester (BSc, PhD); *m* 1976, Gilly Bonny; 1 s (Samuel b 1988); *Career* temp lectr in physics Victoria Univ of Manchester 1974–75, mass spectrometry physicist VG Micromass Ltd 1976–78; Univ of Strathclyde: lectr in applied physics 1978, sr lectr in physics and applied physics 1987, reader in physics and applied physics 1990, prof of photophysics 1993–, dir Femtosecond Research Centre 1994–, head Dept of Physics 2004–; visiting scientist Univ of Perugia 1975, Sir C V Raman Endowment visiting chair Univ of Madras 1999, visiting prof Kyoto Inst of Technol 2000, visiting prof of applied physics Czech Tech Univ Prague 2002–; Royal Soc industrial research fell 1987 and 1989, Nuffield Fndn science research fell 1988, Japanese Soc for the Promotion of Science visiting research fell 2000; memb: EPSRC Control and Instrumentation Coll 1996, Scientific Advsy Bd Kalibrant Ltd 1997–2002, Physics and Astronomy Sectional Ctee Royal Soc of Edinburgh 2003–, Enterprise Fellowships Ctee Royal Soc of Edinburgh 2003–; memb Editorial Bd: Jl of Fluorescence 1990–2002, Jl of Biomedical Optics 1995–, Measurement Science and Technology 2000–, Research on Chemical Intermediates 2002–; author of over 160 jl pubns on molecular fluorescence, sensors, optical techniques and soft solids; fndr co-dir IBH Ltd 1977–2003, dir Jobin Yvon IBH Ltd 2004–; FInstP, CPhys 1986, FRSC, CChem 2001, FRSE 2003; *Style*— Prof David Birch; ✉ University of Strathclyde, Glasgow G4 0NG (tel 0141 548 3377, e-mail djs.birch@strath.ac.uk)

BIRCH, Dr John Anthony; s of Charles Aylmer Birch (d 1966), of Leek, Staffs, and Mabel, *née* Greenwood (d 1971); *b* 9 July 1929; *Educ* Trent Coll, RCM (RCO Pitcher scholar); *Career* Nat Serv RCS 1949–50; organist and choirmaster St Thomas's Church Regent St 1950–53, accompanist St Michael's Singers 1952–58, organist and choirmaster All Saints Church Margaret St London 1953–58, sub-organist HM Chapels Royal 1957–58, organist and master of the choristers Chichester Cathedral 1958–80, prof RCM 1959–97 (conslt 1997–), re-established the Southern Cathedrals Festival with Cathedral Organists of Salisbury and Winchester 1960, musical advsr Chichester Festival Theatre 1962–80, choirmaster Bishop Otter Coll Chichester 1963–69, organist Royal Choral Soc 1966– (accompanist 1965–70), md CA Birch Ltd Staffs 1966–73 (rep 1950–66), univ organist Univ of Sussex 1967–94 (visiting lectr in music 1971–83), special cmmr Royal Sch of Church Music, organist and dir of choir Temple Church 1982–97, organist Royal Philharmonic Orchestra 1983–, curator-organist Royal Albert Hall 1984–; concert appearances: France, Belgium, Austria, Germany, Italy, Switzerland, Netherlands, Spain, Portugal, Poland, Romania, Scandinavia, Japan, USA, Mexico, Far East; recital tours: Canada and US 1966 and 1967, Aust and NZ 1969, SA 1978; examiner Assoc Bd Royal Schs of Music 1958–77, a gen ed Novello & Co 1967–77, fell Corp of SS Mary and Nicolas (Woodard Schs) 1973–99; govr Hurstpierpoint Coll 1974–93, memb Cncl Corp of the Cranleigh and Bramley Schs (govr St Catherine's Bramley 1981–89); tstee Ouseley Trust 1989–; pres RCO 1984–86 (memb Cncl 1964–2003 and 2005–, vice-pres 1986–, hon treas 1997–2002), pres The Burgon Soc 2001– (hon fell); waywarden of the Liberty of the Close Salisbury Cathedral 1997–2004; underwriting memb Lloyd's 1976–2002; Freeman City of London 1991, Freeman Worshipful Co of Glaziers and Painters of Glass 2006; Hon MA Univ of Sussex 1971, DMus Lambeth 1989, hon bencher Middle Temple 1998; ARCM, LRAM, FRCO (dipCHM), FRCM 1981; *Recreations* gardening, collecting pictures; *Clubs* Garrick, New (Edinburgh); *Style*— Dr John Birch; ✉ 2 The Chantry, Canon Lane, Chichester, West Sussex PO19 1PZ (tel 01243 537333, fax 01243 537377, e-mail drjohnbirch@aol.com)

BIRCH, Paul; s of Ronald Arthur Birch (d 1997), and Dorothy, *née* Channer; *b* 22 March 1952; *Educ* Dr Challoner's GS, AA Sch of Architecture (AADipl); *m* 1988, Janet, *née* Simpson; 1 s (James b 1989); *Career* architect; with GMW Partnership 1976–82 (projects incl Univ of Riyadh Saudi Arabia, Mobil HQ Strand London and office building Monument London), gp ldr Covell Matthews Wheatley Partnership 1982–88 (projects incl offices in Ropemaker St London, Appold St London and Swindon), dir Hamilton Assocs Architects Ltd 1988– (projects incl offices in Bow churchyard London and Leadenhall St London, Plough Place London (Commerical Bldg of the Year 2001), and HQs for Burmah Castrol, AIT and Perpetual); sometime contrib of articles on commercial office buildings Property Week magazine; RIBA 1982, ARB 1982, FRSA 2006; *Recreations* motor racing, football, theatre, cinema, travel; *Style*— Paul Birch, Esq; ✉ Hamilton Associates Architects Ltd, 280 Kings Road, London SW3 5AW (tel 020 7351 5432, e-mail p.birch@hamilton-assoc.com)

BIRCH, Paul John; JP (West Midlands 1999); s of Harrold James Birch, and Beryl, *née* Saul (d 1994); *b* 12 November 1954, Croydon; *Educ* Aston Univ, J L Kellogg Business Sch Northwestern Univ Chicago, Richard Ivey Business Sch Univ of Western Ontario (ATCO Calgary RD Southern scholar), Univ of Wolverhampton Business Sch (MBA); *m* 12 Sept 1992, Olivia, *née* Darling; 1 s (Joshua Harrison b 22 Sept 1991), 2 da (Hannah Rachael b 20 Jan 1995, Eleanor Louise b 17 Sept 2003); *Career* cr Heavy Metal Records 1979, cr Revolver Records 1980 (acts incl Stone Roses, Jayne's Addiction, Diamond Head, UFO, Misfits, Scorpions, UK Subs and Vibrators, catalogue of 2500 copyrights), developed Revolver Recording studios 1990, awarded more than 20 gold discs; cr MIDEM venture and trade show, launched Br Midlands Music 2007; memb Bd: BPI 1990– (former chair Educn Ctee and Int Ctee, former memb Copyright Strategy Ctee), Phonographic Performance Ltd 1998 (co-chair Int Ctee until 2005, memb New Business Ctee), IFPI (memb European Exec Ctee and Main Bd); sec UK Trade Investment North American Alumni Assoc DTI, memb Bd Birmingham-Chicago Sister City Ctee; former chair Victim Support charity; govr Wolverhampton GS, helped launch Birmingham Univ Business Sch's Innovation Exchange; MBPI 1981, FCIM 1995, AIM 1996 (fndr memb); *Style*— Paul Birch, Esq; ✉ Revolver Music Ltd, 152 Goldthorn Hill, Penn, Wolverhampton WV2 3JA (tel 01902 345345, fax 01902 345155, e-mail paul.birch@revolverrecords.com)

BIRCH, Peter Gibbs; CBE (1992); s of William Birch (d 1971), and Gladys, *née* Gibbs (d 1971); *b* 4 December 1937; *Educ* Allhallows Sch; *m* 17 March 1962, Gillian Heather, da of Leonard Brace Sale Benge; 3 s (James b 1964, Simon b 1967, Alexander b 1970), 1 da (Sophie b 1972); *Career* Nat Serv 2 Lt Royal West Kent Regt 1956–58, seconded to Jamaica Regt; with Nestlé in UK, Switzerland, Singapore and Malaya 1958–65; Gillette: with Gillette UK 1965–68, Gillette Australia (Melbourne) 1969–71, gen mangr Gillette NZ 1971–73, gen mangr Gillette SE Asia 1973–75, gp gen mangr Gillette Africa, ME and Eastern Europe 1975–81, md Gillette (UK) 1981–84; chief exec Abbey National plc (formerly Abbey National Building Society) 1984–98; chm: Land Securities plc 1998–2007, Kensington Gp plc 2000–, UCTX Ltd 2001–03, Sainsbury's Bank plc 2002–06; non-exec dir: Argos plc 1990–98, Dalgety plc 1993–98, Trinity Mirror plc (formerly Trinity plc) 1998–2007 (non-exec chm 1998–99), N M Rothschild & Sons 1998–, Coca-Cola Beverages plc 1998–2000, Travelex 1999–, Trigold 2007–, Lampull 2007–, Banca Finantia 2007–; chm Legal Services Cmmn 2000–02; pres Middx Young People's Clubs; *Recreations* swimming, cycling, skiing; *Style*— Peter G Birch, Esq, CBE; ✉ c/o N M Rothschild & Sons Ltd, New Court, St Swithin's Lane, London EC4P 4DU (tel 020 7280 5000, fax 020 7280 5562)

BIRD, A John; MBE (1995); s of Alfred Ernest Bird (d 1983), and Eileen Mary, *née* Dunne (d 1973); *b* 30 January 1946; *Educ* St Thomas More's Secdy Modern, Chelsea Sch of Art, Ealing Coll of HE (BA); *m* 1, 30 August 1965 (m dis 1971), Linda, *née* Haston; 1 da (Emily Jane b 3 April 1966); m 2, 10 March 1973 (m dis 2004), Isobel Theresa, *née*

Ricketts; 1 s (Patrick Jack b 12 August 1975), 1 da (Eileen Diana b 15 November 1977); m 3, Parveen Kaur Sodhi; 1 s (Sonny John b 2005), 1 da (Ishpriya Maria b 2006); *Career* currently prop and ed-in-chief The Big Issue; pres Oxford Univ Homeless Action Gp; Eds' Ed of the Year Award 1994; advsr Sch for Social Entrepreneurs; ind candidate for Mayor of London 2008; pres Friends of 18th Century Soc; Hon Dr Oxford Brookes Univ 2001; fell Liverpool John Moores Univ; MInstD 1998; *Recreations* cycling, reading, writing, dancing, walking; *Style—* John Bird, Esq, MBE; ✉ The Big Issue, 1–5 Wandsworth Road, London SW8 2LN (tel 020 7526 3200, fax 020 7526 3261, e-mail john.bird@bigissue.com, website www.bigissue.com)

BIRD, Prof Colin Carmichael; CBE (2000); s of John G C Bird (ka Italy 1943), and Sarah, *née* Carmichael; *b* 5 March 1938; *Educ* Lenzie Acad, Univ of Glasgow (MB ChB, PhD); *m* 20 March 1964, Ailsa Mary, *née* Ross; 1 da (Elayne b 10 Jan 1965), 2 s (Scott b 4 May 1966, Alan b 7 Dec 1971); *Career* lectr in pathology: Univ of Glasgow 1965–67 (McGhie cancer research fell 1963–65), Univ of Aberdeen 1967–72; MRC (Goldsmith's) travelling fell Univ of Chicago 1970–71; sr lectr in pathology Univ of Edinburgh 1972–75, prof and head Dept of Pathology Univ of Leeds 1975–86; Univ of Edinburgh: prof and head Dept of Pathology 1986–95, provost Faculty of Med and Veterinary Med 1995–2002, dean Faculty of Med 1995–2002; author of approx 200 pubns in various scientific jls on cancer and cancer genetics; memb: Pathological Soc of GB and I 1964, Assoc of Clinical Pathologists 1976 (hon fell 2001); Dr (hc) Univ of Edinburgh 2004; FRCPath 1978, FRCPEd 1989, FRSE 1992, FRCSEd 1995, FAMS 1998; *Recreations* golf, walking, reading and music; *Clubs* New (Edinburgh), various golf clubs; *Style—* Prof Colin C Bird, CBE, FRSE; ✉ 45 Ann Street, Edinburgh EH4 1PL (tel 0131 332 5568, e-mail colin@colincbird.com)

BIRD, Harold Dennis (Dickie); MBE (1986); s of James Harold Bird (d 1969), and Ethel, *née* Smith (d 1978); *b* 19 April 1933; *Educ* Raley Sch Barnsley; *Career* cricket umpire, ret 1998; umpired in four World Cups, only man to umpire 3 World Cup finals (WI v Aust Lord's 1975, WI v England Lord's 1979, WI v India Lord's 1983); other major matches umpired incl: World Cup India 1987, Queen's Silver Jubilee Test Match (England v Aust Lord's 1977), Centenary Test Match (England v Aust Lord's 1980), Bi-centenary Test Match (MCC v Rest of World Lord's 1987); only umpire of both men's and women's World Cup Finals (women's World Cup NZ 1982), umpire of 68 test matches and 92 one-day internationals (world record) and many other cricketing events (incl Gillette, Nat West, Benson and Hedges and Refuge Assurance Cup Finals, int tournaments Sharjah (EAE), Best Batsman in the World, World Double Wicket and Best All-Rounder in the World competitions), umpire of 159 int matches (world record); other matches umpired incl: Ashia Cup in Sri Lanka 1984, ind umpire Zimbabwe v India and NZ 1992, ind umpire test series WI v Pakistan 1993, test series Zimbabwe v NZ 1993, test series NZ v Pakistan 1994, test match Pakistan v Aust 1994, 60th diamond test match Pakistan v Aust Karachi 1994, test match India v WI 1994, test series Aust v Pakistan 1996; ret as test umpire 1996; qualified MCC advanced cricket coach, former player Yorkshire and Leicestershire CCCs; declined: Kerry Packer's breakaway league World Series Cricket 1977, rebel tour to SA 1980s; hon life memb Yorkshire CCC and Leicestershire CCC; subject of BBC documentary 1996; appeared on TV programmes incl: This Is Your Life, Through The Keyhole, Breakfast with Frost, Desert Island Discs, Songs of Praise, Clive James Show, Clive Anderson Show, A Question of Sport, Grandstand, News Night, They Think It's All Over; fndr Dickie Bird Fndn 2004; Freeman Borough of Barnsley 2000; Hon Dr Sheffield Hallam Univ 1996, Hon LLD Univ of Leeds 1997; *Awards* Yorkshire Personality of the Year 1977, Rose Bowl Barnsley Cncl (for 100th int match) 1988, Variety Club of GB Yorkshire Award 1988, Nat Grid Award to commemorate world record 49th Test Zimbabwe v NZ 1992, Yorkshireman of the Year 1996, People of the Year Award 1996, Variety Club of GB Special Award 1997, Cricket Writers Award for Outstanding Service to Cricket 1997, Lifelong Achievement Award 1998, Special Merit Award Professional Cricketers Assoc 1998, Services to Cricket Yorkshire CC 1998, Services to Warwickshire CC 1998, 25 Years of Service TCCB, 30 Years of Service ECB, Anglo American Sporting Club award, Barnsley Millennium Award of Merit 2000, Commemorative Clock Headingley 2002; *Books* Not Out (1978), That's Out (1985), From The Pavillion End (1988), Dickie Bird My Autobiography (1997, best selling sports autobiography in history), White Cap and Bails (1999), Dickie Bird's Britain (2002); *Clubs* Lord's Taverners, MCC, Cambridge Univ Cricket, Yorkshire CCC, Leicestershire CCC, Barnsley FC; *Style—* Dickie Bird, Esq, MBE; ✉ White Rose Cottage, 40 Paddock Road, Staincross, Barnsley, South Yorkshire S75 6LE (tel 01226 384491); England and Wales Cricket Board, Lord's Cricket Ground, London NW8 8QN (tel 020 7286 4405)

BIRD, John; *b* 22 November 1936, Nottingham; *Educ* High Pavement GS Nottingham, King's Coll Cambridge; *Career* comedian and writer; sometime assoc artistic dir Royal Court Theatre; BAFTA Best Light Entertainment Performance 1966; hon degree Univ of Nottingham 2002; *Television* as writer incl: That Was The Week That Was 1962, The Late Show 1966; as writer and performer incl: A Series of Bird's 1967, With Bird Will Travel 1968, After That, This 1975, Pleasure At Her Majesty's 1976, Rory Bremner 1989, Rory Bremner...Who Else? 1993, Bremner, Bird and Fortune: Three Men And A Vote 1997, Bremner, Bird and Fortune: Between Iraq and a Hard Place 2003, Bremner, Bird and Fortune: Trust Me, I'm a Prime Minister 2004, Bremner, Bird and Fortune (series) 2005–07; as performer: Private Eye TV 1971, El Cid 1990–93, Chambers 2000, Absolute Power 2004–05; *Style—* John Bird, Esq; ✉ c/o Chatto & Linnit, 123A Kings Road, London SW3 4PL (tel 020 7352 7722, fax 020 7352 3450)

BIRD, Michael George; OBE (2000); s of George Bird, and Margaret, *née* Stephens; *b* 5 January 1960; *Educ* Bedales (scholar), Emmanuel Coll Cambridge (senior scholar, MA), Voronezh Univ (British Cncl scholar), Harvard Univ (Kennedy scholar); *m* 12 April 2003, Simone Lees; *Career* British Council: London 1985–87, Moscow 1987–91, UK Research and HE Liaison Office Brussels 1991–93, regional dir St Petersburg and North-West Russia 1993–97, dir Ukraine 1997–2001, dir Scotland 2001–05, dir Germany 2005–; *Style—* Michael Bird, Esq, OBE; ✉ British Council, Hackescher Markt 1, 10178 Berlin, Germany (e-mail michael.bird@britishcouncil.de)

BIRD, Richard; s of Desmond Bird, and Betty, *née* Brookman; *b* 12 February 1950; *Educ* King's Sch Canterbury, Magdalen Coll Oxford (MA, represented Britain at fencing); *m* July 1973, Penelope Anne, da of Dennis and Joan Frudd; 1 s (Martin b Sept 1977), 1 da (Eleanor b Feb 1980); *Career* DOE: admin trainee 1971–73, asst private sec to Min of Planning and Local Govt 1974–75; Dept of Tport: princ 1975–78, first sec UK Perm Representation to EC Brussels 1978–82, princ private sec to Sec of State for Tport 1982–83, asst sec 1983–90, under sec and head of Road Safety Directorate 1990–92; under sec Cabinet Office 1992–94, dir of personnel Dept of Tport 1994–97, dir of integrated and local tport DETR 1997–2001, dir of environment quality and waste DEFRA 2001–03, dir Water DEFRA 2003–; *Recreations* choral singing, summer sports; *Style—* Richard Bird, Esq

BIRD, Sir Richard Geoffrey Chapman; 4 Bt (UK 1922), of Solihull, Co Warwick; s of Sir Donald Geoffrey Bird, 3 Bt (d 1963); *b* 3 November 1935; *Educ* Beaumont; *m* 1, 1957, Gillian Frances (d 1966), da of Bernard Haggett, of Solihull; 4 da (Cecilia Mary b 1957, Frances Bernadette b 1959, Brigitte Ann b 1960, Rowena Clare b 1962), 2 s (John Andrew b 1964, Mark Richard b 1965); m 2, 1968, Helen Patricia, o da of Frank Beaumont, of Pontefract; 2 da (Catherine Veronica b 1970, Denise Helen b 1972); *Heir* s, John Bird; *Style—* Sir Richard Bird, Bt; ✉ 20 Milcote Road, Solihull B91 1JN

BIRD, Prof Richard Simpson; s of John William Bird (d 1990), and Martha, *née* Solar; *b* 13 February 1943; *Educ* St Olave's GS, Gonville & Caius Coll Cambridge (MA), Inst of Computer Science Univ of London (MSc, PhD); *m* 26 August 1967, Norma Christine, da of Percy Lapworth; *Career* lectr in computer science Univ of Reading 1972–83; Univ of Oxford: lectr in computer science 1983–88, reader in computation 1988–96, prof of computation 1996–, dir computing lab 1998–2003; fell Lincoln Coll Oxford 1988–; *Books* Programs and Machines (1977), Introduction to Functional Programming (1988, 2 edn 1997), Algebra of Programming (1996); *Recreations* jogging, bridge; *Style—* Prof Richard Bird; ✉ Stocks, Chapel Lane, Blewbury, Oxfordshire OX11 9PQ (tel 01235 850258); Lincoln College, Oxford OX1 3DR (tel 01865 273840, e-mail bird@comlab.ox.ac.uk)

BIRD, (Irene) Veronica; OBE (2002); da of late George Bird, and late Ethel, *née* Goodlad; *Educ* Ackworth Sch Pontefract; *Career* prison offr HMP Holloway and HMP Pucklechurch 1968–73, princ offr HMP Styal 1973–78, chief offr HMP Risley 1978–82; dep govr: HMP Styal 1982–87, HMP Thorn Cross 1987–91, HMP Armley 1991–94; controller HMP Buckley Hall 1994–98; govr: HMP Brock Hill 1998–2000, HMP New Hall 2000–; Butler Tst: fundraiser, volunteer co-ordinator, winner Butler Tst Award 2000; tstee Shannon Tst; memb Prison Govrs Assoc 1982; *Recreations* gardening, swimming, interior design, photography, travel; *Clubs* Westminster Dining; *Style—* Miss Veronica Bird, OBE; ✉ 100 Cornwall Road, Harrogate, North Yorkshire HG1 2NG (tel 01423 569316)

BIRDWOOD, 3 Baron (UK 1938), of Anzac and of Totnes, Devon; Sir Mark William Ogilvie Birdwood; 3 Bt (UK 1919); s of 2 Baron, MVO (d 1962), and (Elizabeth) Vere Drummond, CVO (d 1997), da of Lt-Col Sir George Drummond Ogilvie, KCIE, CSI; *b* 23 November 1938; *Educ* Radley, Trinity Coll Cambridge; *m* 27 April 1963, Judith Helen, er da of Reginald Gordon Seymour Roberts; 1 da (Sophie); *Career* former 2 Lt RHG; chm: Martlet Ltd 1986–, Fiortho Ltd 1992–2002, Steeltower Ltd; dir: IMS plc 1997–2000, The Character Group plc 1997–, Jasmin plc 1998–2000; memb House of Lords Select Ctee on Sci and Technol 1999–2000; res assoc Centre for Philosophy of Natural and Social Sci; memb Terra Consilia (Terra Firma Capital Partners strategy cncl); Liveryman Worshipful Co of Glaziers & Painters of Glass; *Clubs* Brooks's; *Style—* The Rt Hon the Lord Birdwood; ✉ Russell House, Broadway, Worcestershire WR12 7BU; 5 Holbein Mews, London SW1W 8NW

BIRKBECK, John Oliver Charles; yr s of Lt-Col Oliver Birkbeck (d 1952), and Lady (Mary) Joan Wilhelmina Cator, *née* Fitzclarence, sis of 5 Earl of Munster, direct descendent ofWilliam IV and the actress Dorothy Jordan; *b* 22 June 1936; *Educ* Gordonstoun, RAC Cirencester; *m* 2 May 1964, Hermione Anne, o da of Maj D'Arcy Dawes (d 1967), of Leacon Hall, Warehorne, Ashford, Kent; 2 da (Lucy Claire (Mrs Leitaõ) b 1966, Rosanna Mary (Mrs Tremayne) b 1974), 1 s (Oliver Benjamin b 1973); *Career* chm: Breckland Dist Cncl 1987–88 (memb 1969–95), Norfolk County Cncl 1989 (memb 1970–93 and 1997–2001, chm Planning Ctee), Norfolk Historic Buildings Tst 1987–, Norfolk Windmills Tst 1988–2002, Norfolk Churches Tst 1992–95 (vice-chm 1990–92); Norfolk rep Tennants of Yorkshire Auctioneers, church warden Litcham All Saints 1980–; pres: Norfolk Club 1998–99, Mid Norfolk Cons Assoc 2002–; High Sheriff Co of Norfolk 1995; patron of the living of Kempstone; *Recreations* shooting, gardening, looking at old buildings; *Clubs* Norfolk (Norwich), All Sorts; *Style—* John Birkbeck, Esq; ✉ Litcham Hall, King's Lynn, Norfolk PE32 2QQ (tel 01328 701389, fax 01328 701164)

BIRKBY, Roger; s of John Robert Howarth Birkby (d 1978), and Vera Mary, *née* Hirst; *b* 21 November 1945; *Educ* Bradford GS, Christ's Coll Cambridge (MA, LLB); *m* 1974, Wendy, *née* Godfree; 2 da (Miranda b 1985, Olivia b 1987); *Career* articled clerk Lovell White & King 1969–71; Norton Rose: joined 1971, ptnr 1976–, resident ptnr Bahrain office 1982–84, Hong Kong office 1985–88, managing ptnr 1994–2002; memb City of London Slrs' Co; memb: Law Soc, Int Bar Assoc; *Recreations* golf, tennis, walking, music; *Style—* Roger Birkby, Esq; ✉ Norton Rose, Kempson House, Camomile Street, London EC3A 7AN (tel 020 7283 6000, fax 020 7283 6500, e-mail roger.birkby@nortonrose.com)

BIRKENHEAD, Brian; *Career* fin dir Shell UK Oil 1983–87, fin dir Johnson Matthey plc 1987–89; National Power plc: joined National Power Div CEGB 1989, gp fin dir National Power plc until 1996; non-exec dir: De La Rue plc 1994–2000, ITnet plc 1998–, Oil Tools International Ltd 1998–2000, API Gp plc 2006–; chm 100 Gp of Finance Dirs 1995–97 (dep chm 1997–98), tstee BT Pension Scheme 1998–; *Style—* Brian Birkenhead, Esq; ✉ 14 President's Quay, St Katharine's Way, London E1W 1UF (tel 020 7480 5668, e-mail brian.birkenhead@which.net)

BIRKENHEAD, Bishop of 2007–; Rt Rev (Gordon) Keith Sinclair; s of Donald Sinclair (d 1975), and Joyce, *née* Ellis; *b* 3 December 1952, Westminster; *Educ* ChCh Oxford (MA), St John's Coll and Cranmer Hall Univ of Durham (BA); *m* 6 May 1989, Rosemary, *née* Jones; 2 s (Peter b 10 June 1992, David b 6 Sept 1996), 1 da (Anna b 14 Sept 1993); *Career* admitted slr 1979; ordained church min 1984; formerly vicar: Birmingham, Coventry; chair Govt Interim Partnership Bd New Deal for Communities Aston; *Style—* The Rt Rev the Bishop of Birkenhead; ✉ Bishop's Lodge, 67 Bidston Road, Prenton, Wirral, Merseyside CH43 6TR (tel 0151 652 2741, fax 0151 651 2330, e-mail bpbirkenhead@chester.anglican.org)

BIRKETT, Aidan; *b* 22 February 1953; *Educ* St Cuthbert's GS Newcastle upon Tyne; *m* Maureen; 2 c (Alex, Thomas); *Career* global head of business recovery servs PricewaterhouseCoopers until 2001, currently managing ptnr corporate finance and memb Exec Ctee Deloitte; Professional of the Year Soc of Turnaround Professionals 2002; ACA 1977, ACT 1980; *Recreations* food, drink, music, opera, travel, motor cars; *Style—* Aidan Birkett, Esq; ✉ Deloitte & Touche LLP, Athene Place, 66 Shoe Lane, London EC4A 3BQ

BIRKETT, 2 Baron (UK 1958); Michael Birkett; s of 1 Baron Birkett (d 1962); *b* 22 October 1929; *Educ* Stowe, Trinity Coll Cambridge; *m* 1978, Gloria (d 2001), da of Thomas Taylor, of Queen's Gate, London; 1 s (Hon Thomas b 25 July 1982); *Heir* s, Hon Thomas Birkett; *Career* film prodr 1961–; prodns incl: The Caretaker, Marat/Sade, A Midsummer Night's Dream, King Lear; dep dir Nat Theatre 1975–77, conslt to Nat Theatre on films, TV and sponsorship 1977–79, dir Recreation and the Arts GLC 1979–86; govr BRIT Sch for Performing Arts and Technol Croydon 1980–; chm Donatella Flick Conducting Competition; Master Worshipful Co of Curriers' 1975–76; *Recreations* the arts; *Style—* The Rt Hon the Lord Birkett; ✉ Great Allfields, Balls Cross, Petworth, West Sussex GU28 9JR (tel 01403 820226)

BIRKETT, Peter Vidler; QC (1989); s of Neville Lawn Birkett, JP, of Kendal, Cumbria, and Marjorie Joy, *née* Vidler; *b* 13 July 1948; *Educ* Sedbergh, Univ of Leicester (LLB); *m* 11 Dec 1976, Jane Elizabeth, da of Robert Hall Fell, MBE (d 1981); 2 s (Nicholas Robert b 12 Dec 1984, Michael Peter Vidler b 20 Dec 1986); *Career* called to the Bar Inner Temple 1972 (bencher 1996); barr N Circuit 1972–, recorder of the Crown Court 1989–, leader N Circuit 1999–2001; actg deemster IOM; memb Gen Cncl of the Bar; *Recreations* golf, skiing, music; *Clubs* Wilmslow Golf; *Style—* Peter Birkett, Esq, QC; ✉ 18 St John Street, Manchester M3 4EA (tel 0161 278 1800)

BIRKHEAD, Prof Timothy Robert; s of Robert Harold Birkhead, and Nancy Olga, *née* Thomson; *b* 20 February 1950, Leeds; *Educ* Univ of Newcastle upon Tyne (BSc), Wolfson Coll Oxford (DPhil); *m* 25 Sept 1976, Miriam Enid, *née* Appleton; 3 c; *Career* Dept of Animal and Plant Sciences Univ of Sheffield: lectr 1976–86, sr lectr 1986–89, reader 1989–92, prof of behavioural ecology 1992–; pres Int Soc for Behavioural Ecology 1996–98; Nuffield research fell 1990–91, Leverhulme research fell 1995–96; Hon DSc Univ of Newcastle upon Tyne 1989; FRS 2004; *Books* Avian Ecology (with C M Perrins, 1983),

The Atlantic Alcidae (ed with D N Nettleship, 1985), The Survival Factor (with M E Birkhead, 1989), The Magpies (1991), The Cambridge Encyclopedia of Ornithology (1991, McColvin Medal), Sperm Competition in Birds (1992), Great Auk Islands (1993), Sperm Competition and Sexual Selection (1998), Promiscuity (2000), The Red Canary (2003, Consul Cremer Prize); author of articles in pubns incl Nature and Science; *Recreations* art, music, walking; *Style—* Prof Timothy Birkhead; ✉ Department of Animal and Plant Sciences, University of Sheffield, Western Bank, Sheffield S10 2TN (tel 0114 222 4622, fax 0114 222 0002, e-mail t.r.birkhead@sheffield.ac.uk)

BIRKIN, Sir John Christian William; 6 Bt (UK 1905), of Ruddington Grange, Ruddington, Notts; o s of Sir Charles Lloyd Birkin, 5 Bt (d 1985), and Janet Ramsay, *née* Johnson; *b* 2 July 1953; *Educ* Eton, Trinity Coll Dublin, London Film Sch; *m* 25 June 1994, Emma Louise, da of Roger Leonard Gage, of Aveton Gifford, S Devon; 1 s (Benjamin Charles b 4 Nov 1995), 1 da (Daisy Burda b 17 Dec 2000); *Heir* s, Benjamin Birkin; *Career* freelance dir of television commercials, dir Compound Eye Productions Ltd; *Style—* Sir John Birkin, Bt

BIRLEY, Prof Susan Joyce (Sue); *Educ* UCL (BSc), Harvard Univ (Int Teachers Prog scholar), Univ of London (PhD); *Career* advanced and scholarship mathematics teacher Dunsmore Sch 1964–66, lectr in quantitative aspects Dept of Economics and Mgmnt Lanchester Poly 1966–68, sr lectr in business policy Mgmnt Sch Poly of Central London 1970–72 (lectr in quantitative methods 1968–70), sr research fell City Univ 1972–74; London Business Sch: lectr in small business 1974–79, sr research fell Inst of Small Business 1979–82, dir New Enterprise Prog 1979–82; assoc prof of strategy and entrepreneurship Coll of Business Univ of Notre Dame USA 1982–85 (adjunct assoc prof 1978–82), Philip & Pauline Harris prof of entrepreneurship Cranfield Sch of Mgmnt Cranfield Inst of Technology 1985–90 (also dir of research and dir Cranfield Entrepreneurship Research Centre), dir of research and prof of mgmnt in the field of entrepreneurship Mgmnt Sch ICSTM 1990–2003; visiting prof INSEAD 1991 (visiting lectr 1978); fndr dir: The Guidehouse Group plc 1980–85, Greyfriars Ltd 1982–85, Newchurch & Co (chm) 1986–97; non-exec dir: National Westminster Bank plc 1996–2000, PSE Ltd 1997–2003, BAE Systems plc 2000–; advsr Dept of Econ Devpt NI 1985–88, academic dir Euro Fndn for Entrepreneurship Research 1988–90, vice-chm Exec Ctee Br Acad of Mgmnt 1988–89, govr Harris City Technol Coll 1990–92, bd memb Local Enterprise Devpt Unit (LEDU) N Ireland 1991–93 (advsr 1988–89), currently conslt advsr Grant Thornton; memb: Postgrad Bd CNAA 1979–82, Steering Ctee UK Nat Small Firms Policy and Research Conf 1985–90, Adjudication Ctee Prince of Wales' Award for Innovation 1986–, Bd of Dirs Strategic Mgmnt Soc 1987–90, Cncl NI Econ Cncl 1988–94, Deregulation Advsy Bd DTI 1988–90, Polytechnics and Colls Funding Cncl 1988–93, E European Links Advsy Bd British Cncl 1990–91, Advsy Cncl Sheffield Business Sch 1990–93, Growing Business Target Team Business in the Community 1990–91, Enterprise and Econ Devpt Leadership Team Business in the Community 1992–93, Technology Foresight Steering Gp 1998–; Conf of Teachers of Mgmnt 1986 (also chm), Tenth UK Nat Small Firms Policy and Res Conf 1987, Annual Global Conf on Entrepreneurship Research (jtly) 1990–; author of numerous jl articles, conf papers, reports, case studies and books; Freeman City of London; *Books* The Small Business Casebook (1979), New Enterprises (1982), The British Entrepreneur (jtly, 1990), Building European Ventures (ed, 1990), Mastering Enterprise (1997), Franchising: Pathway to Wealth Creation (2003); *Style—* Prof Sue Birley; ✉ The Mill House, Benham Park, Marsh Benham, Newbury, Berkshire RG20 8LX

BIRMINGHAM, Archdeacon of; *see:* Osborne, Ven Hayward

BIRMINGHAM, Archbishop of Birmingham (RC) 2000–; Most Rev Vincent Gerard Nichols; s of Henry Joseph Nichols, and Mary Nichols, *née* Russell; *b* 8 November 1945; *Educ* St Mary's Coll Crosby, Gregorian Univ Rome (STL, PhL), Univ of Manchester (MA), Loyola Univ Chicago (MEd); *Career* chaplain St John Rigby VI Form Coll Wigan 1972–77, priest in the inner city of Liverpool 1978–81, dir of Upholland Northern Inst (with responsibility for the in-service training of clergy and for adult Christian educn 1981–84); advsr Cardinal Hume and Archbishop Worlock at the Int Synods of Bishops 1980, 1983, 1987 and 1991, gen sec Bishops' Conf of England and Wales 1984–92, Catholic bishop in North London 1992–2000; del: Synod of Bishops 1994, Synod of European Bishops 1999; *Publications* Promise of Future Glory: Reflections on the Mass (1997), Missioners: Priests and people today (2007); *Style—* The Most Rev Archbishop of Birmingham; ✉ Archbishop's House, 8 Shadwell Street, Birmingham B4 6EY (tel 0121 236 9090, fax 0121 212 0171, e-mail archbishop@rc-birmingham.org)

BIRO, Val Bálint Stephen; s of Dr Bálint Biro (d 1944), and Margaret, *née* Gyulahazi (d 1982); *b* 6 October 1921, Hungary; *Educ* Cistercian Sch Budapest, Central Sch of Art and Design London; *m* 1, 1945 (m dis), Vivien, da of R V G Woolley; 1 da (Melissa b 1951); m 2, 1970, Marie-Louise Ellaway, da of P Christofas; 1 step s (Philip b 1956), 1 step da (Caroline b 1961); *Career* author and illustrator; memb NFS London 1942–45, studio mangr Sylvan Press London 1944–46, prodn mangr C & J Temple London 1946–48, art dir John Lehmann Ltd London 1948–53; designer of 4000 book jackets 1945–95; contrib weekly illustrations Radio Times 1951–72; cncllr Chesham UDC 1966–70, memb/chm governing bodies Amersham Coll of Art & Design 1974–84, vice-chm Bosham Assoc 1989–91; primary sch visitor as artist and storyteller 1970–; named among Top Hundred Authors in list from PLR 1990; memb Soc of Authors; *Books* author and illustrator of numerous children's books incl: series of 36 Gumdrop books (about his vintage car) 1965–2001, Hungarian Folktales (1981), The Magic Doctor (1982), The Hobyahs (1985), Tobias and the Dragon (1989), Look-and-Find ABC (1990), Miranda's Umbrella (1990), Rub-a-Dub-Dub Nursery Ryhmes (1991), Three Billy Goats Gruff (1993), Jasper's Jungle Journey (1995), Lazy Jack (1995), Bears Can't Fly (1996), Hansel and Gretel (1996), Goldilocks and the Three Bears (1998), Little Red Riding Hood (1999), The Joking Wolf (2001), Hans Christian Andersen's Fairy Tales (2005), Treasury of Aesop's Fables (2007), Grimm's Fairy Tales (2008); illustrator of over 400 books incl: Worlds Without End (Denys Val Baker, 1945), The Prisoner of Zenda (Anthony Hope, 1961), Wizard of Oz books (L Frank Baum, 1965–67), One Man's Happiness (Lord Tweedsmuir, 1968), The Good Food Guide (1971), The Robert Carrier Cookery Course (1974), The Wind in the Willows (Kenneth Grahame, 1983), The King's Jokes (Margaret Mahy, 1987), When I Was Your Age (Ken Adams, 1991), What's Up The Coconut Tree? (A H Benjamin, 1991), The Show-off Mouse (A H Benjamin, 1993), My Oxford Picture Word Book (OUP, 1994), The Dinosaur's Egg (Christina Butler, 1994), The Flying Boot Reading Scheme (Prof Ted Wragg, 1994/95), The Landleagers (Trollope, 1995), The Father Brown Stories (2 Vols, Chesterton, 1996), The Dinosaur's Dinner (Christina Butler, 1997), Carole's Camel (Michael Hardcastle, 1997), Jennings Sounds the Alarm (Anthony Buckeridge, 1999), Jennings Breaks the Record (Anthony Buckeridge, 2000), Jennings Joins the Search Party (Anthony Buckeridge, 2001), Introducing Rex Milligan (Anthony Buckeridge, 2002), Jamaica Primary Curriculum (2004–06); *Exhibitions* Pallant House Chichester 2000, Bath Literature Festival 2003, Ashmolean Museum Oxford 2003, Chris Beetles London 2004, Petworth House Sussex 2004, Uppark House Sussex 2005; *Recreations* vintage car motoring; *Clubs* Vintage Sports Car, Vintage Austin Register; *Style—* Val Biro, Esq; ✉ Bridge Cottage, Brook Avenue, Bosham, West Sussex PO18 8LQ (tel 01243 574195)

BIRRELL, Christopher Ros Stewart; *b* 11 March 1954; *Educ* Radley, Mansfield Coll Oxford (MA); *m* 1984, Georgie; 2 s (Edward b 31 January 1987, Henry b 23 January 1989), 1 da (Claudia b 13 September 1991); *Career* with: Price Waterhouse 1977–82, Matheson & Co Ltd 1982–83, Henderson Admin Ltd 1983–85; gp fin dir SBJ Gp Ltd 1993– (joined 1985); memb: ICAEW 1981–, ACT 1993–; *Recreations* sailing, shooting, fishing, golf, opera; *Clubs* Buck's, City of London; *Style—* Christopher Birrell, Esq; ✉ 25 Turret Grove, London SW4 0ES; SBJ Group Ltd, One Hundred Whitechapel, London E1 1JG (tel 020 7816 2000, fax 020 7816 2247)

BIRRELL, Ian; s of Norman Alistair Birrell, of Sussex, and Patricia Ann, *née* Foll; *b* 30 January 1962; *Educ* Ampleforth, Univ of Aberdeen (MA), City Univ (Dip Journalism); *m* 1990, Linnet, *née* MacIntyre; 1 s (Hamish b 10 Sept 1991), 1 da (Iona b 16 Oct 1993); *Career* Wolverhampton Express & Star 1985–86, Hampstead & Highgate Express 1987–88; Sunday Times 1988–95: news ed, managing ed News Review; dep ed Sunday Express 1996, exec ed Daily Mail 1996–98, dep ed The Independent 1998–; *Recreations* Everton FC, diving, munro-bagging, guitar; *Style—* Ian Birrell, Esq; ✉ The Independent, Independent House, 191 Marsh Wall, London E14 9RS (tel 020 7005 2401, fax 020 7005 2022, e-mail i.birrell@independent.co.uk)

BIRSE, Peter Malcolm; s of Peter Alexander McCauley Birse, of 7 MacKenzie St, Carnoustie, Scotland, and Margaret Cumming, *née* Craib; *b* 24 November 1942; *Educ* Arbroath HS, Univ of St Andrews (BSc); *m* 25 Jan 1969, Helen, da of Paul Stanley Searle, of Bishopston, Bristol; 2 s (James Peter Alexander b 1971, Robert Archibald b 1975), 1 da (Bridget b 1969); *Career* engr John Mowlem Ltd 1963–65, engr and project mangr Gammon Ghana Ltd 1965–67, contract mangr Gammon (UK) Ltd 1967–70, established Birse Gp plc (construction gp) 1970 (currently non-exec chm); chm Peter Birse Charitable Tst; MICE 1971; *Recreations* sailing, skiing, tennis, golf, fishing; *Clubs* Royal Ocean Racing; *Style—* Peter Birse, Esq

BIRSS, Colin Ian; s of Dr Ian Birss, and Davina, *née* Carson; *b* 28 December 1964, Thurso, Caithness; *Educ* Largs Acad, Lancaster Royal GS, Downing Coll Cambridge (MA, exhibitioner), City Univ London (Dip); *m* 1 Aug 1987, Kate, *née* Squibbs; 2 s (Arnot b 27 March 1993, Ned b 27 Dec 1994), 1 da (Dorothea b 31 May 2001); *Career* called to the Bar Middle Temple 1990 (Stanley Levy Prize 1990); UKAEA 1983, Arthur Andersen & Co 1986–88, memb Chambers of Antony Watson, QC (formerly of David Young, QC) 1990–, standing counsel to the Comptroller Gen for Patents Designs and Trade Marks 2004–; *Books* Terrell on the Law of Patents (15th edn 2000, 16th edn 2006); *Recreations* beekeeping; *Style—* Colin Birss, Esq; ✉ 3 New Square, Lincoln's Inn, London WC2A 3RS (tel 020 7405 1111, fax 020 7405 7800, e-mail birss@3newsquare.co.uk)

BIRT, Baron (Life Peer UK 2000), of Liverpool in the County of Merseyside; Sir John Birt; kt (1998); s of Leo Vincent Birt, of Richmond, Surrey, and Ida Birt; *b* 10 December 1944; *Educ* St Mary's Coll Liverpool, St Catherine's Coll Oxford (MA); *m* 14 Sept 1965, Jane Frances, da of James Harris Lake (d 1982, 2 Lt US Navy), of Chevy Chase, Maryland, USA; 1 s (Jonathan b 1968), 1 da (Eliza b 1971); *Career* prodr Nice Time 1968–69, jt ed World in Action 1969–70, prodr The Frost Programme 1971–72, exec prodr Weekend World 1972–74, head of current affairs LWT 1974–77, co-prodr The Nixon Interviews 1977, controller of features and current affairs LWT 1977–81, dir of programmes LWT 1982–87; BBC: dep DG 1987–92, DG 1992–2000; advsr to the PM on Criminal Justice 2000–01, strategy advsr to the PM 2001–05, with Terra Firma 2005–, chm Waste Recycling Gp 2006–; memb: Wilton Park Academic Cncl 1980–83, Media Law Gp 1983–94, Working Pty on the New Technols Broadcasting Research Unit 1981–83 (memb Exec Ctee 1983–87), Opportunity 2000 Target Team 1991–98; visiting fell Nuffield Coll Oxford 1991–99; hon fell St Catherine's Coll Oxford; Hon Doctorate Liverpool John Moores Univ; winner Emmy (for outstanding contrib to int TV) Nov 1995; FRTS (vice-pres 1994–2000); *Style—* The Rt Hon the Lord Birt; ✉ House of Lords, London SW1A 0PW

BIRTLES, His Hon Judge William; s of William George Birtles (d 1976), of Shepperton, Middx, and Dorothy Louisa, *née* Martin (d 1999); *b* 27 October 1944; *Educ* Shene Co GS for Boys, KCL (LLB, AKC, LLM), Harvard Law Sch (Kennedy scholar, LLM), NYU Law Sch; *m* 17 Dec 1981, Rt Hon Patricia Hewitt, MP, *qv*, da of Sir (Cyrus) Lenox Simson Hewitt, OBE, of Sydney, Aust; 1 da (Alexandra Catherine b 1986), 1 s (Nicholas Adam b 1988); *Career* called to the Bar: Gray's Inn 1970, Lincoln's Inn 1986, NI 1998; lectr in law KCL 1968–70, Robert Marshall fell NYU Law Sch 1971–72, lectr in law UCL 1972–74, practising barr 1974–2002, circuit judge (SE Circuit) 2002–; sr assoc memb St Antony's Coll Oxford 1995– (midcareer fell 1992–93); *Publications* Planning and Environmental Law (jtly, 1994), Local Government Finance Law (jtly, 2000), Liability for Environmental Harm (jtly, 2004); *Recreations* opera, classical music, collecting travel books, international relations; *Clubs* New Parks Social; *Style—* His Hon Judge Birtles; ✉ The Mayor's and City of London Court, Guildhall Buildings, Basinghall Street, London EC2V 5AR

BIRTS, His Hon Judge Peter William; QC (1990), QC (NI 1996); s of John Claude Birts (d 1969), of Sussex, and Audrey Lavinia, *née* McIntyre; *b* 9 February 1946; *Educ* Lancing, St John's Coll Cambridge (choral scholar, MA); *m* 1, 24 April 1971 (m dis), Penelope Ann, da of Wing Cdr Anthony Eyre, DFC (d 1946); 2 da (Melanie b 1972, Charlotte b 1975), 1 s (William b 1979); m 2, 3 Oct 1997, Angela Forcer-Evans, *née* Sivell; *Career* called to the Bar Gray's Inn 1968 (bencher 1998); recorder of the Crown Court 1989–2005, dep High Court judge 2000–05, circuit judge (SE Circuit) 2005–; memb: Bar Cncl 1990–95, Judicial Studies Bd 1991–96, County Court Rule Ctee 1991–98; chm Bar Cncl Legal Aid and Fees Ctee 1994–95; asst cmmr Parly Boundary Cmmn for England 1992–2005, legal memb Mental Health Review Tbnls 1994–, legal memb Parole Bd 2006–; govr Benenden Sch 1990–93; Freeman of City of London 1967, Liveryman Worshipful Co of Carpenters 1967; *Books* Trespass: Summary Procedure for Possession of Land (with Alan Willis, 1987), Remedies for Trespass (1990); author of articles on trespass and countryside law; contrib and ed Butterworths Costs Service (2000–); *Recreations* music, shooting, fishing, tennis, walking; *Clubs* Hurlingham; *Style—* His Hon Judge Peter Birts, QC; ✉ Snaresbrook Crown Court, 75 Hollybush Hill, Snaresbrook, London E11 1QW (tel 020 8530 0000, e-mail peter.birts@virgin.net)

BIRTWISTLE, Adam; s of Sir Harrison Birtwistle, CH, *qv*, and Sheila Margaret Wilhelmina, *née* Duff; *b* 1 April 1959; *Educ* Chelsea Coll of Art; *Career* artist; first one-man show Piano Nobile Galleries London 1986; portrait cmmns incl: Sir Harrison Birtwistle, Sir Peter Blake, Richard Borchard, Alfred Brendel, Elvis Costello, Sir George and Lady Christie, Sir Peter Hall, Peter Harper, David Hockney, Sir Michael Hopkins, Jeremy Irons, Sir Patrick Moore, Paul Myners, Dame Marjorie Scardino, David Sylvester, Sir Michael Tippett, Very Rev Archbishop Desmond Tutu; work displayed: Nat Portrait Gallery, Royal Acad of Music, Sadler's Wells, Glyndebourne, Denver Museum and Art Gallery USA; *Publications* Cocks and Faces: recent paintings by Adam Birtwistle (1994), Glyndebourne Programme Book (contrib, 2001), Birtwistle's Beasts: 20 Years of Painting (2006); *Style—* Adam Birtwistle, Esq; ✉ c/o Dr Robert Travers, Piano Nobile Fine Paintings, 129 Portland Road, London W11 4LW (tel and fax 020 7229 1099, e-mail art@paino-nobile.com)

BIRTWISTLE, Sir Harrison; CH (2001), kt (1988); s of Frederick Birtwistle (d 1985), and Margaret, *née* Harrison (d 1970); *b* 15 July 1934; *Educ* Royal Manchester Coll of Music, Royal Acad of Music London (LRAM); *m* 4 Jan 1958, Sheila Margaret Wilhelmina, da of George Duff (d 1986); 3 s (Adam Birtwistle, *qv*, b 1959, Silas b 1963, Thomas b 1965); *Career* composer; associate dir music Nat Theatre London 1976–88, Henry Purcell prof of composition King's Coll London 1995–2001, composer-in-residence LPO, dir of contemporary music Royal Acad of Music; visiting fell Princeton Univ USA 1968, visiting prof of music Swarthmore Coll Pennsylvania USA 1975, Slee visiting prof NY State Univ at Buffalo USA 1977, Harkness fell Univ of Colorado Boulder USA 1969; retrospective Secret Theatres South Bank Centre 1996; Hon FRMCM and ARMCM 1986, Hon FRAM, hon fell Akademie der Kunst Berlin; Chevalier de l'Ordre des Arts et des Lettres (France) 1986; *Works* incl: Secret Theatre (1965), Tragoedia (1965), Punch and Judy (first staged Aldeburgh Festival 1967), Meridian (1971), The Mask of Orpheus, Ritual Fragment, The Triumph of Time (1972), Earth Dances (1986), Gawain (1991), Antiphonies, Nomos, An Imaginary Landscape, The Second Mrs Kong (premiered Glyndebourne 1994), Panic (saxophone concerto premiered BBC Proms 1995), Slow Frieze (1996), Pulse Shadows (1997), Exody (1998), The Woman and the Hare (1999), The Axe Manual (2001), The Shadow of Night (2002), Thesus Game (2003), The Io Passion (2004), Night's Black Bird (2004), Orpheus Elegies (2005), Neruda Madrigales (2006), The Minotaur (2008); *Awards* Evening Standard Award for Opera 1986, Grawemeyer Award Univ Louisville Kentucky USA 1986, Royal Philharmonic Soc Award for large scale composition 1992 (for Gawain), Siemens Prize 1995; *Recreations* fishing, walking; *Style—* Sir Harrison Birtwistle, CH; ✉ c/o Allied Artists Agency, 42 Montpelier Square, London SW7 1JZ (tel 020 7589 6243, fax 020 7581 5269)

BIRTWISTLE, Sue Elizabeth; da of Frank Edgar Birtwistle (d 1987), and Brenda Mary, *née* Higham (d 1998); *m* 14 July 1973, Sir Richard Charles Hastings Eyre, CBE, *qv*, s of Cdr Richard Galfredus Hastings Giles Eyre; 1 da (Lucy b 25 Sept 1974); *Career* theatre dir: Royal Lyceum Theatre in Educn Co 1970–72, Nottingham Playhouse Roundabout Co 1973–78, freelance 1978–80; freelance TV prodr 1980–; work incl: Hotel du Lac (BBC, BAFTA Award 1987, ACE Award 1988), Scoop (LWT), 'v' (Channel 4, RTS Award), Or Shall We Die? (Channel 4), Dutch Girls (LWT), Ball-Trap on the Côte Sauvage (BBC), Anna Lee (LWT) 1993, Pride and Prejudice (BBC, 4 BAFTA nominations, 4 Emmy nominations, 2 ACE Award nominations, TRIC Award, VVL Award 1995/96, Peabody Award 1996, 2 BANFF Awards incl Victor Laudorum Prize, TV Critics of America Award, BVA Award, English Heritage Award) 1995, Emma (ITV) 1996, King Lear (BBC, Peabody Award 1999) 1998, Wives and Daughters (BBC, 3 British Press Guild Awards, 5 BAFTA Awards) 1999, Armadillo (BBC) 2001; memb Drama Panel Arts Cncl 1975–77; *Books* The Making of Pride and Prejudice (1995), The Making of Jane Austen's Emma (1996); *Recreations* the countryside, books, theatre, music, croquet; *Style—* Miss Sue Birtwistle; ✉ c/o Nick Marston, Curtis Brown, 4th Floor, Haymarket House, 28–29 Haymarket, London SW1Y 4SP (tel 020 7396 6600)

BISCHOFF, Sir Winfried Franz Wilhelm (Win); kt (2000); s of late Paul Helmut Bischoff, and Hildegard, *née* Kühne; *b* 10 May 1941; *Educ* Marist Bros Inanda Johannesburg, Univ of the Witwatersrand (BCom); *m* 1972, Rosemary Elizabeth, da of Hon Leslie Leathers; 2 s; *Career* md Schroders Asia Ltd Hong Kong 1971–82; J Henry Schroder & Co Ltd: dir 1978–, chm 1983–94; Schroders plc: dir 1983–, gp chief exec 1984–95, chm 1995–2000; chm Citigroup Europe 2000–; non-exec dir: Cable and Wireless plc 1991–2003 (dep chm 1995–2003), The McGraw-Hill Companies NY 1999–, Land Securities plc 1999–, IFIL Finanziaria di Partecipazioni SpA Italy 1999–2003, Eli Lilly and Co Indianapolis 2000–, Siemens Holdings plc 2001–04; DSc (hc) City Univ 2000; *Recreations* opera, music, golf; *Clubs* Frilford Heath Golf, Swinley Forest Golf, Woking Golf, Annabel's; *Style—* Sir Win Bischoff; ✉ Citigroup Centre, 33 Canada Square, London E14 5LB (tel 020 7986 2600)

BISCOE, Michael; s of Guy Biscoe (d 1967), of London, and Sheila Mary, *née* Seymour Chalk (d 2004); *b* 4 May 1938; *Educ* Westminster, Selwyn Coll Cambridge (MA, DipArch); *m* 28 Jan 1967, Kari Jetten (d 2007), da of late Edward Beresford Davies, MD, of Cambridge, and late Hendriette Marie, *née* Fuglesang; 1 da (Henrietta b 5 Jan 1968), 1 s (Guy b 14 May 1970); *Career* Nat Serv RA, served Cyprus 1956–58; sr ptnr Biscoe & Stanton 1977–97 (ptnr 1967–77), princ Biscoe Assocs 1997–; govr Colfe's Sch 1996– (vice-chm 1999–); Liveryman: Worshipful Co of Leathersellers 1972 (Master 2003), Worshipful Co of Chartered Surveyors 1975–2005; RIBA, FRICS; *Recreations* music, history of art and architecture, shooting, fishing; *Clubs* Chelsea Arts; *Style—* Michael Biscoe, Esq; ✉ Biscoe Associates, 68 Lombard Street, London EC3V 9LJ (tel 020 7861 9515, fax 020 7861 9516, e-mail mb@biscoe-associates.com)

BISH-JONES, Trevor Charles; *b* 23 April 1960; *Educ* Varndean GS Brighton, Portsmouth Sch of Pharmacy (BSc); *m* 8 Sept 1990, Amanda Jane, *née* Zeil; 2 da (Alexa Rose b 12 June 1995, Florence Rose b 8 May 1998); *Career* research chemist The Tosco Corp CO 1980–81; Boots plc: store mangr 1981–84, EPOS project mangr 1984–86, various buying and mktg positions (latterly buying and mktg controller) 1987–94; Dixons Stores Gp: mktg dir PC World and Dixons 1994–97, successively md The Link, Dixons then Currys 1997–2002; ceo Woolworths Gp plc 2002–; non-exec dir Royal London Gp 2005–; patron Macmillan Milton Keynes Appeal; govr Ashridge Mgmnt Coll; memb Mktg Soc 1997, CCMI 2002; *Recreations* riding, golf, travel, football; *Style—* Trevor Bish-Jones, Esq; ✉ Woolworths Group plc, Woolworth House, 242–246 Marylebone Road, London NW1 6JL (tel 020 7706 5503, fax 020 7224 8699, mobile 07765 220965, e-mail tbj@woolworthsgroupplc.co.uk)

BISHOP, Alan; *Educ* Univ of Oxford (MA History); *Career* Hobson Bates 1974–78, fndr ptnr Milton Sharam Gottlieb 1978–81, Foote Cone & Belding 1981–83, bd account dir and new business dir Ted Bates 1983–85; Saatchi & Saatchi: joined as bd dir 1985, gp account dir 1988–90, chief operating offr 1990–91, vice-chm 1991–94, regnl account dir Procter & Gamble Health & Beauty Care Europe and ME 1992–94, chief operating offr Saatchi & Saatchi North America Inc NY 1994–95, pres, chm and ceo Saatchi & Saatchi North America Inc NY 1995–97; chm: Saatchi & Saatchi London 1997–98, Saatchi & Saatchi International 1998–2002; chief exec COI 2002–; *Style—* Alan Bishop, Esq; ✉ Central Office of Information, Hercules House, Hercules Road, London SE1 7DU (tel 020 7261 8210)

BISHOP, Andrew Lawrence; s of Lawrence Bishop, of Bristol, and Maureen, *née* Williams; *b* 28 November 1965, Bristol; *Educ* St Brendan's Coll Bristol, Univ of Exeter (LLB); *m* 16 April 1994, Sarah, *née* Hellier; 3 da (Hannah, Megan, Lily); *Career* admitted slr 1989, slr advocate 1999; ptnr Bishop & Light Slrs 1995–; vice-chm Criminal Law Slrs Assoc 2005–; memb Law Soc 1989– (memb Mental Health Review Tbnl Panel 1996); *Recreations* sailing, football, running; *Style—* Andrew Bishop, Esq; ✉ 56 Bramble Gardens, Burgess Hill RH15 8UQ; Bishop & Light, Cambridge House, Cambridge Grove, Hove BN3 3ED (e-mail andrewbishop@bishopandlight.co.uk)

BISHOP, (Dr) Catherine Jane (Cath); da of Brian Reynold Bishop, and Jean Muriel, *née* Kellie; *b* 22 November 1971; *Educ* Westcliff HS for Girls, Pembroke Coll Cambridge (MA, Rowing blue), Univ of Wales Aberystwyth (MPhil), Univ of Reading (PhD); *Career* amateur rower; memb: Cambridge Univ Boat Club 1991–93 (incl varsity boat races 1991 and 1993), Marlow Rowing Club (hon life memb), GB squad 1995–2004; achievements incl: Bronze medal England eights Cwlth Games Canada 1994, Silver medal coxless pairs World Championships 1998, winner coxless pairs World Cup 1998, 1999 and 2003, Gold medal coxless pairs World Championships 2003, Silver medal coxless pairs Olympic Games Athens 2004; Olympian 1996, 2000 and 2004; indoor rowing: world champion 1999, world record holder 2000–02; after-dinner speaker at rowing clubs and univs; diplomat FCO 2001–; *Recreations* running, fitness training, travel abroad, reading contemporary literature, writing fiction, learning languages, pianist and accompanist; *Style—* Cath Bishop; ✉ mobile 07905 054263, e-mail cjbishop@btinternet.com

BISHOP, Christopher Charles Rigby; s of Michael Rigby Bishop (d 1996), and Beatrice, *née* Villemer; *b* 17 November 1952; *Educ* Stonyhurst, Magdalene Coll Cambridge (MA), St Thomas' Hosp Med Sch (MB BChir, MChir); *m* 17 Sept 1977, Anthea Jane, *née* Tilzey; 2 s (Charles Alexander Rigby b 17 May 1983, Hugo Guy Pierre b 8 July 1984), 2 da (Lucie Marie Henrietta, Gabrielle Marie Susanna (twins) b 11 Sept 1986); *Career* surgical registrar Southampton Univ Hosps 1980–82, sr surgical registrar St Thomas' Hosp 1987–90 (surgical registrar 1982–84, lectr in surgery 1984–87), conslt surgn UCL Hosps 1991–; vascular fell Scripps Clinic and Research Fndn Calif 1989, Hunterian prof RCS 1991; *Recreations* yachting, skiing; *Style—* Christopher Bishop, Esq; ✉ 149 Harley Street, London W1G 6BN (tel 020 7235 6086, mobile 078 3163 1007)

BISHOP, David Charles; s of Kenneth Charles Bishop, MBE (d 1999), of Sedbergh, Cumbria, and Margaret Cecilia, *née* Birtwistle; *b* 6 April 1947, Kendal, Cumbria; *Educ* Sedbergh, Gonville and Caius Coll Cambridge (MA); *m* 6 June 1980, Ann Winifred, da of Leslie Brian Tallon (d 1984), of Blundellsands; 1 s (Michael Richard b 13 March 1983), 1 da (Julia Ann b 28 Dec 1984); *Career* admitted slr 1972; NP 1983; ptnr Laces & Co (latterly Berrymans Lace Mawer) 1974–2000 (articled clerk 1970–72), princ David Bishop & Co 2000–; memb: Law Soc, Soc of Tst and Estate Practitioners, Int Tax Planning Assoc; *Publications* Cohabitation: Law, Practice and Precedents (co-author, 2005), Elderly Clients: A Precedent Manual (contrib, 2005); *Recreations* ornithology, travel; *Style—* David Bishop, Esq; ✉ 27 Victoria Road, Freshfield, Liverpool L37 7AQ (tel 01704 873819, fax 01704 834766, e-mail david_bishop@compuserve.com); David Bishop & Co, 14 Chapel Lane, Formby, Liverpool L37 4DU (tel 01704 878421, fax 01704 878959, e-mail david@david-bishop.co.uk)

BISHOP, Prof Dorothy Vera Margaret; *b* 14 February 1952; *Educ* St Hugh's Coll Oxford (MA), Inst of Psychiatry Univ of London (MPhil), Univ of Oxford (DPhil); *m* 1976, Patrick Michael Anthony Rabbitt; *Career* probationer grade clinical psychologist Maudsley and Bexley Hosps 1973–75; res offr Neuropsychology Unit Univ of Oxford 1975–82, Fulford jr res fell St Anne's Coll Oxford 1976–78, Bowra res fell Wadham Coll Oxford 1980–81, visiting scientist Montreal Neurological Inst 1981, MRC sr res fell Univ of Newcastle upon Tyne 1982–86, MRC sr res fell Univ of Manchester 1986–91, MRC sr res scientist Cognition and Brain Sciences Unit Cambridge 1991–98 (special appt 1998–), sr res fell Churchill Coll Cambridge 1993–98, Wellcome princ res fell Univ of Oxford 1998–, prof of developmental neuropsychology Univ of Oxford 1999–, supernumerary fell St John's Coll Oxford 2006–; adjunct prof Dept of Psychiatry Univ of WA 1999–2002 and 2005–; memb Ctee Experimental Psychology Soc 1986–88, memb Med Educn and Info Unit Spastics Soc 1988–91, memb ctee Assoc for Child Psychology and Psychiatry 1989–92, hon sec Br Neuropsychological Soc 1990–93, bd memb and chair Research Evaluation Ctee ESRC 1996–; assoc ed: Quarterly Jl of Experimental Psychology 1985–89, Br Jl of Disorders of Communication 1987–90, Br Jl of Developmental Psychology 1988–91; memb editorial bd: Developmental Medicine and Child Neurology 1987–97, European Jl of Disorders of Communication 1991–, Laterality 1995–, Autism: Int Jl of Research and Practice 1996–, Developmental Review 1996–, Applied Psycholinguistics 1997–; chief ed Jl of Child Psychology and Psychiatry 1994–97 (co-ed 1990–94); memb: Experimental Psychology Soc, Multiple Births Fndn, Nat Autistic Soc, Br Neuropsychological Soc, BAAS (pres Psychology Section 1999); hon memb Assoc for Child Psychology and Psychiatry, hon fell Coll of Speech and Language Therapists 1992, pres Experimental Psychology Soc 2000; MD (hc) Univ of Lund 2004; FMedSci 2000, FBA 2006; *Books* Language Development in Exceptional Circumstances (jt ed, 1988), Handedness and Developmental Disorders (1990), Uncommon Understanding: development and disorders of language comprehension in children (1997, Br Psychological Soc Annual Book Prize 1999), Speech and Language Impairments in Children: causes, characteristics, intervention and outcome (jt ed, 2000); author of numerous articles and research papers in learned journals; *Recreations* Victorian novels, pre-1945 films; *Style—* Prof Dorothy Bishop, FBA; ✉ Department of Experimental Psychology, South Parks Road, Oxford OX1 3UD (tel 01865 271369, fax 01865 281255)

BISHOP, James Drew; s of Sir (Frank) Patrick Bishop, MBE, MP (d 1972), and his 1 wife Vera Sophie, *née* Drew (d 1953); *b* 18 June 1929; *Educ* Haileybury, CCC Cambridge; *m* 1959, Brenda, da of George Pearson; 2 s; *Career* The Times: foreign corr 1957–64, foreign news ed 1964–66, asst ed features 1966–70; ed Illustrated London News 1971–87; dir: Illustrated London News and Sketch Ltd 1971, International Thomson Publishing Ltd 1980–85; ed-in-chief Illustrated London News Pubns 1987–95; chm: Assoc of Br Editors 1987–95, National Heritage 1998–; memb Advsy Bd Annual Register 1970–, chm Editorial Bd Natural World 1981–97; *Books* A Social History of Edwardian Britain (1977), A Social History of the First World War (1982), The Story of the Times (with Oliver Woods, 1983), Illustrated Counties of England (ed, 1985), The Sedgwick Story (1998); *Recreations* reading, walking; *Clubs* Oxford and Cambridge, MCC; *Style—* James Bishop, Esq; ✉ Black Fen, Stoke by Nayland, Suffolk CO6 4QD (tel 01206 262315, fax 01206 262876)

BISHOP, John Anthony Fremantle; s of Evan Winfrid Bishop, OBE, of Lymington, Hants, and Mary, *née* Godwin-Smith (d 1983); *b* 17 February 1949; *Educ* Warminster Sch, LAMDA; *Career* BBC TV: floor asst 1971, asst floor mangr, then prodn mangr 1974, dir light entertainment 1980, prodr light entertainment 1984, exec prodr 1988, asst head of variety and light entertainment 1988–91; controller of entertainment and comedy Carlton Television 1991–99, TV exec ITV and BBC 2000–; *Recreations* theatre and swimming; *Style—* John Bishop, Esq; ✉ Flat 2, 32 Leather Lane, London EC1N 7SQ (e-mail johnny.bishop@btinternet.com)

BISHOP, His Hon John Edward; s of Albert George Bishop (d 1988), of Banstead, and Frances Marion, *née* Clericetti (d 1984); *b* 9 February 1943; *Educ* St Edward's Sch Oxford; *m* 29 June 1968, Elizabeth Ann, da of Frank Grover; 2 da (Caroline Jane b 20 Nov 1970, Sally Ann b 22 Feb 1973); *Career* articled to Peter Carter-Ruck Messrs Oswald Hickson Collier & Co London WC2 1962–66, admitted slr 1966, ptnr Messrs Copley Clark & Co Sutton Surrey 1969–81, ptnr Messrs Tuck & Mann Epsom Surrey 1981–85; registrar: Woolwich Co Ct 1985–88, Croydon Co Ct 1988–93; recorder 1990–93 (asst recorder 1987–90), district judge 1992–93, circuit judge (SE Circuit) 1993–2004 (dep circuit judge 2004–); memb The Law Soc 1966, pres Mid Surrey Law Soc 1980–81; *Recreations* golf, walking, music, reading, garden, family; *Clubs* Walton Heath Golf; *Style—* His Hon John Bishop

BISHOP, John Maurice; s of Edwin Maurice Bishop, of Paignton, Devon, and Joyce Emily, *née* Edmonds; *b* 6 May 1947; *Educ* Sherborne, QMC London (LLB); *m* 1, 30 March 1970 (m dis 1985), Maureen, *née* Maloney; 1 s (Edward b 19 Dec 1973), 4 da (Laura b 6 March 1976, Sophie b 10 Nov 1979, Alice, Chloe (twins) b 26 July 1982); m 2, 18 April 1986 (m dis 1998), Virginia, *née* Welsh; 1 step da (Sophie b 22 April 1980); m 3, 18 April 2002, Pauline, *née* Crogan; *Career* slr; Masons: articled clerk 1969–71, asst slr 1971, salaried ptnr 1972, equity ptnr 1973, managing ptnr 1987–90, sr ptnr 1991–2003, resident sr ptnr Asia Pacific 2003–; official referee Slrs' Assoc (chm 1990–94, pres 1995–); memb Law Soc 1969, admitted slr Hong Kong 1983B 1975, ACIArb 1980; *Recreations* golf; *Clubs* Rye Golf, Foreign Correspondents; *Style—* John Bishop, Esq; ✉ Masons (Solicitors), 50th Floor, Central Plaza, 18 Harbour Road, Hong Kong (e-mail john.bishop@masons.com)

BISHOP, John Michael; s of Lt Wilfred Charles John Michael Bishop (d 1988), and Margery Bains, *née* Emmerson (d 1990); *b* 1 March 1947; *Educ* Kent Coll Canterbury, LSE (LLB), Inns of Court Sch of Law; *m* 12 Aug 1982 (m dos 2004), Laurie Marie, da of Lyman Charles Harris (d 1980), of Virginia Beach, Virginia, USA; 2 da (Heather Virginia, Lucy Cecilia); *Career* Kent and Co of London Yeomanry (TA) 1965–67; practising barrister, head of chambers at 7 Stone Buildings 1986–99; memb: Hon Soc Middle Temple, Hon Soc Lincoln's Inn; *Recreations* photography, antiquarian books; *Style—* John Bishop, Esq; ✉ Greenfields, Pean Hill, Whitstable, Kent; Clarendon Chambers, 7 Stone Buildings, Lincoln's Inn, London WC2A 3SZ (tel 020 7681 7681, fax 020 7681 7684); Becket

Chambers, 17 New Dover Road, Canterbury, Kent CT1 3AS (tel 01227 786 331, fax 01227 786329)

BISHOP, Kevin John; s of Lindsay Bishop, and Mary Inez, *née* King; *Educ* South Bromley Coll, Plymouth Poly Coll of Art (BA); *Career* ed Entertainment Events BBC TV; dir: Wogan 1984–86, French and Saunders 1987–88, Victoria Wood 1989, HM Queen Mother's 90th Birthday Gala; prodr: Michael Barrymore's Saturday Night Out 1988–89, Rory Bremner 1990–91, Rita Rudner 1991, The Children's Royal Variety Performance 1991, 1993 and 1994, A Bit of Fry and Laurie 1991, The Royal Variety Performance 1992, 1994, 1996, 1998, 2000, 2002 and 2004, Showstoppers 1994 and 1995, The British Acad Awards 1997, Eurovision Song Contest 1998; *Style*— Kevin Bishop, Esq; ✉ BBC TV, Wood Lane, London W12 7RJ (tel 020 8743 8000)

BISHOP, Sir Michael David; kt (1991), CBE (1986); s of Clive Leonard Bishop (d 1980); *b* 10 February 1942; *Educ* Mill Hill Sch; *Career* chm: British Midland plc (joined 1964), British Regional Airlines Group plc 1982–2001, Manx Airlines 1982–2001, Loganair 1983–97, Channel 4 Television 1993–1997 (dep chm 1991–93); dep chm Airtours plc 1996–2001 (dir 1987–2001); dir: Williams plc 1993–2001, Kidde plc 2000–02; memb: E Midlands Electricity Bd 1980–83, E Midlands Bd Central Independent Television plc 1981–90; chm D'Oyly Carte Opera Tst; tstee UK Friends of Royal Flying Doctor Serv of Aust; *Clubs* Brooks's, St James's (Manchester); *Style*— Sir Michael Bishop, CBE; ✉ Donington Hall, Castle Donington, Derby DE74 2SB (tel 01332 854000)

BISHOP, Patrick Joseph; s of Ernest Bishop, of Wimbledon, London, and Kathleen, *née* Kelly; *b* 17 October 1952; *Educ* Wimbledon Coll, CCC Oxford (exhibitioner, BA); *m* 1989 (m dis), Marie, da of William Colvin, of Oyster Bay, NY; partner, Henrietta Miers, da of Col Douglas, and Mrs Richenda Miers, of Lettoch, N Kessock, Inverness; 1 da (Honor Bridget b 3 Dec 2006); *Career* journalist; training scheme Mirror Group Newspapers 1974–76, freelance 1976–78, news reporter Evening Standard 1978–79, The Observer 1979–84 (news reporter, NI corr, corr with Br Forces in Falklands War), reporter ITN Channel Four News 1984–85, reporter and diplomatic corr The Sunday Times 1985–87, sr corr The Sunday Telegraph 1987–88; The Daily Telegraph: Middle East corr 1988–92, sr foreign corr 1992–95, foreign ed 1995–97, assoc ed (foreign) 1997–99, Paris corr 1999–2002, special corr 2002–; dir Medécins sans Frontières (UK) 1992– (chm 1995–2000); *Books* The Winter War (with John Witherow, 1982), The Provisional IRA (with Eamonn Mallie, 1987), Famous Victory (1992), The Irish Empire (1999), Fighter Boys (2003), Bomber Boys: Fighting Back 1940–45 (2007), 3 Para (2007); *Style*— Patrick Bishop, Esq; ✉ c/o David Godwin Associates, 55 Monmouth Street, London WC2H 9DG (e-mail patrickbishop2001@hotmail.com)

BISHOP, Prof Paul; *Educ* Macquarie Univ Sydney (PhD); *Career* Univ of Sydney until 1989, Monash Univ Melbourne 1989–97 (latterly dir Grad Sch of Environmental Science), prof of physical geography Univ of Glasgow 1998–; FRSE 2004; *Style*— Prof Paul Bishop; ✉ Department of Geographical and Earth Sciences, University of Glasgow, University Avenue, Glasgow G12 8QQ

BISHOP, Peter Antony; s of Jack Lionel Thomas Bishop (d 2001), of Eastbourne, and Audrey Florence, *née* Barker; *b* 15 September 1953, London; *Educ* Trinity Sch of John Whitgift, Univ of Manchester (BA, schs open scholar, RTPI Prize, Heywood Medal); *m* 7 Feb 1998, Lesley Williams; 1 da (Freya Clare b 13 Aug 1996), 1 s (Adam Stirling b 24 Aug 1998); *Career* devpt planner: Westminster 1976–78, Newham 1978–80; head of res London Borough of Islington 1980–83, head of planning Tower Hamlets 1984–87 (schemes incl Spitalfields and Canary Wharf), dir of property and planning Haringey 1987–97; dir of environment: London Borough of Hammersmith and Fulham 1997–2001 (i/c White City and Imperial Wharf devpts), London Borough of Camden 2001–06 (devpts incl Kings Cross); dir Design for London 2007–; planning advsr Assoc for London Authorities 1987–91, lectr and teacher in Britain and abroad; memb London Advsy Ctee English Heritage 2007–, communications exec Renate Campbell Tst 1991–2000, fund raising offr Climbers Club of GB 1998–2002; *Recreations* rock climbing, European cinema, antiquarian books; *Style*— Peter Bishop, Esq; ✉ Design for London, Palestra, 197 Blackfriars Road, London SE1 8AA (tel 020 7593 8141, fax 020 7593 8002, e-mail peter.bishop@designforlondon.gov.uk)

BISS, Adele; *b* 18 October 1944; *m* Roger Davies; *Career* grad trainee Consumer Product Mktg Unilever 1968–70, Thomson Holidays 1970–78, dir Biss Lancaster until 1990 (fndr 1978, sold to WCRS, now Aegis Gp Plc); chm BTA and English Tourist Bd 1993–96, fndr chm A S Biss & Co (political and public affrs) 1996–; non-exec dir Eurostar (UK) Ltd, dir Engine 2006–; govr Univ of Middlesex until 2006, memb Cncl UCL until 2006; *Style*— Ms Adele Biss; ✉ A S Biss & Co, 5th Floor, 36 Broadway, Westminster, London SW1H 0BH (tel 020 7340 6200, fax 020 7340 6250)

BISSELL, Frances Mary; da of Robert Maloney, and Mary, *née* Kelly; *b* 19 August 1946; *Educ* Goyt Bank HS, Cape Town HS, Allerton HS Leeds, Univ of Leeds (BA); *m* 12 Dec 1970, Thomas Emery Bissell, s of Thomas Wilson Bissell (d 1975), of Pittsburgh, USA; 1 step da (b 1958); *Career* VSO Nigeria 1965–66, asst École Normale 1968–69, British Cncl 1970–97 (leave of absence 1987–97), freelance writer, author, broadcaster and conslt on cookery and food 1983–, The Times Cook 1987–2000; guest cook: Mandarin Oriental Hong Kong 1987 and 1990, Intercontinental Hotel London 1987 and 1988, Manila Peninsula 1989, Dusit Thani Bangkok 1992, Café Royal 1994–95, George V Paris 1995, The Mark New York 1997, 1999 and 2000; conslt Sloane Club 2006–; TV: Frances Bissell's Westcountry Kitchen 1995, Frances Bissell's Westcountry Christmas; guest speaker: Swan Hellenic 2000–, Hebridean Spirit 2005–; fndr memb Guild of Food Writers 1985, memb Academy of Culinary Arts; Glenfiddich Cookery Writer of the Year 1994, James Beard Fndn Award 1995, Shackleton Ctee Fellowship 2001; FRSA; *Books* A Cook's Calendar (1985), The Pleasures of Cookery (1986), Ten Dinner Parties for Two (1988), The Sainsbury's Book of Food (1989), Oriental Flavours (1990), The Real Meat Cookbook (1992), The Times Cookbook (1993), Frances Bissell's Westcountry Kitchen (1996), An A-Z of Food and Wine in Plain English (with Tom Bissell, 1999), Modern Classics (2000), The Organic Meat Cookbook (2000), Entertaining (2002), Frances Bissell's Country Kitchen (2002), Preserving Nature's Bounty (2006), The Scented Kitchen (2007); *Recreations* travelling, writing and cooking; *Style*— Mrs Thomas Bissell; ✉ 2 Carlingford Road, London NW3 1RX

BITEL, Nicholas Andrew (Nick); s of Max Bitel, of London, and Cecilia, *née* Singer (d 1980); *b* 1959, London; *Educ* St Paul's, Davidson Coll NC (Dean Rusk scholar), Univ of Manchester (LLB); *m* 1982, Sharon, *née* Levan; 3 s (Daniel b 1985, Adam b 1987, Jonathan b 1992); *Career* ptnr Max Bitel Greene 1983–; ceo London Marathon 1995–, memb Cncl UK Sport 2002–; memb Law Soc 1983–; *Recreations* sport, theatre; *Clubs* MCC; *Style*— Nick Bitel, Esq; ✉ Max Bitel Greene, One Canonbury Place, London N1 2NG (tel 020 7354 2767, fax 020 7226 1210)

BJORGOLFSSON, Thor; s of Bjorgolfur Gudmundsson, and Thora Hallgrimsson; *b* 19 March 1967, Reykjavik, Iceland; *Educ* Iceland Coll of Commerce Reykjavik, NY Univ; *partner* Kristin Olafsdottir; 1 s; *Career* mktg dir in brewing industry Iceland and Russia 1992, co-fndr and chm Bravo International Ltd St Petersburg 1996 (sold to Heineken International 2002), chm Pharmaco (latterly Actaris) 2002, co-fndr and chm of the Bd Samson 2002 (also chm Straumur Burdanas), fndr Novator Partners LLP 2004, private investor in telecommunication cos in countries incl Finland, Poland, Bulgaria and Greece 2004–; elected to Young Global Leaders World Econ Forum 2005 and 2006, memb Bd of East West Inst 2006; Man of the Year in Business Vidskiptabladid newspaper 2003, IMARK Award Icelandic Mktg Assoc 2005, Investor of the Year Bulgarian Radio 2006, Business Man of the Year Frettabladid newspaper 2006; *Recreations* skiing, sailing, mountain biking, motorbiking; *Style*— Thor Bjorgolfsson, Esq; ✉ Novator Partners LLP, 25 Park Lane, London W1K 1RA (tel 020 7647 1500, fax 020 7491 1148, e-mail helene@novator.co.uk)

BLACK, Alan William; s of William Black, of Styvechale, Coventry, and Agnes Whyte Buchanan, *née* Wilson; *b* 21 February 1952; *Educ* King Henry VIII Sch, KCL (LLB); *Career* slr; ptnr Linklaters 1983– (head Global Projects and Project Finance Gp 1993–2005); Freeman Worshipful Co of Slrs 1983; memb Law Soc; *Recreations* tennis, golf, opera and early music, Far East, searching for Schrodinger's cat; *Clubs* The Second Eleven, The Inner Theatre; *Style*— Alan Black, Esq; ✉ Linklaters, One Silk Street, London EC2Y 8HQ (tel 020 7456 2000, fax 020 7456 2222)

BLACK, His Hon Barrington; s of Louis L Black, and Millicent, *née* Brash; *b* 16 August 1932; *Educ* Roundhay Sch, Univ of Leeds (LLB); *m* 19 June 1962, Diana Heller, JP, da of Simon Heller; 2 da (Harriette b 1963, Anna b 1971), 2 s (Matthew b 1965, Jonathan b 1968); *Career* admitted slr 1956; cmmnd RASC 1956–58; met stipendiary magistrate 1984–93, chm Inner London Juvenile Court 1986–93, recorder of the Crown Court 1991–93, circuit judge (SE Circuit) 1993–2005 (dep circuit judge 2005–); chm Family Court 1991–93; former pres Univ of Leeds Union, memb Court and Cncl Univ of Leeds; vice-pres NUS; *Recreations* music, opera; *Style*— His Hon Barrington Black

BLACK, Prof Dame Carol Mary; DBE (2005, CBE 2002); da of Edgar Herbert, and Annie Herbert; *b* 26 December 1939; *Educ* Univ of Bristol (BA, Postgrad Dip, pathology travelling scholar, Martin Memorial Pathology Prize, Surgery Prize, Obstetrics Prize, MB ChB, MD); *m* 1, 1973 (m dis 1983), James Black; m 2, 2002, Dr Chris Morley; *Career* conslt rheumatologist W Middx Univ Hosp 1981–89, conslt rheumatologist Royal Free Hosp 1989–94, prof of rheumatology Royal Free & UC Med Sch London 1994–; hon conslt: Crawley Hosp, Heatherwood Hosp Ascot, Royal Brompton Hosp London, Eastbourne Hosp; pres RCP 2002– (memb Cncl, clinical vice-pres 1999–2002); chm RCP Working Pty: on Acute Med 1999–2000, on Women in Med 2000–01, on Conslt Careers 2000–01; memb Editorial Bd Br Jl of Rheumatology, memb Editorial Bd Kuwait Inst for Med Specialisation, section ed Current Opinion in Rheumatology, memb Advsy Bd Arthritis and Rheumatism jl; med dir and memb Bd Royal Free Hampstead NHS Tst 2000–02; Royal Free Hosp: memb R&D Ctee, memb Academic Advsy Bd in Med, former chm Care of the Elderly/Dermatology/Rheumatology Specialty Gp, former memb Med Advsy Ctee; Dept of Health: expert advsr on silicone breast implants and autoimmune diseases Med Devices Agency, memb Modernisation Bd, memb Leadership Centre's Thinking and Planning Gp, memb Academic Bd NHSU, memb Doctors Forum, memb Nat Specialist Commissioning Advsy Gp, First Ind Expert Advsy Gp on silicone gel breast implants; expert advsr on the provision of info by the Govt relating to the safety of breast implants Health of Commons Health Ctee; memb GMC; memb Cncl: Acad of Med Sci, ICRF, NICE Partners (memb NICE Appraisal Ctee 1999–2002); memb: Jt Med Advsy Ctee, Specialist Trg Authy (memb Academic and Research Sub-Gp), Jt Conslts Ctee, Nat Acad of Policy Advsy Gp (NAPAG), NI Ctee, EULAR Clinical Trials Ctee, Clincial Interest Gp Wellcome Tst (former vice-chm), Scientific Co-ordinating Ctee Arthritis Research Campaign, Pulmonary Hypertensions Clinicians Gp, Med Advsy Bd United Scleroderma Fndn USA, Med Advsy Bd Raynaud's and Scleroderma Assoc Tst, Sclerderoma Fedn Med and Scientific Advsy Bd; named lectures and awards incl: Marisa Ara European Prize in Rheumatology 1984, Marsden travelling fell, Parkes Weber lectr RCP 1994, Heberden roundsman 1999, B Shine lectr in rheumatology Haifa 1999, Nanna Svartz lectr Gothenburg 2002, Philip Ellman lectr RSM 2003, Henry Fuller lectr RSM 2003, Convocation lectr Univ of Bristol 2003; chm and fndr memb: European Scleroderma Gp, UK Systemic Sclerosis Gp; memb: Assoc of Physicians, Br Soc for Rheumatology, Assoc of Clinical Profs of Med, RSM (pres Section of Clincial Immunology and Allergy 1998–2000), BMA, Br Soc for Immunology, Br Connective Tissue Soc, American Coll of Rheumatology, Br Health Professionals in Rheumatology, Hunterian Soc; hon memb: Italian Soc of Rheumatology, Turkish Soc of Rheumatology; memb Bd of Govrs Goodenough Coll, memb Cncl London Goodenough Tst; tstee Tancred; hon fell: UCL, Lucy Cavendish Coll Cambridge, Univ of Bristol; CCMI; FRCP 1988 (MRCP 1973), FMedSci 1996, FACP 2002, FRCPEd, FRCPI, FRACP; *Publications* Systemic Sclerosis (jtly, 1985), Scleroderma (jtly, 1988); author of numerous articles, reviews and chapters in books; *Recreations* music, travel, walking, theatre; *Clubs* Athenaeum, RCP Coll; *Style*— Prof Dame Carol Black, DBE, PRCP; ✉ The Royal College of Physicians, 11 St Andrews Place, Regent's Park, London NW1 4LE

BLACK, Sir (Robert) David; 3 Bt (UK 1922), of Midgham, Co Berks; s of Sir Robert Andrew Stransham Black, 2 Bt, ED (d 1979); *b* 29 March 1929; *Educ* Eton; *m* 1, 1953 (m dis 1972), Rosemary Diana, da of Sir Rupert John Hardy, 4 Bt; 2 da (Diana Sarah (Mrs Mark Newton) b 1955, Joanna Rosemary (Mrs Christopher R C Wild) b 1966), and 1 da decd; m 2, 1973, (Dorothy) Maureen, da of Maj Charles Robert Eustace Radclyffe, and wid of Alan Roger Douglas Pilkington; *Career* formerly Maj Royal Horse Gds and Maj Berks and Westminster Dragoon Yeo 1964–67; vice-chm Berks Eastern Wessex TAVR 1985–92; Hon Col 94 (Berks Yeo) Signal Sqdn 1988–98; jt MFH Garth and S Berks Hunt 1964–72; High Sheriff Oxon 1993–94, DL Caithness 1991–2004; *Recreations* shooting, stalking, fishing, gardening; *Clubs* Cavalry and Guards', Flyfishers'; *Style*— Sir David Black, Bt; ✉ Beech Farm House, Woodcote, Reading, Berkshire RG8 0PX (tel 01491 682234, fax 01491 682112)

BLACK, Don; OBE (1999); s of Morris Blackstone (d 1979), of Hackney, London, and Betsy, *née* Kersh (d 1966); *b* 21 June 1938; *Educ* Cassland Rd Sch Hackney; *m* 7 Dec 1958, Shirley Kitty, da of James Berg; 2 s (Grant Howard b 28 Jan 1961, Clive Darren b 24 Aug 1963); *Career* lyricist; office jr New Musical Express 1955, music publisher, professional comedian, agent and mangr for Brian Epstein's NEMS co; chm Br Acad of Songwriters Composers and Authors 1986–, frequent broadcaster and chm of the Vivien Ellis prize held at the Guildhall Sch of Music; worked with well known composers incl: Andrew Lloyd Webber, John Barry, Henry Mancini, Elmer Bernstein, Charles Aznavour, Quincy Jones, Jule Styne, Charles Strouse; Hon Dr of Arts City Univ 2005; *Musicals* incl: Tell Me on Sunday, Billy, Aspects of Love, Song and Dance, Sunset Boulevard, The Goodbye Girl, Bombay Dreams, Romeo and Juliet, Dracula, Brighton Rock; *Films* incl: Born Free, To Sir With Love, Diamonds are Forever, Ben, The Man With The Golden Gun, Thunderball, True Grit, Tomorrow Never Dies, The World Is Not Enough; *Awards* Oscar Award (for Born Free 1966), 5 Oscar nominations, Golden Globe Award, 5 Ivor Novello Awards, 3 Tony Nominations, 2 Tony Awards, numerous Platinum, Gold and Silver discs, inducted into Songwriters Hall of Fame 2007; *Publications* subject of Wrestling with Elephants (2003); *Recreations* swimming, snooker; *Clubs* RAC, Groucho, St James's; *Style*— Don Black, Esq, OBE; ✉ c/o John Cohen, Clintons Solicitors, 55 Drury Lane, London WC2B 5SQ (tel 020 7379 6080, fax 020 7240 9310, e-mail donlyric@aol.com)

BLACK, Dr (Ann) Dora; *b* 2 July 1932; *Educ* Univ of Birmingham (MB ChB), Inst of Psychiatry (DPM); *m* 4 Dec 1955, Jack Black, *qv*; 2 s (David b 1960, Andrew b 1961), 1 da (Sophie b 1963); *Career* conslt child and adolescent psychiatrist: Edgware Gen Hosp 1968–84, Royal Free Hosp 1984–95; dir Traumatic Stress Clinic 1995–97 (hon conslt 1997–); author of chapters and papers on: bereavement and traumatic bereavement in childhood, family therapy, liaison psychiatry; lately assoc ed Br Jl of Psychiatry; chm Inst of Family Therapy London 1989–92, vice-chm Cruse (nat charity for bereavement care) 1980–95; Winston Churchill travelling fell 1993; FRCPsych 1979 (MRCPsych 1971), FRCPCH 1996; *Books* Child Psychiatry and the Law (jtly, 1989, 3 edn 1998), Child and

Adolescent Psychiatry (with D Cottrell, 1993), When Father Kills Mother (jtly, 1993, 2 edn 2000), Psychological Trauma: a developmental approach (jtly, 1997); *Recreations* travel, theatre, friends; *Style*— Dr Dora Black; ✉ Traumatic Stress Clinic, 73 Charlotte Street, London W1T 4PL (tel 020 7530 3666, fax 020 7530 3677, mobile 07831 280568)

BLACK, Air Vice-Marshal George Philip; CB (1987), OBE (1967), AFC (1962, and bar 1971); s of William Black, and Elizabeth Edward, *née* Philip; *b* 10 July 1932; *Educ* Aberdeen Acad, Jt Servs Staff Coll, RCDS; *m* 1954, Ella Ruddiman, da of Edwin Stanley Walker (d 1961); 2 s (Stuart Douglas b 1955, Ian Craig b 1959); *Career* joined RAF 1950, flying trg Canada 1951, serv fighter pilot, carrier pilot (on exchange to FAA), flying instr, HQ Fighter Command, Cdr No 111 (Fighter) Sqdn 1964–66, ldr Lightning Aerobatic Team 1965, Cdr Lightning Operational Conversion Unit 1967–69, Cdr No 5 (Fighter) Sqdn 1969–70, jssc 1970, air plans MOD 1971–72, Station Cdr RAF Wildenrath 1972–74, Harrier Field Force Cdr RAF Germany 1972–74, Gp Capt Ops HQ 38 Gp 1974–76, RCDS 1977, Gp Capt Ops HQ 11 (Fighter) Gp 1978–80, Cdr Allied Air Defence Sector One 1980–83, Commandant ROC 1983–84, DCS (Ops), HQ AAFCE 1984–87, Air ADC to HM The Queen 1981–83; sr def advsr Ferranti Defence Systems Edinburgh 1987–92, dir of mil business Marconi Electronic Systems Ltd 1993–99, def advsr BAE Sensor Systems Division 1999–2000, def conslt BAE Systems (Avionics) 2000–, defence conslt Finmeccanica plc 2005; FIMgt 1977, FRAeS 2000; *Recreations* military aviation, model railways; *Clubs* RAF; *Style*— Air Vice-Marshal George Black, CB, OBE, AFC, FIMgt, FRAeS, RAF (ret); ✉ Selex Sensors and Airborne Systems Limited 300 Capability Green, Luton, Bedfordshire LU1 3PG

BLACK, Guy Vaughan; s of late Thomas Black, and Monica, *née* Drew; *Educ* Brentwood Sch, Peterhouse, Cambridge (John Cosin scholar, MA, Sir Herbert Butterfield prize); *Partner* Mark William Bolland, *qv* (civil partnership, 2006); *Career* with Corp Banking Div BZW 1985–86, with Cons Res Dept 1986–89, special advsr to sec of state for Energy 1989–92, account dir Westminster Strategy 1992–94, assoc dir Lowe Bell Good Relations 1994–96, dir PCC 1996–2003, press sec to Rt Hon Michael Howard, MP (ldr Cons Pty) 2004–05, dir of media Cons Central Office 2004–05, dir of communications Telegraph Media Group 2005–; dir: Advtg Standards Bd of Finance, Press Standards Bd of Finance; tstee Sir Edward Heath's Charitable Fndn; memb (Cons) Brentwood BC 1988–92; patron Peterhouse Politics Soc; FRSA 1997; *Recreations* music (playing and listening), obeying my cats, reading (mainly historical biography), enjoying fine wine; *Clubs* Athenaeum, London Press (hon memb); *Style*— Guy Black, Esq

BLACK, District Judge Helen Mary; da of Denis Clifford, and Carole Clifford; *Educ* Ashburton HS, Coll of Law Chester; *Career* articled clerk Stafford Clark & Co 1978–82, admitted slr 1982, slr and ptnr Addison Madden 1982–2000, dep district judge Princ Registry of the Family Div 1995–2000, district judge Princ Registry of the Family Div 2000–, recorder Western Circuit 2005–; memb: Law Soc 1982–, Slr Family Law Assoc (SFLA) 1990–2000; *Publications* Atkins Court Forms: Husband and Wife/Co-habitation (ed, 2002), Atkins Court Forms: Marriage, Civil Partnership and Cohabitation (ed, 2006), Butterworths Family Law Service (ed); *Recreations* skiing, marathon running, scuba diving, having fun; *Style*— District Judge Black; ✉ c/o Principal Registry of the Family Division, First Avenue House, 42–49 High Holborn, London WC1V 6NP

BLACK, Jack; *b* 9 January 1932; *Educ* Towcester GS, Hendon County Sch, UCL (LLB); *m* 4 Dec 1955, Dr Dora Black, *qv*, *née* Braham; 2 s (David b 1960, Andrew b 1961), 1 da (Sophie b 1963); *Career* Nat Serv RASC Lt, Battalion Courts Martial Offr and Asst Adjutant 1954–56; admitted slr 1954; Heald Nickinson: ptnr 1956–91, sr ptnr 1984–91; conslt Radcliffes 1991–99; memb: Governing Bd Int Copyright Soc (INTERGU) 1980–2004, Legal Ctee German Chamber of Industry and Commerce UK 1984–94, Exec Ctee Assoc Littéraire et Artistique Internationale 1985–2002, Bd London Musici 1988–97, Bd Cheltenham Arts Festivals Ltd 1998–2004; chm: British Literary and Artistic Copyright Assoc 1985–93, Intellectual Property Cmmn Union Internationale des Avocats 1988–94; fndr memb: British-German Jurists' Assoc 1970–97, Slrs' Euro Gp 1970–, Cncl Intellectual Property Inst (formerly Common Law Inst of Intellectual Property) 1980–; chm: Cncl King Alfred Sch Hampstead 1978–82, The Bentham Club UCL 1994–99, Cheltenham Int Festival of Music 1998–2004; FRSA; *Books* An Introduction to EEC Law (contrib, 1972), Halsbury's Laws of England EC vols (contrib 5 edn, 1986), Merkin and Black Copyright and Designs Law (1993–), The Decisions of the UK Performing Right Tribunal and Copyright Tribunal (with M Freegard, 1997); *Recreations* the Arts, travel; *Clubs* Reform, Groucho; *Style*— Jack Black, Esq; ✉ 56 Eyre Court, 3–21 Finchley Road, St John's Wood, London NW8 9TU (tel 020 7722 5088)

BLACK, Prof Sir James Whyte; kt (1981); *b* 14 June 1924; *Educ* Beath HS, Univ of St Andrews (MB ChB); *m* 16 April 1994, Prof Rona McLeod MacKie, FRSE, *qv*, da of Prof J Norman Davidson, FRS (d 1972); *Career* prof and head of Dept of Pharmacology UCL 1973–77; dir of therapeutic research Wellcome Research Laboratories 1978–84; prof of analytical pharmacology KCH Med Sch Univ of London 1984–; chllr Univ of Dundee 1992–; awarded Nobel Prize for Medicine 1988; FRCP, FRS; *Style*— Prof Sir James Black, FRS

BLACK, Hon Mrs Justice; Dame Jill Margaret; DBE (1999); da of Dr James Irvine Currie, of Leeds, and late Margaret Yvonne, *née* Rogers; *b* 1 June 1954; *Educ* Penrhos Coll Colwyn Bay, Trevelyan Coll Durham (BA); *m* 10 June 1978, David Charles Black, s of Norman John Black; 1 da (b 14 Sept 1982), 1 s (b 14 June 1986); *Career* called to the Bar Inner Temple 1976, QC 1994, recorder NE Circuit 1999, judge of the High Court of Justice 1999–; fell Br-American Project; FRSA; *Books* The Working Mother's Survival Guide (1988), Divorce: The Things You Thought You'd Never Need to Know (latest edn 2004), A Practical Approach to Family Law (jtly, latest edition 2004), The Family Court Practice (jtly, latest edn 2006); *Style*— The Hon Mrs Justice Black, DBE; ✉ Royal Courts of Justice, Strand, London WC2A 2LL

BLACK, John Alexander; QC (1998); s of John Alexander Black (d 2000), and Grace Gardiner, *née* Cornock (d 1994); *b* 23 April 1951; *Educ* St James Choir Sch Grimsby, Univ of Hull (LLB); *m* 4 June 1977 (m dis 2007), Penelope Anne Willdig; 3 c (Katherine b 1987, Alistair b 1992, Harriet b 1992); *Career* called to the Bar (Inner Temple) 1975, in practice Criminal Bar 1976–; *Recreations* classical music, motor cars, political history; *Style*— John Black, Esq, QC; ✉ 18 Red Lion Court, London EC4A 3EB (tel 020 7520 6000, fax 020 7520 8248/9)

BLACK, Michael Jonathan; QC (1995); s of Samuel Black (d 1971), and Lillian, *née* Ruben (d 1988); *b* 31 March 1954; *Educ* Stand GS, UCL (LLB); *m* 1984, Ann, da of late Keith Pentol; 2 s (Samuel Simon Joshua b 25 July 1985, Benjamin David Louis b 30 Jan 1989); *Career* pupillage 1977–79, called to the Bar: Middle Temple 1978 (bencher 2006), Dubai Int Financial Centre 2006, Eastern Caribbean Supreme Ct 2007; in practice Deans Court Chambers Manchester 1979–95, trained as mediator Harvard Law Sch 1992, barr, arbitrator and mediator (commercial disputes especially in construction indust) Byrom Chambers Manchester and London 1995–2000, recorder of the Crown Court 1999– (asst recorder 1995–99), dep judge Technol and Construction Court 2000–, barr 2 Temple Gardens 2001–; memb: Civil Procedure Rule Ctee 2000–04, Court of Appeal Panel of Mediators 2001–03, Civil Justice Cncl 2005–; asst cmmr Parly Boundary Cmmn for England; dep judge Grand Court Cayman Islands 2001; visiting research fell Univ of Manchester Inst of Sci and Technol 1996–2002, visiting prof of construction and engrg law Univ of Manchester 2002–; memb: American Bar Assoc, Forum on Construction Indust (USA), Technol and Construction Bar Assoc, Northern Circuit Commercial Bar Assoc, London Court of International Arbitration, Professional Negligence Bar Assoc, Int Bar Assoc; Freeman City of London, Liveryman Worshipful Co of Arbitrators; FCIArb 1991, FInstCES 2000; *Books* The Sanctuary House Case: an Arbitration Workbook (contrib, 1996), New Horizons in Construction Law (contrib, 1998), The Law and Practice of Compromise (contrib, 5 edn 2002, 6 edn 2005), Discovery Deskbook (contrib, 2005); *Clubs* Athenaeum; *Style*— Michael Black, Esq, QC; ✉ 2 Temple Gardens, London EC4Y 9AY (tel 020 7822 1200, fax 020 7822 1300, e-mail mbqc@2tg.co.uk)

BLACK, (Francis) Peter; s of Francis Raymond Black (d 1985), and Rosina Mary, *née* De Burgh; *b* 20 August 1932; *Educ* Gunnersbury GS, Hammersmith Coll of Art; *m* 15 March 1958, Jillian Elsie; 2 da (Susan b 1961, Caroline b 1964); *Career* architect with Norman and Dawbarn for 4 years designing Imperial Coll building; joined Scott Brownrigg and Turner 1961 (ptnr 1970–); buildings include Sport City Dubai and three airports in Iraq, also responsible for biothermal waste to energy plants in Redhill and Cambridge; dir: Building Design Services (BDS) Ltd 1992–, Consolidated Development Group 1992–; conslt Internation Banking Group responsible for devpt of infrastructure in Myanmar, Laos and CIS; pres Chertsey Agric Assoc 1990; govr St Paul's Sch (grant maintained); RIBA, FSIAD, FCSD, FRSA, MBIM, MaPS; Ecclesia et Pontifici (Vatican) 1990; *Recreations* runs a small farm at Englefield Green specialising in breeding and showing Dexters, short-legged rare breed of British cattle; *Style*— Peter Black, Esq; ✉ Peter Black Associates, Sandylands Home Farm, Wick Road, Englefield Green, Surrey TW20 0HJ (tel 01784 437418, fax 01784 437422)

BLACK, Peter Malcolm; AM; s of John Malcolm Black, and Joan Arlene, *née* Phillps, of Saughall Massie, Wirral; *b* 30 January 1960; *Educ* Wirral GS for Boys, UC Swansea (BA); *Career* exec offr Land Registry for Wales 1983–99; memb Nat Assembly for Wales (Lib Dem) South Wales West 1999–; memb: Cwmbwrla/Manselton Community Centre; *Recreations* theatre, poetry, films; *Style*— Peter Black, AM; ✉ National Assembly for Wales, Cardiff Bay, Cardiff CF99 1NA (tel 029 2089 8744, fax 029 2089 8362, minicom 029 2089 8363, e-mail peter.black@wales.gov.uk); Constituency Office: 1st Floor, 70 Mansel Street, Swansea SA1 5TN (tel 01792 536353, fax and minicom 01792 536354)

BLACK, Prof Robert; QC (Scot 1987); s of James Little Black, of Lockerbie, Scot, and Jeannie Findlay, *née* Lyon; *b* 12 June 1947; *Educ* Lockerbie Acad, Dumfries Acad, Univ of Edinburgh (LLB), McGill Univ Montreal (LLM); *Career* advocate of the Scot Bar 1972, sr legal offr Scot Law Cmmn 1975–78, in practice Scot Bar 1978–81, prof of Scots law Univ of Edinburgh 1981–2004, now emeritus (lectr 1972–75); Temp Sheriff 1981–94; gen ed The Laws of Scotland: Stair Meml Encyclopaedia 1988–96 (dep then jt gen ed 1981–88); FRSA 1991, FRSE 1992, FFCS (founding fell Inst of Contemporary Scot) 2001; *Books* An Introduction to Written Pleading (1982), Civil Jurisdiction: The New Rules (1983); *Recreations* beer, wine, tea (not always in that order); *Clubs* Royal Over-Seas League; *Style*— Prof Robert Black, QC, FRSE; ✉ 6/4 Glenogle Road, Edinburgh EH3 5HW (tel 0131 557 3571); The Edinburgh Law School, Old College, South Bridge, Edinburgh EH8 9YL (tel 0131 650 2021, fax 0870 125 4834, e-mail robert.black@ed.ac.uk)

BLACK, Robert William; s of Robert G Black (d 1966), of Aberdeen, and Nell, *née* Gray (d 2000); *b* 6 November 1946; *Educ* Robert Gordon's Coll Aberdeen, Univ of Aberdeen (MA), Heriot-Watt Univ (MSc), Univ of Strathclyde (MSc); *m* 1970, Doreen Mary, da of George Riach; 1 da (Emily Doreen b 1971), 3 s (Angus Robert George b 1974, Duncan Riach b 1978, Colin David William b 1984); *Career* planner Notts CC 1971–73, supervisory planner Glasgow Corp 1973–75, sr exec Strathclyde Regnl Cncl 1975–85; chief exec: Stirling DC 1985–90, Tayside Regnl Cncl 1990–95; controller of Audit for Scotland 1995–99, auditor gen for Scotland 2000–; clerk to the Lord-Lt of Stirling and Falkirk 1985–90; Hon LLD Univ of Aberdeen 2004, Hon DBA Queen Margaret UC 2006; FRSS 1984, FRSE 2006; *Recreations* the Arts, swimming, golf; *Clubs* New (Edinburgh); *Style*— Robert Black, Esq; ✉ Audit Scotland, 110 George Street, Edinburgh EH2 (tel 0131 477 1234)

BLACK, Prof Susan Margaret (Sue); OBE (2001); da of Alasdair Gunn, of Inverness, and Isabel, *née* Bailey; *b* 7 May 1961, Inverness; *Educ* Univ of Aberdeen (BSc, PhD); *m* 26 March 1993, Thomas Black; 3 da (Elizabeth Margaret b 7 March 1984, Grace Alexandra b 7 Feb 1995, Anna Louise b 28 Dec 1996); *Career* lectr in human anatomy St Thomas' Hospital 1987–92, conslt forensic anthropologist Univ of Glasgow 1992–2003, head of profession Br Forensic Team Kosovo 1999–2000, head of anatomy and forensic anthropology Univ of Dundee 2003–, dir Centre for Int Forensic Assistance 2003–; fndr Br Assoc for Human Identification 2002, lead assessor Cncl for the Registration of Forensic Practitioners (CRFP), advsr Disaster Victim Identification Ctee Home Office; memb Cncl RSE 2006 (also memb Young Persons Ctee); memb Br Assoc for Clinical Anatomists 2005; Hon DSc Robert Gordon Univ 2003; FRSE 2005; *Publications* Developmental Juvenile Osteology (2000), The Juvenile Skeleton (2004), An Introduction to Forensic Human Identification (2006); *Style*— Prof Sue Black, OBE; ✉ Anatomy and Forensic Anthropology, Life Sciences, University of Dundee, Dundee DD1 5EH (tel 01382 385776, fax 01382 388825, e-mail s.m.black@dundee.ac.uk)

BLACK, Virginia; da of (Morice) William Black, of Birmingham, and Mabel Florence, *née* Jones; *b* 1 October 1943; *Educ* King's Norton GS Birmingham, Royal Acad of Music; *m* 1965, Howard Davis, s of Howard Davis; 2 s (Guy b 25 Sept 1969, Oliver b 6 Jan 1972); *Career* solo harpsichordist specialising in the virtuoso repertoire; tours abroad incl: USA, NZ, Aust, France, Germany, Austria, Poland, Sweden; appearances at major early music festivals incl: Göttingen Handel Festival, Herne, York, Carmel Bach Festival; major venues incl: South Bank, Carnegie Hall, NY, Vienna's Konzerthaus; half of duo with Howard Davis (baroque violin); many live broadcasts and TV appearances in UK and abroad; concerts with Eng Chamber Orch and Ancient Acad of Music, professor of harpsichord Royal Acad of Music; recordings incl: Scarlatti Sonatas (1985), Soler Sonatas (1987), J C Bach (1987), Mozart Violin and Keyboard Sonatas (with Howard Davis, 1988), Brandenburg 5 with Consort of London (1989), The Essential Harpsichord (1989), J S Bach - Goldberg Variations (1990), First Choice in Gramophone (1992), Collector's Choice in Classic CD (1992), The Convertibility of Lute Strings (1992), Soler Scarlatti (1993), 3 Suites by Rameau (1995); Gramophone's Critics Choice of the Year for Soler Sonatas; assoc bd examiner, trainer and moderator, adjudicator and former mentor Certificate of Teaching Assoc Bd of the Royal Schs of Music (CTABRSM) Course; Royal Acad of Music: postgrad tutor 1999–, ldr of postgrad performance 2001–02, chair Postgrad Dip Studies 2002–; FRAM (DipRAM); *Recreations* interior design, creative cookery, garden design; *Style*— Virginia Black; ✉ 74 Harley Street, London W1G 7HQ (tel 020 7323 0559, e-mail v.black@ram.ac.uk)

BLACK OF CROSSHARBOUR, Baron (Life Peer UK 2001), of Crossharbour in the London Borough of Tower Hamlets; Hon Conrad Moffat Black; PC (Canada, 1992), OC (1990); *b* 25 August 1944; *Educ* Carleton Univ Ottawa (BA), Laval Univ Quebec City (LLL), McGill Univ Montreal (MA); *m* 1, 1978 (m dis 1992), (Shirley) Joanna Catherine Louise Hishon Walters; 2 s, 1 da; m 2, 21 July 1992, Barbara Amiel, newspaper columnist; *Career* chm: Argus Corporation Ltd 1979– (chief exec 1985–), The Ravelston Corporation Ltd 1979– (chief exec 1985–), Hollinger International Inc 1985– (chief exec 1995–2003), The Telegraph Gp Ltd 1987–2004 (dir 1985–); co-chm The Sun-Times Company (Chicago) 1994–, chm and chief exec Southam Inc 1994–2000; dir: Canadian Imperial Bank of Commerce 1977–, Brascan Corp 1986–, The Spectator (1828) Ltd 1990–, Sotheby's Holdings 1997–, Canwest Global Communications 2001–; memb: Advsy Bd The National Interest Washington DC (chm), Chm's Cncl of the Americas Soc, IISS, Trilateral Cmmn, Steering Ctee Bilderberg Meetings, Int Advsy Bd Cncl of Foreign Relations NY, Hudson Inst, Inst for Int Economics Washington DC, Bd Centre for Policy Studies, Fitch Int

Advsy Ctee; patron The Malcolm Muggeridge Fndn; Hon LLD: Carleton Univ 1989, St Francis Xavier 1979, McMaster Univ 1979; Hon LittD Univ of Windsor 1979; KCSG; *Books* Duplessis (1977, revised as Render Unto Caesar 1998), A Life in Progress (1993); *Clubs* Everglades (Palm Beach), Toronto, Toronto Golf, York (Toronto), University, Mount Royal (Montreal), Athenaeum, Beefsteak, White's, Garrick; *Style*— The Lord Black of Crossharbour, PC, OC, KCSG; ✉ c/o 10 Toronto Street, Toronto, Ontario M5C 2B7, Canada (tel 00 1 416 363 8721)

BLACKADDER, Dame Elizabeth Violet; DBE (2003, OBE 1982); da of Thomas Blackadder (d 1941), of Falkirk, and Violet Isabella, *née* Scott (d 1984); *b* 24 September 1931; *Educ* Falkirk HS, Univ of Edinburgh, Edinburgh Coll of Art; *m* 1956, John Houston, OBE, *qv*, s of Alexander Anderson Houston (d 1947); *Career* artist; lectr Sch of Drawing and Painting Edinburgh Coll of Art 1962–86; numerous solo exhibitions since 1960 (Mercury Gallery 1965–), shows regularly at Royal Scottish Acad and Royal Acad, Browse Darby London, Tapestry designs (woven by Dovecot Studios) in private collections Robert Fleming Holdings Ltd, Reckitt & Colman plc; solo exhibitions incl: Retrospective (Scottish Arts Cncl & touring) 1981–82, Retrospective (Aberystwyth Arts Centre & touring) 1989; works in the collections of: Scottish Arts Cncl, Scottish Nat Gallery of Modern Art, Scottish Nat Portrait Gallery, Nat Portrait Gallery, Govt Art Collection, Kettle's Yard Univ of Cambridge, Univ of Edinburgh, Hunterian Art Gallery Univ of Glasgow, Univ of St Andrews, Univ of Stirling, Nat Museum of Women in the Arts Washington DC, McNay Art Museum San Antonio Texas, Heriot-Watt Univ, Robert Fleming Holdings Ltd; Guthrie award Royal Scottish Acad 1963, Pimms award Royal Acad 1983, Watercolour Fndn Royal Acad 1988; HM Painter and Limner in Scotland 2001; memb: Soc of Scottish Artists, Royal Glasgow Inst of the Fine Arts, Royal Scottish Soc of Painters in Watercolours; hon memb: Royal W of Eng Acad, RWS, Royal Soc of Painter-Printmakers; hon fell RIAS; Hon DLitt: Heriot-Watt Univ 1989, Univ of Aberdeen, Univ of Strathclyde 1998, Univ of London 2004; Hon Dr Univ of Edinburgh 1990; Hon LLD: Univ of Glasgow 2001, Univ of St Andrews 2003; Hon DUniv Stirling 2002, DLit (hc) Univ of London 2004; hon fell Edinburgh Coll of Art 2004; Hon FRSE, RSA 1972, RA 1976; *Recreations* gardening and golf; *Style*— Dame Elizabeth Blackadder, DBE, RA, RSA; ✉ 57 Fountainhall Road, Edinburgh EH9 2LH (tel 0131 667 3687)

BLACKBURN, Dr Bonnie Jean; da of John Hall Blackburn (d 1990), and Ruth Gwendolyn, *née* Moore (d 1992); *b* 15 July 1939, Albany, NY; *Educ* Wellesley Coll Mass (BA), Univ of Chicago (MA, PhD); *m* 1, 10 Sept 1971, Edward E Lowinsky (d 1985); m 2, 6 Jan 1990, Leofranc Holford-Strevens; 1 da (Paula Garner b 17 July 1967); *Career* visiting assoc prof Dept of Music Univ of Chicago 1986, lectr Sch of Music Northwestern Univ 1987, visiting assoc prof State Univ of NY at Buffalo 1989–90, freelance ed of scholarly books Oxford 1990–, gen ed Monuments of Renaissance Music 1993–; memb Editorial Bd: Early Music History, Early Music, Saggiatore Musicale, Alamire Fndn Yearbook, Analysis in Context; John Simon Guggenheim Memorial Fndn Fellowship 1989–90; FBA 2005; *Books* author: Music for Treviso Cathedral in the Late Sixteenth Century: A Reconstruction of the Lost Manuscripts 29 and 30 (1987), The Oxford Companion to the Year (jtly, 1999), Composition, Printing and Performance: Studies in Renaissance Music (2000), The Oxford Book of Days (jtly, 2000), The Josquin Companion (contrib, 2000), The New Oxford History of Music (contrib, 2001); ed: Johannis Lupi Opera omnia (3 vols, 1980–89), A Correspondence of Renaissance Musicians (jtly, 1991), The Perfect Musician (jtly, 1995), Théorie et analyse musicales 1450–1650/Music Theory and Analysis: Actes du colloque international Louvain-la-Neuve 23–25 septembre 1999 (jtly, 2001); *Recreations* travel; *Style*— Dr Bonnie Blackburn, FBA; ✉ 67 St Bernard's Road, Oxford OX2 6EJ (tel 01865 552808, fax 01865 512237, e-mail bonnie.blackburn @wolfson.ox.ac.uk)

BLACKBURN, Vice Adm Sir David Anthony James (Tom); KCVO (2004, LVO 1978), CB (1999); s of late Lt J Blackburn, DSC, RN, and late Mrs M J G Pickering-Pick; *b* 18 January 1945; *Educ* Taunton Sch, RNC Dartmouth; *m* 1973, Elizabeth Barstow; 3 da; *Career* cmd HMS Kirkliston 1972–73, Equerry-in-Waiting to HRH The Duke of Edinburgh 1976–78, Exec Offr HMS Antrim 1978–81; Cmd: HMS Birmingham 1983–84, Capt Third Destroyer Sqdn and CO HMS York 1987–88; Cdre and Naval Base Cdr Clyde 1990–92, CO HMS Cornwall and Capt Second Frigate Sqdn 1992–93, Defence Attaché and Head British Defence Staff Washington DC 1994–97, Chief of Staff to Cdr Allied Naval Forces Southern Europe 1997–99; Master HM Household 2000–05; memb Pensions Appeal Tbnl 2005–, chm Marine Soc and Sea Cadets 2006–, chm St John Ambulance London 2006–; *Style*— Vice Adm Sir Tom Blackburn, KCVO, CB

BLACKBURN, David Michael; s of Rudolph Isaac Blackburn, of London, and Esther Sybil, *née* Levy; *b* 23 December 1937; *Educ* City of London Sch, St John's Coll Cambridge (MA, LLM); *m* 1, 11 Jan 1962 (m dis 1969), Louise Joy, da of Louis Courts, of London; 1 da (Deborah b 1963), 1 s (James b 1964); m 2, 30 April 1970, Janice, da of Louis Brown (d 1987); 2 s (Oliver b 1971, Joshua b 1973); *Career* solicitor; ptnr Courts & Co 1962–81; dir: Rosehaugh plc 1979–85, Rosehaugh Stanhope Developments plc 1983–92, Blackburn Associates Ltd 1986–, QVS Developments Ltd 1998–2004, Wartski Ltd 2001–; property project conslt 1985–, CEDR registered mediator 2004–; memb Bd: Nat Opera Studio 1994–, Design Museum 2006–; memb Law Soc 1962; *Style*— David M Blackburn, Esq; ✉ 3 Norland Place, London W11 4QG (tel 020 7792 8288, fax 020 7792 3334, e-mail db@blackburnuk.net)

BLACKBURN, Dean of; *see:* Armstrong, The Very Rev Christopher

BLACKBURN, Elizabeth; QC (1998); da of Robert Arnold Parker, and Edna, *née* Baines; sis of Robert Stewart Parker, CB, *qv*; *b* 5 October 1954; *Educ* City of London Sch for Girls, Univ of Manchester (BA); *m* 1979, John Blackburn, QC; 2 s (David John b 11 May 1986, Jack Alexander b 20 July 1989); *Career* called to the Bar Middle Temple 1978 (Harmsworth scholar), memb Specialist Commercial and Admiralty Chambers 1980–, examiner of the High Court 1987–90; memb: Exec Ctee Br Maritime Law Assoc, Advsy Ctee on Historic Wreck Sites DCMS, UK Delgn 2003 IOPC Supplementary Fund Diplomatic Conf; *Recreations* gardening, family life, France; *Style*— Mrs Elizabeth Blackburn, QC; ✉ Stone Chambers, 4 Field Court, Gray's Inn, London WC1R 5EA (tel 020 7440 6900, fax 020 7242 0197, e-mail mrseblackburn@aol.com)

BLACKBURN, Julia Karen Eugénie; da of Thomas Blackburn (d 1977), of London and N Wales, and Rosalie, *née* De Meric (d 1999); *b* 12 August 1948; *Educ* Putney HS, Univ of York (BA); *m* 1, (m dis 1996), Hein Bonger; 1 da (Natasha b Aug 1978), 1 s (Martin Thomas b Nov 1983); m 2, Herman Makkink; *Career* writer; FRSL; *Books* The White Men (1978), Charles Waterton - Traveller and Conservationist (1989), The Emperor's Last Island (1991), Daisy Bates in the Desert (1994), The Book of Colour (1995), The Leper's Companions (1999), Thomas Blackburn: Selected Poems (ed, 2001), Old Man Goya (2002), With Billie (2005); stories in PN Review 1990–91 and Granta 1998; *Style*— Ms Julia Blackburn; ✉ c/o Gill Coleridge, Rogers Coleridge and White, 20 Powis Mews, London W11 1JN (tel 020 7221 3717)

BLACKBURN, Bishop of 2004–; Rt Rev Nicholas Stewart Reade; s of Sqdn Ldr Charles Sturrock Reade (d 2000), of Staffs, and Eileen Vandermere, *née* Fleming (d 1994); *b* 9 December 1946; *Educ* Elizabeth Coll Guernsey, Univ of Leeds (BA, DipTh), Coll of the Resurrection Mirfield; *m* 17 July 1971, Christine, da of Very Rev R C D Jasper, CBE (d 1990); 1 da (Claire b 4 Jan 1978); *Career* ordained: deacon 1973, priest 1974; curate: St Chad Coseley 1973–75, St Nicholas Codsall and priest i/c Holy Cross Bilbrook 1975–78, vicar St Peter Upper Gornal and chaplain Burton Road Hosp Dudley 1978–82, vicar St Dunstan Mayfield and rural dean of Dallington 1982–88, vicar and rural dean of Eastbourne 1988–97, canon and preb of Chichester Cathedral 1990–97, archdeacon of Lewes and Hastings 1997–2004; chm Chichester Diocesan Liturgical Ctee 1989–97; memb: Bishop's Cncl and Standing Ctee of Chichester 1989–2004, Gen Synod C of E 1995–2000 and 2003–; pres: Eastbourne and Dist Police Court Mission 1994–, Crowhurst Healing Centre 2000–; vice-pres Disabled Living 2005–; tstee: St Wilfrid's Hospice Eastbourne 1995–98, UC Chichester (formerly Bishop Otter Coll) 1997–2004; patron: Sussex Heritage Tst 1998–, Rosemere Cancer Fndn 2004–, Helping Hand 2005–, Derian House Children's Hospice 2006–, Skipton and E Lancs Rail Action Partnership 2006–; govr: Bishop Bell C of E Aided Secdy Sch 1988–97 (chm 1988–92), St Mary's Hall Girls' Sch Brighton 2002–04; *Recreations* reading, particularly ecclesiastical and modern political biographies, cycling and walking; *Style*— The Rt Rev the Bishop of Blackburn; ✉ Bishop's House, Ribchester Road, Blackburn BB1 9EF (tel 01254 248234, fax 01254 246668, e-mail bishop@bishopofblackburn.org.uk)

BLACKBURN, Peter Hugh; CBE (2003); s of Hugh Edward Blackburn (d 1964), of Bradford, W Yorks, and Sarah, *née* Moffatt (d 1996); *b* 17 December 1940; *Educ* Douai Sch, Univ of Leeds (BA), Univ of Poitiers (Dip French), Harvard Business Sch (AMP); *m* 17 Aug 1967, Gillian Mary, da of William Francis Popple, of Yorks; 3 da (Joanna Clare b 1968, Catherine Elizabeth b 1970, Louise Mary b 1973); *Career* articled clerk RS Dawson & Co Chartered Accountants 1962–66, fin controller John Mackintosh & Sons Ltd Norwich 1967–72 (works accountant Halifax 1966–67); Rowntree Mackintosh: fin dir Overseas Div 1972–75, asst md Europe rising to md 1975–84, gp bd dir 1982–88, chm UK and Eire Region 1985–88; Nestle SA (following takeover): md Rowntree UK 1988–91, dir int chocolate & confectionery strategy 1989–90, chm and chief exec Nestle UK Ltd 1991–96 and 1998–2001, pres and dir gen Nestle France SA 1996–97; chm Northern Foods plc 2002–05; non-exec dir: SIG plc 2001–, Compass Gp plc 2002–; pres Food and Drink Fedn 2000–02, pres Incorporated Soc of Br Advertisers (ISBA) 1998–2000; chm Harrogate Int Festival 2004–; memb Cncl York Univ 2001–03; memb Worshipful Co of Merchant Adventurers York 1989–2006; Hon DLitt Univ of Bradford 1991, Hon Dr Leeds Met Univ 2005; Chevalier du Tastevin 1984; Hon FIL 1989, FIGD, FCA 1976 (ACA 1966); *Recreations* fell walking, photography; *Style*— Peter H Blackburn, Esq, CBE

BLACKBURN, Ven Richard Finn; s of William Brow Blackburn (d 1987), of Leeds, and Ingeborg, *née* Lerche-Thomsen (d 1991); *b* 22 January 1952; *Educ* Eastborne Coll, St John's Coll Durham (BA), Univ of Hull (MA), Westcott House Theol Coll Cambridge; *m* 1980, Helen Claire, da of Edward Davies; 3 da (Charlotte b 23 Oct 1982, Emma b 25 Sept 1984, Isabelle b 18 July 1988), 1 s (Robert b 27 Sept 1986); *Career* NatWest Bank 1976–81, curate St Dunstan and All Saints Stepney 1983–87, priest-in-charge St John's Isleworth 1987–92, vicar of Mosborough 1992–99, rural dean of Attercliffe 1996–99, hon canon Sheffield Cathedral 1998–99, archdeacon of Sheffield and Rotherham 1999–, residentiary canon Sheffield Cathedral 1999–2005 (acting dean 2003), dignitary in convocation 2000–05, chair Churches Regnl Cmmn for Yorks and the Humber 2005–, vice-chair Church of England Pensions Bd 2006–; memb Sch Cncl: Worksop Coll 2001–, Ranby Hall Sch 2001–; *Recreations* music, gardening, walking, rowing; *Clubs* Parrs Priory Rowing; *Style*— The Ven the Archdeacon of Sheffield and Rotherham; ✉ Sheffield Diocesan Church House, 95–99 Effingham Street, Rotherham, South Yorkshire S65 1BL (tel 01709 309110, fax 01709 309107, e-mail archdeacons.office@sheffield.anglican.org)

BLACKBURN, Prof Simon Walter; s of Cuthbert Blackburn (d 1984), and Edna, *née* Walton (d 1986); *b* 12 July 1944, Bristol; *Educ* Clifton, Trinity Coll Cambridge (sr scholar); *m* 1968, Angela, *née* Bowles; 1 da (Gwendolen b 1973), 1 s (James b 1975); *Career* jr research fell Churchill Coll Cambridge 1967–69, tutorial fell in philosophy Pembroke Coll Oxford 1969–90, Edna J Koury distinguished prof of philosophy Univ of N Carolina Chapel Hill 1990–2001, prof of philosophy Univ of Cambridge 2001–; vice-pres Br Humanists Assoc; FBA 2001; *Books* Reason and Prediction (1973), Spreading the Word (1984), Essays in Quasi-Realism (1993), The Oxford Dictionary of Philosophy (1994), Ruling Passions (1998), Think (1999), Being Good (2001), Lust (2004), Truth: A Guide for the Perplexed (2005), Plato's Republic (2006); *Recreations* walking, talking; *Style*— Prof Simon Blackburn; ✉ 141 Thornton Road, Girton, Cambridge CB3 0NE (tel 01223 528278); Department of Philosophy, Sidgwick Avenue, Cambridge CB3 9DA (tel 01223 335095, e-mail swb24@cam.ac.uk)

BLACKER, Dr Carmen Elizabeth; OBE (2004); da of Carlos Paton Blacker, and Helen Maud, *née* Pilkington; *b* 13 July 1924; *Educ* Benenden Sch, SOAS Univ of London (BA, PhD), Somerville Coll Oxford (BA), Radcliffe Coll USA, Keio Univ Tokyo; *Career* univ lectr in Japanese Univ of Cambridge 1958–91 (fell Clare Hall 1965–), prof Ueno Gakuen Coll Tokyo 1991; visiting prof: Columbia Univ 1965, Princeton Univ 1979; pres Folklore Soc 1982–84; hon fell Somerville Coll Oxford 1991; Minakata Kumagusu Prize (Japan) 1997; Order of the Precious Crown (Japan); FBA 1989, FSA 2004; *Books* The Japanese Enlightenment: A Study of the Writings of Fukuzawa Yukichi (1964), The Catalpa Bow: A Study of Shamanistic Practices in Japan (1975, revised edns 1986 and 1999), Collected Writings (2000); articles in Monumenta Nipponica, Folklore, Trans of Asiatic Soc of Japan, Asian Folklore Studies; *Recreations* walking, comparative mythology; *Style*— Dr Carmen Blacker, OBE, FBA; ✉ Willow House, Grantchester, Cambridge CB3 9NF (tel 01223 840196); Faculty of Oriental Studies, Sidgwick Avenue, Cambridge

BLACKER, Jacob (Jac); s of Benjamin Blacker (d 1968), of Cape Town, and Rosa Blacker (d 1983); *b* 13 October 1933; *Educ* Matriculation Wynberg Boys' HS Cape Town, Univ of Cape Town (BArch); *m* 14 Jan 1962, Delores Ramona (Del), da of Donald Reynolds (d 1981), of Brisbane, Aust; 3 s (Amos b 1966, Ben b 1968, Adam b 1970); *Career* job architect Chrysos Daneel SA 1957, assoc Ernö Godlinger Architects & Planners 1958–65, fndr Jacob Blacker Architects Designers Planners 1965–; buildings designed and constructed incl: Islamic Art Museum, Jerusalem City Museum; tutor UCL Architecture Sch 1975–79; Furnival site devpt for housing 1989; fndr Intro Course for Overseas Students 1986–; memb: London Regnl Ctee RIBA, Bd of Govrs Building Centre; chm: Educn Gp RIBA, Camden Soc Architects; RIBA 1961, FRSA 1997; *Books* Building Owners Maintenance Manual & Job Diary (1966–82); *Recreations* singing opera, descriptive geometry, drawing, painting, the mathematics of perception; *Style*— Jac Blacker, Esq; ✉ Jacob Blacker Architects, 5 Shepherds Walk, Hampstead, London NW3 5UE (tel 020 7431 1776, fax 020 7435 9739)

BLACKETT, David John; s of Capt Frederick Herbert Blackett, of Edinburgh, and Mary, *née* Watson (d 1982); *b* 22 August 1950; *Educ* Dollar Acad, Univ of Edinburgh (BCom); *m* 1979, Anita Mary, da of Gareth Evans; 1 s (Matthew Gareth b 9 March 1988), 1 da (Sarah Louise b 12 Dec 1983); *Career* trainee CA Graham Smart & Annan 1970–73, N M Rothschild & Sons Ltd: joined 1973, seconded to jt venture in Malaysia with Bumiputera Merchant Bankers 1975–77, md N M Rothschild & Sons (Singapore) Ltd 1979–86, dir N M Rothschild & Sons Ltd 1983–96, md N M Rothschild & Sons (Hong Kong) Ltd 1986–96, chm Asia/Pacific Newcourt Credit Gp Inc 1997–; MICAS 1975; *Recreations* polo, sailing, golf, tennis, photography; *Clubs* Oriental (London), Guards Polo, Hong Kong, Shek-O Golf; *Style*— David Blackett, Esq

BLACKETT, Sir Hugh Francis; 12 Bt (E 1673), of Newcastle, Northumberland; s of Maj Sir Francis Hugh Blackett, 11 Bt (d 1995), and his 1 w Elizabeth Eily (d 1982), *née* Dennison; *b* 11 February 1955; *Educ* Eton; *m* 1982, Anna Margaret, yr da of James St George Coldwell, of Somerton, Oxon; 3 da (Amelia b 1984, Isabella b 1986, Flora b 1988), 1 s (Henry Douglas b 1992); *Heir* s, Henry Blackett; *Career* High Sheriff Northumberland 2007–08; *Style*— Sir Hugh Blackett, Bt; ✉ Halton Castle, Corbridge, Northumberland NE45 5PH

BLACKETT, Thomas Richard (Tom); s of Thomas Blackett (d 1983), of Worthing, W Sussex, and Phyllis Sutcliffe (d 1984); *b* 25 January 1947; *m* Bridget Jane, da of Nick and Barbara Arlidge; 2 s (William b 7 Oct b 1974, Freddie b 10 Dec 1987); *Career* labourer 1968–69, Attwood Statistics 1969–72, Research Bureau Ltd 1972–77, MAS Survey Research 1977–78, Inbucon Management Consultants 1978–83, currently dep chm Interbrand Group Ltd; memb: MRS 1974, ESOMAR 1978, Int Trademarks Assoc 1995; *Books* Trademarks (1997), Co-Branding (jtly, 1999), Brand Medicine (jtly, 2001); *Recreations* family, garden, rugby, cricket, rowing, golf, wine, opera, theatre, good food; *Clubs* Naval and Military, Soc of St George, Windsor Rugby (pres 1993–95); *Style*— Tom Blackett, Esq; ✉ Coutts & Co, 440 Strand, London WC2R 0QS; Interbrand Group Ltd, 85 Strand, London WC2R 0DW (tel 020 7554 1000)

BLACKETT-ORD, His Hon (Andrew) James; CVO (1988); 2 s of John Reginald Blackett-Ord, JP (d 1967), of Whitfield Hall, Hexham, Northumberland, and Lena Mary, *née* Blackett-Ord (d 1961); *b* 21 August 1921; *Educ* Eton, New Coll Oxford (MA); *m* 9 June 1945, Rosemary, da of Edward William Bovill (d 1966), of Moreton, Essex; 4 s (Christopher b and d 13 Feb 1946, Charles b 6 Feb 1948, Mark, b 10 May 1950, Benjamin James b 12 Feb 1963), 1 da (Nicola Mary Lena b 25 Oct 1961); *Career* Lt Scots Guards, served in UK, N Africa and Italy 1941–46 (wounded Anzio, prisoner 1944–45); called to the Bar: Inner Temple 1947, Lincoln's Inn 1948 (bencher 1985); County Court judge 1971; vice-chllr Co Palatine of Lancaster, memb Cncl Duchy of Lancaster and circuit judge (Chancery Div) Northern Area 1973–87; chllr Dio of Newcastle upon Tyne 1971–98; *Recreations* rural life, reading, travel; *Clubs* Garrick, Lansdowne; *Style*— His Honour A J Blackett-Ord, CVO; ✉ Helbeck Hall, Brough, Kirkby Stephen, Cumbria CA17 4DD (tel 017683 41323)

BLACKFORD, Richard; *b* 13 January 1954; *Educ* Royal Coll of Music (Tagore Gold Medal); *Career* composer for theatre, television and film; publishing contracts with Schott, OUP and Novello; composer in residence Balliol Coll Oxford 1982, dir of music Royal Ballet Sch 1990–96, guest prof of film music composition Royal Acad of Music 1995–; *Theatre* credits incl: The Prince's Play (RNT), The Labourers of Herakles (Delphi Int Festival), The Kaisers of Carnuntum (Carnuntum Festival Vienna), The Rose Tattoo (Theatr Clywd), Macbeth (Theatr Clywd), The Devils (Theatr Clywd), Full Moon (Theatr Clywd and Young Vic), King (Piccadilly), Plea to Autumn (ROH), Medea (Lyric Hammersmith); *Opera* incl: The Pig Organ (Royal Opera cmmn for The Round House), Gawain and Ragnall (Radio 3), Metamorphoses (Royal Coll of Music Centenary Cmmn), Sir Gawain and The Green Knight (42 prodns, Argo Records); *Television* Millennium (CNN/BBC, Emmy nomination for Outstanding Achievement in Music), Preston Front (BBC), Degrees of Error (BBC), Pigeon Summer (Channel 4), A Little Bit of Lippy (Edinburgh Film Festival/Screen Two), Ruth Rendell Mysteries (TVS feature), Profound Scoundrels (TVS), Family (Channel 4), Buddy Breathing (TVS), Finding Sarah (Channel 4), Columbus (BBC), The Vanishing Man (ITV), Space Island One (Sky One); 53 television films for German TV; documentary credits for BBC incl: Secrets of Calcutta, Scharansky, St Luke's Gospel, St Mark's Gospel, Richard Strauss Remembered (prodr, 1st prize Huston Int Film Festival), When I Get to Heaven, Shout, Opinions (RTS Award), Great Women of Our Century; for Channel 4 incl: The Shadow of Hiroshima, A Maybe Day in Kazakhstan (with Tony Harrison, *qv*), A Walk Up Fifth Avenue, To The End of The Rhine (with Bernard Levin, CBE); commercials incl: Hilton Hotels Two Little Boys (Saatchi & Saatchi); *Film* City of Joy (Indian compositions, dir Roland Joffe), Prometheus (also with Tony Harrison), Song for a Raggy Boy; *Compositions* Mirror of Perfection (Sony Classical), Sinfonie Poliziane, Music for Carlow; String Quartet Canticles of Light, Concerto for Seven, A Portrait of Hans Sachs, Zodiac Dances, Postumous Leonatus, Carol: Lullay my Liking, Dragon Songs of Granny Chang, Three Cornish Pieces, Voices of Exile; *Style*— Richard Blackford, Esq; ✉ Novello, Promotion Department, 8/9 Frith Street, London W1D 3JB (tel 020 7432 4209, fax 020 7287 6329)

BLACKHAM, Vice Adm Sir Jeremy Joe; KCB (1999); s of Rear Adm Joseph Leslie Blackham, CB, DL, of Bembridge, IOW, and Coreen Shelford, *née* Skinner; *b* 10 September 1943; *Educ* Bradfield Coll, BRNC Dartmouth, Open Univ; *m* 18 Dec 1971, Candy, da of George Carter (d 1992), of Durban, SA; *Career* entered RN 1961; CO HMS Beachampton 1969–70, CO HMS Ashanti 1975–77, promoted Cdr 1977, Capt 1984, CO HMS Nottingham 1984–85; Comdt RN Staff Coll Greenwich 1987–89, Dir of Naval Plans and Progs 1989–92, CO HMS Ark Royal 1992–93 and CO RN Task Force in Adriatic 1993, Rear Adm 1993, DG Naval Personnel Strategy and Plans 1993–95, Asst Chief of Naval Staff 1995–97, Vice Adm 1997, Dep Cdr Fleet and COS to C-in-C Fleet 1997–99, DCDS (Progs and Personnel) 1999, DCDS (Equipment Capability) 1999–2002, ret; county pres and sr military advsr EADS 2003–05, chm ATMAANA plc, chm Sarnmere plc, ed The Naval Review; vice-pres, memb Cncl and assoc fell RUSI 2003–, vice-pres Int Festival of the SEA; memb RIIA; author of numerous articles for professional jls, regular lectr on defence matters; chm Blackheath Conservatoire of Music and Arts 2000–; memb Advsy Bd City Forum, memb Int Advsy Bd Ocean Security Initiative; Freeman City of London 1995, Liveryman Worshipful Company of Shipwrights 1999; FRSA, CRAeS, MInstD; *Recreations* cricket, music, walking, reading, writing, theatre, travel, languages; *Clubs* MCC; *Style*— Vice Adm Sir Jeremy Blackham, KCB

BLACKHURST, Christopher Charles (Chris); s of Donald Blackhurst, of Barrow-in-Furness, Cumbria, and Rose Bestwick, *née* Wood; *b* 24 December 1959; *Educ* Barrow-in-Furness GS, Trinity Hall Cambridge (MA); *m* 1, 1986 (m dis 2003), Lynette Dorothy Wood, da of Philip Grice, and Mollie Grice; 2 s (Harry Max Thomas b 20 Sept 1987, Barnaby Samuel b 15 April 1992), 1 da (Daisy Natasha b 25 Dec 1988); m 2, 2004, Annabelle Sara, da of Norman Fisher, and Mary Fisher; 1 s (Archie Norman Donald b 6 March 2005), 1 da (Grace Rose Frances b 15 Feb 2007); *Career* articled clerk Cameron Markby 1982–84, asst ed International Financial Law Review (Euromoney Publications) 1985–86, sr writer Business Magazine 1987–88 (staff writer 1986–87), dep ed Insight The Sunday Times 1990 (business reporter 1989–90), city ed Sunday Express 1990–92, sr business writer The Independent on Sunday 1992–93, Westminster corr The Independent 1993–94, sr journalist The Observer 1994–95, Westminster corr The Independent 1995–96, asst ed The Independent on Sunday 1996–98; dep ed: The Independent 1998, The Express 1998–2001; city ed Evening Standard 2002–; TSB/PIMS Fin Journalist of the Year 1988, highly commended British Press Awards 1993 and 2007, Feature Writer of the Year Business Journalist Awards 2005, highly commended London Press Club Awards 2006; *Recreations* golf, tennis, watching sport, opera, music, theatre; *Clubs* Reform, Roehampton, Sigi Cornish Tennis; *Style*— Chris Blackhurst; ✉ mobile 07831 237072, e-mail chris.blackhurst@standard.co.uk

BLACKIE, Prof John Walter Graham; s of Walter Graham Blackie (d 1972); *b* 2 October 1946; *Educ* Uppingham, Peterhouse Cambridge, Harvard Univ, Merton Coll Oxford, Univ of Edinburgh; *m* 1972, Jane; *Career* advocate 1974, lectr in Scots law Univ of Edinburgh 1975 (sr lectr 1988–91), visiting lectr Univ of Göttingen 1981 and 1990, prof of law Univ of Strathclyde 1991–; dir Blackie & Son Ltd (Publishers) 1970–93; *Publications* Personal bar (with E Reid), articles and essays on Scottish private law, especially the Law of Obligations, aspects of medical law, comparative law and doctrinal legal history; *Recreations* sailing (especially classic boats), playing the horn; *Style*— Prof John Blackie; ✉ The Old Coach House, 23A Russell Place, Edinburgh EH5 3HW (tel 0131 202 6481); University of Strathclyde, The Law School, The Lord Hope Building, St James' Road, Glasgow G4 0ZT (fax 0141 553 1546, e-mail john.blackie@strath.ac.uk)

BLACKISTON, Galton Benjamin; s of B L J Blackiston, of Morston Hall Hotel, Norfolk, and Anne, *née* Skerrett-Rogers; *b* 13 August 1962; *Educ* Homewood Sch Tenterden Kent; *m* 12 Dec 1987, Tracy Jane Rowe; 2 s (Harry Galton, Sam Henry); *Career* restaurateur and hotelier; weekly Galtons Goodies stall on Rye Market 1979, trained under John Tovey of Miller Howe 1980–86, head chef Miller Howe 1986–90 (involved with public demonstrations for TV and radio and work in USA, SA and Canada), proprietor Morston Hall Hotel Holt 1991–; finalist The Great British Menu (BBC TV); memb RAGB, memb Guild of Food Writers, Master Chef GB; *Awards* AA Best Newcomer Award 1992, Independent Newspaper Country Hotel of the Year, Catey Award for Best Newcomer, 3 Red AA Stars and 3 Rosettes, Michelin Star, Tourist Bd Hotel of the Year (Gold Rated) EATB, Hotel and Restaurant of the Year Craft Guild of Chefs 2001, EDP Norfolk Chef and Restaurant of the Year Awards 2003; *Publications* Morston Hall Cook Book (2002), More from Morston (2005), A Return to Real Cooking (2006); *Recreations* cricket, eating out, wine, reading cookery books old and new, golf; *Style*— Galton Blackiston, Esq; ✉ Morston Hall, Morston, Holt, Norfolk NR25 7AA (tel 01263 741041, fax 01263 740419, e-mail galton@blackiston.com, website www.morstonhall.com)

BLACKLEDGE, Michael Glyn; s of Edward John Blackledge (d 1981), of Bromley, Kent, and Winifred May, *née* Hemsley; *b* 24 October 1954; *Educ* Colfe's GS London, South Bank Poly (Dip Estate Mgmnt), Garnett Coll (Cert Ed), Coll of Estate Management (Dip Arbitration, David Lawrence Prize), Univ of Surrey (PGDip); *m* 21 Aug 1976, Janet May, da of Edward Arthur Connell, of Seaview, Isle of Wight; 2 s (Jonathan b 1984, Alexander b 1990); *Career* surveyor Thames Water Authy 1974–78; valuer: City of Westminster 1978–79, London Borough of Croydon 1979–81; sr lectr: Vauxhall Coll of Bldg and Further Educn 1981–88, Thames Poly 1988–89; sr surveyor King & Co 1989–91; sr lectr: Portsmouth Poly 1991–92, Univ of Portsmouth 1992–; sole princ conslt 1992–; tutor Coll of Estate Mgmnt 1989–; Freeman City of London, memb Worshipful Co of Feltmakers; FRICS 1990 (ARICS 1978); *Recreations* writing, golf, soccer, athletics, military history; *Style*— Michael Blackledge, Esq; ✉ 34 Horestone Drive, Seaview, Isle of Wight, PO34 5DD (tel and fax 01983 567577, mobile 07900 604142, e-mail mike.blackledge@virgin.net)

BLACKLEY, Emma Clare; da of John Barney Blackley (d 1988), and Cecily Clare Coales, *née* Stuart-Prince; *b* 11 June 1956; *Educ* Berkhamsted Sch for Girls, Lady Margaret Hall Oxford (BA); *m* 10 Dec 1988, Dr (Alan) Nicholas Spoliar, s of Stanislas Vjekoslav Spoliar; 1 s (Frederick Francis Blackley b 21 Dec 1992), 1 da (Anna Lucy Faithful b 18 Jan 1995); *Career* sec to dir Old Master Drawings Dept P & D Colnaghi & Co Ltd 1979–80, PA to editorial dir Cassell Ltd 1980–81; Octopus Books Ltd: asst ed Fiction Dept 1981–82, ed Children's and Fiction Depts 1982–84, publishing mangr Children's and Fiction Depts 1984–86, dep publisher Children's and Fiction Depts 1986–87, dep publisher New Edns Div 1987–89, publisher New Edns Div 1989–90; publishing dir Octopus Illustrated Publishing (div of Reed Consumer Books Ltd) 1990–92, divnl md Reed Illustrated Books 1992–93, gp publishing devpt dir Reed Consumer Books 1993–95; publishing conslt 1995–97 (clients incl Ryland Peters & Small Ltd and Phaidon Press Ltd); princ conslt KPMG Consulting 1997–2002, ind conslt 2002–03, commercial devpt mangr KPMG People Services 2003–05, chief operating offr CIM/ICE Advsy KPMG LLP 2005–; *Recreations* walking, tennis, squash, opera, cinema, literature, wine, travel; *Style*— Ms Emma Blackley; ✉ 47 Malvern Road, London E8 3LP (tel 020 7275 8566)

BLACKLEY, Neil Ramsay; s of (Samuel) Ramsay Blackley, OBE, of Beetley, Norfolk, and Deirdre, *née* Wilson; *b* 30 August 1955; *Educ* Malvern Coll, Imperial Coll London (BSc), London Business Sch (MBA); *m* Fiona, *née* Andrews; 3 da (Emily, Natasha (twins) b 1996, Arianne b 2002); *Career* shipping analyst Lindsay Blee (chartering) Ltd 1979–82; investment/media analyst: Esso Pension Fund 1982–83, James Capel 1983–93, Goldman Sachs 1993–96, Merrill Lynch 1996–2003; chm Media Advsy Bd APAX; non-exec dir Freud Communications; memb Business Graduates Assoc; ACGI 1977, MSI, MBIM; *Publications* incl: The Design Consultancy Marketplace, The Global Advertising Marketplace, Electronic Retailing, Broadband Interactive Services, European Pay TV & Cable, Blueprint for Media Investment; *Recreations* squash; *Style*— Neil Blackley, Esq

BLACKLOCK, Telfer George; s of Telfer Blacklock, of Edinburgh, and Mary, *née* Miller (d 2006); *b* 3 March 1958, Edinburgh; *Educ* St Mark's Swaziland, George Heriots Edinburgh, Univ of Edinburgh (MA, LLB, DipLP); *m* 4 June 1988, Mairead Catriona, *née* Black; 4 s (Calum Telfer William b 14 Oct 1990, Angus Telfer b 8 Oct 1992, Struan Miller Macphail b 23 May 1996, Ross Donald b 9 June 1999); *Career* admitted slr 1983; Balfour & Manson: trainee 1982–84, asst 1984–88, ptnr 1988–91; co-fndr Blacklock Thorley (now Blacklocks) 1992–; *Recreations* golf, bridge, cinema; *Clubs* Murrayfield Golf, Kilspindie Golf; *Style*— Telfer Blacklock, Esq; ✉ Blacklocks, 89 Constitution Street, Edinburgh EH6 7AS (tel 0131 555 7500, fax 0131 555 5535, e-mail tgb@blacklocks.co.uk)

BLACKMAN, Elizabeth; MP; *Career* MP (Lab) Erewash 1997–; asst Govt whip 2006–; *Style*— Ms Elizabeth Blackman, MP; ✉ House of Commons, London SW1A 0AA (tel 020 7219 3000)

BLACKMAN-WOODS, Dr Roberta; MP; *b* 16 August 1957, Belfast; *Educ* Univ of Ulster (BSc, PhD); *m* Tim Blackman; 1 da (b 1987); *Career* prof of social policy and assoc dean Univ of Northumbria; MP (Lab) City of Durham 2005–; former chair Newcastle E and Wallsend CLP, chair City of Durham CLP; vol Save the Children, Child Poverty Action Gp; chair of govrs Durham Johnston Sch; memb: GMB, AUT; *Style*— Dr Roberta Blackman-Woods, MP; ✉ House of Commons, London SW1A 0AA

BLACKMORE, Prof Stephen; s of Edwin Arthur Blackmore, and Josephine, *née* Henwood; *b* 30 July 1952; *Educ* Cheltenham GS, St George's Sch Hong Kong, Univ of Reading (BSc, PhD); *m* 7 July 1973, Patricia Jane Melrose, *née* Hawley; 1 da (Elizabeth Jane b 27 Oct 1979), 1 s (Roger Arthur b 20 June 1982); *Career* botanist Royal Soc Aldabra Res Station Seychelles 1976–77, lectr in botany and head Nat Herbarium Univ of Malawi 1978–80; Natural History Museum: head of palynology Dept of Botany 1980–90, keeper of botany 1990–99, assoc dir of life sciences 1992–95; regius keeper Royal Botanic Garden Edinburgh 1999–; pres Systematics Assoc 1994–97, chm UK Systematics Forum 1993; Linnean Soc: Trail Crisp medal 1987, Bicentenary medal 1992; tstee Little Sparta Tst 2000; author of over 100 scientific papers and 7 botanical books; memb Bd of Dirs Edinburgh Coll of Art 2004; FLS 1976, FIBiol 1993, FRSE 2001; *Recreations* photography, blues guitar music, hill walking; *Style*— Prof Stephen Blackmore; ✉ Royal Botanic Garden Edinburgh, 20A Inverleith Row, Edinburgh EH3 5LR (tel 0131 248 2930, fax 0131 248 2903, e-mail s.blackmore@rbge.org.uk)

BLACKMORE, Tim; MBE (1999); s of Rev Harry J Blackmore (d 1964), and Marjorie, *née* Walker; *b* 3 July 1944, Hull; *Educ* King's Sch Pontefract, Blyth GS; *m* 6 May 1967, Margaret, *née* Hughes; 1 da (Joanna b 26 July 1968), 1 s (Simon b 29 Nov 1970); *Career* prodr BBC Radio 1962–77, head of programmes Capital Radio 1977–83, first dir Radio Acad 1987–88, prog dir Unique Broadcasting 1989–2001, editorial dir UBC Media Gp 2001–; chm Sony Radio Acad Awards 1998–; fell Radio Acad 1994; *Recreations* DIY, dining, music, grandchildren; *Style*— Tim Blackmore, Esq, MBE; ✉ 4 Chenies House, Corney Reach Way, London W4 2TR (tel 020 8987 9673); UBC Media Group, 50 Lisson Street, London NW1 5DF (tel 020 7453 1681, fax 020 7723 2274, e-mail tim@ubcmedia.com)

BLACKSHAW, Alan; OBE (1992), VRD (1970); s of Frederick William Blackshaw (d 1983), of Blundellsands, Liverpool, and Elsie, *née* MacDougall (d 1978); *b* 7 April 1933; *Educ* Merchant Taylors', Wadham Coll Oxford (MA); *m* 1, 1956 (m dis 1983), Jane Elizabeth Turner; 1 da (Sara); m 2, 1984, Dr Elspeth Paterson, da of late Rev Gavin C Martin; 1 s (Alasdair b 1985), 2 da (Elsie b 1987, Ruth b 1990); *Career* business conslt; RM 1954–56,

RMR 1954–74, Capt; HM Civil Serv: joined 1956, under sec Dept of Energy 1974–79 (DG Offshore Supplies Office 1976–78, head of Coal Div 1978–79); conslt dir Strategy International Ltd 1979–91, assoc Oakwood Environmental Ltd 1991–96; dir: Paths for All Partnership Ltd 1996–97, Moray, Badenoch and Strathspey Enterprise 1998–2000; memb: Scot Cncl for Devpt and Industry 1974–78, Scot Sports Cncl 1990–95, Scot Natural Heritage 1991–97 (chm: Audit Ctee 1995–97, Access Task Force 1992–94), Adventure Activities Licensing Authy 1996–2007, Sci and Environment Gp Univ of Highlands and Islands Project 1997–2000 (memb Faculty Bd for Environment and Science 2000–04), Cairngorms Partnership Bd 1998–2003 (chm Recreation Forum 1998–2003); pres: Br Mountaineering Cncl 1973–76 (patron 1976–), Scottish Nat Ski Cncl 1994–2000 (chm 1991–94), Ski Club of GB 1997–2003 (hon memb), Alpine Club 2001–04 (hon memb); hon advsr Mountaineering Cncl of Scot 1994–; Mountaineering Cmmn Union Internationale des Associations d'Alpinisme (UIAA): chm Access and Conservation Group 1995–98, chm 1990–2000, special rep UN Mountain Partnership 1999–2005, pres 2005; chm: Br Ski Fedn 1984–86, Nat Mountain Centre Plas y Brenin 1986–95, UK Mountain Trg Bd 1991–94, Scottish Adventure Activities Forum 1999–; sec Edinburgh Branch Oxford Soc 1989–98; Freeman City of London 1966; *Publications* Mountaineering (1965, 3 edn, 1975), The Alpine Journal (ed, 1968–70); *Recreations* mountaineering, skiing, sailing; *Clubs* Alpine; *Style*— Alan Blackshaw, Esq, OBE, VRD; ✉ Rhu Grianach, Kingussie Road, Newtonmore, Inverness-shire PH20 1AY (tel 01540 673239); Les Autannes, Le Tour, F74402 Argentière, France (tel 00 33 4 50 54 12 20)

BLACKSHAW, Ian Stewart; s of late William Parkington Blackshaw, of Derbys; *b* 18 December 1943; *Educ* King Edward VII Sch Lytham St Anne's, Coll of Law London, Madrid Univ, Anglia Ruskin Univ (LLM); *m* 1970, Christine, da of late Thomas Haworth, of Lytham St Anne's; 2 s; *Career* admitted slr 1967, private practice in NW England, London and Madrid and corp practice with Coca-Cola and GKN 1967–80, sec of Bd and legal advsr Monsanto plc 1980–81, counsel for int affrs Gomez-Acebo & Pombo Madrid 1981–86; legal advsr: Br Embassy Madrid 1981–86, Br C of C Spain 1981–86; legal counsel EMEA Div RJR Nabisco Geneva 1986–90, vice-pres (legal affrs) ISL Sports Marketing Group AG Lucerne 1990–91; in int practice London and Spain 1991–96, int sports mktg conslt and academic 1996–; visiting prof of int business law Inst of Int Legal Studies Salzburg, visiting prof Int Sports Studies Centre Neuchatel Univ 2001–; fell: Int Sports Law Centre TMC Asser Instituut The Hague 2000–, UK Sports Dispute Resolution Panel 2001–, Int Court of Arbitration for Sport Lausanne 2002–; memb WIPO Arbitration and Mediation Center Geneva 2004–; contributing ed The Int Sports Law Jl, author of several books and articles on sports law and other legal subjects; memb: Int Bar Assoc, LES Int; *Recreations* music, travel, sport, family pursuits; *Clubs* Travellers, Baur au Lac (Zurich); *Style*— Ian S Blackshaw, Esq; ✉ e-mail cblackshawg@aol.com

BLACKSTONE, Baroness (Life Peer UK 1987), of Stoke Newington in Greater London; Tessa Ann Vosper Blackstone; PC (2001); er da of late Geoffrey Vaughan Blackstone, CBE, GM (d 1989), of Bures, Suffolk, and Joanna, *née* Vosper; *b* 27 September 1942; *Educ* Ware GS for Girls, London Sch of Economics and Political Science (BSc, PhD); *m* 1963 (m dis), Thomas Charles Evans (d 1985); 1 s (Hon Benedict), 1 da (Hon Liesel); *Career* assoc lectr in sociology Enfield Coll of Technol 1965–66, asst lectr then lectr in social admin LSE 1966–75, fell Centre for Studies in Social Policy 1972–74, advsr Central Policy Review Staff Cabinet Office 1975–78, prof of educnl admin Inst of Educn Univ of London 1978–83, dep educn offr (resources) ILEA 1983–86, clerk to the Authy and dir of educn ILEA 1986, Rowntree special research fell Policy Studies Inst 1986–87, master Birkbeck Coll London 1987–97, min of state Dept for Educn and Employment 1997–2001, min of state for the Arts 2001–03; vice-chllr Univ of Greenwich 2004–; chm: Fabian Soc 1984–85, General Advsy Cncl BBC 1987–91, IPPR 1988–97, RIBA Tst 2004–; dir: Fullemploy Group 1984–91, Br Assoc for Central and Eastern Europe 1987–96, Thames Television 1991–92, Granada Learning 2003–06; non-exec dir: VT Gp 2004–, Mott-McDonald 2005–; memb: Arts Cncl Planning Bd 1986–90, Bd Royal Opera House 1987–97 (chm Ballet Bd 1991–97), Mgmnt Ctee King Edward's Hosp Fund for London 1990–95, Panel 2000; tstee Natural History Museum 1992–97; *Books* Students in Conflict: The LSE in 1967 (co-author, 1970), A Fair Start: The Provision of Pre-School Education (1971), The Academic Labour Market: Economic and Social Aspects of a Profession (co-author, 1974), Disadvantage and Education (co-author, 1982), Testing Children: Standardised Testing in Local Education Authorities and Schools (co-author, 1983), Response to Adversity (co-author, 1983), Inside the Think Tank: Advising the Cabinet 1971–83 (co-author, 1988), Prisons and Penal Reform (1990), Race Relations in Britain (1997); *Style*— The Rt Hon the Baroness Blackstone, PC; ✉ House of Lords, London SW1A 0PW (tel 020 7219 3000)

BLACKWELL, Nigel Stirling; s of Richard Blackwell, DSC (d 1980), and Marguerite, *née* Holliday; *b* 18 March 1947; *Educ* Winchester, St Edmund Hall Oxford (MA); *m* 1, 22 Sept 1984, Eliza Pumpelly (d 1995), da of Frank Mauran III, of Rhode Island; 1 da (Georgina Stirling b 27 July 1986), 1 s (Richard Raphael Holliday b 17 June 1989); m 2, 5 Sept 2005, Christina Jane Lowry, da of Rolf Pasold of Geneva, Switzerland; *Career* dep chm and ceo Blackwell N America 1979–86, jt md BH Blackwell 1980–83 (dir 1974), md The Blackwell Gp 1983–89, chm and md Blackwell Retail Gp 1983–89; chm: Blackwell Publishers Ltd (formerly Basil Blackwell Ltd) 1985–2001, Blackwell Science (formerly Blackwell Scientific) 1990–2001 (dir 1980–2001), Munksgaard Publishers Copenhagen 1992–2001 (dir 1987–2001), Blackwell Publishing Ltd 2001–07; vice-pres Western Provident Assoc 2004– (dir 1992–2004); memb York Harbor Vol Veteran Firemens' Assoc; *Recreations* country pursuits; *Clubs* Leander, Dunes (Narragansett RI), Vincent's (Oxford), White's, York Harbor Reading Room (Maine); *Style*— Nigel Blackwell, Esq; ✉ Shakespeare Head Press, Building 7200, The Quorum, Oxford Business Park North, Oxford OX4 2JX (tel 01865 487169, fax 01865 481482 e-mail tds@shakespeareheadpres.com)

BLACKWELL, Baron (Life Peer UK 1997), of Woodcote in the County of Surrey; Dr Norman Roy Blackwell; s of Albert Edward Blackwell (d 1972), and Frances Evelyn, *née* Lutman; *b* 29 July 1952; *Educ* Latymer Upper Sch Hammersmith, Royal Acad of Music (jr exhibitioner), Trinity Coll Cambridge (MA), Wharton Business Sch Univ of Pennsylvania (Thouron Scholar, MBA, PhD); *m* 1974, Brenda, da of Thomas Clucas; 2 da (Hon Jane b 1979, Hon Sarah b 1983); 3 s (Hon Simon b 1981, Hon Richard b 1987, Hon William b 1989); *Career* strategic planning Plessey Co 1976–78, with McKinsey & Co 1978–86, special advsr PM's Policy Unit 1986–87, ptnr McKinsey & Co 1988–95, head PM's Policy Unit 1995–97, dir gp devpt NatWest Group plc 1997–2000; special advsr KPMG Corp Fin 2000–; chm: Centre for Policy Studies 2000–; non-exec chm: Smartstream Technologies Ltd 2001–05, Interserve plc 2005–; non-exec dir: Dixons Gp plc 2000–03, Corporate Services Gp 2000–06, SEGRO plc (formerly Slough Estates plc) 2001–, Standard Life plc 2003–, Office of Fair Trading 2003–; *Recreations* classical music, walking, gardening; *Clubs* Carlton, RAC; *Style*— The Rt Hon Lord Blackwell; ✉ House of Lords, London SW1A 0PW

BLAGG, Nikola Kate; da of Cedric Charles Blagg, of Peterborough, and Enid, *née* Hancock; *b* 27 September 1955; *Educ* Stewards Comp Harlow Essex, UCL (BSc); *m* Kevin Michael O'Connell; 1 s (Sam b 25 Oct 1988), 1 da (Ellen b 4 Nov 1993); *Career* media trainee Albany Advertising International 1979–80, media exec rising to assoc md Int Media Dept D'Arcy MacManus & Masius (now DMB&B) 1980–85; Carat International (int media planning and buying) 1985–: joined 1985, subsequently media dir then md, currently commercial dir; dir Carat UK 1991–96; memb Int Advtg Assoc 1980; *Style*— Ms Nikola Blagg; ✉ Carat International, Broadway House, 2–6 Fulham Broadway, London SW6 1AA (tel 020 7381 8010, fax 020 7385 3233)

BLAHNIK, Manolo; s of E Blahnik (d 1986), and Manuela, *née* Rodrigo-Acosta; *b* 28 November 1942; *Educ* Univ of Geneva, Louvre Art Sch Paris; *Career* designer of shoes and furniture; co-proprietor 1973–; subject of Manolo Blahnik exhbn at Design Museum London 2003; Hon Dr Arts RCA 2001, Hon RDI (RSBA) 2001; La Medalla de Oro en Merito en las Bellas Artes (Spain) 2002; *Awards* CFDA Special Award 1987, Fashion Cncl of America Award 1987, 1990 and 1998, Hispanic Inst Washington Antonio Lopez Award 1990, Br Fashion Cncl Award 1990 and 1999, American Leather New York Award 1991, Houston Museum of Fine Art Silver Slipper Award 1999 (first shoe designer to receive this award), Neiman Marcus Award 2000, La Aguja de Oro (The Golden Needle) Madrid 2001, La Medalla de Oro en Merito en las Bellas Artes Spain 2002, La Medalla de Oro de Canarias Spain 2003, Shoe Designer of the Year Footwear News 2003, Accessory Designer of the Year Lycra British Style Awards 2003, Pinnacle in Art & Design Award Pratt Inst NY 2005; *Publications* subject of: Manolo Blahnik (by Colin McDowell, 2000), Manolo Blahnik Drawings (2003), Blahnik by Boman (by Eric Boman, 2005); *Recreations* travel and painting; *Style*— Manolo Blahnik, Esq; ✉ 49–51 Old Church Street, London SW3 5BS (tel 020 7352 8622 and 020 7352 3863)

BLAIN, Harry Christian Peter; s of Peter Blain, and Sharon-Anne Blain; *b* 12 September 1967; *Educ* De Burgh Sch Epsom; *m* 23 June 2001, Bodil Bjerkvik; 1 da from previous m (Chyna Emma b 27 Aug 1995); *Career* gallery owner; estab Blain's Fine Art 1992, estab (with Graham Southern, *qv*) Haunch of Venison 2002; memb Cncl Serpentine Gallery; *Recreations* skiing, sailing, diving, art; *Style*— Harry Blain, Esq; ✉ Haunch of Venison, 6 Haunch of Venison Yard, London W1K 5ES (tel 020 7495 5050, fax 020 7495 4050, mobile 07973 347744, e-mail harry@haunchofvenison.com)

BLAIR, Rt Hon Anthony Charles Lynton (Tony); PC (1994); s of Leo Charles Lynton Blair and late Hazel Blair; *b* 6 May 1953; *Educ* Durham Choristers Sch, Fettes, St John's Coll Oxford; *m* 1980, Cherie Booth, QC, *qv*, da of Tony Booth, the actor; 3 s (Euan Anthony b 19 Jan 1984, Nicholas John b 6 Dec 1985, Leo George b 20 May 2000), 1 da (Kathryn Hazel b 2 March 1988); *Career* called to the Bar Lincoln's Inn 1976; Parly candidate Beaconsfield by-election 1982, MP (Lab) Sedgefield 1983–2007; memb Shadow Cabinet 1988–97, chief oppn spokesman on energy 1988–89, chief oppn spokesman on employment 1989–92, chief oppn spokesman on home affrs 1992–94, ldr Lab Pty 1994–2007, ldr of HM Oppn 1994–97, Prime Minister, First Lord of the Treasury and Minister for the Civil Service 1997–2007; Middle East envoy on behalf of US, Russia, UN and EU 2007–; *Style*— The Rt Hon Tony Blair

BLAIR, Bruce Graeme Donald; QC (1989); *b* 12 April 1946; *Educ* Harrow, Magdalene Coll Cambridge; *m*; 3 da; *Career* called to the Bar 1969; barr specialising in family law, currently head of chambers 1 Hare Court; recorder 1994–, dep judge of the High Court (Family Div) 1990–; memb Family Law Bar Assoc; *Publications* Practical Matrimonial Precedents (co-author, 1989, 27 edn 2004); *Recreations* bridge, tennis, turf; *Style*— Bruce Blair, Esq, QC; ✉ 1 Hare Court, Temple, London EC4Y 7BE

BLAIR, David Hetherington; s of late George Tallantyre Blair, of Penrith, Cumbria, and late Mary Isobel, *née* Hetherington; *b* 22 December 1943; *Educ* Queen Elizabeth GS Penrith; *m* Vanessa, da of late Albert George Taylor; 2 da (Maxine b 1965, Zoe b 1968), 1 s (Joshua b 1986); *Career* John Laing plc: joined 1962, dir 1988–95, chm 1995–98; chm Laing Construction plc 1995–98, main bd dir John Laing plc 1994–98; chm: Laing Fleet Services plc 1988–92, EPL Ltd 1988–98, O C Summers Ltd 1995–98, John Laing International Ltd 1998 (dir 1988–95); md John Laing ETE Ltd 1988; non-exec chm Potensis 2000–01; dir: Leicester Communications Ltd 1991–95, Lakewoods Ltd 1991–98, CCL Ltd 1991–98, Societé Européan Constructionne 1994–98, Reading Construction Forum 1995–98, John Laing Pension Tst Ltd 2004–; FCIOB, FRICS; *Style*— David H Blair, Esq; ✉ Amberhurst, 1 Broom Close, Esher, Surrey KT10 9ET (tel 01372 462644, e-mail davidhblair@btopenworld.com)

BLAIR, Sir Ian Warwick; kt (2003), QPM (1999); *Educ* Wrekin Coll, Harvard HS LA, ChCh Oxford (MA); *m* Felicity; 1 s, 1 da; *Career* police constable (grad entry) rising to Inspr Met Police 1974–85, DCI CID N London and mangr Met Police Crime Investigation Project 1988–89, Supt Kensington Div 1989–91, Chief Supt and staff offr to HM's Chief Inspr Constabulary Home Office 1991–93, offr i/c Operation Gallery 1993–96, Asst Chief Constable then Dep Chief Constable Thames Valley Police 1994–97, Chief Constable Surrey Police 1998–2000, Metropolitan Police Cmmr 2005– (Dep Cmmr 2000–05); visiting scholar Int Centre for Advanced Studies NYU, visiting fell Nuffield Coll Oxford; hon student ChCh Oxford; *Publications* Investigating Rape: A New Approach for Police (1985); *Recreations* skiing, tennis, theatre; *Style*— Sir Ian Blair, QPM; ✉ New Scotland Yard, Broadway, London SW1H 0BG (tel 020 7230 2346)

BLAIR, Isla Jean; da of Ian Baxter (d 1981), of Horsham, W Sussex, and Violet Barbara Skeoch (d 2005); *Educ* St Marys Dunblane, West Preston Manor Rustington, RADA; *m* 1968, Julian Glover, *qv*; 1 s (Jamie Blair Glover b 1969); *Career* actress; narrator for numerous audio books; Voice of the Year Spoken Word Award 2002; *Theatre* Prospect Theatre Co: The Padlock, Geraldine in What the Butler Saw, Miss in Her Teens, title role in Miss Julie, Regan in King Lear, Lydia Languish in The Rivals, Viola in Twelfth Night, Fanny Burney in Boswell's Life of Johnson, Thieves Carnival; Yvonne Arnaud Theatre Guildford: Amanda in Private Lives (and tour), Nora in A Doll's House (and tour); Bristol Old Vic: Kate in Kiss Me Kate, Heloise in Abelard and Heloise, Maggie in Hobson's Choice, Varya in The Cherry Orchard, Mary in Vivat Regina, Dotty in Jumpers, Desdemona in Othello, Clea in Black Comedy, Millie in The Browning Version; Triumph Prodns: Sarah in Say Who Your Are, Myra in Hay Fever; Palace Theatre Watford: Ruth in So Long on Lonely Street, Linda/Maud in Suite in Two Keys, Mrs Erlynne in Lady Windermere's Fan; RSC: Aglaya in Subject Fits, Emilia in The Man of Mode; other credits incl: Mad, Bad and Dangerous to Know (Ambassadors and Doolittle Theater USA), Belise in The Sisterhood (Minerva Chichester), Marchesa Matilde Spina in Henry IV (Wyndham), Jenny in The Health Farm (King's Head), Regan in King Lear (Compass), Gilda in Design for Living (Nottingham Playhouse), Lydia Languish in The Rivals (American tour), Lady Teazle in The School for Scandal (Thorndike Leatherhead), Philia in A Funny Thing Happened on the Way to the Forum (Strand), Nora in A Doll's House (Thorndike Leatherhead), Rhoda in Popkiss (Globe), Irene Molloy in The Matchmaker (Chichester Theatre), Keyboard Skills (Southampton), Mrs Prentice in What the Butler Saw (RNT), The Verge (Orange Tree), Dotty in Noises Off (Picadilly Theatre), Lydia in In Praise of Love (nat tour), Gertrude in Hamlet, Elmire in Tartuffe, Nurse Ratched in One Flew Over the Cuckoo's Nest, Louisa Kitteridge in Six Degrees of Separation, Mrs Kitty Warren in Mrs Warren's Profession, Helen Lancaster in Waters of the Moon (Salisbury Playhouse), Domina in A Funny Thing Happened on the way to the Forum (RNT), Stuff Happens (RNT), Mrs Patrick Campbell in Mrs Pat (Theatre Royal York), Mrs Lintott in The History Boys (Wyndhams Theatre); *Television* roles for BBC incl: Caroline in A Legacy, Lady Caroline in When the Boat Comes In, title role in Jean Brodie (Open Univ), title role in 'Alexa' Love Story, Flora in The History Man, Jenny in The Beggars' Opera, Ruth in Mother Love (series), In Your Dreams, True Tilda, A Touch of Frost, Heaven on Earth, Claire Carlsen The Final Cut - House of Cards; other credits incl: Sarah in The Liars, Daphne in Present Laughter,Linda in The Doctors, Elizabeth in Off Peak, Laura in The Bounder (series), Caroline in Boon VI, Maggie in The Good Guys, Jenny in 'Cherubim and Seraphim' Inspector Morse VI, Katherine Dunbar in The Advocates (series), Dr Jane Moore in Midsomer Murders; BBC appearances incl: Blake's

Seven, An Englishman's Castle, Forgotten Love Songs, Doctor Who, Holby City, New Tricks, Casualty; other appearances incl: The Avengers, Space 1999, Only When I Laugh, Six Centuries of Verse, C.A.T.S. Eyes, Taggart, Bookie (series), Haggard, The Darling Buds of May, Medics, Dr Finlay, Hellfire, In Suspicious Circumstances, Mrs Bradley Mysteries, The House of Angelo, Heaven on Earth, Dalziel and Pascoe, The Office, Heartbeat, Blakee the home secretary in Quartermas; *Radio* incl: Mary Bannister in The House (series), Titania in A Midsummer Night's Dream, Lady Windermere's Fan; *Film* incl: The Tennis Court, Real Life, Lucy in Taste the Blood of Dracula, Battle of Britain, Mrs Donovan in Indiana Jones and The Last Crusade, Mrs Hawkins in Treasure Island, The Baroness in Valmont, Mother Agatha in The Monk, Sheila in The Match, Matron in Mrs Caldicot's Cabbage War, Dr Jackson in After Life; *Style*— Ms Isla Blair; ✉ c/o Shepherd Management, 13 Radner Walk, London SW3 4BP (tel 020 7352 2200, fax 020 7352 2277)

BLAIR, Michael Campbell; Hon QC (1996); s of Sir Alastair Campbell Blair, KCVO, TD, WS (d 1999); bro of Robin Blair, Esq, LVO, WS, *qv*; *b* 26 August 1941; *Educ* Cargilfield Sch Edinburgh, Rugby, Clare Coll Cambridge (MA, LLM), Yale Univ (MA); *m* 1966, Halldóra Isabel, da of late Richard Anthony Conolly Tunnard, DL, of Lincs; 1 s (Alastair Magnus b 1974); *Career* called to the Bar Middle Temple 1965 (bencher 1995, dep treas 2007); circuit admin Midland & Oxford Circuit 1982–86, under sec Lord Chllr's Dept 1982–87 (joined 1966, private sec to Lord Chllr and dep Serjeant at Arms House of Lords 1968–71); FSA: dir legal servs 1987–91, gen counsel 1991–93, head Policy and Legal Affrs 1993–95, dep chief exec 1996–98, gen counsel to Bd 1998–2000; in ind practice at the Bar and memb of chambers 3 Verulam Buildings 2000–; chm: Personal Investment Authy 2000–02, Investment Mgmnt Regulatory Orgn 2000–02, Securities and Futures Authy 2001–02, Review Body on Doctors' and Dentists' Remuneration 2001–; pres Guernsey Fin Servs Tbnl 2002–, memb Competition Appeal Tbnl 2000–, memb Bd Dubai Financial Servs Authy 2004–; dir Financial Services Compensation Scheme Ltd 2000–05; memb Gen Cncl of the Bar 1989–99 (chm Professional Standards Ctee 1994, treas 1995–98), chm Bar Assoc for Commerce Fin and Indust 1990–91, memb Cncl of Legal Educn 1992–97; dep chm Virt-x Exchange Ltd 2007–; FRSA 1993; *Books* Sale of Goods Act 1979 (1980), Financial Services: the New Core Rules (1991), Butterworths' European Law Service (vol on Banking and Financial Services, conslt ed 1992), Blackstone's Guide to the Bank of England Act 1998 (1998), Blackstone's Guide to the Financial Services and Markets Act 2000 (2001), Butterworths' Financial Regulation Service (gen ed, 2002), Halsbury's Laws of England Financial Services Title (consulting ed, 2003), Financial Services Law (jt ed, 2006), Financial Markets and Exchanges Law (jt ed, 2007); *Recreations* family life, cross-country skiing, croquet; *Clubs* Athenaeum; *Style*— Michael Blair, Esq, QC; ✉ 3 Verulam Buildings, Gray's Inn, London WC1R 5NT (tel 020 7831 8441, fax 020 7831 8479, e-mail mblair@3vb.com)

BLAIR, Robin Orr; LVO (1999), WS (1965); s of Sir Alastair Campbell Blair, KCVO (d 1999); bro of Michael Blair, Esq, QC, *qv*; *b* 1 January 1940; *Educ* Rugby, Univ of St Andrews (MA), Univ of Edinburgh (LLB); *m* 1, 20 May 1972, Caroline, *née* McCallum Webster (d 2000); 2 s (Matthew b 1974, Benjamin b 1976), 1 da (Alice b 1980); m 2, 25 Feb 2005, Lel, *née* Walker; *Career* ptnr Davidson & Syme WS 1967–72, non-exec dir Tullis Russell & Co Ltd 1978–99, chm Top Flight Leisure Group 1987–98 (non-exec dir 1977–98); Dundas & Wilson CS: ptnr 1972–97, managing ptnr 1976–83 and 1988–91; fndr ptnr Turcan Connell WS 1997–2000; Lord Lyon King of Arms 2001–, sec Order of Thistle 2001–; chm Scottish Solicitors' Staff Pension Fund 1985–91; Purse Bearer to the Lord High Cmmr to the Gen Assembly of the Church of Scotland 1988–2002; chm Scotland's Churches Scheme 1998–; memb Ct Univ of Edinburgh 2003–; sec Assoc of Edinburgh Royal Tradesmen 1966–91, memb Queen's Body Guard for Scotland (Royal Co of Archers) 1970–; memb Law Soc of Scotland 1965; *Clubs* New (Edinburgh), Hon Co of Edinburgh Golfers; *Style*— Robin Blair, Esq, LVO, WS, Lord Lyon King of Arms; ✉ Court of the Lord Lyon, HM New Register House, Edinburgh EH1 3YT (tel 0131 556 7255, fax 0131 557 2148)

BLAIR-GOULD, John Anthony; s of Ralph Blair-Gould (d 1984), and Lydia, *née* Geneen (d 1974); *b* 25 January 1942; *Educ* Sherborne; *m* 11 Sept 1982, Margaret Anne, da of Joseph Lewis Bryan (d 2002), of Oakham, Rutland; *Career* admitted slr 1965, called to the Bar Inner Temple 1970, asst recorder and recorder of the Crown Court 1982–, pt/t immigration adjudicator 1998–; pt/t legal memb Immigration Appeal Tbnl 2004–; immigration judge 2005–; inspr DTI 1988–89; asst Parly Boundary Cmmr 1992–95 and 2000–; *Recreations* music; *Style*— John Blair-Gould, Esq; ✉ 3 Raymond Buildings, Gray's Inn, London WC1R 5BH (tel 020 7400 6400, fax 020 7400 6464)

BLAKE, His Hon Judge Andrew Nicholas Hubert; s of John Berchmans Blake, of Clitheroe, Lancs, and Beryl Mary, *née* Murphy; *b* 18 August 1946; *Educ* Ampleforth, Hertford Coll Oxford (MA); *m* 7 July 1978, Joy Ruth, da of Ronald Shevloff (d 1986), of Southport; 1 s (Ben b 4 June 1980); *Career* called to the Bar Inner Temple 1971, recorder of the Crown Court 1988–99, circuit judge (Northern Circuit) 1999–; *Recreations* skiing, the Turf, fishing; *Style*— His Hon Judge Andrew Blake; ✉ Preston Crown Court, Ringway, Preston PR1 2LL

BLAKE, Carole Rae; da of Maisie Lock, *née* Pitt, and step da of Gilbert Lock; *Educ* Pollards Hill Co Secdy Sch; *Career* rights mangr George Rainbird 1963–70, rights and contracts mangr Michael Joseph 1970–74, rights and contracts mangr W H Allen 1974–75, mktg dir Sphere 1975–76, fndr literary agency 1977, merged with Julian Friedmann Agency forming Blake Friedmann 1983, currently head Book Div Blake Friedmann; pres Assoc of Authors' Agents 1992–95; chm Bd of Dirs Book Trade Benevolent Soc 2004– (memb Bd), memb Soc of Bookmen 1991– (chair 1997–98); Advsy Bd: City Univ postgrad publishing course, UCL Centre for Publishing; *Books* From Pitch to Publication (1999); *Recreations* reading, walking, classical music, African wildlife; *Style*— Ms Carole Blake; ✉ Blake Friedmann Literary Agency Ltd, 122 Arlington Road, London NW1 7HP (tel 020 7284 0408, fax 020 7284 0442, e-mail carole@blakefriedmann.co.uk)

BLAKE, David William John; s of William Morley Blake (d 1985), and Winifred Juliet, *née* Virgo (d 1975); *b* 19 October 1946; *Educ* King Henry VIII GS Abergavenny, Univ of Sussex (BSc); *m* 1972 (m dis 1992), Marianne Neville-Rolfe, *qv*; *Career* journalist; roving European economic reporter Sunday Times 1970–72; The Times: joined 1973, foreign ed Business News, economics corr 1977–78, economics ed 1978–82, home ed 1982–86, managing ed Business News 1986–87; fndr then dep ed Sunday Correspondent 1987–91, assoc ed The European 1991–94, exec dir Goldman Sachs 1994–; parly candidate (Lab) East Grinstead 1974, local cncllr 1974–78; *Books* The Economics of Prosperity (ed with P Ormerod, 1980); *Recreations* Arsenal FC, music, travel; *Clubs* Reform; *Style*— David Blake, Esq; ✉ 42 Wilmington Square, London WC1X 0ET (tel 020 7837 4320)

BLAKE, Howard David; OBE (1994); s of Horace Claude Blake (d 1985), of Brighton, E Sussex, and Grace, *née* Benson (d 1990); *b* 28 October 1938; *Educ* Brighton GS, Royal Acad of Music (LRAM); *Career* composer; dir Performing Right Soc 1978–87, fndr memb Assoc of Professional Composers 1980, visiting prof of composition Royal Acad of Music 1992; FRAM 1989; *Film and Theatre* film scores incl: The Duellists 1977, The Riddle of the Sands 1978, The Snowman 1982, The Lords of Discipline 1983, A Month in the Country 1986, Granpa 1989, A Midsummer Night's Dream 1996, The Bear 1998, My Life So Far 1998, The Snowman Theatre Show 1998; theatre: Henry V RSC 1984, As You Like It RSC 1985; stage works: The Annunciation 1979, The Station 1987; ballet: The Annunciation, Reflections, Diversions, Court of Love, The Snowman 1993, Eva (Sweden) 1995; *Instrumental works* orchestral works: Toccata 1976, The Snowman 1982, Concert Dances 1984, Concerto for Clarinet and Orchestra 1984, Nursery Rhyme Overture 1984, Suite, The Up And Down Man 1985, The Conquest of Space 1988, Granpa 1988, Diversions 1989, The Bells 1991, Piano Concerto (cmmnd by The Philharmonia for the birthday of HRH The Princess of Wales) 1991, Violin Concerto (cmmnd by City of Leeds) 1993, The Land of Counterpane 1994, La Belle Dame Sans Merci 1994, Agatha Suite 1994, All God's Creatures 1995, Sleepwalking 1998, The Rise of the House of Usher 2003, Enchantment of Venus 2006; chamber music: Reflections 1974, The Up and Down Man 1974, Concert Dances (wind band) 1988, Serenade for Wind Octet 1991; piano and instrumental music: Penillion 1975, Eight Character Pieces 1976, Dances for Two Pianos 1976, Prelude for Solo Viola 1979; brass ensemble and brass band: Sinfonietta 1981, Fusions 1986; *Vocal works* Three Sussex Songs 1973, A Toccata of Galluppi's 1978, Walking in the Air, Shakespeare Songs 1987, Make Believe; choral music: The Song of St Francis 1976, The New National Songbook 1976, Benedictus 1979, Festival Mass 1987, Four Songs of the Nativity 1991, Song of St Francis (revised, premiered at The Three Choirs Festival Hereford) 1991, Charter for Peace (cmmnd for UN fiftieth anniversary celebrations) 1995, Still Falls The Rain 1996, Stabat Mater 2002, Songs of truth and Glory (The Elgar Cmmn) 2005, Winterdream 2006, To Sleep 2006; *Recordings* The Snowman 1982, Clarinet Concerto 1986, Benedictus 1988, Granpa 1988, Piano Concerto 1990, Violin Concerto 1993, A Midsummer Night's Dream 1996, The Snowman Ballet 1998; *Recreations* reading, walking, swimming; *Clubs* Groucho, Chelsea Arts; *Style*— Howard Blake, Esq, OBE; ✉ Studio 6, 18 Kensington Court Place, London W8 5BJ (e-mail howardblake.obe@virgin.net); c/o Anna Menzies (mobile 07711 617718, e-mail anna@annamenzies.com)

BLAKE, Jeremy Michael; s of Norman Edward Blake (d 1994), of Faversham, Kent, and Betty Mary, *née* Whiting; *b* 10 April 1953; *Educ* Sir Roger Manwood's GS Sandwich, Univ of Newcastle upon Tyne (H B Saint scholarship, BA, BArch), British Sch at Rome (Rome scholar in architecture); *m* 1 Sept 1984, (Eleanor) Katharine Margaret, da of Rev (Francis) John Bacon; 3 s (Matthew David b 8 Feb 1986, Jonathan Paul b 22 April 1989, Timothy Stephen b 4 June 1992); *Career* architect; L J Couves & Partners Newcastle upon Tyne 1972–77, APP Horsham 1978–80, EPR London 1980, own practice Sussex 1980–84, Erith & Terry Dedham 1984–87, Fitzroy Robinson Ltd Cambridge 1987–2000, Fitzroy Robinson Ltd London 2000–05, Aukett Fitzroy Robinson 2005–07, princ Purcell Miller Tritton LLP 2007–; hon sec RIBA Traditional Architecture Gp 2003–07, memb Lime Forum Ctee 2007–; memb: RIBA 1980, Faculty of Architecture Br Sch at Rome 1980, Soc of Architectural Historians of GB; AABC 2003 (memb Bd 2007–); *Books* La Falsa Prospettiva in Italian Renaissance Architecture (1982), Ss Vincenzo e Anastasio at Tre Fontane Near Rome (with Dr Joan E Barclay Lloyd, 2006); *Recreations* classical music, painting, surfing, swimming, gardening, reading; *Style*— Jeremy Blake, Esq; ✉ Purcell Miller Tritton, The Clove Building, Maguire Street, London SE1 2NQ (tel 020 7397 7171, fax 020 7397 7172, e-mail jeremyblake@pmt.co.uk)

BLAKE, John Michael; s of Maj Edwin Francis Blake, MBE (d 1972), of London, and (Evelyn) Joyce, *née* Meadows; *b* 6 November 1948; *Educ* Westminster City GS, NW London Poly; *m* 29 June 1968, Diane Sutherland, da of Peter John Campbell (d 1973), of London; 2 da (Emma b 1969, Charlotte b 1971), 1 s (Adam b 1985); *Career* reporter: Hackney Gazette 1965–68, Evening Post Luton 1968–69, Fleet Street News Agency 1969–71; columnist: London Evening News 1971–80, London Evening Standard 1980–82, The Sun 1982–84; asst ed Daily Mirror 1984–88, ed The People 1988–90, prodr Sky Television 1990; md: Blake Publishing 1991–, John Blake Publishing 2000–, Metro Publishing 2001–; *Books* Up And Down With The Rolling Stones (1979), All You Needed Was Love (1981); *Recreations* messing about in boats; *Clubs* Groucho, Chelsea Arts; *Style*— John Blake, Esq; ✉ John Blake Publishing, 3 Bramber Court, 2 Bramber Road, London W14 9PB (e-mail john@blake.co.uk)

BLAKE, Jonathan Elazar; s of Asher Blake, of London, and Naomi, *née* Düm; *b* 7 July 1954; *Educ* Haberdashers' Aske's, Queens' Coll Cambridge (MA, LLM); *m* 3 Aug 1980, (Marion) Isabel, da of Joseph Horovitz, of London; 1 da (Lucy Esther b 1984), 3 s (David Edward b 1987, Simon Andrew b 1989, Michael Alexander b 1993); *Career* slr; Stephenson Harwood 1977–82, ptnr SJ Berwin 1982– (currently sr ptnr); memb: Law Soc, Inst of Taxation, Br Venture Capital Assoc, Euro Venture Capital Assoc; *Books* Venture Capital Fund Structures in Europe, Venture Capital in Europe (contrib), AIM and EASDAQ: the New Enterprise Markets; *Recreations* family, theatre, walking, skiing; *Style*— Jonathan Blake, Esq; ✉ SJ Berwin LLP, 10 Queen Street Place, London EC4R 1BE (tel 020 7111 2317, fax 020 7111 2000, e-mail jonathan.blake@sjberwin.com)

BLAKE, Sir (Francis) Michael; 3 Bt (UK 1907), of Tillmouth Park, Cornhill-on-Tweed, Co Northumberland; s of Sir (Francis) Edward Colquhoun Blake, 2 Bt (d 1950); *b* 11 July 1943; *Educ* Rugby; *m* 1968, Joan Ashbridge, o da of Frederic Cecil Ashbrige Miller, of Ramsay Lodge, Kelso; 2 s ((Francis) Julian b 1971, Nicholas Winston b 1974); *Heir* s, Julian Blake; *Career* stockbroker; High Sheriff Northumberland 2002; *Style*— Sir Michael Blake, Bt; ✉ The Dower House, Tillmouth Park, Cornhill-on-Tweed, Northumberland TD12 4UR (tel 01890 882443)

BLAKE, Michael David (Mike); *b* 4 July 1954; *Educ* UC Sch London, Univ of Sussex (BA); *m* 1985, Sharon, *née* Millett; 2 da (Hannah, Helena); *Career* KPMG: joined 1976, ptnr 1990–, sr ptnr Reading office 1996, chief ops offr southern offices 1998, chief ops offr UK corp recovery practice 1999, UK chief financial offr 2003, head of infrastructure KPMG Europe 2007, memb UK Bd and Exec; FCA, FABRP; *Recreations* theatre, cinema, France, playing and watching cricket; *Clubs* Farley Hill Cricket; *Style*— Mike Blake, Esq; ✉ KPMG, 8 Salisbury Square, London EC4Y 8BB (tel 020 7694 1855, fax 020 7311 8499, e-mail mike.blake@kpmg.co.uk)

BLAKE, Nicholas John Gorrod; QC (1994); s of Leslie Gorrod Blake (d 1960), and Jean Margaret, *née* Ballinger; *b* 21 June 1949; *Educ* Cranleigh, Magdalene Coll Cambridge (exhibitioner, MA), Inns of Court Sch of Law; *m* 5 July 1986, Clio, da of Chris Whittaker; 4 c (Lydia Beatrice b May 1986, Harrison b and d May 1987, Sophia Isobel b Oct 1988, Sebastian Patrick b June 1991); *Career* called to the Bar Middle Temple 1974 (bencher 2002); recorder 2000–, dep judge of the High Court 2003–; specialist in immigration law and in criminal, civil and admin law concerning human rights; currently memb Cncl JUSTICE; formerly: sec Haldane Soc of Socialist Lawyers, chm Immigration Law Practitioners' Assoc; *Publications* Police, the Law and the People (1978), Wigs and Workers (1980), Policing the Miners' Strike (contrib, 1983), Jury Trial Under Attack (contrib, 1985), The New Nationality Law (with Ian Macdonald, 1983), Immigration Law and Practice (with Ian Macdonald, 1990 and 1995), Immigration Law (contrib, 2002), Human Rights and Immigration Law (co-author, 2002); *Style*— Nicholas Blake, Esq, QC; ✉ Matrix Chambers, Griffin Building, Grays Inn, London WC1R 5LN (tel 020 7404 3447, fax 020 7404 3448, e-mail nickblake@matrixlaw.co.uk)

BLAKE, Sir Peter; kt (2002), CBE (1983); s of Kenneth Blake, and Betty Blake; *b* 25 June 1932, Dartford, Kent; *Educ* Gravesend Sch of Art, RCA; *m* 27 April 1987, Chrissy; 3 da (Liberty, Daisy, Rose); *Career* artist; teacher: St Martin's Sch of Art 1960–62, Harrow Sch of Art 1960–63, Walthamstow Sch of Art 1961–64, RCA 1964–76; fndr memb Brotherhood of Ruralists 1975; album cover designer: Sgt Pepper's Lonely Hearts Club Band by The Beatles 1967, New Boots and Panties by Ian Dury and the Blockheads 1977, Stanley Road by Paul Weller 1995, Gettin' in Over my Head by Brian Wilson 2004, Me and Mr Johnston by Eric Clapton 2004; designer: Live Aid poster 1985, Live 8 poster 2005; assoc artist Nat Gallery London 1994, sr hanger Summer Exhibition (Royal Acad of Arts London) 2001, prof of drawing Royal Acad Schs 2002; Hon Dr RCA London

1998; RA 1981–2005 (ARA 1974), RDI 1981; *Solo Exhibitions* incl: Portal Gallery London 1962, Robert Fraser Gallery London 1965, Leslie Waddington Prints London 1969, Stedelijk Museum (and European tour) 1973–74, Galerie Claude Bernard Paris 1984 and 1995, Nishimura Gallery Tokyo 1988, Govinda Gallery Washington DC 1992, Tabernacle Cultural Centre Machynlleth 1993, Nat Gallery London and Whitworth Art Gallery Manchester 1996–97, Morley Gallery London 1999, Tate Gallery Liverpool 2000, One to Ten (Waddington Gallery London) 2005; *Selected Group Exhibitions* with Brotherhood of Ruralists incl: Summer Exhibition (Royal Acad of Arts London) 1976, Arnolfini Gallery Bristol (and tour) 1981; *Work in Public Collections* incl: Arts Cncl of GB London, Baltimore Museum of Art, Bristol City Art Gallery, Br Cncl London, Leeds City Art Gallery, Museum Ludwig Cologne, Museum Moderner Kunst Vienna, MOMA NY, RCA London, Tate Gallery London, V&A London, Whitworth Art Gallery Manchester; *Clubs* Groucho, Gerry's, Max Miller Appreciation Soc; *Style*— Sir Peter Blake, CBE, RDI; ✉ c/o Waddington Gallery, 11 Cork Street, London W1X 1PD

BLAKE, Prof Quentin Saxby; CBE (2005, OBE 1988); s of William Blake, and Evelyn Blake; *b* 16 December 1932; *Educ* Downing Coll Cambridge (MA); *Career* freelance artist and illustrator; head of Dept of Illustration RCA 1978–86 (visiting prof 1989–); hon fell: Univ of Brighton 1992, Downing Coll Cambridge 2000, Royal Acad of Art 2001; Hon Dr: London Inst 2000, RCA 2001, Univ of Northumbria 2001; Hon DLitt Cantab 2004; first Children's Laureate 1999–2001; RDI, FCSD, sr fell RCA 1988; Chevalier de l'Ordre des Arts et des Lettres (France) 2002; *Books* over 250 books; subject of: Words and Pictures, Laureate's Progress; *Style*— Prof Quentin Blake, CBE, RDI; ✉ 30 Bramham Gardens, London SW5 0HF

BLAKE, Richard John Bowden; s of Frederick Milman Blake (d 1989), of Guildford, Surrey, and Ida Mary (Mollie), *née* Wood (d 1999); *b* 12 March 1936; *Educ* Aldenham; *m* 1, 23 April 1960, Gillian Mary Wagner (d 1986); 1 s (Johnathan Rupert Bowden b 23 July 1962), 2 da (Annabelle Clare, Sophie Alexandra (twins) b 28 Feb 1965); m 2, 12 Aug 1988, Shirley Anne Virginia Edwards, da of Gerald Lee; *Career* Baker Todman: articled clerk 1954, chartered accountant 1960, ptnr 1964–93, sr ptnr 1986–93; chm Baker Tilly 1988–94; dir: Filtronic plc, Attenborough Holdings Gp, Dragon International Studios Ltd, Promenade Productions Ltd, YooMedia plc; FCA; *Recreations* golf, theatre, racing, cricket; *Clubs* MCC, Turf, Saints & Sinners, Lucifers, Surbiton Hockey, Royal Porthcawl Golf; *Style*— Richard Blake, Esq

BLAKE, Sir (Thomas) Richard Valentine; 17 Bt (I 1622), of Menlough, Galway; s of Sir Ulick Temple Blake (d 1963), 16 Bt, of Saltergill, Yarm-on-Tees, and Elizabeth Longley-Cook (d 1978); *b* 7 January 1942; *Educ* Bradfield Coll; *m* 1, 1976, Jacqueline, da of late Desmond E Daroux, and formerly w of Peter Alers Hankey; m 2, 1982 (m dis 1986), as her 3 husband, the singer Bertice Reading; m 3, 1991, Wendy, wid of late Anthony Ronald Roberts, and da of Edward William Gough (d 1965), of Richmond, Surrey; *Heir* kinsman, Anthony Blake; *Career* joined motor trade 1959; dir: Sir Richard Blake & Assocs 1967–75, City Chase Ltd 1980–84 (specialists in Rolls-Royce, Bentley and Gordon-Keeble cars); proprietor Autobart 1988–92, sales assoc Taylor's of Birdham 1995– (Rolls-Royce and Bentley specialists); memb Goodwood Supporters Assoc; *Recreations* gardening, vintage cars; *Clubs* Gordon-Keeble Owners' (hon life memb), Rolls-Royce Enthusiasts', Goodwood Road Racing, Cowdray Park Polo, Chiddingfold, Leconfield, Cowdray Hunt; *Style*— Sir Richard Blake, Bt; ✉ 46 Chemin Du Peylong, Sud 83510, Lorgues Var, France (tel and fax 00 33 4 94 67 61 05)

BLAKEMORE, Prof Colin Brian; s of Cedric Norman Blakemore (d 1987), of Kidlington, Oxford, and Beryl Ann, *née* Smith; *b* 1 June 1944; *Educ* King Henry VIII Sch Coventry, CCC Cambridge (MA), Univ of Calif Berkeley (PhD), Univ of Oxford (MA, DSc), Univ of Cambridge (ScD); *m* 28 Aug 1965, Andrée Elizabeth, da of Ronald George Washbourne (d 1995), of Coventry, Warks; 3 da (Sarah Jayne b 1974, Sophie Ann b 1976, Jessica Katy b 1979); *Career* Univ of Calif Berkeley Harkness fell of the Cwlth Fund 1965–67; Univ of Cambridge: demonstrator in physiology 1967–72, official fell and dir of med studies Downing Coll 1971–79, lectr in physiology 1972–79, Royal Soc Locke res fell 1976–79; Waynflete prof of physiology Univ of Oxford and professorial fellow Magdalen Coll Oxford 1979–; dir: McDonnell-Pew Centre for Cognitive Neuroscience 1990–, MRC Interdisciplinary Research Centre for Cognitive Neuroscience 1996–; visiting prof: Dept of Psychology NY Univ 1970, Dept of Psychology MIT 1971; visiting scientist Salk Inst San Diego 1982, 1983 and 1992, McLaughlin visiting prof McMaster Univ Hamilton Ontario 1992, Regents' prof Univ of Calif Davis 1995–96; memb: BBC Sci Consultative Gp 1975–79, Scientific Advsy Bd Cognitive Neuroscience Inst NY 1981–, Sci Ctee Bristol Exploratory 1983–, Professional Advsy Ctee Schizophrenia: A National Emergency (SANE) 1989– (tstee 2001–), Exec Ctee Dana Alliance for Brain Initiatives NY and Washington DC 1996–, Nat Ctee for the 2000 Forum of Euro Neuroscience Brighton 1998–, UK Forum for Genetics and Insurance 1998–, Sci Advsy Ctee of the Volkswagen Stiftung Germany 1999–, Ind Expert Gp on Mobile Phones established by the Dept of Health 1999–, prog mgmnt ctee of the UK Mobile Telecommunications and Health Res Prog 2000–, strategic advsy ctee of Proseed Capital Holdings 2000–, Royal Soc Sci in Soc Ctee 2001–, cncl COPUS (formerly ctee on the Public Understanding of Sci) 2001–, Royal Soc Michael Faraday Award Ctee 2001–, joint Royal Soc/Acad of Med Sci Working Gp on the Sci of Transmissible Spongiform Encephalopathies (BSE, CJD etc) 2001–; chm Exec Ctee and chief exec Euro Dana Alliance for the Brain 1997–; chm: Royal Soc Public Prog Working Gp 2001–, Royal Soc Partnership Grants Ctee 2001–, Br Assoc for Advancement of Sci 2001–; pres Biosciences Fedn 2002–; patron CORPAL (support gp for families affected by ageneis of the corpus callosum and Aicardi's Syndrome) 1989–, patron and sr advsr at Bristol 1996–, patron Assoc for Art, Sci, Engrg and Technol (ASCENT) 1997–, patron and memb Professional Advsy Panel Headway (Nat Head Injuries Assoc) 1997–, patron Clifton Scientific Tst Bristol 1999–, patron Oxford Univ Scientific Soc 2000–, tstee Brain Child (charity supporting research into the developmental neuropsychology of cognitive disorders 1991–; conslt to Home Office and Police Fedn on TETRA (police communication) 2001–; memb Home Office/Defence Sci and Technol Lab TETRA Health and Safety Mgmnt Ctee 2001–; chm Weak Electric Field Effects Gp Nat Radiological Protection Bd 2001–; conslt: Wellcome Tst exhbn Head On: Art with the Brain in Mind 2001–, Thriving Child Project JABADAO (Centre for the Study of Movement, Learning and Health) 2002–, Electromagnetic Fields and Neurological Disease WHO 2002–03; participant 'Bright Sparks' Festival of Br Science India 1999; presenter The Next Big Thing (10 debates on current issues in sci, BBC) 2000; advsr Y Touring Theatre of Science project (sci drama for inner city schs) 2000–; memb Advsy Gp Dana Centre at the Wellcome Wolfson Building Science Museum 2002; memb Exec Cncl Novartis Fndn 2002–; fell World Innovation Fndn 2002–; conslt Wellcome Tst Exhbn Head On - Art with the Brain in Mind 2001–02; numerous named lectures, hon appointments and awards incl: BBC Reith lectr 1976, Lethaby prof RCA 1978–79, Royal Soc Michael Faraday Award and Medal 1989, Osler Medal (RCP) 1993, Ellison-Cliffe Medal (RSM) 1993, Royal Soc lectr (Assoc for Sci Educn) 1995, Physiological Soc Prize Review Lecture 1995, Leverhulme Research Grant 1995–96, Alcon Prize Alcon Research Inst 1996, Memorial Medal Charles Univ Prague 1998, Alfred Meyer Award (Br Neuropathological Soc) 2001, Inst of Biology Charter Award and Medal 2001, Baly Medal RCP (Dyster Tst) for distinction in the sci of physiology 2001, Outstanding Contribution to Neuroscience Award (Br Neuroscience Assoc) 2001, Menzies Medal Menzies Fndn Aust 2001; Liveryman Worshipful Co of Spectacle Makers 1998–; memb: Br Neuroscience Assoc 1968 (memb Nat Ctee 1973–77 and 1997–, pres 1997–), Physiological Soc 1968 (hon memb 1998–, pres 2001–), Experimental Psychological Soc 1968, Euro Brain and Behaviour Soc 1972 (memb Ctee 1974–76), Int Brain Res Orgn 1973 (memb Governing Cncl 1973–, memb Exec Ctee 1979–91), Cambridge Philosophical Soc 1975–79, Euro Neuroscience Assoc 1977 (memb Nominating Ctee 1988), Soc for Neuroscience 1981, Oxford Med Soc 1986, Child Vision Res Soc 1986 (memb Organising Ctee 1986–), Nat Conf of Univ Profs 1989, Br Assoc for the Advancement of Science 1990 (vice-pres 1990–, treas 1993, pres 1997–98, hon memb 2001–), Euro Biomedical Research Assoc (fndr memb) 1994, Academia Europaea 1995, Cncl of Fedn of European Neuroscience Socs 1998–, Int Soc on Infant Studies 2001–, Interim Exec Ctee for UK Fedn of Life Sciences 2002–, Advsy Gp Sense about Science 2002–, Med Panel (Seriously Ill for Medical Research) SIMR 2002–, Sci, Engrg and Environment Advsy Ctee Br Cncl 2003–; hon patron Wrexham Sci Festival 2002–; foreign memb Royal Netherlands Acad of Arts and Sciences 1993, hon memb Maverick Club 1999–, hon assoc Rationalist Int 2000–, hon assoc Cheltenham Festival of Sci 2001–; Hon DSc: Aston Univ 1992, Univ of Salford 1994; hon fell: CCC Coll Cambridge 1994, Cardiff Univ of Wales 1998, Downing Coll Cambridge 1999; fell World Economic Forum 1994–98; fndr FMedSci 1998; FRS 1992, FIBiol, CBiol; *Books* Handbook of Psychobiology (1975), Mechanics of the Mind (1977), Mindwaves (1987), The Mind Machine (1988), Images and Understanding (1990), Vision: Coding and Efficiency (1990), Gender & Society (1999), The Oxford Companion to the Body (2001); *Publications* varied editorial work incl: memb Editorial Bds Vision Research and Int Review of Neurobiology, assoc ed NeuroReport 1989–, ed-in-chief Oxford Companion to the Body (OUP) 1996–; *Recreations* running, the arts; *Clubs* Chelsea Arts; *Style*— Prof Colin Blakemore, FRS; ✉ University Laboratory of Physiology, Parks Road, Oxford OX1 3PT (tel 01865 272470, fax 01865 272488, e-mail blakemore@physiol.ox.ac.uk)

BLAKEMORE, Michael Howell; AO (2003), OBE (2003); s of Dr Conrad Howell Blakemore (d 1976), and Una Mary, *née* Litchfield (later Mrs Heyworth, d 1982); *b* 18 June 1928, Sydney, NSW; *Educ* Cranbrook Sch, The King's Sch, Univ of Sydney, RADA; *m* 1, 1960 (m dis 1986), Shirley Mary Bush; 1 s (Conrad); m 2, 1986, Tanya McCallin, *qv*, da of Clement McCallin (actor, d 1978); 2 da (Beatrice b 1981, Clementine b 1984); *Career* stage and film director (occasional writer and actor); co-artistic dir Glasgow Citizen's Theatre 1966–68, assoc dir NT 1971–76, resident dir Lyric Theatre Hammersmith 1980; freelance dir of prize winning prodns: A Day in the Death of Joe Egg 1968, Arturo Ui 1969, Forget-Me-Not-Lane 1971; also dir of: The National Health 1969, Plunder 1975, Long Day's Journey Into Night 1971, The Front Page 1972 (Plays and Players Best Dir Award for the latter two prodns), The Wild Duck, Make and Break, Noises Off, Design for Living, Knuckle, Candida, Separate Tables, Privates on Parade (also the film), Deathtrap, All My Sons, Benefactors (London and Broadway), Made in Bangkok, Lettice and Lovage (London and Broadway), Uncle Vanya, After The Fall, City of Angels (Broadway and London), Noises Off (London and Broadway, received Drama Desk Award 1984), The Sisters Rosensweig (Old Vic), Death Defying Acts (off-Broadway 1995), The Life (Broadway 1997), Alarms and Excursions (London) 1998, Kiss Me Kate (Broadway) 1999 (Tony and Drama Desk Awards 2000) and 2001 (Victoria Palace Theatre London), Copenhagen (RNT 1998, London 1999, Paris 1999 (Moliere Award) and Broadway 2000 (Tony and Drama Desk Awards)), Three Sisters (London) 2003, Democracy (NT) 2003, Embers (Duke of York's) 2006; film A Personal History of the Australian Surf (also wrote and acted in the latter, Peter Seller's Award for Comedy in the Standard Film Awards); actor The Last Bastion for Channel 10 television in Australia 1984; film actor/writer/dir Country Life (Aust) 1994; *Books* Next Season (1969), Arguments with England (2004); *Clubs* RAC; *Style*— Michael Blakemore, AO, OBE; ✉ 3 Hampstead Hill Mansions, Downshire Hill, London NW3 1NY (tel 020 7431 1663, fax 020 7431 2860)

BLAKENHAM, 2 Viscount (UK 1963); Michael John Hare; s of 1 Viscount Blakenham, OBE, PC, VMH (d 1982, 3 s of 4 Earl of Listowel), and (Beryl) Nancy, *née* Pearson, da of 2 Viscount Cowdray; *b* 25 January 1938; *Educ* Eton, Harvard Univ (AB Econ); *m* 12 Jan 1965, his 1 cous, Marcia Persephone, da of Maj Hon Alan Victor Hare, MC (d 1995); 1 s, 2 da; *Career* 2 Lt The Life Gds 1956–57; English Electric 1958, Lazard Bros 1961–63, Standard Industrial Group 1963–71, Royal Doulton 1972–77, CE Pearson plc 1978–83; chm: Pearson plc 1983–97, Financial Times Group Ltd 1983–93, MEPC plc 1993–98 (dir 1990–98), Japan 2001 1999–; ptnr Lazard Ptnrs 1984–97 (dir 1975–97); dir: Sotheby's Holdings Inc 1987–, UK-Japan 21st Century Gp 1990–, Lafarge 1997–; memb: Int Advsy Bd Lafarge 1979–97, Int Advsy Gp Toshiba Corporation 1997–; memb House of Lords Select Ctee on: Sci and Technol 1985–88, Sustainable Development 1994–95; memb Nature Conservancy Cncl 1986–90, pres Sussex Wildlife Tst 1983–, vice-pres Royal Soc for the Protection of Birds 1986– (chm 1981–86), chm Royal Botanic Gardens Kew and Wakehurst Place 1997– (tstee 1991–); *Style*— The Rt Hon Viscount Blakenham; ✉ 1 St Leonard's Studios, London SW3 4EN

BLAKER, Sir John; 3 Bt (UK 1919), of Brighton, Sussex; s of Maj Sir Reginald Blaker, 2 Bt, TD (d 1975), and Sheila Kellas, *née* Cran; *b* 22 March 1935; *m* 1, 1960 (m dis 1965), Catherine Ann, da of late Francis John Anselm Thorold; m 2, 1968, Elizabeth Katherine, da of Col John Tinsley Russell, DSO; *Heir* none; *Style*— Sir John Blaker, Bt; ✉ Stantons Farm, East Chiltington, Lewes, East Sussex

BLAKER, Michael; *b* 19 January 1928; *Educ* Brighton Coll of Art (NDD); *m* 1977, Catriona McTurk; *Career* artist, writer, printmaker; proprietor own gallery, Avery Row, New Bond St London 1951–53; contrib articles: The Artist, Leisure Painter; editorial conslt and contrib Printmaking Today, ed and designer Printmakers' Jl 1983–93; ret sr fell Royal Soc Painter-Printmakers, past fell Royal West of England Acad; *Exhibitions* solo exhbns: Hove Library 1949 and 1951, Foyles Gallery 1951, Bedford Coll London 1976, St Edmunds Art Centre Salisbury 1981, Medici Gallery 1986, Nevill Gallery Canterbury 1990, John Davies Stow on the Wold 1997; larger gp exhbns incl: RA, RE exhbn Bankside Gallery (featured artist 1992); *Collections* work in public and private collections incl: Tate Gallery, V&A, S London Art Gallery, Brighton Gallery, The Oriana Collection; *Books* The Autobiography of a Painter-Etcher (1985), A Beginner's Guide to Oil Painting (1994); published own novels: Out of Place Angel (1999), An Architect Unleashed (1999), Artists At Large (1999), We Who Follow the Guns (2000), The Lost Hour of Spring (2000), Not So Black a Widow (2000), Two Tales of the Sixties (2000), Disenchanted George (2000), Soupcons and Stories (2002), Three Plays (2002), The Last Confession (2002); *Recreations* early jazz, sequential graphic art (comics), collecting early 20th century etchings, photography; *Style*— Michael Blaker; ✉ 122 Grange Road, Ramsgate, Kent CT11 9PT (tel 01843 596401, website www.michael.blaker.co.uk)

BLAKER, Lt-Col (Guy) Peter; s of Guy Stewart Blaker (d 1969), of Rotherfield Greys, Henley-on-Thames, and Dawn Laetitia Prudence, *née* Watson (d 1997), gda of Gen Sir John Watson, VC, GCB (d 1919); *b* 10 November 1936; *Educ* Boxgrove Sch, Lancing, Jesus Coll Cambridge (MA, LLB); *m* 18 Jan 1969, Hiltegund Maria, da of Dr Hermann Bastian (d 1945), of Freiburg-im-Breisgau; 1 da (Alexandra b 1970), 2 s (Dominic b 1971, Nicholas b 1975); *Career* Nat Serv, cmmnd W Yorks Regt 1957, Royal Green Jackets 1961–84, served Malaya, Borneo, Singapore, Cyprus, UK, Germany, Belgium (SHAPE); Army Aviation Pilot 1964–67, Staff Coll 1968, cmd Cambridge Univ Offrs Trg Corps 1979–82; Queen's Messenger 1984–85; gen mangr Newdata Publishing 1985–86; sec Gen Cncl and Register of Osteopaths 1987–95, sec Blackie Fndn Tst 1996–98; co-ordinator Br Southern Slav Soc 1998–99; regnl dir Ormonde Advsy Service 1998–; lay chm Rotherfield Greys PCC 1985–97; chm Berkshire Automobile Club 1990–; *Recreations* classical music, history, languages, ornithology, fly fishing, bee-keeping, rowing; *Clubs* Naval and

Military, MCC, Leander (assoc), Phyllis Court; *Style—* Lt-Col Peter Blaker; ✉ Greys Piece, Rotherfield Greys, Henley-on-Thames, Oxfordshire RG9 4QG (tel 01491 628308, e-mail pblaker@globalnet.co.uk)

BLAKER, Baron (Life Peer UK 1994), of Blackpool in the County of Lancashire, and of Lindfield, in the County of West Sussex; Sir Peter Allan Renshaw Blaker; KCMG (1983), PC (1983); s of Cedric Blaker, CBE, MC, ED (d 1965), of Scaynes Hill, W Sussex, and Louise Douglas, *née* Chapple (d 1985); *b* 4 October 1922; *Educ* Shrewsbury, Trinity Coll Toronto (BA), New Coll Oxford (MA); *m* 1953, Jennifer, er da of Sir Pierson John Dixon, GCMG, CB (d 1965); 2 da (Hon Antonia Helena Renshaw b 1957, Hon Candida Juliet Renshaw b 1961), 1 s (Hon Adam Pierson Renshaw b 1963); *Career* WWII Capt Argyll and Sutherland Highlanders Canada (wounded); admitted slr 1948, called to the Bar 1952; Foreign Serv 1953–64; MP (Cons) Blackpool S 1964–92; Parly under sec Army 1972–74 and FCO 1974, min of state FCO 1979–81, min of state for Armed Forces 1981–83; chm Cons Pty Foreign and Cwlth Affairs Ctee 1983–92 (vice-chm 1974–79); memb: Select Ctee on Conduct of Members 1976–77, Public Accounts Cmmn 1987–92, Intelligence and Security Ctee 1996–97; *Recreations* tennis, sailing, swimming, opera; *Style—* The Rt Hon Lord Blaker, KCMG, PC

BLAKEY, Ian Johnston; s of Walter James Blakey, BEM, of Cottingham, N Humberside, and Freda Blakey, *née* Johnston; *b* 25 August 1932; *Educ* Hull GS; *m* 9 June 1956, Pamela Mary, da of late George Edward McMurran; 1 s (Jeremy Sean b 1961), 1 da (Zelda Rebecca b 1965); *Career* Nat Serv RN 1950–52; dir: Rediffusion Holdings Singapore (PTE) Ltd, Nisa Today Central Distribution Ltd 1986–, The Health Scheme 1987–; chm: I J Blakey Haulage Co Ltd 1962–, Humberside Wishing Well Appeal 1995–, Hull and East Yorkshire Hospitals NHS Tst 1999–2003; Liveryman Worshipful Co of Carmen; FCIT 1981, FInstTA 1976, FSA 1999; OStJ; *Recreations* golf, horse racing, charity fund raising; *Style—* Ian Blakey, Esq; ✉ Beech House, Northgate, Cottingham, North Humberside HU16 5QL (tel 01482 846131); Woodhouse Street, Hedon Road, Hull (tel 01482 327359, fax 01482 216489)

BLAKISTON, Sir Ferguson Arthur James; 9 Bt (GB 1763), of the City of London; s of Sir (Arthur) Norman Hunter Blakiston, 8 Bt (d 1977); *b* 19 February 1963; *Educ* Lincoln Coll NZ (DipAg), Auckland Inst of Technology (Cert Marketing), NZ Inst of Business Studies (Dip Travel Writing and Photography); *m* 3 April 1993, Linda Jane, da of late Robert John Key, of Queenstown, NZ; 2 da (Lydia Mary Ann b 28 Nov 1996, Emma Charlotte Helen b 21 Oct 1999); *Heir* bro, John Blakiston; *Career* builder, farmer, freelance writer and photographer; *Style—* Sir Ferguson Blakiston, Bt; ✉ Cortington, 8 Waihi Terrace, Geraldine, South Canterbury, New Zealand

BLAKISTON, Lt Col John Alan Cubitt; s of John Francis Blakiston, CIE (d 1965), of Aberdaron, Gwynedd, and Margaret Dora, *née* Ward-Jackson (d 1991); descended from Sir Matthew Blakiston, Lord Mayor of London 1760; *b* 15 July 1938; *Educ* Wellington, Univ of London; *m* 30 May 1975, Sally Ann, da of Lt-Col J D L Dickson, MC (d 1958); 2 da (Caroline b 22 Nov 1979, Emma b 1 July 1981), 1 s (Matthew b 11 Nov 1982); *Career* RNVR 1956–60, cmmnd 13/18 Royal Hussars (QMO) 1961, seconded to 4 Royal Tank Regt in Borneo 1965, seconded to UN Forces Cyprus 1966–67, Staff Coll RMCS and Camberley 1969–71, regtl duty in NI 1972, cmd Demonstration Sqdn Sch of Infantry 1972–74, SO2 (W) Def Intelligence Staff 1974–76, regtl duty in BAOR and NI 1976–78, German Staff Coll 1979–81, SO1 Def Intelligence Staff 1981–85, SO1 Ops HQ AFCENT 1985–88; sr mil rep AWE Aldermaston, chm NATO and FINABEL (Euro) Nuclear Defence Ctees 1988–93; underwriting memb Lloyds; *Recreations* riding; *Clubs* Cavalry and Guards'; *Style—* Lt Col John A C Blakiston; ✉ Grove House, Lydiard Millicent, Swindon, Wiltshire SN5 3LP (tel 01793 770450)

BLAKSTAD, Michael Björn; s of Gabriel Clifford Clark Blakstad, and Alice Blakstad; *b* 18 April 1940; *Educ* Ampleforth, Oriel Coll Oxford (MA); *m* 1965, Patricia Marilyn, da of Robert Andrew Wotherspoon, DL (d 1977); 1 s, 2 da (twins); *Career* trainee BBC 1962–68, prodr Yorkshire TV 1968–71, freelance prodr 1971–74, ed BBC 1974–80 (progs incl Tomorrow's World and The Risk Business), dir of progs Television South plc 1981–84, fndr and md Blackrod 1980 (sometime chm), fndr Workhouse Ltd 1984, chm and chief exec Workhouse Prodns Ltd 1984–88, jt chief exec Videodisc Co 1984–88, chm Friday Prodns 1984–88, chm Filmscreen Int Ltd 1984–86, chm and chief exec Chrysalis Television Ltd and dir Chrysalis Group plc 1988–90; chm: Workday Ltd 1988–90, Blackrod Interactive Services 1988–90, Workhouse Ltd 1990–2003, Winchester Independent Radio Ltd 1995–98; dir michaelblakstad ltd 2002–, external prof of digital media Univ of Glamorgan 2002–; dir: Televison Enterprise and Asset Mgmnt plc 1991–98, Zenith Entertainment plc 1998; chm: Southern Screen 1998–2004, Exec Steering Gp The Broadbandshow 2002–04; dir: IPPA 1986–90, Int Video Communications Assoc 1988–90 and 1999–2001; chm Winchester Theatre Royal 1990–95 (dir 1988–95), chm of govrs Bedales Sch 2001–05; *Books* The Risk Business (1979), Tomorrow's World Looks to the Eighties (1979), The Communicating Organisation (jtly, 1995), The Liphook Story (2004); *Recreations* golf, opera, theatre, writing; *Clubs* Reform; *Style—* Michael Blakstad, Esq

BLANC, Raymond René Alfred; s of Maurice Blanc, and Anne-Marie, *née* Tournier; *b* 19 November 1949; *Educ* Besançon Coll France (Dip BEPC); *m* 1, 14 Jan 1974 (m dis 1986), Jennifer Colbeck; 2 s (Olivier b 18 Oct 1974, Sebastien b 15 April 1981); m 2, 18 Dec 1990 (sep), Katalin Szoke; *Career* chef; chef patron: Les Quat'Saisons Oxford 1977, Maison Blanc 1978–88, Le Manoir Aux Quat'Saisons 1984–, Le Petit Blanc Oxford 1996, Cheltenham 1997, Birmingham 1999, Manchester 2000, Tunbridge Wells 2004; chef patron and chm Blanc Restaurants Ltd 1984–; TV appearances incl: Food and Drink 1987, In At the Deep End 1989, Chef's Apprentice 1989; own TV series Blanc Mange (BBC 2) 1994; memb: Academy of Culinary Arts, Syndicat de l'Haute Cuisine Française, Relais Et Chateaux Tradition Et Qualité; Personalité de l'année 1990; 2 Michelin stars 1999; Hon DBA Oxford Brookes Univ 1999; Cdr de l'Assoc Int des Maîtres Conseils en Gastronomie Française; *Books* Le Manoir Aux Quat'Saisons (1988), Cooking for Friends (1991), Blanc Mange (1994), A Blanc Christmas (1996), Blanc Vite (1998), Foolproof French Cookery (2002); *Recreations* reading, music, tennis, swimming; *Style—* Raymond Blanc, Esq; ✉ Le Manoir Aux Quat'Saisons, Church Road, Great Milton, Oxfordshire OX44 7PD (tel 01844 278881, fax 01844 278847)

BLAND, Sir (Francis) Christopher Buchan; kt (1993); eldest s of James Franklin MacMahon Bland, of Co Down, and Jess Buchan, *née* Brodie; *b* 29 May 1938; *Educ* Sedbergh, The Queen's Coll Oxford; *m* 1981, Jennifer Mary Denise, elder da of late Rt Hon William Morrison May, MP, of Co Down, and formerly w of Viscount Enfield (now 8 Earl of Strafford); 1 s; *Career* chm: Sir Joseph Causton & Sons 1977–85, LWT Holdings plc 1984–94, Life Sciences International, NFC plc 1995–, Bd of Govrs BBC 1996–2001, British Telecom plc 2001–07; dep chm Independent Broadcasting Authy (IBA) 1972–79; *Recreations* fishing, skiing; *Clubs* Beefsteak; *Style—* Sir Christopher Bland

BLAND, Prof David Edward; OBE (1998); s of Rev Albert Edward Bland, of Blackburn, and Lily, *née* Simmons; *b* 9 December 1940; *Educ* Queen Elizabeth GS Blackburn, UC Durham (BA, MLitt), Univ of Sheffield (PhD); *Career* warden of Sorby Hall and pro-vice-chllr Univ of Sheffield 1964–89, DG Chartered Insurance Inst 1989–2000, head E London Business Sch Univ of E London 2000–02; visiting prof City Univ 1994–; chm: Postwatch SE England 2002–, Thames Region CCWater 2005; CII Gold Medal 2000; Master: Worshipful Co of Insurers, Worshipful Co of Firefighters 1999–2000; fell Inst of Co Accountants 1970 (pres 1990–91), FSCA, FCIPD 1991, FCII 1994, FIRM (memb 2000); *Books* Can Britain Survive? (with KW Watkins, 1971), Managing Higher Education (1990), Principles and Practice of Insurance (1994), Treasury Risk (2000); *Recreations* walking, music; *Clubs* Athenaeum; *Style—* Prof David Bland, OBE; ✉ 31 Dundee Court, 73 Wapping High Street, London E1 9YG (tel 020 7533 0086, fax 020 7553 2963, e-mail davidbland@dunelm.org.uk

BLAND, Jeff; s of Albert Bland, and Marjory Bland; *b* 17 August 1953; *Educ* Carlton GS Bradford, Bradford Tech Coll (City & Guilds, Student of the Year); *m* Jill, *née* Hepburn; *Career* various positions rising to sous chef Gleneagles Hotel 1973–77, relief chef Br Transport Hotels 1978–80, chef Station Hotel Inverness 1980–82; exec chef: Gosforth Park Newcastle 1982–87, Caledonian Edinburgh 1987–90, Cameron House Hotel Alexandria 1990–97 (Scottish Hotel of the Year 1991, 3 AA Rosettes, Egon Ronay Award, Macallan Decanter Restaurant of the Year 1992, RAC Blue Ribbon 1994, Michelin Star 1995 and 1996, AA Hotel of the Year 1995), Balmoral Hotel Edinburgh 1997– (Michelin Star 2003, 2004, 2005 and 2006); demonstrator Good Food Show 1995; guest appearances: Square Meals, Junior Masterchef; guest chef fundraising dinner Michigan USA (raised 1 million dollars); memb: Craft Guild of Chefs 1974, Académie Culinaire de France 1988 (mentor, chm Scottish branch); Craft Guild Chef of the Year 1995, Chefs of GB Chef of the Year 1995, Scottish Chef of the Year Scottish Chef Awards 2003, Icon of Scotland Award 2004; *Recreations* eating out, wine, entertaining friends, running (completed various half marathons and London marathon); *Style—* Jeff Bland, Esq; ✉ Balmoral Hotel, Princes Street, Edinburgh EH2 2EQ (tel 0131 556 2414)

BLANDFORD, Marquess of; (Charles) James Spencer-Churchill; s and h (by 1 w, *see* Mrs John Gough), of 11 Duke of Marlborough, JP, DL, *qv*; *b* 24 November 1955; *Educ* Pinewood, Harrow, RAC Cirencester; *m* 1, 1990 (m dis 2001), Rebecca Mary, da of Peter Few Brown and Mrs John Winnington-Ingram; 1 s (George, Earl of Sunderland b 28 July 1992); m 2, 1 March 2002, Edla Griffiths, da of Alun Griffiths, of Monmouthshire; *Career* insurance broker and helicopter pilot; freelance journalist for Sunday Times, Sunday Mail travel writer, Formula One hospitality and marketing co-ordinator; *Recreations* skiing, flying, shooting; *Clubs* Turf, Annabel's; *Style—* Marquess of Blandford; ✉ Blenheim Palace, Woodstock, Oxfordshire OX20 1PS (mobile 07785 795838); 16 Lawrence Street, London SW3 5NE (tel 020 7351 2730); Woottondown Farmhouse, Wootton, Woodstock, Oxfordshire OX20 1AF (tel 01869 331222, e-mail lordblandford@aol.com)

BLANDFORD, Mark Robert; s of Roy Blandford, of Brobury, Herefordshire, and June, *née* Farr; *b* 25 November 1957, Hereford; *Educ* Hereford Cathedral Sch, Wolverhampton Poly (HND, DipM); *m* 16 May 1981, Patricia, *née* Bowen; 2 da (Lucy b 22 Nov 1987, Sophie b 27 March 1989); *Career* mktg asst Star Aluminium 1979–80, mktg exec Sun Valley Poultry 1980–82, sales exec Radio Wyvern 1982–84, fndr Blandford Betting 1984–97, fndr and exec dir Sportinget plc 1997–2007; nat finalist Entrepreneur of the Year 2000; memb Inst of Mktg 1979; *Recreations* football (Hereford United), poker, horse racing (owner); *Style—* Mark Blandford, Esq

BLANDFORD, Prof Roger David; s of Jack George Blandford, and Janet Margaret Blandford; *b* 28 August 1949; *Educ* King Edward's Sch Birmingham, Magdalene Coll Cambridge (BA, Charles Kingsley Bye Fell, MA, PhD); *m* 1972, Elizabeth Denise Kellett; 2 s; *Career* res fell St John's Coll Cambridge 1973–76, memb Inst for Advanced Study Princeton 1974–75; Caltech: asst prof 1976–79, prof 1979–88, Richard Chace Tolman prof of theoretical astrophysics 1989–94, Pehong & Adele Chen prof of particle astrophysics and cosmology Stanford Univ 1993–, dir Kavli Inst for Particle Astrophysics and Cosmology 1993–; Alfred P Sloan res fell 1980–84, Guggenheim fell 1988–89; FRS, FRAS, FAAAS; *Style—* Prof Roger Blandford, FRS

BLANE, Michael Lawrence; *b* 17 August 1938; *Educ* Washington and Lee Univ, Case Western Reserve Univ (BA, LLB); *Career* enforcement counsel US Securities and Exchange Cmmn 1967–70, vice-pres and asst gen counsel Dean Witter Reynolds Inc 1973–81, sr counsel Merrill Lynch Europe Ltd 1981–90, dir Int Securities Regulatory Orgn 1985–86, gp compliance offr Banque Nationale de Paris 1990–; dir Securities Assoc 1986–88: Rules Ctee, Enforcement Ctee, Authorisation Ctee Bd; memb: 1992 Ctee Int Stock Exchange, Nat Assoc of Securities Dealers, American Arbitration Assoc, Commodity Futures Indust Assoc; *Style—* Michael L Blane, Esq; ✉ Banque Nationale de Paris London, 8–13 King William Street, London EC4P 4HS (tel 020 7895 7216, fax 020 7895 7013)

BLANK, Sir (Maurice) Victor; kt (1999); s of Joseph Blank, and Ruth, *née* Levey; *b* 9 November 1942; *Educ* Stockport GS, St Catherine's Coll Oxford (MA); *m* 29 June 1977, Sylvia Helen, *née* Richford; 2 s (Simon b 1 May 1978, Robert b 23 June 1984), 1 da (Anna b 16 Sept 1979); *Career* ptnr Clifford-Turner (slrs) 1969–81; Charterhouse plc: head of corporate finance and md Charterhouse Bank Ltd 1981–85, chief exec 1985–96, chm 1991–97, chm Charterhouse Bank Ltd 1985–97; chm Mirror Gp 1998–99, chm Trinity Mirror plc 1999–2006, dep chm Coats plc (formerly Coats Viyella plc) 1999–2003 (non-exec dir 1989–2003); GUS plc (formerly The Great Universal Stores plc): non-exec dir 1993–, dep chm 1996–2000, chm 2000–; chm Lloyds TSB Gp plc 2006–; non-exec dir: Williams plc 1995–2000, Chubb plc 2000–04; chm: WellBeing of Women (formerly Birthright) 1989–, Industrial and Devpt Advsy Bd 1999–2004; memb: Cncl Univ of Oxford 2000–, Fin Reporting Cncl 2003–, Advsy Cncl Orch of the Age of Enlightenment; tstee Oxford Univ Law Fndn 1998–2001; advsr: Oxford Environmental Change Unit, RSA; vice-pres Oxford Philomusica; chm of govrs UCS; Freeman City of London; hon fell St Catherine's Coll Oxford 2003–; memb: City of London Slrs' Co, Law Soc; CIMgt, Hon FRCOG 1998; *Books* Weinberg and Blank on Takeovers and Mergers; *Recreations* family, cricket, tennis, theatre; *Clubs* IOD; *Style—* Sir Victor Blank; ✉ GUS plc, One Stanhope Gate, London W1K 1AF (tel 020 7318 6209, fax 020 7318 6233); Lloyds TSB Group plc, 25 Gresham Street, London EC2V 7HN

BLANKSTONE, Michael David; s of Solomon Julius Blankstone (d 1981), and Isabel, *née* Franklin (d 1979); *b* 20 November 1936; *Educ* Quarry Bank HS Liverpool; *m* 17 June 1963, Anne, *née* Harrison; 2 s (Mark Lewis b 13 April 1964, Neil Simon b 6 Jan 1968); *Career* with family furniture mfrg business 1953–59, trainee then stockbroker Hornby Tobin & Ockleston 1959–66, ptnr Neilson Hornby Crichton 1966–75, sr ptnr Blankstone Sington & Co 1975–89 (co-fndr), chm Blankstone Sington Ltd 1989–; chm Blankstone Investments Ltd; chm The Stock Exchange Liverpool 1988–90 (vice-chm 1986–88), former memb Stock Exchange NW Advsy Gp, former chm Liverpool Stock Exchange Benevolent Fund, memb London Stock Exchange Benevolent Fund 1999; former memb: Cncl Liverpool Sch of Tropical Med, Nat Museums and Galleries on Merseyside Devpt Tst; tstee Liverpool Jewish Youth & Community Centre; past tstee: Hillsborough Disaster Appeal, Royal Liverpool Philharmonic Soc Jubilee Fndn Tst; MSI (memb Stock Exchange 1964), FInstD 1975; *Recreations* travel, reading, charity work; *Style—* Michael D Blankstone, Esq; ✉ Blankstone Sington Ltd, 91 Duke Street, Liverpool L1 5AA (tel 0151 707 1707, fax 0151 707 1247)

BLANNING, Prof Timothy Charles William (Tim); s of Thomas Walter Blanning, and Gwendolyn Marchant, *née* Jones; *b* 21 April 1942; *Educ* King's Sch Bruton, Sidney Sussex Coll Cambridge (MA, PhD, LittD); *m* 1988, Nicky Jones; 1 s (b 2001), 1 da (b 2004); *Career* Univ of Cambridge: asst lectr in history 1972–76, lectr in history 1976–87, reader in modern European history 1987–92, prof of modern European history 1992–; fell Sidney Sussex Coll Cambridge 1968– (res fell 1965–68); FBA 1990; *Books* Joseph II and Enlightened Despotism (1970), Reform and Revolution in Mainz 1740–1803 (1974), The French Revolution in Germany (1983), The Origins of the French Revolutionary Wars (1986), The French Revolution: Aristocrats versus Bourgeois? (1987), Joseph II (1994),

The Oxford Illustrated History of Modern Europe (ed, 1996), The French Revolutionary Wars 1787–1802 (1996), The Rise and Fall of the French Revolution (ed, 1996), History and Biography: Essays in Honour of Derek Beales (ed, 1996), The French Revolution: Class War or Culture Clash? (1998), The Short Oxford History of Europe: The Eighteenth Century (ed, 2000), The Short Oxford History of Europe: The Nineteenth Century (ed, 2000), The Oxford History of Modern Europe (ed, 2000), The Culture of Power and the Power of Culture: Old Regime Europe 1660–1789 (2002), Unity and Diversity in European Culture c 1800 (ed, 2006), The Pursuit of Glory: Europe 1648–1815 (2007); *Recreations* gardening, music, dog walking; *Clubs* Athenaeum; *Style*— Prof Tim Blanning, FBA, ✉ Faculty of History, West Road, Cambridge CB3 9EF (tel 01223 335308, fax 01223 335968, e-mail tcb1000@cam.ac.uk)

BLASHFORD-SNELL, Col John Nicholas; OBE (1996, MBE 1969); s of Alderman the Rev Prebendary Leland John Blashford-Snell, MBE, TD (d 1978), of Angmering-on-Sea, W Sussex, and Gwendolen Ives, *née* Sadler (d 1968); *b* 22 October 1936; *Educ* Victoria Coll Jersey, RMA Sandhurst, Staff Coll Camberley; *m* 27 Aug 1960, Judith (Frances), da of Lt-Col Beresford Thomas Sherman, OBE (d 1982), of Tivoli Court, Westbourne, Dorset; 2 da (Emma b 1964, Victoria b 1967); *Career* cmmnd RE 1957, Trg Adj 33 Ind Field Sqdn RE Cyprus 1959–62 (Troop Cdr 1958–59), Troop Cdr Junior Leaders Regt RE 1962–63, Instr & Adventure Trg Offr RMA Sandhurst 1963–66, Adj 3 Div Engrs 1966–67, leader Gt Abbai (Blue Nile) Expdn 1968, Staff Coll (RMCS and Camberley) 1968–69, GSO2 MOD 1970–72, leader Br Trans-Americas Expdn 1972, OC 48 Field Sqdn RE (Belize, Oman, N Ireland) 1972–74, leader Zaïre River Expdn 1974–75, GSO1 MOD 1975–76, CO Junior Leaders Regt RE 1976–78, Cdr Operation Drake 1978–81, ACPR MOD 1981–82, Cdr Fort George Volunteers 1983, Cdr Operation Raleigh 1984–89 (DG 1989–91); lectr MOD 1991–; leader: Kalahari Quest Expdn 1990, Karnali Quest Expdn 1991, Karnali Gorge Expdn 1992, Mongolia Amarsana Expdn 1992 and numerous other expdns since; chm: Starting Point Appeal The Merseyside Youth Assoc 1993–2001, The Scientific Exploration Soc; tstee Operation New World; pres: Liverpool Construction Crafts Guild, Galley Hill Gun Club, Just A Drop, The Vole Club, Centre for Fortean Zoology; hon vice-pres St George's Day Club; Darien Medal (Colombia) 1972, The Segrave Trophy 1974, Livingstone Medal RSGS 1975, Paul Harris Fellow Rotary Int 1981, Patron's Medal RGS 1993, Gold Medal Inst of Royal Engrs 1994, La Paz Medal (Bolivia) 2000; Freeman City of Hereford 1984; Hon DSc Univ of Durham 1986, Hon DEng Bournemouth Univ 1997; FRSGS 1976; *Books* Weapons and Tactics (with Tom Wintringham, 1973), Where the Trails Run Out (1974), In the Steps of Stanley (1975), Expeditions the Experts' Way (with Alistair Ballantine, 1977), A Taste for Adventure (1978), In the Wake of Drake (with Mike Cable, 1980), Operation Drake (with Mike Cable, 1981), Mysteries, Encounters with the Unexplained (1983), Operation Raleigh - The Start of an Adventure (1987), Operation Raleigh, Adventure Challenge (with Ann Tweedy, 1988), Operation Raleigh, Adventure Unlimited (with Ann Tweedy), Something Lost Behind the Ranges (1994), Mammoth Hunt (with Rula Lenska, 1996), Kota Mama (with Richard Snailham, 2000), East to the Amazon (with Richard Snailham, 2002); *Recreations* shooting, travel, food and wine, photography; *Clubs* Explorers, Artists' (Liverpool), Buck's, Travellers, Jersey Pistol; *Style*— Col John Blashford-Snell, OBE; ✉ c/o Scientific Exploration Society, Expedition Base, Motcombe, Dorset SP7 9PB (tel 01747 854456, fax 01747 851351, e-mail jbs@ses-explore.org)

BLATCHFORD, Ian; *b* 17 August 1965; *Educ* Mansfield Coll Oxford (MA); *Career* grad trainee Bank of England 1986–88, corp finance exec Barclays de Zoete Wedd 1988, financial controller and deputy finance dir Arts Cncl of GB 1989–94, financial controller Cricket Communications 1994–96, dir of finance and projects Royal Acad of Arts 1996–2002, dep dir V&A 2002–; tstee: London Sch of Osteopathy, Sonic Arts Network, American Friends of the V&A; FCMA 2002 (ACMA 1994); *Style*— Ian Blatchford, Esq; ✉ Victoria and Albert Museum, Cromwell Road, South Kensington, London SW7 2RL (tel 020 7942 2259, e-mail i.blatchford@vam.ac.uk)

BLATHERWICK, Sir David Elliott Spiby; KCMG (1997, CMG 1990), OBE (1973); s of late Edward S Blatherwick; *b* 13 July 1941; *Educ* Lincoln Sch, Wadham Coll Oxford; *m* 1964, (Margaret) Clare, *née* Crompton; 1 da (b 1969), 1 s (b 1972); *Career* HM Dip Serv (ret); MECAS 1964, third later second sec Foreign Office 1966–68, second sec Kuwait 1968–70, first sec Dublin 1970–73, first sec FCO 1973–77, first sec and head of Chancery Cairo 1977–81, cnsllr and head of Political Affrs Div Northern Ireland Office 1981–83, head of Energy, Sci and Space Dept 1983–85, on leave to Stanford Univ California 1985–86, cnsllr and head of Chancery UK Mission to UN NY 1986–89, princ fin offr and chief inspector FCO 1989–91: HM ambass: Dublin 1991–95, Cairo 1995–99; chm Egyptian Br Chamber of Commerce 1999–; jt chm Anglo-Irish Encounter 2003–; *Clubs* Athenaeum; *Style*— Sir David Blatherwick, KCMG, OBE; ✉ Egyptian British Chamber of Commerce, 299 Oxford Street, London W1A 4EG

BLATTLER, Daniel; s of Bruno Blattler, of Switzerland, and Adelheid Blattler; *m* 7 Dec 1990, Norma, da of Clifford Wint; 1 s (Louis), 1 da (Gemma); *Career* apprenticeship as reproduction specialist Switzerland; fndr memb Lith-Work Switzerland 1988–92, diploma lectr in pre-press prodn Switzerland 1990, md e-fact London 1997– (prodn mangr 1996–97), fndr blattler ltd (brand and mktg consultancy and print mgmnt) 2003; recipient: numerous awards annually for best poster and fine art reproduction 1988–92, various awards for best catalogue prodn 1996–2003; e-fact recipient of numerous awards for design and photography 1996–2003; MInstD, memb Mktg Soc; *Style*— Daniel Blattler, Esq; ✉ 31 Whitmore Road, Beckenham, Kent BR3 3NU (tel 020 8663 3261, fax 020 8663 1842, e-mail daniel@blattler.com)

BLAU, Dr Joseph Norman; s of Abraham Moses Blau (d 1942), and Reisla, *née* Vogel (d 1942); *b* 5 October 1928; *Educ* Dame Alice Owens Sch, Bart's Med Coll Univ of London (MB BS, MD); *m* 19 Dec 1968, Jill Elise, da of Geoffrey C Seligman; 2 s (Justin b 15 Jan 1970, Adrian b 27 April 1972), 1 da (Rosie b 9 Sept 1975); *Career* Nat Serv Lt and Capt RAMC 1953–55; med offr: SW Dist HQ Taunton 1954, Army Neurological Unit Wheatley Oxon 1955; middle and sr registrar London and Maida Vale Hosp 1960–61, Nuffield Med Research Fellowship Mass Gen Hosp Boston USA 1962; conslt neurologist: Nat Hosps for Neurology and Neurosurgery Queen Square and Maida Vale 1962–93, Royal Nat Throat Nose and Ear Hosp 1965–93, Northwick Park Hosp Harrow Middx 1972–93; hon sr lectr Histopathology Dept Guy's Med Sch 1970–89, hon dir and conslt neurologist City of London Migraine Clinic 1980–, hon conslt neurologist Nat Hosp for Neurology and Neurosurgery Queen Square 1993–, conslt neurologist King George Hosp Ilford 1995–2003, conslt neurologist Hosp of St John and St Elizabeth London 1999–2003, conslt neurologist St Luke's Hosp for the Clergy 2003–; chm: Soc of Authors Writer Gp (Med Writers Gp) 1989–91, Br Assoc Study of Headache 1997–; former pres London Jewish Med Soc, hon med advsr Br Migraine Assoc 1980–; memb: Cncl Neurological Section RSM 1984–87 and 1994–97, Scientific Advsy Ctee Migraine Tst 1989–92, Professional and Linguistic Assessment Bd General Med Cncl 1990–93, Assoc of Br Neurologists, Advsy Cncl Br Soc of Music Therapy, Cncl Br Assoc for Performing Arts Med 1993–97, Cncl Anglo-Dutch Migraine Assoc 2000–02; memb Editorial Bd Headache Quarterly; memb RSM; FRCP, FRCPath; *Publications* Migraine - Clinical, Therapeutic, Conceptual and Research Aspects (ed and contrib, 1987), Migraine (with J F Drummond, 1991), Behaviour During a Cluster Headache (1993); author of chapters in books and original articles on headache, migraine and other neurological topics; *Recreations* cello playing, history of ideas; *Style*— Dr J N Blau; ✉ 5 Marlborough Hill, London NW8 0NN (tel 020 7586 3804); Private Consulting Rooms, National Hospital for Neurology and Neurosurgery, Queen Square, London WC1N 3BG (tel 020 7829 8792, fax 020 7833 8658); St Luke's Hospital for the Clergy, 14 Fitzroy Square, London W1T 6AH (tel 020 7388 4954, fax 020 7383 4812)

BLAUG, Prof Mark; s of Bernard Blaug (d 1949), and Sarah, *née* Toeman (d 1974); *b* 3 April 1927; *Educ* Queen's Coll NY (BA), Columbia Univ NY (MA, PhD); *m* 1, 1946 (m dis 1951), Rose Lapone; *m* 2, 1954 (m dis 1960), Brenda M Ellis; 1 s (David Ricardo b 1956); *m* 3, 1969, Ruth Marilyn, da of Ronald Towse (d 1971); 1 s (Tristan Bernard b 1971); *Career* asst prof Yale Univ 1954–62, Inst of Educn Univ of London 1963–84 (sr lectr, reader, prof), lectr LSE 1963–78; prof emeritus: Univ of London 1984, Univ of Buckingham 1984; visiting prof: Univ of Exeter 1989–99, Univ of Amsterdam 1999–, Erasmus Univ Rotterdam 2001–; conslt 1964–90 (World Bank, UNESCO, ILO, Ford Fndn), editorial conslt Edward Elgar Publishing 1986–; memb: American Econ Assoc, Royal Econ Soc; Hon DSc Univ of Buckingham 1994; foreign hon memb Royal Netherlands Acad of Arts and Scis 1986, distinguished fell History of Economics Soc 1990; FBA 1989; *Books* Ricardian Economics (1958), The Causes of Graduate Employment in India (1969), Introduction to the Economics of Education (1970), Education and The Employment Problem in Developing Countries (1973), Economic History and the History of Economics (1986), The Economics of Education and the Education of an Economist (1987), John Maynard Keynes, Life, Ideas, Legacy (1990), Economic Theories: True or False? (1990), The Methodology of Economics (1992), Economic Theory in Retrospect (1996), Not Only an Economist (1997), Great Economists Before Keynes (1997), Great Economists Since Keynes (1998), Who's Who in Economics (ed, 4 edn 2003); *Recreations* talking, walking, sailing; *Style*— Prof Mark Blaug, FBA; ✉ Langsford Barn, Peter Tavy, Tavistock, Devon PL19 9LY (tel 01822 810562); 5E Binnenvestgracht 9, 2311 VH Leiden, The Netherlands (tel 00 31 071 566 3222)

BLAXTER, Prof John Harry Savage; s of Kenneth William Blaxter, CMG (d 1964), and Janet Hollis (d 1981); *b* 6 January 1929; *Educ* Berkhamsted Sch, Univ of Oxford (MA, DSc); *m* 20 Dec 1952, Valerie Ann, da of Gerald McElligott; 1 da (Julia b 1955), 1 s (Timothy b 1958); *Career* sci offr then sr sci offr Marine Lab Aberdeen 1952–64, lectr Zoology Dept Univ of Aberdeen 1964–69; Scot Marine Biological Assoc Dunstaffnage Marine Lab Oban: princ sci offr 1969–74, sr princ sci offr special merit 1974–85, dep chief sci offr special merit 1985–91, res fell 1991–2001; memb Cncl Marine Biological Assoc: 1973–76, 1977–80, 1983–86 and 1989–93; pres Fisheries Soc of the Br Isles 1992–97 (Beverton Medal 1998); tstee Argyll Fisheries Tst 1999–; emeritus fell The Leverhulme Tst 1991–93, hon prof Dept of Molecular and Biological Sci and Inst of Aquaculture Univ of Stirling 1986–, hon prof Dept of Biology and Preclinical Med Univ of St Andrews 1990–2000; ed: Advances in Marine Biology 1977–98, ICES Journal of Marine Science 1991–98; Highest Achievement Award American Inst of Fishery Biologists 1998; Hon DUniv Stirling 1994; FIBiol, FRSE 1974; *Publications* over 130 papers in learned journals on fish behaviour and physiology; *Recreations* sailing, gardening, golf; *Style*— Prof John H S Blaxter, FRSE; ✉ Dems Lodge, Barcaldine, Oban, Argyll PA37 1SF (tel 01631 720228)

BLEARS, Hazel; PC (2005), MP; *Career* MP (Lab) Salford 1997–; Parly under-sec of state: for Health 2001–02, for Public Health 2002–03, min of state Home Office 2003–06, chair Lab Party and min without portfolio 2006–07; sec of state for the community and local govt 2007–; *Style*— The Rt Hon Hazel Blears, MP; ✉ House of Commons, London SW1A 0AA (tel 020 7219 3000)

BLEASDALE, Cyril; OBE (1988); s of Frederick Bleasdale (d 2001), and Alice Bleasdale (d 1976); *b* 8 July 1934; *Educ* Stanford Business Sch; *m* 1970, Catherine Valerie; 2 da (Jane b 1970, Emma b 1972); *Career* md Freightliner 1975–82, dir BR Intercity 1982–86, gen mangr BR LM 1986–89, dir Scotrail 1990–94; md Railnews Ltd 1997–, DG Chartered Inst of Logistics and Tport 1999–; chm Hertford Business Incubation Centre 2002–; FCILT, FIMgt; *Recreations* squash, keep fit; *Style*— Cyril Bleasdale, Esq, OBE; ✉ 22 Trafalgar Street, Cheltenham GL50 1UH (tel 01698 854 008)

BLEASE, Hon (William) Victor; eldest s of Baron Blease, JP (Life Peer), qv; *b* 1942; *m* 1969, Rose Mary, da of Alan Seaton; 2 s, 2 da; *Career* chief exec NI Housing Exec until 1999, subsequently visiting prof of housing Univ of Ulster; *Style*— The Hon W Victor Blease

BLEASE, Baron (Life Peer UK 1978), of Cromac in the City of Belfast; William John Blease; JP (Belfast 1974); s of late William John Blease, and Sarah Blease; *b* 28 May 1914; *Educ* Belfast Tech, New Univ of Ulster; *m* 1939, Sarah Evelyn (d 1995), da of William Caldwell; 3 s, 1 da; *Career* industrial rels conslt, former union official; memb IBA 1974–79; Hon DLitt Univ of Ulster 1972, Hon LLD Queen's Univ Belfast 1982; *Recreations* reading, DIY; *Style*— The Rt Hon Lord Blease; ✉ House of Lords, London SW1A 0PW

BLEDISLOE, 3 Viscount (1935 UK); Christopher Hiley Ludlow Bathurst; QC (1978); s of 2 Viscount Bledisloe, QC (d 1979); *b* 24 June 1934; *Educ* Eton, Trinity Coll Oxford; *m* 1962 (m dis 1986), Elizabeth Mary, da of late Sir Edward Thompson; 2 s (Hon Rupert Edward Ludlow b 13 March 1964, Hon Otto Benjamin Charles b 16 June 1971), 1 da (Hon Matilda Blanche (Hon Mrs Clark) b 16 Feb 1967); *Heir* s, Hon Rupert Bathurst; *Career* called to the Bar Gray's Inn 1959; sits as ind peer in House of Lords, elected hereditary peer 1999; *Clubs* Garrick; *Style*— The Rt Hon the Viscount Bledisloe, QC; ✉ Fountain Court, Temple, London EC4Y 9DH (tel 020 7583 3335, fax 020 7353 0329)

BLENNERHASSETT, Sir (Marmaduke) Adrian Francis William; 7 Bt (UK 1809), of Blennerville, Co Kerry; s of Lt Sir Marmaduke Charles Henry Joseph Casimir Blennerhassett, 6 Bt, RNVR (d 1940), and Gwenfra Mary, *née* Harrington-Morgan; *b* 25 May 1940; *Educ* Michael Hall, McGill Univ Montreal (BSc), Imperial Coll London (MSc), Cranfield Business Sch (MBA); *m* 1972, Carolyn Margaret, da of late Gilbert Brown; 1 da (Celina Mary Charlotte b 1973), 1 s (Charles Henry Marmaduke b 1975); *Heir* s, Charles Blennerhassett; *Clubs* Travellers; *Style*— Sir Adrian Blennerhassett, Bt

BLESSED, Brian; s of William Blessed, of Bolton-on-Dearne, S Yorks, and Hilda, *née* Wall; *b* 9 October 1936; *Educ* Bolton-on-Dearne Secondary Modern; *m* 28 Dec 1978, Hildegard Neil *née* Zimmermann; 1 da (Rosalind Josephine b 16 April 1975); *Career* actor; pres: Cncl for Nat Parks, Yorkshire Wildlife Tst; tstee Bowles Rocks Tst; patron: Freshfields, Kinder Mountain Rescue, The Nepal Tst, Scope; *Theatre* RSC: Claudius in Hamlet, Hastings in Richard III, Exeter in Henry V; other roles incl: Maxim Gorky in State of Revolution, John Freeman in Metropolis, Old Deuteronomy in Cats, Henry II in The Lion in Winter; An Evening with Brian Blessed (one man show) 1992–93 & 1995–96, Hard Times (West End), Sir Tunbelly Clumsey in The Relapse (RNT), Baron Bomburst in Chitty, Chitty, Bang, Bang (London Palladium) 2002–03; *Television* PC Fancy Smith in Z Cars, Augustus Caesar in I Claudius, Albert in George's Sand, King Guthram in Churchill's People, Porthos in The Three Musketeers, Pepone in The Little World of Don Camillo, Spiro in My Family and Other Animals, King Richard in Blackadder (first series), The Boy Dominic, Prof Atticus in Magyver - Lost Treasure of Atlantis, Squire Western in Tom Jones; *Films* Prince Vultan in Flash Gordon, Long John Silver in Return to Treasure Island, Talthybius in Trojan Women, Pedro in Man of La Mancha, Exeter in Henry V, General Zukov in War and Remembrance, Lord Locksley in Robin Hood Prince of Thieves, General Gonse in Prisoners of Honour, Antonio in Much Ado About Nothing, The Ghost in Hamlet, Lear (also dir), Clayton in Walt Disney's Tarzan, Boss Nass in Star Wars - The Phantom Menace, Leonidas in Alexander The Great; *Books* The Turquoise Mountain, The Dynamite Kid, Nothing's Impossible, Blessed Everest, Quest for the Lost World; *Style*— Brian Blessed, Esq; ✉ c/o Derek Webster, Associated International Management, 1 Blythe Road, London W14 0HG (tel 020 7348 4850, fax 020 7348 4851, e-mail info@aimagent.com, website www.aimagent.com)

BLETHYN, Brenda; OBE (2003); *Educ* Guildford Sch of Dance and Drama; *Career* actress; Hon DLitt Univ of Kent at Canterbury 1999; *Theatre* NT incl: Beaux Stratagem (Best Actress nomination), Troilus and Cressida, Tambourlaine, Tales From the Vienna Woods, Madras House, The Passion, Bedroom Farce, The Double Dealer, Fruits of Enlightenment, Strife, A Midsummer Night's Dream, The Guardsman, The Provoked Wife, Dalliance; other roles incl: Steaming (Comedy Theatre, Best Supporting Actress Award), Benefactors (Vaudeville, Best Actress nomination), Crimes of the Heart (Bush), A Doll's House (Royal Exchange), Born Yesterday (Royal Exchange Manchester), An Ideal Husband (Royal Exchange Manchester), The Dramatic Attitudes of Miss Fanny Kemble (Southampton), Absent Friends (Manhattan Theater NY, Theater World Award for Outstanding Performance), Wildest Dreams (RSC), The Bed Before Yesterday (Almeida), Habeas Corpus (Donmar), Mrs Warren's Profession (Strand); *Television* incl: The Labours of Erica (2 series), Death of An Expert Witness, A Chance in a Million (3 series, Comedy Award), Alas Smith and Jones, Tales of the Unexpected, The Shawl, All Good Things, Bedroom Farce, Play for Today (Grown Ups), The Richest Woman In The World, Yes Minister, King Lear, Henry VI, The Story Teller, The Bullion Boys, The Buddha of Suburbia, Sleeping with Mickey, Outside Edge (3 series, Best TV Comedy Actress Award), Between the Sheets, Belonging; *Film* incl: The Witches, A River Runs Through It 1992, Secrets and Lies 1996 (Best Actress Award Cannes 1996, Golden Globe Award for Best Actress 1997, London Film Critics' Circle Award for Best British Actress 1997, Oscar nomination for Best Actress 1997, BAFTA Award for Best Actress 1997), Remember Me 1996, Girl's Night 1997, Music From Another Room 1997, In the Winter Dark 1997, Little Voice 1997 (Oscar, Golden Globe, Screen Actors Guild, and BAFTA nominations for Best Supporting Actress 1999), Night Train 1998, Daddy and Them 1998, RKO 281 1999, Saving Grace 1999 (Golden Globe nomination for Best Actress 2001, Variety Club (GB) Best Actress Award 2001), On the Nose 2000, The Sleeping Dictionary 2000, Anne Frank 2001 (Emmy nomination for Best Supporting Actress 2001), Lovely and Amazing 2002, Pumpkin 2002, Plots with a View 2002, Sonny 2002, Blizzard 2002, The Sleeping Dictionary 2003, Beyond the Sea 2004, A Way of Life 2004, Pride & Prejudice 2005; *Style*— Miss Brenda Blethyn, OBE; ✉ c/o ICM, Oxford House, 76 Oxford Street, London W1N 0AX (tel 020 7636 6565, fax 020 7323 0101, e-mail b.blethyn@btinternet.com)

BLEWITT, Maj Sir Shane Gabriel Basil; GCVO (1996, KCVO 1989, CVO 1987, LVO 1981); s of late Col Basil Blewitt; *b* 25 March 1935; *Educ* Ampleforth, ChCh Oxford (MA); *m* 1969, Julia, da of late Robert Henry Calvert, and wid of Maj John Morrogh-Bernard, of the Irish Gds; 1 s, 1 da, 1 step s, 1 step da; *Career* Army Service Irish Gds 1956–74 (BAOR, Germany, NI, Aden, Hong Kong); Antony Gibbs & Sons Ltd 1974; Keeper of the Privy Purse and Treas to HM The Queen 1988–96 (Asst Keeper 1975–85, Dep Keeper 1985–87), Extra Equerry to HM The Queen 1996–; memb: Kings Fund Gen Cncl 1989–, Cncl King Edward VII Hosp for Officers 1989–; *Clubs* White's, Army and Navy; *Style*— Maj Sir Shane Blewitt, GCVO; ✉ tel 01798 342143, e-mail blewittshane@aol.com

BLIN, Raymond Ellis; s of Arnold Blin, of Newton Mearns, Glasgow, and Helen, *née* Shenken; *b* 6 October 1950; *Educ* Hutchesons' GS, Univ of Aberdeen; *m* 3 Aug 1982, Shoana Marshall, da of John Marsh; 1 da (Francesca Anna Kimberley b 28 May 1990); *Career* articled clerk Kerr McLeod & Co (now Deloitte & Co) 1969–76, CA 1976, ptnr Insolvency Douglas Laing and Jackson CA's 1977–81; Pannell Kerr Forster: local managing ptnr 1981–89, regnl managing ptnr Scotland 1990–92, exec ptnr Nat Firm 1992–98, nat ops ptnr until 1998; nat ops ptnr Baker Tilly 1998–; dir Inside Out Devpt Ltd 1993–; ICAS, IPA, MCIM, SPI; *Recreations* showjumping and breeding horses, bridge; *Style*— Raymond Blin, Esq

BLISS, Prof Christopher John Emile; s of John Llwelyn Bliss of London (d 1978), a founder of the BBC TV service from 1936, working as a "boffin" designer, etc, and Patricia Paula, *née* Dubern; *b* 17 February 1940, London; *Educ* Finchley Catholic GS, King's Coll Cambridge (BA, PhD); *m* 1, 1964, Heather, da of Cyril Midmer, of Dublin; 1 s (John Benet b 1966), 2 da (Anna Katharine b 1968, Madeline Frances b 1974); m 2, 1983, Ghada, da of Adel Saqf El Hait, of Jordan; 1 s (Larry Kareem b 1996); *Career* fell Christ's College Cambridge 1965–71, lecturer in economics Univ of Cambridge 1967–71 (asst lecturer 1965–67), prof of economics Univ of Essex 1971–77; fell Nuffield Coll Oxford 1977–, Nuffield prof of economics Univ of Oxford 1992– (Nuffield reader in economics 1977–92); ed: Review of Economic Studies 1967–71, Oxford Economic Papers 1989–96, Economic Jl 1996–2004; fell Econometric Soc 1978, FBA 1988; *Books* Capital Theory of the Distribution of Income (1975), Palanpur: the Economy of an Indian Village (with N H Stern), Trade, Growth and Inequalit (2007); *Recreations* music; *Style*— Prof Christopher Bliss, FBA; ✉ 11 Heyford Road, Steeple Aston, Oxfordshire OX25 4SU; Nuffield College, Oxford OX1 1NF (tel 01865 278573, e-mail christopher.bliss@nuffield.ox.ac.uk)

BLISS, Dr Timothy Vivian Pelham; s of late Cdr Pelham Marryat Bliss, RN, and Elizabeth Cotton, *née* Sproule; *b* 27 July 1940; *Educ* Dean Close Sch Cheltenham, McGill Univ Montreal (BSc, PhD), Imperial Coll London, Hatfield Poly (BSc); *m* 1, 1975 (m dis 1994), Virginia Catherine Morton-Evans; 2 step da (Clara, Catherine), 1 step s (James); m 2, 1994, Isabel Frances Vasseur; 2 step s (Roman, Blaise); 1 da by Katherine Sarah Clough (Linnea Ann Susan b 4 Feb 1981); *Career* memb scientific staff MRC 1967–2006, head Div of Neurophysiology Nat Inst for Medical Research 1988–2006; visiting prof: Dept of Physiology UCL 1993–, Univ of Paris Sud Orsay 1996; Bristol Myers Squibb Award for Neuroscience (with E R Kandel) 1991, Feldberg Prize 1994, Br Neuroscience Assoc Award 2003; memb: Brain Research Assoc 1967–, Physiological Soc 1968–, European Neuroscience Assoc (memb Scientific Program Ctee 1994–98); tstee Sir John Soane's Museum 2004–; FRS 1994, FMedSci 1998; *Recreations* naval history, travelling; *Clubs* Academy; *Style*— Dr T V P Bliss, FRS; ✉ National Institute for Medical Research, Mill Hill, London NW7 1AA (tel 020 8816 2382, fax 020 8906 4477, e-mail tbliss@nimr.mrc.ac.uk)

BLIZZARD, Robert John (Bob); MP; s of Arthur Blizzard (d 2001), and Joan Blizzard (d 1994); *b* 31 May 1950; *Educ* Culford Sch Bury St Edmunds, Univ of Birmingham (BA); *m* 1978, Lyn; 1 s (Christopher), 1 da (Laura); *Career* head of English: Crayford Sch Bexley 1976–86, Lynn Grove HS Gorleston Norfolk 1986–97; MP (Lab) Waveney 1997–; PPS to: Baroness Hayman 1999–2001, Rt Hon Nicholas Brown, MP 2001–03, Rt Hon Douglas Alexander, MP 2005–; chair: Br Brazilian All-Pty Gp, All-Pty Gp on Oil and Gas Industry, Br Chile All-Pty Gp, Latin America All-Pty Gp, Renewable Tport Fuels All-Pty Gp; sec All-Pty Jazz Appreciation Gp; cncllr Waveney DC 1987–97 (ldr 1991–97); memb: NUT, GMB; *Recreations* walking, skiing, listening to jazz, watching rugby and cricket; *Clubs* Royal Norfolk & Suffolk Yacht, Ronnie Scott's, 606; *Style*— Bob Blizzard, Esq, MP; ✉ House of Commons, London SW1A 0AA (e-mail blizzardb@parliament.uk, website www.bobblizzardmp.co.uk); tel 01502 514913, fax 01502 580674

BLOCH, (Andrew Charles) Danby; s of late Prof Moishe Rudolf Bloch, and Mary Hall Bloch; *b* 19 December 1945; *Educ* Tonbridge, Wadham Coll Oxford (MA); *m* 1968, Sandra, da of late William Wilkinson; 1 s (Adam b 1972), 1 da (Hester b 1974); *Career* researcher Oxford Centre for Mgmnt Studies (now Templeton Coll) 1968–70; dir: Grosvenor Advisory Services Ltd 1971–74, Oxford Fine Arts Ltd 1975–85, Raymond Godfrey & Partners Ltd 1974–, Taxbriefs Ltd 1975–; chm Rivington Street Hldgs Ltd (formerly T1PS.com) 2000–07, chm Helm Godfrey Ptnrs 2000–; memb Steering Ctee for Investment Advsrs' Cert of Securities Inst; regular weekly column on taxation (and related topics): The Times 1979–82 and 1986–88, Sunday Times 1988–91; regular fin column in Daily Telegraph 1982–86; chm Bd of Govrs Oxford Brookes Univ (formerly Oxford Poly) 1998–2004 (memb 1990–, dep chm 1993–98), pro-chllr Oxford Brookes Univ 2004–; tstee Oxford Inst of Legal Practice 1993–98 (chm 1994–95 and 1996–97), patron Friends of the Pitt Rivers Museum Oxford 2000–, chm Oxfordshire Visual Arts Devpt Assoc (OVADA) 2004–, memb Advsy Bd Modern Art Oxford (formerly MOMA Oxford) 2006– (memb Cncl 1990–2006); memb Personal Fin Soc; Hon DUniv Oxford Brookes 2004; *Books* Providing Financial Advice, Financial Advice, Planning for School and College Fees (co-author); ed CII dip in financial planning learning texts: Taxation, Trusts, Tax and the Legal Aspects of Business, Pension Income Options, Pension Funding Options, Investments; *Style*— Danby Bloch, Esq; ✉ 17 Norham Road, Oxford OX2 6SF (tel 01865 512661, fax 01865 558308); Taxbriefs Ltd, 2–5 Benjamin Street, London EC1M 5QL (tel 020 7250 0967, fax 020 7251 8867, e-mail danby@bloch.com)

BLOCH, Prof Maurice E F; *b* 21 October 1939, Caen, France; *Educ* sch in Paris, LSE (BA), Univ of Cambridge (PhD); *m*; 2 c; *Career* lectr Univ of Wales Swansea 1967–68, lectr LSE 1968–76, reader Univ of London 1976–83, prof of anthropology Univ of London 1983–; convenor Anthropology Dept LSE 1985–88 and 1990–; visiting prof: Univ of Calif Berkeley 1974–75, Univ of Paris Nanterre 1979, Univ of Stockholm 1980–81, Nat Ethnology Museum of Japan 1984; dir d'études associé École des Hautes Études en Sciences Sociales France 1982–83; Rivers Medal Royal Anthropological Inst 1983; fell Danish Centre for the Humanities Copenhagen 1988; FBA 1990; *Books* Placing the Dead: Tombs, Ancestral Villages and Kinship Organization in Madagascar (1971), Political Laguage, Oratory and Traditional Society (ed, 1975), Marxist Analyses and Social Anthropology (ed, 1975), Death and the Regeneration of Life (ed, 1982), Marxism and Anthropology: The History of a Relationship (1983), From Blessing to Violence: History and Ideology in the Circumcision Ritual of the Merina of Madagascar (1986), Ritual, History and Power - Selected Papers in Anthropology (1989), Money and the Morality of Exchange (ed, 1989), Prey into Hunter: The Politics of Religious Experience (1991); author of numerous articles in publications and jls; *Style*— Prof Maurice Bloch, FBA; ✉ Department of Anthropology, London School of Economics and Political Science, Houghton Street, London WC2A 2AE (tel 020 7405 7686, fax 020 7242 0392)

BLOCH, Michael Anthony; s of Richard Bloch, and Ruth, *née* Grant; *b* 24 September 1953; *Educ* Portadown Coll, St John's Coll Cambridge (MA, LLB); *Career* called to the Bar Inner Temple 1978; assisted Maître Suzanne Blum of Paris with affairs of the Duchess of Windsor and her Estate 1979–88; literary executor of James Lees-Milne (d 1997), cr website www.jameslessmilne.com; author; *Books* The Duke of Windsor's War (1982), Operation Willi (1984), Wallis and Edward (1986), The Secret File of the Duke of Windsor (1988), The Reign and Abdication of Edward VIII (1990), Ribbentrop (1992, new edn 2003), The Duchess of Windsor (1996), FM: The Life of Frederick Matthias Alexander (2004); ed later diaries of James Lees-Milne: Deep Romantic Chasm 1979–81 (2000), Holy Dread 1982–84 (2001), Beneath a Waning Moon 1985–87 (2003), Ceaseless Turmoil 1988–92 (2004), The Milk of Paradise 1993–97 (2005); *Recreations* eating, bridge, playing Chopin; *Clubs* Savile, Oxford and Cambridge, Cambridge Union Soc; *Style*— Michael Bloch, Esq; ✉ 2 Strathearn Place, London W2 2NQ (tel and fax 020 7723 2220, e-mail padders@dircon.co.uk); c/o Andrew Hewson, Esq, Johnson & Alcock, 45 Clerkenwell Green, London EC1R 0HT

BLOCH, Michael Gordon; QC (1998); s of John Bloch, of Hants, and Thelma Bloch; *b* 18 October 1951; *Educ* Bedales, Univ of Cambridge (MA), UEA (MPhil); *m* 1, (m dis), Caroline, da of Sir Leonard Williams; 2 da (Susannah, Claudia); m 2, 12 Sept 1998, Lady Camilla Bingham, da of 7 Earl of Lucan; 2 s (Cameron Charles b 28 Feb 2002, Angus John Patrick b 31 July 2003); *Career* called to the Bar 1979; tstee Childline; govr Bedales; *Clubs* RAC; *Style*— Michael Bloch, Esq, QC; ✉ Wilberforce Chambers, 8 New Square, Lincolns Inn, London WC2A 3QP (tel 020 7306 0102, fax 020 7306 0095, e-mail chambers@wilberforce.co.uk)

BLOCH, Selwyn; QC (2000); *Educ* Univ of Stellenbosch SA (BA, LLB); *Career* called to the Bar 1982; practising barr specialising in employment and commercial law; int banking Allen & Overy, slr Webber Wentzel, memb Littleton Chambers 1982–; *Publications* Restrictive Covenants and Confidential Information (co-author, 2 edn 1999); *Style*— Selwyn Bloch, Esq, QC; ✉ Littleton Chambers, 3 King's Bench Walk North, Temple, London EC4Y 7HR

BLOCK, Simon Jonathan; s of Abraham Hyman (Michael) Block (d 1999), and Winifred Joy Harris; *b* 13 February 1950, London; *Educ* Sunbury GS, East Grinstead GS, Crawley Coll of FE; *m* 26 June 1998, Annette Mary Dunphy; 1 s (Robin Timothy b 14 Dec 1977), 1 step da (Cheryl Ann Parkinson b 10 May 1972); *Career* boxer Crawley Amateur Boxing Club 1965–68; Br Boxing Bd of Control: joined 1979, sec Southern Area Cncl 1981–96, gen sec 2000–, sec charitable tst 2000–; hon sec Cwlth Boxing Cncl 1980–; co-sec European Boxing Union 2000–; vice-pres: Sussex Ex-Boxers' Assoc, Kent Ex-Boxers' Assoc; hon memb London Ex-Boxers' Assoc; memb Soc of Friends Ashdown Forest; *Recreations* walking, riding, music, food; *Clubs* St George's Day; *Style*— Simon Block, Esq; ✉ British Boxing Board of Control, The Old Library, Trinity Street, Cardiff CF10 1BH (tel 02920 367000, fax 02920 367019, e-mail sblock@bbbofc.com)

BLOCKLEY, Prof David Ian; s of Harold Gwynne Blockley (d 1972), and Olive Lydia Blockley (d 1979); *b* 18 September 1941; *Educ* Bemrose Sch Derby, Univ of Sheffield (BEng, PhD), Univ of Bristol (DSc); *m* 6 Aug 1966, Karen Elisabeth Blockley; 1 s (Andrew David b 1968), 1 da (Alison Mary b 1973); *Career* devpt engr BCSA Ltd London 1967–69; Univ of Bristol: lectr 1969–82, reader 1982–89, prof 1989–, head Dept of Civil Engrg 1989–95 and 2002–, dean of engrg 1994–98; pres Inst of Structural Engrs 2001–02; corresponding memb: Argentinian Acad of Engrs, Argentinian Acad of Science; Telford Gold Medal Inst of Civil Engrs 1978, George Stephenson Medal Inst of Civil Engrs 1981, Oscar Faber Dip Inst of Structural Engrs 1986; FREng 1992, FICE, FIStructE, FRSA; *Books* The Nature of Structural Design and Safety (1980), Engineering Safety (1992), Doing it Differently (2000), Penguin Dictionary of Civil Engineering (2005); *Recreations* reading, gardening, watching sport (esp soccer and cricket); *Style*— Professor D I Blockley, FREng; ✉ Department of Civil Engineering, University of Bristol, Bristol BS8 1TR (fax 0117 928 7783)

BLOIS, Sir Charles Nicholas Gervase; 11 Bt (E 1686), of Grundisburgh Hall, Suffolk; er s of Capt Sir Gervase Blois, 10 Bt, MC (d 1968), and Audrey Winifred, *née* Johnson; *b* 25 December 1939; *Educ* Harrow, TCD, Royal Agricultural Coll; *m* 8 July 1967, Celia Helen Mary, o da of late Cyril George Francis Pritchett, CBE, of Aldeburgh, Suffolk; 1 s (Andrew Charles David b 1971), 1 da (Helen Janet b 1974); *Heir* s, Andrew Blois; *Career* farmer and landowner; memb Scientific Exploration Soc (SES); FRGS; *Recreations* yacht cruising (yacht 'Caleta'), travel, shooting, rigid inflatable boat (RIB) cruising; *Clubs* Cruising Assoc, Ocean Cruising; *Style*— Sir Charles Blois, Bt; ✉ Benacre Hall, Benacre, Beccles, Suffolk NR34 7LJ (tel 01502 676116)

BLOMEFIELD, Sir (Thomas) Charles Peregrine; 6 Bt (UK 1807), of Attleborough, Co Norfolk; s of Sir Thomas Edward Peregrine Blomefield, 5 Bt (d 1984), and Ginette, *née* Massart; *b* 24 July 1948; *Educ* Wellington, Mansfield Coll Oxford; *m* 1975, Georgina Geraldine, da of late Cdr Charles Over, RN, of Lugger End, Portscatho, Cornwall; 2 da (Emma Georgina b 1980, Harriet Elizabeth b 1986), 1 s ((Thomas) William Peregrine b 1983); *Heir* s, William Blomefield; *Career* fine art conslt; Christies 1970–75, Wildenstein and Co 1975–76; dir: Lidchi Art Gallery Johannesburg 1976–78, Thomas Heneage and Co 1981–87, Fleetwood-Hesketh Ltd 1982–; md Charles Blomefield and Co 1980–; *Recreations* travel; *Style*— Sir Charles Blomefield, Bt; ✉ Attlepin Farm, Chipping Campden, Gloucestershire GL55 6PP

BLOOD, Baroness (Life Peer UK 1999), of Blackwatertown in the County of Armagh; May Blood; MBE (1995); da of William Blood (d 1978), of Belfast, and Mary, *née* McKeen (d 1978); *b* 26 May 1938; *Educ* Linfield Secdy Sch; *Career* community worker; memb: NI Women's Coalition, GI Shankill Partnership; non-exec dir North and West Health and Social Services Bd; memb Senate Queen's Univ Belfast; Catherine Dunfey Peace Award (USA) 1997; Hon DUniv: Ulster 1998, Queen's Belfast 2000, Open Univ 2001; *Recreations* gardening, reading, DIY; *Style*— The Rt Hon the Baroness Blood, MBE; ✉ 7 Blackmountain Place, Belfast BT13 3TT (tel 028 9032 6514); Alessie Centre, 60 Shankill Road, Belfast BT13 3BB (tel 028 9087 4000, fax 028 9087 4009, mobile 07752 475883)

BLOOM, Alan; s of Ronnie Bloom, of Spain, and Anne, *née* Needleman (d 2004); *b* 9 November 1955, London; *Educ* Haberdashers' Aske's; *m* 18 April 1982, Gillian, *née* Galler; 2 s (Mark b 27 Nov 1983, Richard b 28 Jan 1987); *Career* CA 1980; Ernst & Young: joined 1981, ptnr 1988–, head of UK corporate restructuring 1996–; pres Soc of Practitioners of Insolvency; author of many articles and presentations on corporate restructuring and insolvency; fundraiser for Aspire; FCA; *Recreations* golf, watching football, theatre; *Style*— Alan Bloom, Esq; ✉ Ernst & Young, 1 More London Place, London SE1 2AF (tel 020 7951 9898, e-mail abloom@uk.ey.com)

BLOOM, Anthony Herbert; s of Joseph Bloom, and Margaret Roslyn Bloom; *b* 15 February 1939; *Educ* King Edward VII HS, Univ of the Witwatersrand (BCom, LLB), Harvard Law Sch (LLM), Stanford Univ Graduate Sch of Business (Sloan fell); *m* 10 Jan 1973, Gisela; 2 da (Rosemary Claire b 24 Jan 1963, Alexis Monica b 27 May 1975), 2 s (Andrew Martin b 7 Sept 1965, Nicholas Peter b 10 Dec 1973); *Career* with Hayman Godfrey & Sanderson 1960–64; Premier Group Ltd: joined 1966, dir 1969, dep chm 1975, chm 1979–87; dir: Barclays Nat Bank and First Nat Bank of Southern Africa Ltd 1980–88, Liberty Life Association 1982–88, The South African Breweries Ltd 1983–89, CNA Gallo Ltd 1983–89; former non-exec dir Sketchley plc, former dir RIT Capital Partners plc; currently chm Cine-UK Ltd, memb Devpt Cncl RNT; LLD (hc) Harvard Law Sch; *Recreations* karate, opera, ballet, theatre, music; *Style*— Anthony Bloom, Esq; ✉ 8 Hanover Terrace, London NW1 4RJ (tel 020 7723 3422); RIT Capital Partners plc, 27 St James's Place, London SW1A 1NR (tel 020 7493 8111)

BLOOM, His Hon Judge Charles; QC (1987); s of Abraham Barnet Bloom (d 1973), of Manchester, and Freda, *née* Craft (d 1994); *b* 6 November 1940; *Educ* Manchester Central GS, Manchester Univ (LLB); *m* 16 Aug 1967, Janice Rachelle, da of Reuben and Lily Goldberg, of Crumpsal, Manchester; 1 da (Sarah Rebecca b 10 July 1969), 1 s (David Benjamin b 31 Aug 1972); *Career* called to the Bar Gray's Inn 1963, chm Med Appeal Tbnls 1979–97, dep circuit judge 1979–83, recorder of the Crown Court 1983–97, head of chambers 1985–97, dep High Court judge 1992, circuit judge (Northern Circuit) 1997–; co-fndr Rhodes Seventh Day Intellectual Debating Forum; *Recreations* gardening, tennis, running; *Clubs* Friedland Postmusaf Tennis, Larner Viniflora Appreciation Soc; *Style*— His Hon Judge Charles Bloom, QC; ✉ Northern Circuit Office, 15 Quay Street, Manchester M60 9FD

BLOOM, Claire; da of late Edward Bloom and Elizabeth Bloom; *b* 15 February 1931; *Educ* Badminton, USA and privately; *m* 1, 1959 (m dis 1969), Rod Steiger; 1 da (Anna Steiger b 1960); m 2, 1969 (m dis 1976); m3, 1990 (m dis 1995), Philip Roth; *Career* actress; *Theatre* The Condemned of Altona (Royal Court), Duel of Angels (Globe), The Lady's Not For Burning (Globe), Ring Around the Moon (Globe), various Shakespeare, Ivanov, A Doll's House (NY and London), The Cherry Orchard (Chichester Festival Theatre), A Streetcar Named Desire, Hedda Gabler, Vivat! Vivat Regina!, The Turn of the Screw (NY), Till We Awaken the Dead (Almeida), King John, Hamlet and A Winter's Tale (Stratford), The Cherry Orchard 1993, A Long Day's Journey into Night 1996, Electra 1998, Conversations After a Burial (Almeida) 2000, A Little Night Music (NYC) 2003; *Television* Henry VIII, Hamlet, Cymbeline and King John (BBC Shakespeare series), Brideshead Revisited, Time and the Conways, Shadowlands (BAFTA Best Actress Award), Oedipus the King, The Ghost Writer, Anne & Debbie, The Belle of Amhurst (Int Emmy Award), Intimate Contact, Queenie, Anastasia, Liberty, The Camomile Law (Channel 4), Miss Marple - The Mirror Cracked (BBC), Family Money (Channel 4), The Lady in Question, Love and Murder, Yesterday's Children; *Films* Limelight, The Man Between, Alexander the Great, Richard III, Look Back in Anger, The Spy Who Came in From the Cold, The Outrage, The Brother Karamazov, The Buccaneer, Charly, The Brothers Grimm, A Doll's House, Islands in the Stream, Clash of the Titans, Sammie & Rosie Get Laid, Crimes and Misdemeanours, Shakespeare's Women and Claire Bloom, The Book of Eve, Imagining Argentina; *Books* Limelight and After, Leaving A Doll's House; *Style*— Miss Claire Bloom; ✉ c/o Conway van Gelder Ltd, 18–21 Jermyn Street, London SW1Y 6HP (tel 020 7287 0077, fax 020 7287 1940)

BLOOM, Godfrey William; TD (1984), MEP; s of Alan Bloom, and Phyllis Bloom; *b* 22 November 1949, London; *Educ* St Olave's Sch; *m* 5 July 1986, Katryna, *née* Skowronek; *Career* fund mangr Mercury Asset Mgmnt 1987–93 (Micropal Award for Fund Mgmnt 1992), currently chief economist TBO Gp of Cos; MEP (UKIP) Yorks & N Lincs 2004–; memb Inst of Economic Affrs; memb: British Charolais Soc, Campaign against Political Correctness; grad AFPS RN and RAF; *Books* Beyond the Fridge; *Clubs* East India, Royal Cornish, Gadfly, Horsehouse Formals CC (pres), Pocklington RFC (vice-pres), Old Olavians RFC, Cambridge Univ WRFC, Bentley Drivers'; *Style*— Godfrey Bloom, Esq, TD, MEP; ✉ TBO Group, Devlin House, 36 St George Street, London W1S 2FW (tel 01757 630778, fax 01757 630395)

BLOOM, Prof Margaret Janet; CBE (2003); da of John Sturrock (d 1992), and Jean Elizabeth, *née* Ranken (d 1997); *b* 28 July 1943; *Educ* Sherborne, Girton Coll Cambridge (MA); *m* 1965, Prof Stephen Bloom, s of Dr Arnold Bloom (d 1992); 2 da (Sarah Elizabeth b 1970, Chloë Isabel b 1976), 2 s (Nicholas Alexander b 1973, James Duncan b 1978); *Career* economist rising to dep gp economist John Laing & Son plc 1965–69, gp economist Tarmac plc 1969–70, Nat Econ Devpt Office 1970–86, Sci & Technol Secretariat Cabinet Office 1986–89, grade 5 DTI 1989–95, grade 4 rising to grade 3 Agencies Gp Cabinet Office 1995–96, dir of competition enforcement OFT 1997–2003; sr conslt Freshfields Bruckhaus Deringer 2003–; pt/t lectr UCL 1977–80, external examiner UCL 1985–88, visiting prof KCL 2002–; tstee Money Advice Tst 2004–, ind memb Link Standing Ctee on Consumer Issues 2006–; *Recreations* family, foreign travel, eating out, rambling; *Style*— Prof Margaret Bloom, CBE; ✉ School of Law, King's College London, Strand, London WC2R 2LS (tel 020 7435 0912, e-mail margaret.bloom@kcl.ac.uk)

BLOOM, Prof Stephen Robert (Steve); *b* 24 October 1942, Maidstone, Kent; *Educ* Mill Hill Sch London, Univ of Cambridge (Science Prize, Walter Knox Chemistry Prize, Bacteriology Prize, Histology Cert, Ophthalmology Prize, Radiotherapy and Radiology Prize, MB BChir, MA, MD), Middx Hosp Med Sch London (DSc); *m* 1965, Margaret Janet, *née* Sturrock; 2 da (Sarah Elizabeth b 1970, Chloe Isabel b 1976), 2 s (Nicholas Alexander b 1973, James Duncan b 1978); *Career* Middx Hosp London: gastroenterology house physician 1967–68, cardiology house physician 1968; house surgn Mount Vernon Hosp London 1968–69, casualty MO Middx Hosp London 1969, endocrinology house physician Hammersmith Hosp London 1969–70; Middx Hosp London: Leverhulme research scholar Inst of Clinical Research 1970, registrar Med Unit 1970–72, MRC clinical research fell Inst of Clinical Research 1972–74; Hammersmith Hosp London: sr lectr and conslt physician Royal Postgrad Med Sch (RPMS) 1974–78, reader in med RPMS 1978–82, prof of med and conslt physician Faculty of Med Imperial Coll 1982–, dir of endocrinology 1982–, dep dir Dept of Med RPMS 1984–97, dir of chemical pathology 1994–, clinical dir Pathology and Therapy Servs 1996–; chm Div of Investigative Science Imperial Coll London 1997–; chm Higher Degrees Ctee RPMS 1991–96, chm Academic Bd RPMS 1995–97; Hammersmith Hosps Tst: chm Jr Doctors Hours Ctee 1995–2000, chm Hosp Med Ctee 1995–, memb Tst Bd 1996–; chm Local Negotiating Ctee BMA 1995–, memb Mgmnt Planning Gp Imperial Coll London 1997–2001, memb Princs Advsy Gp Faculty of Med Imperial Coll London 1997–; RCP: sr examiner MRCP 1987–, memb Ethics Ctee 1991–96, pro-censor 1993–95, second censor 1994–97, academic vice-pres 1999–2001; referee Queen's Univ Belfast 1994–; memb: Int Steering Ctee GI Hormones 1980–87, Nat Inst Biological Standards Bd 1985–99 (memb Reorganisation Ctee 1991, chm Scientific Ctee 1993–99), Research Corp Tst Med Sciences Bd 1986–88, Scientific Steering Ctee Int Endocrine Soc 1986–89, WHO Expert Advsy Ctee on Biological Standardization 1989–, Global Assessment Ctee Inst of Child Health 1990, Clinical Specialities Liaison Ctee 1991–93, Regional Med Advsy Ctee 1991–95, Sub-Ctee on Biologicals Ctee on Safety of Meds 1992–95, Fin and Gen Purposes Ctee Nat Inst for Biological Standards and Control (NIBSC) 1992–99, Subject Panel in Gen Med Univ of London 1993–96; chm Bioscientifica 2005, dir Thiakis Ltd 2006; selected summaries corr Gastroenterology 1979–83, fndr and ed-in-chief Regulatory Peptides 1979–84, ed Endocrinology 1995–98; memb Editorial Bd: Jl of Developmental Physiology 1980–85, Excerpta Medica Endocrinolgy 1981–86, Gut 1982–86, European Jl of Clinical Pharmacology 1982–86, Jl of Endocrinology 1983–87, Diabetes Research and Clinical Practice 1986–90, Archives Internationale de Pharmacodynamie et de Therapie 1987–, Biomedical Research 1988–91, Clinical Autonomic Research 1989–92, Jl of Neuroendocrinology 1990–92; author of numerous articles in learned jls incl: Nature, Science, Diabetes, Neuroscience, Lancet, BMJ; Lawrence lectr Br Diabetic Assoc 1976, Copp lectr American Diabetic Assoc 1978, Goulstonian lectr RCP 1979, Bengt Ihre lectr Swedish Acad of Science 1979, Prossor White oration 1981, Transatlantic lectr American Soc for Endocrinology 1985, Arnold Bloom lectr Br Diabetic Assoc 1995; Br Soc of Gastroenterology Research Medal 1977, Eric-Sharpe Prize for Oncology, Dale Medal Soc for Endocrinology 2003; memb: American Diabetic Assoc, Assoc of Physicians, Bayliss & Starling Soc (chm 1980–92), Br Diabetic Assoc (memb Scientific Ctee 1991–95, chm Research Ctee 1996–99), Endocrine Soc (American), European Assoc for the Study of Diabetes, European Neuroscience Assoc, Med Research Soc (memb Ctee 1992–95, chm 1995–99), Physiological Soc, RSM, Soc for Endocrinology (memb Ctee 1983–87 and 1994–99, sec-gen 1999–2002, chm 2002–), Soc of Gastroenterology (Br and American); FRCP 1978, FRCPath 1993, FMedSci 1997; *Books* Gut Hormones (ed, 1978, 2 edn (jtly) 1981), Gastrointestinal and Related Hormones (jt ed, 1979), Radioimmunoassay of Gut Regulatory Peptides (jt ed, 1981), Basic Science in Gastroenterology (jt ed, 1982), Systemic Role of Regulatory Peptides (jt ed, 1982), Gastrointestinal and Hepatobiliary Cancer (jt ed, 1983), Endocrine Tumours (jt ed, 1985), Toohey's Medicine for Nurses (14 edn (jtly) 1986, 15 edn 1995), Somatostatin (jt ed, 1986), Therapeutic Applications of LHRH (jt ed, 1986), Peptides: A Target for New Drug Development (jt ed, 1991), Surgical Endocrinology (jt ed, 1993); *Style*— Prof Steve Bloom; ✉ Department of Metabolic Medicine, Division of Investigative Science, Imperial College Faculty of Medicine, Hammersmith Hospital Campus, Du Cane Road, London W12 0NN (tel 020 8383 3242, fax 020 8383 3142, e-mail s.bloom@imperial.ac.uk)

BLOOMER, Jonathan William; *b* 23 March 1954; *Educ* Imperial Coll London (BSc, ARCS); *m* Sept 1977, Judy; 3 c; *Career* Arthur Andersen: joined 1974, ptnr Fin Mkts Div Audit and Business Advsy Practice 1987–91, managing ptnr Euro Insurance Practice 1991–94; Prudential plc: gp fin dir 1995–99, dep gp chief exec 1999–2000, chief exec 2000–05, md Cerberus UK Advsrs LLP 2005–; memb: Urgent Issues Task Force 1995–99, Financial Services Practitioner Panel 2001– (chm 2003–05), Bd Assoc of Br Insurers 2001–05; FCA; *Recreations* sailing, rugby; *Style*— Jonathan Bloomer, Esq

BLOOMFIELD, Keith George; CMG (2007); *b* 2 June 1947; *m* 1976, Geneviève, *née* Charbonneau; 3 da; *Career* diplomat; early career with ODA and MOD, entered HM Dip Serv 1980, posted UKREP Brussels 1980–85, EC Dept (Internal) FCO 1985–87, head of Chancery Cairo 1987–90, dep head of mission Algiers 1990–94, cnsllr (political and mgmnt) Rome 1994–96, min and dep head of mission Rome 1996–98, head Counter Terrorism Policy Dept FCO 1999–2002, ambass to Nepal 2002–06; *Style*— Keith Bloomfield, Esq, CMG

BLOOMFIELD, Robin Russell Clive; CBE (1993); s of Cyril George Bloomfield (d 1984), of Aldenham, Watford, and Gwendolen Lucy, *née* Hall (d 1997); *b* 2 October 1933; *Educ* Univ Coll Sch, Shuttleworth Agric Coll (NDA); *m* 1, 1968, Janet Cecily (d 1991); 2 da (Justine Anne b 9 Dec 1971, Philippa Lucy b 8 March 1975), 1 s (Russell George b 2 May 1976); m 2, 1994, Angela Rae; *Career* began farming 1953, fndr Oakridge Farms 1958, variously farming up to 1,700 acres (currently 600); built own golf course Aldenham 1973 (also designed three others); chm Eastern Counties Farmers 1979–84, memb Cncl NFU HQ 1974–88 (memb SE Planning Cncl 1971–76), chm Eastern Region MAFF 1986–93, memb Govt Deregulation Task Force 1994; former govr Royal Agric Assoc of England, Agric Research Inst Assoc; parish cncllr 1968–77, JP Watford Bench 1972–85; Master Worshipful Co of Barbers 1996–97, memb Ct of Assts Worshipful Co of Farmers, Freeman City of London; past govr Capel Manor Horticultural and Environmental Centre; memb NFU 1953; ctee memb Dorset CLA; *Recreations* fishing, shooting, golf, walking; *Clubs* Farmers'; *Style*— Robin Bloomfield, Esq, CBE; ✉ RRC Bloomfield, The Mill House, Chamberlayne's Farm, Bere Regis, Dorset BH20 7LS (tel 01929 472438, fax 01929 472626, e-mail chamber@gotadsl.co.uk)

BLOSSE, *see*: Lynch-Blosse

BLOW, Selina (Mrs Levinson); da of Jonathan Blow (d 1977), and Helga, *née* de Silva; *b* 19 September 1966; *Educ* Hatherop Castle Sch, Queen's Coll London; *m* 1998, Charles Levinson; 1 s (Augustus b Dec 1998), 1 da (Violet b July 2002); *Career* fashion designer: ready-to-wear collection 1992, new generation 1992, opened Selina Blow shop 1993, menswear and childrenswear launched 2000; memb Countryside Alliance; *Recreations* film, painting, gardens, cooking, Sri Lanka; *Style*— Ms Selina Blow; ✉ 1 Ellis Street, Sloane Street, London SW1X 9AL (tel 020 7730 2077, e-mail sb@selinablow.fsnet.co.uk)

BLOWERS, Dr Anthony John; CBE (1985), JP (Surrey 1970), DL (Surrey 1986); s of Geoffrey Hathaway Blowers (d 1973), of Chertsey, Surrey, and Louise, *née* Jux (d 1998); *b* 11 August 1926; *Educ* Sloane GS Chelsea, Sir John Cass Coll London, Univ of Surrey (PhD), Univ of Surrey Roehampton (Cert Drugs: Prevention and Educn); *m* 4 Sept 1948, Yvonne, da of Capt Alan Victor Boiteux-Buchanan (d 1986); 1 da (Anne (Mrs Ricketts) b 1951), 2 s (Colin b 1953, Christopher b 1955); *Career* RCS 1944–45, RAMC 1945–46, RWAFF (served Nigeria) 1946–48; experimental offr Miny of Agric 1953–59 (sr sci asst 1949–53); Sandoz Pharmaceuticals: joined 1959, sr research offr 1973–87, conslt in psychopharmacology 1987–91; conslt in bacteriology Mansi Laboratories 1973–95, dir of corp affrs Magellan Medical Communications 1990–99, dir Ogilvy Public Relations 1999–; visiting research fell Roehampton Inst (now Univ of Surrey Roehampton) 1998–; visiting lectr Dept of Addictive Behaviour and Psychiatry St George's Hosp Med Sch London; vice-chm Surrey AHA 1976–77 (memb 1973–80), memb SW Thames RHA 1980–81, chm W Surrey and NE Hants HA 1981–86; memb Mental Health Review Tbnl 1975–99, cmmr Mental Health Act Cmmn 1987–96, Mental Health Act mangr Heathlands Mental Health NHS Tst 1994–; memb Cons Policy Gp on Mental Health 1978–81, admin sec Parly Gp for Res and Devpt in Fertility and Contraception 1994–; vice-pres: Hosp Saving Assoc 1994–2000, Parkinson's Disease Soc 1995– (actg chief exec 1995); chm: Surrey Drug Action Team 1995–2001, The Knight Fndn for Cystic Fibrosis 1997–; memb: Scientific Bd Worthing Mental Health Fndn, Cncl Psychiatry Res Tst 1986– (tstee 1995–), Health Servs Ctee CNAA 1989–94, Devpt Gp MA/MSc in Drugs Policy, Prevention and Educn

Roehampton Inst 1995–2000; cncllr: Chertsey UDC 1964–74 (chm 1969–70 and 1973–74), Surrey CC 1970–85 (vice-chm Social Servs Ctee 1973–77), Runnymede BC 1973–84 (chm 1973–74); memb Bd of Visitors Coldingley Prison 1978–92; chm Surrey Police Authy 1981–85 (memb 1973–90), vice-chm Farnham Police Community Liaison Ctee 1985–94; chm: Runnymede and Elmbridge Police Community Liaison Ctee 1983–94, SW Surrey Crime Prevention Ctee 1986–92, Surrey Ctee Police Convalescence and Rehabilitation Tst 1986–88, London and SE Young Offenders Working Gp 1991–95, Runnymede and Elmbridge Ctee Wishing Well Appeal; Duke of Edinburgh Award Scheme: vice-chm Woking Ctee 1987–92, chm SE Region 1990–98, memb Nat Advsy Cncl 1990–98; memb Cncl Magistrates' Assoc 1986–91, chm Surrey Magistrates' Soc 1988–94; memb: Surrey Magistrates' Club, Middlesex and Surrey Soc; patron The Addiction Appeal Chaucer Clinic 2004–; govr: Fullbrook Sch 1967–85 (chm 1981–85), Ottershaw Sch 1975–81 (chm 1979–81), More House Sch Frensham 2003–; memb Ct Univ of Surrey 1986–; pres Runnymede Scout Cncl 1970–84; St John Ambulance: cdr Surrey 1987–91, asst DG 1985–91, DG 1991–94; Order of St John: memb Chapter-Gen 1990–99, memb Priory Chapter England and the Islands 1999–, vice-pres St John Fellowship 2001– (chm 1995–2001); High Sheriff Surrey 1990–91; Freeman: Borough of Runnymede 1985, City of London 1983; Liveryman Worshipful Soc of Apothecaries 1988 (Yeoman 1983–88); CBiol 1983, FIMLS 1983; KStJ 1991; *Books* The Isolation of Salmonellae (1978), Tardive Dyskinesia (1982); numerous contributions to science books and jls; *Recreations* tackling drug misuse, fund raising, gardening; *Clubs* Country Gentlemen's Assoc; *Style*— Dr Anthony Blowers, CBE, DL; ✉ Westward, 12 Birch Close, Boundstone, Farnham, Surrey GU10 4TJ (tel 01252 792769); Ogilvy Public Relations, Porters Place, 11–33 St John Street, London EC1M 4GB (tel 020 7309 1000, fax 020 7309 1001)

BLOXHAM, Tom; MBE (2009); *b* 20 December 1963, Fleet, Lincs; *Career* chm and co-fndr (with Jonathan Falkingham) Urban Splash 1993–; chair: Manchester Int Arts Festival, IPPR Centre for Cities Think Tank; memb: Arts Cncl England (chair NW), Urban Sounding Bd ODPM, Property Advsy Gp ODPM, Govt's Urban Task Force Working Gps; dir Liverpool Capital of Culture; UK Property Entrepreneur of the Year Property Week 1998 and 2002, Ernst & Young Young Entrepreneur of the Year 1999, Young Entrepreneur of the YEar IOD NW 1999, Manchester Evening News Business of the Year 2002, RIBA Client of the Year 2002, Property Entrepreneur of the Year Building Magazine 2003, Property Personality of the Year Insider Awards 2004, Property Entrepreneur of the Year EN magazine 2004; hon fell: John Moores Univ Liverpool 2001, Univ of Central Lancashire 2003; Hon DDes Oxford Brookes Univ 2004; Hon FRIBA 2000, hon fell Royal Soc of Architects; *Style*— Tom Bloxham, Esq, MBE; ✉ Urban Splash, Timber Wharf, 16–22 Worsley Street, Manchester M15 4LD (tel 0161 839 2999, fax 0161 839 8999, e-mail tombloxham@urbansplash.co.uk)

BLUE, Rabbi Lionel; OBE (1994); s of Harry Blue (d 1965), and Hetty Blue; *b* 6 February 1930; *Educ* Westminster City Sch, Hendon Co Sch, Balliol Coll Oxford (MA), UCL (BA), Leo Baeck Coll (Rabbinical Dip, fell); *Career* minister Settlement Synagogue 1957, rabbi Middx New Synagogue 1959, religious dir for Euro Bd World Union for Progressive Judaism 1963–66, lectr Leo Baeck Coll 1963–, convener Ecclesiastical Ct Reformed Synagogues of GB 1969–89; broadcaster: Prayer for the Day, Thought for the Day, Pause for Thought, In Search of Holy England; writer, columnist The Tablet, co-ed Forms of Prayer 1969–, retreat leader; memb Rabbinical Assembly Reformed Synagogues of GB (hon vice-pres), vice-chm Standing Conf of Jews, Christians and Moslems in Europe; Hon DUniv Open Univ 1998; FRSA; *Books* To Heaven with Scribes and Pharisees (1975), Forms of Prayer Vols 1 and 2 (1977), A Backdoor to Heaven (1978), Kitchen Blues (1985), Bright Blue (1985), Blue Heaven (1987), Guide to Here and Hereafter (jtly, 1988), Blue Horizons (1989), Bedside Manna (1991), How to get up when life gets you down (jtly, 1992), The Little Blue Book of Prayer (jtly, 1993), Tales of Body and Soul (1994), Kindred Spirits (jtly, 1995), My Affair with Christianity (1998), Sun, Sand and Soul (jtly, 1999), Little Book of Blue Thoughts (2001), Blue's Jokes (2001), Hitchhiking to Heaven (2004); *Recreations* monasteries, charity shops, painting, travelling; *Style*— Rabbi Lionel Blue, OBE; ✉ Leo Baeck College, 80 East End Road, London N3 2SY (tel 020 8349 4525)

BLUMENTHAL, Heston Marc; OBE (2006); s of Stephen Jeffrey Blumenthal, and Celia Blumenthal; *b* 27 May 1966; *Educ* Latymer Upper Sch, John Hampden GS; *m* 10 Aug 1991, Susanna Clare; 1 s (Jack Stephen b 18 Jan 1993), 2 da (Jessica Ella b 19 Dec 1994, Joy Mae b 6 Oct 1997); *Career* credit controller Team Leasing (family equipment leasing co) for nine years; self taught chef; chef/prop The Fat Duck 1995–; *Awards* Michelin Star 1999, 2 Michelin Stars 2002, 3 Michelin Stars 2004; Good Food Guide: Restaurant of the Year 1997, 9 out of 10 1999, Chef of the Year 2001, 8 out of 10 2002; AA Restaurant Guide: 4 Rosettes 1997, Restaurant of the Year 2001, Chefs' Chef of the Year 2002, Wine Award (nat winner and winner for England) 2002, 5 Rosettes 2002, 2003, 2004 and 2006; Time Out Eating and Drinking Guide (one of best restaurants in London area) 1997, Egon Ronay Guide 1997, Decanter Magazine Restaurant of the Year 1997–98, Evening Standard London Restaurant Guide, Harpers & Queen Premier Crew Award for Service 2001, Chef of the Year Catey Awards 2004, Best Out of Town Restaurant Tatler Magazine Awards 2004, Best Out of Town Restaurant Square Meal/BMW Awards 2004, Best Restaurant Observer Food Monthly Awards 2004, Restaurant Magazine World's Best Restaurant 2005 (Second Best 2004), 19/20 Gault Millau Guide 2005; *Books* Family Food (2002); *Recreations* food, wine, sport, family; *Style*— Heston Blumenthal, Esq, OBE; ✉ The Fat Duck, High Street, Bray, Berkshire SL6 2AQ (tel 01628 580333, fax 01628 776188)

BLUMENTHAL, Dr Ivan; *b* 16 January 1947; *Educ* Queen's Coll Queenstown, Univ of Cape Town (MB ChB); *m* 16 Dec 1973, Janet Helen; 2 s (Morris b 4 Oct 1974, Toby b 3 Sept 1976); *Career* med trg in paediatrics: South Africa, UK, USA; currently conslt paediatrician Highfield Hosp; contrib med jls; MRCP 1975, DCH 1974; *Books* Your Child's Health (1987), Child Abuse - A Handbook for Health Care Practitioners (1994); *Recreations* bridge; *Style*— Dr Ivan Blumenthal; ✉ 38 Norford Way, Bamford, Rochdale OL11 5QS (tel 01706 358954, fax 01706 646888, e-mail ivan.blumenthal@norford.fsbusiness.co.uk); Highfield Hospital, Manchester Road, Rochdale OL11 4LZ (tel 01706 655121, fax 01706 356759)

BLUNDELL, Prof Derek John; s of Frank Herbert Blundell (d 1978), and Irene Mary, *née* Davie (d 1963); *b* 30 June 1933; *Educ* East Grinstead GS, Univ of Birmingham (BSc), Imperial Coll London (PhD, DIC); *m* 15 Sept 1960, Mary Patricia, da of Archibald James Leonard (d 1968); *Career* lectr in geology Univ of Birmingham 1959–70, reader in geophysics Lancaster Univ 1971–75 (sr lectr 1970–71), prof of environmental geology Univ of London 1975–98 (emeritus prof of geophysics 1998–); head Dept of Geology: Chelsea Coll London 1975–85, Royal Holloway Coll London 1992–97 (dean of Research and Enterprise 1995–98); Leverhulme emeritus fell 1998–2000; pres Geological Soc 1988–90; Coke Medal Geological Soc 1993; hon fell Royal Holloway Coll London 2005; memb Academia Europaea; FGS 1956, CGeol 1990; *Publications* A Continent Revealed - The European Geotraverse (1992), Tectonic Evolution of Southeast Asia (Geological Soc Special Pubn 106, 1996), Lyell: The Past is the Key to the Present (Geological Soc Special Pubn 143, 1998), The Timing and Location of Major Ore Desposits in an Evolving Orogen (Geological Soc Special Pubn 204, 2002); Geodynamics and Ore Deposit Evolution in Europe (2005); contrib to various jls on seismic exploration, earthquake hazards, mountain building and mineral deposits; *Recreations* cycling, golf; *Clubs* Athenaeum; *Style*— Prof Derek Blundell; ✉ Geology Department, Royal Holloway, University of London, Egham, Surrey TW20 0EX (tel 01784 443811, fax 01784 471780, e-mail d.blundell@gl.rhul.ac.uk)

BLUNDELL, John; s of James Blundell (d 2000), and Alice Margaret, *née* Taylor (d 1996); *b* 9 October 1952, Congleton, Cheshire; *Educ* King's Sch Macclesfied, LSE (BSc (Econ)); *m* 1977, Christine Violet, da of Charles Henry Lowry; 2 s (Miles John b 1982, James Lowry b 1989); *Career* head Parly Press Office Fedn of Small Business 1976–82; pres: Inst for Humane Studies 1982–91, Atlas Economic Research Fndn 1987–91, CG Koch Fndn 1991–93; DG IEA 1993–; memb of various economic research orgns in UK, USA, India and Peru; memb: Fairbridge Cncl 1998–, John Templeton Fndn Radnor PA 2001–, Selection Ctee Milton Friedman Prize 2002–; Nat Free Enterprise Award 2000; *Publications* Beyond Left and Right (1998), Regulation without the State (1999), Regulation without the State: The Debate Continues (2000), Waging the War of Ideas (2001, expanded 3 edn 2007), A Tribute to Peter Bauer (2002), Friend or Foe? What Americans should know about the European Union (2004); *Recreations* golf, cricket, American football, genealogy, writing; *Clubs* Marin Cricket; *Style*— John Blundell, Esq; ✉ 43 Ponsonby Place, Wesminster, London SW1P 4PS (tel 020 7828 8431); Institute of Economic Affairs, 2 Lord North Street, Westminster, London SW1P 3LB (tel 020 7799 8900, fax 020 7799 2137, e-mail jblundell@iea.org.uk)

BLUNDELL, Prof Richard William; CBE (2006); *b* 1 May 1952; *Educ* Univ of Bristol (BSc), LSE (MSc); *Career* lectr in econometrics Univ of Manchester 1975–84, prof of economics UCL 1984–; dir of research Inst for Fiscal Studies 1986–; dir: Society for Economic Analysis Ltd 1988–93, ESRC Centre for Micro-Economic Analysis of Fiscal Policy 1991–; visiting assoc prof Univ of Br Columbia 1980; visiting prof: MIT 1993, Univ of Calif Berkeley 1994 and 1999; elected Leverhulme personal research prof 1999; memb Cncl: Royal Economic Soc 1990–94, European Economic Assoc 1997–, Econometric Soc 1998; memb Advsy Bd: Dept of Applied Economics Univ of Cambridge, Br Household Panel Study Univ of Essex; ed Jl of Econometrics 1991–97, co-ed Econometrica 1997–2001; memb Editorial Bd: Jl of Applied Econometrics 1985–89, Fiscal Studies 1986–, Ricerche Economiche 1993–, Int Jl of Taxation 1993–; Jrjö Jahnsson Prize 1995, Frisch Prize 2000; Hon Dr Univ of St Gallen; pres Euro Economics Assoc 2004 (vice-pres 2002), hon memb American Economic Assoc 2001; fell Econometric Soc 1991 (memb Cncl 1999, pres 2006), FBA 1997, FAAAS 2002, Hon FIA 2003; *Books* Unemployment, Search and Labour Supply (with I Walker, 1986), The Measurement of Household Welfare (with I Preston and I Walker, 1994); author of numerous articles in books and jls; *Style*— Prof Richard Blundell, CBE, FBA; ✉ Department of Economics, University College London, Gower Street, London WC1E 6BT (tel 020 7679 5863, fax 020 7916 2773, e-mail r.blundell@ucl.ac.uk)

BLUNDELL, Prof Stephen; *b* 1967; *Educ* Univ of Cambridge (MA, PhD); *Career* prof of physics Univ of Oxford 2004–, professorial fell Mansfield Coll Oxford, lectr CCC Oxford; CPhys, MInstP; *Books* Magnetism in Condensed Matter (2001), Concepts in Thermal Physics (with K Blundell, 2006); *Style*— Prof Stephen Blundell; ✉ Oxford University Department of Physics, Clarendon Laboratory, Parks Road, Oxford OX1 3PU

BLUNDELL, Prof Sir Thomas Leon (Tom); kt (1997); s of Horace Leon Blundell, of Sussex, and Marjorie, *née* Davis; *b* 7 July 1942; *Educ* Steyning GS, BNC Oxford (BA, DPhil); *m* 1, 1964 (m dis 1973), Lesley; 1 s (Ricky b 19 Nov 1969); m 2, 1973 (m dis 1983), Reiko; m 3, 22 May 1987, Lynn Bancinyane, da of Phineas Sibanda, of Zimbabwe; 2 da (Sichelesile 5 Jan 1988, Samkeliso b 25 June 1989); *Career* postdoctoral res fell Molecular Biophysics Laboratory Univ of Oxford 1967–72 (jr res fell Linacre Coll 1968–70), lectr in biological sci Univ of Sussex 1973–76, prof of crystallography Birkbeck Coll London 1976–90 (govr 1985–89), DG Agric and Food Research Cncl 1991–94, chief exec BBSRC 1994–96, Sir William Dunn prof of biochemistry and head of Dept Univ of Cambridge 1996–, chair Sch of Biological Sciences Univ of Cambridge 2003–; professorial fell Sidney Sussex Coll Cambridge 1995–; chm Royal Cmmn on Environmental Pollution 1998–2005; chm Biofabrica 1989–91; industrial consltt: CellTech 1981–86, Pfizer Central Research 1984–90, Abingworth Management Ltd 1988–90 and 1997–; scientific advsr Oxford Molecular Ltd 1996–99; memb Research Bd: SmithKline Beecham plc 1997–2000, Bioprocessing Ltd 1997–99; memb Scientific Advsy Bd: Protein Mechanics Calif 2001–, Teraview 2002–; non-exec dir Celltech plc 1997–2004 (chm Scientific Advsy Bd 1998–2004), co-fndr and non-exec dir Astex technol Cambridge 1999– (also chm Sci Advsy Bd); hon dir ICRF Structural Molecular Biology Unit 1989–96, dir Int Sch of Crystallography Erice Italy 1982–, chm Biological Sci Ctee SERC 1983–87 (memb Cncl 1989–90); memb: Cncl AFRC 1985–90, Advsy Cncl on Science and Technol 1988–90, Advsy Bd Research Cncls 1991–94, European Sci and Technol Assembly (ESTA) 1995–97, Bd Babraham Inst 1997–2003; memb Editorial Advsy Bd: Biochemistry 1986–89, Protein Science 1992–98; jt ed Progress in Biophysics and Molecular Biology 1979–; pres UK Biosciences Fedn 2004–08; cncllr Oxford CBC 1970–73 (chm Planning Ctee 1972–73); tstee Lawes Tst 1998–; Hon DSc: Univ of Edinburgh 1993, UEA 1993, Univ of Sheffield 1994, Univ of Strathclyde 1994, Univ of Warwick 1995, Univ of Antwerp 1995, Univ of Nottingham 1996, Univ of South West England 1997, Univ of Stirling 2000, Univ of Sussex 2001, Univ of St Andrews 2002, Univ of Pavia 2002, Univ of London 2003, Univ of Dundee 2007; Alcon Award 1985, Gold Medal Inst of Biotechnological Studies 1987, Sir Hans Krebs Medal Fedn of Euro Biochemical Socs 1987, Ciba Medal UK Biochemical Soc 1988, Feldberg Prize in biology and medicine 1988, Gold Medal Soc for Chem Indust 1995, Bernal Medal Royal Soc 1998, European Prize for Innovative Science 1998; hon fell: Birkbeck Coll London 1989, BNC Oxford, Linacre Coll Oxford 1991; fell Indian Nat Acad 1994; memb: EMBO 1984, Academia Europaea 1993; FRS 1984 (memb Cncl 1997–98), Hon FRASE 1993, FMedSci 1998; *Books* Protein Crystallography (1976); *Recreations* playing jazz, listening to opera, walking; *Style*— Prof Sir Tom Blundell, FRS; ✉ Department of Biochemistry, University of Cambridge, Tennis Court Road, Cambridge CB2 1GA (tel 01223 333628, fax 01223 766082, e-mail tom@cryst.bioc.cam.ac.uk)

BLUNDEN, George Patrick; s of Sir George Blunden, of Gunthorpe, Norfolk, and Anne, *née* Bulford; *b* 21 February 1952; *Educ* St Edward's Sch Oxford, UC Oxford (BA); *m* 8 July 1978, Jane Rosemary, da of Gp Capt Charles Eric Hunter (d 1986); 2 da (Victoria Jane b 10 Sept 1980, Eleanor Louise b 18 Sept 1985), 1 s (George Edward Paul b 4 Aug 1982); *Career* dir: Seccombe Marshall & Campion 1983–86, S G Warburg Securities 1986–92, S G Warburg Discount 1989–92; chief exec Union plc 1992–97, dir Alliance Capital Whittingdale Ltd 1997–2004; non-exec dir Beazley Furlonge Ltd 1994–; chm and tstee Southern Housing Group 1990–2004; Freeman City of London 1988; Liveryman Worshipful Co of Goldsmiths; *Clubs* Reform, MCC; *Style*— George Blunden, Esq; ✉ Alliance Bernstein Ltd, 1 Mayfair Place, London W1X 6JJ (tel 020 7470 1645, e-mail george.blunden@alliancebernstein.com)

BLUNDEN, Sir Philip Overington; 7 Bt (I 1766), of Castle Blunden, Kilkenny; s of Sir John Blunden, 5 Bt (d 1923); suc bro Sir William Blunden, 6 Bt (d 1985); *b* 27 January 1922; *Educ* Repton; *m* 1945, Jeanette Francesca Alexandra (d 1999), da of Capt Duncan Macdonald, RNR, of Portree, Isle of Skye; 2 s (Hubert Chisholm b 1948, John Maurice Patrick b 1955), 1 da (Marguerite Eugenie b 1967); *Heir* s, Hubert Blunden; *Career* served RN 1942–45; estate mangr Castle Blunden 1948–62, mktg of industrial plastics 1962–83, engaged in fine art restoration and painting 1976–; artist; *Recreations* gardening, fishing, field sports, reading, painting; *Clubs* Royal Dublin Soc (life memb); *Style*— Sir Philip Blunden, Bt

BLUNKETT, Rt Hon David; PC (1997), MP (Lab) Sheffield Brightside (majority 17,049); s of Arthur Blunkett (d 1960), and Doris Matilda Elizabeth, *née* Williams (d 1983); *b* 6 June 1947; *Educ* Univ of Sheffield (BA), Huddersfield Holly Bank Coll of Educn (PGCE); *Children* 4 s (Alastair Todd b 27 March 1977, Hugh Sanders b 13 July 1980, Andrew Keir b 31 Oct 1982, William Saunders b 20 Sept 2002); *Career* clerk typist 1967–69, lectr and tutor in industrial rels and political admin Barnsley Coll of Technol 1973–87, on secondment as ldr Sheffield City Cncl 1981–87, dep chm AMA 1984–87; Sheffield City Cncl: memb 1970–88, chm Family and Community Servs Ctee 1976–80, ldr 1980–87; memb S Yorks Metropolitan CC 1973–77; memb Lab Pty NEC 1983–98, chm Lab Pty Ctee on Local Govt 1984–92, MP (Lab) Sheffield Brightside 1987–, oppn front bench spokesman on the environment 1988–92, memb Shadow Cabinet 1992–97; chief oppn spokesman on: health 1992–94, educn 1994–95, educn and employment 1995–97; sec of state for educn and employment 1997–2001, sec of state Home Office 2001–04, sec of state for work and pensions 2005; chm Labour Party 1993–94 (vice-chm 1992–93); *Books* Local Enterprise and Worker's Plans (1981), Building from the Bottom: the Sheffield Experience (1983), Democracy in Crisis: the town halls respond (1987), On a Clear Day (1995, revised edn 2002), Politics and Progress (2001), The Blunkett Tapes - My Life in the Bear Pit (2006); *Recreations* walking, music, sailing, being with friends; *Style*— The Rt Hon David Blunkett, MP; ✉ 4th Floor, Palatine Chambers, Sheffield S1 2HN (tel 0114 2735987); House of Commons, London SW1A 0AA (tel 020 7219 3000)

BLUNOS, Martin Lauris; s of Leon Karl Blunos, of Thornbury, Bristol, and Venita, *née* Kalnins; *b* 11 April 1960; *Educ* Castle Sch Thornbury Bristol, Gloucestershire Coll of Arts and Technol Cheltenham (City & Guilds), Cambridge Catering Coll (City & Guilds); *m* 27 April 1989, Siân Eulyned, da of William Gilbert Williams; 2 s (Leon William Lauris b 12 Dec 1989, Max Elwyn Harijs b 2 Nov 1991); *Career* restaurateur; early catering experience working in Switzerland (Rorschach and Zurich) and on private yacht in Athens, subsequent experience working in hotels and restaurants in London; fndr proprietor Lettonie 1988–2001, Blinis Bath 2001–; head chef The Lygon Arms 2004–; *Awards* for Lettonie: 4 out of 5 Good Food Guide 1997, Restaurant of the Year 1997, 4 AA Rosettes, 2 Michelin stars, 1 Egon Ronay star; *Recreations* family; *Style*— Martin Blunos, Esq; ✉ The Lygon Arms, Broadway, Worcestershire WR12 7DU

BLUNT, Crispin Jeremy Rupert; MP; s of late Maj Gen Peter Blunt, CB, MBE, GM, and late Adrienne, *née* Richardson; bro of Oliver Blunt, QC, *qv*; *b* 15 July 1960; *Educ* Wellington, RMA Sandhurst, UC Durham (BA), Cranfield Inst of Technol (MBA); *m* 15 Sept 1990, Victoria Ainsley, *née* Jenkins; 1 da (Claudia b 22 Feb 1992), 1 s (Frederick b 22 Aug 1994); *Career* cmmnd 13/18 Royal Hussars 1980; troop ldr: UK and Cyprus 1980–81, BAOR 1984–85; regimental signals offr/ops offr BAOR/UK 1985–87, sqdn ldr, 2 i/c UK 1987–89, resigned cmmn 1990, representative Forum of Private Business 1991–92, conslt Politics International 1993; special advsr to: sec of state for Defence 1993–95, foreign sec 1995–97: MP (Cons) Reigate 1997–; oppn frontbench spokesman on NI 2001–02, shadow min for trade and industry 2002–03, oppn whip 2004–; memb House of Commons Select Ctee on: Def 1997–2000 and 2003–04, Environment Tport and Regions 2000–01; *Recreations* cricket, sport, travel, bridge, food and wine; *Clubs* Reigate Priory Cricket, RAC, MCC; *Style*— Crispin Blunt, Esq, MP; ✉ House of Commons, London SW1A 0AA (tel 020 7219 2254, website www.crispinbluntmp.com)

BLUNT, David John; QC (1991); s of Vernon Egerton Rowland Blunt (d 1990), of Staunton-on-Wye, Hereford, and Catherine Vera, *née* Jones; *b* 25 October 1944; *Educ* Farnham GS, Trinity Hall Cambridge (MA), Inns of Court Sch of Law (Colombos Prize for Public Int Law); *m* 28 Feb 1976, Zaibonisa, da of Isaak Ebrahim (d 1962), of Cape Town, South Africa; 1 da (Dr Nadia Shaida b 1980), 1 s (Joseph Isaac b 1987); *Career* called to the Bar Middle Temple 1967 (bencher 2000); asst recorder 1985–90, recorder of the Crown Court 1990–, dep judge of Tech and Construction Court 1993, dep High Court judge 2003; chm Bonhams Gp Ltd 1990–2000; memb Lib Dem Pty; Parly candidate (Lib): Lambeth Central 1978 and 1979, Cornwall SE 1983; *Recreations* reading, writing, running, cycling, gardening, old cars; *Clubs* Thames Hare and Hounds; *Style*— David Blunt, Esq, QC; ✉ 4 Pump Court, Temple, London EC4Y 7AN (tel 020 7842 5555)

BLUNT, Sir David Richard Reginald Harvey; 12 Bt (GB 1720), of London; s of Sir Richard David Harvey Blunt, 11 Bt (d 1975); *b* 8 November 1938; *m* 1969, Sonia Tudor Rosemary, da of late Albert Edward Day; 1 da (Davina Angela Rosemary b 1972); *Heir* kinsman, Robin Blunt; *Style*— Sir David Blunt, Bt; ✉ 74 Kirkstall Road, London SW2 4HF

BLUNT, James; né James Hillier Blount; *b* 22 February 1974, Tidworth, Wilts; *Educ* Harrow, Univ of Bristol (BEng), RMA Sandhurst; *Career* singer and songwriter; cmmnd offr Household Cavalry (The Life Gds), armoured reconnaissance offr rising to Capt NATO Peacekeeping Force Kosovo; solo artist 2004–; Back to Bedlam (album) 2004; singles: High 2004, Wisemen 2005, You're Beautiful 2005, Goodbye My Lover 2005, No Bravery 2006; *Awards* Best New Act MTV Europe Music Awards 2005, Best New Act Q Awards 2005, Best Pop Act Digital Music Awards 2005, Best Int Newcomer NRJ Music Awards (France) 2006, Best Pop Act and Best Male Brit Awards 2006, Best Int Newcomer ECHO Awards (Germany) 2006, Song of the Year MTV Australia Video Music Awards 2006, Most Performed Work and Int Hit of the Year Ivor Novello Awards 2006; *Style*— James Blunt, Esq; ✉ c/o Twenty-First Artists Limited, 1 Blythe Road, London W14 0HG

BLUNT, Oliver Simon Peter; QC (1994); s of late Maj-Gen Peter John Blunt, CB, MBE, GM, of Ramsbury, Wilts, and Adrienne, *née* Richardson; bro of Crispin Blunt, MP, *qv*; *b* 8 March 1951; *Educ* Bedford Sch, Univ of Southampton (LLB); *m* 29 Sept 1979, Joanna Margaret, da of Robert Dixon (d 1985); 3 da (Felicity b 1981, Emily b 1983, Susannah b 1991), 1 s (Sebastian b 1989); *Career* called to the Bar Middle Temple 1974; asst recorder 1991, recorder 1995; *Recreations* cricket, squash, golf; *Clubs* Roehampton, Barnes Sports, Rosslyn Park; *Style*— Oliver Blunt, Esq, QC; ✉ 106 Priory Lane, Roehampton, London SW15 5JL (tel 020 8876 3369); Furnival Chambers, 32 Furnival Street, London EC4A 1JQ (tel 020 7405 3232)

BLUNT, Dr Stavia Brigitte; da of Harry Blunt, of Kenya, and Elly, *née* Sfalagacos (d 1981); *Educ* Malvern Girls' Coll (head girl), Univ of Oxford (BA, John Llewellyn scholarship, John Cooney scholarship, Martin Wronker Prize), Westminster Med Sch, Inst of Neurology (PhD); *m* 12 Sept 1987, George Leggatt, QC, *qv*, s of Rt Hon Sir Andrew Leggatt, *qv*; 1 s (Peter b 4 April 1990), 1 da (Elly b 25 Feb 1993); *Career* jr dr at various London teaching hosps; neurology specialist trg: Hammersmith Hosp, Nat Hosp for Neurology, Charing Cross Hosp, Atkinson Morley's Hosp; conslt and sr lectr in neurology Hammersmith Hosp 1994–98; conslt: Charing Cross Hosp 1998–, Parkside Hosp 1998–; former sec Neurology Section RSM; memb Bd Research Advsy Ctee Royal Hosp for Neurodisability; MRC Trg fell 1988–91, Vera Down Res Award BMA 1993, Royal Soc Res Award 1994; FRCP 2000 (MRCP 1987); *Publications* Having a Baby (1997), Shaping Up During and After Pregnancy (1998), Working Mother (1999); author of numerous book chapters and over 50 medical papers in peer-reviewed jls; *Recreations* songwriting (www.stavia.co.uk; albums recorded: Magic Garden, Forbidden Fruit, The Way You Are, Deep Waters), swimming, web design; *Style*— Dr Stavia Blunt; ✉ Department of Neurology, Charing Cross Hospital, Fulham Palace Road, Hammersmith, London W6 8RF

BLYTH, 4 Baron (1907 UK); Sir Anthony Audley Rupert Blyth; 4 Bt (1895); s of 3 Baron Blyth (d 1977); *b* 3 June 1931; *Educ* St Columba's Coll Dublin; *m* 1, 1954 (m dis 1962), Elizabeth Dorothea, da of Robert T Sparrow, of Vancouver, BC, Canada; 1 s (Hon Riley Audley John b 4 March 1955 d 1996), 2 da (Hon Marcia Edna Dorothea b 1956, Hon Alexandra b 1957); m 2, 1963, Oonagh Elizabeth Ann, yr da of late William Henry Conway, of Dundrum, Dublin; 1 da (Hon Lucinda Audley Jane b 1966), 1 s (Hon James Audley Ian b 1970); *Heir* s, Hon James Blyth; *Style*— The Rt Hon the Lord Blyth; ✉ Blythwood Estate, Athenry, Co Galway, Republic of Ireland

BLYTH, Sir Charles (Chay); kt (1997), CBE (1972), BEM (1967); s of Robert Blyth (d 1971), and Jessie Pat, *née* Patterson (d 1965); *b* 14 May 1940; *Educ* Hawick HS; *m* 1, 1962 (m dis 1992), Maureen Margaret, da of Albert Morris (d 1956); 1 da (Samantha b 1967); m 2, 1995, Felicity Rayson; *Career* served 3 Bn Para Regt 1958–67, Sgt; Cadbury Schweppes 1968–69, dir Sailing Ventures (Hampshire) Ltd 1969–73; md: Rainbow Charters Ltd 1974–, South West Properties Ltd 1978–94, The Challenge Business Ltd 1989–2006; conslt Hill & Knowlton Ltd 1983–92; rowed N Atlantic with Capt John Ridgeway 1966, circumnavigated world westwards solo in yacht British Steel 1970–71, circumnavigated world eastwards with crew of paratroopers in yacht Great Britain II Whitbread Round the World Yacht Race 1973–74 (winner Elapsed Time prize), Atlantic sailing record Cape Verde to Antigua 1977, winner Round Britain Race in yacht Great Britain IV (crew Robert James) 1978, winner Observer/Europe 1 Doublehanded Transatlantic Race in record time (crew Robert James) 1981, captained yacht United Friendly (first British yacht home) Whitbread Round the World Race 1981/82, in yacht Brittany Ferries GB came 2nd overall and first in Class I Round Britain and Ireland Race 1982 and first in Class Plymouth Vilamoura Plymouth Race 1983, in trimaran Beefeater II (with Eric Blunn) capsized off Cape Horn during NY-San Francisco record attempt and spent 19 hours in water before rescue 1984, co-skipper Virgin Atlantic Challenger I 1985, co-skipper Virgin Atlantic Challenge II on the successful Blue Riband 1986; chm: Silk Cut Awards Ctee 1983–92, British Steel Challenge Round the World Yacht Race 1992–93, BT Global Challenge Round the World Yacht Race 1996/97; Man of the Year 1966; Yachting Journalists' Assoc: Yachtsman of the Year 1971, Special Award for Outstanding Servs to Yachting 1994; Chichester Trophy RYS 1971; pres Inst of Professional Sales 1999, pres CIM (Wessex Branch) 1999; Hon DTech Univ of Plymouth 1994, Hon LLD Univ of Portsmouth 1999; *Books* A Fighting Chance (1966), Innocent Aboard (1968), The Impossible Voyage (1971), Theirs is the Glory (1974), Challenge (1993); *Recreations* horse riding, skiing; *Clubs* Royal Southern Yacht, Royal Ocean Racing, Special Forces, Leander, Henley; *Style*— Sir Chay Blyth, CBE, BEM; ✉ Box End Farm, Box, Minchinhampton, Gloucestershire GL6 9HA (tel 01453 836333)

BLYTH, Mark Terence; s of Terence Blyth, of Esher, Surrey, and Patricia, *née* Vincent; *b* 2 September 1965, Woking; *Educ* Poole GS, Univ of Warwick (LLB), Guildford Coll of Law; *m* 20 Aug 1989, Melanie, da of Frank Russell; 2 da (Alexandra Charlotte b 22 May 1998, Helena Catherine b 27 Aug 1999); *Career* articled clerk Allen & Overy 1988–90; Linklaters: slr 1990–2000, ptnr 2000–, currently head of pensions litigation; author of numerous articles relating to pensions litigation; memb: Assoc of Pension Lawyers, Assoc of Contentious Tst and Probate Specialists, Law Soc; *Recreations* jogging, gardening; *Style*— Mark Blyth, Esq; ✉ Linklaters, One Silk Street, London EC2Y 8HQ (tel 020 7456 2000, fax 020 7456 2222, e-mail mark.blyth@linklaters.com)

BLYTH, (William) Michael; s of William Paterson Blyth (d 1993), and Bertha Margaret, *née* Roxburgh; *b* 12 May 1950; *Educ* Sedbergh, Univ of St Andrews (BSc); *m* 1972, Carolyn, da of Samuel Alexander Haig Haddow; 2 s (Christopher Michael b 1974, Mark Alexander b 1978); *Career* Thomson McLintock & Co (now KPMG): apprentice 1972–76, audit mangr 1977–79; S Easton Simmers & Co: audit mangr 1979–81, ptnr 1981–86; Baker Tilly (formerly HLB Kidsons): ptnr 1986–, nat dir Staff Resources 1990–93, office managing ptnr (Glasgow) 1991–96, regnl managing ptnr (Scotland) 1994–97, nat dir Professional Servs 1997–2002; dir Erskine Hosp, dir Merchants House of Glasgow; memb Incorporation of Bakers (Glasgow) 1963; MICAS 1976; *Recreations* skiing, tennis, gardening; *Style*— Michael Blyth, Esq; ✉ Low Borland, Dunlop, Ayrshire KA3 4BU (tel 01560 484846); Baker Tilly, Breckenridge House, 274 Sauchiehall Street, Glasgow G2 3EH (tel 0141 307 5000, fax 0141 307 5005, e-mail mike.blyth@bakertilly.co.uk)

BLYTHE, Ronald George; s of Albert George Blythe (d 1957), and Matilda Elizabeth Elkins (d 1976); *b* 6 November 1922; *Educ* St Peter's and St Gregory's Sch Sudbury, Lambeth (MLitt); *Career* writer; reference librarian until 1954, full-time writer 1955–; memb Centre of E Anglian Studies UEA 1972–76; pres John Clare Soc 1981–, pres Robert Bloomfield Soc 2001, vice-pres Hazlitt Soc 2004, pres Kilvert Soc 2006; chm Essex Festival 1981–83; memb Soc of Authors (memb Mgmnt Ctee 1970–79), memb Eastern Arts Lit Panel; lay canon St Edmundsbury Cathedral 2003; Hon MA UEA 1990, Hon DLitt Anglia Ruskin Univ 2001, Hon DLitt Univ of Essex 2002; FRSL 1969; *Books* incl: A Treasonable Growth (1960), Immediate Possession: Short Stories (1961), The Age of Illusion (history, 1963), Components of the Scene: Poems, Essays and Stories of the Second World War (1965), Akenfield (1969), Aldeburgh Anthology (1972), The View in Winter (1979), Places (1981), From the Headlands (1982), The Stories of Ronald Blythe (1985), Divine Landscapes (1986), The Pleasure of Diaries (1989), Private Words: Letters and Diaries of the Second World War (1991), Word from Wormingford (1997), First Friends: Paul and Bunty, John and Christine and Carrington (1999), Talking About John Clare (1999), Out of The Valley (1999), Going to See George (1999), The Circling Year (2001), Talking to the Neighbours (2002), The Nash Cats' Story (2003), George Herbert: A Priest to the Temple: the Country Parson, and Selected Poems (ed, 2003), The Assassin (novel, 2004), Borderland (2004), A Year at Bottengoms Farm 2006, A Writer's Day Book (2006); author of essays, stories, poems, reviews in newspapers and magazines and critical studies of: Jane Austen, Leo Tolstoy, Henry James, J C Powys, William Hazlitt, Thomas Hardy; *Films* A Painter in the Country (BBC2) 1968, Constable Observed 1969, Akenfield 1974; *Awards* Heinemann Award 1969, Angel Prize 1985, Benson Medal for Lit 2006; *Recreations* gardening, walking, looking at architecture, plants and landscape; *Style*— Dr Ronald Blythe; ✉ Bottengoms Farm, Wormingford, Colchester, Essex CO6 3AP (tel 01206 271308); c/o Andrew Hewson, Johnson and Alcock Limited, Clerkenwell House, 45/47 Clerkenwell Grove, London EC1K 0HT (tel 020 7251 0125)

BNINSKI, Dr Kazimierz Andrzej; s of Count Charles Felix Bninski-Mizgalski (d 1983), Lt Cdr Polish Navy (and POW), of Sopot, Poland, and Countess Sophie, *née* de Saryusz-Woyciechowska (descends from ancient Polish Jelita clan, and descendant of Floryan Saryusz who fought against the Teutonic Knights in the Battle of Plowce in 1331); paternal gggf Count Pawel Bninski (b 1773, s of Count Lucas Victor Bninski) was a distinguished cavalry officer who fought against the Russian army of Catherine II in 1794 and afterwards temporarily sought refuge under the pseudonym Mizgalski; *b* 28 February 1939; *Educ* Univ of Gdańsk Poland (MD); *m* 2 July 1988, Teresa Maria, da of Baron Adam Andrzej Maria de Gallen-Bisping, and a cous of King Juan Carlos of Spain; 2 s (Paul Charles b 11 Oct 1989, Adam Charles b 9 June 1994), 1 da (Maria Elizabeth Sophie b 17 Oct 1992); *Career* SHO Nelson Hosp London 1967–68, SHO St Mary Abbots Hosp London 1969–71, registrar in med St Mary's Hosp and St Charles' Hosp London 1972–76, physician 7 US Army Germany 1977–80, jr ptnr gen practice 1981–87, dir i/c Polish Clinic Harley Street London 1988–; *Style*— Dr Kazimierz Bninski; ✉ The Polish Clinic, 131 Harley Street, London W1G 6BB (tel 020 7580 4693)

BOADEN, Helen; da of William John Boaden, and Barbara Mary Boaden; *b* 1 March 1956; *Educ* Univ of Sussex (BA); *m* 1994, Stephen Burley; *Career* care asst Hackney Social Servs 1978, reporter Radio WBAI NY 1979, reporter Radio Tees and Radio Aire 1980–83, prodr BBC Radio Leeds 1983–85, reporter File on 4 (BBC Radio 4) and Brass Tacks (BBC2) and presenter Woman's Hour (BBC Radio 4) 1985–91, presenter Verdict (Channel 4) 1991–, ed File on 4 (BBC Radio 4) 1991–94, head of network current affrs BBC Manchester 1994–97, head of business progs BBC News 1997, head of current affrs and business progs BBC 1998–2000, controller BBC Radio 4 2000–04, controller BBC7 2002–04, dir BBC News 2004–; chair Radio Acad 2003–; Sony Gold Awards for: investigation into AIDS in Africa (File on 4) 1987, investigation into bullying in Feltham Young Offenders Inst (File on 4) 1993, Radio Station of the Year (BBC Radio 4) 2003 and 2004; Hon Dr: UEA,Univ of Sussex, Univ of York; *Style*— Ms Helen Boaden; ✉ c/o BBC, Television Centre, Wood Lane, London W12 7RJ (tel 020 8743 8000)

BOAITEY, Charlotte; da of Kwaku Yentumi Boaitey (d 1944), and Lydia, *née* Sarpong (d 1989); *b* 21 March 1944; *Educ* Aburi Girls' Sch Ghana, Univ of London (LLB), Lady Margaret Hall Oxford (MPhil Social Anthropology); *m* 19 Oct 1972, Alfred Kwasi Kwarteng, s of Kodua Kwarteng; 1 s (Kwasi Addob b 26 May 1975); *Career* barrister; fndr memb Legal Dept of Community Relations Cmmn (now Cmmn for Racial Equality) 1972–75, called to the Bar Middle Temple 1976, currently head of chambers 12 Old Square; asst boundary cmmr, chm Review Cncllr Renumeration, pt/t legal chm Mental Health Review Tbnl; conslt anthropologist Granada TV series Disappearing World 1982; chm Queensbury Methodist Home and Overseas Mission; tstee of various charities; *Recreations* gardening, house keeping; *Style*— Miss Charlotte Boaitey; ✉ 12 Old Square, 1st Floor, Lincoln's Inn, London WC2A 3TX (tel 020 7404 0875)

BOAL, His Hon (John) Graham; QC (1993); s of Surgn-Capt Jackson Graham Boal (d 1958), and Dorothy Kenley, *née* Hall (d 1984); *b* 24 October 1943; *Educ* Eastbourne Coll, KCL (LLB); *m* 28 June 1978, Elizabeth Mary, da of Col L C East, DSO, OBE; 1 s (Thomas Henry b 1980); *Career* called to the Bar Gray's Inn 1966 (bencher 1991); jr Treasury counsel 1977–85, sr prosecuting counsel to Crown at Central Criminal Court 1985–91, first sr prosecuting counsel to the Crown at Central Criminal Court 1991–93; recorder of the Crown Court 1985–96, sr circuit judge (SE Circuit) 1996–2005, perm judge at Central Criminal Court 1996–2005; vice-chm Criminal Bar Assoc 1991–93, judicial memb Parole Bd 2001–05; chm Orchid Cancer Appeal 1999–2005; *Recreations* golf, theatre, walking, watching sport; *Clubs* Garrick, New Zealand Golf, Royal West Norfolk Golf, MCC; *Style*— His Hon Graham Boal, QC; ✉ c/o Central Criminal Court, Old Bailey, London EC4M 7EH (tel 020 7248 3277)

BOARD, Kathryn; OBE (1999); da of Nicholas Llewellyn Board, of Southampton, and Eileen Mary, *née* Gleeson (d 1992); *b* 24 December 1952; *Educ* La Sagesse Convent Romsey, Royal Holloway Coll London (BA), Univ of Leeds (MA); *m* Dec 1987 (m dis 1996); 1 da (Ellen Lucia b 1 Oct 1988), 1 s (Nicolas Gonzalo b 6 July 1991); *Career* teacher Br Cncl Afghanistan 1975–79, lectr in linguistics and phonetics Univ of Ghent 1980–84; Br Cncl: English language teaching (ELT) conslt 1984–86, English language offr Peru 1986–89, regnl dir Basque Country Spain 1989–92, teaching centre mangr Ecuador 1992–95, dir Colombia 1995–99, dir Argentina 1999–2000, policy dir (Americas) 2000–02, dir Germany 2002–05, geographical dir Europe, Americas, Middle East and North Africa 2005–; *Recreations* travelling, reading, world history, politics; *Style*— Ms Kathryn Board, OBE; ✉ British Council, 10 Spring Gardens, London SW1A 2AH (tel 020 7930 8466, e-mail kathryn.board@britishcouncil.org)

BOARD, Prof Kenneth; s of George Herbert Board, of Llanelli, and Beryl, *née* Roberts; *b* 15 April 1941; *Educ* Llanelli Boys' GS, Univ of Wales Swansea (BSc, MSc, DSc), Univ of Bangor (PhD); *m* 30 July 1966, Meriel, da of Gwilym Leonard Jones, of Bynea, Llanelli, Dyfed; 2 s (Meirion b 1973, Alun b 1976); *Career* research scientist: GEC Hirst Research Centre, Philips Research Lab 1969–75; Dept of Electrical Engrg Univ of Wales Swansea: lectr 1975–82, sr lectr 1982–84, reader 1984–86, prof 1986–, head of dept 1992–99, chm of faculty 1996–97, Technium chair of entrepreneurship 1998–2003, dir Knowledge Exploitation Centre; co-fndr and dir Enfis Ltd 2001–; MIEEE 1982, FIEE 1997, FREng 2001; *Books* Introduction to Semiconductor Microtechnology (1983); *Recreations* squash, running, music; *Clubs* Clyne Golf; *Style*— Prof Kenneth Board; ✉ Knowledge Exploitation Centre, Department of Electrical Engineering, University of Wales Swansea, Singleton Park, Swansea SA2 8PP (tel 01792 295415, fax 01792 513398, e-mail k.board@swansea.ac.uk)

BOARDMAN, Christopher Miles (Chris); MBE (1993); s of Keith Boardman, and Carol, *née* Lindfield; *b* 26 August 1968; *Educ* Hilbre Secdy Sch, Withens Coll; *m* 22 Oct 1988, Sally-Anne, *née* Edwards; 4 s (Edward Thomas b 11 March 1989, George Douglas b 15 Jan 1994, Oscar Miles b 13 July 1995, Sonny b 27 Feb 2002), 1 da (Harriet Lydia b 1 June 1991); *Career* cyclist (individual); int debut Jr World Championships Stuttgart 1985; achievements incl: Bronze medal Cwlth Games Edinburgh 1986, 2 Bronze medals Cwlth Games Auckland 1990, Gold medal 4000m individual pursuit Olympic Games Barcelona 1992, Double World champion 1994 (individual pursuit and individual time trial), Bronze medal individual time trial Olympic Games Atlanta 1996; professional cyclist; with French Gan Team (world rank number 12), winner Tour de France Prologue and holder Yellow Jersey 1994 and 1998; with French Credit Agricole team, winner time trial PruTour 1999; competed in 9 World Championships, world champion and world record holder; dir: Beyond Level Four Ltd, NWV Racing Team (GB); vice-pres: Sports Aid Fndn NW, Claire House Charity; *Recreations* swimming, family; *Style*— Chris Boardman, Esq, MBE; ✉ c/o Beyond Level Four Ltd, St Andrews, Bertram Drive, Wirral CH47 0LJ (fax 0151 632 0742, e-mail chrisb24@btinternet.com)

BOARDMAN, Sir John; kt (1989); s of Frederick Archibald Boardman (d 1938), and Clare, *née* Wells (d 1975); *b* 20 August 1927; *Educ* Chigwell Sch, Magdalene Coll Cambridge (MA, Walston student); *m* 26 Oct 1952, Sheila Joan Lyndon Stanford; 2 c (Julia b 1955, Mark b 1957); *Career* Mil Serv 2 Lt Intelligence Corps 1950–52; asst dir Br Sch of Athens 1952–55 (vice-pres), asst keeper Ashmolean Museum Oxford 1955–59, reader in classical archaeology Univ of Oxford 1959–78, Lincoln prof of classical archaeology and art Univ of Oxford 1978–94; Merton Coll Oxford: fell 1963–78, subwarden 1975–78, hon fell 1978; Geddes-Harrower prof Univ of Aberdeen 1974; visiting prof: Columbia Univ 1965, Aust Inst of Archaeology 1987; prof of ancient history Royal Acad of Arts 1990–; ed: Jl of Hellenic Studies 1958–65, Lexicon Iconographicum 1972–; conducted excavations on: Chios 1953–55, Crete, Tocra in Libya 1964–65; vice-pres Archaeological Soc of Athens 1998; delg OUP 1979–89; Cromer Greek prize Br Acad 1959, Kenyon Medal British Acad 1995; corr fell: Bavarian Acad of Sciences 1969, Athens Acad 1997; fell: Inst of Etruscan Studies Florence 1983, Austrian and German Archaeological Insts; hon fell: Magdalene Coll Cambridge 1984, Lincoln Coll Oxford 1995; Hon Dr: Univ of Athens 1991, Univ of Paris (Sorbonne) 1994; foreign memb: Royal Danish Acad 1979, American Philosophical Soc 1999, Acad dei Lincei Rome 1999, Russian Acad of Sciences 2003; membre associé Académie des Inscriptions et Belles Lettres Institut de France 1991; Hon MRIA 1986; FSA 1957, FBA 1969; Hon RA; *Publications* incl: Cretan Collection in Oxford (1961), Island Gems (1963), Archaic Greek Gems (1968), Athenian Black Figure Vases (1974), Harari Collection of Finger Rings (with D Scarisbrick, 1978), The Greeks Overseas (1980), Escarabeos de Piedra de Ibiza (1984), The Oxford History of the Classical World (jtly 1986), Athenian Red Figure Vases, Classical Period (1989), The Oxford History of Classical Art (jtly 1993), The Diffusion of Classical Art in Antiquity (1994), Greek Art (1996), The Great God Pan (1997), Early Greek Vase Painting (1998), Persia and the West (2000), The History of Greek Vases (2001), The Archaeology of Nostalgia (2002), The World of Ancient Art (2006); articles in various learned jls; *Clubs* Athenaeum; *Style*— Sir John Boardman, FBA; ✉ 11 Park Street, Woodstock, Oxfordshire OX20 1SJ (tel 01993 811259, fax 01865 278082)

BOARDMAN, Hon Nigel Patrick Gray; s of Baron Boardman, MC, TD, DL (Life Peer, d 2003); *b* 1950; *Educ* Ampleforth, Univ of Bristol; *m* 1975, Sarah, da of T A Coslett, of Cambridge; 5 da (Tamsin b 1980, Charlotte b 1981, Rebecca b 1984, Cordelia b 1987, Elizabeth b 1992), 1 s (Hugo b 1990); *Career* admitted slr 1975; ptnr Slaughter and May; govr Highgate Sch; *Style*— The Hon Nigel Boardman; ✉ Slaughter and May, 1 Bunhill Row, London EC1Y 8YY (tel 020 7090 3418, fax 020 7090 5000)

BOARDMAN, Royston James (Roy); MBE (1990); s of Herbert James Boardman (d 1969), of London, and Alice Paulin (d 1967); *b* 2 February 1937; *Educ* Walworth Secdy Sch, Borough Rd Training Coll Univ of London, Univ of Essex (MA); *m* Nov 1975, Saverina, da of Dr Aniello Curzio; 2 s (Michael b 21 Dec 1962, Arthur b 17 Aug 1964), 1 da (Luisa b 25 Sept 1973); *Career* Nat Serv RAPC 1955–57; jr librarian Islington Public Libraries 1953–55, head of English Sandon Secdy Sch Essex 1961–65 (joined 1959), lectr in English language & lit British Council Naples and L'Università di Napoli L'Orientale Naples 1965–69, linguistic and cultural researcher Naples 1969–71, lectr Univ of Bari 1972–75; British Council Naples: English language offr South Italy 1975–80, regnl dir South Italy 1980–95; dir St Peter's English Language Centre 1997–, lectr in English for int rels L'Università di Napoli L'Orientale Naples 1998–; *Awards* Premio Calabria 1987 (for cultural rels), Premio Sebetia-Ter 1992; *Books* In the Web (poems, 1961), Over to You (1978), Variety (1982), Springboard 1 (1982), Reading Between the Lines (with John McRae, 1984), My Generation (1994), Literature in Foreign Language Education (1995), Naples and its Environs (1995); *Recreations* reading, poetry, travel, theatre; *Style*— Roy Boardman, Esq, MBE; ✉ Vico S. Geronimo alle Monache 6, 80134 Naples; St Peter's English Language Centre, Riviera di Chiaia 124, 80122 Naples (tel 00 39 081 5526866, fax 00 39 081 682721, e-mail royboardman@hotmail.com)

BOAS, (John) Robert Sotheby; s of Edgar Henry Boas, of Teddington, Middx, and Mary Katherine, *née* Beattie; *b* 28 February 1937; *Educ* Clifton, CCC Cambridge; *m* 25 Sept 1965, (Karen) Elisabeth, da of Gunnar Gersted, of Copenhagen, Denmark; 1 da (Helena b 1970), 2 s (Christopher b 1972, Nicholas b 1975 d 1998); *Career* 2 Lt Royal Signals 1955–57; merchant banker; Price Waterhouse 1960–64, ICI 1964–65, S G Warburg & Co Ltd 1965–95, md SBC Warburg Dillon Read 1995–98, advsr UBS Warburg 1998–2002; non-exec dir: Chesterfield Properties 1978–99, Norwich Union 1998–2000, Trident Safeguards 1998–2002, Invesco Smaller Continental Companies Tst 1998–2004, Prospect Publishing 2000–, Telecom Italia 2004–07; memb Bd Securities Assoc (now Securities and Futures Authy) 1988–96; dir: ENO 1990–99, Donmar Warehouse 1997–2001; memb Bd Cncl The English Stage Co 1978–83; chm Fedn of Br Artists 2001–07; tstee: Nat Heritage Meml Fund and Heritage Lottery Fund 1998–2002, Paintings in Hosp 1998–2007, Natural Life Story Fndn 1998–, Guildhall Sch Tst 2000–, Classical Opera Co 2001–, Gabrieli Tst 2001–, Paul Hamlyn Fndn 2002–; chm London String Quartet Fndn 2006–; FCA; *Recreations* music, painting, theatre, reading; *Style*— Robert Boas, Esq; ✉ 22 Mansfield Street, London W1G 9NR

BOASE, Martin; s of Prof Alan Martin Boase (d 1982), of Edinburgh, and Elizabeth Grizelle, *née* Forster (d 1977); *b* 14 July 1932; *Educ* Rendcomb Coll, New Coll Oxford (MA); *m* 1, 1960 (m dis 1971), Terry-Ann, *née* Moir; 1 s (Daniel b 1962), 1 da (Rachel b 1964); m 2, 1974, Pauline Valerie, da of Lt-Col Philip Henry Akerman Brownrigg, CMG, DSO, OBE, TD, of Checkendon, Berks; 1 da (Hannah b 1976), 1 s (Luke b 1981); *Career* Russian interpreter Intelligence Corps 1951–53; exec London Press Exchange Ltd 1958–60, md Pritchard Wood & Partners Ltd 1967–68 (joined 1961), fndr ptnr The Boase Massimi Pollitt Partnership Ltd 1968; chm: Boase Massimi Pollitt plc 1979–89 (jt chm 1977–79), Omnicom UK plc 1989–95, Kiss FM 1993–2000, Maiden Outdoor plc 1993–2006, Herald Investment Trust 1994–, Investment Trust of Investment Trusts 1995–2005, Heal's plc 1997–2002; dir: Omnicom Group Inc 1989–94, EMAP plc 1991–2000, Matthew Clark plc 1995–98; chm: Advertising Assoc 1987–92, British Television Advertising Awards Ltd 1993–2000, Jupiter Dividend and Growth Tst 1999, NewStar Investment Tst 2000–06, New Media Industries plc 2001–05; dir Oxford Playhouse Tst 1991–97; FIPA 1976; *Recreations* the Turf; *Style*— Martin Boase; ✉ 12 Bishops Bridge Road, London W2 6AA (tel 020 7258 3979, fax 020 7706 3854)

BOATENG, Ozwald; OBE (2006); s of Kwasi Domfeh, of London, and Mary Domfeh; *b* 22 February 1967; *Educ* Southgate Coll (Dip Fashion); *m* 1 Sept 1999, Gyunel; 1 da (Emilia); *Career* fashion designer; fndr Bespoke Couture; produces two ready-to-wear collections each year, designer Givenchy men's collections 2003–; *Awards* Best Male Designer Trophées de la Mode Paris 1996, Br Fashion Award Best Menswear Designer 2000, Cologne Fashion Award for Menswear 2002, nominated Best Dressed Man GQ Magazine Awards 2002, Best Dressed Male Vanity Fair 2006; *Recreations* film, tailoring and fashion; *Style*— Ozwald Boateng, Esq, OBE; ✉ 12A Savile Row, London W1S 3PQ (tel 020 7563 9800, fax 020 7487 5737)

BOATENG, HE the Rt Hon Paul Yaw; PC (1999); s of Kwaku Boateng, of Ghana and England, and Eleanor, *née* McCombie; *b* 14 June 1951; *Educ* Accra Acad, Apsley GS, Univ of Bristol (LLB); *m* 1980, Janet, da of Leonard Alleyne; 3 da (Mirabelle b 1980, Beth b 1982, Charlotte b 1983), 2 s (Benjamin b 1984, Seth b 1987); *Career* admitted slr 1976, slr Paddington Law Centre 1976–79, slr and ptnr BM Birnberg & Co 1979–87; called to the Bar Gray's Inn 1989; legal advsr Scrap Sus Campaign 1977–81, memb (Lab) for Walthamstow GLC 1981–85 (chm Police Ctee 1981–85, vice-chm Ethnic Minorities Ctee 1981–85); Parly candidate (Lab) Herts W 1983, MP (Lab) Brent S 1987–2005; memb House of Commons Environment Ctee 1987–89, oppn spokesman on Treasy and Economic Affairs 1989–92, oppn spokesman on Legal Affairs (Lord Chllr's Dept) 1992–97; Parly under sec of state Dept of Health 1997–98, min of state Home Office 1998–2001, fin sec to the Treasy 2001–02, chief sec to the Treasy 2002–05; high cmmr to South Africa 2005–; broadcaster; presenter: Looking Forward to the Past (BBC Radio 4), Nothing But The Truth (Channel 4), Behind the Headlines (BBC2); chm Afro-Caribbean Educn Resource Project 1978–86; memb Bd: ENO 1984–97, English Touring Opera 1993–97; memb: Exec NCCL 1980–86, World Cncl of Churches Cmmn Prog to Combat Racism 1984–91; chm of govrs Priory Park Sch 1978–84, govr Police Staff Coll Bramshill 1981–84; Hon DL Univ of Lincoln USA, Hon DL Univ of Bristol; *Books* Reclaiming the Ground (contrib with Rt Hon John Smith, QC, MP), contrib foreword to Sense and Sensibility (in Complete Works of Jane Austen, HarperCollins); *Style*— HE the Rt Hon Paul Boateng; ✉ c/o Foreign & Commonwealth Office (Pretoria), King Charles Street, London SW1A 2AH

BOBROW, Dr Lynda Geraldine; da of Jakobus Gideon Nel Strauss, QC (d 1990), of South Africa, and Joy, *née* Carpenter; *b* 23 October 1939; *Educ* Barnato Park Johannesburg, Univ of the Witwatersrand Med Sch (MB BCh); *m* 1963, Prof Martin Bobrow, CBE, *qv*; 3 da (Catherine Sue (Mrs Nicholls) b 1969, Gina b 1971, Jennifer Loren b 1975); *Career* house physician and surgeon Rambam Hosp Haifa 1963–64, house physician Western Gen Hosp Edinburgh 1964–65, patholgy trg Churchill, Radcliffe and John Radcliffe Hosps Oxford 1965–75; conslt histopathologist: Leiden 1981–83, UCL and ICRF London 1983–91, Guy's Hosp London 1991–95, Addenbrooke's Hosp Cambridge 1995–; memb Br Breast Gp 1993–; FRCPath 1989 (MRCPath 1977); *Recreations* walking, reading, theatre, scuba diving; *Style*— Dr Lynda Bobrow; ✉ The Old School, Balsham, Cambridge CB21 6DJ (e-mail lgb21@cam.ac.uk)

BOBROW, Prof Martin; CBE (1995); s of late Joe Bobrow, of Ontario, Canada, and Bessie, *née* Rosin; *b* 6 February 1938; *Educ* Johannesburg, Univ of the Witwatersrand (BSc, MB BCh, DSc); *m* 1963, Dr Lynda Geraldine Bobrow, *qv*, da of Jakobus Strauss, QC, of South Africa; 3 da (Catherine, Gina, Jennifer); *Career* MRC Population Genetics Res Unit 1965–72, Genetics Lab Univ of Oxford 1972–74, prof of human genetics Univ of Amsterdam 1981–82, Prince Philip prof of paediatric res Guy's Hosp 1982–95, prof of med genetics Univ of Cambridge 1995–2005 (emeritus prof 2005–); memb Editorial Bd

Jl of Med Genetics 1976–89 and 1995–98 (ed 1995–98); series ed: Monographs in Med Genetics 1984–2005; author of numerous articles on clinical and molecular genetics; memb: Cncl MRC 1988–92 and 1993–94, Ctee to Examine the Ethical Implications of Gene Therapy and Gene Therapy Advsy Ctee Dept of Health 1989–95, Central Res and Devpt Ctee Dept of Health 1991–96, Acad of Med Sci 1998–2002; non-exec memb: Lewisham NHS Tst Bd 1993–95, Human Genetics Advsy Cmmn 1996–99, Nuffield Cncl on Bioethics 1998–2003 (dep chm 2001–03), Bd Cambridge Univ Hosp NHS Fndn Tst 2004–; chm: Ctee on the Med Aspects of Radiation in the Environment Dept of Health 1985–92, Unrelated Living Transplant Regulatory Authy 1990–99, Molecular and Cellular Med Bd MRC 1992–94, Muscular Dystrophy Gp 1995–; pres Clinical Genetics Soc 1993–94 (vice-pres 1992–93 and 1995–96); govr Wellcome Tst 1996–2007 (dep chm 2004–07); FRCPath 1990 (MRCPath 1978), FRCP, FRCPH, FMedSci (founding fell), FRS; *Style—* Prof Martin Bobrow, CBE, FRS; ✉ Department of Medical Genetics, Wellcome/MRC Building, Addenbrooke's Hospital, Cambridge CB2 2XY (tel 01223 331154, fax 01223 331206)

BOBROWSKI, Dr Jan Jozef; s of Aleksander Bobrowski (d 1987), of Poland, and Antonina, *née* Kandefer (d 1978); *b* 31 March 1925; *Educ* Univ of London, Battersea Coll of Advanced Technol (BSc), ACT (Battersea), Univ of Surrey (PhD); *m* 28 Aug 1954, Zofia, da of Boleslaw Kowalski (d 1972), of Poland; 1 da (Izabella Cecylia Antonina b 3 June 1957); *Career* Polish Corps 1942–47, Lt 1945; practical design trg with Twisteel Reinforcement Ltd 1952–53, pt/t lectr Battersea Coll of Advanced Technol 1952–58, engrg asst C J Pell & Partners 1953–58; chief engr: Pierhead Engrg Div Unit Construction Co 1958–59, Pierhead Ltd 1959–62, Unit Construction Co 1961–62, Jan Bobrowski and Partners 1962–; medal for contribs to pre-stressed concrete 1978, currently holds record for longest span concrete shell constructed at the Olympic Saddledome Calgary; visiting prof Imperial Coll of Sci and Technol London 1981; pres Concrete Soc 1986–87; vice-pres: Inst of Structural Engrs 1985–86, (UK) Fedn Internationale Precontrainte, Univ of Surrey Soc; memb Euro-International Du Beton Econ Devpt Ctee; Freeman City of London 1977, Liveryman Worshipful Co of Constructors 1977; FREng 1983, FICE 1962, FIStructE 1973, MCSCE, Hon FICT (Inst of Concrete Technologists), MConsE, MSocIS (France), PEng (Alberta BC); Sovereign Military Order of St John of Jerusalem Knights of Malta 1984, Polish Army Medal 1945, Cross of Monte Cassino 1945, Polish Defence Medal 1945; *Publications* author of numerous articles to tech jls; *Recreations* equestrianism, fishing; *Style—* Dr Jan Bobrowski, FREng; ✉ Jan Bobrowski and Partners Consulting Engineers, Grosvenor House, Grosvenor Road, Twickenham, Middlesex TW1 4AA (tel 020 8892 7627, fax 020 8891 3151, e-mail janbobpart@aol.com)

BODDY, Dr (Francis) Andrew; s of William Boddy (d 1966), and Janet Hogg, *née* Noble (d 1991); *b* 1 March 1935; *Educ* Prince Henry's GS Otley, Univ of Edinburgh (MB ChB); *m* 1965, Adele, da of Arnold Wirszubski; 2 da (Kasia b 1966, Janet b 1969); *Career* asst lectr Dept of Public Health and Social Med Univ of Edinburgh 1960–63, research assoc NY City Dept of Health 1963–65, lectr Dept of Social Med Univ of Aberdeen 1966–69; Univ of Glasgow: sr lectr Dept of Community Med 1969–78, dir Social Paediatric and Obstetric Research Unit 1978–91, dir Public Health Research Unit 1991–98, sr lectr Dept of Public Health 1998–99, ret; convenor Scottish Affrs Ctee Faculty of Public Health Med 1991–94; Soc for Social Med: memb 1963, hon sec 1982–87, chm 1996; author of pubns on socio-medical and public health topics; FFPHM 1976, FRCPEd 1981; *Recreations* fishing, photography; *Style—* Dr Andrew Boddy; ✉ 26 Rowallan Gardens, Glasgow G11 7LJ (tel 0141 339 4644, e-mail faboddy@btinternet.com)

BODDY, Su-Anna Margaret; da of Bernard Henry Peter Boddy, of Woking, Surrey, and late Audrey May, *née* Murphy; *b* 7 September 1952; *Educ* Brighton and Hove HS, St Bartholomew's Hosp London (BSc, MB, BS); *m* 11 Sept 1982, Nicholas Paul Madden, *qv*; 1 s (Christopher Paul b 6 Feb 1987), 1 da (Katherine Anna b 15 Sept 1988); *Career* house physician gastroenterology & nephrology St Bartholomew's Hosp London 1977, house surgn general surgery Luton & Dunstable Hosp 1977–78, temporary lectr in anatomy St Bartholomew's Hosp London 1978; SHO: accident service & Orthopaedics Luton & Dunstable Hosp 1978–79, paediatric surgery & urology Great Ormond Street Hosp for Sick Children 1979, general & oncological surgery Royal Marsden Hosp London 1979–80, neurosurgery National Hosp for Nervous Diseases London 1980; jr registrar St Bartholomew's Hosp 1980–81; registrar: Luton & Dunstable Hosp 1981–83, Birmingham Children's Hosp 1983–85; research registrar in urology St Bartholomew's Hosp London 1985–88 (MS 1992); sr registrar in paediatric surgery: Leeds General Infirmary and St James's Univ Hosp Leeds 1988–91, St George's Hosp London and Queen Mary's Hosp Carshalton 1992; locum conslt paediatric surgn 1992–93, conslt paediatric surgn and paediatric urologist St George's Hosp London 1993–; flexible trg advsr RCS 1998–2005; treas Br Assoc of Paediatric Urology 2004–07, memb Cncl RCS 2007–; memb: Br Assoc of Paediatric Surgns, Br Assoc of Paediatric Urologists, Br Assoc of Urologists, Euro Soc of Paediatric Urologists, Medical Womens' Fedn, Women in Surgical Trg; FRCS 1983; *Publications* author of several articles in various learned jls; *Recreations* swimming, skiing, cooking; *Style—* Miss Su-Anna Boddy; ✉ 15 Bridgefield Road, Cheam, Surrey SM1 2DG; Department of Paediatric Surgery, St George's Hospital, Blackshaw Road, London SW17 0QT (tel 020 8725 2097, fax 020 8725 2926)

BODEN, John Peter (Johnnie); s of Lt Col Patrick Anthony Drummond Boden (d 2000), of Twyford, Hants, and Rosemary Jane, *née* Huttenbach (d 2003); *b* 1 June 1961; *Educ* Eton, Oriel Coll Oxford; *m* 1992, Sophia Henrietta, da of Martin Lampard; 3 da (Anna Edith b 1994, Katherine Nathalie b 1996, Stella Lucinda b 2000); *Career* with Barclays Merchant Bank (later BZW) 1983–86, with SG Warburg Securities 1986–88, fndr and exec chm JP Boden & Co 1991–; Best Overall Consumer Catalogue and Best Internet Site for Consumer Business ECMOD 2001, Rising Star Award Retail Week 2002, Best E-Business Application European Retail Solutions 2002; incl in: Virgin Top 100 Fastest Growing Companies in UK 1998, 1999 and 2000, Deloitte & Touche/Independent on Sunday Top 100 Fastest Growing Companies in the UK 2001 and 2002; *Recreations* family, riding, gardening, DJing; *Style—* Johnnie Boden, Esq; ✉ JP Boden & Co, Boden House, 114–120 Victoria Road, London NW10 6NY (tel 020 8453 4377, fax 020 8453 1445, e-mail jboden@boden.co.uk)

BODEN, Prof Margaret Ann; OBE (2002); da of Leonard Forbes Boden, OBE (d 1986), and Violet Dorothy, *née* Dawson (d 1967); *b* 26 November 1936; *Educ* City of London Sch for Girls, Newnham Coll Cambridge (MA), Harvard Graduate Sch for Arts and Scis (AM, PhD), Univ of Cambridge (ScD); *m* 24 June 1967 (m dis 1981), John Raymond Spiers, *qv*; 1 s (Ruskin b 1968), 1 da (Jehane b 1972); *Career* lectr in philosophy Univ of Birmingham 1959–65, res prof of cognitive science Univ of Sussex 2002– (lectr and reader 1959–65, prof of philosophy and psychology 1980–2002), founding dean Sch of Cognitive and Computing Science Univ of Sussex 1987–; visiting scientist Yale Univ 1979; Duijker Lecture Amsterdam 1985, Templeton Lecture Sydney 1994, Dacre Lecture Peterhouse Cambridge 1994; co-fndr and dir Harvester Press Ltd 1968–85 (sec 1968–79); chm Cncl and vice-pres Royal Inst of GB 1993–95 (memb Cncl 1992–95), pres General Section BAAS 1992–93; memb: Advsy Bd Res Cncls 1989–91, Animal Procedures Ctee (Home Office) 1994–98; tstee Cncl for Science and Society (chm Working Pty on Benefits and Dangers of Knowledge-Based Systems 1987–88); memb: Mind Assoc, Aristotelian Soc, Royal Inst of Philosophy (memb Cncl 1988–), Br Soc for Philosophy of Science; Hon DSc: Univ of Sussex 2001, Univ of Bristol 2002, Open Univ 2004; FBA 1983 (memb Cncl 1988–, vice-pres 1989–91), FRSA 1992, fell American Assoc for Artificial Intelligence 1993, memb Academia Europaea 1993; *Books* Purposive Explanation in Psychology (1972), Artificial Intelligence and Natural Man (1977/1987), Piaget (1979), Minds and Mechanisms (1981), Computer Models of Mind (1988), Artificial Intelligence in Psychology (1989), The Philosophy of Artificial Intelligence (ed, 1990), The Creative Mind (1990/2004), Dimensions of Creativity (ed, 1994), The Philosophy of Artificial Life (ed, 1996), Artificial Intelligence (ed, 1996), Mind as Machine (2006); *Recreations* dressmaking, travel; *Clubs* Reform; *Style—* Prof Margaret Boden, OBE; ✉ Centre for Research in Cognitive Science, University of Sussex, Falmer, Brighton, East Sussex BN1 9QH (tel 01273 678386, fax 01273 671320, e-mail m.a.boden@sussex.ac.uk)

BODEN, Richard; s of Leslie Boden, and Katherine, *née* Hurst; *b* 4 January 1953; *Educ* St Philip's GS Birmingham, Bournville Coll of FE, Univ of Exeter (BA); *m* 16 April 1983, Sylvie, da of William McRoberts; 2 s (James b 8 Jan 1987, Edward b 3 March 1989); *Career* BBC TV: floor asst 1974–76, asst floor mangr 1976–79, light entertainment prodn mangr 1979–83, dir of light entertainment 1983–89, prodr of light entertainment 1989–95; head of comedy Carlton TV and Central TV 1995–, dir Columbia TriStar Carlton UK Prodns 1995–99, freelance prodr and dir 1999–, fndr memb and ptnr Good TV Prodn 2005–; prodr and dir: Best of British Comedy (BBC TV, 1983), No Place Like Home (BBC TV, 1983–84), I Woke Up One Morning (BBC TV, 1984), Birds of a Feather (BBC TV, 1985), In Sickness and in Health (BBC TV, 1986–90), Cabaret at Jongleurs (BBC TV, 1987), You Must be the Husband (BBC TV, 1987–88), Blackadder (BBC TV, 1988–89), Allo Allo (BBC TV, 1988), 2 Point 4 Children (BBC TV, 1991–95), Health and Efficiency (BBC TV, 1993–94), Every Silver Lining (BBC TV, 1993), Loved By You (Carlton TV, 1996–97), Paul Merton in Galton & Simpson's..... (Carlton TV, 1996–97), Time Gentlemen Please (Sky TV, 2000 and 2001–02), Just Shoot Me (Universal Studios, 2001), The Sketch Show (ITV, 2001); memb: Comedy Jury Golden Rose of Montreux 1996, SitCom Jury Golden Rose of Montreux 1998; *Recreations* sports; *Clubs* BAFTA, RTS, Mensa; *Style—* Richard Boden, Esq; ✉ c/o Nick Marston, Curtis Brown, Haymarket House, 28–29 Haymarket, London SW1Y 4SP (tel 020 7393 4400)

BODEY, Hon Mr Justice; Sir David Roderick Lessiter Bodey; kt (1999); s of Reginald Augustus Bodey (d 1987), and Betty Frances Ada, *née* Lessiter (d 1987); *b* 14 October 1947; *Educ* King's Sch Canterbury, Univ of Bristol (LLB); *m* 28 Feb 1976, Ruth, da of Dr Denis MacAdorey, of Healing, Lincs; 1 s (Simon Christopher b 13 Jan 1980), 1 da (Katherine Sarah b 29 April 1982); *Career* called to the Bar Middle Temple (Harmsworth scholar) 1970; legal assessor to UK Central Cncl for Nursing Midwifery and Health Visiting 1983; QC 1991, recorder of the Crown Court 1993–98 (asst recorder 1989–93), dep judge of the High Court (Family Div) 1995, judge of the High Court of Justice (Family Div) 1999–, liaison judge for London (Family Div) 1999–2001, liaison judge for NE Circuit (Family Div) 2001–; chm Family Law Bar Assoc 1997 (sec 1995); fell Int Acad of Matrimonial Lawyers 1995, memb Family Ctee of Justice 1995–98, memb Supreme Court Procedure Ctee 1995–97; *Recreations* music,sometime marathon running, attempting to keep Triumph TR3 on the road; *Style—* The Hon Mr Justice Bodey; ✉ Royal Courts of Justice, Strand, London WC2A 2LL

BODIWALA, Gautam Govindlal; CBE (2000), JP, DL (2001); s of Dr Govindlal R Bodiwala (d 1983), and Sumanben, *née* Parikh; *b* 11 October 1943; *Educ* Univ of Gujarat (MS); *m* 28 Dec 1969, Gita, da of Prabhulal G Thanawala, of Thana, India; 1 s (Dhaval b 1973), 1 da (Janki b 1977); *Career* conslt and head A&E Serv Leicester 1977–2003; chm Jt Ctee on Higher Trg in A&E Med; sr examiner: Faculty of A&E Med, Fellowship of Royal College of Surgeons Edinburgh; int co-ordinator Br Assoc for A&E Med; lectr: Europe, Israel, India, Australia, USA, Canada, Africa; hon treas British Assoc for A&E Med, memb Rotary Int, fndr pres Leics Medico-Legal Soc; memb: BMA, American Coll of Emergency Physicians; founding fell and treas Faculty of A&E Med; fell: Int Coll of Surgns, Int Coll of Angiology, Int Fedn of Emergency Med (world pres); Hon DSc Univ of Leicester 2000; FCEM, FRCS, FRCP, FRSM, FICS, FICA, FRSA; *Publications* author of over 65 scientific papers and one book; *Recreations* music and reading; *Clubs* Rotary (Oadby); *Style—* Gautam Bodiwala, Esq, CBE, DL; ✉ Lykkebo, 7 Blackthorn Lane, Oadby, Leicester LE2 4FA (tel 0116 271 8899)

BODMER, Sir Walter Fred; kt (1986); s of Dr Ernest Julius Bodmer (d 1968), and Sylvia Emily, *née* Bodmer; *b* 10 January 1936; *Educ* Manchester Grammar, Univ of Cambridge (BA, PhD); *m* 1956, Julia Gwynaeth (d 2001), da of William Gwyn Pilkington (d 1976); 2 s (Mark, Charles), 1 da (Helen); *Career* Univ of Cambridge: research fell Clare Coll 1958–60, official fell 1961, demonstrator Dept of Genetics 1960–61; prof Dept of Genetics Stanford Univ Sch of Med 1968–70 (asst prof 1962–66, assoc prof 1966–68), prof of genetics Univ of Oxford 1970–79; ICRF: dir of research 1979–91, DG 1991–96; princ Hertford Coll Oxford 1996–2005, head Cancer Research UK (formerly ICRF) Cancer and Immunogenetics Lab Weatherall Inst of Molecular Medicine Oxford 1996–; chm: Ctee on Public Understanding of Science 1990–93, Science Consultative Gp BBC 1981–87, Nat Radiological Protection Bd 1998–2003, Orgn of Euro Cancer Insts 1990–93; pres: Royal Statistical Soc 1984–85, BAAS 1987–88 (chm Cncl 1996–2001), Assoc for Science Educn 1989, Br Soc for Histocompatibility and Immunogenetics 1990–91, Human Genome Orgn 1990–92, Int Fedn of Assocs for the Advancement of Science and Technol 1992 (first pres), Br Assoc for Cancer Research 1998–2002; tstee: Natural History Museum (formerly Br Museum (Natural History)) 1983–93 (chm 1988–93), Sir John Soane's Museum 1982–2003, Gtr Manchester Museum of Science and Industry 1989–90; vice-pres Royal Instn 1981–82, memb Advsy Bd for the Research Cncls 1983–88, memb Bd of Patrons St Mark's Hosp and Academic Inst London 1996; chllr Univ of Salford 1995–2005; non-exec dir Fisons plc 1990–96; chm Bd of Dirs Laban London 2000–05, memb Bd Trinity Laban 2005–; chm Leukaemia Research Fund Medical and Scientific Advsy Panel 2003–, tstee Porter Fndn 2006–; William Allan Meml Award 1980, Conway Evans Prize 1982, Rabbi Shai Shacknai Meml Prize Lectureship in Immunology and Cancer Research 1983, John Alexander Meml Prize Lectureship 1984, Rose Payne Distinguished Scientist Lectureship 1985, Michael Faraday Award Royal Soc 1994, Romanes Lecture Univ of Oxford 1995, Harveian Orator Royal Coll of Physicians 1996, Dalton Medal Manchester Literary and Philosophical Soc 2002, D K Ludwig Award 2002, Seroussi Award 2003; hon memb: American Assoc of Immunologists, St Mark's Assoc London 1995; Liveryman Worshipful Co of Scientific Instrument Makers, Hon Freeman Drapers' Co; hon fell: Keble Coll Oxford 1981, Clare Coll Cambridge 1989, Green Coll Oxford 1993, Hertford Coll Oxford 2005; Laurea (hc) in Med and Surgery Univ of Bologna 1987; Hon DSc: Univ of Bath 1988, Univ of Oxford 1988, Univ of Edinburgh 1990, Univ of Hull 1990, Univ of Bristol 1991, Loughborough Univ of Technol 1993, Lancaster Univ 1994, Univ of Aberdeen 1994, Univ of Plymouth 1995, Univ of Salford 1996, Univ of London 1996, UMIST 1997, Univ of the Witwatersrand 1998; Hon MD Univ of Birmingham 1992, Dr (hc) Univ of Leuven 1992, Hon LLD Univ of Dundee 1993, Dr (hc) Masaryk Univ Brno 1994, Dr (hc) Univ of Haifa 1998; foreign memb American Philisophical Soc USA 1989; foreign hon memb American Acad of Arts and Scis 1972, foreign assoc US Nat Acad Scis 1981; fell: Br Soc for Histocompatibility and Immunogenetics, Br Transplantation Soc (hon memb 2002), Royal Statistical Soc, Pathological Soc, Br Soc of Immunology; CBiol, FIBiol, FRCPath, FRS 1974, Hon FRCP, Hon FRCS, Hon FRSE 1992, Hon FRSM 1994, FMedSci 1998, hon fell BAAS 2006; *Books* The Genetics of Human Populations (with L Cavalli-Sforza, 1971, 2 edn 1999), Our Future Inheritance: Choice or Chance? (with A Jones, 1974), Genetics, Evolution and Man (with L Cavalli-Sforza, 1976), The Book of Man (with Robin McKie, 1994); *Recreations* playing the piano, riding, swimming, scuba diving; *Clubs* Athenaeum, Oxford and Cambridge; *Style—* Sir Walter Bodmer, FRS, FRCPath; ✉ Cancer Research UK, Cancer and Immunogenetics Laboratory,

Weatherall Institute of Molecular Medicine, John Radcliffe Hospital, Oxford OX3 9DS (tel 01865 222356, fax 01865 222431, e-mail walter.bodmer@hertford.ox.ac.uk)

BODMIN, Archdeacon of; *see:* Cohen, Ven Clive Ronald Franklin

BODY, Sir Richard Bernard Frank Stewart; kt (1986); s of Lt-Col Bernard Richard Body, of Donnington, Berks, and Daphne Mary Eleanor, *née* Corbett; *b* 18 May 1927; *Educ* Reading Sch; *m* 1959, (Doris) Marion, da of late Maj Harold John Graham, OBE, of Midhurst Sussex; 1 s, 1 da; *Career* called to the Bar Middle Temple 1949; MP (Cons): Billericay 1955–59, Holland with Boston 1966–97, Boston and Skegness 1997–2001 (contested (Cons): Rotherham 1950, Abertillery by-election 1950, Leek 1951); memb Commons Select Ctee on Agric 1979–87 (chm 1986–87); jt chm Cncl Get Britain Out referendum campaign 1975, chm Open Seas Forum 1971–84, chm of tstees Centre for European Studies 1992–; dir New European Publications Ltd 1986–, ed World Review 1996–, dir Salisbury Review Ltd; pres: William Cobbett Soc 1996–, Ruskin Soc 2002– (chm 1997–2002); chm Int Assoc of Masters of Bloodhounds 1997–2003; Hon Freeman Borough of Boston 2002; *Books* Agriculture - The Triumph and the Shame (1982), Farming in the Clouds (1984), Red or Green for Farmers (and the Rest of Us) (1987), Europe of Many Circles (1990), Our Food, Our Land (1991), The Breakdown of Europe (1998), England for the English? (2001); *Recreations* fishing; *Clubs* Carlton, Athenaeum, Pratt's; *Style—* Sir Richard Body; ✉ Jewell's Farm, Stanford Dingley, Reading, Berkshire RG7 6LX (tel 0118 974 4295)

BOEVEY, *see:* Crawley-Boevey

BOGDANOR, Prof Vernon; CBE (1998); s of Harry Bogdanor (d 1971), and Rosa, *née* Weinger (d 1987); *b* 16 July 1943; *Educ* The Queen's Coll Oxford (MA); *m* 23 July 1972 (m dis 2000), Judith Evelyn, da of Frederick Beckett (d 1985); 2 s; *Career* fell Brasenose Coll Oxford 1966– (sr tutor 1979–85 and 1996–97), reader in govt Univ of Oxford 1990–96, prof of govt and politics Univ of Oxford 1996–; prof of law Gresham Coll London; special advsr: House of Lords Select Ctee on Euro Communities 1982–83, House of Commons Public Service Ctee; memb: Political Studies Assoc 1966–, Cncl Hansard Soc for Parly Govt, Nat Ctee for Electoral Reform 1981–, Court Univ of Essex 1982–84, UK delgn CSCE Conf Oslo 1991, Cncl Inst of Jewish Affairs 1991–, Cncl Euro Movement 1994–; hon fell Soc for Advanced Legal Studies 1997; FRSA 1992, FBA 1997; *Books* incl: The Age of Affluence 1951–64 (jt ed, 1970), Devolution (1979), The People and the Party System (1981), Liberal Party Politics (ed, 1983), Multi-Party Politics and the Constitution (1983), Science and Politics (ed, 1984), The Blackwell Encyclopaedia of Political Institutions (ed, 1987), Comparing Constitutions (jtly, 1994), The Monarchy and the Constitution (1995), Essays on Politics and the Constitution (1996), Power and the People: A Guide to Constitutional Reform (1997), Devolution in the United Kingdom (1999), The British Constitution in the Twentieth Century (ed, 2003), Joined-Up Government (2005); *Recreations* music, walking, talking; *Style—* Prof Vernon Bogdanor, CBE, FBA; ✉ Brasenose College, Oxford OX1 4AJ (tel 01865 277830, fax 01865 277822)

BOGDANOV, Dr Michael; s of Francis Benzion Bogdin (d 1962), and Rhoda, *née* Rees (d 1988); *b* 15 December 1938; *Educ* Lower Sch of John Lyon, Harrow, Trinity Coll Dublin (MA), Univ of Munich, Sorbonne; *m* 1, 17 Dec 1966 (sep 2000), Patricia Ann, da of Walter Stanley Warwick (d 1985); 2 s (Jethro Rhys Warwick b 1968, Malachi Taplin b 1969), 1 da (Ffion b 1971); m 2, 22 Sept 2000, Ulrike Engelbrecht; 1 da (Pia Caitlin b 1997), 1 s (Cai Johann b 1999); *Career* director and producer; dir and prodr Radio Telifis Éireann (RTE) 1966–69; artistic dir: Phoenix Theatre Leicester 1973–77, Young Vic 1978–80; assoc dir RNT 1980–88, fndr and artistic dir English Shakespeare Co 1986–98, artistic dir and exec prodr Deutsches Schauspielhaus Hamburg 1989–92; fndr and artistic dir Wales Theatre Co 2003; awarded Sr Academic Fellowship by Leicester Poly (now De Montfort Univ) 1992 and Univ of Wales Cardiff 1993; fell: Welsh Coll for Music and Drama, Univ Sunderland; hon fell TCD, Hon DLitt TCD 2005; *Awards* SWET Award (for dir of the year) 1979, Olivier Award (for dir of the year) 1989, Drama Award (for outstanding achievement) 1987, Melbourne Spoleto Golden Pegasus Award 1988, BAFTA nomination and RTS Award (for Shakespeare on the Estate, BBC documentary) 1994 Best Drama Documentary Banff Film Festival (for Shakespeare on the Estate) 1995, Best Director/Best Production (Timon of Athens, Chicago Shakespeare Rep Theatre) 1997, RTS Award for Best Regional Film (A Light in the Valley, BBC TV) 1999; *Recreations* sport, music, Celtic languages, wine; *Clubs* Lord's Taverners, MCC; *Style—* Dr Michael Bogdanov; ✉ Coach House Productions Limited, 21 Dogo Street, Pontcanna, Cardiff CF11 9JJ (tel and fax 029 2064 0069, e-mail info@walestheatrecompany.com)

BOGGIS, Andrew Gurdon; s of Edmund Alan Theodore Boggis (d 1974), of Devizes, Wilts, and Myrtle Eirene, *née* Donald; *b* 1 April 1954; *Educ* Marlborough, New Coll Oxford (MA), King's Coll Cambridge (PGCE); *m* 23 July 1983, Fiona Mary, da of Rev James Edmund Cocke; 2 da (Rosie b 14 March 1987, Lucy b 10 Oct 1988), 1 s (Edmund b 27 April 1991); *Career* teacher; Eng language asst Salzburg 1975–76, asst master Hitchin Boys' Sch 1978–79, asst master Eton Coll 1979–92, master-in-coll Eton Coll 1984–92, warden Forest Sch 1992–; HMC: memb Ctee 2001–, chm N London Div 2002–03, chm 2006; inspr HMC/Independent Sch's Inspectorate 1998–, memb Independent Schs Examination Bd (ISEB) (chm Languages Sub-Ctee 1995–2001), memb Educn Ctee ESU; dir Common Entrance Publications Ltd 1993–2001; govr: King's Coll Sch Cambridge 1994–99, Skinner's Co's Sch for Girls 1997– (memb Educn and Devpt and Staff Sub-Ctees); memb Ct Univ of Essex 1997–2002; Liveryman Worshipful Co of Skinners 1990 (extra memb Ct of Assts 2004–06); memb HMC 1992, memb ASCL 1992; *Publications* contrib to educational publications incl Conference & Common Room; *Recreations* Austria, Scotland, music (particularly opera), poetry, philosophy, cookery, football (West Ham) and other sports; *Clubs* East India; *Style—* Andrew Boggis, Esq; ✉ The Warden's House, Forest School, College Place, Snaresbrook, London E17 3PY (tel 020 8520 1744, fax 020 8520 3656, e-mail warden@forest.org.uk)

BOGGIS-ROLFE, Richard; s of Paul Boggis-Rolfe (d 1988), of Paris, France, and (Anne) Verena, *née* Collins; *b* 5 April 1950; *Educ* Eton, Trinity Coll Cambridge (MA), London Business Sch; *m* 7 March 1987, Lucy Elisabeth, da of Lt-Col Stephen Jenkins, MC, DL, of Hampnett, Glos; 2 da (Elisabeth Verena b 30 Aug 1988, Alice Catherine b 8 Jan 1990), 1 s (James Edward b 22 Jan 1994); *Career* cmmnd Coldstream Gds 1970, ADC to Lt Gen Sir Richard Worsley (GOC 1 (Br) Corps) 1975–77, Co Cdr 1977–79, Staff Capt QMG MOD 1979–80, ret Hon Maj 1980; dir: Russell Reynolds Associates 1983, Norman Broadbent International Ltd 1984–97; md Norman Broadbent (Hong Kong) 1986; chm Barkers Human Resource Advertising Ltd 1992–97, chm NB Selection Ltd 1995–97 (chief exec 1987–95), gp md BNB Resources plc 1995–97, chief exec Odgers Ray and Berndtson 1998–, chm Ray & Berndtson Int 2004–, dir OPD plc 2005–; govr Westonbirt Sch 2003–; Freeman City of London, memb Ct of Assts Worshipful Co of Pewterers; *Recreations* hunting, gardening, travel; *Clubs* Brooks's, Beefsteak, Pratt's; *Style—* Richard Boggis-Rolfe, Esq; ✉ The Glebe House, Shipton Moyne, Tetbury, Gloucestershire (tel 01666 880441, e-mail richard.boggis-rolfe@odgers.com); L'Hermitage, Basse Nouailette, Hautefort, Dordogne, France (tel 00 33 5 53 50 43 71)

BOGLE, Prof (Ian) David Lockhart; s of Brig Bruce Lockhart Bogle, of Porlock, Somerset, and Susan Gowan, *née* Christie; *b* 22 December 1957, Sydney, Aust; *Educ* Peninsula Sch Mt Eliza Aust, Imperial Coll London (BSc, MSc, PhD); *m* 6 Sept 1996, Jenny Elizabeth, *née* Brown; 1 da (Eleanor May Lockhart b 15 Jan 1999); *Career* sr scientist Br Gas Corp 1983–86, lectr Univ of Adelaide 1986–90; UCL: lectr 1990–94, sr lectr 1994–97, reader 1997–2000, prof 2000–, head Grad Sch 2005–; memb Cncl IChemE, memb Natural Sciences Ctee UK Nat Cmmn for UNESCO, UK rep Working Pty on Computer Aided Process Engrg European Fedn of Chem Engrs; author of over 100 pubns; Cncl Medal IChemE 2005; CEng 1993, FIChemE 1997, FREng 2005; *Recreations* playing the violin; *Style—* Prof David Bogle; ✉ The Graduate School, North Cloisters, University College London, Gower Street, London WC1E 6BT (tel 020 7679 7844, fax 020 7679 7043, e-mail gradschoolhead@ucl.ac.uk)

BOGLE, Dr Ian Gibb; CBE (2003); s of Dr John Bogle (d 1991), and Muriel, *née* Stoll (d 1990); *b* 11 December 1938; *Educ* Liverpool Coll, Univ of Liverpool (MB ChB); *m* 1, 10 Feb 1962 (m dis 2001), Dorothy; 2 da (Karen (Mrs Segal) b 4 Nov 1962, Amanda (Mrs Watts) b 30 April 1965); m 2, 21 Sept 2001, Julie, da of Roy and Rosemary Coulson; *Career* house jobs: (surgery) Stanley Hosp Liverpool, (med) Sefton Gen Hosp Liverpool; princ in Gen Practice Anfield Liverpool 1962–2000; sec Liverpool Local Med Ctee 1972–90, chm Liverpool Area Med Ctee 1976–78, memb Liverpool HA 1978–90, vice-chm Liverpool Family Practitioner Ctee 1987–88, memb NHS Modernisation Bd 2000–03; sec Jt Ctee on Postgrad Trg for Gen Practice 1985–90; chm Cncl BMA 1998–2003 (memb Cncl 1988–2004, chm Gen Med Servs Ctee 1990–97, former sec and pres Liverpool Div); hon md Univ of Liverpool 1999; fell BMA, FRSM, FRCGP 1997; *Recreations* music (especially classical, country and musical comedy), photography, golf, football, travel; *Style—* Dr Ian G Bogle, CBE; ✉ Peach Cottage, Burnt Oak Corner, East Bergholt, Suffolk CO7 6TS (tel 01206 298073)

BOHM, Nicholas David Frederick; s of Franz Bohm (d 1993), and Johanna Cecilia, *née* Bauer (d 1996); *b* 12 July 1943; *Educ* Leighton Park Sch Reading, St John's Coll Cambridge (MA); *m* Carola Ann, *née* Freeman; 5 c; *Career* asst slr Gregory Rowcliffe & Co 1968–70 (articled clerk 1966–68); ptnr: Edward Moeran & Partners 1970–72, Norton Rose 1975–94 (asst slr 1972–75); independent conslt slr 1994–2006; conslt Fox Williams 2001–06; tstee Fndn for Information Policy Research; memb Law Soc (memb Electronic Law Ctee); Freeman City of London; *Recreations* skiing, computers, rough gardening; *Style—* Nicholas Bohm, Esq; ✉ Salkyns, Great Canfield, via Takeley, Bishop's Stortford CM22 6SX (tel 01279 870285, e-mail nbohm@ernest.net)

BOHT, Jean; da of Thomas Herbert Dance (d 1970), of Birkenhead, and Edna May, *née* McDonald (d 1989); *b* 6 March 1936; *Educ* Wirral GS for Girls Bebington, Hilary Burrow's Ballet Sch Liverpool; *m* 1 (m dis 1970), William P Boht (d 1975); m 2, 1971, Carl Davis, *qv*, s of Irving Davis (d 1988); 2 da (Hannah Louise b 1 Jan 1972, Jessie Jo b 3 May 1974); *Career* actress; patron: Br Homoeopathic Assoc, CMV Fndn, Health Unlimited, Clare's Children's Hospice, Thornberry Animal Sanctuary, SOS, Hoylake Cottage Hosp, Parents for Safe Food, Tommy's Campaign, Lung Cancer Appeal, Merseyside Kidney Fndn, Vera Gray Tst, Wirral NHS Jellybean Appeal; hon Lady Taverner; hon fell John Moores Univ 1992; *Theatre* Liverpool Playhouse 1962–64, Bristol Old Vic Co 1964, Royal Court 1965–66, Library Theatre Manchester 1966–67, NT 1968 and 1971, Lincoln Theatre Royal 1969, Joan Littlewood's Theatre Workshop 1969–71, Chichester Festival 1992–94; West End credits incl: St Joan of the Stockyards (Queens) 1964, Steel Magnolias (Lyric) 1990, Bread (Dominion) 1990–91, Dangerous Corner (Whitehall) 1995, Kindertransport (Vaudeville) 1996, The Countess (Criterion) 2005, Embers (Duke of York's Theatre) 2006, White Open Spaces (Soho Theatre) 2006; fringe incl: Kennedy's Children (Kings Head Islington) 1974, Mecca (Open Space) 1977, Wednesday (Bush) 1979, Touched and To Come Home To This (Royal Court) 1980, Birds of Passage (Hampstead) 1983, Lost (Bush) 1986; tours incl: Dangerous Corner 1994–95, Pride and Prejudice 1995, All My Sons 1997, Talking Heads (A Lady of Letters, Soldiering On, and Cream Cracker under the Settee) 1998, Switchboard (Latchmere) 1999, Maria in Twelfth Night (Stafford Castle) 2000, Lil in Why Me 2000, Viva La Diva (Edinburgh Festival) 2001, Just Between Ourselves (nat tour) 2002, The Real Inspector Hound and Black Comedy 2002, Vagina Monologues (tour) 2003–04, Daisy Miller (tour); pantomime appearances incl: Croydon, Piccadilly Theatre, Guildford, High Wycombe, Cambridge Arts; *Television* plays incl: Where Adam Stood, Cranford, Eskimos Do It; series incl: Funny Man, Spyship, Sons and Lovers, Boys From The Black Stuff, Scully, I Woke Up One Morning, Bread, Brighton Belles, Holby City, The Bill; many guest appearances in comedy series, game shows, charity TV shows and radio plays; *Recordings* The Pigeon (by Carla Lane) 1990; *Films* incl: Meddle Not With Change, Distant Voices, Girl On A Swing, Arthur's Hallowed Ground, The Big Game, Jim's Gift, Mothers and Daughters, Little Film, The Feis, Raising Cain, The Understudy; *Awards* incl: BBC TV Personality 1988 (Variety Club of GB), Top Comedy Television Actress 1990 (The Br Comedy Awards), Top Television Personality 1990 (Whitbread Scouseology Awards); *Recreations* fndr Barnes Theatre Co (an amateur gp for teenagers formed in 1985); *Style—* Miss Jean Boht; ✉ c/o AIM (tel 020 7637 1700)

BOILEAU, Lt-Col Sir Guy Francis; 8 Bt (UK 1838), of Tacolnestone Hall, Norfolk; s of Sir Edmond Charles Boileau, 7 Bt (d 1980), and Marjorie Lyle, *née* D'Arcy (d 1997); *b* 23 February 1935; *Educ* Xavier Coll Melbourne, RMC Duntroon; *m* 1962, Judith Frances, da of Sen George Conrad Hannan, of Glen Iris, Victoria; 3 da (Simone Teresa b 1963, Caroline Virginia b 1968, Antonia Josephine b 1975), 2 s (Nicolas Edmond George b 1964, Christopher Guy b 1969); *Heir* s, Nicolas Boileau; *Career* Lt-Col Australian Army; co dir, sports administrator, dealer in antiques; *Recreations* boating, fishing; *Clubs* The Heroes (Victoria); *Style—* Lt-Col Sir Guy Boileau, Bt; ✉ 14 Faircroft Avenue, Glen Iris, Victoria 3146, Australia

BOISSIER, Roger Humphrey; CBE (1992); 3 and yst s of Ernest Gabriel Boissier, DSC, CEng, FIEE (d 1976), of Derby, and Doris Mary, *née* Bingham (d 1958), of Bingham's Melcombe, Dorset; descended from Gaspard Boissier (d 1705), of Geneva, whose grandson Jean-Daniel Boissier (d 1770), settled in England at Lime Grove, Putney (*see* Burke's Landed Gentry, 18 edn, vol I, 1965); *b* 30 June 1930; *Educ* Harrow; *m* 30 Oct 1965, (Elizabeth) Bridget (Rhoda), eldest da of Sir Gerald Gordon Ley, 3 Bt, TD (d 1980) (see Debrett's Peerage & Baronetage, 1980); 1 s (Rupert John b 25 May 1967), 1 da (Clare Louise b 16 Nov 1968); *Career* md Aiton & Co Ltd 1975–83 (joined 1955), exec dir Whessoe plc 1975–83; chm Pressac plc 1990–2002 (dir 1984–2002), chm The Royal Crown Derby Porcelain Co Ltd 2000–; non-exec dir: Derbyshire Building Society 1972–81, Simmonds Precision NV (Holland) 1976–82, Ley's Foundries and Engineering plc 1977–82, British Gas plc (formerly British Gas Corporation) 1981–96, Severn Trent plc 1986–98, T & N plc 1987–98, Edward Lumley Holdings Ltd 1988–2004, Kalon Group plc 1992–99 (chm 1992–95), AMEC Power M&E Services Ltd 1992–96, Allott & Lomax Holdings Ltd 1996–2000; memb Br Nat Ctee (now Br Energy Assoc) World Energy Cncl 1971–2005 (chm 1977–80); High Sheriff of Derbyshire 1987–88; pres Harrow Assoc 2006–; govr: Harrow Sch 1976–96 (dep chm 1988–96), Landau Forte Coll Derby 1995–; pro-chllr and dep chm of Cncl Loughborough Univ 2000–07 (memb Cncl 1991–2007), memb Ct Univ of Derby 1998–; Freeman City of London 1971, Master Worshipful Co of Tin Plate Workers alias Wire Workers 1988–89; Hon DTech Loughborough Univ 2001; CIGEM 1983, FInstD 1984–2007, FRSA 1987, Hon FEI 1991; *Recreations* cars, reading, foreign travel, meeting people; *Clubs* Brooks's, MCC, Surrey CCC; *Style—* Roger Boissier, Esq, CBE; ✉ Low Baronwood, Armathwaite, Carlisle, Cumbria CA4 9TW (tel 01697 472347, fax 01697 472348, e-mail rogerboissier@btinternet.com)

BOIZOT, Peter James; MBE (1986), DL (Cambridgeshire 1998); s of Gaston Charles Boizot, and Susannah, *née* Culshaw; *b* 16 November 1929; *Educ* King's Sch Peterborough (chorister Peterborough Cathedral 1940–44), St Catharine's Coll Cambridge (MA, fell commoner 1996); *Career* Nat Serv 1948–50, cmmnd RASC; capt MV YARVIC 1951; various sales jobs 1953–64; PizzaExpress: fndr 1965, chm and md 1965–93, chm PizzaExpress plc (following flotation) 1993–96, pres 1996–; proprietor: Pizza on the Park 1976–, Great Northern Hotel (Peterborough) 1993–, The Broadway 2000– (Peterborough),

Miss Pears 2001– (Peterborough); dir Connoisseur Casino 1970–82; former owner and chm Peterborough United FC; former publisher: Jazz Express magazine, Boz magazine, Hockey Sport, World Hockey; pres Hampstead & Westminster Hockey Club 1986, vice-pres Hockey Assoc 1990, hon vice-pres English Hockey Assoc; fndr memb Soho Soc, fndr chm Soho Restaurateurs' Assoc 1980, former dir Soho Jazz Festival; chm Westminster Chamber of Commerce 1992–94, memb Cncl London Chamber of Commerce 1992–; Parliamentary candidate (Lib) Peterborough Gen Elections Feb and Oct 1974, former pres Eastern Region Liberal Party; Bolla Award 1983, Hotel and Caterer Food Service Award 1989, Hon LLD Westminster Univ 1995, Hon DLitt Loughborough Univ; Commendatore dell'Ordine al Merito della Repubblica Italiana 1996; *Books* Pizza Express Cook Book (1976, new edn 1991); *Recreations* few and far between; *Clubs* RAC, National Liberal, Hawks' (Cambridge); *Style—* Peter Boizot, Esq, MBE, DL; ✉ Great Northern Hotel, Station Approach, Peterborough, Cambridgeshire PE1 1QL (tel 01733 552331, fax 01733 345279)

BOKSENBERG, Prof Alexander; CBE (1996); s of Julius Boksenberg, and Ernestina Steinberg; *b* 18 March 1936; *Educ* Stationers' Co Sch, Univ of London (BSc, PhD), Univ of Cambridge (MA); *m* 1960, Adella Coren; 1 s, 1 da; *Career* Career Dept of Physics and Astronomy UCL: SRC research asst 1960–65, lectr in physics 1965–75, head Optical and Ultraviolet Astronomy Research Gp 1969–81, reader in physics 1975–78, SRC sr fell 1976–81, prof of physics 1978–81, visiting prof 1981–; dir: Royal Greenwich Observatory 1981–93, Royal Observatories (Royal Greenwich Observatory Cambridge, Royal Observatory Edinburgh, Isaac Newton Gp of Optical Telescopes Canary Islands, Jt Astronomy Centre Hawaii (UK dir Gemini Telescopes Project)) 1993–96; hon prof of experimental astronomy 1991–, research prof Inst of Astronomy Univ of Cambridge and PPARC sr research fell Univ of Cambridge and Univ of London 1996–99, extraordinary fell Churchill Coll Cambridge 1996–; exec ed Experimental Astronomy 1995–; Sherman Fairchild distinguished scholar Caltech 1981–82, visiting prof Univ of Sussex 1981–89, hon prof of experimental astronomy Univ of Cambridge 1991–; lectr tours: Russia (Royal Soc and Russian Acad of Sciences 1989, China (Royal Soc and Chinese Acad of Sciences) 1995, India (Br Cncl) 1999, Japan (Royal Soc and Japan Acad) 1999; pres W London Astronomical Soc 1978–, pres and memb Int Scientific Ctee Canary Islands Observatories 1981–, pres Br Horological Inst 2000–01; hon pres Astronomical Soc of Glasgow; chm: New Industrial Concepts Ltd 1969–81, SRC Astronomy Ctee 1980–81, Int Expert Ctee Gemini Telescopes Project 1992, UK Gemini Telescopes Steering Ctee; memb and dep chm Anglo-Aust Telescope Bd 1989–92; Royal Soc: memb Cncl and tstee 1995–97, memb Tech Support Steering Gp 1997–98, memb Int Exchanges Far East Panel 2000–; UK Nat Cmmn UNESCO: memb Fndn Ctee 1999–2000, chm Sci Ctee 2000–03, memb Cncl 2000–03, chm Steering Ctee Campaign Gp 2003–04; UNESCO: memb Sci Sector Ctee on Int Basic Scis Prog 2002–, memb World Heritage Centre Ctee of Int Experts on Archeo-Astronomical Sites and Observatories 2004–; UK Sci Sector rep UNESCO Gen Conf 2003; UNESCO Regnl Bureau for Sci in Europe (ROSTE): memb Sci Cncl 2000, memb Task Force for Reconstruction of Scientific Cooperation in SE Europe 2000–03, chm Working Gp on Restoring Human Potential in SE Europe 2002–03, memb ISCU Working Gp on Basic Sciences and Basic Research 2004–; RAS: memb Cncl, vice-pres and tstee 2000–03, chm Awards Ctee A 2002–03; InstP: memb Cncl 2001–03, memb Women in Physics Ctee 2002–03, chm Ethics Ctee 2004–; memb: Instrument Definition Team Hubble Space Telescope Euro Space Agency 1973–95, Advsy Ctee South African Astronomical Observatory 1978–85, Science Advsy Ctee Br Cncl 1987–91, Hubble Space Telescope Users Ctee 1990–91, Fachbeirat Max-Planck-Institut für Astronomie 1991–, USA Gemini Telescopes Oversight Ctee 1993–94, Visiting Ctee Euro Southern Observatory 1993–95, Int Astronomical Union Fin Ctee 1997–2000, UK-Japan N+N Bd on Co-operation in Astronomy 1997–, PPARC VISTA Review Bd 1999–2000; memb and or chm of more than 40 other bds or ctees; exec ed Experimental Astronomy 1995–; lecture tours: Royal Soc and Russian Acad of Sciences 1989, Royal Soc and Chinese Acad of Sciences 1995, Br Cncl 'Bright Sparks' India 1999, Royal Soc and Japan Acad 1999; memb: Cambridge Philosophical Soc 1996–, Cncl Churchill Coll Cambridge 1998–2003, Language Centre Mgmnt Ctee Univ of Cambridge 2003–; Hannah Jackson Medal and Gift RAS 1998, Hughes Medal Royal Soc 1999, Glazebrook Medal and Prize InstP 2000; asteroid (3205) Boksenberg named 1988, 37th Herstmonceux Conf (The Hubble Space Telescope and the High Redshift Universe) in personal honour 1996; Worshipful Co of Clockmakers: Freeman 1984, Liveryman 1989, memb Ct of Assts 1994–, Master 2000, Past Master 2001–; Dr (hc) l'Observatoire de Paris 1982, Hon DSc Univ of Sussex 1991; memb Academia Europaea 1989, fell UCL 1991; FRAS 1965, FRS 1978, FRSA 1984, FInstP; *Books* Modern Technology and its Influence on Astronomy (jt ed, 1990); contrib to various learned jls; *Recreations* skiing; *Clubs* Athenaeum; *Style—* Prof Alexander Boksenberg, CBE, FRS; ✉ University of Cambridge, Institute of Astronomy, The Observatories, Madingley Road, Cambridge CB3 0HA (tel 01223 339909, fax 01223 339910)

BOLADUADUA, HE Emitai Lausiki; *m* Asinate; *Career* diplomat; high cmmr to UK 2002– (concurrently non-resident ambass to Holy See, Germany, Denmark, Ireland, Egypt and Israel); *Style—* HE Mr Emitai Boladuadua; ✉ High Commission of the Republic of the Fiji Islands, 34 Hyde Park Gate, London SW7 5DN

BOLAM, Simon; s of Alexander Crossman Bolam (d 1963), of Berwick-upon-Tweed, and Elizabeth Mary, *née* Drybrough (d 1990); *b* 5 September 1942; *Educ* St Mary's Sch Melrose, Glenalmond Coll; *m* 6 July 1968, Sylvia Forsyth, da of Sidney Dawson Ranson; 2 da (Caroline b 5 March 1970, Valerie b 5 May 1971); *Career* with Royal Insurance Edinburgh then Liverpool 1961–70; E H Ranson & Co Insurance Brokers: joined 1970, ptnr 1971, owner 1972–; Insurance Soc of Edinburgh: sec 1986, dep pres 1988, pres 1989, a vice-pres 1990–; Chartered Insurance Inst: memb Cncl 1988–99, chm Mktg and Pubns Ctee and hon ed CII Jl 1989, chm Educn Ctee and a govr CII's Coll of Insurance 1992, dep pres 1993, pres 1994–95, chm CII Audit Ctee 2000–04; Br Insurance Brokers' Assoc: chm Scottish Ctee 1986, chm Motor Ctee 1986, chm Educn and Employment Policy Ctee 1996–98, memb Nat Bd 1996–2000, chm Gen Insurance Broking Ctee 1997–98 (dep chm 1996–97), nat dep chm 1997–98, chm 1998–2000; memb: Nat Exec Round Table 1981–83, Cncl Insurance Brokers Registration Cncl 1997–2001, Bd Gen Insurance Standards Cncl 1999–2005 (chm Smaller Practitioners' Ctee 2001–04), Bd Fin Servs NTO 2000–02; underwriting memb Lloyd's 1989–99; chm Church of Scotland Insurance Co 2006–; Liveryman Worshipful Co of Insurers 1990; Moderator of High Constable City of Edinburgh 1997–99; FCII 1971 (ACII 1961); *Recreations* hill walking, cycling; *Style—* Mr Simon Bolam; ✉ 14 Ramsay Garden, Edinburgh EH1 2NA (tel 0131 225 1849); E H Ranson & Co, 11 Coates Crescent, Edinburgh EH3 7AT (tel 0131 225 9136, fax 0131 220 6149, e-mail sbolam@ehranson.co.uk)

BOLD, Dr (Richard) Andrew; s of Rev W E and Mrs K M Bold; *Educ* Monmouth, Howardian HS Cardiff, ChCh Oxford (BA), Univ of Wales Cardiff (MSc), Centre for Euro Industrial Studies Univ of Bath (PhD); *Career* res offr Greater London Trade Union Resource Unit 1985–87, researcher to Barry Jones, MP (shadow sec of state for Wales) 1987, sr researcher to Lab Peers House of Lords 1987–89, res offr Wales Lab Pty 1989–94, asst gen sec (policy) Wales Lab Pty 1994–99; special advsr to: Rt Hon Alun Michael, MP 1999–2000, Rt Hon Paul Murphy, MP 2000–02, Rt Hon Peter Hain, MP 2002–; *Style—* Dr Andrew Bold; ✉ Office of the Secretary of State for Wales, National Assembly Building, Cardiff Bay, Cardiff CF99 1NA (tel 029 2089 8549, fax 029 2089 8138)

BOLDY, Dr Steven; *Career* fell Emmanuel Coll Cambridge, univ sr lectr and head Dept of Spanish and Portuguese Univ of Cambridge; *Books* The Novels of Julio Cortázar (1980), Before the Boom: Four Essays on Latin-American Literature before 1940 (ed, 1991), Memoria Mexicana (1998), The Narrative of Carlos Fuentes: Family, Text, Nation (2002); *Style—* Dr Steven Boldy; ✉ Department of Spanish and Portuguese, Faculty of Modern and Medieval Languages, University of Cambridge, Sidgwick Avenue, Cambridge CB3 9DA

BOLÉAT, Mark John; s of Paul John Boléat, and Edith Maud, *née* Still; *b* 21 January 1949, Jersey; *Educ* Victoria Coll Jersey, Coventry Univ (BA), Univ of Reading (MA); *m* 13 May 1991, Elizabeth Ann, *née* Barker; *Career* asst master Dulwich Coll 1972, economist Industry Policy Gp 1973; Building Societies Assoc: asst sec 1974–76, under sec 1976–79, dep sec 1979–81, dep sec gen 1981–86, sec gen 1986–87, DG 1987–93; sec gen Int Union of Housing Finance Instns 1986–89; DG: Cncl of Mortgage Lenders 1989–93, Assoc of Br Insurers 1993–99; prop Boleat Consulting 1999–; dir: Scottish Mutual and Abbey National Life 1999–2004, Comino Gp 2000–05, Countryside Properties 2001–05, St Paul Travelers Insurance Co 2005–; chm Assoc of Labour Providers 2004–; memb: Nat Consumer Cncl 2000–05, Gibraltar Finance Services Cmmn 2000–; chm Code of Practice Scrutiny Ctee Retail Motor Industry 2003–05; chm: Circle 33 Housing Tst 1990–93, Hillingdon Community Tst 2003–; memb Ct of Common Cncl City of London 2002–; FCIB; *Books* The Building Society Industry (1982, 2 edn 1986), National Housing Finance Systems - A Comparative Study (1985), The Mortgage Market (with Adrian Coles, 1987), Building Societies - The Regulatory Framework (1992), Housing in Britain (1993), Trade Association Strategy and Management (1996), Models of Trade Association Co-operation (2000), Good Practice in Trade Association Governance (2001), Trade Association Mgmnt (2003); *Recreations* squash, golf, reading; *Clubs* Moor Park Golf; *Style—* Mark Boléat, Esq; ✉ 26 Westbury Road, Northwood, Middlesex HA6 3BU (tel 07770 441377, e-mail mark.boleat@btinternet.com)

BOLES, Sir Jeremy John Fortescue; 3 Bt (UK 1922), of Bishop's Lydeard, Somerset; s of Capt Sir Gerald Fortescue Boles, 2 Bt (d 1945); *b* 9 January 1932; *Educ* Stowe; *m* 1, 1955 (m dis 1970), Dorothy Jane, yr da of James Alexander Worswick, of Enmore, Somerset; 1 da (Sarah Jane (Mrs Paul Bird) b 1956), 2 s (Richard Fortescue b 1958, David Hastings Fortescue b 1967); m 2, 1970 (m dis 1981), Elisabeth Gildroy, yr da of Edward Phillip Shaw, of Englefield Green, Surrey, and wid of Oliver Simon Willis Fleming; 1 da (Jessica Blanche Mary b 1971); m 3, 1982, Marigold Aspey, eld da of Donald Seckington, of Clevedon, Avon; *Heir* s, Richard Boles; *Style—* Sir Jeremy Boles, Bt; ✉ Heriots, Brendon Close, Taunton, Somerset TA23 0RG (tel 01984 640611)

BOLGER, Dermot; s of Roger Bolger, of Dublin, and Bridie, *née* Flanagan (d 1969); *b* 6 February 1959; *Educ* St Canice's Boys' Sch, Nat Sch Finglas, Beneavin Coll Finglas; *m* 17 Dec 1988, Bernadette, da of Vincent Clifton; 2 s (Donnacha b 30 Nov 1990, Diarmuid b 1 May 1992); *Career* writer; factory hand 1978–79, library asst 1979–84, ed and fndr Raven Arts Press 1979–92, exec ed New Island Books 1992–, playwright in assoc Abbey Theatre Dublin 1997; memb: Arts Cncl of Ireland 1989–93, Aosdána 1991–; ed of numerous poetry and prose anthologies incl The Picador Book of Contemporary Irish Fiction (1993, revised edn 2000); *Novels* Night Shift (1985, A E Meml prize 1986), The Woman's Daughter (1987, extended version 1991, Macaulay fell 1987, shortlisted Hughes Fiction prize 1988), The Journey Home (1990, shortlisted Irish Times/Aer Lingus prize 1992, shortlisted Hughes Fiction prize 1990), Emily's Shoes (1992), A Second Life (1994), Father's Music (1997), Finbar's Hotel (ed and co-author, 1997), Ladies Night at Finbar's Hotel (ed, 1999), Temptation (2000), The Valparaiso Voyage (2001), The Family on Paradise Pier (2005); *Poetry* The Habit of Flesh (1979), Finglas Lilies (1980), No Waiting America (1981), Internal Exile (1986), Leinster Street Ghosts (1989), Taking My Letters Back: New and Selected Poems (1998), The Chosen Moment (2004); *Plays* The Lament for Arthur Cleary (first staged Dublin Theatre Festival 1989, Samuel Beckett award, Stewart Parker BBC award, Edinburgh Fringe First), Blinded by the Light (Abbey Theatre Dublin 1990, A Z Whitehead prize), In High Germany (Dublin Theatre Festival 1990, filmed for RTE TV) 1993, The Holy Ground (Gate Theatre Dublin) 1990, One Last White Horse (Dublin Theatre Festival and Abbey Theatre) 1992, April Bright (Abbey Theatre) 1995, The Passion of Jerome (Abbey Theatre) 1999, Consulting Adults (Fishamble) 2000; *Films* The Disappearance of Finbar (C4) 1996; *Recreations* soccer, golf; *Clubs* Donabate Golf (Dublin); *Style—* Dermot Bolger, Esq; ✉ c/o A P Watt, 20 John Street, London WC1N 2DR (tel 020 7405 6774, fax 020 7831 2154)

BOLINGBROKE AND ST JOHN, 7 Viscount (GB 1712); Sir Kenneth Oliver Musgrave St John; 11 Bt (E 1611); also Baron St John of Lydiard Tregoze (GB 1712), Viscount St John and Baron St John of Battersea (GB 1716); s of Capt Geoffrey St John, MC (d 1972); suc kinsman 1974; *b* 22 March 1927; *Educ* Eton; *m* 1, 1953 (m dis 1972), Patricia Mary, da of B J McKenna, of Christchurch, NZ; 1 s (Hon Henry b 1957); m 2, 1972 (m dis 1987) Jainey Anne, da of late Alexander Duncan McRae, of Timaru, NZ; 2 s (Hon Oliver b 1972, Hon Nicholas b 1974); *Heir* s, Hon Henry St John; *Career* pres Travel Agents Assoc of NZ 1965–67, dir World Assoc of Travel Agencies 1967–75; fndr, chm and jt md Atlantic & Pacific Travel Gp of Cos 1956–76, chm Australian Cncl of Tour Wholesalers 1972–75; dir Bolingbroke and Ptnrs Ltd; fell of Aust Inst of Travel; *Recreations* tennis, history, cricket; *Style—* The Rt Hon The Viscount Bolingbroke and St John

BOLLAND, Alexander; QC (1992); s of James Bolland, of Kilmarnock, and Agnes Elizabeth, *née* Anderson; *b* 21 November 1950; *Educ* Kilmarnock Acad, Univ of St Andrews (BD), Univ of Glasgow (LLB); *m* 4 July 1973, Agnes Hunter Pate, da of George Pate Moffat; 2 da (Hilary Louise b 11 Sept 1980, Sophia Francesca b 1 Sept 1984), 1 s (Miles Louis James b 6 Aug 1991); *Career* apprentice Maclay, Murray & Spens 1976–77, pupil advocate 1977–78, admitted Scottish Bar 1978, capt Army Legal Services (later Army Legal Corps) BAOR and UKLF 1978–80, procurator fiscal depute 1980–82, in private practice Scottish Bar 1982–, standing jr counsel to Dept of Employment 1988–92, temp sheriff 1989–99; pt/t chm Employment Tbnls 1992–; *Recreations* reading, hellenistics; *Clubs* Naval and Military, New (Edinburgh); *Style—* Alexander Bolland, Esq, QC; ✉ 60 North Street, St Andrews, Fife KY16 9AH (tel 01334 474599); Advocates' Library, Parliament House, Edinburgh EH1 1RF

BOLLAND, Mark William; s of Robert Arthur Bolland (d 1993), and Joan, *née* Barker; *b* 10 April 1966; *Educ* King's Manor Sch Middlesbrough, Univ of York (BSc); *Partner* Guy Vaughan Black, *qv* (civil partnership, 2006); *Career* public affairs exec Public Affairs Int Ltd Toronto 1986–87, mktg exec IBM (UK) Ltd 1987–88, advsr to DG Advtg Standards Authy 1988–91; Press Complaints Cmmn: exec asst to Chm 1991–92, dir 1992–96; dep private sec to HRH The Prince of Wales 1997–2002 (asst private sec 1996–97); media and mktg communications conslt 2002–; columnist: News of the World 2003–05, Evening Standard 2006–; *Recreations* reading, theatre, music, walking; *Clubs* Garrick; *Style—* Mark Bolland, Esq; ✉ Mark Bolland Associates, 26–27 Great Sutton Street, London EC1V 0DS (e-mail mark@markbolland.com)

BOLT, Chris; *Career* joined civil service 1975, with Department of the Environment 1988–89, head of economic regulation Ofwat 1989–94, rail regulator Office of the Rail Regulator 1998–99 (joined 1994), regulation and corp affrs dir Transco plc 1999–2001, gp dir Regulation and Public Policy Lattice Gp 2001–02, arbiter London Underground PPP Agreements 2002–, chm Office of Rail Regulation 2004–; *Style—* Chris Bolt, Esq; ✉ Office of the PPP Arbiter, One Kemble Street, London WC2B 4AN (tel 020 7282 2170, e-mail chrisbolt@ppparbiter.org.uk)

BOLT, William Norris; s of William Clayton Bolt (d 1984), of Hadley Wood, Herts, and May Gertrude, *née* Norris (d 1973); *Educ* Queen Elizabeth's Sch Barnet, Univ of London (BSc); *m* 1962, Judy Rae, da of John Hanson Greville-Williams; 1 da (Lucinda Jane (Lucy) b 9 June 1969); *Career* ptnr Chesterton Int plc (formerly Chesterton & Sons) 1960–91; govr Suttons Hosp Charterhouse 1994–2002, former pres and chm Hanover Housing Assoc; former chm David Shepherd Wildlife Fndn Trading Co (DSWF), former dir of various property and house building cos; vice-patron Almshouse Assoc; Master Worshipful Co of Wheelwrights 1998; FRICS 1965; *Recreations* gardening, fishing, shooting, books; *Clubs* Flyfishers', Brooks's; *Style—* William Bolt, Esq; ✉ Lodkin, Lodkin Hill, Hascombe, Godalming, Surrey GU8 4JP

BOLT-ORR, Annabelle Elizabeth; da of Harry Collett Bolt (d 1995), and Eileen Nellie, *née* Ellicott (d 2003); *Educ* Oakdene Sch, Univ of York; *m* 16 Sept 1978, George William Michael Orr; 2 s (Alexander Dundas b 8 Nov 1979, James Harry b 3 Feb 1981), 2 da (Lucinda Emily b 19 Oct 1982, Sophie Olivia b 14 July 1984); *Career* called to the Bar Gray's Inn 1970; in practice Commercial Bar 1970–72; HM Customs and Excise: advsr VAT 1972–81, head Int Criminal Div 1990–, advsr prosecuted customs crime (involving drugs and arms trafficking); memb: Int Assoc of Prosecutors, UN Drugs Control Prog, Bar Cncl; author of papers on transnational co-operation in crime and maritime drug trafficking; *Recreations* travel, skiing, gardening; *Clubs* New Cavendish; *Style—* Mrs Annabelle Bolt-Orr; ✉ Solicitor's Office, Her Majesty's Revenue and Customs, Somerset House, West Wing, Strand WC2R 1LB (mobile 07771 976306, e-mail annabelle.bolt@hmrc.gsi.gov.uk)

BOLTON, Bishop of 1999–; Rt Rev David Keith Gillett; s of Norman Arthur Gillett (d 1996), of Rushden, Northants, and Kathleen, *née* Pitts; *b* 25 January 1945; *Educ* Wellingborough GS, Univ of Leeds (BA, MPhil); *m* 3 Sept 1988, (Susan) Valerie, da of Samuel Vernon Shannon (d 1981); *Career* curate St Luke's Watford 1968–71, northern sec Pathfinders and CYFA 1971–74, lectr St John's Coll Nottingham 1974–79, co-leader Christian Renewal Centre NI 1979–82, vicar St Hugh Lewsey Luton 1982–88, princ Trinity Coll Bristol 1988–99, hon canon Bristol Cathedral 1991–99; chair Nat Christian Muslim Forum 2006–; memb: Gen Synod C of E 1985–88 and 1990–99, Gen Synod Bd of Mission 1990–96, C of E Inter-Faith Consultancy 1990–96, Gen Synod Advsy Bd of Ministry 1995–99, Gen Synod Ctee for Minority Ethnic Anglican Concerns 1995–99, Working Pty on Women in the Episcopate 2001–05; chair Southern NW Trg Partnership 2006–; *Books* How Congregations Learn (1979), A Place in the Family (co-author, 1981), The Darkness where God is (1982), Whose Hand on the Tiller (co-author, 1984), Trust and Obey: Explorations in Evangelical Spirituality (1993), Treasure in the Field: The Archbishops' Companion for the Decade of Evangelism (jtly, 1993); *Recreations* gardening, photography, travel; *Style—* The Rt Rev the Bishop of Bolton; ✉ Bishop's Lodge, Bolton Road, Hawkshaw, Bury, Lancashire BL8 4JN (tel 01204 882955, fax 01204 882988, e-mail david.gillett@ukgateway.net)

BOLTON, 8 Baron (GB 1797); Harry Algar Nigel Orde-Powlett; s of 7 Baron Bolton (d 2001), and his 1 w, Hon Christine Helena, *née* Weld-Forester (now Hon Mrs Miles), da of 7 Baron Forester; *b* 14 February 1954; *Educ* Eton; *m* 1977, Philippa, da of Maj Peter Tapply; 3 s (Hon Thomas Peter Algar b 16 July 1979, Hon William Benjamin b 1981, Hon Nicholas Mark b 1985); *Heir* s, Capt the Hon Thomas Orde-Powlett, MC; *Style—* The Rt Hon the Lord Bolton

BOLTON, Ivor; *b* 17 May 1958; *Educ* Clare Coll Cambridge, RCM, Nat Opera Studio; *m* Dr T Knighton (musicologist, journalist and broadcaster); 1 s (Sam b 26 June 1991); *Career* conductor Schola Cantorum Oxford, fndr St James's Baroque Players 1984; music dir: Eng Touring Opera 1991–93, Glyndebourne Touring Opera 1992–97 (joined 1982); chief conductor Scottish Chamber Orch 1994–96; reg conductor: Bayerische Staatsoper Munich, Teatro Comunale Florence; chief conductor Mozarteum Orch Salzburg 2004; conducting debut ENO 1992 (Handel's Xerxes), debut BBC Proms 1993 (with St James's Baroque Players), returned to Proms 2000; *Opera* Glyndebourne Festival incl: Gluck's Orfeo 1989, Don Giovanni 1994, Le Nozze di Figaro 1994, Owen Wingrove 1997, Iphigenie en Aulide 2002; with Glyndebourne Touring Opera: Il Barbiere di Siviglia, The Magic Flute, The Rake's Progress, La Clemenza di Tito, Eugene Onegin, Owen Wingrave; work for other cos incl: La Cenerentola and Carmen (English Touring Opera), Rossini's La Gazza Ladra (Opera North), Mozart's La Finta Giardinera (WNO), Ariadne (Garsington), Giulio Cesare, Cosi Fan Tutte, Serse, Poppea, Marriage of Figaro, Ariodante, Don Giovanni, Orfeo, Ulisse, Clemenza di Tito, Rinaldo and The Rake's Progress (Bayerische Staatsoper), Poppea (Teatro Communale Bologna with Graham Vick), Iphigenie en Tauride (Teatro Colon Buenos Aires), Il Barbiere di Siviglia (Australian Opera), Ariadne (Opera Zuid Netherlands), Goehr's Arianna (world première Royal Opera House), Paisiello's La Molinara (Bologna), Ariodante (ENO, to be televised by BBC), Giulio Cesare (Paris Opera) 1997; *Concert performances* with LSO, BBC Scottish Symphony Orch, London Mozart Players, English Chamber Orch, English Northern Philharmonia, Bournemouth Sinfonietta, Ulster Orch, BBC Symphony Orch (recording), Montreal Symphony, Nat Arts Centre Orch Ottawa, Netherlands Chamber Orch (series Concertgebouw Amsterdam), Salzburg Orch, Munich Orch; *Recordings* with St James's Baroque Players: all Bach Harpsichord Concertos, Purcell's Dido and Aeneas, Baroque Music from Bologna; Brahms and Mendelssohn violin concertos (with London Philharmonic and Xue Wei), Popular Operatic Arias (with Lesley Garrett), Saxophone Concerti (with John Harle), Vivaldi's Stabat Mater (for Thames TV), Poppea and Ariodante (Munich Opera), Bruckner Symphonies 5, 7 and 9 (with Salzberg Mozarten Orch); *DVDs* Mozart Die Entführung (Salzburg Festival), Zaide (Salzburg Festival), La Finta Giardiniera (Salzburg Festival) *Awards* Bayerischer Theaterpreis (awarded by Prime Minister of Bavaria) 1998; *Style—* Ivor Bolton, Esq; ✉ c/o Ingpen & Williams Ltd, 7 St George's Court, 131 Putney Bridge Road, London SW15 2PA

BOLTON, Roger John; s of Harold Bolton, and Olive Yarker, *née* Buck; *b* 13 November 1945; *Educ* Carlisle GS, Univ of Liverpool (BA); *m* 1 (m dis); 2 s (Alexander b 1970, Giles b 1973); m 2, 1987, Julia Helene McLaren; 2 da (Olivia b 1988, Jessica b 1989); *Career* BBC TV: gen trainee 1967, ed Tonight Prog 1977–79, ed Panorama 1979–81, ed Nationwide 1981–83, head Manchester Network Prodn Centre 1983–86; Thames TV: ed This Week 1986–89, controller of network factual progs 1989–92; fndr Roger Bolton Productions Ltd 1993–, currently chm Flame Group; ind prodr BBC's Heart of the Matter series 1992–; former presenter Right to Reply (Channel 4), currently presenter Sunday and Feedback (BBC Radio 4); former chair Edinburgh TV Festival, memb Cncl PACT; FRTS; *Books* Death on the Rock and Other Stories (1990); *Recreations* reading history, visiting churches, walking, five-a-side football; *Style—* Roger Bolton, Esq

BOLTON, Prof Thomas Bruce; *b* 14 November 1941; *Educ* Woodhouse Grove Sch (State scholar), RVC Univ of London (BSc, BVetMed, biology, physiology, biochemistry and pharmacology medals, 2 Centenary prizes, Thomson prize, Cecil Aldin prize), Univ of London (PhD), Univ of Oxford (MA), MRCVS; *m*; 3 c; *Career* veterinary surgn; lectr RVC 1965–66, Royal Soc Locke research fell Brasenose Coll and Dept of Pharmacology Oxford 1969–76; St George's Hosp Med Sch: sr lectr 1976–80, prof 1980–, head Dept of Pharmacology and Clinical Pharmacology 1985–2003, dean of R&D 1997–2001, chm and memb Cncl Academic Bd 1989–91 and 1995–2001; memb Int Interest Gp Wellcome Tst 1992–94 (Physiology and Pharmacology Panel 1985–90), memb Physiological Sciences Funding Ctee 2004–06, memb and vice-chm Horserace Scientific Advsy Ctee for British Racing 1971–85, chm Basic Med and Dental Sciences Assessment Panel Research Assessment Exercise 1992 and 1996, memb UFC and HEFCE Jt Medical Advsy Ctee 1993–95; memb: EC Biomed Panel 1995, Chairs and Programme Grants Ctee British Heart Fndn 1995–98; ed: British Jl of Pharmacology 1975–81, Jl of Physiology 1985–92; memb: British Pharmacological Soc 1970, Research Defence Soc 1971, Univ Fedn of Animal Welfare 1971, Physiological Soc 1971, Biochemical Soc 1987, American Biophysical Soc 1988, Academia Europaea 1998; FMedSci 1998; *Books* Biography of Edith Bülbring (with A F Brading, 1992), Smooth Muscle Excitation (with T Tomita, 1996); *Recreations* sport and building; *Style—* Prof Thomas B Bolton; ✉ Ion Channels and Cell Signalling Division of Basic Medical Sciences, St George's University of London, Cranmer Terrace, London SW17 0RE (tel 020 8725 5617, fax 020 8725 3581, e-mail t.bolton@sgul.ac.uk)

BOMPAS, (Anthony) George; QC (1994); s of Donald George Bompas, and Freda Vice, *née* Smithyman; *b* 6 November 1951; *Educ* Merchant Taylors', Oriel Coll Oxford (scholar, MA); *m* 16 Jan 1981, Donna Linda, da of John Oscar Schmidt; 2 s (Samuel Henry b 13 July 1983, Caleb George b 6 Aug 1989), 1 da (Abra Mae b 8 Aug 1985); *Career* called to the Bar Middle Temple 1975, jr counsel to DTI (Chancery) 1989–94; Liveryman Worshipful Co of Merchant Taylors 1982; *Style—* George Bompas, Esq, QC; ✉ 4 Stone Buildings, Ground Floor, Lincoln's Inn, London WC2A 3XT (tel 020 7242 5524, fax 020 7834 7907)

BONALLACK, Sir Michael Francis; kt (1998), OBE (1971); s of Col Sir Richard Frank Bonallack, CBE (d 1996), and (Winifred) Evelyn Mary, *née* Esplen (d 1986); *b* 31 December 1934; *Educ* Chigwell Sch, Haileybury; *m* 8 Feb 1958, Angela, da of Harry Vivian Ward, of Birchington, Kent; 3 da (Glenna (Mrs Beasley) b 1959, Jane (Mrs Baker) b 1961, Sara (Mrs Stocks) b 1965), 1 s (Robert Richard Ward b 1967); *Career* Nat Serv 2 Lt RASC 1953–55; dir: Bonallack & Sons Ltd (later Freight Bonallack Ltd) 1962–74 (joined 1955), Miller Buckley and Buckley Investments Ltd 1976–84; chm: Cotton (CK) Pennink & Ptnrs Ltd 1980–83, Miller Buckley Leisure Ltd 1980–83; dir Sea Island Co (USA) 2001–; sec Royal and Ancient Golf Club St Andrews 1983–99 (capt 1999–2000); 5 times Br Amateur Golf Champion, 5 times Eng Amateur Golf Champion, 4 times Eng Amateur Stroke Play Champion, twice Leading Amateur in Open Golf Championship, played for Eng 1957–74 (Capt 1962–67), played for Br Walker Cup Team 1957–73 (Capt 1969–71), awarded Bobby Jones Trophy by US Golf Assoc 1972; pres: Eng Golf Union 1982, Golf Fndn 2001–, PGA Europe 2002–; dir: World Golf Fndn 2001–, Euro PGA Tour 2001–; chm: Golf Fndn 1977–83, PGA 1976–82; Freeman City of London, Liveryman Worshipful Co of Coachmakers and Coach Harness Makers 1962; fell Myerscough Agric Coll 2000; Hon Dr Univ of Stirling 1994, Hon Dr jur Dundee Abertay Univ 2000, Hon Dr jur Univ of St Andrews 2003; *Recreations* all sports, reading; *Clubs* Chantilly (France), Pine Valley (USA), Royal and Ancient, Augusta National (USA), Ocean Forest (USA); *Style—* Sir Michael Bonallack, OBE; ✉ Clatto Lodge, Blebo Craigs, Cupar, Fife KY15 5UF (tel 01334 850600)

BONAS, Ian George; DL (Co Durham 1985); s of Harry Bonas (d 1984), and Winifred Bonas; *b* 13 July 1942; *Educ* Harrow, Univ of Oxford (MA, DipEcon); *m* 23 Sept 1967, Katharine Anne, *née* Steel; 2 da (Anna Katharine b 25 May 1969, Sophie Katharine b 23 May 1971), 2 s (James Henry b 19 April 1972, William Ian b 7 June 1978); *Career* Ferguson International plc 1988–95; chm and md: Bonas Machine Co Ltd 1973–84 (md 1969–83), Bonas Griffith Ltd 1985–88; chm: Bentley Group Ltd 1989–96, Crane Electronics Ltd 1992–2002; memb: Northern Econ Planning Cncl 1973–79, Ctee in Fin for Industry NEDC 1978–, Cncl Univ of Durham 1983–89; dir Washington Devpt Corp 1979–83, chm Northern Region CBI 1981–83 (memb Nat Ctee 1973–84), dir Civic Tst for NE 1980–89, chm Durham Family Health Servs Ctee 1989–96; chm NE Region REPAC 1996–2005, md Thomas Swan & Co 2005–06; High Sheriff Co Durham 1987–88; *Recreations* music, books, painting, forestry, gardening, skiing, machine building, joinery; *Clubs* Northern Counties; *Style—* Ian Bonas, Esq, DL; ✉ Bedburn Hall, Hamsterley, Bishop Auckland, Co Durham DL13 3NN

BOND, Annabelle Sarah; OBE (2006); da of Sir John Bond, *qv*, and Elizabeth Caroline, *née* Parker; *b* 12 July 1969, Singapore; *Educ* Riddlesworth Hall, Cobham Hall, Inst Alpin Vidamanette Switzerland; *Career* mountaineer; fastest woman and fourth fastest person to climb seven summits (highest mountains on seven continents) 2004–05, N Pole with Prince Albert of Monaco 2006; FPD Savills Hong Kong 1991–2000; fundraiser: Eve Appeal, Laureus Sports Awards; award from the Chilean Army for Everest Expedition 2004; *Style—* Ms Annabelle Bond, OBE; ✉ c/o IMG (tel 020 8233 5065, e-mail clacy@imgworld.com)

BOND, Christopher Michael; s of Lt-Col James Hugh Bond, MC (d 1983), and Winifred Dodman, *née* Goodall (d 1989); *b* 28 June 1943; *Educ* Wellington, Trinity Hall Cambridge (BA); *m* 19 Feb 1966, Lindsay, da of late Arthur Lewis Cruickshank; 1 s (Neil Alexander), 1 da (Lara Marianne Addison); *Career* admitted slr 1969, gen counsel and asst co sec Reuters plc 1972–76, ptnr Field Fisher Waterhouse 1979–2005; sr advsr Securities & Investment Inst 2005–, conslt Raymond James Investment Services Ltd 2005–, conslt Mitsubishi UFJ Tst Int 2005–; non-exec dir: FM Consult 2005–, Westpac Europe Ltd 2006–; chm Exec Ctee European Legal Alliance 2002–05, memb Cncl Compliance Inst 2001–05 (chm Professional Educn Bd 2003–05); lectr int law confs in: America, Europe, Japan, Korea, Taiwan, UK; hon advsr Taipei Representative Office 2002–; author of articles in: Securities & Investments Review, Compliance Inst Gazette, Compliance Monitor, Complinet; Guild of Int Bankers; memb Law Soc 1969–2005; *Books* Investing in the United Kingdom (1986), Investing in the United Kingdom: The Basic Issues (1987); *Recreations* music, reading, gardening; *Style—* Christopher Bond, Esq

BOND, Edward; *b* 18 July 1934, London; *m* 1971, Elisabeth Pablé; *Career* playwright and director; Northern Arts literary fell 1977–79, George Devine award 1968, John Whiting award 1968, Obie 1976; Hon DLitt Yale 1977; City of Lyon Medal 2007; *Plays* The Pope's Wedding (1962), Saved (1965), Narrow Road to the Deep North (1968), Early Morning (1968), Passion (1971), Black Mass (1971), Lear (1972), The Sea: A Comedy (1973), Bingo (1974), The Fool (1976), A-A-America! (1976), Grandma Faust and The Swing, Stone (1976), The Bundle (1978), The Woman (1979), The Worlds with The Activist Papers (1980), Restoration (1981), Summer: a play for Europe, and Fables (short stories) (1982), Derek (1983), Human Cannon (1984), The War Plays (part 1 Red Black and Ignorant, part 2 The Tin Can People, part 3 Great Peace, 1985), Jackets (1989), In the Company of Men (1990), September (1990), Olly's Prison (1993), Tuesday (1993), Coffee: A Tragedy (1995), At the Inland Sea (a play for young people, 1996), Eleven Vests (1997), The Crime of the Twenty-first Century (1998), The Children (a play for two adults and sixteen children, 2000), Chair (2000), Have I None (2000), Existence (2002), The Balancing Act (2003), The Short Electra (2004), The Under Room (2005), My Day: A Song Cycle for young people (2005), Arcade (2006), Born, (2006), Tune (2007), People (2008), Collected Plays (8 vols, 1977–2006); *Opera Libretti* We Come to the River (1976), The English Cat (1983); *Ballet Libretto* Orpheus (1982), the latter Three: music by Hans Werner Henze; *Translations* Chekhov's The Three Sisters (1967), Wedekind's Spring Awakening (1974), Lùlú (with Elisabeth Bond-Pablé, 1992); *Other Publications* Theatre Poems and Songs (1978), Collected Poems 1978–85 (1987), Notes on Post-Modernism (1990), Letters (5 Vols, 1994–2001), Notes on Imagination (1995), The Hidden Plot: Notes on Theatre and the State (2000), Selected Notebooks (Vol 1, 2000, Vol II, 2001), Edward Bond and the Dramatic Child (2005); *Style—* Edward Bond, Esq; ✉ c/o Casarotto Ramsay Ltd, Waverley House, 7–12 Noel Street, London W1F 8GQ

BOND, Graham; s of Thomas Carlile (d 1980), of Blackburn, Lancs, and Mary, *née* Dixon (d 1999); *Educ* Queen Elizabeth's GS Blackburn, Royal Coll of Music (exhibition scholar, various prizes); *Career* repetiteur London Opera Centre 1970; London Festival Ballet/English Nat Ballet: conductor 1970–76, princ conductor 1976–94, music dir 1983–94; chief conductor Royal Danish Ballet 1994–; tours incl: Australia, France, Spain, Italy, Germany, Yugoslavia, Greece, Denmark, Venezuela, Turkey, China, USA; orchs worked with incl: Monte Carlo Philharmonic, Tivoli Symphony Copenhagen, Stanislavsky Theatre Moscow, Opera House Turin, Hong Kong Philharmonic, Danish Radio, Royal Opera Copenhagen, Opera Teatro Massimo Sicily, Cairo Symphony; guest conductor: Stuttgart Ballet, San Carlo Opera Orch Naples, Metropolitan Opera NY 1989, Deutsche Oper Berlin 1990–93, Bolshoi Ballet tour of England 1990, Opera House Budapest 1992, Palacio de Bella Artes Mexico 1993, Sofia Opera Orch 1993, Bergen Festival 1996, Royal Opera House 1995, Dutch Nat Ballet 1996 and 1997, Teatro Real Madrid 1997, Royal Ballet in China 1999, Paris Opera 1999, Royal Opera House 2000–2004, Bolshoi and Maryinsky Russia 2003, Royal Opera Stockholm 2003–05; memb conducting staff Royal Coll of Music 1985–94; awards incl: Worshipful Co of Musicians medal for a Distinguished Student Royal Coll of Music, Adrian Boult scholarship for study at the Accademia Chigiana Siena; Hon RCM 1994; *Recreations* theatre, walking; *Style*— Graham Bond, Esq; ✉ 8 Calverley Park Crescent, Tunbridge Wells, Kent TN1 2NB (tel and fax 01892 536994); c/o Royal Theatre, Copenhagen, Denmark (tel 00 45 33 69 69 33)

BOND, Jane Alison Mary; da of Geoffrey Macdonald Mallock Bond (d 1984), of Budleigh Salterton, Devon, and Louise Margurite, *née* Houssemayne du Boulay; *b* 1 April 1939; *Educ* Kinnaird Park Sch Bromley, St Martin's Sch of Art, City and Guilds Sch of Art (Rodney Burns drawing award), RA Schs (Henfield figure painting award, S J Soloman Bronze medal, Duff Greet prize); *Career* TV, theatre and film costume designer for WNO, ENO and many LWT prodns until 1978, currently full time artist; *Exhibitions* Imperial Tobacco Award (Nat Portrait Gall) 1981, British Drawing (Hayward Gall) 1982, Spirit of London (Royal Festival Hall) 1982 and 1986, Cleveland Int Drawing Biennale 1983, The Pick of New Graduate Art (Christie's) 1984, Riverside Open (Riverside Studios) 1985 and 1987, Drawings (Holland Gall) 1987, The Discerning Eye (Mall Galls) 1991, 1992 and 1997, Selected Drawings (Glyndebourne Opera House) 1992–2001, Making A Mark (Mall Galls) 1993; exhibits regularly at New English Art Club, Royal Soc of Portrait Painters and Royal Academy of Arts Summer Exhbns; Ernest Kleinwort Meml prize New English Art Club 1989, House & Garden Interior prize RA Summer Exhbn 1993; elected memb: New English Art Club 1989, Royal Soc of Portrait Painters 1992; *Recreations* travel, opera, antique dolls houses; *Clubs* Two Brydges; *Style*— Miss Jane Bond, RP, NEAC; ✉ 8 Ceylon Road, London W14 0PY (tel 020 7603 8308)

BOND, Jennie; da of Kenneth Bond, and Pamela, *née* Collins; *b* 19 August 1950; *Educ* St Francis' Coll Letchworth, Univ of Warwick (BA); *m* 1982, Jim Keltz; 1 da (Emma b 17 Feb 1990); 2 step c (Stephen, Danielle); *Career* broadcaster, news presenter and royal correspondent; reporter: Richmond Herald 1972–75, Evening Mail (Slough & Hounslow) 1975–77; BBC Radio 1977–88 (incl Woman's Hour, Today), BBC TV News 1988–2003; patron Nat Assoc of Ladies Circles; *Publications* Reporting Royalty (2001), Elizabeth: Fifty Glorious Years (2002), Elizabeth: 80 Glorious Years (2006); *Recreations* dancing, walking, drinking wine as the moon rises over the sea; *Style*— Ms Jennie Bond; ✉ c/o Knight Ayton Management, 114 St Martin's Lane London WC2N 4BE

BOND, Sir John Reginald Hartnell; kt (1999); s of Cdre Reginald Harold Arthur Bond, OBE (d 1978), of Hampshire, and Edith Christine Alice, *née* Powell; *b* 24 July 1941; *Educ* Tonbridge, Cate Sch Calif (ESU scholar); *m* 27 April 1968, Elizabeth Caroline, da of John Anthony Parker; 2 da (Annabelle Sarah b 12 July 1969, Lucy Candida b 18 Dec 1972), 1 s (Jonathan Simon b 13 Nov 1976); *Career* Hongkong and Shanghai Banking Corporation: joined Hongkong Bank 1961, chief exec Wardley Ltd (HSBC subsid) Hong Kong 1983–87 (dep md 1982–83), exec dir and chief exec Americas Regnl Office USA 1988–90 (gen mangr and chief exec 1987–88), exec dir banking Gp Head Office Hong Kong 1990–91, pres and chief exec Marine Midland Banks Inc Buffalo 1991–92, gp chief exec HSBC Holdings plc London 1993–98, gp chm HSBC Holdings 1998–2006, chm HSBC Bank USA 1997–2006, chm HSBC Americas Inc 1997–2006, chm HSBC Bank plc 1998–2006; non-exec chm Vodafone 2006– (non-exec dir 2005–); non-exec dir: Ford Motor Co 2000–, Bank of England 2001–04; chm Inst of Int Fin Washington DC 1998–2003, pres Int Monetary Conf 2001–02; hon fell London Business Sch 2003; Hon DEc Richmond American Int Univ in London 1998, Hon DLitt Loughborough Univ 2000; Hon LLD: South Bank Univ 2000, Univ of Bristol 2005, Univ of Nottingham 2005; Hon DLitt Univ of Sheffield 2002, Hon DSc City Univ London 2004, Hon Dr London Met Univ 2004; FCIB 1983, CIMgt 1993; Magnolia Gold Award Shanghai Municipal People's Govt 2003, Foreign Policy Assoc Medal NY 2003; *Recreations* skiing, golf and reading biography; *Clubs* MCC, Hong Kong, Royal Ashdown Forest Golf, John's Island (Florida); *Style*— Sir John Bond

BOND, (Thomas) Michael; OBE (1997); s of Norman Robert Bond, and Frances Mary, *née* Offer; *Educ* Presentation Coll Reading; *Career* served: RAF 1943–44, Middx Regt 1944–47; with BBC 1941–43, BBC Monitoring Serv 1947–50, TV cameraman BBC 1950–65, full-time writer 1965–; patron Action Research; *Books* Paddington novels: A Bear Called Paddington (1958), More about Paddington (1959), Paddington Helps Out (1960), Paddington Abroad (1961), Paddington at Large (1962), Paddington Marches On (1964), Paddington at Work (1966), Paddington Goes to Town (1968), Paddington Takes the Air (1970), Paddington's Blue Peter Story Book (1973), Paddington on Top (1974), Paddington Takes the Test (1979), Paddington on Screen (1981), Paddington - A Classic Collection (1998), Paddington Treasury (2001); Paddington picture books: Paddington and the Christmas Surprise (1997), Paddington Bear (1998), Paddington at the Zoo (1998), Paddington the Artist (1998), Paddington and the Tutti Frutti Rainbow (1998), Paddington at the Fair (1998), Paddington at the Carnival (1998), Paddington - My Scrapbook (1999), Paddington Minds the House (1999), Paddington at the Palace (1999), Paddington and the Marmalade Maze (1999), Padington's Busy Day (1999), Paddington's Party Tricks (2000), Paddington in Hot Water (2000), Paddington at the Circus (2000), Paddington Goes to Hospital (2001), Paddington's Garden (2002), Paddington and the Grand Tour (2003); other children's books: Here Comes Thursday! (1966), Thursday Rides Again (1968), Thursday Ahoy! (1969), Parsley's Tail (1969), Parsley's Good Deed (1969), Parsley's Last Stand (1970), Parsley's Problem Present (1970), Thursday in Paris (1971), The Tales of Olga Da Polga (1971, 2 edn 2001), Parsley's Parade (1972), The Day the Animals Went on Strike (1972), Parsley the Lion (1972), Olga Meets Her Match (1973, 2 edn 2001), Windmill (1975), Mr Cram's Magic Bubbles (1975), Parsley and Herbs (1976), Olga Carries On (1976, 2 edn 2001), J D Polson and the Liberty Head Dime (1980), J D Polson and the Dillogate Affair (1981), Olga Takes Charge (1982, 2 edn 2001), The Caravan Puppets (1983), Olga Moves House (2001), Olga Follows her Nose (2002); adult novels: Monsieur Pamplemousse (1983), Monsieur Pamplemousse and the Secret Mission (1984), Monsieur Pamplemousse on the Spot (1986), Monsieur Pamplemousse Takes the Cure (1987), Monsieur Pamplemousse Aloft (1989), Monsieur Pamplemousse Investigates (1990), Monsieur Pamplemousse Rests His Case (1991), Monsieur Pamplemousse Stands Firm (1992), Monsieur Pamplemousse on Location (1992), Monsieur Pamplemousse Takes the Train (1993), Monsieur Pamplemousse Afloat (1998), Monsieur Pamplemousse on Probation (2000), Monsieur Pamplemousse on Vacation (2002), Monsieur Pamplemousse Hits the Headlines (2003), Monsieur Pamplemousse and the Militant Midwives (2006); non-fiction: The Pleasures of Paris (1987), Bears and Forebears: A Life So Far (1996); *Television* Paddington animated series (56 episodes), The Herbs (13 episodes), The Adventures of Parsley (32 episodes); *Style*— Michael Bond, Esq, OBE; ✉ The Agency, 24 Pottery Lane, Holland Park, London W11 4LZ (tel 020 7727 1346, fax 020 7727 9037)

BOND, Prof Sir Michael Richard; kt (1995); s of Frederick Richard Bond (d 1999), and Dorothy, *née* Gardner (d 1988); *b* 15 April 1936; *Educ* Magnus GS Newark, Univ of Sheffield (MB ChB, MD, PhD); *m* 24 June 1961, Jane, da of Charles Issitt (d 1962); 1 s (Matthew b 9 Aug 1970), 1 da (Lucy b 2 June 1975); *Career* lectr in psychiatry Univ of Sheffield 1964–67 (asst lectr and res registrar surgery 1961–64); Univ of Glasgow: sr house offr, registrar then sr registrar in neurosurgery 1967–71, lectr then sr lectr in neurosurgery 1971–73, prof of psychological med 1973–98, vice-princ 1986–97, admin dean Faculty of Med 1991–97; memb: University Grants Ctee Medical Ctee 1982–91, Universities Funding Cncl 1991–93 (on dissolution), London Inquiry Gp 1992–93, Cncl Higher Educn Funding Cncl for Scotland 1993–96; chm Jt Med Advsy Ctee Higher Educn Funding Cncls for England, Scotland and Wales 1993–95; tstee Lloyds TSB Tst (Scotland) 1999–2005; pres Int Assoc for the Study of Pain 2002–05; memb Cncl Prince and Princess of Wales Hospice Glasgow 1997–2002; chm of govrs Glasgow HS 2001–06, dir and former chm Head Injury Tst Scotland 1988–99, vice-pres St Andrews Ambulance Assoc 1998– (memb Cncl 1995–99, CMO 1997–99); Hon DSc Univ of Leicester 1996, Hon DUniv Glasgow 2001; Hon FRCA 1999; FRCSEd 1969, FRCPsych 1981, FRCPS 1981, FRSE 1998, FRSA; *Books* Pain: Its Nature Analysis Treatment (2 edns 1979, 1984), Pain and its Treatment (2006); *Recreations* painting, forest walking, physical fitness, antique book collecting; *Clubs* Athenaeum; *Style*— Prof Sir Michael R Bond, FRSE; ✉ 33 Ralston Road, Bearsden, Glasgow G61 3BA (tel 0141 942 4391, e-mail m.bond@admin.gla.ac.uk)

BOND, Richard Douglas; s of Douglas Charles Bond, and Vera Eileen, *née* Richards; *b* 23 July 1946; *Educ* Berkhamsted Sch, London Coll of Law; *m* 27 Oct 1973, Anthea Mary (d 1996), da of Harold Francis Charrington, GC; 2 da (Charlotte Emma b 3 May 1976, Suzanne Claire b 1 Sept 1980); *Career* articled clerk Halsey Lightly & Hemsley 1964–69; Herbert Smith: joined as slr 1969, seconded to British National Oil Corporation 1976–78, ptnr 1977–2005, head of corporate 1993–2000, sr ptnr 2000–05; *Clubs* MCC; *Style*— Richard Bond, Esq; ✉ tel 020 7823 7026

BOND, His Hon Judge Richard Henry; s of Lt-Col Ashley Raymond Bond, MBE, DL, JP (d 1975), of Wareham, Dorset, and Mary, *née* Bowles (d 1952); *b* 15 April 1947; *Educ* Sherborne; *m* 25 April 1987, (Annabel) Susan, da of Brig John Henry Peter Curtis, MC (d 1999); 1 s (Henry b 30 Oct 1988), 1 da (Annabel b 27 Feb 1990); *Career* called to the Bar Inner Temple 1970; recorder of the Crown Court 1995–97, circuit judge (Western Circuit) 1997–; *Recreations* gardening, walking; *Clubs* Travellers; *Style*— His Hon Judge Bond; ✉ The Courts of Justice, Deansleigh Road, Bournemouth BH7 7DS (tel 01202 502800)

BOND, Samantha; da of Philip Bond, of Abergwynfi, and Pat Sandys, *née* Trotter (d 2000); *b* 27 November 1961; *Educ* Godolphin & Latymer Sch, Bristol Old Vic Theatre Sch; *m* 1989, Alexander Hanson; 1 da (Molly b 22 Oct 1991), 1 s (Arthur (Tom) b 12 Jan 1993); *Career* actor; patron Shooting Star Tst, ambass Prince's Tst, ambass Macmillan Cancer Support; *Theatre* repertory incl: Coventry, Southampton, Edinburgh, Derby, Bristol; credits incl: Juliet in Romeo and Juliet (Lyric Hammersmith) 1986, Beatrice in Much Ado About Nothing (Phoenix and tour) 1988, Infanta in Le Cid (RNT) 1994 (nomination Olivier Award), C in Three Tall Women (Wyndham's) 1995, Amy in Amy's View (RNT and Broadway) 1997 (nomination Tony Award), Mary in Memory of Water (Vaudeville) 1998, Lady Macbeth in Macbeth (Albery) 2002, Karen in Dinner with Friends (Hampstead) 2001, title role in A Woman of No Importance (Theatre Royal Haymarket) 2003, Esther Rubenstein in The Rubenstein Kiss (Hampstead) 2005, Lady Driver in Donkeys' Years (Comedy) 2006 (nomination Olivier Award); RSC 1992–93 incl: Hermione in The Winter's Tale, Rosalind in As You Like It; *Television* incl: The Ginger Tree, Emma, Family Money, Tears Before Bedtime, Morse, NCS Manhunt, The Hunt, Donovan (2 series), Distant Shores (2 series), The Murder Room; *Film* Eric The Viking 1989, What Rats Won't Do 1998, Blinded 2003, Yes 2003; Moneypenny in: GoldenEye 1995, Tomorrow Never Dies 1997, The World is Not Enough 1999, Die Another Day 2002, Wolfenden, Clapham Junction, Outnumbered; *Recreations* playing with children, watching cricket, Scrabble, winner ITV Celebrity Spelling Bee 2005; *Style*— Miss Samantha Bond; ✉ c/o Conway van Gelder Ltd, 18–21 Jermyn Street, London SW1Y 6HP (tel 020 7287 0077, fax 020 7287 1940)

BONE, Charles William Henry; s of William Stanley Bone (d 1966), and Elizabeth, *née* Burfoot; *b* 15 September 1926; *Educ* Farnham Coll of Art, RCA; *m* 1950, Sheila Mary, da of Lionel Mitchell (d 1956); 2 s (Richard, Sebastian); *Career* artist; lectr Brighton Coll of Art 1950–86, conslt COSIRA 1952–70; craft advsr Malta Industries Assoc 1952–78, designer Stourhead Ball 1959–69, dir RI Galleries Piccadilly 1965–70; critic for Arts Review; memb Cncl RI 1964 (vice-pres 1974), govr Fedn of Br Artists 1976–81 and 1983– (memb Exec Cncl 1983–84 and 1986–88), pres Royal Inst of Painters in Water Colours 1979–89 (vice-pres 1974–79); Hunting Gp Prize for the Most Outstanding Watercolour by a Br Artist 1984; hon memb: Botanical Artists, Medical Art Soc, Fedn of Canadian Artists; ARCA; *Exhibitions* oils and water colours in exhibitions: Medici Gallery 1950–, London Gp, NEAC, RBA 1950–, RA 1950–; 39 one man exhibitions 1950–; *Works in Private Collections* France, Italy, Malta, America, Canada, Japan, Aust, Norway, Sweden, Germany; *Other Work* incl: ceramic mural on the history of aerial photography, other murals in Italy and Spain, film on painting for Castle Communications plc 1990, book on Waverley Surrey 1991; *Books* The Author's Circle (1998), Anglican Cathedrals (2000); *Clubs* Chelsea Arts; *Style*— Charles Bone, Esq; ✉ Winters Farm, Puttenham, Guildford, Surrey GU3 1AR (tel 01483 810226); 17 Carlton House Terrace, London SW1

BONE, Prof (James) Drummond; s of William Drummond Bone (d 1979), and Helen, *née* Yuill (d 1973); *b* 11 July 1947; *Educ* Ayr Acad, Univ of Glasgow, Balliol Coll Oxford (Snell exhibitioner); *m* 1970, Vivian Clare, *née* Kindon; *Career* lectr Dept of English and Comparative Literary Studies Univ of Warwick 1972–80; Univ of Glasgow: lectr then sr lectr Dept of English 1980–95, prof of English literature 1995–, dean Faculty of Arts 1992–95, vice-princ 1995–99; princ Royal Holloway Univ of London 2000–02, vice-chllr Univ of Liverpool 2002–; pres Univ UK 2005–07; academic ed The Byron Jl 1978–88, co-ed Romanticism 1995–, author of many articles on Romanticism and also the occasional short story; chm Liverpool Culture Co 2005–; chm FACT (Fndn for Art and Creative Technol) 2004–, chm Graduate Prospects 2005–; hon fell Royal Holloway and Bedford New Coll 2004; Freeman Worshipful Co of Coachmakers and Coach Harness Makers; FRSA 1995; *Publications* Writers and their Work: Byron (2000), Cambridge Companion to Byron (ed, 2004); *Recreations* music, skiing, Maseratis (chm Maserati Club); *Clubs* Athenaeum, Savile; *Style*— Prof Drummond Bone; ✉ University of Liverpool, Foundation Building, 765 Brownlow Hill, Liverpool L69 7ZX (tel 0151 794 2003, fax 0151 708 7092)

BONE, Peter; MP; *b* 19 October 1952, Billericay, Essex; *Educ* Westcliff-on-Sea GS; *Career* chartered accountant 1977, finance dir Essex Electronics and Precision Engrg Gp 1977–83, chief exec High Tech Electronic Co 1983–90; cncllr (Cons) Southend-on-Sea BC 1977–86; Parly candidate (Cons): Islwyn 1992, Pudsey 1997, Wellingborough 2001; MP (Cons) Wellingborough 2005–; *Style*— Peter Bone, Esq, MP; ✉ House of Commons, London SW1A 0AA

BONE, Dr Quentin; JP; s of Stephen Bone (d 1958), and Sylvia Mary, *née* Adshead (d 1995); *b* 17 August 1931; *Educ* Warwick Sch, St John's Coll and Magdalen Coll Oxford (DPhil); *m* 9 Aug 1958, Susan Elizabeth, da of Sidney Smith (d 1963), of Witney, Oxon; 4 s (Matthew b 5 June 1959, Oliver b 2 Jan 1961, Alexander b 13 Aug 1963, Daniel b 21

Nov 1965); *Career* Plymouth Lab of the Marine Biological Assoc UK: zoologist 1959–, dep chief scientific offr 1987–91, emeritus res fell 1992–; ed Philosophical Transactions of the Royal Soc - Biological Sciences 1988–94; Gold Medal for Zoology Linnean Soc 1999, Frick Medal Zoological Soc of London 2004; FRS 1984; *Books* Biology of Fishes (with N B Marshall and J S Blaxter, 1994, 3 edn with R Moore, 2007), Biology of Pelagic Tunicates (1998); *Recreations* botany, travel, repairing machines; *Style—* Dr Quentin Bone, FRS; ✉ Marchant House, Church Road, Plymstock, Plymouth PL9 9BG; The Marine Laboratory, Citadel Hill, Plymouth PL1 2PB (tel 01752 633100, e-mail qb@mba.ac.uk)

BONE, Vivian Clare; da of Keith Dudley Kindon (d 1958), and Matilda Mary, *née* Nash (d 1998); *b* 15 May 1946; *Educ* Channing Sch Highgate, Univ of Sussex (BSc); *m* 1970, (James) Drummond Bone, s of William Drummond Bone; *Career* maths and physics ed Academic Div OUP 1968–79; Edinburgh Univ Press: sr ed and asst sec 1980, acting sec 1990, publisher 1991–96, md 1992–96, non-exec dir and conslt 1996–2001, conslt 2001–06; non-exec dir Liverpool Univ Press 2004– (conslt 2002–04); memb Editorial Bd Learned Publishing 2003–, contrib Being Scottish 2002; FRSA 2002; *Style—* Mrs Vivian Bone; ✉ e-mail vivianbone@hotmail.com

BONELLI, Federico; *b* Italy; *Educ* Turin Dance Acad; *Career* ballet dancer; soloist Zürich Ballet 1997–99 (joined 1996), princ Dutch Nat Ballet 2002–04 (joined 1999), princ Royal Ballet 2004–; second prize Concour Int de Havana Cuba, first prize Reiti Int Ballet Competition, Prix de Lausanne scholarship 1996; *Performances* incl: Cinderella, Romeo and Juliet, La Sylphide, Onegin; roles with the Royal Ballet incl: Romeo, the Prince in Cinderella, Albrecht, Daphnis, Lensky, Polyphonia, Agon; danced in works by: Balanchine, Forsythe, Van Manen, Massine, Robbins, Tetley; *Style—* Federico Bonelli, Esq; ✉ c/o The Royal Ballet, Royal Opera House, Covent Garden, London WC2E 9DD

BONEY, His Hon Judge Guy Thomas Knowles; QC (1990); s of Lt-Col Thomas Knowles Boney (d 1975), of Llandudno, and Muriel Hilary Eileen, *née* Long (d 1984); *b* 28 December 1944; *Educ* Winchester, New Coll Oxford (MA); *m* 4 Dec 1976, Jean Ritchie, QC, *qv*, da of Walter Ritchie (d 1979), of Solihull; 2 s (R Oliver *b* 21 Jan 1979, Christian V K *b* 29 March 1981); *Career* called to the Bar Middle Temple 1968 (bencher 1997); in practice Western Circuit 1969–2003, recorder of the Crown Court 1985–2003, head Pump Court Chambers 1992–2001, dep judge of the High Court 1994–2003, circuit judge (Western Circuit) 2003–; chm Friends of Winchester Coll 2001–; contrib to horological jls; Lord of the Manor of Stockbridge (Nat Tst appt) 2003–; *Books* The Road Safety Act 1967 (1971), Halsbury's Laws of England vol 40 (contrib); *Recreations* horology, music, amateur drama; *Clubs* Reform, Garrick; *Style—* His Hon Judge Boney, QC; ✉ 31 Southgate Street, Winchester, Hampshire SO23 9EB (tel 01962 868161, fax 01264 811180)

BONFIELD, Andrew Robert John; s of Terence Bonfield, and Roberta Alexandra, *née* Stackhouse; *b* 17 August 1962; *Educ* Univ of Natal (BCom, Postgrad Dip Accountancy); *m* Sandra; 2 s (Cameron, Scott); *Career* Price Waterhouse: South Africa 1984–87, London 1987–90; SmithKline Beecham plc: exec Corporate Planning 1990–91, dir and vice-pres Corporate Accounts 1991–95, corp controller 1995–97, dep fin dir and sr vice-pres 1997–99, chief fin offr 1999–2000; exec dir BG Gp plc 2001–02, sr vice-pres and chief fin offr Bristol-Myers Squibb 2002–; memb South African ICA; *Recreations* golf; *Style—* Andrew Bonfield, Esq

BONFIELD, Sir Peter Leahy; kt (1996), CBE (1989); s of George Bonfield, and Patricia Bonfield; *b* 3 June 1944; *Educ* Hitchin Boys' GS, Loughborough Univ (BTech); *m* 1968, Josephine Houghton; *Career* Texas Instruments Inc Dallas USA 1966–81, dep chief exec STC plc 1987–90, chief exec British Telecommunications plc 1996–2002; dir: BICC plc 1992–96, MCI Inc 1996–98, LM Ericsson Sweden 2002–, Mentor Graphics Corp Inc USA 2002–, TSMC Taiwan 2002–; dep chm ICL plc 1997–2000 (chm and chief exec 1985–96), memb Advsy Bd Sony Corp 2004–, memb Supervisory Bd Actis LLP 2005–, non-exec dir Corporate Bd DCA 2005–, chm Supervisory Bd NXP 2006–, non-exec dir Dubai Int LLP 2006–; vice-pres Br Quality Fndn 1993–; memb Int Advsy Bd Citigroup; former memb: Euro Round Table, EU-Japan Business Dialogue Round Table; ambass for Br business; Nat Electronics Cncl Mountbatten Medal 1995, Inst of Mgmnt Gold Medal 1996; Freeman City of London 1990, Liveryman Worshipful Co of Information Technologists 1992; hon citizen of Dallas; hon doctorates from Univs of: Loughborough, Surrey, Mid Glamorgan, Nottingham Trent, Brunel, Open Univ, Northumbria at Newcastle, London (Royal Holloway), Kingston, Cranfield, Essex; FIEE 1990, FBCS 1990, FCIM 1990, FRSA 1992, FREng; Cdr of the Order of the Lion of Finland 1995; *Recreations* music, sailing, skiing; *Clubs* RAC, Royal Thames Yacht; *Style—* Sir Peter Bonfield, CBE, FREng; ✉ PO Box 129, Shepperton, Middlesex TW17 9WL

BONFIELD, Prof William; CBE (1998); s of Cecil William Bonfield (d 2001), of Baldock, Herts, and Ellen Gertrude, *née* Hawkes (d 1981); *b* 6 March 1937; *Educ* Imperial Coll London (Perry Meml medal, Bessemer Medal, Ernest Edward Glorney Prize, BSc(Eng), PhD, ARSM, DIC); *m* 18 June 1960, Gillian Winifred Edith, da of John Hamilton Cross; 1 s (Peter William *b* 25 June 1963), 2 da (Stephanie Jane *b* 10 Sept 1965, Astrid Elizabeth *b* 21 May 1969); *Career* Honeywell Res Center Minnesota 1961–68; Queen Mary Univ of London 1968–99: head Dept of Materials 1980–90, chm Sch of Engrg 1981–88, govr 1984–87, dean of engrg 1985–89, prof of materials 1974–99 and dir Interdisciplinary Res Centre in Biomedical Materials 1990–99; Univ of Cambridge: prof of med materials 2000–05, dir Pfizer Inst for Pharmaceutical Materials Science 2002–05, emeritus prof 2005–; distinguished visiting prof Univ of Toronto 1990, visiting prof Henry Ford Hosp Detroit 1992, hon prof Univ of Sichuan China 1992–, adjunct prof Univ of Naples 1993–; dir Apatech Ltd 2001–; ed: Jl of Materials Science 1973–2002, Jl of Materials Science Letters 1981–2002, Materials in Medicine 1990–, Jl of the Royal Soc of London: Interface 2004–; A A Griffith Silver Medal Inst of Metals 1991, Royal Soc Armourers and Brasiers' Co Medal 1991, George Winter Award Euro Soc for Biomaterials 1994, Kelvin Medal Instn of Civil Engrs 1995, Acta Metallurgica J Herbert Holloman Award 2000, Chapman Medal IMMM 2003, Japanese Soc for Biomaterials Medal 2003, Prince Philip Gold Medal Royal Acad of Engrg 2004, President's Prize UK Soc for Biomaterials 2004; Freeman City of London 1998, Liveryman Worshipful Co of Armourers and Brasiers 1999 (Freeman 1994, memb Ct of Assts 2001, Renter Warden 2005, Upper Warden 2006); hon memb: Canadian Orthopaedic Res Soc 1984, Indian Materials Res Soc 1993; memb: Royal Instn, Euro Soc for Biomaterials; Hon DSc Univ of Aberdeen 2002; CEng 1972, FIM 1972, FREng 1993, founding fell in biomaterials, sci and engrg (FBSE) Euro Soc for Biomaterials 1995, FRS 2003, CPhys 2003, FIPEM 2003, FInstP, FRSC 2005; *Publications* Bioceramics (with G W Hastings and K E Tanner, 1991); author of over 400 scientific papers; *Recreations* cycling, gardening; *Clubs* Athenaeum, North Road Cycling, Gosling Sports Park; *Style—* Prof William Bonfield, CBE, FRS, FREng; ✉ Department of Materials Science and Metallurgy, University of Cambridge, Pembroke Street, Cambridge CB2 3QZ (tel 01223 334435, fax 01223 334567, e-mail wb210@hermes.cam.ac.uk)

BONHAM, Sir Antony Lionel Thomas; 4 Bt (UK 1852); DL (Glos 1983); s of Maj Sir Eric Henry Bonham, 3 Bt, CVO, JP (d 1937), and Ethel (d 1962), da of Lt-Col Leopold Seymour (s of Rt Hon Sir George Seymour, GCB, GCH, PC, and Hon Gertrude, da of 21 Baron Dacre; Sir George Seymour was s of Lord George Seymour, MP, s of 1 Marquess of Hertford); Sir Samuel George Bonham, 1 Bt, KCB, was govr and C-in-C Hong Kong and chief supt Br Trade in China 1847–53; *b* 21 October 1916; *Educ* Eton, RMC Sandhurst; *m* 19 Feb 1944, Felicity (d 2003), o da of Col Frank Lionel Pardoe, DSO (d 1947); 3 s ((George) Martin Antony *b* 1945, Simon Philip *b* 1947, Timothy Eric *b* 1952); *Heir* s, Martin Bonham; *Career* serv Royal Scots Greys 1937–49, Maj; dir wine merchants

1950–70, ret; *Style—* Sir Antony Bonham, Bt, DL; ✉ Greystones, The Croft, Fairford, Gloucestershire (tel 01285 712258)

BONHAM, Nicholas; s of late Leonard Charles Bonham, and Diana Maureen, *née* Magwood (d 1995); *b* 7 September 1948; *Educ* Trent Coll; *m* 7 April 1977 (m dis), Kaye Eleanor Ivett; 2 da (Katie *b* 1981, Jessica *b* 1982); *m* 2, 25 Sept 2003, Susan Angela Chester; *Career* dir Bonhams Group Ltd 1970–2004, md 1975–87, dep chm Bonhams 1987–2004; Freeman City of London 1970, memb Worshipful Co of Pewterers; *Recreations* sailing, tobogganing, skiing, scuba diving; *Clubs* South West Shingles Yacht, Acton Turville Bobsleigh, St Moritz Toboggan, Royal Thames Yacht, Seaview Yacht, Kennel; *Style—* Nicholas Bonham, Esq; ✉ Prospect Quay, Point Pleasant, London SW18 1PS (e-mail nbonham@lycos.co.uk)

BONHAM CARTER, Edward Henry; s of Hon Raymond Bonham Carter (d 2004), and Elena, *née* Propper de Callejon; bro of Helena Bonham Carter, *qv*; *b* 24 May 1960, London; *Educ* Harrow, Univ of Manchester; *m* Victoria; 2 s (Harry *b* 1996, Tobias *b* 2004), 1 da (Maud *b* 2000); *Career* fund mangr and analyst Schroders 1982–86, fund mangr and dir Electra Investment Tst 1986–94; Jupiter Asset Management: dir 1994–, chief investment offr 1999–, jt chief exec 2000–; memb Bd Investment Mgmnt Assoc; *Recreations* ping pong; *Clubs* Brooks's; *Style—* Edward Bonham Carter, Esq; ✉ Jupiter Asset Management, 1 Grosvenor Place, London SW1X 7JJ (tel 020 7314 4746, fax 020 7314 4902, e-mail ebc@jupitergroup.co.uk)

BONHAM CARTER, Helena; da of Hon Raymond Bonham Carter (d 2004), and Elena, *née* Propper de Callejon; sis of Edward Bonham Carter, *qv*; *b* 26 May 1966; *Educ* S Hampstead HS, Westminster; *Career* actress; *Theatre* incl: Woman in White (Greenwich), The Chalk Garden (Windsor), The House of Bernarda Alba (Nottingham Playhouse), Barber of Seville (Palace Theatre Watford) 1992, Trelawney of the Wells (Triumph, Guildford, Brighton and West End); *Television* incl: The Vision (BBC) 1987, Arms and the Man (BBC) 1988, Beatrix Potter 1989, Dancing Queen (Granada) 1993, A Dark Adapted Eye (BBC) 1993, Absolutely Fabulous (BBC), Jo Brand Through the Cakehole (Noel Gay TV); *Radio* incl: The Reluctant Debutant, Marie Antoinette, The Seagull; *Film* incl: Lady Jane (Paramount) 1985, A Room with a View (Merchant Ivory) 1986, A Hazard of Hearts 1987, Francesco 1988, Hamlet (Nelson Ent) 1990, Where Angels Fear to Tread (Merchant Ivory) 1990, Howard's End (Merchant Ivory) 1990, Fatal Deception (Eliott Friedgen & Co) 1992, Frankenstein 1993, Butter (Sundial Pictures), The Gallery (Talking Pictures), Margaret's Museum (Glace Bay Pics Inc) 1994, Mighty Aphrodite (Sweetheart Prodn) 1995, Chinese Portraits (IMA Prodn) 1995, Twelfth Night 1996, The Wings of the Dove (Renaissance Films/Miramax, Oscar nomination for Best Actress 1998) 1996, The Revenger's Comedies (Artisan Films) 1996, The Theory of Flight 1997, Keep the Aspidistra Flying 1997, Fight Club 1998, Women Talking Dirty 1999, Carnivale 1999, Novocaine 2000, Planet of the Apes 2001, Till Human Voices Wake Us 2001, The Heart of Me 2001, Big Fish 2003, Wallace and Gromit: The Curse of the Were-Rabbit 2005, Corpse Bride 2005; *Style—* Miss Helena Bonham Carter; ✉ c/o Conway van Gelder Ltd, 18–21 Jermyn Street, London SW1Y 6HP (tel 020 7287 0077, fax 020 7287 1940)

BONHAM-CARTER OF YARNBURY, Baroness (Life Peer UK 2004), of Yarnbury in the County of Wiltshire; Jane Mary Bonham Carter; da of Baron Bonham-Carter (Life Peer, d 1994), and Leslie Adrienne, da of late Condé Nast; *b* 20 October 1957, London; *Educ* St Paul's Girls' Sch, UCL (BA); *Partner* Baron Razzall, *qv*; *Career* prodr Panorama and Newsnight (both BBC) 1988–93, prog ed A Week in Politics (Channel 4) 1993–96, dir of communications Lib Dem Pty 1996–98 (memb Lib Dem Communications and Campaigns Ctee 1998–2006), ind prodr Brook Lapping Prodns (latterly part of Ten Alps plc) 1998–2004 (assoc 2004–); sits as Lib Dem in House of Lords 2004–, memb Sub-Ctee on Home Affrs 2004–07, memb Select Ctee on the BBC Charter Review 2005–06, memb Select Ctee on Communications 2007–; assoc memb Cncl Britain in Europe 1998–2005 (memb Referendum Campaign Team 2004–05); memb Advsy Ctee Centre Forum (formerly Centre for Reform) 1998–; involvement with RAPt (Rehabilitation for Addicted Prisoners Trust) 1999–; *Clubs* Groucho, Electric; *Style—* The Rt Hon the Lady Bonham-Carter of Yarnbury; ✉ House of Lords, London SW1A 1PW (tel 020 7428 4734)

BONINGTON, Sir Christian John Storey (Chris); kt (1996), CBE (1976), DL (Cumbria 2004); s of Charles Bonington (d 1983), and Helen Anne, *née* Storey (d 1999); *b* 6 August 1934; *Educ* UCS London, RMA Sandhurst; *m* 1962, (Muriel) Wendy, da of Leslie Marchant; 2 s (and 1 s decd); *Career* cmmnd RTR 1956, served in N Germany, Army Outward Bound Sch (mountaineering instr); mgmnt trainee Unilever 1961–62; freelance writer, photographer and mountaineer 1962–; non-exec dir Berghaus Ltd 1997– (chm 1998–); pres: LEPRA 1983–, Br Orienteering Fedn 1985–, Br Mountaineering Cncl 1988–91 (vice-pres 1976–79 and 1985–88), Nat Tst Lake Dist Appeal, Cncl for National Parks 1992–99, The Alpine Club 1996–98; chm Cncl of Mgmnt Mount Everest Fndn 1999–2001, chm Mountain Heritage Trust 2000–05; chllr Lancaster Univ 2005–; vice-pres: Army Mountaineering Assoc 1980–, Young Explorers' Trust, Youth Hostels Assoc, Br Lung Fndn; tstee: Outward Bound Tst, Himalayan Adventure Tst; hon fell UMIST 1976; Hon MA Univ of Salford 1973, Hon DSc Univ of Sheffield 1976, Hon DSc Lancaster Univ 1983, Hon Dr of Common Law Univ of Northumbria 1996, Hon DUniv Sheffield Hallam 1998, Hon DLitt Univ of Bradford 2002; Lawrence of Arabia Medal RSAA 1986, David Livingstone Medal RSGS 1991; FRGS (Founder's Medal 1974); *Ascents and Expeditions* first ascent: Annapurna II (26,041 feet) Nepal with Dick Grant 1960, Nuptse (25,850 feet), third peak of Everest with Sherpa Ang Pemba 1961, Central Pillar of Freney Mont Blanc with Whillans, Clough and Djuclosz 1961; first Br ascent North Wall of the Eiger with Clough 1962; first ascent: Central Tower of Paine Patagonia with Whillans 1963, Old Man of Hoy with Patey and Bailey 1966; ascent Sangay in Ecuador (highest active volcano in the world) 1966; ldr: Annapurna South Face Expdn 1970, Br Everest Expdn 1972; first ascent: Brammah (21,036 feet) Kashmir with Estcourt 1973, Changabang Garhwal Himalayas with Boysen, Haston, Scott and Sandhu 1974; ldr Br K2 Expdn 1978, climbing ldr Br Mount Kongur Expdn 1981 (first ascent with Boardman, Rouse and Tasker 1981), ldr Br Everest Expdn NE Ridge 1982, first ascent W Summit of Shivling (21,330 feet) Gangotri with Fotheringham 1983, first Br ascent (solo) Mount Vinson (highest in Antarctica) 1983, ascent of Mount Everest (29,028 feet) as a memb of 1985 Norwegian Everest Expdn, ldr Norwegian-Br Menlungtse Expdn 1987, ldr Tibet Expdn 1988 which made first ascent West Summit Menlungtse, first ascent W Ridge Panch Chuli II Kumoan Himalayas 1992, first ascent Meslin in Lemon Mountains 1993, first ascent Rangrik Rang Kinnaur Himalayas 1994, first ascent Drangnag-Ri 1995, ldr Sepu Kangri Expdn to Tibet 1997 and 1998, first ascent Danga II (6,194 metres) 2000, first ascent Jaraun Peak Kullu (5,205 metres) 2003; *Books* I Chose to Climb (autobiography, 1966), Annapurna South Face (1971), The Next Horizon (autobiography, 1973), Everest South West Face (1973), Changabang (jt author), Everest the Hard Way (1976), Quest for Adventure (1981), Kongur - China's Elusive Summit (1982), Everest - The Unclimbed Ridge (with Dr Charles Clarke, *qv*, 1983), The Everest Years (1986), Mountaineer - Thirty Years of Climbing on the World's Great Peaks (autobiography, 1989), The Climbers (1992), Sea, Ice and Rock (with Sir Robin Knox-Johnston, CBE, RD, *qv*, 1992), Great Climbs (gen ed, 1994), Tibet's Secret Mountain (with Dr Charles Clarke, 1999), Boundless Horizons (compendium of earlier autobiographies, 2000), Chris Bonington's Everest (2002), Everest Expeditions (2003); *Recreations* mountaineering, skiing, orienteering; *Clubs* Alpine (pres 1996–99), Climbers', Fell and Rock Climbing, Army and Navy, Travellers; *Style—* Sir Christian Bonington, CBE, DL; ✉ Badger Hill,

Hesket Newmarket, Wigton, Cumbria CA7 8LA (tel 01697 478286, fax 01697 478238, e-mail chris@bonington.com, website www.bonington.com)

BONNER, Paul Max; OBE (1999); s of Frank Max Bonner (d 1985), and Lily Elizabeth Marchant, *née* Jupp; *b* 30 November 1934; *Educ* Felsted; *m* 26 July 1956, (Nora) Jenifer, da of Dr George Raymond Hubbard; 2 s (Neil b 6 Jan 1957, Mark b 27 May 1959), 1 da (Alison b 27 June 1962); *Career* Nat Serv 1953–55, cmmnd 2 Lt RASC 1953, Acting Capt 1955, served in Egypt; BBC: radio studio mangr Bristol 1955–57, TV prodn Bristol 1957–59, current affairs prodr Lime Grove 1960–62, documentary prodr 1962–74, ed community progs 1974–77, head of sci and feature progs 1977–80; Channel Four TV: channel controller 1980–83, exec dir and prog controller 1983–87; dir Programme Planning Secretariat ITVA 1987–92, dir of secretariat ITV Network Centre 1992–94; memb: Ctee for Public Understanding of Sci 1986–92, Bd Children's Film Unit 1989–98; chm COPUS Broadcast 1995–98; dir: Broadcasting Support Services 1987–94 (vice-pres 1995–2004), House of Commons Broadcasting Unit Ltd 1989–94; govr Nat Film and TV Sch 1983–88; FRTS 1989; *Books* The Third Age of Broadcasting (jtly), Independent Television in Britain Vol 5: ITV and the IBA 1981–92 (1998), Independent Television in Britain Vol 6: New Developments 1981–92: Channel Four, TV-am, Cable and Satellite (2002); *Recreations* walking, photography; *Clubs* Chelsea Arts, Reform; *Style—* Paul Bonner, Esq, OBE; ✉ 5 North View, Wimbledon Common, London SW19 4UJ

BONNET, Robert (Rob); s of Harold Geoffrey Bonnet (d 1990), of Beckenham, Kent, and Margaret Mary, *née* Beevers; *b* 27 September 1952; *Educ* Dulwich Coll, Univ of Sussex (BA); *m* 1980, Margaret Suzanne, *née* Harvey; 2 da (Clare Louise b 1981, Eleanor Jane b 1983); *Career* media buyer Benton and Bowles advtg agency 1976–77, disc jockey Evian-les-Bains 1977; BBC: station asst BBC Radio Brighton 1978–80, prodr BBC Radio Norfolk 1980–82, prodr BBC Radio Sport 1982–85, sports reporter BBC East (Norwich) 1985–87, sports corr BBC TV News 1989–95 (sports reporter 1987–89), sports presenter/reporter BBC TV News and Radio Sport 1995–; RTS Sports Report of the Year (for 9 O'Clock News coverage of Sydney winning Olympic Games for 2000) 1993; *Recreations* golf, travel; *Clubs* Studley Wood Golf; *Style—* Rob Bonnet, Esq; ✉ BBC TV News and Current Affairs, Television Centre, London W12 7RJ

BONNET, Tim; s of Maj-Gen Peter Bonnet, CB, MBE, of East Anstey, Devon, and Sylvia Mary, *née* Coy; *b* 6 June 1964; *Educ* Monkton Combe Sch, Kingston Business Sch (BA); *Career* with Aer Lingus gp of cos 1989–91; TEQUILA\London: md 1992–2004, ceo 2004–; memb Business Advsy Gp Comic Relief; memb Bd Mktg Communications Consulting Assoc (MCCA) 2000; fndr and tstee Tusk Force; *Recreations* skiing, sailing, waterskiing, travel, tennis; *Style—* Tim Bonnet, Esq; ✉ TEQUILA, 82 Dean Street, London W1D 3HA (tel 020 7440 1100, fax 020 7440 1101, e-mail tim.bonnet@tequila-uk.com)

BONNEVILLE, Hugh Richard (né Williams); s of John Pritchard Williams, FRCS, of W Sussex, and Patricia Adèle, *née* Freeman; *b* 10 November 1963; *Educ* Sherborne, CCC, Webber Douglas Acad; *m* 4 Nov 1998, Lulu Evans, *née* Conner; 1 s (Felix b 2 Nov 2001); *Career* actor; theatrical prodr: Beautiful Thing (Duke of York's Theatre), Half Time (Donmar Warehouse); *Theatre* RNT roles incl: The Devil's Disciple, School for Scandal, Juno and the Paycock, School for Wives, Entertaining Strangers, Yerma; RSC (nominee Ian Charleson Award) incl: Hamlet, Amphibians, The Alchemist, 'Tis Pity She's a Whore, Two Gentlemen of Verona, The Virtuoso; other credits incl: Us and Them (Hampstead), Habeas Corpus (Donmar), My Night With Reg (Criterion), The Handyman (Chichester), Cloaca (Old Vic); rep work at Leicester Haymarket and Colchester Mercury; *Television* incl: Mosley, Madame Bovary, Take a Girl Like You, The Cazalets, Armadillo, Impact, Tipping the Velvet, Dr Zhivago, Daniel Deronda, The Commander, Love Again, Hear the Silence, The Robinsons, Courting Alex, Beau Brummell, Tsunami: The Aftermath, Five Days, Freezing, Diary of a Nobody, Filth: the Mary Whitehouse Story; *Radio* incl: People Like Us, Married, Romantic Friction; *Film* incl: Frankenstein, Mansfield Park, Notting Hill, Tomorrow Never Dies, Blow Dry, Iris (BAFTA nomination Best Supporting Actor, Berlin Film Festival Award Best Young Talent), Conspiracy of Silence, Stage Beauty, Asylum, Underclassman, Piccadilly Jim, Man to Man, Four Last Songs, Scenes of a Sexual Nature, French Film; *Recreations* studying jobsworths in their natural habitat; *Clubs* Garrick, Soho House; *Style—* Hugh Bonneville, Esq; ✉ c/o Gordon and French, 12–13 Poland Street, London W1F 8QB (tel 020 7734 4818, fax 020 7734 4832)

BONO, (Paul Hewson); Hon KBE (2007); s of Robert (Bob) Hewson, and Iris Hewson; *b* 10 May 1960; *Educ* Mount Temple Sch; *m* Alison (Ali); 2 da (Jordan b 10 May 1989, Eve); *Career* lead singer and fndr memb U2 1978– (with The Edge, Adam Clayton, and Larry Mullen, Jr, *qqv*); first U2 release U23 (EP) 1979; *Albums* Boy 1980, October 1981, War 1983 (entered UK chart at no 1), Under A Blood Red Sky 1983 (live album), The Unforgettable Fire 1984 (entered UK charts at no 1), Wide Awake in America 1985, The Joshua Tree 1987 (entered UK charts at no 1, fastest selling album ever in UK, Album of the Year Grammy Awards 1987), The Joshua Tree Singles 1988, Rattle & Hum 1988 (entered UK charts at no 1), Achtung Baby 1991, Zooropa 1993 (no 1 in 18 countries, Best Alternative Album Grammy Awards 1993), Pop 1997 (no 1), The Best of 1980–1990 1998, All That You Can't Leave Behind 2000 (no 1, Best Rock Album Grammy Awards 2002), The Best of 1990–2000 2002, How To Dismantle An Atomic Bomb 2004 (Album of the Year and Best Rock Album Grammy Awards 2006); *Singles* incl: Fire 1981, New Year's Day (first UK Top Ten hit) 1983, Pride (In the Name of Love) 1984, Unforgettable Fire 1985, With or Without You 1987, I Still Haven't Found What I'm Looking For 1987, Where The Streets Have No Name 1987 (Best Video Grammy Awards 1989), Desire (first UK no 1 single) 1988 (Best Rock Performance Grammy Awards 1989), Angel of Harlem 1988, When Love Comes to Town 1989, All I Want Is You 1989, Night & Day (for AIDS benefit LP Red Hot & Blue) 1990, The Fly (UK no 1) 1991, Stay 1993, Discotheque (UK no 1) 1997, Staring at the Sun 1997, Sweetest Thing 1998, Beautiful Day (UK no 1) 2000 (Record of the Year, Song of the Year and Best Rock Performance by a Duo or Group with Vocal Grammy Awards 2001), Stuck in a Moment You Can't Get Out Of 2001 (Best Song by a Pop Duo or Group Grammy Awards 2002), Elevation 2001 (Best Rock Performance by a Duo or Group with Vocal Grammy Awards 2002), Walk On 2001 (Record of the Year Grammy Awards 2002), Electrical Storm 2002, Vertigo (UK no 1) 2004 (Best Rock Performance by a Duo or Group with Vocal, Best Rock Song and Best Short Form Music Video Grammy Awards 2005), Sometimes You Can't Make It On Your Own (UK no 1) 2005 (Song of the Year, Best Rock Duo or Group Vocal and Best Rock Song Grammy Awards 2006); also duet with Frank Sinatra I've Got You Under My Skin 1993; *Film* Rattle & Hum 1988; *Tours* incl: UK, US, Belgium and Holland 1980, UK, US, Ireland and Europe 1981–83, Aust, NZ and Europe 1984, A Conspiracy of Hope (Amnesty International Tour) 1986, Joshua Tree tour 1987 (Best Rock Performance Grammy Awards 1987), Rattle & Hum tour 1988, Zoo TV tour (played to 5 million people) 1992–93, Popmart tour 1997–98, Elevation tour 2001, Vertigo tour 2005; also appeared at: Live Aid 1985 (Best Live Aid Performance Rolling Stone Readers' Poll 1986), Self Aid Dublin, Smile Jamaica (Dominion Theatre, in aid of hurricane disaster relief) 1988, New Year's Eve concert Dublin (broadcast live to Europe and USSR) 1989; performed at venues incl: Wembley Stadium, Madison Square Garden NY, Longest Day Festival Milton Keynes Bowl, Croke Park Dublin, Sun Devil Stadium AZ; *Awards* Best Band Rolling Stone Readers' Poll 1986 (also jt winner Critics' Poll), Band of the Year Rolling Stone Writers' Poll 1984, Best International Act BPI Awards 1989 and 1990, Best Live Act BPI Awards 1993, Best International Group Brit Awards 2001, Outstanding Contribution to the Music Industry Brit Awards 2001, Outstanding Song Collection Ivor Novello Awards 2003, Golden Globe Award (for Hands that Built America) 2003, Oscar nomination (for Hands that Built America) 2003; *Style—* Bono; ✉ c/o Regine Moylett Publicity, 2C Woodstock Studios, Woodstock Grove, London W12 8LE (tel 020 8749 7999)

BONSALL, David Charles; s of Leonard Dale Bonsall (d 1984), and Nellie Bonsall; *b* 26 July 1956; *Educ* Winchester, St John's Coll Cambridge (MA, LLM); *m* 11 Oct 1980, Margaret Ruth, da of Arthur George Shaw, OBE (d 2003), of St Albans, Herts; 2 da (Philippa Ruth b 25 Sept 1989, Kathryn Penelope b 20 June 1992); *Career* admitted slr 1981; ptnr Freshfields 1987–93 (articled clerk 1979–81), global head Asset Backed Fin UBS Ltd 1993–98, int head of asset securitisation CIBC World Markets 1998–2000, Bonsall Conslt 2001–; chm Trade Receivables Mgmnt Servs, dir AIG Trade Finance Ltd; Freeman Worshipful Co of Slrs; *Books* Securitisation (1990); *Recreations* golf, skiing, music; *Clubs* The Royal St George's Golf (capt 2003–04), R&A (memb Championship Ctee 2006–), Rye Golf, Sunningdale Golf, Royal Worlington and Newmarket Golf, Pine Valley Golf; *Style—* David Bonsall, Esq; ✉ Horton Priory, Monks Horton, Ashford, Kent TN25 6DZ (tel 01303 814154, fax 01303 814971, e-mail davidbonsall@aol.com)

BONSOR, Anthony Miles; s of David Victor Bonsor, of Herts, and late Sheila Valerie, *née* Graham; *b* 3 May 1948; *Educ* Eton, Univ of Southampton (LLB); *m* 1980, Frances Elizabeth, da of David Bankes; 2 da (Sophie Elizabeth b 27 Aug 1982, Laura Frances b 17 June 1988), 1 s (Miles David b 12 Sept 1984); *Career* articled clerk Farrer & Co 1971–73, admitted slr 1974, Richards Butler & Co 1975–76; Denton Hall 1976–79, ptnr Hong Kong Office 1979–83, ptnr Denton Wilde Sapte (formerly Denton Hall) 1983–; memb Law Soc; *Style—* Anthony Bonsor, Esq; ✉ Denton Wilde Sapte, 1 Fleet Place, London EC4M 7WS (tel 020 7242 1212, fax 020 7246 7777)

BONSOR, Sir Nicholas Cosmo; 4 Bt (UK 1925), of Kingswood, Epsom, Surrey; DL (Bucks 2007); s of Sir Bryan Cosmo Bonsor, 3 Bt, MC, TD (d 1977), and Elizabeth, *née* Hambro (d 1995); *b* 9 December 1942; *Educ* Eton, Keble Coll Oxford (MA); *m* 4 Sept 1969, Hon Nadine Marisa Lampson, da of 2 Baron Killearn (d 1996); 3 da (Sacha Henrietta b 1975, Elizabeth Nadine, Mary Catherine (twins) b 1987), 2 s (Alexander Cosmo b 1976, James Charles b 1983); *Heir* s, Alexander Bonsor; *Career* served The Royal Bucks Yeo (RA TA) 1964–69; called to the Bar Inner Temple 1967; in practice 1967–75 and 2003–, jt head of chambers 2004–; MP (Cons): Nantwich 1979–83, Upminster 1983–97; min of state FCO 1995–97; vice-chm Tourism Sub-Ctee 1980–83, vice-chm Cons Parly Foreign Affrs Ctee 1981–83, vice-chm Cons Parly Defence Ctee 1987–90, chm Commons Select Ctee on Defence 1992–95, memb Select Ctee on Broadcasting 1992–95, memb Liaison Ctee 1992–95, vice-chm Cons Parly Constitutional Ctee 1992–95; chm: Verdin Tst for the Mentally Handicapped 1982–91, Cyclotron Tst for Cancer Treatment 1984–92 (pres 1992–), Food Hygiene Bureau Ltd 1986–95, Br Field Sports Soc 1988–94, Baronets' Tst 1993–95, Leadership (UK) Ltd 2000–05, You to Coach plc 2000–03; dir Govt Rels Crosby MTM 1998–2003; memb Cncl: Lloyd's 1987–92, RUSI 1992–95 and 1997–99, China Br Business Cncl 2000–03; chm Standing Cncl of the Baronetage 1990–93 (vice-chm 1987–89), dir Blue Note Mining.ca 2007–; Hon Col 60 Signals Sqdn (V) 2000–; chm Bucks RFCA 2001–; Freeman City of London 1988; FRSA 1970; *Recreations* sailing, military history, shooting; *Clubs* White's, Royal Yacht Sqdn, House of Commons Yacht (Cdre 1985–86), Pratt's; *Style—* Sir Nicholas Bonsor, Bt; ✉ c/o White's Club, St James's, London SW1A 1JG (e-mail bonsors@yahoo.co.uk)

BONSOR, (Angus) Richard; s of Sir Bryan Cosmo Bonsor, 3 Bt, MC, TD (d 1977), of Leighton Buzzard, Beds, and Elizabeth, *née* Hambro (d 1995); *b* 3 February 1947; *Educ* Eton, Keble Coll Oxford (BA); *m* 14 Jan 1971, Susan Anne, da of David Henry Lewis Wigan, of Diss, Norfolk; 2 s (Rupert James b 26 Sept 1974, Edward Richard b 16 July 1976), 1 da (Clare Lucinda b 3 Sept 1981); *Career* ptnr Rowe & Pitman 1978 (joined 1968); dir: S G Warburg Securities 1986, associated to Matheson Securities 1989–92, UBS Ltd 1992–95, J O Hambro Investment Management 1995–; MSI; *Recreations* golf, racquets; *Clubs* White's, Turf, Pratt's, Sunningdale, Royal West Norfolk Golf; *Style—* Richard Bonsor, Esq; ✉ J O Hambro Investment Management, 21 St James's Square, London SW1Y 4HB

BONVIN, Her Hon Judge Jane Anne Marie (Mrs S M Poulter); DL (Hants 2003); da of Jean Albert Bonvin (d 1989), and Phyllis Margaret, *née* Boyd (d 1992); *b* 15 December 1946; *Educ* Putney HS GPDST, Univ of Bristol (LLB); *m* 19 Aug 1972, Sebastian Murray Poulter (d 1998); *Career* volunteer law lectr IVS Lesotho 1969–71; called to the Bar Gray's Inn 1971; barr Western Circuit 1972–77 and 1979–95, recorder 1992–95 (asst recorder 1989–92), circuit judge (Western Circuit) 1995–; ed Lesotho Law Reports 1977–79; FRSA; *Publications* Lesotho Law Reports (2 Vols, 1971–73 and 1974–75); *Recreations* gardening, travel, walking, horseracing; *Clubs* Univ Women's; *Style—* Her Hon Judge Bonvin; ✉ c/o Third Floor, South Side Offices, The Law Courts, Winchester, Hampshire SO23 9EL (tel 01962 876004/5)

BONYNGE, Richard; AO (1983), CBE (1977); s of C A Bonynge, of Epping, NSW; *b* 29 September 1930; *Educ* Sydney HS, Sydney Conservatorium, Royal Coll of Music; *m* 1954, Dame Joan Sutherland, *qv*; 1 s; *Career* opera conductor; official debut as conductor Santa Cecilia Orch Rome 1962; artistic dir: Sutherland/Williamson Int Grand Opera Co Aust 1965, Vancouver Opera 1974–77; musical dir Aust Opera 1976–86; conducted many operas in: Metropolitan Opera, San Francisco, Chicago Lyric Opera, Teatro Liceo, Barcelona, Royal Opera House Covent Garden, San Diego Opera, Sydney Opera; has made numerous recordings of opera and ballet; Commandeur L'Ordre des Arts et des Lettres France 1989; *Style—* Richard Bonynge, Esq, AO, CBE; ✉ c/o Ingpen & Williams Ltd, 7 St Georges Court, 131 Putney Bridge Road, London SW15 2PA

BOOBIER, Nigel John; s of Derek James Boobier, of Exeter, Devon, and Ruth Mary, *née* Gresswell; *b* Okehampton, Devon; *Educ* Exeter Coll, Univ of Birmingham (LLB); *m* 28 Dec 1991, Michelle Maria-Theresa, *née* Gore; 1 da (Chloe Victoria), 3 s (Joseph Michael, Laurence Daniel, Edward James); *Career* slr; trainee slr Anstey Sargent and Probert 1992–95, slr Dibb Lupton Broomhead 1995–97; Osborne Clarke: slr and assoc 1997–2002, ptnr 2002–; licensed insolvency practitioner 1998, regular speaker at conferences on restructuring and insolvency, contrib to jls on restructuring and insolvency; memb Law Soc; fell Assoc of Business Recovery Professionals (vice-chm S Wales and SW branch); *Recreations* family, cricket, rugby, food and drink; *Style—* Nigel Boobier, Esq; ✉ Osborne Clarke, 2 Temple Back East, Temple Quay, Bristol BS1 6EG (tel 0117 917 4164, fax 0117 917 4165, e-mail nigel.boobier@osborneclarke.com)

BOOKBINDER, Alan Peter; s of Geoffrey Ellis Bookbinder (d 1990), and Bridget Mary, *née* Doran (d 2006); *b* 16 March 1956; *Educ* Manchester Grammar, St Catherine's Coll Oxford (BA), Voronezh Univ (Br Cncl scholar), Harvard Univ (MA); *m* Victoria, *née* Ambery-Smith; 1 s (Joe Ambery b 9 June 1993), 1 da (Holly Ambery b 7 June 1996); *Career* BBC: joined as trainee asst prodr 1980, asst prodr (current affrs) 1982–85, prodr (documentaries) 1985–86, series prodr (documentaries) 1986–92, series ed Under the Sun 1992–96, exec prodr (science) 1997–2001, head of religion and ethics 2001–06; dir Sainsbury Family Charitable Tsts 2006–; contrib to newspapers and magazines; *Books* Comrades (1985); *Style—* Alan Bookbinder, Esq; ✉ Sainsbury Family Charitable Trusts, 1st Flooor, Allington House, 150 Victoria Street, London SW1E 5AE (tel 020 7410 7035, e-mail alan.bookbinder@sfct.org.uk)

BOOKER, Christopher John Penrice; s of late John Mackarness Booker, of Shillingstone, Dorset, and Margaret Booker (d 1991); *b* 7 October 1937; *Educ* Shrewsbury, CCC Cambridge; *m* 1, 1963 (m dis), Hon Mrs Emma C Tennant, *qv*; m 2, 1972 (m dis), Christine Verity; m 3, 1979, Valerie, da of late Dr M S Patrick, OBE; 2 s; *Career* author, journalist and broadcaster; Liberal News 1960, jazz critic Sunday Telegraph 1961, ed Private Eye

1961–63 (contrib 1965–); resident scriptwriter: That Was The Week That Was 1962–63, Not So Much A Programme 1963–64; contrib Daily Mail 1969–, columnist Sunday Telegraph 1990–; former contrib: Spectator, Daily Telegraph (Way of the World column as Peter Simple II 1987–90); wrote extensively on property devpt, planning and housing 1972–77, TV prog City of Towers: the Rise and Fall of a Twentieth Century Dream (1979); memb Cowgill Enquiry into post-war repatriations from Austria 1986–90; *Books* The Neophiliacs: A Study of the Revolution in English Life in the 50's and 60's (1969), Goodbye London (with Candida Lycett-Green, 1973), The Booker Quiz (1976), The Seventies (1980), The Games War: A Moscow Journal (1981), Repatriations from Austria in 1945 (jtly, 1990), The Mad Officials (with Richard North, 1994), The Castle of Lies: Why Britain Must Get Out of Europe (1996), A Looking Glass Tragedy (1997), The Great Deception: A Secret History of the European Union (with Richard North, 2003), The Seven Basic Plots: Why Do We Tell Stories? (2004), The Great Deception: Can the European Union Survive? (2005), Scared to Death: The Anatomy of a Modern Madness (2007); contrib to Private Eye anthologies incl John Major Diaries and St Albion's Parish News; *Recreations* the psychology of storytelling, nature, music, playing village cricket; *Style*— Christopher Booker, Esq; ✉ The Old Rectory, Litton, Bath, Somerset (tel 01761 241263)

BOOKER, Michael William; s of Donald Booker, of Great Longstone, Derbys, and Mary Elizabeth, *née* Trickett; *b* 5 October 1955; *Educ* King Edward VII Sch Sheffield, Univ of Liverpool Med Sch (BM BCh); *m* 1, 1979 (m dis 1991), Judith Anne, da of Donald Ryder; 2 da (Laurie Anne b 15 Sept 1982, Chloe Maxine b 5 June 1985); m 2, 1994, Elizabeth Mary, da of Gordon Ball; 2 s (James Michael b 14 April 1996, Thomas William b 3 Nov 1998); *Career* research fell then lectr in obstetrics and gynaecology King's Coll Sch of Med and Dentistry 1984–89; conslt in obstetrics and gynaecology: Singapore Gen Hosp 1989–90, Mayday Univ Hosp Croydon 1990– (estab centre for reproductive med and in-vitro fertilization and embryo transfer clinic (transport IVF prog) 1992); district tutor (Croydon Health Dist) RCOG; author of numerous contribs to med jls; memb: BMA 1978, RSM 1988, AFS 1988, BFS 1991, ESHRE 1994, FRCOG; *Recreations* windsurfing, scuba diving, jazz; *Style*— Michael Booker, Esq; ✉ Mayday Hospital, Mayday Road, Croydon, Surrey CR7 7YE (tel 020 8657 6155, fax 020 8657 0755, e-mail mbooker@uk-consultants.co.uk)

BOON, Dr Nicholas Antony; s of Capt John Nicholas Boon, MC, of Loudwater, nr Rickmansworth, Herts, and Doreen Myrtle, *née* Francke; *b* 31 December 1950; *Educ* Canford, Gonville & Caius Coll Cambridge (MA, MB BChir), Middx Hosp Med Sch (MD); *m* 19 May 1979, (Grace) Anne, da of Prof W B Robertson, of Wimbledon; 2 da (Victoria b 11 Aug 1982, Sarah Jane b 15 March 1984); *Career* clinical lectr and sr registrar John Radcliffe Hosp Oxford 1983–86, conslt cardiologist Royal Infirmary of Edinburgh 1986–, hon reader Univ of Edinburgh 2005– (hon sr lectr 1986–2005); pres elect Br Cardiac Soc 2005–; FRCP 1988, FESC 1996; *Publications* author of numerous scientific pubns and contrib to various med textbooks incl Oxford Textbook of Medicine and Davidson's Principles and Practice of Medicine (co-ed); *Recreations* golf, skiing; *Clubs* Luffness New; *Style*— Dr Nicholas Boon; ✉ 7 Cobden Crescent, Edinburgh EH9 2BG (tel 0131 667 3917, fax 0131 622 0184, e-mail boons@lineone.net); Department of Cardiology, Royal Infirmary of Edinburgh, 51 Little France Crescent, Edinburgh EH16 4SU (tel 0131 242 1848/9, fax 0131 242 1824)

BOONHAM, Nigel Francis; *b* 30 May 1953; *Educ* Kent Coll Canterbury, Brighton Tech Coll, Woolwich Adult Educn Inst; *m* Mayuri; *Career* sculptor; early career as asst to Oscar Nemon; commissions incl: portrait sculptures and monuments to John Hunter 1979, Lord Runcie 1981, Dr Joseph Needham 1985, Diana Princess of Wales 1991, Archbishop Daniel Mannix and Boadicea 1999, Dame Cicely Saunders OM 2001, The Basil Hume Memorial Garden and Statue (unveiled by HM The Queen) 2002; work features in collections incl: Nat Portrait Gall, Manchester Free Trade Hall, Int Courts of Justice The Hague, Worshipful Co of Goldsmiths; pres Soc of Portrait Sculptors 2004– (memb 1996–, vice-pres 1999–2004); FRBS 1983 (ARBS 1980); *Exhibitions* Royal Acad Summer Exhbn 1975 and 1976, Soc of Portrait Sculptors 1976, 1977 and annually 1996–2007, Portraits of Today (Nat Portrait Gall London) 1981, Phoenix Gall Lavenham 1982, Royal Soc of Br Sculptors (Scone Palace Scotland) 1983, Vauxhall Studio London 1984, Notting Hill London 1989 and 1990, 20th Century Portraits (Nat Portrait Gall) 1995, Markovitch Gall London 1996 and 1997, Addison-Ross Gall London 1998; *Recreations* books, music, sculpture, dance; *Style*— Nigel Boonham, FRBS; ✉ 5 Havelock Walk, Forest Hill, London SE23 3HG (tel 020 8291 3604, e-mail nigelboonham@hotmail.com)

BOORD, Sir Nicolas John Charles; 4 Bt (UK 1896), of Wakehurst Place, Ardingly, Sussex; s of Sqdn Ldr Sir Richard William Boord, 3 Bt (d 1975), and Yvonne Swingler, *née* Bird; *b* 10 June 1936; *Educ* Eton, Sorbonne, Societa Dante Alighieri Italy, Univ of Santander Spain; *m* 1, 1960 (m dis 1965), Françoise, da of Giuseppe Tempra; m 2, 1965, Françoise Renée Louise, da of Marcel Clovis Mouret, of Marseilles, France; *Heir* bro, Antony Boord; *Career* scientific translator/English trg specialist; jt translator: The History of Physics and The Philosophy of Science (1972), numerous scientific papers for English and American scientific and tech jls; *Recreations* English and French literature and linguistics; *Style*— Sir Nicolas Boord, Bt; ✉ 61 Traverse le Mée, 13009 Marseilles, France

BOORMAN, Edwin Roy Pratt; OBE (2002), DL (Kent); s of Henry Roy Pratt Boorman, CBE (d 1992), and his 1 w, Enid Margaret, *née* Starke; *b* 7 November 1935; *Educ* Rydal Sch, Queens' Coll Cambridge (MA); *m* 1 (m dis 1982), Merrilyn Ruth Pettit; 4 da; m 2, 1983, Janine Mary, da of William Craske, of Penenden Heath, Maidstone; 1 s; *Career* Kent Messenger Group: joined 1959, ed South Eastern Gazette 1960–62, ed Kent Messenger 1962–65, md 1965–86, chm and chief exec 1986–2002, chm 2002–; chm Messenger Print Ltd 1972–98; chm: Kent Youth Tst 1988–2001 (dep pres 2002–), Kent Branch IOD 1993–96, North Kent Success 1993–96, Royal Br Legion Industries 2000, Kent River Walk 1998–; tstee: Chatham Historic Dockyard 1992–97, Kent Air Ambulance Appeal 1993–, On the Move 1998–; pres Loose Amenities Assoc 1989–, life vice-pres Kent Co Royal British Legion 2003–, patron Kent Child Witness Service; govr: Sutton Valence Sch 1976–2002, Canterbury Christ Church Coll 1996–; chm Cncl Order of St John for Kent 1997–, High Sheriff for Kent 1997–98; memb Ct of Assts Worshipful Co of Stationers and Newspapermakers 1986–2000 (memb emeritus list 2001); pres Newspaper Soc 2001–02; *Recreations* sailing (yacht 'Messenger'); *Clubs* Ocean Cruising, Medway Yacht, Kent CCC, Carlton; *Style*— Edwin Boorman, Esq, OBE, DL; ✉ Redhill Farm, 339 Redhill, Wateringbury, Kent; Kent Messenger, Messenger House, New Hythe Lane, Larkfield, Kent ME20 6SG (tel 01622 717880, fax 01622 710937)

BOORMAN, John; CBE (1994); s of George Boorman, and Ivy, *née* Chapman; *b* 18 January 1933; *Educ* Salesian Coll Chertsey; *Career* film director; contrib articles to Manchester Guardian and various magazines 1950–54, successively broadcaster, critic BBC radio, film ed ITN London 1955–58, dir/prodr Southern TV 1958–60, head of documentaries BBC TV Bristol (dir The Citizens series and The Newcomers documentaries) 1960–64, Lee Marvin: A Personal Portrait by John Boorman 1998; fell BAFTA 2004; *Films* Catch us if you can 1965, Point Blank 1967, Hell in the Pacific 1968, Leo the Last 1969, Deliverance 1970, Zardoz 1973, The Heretic 1976, Excalibur 1981, The Emerald Forest 1985, Hope and Glory 1987, Where the Heart is 1989, I Dreamt I Woke Up 1991, Beyond Rangoon 1994, Two Nudes Bathing 1995, The General 1997 (Best Film Evening Standard British Film Awards 1999, Best Dir Cannes), The Tailor of Panama 2000, Country of my Skill (retitled, formerly Truth) 2003; *Books* The Legend of Zardoz (1973), Money into Light (1985), Hope and Glory (1987), Projections 1–7 (1992), Projections 1–13 (1992–1999), Adventures of a Suburban Boy (2003); *Style*— John Boorman, Esq, CBE

BOOTE, Charles Richard Michael; TD (1971, and two clasps 1978 and 1983), DL (Staffs 1988); s of Col (Charles Geoffrey) Michael Boote, MBE, TD, JP, DL (d 1999), and Elizabeth Gertrude, *née* Davies (d 1980); *b* 7 August 1939; *Educ* Cheltenham Coll; *m* 9 Oct 1965, Alison Brookes, da of Charles Kenneth Stott (d 1979), of Stafford; 2 da (Vanessa b 1967, Emma b 1970), 1 s (James b 1974); *Career* Maj TA cmd B (Staffs Yeo), The Queen's Own Mercian Yeo 1974–78, 2 i/c The Queen's Own Mercian Yeo 1978–80; md Armitage Shanks Integrated Systems 1988–90, corp devpt dir Home Products Div Blue Circle Industries plc 1987–89; chm: Staffs Ctee of the Rural Devpt Cmmn 1984–97 (memb Cmmn's Econ Advsy Panel 1988–96), Staffs Ambulance Serv NHS Tst 1991–93, Stafford Enterprise Ltd (dir 1990–97); dir: Staffs Trg and Enterprise Cncl 1989–94, Field Inns Ltd 2000–, Team GBS Ltd 2001–; chm and chief exec EC Gp Int 1991–; chm GP Net Ltd 2000–03; memb: Exec Ctee Staffs Devpt Assoc 1991–94, Staffs Ctee Country Landowners Assoc 1988–95; gen cmmr of taxes Stafford Div 1993–; treas Staffs Assoc of Clubs for Young People (formerly Staff Assoc of Boys' Clubs) 1968– (vice-chm 1968–2003), employers rep W Midlands TAVR Assoc Ctee 1983–97; High Sheriff of Staffs 1990–91; FCA, FCMA, CMI; *Recreations* skiing, tennis, squash; *Style*— Charles Boote, Esq, TD, DL; ✉ Enson Moor House, Sandon, Stafford ST18 9TA (home tel 01889 508223, office tel 01889 508008, fax 01889 508405, e-mail charles@charlesboote.com)

BOOTH, *see also*: Gore-Booth

BOOTH, Anthony John; CBE (1993); s of Benjamin Booth, and Una Lavinia, *née* Cumberpatch; *b* 18 March 1939; *Educ* Bungay GS, Univ of London (BSc (Eng)), Ealing Coll (DMS); *m* 4 Sept 1965, Elspeth Marjorie, da of Rev Francis Stewart Gordon Fraser, MBE, TD (d 1962); 1 da (Caroline Ruth b 1968), 1 s (Richard Mark b 1970); *Career* British Telecom (formerly GPO): scientific asst Res Dept PO 1957, exec engr then sr exec engr Telecom HQ 1965–71, asst staff engr Central HQ Appts 1971–74, head of section and div External Telecom Exec 1974–78, head of div Telecommunications HQ 1978–79, dir of int networks 1979–80, regnl dir London Region 1980–83, md British Telecom International 1983–91, corp dir British Telecommunications plc 1984–94, md BT Business Communications 1991–92, md BT Special Businesses and International Affairs 1992–94; chm Ericsson Ltd 1994–2002; dir RB Phusion Ltd 2001–; dir and tstee AQA (Assessment and Qualifications Alliance Ltd) 2000–06 (vice-chm 2003–06); memb: Regnl Affairs Ctee C of C and Industry 1980–84, London Regnl Ctee CBI 1982–84, Overseas Ctee CBI 1984–94; govr Ealing Coll 1989–91, chm Bd of Govrs Thames Valley Univ 1992–96; memb: Bd HEFCE 1996–2001, Cncl Univ of Surrey 1998–2004, Bd of Companions CMI 1999–; chm: SE Regn RLSS UK 1997–2001, IOD W Surrey 1999–2002 (pres 2002–); memb Guild of Freemen of the City of London 1982; Hon DPhil Thames Valley Univ 1995; CEng 1985, FIEE 1985, CCMI (CIMgt 1986), FRSA 1991, FInstD 1997; *Recreations* opera, golf; *Clubs* Caledonian, Camberley Heath Golf; *Style*— Anthony Booth, Esq, CBE; ✉ 63 Hillsborough Park, Camberley, Surrey GU15 1HG

BOOTH, Cherie; QC (1995); da of Anthony George Booth, of Co Cavan, Ireland, and Gale, *née* Smith; *b* 23 September 1954, Bury; *Educ* Seafield Convent GS Liverpool, LSE (LLB); *m* 29 March 1980, Rt Hon Tony Blair, MP, *qv*, s of Leo Charles Lynton Blair; 3 s (Euan Anthony b 19 Jan 1984, Nicholas John b 6 Dec 1985, Leo George b 20 May 2000), 1 da (Kathryn Hazel b 2 March 1988); *Career* called to the Bar Lincoln's Inn 1976 (Hardwicke and Kennedy scholar, Ede & Ravenscroft Prize for highest bar finals results, bencher); in practice: Alexander Irvine (now Baron Irvine of Lairg, PC (Life Peer), *qv*) 1976–77, New Court Chambers 1977–91, Gray's Inn Square Chambers 1991–2000, Matrix Chambers 2000–; recorder 1999– (asst recorder 1996–99); chair IT Ctee Bar Cncl 1991, vice-chair (IT) Bar Services and Information Technology Ctee 1995–96, chair Bar Conf 1997; Parly candidate (Lab) Thanet North Gen Election 1983; pres Barnardo's and Loomba tst, vice-pres 4Children, St Joseph's Hospice and Family Mediators Assoc, tstee Citizenship Fndn, ambass London 2012 and Weston Spirit, patron of numerous charities; govr LSE; Legal Personality of the Year (The Lawyer magazine) 1997; chllr and hon fell Liverpool John Moores Univ; govr and hon fell: LSE, Open Univ; Hon LLD: Univ of Westminster, Univ of Liverpool 2003; Hon DLitt UMIST 2003; Freeman City of London 2006; hon bencher King's Inn Dublin 2002; hon fell Inst of Advanced Legal Studies, FRSA; *Recreations* reading, keeping fit, the arts, spending as much time as possible with my children; *Style*— Ms Cherie Booth, QC; ✉ Matrix Chambers, Griffin Building, Gray's Inn, London WC1R 5LN

BOOTH, Sir Christopher Charles; kt (1982); s of Lionel Barton Booth (MB, MD) and Phyllis Petley, *née* Duncan; *b* 22 June 1924; *Educ* Sedbergh, Univ of St Andrews (MB, MD); *m* 1, 1959, Lavinia Loughridge, of Belfast; 1 s, 1 da; m 2, 1970, Prof Soad Tabaqchali, *qv*; 1 da; m 3, 2001, Joyce Singleton; *Career* formerly med tutor, lectr then sr lectr London Postgrad Med Sch, prof and dir Dept of Med RPMS Univ of London 1966–77, dir Clinical Research Centre MRC 1978–88; Harveian librarian Royal Coll of Physicians 1989–97; memb: Advsy Bd to Res Cncls 1976–78, MRC 1981–84; chm: Med Advsy Ctee Br Cncl 1979–85, Royal Naval Personnel Ctee 1985–92; pres: Br Soc of Gastroenterology 1978–79, BMA 1986–87, Johnson Soc 1987–88, RSM 1988; foreign memb American Philosophical Soc 1982; Hon FACP 1973, Hon FRSM 1991; Dr (hc): Paris 1975, Poitiers 1981, Bologna 1991; Hon LLD Univ of Dundee 1982; FRCP 1964, FRCPEd 1967; Chevalier de l'Ordre National du Mérite (France) 1977; *Books* Chain of Friendship: Letters of Dr John Fothergill of London 1735–1780 (with Betsy C Corner, 1971), Disorders of the Small Intestine (with G Neale, 1985), Doctors in Science and Society (1987), Take Time by the Forelock (with Christopher Lawrence and Paul Luger, 1999), A Physician Reflects (2003), John Haygarth, FRS, A Physician of the Enlightenment (2005); *Recreations* fishing, history; *Style*— Sir Christopher Booth

BOOTH, Prof Sir Clive; kt (2003); s of Henry Booth and Freda Frankland; *b* 18 April 1943; *Educ* King's Sch Macclesfield, Trinity Coll Cambridge (MA), Univ of Calif Berkeley (Harkness fell, MA, PhD); *m* 1969, Margaret Sardeson; *Career* joined DES 1965, princ private sec to Sec of State for Educn and Sci 1975–77, asst sec 1977–81; dep dir Plymouth Poly 1981–84, memb HM Inspectorate DES 1984–86, vice-chllr Oxford Brookes Univ (formerly Oxford Poly) 1986–97; asst cmmr Nat Cmmn on Educn 1992–94, chm Teacher Trg Agency 1997–2003, sr advsr to Br Cncl 1997–2003; chm Review Body for Nurses and Professions Allied to Med 1998–2004, dep chm SE England Devpt Agency (SEEDA) 1999–2004, chm Central Police Trg and Devpt Authy (CENTREX) 2002–, interim chm (overseeing merger) New Opportunities Fund and Community Fund 2004–; memb: Governing Cncl SRHE 1981–90, Advsy Ctee Brunel Univ Educn Policy Centre 1986–90, Computer Bd for Univs and Res Cncls 1987–92, CNAA Ctee for Info and Devpt Servs 1987–91, Fulbright Academic Administrators Selection Ctee 1988–97, Br Cncl Ctee for Int Cooperation in Higher Educn 1988–97, Cncl for Indust and Higher Educn 1990, Fulbright Cmmn 1992–97, Oxford Inst of Nursing Bd 1991–96, Cwlth Scholarships Cmmn 1992–97, UK ERASMUS Cncl 1992–97, Br Cncl Bd 1995–97, LSC for Milton Keynes, Oxon and Bucks 2001–05; dir: Thames Action Resource Gp for Educn and Trg 1986–97, Thames Valley Technol Centre 1989–97, Oxfordshire Business Link 1995–2003; chm: Oxfordshire Learning Partnership Ltd 1999–, Oxfordshire Connexions Mgmnt Ctee 2000–03, The PhD Consortium 2000–04, The Big Lottery Fund Bd 2004–; vice-chm Ctee of Vice-Chllrs and Princs 1992–94; Leverhulme res fell 1983; govr Headington and Wheatley Park Schs, jt ed Higher Educn Quarterly 1986, memb Ed Bd Oxford Review of Educn 1990–; *Recreations* cycling, walking, bridge, opera; *Style*— Prof Sir Clive Booth; ✉ 43 St John Street, Oxford OX1 2LH (tel 01865 557762, fax 01865 558886)

BOOTH, Prof Derek Blake; s of Sir Philip Booth, 2 Bt (d 1960); h to Btcy of bro, Sir Douglas Booth, 3 Bt, *qv*; *b* 7 April 1953; *Educ* Hampshire Coll Amherst (BA), Univ of Calif at Berkeley (BA), Stanford Univ (MS), Univ of Washington (PhD); *m* 1981, Elizabeth Dreisbach; 1 s (Colin b 1982), 1 da (Rachel b 1986); *Career* geologist; currently affiliate prof Depts of Civil and Environmental Engrg and of Earth and Space Sciences Univ of Washington; sr geologist Stillwater Sciences Inc; author of articles in jls and chapters in books; *Style—* Prof Derek Booth

BOOTH, Sir Douglas Allen; 3 Bt (UK 1916), of Allerton Beeches, City of Liverpool; s of Sir Philip Booth, 2 Bt (d 1960), and his 2 w, Ethel, *née* Greenfield; *b* 2 December 1949; *Educ* Gaspar de Portolà Junior HS, Beverley Hills HS CA, Harvard Univ; *m* 17 Nov 1991, Yolanda Marcella, *née* Scantlebury; 1 da (Zahra Jessica b 13 Aug 1993); *Heir* bro, Derek Booth; *Career* TV and film writer/prodr; *Recreations* music, backpacking; *Style—* Sir Douglas Booth, Bt

BOOTH, Graham; MEP (UKIP) SW Region; s of Harry Booth (d 1963), and Dinx, *née* Prout; *b* 29 March 1940; *Educ* Torquay Boys' GS; *m* 1; 2 s (Gary b 1962, Terry b 1965); m 2, 10 Sept 1982, Pamela, da of Alfred Jones; *Career* Lloyds Bank 1956–60, family holiday business 1960–; UKIP: joined 1996, dep ldr 2001–02; MEP (UKIP) SW Region 2002–; *Recreations* golf, astronomy, poetry, coin collecting; *Style—* Graham Booth, Esq, MEP; ✉ 41 Oyster Bend, Paignton, Devon TQ4 6NL (tel and fax 01803 557433, mobile 07968 848991, e-mail mrgrahambooth@aol.com)

BOOTH, Dr (Vernon Edward) Hartley; s of Vernon William Hartley Booth, and Eilish, *née* Morrow; *b* 17 July 1946; *Educ* Queens Coll Taunton, Univ of Bristol (LLB), Downing Coll Cambridge (LLM, Dip Int Law, PhD); *m* 30 July 1977, Adrianne Claire Cranefield, da of Knivett Garton Cranefield, DFC; 1 da (Emily Claire Hartley b 1982), 2 s (Peter Toby Hartley b 1985, Thomas Edward Hartley b 1988); *Career* called to the Bar Inner Temple; practising 1970–84, special advsr to PM and memb 10 Downing St Policy Unit 1984–88, chief exec and md Br Urban Devpt Ltd 1988–90, chm British Urban Regeneration Assoc 1990–92; Parly candidate (Cons) Hackney and Stoke Newington 1983, MP (Cons) Finchley 1992–97; PPS to: Rt Hon Douglas Hogg, QC, MP 1992–94, Eric Forth, MP 1996–97; memb: Select Ctee on European Legislation 1992, Select Ctee on Home Affairs 1992, Euro Standing Ctee 1995–97; chm: Urban Affrs Ctee 1994–97, All-Pty Central Asia Ctee 1995–97; dir Canford Gp plc 1978–; conslt: Berwin Leighton 1991–2000, Fenners Solicitors 2001–03, Maclay Murray Spens 2003–; external dir Edexcel Fndn 1999–2002; co-chm Uzbek br Trade Cncl 2000–; former leader writer Daily Telegraph; vice-pres RLSS; pres: Resources for Autism 1997–, Br Uzbeck Soc 2001–; *Books* British Extradition Law and Procedure (volume I 1980, volume II 1981), Victims of Crime (1992), Into the Voids (1993), There Goes the Neighbourhood (1994), Return Ticket (1994); *Style—* Dr Hartley Booth; ✉ c/o Maclay Murray Spens Solicitors, 10 Foster Lane, London EC2V 6HR

BOOTH, Michael John; QC (1999); s of Eric Charles Booth of Hale, and Iris, *née* Race; *b* 24 May 1958; *Educ* Manchester Grammar (scholarship), Trinity Coll Cambridge (open scholarship, MA); *Family* 1 da (Abigail b 22 July 1992), 2 s (Henry b 31 Oct 1994, Freddie b 27 Oct 1997); *Career* called to the Bar Lincoln's Inn 1981, memb Bar Cayman Islands; *Recreations* walking, reading, swimming, football, wine, history in general, Alexander the Great in particular; *Style—* Michael J Booth, Esq, QC; ✉ King's Chambers, 40 King Street, Manchester M2 6BA (tel 0161 832 9082, fax 0161 835 2139, e-mail mbooth@kingschambers.com)

BOOTH, Peter John Richard; s of Eric Albert Booth, and Edith, *née* Brown; *b* 27 March 1949; *Educ* Benton Park Secdy Modern Sch; *m* 27 July 1970, Edwina Ivy; 3 s (Peter Tristan b 24 Jan 1971, Jonathen Richard b 11 Sept 1972, James Lee b 19 Sept 1978); *Career* Dyers Operative 1964; Nat Union of Dyers Bleachers and Textile Workers: dist offr 1973, nat res offr 1975, nat organiser 1980; TGWU: joined 1982, nat trade gp organiser 1982, textile nat gp sec 1986–93, nat organiser (mfrg) 1999–; pres Int Textile Garment & Leather Workers' Fedn 1996–2004 (memb Exec Ctee); vice-pres Br Textile Confedn 1989–97, vice-pres Euro Trade Union Ctee of Textiles Clothing and Leather; dir: Apparel Knitting and Textiles Alliance 1989–, Man-Made Fibres Industry Trg Advsy Bd 1986–, Nat Textile Trg Gp 1988–; chm Carpet Industry Trg Cncl 1986–; memb: Presidium 1982–96, Textiles Clothing and Footwear Industries Ctee TUC 1976–, Confedn of Br Wool Textiles Trg Bd 1986–, Health and Safety Ctee Cotton and Allied Textiles Industries Advsy Ctee, Health and Safety Cmmn Texile Industry Advsy Ctee, Textiles Industry Advsy Cmmn (TEXIAC), Skillfast UK, Textile Clothing and Strategy Gp, DTI Manufacturing Forum, TUC Manufacturing Task Gp; tstee Cotton War Meml Tst; FRSA; *Books* The Old Dog Strike (1985); *Recreations* walking, gardening, dominoes, chess; *Clubs* Yeadon Trades Hall; *Style—* Peter Booth, Esq

BOOTH, Robin Godfrey; s of Frank Booth (d 1990), of York, and Dorothy, *née* Johnson; *b* 11 August 1942; *Educ* Winchester, King's Coll Cambridge (DipArch, MA), Univ of Edinburgh (MSc); *m* 10 July 1971, Katherine, da of Arthur Middleton, of Lynchburg, VA; 1 da (Emily b 1974), 1 s (Richard b 1977); *Career* architect and town planner; master planner and job architect Devpt Dept of Architecture and Civic Design GLC 1965–71, architect planner for South West Area Traffic and Devpt Branch GLC 1971–72, project architect for New County HQ for Hereford-Worcester (RIBA commendation 1978) Robert Matthew Johnson-Marshall & Partners 1972–76, sr architect concerned with design of various projects overseas and in London John S Bonnington Partnership 1976–80, project architect then ptnr for Standard Chartered Bank's HQ (special award Marble Architectural Awards West Europe 1987), Fitzroy Robinson Ltd 1980–2001 (formerly ptnr then dir Thames Exchange and Scottish Widows London Wall projects and dir i/c of works on the Union Bank of Switzerland in London and Barclaycard HQ Northampton), architect dir Building Design Partnership London Corp Gp 2001–; author of various articles in Architects Jl and RIBA Jl; Plasterers' trophy for fibrous plasterwork 1985, Br Assoc of Landscape Industries principal award for interior landscaping 1986; RIBA 1970 (memb Eastern Regions Competitions Ctee 1979–80), MRTPI 1978; *Books* Neufert: Architectural Data (contrib 1980 edn); *Recreations* music, theatre, travel, photography; *Clubs* Baconian Society (St Albans); *Style—* Robin Booth; ✉ Robin Booth Architect and Planning Consultant, 23 Hill Street, St Albans, Hertfordshire AL3 4QS (tel and fax 01727 856504)

BOOTH-JONES, Christopher Charles; *b* 4 October 1943; *Educ* Dover Coll, RAM (ARAM); *m* 15 April 1995, Leonora Lane, da of late Frank Colin Bagnall; 2 s from previous m (Benedict b 1 Jan 1982, Luke b 20 Sept 1984), 4 step c (Hannah, Emily, Polly, William); *Career* baritone; joined WNO 1971, ENO 1983– (princ baritone for 18 years); worked with: Glyndebourne Festival and Touring Opera, English Music Theatre, Kent Opera, Opera North, Royal Opera House, Monteverdi Choir; worked in many countries and festivals incl: Russia, Hong Kong, USA, Brazil, Italy, Festival Estival Paris; *Roles* with ENO: Papageno in The Magic Flute, Guglielmo in Cosi fan Tutte, Dr Falke in Die Fledermaus, Schaunard in La Bohème, Grosvenor in Patience, Silvio in Pagliacci, Novice's Friend in Billy Budd, Elviro in Xerxes, Music Master in Ariadne, Yeletsky in Queen of Spades, Herald in Lohengrin, Faninal in Rosenkavalier, Demetrius in Midsummer Night's Dream, Count in The Marriage of Figaro, Germont in La Traviata, Sharpless in Madam Butterfly; also Narrator in Caucasian Chalk Circle (Newcastle Festival) and Morales in Carmen (Royal Opera House), Melot in Trisan and Isolde (Royal Opera House), Spirit Messenger in Die Frau ohne Schatten (Royal Opera House); *Concerts* appearances incl: Carmina Burana, Messiah, Bach's Mass in B minor, St John's Passion, St Matthew Passion, Handel's Samson, Faure's Requiem, Brahms' Requiem, Vaughan Williams' Sea Symphony; *Recordings* Julius Caesar and Pacific Overtures, Tosca, Great Things (album of English song); videos of The Gondoliers, Rusalka, Xerxes, Billy Budd, Carmen; *Recreations* mountain and hill walking, gadgets, wines, reading; *Style—* Christopher Booth-Jones, Esq; ✉ c/o Helen Sykes Artists' Management, 100 Felsham Road, London SW5 1DQ (tel 020 8780 0060, fax 020 8780 8772)

BOOTHBY, Sir Brooke Charles; 16 Bt (1660), of Broadlow Ash; s of Sir Hugo Boothby, 15 Bt (d 1986); *b* 6 April 1949; *Educ* Eton, Trinity Coll Cambridge (BA); *m* 1976, Georgiana Alexandra (d 2002), da of Sir John Wriothesley Russell, GCVO, CMG (d 1984), and Lady (Aliki) Russell; 2 da; *Heir* kinsman, George Boothby; *Career* Fontygary Parks Ltd: md 1979–95, vice-chm 1995–2003, chm 2004–; chm: Tourism Quality Services Ltd 1990–, Associated Quality Services Ltd 1994–, TQS (1994) Ltd 1994–2002, TQS (Ireland) Ltd 1995–2002, AQS Ltd 1998–2007; dir: Wales Tourism Alliance Ltd 2001–, Bradford Rural Estates Ltd 2001–; chm: Historic Houses Assoc Inheritance Ctee 1984–86, Nat Caravan Cncl Parks Div 1987–90, Adventure Activities Licensing Authy 1996–, Capital Region Tourism Ltd 2002–03; pres: Glamorgan Branch Country Landowners Assoc 1991–94, Vale of Glamorgan Nat Tst 1998–; govr United World Coll of the Atlantic 2003–06 (dir UWC Ltd, tstee of fndn); High Sheriff S Glamorgan 1986–87; hon consul of Malta for Wales; *Recreations* gardening; *Style—* Sir Brooke Boothby, Bt; ✉ Fonmon Castle, Barry, Vale of Glamorgan CF62 3ZN (tel 01446 710206, fax 01446 711687, e-mail fonmon_castle@msn.com)

BOOTHBY, Richard Charles Brooke; s of George William Bernard Boothby (d 1972), and Avril Alice (d 1993), *née* Innell; *b* 16 December 1955; *Educ* Barry Boys' Comp Sch, Univ of Manchester (MusB, postgrad study with David Fallows), Salzburg Mozarteum (with Nikolaus Harnoncourt); *m* 23 May 1992 (m dis 2001), Fiona Clare, da of Peter Padfield; 1 s (Maximillian Brooke b 31 Jan 1995), 1 da (Megan Miranda b 3 Feb 1998); m 2, 6 April 2005, Giovanna del Parugia; *Career* viola da gamba player and 'cellist; fndr and memb Purcell Quartet 1984–; fndr memb Fretwork 1985–; regularly tours Europe, Japan and US with these ensembles, has also played with other ensembles incl Taverner Players, and as soloist; prof of viola da gamba RCM, prof of viola da gamba and baroque cello WCMD; *Recordings* 6 in La Folia series on Hyperion, 28 with Chandos Records incl discs devoted to Purcell, Biber, Corelli, Lawes, Reclair, Schütz, Vivaldi and Bach (1st solo disc Bach Sonatas for viola da gamba and harpsichord); with Fretwork 14 discs on Virgin Clasics incl music by Byrd, Gibbons, Dowland, Lawes and Purcell; recordings with Fretwork of contemporary music by George Benjamin, Michael Nyman and Elvis Costello; *Style—* Richard Boothby, Esq; ✉ e-mail forqueray1@mac.com

BOOTHMAN, Clive Nicholas; s of Thomas Hague Boothman (d 1996), and Margaret, *née* Knox; *b* 28 May 1955; *Educ* Charterhouse, Trinity Coll Oxford (BA); *m* 28 May 1983, Anne, da of Wace Philo; 2 s (Alexander b 4 July 1986, Harry b 9 July 1988), 1 da (Georgina b 1 Aug 1990); *Career* Arthur Young McClelland Moores Jersey CI 1976–81, accountant Moore Stephens & Butterfield Bermuda 1982–83; Schroder Gp: joined 1983, asst dir J Henry Schroder Wagg & Co Ltd 1986–87 (mangr 1985–86, investment res 1983–85), md Schroder Unit Tsts Ltd 1988–98, md Schroder Private Client Gp 1998–, dir Schroder Investment Mgmnt Ltd 1992–2000; ceo Gerrard Ltd 2000–01, ceo Cofunds Ltd 2002–03; chm Fundsdirect 2005–; chm Assoc of Unit Tsts and Investment Funds until 1997; ACA 1980, AIIMR 1984; *Recreations* sailing, windsurfing, tennis, vintage cars; *Style—* Clive Boothman, Esq; ✉ 331 Riverside Walk, Smugglers Way, London SW18 1ED (tel 020 8871 9048, e-mail cliveboothman@hotmail.com)

BOOTHROYD, Baroness (Life Peer UK 2001), of Sandwell in the County of West Midlands; Betty Boothroyd; OM (2005), PC (1992); da of Archibald Boothroyd (d 1948), of Dewsbury, W Yorks, and Mary Boothroyd (d 1982); *b* 8 October 1929; *Educ* Dewsbury Coll of Commerce and Art; *Career* MP (Lab): West Bromwich 1973–74, West Bromwich West 1974–2000 (Parly candidate (Lab): Leicester SE (by-election) 1957, Peterborough 1959, Nelson and Colne (by-election) 1968, Rossendale 1970); asst Govt whip 1974–76, UK memb European Parl 1975–77, former memb Select Ctee on Foreign Affrs, memb Speaker's Panel of Chairmen 1979–87, Lab Pty Nat Exec Ctee 1981–87, House of Commons Cmmn 1983–87, second dep chm Ways and Means and dep speaker 1987–92; Speaker House of Commons 1992–2000; memb Hammersmith Borough Cncl 1965–68; memb Ct Univ of Birmingham 1982–, chllr Open Univ 1994–2006; The Spectator Parliamentarian of the Year Award 1992; Liveryman Worshipful Co of Feltmakers; Hon Liveryman Worshipful Co of Grocers 2005; Hon LLD: Univ of Birmingham, Leeds Metropolitan Univ, Leicester South Bank Univ, Univ of Cambridge, North London Univ, Univ of Oxford, Univ of St Andrews 2003; Hon FCGI; *Publications* Betty Boothroyd - The Autobiography (2001); *Recreations* reading, walking and gardening; *Style—* The Rt Hon the Baroness Boothroyd, OM, PC; ✉ House of Lords, London SW1A 0PW (tel 020 7219 3000)

BOOTLE, Roger Paul; s of David Bootle, MBE (d 1972), and Florence Ethel, *née* Denman (d 1982); *b* 22 June 1952; *Educ* Downer GS, Merton Coll Oxford (BA), Nuffield Coll Oxford (MPhil); *Career* lectr in economics St Anne's Coll Oxford 1976–78, with Citibank 1978–79, dep head economic policy CBI 1979–81; chief economist: Capel Cure Myers 1982–86, Lloyds Merchant Bank 1986–87 (dir 1986–87); conslt 1987–89; chief economist and dir of research HSBC Greenwell (formerly Greenwell Montagu Gilt Edged) 1989–96, gp chief economist HSBC Holdings plc 1996–98; md Capital Economics Ltd 1999–; specialist advsr House of Commons Treasy Select Ctee 1997–; econ advsr Deloitte & Touche 1999–; visiting prof Manchester Business Sch 1995–; memb HM Treasy ind panel of economic forecasting advsrs 1996–97; columnist Sunday Telegraph 2000–06, columnist Daily Telegraph 2006–; contrib: Financial Times, Times, numerous pubns; various TV and radio appearances as commentator on economic affairs; *Books* Theory of Money (jtly, 1978), Index-Linked Gilts (1986, 2 edn 1991), The Death of Inflation (1996), Money for Nothing: Real Wealth, Financial Fantasies and the Economy of the Future (2003); *Recreations* bridge, squash, horseracing, classical music, theatre; *Style—* Roger Bootle, Esq; ✉ Capital Economics, 150 Buckingham Palace Road, London SW1W 9TR (tel 020 7823 5000, fax 020 7823 6666, e-mail roger.bootle@capitaleconomics.com)

BOOTON, Dr Paul; s of Arthur Terence Booton, and Jean Brunhilde Mary, *née* Price; *b* 11 May 1955; *Educ* Hornchurch GS, The London Hosp Med Coll (BSc, MB BS); *Children* 1 da (Caitlin Margaret b 1998), 1 s (Keir Thomas b 2000); *Career* physician to Prof J M Ledingham London Hosp 1980, MO to Kaitak and Sham Shui Po refugee camps UN High Cmmn on Refugees 1981, SHO and registrar med Oldchurch Hosp Romford 1982–86, lectr gen practice UMDS 1988–90; King's Coll Sch of Med and Dentistry: lectr Dept of Gen Practice 1990–94, curriculum sub-dean 1991–94, sr lectr in med educn 1994–2004, undergrad sub-dean 1994–98, head of Dept of Med & Dental Educn and asst clinical dean 1998–2002; currently dir of undergrad educn in primary care Imperial Coll London; memb Lab Pty; MRCP 1984, MRCGP 1988; *Recreations* walking, skiing, cycling, theatre, music; *Style—* Dr Paul Booton; ✉ Primary Care and Social Medicine, Reynolds Building, Charing Cross Campus, Imperial College, London W6 8RP (tel 020 7594 3352, fax 020 7594 0854, e-mail p.booton@imperial.ac.uk)

BORDEN, Prof Iain Michael; s of Anthony Ian Borden, of Oxford, and Shelagh Mary, *née* Birks; *b* 9 November 1962; *Educ* Univ of Newcastle upon Tyne (BA), UCL (MSc), UCLA (MA), Univ of London (PhD); *m* Claire, *née* Haywood; 1 s (Samuel Anthony Alan b 11 Aug 2006); *Career* UCL: sub-dean Faculty of the Built Environment 1996–99, dir architectural history and theory 1999–, reader in architecture and urban culture 1999–2002, head Bartlett Sch of Architecture 2001–, prof of architecture and urban culture 2002–; Freeman City of Oxford; Hon FRIBA; *Books* Architecture & the Sites of

History (co-ed, 1995), Strangely Familiar (co-ed, 1996), City Culture Reader (co-ed, 2000), Gender Space Architecture (co-ed, 2000), The Dissertation (co-author, 2000), Intersections (co-ed, 2000), Skateboarding, Space and the City (2001), The Unknown City (co-ed, 2001), Manual: The Architecture and Office of Allford Hall Monaghan Morris (2003), Bartlett Works (co-ed, 2004), Transculturation (co-ed, 2005); *Style*— Prof Iain Borden; ✉ Bartlett School of Architecture, University College London, 22 Gordon Street, London WC1H 0QB (tel 020 7679 4821, fax 020 7380 4831, e-mail i.borden@ucl.ac.uk)

BORDISS, Andrew Raymond; s of Raymond George Bordiss, of Brockworth, Glos, and Joyce, *née* Edwards; *b* 12 February 1957; *Educ* Brockworth Sch; *m* 17 Sept 1983, Deborah Anne, da of Robert Ellis; 2 s (Samuel Andrew b 1984, John George b 1988), 1 da (Isabelle Megan b 1990); *Career* journalist; night ed Today 1986–89, ed Auto Express 1989–93, assoc night ed Daily Telegraph 1993–98, dep ed Evening Standard 1998–; memb Cncl IAM 1992–2001; *Recreations* golf, cycling, rugby; *Clubs* Press Golfing Soc, Surrey RFC, Rosslyn Park RFC; *Style*— Andrew Bordiss, Esq; ✉ Evening Standard, 2 Derry Street, London W8 5EE

BOREEL, Jonkheer Sir Stephan Gerard; 14 Bt (E 1645), of Amsterdam, Holland; s of Jonkheer Gerard Lucas Boreel (d 1970), and Virginia Rae, *née* Bright (d 1972); succ kinsman, Jonkheer Sir Francis David Boreel, 13 Bt (d 2001); *b* 9 February 1945; *m* Francien P Kooijman; 1 s (Jacob Lucas Cornelis b 29 Sept 1974); *Style*— Jonkheer Sir Stephan Boreel, Bt; ✉ Elzenoord 30, 8172 AZ, Vaassen, Holland (tel 0578 57 25 64, e-mail s.boreel@xsyall.nl)

BORENIOK, Heinrich Robert; s of Hans Peter Boreniok (d 1984), and Helga Margarete, *née* Rupp; *b* 6 July 1957; *Educ* Ratskeller Frauenaurach; *m* 7 May 1988, Dorothy Patricia, da of Frederick Scroggie; *Career* Nat Serv German Air Force 1976–78; German diplommaster chef (Kuechen meister); first commis chef Great Western Royal Hotel 1978–79, chef de partie saucier Steigenberger Kurhaus Hotel Bad Kissingen summer 1979, chef de partie saucier La Riva Lenzerheide winter 1979, jr sous chef Dunloe Castle summer 1980 (joined as chef gardemanger), sous chef Hotel Forsthaus Furth 1980–83, sous chef rising to premier sous chef The Savoy London 1983–86, maitre chef de cuisine A l'ecu de France London 1986–89, chef de cuisine Staple Ford Park 1989, exec chef Berkshire Hotel London 1990, exec chef de cuisine Edwardian Int until 1992, exec chef de cuisine Naval and Military Club 1992–; memb: Assoc Culinaire Française UK 1983, Acad Culinaire de France GB 1994, Scotch Beef Club 1995, Acad of Culinary Arts 1998, Conseil Culinaire Français de Grand Bretagne 1999; Palmes Culinaire 1999, Maitrise Escoffier 2004; Ordre International des Disciples d'Auguste Escoffier 1998; *Books* Readers Digest Cooks Scrapbook (contrib, 1995); *Recreations* cooking, reading, music, the outdoors, travelling, spectating and following equestrian and motor racing sports; *Style*— Heinrich Boreniok, Esq; ✉ Naval and Military Club, In and Out Ltd, 4 St James's Square, London SW1Y 4JU (tel 020 7827 5757 ext 268, fax 020 7827 5758)

BORG, Dr Alan Charles Nelson; CBE (1991); s of Charles John Nelson Borg (d 1986), and Frances Mary Olive, *née* Hughes (d 1985); *b* 21 January 1942; *Educ* Westminster, BNC Oxford (MA, Fencing blue), Courtauld Inst of Art London (MA, PhD); *m* 1, 1964; 1 s (Giles b 1965), 1 da (Emma b 1970); *m* 2, 1976, Lady Caroline Sylvia Hill (raised to the rank of a Marquess's da 1992), da of Lord Francis Hill and sis of late 8 Marquess of Downshire; 2 da (Leonora b 1980, Helen b 1982); *Career* lectr in English Univ d'Aix-Marseille 1964–65, lectr in history of art Univ of Indiana 1967–69, asst prof of history of art Princeton Univ 1969–70, asst keeper Royal Armouries HM Tower of London 1970–78, keeper Sainsbury Centre for Visual Arts UEA 1978–82, DG Imperial War Museum 1982–95, dir V&A 1995–2001, librarian St John's Gate 2007– (dep librarian 2004–07); chm Conf of Dirs of Nat Museums and Galleries 1998–2001; pres: Meyrick Soc 1994–, Elizabethan Club 1995–2000; govr: Coram Family 1995–2006, Westminster Sch 1998–; tstee: The Foundling Museum 1998– (chm 2006–), St Paul's Cathedral Fndn 2001–06, Handel House Museum 2002–; memb Bd of Dirs Musée du Louvre 1999–2001; Freeman City of London 1997, Liveryman Worshipful Co of Painter-Stainers 1997; Hon Dr Sheffield Hallam Univ 2000; Hon FRCA 1991, Hon FRIBA 2001, FSA; *Books* Architectural Sculpture in Romanesque Provence (1972), European Swords and Daggers in the Tower of London (1974), Torture and Punishment (1975), Heads and Horses (1976), Arms and Armour in Britain (1979), War Memorials (1991), The History of the Painters' Company (2005); *Recreations* music, travel; *Clubs* Special Forces, Beefsteak; *Style*— Dr A C N Borg, CBE, FSA; ✉ Telegraph House, 36 West Square, London SE11 4SP (tel 020 7582 8122)

BÖRJESSON, Rolf Libert; s of Stig Allan Börjesson (d 1992), and Brita Ahlström (d 2004); *b* 29 September 1942, Helsingborg, Sweden; *Educ* Chalmers Univ of Technol Gothenburg (MSc); *m* 1969, Kristina; 2 da (Jenny b 10 May 1973, Katya b 13 May 1976); *Career* PLM AB: exec vice-pres 1987–88, chief operating offr 1988–90, pres and ceo 1990–96; Rexam plc: chief exec 1996–2004, chm 2004–; memb Bd: Copenhagen Airports 2002–, SCA Sweden 2003–; *Recreations* horse riding, shooting; *Style*— Rolf Börjesson, Esq; ✉ Rexam plc, 4 Millbank, London SW1P 3XR (tel 020 7227 4100)

BORMAN, Dr Edwin Miles; s of David Bevil Borman (b 1936), and Sophia, *née* Miller; *b* 9 September 1961; *Educ* Theodor Herzl HS Port Elizabeth, Univ of Cape Town Med Sch (MB ChB); *Career* house offr Groote Schuur Hosp Cape Town 1985; Plymouth HA 1986–91 (SHO posts in surgical and med specialities 1986–90), S Birmingham HA 1991–94 (registrar posts in anaesthetics and intensive care, sr registrar posts in anaesthetics and intensive care Coventry and Birmingham rotation 1995–97, conslt anaesthetist Walsgrave Hosp Coventry 1997–, chm LNC Walsgrave Hosp 1998–; BMA: chm Jr Doctors Ctee 1991–94, memb Cncl 1991–, memb Jt Conslts Ctee 1991–94 and 1999–, chm Int Ctee 1999–; GMC: memb Cncl 1994–, chm Ctee for Diversity and Equality 2003–, chm Working Gp on Consent 2006–; memb: Ministerial Gps on 'Achieving a Balance' and 'The New Deal' 1991–94, CMO's Working Gps on Specialist Med Trg 1992–93 and on Overseas Doctors in the UK 1994, Perm Working Gp of Euro Jr Hosp Doctors 1993–96, Euro Bd of Anaesthesiology and Reanimation 1995–97, Dept of Health Steering Gp on Refugee Health Professionals 2001–06, Dept of Health Steering Gp Working Time Directive 2001–03; European Union of Med Specialists (UEMS): UK memb 1998–, vice-pres 2006–, chm Working Gp on Continuing Professional Devpt 2000–; dep chm Central Conslts and Specialists Ctee 2002–04, ldr UK delgn Comité Permanent des Médicins Européens 2001–; memb Bd Global Alliance for Medical Educn 2004–; invited lectr Canada, USA, India and Europe; memb BMA 1986, FFARCSI 1993, FRCA 1994; *Recreations* classical music, Eastern art; *Style*— Dr Edwin Borman; ✉ 30 Clover Drive, Bartley Green, Birmingham B32 3DJ (tel 0121 426 5760); Anaesthetic Department, University Hospitals, Coventry CV2 2DX (tel 024 7696 5893, e-mail edwin@borman.demon.co.uk)

BORN, Gary Brian; s of Clyde R Born, of Camden, SC, and Eleanor Born; *b* 14 September 1955, NY; *Educ* Haverford Coll (BA), Univ of Pennsylvania (JD); *m* 1988, Beatrix von Wedel-Goedens; 1 da (Natascha b 1988), 1 s (Henrik b 1990); *Career* memb DC Bar 1984; law clerk to Henry J Friendly (circuit judge Second Circuit Court of Appeal) 1981–82, law clerk to William H Rehnquist (assoc justice US Supreme Court) 1982–83, assoc Wilmer Cutler & Pickering 1984–88, ptnr Wilmer Cutler & Pickering Washington DC 1988–91, sr ptnr Wilmer Cutler Pickering Hale and Dorr LLP London 1991–; adjunct prof of law: Univ of Arizona Coll of Law 1987–90, Georgetown Law Sch 1987–91, Pepperdine Univ Law Sch London 1994–98; visiting lectr UCL 1991–94; memb: Exec Cncl American Soc of Int Law 1991–94, Bd Inst for US Studies 1996–; memb American Law Inst 1999–; *Books* The Extraterritorial Application of National Laws (co-author, 1987), International Civil Litigation in United States Courts (3 edn 1996, 4 edn 2007), International Arbitration and Forum Selection Agreements: Drafting and Enforcing (1999, 2 edn 2006), International Commercial Arbitration: Commentary and Materials (2 edn, 2000); *Recreations* scuba diving, hiking; *Clubs* Athenaeum; *Style*— Gary Born, Esq; ✉ Wilmer Cutler Pickering Hale and Dorr LLP, 4 Carlton Gardens, London SW1Y 5AA (tel 020 7872 1000, fax 020 7389 3537, e-mail gary.born@wilmerhale.com)

BORN, Prof Gustav Victor Rudolf; *b* 29 July 1921; *Educ* Univ of Edinburgh (MB ChB), Univ of Oxford (DPhil, MA); *m* 1, 1950 (m dis 1961), Wilfrida Ann Plowden-Wardlaw; 2 s, 1 da; *m* 2, 1962, Dr Faith Elizabeth Maurice-Williams; 1 s, 1 da; *Career* Vandervell prof of pharmacology RCS and Univ of London 1960–73, Sheild prof of pharmacology Univ of Cambridge and fell Gonville & Caius Coll Cambridge 1973–78, prof of pharmacology KCL 1978–86, currently prof William Harvey Research Inst Bart's Med Coll and emeritus prof of pharmacology Univ of London; prof Fondation de France Paris 1982–84, visiting prof Univ of Tübingen 1963, visiting prof in chemistry Northwestern Univ IL, formerly William Creasy visiting prof in clinical pharmacology Brown Univ RI; hon dir Thrombosis Research Gp MRC 1964–73; scientific advsr Vandervell Fndn 1968–2000, currently advsr Heineman Med Research Center Charlotte NC; chm: Scientific Advsy Bd Chemie Grünenthal 1981–96, Advsy Bd Biorex Co Budapest 1992–2002; conslt: Reckitt and Colman plc 1962–88, ICI 1965–70, Thomae-Boehringer Ingelheim 1965–90, Merck, Sharp and Dohme 1970–80 (memb Bd of Advsrs 1975–80), Miles Labs Inc 1980–90, Bayer AG 1980–2000, Bayer UK Ltd 1987–2000; memb Editorial Bd: Pharmacological Reviews, Heffter's Handbook of Experimental Pharmacology, Clinical Hemorheology and Microcirculation; author of over 300 articles in learned jls; former examiner in pharmacology: Univ of Edinburgh, Univ of Cambridge, Univ of Oxford; former memb: Cmmn on Review of Med DHSS, Scientific Advsy Gp Forensic Science Serv Home Office, Med Cmmn Fritz Thyssen Fndn, Cncl on Thrombosis American Heart Assoc, Sainsbury Ctee (Official Ctee of Enquiry into the Relationship of the Pharmaceutical Industry with the NHS), Working Pty on Antihaemophilic Globulin MRC, Scientific Ctee Nuffield Inst of Comparative Med Zoological Soc of London, Scientific Cncl Fondation Cardiologique Princesse Liliane Belgium, Research Grants Ctee Br Heart Fndn, Int Ctee on Thrombosis and Haemostasis; pres Int Soc on Thrombosis and Haemostasis 1979–81 (sometime memb Cncl, hon life memb 2000–), fndn pres Br Soc for Thrombosis and Haemostasis 1980–81, currently patron Alzheimer Research Tst; memb: Akademie Leopoldina 1971, Rheinisch-Westfälische Akademie Düsseldorf 1982, German Pharmacological Soc 1992; corresponding memb: Belgian Royal Acad of Med 1982, Société de Biologie 1993; hon life memb NY Acad of Sciences 1981; hon memb: Soc for Advances in Internal Med (Heilmeyer Soc) 1994, European Thrombosis Research Orgn 1996, Br Atherosclerosis Soc 2001, Club of Rome; former memb: Jung Prize Kuratorium, Shakespeare Prize Kuratorium, German Lipid League Kuratorium; Albrecht von Haller Medal Univ of Göttingen 1979, Ratschow Meml Medal Int Angiology Curatorium 1980, Paul Morawitz Prize 1980, Auenbrugger Medal Univ of Graz 1984, Royal Medal Royal Soc 1987, Robert Pfleger Prize 1990, Alexander von Humboldt Award 1994, Int Aspirin Sr Award 1995, Distinguished Career Award Int Soc on Thrombosis and Haemostasis 1997, Fahraeus Medal 2000, Gold Medal for Med Ernst Jung Fndn 2001; Hon DSc: Univ of Bordeaux 1979, Univ of Paris 1987, Loyola Univ Chicago 1995; Hon MD: Univ of Münster 1980, Univ of Leuven 1981, Univ of Edinburgh 1982, Brown Univ RI 1987, Univ of München 1989, Univ of Düsseldorf 2001, Univ of London 2006; hon fell St Peter's Coll Oxford 1979, FKC 1988; FRS 1972, FRCP 1979, Hon FRCS 2002; Chevalier de l'Ordre National du Mérite (France) 1979; *Style*— Prof Gustav Born; ✉ The William Harvey Research Institute, St Bartholomew's and the Royal London School of Medicine and Dentistry, Charterhouse Square, London EC1M 6BQ (tel 020 7882 6070, fax 020 7882 6071)

BORRETT, Neil Edgar; s of Edgar Edward Borrett (d 1975), and Winifred, *née* Mowbray (d 1992); *b* 10 March 1940; *Educ* Dartford GS, Woolwich Poly, Coll of Estate Mgmnt; *m* 1965, Jane, da of Francis Wallace Chapman; 2 da (Deanna Jane b 31 July 1966, Joanne Emma b 23 July 1971); *Career* various positions in Reconstruction and Purchasing Depts NCB 1958–62, dir Alliance Property Co Ltd (later Argyle Securities) 1963–77, md Morgan Grenfell Property Servs 1977–87, ptnr Vigers 1987–90, dir of Property Holdings DOE 1990–96, chief exec Property Advisors to the Civil Estate (PACE) 1996–97, chm Matek Business Media 1997–2004, head Crown Estate's commercial property portfolio 1997–2000, dir London and Regional Properties 2000–02; ind memb Property Project Bd Home Office 2002–05; chm Forentech 2004–; govr: South Bank Univ 1996–2004, Hillcroft Coll 2005–; FRICS 1968; *Recreations* golf, boating, photography; *Clubs* Bramley Golf; *Style*— Neil Borrett, Esq; ✉ e-mail borrett@tesco.net

BORRIE, Baron (Life Peer UK 1995), of Abbots Morton in the County of Hereford and Worcester; Sir Gordon Johnson Borrie; kt (1982), QC (1986); s of Stanley Borrie, of Croydon, Surrey; *b* 13 March 1931; *Educ* John Bright GS Llandudno, Univ of Manchester (LLB, LLM); *m* 1960, Dorene, da of Herbert Toland, of Toronto; *Career* Nat Serv Army Legal Servs, HQ Br Cwlth Forces Korea 1952–54; called to the Bar Middle Temple 1952, bencher 1980, in practice 1954–57, lectr then sr lectr Coll of Law 1957–64; Univ of Birmingham: sr lectr 1965–68, prof of Eng law and dir Inst of Judicial Admin 1969–76, dean Law Faculty 1974–76; DG Office of Fair Trading 1976–92, chm Commission on Social Justice 1992–94, pres Inst of Trading Standards Admin 1992–97, chm Direct Mktg Authy 1997–2000; dir: Woolwich Building Society (now Woolwich plc) 1992–2000, Three Valleys Water Services plc 1992–2003, Mirror Group Newspapers plc 1993–99, Telewest plc 1994–2001, General Utilities plc 1998–2003; chm: Accountancy Fndn 2000–03, Advtg Standards Authy 2001–07, Cncl Ombudsman for Estate Agents 2007–; govr Birmingham Coll of Commerce 1966–70; former memb Law Cmmn Advsy Panel for Contract Law; memb: Parole Bd 1971–74, Cncl Consumers' Assoc 1972–75, Equal Opportunities Cmmn 1975–76; contested: (Lab) Croydon NE 1955, Ilford South 1959; Hon LLD: City of London Poly (now City of London Univ) 1989, Univ of Manchester 1990, Univ of Hull 1991, Univ of Dundee 1993, UWE 1997, Univ of Nottingham 2005; hon dr Nottingham Trent Univ 1996; hon memb SPTL 1989, FRSA 1982; *Books* Commercial Law (1962, 6 edn 1988), The Development of Consumer Law and Policy (1984), others in joint authorship; *Recreations* gastronomy, piano playing, travel; *Clubs* Reform, Garrick, Pratt's; *Style*— The Rt Hon Lord Borrie, QC; ✉ Manor Farm, Abbots Morton, Worcestershire (tel 01386 792330); 4 Brick Court, Temple, London EC4 (tel 020 7353 4434, fax 020 7583 6148)

BORROW, David Stanley; MP; s of James Borrow, and Nancy, *née* Crawshaw; *b* 2 August 1952; *Educ* Mirfield GS, Coventry Univ (BA); *Career* grad trainee Yorkshire Bank 1973–75, Valuation Tbnl Service 1975–97 (clerk to Merseyside Valuation Tbnl 1983–97); MP (Lab) S Ribble 1997–; PPS: to Tport Min 2003–, to Higher Educn Min 2004–05; chair Back Bench Ctee on: Trade & Industry, Defence, Agric; vice-chair All-Pty Gp on: Aids and HIV, Penal Affrs; sec PLP Regnl Govt Gp; cncllr Preston BC 1987 (leader 1992–94 and 1995–97); memb: Inst of Rating, Revenues & Valuation, Soc of Clerks of Valuation Tbnls (pres 1990–92 and 1996–97), All-Pty Aerospace Gp 1999– (chair 1999–), Agric Select Ctee 1999; memb Labour Campaign for Electoral Reform; *Style*— David Borrow, Esq, MP; ✉ House of Commons, London SW1A 0AA (tel and fax 020 7219 4126); constituency (tel 01772 454727, fax 01772 422982)

BORROWS, Simon Alexander; s of Kenneth Ambrose Borrows (d 2004), and Ailsa Nancy, *née* McLeod; *b* 24 January 1959, Taplow, Bucks; *Educ* Rossall Sch, Univ of London (LLB), London Business Sch (MBA); *m* 31 Oct 1987, Sally Ann, *née* Weston; 2 da (Polly Louise b 2 Jan 1990, Maisie Ellen b 13 March 1992), 1 s (George Henry b 1 Oct 1993); *Career* dir Baring Bros & Co Ltd 1988–98 (head of M&A 1995–98), ptnr Greenhill & Co 1998–

(founding ptnr London office), co-pres Greenhill & Co Inc 2004–; memb Advsy Bd London Business Sch 2000–03; *Recreations* family, golf, skiing, shooting, theatre; *Clubs* Hankley Common Golf, Queenwood Golf, Rye Golf; *Style*— Simon Borrows, Esq; ✉ Greenhill & Co, Lansdowne House, 57 Berkeley Square, London W1J 6ER (tel 020 7198 7400, fax 020 7198 7500, e-mail sborrows@greenhill.com)

BORTHWICK, Sir Antony Thomas; 4 Bt (UK 1908), of Whitburgh, Co Haddington; s of Sir John Thomas Borthwick, 3 Bt, MBE (d 2002); *b* 12 February 1941; *Educ* Eton; *m* 1, 1966 (m dis), Gillian Deirdre Broke, twin da of late Nigel Vere Broke Thurston, RN; 1 s (Matthew Thomas Thurston b 1968), 2 da (Suzanna Claire Irene b 1970, Camilla Fay Broke b 1973); m 2, 2002, Martha Wheeler Donner, of Dyersburg TN; *Heir* s, Matthew Borthwick; *Style*— Sir Antony Borthwick, Bt

BORTHWICK, 24 Lord (S 1450); John Hugh Borthwick of that Ilk; DL; Baron (territorial) of Heriotmuir; er (twin) s of 23 Lord Borthwick, TD, JP, DL (d 1996), and Margaret, *née* Cormack (d 1976); *b* 14 November 1940; *Educ* Gordonstoun, Edinburgh Sch of Agric (SDA, NDA); *m* 1974, Adelaide, o da of Archy Birkmyre, of Comrie, Perthshire; 2 da (Hon Georgina b 18 Dec 1975, Hon Alexandra b 25 Aug 1977); *Heir* twin bro, Hon James Borthwick of Glengelt; *Career* landowner and former farmer; *Recreations* trout fishing, stalking; *Clubs* New (Edinburgh); *Style*— The Rt Hon the Lord Borthwick, DL; ✉ Crookston, Heriot, Midlothian EH38 5YS (tel 01875 835236)

BORTHWICK, Stephen Robert; s of Sidney Borthwick, and Edna, *née* Robinson (d 1997); *b* 23 September 1951; *Educ* Strode's GS Egham Surrey, UNCW Bangor (open scholar, BSc), CCC Cambridge (PGCE); *m* 1974, Glynis Hannah, da of J A Francis (d 1987); *Career* asst master: Bloxham Sch 1974–80, Rugby Sch 1980–84; head Depts of Physics and Technology Marlborough Coll 1984–89, dep headmaster and dir of studies Bishop's Stortford Coll 1989–94, headmaster Aldenham Sch 1994–2000, headmaster Epsom Coll 2000–; memb: Secdy Heads Assoc 1989–, HMC 1994–; Freeman City of London 2000; MInstP 1974, CPhys 1977, FRSA 1997; *Books* Revised Nuffield A Level Physics Course (co-author, 4 vols 1980); *Recreations* photography (landscape, portrait), collector of gramophone music, golf; *Clubs* East India; *Style*— Stephen Borthwick, Esq; ✉ The Headmaster's House, Epsom College, Epsom, Surrey KT17 4JQ (tel 01372 821242, fax 01372 821292, e-mail headmaster@epsomcollege.org.uk)

BORWICK, 5 Baron (UK 1922); Sir Geoffrey Robert James (Jamie) Borwick; 5 Bt (UK 1916); s of Hon Robin Sandbach Borwick (d 2003), of Wells, Somerset, and Hon Patricia Borwick, *née* McAlpine; suc half-unc 4 Baron Borwick (d 2007); *b* 7 March 1955; *Educ* Eton; *m* 1981, Victoria Lorne Peta, da of R Dennis Poore (d 1987), of London; 3 s (Edwin b 1984, Thomas b 1987, William b 1997), 1 da (Alexandra b 1990); *Heir* s, Edwin Borwick; *Career* chm: Federated Trust Corporation Ltd 1981–, London Taxis International Ltd 1984–2003, Hansa Trust plc 1985–, Manganese Bronze Holdings plc 2001–03 (chief exec 1984–2001), Modec Ltd 2004–; md Love Lane Investments Ltd 1984–; memb FSA Listing Authy Advsy Ctee 1997–2003; *Recreations* travel; *Clubs* Garrick, Bohemian (San Francisco); *Style*— The Lord Borwick

BOSANQUET, Prof Nicholas Francis Gustavus; s of Lt-Col Neville Richard Gustavus Bosanquet (d 2003), of Wilts, and Nancy Bosanquet, *née* Mason (d 2003); *b* 17 January 1942; *Educ* Winchester, Clare Coll Cambridge, Yale Univ, LSE; *m* 31 Aug 1974 (m dis 1993), Anne Connolly; 2 da (Kate b 1978, Helen b 1981); m 2, 9 Nov 1996, Anna Zarzecka; *Career* sr res fell Centre for Health Econ Univ of York, lectr in economics LSE and City Univ, prof of health policy Royal Holloway and Bedford New Coll London 1988–93, prof of health policy Imperial Coll London 1993–; special advsr to Health Ctee House of Commons; econ advsr: Nat Bd for Prices and Incomes, Royal Cmmn on Distribution of Income and Wealth; conslt: World Bank, OECD, health authorities and cos in Britain; arbitrator ACAS; dir: Reform, TBS GB; contrib to Economic Jl, BMJ; *Books* Industrial Relations in the NHS: The Search for a System (1980), After the New Right (1983), Family Doctors and Economic Incentives (1989), The Economics of Cancer Care (2006); *Recreations* collecting books on WWI; *Style*— Prof Nick F G Bosanquet; ✉ Department of Bioengineering, Imperial College, Bagrit Centre, Exhibition Road, London SW7 2AZ (tel 020 7594 3355, fax 020 7584 4297)

BOSCAWEN, Hon Evelyn Arthur Hugh; s and h of 9 Viscount Falmouth; *b* 13 May 1955; *Educ* Eton, RAC Cirencester, Harvard Business Sch; *m* 1977 (m dis 1995), Lucia Caroline, da of Ralph Vivian-Neal, of Poundisford Park, Somerset; 1 s ((Evelyn George) William b 1979), 1 da (Laura Frances b 1982); m 2, 1995, Katharine Helen, eldest da of Mark Maley, of Nayland, Suffolk; 2 s (Frederick Mark b 1996, Archard Hugh b 1998), 1 da (Cecilia Rose b 2001); *Career* dep chm Goonvean 1979–; dir: F H Wrigley, Cornish Grain; chm Kent branch CLA 1996–98; Liveryman Worshipful Co of Clockmakers; High Sheriff Cornwall 2007–08; *Style*— The Hon Evelyn Boscawen; ✉ c/o Tregothnan Estate Office, Truro, Cornwall

BOSE, Mihir; s of Kiran Chandra Bose, and Sova Rani Bose; *m* 1, 1986 (m dis 1999), Kalpana; 1 da (Indira); m 2, 2002, Caroline Alison Gascoyne-Cecil; *Career* journalist; corr LBC 1974–75, foreign corr Sunday Times 1975–78, reporter Accountancy 1978–80, ed Property Guide 1980–81, ed Pensions 1981–83, city ed and dep ed Financial Weekly 1983–86, city features ed London Daily News 1987, sports news reporter Sunday Times 1987–95, sports columnist Daily Telegraph 1995–2006, sports ed BBC News 2007–; Business Columnist of the Year 1990, Sports Story of the Year 1997, Sports News Reporter of the Year 1999, jt winner (with Daily Telegraph) Team Award Sports Journalists' Assoc Sports Writer and Photographer Awards; FCA 1974; *Books* cricket titles: Keith Miller: A Cricketing Biography, All in a Day: Great Moments in Cup Cricket, A Maiden View: The Magic of Indian Cricket, Cricket Voices, A History of Indian Cricket (Cricket Soc Literary Award 1990); football titles: Behind Closed Doors: Dreams and Nightmares at Spurs, Manchester Unlimited, The Rise and Rise of Manchester United; general sporting titles: Sporting Colours: Sport and Politics in South Africa (runner-up William Hill Sports Book of the Year 1994), Sporting Babylon; history and biography titles: The Lost Hero: A Biography of Subhas Bose, The Aga Khans, Michael Grade: Screening the Image, Memons, False Messiah: The Life and Times of Terry Venables, Raj, Spies, Rebellion, Bollywood: A History; business titles: The Crash: The 1987–88 World Market Slump, A New Money Crisis: A Children's Guide to Money, Are You Covered? An Insurance Guide, Fraud - The Growth Industry of the 1980s, How to Invest in a Bear Market; autobiography: The Sporting Alien; *Recreations* organising my own cricket team, cinema, walking, travel; *Clubs* Reform, MCC; *Style*— Mihir Bose, Esq; ✉ 30 Poplar Grove, London W6 7RE (tel 020 7371 3976, fax 020 7610 4111, e-mail mbose@mbose.demon.co.uk)

BOSEL, Charles Henry; s of Douglas Henry Bosel (d 1985), of Brisbane, Aust, and Edith May, *née* Bouel (d 1987); *b* 4 July 1937; *Educ* Univ of Queensland (BArch), Univ of Liverpool (Master of Civic Design), Academica Britannica Rome (Rome Scholar in Architecture); *m* 6 Feb 1960, Betty Eunice, da of Cyril Allan Asplin (d 1977), of Tully, Aust; 2 s (Michael Charles b 1964, Stuart Allan b 1966), 2 da (Juliet Ann b 1971, Nicole Betty b 1975); *Career* architect and town planner; chm: St George's Hill Ltd 1981–2002, SSC Overseas Ltd 1986–2002, Ecinue Holdings Ltd 1987–2003, Claverton House (Bridgwater) Ltd 1993–2003, Avalon Homes (Minehead) Ltd 1993–2003, Claverton House (Axbridge) Ltd 1995; dir Al Marzouk and Abi Hanna 1980–2003; pres Cor-Dor Group Holdings NV 1986–2003; memb: Royal Town Planning Inst, RIBA, Royal Aust Inst Architects, Royal Aust Planning Inst, Soc of Rome Scholars, Kuwait Soc of Engrs; *Recreations* tennis, squash; *Style*— Charles Bosel, Esq; ✉ 116 Meridian Place, London E14 9FE (tel 020 7515 3553, fax 020 7537 7779, e-mail charles.bosel@btinternet.com)

BOSSOM, Bruce Charles; s and h of Hon Sir Clive Bossom, 2 Bt, *qv*, and Lady Barbara, *née* North, of London; *b* 22 August 1952; *Educ* Eton, Coll of Estate Mgmnt, Harvard Business Sch (PMD); *m* 1985, Penelope Jane, da of Edward Holland-Martin (d 1981), of Overbury Court, Glos; 2 da (Rosanna Emily b 1986, Amanda Lucy b 1988), 1 s (George Edward Martin b 1992); *Career* Jones Lang Wootton 1972–86 (ptnr 1981); dir: Phoenix Properties & Finance plc 1986–89, Mountleigh Group plc 1989–93, LaSalle Partners 1993–99; fndr Orion Capital Managers; Liveryman Worshipful Co of Grocers; FRICS, FRSA; *Clubs* White's; *Style*— Bruce Bossom, Esq; ✉ Overbury Court, Tewkesbury, Gloucestershire GL20 7NP (tel 01386 725312, fax 01386 725528); 34 Princedale Road, London W11 4NJ (tel 020 7727 5127, fax 020 7243 4163); Orion Capital Managers, 2 Cavendish Square, London W1G 0PD (tel 020 7612 9360, fax 020 7612 9398, e-mail bbossom@orioncapman.com)

BOSSOM, Hon Sir Clive; 2 Bt (UK 1953), of Maidstone, Kent; s of Baron Bossom (Life Peer and 1 Bt), by his 1 w Emily, *née* Bayne (d 1932); Sir Clive suc to Btcy 1965; *b* 4 February 1918; *Educ* Eton; *m* 1951, Lady Barbara Joan, da of late Lord North and sis of 9 Earl of Guilford (d 1999); 3 s (Bruce Charles b 1952, Andrew Clive b 1954, James Edward b 1962), 1 da (Arabella Emily b 1968); *Heir* s, Bruce Bossom, *qv*; *Career* Maj Europe and Far East (regular soldier The Buffs 1939–48); cncllr Kent CC 1949–51; MP (Cons) Leominster 1959–74; PPS to: Jt Parly Secs of Mins of Pensions 1960, Sec of State for Air 1962–64, Home Sec 1970–72; chm Europ Assistance Ltd 1972–88, past chm Anglo-Eastern Bank, dir Northern Star Insurance Co, dir Vosper Ltd 1973–83; chm Br Motor Sports Cncl 1975–82, vice-chm Br Road Fedn 1975–82, int pres Int Social Service for Refugees (ISS) 1984–89; pres: IFPA 1969–81, Anglo-Netherlands Soc 1978–89, Anglo-Belgian Soc 1983–85; vice-pres: (d'honneur) FIA, Iran Soc (past pres); chm Ex-Servs War Disabled Help Ctee 1973–88, vice-chm Jt Ctee Red Cross and St John 1987–92; master Worshipful Co of Grocers 1979–80; FRSA, FRGS; KStJ 1961, Almoner OStJ 1987–93; Cdr of Leopold II (Belgium), Cdr Order of Crown (Belgium), Knight Cdr Order of Orange Nassau (Netherlands), Order of Homayoun (Iran); *Recreations* travel; *Clubs* Carlton, RAC (chm 1975–78), BARC (pres 1984–90), Ends of the Earth (pres); *Style*— The Hon Sir Clive Bossom, Bt; ✉ 97 Cadogan Lane, London SW1X 9DU (tel and fax 020 7245 6531); Rotherdown, Petworth, West Sussex GU28 0BT (tel and fax 01798 342329)

BOSTELMANN, Michael John; s of Martin Horst Bostelmann; *b* 16 November 1947; *Educ* Bradfield; *m* 1973, Gillian, da of Allan Vickery; 2 s (Richard b 1979, David b 1981); *Career* sr ptnr Arnold Hill & Co CAs London; dir: British Paper Co 1974–2003, Quadrem Hope Ltd 1977–2003; gp md Fandstan Electric Gp 1998–; treas Royal Commonwealth Soc, pres Thames Hare and Hounds; FCA; *Recreations* long distance running (fastest marathon 2 hrs 37 mins 1983), music, gardening; *Clubs* Thames Hare and Hounds, Hurlingham, Royal Commonwealth; *Style*— Michael Bostelmann, Esq; ✉ 33 West Temple Sheen, East Sheen, London SW14 7AP; Craven House, 16 Northumberland Avenue, London WC2N 5AP (tel 020 7306 9100)

BOSTOCK, Martin James; s of Alfred William Bostock, and Muriel Mary, *née* Alder; *Educ* Churcher's Coll Petersfield, Univ of Hull (BA); *m* 1988, Sue Batcheler; 1 da (Poppy b 1990), 1 s (Charlie b 1993); *Career* VSO teacher Thailand 1971–72, asst mangr El Vino Wine Bar London 1975–6; account dir: Extel Advertising and PR 1977–82, Abel Hadden Assoc 1982–83; gp account dir Good Relations 1983–84, head of press and publicity London Borough of Hackney 1984–86, chm Nelson Bostock Communications 1987–; memb PRCA 1989; *Recreations* collecting vintage guitars and playing the blues, tennis; *Style*— Martin Bostock; ✉ Nelson Bostock Communications, Compass House, 22 Redan Place, London W2 4SA (tel 020 7229 4400)

BOSTOCK, Thomas Geoffrey (Tom); *b* 14 December 1949; *Educ* St Lawrence Coll Ramsgate, Univ of Edinburgh (BArch); *Career* architect; architectural asst Oxford Architects Partnership 1971–72; Reiach and Hall Ltd (formerly Alan Reiach Eric Hall & Partners): architectural asst 1974–75, architect 1975–80, assoc 1980–83, ptnr 1983–93 (i/c opening Glasgow office 1986), dir and co sec 1993–; RIBA Regnl Awards (for British Steel Corporation office bldg Airdrie 1978 and Strathclyde Graduate Business Sch 1992); memb: Cncl Edinburgh Architectural Assoc 1982–85, Awards Ctee RIAS 1985–90; various lectures on practice mgmnt Univ of Edinburgh and Edinburgh Coll of Art 1986–, examiner RIBA Part III 1989–2000; RIBA, ARIAS; *Style*— Tom Bostock, Esq; ✉ Reiach and Hall Architects, 6 Darnaway Street, Edinburgh EH3 6BG (tel 0131 225 8444, fax 0131 225 5079, e-mail tom.bostock@reiachandhall.co.uk)

BOSTON, Dr Kenneth George (Ken); AO (2001); s of Kenneth Francis Boston (d 1960), and Enid Beatrice, *née* Taylor; *b* 9 September 1942, Melbourne, Aust; *Educ* Univ of Melbourne (MA, PhD); *m* 13 May 1978, Yvonne, *née* Roep; 1 da (Nathalie b 27 June 1981); *Career* DG of educn S Aust 1988–91, DG of educn and trg NSW 1991–2002, chief exec Qualifications and Curriculum Authy England 2002–; pres Aust Coll of Educn 2001–02; *Clubs* Royal Sydney Yacht Sqdn, Sydney Cricket; *Style*— Dr Ken Boston, AO; ✉ Qualifications and Curriculum Authority, 83 Piccadilly, London W1J 8QA (tel 020 7509 5280, fax 020 7509 6975, e-mail bostonk@qca.org.uk)

BOSTON OF FAVERSHAM, Baron (Life Peer UK 1976), of Faversham in the County of Kent; Terence George; QC (1981); s of George Thomas Boston (d 1986), and Kate, *née* Bellati (d 1995); *b* 21 March 1930; *Educ* Woolwich Polytechnic Sch, KCL; *m* 1962, Margaret Joyce, da of Rowley Henry Jack Head (d 1932), of Aust; *Career* sits as a cross-bench Peer in Lords; Flt Lt RAF 1950–52; called to the Bar Inner Temple 1960 (Gray's Inn 1973); news sub-ed BBC External Services 1957–60, sr prodr BBC (current affairs) 1960–64, chm TVS (later TVS Entertainment plc) 1980–90; MP (Lab) Faversham Kent 1964–70; PPS to: Min of Public Bldg and Works 1964–66, Min of Power 1966–68, Min of Tport 1968–69; asst govt whip 1969–70; min of state Home Office 1979; oppn front bench spokesman on: Home Office Affrs 1979–84, Defence 1984–86; a dep speaker House of Lords 1991–, princ dep chm of ctees House of Lords 1992–94, chm Select Ctee on the European Communities House of Lords 1992–94, chm of Ctees House of Lords 1994–2000; tstee Leeds Castle (Kent) Fndn 1991–, chm Leeds Castle Enterprises Ltd 2005–; *Recreations* opera, fell walking; *Style*— The Rt Hon The Lord Boston of Faversham, QC; ✉ House of Lords, London SW1A 0PW

BOSTRIDGE, Dr Ian Charles; CBE (2004); s of late Leslie John Bostridge, and Lilian Winifred, *née* Clark; *b* 25 December 1964; *Educ* Westminster (Queen's scholar), St John's Coll Oxford (scholar, MA, DPhil), St John's Coll Cambridge (MPhil); *m* 1992, Lucasta Frances Elizabeth, da of late Tim Miller; 1 s (Oliver Timothy b 28 July 2000); *Career* tenor; débuts: Royal Festival Hall (young sailor in Tristan und Isolde) 1993, Barbican (Hylas in Les Troyens) 1994, Wigmore Hall (recital) 1995, Royal Opera House (Third Jew in Salome) 1995, ENO (Tamino in The Magic Flute) 1996, Bavarian State Opera (Nerone in L'Incoronazione di Poppea) 1998, Carnegie Hall (Les Nuits d'Été and serenade for tenor, horn and strings) 1999; roles incl: Tom Rakewell, Peter Quint, Belmonte, Tamino, Young Man in Janáček's Diary of One Who Vanished, Idomeneo, Monteverdi's Orfeo; numerous recitals and concerts in Berlin, Paris, Sydney, NY, Brussels, Amsterdam, Edinburgh, Vienna, San Francisco, Salzburg, Florence and Milan; exclusive contract with EMI 1997–; lectr Music and Magic Univ of Edinburgh Festival Lecture 2000; dedicatee Hans Werner Henze's Sechs Gesänge aus dem Arabischen; hon fell CCC Oxford 2001, Hon DMus Univ of St Andrews 2004; Hon RAM 2002; *Awards* NFMS Award 1991, Young Concert Artists' Tst Award 1992, Royal Philharmonic Soc Debut Award 1995, Gramophone Solo Vocal Award 1996 and 1998, South Bank Show Classical Music Award 1996, Echo Award 1997 and 1999, Munich Festival Prize 1998, Le Monde de la Musique

Prize 1998, Opernwelt Male Singer of the Year 1998, Edison Award 1998 and 2001, Grammy 1999 (nominee 2001, 2002 and 2003), Time Out Award 1999, Brit Award 2000, Prix Caecilia 2001, Preis der Deutscher Schallplattenkritik 2001, Japanese Recording Acad Award 2001, Gramophone Opera Award 2003; *Books* Witchcraft and its Transformations c1650–c1750 (1997); *Recreations* reading, cooking, looking at pictures; *Style*— Dr Ian Bostridge, CBE; ✉ c/o Askonas Holt, Lonsdale Chambers, 27 Chancery Lane, London WC2E 8LA

BOSVILLE MACDONALD OF SLEAT, Sir Ian Godfrey; 17 Bt (NS 1625), of Sleat, Isle of Skye; also 25 Chief of Sleat; DL (East Riding of Yorkshire 1997); s of Sir (Alexander) Somerled Angus Bosville Macdonald of Sleat, 16 Bt, MC (24 Chief of Sleat, d 1958), and Mary Elizabeth, *née* Gibbs (d 2004); *b* 18 July 1947; *Educ* Pinewood Sch, Eton, RAC Cirencester; *m* 1970, Juliet Fleury, o da of late Maj-Gen John Ward-Harrison, OBE, MC; 2 da (Deborah Fleury b 1973, Isabel Mary b 1983), 1 s (Somerled Alexander b 1976); *Heir* s, Somerled Alexander Bosville Macdonald, yr of Sleat; *Career* chartered surveyor; memb: Royal Soc of Health 1972, Economic Research Cncl 1979–; memb (for Bridlington S) Humberside CC 1981–85; pres: Humberside Branch Br Red Cross 1988–96, Br Food and Farming Humberside 1989, Hull and East Riding Branch Br Red Cross 1996–2003, Humber and Wolds Rural Community Cncl 1997–, Humberside Young Farmers; chm: Rural Devpt Cmmn Humberside 1988–95, East Riding of Yorkshire Cncl Rural Partnership 1999–, Northern Region Br Red Cross 2000–03; memb Bd of Tstees Br Red Cross 2001–06; High Sheriff Humberside 1988–89; FRICS 1986 (ARICS 1972), MRSH 1972; *Recreations* ornithology; *Clubs* White's, New, Puffins, Lansdowne; *Style*— Sir Ian Bosville Macdonald of Sleat, Bt, DL; ✉ Thorpe Hall, Rudston, Driffield, East Yorkshire YO25 4JE (tel 01262 420239, e-mail sleat01@btinternet.com)

BOSWALL, *see:* Houstoun-Boswall

BOSWELL, Lindsay; *Educ* Merchiston Castle Sch Edinburgh; *m*; 2 da; *Career* offr rising to maj Argyll and Sutherland Highlanders Inf Regt 1978–89; Raleigh Int: co dir for Zimbabwe, Botswana, Chile and Malaysia 1990–94, prog dir 1994–98; London dir Prince's Tst Volunteers 2000–, chief exec Inst of Fundraising 2000–; memb Steering Ctee Legacy Promotion Campaign, chair Advsy Bd Giving Nation; *Recreations* gardening; *Style*— Lindsay Boswell, Esq; ✉ Institute of Fundraising, Park Place, 12 Lawn Lane, London SW8 1UD (tel 020 7840 1000, fax 020 7840 1001)

BOSWELL, Lindsay Alice; QC (1997); da of Graham Leonard William Boswell, OBE (d 1988), and Erica Margaret Boswell (d 1996); *b* 22 November 1958, Nairobi; *Educ* St Mary's Ascot, Brooke Hse Market Harborough, UCL (BSc), City Univ London (Dip Law); *m* 23 March 1987, Jonathan James Acton Davis, QC, *qv*; 1 s (Matthew James Acton Davis b 30 May 1987); *Career* called to the Bar Gray's Inn 1982; *Recreations* gardens; *Clubs* Aviation Club of UK; *Style*— Miss Lindsay Boswell, QC; ✉ Quadrant Chambers, 10 Fleet Street, London EC4Y 1AU (tel 020 7583 4444, fax 020 7583 4455, e-mail lindsay.boswell@quadrantchambers.com)

BOSWELL, Timothy Eric; MP; s of Eric New Boswell (d 1974), of Banbury, and Joan Winifred Caroline, *née* Jones (d 2003); *b* 2 December 1942; *Educ* Marlborough, New Coll Oxford (MA, post grad dip); *m* 2 Aug 1969, Helen Delahay, da of Rev Arthur Delahay Rees (d 1954), of Swansea; 3 da (Victoria b 1971, Emily b 1975, Caroline b 1978); *Career* head of Econ Section Cons Res Dept 1970–73 (agric and economics advsr 1966–73); managed family farm from father's death in 1974; MP (Cons) Daventry 1987–; PPS to fin sec to the Treasy 1989–90, asst Govt whip 1990–92, a Lord Cmmr of the Treasury (sr whip) 1992; Parly under sec of state: Dept for Education 1992–95, MAFF 1995–97; oppn frontbench spokesman on: Treasy 1997, DTI matters 1997–99, educn and employment 1999–2001, people with disabilities 1999–2003, work and pensions 2001–02; shadow min: for educn and skills 2002–03, for legal, constitutional and home affrs 2003–04, for work 2004–06; PPS to Party Chm 2005–; memb Commons Select Ctee on Agriculture 1987–89; chm Parly Charity Law Reform Panel 1988–90; chm Daventry Constituency Cons Assoc 1979–83 (treas 1976–79); chm Northants Leics and Rutland Counties branch NFU 1983; memb: Cncl Perry Fndn for Agric Research 1966–90 (pres 1984–90), AFRC 1988–90; govr Univ of Wales Inst Cardiff 2007–; *Recreations* shooting, countryside, snooker, poetry; *Clubs* Farmers'; *Style*— Timothy Boswell, Esq, MP; ✉ House of Commons, London SW1A 0AA (tel 020 7219 3000)

BOSWOOD, Anthony Richard; QC (1986); s of late Noel Gordon Paul Boswood, of Radnage, Bucks, and Cicily Ann, *née* Watson; *b* 1 October 1947; *Educ* St Paul's, New Coll Oxford (BCL, MA); *m* 4 Jan 1973, Sarah Bridget, da of Sir John Lindsay Alexander; 3 da (Eleanor b 1976, Louise b 1978, Grace b 1983); *Career* called to the Bar Middle Temple 1970; *Recreations* opera, riding, tennis, racing; *Style*— Anthony Boswood, Esq, QC; ✉ Fountain Court, Temple, London EC4Y 9DH (tel 020 7583 3335, fax 020 7353 0329/1794, mobile 07713 106918, e-mail a.boswood@dial.pipex.com); Podere Casanuova, Pieveasciata, Castelnuovo Berardenga (SI), Italy; South Hay House, Kingsley, Bordon, Hampshire GU35 9NR

BOSWORTH, Simon Charles Neville; s of Sir Neville Bruce Alfred Bosworth, CBE, and Lady Charlotte Marian Bosworth (d 2003); *b* 6 August 1946; *Educ* Stouts Hill Gloucester, Bradfield; *m* 2 Feb 1979, Evelyn Fay, da of William Leslie Wallace (d 1984); 1 da (Claudia b 1984); *Career* dir: W H Cutler (Midlands) Ltd 1968–70, Sutton (Wine Bars) Ltd 1972–74, Hill Alveston & Co Ltd 1973–98, Luttrell Park Investments Ltd 1974–, Berkswell Properties Ltd 1983–, Berkswell Investments Ltd 1984–; *Recreations* football, gardening; *Style*— Simon C N Bosworth, Esq; ✉ Willowbrook House, Preston Road, Lowsonford, Henley-in-Arden, Warwickshire B95 5EZ (tel 01926 842995)

BOTHAM, Sir Ian Terence; kt (2007), OBE (1992); s of Les Botham, and Marie Botham; *b* 24 November 1955; *Educ* Buckler's Mead Secdy Sch Yeovil; *m* 31 Jan 1976, Kathryn; 1 s (Liam James b 26 Aug 1977), 2 da (Sarah Lianne b 3 Feb 1979, Rebecca Kate b 13 Nov 1985); *Career* former professional cricketer; Somerset CCC: second XI 1971, first class debut 1974, awarded county cap 1976, capt 1984–85, benefit 1984; Worcestershire CCC 1987–91 (capped 1987), Queensland Aust off-season 1987–88, Durham CCC 1992–93 (capped 1992); England: 116 one day ints, 102 test matches 1977–92, capt 12 tests 1980–81, highest score 208 v India Oval 1982, best bowling 8 for 34 v Pakistan Lord's 1978; tours: Pakistan/NZ 1977–78, Aust 1978–79, Aust and India 1979–80, W Indies 1980–81, India 1981–82, Aust/NZ 1982–83, W Indies 1985–86, Aust 1986–87, NZ/Aust 1991–92; pt/t technical advsr England squad Zimbabwe and New Zealand 1996–97; test records incl: scored 1000 runs and took 100 wickets in fewest matches, first player to score a century and take 8 wickets in an innings (v Pakistan Lord's 1978), scored third fastest double century by Englishman (200 in 272 minutes v India Oval 1982); BBC TV Sporting Personality of the Year 1981; team capt Question of Sport (BBC 1) until 1996, currently cricket commentator Sky TV, various appearances in pantomime, raised over £3m for Leukaemia Research through long-distance walks; *Books* incl: Botham Down Under, High, Wide and Handsome, It Sort of Clicks (with Peter Roebuck), Cricket My Way (with Jack Bannister), The Incredible Tests (with late Peter Smith), Botham: My Autobiography (with Peter Hayter, 1994), The Botham Report (1997), Botham's Century (2001); *Recreations* golf, shooting, salmon and trout fishing, flying; *Style*— Sir Ian Botham, OBE; ✉ c/o Mission Sports Management Ltd, Kirmington Vale, Barnetby, North Lincolnshire DN36 6AF (tel 01682 688900, fax 01652 688899)

BOTSFORD, Keith; s of Willard Hudson Botsford (d 1947), and Carolina Romani, *née* Rangoni-Machiavelli-Publicola-Santacroce (d 1995); *b* 29 March 1928; *Educ* Portsmouth Abbey Sch, Univ of Iowa (AB), Yale Univ (AM), Columbia Univ, Manhattan Sch of Music, Holborn Coll of Law, Strasbourg Univ; *m* 1 (m dis), Ann Winchester; 3 s (Aubrey b 1957, Giannandrea b 1960, Josue b 1962), 2 da (Clarissa b 1959, Flora b 1964); *m* 2 (m dis), Sally Elwina Weekes; 1 s (Matthew b 1968), 1 da (Polly b 1972); *m* 3, Nathalie Favre-Gilly, da of Paul Favre-Gilly; 1 s (Thomas b 1987), 1 da (Xenia b 1987 (decd)); *Career* writer, ed, prof and newspaper corr; 970 Counter Intelligence 1945–47; reporter France-Amerique 1945; instr in French: Yale Univ 1948–49, Univ of Iowa 1949–50; translator Human Relations Area Files 1949–51, asst prof Bard Coll 1953–56; asst prodr: CBS TV 1955–57, Stratford Shakespeare Festival 1958; assoc prof Univ of Puerto Rico 1958–61 (asst to chllr 1958–61), Latin American corr New Leader 1962–65, dep sec Int PEN 1965–66, dir Nat Translation Centre and prof of English Univ of Texas 1966–71, chm Kolokol Press 1971–, writer in residence Deutsche Austauch Dienst Berlin 1973, corr Sunday Times 1973–86; Boston Univ: prof of journalism and lectr in history 1978–81 and 1988–, asst to pres 1978–81, dir public affrs publications 1989–94; ed-in-chief Grand Prix International 1981–83, pres Int Racing Press Assoc 1981–84, corr and columnist The Independent 1987–98, publisher and ed-in-chief Bostonia Magazine 1989–94, corr La Stampa 1992–98; ed: Yale Poetry Review, Poetry New York, The Noble Savage, Delos, Anon, Kolokol, The Republic of Letters; Translation Medal City of Rimini, PEN Translation Prize; grantee: Ford Fndn 1961–65, Rockefeller Fndn, Moody Fndn; memb Soc of Editors, Magazine Publishers' Assoc; *Books* Novels: The Master Race (1955), The Eighth-best-dressed Man in the World (1957), Benvenuto (1961), The March-Man (1964), The Search for Anderson (as I I Magdalen, 1982), Ana P (as I I Magdalen, 1985), Cockpits (as Liam Frey, 1987), Out of Nowhere (2000), The Mothers (2002), Lennie & Vance & Benji (as I I Magdalen, 2002), Emma H (as I I Magdalen, 2003); Non-Fiction: Dominguin (1972), Driving Ambition (1981), Keke (1985), Champions of Formula One (1988), Bellow & Botsford: Editors (2000); Michelet, History of the French Revolution (trans, 1975–), House of Others (trans, 1994), Sacralization of Politics in Fascist Italy (trans, 1998), Marcello Olschki: Sixth Form, 1939 (trans, 2002); *Recreations* law, musical composition; *Style*— Keith Botsford, Esq; ✉ 120 Cushing Avenue, Dorchester, Massachusetts, MA 02125, USA (tel 00 1 617 265 5019); College of Communication, 640 Commonwealth Avenue, Boston, Massachusetts, MA 02215, USA

BOTT, Alan John; OBE (1995); s of Albert Henry John Bott, and Eileen Mary, *née* Spiers; *b* 30 March 1935; *Educ* KCS Wimbledon, Merton Coll Oxford (MA, postmaster); *m* 10 Sept 1966, Caroline Gaenor, da of Frank Leslie Williams (d 1943); 2 s (Jonathan b 3 April 1968, Simon b 26 June 1970), 1 da (Alison b 24 March 1972); *Career* dir: The NZ Shipping Co 1971 (joined 1956), P&O Containers Ltd (formerly Overseas Containers Ltd) 1976–96; chm: The Aust and NZ Shipping Confs 1978–94, The Europe Southern Africa Shipping Conf 1990–96, NZ/UK C of C and Indust 1990–96; dir and vice-pres ECSA, dir and vice-chm CENSA until 1996; extra mural univ lectr in architecture 1962–, NADFAS lectr 1997–, memb Guildford Diocesan Advsy Ctee 2001–, memb Surrey Archaeological Soc Cncl 2000–03 and 2005–; Swan Hellenic lectr 2000–; churchwarden Godalming Parish Church 1979–2002 (dep churchwarden 2002–), tstee Godalming Museum 1986– (chm 1994–); Bodley fell Merton Coll Oxford 2001 (memb SCR 1993–); FSA 1965; FCIT 1990; *Books* Monuments in Merton College Chapel (1964), Sailing Ships of The NZSCO (1973), Godalming Parish Church (1978, 3 edn 1997), Baptisms and Marriages at Merton College Oxford (1981), Rake Manor, Godalming (1990), Merton College, A Short History of the Buildings (1993), Wall Paintings in Godalming Church (1996), The Ancient Roofs and Heraldic Bosses in Godalming Church (1999), Compton Parish Church (2000), The Heraldry in Merton College Oxford (2001), Witley and Thursley Parish Churches (2003), Beddgelert Parish Church (2004), Dunsfold and Hascombe Parish Churches (2005), Peper Harow and Shackleford Parish Churches (2007); *Recreations* tennis, golf, gardening, writing and lecturing on the history of European architecture; *Clubs* Travellers; *Style*— Alan Bott, Esq, OBE; ✉ Rake Court, Milford, Godalming, Surrey GU8 5AD (tel 01483 416546)

BOTT, Valerie; da of Rowland Bott (d 1993), and Joan Evelyn, *née* Lydeard (d 2003); *b* 16 December 1948; *Educ* Thistley Hough Sch for Girls Stoke-on-Trent, UCL (BA), Univ of Leicester (Dip Museum Studies, MA); *Partner* 1967–, James Wisdom; *Career* sr asst Vestry House Museum Waltham Forest 1971–75, keeper Grange Museum Brent 1975–86, museum devpt offr Wandsworth 1986–88, head Newham Museum Service 1988–93, conslt curator to Fairground Heritage Tst 1994–96 (also freelance cmmns), dep dir Museums & Galleries Commission 1996–2000, Museum Consultancy 2000–; chair Museum Professionals Gp 1979–80, pres London Fedn of Museums & Galleries 1988–91, chair London Museums Consultative Ctee 1990–93, hon treas Thames Explorer Tst, memb London Regnl Ctee Heritage Lottery Fund 2001–07, chair William Hogarth Tst 2001–; FMA 1980 (AMA 1974); *Recreations* keeping ducks, gardening, museums; *Style*— Ms Valerie Bott; ✉ 25 Hartington Road, Chiswick, London W4 3TL (tel and fax 020 8995 7413, e-mail valbott@museums.freeserve.co.uk)

BOTTAZZO, Prof Gian Franco; *b* 1 August 1946, Venice, Italy; *Educ* Univ of Padua (MD); *Career* univ contract award Inst of Med Semeiology Univ of Padua 1972–73; Dept of Immunology Middx Hosp Med Sch: Br Cncl research fell 1974–75, Wellcome research fell 1974–75, lectr in clinical immunology 1977–80, sr lectr 1980–83, reader 1984–89, prof of clinical immunology 1989–90; hon sr lectr St Bartholomew's Hosp Med Coll 1982, temp dir Dept of Diabetes and Immunogenetics St Bartholomew's Hosp 1982–84; prof of immunology and clinical immunology and head Dept of Immunology (Whitechapel): The London Hosp Med Coll 1991–95, St Bartholomew's and The Royal London Sch of Med and Dentistry 1996–97; med and scientific dir Autoimmune Diseases Charitable Tst (ADCT) London 1992–2000, scientific dir Ospedale Pediatrico Bambino Gesú Scientific Inst Rome 1998–; Minkowsky Award Euro Assoc for Studies of Diabetes 1982, R D Lawrence Award Br Diabetic Assoc 1985, Diaz Cristobal Award Int Diabetes Fed 1985, King Faisal Prize for Med 1986, Mack-Forster Award Euro Soc for Clinical Investigation 1987, David Rumbrough Award Juvenile Diabetes Fndn Int 1987, Harington de Visscher Prize Euro Thyroid Assoc 1988, Laurea (hc) Nantes 1990, Banting Meml Award American Diabetes Assoc 1992, Ely Lilly (SA) Travel Fellowship 1993, 8th S A Berson Lecture Tel Aviv 1993; author of numerous papers, reviews, chapters and commentaries on human autoimmune diseases, with particular reference to the pathogenesis of insulin-dependent diabetes mellitus and other endocrine autoimmune diseases; FRCP, FRCPath; *Style*— Prof Gian Franco Bottazzo; ✉ Ospedale Pediatrico Bambino Gesú, Piazza S. Onofrio, 4 00165 Roma (tel 00 39 06 6859 2277, fax 00 39 06 6859 2101, e-mail bottazzo@opbg.net)

BOTTING, (Elizabeth) Louise; CBE (1993); da of Robert Young (d 1956), and Edith, *née* Roberts (d 1981); sis of John R C Young, CBE, *qv*; *b* 19 September 1939; *Educ* Sutton Coldfield HS, LSE (BSc Econ); *m* 1, 1964 (m dis 1986), Douglas Botting; 2 da (Catherine b 1966, Anna b 1967); *m* 2, 23 May 1989, Leslie Carpenter, *qv*; *Career* broadcaster and financial journalist; investment analyst Kleinwort Benson 1961–65, columnist Daily Mail 1970–75, Br Forces Broadcasting 1971–83; Douglas Deakin Young fin consultancy: joined 1975, md 1982–88, chm 1988–; presenter Money Box (BBC Radio 4) 1977–92; chm New 102 Ltd 1996–2001; non-exec dir: Trinity Mirror (formerly Trinity plc) 1991–99, London Weekend Television (Holdings) plc 1992–94, General Accident 1992–98, CGU plc 1998–2000 (following merger with Commercial Union); memb Bd Camelot 1999–; memb Senior Salaries Review Body 1987–94; *Style*— Louise Botting, CBE; ✉ Douglas Deakin Young Ltd, 1 Hobart Place, London SW1 0HU (tel 020 7201 3030)

BOTTOMLEY, Peter James; MP; s of Sir James Bottomley, KCMG; bro of Susan Whitfield, *qv*; *b* 30 July 1944; *Educ* Westminster, Trinity Coll Cambridge (MA); *m* 1967, Virginia Hilda Brunette Maxwell (Baroness Bottomley of Nettlestone, PC (Life Peer)), *qv*, da of

John Garnett, CBE (d 1997); 1 s, 2 da; *Career* MP (Cons): Greenwich, Woolwich W June 1975–83 (also contested both 1974 gen elections), Eltham 1983–97, Worthing West 1997–; PPS to: Min of State FCO 1982–83, Sec of State for Social Servs 1983–84, Sec of State for NI 1990; Parly under sec of state: Dept of Employment 1984–86, Dept of Transport (min for roads) 1986–89, NI Office (min for agriculture and for environment) 1989–90; chm: Br Union of Family Orgns 1973–80, Family Forum 1980–82, C of E Children's Soc 1983–84; tstee Christian Aid 1978–84; memb Ct of Assts Worshipful Co of Drapers; *Recreations* children; *Style*— Peter Bottomley, Esq, MP; ✉ House of Commons, London SW1A 0AA

BOTTOMLEY, Stephen John; s of Frederick John Bottomley, of Norwich, and Jean Mary, *née* Moore; *b* 23 October 1954; *Educ* Sutton Valence, UEA (BA); *m* 8 June 1984, Gail Barbara, da of Grenville Herbert Ryder (d 1989), of Crosby, Liverpool; 2 da (Clare b 1987, Emma b 1989), 1 s (Charles b 1991); *Career* admitted slr 1980; ptnr Bartletts De Reya 1984–88, dir Johnson Fry Corporate Finance Ltd 1988, ptnr Mayer Brown Rowe & Maw (formerly Rowe & Maw) 1988–; Freeman Worshipful Co of Slrs; memb Law Soc; *Recreations* golf; *Style*— Stephen Bottomley, Esq; ✉ 22B Taggart House, 109 Repulse Bay, Hong Kong (tel 00 852 2812 2063); Mayer Brown Rowe & Maw LLP, 7th Floor, Gloucester Tower, The Landmark, 15 Queen's Road, Central, Hong Kong (tel 00 852 3763 7006, fax 00 852 3763 7500, e-mail sbottomley@mayerbrownrowe.com)

BOTTOMLEY OF NETTLESTONE, Baroness (Life Peer UK 2005), of St Helens in the County of Isle of Wight; Virginia Hilda Brunette Maxwell Bottomley; PC (1992), DL (Surrey 2006); da of John Garnett, CBE (d 1997); *b* 12 March 1948; *Educ* LSE (MSc); *m* 1967, Peter James Bottomley, MP, *qv*; 1 s, 2 da; *Career* social scientist 1971–84, chm Lambeth Juvenile Court 1981–84; Parly candidate (Cons) IOW 1983, MP (Cons) Surrey SW 1984–2005; PPS to: Min of State for Educn and Sci 1985–86, Min for Overseas Devpt 1986–87, Sec of State for Foreign and Cwlth Affrs 1987–88; Parly under sec of state DOE 1988–89, min of state Dept of Health 1989–92, sec of state for health 1992–95, sec of state for nat heritage 1995–97, memb Foreign Affrs Select Ctee 1997–99; chm Millennium Cmmn 1995–97, vice-chair Br Cncl (memb Bd 1997–2000), pres Centre for Int Briefing; pro-chllr Univ of Surrey 2005–, chllr Univ of Hull 2006–; memb: Ct of Govrs LSE 1985–, MRC 1987–88, Bd Prince of Wales International Business Leaders Forum, Governing Body ICC UK, Advsy Cncl Judge Sch of Mgmnt Univ of Cambridge; govr: London Univ of the Arts 2000–06, Ditchley Fndn 1991–; chair brand practice Odgers Ray and Berndtson, dir Mid Southern Water Co 1987–88, memb Supervisory Bd Akzo Nobel NV 2000–, non-exec dir BUPA 2007–; ind tstee The Economist 2006–; JP Inner London 1975–84; pres: Abbeyfield Soc, Farnham Castle; lay canon Guildford Cathedral 2004–; fell Industry and Parliament Tst 1987; Freeman City of London 1989; *Recreations* family; *Style*— The Rt Hon the Lady Bottomley of Nettlestone, DL; ✉ House of Lords, London SW1A 0PW

BOTTOMS, Prof Sir Anthony Edward; kt (2001); s of Dr James William Bottoms (d 1980), and Dorothy Ethel, *née* Barnes (d 1983); *b* 29 August 1939; *Educ* Eltham Coll, Corpus Christi Coll Oxford (MA), Corpus Christi Coll Cambridge (MA), Univ of Sheffield (PhD); *m* 1962, Janet Freda, da of Rev E L Wenger; 2 da (Catharine b 1966, Erica b 1970), 1 s (Stephen b 1968); *Career* probation officer 1962–64, research officer Inst of Criminology Univ of Cambridge 1964–68; Univ of Sheffield: lectr 1968–72, sr lectr 1972–76, prof of criminology 1976–84, dean of Faculty of Law 1981–84; dir Inst of Criminology Univ of Cambridge 1984–98, Wolfson prof of criminology Univ of Cambridge 1984–2006 (emeritus prof 2006–), professorial fell Univ of Sheffield 2002–07; visiting fell Simon Fraser Univ BC Canada 1982, visiting prof Queen's Univ Belfast 1999–2000, life fell Fitzwilliam Coll Cambridge 2006– (pres 1994–98, fell 1984–2006); ed Howard Journal of Penology and Crime Prevention 1975–81; memb: Parole Bd for England and Wales 1974–76, Home Office Research and Advsy Gp on Long-term Prison System 1984–90; Sellin-Glueck Award American Soc of Criminology 1996; Hon LLD Queen's Univ Belfast 2003; FBA 1997; *Publications* Criminals Coming of Age (jtly, 1973), The Urban Criminal (jtly, 1976), Defendants in the Criminal Process (jtly, 1976), The Coming Penal Crisis (ed jtly, 1980), Problems of Long-Term Imprisonment (ed jtly, 1987), Social Inquiry Reports (jtly, 1988), Intermediate Treatment and Juvenile Justice (jtly, 1990), Intensive Community Supervision for Young Offenders (1995), Prisons and the Problem of Order (jtly, 1996), Criminal Deterrence and Sentence Severity (jtly, 1999), Community Penalties (ed jtly, 2001), Ideology, Crime and Criminal Justice (ed jtly, 2002), Alternatives to Prison (jt ed, 2004; also author of numerous articles in academic books and jls; *Style*— Prof Sir Anthony Bottoms, FBA; ✉ Institute of Criminology, Sidgwick Avenue, Cambridge CB3 9DT (tel 01223 335366/60, fax 01223 335356, e-mail aeb11@cam.ac.uk); Department of Law, University of Sheffield, Crookesmoor Building, Conduit Road, Sheffield S10 1FL (tel 0114 222 6839, fax 0114 222 6832, e-mail a.e.bottoms@sheffield.ac.uk)

BOTTONE, Bonaventura; s of Bonaventura Bottone, of Harrow, and Kathleen, *née* Barnes; *b* 19 September 1950; *Educ* Lascelles Secdy Modern Sch Harrow, Royal Acad of Music London; *m* 28 April 1973, Jennifer, da of Ralph Dakin (d 1973); 2 s (Benjamin Nicholas b 13 Jan 1978, Jonathan Samuel b 16 March 1984), 2 da (Francesca Louise, Rebecca Charlotte (twins) b 23 Nov 1979); *Career* tenor; appeared at numerous international venues incl: Royal Opera House Covent Garden, London Coliseum, Glyndebourne Festival, Nice Opera, Batignano Festival Opera, Houston Opera, Met Opera NY, Munich Bavarian State Opera, Cleveland Symphony Orch Blossom Festival 1997, Santiago Chile 1998; frequent BBC broadcaster; FRAM 1998; *Roles* with ENO incl: David in Die Meistersinger, The Duke of Mantua in Rigoletto, Alfred in La Traviata, Beppe in I Pagliacci, Nanki-Poo in The Mikado, Sam Kaplan in Street Scene, Truffaldino in The Love for Three Oranges, Lenski in Eugene Onegin 1994, Rodolfo in La Boheme, title role in Dr Ox by Gavin Bryars (premier) 1998; with Royal Opera Co incl: the Italian Tenor in Der Rosenkavalier (Covent Garden debut), Alfredo in Die Fledermaus, the Italian Tenor in Capriccio, Raoul de Nanzis in Les Hugenots, Comte Liebenskof in Viaggio a Reims; with Scottish Opera incl: Governor General in Candide, Loge in Das Rheingold, Narraboth in Salome; others incl: Italian Tenor in Capriccio (Glyndebourne Festival Opera) 1990, Alfredo in La Traviata (Opera North) 1990, title role in Le Comte Ory (WNO) 1992, Pedrillo in Die Entführung aus dem Serail (Houston Opera, US debut), Fernando in La Favorita (WNO) 1993, Dream of Gerontius (Royal Festival Hall) 1994, the Italian Tenor in Capriccio (Chicago Lyric Opera debut) 1994, Governor General in Candide (Lisbon debut) 1994, BBC Proms 1996, Turiddu in Cavelleria Rusticana (WNO) 1996, Faust in Damnation of Faust 1997, Pinkerton in Madama Butterfly (Florentine Opera Milwaukee) 2000, Alfred in Die Fledermaus (Opéra National de Paris Bastille) 2000, Riccardo in Un Ballo in Maschera (Atlanta Opera debut, 2001), Damnation de Faust (Brisbane Symphony Orchestra) 2002, Troilus in Troilus and Cressida (Philharmonia Orchestra) 2002, Faust in Faust et Hélèn (Deutsches Symphonic Orchestra Berlin) 2002, Nanki Poo Mikado (La Fenice Venice) 2003, Loge in Das Rheingold (Lyric Opera Chicago) 2005, Rodolfo in La Bohèmè (Opera Queensland) 2005, Memlaus in La Belle Hélèn (ENO) 2006, Alfred in Die Fledermaus (Glyndebourne Festival and Chicago Lyric Opera) 2006, Govr in Candide (La Scala Milan debut) 2007; *Recordings* incl: Cassio in Otello, Arturo in Lucia di Lammermoor, Nanki-Poo in The Mikado (with ENO (highlights), also with D'Oyly Carte), The Student Prince, Orpheus In The Underworld (with ENO), Sondheim's A Little Night Music, Weill's Street Scene, Tippett's The Ice Break, Vaughan Williams' Hugh the Drover (Hyperion), Lily Boulanger's Faust et Hélène (Chandos); *Recreations* gardening, cycling, boating; *Style*— Bonaventura Bottone, Esq; ✉ c/o Stafford Law Associates, Candleway, Broadstreet, Sutton Valence, Kent ME17 3AT (tel 01622 840038, fax 01622 840039, e-mail staffordlaw@btinternet.com, website stafford-law.com); website www.bonaventurabottone.com

BOUCH, Dr (Dennis) Clive; s of Tom Bouch (d 1967), of Aspatria, Cumbria, and Elizabeth Anderson, *née* Errington; *b* 12 September 1939; *Educ* Nelson Thomlinson GS Wigton, Univ of Edinburgh (BSc, MB ChB); *m* 12 Sept 1968, (Valerie Alexander) Sandra, da of Alexander Lamb (d 1983), of Edinburgh; 2 s (David Christopher b 1972, Jeremy Clive b 1973), 2 da (Caroline Anne b 1975, Katharine Mary b 1978); *Career* lectr in pathology Univ of Edinburgh 1966–75, conslt pathologist to Leics HA 1976–2004, head of dist pathology serv 1985–94, Home Office pathologist 1984–, dir of forensic pathology Univ of Leicester 1990–; chm: Dist Hosps Med Staff Ctee Leics HA 1984–88, Dist Med Advsy Ctee Leics HA 1990–94; conslt memb Policy Advsy Gp Leics HA 1990–94; memb Home Office Policy Advsy Bd for Forensic Pathology 2000–07; FRCPath 1985; *Style*— Dr Clive Bouch; ✉ Department of Pathology, The Leicester Royal Infirmary, Leicester LE1 5WW (tel 0116 258 6581)

BOUCHER, Prof Robert Francis (Bob); CBE (2000); s of Robert Boucher (d 1987), of London, and Johanna, *née* Fox (d 1982); *b* 25 April 1940; *Educ* St Ignatius Coll Stamford Hill, Borough Poly London, Univ of Nottingham (PhD); *m* 16 Aug 1965, Rosemary Ellen, *née* Maskell; 3 s (Jeremy Robert Philip b 4 Sept 1968, Jonathan Francis b 26 Jan 1971 (decd), Timothy James b 19 June 1972), 1 da (Justine Louise Julia b 20 Nov 1974); *Career* ICI postdoctoral fell Univ of Nottingham 1966, lectr Queen's Univ Belfast 1968–70 (res fell 1966–68); Univ of Sheffield: lectr 1970–76, sr lectr 1976–85, prof 1985–95, pro-vice-chllr 1992–95, vice-chllr 2001–; princ and vice-chllr UMIST 1995–2000, vice-chllr Univ of Sheffield 2001–07; dir: HEQC 1995–97, Univs and Colls Staff Devpt Agency 1995–99, e-Learning Co Ltd 2001–05; chm: Engrg Professors' Cncl 1993–95, DTI Action for Engrg Task Force 1994–96, HEQC Quality Enhancement Gp 1995–97, HEQC Grad Standards Prog 1995–97, CVCP/UUK Int Sector Gp 1995–2006, Graduate Prospects Ltd 1998–2004, Marketing Manchester 1999–2000; memb: Senate Engrg Cncl 1995–99, Bd Br Cncl 1996–2003 (chm Ctee for Int Co-operation in HE 1996–2003), Cncl Assoc Cwlth Univs 1999– (treas 2004–), Univs UK Bd 2002–, chm White Rose Univ Consortium 2003–; tstee Nat Portrait Gallery 2003–, memb Bd Yorkshire Forward 2003–06; author of various articles for engrg jls, confs and papers; recipient Felber Medal CVUT Prague 1998; Hon DHL SUNY 1998; MIEEE 1986, FIMechE 1992, FREng 1994, FASME 1997, FGCI 2006; *Recreations* hill walking, music, exercise; *Clubs* Athenaeum; *Style*— Prof R F Boucher, CBE, FREng; ✉ 18 Endcliffe Hall Avenue, Sheffield S10 3EL (e-mail r.boucher@sheffield.ac.uk)

BOUGHEY, Dr Sir John George Fletcher; 11 Bt (GB 1798), of Newcastle-under-Lyme, Staffordshire; s of Sir Richard James Boughey, 10 Bt, JP, DL (d 1978); *b* 12 August 1959; *Educ* Eton, Univ of Zimbabwe; *Heir* bro, James Boughey; *Career* medical; MRCPI 1994; *Clubs* Boodle's; *Style*— Dr Sir John Boughey, Bt

BOUKAMEL, Bassam; s of Rafic Yusuf Boukamel (d 1989), and Vasima, *née* Kazou; *b* 2 June 1948; *Educ* International Coll Beirut, American Univ of Beirut (BA), Fordham Univ NY (MA); *Career* economist 1975–85, dir Raab Boukamel Art Resources Limited (renamed Boukamel Contemporary Art in 1996) 1986–, promoter of 1980's exponents of Euro art (Rainer Fetting, Luciano Castelli, Ernesto Tatafiore), lead promoter of Scot contemporary artists (Ken Currie, Philip Braham), curator of survey exhibitions on contemporary Scot art and American contemporary photography; publisher of art books; *Style*— Bassam Boukamel, Esq

BOULDING, Philip Vincent; QC (1996); s of Vincent Fergusson Boulding, of Cambridge, and Sylvia Boulding; *b* 1 February 1954; *Educ* Downing Coll Cambridge (scholar, MA, LLM, Rugby blue, pres CU Amateur Boxing Club); *m* Helen Elizabeth, da of Joseph William Richardson; 1 s (Joseph William b 1993), 1 da (Harriet Helen b 1995); *Career* called to the Bar: Gray's Inn 1979 (Holker Entrance Award 1978, Sr Holker Award 1979, bencher 2004), Hong Kong Bar 1997; specialist in construction and engrg law worldwide, regularly sits as an arbitrator, adjudicator and mediator in construction and engrg disputes; practising in Hong Kong (dealing with disputes arising out of the construction of the new airport and other large infrastructure projects, such as the strategic sewage disposal scheme) since 1997 in addition to practising in the UK; former memb Ctee Official Referees' Bar Assoc; memb London Common Law and Commercial Bar Assoc; appointed govr Hills Road VI Form Coll Cambridge 1997–2000; played rugby for England (at under 23 level) 1977 and Bedford RUFC; sr pres Downing Coll Griffins Club 2003–; *Recreations* sport generally, fine wine, cutting grass; *Clubs* Hawks' (Cambridge), RAC; *Style*— Philip Boulding, Esq, QC; ✉ Keating Chambers, 15 Essex Street, Outer Temple, London WC2R 3AU (tel 020 7544 2600, fax 020 7240 7722, e-mail pboulding@keatingchambers.com)

BOULOS, Prof Paul Bernard; s of Bernard Boulos (d 1964), of Khartoum, Sudan, and Evelyn, *née* Haggar; *b* 10 March 1944; *Educ* Comboni Coll Khartoum, Univ of Khartoum (MB BS); *m* 1 March 1979, Marilyn Lesley, da of Ronald Robert Went (d 1994), of Highgate, London; 1 s (Mark Ronald b 22 Aug 1980), 2 da (Sarah-Jane b 15 Sept 1981, Paula Louise b 28 Dec 1984); *Career* surgical registrar UCH 1970–73; lectr in surgery Faculty of Med Univ of Khartoum 1973–76, res fell Dept of Surgical Studies Middx Hosp 1976–77, sr surgical registrar UCH 1977–80 and St Mark's Hosp 1980–81; UCL: sr lectr in surgery 1981–92, reader in surgery 1992–97, prof of surgery 1997–; conslt surgn: UCH 1981–, The Middlesex Hosp 1993–; memb: RSM (memb Cncl Coloproctology Section), Assoc of Surgns of GB and I, Br Soc of Gastroenterology, Assoc of Coloproctology of GB and I, Surgical Res Soc, BMA, American Soc of Colon Rectal Surgns, Soc of Expert Witnesses; RCSEng surgical tutor; RCSEd examiner; NE Thames coll rep, coll tutor Hong Kong, Univ of London examiner; MS, FRCS, FRCSEd, Hon FCS (Hong Kong); *Style*— Prof Paul Boulos; ✉ St Anne, 15 Richmond Road, New Barnet, Hertfordshire EN5 1SA (tel 020 8449 6552, fax 020 8449 6252); Department of Surgery, Royal Free and University College Medical School, The Medical School Building, 74 Huntley Street, London WC1E 6AU (tel 020 7679 6490, fax 020 7679 6470, e-mail p.boulos@ucl.ac.uk)

BOULT, Geoffrey Pattisson; *b* 6 June 1957; *Educ* St Edward's Sch Oxford, Hatfield Coll Durham (BA), Univ of Durham (PGCE); *m* 27 July 1984, Katie, *née* Goddard; 4 da (Alice b 2 March 1986, Tessa b 30 April 1988, Zoë b 28 Aug 1991, Matilda b 2 Aug 1997); *Career* geography teacher Canford Sch 1980–87, teacher Geelong GS Australia 1984–85, head of geography Cranleigh Sch 1987–92, housemaster Field House St Edward's Sch Oxford 1994–2001, headmaster Giggleswick Sch 2001–; sec Oxford Conf in Educn 1986–88; chm Boarding Schs Assoc 2007–; *Recreations* golf, walking, hockey, reading, music; *Clubs* Pedagogues, Cryptics; *Style*— Geoffrey Boult, Esq; ✉ Giggleswick School, Settle, North Yorkshire BD24 0DE (tel 01729 893005, fax 01729 893150, e-mail headmaster@giggleswick.org.uk)

BOULTER, Prof Patrick Stewart; s of Frederick Charles Boulter, MC (d 1961), of Annan, Scotland, and Flora Victoria, *née* Black (d 1965); *b* 28 May 1927; *Educ* King's Coll Sch, Carlisle GS, Guy's Hosp Med Sch (MB BS, Gold medal); *m* 3 Oct 1946, (Patricia) Mary Eckersley, da of Samuel Gordon Barlow (d 1966), of Lowton, Lancs; 2 da (Jennifer (Mrs Bond), Anne (Mrs Wood)); *Career* registrar Dept of Surgical Studies Middx Hosp 1957–59, sr surgical registrar Guy's Hosp 1959–62 (hon conslt surgn 1962–66), conslt surgn Guildford Hosps and Regnl Cancer Unit 1962–91, emeritus conslt oncological and gen surgn Royal Surrey Co Hosp and Regnl Radiotherapy Centre; visiting prof: Univ of Surrey 1986– (hon reader 1968–80), Univ of Madras, Univ of Brunei Darussalam 1992–; RCS (England): surgical tutor 1964, regnl advsr 1975, Penrose-May teacher 1985–; RCS (Edinburgh): examiner 1979, memb Cncl 1984–, vice-pres 1989–91, pres 1991–94, regent

1995; hon citizen State of Nebraska 1967; memb Br Breast Gp and hon memb Surgical Res Soc, memb Med Advsy Cmmn Health Risk Resources International (HRRI); tstee Thalidomide Tst (chm Health and Welfare Ctee); Hon DUniv Surrey 1996; hon memb: N Pacific Surgical Assoc 1991, Assoc of Surgns India 1993, Soc of Surgns of Nepal 1994; hon fell Royal Aust Coll of Surgns 1984, Hon FCS South Africa 1992, Hon FCS Sri Lanka 1992, Hon FRCSI 1993, Hon FCSHK 1993; memb Acad of Med of Malaysia 1993; fell Assoc of Surgns of GB and I (former chm Educnl Ctee), FRCS, FRCS (Edinburgh), FRCP (Edinburgh), FRCP 1997, FRCPS (Glasgow) 1993, FCPS (Pakistan) 1994, fell Acad of Med Singapore 1994, Int Master Surgn (Int Coll of Surgns) 1994, Hon FFAEM 1996; *Publications* articles and chapters on surgical subjects incl breast disease, surgical oncology and endocrine surgery; *Recreations* mountaineering, skiing, fishing, gardening; *Clubs* Alpine, Caledonian, Swiss Alpine, New (Edinburgh); *Style—* Prof Patrick Boulter; ✉ Quarry Cottage, Salkeld Dykes, Penrith, Cumbria CA11 9LL (tel and fax 01768 898822, e-mail psboulter@aol.com); Royal College of Surgeons, Nicolson Street, Edinburgh EH8 9DW

BOULTON, Prof Andrew James Michael; s of Prof James Thompson Boulton, and Margaret Helen, *née* Leary; *b* 21 February 1953; *Educ* Nottingham HS, Univ of Newcastle upon Tyne (MB BS, MD); *m* 1, 3 July 1976 (m dis 1996), Helen Frances; 1 s (Jonathan David b 1 July 1978), 2 da (Caroline Helen b 14 Sept 1979, Sarah Elizabeth b 24 July 1985); m 2, 18 Aug 1997, Dr Loretta Vileikyte; *Career* sr med registrar Royal Hallamshire Hosp 1981–86 (diabetes res fell 1979–81), visiting asst prof of med Univ of Miami Florida 1983–84, conslt and prof in med Manchester Royal Infirmary 1995– (conslt and sr lectr 1986–91, reader and conslt 1991–95); R D Lawrence lectr Br Diabetic Assoc 1990, Pecoraro lectr American Diabetes Assoc 1996, Camillo Gogli lectr European Diabetes Assoc 2003; ed Diabetic Medicine 1991–95 (formerly dep ed); chm: Postgrad Educn Euro Diabetes Assoc 1995–2001, Diabetic Foot Study Gp Europe 1998–2001; hon sec Euro Diabetes Assoc 2001–04, chair Foot Cncl American Diabetes Assoc 2005–; author numerous papers on diabetic complications; Hon DSc Univ of Cluj-Napoca Romania 2003; FRCP 1992 (MRCP 1979); *Books* The Foot In Diabetes (jtly, 1987, 4 edn 2006), Diabetes In Practice (jtly, 1989), Diabetic Neuropathy (1997); *Recreations* campanology, classical music; *Style—* Prof Andrew Boulton; ✉ Department of Medicine, Manchester Royal Infirmary, Oxford Road, Manchester M13 9WL (tel 0161 276 4452, fax 0161 274 4740, e-mail andrew.j.boulton@man.ac.uk)

BOULTON, Fiona Jane; da of Michael Harry Lockton, and (Elizabeth) Iona, *née* Williams; *b* 11 April 1964, Sutton Coldfield, W Midlands; *Educ* UC Cardiff (BSc), Exeter Coll Oxford (PGCE), Inst of Educn Univ of London (MA, NPQH); *m* 23 July 1994, Richard Edward Stanley Boulton, *qv*, s of Sir Clifford Boulton, GCB, DL; 2 da (Honor Olivia Anne b 26 April 1998, Katia Jane Imogen b 23 Sept 2001), 1 s (Fraser William James b 22 Jan 2000); *Career* housemistress: Stowe Sch 1989–91, Marlborough Coll 1991–95; headmistress Guildford HS 2002– (dep head 1996–2002); *Recreations* family, cooking, walking, reading, art; *Style—* Mrs Fiona Boulton; ✉ Guildford High School, London Road, Guildford, Surrey GU1 1SJ (tel 01483 561440, mobile 07769 705010, e-mail fiona.boulton@church-schools.co.uk)

BOULTON, Prof Geoffrey Stewart; OBE (2000); s of George Stewart Boulton (d 2000), of Forsbrook, Staffs, and Rose Boulton (d 1990); *b* 28 November 1940; *Educ* Longton HS, Univ of Birmingham (BSc, PhD, DSc); *m* Denise Bryers, da of Joseph Lawns; 2 da (Katherine Elisabeth b 7 March 1973, Olivia Frances b 28 April 1976); *Career* Br Geological Survey 1962–64, Keele Univ 1964–65, Univ of Birmingham 1965–67, Water Dept Nairobi 1968, lectr then reader Sch of Environmental Science UEA 1968–86, prof Univ of Amsterdam 1980–86; Univ of Edinburgh: regius prof of geology and mineralogy 1986–, provost and dean Faculty of Science 1994–99 (vice-princ 1999–); chm: NERC Polar Science Bd until 1994, NERC Earth Science and Technol Bd, Royal Soc Section Ctee for Earth Science and Astronomy; memb: Natural Environment Research Cncl, Nature Conservancy Cncl for Scotland Science Bd until 1992, Royal Cmmn on Environmental Pollution 1994–2000, Cncl Royal Soc 1997–2000, Scottish Higher Educn Funding Cncl 1997–2003, Scottish Science Advsy Ctee 2002–, Cncl for Science and Technol 2004–; contrib to numerous books and papers in glaciology, Polar science and global environmental change; Kirk Bryan Medal Geological Soc of America, Seligman Crystal Int Glaciological Soc, Lyell Medal Geological Soc of London 2006, Tedford Medal for Science Inst for Contemporary Scotland 2006; Hon DTech Chalmers Univ, Hon DSc Univ of Birmingham, Hon DSc Univ of Keele; FRS 1991, FRSE 1989, FGS; *Recreations* climbing, violin, sailing; *Style—* Prof Geoffrey Boulton; ✉ 19 Lygon Road, Edinburgh EH16 5QD (tel 0131 667 2531); Department of Geology and Geophysics, Grant Institute, Kings Buildings, University of Edinburgh, Edinburgh EH9 3JW (tel 0131 650 4844, fax 0131 668 3184, e-mail g.boulton@ed.ac.uk)

BOULTON, Prof James Thompson; s of Harry Boulton, MM (d 1951), of Pickering, N Yorks, and Annie Mary Penty, *née* Thompson (d 1974); *b* 17 February 1924; *Educ* UC Durham (BA), Lincoln Coll Oxford (BLitt), Univ of Nottingham (PhD); *m* 6 Aug 1949, Margaret Helen, da of Arthur Haydn Leary (d 1966), of Stockton-on-Tees, Cleveland; 1 s (Andrew b 1953), 1 da (Helen b 1955); *Career* RAF Flt Lt pilot 1943–46; Univ of Nottingham: lectr, sr lectr, reader in English 1951–64, prof 1964–75, dean Faculty of Arts 1970–73; John Cranford Adams prof of English Hofstra Univ NY 1967; Univ of Birmingham: prof of English studies and head of dept 1975–88, dean Faculty of Arts 1981–84, public orator 1984–88, emeritus prof 1988, dep dir Inst for Advanced Research in Arts and Social Sciences 2000– (dir 1988–2000); Hon DLitt: Univ of Durham 1991, Univ of Nottingham 1993; FRSL, FBA; *Books* Burke's Sublime and Beautiful (ed, 1958, 2 edn 1987), The Language of Politics In The Age of Wilkes and Burke (1963, 2 edn 1975), Johnson: The Critical Heritage (1971), Letters of D H Lawrence, Vols 1–8 (ed, 1979–2001), Selected Letters of D H Lawrence (1997, 2 edn 1999), Edmund Burke, The Early Writings (ed, 1998), D H Lawrence: Late Essays and Articles (ed, 2003), James Boswell: An Account of Corsica (ed, 2006); *Recreations* gardening; *Style—* Prof James Boulton, FBA, FRSL; ✉ Institute for Advanced Research in Arts and Social Sciences, University of Birmingham, Edgbaston, Birmingham B15 2TT (tel 0121 414 5850)

BOULTON, Richard Edward Stanley; s of Sir Clifford Boulton, GCB, DL, and Anne, *née* Raven; *b* 3 May 1959; *Educ* Marlborough (Wedgwood scholar), Oriel Coll Oxford (MA, half blue), Guildford Coll of Law (Dip Law), BPP Law Sch (Bar vocational course); *m* 23 July 1994, Fiona Jane Boulton, *qv*, da of Michael Harry Lockton; 2 da (Honor Olivia Anne b 26 April 1998, Katia Jane Imogen b 23 Sept 2001), 1 s (Fraser William James b 22 Jan 2000); *Career* Arthur Andersen 1981–2001: joined 1981, ptnr 1990, head of Econ and Fin Consulting 1994–97, head of Business Consulting 1995–97, global managing ptnr strategy and planning 1997–2000, global managing ptnr Business Consulting 2000–01, chief info offr 2000–01; dir LECG 2002–; barr One Essex Court 2003–; advsr to Office of Rail Regulator 1994, conslt to Scott Inquiry 1995; treas Friends of the Tate Gallery; FAE 1994, FCA 1996 (ACA 1984); *Publications* co-author Cracking the Value Code: How Successful Businesses are Creating Wealth in the New Economy (2000); *Recreations* golf, running, travel, wine, modern art; *Clubs* MCC, Wisley Golf; *Style—* Richard Boulton, Esq; ✉ Waterton, Cleardown, Woking, Surrey GU22 7HH (tel 01483 760258, fax 01483 771272, e-mail richardeboulton@hotmail.com)

BOURDILLON, Dr Peter John; s of John Francis Bourdillon (d 1992), of Bradford-on-Avon, Wilts, and Pamela Maud, *née* Chetham (d 1992); *b* 10 July 1941; *Educ* Rugby, Middlesex Hospital Med Sch (MB, BS); *m* 1964, Catriona Charmian Cecil, da of Brig Walter Glencairn-Campbell OBE; 2 da (Charmian Xenia (Mrs Andrew H Findlay) b 4 Feb 1968, Helena Maude b 30 April 1974), 1 s (Paul Charles Chetham b 14 April 1972); *Career* house physician and surgeon posts in London 1965–68, med registrar Middlesex Hosp 1969–70; Hammersmith Hosp: med registrar 1970–72, sr registrar in cardiology 1972–74, pt/t conslt in cardiology 1975–2006; Dept of Health (formerly DHSS): pt/t med offr 1975–81, pt/t sr med offr 1981–91, head of Medical Manpower and Educn Div NHS Mgmnt Exec 1991–93, head Health Care Medical Div 1993–95, head Specialist Clinical Services Div 1995–97, seconded to Acad of Med Royal Colls 1997–2001; hon sr lectr Univ of London 1979–; pt/t cardiologist Hertford Cardiology 2002–07; pt/t med awards administrator Assoc of Cwlth Univs 2001–; numerous articles in med jls; memb: BMA 1965, British Cardiac Soc 1972; FRCP 1983 (MRCP 1968), QHP 1996–99; *Recreations* writing software, golf, skiing; *Clubs* Highgate Golf; *Style—* Dr Peter Bourdillon; ✉ 13 Grove Terrace London NW5 1PH (tel 020 7485 6839, e-mail pbourdillon@msn.com)

BOURKE, Dr Brian Eamonn; s of Edmund Egan Bourke (d 1961), and Joan Eileen, *née* Kiernan; *b* 29 April 1948; *Educ* Beaumont Coll, King's Coll and King's Coll Hosp Univ of London (MB BS); *m* 25 March 1972, Elisabeth Janie, da of Brig Christopher Percy Sibthorpe Bright, CBE (d 1988), of Henley-on-Thames, Oxon; 2 da (Serena Katherine b 15 March 1974, Imogen Elisabeth b 6 July 1984), 2 s (Henry Edmund b 12 April 1976, Piers Christopher b 18 Aug 1978); *Career* house surgn KCH London 1972, house physician Royal Berks Hosp Reading 1972, sr house offr in med The London Hosp 1972–74, med registrar St Stephen's Hosp London 1974–76, registrar and sr registrar Charing Cross Hosp London 1976–81, conslt physician and hon sr lectr St George's Hosp and Med Sch London 1981–; hon sec Br Soc for Rheumatology 1990–94, memb BR Soc for Immunology; pres Section of Rheumatology Royal Soc of Med, MRCP 1974, FRCP 1989; *Recreations* tennis, swimming, skiing; *Clubs* Hurlingham, Queen's; *Style—* Dr Brian Bourke; ✉ 152 Harley Street, London W1G 7LH (tel 020 7935 2477); St George's Hospital, London SW17 0QT (tel 020 8672 1255)

BOURKE, Rt Rev Michael Gay; *see:* Wolverhampton, Bishop of

BOURN, Sir John Bryant; KCB (1991, CB 1986); s of Henry Thomas Bryant Bourn (d 1997), and Beatrice Grace, *née* Pope (d 1979); *b* 21 February 1934; *Educ* Southgate County GS, London Sch of Economics (BSc, PhD); *m* 21 March 1959, Ardita Ann, da of Maurice Wilfred Fleming (d 1940); 1 s (Jonathan b 1967), 1 da (Sherida b 1962); *Career* Air Miny 1956–63, HM Treasy 1963–64, private sec to Permanent Under Sec MOD 1964–69, asst sec and dir of programmes Civil Serv Coll 1969–72, asst sec MOD 1972–74, under sec N Ireland Office 1974–77, asst under sec of state MOD 1977–82, dep sec N Ireland Office 1982–84, dep under sec of state (Defence Procurement) MOD 1985–88, comptroller and auditor gen 1988–, auditor gen for Wales 1999–2005, PM's ind advsr on mins' intersts 2006–; chm Professional Oversight Bd 2003–; visiting prof LSE 1983–; *Recreations* swimming; *Style—* Sir John Bourn, KCB; ✉ National Audit Office, 159–197 Buckingham Palace Road, Victoria, London SW1W 9SP

BOURN, Prof (Alan) Michael; s of Ernest James Bourn (d 1988), and Frances Mary, *née* Fones (d 1977); *b* 10 June 1934; *Educ* Southgate County GS London, LSE (BSc); *m* 1, 4 April 1960 (m dis 1986), (Karoline) Sigrid, *née* Hegmann; 2 s (Alexander b 1961, Jeremy b 1962); m 2, 21 August 1998, Eileen Dorothy, *née* Walker; 1 step da (Sarah b 1973); *Career* Nat Serv 2 Lt RAPC 1958–60; professional accounting 1954–58, IBM UK Ltd 1960–61; various academic appts in London, Liverpool and Manchester 1962–69; prof of industrial admin Univ of Canterbury NZ 1969–72, prof of business studies Univ of Liverpool 1972–80, chm Liverpool University Press 1976–80, govr Chester Coll 1977–80; Univ of Southampton: prof of accounting 1980–99, dean Faculty of Social Sciences 1983–86, dep vice-chllr 1986–90, prof emeritus 1999–; visiting prof Queen's Univ Belfast 2000 and 2001; pres Assoc of Univ Teachers of Accounting 1982–83, chm Conf of Profs of Accounting 1987–90; memb Bd Nuffield Theatre Tst 1991–94; chm Multicosm Ltd (now Active Navigation Ltd) 1995–97; conslt: DTI 1992–2006, Burnett Swayne & Numerica 1994–, CSSO Ireland 2000, QAA 2000–05, DETE Ireland 2001–02, UNDP 2003–05, Br Univs Finance Dirs' Gp (BUFDG) 2005–; FCA 1968 (ACA 1958); *Books* Shipping Enterprise and Management 1830–1939 (with F E Hyde and J R Harris, 1967), Studies In Accounting for Management Decision (1969), Favell's Book-keeping & Accounts (7 edn, 1980), Industrial Development In Merseyside (with P Stoney, 1984), Management Accounting in Healthcare (with C M S Sutcliffe, 1996); *Recreations* trumpet-playing, leader of Mardi Gras jazz band, golf; *Style—* Prof Michael Bourn; ✉ Centre for Higher Education Management and Policy, School of Managment, University of Southampton, Southampton SO17 1BJ (tel 023 8059 7797, fax 023 8059 3844, e-mail michaelbourn@beeb.net)

BOURNE, Adrian Rodney; s of Leslie Bourne, and Marjorie Bourne; *b* 5 July 1944; *Educ* King Edward's Five Ways GS Birmingham; *m*; 1 c; *Career* sales rep Pan Books Ltd 1970–72; Hodder and Stoughton Ltd: sales rep 1972–74, paperback sales mangr H&S NZ 1974–78, paperback export sales mangr/dir 1978–85, paperback sales and mktg dir 1985–87, md (paperbacks) 1987–91; HarperCollins Publishers: md Int Sales Div 1991–93, md Trade Gp Sales Div 1993–96, md Trade Div 1996–2001; md Weidenfeld & Nicolson 2002–05; *Recreations* golf, wine, gardening, computing; *Clubs* RAC, 50 St James's, Bletchingley Golf, Manor House Castle Coombe, Autowink; *Style—* Adrian Bourne, Esq

BOURNE, Debra Lysette; da of Brian Neville Bourne, and Leila Ruby Simcovitch; *b* 12 February 1964; *Educ* Ilford Co HS for Girls, E Ham Tech Coll, NE London Poly; *m* 9 Sept 2001, David Henry Rosen; 1 s (Johnny Curtis Bourne Rosen b June 1999); *Career* co dir Lynne Franks PR 1990–92 (joined 1984), PR conslt 1993–; specialist in consumer public relations focusing on youth market, brand positioning, image creation and promotion, clients incl: Katharine Hamnett, Jean Paul Gaultier, Pepe Jeans, Knickerbox, Coca Cola Clothes, Ghost, Swatch, Fiorucci; creative conslt 1997–, clients incl: The Beatles, Donna Karan, Frank Magazine; exec fashion ed Arena and Arena Homme Plus magazines 1995–99, contrib ed GQ magazine 2000–; *Style—* Ms Debra Bourne; ✉ 12a Clifton Gardens, London W9 1DT (tel 020 7289 6588, fax 020 7289 6230, e-mail debra.bourne@mailbox.co.uk)

BOURNE, Henry; s of Prof Kenneth Bourne (d 1992), and Eleanor Anne, *née* Wells (d 1996); *b* 10 May 1963; *Educ* City of London Sch, Crown Woods Sch; *m* 2002, Harriet Anstruther; *Career* photographer; photographic asst to Michael Joseph 1982–84, freelance photographic asst 1984–86, freelance photographer of portraits, fashion, interiors, still life and reportage; cmmns incl contribs to: Arena Homme Plus, Elle, Elle Decoration, Esquire, GQ, The Guardian, Harper's Bazaar (US), The Independent, Vanity Fair, Vogue, W, Wallpaper, World of Interiors; exhbns: Fashion Acts 1996, 1997 and 1998, Condé Nast Traveller 1999 and 2002, DIFFA NY 2000–01; Gold Medal Photography Award Soc of Pubn Designers USA 1997; *Books* The Ivy: The Restaurant and its Recipes, Le Caprice; *Style—* Henry Bourne, Esq; ✉ 43 Thurloe Square, London SW7 2SR (tel 020 7225 0044, e-mail info@henrybourne.com, website www.henrybourne.com)

BOURNE, Prof (Frederick) John; CBE; s of Sydney John Bourne (d 1960), of Evesham, Worcs, and Florence Beatrice, *née* Craven (d 1988); *b* 3 January 1937; *Educ* Prince Henry's GS Evesham, RVC (BVetMed, MRCVS), Univ of Bristol (PhD); *m* 12 Sept 1959, Mary Angela, da of William Reginald Minter (d 1990); 2 s (Stephen b 1962, Nigel b 1964); *Career* asst in gen vet practice Cornwall 1961–62, jr ptnr in 2–man vet practice Glos 1962–66; Univ of Bristol: lectr in animal husbandry 1966–74, reader in animal husbandry 1974–80, prof and head Dept of Vet Med 1980–88, BBSRC prof of animal health 1988–97; visiting prof Univ of Reading 1988–97; dir BBSRC Inst for Animal Health 1988–97; chm Govt Ind Scientific Gp on Control of Cattle TB 1998–; memb: Technol Interaction Bd BBSRC 1992–97, Agric and Veterinary Ctee Br Cncl 1994–98; hon fell Edward Jenner

Inst for Vaccine Res 2001–; foreign memb Polish Acad of Scis; *Books* Advances in Veterinary Immunology (1984 and 1985); chapters in over 20 books; *Recreations* golf, fishing; *Style*— Prof John Bourne, CBE; ✉ Westlands, Jubilee Lane, Langford, Bristol BS40 5EJ (tel and fax 01934 852464, e-mail johnbourne@westlands68.freeserve.co.uk)

BOURNE, Matthew Christopher; OBE (2001); s of Harold Jeffrey (Jim) Bourne, of London, and June Lillian, *née* Handley; *b* 13 January 1960; *Educ* Sir George Monoux Sch London, The Laban Centre (BA); *Career* dancer Transitions Dance Co 1986, fndr, artistic dir, resident choreographer and performer Adventures In Motion Pictures (AMP) 1987, artistic dir New Adventures 2001–; hon fell Laban Centre 1997 (memb bd of dirs 2000–); *Choreography* for AMP incl: Overlap Lovers 1987, Buck and Wing 1988, Spitfire 1988, The Infernal Galop 1989 (revived 1992), Green Fingers 1990, Town and Country 1991, Deadly Serious 1992, Nutcracker (co-prodn with Opera North 1992, revived 1993), The Percys of Fitzrovia 1992, Highland Fling 1994, Swan Lake 1995 (TV 1996, revised for LA 1997 and NY 1998–99), Cinderella 1997 (revised for LA 1999), The Car Man (2000/01); performed with choreographers incl: Jacob Marley, Brigitte Farges, Ashley Page; fndr memb Lea Anderson's Featherstonehaughs 1988; choreography for theatre incl: As You Like It (RSC, Stratford and Barbican) 1989, Singer (RSC, Stratford and Barbican) 1989, Leonce and Lena (Crucible Sheffield) 1989, Children of Eden (Prince Edward Theatre) 1991, A Midsummer Night's Dream (Aix-en-Provence Opera Festival) 1991, The Tempest (Nat Youth Theatre 1991, revived 1993), Show Boat (Malmö Stadsteater Sweden) 1991, Peer Gynt (Ninagawa Co Oslo, Barbican and World Tour) 1994, Watch with Mother (Nat Youth Dance Co) 1994, Cameron Mackintosh's revival of Oliver! (London Palladium) 1994, Boutique (Images of Dance) 1995, Watch Your Step (Irving Berlin Gala) 1995, Franch and Saunders Live 2000, My Fair Lady (RNT and Drury Lane) 2001, South Pacific (RNT) 2002, Dearest Love (George Piper Dances) 2003; with New Adventures: Play without Words (RNT) 2002, Nutcracker! (Sadlers Wells) 2002; *Television* incl: Late Flowering Lust (BBC/Ecosse Films) 1993, Drip: A Self-Love Story (BBC) 1993, Roald Dahl's Little Red Riding Hood (BBC) 1995, Swan Lake (BBC) 1996, subject of South Bank Show 1997, presenter Channel 4 Dance 1999, The Car Man (Channel 4), Bourne to Dance (Channel 4) 2002, Nutcracker! (BBC 1) 2003; *Awards* incl: Place Portfolio Award 1989, Bonnie Bird Choreography Award 1989, Barclays New Stages Award 1990, nominated for Most Outstanding Achievement in Dance Olivier Award 1992, nominated for Best New Dance Prodn (The Nutcracker) Olivier Awards 1994; over 25 awards for Swan Lake incl: Olivier Award for Swan Lake 1996, Los Angeles Drama Critics Circle and Dramalogue Awards for Swan Lake 1997, Time Out Special Award 1997, SouthBank Show Award 1998, 2 Drama Desk Awards 1999, 2 Outer Critics Circle Awards 1999, 2 Tony Awards (dir and choreographer) 1999, Astaire Award 1999, Olivier Award for Outstanding Choreography 2002, Hamburg Shakespeare Prize 2003, Olivier Awards for Outstanding Choreography and Best Entertainment for Play Without Words 2003; *Publications* Matthew Bourne & His Adventures in Motion Pictures (ed Alastair Macauley, 1999); *Recreations* theatre, cinema, the choreography of Frederick Ashton and Fred Astaire, the music of Percy Grainger, Ella Fitzgerald and most pre-1950 singers; *Clubs* Soho House; *Style*— Matthew Bourne, Esq, OBE; ✉ 21 Stamford Road, London N1 4JP (e-mail mattbourneathome@aol.com); c/o Jessica Sykes, ICM, Oxford House, 76 Oxford Street, London W1 2SH (tel 020 7636 6565, fax 020 7323 0701)

BOURNE, Nicholas; AM; *b* 1 January 1952; *Educ* King Edward VI GS Chelmsford, UCW Aberystwyth (LLB), Univ of Cambridge (LLM), Univ of Wales (LLM); *Career* called to the Bar Grays Inn 1972 (Bacon Holt and Uthwatt entrance scholar, Lee essay prize, Holker sr scholar, Arden Atken and Reid prize); formerly dean of Swansea Law Sch, asst princ Swansea Inst of HE; supervisor in law: CCC Cambridge 1974–80, St Catharine's Coll Cambridge 1974–82, LSE 1975–79; princ Chart University Tutors Ltd 1979–88, co sec and dir Chart Foulks Lynch plc 1984–88, dir Holborn Gp Ltd 1988–91, dir of studies Holborn Law Tutors Ltd 1988–91, sr lectr in law South Bank Univ 1991–92, lectr in company law UCL 1991–96; lecture tours in Singapore and Malaysia 1980–1992, visiting lectr Univ of Hong Kong 1996–; consultancies incl: external examiner Univ of London LLB 1991–2000, editorial bd Malaysian Law News 1991–2004, editorial advsy bd Business Law Review 1991–, West Wales TEC for the provision of legal advice 1992–96; memb Nat Assembly for Wales (Cons) Wales Mid & West (regnl list) 1999–, ldr Cons Pty Nat Assembly for Wales 1999–; memb: NE Thames RHA 1990–92, W Glamorgan HA 1994–97; MInstD 1984; *Publications* Duties and Responsiblities of British Company Directors (1982), British Company Law and Practice (1983), Business British Law for Accountants (1987), Lecture Notes for Company Law (3rd edn, 1998), Scottish Company Law (with Brian Pillans, 1996, 2nd edn, 1999), Essential Company Law (2nd edn, 1997), Business Law and Practice (1994); regular contrib to business and company law journals; *Recreations* walking, tennis, badminton, squash, cricket, theatre, rugby, travel, cinema, Nat Tst, NSPCC, The British Heart Fndn; *Clubs* Oxford and Cambridge; *Style*— Nicholas Bourne, Esq, AM; ✉ National Assembly for Wales, Cardiff Bay, Cardiff CF99 1NA (tel 029 2089 8351, fax 029 2089 8350, e-mail nicholas.bourne@wales.gov.uk)

BOURNE, Stephen Robert Richard; s of Colyn Morton Bourne, and Kathleen, *née* Turner; *Educ* Berkhamsted Sch, Univ of Edinburgh (MA), Univ of Cambridge (MA); *m* 1978, Stephanie Ann Bickford; 1 da (Jessica b 1985), 1 s (Robert b 1987); *Career* various posts: Deloitte Haskins & Sells 1974–80, Exxon Chemical Asia-Pacific Ltd 1980–86, Dow Jones Telerate 1986–94; md Burrups Ltd and Westerham Press Ltd 1994–96, with Cambridge Univ Press 1997– (chief exec and univ printer 2002–); dir Britten Sinfonia Ltd; dir Wine Soc; Liveryman Worshipful Co of Stationers and Newspaper Makers (memb Ct of Assts); official fell Clare Hall Cambridge; memb Inst of Paper, Printing and Publishing (IP3); FCA 1977 (ACA 1974), FRSA; *Recreations* performing arts, cricket, skiing, fine wines; *Clubs* Athenaeum, Wynkyn de Worde Soc, Hong Kong, Hong Kong Soc, Aberdeen BC (Hong Kong), Royal Cwlth Soc, Kent CCC, Middlesex CCC, Exning CC, Cambridge Univ Real Tennis, Cambridge Univ Lawn Tennis (hon vice-pres); *Style*— Stephen Bourne, Esq; ✉ Falmouth Lodge, Snailwell Road, Newmarket, Suffolk CB8 7DN (tel 01638 667006, fax 01638 667005, e-mail bournesnewmarket@btinternet.com); Cambridge University Press, Shaftesbury Road, Cambridge CB2 2RU (tel 01223 312393, fax 01223 325701, e-mail sbourne@cambridge.org)

BOURNE, Valerie (Val); CBE (2004, OBE 1991); *Educ* Elmhurst Ballet Sch, Royal Ballet Sch (also with Cleo Nordi, Anna Northcote and Andrew Hardie); *Career* performed with: Royal Ballet and Opera Ballet in final year at Royal Ballet Sch 1960–61, Sadlers Wells Opera Ballet 1961–63; Wilfred Stiff Assocs PR (clients incl: Ballet Rambert, Owen Brannigan, Daniel Barenboim, John Ogden, Cyril and Phyllis Sellick); press and publicity offr: London Festival Ballet 1967, Ballet Rambert 1968–76; asst to offr i/c dance Music Dept Arts Cncl of GB 1976–77, dance offr Gtr London Arts 1977–80, artistic dir Dance Umbrella 1980– (organised first Dance Umbrella Festival 1978); Digital Dance Premier Award 1989, Int Theatre Inst Award 1990; Chevalier de l'Ordre des Arts et des Lettres (France) 1996; *Style*— Ms Val Bourne, CBE; ✉ Dance Umbrella, 20 Chancellor's Street, London W6 9RN (tel 020 8741 4040, fax 020 8741 7902)

BOURNE-ARTON, Simon Nicholas; QC (1994); yr s of Maj Anthony Temple Bourne-Arton, MBE (d 1996), of West Tanfield, N Yorks, and (Margaret) Elaine (d 2001), da of W Denby Arton, of Sleningford Park, N Yorks; *b* 5 September 1949; *Educ* Harrow, Teesside Poly (HND), Univ of Leeds (LLB); *m* 1974, Diana Carr-Walker; 2 s (James b 3 Aug 1977, Tom b 19 March 1980), 1 da (Isabel b 15 Aug 1983); *Career* called to the Bar Inner Temple 1975 (bencher 2003); in practice NE Circuit, recorder of the Crown Court 1993–; *Recreations* golf, tennis, walking, wine, family and friends; *Style*— Simon Bourne-Arton, Esq, QC; ✉ Park Court Chambers, 16 Park Place, Leeds LS1 2SJ (tel 0113 243 3277, fax 0113 242 1285)

BOURNEMOUTH, Archdeacon of; *see:* Harbidge, Ven Adrian Guy

BOURSNELL, Clive; s of Raymond Robert Morgan, of Sunningdale, Berks, and Vera, *née* Kossick; *b* 2 June 1942; *Educ* Corona Stage Sch; *Career* professional photographer (initially working in fashion, currently specialising in portraits and feature work); child actor appearing on TV and in films: Hunted (with Dirk Bogarde) 1952, The Beggar's Opera (with Laurence Olivier) 1952; woodman Windsor Great Park Berks 1958–60; extensive travelling throughout Canada 1960–64: successively dairy farmer, pit labourer in uranium and gold mines, door-to-door magazines salesman, prospector for natural gas and oil, asst glaciologist Geography Dept McGill Univ Montreal, mountaineer High Arctic 1964–67; fashion photographer's asst London, staff photographer Ambassador Magazine 1968–69, freelance photographer 1969–; work featured in various pubns incl: The Observer, Vogue and Honey magazines, Sunday Times and Telegraph magazines, Independent on Sunday, Illustrated London News, Country Living, Country Life; nat and int lectures and slide shows on English gardens and photographing gardens; fndr memb Photographers Assoc 1968 (variously memb Cncl); *Books* Covent Garden Market (1977), The Royal Opera House (1982), English Herb Gardens (1986), English Water Gardens (1987), Making of the English Garden (1989), The Curious Gardener (2001 and 2002); *Recreations* photography, opera, dance, walking, climbing (lone attempt of Mt McKinley Alaska, mountaineer on Arctic expedition to Alex Hieberg), being me; *Style*— Clive Boursnell, Esq; ✉ 5A Borneo Street, London SW15 1QQ (tel 020 8789 8956, fax 020 8785 1110, mobile 078 3164 7244); The Old Chapel, Bucks Mill, Bideford, Devon EX39 5DY

BOUTWOOD, Nigel Peter Ralph; *b* 12 May 1951; *Educ* Lancing; *m* 2 April 1977, Jeanette Elsma, da of Jeffery Warner Etherington; 2 da (Emma Jane Elsma b 1980, Tiffany Roberta b 1982), 1 s (Charles Peter Warner b 1991); *Career* J Walter Thompson 1970, Thames TV 1971–78, Southern TV 1978–82, TVS 1982–85, chm and md Boutwood Advertising Ltd 1985–; chm of tstees Charlie's Challenge Charity (raising funds for research into children's brain tumours) 1995–; *Recreations* sailing, skiing, tennis; *Clubs* Aspinall's; *Style*— Nigel Boutwood, Esq; ✉ Boutwood Advertising Ltd, 37 Terminus Road, Eastbourne, East Sussex BN21 3QL (tel 01323 640212, fax 01323 411999, e-mail info@boutwood.com)

BOVEY, Barry William Vincent; OBE (1979); s of William Vincent Bovey (d 1965), of Worcester, and Irene Ida, *née* Holderness (d 1982); *b* 29 October 1929; *Educ* Haileybury, Univ of London; *m* 1, 23 June 1954 (m dis 1978), Daphne Joan, da of Cdr Arthur Gordon Marshall, RNR (d 1981), of Hampton Court; 2 s (Michael b 1957, Nigel b 1961); *m* 2, 22 Dec 1979, Jean Christine, da of Ronald Yeardley Goddard (d 1991), of Sheffield; *Career* Nat Serv RA 1951–53, Capt RA (TA) 1953–57; gp sales dir Robert Jenkins Ltd 1967–72, chm Orbit Valve plc 1974–95 (md 1972–74); vice-pres Energy Industries Cncl 1984–93 and 1996– (chm 1980–84 and 1993–96); Process Plant EDC: memb Nat Econ Devpt Office 1980–87, chm Int Mktg Gp 1981–87; Freeman City of London, memb Ct of Assts Worshipful Co of Glovers; FCIM 1980, FIEx 1987, FInstD 1979; *Recreations* yachting, golf, tennis; *Clubs* Royal Thames Yacht; *Style*— Barry Bovey, Esq, OBE; ✉ Chadmore House, Willersey, Broadway, Worcestershire WR12 7PH (tel 01386 858 922, fax 01386 858305, mobile 07711 105701)

BOVEY, Dr Leonard; s of Alfred Bovey (d 1968, twice Mayor of Exeter), and Gladys, *née* Brereton; *b* 9 May 1924; *Educ* Hele's Sch Exeter, Emmanuel Coll Cambridge (BA, PhD); *m* Nov 1944, Constance (d 1987), da of Thomas Hudson (d 1960); 1 s (Christopher b 1951), 1 da (Jennifer b 1955); *Career* postdoctoral fell Nat Res Cncl Ottawa 1950–52, AERE Harwell 1952–65; dir: W Midlands Regnl Office Miny of Tech 1966–70, Yorks & Humberside DTI 1970–73; cnsllr scientific and technol affrs High Cmmn Ottawa 1974–77, head Technol Requirements Branch DTI 1977–84; ed Materials & Design (Butterworth Heinemann) 1985–; CPhys, FInstP; *Recreations* theatre, music; *Clubs* Civil Service, London Scientific Diplomat; *Style*— Dr Leonard Bovey; ✉ 32 Radnor Walk, London SW3 4BN (tel 020 7352 4142)

BOVEY, Philip Henry; s of Cdr Norman Henry Bovey, OBE, DSC, VRD (d 2005), and Dorothy Yvonne, *née* Kent Williams (d 2003); *b* 11 July 1948; *Educ* Rugby, Peterhouse Cambridge (scholar, MA); *m* 14 Sept 1974, Jenet Alison, da of Canon James Mitchell McTear (d 1973); 2 c (Katherine b 1976, Stephen b 1978); *Career* FCO 1970–71; admitted slr 1974; Slaughter & May 1972–75, DTI 1976–77, Cabinet Office 1977–78; DTI 1978–: under sec 1985–, dir of legal servs 1996–2004, dir Co Law Reform Bill Project 2005–07; inspr Companies Act 1984–88; *Recreations* photography; *Style*— Philip Bovey, Esq; ✉ 102 Cleveland Gardens, Barnes, London SW13 0AH (tel 020 8876 3710)

BOWATER, Sir John Vansittart; 4 Bt (UK 1914), of Hill Crest, Borough of Croydon; s of Capt Victor Spencer Bowater (d 1967), 3 s of 1 Bt; suc unc, Sir (Thomas) Dudley (Blennerhassett) Bowater, 3 Bt, 1972; *b* 6 April 1918; *m* 1943, Joan Kathleen (d 1982), da of Wilfrid Ernest Henry Scullard (d 1963), of Boscombe; 1 s (Michael Patrick b 1949), 1 da (Penelope Ann (Mrs Martin Doughty) b 1954); *Heir* s, Michael Bowater; *Career* dir Oswald Bailey Gp of Cos; cncllr Bournemouth Town Cncl 1983–91; *Style*— Sir John Bowater, Bt; ✉ 214 Runnymede Avenue, Bearwood, Bournemouth, Dorset (tel 01202 571782)

BOWDEN, Sir Andrew; kt (1994) MBE (1961); s of William Victor Bowden, of Brighton, E Sussex, and Francesa Wilson; *b* 8 April 1930; *Educ* Ardingly; *m* 1970, Benita, da of B A Napier, of Brighton, E Sussex; 1 s, 1 da; *Career* worked in paint industry 1955–68, personnel conslt 1967–; memb Wandsworth BC 1956–62, nat chm Young Cons 1960–61; Parly candidate (Cons): N Hammersmith 1955, N Kensington 1964, Kemptown Brighton 1966; MP (Cons) Brighton Kemptown 1970–97; memb Select Ctees on: Expenditure 1973–74, Abortion 1975, Employment 1979–97; jt chm All-Pty Parly Gp for Pensioners 1971–97, int chm People to People 1981–83, memb Cncl of Europe 1987–97; int conslt to Global Equities Corp NY 2004–; nat pres Captive Animals Protection Soc 1975–97; *Books* Dare We Trust Them - A New Vision for Europe (jtly, 2005); *Recreations* chess, golf, poker; *Clubs* Carlton; *Style*— Sir Andrew Bowden, MBE; ✉ Ashdene, 4 Carden Avenue, Brighton, East Sussex BN1 8NA (tel 01273 552136)

BOWDEN, Gerald Francis; TD; s of Frank Albert Bowden, and Elsie, *née* Burrill; *b* 26 August 1935; *Educ* Battersea GS, Magdalen Coll Oxford, Coll of Estate Mgmnt; *m* 1967, Heather Elizabeth Hill, *née* Hall (d 1984); 2 da, 1 step s, 1 step da; *Career* called to the Bar Gray's Inn 1963, chartered surveyor; cncllr Dulwich Div GLC 1977–81, MP (Cons) Dulwich 1983–92; in practice as barrister 1992–; univ lectr 1992–; chm Leasehold Valuation Tbnl and Rent Assessment Panel 1994–; princ lectr in law Dept of Estate Mgmnt South Bank Univ (formerly South Bank Poly) 1972–83; *Style*— Gerald Bowden, Esq, TD

BOWDEN, Sir Nicholas Richard; 4 Bt (UK 1915), of City of Nottingham; s of Sir Frank Houston Bowden, 3 Bt (d 2001); *b* 13 August 1935; *Educ* Millfield; *Career* Nat Serv, former trooper Life Gds; farmer; *Recreations* riding; *Style*— Sir Nicholas Bowden, Bt; ✉ 4 Hensting Farm Cottages, Hensting Lane, Fishers Pond, Eastleigh, Hampshire SO50 7HH (tel 01962 777260)

BOWDLER, Timothy John (Tim); CBE (2006); s of Henry Neville Bowdler (d 2003), and Barbara Mary, *née* Richardson; *b* 16 May 1947, Wolverhampton; *Educ* Wrekin Coll, Univ of Birmingham (BSc), London Business Sch (MBA); *m* 1976, Brita Margaretha, *née* Eklund; 2 da (Emma b 27 May 1978, Anna b 17 July 1980); *Career* grad mgmnt trainee rising to branch admin mangr GKN Stanley Ltd 1969–73; RHP Bearings Ltd: commercial mangr 1975–77, gen mangr Business Ops 1977–81; Sandvik Ltd: dir and gen mangr Sandvik Steel 1981–84, md Spooner Industries Ltd 1984–87; md Chloride Motive Power Chloride Gp plc 1987–88, dir Northern Div Tyzack & Partners Ltd 1989–90; Cape plc: divnl md Cape Architectural Products 1990–92, divnl md Cape Building and Architectural Products 1992–94; Johnston Press plc: gp md 1994–97, chief exec 1997–; chm Press Standards Bd of Finance Ltd 2000–; non-exec dir: Assoc Br Ports Holdings plc 2001–06, Press Assoc 2001–, Miller Gp 2004–; Newspaper Soc: pres 2002–03, memb Cncl, chm Political, Editorial and Regulatory Affrs (PERA) Ctee; FRSA 2003; *Recreations* golf, skiing, Swedish summerhouse, sailing, fishing; *Clubs* Bruntsfield Links Golfing Soc, New (Edinburgh); *Style—* Tim Bowdler, Esq, CBE; ✉ Johnston Press plc, 53 Manor Place, Edinburgh EH3 7EG (tel 01312 253 361, fax 01312 267 230, e-mail tbowdler@johnstonpress.co.uk)

BOWE, Prof Michael; *Educ* Univ of Oxford, Univ of Manchester, Carleton Univ Ottawa; *Career* asst prof of economics Simon Fraser Univ 1984–93, joined Manchester Sch of Mgmnt 1993, currently prof of int finance Univ of Manchester; Bank of Valletta prof of int banking and finance Univ of Malta 1993–2007; visiting prof: Helsinki Sch of Economics and Business Admin 1988–2000, Univ of Vienna 1996, Emory Univ 1999, Nat Univ of the Ukraine Kyiv-Mohyla Inst 2003; research assoc Columbia Univ NY 1986–89, fell Nat Univ of Singapore 1992–93; conslt to various instns incl: World Bank, Canadian Int Dept Agency, Govt of BC, Union Bank of Finland Ltd, Den Danske Bank, Kansallis-Osake-Pankki, Bank of Valletta, Singapore Stock Exchange, Finnish Options Market; memb: Royal Economic Soc, American Economics Assoc, Canadian Economics Assoc, European Finance Assoc, European International Business Acad; FCIB; *Books* incl: Eurobonds (1988), Has the Market Solved the Sovereign-Debt Crisis? (jtly, 1997), Banking and Finance in Islands and Small States (jt ed, 1998); *Style—* Prof Michael Bowe; ✉ Manchester Business School, The University of Manchester, Booth Street West, Manchester M15 6PB

BOWEN, Anthony James George; JP (1972), DL (2006); s of Howard James Bowen (d 1976), of Saundersfoot, Dyfed, and Georgina Ann, *née* Morris (d 2005); *b* 29 January 1941; *Educ* Narbeth GS, Loughborough Coll of Advanced Tech (DLC); *m* 1 June 1973, Patricia Ann, da of Douglas Edward Watson Hutchinson (d 1964), of Nottingham; 1 step s (Simon Miles Barrett b 30 April 1967), 1 step da (Lisa Ellen Kessels b 29 April 1970); *Career* chm and md Green Bower Garages Ltd (BMW main dealers Dyfed) 1963–; chm: Pembrokeshire NHS Tst 1992–95, Pembrokeshire Petty Sessions Div; memb Cncl The Prince's Trust Cymru 2001–; sub prior Priory for Wales Order of St John 1991–98; memb Rotary Int, former memb Round Table; FIMI 1984; KStJ 1988; *Recreations* golf, skiing, walking; *Style—* Anthony Bowen, Esq, DL; ✉ St Giles, Uzmaston Road, Haverfordwest, Pembrokeshire SA61 1TZ (tel 01437 762792); Green Bower Garages Ltd, Slebech, Haverfordwest, Pembrokeshire SA62 4PD (tel 01437 771122, fax 01437 751373)

BOWEN, Christopher Richard Croasdaile (Kit); s of Christopher James Croasdaile Bowen (ka 1944), and Helen Florence Anderton, *née* Lyons; *b* 7 October 1944; *Educ* Rugby; *m* 22 April 1972, Janet Margaret, da of Capt Alexander Francis Matheson, RN; 1 da (Nicola Frances b 26 March 1976), 1 s (Robert James Croasdaile b 28 April 1978); *Career* Royal Tank Regt 1963–68; IBM (UK) 1969–79; chartered accountant 1983; Saffery Champness: joined 1980, ptnr 1983–, dep chm 1993–95, chm 1995–97; FCCA 1979; *Recreations* the countryside; *Style—* Christopher Bowen, Esq; ✉ Kinellan House, Strathpeffer, Ross-shire IV14 9ET (tel 01997 421476, e-mail kit.bowen@saffery.com); Saffery Champness, Lion House, Red Lion Street, London WC1R 4GB (tel 020 7841 4000, fax 020 7841 4100); Saffery Champness, Kintail House, Beechwood Park, Inverness IV2 3BW (tel 01463 246300, fax 01463 246301)

BOWEN, Prof David Quentin; s of William Esmond Bowen (d 1984), of Heddlys, Glasfryn, Llanelli, and Jane, *née* Williams (d 1992); *b* 14 February 1938; *Educ* Llanelli GS, UCL (BSc, PhD); *m* 18 Sept 1965, Elizabeth, da of David Islwyn Williams (d 1989); 2 s (Huw b 1966, Wyn b 1969); *Career* prof of physical geography UCW Aberystwyth 1983–85, prof of geography Royal Holloway Coll London 1985–88; prof and dir Inst of Earth Studies UCW 1988–93; Univ of Wales Cardiff: prof of quaternary geology 1994–2004, emeritus prof 2005–, Leverhulme emeritus fell 2005–07; fndr ed-in-chief Quaternary Sci Review 1982–94, pres Quaternary Res Assoc (UK) 1979–81, pres INQUA Stratigraphy Cmmn (Int Union for Quaternary Res) 1991–93; memb: NERC Ctees 1978–96, UGC Earth Sci Review 1988, Nature Conservancy Cncl 1986–91, Jt Nature Conservation Ctee (GB) 1990–97, Dutch Univs Earth Sci Review 1996, Sci Advsy Panel Nat Museum of Wales, American Geophysical Union; chm Llanelli Millennium Coastal Park Forum 1996–2001, dep chm Countryside Cncl for Wales 1990–2000; BBC Wales Annual Lecture 1996; hon memb INQUA 1999; *Books* Quaternary Geology (1978, Russian edn 1982), The Llanelli Landscape (1980), Glaciations in the Northern Hemisphere (1986); *Recreations* music, rugby, cricket; *Style—* Prof David Bowen; ✉ School of Earth, Ocean and Planetary Sciences, Cardiff University, Cardiff CF10 3YE (tel 029 2087 4337, fax 029 2087 4326, e-mail bowendq@cardiff.ac.uk)

BOWEN, Sheriff Principal Edward Farquharson; TD (1977), QC (Scot 1992); s of Stanley Bowen, CBE; *b* 1 May 1945; *Educ* Melville Coll Edinburgh, Univ of Edinburgh (LLB); *m* 1975, Patricia Margaret, da of Rev Robert Russell Brown, of Perth; 2 s (James, David), 2 da (Helen, Alexandra); *Career* admitted slr 1968, passed advocate 1970; advocate depute 1979–83, Sheriff of Tayside Central and Fife at Dundee 1983–90, ptnr Thorntons WS 1990–91, resumed practice at Scottish Bar 1991; Sheriff Princ of: Glasgow and Strathkelvin 1997–2005, Lothian and Borders 2005–; temp judge Court of Session 2000–; memb Criminal Injuries Compensation Bd 1996; chm Northern Lighthouse Bd 2003–05; *Recreations* golf, curling; *Clubs* New (Edinburgh), Hon Co of Edinburgh Golfers, Panmure Golf, R&A; *Style—* Sheriff Principal Edward Bowen, TD, QC; ✉ Sheriff Courthouse, 27 Chambers Street, Edinburgh EH1 1LB (tel 0131 225 2525)

BOWEN, Jeremy; s of Gareth Bowen, of Cardiff, and Jennifer, *née* Delany; *b* 6 February 1960; *Educ* Cardiff HS, UCL (BA), Johns Hopkins Sch of Advanced International Studies Washington DC and Bologna (MA); *Career* BBC News: news trainee 1984–86, fin reporter 1986, corr Geneva 1987, sometime presenter Breakfast News, foreign affrs corr 1988–95, corr Middle East 1995–2000, presenter Breakfast from BBC News 2000–02, Middle East ed 2005–; special corr BBC News pubns Six Days 2003; presenter documentaries for BBC1 incl: Son of God 2000, Moses 2002, Booze 2002, Noah 2003, Jeremy Bowen on the Frontline 2005; winner: Silver Nymph Monte Carlo TV Festival 1994, Gold Medal NY TV Festival, RTS Award 1996, Sony Gold Award 2004; *Publications* War Stories (2006); *Style—* Jeremy Bowen, Esq

BOWEN, John; s of John Thomas Bowen (d 1964), and Marjorie Mabel, *née* George (d 1973); *b* 7 June 1937; *Educ* Aberdare Boys' Co GS, UC Wales (LLB); *m* 6 Sept 1969, Helen Margaret, da of Dudley Guildford Keay; 1 s (Thomas Huw David b 1 July 1975); *Career* slr; articled clerk Marchant Harries & Co Slrs Aberdare 1957–60; asst slr: G Houghton & Son London EC2 1960, Gamlen Bowerman & Forward Lincoln's Inn London 1960–64; Morgan Cole Slrs Cardiff: asst slr 1964–66, ptnr 1966–99, chm Mgmnt Bd 1989–99, conslt 1999–; dir: Principality Building Society 1996–, Finance Wales Investments Ltd 1999–, Peter Alan Ltd 1999–, Wales Innovation Fund 1999–; co sec CRC Gp plc 1999–; chm Employment Tbnl 2000; audit cmmr 2001–; assessor legal practice course The Law Soc 1996; memb Law Soc 1960; fell Univ of Cardiff 1999; *Recreations* English literature, music, industrial history, contract bridge; *Style—* John Bowen, Esq; ✉ Morgan Cole Solicitors, Bradley Court, Park Place, Cardiff CF1 3DP (tel 029 2052 1786, fax 029 2052 1095, e-mail john.bowen@morgan-cole.com)

BOWEN, Kenneth John; s of Hector John Bowen (d 1980), of Llanelli, Carmarthenshire, and Sarah Ann (Sally), *née* Davies (d 1939); *b* 3 August 1932; *Educ* Llanelli GS, UC Wales Aberystwyth (BA), St John's Coll Cambridge (MA, MusB), Inst of Educn Univ of London; *m* 31 March 1959, Angela Mary, da of George Stanley Evenden, of Morecambe, Lancs; 2 s (Geraint, Meurig); *Career* Flying Offr Educn Branch RAF 1958–60; prof of singing Royal Acad of Music 1967–98 (head of vocal studies 1987–91); conductor: London Welsh Chorale 1983–, London Welsh Festival Chorus 1987–90; former concert and operatic tenor (ret 1988); debut Tom Rakewell New Opera Co Sadler's Wells 1957; appeared: Promenade concerts, Three Choirs Festival, Aldeburgh and other maj festivals; performed at: Royal Opera House, ENO, WNO, Glyndebourne Touring Opera, English Opera Gp, English Music Theatre, Kent Opera, Handel Opera Soc; numerous recordings and int appearances (Europe, USA, Canada, Israel, Far East), winner first prize Munich Int Competition and Queen's prize; adjudicator Royal Nat Eisteddfod of Wales and Llangollen Int Eisteddfod; dir Br Youth Opera; patron Welsh Music Guild, vice-pres Hon Soc of Cymmrodorion, vice-pres London Welsh Tst, former chm Assoc of Teachers of Singing, former pres RAM Club; memb Gorsedd of Bards; Hon DMus Univ of Wales 2003; Hon RAM, FRSA; *Recreations* golf, walking, theatre, wine; *Style—* Dr Kenneth Bowen; ✉ 61 Queens Crescent, London NW5 3QG (tel and fax 020 7267 4700)

BOWEN, Sir Mark Edward Mortimer; 5 Bt (UK 1921), of Colworth, Co Bedford; o s of Sir Thomas Frederic Charles Bowen, 4 Bt (d 1989), and Jill Claude Murray, *née* Evans (d 1999); *b* 17 October 1958; *Educ* Wellington; *m* 1983, Kerry Tessa, da of Michael John Moriarty, of Rustington, W Sussex; 1 s (George Edward Michael b 27 Dec 1987), 1 da (Grace Francesca b 3 March 1989); *Heir* s, George Bowen; *Career* Lloyd's broker 1978–; *Style—* Sir Mark Bowen, Bt

BOWEN, William George (Will); s of Humphry John Moule Bowen, and Ursula Hill; *b* 30 October 1957; *Educ* Marlborough (jr scholarship), Balliol Coll Oxford (BA, DPhil); *Career* stage designer; res chemist Borax Consolidation Ltd 1975–79; fndr Almeida Theatre Islington (with Pierre Audi and Chris Naylor 1979); set builder Oxford Playhouse Co 1979–82; memb: SBTD 2000, Royal Inst 2004; *Theatre* as prodn carpenter: Camelot (Apollo Victoria Theatre London) 1982, The Boyfriend (Old Vic and UK tour) 1984, Guys & Dolls (NT UK tour) 1985; as prodn mangr: Charley's Aunt (Aldwych Theatre) 1983, Trumpets & Raspberries (The Phoenix Theatre) 1984, The Nerd (Aldwych Theatre) 1984, Torch Song Trilogy (Albery Theatre) 1985, Kiss Me Kate (Old Vic and UK tour) 1987, Henry IV (nat tour) 1990, The Rehearsal (Garrick Theatre) 1990; as design co-ordinator: Phantom of the Opera (Her Majesty's Theatre) 1986, Aspects of Love (Prince of Wales Theatre) 1989, The Hunting of the Snark (Prince Edward Theatre) 1991, Oliver! (Palladium Theatre) 1994; as tech designer: The Wind in the Willows (NT) 1990, Sunset Boulevard (Adelphi Theatre) 1993, Jesus Christ Superstar (Lyceum Theatre) 1996, Chitty Chitty Bang Bang (Palladium Theatre) 2002, His Dark Mateials (NT) 2003; as theatre designer: Waking Hours (Lyric Hammersmith) 1984, Born in the Gardens (Questors Theatre) 1988, Under Milk Wood 1992, Julius Caesar (NYT) 1992, Helping Harry 2001; as musical designer: Days of Hope (Oxford Playhouse and Hampstead Theatre) 1991, Girlfriends (Arts Theatre) 1992, Romance/Romance (Gielgud Theatre) 1997, The Canterville Ghost (Northcott Theatre Exeter) 1998, Peter Pan (Royal Festival Hall) 2002; as comedy designer: Rowan Atkinson (also designer and prodn mangr, West End, Broadway and world tours) 1980–92, Mel Smith & Griff Rhys Jones (Cabaret) 1983, Eddie Izzard (West End and UK tour) 1996, One Word Improv (Albery Theatre) 1997, Derren Brown (Palace Theatre) 2004, (Cambridge Theatre) 2005 and (UK tour) 2007; as concert designer: Fairuz (Royal Festival Hall) 1986, John Harle (Queen Elizabeth Hall) 1987, The Music of Andrew Lloyd Webber (Seville) 1992; as lighting designer: Rowan Atkinson (UK tour) 1983–88, John Harle's Berliner Band (London and Aldeburgh) 1986–90, Ute Lemper (Barbican Concert Hall) 1990; as theatre conslt: Royal Albert Hall (stage extension project) 1992, Soho Theatre London 1996–98, Olivier Environment (NT) 1999, Abbey Theatre Dublin 2007; as theatre building designer: Combe Barns 1987, Sydmonton Court 1991, Great Offley Barns 1995, Lyttelton Theatre Transformation (NT) 2002; *Opera* Evenings at Combe 1987–2006, Don Pasquale (Holland Park 1997), La Fedelta Premiata (Guidhall) 1997, La Traviata (Stowe Opera) 1997, Lucia di Lammermoor (Stowe Opera) 1998, Carmen (Clonter Opera 1998), Il Tabarro (Clonter Opera) 1999, Falstaff (British Youth Opera (BYO)) 1999, The Barber of Seville (BYO) 1999, May We Borrow Your Husband (Lichfield Festival) 1999, Don Pasquale (Clonter Opera) 1999, Seraglio (BYO) 2000, Xerxes (BYO) 2000, The Rape of Lucretia (BYO) 2000, Carmen (Holland Park Opera) 2001, Bevenuto Cellini (Bloomsbury Theatre) 2002, Suor Anjelica (Holland Park) 2002, I Pagliacci (Holland Park) 2002, Macbeth (Icelandic Opera) 2003, Norma (Holland Park) 2004, La Fanciulla del West (Holland Park) 2004, Tosca (Icelandic Opera) 2005; *Television* Comic Relief 1986, Hysteria 1989, Rowan Atkinson HBO Special 1991, Derren Brown - Something Wicked This Way Comes 2006; *Film* The Girl in the Red Dress 2002; *Recreations* mathematics, landscape, natural history, photography, travel; *Style—* Will Bowen, Esq; ✉ c/o Noel Gay Artists, 19 Denmark Street, London WC2H 8NA (tel 020 7836 3941, fax 020 7287 1816)

BOWEN-SIMPKINS, Peter; s of Horace John Bowen-Simpkins (d 1969), and Christine Dulce, *née* Clarke; *b* 28 October 1941; *Educ* Malvern Coll, Selwyn Coll Cambridge (MA, MB, BChir), Guy's Hosp; *m* 19 Aug 1967, Kathrin, da of Karl Otto Ganguin (d 1987), of Chelmsford, Essex; 2 da (Emma Jane b 6 Nov 1969, Philippa b 28 Dec 1971); *Career* resident MO Queen Charlotte's Maternity Hosp London 1971, resident surgical offr Samaritan Hosp for Women London 1972, sr registrar and lectr in obstetrics and gynaecology Middx Hosp and Hosp for Women 1972–78, conslt gynaecologist Singleton Hosp Swansea 1979–2005, medical dir London Women's Clinic London, Swansea and Cardiff, inspr of nullity for Wales, lectr in family planning Margaret Pyke Centre London; contrib chapters in various books on obstetrics and gynaecology, and author of papers and pubns in med jls incl: Br Med Jl, Br Jl of Obstetrics and Gynaecology (BJOG); examiner: Royal Coll of Obstetricians and Gynaecologists, Univ of Wales, Univ of Hong Kong, Univ of Kartoum Sudan, Coll of Physicians and Surgeons of Pakistan, GMC; RCOG: memb Cncl 1993–2005, memb Fndn Bd Faculty of Family Planning 1994–97, hon treas 1998–2005, press offr 2000–05; exec chm BJOG; Handcock Prize for Surgery RCS 1966; co-fndr and past pres Victor Bonney Soc, ldr Cambridge Expedition to Eritrea 1963; Freeman City of London, Liveryman Worshipful Soc of Apothecaries 1976, Liveryman Welsh Livery Guild (Urdd Lifrai Cymru) 1995; LRCP 1966, MRCS 1966, MRCOG 1973, FRCOG 1985, FFFP 2005 (MFFP 1993); *Books* Pocket Examiner in Obstetrics & Gynaecology (1983), A Practice of Obstetrics and Gynaecology (2000); *Recreations* fly fishing, skiing, golf, sailing, tennis; *Clubs* Flyfishers; *Style—* Peter Bowen-Simpkins, Esq; ✉ Sancta Maria Hospital, Swansea SA1 6DF (tel 01792 479040, fax 01792 390458, e-mail pbs@reynoldston.com); Royal College of Obstetricians and Gynaecologists (tel 020 7772 6285, e-mail pbs@rcog.org.uk)

BOWER, Prof (Daphne) Jane; da of William Hughes, and Mary, *née* Younger; *b* 7 September 1945, Dunfermline, Fife; *Educ* Dunfermline HS, Harvard Univ, Univ of Edinburgh (Carnegie fell, BSc, Sir David Baxter fell, PhD, Walter Scott & Ptnrs fell, MBA), Univ of Lancaster and L'Ecole Supérieure de Commerce de Lyon (Fndn for Mgmnt Educn fell, MA/FPM, Cert); *m* 1; 1 s (Nicholas b 30 Sept 1964), 3 da (Elanor b 15 Jan 1966, Penelope, Clio (twins) b 13 Jan 1970); m 2, Jan 1989, Dr Kenneth Lyall; *Career* res fell Stanford Univ Med Sch 1974–75, sr res fell Genetics Dept Univ of Edinburgh 1975–84, project ldr biotech R&D MRC Human Genetics Unit Edinburgh 1984–90, lectr in technol mgmnt Heriot-Watt Univ 1990–94 (dep head of dept 1992–93), sr lectr and dir Centre for

Entrepreneurship Univ of Aberdeen 1994–97, dir Kinnell Technologies 1997–99, prof of entrepreneurship Glasgow Caledonian Univ 1999–2005; Univ of Dundee: dir Centre for Enterprise Mgmnt 2005–, dean Postgraduate Sch of Mgmnt and Policy 2006–; Royal Soc sr res fell Univ of Nagoya Japan 1989–90, visiting lectr in tech mgmnt Budapest Technol Univ 1993–94; founding dir Biohorizon Ltd 1988–90; memb: Editorial Bd Int Jl of Innovation Mgmnt 1996–, Editorial Advsy Bd Int Jl of Entrepreneurship and Innovation 2004–; chm Scot Stem Cell Network 2005–06 (memb Advsy Gp 2003–06); memb: Awards Panel Nat Assoc of Colitis and Crohn's Disease 1997–2004, RSA Scot Ctee 1999–2005, Scot HE Funding Cncl 2001–05, Scot Hosps Endowment Res Tst 2001–05, Scot Science Advsy Ctee 2002–04; expert conslt EC's European Innovation Monitoring System 1993–96; CRINE Network Premier Award; FRSA 1993, FRSE 2005; *Publications* Company and Campus Partnership: Supporting technology transfer (1992); author of over 65 articles in professional jls, 10 published reports; *Clubs* Aberdeen Business (fndr memb); *Style*— Prof Jane Bower; ✉ Postgraduate School of Management and Policy, University of Dundee, Dundee DD1 4HN (e-mail d.j.bower@dundee.ac.uk)

BOWERING, Christine; DL (Notts 2000); da of Kenneth Soper (d 1978), and Florence Evelyn Winifred, *née* Kruse (d 1982); *b* 30 June 1936; *Educ* St Bernard's Convent Westcliff, Newnham Coll Cambridge; *m* 23 July 1960, Rev (John) Anthony Bowering, s of John Bowering; 1 s (John Robert b 1962), 1 da (Eleanor Jane (Mrs Power) b 1964); *Career* teacher: St Bernard's Convent Westcliff 1959–60, Ursuline Convent Brentwood 1960–62; various pt/t occupations 1962–72, teacher then second mistress Sheffield HS for Girls GPDST 1972–84, headmistress Nottingham HS for Girls GPDST 1984–96; memb: Engrg Cncl 1988–91, Educn Ctee GSA 1989–96 (chm 1989–93), Cncl GSA, Cncl Standing Conf on Schools Sci and Technol (SCSST), Ind Schs Curriculum Ctee 1990–94 (chm 1992–94), Educn Ctee Goldsmiths' Co 1992–98 and 2002–; non-exec dir Queens' Med Centre Hosp Tst Nottingham 1993–98, chm Nottingham City Hosp NHS Tst 1998–; chm Dio of Southwell and Nottingham Family Care 1998–2006, memb Southwell Diocesan Synod 2000–; govr: Nottingham Trent Univ (formerly Nottingham Poly) 1989–96, Minster Sch Southwell; assoc memb Newnham Coll Cambridge 1991–2002, hon memb GSA 1996–; Hon DLitt Univ of Nottingham; FRSA; *Recreations* holidaying in France, church and family activities; *Style*— Mrs Christine Bowering, DL; ✉ Linthwaite Cottage, Main Street, Kirklington, Newark NG22 8ND (tel 01636 816995)

BOWERMAN, David William; CBE (2004), JP (1970), DL (W Sussex 1992); s of Alfred Hosegood Bowerman (d 1982), of Champs Hill, Coldwaltham, and Margaret, *née* Vellacott; *b* 9 January 1936; *Educ* Monkton Combe Sch, Univ of Reading (BSc); *m* 9 Sept 1961, (Clarice) Mary, da of Prof William Melville Capper (d 1975), of Clifton, Bristol; 3 da (Janet Mary (Mrs William Taylor) b 28 June 1962, Katharine Emma b 9 July 1964, Anna Margaret (Mrs Simon Downham) b 28 May 1966); *Career* farmer; chm: Arundel Bench 1985–89 (memb 1970–96), Arundel Juvenile Bench 1980–85 (memb 1972–86), Bd of Visitors HM Prison Ford 1979–82 (memb 1970–85), W Sussex Probation Ctee 1988–94 (memb 1975–94), W Sussex Forum for Offender Accommodation 1979–94, Exec Bd Sussex Crime Reduction Initiative (CRI) 1995–2001 (memb and vice-chm 1979–2001), Music at Boxgrove 1991–2003, Chichester Cathedral Millennium Endowment Tst 1997–2005, Bowerman Charitable Tst 1982–, Elgar Fndn and Birthplace Tst 1998–2005; tstee: Mary How Tst, Chichester Cathedral Tst, Chichester Cathedral Cncl, Royal Coll of Organists, English Chamber Orchestra and Music Soc, Cncl Royal Philharmonic Soc, King Edward VII Hosp Midhurst (memb Instn); High Sheriff W Sussex 1990–91; Hon RCM 2005; *Recreations* music, fly fishing, art; *Clubs* Mosimann's; *Style*— David Bowerman, Esq, CBE, JP, DL; ✉ Champs Hill, Coldwaltham, Pulborough, West Sussex RH20 1LY (tel 01798 831868/831205, fax 01798 831536)

BOWERMAN, John Ernest; s of Ernest James Bowerman (d 1973), and Irene May, *née* Partridge (d 1993); *b* 13 March 1931; *Educ* Torquay GS, Dental and Med Schs Univ of Bristol (scholar, BDS, MB ChB, numerous prizes and awards, Badminton colours); *m* 20 March 1955, Hilary Winifred, da of Charles Frederick Hazlewood; 1 s (Martin John b 15 Aug 1959), 1 da (Sarah Jane b 2 May 1962); *Career* Lt RADC 1954–55, ret Capt 1956; house surgn Univ of Bristol Dental Sch 1954, in gen dental practice 1955–60, dental surgn Marlpitts Geriatric Hosp Honiton Devon 1958–59, registrar in dental surgery Univ of Bristol Dental Sch and Maxillofacial Unit Frenchay Hosp Bristol 1960–61, house physician in gen med Professorial Med Unit United Bristol Hosps 1965–66, house surgn in gen and ENT surgery Frenchay Hosp Bristol 1966; sr registrar in oral surgery 1967–69: Westminster Hosp and Queen Mary's Univ Hosp Roehampton (registrar in oral surgery 1966–67), UCH Dental Sch; hon conslt in oral and maxillofacial surgery Royal Dental Hosp of London and St George's Hosp Tooting London 1974–81; conslt in maxillofacial surgery: Westminster Hosp 1969–91, Queen Mary's Univ Hosp 1969–94, Epsom Dist Hosp 1978–94; currently: hon consulting surgeon in maxillofacial surgery Chelsea and Westminster Hosp & Queen Mary's Univ Hosp, in private practice London; visiting prof: Univ of Cairo and Egyptian Air Force Hosp 1984, Univ of Alexandria and Maadi Armed Forces Hosp 1985, Univ Dental Sch Kenyatta Nat Hosp 1988; dental clinical tutor Roehampton Postgrad Med Centre 1977–93, examiner RCS 1983–89; memb: Euro Assoc for Cranio-Maxillofacial Surgery (memb Cncl 1986–92), Regional Hosp Dental Surgery Ctee SW Thames RHA (chm 1975–83); memb: BDA, BMA; FDS RCS 1964, FRCSEd 1985, fell BAOMS (memb Cncl 1983–84); *Publications* Dental Manifestations of Systemic Disease (Radiology in Clinical Diagnosis Series, with D H Trapnell, 1973); contrib chapters to numerous med and dental textbooks, author of numerous published articles in learned jls; *Recreations* salmon fishing, skiing, DIY; *Style*— John Bowerman, Esq; ✉ Pond Cottage, Whitmore Vale, Grayshott, Hampshire GU26 6JB (tel and fax 01428 713314); Princess Grace Hospital, London W1U 5NY (tel 020 7908 2149)

BOWERS, Daniel Selwyn (Danny); s of Philip Louis Bowers, and Iris, *née* Pash; *b* 13 October 1958; *Educ* Manchester Poly (BA), London Coll of Printing (Dip Radio Journalism); *m* 12 March 1989, Elizabeth, da of Lawrence Abramson; 1 s (Adam Benjamin b 4 March 1992), 1 da (Emma Sarah b 19 Sept 1994); *Career* news reporter and prodr (Midlands) BBC Radio 1980–83, dep news ed and sports ed (Staffs and Cheshire) Signal Radio 1983–85, news/business reporter LBC/IRN 1985–86, fin corr LBC Radio 1986–90; freelance: Pink Section London Evening Standard 1990–91, Business Daily (C4) 1990–91; fin ed Independent Radio News (ITN Radio) 1991–95; co-fndr Electronic Media Relations 1989–91 (resigned as dir 1991), md MoneyWorld UK (formerly Lizdan Ltd) 1995– (dir 1991–); *Recreations* playing tennis, running and playing with the children, pony trekking; *Style*— Danny Bowers, Esq

BOWERS, John Simon; QC (1998); s of Alf Bowers, and Irene Bowers, of Cleethorpes, Humberside; *b* 2 January 1956; *Educ* Matthew Humberstone Comp Sch Cleethorpes, Lincoln Coll Oxford (open scholar, BA, BCL); *m* Suzanne Franks; 3 c (Emma, Hannah, Benjamin); *Career* called to the Bar 1978; recorder Midland Circuit 2003–; chair Employer Law Bar Assoc; memb: Home Office Task Force on Human Rights, Bar Cncl Race Relations Ctee, Employer Law Assoc 1990, Standards Bd for Eng 2001–; hon legal advisor Public Concern at Work; hon prof Univ of Hull 2002–; *Publications* Bowers on Employment Law (1980), Atkins Court Forms Volume 38 (1986), Modern Law of Strikes (1987), Employment Tribunal Procedure (1987), The Employment Act 1988, Termination of Employment (1988), Basic Procedure in Courts and Tribunals (1990), Textbook on Employment Law (1990), Employment Law Updates (1991), Transfer of Undertakings: the Legal Pitfalls (1996); *Style*— John Bowers, Esq, QC; ✉ Littleton Chambers, 3 King's Bench Walk North, Temple, London EC4Y 7HR (tel 020 7797 8600, fax 020 7797 8600)

BOWERS, His Hon Judge Peter Hammond; s of Edward Hammond Bowers (d 1993), of Cleveland, and Elsie, *née* Wharton; *b* 22 June 1945; *Educ* Acklam Hall Sch Middlesbrough, Coll of Law London; *m* 26 Aug 1970, Brenda Janet, da of Alistair Gordon Burgess (d 1969); 2 s (Richard Peter b 8 Oct 1976, Martin James b 31 May 1978), 1 da (Jayne Elizabeth (twin) b 31 May 1978); *Career* articled clerk Alex Lauriston & Son Middlesbrough, admitted slr 1966, in private practice 1966–70, prosecuting slr 1970–72, transferred to the Bar (Inner Temple) 1972, recorder of the Crown Court 1989–95 (asst recorder 1984), circuit judge (NE Circuit) 1995–; memb Law Soc 1966–72; *Recreations* cricket and armchair spectator, paintings and antiques, aspiring artist; *Style*— His Hon Judge Bowers

BOWERS, Dr Peter John; s of Dr Arthur Clifford Bowers (d 1947), and Doris Bowers (d 2005); *b* 2 June 1946; *Educ* Queen Elizabeth GS, Univ of London (BSc, AKC), Univ of Manchester (MB ChB, MSc); *m* 1 Aug 1970, (Patricia) Lesley, da of Philip Bethell, of Darlington, Co Durham; 1 da (Juliet b 1974), 2 s (Jonathan b 1975, Anthony b 1982); *Career* house physician and surgn Central Manchester Hosps 1973–74, sr house offr in paediatrics Booth Hall Hosp 1974–75, sr registrar in child psychiatry S Manchester Hosp 1978–81 (registrar in psychiatry 1975–78), tutor Dept of Child Psychiatry Univ of Manchester 1981–82, conslt in child and adolescent psychiatry NW RHA 1983–94, conslt in child and adolescent psychiatry and med dir Tameside and Glossop Community and Priority Servs NHS Tst 1994–2002, conslt in child and asolescent psychiatry Pennine Care NHS Tst 2002– (lead conslt Child and Adolescent Mental Health Services 2005–); expert witness for official slr and guardian-ad-litems 1984–; memb: Manchester Med Soc, Assoc of Family Therapists, Assoc for Child and Adolescent Mental Health; FRCPsych; *Recreations* amateur dramatics and operatics, theatre, jogging, travel; *Style*— Dr Peter Bowers; ✉ 6 Clifton Avenue, Fallowfield, Manchester M14 6UB (tel 0161 224 9508, e-mail peterjohnbowers@doctors.org.uk); Springleigh, Child and Family Therapy Service, Waterloo Road, Stalybridge SK15 2AU (tel 0161 303 4902, e-mail peter.bowers@penninecare.nhs.uk)

BOWERS-BROADBENT, Christopher Joseph St George; s of Henry William Bowers-Broadbent (d 1965), of Ilfracombe, Devon, and Doris E, *née* Mizen; *b* 13 January 1945; *Educ* King's Coll Cambridge (chorister), Berkhamsted Sch, Royal Acad of Music; *m* 17 Oct 1970, Deirdre Ann, da of Norman Cape, of Kimbolton, Cambs; 1 da (Tabitha Jane b 2 May 1971), 1 s (Henry William b 10 Jan 1975); *Career* int concert organist; organist and choirmaster St Pancras Parish Church 1965–88, concert organist debut Camden Festival 1966, organist W London Synagogue 1973–, prof Royal Acad of Music 1976–92, organist and choirmaster Gray's Inn 1983–; many sacred and secular compositions; operas incl: The Pied Piper 1972, The Seacock Bane 1979, The Last Man 1983; FRAM; *Recreations* silence; *Style*— Christopher Bowers-Broadbent, Esq; ✉ 94 Colney Hatch Lane, Muswell Hill, London N10 1EA (tel 020 8883 1933, fax 020 8883 8434, e-mail chris@christopherbowers-broadbent.com)

BOWERY, Prof Norman George; s of George Bowery (d 1971), and Olga, *née* Beevers (d 1991); *b* 23 June 1944; *Educ* Christ's Coll Finchley, Univ of London (PhD, DSc); *m* 14 Feb 1970, Barbara Joyce, da of Eric Norman Westcott, of Goring-by-Sea, W Sussex; 2 da (Nicole Louise b 1973, Annette Jane b 1977), 1 s (Andrew James b 1975); *Career* sr lectr St Thomas' Hosp London 1982–84 (lectr 1975–82), section ldr Neuroscience Res Centre MSD Harlow 1984–87, Wellcome prof of pharmacology Univ of London 1987–95, prof of pharmacology The Med Sch Univ of Birmingham 1995–2004 (now emeritus); head of biology GlaxoSmithKline Psychiatric CEDD Verona 2004–06; memb and vice-chm Biological Cncl 1988–91; ed-in-chief Current Opinion in Pharmacology; memb: MRC Neuroscience Ctee 1983–87 and 1995–97, SERC Link Ctee 1988–90; memb: Br Pharmacological Soc (hon gen sec 1995–97, pres 1999–2000), American Neuroscience Assoc, Br Neuroscience Assoc; Laurea (hc) Univ of Florence; *Books* Actions and Interactions of GABA and Benzodiazepines (1984), GABAergic Mechanisms on the Periphery (1986), GABA Basic Research and Clinical Applications (1989), GABAB Receptors in Mammalian Function (1990), The GABA Receptors (1996), GABA: Receptors, Transporters and Metabolism (1996), Allosteric Receptor Modulation in Drug Targeting (2006); *Recreations* walking, gardening, socialising; *Style*— Prof Norman Bowery; ✉ e-mail n.g.bowery@bham.ac.uk

BOWES, Roger Norman; s of Russell Ernest Bowes, and Sybil Caroline Rose, *née* Bell; *b* 28 January 1943; *Educ* Chiswick GS, Dorking GS; *m* 1 (m dis 1974), Denise Hume Windsor; 1 da (Virginia Lynsey b 1961); m 2 (m dis 1988), Ann Rosemary O'Connor, *née* Hamstead; *Career* sales mangr Mirror Group Newspapers 1970–75, media dir McCann Erickson Advertising 1976–78; Mirror Group Newspapers: advtg dir 1978–81, dep chief exec 1982–83, chief exec 1984; md Guinness Enterprises 1985, chief exec Express Group Newspapers 1985–86, chm Citybridge 1987–95, chief exec ASLIB (Assoc for Information Management) 1989–; memb Euro Cncl of Info Assocs; FRSA; *Recreations* political and military history, cookery, classic cars; *Style*— Roger Bowes, Esq; ✉ ASLIB, Temple Chambers, 3–7 Temple Avenue, London EC4Y 0HP (e-mail rbowes@aslib.com)

BOWES-LYON, David James; DL (Midlothian, 1992); s of Maj-Gen Sir James Bowes-Lyon, KCVO, CB, OBE, MC (d 1977), and Mary, *née* De Trafford; *b* 21 July 1947; *Educ* Ampleforth; *m* 1976, Elizabeth Harriet Bowes-Lyon (Lady-in-Waiting to HRH The Princess Royal), da of Sir John Colville, CB, CVO, of Broughton, Hants; 2 da (Georgina b 1977, Alexandra b 1986), 2 s (James b 1979 (Page of Honour to HM The Queen), Charles b 1989); *Career* Capt 14/20 Kings Hussars 1970–78 NI, W Germany, Cyprus, Zaïre; The Union Discount Co of London 1979–92 (dir various subsid cos); dir: Scottish Business Achievement Tst 1981–, Aitken Campbell and Co Ltd 1987–96, Lothian Racecourse Ltd (Edinburgh) 1987–, Independent Pension Trustees plc 1993–, Christies International UK Ltd 1994–; chm Queen Mother's Meml Fund for Scotland 2003–; offr Queen's Body Guard for Scotland (Royal Co of Archers); *Recreations* shooting, fishing, racing; *Clubs* White's, New (Edinburgh, chm 2004); *Style*— David Bowes-Lyon, Esq, DL; ✉ Heriot Water, Heriot, Midlothian EH38 5YE

BOWES LYON, Sir Simon Alexander; KCVO (2005); s of Hon Sir David Bowes Lyon, KCVO (d 1961), and Rachel Pauline, *née* Spender Clay (d 1996); *b* 17 June 1932; *Educ* Eton, Magdalen Coll Oxford; *m* 11 April 1966, Caroline Mary Victoria, er da of Rt Rev Victor Joseph Pike, CB, CBE, MA, DD, Bishop of Sherborne 1959–76; 1 da (Rosie (Mrs David Glazebrook) b 1968), 3 s (Fergus b 1970, David b 1973, Andrew b 1979); *Career* dir SPW Securities Ltd and other cos; HM Lord-Lt Herts 1986–2007; FCA 1959; KStJ 1996; *Recreations* shooting, gardening, walking, music; *Clubs* Brooks's; *Style*— Sir Simon Bowes Lyon, KCVO; ✉ St Paul's Walden Bury, Hitchin, Hertfordshire SG4 8BP (tel 01438 871218, fax 01438 871341, e-mail spw@boweslyon.demon.co.uk); 12 Morpeth Mansions, London SW1P 1ER (tel 020 7828 8057)

BOWIE, David (*né* David Robert Jones); *b* 8 January 1947; *m* Iman Abdulmajid; 1 da (Alexandria Zahra Jones b 2000); *Career* singer; formerly with: The Kon-Rads 1964, The Manish Boys 1964–65, The Lower Third 1965–66, Tin Machine 1989–92 (album Tin Machine 1989, UK no 3); 25 UK top ten singles incl 4 no 1's (Space Oddity 1975, Under Pressure 1981, Let's Dance 1983, Dancing in the Street 1985), 7 US top ten singles incl 2 no 1's (Fame 1975, Let's Dance 1983); solo albums incl: David Bowie (1967), Man of Words, Man of Music/Space Oddity (1969), The Man Who Sold the World (1971), Hunky Dory (1971), The Rise and Fall of Ziggy Stardust and the Spiders from Mars (1972, UK no 5), Hunky Dory (1972, UK no 3), Space Oddity (1972, UK no 26), Images 1966–67 (1973), Aladdin Sane (1973, UK no 3), Pin-Ups (1973, UK no 3), Diamond Dogs (1974, UK no 1, US no 5), David Live (1974, UK no 2, US no 8), Young Americans (1975, UK no 2, US no 9), Station to Station (1976, UK no 5, US no 3), Changesonebowie (compilation 1976, UK no 2, US no 10), Low (1977, UK no 2, US no 11), Heroes (1977, UK no 3), Stage (1978, UK no 5), Lodger (1979, UK no 4), Scary Monsters and Super Creeps (1980, UK no 10), The Very Best of David Bowie (1981, UK no 3), Christiane F. (film soundtrack, 1982), Let's Dance (1983, UK no 1, US no 4), Golden Years (compilation 1983, UK no 33), Ziggy Stardust - The Motion Picture (1983, UK no 17), Fame and Fashion (1984, UK no 40), Love You Till Tuesday (1984, UK no 53), Tonight (1984, UK no 1), Absolute Beginners (1986), Never Let Me Down (1987, UK no 6), Sound and Vision (1989), Changesbowie (1990, UK no 1), Black Tie White Noise (1993, UK no 1), Bowie: The Singles Collection (1993), Santa Monica (1994), Outside (1995, UK no 8), Earthling (1997), After Hours (1999), Heathen (2002), Reality (2003); soundtrack for The Buddha of Suburbia (1993); *Awards* Ivor Novello Award (for Space Oddity) 1969, Best Male Singer UK Rock and Pop Awards 1981, Best British Male Artist BRIT Awards 1984, Int Hit of the Year and Best Rock Song (for Let's Dance) Ivor Novello Awards 1984, Best Album Package (for Sound and Vision) Grammy Awards 1990, Q Award (for Inspiration with Brian Eno) 1995, Outstanding Contribution BRIT Award 1996; album prodr for: Iggy Pop, Lou Reed, Mott the Hoople; actor; *Films* The Man Who Fell to Earth, Just A Gigolo, The Hunger, BAAL, Merry Christmas Mr Lawrence, Ziggy Stardust and the Spiders from Mars, Into the Night, Absolute Beginners, Labyrinth, Twin Peaks: Fire Walk With Me, The Last Temptation of Christ, Basquiat; *Stage* The Elephant Man (1980); artist and publisher; exhibited installation art Florence Biennale 1996, fndr 21 (art publishing house) 1997; *Style*— David Bowie, Esq; ✉ c/o The Outside Organisation, Queens House, 180–182 Tottenham Court Road, London W1P 9LE (tel 020 7436 3633, fax 020 7436 3632)

BOWIE, James; s of James Bowie (d 1991), of Leicester, and Olive May, *née* Elcock; *b* 22 January 1947; *Educ* Oakham Sch, Westminster Tech Coll London (HND Hotel Mgmnt); *m* 1, 1972 (m dis), Anne Margaret Stephens; 1 s (James b 15 Nov 1975); m 2, 1988, Susan Elizabeth, *née* Messenger; 1 s (Nicolas Edward b 24 June 1984), 1 da (Rosie Victoria b 27 Jan 1982); *Career* food service trg Hotel Normandie Le Havre 1964, food preparation and service Moëvenpick Zurich 1967, mgmnt trainee Plough & Harrow Birmingham then Vendage Pommerol 1968; Belmont Hotel (family business): joined 1969, gen mangr 1971, md 1975; mangr Hathersage Inn Hathersage; chm: Leicester Hoteliers 1974, 1977 and 1985, Best Western Hotels 1988–90 (memb 1971–); dir Leicester Promotions Ltd 1993–; vice-chm Leicester Tourism TDAP 1989–92; active in: BHA 1970–, Leicester Assoc of Hotels 1972–; chm Heart of Eng Divnl Ctee BHA 1993–94; FHCIMA 1980, Master Innholder 1986; *Recreations* hunting, eating, drinking, skiing, rugby; *Style*— James Bowie, Esq; ✉ Belmont House Hotel, Leicester LE1 7GR (tel 0116 254 4773)

BOWIS, John Crocket; OBE (1981), MEP (Cons) London; s of Thomas Palin Bowis (d 1957), of Brighton, and Georgiana Joyce Bowis, *née* Crocket; *b* 2 August 1945; *Educ* Tonbridge, BNC Oxford (MA); *m* 1968, Caroline Taylor, of Oxon; 1 da (Imogen b 1970), 2 s (Duncan b 1972, Alistair b 1978); *Career* Cons Central Office 1972–80, public affrs dir Br Insurance Brokers' Assoc 1981–86, cncllr Royal Borough of Kingston upon Thames 1982–86 (chm of educn 1984–86); MP (Cons) Battersea 1987–97, memb Select Ctee on Membs Interests 1987–90; PPS to: Min for Inner Cities and Local Govt 1989–90, Sec of State for Wales 1990–93; Parly under-sec of state Dept of Health 1993–96, Min for Road Safety and Transport in London Dept of Transport 1996–97; MEP (Cons) London 1999–, spokesman Environment Health and Consumer Ctee of Euro Parl, dep ldr Cons MEPs 2002–; int policy advsr to WHO on mental health 1997–; pres: Br Youth Cncl 1987–92, Cons Trade Unionists 1990–94, Torche 1999–; vice-pres: Br Epilepsy Assoc, Battersea Soc, Apex, Wandsworth Symphony Orch, Friends of Battersea Parish Church, Battersea Army Cadet League; chm Nat Cncl for Civil Protection 1990–93, vice-chm Int Soc for Human Rights 1989–92; memb Bd: RNT 1990–93, South Bank 1990–93, Royal Acad of Dancing 1992–98, CARA 1995–, International Social Services 1997–; tstee: Nat Aids Tst 1997–, Epilepsy Research Fndn 1997–, Share Community 1997–, Mosaic Clubhouse 1997–, Int Inst of Special Needs Offenders 1998–; memb Inst of Psychiatry 1997; Hon FRCPsych 2003; *Recreations* theatre, music, art, sport; *Style*— John Bowis, OBE, MEP; ✉ PO Box 262, New Malden KT3 4WJ (tel 020 8949 2555, fax 020 8395 7463, e-mail johnbowis@aol.com, website www.johnbowis.com)

BOWKER, Prof John Westerdale; s of Gordon Westerdale Bowker, and Marguerite, *née* Burdick; *b* 30 July 1935; *Educ* St John's Sch Leatherhead, Worcester Coll Oxford (MA), Ripon Hall Oxford; *m* 1963, Margaret Roper; 1 s; *Career* Nat Serv RWAFF N Nigeria 1953–55; Henry Stephenson research fell Univ of Sheffield and deacon and curate of St Augustine's Brocco Bank 1961–62, fell, dir of studies and dean of chapel CCC Cambridge 1962–74, lectr Faculty of Theology Univ of Cambridge 1965–74, Wilde lectr Univ of Oxford 1972–75, prof of religious studies Lancaster Univ 1974–85, fell, dir of studies and dean of chapel Trinity Coll Cambridge 1984–94, hon canon of Canterbury 1985–; Gresham prof Gresham Coll 1992–97 (fell 1998–), fell Acad of Moral Science Beijing 1998; Staley lectr Rollins Coll Florida 1978–79, public lectr Univ of Cardiff 1984, Riddell lectr Univ of Newcastle upon Tyne and Boutwood lectr Univ of Cambridge 1985, Philippa Harris lectr Ontario Cancer Inst 1986, adjunct prof N Carolina State Univ and Univ of Pennsylvania 1986, CIBA Fndn lectr in religion and embryo research 1986, Boardman lectr Univ of Pennsylvania and Bicentenary lectr Georgetown Univ 1988, Scott Holland lectr Univ of London and Montefiore lectr Univ of Southampton 1989, Hensley Henson lectr Univ of Oxford 2003; memb: Durham Cmmn on Religious Educn 1967–70, Root Cmmn on Marriage and Divorce 1967–71, Archbishops' Cmmn on Doctrine 1977–86; conslt Marriage Research Inst 1981; vice-pres Culture and Animals Fndn 1986, pres Christian Action AIDS 1986; hon pres Stauros (Euro/American inst concerned with med ethics) 1980; European ed Zygon (jl of religion and sci) 1980; contrib numerous and varied documentary progs for BBC and ITV incl: The Nature of Religious Experience, AIDS - the Issues and the Actions, Evil (series awarded Sandford St Martin prize), Places of Poetry and Praise (BBC series), An Alphabet of Faith, The Poetry of Presence; *Books* The Targums and Rabbinic Literature: An Introduction to Jewish Interpretations of Scripture (1969 and 1979), Problems of Suffering in Religions of the World (1970, 3 edn 1990), Jesus and the Pharisees (1973), The Sense of God: Sociological, Anthropological and Psychological Approaches to the Origin of the Sense of God (1973, 2 edn 1995), The Religious Imagination and the Sense of God (1978), Worlds of Faith: Religious Belief and Practice in Britain Today (1983), The Origins, Functions and Management of Aggression in Biocultural Evolution - Zygon (ed with introduction, 1983), Licensed Insanities: Religions and Belief in God in the Contemporary World (1987), The Meanings of Death (1991, HarperCollins Prize 1993), A Year to Live (1991), Hallowed Ground: The Religious Poetry of Place (1993), Is God a Virus? Genes, Culture and Religion (1995), Voices of Islam (1995), The Oxford Dictionary of World Religions (1997), World Religions (1997), The Complete Bible Handbook (1998, Benjamin Franklin Award 1999), The Concise Dictionary of World Religions (2000), God: A Brief History (2002), The Cambridge Illustrated History of Religions (2002), The Sacred Neuron (2005), Beliefs that Changed the World (2007); for children: Uncle Bolpenny Tries Things Out (1973); *Recreations* walking, books, gardening, cooking, painting, poetry; *Style*— Prof John Bowker; ✉ 14 Bowers Croft, Cambridge CB1 8RP

BOWKER, (Steven) Richard; CBE (2005); s of Roger William Bowker, and Dr Sylvia Grace Bowker, *née* Walker; *b* 23 April 1966, Oldham, Lancs; *Educ* Queen Elizabeth's GS Blackburn, Univ of Leicester (BA); *m* 8 June 2002, Madeline Victoria, da of Alan Ivemy; 2 s (William Alexander b 30 Aug 2004, Charles Anthony b 14 Aug 2007); *Career* head of PFI London Underground Ltd to 1996, princ Babcock & Brown 1996–99, founding dir Quasar Associates Ltd 1999–2000, co-chm Virgin Rail Gp Ltd 2000–01 (non-exec dir 1999–2000), gp commercial dir Virgin Gp of Companies 2000–01, chm and chief exec Strategic Rail Authy 2001–04, chief exec Partnership for Schools 2005–06, chief exec National Express Gp plc 2006–; memb Bd: British Waterways 2004–, Countryside Alliance; memb Business Devpt Bd SCOPE; dep pres Heritage Railway Assoc; tstee: Settle and Carlisle Railway Tst, Greengauge; vice-pres London Int Piano Competition; FILT, FCIT 2002 (MCIT 1996), FCMA 2003 (ACMA 1993), CCMI 2003, FRSA 2006; *Recreations* Blackburn Rovers FC, music, hill walking, canal boating and inland waterways, wine, reading; *Style*— Richard Bowker, Esq, CBE; ✉ National Express Group plc, 75 Davies Street, London W1K 5HT (tel 020 7529 2000, fax 020 7529 2100)

BOWKETT, Alan John; s of John Bowkett, and Margaret, *née* Nicholson; *b* 6 January 1951, Bilsthorpe, Notts; *Educ* King Charles I GS, UCL (BSc), London Business Sch (MSc); *m* 1 Aug 1975, Joy Dianne, *née* Neale; 2 da (Alexandra b 22 Sept 1980, Camilla b 24 July 1982); 3 s (Rupert b 15 March 1984, Hugo b 2 Feb 1986, Charlie b 2 May 1996); *Career* md Boulton & Paul plc 1985–87; ceo: RHP Bearings Ltd 1987–91, Berisford plc 1992–99; chm: Metzeller APS SA 2000–05, Acordis BV 2000–04, Doncaster Gp 2003–06, Seton House (formerly Britax plc) 2005–, Redrow plc 2007–; non-exec dir Greene King plc 1994–2006; chm London Borough of Ealing Social Servs 1978–82; fell UEA 1993 (treas 1988–93); *Recreations* shooting, salmon fishing, opera, everything Italian, growing vegetables; *Clubs* Carlton, RAC; *Style*— Alan Bowkett, Esq; ✉ Croxton Park, Croxton, Cambridgeshire PE19 6SY (tel 01480 880058, fax 01480 880345); Seton House, Gallows Hill, Warwick CV34 6DE (tel 01926 406309, fax 01926 406308)

BOWLBY, Sir Richard Peregrine Longstaff; 3 Bt (UK 1923), of Manchester Square, Borough of St Marylebone; s of (Edward) John Mostyn Bowlby, CBE, MD (d 1990), and Ursula, *née* Longstaff; suc unc, Sir Anthony Hugh Mostyn Bowlby, 2 Bt, 1993; *b* 11 August 1941; *Educ* Dauntsey's Sch West Lavington; *m* 27 April 1963, Xenia, o da of Roderick Paul Agnew Garrett, of London; 1 s (Benjamin b 1966), 1 da (Sophia b 1969); *Heir* s, Benjamin Bowlby; *Style*— Sir Richard Bowlby, Bt; ✉ Boundary House, Wyldes Close, London NW11 7JB (tel 020 8458 8474)

BOWLER, Dr John Vaughan; *b* 22 March 1959; *Educ* King George V Sch Hong Kong, Worksop Coll, St Thomas' Hosp Med Sch (BSc, MB BS, MD, Cochrane prize, MRC scholarship, Third Beaney prize, Mead medal, Perkins prize); *Career* house surgn St Helier Hosp Carshalton 1984–85, house physician Dept of Med St Thomas' Hosp London 1985; SHO: intensive therapy St Thomas' Hosp London 1985–86, neurology Hammersmith Hosp 1986, cardiology Nat Heart Hosp 1986–87; registrar: gen med Queen Mary's Hosp Sidcup 1987, neurology Atkinson Morley's Hosp 1987–88; Chest, Heart and Stroke Assoc res fell in neurology Dept of Clinical Neuroscience Charing Cross and Westminster Med Sch 1988–90, registrar in neurology Regnl Neurosciences Centre Charing Cross Hosp 1991–92, clinical fell in neurology Dept of Clinical Neurological Sciences Univ of Western Ontario 1992–95, lectr (hon sr registrar) in clinical neurology Dept of Clinical Neurosciences Charing Cross and Westminster Med Sch 1995–98, conslt neurologist and hon sr lectr in neurology Royal Free Hosp, Royal Free and UC Med Sch and N Middx Hosp 1998–; memb Assoc of Br Neurologists, fndr memb Int Soc for Vascular Behavioural and Cognitive Disorders; corresponding assoc memb American Acad of Neurology; int fell Stroke Cncl American Stroke Assoc, fell American Heart Assoc; FRCP (MRCP 1987); *Publications* ed one book on vascular dementia; author of numerous refereed papers, reports, review articles, editorials, abstracts and book chapters; *Recreations* current affairs, classical music, wine, computers; *Style*— Dr J V Bowler; ✉ Royal Free Hospital, Pond Street, London NW3 2QG (tel 020 7830 2387, e-mail john.bowler@ucl.ac.uk)

BOWLER, Prof Peter J; *Educ* Univ of Toronto (PhD); *Career* MRIA, fell AAAS, FBA; *Books* The Fontana History of Environmental Sciences (1992), Evolution: The History of an Idea (3 edn 2003), Making Modern Science: A Historical Survey (2005); *Style*— Prof Peter Bowler; ✉ School of History and Anthropology, The Queen's University, Belfast BT7 1NN

BOWLES, Andrew Graham; s of John Russell Bowles (decd), and Anne Bowles; *b* 28 June 1960; *Educ* Uppingham, Oxford Poly Sch of Architecture (BA, DipArch); *m* Claire Etienne, *née* Brown; 3 s (Henry Worthington b 1992, Charles Andrew John b 1995, Maxwell Alexander b 1998); *Career* architect; Wyn Jones Paul Andrews Associates 1983–84; Sheppard Robson (architects, planners and interior designers) London: joined 1986, assoc 1997–98, ptnr 1998–, currently head of science; projects incl: Swan Theatre High Wycombe 1991–92, 55 King William St London for Skansa AB 1992, The Helicon EC2 for London & Manchester 1992–95 (RIBA Regnl Award for Architecture and Civic Tst Award commendation 1998), The BAA Project Process 1995, office devpt Chiswell St for City Univ 1996, office devpt 59–67 Gresham St EC2 for Legal & General and Stanhope 1998; chm London Constructing Excellence Club; RIBA; *Recreations* mountains, cricket, music, wine; *Style*— Andrew Bowles, Esq; ✉ Sheppard Robson, 77 Parkway, London NW1 7PU

BOWLES, Hamish Philip; s of David Victor Bowles, of London, and Anne, *née* Burmester; *b* 23 July 1963; *Educ* Simon Langton Boys' GS Canterbury, William Ellis Sch Highgate, St Martin's Sch of Art; *Career* guest fashion ed Teenage Issue Harpers & Queen 1983, London and Paris ed Harpers' Bazaar Australia 1983–84, contributing ed 1983–84 (Harpers & Queen, The Face, Arena, GQ, Vanity Fair); Harpers & Queen: jr fashion ed 1985, fashion dir 1987, style dir 1989–92; style ed American Vogue 1992–; creative conslt Met Museum of Art; memb The Costume Soc 1976; *Recreations* collecting vintage couture, travel, theatre; *Style*— Hamish Bowles, Esq

BOWLES, Peter John; s of Herbert Reginald Bowles, and Sarah Jane, *née* Harrison; *b* 16 October 1936; *Educ* High Pavement GS Nottingham, RADA (scholar, Kendal prize); *m* 8 April 1961, Susan Alexandra, da of David Cyril Bennett; 2 s (Guy Rupert b 24 Sept 1962, Adam Peter b 26 Jan 1964); 1 da (Sasha Jane b 12 Oct 1966); *Career* actor; Comedy Actor of the Year Pye Awards 1984, ITV Personality of the Year Variety Club 1984; Hon DLitt Nottingham Trent Univ 2002; *Theatre* London debut in Romeo and Juliet (Old Vic) 1956; other work incl: Happy Haven and Platonov (Royal Court) 1960, Afternoon Men (Arts Theatre) 1961, Absent Friends (Garrick) 1975, Dirty Linen (Arts Theatre) 1976, Born In the Gardens (Globe) 1980, Some of My Best Friends are Husbands (Haymarket Leicester and nat tour) 1985, The Entertainer (Shaftesbury) 1986, Canaries Sometimes Sing (Albery) 1987, Man of The Moment (Globe) 1990, Otherwise Engaged (nat tour) 1992, Seperate Tables (Albery) 1993, Pygmalion (Chichester) 1994, In Praise of Love (Apollo) 1995, Gangster No1 (Almeida) 1995, Present Laughter (Wyndhams) 1996, The School for Wives (Piccadilly) 1997, The Misanthrope, Major Barbara (Piccadilly) 1998, Sleuth (Mobile UK tour) 1999, Hedda Gabler (UK Tour) 1999, The Beau (Theatre Royal Haymarket) 2001, The Royal Family (Haymarket) 2001, Sleuth (Apollo) 2002, Our Song (UK tour) 2003, Wait Until Dark (Garrick) 2003, The Old Masters (Comedy) 2004, The Unexpected Man (nat tour) 2005, Joe & I (Kings Head) 2005, Hay Fever (Haymarket) 2006, Waltz of the Toreadors (Chichester) 2007; *Television* incl: The Avengers, The Prisoner, The Persuaders, The Protectors, Danger Man, Rumpole of The Bailey, To The Manor Born, Only When I Laugh, The Bounder, The Irish RM, Lytton's Diary (devised series), Executive Stress, Perfect Scoundrels (co-devised series), Running Late (TV film, also co-prodr, winner The Golden Gate Award San Francisco), Little White Lies; *Film* incl: Blow Up, The Charge of the Light Brigade, Laughter In The Dark, A Day in the Death of Joe Egg, The Hollywood Ten, Love and War in the Appennines, Colour Me

B

Kubrick, Freebird, Baker Street 2007; exec prodr Gangster No1; *Recreations* motoring and physical jerks; *Clubs* Garrick, Chelsea Arts; *Style*— Peter Bowles, Esq; ✉ c/o Jeremy Conway, Conway van Gelder, 18–21 Jermyn Street, London SW1 6HP (tel 020 7287 0077, fax 020 7287 1940)

BOWMAN, Angela Dawn; *b* 17 March 1971; *Educ* Chiltern Edge Secdy Sch, Henley Coll, Univ of Southampton (LLB), Guildford Coll of Law (DipLP); *Career* slr specialising in trust and probate disputes for nat and local charities; trainee slr Kidd Rapinet 1995–97, ptnr and head Charities Probate Litigation Dept Henmans Slrs 2004– (joined 1997); memb Assoc of Contentious Tst and Probate Specialists (ACTAPS); memb: European Assoc of Planned Giving (EAPG), Charity Law Assoc; *Recreations* tennis, golf, skiing and snowboarding, piano; *Style*— Ms Angela Bowman; ✉ Henmans LLP, 5000 Oxford Business Park South, Oxford OX4 2BH (tel 01865 781000, fax 01865 778504, e-mail angela.bowman@henmansllp.co.uk)

BOWMAN, James Thomas; CBE (1997); s of Benjamin and Cecilia Bowman, *née* Coote; *b* 6 November 1941; *Educ* Ely Cathedral Choir Sch, King's Sch Ely, New Coll Oxford; *Career* counter-tenor; operatic debuts incl: Glyndebourne Festival 1970, Scottish Opera 1971, Royal Opera House Covent Garden 1972, Sydney Opera 1978, Opéra Comique Paris 1979, Theatre du Châtelet Paris 1983, Badisches Staatstheater Karlsruhe 1984, ENO 1985, La Scala Milan 1987; Gentleman-in-Ordinary HM Chapels Royal St James's Palace 2000; pres: Dorking Halls Concertgoers Soc 1994–, The Holst Singers 1995–; vice-pres Bach Choir 2006–; patron New Chamber Opera Oxford 1995–; Medal of Honour City of Paris 1992, Officier de l'Ordre des Arts et des Lettres (France) 1995 (Chevalier 1992), Hon DMus Univ of Newcastle upon Tyne 1996; hon fell New Coll Oxford 1998; *Clubs* Athenaeum; *Style*— James Bowman, Esq, CBE; ✉ 4 Brownlow Road, Redhill, Surrey RH1 6AW (e-mail jamestbowman@hotmail.com)

BOWMAN, Philip; s of Thomas Patrick Bowman (d 1987), and Norma Elizabeth, *née* Deravin; *b* 14 December 1952; *Educ* Westminster, Pembroke Coll Cambridge (MA); *Career* Price Waterhouse London 1974–78, Gibbs Bright & Co Pty Ltd Melbourne 1978–83; Bass plc: joined 1985, fin dir Bass plc 1991–94, chief exec Retail Div 1994–95; fin dir Coles Myer Ltd Melbourne 1995–96; Allied Domecq plc: fin dir 1998–99, chief exec 1999–2005; chief exec Scottish Power plc 2006–; chm: Chateau Lascombes 1994–95, Liberty plc 1998–2000, Coral Eurobet 2004–05; non-exec dir: British Sky Broadcasting Gp 1994–2003, Burberry Gp plc 2002–, Scottish & Newcastle 2006–07; memb Advsy Bd Alchemy Partners 2000–; FCA 1983; *Recreations* opera, entomology, scuba diving, computers and electronics; *Clubs* Victoria Racing, Royal Automobile of Victoria (Melbourne), National Golf (Victoria); *Style*— Philip Bowman, Esq

BOWMAN, Victoria Jane; *née* Robinson; *b* 12 June 1966; *Career* diplomat; entered HM Dip Serv 1988, third then second sec Rangoon 1990–93, first sec FCO 1993, first sec (info and press) UKREP Brussels 1996–99, Cabinet of European Cmmr (Rt Hon Chris Patten, now Baron Patten of Barnes, CH, PC (Life Peer), *qv*) 1999–2002, ambass to Burma 2002–06; *Style*— Ms Victoria Bowman; ✉ c/o Foreign & Commonwealth Office, King Charles Street, London SW1A 2AH

BOWMAN, William Archibald (Bill); s of Archibald George Bowman (d 1978), of Auchtermuchty, and Eleanor Little, *née* Ratcliff; *b* 30 May 1950; *Educ* George Watson's Coll Edinburgh, Univ of Edinburgh (BCom); *m* 10 April 1973, Helen Macaulay, da of Malcolm Macleod, of Strathkinness; *Career* CA; dep sr ptnr KPMG Romania; memb Supervisory Bd KPMG CEE; *Clubs* Royal Northern & Univ (Aberdeen); *Style*— W A Bowman, CA; ✉ e-mail bbowman@kpmg.com

BOWMAN-SHAW, Sir (George) Neville; kt (1984), DL (2002); s of George Bowman-Shaw; *b* 4 October 1930; *Educ* privately; *m* 1962, Georgina, da of John Blundell; 3 s (Andrew, Justin, Fergus Neville (d 1996)), 1 da (Annabelle); *Career* exec chm Lancer Boss Group 1966–94; chm Lancer Boss subsids: Boss Trucks 1959–94, Boss Engineers 1961–94, Lancer Boss International SA Lausanne 1962–94, Lancer Boss Austria 1966–94, Lancer Boss France 1967–94, Boss France 1968–94, Tamefire Ltd 1983–94, Boss España 1984–94, Boss Trucks España 1984–94, Steinbock GmbH Moosburg 1984–94; also chm: Forexia Ltd 1994–96, Stephensons BMH Ltd 1994–2000, BMH Ltd 1994–2005, Avanti BMH Ltd 1995–2002, Bowman Lift Trucks Ltd 1996–2005, Samuk Ltd 1997–, Apollo BMH Ltd 1998–, Samuk HC Ltd 2004–; memb: Design Cncl 1979–84, Br Overseas Trade Bd 1982–85; Liveryman: Worshipful Co of Feltmakers, Worshipful Co of Coachmakers & Coach Harness Makers; *Recreations* shooting, farming, rare breeds and vintage tractors collections; *Clubs* Cavalry and Guards', MCC, Buck's; *Style*— Sir Neville Bowman-Shaw, DL; ✉ Toddington Manor, Toddington, Bedfordshire LU5 6HJ (tel 01525 872576, fax 01525 874555, e-mail nbs@samuk.net)

BOWN, Christopher Michael; s of Michael John David Bown, of Le Touquet, France, and Dora Winifred, *née* Horsfall; *b* 25 August 1956; *Educ* Haileybury, Queens' Coll Cambridge (exhibitioner), Coll of Law; *m* 17 Oct 1987, Lorna Mary, da of Arthur Southcombe Parker; 2 s (Alexander b 27 April 1989, Dominic b 24 June 1995), 2 da (Sophia b 25 March 1991, Florence b 19 April 1993); *Career* Baker & McKenzie: articled clerk 1979, assoc London 1981–82 and 1984–87, seconded to Frankfurt 1983, ptnr 1987–98; ptnr Freshfields Bruckhaus Deringer 1998–; *Recreations* sailing, rowing; *Style*— Christopher Bown, Esq; ✉ Freshfields Bruckhaus Deringer, 65 Fleet Street, London EC4Y 1HS (tel 020 7936 4000, e-mail christopher.bown@freshfields.com)

BOWN, Prof Lalage Jean; OBE (1977); da of Arthur Mervyn Bown, MC (d 1969), of Woolstaston Hall, Salop, and Dorothy Ethel, *née* Watson (d 2002); *b* 1 April 1927; *Educ* Wycombe Abbey, Cheltenham Ladies' Coll, Somerville Coll Oxford (MA); *Children* 2 foster da (Taiwo b 1956, Kehinde b 1956); *Career* resident tutor Univ Coll of the Gold Coast (now Univ of Ghana) 1949–55, res tutor Makerere Univ Coll Uganda 1955–59, tutorial advsr, asst dir and dep dir Extra-Mural Dept Univ of Ibadan Nigeria 1960–66 (assoc prof 1962), dir of extra-mural studies and prof Univ of Zambia 1966–70, prof of adult educn Ahmadu Bello Univ Nigeria 1971–76, prof of adult educn Univ of Lagos Nigeria 1977–80 (dean of educn 1979–80), dir and titular prof Dept of Adult and Continuing Educn Univ of Glasgow 1981–92 (currently emeritus prof), hon prof Dept of Continuing Educn Univ of Warwick 1992–97, visiting professorial fell Inst of Educn Univ of London 1997–99; author of several academic books, monographs and articles; Cwlth visiting prof Univ of Edinburgh 1974, visiting fell Inst of Devpt Studies Univ of Sussex 1980–81, faculty fell Univ of Southampton 1981, distinguished visiting fell Curtin Univ of Technol Perth Aust 1995, visiting lectr Friedrich Schiller Univ Jena 1999; jt sec Int Congress of Africanists 1961–67, sec Int Congress of Univ Adult Educn 1976–81; hon life memb People's Educn Assoc Ghana 1973, hon life memb African Adult Educn Assoc 1976; memb: Bd Int Cncl for Adult Educn 1975–79, Bd Br Cncl 1981–89, Scottish Community Educn Cncl 1982–89, Governing Body Inst of Devpt Studies 1982–91; Br memb Cwlth Standing Ctee for Student Mobility and Higher Educn Co-operation 1989–94, chair Scottish Museums Cncl 1993–96, memb Cncl Royal Soc of Edinburgh 1995–99, chair Cncl for Educn in the Cwlth Working Gp on Student Mobility 1999–2000, exec memb Cncl for Educn in the Cwlth 2000–06 (jt dep chair 2003–06); pres: Devpt Studies Assoc 1984–86, Br Comparative Int Educn Soc 1985–86; hon pres British Assoc for Literacy in Devpt 1992–98; vice-pres: Nat Union of Townswomen's Guilds 1984–2005, Workers' Educnl Assoc 1984–95; hon vice-pres Education Action Int (formerly World Univ Service (UK)) 2004– (tstee 1997–2003); memb Bd of Tstees of Nat Museums of Scotland 1987–97, tstee Womankind Worldwide 1988–96, patron African Families Fndn 2000–, tstee Alhaji Sir Tafawa Balewa Memorial Tst 2005–; chair Shrewsbury Town Centre Residents Assoc 2002–05; William Pearson Tolley Medal Syracuse Univ 1975, Symons Medal Assoc of Cwlth Univs 2001, Cwlth World Teachers' Day Lifetime Achievement Award 2003; Hon DUniv: Open Univ 1975, Paisley 1993, Stirling 1994; Dr (hc) Univ of Edinburgh 1993, Hon DLitt Univ of Glasgow 2002, Hon CIPD 1993, FRSA 1984, FEIS 1990, FRSE 1991, AcSS 2000; *Recreations* travel, entertaining friends; *Clubs* Royal Over-Seas League, Cwlth; *Style*— Prof Lalage Bown, OBE, FRSE; ✉ 1 Dogpole Court, Dogpole, Shrewsbury SY1 1ES (tel 01743 356155, fax 01743 233626)

BOWN, Prof Stephen Glendening; s of Eric Inston Bown (d 1988), of Bexhill-on-Sea, and Olive Mary Kirkman, *née* Payne; *b* 13 December 1944; *Educ* St Dunstan's Coll Catford, Univ of Cambridge (MA, MB BChir, MD), Harvard Univ (AM); *m* 3 April 1982, Sheila Alyson, da of Peter Taylor (d 1991), of Bexhill-on-Sea; 2 da (Philippa Lucy b 1989, Sophie Elizabeth b 1991); *Career* Nat Med Laser Centre UCL Med Sch: dir 1986–, prof of laser med and surgery 1990–; conslt physician UCL Hosps NHS Tst 1987–; memb Bd Int Photodynamic Assoc 1992–, past pres Br Med Laser Assoc; over 250 sci pubns on med applications of lasers, past ed Lasers in Medical Science; Freeman City of London 1982; memb: Br Soc of Gastroenterology 1977, BMA 1974; MRCP 1974, FRCP 1991; *Recreations* squash, travel; *Style*— Prof Stephen Bown; ✉ 10 Watling Street, St Albans, Hertfordshire AL1 2PX (tel 01727 833701); National Medical Laser Centre, Department of Surgery, The Institute of Surgical Studies, Charles Bell House, 67–73 Riding House Street, London W1W 7EJ (tel 020 7679 9090, fax 020 7813 2828, e-mail s.bown@ucl.ac.uk)

BOWNE, Anthony; *Educ* Univ of Southampton (BSc), Laban Centre for Movement and Dance (Dip), Bartlett Sch of Architecture UCL (MSc); *Career* Laban: lectr in lighting design 1983–86, sr lectr 1987–94, dep chief exec 1994–2003, chief exec 2003–, chief exec Trinity Laban 2003–; tech/admin dir Transitions Dance Co 1983–94, tech dir GB tour Nat Youth Dance Co 1986–87, sr lectr in theatre lighting design Hong Kong Acad for Performing Arts 1996–98, prof of dance Lasalle Coll Singapore 2004–; lighting designer 1993–, prodns in UK, Taiwan, Hong Kong, Singapore and Shanghai; London Dance and Performance Award for Lighting Design of No Respite 1992; one of ten lighting designers chosen as "ones to watch" in the next decade Designer for the 90's 1990; guest teacher: Social Hall of Education Taipei 1988, Keene State Coll NH 1991, 1993 and 1995, Univ of the Arts Philadelphia 1991 and 1993, Poly Univ Hong Kong 1997, Arts Cncl England/CABE 2004; memb: Scholarship Review Panel Western Australia Acad for Performing Arts, Govt Dance Forum, All Party Parly Dance Gp; chair Cholmondeleys and Featherstoneshaughs dance cos; memb Bd: Bonnie Bird Choreography Fund, Granada/Univ of California Davis Artists-in-Residence program, Bird Coll Sidcup; govr Finnish Inst London; FRSA 2002; *Style*— Anthony Bowne, Esq; ✉ Laban, Creekside, London SE8 3DZ (tel 020 8691 8600, fax 020 8691 8400, e-mail a.bowne@laban.org)

BOWNES, Prof Mary; OBE (2006); *b* 14 November 1948, Drewsteignton, Devon; *Educ* Univ of Sussex (BSc, DPhil); *Career* postdoctoral assoc Univ of Freiburg and Univ of Calif Irvine 1973–76, lectr in genetics and developmental biology Univ of Essex 1976–79; Univ of Edinburgh: lectr in molecular biology 1979–89, sr lectr 1989–91, reader 1991–94, personal chair in developmental biology 1994–, assoc dean for postgrads Faculty of Science and Engrg 1997–98, head Inst of Cell and Molecular Biology 1998–2001, vice-princ 2003–, memb numerous univ ctees and gps; dir Scottish Initiative for Biotechnology Educn 2002–; memb Editorial Advsy Bd Jl of Embryology and Experimental Morphology/Development 1982–88, memb Editorial Bd Insect Molecular Biology 1990–, assoc ed Developmental Biology 1992–95, memb Editorial Bd Jl of Endocrinology 2000–; author of numerous papers in jls, book chapters and review articles; external examiner: Univ of Sussex 1996–2000, Univ of Oxford 2001–03, Univ of York 2004–06, Univ of Glasgow 2005–; chair: Steering Ctee Science and Plants for Schs (SAPS) Biotechnology Scotland Project 2000– (memb 1998–), Bd Edinburgh Centre for Rural Research 2003– (memb 1999, memb Exec Ctee 2000–03), Strategy Bd BBSRC 2004–, Studentships and Fellowships Strategy Panel BBSRC 2004–; memb: Bd Genetics Soc 1980–83, Ctee Br Soc for Developmental Biology 1982–87 (treas 1984–89), Advsy Bd Inst for Science Educn Scotland 2002–03, Advsy Bd MRC 2002–03, Cell and Molecular Biology Section Ctee RSE 2004–, Young People's Ctee RSE 2004–; CBiol, FIBiol, FRES, FRSE; *Books* Metamorphosis (jt ed, 1985), Ecdysone from Metabolism to Regulation of Gene Expression (ed, 1986); *Style*— Prof Mary Bownes, OBE; ✉ Institute of Cell Biology, The University of Edinburgh, Darwin Building, The King's Buildings, Edinburgh EH9 3JR

BOWNESS, Baron (Life Peer UK 1995), of Warlingham in the County of Surrey and of Croydon in the London Borough of Croydon; Sir Peter Spencer Bowness; kt (1987), CBE (1981), DL (Greater London 1982); s of Hubert Spencer Bowness (d 1981), of Cardiff, and Doreen (Peggy) Blundell, *née* Davies; *b* 19 May 1943; *Educ* Whitgift Sch Croydon; *m* 1, 27 July 1969 (m dis 1983), Marianne, da of Robert Hall, of Croydon; 1 da (Hon Caroline b 1978); m 2, 6 June 1984, Mrs Patricia Jane Cook, da of John Cullis, of Abergavenny; *Career* slr and Notary Public; ptnr Weightman Sadler Solicitors Purley 1970–2002, conslt Streeter Marshall Solicitors Croydon, Purley and Warlingham 2002–; ldr Croydon Cncl 1976–79 and 1980–94, ldr Opposition Croydon Cncl 1994–96, chm London Boroughs Assoc 1978–94, dep chm Assoc of Metropolitan Authorities 1978–80; memb: Audit Cmmn England & Wales 1983–95, London Residuary Body 1985–93, Nat Trg Task Force 1989–92, Congress (formerly Standing Conf) of Local and Regnl Authorities of Europe (Cncl of Europe) 1990–98, UK Delgn Ctee of Regions Euro Union 1993–98, Bureau COR 1993–98; memb Bd London First/London Forum 1993–94; sits as Cons House of Lords, oppn spokesman on local govt 1997–98, House of Lords rep UK delgn to EU Charter of Fundamental Rights Drafting Cmmn 1999–2000; chm of Sub-Ctee House of Lords Foreign Policy Defence and Developmental Aid of the EU Select Ctee 2003–06; memb OSCE Parly Assembly 2007–; former govr Whitgift Fndn; Freeman City of London 1987, Hon Freeman London Borough of Croydon 2002; Hon Col 151 (Greater London) Tport Regt (V) 1988–93; *Recreations* travel, gardening; *Style*— The Rt Hon Lord Bowness, CBE, DL; ✉ House of Lords, London SW1A 0PW (e-mail lordbowness@btinternet.com); office tel 01883 622433

BOWRAN, Peter Anthony Graham (Tony); s of James Eric Bowran, and Charlotte, *née* Peacock (d 1981); *b* 23 August 1953, Middlesbrugh; *Educ* Calday Grange GS, London Coll of Printing; *m* Linda Rosena Peryer; *Career* photographer; commissioned by London and worldwide advertising agencies; personal work published in several books on photography and exhibited in London and Cornwall; photography awards incl: Assoc of Photographers (AFAEP) Gold, Silver and Merit certs, D&AD, Creative Circle, Clio Communication Arts, One Show and London Photographic; fencer (fenced for GB in several Fedn Int Escrime World Cup events); *Clubs* Lansdowne, Épée, Soho House; *Style*— Tony Bowran, Esq; ✉ 5 Wandon Road, London SW6 2JF (tel 020 7731 2689, e-mail ltb.studio1@talktalk.net, website www.tonybowran.com)

BOWRING, Clive John; s of George Edward Bowring (d 1997), of Guernsey, and Kathleen Elma (Jane), *née* Tyte (d 1993); *b* 1 September 1937; *Educ* Rugby; *Career* Nat Serv 1956–58, Lt RNR; C T Bowring & Co Ltd 1958–80 (dir C T Bowring (Insurance) Holdings Ltd 1976), dir Robert Fleming Insurance Brokers Ltd 1980– (chm 1996–); dir: Forest North Holdings Ltd, New Hurlingham Court Ltd; tstee New Forest Ninth Centenary Tst, govr Queen Elizabeth's Fndn 1984; Freeman City of London 1984, Liveryman Worshipful Co of Insurers 1984; *Recreations* sailing, travel, the countryside; *Clubs* City of London, Royal Ocean Racing, Hurlingham, Poole Yacht, Lloyds Yacht, Pilgrims; *Style*— Clive Bowring, Esq; ✉ Robert Fleming Insurance Brokers Ltd, Staple Hall, Stone House Court, London EC3A 7NP (tel 020 7621 1263, fax 020 7626 5692, e-mail clive.bowring@rfib.co.uk)

BOWRING, Rev Lyndon; s of Arthur Bowing, of Caerphilly, Mid Glam, and Ellen May, *née* Gardner; *b* 15 February 1948; *Educ* Caerphilly GS, London Bible Coll; *m* 25 May 1974, Celia Joan, da of Capt Edward Ernest Bartholomew (d 1983), of Shoreham-by-Sea; 2 s (Daniel Alexander, Andrew Gareth), 1 da (Emma Charlotte); *Career* Elim pentecostal minister Kensington Temple 1972–80, chm NFOL 1981–83, exec chm CARE 1983–; vice-chm: Luis Palau's Mission 1984, Billy Graham's Mission 1989; chm Maranatha Christian Tst, dir London and Nationwide Missions; public speaker; *Recreations* family, reading, walking, gardening, exploring London; *Style*— The Rev Lyndon Bowring; ✉ 22 Thornton Avenue, Chiswick, London W4 (tel 020 8747 3796); CARE, 53 Romney Street, London SW1 (tel 020 7233 0455, fax 017 233 0983)

BOWRING, Peter; CBE (1993); eld s of Frederick Clive Bowring (d 1965), and Agnes Walker, *née* Cairns (d 1961); *b* 22 April 1923; *Educ* Shrewsbury; *m* 1, 1946 (m dis), Barbara Ekaterina Brewis (d 2005); 1 s (Antony), 1 da (Thérèsa); m 2, 1979 (m dis), Carol Hutchings; m 3, 1986, Carole M Dear; *Career* served WWII 1941–46, cmmnd Rifle Brigade 1942, served Egypt, N Africa, Italy, Austria (despatches); C T Bowring & Co Ltd: joined 1947, dir 1956–84, dep chm 1973–78, chm 1978–82; chm: C T Bowring Trading (Holdings) Ltd 1967–84, Bowmaker Plant Ltd 1972–83, Bowring Steamship Co Ltd 1974–82, Bowmaker Ltd 1978–82, C T Bowring UK Ltd 1980–84; vice-chm Marsh & McLennan 1982–84 (dir 1980–84); memb Lloyd's 1968–98; dir: Rhein Chemie Holding GmbH 1968–, Centre for Policy Studies 1983–88, Ind Primary and Secdy Educn Tst 1986–2006; pres Help the Aged 1988–2000 (chm 1977–87); chm: Aldeburgh Fndn 1982–89, City Arts Tst 1987–94 (dep chm 1986–87), Inter-Action Social Enterprise Tst Ltd 1989–91, Bd of Govrs St Dunstan's Educnl Fndn 1977–90 (govr 1974–95, companion 1998), Transglobe Expedition Tst 1993–; memb Bd of Govrs Shrewsbury Sch 1969–97; tstee: Wakefield (Tower Hill, Trinity Square) Tst 1986–2006 (chm 2002–05), Zoological Soc Devpt Tst 1987–1990, Ironbridge Gorge Museum Devpt Tst 1989–93 (companion 1993), The SPRY Tst (formerly Upper Severn Navigation Tst) 1989–, Third Age Challenge Tst 1991–2000; memb Guild of Freemen of City of London, Freeman Worshipful Co of Watermen and Lightermen, Liveryman Worshipful Co of Insurers, Master Worshipful Co of World Traders 1989–90 (Sr Warden 1988–89); FRSA, FInstD; *Publications* The Last Minute, A Thicket of Business; *Recreations* sailing, motoring, listening to music, cooking, photography; *Clubs* Royal Thames Yacht, Royal Green Jackets, Little Ship; *Style*— Peter Bowring, Esq, CBE; ✉ 79 New Concordia Wharf, Mill Street, London SE1 2BB (tel and fax 020 7237 0818)

BOWRING, Prof Richard John; s of Richard Arthur Bowring (d 1987), and Mabel, *née* Eddy; *b* 6 February 1947; *Educ* Blundell's, Downing Coll Cambridge (BA, PhD, LittD); *m* 30 Jan 1970, Susan, da of Wilfred Raymond Povey, of Stoke-on-Trent, Staffs; 1 da (Imogen Clare b 17 May 1977); *Career* mgmnt trainee Cathay Pacific Airways 1968–70, lectr in Japanese Monash Univ Melbourne 1976–78, asst prof of Japanese Columbia Univ NY 1978–79, assoc prof of Japanese Princeton Univ 1979–84, prof of Japanese studies Univ of Cambridge 1985– (lectr in Japanese 1984), fell Downing Coll Cambridge 1985–2000 (hon fell 2000–), Master Selwyn Coll Cambridge 2000–; readership British Acad 1995–97; memb Review Ctee for Oriental Studies Univ of Oxford 2000; tstee Cambridge Fndn 1989–98, advsr to UFC 1991–92, Crown rep Governing Body SOAS Univ of London 1994–99, chm HEFCE Working Pty on Funding of SOAS 2000; *Books* Mori Ogai and the Modernisation of Japanese Culture (1979), Murasaki Shikibu: Her Diary and Poetic Memoirs (1982), Murasaki Shikibu: The Tale of Genji (1988), Introduction to Modern Japanese (1992), Cambridge Encyclopedia of Japan (1993), The Diary of Lady Murasaki (1996), Fifty Years of Japanese at Cambridge (1998), Cambridge Intermediate Japanese (2002), The Religious Traditions of Japan, 500–1600 (2005); *Style*— Prof Richard Bowring; ✉ Master's Lodge, Selwyn College, Grange Road, Cambridge CB3 9DQ

BOWSHER, Dr David Richard; s of Reginald William George Bowsher (d 1971), of Bishop's Cleeve, Glos, and Marion, *née* Scott (d 1966); *b* 23 February 1925; *Educ* Haileybury, Gonville & Caius Coll Cambridge (MA, ScD, MD), UCH, Univ of Liverpool (PhD), Harvard Med Sch Boston USA; *m* 1, 1952 (m dis 1959), (Anna) Meryl, *née* Reid; 1 s (Julian Michael Charles b 1953); m 2, 1 April 1969, Doreen, da of Laurence Arthur (d 1971); *Career* Cncl of Europe research fell: Oslo and Leyden 1958, Uppsala 1970; Royal Soc Euro fell: Paris 1968–69, Marseilles 1974; reader and hon conslt neurologist Faculty of Med Univ of Liverpool 1972–90 (research fell 1952–54, asst lectr 1954–56, lectr 1956–64, sr lectr 1964–72); professeur associé Faculté des Sciences: de Paris 1961–62, de Marseille 1986; currently hon sr research fell and hon conslt neurologist Pain Res Inst and tstee Pain Relief Fndn; hon sr research fell Dept of Neurological Sci Univ of Liverpool; former pres: Br and Irish Chapter Int Assoc for the Study of Pain, North of England Neurological Assoc, Liverpool Div BMA; pres Burke and Hare Soc, Neuroscience ed Clinical Anatomy, former chm Merseyside and N Wales Pain Gp; author of over 250 articles in med and scientific jls; fndr memb Int Assoc Study of Pain; memb: Physiological Soc, Assoc des Physiologistes de Langue Française, Brain Res Assoc; FRCPEd, FRCPath; *Books* Cerebrospinal Fluid Dynamics in Health and Disease (1960), Mechanisms of Nervous Disorder: An Introduction (1978), Introduction to the Anatomy and Physiology of the Nervous System (5 edn, 1988), Pain: Management and Control in Physiotherapy (jtly, 1988), Neurological Emergencies in Medical Practice (jtly, 1988), Pain Control in Nursing Practice (jtly, 1994); *Recreations* walking, language and languages, opera and music, history, uxoriousness; *Style*— Dr David Bowsher; ✉ Pain Research Institute, Clinical Sciences Building, University Hospital Aintree, Liverpool L9 7AL (tel 0151 529 5820, fax 0151 529 5821, e-mail bowsher@liv.ac.uk)

BOWSHER, His Hon Peter Charles; QC (1978); s of Charles Bowsher, and Ellen Bowsher; *b* 9 February 1935; *Educ* Ardingly, Oriel Coll Oxford (MA); *m* 1960, Deborah, da of Frederick Wilkins, of Vancouver; 2 s; *Career* cmmnd RA 1954; called to the Bar Middle Temple 1959 (bencher 1985); recorder (SE Circuit) 1983–87, official referee and circuit judge (SE Circuit) 1987–98, judge of the Technology and Construction Court of High Court of Justice 1998–2003, in private practice as arbitrator and adjudicator 2003–; memb: Cncl Soc for Computers and Law 1990–95, Judicial Ctee Acad of Experts 1992–2003; FCIArb 1990 (Chartered Arbitrator 2003–); *Recreations* music, photography; *Clubs* Brooks's, RAC; *Style*— His Hon Peter Bowsher, QC; ✉ Keating Chambers, 15 Essex Street, London WC2R 3AU

BOWTELL, Dame Ann Elizabeth; DCB (1997, CB 1989); da of John Albert Kewell, of Hove, E Sussex, and Olive Rose, *née* Sims; *b* 25 April 1938; *Educ* Kendrick Girls' Sch Reading, Girton Coll Cambridge (MA), Royal Holloway Univ of London (MA); *m* 11 Feb 1961, Michael John Bowtell, s of Norman Bowtell; 2 s (Thomas, Samuel), 2 da (Sophie, Harriet); *Career* asst princ Nat Assistance Bd 1960–64; DHSS: princ 1964–73, asst sec 1973–80, under sec 1980–86, dep sec 1986–88; DSS 1988–90, princ estab and fin offr Dept of Health 1990–93, first civil serv cmmr Cabinet Office 1993–95, dep then perm sec DSS 1995–99; tstee Joseph Rowntree Fndn; hon fell Girton Coll Cambridge, Hon DUniv Middx; FRSA; *Recreations* walking, bird watching, medieval history, classical music; *Style*— Dame Ann Bowtell, DCB; ✉ tel 01932 229260, e-mail ann@annbowtell.free-online.co.uk

BOWYER, (Arthur) David; s of Sir Eric Blacklock Bowyer, KCB, KBE (d 1964), and late Elizabeth Crane, *née* Nicholls (who m 2, Sir Sidney Caine, KCMG (d 1991)); *b* 27 August 1940; *Educ* Tonbridge, Trinity Hall Cambridge (BA); *m* 6 Dec 1969, Ann Victoria, da of His Hon Herbert Christopher Beaumont, MBE (d 2002), of Bradfield, Berks; 1 da (Katharine Sarah (Mrs Foster-Brown) b 1971), 2 s (Edward Christopher b 1972, Andrew Mark b 1975); *Career* admitted slr 1965; ptnr Clifford Chance (formerly Clifford-Turner) 1968–91, ptnr Withers 1991–99 (conslt 1999–2000), sole practitioner 2001–; memb: Law Society 1976; *Recreations* skiing, golf, shooting and travel; *Clubs* Boodle's, Huntercombe Golf; *Style*— David Bowyer, Esq; ✉ Ashe Warren House, Ashe Warren, Overton, Basingstoke, Hampshire RG25 3AW (tel 01256 770215, e-mail davidbowyer@compuserve.com)

BOWYER, (Arthur) William; s of Arthur Bowyer (d 1979), of Leek, Staffs, and Emma Bowyer (d 1983); *b* 25 May 1926; *Educ* Burslem Sch of Art, Royal Coll of Art (ARCA); *m* Vera Mary, da of William Norman Small (d 1986); 2 s (Francis David b 1951, Jason Richard b 1957), 1 da (Emma Jane b 1966); *Career* painter; Bevin Boy Sneyd Colliery Burslem 1942–44; teacher: Gravesend Sch of Art, Central Sch of Art, Walthamstow Sch of Art; Sir John Cass head of fine art Maidstone Coll of Art 1971–81, ret to paint; work in collections: Royal Acad, Royal Soc of Painters in Watercolour, Nat Portrait Gallery, Graves Gallery Sheffield, Arts Cncl of GB, many private collections; hon sec New English Art Club 1964–99; RA 1981 (ARA 1974), RP, RBA, RWS; *Recreations* cricket, swimming; *Clubs* Arts; *Style*— William Bowyer, Esq, RA; ✉ 12 Cleveland Avenue, Chiswick, London W4 (tel 020 8994 0346); Studio, 8 Gainsborough Road, Chiswick, London W4

BOWYER-SMYTH, (Sir) Thomas Weyland; 15 Bt (E 1661), of Hill Hall, Essex; s of Capt Sir Philip Weyland Bowyer-Smyth, 14 Bt, RN (d 1978); *b* 25 June 1960; *m* 14 Aug 1992 (m dis 1996), Sara Louise, *née* Breinlinger; m 2, 25 July 1998, Mary Rose Helen, *née* Giedroyc; 1 s (Casimir Stanley Giedroyc Bowyer b 13 September 1997), 1 step s (Zygmunt Lawrence Giedroyc Heath b 19 March 1991); *Heir* kinsman, John Windham; *Style*— Mr Thomas Bowyer

BOX, Stephen John; s of Ronald Tully Box (d 1981), and Mollie Rita, *née* Clarke (d 2000); *b* 13 September 1950; *Educ* Ardingly; *m* 25 April 1992, Christine Elisabeth, da of Robert Beevers (d 1989), of Rockhampton, Qld, Aust; *Career* CA; articled clerk Hilton Sharp & Clarke 1967–71; Coopers & Lybrand: sr 1971–73, mangr 1973–82, ptnr 1982–97; fin dir National Grid Gp plc 1997–2002; non-exec dir: Michael Page International plc 2001–, South East Water Ltd, Wales and West Utilities Ltd; memb Financial Reporting Review Panel; FCA 1971; *Recreations* opera, theatre, travel, gardening, bridge, reading, swimming; *Style*— Stephen Box, Esq

BOX, Stephen Thomas; s of Thomas George, of Nuneaton, Warks, and Edith Helen, *née* Reid; *Educ* Queen Elizabeth GS Atherstone, Univ of Salford (BSc), Physical Electronics City Business Sch (DipBA); *m* 8 Jan 1988 (m dis 1995), Sarah, da of Dennis Grimwood Roscow; 2 da (Daisy Philippa b 24 Aug 1988, Imogen Poppy b 9 Aug 1990); *Career* sci offr AERE Harwell 1968–74, computer conslt CSI Ltd 1974–76, systems analyst Chase Manhattan Bank 1976–78, head int systems devpt Citicorp 1978–80, freelance mgmnt conslt 1980–86, dir debt securities ops Kleinwort Benson Ltd 1987–89, mgmnt conslt and corp financier Stephen Box & Co 1989–90, co-fndr and dir Blue Skies Corporation plc 1990–94, dir UNIVEST Corporation Ltd 1995–; contrib to Manuale del Project Finance 1999; Liveryman Worshipful Co of Gunmakers 2003; *Recreations* shooting, tennis, golf, music, opera; *Style*— Stephen Box, Esq; ✉ Farthing Lodge, 20 Stamford Road, Weldon, Northamptonshire NN17 3JL (tel 01536 402960, fax 01536 401528, e-mail stephen.box@btinternet.com)

BOXER, Prof David Howell; s of William H S Boxer, of Aberdare, and Sarah, *née* Davies; *b* 11 June 1947; *Educ* Aberdare Boys' GS, Univ of Bristol (univ scholar, Lord Kitchener Nat Meml Fund scholar, BSc, PhD, CertEd); *m* Dr Maureen Boxer, da of Matthew McGuckin; 1 s (Iain b 6 Oct 1983); *Career* Univ of Dundee: Nuffield Fndn sci res fell 1982–83, head Dept of Biochemistry 1988–93, personal chair 1991, prof of microbial biochemistry 1991–2002, dean Science and Engrg Faculty 1994–99, dep princ 2000–02, vice-princ (research and enterprise) 2002–; SERC: memb Molecular Recognition Initiative Ctee 1989–93, chm Biochemistry and Biophysics Sub Ctee 1991–93; external examiner: Univ of Stirling 1992–, Univ of Edinburgh 1992–, Univ of Newcastle upon Tyne 1993–, Univ of Sheffield 1994–; ed: Molecular Microbiology 1986–91, Biochemical Jl 1989–90, Methods in Microbiology 1991–; author of numerous pubns in scientific jls, regular invited speaker at Univs and int meetings; memb: Biochemical Soc 1974–, Soc for General Microbiology 1980–, Br Biophysical Soc 1980–, American Soc for Microbiology 1981–, Inorganic Biochemistry Discussion Gp 1983–, American Chemical Soc 1990–; *Recreations* walking, cycling, skiing; *Style*— Prof David Boxer

BOYACK, Sarah; MSP; da of James Boyack (d 1989), and Alma Boyack, *née* Graham; *b* 16 May 1961; *Educ* Royal HS Edinburgh, Univ of Glasgow (MA), Heriot-Watt Univ (Dip Town & Country Planning); *Career* planning asst London Borough of Brent 1986–88, sr planning offr Central Regional Cncl 1988–92, lectr in planning Edinburgh Coll of Art Heriot-Watt Univ 1992–99; MSP (Lab) Edinburgh Central 1999–; min for tport and environment 1999–2001, min for tport and planning 2001, memb European Ctee; *Style*— Ms Sarah Boyack, MSP; ✉ Constituency Office, 15A Stafford Street, Edinburgh EH3 7BU (tel 0131 476 2539, fax 0131 467 3574); The Scottish Parliament, Edinburgh EH99 1SP (tel 0131 348 5751, fax 0131 348 5974, e-mail sarah.boyack.msp@scottish.parliament.uk)

BOYCE, Sir Graham Hugh; KCMG (2001, CMG 1991); s of Cdr Hugh Boyce, DSC, RN, and Madeline Millicent, *née* Manley; *b* 6 October 1945; *Educ* Hurstpierpoint Coll, Jesus Coll Cambridge (MA); *m* 11 April 1970, Janet Elizabeth (Lady Boyce), da of Rev Gordon Charles Craig Spencer, of Bath; 1 s (James b 1971), 3 da (Rachel b 1974, Sara b 1980, Josephine b 1984); *Career* VSO Antigua 1967; FCO: HM Dip Serv 1968, third then second sec Ottawa 1971, MECAS Shemlan 1972–74, first sec Tripoli 1974–77, FCO 1977–81, first sec Kuwait 1981–85, asst head ME Dept 1985–86, cnsllr and consul-gen Stockholm 1987–90, ambass and consul-gen Doha 1990–93, head Environment Science and Energy Dept 1993–96, ambass to Kuwait 1996–99, ambass to Egypt 1999–2001; vice-chm VT Int Servs 2002–06, jt chm Windsor Energy Gp 2005–; chm Middle East Advsy Bd: Invensys 2005–, Lehman Bros 2006–; memb: Int Advsy Cncl Kuwait Investment Office 2004–, Int Advsy Bd SOAS 2007–, European Advsy Cncl Air Products 2007–; vice-chm Middle East Assoc 2004–; *Recreations* tennis, reading, golf; *Style*— Sir Graham Boyce, KCMG; ✉ e-mail ghbhc@aol.com

BOYCE, Baron (Life Peer UK 2003), of Pimlico in the City of Westminster; Adm (Sir) Michael Cecil Boyce; GCB (1999), OBE (1982), DL (Gtr London 2003); *b* 2 April 1943; *Career* joined RN 1961, submariner 1965, served HM Submarines Anchorite, Valiant and Conqueror 1965–72; cmd HM Submarines: Oberon 1973–74, Opossum 1974–75, Superb 1979–81; cmd HMS Brilliant 1983–84, Capt (SM) Submarine Sea Trg 1984–86, RCDS 1988, Cdre 1988, Sr Naval Offr Middle East 1989, Dir Naval Staff Duties 1989–91; Rear Adm 1991; Flag Offr: Sea Trg 1991–92, Surface Flotilla 1992–95; Cdr Anti-Submarine Warfare Striking Force 1992–94, Vice Adm 1994, Adm 1995, Second Sea Lord and C-in-C Naval Home Cmd 1995–97, C-in-C Fleet, C-in-C Eastern Atlantic, Cdr Allied Naval Forces North Western Europe 1997–98, First Sea Lord and Chief of the Naval Staff 1998–2001, Chief of the Defence Staff 2001–03, Col Cmdt SBS 2003–; Lord Warden of the Cinque Ports and Constable Dover Castle 2004–; pres: Officers Assoc 2003–, RN Submarine Museum 2004–; memb Cncl: White Ensign Assoc 2003– (chm 2008–), RNLI 2004– (tstee 2006–); patron Submariners Assoc 2003–, tstee Nat Maritime Museum 2005–, dir Naval and Military Club 2003–; non-exec dir: WS Atkins 2004–, VT Group plc 2004–; pres London Dist St John Ambulance 2003–; Freeman City of London 1999; elder bro Trinity House 2006–; KStJ 2002; *Style*— The Rt Hon the Lord Boyce, GCB, OBE, DL; ✉ House of Lords, London SW1A 0PW

BOYCE, Sir Robert Charles Leslie; 3 Bt (UK 1952), of Badgeworth, Co Gloucester; s of Sir Richard (Leslie) Boyce, 2 Bt (d 1968), and Jacqueline Anne Boyce-Dennis, *née* Hill; *b* 2

May 1962; *Educ* Cheltenham Coll, Univ of Salford (BSc), Univ of Nottingham (BMedSci, BM BS); *m* 1985, Fiona Margaret, 2 da of John Savage, of Coventry, Warks; 1 s (Thomas Leslie b 3 Sept 1993), 1 da (Amelia Moira b 23 March 1996); *Heir* s, Thomas Boyce; *Career* conslt ophthalmic and oculoplastic surgn; FRCSEd; *Clubs* BMA; *Style*— Sir Robert Boyce, Bt

BOYCE, William; QC (2001); *b* 29 July 1951; *Educ* St Joseph's Acad GS Blackheath, Univ of Kent (BA); *Career* called to the Bar Gray's Inn 1976, recorder 1997–, bencher 2007; sr Treasy counsel Central Criminal Court 1997–2001 (jr Treasy counsel 1991–97); *Style*— William Boyce, Esq, QC; ✉ Queen Elizabeth Building, Temple, London EC4Y 9BS (tel 020 7583 5766)

BOYCOTT, Geoffrey (Geoff); OBE (1981); s of late Thomas Wilfred Boycott, and Jane, *née* Speight; *b* 21 October 1940; *Educ* Kinsley Secdy Modern, Hemsworth GS; *m* 26 Feb 2003, Rachael, *née* Swinglehurst; 1 da (Emma Jane); *Career* former cricketer; played for: Yorks CCC 1962–86 (co cap 1963, capt 1971–78), England 1964–74 and 1977–82 (capt 1977–78, 4 tests); scored one hundredth first class century 1977 (England v Australia), scored one hundred and fiftieth century 1986, exceeded world record no of runs scored in Test Matches Delhi 1982; hon life memb and memb Bd Yorks CCC; sometime commentator: BBC, TW1, World Tel, Espn/Star Sports, Talk Radio, SABC, Channel 4, BBC Radio, Channel 9 (Aust), Channel 5 TV (Aust), NZTV; *Books* Geoff Boycott's Book for Young Cricketers (1976), Put to the Test: England in Australia 1978–79 (1979), Geoff Boycott's Cricket Quiz (1979), Boycott On Batting (1980), Opening Up (1980), In the Fast Lane: England in the West Indies (1981), Master Class (1982), Boycott, The Autobiography (1987), Boycott on Cricket (1990); *Videos* Boycott on Batting (1990), Geoff Boycott's Greatest England Team (1991), Geoffrey Boycott on Cricket (1999); *Recreations* golf; *Style*— Geoff Boycott, Esq, OBE; ✉ Yorkshire County Cricket Club, Headingley Cricket Ground, Leeds LS6 3BY

BOYCOTT, Rosel Marie (Rosie); da of Maj Charles Boycott, and Betty, *née* Le Sueur (d 1981); *b* 13 May 1951; *Educ* Cheltenham Ladies' Coll, Univ of Kent; *m* 1, (m dis 1998), David Leitch; 1 da (Daisy Anna b 9 Aug 1983); m 2, 1999, Charles Howard, QC, *qv*; *Career* journalist and author; fndr: Spare Rib magazine 1972, Virago Press 1973; ed Osrati (Kuwaiti women's magazine) 1976–79, freelance contrib to various nat newspapers, full-time appts at Daily Mail, Daily Telegraph and Harpers & Queen, ed British Esquire 1992–96; ed: Independent on Sunday 1996–98, The Independent 1998, The Daily Express 1998–2001; contrib to progs on TV and radio and to Daily Mail and The Observer; *Books* Loka: The Buddhist Journal of Naropa (ed, 1975), Batty, Bloomers and Boycott (1981), A Nice Girl Like Me (autobiography, 1983), All For Love (novel, 1985); *Recreations* sailing, tennis, riding; *Clubs* Globe, Groucho, Academy; *Style*— Ms Rosie Boycott

BOYD, Alan Robb; s of Alexander Boyd (d 1963), and Mary Herd, *née* Robb (d 1998); *b* 30 July 1953; *Educ* Irvine Royal Acad, Univ of Dundee (LLB), Open Univ (BA); *m* 1973, Frances Helen, da of Joseph Donaldson; 2 da (Carol Jane b 10 Sept 1975, Fiona Anne b 22 March 1979); *Career* admitted slr 1976, princ legal asst Shetland Islands Cncl 1979–81, princ slr Glenrothes Development Corporation 1981–84, legal advsr Irvine Development Corporation 1984–97, dir of Public Law McGrigors LLP Slrs 1997–, dir McGrigors Public Policy 1999–; pres Euro Co Lawyers' Assoc 1992–94, pres Law Soc of Scotland 1995–96 (vice-pres 1994–95, memb Cncl 1985–97); NP 1982, SSC; *Recreations* golf, music, gardening; *Clubs* Turnberry Golf; *Style*— Alan Boyd, Esq; ✉ 45 Craigholm Road, Ayr KA7 3LJ (tel 01292 262542, e-mail alanrboyd@aol.com); McGrigors LLP, Pacific House, 70 Wellington Street, Glasgow G2 6SB (tel 0141 248 6677, fax 0141 204 1351, e-mail alan.boyd@mcgrigors.com)

BOYD, Sir Alexander Walter; 3 Bt (UK 1916), of Howth House, Howth, Co Dublin; s of late Maj Cecil Anderson Boyd, MC, MD, late RAMC, 2 s of 1 Bt; suc unc, Sir Walter Herbert Boyd, 2 Bt, 1948; *b* 16 June 1934; *m* 1958, Molly Madeline, da of late Ernest Arthur Rendell, of Vernon, BC, Canada; 3 da (Heather Lynn b 1959, Susan Christine b 1961, Sandra Molly b 1967), 2 s (Ian Walter Rendell b 1964, Robert Alexander Rendell b 1966); *Heir* s, Ian Boyd; *Style*— Sir Alexander Boyd, Bt

BOYD, (Morgan) Alistair; CMG (1990); s of Preb Norman Robert Boyd (d 1945), and Muriel Katherine, *née* Humby (d 1984); *b* 1 May 1934; *Educ* Marlborough, Wadham Coll Oxford (MA); *m* 26 May 1959, Judith Mary, da of Preb Henry Wilfred Lawrence Martin, of Christ Church, Jerusalem; *Career* Commonwealth Devpt Corp: mgmnt trainee 1957, investigations exec Malaysia and rep Economist Intelligence Unit Liaison Office for the Fedn of Br Industry 1961, mangr E Caribbean Housing and related mortgage fin cos in the Caribbean 1967, attached to FO for mission to Turks and Caicos Islands 1970, gen mangr Tanganyika Development Finance Co Tanzania 1970–74, seconded as advsr on establishing Industrial Devpt Bank to Kenya Govt 1975, regnl controller Central Africa Lusaka 1976–80, regional controller E Africa Nairobi 1980–83, head of new business worldwide London 1983, dir of operations in Africa London 1985, dep chief exec 1991–94, advsr 1994–2000; memb Cncl Africa Centre 1995–2004, chm UK Southern Africa Business Assoc 1995–, vice-chm Royal African Soc 1996–; dir AMREF UK 1999– (chm 2001), chm Gateway to Growth 2005–; memb Bd: Hub River Power Co Pakistan 1994–96, EDESA Management AG Switzerland 1994–97, Tea Plantations Investment Trust plc 1998–; memb: Ctee on South African Trade 1995–2001, Steering Ctee World Congress (1998) Land Ownership and Resource Mgmnt 1996–2000, Directorate of Tropical Africa Advsy Gp 1997–2000; tstee CDC Pension Fund 1995–2001; lectr for Maurice Frost Lecture Agency and ESU 1956–62 (USA tour 1961), Malaysia corr Far Eastern Economic Review 1963–66; FRGS 1959, FRSA (memb 1990); *Books* Royal Challenge Accepted (1961); *Recreations* sailing, music; *Clubs* Naval, ESU; *Style*— Alistair Boyd, Esq, CMG; ✉ 7 South Hill Mansions, South Hill Park, London NW3 2SL (e-mail morgaliboyd@yahoo.com)

BOYD, Don; s of Donald John Boyd (d 1991), of Tollard Royal, Dorset, and Lubov Petrovna Drosdovo (d 2001); *Educ* Loretto, London Film Sch; *m* 1, 1970 (m dis 1973), Vivien; 1 da (Amanda Cara (Mrs Bailey) b 6 May 1971); m 2, 1973, Hilary, da of Maj John Heale Sandeman-Allen; 2 da (Clare (Mrs Clark) b 1 July 1974, Katherine b 12 Aug 1977); *Career* film director and producer; fndr: Boyd's Co 1978, Anglo Int Films 1988, Tartan Films 1988, Lexington Films 1996; season of films presented at Nat Film Theatre 1982, delivered Guardian Lecture 1982; visiting prof Univ of Exeter; occasional contrib: The Guardian, The Observer, New Statesman, The Sunday Times; govr London Film Sch; Freeman: City of Mount Dora Florida 1981, State of Florida 1981; memb Cncl Directors' Guild of GB; FRSA; *Television* documentaries as dir incl: Man, God and Africa 1992, Vicars 1993, The Babe Business 1993, The Last Afrikaner 1994, Ruby's Health Quest (series, BBC) 1995, Ruby Does the Season (series, ITV, also prodr) 1995, Ruby With...(series, BBC, nominated BAFTA 1997) 1996, Sir Norman Foster (BBC) 1996, Full Frontal in Flip Flops (ITV) 1998, Donald and Luba: A Family Movie (BBC) 1999/2000, The Susan Smith Story (ITV) 2000, My Gay Husband (Channel 4) 2000, The Passions of Louis Malle (BBC) 2003, The Highest Bidder - The Windsors (BBC) 2003; *Films* as writer and dir incl: Intimate Reflections 1974, East of Elephant Rock 1975/76, The Four Seasons 1977, Goldeneye 1989, Twenty-One 1990 (nomination Grand Prize Sundance 1991), Kleptomania 1993, Lucia 1998–99, My Kingdom 2002, Andrew and Jeremy Get Married 2005 (nomination Best Documentary BIFA 2005); as exec prodr incl: Sweet William 1978, Scum 1978, The Tempest 1979, Hussy 1979, Blue Suede Shoes 1979, The Great Rock'n'Roll Swindle 1980, Anticlock 1980, An Unsuitable Job for Woman 1981; as prodr (with Boyd's Co) incl: Honky Tonk Freeway 1980/81, Look Back in Anger 1980, Scrubbers 1982, Captive 1985, Aria (closing night film Cannes Film Festival 1987) 1986–87; Anglo International Films, as prodr incl: The Last of England 1987, War Requiem 1988, The Girl With Brains in Her Feet, Crossmaheart; *Recreations* cinema and all other arts in particular opera and theatre; *Clubs* Groucho; *Style*— Don Boyd, Esq; ✉ c/o Caroline Michel, William Morris Agency, London

BOYD, Douglas; s of Marcus Alexander Boyd (d 1985), and Agnes (Nan), *née* Hollis (d 2001); *b* 1 March 1959; *Educ* RAM under Janet Craxton, studied with Maurice Bourgue in Paris; *m* 1, 1986 (m dis 1990), Gabielle Lester; 1 s (Samuel Marcus b 1988); m 2, 1994, Sally Pendlebury, cellist; 1 da (Iona Elizabeth b 1999), 1 s (Sebastian Alexander b 15 May 2003); *Career* former professional oboist, currently conductor; *As Oboist* debut Salzburg Festival 1990; soloist in important musical centres of Europe, Far East and America; co-fndr Chamber Orch of Europe (princ oboist, leading memb Wind Soloists); prof RAM (Hon ARAM 1990); concerto appearances incl: Chamber Orch of Europe, Scottish Chamber Orch, Vienna Symphony Orch, BBC Scottish Symphony, Bournemouth Sinfonietta, Orch of St Johns Smith Square, Acad of St Martin in the Fields, Moscow Virtuosi, Hong Kong Philarmonic, Basle Radio Symphony, Nat Arts Centre Orch Ottawa, Royal Scot Nat Orch, Northern Sinfonia of England, Winterthur Orch, Orchestre National de Lyon (debut), Cincinnati Symphony Orch (debut), Budapest Festival Orch; work with conductors incl: Claudio Abbado, Paavo Berglund, Sir Yehudi Menuhin, Alexander Schneider, Michael Tilson Thomas; int festivals incl: Berlin, City of London, Edinburgh, Korsholm, Vancouver, Charleston, Spoleto; *Recordings* Bach Oboe Concerto (dir and soloist, Deutsche Grammophon) 1990, Vivaldi Oboe Concerti (dir and soloist, Deutsche Grammophon) 1992, Schumann Recital (with Joao Maria Pires, Deutsche Grammophon) 1995; Strauss Oboe Concerto (ASV) 1990, Zelenka Trio Sonatas (claves) 1998, Ligeti Double Concerto (Jaques Zoon and Claudio Abbado, Deutsche Grammophon) 1998; as conductor: Beethoven Symphonies 2 & 5 (with Manchester Camerata, Avie Records), Mahler Symphony No 4 (with Manchester Camerata, Avie Records); *As Conductor* princ conductor Manchester Camerate 2001– (also music dir), princ guest conductor City of London Sinfonia 2002–, artistic ptnr St Paul Chamber Orch Minnesota; appearances incl: Scottish Chamber Orch, Manchester Camerata, Hong Kong Philharmonic, City of London Sinfonia, Orchestre National de Lyon, Upsalla Chamber Orch, Royal Scottish Nat Orch, St Paul Chamber Orch Minnesota, Baltimore Symphony, Seattle Symphony, BBC Symphony, BBC Philharmonic, City of Birmingham Symphony Orch, Toronot Symphony Orch, Dallas Symphony Orch, Detroit Symphony Orch; *Style*— Douglas Boyd, Esq; ✉ c/o Ingpen & Williams Ltd, 7 St George's Court, 131 Putney Bridge Road, London SW15 2PA (tel 020 8874 3222, e-mail dougieboyd@dial.pipex.com)

BOYD, Douglas Turner; OBE (2006); s of David Findlay Boyd (d 1979), and Edith May, *née* Turner (d 1981); *b* 7 April 1939; *Educ* Hutchesons' GS; *m* 2 Sept 1968, Sheena Lynam Park, da of John Lynam Henderson (d 1970); 2 da (Catriona Henderson b 8 April 1970, Aileen Elizabeth b 30 Aug 1971); *Career* qualified CA (ICAS); KPMG 1956–98; dir: Hanover (Scotland) Housing Association Ltd 1998– (chm 2004–), Scottish Food Quality Certification Ltd 1998–2005, Taylor Clark plc 2000–, Checkmate International plc 2001–, Cairnstar Ltd 2001–; memb: Doctors and Dentists' Pay Review Body 1987–92, Scottish Milk Mktg Bd 1994–2002; lay memb General Optical Cncl 1986–2001; govr: Macaulay Land Use Research Inst 1997–2003, Royal Scottish Acad of Music and Drama 1998–2007 (vice-chm 2003–07); memb: Incorporation of Gardeners (Glasgow) 1986, Incorporation of the Weavers of Anderston 1987, The Merchants' House of Glasgow 1990 (dir 2001–07); FRSAMD 2006; *Recreations* keep fit, golf; *Clubs* Western (Glasgow), Lenzie, Lenzie Golf; *Style*— Douglas T Boyd, Esq, OBE, FRSAMD; ✉ 5 Laurel Avenue, Lenzie, Kirkintilloch, Glasgow G66 4RX (tel 0141 776 5625, fax 0141 578 3827, e-mail douglas.boyd2@ntlworld.com)

BOYD, Fionnuala; da of Joseph Douglas Allen Boyd (d 1990), and Doreen, *née* Wilson; *b* 13 April 1944; *Educ* The Grammar Sch Welwyn Garden City, St Albans Art Sch, Univ of Leeds (BA); *m* 1965, Leslie Douglas Evans, *qv*, s of Leslie Edward Evans; 1 s (Jack Luis b 1969), 1 da (Ruby Rose b 1971); *Career* artist; began working with Leslie Evans 1968, Bi-Centennial fellow USA 1977–78; artist in residence: Milton Keynes Devpt Corp 1982–84, Brunei Rainforest Project 1991–92; *Exhibitions* with Leslie Evans: Angela Flowers Gallery 1972, 1974, 1977, 1979, 1980, 1982, 1984, 1986, 1988, 1990, 1992, 1994, 1996, 1998, 2000, 2002 and 2003, Park Square Gallery Leeds 1972, Boyd and Evans 1970–75 (Turnpike Gallery Leigh) 1976, Fendrick Gallery Washington DC 1978, Graves Art Gallery Sheffield 1978, Spectro Arts Workshop Newcastle 1980, Ton Peek Utrecht 1981, A Decade of Paintings (Milton Keynes Exhibition Gallery) 1982–83, Drumcroon Art Centre Wigan 1985, Bird (Flowers East, London) 1990, English Paintings (Brendan Walter Gallery Santa Monica) 1990, Angela Flowers (Ireland) Inc Rosscarberry Ireland 1990, Flowers East London 1991, Brunei Rainforest (Milton Keynes, Brunei, Malaysia & Singapore) 1993, New Rain Forest Paintings (Flowers East) 1994, Portrayal (Flowers East) 1996, Western Photographs (Flowers East) 1999, Natural Wonder (Flowers West Santa Monica) 1999, solo show (Flowers West Santa Monica) 1999 and 2001, solo show (Flowers East London) 2000, Colour in Black & White (Flowers Graphics London and Keller & Greene LA) 2003, Landmarks (Milton Keynes Gallery and Flowers Central London) 2005, Color in Black & White (Flowers NY) 2006, Boyd & Evans (Galerie d'Art Int Solana Beach CA) 2006, Looking Differently (Flowers East London) 2007; *Group Exhibitions* incl: Postcards (Angela Flowers Gallery) 1970, British Drawing 1952–72 (Angela Flowers Gallery) 1972, Imagini Come Strumenta di Realta (Studio la Citta Verona) 1973, New Image Painting (First Tokyo Int Biennale of Figurative Art) 1974, Body and Soul (Peter Moores, Liverpool) 1975, British Realist Show (Ikon Gallery) 1976, Aspects of Realism (Rothmans of Pall Mall, Canada) 1976–78, The Real British (Fischer Fine Art) 1981, Black and White Show (Angela Flowers Gallery) 1985, Sixteen (Angela Flowers Gallery) 1986, State of the Nation (Herbert Gallery, Coventry) 1987, Contemporary Portraits (Flowers East) 1988, The Thatcher Years (Flowers East) 1989, Picturing People: British Figurative Art since 1945 (touring exhibition Far East) 1989–90, Art '90 London (Business Design Centre) 1990, 25th Anniversary Exhibition (Flowers East) 1995, Wheels on Fire (Wolverhampton Stoke-on-Trent) 1996, Sight Lines (Honiton Festival) 1996, Contemporary British Landscape (Flowers East) 1999; work in public collections of: Arts Cncl of GB, Br Cncl, MOMA NY, Metropolitan Museum NY, Sheffield City Art Gallery, Wolverhampton City Art Gallery, Leeds City Art Gallery, Contemporary Art Soc, Leicester Educn Authy, Manchester City Art Gallery, Unilever plc, Tate Gallery, Williamson Art Gallery, Borough of Milton Keynes; *Awards* prizewinner Bradford Print Biennale, first prize 6th Festival Int de la Peinture Cagnes-sur-Mer; *Recreations* books, films, hills, friends, exercise, music; *Style*— Fionnuala Boyd; ✉ Boyd & Evans, Flowers East, 82 Kingsland Road, London E2 8DP (tel 020 7920 7777, e-mail gallery@flowerseast.com, website www.flowerseast.com)

BOYD, Prof Ian Lamont; s of J Morton Boyd (d 1998), and Winifred, *née* Rome; *b* 9 February 1957; *Educ* George Heriot's Sch Edinburgh, Univ of Aberdeen (BSc, DSc), Univ of Cambridge (PhD); *m* 4 Sept 1982, Sheila, *née* Aitken; 1 s (Euan b 6 April 1985), 2 da (Helen b 1 Dec 1986, Lauren b 6 April 1989); *Career* res scientist NERC Inst of Terrestrial Ecology 1982–87, memb Br Antarctic Survey 1987–2001, prof of biology Univ of St Andrews 2001–, dir NERC Sea Mammal Res Unit 2001–, chief exec SMRU Ltd 2006–; ed Jl of Zoology, memb Cncl of Mgmnt Hebridean Tst; Bruce Medal Royal Soc of Edinburgh 1995, Scientific Medal Zoological Soc of London 1998, Marshall Award Zoological Soc of London 2006; hon prof Univ of Birmingham 1997; FRSE 2002; *Publications* author or ed of 8 books and over 130 scientific pubns; *Recreations* walking, sailing; *Style*— Prof Ian Boyd; ✉ Sea Mammal Research Unit, Gatty Marine Laboratory, St Andrews, Fife KY16 8LB (tel 01334 462630, fax 01334 462632, e-mail ilb@st-andrews.ac.uk)

BOYD, Ian Mair; s of John Telfer Boyd (d 1976), and Margaret Mair, *née* Murdoch (d 2001); *b* 4 September 1944; *Educ* Ayr Acad, London Business Sch (MSc); *m* 20 Dec 1975, Theodora (Toody), da of Theodor Georgopoulos, of Athens; 2 s (Telfer, Fraser), 1 da (Amber); *Career* CA 1966, gp fin dir The Weir Group plc 1981–2004; chm Braid Gp (Hldgs) Ltd 2007–; dir: Glasgow Income Trust plc 1990–, Inveresk plc 1993–2001; memb Cncl ICAS 1987–93, chm Gp of Scot Fin Dirs 1990–92; *Recreations* golf, hill walking, skiing, bird watching, fishing; *Clubs* Prestwick Golf; *Style*— Ian M Boyd, Esq; ✉ 34 Newark Drive, Glasgow G41 4PZ (tel 0141 423 7850)

BOYD, James Edward (Teddy); s of Robert Edward Boyd, and Elizabeth Reid Sinclair; *b* 14 September 1928; *Educ* Kelvinside Acad, The Leys Sch Cambridge; *m* Judy Ann Christey Scott; 2 s, 2 da (1 decd); *Career* CA Scot (dist) 1951; ptnr McClelland Ker & Co 1953–61; fin dir: Lithgows Ltd 1962–69, Scott Lithgow Ltd 1970–78; dir and fin advsr Denholm Gp of Cos 1968–96; dir: Lithgows (Hldgs) Ltd 1962–87, Ayrshire Metal Products plc 1965–94 (dep chm 1989–91, chm 1991–94), Invergordon Distillers (Hldgs) plc 1966–88 (md 1966–67), Nairn & Williamson (Hldgs) Ltd 1968–75, GB Papers plc 1977–87, Carlton Industries plc 1978–84, James River UK Hldgs Ltd 1987–90, Jebsens Drilling plc 1978–85, Save & Prosper Gp Ltd 1987–89; Scottish Widows' Fund & Life Assurance Soc 1981–94 (dep chm 1988–93), Br Linen Bank Ltd 1983–94 (govr 1986–94), Shanks & McEwan Gp plc 1983–94, Scottish Exhibition Centre 1983–89, Civil Aviation Authy 1984–85, Bank of Scotland 1984–94, Bank of Wales 1986–88, dep chm BAA plc (formerly British Airports Authy) 1985–94; chm: Fairfield Shipbuilding & Engrg Co Ltd 1964–65, Gartmore European Investment Tst plc 1978–91, English & Caledonian Investment plc 1981–91, Yarrow plc 1984–86; memb: Clyde Port Authy 1974–80, Cncl Inst of Chartered Accountants of Scotland 1977–83 (vice-pres 1980–82, pres 1982–83), Exec Ctee Accountants Jt Disciplinary Scheme 1979–81; memb Cncl Glenalmond Coll 1983–92; *Recreations* tennis, golf, gardening, painting; *Style*— J E Boyd, Esq; ✉ Dunard, Station Road, Rhu, Dunbartonshire G84 8LW (tel 01436 820441, e-mail judy.teddy.boyd@amserve.net); The Denholm Group, 18 Woodside Crescent, Glasgow (tel 0141 353 2090)

BOYD, Prof (Thomas) James Morrow; s of Thomas James Boyd (d 1979), and Isobel Cameron, *née* Morrow (d 1998); *b* 21 June 1932; *Educ* Larne GS, Queen's Univ Belfast (BSc, PhD); *m* 5 Sept 1959, Marguerite Bridget, da of William Snelson (d 1980), of Drayton Manor, Stafford; 2 da (Rebecca b 1964, Marguerite b 1968); *Career* res fell Univ of Birmingham 1957–59, asst res prof Univ of Maryland 1959–61, Ford fndn fell Princeton Univ 1962, sr res assoc UKAEA Culham Lab 1962–65, sr lectr Univ of St Andrews 1965–68; Univ of Wales Bangor: prof of applied mathematics and computation 1968–82, prof of theoretical physics 1982–90, dean Faculty of Science 1981–85; prof of physics Univ of Essex 1990–99 (visiting res prof of physics 1999–); visiting prof of physics Univ of Br Columbia 1975, Fulbright sr fell and visiting prof of physics Dartmouth Coll 1987–88, visiting prof Instituto Nacional de Investigaciones Nucleares Mexico 2002–; memb UK-Austrian Mixed Cmmn 1977–87; memb NY Acad of Sciences 1987; CPhys, FInstP 1974 (chm Plasma Physics Gp 1975–77); *Books* Plasma Dynamics (with J J Sanderson, 1969, Chinese edn 1977), Electricity (with C A Coulson, 1979), The Physics of Plasmas (with J J Sanderson, 2002, Chinese edn 2005); *Recreations* skiing, climbing, travel, choral music; *Style*— Prof James Boyd; ✉ 6 Frog Meadow, Brook Street, Dedham, Colchester CO7 6AD (tel 01206 323170); Mullion Cottage, Meirion Lane, Bangor, Gwynedd LL57 2BU (tel 01248 364108); Centre for Physics, University of Essex, Wivenhoe Park, Colchester, Essex CO4 3SQ (tel 01206 872873, fax 01206 873598, e-mail tjmb@essex.ac.uk)

BOYD, (David) John; QC (1982); s of David Boyd (d 1964), and Ellen Jane, *née* Gruer (d 1953); *b* 11 February 1935; *Educ* Eastbourne Coll, St George's Sch Newport RI, Gonville & Caius Coll Cambridge (MA); *m* 1960, Raija Sinikka, da of Onni Lindholm (d 1952), of Finland, 1 da (Karin b 1969), 1 s (Roderick b 1972); *Career* called to the Bar Gray's Inn 1963 (bencher 1988); sec asst ICI 1957–62, legal asst Pfizer 1962–66, legal offr Henry Wiggin and Co 1966–68; joined Inco Europe Ltd 1968, sec and chief legal offr Inco Europe Ltd 1972–86 (dir 1984–86); in private practice at Bar 1986; Digital Equipment Co: dir of legal servs 1986–93, dir of public affrs and communications 1993–95; dir Digital Equipment Scotland Ltd 1987–95, chm AXXIA Systems Ltd 1995–; immigration adjudicator 1995–2005, immigration judge 2005–; chm Competition Panel CBI 1988–93, dir Impala Platinum 1972–78, gen cmmr of Income Tax 1978–81, memb Senate of Inns of Court and Bar 1978–81, chm Bar Assoc for Commerce Finance and Industry 1980–81, sec-gen Assoc des Juristes d'Enterprise Européens 1983–84, legal advsr Review Bd for Govt Contracts 1984–91, memb Monopolies and Mergers Cmmn Electricity Panel 1991–98, dir Centre for Euro Dispute Resolution 1991–94; vice-pres Cncl of Immigration Judges 1998–99; memb: Cncl Centre for Commercial Law Studies Queen Mary & Westfield Coll London 1989–93, Exec Ctee Royal Acad of Dance 1991–99; chm Contemporary Dance Tst and The Place theatre London 1995–98, dir Oxford Orchestra da Camera 1996–2001; treas Upton Bishop PCC 2004–; fndn govr Gorsley Goffs Sch 2006–; FCIArb; *Recreations* viticulture, France; *Clubs* Leander; *Style*— John Boyd, Esq, QC; ✉ Beeches, Upton Bishop, Ross-on-Wye, Herefordshire HR9 7UD (tel 01989 780214, fax 01989 780538)

BOYD, Sir John Dixon Iklé; KCMG (1992, CMG 1985); s of Prof James Dixon Boyd (d 1968), of Cambridge, and Amélie, *née* Lowenthal (d 1998); *b* 17 January 1936; *Educ* Westminster, Clare Coll Cambridge (BA), Yale Univ (MA); *m* 1, 28 Jan 1968 (m dis 1977), Gunilla Kristina Ingegerd, da of Gösta Rönngren, of Västerås, Sweden; 1 s (Jonathan b 1969), 1 da (Emily b 1971); m 2, 11 Nov 1977, Julia Daphne, da of Capt Antony Edward Montague Raynsford, DL, RN (d 1993), of Milton Malsor Manor, Northampton; 3 da (Jessica b 1978, Alice b 1979, Olivia b 1981); *Career* HM Dip Serv: Hong Kong 1962–64, Peking 1965–67, FCO 1967–69, Washington 1969–73, Peking 1973–75, HM Treasy (on loan) 1976, Bonn 1977–81, UK Mission to UN 1981–84, political advsr Hong Kong 1985–87, dep under-sec of state FCO 1987–89, chief clerk 1989–92, ambass to Japan 1992–96; master Churchill Coll Cambridge 1996–2006 (fell 2006–), advsr East Asia Inst Univ of Cambridge 1998–; emeritus fell Br Assoc for Japanese Studies 2007–; non-exec dir BNFL 1997–2000, memb ASEM Vision Group 1998–2000; vice-chm Menuhin Prize 1996–, chm David Davies Memorial Inst 1997–2000, co-chm Nuffield Languages Inquiry 1998–2000, memb ANA Advsy Panel 2003–; govr RSC 1996–2006, chm of govrs Bedales Sch 1996–2001; chm of tstees Cambridge Union Soc 1997–2006; tstee: Br Museum 1996–2006 (chm 2002–06, tstee emeritus 2007–), Wordsworth Tst 1997–, RAND (Europe) UK 2001–, GB Sasakawa Fndn 2001–, Dr Busby's Tst 2004–, Joseph Needham Research Inst 2005–; hon fell Clare Coll Cambridge 1994; Grand Cordon Order of the Rising Sun (Japan) 2007; *Recreations* music, fly fishing; *Clubs* Hawks' (Cambridge), Hong Kong, Athenaeum, Beefsteak; *Style*— Sir John Boyd, KCMG; ✉ Churchill College, Cambridge CB3 0DS

BOYD, Michael Neil Murray; s of late Lt Cdr Neil Kenneth Boyd, DSC*, of New Milton, Hants, and Felicity Victoria, *née* Weston; *b* 17 August 1946; *Educ* Bryanston; *m* 30 May 1970, Belinda Rachel Elizabeth, da of Capt Basil Harry Lawrence (d 1973); 1 da (Zara b 18 Sept 1975), 1 s (Ashleigh b 21 June 1980); *Career* Ernst & Young (formerly Ernst & Whinney): ptnr London 1975, NY 1979–82, ptnr i/c London Audit Dept 1984–86, memb Exec and Firm's Cncl 1986–89 and 1992–2000, fin ptnr 1987–89, chm Int Extractive Industries Ctee 1988–92, chm Ernst & Young Eastern Europe 1988–90, nat audit ptnr 1989–92, managing ptnr London Office 1992–95, vice-chm (global accounts) Ernst & Young Global 1999–2003, global managing ptnr (quality and risk mgmnt) 2003–05, chm and area managing ptnr Ernst & Young Far East 2005–07, managing ptnr strategic accounts and sectors London 2005–; vice-chm Auditing Practices Bd 1991–94; memb: Cncl Corp of Cranleigh Sch and St Catherine's Bramley 1975–99, Oil Industry Accounting Ctee 1988–94, Cncl E Euro Trade Cncl 1989–92; govr Cranleigh Sch 1975–79 and 1985–99; MInstPet 1983, FCA 1975 (memb 1969); *Recreations* tennis, skiing, sailing, opera; *Clubs* City of London, Salcombe Yacht, China, Hong Kong, Hong Kong Jockey; *Style*— Michael Boyd, Esq; ✉ Ernst & Young LLP, 1 More London Place, London SE1 2AF (tel 020 7951 0738, e-mail michael.boyd@uk.ey.com)

BOYD, Prof Sir Robert David Hugh; kt (2004); s of Prof James Dixon Boyd (d 1968), of Cambridge, and Dr Amélie Boyd (d 1998); *b* 14 May 1938; *Educ* Univ of Cambridge, UCH London; *m* 1 April 1966, Meriel Cornelia, da of T G Talbot, CB, QC, of Edenbridge, Kent; 1 s (Thomas b 1967), 2 da (Diana b 1969, Lucy b 1974); *Career* med posts: UCH, Brompton Hosp, Gt Ormond St Hosp; res fell and sr lectr UCH 1967–80; Faculty of Med Univ of Manchester: prof of child health and paediatrics 1981–96, dean 1989–93; princ St George's Hosp Med Sch London 1996–2003; pro-vice chllr Univ of London 2000–03; chair: Manchester HA 1994–96, Nat Centre for Research and Development in Primary Care 1994–96, Cncl of Heads of UK Med Schs 2001–03, Lloyds TSB Fndn England and Wales 2003–, Campaign for Assisting Refugee Academic 2004–; Hon DSc: Kingston Univ, Keele Univ; FRCP, FRCPCH, FMedSci, FFPH; *Publications* Placental Transfer-Methods and Interpretations (co-ed, 1981), Perinatal Medicine (co-ed, 1983), Paediatric Problems in General Practice (jtly, 1989, 3 edn 1997), Placenta (ed, 1989–95); numerous pubns on healthcare systems, child health, gen practice, and foetal and placental physiology; *Style*— Prof Sir Robert Boyd; ✉ Stone House, Adlington, Cheshire SK10 4NU (tel and fax 01625 872400); Lloyds TSB Foundation for England and Wales, PO Box 46156, 3rd Floor, 4 St Dunstan's Hill, London EC3R 8WQ (e-mail rboyd@doctors.org.uk)

BOYD, Robert Nathaniel; CBE (1971); s of Peter Ferguson Boyd (d 2007), and Annie Jane, *née* Newton; *b* 17 November 1918; *Educ* Boys' GS Suva Fiji, Churcher's Coll Petersfield; *m* 1947, Carrie, da of Harry Squires; 2 s; *Career* Lt-Col (ret) Br Somaliland 1940, Abyssinia, Madagascar and Burma, 30 years Territorial and Res Service; served Central Africa Civil Serv 1947–68; auditor gen Zambia 1966–68, sec and fin controller Air Tport and Travel Indust Trg Bd 1969–77; practising arbitrator (1983–97) and co dir; chm Dist Fin Ctee Wokingham Dist Cncl 1974–77 (memb Cncl 1972–77); vice-pres United Soc for Propagation of Gospel 1992– (vice-chm 1982–90, treas 1982–96, govr 1996–99, memb Cncl 1999–2006); FCIS, FCIArb, FCMI; Efficiency Decoration Zambia 1968, Order of the Epiphany Anglican Church in Central Africa 1968; *Books* A Colonial Odyssey (1996); *Recreations* bowls; *Clubs* Hurst Bowling, Royal Cwlth Soc; *Style*— Robert Boyd, Esq, CBE; ✉ 8 Pegasus Court, North Street, Heavitree, Exeter EX1 2RP (tel 01392 479418)

BOYD, Robert Patrick; s of William Henry Boyd, of Farnham, Surrey (d 1978), and Dorothy, *née* Cole (d 1989); *b* 21 December 1946, Finedon; *Educ* Stonyhurst Coll, Univ of Birmingham (LLB), Coll of Law London; *m* 15 Sept 1984, Marilyn Elizabeth, *née* Thomas; 2 s (James b 11 May 1986, Alexander b 19 Aug 1988), 1 da (Eleanor b 18 May 1990); *Career* admitted slr 1972; slr specialising in law relating to ind schs; princ Robert Boyd and Co 1976–88, ptnr Veale Wasbrough 1988–; memb: Law Soc, Bristol Law Soc, Bristol Medico-Legal Soc; charity pianist for St Peter's Hospice and Bristol Savages; jt winner Nat Mooting Competition 1971; *Publications* Independent Schools: Law, Custom and Practice (1998), Running a School Boarding House (2000), Bursars' Handbook (contrib, 2000); author of various articles; *Recreations* piano (and musical saw), carpentry, sailing, writing, family; *Clubs* East India, Bristol Savages; *Style*— Robert Boyd, Esq; ✉ Veale Wasbrough, Orchard Court, Orchard Lane, Bristol BS1 5WS (tel 0117 314 5334, fax 0117 925 2025, e-mail rboyd@vwl.co.uk)

BOYD, Stewart Craufurd; CBE (2005), QC (1981); s of late Leslie Balfour Boyd, OBE, and Wendy, *née* Blake; *b* 25 October 1943; *Educ* Winchester, Trinity Coll Cambridge (MA); *m* 1970, Catherine (Hon Mrs Boyd), da of late Baron Jay, PC (Life Peer); 1 s (Matthew b 1975), 3 da (Rachel b 1972, Emily b 1973, Hannah b 1987); *Career* called to the Bar Middle Temple 1967 (bencher 1990); non-exec dep chm and dir FSA 1999–; *Books* Scrutton on Charterparties and Bills of Lading (jt ed), Commercial Arbitration (jtly with The Rt Hon Lord Mustill); *Recreations* sailing, gardening, music; *Style*— Stewart Boyd, Esq, CBE, QC; ✉ 1 Gayton Crescent, London NW3 1TT (tel 020 7431 1581); Wraxall Manor, Higher Wraxall, Dorchester, Dorset DT2 0HP (tel 01935 83283); Essex Court Chambers, 24 Lincoln's Inn Fields, London WC2A 3ED (tel 020 7813 8000, fax 020 7813 8080)

BOYD, William Andrew Murray; CBE (2005); s of Alexander Murray Boyd (d 1979), and Evelyn, *née* Smith; *b* 7 March 1952; *Educ* Gordonstoun, Univ of Nice (Dip), Univ of Glasgow (MA), Jesus Coll Oxford; *m* Susan Anne, da of David Leslie Wilson (d 2003), of Maxwell Park, Glasgow; *Career* lectr in English literature St Hilda's Coll Oxford 1980–83, TV critic New Statesman 1981–83; author; Hon DLitt: Univ of St Andrews 1997, Univ of Stirling 1997, Univ of Glasgow 2000; FRSL 1982; Officier de l'Ordre des Arts et des Lettres (France) 2005; *Films* Good and Bad at Games (1983), Dutch Girls (1985), Scoop (adaptation from Evelyn Waugh novel, 1986), Stars and Bars (1988), Aunt Julia and the Scriptwriter (adaptation from Mario Vargas Llosa novel, 1990), Mister Johnson (adaptation from Joyce Cary novel, 1990), Chaplin (1992), A Good Man in Africa (1994), The Trench (dir,1999), Sword of Honour (adaptation from the novels of Evelyn Waugh, 2001), Armadillo (2001), Man to Man (2005), A Waste of Shame (2005); *Novels* A Good Man in Africa (1981, Somerset Maugham Award, Whitbread Prize first novel 1981), On the Yankee Station (1981), An Ice-Cream War (1982, John Llewelyn Rhys Prize 1982), Stars and Bars (1984), School Ties (1985), The New Confessions (1987), Brazzaville Beach (1990, James Tait Black Meml Prize 1991, McVitie's Prize 1991, Scottish Writer of the Year 1991), The Blue Afternoon (1993, Sunday Express Book of the Year 1993, Los Angeles Times Award for Fiction 1995), The Destiny of Nathalie 'X' (1995), Armadillo (1998), Nat Tate: an American Artist (1998), Any Human Heart (2002, Prix Jean Monnet 2003), Fascination (2004), Bamboo (2005), Restless (2006, Costa Novel of the Year); *Clubs* Chelsea Arts, Two Brydges Place, Groucho; *Style*— William Boyd, Esq, CBE, FRSL; ✉ c/o The Agency, 24 Pottery Lane, Holland Park, London W11 4LZ

BOYD-CARPENTER, Sir (Marsom) Henry; KCVO (2002, CVO 1994); s of Francis Henry Boyd-Carpenter (d 1984), of East Lambrook Manor, Somerset, and Nina, *née* Townshend (d 1982); *b* 11 October 1939; *Educ* Charterhouse, Balliol Coll Oxford (MA); *m* 18 Sept 1971, Lesley Ann, da of William Henry Davies (d 1986), of Billericay, Essex; 1 s (William Henry Francis b 28 July 1975), 1 da (Alexandra Mary b 28 June 1979); *Career* admitted slr 1966; ptnr Farrer & Co 1968–2002 (sr ptnr 2000–02), slr Duchy of Cornwall 1976–94, private slr to HM The Queen 1995–2002; govr St Mary's Sch Gerrards Cross 1967–70, hon auditor Law Soc 1979–81, hon steward Westminster Abbey 1980–, memb Governing Body Charterhouse Sch 1981–2004 (chm 2000–04), memb Cncl Chelsea Physic Garden 1983–2002, memb Bd of Govrs Sutton's Hosp 1994–2004, hon legal advsr Canterbury Cathedral Appeal Fund 1994–2001, memb Cncl Prince of Wales Inst of Architecture 1995–99, memb Bd Br Library 1999–2007 (dep chm 2003–2007), memb Cncl Inst of Cancer Research 2001–06; tstee: Nat Gardens Scheme 1998–2003, The Merlin Tst 1998–2004; memb RHS Governance Working Pty 2000–01; pres Wood Green Animal Shelters 2001–; memb Law Soc 1966; *Recreations* reading, listening to music, hill walking, gardening; *Style*— Sir Henry Boyd-Carpenter, KCVO; ✉ Llanvapley Court, Llanvapley, Abergavenny, Monmouthshire NP7 8SG (tel 01600 780250)

BOYD-CARPENTER, (Lt-Gen the Hon) Sir Thomas Patrick John; KBE (Mil 1993, MBE (Mil) 1973); s of Baron Boyd-Carpenter, PC, DL (Life Peer, d 1998); *b* 1938; *Educ* Stowe; *m* 1972, Mary-Jean, da of John Elwes Duffield; 3 c; *Career* Scots Gds, Col GSAT3 MOD 1981, Cmd 24 Inf Bde 1983–84, D DEF Pol MOD 1985–87, COS HQ BAOR 1988–89, ACDS (Prog) MOD 1989–92, DCDS (P & P) MOD 1992–96; chm: Social Security Advsy Ctee 1995–2004, Kensington, Chelsea and Westminster HA 1996–2001, Moorfields Eye Hosp 2001–08, Lord Chancellor's Advsy Bd on Family Law 1997–2002; dir People in Business 1996–; *Style*— Sir Thomas Boyd-Carpenter, KBE

BOYD OF DUNCANSBY, Baron (Life Peer 2006), of Duncansby in Caithness Colin David Boyd; PC (2000), QC (Scot 1995); s of Dr David Hugh Aird Boyd, of Edinburgh, and Betty Meldrum, *née* Mutch; *b* 7 June 1953; *Educ* Wick HS Caithness, George Watson's Coll Edinburgh, Univ of Manchester (BA), Univ of Edinburgh (LLB); *m* 1979, Fiona Margaret, da of Archibald MacLeod; 1 da, 2 s; *Career* slr 1978–82 and 2007–, admitted Faculty of Advocates 1983, advocate depute 1993–95, slr-gen for Scotland 1997–2000, Lord Advocate of Scotland 2000–06, conslt and head of public law Dundas & Wilson LLP 2007–; legal assoc RTPI 1991; memb House of Lords Select Ctee on Delegated Powers and Regulatory Reform; FRSA 2000, memb Law Soc of Scotland 2007; *Books* The Legal Aspects of Devolution (contrib, 1997); *Recreations* reading, hill walking, watching rugby; *Style*— The Rt Hon the Lord Boyd of Duncansby, PC, QC; ✉ House of Lords, London SW1A 0PW (tel 020 7219 6987)

BOYD OF MERTON, 2 Viscount (UK 1960); Simon Donald Rupert Neville Lennox-Boyd; s of 1 Viscount Boyd of Merton, CH, PC, DL (d 1983), and Patricia, Viscountess Boyd of Merton (d 2001); *b* 7 December 1939; *Educ* Eton, ChCh Oxford (MA); *m* 1962, Alice Mary, JP (High Sheriff of Cornwall 1987), DL (Cornwall 1995), da of Maj Meysey George Dallas Clive (ka 1943); 2 da (Hon Charlotte b 1963, Hon Philippa b 1970), 2 s (Hon Benjamin b 21 Oct 1964, Hon Edward b 30 March 1968); *Heir* s, Hon Benjamin Lennox-Boyd; *Career* dep chm Arthur Guinness & Sons 1981–86, chm The Iveagh Tstees Ltd 1993–2003 (dir 1967–2003); chm: Save the Children Fund 1987–92, Stonham Housing Assoc 1992–98; vice-chm Guinness Tst 1993–2004 (tstee 1974–2004); Liveryman Worshipful Co of Goldsmiths; *Recreations* planting trees; *Style*— The Rt Hon the Viscount Boyd of Merton; ✉ Ince Castle, Saltash, Cornwall (tel 01752 842672, fax 01752 847134, e-mail boydince@aol.com)

BOYES, Roger F; *Career* fin dir Linpac Containers International Ltd until 1986, gp fin dir Fenner plc 1986–90; Leeds Permanent Building Society: fin dir 1990–93, actg chief exec 1993–94, chief exec 1994–95; gp fin dir Halifax plc 1995–2001; Heywood Williams Gp plc: non-exec dir 2002–03, exec chm 2003–04, non-exec chm 2004–; non-exec dir: Expro International Gp plc 2002–, British Vita plc; chm British Vita Pension Trust Ltd; CIMgt; FCMA, MInstD; *Style*— Roger Boyes, Esq

BOYLAN, Brian; *Educ* Glasgow Sch of Art; *Career* Wolff Olins: joined as designer 1970, dep chm until 1997, chm (following MBO) 1997–; former/current clients incl: ICI, National Power, Citibank, Coopers and Lybrand, General Motors, Halifax, NatWest, Vauxhall, Credit Suisse Group, Heathrow Express, Inland Revenue, Allied Irish Bank; int speaker on corp identity; FRSA; *Style*— Brian Boylan, Esq; ✉ Wolff Olins, 10 Regents Wharf, All Saints Street, London N1 9RL (tel 020 7713 7733, fax 020 7713 0217)

BOYLE, Alan Gordon; QC (1991); s of Dr M M Boyle, and Mrs H I Boyle, *née* Hallworth, of Keswick, Cumbria; *b* 31 March 1949; *Educ* Shrewsbury, St Catherine's Coll Oxford (open exhbn, MA), Inns of Court Sch of Law; *m* 1981, Claudine-Aimée, *née* Minne-Vercruysse; 2 da (Julia b 17 July 1981, Zoe b 26 May 1984); *Career* called to the Bar Lincoln's Inn 1972 (Hardwicke scholar); memb: Chancery Bar Assoc, Assoc of Trusts and Probate Specialists, Insolvency Lawyers' Assoc; *Publications* The Practice and Procedure of the Companies Court (1997); *Recreations* music, hill walking, photography; *Style*— Alan Boyle, Esq, QC; ✉ Serle Court, 6 New Square, Lincoln's Inn, London WC2A 3QS (tel 020 7242 6105, fax 020 7405 4004, e-mail aboyle@serlecourt.co.uk)

BOYLE, Gerard Paul; s of Edward Boyle, of Glasgow; *b* 29 June 1971; *Educ* Univ of Strathclyde (BA); *m* 21 Oct 2001, Caroline; *Career* media manager Leo Burnett Advtg 1994–97, strategist Michaelides & Bednash 1997–99; ZenithOptimedia: managing ptnr Zenith Media 1999, md 2003–07, UK chief exec 2007–; *Recreations* golf, cooking, wine appreciation, travel; *Style*— Gerard Boyle, Esq; ✉ ZenithOptimedia, 24 Percy Street, London W1T 2BS (e-mail gerry.boyle@zenithmedia.co.uk)

BOYLE, Capt Michael Patrick Radcliffe; DL (Hants 1982); s of Patrick Spencer Boyle (s of late Capt Hon E Spencer H Boyle, RN, 5 s of 5 Earl of Shannon, by his 2 w, Julia, da of Sir William Hartopp, 3 Bt), and Vera Maud *née* Radcliffe, da of late Daniel Radcliffe, Esq, JP, LLD, of Pen-Y-Lan, Cardiff; *b* 25 January 1934; *Educ* Eton; *m* 1, 1962 (m dis 1995), Lady Nell Carleton Harris, da of 6 Earl of Malmesbury, TD, DL, and Hon Diana Carleton, da of 2 Baron Dorchester; 2 s, 1 da; m 2, 1 June 1995, Mrs Alexandra Mary Hilda Seymour, da of Maj Sir Victor Basil John Seely, 4 Bt (d 1980); *Career* cmmnd Irish Gds 1953, Capt 1961, ret 1966; High Sheriff Hants 1976–77; Hants CC: memb 1970–2001, chm 1997–99, Alderman 2001–; memb Hants Police Authy 1970–2001 (chm 1976–88); cmmr St John Ambulance Bde Hants 1969–75; Freeman City of London, Liveryman Worshipful Co of Gunmakers; CStJ; *Recreations* shooting, sailing; *Clubs* Boodle's, Royal Yacht Sqdn; *Style*— Capt M P R Boyle, DL; ✉ Saint Cross House, Whitchurch, Hampshire RG28 7AS (tel 01256 895505)

BOYLE, Prof Nicholas; s of Hugh Boyle (d 1955), and Margaret Mary Faith, *née* Hopkins (latterly Mrs Boothroyd, d 2003); *b* 18 June 1946, London; *Educ* King's Sch Worcester, Magdalene Coll Cambridge (open scholar, MA), Univ of Cambridge (PhD, LittD); *m* 1983, Rosemary Angela, *née* Devlin; 3 da (Mary Rose b 1986, Elisabeth Doran b 1992, Angela Margaret b 1996), 1 s (Michael Hugh b 1989); *Career* Magdalene Coll Cambridge: research fell 1968–72, official fell 1972–2000, coll lectr in German (also Girton Coll) 1972–74, dir of studies in modern languages 1972–90, dean 1979–82, tutor 1984–93, garden steward 1987–, professorial fell 2000–, pres 2006–; Univ of Cambridge: lectr 1979–93 (asst lectr 1974–79), reader in German literary and intellectual history 1993–2000, prof of German literary and intellectual history 2000–, memb Faculty Bd Modern and Medieval Languages 1982–90 and 1996–2001 (sec 1982–85), head Dept of German 1996–2001; scholar Alexander von Humboldt Fndn Göttingen Univ 1978 and 1980–81, Br Acad research reader in the humanities 1990–92, research fell John Rylands Research Inst Univ of Manchester 1993, fell Wissenschaftskolleg zu Berlin 1994–95, third Erasmus lectr Univ of Notre Dame 2002–03; memb Cncl English Goethe Soc 1993–; pres Cambridge Modern Language Soc 1987–90, chm Cambridge Cyrenians 1970–71; Goethe Medal Goethe-Institut 2000; FBA 2001; *Books* Realism in European Literature: Essays in honour of J P Stern (jt ed, 1986), Goethe: Faust, Part One (1987), Goethe: The Poet and the Age, Vol One The Poetry of Desire (1749–1790) (1991, W Heinemann Prize RSL, J G Robertson Meml Prize Univ of London), Goethes Werke auf CD-ROM (editorial conslt, 1995), Who Are We Now? Christian Humanism and the Global Market from Hegel to Heaney (1998), J W von Goethe: Selected Works (ed, 1999), Goethe: The Poet and the Age, Vol Two Revolution and Renunciation (1790–1803) (2000, Annibel Jenkins Prize American Soc of Eighteenth Century Studies), Goethe and the English-Speaking World (jt ed, 2002), Sacred and Secular Scriptures: A Catholic Approach to Literature (2004); author of numerous articles in learned jls; *Recreations* visiting gardens; *Style*— Prof Nicholas Boyle, FBA; ✉ 20 Alpha Road, Cambridge CB4 3DG (tel 01223 364310, e-mail nicholas.boyle@ntlworld.com); Magdalene College, Cambridge CB3 0AG (tel 01223 332137, e-mail nb215@cam.ac.uk)

BOYLE, Prof Roger Michael; CBE (2004); Dr Michael Boyle (d 2001), and Hazel, *née* Hallworth; *b* 27 January 1948; *Educ* Shrewsbury, London Hosp Med Coll (MB BS); *m* Margo, da of F Gardner Cox, of Philadelphia, USA; 3 s (Peter b 1 Nov 1977, Thomas b 2 April 1979, Edward b 20 Oct 1981), 1 da (Amy b 13 October 2002); *Career* The London Hosp: house physician Cardiac and Haematology Depts 1972–73, house surgn Dept of Surgery 1973, SHO Dept of Med 1973–75, SHO in cardiology 1975; Chelmsford and Essex Hosp: registrar in gen med and neurology 1975–77, research registrar 1977–78; research registrar (Br Heart Fndn) Regional Cardiac Centre Wythenshawe Hosp Manchester 1978–80, lectr in cardiology Dept of Cardiovascular Studies Univ of Leeds and hon sr registrar in cardiology Leeds Gen Infirmary, Univ Hosp of St James and Killingbeck Hosp Leeds 1980–83, conslt cardiologist York District Hosp; York Health Servs NHS Tst: chm Med Servs Div of Med York Dist Hosp 1988–96, pt/t gen mangr Med Servs York Health Servs Tsts 1996–98, memb Exec Bd 1996–99, memb Med Advsy Gp 1991–98, memb Computer Systems Programme Bd 1994–98, memb Tst Strategy Gp 1995–99, currently conslt cardiologist and physician; nat dir for heart disease and stroke Dept of Health 2000–; hon conslt cardiologist St Mary's Hosp NHS Tst London 2003–, hon chair UCL 2006–; conslt med advsr General Accident Life Assurance 1985–96, chief med offr Leeds Life 1994–96; advsr: W Cumbria HA 1992–93, W Surrey HA 1996, S Essex HA 1997, Havering Hosps Tst 1999; memb Med Advsy Ctee Purey Cust Nuffield Hosp York 1995–2000, memb Advsy Panel: Pfizer UK 1994–2000, BUPA 1995, Schering Plough 1996–97, Roche Products Ltd 1997–98; visiting prof Dept of Cardiology Cornell Med Center NY 1987; external examiner Univ of Newcastle upon Tyne 1996; Dept of Health: advsr Nat Casemix Office 1993–96, chm Nat Coronary Heart Disease Task Force 2000–, memb Expert Design Panel Primary Care Collaborative 2000–, memb NHS Top Team, memb Cross Taskforce Prevention Gp, memb Clinical Priorities Gp, memb Cardiovascular Research Funders Gp, memb Coronary Heart Disease Collaborative Core Gp, memb Coronary Heart Disease Beacons Selection Panel; memb Editorial Bd and regular reviewer of papers Br Heart Jl (now Heart) 1991–, reviewer European Heart Jl 1994–; RCP: co-opted memb Specialty Advsy Ctee in Cardiology Calman Report 1993, memb Jt Cardiology Ctee RCP/Br Cardiac Soc 1993–, sec Specialty Advsy Ctee 1994–97 (chm 1997–2000), memb Jt Ctee on Higher Med Trg 1994–2000; Br Cardiac Soc: memb 1984–, memb Cncl 1991–96 (ex officio memb 1998–), memb Sub-Ctee on Radiation Hazards Protection for Cardiologists 1992, sec Sub-Ctee on Cardiology in Dist Gen Hosps 1992–94, memb Advsy Ctee to Tomlinson Report 1993, memb Abstract Selection Panel AGM 1994–2000, memb Trg and Manpower Ctee 1995– (chm 1997–98), rep to Specialty Workforce Advsy Gp NHSE 1995–; advsr on trg issues Irish Cardiology Bd 1998–2000; author of numerous presentations to learned socs and of articles in jls incl Br Heart Jl, BMJ, Jl of the RCP, European Heart Jl and Int Jl of Cardiology; memb: Yorks Thoracic Soc 1982–, York Med Soc 1983– (sec 1983–90), Med Research Soc, RSM; FRCP 1991 (MRCP 1976), FESC 1994, FRCPEd 2002; *Recreations* piano, walking, sailing; *Clubs* Corinthian Yacht (Philadelphia), Percuil Sailing (Portscatho), Mantoloking Yacht (New Jersey); *Style*— Prof Roger Boyle, CBE; ✉ Department of Health, Wellington House, 133–155 Waterloo Road, London SE1 8UG (tel 020 7972 4821, fax 020 7972 4063, e-mail roger.boyle@doh.gsi.gov.uk)

BOYLE, Simon; JP (2002); s of Lt-Col P J S Boyle (ka 1944), and Mrs Charles Floyd, *née* Fuller (d 1996); *b* 22 March 1941; *Educ* Eton; *m* 10 Oct 1970, Catriona, da of Maj W G Gordon, DFC; 4 da (Alice b 1972, Mary b 1974, Susannah b 1977, Christian b 1982); *Career* Stewarts and Lloyds Ltd 1959–65, Avon Rubber Co Ltd 1966–70, British Steel 1970–2001, ret; chm Monmouth Diocesan Parsonage Bd, vice-chm Monmouth Diocesan Bd of Fin, tstee St David's Fndn Hospice Care; HM Lord-Lt Gwent (DL 1997); CStJ 2002; *Recreations* gardening, sailing; *Style*— Simon Boyle, Esq; ✉ Penpergwm Lodge, Abergavenny, Gwent NP7 9AS (tel and fax 01873 840208, e-mail boyle@penpergwm.co.uk)

BOYLE, Sir Stephen Gurney; 5 Bt (UK 1904), of Ockham, Salehurst, Sussex; er s of Sir Richard Gurney Boyle, 4 Bt (d 1983, s of Sir Edward Boyle, 2 Bt; suc to Btcy only of bro, Baron Boyle of Handsworth 1981), and Elizabeth Anne, yr da of Norman Dennes; *b* 15 January 1962; *Heir* bro, Michael Boyle; *Style*— Sir Stephen Boyle, Bt

BOYLSTON, Prof Arthur William; s of George Arthur Boylston, and Marie, *née* Showers; *b* 16 November 1942; *Educ* Phillips Exeter Acad, Yale Univ (BA), Harvard Univ (MD); *m* 1 July 1978, Anthea, da of John Murray Phelps; 2 s (Thomas Arthur b 1980, Nicholas John b 1984); *Career* sr asst surgn US Public Health Serv 1970–72, lectr, sr lectr then reader St Mary's Hosp Med Sch London 1972–88, prof of pathology Univ of Leeds 1988–; FRCPath 1988; *Recreations* gardening, walking; *Clubs* Athenaeum; *Style*— Prof Arthur Boylston; ✉ Molecular Medicine Unit, Clinical Sciences Building, St James's Hospital, Leeds LS9 7TH (tel 0113 206 5681, fax 0113 244 4475)

BOYNE, 11 Viscount (I 1717); Gustavus Michael Stucley (Tavie) Hamilton-Russell; also Baron Hamilton of Stackallen (I 1715) and Baron Brancepeth (UK 1866); sits as Baron Brancepeth; s of 10 Viscount Boyne, KCVO, JP (d 1995), and Rosemary Anne, *née* Stucley; *b* 27 May 1965; *Educ* Harrow, RAC Cirencester (Dip Rural Estate Mgmnt); *m* 1 June 1991, Lucy, da of George Potter, of Foxdale, Bunbury, Cheshire; 1 da (Hon Emelia Rose b 25 Jan 1994), 3 s (Frederick Gustavus George b 23 March 1997, Hon (Gustavus) Archie Edward b 30 June 1999, Hon Jack Gustavus Michael b 30 June 1999); *Heir* s, Hon Archie Hamilton-Russell; *Career* dir Carter Jones Chartered Surveyors; MRICS; *Recreations* cricket, skiing, travel; *Clubs* Turf; *Style*— The Rt Hon the Viscount Boyne; ✉ Burwarton House, Bridgnorth, Shropshire WV16 6QH (tel 01746 787221)

BOYS, Penelope Ann; CB (2005); da of late Hubert John Boys, and late Mollie, *née* Harnett; *b* 11 June 1947; *Educ* Guildford Co Sch for Girls; *m* 1977, David Charles Henshaw Wright; *Career* exec offr DES (now DFE) 1966–69, asst princ Miny of Power 1969–72, private sec to min without portfolio 1972–73; Dept of Energy: princ 1973–78, seconded to British Nat Oil Corp 1978–80, head of Int Unit 1981–85, seconded as head ST2 Div HM Treasy 1985–87, dir of personnel Dept of Energy 1987–89, dep DG Office of Electricity Regulation 1989–93; head of personnel Dept of Trade and Industry 1993–96, sec to the Competition Cmmn (formerly Monopolies and Mergers Cmmn) 1996–2000, exec dir Office of Fair Trading 2003– (dep DG 2000–03); *Recreations* cooking, walking, racing; *Style*— Miss Penelope Boys, CB; ✉ Office of Fair Trading, Fleetbank House, 2–6 Salisbury Square, London EC4Y 8JX (tel 020 7211 8350)

BOYS SMITH, Stephen Wynn; CB (2001); s of John Boys Smith (d 1991), and Gwendolen Sara, *née* Wynn (d 1994); *b* 4 May 1946; *Educ* Sherborne, St John's Coll Cambridge (MA), Univ of British Columbia (MA); *m* 1971, Linda Elaine, da of Ronald Price; 1 s (Nicholas John b 16 Oct 1973), 1 da (Sarah Jane b 9 March 1977); *Career* teaching asst Univ of British Columbia 1967–68; Home Office: joined 1968, asst private sec to Home Sec 1971–73; Central Policy Review Staff Cabinet Office 1977–79, Home Office 1979–81, asst sec NI Office 1981, princ private sec to Sec of State for NI 1981–82, Home Office 1984, princ private sec to Home Sec 1985–87, under sec Home Office Police Dept 1989–92, under sec HM Treasy 1992–95, dep sec (head of Police Dept) Home Office 1995–96, dir of police policy Home Office 1996–98, DG immigration and nationality Home Office 1998–2002, DG Organised Crime, Drugs and International Directorate 2002–03, ret; jt sec Ind Monitoring Cmmn 2004–; Ind Review of Coal Health Compensation Schemes DTI 2005, Ind Review of Airport Policing Home Office and Dept for Tport 2006; *Style*—

Stephen Boys Smith, Esq, CB; ✉ 23 Church Street, Ampthill, Bedfordshire MK45 2PL (tel 01525 403800)

BRABAZON, James; s of Leslie Moffatt Seth-Smith (d 1955), and Ursula Mary Seth-Smith (d 1968); *b* 12 January 1923, Kampala, Uganda; *Educ* Uppingham, Univ of London (BA); *m* 1, 1950, Elizabeth Marka, *née* Webb (decd); 2 da (Elizabeth Naomi b 1951, Penelope Marka b 1957), 1 s (Nigel James b 1953); m 2, 1974, Margaret Lilian, *née* Lord (decd); 1 da (Helena Margaret b 1976); *Career* statistical section Admiralty Merchant Shipping Dept 1941–45, actor in rep 1948–54, playwright 1958– (plays performed on stage and TV); story ed then dir Drama Dept BBC 1963–70, drama prodr Granada TV 1970–76, drama prodr LWT 1976; prodr The Law of Love (documentary) 1988, co-writer and co-prodr Lost in Siberia (feature film) 1990, co-prodr Karzan's Brothers (documentary) 1996; supporter: Dr Schweitzer's Hosp Fund, Friends of Albert Schweizer; FRSL 1980; *Publications* People of Nowhere (play, 1960, official play World Refugee Year), Albert Schweizer (biography, 1976, revised edn 2000), Dorothy L Sayers (biography, 1981); *Recreations* trying to walk (arthritis); *Style*— James Brabazon, Esq; ✉ c/o Conrad Williams, Blake Friedmann Ltd, 122 Arlington Road, London NW11 7AP (tel 020 7284 0408, fax 020 7284 0442, e-mail conrad@blakefriedmann.co.uk)

BRABAZON OF TARA, 3 Baron (UK 1942); Ivon Anthony Moore-Brabazon; DL (IOW 1993); s of 2 Baron Brabazon of Tara, CBE (d 1974, whose f, 1 Baron, was Min of Aircraft Production after Beaverbrook; the Bristol-Brabazon airliner was named after him); *b* 20 December 1946; *Educ* Harrow; *m* 8 Sept 1979, Harriet, da of Mervyn de Courcy Hamilton, of Harare, Zimbabwe, by his w, Lovell Ann, da of Rowland Cullinan, of Olifantsfontein, Transvaal; 1 s (Hon Benjamin Ralph b 1983), 1 da (Hon Anabel Mary b 1985); *Heir* s, Hon Benjamin Moore-Brabazon; *Career* memb London Stock Exchange 1972–84; a Lord in Waiting (government whip) 1984–86; spokesman for Dept of Transport 1984–85, and for Treasy, Dept of Trade and Industry, Energy 1985–86; Parly under-sec of state for Transport and min for Aviation and Shipping 1986–89, min of state Foreign and Commonwealth Office 1989–90, min of state Dept of Tport 1990–92, oppn spokesman environment, tport and the regions 1998–2001, chm of ctees House of Lords 2003– (princ dep chm 2001–03); pres UK Warehousing Assoc 1992–, dep chm Fndn for Sport and the Arts 1992–, memb RAC Public Policy Ctee 1992–99, memb Cncl Shipwrecked Mariners Soc 1993–, tstee Medical Cmmn on Accident Prevention 1994–99; pres: Br Int Freight Assoc 1997–99, Inst of the Motor Indust 1998– (dep pres 1997–98); *Recreations* sailing, Cresta Run, golf; *Clubs* Royal Yacht Sqdn; *Style*— The Rt Hon the Lord Brabazon, DL; ✉ House of Lords, London SW1A 0PW (e-mail brabazoni@parliament.uk)

BRABBINS, Martyn Charles; s of Herbert Henry Brabbins (d 1985), and Enid Caroline, *née* Pope (d 1985); *b* 13 August 1959; *Educ* Sponne Sch Towcester, Goldsmiths Coll London, Leningrad State Conservatoire; *m* 31 August 1985, Karen Maria, da of John Christopher Evans; 2 s (Alexander John b 17 June 1989, Leo John b 30 June 1992), 1 da (Nina Pamela b 13 Sept 1994); *Career* conductor; winner Leeds Conductors Competition 1988; professional debut Scottish Chamber Orch 1988; assoc princ conductor BBC Scottish Symphony Orch 1992–, princ conductor Sinfonia 21 1994–, princ conductor Huddersfield Choral Soc; artistic dir Cheltenham Int Festival of Music 2005–; conductor: RPO, LPO, Philharmonia Orch, BBC Symphony Orch, Royal Liverpool Philharmonic Orch, BBC Nat Orch of Wales, Ulster Orch, North German Radio Orch, St Petersburg Philharmonic, Australian Youth Orch, English Chamber Orch, Northern Sinfonia, ENO, Opera North, Scottish Opera, English Touring Opera, Kirov Opera, Nash Ensemble, Bavarian Radio Symphony Orch, Lahti Symphony; *Recordings* Henselt Piano Concerto, Hindemith Viola Concertos, Britten War Requiem, Parry Piano Concerto, Stanford Piano Concerto, orchestral works by Mackenzie, Wallace and Maccunn, Korngold Die Katrin (winner of the Opera Section Cannes Music Awards, Birtwistle, Woolrich, Crosse, Keal, Finissy, Bedford, Bainbridge); *Publications* Cambridge University Press Handbook of Conducting (contrib, 2003); *Recreations* cooking, running, travelling, reading, being with my family; *Style*— Martyn Brabbins, Esq; ✉ c/o Stephen Lumsden, Intermusica, 16 Duncan Terrace, London N1 8BZ

BRABOURNE, 8 Baron (UK 1880); Norton Louis Phillip Knatchbull; 17 Bt (E 1641); s and h of Countess Mountbatten of Burma, *qv*, and s of 7 Baron Brabourne (d 2005); *b* 8 October 1947; *Educ* Gordonstoun, Univ of Kent; *m* 1979, Penelope, da of late R W E Eastwood, of Lausanne, Switzerland; 1 s (Nicholas, Lord Romsey b 1981), 2 da (Hon Alexandra b 1982, Hon Leonora b 1986 d 1991); *Heir* s, Lord Romsey; *Career* film and TV prodr 1971–80; High Steward Romsey 1980; Liveryman Worshipful Co of Mercers; *Clubs* Royal Motor Yacht (Vice Adm 1985); *Style*— The Rt Hon the Lord Brabourne; ✉ Broadlands, Romsey, Hampshire SO51 9ZD (tel 01794 505030)

BRACEWELL-SMITH, Sir Charles; 4 Bt (UK 1947), of Keighley, Co York; s of Sir George Bracewell Smith, 2 Bt, MBE (d 1976); suc bro, Sir Guy Bracewell Smith, 3 Bt 1983; *b* 13 October 1955; *Educ* Harrow; *m* 1; m 2, 25 July 1996, Nina, *qv*, da of K C Kakkar, of New Delhi, India; 1 adopted da; *Heir* none; *Career* former dir Park Lane Hotel; fndr The Homestead Charitable Tst; *Books* as Francis O'Donovan: The Song of Saints, The Eternal Triangle; *Recreations* comparative religion, mystical theology, philosophy, psychology, Arsenal FC; *Clubs* RAC; *Style*— Sir Charles Bracewell-Smith, Bt; ✉ 7 Clarence Gate Gardens, Glentworth Street, London NW1 6AY

BRACEWELL-SMITH, Lady; Nina Bracewell-Smith; da of K C Kakkar, and Swadesh, *née* Kapoor; *b* 14 November 1965, Bonn, Germany; *Educ* BBA; *m* 25 July 1996, Sir Charles Bracewell-Smith, Bt, *qv*; *Career* dir: Tymals Investment Co 1994–2001, Sheraton Park Lane 1996–97, Arsenal FC 2005–; tstee Homestead Charitable Tst; *Recreations* bridge, tennis, travelling; *Clubs* RAC; *Style*— Lady Bracewell-Smith

BRACK, Peter Kenneth; s of Rev Martin Brack (d 1953), rector of Wolviston, Co Durham 1906–50, private chaplain to Marquess of Londonderry 1908–14, and Dorothea, *née* Martin (d 1977); *b* 13 April 1922; *Educ* Trent Coll Derbys; *Family* 1 da (Michelle Diana Haines-Brack b 6 May 1946); m, 1 April 1961, Nora (d 2001), da of Francis Kilmartin, MM (d 1957), of Cheadle, Cheshire; *Career* Rolls Royce Ltd (Derby) 1940–71; engrg apprenticeship followed by various duties home and abroad: Cordoba Argentina 1950–52, Venezuela 1953–56, France and Italy 1957–59; md Rolls Royce De España SA Barcelona 1963–71; memb Ctee of Inspection of the liquidation of Rolls Royce Realisations Ltd 1971–2004; dir: Bennett's Machine Co 1973–75, TTI Ltd (Translations Co) 1975–77; chm Brack & Assocs Ltd 2006– (md 1977–2006), md Pennack Ltd 2006–; Derbys delg Int C of C London 1972–82; pres Br Club Barcelona 1966–71; life memb: Nat Tst, Nat Philatelic Soc, CGA; CEng, FRAeS, FCMI; *Recreations* philately (South American specialist and a recognised authority on Venezuelan stamps), golf, chess, antiques, natural history; *Clubs* Canning, In & Out, Chevin Golf; *Style*— Peter Brack, Esq; ✉ Chrysalis, Windley, Belper, Derbyshire DE56 2LP (tel 01773 550364); Brack & Associates Ltd, Southgate Business Centre, Normanton Road, Derby DE23 6UQ (tel 01332 360242, fax 01332 291551, e-mail sales@bracktranslations.co.uk)

BRACKLEY, Rt Rev Ian James; *see:* Dorking, Bishop of

BRADBEER, Sir (John) Derek (Richardson); kt (1988), OBE (1973), TD (1964), DL (1988); s of William Bertram Bradbeer (d 1992), of Hexham, Northumberland, and Winifred, *née* Richardson (d 1985); *b* 29 October 1931; *Educ* Canford, Sidney Sussex Coll Cambridge (MA); *m* 6 April 1962, Margaret Elizabeth, da of Gerald Frederick Chantler, TD (d 1994), of Ponteland, Northumberland; 1 s (Jeremy b 1962), 1 da (Amanda b 1963); *Career* cmmnd RA 1951, TA, 1952–77, CO 101 (N) Med Regt RA (V) 1970–73, Dep Cdr 21 and 23 Bdes 1973–77, Hon Col 101 (N) FD Regt RA (V) 1986–91; chm TAVR Assoc North of England 1990–96; admitted slr 1959; ptnr Wilkinson Maughan Newcastle 1961–97, conslt Eversheds (following merger) 1997–; Law Soc: memb Cncl 1973–94, vice-pres 1986–87, pres 1987–88; pres Newcastle Law Soc 1980, govr Coll of Law 1983–2002 (chm 1990–99), UK vice-pres Union Internationale des Avocats 1989–93; memb: Criminal Injuries Compensation Bd 1988–2000, Criminal Injuries Compensation Appeals Panel 1996–, Disciplinary Ctee Inst of Actuaries 1989–96, Insurance Brokers Registration Cncl 1990–97; dir JT Dove Pensions Tst Ltd 1975–97; chm North East Water plc 1992–2002 (dir 1990–92), dep chm Northumbrian Water Group plc 1996–2002; dir: Newcastle and Gateshead Water plc 1978–90, Sunderland and South Shields Water 1990–2002; *Recreations* gardening, reading, tennis, general sport; *Clubs* Army and Navy, Northern Counties; *Style*— Sir Derek Bradbeer, OBE, TD, DL

BRADBEER, Harry James; s of Thomas Linthorn Bradbeer, of Devon, and Vivyen Elise, *née* Atterbury; *b* 21 September 1966; *Educ* Marlborough, UCL (BA), Univ of Michigan; *m* 1998, Hon Nino Natalia O'Hagan Strachey, da of 4 Baron O'Hagan , *qv*, and Princess Tamara Imeretinsky; 1 s (Caspian Thomas Charles b 20 July 2001); *Career* TV and film dir; script reader to John Schlesinger 1991–93; *Television* credits incl: The Bill 1996, This Life 1997, The Cops 1998–99 (Best Drama Series BAFTA Awards 1998–99, Best Drama Series RTS Awards 1999), Attachments 2000, A is for Acid 2002, The Brides in the Bath 2003, Outlaws 2004 (nominee Best Drama Serial BAFTA Awards 2004), No Angels 2004–05, Sugar Rush 2005–06 (Int Emmy 2006, nominee Best Drama Series BAFTA Awards 2006), Perfect Day 2006 (nominee Best Comedy Prog Rose d'Or Montreux Festival 2007), Messiah 2007; *Films* A Night with a Woman. A Day with Charlie 1994, As The Beast Sleeps 2001 (Best Single Drama Belfast Arts Awards 2002, nominee Best Single Drama IFTA Awards 2002); *Recreations* skiing, sailing, cooking; *Clubs* Soho House; *Style*— Harry Bradbeer, Esq; ✉ c/o St John Donald, PFD, Drury House, 34–43 Russell Street, London WC2B 5HA (tel 020 7344 1000)

BRADBOURN, Philip Charles; OBE (1994), MEP; s of Horace Bradbourn (d 1978), and Elizabeth, *née* Cox (d 1992); *b* 9 August 1951, Tipton, Staffordshire; *Educ* Tipton GS, Wulfrun Coll, Worcester Coll (Dip); *Career* local govt offr 1967–87, political advsr Wolverhampton City Cncl 1987–99, MEP (Cons) W Midlands 1999–, Cons chief whip European Parl 2003–07, Cons spokesman on justice and home affairs 2007–; nat chm Cons Political Centre 1990–93, regnl chm W Midlands Cons Pty 1997–99, 1 vice chm Civil Liberties, Justice and Home Affairs Ctee 2007–; *Recreations* gardening; *Style*— Philip Bradbourn, Esq, OBE, MEP; ✉ 285 Kenilworth Road, Balsall Common, Coventry CV7 7EL (tel 01676 530621, fax 01676 530658); European Parliament, ASP-14E169, Rue Wiertz, 1047 Brussels, Belgium (tel and fax 00 322 284 7407, e-mail pbradbourn@europarl.eu.int)

BRADBURY, His Hon Anthony Vincent; s of Alfred Charles Bradbury (d 1955), and Noreen, *née* Vincent Jones (d 1997); *b* 29 September 1941; *Educ* Kent Coll Canterbury, Univ of Birmingham (LLB, Sir Henry Barber law scholar); *m* 22 Jan 1966, Rosalie Anne, *née* Buttrey; 1 da (Irene Jane b 18 Jan 1973); *Career* admitted slr 1965, asst slr Frere Cholmeley 1965–67 (articled clerk 1963–65), asst slr Abbott Thomas & Co 1967–70, princ Bradbury & Co 1970–81, dep registrar 1978–81, registrar Ilford Co Ct 1981–91, asst recorder 1985–90, recorder 1990–92, district judge Chelmsford Co Ct 1991–92, circuit judge (SE Circuit) 1992–2006 (dep circuit judge 2006–), dep judge of the High Court 2001–06; memb GLC and ILEA for Wandsworth 1967–70; Parly candidate (Cons): Battersea N 1970, Battersea S Feb 1974; contrib articles to Wisden's Cricketers Almanack and other cricket publications; *Recreations* walking, travel, supporting Yorkshire cricket; *Clubs* MCC, Yorkshire CCC, Cricket Writers', Reform; *Style*— His Hon Anthony Bradbury

BRADBURY, 3 Baron (UK 1925); John Bradbury; s of 2 Baron Bradbury (d 1994), and his 1 w, Joan, *née* Knight; *b* 17 March 1940; *Educ* Gresham's, Univ of Bristol; *m* 1968 Susan, da of late W Liddiard, of East Shefford, Berks; 2 s (Hon John b 1973, Hon Ben b 1975); *Heir* s, Hon John Bradbury; *Style*— The Rt Hon the Lord Bradbury

BRADBURY, Michael Raymond; s of Arnold Needham Bradbury, of Wetherby, W Yorks, and Rita Ann, *née* Fenwick; *b* 26 April 1952; *Educ* Leeds GS, Liverpool Univ Sch of Architecture (BA, BArch); *m* 1, (m dis); 1 s (Augustus William b 16 Oct 1978), 2 da (Sally Elizabeth Rose b 21 April 1983, Laura Jane b 26 Feb 1986); m 2, July 2005, Janet White; *Career* Poynton Bradbury Wynter Cole (formerly Poynton Bradbury Wynter): joined Robert A Poynton, RIBA as architectural asst 1976, qualified 1977, assoc 1979, equal ptnr 1983–; RIBA: chm Cornwall Branch 1989–91 (sec 1995–98), chm South Western Region 1993–95 (vice-chm 1991–93), elected to Nat Cncl 1999–2002; memb Exec Ctee Cornwall Branch CPRE 1991–; winner various CPRE and RIBA awards; ARCUK 1977, RIBA 1977, MFB 1995; *Recreations* sailing, windsurfing, squash; *Clubs* Mounts Bay Sailing; *Style*— Michael R Bradbury, Esq; ✉ 1 Bellair House, Madron, Penzance TR20 8SP (tel 01736 792000, fax 01736 792001, e-mail architects@pbwc.co.uk)

BRADES, *see:* Ferleger Brades

BRADFIELD, James Dean; *b* 21 February 1969; *Educ* Oakdale Comp Sch; *Family* 1 c; *Career* pop singer; lead singer of Manic Street Preachers; signed to Sony 1991–; *Albums* New Art Riot (EP, 1989), Generation Terrorists (1991), Gold Against the Soul (1993), The Holy Bible (1994), Everything Must Go (1996), This Is My Truth Tell Me Yours (1998), Know Your Enemy (2001), Forever Delayed (2002), Lipstick Traces (2003); *Singles* Motown Junk (1990), You Love Us (1990), Stay Beautiful (1991), Love's Sweet Exile (1991), Slash 'N' Burn (1992), Motorcycle Emptiness (1992), Suicide is Painless (1992), Little Baby Nothing (1992), From Despair to Where (1993), La Tristesse Durera (1993), Roses in the Hospital (1993), Life Becoming a Landslide (1994), Faster (1994), Revol (1994), She is Suffering (1994), Design for Life (UK no 2, 1996), Everything Must Go (1996), Kevin Carter (1996), Australia (1996), If You Tolerate This Your Children Will Be Next (UK no 1, 1998), The Everlasting (1998), You Stole The Sun From My Heart (1999), Tsunami (1999), The Masses Against the Classes (UK no 1, 2000), So Why So Sad (2001), Found That Soul (2001); *Awards* incl: Best Band Brit Awards 1997, Best Album (Everything Must Go) Brit Awards 1997, Best British Group Brit Awards 1999, Best British Album (This is My Truth Tell Me Yours) Brit Awards 1999; *Recreations* football; *Style*— James Bradfield; ✉ c/o Terri Hall, Hall or Nothing Press, 11 Poplar Mews, Uxbridge Road, London W12 (tel 020 8740 6288, fax 020 8749 5982)

BRADFORD, Barbara Taylor; OBE (2007); da of Winston Taylor (d 1981), and Freda Walker Taylor (d 1981); *Educ* Northcote Sch for Girls; *m* 24 Dec 1963, Robert Bradford; *Career* author and journalist; women's ed Yorkshire Evening Post 1951–53 (reporter 1949–51), fashion ed Woman's Own 1953–54, columnist London Evening News 1955–57, exec ed The London American 1959–62, ed National Design Center Magazine USA 1965–69; nationally syndicated columnist: Newsday (New York) 1968–70, Chicago Tribune/New York Daily News Syndicate 1970–75, Los Angeles Times Syndicate (New York) 1975–81; memb: Cncl The Authors' Guild Inc USA 1989, PEN USA; inductee literary legend Writers Hall of Fame of America 2003; Hon DLitt Univ of Leeds 1992, Hon DLitt Univ of Bradford 1995; *Novels* A Woman of Substance (1980, Matrix Award for books from New York Women in Communications 1985, Prix Litteraire Deauville Film Festival 1994), Voice of the Heart (1983), Hold the Dream (1985, screen adaptation 1986), Act of Will (1986), To Be The Best (1988), The Women in his Life (1990), Remember (1991), Angel (1993), Everything to Gain (1994), Dangerous to Know (1995), Love In Another Town (1995), Her Own Rules (1996), Power of a Woman (1997), A Secret Affair (1998), A Sudden Change of Heart (1999), Where You Belong (2000), The Triumph of Katie Byrne (2001), Three Weeks in Paris (2002), Emma's Secret (2003), Unexpected Blessings (2004), Just Rewards (2005), The Ravenscar Dynasty (2006), The Ravenscar Heir (2007); *Non-fiction* published in USA incl: Complete Encyclopedia of Homemaking Ideas (1968), How To Be The Perfect Wife (1969), How to Solve Your Decorating Problems (1976), Luxury Designs for Apartment Living (1981); *Style*— Mrs Barbara Taylor Bradford, OBE; ✉ Bradford Enterprises, 450 Park Avenue # 1903, New York NY 10022 2605, USA (tel 00 1 212 308 7390, fax 00 1 212 935 1636)

BRADFORD, Prof Henry Francis; s of Henry Bradford (d 1996), and Rose Bradford (d 2003); *b* 9 March 1938; *Educ* Dartford GS, UCL (2nd MB BS), Univ of Birmingham (BSc), Inst of Psychiatry Univ of London (PhD, DSc); *m* 1, 28 March 1964, Helen (d 1999), da of Benjamin Caplan (d 1985); 1 da (Sonya Helen b 25 Jan 1968), 1 s (Daniel Benjamin Alexander b 24 Aug 1969); m 2, 4 Sept 1999, Mary-Thérèse, da of Harold Nazareth (d 1987), and Isabel Nazareth (d 2002); *Career* MRC research fell in neuroscience Instn of Psychiatry Univ of London 1964–65; Imperial Coll London: lectr in biochemistry 1965–, reader in biochemistry 1975–, prof of neurochemistry 1979–2003 (emeritus prof and sr res fell 2003–), dir of undergraduate studies 1988–; ed: Jl of Neurochemistry 1973–81, The Biochemist 1989–95 (chief ed 1988–95), Jl of Brain Science 1995–; Silver Jubilee lectr Indian Inst of Chemical Biology Calcutta 1982, Sandoz lectr Inst of Neurology London 1976 and 1985, guest lectr Int Soc for Neurochemistry Japan 1985, 1995 and 1997, Harold Chaffer Meml lectr Univ of Otago NZ 1987, plenary lectr Japanese Brain Science and Neurosurgery Congress Okinawa 1997; author of about 400 scientific papers (incl 10 scientific reviews), ed 3 vols of scientific reviews 1981–88; awarded £7 million in neuroscience/med res grants 1971–2003; chm MRC Epilepsy Res Co-ordinating Ctee 1978–88 (memb Neuroscience Ctee and Bd 1973–82), scientific advsr Brain Res Tst 1985–95, hon archivist UK Biochemical Soc 1988–98 (hon sec 1973–81), memb Wellcome Tst Ctee for the History of Med 1985–; Bronze medal for contrib to neurochemistry Univ of Okayama Japan 1985; memb: UK Biochemical Soc, Int Soc Neurochemistry, Brain Res Assoc; FRCPath 1988 (MRCPath 1976); *Books* Chemical Neurobiology (1985); *Recreations* history of science, natural history, music; *Style*— Prof Henry Bradford; ✉ Division of Cell and Molecular Biology, Department of Life Sciences, Faculty of Natural Sciences, Imperial College, South Kensington, London SW7 2AZ (tel 020 8464 4615, e-mail h.bradford@imperial.ac.uk)

BRADFORD, Katie; da of Frank Bradford, and Thelma, *née* Jones; *Educ* Barrs Hill GS Coventry, UCL (LLB, LLM), Coll of Law; *Career* solicitor; Linklaters: ptnr, head of property and fin litigation; accredited mediator, memb: Law Soc 1982, RICS panels for third party appts; Liveryman City of London Slrs Co; FRSA; *Publications* Butterworths Business Landlord and Tenant Handbook; contrib ed The Conveyancer; various articles in legal and property press; *Recreations* theatre, opera, choral singing, cricket; *Clubs* Middlesex CCC, Surrey CCC, MCC; *Style*— Ms Katie Bradford, FRSA; ✉ Linklaters, One Silk Street, London EC2Y 8HQ (tel 020 7456 4234, fax 020 7456 2222)

BRADFORD, 7 Earl of (UK 1815); The Rt Hon Richard Thomas Orlando Bridgeman; 12 Bt (E 1660); also Baron Bradford (GB 1794) and Viscount Newport (UK 1815); s of 6 Earl of Bradford, TD (d 1981); *b* 3 October 1947; *Educ* Harrow, Trinity Coll Cambridge (MA); *m* 1979 (m dis), Joanne Elizabeth, da of Benjamin Miller, of London; 3 s (Alexander Michael Orlando, Viscount Newport b 6 Sept 1980, Hon Henry Gerald Orlando b 18 April 1982, Hon Benjamin Thomas Orlando b 7 Feb 1987), 1 da (Lady Alicia Rose b 27 Dec 1990); *Heir* s, Viscount Newport; *Career* proprietor Porters English Restaurant Covent Garden 1979–, jt proprietor The Countess's Arms Weston Heath nr Newport 1998–; chm Weston Park Enterprises Ltd 1986–99 (tstee The Weston Park Fndn 1988–99); IOD: memb Midlands Ctee 1989–97, memb Cncl 1997–99; Tidy Britain Gp (now EnCams): chm W Midlands Advsy Ctee 1990–2001, chm Policy and Advsy Ctee 1998–2000 (memb 1994–98), vice-chm 1998–2002, memb Cncl 2002–05; chm: Wrekin Heritage Assoc 1987–2000, Westminster Considerate Restaurateurs Assoc 1992–98; pres: Wrekin Tourism Assoc (now Telford and Shropshire Marketing Partnership) 1980–, Newport Branch RNLI 1981–98, Wolverhampton Friends of the Samaritans 1982–98, Telford Victim Support 1986–99, Master Chefs of GB 1990–2003, Assoc of Conf Execs 1990–95, Stepping Stones Appeal for the Fndn for Conductive Educn 1991–94; vice-pres Re-Solv (The Campaign Against Solvent Abuse) 1989– (pres 1984–89); memb: Ctee Restaurant Assoc 1977–82 and 1992–, GB Great Food Working Pty 1990–95; tstee Castle Bromwich Hall Gardens Tst; patron: Rodbaston Agric Coll 1998–, Miracles 1998–; pres Shropshire Victim Support 1999–2005; *Publications* My Private Parts and The Stuffed Parrot (compilation, 1984), The Eccentric Cookbook (1985), Stately Secrets (1994), Porters English Cookery Bible - Ancient and Modern (with Carol Wilson, 2004); online publications: The Earl of Bradford's London Restaurant Guide (www.london-restaurants.com, 1998), The Traditional English Restaurants of London (www.english-restaurants.com, 1998), Virtual London (www.virtual-london.com, 1999), London Life (www.londonlife.co.uk, 1999), The Restaurant Guide (www.restaurant-guide.com, 2000), The Stately Home Guide (www.statelyhomes.com, 2001), Hotel Guide (www.vip-hotels.com, 2001), Fake Titles (www.faketitles.com); *Recreations* cooking, gardening; *Style*— The Rt Hon the Earl of Bradford; ✉ Woodlands House, Weston-under-Lizard, Shifnal, Shropshire TF11 8PX (tel 01952 850566, fax 01952 850697, e-mail bradfordr@porters.uk.com)

BRADFORD, Sarah Mary Malet (Viscountess Bangor); da of Brig Hilary Anthony Hayes, DSO, OBE (d 1984), and Mary Beatrice de Carteret Malet (who m 2, Keith Murray, and d 1995); *b* 3 September 1938; *Educ* St Mary's Convent Shaftesbury, Lady Margaret Hall Oxford (state scholarship, coll history scholarship); *m* 1, 1959 (m dis), Anthony John Bradford, s of John Frank Bradford; 1 da (Annabella Mary b 1964), 1 s (Edward John Alexander b 1966); m 2, 1976, 8 Viscount Bangor, *qv*; *Career* author, reviewer and journalist; *Books* The Story of Port (1978, new edn 1983, first published as The Englishman's Wine 1969), Portugal and Madeira (1969), Portugal (1973), Cesare Borgia (1976), Disraeli (1982), Princess Grace (1984), King George VI (1989), Sacheverell Sitwell (1993), Elizabeth, A Biography of Her Majesty The Queen (1996), America's Queen: The Life of Jacqueline Kennedy Onassis (2000), Lucrezia Borgia, Life, Love and Death in Renaissance Italy (2004), Diana (2006); *Recreations* reading biographies, diaries and letters, gardening, travelling, watching Liverpool FC; *Style*— Sarah Bradford; ✉ c/o Aitken Alexander Associates, 18–21 Cavaye Place, London SW10 9PT (tel 020 7373 8672, fax 020 7373 6002, e-mail recep@gillonaitken.co.uk)

BRADING, Prof Alison Frances; da of Brig Norman Baldwin Brading (d 1990), and Helen Margaret, *née* Gatey; *b* 26 February 1939, Bexhill on Sea, E Sussex; *Educ* Maynard Sch Exeter, Univ of Bristol (BSc, PhD), Univ of Oxford (MA); *Career* Univ of Oxford: research asst Dept of Pharmacology 1965–71, fell and tutor in physiology Lady Margaret Hall 1968–2005, departmental demonstrator Dept of Pharmacology 1971–72, univ lectr in pharmacology 1972–2005, univ advsr for physiological sciences students 1992–99, memb Libraries Bd 1993–95, titular prof in pharmacology 1996–2005; ed Jl of Physiology 1978–83 (distributing ed 1983–85), advsy ed Jl of Muscle Research and Cell Motility 1980–90, ed Naunyn-Schmiedeberg's Archives of Pharmacological 1993–2000 (advsy ed 1983–93), ed Br Jl of Pharmacology 1988–94, ed Physiological Soc Newsletter 1989–92, ed Br Jl of Urology 1993–2004, section ed Smooth Muscle Cellular Physiology Neurourology and Urodynamics 2002–; assessor RCS Surgical Research Fellowships 1994–; estab Oxford Continence Gp 1981; memb: Grants Panel Nuffield Fndn Undergraduate Research Bursaries 1990–, Grants Panel Action Research 1993–97, Commissioning Team R&D Prog for People with Physical and Complex Disabilities North Thames 1994; memb: Physiological Soc (memb Ctee 1986–92, tstee Benevolent Fund 1997), Br Pharmacological Soc, Biophysical Soc, Urodynamics Soc, Int Continence Soc (memb Scientific Ctee 1998–2000), Int Soc for Autonomic Neuroscience; assoc memb Br Assoc of Urological Surgeons; conslt: Zeneca Pharmaceuticals USA, Wyeth Ayerst Princeton USA, Synthelabo Researche Paris, Glaxo Wellcome North Carolina, Abbott Pharmaceuticals Chicago, Lectus; *Books* The Autonomic Nervous System and its Effectors (1999); *Style*— Prof Alison Brading; ✉ 5 Canal Road, Thrupp, Kidlington, Oxford OX5 1LD (tel 01865 374745); Department of Pharmacology, Mansfield Road, Oxford OX1 3QT (e-mail alison.brading@pham.ox.ac.uk)

BRADING, Prof David Anthony; s of Ernest Arthur Brading, and Amy Mary, *née* Driscoll; *b* 26 August 1936; *Educ* Pembroke Coll Cambridge (BA, LittD), UCL (PhD); *m* 1966, Celia, *née* Wu; 1 s; *Career* asst prof Univ of Calif Berkeley 1965–71, assoc prof Yale Univ 1971–73; Univ of Cambridge: lectr 1973–92, reader in Latin American history 1992–99, prof of Mexican history 1999–2003; fell Clare Hall Cambridge 1995–; hon prof Univ of Lima 1993; FBA 1995; Order of the Aztec Eagle (Mexico) 2002; *Books* Miners and Merchants in Bourbon Mexico (1971), Haciendas and Ranchos in the Mexican Bajio (1979), The Origins of Mexican Nationalism (1985), The First America (1991), Church and State in Bourbon Mexico (1994), Mexican Phoenix (2001); *Recreations* music, walking; *Clubs* Oxford and Cambridge; *Style*— Prof David Brading; ✉ 28 Storey's Way, Cambridge CB3 0DT (tel 01223 352098)

BRADLEY, Prof (John) Andrew; s of Colin Bradley, and Christine Bradley, of Cape Town, SA; *b* 24 October 1950; *Educ* Univ of Leeds (MB ChB), Univ of Glasgow (PhD); *m* 31 May 1987, Eleanor Mary, *née* Bolton; *Career* conslt surgn Western Infirmary Glasgow 1984–97, prof of surgery and immunology Univ of Glasgow 1994–97 (formerly surgical research fell then lectr in surgery), prof of surgery Univ of Cambridge and hon conslt surgn Addenbrooke's Hosp Cambridge 1997–; author of numerous pubns mainly concerned with organ transplantation; FRCSGlas, FRCSEng, FMedSci; *Recreations* skiing, hill walking; *Style*— Prof Andrew Bradley; ✉ University Department of Surgery, Box 202, Level 9, Addenbrooke's Hospital, Cambridge CB2 2QQ (tel 01223 336976, fax 01223 762523, e-mail jab52@cam.ac.uk)

BRADLEY, Anna Louise; da of Donald Ernest Bradley, of London, and Angela Lucy, *née* Bradley; *b* 29 July 1957; *Educ* Univ of Warwick (BA, MBA); *Partner* Norman Howard Jones; 1 da (Natasha Storm b 11 March 1988), 1 s (Nathan Blaze b 12 Oct 1990); *Career* sr sub ed Marshall Cavendish Partworks Ltd 1978–82; Consumers' Assoc: sr project ldr 1982–87, project mangr 1987–88, head of food and health 1988–91, dep res dir 1991–93; exec dir and co sec Inst for the Study of Drug Dependence 1993–98, dir Nat Consumer Cncl 1999–2002, dir of retail themes FSA 2002–05; chm DEFRA Horizon Scanning Advsy Panel 2002–04, chm Organic Standards Bd Soil Assoc 2006–, advsy conslt Fishburn Hedges 2006–, tstee Addaction 2006–, consumer and communications conslt Frontfoot Consultancy 2006–, non-exec dir Soil Assoc Certification Ltd 2007–; jt asst sec All-Pty Parly Gp on Drug Misuse 1994–98; memb: The Patients' Assoc 1985–88, Advsy Cncl on the Misuse of Drugs 1996–98, Consumer Policy Review Advsy Bd 1999–2002, Camelot Ind Advsy Panel on Social Responsibility 2000–02, Agric Economics and Biotechnology Cmmn 2000–2005, DEFRA Chief Scientist's Science Advsy Gp 2002–03, Public Debate on GM Bd 2002–03, Sustainable Farming and Food Implementation Gp 2002–03, Royal Soc Science in Society Ctee 2003–05, Science Advsy Cncl 2004–05; *Books* Healthy Living (co-author, 1985), Understanding Additives (ed, 1988), Healthy Eating (1989), Caring for Someone with AIDS (contrib, 1990); author of numerous articles in jls and research papers; *Style*— Ms Anna Bradley

BRADLEY, Prof Anthony Wilfred; s of David Bradley (d 1970), of Dover, Kent, and Olive Margaret, *née* Bonsey (d 1964); *b* 6 February 1934; *Educ* Dover GS, Emmanuel Coll Cambridge (MA, LLM); *m* 5 Sept 1959, Kathleen, *née* Bryce; 1 s, 3 da; *Career* slr of the Supreme Ct 1960–89, fell Trinity Hall Cambridge 1960–68; Univ of Edinburgh: prof of constitutional law 1968–89, dean Faculty of Law 1979–82, emeritus prof 1990; ed Public Law 1986–92; called to the Bar Inner Temple 1989, in practice 1989–; memb: Ctee of Inquiry into Local Govt in Scotland 1980, Ctee to Review Local Govt in the Islands of Scotland 1983–84; legal advsr House of Lords Ctee on the Constitution 2002–05; vice-pres Int Assoc of Constitutional Law 2004–07; chm Edinburgh Cncl for Single Homeless 1984–88; Hon LLD: Staffs Univ 1993, Univ of Edinburgh 1998; *Books* Justice Discretion and Poverty (with M Adler, 1976), Governmental Liability (with J Bell, 1991), European Human Rights Law (with M Janis and R Kay, 2 edn 2000), Constitutional and Administrative Law (with K Ewing, 13 edn 2002, 14 edn 2006); *Recreations* music; *Style*— Prof Anthony Bradley; ✉ Morland, Sheepstead, Marcham, Abingdon, Oxfordshire OX13 6QG (tel 01865 390774)

BRADLEY, Prof Benjamin Arthur de Burgh; *b* 17 September 1942; *Educ* Silcoates Sch Wakefield, Bilston GS, Univ of Birmingham Med Sch (MB ChB, MSc, PhD), Univ of Cambridge (MA); *m* 27 April 1968, Anne; 4 da (Rachel b 18 Oct 1970, Lucy b 4 Aug 1972, Elise b 8 July 1976, Nicola b 29 Jan 1979); *Career* house surgn and house physician United Birmingham Hosps 1965–66, MRC res scholar and latterly MRC jr res fell Dept of Experimental Pathology Univ of Birmingham 1966–70, asst dir of res Univ of Cambridge and hon sr registrar in transplantation immunology Addenbrooke's Hosp 1970–75, sr lectr Dept of Immunohaematology Rijksuniversiteit and pt/t clinical specialist Academisch Ziekenhuis Leiden 1975–79, dir UK Transplant Service 1979–92; Univ of Bristol: hon clinical lectr in haematology Faculty of Med 1979–92, hon prof of transplantation immunology Faculty of Med 1988–, personal chair 1992–2004, prof of transplantation sciences 1992–2004, dir Dept of Transplantation Sciences 1992–2004, dir of immunology Ximerex Inc (Nebraska USA) 2006–; med dir British Bone Marrow Donor Appeal 1993–95; hon conslt: N Bristol Hosps NHS Tst 1979–, United Bristol Healthcare NHS Tst 1993–; memb Bd of Tstees Jenner Educnl Tst 1992–2000, fndr and memb Bd of Tstees Transplant Tst 1990–; chm Editorial Bd: Euro Jl of Immunogenetics 1989–2004, Transplantation 1999–2001; memb: British Soc for Immunology 1969–, British Transplantation Soc 1972– (memb Ctee 1987–89), Transplantation Soc 1975–, Dutch Soc for Immunology 1976–, Bristol Medico-Chirurgical Soc 1979–, Euro Soc for Organ Transplantation 1986–, Scientific Ctee Anthony Nolan Tst 1987–92, RSM 1987–2000, Euro Bone Marrow Transplant Gp 1989–2004, British Soc of Histocompatibility and Immunogenetics 1989– (pres 1996–98), Exec Ctee World Marrow Donor Assoc 1990–94, Scientific Policy Advsy Ctee Bd Nat Inst for Biological Standards and Control 1991–96, Euro Fndn for Immunogenetics 1991– (pres 1988–89); FRCPath 1986 (MRCPath 1974), FRCP 1999; *Recreations* yachting and dinghy racing; *Style*— Prof Benjamin Bradley; ✉ The East Barn, The Pound, Lower Almondsbury, Bristol BS32 4EF (tel 01454 201077, e-mail benjamin.bradley@btinternet.com)

BRADLEY, Christopher; s of Hugh Bradley (d 1968), of Glasgow, and Jean McQueen, *née* Dunn (d 1987); *b* 29 May 1950; *Educ* St Aloysius Coll, Blackpool and Fylde Coll (HND Hotel Mgmnt); *m* 3 May 1979, Judy Patricia, da of Robin Cousins; *Career* asst mangr Trust House Forte 1971–72, sales mangr Grand Metropolitan & Centre Hotels 1972–75, internal auditor Lord Chllr's Office 1975–78, systems conslt ICL and NCR 1978–80, chef/patron Mr Underhill's 1981– (Michelin star 1994, Etoiles Mondials de la Gastronomie 1994, 4/5 Good Food Guide 1996 and 1997, 8 out of 10 Good Food Guide 1999, Michelin star 1999–); MHCIMA; *Recreations* motor racing, gardening, not cooking; *Style*— Christopher Bradley, Esq; ✉ Mr Underhill's at Dinham Weir, Dinham, Ludlow, Shropshire SY8 1EH (tel 01584 874431)

BRADLEY, Dr (Charles) Clive; s of Charles William Bradley (d 1992), and Winifred, *née* Smith (d 1963); *b* 11 April 1937; *Educ* Longton HS, Univ of Birmingham (BSc), Univ of Cambridge (PhD); *m* 25 Sept 1965, Vivien Audrey, da of Charles Frederick Godley, and

Doris Godley, of Hillsborough, Sheffield; 1 s (Daniel b 5 Sept 1969), 1 da (Abigail b 19 May 1973); *Career* sr scientific offr Nat Physical Laboratory 1961–67, res scientist MIT and Nat Bureau of Standards USA 1967–69, sr and princ scientific offr Nat Physical Laboratory 1969–75, sr princ scientific offr and dep chief scientific offr DTI 1975–82, cnsllr sci and technol Br Embassy Tokyo 1982–88, head Advsy Cncl on Sci and Technol Secretariat Cabinet Office 1988–90, md Sharp Laboratories of Europe Ltd 1990–99 (advsr 1999–2001); visiting prof Dept of Materials Univ of Oxford 1999–2002; dep cmmr gen for UK Sci Expo Japan 1985, chm Industrial Energy Conservation Ctee Int Energy Agency 1980–82; memb: SERC and EC Ctees 1978–82 and 1989–93, Technology and Innovation Ctee CBI 1993–98, Cncl for Continuing Educn Univ of Oxford 1993–2000; memb Wolfson Coll Oxford 1999–2004; dir Birdshill Oxshott Estate Co 2000–; treas and memb Cncl The Japan Soc 2001–; FInstP 1997; *Books* High Pressure Methods in Solid State Research (1969); *Recreations* tennis, gardening; *Clubs* Athenaeum; *Style*— Dr Clive Bradley; ✉ 8 Montrose Gardens, Oxshott, Surrey KT22 0UU (tel 01372 843664)

BRADLEY, Clive; CBE (1996); s of Alfred Bradley (d 1970), and Annie Kathleen, *née* Turner (d 1990); *b* 25 July 1934; *Educ* Felsted, Clare Coll Cambridge (MA), Yale Univ; *Career* PO RAF 1953–55; called to the Bar Middle Temple 1961; BBC 1961–63 and 1965, broadcasting offr Lab Party 1963–64, political ed The Statist and broadcaster 1965–67, gp lab advsr IPC 1967–69, dep gen mangr Daily and Sunday Mirror and controller of admin IPC Newspapers 1969–71, project dir IPC 1971–73, dir The Observer 1973–76, chief exec Publishers Assoc 1976–97; convenor Confederation of Information Communication Industries 1984–; author of various pubns on politics, econs, media, industrial rels and law; dep chm Central London Valuation Panel 1973–2007; govr Felsted Sch; chair Richmond upon Thames Arts Cncl, former chair Age Concern Richmond; *Style*— Clive Bradley, Esq, CBE; ✉ 8 Northumberland Place, Richmond upon Thames, Surrey TW10 6TS (tel 020 8940 7172, fax 020 8940 7603, e-mail bradley_clive@btopenworld.com)

BRADLEY, Prof David John; s of late Harold Robert Bradley, and Mona Bradley; *b* 12 January 1937; *Educ* Wyggeston Sch Leicester, Selwyn Coll Cambridge, UCH Med Sch (Atchison scholar, Magrath scholar, MB BChir, MA, Trotter medal in surgery, Liston gold medal in surgery, Frank Smart prize), Univ of Oxford (DM); *m* 1961, Lorne Natalie, da of late Maj L G Farquhar; 2 s, 2 da; *Career* med res offr Bilharzia Res Unit Tanzania 1961–64, sr lectr Makerere Univ of East Africa Uganda 1966–69 (lectr 1964–66), Royal Soc tropical res fell Sir William Dunn Sch of Pathology Oxford 1969–73, sr res fell and Staines med fell Exeter Coll Oxford 1971–74, clinical reader in pathology Oxford Clinical Med Sch 1973–74, prof of tropical hygiene London Sch of Hygiene and Tropical Med 1974–2000 (Ross prof emeritus 2000–); dir Malaria Reference Laboratory 1974–, hon conslt public health medicine HPA 1974–, hon conslt in tropical and communicable diseases Camden and Islington DHA 1983, Westminster PCT 2002–; memb: WHO Expert Advsy Panel on Parasitic Diseases 1972–, Panel of Experts on Environmental Mgmnt 1981–; chm Div of Communicable and Tropical Diseases LSHTM 1982–88; ed: Jl of Tropical Med and Hygiene 1981–95, Tropical Med and Int Health 1995–98; RSTM&H: Chalmers Medal 1980, Macdonald Medal 1996, pres 1999–2001; foreign corresponding memb Royal Belgian Acad of Med 1984, corresponding memb German Tropenmedizingingesellschaft 1980; Harben Gold Medal RIPHH 2002; FIBiol 1974, FFPHM 1979, Hon FCIWEM 1981, FRCPath 1981, FRCP 1985, FMedSci 1999; *Books* Drawers of Water (with G F and A U White, 1972), Health in Tropical Africa During the Colonial Period (with E E Sabben-Clare and B Kirkwood, 1980), Sanitation and Disease (jtly, 1983), Travel Medicine (jtly, 1992), The Malaria Challenge (with M.Coluzzi, 1999); *Recreations* landscape gardens, natural history, travel; *Style*— Prof David Bradley; ✉ Flat 3, 1 Taviton Street, London WC1H 0BT (tel 020 7383 0228); Department of Infectious and Tropical Diseases, London School of Hygiene and Tropical Medicine, Keppel Street, London WC1E 7HT (tel 020 7927 2233, fax 020 7580 9075)

BRADLEY, David Rice; s of George Leonard Bradley, and Evelyn Annie Bradley; *b* 9 January 1938; *Educ* Christ Coll Brecon, St Catharine's Coll Cambridge (exhibitioner, MA), Univ of Edinburgh (Dip Applied Linguistics); *m* 1962, Josephine Elizabeth Turnbull Fricker, *née* Harries; 2 s; *Career* Nat Serv cmmnd 24 Regt S Wales Borderers 1956–58, served UK, Malaya, Singapore and British N Borneo; Br Cncl: gen serv offr England and Madrid 1961–62, asst educn offr Dhaka E Pakistan 1962–64, educn offr E Pakistan 1964–65, seconded as assoc prof to English Language Teaching Inst Allahabad India 1966–68, educn offr N India (temporarily chief educn offr India) 1968–69, dir of studies Br Inst Madrid, English language offr Spain and dir Br Cncl English Teaching Centre Madrid 1969–73; DOE: princ Directorate Gen of Res Secretariat 1973–76, Planning and Land Use Directorate Devpt Control Div 1976–78, Inner Cities Directorate 1978–79, study offr to devise MINIS (Mgmnt Info System for Ministers) in consultation with Lord Rayner 1979–80, Central Policy Planning Unit 1980–81, study offr (asst sec) Local Govt Fin 1981–82; Nuffield Coll Oxford: Gwilym Gibbon res fell (on leave from DOE) 1982–83, visiting fell 1993–2001; head of fin Environmental Servs Div 1983–86, head London Urban Devpt Div 1986–88, dir (under sec) Merseyside Task Force 1988–90; chief exec London Borough of Havering 1990–95, memb Cncl Sch of Mgmnt Studies Univ of Oxford 1995–98, advsr DETR 1996–98; head Corp Fundraising Univ of Oxford 1997–2000, dir of devpt KCS Wimbledon 2000–06; hon sec London Planning and Devpt Forum 1990–2003; memb Bd E Thames Housing Gp 1997–98, Cncl of Mgmnt Bankside Gallery 2001–03; *Recreations* painting; *Style*— David R Bradley, Esq; ✉ 29 York Court, The Albany, Albany Park Road, Kingston upon Thames, Surrey KT2 5ST (tel 020 8547 1573)

BRADLEY, Jenny; da of John Shannon Kean, of Oxford, and Jean Smith, *née* Coburn; *b* 2 June 1947; *Educ* Headington Sch Oxford, Oxford Poly; *Career* served indentures as journalist Bracknell News Berks 1966–69, PR exec Joan Chesney Frost Publicity Services London 1969–71, pubns mangr Marks & Spencer Ltd 1971–74; ed Thames & Chilterns Tourist Bd Oxon 1974–77, pubns mangr Milk Mktg Bd (Milk Producer) 1977–82, communications dir Dairy Crest Ltd Surrey 1982–90, public affrs dir Heathrow Airport Ltd 1990–2000, public affrs dir BAA Airports 2000–; memb: Int Assoc of Business Communicators 1987, Assoc of Women in PR 1988; *Style*— Ms Jenny Bradley; ✉ Heathrow Airport Ltd, Heathrow Point, 234 Bath Road, Harlington, Middlesex UB3 5AP (tel 020 8745 4108, fax 020 8745 5612)

BRADLEY, Baron (Life Peer 2006), of Withington in the County of Greater Manchester; Keith John Charles Bradley; PC (2001); *Educ* Bishop Vesey's GS, Manchester Poly (BA), York Univ (MPhil); *m*; 2 s, 1 da; *Career* MP (Lab) Manchester Withington 1987–2005; shadow min: for social security 1991–96, for tport 1996–97; Parly under-sec of state DSS 1997–98, dep chief whip and treas HM Household 1998–2001, min of state for Criminal Justice, Sentencing and Law Reform Home Office 2001–02, memb Health Select Ctee 2003; Manchester City Cncl: cncllr 1983–88, chm Environmental Servs Ctee 1984–88; dir: Manchester Ship Canal Co 1984–87, Manchester Airport plc 1984–87; *Style*— The Rt Hon the Lord Bradley, PC; ✉ House of Lords, London SW1A 0PW

BRADLEY, Michael John; CMG (1990), QC (Cayman Islands) 1983; *b* 1933; *Educ* Queen's Univ Belfast (LLB); *m*; 1 s; *Career* attorney gen: British Virgin Islands 1977–78, Turks and Caicos Islands 1980, Montserrat 1981, Cayman Islands 1982–87; govr Turks and Caicos Islands WI 1987–93, law revision cmmr Cayman Islands 1994–, constitutional advsr Overseas Territories Dept FCO 2001–; memb Law Soc NI; *Style*— Mr Michael Bradley, CMG, QC; ✉ 11 The Lays, Goose Street, Beckington, Somerset BA11 6RS (tel and fax 01373 831059)

BRADLEY, Patrick James; s of Gerard Bradley (d 1967), of Dublin, and Nan, *née* O'Leary (d 1990); *b* 10 May 1949; *Educ* Glenstal Abbey Sch Murroe, UCD (MB BCh, BAO, DCH); *m* 17 May 1974, Sheena, da of Frank Kelly (d 1954), of Draperstown, Co Derry; 2 da (Paula b 19 Nov 1975, Caitriona b 5 June 1984), 3 s (Darragh Francis b 19 Nov 1976, Cormac b 12 Dec 1978, Eoin Patrick b 16 Oct 1980); *Career* Nottingham HA: conslt otolaryngologist and head and neck oncologist 1982–, clinical dir Dept of Otolaryngology 1991–96, clinical dir of audit, risk and effectiveness 1996–2000, memb Theatre Users (former chm); nat clinical head Head and Neck Cancer NHS 2003–; vice-chm: Trent Regnl Advsy Ctee (Otolaryngology), ALLEA East Midlands 2003–; chm: Nottingham Section BMA 1994–95, Clinical Practice Br Assoc of Otorhinolaryngologists Head and Neck Surgns 1995–98, Educn and Trg Ctee BAO-HNS 1999–2002; memb Cncl: Otorhinolaryngological Res Soc (treas 1993–96), RSM (memb Section of Laryngology/Rhinology 1991–2000, pres 1998–99); pres: Young Otolaryngologist Head and Neck Surgeons 1993–94 (hon memb 1997), Assoc of Head and Neck Oncologists GB 2003–05 (also Cncl memb and tstee), European Laryngological Soc 2004–06, Midlands Inst Otolaryngology 2005–07; memb Bd: European Head and Neck Soc 2005–, European Acad of Otolaryngology, Head and Neck Surgery 2006– (also vice-pres), European Salivary Gland Gp 2006–; memb: Br Assoc of Surgical Oncologists (memb Cncl 1998–2001, pres 2007–), Br Assoc of Otorhinolaryngologists; corresponding memb: American Laryngological Assoc, Triological Soc, Assoc of Head and Neck Surgns; DCH, FRCSI, FRCSEd, FRCS, Hon FRSSLT, Hon FRACS, FHKCORL; *Books* Ear, Nose and Throat Disease (1989), Robb and Smith (contrib, 1992), Scott-Brown's ORL (contrib, 1994, 1995 and 2006 edns), Mawson's Head and Neck (contrib, 1997), ABC of Ear, Nose and Throat (jt ed, 5 edn 2007); also author of various pubns on head and neck cancer diagnosis and mgmnt; *Recreations* skiing, golf, scuba; *Clubs* Nottingham RFC (vice-pres), Beeston Fields Golf, Notts Golf; *Style*— Patrick Bradley, Esq; ✉ The Park Hospital, Sherwood Lodge Drive, Burnstump Country Park, Nottingham NG5 8RX (tel 0115 9662134, e-mail pjbradley@zoo.co.uk)

BRADLEY, Ven Peter; s of David Noel Bradley, and Doris, *née* Howarth; *b* 4 June 1949, Liverpool; *Educ* Old Swan Tech Coll, Ian Ramsey Coll, Lincoln Theol Coll and Univ of Nottingham (BTh); *m* 1970, Pat; 3 s; *Career* ordained: deacon 1979, priest 1980; asst curate UpHolland Team Miny 1979–83, vicar Holy Spirit Dovecot 1983–94, team rector UpHolland Team Miny 1994–, hon canon Liverpool Cathedral 2000–, archdeacon of Warrington 2001–; dir Continuing Ministerial Educn 1989–2001, dep dir In-Service Trg 1988–89; sec: Diocesan Bd of Miny 1983–88, Gp for Urban Miny and Leadership 1984–88; memb: Gen Synod 1990–, Evangelism and Renewal at Home Ctee Central Bd for Mission and Unity 1992–95 (contrib A Time for Sharing report); pt/t memb of staff: Aston Trg Scheme 1988–97, Diocesan OLM Scheme 1995–; *Recreations* walking, reading, music; *Style*— The Ven the Archdeacon of Warrington; ✉ e-mail archdeacon@peterbradley.fsnet.co.uk

BRADLEY, Peter Richard; CBE (2005); s of Patrick John Bradley, of NZ, and Mary, *née* China; *b* 28 December 1957; *Educ* Temple Moor GS Leeds, Univ of Otago NZ (MBA); *m* 14 Jan 1978 (sep), Mary Elisabeth, *née* Verhoeff; 1 s (Luke Paul b 12 Oct 1979), 2 da (Kathryn Marie b 10 Dec 1980, Allanah Louise b 25 Sept 1984); *Career* Commercial Bank of Aust 1973–76; St John Ambulance Serv Auckland: joined 1976, qualified paramedic 1986, chief ambulance offr 1993–95; London Ambulance Serv: joined 1996, dir of ops 1998–2000, chief exec 2000–; nat ambulance advsr 2004–; pres Ambulance Serv Assoc 2003–04; Queen's Golden Jubilee Medal 2002; MIMgt 1996, fell NZ Inst of Mgmnt (FNZIM) 1999, fell Ambulance Serv Inst (FASI) 2001; OBStJ 1994 (SBStJ 1992); *Recreations* personal fitness, reading, sports; *Style*— Peter Bradley, Esq, CBE; ✉ London Ambulance Service NHS Trust, 220 Waterloo Road London SE1 8SD (tel 020 7463 2567, fax 020 7921 5127, e-mail peter.bradley@lond-amb.nhs.uk)

BRADLEY, Philip Herbert Gilbert; s of Herbert Bradley (d 1981), of S Ireland, and Phyllis Eleanor Josephine, *née* Marshall (d 2003); *b* 11 November 1949; *Educ* Charterhouse, Trinity Coll Dublin (BA, BAI (engrg)); *m* 3 Sept 1977, Charlotte Knollys Olivia, da of Lt-Col John Clairmont Wood, of Coombe Down, Beaminster, Dorset; 3 s (William b 6 Oct 1980, Piers b 9 Dec 1982, Timothy b 14 March 1985); *Career* Coopers & Lybrand chartered accountants 1974–78, Robert Fleming & Co Ltd bankers 1978–79, Jardine Fleming & Co Ltd bankers Hong Kong 1979–81, dir Robert Fleming & Co bankers London 1984–97, dir Chaffeigh Ltd 1998–, chm Hemocorm Ltd, chm ECourier Ltd; tstee: RSM, Northwick Park Inst of Med Res; govr Milton Abbey; ACA; *Recreations* travel, music, opera, fishing, farming, skiing; *Clubs* Kildare Street (Dublin); *Style*— Philip Bradley, Esq; ✉ 30 Smith Terrace, Chelsea, London SW3 4DH (tel 020 7352 6921, mobile 07785 733106, e-mail bradley@smithterrace.fsnet.co.uk)

BRADLEY, Simon Anthony; s of Roy Bradley, and Diane, *née* Bonser; *b* 7 March 1967; *Educ* Wellsway Comp Sch Bristol, St Brendan's Sixth Form Coll; *m* 30 March 1996, Duska, da of Dusan Kovacevic; *Career* chef; The Ritz Hotel Paris 1989–90 (Dip Ritz Escoffier 1989), Le Manoir aux Quat' Saisons 1991–92, L'Ortolan Restaurant 1992, head chef Atlantic Bar and Grill 1993–96, Coast Restaurant 1996–98, head chef Odette's Restaurant 1998– (owner 2002–); dir Artisan Restaurants Ltd; *Recreations* long-distance running, fine wines; *Clubs* Esporta Health; *Style*— Simon Bradley, Esq; ✉ 130 Regent's Park Road, Primrose Hill, London NW1 8XL (tel 020 7586 5486); Odette's, 130 Regent's Park Road, London NW1 8XL (tel 020 7722 5388, fax 020 7586 0508)

BRADLEY, (Philip) Stephen; s of Robert Bradley, of St Annes on Sea, and Hilda, *née* Whalley; *b* 22 August 1949; *Educ* Queen Elizabeth's GS Blackburn; *m* 1, 4 April 1976 (m dis 1985), Janet Elizabeth, da of Eric Hollingworth; 2 s (Richard b 26 Oct 1980, Alexander b 2 Sept 1982); m 2, 21 May 1993, Anne, da of Diana May Hill; *Career* chartered accountant; articled clerk Waterworth Rudd & Hare Blackburn 1967–71; PricewaterhouseCoopers (formerly Price Waterhouse before merger): audit sr Manchester 1972–75, mgmnt conslt Manchester 1975–77, mgmnt conslt Nairobi 1978–84, ptnr 1980, mgmnt conslt ptnr London 1987–2002; ptnr IBM Business Consulting Services 2002–; FCA 1971, FIMC 1980, MILDM 1987; *Style*— Stephen Bradley, Esq

BRADMAN, Godfrey Michael; s of William Isadore Bradman (d 1973), and Anne Brenda, *née* Goldsweig; *b* 9 September 1936; *m* 2, 1975, Susan, da of George Bennett; 1 s (Daniel b 1977), 2 da (Camilla b 1976, Katherine b 1976), 1 step s (Christian), 1 step da (Sophie); *Career* CA 1961; sr ptnr Godfrey Bradman and Co 1961–69, chm and chief exec London Mercantile Corporation 1969, chm Rosehaugh plc 1979–91; chm and jt chief exec European Land & Property Corporation 1992–; chm: European Land and Property Investments Co 1993–, Ashpost Finance 1993–, Pondbridge Europe Ltd 1994–; jt chm Victoria Quay Ltd 1993–; fndr and dir AIDS Policy Unit 1987–90; established: Parents Against Tobacco Campaign (jt chm), Opren Victims Campaign (pres), CLEAR Campaign for Lead Free Air 1981–91, Campaign for Freedom of Information 1983–, Citizen Action and European Citizen Action 1983–91; pres Soc for the Protection of Unborn Children Educnl Research Tst 1987–, chm Friends of the Earth Tst 1983–91; memb: Cncl UN Int Year of Shelter for the Homeless 1987, Governing Body LSHTM 1988–91; Wilkins fell Cambridge; hon fell: KCL, Downing Coll Cambridge 1997; Hon DSc Univ of Salford; FCA; *Recreations* riding, family, reading; *Style*— Godfrey Bradman, Esq

BRADSHAW, Adrian; s of Sydney Bradshaw, of Wilmslow, Cheshire, and Nina, *née* Gerrand; *b* 24 February 1957; *Educ* Urmston GS, Univ of Central England (BA); *m* 12 Sept 1984, Valerie Joy, da of Dr Ivor Citron; 1 da (Charlotte b 16 Jan 1986), 1 s (Benjamin b 11 Oct 1989); *Career* Citicorp Scrimgeour Vickers 1978–81, Bell Lawrie White 1981–82, corp fin Nat West Markets 1982–83, dir Guidehouse Ltd 1983–89, md Corp Fin Div and memb Bd Arbuthnot Latham Bank 1989–91, chm and chief exec Fin Mktg Gp Incepta Gp plc 1991–93; dir: Bradmount Investments Ltd 1994–, Base Gp plc 2000–, Assetco plc 2003–; MInstD; *Recreations* tennis, golf, skiing, theatre, cuisine, travel; *Clubs* Groucho, Riverside Racquet, Annabel's, George, Sketch; *Style*— Adrian Bradshaw, Esq; ✉ Bradmount Investments Ltd, 25 Upper Brook Street, London W1K 7QD (tel 020 7495 5524, fax 020 7495 5521)

BRADSHAW, Benjamin (Ben); MP; s of Canon Peter Bradshaw, and Daphne, *née* Murphy; *b* 30 August 1960; *Educ* Thorpe St Andrew Sch Norwich, Univ of Sussex (BA); *partner* Neal Thomas Dalgleish; *Career* reporter: Express and Echo Exeter 1984–85, Eastern Daily Press Norwich 1985–86, BBC Radio Devon Exeter 1986–89; BBC correspondent Berlin 1989–91, reporter World at One and World This Weekend (BBC Radio 4) 1991–97; MP (Lab) Exeter 1997–; PPS to John Denham MP 2000–01, Parly under sec of state FCO 2001–02, Parly sec Privy Cncl Office 2002–03, Parly under sec of state DEFRA 2003–06, min of state DEFRA 2006–07, min for the SW 2007–; Consumer Journalist of the Year 1988, Anglo-German Fndn Journalist of the Year 1990, Sony News Reporter Award 1993; memb NUJ; *Recreations* cycling, walking in Devon, cooking, gardening; *Clubs* Whipton Labour (Exeter); *Style*— Ben Bradshaw, Esq, MP; ✉ House of Commons, London SW1A 0AA (tel 020 7219 6597, fax 020 7219 0950, e-mail bradshawb@parliament.uk)

BRADSHAW, Stephen Paul; s of Eric Douglas Bradshaw, and Victoria, *née* Gibbons; *b* 26 November 1948; *Educ* Nottingham HS, Queens' Coll Cambridge (MA); *m* 27 May 1972, Jenny, da of Michael Richards; 2 s (Nicholas b 4 Oct 1973, Rusty b 2 May 1977), 1 da (Melissa b 17 Aug 1980); *Career* prodr BBC Radio London 1970–73; reporter and presenter: File on 4 (BBC Radio Four) 1977–80, Newsweek (BBC2) 1980–83, People and Power (BBC1) 1983, Newsnight (BBC2) 1984–87; corr Panorama (BBC1) 1987–2007, BBC Current Affairs 2007–; memb Int Consortium of Investigative Journalists; Amnesty Int Media Award, Outstanding Int Investigative Journalism Award, DuPont Columbia Award, Peabody Award, One World Int Documentary Award, Emmy Award for Investigative Journalism; *Books* Cafe Society (1978); *Recreations* work, children, gardening; *Style*— Stephen Bradshaw, Esq; ✉ c/o Room 1118, BBC White City, 201 Wood Lane, London W12 7TS (e-mail sbflaxmoor@aol.com)

BRADSHAW, William Martin (Bill); s of Leslie Charles Bradshaw (d 1971), of Lobley Hill, Gateshead, and Vera, *née* Beadle; *b* 12 December 1955; *Educ* Gateshead GS and Saltwell HS, Darlington NCTJ Journalism Sch; *m* 13 June 1981, Fiona Judith, da of William MacBeth (d 1974); 1 s (Kit Leslie b 12 Nov 1990), 1 da (Holly b 15 Feb 1993); *Career* jr then sr reporter Halifax Courier 1975–77, news reporter Newcastle Evening Chronicle 1977–79, sports reporter (covering soccer and athletics) Newcastle Journal 1979–83, sports ed The People London 1990–94 (sports reporter Manchester 1983–85 and London 1985–89), ed The Journal Newcastle 1994–96, former asst ed Sunday Mirror, currently sports ed Daily Express; memb: Football Writers' Assoc 1981, SWA 1985; Sports Journalist of the Year 1990, Sports Reporter of the Year 1990; *Recreations* cricket, soccer, water skiing, reading, golf; *Style*— Bill Bradshaw, Esq

BRADSHAW, Baron (Life Peer UK 1999), of Wallingford in the County of Oxfordshire; Prof William Peter Bradshaw; s of Leonard Charles Bradshaw (d 1978), and Ivy Doris, *née* Steele (d 1980); *b* 9 September 1936; *Educ* Slough GS, Univ of Reading (BA, MA); *m* 30 Nov 1957, Jill Elsie (d 2002), da of James Francis Hayward, of Plastow Green, Hants; 1 s (Robert William b 1966), 1 da (Joanna b 1968); m 2, 30 Aug 2003, Diana Mary, da of Leslie Norman Whatley, of Oxford; *Career* Nat Serv 1957–59; BR: mgmnt trainee 1959, div movements mangr Bristol 1967, div mangr Liverpool 1973, chief ops mangr London Midland Region 1976, dep gen mangr London Midland Region 1977, dir of ops BR HQ 1978, dir Policy Unit BR HQ 1980, gen mangr W Region 1983–85; prof of tport mgmnt Univ of Salford 1986–92 (visiting prof Sch of Mgmnt 1992–2000); chm Ulsterbus 1987–93; dir: Northern Ireland Transport Holding Co 1988–93, Lothian Regional Transport 1997–99; special advsr Tport Select Ctee House of Commons 1992–97; memb: Oxfordshire CC 1993–, Thames Valley Police Authy 1997– (vice-chm 1997–2003), Strategic Rail Authy 1999–2001, Cmmn for Integrated Transport 1999–2001; chm Bus Appeals Body 1998–2000; Lib Dem spokesman on transport House of Lords 2003–; hon fell Wolfson Coll Oxford 2004– (supernumerary fell 1988–2003); *Recreations* growing hardy perennial plants, playing memb of brass band; *Clubs* Nat Lib; *Style*— The Rt Hon the Lord Bradshaw; ✉ House of Lords, London SW1A 0PW

BRADSTREET, Philip Lionel Stanton; s of Arthur William Haywood Bradstreet (d 1987), and Catherine Margaret Patricia, *née* Brennan; *b* 14 August 1946; *Educ* Downside, Trinity Coll Cambridge (MA); *m* 5 June 1971, Marie Christine Francoise Dominique, da of Henri Coronat (d 1986); 3 s (Christophe b 1972, Matthieu b 1975, William b 1983), 1 da (Anne-Marie b 1976); *Career* expert Cmmn of the Euro Communities 1981–83, dir Euro Community Servs Price Waterhouse Brussels 1983–94, dir Bossard Consultants Brussels 1994–98, dir Mazars Gp France; memb: de L'Ordre des Experts-Comptables France, de L'Institut des Experts-Comptables Belgium; Freeman City of London 1970; FCA; *Recreations* tennis, rugby, music; *Clubs* Hawks' (Cambridge); *Style*— Philip Bradstreet, Esq; ✉ 38 Avenue Maurice, 1050 Brussels, Belgium (tel 00 322 647 7394); Mazars Group, Le Vinci, 4 Alee de L'Arche, 92075, Paris La Defénse, France (tel 00 33 1 49 97 65 88, fax 00 33 1 49 97 60 18, mobile 00 33 6 13 23 57 96, e-mail philip.bradstreet@mazars-guerard.fr)

BRADWELL, Bishop of 1993–; Rt Rev Dr Laurence Alexander (Laurie) Green; s of Leonard Alexander Green, and Laura Elizabeth, *née* McKee; *b* 26 December 1945; *Educ* East Ham GS, KCL (BD, AKC), NY Theol Seminary (STM), SUNY (DMin), St Augustine's Coll Canterbury; *m* Victoria (Vicki); 2 da (Rebecca b 18 Sept 1974, Hannah b 6 June 1976); *Career* curate St Mark Kingstanding Birmingham 1970–73, vicar St Chad Erdington Birmingham 1973–83, princ Aston Trg Scheme 1983–89, team rector All Saints Poplar 1989–93; formerly: industrial chaplain British Steel Corporation, asst youth offr Birmingham Dio; *Publications* Power to the Powerless (1987), Let's Do Theology (1990), God in the City (jtly, 1995), Jesus and the Jubilee (1997), The Challenge of the Estates (1998), The Impact of the Global (2001), Urban Ministry and the Kingdom of God (2003); *Recreations* jazz piano and classical guitar; *Style*— The Rt Rev the Bishop of Bradwell; ✉ Bishop's House, Orsett Road, Horndon-on-the-Hill, Essex SS17 8NS (tel 01375 673806, fax 01375 674222, e-mail b.bradwell@chelmsford.anglican.org)

BRADY, Angela; *m* 1986, Robin Mallalieu, *qv*; 2 c; *Career* architect; experience in Toronto, Copenhagen and Dublin; ptnr Brady Mallalieu Architects LLP 1987–; architectural advsr: Civic Tst Nat Panel, English Heritage/CABE Urban Panel; RIAI: memb Cncl, chm London Forum; memb: Ctee RIBA Women in Architecture (chair 2000–05), London Devpt Agency as Design Champion, Panel Design for London GLA; tstee dir Building Exploratory Hackney (BEH); ambass STEMnet; dir/author of: Blackbox (Irish TV), Hot Property (Channel 5), BBC 1 London Radio architectural debate, BBC Radio 3, BBC Radio 4, Building The Dream (65 part TV series, ITV); contrib: London Biennale, Architecture Week; curator Diversecity Global Snowball (exhbn promoting women of ethnic minorities in architecture, visited cities incl LA, Chicago, Boston, Brussels, Luxembourg, Paris, Istanbul, Beijing, Zhengzhou, Sydney, Auckland, Dublin, Athens and UK tour, website www.diversecity-architects.com); assist RIBA Architects in Schools Initiative; ARB, RIBA, FRIAI 1998, FRSA 2004; *Awards* RIAI Award for house renovation in Islington London 1991, Irish Post/AIB Bank Personal Achievement Award 1993, RIAI Award for office fitout for Groundwork Hackney London 1995, RIAI Award for Sch of Architecture Univ of North London 1997, RIAI Award for house in Knightsbridge London, Brick Awards for Dublin Foyer Housing and Sports Centre 2003, RIAI Award Barra Park Open Air Theatre 2005, highly commended finalist Women in Construction Alkins Awards Women of Outstanding Achievement 2007, Business Partnership Award Greenwich Educn Business Partnership 2007; *Books* Dublin: a guide to contemporary architecture (with Robin Mallalieu, 1997); *Style*— Ms Angela Brady; ✉ Brady Mallalieu Architects LLP, 90 Queens Drive, London N4 2HW (tel 020 8880 1544, fax 020 8880 2687, e-mail bma@bradymallalieu.com, website www.bradymallalieu.com)

BRADY, Charles William; *b* 11 May 1935; *Educ* Georgia Inst of Technol, Harvard Business Sch; *Career* chm and founding ptnr INVESCO Capital Mgmnt Inc 1979–93, dir INVESCO plc 1986–93, chm AMVESCAP (formerly INVESCO) plc 1993–2006; memb Atlanta Soc of Financial Analysis; *Recreations* skiing, hiking, golf; *Clubs* Commerce, Cherokee Town & Country, Piedmont Driving; *Style*— Charles Brady, Esq, BS

BRADY, Hon Mrs (Charlotte Mary Thérèse); *née* Bingham; da of 7 Baron Clanmorris (d 1988); *b* 29 June 1942; *Educ* The Priory Haywards Heath, Sorbonne; *m* 1964, Terence Joseph Brady, s of Frederick Arthur Noel Brady (d 1985), of Montacute, Somerset; 1 da (Candida b 1965), 1 s (Matthew b 1972); *Career* playwright, novelist; writes as Charlotte Bingham; *Books* Coronet Among the Weeds (1963), Lucinda (1965), Coronet Among the Grass (1972), Rose's Story (with husb Terence Brady 1973), Yes Honestly (1977), Belgravia (1983), Country Life (1984), At Home (1985), To Hear A Nightingale (1988), The Business (1989), In Sunshine or in Shadow (1991), Stardust (1992), By Invitation (1993), Nanny (1993), A Change of Heart (1994), Debutantes (1995), The Nightingale Sings (1996), Country Wedding (1996), Grand Affair (1997), Love Song (1998), The Kissing Garden (1999), The Love Knot (2000), The Blue Note (2000), The Season (2001), Summertime (2001), Distant Music (2002), The Chestnut Tree (2002), The Wind off the Sea (2003), The Moon at Midnight (2003), Daughters of Eden (2003), The House of Flowers (2004); *Plays* I Wish I Wish, Coming of Age, The Shell Seekers (adaptation, with Terence Brady); *TV Series* (with Terence Brady): Take Three Girls, Upstairs Downstairs, No Honestly, Yes Honestly, Play for Today, Thomas and Sarah, Nanny, Pig in the Middle; *TV Films* Love With A Perfect Stranger, This Magic Moment; *Recreations* horse breeding, riding, gardening, racing, swimming; *Style*— The Hon Mrs Brady; ✉ c/o United Authors, 11–15 Betterton Street, London WC2 9BP (tel 020 7470 8886)

BRADY, Graham; MP; s of John Brady, and Maureen Brady; *b* 20 May 1967; *Educ* Altrincham GS, Univ of Durham (BA); *m* 1992, Victoria Anne Lowther; 1 da (Catherine b 1993), 1 s (William b 1998); *Career* trainee Shandwick plc, with Centre for Policy Studies 1990–92, public affrs dir Waterfront Partnership (business consultancy) 1992–97; MP (Cons) Altrincham and Sale West 1997–; PPS to chm Cons Pty 1999–2000; oppn whip 2000, oppn spokesman on educn and employment 2000–01, oppn frontbench spokesman on educn and skills 2001–03, PPS to Rt Hon Michael Howard, QC, MP 2003–; memb Select Ctee on Educn and Employment 1997–2001; memb 1922 Exec Ctee 1998–2000, sec Cons Backbench Educn and Employment Ctee 1997–2000; vice-patron Friends of Rosie; memb Advsy Cncl Centre for Policy Studies; *Recreations* family, garden; *Style*— Graham Brady, Esq, MP; ✉ House of Commons, London SW1A 0AA (tel 020 7219 4604, fax 020 7219 1649)

BRADY, Janet Mary (Jan); da of Allan Frederick Mount, MBE (d 2006), of Oxford, and Doreen Margaret, *née* Hicks; *b* 26 February 1956; *Educ* Rochester GS, Medway and Maidstone Coll of Technol; *Career* legal asst Mobil Oil 1974–77, tax asst Marathon Oil 1977–81, account dir Sterling PR 1982–85, dir PR American Express (UK and Ireland) 1985–87, fndr dir Kinnear PR 1988–89, chief exec Cadogan Management Ltd 1994–95 (md 1989–94), chm Specialtours Ltd 1990–95, md The Albermarle Connection 1995–99; co sec Oxford Sch of Osteopathy 1999–2001; co sec and chief exec SportsAid Southern Region 2001–04; chm Women in Mgmnt 1991–94, pres Soc of Consumer Affrs Professionals UK 1993; gen mangr Mill Court Clinical Centre Oxford Brookes Univ 1999–2001; advsr Independent Public Relations 1999–, sr exec coach and mangr of reputations (people, products and plcs); advsr: Br Sports Assoc for the Disabled (now DSE) 1990–99, East London Partnership 1991–98, Spencer House 1991–, Groundwork UK 1997–2000; dir: Bulgarian Period Properties 2005–, Pest Properties Kft 2006–; ind memb Heathrow Airport Conslt Ctee 1998–2005; *Recreations* stonemasonry, landscape gardening, writing, healing; *Clubs* Bluebird; *Style*— Ms Jan Brady; ✉ 23 Lyne Road, Kidlington, Oxford OX5 1AE (tel 01865 376958, e-mail reputation@swissmail.org)

BRADY, (Helen) Joan; da of Robert Alexander Brady (d 1963), and Mildred Alice, *née* Edie (d 1965); *b* 4 December 1939; *Educ* Columbia Univ (Phi Beta Kappa); *m* 23 Sept 1963, Dexter Wright Masters, s of Thomas Davis Masters; 1 s (Alexander Wright b 12 Oct 1965); *Career* author; formerly dancer: San Francisco Ballet 1955–57, NYC Ballet 1960; awarded Nat Endowment for the Arts (Washington) 1986; *Books* The Impostor (1979), The Unmaking of a Dancer (1982), Theory of War (1993, Whitbread Novel of the Year 1993, Whitbread Book of the Year 1994, Prix de Meilleur Livre Etranger 1995), Prologue (1994), Death Comes For Peter Pan (1996), The Emigre (1999), Bleedout (2005); *Style*— Ms Joan Brady; ✉ c/o John Saddler, The Saddler Literary Agency, 9 Curzon Road, London W5 1NE (tel 020 8991 8082, e-mail js-kg@tiscali.co.uk)

BRADY, Karren; da of Terry Brady, of Enfield, and Rita, *née* Chambers; *b* 4 April 1969; *Educ* Poles Convent Sch, Alderham Sch; *m* 1995, Paolo (Paul) Peschisolido; *Career* jr exec Saatchi & Saatchi 1987–88, sales exec London Broadcasting Company (LBC) 1988–89, mktg and sales dir Sport Newspapers Ltd 1989–93, md Birmingham City Football Club plc 1993–; non-exec dir: Mothercare 2003–, Channel 4 2004–, Kerrang! Radio 2004– (chm); memb Bd Sport England 2005–; *Style*— Miss Karren Brady; ✉ Birmingham City Football Club plc, St Andrews' Ground, Birmingham B9 4NH

BRADY, Prof Sir (John) Michael; kt (2004); s of John Brady, OBE, and Priscilla Mansfield, *née* Clark; *b* 30 April 1945; *Educ* Prescot GS, Univ of Manchester (BSc, MSc), ANU (PhD); *m* 2 Oct 1967, Naomi, *née* Friedlander; 2 da (Sharon b 1971, Carol b 1973); *Career* sr lectr Univ of Essex 1978–80 (lectr 1970–78), sr res scientist MIT 1980–85, prof Univ of Oxford 1985–; memb Bd of Dirs: GCS, Miranda Solutions, Oxford Instruments, AEA Technology; dep chm Oxford Instruments plc 2000–; founding ed International Journal of Robotics Research 1981–99, ed Artificial Intelligence; Hon DUniv: Essex 1996, Manchester 1998, Liverpool 1999, Southampton 1999, Paul Sabatier Toulouse 2000; MIEEE, FRSA, FIEE, FREng 1992, FRS 1997; *Books* Theory of Computer Science (1975), Computer Vision (1981), Robot Motion (1983), Computational Models of Discourse (1983), Robotics (1985), Robotics Science (1989), Mammographic Image Analysis (1999); *Recreations* Dickens, wine, Everton FC; *Style*— Prof Sir Michael Brady, FRS, FREng; ✉ Department of Engineering Science, University of Oxford, Ewert House, Ewert Place, Summertown, Oxford OX2 7BZ (tel 01865 280930, fax 01865 280922, e-mail jmb@robots.ox.ac.uk)

BRADY, Most Rev Sean; *see:* Armagh, Archbishop of (RC)

BRAGG, (Henry) John; s of Henry Bragg, of Torquay, Devon; *b* 28 November 1929; *Educ* Torquay GS, Chelsea Poly, Univ of London; *m* 1, 1954, Jean, *née* Harris (d 1969); 1 s, 2 da; m 2, 1972, Anthea, da of Kew Shelley, QC; 1 step s, 1 step da; *Career* Nat Serv RAMC 1951–53; Glaxo Laboratories 1953–55, Pfizer Ltd 1955–70, md Calor Gas Ltd 1970–80, dir Imperial Continental Gas Assoc 1978–85, md Calor Group 1980–85, dir Advanced Petroleum Technology Ltd 1985–89; chm: Canterbury and Thanet HA 1986–94, E Kent HA 1994–96; memb Professions Allied to Med Whitley Cncl 1990–96; Canterbury Christ Church Univ: govr 1991–2005, chm Bd of Govrs 1999–2005; tstee: Kent Community Housing Tst 1992–, Sandwich United Charities 1992–; mayor of Sandwich 1989–92; memb: Sandwich Town Cncl 1985–, Dover DC 1989–2003; Hon DCL Univ of Kent 1996; hon fell Canterbury Christ Church Univ; FCILT, FRPharmS, DBA;

Recreations golf, books, maps; *Clubs* Royal St George's Golf; *Style*— John Bragg, Esq; ✉ Hideway House, St George's Road, Sandwich, Kent CT13 9LE

BRAGG, Baron (Life Peer UK 1998), of Wigton in the County of Cumbria; Melvyn Bragg; s of Stanley Bragg, of Wigton, Cumbria, and Mary Ethel, *née* Parks; *b* 6 October 1939; *Educ* Nelson Thomlinson GS Wigton, Wadham Coll Oxford (open scholar, MA); *m* 1, 1961, Marie-Elisabeth Roche (decd); 1 da; m 2, 1973, Catherine Mary (see Cate Haste, *qv*), da of Eric Haste, of Crantock, Almondsbury, Avon; 1 da (Hon Alice b 1977), 1 s (Hon Tom b 1980); *Career* writer and broadcaster; general traineeship BBC 1961, prodr on Monitor (BBC) 1963; ed BBC 2 1964: New Release (arts magazine latterly called Review, then Arena), Writers World (documentary), Take It or Leave It (literary programme); presenter: In The Picture (Tyne Tees) 1971, 2nd House (BBC) 1973–77, Start the Week (BBC Radio 4, TRIC Award 1990 and 1994) 1988–98, In Our Time (BBC Radio 4) 1998–, Routes of English (BBC Radio 4) 1999–; presenter and ed: Read All About It (BBC) 1976–77, South Bank Show (ITV) 1978– (BAFTA Prix Italia 5 times, TV Music ad Arts Programme of the Year TV and Radio Industry Awards 2000), Adventure of English (also writer, ITV); dir LWT Productions 1992, controller Arts Dept LWT 1990– (head of arts 1982–90), chm Border Television 1990–96 (dep chm 1985–90); govr LSE 1997–, chllr Univ of Leeds 1999–; pres MIND 2002–; occasional contrib Observer, Sunday Times and Guardian, weekly column Times 1996–98; memb RSL 1977–80, pres Nat Campaign for the Arts; Hon DUniv Open Univ 1988, Hon LLD Univ of St Andrews 1993; Hon DLitt: Liverpool 1986, Lancaster 1990, CNAA 1990, South Bank Univ 1997, Univ of Leeds 2000, Univ of Bradford 2000, Queen's Univ Belfast 2005; Hon DCL Univ of Northumbria 1994; Hon DSc: UMIST 1998, Brunel Univ 2000; Hon DA Univ of Sunderland 2001; hon fell Lancashire Poly; Domus fell St Catherine's Coll Oxford 1990, hon fell Library Assoc 1994, hon fell Wadham Coll Oxford 1995, hon fell Univ of Wales Cardiff 1996; FRSL, FRTS; *Awards* John Llewelyn Rhys Award and PEN Awards for Fiction, BAFTA Richard Dimbleby Award for Outstanding Contribution to TV 1987, RTS Gold Medal 1989, winner BAFTA Huw Wheldon Award for Best Arts Programme or Series (for An Interview with Dennis Potter) 1994, winner BAFTA for Debussy film (with Ken Rusell), Radio Broadcaster of the Year (for In Our Time and Routes of English) Broadcasting Press Guild Radio Awards 1999, VLV Award - Best Individual Contributor to Radio (for In Our Time and Routes of English) 2000, VLV Award - Best New Radio Series (for Routes of English) 2000; *Novels* For Want of a Nail (1965), The Second Inheritance (1966), Without a City Wall (1968), The Hired Man (1969), A Place in England (1970), The Nerve (1971), Josh Lawton (1972), The Silken Net (1974), A Christmas Child (1977), Autumn Manoeuvres (1978), Kingdom Come (1980), Love and Glory (1983), The Cumbrian Trilogy (1984, comprising The Hired Man, A Place in England and Kingdom Come), The Maid of Buttermere (1987), A Time to Dance (1991, BBC TV series 1992), Crystal Rooms (1992), Credo: An Epic Tale of Dark Age Britain (1996), The Soldier's Return (1999, W H Smith Literary Award 2000), A Son of War (2001), Crossing the Lines (2003); *Non fiction* Land of the Lakes (1983), Laurence Olivier (1984), Rich (1988, biog of Richard Burton), Speak for England - oral history of England since 1900 (1976), Ingmar Bergman: The Seventh Seal (1996), On Giant's Shoulders (1998), The Adventure of English (2003); *Musicals* Mardi Gras, Orion (TV, 1976), The Hired Man (W End 1985, Ivor Novello Award 1985); *Screenplays* Isadora, Jesus Christ Superstar, The Music Lovers, Clouds of Glory, Play Dirty; *Stage Play* King Lear in New York 1992; *Recreations* walking, books; *Clubs* Garrick; *Style*— The Rt Hon the Lord Bragg; ✉ 12 Hampstead Hill Gardens, London NW3 2PL; The South Bank Show, The London Television Centre, Upper Ground, London SE1 9LT (tel 020 7261 3128, fax 020 7261 3299, telex 918123)

BRAGGE, Master; Nicolas William; s of Norman Hugh Bragge (d 2001), and Nicolette Hilda, *née* Simms (d 1989); *b* 13 December 1948, Ashford, Kent; *Educ* S Kent Coll of Technol Ashford, Holborn Coll of Law London (LLB), Inns of Court Sch of Law; *m* 22 Dec 1973, Pamela Elizabeth Brett; 3 s (Thomas Hereward b 1976, Christopher Joseph b 1980, Alasdair Charles b 1986); *Career* visiting lectr in law Poly of Central London 1970–73; called to the Bar Inner Temple (Gray's Inn) 1972; in practice at Intellectual Property and Chancery Bars 1973–97; a dep master High Court (Chancery Div) 1993–97, master of the Supreme Court (Chancery Div) 1997–; pt/t chm: Social Security Appeal Tbnls 1990–97, Disability Appeal Tbnls 1992–97; a dep social security cmmr 1996–2000; an ed Civil Procedure 2000–; author of various articles on legal and historical subjects; Freeman City of London 1970, memb Court of Assts Guild of Freemen of the City of London 2005–, Master Worshipful Co of Cutlers 2003–04; *Clubs* City Livery; *Style*— Master Bragge; ✉ Thomas More Building, Royal Courts of Justice, Strand, London WC2A 2LL

BRAHAM, Philip John Cofty; s of Ronald Marcus Braham, of Innellan, Argyll, and Dorothy May, *née* Cofty; *b* 8 April 1959; *Educ* Bearsden Acad, Duncan of Jordanstone Coll of Art Dundee (Br Cncl scholar, Dip Fine Art), Royal Acad of Fine Art The Hague (Greenshields Award, special commendation for postgrad studies); *m* 1, (m dis), Barbara, *née* Campbell; 1 da (Robyn b 13 March 1987); m 2, 2 Aug 2007, Katherine, *née* Ayres; *Career* artist; visiting artist UCLA 1981–82; subject of various exhibition catalogues; lectr in fine art Duncan of Jordanstone College of Art Dundee 2000–; *Solo Exhibitions* Main Fine Art Glasgow 1984, The Scottish Gallery Edinburgh 1985, 1988 and 2005, Glasgow Art Centre 1987, The Raab Gallery London 1989, 1992, 1994 and 1995, Compass Gallery Glasgow 1993 and 1999, Galerie Christian Dam Copenhagen 1994, Galerie Christian Dam Oslo 1997, Boukamel Contemporary Art London 1997, 2000 and 2003, Talbot Rice Gallery Edinburgh 2000, Osborne Samuel Gallery London 2005; *Group Exhibitions* incl: The Human Touch (Fischer Fine Art London) 1985, Artists at Work (Edinburgh Festival Event) 1986, The Vigorous Imagination (Nat Gallery of Modern Art Edinburgh) 1987, Metamorphosis (Raab Gallery London and Berlin) 1989, Landscape and Cityscape (Raab Gallery London) 1990, Cimal (Lucas Gallery Valencia) 1990, Galerie Bureaux et Magasins Ostend 1991, Scottish Art in the 20th Century (Royal W of England Acad Bristol) 1991, Scottish Painters (Flowers East London) 1993, Visions of Albion - Aspects of British Landscape I, II and III (Collyer-Bristow Gallery London) 1992, 1993 and 1994, The Power of the Image (Martin Gropius Bau Berlin) 1995, Aspects of Landscape (Scottish Gallery) 1996, Love and Poetry (Tobias Hirschmann Frankfurt) 1996, Aspects of Landscape (The Scottish Gallery) 1996, The Vigorous Imagination Ten Years on (The Scottish Gallery) 1997, International Kunst (Galerie Christian Dam Copenhagen) 1997, Artaid 98 (City Art Centre Edinburgh) 1998, Art from Scotland (Forbes Building NY) 1998, Art and Nature (Botanic Gardens Cagliari) 1998, Mountain (Wolverhampton Art Gallery and Museum) 1999, New European Artists (Sotheby's Amsterdam) 2001, Artaid (London) 2002, Demarco 40th Anniversary Exhibition (City Arts Centre Edinburgh) 2003, The Call of the Sea (Open Eye Gallery Edinburgh) 2005; *Collections* incl: Scottish Arts Cncl, Scottish Nat Gallery of Modern Art, Aberdeen Art Gallery, BBC, The Contemporary Arts Soc, RCP (Edinburgh), Life Assoc of Scotland, Educnl Inst of Scotland, Fleming Holdings, Texaco Holdings, Rainbow GmbH, Dundee Art Gallery, The City Arts Centre Edinburgh, Pallant House Gallery, Scottish Exec Edinburgh; *Awards* incl: EIS Award 1985, SAC Award 1989, RSA Guthrie Award 1995, Bursary for Research Friends of the Royal Scottish Acad 2003; *Recreations* fitness, walking, music; *Clubs* Scottish Malt Whisky Soc; *Style*— Philip Braham, Esq; ✉ c/o BCA Gallery, 5 Wetherby Gardens, London SW5 0JN (tel 020 7373 0900, e-mail art@bca-gallery.com)

BRAHAMS, Diana Joyce; da of late Gustave Arnold, and late Rita, *née* Rosenberg; *b* 18 February 1944; *Educ* Roedean Sch Johannesburg, Queen's Coll Harley St London; *m* 14 June 1964, Malcolm Henry Brahams, s of Reginald Brahams; 2 s (Nigel Robert b 20 Aug 1966, Gareth Edmund b 25 April 1970), 1 da (Catherine Sophie b 16 July 1968); *Career* called to the Bar Middle Temple 1972; tenant in chambers of John Hendy QC (specialising in clinical negligence, personal injuries and product liability suits); legal practitioner, freelance writer and lectr specialising in med and the law; contrib to: legal and property jls 1977–86, various medical and scientific jls 1981–; legal corr The Lancet 1981–2001, ed Medico-legal Jl 1983–; fndr memb: HealthWatch; memb: Medico-Legal Soc, Professional Negligence Bar Assoc (PNBA), Personal Injury Bar Assoc (PIBA), Assoc of Personal Injury Lawyers (APIL); *Books* contrib: The Law and You (1987), Encyclopaedia Britannica's Medical and Health Annual (1985, 1986, 1989 and 1990), No Fault Compensation in Medicine (1989), Benzodiazepines - Current Concepts (1990), Human Genetic Information, Science Law and Ethics (1990), Orthogeriatrics (1991), Pharmaceutical Medicine (1993), Oxford Medical Companion (1994), Nursing Law & Ethics (1995), Medico-Legal Essentials in Health Care (1996); *Recreations* theatre, travel, reading, portrait painting and drawings, antiques, pictures (esp Victorian), going to and having parties; *Style*— Mrs Diana Brahams; ✉ Old Square Chambers, 10–11 Bedford Row, London WC1R 4BU (tel 020 7269 0300, fax 020 7405 1387, e-mail brahams@oldsquarechambers.co.uk)

BRAIDEN, Prof Paul Mayo; s of Isaac Braiden (d 1966), and Lilian, *née* Mayo; *b* 7 February 1941; *Educ* Dudley GS, Univ of Sheffield (BEng, MEng, PhD); *m* 30 Aug 1993, Lesley, *née* Howard; *Career* Speedicut res scholar Firth Brown Tool Ltd Sheffield 1965–68, asst prof and Ford Fndn fell Dept of Mechanical Engrg Carnegie-Mellon Univ Pittsburgh 1968–70, sr and princ sci offr AERE 1970–76, Univ of Durham 1976–83 (lectr and sr lectr Dept of Engrg Sci, tutor Trevelyan Coll); Univ of Newcastle upon Tyne: head Dept of Mechanical Materials and Manufacturing Engrg 1992–97, Sir James Woodeson prof of mfrg engrg 1983–, John Holmes meml lectr 1989; chm: NE Sector Working Pty on Advanced Mfrg Technol DTI 1986–88, N Region IProdE 1988–90; SERC: chm Ctee of Engrg Design 1990–94, memb Electro-Mechanical Ctee 1989–91, memb Innovative Manufacturing Engrg Panel, memb Engrg Bd 1990–91, memb Engrg Res Ctee 1991–94; Royal Acad of Engrg: hon sec for Mechanical Subjects 1997–2000, memb Cncl 1997–2000; memb Nat Ctee Methodist Hymn Book Revision 1979–82; MInstP 1976, FIMechE 1979, FIProdE 1981, FREng 1994; *Recreations* music (especially opera and oratorio), trained tenor voice, cycling, skiing; *Style*— Prof Paul Braiden, FREng; ✉ School of Mechanical and Systems Engineering, University of Newcastle upon Tyne, Stephenson Building, Claremont Road, Newcastle upon Tyne NE1 7RU (tel 0191 222 6210, fax 0191 222 8600, telex 53654 UNINEW G)

BRAILSFORD, Hon Lord (Sidney) Neil; s of Sidney James Brailsford, of Edinburgh, and Jean Thelma More, *née* Leishman; *b* 15 August 1954; *Educ* Daniel Stewart's Coll Edinburgh, Univ of Stirling (BA), Univ of Edinburgh (LLB); *m* 7 Sept 1984, Elaine Nicola, yr da of late John Mausie Robbie; 3 s (Sidney Joshua Lawrence b 25 Jan 1995, Nathaniel Oliver Robbie b 29 July 1996, Samuel James Liberty b 11 July 1999); *Career* apprentice Messrs Biggart Baillie & Gifford, WS Edinburgh and Glasgow 1979–80, admitted to Faculty of Advocates 1981 (treas 2000–), standing jr counsel Dept of Agric and Fisheries in Scot 1987–92, called to the English Bar Lincoln's Inn 1990, QC (Scot) 1994, advocate depute 1999–2000, senator Coll of Justice 2006–; sec Advocates' Business Law Gp 1988–; chm Discipline Ctee ICAS 2003–; memb Ct Univ of Stirling 2001–06; *Recreations* swimming, travel, food and wine, history (particularly American history and politics); *Clubs* New (Edinburgh); *Style*— The Hon Lord Brailsford; ✉ 29 Warriston Crescent, Edinburgh EH3 (tel 0131 556 8320); c/o Advocates' Library, Parliament House, Edinburgh EH1 1RF (tel 0131 226 5071, fax 0131 225 3642, e-mail lord.brailsford@scotcourts.gov.uk); 135 Kidder Hill Road, Grafton, Vermont 05146, USA (tel 00 1 802 843 2120, fax 00 1 802 843 2118)

BRAIN, 2 Baron (UK 1962); Sir Christopher Langdon Brain; 2 Bt (UK 1954); s of 1 Baron, DM, FRS, FRCP, FRCPI, FRCPE (d 1966), and Stella, *née* Langdon-Down (d 1993); *b* 30 August 1926; *Educ* Leighton Park Sch Reading, New Coll Oxford (MA); *m* 1953, Susan Mary, da of George Philip Morris; 3 da (Hon Nicola Dorothy (Hon Mrs Bashforth) b 1955, Hon (Fiona) Janice (Hon Mrs Proud) b 1958, Hon Naomi Melicent (Hon Mrs Kemp) b 1960); *Heir* bro, Dr Michael C Brain, *qv*; *Career* mgmnt consltr; various posts in photographic industry; RPS: gen mangr 1982–84, memb of Ct 1988–90 and 1992–98; memb: British Copyright Cncl 1989–2001, British Photographers Liaison Ctee 1989–98 (chm 1991–97), Devon Care Tst 1994 (chm 1996–99); past memb House of Lords: Euro Sub-Ctee 1990–97, Euro Select Ctee 1991–95, Science & Technol Sub-Ctee 1997–98; Liveryman Worshipful Co of Weavers (Upper Bailiff 1984–85); *Recreations* sailing, fly fishing; *Clubs* Oxford and Cambridge Sailing Soc, Royal Photographic Soc (ARPS); *Style*— The Rt Hon the Lord Brain; ✉ Alexandra House, 8 Cross Street, Moretonhampstead, Devon TQ13 8NL

BRAIN, Dr (the Hon) Michael Cottrell; s of 1 Baron Brain (d 1966), and hp of bro, 2 Baron Brain, *qv*; *b* 6 August 1928; *Educ* Leighton Park Sch Reading, New Coll Oxford (MA, BCh, DM), London Hosp; *m* 1960, Hon Elizabeth Ann, da of Baron Tangley, KBE (Life Peer, d 1973); 2 da (Hilary Catherine (Mrs Peter Cook) b 1961, Philippa Harriet (Mrs Armando Teves) b 1963), 1 s (Thomas Russell b 1965); *Career* Capt RAMC 1956–58; physician Hammersmith Hosp 1966–69, prof of med McMaster Univ Canada 1969–94 (now emeritus); Univ of Calgary Canada: hon prof of med 1995–2003, hon research prof of biochemistry and molecular biology 2003–; FRCP, FRCP(C); *Recreations* reading; *Style*— Dr Michael C Brain; ✉ 3215 1st Street, SW, Calgary, Alberta, Canada T2S 1P9 (tel 00 1 403 287 3386, fax 00 1 403 243 1468, e-mail brainmc@shaw.ca)

BRAIN, Prof Paul Fredric; s of Frederick Ernest Brain, of Manchester, and Ada, *née* Squirell; *b* 1 July 1945; *Educ* Stretford Coll Manchester, Univ of Hull (BSc, PhD); *m* 4 July 1975, Sonja, da of Johannes Antonius Quirinus Strijbos, of Rotterdam, Holland; 2 s (Vincent Fredric b 1976, Daniel Robert b 1983); *Career* fellowship Univ of Sheffield 1970–71; Dept of Zoology Univ of Wales Swansea: lectr 1971–78, sr lectr 1978–83, reader 1983–87, personal chair in zoology 1987–; head Sch of Biology Univ of Wales Swansea 1995–98; visiting prof in psychology Univ of Hawaii 1986–90, visiting prof in zoology Univ of Kebangsaan Malaysia 1987; vice-pres: Laboratory Animal Science Assoc 1992–96, Assoc for Study of Animal Behaviour; pres Int Soc for Res on Aggression 1982–84; vice-chm Inst of Biology 2002–07; sec Nat Conf of Univ Profs 1996–1999, chm Heads of Univ Biological Scis 1999–2003; Quality Assurance Agency (QAA): assessor Organismal Biosciences 1998–2000, memb Benchmark Panel for Biosciences 2000–06, memb Benchmark Steering Gp 2003–; St Vincent (Italy) Int Prize for Med 1980; FIBiol; *Books* numerous incl: Hormones and Aggression Vol I (1977), Alcohol and Aggression (1986), Ethoexperimental Approaches to the Study Behaviour (with R J Blanchard and S Parmigiani, 1989), Fear and Defence (1989), Heterotypical Behaviour in Man and Animals (jtly, 1991); *Recreations* travel, reading, photography, marathon running; *Style*— Prof Paul Brain; ✉ Department of Biological Sciences, University of Wales Swansea, Swansea SA2 8PP (tel 01792 295444, e-mail p.f.brain@swansea.ac.uk)

BRAIN, Rt Rev Terence John; *see:* Salford, Bishop of (RC)

BRAIN, Dr Timothy John; QPM (2002); s of Roy Brain, of Kingswood, Bristol, and Pearl, *née* Batt (d 1999); *b* 13 July 1954; *Educ* Rodway Sch Bristol, Univ of Wales Aberystwyth (BA, PhD); *m* 19 Oct 1985, Elisabeth Anne, da of Jack Row; 1 s (Richard Timothy John b 31 May 1989); *Career* Avon & Somerset Constabulary 1978–90: Constable 1978, Sgt 1982, Inspr 1983, Chief Inspr 1989 (staff offr to Asst Chief Constable); Hants Constabulary 1990–94: Supt Basingstoke 1990, head Force Re-organisation Team 1993; West Midlands Police 1994–98: Asst Chief Constable (Community Affrs) 1994, Asst Chief Constable (Ops) 1996; Glos Constabulary 1998–: Dep Chief Constable 1998, Chief Constable 2001–; chm

Chief Police Officers' Staff Assoc (CPOSA), memb ACPO 1994– (chm Fin Ctee, spokesperson on prostitution and related vice matters); chm: Br Police Rugby, Br Police Symphony Orch; prof London South Bank Univ 2006; Univ of Wales Aberystwyth: visiting fell 2007, memb Advsy Bd Sch of Mgmnt and Busines Studies, memb Advsy Bd Dept of History and Welsh History; memb Ralph Vaughan Williams Soc; memb Ctee Friends of the Soldiers of Glos Museum 2006; active memb C of E; USAF (Europe) Medal of Distinction 2003; FRSA 2004; *Publications* Operational Policing Review (co-author, 1990); *Recreations* church music, classical music, history, rugby union; *Style*— Dr Timothy Brain, QPM; ✉ Gloucester Constabulary Headquarters, 1 Waterwells, Waterwells Drive, Quedgeley, Gloucester GL2 2AN (tel 01242 276008, fax 01242 276176)

BRAITHWAITE, Althea; da of Air Vice-Marshal Francis Joseph St George Braithwaite (d 1956), and Rosemary, *née* Harris (Lady Earle (d 1978)); *b* 20 June 1940; *Educ* Felixstowe Coll; *m* 1, 1966 (m dis 1974), Malcolm Gordon Graham-Cameron; 1 s (Duncan Charles b 1968); m 2, 1979, Edward James Parker; *Career* artist, writer and illustrator of about 230 books for children 1968–; specialises in information books covering numerous topics; fndr and managing ed Dinosaur Publications Ltd (sold to Collins 1984); artist; first solo exhbn Painted Furniture 1997, Painted Glass 2002, Kiln Fused Glass 2005 and 2007, now specialising in fused and stained glass exhibited in galleries in Lincoln, Stamford and East Anglia incl Stained Glass Museum Ely 2004; *Style*— Ms Althea Braithwaite; ✉ The Studio at Beechcroft House, Over, Cambridge CB4 5NE (e-mail althea@altheabraithwaite.net, website www.altheabraithwaite.net)

BRAITHWAITE, Andrew; s of Norman Braithwaite (d 2005), and Dorina Cox, *née* Soleri; *b* 23 October 1959, Bromley, Kent; *Educ* St Olave's GS, Univ of Southampton (LLB), Nottingham Trent Univ; *m* July 2006, Nicola Webb; *Career* admitted slr 1985; articled clerk Ingledew Brown Bennison & Garrett 1983, slr Stein, Swede, Jay & Bibring (now Finers) 1985 (ptnr 1986), ptnr Wansbroughs (now Beachcrofts) 1989 (head of company commercial 1993), ptnr and head of commercial Osborne Clarke 1997–; chair Bristol Interactive Cluster 2000–04; memb Law Soc 1985, affiliate Br Franchise Assoc 1995; *Recreations* travelling, walking, good food (cooking and eating); *Style*— Andrew Braithwaite, Esq; ✉ Osborne Clarke, 2 Temple Back, Temple Quay, Bristol BS1 6EG (tel 0117 917 4178, fax 0117 917 4179)

BRAITHWAITE, Michael; *b* 10 December 1937; *Educ* City Univ (BSc); *m* 4 Feb 1967, (Pamela) Margaret; 1 da (Sally b 4 Oct 1969), 1 s (James b 7 Jan 1971); *Career* UKAEA 1958–69; ptnr: Deloitte & Touche (formerly Touche Ross) 1969–97, Braithwaite Associates 1997–; Liveryman Worshipful Co of Info Technologists 1988; CEng, MBCS, FInstMC; *Recreations* skiing, scuba diving, gardening; *Style*— Michael Braithwaite, Esq; ✉ Thriplow Manor, Thriplow, Royston, Hertfordshire (tel 01763 208053, fax 01763 208054, e-mail michael-braithwaite@msn.com)

BRAITHWAITE, William Thomas Scatchard (Bill); QC (1992); s of John Vernon Braithwaite (d 1975), and Nancy Phyllis Scatchard (d 1995); *b* 20 January 1948; *Educ* Gordonstoun, Univ of Liverpool (LLB); *m* Sheila, *née* Young; 1 da (Dawn Plint), 1 s (Ross Thomas Vernon); *Career* called to the Bar Gray's Inn 1970, pupil to His Hon Judge Arthur, currently in personal injury litigation practice; memb: Euro Brain Injury Soc, Spinal Injuries Assoc, Headway, Assoc of Personal Injury Lawyers; conslt ed The Quantum of Damages 1995–2004, jt ed Medical Aspects of Personal Injury Litigation; author of articles and lectures on brain and spine litigation in England, Europe and America; *Books* Brain and Spine Injuries - The Fight for Justice; *Recreations* cars and wine; *Style*— Bill Braithwaite, QC; ✉ Exchange Chambers, Pearl Assurance House, Derby Square, Liverpool L2 9XX (tel 0151 236 7747, fax 0151 236 3433, e-mail billbraithwaite.qc@btinternet.com)

BRAKA, Ivor Isaac; s of Joseph Braka, and Margaret Elizabeth, *née* Dodds; *b* 19 December 1954; *Educ* Oundle, Pembroke Coll Oxford (BA); *m* 1991 (m dis 1999), Camilla Mary, da of Duncan Henry Davidson; 1 s (Joseph Duncan b 10 Nov 1996); *Career* art dealer; *Style*— Ivor Braka, Esq; ✉ 63 Cadogan Square, London SW1X 0DY (tel 020 7235 0266)

BRAKE, Thomas (Tom); MP; s of Mike and Judy Brake; *b* 6 May 1962; *Educ* Lycée International Paris, Imperial Coll London (BSc); *m* Candida; 1 da, 1 s; *Career* trainee computer programmer Hoskyns (now Cap Gemini) rising to princ conslt 1983–97, MP (Lib Dem) Carshalton and Wallington 1997– (contested seat 1992); environment spokesman 1997–2001; Lib Dem shadow tport min 2001–03, Lib Dem shadow int devpt sec of state 2003–05, Lib Dem shadow transport sec of state 2005–06, Lib Dem shadow min for Dept of Communities and Local Govt 2006–, Lib Dem London spokesman 2007–; memb: Tport Select Ctee 2002–03, Accommodation and Works Ctee, Franco-Br Parly Relations Gp; cncllr (Lib Dem): London Borough of Hackney (sometime jt lead memb on environment) 1988–90, Sutton (sometime memb Policy and Resources Ctee and vice-chm Policy Sub-Ctee) 1994–98; *Style*— Tom Brake, MP; ✉ Constituency Office, Kennedy House, 5 Nightingale Road, Carshalton, Surrey SM5 2DN (tel 020 8255 8155, fax 020 8395 4453); House of Commons, London SW1A 0AA (tel 020 7219 6491, fax 020 7219 6491, e-mail braket@parliament.uk, website www.tombrake.co.uk)

BRAKEWELL, Jeanette; da of James Joseph Brakewell, of Brindle, Lancs, and Clara May, *née* Scambler; *b* 4 February 1974; *Educ* St Michael's C of E HS Chorley; *Partner* Brook Staples; *Career* three day eventer; achievements (all on Over to You) incl: team Gold medal European Championships 1999, 2001, 2003 and 2005, team Silver medal Olympic Games Sydney 2000, team Bronze medal and individual Silver medal World Equestrian Games 2002, team Silver medal Olympic Games Athens 2004; Horse Trials Support Gp Scholarship 1997, Raymond Brooks-Ward Meml Trophy 1997, British Equestrian Fedn Medal of Honour 2003; *Recreations* skiing, swimming; *Style*— Miss Jeanette Brakewell

BRAMALL, Field Marshal Baron (Life Peer UK 1987), of Bushfield in the County of Hampshire; Edwin Noel Westby; KG (1990), GCB (1979, KCB 1974), OBE (1965), MC (1945) JP (1986); yr s of Maj Edmund Haselden Bramall, RA (d 1964), and Katharine Bridget, *née* Westby (d 1985); bro of Sir Ashley Bramall (d 1999); *b* 18 December 1923; *Educ* Eton; *m* 1949, Dorothy Avril Wentworth, only da of Brig-Gen Henry Albemarle Vernon, DSO, JP (ggggs of Henry Vernon by his w Lady Henrietta Wentworth, yst da of 1 Earl of Strafford, Henry Vernon being himself 2 cous of 1 Baron Vernon); 1 s, 1 da; *Career* 2 Lt KRRC 1943, served NW Europe WWII, Japan 1946–47, Middle East 1953–58, Instr Army Staff Coll 1958–61, staff offr to Lord Mountbatten for re-organising MOD 1963–64, served Malaysia during Indonesian confrontation 1965–66 (CO 2 Greenjackets KRRC), cmd 5 Airportable Bde 1967–69, IDC 1970, GOC 1 Div BAOR 1971–73, Lt-Gen 1973, Cdr Br Forces Hong Kong 1973–76, Gen 1976, Col Cmdt 3 Bn Roy Green Jackets 1973–84, Col 2 Gurkhas 1976–86, C-in-C UKLF 1976–78, Vice-Chief Defence Staff (Personnel and Logistics) 1978–79, Chief General Staff 1979–82, ADC Gen to HM The Queen 1979–82, Field Marshal 1982, Chief of the Defence Staff 1982–85; pres Gurkha Bde Assoc 1987–, pres (Army) Not Forgotten Assoc; tstee Imperial War Museum 1983–98 (chm 1989–98); HM Lord-Lt Greater London 1986–98; pres: MCC 1988–89, Greater London Playing Fields Assoc 1990–, London Age Concern; OStJ; *Books* The Chiefs: The Story of the UK Chiefs of Staff (co-author); *Clubs* MCC, Travellers (chm 1998–), Pratt's; *Style*— Field Marshal the Lord Bramall, KG, GCB, OBE, MC; ✉ House of Lords, London SW1A 0PW

BRAMANTE, Gabriele; *b* 11 March 1957, Munich; *Educ* convent boarding sch Germany, Kingston Poly (BA, RIBA student prize, RIBA Lovell meml award, Michael Nadel scholar), Harvard Univ (MAarch, Rotary Fndn grad scholar); *Career* architect; world authority on Japanese architecture, Japan corr for The Architectural Review for 8 years, freelance contrib to magazines worldwide; estab Bramante Architects 1993 (opened German office 2004); projects incl CAB Chessington (BBC Design Award, Int Innovation Award, subject of BBC documentary); guest lectr at univs in Japan, Oxford, Cambridge and London; Woman of the Year 1997; *Books* Willis Faber and Dumas Building by Sir Norman Foster, Guide to Japanese Architecture; contrib to jls, int books and encyclopaedias, own design work published in various books and int magazines; *Style*— Ms Gabriele Bramante; ✉ Bramante Architects, Piloty Weg 5, 82541 Ambach, Bavaria, Germany

BRAMBLE, Roger John Lawrence; DL (Greater London 1986); s of Courtenay Parker Bramble, CIE (d 1987), of Childer Thornton, Cheshire, and Margaret Louise Bramble, MBE (d 1989), da of Sir Henry Lawrence, KCSI; *b* 3 April 1932; *Educ* Eton, King's Coll Cambridge (MA); *Career* cmmnd Coldstream Gds 1951; chm: Lloyd's Brokers, BDB Ltd; memb Lloyd's 1960–2003; dir ENO 1986–98, dir Eng Nat Ballet 1986–2002 (dep chm 1990–99), memb Cncl Nat Opera Studio 2000–, chm Cncl for Dance Educn and Trg 2000–, chm Young Musicians Symphony Orch 2001–; chm Benesh Inst 1986–97; chm of tstees Debtcred 2002–; tstee: Serpentine Gallery 1990–, Albert Meml 1996–2000, Paddington Devpt Tst 1998; cncllr City of Westminster 1968–98, Lord Mayor of Westminster 1985–86; High Sheriff of Gtr London 1999, chm Assoc of High Sheriffs 2001–04; FRSA 1989; Order of the Aztec Eagle Mexico 1985, Order of Merit Qatar 1985, Order of Southern Cross Brazil 1993, Order of the Stella della Solidarieta Italiana 2003; *Recreations* music, farming, languages; *Clubs* Turf, Mark's; *Style*— Roger Bramble, Esq, DL; ✉ 2 Sutherland Street, London SW1V 4LB (tel and fax 020 7828 2439); Sutton Hosey Manor, Long Sutton, Langport, Somerset TA10 9NA

BRAMLEY, Prof Alan Neville; s of Frederick William Bramley (d 1980), of York, and Hilda, *née* Jackson (d 1991); *b* 7 October 1939; *Educ* Archbishop Holgate's GS York 1950–57, Univ of Liverpool (BEng, PhD), Univ of Birmingham; *m* 1961, Georgina Anne, da of Joseph Thornton; 2 s (Richard Gavin b 1964, Charles Julian b 1969), 1 da (Jill Victoria b 1966); *Career* graduate apprentice Rolls Royce Ltd 1960–62, post-doctoral res fell Univ of Birmingham 1965–68, jt lectr in metal forming Depts of Mech Engrg & Metallurgy Univ of Leeds 1968–79 (jt sr lectr 1979–86); Univ of Bath: prof of mechanical engrg and head Design Manufacture Materials & Structures Gp 1986–2000, head Sch of Mechanical Engrg 1987–90, head Dept of Engrg and Applied Science 2000–04; ed Part B Proceedings IMechE Jl of Engrg Manufacture 1989–; CEng 1970, FIMechE 1984, FIET 1987, FInstF 1994; *Publications* author of over 200 papers in learned jls and int conf proceedings on numerical modelling in manufacturing processes; *Recreations* jazz musician; *Style*— Prof Alan Bramley; ✉ Department of Mechanical Engineering, University of Bath, Claverton Down, Bath BA2 7AY (tel 01225 386196, fax 01225 386928, e-mail a.n.bramley@bath.ac.uk)

BRAMLEY, Andrew; s of Peter Bramley (d 1989), of Ridgeway, Derbys, and Tessa Bramley, *qv*, *née* Hardwick; *b* 18 January 1966; *Educ* Henry Fanshawe Sch Derbys; *m* 27 Sept 1998, Carole Rena, da of Colin Mills, of Derby; *Career* mangr family business until 1985; converted Old Vicarage (family home) into restaurant 1985–87; owner and mangr Old Vicarage 1987– (Good Food Guide Newcomer of Year 1988, Derbyshire Restaurant of the Year 1988–90, Egon Ronay star 1988–94 (2 stars 1995–99), Clover Leaf in Ackerman Guide 1990–95, Northern Restaurant of the Year award Chef Magazine 1991, Egon Ronay Dessert of the Year 1998, Michelin star 1999); featured in major Food and Wine Guides; TV and radio appearances; memb: Restaurant Assoc of GB, Sheffield C of C; *Books* Women Chefs of Great Britain (with Tessa Bramley, 1990); *Recreations* cooking, writing, painting; *Style*— Andrew Bramley, Esq; ✉ The Old Vicarage, Ridgeway Moor, Ridgeway, Derbyshire S12 3XW (tel 0114 247 5814, fax 0114 247 7079, e-mail andrew@theoldvicarage.co.uk)

BRAMLEY, Robin Thomas Todhunter; s of E A Bramley (d 1991), and Mary, *née* Todhunter (d 2001); *b* 16 June 1950; *Educ* Ampleforth, Univ of Exeter (LLB); *m* 20 Oct 1973, Patricia Anne, da of Maj E S L Mason (d 1996), of Bungay, Suffolk; 1 da (Henrietta b 1979), 1 s (George b 1982); *Career* chartered surveyor and mediator; landowner and farmer Gillingham Estate, sr ptnr Francis Hornor & Son chartered surveyors Norwich 1992–97 (ptnr 1976–92), ptnr Francis Hornor Brown & Co 1997–2000, ptnr Brown & Co 2000–; dir Consensus Mediation Ltd 2002–; CEDR accredited mediator 1998; memb of Lord Chllr's Panel of Arbitrators 1992; memb: The Broads Authy 1989–99, Norfolk Police Authy 1994–2001; chm: Broads Soc 1986–87, Waveney Harriers 1995–; JP; FRICS 1978, QDR 1996, MCIArb 1999; *Recreations* shooting, riding, fishing, history, conservation; *Clubs* Norfolk, MCC; *Style*— R T T Bramley, Esq; ✉ Hill Farm, Gillingham, Norfolk NR34 0EE (tel 01502 677256, fax 01502 679050)

BRAMLEY, Tessa; da of Howard Hardwick (d 1990), of Coal Aston, S Yorks, and Irene, *née* Barber; *b* 3 April 1939; *Educ* Henry Fanshawe GS, High Storrs GS Sheffield, London Coll of Home Economics, Totley Hall Trg Coll Sheffield (Dip Domestic Science, DipEd); *m* 8 May 1965, Peter Bramley (d 1989), s of Francis Bramley; 1 s (Andrew Bramley, *qv*, b 18 Jan 1966); *Career* teacher and lectr in domestic sci 1963–75, sales and promotion in food business 1975–81, own restaurant (with husband) 1981–, opened Old Vicarage 1987 (Good Food Guide Newcomer of Year 1988, Derbyshire Restaurant of the Year 1988–90, Egon Ronay star 1988–94 (2 stars 1995–99), Clover Leaf in Ackerman Guide 1990–95, Northern Restaurant of the Year award Chef Magazine 1991, Egon Ronay Dessert of the Year 1998, Michelin star 1999–2007); TV presenter: Here's One I Made Earlier 1996 and 1997 (C4), Tessa Bramley's Country Kitchen 1997 (Carlton), Tessa Bramley's Seasonal Kitchen 1998 (Carlton); Inst of Master Chefs; appeared on Light Lunch 1997 (C4), guest judge on Masterchef 1997 (BBC2), Tessa's Taste Buds (TV series, Carlton Ondigital) 1999–; fell Masterchefs of GB 2003; *Books* Women Chefs of Great Britain (with Andrew Bramley, 1990), The Instinctive Cook (1995), featured in Great British Chefs (II) (1995), A Taste of Tradition (1997), Traditional Puddings (1997), Cassaroles (2000), Perfect Puddings (2002); *Recreations* literature and music; *Style*— Ms Tessa Bramley; ✉ Old Vicarage, Ridgeway Moor, Ridgeway, Derbyshire S12 3XW (tel 0114 247 5814, e-mail eat@theoldvicarage.co.uk)

BRANAGH, Kenneth Charles; s of William Branagh, and Frances Branagh; *b* 10 December 1960, Belfast, NI; *Educ* Meadway Comp Sch Reading, RADA; *Career* actor and dir; assoc memb RADA, Gielgud Golden Quill 2000 (yst ever winner); *Theatre* with RSC 1984–85 (plays incl: Henry V (yst Henry V in RSC history), Hamlet, Love's Labour's Lost), co-fndr (with David Parfitt, *qv*) Renaissance Theatre Co (RTC) 1987 (plays incl: Public Enemy (also writer) 1987, Hamlet 1988, Look Back In Anger 1989, King Lear (also dir) 1990, A Midsummer Night's Dream (also dir) 1990, Uncle Vanya (dir) 1991, Coriolanus 1992); other credits incl: Another Country (Queen's Theatre) London 1982 (SWET Award and Most Promising Newcomer Plays and Players Award), Hamlet (RSC) 1992–93, The Play What I Wrote (dir, West End) 2001, Richard III (Crucible Theatre) 2002, Edmond (Nat Theatre) 2003, Ducktastic (dir, Albery Theatre) 2005; *Television* incl: The Billy Plays 1981–86, Boy in the Bush 1984, Fortunes of War 1987, Look Back in Anger 1989, Conspiracy 2001, Shackleton 2002, Warm Springs 2005; *Film* incl: Coming Through 1985, A Month in the Country 1987, Henry V (also dir and author screenplay) 1989, Dead Again (also dir) 1991, Peter's Friends (also dir and prodr) 1992, Much Ado About Nothing (also dir, prodr and author screenplay) 1993, Frankenstein (also dir and prodr) 1994, Othello 1995, Hamlet (also dir and author screenplay) 1996, The Theory of Flight 1998, The Dance of Shiva 1998, Celebrity 1999, Wild Wild West 1999, Love's Labour's Lost (also dir, prodr and author screenplay) 2000, Rabbit-Proof Fence 2002, Harry Potter and the Chamber of Secrets 2002, Five Children and It 2004; as dir and author screenplay: In the Bleak Midwinter 1995, Listening 2003; *Publications* Public Enemy (1988),

Beginning (1989); *Recreations* reading, playing the guitar; *Style*— Kenneth Branagh; ✉ c/o Kenneth Branagh Limited, Shepperton Studios, Studios Road, Shepperton TW17 0QD (tel 01932 592187, fax 01932 592125)

BRANCH, Prof Michael Arthur; CMG (2000); s of Arthur Frederick Branch (d 1986), and Mahala, *née* Parker; *b* 24 March 1940; *Educ* Shene London, SSEES Univ of London (BA, PhD), Univ of Helsinki; *m* 11 Aug 1963, (Ritva-Riitta) Hannele, da of Erkki Lauri Kari (d 1982), of Heinola, Finland; 3 da (Jane, Jean, Ann); *Career* Univ of London: lectr Finno-Ugrian Studies 1971–73 (asst lectr 1967–71), dir Sch of Slavonic and E Euro Studies 1980–2001, prof of Finnish 1986–2001 (lectr 1973–77, reader 1977–86), fell UCL 2001–, Leverhulme emeritus fell 2004–06; Hon DPhil Univ of Oulu Finland 1983; Commander of the Finnish Lion Finland 1980, Commander of the Order of Merit Poland 1993, St Mary's Land Cross of Estonia 2000, Grand Duke Gedeminas Cross Lithuania 2002; *Books* A J Sjögren: Travels in the North (1973), Finnish Folk Poetry - Epic (jtly, 1977), Student's Glossary of Finnish (jtly, 1981), Kalevala - translated by W F Kirby (ed, 1985), Edith Södergran (jt ed, 1992), The Great Bear (jtly, 1993), Uses of Tradition (jt ed, 1994), Finland and Poland in the Russian Empire (jt ed, 1995), The Writing of National History and Identity (ed, 1999); *Recreations* walking, forestry; *Clubs* Athenaeum; *Style*— Prof Michael Branch, CMG; ✉ 33 St Donatt's Road, New Cross, London SE14 6NU; Hämeentie 28 A3, 00530 Helsinki, Finland

BRAND, Charles David William; s of Michael Brand, and Laura, *née* Smith (d 1999); *b* 1 July 1954; *Educ* Bryanston, Univ of Reading (BA); *m* 20 Jan 1992, Virginia, da of Baron Bonham-Carter (Life Peer, d 1994); 1 s (Henry), 1 da (Violet); *Career* researcher and prodr LWT 1977–87 (progs incl: Sunday Sunday, James Bond - The First 21 Years, An Audience with Mel Brooks, The World According to Smith and Jones), freelance prodr Free Nelson Mandela Concert 1987, prodr Tiger Television 1988–93 (progs incl: The Movie Life of George, Clive James Meets Jane Fonda, The Driven Man, Life of Python, Funny Business); Tiger Aspect Prodns: md and memb Bd 1993– (exec prodr: Kid in the Corner, Births Marriages and Deaths, Playing the Field, Country House, Streetmate), dir Specialist Factual and US dir Documentary & Factual Programming 2002– (progs incl: Human Mutants, Virtual History, Pinochet in Suburbia, Boris Johnson and the Dream of Rome, The Monastery); exec prodr: Billy Elliott 2000, Lib Dem Party political broadcasts; chair Int Edinburgh Television Festival 2002, memb Exec Ctee MediaGuardian Edinburgh Int Television Festival (MGEITF) 2002–, memb Devpt Bd YCTV, chair Channel of the Year Awards; BAFTA 1990; FRTS 2004 (memb 1991); *Recreations* walking, bicycling, tennis; *Clubs* Groucho; *Style*— Charles Brand, Esq; ✉ Tiger Aspect Productions, 5 Soho Square, London W1V 5DE (tel 020 7544 1688, fax 020 7434 1903, mobile 07785 770509, e-mail charlesbrand@tigeraspect.co.uk)

BRAND, Harriett; da of Sam Brand (d 1969), and Ann Weisberg Brand; *b* Brooklyn, NY; *Educ* Brooklyn Coll, City Univ of NY (BA), INSEAD (MBA); *Career* early career in int marketing and promotion EMI Music; currently sr vice-pres Music MTV Networks Europe & Int (joined 1993); memb Nordoff-Robbins Woman of the Year Ctee; UK Music Industry Woman of the Year 2003; supporter Thrangu Tst (involved with Tibetan Buddhist community in Nepal, Tibet and India); FRGS, FRSA; *Style*— Ms Harriett Brand; ✉ Universal Music, 344–346 Kensington High Street, London W14 8NS (tel 020 7471 5322, mobile 07785 353879, e-mail harriett.brand@umusic.com)

BRAND, Jo; *b* 23 July 1957, Clapham, London; *m* 2 c; *Career* psychiatric nurse until 1988, stand-up comedienne 1988–; *Television* incl: Through the Cakehole 1993, Jo Brand Goes Back to Bedlam 1994, All the Way to Worcester 1996, A Big Slice of Jo Brand 1996, Jo Brand Burns Rubber 1997, Commercial Breakdown 1999, Jo Brand's Hot Potatoes 2002; appearances incl: Question Time 2000, What Not to Wear on the Red Carpet 2003, Comic Relief does Fame Academy 2003, Star Spell 2004, Parkinson 2006; *Film* incl Human Traffic; *Radio* regular panellist on Windbags (BBC Radio 1) 1993–94; *Books* A Load of Old Balls 1995, A Load of Old Ball Crunchers 1997, Sorting Out Billy 2004, It's Different for Girls 2005; *Style*— Ms Jo Brand; ✉ c/o The Richard Stone Partnership, 2 Henrietta Street, London WC2E 8PS (tel 020 7497 0849, fax 020 7497 0869)

BRAND, Dr Paul Anthony; s of Thomas Joseph Brand (d 1994), and Marjorie Jean, *née* Smith (d 1999); *Educ* Hampton GS, Magdalen Coll Oxford (MA, DPhil); *m* 1970, Vanessa Carolyn Alexandra, da of J L Rodrigues; *Career* asst keeper Public Record Office London 1970–76, lectr in law Univ Coll Dublin 1976–83, research fell Inst of Historical Research London 1993–; visiting prof Columbia Univ Law Sch 1995 and 2003, sr research fell All Souls Coll Oxford 1999– (fell 1997–99, visiting fell 1995); Donald W Sutherland prize American Soc for Legal History 1988; treas Pipe Roll Soc, memb Cncl and vice-pres (UK) Selden Soc; memb American Law Inst 2000; Gold medal Irish Legal History Soc 2006; FRHistS 1980, FBA 1998; *Books* The Origins of the English Legal Profession (1992), The Making of the Common Law (1992), The Earliest English Law Reports vols I and II (1996) and vol III (2005), Kings, Barons and Justices: The Making and Enforcement of Thirteenth Century Legislation (2003), Plea Rolls of the Exchequer of the Jews vol VI (2006); *Recreations* theatre, looking at buildings; *Style*— Dr Paul Brand, FBA; ✉ 155 Kennington Road, London SE11 6SF (tel 020 7582 4051); All Souls College, Oxford OX1 4AL (tel 01865 279286, e-mail paul.brand@all-souls.oxford.ac.uk)

BRANDON, (David) Stephen; QC (1996); s of James Osbaldeston Brandon (d 1992), and Dorothy, *née* Wright; *b* 18 December 1950; *Educ* Univ of Nottingham (BA), Keele Univ (LLM); *m* 1987, Helen Beatrice, da of Frank Lee; 1 da (Arabella Beatrice May b 1989); *Career* lectr in law Keele Univ 1975–85, called to the Bar Gray's Inn 1978, in practice at Revenue Bar 1981; *Books* Taxation of Migrant and Non-Resident Companies (1989), Taxation of Non-UK Resident Companies and their Shareholders (2002); *Recreations* art (especially collecting early woodcuts), opera, nurturing woodlands; *Style*— Stephen Brandon, Esq, QC; ✉ Clopton Manor, Clopton, Northamptonshire; 24 Old Buildings, 1st Floor, Tax Chambers, Lincoln's Inn, London WC2A 3UU (tel 020 7242 2744, fax 020 7831 8095)

BRANDRETH, Gyles Daubeney; s of Charles Daubeney Brandreth (d 1982), of London, and Alice, *née* Addison; *b* 8 March 1948; *Educ* Bedales, New Coll Oxford (MA); *m* 8 June 1973, Michele, da of Alec Brown; 1 s (Benet Xan b 1975), 2 da (Saethryd Charity b 1976, Aphra Kendal Alice b 1978); *Career* author, broadcaster, producer and publisher; MP (Cons) City of Chester 1992–97; PPS: to Fin Sec to the Treasy 1993–94, to Sec of State for Nat Heritage 1994–95, to Sec of State for Health 1995, govt whip 1995–96, a Lord Cmmr of HM's Treasy (govt whip) 1996–97; journalist, TV and radio presenter 1969–, ed-at-large Sunday Telegraph Review; writer/performer Zipp! The Musical (Edinburgh Festival Most Popular Show Award 2002, Duchess Theatre London 2003, UK tour 2004), Malvolio in Twelfth Night The Musical 2005; fndr: Nat Teddy Bear Museum Stratford-upon-Avon, Nat Scrabble Championships; vice-pres National Playing Fields Assoc 1993– (appeals chm 1984–88, chm 1989–93); co-curator exhbn of children's writers Nat Portrait Gallery 2002; *Books* various incl: Created in Captivity (1972), Under the Jumper (autobiography, 1993), Who is Nick Saint? (novel, 1996), Venice Midnight (novel, 1998), Breaking the Code: Westminster Diaries 1990–97 (1999), John Gielgud: An Actor's Life (2000), Brief Encounters: Meetings with Remarkable People (2001), Philip and Elizabeth: Portrait of a Marriage (2004), Charles and Camilla: Portrait of a Love Affair (2005), Oscar Wilde and the Candlelight Murders (novel, 2007), Oscar Wilde and the Ring of Blood (2008); *Recreations* sometime holder of world record for longest-ever after-dinner speech (12 1/2 hours); *Style*— Gyles Brandreth, Esq; ✉ c/o International Artistes, 4th Floor, Holborn Hall, London WC1V 7BD (tel 020 7025 0600)

BRANKIN, Rhona; MSP; *b* 19 January 1950; *Educ* Jordanhill Coll Sch Glasgow, Univ of Aberdeen (BEd), Moray House Coll of Educn Edinburgh (Dip); *m*; 2 da; *Career* teacher Dingwall Primary Sch 1975–77, learning support teacher Invergordon Acad 1983–84, teacher South Lodge Primary Sch Invergordon 1984–88, sr teacher learning support Alness Acad 1988–90, princ teacher learning support Inverness HS 1990–94, lectr in special educn needs Northern Coll Dundee 1994–99; MSP (Lab) Midlothian 1999–; dep min: Culture and Sport 1999–2000, Rural Devpt 2000–01; former chair Scottish Lab Pty; memb: Nat Tst for Scotland, Socialist Environment and Resources Assoc, Architectural Heritage Assoc fo Scotland; Hon FRIBA; *Recreations* music, theatre, horse riding, golf, outdoor pursuits; *Style*— Ms Rhona Brankin, MSP; ✉ The Scottish Parliament, Edinburgh EH99 1SP (tel 0131 348 5838, fax 0131 348 5988, e-mail rhona.brankin.msp@scottish.parliament.uk, website www.rhonabrankin.com)

BRANNAN, Tom; s of James Brannan, of Bargeddie, Strathclyde, and Rebecca Brannan (d 1994); *b* 21 August 1951; *Educ* St Patrick's Secdy Sch Coatbridge, Univ of Strathclyde (BA); *m* 1, (m dis); 2 da (Kirsty b 14 Dec 1976, Sarah b 11 Aug 1979); m 2, 23 Oct 1999 (re-married), Jacqueline Blenkinsop; *Career* export exec Black & Decker 1971–75, sales dir Hestair Group 1975–81, sales and mktg dir Shelvoke & Drewry 1981–82, mktg dir Lancer Boss 1982–84, client servs dir Primary Contact Advertising (Ogilvy Group) 1984–95; currently: dir YesCity Ltd, Vigorat Ltd, mktg dir Initia Ltd; mktg advsr and speaker for various charities, business gps and other bodies; nat chm CIM 1996; FCIM 1990 (MCIM 1983), FRSA 1996, Chartered Marketer 1998; *Books* The Effective Advertiser (1993), A Practical Guide to Integrated Marketing Communications (1995, 2 edn 1998), Gower Handbook of Marketing (contrib), Profit from Strategic Marketing (contrib); *Recreations* fly fishing, reading, antiquities, antiques; *Style*— Tom Brannan, Esq; ✉ 20A Freegrove Road, London N7 9JN (e-mail tom.brannan@yescity.biz)

BRANSON, Nigel Anthony Chimmo; JP (City of London 1996); s of Anthony Hugh Chimmo (Tony) Branson (d 1989), and Isobel Mary Mearns (d 2000); *b* 1 July 1942; *Educ* Tonbridge; *m* 10 July 1971, Nancy Jane, da of George Sexton Mooney III (d 1980), of Boston, MA; 1 da (Jessica b 1973), 1 s (Douglas b 1974); *Career* Sedgwick Group plc: joined London 1960, Johannesburg 1964–65, Lusaka 1966–68, Edinburgh 1973–79, jt md Sedgwick UK Risk Services Ltd 1996–97, Lark Insurance Broking Group 1997–2000; underwriter Lloyd's 1983–97; vice-chm Haberdashers' Aske's Hatcham City Tech Coll 1995–2002 (govr 1991–2002, responsible offr 1996–2000); chm: Audit Ctee Grant Maintained Schs Fndn 1997–98 (also tstee), Red Cross City Christmas Fayre 1999, SW Kent PCT 2004–06; vice-chm Kent and Medway Strategic HA 2002–04, md Elite Models Ltd 2001–, dir Cathedral Enterprises Ltd 2001–04; tstee: REMAP 1997–2004, English Schs Orch 1998–, League of Mercy 1999–, Royal Humane Soc 2003–05, Reeve Fndn 2004–06; govr Bow Boys' Sch 2002–04; Sheriff City of London 2000; memb Ct of Common Cncl: Bassishaw Ward 1996–99, Langbourn Ward 2002–06; Freeman: City of London 1969, Worshipful Co of Haberdashers 1970 (memb Ct of Assts 1990, Master 2006–07), Worshipful Co of Broderers 2000 (memb Ct of Assts 2004); *Recreations* Lake District, walking, reading, trout fishing, golf; *Clubs* Wildernesse, Pickwick, Langbourn Ward (chm 2000), Wards; *Style*— Nigel Branson, Esq; ✉ Thornhill, Oak Lane, Sevenoaks, Kent TN13 1UF (mobile 07850 332680)

BRANSON, Sir Richard Charles Nicholas; kt (2000); s of Edward James Branson, and Evette Huntley, *née* Flindt; bro of Vanessa Branson, *qv*; *b* 18 July 1950; *Educ* Stowe; *m* 1, 1969 (m dis), Kristen Tomassi; m 2, 20 Dec 1989, Joan Sarah Drummond, da of John Templeman (d 1988), of Glasgow, Scotland; 1 s (Sam Edward Charles b 12 Aug 1985), 1 da (Holly Katy b 20 Nov 1981); *Career* ed Student magazine 1968–69; fndr: Student Advsy Centre (now Help) 1970, Virgin Mail-Order Co 1969, Virgin Retail 1970, Virgin Records 1973, Virgin Atlantic Airways 1984, Voyager Group Ltd 1986; chm and chief exec: Virgin Management, Virgin Retail Group, Virgin Communications, Virgin Holdings, Virgin Radio 1993–97, Virgin Direct 1995–, V2 Music 1996–, Virgin Rail 1996–; life pres Virgin Music 1992–; tstee: Healthcare Fndn (fndr 1987), Charity Projects; patron: Nat Holiday Fund, Paul O'Gorman Fndn, Trevor Jones Tst, London Sch for Performing Arts & Technol; pres Br Disabled Water Ski Assoc, hon vice-pres Operation Raleigh, hon memb Ctee The Friends of the Earth; capt Atlantic Challenger II, winner Blue Riband for fastest crossing of the Atlantic by boat 1986, world record crossings of Atlantic and Pacific by hot air balloon with Per Lindstrand 1987 and 1991; Excellent Hon Prof of Economics Miyazaki Sangyo Keiei Univ Japan, Key to the City of NY, hon Japanese citizen (City of Miyakanojo); Hon DTech Loughborough 1993; *Books* Losing my Virginity: The Autobiography (1998); *Recreations* tennis, skiing, swimming, ballooning; *Clubs* Roof Garden (proprietor), British Balloon and Airship; *Style*— Sir Richard Branson; ✉ Virgin Management Ltd, 120 Campden Hill Road, London W8 7AR

BRANSON, Vanessa Gay; da of Edward James Branson, of Shamley Green, Surrey, and Evette Huntley, *née* Flindt; sis of Sir Richard Branson, *qv*; *b* 3 June 1959; *Educ* Box Hill Sch, New Acad of Art Studies; *m* 1983, Robert Devereux, s of Humphrey Devereux; 3 s (Noah Edward b 1987, Louis-Robert de Lacey b 1991, Ivo Edmund Bouchier b 9 March 1995), 1 da (Florence b 1989); *Career* with: Posterbrokers 1981–83, Picturebrokers 1983–86; prop: Vanessa Devereux Gallery 1986–, Riad el Fenn Marrakech; fndr: Portobello Contemporary Art Festival, Arts in Marrakech (AIM); curator Wonderful Fund Collection; *Recreations* theatre, cinema, sport, food; *Style*— Vanessa Branson; ✉ 5 Ladbroke Terrace, London W11 3PG (tel 020 7229 6485, fax 020 7727 7582)

BRASIER, Prof Martin David; *b* 12 April 1947; *Educ* Univ of London (BSc, PhD), Univ of Oxford (MA); *Career* micropalaeontologist Palaeontology Dept Inst of Geological Sciences 1972–73, lectr Geology Dept Univ of Reading 1973–74; Univ of Hull: lectr Geology Dept 1974–86, reader in palaeobiology 1986–90; tutorial fell St Edmund Hall Oxford 1988–; Earth Sciences Dept Univ of Oxford: lectr in geology 1988–96, reader in earth sciences 1996–2002, prof of palaeobiology 2002–; memb: UK Stratigraphy Cmmn Geological Soc 1991–96, UNESCO-Int Geological Correlation Prog Project 303 on Precambrian-Cambrian Events (chm 1990–94), Int Subcommission on Geochronology (IUGS) 1992–96, Subcommission on Cambrian Stratigraphy IUGS 1992– (chm 1992–96), Int Subcommission on Terminal Neoproterozoic Stratigraphy 1998–, NASA-Lunar and Planetary Assoc Mars Field Geology, Biology and Palaeontology Workshop 1998, Nat Science Fndn (NSF) Panel Washington DC 2003; numerous invited talks and lectures; *Publications* Microfossils (1980, new edn 2003); author of 200 articles and papers in jls and magazines incl Nature, Scientific American, Geological Magazine, Precambrian Research, New Scientist, Science, Science News, Geoscientist and Oxford University Gazette; *Style*— Prof Martin Brasier; ✉ St Edmund Hall, Oxford OX1 4AR

BRASLAVSKY, Dr Nicholas Justin; QC (1999); s of Rev Cyril Braslavsky (d 1980), and Stella, *née* Fisher; *b* 9 February 1959; *Educ* Blackpool GS, High Pavement GS Nottingham, Univ of Birmingham (LLB, MJur, PhD), Inns of Court Sch of Law; *m* 1990, Jane, *née* Margolis; 2 s (Max b 28 April 1992, Miles b 22 July 1996), 1 da (Millie b 7 Feb 1994); *Career* called to the Bar 1983 (Social Sci Research Cncl scholar 1979–82, Inner Temple scholar 1982); recorder 2001–; memb Kings Chambers (formerly 40 King Street); memb: Professional Negligence Bar Assoc 1990, Personal Injuries Bar Assoc 1990, Ctee Northern Circuit Med Law Assoc; *Style*— Dr Nicholas Braslavsky, QC; ✉ Kings Chambers, 36 Young Street, Manchester M3 3FT (tel 0161 832 9082, fax 0161 835 2139)

BRASON, Paul; s of John Ainsley Brason, and Audrey, *née* Wheldon; *b* 17 June 1952; *Educ* King James I GS Newport IOW, Camberwell Coll of Art; *Family* 2 s (Oliver Louis b 11 April 1983, Simon Nicholas b 9 June 1987), 1 da (Anne Louise b 9 June 1987); *Career* artist, portrait painter; has exhibited regularly at Nat Portrait Gall, Royal Acad and

Royal Soc of Portrait Painters; work in many private and public collections incl: Royal Collection Windsor Castle, Nat Portrait Gall, The Duke of Westminster, The Duke of Buccleuch, The Duke of Richmond, The Bodleian Library Oxford, Balliol Coll Oxford, Trinity Coll Oxford, CCC Oxford, Merton Coll Oxford, Eton Coll, Museums and Galleries Cmmn, HSBC Bank, and others; Ondaatje Prize for Portraiture 1998; memb Royal Soc of Portrait Painters 1994, pres RP 2001, elected memb Royal W of Eng Acad (RWA) 2002; *Clubs* Arts, Chelsea Arts; *Style—* Paul Brason, Esq, PPRP, RWA

BRASSEY, Hon Edward; s and h of 3 Baron Brassey of Apethorpe; *b* 9 March 1964; *Educ* Eton, RMA Sandhurst; *m* 1 Feb 2003, Joanna Pardoe; 1 s (Christian Peter b 23 Dec 2003), 1 da (Rose Myrna b 9 Feb 2006); *Career* Capt Grenadier Gds 1985–91, public affrs conslt Ludgate Communications 1992–98, mktg conslt The Montgomery Network 1999–, ceo Children's Fire and Burn Tst 2004–; *Recreations* karate, cricket, fishing; *Style—* The Hon Edward Brassey; ✉ The Manor House, Apethorpe, Peterborough PE8 5DL

BRATHWAITE, James Everett; CBE (2001); s of James Brathwaite (d 2004), and Louise Brathwaite; *b* 31 March 1953, St Lucy, Barbados; *Educ* Univ of Sheffield (BSc), Open Univ (Dip); *m* Barbara; 4 da (Catherine b 14 Nov 1973, Camilla b 9 June 1986, Charlotte b 26 Sept 1988, Cressida b 28 April 1991), 1 s (James b 4 April 1995); *Career* grad trainee accountant then salesman and sales trainer Beecham Pharmaceuticals UK Ltd 1975–79, product mangr then mktg mangr Bayer Pharmaceuticals UK Ltd 1979–82, fndr and ceo Epic Multimedia Gp plc (previously VPS) 1982–97, fndr dir and chief exec XL Entertainment plc 1997–; chm: SEAL Ltd 2000–, Community Alerts Ltd 2002–, Splash FM 2002–, Brighton & Hove Radio Ltd 2003–, Morgan Everett Ltd 2003–; dir: Exam on Demand 1998–, Nat Business Angels Network Ltd 2003–04, Organisational Technol Res 2005–, Regional Satellite TV Ltd 2005–; non-exec chm SEEDA 2002– (memb Bd 2001–); memb: Caribbean Advsy Gp FCO 1998–2002, Small Business Cncl 2000–04, Americas Advsrs Gp Trade Partners UK 2001–03, Int Trade Devpt Advsy Panel UK Trade and Investment 2002–05, Investment Ctee DTI 2002–06, Public Serv Agreements Sounding Bd ODPM 2003–05, Manufacturing Forum DTI 2004–, London 2012 Forum 2004–, Bd Environment Agency 2005–, Sustainable Procurement Taskforce DEFRA 2005–06; non-exec dir Sussex Enterprise Ltd 1994–2002, founding chm Business Link Sussex Ltd 1995–2003 (memb Nat Business Link Accreditation A Advsy Bd 1999–2000), fndr dir Wired Sussex 1996–2002, memb Bd Arundel Festival Ltd 1998–2002 (chm 2001), dir Farnham Castle Tstees and Farnham Castle Briefings Ltd 2004–; patron Asian Business Cncl; business rep Bd Brighton & Hove Sixth Form Coll, memb Ct Univ of Sussex 2002– (memb Cncl 1995–2001), dir Univ of Greenwich 2002–; memb Bd Rockinghorse charity 1994–96, fundraiser Alexandra Hosp for Sick Children Brighton; memb BAFTA; hon fell UC Chichester; MInstD, Hon FCGI 2005, FRSA; *Recreations* music, skiing, watching all sport especially football and Manchester United, coaching rugby; *Clubs* Reform, Cwlth, RSA; *Style—* James Brathwaite, Esq, CBE

BRATZA, Hon Mr Justice; Sir Nicolas Dušan Bratza; kt (1998); s of Milan Bratza (concert violinist, d 1964), and Hon Margaret Bratza, *née* Russell (d 1981); *b* 3 March 1945; *Educ* Wimbledon Coll, Brasenose Coll Oxford (MA); *Career* instr Univ of Pennsylvania Law Sch 1967–68; called to the Bar Lincoln's Inn 1969 (bencher 1993); jr counsel to the Crown (common law) 1978–88, QC 1988, recorder of the Crown Court 1993–98, UK memb European Cmmn of Human Rights 1993–98, judge of the High Court of Justice (Queen's Bench Div) 1998–, judge of the European Court of Human Rights 1998– (section pres 1998–2000 and 2001–07, vice-pres of Ct 2007–); memb: Cncl of Legal Educn 1988–92, Advsy Cncl Br Inst of Human Rights 2004– (vice-chm 1989–98, govr 1985–2004), Advsy Bd Br Inst of Int and Comparative Law 2005– (memb Cncl 1999–2005); memb Editorial Bd European Human Rights Law Review 1996–, memb Editorial Bd European Law Review 2004–; Hon DUniv Essex; *Books* Halsbury's Laws of England (4 edn, jt contrib of titles Contempt of Court and Crown Proceedings); *Recreations* music, cricket; *Clubs* Garrick, MCC; *Style—* The Hon Sir Nicolas Bratza; ✉ European Court of Human Rights, Council of Europe, F-67075 Strasbourg Cedex, France

BRAUDE, Prof Peter Riven; s of Barnett Braude (d 1988), and Sylvia Carmen, *née* Grumberg (d 2001); *b* 29 May 1948; *Educ* King Edward VII Sch Johannesburg, Univ of the Witwatersrand (BSc, MB BCh), Univ of Cambridge (MA, PhD), Soc of Apothecaries (Dip Philosophy of Med (DPMSA)); *m* 1973, Beatrice Louise, *née* Roselaar; 2 s (Philip Roselaar b 1983, Richard Roselaar b 1986); *Career* demonstrator in anatomy Univ of Cambridge 1974–79, SHO St Mary's Hosp London and Addenbrooke's Hosp Cambridge 1979–81, sr research assoc Dept of Obstetrics and Gynaecology Univ of Cambridge 1981–83, registrar in obstetrics and gynaecology Rosie Maternity Hosp Cambridge 1983–85; Univ of Cambridge: MRC clinical research conslt in obstetrics and gynaecology 1986–89, conslt sr lectr in obstetrics and gynaecology 1989–91; prof of obstetrics and gynaecology UMDS (GKT 1998–) 1991–, currently head Dept of Women's Health Sch of Med KCL (formerly head Dept of Obstetrics and Gynaecology UMDS); Guy's and St Thomas' Hosp: clinical dir Women's Servs 1993–94, dir Assisted Conception Unit and Fertility Serv 1993–99, dir Centre for Pre-implantation Genetic Diagnosis Guy's and St Thomas' Fndn Tst 1999–; memb HFEA 1999–2004, chair Scientific Advsy Ctee RCOG; 75th Jubilee Gold Medal for achievement in sci Univ of the Witwatersrand 1997; FRCOG 1993 (MRCOG 1982), FMedSci 2006; *Publications* ABC of Superfertility (jtly); author of various publications on human developmental embryology, male and female infertility and preimplantation genetics; *Recreations* narrowboating, gardening, skiing; *Style—* Prof Peter Braude; ✉ Department of Women's Health, Guy's, King's and St Thomas' School of Medicine, King's College London, 10th Floor, North Wing, St Thomas' Hospital, London SE1 7EH (tel 020 7188 4138, fax 020 7620 1227, e-mail obgyn@kcl.ac.uk)

BRAUER, Irving; s of Jack Brauer (d 1972), of Hackney, London, and Lily, *née* Croll (d 1978); *b* 8 August 1939; *Educ* Davenant Fndn, Northern Poly (DipArch); *m* 21 April 1964, Stephanie Margaret, da of Edwin Sherwood, of Florida, USA; 1 da (Amelia b 1965), 1s (Marlow b 1975); *Career* architect and designer, worked in London and NY 1960–63, partnership Beryl Gollins 1963–76, ptnr Brauer Associates 1976–; chm PIA (Product Innovation in Archtecture) 2002–; visiting tutor: Canterbury Sch of Architecture 1967–70, Central London Poly 1968–71; elected memb CSD 1967 (elected fell 1976–2005); RIBA; *Recreations* house renovation, theatre, reading, travel; *Style—* Irving Brauer, Esq; ✉ Apartment 1, Paramount Building, 212 St John Street, London EC1V 4JY (tel 020 7251 6210), London; Brauer Associates, 11–29 Fashion Street, London E1 6PX (tel 020 7377 2090, fax 020 7377 5253, e-mail irving@brauerassociates.co.uk)

BRAWER, Rabbi Dr Naftali Yosef; *b* 5 February 1970; *Educ* Rabbinical Coll of America Morristown NJ, Yeshiva Tomchei Tmimim Brooklyn NY, London Sch of Jewish Studies Univ of London (Dip, MA), UCL (PhD); *m* Dina, *née* Elmaleh; 4 c; *Career* ordained rabbi 1992; rabbi and educnl dir Friends of Lubavitch of Bergen Co NJ 1992–96 (also assoc chaplain Bergen Co Prison Annex), rabbi Northwood United Synagogue London 1996– (also chaplain Mt Vernon Hosp); teacher Hasmonean HS for Girls 2005, lectr London Sch of Jewish Studies 2005–; memb Advsy Bd: Consultative Cncl of Jewish Orgns René Cassin, Children of Abraham, Home Office Steering Ctee on Muslim-Jewish Dialogue Conf; fndr orgns incl Jewish Business Network (New Jersey); speaker at int confs; contrib to progs on BBC Radio 4, World Serv and BBC 2; contrib: The Jewish Standard 1994–96, The Jewish Chronicle 1998– (monthly columnist 2003–); memb: Assoc for Jewish Studies, Rabbinical Cncl of America, Rabbinical Cncl of the United Synagogue (UK), Chief Rabbi's Cabinet UK (Social Ethics Portfolio 1999–2004, Jewish-Muslim Rels Portfolio 2004–); *Style—* Rabbi Dr Naftali Brawer; ✉ 21–23 Murray Road, Northwood, Middlesex HA6 2YP (tel 01923 820004)

BRAY, (Richard) Andrew; s of John Frederick Arthur Bray (d 1962), and Dorothy Agnes Bray (d 1981); *b* 5 December 1938; *Educ* Sandown Sch Bexhill-on-Sea, Canterbury Coll of Art (NDD), RCA Sch of Silversmithing and Jewellery Design (scholar); *m* 1965, Margaret Anne, da of James Norman Hope; 2 da (Emma Claire b 1970, Shuna Anne b 1974); *Career* silversmith; visiting tutor Dip AD Silversmithing: Canterbury Coll of Art 1965–67, Camberwell Sch of Art and Crafts 1963–73; head of Art Kent Coll Canterbury 1976–77; Silversmithing and Metalwork Dept Camberwell Sch of Art and Crafts: lectr 1977, sr lectr 1983, princ lectr 1989–, course dir to 1998; design work 1965–89 (freelance for various firms, numerous cmmnd pieces of jewellery and silverplate for private and public bodies), involved in res 1983–85; cmmns incl: Royal Ascot Gold Cup 1960, independence gifts for FCO 1966, centenary gifts for Br Assurance Assoc 1967, univ plate incl King's, Churchill, Corpus Christi and Clare Colls Cambridge, livery plate incl Goldsmiths, Armourers and Brasiers, Dyers and Watermen and Lightermen Cos, product design incl Dunhill's and Ronson lighters, best products, Pifco electrical appliances, Kitchen Devil and Sipelia Sheffield cutlery; participant in exhibitions at: The Commonwealth Institute London 1967, The Greenwich Museum London 1968, Two Man Exhibitions Silver Plate London Wall 1969, The Fitzwilliam Museum Cambridge 1973, The Victoria and Albert Museum London 1977, The Goldsmiths Hall London 1982, The Rufford Craft Centre 1985, Twentieth Century European Silver Crafts Cncl 1993, Br Cnl touring exhibition Europe, Goldsmiths Co Silver and Tea exhibition, Mappin and Webb, International Jewellery Show London 1998, Int Silver Touring Exhbn Poland and E Euro 2000, Int Silver Exhbn Holland 2002 (by invitation), AVA Ashford 2002 and 2004 (by invitation), Stables Art Gallery Hastings 2003; solo exhibition KCC Ashford 2002; selected designer/maker Nat Forum for New British Silver 1995; co-designer maker: civic regalia for Ashford BC 1972, public arts performance area Ashford BC 2000; winner Ascot Gold Cup National Design Competition 1960; fndr memb Assoc of Br Designer Silversmiths 1997 (co-opted memb Ctee 2002); chm Ashford Visual Artists 2000; memb Cultural and Heritage Forum: Ashford's Future Vision 2003, Ashford's New Architectural Landmarks Ashford BC and Kent CC 2004 (by invitation); Kent Fedn of Master Builders Award 1964, Jurisprudence Prize Royal Soc of Arts 1968; fell Soc Designer Craftsmen 1969; Freeman Worshipful Co of Goldsmiths 1989, Freeman City of London 1992; *Style—* Andrew Bray, Esq

BRAY, Angie; AM; da of Benedict G C T Bray (d 1987), of the Isle of Man, and Patricia, *née* Measures; *b* 13 October 1953; *Educ* Downe House, Fairlawn Sch Cambridge, Univ of St Andrews (MA); *Partner* Nigel Hugh-Smith; *Career* radio presenter and reporter LBC Radio 1981–88; head of broadcasting Cons Pty and press sec to Pty Chm 1989–92, sr conslt in public affrs 1992–2000; GLA: memb London Assembly (Cons) W Central 2000–, Cons spokesman for the congestion charge, memb Tport, Environment and Business Mgmnt and Appts Ctees; vice-pres Hammersmith & Fulham Cons Assoc, Parly candidate (Cons) East Ham 1996–97; *Recreations* tennis, history, music, walking my dogs; *Style—* Angie Bray, AM; ✉ London Assembly, City Hall, Queens Walk, Southwark, London SE1 2AA (e-mail angie.bray@london.gov.uk)

BRAY, Julian Charles; s of Flt Lt Reginald Charles Julian Bray, and Irene Audrey, *née* Stewart; *b* 23 May 1945; *Educ* Ayr Acad; *m* 1, 1965 (m dis 1970), Julie; 1 da (Amanda Caroline); m 2, 1971 (m dis 1981), Judith Marina; 2 s (Dominic Julian b 13 Oct 1977, Oliver William b 13 June 1980); m 3, 1985 (m dis 2001), Vivienne Margaret Carlton; 1 s (William Charles b 18 Aug 1989); *Career* independent TV prodr and presenter, broadcaster, writer and journalist; prodr/dir ASM Productions; md: Leadenhall Associates Ltd 1986–90, Alpha Strategy Management Ltd 1991–92; non-exec dir CNS (City News Service) 1986–90 (ed 1990–); dir: NTN TV News Ltd 1988, DTI Eureka Information Bureau 1990, Marketmetro Ltd 2002–; business devpt dir Extel PR, head of media relations Welbeck PR Ltd; sr ptnr Carlton Consulting 1993–2001, ceo Media Assocs, exec prodr Rascal TV & Film Prodns Inc 2007–; int lectr and writer on econ and European affrs 1994–; memb: Equity, NUJ, The Magic Circle, Int Brotherhood of Magicians USA (sec Eng Ring 1999, memb Br Ring No 25); MCIPR, MBII (memb Cncl E Anglia); *Books* Information Technology in the Corporate Environment (1980); *Recreations* theatre, microbreweries and fine wine, travel, magic; *Clubs* The Magic Castle (Hollywood), Peterborough City; *Style—* Julian Bray, MCIPR, MMC, MBII; ✉ 17 Kedleston, Heritage Park, Peterborough PE2 8XL (tel 01733 345581, fax 01733 892677, mobile 07944 217476, e-mail julianbray@aol.com)

BRAY, Kelvin Arthur; CBE (1990, OBE 1982); s of Arthur William Stretton Bray (d 1979), of Leicester, and Clarice May, *née* Perrin (d 1985); *b* 4 February 1935; *Educ* Leicester City Boys' Sch, King's Coll Cambridge (MA); *m* 1959, Grace Elizabeth, da of Dr Matthew Millar Tannahill (d 1981), of Lincoln; 2 s (Adam Kelvin b 9 March 1966, Julian Dominic b 27 February 1968); *Career* sales mangr (Gas Turbine Div) Ruston & Hornsby Ltd 1963; md: Ruston Gas Turbines Ltd 1969–98 (Queen's Award for Export 1969, 1977, 1978 and 1982, Queen's Award for Technol 1986), GEC Gas Turbines Ltd 1983–89, GEC ALSTHOM Gas Turbine & Diesel Div 1989–94, GEC ALSTHOM NV 1991–98, GEC ALSTHOM Power Gen Div 1994–97; chm GEC ALSTHOM Ltd 1997–98; assoc dir GEC 1985–98; chm: Napier Turbochargers Ltd, Euro Gas Turbines NV 1989–98; Univ of Lincoln: dep chm 1998, chm of govrs 2001–04, pro-chllr 2003–, visiting prof Lincoln Business Sch 2005–; Royal Soc Esso Medal 1974, MacRobert Award 1983, Gold Medal Inst of Gas Engrs 1994, Lincoln Civic Award 1995; Freeman City of Lincoln 2005; Hon DSc Univ of Lincoln 2005; FIMechE 1957, FREng 1979; *Recreations* golf, swimming; *Style—* Kelvin A Bray, Esq, CBE, MA, FREng, FIMechE; ✉ 17 Cherry Tree Lane, Nettleham, Lincoln LN2 2PR

BRAY, Michael Peter; s of Sqdn Ldr William Charles Thomas Bray, DFC (d 1985), and Ivy Isobel, *née* Ellison (d 1986); *b* 27 March 1947; *Educ* Caterham Sch, Univ of Liverpool (LLB); *m* 25 July 1970, Elizabeth-Ann, da of Hubert John Harrington (d 1981); 2 da (Natasha Jane b 13 April 1977, Samantha Louise b 13 April 1984); *Career* slr; ptnr Clifford Chance 1976– (formerly Coward Chance, joined 1970), chief exec Clifford Chance 2000–03; memb Jt Working Pty on Banking Law of the Law Reform Ctees of the Law Soc and Bar Cncl; Freeman City of London Slrs' Co 1976; memb Law Soc; *Recreations* theatre, reading, skiing, photography, golf; *Style—* Michael Bray, Esq; ✉ Clifford Chance, 10 Upper Bank Street, London E14 5JJ (tel 020 7600 1000, fax 020 7600 5555)

BRAY, Noreen; OBE (1996); *Educ* Heathfield House RC HS, Univ of Wales (BA); *Children* 2 s; *Career* PR conslt; grad trainee BBC 1971–73, TV and radio news and current affairs journalist BBC Wales 1976–89, bd dir Good Relations Ltd (part of Chime Communications) 1989– (currently md Cardiff Office); cmmr for Wales Equal Opportunities Cmmn 1990–95, pres SCOPE (formerly Spastics Soc) Wales 1996–2000; dir Bank of Wales 1999–2001, dir Real Radio 2000–02, memb Prince's Tst Cncl for Wales, govr Univ of Wales Inst Cardiff (UWIC), Privy Cncl nominee Ct Univ of Cardiff, memb Bd Br Chambers of Commerce 2006–; memb NUJ; MIPR, FRSA; *Recreations* reading, music, exercise; *Style—* Mrs Noreen Bray, OBE; ✉ Windsor House, Windsor Lane, Cardiff CF1 3DE (tel 029 2034 4888)

BRAY, His Hon Judge Richard Winston Atherton; s of Winston Bray, CBE (d 2003), and Betty Atherton, *née* Miller; *b* 10 April 1945; *Educ* Rugby, CCC Oxford; *m* 6 Jan 1978, Judith Elizabeth Margaret, da of Maj C B Ferguson (d 1980); 1 s (Edward b 2 Oct 1984), 3 da (Hester b 24 May 1981, Miranda b 12 Sept 1986, Rosalind b 23 Aug 1989); *Career* called to the Bar Middle Temple 1970; recorder Midland & Oxford circuit 1987–93; circuit judge (Midland & Oxford Circuit) 1993–; *Recreations* cricket, real tennis, gardening; *Clubs* MCC, Frogs; *Style—* His Hon Judge Bray

BRAYBROOKE, 10 Baron (GB 1788); Robin Henry Charles Neville; JP, DL (Essex); hereditary visitor Magdalene Coll Cambridge; s of 9 Baron Braybrooke, JP, DL (d 1990), and his 1 w, Muriel Evelyn, *née* Manning (d 1962); *b* 29 January 1932; *Educ* Eton, Magdalene Coll Cambridge (MA), RAC Cirencester; *m* 1, 1955 (m dis 1974), Robin Helen, o da of late T A Brockhoff, of Rose Bay, NSW; 4 da (Hon Amanda Muriel Mary (Hon Mrs Murray) b 1962, Hon Caroline Emma (Countess of Derby) b 1963, Hon Victoria (Hon Mrs Bromet), Hon Arabella (Hon Mrs Potter) (twins) b 1970) and 1 da decd (Hon Henrietta Jane b 1965 d 1980); m 2, 1974 (m dis 1998), Linda, 2 da of Arthur Norman, of Saffron Walden, Essex; 3 da (Hon Sara Lucy b 1975, Hon Emma Charlotte (Hon Mrs Carboni) b 1979, Hon Lucinda Octavia b 1984); m 3, 1998, Perina, da of Augustine Courtauld (d 1959), and The Lady Butler of Saffron Walden, of Great Yeldham, Essex; *Heir* kinsman, Richard Neville; *Career* cmmnd Rifle Bde 1951, served with 3 Bn King's African Rifles in Kenya and Malaya 1951–52; farmer and landowner; RDC cncllr 1959–69, CC for Stansted 1969–72; memb: Cncl CLA 1965–83, Agric Land Tbnl Eastern Area 1975–; chm: Price Tst 1983–94, Rural Devpt Cmmn for Essex 1984–90; dir Essex and Suffolk Insurance Co until taken over by Guardian Royal Exchange; HM Lord-Lt Essex 1992–2002; Hon DUniv Essex 2000; KStJ; *Recreations* railways, motorcycling, photography; *Clubs* Boodle's, Farmers'; *Style—* The Rt Hon the Lord Braybrooke; ✉ Abbey Farm House, Audley End, Saffron Walden, Essex CB11 4JB (tel 01799 522484, office 01799 541354/541956, fax 01799 542134, e-mail aee@farming.co.uk)

BRAYFIELD, Celia Frances; da of Felix Francis Brayfield (d 1975), and Ada Ellen, *née* Jakeman (d 1995); *b* 21 August 1945; *Educ* St Paul's Girls' Sch, Universitaire de Grenoble; *Children* 1 da (Chloe Elizabeth b 8 Oct 1980); *Career* writer and broadcaster; trainee Nova IPC Magazines 1968–69, asst to women's ed The Observer 1969, feature writer Daily Mail 1969–71, TV critic Evening Standard 1974–82, TV critic The Times 1983–88, columnist Sunday Telegraph 1989–90; dir Nat Acad of Writing 2000–03; reader in creative writing Brunel Univ 2007– (sr lectr 2005–07), vice-pres One Parent Families 2007–; tstee One Parent Families 1990–2007, memb Mgmnt Ctee Soc of Authors 1995–98; *Books* The Body Show Book (co-author, 1982), Pineapple Dance Book (co-author, 1984), Glitter - The Truth About Fame (1985), Pearls (1987), The Prince (1990), White Ice (1993), Harvest (1995), Bestseller (1996), Getting Home (1998), Sunset (1999), Heartswap (2000), Mister Fabulous and Friends (2003), Wild Weekend (2004), Deep France (2004); *Recreations* family life; *Clubs* Chelsea Arts; *Style—* Ms Celia Brayfield; ✉ c/o Curtis Brown Ltd, 28/29 Haymarket, London SW1Y 4SP (tel 020 7396 6600, e-mail celia@celiabrayfield.com)

BRAYNE, Mark Lugard; s of Thomas Lugard Brayne, of Harborne, Birmingham, and Audrey Diana, *née* Thompson; *b* 17 April 1950; *Educ* Gresham's, Wymondham Coll, Univ of Leeds (BA), De Montfort Univ (MA); *m* 1, 25 March 1977 (m dis), Jutta, da of Fritz Hartung, of Oberammergau, Germany; 2 s (Christopher b 1980, Alastair b 1982), 1 da (Katharine b 1987); m 2, 20 Sept 2002, Sue, da of John Bowes, of Cheltenham, Glos; *Career* Moscow and E Berlin Reuters News Agency 1973–78; BBC: German service corr Berlin 1979–81, Central Euro corr Vienna 1981–84, Beijing corr China 1984–87; BBC World Service: dip corr 1988–92, dep head Central European Serv 1992–93, dep head Russian Serv 1993–94, regnl ed Europe 1994–2002; dir BBC project for journalism and trauma 2002–03, dir Europe Dart Centre for Journalism and Trauma; UK Cncl for Psychotherapy (UKCP) reg psychotherapist, writer and lectr on journalism, trauma and ethics, memb Bd Euro Soc for Traumatic Stress Studies (ESTSS); *Recreations* singing, people, cycling; *Style—* Mark Brayne, Esq; ✉ e-mail mark@braynework.org

BRAYTON, Margaret Abigail; MBE (1989); da of Thomas George Brayton (d 1965), of Cumbria, and Sybella, *née* Little (d 1974); *b* 6 July 1919; *Educ* White House GS Brampton, City of Carlisle GS, Newcastle Gen Sch of Nursing (SRN), Simpson Meml Maternity Pavilion Royal Infirmary of Edinburgh (SCM), Hosp for Sick Children Great Ormond St London (RSCN), Yale Univ, McGill Univ Montreal (Br Cwlth Nurses War Meml scholar), RCN (Br Red Cross and St John Jt Ctee scholar, NsgMD); *Career* Br Red Cross vol with Royal Naval Nursing Serv 1939–40, qualified nurse working with med relief teams in Europe 1944–45; nursing offr Paediatric Unit Newcastle Gen Hosp 1946–47, sister Nuffield Dept of Child Health Babies Hosp Royal Victoria Infirmary and Newcastle Gen Hosp 1949–53, assignments with WHO and UNICEF in India, Malaysia, Singapore, Hong Kong, Sri Lanka, Pakistan and Uganda 1949–55, James Mackenzie Child Health Unit Fife CC and Univ of St Andrews 1953–55, matron and princ of nursing educn Whitehaven and West Cumberland Hosp 1956–59, asst regnl nursing offr South Eastern Regnl Hosp Bd Edinburgh and Eastern Regnl Hosp Bd Dundee 1959–60, chief regnl nursing offr South Eastern Regnl Hosp Bd Edinburgh Scotland 1960–72, exec sec Cwlth Nurses Fedn (and ed Newsletter) 1973–93; formerly: vice-chm RCN Scotland, memb Cncl RCN London, vice-pres Assoc of State Enrolled Nurses (now amalgamated with RCN), chm Extension Servs Scottish Nursing Servs Ctee, memb Advsy Ctee Nursing Degree Prog Dept of Nursing Studies Univ of Edinburgh, pres Soroptimist Int of Edinburgh and Central London; fndr chm and memb Cwlth Professional Assoc Meetings (now Assoc of Cwlth Orgns), memb Cwlth Fndn Gp to visit Zimbabwe; pres Divnl Union Soroptimist Int South Scotland, vice-pres Royal Cwlth Soc, vice-pres Cwlth Countries League (ed Newsletter and former chairwoman), life vice-pres Corona Worldwide, patron Assoc of Guyanese Nurses and Allied Professionals (UK), patron Confedn of Black and Ethnic Minority Nurses 2005; Distinguished Service Award Trinidad and Tobago Registered Nurses Assoc 1990; Freeman City of London 1980; hon fell West African Coll of Nursing 1982; FRSA 1982; hon chiefdom title Western Samoa 1975; *Recreations* the Arts, archeological digs, hill climbing, unusual train journeys, sailing, reading; *Clubs* Royal Cwlth Soc, Soroptimist Int of Central London; *Style—* Miss Margaret Brayton, MBE; ✉ 22 Dean Abbott House, 70 Vincent Street, London SW1P 4HS (tel and fax 020 7931 9248)

BRAZIER, Julian William Hendy; TD, MP; s of Lt-Col Peter Hendy Brazier, and Patricia Audrey Helen, *née* Stubbs, ggda of Bishop Stubbs of Oxford noted lectr and author of the Stubbs Charters (Constitutional History of England); *b* 24 July 1953; *Educ* Dragon Sch Oxford, Wellington, BNC Oxford (scholar, MA), London Business Sch; *m* 21 July 1984, Katharine Elizabeth, da of Brig Patrick Blagden, CBE; 3 s (William, Alexander (twin), John b 3 Dec 1992); *Career* SSLC with RE and Capt TA in Airborne Forces; with Charter Consolidated Ltd (now plc) 1975–84 (sec to Exec Ctee of the Bd of Dirs 1981–84), H B Maynard Int Mgmnt Conslts 1984–87; MP (Cons) Canterbury 1987–; PPS to Rt Hon Gillian Shephard, MP, *qv*, 1990–93; oppn whip 2001–02, shadow min for Work and Pensions 2002–03, shadow min for Trade and Int Devpt 2003–; memb House of Commons Defence Select Ctee 1997–2001; *Recreations* cross country running, history, science, philosophy; *Clubs* Travellers; *Style—* Julian Brazier, Esq, TD, MP; ✉ House of Commons, London SW1A 0AA

BRAZIER, Paul; *b* 29 July 1962; *Career* advtg exec; art dir Cogent Elliott 1984–87, WCRS 1987–91; Abbott Mead Vickers BBDO: joined 1991, now exec creative dir; awards for: RSPCA, Volvo SIPS, Volvo, The Economist, QEFDP, Sainsbury's, Cellnet, Pizza Hut, Aer Lingus, DETR, Dulux, Wrangler, Road Safety, COI/DFT, Kaliber, Guinness, BBC World, BT; Hon Degree in Visual Arts (Graphics) Wolverhampton; *Style—* Paul Brazier, Esq; ✉ Abbott Mead Vickers BBDO Ltd, 151 Marylebone Road, London NW1 5QE (tel 020 7616 3500, fax 020 7616 3600)

BREACH, Peter John Freeman; s of Andrew Breach, CBE, LLD (d 1992), and Christine Ruth, *née* Watson (d 1973); *b* 12 January 1942; *Educ* Clifton, Univ of Bristol (BA); *m* 17 Dec 1966, Joan, da of (William) Raymond Livesey, of Clitheroe, Lancs; 3 s (Harry William Freeman b 1972, Christopher Andrew Talbot (Kit) b 1974, Alexander Robin Livesey b 1989); *Career* Coopers & Lybrand 1963–68, Hoare Govett 1968–69, County Bank Ltd 1969–70, JH Vavasseur & Co Ltd 1970–73, pres and ceo Major Holdings & Devpts Ltd 1972–73, divnl md Bath & Portland Gp Ltd 1974–78, md James Dixon/Viners Ltd 1978–82, fin dir Bristol & West Building Soc 1988–91 (dir 1976–91, exec dir 1983–91); chm 1992–: Hawksworth Securities plc (dir 1988), Principality Holdings Gp (dir 1972), Farthingford Properties Ltd (dir 1972), Surthurst Ltd (dir 1983); chm Coffee Republic plc 2006–; govr and chm Redland HS for Girls; Freeman: City of London, City of Bristol; Liveryman Worshipful Co of Basketmakers; FCA, CTA, MCT, ASIP; *Recreations* sailing, skiing, gardens, historic homes; *Clubs* Royal Dart Yacht, Naval; *Style—* Peter Breach, Esq; ✉ 7 Park Street, Bristol BS1 5NF (tel 0117 925 9494, fax 0117 927 2462, mobile 07779 330706, e-mail peter.breach@hawksworthplc.com)

BREADEN, Very Rev Robert William; s of Moses Breaden (d 1958), of Magheracloone, Co Monaghan, and Martha Jane, *née* Hall (d 1988); *b* 7 November 1937; *Educ* The King's Hosp Dublin, Edinburgh Theol Coll; *m* 3 July 1970, Glenice Sutton, da of Douglas Martin (d 1990), of Dundee, and Joyce, *née* Sutton; 1 s (Patrick b 1971), 4 da (Sarah b 1973, Kathleen b 1979, Christina b 1981, Ann-Louise b 1987); *Career* ordained 1961, asst curate St Mary's Broughty Ferry 1961–65; rector: Church of the Holy Rood Carnoustie 1965–72, St Mary's Broughty Ferry 1972–; canon St Paul's Cathedral Dundee 1977, dean Dio of Brechin 1984–; OStJ 2001; *Recreations* gardening, horse-riding; *Clubs* Rotary of Abertay (pres 1979–80); *Style—* The Very Rev the Dean of Brechin; ✉ 46 Seafield Road, Broughty Ferry, Dundee DD5 3AN (tel 01382 477477, fax 01382 477434, e-mail ateallach@aol.com)

BREAKS, Michael Lenox; s of Cdr John Lenox Breaks, OBE, RN (d 2001), of Denmead, Portsmouth, and Madeleine Henrietta, *née* Page (d 1997); *b* 12 January 1945; *Educ* St George's Coll Weybridge, Univ of Leeds (BA), UC Aberystwyth (Dip Lib); *m* 12 April 1970, Barbara Monica, da of Charles Lawson (d 1984); 1 s (Jeremy Lenox b 1 March 1973), 1 da (Sarah Jessica b 15 May 1975); *Career* asst librarian: Univ Coll Swansea 1971–72, Univ of York 1972–73; social scis librarian Univ Coll Cardiff 1977–81, dep librarian Univ Coll Dublin 1981–85, univ librarian Heriot-Watt Univ 1985–; chm Joint Academic Network (JANET) Nat User Gp 1991–93, pres Int Assoc of Technological Univ Libraries 2000–04 (sec 1992–98, vice-pres 1998–2000); non-exec dir UK Education and Research Networking Assoc 1993–97; chair Archive Hub Steering Ctee 2000–; memb: Advsy Ctee on Networking 1991–93, Advsy Ctee on Br Library Document Supply Centre 1992–96, Cncl SCONUL 1993–97 and 2006–, Scot Library and Information Cncl Mgmnt Ctee 1995–2001, Library and Information Cmmn Research Ctee 1996–2000, Bd of Tstees EduServe 1999–, Joint Info Systems Ctee (JISC) on Electronic Info 1999–2001, Br Library Advsy Cncl 1999–2002; ed New Review of Information Networking; *Recreations* gardening, horse riding, walking; *Style—* Michael Breaks, Esq; ✉ 2 Corrennie Gardens, Edinburgh EH10 6DG (tel 0131 447 7193); Heriot-Watt University, Riccarton, Edinburgh EH14 4AS (tel 0131 451 3570, fax 0131 451 3164, e-mail m.l.breaks@hw.ac.uk)

BREAKWELL, Prof Glynis Marie; da of Harold Breakwell, of Tipton, and Vera, *née* Woodhall (d 1993); *b* 26 July 1952; *Educ* Univ of Leicester (BA), Univ of Strathclyde (MSc), Univ of Bristol (PhD), Univ of Oxford (DSc); *Career* lectr in social psychology Univ of Bradford 1976–78, prize fell in social psychology Nuffield Coll Oxford 1978–82; Univ of Surrey: lectr in social psychology 1981–87, sr lectr in psychology 1987–88, reader 1988–91, prof of psychology 1991–2001, head Dept of Psychology 1990–95, pro-vice-chllr (staff devpt and continuing educn) 1994–95, pro-vice-chllr (research and enterprise) 1995–2001, head Sch of Human Sciences 1997–2001; vice-chllr Univ of Bath 2001–; pres Psychology Section Br Assoc for the Advancement of Sci 1994–95 (vice-pres 1995–96); Br Psychological Soc: Young Social Psychologist Award 1978, assoc fell 1984, fell 1987, Myers Award 1993, memb Social Psychology Section Ctee 1995–99 (chair 1997–99); dir New Swindon Co 2002–07; tstee Theatre Royal Bath 2002–06, chair Bath Festivals Ltd 2006–, chair HERDA SW 2006–; MA (by special resolution) Univ of Oxford 1978; Hon LLD Univ of Bristol 2003; CPsychol 1988; FRSA 1997, AcSS 2002; *Books* Social Work: The Social Psychological Approach (with C Rowett, 1982), The Quiet Rebel (1985), Coping with Threatened Identities (1986), Facing Physical Violence (1989), Interviewing (1990), Social Psychology of Political and Economic Cognition (ed, 1991), Managing Violence at Work: Course Leader's Guide (with C Rowett, 1992), Managing Violence at Work: Workbook (with C Rowett, 1992), Careers and Identities (jtly, 1992), Social Psychology of Identity and the Self Concept (ed, 1992), Empirical Approaches to Social Representations (with D V Canter, 1993), Basic Evaluation Methods (with L Millward, 1995), Research Methods in Psychology (with S Hammond and C Fife-Schaw, 1995, 3 edn 2006), Changing European Identities: Social Psychological Analyses of Change (jtly ed with E Lyons, 1996), Coping with Aggressive Behaviour (1997), Doing Social Psychology Research (ed, 2003), The Psychology of Risk (2007); also author of numerous journal articles, monographs and book chapters; *Recreations* painting; *Clubs* Athenaeum; *Style—* Prof Glynis Breakwell; ✉ University of Bath, Claverton Down, Bath BA2 7AY (tel 01225 386262, fax 01225 386626, e-mail g.breakwell@bath.ac.uk)

BREALEY, Prof Richard Arthur; s of Albert Brealey (d 1974), and Irene Brealey (d 1994); *b* 9 June 1936; *Educ* Queen Elizabeth's Sch Barnet, Exeter Coll Oxford (MA); *m* 10 Feb 1967, Diana Cecily, da of Derek Brown-Kelly (d 2003); 2 s (David Andrew b 1970, Charles Richard b 1972); *Career* Investment Dept Sun Life Assurance Co of Canada 1959–66, mangr computer applications Keystone Custodian Funds of Boston 1966–68; London Business Sch: prof of fin 1973–98, dir Inst of Fin and Accounting 1974–84, memb Body of Govrs, dep princ and academic dean 1984–88, visiting prof 1998–2001, emeritus prof 2001–; visiting prof: Univ of Calif Berkeley, Univ of Br Colombia, Univ of Hawaii, Aust Grad Sch of Mgmnt; advsr to Govr Bank of England 1998–2001; tstee HSBC Investor Funds; former dir: Sun Life Assurance Co of Canada UK Holdings plc, Swiss Helvetia Fund, Tokai Derivative Products; dep chm Balancing and Settlement Code Panel 1998–; former: pres European Fin Assoc, dir American Fin Assoc; FBA; *Books* incl: Introduction to Risk and Return from Common Stocks (2 edn, 1983), Fundamentals of Corporate Finance (jtly, 1994, 5 edn 2007), Principles of Corporate Finance (with S C Myers and F Allen, 9 edn, 2007); *Recreations* rock climbing, skiing, horse riding; *Style—* Prof Richard Brealey, FBA; ✉ Haydens Cottage, The Pound, Cookham, Berkshire SL6 9QE (tel 01628 520143); London Business School, Sussex Place, Regent's Park, London NW1 4SA (tel 020 7262 5050, fax 020 7724 3317)

BREAM, Julian; CBE (1985, OBE 1964); *b* 15 July 1933; *Educ* RCM; *m* 1, Margaret Williamson; m 2, 1980 (m dis), Isobel, *née* Sanchez; *Career* guitarist and lutanist; professional debut Cheltenham 1947, London debut Cowdray Hall 1950; fndr Julian Bream Consort 1960, organiser own summer arts festival, estab workshops in Wiltshire for manufacture of guitars, lutes and harpsichords; subject of biographical film A Life in the Country BBC TV 1976, gave series of masterclasses on BBC TV, made series of films on location on devpt of Spanish lute and guitar music 1984, made film of Elizabethan music and poetry with Dame Peggy Ashcroft for BBC TV 1987; performed with: BBC Symphony Orch, Scottish Chamber, London Symphony Orch, various string quartets and chamber ensembles, internationally known duo with John Williams; venues incl: Toronto, Boston, Chicago, Belgium, Concertgebouw Amsterdam, Musikverein Vienna, Milan, Rome, Venice, Berlin, Munich, Frankfurt, Zurich, Geneva, Japan, Hong Kong, Aust, NZ, Madrid, Athens, Paris, Bratislava, Prague, Warsaw, India, S America; performed at festivals incl: Aldeburgh, Bath, Three Choirs, Echternach, Ansbach, Ludwigsburg, Bergen, Prague Spring, Stresa, Helsinki; winner various int recording awards incl: six from Nat Acad of Recording Arts and Scis USA, two Edison Awards, various prizes from Gramophone magazine, platinum disc, various gold and silver discs for recordings made with John Williams; exclusive artist EMI 1990–; cmmnd new works from composers incl: Britten, Henze, Arnold, Walton, Brouwer; Hon DUniv Surrey 1968, Hon DMus Univ of Leeds 1984, PhD London Guildhall Univ 1999; Villa-Lobos Gold medal 1976; ARAM 1969, FRCM 1981, FRNCM 1983; *Performances* incl: first UK public performance of Brouwer's Concerto Elegiaco (written especially for him) St John's Smith Square 1986, George Malcolm's 70th Birthday Concert (with Dame Janet Baker and Sir Yehudi Menuhin) Wigmore Hall 1987, concert on centenary of Villa-Lobos' birth Wigmore Hall 1987, BBC Proms Concerts 1987, 1989, 1991 and 1993, recitals with Dame Peggy Ashcroft at Greenwich and Aldeburgh Festivals 1990, Japan Festival London 1991, 60th birthday season recitals Amsterdam and UK 1992/93, 50th anniversary concert Wigmore Hall 2001, continues to perform at prestigious festivals and venues throughout the UK; *Style*— Julian Bream, Esq, CBE; ✉ c/o Hazard Chase Ltd, 25 City Road, Cambridge CB1 1DP

BREARLEY, Christopher John Scott; CB (1994), DL (Herts 2007); s of Geoffrey William Brearley (d 1968), and Winifred Marion, *née* Scott (d 1995); *b* 25 May 1943; *Educ* King Edward VII Sch Sheffield, Trinity Coll Oxford (MA, BPhil); *m* 1971, Rosemary Nanette, da of Lt-Col Wilfrid Sydney Stockbridge (d 1993), and Dorothea Stockbridge (d 2001); 2 s (Thomas b 1973, William b 1976); *Career* civil servant; former dir: Scottish Servs, Property Servs Agency 1981–83; under sec Cabinet Office 1983–85; DOE: dir Local Govt Fin 1985–88, dir Planning and Devpt Control 1988–89, dep sec Local Govt 1990–93, Local Govt and Planning 1994–95, Local Devpt Gp 1996–97, DG Planning, Roads and Local Transport Gp DETR 1997–2000; chair Nat Retail Planning Forum 2005–; cncllr Three Rivers DC 2003–07 (chm Licensing Ctee 2004–07, memb Chiltern Conservation Bd 2004–07); non-exec dir John Maclean & Son 1986–88; govr and tstee Watford GS for Boys 1988–2004 (chm of govrs 1998–2004); tstee Motability Tenth Anniversary Tst 2001–, memb Policy Ctee CPRE 2001–07; chm: CPRS - The Hertfordshire Soc 2004–, SW Herts Lib Dems 2004–; Freeman City of London; *Recreations* walking, crosswords; *Clubs* Oxford and Cambridge, New (Edinburgh); *Style*— Christopher Brearley, Esq, CB, DL; ✉ Middlemount, 35 South Road, Chorleywood, Hertfordshire WD3 5AS (tel 01923 283848, e-mail cjsbrearley@ntlworld.com)

BREARLEY, Stephen; s of Roger Brearley, of Mossley Hill, Liverpool, and Joyce Mary, *née* Hewitt; *b* 17 March 1953; *Educ* Liverpool Coll, Gonville & Caius Coll Cambridge (MA), Middx Hosp Med Sch (MB BChir, MChir (Cantab)); *m* 1980, Margaret Faith, da of Edward Collier; 2 s (Jonathan Joshua b 5 March 1982 d 2002, Samuel Sebastian James b 1 Dec 1985); *Career* research fell Birmingham Gen Hosp 1983–84, surgical sr registrar W Midlands Region 1988–91; conslt gen and vascular surgn: Whipps Cross Univ Hosp London 1992– (chm Med Staff Assoc 1998–2006), BUPA Roding Hosp Ilford, Holly House Hosp Buckhurst Hill; hon sr lectr Jt Medical Sch of St Bart's and the Royal London Hosp Univ of London, RCS surgical tutor Whipps Cross Hosp 1992–98, organiser Whipps Cross Higher Surgery Course, memb Redbridge and Waltham Forest Research Ethics Ctee 1993–99; memb: Jr Doctors' Ctee BMA 1979–91 (chm 1983–84), GMC 1984– (chm Registration Ctee 1998–), Permanent Working Gp of Euro Jr Hosp Doctors 1985–91 (chm Educn Sub-Ctee), Standing Ctee on Postgraduate Med Educn 1989–92 (fndr memb), Assoc of Surgns of GB and I, Vascular Surgical Soc, RSM; fndr memb Expert Witness Inst; FRCS 1981; *Publications* author of articles on med educn, med manpower and medicine in Europe; *Recreations* playing, conducting and listening to music, flying, cricket, golf; *Style*— Stephen Brearley, Esq; ✉ Whipps Cross University Hospital, London E11 1NR (tel 020 8535 6670, fax 020 8535 6670, mobile 077 7098 1609, e-mail vascusurg@btconnect.com)

BREARS, Peter Charles David; s of Charles Henry, and Mary Theresa Margaret, Brears; *b* 30 August 1944; *Educ* Castleford Tech HS, Leeds Coll of Art (dipAD); *Career* keeper of folk life Hampshire Co Cncl 1967–69; curator: Shibden Hall Halifax 1969–72, Clarke Hall Wakefield 1972–75, Castle Museum York 1975–79; dir Leeds City Museums 1979–94, museum conslt and writer 1994–; pres Soc for Folk Life Studies 1992; FMA 1980, FSA 1980; *Books* The English Country Pottery (1971), Yorkshire Probate Inventories (1972), The Collectors' Book of English Country Pottery (1974), Horse Brasses (1981), The Gentlewoman's Kitchen (1984), Traditional Food in Yorkshire (1987), North Country Folk Art (1989), Of Curiosities and Rare Things (1989), Treasures for the People (1989), Images of Leeds (1992), Leeds Described (1993), Leeds Waterfront Heritage (1993), The Country House Kitchen (1996), The Old Devon Farmhouse (1998), Ryedale Recipes (1998), A Taste of Leeds (1998), All the King's Cooks (1999), The Compleat Housekeeper (2000), The Boke of Keruynge (2003), A New and Easy Method of Cookery (ed, 2005); numerous articles in Folk Life, Post-Medieval Archaeology and others; *Recreations* hill walking, drawing, cooking; *Style*— Peter Brears, Esq, FSA; ✉ 4 Woodbine Terrace, Headingley, Leeds LS6 4AF (tel 0113 275 6537)

BRECHER, David John; s of William Brecher (d 1974), and Rachel, *née* Teitelbaum (d 1979); *b* 4 May 1927; *Educ* Haberdashers' Aske's, Trinity Coll Cambridge (MA); *m* 8 April 1953, Marjorie, da of Samuel Gordon; 1 da (Valerie Zara b 1955), 1 s (Andrew Justin b 1965); *Career* Nat Serv Army 1946–48; admitted slr 1952, fndr and sr ptnr Brecher & Co slrs 1952–95, currently conslt to Brecher Abram; formerly chm Thompson Property Co, non-exec dir Alba plc 1987–; memb Exec Cystic Fibrosis Res Tst; Freeman City of London 1963, Liveryman Worshipful Co of Blacksmiths; memb Law Soc; *Recreations* golf, bridge, boating, reading; *Clubs* Athenaeum, Estates Golfing Soc, Coombe Hill Golf, Mark's, Annabel's, Harry's Bar, Cambridge Union; *Style*— David Brecher, Esq; ✉ Brecher Abram, Heron Place, 3 George Street, London W1U 3QG (tel 020 7563 1000, fax 020 7486 7796)

BRECHIN, Rt Rev Neville Chamberlain; *b* 24 October 1939; *Educ* Salford GS, Univ of Nottingham (BA Theol, MA Applied Social Studies), Ripon Hall Oxford; *Family* m with 4 c; *Career* curate St Paul's Birmingham 1963–64, priest-in-charge St Michael's Gospel Lane Birmingham 1964–69, rector Deer Creek Parish USA 1967–68, vicar St Michael's Anglican Methodist Church Birmingham 1962–72, exec sec Lincoln Social Responsibility Ctee 1974–82, canon and prebend Lincoln Cathedral 1979–96, rector Church of St John the Evangelist Edinburgh 1982–97, bishop of Brechin 1997–2005; master Hugh Sexey's Hosp 2005–; *Style*— The Rt Rev Neville Chamberlain; ✉ Hugh Sexey's Hospital, High Street, Bruton, Somerset BA10 0AS (tel 01749 813911)

BRECKENRIDGE, Prof Sir Alasdair Muir; kt (2004), CBE (1995); s of Thomas Breckenridge (d 1973), of Arbroath, Scotland, and Jane, *née* Mackay (d 1986); *b* 7 May 1937; *Educ* Bell Baxter Sch, Univ of St Andrews (MB ChB, MD); *m* 28 Feb 1967, Jean Margaret, da of Trevor Charles William Boyle, of East London, South Africa; 2 s (Ross Alexander b 1969, Bruce Gordon b 1971); *Career* Dundee Royal Infirmary 1961–62 (house physician); Hammersmith Hosp and Royal Postgrad Med Sch London 1962–74: house physician, res fell, registrar, sr registrar, lectr, sr lectr; prof of clinical pharmacology Univ of Liverpool 1974–2002; chm: Jt Med Advsy Ctee HEFCE 1997–2002, Ctee on Safety of Medicines 1999–2003, Medicines and Healthcare Products Regulatory Agency 2003–; FRCP 1974, FRSE 1991; *Recreations* golf; *Style*— Prof Sir Alasdair Breckenridge, CBE, FRSE; ✉ Cree Cottage, Feather Lane, Heswall, Wirral L60 4RL (tel 0151 342 1096)

BREED, Colin Edward; MP; s of Alfred Breed (d 1995), and Edith Violet Breed (d 1984); *b* 4 May 1947; *Educ* Torquay Boys' GS; *m* 6 July 1968, Janet, *née* Courtiour; 1 da (Esther Janet b 21 Dec 1972), 1 s (Matthew James b 17 April 1975); *Career* mangr Midland Bank 1964–81, md Dartington & Co Ltd 1981–91, dir Gemini Abrasives Ltd 1991–97; MP (Lib

Dem) Cornwall SE 1997–, memb Lib Dem Trade & Industry Team 1997–99, Lib Dem spokesman on competition and consumer affrs; shadow min: agric and rural affrs 1999–, defence 2005–, Treasy 2006–; memb Select Ctee: Euro Scrutiny, Environment, Food and Rural Affairs 2001–04, Defence 2004–06, Treasury 2006–; lay memb GMC 1999–; local Methodist preacher; ACIB; *Recreations* golf, charitable orgns; *Clubs* National Liberal; *Style*— Colin Breed, Esq, MP; ✉ House of Commons, London SW1A 0AA (tel 020 7219 2588, fax 020 7219 5905, e-mail breedc@parliament.uk, website www.colinbreed.org.uk)

BREEDON, Timothy James (Tim); s of Peter Breedon (d 2003), and Ruth, *née* Davis; *b* 14 February 1958; *Educ* Calthorpe Park Comp Sch Fleet, Farnborough Sixth Form Coll, Worcester Coll Oxford (MA), London Business Sch (MSc); *m* 1982, Susan Margaret, *née* Hopkins; 3 s (Alexander b 1988, Matthew b 1990, William b 1996); *Career* Legal & General Investment Mgmnt Ltd: joined 1987, dir 1994–; Legal & General Gp plc: gp dir (investments) 2002–05, dep chief exec 2005, chief exec 2006–; dir Financial Reporting Cncl (FRC) 2004–; *Style*— Tim Breedon, Esq; ✉ Legal & General Group plc, Temple Court, 11 Queen Victoria Street, London EC4N 4TP (tel 020 7489 1888)

BREEN, His Hon Judge Geoffrey Brian; s of Ivor James Breen, and Doreen Odessa Breen (d 1995); *b* 3 June 1944; *Educ* Harrow HS, Coll of Law; *m* 8 April 1978 (m dis 1999), Lucy, da of Serafin Cabrera (d 1984), of Bogotá, Colombia; 1 s (Christopher b 1977), 1 da (Deborah b 1979); *Career* Stiles Breen & Partners: articled clerk 1962–67, admitted slr 1967, ptnr 1970–75, sr ptnr 1976–86; ptnr Blaser Mills & Newman 1976–86; metropolitan stipendiary magistrate 1986–2000, recorder of the Crown Court 1993–2000, circuit judge 2000–; pres Mental Health Review Tbnls (Restricted Patients Panel) 2006–; chm Youth Cts 1989–93, chm Family Proceedings Cts 1991–2000; former memb Ctee: Central and S Middx Law Soc, London Criminal Cts Slrs' Assoc; fell and former memb Cncl Br Acad of Forensic Sciences; *Recreations* classical guitar, DIY, reading; *Style*— His Hon Judge Breen; ✉ Luton Crown Court, 7 George Street, Luton, Bedfordshire LU1 2AA (tel 01582 522000)

BREEN, Kieran; s of Patrick Breen (d 1999), and Mary, *née* McLoughlin (d 2004); *b* 18 February 1955; *Educ* St Michael's Coll Enniskillen, UCD (BArch); *Career* architect; with Richard Rogers Partnership 1979–89; projects incl: Lloyds of London, Linn Products Glasgow, Wellcome Fndn Beckenham, Centre Commercial Nantes, Fujisawa & Iikura Tokyo; dir David Marks Julia Barfield Architects 1989–91; projects incl: Thames Valley Park, Information Age Centre, Battlebridge Basin; assoc Scottish office RMJM 1991–94, sr assoc ptnr KPF 1994–2002; projects incl: Wave Tower Bangkok, Filinvest Corp City Manila, Abu Dhabi Investment Authy HQ, AIG Europe HQ London, Bur Juman Centre Dubai; md: RMJM London Ltd 2002–05, Anshen & Allen 2006–; memb ARB 1984, RIBA 1987; *Recreations* travel, food, architecture; *Style*— Kieran Breen, Esq; ✉ Anshen & Allen, One Oliver's Yard, City Road, London, EC1Y 1DT (tel 020 7017 3100, e-mail kieran.breen@anshen.co.uk)

BREEN, Mary; *Career* former head of physics Eton Coll, headmistress St Mary's Sch Ascot 1999– (first lay headmistress); *Style*— Mrs Mary Breen; ✉ St Mary's School, St Mary's Road, Ascot, Berkshire SL5 9JF

BREEZE, Prof David John; s of Reginald Coulson Breeze, of Blackpool, and Marian, *née* Lawson; *b* 25 July 1944; *Educ* Blackpool GS, Univ of Durham (BA, PhD); *m* 22 July 1972, Pamela Diane, da of Victor James William Silvester; 2 s (Simon David b 10 March 1976, Christopher John b 16 Jan 1979); *Career* pt/t lectr Dept of Archaeology Univ of Durham 1968–69, successively asst inspr of ancient monuments, inspr then princ inspr Scottish Office (formerly DOE) 1969–89, chief inspr ancient monuments Historic Scotland 1989–2005, head of special heritage projects Historic Scotland 2005–; visiting prof Dept of Archaeology Univ of Durham 1994–, hon prof Univ of Edinburgh 1996–, hon prof Univ of Newcastle upon Tyne 2003–; pres: South Shields Archaeological and Historical Soc 1983–85, Soc of Antiquaries of Scotland 1987–90 (vice-pres 1984–87); vice-pres: Royal Archaeological Inst 2002–07, Cumberland and Westmorland Antiquarian and Archaeological Soc 2002–, Soc of Antiquaries of Newcastle upon Tyne 2007–; tstee Senhouse Museum Trust 1985–; chm: Hadrian's Wall Pilgrimages 1989 and 1999, British Archaeological Awards 1993– memb: Int Ctee of the Congress of Roman Frontier Studies 1983–, Hadrian's Wall Advsy Ctee 1977–97; author of many articles in British and foreign jls; corresponding memb German Archaeological Inst 1979; FSA 1975, FRSE 1991, FRSA 1999, Hon FSA Scot 2005 (FSA Scot 1970), Hon MIFA 2006 (MIFA 1990); *Books* incl: Hadrian's Wall (with B Dobson, 1976, 4 edn 2000), The Romans in Scotland - An Introduction to the Collections of The National Museum of Scotland (with D V Clarke and G MacKay, 1980), The Northern Frontiers of Roman Britain (1982), Roman Forts in Britain (1983), Hadrian's Wall - A Souvenir Guide to the Roman Wall (1987), A Queen's Progress (1987), Invaders of Scotland (with Anna Ritchie, 1991), Roman Officers and Frontiers (with B Dobson, 1993), Roman Scotland: Frontier Country (1996, 2 edn 2006), The Stone of Destiny (with G Munro, 1997), Historic Scotland (1998), Historic Scotland, People and Places (2002), The Stone of Destiny: Artefact and Icon (with R Welander and T Clancy, 2003), The Antonine Wall (2004), Frontiers of the Roman Empire (with S Jilek and A Thiel, 2005), J Collingwood Bruce's Handbook to the Roman Wall (14 edn, 2006); *Recreations* reading, travel; *Style*— Prof David Breeze, FSA, FRSE; ✉ 36 Granby Road, Edinburgh EH16 5NL (tel 0131 667 8876); Historic Scotland, Longmore House, Salisbury Place, Edinburgh EH9 1SH (tel 0131 668 8724, fax 0131 668 8730)

BREMNER, Charles John Fraser; s of John Fraser Bremner, and Rosemary, *née* Ives; *b* 16 June 1951; *Educ* Blairmore Sch, St Peter's Coll S Aust, New Coll Oxford (BA), UC Cardiff (Dip Journalism Studies); *m* 1, 1973 (m dis 1982), Valeria, *née* Gaidukowski; 1 da (Anna Lucy b 1977); *m* 2, 1987 (m dis 2006), Fariba, da of Abbas Shirdel; 1 s (James Charles Farhad b 1991), 1 da (Leila Jenny b 1993); *Career* Reuters: trainee 1975–77, Moscow corr 1977–79, Mexico City corr 1979–80, Paris corr 1981–83, bureau chief Moscow 1983–86; The Times: New York corr 1987–92, Paris corr 1992–95 and 1999–, Europe corr 1995–99; *Recreations* flying, sailing, music; *Style*— Charles Bremner, Esq; ✉ c/o The Times, 1 Pennington Street, Wapping, London E1 9XN (e-mail charles.bremner@thetimes.co.uk)

BREMNER, Eric; s of Hamish Bremner, of Edinburgh, and Mary Wotherspoon Thomson, *née* Ross; *b* 9 July 1958; *Educ* Trinity Acad Edinburgh, Grays Sch of Art Aberdeen, Harrow Coll of Further Educn (Dip Fashion Design), RCA (MA); *m* 1 Sept 1979, Jane Catherine Mary, da of Donald Bruce Scott; 2 s (Hamish Scott b 10 May 1986, Fergus Ross b 1 Sept 1996), 1 da (Grace Francine b 5 March 1991); *Career* design asst Margaret Howell 1984; design dir Laura Ashley 1993–94, sr designer Sportmax/Max Mara Italy 1994– (designer 1984–94); design conslt: Marina Rinaldi Italy 1986–93, Prisma Commerciale Abbigliamento Italy 1987–93; pt/t tutor Fashion Sch RCA 1987–; external assessor: fashion (MDes) Edinburgh Coll of Art 1989–94, fashion (BA) Nat Coll of Art and Design Dublin 1989–94; *Recreations* cooking, music; *Style*— Eric Bremner, Esq; ✉ 9 High Street, Sutton Courtenay, Oxfordshire OX14 4AW (tel 01235 848620)

BREMNER, Rory Keith Ogilvy; s of Maj Donald Stuart Ogilvy Bremner (d 1979), and Anne Ulithorne, *née* Simpson (d 2000); *b* 6 April 1961; *Educ* Wellington, KCL (BA); *m* 1, 8 Jan 1987 (m dis 1996), Susan Catherine, *née* Shackleton; *m* 2, 11 Sept 1999, Tessa Elizabeth, *née* Campbell Fraser; 2 da (Ava b 9 June 2001, Lila b 4 Aug 2003); *Career* satirical impressionist, writer and performer 1984–; tours and one-man shows 1985–, series BBC TV 1986–92, series Rory Bremner - Who Else? (Channel 4) 1992–98, Bremner, Bird and Fortune 1998–, Between Iraq and a Hard Place 2003; opera translations for Broomhill Opera: Der Silbersee 1999, Carmen 2001; columnist New Statesman 2005–; Press Prize (Montreux) 1987, Top Male Comedy Performer (BCA) 1992, BAFTA 1994, 1995 and 1996, RTS Award 1995, 1998 and 1999; FKC 2005; *Recreations* cricket, travel, tennis, opera, country sports, golf; *Clubs* Lord's Taverners; *Style*— Rory Bremner, Esq; ✉ c/o The Richard Stone Partnership, 2 Henrietta Street, London WC2E 8PS (tel 020 7497 0849, fax 020 7497 0869)

BRENDEL, Alfred; Hon KBE (1989); s of Albert Brendel, and Ida, *née* Wieltschnig; *b* 5 January 1931; *m* 1, 1960 (m dis 1972), Iris Heymann-Gonzala; 1 da (Doris); m 2, 1975, Irene, da of Dr Johannes Semler; 1 s (Adrian), 2 da (Anna-Sophie, Katharina); *Career* pianist and writer; concert career since 1949; recordings for Vox, Turnabout, Vanguard, Philips; Evening Standard Outstanding Artistic Achievement Award 1995, Léonie Sonning Music Prize 2002, Ernst von Siemens Prize 2004; Hon DMus: Univ of London 1978, Univ of Sussex 1980, Univ of Oxford 1983, Univ of Warwick 1991, Yale Univ 1992, Univ of Cologne 1995, Univ of Exeter 1998; fell Exeter Coll Oxford; memb Acad of Arts and Sciences USA 1989; Hon RAM, FRNCM 1990; Ordre pour le Mérite (Germany) 1991, Chevalier de l'Ordre des Arts et des Lettres (France) 2003 (Commandeur 1985); *Books* Musical Thoughts and Afterthoughts (essays, 1976), Music Sounded Out (essays, 1990), Fingerzeig (45 texts, German, 1996), Störendes Lachen Während des Jaworts (44 texts, German, 1997), One Finger Too Many (poetry, London 1998, New York 1999), Kleine Teufel (poems, German, 1999), Collected Essays on Music (a cappella, 2000), Ausgerechnet Ich (2001), The Veil of Order (2002), Spiegelbild und schwarzer Spick (collected poems, German, 2003); *Recreations* reading, theatre, films, unintentional humour, kitsch; *Style*— Alfred Brendel, Esq, KBE; ✉ c/o Ingpen & Williams Ltd, 7 St George's Court, 131 Putney Bridge Road, London SW15 2PA (tel 020 8874 3222, fax 020 8877 3113)

BRENDON, John Patrick; *b* 27 March 1947; *Educ* Tonbridge, Univ of Manchester (BA); *Children* 1 da (Camilla b 4 Oct 1985), 1 s (Richard b 2 May 1987); *Career* PricewaterhouseCoopers (formerly Price Waterhouse): joined London office 1968, ptnr 1980–, NY office 1984–87, memb UK firm Supervisory Bd 1998–, memb Global Oversight Bd 2000–01, UK ethics ptnr 2004–06, global chief accountant 2004–; FCA (ACA 1972); *Clubs* MCC, Hever Castle Golf; *Style*— John Brendon, Esq; ✉ PricewaterhouseCoopers, 1 Embankment Place, London WC2N 6RH (tel 020 7804 4816)

BRENMAN, Greg; *Career* co-chm Tiger Aspect Pictures, head of drama and memb Bd of Dirs Tiger Aspect Prodns; *Television* prodr: Jane Eyre (ITV), Deacon Brodie (BBC1), Births Marriages and Deaths, (BBC2, Best Drama Broadcast Awards, nominee BAFTA Award and Indie Award), Kid in the Corner (Channel 4, three Golden Nymph Awards, Mental Health Award, nominee BAFTA Award), Playing The Field (BBC1, Best Indie Drama, nominee RTS Award and BAFTA Award), Shockers (Channel 4), Hound of The Baskervilles (BBC1), Rescue Me (BBC1), Murphy's Law (BBC1), Fat Friends (ITV), My Fragile Heart, (ITV, nominee RTS Award and Broadcast Award), Bodily Harm, (Channel 4, RTS nomination), Murder, (BBC2, BAFTA Award), Omagh (Channel 4), Family Business (BBC1); *Film* prodr: Billy Elliott 2000 (Best Newcomer Prodr Award Producers Guild of America, nominee Best Picture Golden Globe Award, Best Independent Film Br Independent Film Awards), The Martins 2001, The League of Gentlemen's Apocalypse 2005; *Style*— Greg Brenman, Esq; ✉ Tiger Aspect Productions, 5 Soho Square, London W1V 5DF

BRENNAN, Baron (Life Peer UK 2000), of Bibury in the County of Gloucestershire; Daniel Joseph; QC (1985); s of Daniel Brennan (d 1969), of Bradford, and Mary, *née* Ahearne (d 1966); *b* 19 March 1942; *Educ* St Bede's GS Bradford, Univ of Manchester (LLB); *m* 21 Aug 1968, Pilar, da of Luis Sanchez Hernandez, of Madrid (d 1980), and Nieves Moya Dominguez; 4 s (Daniel b 1971, Patrick b 1972, Michael b 1977, Alexander b 1980); *Career* called to the Bar: Gray's Inn 1967, King's Inn Dublin 1990, NI 2001; recorder of the Crown Court 1982–; memb Criminal Injuries Compensation Bd 1989–97; bencher Gray's Inn 1993; chm Personal Injury Bar Assoc 1995–97; chm Gen Cncl of the Bar 1999 (vice-chm 1998); ind advsr to Home Sec and Min of Def on compensation for miscarriages of justice; pres Catholic Union of GB; Hon LLD Nottingham Trent 1999, Hon LLD Univ of Manchester 2000; FRSA 2000; *Publications* Bullen & Leake on Pleadings (gen ed, 14 edn, 2001); *Style*— Lord Brennan, QC; ✉ Matrix Chambers, Griffin Building, Gray's Inn Road, London WC1R 5LN (tel 020 7611 9359, fax 020 7404 3448)

BRENNAN, Kevin Denis; MP; s of Michael Brennan (d 2006), of Cwmbran, and Beryl, *née* Evans; *b* 16 October 1959; *Educ* St Alban's RC Comp Sch Pontypool, Pembroke Coll Oxford (BA), UC Cardiff (PGCE), Univ of Glamorgan (MSc); *m* 1988, Amy Lynn, da of Charles Wack; 1 da (Siobhán Lynn b 15 March 1994); *Career* head of econ Radyr Comp Sch 1985–94; researcher for Rt Hon Rhodri Morgan, MP 1995–2000, special advsr Nat Assembly for Wales 2000; MP (Lab) Cardiff W 2001–; a Lord Cmmr of HM Treasy (Govt whip) 2006–; memb Select Ctee for Public Admin 2001–05; memb Cardiff City Cncl 1991–2001 (chair Finance, chair Econ Scruntiny); memb Lab Campaign for Electoral Reform; memb: Fabian Soc, Bevan Fndn, Socialist Health Assoc; memb Parly rock band MP4; *Recreations* sport (particularly watching rugby), music; *Clubs* Canton Labour; *Style*— Kevin Brennan, MP; ✉ House of Commons, London SW1A 0AA (tel 029 2022 3207, e-mail brennank@parliament.uk)

BRENNAN, Richard; *Career* formerly with Hutchison Telecom Hong Kong; Orange: gp IT and ops dir 1993, UK gp commercial dir 1999, currently exec vice-pres Global Brand, Mktg and Products; *Style*— Richard Brennan, Esq

BRENNAN, Ursula; *b* 28 October 1952; *Educ* Putney HS, Univ of Kent at Canterbury (BA); *m* 28 June 1975, Denis Brennan; *Career* ILEA 1973–75, various posts rising to gp dir DWP 1999–2004, DG DEFRA 2004–; *Style*— Mrs Ursula Brennan

BRENNAND-ROPER, Dr David Andrew; s of Dr John Hanson Brennand-Roper (d 1974), of Guernsey, CI, and Joyce Brennand-Roper, *née* Deans; *b* 22 August 1946; *Educ* Bryanston, BNC Oxford (MA), Guy's Hosp Med Sch (BM BCh); *m* Sheila Jane, *née* Boswell; 4 c (Tanya Alexandra b 8 June 1982, Anneka Louise b 18 June 1984, Alexander James Boswell b 4 Aug 1992, Giles William John b 24 Aug 1995); *Career* Sir Phillip Oppenheimer res fell in nuclear cardiology 1979–81, sr registrar in cardiology Guy's Hosp 1981–82, conslt cardiologist Guy's and St Thomas' Tst and Dartford Hosps 1982–2002, emeritus conslt cardiologist Guy's and St Thomas' Hosps 2002–; lectr of the Br Heart Fndn; memb European Soc of Cardiology; Freeman City of London 1977, former Freeman Worshipful Co of Tobacco Pipe Makers 1977–82; memb BMA; FRCP; *Recreations* golf, photography, oenology; *Style*— Dr David Brennand-Roper; ✉ Suite 201, Emblem House, London Bridge Hospital, 27 Tooley Street, London SE1 2PR (tel 020 7357 8467, fax 020 7403 1702, e-mail drbroper@virgin.net)

BRENNER, Dr Sydney; CH (1987); *b* 13 January 1927; *Educ* Univ of the Witwatersrand (MSc, MB BCh), Univ of Oxford (DPhil); *Family* 3 c, 1 step s; *Career* Carnegie Corp fell USA 1954, Virus Laboratory Univ of Calif Berkeley 1954, lectr in physiology Univ of the Witwatersrand 1955–56, fell King's Coll Cambridge 1959–; MRC: memb scientific staff 1957–92, memb Cncl 1978–82 and 1986–90; dir Laboratory of Molecular Biology Cambridge 1979–86, dir Molecular Genetics Unit 1986–91; non-resident fell The Salk Inst San Diego 1981–85, visiting fell Central Res and Devpt Dept E 1 du Pont de Nemours & Co Wilmington 1985–99, visiting prof in med Royal Free Hosp Sch of Med Univ of London 1987–91, hon prof of genetic med Univ of Cambridge Clinical Sch 1989–97, scholar in residence Scripps Res Inst La Jolla 1989–91 (memb 1991–), research worker Dept of Med Univ of Cambridge Sch of Clinical Med 1992–96, pres The Neuroscience Res Program NY 1992–96, pres Molecular Sciences Inst La Jolla 1996–2001, distinguished research prof Salk Inst La Jolla 2001–, adjunct prof Univ of Calif San Diego 2001–03; Warren Triennial prize 1968, William Bate Hardy Prize Cambridge Philosophical Soc 1969, Gregory Endel Medal German Acad of Sci Leopoldina 1970, Albert Lasker Medical Research award 1971, Royal medal Royal Soc of London 1974, Charles-Leopold Mayer prize (French Acad) 1975, Gairdner Fndn Int award Canada 1978 and 1991, Krebs medal Fedn of European Biomedical Scis 1980, Ciba medal (Biochemical Soc) 1981, Feldberg Fndn prize 1983, Neil Hamilton Fairley medal (RCP) 1985, Croonian lectr Royal Soc of London 1986, Rosenstiel award Brandeis Univ USA 1986, Genetics Soc of America Medal 1987, Prix Louis Jeantet de Med (Fndn Louis Jeantet de Med Switzerland) 1987, Harvey prize Technion - Israel Inst of Technol 1987, Hughlings Jackson medal (Royal Soc of Med London) 1987, Waterford Bio-Medical Sci award (Res Inst of Scripps Clinic La Jolla) 1988, Kyoto prize 1990, Copley medal Royal Soc of London 1991, King Faisal Int prize for Science King Faisal Fndn Saudi Arabia 1992, Bristol-Myers Squibb award for Distinguished Achievement in Neuroscience Res 1992, Albert Lasker Award for Special Achievement in Med Sci 2000, Novartis Drew Medal in Biomedical Research 2001, Distinguished Service Award of The Miami Nature of Winter Biotechnology Symposia 2002, March of Dimes Prize in Developmental Biology 2002, Dan David Prize 2002, Nobel Prize in Physiology or Med 2002 (with Dr Sir John E Sulston and Prof H Robert Horvitz), UCL Prize in Clinical Science 2003 Nat Science Prize Singapore 2004, UC San Diego/Merck Life Sciences Achievement Award 2005; Hon DSc: Trinity Coll Dublin 1967, Univ of the Witwatersrand 1972, Univ of Chicago 1976, Univ of London 1982, Univ of Leicester 1983, Univ of Oxford 1985, Rockefeller Univ 1996, Columbia Univ 1997, La Trobe Univ 1999, Harvard Univ 2002, Yale Univ 2003, Univ of Br Columbia 2004, Toronto Univ 2005; Hon DLitt Nat Univ of Singapore 1995; Hon LLD: Univ of Glasgow 1981, Univ of Cambridge 2001; Hon Dr: Nat Friederich Schiller Univ Jena 1998, Univ of Oporto 2003; hon memb: Deutsche Akademie der Natursforscher Leopoldina 1975, Soc for Biological Chemists 1975, The Chinese Soc of Genetics (Taiwan) 1989, Assoc of Physicians of GB and Ireland 1991, Alpha Omega Alpha Honor Med Soc 1994, German Soc of Cell Biology 1999, Japan Genetics Soc 2001; fell American Acad of Microbiology 1996; hon fell: Exeter Coll Oxford 1985, Indian Acad of Scis 1989, Acad of Med Scis London 1999; hon memb: German Soc of Cell Biology 1999, Genetics Soc of Japan 2001, Biochemical Soc UK 2003, Cambridge Philosophical Soc 2003, Physiological Soc 2003, Biophysical Soc 2003, European Acad of Science 2004; foreign assoc: US Nat Acad of Scis 1977, Royal Soc of South Africa 1983; foreign hon memb American Acad Arts and Science 1965, fell AAAS 1966; foreign memb: American Philosophical Soc 1979, Real Academia de Ciencias (Spain) 1985; external scientific memb Max Planck Soc 1988, memb Academia Europaea 1989, Correspondant Scientifique Emérite de l'INSERM Paris 1991, Associé Étranger Académie des Sciences Institut de France Paris 1992; FRS 1965, FRCP 1979, Hon FRSE 1979, Hon FRCPath 1990; National Day Public Service Star Repub of Singapore 2000, Hon Citizen Republic of Singapore 2003, Officier de la Legion d'Honneur 2003, Order of Mapungubuse (South Africa) 2004; *Style*— Dr Sydney Brenner, CH, FRS

BRENT, Lucy Elizabeth; da of Allan Henry David George Brent (d 1978), and Irene Dorothy, *née* Jameson; *b* 7 January 1947; *Educ* Oak Hall; *Career* dep chm Trimite Ltd; FIMgt; *Recreations* skiing, bridge, golf, theatre, opera; *Clubs* Wentworth Golf; *Style*— Miss Lucy Brent; ✉ c/o Midland Bank, 28 High Street, PO Box 41, Uxbridge, Middlesex UB8 1JN

BRENT, Michael Hamilton; s of Allan Henry David George Brent (d 1978), and Irene Dorothy, *née* Jameson; *b* 18 March 1943; *Educ* Charterhouse; *m* 1973, Janet, da of Irvine McBeath; 1 s, 2 da; *Career* chm and md Trimite Ltd 1975–; FCA; *Recreations* bridge, chess, golf, sailing, skiing, tennis; *Clubs* Wentworth Golf; *Style*— Michael Brent, Esq, FCA; ✉ Trimite Ltd, Arundel Road, Uxbridge, Middlesex UB8 2SD (tel 01895 251234, fax 01895 256789); c/o HSBC, PO Box 41, High Street, Uxbridge, Middlesex

BRENTFORD, 4 Viscount (UK 1929), of Newick, Sussex; Sir Crispin William Joynson-Hicks; 4 Bt of Holmbury (UK 1919), 2 Bt of Newick (UK 1956); s of 3 Viscount Brentford, DL (d 1983) and Phyllis, *née* Allfrey (d 1979); *b* 7 April 1933; *Educ* Eton, New Coll Oxford; *m* 1964, Gillian Evelyn, OBE (1996), er da of late Gerald Edward Schluter, OBE, of Nairobi, Kenya; 3 da (Hon Emma b 1966, Hon Rowena (Hon Mrs Banks) b 1967, Hon Amy b 1978), 1 s (Hon Paul William b 1971); *Heir* s, Hon Paul Joynson-Hicks; *Career* late Lt 9 Lancers; slr 1960; ptnr in legal firm of Taylor Joynson Garrett 1961–95; memb Ct of Assts Worshipful Co of Girdlers (Master 1983–84); *Style*— The Rt Hon the Viscount Brentford; ✉ Springhill, Broad Oak, Heathfield, East Sussex TN21 8XJ (tel 01435 867161)

BRENTON, Howard John; s of Donald Henry Brenton, and Rose Lilian, *née* Lewis; *b* 13 December 1942; *Educ* Chichester HS for Boys, St Catharine's Coll Cambridge (BA); *m* 31 Jan 1970, Jane Margaret, da of William Alfred Fry; 2 s (Samuel John b 23 Sept 1974, Harry William Donald b 6 Sept 1976); *Career* playwright; plays incl: Christie in Love (Portable Theatre) 1969, Revenge (Royal Court Theatre Upstairs) 1969, Hitler Dances (Traverse Theatre Workshop Edinburgh) 1972, Measure for Measure, after Shakespeare (Northcott Theatre Exeter) 1972, Magnificence (Royal Court Theatre) 1973, Brassneck (with David Hare, Nottingham Playhouse) 1973, The Churchill Play (Nottingham Playhouse) 1974 and twice revived by the RSC in 1978 and 1988, Government Property (Aarhus Theatre Denmark) 1975, Weapons of Happiness (NT) 1976 (winner of the Evening Standard Best Play of the Year award), Epsom Downs (Jt Stock Theatre Co) 1977, Sore Throats (RSC) 1979, The Romans in Britain (NT) 1980, Thirteenth Night (RSC) 1981, The Genius (Royal Court Theatre) 1983, Bloody Poetry (Foco Novo Theatre) 1984 and revived by the Royal Court Theatre 1988, Pravda (with David Hare, NT) 1985 (winner of the Evening Standard Best Play of the Year award), Greenland (Royal Court Theatre) 1988, Iranian Nights (with Tariq Ali, Royal Court Theatre) 1989, HID - Hess is Dead (RSC and Mickery Theatre Amsterdam) 1989, Moscow Gold (with Tariq Ali, RSC) 1990, Berlin Bertie (Royal Court) 1992, Playing Away (opera libretto, Opera North) 1994, Faust (RSC) 1995, In Extremis (Univ of Calif) 1997, Ugly Rumours (with Tariq Ali, Tricycle Theatre) 1998, Nasser's Eden (BBC Radio) 1998, Collateral Damage (with Tariq Ali and Andy de la Tour, Tricycle Theatre) 1999, Snogging Ken (with Tariq Ali and Andy de la Tour, Almeida Theatre) 2000, Kit's Play (RADA Jerwood Theatre) 2001, Paul (RNT) 2005, In Extremis (Shakespeare's Globe) 2006; TV plays incl: A Saliva Milkshake (BBC) 1975, The Paradise Run (Thames) 1976, Desert of Lies (BBC) 1984, the four part series Dead Head (BBC) 1986, Spooks (writer of several episodes, BBC) 2002, 2003, 2004 and 2005 (Best Drama Series BAFTA Awards); Arts and Humanities Research Bd Fellowship Univ of Birmingham 2000–03; Freeman City of Buffalo NY; Hon Dr Univ of North London, Hon DLitt Univ of Westminster; *Books* Diving for Pearls (1989), Hot Irons (1995, 2 edn 1998); *Recreations* painting; *Style*— Howard Brenton, Esq; ✉ c/o Casarotto Ramsay Ltd, National House, 4th Floor, 60–66 Wardour Street, London W1V 3HP (tel 020 7287 4450, fax 020 7287 9128)

BRENTON, Timothy Deane; QC 1998; s of Cdr Ronald William Brenton, MBE (d 1982), and Peggy Cecilia Deane, *née* Biggs; *b* 4 November 1957; *Educ* King's Sch Rochester, BRNC Dartmouth, Univ of Bristol (LLB); *m* 29 Aug 1981, Annabel Louisa, da of Alan Harry Robson, of Sharrington, Norfolk; 1 da (Louisa Elizabeth b 8 April 1990), 1 s (Benjamin Alexander b 27 April 1993); *Career* RN 1975–79; lectr in law KCL 1980, called to the Bar Middle Temple 1981, standing counsel to Treas Slr in Admiralty matters 1991–98, hon counsel to King George's Fund for Sailors 2000–; memb Commercial Bar Assoc, supporting memb London Marine Arbitrators Assoc; *Recreations* golf, fishing, country pursuits, music; *Style*— Timothy Brenton, Esq, QC; ✉ 7 King's Bench Walk, Temple, London EC4Y 7DS (tel 020 7910 8300, fax 020 7583 0950, e-mail tbrenton@7kbw.co.uk)

BRENTON, Will; s of John Kenneth Williamson (d 1997), and Doreen Mary Brenton; *b* 11 November 1962, Leeds; *Educ* Old Hall HS Maghull Liverpool, Welsh Coll of Music and

Drama (Dip Dramatic Arts); *Children* 1 da (Ella b 1996); *Career* actor, dir and prodr; co-fndr Tell Tale Prodns 1994–, fndr Wish Films Ltd 2005 (producing Jim Jam & Sunny for ITV); actor: Godspell 1987, Flying Lady 1988, Playdays 1988–90, Inspector Morse 1989, Blood Brothers 1990–91; actor and writer of pantomimes in Coventry 1990–2000; dir: Playdays 1990–94 (and writer), Coronation Street 1996–97, Emmerdale 1997–98, Bitsa 1996; creator, dir and prodr Fun Song Factory 1994–2004; writer, creator and prodr: Tweenies 1998–2004, Tweenies Live 2000–04, Boo! 2001–04, Sprogs 2002–04, Ella 2004; BAFTA (for Tweenies) 2000, nominee BAFTA Award 1999, 2000, 2001, 2002 and 2003; FRTS 2000; *Style*— Will Brenton, Esq; ✉ Wish Films Limited, Elstree Film Studios, Shenley Road, Borehamwood, Hertfordshire WD6 1JG (tel 020 8324 2308, e-mail will@wishfilms.com)

BRENTWOOD, Bishop of (RC) 1980–; Rt Rev Thomas McMahon; *b* 17 June 1936; *Educ* St Bede's GS Manchester, St Sulpice Paris; *Career* ordained Wonersh Surrey 1959, asst priest Colchester 1959–64, priest Westcliff-on-Sea 1964–69, parish priest Stock 1969–, chaplain Univ of Essex 1972–80; hon ecumenical canon Chelmsford Cathedral 2005; former memb Nat Ecumenical Cmmn; chm: Brentwood Ecumenical Cmmn 1979, Ctee for Pastoral Liturgy Bishop's Dept for Christian Life and Worship 1983–97, Essex Churches Consultative Cncl 1984–93, Ctee for Church Music 1985–2001, Bishops' Patrimony Ctee 2001–; vice-pres: Pax Christi 1987–, Friends of Cathedral Music; memb: London Church Leaders Gp, East of England Churches Together, Movement for Christian Democracy (fndr), Int Cmmn for English in Liturgy (representing Bishops of England and Wales on Episcopal Bd) 1983–2002, Churches Together in Essex and East London (chm 1984–93), Cncl of St George's House Windsor 2005– (as Bishops' Conf rep); memb Ct: Univ of Essex, NE London Univ; pres Essex Show 1992; hon fell Hertford Coll Oxford 2005; Hon Doctorate: Univ of Essex 1991, Anglia Poly Univ 2000; *Style*— The Rt Rev the Bishop of Brentwood; ✉ Bishop's House, Stock, Ingatestone, Essex CM4 9BU (tel 01277 840268)

BRERETON, Donald; CB (2001); s of Clarence Vivian Brereton (d 1965), and Alice Gwendolin, *née* Galpin; *b* 18 July 1945; *Educ* Plymouth Coll, Univ of Newcastle upon Tyne (BA); *m* 12 April 1969, Mary Frances, da of William Turley (d 1967); 2 da (Kathryn Vivian b 15 Nov 1972, Sally Clare b 21 Dec 1974), 1 s (Samuel Edward b 21 Feb 1977); *Career* VSO Malaysia 1963–64, asst princ Miny of Health 1968–71, asst private sec to sec of state for Social Servs 1971–72, private sec to Permanent Sec DHSS 1972–73, princ Health Servs Planning 1973–79, princ private sec to Sec of State for Social Servs 1979–82; asst sec: DHSS Policy Strategy Unit 1982–84, Housing Benefit 1984–89; under sec and head PM's Efficiency Unit 1989–93, policy dir DSS 1993–2001, dir Disability and Carers Gp DWP 2001–2003; dir Motability 2004–; chm Carers UK; selector VSO; *Recreations* tennis, holidays, books, bridge; *Style*— Donald Brereton, Esq, CB

BRETSCHER, Dr Mark Steven; s of Egon Bretscher (d 1973), and Hanna, *née* Greminger (d 1993); *b* 8 January 1940; *Educ* Abingdon Sch, Gonville & Caius Coll Cambridge (minor scholar, major scholar, Coll Prize, MA, PhD); *m* 1978, Barbara Mary Frances Pearse; 1 da (Nicola Katherine Pearse b 1978), 1 s (Andrew Jonathan b 1981); *Career* research fell Gonville & Caius Coll Cambridge 1964–70 (research student 1961–64), head Div of Cell Biology MRC Laboratory of Molecular Biology Cambridge 1984–95 (memb Scientific Staff 1965–2005), ret; Jane Coffin Childs Meml fell Stanford Univ 1964–65, visiting prof: Harvard Univ 1975–76, Stanford Univ 1984–85; memb Euro Molecular Biology Orgn; Friedrich Miescher Prize Swiss Biochemical Soc 1979; FRS 1985; *Publications* papers in scientific jls on topics of: the genetic code and protein synthesis 1962–70, membrane structure 1971–, cell locomotion 1976–; *Recreations* planting and cultivating woodland, mountain walking; *Style*— Dr Mark Bretscher, FRS; ✉ Ram Cottage, Commerical End, Swaffham Bulbeck, Cambridgeshire CB5 0ND (tel 01223 811276); MRC Laboratory of Molecular Biology, Hills Road, Cambridge CB2 2QH (tel 01223 248011, fax 01223 412142, e-mail msb@mrc-lmb.cam.ac.uk)

BRETT, Nicholas Richard John; s of Reginald Sydney Brett (d 1993), and Urania Rhoda, *née* Morris; *b* 6 February 1950; *Educ* Abingdon Sch, Bedford Coll London (BA, pres Students' Union), Pennsylvania State Univ (MA), Kellogg Business Sch Northwestern Univ (Exec Prog); *m* 1 (m dis); m 2, 3 Dec 1981, Judith Anne, da of Norman Armitage Miller; 2 da (Camilla Beatrice Brett-Miller b 31 May 1980, Harriet Lucy Brett-Miller b 3 July 1983); *Career* news reporter then news ed East Ender (Stratford Express series) 1977, chief reporter Camden Journal 1978–81, prodn ed Times Health Supplement 1981; The Times: sports sub-ed 1982, chief sub-ed Saturday section 1982, dep ed Saturday section 1983, ed Saturday section 1984, asst features ed 1985, dep features ed 1986, features ed 1986–88; ed Radio Times and editorial dir BBC Magazines 1988–96, publishing dir Radio Times 1996–97, dir Radio Times Arts and Factual Gp 1997–2001, dep md BBC Magazines 2001–; memb Code of Practice Ctee Press Standards Bd of Fin 1992–94; pres European Assoc of TV Magazines 1993–95 (vice-pres 1992–93), chm BSME 1992; Radio Times winner Magazine of the Year Magazine Publishing Awards 1991, Ed of the Year BSME Awards 1993, Ed of the Year PPA Magazines Awards 1996; *Recreations* Arsenal, birdwatching, carpentry, walking; *Clubs* Groucho; *Style*— Nicholas Brett, Esq; ✉ BBC Magazines, Woodlands, 80 Wood Lane, London W12 0TT (tel 020 8433 3065, fax 020 8433 3002, e-mail nicholas.brett@bbc.co.uk)

BRETT, Simon Anthony Lee; s of Alan John Brett (d 1979), and Margaret, *née* Lee (d 2001); *b* 28 October 1945; *Educ* Dulwich Coll, Wadham Coll Oxford (maj scholar, BA, pres OUDS); *m* 27 Nov 1971, Lucy Victoria, da of late Alastair Dixon McLaren; 1 da (Sophie b 9 Oct 1974), 2 s (Alastair b 22 July 1977, Jack b 11 March 1981); *Career* writer; Father Christmas Toy Dept Shinners of Sutton 1967; prodr light entertainment: BBC Radio 1968–77 (worked on progs incl: Week Ending, Frank Muir Goes Into..., The News Huddlines, Lord Peter Wimsey, The Hitch-Hikers Guide to the Galaxy), LWT 1977–79 (worked on progs incl: End of Part One, Maggie and Her, The Glums); full time writer 1979–; writing for TV incl After Henry (nominated for 1988 and 1989 BAFTA Awards), How to be a Little Sod; writing for radio incl: Afternoon Theatre, Frank Muir Goes Into..., Semicircles, Molesworth, After Henry (BPG Award for Outstanding Radio Programme 1987), Dear Diary, No Commitments, Foul Play, Smelling of Roses; Writers' Guild Award for Best Radio Feature Script (with Frank Muir) 1973; pres Detection Club 2001–; chm: Crime Writers' Assoc 1986–87, Soc of Authors 1995–97; memb PLR Advsy Ctee 2003–; *Publications* crime novels featuring actor-detective Charles Paris: Cast, In Order of Disappearance, So Much Blood, Star Trap, An Amateur Corpse, A Comedian Dies, The Dead Side of The Mike, Situation Tragedy, Murder Unprompted, Murder in the Title, Not Dead Only Resting, Dead Giveaway, What Bloody Man is That?, A Series of Murders, Corporate Bodies, A Reconstructed Corpse, Sicken and so Die, Dead Room Farce; other crime novels: A Shock to the System (Best Novel Award nomination by Mystery Writers of America, filmed starring Michael Caine), Dead Romantic, A Nice Class of Corpse, Mrs Presumed Dead, Mrs Pargeter's Package, The Christmas Crimes at Puzzel Manor, Mrs Pargeter's Pound of Flesh, Singled Out, Mrs Pargeter's Plot, Mrs Pargeter's Point of Honour, The Body on the Beach, Death on the Downs, The Torso in the Town, Murder in the Museum, The Hanging in the Hotel, The Witness at the Wedding, The Stabbing in the Stables; crime short stories: A Box of Tricks, Crime Writers and Other Animals; others, incl various humorous books; *Style*— Simon Brett, Esq; ✉ c/o Michael Motley, The Old Vicarage, Tredington, Tewkesbury, Gloucestershire GL20 7BP (tel 01684 276390)

BRETT, Simon Baliol; s of Antony Reginald Forbes Baliol, MBE (d 1981), and Bay Helen, *née* Brownell (d 1989); *b* 27 May 1943; *Educ* Ampleforth, St Martin's Sch of Art; *m* 31 Aug 1974, Juliet Anne, da of Paul Hamilton Wood, OBE (d 1962); 1 da (Emily b 1977); *Career* wood engraver and artist illustrator; pt/t teacher Marlborough Coll Art Sch 1971–89; proprietor Paulinus Press 1981–88; chm Soc of Wood Engravers 1987–92 (treas 1992–2000); winner of Francis Williams Illustration Award 1991; RE 1991 (ARE 1987); *Books* illustrated: numerous for Folio Soc, private presses and commercial publishers incl: Clarissa (1991), The Confessions of St Augustine (1993), Middlemarch (1999), The Poetry of John Keats (2001), Meditations on Marcus Aurelius (2003), Legends of the Ring (2004), Legends of the Grail (2007); written: on history and practice of wood engraving incl: Engravers I (1987), Engravers II (1992), Wood Engraving - How to Do It (1994, 2 edn 2000), An Engraver's Globe (2002); *Style*— Simon Brett, Esq; ✉ 12 Blowhorn Street, Marlborough, Wiltshire SN8 1BT (tel 01672 512905)

BRETT, District Judge Trevor Graham; s of Joseph Brett (d 1986), and Nellie Kathleen, *née* Dean (d 1994); *b* 26 January 1950; *Educ* Borden GS Sittingbourne, Birmingham Poly (LLB London); *m* 5 April 1975, Gillian Margaret, da of Ernest Charles Fluck; 3 s (Mark Graham b 7 July 1978, Andrew Graham b 5 Dec 1980, Oliver Graham b 4 Nov 1985); *Career* articled 1972–74, admitted slr 1974; in private practice: Bradbury & Co Camberwell 1974–75, Basset & Boucher Rochester 1975–85, Dakers Green Brett Chatham 1985–92; district judge Uxbridge, Slough and Reigate Co Cts Apr 1992–93; district judge Bromley Co Cts 1993–; memb Law Soc 1974– (sec Rochester, Chatham and Gillingham Law Soc 1982–92); *Recreations* sport, especially golf, soccer and badminton, reading; *Style*— District Judge Brett

BRETT, Baron (Life Peer UK 1999), of Lydd in the County of Kent; William Henry Brett; *b* 6 March 1942; *m* (m dis 2006), Janet, *née* Grose; 2 da (Judith, Hannah); *Career* former booking clerk British Rail and official Transport Salaried Staffs' Assoc, negotiator bank employees' union (now UNIFI) 1966–68, divnl offr ASTMS 1968–74, also former presenter Union Scene (BBC Radio Nottingham); IPMS (now PROSPECT): joined as asst sec (environment and agric members) 1974–80, asst gen sec (private and public sectors) 1989, gen sec 1989–99, ret; memb Gen Cncl TUC 1989–99 (memb ctees: Fin and Gen Purposes, Int, Public Serv, Employment Policy and Organisation, Energy and Safety Health and Environment), memb Exec Ctee Public Servs Int 1986–99 (memb Steering Gp Euro Public Servs Ctee); cncllr (Lab) London Borough of Lewisham 1964–68; ILO: chm Governing Body 2002–03 (pres Workers' Gp and vice-pres Governing Body 1993–2002), dir London Office (UK and Ireland) 2004–; non-exec dir Docklands Light Railway 1998–2000; Hon Dr and hon sr fell Sullivan Univ Louisville KY 2004; FRSA 1994; *Books* International Labour in the 21st Century (1994); *Style*— The Lord Brett; ✉ 310 Nelson House, Dolphin Square, London SW1V 3NY (tel 020 7798 5681, e-mail billbrett70@hotmail.com or brettw@parliament.uk)

BRETT-HOLT, Alexis Fayrer (Alex); da of Raymond Arthur Brett-Holt (d 2001), of Esher, Surrey, and Jacqueline, *née* Hosken; *b* 7 March 1950; *Educ* Wimbledon HS, St Anne's Coll Oxford (BA); *m* 1980, (John) Gareth Roscoe, *qv*; 1 da (Philippa Claire b 1982), 1 s (Jonathan Hugh b 1983); *Career* called to the Bar Lincoln's Inn 1973; Dept of Environment: legal asst 1974, seconded to Dept of Health 1989–93, asst slr 1993–97, with Whitehall and Industry Gp on secondment to IBM 1995; dir Legal Services C DTI 1997–, legal advsr HSE 2004–; pres Assoc of First Div Civil Servants 1987–89; memb Bar Cncl 1994 and 1997; *Style*— Ms Alex Brett-Holt

BRETTEN, (George) Rex; QC (1980); s of Horace Victor Bretten (d 1954), and Kathleen Edna Betty Bretten; *b* 21 February 1942; *Educ* King Edward VII Sch, King's Lynn, Sidney Sussex Coll Cambridge (MA, LLM); *m* 1965, Maureen Gillian, *née* Crowhurst; 1 da; *Career* called to the Bar Lincoln's Inn 1965; *Clubs* Athenaeum; *Style*— G R Bretten, Esq, QC; ✉ Stonehill House, Horam, Heathfield, East Sussex; 15 Old Square, Lincoln's Inn, London WC2A 3UE (tel 020 7242 2744, fax 020 7831 8095)

BRETTLE, Robert Harvey Linton; s of Robert Edward Brettle (d 1974), and Mabel, *née* Linton (d 1998); *b* 3 April 1935; *Educ* Highgate Sch, ChCh Oxford (MA); *m* 27 May 1964, Lindsay Mary, da of late Sydney Howson; 3 s (Thomas b 1966, Oliver b 1969, Adrian b 1972); *Career* Nat Serv: cmmnd Middx Regt 1955, Royal West Africa Frontier Force 3 Bn Nigeria Regt (later Queen's Own Nigeria Regt) 1955–56, Intelligence and Recruitment Offr asst adj; admitted slr 1963 (insolvency practitioner); sr ptnr: Peard Son and Webster of Croydon 1983–86 (ptnr 1966–83), Peard Webster Pringle and John 1986–96 (conslt 1996–97); currently dep High Court registrar in bankruptcy; pres Croydon and Dist Law Soc 1972–73, chm of govrs St Margaret's Sch for Spastics and Physically Handicapped Children 1972–84; memb Law Soc 1963; *Recreations* bridge, gardening, travel; *Clubs* RAC; *Style*— Robert Brettle, Esq; ✉ 1 Willow Mount, Croydon, Surrey CR0 5LD (tel 020 8688 3307); Glavenside, Holt Road, Letheringsett, Holt, Norfolk NR25 7AR

BREUILLY, Prof John James; s of John Arthur Breuilly (d 1981), and Gwen, *née* Ellis (d 1987); *b* 31 October 1946, London; *Educ* Dunstable GS, Univ of York (BA, DPhil); *m* 1970, Elizabeth Linda; 1 s (b 2 Jan 1977), 1 da (b 30 June 1978); *Career* successively lectr in history, sr lectr, reader and prof Univ of Manchester 1972–95, prof of modern history Univ of Birmingham 1995–2004, prof of nationalism and ethnicity LSE 2004–; visiting prof: Hamburg 1987–88, Bielefeld 1992–93; research fell Wissenschaftskolleg Berlin 2001–02; FRHistS 1981; *Books* Nationalism and the State (2 edn 1993), The Formation of the First German Nation State, 1800–1871 (1996), 19th Century Germany: Politics, Culture and Society, 1780–1918 (ed, 2001); *Recreations* singing, cricket; *Style*— Prof John Breuilly; ✉ Department of Government, London School of Economics, Houghton Street, London WC2A 2AE (tel 020 7955 6153, e-mail j.breuilly@lse.ac.uk)

BREWER, David; s of William Watson Brewer (d 1968), and Eileen, *née* Hall; *b* 24 July 1946; *Educ* Brigg GS, Emmanuel Coll Cambridge (BA); *m* 26 May 1973, Elizabeth Margaret, da of John William Ferguson (d 1986); 1 da (Jane b 1975); *Career* British Coal: area chief accountant South Midlands 1979–85, chief accountant 1985–87, head of fin servs 1987–91, fin controller 1991–93, head of fin 1993–95; fin and operations dir Scottish Coal 1995–97, business conslt 1997–98, dir and UK gen mangr Miller Mining The Miller Gp Ltd 1998–2000, commercial and financial conslt to the mining industry 2000–03, DG Confedn of UK Coal Prodrs 2003–; assoc MIMM 1990, ACMA 1978; *Style*— David Brewer, Esq; ✉ 161 Chelsea Road, Sheffield S11 9BQ (tel 0114 255 8392, e-mail davidbreweris@hotmail.com)

BREWER, Sir David William; kt (2007), CMG (1999), JP (1979); s of Dr H F Brewer, and Elizabeth, *née* Nickell-Lean; *Educ* St Paul's, Univ of Grenoble; *m* 1985, Tessa Suzanne Mary, *née* Jordá; 2 da (Olivia b 1988, Gabriella b 1990); *Career* joined Sedgwick Gp 1959, rep Sedgwick Gp Japan 1976–78; dir: Sedgwick Gp Devpt Cos 1982–98, Sedgwick Far East Ltd 1982–99 (chm 1993–97), Sumitomo Marine & Fire Insurance Co (Europe) Ltd 1985–98, Sedgwick Int Risk Mgmnt Inc 1990–99; chm: Sedgwick Insurance and Risk Mgmnt Conslts (China) Ltd 1993–97, Sedgwick Japan Ltd 1994–97; dir and sr conslt British Invisibles 1998–2001, sr conslt Int Financial Servs London 2001–, conslt Asia Pacific Region Marsh Inc 1999–2007, memb European Advsy Bd Calyon Europe (formerly Credit Lyonnais) 2000–05, dir London Asia Capital plc 2005–, non-exec chm Tinci Holdings Ltd 2006–, ind dir Tullett Prebon SITICO Ltd 2007–, non-exec vice-chm Marsh Ltd 2007–, non-exec dir Canton Property Investment Ltd 2007, dir Securities and Investment Inst 2007–; vice-pres GB-China Centre 2004– (chm 1997–2004), chm Financial Servs Ctee Int Financial Services London/China-Br Business Cncl 1993–, exec chm UK-China Forum 2000–04, chm Bd China-Britain Business Cncl 2007– (hon treas 1991–2007); memb: Action Japan Ctee DTI 1996–2000, UK-Korea Forum for the Future 2000–02, China Prog Advsy Bd Chatham House 2004–; vice-pres City of London Sector Br Red Cross Soc 1986–, pres Insurance Inst of London 2006–07 (vice-pres 2005–06); memb Int Bd of Overseers Cass Business Sch City Univ 2003–; dir: City of London

Sinfonia 1988–, Guildhall Sch Tst 1999–; pres City of London Branch RNLI 2007– (memb 1989–, chm 1997–2006), chm: City of London Branch IoD 1999–, Care for Children UK 2007– (dir 1998–2006); pres London Cornish Assoc 2005–; tstee The Lord Mayor's 800th Anniversary Awards Tst 1997–; tstee Daiwa Anglo-Japanese Fndn 2007–; memb: Cncl Spitalfields Festival 1989–2002 (memb Devpt Ctee 2001–02), Advsy Cncl LSO 1999–, Advsy Bd The Sixteen 2005–; govr: City of London Poly 1979–90, Corp of Sons of the Clergy 1993–, SOAS Univ of London 2000–; int envoy for London Think London Int 2005–; churchwarden St Lawrence Jewry 1996–, almoner Christ's Hosp 1998–2004, memb Parish Clerks' Co 2006–; pres The Soc of Young Freemen 2003–; Hon Master of the Bench Gray's Inn 2004–; HM Cmmr of Lieutenancy for City of London 2005–; Alderman Bassishaw Ward City of London 1996– (memb Ct of Common Cncl 1992–96, pres Bassishaw Ward Club 1996–), Sheriff City of London 2002–03, Lord Mayor of London 2005–06; Liveryman Worshipful Co of Merchant Taylors 1968 (memb Ct of Assts 1985–, Master 2001–02), Liveryman Worshipful Co of Insurers 2001 (memb Ct of Assts 2004–), warden Ct of Assts Worshipful Co of Blacksmiths 2007– (hon memb 2001–), Hon Freeman Co of Security Professionals 2005; Hon DSc City Univ, Hon PhD London Met Univ; FCII 1966, Hon FSII 2006; *Recreations* music (especially opera and choral music), golf, mechanical gardening, chocolate, paronomasia; *Clubs* Garrick, City of London, MCC, St Enodoc Golf; *Style—* Sir David Brewer, CMG, JP; ✉ 16 Cowley Street, London SW1P 3LZ (tel 020 7222 5481, fax 020 7222 2123); International Financial Services London, 29–30 Cornhill, London EC3V 3NF (tel 020 7213 9119, fax 020 7213 9142, e-mail d.brewer@ifsl.org.uk); Orchard Cottage, Hellandbridge, Bodmin, Cornwall PL30 4QR (tel 01208 841268, fax 01208 841668)

BREWER, Prof Derek Stanley; s of Stanley Leonard Brewer, and Winifred Helen, *née* Forbes; *b* 13 July 1923; *Educ* The Crypt GS, Magdalen Coll Oxford (MA), Univ of Birmingham (PhD), Univ of Cambridge (LittD); *m* 1951, Lucie Elisabeth Hoole; 3 s, 2 da; *Career* academic, author and academic publisher; Univ of Cambridge: master Emmanuel Coll 1977–90, prof of English 1983–90, emeritus prof 1990–, life fell 1990–; Seatonian prize 1969, 1972, 1979 (jtly), 1980 (jtly), 1983, 1986, 1988 1992 (jtly) 1993 and 1999; Hon: LLD Keio Univ 1982, LLD Harvard Univ 1983, LittD Univ of Birmingham 1985, DUniv York 1985, DUniv Sorbonne 1988, DLitt Williams Coll 1989, DUniv Liège 1990; hon fell Eng Assoc 2001; hon memb Japan Acad 1981, corresponding fell Medieval Acad of America 1987; *Style—* Prof Derek Brewer; ✉ Emmanuel College, Cambridge (tel 01223 334200, fax 01223 241104, e-mail dsb27@hermes.cam.ac.uk)

BREWERTON, David Robert; s of Ernest John Brewerton (d 1980), and Violet Florence, *née* Smith; *b* 25 February 1943; *Educ* Coopers Company's Sch; *m* 25 May 1963, Patricia Ann, da of James Albert Driscoll, OBE; 2 s (Benjamin David b 27 March 1968, Jake David b 14 April 1970), 1 da (Sarah Ann Jane b 14 Sept 1973); *Career* Stock Exchange red button with Grieveson Grant 1959; sub ed: Extel Statistics 1964, Financial Times 1965; commercial property corr Daily Telegraph 1971 (reporter 1969), ed Policy Holder Insurance News 1977, Questor Daily Telegraph 1978, city ed The Independent 1986, exec ed finance and indust The Times 1988, ptnr Brunswick Group Ltd 1991–2002, writer and freelance journalist 2005–; Financial Journalist of the Year 1986; *Recreations* sailing, cooking, travel; *Style—* David Brewerton, Esq; ✉ 82 Bickenhall Mansions, Bickenhall Street, London W1U 6BS (tel 020 7486 0315)

BREWIN, Daniel Robert (Dan); s of John Stuart Brewin (d 1968), of Sheffield, and Elsie Mary Brewin, *née* Timm (d 1989); *b* 22 August 1946; *Educ* King Edward VII Sch Sheffield, Univ of Salford (BSc), Cranfield Sch of Mgmnt (MBA 1977); *m* 1, 1974 (m dis); 2 s (John b 1976, Timothy b 1980), 1 da (Anna b 1978); m 2, 1993, Lynne Joyce Pontet, da of Frank Harvey Manchester; *Career* British Airways: various appts 1964–81, dir of ops Manchester Airport 1981–84; gen mangr UK sales British Caledonian 1984–87 (sr gen mangr commercial 1987), sr gen mangr Gatwick British Airways plc 1991–93, head UK sales British Airways 1993–98, exec vice-pres sales and marketing USA British Airways 1998–2001, dep chm British Airways Holidays Thomas Cook Holidays Jt Venture Co 2001; currently UK and I gen mangr Jet Airways; FInstTT (pres 1991–93); *Recreations* golf, cinema; *Style—* Dan Brewin, Esq

BREWSTER, Martyn Robert; s of Robert Richard Frederick Brewster of Watford, Herts, and Doreen Violet, *née* Lilburn; *b* 24 January 1952; *Educ* Watford Boys GS, Herts Coll of Art, Brighton Poly (BA, Postgrad Dip Painting and Printmaking, Art Teachers Cert); *m* 1988 (m dis 1997), Hilary Joy, da of Peter John Carter; 1 da (Sophie Roberta b 19 Aug 1988); *Career* artist; lectr in art East Herts Coll 1980–89; sr lectr in fine art Bournemouth Coll of Art and Design 1998–; visiting lectr various arts schs 1980–89 incl: Winchester, Bournemouth, London Coll of Furniture; Space Studio in London 1983, studio in Dorset 1990; Eastern Arts Award 1977, awarded various Regnl Arts Association grants 1979–86, Br Cncl travel award 1991, Arts Cncl devpt grant 1994; memb Brighton Open Studios 1975–79; *Two-man Exhibition* Thumb Gallery Soho 1987–; *Solo Exhibitions* incl: Peterborough City Museum and Art Gallery 1983, London Coll of Furniture 1984, Warwick Arts Tst London 1986, Winchester Gallery 1986, Minories Essex 1986, Woodlands Gallery London 1987, Thumb Gallery (Shadows and Light 1987, Light Falls 1990), Atlanta 1991, Jill George Gallery 1992 (Nature Paintings 1994, Lowick Prints 1995, Beauty and Sadness 1996), Paintings, Prints & Drawings 1969–1997 Russell-Cotes Art Gallery Bournemouth 1997 and tour, Night Music (Jill George Gallery) 1998, Royal West of England Acad 2001, King Alfred's Coll Winchester 2001, Nature Paintings Jill George Gallery 2000 and 2002; *Group Exhibitions* incl: Spirit of London (Festival Hall) 1983, English Expression (Warwick Arts Tst) 1984, Int Art Fair London 1985, Angela Flowers Gallery 1985–86, Int Art Fairs LA 1987–90, London Group (RCA) 1988, Art London (Thumb Gallery) 1989–90, Critics Choice (Air Gallery London and Ianetti Lanzone Gallery San Francisco) 1989; *Works in Collection* of: Warwick Arts Tst, The Open Univ, Wiltshire Educn Authy, Russell-Cotes Art Gallery and Museum, Pallant House Chichester, Study Gallery Poole, Arts Inst Bournemouth, British Museum, Ashmolean Museum Oxford, various hosps, Peterborough Museum, various private collections worldwide; *Books* Monograph on Artist (text by Simon Olding and Mel Gooding, 1997), Re-Inventing The Landscape - Contemporary Painters and Dorset (by Vivienne Light, 2002); *Recreations* reading, walking; *Style—* Martyn Brewster, Esq; ✉ 15 West Road, Boscombe, Bournemouth, Dorset BH5 2AN; c/o Jill George Gallery Ltd, 38 Lexington Street, Soho, London W1R 3HR (tel 020 7439 7319/7343, studio 01202 423300, mobile 07966 259463)

BREWSTER, Richard David; s of David Edward Brewster; *b* 5 January 1946; *Educ* Highgate Sch; *m* Susan Ann; 3 s (Edward, William), 2 da (Emily, Rachel); *Career* CA; fin dir Giltspur plc until 1983; chief exec: David S Smith (Holdings) plc 1983–91, Jarvis Porter Group plc 1991–98, Interbrandpro Holdings plc 2000–06; currently corp finance conslt PKF (UK) LLP; non-exec chm: Bankers Investment Tst plc 1991–, Merrill Lynch British Smaller Companies Tst plc 1998; formerly non-exec chm Welsh Devpt Agency; vice-pres RNIB; memb Ct of Assts Worshipful Co of Stationers and Newspaper Makers; FCA 1968; FInstD, fell Inst of Packaging (vice-pres); *Recreations* sailing, tennis, golf, skiing; *Clubs* Island Cruising, IOD, Little Ship, Richmond Cricket and Tennis; *Style—* Richard Brewster, Esq; ✉ c/o Gate House, 180 Kew Road, Richmond, Surrey TW9 2AS; PKF (UK) LLP (tel 020 7065 0568, fax 020 7065 0527, e-mail richard.brewster@uk.pkf.com)

BREWSTER, Richard Philip; *b* 25 May 1952; *Educ* Leeds GS, Trinity Coll Oxford (open scholar, BA, Cross-Country Running blue); *Career* various posts in commercial mgmnt ICI 1976–86, nat appeals mangr Oxfam 1986–89; SCOPE (formerly Spastics Soc): dir of mktg 1989–95, chief exec 1995–2003; exec dir National Center on Nonprofit Enterprise Reston VA; sr visiting practitioner Center of Public and Nonprofit Leadership Georgetown Univ Washington DC 2003–04, sr visiting research fell Open Univ Business Sch; *Style—* Richard Brewster, Esq

BRIANCE, Richard Henry; o s of John Albert Perceval Briance, CMG (d 1989), and Prunella Mary, *née* Chapman; *b* 23 August 1953; *Educ* Eton, Jesus Coll Cambridge (BA); *m* 13 Oct 1979, Lucille, *née* de Zalduondo; 2 da (Zoe b 1982, Clementine b 1987), 2 s (Henry b 1984, Frederick b 1989); *Career* merchant banker; md Credit Suisse First Boston Ltd until 1991, vice-chm UBS Ltd 1991–97, chief exec West Merchant Bank Ltd 1997–99, chief exec Hawkpoint Partners Ltd 1999–2003 (currently dep chm); non-exec dir Oxford Analytica 1999–; memb Fin Law Panel 2000–02; chm Trinity Hospice; tstee: London Children's Ballet, Policy Exchange; *Clubs* Brooks's, Hawks' (Cambridge), Hurlingham, Pilgrims, Queenwood, Mill Reef; *Style—* Richard Briance, Esq; ✉ The Old House, Holland Street, London W8 4NA (tel 020 7937 2113)

BRICE, (Ann) Nuala; da of William Connor (d 1957), of Manchester, and Rosaleen Gertrude, *née* Gilmartin (d 1991); *b* 22 December 1937; *Educ* Loreto Convent Manchester, UCL (LLB, LLM, PhD); *m* 1 June 1963, Geoffrey James Barrington Groves Brice, QC, s of Lt Cdr John Edgar Leonard Brice, MBE; 1 s (Paul Francis b 17 March 1964); *Career* admitted slr 1963 (awarded Stephen Heelis prize and John Peacock conveyancing prize); The Law Society: asst slr 1963, asst sec 1964, sr asst sec 1973, departmental sec 1982, asst sec-gen 1987–92; chm VAT and Duties Tbnls and dep special cmmr of taxes 1992–, cmmr for the Special Purposes of the Income Tax Acts 1999–, chm Financial Servs and Markets Tbnl 2001, chm Pensions Regulator Tbnl 2005; visiting prof of law: Tulane Univ New Orleans 1990–99, Univ of Natal 1996; Freeman City of London, Liveryman City of London Solicitors' Co; memb Law Soc 1963; *Recreations* reading, music, gardening; *Clubs* Univ Women's, Royal Inst; *Style—* Mrs Nuala Brice; ✉ Finance and Tax Tribunals, 15–19 Bedford Avenue, London WC1B 3AS (tel 020 7612 9700)

BRICHTO, Rabbi Dr Sidney; s of Solomon Brichto (d 1991), and Rivka, *née* Frankel-Thomim (d 1972); *b* 21 July 1936; *Educ* NYU (BA, Phi Beta Kappa), Hebrew Union Coll NY (MA, MHL, DD), UCL (study fell); *m* 1, 1959, Frances Goldstein (decd); 1 da (Anne Eta b 11 Jan 1963), 1 s (Daniel S b 19 April 1966); m 2, 1971, Cathryn, da of Edward Goldhill; 2 s (Adam Haim b 20 May 1974, Jonathan James b 7 July 1978); *Career* assoc min Liberal Jewish Synagogue 1961–64, fndr princ Evening Inst for Study of Judaism 1962–65, sr vice-pres ULPS 1991– (exec vice-pres and dir 1964–89), dir Joseph Levy Charitable Fndn 1989–99; memb: Exec Cncl Leo Baeck Coll 1964–74, Exec Inst of Jewish Policy Research 1992–; chm: Conf of Rabbis ULPS 1969–70 and 1974–75, Cncl of Reform and Liberal Rabbis 1974–76, Chief Rabbi's Consultative Ctee on Jewish-non-Jewish Rels 1976–78; chm Advsy Ctee Israel Diaspora Tst 1982–, hon vice-pres Nat Assoc of Bereavement Servs 1992–96, govr Oxford Centre for Hebrew Studies 1994–2002; Hon DD Hebrew Union Coll Cincinnati Ohio 1984; *Books* Child's Bible (1957), Funny...You Don't Look Jewish - A Guide to Jews and Jewish Life (1994), Two Cheers for Secularism (ed with Bishop Richard Harries, 1998), Ritual Slaughter - Growing Up Jewish in America (2001); The People's Bible translations: Genesis (2000), Samuel (2000), Song of Songs (2000), Luke and Acts of the Apostles (2000), The Genius of Paul (2001), The Conquest of Canaan (2001), He Kissed Him and They Wept (jt ed, 2001), Moses, Man of God (2003), The Laws of Moses (2003), Apocalypse, The Writings of St John (2004), The New Testament (2008); *Recreations* reading and writing, lunching; *Clubs* Athenaeum; *Style—* Rabbi Dr Sidney Brichto; ✉ c/o The Athenaeum, Pall Mall, London SW1Y 5ER (tel 020 8933 6216, fax 020 8429 1498, e-mail sidney@brichto.com, website www.brichto.com)

BRICKWOOD, Prof Alan John; s of Robert James Brickwood (d 1988), of Hants, and Kathleen Agnes Brickwood (d 1978); *b* 16 October 1945; *Educ* Clapham Coll London, RCA (MDes); *Family* 2 s (Benjamin James b 21 Nov 1971, Thomas Alan David b 4 July 1999); *Career* research asst HUSAT (Human Scis and Advanced Technol) Research Gp Loughborough Univ 1970–74, fndr and dir Molehurst Ltd 1974–76, head of tport design Coventry Univ 1976–84, pro-vice-chllr Staffordshire Univ 1984–95, prof Dept of Design Brunel Univ 1996–98, industrial advsr Innovation Unit DTI 1996–98, fndr and princ Alan Brickwood & Associates Ltd 1999–; CNAA: memb Cncl and Gen Ctee 1984–87, chm Ctee for Art and Design 1984–90; auditor HEQC 1992–96; memb Advsy Gps HEFCE 1993–95; chm Conf for HE in Art and Design (CHEAD) 1992–95; memb: Design Ctee RSA 1988–91, Cncl Polytechnics and Colls Funding Cncl (PCFC) 1988–93, Prince of Wales 'Partners in Innovation' Highgrove 1991, Industry 96 1994–97, DTI Task Gp 'Action for Engrg' 1995–96; tstee CNAA Art Collection Tst 2003; CIMechE 1997; FRSA 1980, FCSD 1981; *Style—* Prof Alan Brickwood; ✉ Old Coach House, The Avenue, Stratford-upon-Avon, Warwickshire CV37 0PH (tel 01789 266103, e-mail alan@alanbrickwood.co.uk)

BRICKWOOD, Richard Ian; s of Basil Arthur Brickwood (d 1979), and Hilary Joan Brickwood; *b* 22 December 1947; *Educ* Wesley Coll Dublin, Hele's GS Exeter; *m* 6 March 1971, Susan Vanessa Mary, da of Donald Hugh Galpin (d 1971); 1 da (Sarah Louise b 1977), 1 s (Stephen James b 1979); *Career* Lloyds broker; project dir HSBC Insurance Holdings Ltd; *Recreations* sailing, gliding, canoeing, fishing; *Clubs* Cambridge Gliding; *Style—* Richard I Brickwood, Esq; ✉ Swan House, Widford, Ware, Hertfordshire SG12 8SJ (tel 01279 842425 or 020 7991 0600)

BRIDGE, Andrew; s of Peter Bridge, and Roslyn Bridge; *b* 21 July 1952; *Educ* Port Regis Sch, Bryanston, LAMDA, Theatre Projects London; *m* Susan Bridge; 2 s (Oliver b 1988, Alex b 1994), 1 da (Tessa (twin) b 1994); *Career* lighting designer; numerous projects incl: Siegfried and Roy spectacular (Mirage Hotel Las Vegas), Disneyland's Buffalo Bill's Wild West Show (France), Torvill and Dean, flood lighting Lloyds of London, designer to Shirley Bassey in Concert (for ten years); conslt Imagination (industrial and architectural lighting); memb: Assoc of Lighting Designers (Brit), United Scenic Artist (local 829, USA); *Theatre* UK credits incl: Carte Blanche, The Card, An Evening with Tommy Steele, Bing Crosby and Friends, Time, Oliver (also Broadway), The Boyfriend, Billy Bishop goes to War, Tomfoolery, Little Me, Blondel, The Hunting of the Snark, Five Guys Named Moe (also USA, Aust), Sunset Boulevard, Phantom of the Opera (also USA, Japan, Austria, Canada, Sweden, Germany, Aust, Switzerland, Holland), Joseph and the Amazing Technicolor Dreamcoat (also USA, Canada, Aust, Germany), Heathcliff, Doctor Dolittle; *Awards* for Phantom of the Opera incl: Tony Award, Drama Desk Award (NY), Outer Circle Critics' Award (NY), Dora Mavor Award (Canada), Los Angeles Critics' Award; for Sunset Boulevard incl: Tony Award, Los Angeles Critics' Award and Ovation Award; for Lloyds of London Nat Lighting Award; *Style—* Andrew Bridge, Esq; ✉ c/o Performing Arts Management, 6 Windmill Street, London W1P 1HF (tel 020 7255 1362, fax 020 7631 4631)

BRIDGE, Christopher John; s of Lt-Col J E Bridge, OBE, TD (d 1983), and Jeanne, *née* Pryor; *b* 30 April 1948; *Educ* Mount House Sch Tavistock, Prior Park Coll Bath, Univ of Aberdeen (LLB); *m* 1976, Caroline, da of John Perchard; 2 da (Claire b 7 Aug 1981, Helen b 13 Aug 1984); *Career* industrial rels asst Rolls Royce Glasgow 1968–71, sr personnel offr BBC 1971–77; dist personnel offr: Kensington Chelsea and Westminster AHA 1977–82, Victoria HA 1982–86; assoc gen mangr Charing Cross Hosp 1986–88, gen mangr Mental Health Unit NE Essex HA 1988–91, chief exec NE Essex Mental Health NHS Tst 1991–2001, chief exec Workforce Confedn NHS Eastern Region (E) 2001–02; chm: Equip 2002–, HealthProm 2003–; govr Colchester Inst of Higher and Further Educn 1990; fell Univ of Essex 2002; MIPM 1971; *Recreations* golf, skiing; *Style—* Christopher Bridge, Esq; ✉ 90 High Road, Leavenheath, Colchester, Essex CO6 4PF (tel 01206 262869, e-mail cjbridge@mail.com)

BRIDGE, Prof John William; s of Harry Bridge (d 1985), of Crewkerne, Somerset, and Rebecca, *née* Lilley (d 1983); *b* 2 February 1937; *Educ* Crewkerne Sch, Univ of Bristol (LLB, LLM, PhD); *m* 28 July 1962, Janet Faith, da of Horace George Attew Hearn (d 1985), of Crewkerne, Somerset; 1 da (Susan b 1968); *Career* visiting prof Coll of William and Mary 1977–78 and 1997; Univ of Exeter: lectr then sr lectr 1961–74, prof of public law 1974–2001, dean Faculty of Law 1979–82, head of Dept of Law 1983–88 and 1997–98, dep vice-chllr 1992–94, sr dep vice-chllr 1994–96, head Sch of Law 1998–99, emeritus prof of law 2001–; visiting prof: Univ of Connecticut 1985 and 1991, Univ of Fribourg/Suisse 1990, Univ of Mauritius 1987; visiting fell All Souls Coll Oxford 1988–89; sr Fulbright scholar 1977–78 and 1991–92; hon fell Soc for Advanced Legal Studies 1997–; memb: Int Acad of Comparative Law, Cncl of UK Nat Ctee for Comparative Law (chm 1992–2001), Exec Ctee Int Assoc of Legal Science, Scientific Ctee Inst of Fedm Fribourg Switzerland, Soc of Public Teachers of Law 1961–; pres Exeter Musical Soc 1983–88, memb Cncl St Margaret's Sch Exeter 2002– (custos 2005–), fell The Woodward Corp 2003–; *Books* European Legislation (with E Freeman, 1975), Law and Institutions of the European Union (with D Lasok, 6 edn 1994); *Recreations* singing in choirs, family history, gardening; *Clubs* Royal Over-Seas League; *Style—* Prof John Bridge; ✉ 8 Pennsylvania Close, Exeter, Devon EX4 6DJ (tel 01392 254576, e-mail jandj@bridge3768.fsnet.co.uk)

BRIDGE, Wayne Michael; *b* 5 August 1980, Southampton; *Career* professional footballer; clubs: Southampton FC 1997–2003 (finalists FA Cup 2003), Chelsea FC 2003– (winners FA Premiership 2005 (runners-up 2004 and 2007), League Cup 2005 and 2007, FA Cup 2007), Fulham FC (on loan) 2006; England: 23 caps, debut v Holland 2002, memb squad World Cup 2002 and 2006, memb squad European Championship 2004; *Style—* Mr Wayne Bridge; ✉ c/o Chelsea Football Club, Fulham Road, London SW6 1HS

BRIDGE OF HARWICH, Baron (Life Peer UK 1980), of Harwich in the County of Essex; Nigel Cyprian Bridge; kt (1968), PC (1975); s of Cdr Cyprian Dunscombe Charles Bridge, RN (d 1938); *b* 26 February 1917; *Educ* Marlborough; *m* 1944, Margaret, da of Leonard Heseltine Swinbank, of Weybridge, Surrey; 1 s, 2 da; *Career* barr 1947–68, judge of the High Court of Justice 1968–75, Lord Justice of Appeal 1975–80, Lord of Appeal in Ordinary 1980–92; chm Permanent Security Cmmn 1982–85; *Style—* The Rt Hon Lord Bridge of Harwich, PC; ✉ House of Lords, London SW1A 0PW

BRIDGEMAN, Viscountess; (Victoria) Harriet Lucy; da of Ralph Meredyth Turton, TD (d 1988), of Kildale Hall, Whitby, N Yorks, and Mary Blanche, *née* Chetwynd-Stapylton; *b* 30 March 1942; *Educ* privately, St Mary's Sch Wantage, Trinity Coll Dublin (MA); *m* 10 Dec 1966, 3 Viscount Bridgeman, *qv*; 4 s (1 decd); *Career* exec ed The Masters 1966–68; ed: Discovering Antiques 1968–70, Going, Going, Gone series (Sunday Times Colour Magazine) 1973; fndr and md The Bridgeman Art Library Ltd 1971–; memb Ctee British Assoc of Picture Libraries and Agencies; European Woman of the Year Award (Arts Section) 1997, Int Business Woman of the Year 2005; tstee Br Sporting Art Tst; fndr Artists' Collecting Soc 2006; FRSA; *Books* author and ed of numerous books incl: The Encyclopaedia of Victoriana, The Illustrated Encyclopaedia of Needlework, The Last Word, Society Scandals, Guide to Gardens of Europe; *Recreations* reading, family, travelling; *Clubs* Chelsea Arts, RSA; *Style—* The Viscountess Bridgeman, FRSA; ✉ 19 Chepstow Road, London W2 5BP (tel 020 7727 4065/5400, fax 020 7792 8509, e-mail harriet@bridgeman.co.uk, website www.bridgeman.co.uk); Watley House, Sparsholt, Winchester, Hampshire SO21 2LU (tel and fax 01962 776297)

BRIDGEMAN, John Stuart; CBE (2001), TD (1994), DL (Oxon 1989); s of James Alfred George Bridgeman (d 1961), and Edith Celia, *née* Watkins (d 1994); *b* 5 October 1944; *Educ* Whitchurch Sch Cardiff, UC Swansea (BSc); *m* 1967, Lindy Jane, da of Sidney Fillmore, of Gidea Park, Essex; 3 da (Victoria b 1972, Philippa b 1974, Annabel b 1980); *Career* chm: Audit and Standards Ctee Warwickshire CC 2000–, Howtocomplain.com 2000–, Warwickshire Police Authy 2001–, CCS Enforcement Servs 2004–, Horseracing Regulatory Authy 2005–; chm of tstees Banbury Sunshine Centre 2003–, memb Bd Br Waterways 2006–; vice-pres Trading Standards Inst 2001–; previously with: Alcan Industries 1966, Aluminium Co of Canada 1969, Alcan Australia 1970; commercial dir Alcan (UK) Ltd 1977–80, vice-pres (Europe) Alcan Basic Raw Materials 1978–82, divnl md British Alcan Aluminium plc 1983–91 (divnl md Alcan Aluminium (UK) Ltd 1981–83), dir of corp planning Alcan Aluminium Ltd (Montreal) 1992–93, md British Alcan Aluminium plc 1993–95; memb Monopolies and Mergers Cmmn 1990–95, DG Office of Fair Trading 1995–2000, chm Novares Consortium 2000–01, dir Cardew Chancery 2001–03; advsr to Norton Rose 2000–02; dir Oxford Psychologists Press 2001–06; visiting prof of mgmnt: Keele Univ 1992–, Univ of Surrey 2004–; chm Aluminium Extruders' Assoc 1987–88 (memb Cncl 1982–91), vice-pres Aluminium Fedn 1995 (memb Bauxite Advsy Gp 1977–81); US Aluminium Assoc prize winner 1988; chm: North Oxon Business Gp 1984–92, Enterprise Cherwell Ltd 1985–91, Oxfordshire Economic Partnership 2000–07, Direct Marketing Authy 2001–07; govr North Oxon Coll 1985–98 (chm 1989), memb Bd Heart of England TEC 1990–2002 (chm 2000–02), dir Oxford Orchestra da Camera 1996–2000; tstee: Fndn for Canadian Studies 1995– (vice-chm 2005–), Oxon Community Fndn 1996–2002, Oxfordshire Yeomanry Tst 1997–; pres: Canada-UK C of C 1997–98 (vice-pres 1995–96), Oxford Gliding Club 1998–; memb: Cncl Canada-UK Colloquia 1993–1998 and 2003– (treas 2005), Ctee Canada Club 1994–; TA and Reserve Forces: cmmnd 1978, QOY 1981–84, Maj REME (V) 1985–94, Staff Coll 1986, memb Oxon and E Wessex TAVRA 1985–2000, memb Nat Employer Liaison Ctee for Reserve Forces 1992–2002 (chm 1997–2002), Hon Col 5 (Queen's Own Oxfordshire Hussars) Sqdn 31 (City of London) Signal Regt 1996–, memb South Eastern Reserve Forces and Cadets Assoc (SERFCA) 2001–; memb Def Sci Advsy Cncl 1991–94; High Sheriff Oxon 1995; memb Ct of Assts Worshipful Co of Turners; Hon Dr Sheffield Hallam Univ 1996; hon fell Univ of Wales Swansea 1997; hon memb Inst of Consumer Affairs 1999; CIMgt, FRGS, FRSA, FInstD, Hon FICM 1998; *Recreations* horses, Oxfordshire affairs, Territorial Army, gardening, shooting, skiing; *Clubs* Reform, Glamorgan County Cricket; *Style—* John S Bridgeman, CBE, TD, DL; ✉ Horseracing Regulatory Authority, 151 Shaftesbury Avenue, London WC2H 8AL

BRIDGEMAN, 3 Viscount (UK 1929); Robin John Orlando Bridgeman; s of Brigadier Hon Geoffrey John Orlando Bridgeman, MC, FRCS (d 1974, 2 s of 1 Viscount Bridgeman, sometime Home Sec and First Lord of the Admiralty), and Mary Meriel Gertrude (d 1974), da of Rt Hon Sir George Talbot, a High Court Judge; suc unc, 2 Viscount, 1982; *b* 5 December 1930; *Educ* Eton; *m* 10 Dec 1966, (Victoria) Harriet Lucy (Viscountess Bridgeman, *qv*); 3 da of Ralph Meredyth Turton, TD (d 1988), of Kildale Hall, Whitby; 3 s (and 1 s decd); *Heir* s, Hon Luke Bridgeman; *Career* 2 Lt Rifle Bde 1950–51; CA 1958; ptnr Henderson Crosthwaite & Co Stockbrokers 1973–86; dir: Guinness Mahon & Co Ltd 1988–90, Nestor-BNA plc (now Nestor Healthcare Group plc) 1989–94, SPLIT plc 1996–97; dir The Bridgeman Art Library Ltd 1972–; chm Asset Management Investment Co plc 1994–2001; oppn whip House of Lords 1998–; Reed's Sch: pres Fndn Appeal 1992–93, chm 1995–2002; special tstee Hammersmith Hospitals NHS Tst (formerly Hammersmith and Queen Charlotte's Special HA) 1986–99, chm Friends of Lambeth Palace Library; treas: Florence Nightingale Aid in Sickness Tst 1995–, New England Co 1996–; tstee: Winchester Theatre Fund 1985–2001, Friends of Music at Winchester 1998–; chm Hosp of St John and St Elizabeth 1999–; Knight SMOM; *Recreations* gardening, skiing, shooting, music; *Clubs* MCC, Beefsteak; *Style—* The Rt Hon the Viscount Bridgeman; ✉ 19 Chepstow Road, London W2 5BP (tel 020 7727 5400, fax 020 7792 9178); Watley House, Sparsholt, Winchester SO21 2LU (tel and fax 01962 776297, e-mail bridgemanr@parliament.uk)

BRIDGES, Prof James Wilfrid (Jim); s of Wilfrid Edward Seymour Bridges (d 1994), of Cuxton, Kent, and Mary Winifred, *née* Cameron (d 1987); *b* 9 August 1938; *Educ* Bromley GS, KCL (BSc), St Mary's Hosp Med Sch London (PhD), Univ of London (DSc); *m* Dr Olga Bridges; *Career* lectr St Mary's Hosp Med Sch London 1962–68; Univ of Surrey: reader in biochemistry 1968–78, dir Robens Inst of Industrial and Environmental Health and Safety 1978–95, prof of toxicology and environmental health 1979–2003 (emeritus prof 2003–), dean Faculty of Sci 1988–92, head Euro Inst of Health and Scis 1995–2000, dean for int strategy 2000–03; visiting prof: Univ of Texas 1973 and 1979, Univ of Rochester NY 1974, Centro de Investigacion y de Estudios Avanzados Mexico 1991; visiting sr scientist Nat Inst of Environmental Health Sciences USA 1976; chm Br Toxicology Soc 1980–81, first pres Fedn of Euro Socs of Toxicology 1985–88, memb Exec Ctee Euro Soc of Biochemical Pharmacology 1983–89, fndr Euro Drug Metabolisms Workshops, chm Veterinary Residue Ctee 2000–04; memb: Veterinary Products Ctee MAFF 1982–98, Advsy Ctee on Toxic Substances HSE 1986–89, Air Soil and Water Contaminants Ctee DHSS/DOE 1984–90, UK Shadow Gp on Toxicology DHSS 1984–2000, Watch Ctee HSE 1987–2004, Food Safety and Applied Res Consultative Ctee 1989–90, Advsy Ctee on Irradiated and Novel Foods MAFF 1982–88, Maj Hazards Ctee Working Party (HSE) 1982–84, Corporation of Farnborough Coll of Technology 1992–2000; EEC: memb Scientific Ctee on Animal Nutrition 1990–97, memb Scientific Steering Gp on Consumer Health 1997–2003, chm Scientific Ctee on Toxicity, Ecotoxicity and the Environment 1997–2004, chm Harmonisation of Risk Assesment Task Force 1998–2003, chm Scientific Ctee on Emerging and Newly Identified Health Risks 2004–, memb European Parl/EU Mirror Gp 2006–; expert advsr: European Food Safety Authy 2003–, DG Research 2005–; Inst of Biology: chm Food Policy Gp 1990–93, memb Policy Ctee 1993–97; memb Bd of Dirs Int Life Scis Inst (Europe) 2000–04; chm Environmental Advsy Bd Shanks plc 2004–; elected hon memb Soc of Occupational Med 1989, elected fell Collegium Ramazzini 1990; Hon DSc Baptist Univ Hong Kong; CChem, CBiol 1981, FRSC, FIBiol, MInstEnvSci 1980, MRCPath 1984, FRSA 1989, FIOSH 1990; *Publications* incl: Progress in Drug Metabolism (ed with Dr L Chasseaud, Vols 1–10), Watershed 89 The Future for Water Quality in Europe Vols I and II (ed with M L Richardson and D Wheeler), Animals and Alternatives in Toxicology (ed with M Balls and J Southee), Losing Hope: The Environment and Health in Russia (with Dr Olga Bridges, 1996); jt ed of 17 books and over 370 res pubns and reviews in scientific jls; *Recreations* theatre, concerts, travel; *Style—* Prof Jim Bridges; ✉ Research for Sustainability, Liddington Hall Drive, Guildford, Surrey GU3 3AE (mobile 07768 004595, e-mail j.bridges@surrey.ac.uk)

BRIDGES, Hon Mark Thomas; er s and h of 2 Baron Bridges, GCMG, *qv*; *b* 25 July 1954; *Educ* Eton, CCC Cambridge; *m* 1978, Angela Margaret, da of J L Collinson (d 1997); 3 da (Venetia Rachel Lucy b 21 Feb 1982, Camilla Frances Iona b 22 June 1985, Drusilla Katharine Anne b 12 July 1988), 1 s (Miles Edmund Farrer b 1 July 1992); *Career* slr; dir The Abinger Hall Estate Co 1984–92, ptnr Farrer & Co 1985–; slr to the Duchy of Lancaster 1998–, private slr to HM The Queen 2002–; memb Cncl Royal Sch of Church Music 1989–97, treas The Bach Choir 1992–97, chm Music in Country Churches 2006; tstee UCHL Charities 1992–; govr: Purcell Sch 2000–, Sherborne Sch for Girls 2001–, Hanford Sch 2004–; academician Int Acad of Estate and Tst Law; memb Ct of Assts Worshipful Co of Goldsmiths; *Recreations* sailing (yacht 'Makai'), reading, music; *Clubs* Brooks's, House of Lords' Yacht, Noblemen and Gentlemen's Catch; *Style—* The Hon Mark Bridges; ✉ 66 Lincoln's Inn Fields, London WC2A 3LH

BRIDGES, Stephen John; LVO (1998); s of Gordon Alfred Richard Bridges, of Wembury, Devon, and Audrey Middleton Bridges; *b* 19 June 1960; *Educ* Devonport HS, Plymouth Poly (Dip Law and Accounting), LSE, Leeds (MA); *m* 30 June 1990, Kyung Mi, da of Chan Young Yoon; *Career* joined FCO 1980, third sec Luanda 1984–87, third then second sec Seoul 1987–91, second then first sec UN and SE Asia Depts 1991–96, first sec and head of political section Kuala Lumpar 1996–2000, ambass to Cambodia 2000–05, dep high cmmr Bangladesh until 2007; with Mining House Ltd 2007–; *Recreations* golf, food and wine, Coco and Montague the dogs; *Style—* Stephen Bridges, Esq, LVO

BRIDGES, Stuart John; s of Frederick Francis Bridges, of Lymington, Hants, and Gladys Mary, *née* Hayhoe (d 2004); *b* 16 September 1960; *Educ* Dalriada Sch, Gonville & Caius Coll Cambridge (nat engrg scholar, MA); *m* 14 Sept 1996, Diane Leonie, *née* Forrester; 2 s (Sebastian Charles Henry b 18 April 1997, Alexander George Richard b 29 April 2000); *Career* Arthur Andersen & Co 1983–89, Richard Ellis 1989–91, Henderson Investors 1991–94, exec dir Jacobs Holdings plc 1995–97, gp fin dir Hiscox plc 1999–; ACA 1987; *Recreations* golf, sailing; *Style—* Stuart Bridges, Esq; ✉ Hiscox plc, 1 Great St Helen's, London EC3A 6HX (tel 020 7448 6000, fax 020 7448 6900, e-mail stuart.bridges@hiscox.com)

BRIDGES, 2 Baron (UK 1957), of Headley, Co Surrey and of St Nicholas-at-Wade, Co Kent; Sir Thomas Edward Bridges; GCMG (1988, KCMG 1983, CMG 1975); s of 1 Baron Bridges, KG, GCB, GCVO, MC (d 1969), and Hon Katherine, da of 2 Baron Farrer (d 1986); *b* 27 November 1927; *Educ* Eton, New Coll Oxford (MA); *m* 1953, Rachel Mary (d 2005), da of Sir Henry Bunbury, KCB (d 1968), of Ewell, Surrey; 2 s, 1 da; *Heir* s, Hon Mark Bridges, *qv*; *Career* entered HM Foreign Serv 1951; served: Bonn, Berlin, Rio de Janeiro, Athens, Moscow, Foreign Office; private sec (overseas affrs) to PM 1972–74, min (commercial) Washington 1975–79, dep sec FCO 1979–83, ambass to Italy 1983–87, ret; elected memb House of Lords 1999; memb Select Ctee on Euro Communities House of Lords 1988–92 and 1994–98, intl bd memb Securities and Futures Authy 1989–97; chm: UK Nat Ctee for UNICEF 1989–97, British-Italian Soc 1991–97; vice-pres Cncl for Nat Parks 2000–; tstee Rayne Fndn 1995–; FRSA; *Style—* The Rt Hon the Lord Bridges, GCMG; ✉ 56 Church Street, Orford, Woodbridge, Suffolk IP12 2NT (tel and fax 01394 450235)

BRIDGEWATER, Adrian Alexander; s of Maj Philip Alexander Clement Bridgewater (d 1980), of Southdown, Crease Lane, Tavistock, Devon, and Hon Ursula Vanda Maud Vivian (d 1984); *b* 24 July 1936; *Educ* Eton, Magdalene Coll Cambridge (MA); *m* 1, 11 April 1958 (m dis 1968), Charlotte, da of Rev Michael Ernest Christopher Pumphrey (d 1982); 2 da (Emma Mary b 23 Dec 1960, Sophy Charlotte b 31 July 1962), 1 s (Thomas Michael George b 12 Nov 1963); m 2, 7 Nov 1969, Lucy Le Breton (d 2006), da of Sir Basil Bartlett, 2 Bt (d 1986); 2 da (Nancy Le Breton b 10 Aug 1971, Daisy Maud b 27 Jan 1973), 1 s (Benjamin Hardington b 20 March 1979); *Career* founder and dir CRAC 1963–74, founder and chm Hobsons Press Ltd 1974–87; chm: Hobsons Publishing plc 1987–92, Johansens Ltd 1987–92, Care Choices Ltd 1993–, Connect Publishing Ltd 1993–, ECCTIS Ltd 1991–, Elephant Design Ltd 2004–; dep chm Papworth Tst 1989–; memb Cncl: Inst for Manpower Studies 1966–67, Open Univ 1974–80, RCA 1979–81, Nat Inst Careers Education and Counselling 1966–92, VSO 1980–82, Br Sch Osteopathy 1989–91, Careers Res and Advsy Centre (CRAC) 1993–, Ind Schs Careers Orgn 1994–2003; govr King's Coll Choir Sch Cambridge 1988–92; *Recreations* walking, surfing, racing; *Clubs* Garrick; *Style—* Adrian Bridgewater, Esq; ✉ Manor Farm, Great Eversden, Cambridgeshire CB23 1HW (tel 01223 263229); 2 Carlton Mansions, Randolph Avenue, London W9 1NP (e-mail adrianbridgewater@ukonline.co.uk)

BRIDGWATER, Prof John; s of Eric Bridgwater, of Birmingham, and Mabel Mary, *née* Thornley; *b* 10 January 1938; *Educ* Solihull Sch, Univ of Cambridge (MA, PhD, ScD), Princeton Univ (MSE); *m* 29 Dec 1962, Diane, da of Arthur Edgarton Tucker (d 1965); 1

s (Eric Arthur b 1966), 1 da (Caroline Mary b 1967); *Career* chemical engr Courtaulds Ltd 1961–64; Univ of Cambridge 1964–71: demonstrator and lectr in chemical engrg, fell St Catharine's Coll; visiting assoc prof Univ of British Columbia 1970–71; Univ of Oxford 1971–80: fell Balliol Coll (former fell Hertford Coll), lectr in engrg sci; dean Faculty of Engrg Univ of Birmingham 1989–92 (prof 1980–93, head Sch of Chemical Engrg 1983–89); Univ of Cambridge: head Dept of Chemical Engrg 1993–98, sr tutor St Catharine's Coll 2004, currently emeritus prof of chemical engrg; visiting prof Univ of Calif Berkeley 1992–93, visiting Erskine fell Univ of Canterbury 2002; pres Instn of Chemical Engrs 1997–98; chm Bd Chemical Engrg Sci 1983–2003; memb Engrg Bd SERC 1986–89; pres World Cncl for Particle Technol 1999–2002; dir Tunku Abdul Rahman Centenary Fund 2004–06; FIChemE 1974, FREng 1987; *Recreations* travel, gardening, mountain walking; *Style—* Prof John Bridgwater, FREng; ✉ Department of Chemical Engineering, University of Cambridge, Pembroke Street, Cambridge CB2 3RA (tel 01223 334777, fax 01223 334796)

BRIDPORT, 4 Viscount (UK 1868); Alexander Nelson Hood; also Baron Bridport (I 1794) and 7 Duke of Bronte in Sicily (cr 1799 by Ferdinand IV, the 'Lazzarone' King of the Two Sicilies, largely for Nelson's role in exterminating the Parthenopean Republic). In 1801 a Br Royal Licence was issued to Admiral Lord Nelson allowing him to accept for himself and his heirs the Dukedom of Bronte; s of 3 Viscount (d 1969, fourth in descent from the union of 2 Baron Bridport (2 s of 2 Viscount Hood) and Lady Charlotte Nelson, da of 1 Earl and niece of the great Admiral), and Sheila Jeanne Agatha, *née* van Meurs (d 1996); *b* 17 March 1948; *Educ* Eton, Sorbonne; *m* 1, 1972 (m dis 1979), Linda Jacqueline, da of Lt-Col Vincent Rudolph Paravicini; 1 s (Hon Peregrine Alexander Nelson b 30 Aug 1974); m 2, 1979 (m dis 1999), Mrs Nina Rindt, da of Curt Lincoln; 1 s (Hon Anthony Nelson b 7 Jan 1983); *Heir* s, Hon Peregrine Hood; *Career* with Kleinwort Benson Ltd 1967–80, Robert Fraser & Ptnrs 1980–83, exec dir Chase Manhattan Ltd 1983–85, gen mangr Chase Manhattan Bank (Suisse) 1985–86, md Shearson Lehman Hutton Finance (Switzerland) 1986–90, managing ptnr Bridport & Cie SA 1991–; *Recreations* skiing, diving, bridge; *Clubs* Brooks's; *Style—* The Rt Hon the Viscount Bridport; ✉ 1 Place Longemalle, 1204 Geneva, Switzerland (tel 00 41 22 817 7000, fax 00 41 22 817 7050, e-mail bridport@bridport.ch)

BRIEN, Nicolas Frederich; s of Hubert Barrie Brien, of London, and Ursula, *née* Pfaller; *b* 18 January 1962; *Educ* King's Coll Wimbledon, Coll for Distributive Trades London; *m* Anastasia; 1 s (Lucas Barrie); *Career* Lerner & Grey June-Dec 1982, Grey Advertising 1983–84, Benton & Bowles 1984–85, WCRS 1985–89, BBJ Media Services 1989–92; Leo Burnett: exec media dir 1992–96, dep md 1994–96, md 1996–98, chief exec 1997–; memb Media Res Gp IPA; MInstD; *Recreations* polo, skiing, tennis, golf, squash, tae kwon do (former UK nat champion), theatre, ballet, opera, reading; *Clubs* RAC; *Style—* Nicolas Brien, Esq; ✉ Starcom Mediavest Group, 35 West Wacker Drive, Chicago, IL 606 01, USA (tel 00 1 312 220 1589)

BRIER, Norma; *b* 23 December 1949; *Educ* Henrietta Barnet Sch, Goldsmiths Coll London (BA), LSE (MSc, CQSW); *m* Sam Brier; 2 c; *Career* social worker and supervisor Student Unit London Borough of Camden 1971–76 (LSE 1973–74), pt/t lectr in social work and sociology and course organiser Counselling Skills for Teachers London Borough of Harrow 1976–83, charity work for learning-disabled children 1983–85; Ravenswood Fndn (now Norwood Ravenswood): joined as dir of community and social servs 1985, exec dir 1989–96, jt exec dir (following merger with Norwood) 1996–99, chief exec 1999–; conslt Aid for Belarussian Children Project, chair Voluntary Organisations Disability Gp 1998–2001; tstee Karten CTec 1997; memb: Panel of Ind Inquiry into Royal Brompton and Harefield Cardiology Services 1999–2001, Learning Disability Advsy Gp Dept of Health 1999–2001; Office for Public Mgmnt Prize for Leadership 1994; *Recreations* cycling, tennis, gardening, theatre, cinema; *Style—* Mrs Norma Brier; ✉ Norwood, Broadway House, 80–82 Broadway, Stanmore, Middlesex HA7 4HB (tel 020 8954 4555, fax 020 8420 6800)

BRIERLEY, Anthony William Wallace (Tony); s of William Derrick Brierley (d 1993), and Rosemary, *née* Woodford; *b* 1 October 1949, Nottingham; *Educ* Forest Fields GS Nottingham, Trent Poly Nottingham (BA), Inns of Court Sch of Law London; *Career* called to the Bar Inner Temple 1981; admitted slr 1990; W E Brierley & Sons Ltd 1968–77, legal advsr Notts Magistrates Courts 1981–83; 3i Gp plc: legal advsr 1983–90, head of legal 1990–94, dep co sec 1994–95, gen counsel and co sec 1996–, dir legal and regulatory 1996–, memb Exec Ctee 1996–; dir: Ship Mortgage Finance Co plc 1995–, 3i Europe plc 1995–, Baronsmead Investment Tst 1998–, 3i Asia Pacific plc 2000–; memb Leadership Team Business in the Environment 2002–; memb Commerce and Industry Gp Law Soc 2002– (memb Corp Governance Ctee 2002–05, chm Trg Ctee 2004–); *Recreations* golf, ballet, collecting; *Clubs* Reform, Bentley Drivers; *Style—* Tony Brierley, Esq; ✉ 3i Group plc, 16 Palace Street, London SW1E 5JD (tel 020 7928 3131, fax 020 7620 2805)

BRIERLEY, David; CBE (1986); s of Ernest William Brierley (d 1982), of Romiley, Stockport, Cheshire, and Jessie, *née* Stanway (d 1991); *b* 26 July 1936; *Educ* Stockport GS, Clare Coll Cambridge (MA, CertEd); *m* 7 Dec 1962, Ann, da of Charles Rossell Fosbrooke Potter; 2 s (Benedict b 1964, Crispin b 1966); *Career* teacher 1959–61; RSC: stage mangr 1961–63, gen stage mangr 1963–66, asst to the dir 1966–68, gen mangr 1968–96, hon assoc artist 1996–; Arts Cncl of England: Capital Advsy Panel 1996–2005, chm Stabilisation Advsy Panel 1996–2006, memb Cncl 1997–2002, memb Audit Ctee 1998–; memb Bd and Exec Ctee Theatre Royal Plymouth 1997–; Br Cncl: chm Drama and Dance Advsy Ctee 1997–2006, chm Arts Advsy Ctee 2002–06; tstee Hall for Cornwall Tst 1999– (chm 2003–); govr Clwyd Theatr Cymru 1997–; Hon DLitt; *Recreations* reading; *Style—* David Brierley, CBE; ✉ Headland, 8 Pear Tree Close, Chipping Campden, Gloucestershire GL55 6DB (tel 01386 840361, fax 01386 840805, e-mail david.brierley@virgin.net)

BRIERS, Richard David; CBE (2003, OBE 1989); s of Joseph Benjamin Briers (d 1980), and Morna Phyllis, *née* Richardson (d 1992); *b* 14 January 1934; *Educ* Ridgeways Co-Educnl Sch Wimbledon, RADA; *m* 24 Feb 1957, Ann Cuerton, da of Ronald Horace Davies (d 1980); 2 da (Katy Ann b 10 Aug 1963, Lucy Jane b 19 Aug 1967); *Career* actor 1955–; Nat Serv RAF 1951–53; London debut Gilt and Gingerbread (Duke of York's) 1959; *Theatre* incl: Arsenic and Old Lace 1965, Relatively Speaking 1966, The Real Inspector Hound 1968, Cat Among the Pigeons 1969, The Two of Us 1970, Butley 1972, Absurd Person Singular 1973, Absent Friends 1975, Middle Age Spread 1979, The Wild Duck 1980, Arms and the Man 1981, Run For Your Wife 1983, Why Me? 1985, The Relapse 1986, Twelfth Night 1987 (tv 1988), A Midsummer Night's Dream 1990, King Lear 1990, Wind in the Willows 1991, Uncle Vanya 1991, Home 1994, A Christmas Carol 1996–97, The Chairs 1997–98, Spike 2001, Bedroom Farce 2002, The Tempest 2002; *Television* series incl: Brothers-in-Law, Marriage Lines, The Good Life, OneUpManShip, The Other One, Norman Conquests, Ever-Decreasing Circles, All In Good Faith, Monarch of the Glen, Dad; *Films* incl: Henry V 1989, Much Ado About Nothing 1992, Swansong 1993, Frankenstein 1994, In the Bleak Midwinter 1995, Hamlet 1996, Love's Labour's Lost 1999, Peter Pan 2003, As You Like It 2005; *Books* Natter Natter (1981), Coward and Company (1987), A Little Light Weeding (1993), A Taste of the Good Life (1995); *Recreations* gardening, reading; *Style—* Richard Briers, Esq, CBE; ✉ c/o Hamilton Hodell Ltd, 5th Floor, 66–68 Margaret Street, London W1W 8SR (tel 020 7636 1221, fax 020 7636 1226)

BRIGGS, Prof (George) Andrew Davidson; s of John Davidson Briggs, of Cambridge, and Catherine Mary, *née* Lormer; *b* 3 June 1950, Dorchester, Dorset; *Educ* The Leys Sch Cambridge (scholar), St Catherine's Coll Oxford (Clothworkers' scholar, MA), Queens' Coll Cambridge (PhD, Chase Prize for Greek), Ridley Hall Cambridge; *m* 1981, Diana Margaret Ashley, *née* Johnson; 2 da (Felicity Claire Davidson b 22 June 1983, Elizabeth Catherine Davidson b 29 July 1985); *Career* Royal Soc research fell in the physical sciences 1982–84; Univ of Oxford: lectr in metallurgy and science of materials 1984–96, reader in materials 1996–99, prof of materials 1999–2002, prof of nanomaterials 2002–; fell Wolfson Coll Oxford 1984–2002 (emeritus fell 2003), professorial fell St Anne's Coll Oxford 2003–; dir Quantum Info Processing Interdisciplinary Research Collaboration and professorial research fell EPSRC 2002–; professeur invité Ecole polytechnique fédérale de Lausanne 1992–2002, visiting prof Univ of NSW 2002; memb Editorial Bd: Science and Christian Belief 2001, Current Opinion in Solid State and Materials Science 2002, Nanotechnology; Holliday Prize Inst of Metals 1986, Buehler Tech Paper Merit Award for Excellence 1994, Metrology for World Class Mfrg Award 1999; involved with: St Andrew's Church Oxford, Christians in Science; Freeman City of London, Liveryman Worshipful Co of Clothworkers; Hon FRMS 1999, FInstP 2004; *Publications* An Introduction to Scanning Acoustic Microscopy (1985), Acoustic Microscopy (1992), The Science of New Materials (ed, 1992), Advances in Acoustic Microscopy 1 (1995), Advances in Acoustic Microscopy 2 (1996); also author of numerous contribs to learned jls; *Recreations* Christian theology, opera, skiing, sailing, flying; *Style—* Professor Andrew Briggs; ✉ University of Oxford, Department of Materials, Parks Road, Oxford OX1 3PH (tel 01865 273725, fax 01865 273730, e-mail andrew.briggs@materials.ox.ac.uk)

BRIGGS, Prof Anthony David Peach; s of Horace Briggs (d 1972), and Doris Lily, *née* Peach; *b* 4 March 1938; *Educ* King Edward VII Sch Sheffield, Trinity Hall Cambridge (MA), Univ of London (PhD); *m* 28 July 1962, Pamela Anne, da of Harry Metcalfe; 2 da (Fiona b 4 Nov 1966, Antonia 15 Aug 1970), 1 s (Julian b 2 Jan 1974); *Career* Nat Serv 1956–58, trained as Russian interpreter CSC interpretership 1958; Univ of Bristol 1968–87: lectr in Russian, sr lectr, reader, head Russian Dept; prof of Russian language and lit Univ of Birmingham 1987–99; memb Br Assoc for Slavonic and E Euro Studies; *Books* Mayakovsky, A Tragedy (1979), Alexander Pushkin: A Critical Study (1983), A Wicked Irony (Lermontov's A Hero of Our Time) (with Andrew Barratt, 1989), The Wild World (Pushkin, Nekrasov, Blok) (1990), Eugene Onegin (1992), Mikhail Lermontov: Commemorative Essays (1992), Alexander Pushkin (1997), Omar Khayyam (1998), English Sonnets (1999), Shakespeare's Love Poetry (1999), Alexander Pushkin: a Celebration (1999), Love, Please! (2001), Tolstoy's War and Peace (transl, 2005), Remember: Poems of Childhood (2005); *Recreations* Mozart, housebuilding and restoration, country walking with large dogs; *Style—* Prof Anthony Briggs; ✉ Custard Mead, Stoppers Hill, Brinkworth, Wiltshire SN15 5AW (tel 01666 510075, e-mail adpbriggs@aol.com)

BRIGGS, Baron (Life Peer UK 1976), of Lewes in the County of East Sussex; Asa Briggs; o s of William Walker Briggs (d 1952), of Keighley, W Yorks, and Jane Briggs; *b* 7 May 1921; *Educ* Keighley GS, Sidney Sussex Coll Cambridge (BA), LSE (BSc); *m* 1955, Susan Anne, da of Donald Ivor Banwell (d 1980), of Keevil, Wilts; 2 s, 2 da; *Career* served Intelligence Corps (Bletchley) 1942–45; historian and writer; prof of history Univ of Sussex 1961–76 (vice-chllr 1967–76), provost Worcester Coll Oxford 1976–91, chllr Open Univ 1978–94; chm Cwlth of Learning 1988–93; Marconi medal, French Acad of Architecture's medal for formation and teaching 1982, Snow medal 1991, Wolfson prize for history 2000; Liveryman Worshipful Co of Spectacle Makers; FBA; *Recreations* travel; *Clubs* Beefsteak, Oxford and Cambridge; *Style—* The Rt Hon the Lord Briggs, FBA; ✉ The Caprons, Keere Street, Lewes, East Sussex BN7 1TY (tel 01273 474704)

BRIGGS, Johnny Ernest; MBE (2007); s of Ernest Briggs, and Rose, *née* Good; *b* 5 September 1935; *Educ* Singlegate Secdy Sch, Italia Conti Stage Sch; *m* 1, 1961 (m dis 1977), Caroline, *née* Hoover; 1 s (Mark b 1963), 1 da (Karen b 1965); m 2, 1977, Christine (m dis 2006), da of Maurice Allsop; 2 da (Jennifer b 1978, Stephanie b 1982), 2 s (Michael b 1980, Anthony b 1989); *Career* actor; Nat Serv 8 Royal Tank Regt 1953–55; *Theatre* began in Italian Opera at Cambridge Theatre 1947; rep: Amersham, Northampton, Dewsbury, Barrow-in-Furness, Bromley, Windsor; numerous tours and West End appearances; *Television* Mike Baldwin in Coronation Street (Granada) 1976–2006; *Film* over 50 incl: Carry On films, Cosh Boy, Light up the Sky, Wind of Change, HMS Defiant, The Last Escape; *Awards* Best Storyline Soap Award 2000, Best Soap Actor of the Year Award Manchester Evening News 2001, Life Achievement Award 2006, Gold Heritage Award 2006; *Recreations* golf; *Clubs* Stourbridge Golf; hon memb: Mottram Hall Golf, Patshall Park Golf, St Pierre Golf, IOM Golf, Northop Country Park Golf, Bowood Golf and Country, The Marriott (Manchester); *Style—* Johnny Briggs, Esq, MBE; ✉ c/o Derek Webster, AIM Agency, 903 Imperial Point, Salford Quays, Salford M50 3RB (tel 0161 848 0664)

BRIGGS, Martin; *m* Angela; *Career* early career in private sector; Civil Service: former economist DTI, dir English Unit Invest in Britain Bureau 1991, dir Competitiveness, Trade and Industry Govt Office for the E Midlands 1994, dir Competitiveness DTI, dir Business Links and Operations 1998, chief exec E Midlands Devpt Agency (emda) 1999–2005; special prof Univ of Nottingham for Innovation; *Recreations* music, philosophy, reading; *Style—* Martin Briggs, Esq

BRIGGS, Hon Mr Justice; Sir Michael Townley Featherstone; kt (2006); s of Capt James William Featherstone Briggs, and late Barbara Nadine, *née* Pelham Groom; *b* 23 December 1954; *Educ* Charterhouse, Magdalen Coll Oxford (MB); *m* 1981, Beverly Ann, da of late Gerald Alan Rogers; 3 s (Nicholas b 1984, James b 1986, Richard b 1988), 1 da (Jessica Molly b 1992); *Career* called to the Bar Lincoln's Inn 1978; jr counsel to the Crown in Chancery 1990–94, QC 1994, attorney gen to Duchy of Lancaster 2001–, judge of the High Court of Justice (Chancery Div) 2006–; *Recreations* sailing, singing, garden steam railways, cooking; *Clubs* Royal Yacht Sqdn, Bar Yacht, Goodwood Road Racing; *Style—* The Hon Mr Justice Briggs; ✉ Royal Courts of Justice, Strand, London WC2A 2LL

BRIGGS, Dr (Michael) Peter; s of Hewieson Briggs (d 1992), and Doris, *née* Habberley (d 1999); *b* 3 December 1944; *Educ* Abbeydale Boys' GS Sheffield, Univ of Sussex (BSc, DPhil); *m* 1969, Jennifer Elizabeth, da of late Donald Watts; 1 da (Alison Mary b 26 Jan 1976), 1 s (Andrew Peter b 30 July 1981); *Career* jr research fell Dept of Chemistry Univ of Sheffield 1969–71, research asst Dept of Architecture Univ of Bristol 1971–73, deputation sec Methodist Church Overseas Div 1973–77, area sec (Herts and Essex) Christian Aid Br Cncl of Churches 1977–80; BAAS: educn mangr 1980–86, public affrs mangr 1986–88, dep sec 1988–90, exec sec 1990–97, chief exec 1997–2002; princ Southlands Coll and pro-rector Univ of Surrey Roehampton 2002–04, pro-vice-chllr and princ Southlands Coll Roehampton Univ 2004–07, special advsr to the Vice-Chllr and Princ Southlands Coll Roehampton Univ 2007; chm Mgmnt Ctee Methodist Church Div of Social Responsibility 1983–86, exec memb Ctee on the Public Understanding of Science 1986–2002, memb Prog Cncl Int Center for the Advancement of Scientific Literacy 1992–; Hon DSc Univ of Leicester 2002; FRSA 1990; *Recreations* walking; *Clubs* Athenaeum; *Style—* Dr Peter Briggs; ✉ Southlands College, Roehampton University, 80 Roehampton Lane, London SW15 5SL (tel 020 8392 3411, fax 020 8392 3431)

BRIGGS, Raymond Redvers; s of Ernest Redvers Briggs, and Ethel, *née* Bowyer; *b* 18 January 1934; *Educ* Rutlish Sch Merton, Wimbledon Sch of Art, Slade Sch of Fine Art (DFA); *m* 1963, Jean Patricia (d 1973), da of Arthur Taprell Clark; *Career* author, book illustrator and designer; FRSL; *Books* Father Christmas (1973), Fungus the Bogeyman (1977), The Snowman (1978), When the Wind Blows (book, radio play and stage play,

1982–83), The Man (1992), The Bear (1994), Ethel and Ernest (1998), Ug, Boy Genius of the Stone Age (2001), Blooming Books (2003), The Puddleman (2004); *Clubs* Groucho; *Style*— Raymond Briggs, Esq; ✉ e-mail raymondbriggs@hotmail.com

BRIGHT, Christopher Reuben; s of Eric Bright, OBE (d 1988), and Anne Bright (d 1985); *b* 12 April 1959; *Educ* Univ of Wales (BSc), Dalhousie Law Sch (LLM), Jesus Coll Oxford (BCL); *m* 1985, Susan; 3 s (Samuel b 1987, Thomas b 1989, Jacob b 2000); *Career* teaching asst Dalhousie Law Sch 1980–81, lectr in law Jesus Coll Oxford 1984–86; admitted slr 1985; Linklaters & Paines: slr 1992–99, ptnr 1992–2001, head of EU competition and regulation 1999–2001; conslt Shearman & Sterling LLP 2001–; memb Advsy Cncl: Oxford Inst of Euro and Comparative Law 1996–, Oxford Law Fndn; non-exec dir Jersey Competition Regulators Assoc 2004–; memb: Disciplinary Tbnl Accountancy Investigation and Discipline Bd 2004–, Competition Cmmn 2006–; sr visiting research fell in law Univ of Oxford 2004–; memb City of London Slrs' Co; *Books* Public Procurement Handbook (1994), Understanding the Brussels Process (1995); *Recreations* daydreaming and gardening; *Style*— Christopher Bright, Esq; ✉ 27 Lathbury Road, Oxford OX2 7AT (tel 01865 451199); Shearman & Sterling LLP, 9 Appold Street, London EC2A 2AP (tel 020 7655 5000, fax 020 7655 5500, e-mail cbright@shearman.com)

BRIGHT, Sir Graham Frank James; kt (1994); s of late Robert Frank Bright, and Agnes Mary, *née* Graham; *b* 2 April 1942; *Educ* Hassenbrook Comp Sch, Thurrock Tech Coll; *m* 16 Dec 1972, Valerie, da of late Ernest Henry Woolliams; 1 s (Rupert b 1984); *Career* chm and md Dietary Foods Ltd 1977–; chm Int Sweetness Assoc Brussels 1997–2004; Parly candidate (Cons): Thurrock 1970 and 1973, Dartford 1974; MP (Cons): Luton E 1979–83, Luton S 1983–97; PPS to: David Waddington QC MP and Patrick Mayhew QC MP as Mins of State Home Office March-June 1983, David Waddington and Douglas Hurd MP as Mins of State Home Office June-July 1983, David Waddington and Giles Shaw MP 1984–86, Earl of Caithness at DOE 1988–89 and as Paymaster Gen 1989–90, John Major as Chllr of the Exchequer and as PM 1990–94; vice-chm Cons Pty 1994–97; sec Backbench Cons Smaller Business Ctee 1979–80 (vice-chm 1980–83), sec Backbench Aviation Ctee 1980–83, memb Select Ctee on House of Commons Servs 1982–84, chm Cons Smaller Businesses Ctee 1983–84 and 1987–88, vice-chm Cons Aviation Ctee 1983–85, sec Backbench Food and Drink Sub-Ctee 1983–85; introduced Private Members Bills: Video Recordings Act 1984, Entertainments (Increased Penalties) Act 1990; jt sec Parly Aviation Gp 1984, vice-chm Aviation Ctee 1987–88; candidate Euro Parly elections eastern region 1999; memb: Thurrock BC 1966–79, Essex CC 1967–70; Cons Pty: chm Eastern Region 2006– (dep regnl chm 2002–06), area chm Cambs and Beds 2003–07; former nat vice-chm Young Cons; former dir Small Business Bureau Ltd 1989, dir and treas Mainstream Tst 2001–07, treas Former Membs of Parliament Assoc 2004–, tstee Parly Pension Fund 2007–; cchm Hassenbrook Technol Coll 2005–; *Recreations* gardening and golf; *Clubs* Carlton; *Style*— Sir Graham Bright; ✉ e-mail graham@grahambright.com

BRIGHT, Prof Simon; *Educ* Univ of Cambridge (PhD); *Career* research scientist then princ scientist Rothamsted Research 1974–86, plant biotechnology mangr ICI Seeds (later Zeneca Plant Science) 1987–96, technol interaction mangr Zeneca Agrochemicals 1996–2000, head of European genomics Syngenta 2000–02, head of technol interaction Syngenta 2002–04, dir Warwick HRI (formerly Horticulture Research Int) Univ of Warwick 2004–; memb BBSRC; *Style*— Prof Simon Bright; ✉ Warwick HRI, Wellesbourne, Warwickshire CV35 9EF

BRIGHTMAN, Dr David Kenneth; s of Brian George Brightman (d 2004), and Dorothy Brightman (d 1969); *b* 12 August 1954, Luton, Beds; *Educ* Univ of Nottingham (PhD); *m* 1982 (m dis 1991); 2 s (Samuel Theodore b 15 April 1983, Oliver William b 6 March 1985); *Partner* Gillian Theresa Bolton; *Career* early career as lectr in crop prodn, worked on family farm 1982–; dir and co sec Arable Crop Storage Ltd, co sec Arable Crop Services Ltd, dir Centaur Producers Ltd, dir Rothamsted Research 2005–; memb Cncl BBSRC 2003–, monitor DEFRA SA LINK prog; current and former memb several ctees and consultation panels NFU, local farming interest gps and MAFF, DEFRA and DETR projects; CBiol, FIBiol 2005, ARAgS 2005; *Recreations* skiing, golf; *Style*— Dr David Brightman

BRIGNELL, Prof John Ernest; s of Patrick John Brignell, and Marjorie Beatrice, *née* Acock; *b* 13 July 1937; *Educ* Stationers' Company's Sch Hornsey, Univ of London (BSc, PhD); *m* 1 July 1965, Gillian, da of Harry Wright (d 1985), of Nether Wallop; 1 da (Penelope b 1971); *Career* student apprentice STC Ltd 1955–59; City Univ London: res asst Northampton Coll 1959–64, res fell and res tutor 1964–67, lectr 1967–70, reader in electronics 1970–80; Univ of Southampton: prof of electronics 1980–85, prof of industrial instrumentation 1985–2001, prof emeritus 2001–; Goldsmiths travelling fell 1969: Grenoble, Gdansk, Geneva; Callendar Silver Medal (InstMC) 1994; FIEE, FInstP, FInstMC, FRSA; *Books* Laboratory on-line computing (1975), Intelligent sensor systems (1994), Sorry, Wrong Number! (2000), The Epidemiologists (2004); *Recreations* fly fishing, horticulture; *Style*— Prof John Brignell; ✉ 5 Ash Grove, Mere, Wiltshire BA12 6BX (tel 01747 861114, e-mail jeb@numberwatch.co.uk)

BRIGSTOCKE, Dr Hugh; s of Canon G E Brigstocke (d 1971), and Mollie, *née* Sandford (d 2002); *b* 1943; *Educ* Marlborough, Magdalene Coll Cambridge (MA), Univ of Edinburgh (PhD); *m* 1969, Anthea, née White; 1 s (Julian), 1 da (Sophie); *Career* curator of Italian, French and Spanish pictures National Gallery of Scotland 1968–83; ed-in-chief Grove Dictionary of Art 1983–87 (consulting ed 1987–96); Dept of Old Master Paintings Sothebys: conslt 1989, dir 1990, head of dept 1993–94, sr expert 1994–95; freelance writer, ed and art historian 1995–, ed The Oxford Companion to Western Art 1995–2001, ed The Walpole Soc 2000–; guest scholar Getty Museum CA 1983–84, hon visiting fell in history of art Univ of York 1996, Paul Mellon fell Br Sch Rome 2001; *Publications* A Critical Catalogue to the Italian and Spanish Paintings in the National Gallery of Scotland (1978, 2 edn 1993), William Buchanan and the 19th Century Art Trade: 100 letters to his agent in London and Italy (1979), Poussin Bacchanals and Sacraments (exhbn catalogue National Gallery of Scotland, 1981), A Loan Exhibition of Drawings by Nicolas Poussin from British Collections (exhbn catalogue Ashmolean Museum, 1990), Masterpieces from Yorkshire Houses - Yorkshire Families at Home and Abroad 1700–1850 (jtly, exhbn catalogue York City Art Gallery, 1994), Italian Paintings from Burghley House (jtly, exhbn catalogue Frick Art Museum Pittsburgh and five other museums in USA 1995–96), En torno a Velázquez (jtly, exhbn catalogue Museo de Bellas Artes de Asturias Oviedo, 1999), A Poet in Paradise: Lord Lindsay and Christian Art (jtly, exhbn catalogue Nat Gall of Scotland Edinburgh, 2000), Oxford Companion to Western Art (2001), Procaccini in America (exhbn catalogue, NY, 2002); author of numerous articles on Italian and French painting in various jls incl Burlington Magazine, Apollo, British Art Jl, Revue de l'Art, Revue du Louvre and Paragone; *Recreations* opera, theatre, wine, horse racing; *Style*— Dr Hugh Brigstocke; ✉ 118 Micklegate, York YO1 6JX (tel 01904 627019, e-mail hughbrigstocke@hotmail.com)

BRIGSTOCKE, Adm Sir John Richard; KCB (1997); s of Canon G E Brigstocke (d 1971), and Molly, *née* Sandford (d 2002); *b* 30 July 1945; *Educ* Marlborough, BRNC Dartmouth, Royal Naval Coll Greenwich, RCDS; *m* 21 April 1979, Heather, da of Dennis Day (d 2004), and Muriel Day (d 1995); 2 s (Tom b 1981, Jamie b 1984); *Career* RN: joined 1962, Cdr 1977, Capt 1982, Rear Adm 1991, Vice Adm 1995, Adm 1997; sea cmds: HMS Upton 1970–71, HMS Bacchante 1978–79, HMS York and 3rd Destroyer Sqdn 1986–87, HMS Ark Royal 1989–90, Flag Offr Flotilla Two 1991–92, Cdr UK Task Gp 1992–93, Flag Offr Surface Flotilla 1995–97; shore appts: Naval Plans MOD 1980–81 and 1982–84, Capt BRNC Dartmouth 1987–88, Asst Chief of Naval Staff and memb of Admiralty Bd 1993–95, Adm pres RNC Greenwich 1994–95, Second Sea Lord C-in-C Naval Home Cmd and memb of Admiralty Bd 1997–2000, Flag ADC to HM The Queen 1997–2000; gp chief exec St Andrew's Gp of Hosps 2000–04; judicial appts and conduct ombudsman 2006–; chm Cncl Univ of Buckingham 2005–; chm NHS East Midlands 2006–; younger bro Trinity House; Freeman City of London; *Recreations* skiing, equestrianism; *Style*— Adm Sir John Brigstocke, KCB; ✉ Ministry of Defence, (c/o Naval Secretary), Leach Building, Whale Island, Portsmouth PO2 8BY

BRIGSTOCKE, Nicholas Owen; s of Mervyn Owen Brigstocke, and Janet Mary, *née* Singleton; *b* 25 June 1942; *Educ* Epsom Coll; *m* 17 May 1969, Carol Barbara, da of Air Marshal Sir Walter Philip George Pretty, CB, KBE (d 1975); 1 da (Lucinda b 1971), 2 s (Marcus b 1973, Henry b 1981); *Career* Shell Mex and BP Ltd 1961–69, de Zoete and Bevan Ltd 1969–78, ptnr de Zoete and Bevan Ltd 1978–86; Barclays de Zoete Wedd Securities Ltd: dir and head of UK equity sales 1986–89, md corporate broking 1989; chm: de Zoete and Bevan Ltd 1994–97 (dep chm 1991–94), Credit Suisse First Boston de Zoete and Bevan Ltd 1997–2001, Sentry Select (UK) Ltd; non-exec dir: Turbo Genset plc, Bridgewell Gp plc, Dynamic Digital Depth Co Ltd, Azure Dynamics Corp, Healthcare Enterprise Gp plc, Capital Accumulation Ltd, Inter Pipeline Fund; MInstD; MSI Dip; *Recreations* tennis, cricket, golf; *Clubs* MCC, City of London, Turf; *Style*— Nicholas Brigstocke, Esq; ✉ St Ann's, Sheep Lane, Midhurst, West Sussex GU29 9NT (fax 020 7376 7099, mobile 07860 834485, e-mail nbrigstocke@hcegroup.com)

BRILL, John; s of late Eric William Brill, of Bramhall, Cheshire, and late Barbara Brill; *b* 21 August 1935; *Educ* King's Sch Macclesfield, Jesus Coll Cambridge (MA); *m* 10 Sept 1960, Elizabeth, da of late David James Hughes-Morgan; 3 s (Timothy, Jonathon, James); *Career* Nat Serv RN 1954–56; mgmnt trainee and dep PR mangr Rank Organisation 1959–64, account exec London Press Exchange 1964–66, md Brian Dowling Ltd 1966–76; chm GCI London (formerly Sterling Public Relations) 1976–93, dir Hanson Green 1993–96, md KREAB Communications Ltd 1999–2002; princ John Brill Consulting 1993–; FIPR; *Recreations* golf, tennis, pole vaulting; *Clubs* Savile, Buck's, MCC; *Style*— John Brill, Esq; ✉ Lower Street House, Lower Street, Fittleworth, West Sussex RH20 1EP (tel 01306 712969, e-mail john@brillconsulting.fsnet.co.uk)

BRIMACOMBE, Michael William; s of Lt-Col Winston Brimacombe, OBE (d 1995), of Torquay, Devon, and Marjorie Gertrude, *née* Ling (d 1998); *b* 6 March 1944; *Educ* Kelly Coll London (LLB); *m* 8 April 1968, Pamela Jean, da of Charles Mark Stone, of Grouville, Jersey; 1 s (John Mark b 1969), 2 da (Ruth Michelle b 1972, Helen Marie-Anne b 1976); *Career* sr ptnr Norman Allport & Co 1972–, ptnr Price Waterhouse (UK and Jersey) 1975–85; md Legal Tstees (Jersey) Ltd 1985–2000, chm Jobstream Group plc 1993–, chm nGame Ltd 1998–2002, dir MForma Group Inc 2002–04; FCA 1968, FRSA 1987; *Recreations* reading, travelling, walking; *Style*— Michael Brimacombe, Esq; ✉ Temple View, Rue des Marettes, Faldouet, St Martin, Jersey JE3 6DS (tel 01534 851087); L T Group Ltd, PO Box 779, Jersey JE4 0SE (tel 01534 856442, fax 01534 856576)

BRIMBLECOMBE, Prof Peter; s of Arthur Brimblecombe, of Kaitaia, NZ, and Betty Brimblecombe; *b* 23 January 1949, Australia; *Educ* Univ of Auckland (BSc, MSc, PhD); *m* 16 Dec 1995, Caroline; *Career* prof of atmospheric chemistry Sch of Environmental Sciences UEA; sr ed Atmospheric Environment 1990–; *Books* incl: Air Composition and Chemistry (1986), The Big Smoke (1987), Evolution of the Global Biogeochemical Sulphur Cycle (co-ed, 1989), The Silent Countdown: Essays in European Environmental History (co-ed, 1990), The Science, Responsibility, and Cost of Sustaining Cultural Heritage (jtly, 1994), The Urban Atmosphere and its Effects (co-ed, 2001), The Effects of Air Pollution on the Built Environment (ed, 2003), Air Pollution Science for the 21st Century (co-ed, 2003), An Introduction to Environmental Chemistry (jtly, 2003); *Recreations* cycling, running, photography; *Style*— Prof Peter Brimblecombe; ✉ School of Environmental Sciences, University of East Anglia, Norwich NR4 7TJ (tel 01603 593003, fax 01603 591327, e-mail p.brimblecombe@uea.ac.uk)

BRIMS, Charles David; s of David Vaughan Brims (d 1993), and Eve Georgina Mary, *née* Barrett; *b* 5 May 1950; *Educ* Winchester, Brasenose Coll Oxford; *m* 1973, Patricia Catherine, da of John Desmond Henderson, of Brimpton; 2 s (David b 1980, Edward b 1982); *Career* dir: Courage (Western) Ltd 1980–83, Imperial Inns and Taverns Ltd 1983–86, Imperial Leisure and Retailing Ltd 1985–86; chief exec Portsmouth and Sunderland Newspapers plc 1986–99; chm: Balfour 2000 Ltd 2000–03, George Gale & Co Ltd 2003–06, McMullen & Sons Ltd 2003–; non-exec dir: Claverley Co 1999–, Midland News Assoc Ltd 1999–, CN Gp Ltd 1999–, Blacket Turner & Co Ltd 1999–; pres Newspaper Soc 1998–99; tstee Stable Family Home Tst 2002–; Liveryman Worshipful Co of Brewers; *Recreations* sport; *Clubs* MCC, Vincent's (Oxford); *Style*— Charles Brims, Esq; ✉ Brimpton Lodge, Brimpton, Berkshire RG7 4TG

BRIMSON LEWIS, Stephen John; s of David Raymond Lewis (d 1969), and Doris Agnes, *née* West; *b* 15 February 1963; *Educ* The Barclay Sch, Herts Coll of Art and Design, Central Sch of Art and Design (BA); *Career* set and costume designer; memb United Scenic Artists *Theatre* credits as designer incl: Once In A While The Odd Thing Happens (RNT), Uncle Vanya (RNT), Design for Living (Donmar Warehouse and Gielgud, winner Olivier Award 1995), Les Parents Terribles (RNT (Indiscretions on Broadway, winner Olivier Award 1995, Tony and Drama Desk nominations for set and costume)), A Little Night Music (RNT) 1995, Private Lives (RNT) 1999, Timon of Athens (RSC) 1999, Macbeth (RSC) 2000, Rose (Broadway) 2000, King John (RSC) 2001, Much Ado About Nothing (RSC, Evening Standard Award nomination) 2002, The Taming of the Shrew (RSC) 2003, The Tamer Tamed (RSC) 2003, Arsenic and Old Lace (West End) 2003, All's Well That Ends Well (RSC, West End) 2004, Othello (RSC) 2004, A Midsummer Night's Dream (RSC) 2005, Antony and Cleopatra (RSC) 2006, Julius Caesar (RSC) 2006, Merry Wives of Windsor (RSC) 2006; sets for: Otello (Vienna State Opera), Turn of the Screw (Aust Opera), Tales of Hoffman (Aust Opera), Dorian Gray (Monte Carlo Opera), Dirty Dancing (London and Hamburg) 2006; costumes for: Acorn Antiques (West End), Mrs Klein (RNT), American Clock (RNT), Jeffrey Bernard Is Unwell (West End), Vanilla (West End), L'Elisir D'Amore (Dallas Opera), The Barber of Seville (ROH); *Television* incls costumes for The Nightmare Years (TTN Cable USA); *Exhibitions* work incl Making Their Mark; *Film* Bent (Film Four Int) 1996, Macbeth (Channel 4/RSC/Illuminations)2001; *Style*— Stephen Brimson Lewis, Esq; ✉ c/o Clare Vidal-Hall, 57 Carthew Road, London W6 0DU (tel 020 8741 7647, fax 020 8741 9459, e-mail clarevidalhall@email.com, website www.clarevidalhall.com)

BRINCKMAN, Sir Theodore George Roderick; 6 Bt (UK 1831), of Burton or Monk Bretton, Yorkshire; s of Col Sir Roderick Napoleon Brinckman, 5 Bt, DSO, MC, Grenadier Guards (d 1985), and his 1 w, Margaret Wilson (d 1977), da of Wilson Southam, of Ottawa, Canada; *b* 20 March 1932; *Educ* Millfield, Trinity Coll Sch Port Hope Ontario, ChCh Oxford, Trinity Coll Univ of Toronto; *m* 1, 11 June 1958 (m dis 1983), Helen Mary Anne, da of late Arnold Elliot Cook, of Toronto, Canada; 2 s ((Theodore) Jonathan b 1960, Roderick Nicholas b 1964), 1 da (Sophia Theresa b 1963); m 2, 7 Dec 1983 (m dis 2001), Hon (Greta) Sheira Bernadette Grant-Ferris, da of late Baron Harvington; m 3, 29 Sept 2001, Margaret Diana Davidson, da of late Hugh Wakefield and former w of Gay Kindersley; *Heir* s, Jonathan Brinckman; *Career* publisher and antiquarian bookseller; *Style*— Sir Theodore Brinckman, Bt; ✉ Monk Bretton, Barnsley, Cirencester, Gloucestershire GL7 5EJ (tel 01285 740564)

BRINDLE, Ian; *b* 17 August 1943; *Educ* Rossall Sch, Blundell's, Univ of Manchester (BA); *m* Elisabeth; 2 s (Michael, Andrew), 1 da (Jennie); *Career* chartered accountant;

PricewaterhouseCoopers (formerly Price Waterhouse before merger): articled in London 1965 (Toronto 1971), ptnr 1976–2001, memb Supervisory Ctee 1988–2001, dir Audit & Business Advsy Servs 1990–91, memb UK Exec 1990–2001, sr ptnr UK 1991–2001, chm UK 1997–2001, dep chm Europe; non-exec dir: 4Imprint Group plc 2003–, Elementis plc 2005–, Spirent Communications plc 2006–; dep chm Financial Reporting Review Panel 2001–; memb: Auditing Practices Ctee 1986–90 (chm 1990), Urgent Issues Task Force Accounting Standards Bd 1991–93, Accounting Standards Bd 1993–, Cncl ICAEW; FCA; *Recreations* tennis and golf; *Style*— Ian Brindle, Esq

BRINDLE, Michael John; QC (1992); s of John Arthur Brindle, and Muriel, *née* Jones (d 1975); *b* 23 June 1952; *Educ* Westminster, New Coll Oxford (BA, Ella Stephen scholar); *Career* called to the Bar Lincoln's Inn (Hardwicke scholar) 1975, pupillage with Denis Henry (now Lord Justice Henry) at 2 Crown Office Row Temple 1975–76, tenancy Fountain Court 1976–, asst recorder 1999, recorder 2000; chm of tstees Public Concern at Work 1997–2001, memb Fin Reporting Review Panel 1998–, chm Commercial Bar Assoc 2001 (treas 1999–2000), memb Financial Markets Law Ctee 2002–; *Recreations* classical music, travel, bridge; *Style*— Michael Brindle, Esq, QC; ✉ Fountain Court, Temple, London EC4 9DH (tel 020 7583 3335, e-mail mbrindle@fountaincourt.co.uk)

BRINDLEY, Lynne Janie; adopted da of Ronald Williams, and Elaine, *née* Chapman; *b* 2 July 1950; *Educ* Truro HS, Univ of Reading (BA), UCL (MA); *m* 1972, Timothy Stuart Brindley; *Career* head of mktg and chief exec's office British Library 1979–85, dir of library and info services and pro-vice-chllr Aston Univ 1985–90, princ conslt KPMG 1990–92, librarian and dir of info services LSE 1992–97; Univ of Leeds: librarian 1997–2000, pro-vice-chllr 1997–2000, visiting prof of knowledge mgmnt 2000–; visiting prof of info mgmnt Leeds Metropolitan Univ 2000–03; chief exec British Library 2000–; memb: Lord Chancellor's Advsy Ctee on Public Records 1992–98, Jt Info Systems Ctee HEFCE 1992–98, Int Ctee on Soc Sci Info UNESCO 1992–97, Research Resources Bd ESRC 1997–, Library and Info Cmmn DCMS 1999–2000, Stanford Univ Advsy Cncl for Libraries and Info Resources 1999–, Bd Museums, Libraries and Archives Cncl 2003–; chair Electronic Libraries Prog HEFCE Review of HE Libraries 1992–93; tstee Thackray Med Museum Leeds 1999–2001; Freeman City of London 1989, Liveryman Worshipful Co of Goldsmiths and Silversmiths 1993; hon fell: UCL 2002, Univ of Wales Aberystwyth 2007; Hon DLitt: Nottingham Trent Univ 2001, Univ of Leicester 2002, Univ of Oxford 2002, Univ of Sheffield 2004, Univ of Reading 2004, Univ of Leeds 2006, Open Univ 2006; Hon DPhil London Guildhall Univ 2002, Hon DSc City Univ 2005; fell Inst of Info Sci 1990, FLA 1990, FRSA 1993; *Recreations* classical music, theatre, modern art, hill walking; *Clubs* Reform; *Style*— Mrs Lynne Brindley; ✉ The British Library, 96 Euston Road, London NW1 2DB (tel 020 7412 7273, fax 020 7412 7268, e-mail chief-executive@bl.uk)

BRINDLEY, Richard Graham; s of John G Brindley (d 1990), and Dorothy Jean, *née* Smith; *b* 31 July 1954; *Educ* Jamaica Coll Kingston Jamaica, Denstone Coll, UCL (BSc, DipArch); *m* 20 June 1980, Prof Nicola Brindley, da of Hallimond Robinson; 2 s (James (Hal) b 25 April 1985, Jack W b 17 May 1987); *Career* architect; assoc Eric Cole & Partners 1980–84, co architect Prowting Homes 1984–88, ops dir Boyer Design Gp 1988–89, dir Llewelyn-Davies 1990–99, dir Broadway Malyan 1999–2001, dir Clague 2001–03; RIBA: chm London Region 1994–96, memb Cncl 1996–, vice-pres services 1999–2000, hon treas 2000–02, dir Practice 2003–; RIBA 1979, MIMgt 1989; *Recreations* theatre, swimming; *Style*— Richard Brindley, Esq; ✉ 27 Milman Road, Queens Park, London NW6 6EG (tel 020 8969 4943, e-mail richardbrindley@btinternet.com)

BRINE, Roger Ernest William; s of Ernest Albert Brine (d 1997), and Ivy, *née* Funnell (d 1993); *b* 13 November 1943; *Educ* Purley GS, Coll of Law; *m* 12 May 1973, Monica, da of Erich Bredenbrucher (d 1945), of Herdecke, Germany; 1 s (Martin b 1974), 1 da (Katharine b 1977); *Career* admitted slr 1969; ptnr: Vallis and Struthers 1971–87, Amhurst Brown Colombotti 1988–2001; conslt Charles Russell 2001–; memb: Law Soc, Soc of Tst and Estate Practitioners, Sevenoaks Round Table 1974–84; monitor of trg establishments Law Soc; Best Mentor of Trainee Slrs Award 2000 Coll of Law; *Style*— Roger Brine, Esq; ✉ Charles Russell, Buryfields House, Bury Fields, Guildford, Surrey GU2 4AZ (tel 01483 252525, fax 01483 252550)

BRINING, James; s of Colin Brining, of Leeds, and Christine, *née* Wells; *b* 10 June 1968, Leeds; *Educ* Leeds GS, Girton Coll Cambridge (BA); *m* 9 July 2004, Beverley, *née* Meason; 1 s (Cameron), 1 da (Ellie); *Career* theatre dir; artistic dir Rendezvous Theatre Co 1989–90, artistic dir Proteus Theatre Co 1991–95 (administrative dir 1990–91), community dir Orange Tree Theatre 1995–97, artistic dir Tag Theatre Co 1997–2003, artistic dir and chief exec Dundee Rep Theatre 2003–; vice-chair Fedn of Scottish Theatre; memb Bd: Playwright's Studio Scotland, Ek Theatre, East Glasgow Youth Theatre; memb Dir's Guild of GB; *Recreations* football (playing and watching); *Style*— James Brining, Esq; ✉ Dundee Repertory Theatre, Tay Square, Dundee DD1 1PB (tel 01382 227684)

BRINK, Adrian Charles; s of Charles Oscar Brink (*né* Karl Oskar Levy), and Daphne Hope, *née* Harvey; *Educ* Gordonstoun, Trinity Coll Cambridge (BA, MA); *Career* journalist Time and Tide 1967–69, sub ed Country Life 1969–71, ed Weidenfeld & Nicolson 1971–73, md James Clarke & Co 1973–; *Recreations* flying; *Style*— Adrian Brink, Esq; ✉ James Clarke & Co, PO Box 60, Cambridge CB1 2NT (tel 01223 350865, fax 01223 366951, e-mail adrian@lutterworth.com)

BRINKLEY, HE Robert Edward; CMG (2006); s of Thomas Edward Brinkley, and Sheila, *née* Gearing; *b* 21 January 1954; *Educ* Stonyhurst, CCC Oxford (MA); *m* 20 Feb 1982, Frances Mary, *née* Edwards; 3 s (Andrew b 1982, Francis b 1984, Mark b 1989); *Career* joined HM Dip Serv 1977, memb UK delgn to UK/US/USSR comprehensive test ban negotiations Geneva 1978, second sec (commercial) Moscow 1979–82, first sec FCO 1982–88, first sec (politico-military) Bonn 1988–92, first sec later cnsllr FCO 1992–96, cnsllr (political) Moscow 1996–99, head FCO/Home Office Jt Entry Clearance Unit 2000–02, ambass to Ukraine 2002–06, high cmmr to Pakistan 2006–; *Recreations* reading, walking, music (violin); *Style*— HE Mr Robert Brinkley, CMG; ✉ c/o Foreign & Commonwealth Office (Islamabad), King Charles Street, London SW1A 2AH

BRINTON, Michael Ashley Cecil; s of Maj Sir (Esme) Tatton Cecil Brinton, DL (d 1985), of London, and his 1 wife Mary Elizabeth, *née* Fahnestock (d 1960); *b* 6 October 1941; *Educ* Eton, Vienna, Perugia, Aix-en-Provence; *m* 1966, Angela, da of John Ludlow, of High Wycombe, Bucks; 2 s, 1 da; *Career* Brintons Ltd: dir 1970–, mktg and sales dir 1988–, chm 1991–; pres: Confedn Int des Tapis et Tissus D'Ameublement 1987–91, Qualitas Furnishing Standards 1992–95, Birmingham Branch Chartered Inst of Mktg 1994–95, Furnishing Trades Benevolent Assoc 1995–96, Br Carpet Manufacturers Assoc 1998–2000; chm CBI Hereford and Worcester 1998–; High Sheriff Hereford and Worcester 1990–91, HM Lord-Lt Worcs 2001– (DL Hereford and Worcester 1991); FRSA 1996–2007; KStJ 2002 (OStJ 2001); *Recreations* shooting, fishing; *Style*— Michael Brinton, Esq, KStJ; ✉ The Old Rectory, Pudleston, Leominster, Herefordshire HR6 0RA (tel 01568 760234, fax 01568 760399)

BRISBY, John Constant Shannon McBurney; QC (1996); s of Michael Douglas James McBurney Brisby (d 1965), of London, and Liliana, *née* Daneva (d 1998); *b* 8 May 1956; *Educ* Westminster, ChCh Oxford (MA); *m* 20 April 1985, Claire Alexandra Anne, da of Sir Donald Arthur Logan, KCMG, of London; *Career* 2 Lt 5 Royal Inniskilling Dragoon Gds 1974, transferred Reserve 1975–77; called to the Bar Lincoln's Inn 1978 (bencher 2005), dep high ct judge 2004; memb Exec Cncl Friends of Bulgaria (Charitable Orgn); *Style*— John Brisby, Esq, QC; ✉ 4 Stone Buildings, Lincoln's Inn, London WC2A 3XT

BRISCO, Sir Campbell Howard; 9 Bt (GB 1782), of Crofton Place, Cumberland; s of Gilfred Rimington Brisco (d 1981), and Constance Freda, *née* Polson (d 1980); suc cousin, Sir Donald Gilfrid Brisco, 8 Bt (d 1995); *b* 11 December 1944; *m* 1969, Kaye Janette, da of Ewan William McFadzien, of Winton, NZ; 2 s (Kent Rimington b 1972, Shannon Gregory b 1974), 1 da (Rebecca Kaye (Mrs Robert Haynes) b 1978); *Heir* s, Kent Brisco; *Style*— Sir Campbell Brisco, Bt; ✉ 134 Park Street, Winton, Southland, New Zealand

BRISCOE, Dr John Hubert Daly; LVO (1997); s of Dr Arnold Daly Briscoe, TD (d 2002), of Woodbridge, Suffolk, and Doris Winifred, *née* Nicholson (d 1985); *b* 19 March 1933; *Educ* Winchester, St John's Coll Cambridge, St Thomas' Hosp London (BA, MB BChir, MA); *m* 1 Feb 1958, Janet Anne, da of James Douglas Earlam (d 1958), of Bayfield, Surrey; 4 da (Sarah b 1959, Emma b 1960, Lucy b 1961, Martha b 1967), 1 s (James b 1964); *Career* MO Overseas Civil Serv Basutoland 1959–62, asst in gen practice Aldeburgh 1963–65, princ in gen practice Eton 1965–97; MO: Eton Coll 1965–97, St George's Sch Windsor 1976–97; apothecary to: HM Household Windsor, HM The Queen Mother's Household Royal Lodge 1986–97; hon memb Windsor and Dist Med Soc 1999, Hon MO Guards Polo Club 1966–83, bridgemaster Baldwin's Bridge Tst Eton 1988 and 2002, pres MOs of Schools Assoc 1989–91 (hon sec 1980–85, hon tstee 1992–, fell 2002–); hon auditor Euro Union of Sch and Univ Health and Med 1981–89; lay steward St George's Chapel Windsor Castle 1999–; Freeman City of London 1956, Master Worshipful Soc of Apothecaries of London 2000–01 (Apprentice 1952, Yeoman 1956, Liveryman 1966, memb Ct of Assts 1984–); DObstRCOG 1959, FRSM 1995, Hon LAH 2001, FRCGP 2006 (MRCGP 1968); *Recreations* growing vegetables; *Clubs* Omar Khayyam (pres 2005–06), Athenaeum; *Style*— Dr John Briscoe, LVO; ✉ Wistaria House, 54–56 Kings Road, Windsor, Berkshire SL4 2AH (tel 01753 855321, e-mail briscoe395@btinternet.com)

BRISE, *see:* Ruggles-Brise

BRISTER, Graeme Roy; s of Royston George Brister, of Cambridge, and Eileen Gladys Brister; *b* 5 May 1955; *Educ* Forest Sch, Phillips Exeter Acad New Hampshire, BNC Oxford (MA); *m* 1, 26 July 1986 (m dis 1999), Ashley Fiona; 1 da (Leander b 1988), 1 s (Hugo b 1992); m 2, 28 May 2001, Anita Maria; 1 da (Caitlin b 2003); *Career* admitted slr 1979, ptnr Linklaters and Paines 1985–96, managing ptnr (London) Pinsent Curtis 1997–2000, princ GRB Consultants, dir Blaqwell Inc 2001–, dir First Tracks Ltd 2003–04; tstee The Inst for Citizenship 1997– (chm 2000–); memb: Law Soc 1979, City of London Slr's Co 1981, American Bar Assoc; MCIArb; *Recreations* country, sport, travel, food and wine; *Clubs* Lord's Taverners, Travellers; *Style*— Graeme R Brister, Esq

BRISTOL, Archdeacon of; *see:* McClure, Ven Timothy (Tim)

BRISTOL, Dean of; *see:* Grimley, Very Rev Robert

BRISTOL, 8 Marquess of (UK 1826); Frederick William Augustus Hervey; also Baron Hervey of Ickworth (E 1703), Earl of Bristol (GB 1714) and Earl Jermyn (UK 1826); Hereditary High Steward of the Liberty of St Edmund; patron of thirty livings; s of 6 Marquess of Bristol (d 1985); suc half-bro, 7 Marquess of Bristol (d 1999); *b* 19 October 1979; *Educ* Eton, Univ of Edinburgh; *Career* dir Bristol & Stone Baltic Real Estate; patron: Gwrych Castle Preservation Tst 2002–, The Atheaeum Bury St Edmunds 2005–A Heart for Russia Fndn; tstee children's fire and burn tst Estonia 2003–06; *Recreations* shooting, skiing, stalking, travel, reading, emerging markets; *Clubs* Turf; *Style*— The Most Hon the Marquess of Bristol; ✉ Flat B, 65 Eaton Square, London SW1W 9BQ (e-mail bristol@bristolandstone.com)

BRISTOL, Bishop of 2003–; Rt Rev Michael Arthur Hill; s of Arthur Hill, of Congleton, Cheshire, and Hilda, *née* Fisher; *b* 17 April 1949; *Educ* Wilmslow Co GS, N Cheshire Coll of FE (Dip Business Studies), Ridley Hall Cambridge, Fitzwilliam Coll Cambridge (CertTheol); *m* Anthea Jean, da of Michael Longridge (d 1958); 4 da (Naomi Annabel, Charis Rebeccah, Alexa Helen, Eleanor Fay), 1 s (Nicholas Michael); *Career* mgmnt trainee/jr exec in printing industry 1969–72, memb Scargill House Community 1972–73; theol educn 1973–77 (ordained 1977); asst curate St Mary Magdalene Croydon (then Dio of Canterbury) 1977–80, curate-in-charge Christ Church Slough (Dio of Oxford) 1980–83, priest-in-charge St Leonard Chesham Bois (Dio of Oxford) 1983–90, rector of Chesham Bois 1990–92, archdeacon of Berkshire 1992–98, bishop of Buckingham 1998–2003; *Recreations* sport, reading, civil aircraft; *Style*— The Rt Rev the Bishop of Bristol; ✉ Wethered House, 11 The Avenue, Clifton, Bristol BS8 3HG (tel 0117 973 0222, fax 0117 923 9670, e-mail bishop@bristoldiocese.org)

BRISTOL, Timothy Arnold Neil; s of Arnold Charles Verity Bristol (d 1984), of Wotton, Surrey, and Lillias Nina Maud, *née* Francis-Hawkins (d 1990); *b* 21 February 1941; *Educ* Cranleigh Sch, Guildford Art Sch, RMA Sandhurst; *m* 7 Sept 1968, Elizabeth Olivia, da of late John Gurney, of Walsingham Abbey, Norfolk; 1 da (Arabella b 19 Aug 1970), 2 s (Benjamin b 7 Nov 1972, Samuel b 3 Sept 1983); *Career* 1 Bn KOSB 1960–67, served in the Radfan, Borneo, S Arabia and Dhofar campaigns, seconded to the Sultan of Muscat's Forces 1966–67, ret as Capt; diamond valuer De Beers, seconded to the Sierra Leone Govt Diamond Office 1967–70; publishing mangr Medici Society Ltd 1970–72, chm and chief exec Eastern Counties Printers and Publishing Gp 1972–85, dir Marlar International Ltd 1986–90; chm and ceo Sheffield International (Hldgs) Ltd 1990–2005, md: Sheffield International Selection Ltd 1995–2004, Sheffield International Ltd 2004–; dir Meroncroft Ltd 1992–, chm Meroncroft Investments Ltd 1994–2005; memb Ely Cathedral Finance Ctee 2000–; *Recreations* riding, gardening, reading, flying, travel; *Style*— Timothy Bristol, Esq; ✉ Sheffield International Ltd, 88 Wood Street, London EC2V 7RS (tel 020 7332 0032)

BRITNELL, Mark Douglas; s of Robert Douglas Britnell (d 1991), and Veronica Leigh, *née* Higgins; *b* 5 January 1966, Chester; *Educ* Queens Park HS Chester, Univ of Warwick (BA); *m* 30 July 2005, Stephanie, *née* Joy; 1 da (Beatrix Ella b 19 Feb 2005); *Career* NHS mgmnt trg scheme 1989–91, gen mangr St Mary's Hosp 1991–95, dir Central Middx Hosp 1995–98; Univ Hosp Birmingham: dir 1998–2000, chief exec 2000–06; chief exec South Central SHA 2006–; non-exec dir Dr Foster, memb Advsy Bd Nat Consumer Cncl, sr assoc Kings Fund; columnist for Health Serv Jl; memb: Nat Leadership Network, NHS; *Recreations* sport, politics, history, family; *Clubs* Reform; *Style*— Mark Britnell, Esq; ✉ 45 Frederick Road, Edgbaston, Birmingham B15 1HN (tel 0121 454 4106)

BRITNELL, Prof Richard Hugh; s of Ronald Frank Britnell (d 1987), and Edith, *née* Manson; *b* 21 April 1944, Wrexham; *Educ* Sir William Borlase GS Marlow, Bedford Modern Sch, Clare Coll Cambridge (BA, PhD); *m* 24 March 1973, Jennifer Joan, *née* Beard; 2 s (John Richard b 12 Sept 1976, David James b 16 Sept 1978); *Career* Univ of Durham: lectr in economic history 1966–85, lectr in history 1985–86, sr lectr in history 1986–94, reader in history 1994–97, prof of history 1997–2003, emeritus prof 2003–; FRHistS 1988, FBA 2005; *Books* Growth and Decline in Colchester, 1300–1525 (1986), The Commercialisation of English Society, 1000–1500 (1993, 2 edn 1996), The Closing of the Middle Ages? England 1471–1529 (1997), Britain and Ireland, 1050–1530: Economy and Society (2004); *Recreations* amateur dramatics, keyboard playing (clavichord, piano, organ), cooking, gardening, swimming, walking; *Style*— Prof Richard Britnell; ✉ 2 Parkside, Durham DH1 4RE (tel 0191 384 2017); 25 Orchard House, New Elvet, Durham DH1 3DB (tel 0191 383 0409, e-mail r.h.britnell@durham.ac.uk)

BRITTAIN, Clive Edward; s of Edward John Brittain (d 1948), of Calne, Wilts, and Priscilla Rosalind, *née* Winzer (d 1990); *b* 15 December 1933; *Educ* Calne Secdy Modern Sch; *m* 23 Feb 1957, Maureen Helen, *née* Robinson; *Career* Nat Serv 1954–56; racehorse trainer 1972–; major races won incl: 1000 Guineas 1984, Eclipse Stakes, Dubai Champion Stakes and Breeders Cup Turf USA 1985 (Pebbles), Japan Cup Tokyo 1986 (Jupiter Island), St Léger 1978 (Julio Mariner), 2000 Guineas 1991 (Mystiko), Oaks Stakes Epsom, Irish Oaks,

The Curragh, St Leger Doncaster 1992 (User Friendly), 1000 Guineas 1993 (Sayyedati), Hong Kong International Vase 1996 and 1997 (Luso), Queen Elizabeth Stakes Ascot 1997 (Air Express), Coronation Stakes Ascot 2000 (Crimpelene), Coronation Cup Epsom 2003 and 2004 (Warrsan); *Recreations* shooting; *Clubs* Jockey Club Rooms; *Style*— Clive Brittain, Esq; ✉ Carlburg, 49 Bury Road, Newmarket, Suffolk CB8 7BY (tel 01638 663739); Carlburg Stables, 49 Bury Road, Newmarket, Suffolk CB8 7BY (tel 01638 664347, fax 01638 661744, mobile 077 8530 2121, e-mail carlburgst@aol.com)

BRITTAIN, Nicholas John; s of Denis Jack Brittain, MBE (d 1977), of Hungerford, Berks, and Irene Jane, *née* Williams (d 1945); *b* 8 September 1938; *Educ* Lord Wandsworth Coll, Jesus Coll Oxford (MA); *m* 1964, Patricia Mary, da of Alan Francis John Hopewell (d 1957); 1 s (James b 1969), 2 da (Charlotte b 1971, Rebecca b 1973); *Career* Unilever plc 1960–82, head of gp fin Legal and General plc 1982–86, chief accountant Barclays plc, Barclays Bank plc and dir of various subsid cos 1986–96; with London First 1997–98; Cncl The Bow Gp 1973–75; govr Alexandra Tst 1980–; chm Accounting Ctee BBA 1987–96; ACCA: Cncl 1988–97, Small Business Ctee 1992–2001 (chm 1992–96), Fin Servs Network Panel 1997–2003 (vice-chm 2000–03); dir: Providence Row Housing Assoc 1981– (chm Fin Ctee 1986–), Project Fullemploy 1990–91; memb: Accounting Standards Bd FSOSIC 1994–96, Cncl Speakability (Action for Dysphasic Adults) 1998– (memb Appeal Ctee 2000–, memb Finance and Gen Ctee 2001–); pres Witley branch Cons Assoc 2000– (chm 1978–80 and 1995–97), Cncl SW Surrey Cons Assoc 1987–93 (CPC chm 1987–90, pres 1990–93); Freeman City of London 1993, Liveryman Worshipful Co of Painter-Stainers; FCCA, FRSA; *Recreations* learning to speak and write, watching cricket and rugby, gardening, cooking, church, politics, charitable work; *Clubs* MCC, Surrey CCC, Brook CC, Privateers CC, Hungerford CC, 59, Walbrook Ward (chm 1993–95), Royal Soc of St George, National; *Style*— Nicholas J Brittain, Esq; ✉ Churchfields, Church Lane, Witley, Godalming, Surrey GU8 5PP (tel 01428 682509)

BRITTAN, Lady; Diana Brittan; DBE (2004, CBE 1995); da of Leslie Howell Clemetson (d 1964), and Elizabeth Agnes, *née* Leonard (d 1996); *b* 14 October 1940; *Educ* Westonbirt Sch, Univ of Grenoble, Hartwell House; *m* 1, 1965 (m dis 1980), Dr Richard Peterson; 2 da (Katharine b 10 Sept 1966, Victoria b 12 Sept 1968); m 2, 1980, Baron Brittan of Spennithorne, PC, QC, DL (Life Peer), *qv*; *Career* managing ed EIBIS International (int tech press agency) 1977–88; Equal Opportunities Commission (EOC): cmmr 1988–96, chair Legal Ctee 1994–96 (memb 1988–96), dep chair EOC 1994–96; magistrate City of London Magistrates' Court 1984– (chair of Bench 1990–), dep chair Human Fertilisation and Embryology Authy (HFEA) 1990–97 (also chair Licensing and Fees Ctee and Communications Working Gp), memb Lord Chancellor's Advsy Ctee on Legal Educn and Conduct 1997–99, chair Community Fund 1999–2004; pres Nat Assoc for Connexions Partnerships 2005–, chair The Connexion at St Martins 2005–, chair Carnegie Cmmn for Rural Community Devpt 2006–, chair The Dales Festival of Food and Drink 2006–; memb Bd of Mgmnt Br Sch of Brussels 1990–99; tstee: Action on Addiction 1993–98, Open Univ Fndn 1995–2000, Rathbone Training 1992–2004 (non exec chair 1992–2001), Runnymede Tst until 2007; pres Townwomen's Guilds 1995–, chair Nat Family Mediation 2001–07; distinguished assoc Darwin Coll Cambridge 1998; *Recreations* travel, walking, botany, writing, keeping up with friends; *Style*— Lady Brittan, DBE; ✉ 79 Alderney Street, London SW1V 4HF

BRITTAN, Sir Samuel; kt (1993); s of Dr Joseph Brittan and Rebecca, *née* Lipetz; er bro of Baron Brittan of Spennithorne, PC, QC, DL (Life Peer), *qv*; *b* 29 December 1933; *Educ* Kilburn GS, Jesus Coll Cambridge; *Career* with Financial Times 1955–61, economics ed Observer 1961–64, advsr Dept of Econ Affairs 1965, econ commentator Financial Times 1966–, asst ed Financial Times 1978–96, visiting fell Nuffield Coll 1974–82, visiting prof Chicago Law Sch 1978; hon prof of politics Univ of Warwick 1987–92, hon fell Jesus Coll Cambridge 1988–; memb: Peacock Ctee on the Finance of the BBC 1985–86; Sr Wincott Prize for Financial Journalism 1971, George Orwell Prize 1980, Ludwig Erhard Prize for Econ Writing 1988; Hon DLitt Heriot-Watt Univ 1985, Hon DUniv Essex 1994; *Books* Left or Right - The Bogus Dilemma (1968), The Price of Economic Freedom - A Guide to Flexible Rates (1970), Steering the Economy (1971), Is There an Economic Consensus? (1973), Capitalism and the Permissive Society (1973, revised edn entitled A Restatement of Economic Liberalism, 1988), The Delusion of Incomes Policy (with Peter Lilley, 1977), The Economic Consequences of Democracy (1977), The Role and Limits of Government - Essays in Political Economy (1983), Capitalism with a Human Face (1995), Essays, Moral, Political and Economic (1998), Against the Flow (2005); *Style*— Sir Samuel Brittan; ✉ The Financial Times, Number One, Southwark Bridge, London SE1 9HL (tel 020 7873 3000, fax 020 7873 4343)

BRITTAN OF SPENNITHORNE, Baron (Life Peer UK 2000), of Spennithorne in the County of North Yorkshire; Sir Leon; kt (1989), PC (1981), QC (1978), DL (N Yorks); s of Dr Joseph Brittan, and Rebecca, *née* Lipetz; yr bro of Sir Samuel Brittan, *qv*; *b* 25 September 1939; *Educ* Haberdashers' Aske's, Trinity Coll Cambridge (MA, pres Cambridge Union, chm Cambridge Univ Cons Assoc), Yale Univ (Henry fell); *m* 1980, Diana (Lady Brittan, DBE, *qv*); 2 step da (Katharine b 10 Sept 1966, Victoria b 12 Sept 1968); *Career* called to the Bar Inner Temple 1962 (bencher 1983); chm Bow Gp 1964–65, editor Crossbow 1966–67; MP (Cons): Cleveland and Whitby Feb 1974–83, Richmond N Yorks 1983–88 (Parly candidate (Cons) Kensington N 1966 and 1970); oppn spokesman: Devolution and House of Commons Affrs 1976–78, Devolution and Employment 1978–79; min of state Home Office 1979–81, chief sec to Treasy 1981–83, sec of state for the Home Dept 1983–85, sec of state for Trade and Industry 1985–86; memb European Cmmn 1989–99 (vice-pres 1989–92 and 1995–99), chm Lotis gp of International Financial Services London (IFSL) 2001–; also currently: vice-chm UBS Investment Bank, non-exec dir Unilever; chm Soc of Cons Lawyers 1986–88, chm Conservation Gp for Europe 2000–03, vice-chm Nat Assoc of Sch Govrs and Mangrs 1970–78, memb Ctee Br Atlantic Gp of Young Politicians 1970–78; distinguished visiting fell Policy Studies Inst 1988, Hersch Lauterpacht Meml lectures Univ of Cambridge 1990, distinguished visiting scholar Yale Univ 2000–02; chllr Teeside Univ 1993–; Hon DCL: Univ of Newcastle upon Tyne 1990, Univ of Durham 1992; Hon LLD: Univ of Hull 1990, Univ of Bath 1995; Hon DL Univ of Bradford 1992; Dr (hc) Edinburgh 1991, Dr of Econs (hc) Korea Univ 1997; *Publications* incl: The Conservative Opportunity (contrib), Millstones for the Sixties (jtly), Rough Justice, Infancy and the Law, How to Save your Schools, A New Deal for Health Care (1988), Defence and Arms Control in a Changing Era (1988), Discussions on Policy (1989), Europe: Our Sort of Community (Granada Guildhall Lecture, 1989), Monetary Union: the issues and the impact (1989), European Competition Policy (1992), Europe: The Europe We Need (1994), Globalisation vs Sovereignty? The European Response (Rede Lecture and related speeches, 1997), A Diet of Brussels (2000); *Clubs* White's, Carlton, Pratt's, MCC; *Style*— The Rt Hon the Lord Brittan of Spennithorne, PC, QC, DL; ✉ House of Lords, London SW1A 0PW

BRITTEN, Alan Edward Marsh; CBE (2003); s of Robert Harry Marsh Britten (d 1987), and Helen Marjorie, *née* Goldson; *b* 26 February 1938; *Educ* Radley, Emmanuel Coll Cambridge (MA), Williams Coll Massachusetts, Princeton Univ NJ; *m* 23 Sept 1967, Judith Clare, da of Cdr Anthony Charles Akerman, OBE, DSC, RN, of Edinburgh; 2 da (Tamara b 22 July 1970, Sophie b 29 Feb 1972); *Career* Northamptonshire Regt 1956–57, 2 Lt Cheshire Regt 1957–58, served Malaya; md Mobil Oil Co Ltd UK 1987–89 (joined 1961), vice-pres Mobil Europe Ltd 1990–96 (co assignments USA and Italy); md: Mobil Oil Kenya Group, Mobil Oil A/S Denmark, Mobil Oil Portuguesa SARL, Mobil Oil BV Group Rotterdam, Mobil Oil Co Ltd; dir Br Tourist Authy 1997–2003; chm English Tourism Cncl 1999–2003; chair: Tourism Quality Review Gp 2002–, Tourism Attractions Review 2006–, Tourism Sustainability Review 2007–; memb Cncl Royal Warrant Holders Assoc (pres 1997–98), commissioning ed A Peerage for Trade (2002); tstee Queen Elizabeth Scholarship Tst 1997–2002 (chm 1998–2002); UEA: memb Cncl 1996–2005 (vice-chm 2003–05), tstee dir Overseas Devpt Gp 1997–2007, chm Learning Through Earning Steering Ctee 1998–2000, chm Careers Centre Advsy Bd 1997–99; memb Cncl Aldeburgh Fndn 1989–99, pres Friends of Aldeburgh Productions 2000–; memb Advsy Bd 10 Days At Princeton; govr Trinity Coll of Music 2001–, memb Bd Trinity Coll London 2003–; tstee: Leeds Castle 2004–, Integrated Neurological Services 2006–, Transglobe Expedition Tst 2006–; *Recreations* music, travel, gardening; *Clubs* Garrick, Noblemen and Gentlemen's Catch and Glee, Aldeburgh Golf; *Style*— Alan Britten, Esq, CBE

B

BRITTEN, Philip Stanley; s of Keith Stanley Britten, of Deal, Kent, and Kathleen Josephine, *née* Burton; *b* 29 August 1957; *Educ* Queen Elizabeth GS Faversham, Ealing Tech Coll London (City & Guilds); *Career* chef; Dorchester Hotel London 1973–78, Kulm Hotel St Moritz and Victoria Jungfrau Interlaken 1978–80; sous chef Hambleton Hall Leics 1980–82, head chef Dans Restaurant London 1982–83; Chez Nico London: sous chef 1983–85 (2 Michelin stars), chef patron 1985–87 (1 Michelin star); head chef Capital Hotel London 1988–99 (1 Michelin star, 4 out of 5 Good Food Guide 1999); The Carlton London Restaurant Awards Outstanding London Chef 1999–; md Oscar Samuel Ltd 1993–, dir Solstice Ltd 1996–; *Recreations* driving/motor sports; *Style*— Philip Britten, Esq

BRITTENDEN, (Charles) Arthur; s of late Tom Edwin Brittenden and Caroline, *née* Scrivener; *b* 23 October 1924; *Educ* Leeds GS; *m* 1, 1953 (m dis 1960), Sylvia Penelope Cadman; m 2, 1966 (m dis 1972), Ann Patricia Kenny; m 3, 1975, Val Arnison (d 2002); *Career* northern ed Daily Express 1962–63, dep ed Sunday Express 1963–64, ed Daily Mail 1966–71, dep ed The Sun 1972–81, dir of corp rel News International plc 1982–87, dir Times Newspapers Ltd 1982–87, sr conslt Bell Pottinger Communications Ltd (formerly Lowe Bell Communications Ltd) 1988–2003, dir Dowson-Shurman Associates Ltd 1990–97; memb Press Cncl 1982–86 (jt vice-chm 1983–86); *Style*— Arthur Brittenden, Esq; ✉ 22 Park Street, Woodstock, Oxfordshire OX20 1SP (tel 01993 811425)

BRITTER, Prof Rex Edward; *b* 1946; *Educ* Monash Univ Aust (BE, PhD); *Career* engr Gutteridge Haskins Davey Aust 1968, pt/t lectr in fluid mechanics Royal Melbourne Inst of Technol 1971–72, sr teaching fell Monash Univ 1973–74; Univ of Cambridge: postdoctoral research assoc Dept of Applied Mathematics and Theoretical Physics 1975–78 (SRC sr visiting fell 1979), lectr Dept of Engrg 1979–91, reader in environmental fluid dynamics 1991–2001, prof of environmental fluid dynamics 2001–; official fell Pembroke Coll Cambridge 1979 (asst dir of studies 1980–); CNRS visiting fell Université Scientifique et Medicale de Grenoble 1977, visiting asst prof N Carolina State Univ Raleigh and visiting scientist US Environmental Protection Agency Fluid Modelling Facility 1978, 1979, 1983, 1986 and 1989, visiting sr lectr Dept of Mathematics Monash Univ 1980; founding dir Cambridge Environmental Research Ltd 1985; ed Jl of Hazardous Materials 1984–95; Sugden Award Combustion Inst (British Section) 1990 (jtly); FIMA 1985; *Books* Gas Dispersion (jt ed, 1982), Workbook on the Dispersion of Dense Gases (jtly, 1988), Recent Research on the Dispersion of Hazardous Materials (1998), Wind Flow and Vapor Cloud Dispersion at Industrial and Urban Sites (jtly, 2002); *Style*— Prof Rex Britter; ✉ Department of Engineering, Trumpington Street, Cambridge CB2 1RZ

BRITTON, Prof Celia Margaret; da of James Nimmo Britton (d 1994), of London, and Jessie Muriel, *née* Robertson (d 1991); *b* 20 March 1946; *Educ* N London Collegiate Sch, New Hall Cambridge (MA, Dip Linguistics), Univ of Essex (PhD); *Career* lectr: KCL 1972–74, Univ of Reading 1974–91; Carnegie chair of French Univ of Aberdeen 1991–2002, pt/t chair of French UCL 2003–; pres Soc for French Studies 1996–98, chair French Panel HEFCE Res Assessment Exercise 2001, memb Scottish Academic Awards Scheme Panel 1992–2001; FBA 2001; Chevalier dans l'Ordre des Palmes Académiques 2003; *Books* Claude Simon: Writing the Visible (1987), The Nouveau Roman: Fiction, Theory and Politics (1992), Claude Simon (ed, 1993), Edouard Glissant and Postcolonial Theory (1999), Race and the Unconscious: Freudianism in French Caribbean Thought (2003); *Recreations* travel, cinema, cookery; *Style*— Prof Celia Britton; ✉ University College London, Gower Street, London WC1E 6BT (tel 020 7679 2000, e-mail celiabritton@talk21.com)

BRITTON, Fern Mary Philomena; da of Tony Britton, of London, and Ruth Aves, *née* Hawkins; *b* 17 July 1957; *Educ* Dr Challoner's HS, Central Sch of Speech and Drama; *m* 24 May 2000, Phil Vickery; 2 s (Jack, Harry (twins) b 1993), 2 da (Grace b 1997, Winifred b 2001); *Career* television presenter; stage mangr Cambridge Theatre Co 1977–80; presenter: Spotlight (BBC Plymouth) 1981–83, BBC News 1983, BBC Breakfast Time 1983, Coast to Coast (TVS) 1985–92, London Tonight 1992–93, GMTV 1993, Ready Steady Cook 1993, This Morning 1998– (nominated Best Factual Presenter RTS 2003); *Publications* Fern's Family Food (1997), Winter Treats and Summer Delights (1999), Phil and Fern's Family Food (2003); *Recreations* gardening, yoga, motorcycling; *Clubs* Mensa; *Style*— Ms Fern Britton

BRITTON, Jonathan; s of Gerald Percy Britton (d 1978), and Jean, *née* Bowler; *b* 23 May 1954; *Educ* King's Sch Worcester, Keble Coll Oxford (MA); *m* 21 Sept 1985, Dr Helen Florence Drake, da of Reginald George Drake; 3 s (Thomas Charles b 5 Nov 1987, Henry Robert b 31 July 1991, Joshua William Jonathan b 16 Jan 2000), 2 da (Emma Katherine b 6 March 1990, Charlotte Rebecca b 28 Nov 1994); *Career* CA; Peat Marwick Mitchell & Co 1977–80, Financial Training Ltd 1980–82; mgmnt conslt: Arthur Andersen & Co 1982–84, Morgan Stanley International 1984–86; Swiss Bank Corporation London: fin dir 1986–90, chief operating offr Capital Markets and Treasy Div 1990–92, head of logistics Asia/Pacific Region Hong Kong 1993–95; global controller Warburg Dillon Read 1996–98 (chief operating offr EMEA 1995–96), global chief fin offr UBS Investment Bank 1998–2005, gp financial controller Barclays plc 2006–; memb ICAEW; *Recreations* opera, golf, sailing, running, wine, tennis; *Clubs* Vincent's (Oxford), Salcombe Yacht, Malden Golf, Piltdown Golf, Royal Ocean Racing, Oriental; *Style*— Jonathan Britton, Esq

BRITTON, (Berry) Julian; s of Capt Gordon Berry Cowley Britton, CBE, RN (d 1979), of Southampton, and Vera, *née* Hyman (d 1988); *b* 9 November 1941; *Educ* Taunton Sch Southampton, Bart's Med Sch (MB BS, MS, MA); *m* 20 April 1968, (Edith) Mona, da of Robert Cowans (d 1967), of Gateshead; 1 da (Rachel b 1970), 1 s (Jonathan b 1972); *Career* lectr in surgery Bart's 1972–74, reader in surgery Univ of Oxford 1976–80, conslt surgn Oxford Radcliffe Hosp 1980–2004; Green Coll Oxford: fell 1979–2004 (emeritus fell 2005–), sr tutor 1979–83, vice-warden 1989–92; dir clinical studies Univ of Oxford 1985–88; memb: BMA, RSM; FRCS; *Recreations* fly fishing, carpentry; *Style*— Julian Britton, Esq; ✉ Humphries House, Scaleby Hill, Carlisle CA6 4NB (tel 01228 675987, e-mail bj.britton@tiscali.co.uk)

BRITTON, Moira Jean; OBE (2003); da of Douglas Barker, and Jeannie, *née* Thomson; *b* 20 February 1953; *Educ* Roundhay HS, Univ of Leeds (MBA); *m* 2 Sept 1972, Stephen Britton; 2 da (Heather b 1981, Stephanie b 1987), 1 s (Christopher b 1989); *Career* sr admin asst Leeds AHA 1975–79, unit administrator then unit gen mangr S Tees DHA 1979–83, chief exec S Tees Community and Mental Health NHS Tst 1993–99, chief exec Tees and NE Yorks NHS Tst 1999–2006; memb Inst of Health Serv Admin 1977; Hon Dr Univ of Teesside 2006; *Recreations* aerobics, travel, wining and dining, gardening, reading; *Style*— Mrs Moira Britton, OBE; ✉ tel 01642 701445

BRIXWORTH, Bishop of 2002–; Rt Rev Frank White; s of John Edward White (d 1996), and Mary Ellen, *née* Nicholls (d 1989); *Educ* St Cuthbert's GS Newcastle upon Tyne, Consett Tech Coll, Univ of Wales Inst of Science and Technol (BScEcon), Univ of Wales Cardiff (Dip Social Science), Univ of Nottingham (DipTheol), St John's Coll Nottingham

(Dip Pastoral Studies); *m* 1982, Alison Mary, da of Prof Keith Rodney Dumbell; *Career* dir Youth Action York 1971–73, detached youth worker Manchester Catacombs Tst 1973–77, asst curate St Nicholas' Durham 1980–84, sr curate St Mary and St Cuthbert Chester-le-Street 1984–87, full time hosp chaplain Durham HA 1987–89, vicar St John the Evangelist Birtley 1989–97, rural dean Chester-le-Street 1993–97, archdeacon of Sunderland 1997–2002, hon canon Durham Cathedral 1997–2002, hon canon Peterborough Cathedral 2002–; proctor in convocation Gen Synod C of E 1987–2000; *Recreations* birdwatching, walking, motor cars, theatre, football, history and local studies; *Style*— The Rt Rev the Bishop of Brixworth; ✉ 4 The Avenue, Dallington, Northampton NN5 7AN (tel 01604 759423)

BROACKES, Simon Nigel; s of Sir Nigel Broackes (d 1999), and late Joyce Edith, *née* Horne; *b* 31 July 1966; *Educ* Eton; *Children* 1 da (Nigella Elizabeth b 29 Dec 2004); *Career* quantity surveyor Trollope and Colls Ltd (awarded BEC mgmnt trg prize 1985), sr conslt to Sir Robert McAlpine Ltd (previous roles incl mgmnt of special projects div 1987–95), co-fndr and chm Neptune Land Ltd 2004–; exec dir SQ Group of Cos; dir: London International Exhibition Centre Ltd (ExCel), Greycoat Victoria plc, Madisons Coffee plc, Lanica plc, Newultra Ltd, BHW Investments Ltd, Q.ton Ltd, Carwardines of Bristol Ltd, Expovenue Ltd, Richoux Restaurants Ltd; memb: Gen Cncl Westminster Property Owners' Assoc 1987–92, Lime St Ward Club 1986, Land Inst 1988, Met Special Constabulary 1986–91; *Recreations* classic cars, tennis; *Clubs* Lansdowne, Bluebird, Harrington; *Style*— Simon Broackes, Esq; ✉ Neptune Land Ltd, 102 Sydney Street, London SW3 6NJ (tel 020 7349 1670, fax 020 7349 1671, e-mail simon.broackes@neptuneland.co.uk)

BROADBENT, Sir Andrew George; 5 Bt (UK 1893), of Brook Street, Co London, and Longwood, Yorkshire; o s of Sir George Walter Broadbent, 4 Bt, AFC (d 1992), and Valerie Anne, *née* Ward (d 2001); *b* 26 January 1963; *Educ* Monkton Combe; *Heir* unc, Robert Broadbent; *Career* late The Prince of Wales's Own Regt of Yorkshire, currently studying furniture restoration; *Style*— Sir Andrew Broadbent, Bt

BROADBENT, Prof Edward Granville; s of Joseph Charles Fletcher Broadbent (d 1963), and Lucetta, *née* Riley (d 1968); *b* 27 June 1923; *Educ* Huddersfield Coll, St Catharine's Coll Cambridge (MA, ScD); *m* 7 Sept 1949, Elizabeth Barbara (d 2001), da of Percy Charles Puttick (d 1975); *Career* dep CSO RAE 1969–83 (govt scientist 1943–83), visiting prof Mathematics Dept Imperial Coll London 1983–; author numerous scientific papers in learned jls on theory of aero-elasticity, aerodynamics, magnetohydrodynamics, acoustics and propulsion; FRAeS 1959, FIMA 1965, FRS 1977, FREng 1978; *Books* The Elementary Theory of Aeroelasticity (1953); *Recreations* gardening, theatre, concerts, bridge, chess; *Style*— Prof Edward Broadbent, FRS, FREng; ✉ 11 Three Stiles Road, Farnham, Surrey GU9 7DE (tel 01252 714621); Mathematics Department, Imperial College, Huxley Building, Queens Gate, London SW7 2BZ (tel 020 7594 8501)

BROADBENT, Jim; *b* 24 May 1949; *Career* actor; *Theatre* incl Theatre of Blood (RNT) 2005; *Television* incl: Bird of Prey 1982, Birth of a Nation 1982, Black Adder 1983, Only Fools and Horses 1983–91, Happy Families 1985, The Insurance Man 1985, Tales of the Unexpected 1988, Blackadder's Christmas Carol 1988, Work! 1990, Murder Most Horrid 1991, A Sense of History 1992 (also writer), Gone to Seed 1992, Inspector Morse 1992, The Last Englishman 1995, The Peter Principle 1997, The Gathering Storm 2002, The Young Visiters 2003, Pride 2004, Longford 2006; *Film* incl: The Shout 1978, The Passage 1979, The Dogs of War 1980, Breaking Glass 1980, Time Bandits 1981, The Hit 1984, Brazil 1985, Superman IV: The Quest for Peace 1987, The Good Father 1987, Vroom 1988, Erik the Viking 1989, Life is Sweet 1990, Enchanted April 1992, The Crying Game 1992, Bullets Over Broadway 1994, Princess Caraboo 1994, Widow's Peak 1994, Wide-Eyed and Legless 1994, Richard III 1995, Rough Magic 1995, Smilla's Feeling for Snow 1997, The Borrowers 1997, The Avengers 1997, Little Voice 1998, Topsy-Turvy 1999 (BAFTA nomination), Bridget Jones's Diary 2001, Moulin Rouge 2001 (BAFTA Award for Best Supporting Actor 2002), Gangs of New York 2001, Iris 2001 (Oscar for Best Supporting Actor 2002, Golden Globe for Best Supporting Actor 2002), Nicholas Nickelby 2002, Bright Young Things 2003, Tooth 2004, Around the World in 80 Days 2004, Vanity Fair 2004, Vera Drake 2004, Bridget Jones: The Edge of Reason 2004, The Magic Roundabout 2005, Robots 2005, Valiant 2005; *Style*— Jim Broadbent, Esq; ✉ c/o Harriet Robinson, ICM, Oxford House, 76 Oxford Street, London W1D 1BS

BROADBENT, John Michael (Mike); s of Ronald William Percy Broadbent (d 1979), and Marion, *née* White (d 1963); *b* 24 November 1933; *Educ* Manchester Grammar; *m* 29 July 1961, Sandra Elizabeth, da of Lewis Phillips (d 1966), of Runcorn, Cheshire; 3 da (Maryan b 1965, Jane b 1969, Philippa b 1971 d 1972), 2 s (Adam b 1971, Simon b and d 1967); *Career* Nat Serv Bombardier RA 1953–55; journalist: Kemsley Newspapers 1950–57, Star Newspaper 1957–59; BBC 1959–91: scriptwriter TV News, prodr (later ed) Westminster 1968–72, ed Nine O'Clock News, ed (news) Sixty Minutes, founding ed One O'Clock News, ed Commons TV, asst to Head of BBC Westminster; freelance journalist, broadcasting conslt and lectr 1991–; accompanying offr FCO (OVIS) 1991–95; fndr and former chm Whitehill Ave Luton Res Assoc, memb Luton Town Supporters Club; *Recreations* supporting Luton Town FC, cinema, hospice volunteer; *Style*— Mike Broadbent, Esq; ✉ 382 Icknield Way, Luton, Bedfordshire LU3 2JX (tel 01582 527470, e-mail mike_broadbent@yahoo.com)

BROADBENT, (John) Michael; s of John Fred Broadbent (d 1973), and Hilary Louise, *née* Batty (d 1998); *b* 2 May 1927; *Educ* Rishworth Sch, Bartlett Sch of Architecture, UCL (Certificate in Architecture); *m* 19 June 1954, Mary Daphne, da of Edgar Lionel Joste (d 1985); 1 da (Emma b 9 Jan 1959), 1 s (Bartholomew b 11 Jan 1962); *Career* Nat Serv RA 1945–48 (2 Lt and asst adj Dover Castle 1947–48); trainee Laytons Wine Merchants London 1952–53, Saccone and Speed London 1953–55, John Harvey and Sons Ltd 1955–66 (dir 1963–66); Christie Manson and Woods Ltd: dir 1967–97, head of Wine Dept 1966–92, dir Christie's Wine Course; non-exec dir: Christie's Fine Art Ltd 1998–2001, Wineworld plc 1998–2000, Christie's Int (UK) Ltd 2001–07; chm Wine Trade Art Soc 1972–2007, pres Int Wine and Food Soc 1985–92, chm Wine & Spirit Trades' Benevolent Soc 1991–92; Master Worshipful Company of Distillers 1990–91 (Liveryman 1964, memb Ct of Assts 1969), Liveryman Worshipful Co of Vintners 2006 (Freeman (hc) 2001); Master of Wine 1960, memb Inst Masters of Wine (chm 1971–72); Membre d'Honneur l'Académie du Vin de Bordeaux 1973, Chevalier dans l'Ordre National du Mérite 1979, La Medaille de la Ville de Paris Echelon Vermeil 1989, Membre d'Honneur L'Académie International du Vin 1994; *Books* Wine Tasting (1968–), The Great Vintage Wine Book (1980, II 1991), Pocketbook of Vintages (1992–), Vintage Wine (2002, The James Beard Fndn Best Book on Wine 2003, The Best Wine Book in the World Gourmand World Awards 2003, Golden Laurel Historia Gastronomica Helvetica (Best Wine Book of the Year) 2004, Goldener Feder Gastronomische Akademie Deutschlands 2005); *Recreations* drawing, piano playing; *Clubs* Brooks's; *Style*— Michael Broadbent, Esq; ✉ 87 Rosebank, London SW6 6LJ (tel 020 7381 0858, fax 020 7386 9723); Christie's, 85 Old Brompton Road, London SW7 3LD (tel 020 7752 3295, fax 020 7752 3023)

BROADBENT, Rt Rev Peter Alan (Pete); *see:* Willesden, Bishop of

BROADBENT, (Sir) Richard; KCB (2003); s of John Barclay Broadbent, of Norwich, and Faith Joan Laurie, *née* Fisher; *b* 22 April 1953; *Educ* Univ of London (BSc), Univ of Manchester (MA), Stanford Business Sch (Harkness fell); *Children* 1 s (Alexander Brooke b 25 Jan 1980), 1 da (Louise Rosalind b 19 Oct 1981); *Career* HM Treasy 1975–86, Schroders plc 1986–99, chm HM Customs and Excise 2000–03, chm Arriva plc 2003–; sr ind dir Barclays plc 2003–; chm The GSB Tst; MSI; *Clubs* 2 Brydges Place; *Style*— Richard Broadbent

BROADBRIDGE, 4 Baron (UK 1945); Sir Martin Hugh Broadbridge; 4 Bt (UK 1937); s of Hon Hugh Trevor Broadbridge (d 1979), and Anne Marjorie, *née* Elfick (d 1979); suc cous, 3 Baron 2000; *b* 29 November 1929, Purley, Surrey; *Educ* St George's Coll Weybridge, Univ of Birmingham (BSc); *m* 1, 1954 (m dis 1967), Norma, da of late Maj Herbert Sheffield, MC; 1 da (Hon Katharine Mary Patching b 13 Dec 1956), 1 s (Hon Richard John Martin b 20 Jan 1959); m 2, 1968, Mary Elizabeth, da of Joseph Emlyn Trotman; *Heir* s, Dr the Hon Richard Broadbridge; *Career* HM Overseas Civil Serv dist offr Northern Nigeria 1954–63, road surfacing contractor and specialist in advanced road surface treatments 1963–97; memb Cncl Lincolnshire Wildlife Tst; dir Humber Industry Nature Conservation Assoc (HINCA); pres Northern Lincs CPRE 2004– (chm 2002–04); *Recreations* natural history, game fishing; *Style*— The Rt Hon the Lord Broadbridge; ✉ 23A Westfield Road, Barton on Humber DN18 5AA (tel 01652 632895)

BROADFOOT, Prof Patricia Mary; CBE (2006); da of Norman John Cole (d 1977), and Margaret Grace, *née* Potter (d 1997); *b* 13 July 1949, London; *Educ* Queen Elizabeth's Girls' GS Barnet, Univ of Leeds (BA), Garnett Coll London (PGCE), Univ of Edinburgh (MEd), Open Univ (PhD), Univ of Bristol (DSc); *m* 9 Aug 1980, David Charles Rockey, s of Prof Kenneth Rockey; 2 s (James Charles b 1981, Aurin Laurence b 1983), 1 da (Elanwy Grace b 1987); *Career* teacher Wolmer's Boys' HS Kingston Jamaica 1971–73, research asst rising to research offr Scottish Cncl for Research in Educn 1973–77, pt/t tutor Open Univ 1976–77, lectr rising to sr lectr Westhill Coll Birmingham 1977–81; Univ of Bristol: lectr in educn 1981–90, reader in educn 1990–91, prof of educn 1991–, head Grad Sch of Educn 1993–97, dean of social sciences 1993–98, pro-vice-chllr (educn and widening participation) 2002–; visiting prof Macquarie Univ Sydney 1986, visiting prof Univ of Western Sydney 1991, visiting distinguished scholar Queen's Univ Belfast 1998; BERA: memb 1977–, pres 1987–88; Br Assoc for Int and Comparative Educn: memb 1977–2007, pres 1997; ESRC: memb Cncl 2001–06, chair Int Advsy Ctee 2001–03, chair Research Resources Bd 2003–06; memb: Coll of Fells Int Bureau of Educn Geneva 1999–, Int Consultative Ctee EURYDICE EU Information Network 2002–, HE Acad Research Ctee 2004– (Bd 2007–), Leadership Fndn Research Advsy Panel 2004–, Leadership Tap Mgmnt Prog Advsy Gp 2004–, Burgess Ctee on Assessment in HE 2005–07, HEFCE Quality Assessment Learning and Teaching Ctee 2005–; tstee St Monica Tst Bristol 2005–; hon lay canon Glocester Cathedral 2007; Standing Conf for Studies in Educn Annual Book Prize 1979, Samuel J Messick Meml Lecture Award Educnl Testing Serv (ETS) Princeton 2003; FRSA 1992, AcSS 1999; *Books* incl: Assessment, Schools and Society (1979), The Impact of Research on Policy and Practice in Education (jtly, 1980), Politics and Educational Change: An International Survey (jt ed, 1981), Keeping Track of Teaching: Assessment in the Modern Classroom (jtly, 1982), Selection, Certification and Control: Social Issues in Educational Assessment (ed, 1984), Profiles and Records of Achievement: A Review of Issues and Practice (ed, 1986), Introducing Profiling: A Practical Manual (1987), Profiling in TVEI: A Research Report (jtly, 1989), Changing Educational Assessment: International Perspectives and Trends (jt ed, 1990), Policy Issues in National Assessment (jt ed, 1993), Perceptions of Teaching: Primary School Teachers in England and France (jtly, 1993), Education, Assessment, and Society: A Sociological Analysis (1996), Promoting Quality in Learning: Does England Have the Answer? (jtly, 2000), What Teachers Do: Changing Policy and Practice in Primary Education (jtly, 2000), What Pupils Say (jtly, 2000), Culture Learning and Comparison: Lawrence Stenhouse's Vision of Education for Empowerment (2000), Assessment: What's in it for Schools? (jtly, 2002), A World of Difference: Comparing Learners Across Europe (jtly, 2003), An Introduction to Assessment (2007), 50 Years of Comparitive Education (jntly, 2007); *Recreations* riding, gardening; *Clubs* Athenaeum; *Style*— Prof Patricia Broadfoot, CBE; ✉ Amercombe, Kingswood, Gloucestershire GL12 8RS (tel 01453 844436); University of Gloucestershire, The Park, Cheltenham, Gloucestershire GL50 2RH (tel 01242 714169, fax 02142 714489, e-mail vc@glos.ac.uk)

BROADHURST, Dr Alan Desmond; s of Sydney Broadhurst (d 1980), of Thurmaston, Leics, and Grace Ellen, *née* Kettle (d 1990); *b* 24 February 1926; *Educ* Wyggeston Sch Leicester, Univ of London, Univ of Sheffield, Univ of Cambridge (MB ChB, MRCS, LRCP); *m* 11 Oct 1969, Lotte, da of Hans Zingrich, of Kt Aargau, Switzerland; 2 s (Mark b 2 July 1970, Peter b 28 Dec 1971); *Career* Staff Capt ME Forces 1947–49; pharmacologist/scientific advsr 1949–55, clinical pharmacologist/med advsr Geigy, Manchester and Basle 1955–60 (memb small research gp which discovered imipramine, the first anti-depressant drug), registrar in psychological med Fulbourn Hosp Cambridge 1960–62, sr res in med American Hosp of Paris 1963–64, med registrar Papworth Hosp Cambridge 1964–66, sr registrar in psychiatry and med Addenbrooke's Hosp Cambridge 1966–70, conslt physician Addenbrooke's Hosp Cambridge 1970–89, sr conslt psychiatrist W Suffolk Hosp Bury St Edmunds 1970–91, private practice in psychiatry 1970–; Univ of Cambridge: memb Faculty of Clinical Med 1970–, clinical teacher in psychopharmacology 1984–; author of papers and chapters in books on psychopharmacology and the effects of drugs on human performance and in aviation med, appearances in various TV documentaries about psychopharmacology; memb: Exec Ctee Eastern Div RCPsych 1984–89, E Anglian Thoracic Soc, Oxford Postgrad Inst of Psychiatry, Cambridge Med Soc, Suffolk Med History Soc, RSM, BMA; fndr memb: Royal Coll of Psychiatrists 1971, Br Assoc for Psychopharmacology; Freeman City of London 1997, Liveryman Worshipful Soc of Apothecaries 1997; DPM 1963, FRCPsych 1984, FIBiol 1998, FRSM 2006; *Recreations* motor cruising, sailing, travelling; *Clubs* Athenaeum; *Style*— Dr Alan Broadhurst; ✉ Vicarage Grove, The Park, Great Barton, Suffolk IP31 2SU (tel 01284 787288)

BROADHURST, John Charles; *see:* Fulham, Suffragan Bishop of

BROADHURST, Norman Neill; s of Samuel Herbert Broadhurst, and Ruth Broadhurst; *m* 1964, Kathleen Muriel Joyce; 2 da; *Career* Platt Saco Lowell 1970–81 (latterly finance dir), financial controller then divnl mangr (finance and admin) China Light and Power 1981–86, finance dir United Engineering Steels 1986–90, finance dir then jt dep chief executive (finance/commercial) VSEL plc 1990–94, finance dir Railtrack 1994–2000; non-exec chm: Chloride Gp plc 2001– (non-exec dir 1998–), Freightliner Gp Ltd 2001–, Cattles plc 2006– (non-exec dir 2001–); non-exec dir: Clubhaus 1997–2000, Taylor Woodrow plc 2000–03 (dep chm 2003), Old Mutual plc 1999–, United Utilities plc 1999–, Tomkins plc 2000–06; FCA 1975, FCT 1995; *Style*— Mr Norman Broadhurst; ✉ Chloride Group plc, Ebury Gate, 23 Lower Belgrave Street, London SW1W 0NR

BROADIE, Prof Alexander; *Educ* Royal HS Edinburgh, Univ of Edinburgh (MA), Balliol Coll Oxford (BLitt), Univ of Glasgow (PhD, DLitt); *Career* prof of logic and rhetoric Univ of Glasgow; RSE Henry Duncan prize lectr in Scottish studies 1990–93; Gifford lectr in natural theology Univ of Aberdeen 1994; Hon DUniv Blaise Pacal Univ 2007, DUniv (hc) Blaise Pascal Unv; FRSE 1991; *Books* A Samaritan Philosophy (1981), George Lokert: Late Scholastic Logician (1983), The Circle of John Mair (1985), Notion and Object: Aspects of Late Medieval Epistemology (1989), The Tradition of Scottish Philosophy (1990), Paul of Venice: Logica Magna (1990), Robert Kilwardby OP: On Time and Imagination (1993), Introduction to Medieval Logic (2 edn, 1993), The Shadow of Scotus (1995), The Scottish Enlightenment: An Anthology (1997), Why Scottish Philosophy Matters (2000), The Scottish Enlightenment: The Historical Age of the Historical Nation (2001), The Cambridge Companion to the Scottish Enlightenment (2003), Thomas Reid on Logic, Rhetoric and the Fine Arts (2005), George Turnbull: Principles of Moral and

Christian Philosophy (2005); *Style*— Prof Alexander Broadie, FRSE; ✉ University of Glasgow, Glasgow G12 8QQ (tel 0141 339 8855 ext 4078 and 4509, fax 0141 330 5000, e-mail a.broadie@philosophy.arts.gla.ac.uk)

BROADIE, Prof Sarah Jean; da of J C Waterlow, and A P C Waterlow, *née* Gray; *Educ* Univ of Oxford (MA, BPhil), Univ of Edinburgh (PhD); *m* 2 March 1984, Frederick Broadie, s of I Broadie; *Career* lectr Univ of Edinburgh 1967–84; prof of philosophy: Univ of Texas at Austin 1984–86, Yale Univ 1987–91, Rutgers Univ 1991–93, Princeton Univ 1993–2001, Univ of St Andrews 2001–; John Simon Guggenheim Meml Fellowship 1986–87; FAAAS 1991, FRSE 2002, FBA 2003; *Books* as Sarah Waterlow: Nature, Change, and Agency in Aristotle's Physics (1982), Passage and Possibility (1982); as Sarah Broadie: Ethics with Aristotle (1991), Aristotle: the Nicomachean Ethics (with Christopher Rowe, 2001); *Style*— Prof Sarah Broadie; ✉ Department of Moral Philosophy, University of St Andrews, Edgecliffe, The Scores, St Andrews, Fife KY16 9AL (tel 01334 462486, fax 01334 462485, e-mail sjb15@st-andrews.ac.uk)

BROADLEY, Philip Arthur John; s of Jack Broadley, and Daphne Broadley; *b* 31 January 1961; *Educ* Eastbourne Coll, St Edmund Hall Oxford (MA), Warwick Univ Business Sch (Dip BA); *m* 1989, Gillian, *née* Barlow; 1 da, 1 s; *Career* Arthur Andersen 1983–2000 (ptnr 1993–2000), gp finance dir Prudential plc 2000–; non-exec dir Egg plc 2005–07; chm Hundred Gp of Finance Dirs 2005–07; vice-chm Cncl Eastbourne Coll; FCA, FRSA; *Recreations* skiing, flying, music; *Clubs* Naval and Military; *Style*— Philip Broadley, Esq; ✉ Prudential plc, Laurence Pountney Hill, London EC4R 0HH (tel 020 7548 3905, fax 020 7548 3303, e-mail philip.broadley@prudential.co.uk)

BROADLEY, Simon; s of Donald Broadley, of Beverley, E Yorks, and Betty Broadley; *b* 17 May 1958; *Educ* Pocklington Sch, CCC Oxford (MA); *m* 8 April 1995, Dorothy Reid; *Career* civil servant; DCMS: head Sports Div 1995–99, head Tourism Div 1999–2003, head Lottery Funding Div 2003–; *Recreations* walking, gardening, skiing, film; *Style*— Simon Broadley, Esq; ✉ Department for Culture, Media and Sport, 2–4 Cockspur Street, London SW1Y 5DH (tel 020 7211 6526, fax 020 7211 6530, e-mail simon.broadley@culture.gsi.gov.uk)

BROCK, George Laurence; s of Michael Brock, of Oxford, and Eleanor, *née* Morrison; *b* 7 November 1951, Oxford; *Educ* Winchester, CCC Oxford (MA); *m* 1 July 1978, Kay, *née* Sandeman; 2 s (Patrick b 6 April 1983, Oliver b 8 May 1985); *Career* grad trainee reporter Yorkshire Evening Press 1973–76, reporter The Observer 1976–81; The Times: feature writer 1981–84, opinion page ed 1984–87, foreign ed 1987–90, bureau chief Brussels 1991–95, European ed 1995–97, managing ed 1997–2004, Saturday ed 2004–; pres World Eds Forum 2004– (memb Bd 2001–04), memb Defence, Press and Broadcasting Advsy Ctee 1998–2004, memb Br Exec Int Press Inst; theatre panel judge Olivier Awards 2004; govr The Ditchley Fndn; *Publications* Siege: Seven Days at the Iranian Embassy (co-author, 1980), Thatcher (co-author, 1983); *Recreations* music, walking, theatre, travel; *Style*— George Brock, Esq; ✉ The Times, 1 Pennington Street, London E98 1TT (tel 020 7782 5000)

BROCK, Kay; LVO (2002); da of George Roland Stewart Sandeman (d 1992), and Helen, *née* McLaren (d 2004); *b* 23 May 1953; *Educ* Sherborne Sch for Girls, Somerville Coll Oxford (MA), London Business Sch (MBA); *m* 1 July 1978, George Laurence Brock; 2 s (Patrick Michael b 6 April 1983, Oliver Roland b 8 May 1985); *Career* MAFF 1975–85 (private sec to the Perm Sec 1980–81), conslt in int trade 1985–88, Spicers Consulting Gp 1988–89, dir PDN Ltd 1990–91, European Cmmn 1992–95, advsr UK Knowhow Fund and EBRD 1995–99, asst private sec to HM The Queen 1999–2002, private sec to Lord Mayor of London 2004–; memb Ind Monitoring Bd HMP Wandsworth 2003–04; pres Somerville Coll Alumni Assoc 2004–; Liveryman Worshipful Co of Founders 2005–; *Recreations* music, Italy, cycling; *Clubs* Farmers, Walbrook; *Style*— Mrs Kay Brock, LVO; ✉ The Mansion House, London EC4N 8BH (tel 020 7626 2500)

BROCK, Michael George; CBE (1981); s of Sir Laurence George Brock, CB (d 1949), and Ellen Margery, *née* Williams; *b* 9 March 1920; *Educ* Wellington, CCC Oxford, Univ of Oxford (DLitt 2002); *m* 1949, Eleanor Hope Morrison; 3 s; *Career* historian; pro-vice-chllr Univ of Oxford 1980–88; warden: Nuffield Coll Oxford 1978–88, St George's House Windsor Castle 1988–93; hon fell: Wolfson Coll Oxford 1977, CCC Oxford 1982, Nuffield Coll Oxford 1988; Hon DLitt Univ of Exeter 1982; FRHistS, FRSL; *Style*— Dr Michael Brock, CBE, FRSL; ✉ Flat 1, Ritchie Court, 380 Banbury Road, Oxford OX2 7PW (tel 01865 515075)

BROCKBANK, Anthony Lionel; s of Maj-Gen Robin Brockbank (d 2006), and Gillian, *née* Findlay; *b* 17 December 1960, London; *Educ* Eton, ChCh Oxford (BA), Coll of Law; *m* 17 May 1997, Caroline, *née* Walford; 2 da (Eleanor b 15 Sept 2000, Rosanna b 23 Feb 2002); *Career* slr; Linklaters 1984–89, Hobson Audley 1989–2000 (ptnr 1993), ptnr Field Fisher Waterhouse 2000–; *Style*— Anthony Brockbank, Esq; ✉ Field Fisher Waterhouse LLP, 35 Vine Street, London EC3N 2AA (tel 020 7861 4000, fax 020 7488 0084, e-mail anthony.brockbank@ffw.com)

BROCKBANK, Mark Ellwood; s of John Ellwood Brockbank, of Westward Park, Wigton, Cumbria, and Elizabeth, *née* Allen; *b* 2 April 1952; *Educ* Bootham Sch York; *Career* underwriter Lloyd's 1983–; chief exec Brockbank Group plc 1995– (dir 1988–); non-exec chm Brockbank Syndicate Management Ltd 1982–; chm Brockbank Personal Lines 1997; exec vice-pres XL Capital Ltd Bermuda; *Recreations* the arts, shooting, bridge; *Style*— Mark Brockbank, Esq

BROCKBANK, Thomas Frederick; s of John Bowman Brockbank (d 1990), of Hilton, and Alice Margaret, *née* Parker (d 1987); *b* 6 March 1938; *Educ* Bootham Sch York, Loughborough Coll (DLC Mech Engrg); *m* 16 Dec 1967 (m dis 1992), Joan Emma, da of Martin Israelski, of Leamington; 3 da (Eleanor Clare b 1970, Laura Katherine b 1973, Harriet Elisabeth b 1975); *Career* merchant banker; Courtaulds Ltd 1960–65, mgmnt conslt Arthur Andersen & Co London 1965–68, RTZ Conslts (part of RTZ Corp) 1968–73, Hill Samuel Bank Ltd 1973–93 (dir of corp fin 1985–93); currently: company dir and mgmnt conslt, chm Nightingale Square Properties plc, tstee Buskaid; author of numerous lectures and articles, particularly on finance for growing companies, flotation and general strategy; MIMC, MSI, FRSA; *Recreations* music, theatre, art, photography, travel; *Style*— Thomas Brockbank, Esq; ✉ Nightingale Square Properties plc, 30A Edgarley Terrace, London SW6 6QD (tel 020 7731 7343, fax 020 7731 7420)

BROCKES, Prof Jeremy Patrick; s of Bernard Arthur Brockes, of Stonor, Henley-on-Thames, and Edna, *née* Heaney (d 1959); *b* 29 February 1948; *Educ* Winchester, St John's Coll Cambridge (BA), Univ of Edinburgh (PhD); *Career* postdoctoral fell Harvard Medical Sch 1972–75, research assoc UCL 1975–78, assoc prof of biology California Inst of Tech 1981–83 (asst prof of biology 1978–81); memb MRC Biophysics Unit KCL 1983–88, memb Ludwig Inst for Cancer Research 1988–97, prof UCL 1991–97, MRC research prof UCL 1997–; scientific medals: Zoological Soc of London 1985, Biological Cncl 1990; memb: EMBO 1988, Academia Europaea 1989; FRS 1994; *Recreations* soprano saxophone; *Style*— Prof Jeremy Brockes, FRS; ✉ Department of Biochemistry, UCL, Gower Street, London WC1E 6BT (tel 020 7679 4483, e-mail j.brockes@ucl.ac.uk)

BROCKHURST, Rowan Benford; s of Geoffrey Thomas Brockhurst (d 1997), and Barbara, *née* Wickens (d 1994); *b* 23 June 1936; *Educ* Sutton Valence, Coll of Law London; *m* 1, 8 April 1961 (m dis 1984), Eve, da of Maj William Tristram (d 1942); 1 da (Harriet b 1963), 1 s (Nicholas b 1965); m 2, 13 May 1987, Fiona Daphne, da of John Cunningham (d 1985); *Career* Nat Serv 2 Lt RASC 1959–60, Capt Army Emergency Res of Offrs; admitted slr 1958; sr ptnr Meesons Ringwood and Fordingbridge 1979–2002; pres Hants Inc Law Soc 1978–79, dir Slrs' Benevolent Assoc 1982–94; memb Law Soc 1958; pres: Ringwood and Dist Community Assoc 1992–95, Fordingbridge Soc, Ringwood Philatelic Soc, Ringwood and Fordingbridge Footpath Soc; vice-patron Trade Aid; *Recreations* walking, gardening, reading, inland waterways; *Style*— Rowan Brockhurst, Esq; ✉ 78 Allen Water Drive, Fordingbridge, Hampshire SP6 1RE (tel 01425 653748)

BROCKINGTON, Prof John Leonard; s of Rev Leonard Herbert Brockington (d 1978), and Florence Edith, *née* Woodward; *b* 5 December 1940; *Educ* Mill Hill Sch, CCC Oxford (MA, DPhil); *m* 2 Aug 1966, Mary, da of Joseph Gascoigne Fairweather (d 1988); 1 da (Anne b 1967), 1 s (Michael b 1971); *Career* Univ of Edinburgh: lectr in Sanskrit 1965–82, head of dept 1975–99, sr lectr 1982–89, reader 1989–98, prof of Sanskrit 1998–2005; elected sec gen of the Int Assoc of Sanskrit Studies 2000; FRSE 2001; *Books* The Sacred Thread - Hinduism in its Continuity and Diversity (1981), Righteous Rama: The Evolution of an Epic (1985), Hinduism and Christianity (1992), The Sanskrit Epics (1998), Epic Threads: John Brockington on the Sanskrit Epics (with Greg Bailey and Mary Brockington, 2000), Rama the Steadfast: An early form of Ramayana (with Mary Brockington, 2006); *Style*— Prof John Brockington; ✉ 3 Eskvale Court, Penicuik, Midlothian EH26 8HT (tel 01968 678709); Sanskrit, School of Asian Studies, University of Edinburgh, 7 Buccleuch Place, Edinburgh EH8 9LW (tel 0131 650 3985, e-mail j.l.brockington@ed.ac.uk)

BROCKLEBANK, Sir Aubrey Thomas; 6 Bt (UK 1885), of Greenlands, Co Cumberland and Springwood, Co Lancaster; s of Sir John Montague Brocklebank, 5 Bt, TD (d 1974), and Pamela Sue, *née* Pierce (d 2005); *b* 29 January 1952; *Educ* Eton, UC Durham (BSc); *m* 1979 (m dis 1990), Dr Anna-Marie, da of Dr William Dunnet; 2 s (Aubrey William Thomas b 1980, Hamish John b 1987); m 2, Hazel, da of Brian Roden; 1 s (Archie Thomas b 1999); *Heir* s, Aubrey Brocklebank; *Career* financial conslt; chm: The Aim Distribution Tst plc, Keydata Aim VCT plc, Puma VCT plc, Top Ten Holdings plc, dir various other cos; *Clubs* Brooks's; *Style*— Sir Aubrey Brocklebank, Bt; ✉ Hunters Lodge, St Andrews Lane, Titchmarsh, Northamptonshire NN14 3DN

BROCKLEBANK, Edward (Ted); MSP; s of Flt Lt Fred Brocklebank (d 1994), of Ballater, Grampian, and Agnes Mitchell, *née* Ainslie (d 1969); *b* 24 September 1942; *Educ* Madras Coll St Andrews; *m* 21 Aug 1965 (m dis 1979), Lesley Beverley, da of Dr Ronald Beverley Davidson (d 1975), of Dundee; 2 s (Andrew Edward, Jonathan Ainslie); *Career* trainee journalist DC Thomson & Co Ltd Dundee 1960–63, freelance 1963–65, journalist Scot TV Glasgow 1965–70; Grampian TV: in vision journalist/presenter Aberdeen 1970–77, head of news and current affrs 1977–85, head of documentaries and features 1985–95, prodns incl What Price Oil? (BAFTA Award 1974), Tale of Two Cities (TRICS Award 1977) and Oil (8 pt series for Channel 4, AMANDA Documentary Award 1988); fndr and md Greyfriars Productions 1995–2003; MSP (Cons) Mid Scotland and Fife 2003–; *Recreations* ornithology, golf, oil painting; *Clubs* New (Edinburgh), R&A; *Style*— Ted Brocklebank, Esq, MSP

BROCKLEBANK-FOWLER, Simon Edward; *b* 29 September 1961; *Educ* Westminster, Jesus Coll Cambridge (exhibitioner, MA); *m* 24 April 1993, Alexandra Robson, *qv*, da of Sir John Robson, KCMG; 1 da; *Career* FCO 1982–86, investment banker 1986–92, dir Shandwick Consultants Ltd 1992–94, md Citigate Communications Ltd 1995–98, fndr and chm Cubitt Consulting 1998–; memb Advsy Bd Cass Business Sch 2004–; fell Investor Rels Soc 1998–, FRSA 2004; *Recreations* shooting, tennis; *Clubs* Brooks's, Leander, Buck's; *Style*— Simon Brocklebank-Fowler, Esq; ✉ Cubitt Consulting Ltd, 30 Coleman Street, London EC2R 5AL (tel 020 7367 5100, e-mail simon.brocklebank-fowler@cubitt.com)

BRODIE, Alan; s of Maxwell Brodie (d 1998), of Glasgow, Scotland, and Judy, *née* Jacobson; *b* 11 January 1955; *Educ* HS of Glasgow, Univ of Edinburgh (BA, LLB); *m* 1, 15 Nov 1982 (m dis 1994), Rosemary Anne Squire; 1 s (Daniel Henry b 1987), 1 da (Jennifer b 1986); m 2, 20 Oct 1996 (m dis 2000), Caroline Louise Diprose; *Career* dir Michael Imison Playwrights Ltd (Literary Agents) 1981–89, fndr Alan Brodie Representation 1989–93 and 1996–, dir International Creative Management Ltd 1993–96; co-chair Personal Managers Assoc; chair of tstees Noël Coward Fndn, patron Chicken Shed Theatre Co, memb Down's Syndrome Assoc; *Style*— Alan Brodie, Esq; ✉ 6th Floor, Fairgate House, 78 New Oxford Street, London WC1A 1HB

BRODIE, Sir Benjamin David Ross; 5 Bt (UK 1834), of Boxford, Suffolk; s of Sir Benjamin Collins Brodie, 4 Bt, MC (d 1971); *b* 29 May 1925; *Educ* Eton; *m* 19 Sept 1956 (m dis), Ludmilla Maria, da of August Adamer; 1 s (Alan Ross), 1 da (Sonja Mary Brodie-Fairhead); *Heir* s, Alan Brodie; *Career* late Royal Signals; *Style*— Sir Benjamin Brodie, Bt

BRODIE, (James) Bruce; s of John Hobson Brodie (d 1979), of Graaff-Reinet, South Africa, and Edith Florence, *née* Murray (d 2001); *b* 19 March 1937; *Educ* Union HS, Univ of Natal (BA), Fitzwilliam Coll Cambridge (MA); *m* 15 Dec 1962, (Amie) Louise, da of Kenneth Turner James, MBE (d 1964), of Fetcham, Surrey; 2 da (Sarah b 1964, Nicola b 1966); *Career* former slr and ptnr Frere Cholmeley (chm 1990–92), barr and arbitrator 1993–; *Recreations* cricket, fishing; *Clubs* Hawks' (Cambridge), MCC, groucho, Western Province Cricket, Kelvin Grove; *Style*— Bruce Brodie, Esq; ✉ 39 Essex Street, London WC2R 3AT (tel 020 7832 1111, fax 020 7353 3978, e-mail bruce.brodie@39essex.co.uk)

BRODIE, Prof David Alan; s of William Brodie, and Margaret, *née* Blackwell; *b* 24 June 1946; *Educ* King's Sch Worcester, Univ of Nottingham (BEd), Loughborough Univ (MSc, PhD); *m* 1971, Megan Elizabeth, da of Elvet Plummer; 1 da (Jo-Anne Beth b 1973), 1 s (Tom David b 1977); *Career* dir of physical welfare Abingdon Sch 1969–72, lectr in physical educn Saltley Coll 1972–74, sr res fell Carnegie Sch Leeds Poly 1974–81, prof and head Dept of Movement Sci and Physical Educn Univ of Liverpool 1990–2001 (dir of physical educn and recreation 1981–90); head Research Centre for Society and Health Buckinghamshire Chilterns UC 2001–; memb: Int Soc for the Advancement of Kinanthropometry 1991, Br Cardiac Soc 2002, Physiological Soc 2003, RSM 2007; *Books* Fitness Training for Rugby (jtly, 1978), Get Fit for Badminton (with J Downey, 1980), Microcomputing in Sport and Physical Education (with J J Thornhill, 1983), Citysport Challenge (jtly, 1992), Inner City Sport: who plays, what are the benefits? (with K Roberts, 1992), HE Departmental Leadership/Management - An Exploration of Roles and Responsibilities (with P Partington, 1992), Research Methods in Health Sciences (jtly, 1994), Health Matters at Work (1995); *Recreations* exercise, gardening, travel; *Clubs* Pensby Runners; *Style*— Prof David Brodie; ✉ Research Centre for Society and Health, Buckinghamshire Chilterns University College, Chalfont St Giles, Buckinghamshire HP8 4AD (tel 01494 605128, fax 01494 605212, e-mail david.brodie@bcuc.ac.uk)

BRODIE, Hon Lord; Philip Hope; s of Very Rev Dr Peter Philip Brodie (d 1990), of Stirling, and Constance Lindsay, *née* Hope; *b* 14 July 1950; *Educ* Dollar Acad, Univ of Edinburgh (LLB), Univ of Virginia (LLM); *m* 16 April 1983, Carol Dora, da of Dr Ian Stanley McLeish, of Bearsden, Glasgow; 2 s (Alexander b 1984, Peter b 1986), 1 da (Alice b 1988); *Career* admitted Faculty of Advocates 1976; standing jr counsel (Scot) MOD (Procurement) Health and Safety at Work Exec 1983–87, QC (Scot) 1987, pt/t chm Industrial Tbnls 1987–91, pt/t chm Med Appeal Tbnls 1991–96, memb Mental Welfare Cmmn for Scot 1985–96, advocate depute 1997–99, senator Coll of Justice 2002–, chm Judicial Studies Ctee 2006; called to the Bar Lincoln's Inn 1991; *Style*— The Hon Lord Brodie; ✉ 2 Cobden Crescent, Edinburgh EH9 2BG (tel 0131 667 2651); The Court of Session, Parliament House, Edinburgh EH1 1RQ (tel 0131 225 2595)

BRODIE, Robert; CB (1990), WS (2002); s of Robert Brodie, MBE (d 1966), and Helen Ford Bayne, *née* Grieve (d 1997); *b* 9 April 1938; *Educ* Morgan Acad Dundee, Univ of St Andrews (MA, LLB); *m* 26 Sept 1970, Jean Margaret, da of Sheriff Princ Thomas Pringle McDonald, QC (d 1969); 2 s (Robert b 1971, James b 1980), 2 da (Alison b 1973, Ruth b

1978); *Career* legal asst to Sec of State for Scotland 1965 (dep slr 1984–87, slr 1987–98), dep dir of Scottish Cts admin 1975–82; temp sheriff 1999–2000; memb: Sheriff Court Rules Cncl 1975–82, Scottish Ctee on Jurisdiction and Enforcement 1977–80, Working Party on Divorce Procedure 1979–80; session clerk Wardie Parish Church 1981–91; chm Scottish Assoc of CAB 1999–2004; pt/t chm Employment Tbnl (Scotland) 2000–02; pt/t sheriff 2000; memb Law Soc of Scotland; *Recreations* music, hill walking, making jam; *Style*— Robert Brodie, Esq, CB; ✉ 8 York Road, Edinburgh EH5 3EH (tel and fax 0131 552 2028, e-mail bob.brodie@blueyonder.co.uk)

BRODIE, Stanley Eric; QC (1975); s of Dr Abraham Brodie (d 1978), of Allerton, Bradford, and Cissie Rachel Garstein (d 1998); uncle Sir Israel Brodie, former chief rabbi of GB and The Cwlth; *b* 2 July 1930; *Educ* Bradford GS, Balliol Coll Oxford (MA); *m* 1, 31 July 1956, Gillian Rosemary, da of Sir Maxwell Joseph; 2 da (Henrietta b 1957, Charlotte b 1960); m 2, 29 Oct 1973, Elizabeth (Hon Mrs Justice Gloster, DBE), *qv*, da of Peter Gloster; 1 da (Sophie b 1978), 1 s (Samuel b 1981); *Career* called to the Bar Inner Temple 1954, recorder Crown Court 1975, bencher Inner Temple 1984 (reader 1999, treas 2000), memb Bar Cncl 1987; *Recreations* fishing, boating, opera, holidays; *Clubs* Flyfishers', Athenaeum, Beefsteak; *Style*— Stanley Brodie, Esq, QC; ✉ Blackstone Chambers, Blackstone House, Temple, London EC4Y 9BW (tel 020 7583 1770)

BRODIE OF LETHEN, Ewen John; s of David James Brodie of Lethen (d 1966), and Diana Davidson (d 1991); *b* 16 December 1942; *Educ* Harrow; *m* 4 Aug 1967, Mariota, yr da of Lt Col Ronald Steuart Menzies, of Culdares; 3 da (Sarah b 30 Dec 1967, Jane b 5 May 1970, Katherine b 21 Jan 1972); *Career* Lt Grenadier Guards 1961–64; mktg mangr IBM (UK) Ltd 1965–74; estate mgmnt 1975–; memb Regnl Advsy Ctee (N Scotland) Forestry Cmmn 1977–89, vice-chm Timber Growers Scotland 1979–82; dir John Gordon & Son Ltd 1992–; HM Lord-Lt Nairnshire 1999– (DL 1980–99); *Recreations* countryside sports; *Clubs* New (Edinburgh); *Style*— Ewen Brodie of Lethen; ✉ Lethen House, Nairn IV12 5PR (tel 01667 452079, fax 01667 456449, e-mail ejbrodie@supanet.com)

BRODRICK, His Hon Judge Michael John Lee; s of His Hon Norman John Lee Brodrick, QC, JP (d 1992), and Ruth Severn (d 1998), da of Sir Stanley Unwin, KCMG, the publisher; *b* 12 October 1941; *Educ* Charterhouse, Merton Coll Oxford; *m* 1969, Valerie Lois, da of Gerald Max Stroud; 2 c; *Career* called to the Bar Lincoln's Inn 1965 (bencher 2000); memb Western Circuit; elected to Senate of Inns of Court and the Bar 1979–82, recorder 1981–87, circuit judge (Western Circuit) 1987–, resident judge Winchester Combined Court 1999–, sr circuit judge 2002–, hon recorder of Winchester 2005–; liaison judge to: SE Hants Magistrates 1989–93, IOW Magistrates 1989–94, NE and NW Hants Magistrates 1999–2007; pres Cncl of HM Circuit Judges 2003 (memb Ctee 1991–2003); judicial memb Tport Tbnl 1986; memb Lord Chllr's Advsy Ctee for Appt of Magistrates for SE Hants 1993–2000 (Portsmouth 1990–93); cnsllr to the Dean and Chapter of Winchester Cathedral 1993–; memb Wine Ctee Western Circuit 1982–86; *Recreations* gardening; *Style*— His Hon Judge Brodrick

BROERS, Baron (Life Peer UK 2004), of Cambridge in the County of Cambridgeshire; Prof Sir Alec Nigel Broers; kt (1998), DL (Cambs 2000); s of Alec William Broers (d 1987), of Melbourne, Aust, and Constance Amy, *née* Cox (d 2001); *b* 17 September 1938; *Educ* Geelong GS, Univ of Melbourne (BSc), Gonville & Caius Coll Cambridge (BA, PhD); *m* 1964, Mary Therese, da of Michael Phelan (d 1944); 2 s (Hon Mark b 1965, Hon Christopher b 1967); *Career* numerous managerial positions incl mangr Photon and Electron Optics IBM T J Watson Res Lab 1965–81; mangr: Lithography and Technology Tools 1981–82, Advanced Devpt IBM E Fishkill Lab 1983–84; prof of electrical engrg and head Electrical Div Engrg Dept Univ of Cambridge 1984–92 (head of dept 1992–96), master Churchill Coll Cambridge 1990–96, vice-chllr Univ of Cambridge 1996–2003; pres Royal Acad of Engrg 2001–06 (memb Cncl 1993–), memb IBM Corp Tech Ctee 1984; memb Cncl: EPSRC 1994–2000, Univ of Melbourne 2000–02; chm Plastic Logic Ltd 2004–; non-exec dir: Lucas Industries 1995–96, Vodafone 1998–2007, R J Mears LLC 2003–; sr advsr to Warburg Pincus 2004–; chm House of Lords Select Ctee for Science and Technol 2004–; IEEE Cledo Brunetti Award 1985, American Inst of Physics Prize for Industrial Applications of Physics 1982, Prince Philip Medal Royal Acad of Engrg 2000; memb American Philosophical Soc; tstee Br Museum 2004–; IBM fell 1977; fell: Trinity Coll Cambridge 1985–90, Churchill Coll Cambridge, Imperial Coll London 2004; hon fell: Gonville & Caius Coll Cambridge, Trinity Coll Cambridge, St Edmund's Coll Cambridge, Aust Acad of Technological Sciences and Engrg, Cardiff Univ 2001; ScD Univ of Cambridge 1991; Hon DEng Univ of Glasgow 1996, Hon DSc Univ of Warwick 1997, Hon DUniv Anglia Poly, Hon DTech Univ of Greenwich 2000, Hon PhD Univ of Peking 2002, Hon DEng UMIST 2002, Hon LLD Univ of Melbourne 2002, Hon LLD Univ of Cambridge 2004; foreign assoc Nat Acad of Engrg USA; Hon FMedSci, Hon FIEE, FInstP, FRS, FREng 1985, Hon FIMechE 2004; *Publications* author of BBC Reith Lectures 2005, also numerous papers, book chapters and patents on integrated circuit microfabrication and related subjects; *Recreations* music, sailing, skiing, tennis; *Style*— The Rt Hon the Lord Broers, DL, FRS, FREng; ✉ The Royal Academy of Engineering, 29 Great Peter Street, Westminster, London SW1P 3LW (tel 020 7222 2688, fax 020 7233 0054)

BROKE, Adam Vere Balfour; s of Charles Vere Broke (d 1944), and Violet Rosemary, *née* Balfour; *b* 16 April 1941; *Educ* Eton; *m* 27 March 1965, Sarah Penelope, da of Norman Lanyon, DSC (d 1981); 3 da; *Career* chartered accountant; conslt Mercer & Hole; former pres Inst of Taxation; Past Master Worshipful Co of Tax Advsrs; FCA 1964, fell CTA 1971; *Recreations* music, gardening, shooting; *Clubs* Boodle's; *Style*— Adam Broke, Esq; ✉ Mercer & Hole, 76 Shoe Lane, London EC4A 3JB (tel 020 7353 1597)

BROKENSHIRE, James; MP; *b* 1968, Southend-on-Sea, Essex; *Educ* Davenant Fndn GS Loughton, Cambridge Centre for Sixth Form Studies, Univ of Exeter (LLB); *Career* slr; ptnr Jones Day Gouldens 1999–2005; MP (Cons) Hornchurch 2005–, shadow home affrs min 2006–; former nat vice-chm Young Conservatives; *Style*— James Brokenshire, Esq, MP; ✉ House of Commons, London SW1A 0AA

BROMHEAD, Brig David de Gonville; CBE (1994, OBE 1988), LVO (1984); 2 s of Lt-Col Edmund de Gonville Hosking Bromhead (d 1976, himself yr bro of Sir Benjamin Bromhead, 5 Bt, OBE, and great nephew of Lt-Col Gonville Bromhead, VC, who defended Rorke's Drift in the Zulu War of 1879), and Joan, da of late Brig Sir Henry Scott, CB, DSO, MC; *b* 16 September 1944; *Educ* St Andrew's Grahamstown, RMA; *m* 1970, Susan, da of Cdr Richard Furley Fyson, DSC, JP, RN; 2 da (Annabel Suzanne de Gonville b 1973, Antonia Diana de Gonville b 1978), 1 s (James Henry de Gonville b 1974); *Career* Royal Regt of Wales, Gen Serv Medal (Clasps) S Arabia and NI; has taken part in expeditions under John Blashford-Snell down Blue Nile (1968) and led reconnaissance party through Darien Gap during Trans-America Expedition 1971; equerry to HRH The Prince of Wales 1982–84, Lt-Col 1983, cmd 1 Bn Royal Regt of Wales, Col 1987, Brig 1991; cmd Berlin Inf Bde 1990–94; cmd Br Mil Mission to the Saudi Arabian Nat Guard 1996–2000; Freeman of the Bezirk of Wilmersdorf Berlin; FRGS; *Recreations* fishing; *Style*— Brig David Bromhead, CBE, LVO; ✉ e-mail david@bromhead.org

BROMLEY, Sir Rupert Charles; 10 Bt (GB 1757), of East Stoke, Nottinghamshire; s of Maj Sir Rupert Howe Bromley, 9 Bt, MC (d 1966, fifth in descent from Sir George Bromley, 2 Bt, who changed his name to Bromley from Smith); *b* 2 April 1936; *Educ* Michaelhouse Natal, Rhodes Univ, ChCh Oxford; *m* 26 April 1962, Priscilla Hazel, o da of late Maj Howard Bourne, HAC; 3 s (Charles Howard b 1963, Philip Anthony b 1964, Henry Walford b 1970); *Heir* s, Charles Bromley; *Career* barrister at law Inner Temple 1959; dir Aggregate and Sand Producers' Assoc of South Africa 1991–99; diocesan registrar Dio of Johannesburg 1985–2000; *Recreations* golf; *Clubs* Kelvin Grove, Seven Seas; *Style*— Sir Rupert Bromley, Bt; ✉ The Old Manse, Glen Road, Glencairn 7975, South Africa (tel 00 27 21 782 6400, fax 00 27 21 782 5016, e-mail cilla@bromley.co.za)

BROMLEY-DAVENPORT, William Arthur; JP (Cheshire 1975); only s of Lt-Col Sir Walter Bromley-Davenport, TD, DL (d 1989), of Capesthorne Hall, and Lenette, *née* Jeanes (d 1989); *b* 7 March 1935; *Educ* Eton, Cornell Univ; *m* 29 Dec 1962, Elizabeth Boies, da of John Watts, of Oldwick, NJ; 1 s (Nicholas Walter b 11 June 1964), 1 da (Liberty Charlotte b 25 Dec 1970); *Career* Nat Serv 2 Bn Grenadier Guards 1953–54, Hon Col 3 (Vol) Bn 22 Cheshire Regt 1985–99, Hon Col (Cheshire) The King's and Cheshire Regt 1999–2005; pres TAVRA NW of England and IOM 1998–2003; landowner (UK and Norway); county pres: Cheshire Magistrates' Assoc 1990–, Youth Fedn for Cheshire, Halton, Warrington and Wirral 1990–, Cheshire Branch SSAFA - Forces Help 1992–, Cheshire Branch RBL 1998–, Reaseheath Coll Tst 1991–; pres: Cheshire Scout Cncl 1990– (chm 1981–90), Cheshire Agricultural Soc 1993–96 (patron 2001–), Cheshire Cncl Order of St John 1998–; chm of govrs King's Sch Macclesfield 1986–2005; Hon DLitt Univ of Chester 2006; High Sheriff Cheshire 1983–84, HM Lord-Lt Cheshire 1990– (DL 1982); ACA 1966; *Style*— William A Bromley-Davenport, Esq; ✉ The Kennels, Capesthorne, Macclesfield, Cheshire SK11 9LB; Fiva, 6300 Aandalsnes, Norway

BROMLEY-MARTIN, Michael Granville; QC (2002); s of David Eliot Bromley-Martin (d 2002), and Angela Felicity, *née* Hampden-Ross; *b* 27 April 1955, Bosham, Sussex; *Educ* Eton, Univ of Southampton (BSc); *m* 26 Nov 1983, Anna Frances, *née* Birley; 1 s (Charles b 28 May 1988), 2 da (Alexandra b 22 May 1990, Olivia b 10 July 1994); *Career* called to the Bar 1979; memb of chambers 3 Raymond Buildings 1980–; inspr DTI 1989–90, recorder of the Crown Court 2003–; *Recreations* sailing, shooting, fishing, tennis; *Clubs* Royal Ocean Racing, Garrick, Itchenor Sailing; *Style*— Michael Bromley-Martin, Esq, QC; ✉ 3 Raymond Buildings, Gray's Inn, London WC1R 5BH (tel 020 7400 6400, fax 020 7400 6464, e-mail mbm@raymondbuildings.com)

BROMWICH, Prof Michael; s of William James Bromwich (d 1982), and Margery, *née* Townley (d 1977); *b* 29 January 1941; *Educ* Wentworth Secdy Modern Southend, LSE (BSc); *m* 10 Aug 1972, Prof Christine Margaret Elizabeth Whitehead, OBE, da of Edward Daniel Whitehead, MBE, of Tunbridge Wells, Kent; *Career* mangr Ford Motor Co Ltd 1965–66 (accountant 1958–62); lectr LSE 1966–70, prof UWIST 1970–77, prof Univ of Reading 1977–85, CIMA prof LSE 1985–2006 (emeritus 2006–); chm Bd of Accreditation of Educnl Courses 1987–89, pres CIMA 1987–88; Distinguished Academic of the Year 1999; memb: Industry and Employment Ctee SSRC/ESRC 1980–84, Accounting Standards Ctee 1981–84, Research Grants Bd ESRC 1992–96, Academic Panel OFT 2002–; additional memb Monopolies and Mergers Cmmn 1992–2000, accounting advsr OFT; Hon DSc Lund Univ; assoc memb CIPFA 1977, FCMA (ACMA 1963); *Books* Economics of Capital Budgeting (1976), Economics of Accounting Standards (1985), Financial Reporting Information and Capital Markets (1992), Management Accounting: Pathways to Progress (1994), Accounting for Overheads: Critique and Reforms (1997), Following the Money: The Economic Failure and the State of Corporate Disclosure (jtly, 2003), Worldwide Financial Reporting: The Development and Future of Accounting Standards (2006); *Recreations* work, eating in restaurants; *Style*— Prof Michael Bromwich; ✉ London School of Economics and Political Science, Houghton Street, London WC2A 2AE (tel 020 7955 7323, fax 020 7955 7420, e-mail m.bromwich@lse.ac.uk)

BRON, Eleanor; da of Sydney Bron (d 1995), and Fagah Bron (d 1990); *b* 14 March 1938; *Educ* N London Collegiate Sch, Newnham Coll Cambridge (BA); *Career* actress and writer; with De La Rue Co 1961, subsequent revue work and appearances at Establishment Nightclub Soho 1962 and in NY 1963; dir: Actor's Centre Bd 1982–93, Soho Theatre Co Bd 1993–2000; *Theatre* incl: Jennifer Dubedat in The Doctor's Dilemma, 1966, title role in The Prime of Miss Jean Brodie 1967 and 1984, title role in Hedda Gabler 1969, Portia in The Merchant of Venice 1975, Amanda in Private Lives 1976, Elena in Uncle Vanya 1977, Charlotte in The Cherry Orchard 1978 (also Varya 1985), Margaret in A Family 1978, On Her Own 1980, Goody Biddy Bean in The Amusing Spectacle of Cinderella and her Naughty, Naughty Sisters 1980, Betrayal 1981, Heartbreak House 1981, Duet for One 1982, The Duchess of Malfi 1985, The Real Inspector Hound and The Critic (double bill) 1985, Jocasta/Ismene in Oedipus and Oedipus at Colonus 1987, Infidelities 1987, The Madwoman of Chaillot 1988, The Chalk Garden 1989, Frosine in The Miser 1991, Isabella in The White Devil 1991, Gertrude in Hamlet 1993, Agnes in A Delicate Balance 1996, Katherine in A Perfect Ganesh 1996, Dona Rosita (Almeida) 1997, Be My Baby 1998, Making Noise Quietly 1999, Tuppence to Cross the Mersey 2005, The Clean House 2006, In Extremis 2007; other performances incl: Façade by Walton, Oral Treason by Kagel (Almeida Festival of Contemporary Music) 1987, Die Glückliche Hand by Schönberg (Nederlandse Opera) 1990, Desdemona - If You Had Only Spoken (one-woman show, Almeida 1991, Edinburgh Festival 1992); *Music* author of lyrics for song-cycle with John Dankworth 1973 and verses for Saint-Saens' Carnival of the Animals 1975; *Television* appearances in Not So Much a Programme More a Way of Life (BBC) 1964 and several TV series written with John Fortune; other TV progs and series incl: Making Faces (by Michael Frayn) 1976, Pinkerton's Progress 1983, Inspector Alleyn 1992, Absolutely Fabulous 1992 and 1993, Fat Friends 2000 and 2002, Gypsy Girl 2000, Randall and Hopkirk 2001, Ted and Alice 2002; TV plays incl: Nina 1978, My Dear Palestrina 1980, A Month in the Country 1985, Quartermaine's Terms 1987, Changing Step 1989, The Hour of the Lynx 1990, The Strawberry Tree 1993, The Blue Boy 1994, The Saint Exupéry Story 1994, Wycliffe 1995, Vanity Fair 1998; *Film* Help! 1965, Alfie 1966, Two for the Road 1967, Bedazzled 1967, Women in Love 1969, The National Health 1973, The Day That Christ Died 1980, Turtle Diary 1985, Little Dorrit 1988, Black Beauty 1993, Deadly Advice 1994, A Little Princess 1994, The House of Mirth 2000, Iris 2001, The Heart of Me 2002, Wimbledon 2003; *Books* Is Your Marriage Really Necessary (with John Fortune, 1972), My Cambridge (contrib, 1976), More Words (contrib, 1977), Life and Other Punctures (1978), The Pillow Book of Eleanor Bron (1985), Desdemona - If You Had Only Spoken (by Christine Brückner, trans 1992), Double Take (novel, 1996), Cedric Price Retriever (co-ed, 2006); *Style*— Miss Eleanor Bron; ✉ c/o Rebecca Blond Associates, 69A King's Road, London SW3 4NX (tel 020 7351 4100, fax 020 7451 4600)

BRONDER, Peter; s of Johann Bronder, and Gertrude, *née* Kastl; *b* 22 October 1953; *Educ* Letchworth GS, RAM; *Career* tenor; Bayreuth Festival Chorus 1983, Glyndebourne Festival Chorus 1985, princ tenor WNO 1986–90 (performances for WNO in NY and Milan 1989, Tokyo 1990), freelance 1991–, regular guest appearances with major UK Opera cos; debut: Royal Opera Covent Garden 1986, ENO 1989, Glyndebourne Festival 1990, Theâtre Champs Elysées Paris 1991, Bavarian State Opera 1995, Int Festival Istanbul 1995, Brussels La Mounaie 1999; live on BBC Radio 3: Snape Maltings Concert 1987, Richard Strauss' Salome 1988, Bellini's Somnambula 1989, Gluck's Iphigenie en Tauride 1992, Donizetti's Maria Stuarda 1994, Strauss' Der Rosenkavalier 1994, Beethoven's Choral Symphony 1995, Tchaikovsky's Enchantress 1998, Wagner's Parsifal 1998, Berg's Wozzeck 1998, Love Cries (Birtwistle and Berkeley, World Premiere) 1999, Clemenza di Tito (Glyndebourne) 1999; recordings: Kiri Te Kanawa recital 1988, Adriana Lecouvreur Cilea 1988, Osud Janácek 1989, Weill's Street Scene 1991, Beethoven's Choral Symphony 1991, Rossini's Turco in Italia 1992, Stravinsky's Rake's Progress 1997, Leoncavallo's I Pagliacci 1997, Verdi's Falstaff 1998; many appearances on TV and radio incl: BBC TV Laurence Olivier Awards 1985, Verdi's Falstaff (with WNO) 1989, Berg's Wozzeck (with ENO) 1990, Salome (ROH) 1997; ARAM, LRAM, LGSM; *Recreations* sports, photography, electronics, motorcycling; *Style*— Peter Bronder, Esq; ✉ c/o Allied Artists Agency, 42 Montpelier Square, London SW7 1JZ (tel 020 7589 6243, fax 020 7581 5269)

BROOK, Anthony Donald; s of Donald Charles Brook (d 1976), and Doris Ellen, *née* Emmett (d 1987); *b* 24 September 1936; *Educ* Eastbourne Coll; *m* 1, 18 March 1964, Ann Mary (d 2000), da of Edwin Reeves (d 1991); 2 da (Clare b 30 June 1966, Joanne b 26 April 1970); m 2, 18 Feb 2005, Jean Curtis; *Career* CA Peat Marwick Mitchell CAs (now KPMG) 1960–65 (articled clerk 1955–60), mgmnt accountant Associated Television Ltd 1966–68, fin controller ATV Network Ltd 1969–74, dir external fin IBA 1975–77, fin dir and gen mangr ITC Entertainment Ltd 1978–80, dep chair and md TVS Entertainment plc and TVS Television Ltd 1981–93; chair: SelecTV plc 1993–95, Ocean Radio Group Ltd 1994–2000, Southern Screen Cmmn 1995–99 dir: Southern Radio plc 1984–94, Independent Television Assoc Ltd 1991–92, Independent Television News Ltd 1991–93, Telemagination Ltd 1992–2000, Meridian Broadcasting 1993–95, AAB Management Ltd 1993–2007; FCA 1970; *Recreations* travel, sailing, golf; *Clubs* Royal Southern Yacht, Meon Valley Golf; *Style*— Anthony Brook, Esq; ✉ e-mail anthony@brook8448.fsnet.co.uk

BROOK, Prof Charles Groves Darville; JP (Avon and Somerset 2003); s of Air Vice-Marshal William Arthur Darville Brook, CB, CBE (d 1953), and Marjorie Jean Hamilton, *née* Grant (d 2004); *b* 15 January 1940; *Educ* Rugby, Magdalene Coll Cambridge (MA, MD), St Thomas' Hosp Med Sch (MB BChir, DCH); *m* 16 March 1963, Hon Catherine Mary, da of late Lord Hawke, of Northwich, Cheshire; 2 da (Charlotte b 1965, Henrietta b 1968); *Career* resident posts: St Thomas' Hosp 1964–68, Hosp for Sick Children Gt Ormond St 1968–74; Wellcome travelling res fell Kinderspital Zurich 1972–73, conslt paediatrician Middx Hosp 1974–2000 (emeritus 2000–), prof of paediatric endocrinology UCL 1989–2000 (emeritus 2000–); dir London Centre of Paediatric Endocrinology Middx and Gt Ormond St Hosps 1994–2000 (hon 2000–); chief examiner in med UCL Med Sch 1994–99; chm Richmond Soc 1968–74, special tstee Middx Hosp 1984–97, tstee Richmond Parish Land Charity 1988–94; memb Ctee of Mgmnt Royal Med Benevolent Fund 1976–96 (treas 1989–96); memb: St Leonard's Pitcombe Parochial Church Cncl 2000–, Pitcombe Parish Cncl 2001–07 (vice-chair 2002, chair 2003–07); tstee St Margaret's Somerset Hospice 2006– (vice-pres 2005–06) FRCP 1979, FRCPCH 1997; *Books* Clinical Paediatric Endocrinology (5 edn, 2005), All About Adolescence (1985), Current Concepts in Paediatric Endocrinology (1988), The Practice of Medicine in Adolescence (1993), A Guide to the Practice of Paediatric Endrocrinology (1993), Essential Endocrinology (4 edn, 2001); *Recreations* DIY, gardening, fishing; *Style*— Prof Charles Brook; ✉ Hadspen Farm, Castle Cary, Somerset BA7 7LX (tel and fax 01963 351492, e-mail c.brook@ucl.ac.uk)

BROOK, Michael; s of John Brook (d 1981), and Mary, *née* Gilpin (d 2001); *b* 1 September 1949; *Educ* Batley GS, Leeds Poly (BA); *m* 21 April 1973, Lynn, da of Leonard Sargeant Allan; 2 da (Alison Judith b 7 Feb 1976, Joanne Elizabeth b 25 May 1977); *Career* asst sales mangr British Jeffrey Diamond Wakefield 1972–73, asst mktg controller Yorkshire Electricity Bd 1974–76, brands mangr Thomas Eastham & Sons 1976–79; Graham Poulter Partnership: account mangr 1979–80, account dir 1980–82, assoc dir 1982–83, dir and ptnr 1983–91; md Ken Geddes Associates Ltd 1991–92, dir Lumley Warranty Services 1992–93; Creative Communications: account dir 1993–, md 1994–96; project dir On Demand Information: Internet 2 1996–97, mktg dir New Media Publishing Div 1997–98; md Whitaker's Advertising 1998–99, product devpt dir IQ Business Ltd 1999–; MCIM 1976; *Recreations* golf, cricket, photography, music; *Clubs* Howley Hall Golf; *Style*— Michael Brook, Esq; ✉ 3 Woodkirk Gardens, Leeds Road, Dewsbury, West Yorkshire WF12 7HZ (tel 01924 475544, e-mail mikebrook@talktalk.net); IQ Business Ltd, Oakgate House, 25 Market Place, Wetherby, West Yorkshire LS22 6LQ (tel 01937 587798, fax 01937 584525, e-mail mike.brook@iq-business.co.uk)

BROOK, Nigel Geoffrey; s of Basil William Brook, of Coventry, and Dorothy, *née* Botting; *b* 13 December 1956; *Educ* Bablake Sch Coventry (scholarship), St Catherine's Coll Oxford (David Blank open scholarship, BA); *m* 28 April 1984, Ann, da of Edwin Carrington; 1 da (Emma Mary Carrington Brook b 2 March 1988); *Career* Clyde & Co: articled clerk 1979–81, ptnr 1985–; *Recreations* running; *Style*— Nigel Brook, Esq; ✉ Clyde & Co, 51 Eastcheap, London EC3M 1JP (tel 020 7623 1244, fax 020 7623 5427)

BROOK, Prof Peter; s of Ernest John Brook (d 1986), and Jenny, *née* Waters; *b* 17 January 1947; *Educ* Barry GS, Univ of Swansea (BSc), Univ of London (MSc); *m* 1978, Deirdre Teresa, da of Terence Handley; 2 da (Jessica Frances b 3 Dec 1982, Elizabeth Mary b 2 April 1987); *Career* head Computer Networks Div RSRE 1981–85, head Air Defence & ATC Gp RSRE 1985–87, dir of sci (Land) MOD 1987–89, head Battlefield Systems Gp DRA 1989–94, chief scientist CIS DERA 1994–96, chief scientist Land Systems DERA 1996–98, dir Int Cncl on Systems Engrg (INCOSE) 1997–, dir Systems Engrg DERA 1998–2000, head Integration Authy DPA 2000–05, strategic conslt QinetiQ Ltd 2005–; visiting prof Cranfield Univ (RMCS Shrivenham); FIEE, FREng 1999; *Publications* Systems Engineering - Coping with Complexity (1998); numerous technical publications: microwave systems, military command and control and systems engrg; *Recreations* choral and solo singing, walking, theatre, concerts; *Style*— Prof Peter Brook, FREng; ✉ Dashwood House, Manby Road, Malvern, Worcestershire WR14 3BB (tel 01684 893472, e-mail dashwoodbrook@aol.com); Woodward Building, Malvern Technology Park, St Andrews Malvern, Worcestershire WR14 3PS

BROOK, Richard; *Career* successively: asst dir Thames Reach Housing Assoc, dir of community services Heritage Care, dir of care and community services The Shaftesbury Soc; chief exec: Christian Alliance Housing Assoc 1999–2001, Mind 2001–05; public guardian designate and chief exec Public Guardianship Office 2005–; *Style*— Richard Brook; ✉ Public Guardianship Office, Archway Tower, 2 Junction Road, London N19 5SZ

BROOK, Prof Sir Richard John; kt (2002), OBE (1988); s of late Frank Brook, and late Emily Sarah, *née* Lytle; *b* 12 March 1938; *Educ* Univ of Leeds (BSc), MIT (ScD); *m* 3 March 1961, Elizabeth Christine, da of Thomas Aldred; 1 da (Madeline Sarah b 13 June 1965), 1 s (Jonathan Henry b 21 Dec 1967); *Career* res asst MIT 1962–66, asst prof Univ of Southern California 1966–70, gp ldr AERE Harwell 1970–74, prof and head Dept of Ceramics Univ of Leeds 1974–88, dir Max Planck Institut for Metals Research Stuttgart 1988–91, fell St Cross Coll Oxford 1991–, prof of materials Univ of Oxford 1991–, chief exec EPSRC 1994–2001, dir Leverhulme Tst 2001–; non-exec dir and memb Bd: Carbon Tst 2002–, ERA Fndn 2002–; hon prof Univ of Stuttgart 1988–, memb Senate Max Planck Soc 1999–; author of res pubns (on ceramic sci and engrg), 11 patents; ed Jl of the European Ceramic Soc 1989–; Dr (hc) Univ of Aveiro Portugal; DSc (hc): Univ of Bradford, Loughborough Univ, Nottingham Trent Univ, Brunel Univ, Univ of Strathclyde, Limoges Univ France; membre d'honneur Société Française de la Métallurgie et des Matériaux 1995, distinguished life fell American Ceramic Soc 1995, memb Deutsche Akademie der Naturforscher Leopoldina 2002; CEng; FIM 1986, FREng 1998; *Style*— Prof Sir Richard Brook, OBE, FREng; ✉ Leverhulme Trust, 1 Pemberton Row, London EC4A 3BG

BROOK, Rosemary Helen (Mrs Dickie Arbiter); da of Charles Rex Brook (d 1971), and Nellie Beatrice, *née* Yare (d 1998); *b* 7 February 1946; *Educ* Gravesend Sch for Girls, Newnham Coll Cambridge (MA); *m* 1, 1970 (m dis 1979), Roger John Gross; m 2, 1984, Richard Winston Arbiter, LVO; 1 step da (Victoria b 1974); *Career* account mangr McCann Erickson Ltd 1975–77, head of public affrs Wiggins Teape Gp Ltd 1977–82 (Euro mktg co-ordinator 1968–75), Euro gen mangr Edelman Public Relations Worldwide 1992–94, UK chm and chief exec Edelman (UK) 1982–94, chm Brook Wilkinson Ltd 1994–2001, exec chm Argyll Consultancies plc 2005– (dir 2001–); chm Exec Ctee Industry and Parly Tst 2007 (memb 1998–, tstee 2006); Freeman City of London 1985, Master Guild of PR Practitioners 2003–04; assoc fell Newnham Coll Cambridge 1999–2003; FCIPR (FIPR 1977, pres 1996); *Recreations* opera, ballet, reading, music; *Clubs* Reform; *Style*— Miss Rosemary Brook; ✉ Apartment 3, 16 Marloes Road, London W8 5LH; Argyll Consultancies plc, Central Court, 25 Southampton Buildings, London WC2A 1AL (tel 020 3043 4151, fax 020 3043 4154, e-mail rosemary.brook@kaizo.net)

BROOK-PARTRIDGE, Bernard; s of Leslie Brook-Partridge (d 1933), and Gladys Vere, *née* Brooks, later Mrs Burchell (d 1989); *Educ* Selsdon Co GS, Cambs Tech Coll, Univ of Cambridge, Univ of London; *m* 1, 3 Nov 1951 (m dis 1965), (Enid) Elizabeth, da of Frederick Edmund Hatfield (d 1951); 2 da (Eva Katharine Helen (Mrs New) b 6 Dec 1952 d 2001, Katrina Elizabeth Jane b 18 Aug 1954); m 2, 14 Oct 1967, Carol Devonald, da of Arnold Devonald Francis Lewis (d 1989); 2 s (Charles Gareth Devonald b 21 Dec 1969, James Edward Devonald b 4 June 1974); *Career* Nat Serv 1944–49; memb Gray's Inn 1950, cashier and accountant Dominion Rubber Co Ltd 1950–51, asst export mangr British & General Tube Co Ltd 1951–52, asst sec Assoc of Int Accountants 1952–59, sec-gen Inst of Linguists 1959–62, various teaching posts FRG 1962–66, special asst to md M G Scott Ltd 1966–68, business conslt (incl various directorships) 1968–72, memb Peterborough Devpt Corp 1972–88, ptnr Carsons, Brook-Partridge & Co 1972–2004, dir and sec Roban Engineering Ltd 1975–96, chm Queensgate Management Services Ltd 1981–87; dir: Brompton Troika Ltd 1985–, Edmund Nuttall Ltd 1986–92, PEG Management Consultants plc 1988–92, Kyle Stewart Ltd 1989–92, Lucknam Park Hotels Ltd 1994–95, Wilding Properties Ltd 1995–2003, UK Immigration Services Ltd 1999–2004, Ethical Developments Ltd 1999–2002; chm: Daldorch Estates Ltd 1995–98, Dick Robson plc 1996–97, Robson Dunk Ltd 1996–98; dep chm World Trade Centre Ltd 1997–2001; conslt Paul Whitley Architects 1998–2002; memb Cncl ICSA 1982–97 (pres 1986); local govt and political advsr Transmanche-Link 1988 and 1989; contested (Cons) St Pancras N LCC 1958, memb (Cons) St Pancras MBC 1959–62, prospective parly candidate (Cons) Shoreditch and Finsbury 1960–62, contested (Cons) Nottingham Central 1970; GLC: memb for Havering 1967–73, memb for Havering (Romford) 1973–85, chm of Cncl 1980–81; chm: Environmental Planning (NE) Area Ctee 1967–71, Town Devpt Ctee 1971–73, Arts Ctee 1977–79, Public Servs and Safety Ctee 1978–79; oppn spokesman: on arts and recreation 1973–74, on police matters 1983–85; memb: Exec Ctee Gtr London Arts Assoc 1973–78, Exec Cncl Area Museums Serv for SE England 1977–78, Cncl and Exec Gtr London and SE Cncl for Sport and Recreation 1977–78, GLC Ldrs Ctee with special responsibility for law and order and police liaison matters 1977–79; dep ldr Recreation and Community Servs Policy Ctee 1977–79; memb: Exec Ctee Exmoor Soc 1974–79, BBC Radio London Advsy Cncl 1974–79, Gen Cncl Poetry Soc 1977–86 (treas 1982–86), London Orchestral Concert Bd Ltd 1977–78, LCDT 1979–84; dir ENO 1977–79; tstee: London Festival Ballet 1977–79, Sadler's Wells Fndn 1977–79; chm: London Symphony Chorus Devpt Ctee 1981–88, The Young Vic Theatre 1983–87 (dir 1977–88), London Music Hall Tst Ltd 1983–90, Royal Philharmonic Soc 1991–95; vice-chm London Music Hall Protection Soc Ltd (Wilton's Music Hall) 1983–97 (memb Bd 1978–, chm 1981–83); chm: Samuel Lewis Housing Tst Ltd 1985–92 (tstee 1976–94), City & Coastal Housing Association Ltd 1991–94, St George's Housing Association Ltd 1985–92, Shipworkers Jubilee Housing Tst 1985–92 (both now part of Samuel Lewis Housing Tst Ltd), Spearhead Housing Tst 1986–92; govr and tstee SPCK 1976–95 (vice-pres 1995–); pres: Br Sch of Osteopathy Appeal Fund 1980–84, Witan Rifle Club 1979–92, City of London Rifle League 1980–2004, Gtr London Horse Show 1982–86, GLA City Hall branch (formerly Gtr London Co Hall branch) Royal Br Legion 1988–2005; hon sec The Henley Soc 1998–2000; dir Central London Masonic Centre Ltd 1999– (dep chm 2000–); Freemason 1973–; hon fell and Hon PhD Columbia Pacific Univ USA 1984; FCIS 1970–2007, FCPU 1984, MCMI 1978, hon fell Inst of Incorporated Engrgs; Order of Gorkha Dakshina Bahu (second class, Nepal) 1981; *Books* Europe - Power and Responsibility - Direct Elections to the European Parliament (with David Baker, 1972), author of numerous contribs to learned jls and periodicals on various subjects; *Recreations* conversation, opera, classical music, being difficult; *Clubs* Athenaeum, Leander; *Style*— Bernard Brook-Partridge, Esq; ✉ 28 Elizabeth Road, Henley-on-Thames, Oxfordshire RG9 1RG (tel 01491 412080, fax 01491 412090, e-mail bernard@brook-partridge.freeserve.co.uk)

BROOKE, Sir Alistair Weston; 4 Bt (UK 1919), of Almondbury, W Riding of Yorkshire; s of Sir John Weston Brooke, 3 Bt (d 1983), and his 1 w Rosemary, da of late Percy Llewelyn Nevill (gs of 4 Earl of Abergavenny); *b* 12 September 1947; *Educ* Repton, RAC Cirencester; *m* 1982, Susan Mary, o da of Barry Griffiths, of Orchards End, Norton, Powys; 1 da (Lorna Rosemary Weston b 1983); *Heir* bro, Charles Brooke; *Style*— Sir Alistair Brooke, Bt; ✉ Fearn Lodge, Ardgay, Ross-shire

BROOKE, Annette; MP; da of Ernest Henry Kelly, and Edna Mabel Kelley; *b* 7 June 1947; *Educ* Romford Tech Coll, LSE (BSc), Hughes Hall Cambridge (CEd); *m* Mike Brooke; 2 da; *Career* lectr and teacher of economics and social sciences Open Univ and various local schs incl Talbot Heath Sch until 1995; cncllr Broadstone Poole BC 1986–2003, dep ldr Lib Dem Gp 1995–97 and 1998–2000, chair of planning 1991–96, chair Environment Strategy Working Pty 1995–97, chair of educn 1996–2000, sheriff 1996–97, mayor 1997–98, dep mayor 1998–99; MP (Lib Dem) Dorset Mid and N Poole 2001–; memb Lib Dem Home Affrs team 2001–03, spokesperson for Children in Educn team 2004–; memb Public Accounts Select Ctee, chair All-Pty Parly Gp on Microfinance and Microcredit, vice-chair All-Pty Parly Gp on Endometriosis, vice-chair All-Pty Parly Gp on Children; jt owner of small family business (rocks, minerals and gemstones); *Style*— Mrs Annette Brooke, MP; ✉ House of Commons, London SW1A 0AA (tel 020 7219 8193, fax 020 7219 1898, e-mail brookea@parliament.uk); Constituency Office, 14 York Road, Broadstone, Dorset BH18 8ET (tel 01202 693555, fax 01202 658420)

BROOKE, Prof Christopher Nugent Lawrence; CBE (1995); s of Prof Zachary Nugent Brooke (d 1946), of Cambridge, and Rosa Grace Stanton (d 1964); *b* 23 June 1927; *Educ* Gonville & Caius Coll Cambridge (MA, DLitt); *m* 18 Aug 1951, Dr Rosalind Beckford Clark, da of Leslie Herman Septimus Clark; 3 s (Francis Christopher b 23 July 1953 d 1996, Philip David Beckford b 19 April 1956, Patrick Lawrence Harvey b 23 May 1959); *Career* Nat Serv 1948–50, RAEC temp Capt 1949–50; Univ of Cambridge: fell Gonville & Caius Coll 1949–56 and 1977–, asst lectr in history 1953–54, lectr in history 1954–56, praelector rhetoricus 1955–56, Dixie prof of ecclesiastical history 1977–94; prof of medieval history Univ of Liverpool 1956–67, prof of history Westfield Coll London 1967–77; vice-pres Royal Historical Soc 1971–74 (hon vice-pres 2002–); memb: Royal Cmmn on Historical Monuments 1977–84, Reviewing Ctee on Export of Works of Art 1979–82; pres Soc of Antiquaries 1981–84; vice-pres: Cumberland and Westmorland Antiquarian and Archaeological Soc 1985–89, Northants Record Soc 1987–; corresponding fell Medieval Acad of America 1981, corresponding memb Monumenta Germaniae Historica 1988, fell Società Internazionale di Studi Francescani, corresponding memb Bavarian Acad of Scis 1997; Hon DUniv York; FSA, FBA 1970, FRHistS; *Books* The Letters of John of Salisbury (with W J Millor and H E Butler, 1955 and 1979), Carte Nativorum - a Peterborough Abbey Cartulary of the fourteenth Century (with M M Postan, 1960), From Alfred to Henry III (1961), The Saxon and Norman Kings (1963, 3 edn 2001), Europe in the Central Middle Ages (1964, 3 edn 2000), Gilbert Foliot and his Letters (with A Morey, 1965), Letters and Charters of Gilbert Foliot (with A Morey,

1967), The Twelfth Century Renaissance (1969–70), The Heads of Religious Houses, England and Wales, 940–1216 (with D Knowles and VCM London, 1972, 2 edn 2001), The Monastic World 1000–1300 (with Wim Swaan, 1974, 2 edn (as The Age of the Cloister) 2003, 3 edn (as The Rise and Fall of the Medieval Monastery) 2006), A History of Gonville & Caius Coll (1985), Oxford and Cambridge (with Roger Highfield and Wim Swaan, 1988), The Medieval Idea of Marriage (1989), David Knowles Remembered (jtly, 1991), A History of the University of Cambridge, IV, 1870–1990 (1993), Jane Austen, Illusion and Reality (1999), A History of Emmanuel College, Cambridge (with S Bendall and P Collinson, 1999), Churches and Churchmen in Medieval Europe (1999), The Monastic Constitutions of Lanfranc (with D Knowles, 2002); *Style*— Prof Christopher Brooke, CBE; ✉ Gonville & Caius College, Cambridge CB2 1TA

BROOKE, Sir Francis George Windham; 4 Bt (UK 1903), of Summerton, Castleknock, Co Dublin; s of Sir George Cecil Francis Brooke, 3 Bt, MBE (d 1982), and Lady Melissa Eva Caroline Brooke; *b* 15 October 1963; *Educ* Eton, Univ of Edinburgh (MA); *m* 8 April 1989, Hon Katharine Elizabeth Hussey, o da of Baron Hussey of North Bradley, and Lady Susan Hussey, DCVO, *qv*; 1 s (George Francis Geoffrey b 10 Sept 1991), 2 da (Olivia Nancy b 12 Jan 1994, Sarah Mary b 20 March 1996); *Heir* s, George Brooke; *Career* Foreign and Colonial Management 1989–97, Merrill Lynch Investment Managers 1997–2004, Troy Asset Management 2004–; *Clubs* Turf, White's, Royal St George's; *Style*— Sir Francis Brooke, Bt; ✉ 65 Sterndale Road, London W14 OHU; Glenbevan, Croom, Co Limerick, Ireland

BROOKE, Rt Hon Sir Henry; kt (1988); yr s of Baron Brooke of Cumnor, CH, PC (Life Peer, d 1984), and Baroness Brooke of Ystradfellte, DBE (Life Peer, d 2000); bro of Baron Brooke of Sutton Mandeville, CH, PC (Life Peer), *qv*; *b* 19 July 1936; *Educ* Marlborough, Balliol Coll Oxford (MA); *m* 16 April 1966, Bridget Mary, da of Wilfrid George Kalaugher (d 1999), of Jesmond, Newcastle upon Tyne; 3 s (Michael John b 1967, Nicholas George b 1968, Christopher Robert b 1973), 1 da (Caroline Mary b 1973); *Career* Nat Serv 2 Lt RE 1955–57; called to the Bar Inner Temple 1963 (bencher 1987); jr counsel to the Crown (Common Law) 1978–81, QC 1981, counsel to Sizewell B Nuclear Reactor Inquiry 1983–85, recorder SE Circuit 1983–88, a judge of the High Court of Justice (Queen's Bench Div) 1988–96, a Lord Justice of Appeal 1996–2006, judge in charge of modernisation 2001–04; vice-pres Court of Appeal (Civil Div) 2003–06; DTI inspr into the affairs of House of Fraser Holdings plc 1987–88; chm: Professional Standards Ctee Bar Cncl 1987–88, Ethnic Minorities Advsy Ctee Judicial Studies Bd 1991–94, Law Commission 1993–95, Cncl Centre for Crime and Justice Studies 1997–2001, Judges' Standing Ctee on IT 1997–2001; pres Soc for Computers and Law 1992–2001; tstee Wordsworth Tst 1995–2001, chm of tstees Br and Irish Legal Info Inst 2001–; gen ed The White Book (Sweet & Maxwell's Civil Procedure) 2004–; *Clubs* Brooks's; *Style*— The Rt Hon Sir Henry Brooke; ✉ Royal Courts of Justice, Strand, London WC2A 2LL

BROOKE, Prof John Hedley; s of Hedley Joseph Brooke, and Margaret, *née* Brown; *b* 20 May 1944; *Educ* King Edward VI GS Retford, Fitzwilliam Coll Cambridge (Wallerstein exhbn, sr scholarship, BA, MA, PhD); *m* 30 Aug 1972, Janice Marian, da of Albert Heffer; *Career* res fell Fitzwilliam Coll Cambridge 1967–68, tutorial fell Univ of Sussex 1968–69; Lancaster Univ: lectr 1969–80, sr lectr 1980–91, reader 1991–92, prof of history of science 1992–99; Gifford lectr Univ of Glasgow 1995–96; Univ of Oxford: Andreas Idreos prof of science and religion 1999–2006, dir Ian Ramsey Centre, fell Harris Manchester Coll; Inst of Advanced Study distinguished fell Univ of Durham 2007–; ed Br Jl for the History of Science 1989–93, corresponding memb Int Acad of History of Science 1993; pres Science and Religion Forum 2006–; conslt Open Univ; memb: Center for Theological Inquiry Princeton, Center for Theology and the Natural Sciences Berkeley; coordinator European Science Fndn Network: Science and Human Values 2001–04; Templeton Prize for Outstanding Books in Science and Religion 1992; memb: BAAS (pres historical section 1996–97), Br Soc for the History of Science (pres 1996–98), Br Soc for the History of Philosophy, History of Science Soc (Watson Davis Prize 1992), Soc for the History of Alchemy and Chemistry, Int Soc for Science and Religion; *Books* Science and Religion: Some Historical Perspectives (1991), Thinking About Matter (1995), Reconstructing Nature: The Engagement of Science and Religion (jtly, 1998), Science in Theistic Contexts (ed, 2001), Heterodoxy in Early Modern Science and Religion (ed, 2005), Religious Values and the Rise of Science in Europe (ed, 2005); *Recreations* music (opera), foreign travel, walking in the Lake District, chess, rhododendrons; *Style*— Prof John Brooke; ✉ Harris Manchester College, Oxford OX1 3TD (tel 01865 271019, fax 01865 271012, e-mail john.brooke@theology.ox.ac.uk)

BROOKE, Martin Montague; s of Montague Brooke (d 1957), of Kew Gardens, Surrey, and Sybil Katharine, *née* Martin (d 1959); *b* 25 August 1923; *Educ* Eastbourne Coll, Magdalene Coll Cambridge (MA); *m* 1950, Judith Mary, da of Rev Truman Tanqueray (d 1960), of Peaslake, Surrey, late headmaster of Ipswich Sch; 2 s (Anthony, Samuel), 1 da (Katharine); *Career* Lt RNVR, served Atlantic and Indian Oceans 1942–45; banker; dir Guinness Mahon 1963–72, chm Druidale Securities 1972–; dir: Emperor Fund NV 1968–90, Cannon Assurance 1969–84, Cannon Lincoln Investment Management 1991–95; fund mangr M&G Investment Management 1996–97; memb Cncl Distressed Gentlefolk's Aid Assoc 1969–94; *Recreations* gardening, walking; *Clubs* Naval; *Style*— Martin Brooke, Esq; ✉ Duxbury House, 53 Chantry View Road, Guildford, Surrey GU1 3XT (tel 01483 504777, fax 01483 564046, e-mail druidale@btopenworld.com); Johnson's Cottage, Druidale, Ballaugh, Isle of Man IM7 5JA (tel 01624 897908)

BROOKE, His Hon Judge Michael Eccles Macklin; QC (1994); s of Reginald Eccles Joseph Brooke (d 1978), and of Beryl Cicely, *née* Riggs (d 1988); *b* 8 May 1942; *Educ* Lycée Français de Londres, Univ of Edinburgh (LLB); *m* 1, 21 Oct 1972 (m dis 1985), Annie Sophie, da of André Vautier; 3 s (Nicholas b 1975, Anthony b 1977, Benjamin b 1979); m 2, 28 June 1996, Mireille, da of late Colin Colahan; 2 step da; *Career* called to the Bar Gray's Inn 1968 (bencher 2003), in practice 1968–2004, admitted avocat a la Cour d'Appel de Paris and in practice 1987–2004, circuit judge (South Eastern Circuit) 2004–; *Recreations* boating, England and France; *Clubs* Travellers; *Style*— His Hon Judge Brooke, QC

BROOKE, Patrick Thomas Joseph; s of Robert Samuel Brooke (d 1974), and Mary Agnes, *née* Coleman (d 1987); *b* 4 February 1947; *Educ* Ross GS; *m* Rosemary Elizabeth Joyce; 2 s (Daniel Patrick Coleman b 31 Oct 1983, Lewis Samuel Joseph b 9 Oct 1985); *Career* qualified CA 1970; ptnr Waugh Haines Rigby 1974 (merged Cheltenham office with Grant Thornton 1986), managing ptnr 1986–92 and 1998–2003, nat ptnr responsible for Single Euro Market Servs 1989–2001, regnl sales and mktg ptnr 1992–2004; chm of tstees Cotswold Hosp Radio 1988–, chm Local Support Gp for Cotswold Nuffield Hosp 1992–2005; non-exec dir: Glos TEC 1991–2001 (resigned), Glos Devpt Agency 1998–2000 (resigned); Cheltenham Arts Festivals: memb Devpt Ctee 1996–2000, memb Fin Advsy Gp 2000–; Univ of Glos: memb Devpt Advsy Bd 2001–02, ind memb Cncl 2003–; ATII 1972, FCA 1979 (ACA 1970); *Recreations* golf, tennis, music, reading; *Clubs* The New Cheltenham, East Gloucestershire, Cotswold Hills Golf (capt 2005); *Style*— Patrick Brooke, Esq; ✉ Grant Thornton, Chartered Accountants, The Quadrangle, Imperial Square, Cheltenham, Gloucestershire GL50 1PZ (tel 0845 026 1251, fax 01242 222330, mobile 07973 252823)

BROOKE, Sir Richard David Christopher; 11 Bt (E 1662), of Norton Priory, Cheshire; s of Sir Richard Neville Brooke, 10 Bt (d 1997), and his 1 w, Lady Mabel Kathleen, *née* Jocelyn (d 1985), da of 8 Earl of Roden; *b* 23 October 1938; *Educ* Eton; *m* 1, 1963 (m dis 1978), Carola Marion, eldest da of Sir Robert Erskine-Hill, 2 Bt (d 1989); 2 s (Richard Christopher b 1966, Edward Marcus b 1970); m 2, 1979, Lucinda, o da of John Frederick Voelcker, of Happy Hill, Lidgetton, Natal, and formerly wife of William Barlow; *Heir* s, Richard Brooke; *Career* Lt Scots Gds 1957–58; ptnr Rowe & Pitman 1968–86, dir S G Warburg Group plc and dep chm Warburg Securities 1986–90, pres and chm S G Warburg (USA) Inc 1988–90; dir: J O Hambro & Co 1990–98, Govett Atlantic Investment Trust plc 1990–92, Contra Cyclical Investment Trust plc 1991–96, Exeter Preferred Capital Investment Trust plc 1991–2001, Gartmore American Securities plc 1991–95, Contra-Cyclical Trading Ltd 1992–96, Govett American Smaller Companies Investment Trust plc 1992–98, HCG Lloyd's Investment Trust plc 1993–96, Templeton Latin America Investment Trust plc 1994–2000, Templeton Emerging Markets Investment Trust plc 1994–2003, Mercury International Investment Trust plc 1995–98, Fidelity Special Values Investment Trust plc 1995–, Avocet Mining plc 1995–, Templeton Central & European Investment Co 1996–98, Exeter Selective Assets Investment Trust plc 2001–03, The Languedoc House (UK) Ltd 2006–; chm: Brooke & Pntrs 1990–, Armstrong International Ltd 1990–2001, North Atlantic Smaller Companies Investment Trust plc 1993–98, Govett Global Smaller Companies Investment Trust plc 1994–97, Brooke Restaurants Ltd 1996–98, Tai Chi Fund LP 2006, IDF Fund LP 2006–; memb Int Capital Markets Advsy Ctee NY Stock Exchange 1987–90, chm Int Markets Advsy Bd 1992–95, vice-chm Bd of Govrs Nat Assoc of Securities Dealers Inc 1994–95; *Recreations* boating, fine art, travel; *Clubs* Boodle's (chm of tstees 2007), Pratt's, Taporley Hunt, The Pilgrims, Soc of Merchants Trading with the Continent; *Style*— Sir Richard Brooke, Bt; ✉ Château Rouzaud, St Victor-Rouzaud, 09100 Pamiers, France

BROOKE, Sir Rodney George; kt (2007), CBE (1996), DL (1989); s of George Sidney Brooke (d 1967), of Morley, W Yorks, and Amy, *née* Grant; *b* 22 October 1939; *Educ* Queen Elizabeth GS Wakefield; *m* 2 Sept 1967, Dr Clare Margaret Brooke, da of William Martin Cox (d 1985), of Moseley, Birmingham; 1 s (Magnus b 1971), 1 da (Antonia b 1973); *Career* asst slr: Rochdale CBC 1962–63, Leicester City Cncl 1963–65; dir of admin Stockport CBC 1971–73 (sr asst slr 1965–67, asst town clerk 1967–69, dep town clerk 1969–71), chief exec and clerk W Yorks CC 1981–84 (dir of admin 1973–81), clerk to W Yorks Lieutenancy 1981–84, chief exec Westminster City Cncl 1984–89, hon sec London Boroughs Assoc 1984–90, clerk to Gtr London Lieutenancy 1987–89, chm Bradford HA 1989–90, assoc Ernst and Young 1989–90, advsr Longman Group 1989–90, sec Assoc of Metropolitan Authorities 1990–97, chm Electricity Consumers' Ctee (Yorks) 1997–2001, chm Cmmn on Accessible Transport in London 1998–2003, chm National Electricity Consumers Cncl 1999–2001; visiting res fell: Royal Inst of Public Admin 1989–91, Nuffield Inst for Health Service Studies Univ of Leeds 1989–; sr visiting res fell Univ of Birmingham 1997–; chm: Durham Univ Public Serv Devpt Fndn 1994–98, Dolphin Square Tst 2002– (dir 1987–), Gen Social Care Cncl 2002–; dir: Fndn for IT in Local Govt 1988–91, Riverside Community Health Tst 2000–02, Westminster Primary Care Tst 2002–06; memb Ethics Standards Bd for Accountants 2001–04; tstee: Community Devpt Fndn 1996–99, Dolphin Square Charitable Fndn 2006–; assoc Local Govt Mgmnt Bd 1997–99; chm Pimlico Sch (govr 2000–07), memb Cncl Tavistock Inst 2006–; Freeman City of London 1993; hon fell Inst of Local Govt Univ of Birmingham 1987; FRSA; OM (France) 1984, Order of Aztec Eagle (Mexico) 1985, Medal of Merit (Qatar) 1985, Order of Merit (Germany) 1986, Order of Merit (Senegal) 1988; *Books* Managing the Enabling Authority (1989), The Environmental Role of Local Government (1990), City Futures in Britain and Canada (jtly, 1991), The Handbook of Public Services Management (jtly, 1992), A Fresh Start for Local Government (jtly, 1997), The Utilities: A Consumers Eye View (2000), Councillors (2005); *Recreations* skiing, opera, Byzantium; *Clubs* Athenaeum, Ski of GB; *Style*— Sir Rodney Brooke, CBE, DL; ✉ Stubham Lodge, Middleton, Ilkley, West Yorkshire LS29 0AX (tel 01943 601869, fax 01943 816731); 706 Grenville House, Dolphin Square, London SW1V 3LR (tel and fax 020 7798 8086, e-mail rodney.brooke@gscc.org.uk)

BROOKE, (Christopher) Roger Ettrick; OBE (2005); s of Maj Ralph Brooke, RAMC; *b* 2 February 1931; *Educ* Tonbridge, Trinity Coll Oxford; *m* 1958, Nancy; 3 s, 1 da; *Career* HM Dip Serv 1955–66; dep md IRC 1966–69, dir Pearson Group Ltd 1971–79, gp md EMI Ltd 1979–80; Candover Investments plc: chief exec 1981–91, chm 1991–99; chm: The Audit Cmmn 1995–98, Innisfree Ltd 1998–2006, Advent 2VCT plc 1998–2005, Accord plc 1999–2005, Foresight4VCT plc 2005–; dep chm Carillion plc 1999–2001; dir: Slough Estates plc 1980–2001, Beeson Gregory Gp plc 2000–02, IP Group plc (formerly IP2IPO plc) 2002–; *Recreations* theatre, golf; *Style*— Roger Brooke, Esq, OBE; ✉ Watermeadow, Swarraton, Alresford, Hampshire SO24 9TQ

BROOKE OF SUTTON MANDEVILLE, Baron (Life Peer UK 2001), of Sutton Mandeville in the County of Wiltshire; Peter Leonard Brooke; CH (1992), PC (1988); s of Baron Brooke of Cumnor, CH, PC (Life Peer, d 1984), and Baroness Brooke of Ystradfellte, DBE (Life Peer, d 2000); bro of Rt Hon Lord Justice Brooke, *qv*; *b* 3 March 1934; *Educ* Marlborough, Balliol Coll Oxford (MA), Harvard Business Sch (MBA); *m* 1, 1964, Joan (d 1985), da of Frederick Smith, of São Paulo, Brazil; 3 s (and 1 s decd); m 2, 1991, Mrs Lindsay Allinson; *Career* Royal Engineers 1952–53 (invalided out); res assoc IMEDE Lausanne and Swiss corr Financial Times 1960–61, with Spencer Stuart Management Consultants 1961–79 (chm 1974–79); MP (Cons): City of London and Westminster S 1977–97, Cities of London and Westminster 1997–2001; asst Govt whip 1979–81, Lord Cmmr of the Treasy (Govt whip) 1981–83, under sec of state for educn and sci 1983–85, min of state Treasy 1985–87, Paymaster Gen Treasy 1987–89, chm Cons Pty 1987–89, sec of state for NI 1989–92, sec of state for nat heritage 1992–94; chm: Cusichaca Project 1978–98, Churches Conservation Tst 1995–98, Conf on Trg for Architectural Conservation 1995–98, Building Socs Ombudsman Cncl 1996–2001, Select Ctee on NI Affairs 1997–2001, Assoc of Cons Peers 2004–; pres Br Antique Dealers Assoc 1995–2005, pres Br Art Market Fedn 1996–; chm and pro-chllr Univ of London 2002– (memb Cncl 1994–, dep chm 2001–02); sr fell RCA 1987, presentation fell KCL 1989; Liveryman Worshipful Co of Drapers; hon fell Queen Mary & Westfield Coll London 1996; Hon DLitt Univ of Westminster 1999, Hon DLitt London Guildhall Univ 2001; FSA 1998; *Recreations* cricket, walking; *Clubs* Beefsteak, Brooks's, City Livery, Coningsby (pres), Grillions, I Zingari, MCC, St Andrew's (pres); *Style*— The Rt Hon the Lord Brooke of Sutton Mandeville, CH, PC

BROOKE-ROSE, Prof Christine; da of Alfred Northbrook Rose (d 1934), and Evelyn Brooke (d 1984); *b* 16 January 1923; *Educ* St Stephen's Coll Folkestone, Univ of Oxford (MA), Univ of London (PhD); *m* 1948 (m dis 1975), Jerzy Peterkiewicz; *Career* novelist and critic; Flt Offr WAAF 1941–45; freelance journalist 1955–68, prof of English language and lit Univ of Paris Vincennes 1975–88 (lectr 1968–75); hon fell Somerville Coll Oxford 1997; Hon DLitt UEA 1988; travelling prize Soc of Authors 1964, James Tait Black Meml Prize 1966, translation prize Arts Cncl 1969; *Books* criticism: A Grammar of Metaphor (1958), A ZBC of Ezra Pound (1971), A Rhetoric of the Unreal (1981), Stories, Theories and Things (1991); novels: The Languages of Love (1957), The Sycamore Tree (1958), The Dear Deceit (1960), The Middlemen (1961), Out (1964), Such (1965), Between (1968), Thru (1975), Amalgamemnon (1984), Xorandor (1986), Verbivore (1990), Textermination (1991), Remake (1996), Next (1998), Subscript (1999); also short stories and essays incl: Go When You See the Green Man Walking (1969); *Recreations* people, travel; *Style*— Prof Christine Brooke-Rose; ✉ c/o Cambridge University Press, PO Box 110, Cambridge CB2 3RL

BROOKE-TAYLOR, Timothy Julian (Tim); s of Edward Mallalieu Brooke-Taylor (d 1953), of Buxton, Derbys, and Rachel Frances, *née* Pawson (d 1995); *b* 17 July 1940; *Educ* Winchester, Pembroke Coll Cambridge (MA); *m* 20 July 1968, Christine Margaret, da of

Denis Wheadon; 2 s (Ben b 27 Nov 1969, Edward b 7 May 1971); *Career* actor; dir Derby County FC, rector Univ of St Andrews; Hon LLD Univ of St Andrews, Hon Dr Univ of Derby; *Theatre* West End: The Unvarnished Truth, Run For Your Wife, The Philanthropist; other: You Must Be The Husband (tour), My Fat Friend and Privates on Parade (Aust), Table Manners (Far and Middle East, Nat UK Tour 1999), The Lady Killers, Why Me!; *Television* The Braden Beat, At Last the 1948 Show, Broaden Your Mind, The Goodies, Me and My Girl, The Rough With The Smooth, You Must Be The Husband, One Foot in the Grave, tlc, Beat the Nation, Golf Clubs with Tim Brooke-Taylor; *Films* 12 + 1, The Statue, Willy Wonka and the Chocolate Factory; *Radio* I'm Sorry I'll Read That Again, Hoax, I'm Sorry I Haven't A Clue; *Books* Rule Britannia, Tim Brooke-Taylor's Cricket Box, Tim Brooke-Taylor's Golf Bag, The Almost Complete I'm Sorry Haven't A Clue; *Recreations* golf, Derby County; *Clubs* Temple and Bearwood Lakes, Cookham Dean Nomads; *Style*— Tim Brooke-Taylor, Esq; ✉ c/o Jill Foster Ltd, 9 Barb Mews, London W6 7PA (tel 020 7602 1263, fax 020 7602 9536, e-mail agents@jfl.uninet.co.uk)

BROOKEBOROUGH, 3 Viscount (UK 1952); Sir Alan Henry Brooke; 7 Bt (UK 1822), DL (Co Fermanagh 1987); er s of 2 Viscount Brookeborough, PC, DL (d 1987), and Rosemary, Viscountess Brookeborough; *b* 30 June 1952; *Educ* Harrow, Millfield; *m* 12 April 1980, Janet Elizabeth, o da of John Cooke, of Doagh, Co Antrim; *Heir* bro, Hon Christopher Brooke; *Career* cmmnd 17/21 Lancers 1972, transferred to UDR pt/t 1977, Co Cdr 4 Bn UDR 1980–83, transfer UDR pt/t 1983, Maj-Co Cdr UDR 1988–93, Lt Col Royal Irish Regt 1993–, Hon Col 4/5 Bn The Royal Irish Rangers TAVR 1997–; non-exec dir Basel International (Jersey) 2000– (chm 1996–2001); non-exec dir Green Park Healthcare Tst 1992–2001; farmer; memb: EEC Agric Sub-Ctee House of Lords 1988–97, Select Ctee on European Communities 1998–2002, Sub-Ctee Br Energy Industry and Transport 1998–2002, NI Policing Bd 2001–06; memb Nat Employer Advsy Bd (NEAB) 2005–; pres Army Benevolent Fund NI 1995–; High Sheriff Co Fermanagh 1995; Lord in Waiting to HM The Queen 1997–; *Recreations* riding, fishing, shooting, skiing; *Clubs* Cavalry and Guards'; *Style*— The Rt Hon the Viscount Brookeborough, DL; ✉ Colebrooke, Brookeborough, Co Fermanagh (tel 028 895 31402)

BROOKES, Eur Ing James Robert (Jim); s of James Brookes, of Worsley, Lancs, and Hettie, *née* Colley; *b* 2 September 1941; *Educ* Manchester Grammar, CCC Oxford (MA); *m* 30 May 1964, Patricia, da of John Gaskell, MBE, of Knutsford, Cheshire; 3 da (Diane (Mrs Chambers) b 9 Oct 1965, Gail (Mrs Crocker) b 28 June 1967, Maura (Mrs Grubb) b 8 July 1969); *Career* various posts in UK and USA as systems and applications programmer in devpt, tech support and sales; branch mangr Univ and Nat Res Region Ferranti Int Computers 1962–67, computer servs mangr Queen's Univ Belfast 1967–69, mangr Univ of Manchester Regnl Computer Centre 1969–75, dir SW Univs Regnl Computer Centre 1975–87, dir Univ of Bath Computer Servs 1983–87, chief exec Br Computer Soc 1986–91, chm BISL 1988–91, visiting prof Strathclyde Univ Business Sch 1991–95, dir of info servs Univ of Portsmouth 1992–95, head of information systems Avon and Somerset Constabulary 1995–98, ind conslt 1998–, non-exec dir The Knowledge Group 1998–2002 and 2006–, non-exec dir Smart South West 1999–2005, non-exec chm Homeworkbase Ltd 2005–; memb PITCOM Cncl 1990– (memb Prog Exec 1997–2000); Liveryman Worshipful Co of Info Technologists 1992 (memb 1988), Freeman City of London 1989; CEng, FBCS 1973, FRSA, Eur Ing 1991; *Recreations* sailing, fell walking, cycling, bridge, music, reading, badminton; *Clubs* Oxford and Cambridge; *Style*— Eur Ing Jim Brookes; ✉ 29 High Street, Marshfield, Chippenham, Wiltshire SN14 8LR (tel 01225 891294, e-mail jr.brookes@btinternet.com)

BROOKES, John A; MBE; s of Edward Percy Brookes (d 1982), and Margaret Alexandra, *née* Reid; *b* 11 October 1933; *Educ* Durham Sch, Durham Co Sch of Horticulture, UCL (DipLD); *Career* landscape designer; formerly apprentice with/to: Parks Dept Nottingham Corp, Brenda Colvin, Dame Sylvia Crowe; in private practice 1964–; work currently in progress incl private gardens in USA, GB, Japan and Argentina; formerly: lectr in landscape design Inst of Park Admin, asst lectr in landscape design Regent Street Poly, dir Inchbald Sch of Garden Design; lectr in landscape design Royal Botanic Gardens Kew; fndr: Inchbald Sch of Interior Design Teheran Iran 1978, Clock House Sch of Garden Design (within estab garden of Denmans W Sussex) 1980; regular lectr on garden design worldwide; past chm Soc of Garden Designers; Hon DUniv Essex; FSGD; *Books* Room Outside (1969, reprint 1979), Gardens for Small Spaces (1970), Garden Design and Layout (1970), Living in the Garden (1971), Financial Times Book of Garden Design (1975), Improve Your Lot (1977), The Small Garden (1977, reprint 1984), The Garden Book (1984), A Place in the Country (1984), The Indoor Garden Book (1986), Gardens of Paradise (1987), The Country Garden (1987), The New Small Garden Book (1989), John Brookes' Garden Design Book (1991), Planting the Country Way (1994), John Brookes' Garden Design Workbook (1994), The New Garden (1998), John Brookes Garden Masterclass (2002), John Brookes' Garden Design Course (2007); *Style*— John Brookes, Esq, MBE; ✉ Clock House, Denmans, Fontwell, Arundel, West Sussex BN18 0SU (tel 01243 542808, fax 01243 544064, e-mail jbrookes@denmans-garden.co.uk)

BROOKES, Mike; s of late Lt-Col G K Brookes, MBE, RAMC, and Mrs Brookes; *b* 20 May 1940; *Educ* Univ of Exeter (BSc); *m* 1962, Maureen; 2 c; *Career* Ford of Europe 1962–94: various positions rising to dir of Euro gen servs 1977–90, dir of material planning and transportation 1990–94; chm: Southend Hosp NHS Tst 1996–2000, S Essex HA 2000–02, Essex Strategic HA 2002–; *Recreations* golf, rugby, cricket, reading; *Style*— Mike Brookes, Esq

BROOKES, Nicholas Kelvin; s of Stanley Brookes (d 2004), and Jean, *née* Wigley; *b* 19 May 1947, London; *Educ* Harrow; *m* 22 Aug 1968, Maria, *née* Crespo; 1 da (Katrina b 8 Aug 1969), 2 s (David b 14 Jan 1971, Miguel b 3 Sept 1973); *Career* Texas Instruments Inc: fin dir Spain 1974–80, md Canada 1980–84, European md and gp vice-pres 1985–91, vice-pres and gp pres 1991–95; ceo Spirent plc 1995–2004, chm De La Rue plc 2004–; non-exec dir: Axel Johnson Inc Corporacion Financiera Alba SA; memb Cncl IOD 2006–, CCMI, FCA 1973, FInstD 1998; *Recreations* tennis, golf, chess; *Clubs* Reform; *Style*— Nicholas Brookes, Esq; ✉ Wolvers Hall, Ironsbottom Lane, Reigate, Surrey RH2 8PU (tel 01293 862335, fax 01293 862384); De La Rue plc, Jays Close, Viables, Basingstoke, Hants RG22 4BS (tel 01256 605326, fax 01256 605347, e-mail nicholas.brookes@uk.delarue.com)

BROOKES, Nicola; da of Leon Bernard (d 1954), of Ruislip, and Violet Charlotte, *née* Farrar; *b* 25 December 1951; *Educ* Wycombe HS, Univ of Warwick (BSc); *m* 27 Sept 1980, Ian Thomas Burns, s of Thomas George Burns, of West Kirby, Wirral; 1 da (Laura Kathryn b 1988), 1 s (Thomas Leon Phillip b 1990); *Career* trainee accountant Arthur Andersen & Co 1973–76; Amari plc: joined 1976, corporate devpt dir 1984–86, fin dir 1986–89; dir VIA International Ltd 1989–99 (formerly fin dir), fin dir Barnes Tst Television Ltd 1997–2000, fin dir Vitesse Media plc 2001–05, currently fin dir Chaco plc; selected by Business magazine as one of Britain's Top 40 young leaders, finalist Business Woman of the Year 1988; FCA 1981; *Recreations* swimming, skiing, reading, music and opera; *Style*— Ms Nicola Brookes

BROOKES, Peter; s of late G H Brookes, and late J E Brookes, *née* Owen; *b* 28 September 1943; *Educ* Heversham GS, RAF Coll Cranwell (BA), Central Sch of Art & Design (BA); *m* 1971, Angela, *née* Harrison; 2 s (Ben, Will); *Career* freelance illustrator and cartoonist 1969–; tutor: Central Sch of Art & Design 1977–79, RCA 1979–89; cover artist The Spectator 1986–, political cartoonist The Times 1995–, contrib to numerous pubns incl The Listener, Radio Times and TLS; stamp designs for Royal Mail 1995, 1999 and 2003; Political Cartoonist of the Year Cartoon Art Tst Awards 1996, 1998 and 2006, Cartoonist of the Year Br Press Awards 2002, Cartoonist of the Year Political Cartoon Soc 2006; memb Alliance Graphique Internationale (AGI) 1988, FRSA 2000, RDI 2002; *Publications* Nature Notes (1997), Nature Notes: The New Collection (1999), Nature Notes III (2001), Peter Brookes of The Times (2002), Nature Notes: The Natural Selection (2004); *Recreations* music, arguing; *Clubs* Queens Park Rangers FC; *Style*— Peter Brookes, Esq, RDI; ✉ The Times, 1 Pennington Street, London E98 1TT (tel 020 7782 5074, fax 020 7782 5639, e-mail peter.brookes@the-times.co.uk)

BROOKING, Sir Trevor David; kt (2004), CBE (1999, MBE 1981); *b* 2 October 1948; *m* 1970, Hilkka Helakorpi; 2 c; *Career* former professional footballer; with West Ham United 1965–84, over 500 appearances, FA Cup winners' medal 1975 and 1980; England: debut 1974, 47 caps, scored 5 goals, ret 1982; football commentator, analyst and presenter BBC TV and Radio 1988–2004; Sport England (formerly Sports Cncl): memb 1989–, chm 1999–2002 (actg chm 1998–99); co-chm Lottery Sports Panel; non-exec dir West Ham United FC until 2004 (sometime actg coach 2003), dir of football devpt FA 2004–; *Style*— Sir Trevor Brooking, CBE; ✉ c/o Jane Morgan Management, Thames Wharf Studios, Rainville Road, London W6 9HA (tel 020 7386 5345, fax 020 7386 0338, e-mail enquiries@janemorganmgt.com)

BROOKMAN, Baron (Life Peer UK 1998), of Ebbw Vale in the County of Gwent; (David) Keith Brookman; *b* 3 January 1937; *Educ* Nantyglo GS Gwent; *Career* Nat Serv RAF; steel worker Richard Thomas & Baldwin Ltd Ebbw Vale 1953–73; Iron and Steel Trades Confedn: divnl organiser 1973, asst gen sec 1985–93, gen sec 1993–99; memb Exec Cncl Confedn of Shipbuilding and Engrg Unions 1989–95; chm Nat Steel Co-ordinating Ctee 1993–99 (memb 1991–93); TUC: memb Educn Advsy Ctee for Wales 1976–82, memb Steel Ctee 1985–90, memb Gen Cncl 1992–99; British Steel: memb Jt Accident Prevention Advsy Ctee (JAPAC) 1985–93, memb Advsy Ctee on Educn and Trg (ACET) 1986–93, operatives' sec Long Products General Steels Jt Standing Ctee 1993–98, operatives' sec Strip Trade Bd 1993–98, memb Bd UK Steel Enterprise 1993–; Labour Pty: memb Exec Ctee Wales 1982–85, memb Nat Constitutional Ctee 1987–91, memb NEC 1991–92; International Metalworkers' Fedn: hon sec IMF British Section 1993–99, pres IMF Iron and Steel and Non-Ferrous Metals Dept 1993–99; operatives' sec Jt Industrial Cncl for the Slag Industry 1985–93; memb: Exec Cncl European Metalworkers' Fedn 1985–95, Euro Coal and Steel Community Consultative Ctee 1993–2002; employees' sec Euro Works Cncl British Steel 1996–98; govr Gwent Coll of HE 1980–84, tstee Julian Melchett Tst 1985–95; *Style*— The Lord Brookman; ✉ House of Lords, London SW1A 0PW (tel 020 7219 8633)

BROOKNER, Dr Anita; CBE (1990); da of Newson Brookner, and Maude, *née* Schiska; *b* 16 July 1928; *Educ* James Allen's Girls' Sch, KCL (BA), Courtauld Inst of Art (PhD); *Career* lectr then reader Courtauld Inst of Art 1964–88, Slade prof of art Univ of Cambridge 1967–68; fell New Hall Cambridge; FRSL; *Books* Watteau (1964), The Genius of the Future (1971), J B Greuze (1972), Jacques Louis David (1980), The Stories of Edith Wharton Vol I (ed, 1988) Vol II (ed, 1989), Soundings (1997), Romanticism and its Discontents (2000); *Novels* A Start in Life (1981), Providence (1982), Look At Me (1983), Family and Friends (1983), Hotel du Lac (1984, Booker-McConnell prize, filmed for TV 1986), A Misalliance (1986), A Friend from England (1987), Latecomers (1988), Lewis Percy (1989), Brief Lives (1990), A Closed Eye (1991), Fraud (1992), A Family Romance (1993), Altered States (1996), Visitors (1997), Falling Slowly (1998), Undue Influence (1999), The Bay of Angels (2001), The Next Big Thing (2002), The Rules of Engagement (2003); many articles in Apollo, Burlington Magazine, TLS; *Recreations* walking, reading; *Style*— Dr Anita Brookner, CBE, FRSL

BROOKS, (Francis) David; s of Francis Brooks (d 1945), of Great Haywood, Staffs, and Alice Ida, *née* Jones (d 1984); *b* 18 January 1934; *Educ* Ackworth Sch, ChCh Oxford (MA); *m* 19 July 1958, Jennifer Mary, da of Edward Line; 2 s (Julian Francis b 3 Nov 1961, Peter Edward b 15 Sept 1963), 2 da (Ruth Marguerite b 19 Jan 1967, Hilary Jennifer b 25 July 1969); *Career* Cadbury Bros/Cadbury Schweppes: personnel mangr Confectionery Gp 1974, Bournville Factory dir Cadbury Ltd 1976, vice-pres tech Peter Paul Cadbury (USA) Inc 1982, sr vice-pres confectionery ops Cadbury Schweppes (USA) Inc 1984, chm and md Cadbury Ltd 1990–94 (ops dir 1987, md 1989); memb: Exec Ctee Food and Drink Fedn 1990–93, President's Ctee Biscuit Cocoa Chocolate and Confectionery Alliance 1990–94; dir: Birmingham TEC 1992–94, Newtown/S Aston City Challenge Co 1995–98, Aston Reinvestment Tst 1995–2005; non-exec dir Birmingham Heartlands Development Corp 1993–98; chm: Cncl Birmingham Common Purpose 1993, Groundwork Birmingham Ltd 1994–97, Birmingham Settlement 1994–2000, Prince's Youth Business Tst (W Midlands and Warks) 1996–99, Cncl Selly Oak Colls 1997–2000, Selly Oak Colls Endowment Tst 2000–03 (tstee 1997–2003), Prince's Tst W Midlands Region 2000–05, ART Homes Ltd 2000–07; non-exec chm Lyalvale Express Ltd 1997–; chm Mercian Housing Assoc 2005– (memb Bd 2003–); tstee: Woodbrooke Coll 1994–2000, HCI (Birmingham) Ltd 1997–99; memb Cncl Univ of Birmingham 2000–07; FRSA 1992; *Recreations* music, history, countryside; *Style*— David Brooks, Esq; ✉ 1 Alexandra House, 44 Farquhar Road, Edgbaston, Birmingham B15 3RE (tel 0121 455 8097, fax 0121 455 8098)

BROOKS, Prof David James; *b* 4 December 1949; *Educ* ChCh Oxford (open scholar, BA), UCH Med Sch London (MB BS), Univ of London (MD, DSc); *Career* jr res fell Wolfson Coll Oxford 1973–74; house surgn rising to conslt and sr lectr at various hosps, hon conslt and Hartnett prof of neurology Imperial Coll Sch of Med London, Hammersmith Hosps and Inst of Neurology 1993–, head of neurology MRC Clinical Sciences Centre Hammersmith Hosp 1993–, hon sr lectr Inst of Psychiatry 1993–; Div of Neuroscience and Psychological Med Imperial Coll London: head Sensorimotor Systems Dept; visiting prof Univ of Innsbruck; clinical dir Hammersmith Imanet Ltd Hammersmith Hosp 2001–; head of neurology medical diagnostics and CMO Imanet GE Healthcare plc 2002–; chm: Cncl of Mgmnt UK Parkinson's Disease Assoc 1997–98 (tstee 1996–99), Scientific Issues Ctee Movement Disorder Soc 1998–2002; memb: Grants Ctee MRC Neurosciences and Mental Health Bd 1995–97, Med Advsy Panel UK Parkinson's Disease Soc 1995– (chm 1996–97), Med Advsy Panel UK Huntington's Disease Assoc 1996–, MRC Med Advsy Bd 1997–2000, Neuroscience Panel Wellcome Tst 2000–03, Int Advsy Bd German Parkinson Network 2000–06, Int Advsy Bd Dementia Network 2007–, Advsy Bd European Soc for Clinical Neuropharmacology, European Multiple Systems Atrophy Steering Gp, Int Advsy Bd Michael J Fox Fndn 2002–, EC Concerted Actions on Neural Transplantation (NECTAR/NEST), Bd MRC Neuroscience 2004–; memb industrial advsy bds: Glaxo SmithKline, Orion-Pharma, Aventis, Astra-Zeneca, Novartis, Solvay, TEVA; conslt: Shire, Motac Neuroscience, Lundbeck; memb Editorial Bd: Jl of Neural Transmission, Jl of Neurology, Neurosurgery and Psychiatry, Synapse, Movement Disorders; patron Alzheimer's Soc 2007–; Stanley Fahn lectr 2002, Cotzias lectr 2003, Charles Wilson lectr 2004, Kuhl-Lassen lectr 2005, Sprague lectr 2006; memb: Assoc of Br Neurologists, BMA, European Neurological Soc, American Assoc of Neurology, Movement Disorder Soc, American Neurological Assoc, Assoc of Physicians (UK), Int Soc of Cerebral Blood Flow and Metabolism (a dir 1993–97), Soc for Neuroscience, Int Basal Ganglia Soc, Australian and NZ Assoc of Neurologists, Atlanto-Euro-Mediterranean Acad of Med Scis; FRCP 1993 (MRCP 1982), FMedSci 2001; *Publications* author of over 280 papers in peer-reviewed jls, symposia proceedings, reviews and abstracts; *Clubs* Athenaeum; *Style*— Prof David J Brooks; ✉ 186 Jersey Road, Osterley, Middlesex TW7 4QN (e-mail david.brooks@csc.mrc.ac.uk)

BROOKS, Harry; Jr; eld s of Harry Brooks Sr (d 1978), of Peover Hall, Knutsford, Cheshire, and Norah Brooks (d 1991); *b* 16 February 1936; *m* 23 July 1977, Lela; 1 da (Milanka b 12 Sept 1983); *Career* actor, prodr, photographer, writer, entrepreneur; started career at Liverpool Playhouse, performed in many stage prodns, TV progs and films; prodr Harry Brooks Productions, Pinewood Studios (work incl features, TV commercials and corporate videos); writer of original prodns: Mice (musical), The Lady of Light (stage and book), Disguise (screenplay), Les Aventures des Duchesses (screenplay), Pistol (screenplay), Play on Words (stage), Dance on Tap (musical), Inheritance & Loyalty (autobiography); fndr and chm The MIDAS Consortium (Multimedia Interactive Data Access Systems, project to provide a syndication of global mobile phone subsidiaries for internet shopping and multimedia services); *Recreations* reading, languages, writing, classical music, traditional jazz, photographing classically beautiful women, talking passionately about his wonderful Dad (pioneer of hire-purchase in the 1920s with New Day Furniture Gp); *Clubs* Beaufort Polo; *Style*— Harry Brooks, Jr, Esq; ✉ tel 07000 700011 or 01753 561700, Pinewood Studios, e-mail harry@harrybrooks.com, website www.harrybrooks.com; tel 01753 656825, website www.midascash.com

BROOKS, Jason; s of Michael David Brooks, and Patricia, *née* Morgan; *b* 1968; *Educ* Oakwood Comp Sch Rotherham, Thomas Rotherham Coll, Rotherham Coll of Arts and Technol, Cheltenham and Gloucester Coll of Art and Design, Chelsea Coll of Art and Design; *Career* artist; *Solo Exhibitions* Entwistle London 1997–98, 2000 and 2003, Harewood House Leeds 2001, Archimede Staffolini Gallery Nicosia 2002, Auto (Max Wigram Gallery London) 2005, Stellan Holm Gallery NY 2006; *Selected Group Exhibitions* Get Real (Riverside Studios London) 1992, Abstractions from the Domestic Suburb Scene (SIN) (Benjamin Rhodes Gallery London) 1992, SS Excess (Factual Nonsense London) 1993, To Boldly Go... (Cubitt Street Gallery London) 1993, BT New Contemporaries (Serpentine Gallery London and tour) 1993, Likeness: Representing Sexualities (Manchester City Art Galleries) 1997, John Moores 20 Liverpool Exhibition (Walker Art Gallery Liverpool) 1997, The Whitechapel Open (Whitechapel Art Gallery London) 1998, Postcards on Photography (Cambridge Darkroom and tour) 1998, Near (Sharjah Art Museum UAE), Painting Lab (Entwistle London) 1999, The Flower Show (Harewood House) 1999, John Moores 21 Liverpool Exhibition (Walker Art Gallery Liverpool) 1999, Fresh Paint (Scottish Gallery of Modern Art Glasgow) 1999, Natural Dependency (Jerwood Gallery London) 1999, Psycho Soma (Lombard Freid NY) 2000, I Am A Camera (Saatchi Gallery London) 2001, Besides, It Is Always Others Who Die (291 London) 2001, Open Plan (Alphadelta Gallery and Artio Gallery Athens) 2001, Babel (Nat Museum of Contemporary Art Korea) 2002, Yes I Am a Long Way from Home (Wolverhampton Museum and Art Gallery, The Nunnery London, and Northern Centre for Contemporary Art Sunderland) 2003, The Flower Show (Rhodes & Mann London) 2003, Pale Fire (Galerie Nordenhake Berlin) 2003, Blow Up: New Painting and Photoreality (St Paul's Gallery Birmingham) 2004, John Moores 23 Liverpool Exhibition (Walker Art Gallery Liverpool) 2004, Appearance (Whitewall Waterfront Leeds) 2005, Darkness Visible (Ferens Art Gallery Hull and Southampton City Art Gallery) 2006, Heads (Flowers East London) 2006, Harewood House 2006, Museum of Art Donna Regina Naples 2006, Timer (Triennale Bovisa Milan) 2007; *Work in Collections* The Berardo Collection MOMA Sintra, British Telecom London, Cheltenham & Gloucester Building Soc Cheltenham, Coopers & Lybrand London, James Moores Collection Liverpool, William Morris Agency LA, Saatchi Collection London, Speyer Collection NY, Unilever London, ABN AMRO London, Neuberger Berman NY, Ferens Art Gallery Hull, Harewood House Tst, Dakis Collection; *Awards* Rome Travel Bursary Br Sch in Rome 1990, British Telecom artist-in-residence 1994, co-prizewinner John Moores Exhbn 1997, winner NatWest Art Prize 1999; *Recreations* golf, tennis, sports cars; *Style*— Jason Brooks, Esq

BROOKS, Jermyn Paul; *b* 23 February 1939; *Educ* Northampton GS, Lincoln Coll Oxford (MA), Free Univ Berlin; *m* Val; 1 s (Robin b 1970), 1 da (Victoria b 1976); *Career* PricewaterhouseCoopers (formerly Price Waterhouse before merger): joined 1962, Frankfurt office 1967, ptnr 1973–2000, ptnr i/c Iranian practice 1976–79, Frankfurt 1979–93, involved in establishment of Turkey office 1980–84, ptnr i/c Mgmnt Consultancy practice 1987–88 (Audit practice Frankfurt 1986–87), sr ptnr Germany 1989–93, memb Bd European Mgmnt, chm Eastern Europe Jt Venture Bd 1992–93, chm Price Waterhouse Europe 1993–98, dep chm Price Waterhouse World Firm 1993–97 and chm 1997–98, global managing ptnr 1998–2000; dir Transparency Int Berlin and London 2000–03 (memb Int Bd of Dirs 2003–); memb Exec Ctee and treas American C of C Germany 1988–93; non-exec dir Mott MacDonald Gp Ltd 2003–; dir Int IDEA Stockholm 2003–; German Wirtschaftsprüfer; FCA, FIL; frequent speaker on accounting and auditing issues, bribery and corruption and social responsibility of business; author of 3 books on German accounting law and articles on bribery and corruption; *Recreations* tennis, gardening, music; *Style*— Jermyn Brooks, Esq; ✉ 26 Shouldham Street, London W1H 5FL (tel 020 7723 9141); Ulmenweg 4, 61381 Friedrichsdorf, Germany (tel 00 49 6172 71384, e-mail jbrooks@transparency.org)

BROOKS, Prof John Stuart; s of Ernest Brooks (d 2005), and Maude, *née* Langford (d 1981); *b* 8 March 1949, Holloway, London; *Educ* Cheshunt GS, Univ of Sheffield (BSc, PhD, DSc); *m* 14 Aug 1971, Jill, *née* Pusey; 2 s (Thomas David b 3 Jan 1998, Christopher John b 12 Nov 1999); *Career* Sheffield City Poly: lectr 1973–84, head Applied Physics Dept 1984–90, dir Materials Research Inst 1990–92; asst princ Sheffield Hallam Univ 1992–98, vice-chllr Univ of Wolverhampton 1998–2005, vice-chllr Manchester Met Univ 2005–; author of 75 papers on materials, spectroscopy and surface engrg; CPhys 1985, FInstP 1985, CEng 1992; *Recreations* travel, walking, music, bridge; *Style*— Prof John Brooks; ✉ Manchester Metropolitan University, All Saints Building, All Saints, Manchester M15 6BH (tel 0161 247 1560, e-mail john.brooks@mmu.ac.uk)

BROOKS, Dr Nicholas Hugh; s of Lt-Col A Brooks, of Great Missenden, Bucks, and Mary, *née* Gerrard; *b* 6 July 1947; *Educ* Perse Sch Cambridge, Bart's Med Coll and Univ of London (MB BS, MD); *m* 16 March 1974, Barbara Mary, da of Dr Robert Boal, of Southampton, Hants; 1 s (Alexander James b 1977), 1 da (Victoria Jane b 1979); *Career* Bart's: house surgn Surgical Professional Unit 1971, house surgn in cardiothoracic surgery then SHO in gen med 1972, registrar in cardiology 1973–74; house physician Southampton Gen Hosp 1971, Br Heart Fndn res fell St George's Hosp 1976–77 (registrar in med 1975), clinical lectr and hon sr registrar London Chest Hosp and London Hosp 1977, conslt cardiologist Wythenshawe Hosp Manchester 1984–; chm Specialist Advsy Ctee JCHMT 2000–03 (sec 1998–2000); hon sec Cardiology Ctee RCP 1988–93, hon sec Br Cardiac Soc 1996–98 (hon asst sec 1994–96); pres Br Cardiac Soc 2005–07 (pres-elect 2003–05); FRCP 1990 (MRCP), FESC 1996; *Books* Diseases of the Heart (contrib, 1989 and 1996); *Recreations* tennis, skiing, music; *Style*— Dr Nicholas Brooks; ✉ Oldcroft House, Elm Grove, Alderley Edge, Cheshire SK9 7PD (tel 01625 582853, e-mail nhbrooks@talk21.com); South Manchester University Hospitals Trust, Wythenshawe Hospital, Manchester M23 9LT (tel 0161 291 2387, e-mail nicholas.brooks@smtr.nhs.uk)

BROOKS, Prof Nicholas Peter; s of Dr (William) Donald Wykeham Brooks, CBE (d 1993), of Storrington, W Sussex, and Phyllis Kathleen, *née* Juler (d 1988); *b* 14 January 1941; *Educ* Winchester, Magdalen Coll Oxford (MA, DPhil); *m* 16 Sept 1967, Chloë Carolyn, da of Rev Sidney C Willis (d 1978); 1 da (Ebba b 31 Jan 1969), 1 s (Crispin b 29 Dec 1970); *Career* sr lectr in medieval history Univ of St Andrews 1978–85 (lectr 1964–78); Univ of Birmingham: prof of medieval history 1985–2004 (emeritus prof 2004–), dean Faculty of Arts 1992–95, assoc dean 1996–97; chm St Andrews Preservation Tst 1977–83; FBA, FRHistS; *Books* Latin and the Vernacular Languages in Early Medieval Britain (1982),

The Early History of the Church of Canterbury (1984), St Oswald of Worcester: Life and Influence (1996), Anglo-Saxon Myths: State and Church 400–1066 (2000), Communities and Warfare 700–1400 (2000), St Wulfstan and his World (2005); *Recreations* gardening, walking; *Style*— Prof Nicholas Brooks, FBA; ✉ Department of Medieval History, University of Birmingham, Edgbaston, Birmingham B15 2TT (tel 0121 414 5736, e-mail n.p.brooks@bham.ac.uk)

BROOKS, Peter Malcolm; s of Roger Morrison Brooks (d 1968), of Winchester, Hants, and Phyllis Fuller, *née* Hopkinson (d 2000); *b* 12 February 1947; *Educ* Marlborough, Univ of Southampton (LLB, Eng and Br Univs squash team rep); *m* 1, 1974 (m dis); 1 s (Matthew Harry Morrison b 21 July 1980); *m* 2, 1987, Patricia Margaret; 1 s (Nicholas John Morrison b 27 Nov 1987); *Career* VSO Sarawak 1965–66; admitted slr 1971; ptnr: Macfarlanes 1977–84, Clifford Chance 1984–96 (latterly head of Corp Practice); gen counsel to the Global Corporates & Instns (GCI) Bd Deutsche Bank AG 1997–99; chm Euro Corp Coverage Clifford Chance 1999–2002; dir Gentin Int UK; non-exec dir: Enodis plc 1998– (chm 2000–), Chesterton Int plc 2000– (chm 2000–03), Code Securities Ltd; *Recreations* rackets, cricket, opera, theatre, travel; *Clubs* Brooks's; *Style*— Peter Brooks, Esq; ✉ Enodis plc, Washington House, 40–41 Conduit Street, London W1S 2YQ (e-mail peter.brooks@enodis.com)

BROOKS, Richard John; s of Peter John Brooks (d 2000), and Joan, *née* Maxwell (d 1965); *b* 5 February 1946; *Educ* Univ of Bristol (BA); *m* Jane Elizabeth; 2 da (Kate b 13 July 1981, Anna b 5 Dec 1984); *Career* journalist; Bristol Evening Post 1968–71, Daily Mail 1971, BBC 1971–79, The Economist 1979–80, Sunday Times 1980–85, media ed The Observer 1985–99, arts ed Sunday Times 1999–; *Recreations* watching films, playing sport; *Style*— Richard Brooks, Esq; ✉ Sunday Times, 1 Pennington Street, London E1 (tel 020 7782 5735)

BROOKS, Richard William; s of Roger William Brooks, of Lancs, and Jennifer Ann, *née* Hawkard; *b* 18 February 1969, Malta; *Educ* Arnold Sch Blackpool, Univ of Warwick (LLB), Chester Sch of Law; *m* 1 May 2004, Victoria Jane, *née* Hopwell; *Career* slr; ptnr: Chalk Smith Brooks 1999, Withy King Slrs 2004–; memb Law Soc; *Recreations* rugby, horseracing; *Style*— Richard Brooks, Esq; ✉ 27 Newbury Street, Lambourn, Berkshire RG17 8PB (tel 07775 918757); Withy King, Ailesbury Court, High Street, Marlborough SN8 1AA (e-mail richard.brooks@withyking.co.uk)

BROOKS, Robert; s of William Frederick Brooks, of Enton, Surrey, and Joan Patricia, *née* Marshall; *b* 1 October 1956; *Educ* St Benedict's Sch Ealing; *Career* dir: Christie's S Kensington Ltd 1984–87 (joined 1975), Christie Manson and Woods Ltd 1987–89; estab Brooks (Auctioneers) Ltd 1989, chm W & F C Bonham & Sons Ltd; FIA Gp N Euro Touring Car champion 1999; *Recreations* motor sport, golf, cricket; *Clubs* British Racing Drivers (chm); *Style*— Robert Brooks, Esq

BROOKS, Prof Stephen Peter; s of Peter Brooks, of Cyprus, and Adrienne, *née* Randall; *b* 31 July 1970, Crawley, W Sussex; *Educ* Univ of Bristol (BSc), Univ of Kent at Canterbury (MSc, Shell Prize), Univ of Cambridge (PhD, J T Knight Prize); *m* 3 June 2002, Kari O'Nions; 1 da (Amelie Clare b 14 March 2006); *Career* research asst Univ of Kent at Canterbury 1992–93, lectr in statistics Univ of Bristol 1996–99, sr lectr in statistics Univ of Surrey 1999–2000, EPSRC advanced res fell and reader in statistics then prof of statistics Univ of Cambridge 2000–; visiting scholar Stanford Univ 1997, visiting fell Univ of Bristol 1999–2001; memb Inst for Learning and Teaching in HE; RSS: chm Grad Trg Ctee 2000–02, memb Cncl 2001–05, assoc ed Jl of RSS Series D 1996–99 and Series B 2000–04, book reviews ed 1996–99, memb Res Section Ctee 1999–2002; assoc ed Biometrics 2004–07; author of numerous jl articles and papers; referee for various int statistical jls, books and grant proposals; memb: EPSRC Mathematics Coll 2000–, European Regnl Ctee Bernoulli Soc 2002–05, Br region Int Biometric Soc Ctee, Environmental Mathematics and Statistics Prog Steering Ctee NERC/EPSRC 2002–05, Mathematics Strategic Advsy Team EPSRC 2003–04; memb Ct Univ of Surrey 2003–; RSS Research Prize 1999, Philip Leverhulme Prize 2004, RSS Guy Medal in Bronze 2005; CStat 1999, CMath, CSci, FRSS 1992; *Recreations* scuba diving; *Style*— Prof Stephen Brooks; ✉ Department of Pure Mathematics and Mathematical Statistics, Faculty of Maths, Centre for Mathematical Sciences, Wilberforce Road, Cambridge CB3 0WB (tel 01223 766535, e-mail steve@statslab.cam.ac.uk)

BROOKS OF TREMORFA, Baron (Life Peer UK 1979), of Tremorfa in the County of South Glamorgan; John Edward Brooks; s of Edward George Brooks, and Rachel, *née* White; *b* 12 April 1927; *Educ* Coleg Harlech; *m* 1, 1948 (m dis 1956); 1 s, 1 da; *m* 2, 1958, Margaret Pringle; 2 s; *Career* sec Cardiff SE Lab Pty 1966–84, contested (Lab) Barry Feb and Oct 1974, Parly agent to Rt Hon James Callaghan, MP, at Gen Elections 1970 and 1979; S Glamorgan CC: memb 1973–93, leader 1973–77 and 1986–92, chm 1981–82; chm Lab Pty Wales 1978–79, oppn def spokesman 1980; dep chm Cardiff Bay Devpt Corp (memb 1987–); *Recreations* most sports, reading; *Style*— The Rt Hon the Lord Brooks of Tremorfa; ✉ 46 Kennerleigh Road, Rumney, Cardiff CF3 9BJ (tel 029 2079 1848)

BROOKSBANK, David Wadsworth; MBE (1974); s of Henry Wadsworth Brooksbank (d 1973), of Harrow, and Clarice Hilda, *née* Sear, MBE (d 1990); *b* 26 March 1942; *Educ* Kings Sch Harrow; *m* 1966, Judith Mary, *née* Lammas; 1 s (John Robert b 1967), 1 da (Angela Mary b 1970); *Career* gen mangr of cargo British Caledonian Airways 1978–88, md Scan International Gp 1988–91, gen mangr of cargo Dan Air 1991–92, sr mktg dir Europe, Middle East and Africa Airmax Airlines 1992–97, chm East-West-Jet Ltd 1997–2004; *Recreations* music, cricket, country walks, ornithology; *Clubs* Aviation; *Style*— David Brooksbank, Esq, MBE; ✉ 57 The Close, Norwich, Norfolk NR1 4EH

BROOKSBANK, Sir (Edward) Nicholas; 3 Bt (UK 1919), of Healaugh Manor, Healaugh, W Riding of Yorks; Lord of the Manor of Healaugh; s of Lt-Col Sir (Edward) William Brooksbank, 2 Bt, TD, JP, DL (d 1983), and Ann, Lady Brooksbank; *b* 4 October 1944; *Educ* Eton; *m* 1970, Hon Emma Myrtle Mary Anne, o da of Baron Holderness, PC, DL (d 2002); 1 s (Florian Tom Charles b 1982), 1 da (Victoria Mary Grania b 1985); *Heir* s, Florian Brooksbank; *Career* Capt The Blues and Royals, ret; Christie's rep York 1974–97; *Style*— Sir Nicholas Brooksbank, Bt

BROOM, Prof Donald Maurice; s of Donald Edward Broom (d 1971), and Mavis Edith Rose, *née* Thompson (d 2002); *b* 14 July 1942; *Educ* Whitgift Sch, St Catharine's Coll Cambridge (MA, PhD, ScD); *m* 31 May 1971, Sally Elizabeth Mary, da of Thomas Edward Fisher (d 1969), of Ufton Nervet, Berks; 3 s (Oliver b 1973, Tom b 1976, Giles b 1981); *Career* lectr (later reader) Dept of Pure and Applied Zoology Univ of Reading 1967–86, Colleen Macleod prof of animal welfare Dept of Veterinary Med Univ of Cambridge 1986–, fell St Catharine's Coll Cambridge 1987– (pres 2001–04); visiting asst prof Dept of Zoology Univ of Calif 1969, visiting lectr Dept of Biology Univ of WI Trinidad 1972, visiting scientist Div of Animal Prodn Cwlth Sci and Industrial Res Orgn Perth 1983, memb NERC Ctee on Seals 1986–97, invited advsr Cncl of Euro Standing Ctee on Welfare of Animals Kept for Farming Purposes 1987–2000, chm Euro Union Scientific Veterinary Ctee (Animal Welfare) 1990–97, memb Euro Union Sci Ctee on Animal Health and Animal Welfare 1997–2003, vice-chm Euro Food Safety Authy Panel on Animal Health and Welfare 2003–, Euro Union rep on Quadripartite Working Gp on Humane Trapping Standard 1995–96; chm Orgn Int des Epizooties (OIE) Gp on Animal Welfare During Land Tport 2003–; memb: UK Miny of Agric Farm Animal Welfare Cncl 1991–99, UK Home Office Animal Procedures Ctee 1998–; hon res assoc Inst of Grassland and Environmental Res 1985–, tstee Farm Animal Care Tst 1986– (chm 1999–), hon treas Assoc for the Study of Animal Behaviour 1971–80 (memb Cncl 1971–83); pres Int Soc for Applied Ethology 1987–89 (memb Cncl 1981–84, vice-pres

1986–87 and 1989–91); memb: Int Ethological Ctee 1976–79, Br Tst for Ornithology, Br Soc of Animal Sci, Assoc of Veterinary Teachers and Res Workers, Int Soc of Anthrozoology; pres St Catharine's Soc 2005–06 (vice-pres 2004–05 and 2006–07), vice-pres Old Whitgiftian Assoc 2000; George Fleming prize for best paper in Br Veterinary Jl 1990, Br Soc of Animal Sci/RSPCA Award for innovative devpts in animal welfare 2001, Eurogroup Medal for work to improve the welfare of animals 2001, RSPCA Michael Kay Award for servs to animal welfare in Europe 2007; hon coll fell Myerscough Coll Univ of Central Lancs 1999, Hon DSc De Montfort Univ 2000; prof (hc) Univ of Salvador Argentina 2004, Hon Dr Norwegian Univ of Life Sciences 2005; hon socio corrispondanti Accademia Peloritana di Pericolanti Messina 2005; FIBiol 1986, FZS (memb Animal Welfare Ctee 1986–95); *Books* Birds and their Behaviour (1977), Biology of Behaviour (1981), Encyclopaedia of Domestic Animals (ed, with P A Messent, 1986), Farmed Animals (ed, 1986), Farm Animal Behaviour and Welfare (with A F Fraser, 1990), Stress and Animal Welfare (with K G Johnson, 1993), Coping with Challenge: Welfare in Animals Including Humans (ed, 2001), The Evolution of Morality and Religion (2003), Domestic Animal Behaviour and Welfare (with A F Fraser, 2007); *Recreations* squash, modern pentathlon, ornithology; *Clubs* Hawks' (Cambridge); *Style—* Prof Donald Broom; ✉ Department of Veterinary Medicine, University of Cambridge, Madingley Road, Cambridge CB3 0ES; St Catharine's College, Cambridge CB2 1RL (tel 01223 337697, fax 01223 337610, e-mail dmb16@cam.ac.uk, website www.vet.cam.ac.uk/research/welfare/)

BROOM, Douglas Philip; s of late George Edward Shirley Broom, of Haxey, Lincs, and late Joyce Elizabeth, *née* Williams; *b* 27 December 1956; *Educ* Holy Trinity Sch Crawley, Highbury Coll Portsmouth (NCTJ course); *m* 20 Oct 1979, Susan Mary, da of Kenneth Dudley, of Harrold, Beds; 1 s (Thomas Edward b 16 Feb 1989), 1 da (Sophia Elizabeth b 22 July 1991); *Career* The News Portsmouth 1976–79 (joined as trainee, later dist chief reporter), dep news ed Bury Free Press Bury St Edmunds 1979–80, chief law courts reporter Cambridge Evening News 1980–82, law courts reporter Press Assoc 1982–86 (educn correspondent 1986–88); The Times: educn reporter 1988–90, local govt correspondent 1990–92, contrib 1992–; ed Public Finance magazine 1993–97 (asst ed 1992); VNU Business Pubns: ed Accountancy Age 1997–99, ed dir Business and Finance 1999–2000, gen mangr Learned Information (Europe) Ltd 2000–01, publisher Business and Finance 2001–02; dir CCH Magazines 2002–; memb: High Court Journalists' Assoc 1982–86 (chm 1985–86), Educn Correspondents' Gp 1986–90, Ctee Br Soc of Magazine Eds 1997–2000; FRSA 1995; *Recreations* reading, walking, opera; *Style—* Douglas Broom, Esq; ✉ Wolters Kluwer (UK) Ltd, 145 London Road, Kingston upon Thames, Surrey KT2 6SR (tel 020 8247 1372, e-mail douglas.broom@cch.co.uk)

BROOME, Prof John; s of Richard Broome (d 1986), of Corfe Castle, Dorset, and Tamsin, *née* Luckham (d 1994); *b* 17 May 1947; *Educ* Trinity Hall Cambridge (BA), MIT (PhD), Bedford Coll London (MA); *m* 1970, Ann, da of Herbert Rowland; 1 da (Kitty b 1975), 1 s (Richard b 1978); *Career* lectr in economics Birkbeck Coll London 1972–78; Univ of Bristol: reader 1979–91, prof of economics 1991–95; prof of philosophy Univ of St Andrews 1996–2000, White's prof of moral philosophy Univ of Oxford 2000–; FRSE 1999, FBA 2000; *Books* The Microeconomics of Capitalism (1983), Weighing Goods: Equality, Uncertainty and Time (1991), Counting the Cost of Global Warming (1992), Ethics out of Economics (1999), Weighing Lives (2004); *Recreations* sailing; *Style—* Prof John Broome; ✉ Corpus Christi College, Oxford OX1 4JF (tel 01865 276731, e-mail john.broome@philosophy.ox.ac.uk)

BROOMFIELD, Graham Martin; s of Herbert Broomfield (d 1989), of W Sussex, and Muriel Joyce, *née* Robinson (d 1994); *b* 12 February 1945; *Educ* Dorking County GS, Chelsea Coll London (BSc); *m* 5 Oct 1974, Wai Yu (Miranda), da of Leung Fu Ping (d 1972); 1 s (Lee b 1978), 1 da (Amy b 1981); *Career* CA; Charles Comins & Co (now Baker Tilly) 1967–72, Peat Marwick Mitchell & Co (now KPMG) 1972–76, Warner Communications Inc (now AOL Time Warner) 1977–81, Prager & Fenton 1981–87, Broomfield & Co 1983–; govr St Clements & St James Sch; *Recreations* politics, history; *Style—* Graham M Broomfield, Esq; ✉ 17 Cromwell Grove, London W6 7RQ (tel 020 7603 4487, fax 020 7371 4908, e-mail 106051.1243@compuserve.com)

BROOMFIELD, Nicholas (Nick); *b* 30 January 1948, London; *Educ* Univ of Cardiff, Univ of Essex, Nat Film Sch; *Partner* Joan Churchill; 1 s; *Career* documentary filmmaker; *Films* Who Cares 1970, Proud to Be British 1973, Behind the Rent Strike 1974, Whittingham 1975, Juvenile Liaison 1976, Fort Augustus 1976, Marriage Guidance 1977, Tattoed Tears 1978, Soldier Girls 1980, Chicken Ranch 1982, Lily Tomlin 1986, Driving Me Crazy 1988, Diamond Skulls 1989, Juvenile Liaison 2 1990, The Leader, His Driver, The Driver's Wife 1990, Monster in a Box 1991, Too White For Me 1992, Aileen Wuornos: The Selling of a Serial Killer 1993, Tracking Down Maggie 1994, Heidi Fleiss: Hollywood Madam 1995, Fetishes 1996, Kurt & Courtney 1997, Biggie and Tupac 2002, Aileen: Life and Death of a Serial Killer 2003, His Big White Self 2006, Ghosts 2007; *Awards* Robert Flaherty Award BAFTA, Prix Italia, Dupont Columbia Award For Outstanding Journalism, Peabody Award, RTS Award, John Grierson Award, The Hague Peace Prize, Chris Award, Amnesty Int Award DOEN, Special Jury Award Melbourne Film Festival; First Prize: Sundance Film Festival, US Film Festival, Chicago Film Festival, Festival of Mannheim, Fesitval di Popoli; *Style—* Nick Broomfield, Esq; ✉ Lafayette Films, PO Box 5048, Santa Monica, CA 90409, USA (e-mail nick@nickbroomfield.com)

BROOMFIELD, Sir Nigel Hugh Robert Allen; KCMG (1993, CMG 1986); s of Col Arthur Allen Broomfield, OBE, MC (d 1970), and Ruth Sheilagh, *née* Anderson (d 1974); *b* 19 March 1937; *Educ* Haileybury, Trinity Coll Cambridge (BA); *m* 8 June 1963, Valerie, da of G Fenton, of Noirmont, Jersey; 2 s (Alexander Allen b 29 April 1970, Nicholas Richard Allen b 2 Oct 1976); *Career* Maj 17/21 Lancers 1958–68; first sec: FCO 1969, Bonn 1970, Moscow 1973, FCO 1975; RCDS 1978, cnsllr and head of Chancery BMG Berlin 1979, head E Euro and Soviet Dept FCO 1981, dep high cmmr New Delhi 1986, ambass to GDR E Berlin 1988, dep under sec of state (defence) FCO 1990; ambass to Germany 1993–97; advsr Andersen 1997–2001, chm Yatra Ltd 2007–, conslt Swilts Gp plc 2007–; dir Ditchley Fndn 1999–2004, chm Leonard Cheshire 2005–; Br Amateur Squash Champion 1957–58; *Recreations* reading, music, sport; *Clubs* MCC, RAC, All England Lawn Tennis; *Style—* Sir Nigel Broomfield, KCMG

BROTHERHOOD, James; s of Frederick Arthur Brotherhood (d 1974), and Isabel, *née* Bradley (d 1991); *b* 5 June 1946; *Educ* King's Sch Chester; *m* 1, 2 Aug 1969, Susan Elizabeth, da of Thomas Ian Jodrell Toler, of Cheshire; 3 s (Jonathan Alexander Jodrell b 1973, Philip Richard Thomas b 1975, Michael Rupert Benjamin b 1981), 2 da (Katherine Mary b 1978, Eleanor Elizabeth b 1984); *m* 2, 11 March 1989, Rosalind Ann, da of late Dr Robert Alan Blyth, of Cheshire; 1 da (Emily Victoria b 1991); *Career* architect; fndr James Brotherhood & Associates; pres Cheshire Soc of Architects 1978–80, chm NW Region RIBA 1983; RIBA: memb ctee 1982, prof practice external examiner; pres Chester Assoc of Old King's Scholars 1998; fndr Chester Heritage Trust 1997; Dip Arch (Hons) 1973, RIBA 1974, AABC 1999; *Recreations* shooting, fishing; *Clubs* City (Chester), Artist's Liverpool, Pitt; *Style—* James Brotherhood, Esq; ✉ James Brotherhood & Associates, Golly Farm, Golly, Burton, Rossett, Wrexham LL12 0AL (tel 01244 579000, fax 01244 571133, e-mail info@jba-architects.co.uk)

BROTHERSTON, Lez; s of Leslie Brotherston, of Liverpool, and Irene, *née* Richardson; *b* 6 October 1961; *Educ* Prescot GS, St Helens Sch of Art, Central Sch of Art and Design (BA); *Career* set and costume designer; artistic assoc New Adventures Theatre; *Theatre* for Greenwich Theatre: Northanger Abbey, The Last Romantics, Handling Bach, The Sisters Rosensweig (also Old Vic), Falling over England, Under the Stars, The Prisoner of Zenda, Schippel the Plumber (also Edinburgh Festival), The Government Inspector, Side by Side by Sondheim; for Actors' Touring Co: No Way Out, The Maids, The Triumph of Love, Hamlet, Princess Ivona, Dr Faustus, Heaven Bent Hellbound; for Oldham Coliseum: Wuthering Heights, Love on the Dole; other prodns incl: Hindle Wakes (Manchester Royal Exchange), Rosencrantz and Guildenstern are Dead (RNT), Enjoy (Nottingham Playhouse), Neville's Island (Apollo West End), The Schoolmistress (Chichester Festival Theatre), Jane Eyre (Playhouse West End), Comedians (West Yorkshire Playhouse and Lyric Hammersmith), Jane Eyre (Theatr Clwyd and Thorndike), Mystery Plays (Coventry Belgrade), The School for Wives (Belfast Arts), Jane Eyre (Derby Playhouse), A Midsummer Night's Dream (Royal Exchange), Speedking (Liverpool Playhouse), The Daughter-In-Law (Bristol Old Vic), The Little Foxes (Leeds Playhouse), The Beaux Stratagem (Stephen Joseph Theatre), The Man of Mode (Swan Theatre Worcester), Pinocchio Boys (Paines Plough), The Eleventh Commandment (Hampstead), Alarms & Excursions (Gielgud Theatre), Hindle Wakes (Royal Exchange), Nude With Violin (Royal Exchange), A Midsummer Night's Dream (Albery), French & Saunders Live (UK tour), Little Foxes (Donmar Warehouse), Victoria Wood At It Again (Royal Albert Hall), Bedroom Farce (Aldwych), Design for Living (Manchester Royal Exchange), Text Without Words (RNT), The Crucible (Sheffield Crucible), The Miracle Worker (Charlotte Rep Theatre), The Dark (Donmar Warehouse), Tonight's the Night (Victoria Palace Theatre), The Crucible (Sheffield Crucible), Play Without Words (RNT), Playing With Fire (RNT); *Musicals* incl: Camelot (BOC Covent Garden Festival), Face (Queen's Theatre Hornchurch and tour), Maria Friedman by Special Arrangement (Donmar Warehouse), Annie (Liverpool Playhouse), Cabaret (Sheffield Crucible), Closer than Ever (Manchester Library Theatre), High Society (West Yorkshire Playhouse), Songbook (Watermill Newbury), Spend Spend Spend (Picadilly Theatre West End and UK tour), My One and Only (UK premiere Chichester Festival Theatre, also at Piccadilly Theatre), Tonight's the Night (Phil McIntyre Prodns), Acorn Antiques (Haymarket London), Far Pavillions (Shaftesbury Theatre London), The Pirate Queen (The Point Dublin); *Dance* for Northern Ballet Theatre: Dracula, The Brontës, A Christmas Carol (also BBC), Swan Lake, Romeo and Juliet (also BBC), Strange Meeting, Giselle, Hunchback of Notre Dame, Carmen; for Adventures in Motion Pictures: Swan Lake (Olivier Award Best New Dance Prodn, London, LA and Broadway), Highland Fling, Cinderella (Piccadilly and LA), The Car Man (Old Vic and UK tour); other credits incl: Grey Matter (Ballet Rambert), Just Scratchin the Surface and Night Life (Scottish Ballet), Bounce (Stockholm, Sweden and The Roundhouse, London), 6 Faces (K Ballet Japan), Edqard Scissorhands (New Adventures Theatre), Soldiers Tale (ROH), wroter, dir and designer Les Liasons Dangereuses (Tokyo and Sadlers Wells); *Opera* for Opera North: Le Roi Malgre Lui, Madam Butterfly (set only), Masquerade, The Flying Dutchman; for Buxton Festival Opera: The Impresario, Il Sogno Di Scipione, David and Goliath, Sir Gawain and the Green Knight, Maria Padilla; for Opera Zuid: Hänsel and Gretel, A Cunning Little Vixon, Ariadne Auf Naxos, Werther; for Hong Kong Arts Festival: Der Rosenkavalier, The Marriage of Figaro; for Camden Festival: Silver Lake, The Tsar has his Photograph Taken, The Protagonists; other prodns incl: Falstaff (Teatro Bellini, Sicily and Copenhagan), Dido and Aeneas/Venus and Adonis (Festwochen der Alten Musik, Innsbruck & De Vlaamse Opera, Antwerp), Cornet Christoph Rilke's Song of Love and Death (Glyndebourne Touring Opera), L'Italiana in Algeri (Dublin Grand Opera), Rigoletto (Opera Northern Ireland), Don Giovanni (Opera 80), Hänsel and Gretel (set only, WNO), Die Fledermaus (Opera East), La Traviata (Phoenix Opera), Don Giovanni (Surrey Opera), Hänsel and Gretel (Opera Northern Ireland), La Somnambula (Teatro Municipale, Rio de Janeiro); *Film* Swan Lake (AMP/BBC/NVC), Letter to Brezhnev (Palace Pictures), The Car Man (AMP/Channel 4); *Costume and Props* for BBC: Dr Who, The Cleopatras, Richard III, Henry VI (parts I, II and III), King Lear, Antony and Cleopatra, The Merchant of Venice; for ITV: Deceptions (mini-series), The Far Pavilions; other prodns incl: Highlander, Bullshot Drummond, Brazil, Young Sherlock and the Pyramid of Fear, The Last Emperor; *Awards* winner Outstanding Achievement in Dance Olivier Award for Cinderella (Piccadilly Theatre) 1998; Olivier Award nominations incl: Outstanding Achievement in Dance (for Northern Ballet Theatre Season at the Royalty Theatre), Best Set Design (for Neville's Island), Best Set Design (for Spend Spend Spend), Best Design (for Play Without Words); Manchester Evening News and Br Regional Theatre nomination for Best Designer (for Hindle Wakes), Outstanding Set and Costume Design (for Little Foxes); for Swan Lake on Broadway: Drama Desk Award for Best Costume Design, Drama Desk Award for Best Set Design for a Musical, Outer Critic Circle Award for Best Costume Design, Tony Award for Best Costume Design; Drama Critics Circle Award for Outstanding Costume Design (for Cinderella, LA), Critics Circle Dance Award for Achievement in Design, Drama Desk Nomination for Best Set and Costumes (for Play Without Words NY); *Style—* Lez Brotherston, Esq; ✉ c/o Cassie Mayer Ltd, 5 Old Garden House, The Lanterns, Bridge Lane, London SW11 3AD

BROUCHER, David Stuart; s of late Clifford Broucher, of Ewenny, Glamorgan, and Betty Elma, *née* Jordan; *b* 5 October 1944; *Educ* Manchester Grammar, Trinity Hall Cambridge (BA); *m* 25 Nov 1971, Marion Monika, da of late Mr Wilkinson Gill, of Stagshaw, Northumberland; 1 s (Nicholas David b 1972); *Career* Foreign Office 1966–68, Br Mil Govt Berlin 1968–72, Cabinet Office 1972–75, Br Embassy Prague 1975–78, FCO 1978–83, UK perm rep to the EC 1983–85, cnsllr Jakarta 1985–89, cnsllr (economic) Bonn 1989–93, FCO 1994–97, ambass to Czech Republic 1997–2001, ambass to Conf on Disarmament 2001–04, personal advsr to pres of Romania 2005, visiting fell Univ of Southampton 2006–; *Recreations* golf, music, sailing; *Style—* David Broucher, Esq

BROUGH, Paul; s of Douglas Brough of London, and Liese Cattle, *née* Banks; *b* 15 July 1963, London; *Educ* Dulwich Coll, RCM, St Michael's Coll Tenbury, Magdalen Coll Oxford (MA, Mackinnon scholar), Royal Acad of Music (Henry Wood scholar); *Career* freelance choral orchestral and operatic conductor 1986–, conductor The Hanover Band 2004– (princ conductor 2007, projects incl Mozart's World, Imperial Vienna and The Genius of Mozart, concert at Cadogan Hall London and Haydnfestpiele Eisenstadt), conducting tutor and acad studies lectr Royal Acad of Music 2004–, dir of music All Saints Margaret St London 2004–, various BBC Radio and TV broadcasts; Boult Mem Prize 1986, Ernest Read Prize 1997; ARAM 2007; *Recreations* friends, solitude; *Style—* Paul Brough, Esq; ✉ website www.paulbrough.com

BROUGHAM, Hon David Peter; s of 4 Baron Brougham and Vaux (d 1967); *b* 22 August 1940; *Educ* Sedbergh; *m* 1, 1969, Moussie Christina Margareta Hallström, da of Sven Hörnblad, of Stockholm, Sweden; 1 s (Henry b 1971); *m* 2, 1977, Caroline Susan, only da of Lt-Col James Michael Heigham Royce Tomkin, MC, of Wissett, Suffolk, by his w Margaret Elinor, da of Sir Charles Henry Napier Bunbury, 11 B, and former w of Julian Dixon; 1 s (Oliver b 1978); *Career* dir Standard Chartered plc 1993–98 (joined as head of credit 1989), responsible for banking activities in Europe, America, Africa, ME and S Asia; non-exec dir: Asia Pacific Debt Recovery Co Hong Kong, Alliance and Leicester plc, Hamden Holdings plc, Matrix e-ventures Fund VCT plc; *Style—* The Hon David Brougham; ✉ 3 Chancellor House, Hyde Park Gate, London SW7 5DQ (tel and fax 020 7589 1634)

BROUGHAM AND VAUX, 5 Baron (UK 1860); Michael John Brougham; CBE (1995); s of 4 Baron (d 1967) by his 2 w, Jean (d 1992), da of late Brig-Gen Gilbert Follett, DSO, MVO, and Lady Mildred, *née* Murray (d 1972), da of 7 Earl of Dunmore, DL; *b* 2 August 1938; *Educ* Lycée Jaccard Lausanne, Millfield, Northampton Inst of Agric; *m* 1, 1963 (m

B

dis 1968), Olivia Susan (d 1986), da of Rear Adm Gordon Thomas Seccombe Gray, DSC (d 1997); 1 da; m 2, 1969 (m dis 1981), Catherine (who m 1981 Rupert Edward Odo Russell, gs of Sir Odo Russell, KCMG, KCVO, CB, himself 2 s of 1 Baron Ampthill), da of William Gulliver (d 1967); 1 s; *Heir* s, Hon Charles Brougham; *Career* Parly conslt and co dir; pres RoSPA 1986–89; former chm Tax Payers' Soc; a dep chm House of Lords 1993–, a dep speaker House of Lords 1995–; memb Select Ctee on House of Lords Officers 1997; memb Exec Gp Assoc of Cons Peers 1991–98 (dep chm 1998–2007); chm European Secure Vehicle Alliance (ESVA) 1993–; pres: Nat Health and Safety Gps Cncl 1994, London Occupational Health Safety and Hygiene Gp 2000; *Recreations* rugger, tennis, photography; *Style—* The Rt Hon the Lord Brougham and Vaux, CBE; ✉ 11 Westminster Gardens, Marsham Street, London SW1P 4JA

BROUGHTON, Sir David Delves; 13 Bt (E 1660), of Broughton, Staffs; s of Lt Cdr Peter John Delves Broughton, RN (d 1963), and his 1 w, Nancy Rosemary, *née* Paterson; suc kinsman, Sir (Evelyn) Delves Broughton, 12 Bt (d 1993); *b* 7 May 1942; *m* 1969, Diane, da of late Ronald Lindsay Nicol, of Victoria, Aust; (by Hildegard Weitzel) 1 da (Jennifer Zoë Weitzel b 1977); *Heir* half-bro, Geoffrey Delves Broughton; *Style—* Sir David Broughton, Bt; ✉ 31 Mayfield Court, Sandy, Bedfordshire SG19 1NF (tel 01767 691750, e-mail davebro@madasafish.com)

BROUGHTON, Hon James Henry Ailwyn; s and h of 3 Baron Fairhaven, JP; *b* 25 May 1963; *Educ* Harrow; *m* 22 March 1990, Sarah Olivia, da of Harold Digby Fitzgerald Creighton; 2 da (Sophie Rose b 30 April 1992, Emily Patricia b 15 May 1995), 1 s (George Ailwyn James b 17 March 1997); *Career* Capt Blues and Royals 1984–94; Baring Asset Management Ltd 1994–97, currently owner and mangr Barton Stud; *Recreations* racing, gardening, shooting; *Style—* The Hon James Broughton; ✉ Barton Stud, Great Barton, Bury St Edmunds, Suffolk IP31 2SH (tel 01284 787226, fax 01284 787231)

BROUGHTON, Martin Faulkner; *b* 1947; *Educ* Westminster City GS; *m* 1974, Jocelyn Mary, *née* Rodgers; 1 s, 1 da; *Career* British American Tobacco plc: joined 1971, fin dir BAT Industries plc 1988–92, chm Wiggins Teape Gp 1989–90, chm Eagle Star 1992–93, gp chief exec and dep chm 1993–98, chm 1998–2004; chm British Airways plc 2004– (non-exec dir 2000–); non-exec dir Whitbread plc 1993–2000; pres CBI 2007–; memb: Takeover Panel 1996–2000, Fin Reporting Cncl 1998–2004; chm British Horseracing Bd 2004–07 (ind dir 2000–07); co-chm TransAtlantic Business Dialogue 2006–; FCA; *Recreations* theatre, golf, horseracing; *Clubs* Tandridge Golf; *Style—* Martin Broughton, Esq; ✉ British Airways plc, Waterside, PO Box 365, Harmondsworth, Middlesex UB7 0GB

BROUGHTON, Dr Peter; s of Thomas Frederick Broughton (d 1983), of Skipton, and Mary Theodosia, *née* Bracewell (d 1993); *b* 8 September 1944; *Educ* Univ of Manchester (BSc, PhD); *m* Aug 1968, Janet Mary, da of Ronald George Silveston (d 1996); 2 s (Jonathan b 3 May 1971, Nicholas b 8 Jan 1974); *Career* research student then research asst in structural engrg Univ of Manchester 1966–71, structural engrg surveyor Lloyds Register of Shipping 1971–74, ptnr subsid of Campbell Reith and Partners (chartered engrs) 1974–75, soils/structural engr Burmah Oil Trading Ltd 1975–76, sr soils/structural engr rising to supervising structural engr British National Oil Corporation 1977–79; Phillips Petroleum Co: sr structural engr UK Div 1979–82, civil engrg supervisor UK Div 1982–86, princ project engr and co rep (for Ekofisk Protective Barrier Project) Norway Div 1986–90, princ project engr and co rep then engrg and procurement mangr UK Div 1990–93, engrg and construction project mangr for sub-structures Norway Div 1994–98, Maureen Platform refloat and decommissioning project mangr UK Div 1998–2003; conslt to Peter Fraenkel and Ptnrs Ltd 2003–, assoc to Gaffney Cline and Assocs Ltd 2007–; visiting prof Dept of Civil Engrg Imperial Coll London 1991–2005, Royal Acad of Engrg visiting prof Dept of Engrg Sci Univ of Oxford 2004–07; CEng, FICE, FIMarEST, FIStructE, FRINA, FREng 1996; *Awards* Special Award Instn of Structural Engrs 1990, Stanley Gray Award Inst of Marine Engrg, Sci and Technol 1992, George Stephenson Medal ICE 1993, Bill Curtin Medal ICE 1997, Overseas Premium ICE 1998, David Hislop Award ICE 1999, Contribution to Institution Activity Award ICE 2002; *Publications* The Ekofisk Protective Barrier (1992), The Analysis of Cable and Catenary Structures (1994), The Effects of Subsidence on the Steel Jacket and Piled Foundation Design for the Ekofisk 2/4X and 2/4J Platforms (1996), Challenges of Subsidence at the Norwegian Ekofisk Oil Field (Royal Soc of Edinburgh/Royal Acad of Engrg lectr, 1998), Steel Jacket Structures for the New Ekofisk Complex in the North Sea (1998), The Removal of the Maureen Steel Gravity Platform (1999), Decommissioning of the Maureen Oil Platform (2000), Foundation Design for the Refloat of the Maureen Steel Gravity Platform (2002), Refloating the Maureen Platform (2002); also author of numerous other pubns; *Recreations* gardening, walking, swimming, trout fishing; *Style—* Dr Peter Broughton, FREng; ✉ Peter Fraental and Partners Ltd, South House, 21–37 South Street, Dorking, Surrey RH4 2JZ

BROWETT, John Peter; s of Peter Harry James Browett, and Florence Margaret, *née* Kingdom; *b* 12 June 1946; *Educ* Wyggeston Boys' GS Leicester, Bart's Med Coll London; *m* 6 Sept 1969, Penelope Anne, da of Alan Ross Land; 1 s (Oliver Peter Ross), 1 da (Deborah Louise); *Career* conslt orthopaedic surgn Bart's 1980–95, orthopaedic conslt to Tottenham Hotspur FC 1980–94, conslt orthopaedic and knee surgeon 95 Harley St and the Princess Grace Hosp; Freeman City of London 1988; Liveryman Worshipful Co of Barber Surgns 1989; memb: Br Assoc Surgery of the Knee, Br Orthopaedic Sports Trauma Assoc, Int Soc of Arthroscopy Knee Surgery and Orthopaedic Sports Med (ISAKOS), European Society of Sports, Knee Surgery & Arthroscopy (ESSKA); FRCS; *Recreations* skiing, wildlife, sailing; *Style—* John Browett, Esq; ✉ 101 Harley Street, London W1G 6AH (tel 020 7486 9323, fax 01707 876218)

BROWN, *see also:* Holden-Brown

BROWN, Prof Alice; da of Robert Wilson (d 1998), and Alice, *née* Morgan; *b* 30 September 1946; *Educ* Univ of Edinburgh (MA, PhD, Medal for Int Business, D P Heatley Prize); *m* 26 June 1965, Alan James Brown; 2 da (Julie Anne b 1968, Jill Doreen b 1971); *Career* temp lectr Univ of Stirling 1984–85, Univ of Edinburgh: temp lectr Univ of Edinburgh 1985–90, lectr in politics 1990–92, sr lectr Dept of Politics 1992, head Dept of Politics 1995, head Planning Unit 1996, prof of politics (personal chair) 1997–, co-dir Governance for Scotland Forum (now Inst of Governance) 1998–2002, vice-princ 1999–2002; Scottish public servs ombudsman 2002–; memb: Exec Political Studies Assoc 1996–99 (chair Sub-Ctee on Educn, memb Research Sub-Ctee), memb ESRC Politics, Economics, Geography (PEG) Virtual Reality Coll 1997–99, memb ESRC Evidence-Based Policy Ctee 2001; advsr to Standing Cmmn on the Scottish Economy 1987–89, advsr Scottish Constitutional Convention on Electoral Reform 1991, advsr to min for Women's Issues Scottish Office 1997–99, ind advsr to Lab Pty as memb Scottish Parl Selections Bd 1998–99; cmmr Scottish Constitutional Cmmn 1993–94 (chair Sub-Ctee on Gender Equality), convenor Scottish Gender Research Network 1997–2001; chair: Cmmn on Equal Opportunities Policy for a Scottish Parl 1996–97, Community Planning Taskforce 2000–02; memb Bd: Scottish Low Pay Unit 1992–95, John Wheatley Centre (Centre for Scottish Public Policy) 1992–2002, Lothian Trade Union Community Resource Centre 1993–98; memb: Advsy Gp Equal Opportunities Cmmn (EOC) in Scotland 1995–2002, Cmmn on Quangos 1996–97, 1996–97, Cross-Pty Consultative Steering Gp Scottish Office 1997–98, Acadmic Advsy Panel Hansard Soc 1998–2000, Scottish Ctee Br Cncl 1998–2002, Scottish HE Funding Cncl (SHEFC) 1998–2002 (chair Mergers Ctee 2000–02), Hansard Soc Cmmn on the Scrutiny Role of Parl 1999–2001, Neill Ctee on Standards in Public Life (now Wicks Ctee) 1999–2001 and 2001–03, Hansard Soc Scotland 2000–02, Public Sector Taskforce 2001–03, memb Lay Advsy Gp RCPEd 2003–, memb Advsy Bd Cmmn for Racial Equality in Scotland 2003–; academic memb Women's Issues Research Advsy Gp Scottish Exec 1998–2001; fndr memb: Engender (women's research and campaigning gp) 1991, Scottish Women's Co-ordination Gp 1992; co-ed The Scottish Government Yearbook 1989–91, asst ed Scottish Affairs 1992–2002; memb Editorial Bd: Edinburgh Univ Press 1992–94 and 1998, Scotland Forum 1998–99; AcSS, FRSE 2002, memb CIPFA 2004; *Publications* The MSC in Scotland (jt ed and contrib, 1989), Restructuring Education in Ireland (jtly, 1993), A Major Crisis: The Politics of Economic Policy in Britain in the 1990s (jtly, 1996), Politics and Society in Scotland (jtly, 1996), Politics and Society in Scotland (jtly 2 edn, 1998), The Scottish Electorate (jtly, 1999), New Scotland, New Politics (jtly, 2001), The Changing Politics of Gender Equality in Britain (jt ed, 2002); author of numerous book chapters, articles, papers and reports; *Recreations* reading, music, cooking; *Style—* Prof Alice Brown; ✉ Scottish Public Services Ombudsman, 4 Melville Street, Edinburgh EH3 7NS

BROWN, Rev Dr (James) Alistair; *b* 9 September 1950; *Educ* Bell Baxter Sr HS Cupar, Edinburgh Coll of Commerce (Journalism course), Univ of Edinburgh (BA, BD, PhD); *m* Alison; 4 c; *Career* reporter and sub-ed The Scotsman and Evening News (Glasgow and Edinburgh) 1967–70 (pt/t sub-ed Evening News while at univ 1970–78), clerical worker local govt 1974–75, student asst pastor Craigmillar Baptist Centre Edinburgh 1975–78; pastor: Livingston Baptist Church - Dedridge Congregation 1981–86 (pt/t pastor 1979–81), Gerrard Street Baptist Church Aberdeen 1986–96; gen dir Baptist Missionary Society Nov 1996–; accredited min Baptist Union of Scot (former memb Cncl and Exec); sometime pt/t lectr in New Testament studies Univs of Edinburgh and Aberdeen, former memb Scot Cncl of Interserve, former tstee Aberdeen Sch of Christian Studies, former baptist chaplain Univ of Aberdeen; *Books* To Illustrate That (1989), Late Night Extra (1991), Save Sam (1993), Worship: Adoration and Action (contrib, 1993), The Runaway (1994), Near Christianity (1996), I Believe in Mission (1997); *Recreations* golf, photography, hill walking, advanced driving and motorcycling, lapidary; *Style—* Rev Dr Alistair Brown; ✉ BMS World Mission, Baptist House, PO Box 49, 129 Broadway, Didcot, Oxfordshire OX11 8XA (tel 01235 517700, fax 01235 517601)

BROWN, Andrew William; s of Harry Eugene Brown (d 1971), of Ballygarvan House, Ballygarvan, Co Cork, and Geraldine, *née* O'Leary; *b* 3 March 1946; *Educ* St Edmund's Coll Ware; *m* Shelby Ann, *née* Hill; *Career* J Walter Thompson Co Ltd: joined 1965, account planner 1973–76, head of trg 1980–86, bd dir 1982–93, head of account mgmnt 1986–88, gp dir 1987–93; DG Advertising Assoc 1993–; memb Cncl IPA 1991–93 (memb Trg Ctee 1980–93); chm: CAM Fndn 1994–96, Committee of Advtg Practice (CAP) 1999–; dir Advtg Standards Bd of Finance (ASBOF) 1993–; *Recreations* reading, theatre, sport; *Clubs* Reform, MCC, XL; *Style—* Andrew Brown, Esq; ✉ Advertising Association, Abford House, 15 Wilton Road, London SW1V 1NJ (tel 020 7828 2771, fax 020 7931 0376)

BROWN, Anthony Nigel; s of Sydney Brown, of Birmingham, and Gene, *née* Laitner; *b* 12 June 1955; *Educ* Clifton, Univ of Manchester (LLB); *m* 16 April 1989, Gail Denise, da of Dr Nathaniel Rifkind, of Glasgow; 2 s (Joshua Jack b 10 April 1991, Nathan Avi b 15 Jan 2000), 1 da (Sasha Jade b 14 Oct 1993); *Career* admitted slr 1980; voluntary asst Artlaw 1978–81, asst slr Janners 1980–84; fndr and md: Connaught Brown 1984–, The Affordable Art Company Ltd 1991–99; exhibitions: Northern Spirit 1986, Georges d'Espagnat Retrospective 1995, Aspects of Post-Impressionism 2000, Raoul Dufy 2001, The Year of the Horse 2002, Henry Moore: Mother and Child 2003; organised Artlaw auction Royal Acad 1981 and Dulwich Art '90; memb: Educn Advsy Ctee Dulwich Art Gallery, Soc of London Art Dealers; chm Br Friends of the Art Museums Israel; FRSA; *Recreations* looking at art, reading, swimming; *Clubs* RAC; *Style—* Anthony Brown, Esq; ✉ Connaught Brown, 2 Albemarle Street, London W1X 3HF (tel 020 7408 0362, fax 020 7495 3137, e-mail art@connaughtbrown.co.uk)

BROWN, Prof Archibald Haworth (Archie); CMG (2005); s of Rev Alexander Douglas Brown (d 1979), of Darvel, Ayrshire, and Mary, *née* Yates (d 2006); *b* 10 May 1938; *Educ* Annan Acad, Dumfries Acad, City of Westminster Coll, LSE (BSc(Econ)), Univ of Oxford (MA); *m* 23 March 1963, Patricia Susan, da of Percival Walter Leslie Cornwell (d 1970); 1 da (Susan Woolford b 19 Jan 1969), 1 s (Alexander Douglas b 19 Oct 1971); *Career* Nat Serv 1956–58; reporter Annandale Herald and Annandale Observer 1954–56; lectr in politics Univ of Glasgow 1964–71 (Br Cncl exchange scholar Moscow Univ 1967–68); Univ of Oxford: lectr in Soviet institutions 1971–89, prof of politics 1989–2005, emeritus prof 2005; St Antony's Coll Oxford: faculty fell 1971–89, professorial fell 1989–2005 (emeritus fell 2005–), dir Russian and East Euro Centre, sub-warden 1995–97; distinguished visiting fell Kellog Inst for Int Studies Univ of Notre Dame 1998; visiting prof of political science: Yale Univ and Univ of Connecticut 1980, Columbia Univ NY 1985; visiting prof (Frank C Erwin Jr centennial chair of govt) Univ of Texas at Austin 1990–91; Henry L Stimson Lectures Yale Univ 1980, Arnold Wolfers Visiting Fell Lecture Yale Univ 1989, Lothian Euro Lecture Edinburgh 1999; memb Cncl SSEES 1992–98; memb: Political Studies Assoc, American Political Science Assoc, British Assoc of Slavonic and E Euro Studies, American Assoc for the Advancement of Slavonic Studies; foreign hon memb American Acad of Arts and Sciences 2003; elected founding AcSS 1999; FBA 1991; *Books* Soviet Politics and Political Science (1974), The Soviet Union Since the Fall of Khrushchev (co-ed and contrib, 1975, 2 edn 1978), Political Culture and Political Change in Communist States (co-ed and contrib, 1977, 2 edn 1979), Authority, Power and Policy in the USSR: Essays dedicated to Leonard Schapiro (co-ed and contrib, 1980), The Cambridge Encyclopedia of Russia and the Former Soviet Union (co-ed and contrib, 1982, 2 edn 1994), Soviet Policy for the 1980s (co-ed and contrib, 1982), Political Culture and Communist Studies (ed and contrib, 1984), Political Leadership in the Soviet Union (ed and contrib, 1989), The Soviet Union: A Biographical Dictionary (ed and contrib, 1990), New Thinking in Soviet Politics (ed and contrib, 1992), The Gorbachev Factor (1996, W J M Mackenzie Prize, Alec Nove Prize), The British Study of Politics in the Twentieth Century (co-ed and contrib, 1999), Contemporary Russian Politics: A Reader (ed and contrib, 2001), Gorbachev, Yeltsin, and Putin: Political Leadership in Russia's Transition (co-ed and contrib, 2001), The Demise of Marxism-Leninism in Russia (ed and contrib, 2004), Seven Years that Changed the World: Perestoika in Perspective (2007); *Recreations* novels and political memoirs, opera, ballet, watching cricket and football; *Style—* Prof Archie Brown, CMG, FBA; ✉ St Antony's College, Oxford OX2 6JF (e-mail archie.brown@sant.ox.ac.uk)

BROWN, Ben Robert; s of Antony Victor Brown, of Smarden, Kent, and Sheila Mary, *née* McCormack; *b* 26 May 1960; *Educ* Sutton Valence, Keble Coll Oxford (open scholar, BA), UC Cardiff (Dip Journalism); *m* Geraldine Anne, *née* Ryan; 1 da (Ella Olivia b 31 Oct 1992); *Career* journalist; reporter: Radio Clyde Glasgow 1982–83, Radio City Liverpool 1983–85, Radio London 1985–86, Independent Radio News 1986–88; BBC TV News: gen reporter 1988–90, foreign affrs corr 1990–91, Moscow corr 1991–94, gen corr then foreign affrs corr 1994–; major assignments incl: fall of the Berlin Wall, Gulf War (from Riyadh and Kuwait), collapse of the Soviet Union; *Books* All Necessary Means - Inside the Gulf War (with David Shukman, 1991); *Recreations* theatre, cinema, soccer, reading novels and biographies; *Style—* Ben Brown, Esq; ✉ BBC Television News, BBC Television Centre, Wood Lane, London W12 7RJ (tel 020 8743 8000)

BROWN, Brian Michael John; s of Arthur John Frederick Brown (d 1978), and Ethel Louise, *née* Redsull (d 1982); *b* 11 February 1937; *Educ* Sir Roger Manwoods GS Kent; *m* 1, 22 Feb 1960 (m dis 1989), Maureen Ivy Ticehurst (d 1994); 1 da (Rachel Suzanne b 17 March

1961), 2 s (Mark Stephen John b 12 March 1964, Timothy John Michael b 18 Jan 1967); m 2, 20 April 1989, Elizabeth Charlotte, da of Maj Thomas John Saywell; *Career* serv Royal Hampshire Regt 1955–57, Intelligence Corps 1957–58; Trustee Savings Bank: London 1959–60, South Eastern 1960–67; TSB Trust Company Ltd: mktg mangr 1967–71, gen mangr 1971–83, dir 1976, md 1983–88, chief exec 1988–91; conslt and lectr in bancassurance Zebu Consultants 1991–2007; chm: Protection & Investment Ltd 1999–2005 (dir 1999–), Conker Financial Servs Ltd 2004–; memb: Unit Trust Assoc Exec Ctee 1980–88, Lautro Selling Practices Ctee 1989–91, SIB Trg and Competence Panel 1992–94, Chartered Insurance Inst Accreditation Bd 1995–97; chm Andover Dist Community Health Care NHS Tst 1992–97; govr: Cricklade Coll Andover 1989–94 (chm 1991), Wherwell Primary Sch 1998–2003, King Alfred's Coll Winchester 1999–2004, UC Winchester 2004–05, Univ of Winchester 2005–; vice-pres: Deal Wanderers RFC 1972–2005, Deal and Betteshanger Rugby Club 2005–, Winchester and Dist Macmillan Servs Appeal 1986–98, Countess of Brecknock House Charitable Tst 1998–; FIMgt 1976, FCIB 1977; *Publications* Allfinanz Without Limits (1991); *Recreations* railways, coin and stamp collecting, walking, reading, concerts and theatre, eating out; *Style—* Brian Brown, Esq; ✉ The Granaries, Village Street, Chilbolton, Stockbridge, Hampshire SO20 6BE (tel 01264 860127)

BROWN, Adm Sir Brian Thomas; KCB (1989), CBE (1983); s of Walter Thomas Brown (d 1984), and Gladys, *née* Baddeley (d 1989); *b* 31 August 1934; *Educ* Peter Symonds Sch Winchester; *m* 1 Aug 1959, Veronica Mary Elizabeth, da of Wing Cdr J D Bird (d 1982); 2 s (Mark b 1960, Matthew b 1962); *Career* served RN 1952–91, RCDS 1983, Capt HMS Raleigh 1984–86, DGNPS 1986, Chief Naval S & S Offr 1986–88, DGNMT 1987–88, Second Sea Lord and Adm Pres RNC Greenwich 1988–91; non-exec dir: Cray Electronic Holdings 1991–96, Lorien plc 1996–2007; pres: Friends of RN Muesum and HMS Victory 1992–2002, Victory Services Assoc 1993–2002, Portsmouth Servs Fly Fishing Assoc 2006–; chm: King George's Fund for Sailors 1993–2003, Michael May Young Cricketers; Fndn 1993–, P E International 1995–98, Exec Ctee Nuffield Tst for the Forces of the Crown 1996–2003; churchwarden Froxfield with Privett 1999–; jt master Clinkard Meon Valley Beagles 2003–; Freeman City of London 1989, Liveryman Worshipful Co of Gardeners 1991; Hon DEd; FIPD, CIMgt; *Recreations* cricket, gardening, fishing; *Clubs* Army and Navy; *Style—* Adm Sir Brian Brown, KCB, CBE; ✉ The Old Dairy, Stoner Hill Road, Froxfield, Petersfield, Hampshire GU32 1DX (tel 01730 262041)

BROWN, Bryan Wyman; s of Lionel Bruce Brown (d 1967), and Rosina, *née* Puffet (d 1970); *b* 18 April 1947; *Educ* Cheney Sch Oxford, Oxford Sch of Art, Manchester Coll of Art and Design (DipAD, BA), INSEAD Business Sch Fontainebleau; *m* 1970, Elizabeth Margaret, da of Richard Arthur Mills (d 1994); 1 da (Polly b 1974), 2 s (Dominic b 1976, Peter b 1979); *Career* graphic designer Graphic Display Unit 1969–70, art dir McGougan Bowler Associates 1970, sr designer Christian Brann Ltd 1970–71, sr designer then chm Allied International Designers Ltd and dir AIDCOM International plc (chm Design Div) 1971–86, md and chm Marketplace Design Ltd 1987–2004 (projects incl consultancy and design for BAA, Cadbury, Lexus/Toyota, WH Smith); chm: Design Mgmnt Gp CSD 1986–92, Design Gp CBI 1986–90; memb: Design Bd RSA 1984–90, Consumer Mktg Affairs Ctee CBI 1986–92; dir: Design Business Assoc 1990–92, MOMA Oxford 2002–05; external examiner Oxford Brookes Univ 1997–2001 (formerly Northumbria and Kingston Univs); lectr: at numerous schs of art and design incl RCA and Eindhoven Sch of Design Holland 1974–, MBA Progs London and Manchester Business Schs 1979–86; memb Ct Oxford Brookes Univ; govr Cokethorpe Sch Oxon 1994–; memb Victorian Soc; FRSA 1981, FCSD 1979; *Books* The England of Henry Taunt (1973); *Recreations* 19th Century history, conservation, natural history, ornithology, game fishing, gardening and gardening design, walking, real and lawn tennis; *Clubs* D&AD (UK), Oxford Unicorns; *Style—* Bryan Brown, Esq; ✉ Clanfield House, 16 Park Crescent, Abingdon-on-Thames, Oxfordshire OX14 1DF (tel 01235 520278)

BROWN, Cedric Harold; s of late William Herbert Brown, and Constance Dorothy, *née* Frances; *b* 7 March 1935; *Educ* Sheffield, Rotherham and Derby Coll of Technol; *m* 1956, Joan Hendry; 1 s, 3 da; *Career* East Midlands Gas Bd: pupil gas distribution engr 1953–58, various engrg posts 1958–75; engr asst Tunbridge Wells Borough Cncl 1959–60, dir of engr E Midlands Gas 1975–78; British Gas Corporation: asst dir ops and dir construction 1978–79, dir Morecambe Bay Project 1980–87, regnl chm British Gas West Midlands 1987–89; British Gas plc: dir of exploration and prodn 1989–90, memb Bd and md 1989–91, sr md 1991–92, chief exec 1992–96; prop C B Consultants Ltd 1996–, chm Atlantic Caspian Resources plc 1999–, chm Intellipower 2003–; Freeman City of London 1989, Liveryman Worshipful Co of Engrs 1988; FREng 1990, CEng, FIGasE (pres 1996–), FICE; *Publications* author of various tech papers to professional bodies; *Recreations* sport, countryside, places of historic interest; *Style—* Cedric Brown, Esq, FREng; ✉ Atlantic Caspian Resources plc, Ternion Court, 264–268 Upper Fourth Street, Milton Keynes MK9 1DP

BROWN, Prof Charles Malcolm; s of Capt Charles Brown (d 1978), and Beatrice Lily, *née* Haddrick (d 1988); *b* 21 September 1941; *Educ* Houghton-Le-Spring GS, Univ of Birmingham (BSc, PhD, DSc); *m* 16 July 1966, Diane Mary, da of Joseph Bryant (d 1962); 3 da (Sara b 1969, Ann b 1971, Liz b 1976); *Career* lectr Univ of Newcastle upon Tyne 1966–73, sr lectr Univ of Dundee 1973–79; Heriot-Watt Univ: prof 1979–, head of Dept of Biological Sciences 1988–93, dean of science 1993–95, vice-princ 1995–; dir: S Marine Biological Assoc 1975–81, Bioscot Ltd 1982–86, Fermentech Ltd 1983–85; memb: Int Centre for Brewing and Distilling 1988–90, Microbiological Research Authy 1996–, Advsy Ctee on Novel Foods and Processes 1997–; FIBiol 1979, FRSE 1982, FIBrew 1993; *Books* Sediment Microbiology (jtly, 1981), Introduction to Biotechnology (jtly, 1987); *Recreations* music, walking, gardening; *Style—* Prof Charles Brown, FRSE; ✉ 19 Burnside Park, Balerno, Edinburgh EH14 7LY (tel 0131 449 7125); Department of Biological Sciences, Heriot-Watt University, Riccarton, Edinburgh EH14 4AS (tel 0131 451 3362, fax 0131 451 3009, e-mail c.m.brown@hw.ac.uk)

BROWN, Christina Hambley (Tina) (Lady Evans); CBE (2000); da of George Hambley Brown, and Bettina Iris Mary, *née* Kohr (d 1998); *b* 21 November 1953; *Educ* Univ of Oxford (MA); *m* 20 Aug 1981, Sir Harold Matthew Evans, s of Frederick Albert Evans (d 1982); 1 s (George Frederick Evans b 26 Jan 1986), 1 da (Isabel Harriet Evans b 22 Oct 1990); *Career* columnist Punch 1978, ed Tatler 1979–83; ed-in-chief: Vanity Fair 1984–92, The New Yorker 1992–98; chm Miramax/Talk Media 1998–, ed-in-chief Talk magazine 1998–2002; columnist: The Times 2002, Washington Post 2003–; Catherine Pakenham Prize Most Promising Female Journalist (Sunday Times) 1973, Young Journalist of the Year 1978, Advertising Age Magazine Editor of the Year Award 1988, USC Journalism Alumni Assoc Distinguished Achievement in Journalism Award 1994; Hon Dr London Inst 2001; *Books* Loose Talk (1979), Life as a Party (1983), Under the Bamboo Tree (play, 1973), Happy Yellow (play, 1977); *Style—* Ms Tina Brown, CBE; ✉ c/o Margaret Aro, Miramax /Talk Media, 118 West 20th Street, 3rd Floor, New York, NY 10011 USA

BROWN, Dr Christopher Paul Hadley; *b* 15 April 1948; *Educ* Merchant Taylors' Sch, St Catherine's Coll Oxford (MA, Dip Art History), Courtauld Inst (PhD); *m*; 2 c; *Career* National Gallery London: asst keeper 1971–79, dep keeper 1979, curator Dutch and Flemish 17th c paintings, chief curator 1989–98; undergraduate and postgrad teaching and external examiner Courtauld Inst and UCL; fell Netherlands Inst for Advanced Study in the Humanities and Social Scis Wassenaar 1993–94; lectures at: Univ of London, Univ of Cambridge, Univ of Oxford, Univ of Utrecht, Harvard Univ, Yale Univ, Princeton Univ, NY Inst of Fine Art; memb Ctee: Assoc of Art Historians 1978–81, Art Galls Assoc 1978–80; memb British Ctee of Comité Int d'Histoire de l'Art; chm: Art History Seminar Centre for Low Countries Studies; tstee Dulwich Picture Gall; dir Ashmolean Museum Oxford 1998–; *Books* Bruegel (1975), Dutch Painting (1976), Burgundy (co-author, 1977), Rembrandt - The Complete Paintings (2 vols, 1980), Carel Fabritius - Complete Edition with a Catalogue Raisonne (1981), A Chatelet - Early Dutch Painting (co-trans, 1981), Van Dyck (1982), Scenes of Everyday Life - Seventeenth-Century Dutch Genre Painting (1984), Anthony Van Dyck: Drawings (1991), Rubens's Landscapes (1996), Van Dyck 1599–1641 (with Hans Vlieghe, 1999); author of numerous exhbn catalogues and articles in The Times, TLS, Burlington Magazine, Apollo, Nat Gall Technical Bulletin and other jls; *Style—* Dr Christopher Brown; ✉ Ashmolean Museum, Beaumont Street, Oxford OX1 2PH (tel 01865 278005)

B

BROWN, Colin; s of George Wilfred Brown (d 1970), and Gladys Lilian, *née* Carter (d 1963); *b* 8 April 1950; *Educ* Burscough Secdy Sch, Wigan Tech Coll; *m* Dorothy Amanda Golding; *Career* municipal corr: Southport Visiter 1968–73, Sheffield Star 1973–78; political corr: Yorkshire Post 1978–79, The Guardian 1978–86, The Independent 1986–; political ed: Independent on Sunday 2000–02, Sunday Telegraph 2002–04; dep political ed The Independent 2004–; chm Parly Lobby Journalists 1999–2000; *Books* Fighting Talk: The Biography of John Prescott (1997); *Recreations* skiing, windsurfing; *Clubs* Ski Club of GB, Whitstable Yacht, RYA, Soho House; *Style—* Colin Brown, Esq; ✉ The Independent, 191 Marsh Wall, London E14 9RS (tel 020 7005 2000)

BROWN, Prof Colin Bertram; s of Prof Leslie Julius Brown (d 1981), of South Africa, and Adolfinna Anna, *née* Rose (d 1985); *b* 24 May 1942; *Educ* King David HS South Africa, Guy's Hosp Med Sch London (BSc, MB BS, MRCS, LRCP); *m* 1, Barbara Alice, *née* Fink; 2 s (Nicholas Daniel b 1966, Jason Peter b 1971); m 2, 22 Sept 1975, Jacquelynne Anne, *née* Baldwin; 2 da (Kate Victoria b 1978, Hannah Camilla Lester b 1982); *Career* res fell Harvard Med Sch 1974–75, sr registrar Guy's Hosp 1973–78, conslt renal physician Sheffield Kidney Inst and hon prof Univ of Sheffield 1979–, dir ML Laboratories plc 1997–2005; chm Public Cmmn of Peritoneal Dialysis; memb: Ctee on Renal Diseases RCP, Section on Renal Disease MRC, Int Soc of Nephrology, Euro Dialysis and Transplant Assoc, Int Soc of Peritoneal Dialysis, Registry Ctee Renal Assoc of GB (sec); inventor of Adept (for abdominal adhesion prevention); FRCP 1985; *Books* incl: Manual of Renal Disease (1984); contrib incl: Guy's Hospital Reports (1965), Lancet (1970), British Journal of Urology (1972), American Journal of Physiology (1977), Cornell Seminars in Nephrology (1978), Journal of Infection (1983), British Medical Journal (1984), Transplantation (1986), Bone (1981), Clinica Chimica Acta (1988), Nephron (1989), Kidney International (1990), Nephrology Dialysis and Transplantation (1995), American Journal of Kidney Disease (1999), Harrison's Textbook of Medicine On-Line (2000), Human Reproduction (2002), Nephron (2003), Transplantation (2004), Clinical Nephrology (2006); *Recreations* sailing, golf; *Style—* Prof C B Brown; ✉ Sheffield Kidney Institute, Regional Renal Unit, Northern General Hospital, University of Sheffield Medical School, Herries Road, Sheffield, South Yorkshire S5 7AU (tel 0114 271 5309, fax 0114 261 7397, e-mail cbbrown1@compuserve.com)

BROWN, Craig Edward Moncrieff; s of Edward Peter Moncrieff Brown (d 2001), of Duncton, W Sussex, and Hon Jennifer Mary, *née* Bethell, da of 2 Baron Bethell; *b* 23 May 1957; *Educ* Eton, Univ of Bristol; *m* 1987, Frances J M, da of (James) Colin Ross Welch (d 1997), of Aldbourne, Wilts; 1 da (Tallulah b 1988), 1 s (Silas b 1990); *Career* freelance journalist and columnist; articles for numerous newspapers and magazines incl: New Statesman, The Observer, TLS, Mail on Sunday, New York, Stern, Corrière della Serra; columnist The Times 1988– (Parly sketch writer 1987–88), restaurant critic Sunday Times 1988–93; columnist (as Wallace Arnold): The Spectator 1987–, Private Eye 1989–, The Independent on Sunday 1991–; columnist: Evening Standard (as Craig Brown) 1993–, The Guardian (as Bel Littlejohn) 1995–; *Books* The Marsh Marlowe Letters (1983), A Year Inside (1988), The Agreeable World of Wallace Arnold (1990), Rear Columns (1992), Welcome to My Worlds (1993), Craig Brown's Greatest Hits (1993), The Hounding of John Thenos (1994), The Private Eye Book of Craig Brown Parodies (1995), The Marsh-Marlowe Letters (2001), This is Craig Brown (2003), Craig Brown's Imaginary Friends: The Collected Parodies 2000–2004 (2004), 1966 and All That (2005), This is Tony's Britain: Craig Brown's Blair Years (2005); *Recreations* flower arrangement, needlework, tidying, deportment, macramé; *Clubs* The Academy; *Style—* Craig Brown, Esq

BROWN, Daniel; s of Paul Graham Brown, and Christine Malvern; *b* 30 May 1977, 1977, Liverpool; *Career* creative technologist; early work with Liverpool John Moores Univ's Learning Methods Unit 1993–95, joined Amaze Ltd 1996, multimedia dir SHOWstudio (with Nick Knight, *qv*) 2002–, launched Play/Create 2002–; projects incl: MTV, Warp Records, BBC, Volkswagen, Hi-Res!, TBWA, Pop Magazine, Kleber, Nick Knight, Saatchi and Saatchi, Amaze, SHOWstudio, Play-Create, Noodlebox.com, ADAADAT Recordings, Sony Playstation, Software as Furniture IDEO; exhbns incl: Great Expectations (organised by Design Cncl, Grand Central Station NY) 2000, Web Wizards: Designers Who Define the Web (Design Museum London) 2001, Virtual Accessories (Hyeres Fashion Festival France) 2002, SHOWstudio Interactive projects (ICA London) 2002, Software as Furniture at Great Brits (organised by Br Cncl and Design Museum London, Milan and Tokyo) 2003, Somewhere Totally Else (Design Museum) London 2003; *Awards* incl: Creative Futures: Stars of the New Millennium Creative Review 1999, Top Ten Web Designers Internet Business Magazine 2001, Webby Award (for SHOWstudio) 2003, Designer of Year Design Museum London 2004; *Style—* Daniel Brown, Esq; ✉ website www.danielbrowns.com

BROWN, Sir David; kt (2001); s of Alan Brown, of Hereford, and Laura Marjorie, *née* Richardson; *b* 14 May 1950; *m* 1975, Denise Frances Brown, da of Edward John Bowers; 2 s (Matthew David b 1982, Andrew James b 1986); *Career* chm Motorola Ltd 1997–; non-exec dir Peninsular and Oriental Steam Navigation Co 2002–06; pres: Assoc for Sci Educn 1998, Fedn of the Electronics Industry 1999–2000, IEE 2003–04, Chartered Quality Inst 2007–; Faraday lectr IEE 1982–83 and 1994–95; visiting fell Kellogg Coll Univ of Oxford; Hon Dr: Univ of Bath, Univ of Kingston, Univ of Portsmouth, Univ of Surrey; CIMgt, CEng, FIET, FREng 1999, fell Chartered Quality Inst (FCQI); *Recreations* literature, art, theatre; *Clubs* Athenaeum; *Style—* Sir David Brown, FREng; ✉ Motorola Ltd, Midpoint, Alencon Link, Basingstoke, Hampshire RG21 7PL (tel 01256 790050, fax 01256 790072, mobile 07802 350136, e-mail david.m.brown@motorola.com)

BROWN, Prof David William; s of David William Brown, and Catherine, *née* Smith; *b* 1 July 1948; *Educ* Keil Sch Dunbarton, Univ of Edinburgh (MA), Oriel Coll Oxford (MA), Clare Coll Cambridge (PhD); *Career* fell, chaplain and tutor in theology and philosophy Oriel Coll Oxford 1976–90, lectr in ethics and philosophical theology Univ of Oxford 1984–90, Van Mildert prof of divinity Univ of Durham 1990–; canon residentiary Durham Cathedral 1990–; C of E: memb Doctrine Cmmn 1985–95, memb Gen Synod 1991–95; tstee Scott Holland Tst 1983–, govr St Stephen's House Oxford 1984–; FBA 2002; *Books* Choices: Ethics and the Christian (1983), The Divine Trinity (1985), Continental Philosophy and Modern Theology (1987), Signs of Grace (with D Fuller, 1995), Tradition and Imagination (1999), Discipleship and Imagination (2000), God and Enchantment of Place (2004), Through the Eyes of the Saints (2005), God and Grace of Body (2007); *Recreations* listening to music, gardening; *Style—* Prof David Brown; ✉ 14 The College, Durham DH1 3EQ (tel 0191 386 4657); Department of Theology and Religion, Abbey House, Palace Green, Durham DH1 3RS

BROWN, Derren; *b* 27 February 1971, Croydon, Surrey; *Educ* Whitgift Sch, Univ of Bristol; *Career* psychological illusionist; *Theatre* incl: Derren Brown Live 2003 and 2004, Something Wicked This Way Comes (UK tour) 2005 and 2006 (Olivier Award 2005); *Television* incl: Mind Control 2000–01, Derren Brown Plays Russian Roulette Live 2003, Trick of the Mind 2004–06, Séance 2004, Messiah 2005, The Gathering 2005, The Heist 2006; *Books* Pure Effect (2000), Absolute Magic (2003), Tricks of the Mind (2006); *Recreations* taxidermy, parrots, single malts; *Style*— Derren Brown; ✉ c/o Michael Vine Associates, 29 Mount View Road, London N4 4SS (tel 020 8348 5899, fax 020 8348 3277)

BROWN, Edward Forrest (Ted); s of George J Brown (d 1971), of Aberdeen, and Margaret, *née* Forrest (d 1996); *b* 14 August 1951; *Educ* Warwick Sch, Lanchester Poly Coventry (BA); *m* 1980, Frances Mary, da of Brian Houlden; 2 da (Catherine b 17 Oct 1983, Lyndsay b 26 Sept 1986), 1 s (Douglas b 24 Aug 1988); *Career* commercial trainee British Steel 1970–74; mktg mangr: Kwikform Ltd 1974–79, Bland Payne UK/Segwick Gp 1979–1981; successively trainee exec, branch mangr, mktg mangr, divisional mangr, divisional md, area md, regnl md, chief operating offr and sector md Rentokil Ltd/Rentokil Initial plc 1981–2006; ceo Morgan Everett plc 2006–, chm Cophall Associates Ltd 2006–; memb IOD 1999; Freeman Worshipful Co of World Traders 2007; MInstD 1999; *Recreations* music, tennis, riding; *Clubs* RAC; *Style*— Ted Brown, Esq; ✉ Cophall Associates, Cophall, Fairwarp, East Sussex TN22 3BU (tel 01825 713472, e-mail edwardbrown@cophall.com)

BROWN, Geoffrey Howard; s of John Howard Brown (d 1983), and Nancy, *née* Fardoe (d 1996); *b* 1 March 1949; *Educ* King Henry VIII GS Coventry, Pembroke Coll Cambridge (BA), Sch of Film and TV RCA (MA); *m* 16 Sept 1985, Catherine Ann, da of Adolf Surowiec; *Career* contrib to Time Out 1974–81, contrib to Monthly Film Bulletin 1974–91, dep film critic Financial Times 1977–81, film critic Radio Times 1981–89, music critic The Times 1999– (dep film critic 1981–90, film critic 1990–98); *Books* Walter Forde (1977), Launder and Gilliat (1977), Der Produzent - Michael Balcon und der Englische Film (1981), Michael Balcon - The Pursuit of British Cinema (lead essay, 1984), The Common Touch - The Films of John Baxter (1989), Directors in British and Irish Cinema (assoc ed, 2006); *Recreations* art exhibitions, children's books; *Style*— Geoffrey Brown, Esq

BROWN, Sir George Francis Richmond; 5 Bt (UK 1863), of Richmond Hill; s of Sir Charles Frederick Richmond Brown, 4 Bt, TD, DL (d 1995), and his 1 w, Audrey, *née* Baring (d 1996); *b* 3 February 1938; *Educ* Eton; *m* 1978, Philippa Jane, da of late Capt Edward Joseph W Willcox: 3 s (Sam George Richmond b 27 Dec 1979, Harry Richmond b 7 May 1982, Edward Richmond b 19 April 1987); *Heir* s, Sam Richmond Brown; *Career* Maj Welsh Guards; extra equerry to HRH the Duke of Edinburgh 1961–63, ADC to Govr of Queensland 1963–65; *Clubs* Pratt's, Cavalry and Guards'; *Style*— Sir George Richmond Brown, Bt; ✉ Mas de Sudre, 81600 Gaillac, France (tel 05 63 41 01 32, e-mail masdesudre@wanadoo.fr)

BROWN, Prof Gillian; CBE (1992); da of Geoffrey Rencher Read (d 1969), and Elsie Olive Read (d 1995); *b* 23 January 1937; *Educ* Perse Sch for Girls Cambridge, Girton Coll Cambridge (exhibitioner, MA), Univ of Edinburgh (PhD), Univ of Cambridge (LittD); *m* 21 Aug 1959, Prof (Edward) Keith Brown, s of Rev Reginald John Brown (d 1978); 3 da (Jane Caroline (Mrs Whitgift) b 1960, Katherine Victoria (Mrs Ruttle) b 1961, Sarah Harriett (Mrs Fleming) b 1962); *Career* lectr Univ Coll of Cape Coast Ghana 1962–64, reader Dept of Linguistics Univ of Edinburgh 1981–83 (lectr 1965–81), prof of applied linguistics Univ of Essex 1983–88; Univ of Cambridge: prof of English as an int language 1988–2004, dir Res Centre for English and Applied Linguistics 1988–2004, fell Clare Coll 1988–; memb: Ctee for Linguistics in Educn 1985–88, Kingman Ctee of Inquiry into the Teaching of English Language 1987–88, ESRC Council 1987–90, Br Cncl English Teaching Advsy Ctee 1987–94, Univ Grants Ctee 1987–89, Univ Funding Cncl 1989–91, Cncl of the Philological Soc; chm: ESRC Res Grants Bd 1987–90, Bd Br Inst in Paris 1992–2004; Univ of London: curator Sch of Advanced Study 1994–2005, external memb Cncl 1998–2005; Hon Doctorate Univ of Lyon 1987; *Books* Phonological Rules and Dialect Variation (1972), Listening to Spoken English (1977), Discourse Analysis (with G Yule, 1983), Teaching the Spoken Language (with G Yule, 1983), Speakers, Listeners and Communication (1995); *Style*— Prof Gillian Brown, CBE; ✉ Clare College, Cambridge CB2 1TL (e-mail gb115@cam.ac.uk)

BROWN, Rt Hon (James) Gordon; PC (1996), MP; s of Rev Dr John Brown (d 1998), and J Elizabeth Brown (d 2004); *b* 20 February 1951; *Educ* Kirkcaldy HS, Univ of Edinburgh (MA, PhD); *m* 3 Aug 2000, Sarah Jane, da of Ian Macauley; *Career* rector Univ of Edinburgh 1972–75 (temp lectr 1975–76), lectr in politics Glasgow Coll of Technol 1976–80, journalist then ed Current Affairs Dept Scottish TV 1980–83; memb Scottish Exec Lab Party 1977–83, Parly candidate (Lab) S Edinburgh 1979, MP (Lab) Dunfermline E 1983–2005, Kirkcaldy & Cowdenbeath 2005–, chm Lab Party in Scotland 1983–, oppn front bench spokesman on trade and industry 1985–87, memb Shadow Cabinet 1987–97, shadow chief sec to the Treasy 1987–89, chief oppn spokesman on trade and industry 1989–92, chief oppn spokesman on Treasy and econ affrs (shadow chllr) 1992–97, chllr of the Exchequer 1997–2007, Prime Minister, First Lord of the Treasury and Minister for the Civil Service 2007–; memb TGWU; Hon DCL Univ of Newcastle upon Tyne 2007; *Books* Maxton (1986), Where There Is Greed (1989), John Smith: Life and Soul of the Party (1994), Values Visions and Voices: An Anthology of Socialism (1995); *Recreations* tennis, films, reading; *Style*— The Rt Hon Gordon Brown, MP

BROWN, Graham Austin; s of James Austin Brown, and Jean Marie, *née* Osborne; *b* 23 December 1956; *Educ* Grey Coll Durham (BSc); *m* 2 Sept 1978, Christine Wynne, *née* Bell; 2 da (Amy b 11 Jan 1985, Emma b 29 Aug 1986); *Career* British Petroleum Co plc: various commercial appts UK and overseas 1978–88, seconded PM's Office 1988–90, mangr Marine Lubricants Business 1990–92, mangr Int Oil Trading Business 1992–94; Nat Power: commercial dir 1994, memb Bd 1996, md 1998, chief operating offr 1999; chief operating offr Ontario Power Generation 2000–; *Recreations* gardening, walking; *Style*— Graham Brown, Esq

BROWN, Graham Stephen; s of Frank George John Brown, and Gwen, *née* Thompson; *b* 28 November 1944; *Educ* Farnborough Sch, Univ of Bristol (LLB), KCL (LLM), Catholic Univ of Louvain (Dip); *m* 1972, Jacqueline, da of John Purtill, of Dublin; *Career* Payne Hicks Beach Solicitors: admitted slr 1969, ptnr 1972, sr ptnr 1994–; sometime memb: Capital Taxes Sub-Ctee and Fin Servs Act Working Party of Law Soc, Ctee Holborn Law Soc; chair Advsy Bd The Sixteen; tstee: Arthritis Research Campaign, Nat Churches Tst; Liveryman Worshipful Co of Clockmakers; FRSA; *Recreations* music, theatre, fine arts and architecture; *Clubs* Farmers'; *Style*— Graham Brown; ✉ Payne Hicks Beach, 10 New Square, Lincoln's Inn, London WC2A 3QG (tel 020 7465 4300, fax 020 7465 4400, e-mail gbrown@phb.co.uk)

BROWN, Hamish Macmillan; MBE (2001); s of William Dick Brown (d 1968), of Dollar and Kinghorn, and Effie Grace, *née* Swanson (d 1988); *b* 13 August 1934; *Educ* Dollar Acad; *Career* Nat Serv RAF Egypt and E Africa; asst Martyrs Meml Church Paisley 1958–59, outdoor educn Braehead Sch 1960–71, outdoor activities adviser Fife 1972–73; freelance author, photographer, lectr, poet, mountaineer, traveller and authority on Morocco 1974–; served SMLTB, dir SROW, creator TGO Challenge event; expeditions to: Morocco, Andes, Himalayas, Arctic, Africa, etc; contribs in over 100 pubns; Hon DLitt Univ of St Andrews 1997; FRSGS 1990; *Books* Hamish's Mountain Walk (1978, SAC Award), Hamish's Groats End Walk (1981, shortlist for W H Smith Travel Prize), Poems of the Scottish Hills (1982), Speak to the Hills (1985), The Great Walking Adventure (1986), Travels (1986), Hamish Brown's Scotland (1988), The Island of Rhum (1988), Climbing the Corbetts (1988), Scotland Coast to Coast (1990), Walking the Summits of Somerset and Avon (1991), From the Pennines to the Highlands (1992), Fort William and Glen Coe Walks (1992), The Bothy Brew (short stories, 1993), The Last Hundred (1994), Hamish's Mountain Walk & Climbing the Corbetts (compendium, 1997), 25 Walks Skye & Kintail (2000), Along the Fife Coast Path (2004), 25 Walks Fife (2005), Seton Gordon's Scotland (2005), Exploring the Edinburgh to Glasgow Canal (2006); *Recreations* skiing, canoeing, alpine flowers, gardening, music, books; *Clubs* Alpine, Scottish Mountaineering; *Style*— Dr Hamish M Brown, MBE; ✉ 26 Kirkcaldy Road, Burntisland, Fife KY3 9HQ (tel 01592 873546, fax 01592 741774)

BROWN, Heath; s of Frederick Brown, and Marina May, *née* Ward; *Educ* The Derby Sch Radcliffe, Rochdale Coll of Art, St Martin's Sch of Art (BA); *Career* concurrently freelance journalist London Evening Standard, You magazine, German Vogue and British W 1991–92, dep ed-in-chief International Collections Magazine (menswear lifestyle quarterly) 1992–94, contributing fashion ed Financial Times and The Times Saturday magazine 1994–95, fashion news ed FHM magazine 1995–96, fashion dir The Times Magazine 1996–; memb Press Ctee Br Fashion Cncl, memb Lab Pty; *Recreations* hill walking, travel, sculpture, photography; *Clubs* Met Bar, Soho House; *Style*— Heath Brown, Esq; ✉ The Times, Times House, 2 Pennington Street, London E98 1TD (tel 020 7782 5842, fax 020 7782 5075)

BROWN, Prof Hilda Meldrum; da of Adam Imlach, and Hilda Meldrum; *b* 28 February 1939; *Educ* Albyn Sch for Girls Aberdeen, Univ of W Aust (BA), Univ of Oxford (MA, BLitt, DLitt); *m* 1963, Dr Ben R Brown (d 1992); *Career* Univ of Oxford: lectr in German 1965–2006, univ assessor 1982–83, prof of German 1999–; St Hilda's Coll Oxford: fell and tutor in German 1966–2006, vice-princ 2000–, sr research fell 2006–; memb: Heinrich-von-Kleist-Gesellschaft 1969–, E T A Hoffman-Gesellschaft 2000–03, Goethe Soc 2001–; sometime memb: Cncl Cheltenham Ladies' Coll, Governing Body Sch of Sts Helen and Katharine Abingdon; tstee Alpha Charity Fund; Leverhulme emeritus fell; *Books* Kleist's "Lost Year" (with R H Samuel, 1981), Leitmotiv and Drama: Wagner, Brecht and the Limits of "Epic" Theatre (1991), Heinrich von Kleist: The Ambiguity of Art and the Necessity of Form (1998), E T A Hoffmann and the Serapiontic Principle: Critique and Creativity (2006); *Recreations* piano playing, opera (especially Wagner), hill walking, golf, travel; *Clubs* Athenaeum; *Style*— Prof Hilda Brown; ✉ Bedwell Barn, Farmington, Cheltenham, Gloucestershire GL54 3LU (tel 01451 860418); St Hilda's College, Oxford OX4 1DY (tel 01865 276863, fax 01865 276816, e-mail hilda.brown@st-hildas.ox.ac.uk)

BROWN, Dr Iain Gordon; s of Reginald Sydney Brown (d 1982), of Durban, South Africa and Edinburgh, and Irene, *née* Young; *b* 10 October 1950; *Educ* George Watson's Coll, Univ of Edinburgh (MA), St John's Coll Cambridge (PhD); *m* 2006, Dr Patricia Rosalind, da of late Prof E Raymond Andrew, FRS; *Career* pt/t lectr Dept of Extra-Mural Studies Univ of Edinburgh 1975–76, asst keeper Dept of Manuscripts Nat Library of Scotland 1977–99; curator of seven major and many smaller exhbns 1978–, princ curator Manuscripts Division 1999–; author of approx 185 articles in learned jls, essays, reviews, exhbn catalogues and book chapters, contrib to several major standard works of reference; Scottish rep Friends of the Nat Libraries 1985–, memb Advsy Ctee Yale Edns of the Private Papers of James Boswell 1987–, vice-pres Edinburgh Decorative and Fine Arts Soc (NADFAS) 1990–; Old Edinburgh Club: memb Cncl 1989–93 and 1995–, memb Editorial Bd 1991–, vice-pres 1996–2003 and 2005–; chm James Craig Bicentenary Publications Ctee 1994–95; memb David Hume Commemoration Ctee Saltire Soc 1993–98; memb Editorial Advsy Bd The History of the Book in Scotland 1998–; memb Cncl Scottish Records Assoc 1998–2004 and 2006–; tstee Penicuik House Preservation Tst; memb Incorporation of Hammermen of Edinburgh; Burgess and Free Citizen of Edinburgh 2007; FSA Scot (memb Cncl 1989–92, memb Editorial Bd of Soc's Proceedings 1992–), FRSA 1980, FSA 1985 (memb Cncl 2000–03), FRSE 1997; *Books* Scottish Architects at Home and Abroad (with T A Cherry, 1978), The Hobby-Horsical Antiquary (1980), Poet and Painter: Allan Ramsay, Father and Son 1684–1784 (1984), The Clerks of Penicuik: Portraits of Taste and Talent (1987), History of Scottish Literature, vol II: 1660–1800 (contrib, 1987), Scott's Interleaved Waverley Novels: An Introduction and Commentary (ed and princ contrb, 1987), Building for Books: The Architectural Evolution of the Advocates' Library 1689–1925 (1989), For the Encouragement of Learning: Scotland's National Library (contrib, 1989), Monumental Reputation: Robert Adam and the Emperor's Palace (1992), The Role of the Amateur Architect (contrib, 1994), The Todholes Aisle (ed, 1994), Scottish Country Houses (contrib, 1995), James Craig 1744–1795 (contrib, 1995), Elegance and Entertainment in the New Town of Edinburgh (1995, reprinted 1997 and 2002), Antonio Canova: The Three Graces (contrib, 1995), Witness to Rebellion (with H Cheape, 1996), The Tiger and the Thistle (contrib, 1999), Allan Ramsay and the Search for Horace's Villa (ed and contrib, 2001), International Dictionary of Library Histories (contrib, 2001), Egypt through the Eyes of Travellers (contrib, 2002), Abbotsford and Sir Walter Scott: The Image and the Influence (ed and contrib, 2003), Archives and Excavations (contrib, 2004); *Recreations* travel, the Mediterranean world, looking at buildings, military history, books, antiquarian pursuits, buying ties, raking in skips; *Clubs* New (Edinburgh); *Style*— Dr Iain Gordon Brown, FSA, FRSE; ✉ 1 Bellevue Crescent, Edinburgh EH3 6ND (tel 0131 556 6929); National Library of Scotland, George IV Bridge, Edinburgh EH1 1EW (tel 0131 226 4531, fax 0131 466 2811, e-mail i.brown@nls.uk)

BROWN, Ian; s of George Brown, and Jean Brown; *b* 20 February 1963, Warrington, Cheshire; *m* Fabiola; 1 s (Emilio), 2 other s (Frankie, Casey); *Career* musician; lead vocalist Stone Roses 1984–96, solo artist 1996–; top 20 singles incl: My Star 1998, Corpses in Their Mouths 1998, Be There (UNKLE featuring Ian Brown) 1999, Dolphins Were Monkeys 2000, F.E.A.R 2001, Keep What Ya Got 2004, Time is My Everything 2005, All Ablaze 2005; albums: Unfinished Monkey Business 1998, Golden Greats 1999, Music of the Spheres 2001, Remixes of the Spheres 2002, Solarized 2004, The Greatest (compilation) 2005; Godlike Genius NME Award 2006; *Style*— Ian Brown, Esq; ✉ c/o Paul Smernicki, Fiction Records (Polydor), 364–366 Kensington High Street, London W14 8NS (tel 020 7471 5494)

BROWN, Ian; s of Ronald Brown (d 1983), and Jessie, *née* Bowtell (d 2002); *b* 8 March 1951; *Educ* King's Sch Ely, Central Sch of Speech and Drama (Dip Dramatic Art); *Career* artistic dir Tag Theatre Co Glasgow 1984–88, artistic dir Traverse Theatre Edinburgh 1988–96, artistic dir and chief exec West Yorkshire Playhouse 2002–; *Recreations* travel, architecture, design, film, theatre, opera, art; *Style*— Ian Brown, Esq; ✉ West Yorkshire Playhouse, Quarry Hill, Leeds LS2 7UP (tel 0113 213 7800, fax 0113 213 7250, e-mail ian.brown@wyp.org.uk)

BROWN, Prof Ian James Morris; s of Bruce Beveridge Brown (d 1957), of Alloa, Scotland, and Eileen Frances, *née* Carnegie (d 1986); *b* 28 February 1945; *Educ* Dollar Acad, Univ of Edinburgh and Crewe and Alsager Coll (MA, DipEd, MLitt, PhD); *m* 8 June 1968 (m dis 1997), Judith Ellen, da of George Woodall Sidaway, of Adelaide; 1 da (Emily b 1972), 1 s (Joshua b 1977); m 2, 7 June 1997, Nicola Dawn, da of Donald Robert Axford; *Career* playwright 1967–; sch teacher 1967–69 and 1970–71; lectr in drama: Dunfermline Coll Edinburgh 1971–76, Br Cncl Edinburgh and Istanbul 1976–78; princ lectr Crewe and Alsager Coll 1978–86 (seconded as sec Cork Enq into Professional Theatre 1985–86); drama dir Arts Cncl of GB 1986–94; prof and dean Faculty of Arts Queen Margaret UC Edinburgh 1999–2002 (reader in drama 1994–95, head Drama Dept 1995–99); dir Scottish Centre for Cultural Management and Policy 1996–2002; int arts and educn conslt 2002–;

prog dir Alsager Arts Centre 1980–86; chm Scot Soc of Playwrights 1973–75, 1984–87 and 1997–99, convenor NW Playwrights' Workshop 1982–85; chm: British Theatre Inst 1985–87 (vice-chm 1983–85), Dionysia Chianti World Festival of Theatre 1991–93; chm: Highlands and Islands Theatre Network 2005–, Dràma Na h-Alba theatre festival 2005–; FRSA 1991; *Books* Antoloija Auvremene Škotske Drame (An Anthology of Contemporary Scottish Drama, ed, 1999), Kulturnig Turizm: Konvergentsiga Kultury Turizmana Poroge XXI veka (Cultural Tourism: the convergence of culture and tourism at the start of the 21st Century) (ed, 2001), Poems for Joan (2001), Journey's Beginning: The Gateway Theatre Building and Company, 1884–1965 (ed, 2004), The Edinburgh History of Scottish Literature (3 vols, gen ed, 2006), Changing Identities: Ancient Roots (ed, 2006), The Edinburgh Companions to Scottish Literature (series ed, 2007–); *Plays* incl: Antigone 1969, Mother Earth 1970, The Bacchae 1972, Positively the Last Final Farewell Performance (ballet scenario) 1972, Carnegie 1973, Rune (choral work) 1973, The Knife 1973, Rabelais 1973, The Fork 1976, New Reekie 1977, Mary 1977, Runners 1978, Mary Queen and the Loch Tower 1979, Pottersville 1982, Joker in the Pack 1983, Beatrice 1989, First Strike 1990, The Scotch Play 1991, Bacchai 1991, Wasting Reality 1992, Margaret 2000, A Great Reckonin 2000; *Recreations* theatre, cooking, sport, travel; *Style*— Prof Ian Brown; ✉ New Balghoulan, 5 Fenton Terrace, Pitlochry, Perthshire PH16 5DP

BROWN, Janet; *Educ* Gallowflat Sch, Rutherglen Acad; *m* Peter Butterworth (decd); 1 s (Tyler), 1 da (Emma (decd)); *Career* actress/impressionist; began career with amateur concerts in Glasgow, first engagement Children's Hour BBC Radio; *Theatre* incl: Happy Holidays (Palace Theatre), Mr Gillie (Garrick), The Bargain (St Martin's), Odd Man Out (UK tour), Plaza Suite (Australia and Nottingham Playhouse), Hard Times (Good Co tour) 1996, A Woman of No Importance (Haymarket, Leicester) 1997, A Cream Cracker Under the Settee (Watermill Theatre Newbury) 1999; *Television* incl: Who Do You Do (series, Thames TV), Meet Janet Brown (special for Thames TV), two series of Janet and Company 1983, Cats Eyes (BBC) 1994–95, Roger Roger (BBC) 1997, Millport (BBC) 1997, Rhona (series, BBC) 2000, Doctors (BBC) 2003, The Impressionable Jon Cullishaw 2004, Revolver! (BBC Scotland) 2004, Midsomer Murders (ITV) 2005, Casualty (BBC) 2005; guest appearances on: Parkinson, Aspel & Co, The Johnny Carson Show (USA), two Royal Command Performances, That's Life 1994 (guest presenter); subject of This is Your Life; *Radio* Just Janet (series, BBC Radio) 1992, Millport (three series, BBC Radio 4) 2001–02, Kindling (BBC) 2003, Penelope's Adventures in Scotland (BBC) 2003, Voices from the Grave (BBC Radio 4) 2005; *Films* incl: Folly to be Wise, Bless This House, For Your Eyes Only; *Books* Prime Mimicker (autobiography, 1986); *Style*— Ms Janet Brown; ✉ c/o Susan Angel & Kevin Francis Ltd, 1st Floor, 12 D'Arblay Street, London W1F 8DU (tel 020 7439 3086, fax 020 7437 1712)

BROWN, Jeremy Ronald Coventry; s of Kenneth Coventry Brown, MBE (d 1987), of Durban, South Africa, and Mavis Kathleen, *née* Keal; *b* 2 May 1948; *Educ* Westville Boys HS, Univ of Natal (MSc), Univ of South Africa (B Iuris); *m* 23 Nov 1996, Stephanie, *née* Pollak; *Career* Spoor and Fisher (patent attorneys) South Africa 1971–78, Linklaters London 1978–; pres Licensing Execs Soc Int 1995–96; memb: Licensing Execs Soc Br and Ireland (pres 1991–92), Cncl AIPPI UK; *Recreations* tennis, travel, the Arts; *Clubs* Roehampton, Kelvin Grove (Cape Town), Durban Country; *Style*— Jeremy Brown, Esq; ✉ Linklaters, One Silk Street, London EC2Y 8HQ (tel 020 7456 2000)

BROWN, Prof John Campbell; s of John Brown, of Dumbarton, and Jane Livingstone Stewart, *née* Campbell; *b* 4 February 1947; *Educ* Dumbarton Acad, Univ of Glasgow (numerous undergraduate prizes and bursaries, Denny Medal, Kelvin Prize and Medal, BSc, PhD, DSc); *m* 18 Aug 1972, Dr Margaret Isobel Logan, da of Dr James Cameron Purse Logan; 1 s (Stuart John Logan b 30 June 1976), 1 da (Lorna Margaret b 9 May 1979); *Career* Univ of Glasgow: lectr in astronomy 1968–78, sr lectr 1978–80, reader 1980–84, prof of astrophysics 1984–96, regius prof of astronomy 1996–; hon prof: Univ of Edinburgh 1996–, Univ of Aberdeen 1997–; Astronomer Royal for Scotland 1995–; visitorships: Harvard-Smithsonian Observatory Massachusetts 1967 and 1969, Univ of Tübingen 1971–72, Univ of Utrecht 1973–74, Australian Nat Univ 1975, Ncar High Altitude Observatory Colorado 1977, Univ of Maryland 1980, Nuffield science research fell Univ of Amsterdam and Univ of Calif San Diego 1984, Brittingham prof Univ of Wisconsin Madison 1987, Univ of Sydney 1993, Spinoza visiting fell Univ of Amsterdam 1999; visiting fell: Eigenodische Technische Hochschule (ETH) Zürich 1999, Centre Nationale de Recherche Spatial (CNRS) Paris Observatory 1999, Universities Space Research Assoc (USRA) NASA Goddard 1999; visiting prof Univ of Alabama Huntsville 2003–, visiting scientist Univ of California Berkeley; memb Cncl RSE 1997–; Marlar lectr Rice Univ TX 2006; Inst of Physics Award for Promoting Public Understanding of Physics 2003; FRAS 1973, FRSE 1984, FInstP 1996; *Books* Inverse Problems in Astronomy (with I J D Craig, 1986), The Sun: A Laboratory for Astrophysics (ed with J T Schmelz, 1993); *Recreations* oil painting, jewellery making, woodwork, magic, cycling, walking, photography, reading; *Style*— Prof John C Brown, FRSE; ✉ 21 Bradfield Avenue, Glasgow G12 0QH (tel 0141 581 6789); Astronomy and Astrophysics Group, Department of Physics and Astronomy, University of Glasgow, Glasgow G12 8QQ (tel 0141 330 5182, fax 0141 330 5183, e-mail john@astro.gla.ac.uk)

BROWN, John David; s of Alfred Stanley Brown (d 2000), Little Billing, Northampton, and Joan Mary, *née* Ogle (d 2004); *b* 13 October 1942; *Educ* Northampton GS, Univ of Nottingham (BSc); *m* 24 Sept 1966, Diane Elaine, da of Eric Edmund Hatton (d 1987); *Career* entered patent agent profession 1964, qualified patent agent 1969, ptnr Forrester Ketley & Co London 1972–2006, fndr ptnr Forrester & Boehmert London, Munich, Bremen 1977–2006; formerly chm and memb Jt Examination Bd of the Chartered Inst of Patent Agents and the Inst of Trade Mark Attorneys; past pres Chartered Inst of Patent Agents (memb Cncl); sec Harmonisation Ctee European Patent Inst; SCI 1964, RSC 1964, CIPA 1969; *Recreations* walking, skiing; *Style*— John D Brown, Esq; ✉ Hesket Hall, Hesket Newmarket, Wigton, Cumbria CA7 8JG (tel 01697 478152, fax 01697 478153)

BROWN, John Domenic Weare; s of Sir John Gilbert Newton Brown, CBE (d 2003), and Virginia, *née* Braddell; *b* 29 May 1953, London; *Educ* Westminster, London Coll of Printing (HND); *m* 14 Dec 1987, Claudia Frances, *née* Zeff; 1 da (Lily Rebecca Zeff b 17 Sept 1989), 1 s (Jack Samuel Darcy b 6 April 1993); *Career* book publishing various companies 1975–82, md Virgin Books 1982–87, fndr and chm John Brown Publishing 1987–2004, fndr and chm John Brown Enterprises 2004–, chm Bob Books Ltd 2006–; dir: The Wisden Gp 2003–, Wanderlust Publications 2004–; chm Portobello Business Trust, dir Notting Hill Prep Sch, tstee Keiskamma Tst; memb PPA 1998–2004; Marcus Morris Award 1997; *Recreations* music, cars, travel, sport; *Clubs* Garrick, Soho House; *Style*— John Brown, Esq; ✉ c/o John Brown Enterprises, 241A Portobello Road, London W11 1LT (tel 020 7243 7400, fax 020 7243 7433, e-mail john@johnbrown.co.uk)

BROWN, John Neville; CBE (1995); s of Alfred Herbert Brown (d 1978), of Tutbury, Staffs, and Jessie Wright (d 1991); *b* 18 November 1935; *Educ* Denstone Coll, Selwyn Coll Cambridge (MA); *m* 3 April 1965, Ann Hilliar (d 2002), da of George William Hubert Edmonds; 1 da (Sara Elizabeth Hilliar b 2 July 1966), 1 s (Hamish John Benedict b 19 Dec 1968); *Career* articled clerk Shipley Blackburn Sutton & Co (Chartered Accountants) 1960–63; Ernst & Young (and predecessors): sr 1965, mangr 1968, ptnr 1986–94; princ VAT conslt Binder Hamlyn 1994–95; pres VAT Practitioners' Gp 1992–96; pt/t memb VAT and Duties Tbnls; pres Old Denstonian Club 1997–98, vice-pres World Pheasant Assoc; fin advsr and memb Cncl Staffordshire Regt, chm Bucks Army Cadet League 1995–2001; chm Friends of the Vale of Aylesbury 2003–; hon treas and chm Leonard Cheshire Thames Valley Care at Home Service, hon treas and memb Cncl The Calvert Tst 2000–03, tstee Hindu Kush Conservation Assoc, churchwarden St Margaret Lothbury; Liveryman Worshipful Co of Tax Advsrs, Master Worshipful Co of Glovers 2007–08; FCA 1964, AInsT 1966, FRGS 1988; *Recreations* photography, travel, fishing, reading, ornithology, conservation; *Clubs* Royal Over-Seas League; *Style*— John Brown, Esq, CBE; ✉ 22 Wykeham Way, Haddenham, Aylesbury, Buckinghamshire HP17 8BX (tel and fax 01844 290430, e-mail john.n.brown@btinternet.com)

B

BROWN, Prof Judith Margaret (Mrs P J Diggle); da of Rev W G Brown (d 1968), of London, and late Joan Margaret, *née* Adams; sis of Peter Brown, CBE, *qv*; *b* 9 July 1944, India; *Educ* Sherborne Sch for Girls, Girton Coll Cambridge (exhibitioner, MA, PhD, research studentship); *m* 21 July 1984, Peter James Diggle, s of late J Diggle; 1 s (James Wilfred Lachlan b 9 Nov 1986); *Career* Girton Coll Cambridge: research fell 1968–70, official fell 1970–71, dir of studies in history 1969–71; Univ of Manchester: lectr in history 1971–82, sr lectr 1982–90, reader-elect 1990; Beit prof of cwlth history Univ of Oxford and fell Balliol Coll 1990–; tstee Charles Wallace (India) Tst, memb Scholars' Cncl Library of Congress Washington DC 2001–; govr: Bath Spa Univ (formerly Bath Coll of HE) 1997, SOAS Univ of London 1999–, Sherborne Sch for Girls 2003–; Hon DSSc Univ of Natal 2001; FRHistS 1972; *Books* Gandhi's Rise to Power: Indian Politics 1915–22 (1972), Gandhi and Civil Disobedience. The Mahatma in Indian Politics 1928–34 (1977), Men and Gods in a Changing World (1980), Modern India: The Origins of an Asian Democracy (1984, 2 edn 1994), Gandhi. Prisoner of Hope (1989, Italian trans 1995), Migration. The Asian Experience (ed with Prof Rosemary Foot, *qv*, 1994), Gandhi and South Africa. Principles and Politics (ed with Prof Martin Prozesky, 1996), Hong Kong's Transitions, 1842–1997 (ed with Prof Rosemary Foot, 1997), Nehru (1999), The Oxford History of the British Empire Vol IV: 20th Century (ed with WR Louis, 1999), Christians, Culture and India's Religious Traditions (ed with R E Frykenberg, 2002), Nehru: A Political Life (2003), Global South Asians: Introducing the Modern Diaspora (2006); *Recreations* gardening, classical music; *Style*— Prof Judith M Brown; ✉ Balliol College, Oxford OX1 3BJ (tel 01865 277736, fax 01865 277803)

BROWN, Karen Veronica; da of John David Jennings, and Katherine Veronica Mary, *née* Pollok (d 1996); *b* 13 July 1952; *Educ* Benenden Sch, Univ of Bristol (LLB); *m* 1999, John Blake; *Career* with Granada TV 1979–87; Channel Four TV: Dispatches 1987–92, commissioning ed for educn 1992–96, controller of factual progs 1996–97, dep dir of progs (responsible for multicultural, independent film and video, sport, daytime, nighttime, children's schools progs) 1997–2001, md 4Learning 2000–01, non-exec dir The Television Corp until 2006, accredited mediator Centre for Effective Dispute Resolution, ind conslt in media and communication, conslt Digital Public, memb Gen Teaching Cncl for England 2002–05, Learning Champion Royal Botanical Gardens Kew 2006–07, chair Action Aid, tstee Action Aid Int, assoc PMDU; FRSA 1998; *Recreations* painting, Scotland; *Style*— Ms Karen Brown

BROWN, Keith Clark; s of George Harold Brown (d 1970), and Sophie Eleanor, *née* Clark; *b* 14 January 1943; *Educ* Forest Sch, City of London Coll; *m* Rita Hildegard, da of Jack Stanley Rolfe (d 1977); 1 da (Lucy b 1976), 1 s (Timothy b 1979); *Career* stockbroker and investment banker; ptnr W Greenwell & Co 1978–86, md Greenwell Montagu Securities 1987, md Morgan Stanley Dean Witter 1987–99; chm Int Advsy Bd Bipop-Carire 2000–02, dir Elysian Fund plc 2001–; memb Bd London Regional Transport 1984–94, dir British Aerospace plc 1989–2003; cncllr Brentwood DC 1976–86 (chm 1983–84); chm Racecourse Assoc 2001–04; memb: Br Horseracing Bd 2001–04, Betting Levy Bd 2001–04; treas Essex CCC; govr Brentwood Sch Essex; tstee Fryerning Fndn; Liveryman, treas and memb Ct of Assts Worshipful Co of Coopers (Master 2002–03), memb Master's Court Incorporation of Coopers of Glasgow; FSI, ASIP; *Recreations* cricket, racing and charitable affairs; *Clubs* Carlton, Royal Ascot Racing; *Style*— Keith C Brown, Esq; ✉ Fryerning House, Ingatestone, Essex CM4 0PF (tel 01277 352959, fax 01277 355051, e-mail keith@fryerning.com, website www.fryerning.com)

BROWN, Kenneth Edward Lindsay; s of Col Thomas Pyne Brown, OBE (d 1957); *b* 17 October 1940; *Educ* Sherborne; *m* 1968, Mary Ruth, da of Thomas Forrester (d 1969); 3 s; *Career* dir A R Brown McFarlane & Co Ltd 1967– (chm 1972–2004); FCA; *Recreations* antiques; *Clubs* Royal Ocean Racing; *Style*— Kenneth Brown Esq; ✉ 65 St Andrews Drive, Glasgow G41 4HP (tel 0141 423 8381, fax 0141 423 8946, e-mail pbroawn@aol.com); A R Brown McFarlane & Co Ltd, Suite 1/1, Brook Street Studios, 60 Brook Street, Glasgow G40 2AB (tel 0141 551 8281, fax 0141 551 1518)

BROWN, Prof Kenneth Joseph; s of Charles Brown, of Aberdeenshire, and Dorothy, *née* Duncan; *b* 20 December 1945; *Educ* Robert Gordon's Coll, Univ of Aberdeen (BSc), Univ of Dundee (PhD); *m* 6 Oct 1971, Elizabeth, da of James Lobban; 2 da (Sheila b 30 Jan 1975, Jenny b 29 March 1977), 1 s (Colin b 14 Aug 1980); *Career* Dept of Mathematics Heriot-Watt Univ: lectr 1970–81, sr lectr 1981–91, head of dept 1989–92 and 1999–2002, reader 1991–93, prof 1993–; memb: Inst for Mathematics and its Applications, American Mathematical Soc, Edinburgh Mathematical Soc; FRSE 1991; *Books* Reaction-Diffusion Equations (jt ed with A A Lacey, 1990); *Recreations* reading, tennis; *Style*— Prof Kenneth Brown, FRSE; ✉ 3 Highlea Grove, Balerno, Edinburgh EH14 7HQ (tel 0131 449 5314); School of Mathematical and Computer Sciences, Heriot-Watt University, Riccarton, Edinburgh EH14 4AS (tel 0131 451 3239, fax 0131 451 3249, e-mail k.j.brown@ma.hw.ac.uk)

BROWN, Kenneth Thomas; s of Thomas Alfred Charles Brown (d 1966), and Lilian Florence, *née* Porter (d 1986); *b* 28 November 1928; *Educ* Christ's Coll Finchley; *m* 4 Feb 1956, Barbara Hooper; 3 s (Stephen b 9 Dec 1956, Martin b 11 July 1959, Julian b 16 Jan 1962); *Career* reporter Barnet Press 1945–47 and 1949–51, sub ed and picture ed Gloucestershire Echo 1951–54, features ed Birmingham Gazette 1954–56, sub ed London Evening News and News Chronicle 1956–58, asst night ed and gardening ed Daily Mail 1958–90, gardening editorial conslt 1991–2001; gardening tours conslt RHS 1995–96; churchwarden All Saints Bisley 2004–06; *Recreations* gardening, travel; *Clubs* Farmers; *Style*— Kenneth Brown, Esq; ✉ Parlour Farm House, Bisley, Stroud, Gloucestershire GL6 7BH (tel 01452 770878)

BROWN, Prof Lawrence Michael (Mick); s of Bertson Waterworth Brown, and Edith, *née* Waghorne (d 1989); *b* 18 March 1936; *Educ* Univ of Toronto (BASc), Univ of Cambridge (MA, DSc), Univ of Birmingham (PhD); *m* Dr Susan Drucker Brown, da of David Drucker, of Oronoque Village, Connecticut, USA; 2 da (Sarah May b 1969, Isabel b 1971), 1 s (Toby Solomon b 1974); *Career* Univ of Cambridge: W M Tapp fellowship Gonville & Caius Coll 1963, demonstrator 1965, lectr 1970, fndr fell Robinson Coll 1977–, reader 1982–90, prof 1990–2001, prof emeritus 2001–; Rosenhain Medal (Inst of Metals), R F Mehl Medal (Metals Soc and Inst of Metals), Guthrie Medal and Prize (Inst of Physics); FRS 1981, FInstP, FIM; *Style*— Prof Mick Brown, FRS; ✉ Robinson College, Cambridge CB3 9AN

BROWN, Lyn Carol; MP; da of Joseph Brown, of London, and Iris Brown; *b* 13 April 1960, London; *Educ* Plashet Comp, Whitelands Coll Roehampton Inst (BA); *Partner* John Cullen; *Career* residential social work: London Borough of Ealing 1984, Newham Vol Agencies Cncl 1984–8, London Borough of Waltham Forest 1987–2005; MP (Lab) West Ham 2005–; chair: London Library Devpt Agency 1999–2005, Cultural Servs Exec Local Govt Assoc (LGA) 2000–03, Culture and Tourism Panel Assoc of London Govt (ALG) 2002–05; memb: London Region Sports Bd until 2007, London Arts Bd until 2007, Museums, Libraries and Archives Cncl London until 2007, Co-op Pty, Fabian Soc, Unison;

Recreations reading crime fiction (judge Golden Dagger Award 2005, 2006 and 2007), walking, relaxing with friends; *Style*— Ms Lyn Brown, MP; ✉ House of Commons, London SW1A 0AA (tel 020 7219 6999, fax 020 7219 0889, e-mail brownl@parliament.uk or lyn@lynbrown.org.uk)

BROWN, Maggie; da of Cecil Walter Brown and Marian, *née* Evans; *b* 7 September 1950; *Educ* Colston's Girls' Sch, Univ of Sussex, Univ of Bristol (BA), Univ of Cardiff (Dip Journalism); *m* 22 June 1979, Charles John Giuseppe Harvey, s of Hon John Wynn Harvey, of Coed-y-Maen, Meifod, Powys (s of 1 Baron Harvey of Tasburgh); 3 da (Elena b 27 Dec 1982, Nina b 11 Aug 1985, Stephanie b 8 May 1989), 1 s (John b 1 May 1993); *Career* trainee journalist Birmingham Post & Mail 1972–74; staff writer: Birmingham Post 1974–77, Reuters 1977–78; news editor: Financial Weekly 1979–80, Guardian 1980–86; media editor The Independent 1986; media commentator Guardian Media section, reg contrib BBC radio; reg weekly columnist Media Week and Stage, contrib Evening Standard Media section; *Recreations* reading, gardening, being a mother, horse riding; *Style*— Ms Maggie Brown; ✉ c/o The Guardian, 119 Farringdon Road, London EC1R 3ER

BROWN, Malcolm Carey; s of Rev William George Brown (d 1978), and Bernice Nellie Cordelia, *née* Radcliffe (d 1978); *b* 7 May 1930; *Educ* Nelson GS Lancashire, Poole GS Dorset, St John's Coll Oxford (scholar, MA); *m* 1953, Beatrice Elsie Rose, da of Austin Albert George Light; 2 s (Martin John Carey b 1959, Michael Paul b 1961), 1 da (Catherine Mary b 1963); *Career* Nat Serv Midshipman, later Sub Lt RNVR 1953–54; BBC: gen trainee 1955–57, TV prodn asst 1957–60, documentary film prodr 1960–86; freelance writer 1986– (pt/t freelance writer 1968–86), freelance historian Imperial War Museum 1989–; hon res fell Centre for First World War Studies Univ of Birmingham 2002–; *Television* documentary films as prodr/dir incl: T E Lawrence 1962, I'm a Stranger Here Myself 1963, Horseman Pass By 1966 (British entry in Cork Film Festival), Scapa Flow 1966, The World Turned Upside Down 1967, The Chalfont Profiles 1970–75, Battle of the Somme (short-listed for Int Emmy Award) 1976, Armistice and After 1978, Graf Spee 1979, Checkpoint Berlin 1981, Peace in No Man's Land 1981, Gordon of Khartoum 1983; *Books* Scapa Flow (jtly, 1968), Tommy Goes To War (1978, 2 edn 1999), Christmas Truce (jtly, 1984, 1994), A Touch of Genius (jtly, 1988, short-listed NCR Non-Fiction Book Award 1989 and Nelson Hurst and Marsh Biography Award 1989), The Letters of T E Lawrence (ed, 1988), The Imperial War Museum Book of the First World War (1991, 2002), Secret Despatches from Arabia and Other Writings by T E Lawrence (ed, 1991), The Imperial War Museum Book of the Western Front (1993), The Imperial War Museum Book of the Somme (1996, 2002), The Imperial War Museum Book of 1918: Year of Victory (1998), Verdun 1916 (1999, 2003, French edn 2006), Spitfire Summer (2000, 2003), TE Lawrence (Br Library Historic Lives series, 2003), Lawrence of Arabia, The Life, The Legend (2005), T E Lawrence in War and Peace (2005); *Recreations* walking, the making and keeping of friends; *Style*— Malcolm Brown, Esq; ✉ 4 Northbury Avenue, Ruscombe, Reading, Berkshire RG10 9LG (tel 0118 934 0370, e-mail mcbrown@freenetname.co.uk); c/o Department of Documents, Imperial War Museum, Lambeth Road, London SE1 6HZ (tel 020 7416 5222)

BROWN, Malcolm Ronald; s of Ronald Ernest Charles Brown, MBE (d 1988), of Orpington, Kent, and Peggy Elizabeth, *née* Mitchener; *b* 2 August 1946; *Educ* Quintin GS, Univ of London (BSc); *m* 3 Oct 1970, Lyntina Sydnie, da of Clinton Sydney Squire; 1 da (Samantha Anne b 13 Feb 1972), 1 s (Philip Clinton b 18 May 1975); *Career* construction analyst: de Zoete & Gorton 1968–72, James Capel & Co 1972– (ptnr 1981, sr exec 1984), dir HSBC Investment Bank 1997–2006; AIIMR; *Recreations* ocean racing, chess, gardening; *Style*— Malcolm Brown, Esq; ✉ Carbery House, Carbery Lane, Ascot, Berkshire (tel 01344 622620)

BROWN, Prof Malcolm Watson; s of Denis Brown (d 2001), and Vivian Irene, *née* Watson (d 2001); *b* 24 February 1946, Sheffield; *Educ* St John's Coll Cambridge (open scholarship, Wright Prize, Hockin Prize, research scholarship, MA), Univ of Cambridge (PhD); *m* 6 April 1974, Geraldine Ruth, *née* Hassall; 1 s (Roger Hassall b 7 July 1982), 1 da (Andrea Francesca b 4 May 1985); *Career* asst in research Dept of Anatomy Univ of Cambridge 1972–74, visiting research scientist NIH 1973, research fell Downing Coll Cambridge 1973–74; Dept of Anatomy Univ of Bristol: research asst 1974–75, lectr in anatomy 1975–91, sr lectr in anatomy 1991–94, reader in anatomy and cognitive neuroscience 1994–98, prof of anatomy and cognitive neuroscience 1998–, head of dept 1998–2004 (dep head 1996–98), exec memb MRC Centre for Synaptic Plasticity 1999–; research dir Faculty of Med and Vet Sciences Univ of Bristol 2003–; BBSRC: memb Animal Sciences and Psychology Grants Ctee 1994–97, memb Network Panel 1997–2000; MRC: panel referee for the allocation of research studentships 1991–94, panel referee for clincal research fellowships 1997–99, memb MRC Advsy Bd (MAB) 2000–; delivered numerous lectures at univ depts and int scientific meetings worldwide; author of numerous academic jl papers and research chapters in books; memb: Br Neuroscience Assoc 1973–, European Brain and Behaviour Soc 1984–, Anatomical Soc of GB and I 1998–; Univ of Bristol Merit Awards 1989, 1990 and 1997, AFRC Special Research Fellowship 1991–92; memb and elder Christ Church Nailsworth; FRS 2004; *Recreations* travel; *Style*— Prof Malcolm Brown; ✉ University of Bristol and MRC Centre for Synaptic Plasticity, Department of Anatomy, School of Medical Sciences, University Walk, Bristol BS8 1TD (tel 0117 331 1909, fax 0117 929 1687, e-mail m.w.brown@bris.ac.uk)

BROWN, Prof Margaret Louise; da of (Frederick) Harold Seed (d 1960), and Louisa, *née* Shearer (d 1991); *b* 30 September 1943, Liverpool; *Educ* Merchant Taylors' Sch for Girls Crosby, Newnham Coll Cambridge (MA), Inst of Educn Univ of London (PGCE), Chelsea Coll Univ of London (PhD); *m* 1970, Hugh Palmer Brown; 3 s (Richard Christopher b 24 Oct 1977, Michael Philip b 13 Nov 1979, Peter Nicholas b 16 March 1983); *Career* mathematics teacher Cavendish Sch Hemel Hempstead 1966–69, lectr then sr lectr Chelsea Coll Univ of London 1969–86; KCL: reader 1986–90, prof of mathematics educn 1990–, head Sch of Educn 1992–96; chair: Jt Mathematical Cncl of the UK 1991–95, of tstees Sch Mathematics Project 1996–2006, Educn Supplementary Panel Research Assessment Exercise 2008 2004–08; pres: Mathematical Assoc 1990–91, Br Educnl Research Assoc 1997–98; memb: Nat Curriculum Mathematics Working Gp 1987–88, Numeracy Task Force 1997–98, Advsy Ctee on Mathematics Educn 2005–; Hon EdD Kingston Univ 2002; FKC 1996, AcSS 2000; *Publications* Statistics and Probability (jtly, 1972), Low Attainers in Mathematics 5–16 (jtly, 1982), Children Learning Mathematics (jtly, 1984), Graded Assessment in Mathematics (1992), Intuition or Evidence? (jtly, 1995), Effective Teachers of Numeracy (jtly, 1997); author of numerous jl articles and chapters in books; *Recreations* walking, music; *Style*— Prof Margaret Brown; ✉ 34 Girdwood Road, Southfields, London SW18 5QS (tel and fax 020 8789 4344); Department of Education and Professional Studies, King's College London, Franklin-Wilkins Building, Waterloo Bridge, London SE1 9NH (e-mail margaret.brown@kcl.ac.uk)

BROWN, His Hon Judge (Laurence Frederick) Mark; s of Rt Rev Ronald Brown, of Lancs, and Joyce, *née* Hymers (d 1987); *b* 16 March 1953; *Educ* Bolton Sch, Univ of Durham (BA, Adam Smith Prize for Economics); *m* 5 Aug 1978, Jane Margaret, da of Rev Dr F H Boardman, of Great Sankey, Cheshire; 1 s (Nicholas Edward b 29 April 1984); *Career* called to the Bar Inner Temple 1975; pt/t tutor in law Univ of Liverpool 1976–83, in practice Northern Circuit 1976–2000, recorder 1997–2000 (asst recorder 1993–97), asst boundary cmmr 2000, circuit judge (Northern Circuit) 2000–, ethnic minority liaison judge for Liverpool 2002, liaison judge for Knowsley Magistrates' Court 2002; counsel to Chief Constable Police Disciplinary Tbnls 1989–2000; memb Panel Inns of Court Disciplinary Tbnls 1994–2000, memb Merseyside Area Criminal Justice Strategy Ctee 1997–2000, head of advocacy training on the N Circuit 1998–2001, memb Parole Bd for Eng and Wales 2003–, memb Panel for Judicial Appts 2005–, investigating judge (judicial discipline) 2007–; *Recreations* golf, gardening, ballroom dancing; *Clubs* Royal Liverpool Golf; *Style*— His Hon Judge Mark Brown; ✉ The QE II Law Courts, Derby Square, Liverpool L2 1XA (tel 0151 471 1026)

BROWN, Mark Finlay; *b* 16 March 1963; *Educ* Loughborough Univ of Technol (BScEcon); *Career* economist; equity market strategist and investment banker: CBI 1984, HM Treasy 1985–87, Phillips & Drew 1987–89; strategist UBS 1990–93; ABN AMRO Hoare Govett: head of strategy and economics 1994–96, head of research 1996–98, chief exec ABN AMRO Equities (UK) Ltd 1998–2000; global head of research HSBC plc 2000–02, global head of research ABN AMRO 2002–04, chief exec Arbuthnot Securities 2004–; *Recreations* rugby, mountaineering; *Style*— Mark Brown, Esq

BROWN, Martin; s of Clarence Brown (d 1981), and Anne, *née* Gray (d 2002); *b* 26 January 1949; *Educ* Bolton Sch, New Coll Oxford (MA); *m* 1971, Frances *née* Leithead; 2 s; *Career* civil servant; with HM Customs and Excise (now HM Revenue and Customs) 1971–; postings incl: VAT policy, anti-smuggling controls and excise duties, outfield operational mgmnt (Manchester Airport and Computer Audit Unit), various secondments (private sec to Treasy Min, customs advsr Barbados), dir Customs 1993–94, dir Central Ops 1994–96, dir VAT Policy 1996–2000, head of Tax Practice 2000–01, dir Customs and Tax Practice 2001–02; dir (secondment) Eurocustoms 2002–; *Recreations* the arts, walking, travel, wine, cycling; *Style*— Martin Brown; ✉ Eurocustoms, 8 rue de la Tour des Dames, 75436 Paris Cedex 09, France (tel 00 33 01 55 07 49 90, e-mail martin.brown@eurocustoms.org)

BROWN, Martin Ernest; TD (1999); *b* 9 June 1966; *Educ* Whitgift Sch Croydon; *m* 6 June 1998, Helen, *née* O'Connor; *Career* private sec to the Sec of State for Transport 1987–89, with Westminster Strategy (govt and media conslts) 1989–95; Design Cncl: head of corp affrs 1995–98, dir Govt & Communication 1998–2002; dir Fishburn Hedges (cmmn conslts) 2002–; FRSA; *Style*— Martin Brown, Esq, TD

BROWN, Michael John; s of Lt Cdr S R Brown (d 1976), of Aylesbury, Bucks, and Ada Phyllis, *née* Evett (d 1993); *b* 23 September 1932; *Educ* Berkhamsted Sch, New Coll Oxford (MA, fndr pres Oxford Univ Gymnastics Club); *m* 1, 20 Sept 1963, Margaret Jordan, JP (d 1988), da of William C Jordan (d 1999); 4 s (Edward b 1964, Thomas b 1966, Robert b and d 1968, Adam b 1970); m 2, 24 May 1996, Valetta Radgosky, da of Edward Lucey (d 2002); *Career* admitted slr 1957; ptnr Denton Hall and Burgin 1959–80, sr ptnr Brown Cooper 1981–96 (conslt 1996–2003); dir: Urwick Orr and Partners Ltd (chm 1981–84), Channel Islands TV 1972–77, Purcell Graham and Co 1978–88, Paulstra Ltd 1977–95; hon slr Variety Club of GB 1966–2000, chm Pooh Properties Tst 1972–, chm Clare Milne Tst 2000–; pres: Soc of Eng and American Lawyers 1989–93 (chm 1985–88), Copinger Soc 1992–93; memb Arbitration Panel: American Film Market Assoc 1990–99, World Intellectual Property Orgn 1995–2001, Radnage PCC 2000–03; memb Law Soc 1957–; *Recreations* diverse; *Clubs* Garrick (hon life memb), Pilgrims; *Style*— Michael Brown, Esq; ✉ The Old Dairy, Chapel Hill, Speen, Buckinghamshire HP27 0SP

BROWN, Michael Russell; s of Frederick Alfred Brown, and Greta Mary Brown, OBE, *née* Russell; *b* 3 July 1951; *Educ* Littlehampton, Univ of York; *Career* memb Middle Temple; mgmnt trainee Barclays Bank 1972–74; lectr Swinton Cons Coll 1974–76, res asst to Michael Marshall MP 1975–77, Parly research asst to Nicholas Winterton MP 1977–79; MP (Cons): Brigg and Scunthorpe 1979–83, Brigg and Cleethorpes 1983–97; sec Parly NI Ctee 1981–87 (vice-chm 1987), PPS to Hon Douglas Hogg MP as min of state DTI 1989–90, min of state FCO 1990–92, PPS to Sir Patrick Mayhew as sec of state for NI 1992–93, asst Govt whip 1993–94; political columnist The Independent 1998–; *Style*— Michael Brown, Esq

BROWN, Prof Morris Jonathan; s of Arnold Aaron Brown (d 1970), and Irene Joyce, *née* Goodman; *b* 18 January 1951; *Educ* Edinburgh Acad, Harrow, Trinity Coll Cambridge (scholar, MA, MD), UCH Med Sch (scholar, MSc); *m* 31 July 1977, Diana Costa, da of Kostas Phylactou, of Cyprus; 3 da (Emily Irene Annie b 1981, Chrysothemis Celia Margaret b 1982, Ophelia Wendy Elizabeth b 1986); *Career* MRC sr fell Royal Postgrad Med Sch 1982–85, conslt physician Addenbrooke's Hosp Cambridge 1985–; Univ of Cambridge: prof of clinical pharmacology 1985–, fell Gonville & Caius Coll 1989–, dir of studies (clinical med); chm MRS 1990–96; pres Br Hypertension Soc 2005– (vice-pres 2003–05); author of papers on hypertension; Lilly Gold Medal Br Pharmacological Soc 2001, Walter Somerville Medal Br Card Soc 2006; FRCP 1986, FMedSci 1999, FAHA 2003; *Books* Advanced Medicine (1986), Clinical Pharmacology (jtly, 1997 and 2003); *Recreations* violin and oboe; *Clubs* RSM; *Style*— Prof Morris Brown; ✉ Clinical Pharmacology Unit, University of Cambridge, Level 6, ACCI, Addenbrooke's Hospital, Box 110, Cambridge CB2 2QQ (tel 01223 762577, fax 01223 762576, e-mail mjb14@medschl.cam.ac.uk)

BROWN, Nicholas (Anthony) Phelps; s of Prof Sir Henry Phelps Brown, of Oxford, and Dorothy Evelyn Mostyn, *née* Bowlby; *b* 5 May 1936; *Educ* Westminster, Trinity Coll Cambridge (exhbn, MA, MD), Middlesex Hosp (DO); *m* 12 Dec 1960, Heather Mary, da of Ronald Hubert White; 2 da (Emily Sarah b 1 June 1967, Lucy Kate b 8 Oct 1969), 1 s (Giles Nicholas b 22 May 1972); *Career* Nat Serv 1955–57 (cmmnd RA); The Middlesex Hosp: house surgn 1964, house physician 1964, house offr 1965, clinical asst Univ Coll Hosp 1966–67; Moorfields Eye Hosp: out patient offr 1966–67, resident surgical offr 1967–70, chief clinical asst 1970–71, res fellow to Contact Lens Dept 1971–73, lectr then sr lectr Depts of Clinical Ophthalmology and Experimental Ophthalmology 1971–76 (and Inst of Ophthalmology), hon conslt 1975–76; clinical asst The Hammersmith Hosp 1971–75, private practice 1977–, pt/t teaching at Inst of Ophthalmology and with Univ Examination Postal Inst 1977–, hon conslt The Radcliffe Infirmary Oxford 1983–, dir Clinical Cataract Res Unit Nuffield Laboratory of Ophthalmology Oxford 1989– (res assoc 1983–); Kodak Res Award: slit-image camera devpt 1971, MRC Res Grant: study of the diabetic lens 1974–75, Nuffield Fndn Res Award: computerised analysis of the image of the lens of the eye 1987, Iris Fund for Eye Res: Glaucoma disc assessment by computerised image analysis 1989, Violt M Richards Charity: spoke cataract study 1990, Scheimpflug Award Osaka 1995; FRCS 1969, FCOphth; memb: RSM, BMA, Assoc for Eye Res, Oxford Ophthalmological Congress, Ophthalmological Soc of UK; *Publications* author of numerous papers and articles in ophthalmology journals; chapters in: Medical Ophthalmology, (ed Clifford Rose, 1975), Scientific Foundations of Ophthalmology (1977); Lens Disorders: A Clinical Manual of Cataract Diagnosis (with A J Bron, 1996); *Recreations* natural history, photography; *Style*— Nicholas Phelps Brown, Esq; ✉ 69 Harley Street, London W1N 1DE (tel 020 7636 7153, fax 020 7487 3901, website www.eyes-right.com)

BROWN, Rt Hon Nicholas Hugh; PC (1997), MP; s of late R C Brown, and late G K Brown, *née* Tester; *b* 13 June 1950; *Educ* Tunbridge Wells Tech HS, Univ of Manchester (BA); *Career* memb Newcastle upon Tyne City Cncl 1980–84; MP (Lab): Newcastle upon Tyne E 1983–97, Newcastle upon Tyne E and Wallsend 1997–; oppn frontbench dep spokesman on legal affrs 1985–87, oppn frontbench Treasy spokesman 1987–94, dep to Margaret Beckett, MP as Shadow Ldr of the Commons 1992–94, oppn spokesman on health 1994–95, oppn dep chief whip 1995–97, Parly sec to the Treasy (Govt chief whip) 1997–98, sec of state for Agriculture, Fisheries and Food 1998–2001, min of state for Work 2001–; memb Select Ctee on Broadcasting 1994–95; *Style*— The Rt Hon Nicholas Brown, MP; ✉ House of Commons, London SW1A 0AA; tel 0191 272 0843

BROWN, Prof Nigel Leslie; s of Leslie Charles Brown (d 1983), of Beverley, E Yorks, and Beryl, *née* Brown (d 2004); *b* 19 December 1948; *Educ* Beverley GS, Univ of Leeds (BSc, PhD); *m* 7 Aug 1971, Gayle Lynnette, da of John Wallace Blackah (d 2001), of Beverley, E Yorks; 3 da (Sally b 1975, Louise b 1976, Katie b 1977); *Career* ICI fell MRC Lab of Molecular Biology 1974–76; lectr in biochemistry Univ of Bristol 1976–81, Royal Soc sr research fell 1981–88, visiting fell in genetics Univ of Melbourne 1987–88; Univ of Birmingham: prof of molecular genetics and microbiology 1988–2004, head of biology 1994–99, dep head of biosciences 1999–2000, Leverhulme Tst research fell 2000–01, head of chemistry 2003–04; dir of science and technol BBSRC 2004–; memb Editorial Bd Molecular Microbiology 1986–97, chief ed Fedn of European Microbiology Socs (FEMS) Microbiology Reviews 2000–04; chm: BBSRC Genes & Developmental Biology Ctee 1997–2000, BBSRC Ctee Studentships & Fellowships 2000–04; memb: Research Careers Initiative 1997–98, Governing Cncl John Innes Centre 1999–2004; hon pres W Midlands Assoc for Science Educn 1997–98; memb: Soc of Gen Microbiology, Biochemical Soc, Genetical Soc; FIBiol 1989, FRSC 1990, FRSA 2001; *Recreations* house renovation, travel; *Style*— Prof Nigel Brown; ✉ BBSRC, Polaris House, North Star Avenue, Swindon SN2 1UH (tel 01793 413267, fax 01793 413234)

BROWN, Sir (Austen) Patrick; KCB (1995); *b* 14 April 1940; *Educ* Royal GS Newcastle upon Tyne, SSEES Univ of London; *m* 1966, Mary; 1 da; *Career* Carreras Ltd until 1969: joined 1961, Cyprus office 1965–66, Belgium office 1967–68; mgmnt conslt Urwick Orr & Partners 1969–72, DOE 1972–76, asst sec Property Services Agency (PSA) 1976–80; Dept of Tport: asst sec 1980–83, under sec (fin and ports & buses privatisation) 1983–88; dep sec (privatisation of water industry) DOE 1988–90, chief exec PSA 1990–91, perm sec Dept of Tport 1991–97; dep chm: Kvaerner Corp Devpt Ltd 1998–99, Review of Ex-Service Charities 2000; non-exec chm: Go-Ahead Group plc 2002– (non-exec dir 1999–), Amey plc 2004–; non-exec dir: Hunting plc 1998–2001, Arlington Securities plc 1999–2004, Northumbrian Water Gp plc 2003–; chm: Mobility Choice 1998–, Ind Tport Cmmn 1999–2007; tstee Charities Aid Fndn 1998–2006; visiting prof Univ of Newcastle upon Tyne 1998–; *Clubs* RAC; *Style*— Sir Patrick Brown, KCB

BROWN, Paul; s of Alan Tertius Brown, of Wales, and Enfys Ann, *née* Jones; *b* 13 May 1960; *Educ* Univ of St Andrews; *Career* theatre designer; trained under Margaret Harris; Diploma of Honour Praque Quadrennial 1999; *Theatre* designs for: Almeida, Royal Court, Traverse, Bush, Lincoln Centre NY; prodns 1985–87: A Lie of the Mind, Ourselves Alone, Road; Almeida (at the Gainsborough Studios), Richard II, Coriolanus, The Tempest (Critic Circle Award for Best Designer 2000), Platanov (Critic Circle Award for Best Designer 2001, Evening Standard Award for Best Designer 2001), King Lear, Man of La Mancha (Broadway), Hamlet (Setagua Theatre Tokyo, Sadlers Wells London), False Servant (RNT), As You Desire Me (West End); *Opera* prodns incl: Mitridate (Covent Garden) 1991, Hamlet (Monte Carlo) 1993, L'Incoronazione di Poppea (Bologna) 1993, Zemire et Azor 1993 (Drottningholm Court Theatre Sweden), King Arthur (Paris Châtalet and Covent Garden) 1995, Lady Macbeth of Mtsensk (Met NY) 1995, Tom Jones (Drottningholm Court Theatre Sweden) 1995, The Midsummer Marriage (ROH) 1996, Fidelio (ENO) 1996, Lulu (Glyndebourne) 1996, Parsifal (Bastille Paris) 1997, I Masnadieri (Covent Garden) 1999, Moses und Aron (Metropolitan NY) 1999, Pelléas et Mélislande (Glyndebourne) 1999, Don Carlos (Sydney Opera House) 1999, Falstaff (re-opening Covent Garden) 1999, Peter Grimes (Bastille Paris) 2001, Vanessa (Monte Carlo) 2001, Rigoletto (Madrid) 2001, Thias (Lyric Opera Chicago), Katya Kabanova (Santa Fe), La Traviata (Verona Arena), Mefistofele (Amsterdam) 2004, Die Zauberflöte (Festspielhaus Saltzburg) 2005, The Magic Flute (Bolshoi Moscow) 2005, Lucio Silla (Santa Fe) 2005, Tosca (ROH) 2006, The Tempest (Santa Fe) 2006, Turn of the Screw (Glyndebourne) 2006; *Ballet* Giselle (La Scala Milan) 2001; *Films* Angels and Insects (Oscar nomination 1997), Up At the Villa; *Style*— Paul Brown, Esq; ✉ c/o Megan Willis, Garricks, 5 The Old School House, Lanterns, Bridge Lane, London SW11 3AD (tel 020 7738 1600)

BROWN, Paul Campbell; CBE (2003); s of James Brown (decd), and Edna, *née* Howell (decd); *b* 6 November 1945; *Educ* Portsmouth GS, RMA Sandhurst, Balliol Coll Oxford (BA); *m* 1970, Sarah, da of Jack Hunter Bailey; 2 s (Matthew b 1976, Duncan b 1979); *Career* army offr (UK, Cyprus, Germany) 1966–74; broadcaster/mangr forces and commercial radio 1973–84, head Radio Programming IBA 1984–90, dep chief exec Radio Authy 1990–95, chief exec Commercial Radio Companies Association (CRCA) 1995–2006 (chm CRCA 1999–2000), chm RadioCentre 2006–; chm Steering Bd UK Digital Radio Forum 1998–2001, memb Bd RAJAR 1998–2006, memb Bd Skillset 2004–; pres Assoc of European Radios 1998–2000, chm Radio Acad 2001–04, dep pres World DAB 1999–2005; fell Radio Acad 1996; *Recreations* tennis, boating, hill walking; *Clubs* Army and Navy, Hampshire, Thorney Island Sailing (Vice-Cdre); *Style*— Paul Brown; ✉ RadioCentre, 77 Shaftesbury Avenue, London W1D 5DU (mobile 07930 405323, e-mail paul@westernparade.co.uk)

BROWN, Paul Ray Beck; s of Sqdn Ldr Frederick Beck Brown (d 1997), of Linslade, Beds, and Kathleen, *née* May; *b* 20 July 1944; *Educ* Churcher's Coll Petersfield; *m* 1964, Maureen Ellen Ann, da of Joseph Archibald McMillan (d 1982); 2 da (Lucy Elizabeth Beck b 10 Feb 1965 d 2001, Clara Louise Beck b 20 Jan 1968); *Career* indentured: East Grinstead Courier 1963–65, Lincolnshire Standard 1965–66, Leicester Mercury 1966–68; investigative reporter Birmingham Post 1968–74, news ed Evening Post-Echo Hemel Hempstead 1980–81 (joined 1974), The Sun 1981–82, environment correspondent The Guardian 1989–2005 (joined 1982), currently columnist The Guardian and House and Garden magazine; tutor Guardian Fndn and UN Environment Prog (UNEP) courses in journalism; Midlands Journalist of the Year 1974; memb The Geologists' Assoc; FRGS, FRSA; *Books* The Last Wilderness, 80 Days in Antarctica (1991), Greenpeace (1993), Global Warming, Can Civilisation Survive (1996), Anita Roddick and the Body Shop (1996), Energy and Resources (1998), Just the Facts, Pollution (2002), North South East West (2005), Global Warning: Last Chance for Change (2006); *Recreations* badminton, travel, geology; *Style*— Paul Brown, Esq; ✉ 25 Rothschild Road, Linslade, Leighton Buzzard, Bedfordshire LU7 2SY (tel 01525 374050, e-mail paulbrown5@mac.com)

BROWN, Prof Peter; s of John Brown, of Sutton, Surrey, and Eugenie, *née* Karazeri; *b* 3 August 1960; *Educ* KCS Wimbledon, Trinity Coll Cambridge, Middlesex Hosp Med Sch; *m* 10 Jan 1987, Pauline Lilian, da of Harold Buchanan; 2 da (Alexandra Eugenie b 8 Dec 1993, Alisha Helen b 20 July 1995); *Career* sr clinical scientist MRC 1995–2001, conslt neurologist Nat Hosp for Neurology and Neurosurgery 1995–, reader UCL 2001–04; FRCP 1999; *Publications* over 200 publications on clinical neuroscience in learned jls; *Style*— Prof Peter Brown; ✉ National Hospital for Neurology and Neurosurgery, Queen Square, London WC1N 3BG (tel 020 7837 3611)

BROWN, Peter Michael; s of Michael George Harold Brown (d 1969), of Sussex, and Dorothy Margaret, *née* Douty; *b* 11 July 1934; *Educ* Rugby; *m* 1963, Rosemary Anne Brown, OBE, da of Hubert Simon (d 1979), of Geneva and Baden-Baden; 2 s (Hugo Michael Hubert b 1964, Dominic Peter b 1965); *Career* Nat Serv 2 Lt Somerset Light Infantry; chm: Enterprise Dynamics Ltd, Synergy Holdings Ltd, Charity and Fundraising Appointments Ltd, Gabbitas Educational Consultants Ltd, Independent Remuneration Solutions plc; ind dir: Goldshield Gp plc, County Contact Centres plc; pres Coram Family; chm Fountain Soc; tstee Tomorrow's Achievers; Liveryman Worshipful Co of Skinners; memb MRS, FInstD, FIPD, FRSA, FCA, FILog, FCIM; *Recreations* charity work, tennis, opera; *Clubs* Hurlingham, Lansdowne; *Style*— Peter Michael Brown, Esq; ✉ 12 Hyde Park Place, London W2 2LH; 9 Savoy Street, London WC2R 0BA (tel 020 7402 6050, fax 020 7706 7666, e-mail peter@synergyholdings.co.uk)

BROWN, Peter Wilfred Henry; CBE (1996); s of Rev Wilfred George Brown (d 1968), and Joan Margaret, *née* Adams (d 1998); bro of Prof Judith M Brown, *qv*; *b* 4 June 1941; *Educ* Marlborough, Jesus Coll Cambridge (MA); *m* 29 March 1969 (m dis), Kathleen, da of Hugh Clarke, of Freetown (d 1982); 1 da (Sonya b 1971); *Career* asst master in classics Birkenhead Sch 1963–66, lectr in classics Fourah Bay Coll Univ of Sierra Leone 1966–68, asst sec SOAS Univ of London 1968–75, sec Br Acad 1983–2006 (dep sec 1975–83, acting sec 1976–77); memb: Cncl Br Inst in Eastern Africa 1983–, Br Assoc for Central and Eastern Europe Governing Body 1983–96, Br Library Advsy Cncl 1983–89, Cncl SSEES Univ of London 1984–92 and 1993–99, Warburg Inst Univ of London 1987–93, Inst of Historical Research 1994–98, Cncl for Assisting Refugee Academics 1996–; fell Nat Humanities Center NC 1978; Hon DLitt: Univ of Birmingham, Univ of Sheffield; Knight Cross Order of Merit of the Republic of Poland; *Recreations* sedentary pursuits, musical, bookish; *Clubs* Athenaeum; *Style*— P W H Brown, Esq, CBE; ✉ 34 Victoria Road, London NW6 6PX

BROWN, Ralph; *b* 24 April 1928; *Educ* Leeds GS, Leeds Sch of Art, Hammersmith Sch of Art, RCA; *m* 1, 1952 (m dis 1962), Margaret Elizabeth Taylor; 1 s (Matthew b 1953), 1 da (Sara b 1955); m 2, 1964, Caroline Ann, *née* Clifton-Trigg; 1 s (Jasper b 1965); *Career* sculptor; exhibited widely in UK and worldwide 1953–, pt/t tutor RCA 1958–69; work purchased by many public collections incl: Tate Gallery, Leeds, Liverpool, Bristol, Arts Cncl of GB, RCA, Cardiff, Rijksmuseum, Kröller-Müller, Stuyvesant Fndn SA, Art Gallery of NSW, Contemporary Art Soc; ARA 1968, RA 1972, RWA 1997; *Style*— Ralph Brown, Esq, RA; ✉ Southanger Farm, Chalford, Gloucestershire GL6 8HP (tel 01285 760243, website www.ralphbrown.co.uk)

BROWN, Rt Rev Mgr Ralph; s of John William Brown, and Elizabeth Josephine Brown; *b* 30 June 1931; *Educ* Highgate Sch, St Edmund's Coll Old Hall Green, Pontifical Gregorian Univ Rome (Dr Canon Law JCD); *Career* Middx Regt 1949, served Korea 1950–51; ordained priest Westminster Cathedral 1959; Dio of Westminster: vice-chllr, vice-officialis 1964–69, judicial vicar 1969–76 and 1987–2006, vicar gen 1976–2001; papal chamberlain 1972, sec Canon Law Soc of GB and I 1974–80 and 1986–89 (pres 1980–86), nat co-ordinator for Papal visit to England and Wales 1982, prelate of honour to HH The Pope 1987, canonical advsr to Br Mil Ordinariate 1987–; sec Old Brotherhood of English Secular Clergy 1992 (memb 1987); hon memb Canon Law Soc: Aust and NZ 1975, Canada 1979, America 1979, GB and I 2006; Equestrian Order of the Holy Sepulchre: Knight 1984, Knight Commander 1991, prior Westminster Section 1996; Protonotary Apostolic 1999, Silver Palm of Jerusalem, Cross Pro Piis Meritis SMOM; *Books* Marriage Annulment (1969, 3 edn 1990), Matrimonial Decisions of Great Britain and Ireland (ed, 1969–), The Code of Canon Law in English Translation (co-translator, 1983), The Canon Law: Letter and Spirit (co-ed, 1995); *Publications* Canon Law Society Newsletter (ed, 1986–); various articles in Heythrop Jl, Studia Canonica, Theological Digest, The Jurist; *Clubs* Anglo-Belgian; *Style*— The Rt Rev Mgr Ralph Brown, Prot Ap; ✉ Flat 3, No 8 Morpeth Terrace, London SW1P 1EQ (tel 020 7798 9020, fax 020 7630 8805)

BROWN, Ralph William John Jules; s of John F W Brown, and Heather R Laming; *b* 18 June 1957; *Educ* LSE (LLB); *m* 25 July 1992, Jennifer Jules; *Career* actor, writer, director and producer; musician with Brighton Beach Boys (live shows incl Pet Sounds v Sgt Pepper); *Theatre* incl: West 1985, Deadlines 1986, Panic 1987, Macbeth 1987, Earwig 1990; *Television* incl: West 1986, Christabel 1988, Rules of Engagement 1989, The Black & Blue Lamp 1989, Say Hello to the Real Dr Snide 1990, Requiem Apache 1993, Devil's Advocate 1994, Karaoke 1995, Place of the Dead 1995, Ivanhoe 1996, A Respectable Trade 1997, The Last Train 1998, Cleopatra 1998, Extremely Dangerous 1999, Lock, Stock and Four Stolen Hooves etc 1999–2000, NCS Manhunt 2001, Lenny Blue 2001, Julius Caesar 2002, The Agency 2003, Footballer's Lives 2004, Lawless 2004, Big Dippers 2004, Nighty Night 2005, Rich Hall's Cattle Drive 2005, Spooks 2005, Coronation Street 2005, The Flood 2006, Cold Blood 2006, Cape Wrath 2006–07, Life on Mars 2007; *Film* incl: Withnail and I 1986, Buster 1987, Diamond Skulls 1988, Impromptu 1989, Alien III 1991, The Crying Game 1991, Undercover Blues 1992, Psychotherapy 1992, Wayne's World II 1993, Up N Under 1997, Amistad 1997, Star Wars: Episode 1 - The Phantom Menace 1997, New Year's Day 1999, The Final Curtain 2000, The Man Outside 2000, Mean Machine 2001, I'll Be There 2002, Exorcist - The Beginning 2003, Puritan 2004, Stoned 2004, Straightheads 2005, The Shooter 2006; as writer: Sanctuary (Samuel Beckett Award for Best First Play) 1987, Drive Away the Darkness 1988, Sanctuary DC 1989, Zone 1991, The Passion 1992–94, New Year's Day 1995–98 (also assoc prodr 1999; award winner Raindance Film Festival 2001, award winner Sapporo Film Festival 2001), Black Madonna 2001, High Times 2003, Red Light Runners 2003, In God's Footsteps 2004, Willing and Able 2004; dir: Danny and the Deep Blue Sea 1995, Host (The Crocketts) Pop Promo, The Murmuration 2001, The Last of the Toothpaste 2002; *Style*— Ralph Brown, Esq; ✉ c/o ARG Talent, 4 Great Portland Street, London W1W 8PA (tel 020 7436 6400, fax 020 7436 6700)

BROWN, His Hon Judge Richard George; DL (E Sussex 2004); *b* 10 April 1945, Durham; *Educ* Bournville Grammar/Tech Sch Birmingham, LSE (LLB), Inns of Court Sch of Law (Blackstone entrance exhbn); *m* 1 Jan 1969, Ann Patricia, *née* Wade; 2 s (Lawrence Richard b 14 Sept 1977 d 18 Nov 1980, Jeremy Lawrence Richard b 19 July 1985), 1 da (Elizabeth Ann b 23 April 1982); *Career* insurance clerk 1961–62, shop asst 1962–63, bus conductor 1963–64, trainee radio offr Merchant Navy 1964–65, taxi driver 1965–66, asst in maladjusted sch 1966–67, bus driver 1967–68; called to the Bar Middle Temple 1972, in practice 1972–92, recorder 1990–92 (asst recorder 1986–90), circuit judge (SE Circuit) 1992–, resident and liaison judge Lewes Combined Court Centre 1996–, sr circuit judge 2007–; vice-pres E Sussex Magistrates Assoc 1997–; chm Bd of Govrs Farney Close Sch Bolney 1984–86; *Recreations* travel, sport, being with the family; *Style*— His Hon Judge Richard Brown, DL; ✉ c/o Lewes Crown Court, High Street, Lewes, East Sussex (tel 01273 480400)

BROWN, Richard Howard; CBE (2007); *b* 23 February 1953; *Educ* Marlborough, Trinity Hall Cambridge (MA), UCL (MPhil), Harvard Business Sch; *m*; 3 c; *Career* grad trainee British Railways Bd 1977–79, corp planning asst rising to nat account sales mangr Freightliners Ltd 1979–84; British Railways Bd 1984–96: PA, business planning mangr InterCity HQ, mangr InterCity West Coast and Midland Main Lines, dir InterCity Midland Cross Country, md Midland Mainline Ltd; National Express Gp plc 1996–2002: chief exec Trains Div, gp commercial dir and memb Bd; ceo Eurostar Gp Ltd 2002–; vice-pres Chartered Inst of Logistics and Tport, chm Assoc of Train Operating Cos 2000–02; memb: Derby City Partnership 1995–99, Bd Derby and Derbys Economic Partnership; fndr memb Derby Rail Forum; tstee White Rose charity; FRSA, FCILT; *Recreations* sailing, skiing, walking, gardening; *Style*— Richard Brown, Esq, CBE; ✉ Eurostar UK and Group Ltd, Eurostar House, Waterloo Station, London SE1 8SE (tel 020 7922 4422, fax 020 7922 4482, e-mail richard.brown@eurostar.co.uk)

BROWN, His Hon Judge Robert; s of Robert Brown (d 1966), and Mary Lily, *née* Pullen (d 1995); *Educ* Arnold Sch Blackpool, Downing Coll Cambridge (BA, LLB); *m* 1, 1964 (m dis 1971) Susan; 1 s (Andrew Justin b 20 June 1964), 1 da (Jocelyn Fiona 15 Sept 1970), m 2, 3 Nov 1973 Carole, *née* Tait; 2 step s (James Francis b 12 May 1965, Benjamin William b 1 May 1967); *Career* called to the Bar Inner Temple 1968, standing counsel to DHSS Northern Circuit 1983–88, recorder of the Crown Court 1983–88, circuit judge (Northern Circuit) 1988–; *Recreations* golf; *Clubs* Royal Lytham St Anne's Golf; *Style*— His Hon Judge Robert Brown

BROWN, Robert Edward; MSP; s of Albert Edward Brown (d 2006), of Carlisle, and Joan, *née* Powton (d 1991); *b* 25 December 1947; *Educ* Gordon Schs Huntly, Univ of Aberdeen (LLB); *m* 28 Dec 1977, Gwen Wilson, *née* Morris; 1 da (Julie Elizabeth b 2 Jan 1979), 1 s (David Andrew b 17 Oct 1981); *Career* legal apprentice rising to legal asst Edmonds and Ledingham Aberdeen 1969–72, procurator fiscal depute Dumbarton 1972–74; Ross Harper & Murphy: legal asst 1974–75, ptnr 1975–99, legal conslt 1999–2005; MSP (Lib Dem) Glasgow 1999–, convenor Educn and Young People Ctee 2003–05, dep min for educn and young people 2005–07; memb Glasgow DC (Lib then Lib Dem) 1977–92; Parly candidate (Lib) Rutherglen 1974, 1979, 1983, 1987, 1997, 2003 and 2007, vice-chm Policy Ctee Scottish Lib Dems 1995–2002, policy convenor 2002–; chm Rutherglen CAB 1993–98; memb: Law Soc of Scot 1971, Scot Law Agents' Soc 1975, Glasgow Bar Assoc 1975, Royal Faculty of Procurators 1992; *Recreations* politics, history; *Style—* Robert Brown, Esq, MSP; ✉ 1 Douglas Avenue, Burnside, Rutherglen, Glasgow G73 4RA (tel 0141 634 2353); The Scottish Parliament, Edinburgh EH99 1SP; Constituency Office, Olympic House, Suite 5, 2nd Floor, 142 Queen Street, Glasgow G1 3PU (tel 0141 243 2421, fax 0141 243 2451)

BROWN, Roy Drysdale; s of William Andrew Brown (d 1975), of Cambridge, and Isabelle Drysdale, *née* Davidson (d 1987); *b* 4 December 1946; *Educ* Tonbridge, UCL (BSc), Harvard Business Sch (MBA); *m* 1978, Carol Jane, da of Dr Keene Manning Wallace, of Charleston, S Carolina; 2 s (Alexander b 1980, Cameron b 1984); *Career* Univ Scholarship course GEC 1965–69, commercial gen mangr Vosper Thornycroft Ltd 1972–74; Unilever plc: industrial conslt 1975–77, mktg mangr Uracem Div 1978–80, commercial dir Food Industries Ltd 1981–82, chm Pamol Plantations Sdn Bhd 1982–86, chm PBI Cambridge Ltd 1987–88, tech dir Birds Eye Walls Ltd 1988–90, chm Lever Brothers Ltd 1991–92; Unilever plc/NV: regnl dir Africa, Middle E and Agribusiness 1992–96 (with additional responsibilty for Central and Eastern Europe 1994 and Turkey 1995), pres for Food and Beverages Europe 1996–2001, main bd dir 1992–2001, ret 2001; non-exec dir: GKN plc 1996– (non-exec chm 2004–), Brambles Industries plc 2001–07, BUPA 2001–, HMV Gp plc 2002–, Lloyd's Franchise Bd 2003–, Alliance & Leicester plc 2007– (dep chm); CEng 1983, FIMechE 1983, FIEE 1990; *Recreations* classical music, opera, carpentry, photography, military history; *Style—* Roy Brown, Esq; ✉ GKN plc, 2nd Floor, 50 Pall Mall, London SW1Y 5JH

BROWN, Russell Leslie; MP; s of Howard Russell Brown (d 1987), and Muriel, *née* Anderson (d 2002); *b* 17 September 1951; *Educ* Annan Acad; *m* 3 March 1973, Christine Margaret Calvert; 2 da (Sarah Ann b 12 Aug 1977, Gillian b 8 April 1979); *Career* cncllr: Dumfries & Galloway Regnl Cncl 1986–96 (chm Public Protection Cmmn 1990–94), Annandale & Eskdale DC 1988–96, Dumfries & Galloway Unitary Cncl 1995–97; MP (Lab): Dumfries 1997–2005, Dumfries & Galloway 2005–; PPS to: Rt Hon Lord Williams of Mostyn, PC, QC 2002–03, Rt Hon Baroness Amos, PC 2003–05; memb House of Commons Select Ctee on: Euro Legislation 1997–99, Deregulation and Regulatory Reform 1999–2001, Scottish Affairs 2000–01, Standards and Privileges 2001–03, Regulatory Reform 2001–05; memb Scottish Lab Pty; *Recreations* walking, sport (as a spectator); *Style—* Russell Brown, Esq, MP; ✉ House of Commons, London SW1A 0AA (tel 020 7219 4429, fax 020 7219 0922, e-mail brownr@parliament.uk)

BROWN, Prof (James) Scott; *b* 28 November 1954, Glasgow; *Educ* Queen's Univ Belfast (MB BCh, BAO, MD); *m* Anne; 2 da (Susan, Alison), 1 s (Finlay); *Career* SHO: in gen med Royal Victoria Hosp Belfast 1980–81 (jr house offr 1979–80), in paediatrics Royal Belfast Hosp for Sick Children 1981–82, in obstetrics and gynaecology Waveney Hosp Ballymena 1982–83; GP registrar Portglenone Health Centre 1983–84, princ in gen practice Coleraine and MO to Univ of Ulster at Coleraine 1984–; GP trainer 1989–98, GP postgrad tutor 1992–98; chair of Gen Practice Studies Inst of Postgraduate Med and Health Services Univ of Ulster; Royal Coll of Gen Practitioners: NI Faculty rep on London Cncl 1989–, memb Clinical Research Div 1990–93, memb AIDS/HIV Working Pty 1991–93, chm Servs to Membs and Faculties Div 1992–93, chm Publishing Mgmnt Gp 1992–, chm PR Gp 1993–94, chm Services Network 1993–, memb Central Exec Ctee 1993–, memb RCGP/DOH Stress Fellowship Steering Gp 1995–97, memb RCGP Reaccreditation Fellowship Steering Gp 1995–, vice-chm RCGP 1996–99, memb RCGP Int Ctee 1997–; Astra/Shell Research Trg Fellowship (RCGP) 1988–90, Campbell Young Prize (NI Faculty RCGP) 1988 and 1990, hon research fell Dept of Gen Practice Queen's Univ Belfast 1988–94; author of various articles in peer-reviewed jls; DRCOG, DCH (RCPSI), FRCGP; *Recreations* golf, choral music singing, theatre; *Style—* Prof Scott Brown; ✉ Mountsandel Surgery, 4 Mountsandel Road, Coleraine, Co Londonderry BT52 1JB (tel 02870 342650, fax 02870 321000, e-mail jsbdoc@btopenworld.com)

BROWN, Simon John Saville; s of Ven Robert Saville Brown, and Charlotte, *née* Furber; *b* 6 July 1950; *Educ* Berkhamsted Sch, Selwyn Coll Cambridge (MA); *m*; 2 c; *Career* with Slaughter and May 1972–77 (admitted slr 1974), ptnr Denton Wilde Sapte (formerly Denton Hall) 1980– (joined 1977); *Recreations* jogging, music; *Style—* Simon Brown, Esq; ✉ Denton Wilde Sapte, 1 Fleet Place, London EC4M 7WS

BROWN, Rt Hon Sir Stephen; kt (1975), PC (1983), GBE (1999); s of Wilfrid Brown (d 1972), of Longdon Green, Staffs, and Nora Elizabeth Brown; *b* 3 October 1924; *Educ* Malvern Coll, Queens' Coll Cambridge; *m* 1951, Patricia Ann, da of Richard Good, of Tenbury Wells, Worcs; 2 s (twins), 3 da; *Career* served WWII as Lt RNVR; called to the Bar Inner Temple 1949 (bencher 1974, treas 1994); dep chm Staffs QS 1963–71, recorder West Bromwich 1965–71, QC 1966, a recorder and hon recorder West Bromwich 1972–75, judge of the High Court of Justice (Queen's Bench) 1977–83 (Family Div 1975–77), presiding judge Midland & Oxford Circuit 1977–81, Lord Justice of Appeal 1983–88, pres Family Div 1988–99; former memb Parole Bd England and Wales; memb Butler Ctee on Mentally Abnormal Offenders 1972–75, memb Advsy Cncl on Penal System 1977; chm Cncl Malvern Coll 1976–94, pres Edgbaston HS 1988–; *Recreations* sailing; *Clubs* Garrick; *Style—* The Rt Hon Sir Stephen Brown, GBE; ✉ 78 Hamilton Avenue, Harborne, Birmingham B17 8AR

BROWN, Prof Stephen Frederick; OBE (2005); s of Francis Maurice Brown (d 1989), of Pembroke, and Ruth Audrey, *née* Swallow (d 1987); *b* 29 September 1939; *Educ* Pembroke GS, Univ of Nottingham (BSc, PhD, DSc); *m* 27 April 1963, Marie Josephe Maryse, da of Jean Jacques André la Hausse de Lalouvière; 3 s (Andrew Stephen Francis la Hausse b 9 March 1964, Timothy Peter la Hausse b 4 Jan 1966, Christopher Giles la Hausse b 15 Aug 1967), 1 da (Michelle Anne la Hausse b 22 Sept 1969); *Career* jr engr Sir Robert McAlpine (S Wales) Ltd 1960–61; jr asst engr: Dormon Long (Africa) Ltd 1961–62, Scott Wilson Kirkpatrick and Partners 1962–63; Univ of Nottingham: sr research asst Dept of Civil Engrg 1963–65, lectr in civil engrg 1965–74, sr lectr 1974–78, reader 1978–82, prof of civil engrg 1982–2005, head of dept 1989–94 and 1999–2003, dean of engrg 1992–94, pro-vice-chllr 1994–98, dir Nottingham Centre for Pavement Engineering 2001–05, emeritus prof of civil engrg 2005–; chm Scott Wilson Pavement Engineering Ltd 2003–06 (dir 1985–2003), dir and pres SWK Pavement Engineering Inc 1993–2000; dir: Int Soc for Asphalt Pavements 1987– (chm 2000–02, hon memb 2006), Notice Ltd 1994–2002, Scott Wilson Pavement Engineering SDN BHD 1997–2003, Assoc of Asphalt Paving Technologists 1999–2000 and 2004– (hon memb 2004, pres 2007–08); Br Geotechnical Soc: Prize 1976, Rankine lectr 1996 (chm 1986–88); Instn of Highways and Tport Croda Award 1980, 1984 and 1989 (memb Cncl 1984–86); Inst of Civil Engrs: James Alfred Ewing Medal 1997, Webb Prize 1997, memb Cncl 2000–03; memb Civil Engrg Sub-Ctee HEFCE Research Assessment Exercise 2005–08; Kenyon Research and Educn Award US Nat Asphalt Pavement Assoc 2005; govr Loughborough Endowed Schs 1987– (chm Estates and Health and Safety Ctee 2005–); Liveryman Worshipful Co of Paviors 1996– (Liverymen's Ctee 1997–2004, treas 2001–04, Charity Ctee 2005–, Industry Ctee 2005–07, Paviors Medal 2004); hon fell Inst of Asphalt Pavement Technologists 2004; FIHT 1979, FICE 1982, FREng 1992; *Publications* An Introduction to the Analytical Design of Bituminous Pavements (1980), Cycling Loading of Soils (jt ed, 1991), over 220 technical papers on pavement engrg and soil mechanics; *Recreations* house maintenance, gardening, photography; *Clubs* Univ of Nottingham; *Style—* Prof Stephen Brown, OBE, FREng, DSc; ✉ School of Civil Engineering, University of Nottingham, University Park, Nottingham NG7 2RD (tel 0115 951 3900, fax 0115 951 3909, e-mail stephen.brown@nottingham.ac.uk)

BROWN, Dr Stewart; *Educ* Falmouth Sch of Art (BA), Univ of Sussex (MA), Univ of Wales (PhD), Univ of Nottingham (CertEd); *Career* teacher: Bayero Univ Kano Nigeria, Univ of the WI Barbados; currently dir Centre of West African Studies Univ of Birmingham; *Books* incl: Beasts (1975), Room Service: Poems (1977), Specimens (1979), Caribbean Poetry Now (ed, 1984, 2 edn 1992), Zinder (1986), Voiceprint: An Anthology of Oral and Related Poetry from the Caribbean (jt ed, 1989), Writers from Africa (1989), Lugard's Bridge (1989), Caribbean New Wave: Contemporary Short Stories (ed, 1990), James Berry (1991), The Art of Derek Walcott (ed, 1991), The Pressures of the Text: Orality, Texts and the Telling of Tales (ed, 1995), The Art of Kamau Brathwaite (ed, 1995), African New Voices (ed, 1997), Elsewhere: New and Selected Poems (1999), Kiss and Quarrel: Yorùbá/English Strategies of Mediation (2000), All Are Involved: The Art of Martin Carter (2000), The Oxford Book of Caribbean Short Stories (ed with John Wickham, 2000), The Oxford Book of Caribbean Verse (ed with Mark McWatt, 2005), Poems: Martin Carter (ed with Ian McDonald, 2006); *Style—* Dr Stewart Brown; ✉ Centre of West African Studies, School of Historical Studies, The University of Birmingham, Edgbaston, Birmingham B15 2TT

BROWN, Prof Stewart Jay; s of Vernon George Brown, of St Charles, Illinois, and Marion Eleanor, *née* Little; *b* 8 July 1951; *Educ* Glenbard West HS, Univ of Illinois (BA), Univ of Chicago (MA, PhD); *m* 2 Sept 1972, Teri Beth, da of Thomas Dorsey Hopkins (d 1981); 1 s (Adam b 1977), 1 da (Elizabeth b 1980); *Career* Whiting fell in humanities Univ of Chicago 1979–80, asst to dean and lectr in history Northwestern Univ 1980–82, assoc prof and asst head Dept of History Univ of Georgia 1982–88, prof of ecclesiastical history Univ of Edinburgh 1988–, dean Faculty of Divinity Univ of Edinburgh 2000–04; ed Scottish Historical Review 1993–99; memb Cncl: Scot Church History Soc, Scot Catholic Historical Assoc; FRHistS, FRSE; *Books* Thomas Chalmers and the Godly Commonwealth in Scotland (1982), Scotland in the Age of the Disruption (jtly, 1993), William Robertson and the Expansion of Empire (1997), Piety and Power in Ireland 1760–1960 (jtly, 2000), Scottish Christianity in the Modern World (jtly, 2000), The National Churches of England, Ireland and Scotland 1801–1846 (2001), Cambridge History of Christianity vol VII: Enlightenment, Reawakening and Revolution 1660–1815 (jtly, 2006), Providence and Empire: Religion, Politics and Society in the United Kingdom, 1815–1914 (2007); *Recreations* swimming, hill walking; *Style—* Prof Stewart J Brown; ✉ 160 Craigleith Hill Avenue, Edinburgh EH4 2NB (tel 0131 539 2863); Department of Ecclesiastical History, University of Edinburgh, New College, Mound Place, Edinburgh EH1 2LU (tel 0131 650 8958, e-mail s.j.brown@ed.ac.uk)

BROWN, Stuart Christopher; QC (1991); s of Geoffrey Howard Brown (d 1960), and Olive Lilian Baum, *née* Ford; *b* 4 September 1950; *Educ* Acklam HS Middlesbrough, Worcester Coll Oxford (BA, BCL); *m* 7 July 1973, Dr Imogen Brown, da of Edward Arthur Lucas, of London; 2 da (Sophie b 1976, Katherine b 1979); *Career* called to the Bar Inner Temple 1974, in practice N Eastern Circuit, recorder of the Crown Court 1992–, dep judge of the High Ct 1994–; memb Leeds & W Riding Medico-Legal Soc (pres 1988–90); *Recreations* theatre, travel; *Style—* Stuart C Brown, Esq, QC; ✉ Park Lane Chambers, 19 Park Lane, Leeds LS1 2RD (tel 0113 228 5000, fax 0113 228 1500)

BROWN, Terence Gibbin; s of Rex Brown (d 1990), and Mary Kathleen, *née* Gibbin (d 1971); *b* 14 September 1943; *Educ* All Souls Roman Catholic Sch Peterborough, King's Sch Peterborough, Sch of Architecture Architectural Assoc (Mastic Asphalt Assoc scholar, AA Dipl, RIBA pt III); *m* 1, 10 June 1972 (m dis 1991), Jacqueline Lesley Chinnery; 1 da (Sophie Madelaine b 26 June 1975), 1 s (Edric Samuel b 29 Sept 1977); m 2, 29 Aug 1992, Lucille Julia Cooper, da of Thomas Higgins; *Career* worked for Howard V Lobb & Partners (before completion of AA course); GMW Partnership: joined 1969, assoc 1979, design ptnr 1984, a sr ptnr 1991–; work incl: Zurich Insurance Portsmouth 1977, Minster Ct London 1991, Barclays Bank HQ London 1993, Midsummer Place Milton Keynes 2000, CIPD HQ Wimbledon 2002, Tower 42 London, 41 Lothbury London 2005; highly commended Br Construction Industry Awards 1990, MIPIM Euro Shopping Centre of the Year (St Enoch Centre Glasgow) 1991; memb: ARB (formerly ARCUK) 1971, RIBA 1971, AA 1969, Assoc of Conslt Architects 1989 (memb Cncl 2005), Twentieth Century Soc 1993, Town & Country Planning Assoc 1993, Urban Design Gp 1998; MInstD 1990, FRSA 1995; *Style—* Terence Brown, Esq; ✉ 24 West Hill Road, London SW18 1LN (tel and fax 020 8874 3805); GMW Architects, PO Box 1613, 239 Kensington High Street, London W8 6SL (tel 020 7937 8020, fax 020 7937 5815, e-mail terry.brown@gmw-architects.com, website www.gmw-architects.com)

BROWN, Timothy Colin; s of Peter Brindley Brown (d 2005), and Margaret Jean, *née* McIntosh; *b* 20 September 1957; *Educ* Eton, RMA Sandhurst; *m* 1, 24 Jan 1987 (m dis 1995), Lady Vanessa Petronel Pelham, yst da of 7 Earl of Yarborough; m 2, 19 March 2004, Melissa Stimpson, *née* Currie; 2 da (Annabel Georgina b 16 Dec 2004, Alexandra Siena b 8 July 2006); *Career* 4/7 Royal Dragoon Gds 1976–82 (A/Capt 1980); City & Commercial Communications plc 1983–91 (dir 1987–91), jt chief exec Tavistock Communications Ltd 1992–99 (dir 1991–99), investor relations dir Vodafone AirTouch 1999–2000, gp corp affrs dir Vodafone Gp 2000–04, Mere Consultancy 2004–; *Recreations* equestrian sports, skiing, shooting, backgammon; *Clubs* Cavalry and Guards', Lansdowne; *Style—* Timothy Brown, Esq

BROWN, Prof Tom; s of Tom Brown, of Barnsley, S Yorks, and Catherine, *née* Beardshall; *b* 10 November 1952; *Educ* Broadway GS Barnsley, Univ of Bradford (BTech, PhD); *m* Dorcas Jemema Selverani, da of Jacob Samuel; 1 s (Tom b 23 Sept 1982), 1 da (Asha b 20 April 1984); *Career* postdoctoral research: Dept of Chemistry Univ of Nottingham 1978–79, Dyson Perrins Laboratory Univ of Oxford 1979–82, Chemical Laboratory Univ of Cambridge 1982–85; prof of nucleic acid chemistry Univ of Edinburgh 1985–94, prof of bio-organic chemistry Univ of Southampton 1995–; dir Oligonucleotide Service Wellcome Trust (OSWEL) 1986–2001, conslt Chemistry Ctee SERC 1986; memb Ctee Edinburgh Centre for Molecular Recognition; Griffin and George Prize Univ of Bradford 1975, MakDougall-Brisbane Prize RSE 1992, Josef Loschmidt Award RSC 1992, Caledonian research fell RSE 1993, Royal Soc sr research fell 2005; author of numerous pubns; CChem, FRSC, FRSE; *Style—* Prof Tom Brown, FRSE; ✉ Department of Chemistry, University of Southampton, Highfield, Southampton SO17 1BJ (tel 023 8059 2974, fax 023 8059 2991, e-mail tb2@soton.ac.uk)

BROWN, (Harold) Vivian Bigley; CB (2004); s of Alec Sidney Brown, of Leeds, and Joyce, *née* Bigley; *b* 20 August 1945; *Educ* Leeds GS, St John's Coll Oxford (BA), St Cross Coll Oxford (BPhil); *m* 25 July 1970, Jean Josephine, da of Sir Eric Blacklock Bowyer, KCB (d 1963); 2 s (Matthew b 27 Feb 1973, Oliver b 30 Dec 1974); *Career* with Miny of Technol 1970–75, private sec to Perm Sec DTI 1972–74; commercial sec: Br Embassy Jedda FCO 1975–79, with DTI 1979–86, head Science and Technol Assesment Office Cabinet Office 1986–89; rejoined DTI 1989, chief exec ECGD 1997–2004, advsr to Miny of Fin and Nat Economy Bahrain 2004–; *Books* Islamic Philosophy and The Classical Tradition (with S M Stern and A Hourani, 1972); *Recreations* cycling, canoeing, piano; *Style—* Vivian Brown, Esq, CB; ✉ Ministry of Finance and National Economy, PO Box 333, Manama, Bahrain

BROWN, Prof William Arthur; CBE (2002); s of Prof Arthur Joseph Brown, of Leeds, and Joan Hannah Margaret Brown; *b* 22 April 1945; *Educ* Leeds GS, Wadham Coll Oxford (BA); *m* 1993, Kim Barbara, *née* Saunders; *Career* economic asst NBPI 1966–68, res assoc Univ of Warwick 1968–70; SSRC's Industrial Res Unit Univ of Warwick: res fell 1970–79, dep dir 1979–81, dir 1981–85; Univ of Cambridge: Montague Burton prof of industrial relations 1985–, fell Wolfson Coll 1985–2000, chm Faculty of Economics and Politics 1992–96, chm Sch of Humanities and Social Sciences 1993–96, chm Bd of Graduate Studies 2000–, master Darwin Coll 2000–, chm Faculty of Social and Political Science 2003–; memb: Low Pay Cmmn 1997–, ACAS 1998–2004; *Books* Piecework Bargaining (1973), The Changing Contours of British Industrial Relations (1981), The Individualisation of Employment Contracts in Britain (jtly, 1999); *Recreations* gardening, walking; *Style—* Prof William A Brown, CBE; ✉ Darwin College, Silver Street, Cambridge CB3 9EU (tel 01223 335668); Faculty of Economics and Politics, Cambridge CB3 9DD (e-mail wab10@econ.cam.ac.uk)

BROWN OF EATON-UNDER-HEYWOOD, Baron (Life Peer UK 2003), of Eaton-under-Heywood in the County of Shropshire; Sir Simon Denis Brown; kt (1984), PC (1992); s of Denis Baer Brown (d 1981), and Edna Elizabeth, *née* Abrahams; *b* 9 April 1937; *Educ* Stowe Sch, Worcester Coll Oxford (BA); *m* 31 May 1963, Jennifer, da of (Robert) Prosper Gedye Buddicom (d 1968); 1 da (Abigail b 1964), 2 s (Daniel b 1966, Benedict 1969); *Career* called to the Bar Middle Temple 1961 (Harmsworth scholar, bencher 1980), recorder of the Crown Court 1979–84, first jr treas counsel Common Law 1979–84, judge of the High Court of Justice (Queen's Bench Div) 1984–92, Lord Justice of Appeal 1992–2004, a Lord of Appeal in Ordinary 2004–; vice-pres Court of Appeal (Civil Div) 2001–03; intelligence services cmmr 2000–06; Liveryman Worshipful Co of Butchers; hon fell Worcester Coll Oxford 1993; *Recreations* golf, theatre, reading; *Clubs* Denham Golf, Garrick; *Style—* The Rt Hon the Lord Brown of Eaton-under-Heywood, PC; ✉ House of Lords, London SW1A 0PW

BROWNE, *see also:* Gore Browne

BROWNE, Anthony George; s of late Aloysious Browne, of London, and Frances, *née* Gurney (d 1997); *b* 18 June 1950; *Educ* Downside, BNC Oxford (MA); *m* 15 Nov 1969, Monique Odette, da of Maxime Marnat (d 1965), of Paris; 2 da (Geraldine b 1970, Emily b 1972); *Career* CA 1974; PricewaterhouseCoopers (formerly Price Waterhouse before merger): joined 1971, Exchequer and Audit Dept 1980–82, ptnr i/c privatisation servs 1983–89, ptnr i/c corp fin Australasia 1990–92, ptnr i/c corp fin and recovery UK 1992–94, memb UK Exec 1992–94, head of corp fin and recovery Europe 1994–98, memb Euro Mgmnt Bd 1994–98, world head of corp fin 1996–; memb Gen Cncl United World Coll of the Atlantic 1996–2001; FCA 1975; *Books* Guide to Evaluating Policy Effectiveness; *Recreations* sailing, walking, opera, art, literature; *Clubs* Reform, Royal Cruising; *Style—* Anthony Browne, Esq; ✉ PricewaterhouseCoopers, 1 Embankment Place, London WC2N 6RH (tel 020 7583 5000, fax 020 7804 2528)

BROWNE, Anthony Percy Scott; s of Percy Basil Browne (d 2004), of Semington, Wilts, and Pamela, *née* Exham (d 1951); *b* 8 January 1949; *Educ* Eton, ChCh Oxford (MA); *m* 8 May 1976, Annabel Louise, *née* Hankinson; 3 da (Eleanor b 9 Sept 1981, Cornelia b 17 May 1983, Molly b 29 Nov 1985); *Career* dir Christie's 1978–96, chm Br Art Market Fedn 1996–; memb: Cultural Industries Export Advsy Gp 1998–2001, Ministerial Advsy Panel on Illicit Trade 1999–2003, Bd European Fine Art Fndn 1999–; tstee Raise from Ruins 1978–80; vice-chm Art Fortnight London 2004–05; *Recreations* fishing, gardening; *Clubs* Turf, Pratt's; *Style—* Anthony Browne, Esq; ✉ British Art Market Federation, 10 Bury Street, London SW1Y 6AA (tel 020 7389 2148, fax 020 7839 6599)

BROWNE, Benjamin Chapman; s of Benjamin Chapman Browne (d 1968), of Balsham, Cambs, and Marjorie Grace Hope, *née* Hope-Gill (later Lady Wade; d 2001); *b* 18 May 1953; *Educ* Eton, Trinity Coll Cambridge (MA); *m* 28 July 1979, Sara Katharine, da of Brian Pangbourne, of Petersfield, Hants; 2 s (Benjamin Chapman b 22 Dec 1982, Edward Pangbourne b 1 April 1985), 1 da (Rebecca Katharine b 24 April 1989); *Career* admitted slr 1978; Lovell White and King 1976–79, Morrell Peel and Gamlen Oxford 1979–81; Clyde and Co: joined 1981, ptnr London 1985–2001, res ptnr Dubai 1989–90; ptnr (specialising in shipping and trade) Shaw and Croft 2001–; memb: Br Maritime Law Assoc, Comite Maritime Internationale, Lloyd's Form Working Party, Salvage Liaison Gp; *Recreations* walking, gardening, football; *Style—* Benjamin Browne, Esq; ✉ The Old Vicarage, Church Road, Steep, Petersfield, Hampshire GU32 2DB (tel 01730 233050); Shaw and Croft, 115 Houndsditch, London EC3A 7BR (tel 020 7645 9000, fax 020 7645 9001, e-mail ben.browne@shawandcroft.com)

BROWNE, Benjamin James; QC (1996); s of Percy Basil Browne, of Newtown Farm, Semington, Trowbridge, Wilts, and Jenefer Mary, *née* Petherick; *b* 25 April 1954; *Educ* Eton, Christ Church Oxford (MA); *m* 30 May 1987, Juliet Mary, da of Maj Geoffrey Beresford Heywood; 1 s (Samuel James Timothy b 14 July 1992), 1 da (Matilda Jane b 4 Oct 1989); *Career* called to the Bar Inner Temple 1976; *Recreations* country pursuits, gardening; *Clubs* Boodle's; *Style—* Benjamin Browne, Esq, QC; ✉ 2 Temple Gardens, Temple, London EC4Y 9AY (tel 020 7583 6041, fax 020 7583 2094)

BROWNE, HE Dr Carolyn; da of Brig Christopher Charles Lloyd Browne (d 1972), and Margaret, *née* Howard; *b* 19 October 1958, Yorks; *Educ* Univ of Bristol (BSc), Linacre Coll Oxford (DPhil); *Career* diplomat; desk offr Repub of Ireland FCO 1986–87, second sec then first sec Moscow 1988–91, EU Dept FCO 1991–93, UK Mission to the UN NY 1993–97, dep head Southern European Dept FCO 1997–99, head Human Rights Policy Dept FCO 1999–2002, UK rep Brussels 2002–04, advsr to Dir of Int Security FCO 2005–06, ambass to Repub of Azerbaijan 2007–; *Style—* HE Dr Carolyn Browne; ✉ c/o FCO (Baku), King Charles Street, London SW1A 2AH

BROWNE, (John) Colin Clarke; s of Ernest Browne, JP (d 1964), of Lisburn, Co Antrim, N Ireland, and Isobel Sarah, *née* McVitie (d 1996); *b* 25 October 1945; *Educ* Wallace HS Lisburn, Trinity Coll Dublin (BA); *m* 3 March 1984, Karen Lascelles Barr, da of Ian Barr (d 1995), of Edinburgh; 1 s; *Career* joined Post Office 1969, head of Bd Secretariat Post Office 1977–80, dir Chm's Office BT 1981–85, chief exec Broadband Servs BT 1985–86, dir of corp relations BT 1986–94, dir of corp affrs BBC 1994–2000; ptnr Maitland Consultancy 2000–; former dir MTV Europe and chm Children's Channel; memb: Cncl ISBA 1990–94, Health Educn Authy (later Health Devpt Agency) 1996–2003, Spongiform Encephalopathy Ctee (SEAC) 2003–04; tstee: BBC Children in Need 1994–2000, One World Broadcasting Tst 1997–2002, IIC 1998–2000; dir Cwlth Broadcasting Assoc 1997–2000; memb Govt Communications Review Gp 2003; FIPR; *Recreations* sport, music, reading; *Style—* Colin Browne, Esq; ✉ The Maitland Consultancy, Orion House, London WC2H 9EA (tel 020 7379 5151)

BROWNE, Desmond (Des); PC (2005), MP; *Career* MP (Lab) Kilmarnock and Loudoun 1997–, PPS to Sec of State for Scotland 1998–2001, PPS to Min of State for NI 2000, Parly under-sec of state NI Office 2001–03, min of state Dept of Work and Pensions 2003–04, min of state Home Office 2004–05, chief sec to the Treasy 2005–07, sec of state for def 2007–, sec of state for Scot 2007–; *Style—* The Rt Hon Des Browne, MP; ✉ House of Commons, London SW1A 0AA (tel 020 7219 3000)

BROWNE, Desmond John Michael; QC (1990); s of Sir Denis Browne, KCVO, FRCS (d 1967), of London, and Lady Moyra Browne, DBE, *née* Ponsonby; *b* 5 April 1947; *Educ* Eton, New Coll Oxford; *m* 1 Sept 1973, Jennifer Mary, da of Frank Wilmore, of Brierfield, Lancs; 2 da (Natasha b 1974, Harriet b 1976); *Career* called to the Bar Gray's Inn 1969 (bencher 1999), recorder of the Crown Court 1994–; *Recreations* Australiana, Venice, the South Downs; *Clubs* Brooks's, Beefsteak; *Style—* Desmond Browne, Esq, QC; ✉ 5 Raymond Buildings, Gray's Inn, London WC1R 5BP (tel 020 7242 2902, fax 020 7831 2686)

B

BROWNE, Henry; s of Henry Clarence Browne (d 1974), and Veva Helen, *née* Symons (d 1978); *b* 11 July 1944; *Educ* Felsted, Gstaad International; *m* 30 May 1969, Marion Carole, da of Charles Anthony Wenninger (d 1991), of Poole, Dorset; 1 da (Juliette Caroline b 30 Nov 1971), 1 s (Stephen Henry b 15 Dec 1975); *Career* chm Falcon Holdings plc 1974–; Freeman City of London 1990, Liveryman Worshipful Co of Painter-Stainers 1991; *Recreations* golf; *Clubs* RAC, Moor Park Golf; *Style—* Henry Browne, Esq

BROWNE, Jeremy; MP; s of HE Sir Nicholas Browne, KBE, CMG, *qv*, and Diana, née Aldwinckle; *b* 17 May 1970; *Educ* Univ of Nottingham; *Career* former Parly asst to Alan Beith MP, Dewe Rogerson 1994–96, dir of press and broadcasting Lib Dem Pty 1997–2000, Edelman Communications Worldwide 2000–02, ReputationInc 2003–; Parly candidate (Lib Dem) Enfield Southgate 1997, MP (Lib Dem) Taunton 2005–; *Style—* Jeremy Browne, Esq, MP; ✉ House of Commons, London SW1A 0AA

BROWNE, John Ernest Douglas de la Valette; s of Col Ernest Coigny de la Valette Browne, OBE, of Freshford, nr Bath, and late Victoria Mary Eugene, *née* Douglas; *b* 17 October 1938; *Educ* Malvern Coll, RMA Sandhurst, Cranfield Inst of Technol (MSc), Harvard Business Sch (MBA); *m* 1, 1965 (m dis 1983), Elizabeth Jeannette Marguerite, *née* Garthwaite; m 2, 1986, Elaine Margaret Boylen, *née* Schmid; *Career* served Grenadier Gds: Br Guyana (bn pilot), Cyprus, BAOR 1959–67, Capt 1963, TA Grenadier Gds (Vol) 1981–91, Maj 1986; associate: Morgan Stanley & Co NY 1969–72, Pember & Boyle London 1972–74; dir ME ops European Banking Co Ltd 1974–78; memb Westminster City Cncl 1974–78, MP (Cons) Winchester 1979–92; memb: Treasy Select Ctee 1982–87, Social Security Select Ctee 1990–92, Lords and Commons Anglo-Swiss All-Pty Gp 1979–92 (treas 1984–87, sec 1987–92), Lords and Commons Golf Soc 1988–92, Lords and Commons Yacht Club 1989–92; chm Cons Backbench Smaller Business Ctee 1984–87 (vice-chm 1983–84); sec: Cons Backbench Fin Ctee 1981–84, Cons Backbench Def Ctee 1982–84; introduced: Trades Description Act (Amendment) Bill 1988, Protection of Animals (Amendment) Act 1989, Protection of Privacy Bill 1989, Armed Forces (Liability for Injury) Bill 1991; UK delg N Atlantic Assembly 1986–92, elected rapporteur on human rights 1989–92; vice-pres investments Salomon Smith Barney Inc (Citigroup) 1995–, md Falcon Finance Management Ltd 1978–95, advsr Barclays Bank 1978–83, advsr Control Risks 1980–87; dir: The Churchill Clinic 1980–91, Worms Investment Ltd 1981–83, Tijari Finance Ltd 1985–92, TV3 Broadcasting Gp Ltd 1987–92, Int Bd of World Times 1988–2000, Scientific Component Systems NRG Inc 1990–91; tstee: Household Div Funds 1979–83, Winmall Community Assoc 1985–94; dir Drug Free America 1998–; hon Bd memb Greater Palm Beach Symphony 1998–; memb Ct Univ of Southampton 1979–90; patron Winchester Gp for Disabled People 1982–92; tstee Hursley Park CC 1985–92; govr Malvern Coll 1981–; Liveryman Worshipful Co of Goldsmiths 1982–; OStJ 1979 (memb Chapter Gen 1985–90); *Books* Tarantula - An Anglo American Special Forces Hunt for bin Laden (2002), Representation of The People in the 21st Century (2002); *Recreations* riding, sailing, shooting, skiing, golf; *Clubs* Boodle's, Turf, Fishers Island (NY), Ocean (Florida), Special Forces; *Style—* John Browne, Esq; ✉ 20 Sutton Place South, New York, NY 10022, USA (website www.ssbfcs.com/john_browne)

BROWNE, Brig Michael Edward; CBE (1994), TD (and three Bars), DL (1989); s of John Edward Stevenson Browne, CBE (d 1976), and Muriel May, *née* Lambert (d 1965); *b* 6 December 1942; *Educ* Uppingham; *m* 11 Dec 1970, Susan Elizabeth, da of Sir Hugh Neill, CBE; 2 da (Anna Jane b 27 April 1974, Nicola Catherine b 6 Sept 1975); *Career* TA 1961–94, cmd 3 WFR 1982–84, Brig TA UKLF 1991–94; admitted slr 1966, dep coroner Retford Dist 1970–80, dep dist judge Supreme Ct of Judicature 1986–; former chm Bassetlaw Cons Assoc; chm: Reserve Forces Assoc 1993–96 (pres 1999–2004), E Midlands Reserve Forces and Cadets Assoc (RFCA) 1994–2003; pres CIOR (Interallied Confedn of Reserve Offrs) 1996–98, chm Cncl Reserve Forces and Cadets Assoc 2004–; memb Law Soc 1966; *Recreations* tennis; *Clubs* Army and Navy; *Style—* Brig Michael Browne, CBE, TD, DL; ✉ Firdene, Church Street, Headon, Retford, Nottinghamshire DN22 0RD (tel 01777 249552); 19 Churchgate, Retford, Nottinghamshire DN22 6PF (tel 01777 707401, fax 01777 7713377, mobile 07774 233223, e-mail me.browne@btinternet.com)

BROWNE, His Hon Judge (James) Nicholas; QC (1995); s of James Christopher Browne, MC (d 1952), of London, and Winifred Jessie, *née* Pirie; *b* 25 April 1947; *Educ* Cheltenham Coll, Univ of Liverpool (LLB); *m* 28 March 1981, Angelica Elizabeth (Her Hon Judge Mitchell, d 2006), da of Sir George Mitchell, CB, QC, and Lady Elizabeth Mitchell; 2 da (Emily Elizabeth b 27 Nov 1981, Cassandra Lucy b 10 Dec 1983); *Career* called to the Bar Inner Temple 1971 (Duke of Edinburgh entrance scholar, bencher 2002), criminal practice Midland Circuit and SE Circuit, recorder of the Crown Court (Midland Circuit) 1993–2006 (asst recorder 1990–93), circuit judge (SE Circuit) 2006–; chm Code of Practice Appeal Bd Assoc of the Br Pharmaceutical Industry 2000–06; memb: Criminal Bar Assoc, Midland Circuit; *Recreations* squash, cricket, theatre, spending time with family and friends; *Clubs* Cumberland Lawn Tennis, MCC; *Style—* His Hon Judge Browne, QC; ✉ e-mail nbrowneqc@hotmail.com

BROWNE, Sir Nicholas Walker; KBE (2002), CMG (1999); s of Gordon Browne, and Molly, *née* Gray; *b* 17 December 1947; *Educ* Cheltenham Coll, UC Oxford (open scholar); *m* 1969, Diana, *née* Aldwinckle; 2 s, 2 da; *Career* HM Dip Serv: FCO 1969–71, Tehran 1971–74, second later first sec FCO 1974–76, on loan to Cabinet Office 1976–80, first sec and head of Chancery Salisbury 1980–81, first sec FCO 1981–84, first sec UK rep Brussels 1984–89, chargé d'affaires Tehran 1989, cnsllr FCO 1989–90, cnsllr (press and public affairrs) Washington and head of Br Info Services NY 1990–94, head Middle East Dept FCO 1994–97, chargé d'affaires Tehran 1997–99, ambass to Iran 1999–2001; sr dir (civil) Royal College of Defence Studies 2002–03, ambass to Denmark 2003–06; *Recreations* travel, theatre, happy gatherings; *Style—* Sir Nicholas Browne, KBE, CMG; ✉ c/o Foreign & Commonwealth Office, King Charles Street, London SW1A 2AH

BROWNE OF BELMONT, Baron (Life Peer 2006), of Belmont in the County of Antrim; Wallace Hamilton Browne; MLA; s of Gerald Browne, and Phyllis Hamilton, *née* Smyth; *b* 29 October 1947, Belfast; *Educ* Campbell Coll Belfast, Queen's Univ Belfast (BSc); *Career* biology teacher Rainey Endowed Sch Magherafelt 1970–2000; memb (DUP) Belfast City Cncl 1985– (alderman 1993), MLA (DUP) E Belfast 2007–; Lord Mayor of Belfast 2005–06; sits in House of Lords as crossbench peer 2006–; tstee Somme Assoc; memb NASUWT 1972; High Sheriff Belfast 2002–03; *Recreations* golf, football, cricket, rugby; *Clubs* Army and Navy; *Style—* The Lord Browne of Belmont; ✉ Northern Ireland Assembly, Parliament Buildings, Stormont, Belfast BT4 3XX; House of Lords, London SW1A 0PW

BROWNE OF MADINGLEY, Baron (Life Peer UK 2001), of Madingley in the County of Cambridgeshire; Sir (Edmund) John Phillip Browne; kt (1998); s of late Edmund Browne, and Paula Browne; *b* 20 February 1948, Hamburg; *Educ* King's Sch Ely, Univ of Cambridge (MA), Stanford Univ (MS); *Career* British Petroleum Company plc: joined as univ apprentice 1966, various exploration and prodn posts Anchorage, NY, San Francisco, London and Canada 1969–83, gp treas and chief exec BP Finance International 1984–86, exec vice-pres and chief fin offr Standard Oil Co Ohio 1987–89 (chief fin offr 1986–87); BP Amoco plc (formerly BP plc): chief exec and md 1989–95, main bd dir

1991–2007, gp chief exec 1995–2007; non-exec dir: Redland plc 1993–96, SmithKline Beecham plc 1996–99, Intel Corporation 1997–, Goldman Sachs 1999–; chm Advsy Bd Cambridge Judge Business Sch, emeritus chm Advsy Bd Stanford Grad Sch of Business; vice-pres Bd Prince of Wales Business Leaders Forum; tstee The British Museum 1995–2005; hon fell St John's Coll Cambridge; Hon LLD: Univ of Dundee, Notre Dame Univ, Thunderbird; Hon DSc: Univ of Hull, Leuven Univ, Cranfield Univ, Univ of Buckingham; Hon DEng: Heriot-Watt Univ, Colorado Sch of Mines; Hon DTech Robert Gordon Univ, Hon DUniv Sheffield Hallam, Hon Chem Tech Mendeleyev Univ Moscow; FIMM 1987, FREng 1993, CIMgt 1993; *Recreations* ballet, opera, collecting pre-Colombian artefacts; *Style*— The Rt Hon the Lord Browne of Madingley, FREng

BROWNE-WILKINSON, Baron (Life Peer UK 1991), of Camden in the London Borough of Camden; Nicolas Christopher Henry Browne-Wilkinson; kt (1977), PC (1983); s of late Rev Canon Arthur Rupert Browne-Wilkinson, MC, and Mary Theresa Caroline (Molly), *née* Abraham; *b* 30 March 1930; *Educ* Lancing, Magdalen Coll Oxford (BA); *m* 1, 1955, Ursula (d 1987), da of Cedric de Lacy Bacon; 3 s (Hon Simon, Hon Adam (twins) b 1957, Hon Oliver b 1962), 2 da (Hon Henrietta b 1960, Hon Martha b 1964); m 2, 1990, Mrs Hilary Isabella Jane Tuckwell, da of Prof James Wilfred Warburton; *Career* QC 1972, judge Court of Appeal Jersey & Guernsey 1976–77, judge of the High Court of Justice (Chancery Div) 1977, Lord Justice of Appeal 1983–85, vice-chllr Supreme Court 1985–91, a Lord of Appeal in Ordinary 1991–98, Senior Lord of Appeal in Ordinary 1998–2000; hon fell: American Coll of Trial Lawyers, American Law Inst; Hon LLD UEA; hon fell: St Edmund Hall Oxford, Magdalen Coll Oxford; *Recreations* gardening, music; *Style*— The Rt Hon Lord Browne-Wilkinson, PC; ✉ House of Lords, London SW1A 0PW

BROWNING, Angela Frances; MP; da of late Thomas Pearson, and late Linda Chamberlain; *b* 4 December 1946; *Educ* Reading Coll of Technol, Bournemouth Coll of Technol; *m* 1968, David Browning; 2 s; *Career* teacher of home economics in adult educn 1968–74, auxiliary nurse 1976–77, freelance conslt to mfrg indust 1977–85, mgmnt conslt specialising in trg, finance and corp communications 1985–92; MP (Cons): Tiverton 1992–97, Tiverton and Honiton 1997–; PPS Dept of Employment 1993–94, Parly sec Min of Agric Fisheries and Food 1994–97, oppn spokeswoman on education and disability 1997–98, shadow trade and industry sec 1999–2000, shadow Ldr of the House 2000–01, oppn spokeswoman on constitutional affrs until 2001; vice-chm Cons Pty 2001–; dir Small Business Bureau 1985–94 and 1997–99, chm Women into Business 1988–92, memb Dept of Employment Advsy Ctee for Women's Employment 1989–92, govt co-chm Women's Nat Cmmn 1996–97; Parly candidate (Cons) Crewe and Nantwich 1987, former chm Western Area CPC (and memb CPC Nat Advsy Ctee); pres Inst of Home Economics 1997–2000, vice-pres Inst Sales & Mktg Mgmnt 1997–; nat vice-pres Alzheimers Disease Soc 1997–; memb: Nat Autistic Soc, Thomas Hardy Soc; FInstSMM; *Style*— Mrs Angela Browning, MP; ✉ House of Commons, London SW1A 0AA

BROWNING, Frank Sacheverel (Chips); s of Frank Sacheverel Browning (d 1993), and Ivy Mary Jean, *née* Spice (d 1967); *b* 28 October 1941; *Educ* Dulwich Coll, Univ of St Andrews (MB ChB); *m* 1, 9 July 1966 (m dis 1996), (Carol) Angela, da of George Sutcliffe Seed (d 1958); 1 s (Benjamin Sacheverel b 1968), 2 da (Georgina Mary b 1970, Rebecca Louise b 1973); m 2, 23 Aug 1996, Mollie, da of Joseph Hiley (sometime Cons MP, d 1989); *Career* sr registrar in plastic surgery Leeds and Bradford 1971–80, conslt plastic surgn The Gen Infirmary at Leeds and St James's Univ Hosp 1980–99; microsurgery res fell St Vincent's Hosp Melbourne 1975–76; hon surgn Leeds Tykes RUFC, med dir Bramham Three Day Event; Freeman City of London; memb: BAPRAS, BAAPS, Med Equestrian Assoc; FRCS; *Style*— Chips Browning, Esq; ✉ Terry Lug Farmhouse, Bramham Park, Bramham, Wetherby LS23 6LT (tel 0113 289 2970)

BROWNING, (Walter) Geoffrey (Geoff); s of Lt Walter Samuel Browning (d 1992), and Dorothy Gwendoline, *née* Hill (d 1987); *b* 6 November 1938; *Educ* Burnage GS Manchester; *m* 1, 20 June 1964 (m dis 1982), Barbara; 2 da (Helen b 11 May 1965, Claire b 22 April 1969), 1 s (Matthew b 18 Sept 1967), 1 adopted s (Jon b 16 March 1972); m 2, 17 Aug 1983, Pauline Ann, da of William Wilkinson (d 1998); 2 da (Alexandra b 7 June 1984, Danielle b 9 Sept 1985); *Career* chartered accountant; asst gp sr KPMG (formerly Peat Marwick Mitchell and Co) 1961–63 (articled clerk 1955–60), div co sec The Steetly Co Ltd 1963–64, fin dir Syd Abrams Ltd 1964–69, jt md Boalloy Ltd 1969–90; dir: Marling Industries plc 1990–92, Ardsley Ltd 1992–, Habib European Bank Ltd 1995–; conslt Middlemede Consultants Ltd 1993–2000; underwriting memb Lloyd's 1980–96; FCA; *Recreations* sailing, golf, horses; *Style*— Geoff Browning, Esq; ✉ 4 Kermode Road, Eyreton Lea, Crosby, Isle of Man IM4 4BZ (tel 01624 853871)

BROWNING, Prof George Gordon; s of George Gordon Browning, of Glasgow, and Janet Smith Ballantyne, *née* Money; *b* 10 January 1941; *Educ* Kelvinside Acad, Univ of Glasgow (MB ChB, MD); *m* 1971, Annette Campbell, da of William Mallinson; 2 da (Gillian Gordon b 26 Jan 1973, Jennifer Gordon b 24 Oct 1974), 1 s (Grigor Gordon b 20 Sept 1978); *Career* former appts: resident house surgn and physician then research fell Dept of Surgery Western Infirmary Glasgow, MRC Wernher-Piggott travelling fell Harvard Univ and Massachusetts Eye and Ear Infirmary, sr registrar Glasgow Trg Scheme; sr lectr then titular prof in otorhinolaryngology Univ of Glasgow 1990–99; conslt otologist MRC Inst of Hearing Research Glasgow Royal Infirmary 1978–2003, hon conslt N Glasgow Tst 1978–, hon conslt in charge Dept of Otorhinolaryngology and Scottish Sch of Audiology Glasgow Royal Infirmary 1989–99; ed Clinical Otolaryngology 2004–; visiting scholar Sch of Public Health Harvard Univ 1989; Royal Soc of Med: chm Academic Bd 2001–03, vice-pres 2005–07, memb Section of Otology (pres 1999–2000; memb: Otorhinolaryngological Research Soc (sec 1983–86, pres 1992–94), Br Soc of Academics in Otolaryngology (sec 1992–94, pres 1994–99), Br Soc of Otolaryngologists, Scottish Otolaryngological Soc; Leon Goldman Medal Univ of Cape Town 1991, Walter Jobson Horne Prize BMA 1998, George Davey Howells Meml PrizeUniv of London 2000; FRCSEd 1970, FRCSGlas 1976; *Books* Clinical Audiology and Otology (1986, 2 edn 1998), Updated ENT (3 edn, 1994), Otoscopy - a structured approach (1995), Picture Tests in Otolaryngology (jtly, 1999); author of numerous articles in learned jls; *Recreations* silversmithing, skiing, swimming; *Style*— Prof George G Browning; ✉ MRC Institute of Hearing Research, Royal Infirmary, Queen Elizabeth Building, 16 Alexandra Parade, Glasgow G31 2ER (tel 0141 2114695, fax 0141 5528411)

BROWNING, John; *b* 5 June 1956; *Educ* Crown Woods Sch Eltham, Kingston Univ; *m* Linda; 1 s (James Stephen), 1 da (Virginia Elizabeth); *Career* Henry Bath Ltd 1979, Metallgesellschaft Ltd 1986, Kleinwort Benson Ltd (now Dresdner Kleinwort) 1989, Barclays Capital 2004–07, Bear Sterns Asia 2007–; dir London Metal Exchange 2002–04; FRSA; *Clubs* RAC; *Style*— John Browning, Esq; ✉ Bear Sterns Asia, Citibank Tower, 3 Garden Road, Central, Hong Kong

BROWNING, Prof Keith Anthony; s of James Anthony Browning (d 1972), and Amy Hilda, *née* Greenwood; *b* 31 July 1938, Sunderland; *Educ* Commonweal GS Swindon, Imperial Coll London (state scholarship, BSc, PhD, DIC); *m* 4 August 1962, Ann Muriel, *née* Baish; 2 da (Michelle Ann b 19 March 1967, Jacqueline Claire b 15 Sept 1968), 1 s (Julian James b 25 June 1971); *Career* meteorologist; research atmospheric physicist Air Force Cambridge Research Labs USA until 1966, princ meteorological offr Meteorological Office Radar Research Lab 1966–74, chief scientist Nat Hail Research Experiment Nat Center for Atmospheric Research USA 1974–75, chief meteorological offr Meteorological Office Radar Research Lab 1975–84; Meteorological Office: dep dir Physical Research 1985–89, dir of research 1989–91, memb Bd of Dirs 1989–91, dir Jt Centre for Mesoscale Meteorology (JCMM) Univ of Reading 1992–2003; prof of meteorology Univ of Reading 1995–2003, now emeritus; NERC: memb Cncl 1984–87, dir Univs Weather Research Network (UWERN) 1997–2003, dir Univs Facility for Atmospheric Measurements (UFAM) 2000–03, memb various ctees; chm: Int Symposia on Nowcasting (under auspices of Int Assoc of Meteorology and Atmospheric Physics) 1981, 1984 and 1987, Working Gp 1 Inter-Agency Ctee for Global Environmental Change 1990, Task Gp 7 Second World Climate Conf Geneva 1990, UK Interagency Atmospheric Radar Working Gp 1992, Global Energy and Water Cycle Experiment (GEWEX) Cloud System Study 1992–95, Scientific Prog Ctee European Conf on Global Energy and Water Cycles 1993–94, World Weather Research Prog Int Conf on Quantitative Precipitation Forecasting 2002; co-ordinator European Cloud Resolving Modelling Prog 1996–98; memb: American Meteorological Soc (AMS) Severe Local Storms Ctee 1965–67, Inter-Union Cmmn on Radio Meteorology 1975–78, Int Cmmn on Cloud Physics 1976–84, Cncl and Policy Advsy Ctee European Orgn for the Exploitation of Meteorological Satellites (EUMETSAT) 1986–90, Advsy Panel on Environmental Research Central Electricity Research Labs 1986–90, World Climate Research Prog Sci Steering Gp GEWEX 1988–97, Jt World Meteorological Orgn (WMO)/Int Cncl of Scientific Unions (ICSU) Scientific Ctee World Climate Research Prog 1990–94, Review Panel Aust Bureau of Meteorology Research Centre 1992, Scientific Steering Ctee WMO World Weather Research Prog 1996–; RMS: memb 1956–, vice-pres 1979–81, 1987–88 and 1990–91, pres 1988–90, chartered meteorologist 1994–, fndr memb Accreditation Bd (chm 1994–97), sometime memb Cncl; memb Academia Europaea 1989–; foreign assoc US Nat Acad of Engrg 1992–; ARCS 1959, fell AMS 1975, FRS 1978; *Awards* Air Force Cambridge Research Labs: Superior Performance Award 1964, Award for Special Service Accomplished 1965; RMS: L F Richardson Prize 1965, Buchan Prize 1972, William Gaskell Meml Medal 1982, Symons meml lectr 1998, Symons Gold Medal 2001; L G Groves Meml Prize for Meteorology MOD 1969; AMS: Meisinger Award 1974, Jule G Charney Award 1984, Carl Gustaf Rossby Medal 2003; Charles Chree Medal and Prize Inst of Physics 1981; *Publications* Nowcasting (ed), Global Energy and Water Cycles (co-ed); author of over 190 articles in learned jls in the areas of mesoscale meteorology, severe storms, frontal precipitation, radar meteorology and nowcasting; *Recreations* home and garden; *Style*— Prof Keith Browning, FRS; ✉ Department of Meteorology, University of Reading, Whiteknights, PO Box 243, Reading RG6 6BB (tel 0118 931 6521)

BROWNING, Ralph Morgan; s of Lt-Col John Morgan Browning (d 1974), of Coventry, Warks, and Anne, *née* Chalker (d 1971); *b* 9 August 1925; *Educ* Cheltenham Coll, The Queen's Coll Oxford (MA); *m* 6 Dec 1950, Mary Louise, da of Capt Martinell McLachlin (d 1925), and Dorothy, *née* Smith (d 2001), of St Thomas, Ontario; *Career* Lt 1/7 Rajputs IA 1945–47; mktg mangr The Procter & Gamble Co (UK, France, Italy, USA) 1950–66, mktg dir Reynolds Tobacco Co (Europe and ME) 1967–70, dir L'Oréal (UK) 1970–75; Rémy et Associés: jt md 1976–90, chm 1990–91; md Reid Pye and Campbell Ltd 1982–92, chm Eurobrands Ltd 1988–92, dir Rémy Cointreau 1991–97; dir SAFEC s.a. (Rheims) 1997–2003; memb W Dorset Cons Assoc; Liveryman Worshipful Co of Distillers 1987; *Recreations* fishing, stalking, tennis; *Clubs* Turf, Hurlingham; *Style*— Ralph M Browning, Esq; ✉ The Manor House, Martinstown, Dorchester, Dorset DT2 9JN (tel and fax 01305 889821)

BROWNJOHN, Alan Charles; s of Charles Henry Brownjohn (d 1985), of London, and Dorothy, *née* Mulligan (d 1976); *b* 28 July 1931; *Educ* Univ of Oxford (MA); *m* 1 (m dis 1969), Shirley Toulson; 1 s; m 2 (m dis 2005), Sandra Willingham; *Career* formerly sch teacher and lectr in English; freelance author and poet 1979–; chm Poetry Soc 1982–88; poetry critic: New Statesman 1968–76, Encounter 1977–80, Sunday Times 1990–; reg contrib to TLS and BBC Radio poetry progs; memb Cncl of Mgmnt Arvon Fndn 1973–2002; memb: Writers' Guild of GB, Soc of Authors; Cholmondeley Award for Poetry 1979, Soc of Authors travelling scholarship 1985; FRSL; *Books* Torquato Tasso (trans, 1985), The Way You Tell Them (1990, Authors' Club prize), Horace (trans, 1996), The Long Shadows (published in Romanian, 1996, Br edn 1997), A Funny Old Year (2001); poetry: Collected Poems (1988, new edn 2006), The Observation Car (1990), In the Cruel Arcade (1994), The Cat without E-Mail (2001), The Men Around Her Bed (2004); anthologies: First I Say This (ed), New Poems 1970–71 (ed with Seamus Heaney and Jon Stallworthy), New Poetry 3 (ed with Maureen Duffy); *Recreations* walking, travelling, left-wing censoriousness; *Style*— Alan Brownjohn, Esq; ✉ 2 Belsize Park, London NW3 4ET (tel 020 7794 2479); c/o Rosica Colin Ltd, 1 Clareville Grove Mews, London SW7 5AH (tel 020 7370 1080)

BROWNJOHN, John Nevil Maxwell; s of Gen Sir Nevil Charles Dowell Brownjohn, GBE, KCB, CMG, MC (d 1973), and Isabelle, *née* White (d 1984); *Educ* Sherborne, Lincoln Coll Oxford (MA); *m* 19 Nov 1968, Jacqueline Sally Brownjohn, MBE, da of Geoffrey Byrd (d 1952); 1 da (Emma b 1969), 1 s (Jonathan b 1971); *Career* literary translator, screenwriter; cmmnd Somersetshire LI 1948, served Royal W African Frontier Force 1948–49; chm Exec Ctee Translators' Assoc Soc of Authors 1976; Schlegel-Tieck Special Award 1979, US PEN Goethe-House Prize 1981, Schlegel-Tieck Prize 1993, US Christopher Award 1995, US Helen and Kurt Wolff Prize 1998, Schlegel-Tieck Prize 1999; *Books* over 150 book translations from German and French incl: The Night of the Generals (1963), Klemperer Recollections (1964), The Poisoned Stream (1969), The Human Animal (1971), Willy Brandt Memoirs (1978), A German Love Story (1980), Momo (1985), The Marquis of Bolibar (1989), Love Letters from Cell 92 (1994), Acts: The Autobiography of Wolfgang Wagner (1994), The Karnau Tapes (1997), Heroes Like Us (1997), The 13 and a Half Lives of Captain Bluebear (2000), Hidden Hitler (2001), Winston Churchill (2003), My Wounded Heart (2004), Please, Mr Einstein (2006), Elizabeth I and Mary Stuart (2007), The Sinner (2007), A Perfect Waiter (2008); *Screen Credits* Tess (in collaboration with Roman Polanski and Gérard Brach, 1980), The Boat (1981), Pirates (1986), The Name of the Rose (1986), The Bear (1989), Bitter Moon (in collaboration with Roman Polanski, 1992), The Ninth Gate (in collaboration with Roman Polanski, 1999); *Recreations* music; *Style*— John Brownjohn, Esq; ✉ Bookend House, Hound Street, Sherbourne, Dorset DT9 3AA (tel and fax 01935 814553, e-mail johnbrownjohn@tinyworld.co.uk)

BROWNLEE, Derek; MSP; *b* 10 August 1974; *Educ* Selkirk HS, Univ of Aberdeen (LLB); *Career* CA; Ernst & Young 1996–2002, IOD 2002–04, Deloitte 2004–05, MSP (Cons) S of Scotland 2005–; party spokesperson on finance and public servs; memb Scottish Parl: Finance Ctee, Cross-Party Gp on Borders Rail, Cross-Party Gp on the Scottish Economy; *Style*— Derek Brownlee, Esq, MSP; ✉ 72 High Street, Peebles EH45 8SW (tel 01721 729215); The Scottish Parliament, Edinburgh EH99 1SP (tel 0131 348 5635, fax 0131 348 5932, e-mail derek.brownlee.msp@scottish.parliament.uk)

BROWNLIE, Ian; CBE (1993), QC (1979); s of John Nason Brownlie (d 1952), and Amy Isabella, *née* Atherton (d 1975); *b* 19 September 1932; *Educ* Alsop HS Liverpool, Oxford (MA, DPhil, DCL); *m* 1, 1957, Jocelyn Gale; 1 s, 2 da; m 2, 1978, Christine Apperley, LLM; *Career* called to the Bar Gray's Inn 1958 (bencher 1988); in practice 1967–; fell Wadham Coll Oxford 1963–76, prof of int law LSE 1976–80, Chichele prof of public int law Univ of Oxford 1980–99, fell All Souls Coll Oxford 1980–99 (distinguished fell 2004–); sr ed Br Year Book of Int Law, dir of studies Int Law Assoc 1982–91; memb Int Law Commission 1997–; author of various works on public int law 1982–99; FBA 1979; *Style*— Ian Brownlie, CBE, QC, FBA; ✉ Blackstone Chambers, Blackstone House, Temple, London EC4Y 9BW

BROWNLOW, 7 Baron (1776 GB), of Belton; Sir Edward John Peregrine Cust; 10 Bt (1677 E); s of 6 Baron Brownlow (d 1978), by his 1 w, Katherine (d 1952), da of Brig-Gen Sir David Kinloch, 11 Bt, CB, MVO; *b* 25 March 1936; *Educ* Eton; *m* 1964, Shirlie, da of late

John Yeomans, of The Manor Farm, Hill Croome, Upton-on-Severn; 1 s (Hon Peregrine Edward Quintin b 9 July 1974); *Heir* s, Hon Peregrine Cust; *Career* memb Lloyd's 1961–88; dir Hand-in-Hand Fire and Life Insurance Society (branch of Commercial Union Assurance Co Ltd) 1962–82, chm and md Harris & Dixon (Underwriting Agencies) Ltd 1976–82, dir Ermitage International Ltd; High Sheriff Lincs 1978–79; CStJ 2000 (OStJ 1997, chm Cncl Jersey 1996–2005); *Clubs* White's, Pratt's, Victoria (Jersey); *Style*— The Rt Hon the Lord Brownlow; ✉ La Maison des Prés, St Peter, Jersey JE3 7EL

BROZZETTI, Gianluca; *b* 4 March 1954; *Educ* Univ of Perugia; *Career* various positions: Procter & Gamble, McKinsey & Co, Gucci Group; exec dir Watch and Jewellery Div rising to exec vice-pres Fragrance Div Bulgari Group, pres and ceo Louis Vuitton Malletier 1999–2001, group ceo Asprey & Garrard 2001–05, ceo Asprey 2005–; *Style*— Gianluca Brozzetti, Esq

BRUCE, *see also:* Cumming-Bruce

BRUCE, (Robert) Andrew; s of Robert Bruce (d 1965), and Betty, *née* Bowen (d 1988); *b* 23 June 1949, Cardiff; *Educ* Pembroke Coll Cambridge (MA), Manchester Business Sch (MBA); *m* (m dis); 4 s (Robert b 29 April 1978, James b 17 Dec 1979, Alexander b 1 Oct 1984, Edward b 3 May 1987); *Career* J P Morgan: joined 1973, petroleum and project finance 1974–82, corporate finance SW USA 1982–86, head of risk J P Morgan Securities 1986–88, head of corporate financing 1988–2001, European head of credit 2001–2004; Barclays plc: risk dir BZW/Barclays Capital 1994–98, gp credit risk dir 1998–; dir: Clearstream 1996–, Witan Investment Trust 2003–; *Recreations* sailing, skiing, golf; *Clubs* Royal Southern Yacht; *Style*— Andrew Bruce, Esq; ✉ Barclays plc, 1 Churchill Place, Canary Wharf, London E14 5HP (tel 020 7116 8257, e-mail andrew.bruce@barclayscapital.com)

BRUCE, Christopher; CBE (1998); s of Alexander Bruce (d 1970), and Ethel, *née* Parker; *b* 3 October 1945; *Educ* Rambert Sch; *m* 1967, Marian, da of Frank Meadowcroft, MBE (d 1969); 2 s (Mark Sebastian b 1968, Thomas Benjamin b 1970), 1 da (Molly Ellen b 1975); *Career* choreographer; formerly dancer with London Ballet, Ballet Rambert (roles incl: The Poet in Cruel Garden, Prospero in The Tempest, Pierrot in Pierrot Lunaire), English Nat Ballet (roles incl: Tchaikovsky/Drosselmeyer in The Nutcracker and title role in Petrouchka); assoc choreographer: Ballet Rambert 1979–86 (assoc dir 1975–79), Eng Nat Ballet 1986–91; artistic dir Rambert Dance Co 1994–2003, resident/assoc choreographer Houston Ballet 1989–; works as choreographer for Ballet Rambert incl: George Frideric (debut, music by Handel) 1969, Ancient Voices of Children 1975, Cruel Garden (with Lindsay Kemp) 1977, Ghost Dances 1981, Requiem 1982, Intimate Pages 1984, Ceremonies 1986; works for Eng Nat Ballet incl: Land 1985, The World Again 1986, The Dream is Over 1987, Symphony in Three Movements 1989; works for Houston Ballet incl: Guatama Buddha 1989, Journey 1990, Nature Dances 1992, Hush 2006; works for Rambert Dance Co: Crossing 1994, Meeting Point 1995, Quicksilver 1996, Stream 1996, Four Scenes 1998, God's Plenty 1999, A Steel Garden 2005, Grinning in Your Face 2007; works for other companies incl: Unfamiliar Playground (Royal Ballet) 1974, Cantate (Tanz Forum Cologne) 1981, Village Songs (Nederlands Dans Theater) 1981, Silence is the End of our Song (Royal Danish Ballet) 1984, Remembered Dances (Scottish Ballet) 1985, Les Noces (Gulbenkian Ballet Lisbon) 1989, Il Ballo della Ingrate Agrippina and Venus and Adonis (Kent Opera), Rooster (Geneva Ballet) 1991, Three Songs-Two Voices (Royal Ballet) 2005; new ballets created: Kingdom (Geneva) 1993, Moonshine (Nederlands Dans Theater) 1993, Waiting (London Contemporary Dance Theatre) 1993; subject of BBC documentary 1978; Evening Standard Award for Dance 1974, Prix Italia 1982, International Theatre Inst Award for Dance 1993, Evening Standard Ballet Award for Outstanding Artistic Achievement 1996; Hon Dr Art De Montfort Univ 2000, Hon DLitt Univ of Plymouth 2001; *Style*— Christopher Bruce, Esq, CBE; ✉ c/o Rambert Dance Co, 94 Chiswick High Road, London W4 1SH

BRUCE, David Ian Rehbinder; s of Ian Stuart Rae Bruce, MC (d 1967), and Reinhildt Hilda Henriette Reinholdtsdotter, *née* Baroness Rehbinder; *b* 16 August 1946; *Educ* Eton, Oriel Coll Oxford (MA); *m* 4 Dec 1976, Anne Margaret Turquand (Muffyn), da of Col David Frank Turquand Colbeck, OBE (d 1995); 2 s (Edward, Ian (twins) b 1984); *Career* chartered accountant; Peat Marwick Mitchell & Co 1968–72; Cazenove & Co: investment analyst 1972–79, conslt Ctee to Review the Functioning of Fin Inst 1977–79; Royal Dutch/Shell Gp: asst treas advsr Shell Int Petroleum Co Ltd 1979–80, mangr fin planning Shell Canada Ltd 1980–83, treas & controller Shell UK Ltd 1983–86; exec dir fin and admin The Stock Exchange 1986–90, gp fin dir Guinness Mahon Holdings plc 1990–93, dir of fin Lloyd's of London 1993; chm Bolingbroke Mgmnt Consultancy Ltd 1995–; former memb Hundred Gp, memb Tech Ctee of the Assoc of Corporate Treasurers 1988–; Freeman City of London 1977, Liveryman Worshipful Co of Merchant Taylors 1980; FCA, AIIMR, FCT; *Recreations* music, opera (spectator), shooting, fishing; *Clubs* Pratt's, White's; *Style*— David Bruce, Esq; ✉ 5 Bolingbroke Grove, London SW11 6ES (tel 020 8673 1434, fax 020 7787 8144); office (tel 020 7771 0065)

BRUCE, Fiona Elizabeth; da of John Bruce, and Rosemary Bruce; *Educ* Int Sch Milan, Aske's Girls' Sch, Br Inst Paris (scholar), Hertford Coll Oxford (MA); *Career* broadcaster; BBC: reporter Newsnight 1996–98, presenter Six O'Clock News 1999–2002, presenter 10 O'Clock News 2002–; presenter: Antiques Show 1998–2000, Crimewatch 2000–, Real Story 2003–, Call My Bluff 2003; patron Touch UCHL, supporter Refuge; ambass: Childline, Prince's Tst, Action Medical Research; *Recreations* playing with my children; *Style*— Ms Fiona Bruce; ✉ c/o Knight Ayton Management, 114 St Martin's Lane, London WC2N 4BE (tel 020 7836 5333)

BRUCE, Prof Ian Waugh; CBE (2004); s of Thomas Waugh Bruce (d 1980), and Una Nellie, *née* Eagle (d 1987); *b* 21 April 1945; *Educ* King Edward VI Sch Southampton, Central HS Arizona, Univ of Birmingham (BSocSci); *m* 19 June 1971, Anthea Christine (Tina), da of Dr P R Rowland, of London; 1 da (Hannah b 20 Dec 1976), 1 s (William Waugh (Tom) b 18 May 1979); *Career* apprentice chem engr Courtaulds 1964–65, mktg trainee then mangr Unilever 1968–70, appeals and PR offr then asst dir Age Concern England 1970–74, dir Nat Centre for Volunteering 1975–81, controller of secretariat then asst chief exec Borough of Hammersmith and Fulham 1981–83, vice-pres RNIB 2003– (dir gen 1983–2003); Cass Business Sch (formerly City Univ Business Sch): visiting prof 1991–, hon dir VOLPROF (Centre for Vol Sector and Not-for-Profit Mgmnt) 1991–2003, head Centre for Charity Effectiveness 2003–; chm Coventry Int Centre 1964, memb Arts Cncl of GB Art Panel, Art Film Ctee and New Activities Ctee 1967–71, conslt UN Div of Social Affrs 1970–72; spokesman: Artists Now 1973–77, Nat Good Neighbour Campaign 1977–79; founding sec Volunteurope Brussels 1979–81, advsr BBC Community Progs Unit 1979–81, co-chm Disability Benefits Consortium 1987–2001; memb: Exec Ctee NCVO 1978–81 and 1990–94, Cncl Ret Execs Action Clearing House 1978–83, Advsy Cncl Centre for Policies on Ageing 1979–83, Educn Advsy Cncl IBA 1981–83, Steering Ctee Disability Alliance 1985–92, Exec Ctee Age Concern Eng 1986–92, Nat Advsy Cncl on Employment of Disabled People 1987–98, Bd Central London TEC 1990–97 (dep chm 1996–97), Ctee Nat Giving Campaign 2001–04; chair Res Ctee 2001–04; Univ of Birmingham: Cncl 1994–2000, Ct 2001–; Sir Raymond Priestley Expeditionary Award Univ of Birmingham 1968, UK Charity Outstanding Achievement Award 2001 and 2003; Hon DSocSc Univ of Birmingham 1995; memb ICA, MIMgt 1975, FIMgt 1981, CIMgt 1991, FRSA 1991; *Publications* Public Relations and the Social Services (1972), Patronage of the Creative Artist (jtly, 1974, 2 edn 1975), Blind and Partially Sighted Adults in Britain (1991), Managing and Staffing Britain's Largest Charities (jtly, 1992), Management for Tomorrow (jtly, 1993), Access to Written Information (jtly, 2001), Employment and Unemployment Among People with Sight Problems in the UK (jtly, 2003), Charity Marketing - Meeting Need through Customer Focus (3 edn, 2005); author of papers on visual impairment, voluntary and community work, older people, contemporary art and marketing; *Recreations* the arts, the countryside; *Style*— Prof Ian Bruce, CBE; ✉ Ormond House Cottage, Ormond Road, Richmond, Surrey TW10 6TH; Cass Business School, 106 Bunhill Row, London EC1Y 8TZ (tel 020 7040 8667)

B

BRUCE, Kenneth Robertson (Ken); s of Peter Smith Bruce (d 1984), and Williamina McKenzie, *née* Dunbar (d 2000); *b* 2 February 1951; *Educ* Hutchesons' Boys' GS Glasgow; *m* 1 (m dis), Fiona Frater; 2 s (Campbell McKenzie b 20 Nov 1979, Douglas Robertson b 23 March 1981); m 2, (m dis), Anne Gilchrist; 1 da (Kate Anne b 15 Oct 1992); m 3, 16 Sept 2000, Kerith Coldham; 1 s (William Murray b 5 Jan 2002), 1 da (Verity Isobel b 1 April 2005); *Career* broadcaster; BBC staff announcer 1976–80 (progs incl: Good Morning Scotland, SRO Road Show, Ken Bruce's Saturday (BBC Radio Scot), Midday Concert (BBC Radio 3), Music To Remember (BBC Radio 4); freelance broadcaster 1980–, own daily prog BBC Radio Scot 1980–84; BBC Radio 2: reg dep work 1982–83, own Saturday night show 1984, own daily morning prog 1985–90 and 1991–, presenter daily late night prog 1990; weekly prog BBC World Service 1986–93, presenter Breakaway (BBC Radio 4) 1990–92; main presenter Nat Music Day 1992–95; other progs incl: The 'What If' Show, The ABC Quiz, Pop Score, Comedy Classics (BBC Radio 2), Freewheeling, Pick of the Week (BBC Radio 4), Friday Night is Music Night (BBC Radio 2); commentaries: Commonwealth Games 1986, Olympic Games Seoul 1988, Eurovision Song Contest (BBC Radio 2) 1988–; events incl: Wings and Strings, Voice of Musical Theatre 2000, Proms in the Park; *Recreations* films, reading, music, theatre; *Style*— Ken Bruce, Esq; ✉ c/o Jo Gurnett Personal Management, 12 Newburgh Street, London W1F 7RP (tel 020 7440 1850, fax 020 7287 9642)

BRUCE, Rt Hon Malcolm Gray; PC (2006), MP; s of late David Stewart Bruce, of Wirral, and late Kathleen Elmslie, *née* Delf; *b* 17 November 1944; *Educ* Wrekin Coll, Univ of St Andrews (MA), Univ of Strathclyde (MSc), Univ of Middx (CPE); *m* 1, 1969 (m dis 1992), Veronica Jane, da of Henry Coxon Wilson, of West Kirby, Wirral; 1 s (Alexander b 1974), 1 da (Caroline b 1976); m 2, 1998, Rosemary Elizabeth, da of Peter Arthur Vetterlein, of Beckenham, Kent; 1 da (Catriona b 1999), 1 s (Alasdair b 2002); *Career* trainee journalist Liverpool Daily Post, buyer Boots Ltd, res info offr NESDA, journalist and publisher Aberdeen Petroleum Publishing Ltd; called to the Bar Gray's Inn 1995; Parly candidate (Lib): North Angus and Mearns Oct 1974, West Aberdeenshire 1979; MP (Lib 1983–88, Lib Dem 1988–) Gordon 1983–; Lib spokesman Energy 1986–87, Alliance spokesman Employment 1987, Lib spokesman Trade and Indust 1987–88, SLD spokesman Natural Resources 1988–89; Lib Dem spokesman: Environment and Natural Resources 1989–90, Scotland 1990–92, Treasy and Econ Affrs 1994–99 (also Treasy and Civil Serv 1994–95), Trade and Indust; chm Lib Dem Parly Pty 1999–2001, Lib Dem shadow sec of state for the Environment, Food and Rural Affrs 2001–02; memb: Scottish Select Ctee 1983–87, Trade and Industry Ctee 1987–89 and 1992–94, Treasy Ctee 1994–98, Standards and Privileges Select Ctee 1999–2001, Parly Assembly Cncl of Europe 1999–; pres Scot Lib Dems 2000– (ldr 1988–92); occasional journalist and broadcaster; vice-pres Nat Deaf Children's Soc; tstee Royal Nat Inst for the Deaf; rector Univ of Dundee 1984–87; *Style*— The Rt Hon Malcolm Bruce, MP; ✉ House of Commons, London SW1A 0AA

BRUCE, Sir (Francis) Michael Ian; 12 Bt (NS 1628), of Stenhouse, Stirlingshire; s of Sir Michael William Selby Bruce, 11 Bt (d 1957); *b* 3 April 1926; *m* 1, 1947 (m dis 1957), Barbara Stevens, da of Francis J Lynch; 2 s (Michael Ian Richard b 1950, Robert Dudley b 1952); m 2, 1961 (m dis 1963), Frances Keegan; m 3, 1966 (m dis 1975), Marilyn Anne, da of Carter Mullaly; m 4, Patricia Gail, da of Frederich Root; m 5, 1994, Alessandro Conforto, MD; *Heir* s, Michael Bruce; *Career* US Marine Corps 1943–46, memb Sqdn A 7 Regt NY 1948 (ret); ptnr Gossard-Bruce Co 1953–, Master Mariner's Ticket 1968; pres: Newport Sailing Club Inc Calif 1978–, Newport Academy of Sail Inc Calif 1979–, American Maritime Co 1980–; dir Lenders Indemnity Corp 1985–; *Clubs* Balboa Bay (Newport Beach), Vikings of Orange (Newport Beach); *Style*— Sir Michael Bruce, Bt; ✉ 34 Cormorant Circle, Newport Beach, CA 92663, USA; Newport Sailing Club and Academy of Sail, 3432 Via Oporto, Suite 204, Newport Beach, CA 92663, USA (tel 00 1 714 675 7100)

BRUCE, Robert Charles; s of late Maj James Charles, MC (and Bar), and Enid Lilian, *née* Brown; *b* 5 May 1948; *Educ* Belmont House, Solihull Sch, City of London Coll (BSc); *Career* trainee accountant Edward Moore and Sons 1971–75; Accountancy Age: staff writer and news ed 1976–81, ed 1981–90, assoc ed 1990–93; The Times: accountancy columnist 1992–99, accountancy ed 1999–2001; ed: Corporate Financier 1998–2004, Balance Sheet 1999–2004; Accountancy Journalist of the Year 1995, overall winner Inst of Internal Auditors (IIA) Millennium Award for excellence in business and mgmnt press journalism 2000, IIA Award for excellence in business journalism 2001, shortlisted Tax Journalist of the Year 2001, Inst of Financial Accountants (IFA) Business Finance Journalist of the Year 2004, finalist Tax Writer of the Year 2006; FRSA; *Books* Winners - How Small Businesses Achieve Excellence (1986), ICAS: 150 Years - a Celebration (2004); *Recreations* cricket, buying books; *Clubs* MCC, BCC; *Style*— Robert Bruce, Esq; ✉ 87 Marylands Road, London W9 2DS (tel 020 7286 0211, e-mail robertbruce@ntlworld.com)

BRUCE, Steve Roger; s of Joseph Bruce, of Newcastle upon Tyne, and Sheenagh, *née* Creed; *b* 31 December 1960; *Educ* Benfield Comp Sch Newcastle upon Tyne; *m* Janet, da of Lesley Smith; 1 s (Alex b 28 Sept 1984), 1 da (Amy b 24 May 1987); *Career* professional footballer and manager; player: Gillingham 1978–84, Norwich City 1984–87 (League Cup 1985), Manchester United 1987–96 (capt 1994–96, FA Cup 1990, 1994 and 1996, European Cup Winners' Cup 1991, League Cup 1992, FA Premier League Championship 1993, 1994 and 1996, Charity Shield 1993 and 1994), Birmingham City 1996–98; player/mangr Sheffield United FC 1998–99; mangr: Huddersfield Town FC 1999–2001, Birmingham City FC 2001–; England: 8 youth caps, 1 B cap; *Style*— Steve Bruce, Esq

BRUCE, Prof Victoria Geraldine (Vicki); OBE (1997); da of Charles Frederick Bruce, and Geraldine Cordelia Diane, *née* Giffard; *b* 4 January 1953; *Educ* Church HS Newcastle, Newnham Coll Cambridge (MA, PhD); *Career* demonstrator Dept of Psychology Univ of Newcastle upon Tyne 1977–78; Univ of Nottingham: lectr in psychology 1978–88, reader 1988–90, prof of psychology 1990–92; Univ of Stirling: prof of psychology 1992–2002, dep princ (research) 1995–2002; vice-princ and head Coll of Humanities and Social Sci Univ of Edinburgh 2002–; pres Euro Soc for Cognitive Psychology 1996–98 (memb 1987–, memb Ctee 1994–), chm Psychology Panel 1996 and 2001, chair Panel K 2008 Research Assessment Exercise; memb: Neurosciences and Mental Health Bd MRC 1989–92, ESRC 1992–96 (chm Research Programmes Bd 1992–96), SHEFC 1995–2001; memb Editorial Advsy Bd Psychological Research 1988–; memb Editorial Bd: Euro Jl of Cognitive Psychology 1988–, Visual Cognition 1993–, Applied Cognitive Psychology 1994–95; ed British Jl of Psychology 1995–2000; consulting ed Jl of Experimental Psychology: Applied 1994–2001; memb: Experimental Psychology Soc 1980– (memb Ctee 1986–89), Psychonomic Soc 1988–; FBPsS 1989 (hon fell 1997), CPsychol 1989, FRSE 1996, FBA 1999; *Publications* Visual Perception: Psychology and Ecology (jtly, 1985, 4 edn 2003), Recognising Faces (1988), Visual Cognition: computational, experimental and neuropsychological perspectives (jtly, 1989), Face Recognition (ed, 1991), Processing Images of Faces (ed jtly, 1992), Processing the Facial Image (ed jtly, 1992), Object and face recognition (ed jtly, 1994), Perception and Representation (jtly, 1995), Unsolved Mysteries of Mind: tutorial essays in cognition (ed, 1996), In the Eye of the Beholder:

The Science of Face Perception (with A W Young , *qv*, 1998); also author of numerous articles and papers in learned jls; *Recreations* dogs, walking, games; *Style*— Prof Vicki Bruce, OBE, FBA, FRSE; ✉ College of Humanities and Social Science, University of Edinburgh, 55 George Square, Edinburgh EH8 9JU

BRUCE-CLIFTON, Maj Sir Hervey James Hugh; 7 Bt (UK 1804), of Downhill, Londonderry; s of Sir Hervey John William Bruce, 6 Bt (d 1971); assumed the additional surname and arms of Clifton by Royal Licence 1997; *b* 3 September 1952; *Educ* Eton, Mons Officer Cadet Sch; *m* 1, 1979, Charlotte Sara Jane, da of John Temple Gore (s of late Capt Christopher Gore and Lady Barbara, da of 16 Earl of Eglinton); 1 da (Laura Crista b 1984), 1 s (Hervey Hamish Peter b 1986); m 2, 1992, J M (Anna), yst da of Frank Pope, of Tavistock, Devon; *Heir* s, Hervey Bruce-Clifton; *Career* hotelier in South Africa; *Recreations* flying and outdoor living; *Clubs* Cavalry and Guards'; *Style*— Major Sir Hervey Bruce-Clifton, Bt

BRUCE-GARDNER, Sir Robert Henry; 3 Bt (UK 1945), of Frilford, Co Berks; s of Sir Douglas Bruce Bruce-Gardner, 2 Bt (d 1997), by his 1 w, Monica Flumerfelt, *née* Jefferson; *b* 10 June 1943; *Educ* Uppingham, Univ of Reading, Univ of London; *m* 1979, Veronica Ann Hand Oxborrow, da of late Rev W E Hand; 2 s (Edmund Thomas Peter b 28 Jan 1982, Richard Tyndall Jowett b 1983); *Heir* s, Edmund Bruce-Gardner; *Career* asst lectr Univ of Manchester, lectr Univ of London, dir Dept of Conservation and Technology Courtauld Inst of Art 1990–2000, currently ind conslt and conservator of Himalayan art; hon fell Courtauld Inst of Art; *Clubs* Travellers; *Style*— Sir Robert Bruce-Gardner, Bt; ✉ 121 Brackenbury Road, London W6 0BQ (tel 020 8748 7652, fax 020 8932 4627)

BRUCE-JONES, Tom Allan; CBE (2003); s of Tom Bruce-Jones (d 1984), of Blairlogie, Stirlingshire, and Rachel Inglis, *née* Dunlop; *b* 28 August 1941; *Educ* Charterhouse, Lincoln Coll Oxford (BA); *m* 1, 1965 (m dis 1980), R Normand; 1 da (Caroline b 23 Nov 1966), 1 s (Tom b 8 Sept 1968); m 2, 6 March 1981, Stina Birgitta, da of Harry Ossian Ahlgren (d 1982), of Helsinki; *Career* dir Price and Pierce (Woodpulp) Ltd 1973–77, vice-pres Georgia-Pacific International Inc 1977–79; James Jones and Sons Ltd: jt md 1979–87, md 1987–97, chm 1995–; chm Scottish Woodlands Ltd 2005– (dir 1990–2005); dir: Jones and Campbell (Hldgs) Ltd 1988–, Forestry Industry Council of Great Britain Ltd 1989–96, Stella-Jones Inc (Montreal) 1993– (chm 1994–); forestry cmmr 1996–2003, pres Western European Inst for Wood Preservation 1998–2001; consul for Finland Glasgow 1994–; Knight (First Class) Order of the Lion of Finland 2003; *Recreations* fishing, golf, music; *Clubs* Hon Co of Edinburgh Golfers; *Style*— Tom Bruce-Jones, Esq, CBE; ✉ 12/2 The Pinnacle, 160 Bothwell Street, Glasgow G2 7EA; James Jones & Sons Ltd, Broomage Avenue, Larbert, Stirlingshire FK5 4NQ (tel 01324 562241, fax 01324 556642, e-mail t.brucejones@jamesjones.co.uk)

BRUCE-LOCKHART, Baron (Life Peer 2006), of The Weald in the County of Kent; Sir Alexander John (Sandy) Bruce-Lockhart; kt (2003), OBE (1995); s of John McGregor Bruce-Lockhart, CB, CMG, OBE, and Margaret Evelyn, *née* Hone; *b* 4 May 1942, Yorks; *Educ* Sedberg, RAC Cirencester; *m* 1966, Tess *née* Pressland; 2 s (Mark b 1967, Simon b 1973), 1 da (Natasha b 1970); *Career* farmer: Zimbabwe and Australia 1963–65, Kent 1966–; Kent CC: memb 1989–, ldr Cons Gp 1993–2005, ldr 1997–2005; chm Local Govt Assoc 2004–; chair English Heritage 2007–; tstee: Leeds Castle Fndn, Nat Hort Research Inst; pres Kent Care Handicapped Assoc; Hon DCL Univ of Kent, Hon DBA Univ of Greenwich; *Recreations* walking, shooting, family; *Clubs* Carlton; *Style*— The Rt Hon the Lord Bruce-Lockhart, OBE; ✉ House of Lords, London SW1 0PN (e-mail brucelockharts@parliament.uk); tel 01622 890 651, fax 01622 892 044

BRUCE LOCKHART, Robin Norman; s of Sir Robert Hamilton Bruce Lockhart, KCMG (d 1970), and late Jean Haslewood, *née* Turner; *b* 13 April 1920; *Educ* RNC Dartmouth, Pembroke Coll Cambridge (BEcon); *m* 1, 1941, Margaret Crookdake; 1 da (Sheila Margaret b 1951); m 2, 1955, Ginette de Noyelle (d 1985); m 3, 1987, Eila Owen; *Career* WWII Lt RNVR 1939–46; asst to Br Naval Attaché Paris, Naval Intelligence Admty, Flag Lt to C-in-C China, Flag Lt to C-in-C Eastern Fleet, Ceylon, staff C-in-C Plymouth; foreign mangr Financial Times 1946–53, sr exec Beaverbrook Newspapers 1953–61, dep chm Central Wagon Co Ltd 1965–69; chm: Moorgill Properties Ltd 1967–72, Chasebrook Ltd 1967–72, 37/38 Adelaide Crescent (Hove) Ltd 1983–93; memb London Stock Exchange 1962; author; *Books* Reilly Ace of Spies (1967–, TV series 1984–85), Reilly the First Man (1987), Halfway to Heaven (1985), O Bonitas (1996), Listening to Silence (1997); *Recreations* salmon fishing, travel; *Clubs* MCC; *Style*— Robin Bruce Lockhart, Esq; ✉ 37 Adelaide Crescent, Hove, East Sussex BN3 2JL; Quand Meme, Rue Romain Rolland, Collioure, Pyrénées Orientales, France

BRUCE-RADCLIFFE, Godfrey Martin; s of Roy Bruce-Radcliffe (d 1976), and Joyce Evelyn, *née* Shewring (d 1996); *b* 19 June 1945; *Educ* King's Coll Taunton, Guildford Coll of Law; *m* 5 Oct 1974, Claire Miller; 2 c (Edward b 9 Aug 1976, Helen b 2 Nov 1982); *Career* articled clerk Trower Still & Keeling (now Trowers and Hamlins), admitted slr 1970, ptnr D J Freeman 1978–94 (joined 1977), ptnr Hobson Audley 1994–2002, ptnr Thomas Eggar 2002–06, conslt Thomas Eggar 2007–; memb London Regnl Cncl CBI 1999–2005; Freeman City of London 1986, Liveryman Worshipful Co of Basketmakers 1998, Liveryman Worshipful Co of Loriners 2004; memb Law Soc 1970; *Books* Property Development Partnerships (co-author, 1994), Practical Property Development and Finance (1996), Encyclopaedia of Forms and Precedents (contrib author, Vol 38 (2) 2000), Development and the Law: A Guide for Construction and Property Professionals (2005); *Recreations* sailing, walking, gardening, music; *Style*— Godfrey Bruce-Radcliffe, Esq; ✉ Ellacombe, 21 Anstey Lane, Alton, Hampshire GU34 2NB; Thomas Eggar, 76 Shoe Lane, London EC4A 3JB (tel 020 7842 3849 fax 020 7842 3900, e-mail godfrey.bruce-radcliffe@thomaseggar.com)

BRUCK, Steven Mark; s of Herbert Martin Bruck, of London, and Kathe Margot Bruck; *b* 30 September 1947; *Educ* Hendon GS, Univ of Southampton (BSc), LSE (MSc); *m* 1 July 1971, Mirela, da of Alexander Izsak; 1 da (Tamara b 1974), 1 s (Jonathan b 1977); *Career* articled clerk Chalmers Impey CAs 1969–72, gp accountant Halma plc 1972–73, special projects accountant Overseas Containers Ltd 1973–75, Pannell Fitzpatrick 1975–78, ptnr Mercers Bryant 1978–84, corp fin ptnr Pannell Kerr Forster 1984–97, ptnr Blick Rothenberg 1997–; chm Belsize Square Synagogue 1998–2003, chm Delbanco Meyer & Co Ltd 2000–03; FCA 1972; *Recreations* family, theatre, cycling; *Style*— Steven M Bruck, Esq

BRUCKNER, Dr Felix Ernest; s of late William Bruckner, of London, and late Anna, *née* Hahn; *b* 18 April 1937; *Educ* London Hosp Med Coll Univ of London (MB BS); *m* 24 June 1967, Rosalind Dorothy, da of late George Edward Bailey, of Herts; 2 s (James b 1974, Thomas b 1976), 1 da (Catherine b 1981); *Career* conslt physician and rheumatologist St George's Hosp London 1970–2002; pres Rheumatology and Rehabilitation Section RSM 1994–95; FRCP; *Publications* numerous chapters and papers on rheumatological subjects; *Recreations* chess, music, bridge, reading; *Clubs* RSM; *Style*— Dr Felix Bruckner; ✉ 12 Southwood Avenue, Kingston upon Thames, Surrey KT2 7HD (tel 020 8949 3955)

BRUDENELL, Edmund Crispin Stephen James George; DL (Northants 1977); s of George Brudenell (2 s of Cdr Lord Robert Brudenell-Bruce, RN, 4 s of 3 Marquess of Ailesbury); *b* 24 October 1928; *Educ* Harrow, RAC Cirencester; *m* 8 Nov 1955, Hon Marian Cynthia, *née* Manningham-Buller, eldest da of 1 Viscount Dilhorne, PC; 2 s (Robert, Thomas (twins) b 1956), 1 da (Anna Maria b 1960); *Career* contested (Cons) Whitehaven 1964; High Sheriff of Leics 1969, High Sheriff of Northants 1987; landowner; Liveryman Worshipful Co of Fishmongers; *Recreations* reading, travelling; *Clubs* Carlton, Pratt's; *Style*— Edmund Brudenell, Esq, DL; ✉ Deene Park, Corby, Northamptonshire NN17 3EW (tel 01780 450223, fax 01780 450282); 10 Lochmore House, Ebury Street, London SW1W 9JX (tel 020 7730 8715)

BRUDENELL, Thomas Mervyn; s of Edmund Crispin Stephen James George Brudenell, of Deene Park, Corby, Northants, and Marian Cynthia, *née* Manningham-Buller, da of 1 Viscount Dilhorne; *b* 12 August 1956; *Educ* Eton; *m* 1, 5 May 1984, Venetia Jane (d 1993), da of Maj Robert Patricius Chaworth-Musters (d 1992); 2 da (Sophia b 12 April 1985, Victoria b 11 Feb 1987); m 2, 27 June 1996, Mrs Amanda J Skiffington, da of Alick David Yorke Naylor-Leyland, MVO (d 1991), and the Countess of Wilton; *Career* called to the Bar Inner Temple 1977; *Recreations* shooting, stalking, bridge, racing, golf; *Clubs* White's, Pratt's, Royal St George's Golf; *Style*— Thomas Brudenell, Esq; ✉ 70 Alderney Street, London SW1V 4EX (tel 020 7976 5277); Lark Hall, Fordham, Ely, Cambridgeshire CB7 5LS (tel 01638 720590); Queen Elizabeth Building, Temple, London EC4Y 9BS (tel 020 7797 7837, e-mail t.brudenell@qeb.co.uk)

BRUETON, Dr Martin John; s of Neville Frederick William Brueton (d 1981), of Bristol, and Nancy Rushton, *née* Baldwin; *b* 2 February 1944; *Educ* Bristol GS, Bart's Med Sch (MB BS, MD, DCH), Univ of Birmingham (MSc); *m* May 1967, Patricia Ann, da of Geoffrey Oliphant May (d 1994), and Jean, *née* Heyward (d 1986); 2 da (Nicola Ann b 18 June 1969, Catherine Jane b 16 March 1975), 1 s (Mark Richard b 25 May 1971); *Career* jr registrar Bart's 1970–71 (house physician 1968), sr registrar Ahmadu Bello Univ Zaria Nigeria 1971–73, lectr in paediatrics Univ of Birmingham/Children's Hosp Birmingham 1973–78, sr lectr and hon conslt paediatrician Westminster Children's Hosp 1979–93, hon conslt paediatrician Chelsea and Westminster, Charing Cross and Royal Brompton Hosps and reader in child health Imperial Coll Sch of Med (Charing Cross and Westminster Med Sch until merger 1997) 1979–2001, conslt paediatric gastroenterologist Chelsea and Westminster and St Mary's Hosps 2001–, clinical dir Women and Children's Directorate Chelsea and Westminster Healthcare NHS Tst 1994–95; regularly invited to lecture at overseas univs and to participate in meetings/working gps in the fields of paediatric gastroenterology and nutrition; hon reader in child health Imperial Coll Faculty of Med London 2001–, Wellcome Tst jr research fell 1976; memb: Br Soc of Gastroenterology, Br Soc of Paediatric Gastroenterology Hepatology and Nutrition (pres 1998–2001); FRCP, FRCPCH (offr for higher specialist training 1997–2002); *Books* Diseases of Children in Subtropics and Tropics (jt ed, 1991), Practical Paediatric Therapeutics (jtly, 1991); *Recreations* tennis, music, theatre; *Clubs* RSM; *Style*— Dr Martin Brueton; ✉ The Cleve, Castle Hill, Woodgreen, Fordingbridge, Hampshire SP6 2AX (tel 01725 512324)

BRUGES, Jason David; s of John Edward Bruges, and Lynne, *née* Harris; *b* 15 September 1972, Rochford, Essex; *Educ* Tring Sch, Oxford Brookes Univ (BA), Bartlett Sch of Architecture UCL (Dip); *m* 23 Oct 2004, Katayoun Ghahremani; *Career* Foster Asia 1994–95, Sir Norman Foster & Ptnrs 1995–98, sr designer Imagination 1999–2001, fndr and creative dir Jason Bruges Studio 2001–; teacher and visiting lectr: Westminster Univ, UCL, RCA, Middx Univ, Oxford Brookes Univ, Univ of Plymouth, Southern Californian Inst of Architecture and Design Research Lab, Architectural Assoc; sometime lectr: BAFTA, Inst of Physics, ELDA, ICA; exhbns: RIBA, SCIARC, SCP, Victoria Miro Gallery, Habitat (Brilliant), Venice Film Festival, Selfridges, V&A, Tate Britain, Millennium Galleries, London Fashion Week, UBS/Tate Modern London Architectural Biennale, Center for Architecture NY 2007; contrib V&A's 150th Anniversary Album 2007; jt nominee Interactive BAFTA 2004, Int Lighting Design Award (for Hotel Puerta America) 2006; memb BAFTA 2004; *Recreations* food and wine; *Clubs* Shoreditch House (fndr memb); *Style*— Jason Bruges, Esq; ✉ Jason Bruges Studio, Unit 2.08, The Tea Building, 56 Shoreditch High Street, London E1 6JJ (tel 020 7012 1122, fax 020 7012 1199, e-mail jason@jasonbruges.com)

BRUGES, Katharine Georgia (Kate); da of Christopher John Farara, of Guildford, Surrey, and Alison Mary, *née* Duguid; *b* 19 November 1962; *Educ* Queen Elizabeth II Silver Jubilee Sch, Woking Sixth Form Coll, Newnham Coll Cambridge (MA); *m* 7 Sept 1991, Richard Michael Bruges, s of Maj Michael Bruges; 3 s (Max b 16 June 1993, Harry b 16 June 1995, Jim b 17 July 1999); *Career* J Walter Thompson: joined as graduate trainee 1984, youngest bd appointment 1989, currently professional devpt dir; FIPA 2005; *Recreations* riding, pantomime, gardening; *Style*— Mrs Kate Bruges; ✉ JWT, 1 Knightsbridge Green, London SW1X 7NW (tel 020 7656 7000, fax 020 7656 7010, e-mail kate.bruges@jwt.com)

BRUGHA, Prof Traolach Seán; s of Ruairi Brugha, of Dublin, and Maire, *née* MacSwiney; *b* 6 January 1953; *Educ* Gonzaga Coll Dublin, UCD (MB BCh, MD); *m* 3 April 1976, Máire Nic Eoghain; 3 da (Rossa Eoghain, Lia Patricia, Cillian Traolach); *Career* registrar in psychiatry St Vincent's Hosp Elm Park Dublin 1979–80, registrar then sr registrar Bethlem and Maudsley Hosp London 1980–87, clinical scientist MRC Social Psychiatry Unit London 1982–87, hon lectr in psychiatry Inst of Psychiatry London 1984–87, sr lectr Univ of Leicester 1987–2000, prof of psychiatry Univ of Leicester 2000–, hon conslt psychiatrist Leicester Health Authy 1987–, seconded as SMO Dept of Health London 1995–97; FRCPsych 2002 (MRCPsych 1981); *Recreations* photography, cycling, music; *Style*— Prof Traolach Brugha; ✉ Department of Psychiatry, University of Leicester, Leicester (tel 0116 225 6295, fax 0116 225 6235)

BRUINVELS, Peter Nigel Edward; er s of Capt Stanley Bruinvels, of Dorking, Surrey, and Ninette Maud, *née* Kibblewhite (d 2001); *b* 30 March 1950; *Educ* St John's Sch Leatherhead, Univ of London (LLB), Cncl of Legal Educn; *m* 20 Sept 1980, Alison Margaret, da of Maj David Gilmore Bacon, of Lymington, Hants; 2 da (Alexandra Caroline Jane b 6 April 1986, Georgina Emma Kate b 20 Oct 1988); *Career* princ Peter Bruinvels Assocs (media mgmnt corp communications and public affrs conslts) 1986–, managing ed Bruinvels News & Media (press and broadcasting agents) 1993–, political commentator, freelance journalist and author 1987–; special external advsr DTI 1993–95, memb Child Support and Social Security Appeals Tbnls 1994–99; Church Cmmr 1992–; OFSTED Denominational Schs S48/SIAS RE Inspector 1994–; co-opted business representative memb Surrey LEA 1997–2007; MP (Cons) Leicester E 1983–87, memb Cons Home Office and NI Ctees 1983–87; jt vice-chm: Cons Urban Affrs and New Towns Ctee 1984–87, Cons Educn Ctee 1985–87; promoter Crossbows Act 1987; campaign co-ordinator gen election Eastbourne 1992, Parly candidate The Wrekin 1997 (prospective Parly candidate 1995); memb Cons NUEC 1976–81, vice-chm SE Area Conservatives 1977–79, pres Dorking Conservatives 1995–; chm Church Army Remuneration Ctee 1999–2004, dir Church Army 1999–2004, chm Guildford Diocesan Bd of Educn 2005–; ind lay chm NHS Complaints Procedure 1999–2005; pres NW Midlands CIM 1997–98; chm Surrey Schools Orgn Ctee 2000–, Surrey Jt Services' Charities Ctee 2004–; county field offr Surrey The Royal Br Legion 2002–; non-exec dir E Elmbridge and Mid Surrey PCT 2002–07; hon sec Surrey County Appeals Ctee 2002–; elected memb Guildford Crown Nomination Cmmn 2003; memb: Guildford Diocesan Synod 1974– (vice-pres 2003–), Gen Synod C of E 1985–, Bd of Patrons 1985–, Parly Legislative Ctee (C of E) 1991–96 and 2000–, Gen Synod Bd of Educn 1996–, Bd of Govrs Church Cmmns 1998– (Mgmnt Advsy Ctee 1999–), House of Bishops Clergy Discipline (Doctrine) Gp 1999–, Dearing Implementation Follow-Up Gp 2001–, Cathedrals Fabric Cmmn for England 2006–; lay canon Guildford Cathedral 2002–; govr Univ of York St John 1999–, admissions adjudicator Surrey LEA 1999–2007, memb Ct Univ of Sussex 2001–; memb SE England War Pensions Ctee 2003–, memb Cncl Queen Victoria Clergy Fund 2006–; Freeman City of London 1980; fell Industry and Parl Tst; FRSA, FCIM, MCIJ, MCIPR; *Books* Zoning in on Enterprise (1982), Light up the Roads (1984), Sharing in Britain's Success: A Study in Widening Share Ownership Through Privatisation (1987), Investing in Enterprise: A Comprehensive Guide to Inner City Regeneration and Urban Renewal (1989); *Recreations* politics in the C of E, political campaigning, the media; *Clubs* Carlton, Inner Temple, Corporation of Church House, Jersey Wildlife Preservation; *Style—* Canon Peter Bruinvels; ✉ 14 High Meadow Close, St Paul's Road West, Dorking, Surrey RH4 2LG (tel 01306 887082, fax 0870 133 1756, mobile 07721 411688, voicemail 07050 085456, e-mail peterbruinvels@btopenworld.com or pba@supanet.com); office tel 01306 887680 or 01372 386500, fax 01372 375843

BRUMMELL, David; CB (2005); s of Ernest Brummell (d 1997), and Florence Elizabeth, *née* Martin (d 2002); *b* 18 December 1947; *Educ* Nottingham HS, Queens' Coll Cambridge; *Career* articled clerk then asst slr Simmons & Simmons 1971–75; local govt: Devon CC 1975–77, W Sussex CC 1977–79; Govt Legal Service: Office of Fair Trading 1979–84, Treasy Advsy Division 1984–86, Dept of Energy Advsy Division 1986–89, Treasy Slr's Litigation Division 1989–2000 (head of division 1995–2000), legal secretary to the law officers 2000–; *Recreations* music, tennis, walking, languages, poetry; *Clubs* Athenaeum, Thames Hare & Hounds; *Style—* David Brummell, Esq, CB; ✉ The Legal Secretariat to the Law Officers, Attorney General's Chambers, 9 Buckingham Gate, London SW1E 6JP (tel 020 7271 2401, fax 020 7271 2431)

BRUMMELL, HE Paul; s of Robert George Brummell (d 1992), and June, *née* Rawlins (d 2002); *b* 28 August 1965; *Educ* St Albans Sch, St Catharine's Coll Cambridge (MA); *Career* joined HM Dip Serv 1987, third later second sec Islamabad 1989–92, FCO 1993–94, first sec Rome 1995–2000, dep head Eastern Dept FCO 2000–01, ambass to Turkmenistan 2002–05, ambass to Kazakhstan 2005– (concurrently non-resident ambass to Kyrgyzstan); *Books* Turkmenistan: The Bradt Travel Guide (2005); *Recreations* travel, entering writing competitions, glam rock; *Style—* HE Mr Paul Brummell; ✉ c/o Foreign & Commonwealth Office (Astana), King Charles Street, London SW1A 2AH (e-mail paul.brummell@fco.gov.uk)

BRUMMER, Alexander; s of Michael Brummer, of Brighton, E Sussex, and Hilda, *née* Lyons; *b* 25 May 1949; *Educ* Brighton Hove & Sussex GS, Univ of Southampton (BSc), Univ of Bradford Mgmnt Centre (MBA); *m* 26 Oct 1975, Patricia Lyndsey, da of Saul Leopold Magrill; 1 da (Jessica Rachel b 5 Jan 1978), 2 s (Justin Adam b 29 Sept 1980, Gabriel Joseph b 30 Dec 1981); *Career* journalist; De La Rue Company 1971–72, Haymarket Publishing 1972–73; The Guardian: fin corr 1973–79, Washington corr 1979–85, Washington bureau chief 1985–89, foreign ed 1989, fin ed 1990–99, assoc ed 1998–99; ed Financial Mail on Sunday 1999–2000, City ed Daily Mail 2000–; *Awards* Best Foreign Corr in US Overseas Press Club 1989, Financial Journalist of the Year British Press Awards 1999, Best City Journalist Media Awards 2000, Sr Financial Journalist Wincott 2001, Newspaper Journalist of the Year Work Fndn 2002, Business Journalist of the Year World Leadership Forum 2006; *Books* American Destiny (jt author, 1985), Hanson: A Biography (1994), Weinstock: The Life and Times of Britain's Premier Industrialist (1998); *Recreations* reading, antiques; *Style—* Alexander Brummer, Esq; ✉ Associated Newspapers, Northcliffe House, Derry Street, London W8 5TS (tel 020 7938 6000, e-mail alex.brummer@dailymail.co.uk)

BRUMMER, Malcolm Howard; *b* 21 March 1948; *Educ* Haberdashers' Aske's, Downing Coll Cambridge (MA); *m* 12 March 1980, Yvonne Simy, *née* Labos; 1 s (Richard Joseph b 16 Feb 1982), 1 da (Natasha Nina b 1 Dec 1985); *Career* Berwin Leighton (now Berwin Leighton Paisner): articled clerk 1970–72, ptnr 1975–99, head Property Dept 1983–89, chm Fin Ctee 1987–93, chm 1990–94; property governance dir Tesco Stores Ltd 1999–; memb Law Soc 1972; *Recreations* family, opera, stamps; *Style—* Malcolm Brummer, Esq; ✉ 3 Milton Close, Hampstead Garden Suburb, London N2 0QH (tel 020 8209 0213); Tesco plc, Tesco House, Delamare Road, Cheshunt, Hertfordshire EN8 9SL (tel 01992 644231, e-mail malcolm.brummer@uk.tesco.com)

BRUNDLE, Martin John; s of late Alfred Edward John Brundle, and Alma, *née* Coe; *b* 1 June 1959; *Educ* King Edward VII GS Kings Lynn, Norfolk Coll of Arts and Technol; *m* Elizabeth Mary; 1 da (Charlotte Emily b 9 May 1988), 1 s (Alexander Martin b 7 Aug 1990); *Career* motor racing driver and TV presenter; began racing aged 12, turned professional 1984; Formula One teams driven for: Tyrrell, Zakspeed, Williams, Brabham, Benetton, McLaren, Ligier, Jordan; drove for Jaguar in World Sportscar Championship 1985–91; Le Mans driver: Toyota 1998–99, Bentley 2001; achievements incl: runner-up Br Formula 3 1983, fifth place in first ever grand prix 1984, world sportscar champion 1988, winner Le Mans 24–hr Race 1990, runner-up Italian Grand Prix 1992, third place Br, French, Japanese and Australian Grands Prix 1992, third place San Marino Gp 1993, runner-up Monaco Grand Prix 1994, third place Belgian Grand Prix 1995; currently presenter and analyst Formula One ITV; chm: Grand Prix Drivers Assoc 1994–96, Br Racing Drivers' Club 2000–04; awards: Grovewood Award for most promising young driver in Cwlth 1982, Segrave Trophy for exceptional performance on land or sea 1988, Br Racing Drivers' Club Gold Star 1988 and 2004, RTS Sports Commentator of the Year Award 1998, 1999 and 2005; *Recreations* motor cycling, helicopter flying; *Style—* Martin Brundle, Esq

BRUNNER, Adrian John Nelson; QC (1994); s of Cdr Robert Henry Hugh Brunner, DSC, RN (d 1981), and Elizabeth Elliott, *née* Colbé; *b* 18 June 1946; *Educ* Ampleforth, BRNC, Coll of Law; *m* 1970, Christine Anne, da of late Thomas Peter Hughes, of Buntingford, Herts; 4 da (Elizabeth b 1971, Kate b 1972, Sarah b 1974, Samantha b 1981), 1 s (David b 1976); *Career* served RN 1963–66 (RNR 1966–74); called to the Bar Inner Temple 1968 (major scholarship); recorder of the Crown Court 1990–, master of the bench Inner Temple 2006; *Recreations* yachting, shooting; *Clubs* Royal Yacht Squadron, Bar Yacht; *Style—* Adrian Brunner, Esq, QC; ✉ Furneaux Pelham Hall, Buntingford, Hertfordshire SG9 0LB; Holborn Head Farm, Scrabster, Caithness KW14 7UW; Henderson Chambers, 2 Harcourt Buildings, Middle Temple Lane, Temple, London EC4Y 9DB (tel 020 7583 9020, fax 020 7583 2686)

BRUNNER, Hugo Laurence Joseph; JP; s of Sir Felix John Morgan Brunner, 3 Bt (d 1982), of Greys Court, Henley-on-Thames, Oxon, and Elizabeth, Lady Brunner, OBE (d 2003); *b* 17 August 1935; *Educ* Eton, Trinity Coll Oxford (MA); *m* 7 Jan 1967, Mary Rose Catherine, da of Arthur Joseph Lawrence Pollen (d 1968), of Henley-on-Thames, Oxon; 5 s (Joseph b 1967, Samuel b 1972, Magnus b 1974, Philip b 1977, Francis b 1982), 1 da (Isabel b 1969); *Career* various appts OUP 1958–65 and 1977–79, dir Chatto and Windus 1967–76 and 1979–85 (md 1979–82, chm 1982–85); dir Caithness Glass 1966–96 (chm 1985–90), dir Brunner Investment Tst 1987–99; Parly candidate (Lib) Torquay 1964 and 1966; chm Oxford Diocesan Advsy Ctee for Care of Churches 1985–98; High Sheriff Oxon 1988–89; HM Lord-Lt Oxon 1996– (DL 1993–96); dep high steward Univ of Oxford 2001; hon fell Trinity Coll Oxford 1995; Hon LLD Oxford Brookes Univ 1999; memb Order of St Frideswide 2006; *Recreations* hill walking, visiting churches; *Clubs* Reform, Chelsea Arts; *Style—* Hugo Brunner, Esq; ✉ 26 Norham Road, Oxford OX2 6SF (tel and fax 01865 316431)

BRUNNING, His Hon Judge David Wilfrid; s of Wilfred George Brunning (d 1983), of Burton on Trent, and Marion, *née* Humphries; *b* 10 April 1943; *Educ* Burton-upon-Trent GS, Worcester Coll Oxford (BA, DPA); *m* 8 July 1967, Deirdre Ann Shotton; 3 s (b 1972, 1974, 1977); *Career* articled clerk Leicester CC 1966–67, lectr Loughborough Tech Coll 1968, called to the Bar Middle Temple 1969, in practice (Midland & Oxford Circuit) 1970–88, circuit judge (Midland & Oxford Circuit) 1988–, dep judge of the High Court, designated civil judge, designated care judge Nottingham and Derby until 2004, designated family judge Leicester County Ct 2004–, judge Technol and Construction Court; a pres Mental Health Review Tbnl; memb Ct Univ of Leicester 2003–; *Recreations* walking, wine, campanology; *Style—* His Hon Judge Brunning; ✉ Leicester City Court, 90 Wellington Street, Leicester LE1 6ZZ

BRUNSON, Michael John; OBE (2000); *b* 12 August 1940; *Educ* Bedford Sch, The Queen's Coll Oxford (MA); *m* Susan Margaret, *née* Brown; 2 s (Jonathan b 1966, Robin b 1969); *Career* journalist; VSO teacher Prince of Wales Sch Sierra Leone 1963–64, scriptwriter, researcher and broadcaster BBC External Servs 1964, reporter South East (BBC Radio) 1964–66, asst prodr 24 Hours (BBC TV) 1966–68; ITN: joined 1968, US corr 1972–77, gen assignment reporter 1977–79, newscaster 1977–81, Euro corr 1979–80, diplomatic ed 1980–86, political ed 1986–2000; major assignments incl: first Reagan-Gorbachev summit Geneva, various EC summits, overseas visits by PM and foreign sec, gen elections 1979–97 (jt presenter with Jonathan Dimbleby General Election Results Programme ITV 1997), Conservative leadership contests 1990 and 1995; regular contributor Week in Westminster feature Westminster House Magazine; chm: Parly Lobby Journalists 1994, Parly Press Gallery 1999; memb: Govt's Advsy Gp on Citizenship Educn 1997–98, Qualification and Curriculum Authority's Preparation for Adult Life Gp 1998, Learning and Skills Cncl Adult Learning Ctee 2001–03; tstee The Citizenship Fndn 2000–07; columnist Eastern Daily Press (Norwich) 2000–01, political columnist Saga magazine 2000–05; RTS News Event Award 1995 (for coverage on death of John Smith), RTS Judges' Award (for life time achievement) 1999; Hon DLitt UEA 2003; *Books* A Ringside Seat (2000); *Recreations* reading, classical music, gardening, Norwich City FC; *Clubs* Oxford and Cambridge, Norfolk (Norwich); *Style—* Michael Brunson, Esq, OBE; ✉ c/o Knight Ayton Management, 114 St Martin's Lane, London WC2N 4BE (tel 020 7836 5333, e-mail michael.brunson@btinternet.com)

BRUNT, Rev Prof Peter William; CVO (2001), OBE (1994); s of Harry Brunt, of Prestatyn, Clwyd, and Florence Jane Josephine, *née* Airey; *b* 18 January 1936; *Educ* Manchester Grammar, King George V Sch, Univ of Liverpool (MB, ChB, MD); *m* 1961, (Marina Evelyn) Anne, da of Rev Reginald Henry Lewis (d 1974), of Liverpool; 3 da (Kristin, Nicola, Coralie); *Career* house surgn and house physician Liverpool Royal Infirmary 1959–60, med registrar hosps in Liverpool region 1960–64, res fell Dept of Med Genetics Johns Hopkins Hosp and Sch of Med Baltimore 1965–66, lectr in med Univ of Edinburgh 1967–68, sr registrar in gastroenterology Western Gen Hosp Edinburgh 1968–69, hon lectr in med Univ of London 1969–70, conslt physician and gastroenterologist Aberdeen Royal Infirmary 1970–2001, hon clinical prof in med Univ of Aberdeen, physician to HM The Queen (in Scotland) 1983–2001; chm Med Cncl on Alcohol, memb Scottish Advsy Ctee on Alcohol Misuse, med dir Scottish Advsy Ctee on Distinction Awards; author of numerous chapters in books and articles mainly on liver and alimentary diseases and alcohol; non-stipendiary priest Scottish Episcopal Church; FRCP, FRCPEd (memb Cncl); *Books* Diseases of Liver and Biliary System (1984), Gastroenterology (1984); *Recreations* mountaineering, music; *Clubs* Royal Scots, Association of Physicians; *Style—* The Rev Prof Peter Brunt, CVO, OBE; ✉ e-mail brunt.aberdeen@btinternet.com

BRUNTISFIELD, 2 Baron (UK 1942); Sir John Robert Warrender; 9 Bt (GB 1715), OBE (1963), MC (1943), TD (1967), DL (Somerset 1965); s of 1 Baron Bruntisfield, MC (d 1993), and his 1 w, Dorothy Etta, *née* Rawson (d 1975); *b* 7 February 1921; *Educ* Eton, RMC Sandhurst; *m* 1, 1948, Ann Moireen (d 1976), 2 da of Lt-Col Sir Walter Fendall Campbell, KCIE; 2 s (Hon Michael John Victor b 1949, Hon Jonathan James b 1954), 2 da (Hon Julian Mary b 1950, Hon Sarah Jane (Hon Mrs Bune) b 1952); m 2, 1977, Shirley (d 1981), formerly w of Jonathan J Crawley, and da of Sqdn Ldr Edward Ross, RAF ret; 3 step s; m 3, 1985, Joanna (Jan) K, formerly w of Colin Hugh Campbell Graham, and da of late David Chancellor, of Pencaitland, E Lothian; 2 step s, 1 step da; *Heir* s, Hon Michael Warrender; *Career* Col RARO, Brig Queen's Body Guard for Scotland (Royal Co of Archers), ret 1985, late Capt 2 Dragoons, Royal Scots Greys, ADC to Govr of Madras 1946–48 and cmdg N Som Yeo and 44 Royal Tank Regt 1957–62; *Clubs* Puffins; *Style—* The Rt Hon the Lord Bruntisfield, OBE, MC, TD, DL; ✉ 41 Park Road, Trinity, Edinburgh EH6 4LA (tel 0131 551 3709); 151 Skinnet, Melness, by Lairg, Sutherland IV27 4YP (tel 01847 601214)

BRUNTON, Sir (Edward Francis) Lauder; 3 Bt (UK 1908), of Stratford Place, St Marylebone; s of Sir (James) Stopford Lauder Brunton, 2 Bt (d 1943); *b* 10 November 1916; *Educ* Trinity Coll Sch Port Hope Ontario, Bryanston, McGill Univ Montreal (BSc, MD, CM); *m* 1946, Marjorie Grant, only da of David Sclater Lewis, MSc, MD, FRCP (Canada), of Montreal; 1 s (James Lauder b 1947), 1 da (Nancy Elizabeth (Mrs Ian Willson) b 1949); *Heir* s, James Brunton; *Career* hon attending physician: Royal Victoria Hosp Montreal, St Martha's Hosp; life govr Nova Scotia Art Gallery; fell: Int Soc of Hematology, American Coll of Physicians; memb American Soc of Hematology; *Style—* Sir Lauder Brunton, Bt; ✉ PO Box 140, Guysborough, Nova Scotia, Canada

BRUTON, (Victoria) Jane; da of Roger Bruton (d 2000), and Glynnis, *née* Boardman; *b* 21 March 1968, Wigan, Lancs; *Educ* The Byrchall HS Ashton-in-Makerfield, Winstanley Coll Wigan, Univ of Nottingham (BA), City Univ (Dip Journalism); *m* 23 Aug 1996, Johnathan Whitehead; 2 s (Arthur Louis b 8 July 2001, Jonah Alexander b 21 July 2004); *Career* journalist; sub ed then writer Chat 1991–92, freelance 1993–94, dep ed Wedding and Home 1994–97, assoc ed Prima 1997; ed: Living etc 1998–2002, Eve 2002–04, Grazia 2004–; memb Ctee BSME; Ed of the Year BSME 2004 and 2006; fndr memb and tstee Trees for Cities; *Style—* Ms Jane Bruton; ✉ Grazia, Endeavour House, 189 Shaftesbury Avenue, London WC2H 8JG

BRUTON, Prof Michael John; CBE (1995); s of (Patrick) John Bruton, of Hertford, and Louise Ann, *née* Roberts; *b* 28 March 1938; *Educ* Richard Hale Sch Hertford, UCL (BA), Imperial Coll London (MSc, DIC), Regent St Poly (Dip TP); *m* 2 March 1963, Sheila Grace, da of Alexander Kyle Harrison; 2 da (Suzy b 1969, Catherine b 1972); *Career* princ planning offr Bucks CC 1966–67 (Lanarkshire CC 1965–66), princ lectr town planning Oxford Poly 1967–72, head school planning and landscape Birmingham Poly 1972–77, prof of town planning Univ of Wales Cardiff (formerly Univ of Wales Coll of Cardiff) 1977–, dep princ and registrar UWIST 1985–88, registrar Univ of Wales Cardiff 1988–95; chief exec Residuary Body for Wales 1995–; govr Centre for Environmental Studies 1978–81, chm CNAA Town Planning Bd 1978–84; memb: Countryside Cmmn for Wales 1981–85, Univ Grants Ctee Social Studies Sub-Ctee 1985–88, ESRC Post Graduate Bd 1985–93; chm Regnl Rivers Advsy Ctee for Wales 1989–93, planning advsr to Univ Funding Cncl 1989–93; FRTPI, FCIT, MIHT; *Books* Introduction to Transportation Planning (3 edn, 1985), Spirit and Purpose of Planning (2 edn, 1984), Local Planning in Practice (1987); *Recreations* watching rugby and cricket, travel; *Clubs* Cardiff and County; *Style—* Prof Michael Bruton, CBE; ✉ The Residuary Body for Wales, Ffynnon-las, Tŷ Glas Avenue, Llanishen, Cardiff CF4 5DZ (tel 029 2068 1241, fax 029 2068 1308)

BRYAN, Felicity Anne (Mrs Alexander Duncan); da of Sir Paul Bryan, DSO, MC (d 2004), and Betty Mary, *née* Hoyle (d 1968); *b* 16 October 1945; *Educ* Courtauld Inst of Art, Univ of London; *m* 23 Oct 1981, Alexander Duncan, s of Patrick Duncan (d 1967), and Cynthia Duncan; 1 da (Alice Mary b 1982 d 2004), 2 s (Maxim Paul b 1983, Benjamin Patrick b 1987); *Career* journalist: Financial Times 1968–70, The Economist 1970–72; literary agent and dir Curtis Brown Ltd 1972–88, fndr The Felicity Bryan Agency 1988–; Fndr Stern Fellowship with the Washington Post; memb Ct Oxford Brookes Univ; sponsor Oxford Literary Festival, patron Woodstock Literary Festival, tstee Equilibrium - The Bipolar Fndn; *Books* The Town Gardener's Companion (1982), A Garden for Children (1986), Nursery Style (1989); *Recreations* opera, gardening, travel, entertaining; *Clubs* Groucho; *Style—* Ms Felicity Bryan; ✉ The Felicity Bryan Agency, 2A North Parade, Banbury Road, Oxford OX2 6LX (tel 01865 513816, fax 01865 310055)

BRYAN, Rex Victor; s of Bertram Henry Bryan (d 1970), of Purley, Surrey, and Annie Ella Margaret, *née* King; *b* 2 December 1946; *Educ* Wallington GS, Jesus Coll Oxford (MA); *m* 1, 31 July 1971 (m dis 1981), Catherine, da of Samuel Carbery, of Ballymena, Co Antrim, NI; 1 s (Roland Patrick b 1977); m 2, 9 Aug 1982, Mary Elizabeth, da of Brendan Joseph O'Toole, of Frinton-on-Sea, Essex; 2 s (Adam Francis b 1985, Thomas Edward b 1988), 2 da (Victoria Louise b 1986, Leonora Rose b 1991); *Career* called to the Bar Lincoln's Inn 1971, head of chambers 1986–2003, recorder of the Crown Court 1994–; *Recreations* DIY, horticulture; *Style—* Rex Bryan, Esq; ✉ 5 Pump Court, Temple, London EC4Y 7AP (tel 020 7353 2532, fax 020 7353 5321)

BRYANT, Chris; MP; s of Rees Bryant, and Anne Gracie, *née* Goodwin (d 1993); *b* 11 January 1962; *Career* MP (Lab) Rhondda 2001–; *Style—* Chris Bryant, Esq, MP; ✉ House of Commons, London SW1A 0AA (tel 020 7219 8315, fax 020 7219 1792)

BRYANT, Prof Christopher Gordon Alastair; s of Gordon Douglas Clifford Bryant (d 1975), of Bristol, and Edna Mollie, *née* Shrubb (d 1996); *b* 14 April 1944; *Educ* Kingston GS, Univ of Leicester (BA, MA), Univ of Southampton (PhD); *m* Elizabeth Mary, da of George Thomas Martyn Peters; 2 da (Catherine Elizabeth, Lucy Ann); *Career* tutorial asst Dept of Sociology Univ of Leicester 1965–66, lectr Dept of Sociology and Social Admin Univ of Southampton 1968–76 (asst lectr 1966–68); Univ of Salford: sr lectr Dept of Sociology 1976–82, chm Dept of Sociology 1982–90, prof 1982–, dir Inst for Social Research 1993–98, dean Faculty of Arts, Media and Social Sciences 1999–2003, pro-vice-chllr (research) 2004; guest prof Goethe Univ of Frankfurt am Main 1973; visiting fell: Ohio State Univ Columbus 1981, Univ of Utrecht 1986–91; visiting prof Central European Univ Warsaw 1996–99; memb: Br Sociological Assoc 1966–, Exec Ctee Br Sociological Assoc 1987–91 (chm Pubns Ctee 1989–91), Advsy Bd Central European Univ Warsaw 1999–2003; memb Editorial Bd: Br Jl of Sociology 1991–2000, International Sociology 1992–2004, Polish Sociological Review 2000–; AcSS 2005; *Books* Sociology in Action (1976), Positivism in Social Theory and Research (1985), What Has Sociology Achieved? (1990), Giddens' Theory of Structuration (1991), The New Great Transformation? (1994), Practical Sociology (1995), Democracy, Civil Society and Pluralism in Comparative Perspective (1995), Anthony Giddens: Critical Assessments (4 vols, 1997), The Contemporary Giddens (2001), The Nations of Britain (2006); *Recreations* watching football, theatre, concerts, walking, seeing friends; *Style—* Prof Christopher Bryant; ✉ ESRI, Humphrey Booth House, University of Salford, Salford M5 4WT (tel 0161 295 5614, fax 0161 295 2818, e-mail c.g.a.bryant@salford.ac.uk)

BRYANT, His Hon Judge David Michael Arton; s of late Lt-Col Arthur Denis Bryant, and Dorothy Alice, *née* Arton, of West Tanfield, N Yorks; *b* 27 January 1942; *Educ* Wellington, Oriel Coll Oxford (scholar, MA); *m* (Diana) Caroline, da of Brig Charles Walker Sloan, CBE, of Ripon, N Yorks; 2 s (Edward Denis Charles b 1971, William Robert b 1982), 1 da (Lucinda Mary b 1972); *Career* called to the Bar Inner Temple 1964; practised NE Circuit 1965–89, recorder 1985–89, circuit judge (NE Circuit) 1989–; memb Ripon Deanery Synod; *Recreations* gardening, shooting, medieval history, tennis; *Clubs* Carlton; *Style—* His Hon Judge Bryant; ✉ Teeside Combined Court Centre, Middlesbrough, Cleveland TS1 2AE (tel 01642 340000)

BRYANT, Prof Greyham Frank; s of Ernest Noel Bryant (d 1981), and Florence Ivy, *née* Russell (d 1974); *b* 3 June 1931; *Educ* Univ of Reading (BSc), Imperial Coll London (PhD); *m* 2 July 1955, Iris Sybil, da of Albert Edward Jardine (d 1980); 2 s (Mark Greyham b 2 Jan 1963, David Nicholas b 18 Aug 1966); *Career* sr scientific offr Br Iron and Steel Res 1959–64; Imperial Coll London: research fell 1964–67, reader in industrial control 1975–82, prof of control 1982–, res dir and co-fndr Interdisciplinary Research Centre in Systems Engrg 1989–96, sr research fell 1997–; chm: Broner Consits 1979–88, Greycon Consits 1985–97; dir Circulation Research 1989–2007; MIEE, FIMA, FREng 1988; *Books* Automation of Tandem Mills (jtly), Multivariable Control System Design Techniques; *Recreations* music, oil painting; *Clubs* Athenaeum; *Style—* Prof Greyham Bryant, FREng; ✉ 18 Wimborne Avenue, Norwood Green, Middlesex UB2 4HB (tel 020 8574 5648); Department of Electrical Engineering, Imperial College, London SW7 2AZ (tel 020 7589 5111)

BRYANT, Hugh D; *Educ* Oriel Coll Oxford (open exhibitioner, MA); *Career* early positions with Thomas R Miller & Son and GEC Diesels Ltd; currently slr; formerly with: Hill Dickinson & Co Liverpool, Holman Fenwick & Willan, Waltons & Morse (ptnr), Shadbolt & Co slrs (ptnr); former chief underwriter and dir Liverpool and London P & I (protection and indemnity) Management Ltd; former ptnr and head Marine and Aviation Dept Penningtons slrs, Penningtons' team ldr actg for Shetlands Islands Cncl over BRAER oil spill 1993; chief legal advsr for the creation and launch of Shoreline Mutual (Bermuda) Ltd; regular speaker and lectr incl: Master Mariners' Soc of Pakistan, 'Managing the Marine Environment - The Shetland Standard' Conf Lerwick, Tanker Legislation '93 Conf Washington DC, Mariners' Club Houston, Coll of Petroleum and Energy Studies Oxford; memb Br Maritime Law Assoc, supporting memb London Maritime Arbitrators' Assoc; MRAeS; *Clubs* Reform, Anglo-German (Hamburg); *Style—* Hugh Bryant, Esq; ✉ e-mail bryant@cix.co.uk

BRYANT, Prof John Allen; s of Joseph Samuel Bryant (d 1996), of Croydon, Surrey, and (Beatrice Maud) Patricia, *née* Wallace-Page (d 1990); *b* 14 April 1944; *Educ* Whitgift Sch Croydon, Queens' Coll Cambridge (BA, MA, PhD); *m* 27 July 1968, Marjorie Joan, da of Maj Gerald C G Hatch (d 1983), of Hingham, Norfolk; 2 s (Mark b 1 Jan 1972, Simon b 3 Jan 1974); *Career* research fell UEA 1969–70, lectr Univ of Nottingham 1970–74, reader Univ Coll Cardiff 1982–85 (lectr 1974–77, sr lectr 1977–82), prof of biological sciences Univ of Exeter 1985– (head of biology 1986–91, prof emeritus 2001–), visiting prof West Virginia State Univ 1999–2007; Soc for Experimental Biology: memb Cncl 1981–87 and 1992–2005, hon sec 1983–87, memb Cell Biology Ctee 1988–97, vice-pres 2001–03, pres 2003–05; memb: Plant Sci and Microbiology Ctee SERC 1986–89, Bd of Dirs E African Inst for Scientific Res and Devpt 1991–99, Professional and Educn Ctee Biochemical Soc 1994–97; memb Editorial Bd Sci and Christian Belief; chm Christians in Science 2001–07, memb Annals of Botany Co; CBiol 1984, FIBiol 1986 (MIBiol 1970), FRSA 1989; *Recreations* cross-country (formerly at intercounty level) and road running, birdwatching, walking, sailing; *Style—* Prof John Bryant; ✉ School of Bioscience, University of Exeter, Exeter EX4 4PS (tel 01392 264608, fax 01392 263700, e-mail j.a.bryant@exeter.ac.uk)

BRYANT, John Martin; s of William George Bryant (d 1969), and Doris, *née* Martin (d 1972); *b* 28 September 1943; *Educ* West Monmouth Sch Pontypool, St Catharine's Coll Cambridge (state scholarship); *m* 28 August 1965, Andrea Irene, da of John Leslie Emmons; 2 s (David John b 21 February 1967, Matthew James b 1 February 1971), 1 da (Catherine Jane b 26 July 1969); *Career* grad trainee Steel Co of Wales 1965–67; British Steel plc (now Corus Gp plc): asst mangr Port Talbot 1967–70, technical mangr 1970–73, departmental mangr 1973–76, personnel mangr 1976–78, works mangr 1978–88, project mangr 1982–88, dir of Coated Products 1988–90, md of Tin Plate 1990–92, md of Strip Products 1992–96, exec dir 1996–99, chief exec British Steel plc 1999–, jt chief exec Corus Gp plc 1999–2000; dir: ASW Gp plc 1993–95, Bank of Wales plc 1996–2001; non-exec dir: Welsh Water plc 2001–, Glas Cymru 2001–, Costain Gp plc 2002–; DSc Univ of Wales 2000; CEng 1993, FIM 1993, FREng 2000; *Recreations* rugby, cricket, walking, reading, opera, theatre, family; *Clubs* Crawshays Welsh RFC, Bridgend Lawn Tennis and Squash; *Style—* John Bryant, Esq

BRYANT, Julius John Victor; s of Robert John Stanley Bryant (d 1995), of Bristol, and Dena, *née* Bond; *b* 17 December 1957; *Educ* St Alban's Sch, UCL, Courtauld Inst London; *m* 1984, Barbara Ann, *née* Coffey; 1 s (Maximilian Stanley Bond b 10 Sept 1988); *Career* British paintings cataloguer Sotheby's 1980–81, researcher Walt Disney Productions 1981, museum asst Educn Dept V&A 1982–83; English Heritage: asst curator The Iveagh Bequest Kenwood 1983–88, acting curator Kenwood 1989, head Museums Div English Heritage 1990–93, dir Historic Properties London (Kenwood, Chiswick House, Marble Hill House, The Ranger's House, Westminster Abbey Chapter House, The Jewel Tower Westminster, Eltham Palace, Winchester Palace, London Wall, Coombe Conduits) 1993–95, dir of Collections 1995, dir of Museums and Collections 1996–2002, chief curator 2003–; visiting fell Yale Center for British Art USA 1985, Br Cncl research scholar Leningrad 1989, Mayers Fndn fell Huntington Library and Art Gallery Calif 1992; ed English Heritage Collections Review 1997– (4 vol 2003); memb: Ctee of Nat Art Museum Directors, Int Ctee of Historic House Museums (dep chm 2002–), Mgmnt Ctee Arts and Humanities Research Bd Centre for the Study of the Domestic Interior, Advsy Cncl Paul Mellon Centre for Studies in British Art Yale Univ 2004–, Anglo-Sikh Heritage Trail Advsy Gp 2004–; pres Hampstead Heath Decorative and Fine Arts Soc; Freeman City of Varazdin 2002; FSA 1999; *Books* The Victoria and Albert Museum Guide (1986), Finest Prospects: Three Historic Houses (1986), Marble Hill House (1988), Mrs Howard: A Woman of Reason (1988), The Iveagh Bequest Kenwood (1990), The Landscape of Kenwood (with C Colson, 1990), Robert Adam, Architect of Genius (1992), London's Country House Collections (1993), The London Historic House Museums Review 1990–92 (ed, 1993), The Trojan War Sculptures by Anthony Caro (with J Spurling, 1994, 3 edn 1998), Turner: Painting the Nation (1996; highly commended Gulbenkian Museum Pubn of the Year Awards), The Wernher Collection (2002), Kenwood: Catalogue of Paintings in the Iveagh Bequest (2003); contrib entries on 18th C British sculptors to The Dictionary of Art (1996) and to the New Dictionary of National Biography; author of numerous reviews, articles and pamphlets; *Recreations* running, looking, family life; *Style—* Julius Bryant; ✉ c/o English Heritage, 23 Savile Row, London W1S 2ET (tel 020 7973 3535)

BRYANT, Mark; s of David Christopher Bryant, and Shiela, *née* Everitt-Maiden; *b* 20 March 1968; *Educ* Univ of Central England in Birmingham (BA, Dip Arch), RIBA; *Career* architect; Mark Humphries Architects, EGA Arkitekter AB Stockholm Sweden, ptnr Bryant Priest Newman; memb Ctee Birmingham and Five Counties Archl Assoc Tst; *Projects* incl: indoor cricket centre Edgbaston for Warwickshire CCC, The Drum cultural arts centre Newtown Birmingham, business technology units for Sandwell Technical Coll, restoration and conversion to offices of Grade 1 listed building Birmingham, runner up int competition to redevelop Midland Arts Centre; *Style—* Mark Bryant, Esq

BRYANT, Michael Sydney; s of Sydney Cecil Bryant (d 1977), of Keynsham, Avon, and Lily May, *née* Jefferies; *b* 16 March 1944; *Educ* Bristol GS, Univ of Exeter, City of London Coll; *m* 1 Oct 1994, Sheila Daviron; *Career* Estate Duty Office Inland Revenue 1965–70, assoc dir Bevington Lowndes Ltd 1970–75, mktg dir Rathbone Brothers plc 1975–97; chm Hambro Fraser Smith Ltd 1997–2000; taxation and fin consit 1997–; contrib: Daily Telegraph, Sunday Times, Money Mktg, Taxation; memb Cncl FIMBRA 1986–88 and 1990–91, chm Insurance and Compensation Ctee FIMBRA, memb Tax Ctee IFAA, memb Securities Inst IAC Ctee 1998–; Compagnon du Beaujolais 1982–; IBRC 1977; *Recreations* food, wine, bridge, travel; *Clubs* Carlton; *Style—* Michael Bryant, Esq; ✉ Rue St Nicol, 14600 Honfleur, France (tel 00 33 2 31 89 07 51, fax 00 33 2 31 89 16 30, e-mail michael.bryant@wanadoo.fr)

BRYCE, Andrew John; s of John Robert Murray Bryce, of Lymington, Hants, and Eileen Josephine, *née* Denham; *b* 31 August 1947; *Educ* Thorpe GS Norwich, Univ of Newcastle upon Tyne (LLB), Coll of Law Lancaster Gate; *m* 1, 1972 (m dis 1994), Karalee Frances Lovegrove; 1 s (Alexander Henry b 22 June 1977), 1 da (Lucy Charlotte b 21 May 1980); m 2 (m dis 2005), 1994, Rosalind Beverley Hardy; 1 s (Matthew Cameron b 2 Oct 1986); *Career* CMS Cameron McKenna slrs (formerly Cameron Markby Hewitt): articled clerk 1969–71, admitted slr 1971, ptnr 1973–94; in own practice specialising in environmental law Andrew Bryce & Co 1994–; UK Environmental Law Assoc: fndr memb 1986, vice-chm 1987–88, chm 1988–91, memb Cncl 1986–96; former vice-chm Planning and Environmental Sub-Ctee City of London Law Soc; non-exec dir Augean plc 2005–; memb Law Soc 1973; *Recreations* bird watching, travel, decorative arts, music, tennis; *Clubs* Essex Birdwatching Soc, BTO, RSPB; *Style—* Andrew Bryce, Esq; ✉ Andrew Bryce & Co, Unit 23, Cambridge Science Park, Milton Road, Cambridge CB4 0EY (tel 01223 437011, fax 01223 437012, e-mail bryce@ehslaw.co.uk)

BRYCE, Gordon Craigie; s of George Bryce (d 1970), and Annie Macleod (d 1982); *b* 30 June 1943; *Educ* George Watsons Coll Edinburgh, Edinburgh Coll of Art (DA); *m* 1, 1966 (m dis 1976), Margaret Lothian; 2 s (Jon Oliver b 1968, Toby Garrad b 1969); m 2, 1984, Hilary Duthie; 2 da (Emma Louise b 1984, Alice Victoria b 1992), 1 s (Simon Nicholas b 1988); *Career* studied under Sir Robin Philipson and Sir William Gillies; head of fine art Grays Sch of Art 1986–95 (lectr in printmaking 1968–86); full time artist 1995–; RSW 1976, RSA 1995 (ARSA 1976); *Awards* RSA Chalmers Bursary 1965, RSA Keith Prize 1965, winner Pernod Scottish Acad Competition 1967, Arts Cncl Award 1968 and 1971, RSA Latimer Award 1969, May Marshall Brown Award 1977, maj Arts Cncl Award 1980, Educations Inst of Scotland Award 1981, Shell Expo Premier Award 1982, Sir William Gillies travelling scholarship 1984, Scottish Postal Bd Award 1986; *Solo Exhibitions* New 57 Gallery 1966 and 1968, Absalom Gallery 1968, Richard Demarco Gallery 1971, Univ of Aberdeen 1972, McMurray Gallery London 1977, Royal Edinburgh Hosp 1978, Univ of Edinburgh 1984, Sue Rankin Gallery London 1986–93, Grape Lane Gallery York 1988, Kingfisher Gallery Edinburgh 1988, Yperifanos Gallery NY 1988, Macaulay Gallery Stenton E Lothian 1989–94, Ancrum Gallery 1990, Rendezvous Gallery Aberdeen 1990, 1992 and 1996, Bruton Gallery Bath 1993, Thackeray Rankin Gallery London 1993, Jorgensen Fine Art Dublin 1994, Corrymella Scott Gallery Newcastle 1994, Thackeray Gallery London 1995, 1997 and 2005, The Scottish Gallery 1996, Aitken Dott Ltd Edinburgh 1996–2004 and 2006; *Work in Public Collections* incl: Scottish Nat Gallery of Modern Art, Scottish Arts Cncl, Aberdeen Arts Cncl, Edinburgh Civic Collection, Fife Educn Authy, Royal Edinburgh Hosps Collection, Carnegie Dunfermline Tst, Nat Tst for Scotland, Charterhouse Gp London, Flemings Collection, Seaforth Maritime Museum Aberdeen, BP, Argyle Securities London, Elf Oil, Mobile Oil, Bank of Scotland, Enterprise Oil plc, RSA, Grampian Television, George Watsons Coll Edinburgh; *Recreations* fly fishing; *Style—* Gordon Bryce, Esq

BRYCE, Iain Ross; TD, DL (East Riding of Yorkshire); *b* 19 March 1936; *Educ* Bridlington GS; *m* 13 Jan 1962, Janet Elizabeth; 2 da; *Career* Nat Serv, TA 1958–83: 131 Para Engr Regt, cmd 72 Engr Regt (Tynes) 1974–76, Dep Cdr 29 Engr Brigade 1976–79, Col RE, ret; CA 1959, ptnr Ernst & Young and preceding firms 1966–94; memb Eng Advsy Ctee on Telecommunications 1993–98; Prov Grand Master Yorks N & E Ridings 1984–91, Second Grand Princ The Supreme Grand Chapter of Royal Arch Masons 1991–2005, Dep Grand Master United Grand Lodge of England 1991–2004; memb Cncl RNLI 1995–2007, nat treas and tstee RNLI 1999–2006, pres Bridlington RNLI 2000– (chm 1990–98); chm Hull Coll 1993–96, chm of govrs Bridlington Sch 2003–05 (govr 1994–2006), chm Tstees of Bridlington Sch Fndn 2005–; memb: Worshipful Co of Merchant Adventurers of York, Co of Merchants of the Staple of England; FCA; *Recreations* freemasonry, gardening; *Clubs* Boodle's, Army and Navy, Royal Yorkshire Yacht (Bridlington), Yacht (Bridlington); *Style—* Iain R Bryce, Esq, TD, DL, FCA; ✉ Tighvonie, 76 Cardigan Road, Bridlington, East Yorkshire YO15 3JT (tel 01262 672312, e-mail cyber@nande.fsnet.co.uk)

BRYCE, Prof Tom G K; s of Thomas Knox Bryce (d 1974), of Glasgow, and Minnie Josephine, *née* Oswald (d 1984); *b* 27 January 1946; *Educ* King's Park Secdy Sch Glasgow, Univ of

Glasgow (BSc, MEd, PhD); *m* Karen Douglas, *née* Stewart; 1 da (Laura b 24 May 1986), 1 s (Colin b 1 Oct 1988); *Career* teacher of physics Jordanhill Coll Sch 1968–71, princ teacher of physics King's Park Secdy Sch 1971–73, pt/t lectr in psychology Univ of Glasgow 1972–75; Jordanhill Coll of Educn: lectr in psychology 1973–83, head of psychology 1983–87, head Div of Educn and Psychology 1987–94; Univ of Strathclyde Jordanhill Campus: prof Faculty of Educn 1993, vice-dean Research 1997–2002; dir Techniques for the Assessment of Practical Skills in Sci (TAPS) Projects 1980–90 and co-dir Assessment of Achievement Prog (AAP) Sci Projects 1985–97 (funded by SO Educn Dept); chm Editorial Bd Scottish Educational Review 1988–2002; CPsychol 1990; *Publications* author of articles, chapters and texts incl Scottish Education (co-ed, 1999, 2003); *Recreations* mountaineering (Munro completer 2650 2001), badminton; *Style*— Prof Tom Bryce; ✉ Faculty of Education, University of Strathclyde, Jordanhill Campus, Southbrae Drive, Glasgow G13 1PP (tel 0141 950 3536, e-mail t.g.k.bryce@strath.ac.uk)

BRYDEN, William Campbell Rough (Bill); CBE (1993); s of late George Bryden, and Catherine Bryden; *b* 12 April 1942; *Educ* Greenock HS; *m* 1970, Hon (Monica) Deborah, *née* Morris, da of 3 Baron Killanin, MBE, TD; 1 s (Dillon Michael George b 1972), 1 da (Mary Kate b 1975); *Career* television/theatre director; documentary writer Scottish TV 1963–64; asst dir: Belgrade Theatre Coventry 1965–67, Royal Court Theatre London 1967–69; assoc dir: Royal Lyceum Theatre Edinburgh 1971–74, Royal National Theatre 1975; head of drama television BBC Scotland 1984–94; dir: Cottesloe Theatre (Nat Theatre) 1978–80, Royal Opera House Covent Garden (productions include Parsifal 1988 and The Cunning Little Vixen 1990 and 2003), Bernstein's Mass (Guildhall Sch of Music & Drama) 1987, A Life in the Theatre (Haymarket) 1989, The Ship (Glasgow)1990, The Big Picnic (Glasgow) 1994, A Month In the Country (West End) 1995, Uncle Vanya (West End) 1996, The Mysteries (RNT) 1999, The Silver Tassie (ENO) 2000 (revival 2002), The Good Hope (RNT) 2001, The Creeper (West End) 2006; radio 2003–05 incl: HMS Ulysses, The Charge of the Light Brigade; exec producer BBC TV: Tutti Frutti (by John Byrne) 1987 (best series BAFTA awards), The Play on One (series) 1989; dir The Shawl (by David Mamet) BBC TV 1989; winner: Dir of the Year (Laurence Olivier Awards) 1985, Best Dir Award (Evening Standard) for The Mysteries Nat Theatre 1985, Assoc and Drama Magazine Awards 1986, Gulliver Award; Hon DUniv: Queen Margaret Coll Edinburgh 1989, Stirling 1991; memb bd Scottish TV 1979–85; *Plays* Willie Rough (1972), Benny Lynch (1974), Old Movies (1977), The Long Riders (screenplay, 1980), The Ship (1990), The Big Picnic (1994); *Recreations* music; *Style*— Bill Bryden, Esq, CBE; ✉ c/o ICM Ltd, Oxford House, 76 Oxford Street, London W1D 1BS (tel 020 7636 6565, fax 020 7323 0101)

BRYDON, Donald Hood; CBE (2004, OBE 1993); s of James Hood Brydon (d 1975), and Mary Duncanson, *née* Young; *b* 25 May 1945; *Educ* George Watson's Coll Edinburgh, Univ of Edinburgh (BSc); *m* 1996, Corrine; 1 da (Fiona b 1975), 1 s (Angus b 1977); *Career* research asst Dept of Economics Univ of Edinburgh; investment mangr: Airways Pension Scheme (British Airways), Barclays Bank; dir Barclays Investment Management, chm (formerly chief exec) BZW Investment Management Ltd, dep chief exec BZW 1994–96, chm BZW Private Equity 1994–96, chm Axa Investment Managers SA 1997–, chm Axa Real Estate Investment Managers SA 1998–; non-exec chm: Amersham 2003–04 (non-exec dir 1997–2004), Smiths Gp plc 2004–, Taylor Nelson Sofres 2006–; non-exec dir: London Stock Exchange 1991–98, Edinburgh UK Tracker Trust plc 1996–2006, AXA UK plc 1997–2007, Allied Domecq plc 1997–2005, Scottish Power plc 2003–07; chm: Institutional Shareholders Ctee 1989–90, Fund Managers Assoc 1999–2001, Code Ctee Panel on Takeovers and Mergers 2001–06, London Metal Exchange 2003–; vice-chm Nat Assoc of Pension Funds 1988–90, memb Auditing Practices Bd 1991–94, pres Euro Asset Mgmnt Assoc 1999–2001, chm Financial Servs Practitioner Panel 2001–03 (dep chm 2003–04), chm ifs Sch of Finance 2006–; chm EveryChild 2003–; ldr Bracknell DC 1977–80; AIIMR 1972; *Books* Economics of Technical Information Services (jtly, 1972), Pension Fund Investment (jtly, 1988); *Recreations* golf; *Clubs* Caledonian; *Style*— Donald Brydon, Esq, CBE; ✉ AXA Investment Managers Ltd, 7 Newgate Street, London EC1A 7NX (tel 020 7003 1501)

BRYDON, Rob (né Robert Brydon Jones); s of Howard Jones, and Joy Brydon Jones; *b* 3 May 1965, Port Talbot; *Educ* Porthcawl Comp Sch, Welsh Coll of Music and Drama; *Career* actor; early career as radio and TV presenter and voiceover artist; *Television* as writer and actor: Marion and Geoff 2000 (Br Comedy Award Best Newcomer, RTS Best Newcomer, South Bank Award Best Drama, Broadcasting Press Guild of GB Best Entertainment, also stage show West End and Edinburgh Festival), Human Remains 2000 (Br Comedy Award Best Actor, Banff TV Festival Best Comedy), A Small Summer Party 2001, Director's Commentary 2004, The Keith Barret Show 2004 (also stage show nat tour); as actor incl: Eleven Men Against Eleven 1995, Cold Lazarus 1996, The Way We Live Now 2001, Murder in Mind 2002, Black Books 2002, Cruise of the Gods 2002, Marple: 4.50 From Paddington 2004, Kenneth Tynan: In Praise of Hardcore 2005; *Films* Lock, Stock and Two Smoking Barrels 1998, Twenty Four Hour Party People 2002, Mirrormask 2005, A Cock and Bull Story 2005; *Style*— Mr Rob Brydon; ✉ website www.robbrydon.com

BRYER, Prof Anthony Applemore Mornington; s of Gp Capt Gerald Mornington Bryer, OBE, AFC (d 1994), and Joan Evelyn, *née* Grigsby (d 1994); *b* 31 October 1937; *Educ* Canford Sch, Sorbonne, Balliol Coll Oxford (MA, DPhil); *m* 1, 2 Aug 1961, Elizabeth (d 1995), da of John Milman Lipscomb; 3 da (Theodora Jane b 3 Feb 1965, Anna Caroline b 2 Sept 1966, Sarah Katherine b 19 March 1971); m 2, 11 July 1998, Jennifer Ann Banks, da of Geoffrey Alan Franks; *Career* Nat Serv RAF Adjutant 1956–58; emeritus prof of Byzantine studies Univ of Birmingham 1999– (res fell, lectr, sr lectr, reader, prof 1964–99, first dir of Centre for Byzantine Studies 1976–94, public orator 1991–98); res fell Univ of Athens 1961–62, Hellenic Travellers Club guest lectr 1967–97, five times visiting fell Dumbarton Oaks Harvard Univ 1970–85, Loeb lectr Harvard Univ 1980, visiting Byzantinist Medieval Acad of America 1984, visiting fell Merton Coll Oxford 1985, res advsr to Govt of Cyprus 1988; visiting lectr: Finland 1987, Sweden 1988, Aust 1989, Poland 1993, Albania 1999, Latvia 2000; Wiles lectr Belfast 1990; Runciman lectr and visiting sr research fell KCL 1996–; chm: Br Nat Ctee of Int Byzantine Assoc, Soc for The Promotion of Byzantine Studies 1989–95; pres Br Inst of Archaeology at Ankara 2002–; convenor 21st International Congress of Byzantine Studies London 2006; corresponding memb Hellenic Fndn; FSA 1973, FRHistS 1994; *Books* Iconoclasm (1977), The Empire of Trebizond and the Pontos (1980), The Byzantine Monuments and Topography of the Pontos (2 vols, 1985), Continuity and Change in Late Byzantine and Early Ottoman Society (1986), Peoples and Settlement in Anatolia and the Caucasus 800–1900 (1988), From Mantzikert to Lepanto (1991), Mount Athos (1996), The Post-Byzantine Monuments of the Pontos (2002); *Recreations* travel, writing obituaries; *Clubs* Buckland (Birmingham), Lochaline Social (Morvern), Black Sea (Trebizond); *Style*— Prof Anthony Bryer; ✉ 33 Crosbie Road, Harborne, Birmingham B17 9BG (tel 0121 427 1207); Centre for Byzantine, Ottoman and Modern Greek Studies, University of Birmingham, Birmingham B15 2TT

BRYER, Dr David Ronald William; CMG (1996); s of Ronald Bryer, and Betty, *née* Rawlinson; *b* 15 March 1944; *Educ* King's Sch Worcester, Worcester Coll Oxford (MA, DPhil), Univ of Manchester (Dip TEFL); *m* 1980, Margaret Isabel, da of Sir Eric Bowyer, and Elizabeth, *née* Nicholls; 1 da (Helen b 1983), 1 s (Nicholas b 1985); *Career* teacher Lebanon and UK 1964–74 and 1979–81; asst keeper Ashmolean Museum 1972–74; Oxfam: field dir ME 1975–79, co-ordinator Africa 1981–84, overseas dir 1984–91, dir 1992–2001, memb Bd Oxfam America 2003–, chair Oxfam Int 2003–; sr advsr Centre for Humanitarian Dialogue Geneva 2002–03; chm: Eurostep (grouping of 22 Euro devpt agencies) 1993–95, Steering Ctee for Humanitarian Response (SCHR) Geneva 1995–97, BOAG 1998–2000; tstee Save the Children UK 2002–; memb: Cncl VSO 1990–, Ct Oxford Brookes Univ 1999–2003, Wilton Park Academic Cncl 1999–, UN Sec-Gen's High Level Panel on Financing for Devpt UN 2000–01; *Books* The Origins of the Druze Religion (1975); *Style*— Dr David Bryer, CMG; ✉ Bracken Lodge, Eaton Road, Malvern Wells, Worcestershire WR14 4PE

BRYER, (Alastair) Robin Mornington; s of Gp Capt Gerald Mornington Bryer, OBE, AFC (d 1994), and Joan Evelyn, *née* Grigsby (d 1994); *b* 13 May 1944; *Educ* Dauntsey's Sch West Lavington, King's Coll Durham (BA); *m* 16 Sept 1976, Jennifer Sheridan, da of Lt-Col Richard Sheridan Skelton, OBE; 1 s (William b 1977); *Career* sr planning asst Hampshire CC 1967–73, ptnr Inland and Waterside Planners 1973–77, ind chartered town planner (one of the first in private practice) assisting landowners, developers, MPs, conservation bodies and govt depts 1977–; award winner: Tomorrow's New Communities Competition 1991, Best Small Project Class Daily Telegraph Individual Home Builder Awards 1997; exhibited in architectural section of RA 1980, guest lectr Hellenic Travellers' Club 1980–96; chm PEST (Tory pressure gp) 1966–68, memb Consultancy Bd RTPI 1980–83; chm Old Dauntseians' Assoc 1985–86; Freeman City of London 1987, Guildsman City Guild of Old Mercers 1988; MRTPI 1973; *Books* Jolie Brise, A Tall Ships Tale (1982, 2 edn 1997), Roving Commissions (ed 1983–86), Hair, Fashion and Fantasy down the Ages (2000, Chinese edn 2003), Jack: A literary biography of John Connell (2007); *Recreations* sailing; *Clubs* Royal Cruising (sr memb), Royal Lymington Yacht; *Style*— Robin Bryer, Esq; ✉ Princes Place, Closworth, Yeovil, Somerset BA22 9RH (tel 01935 872268, fax 01935 873341)

BRYMER, Timothy; s of Jack Brymer (d 2004), and Joan, *née* Richardson; *b* 7 November 1951, London; *Educ* Dulwich Coll, Coll of Air Training, Coll of Law; *m* 10 Aug 1985, Helen, *née* Cahill; 1 s (Toby James b 22 Jan 1987), 1 da (Lucy Alexandra b 7 Sept 1990); *Career* admitted slr 1977; slr specialising in aviation and aerospace law; sr ptnr Brymer Marland & Co 1985–90; ptnr and head of aviation gp: CMS Cameron McKenna 1991–2004, Clyde & Co 2004–; author of articles in insurance and aviation publications; trained as commercial pilot Br Overseas Airways Corp (BOAC); founding memb Lawyers Flying Assoc, memb Guild of Pilots and Air Navigators; *Recreations* tennis, squash, cycling, flying (holds pilot's license); *Style*— Timothy Brymer, Esq; ✉ Flambards, Northdown Road, Woldingham, Surrey CR3 7BB (tel 01883 652245, fax 01883 652821, e-mail thebrymers@hotmail.com); Clyde & Co, 51 Eastcheap, London EC3M 1JP (tel 020 7648 1912, fax 020 7623 5427, e-mail tim.brymer@clydeco.com)

BRYNING, Charles Frederick; s of Frederick Bryning (d 1982), of Norbreck, Blackpool, and Dorothy Edith Bryning; *b* 17 July 1946; *Educ* Arnold Sch Blackpool; *m* 29 April 1983, Katrina Carol, da of John Carol Boris Ely, of Lytham St Anne's; 1 s (Simon b 1983); *Career* CA; ptnr Jones Harris & Co 1972–, chief exec Alexander Walker Gp of Cos 1987–91; FCA; *Style*— Charles Bryning, Esq; ✉ 17 St Peters Place, Fleetwood, Lancashire FY7 6EB (tel 01253 874255, e-mail charles.bryning@jones-harris.co.uk)

BRYSON, Bill; Hon OBE (2006); *b* 1951, Des Moines, IA; *Educ* Drake Univ IA; *m*; 4 c; *Career* travel writer; formerly newspaper journalist: chief copy ed business section The Times, dep nat news ed business section The Independent; cmmr English Heritage, pres Campaign to Protect Rural England 2007–; chllr Univ of Durham 2005–; James Cameron Meml Lecture City Univ 2005; Hon DCL Univ of Durham 2004; *Books* travel writing: The Lost Continent (1989), Neither Here Nor There (1991), Notes From a Small Island (1995, adapted for TV 1998, voted best portrayal of England World Book Day 2003), A Walk in the Woods (1997), Notes From a Big Country (1998), Down Under (2000), African Diary (charity book for CARE Int, 2002); other books incl: Mother Tongue (1990), Made In America (1994), A Short History of Nearly Everything (2003, winner General Prize Aventis Prizes for Science Books 2004, shortlisted Samuel Johnson Prize 2004), The Life and Times of the Thunderbolt Kid (memoir, 2006); *Style*— Bill Bryson, Esq, OBE; ✉ c/o Doubleday, Transworld Publishers, 61–63 Uxbridge Road, London W5 5SA

BRYSON, Col (James) Graeme; OBE (1954), QCB (1961), TD (1949, and two clasps 1949 and 1955), JP (Liverpool 1956), DL (1968); s of John Conway Bryson (d 1959), of Liverpool, and Oletta, *née* Olsen; *b* 4 February 1913; *Educ* St Edward's Coll Liverpool, Univ of Liverpool (LLB, LLM), Open Univ (BSc); *m* 1938, Jean (d 1981), da of Walter Cook Glendinning, of Liverpool; 2 s (and 1 s decd), 4 da; *Career* cmmnd from Univ of Liverpool OTC to 89 Field Bde RA (TA) 1936, cmdg various units 1939–45, promoted Lt-Col 1944, cmd 470 (3 W Lancs) HAA Regt 1947–52, cmd 626 HAA Regt 1952–55, Bt-Col 1955, Hon Col 33 Signal Regt (V) 1975–81; admitted slr 1935, sr dist registrar High Court of Justice Liverpool and Admiralty Registrar 1947–78, dep circuit judge 1978–82; memb Lord Chllr's (Payne) Ctee for Enforcement of Debts 1965–69, gen cmmr of taxes 1968–79, memb IOM Cmmn for Reform Enforcement Laws 1972–74, chm Med Appeal Tbnl 1978–86; Northwest Cancer Research Fund: tstee 1950–80, pres 1985–2001, life pres 2001–; pres: City of Liverpool Royal Br Legion 1950– (pres NW England 1979–90), Liverpool Law Soc 1970, Liverpool Rotary Club 1970; hon life pres: West Lancs Co Royal Br Legion 1993–, Merseyside Cncl of Ex-Service and Regtl Assocs 1986–; vice-pres: Royal Artillery Offrs Assoc 1998–, Royal Artillery Assoc (Merseyside) 1998–; vice-patron Regular Forces Employment Assoc (memb Cncl 1952–92); memb Catholic Writers' Guild 2002–; HM Vice Lord-Lt Merseyside 1979–89; FRSA 1989; KHS 1974, KCHS 1990, Knight Hon Soc of Knights of the Round Table 1990, KCSG 1996; *Books* Execution in Halsbury's Laws of England (jtly, 3 edn 1976), Shakespeare in Lancashire (1997, 2 edn 1998), A Cathedral in my Time (2000, 2 edn 2001), A Centenary of Liverpool Lawyers (jtly, 2001), There's Poetry in my Veins (2003), Oxford Dictionary of National Biography (contrib, 2004); *Recreations* ex-service interests, local history, boating; *Clubs* Athenaeum (Liverpool, pres 1969); *Style*— Col Graeme Bryson, OBE, QCB, TD, DL; ✉ Sunwards, 2 Thirlmere Road, Hightown, Liverpool L38 3RQ (tel 0151 929 2652)

BUBB, Nicholas Henry (Nick); s of John William Edward Bubb, of Orsett, Essex, and Diana Rosemary, *née* Willetts; *b* 24 March 1955; *Educ* Gillingham GS, ChCh Oxford (MA); *m* 10 April 1982, Susan Mary, da of Joan Dare, of Chichester, W Sussex; 1 s (Alexander Benjamin Thomas b 1985), 1 da (Amy Louise Harriet b 1988); *Career* retailing analyst: Rowe & Pitman & Co 1977–79, Citicorp Scrimgeour Vickers (formerly Kemp-Gee & Co and Scrimgeour Kemp-Gee) 1979–88 (ptnr 1983), Morgan Stanley 1988–95 (exec dir), Mees Pierson 1996–97, SG Securities 1997–2002, Evolution Securities 2003–06, Pali Int 2007–; memb KMPG-SPSL Retail Think-Tank; *Recreations* cricket, travel, golf, reading, films, wine; *Clubs* Oriental, Riverside Sports Chiswick, MCC; *Style*— Nick Bubb, Esq; ✉ 6 Orchard Rise, Richmond, Surrey TW10 5BX (e-mail nick.bubb@palii.com)

BUBB, Stephen John Limrick; JP; s of John William Edward Bubb, of Orsett, Essex, and Diana Rosemary, *née* Willatts; *b* 5 November 1952, Wigmore, Kent; *Educ* Gillingham GS, ChCh Oxford (MA); *Career* economist NEDO 1975–76, res offr TGWU 1976–80, negotiations offr NUT 1980–87, head of pay negotiations for local govt Assoc of Metropolitan Authorities 1987–95, founding dir Nat Lottery Charities Bd 1995–2000, chief exec ACEVO 2000–, sec-gen euclid (Euroepan network of third sector ldrs) 2007–; fndr dir Metropolitan Authorities Recruitment Agency 1990–95, ind assessor for govt appts 1999–, memb Cabinet Sec's Hons Advsy Ctee 2005–; chm Adventure Capital Fund 2006–; memb Tyson Task Force on Non-Exec Dir Appts 2002; memb W Lambeth HA 1982–89, non-exec memb Lambeth, Lewisham and Southwark HA 1998–2002, govr Guy's & St Thomas' Fndn Tst (chm Strategy Ctee 2004–), chief whip Lambeth Cncl 1982–86, youth court magistrate Inner London 1980–2000, founder chm Lambeth Landmark 1982–88; pt/t tutor Open Univ 1982–87; chm City of Oxford Orchestra 1993–95; FCIPD, FRSA; *Publications* People are Key (2003), And Why Not? Tapping the Talent of Not-For-Profit Chief Executives (2004), Only Connect: A Leader's Guide to Networking (2005), Public Matters (contrib, 2007); *Recreations* genealogy, travel, fine art and fine wine, Anglican church, making a difference; *Clubs* Oxford and Cambridge, New Cavendish; *Style*— Stephen Bubb, Esq, JP; ✉ Armada Cottage, Thames Street, Charlbury, Oxfordshire OX7 3QQ (tel 07785 387844); Association of Chief Executives of Voluntary Organisations, 1 New Oxford Street, London WC1A 1NU (tel 0845 345 8496, fax 0845 345 8482, e-mail stephen.bubb@acevo.org.uk)

BUBNOV, Vladislav Bubnov; s of Sergei Bubnov, of Moscow, and Valentina, *née* Tishenko (d 1991); *b* 23 October 1969; *Educ* Bolshoi Sch Moscow, Bolshoi Acad of Dancing (Teaching Cert); *Career* soloist The Bolshoi Ballet 1987–92, first princ Scottish Ballet 1992–2000, princ Leipziger Ballet 2000, princ Eng Nat Ballet 2000–; repertoire incl: Mercutio in Grigorovich's Romeo & Juliet, Jester in Swan Lake, Bronze Idol in La Bayadère, Shepherd in Spartacus, Spanish Harlequin in The Nutcracker, Pan in Lavrovsky's Walpurgisnacht, Barachio in Boccadoro's L'amour pour l'amour, Two Friends in Balanchine's Prodigal Son, princ in Concerto Borocco, princ in Scotch Symphony, soloist in Bournonville's Conservatoire, James in La Sylphide, Combat/Franz in Wright's Coppélia, Prince in Darrell's The Nutcracker and Cinderella, Hoffman in Darrell's Romeo and Juliet, princ in Darrell's Rückert Songs, Albrecht in Darrell's Giselle, Barman in A Cooper's Just Scratching the Surface, Colas in F Ashton's La Fille Mal Gardee, Prince in B Stevenson's Cinderella, princ in K MacMillan's Diversions, Lysander/Puck in Cohan's Midsummer Night's Dream, Spring in Cohan's Four Seasons, princ in North's Troy Game, Red Couple in Tippet's Bruch Violin Concerto No 1, Vronsky/Levin in Prokovsky's Anna Karenina, soloist in Vespri, Peter in Lustig's Peter Pan, Prince Florimund/Bluebird in Samsova's The Sleeping Beauty, princ in Baldwin's Haydn Pieces and Ae Fond Kiss, Le Corsaire Pas de Deux, Belong Pas de Deux, Poet in Fokine's Les Sylphides, Romeo in J Cranko's Romeo and Juliet, Prince in U Scholz's Swan Lake, princ in U Scholz's Pax Questuosa, Prince in D Dean's Swan Lake, Albrecht in D Dean's Gisselle, Romeo in D Dean's Romeo and Juliet, Prince in M Corder's Cinderella, princ in Hampson's Double Concerto; *Style*— Vladislav Bubnov, Esq; ✉ English National Ballet, Markova House, 39 Jay Mews, London SW7 2ES

BUCHAN, Dr Alexander Stewart; s of Samuel Buchan (d 1992), of Carnoustie, and Mary, *née* Stewart (d 1982); *b* 7 September 1942; *Educ* Loretto, Univ of Edinburgh (MB ChB); *m* 24 Feb 1968, Henrietta Young, da of William Constable Dalrymple, of Edinburgh; 1 s (Alexander b 1969); *Career* conslt anaesthetist 1975–: Royal Infirmary Edinburgh, Royal Hosp for Sick Children, Princess Margaret Rose Orthopaedic Hosp; admin conslt for obstetric anaesthesia Simpson Memorial Maternity Pavilion 1988–; vice-pres Medico-Chirurgical Soc of Edinburgh; memb: Scottish Soc of Anaesthetists, Edinburgh and East of Scotland Soc of Anaesthetists (former pres); FFARCS 1970; *Books* Handbook of Obstetric Anaesthesia (1991), Simpson Handbook of Obstetric Anaesthesia (electronic web pub, 2000); *Recreations* fishing, sailing, golf; *Style*— Dr Alexander Buchan

BUCHAN, District Judge; (James Alexander) Bruce; s of James Welsh Ross Buchan (d 1982), and Phyllis Clare, *née* Buckle (d 1990); *b* 4 May 1947; *Educ* Fulneck Boys Sch, Univ of Birmingham (LLB); *Career* admitted slr; ptnr Dibb Lupton Broomhead 1975–92, district judge 1992–; nat chm Young Slrs' Gp Law Soc 1982–83; memb Law Soc, hon memb Leeds Law Soc; *Recreations* walking and golf; *Clubs* The Leeds, Headingly Golf (Leeds); *Style*— District Judge Buchan; ✉ Dewsbury County Court, Eightlands Road, Dewsbury, West Yorkshire WF13 2PE (tel 01924 465860)

BUCHAN, Colin Alexander Mason; s of G H Buchan, of Scotland, and H Buchan, *née* Stewart; *b* 6 December 1954; *Educ* St John's Coll Johannesburg, INSEAD (AMP), Univ of the Witwatersrand (BComm); *m* 28 March 1980, Susan, *née* Monahan; 3 da (Kirsten b 28 Oct 1984, Alexandra b 27 Dec 1987, Caitlin b 6 May 1990); *Career* with African Finance Corp 1980–84; md SG Warburg South Africa 1984–87, md SG Warburg Far East 1987–94, appointed dir SG Warburg plc 1995, memb Exec Bd SBC Warburg 1995, global head of equities and memb Gp Mgmnt Bd UBS AG 1999–2001, ret; memb Bd: Merrill Lynch World Mining Tst 2001–, Standard Life Investments 2002–, Royal Bank of Scotland Gp plc 2002–; dir Royal Scot Nat Orch 2002–; *Recreations* hill walking, farming pedigree Aberdeen Angus cattle; *Clubs* Rand, Oriental, Hong Kong; *Style*— Colin Buchan, Esq

BUCHAN, Dennis Thorne; s of David S Buchan; *b* 25 April 1937; *Educ* Arbroath HS, Dundee Coll of Art (DA); *m* 1965 (m dis 1976), Elizabeth, *née* Watson; 1 da (Wendy), 1 s (John MacGregor); *Career* artist; lectr Duncan of Jordanstone Coll of Art 1965–94; memb Dundee Group Artists Ltd 1975–81; convenor Royal Scottish Academy 177th Annual Exhbn 2003; RSA 1991 (ARSA 1975) *Solo Exhibitions* Douglas and Foulis Gall 1965, Saltire Soc (Edinburgh Festival) 1974, Compass Gall 1975, A Span of Shores (Compass Gall Glasgow) 1994, Traquair House 1996, Various Experiences (Pentagon Business Centre Glasgow) 2001, 2000+ (Meffan Gall Forfar) 2005; *Group Exhibitions* Five Dundee Painters 1961, + - 30 (Hunterian Museum and tour) 1964, Six Coastal Artists (Demarco Gall) 1965, Scottish Contemporary Painting (Aberdeen Art Gall) 1970, Seven Painters in Dundee (Scottish Nat Gall of Modern Art, McManus Gall) 1972, Painters in Parallel (Scottish Arts Cncl Festival Exhbn) 1978, Kindred Spirits (Ancrum Gall) 1990, Compass Contribution (Tramway) 1990, Scottish Contemporary Painting (Flowers East) 1993, Paperworks (Seagate Gall) 1993, Artists in Angus (Meffan Gall) 1993, Five Scottish Artists (Centre d'Art en L'Ile Geneva) 1994, The RSA in London (Albermarle Gall) 1999, RSA Connections (Edinburgh Festival) 1999 and 2000; *Collections* Edinburgh Hosp Gp, Dundee Coll of Educn, Kingsway Tech Coll, Univ of Leicester, Scottish Arts Cncl, Dundee Museum and Art Galls, Vincent Price Collection, Aberdeen Royal Infirmary; *Awards* Keith Prize RSA 1962, Latimer Award RSA 1963, Arts Cncl Award 1973, William McCaully Award for most distinguished work in RSA Exhbn 1988, William Gillies Bequest Fund Award RSA 1991; *Style*— Dennis Buchan, Esq, RSA; ✉ 8 Inchcape Road, Arbroath, Tayside DD11 2DF (tel 01241 873080)

BUCHAN, (Hon) (Charles Walter) Edward Ralph; 2 s of 3 Baron Tweedsmuir, and his 2 wife Barbara Howard, *née* Ensor (d 1969); *b* 5 August 1951; *Educ* Magdalen Coll Sch Oxford, Univ of Southampton (BSc); *m* 27 Nov 1982, Fiona Jane, da of Capt E P Carlisle, of Llanigon, Hay-on-Wye; 1 s (William b 1984), 3 da (Annabel b 1986, Laura b 1988, Amilia b 1992); *Career* Hill Samuel Bank Ltd: joined 1977, dir 1985–96, md 1993–96; exec dir West LB Panmure Ltd 1999–; formerly md Close Brothers Corporate Finance Ltd, non-exec dir Tibbett & Britten Gp plc; FCA 1976; *Clubs* Travellers; *Style*— The Hon Edward Buchan; ✉ West LB Panmure Ltd, Woolgate Exchange, 25 Basinghall Street, London EC2V 5HA

BUCHAN, Hon James Ernest; 3 s of 3 Baron Tweedsmuir, *qv*, and Barbara Howard, *née* Ensor (d 1969); *b* 11 June 1954; *Educ* Eton, Magdalen Coll Oxford (MA); *m* 1986, Lady Evelyn Rose Phipps, da of 4 Marquess of Normanby, KG, CBE (d 1994); 2 da (Elizabeth Blanche b 1989, Rose Barbara Averil b 1995), 1 s (Nicholas Adam b 1992); *Career* Financial Times: corr Saudi Arabia 1978–80, corr Bonn 1982–84, columnist Lex Column 1984–86, corr NY 1987–90; contrib Independent on Sunday Review 1990–94, chief book critic Spectator 1990–94; Harold Wincott Award for Business Journalism 1986; FRGS, FRAS, FRSL, FZS; *Books* The House of Saud (with Richard Johns and David Holden, 1981), A Parish of Rich Women (1984, Whitbread First Novel Award, Yorkshire Post Award, David Higham Award), Davy Chadwick (1987), Slide (1990), Heart's Journey in Winter (1995, Guardian Fiction Award), High Latitudes (1996), Frozen Desire (1997, Duff Cooper Prize), A Good Place to Die (1999), Capital of the Mind (2003); *Style*— The Hon James Buchan; ✉ c/o Caroline Dawnay, PFD, Drury House, 34–43 Russell Street, London WC2B 5HA (tel 020 7344 1000, fax 020 7836 9539)

BUCHAN, 17 Earl of (S 1469); Malcolm Harry Erskine; also Lord Auchterhouse (S 1469), Lord Cardross (S 1610), and Baron Erskine (UK 1806); s of 16 Earl of Buchan (d 1984), and Christina, *née* Woolner (d 1994); *b* 4 July 1930; *Educ* Eton; *m* 1957, Hilary Diana Cecil, da of late Sir Ivan McLannahan Cecil Power, 2 Bt; 2 s (Henry Thomas Alexander, Lord Cardross b 1960, Hon Montagu John b 1966), 2 da (Lady Seraphina Berry b 1961, Lady Arabella Fleur (Lady Arabella Biddle) b 1969); *Heir* s, Lord Cardross; *Career* JP (Westminster) 1972–99; pres Sane Planning in the SE (SPISE) 1995–, former chm The Dogs & cats Home Battersea, memb Rare Breeds Survival Tst; Liveryman Worshipful of Grocers; *Style*— The Rt Hon the Earl of Buchan; ✉ Newnham House, Newnham, Hook, Hampshire RG27 9AS

BUCHAN-HEPBURN, Capt Sir (John) Alastair Trant Kidd; 7 Bt (UK 1815), of Smeaton Hepburn, Haddingtonshire; s of John Trant Buchan-Hepburn (d 1953), and Edith Margaret (Mitchell), *née* Robb (d 1980); suc cousin, Sir Ninian Buchan-Hepburn of Smeaton-Hepburn, 6 Bt (d 1992); *b* 27 June 1931; *Educ* Charterhouse, Univ of St Andrews, RMA Sandhurst; *m* 1957, Georgina Elizabeth Turner, SRN, da of Oswald Morris Turner, MC (d 1953), of Armathwaite, Cumberland; 3 da (Caroline Georgina (Mrs A W P Thomson) b 1958, Sarah Elizabeth (Mrs D A Cox) b 1960, Louise Mary (Mrs A D S Kinnear) b 1966), 1 s ((John) Christopher Alastair b 1963); *Heir* s, Christopher Buchan-Hepburn; *Career* Capt 1st King's Dragoon Gds, ADC to GOC-in-C Malaya Cmd 1954–57, attached to Swiss Army Cavalry, served BAOR and Far East, attached Household Cavalry; brewing sr exec Arthur Guinness & Co Ltd 1958–86; dir: Broughton Brewery Ltd 1987–95, Broughton Ales Ltd 1995–2001, ret; chm: Valentine Marketing Ltd 2002–03, Valentine Holdings Ltd 2002–03; vice-pres Marine Voluntary Services 2002–, tstee Dundee Industrial Heritage Tst 1999–, memb Ctee St Andrews Branch Royal Br Legion 1999–; memb Vestry Ctee All Saints Church St Andrews; life memb: St Andrew Preservation Tst 1957, 1st Queen's Dragoon Gds Assoc, Scottish Licensed Trade Benevolent Soc, Kate Kennedy Club (Univ of St Andrews), After Many Days Club (Univ of St Andrews); memb Baronets' Tst 1992–; memb RMA Sandhurst Fndn 2004–; memb Incorporation of Maltmen; *Recreations* gardening, shooting, fishing, walking, old china and glass, golf, travel in Scottish Islands; *Clubs* Royal and Ancient Golf, Cavalry and Guards', Country Club UK; *Style*— Capt Sir Alastair Buchan-Hepburn, Bt; ✉ Chagford, 60 Argyle Street, St Andrews, Fife KY16 9BU; (tel 01334 472161)

BUCHANAN, *see also:* Macdonald-Buchanan

BUCHANAN, Alistair John; s of John James Buchanan (d 1983), and Phoebe Leonora, *née* Messel (d 1952); *b* 13 December 1935; *Educ* Eton, New Coll Oxford; *m* 1, 1959, Louise Parker (d 1961); m 2, 1963, Ann Hermione, da of Raymond Alexander Baring (d 1967); 3 da (Katie, Tessa, Helen); *Career* 2 Lt 2 Bn Coldstream Guards 1954–56; Layton-Bennett Billingham & Co 1959–62, Allen Harvey & Ross Ltd 1962–81, A Sarasin & Co Ltd 1980–87, chm Cater Allen Holdings plc 1981–85, md Morgan Grenfell Govt Securities 1985–87, dep chm and md Mees & Hope Securities Holdings Ltd 1987–91; chm: Premium Management Ltd 1989–2000, Lorne House Trust Ltd 1991–2006; dir: LIFFE 1981–84, Heritage of London Trust Ltd 1982–98, Eyecare Products plc 1994–97, Mannin Industries Ltd; Worshipful Co of Vintners; *Recreations* golf, gardening; *Clubs* White's, Cavalry and Guards, Swinley Forest Golf; *Style*— Alistair Buchanan, Esq; ✉ 11 London Place, Oxford OX4 1BD (tel 01865 424576, fax 01865 424603)

BUCHANAN, Sir Andrew George; 5 Bt (UK 1878), of Dunburgh, Stirlingshire; s of Maj Sir Charles James Buchanan, 4 Bt (d 1984), and Barbara Helen (d 1986), da of Lt-Col Rt Hon Sir George Frederick Stanley, GCSI, GCIE, CMG; *b* 21 July 1937; *Educ* Eton, Trinity Coll Cambridge, Wye Coll London; *m* 26 April 1966, Belinda Jane Virginia, DL, da of Donald Colquhoun Maclean and wid of Gresham N Vaughan (d 1964); 1 da (Laura Evelyn (Mrs James Mayes) b 1967), 1 s (George Charles Mellish b 1975), 1 step s, 1 step da; *Heir* s, George Buchanan; *Career* 2 Lt Coldstream Guards 1956–58, Major cmd A Sqdn Sherwood Rangers Yeo (TA) 1971–74, Hon Col B Sqdn (Sherwood Rangers Yeo) Queen's Own Yeomanry 1989–94, Hon Col Notts Army Cadet Force 1991–; farmer; High Sheriff Notts 1976–77; chm Bd of Visitors HM Prison Ranby 1983–84; HM Lord-Lt Notts 1991– (DL 1985); KStJ 1991; *Recreations* walking, forestry, bridge; *Clubs* Boodle's; *Style*— Sir Andrew Buchanan, Bt; ✉ Hodsock Priory Farm, Blyth, Worksop, Nottinghamshire S81 0TY (tel 01909 591227, fax 01909 591947, e-mail andrew.buchanan@hodsock.com)

BUCHANAN, Prof (Robert) Angus; OBE (1993); s of Robert Graham Buchanan (d 1975), of Sheffield, and Bertha Buchanan, MBE, JP, *née* Davis (d 1975); *b* 5 June 1930; *Educ* High Storrs GS Sheffield, St Catharine's Coll Cambridge (MA, PhD); *m* 10 Aug 1955, Brenda June, da of George Henry Wade (d 1955), of Sheffield, and Doris Elsie Wade (d 1971); 2 s (Andrew Nassau b 1958, Thomas Claridge b 1960); *Career* Nat Serv RAOC 1948–50, GHQ FARELF 1949–50; educn offr Royal Fndn of St Katharine Stepney 1956–60, co-opted memb London CC Educn Ctee 1958–60; Univ of Bath: formerly lectr, sr lectr and reader, prof 1990–95 (emeritus 1995–), dir Centre for the History of Technol, Science and Soc 1964–; visiting prof ANU 1981, visiting lectr Wuhan People's Republic of China 1983, Jubilee prof Chalmers Univ Sweden 1984; royal cmmr Royal Cmmn for Historical Monuments 1979–93, memb Properties Ctee Nat Tst 1974–2001; pres: Assoc for Industrial Archaeology 1975–77 and 2003–, Newcomen Soc for History of Engrg and Technol 1981–83, Int Ctee for the History of Technol 1993–97 (sec gen 1981–93); vice-pres Soc of Antiquaries of London 1995–99; chm Bath Branch Historical Assoc 1987–90, dir Nat Cataloguing Unit for the Archives of Contemporary Scientists 1987–95; Hon DSc Chalmers Univ Sweden 1986; Leonardo da Vinci Medal Soc for the History of Technol 1989; hon fell Science Museum 1992–; FRHistS 1978, FSA 1990, FRSA 1993–99; *Books* Technology and Social Progress (1965), Industrial Archaeology of the Bristol Region (jtly, 1969), Industrial Archaeology in Britain (1972), Industrial Archaeology of the Stationary Steam Engine (jtly, 1976), History and Industrial Civilisation (1979), Industrial Archaeology of Central Southern England (jtly, 1980), The Engineers - A History of the Engineering Profession in Britain 1750–1914 (1989), The Power of the Machine (1992), Brunel: The Life and Times of Isambard Kingdom Brunel (2002); *Recreations* walking, rambling, travelling; *Style*— Prof R Angus Buchanan, OBE, FSA; ✉ 13 Hensley Road, Bath BA2 2DR (tel 01225 311508); Centre for the History of Technology Science and Society, University of Bath, Claverton Down, Bath BA2 7AY (e-mail hssraab@bath.ac.uk)

BUCHANAN, Cameron Roy Marchand; s of late Maj Alexander Bell Watson Buchanan, MC, TD, of Woking, Surrey, and Katharine Norma, *née* Stiles; *Educ* St Edward's Sch Oxford, Sorbonne; *m* 11 May 1973 (m dis), Diana Frances, da of Hugh Wilson Jones (d 1979); 1 da (Tanya Katharine b 18 Sept 1974), 1 s (Alexander Cameron b 4 April 1977); *Career* md Harrisons of Edinburgh Ltd (formerly George Harrison & Co Edinburgh Ltd) 1985–; dir Br Knitting and Clothing Export Cncl (chm The Forum), dir Br Wool Mktg Bd; Scottish Entrepreneur of the Year 1992; memb Leith High Constables; Freeman Worshipful Co of Merchants Edinburgh; hon consul for Iceland in Scotland; *Recreations* skiing, golf, tennis; *Clubs* New (Edinburgh), Hon Co of Edinburgh Golfers; *Style*— Cameron Buchanan, Esq; ✉ Calax House, 2 Douglas Gardens, Edinburgh EH4 3DA (tel 0131 220 1889); Harrisons of Edinburgh, 45 Queen Street, Edinburgh EH2 3NH (tel 0131 220 5775, fax 0131 225 6317)

BUCHANAN, Dr David John; *b* 27 December 1945; *Educ* Royal HS Edinburgh, Univ of St Andrews (BSc, PhD, DSc); *m* Joan; 1 da (b 1972), 1 s (b 1974); *Career* research assoc Culham Lab UKAEA 1971–73; British Coal (formerly NCB): head of Geophysics Group Mining Research and Development Establishment (MRDE) 1974–82, head of data processing Doncaster Mining Dept 1982–83, head Mining Sciences Division MRDE 1983–87, mangr of tech strategy/dep head of research HQ Tech Dept 1987–89, head of mining research 1989–90, dir of research and scientific servs 1990–93; dir of Int Mining Consultants Ltd (IMCL) 1994–95, chief exec/accounting offr Health and Safety Lab (HSL) 1995–; non-exec dir Complete Computing Ltd 1979–; special prof Dept of Mineral Resources Engrg Univ of Nottingham; past chm Energy Industries Research Liaison Ctee; memb: Safety in Mines Research Advsy Bd, Soc of Exploration Geophysicists, European Assoc of Exploration Geophysicists; FIMMM, CEng, FREng 1997; *Awards* Best Paper in Geophysics Soc of Exploration Geophysicists 1980, JJ Thomson Premium IEE 1980, Elimco/McArthur Award Inst of Mining Engrs 1988, WM Thornton Medal Inst of Mining Electrical and Mining Mechanical Engrs 1992; *Publications* Coal Geophysics (jt ed) and author of 56 technical papers in a variety of jls; *Recreations* golf, reading, travel; *Style*— Dr David Buchanan, FREng

BUCHANAN, Prof Dennis Langston; s of Langston Llewellyn Buchanan (d 1954), and Georgina Vera, *née* Wheatley; *b* 15 April 1947; *Educ* Cambridge High, Rhodes Univ (BSc), Univ of Pretoria (MSc), Univ of London (PhD), Imperial Coll London (DIC); *m* 17 Dec 1970, Vaughan Elizabeth, da of Fritz Reitz Hayward, of Port Elizabeth; 1 s (James George), 1 da (Alexandra Claire); *Career* Union Corp Ltd South Africa 1969–73, res fell Univ of Witwatersrand 1978–79 (res asst 1976–77), prof of mining geology Royal Sch of Mines Imperial Coll London 1984–97 (res asst 1976–77, lectr 1980–83, emeritus prof and sr research fell 1997–); independent consulting minin geologist and dir Altyn-Tas Jt Venture Kazakhstan 1994; vice-pres Inst of Mining and Metallurgy 1995; CEng 1976, FGS (SA) 1986, FIMMM 1989; *Books* Platinum Group Element Exploration (1988); *Recreations* jogging; *Clubs* Royal Sch of Mines Assoc, Chaps; *Style*— Prof Dennis Buchanan; ✉ Department of Earth Science and Engineering, Imperial College, London SW7 2BP (tel 020 7594 6440, fax 020 7594 7444, e-mail d.buchanan@imperial.ac.uk)

BUCHANAN, Prof (John) Grant; s of Robert Downie Buchanan (d 1937), of Dumbarton, and Mary Hobson (Molly), *née* Wilson (d 1999); *b* 26 September 1926; *Educ* Dumbarton Acad, Glasgow Acad, Christ's Coll Cambridge (MA, PhD, ScD); *m* 14 July 1956, Sheila Elena (d 1996), da of Reginald Lugg (d 1961), of London; 3 s (Andrew b 1959, John b 1962, Neil b 1965); *Career* res fell Univ of Calif Berkeley 1951–52, res asst Lister Inst of Preventive Med London 1952–54; Univ of Newcastle upon Tyne: lectr in organic chemistry King's Coll 1955, sr lectr 1962, reader in organic chemistry 1965; Heriot-Watt Univ: prof of organic chemistry 1969–91, head Dept of Chemistry 1987–91, prof emeritus 1991–; professorial fell Univ of Bath 1991–; pres Euro Carbohydrate Orgns 1991–93; FRSC 1981 (memb Cncl 1982–85), FRSE 1972 (memb Cncl 1980–83), CChem 1981; *Publications* over 170 original papers and reviews on organic and bio-organic chemistry; *Recreations* golf, family; *Clubs* Bath Golf; *Style*— Prof Grant Buchanan, FRSE; ✉ 37 Woodland Grove, Claverton Down, Bath BA2 7AT (tel 01225 466118); Department of Chemistry, University of Bath, Claverton Down, Bath BA2 7AY (tel 01225 386138, fax 01225 386231, e-mail chsjgb@bath.ac.uk)

BUCHANAN, James Meredith; s of Donald Geoffrey Buchanan (d 1978), and Violet Hetherington, *née* Bell; *b* 4 March 1943; *Educ* Haberdashers' Aske's, St George's Hosp Med Sch Univ of London (MB BS, AKC); *m* 4 May 1974, Judith, da of James Edward Spence (d 1997), of Sedgefield, Co Durham; 3 da (Helen, Charlotte, Sarah); *Career* registrar: Norfolk and Norwich Hosp 1972, St Mary's Hosp Portsmouth 1973; sr registrar St George's Hosp London 1974–77 (house offr posts 1967), conslt orthopaedic surgn Sunderland Gp of Hosps 1977–; hon clinical lectr Univ of Newcastle upon Tyne 1979; author of paper in RCS annals and multiple presentations on HA hip arthroplasty; LRCP 1967, FRCS 1972, fell Br Orthopaedic Assoc 1977; *Recreations* rugby football; *Clubs* Blaydon RUFC; *Style*— James Buchanan, Esq; ✉ 8 Grange Terrace, Stockton Road, Sunderland, Tyne & Wear SR2 7DF (tel 0191 5100 555, fax 0191 2841 599, e-mail buchanan@dial.pipex.com)

BUCHANAN, Dr John G S; s of Russell Penman Buchanan (d 1993), and Marguerite (Ginette) St. Clair Stuart, *née* Cabouret, of Auckland, NZ; *b* 9 June 1943; *Educ* Auckland GS, Univ of Auckland (MSc, PhD), Wolfson Coll Oxford (research fell), Harvard Business Sch (PMD); *m* 1967, Rosemary June, *née* Johnston; 1 s, 1 da; *Career* BP plc: various operational, commercial and mktg posts 1970–76, seconded to Central Policy Review Staff Cabinet Office 1976–77, gen mangr Group Corp Planning 1985–88, chief operating offr and dep chief exec BP Chemicals 1988–95, gp treas and chief exec BP Finance 1995–96, chief financial offr and exec dir BP plc 1996–2002; chm Smith & Nephew 2006– (non-exec dir 2005–); non-exec dir: Boots Co plc 1997–2002, BHP Billiton plc 2002– (sr ind dir), AstraZeneca plc 2002–, Vodafone Gp plc 2003– (dep chm 2006–); memb Accounting Standards Bd 1997–2001; *Recreations* golf, skiing, Polynesian culture; *Clubs* Tandridge Golf, Remuera Golf (NZ); *Style*— John Buchanan; ✉ Smith & Nephew plc, 15 Adam Street, London WC2N 6LA

BUCHANAN, Nigel James Cubitt; s of Rev Basil Roberts Buchanan (d 1987), of Cambridge, and Elene, *née* Cubitt (d 2005); *b* 13 November 1943; *Educ* Denstone Coll; *m* 6 July 1968, (Katherine) Mary, da of Prof Sir Arthur Llewellyn Armitage (d 1984); 2 da (Katherine Lucy b 21 Sept 1975, Elizabeth Mary b 15 May 1978), 1 s (James Kenyon b 20 Nov 1979); *Career* PricewaterhouseCoopers (formerly Price Waterhouse before merger): ptnr 1978–2001, Euro dir Fin Servs Practice 1988–97, vice-chm World Financial Servs Practice 1989–97, memb Bd E European Firm 1994–97, sr client ptnr 1994–2001; non-exec dir: Leopold Joseph Hldgs plc 2001–04, Amlin plc 2004– (sr ind dir), Butterfield Bank (UK) Ltd 2004–; memb Ethics Standards Bd Accounting Fndn 2001–03; memb Bd Outward Bound Tst 2002– (dep chm 2005); chm of govrs Aldwickbury Sch 2004–; Freeman City of London 2001, Liveryman Worshipful Co of Tylers and Bricklayers 2001; FCA; *Books* Accounting for Pensions (jtly), PW/Euromoney Debt Equity Swap Guide (jtly); *Recreations* tennis, golf; *Clubs* Carlton; *Style*— Nigel Buchanan, Esq; ✉ Longwood, 16 Park Avenue South, Harpenden, Hertfordshire AL5 2EA (tel 01582 763076, fax 01582 760559)

BUCHANAN, Robin William Turnbull; s of Iain Buchanan, and Gillian Pamela, *née* Hughes-Hallett; *b* 2 April 1952; *Educ* Harvard Business Sch (Baker scholar, MBA); *m* 1986, Diana Tei Tanaka; 2 c (Rowan Hisayo Lindsay b 2 June 1989, Iain James Tei-An b 26 Feb 1993); *Career* Deloitte & Touche (formerly Mann Judd Landau) 1970–77, American Express International Banking Corp 1979–82; Bain & Co Inc: Bain Capital 1982–84, managing ptnr London 1990–96, sr ptnr London 1996–2007, sr advsr 2007–; dean London Business Sch 2007–; non-exec dir: Liberty International plc 1997–, Shire plc (formerly Shire Pharmaceuticals Gp plc) 2003–; memb: Trilateral Cmmn, Northern Meeting, Highland Soc, Professional Standards Advsy Bd IOD, Editorial Bd European Business Jl, Advsy Cncl Prince's Tst; fell Salzburg Seminar; Liveryman Worshipful Co of Ironmongers; FCA, FRSA; *Recreations* farming, forestry, shooting, collecting old children's books; *Clubs* Pilgrims, Boodle's, Beefsteak; *Style*— Robin Buchanan, Esq; ✉ London Business School, Regent's Park, London NW1 4SA

BUCHANAN-JARDINE, Sir (Andrew) Rupert John; 4 Bt (UK 1885), of Castle Milk, Co Dumfries; MC (1945), JP (Dumfriesshire 1957), DL (1978); s of Capt Sir John William Buchanan-Jardine, 3 Bt, JP (d 1969), and his 1 w, Jean (d 1989), da of Lord Ernest Hamilton, sometime MP N Tyrone (7 s of 1 Duke of Abercorn, KG, PC, and Lady Louisa Russell, 2 da of 6 Duke of Bedford, KG); *b* 2 February 1923; *Educ* Harrow, RAC Cirencester; *m* 1950 (m dis 1975), Jane Fiona, da of Sir Archibald Charles Edmonstone, 6 Bt, and Gwendolyn, da of Marshall Field, of Chicago; 1 s (John Christopher Rupert b 1952), 1 da (Diana Gwendolyn Jean b 1955); *Heir* s, John Buchanan-Jardine; *Career* farmer and landowner, formerly Maj RHG; MFH Dumfriesshire 1950–2001; KASG; Bronze Lion (The Netherlands) 1945; *Recreations* country pursuits; *Clubs* MCC; *Style*— Sir Rupert Buchanan-Jardine, Bt, MC, DL; ✉ Dixons, Lockerbie, Dumfriesshire (tel 01576 202508, fax 01576 510362)

BUCK, HE John Stephen; s of Frederick Buck, and Amelia Buck; *b* 10 October 1953, London; *Educ* Univ of York (BA), Wolfson Coll Oxford (MSc, CQSW); *m* 25 Oct 1980, Jean Claire, *née* Webb; 1 da (Rachel b 26 July 1985), 1 s (Christopher b 26 June 1989); *Career* diplomat; early career as probation offr and social worker, entered HM Dip Serv 1980, second sec Sofia 1982–84, first sec FCO 1984–88, head of Chancery Lisbon 1988–92, princ private sec Cabinet Office 1994–96, cnsllr and dep head of mission Nicosia 1996–2000, head Public Diplomacy Dept FCO 2000–03, head Govt Communications and Info Centre FCO/10 Downing St 2003, dir Iraq FCO 2003–04, ambass to Portugal 2004–; *Style*— HE Mr John Buck; ✉ c/o Foreign & Commonwealth Office (Lisbon), King Charles Street, London SW1A 2AH

BUCK, Karen Patricia; MP; *b* 30 August 1958; *Educ* Chelmsford County HS, LSE (BSc, MA, MSc); *Career* head of research OUTSET 1979–83, with London Borough of Hackney 1983–87, health policy offr Lab Party 1987–92, actg head Campaigns Dept Lab Party 1994–95 (dep head 1993–97); MP (Lab) Regent's Park and Kensington N 1997–, chair London Gp of Lab MPs 1998–2005, Parly under sec of state Dept of Transport 2005–; memb Social Security Select Ctee 1997–2001, memb Work and Pensions Select Ctee 2001–05, chair All-Pty Parly Gp on Childcare 2004–05; memb: Westminster City Cncl 1990–97; chair of govrs Wilberforce Sch 1992–99; *Style*— Ms Karen Buck, MP; ✉ House of Commons, London SW1A 0AA; constituency office (tel 020 8968 7999, fax 020 8960 0150, e-mail k.buck@rpkn-labour.co.uk)

BUCK, Louisa; da of late Sir Antony Buck, QC, and Judy Breakell, *née* Grant; *b* 10 July 1960; *Educ* Queensgate Sch London, Girton Coll Cambridge (BA), Courtauld Inst of Art Univ of London (MA); *Children* 2 s (Alfred Benedict b 7 Jan 1992, Francis George b 10 April 2002), 1 da (Nancy Eleanor b 23 March 1995); *Career* freelance author, lectr, broadcaster and journalist; freelance lectr on Twentieth Century Art 1983–84 (Tate Gallery, Sotheby's fine art courses, art courses in London and Europe), Tate Gallery 1984–85 (cataloguer of John Banting and Edward Burra material, curator of exhibition of Bantings graphic work, public lectr), ran Bonhams Modern Pictures Dept 1985; freelance journalist, broadcaster lectr and researcher 1986–; arts correspondent, contrib ed and visual arts correspondent The Art Newspaper; contrib to: New Statesman & Society, Guardian arts pages, Tatler, Vogue, Marie Claire, The Evening Standard; radio 1988–90: visual arts critic LBC, currently visual art reviewer Front Row BBC Radio 4; lectr on Twentieth Century art design and culture: Tate Gallery, RCA, Saatchi Collection, Univ of Reading, ICA; *Books* author of catalogue essays for: A Salute to British Surrealism (Minories Gallery Colchester, 1985), The Surrealist Spirit in Britain (Whitford & Hughes, 1988), Sylvia Ziranek: Ici Villa Moi (Watermans Arts Centre, 1989), Jacqueline Morreau: Paradise Now (Odette Gilbert Gallery, 1990), Meret Oppenheim retrospective Barcelona, Relative Values or What's Art Worth? (jtly, 1990), Something the Matter: Helen Chadwick, Cathy de Monchaux, Cornelia Parker (Saô Paulo Bienal, 1994), The Personal Political Art of Grayson Perry (Stedelijk Museum Amsterdam 2002), Tableau Vivant: Jane Simpson (Centre for Contemporary Art Malaga, 2004); Moving Targets: A User's Guide to British Art Now (1997), Moving Targets 2: A User's Guide to British Art Now (2000), Owning Art: The Contemporary Art Collector's Handbook (co-author, 2006); *Recreations* gardening, swimming, travelling; *Style*— Ms Louisa Buck; ✉ 109 Knatchbull Road, London SE5 9QU (tel 020 7737 0511, fax 020 7274 6087, e-mail lbuck@dircon.co.uk)

BUCKBY, Anthony Jonathan; MBE (1996); s of Gordon Harry Buckby (d 1985), of Worcs, and Muriel, *née* Darby; *b* 1 September 1951; *Educ* King's Sch Worcester (scholar), Univ of Nottingham (BA), Univ of Essex (MA); *m* Giuliana, da of Mario Salvagno; *Career* teacher of English in UK, Germany and Italy 1974–76, reader Univ of Naples 1978–79, asst dir of studies Br Cncl Naples 1979–82 (teacher 1976–78, teacher trainer 1978–79), sch dir Br Inst of Florence 1987–90 (acad advsr 1982–86), dir Br Cncl Bologna 1990–96, dir Language Servs Br Cncl 1996–2000, dep dir Br Cncl Italy 2000–; *Books* Variety (jtly, 1985); *Recreations* gardening; *Style*— Anthony Buckby, Esq, MBE; ✉ Via Urbana 156, 00184 Rome, Italy; Faircroft, Aberedw, Builth Wells, Powys; The British Council, Via Quattro Fontane 20, 00184 Rome, Italy

BUCKHAVEN, Simon; *b* 30 September 1944; *Educ* Lancing (music scholar), Manitoba Univ, Cncl of Legal Educn; *m* Sept 1971, Charlotte Vanderlip, da of Sir Robertson Crichton; 1 da (Katie b 4 May 1976), 1 s (Robertson b 4 Aug 1977); *Career* called to the Bar Gray's Inn 1970; asst parly boundary cmmr 1993–96, head of chambers 1993–99; *Recreations* painting, reading; *Clubs* Athenaeum; *Style*— Simon Buckhaven, Esq

BUCKINGHAM, Bishop of 2003–; Rt Rev Dr Alan Thomas Lawrence Wilson; s of Alan Thomas Wilson (d 1990), of Sevenoaks, Kent, and Anna Maria Magdalena, *née* Amfer (d 1994); *b* 27 March 1955, Edinburgh; *Educ* Sevenoaks Sch, St John's Coll Cambridge (open scholar, MA), Wycliffe Hall Oxford (CertTheol), Balliol Coll Oxford (DPhil); *m* 14 July 1984, Lucy Catherine Janet, *née* Richards; 3 da (Catherine Joanna b 10 May 1986, Stephanie Julia b 26 Dec 1987, Anna Maria b 12 Oct 1998), 2 s (Stewart Thomas b 21 March 1995, Nicholas James (twin) b 21 March 1995); *Career* ordained: deacon 1979, priest 1980; non-stipendiary min then asst curate Eynsham 1978–82, priest i/c St John's Caversham and asst curate Caversham and Mapledurham 1982–89, vicar St John the Baptist Caversham 1989–92, subst chaplain HMP Reading 1990–92, rector Sandhurst 1992–2003, area dean of Sonning 1998–2003, hon canon ChCh Oxford 2002–03; memb: Ecclesiastical Law Soc, Howard League for Penal Reform, Nat Tst; *Recreations* running, art and design, photography, singing, France, modern history, penal affairs, adult education; *Style*— The Rt Rev the Bishop of Buckingham; ✉ Sheridan, Grimms Hill, Great Missenden, Buckinghamshire HP16 9BG (tel 01494 862163, fax 01494 890508, e-mail alan.wilson49@btopenworld.com)

BUCKINGHAM, Prof Julia Clare; da of Jack William Harry Buckingham (d 1991), of Feock, Cornwall, and Barbara Joan, *née* Baker; *b* 18 October 1950; *Educ* St Mary's Sch Calne, Univ of Sheffield (BSc), Univ of London (PhD, DSc); *m* 1974, Simon James Smith, s of Sidney George Smith (d 1973); *Career* sr lectr in pharmacology Royal Free Hosp Sch of Med 1980–87 (research fell Dept of Pharmacology 1974–80), prof and head Dept of Pharmacology Charing Cross and Westminster Med Sch London 1988–97, Imperial Coll London at Hammersmith Hosp: head Dept of Neuroendocrinology, vice-chm Academic Div of Neuroscience and Psychological Med 1997–2003, non-clinical dean for med 2000–03, dep head (non-clinical) Undergraduate Med 2002–, prof of pharmacology, head Academic Div of Neuroscience and Mental Health 2003–; memb Cncl Sch of Pharmacy Univ of London 2001–05; chm Bioscientifica Ltd 2002–05; ed-in-chief Jl of Neuroendocrinology 2004–; Gaddum Meml Prize Br Pharmacological Soc 1994, Soc Medal Soc for Endocrinology 1994; memb: Soc for Endocrinology 1975 (treas 1996–2001, gen sec 2005–), Br Pharmacological Soc 1977 (pres 2004–05, fell 2004), Br Soc for Neuroendocrinology 1980, Physiological Soc 1980, Soc for Meds Research 1980, Br Neuroscience Assoc 1985, Biochemical Soc 1988; govr: KCS Wimbledon 1993–97, St Mary's Sch Calne 2003–; FRSA 1995; *Recreations* music, skiing, sailing; *Clubs* Sloane,

Riverside, Royal Cornwall Yacht; *Style*— Prof Julia Buckingham; ✉ Division of Neuroscience and Mental Health, Imperial College London, Hammersmith Hospital Campus, Du Cane Road, London W12 0NN (tel 020 8383 8034, fax 020 8383 8032, e-mail j.buckingham@imperial.ac.uk)

BUCKINGHAMSHIRE, 10 Earl of (GB 1746); Sir (George) Miles Hobart-Hampden; 14 Bt (E 1611); Baron Hobart (GB 1728); s of Cyril Langel Hobart-Hampden (d 1972), ggs of 6 Earl of Buckinghamshire; suc kinsman 1983; *b* 15 December 1944; *Educ* Clifton, Univ of Exeter (BA), Univ of London (MA); *m* 1, 1968 (m dis), Susan Jennifer, o da of late Raymond W Adams, of Halesowen, Worcs; *m* 2, 1975, Alison Wightman, (JP 1990, DL 1995), da of late William Forrest, of Edinburgh; 2 step s; *Heir* kinsman, Sir John Hobart, 3 Bt, *qv; Career* Hongkong and Shanghai Banking Corp 1963–64, Hudson Bay Co 1968–70, Noble Lowndes & Partners Ltd 1970–81; dir: Scottish Pension Trustees Ltd 1979–81, Anthony Gibbs Pension Services 1981–86, The Angel Trustee Co 1983–86, WISLI Nominees Ltd 1986–91, Wardley Investment Services (Luxembourg) SA 1988–91, Wardley Global Selection 1988–91, WISL Bahamas 1988–91; md Wardley Investment Services International Ltd 1988–91; chm: Wardley Unit Trust Managers Ltd 1988–91, Wardley Fund Managers (Jersey) Ltd 1988–91; dir The Wyatt Co (UK) Ltd 1991–95, ptnr Watson Wyatt LLP (formerly Watson Wyatt Ptnrs) 1995–2004, BESTrustees plc 2004 (dir 2005); dir: Gota Global Selection (Sicav) 1988–95, Korea Asia Fund 1990–91, The Russian Pension Tst Co 1994–2001, Hatfield Tennis Court Club Ltd 2001–06; pres Buckingham Cons Constituency Assoc; sat in House of Lords 1984–99; memb House of Lords Select Ctee EC Sub-Ctee: on Social and Consumer Affairs 1985–90, on Fin Trade and External Relations 1990–92; memb All-Pty Parly Gp on Occupational Pensions; memb House of Lords All-Pty Gp of Ageing Issues; pres: Friends of the Vale of Aylesbury, Old Cliftonian Soc 2001–03; patron: Sleep Apnoea Tst 1997–, Hobart Town (1804) Early Settlers Assoc (Tasmania), John Hampden Soc, Chilterns MS Centre 2005; memb Cncl Buckinghamshire Chilterns UC 2001, govr Clifton Coll; dep chm Br-Aust Soc 2006–, chm Cook Soc 2007; affiliate memb Inst of Actuaries 2001; FInstD; *Recreations* real tennis, fishing, music, reading, walking, rugby football; *Clubs* Royal Over-Seas League, Leamington Tennis Court; *Style*— The Earl of Buckinghamshire; ✉ The Old Rectory, Church Lane, Edgcott, Buckinghamshire HP18 0TU

BUCKLAND, Christopher Robert; s of Claude Buckland (d 1987), of Burnley, Lancs, and Vera, *née* Greenwood (d 1949); *b* 4 January 1944; *Educ* Burnley GS, Univ of Birmingham (BSocSc); *Career* reporter Daily Mail Manchester 1964–65 (Belfast 1965–66); Daily Mirror: reporter Dublin 1966–70, bureau chief Belfast 1970–72, home affrs corr London 1972–74, chief political corr 1974–76, corr Washington DC 1976–78, head of US Bureau 1978–81, foreign ed London 1981–82; political ed: Sunday People 1982–85, Today 1985–89; The Express: asst ed (political and foreign) 1989–95, assoc ed and political columnist 1995–98; political columnist Sunday Mirror 1998–2001; News of the World: political columnist 2001–03, special corr 2003–06; special corr The Sun 2006–; *Recreations* music, piano, racing, soccer spectating, travel; *Clubs* Garrick; *Style*— Christopher Buckland; ✉ Press Gallery, House of Commons, London SW1A 0AA (tel 020 7219 4700); tel and fax 020 8340 4453, e-mail expressbk@aol.com

BUCKLAND, David; s of Denis Buckland, of Sydling St Nicholas, Dorset, and Valarie Buckland; *b* 15 June 1949; *Educ* Hardy's GS, Deep River HS, London Coll of Printing; *Partner* Siobhan Davies, CBE , *qv;* 2 c (Piera b 15 Oct 1984, Sean b 13 April 1986); *Career* designer, artist and film-maker; short film Dwell Time broadcast BBC1 Dance for Camera Season 1996, presented one-man show Nat Portrait Gallery London 1999; cmmn incl: MasterCard, Vanguard Insurance, Royal Caribbean; set and costume designs: Siobhan Davies Dance Co, Royal Ballet, Rambert Dance Co, Second Stride, Compagnie Cré-Ange; work in public collections incl: Nat Portrait Gallery London, Center Georges Pompidou Paris, Metropolitan Museum NY, Getty Collection LA; Cape Farewell expedition (environmental sailing voyage to High Arctic, in partnership with Geographical Assoc, NESTA and Southampton Ocoeanography Centre): dir 2003 and 2004, launched new GCSE geography course 2003, winner NESTA Award 2003 and Arts Cncl Award 2004; video installation This Side to Body 2002; Northern Arts Fellowship 1972, Kodak Award 1980, Nesta Award 2001; *Books* David Buckland (mongraph, 1989), Performances (2000), The Last Judgement (with Sir Antony Caro, 2000); *Recreations* sailing; *Style*— David Buckland, Esq; ✉ 239 Royal College Street, London NW1 9LT (tel 020 7209 0610, e-mail buckland@bucklandart.com, website www.bucklandart.com or website www.capefarewell.com)

BUCKLAND, Gerald David; s of Francis G Buckland (d 1994), of Cheshunt, Herts, and Elizabeth, *née* Hamilton-Allen (d 1998); *b* 22 March 1948; *Educ* St Ignatius' Coll, E Herts Coll; *m* 27 May 1975, Paula, da of Mark Gandy (d 1989); 2 da (Marianne Paula Elizabeth b 10 Feb 1980, Isabella Louise Geraldine b 9 June 1983), 1 s (Anthony Francis Gerald b 3 Jan 1988); *Career* press offr BP Chemicals Ltd 1977–80, PR coordinator BP Int Ltd 1980–82, PR mangr Marathon Int Petroleum Inc 1982–88, corporate rels dir TVS Entertainment plc 1988–91, md Sunrise Media Communications 1991–94, chief exec The Buckland Consultancy UK Ltd 1994–; memb: RTS, BAFTA; *Recreations* music, travel, languages; *Clubs* Groucho; *Style*— Gerald Buckland, Esq; ✉ Le Haut Clairvaux, 86140 Scorbe Clairvaux, France (tel 00 33 6 17 57 34 78, e-mail gerrybuckland@mac.com)

BUCKLAND, Sir Ross; kt (1997); s of William Arthur Haverfield Buckland, and Elizabeth, *née* Schmitzer; *b* 19 December 1942; *Educ* Sydney Boys' HS; *m* 22 Jan 1966, Patricia Ann, da of William Stephen Bubb, of Warriewood, NSW, Aust; 2 s (Sean William b 1968, Mark Charles b 1970); *Career* held various positions in companies engaged in banking, engrg, office equipment and food industry 1958–66; dir fin and admin Elizabeth Arden Pty Ltd 1966–73, md Kellogg (Aust) Pty Ltd 1978 (various positions 1973–77), pres and ceo Kellogg Salada Canada Inc 1979–80, vice-pres Kellogg Co USA, chm Kellogg Company of Great Britain Ltd to 1990 (dir European Operations), gp chief exec Uniq plc (formerly Unigate plc) 1990–2001; pres: Food & Drink Fedn 1987–89, Inst of Grocery Distribution 1997–99, Nat Aust Bank Europe Ltd 1999; non-exec dir: Allied Domecq plc 1998–2004, RJB Mining plc 1995–99; memb Medical Research Cncl 1998; hon fell Inst of Logistics 1996; CIMgt, FICS, FCPA, FIGD; *Recreations* walking; *Style*— Sir Ross Buckland

BUCKLAND-WRIGHT, Prof (John) Christopher; s of John Buckland-Wright (d 1954), of Dunedin, NZ, and Mary Elizabeth, *née* Anderson (d 1976); *b* 19 November 1945; *Educ* Lycée Français de Londres, KCL (BSc, AKC, PhD), Univ of London (DSc); *m* 11 Nov 1975, Rosalin, da of Charles W G T Kirk, OBE (d 1986), of Hemel Hempstead, Herts; 2 da (Helen b 1977, Alexandra b 1978); *Career* asst head Dept of Comparative Osteology Centre for Prehistory and Paleontology Nairobi Kenya 1966–67, teacher Lycée Français de Londres 1971–72, anatomy lectr St Mary's Hosp Med Sch London 1973–76; Guy's Hosp Med Sch London: lectr 1976–80, sr lectr 1980–89, reader in radiological anatomy 1989–97, prof of radiological anatomy 1997–; Guy's Hosp: head Macroradiographic Res Unit Guy's Hosp 1981–88, head Arthrology Unit 1988–96, chm Applied Clinical Anatomy 1996–; memb Int Cmmn on Radiation Units and Measurements 1987–93; first Jessie Dobson lectr RCS 1984, Vicary lectr RCS 1999; pioneered med applications of high definition macroradiography and new methods for radiography of the human knee, developed standardised radiographic procedures now employed internationally for clinical trials in knee osteoarthritis, developed novel methods for measuring changes in joint structure including cancellous bone changes in arthritic joints, first to report beneficial effect of bisphosphonate treatment in knee osteoarthritis; author of over 200 scientific pubns radiography and its application to the study of bone and arthritis;

Freeman City of London 1980; Liveryman Worshipful Co of Barbers 1980 (Hon Librarian 1984–2006, memb Ct of Assts 2000, Renter Warden 2004, Middle Warden 2005, Upper Warden 2006, Master 2007–08); memb: Anatomy Soc 1974, Br Soc of Rheumatology 1984, Br Inst of Radiology 1992 (Immation-Mayneord Meml lectr 1998), Osteoarthritis Res Soc 1992; fell Br Assoc of Clinical Anatomists 1996; *Books* Cockerel Cavalcade (1988), The Engravings of John Buckland Wright (1990), Bathers and Dancers (1993), Baigneuses (1995), Surreal Times (2000), Endeavours and Experiments (2004), To Beauty (2007); *Recreations* fine art and antiquarian books, drawing, painting, walking; *Clubs* City Livery; *Style*— Prof Christopher Buckland-Wright; ✉ 50 Beechwood Avenue, Kew, Richmond, Surrey TW9 4DE (tel 020 8876 2011); Department of Applied Clinical Anatomy, King's College London, School of Medicine, Guy's Campus, London Bridge, London SE1 1UL (tel 020 7848 8035, fax 020 7848 8033, e-mail chris.buckland-wright@kcl.ac.uk)

BUCKLE, Alan; s of John Buckle, and Margaret Buckle; *b* 19 May 1959; *Educ* Matthew Humberstone Sch Lincs, Univ of Durham; *Career* CA; currently head of advsy KPMG; memb Bd Br Cncl; *Style*— Alan Buckle, Esq; ✉ KPMG, 8 Salisbury Square, London EC4Y 8BB (tel 020 7311 8468, e-mail alan.buckle@kpmg.co.uk)

BUCKLES, Nicholas Peter (Nick); s of Ronald Peter Buckles, of Great Bentley, Essex, and Sylvia, *née* Sparrow; *b* 1 February 1961; *Educ* Gable Hall Sch Corringham, Coventry Univ (BA); *m* 26 March 1988, Loraine Dawn, da of John Salter; 2 da (Isabel Ella b 26 Feb 1990, Helena Joy b 15 Dec 1993), 1 s (Benjamin Nicholas b 8 Aug 1991); *Career* Securicor: projects accountant 1985, dir for cash services 1991, dep md Securicor Guarding 1993, md Securicor Cash Services 1996, chief exec Europe 1998, chief exec Security Div 1999, gp chief exec Securicor plc 2002–04, gp chief exec Group4Securicor plc 2005– (dep chief exec and chief operating offr 2004–05); non-exec dir Arriva plc 2005–; Freeman City of London, memb Guild of Security Professionals 2001; *Recreations* football; *Style*— Nick Buckles, Esq; ✉ Group4Securicor plc, The Manor, Manor Royal, Crawley, West Sussex RH10 9UN (tel 01293 554493, fax 01293 554500)

BUCKLEY, Prof Adrian Arthur; s of Arthur Penketh Buckley (d 1977), and Beatrice May Buckley (d 1953); *b* 28 December 1938; *Educ* Poole GS, Univ of Sheffield and Open Univ (BA), Univ of Bradford (MSc), Free Univ Amsterdam (PhD); *m* 6 August 1966, Jenny Rosalie Buckley (d 1977); 2 s (Peter James Scott b 24 Dec 1971, David John Scott b 4 April 1974); *Career* Corp Fin Charterhouse Bank 1971–73, gp treas Redland plc 1973–79, prof Cranfield Sch of Mgmnt 1986– (joined 1980); FCA 1963, FCT 1985; *Books* Multinational Finance (1986, 5 edn 2004), The Essence of International Money (1990, 2nd 1996), International Capital Budgeting (1996), International Investment - Value Creation and Appraisal: Real Options Approach (1998), Corporate Finance Europe (1998); *Recreations* skiing, walking, theatre; *Style*— Prof Adrian Buckley; ✉ Cranfield School of Management, Cranfield University, Cranfield, Bedford MK43 0AL (tel 01234 751122, fax 01234 751806, e-mail adrian.buckley@cranfield.ac.uk)

BUCKLEY, Edgar Vincent; CB (1999); s of Michael Joseph Buckley (d 1983), of Ilford, Essex, and Mary, *née* Byrne; *b* 17 November 1946; *Educ* St Ignatius Coll London, NW Poly London, Birkbeck Coll London (BA, PhD); *m* Frances Jacqueline, da of Dr Harry A Cheetham (decd); 3 da (Martha Jane b 11 July 1974, Hannah Katharine b 30 June 1981, Emmeline Jessica b 11 Feb 1987), 2 s (Edgar Jonathan Christopher b 29 June 1976, William Nicholas Quentin b 11 Nov 1978); *Career* MOD: asst dir Strategic Systems Fin 1980–84, asst dir Nuclear Policy 1984–86, head Resources and Progs (Navy) 1986–90, RCDS 1990, head Def Arms Control Unit 1991–92; def cnsllr UK Delgn to NATO 1992–96, asst under sec of state (Home and Overseas) MOD 1996–99, asst sec gen (planning and operations) NATO 1999–2003, sr vice-pres European mktg Thales 2003–; *Recreations* running, swimming; *Style*— Edgar Buckley, Esq, CB

BUCKLEY, Ian Michael; s of Frank Leslie Buckley (d 1973), and Edith Mary, *née* Brown; *b* 16 November 1950; *Educ* Bradfield Coll, Univ of Southampton (BSc); *m* 20 July 1974, Sarah Ann, da of Arthur William Sale; 2 da (Anna Louise b 11 April 1978, Camilla Alice b 8 Aug 1981); *Career* chartered accountant Peat Marwick Mitchell & Co 1972–82 (articled clerk 1972–75); Smith and Williamson: joined 1982, ptnr and dir of securities 1983–86, gp chief exec 1986–95; chief exec EFG Private Bank Ltd 1997–98 (dir 1995, also md Asset Mgmnt subsid), chief exec Tenon Gp plc 2000–03, chief exec Trust Division and exec dir Rathbone Bros plc 2003– (non-exec dir 2001–03); non-exec dir NXT plc; FCA 1975; *Style*— Ian Buckley, Esq

BUCKLEY, James; s of Harold Buckley (d 1966), and Mabel, *née* Taylor; *b* 5 April 1944; *Educ* Sheffield City GS, Imperial Coll of Sci & Technol (BSc, ARCS); *m* 15 Aug 1972, Valerie (Elizabeth), da of Ivor Powles, of Newport, Gwent; 1 da (Louise b 1976); *Career* scientific offr RAF Coastal Cmd MOD 1965, princ CSD 1971, private sec to Min for Civil Service and Ldr House of Lords (successively Lord Peart, Lord Soames and Baroness Young) 1979–82, private sec to Govr Rhodesia 1979–80, sec Civil Service Coll 1982–85, chief exec BVA 1985–87, dep DG Gen Cncl Br Shipping 1987–91, chief exec The Baltic Exchange 1991–2004; *Recreations* photography, painting, tennis; *Style*— Mr James Buckley

BUCKLEY, Sir Michael Sydney; kt (2002); s of Sydney Dowsett Buckley (d 2000), and Grace Bew, *née* Ellison (d 1991); *b* 20 June 1939, Beckenham, Kent; *Educ* Eltham Coll, ChCh Oxford (MA, Cert Statistics); *m* 1, 8 May 1972, Shirley, *née* Stordy (d 1991); 1 s (Robert Sydney b 7 Dec 1972), 1 da (Elizabeth Jane b 3 June 1974); *m* 2, 17 Oct 1992, Judith Mary, *née* Cobb; *Career* asst princ HM Treasy 1962–66, princ Civil Servs Dept HM Treasy 1966–77, grade 5 DTI 1977–80, grade 5 HM Treasy 1980–82, grade 3 Cabinet Office 1982–85, grade 3 Dept of Energy 1985–91; chm Dartford and Gravesham NHS Tst 1995–96, Parly and health servs Ombudsman 1997–2002, memb GMC 2003–; *Recreations* photography, gardening, reading, listening to music; *Style*— Sir Michael Buckley; ✉ 1 Manor Court, Bearsted, Kent ME14 4BZ (tel 01622 735603, e-mail mnjbuckley@btinternet.com)

BUCKLEY, Peter Neville; s of Edward Richard Buckley, and Ina Heather, *née* Cayzer; *b* 23 September 1942; *Educ* Eton, Manchester Business Sch (Dip); *m* 2 Feb 1967, Mary Barabel, *née* Stewart; 2 da (Arabella Mary b 29 July 1970, Roseanna Neville b 26 Jan 1972); *Career* chartered accountant; articled clerk McClelland Moores & Co (later Ernst & Young); British & Commonwealth Shipping Company (later British & Commonwealth Holdings plc): joined 1968, asst to fin dir, exec dir 1974–87, non-exec dir 1987–88; Caledonia Investments plc: dir 1976–, dep chm and chief exec 1987–94, chm and chief exec 1994–2002, chm 2002–; Sterling Industries plc: dir 1973–2005, chm 1988–2005; non-exec chm Bristow Aviation Holdings Ltd 1991–; non-exec dir: Provident Mutual Life Assurance Assocn 1980–1995, Kerzner International Ltd 1994–2006, Bristow Gp Inc (formerly Offshore Logistics Inc) 1995–, Close Brothers Group plc 1995–; memb Investment Ctee The Wellcome Tst 1995–2002; hon treas Feathers Clubs Assoc; pres RHS; memb Ct of Assts Worshipful Co of Shipwrights (Prime Warden 2004–05); *Recreations* gardening, golf, shooting; *Style*— Peter Buckley, Esq; ✉ Caledonia Investments plc, 30 Buckingham Gate, London SW1E 6NN (tel 020 7802 8080, fax 020 7802 8090)

BUCKLEY, Prof Richard Anthony; s of late Alfred Buckley, of Southampton, and late Dorothy Iris, *née* Neale; *b* 16 April 1947; *Educ* Queen Elizabeth GS Wakefield, Merton Coll Oxford (MA, DPhil), Univ of Oxford (DCL); *m* 1993, Alison Mary, *née* Jones; 1 da (Olivia b 26 Nov 1995); *Career* called to the Bar Lincoln's Inn 1969; lectr in law KCL 1970–75, fell and tutor in law Mansfield Coll Oxford 1975–93, prof of law Univ of Reading 1993–; writer of various articles for legal periodicals, memb Edtorial Bd Rights

B

of Way Law Review 1993–2001 (ed 1991–93); Leverhulme res fell 2001; DCL 2006; *Books* The Law of Nuisance (1981, 2 edn 1996), The Modern Law of Negligence (1988, 3 edn 1999), Salmond and Heuston on Torts (21 edn, with R F V Heuston, 1996), Illegality and Public Policy (2002), The Law of Negligence (2005); *Recreations* walking, swimming, working; *Style—* Professor Richard Buckley; ✉ School of Law, Foxhill House, University of Reading, PO Box 217, Whiteknights Road, Reading RG6 7BA (tel 0118 378 6580, e-mail r.a.buckley@reading.ac.uk)

BUCKLEY, Prof Roger John; s of Frederick William Buckley (d 1997), of Mersham, Kent, and Eileen, *née* Street; *b* 11 January 1945; *Educ* Plymouth Coll, Exeter Coll Oxford, St Thomas' Hosp Med Sch (MA, BM BCh); *m* 1 (m dis), Elizabeth Arnold, da of William Joseph Arnold Sykes (d 1986), of Speldhurst, Kent; 1 da (Harriet b 1974), 1 s (Adam b 1978); m 2, Lesley, *née* Reading; *Career* house surgn St Thomas' Hosp London 1970, sr registrar Westminster Hosp 1978; Moorfields Eye Hosp: res surgical offr 1975, conslt ophthalmologist 1981–2004, dir Contact Lens and Prosthesis Dept 1983–97, hon conslt ophthalmologist 2004–; prof of ocular med: City Univ 1997–2005, Anglia Ruskin Univ 2005–; memb: BSI Contact Lens Ctee 1984–89, Ctee on Dental and Surgical Materials DHSS 1983–94, Gen Optical Cncl 1988–, Expert Advsy Panel Ctee on Safety of Medicines 1994–; pres: Med Contact Lens Assoc 1989–92, Br Contact Lens Assoc 2003–04; vice-pres Int Soc for Contact Lens Research 1993–99; hon med advsr: Musicians' Benevolent Fund 1991–, Royal Soc of Musicians 1994–, Br Assoc for Performing Arts Med 1995–; author of a number of papers and chapters on the cornea, contact lenses and ocular allergy; ATCL 1964, FRCS 1978, FRCOphth 1989, Hon FCOptom 2002; *Recreations* music, hill walking; *Clubs* RSM; *Style—* Prof Roger Buckley; ✉ 8 Glisson Road, Cambridge CB1 2HD; Faculty of Science and Technology, Anglia Ruskin University, East Road, Cambridge CB1 1PT (tel 01223 363271, e-mail rjbuckley@aol.com)

BUCKLEY, Prof Stephen; s of Leslie Buckley (d 1972), of Leicester and Nancy Throsby (d 1989); *b* 5 April 1944; *Educ* City of Leicester Boys' GS, King's Coll Newcastle, Univ of Durham (BA), Univ of Reading (MFA); *m* 1973, Stephanie James; 1 da (Scarlet Matilda b 1973), 1 s (Felix Rupert b 1978); *Career* artist in residence King's Coll Cambridge 1972–74, ind work 1974–; prof of fine art Univ of Reading 1994–; over 60 one man shows worldwide to date incl retrospective MOMA Oxford 1985 and Yale Center for British Art Newhaven 1986; prizewinner at: John Moores Liverpool Exhbn 1974 and 1985, Chichester Nat Art Exhbn 1975, Tolly Cobbold Exhbn 1977; work in collections of: Arts Cncl England, British Cncl, Tate Gallery, V&A, Contemporary Arts Soc, Aberdeen Art Gallery, City Art Gallery Bristol, Walker Art Gallery Liverpool, Whitworth Art Gallery Manchester, Southampton City Art Gallery, Metropolitan Museum NY, MOMA Caracas, Australian Nat Gallery Canberra, Nat Gallery Wellington NZ, Kettle's Yard Gallery Univ of Cambridge; in collaboration with Rambert Dance Co 1987 and 1989; *Style—* Prof Stephen Buckley; ✉ Department of Fine Art, University of Reading, 1 Earley Gate, Whiteknights Road, Reading, Berkshire RG6 6AT (tel 0118 378 8051, website www.stephenbuckley.com)

BUCKMAN, Dr Laurence; s of Allan Buckman (d 1979), and Toni Buckman (d 1978); *b* 19 March 1954, London; *Educ* Univ Coll Sch, Univ Coll Hosp Med Sch; *m* 14 June 1978, Elise, *née* Sider; 2 s (Simon b 1981, Robert b 1983); *Career* hosp dr 1977–83; GP: Borehamwood 1984–93 (trainee 1983–84), Temple Fortune London 1993–; tutor Dept of Primary Care UCL Med Sch 1984–; dep chm GP Ctee BMA 2004– (memb 1991–); author of many newspaper articles on medical politics and the NHS; FRCGP; *Recreations* music, photography, cycling; *Style—* Dr Laurence Buckman; ✉ British Medical Association, Tavistock Square, London WC1H 9JP (tel 020 7383 6191, fax 020 7383 6406)

BUCKNALL, Alison Lucy (Ali); da of Lt Col Thomas George Blackford (d 2002), and Anthea Jean, *née* Martin; *b* 27 October 1962, Sussex; *Educ* The Royal Sch Bath, Royal Holloway Coll Univ of London (BA); *m* 18 Dec 1993, Richard Kenneth Lowndes Bucknall; 2 s (Jake Casper Lowndes b 19 Aug 1996, Max Harry Holden b 6 Oct 2000), 1 da (Sophie Tara Kate b 30 April 1998); *Career* advtg account planner Collett Dickenson and Pearce 1983–89, planner Elgie Stewart Smith 1989–90, planner and assoc dir WCRS 1990–95, bd planning dir D'Arcy 1995–2003; Leo Burnett: bd planning dir 2003–05, exec planning dir 2005–; memb: Mktg Soc, Account Planning Gp, Market Research Soc, Women in Advtg Communications London (WACL); APG Account Planning Awards: highly commended 1995, silver and bronze 2001, gold 2003; *Recreations* reading, travelling; *Style—* Mrs Ali Bucknall; ✉ Leo Burnett Ltd, Warwick Building, Kensington Village, Avonmore Road, London W14 8HQ (tel 020 7071 1185)

BUCKNALL, Dr Clifford Adrian (Cliff); s of Eric Bucknall, of Berkswell, W Midlands, and Elsie Constance, *née* Whittaker; *b* 25 February 1956; *Educ* Leamington Coll, KCL, Westminster Med Sch London (MB BS, MD); *m* 1, 30 July 1983 (m dis 1996); 2 s (Sam b 1984, Tom b 1986); m 2, 22 Nov 1997, Clare, *née* Collis; 2 da (Sophie Charlotte b 2002, Phoebe Holly b 2004); *Career* house surgn Warwick 1979–80, house physician Westminster 1980, sr house physician Nottingham 1980–82, research fell Guy's Hosp 1982–84, registrar Brighton 1984–85, registrar then locum sr registrar KCH 1985–87, sr registrar in cardiology Guy's Hosp 1987–89, conslt cardiologist KCH and Dulwich Hosps 1989–92, conslt cardiologist Guy's and St Thomas' Trust (formerly GKT) 1993– (dir of cardiac services 1993–97 and 2002–05); CMO Royal & Sun Alliance 1993–2000; memb Br Cardiac Soc; FRSM 1979, MRCS 1979, FRCP 1994 (MRCP 1982, LRCP 1979), FESC 1997; *Books* Horizons In Medicine no 1 (contrib, 1989); *Recreations* hockey, tennis, swimming; *Style—* Dr Cliff Bucknall; ✉ c/o 4th Floor, St Olaf House, London Bridge Hospital, 27 Tooley Street, London SE1 2PR (tel 020 7407 0292)

BUCKS, Peter; s of Nathan Bucks (d 1959), and Winifred José Beryl, *née* Hooper (d 1959); *b* 30 September 1947; *Educ* Sevenoaks Sch, Univ of Southampton (BSc); *m* 1973, Sarah Ann, da of Leslie Bernard Dobson (d 1983); 2 s (Oliver b 1978, Toby b 1982), 1 da (Eleanor b 1980); *Career* merchant banker; dir Hill Samuel Bank Ltd 1987–98, non-exec dir British Marine Managers Ltd 1997–2000; sr fin advsr Office of Gas and Electricity Markets 1997–, corp fin advsr Office of Water Services 2000–06; non-exec bd memb: Office of Rail Regulation 2004–, Water Servs Regulation Authy 2006–; Hon FSI, FRSA; *Style—* Peter Bucks, Esq; ✉ Bryants Farm, Dowlish Wake, Ilminster, Somerset TA19 0NX (tel 01460 52441, e-mail bryantsfarm@hotmail.com); 9 Millbank, London SW1P 3GE (tel 020 7901 7483, fax 020 7901 7077, e-mail peter.bucks@ofgem.gov.uk)

BUCKS, Simon; s of Nathan Bucks (d 1960), of Oxted, Surrey, and Josie, *née* Hooper (d 1960); *b* 31 July 1952; *Educ* Clifton; *m* 1, 1976 (m dis), Rita, *née* Goldberg; m 2, 1981, Cheryl Armitage *née* Davey; 1 da (Anna), 1 s (Jonathan); *Career* South West News Service Bristol 1972–75, journalist HTV West Bristol 1975–81, sub-ed then chief sub-ed ITN 1981–87, programme ed Weekend News 1987–89, programme ed News At Ten 1989–92, ed Lunchtime News and sr programme ed Independent Television News 1992–94, controller of programmes London News Network 1996–99 (head of news 1994–96), assoc ed Sky News 2004–; conslt and ptnr Armitage Bucks Communications 1999–; pres elect Soc of Eds; memb :Defence, Press and Broadcasting Advsy Ctee; *Style—* Simon Bucks, Esq; ✉ 16 Micheldever Road, London SE12 8LX (tel 020 8297 2858)

BUCKWELL, Allan Edgar; s of George Alfred Donald Buckwell, of Timsbury, Avon, and Jessie Ethel Neave (d 1989); *b* 10 April 1947; *Educ* Gillingham GS, Univ of London (BSc), Univ of Manchester (MA); *m* 1, (m dis 1990); 2 s (Andrew Simon b 1967, Timothy James b 1971); m 2, 12 July 1997, Elizabeth Mitchell; *Career* lectr Univ of Newcastle upon Tyne 1973–84, prof of agric economics Univ of London 1984–99, emeritus prof of agric economics Imperial Coll London 2002–; chief economist CLA 2000–; pres Agric Econs Soc 2004–05, European Assoc of Agric Economists; *Books* Costs of the Common Agricultural Policy (with D R Harley, K Parton and K J Thompson, 1982), Chinese Grain Economy and Policy (with Cheng Liang Yu, 1990), Agricultural Privatisation, Land Reform and Farm Restructuring in Central Europe (with J F M Swinnen and E Mathijs, 1997); *Style—* Allan Buckwell; ✉ CLA, 16 Belgrave Square, London SW1X 8PQ (tel 020 7460 7937, e-mail allan.buckwell@cla.org.uk)

BUCKWELL, Anthony Basil; s of Maj B A Buckwell, DSO, MC (d 1996), and Y E S Buckwell (d 1996); *b* 23 July 1946; *Educ* Winchester, RAC Cirencester; *m* 27 April 1968, Henrietta Judith, da of Ronald K Watson, WS; 2 da (Tara b 1970, Alexia b 1971); *Career* merchant banker; dir: Absentminders Ltd London 1976–, Kleinwort Benson Ltd London 1985–91, Centro Internationale Handelsbank AG Vienna 1985–91, Capital Trust Ltd London 1991–96, CAIC Ltd 1996–2000, The Corn Exchange (Newbury) Tst 2001–, Intermail plc 2003–04; memb Regnl Advsy Cncl BBC 1998–2001; *Recreations* exploration, fishing, riding; *Clubs* Brooks's; *Style—* Anthony B Buckwell, Esq; ✉ The Cygnet House, 30 Park Street, Hungerford, Berkshire RG17 0EA

BUCZACKI, Prof Stefan Tadeusz; s of Tadeusz Buczacki (d 1978), and Madeleine Mary Cato, *née* Fry (d 2000); *b* 16 October 1945; *Educ* Ecclesbourne Sch Duffield, Univ of Southampton (BSc), Linacre Coll Oxford (DPhil); *m* 1970, Beverley Ann, da of Sidney Charman; 2 s (Julian Nicholas Edward b 10 Nov 1973, Simon James Alexander b 25 March 1977); *Career* princ scientific offr Nat Vegetable Res Station Wellesbourne 1970–84, freelance broadcaster and author, expert witness and garden designer 1984–; ptnr Stefan Buczacki Associates Landscape and Garden Design 2001–; hon prof in plant pathology Liverpool John Moores Univ; pres E Midlands Assoc for Science Educn 1996–97; contrib to magazines, newspapers and learned jls; tstee: Brogdale Horticultural Tst, Hestercombe Gardens Tst (chm Estates Ctee); patron: Parrs Wood Rural Studies Centre, Langdon Gardens Tst, Warwick Castle Gardens Tst, Friends of Hestercombe Garden, Southport Flower Show; memb: Bd of Advsrs Gardeners' Royal Benevolent Soc, British Mycological Soc (pres 1999–2000, vice-pres 1994, Benefactor's Medal 1996), Int Trg Fund, CABI Int; hon fell CABI Bioscience; Hon DUniv Derby; CBiol, FIBiol, FIHort, FLS, ARPS; *Radio* incl: Gardeners' Question Time 1982–94 (chm 1993–94), The Gardening Quiz (originator, writer and presenter) 1988–93, Classic Gardening Forum (presenter) 1994–97; *Television* incl: Gardeners' Direct Line 1983–85, Gardeners' World 1990–91, That's Gardening 1989–92, Chelsea Flower Show 1990–91, Bazaar 1989–93, Good Morning 1992–96, Stefan Buczacki's Gardening Britain 1996, Stefan's Garden Roadshow 1997–98 and 2000, Open House 1998–2002, Learn to Garden with Stefan Buczacki 1999, Stefan's Ultimate Gardens 2001; *Books* Collins Guide to the Pests, Diseases and Disorders of Garden Plants (jt, 1981), Gem Guide to Mushrooms and Toadstools (1982), Collins Shorter Guide to the Pests, Diseases and Disorders of Garden Plants (jt, 1983), Zoosporic Plant Pathogens (ed, 1983), Beat Garden Pests and Diseases (1985), Gardener's Questions Answered (1985), Three Men in a Garden (jt, 1986), Ground Rules for Gardeners (1986), Beginners Guide to Gardening (1988), Creating a Victorian Flower Garden (1988), Garden Warfare (1988), New Generation Guide to the Fungi of Britain and Europe (1989), A Garden for all Seasons (1990), Understanding Your Garden (1990), The Essential Gardener (1991), Dr Stefan Buczacki's Gardening Hints (1992), The Plant Care Manual (1992), The Budget Gardening Year (1993), Mushrooms and Toadstools of Britain and Europe (1993), The Gardeners' Handbook (ed, 1993), Best Climbers (1994), Best Foliage Shrubs (1994), Best Shade Plants (1994), Best Soft Fruit (1994), Best Water Plants (1995), Best Herbs (1995), Best Roses (1996), Best Container Plants (1996), Classic FM Garden Planner (jtly, 1996), Stefan Buczacki's Gardening Britain (1996), Best Garden Doctor (1997), Best Summer Flowering Shrubs (1997), Best Winter Plants (1997), Best Geraniums (1998), Best Clematis (1998), Best Pruning (1998), Stefan Buczacki's Gardening Dictionary (1998), Photoguide to the Pests, Diseases and Disorders of Garden Plants (jt, 1998), Stefan Buczacki's Plant Dictionary (1999), Best Fuchsias (1999), Best Evergreen Trees and Shrubs (1999), First Time Gardener (2000), Essential Garden Answers (2000), Best Ground Cover (2000), Best Rock Garden Plants (2000), Best Kitchen Herbs (2000), Best Water Gardens (2000), Plant Problems - Prevention and Control (2000), Hamlyn Encyclopaedia of Gardening (2002), Fauna Britannica (2002), The Commonsense Gardener (2004), Young Gardener (jtly, 2006), Garden Natural History: New Naturalist No 102 (2007), Collins Wildlife Gardener (2007), Churchill and Chartwell (2007); *Recreations* gardening, fishing, riding, travel, live theatre, fine music, Derbyshire porcelain, book collecting, kippers, photography, my Jaguar XK120; *Clubs* Garrick; *Style—* Prof Stefan Buczacki; ✉ c/o Knight Ayton Management, 114 St Martin's Lane, London WC2N 4BE (tel 020 7836 5333, fax 020 7836 8333, e-mail info@knightayton.co.uk)

BUDD, Sir Alan Peter; kt (1997); s of Ernest Frank Budd (d 1981), and Elsie Nora, *née* Hambling (d 1985); *b* 16 November 1937; *Educ* Oundle, LSE (BSc), Churchill Coll Cambridge (PhD); *m* 18 July 1964, Susan, da of late Prof Norman Millott, of Millport, Isle of Cumbrae; 3 s (Joel b 1973, Nathaniel b 1976, Saul b 1978); *Career* lectr Univ of Southampton 1966–69, Ford visiting prof Carnegie-Mellon Univ of Pittsburgh 1969–70, sr econ advsr HM Treasy 1970–74, high level conslt OECD 1976, prof of economics London Business Sch 1981–88 (sr res fell 1974), Res Bank of Australia res prof Univ of NSW 1983, memb Securities and Investments Bd 1987–88, econ advsr Barclays Bank 1988–91, chief economic advsr to HM Treasy and head Govt Economic Service 1991–97, memb Monetary Policy Ctee Bank of England 1997–99, provost The Queen's College Oxford 1999–; chm Gambling Review Body 2000–01; sr advsr Global Res Dept Credit Suisse First Boston 1999–, chm Oxford Biosensors 2001–03, non-exec dir IG Gp Hldgs plc 2005–; govr LSE 1994–2002; memb Bloomsbury DHA 1986–88; *Books* The Politics of Economic Planning (1976); *Recreations* music, gardening; *Clubs* Reform; *Style—* Sir Alan P Budd; ✉ The Provost's Lodgings, The Queen's College, Oxford OX1 4AW (tel 01865 279120)

BUDD, Rt Rev (Hugh) Christopher; *see:* Plymouth, Bishop of (RC)

BUDD, Sir Colin Richard; KCMG (2002, CMG 1991); s of late Bernard Wilfred Budd, QC, and Margaret Alison Budd, MBE, *née* Burgin; *b* 31 August 1945; *Educ* Kingswood Sch Bath, Pembroke Coll Cambridge; *m* 1971, Agnes, *née* Smit; 1 da (Francesca b 1979), 1 s (Nicholas b 1986); *Career* HM Dip Serv: CO 1967–68, asst private sec to Min without Portfolio 1968–69, third sec Warsaw 1969–72, second sec Islamabad 1972–75, first sec FCO 1976–80, head of Chancery The Hague 1980–84, asst private sec to Sec of State FCO 1984–87, on secondment Euro Secretariat Cabinet Office 1987–88, head of Chancery Bonn 1989–92, chef de cabinet to Sir Leon Brittan (vice-pres EC) 1993–96, dep sec Cabinet Office 1996–97, econ and EU dir FCO 1997–2001, ambass to Netherlands 2001–05, currently cmmr Cmmn for Racial Equality; *Recreations* running, mountains, music; *Style—* Sir Colin Budd, KCMG

BUDGE, David; s of Alistair Budge, of Wick, and Elizabeth, *née* Henderson; *b* 18 October 1957; *Educ* Wick HS, Glasgow Coll (SHND, Dip Industrial Admin); *m* 5 Aug 1983, Christine Margaret, da of James Deans Rankin (d 1970); 2 da (Alexandra, Catherine), 1 s (Andrew John); *Career* res exec Consensus Res Pty Brisbane 1979–80, press offr Wolf Electric Tools Ltd London 1980–81, dir PR Consultants Scotland 1987–94 (joined 1982), ptnr Budge Newton 1994–98, md Budge PR 1998–; vice-chair Glasgow Cncl on Alcohol; winner IPR Sword of Excellence 1986; MCIPR; DipCAM; *Recreations* tennis, badminton; *Clubs* Blantyre Sports; *Style—* David Budge, Esq; ✉ 2 Dunclutha Drive, Bothwell G71 8SQ (tel 01698 852900, fax 01698 540222, e-mail david.budge@budgepr.com)

BUDGE, Prof Ian; s of John Elder Budge (d 1985), of Edinburgh, and Elizabeth, *née* Barnet (d 1979); *b* 21 October 1936; *Educ* Wardie Sch Edinburgh, George Heriot's Sch Edinburgh,

Univ of Edinburgh, Yale Univ; *m* 17 July 1964, Judith Beatrice Ruth, da of Richard Franklin Harrison (d 1973), of Preston, Lancs; 1 s (Gavin b 1965), 1 da (Eileen Elizabeth b 1968); *Career* lectr Univ of Strathclyde 1963–66, prof Univ of Essex 1977– (formerly lectr, sr lectr, reader); visiting prof: Univ of Wisconsin Madison 1969–70, Euro Univ Inst Florence 1982–85, Univ of Calif Irvine 1989, Wissenschaftzentrum Berlin 1990, Universitat Autónoma Barcelona 1991, Netherlands Inst for Advanced Study in the Social Sciences (NIAS) 1995–96, SUNY Binghampton 1998, ANU 2001; exec dir Euro Consortium for Political Res 1979–83; FRSA; *Books* jtly: Scottish Political Behaviour (1966), Belfast: Approach to Crisis (1973), Voting and Party Competition (1978), Explaining and Predicting Elections (1983), The New British Political System (1988); Parties and Democracy (1990), Party Policy and Coalition Government (1992), Parties, Policies and Democracy (1994), The New Challenge of Direct Democracy (1996), The Politics of the New Europe (1997), Mapping Policy Preferences (2001), New British Politics (2004), Elections, Parties, Democracy: Conferring The Median Mandate (2005) Mapping Policy Preferences II (2006); *Recreations* gardening, walking, travel, Italy, Scotland; *Style*— Prof Ian Budge; ✉ 4 Oxford Road, Colchester, Essex CO3 3HW (tel 01206 546622); Department of Government, University of Essex, Colchester CO4 3SQ (tel 01206 872149, fax 01206 873598, e-mail budgi@essex.ac.uk)

BUDGE, Keith Joseph; s of William Henry Budge (d 1976), and Megan, *née* Parry; *b* 24 May 1957; *Educ* Rossall Sch, UC Oxford (MA, PGCE); *m* 1983, Caroline; 2 s (Alastair b 1987, Joseph b 1990), 1 da (Lara b 1991); *Career* asst master: Eastbourne Coll 1980–84 and 1989–91, Marlborough Coll 1984–88; instr in English The Stevenson Sch Pebble Beach Calif 1988–89, housemaster (Cotton House) Marlborough Coll 1991–95, headmaster Loretto Sch 1995–2000, headmaster Bedales Sch 2001–; memb HMC; *Recreations* walking, fishing, theatre, reading; *Clubs* Vincent's (Oxford), Lansdowne; *Style*— Keith Budge, Esq; ✉ Headmaster, Bedales School, Steep, Petersfield, Hampshire GU32 2DG (tel 01730 711551, fax 01730 300500)

BUENO, Antonio de Padua Jose Maria; QC (1989); s of Antonio de Padua Bueno (d 1987), and Ana Teresa de Jesus, *née* Zuloaga (d 2001); *b* 28 June 1942; *Educ* Downside, Salamanca Univ; *m* 22 July 1966, Christine Mary, da of late Michael Lees; 3 da (Nicola b 20 July 1967, Julia b 3 April 1972, Emily b 28 Dec 1988); *Career* called to the Bar Middle Temple 1964 (bencher 1998); recorder of the Crown Court 1989– (asst recorder 1984–89), former head of chambers; *Books* Atkin's Court Forms: Banking (jt ed, 1976), Byles On Bills of Exchange (asst ed 1979, jt ed 1988), Paget's Law of Banking (asst ed, 1982); *Recreations* fishing, shooting; *Clubs* Athenaeum, Kildare Street, MCC; *Style*— Antonio Bueno, Esq, QC; ✉ Hamoon House, Sturminster Newton, Dorset DT10 2DB (tel 01258 861704, fax 01258 863553); Equity House, Blackbrook Park Avenue, Taunton, Devon TA1 2PX (tel 0845 083 3000, fax 0845 083 3001, e-mail buenoqc@aol.com)

BUERK, Michael Duncan; s of Capt Gordon Charles Buerk (d 1975), and Betty Mary Buerk (d 1962); *b* 18 February 1946; *Educ* Solihull Sch; *m* 9 Sept 1968, Christine, da of late Bernard Joseph Lilley, of Hereford; 2 s (Simon, Roland (twins) b 30 Nov 1973); *Career* BBC TV News: joined 1973, energy corr 1976–79, Scotland corr 1979–81, special corr 1981–82, corr and presenter 1982–83, Africa corr 1983–87, presenter 1987–2003; presenter: Moral Maze (BBC Radio 4) 1990–, 999 (BBC 1) 1993–2002, The Choice (BBC Radio 4) 1998–; *Awards* RTS Television Journalist of the Year 1984, RTS Int News Award 1984, George Polk Award (US) Foreign TV Reporting 1984, Nat Headlines Award (US) 1984, Int News/Documentary Award Monte Carlo Festival 1984, BAFTA News & Documentary Award 1985, James Cameron Meml Award 1987, Glaxo Science Writer of the Year Award 1989; *Recreations* oenophily; *Style*— Michael Buerk, Esq

BUFFHAM, Prof Bryan Austin; s of William Austin Buffham (d 1979), of Ilford, and Florence Ethel Mary, *née* London (d 1957); *b* 2 November 1936; *Educ* County HS Ilford, UCL (BSc), Yale Univ (MEng), Loughborough Univ of Technol (PhD), Univ of London (DSc); *m* 12 Nov 1960, Dolores Marie, da of Alfred Lane (d 1986), of Allentown Pa, USA; 2 da (Robin b 1961, Christine b 1962), 1 s (Timothy b 1967); *Career* chemical engr Air Products and Chemicals Inc Allentown PA 1959–64; Loughborough Univ (formerly Loughborough Univ of Technol): res fell 1964–65, lectr 1965–71, sr lectr 1971–81, reader 1982–86, prof 1986–2002, emeritus prof 2002–; ed Chemical Engineering Jl 1970–92; FIChemE 1979; *Books* Mixing in Continuous Flow Systems (with E B Nauman, 1983); *Recreations* cycling; *Style*— Prof Bryan Buffham; ✉ 21 Springfield, Kegworth, Derbyshire DE74 2DP (tel 01509 672938); Department of Chemical Engineering, Loughborough University, Loughborough, Leicestershire LE11 3TU (tel 01509 222503, fax 01509 223923)

BUFORD, William Holmes (Bill); s of William Holmes Buford, Jr, of Jonesboro, Louisiana, and Helen McCollough Shiel, of NYC; *b* 6 October 1954; *Educ* Univ of Calif Berkeley (BA), King's Coll Cambridge (Marshall scholar, MA); *m* 1, 6 July 1991 (m dis 2000), Alicja, *née* Kobiernicka; m 2, 18 Oct 2002, Jessica Hawkins Green; 2 s (George Ely, Frederick Hawkins (twins) b 24 Sept 2005); *Career* ed Granta 1979–95, publisher Granta Books 1989–95, chm Granta Publications Ltd until 1995, literary and fiction ed New Yorker 1995–2002, staff writer New Yorker 2006–; *Books* Among the Thugs (1991), The Granta Book of Travel Writing (ed, 1992), The Granta Book of Reportage (1993), The Granta Book of The Family (ed, 1995), Heat: An Amateur's Adventures as Kitchen Slave, Line Cook, Pasta-Maker and Apprentice to a Danté-Quoting Butcher in Tuscany (2006); *Style*— Bill Buford, Esq; ✉ The New Yorker, 4 Times Square, New York, NY 10036, USA (tel 00 1 212 286 2860, fax 00 1 212 997 7852)

BUGDEN, Paul William; s of Frederick William Bugden, and Rosemary Anne Matilda Winifred Bugden (d 1995); *b* 18 April 1953; *Educ* Merchant Taylors', Univ of Kent (BA); *m* 14 Feb 1984, Nicola Ann, da of Peter Raynes, OBE; 1 s (James William b 22 March 1985), 1 da (Jessica Lucy b 29 Sept 1986); *Career* articled clerk Russell-Cooke Potter & Chapman 1976–77; Clyde & Co: articled clerk 1977–78, admitted slr 1978, based Hong Kong 1981–84, ptnr 1982–; memb: Law Soc, Br Insurance Law Assoc; *Recreations* golf, reading, theatre, running; *Clubs* Bramley Golf; *Style*— Paul Bugden, Esq; ✉ Clyde & Co, Beaufort House, Chertsey Street, Guildford, Surrey GU1 4HA (tel 01483 555555, fax 01483 567330, e-mail paul.budgen@clydeco.com)

BUGEJA, Martin Timothy; s of late Capt Paul Bugeja, and Lina, *née* Aquilina; *b* 27 June 1957, Malta; *Educ* St Edward's Coll Malta; *m* 21 Feb 1977, Joanna Juliet, *née* McNally; 1 s (Tom b 17 May 1984), 1 da (Emma b 7 Sept 1985); *Career* fndr and md Sunspot Tours Mercury Direct 1980–; *Recreations* playing: golf, tennis, walking, bridge; watching: football, rugby; *Style*— Martin Bugeja, Esq; ✉ The Five Gables, East Street, Mayfield, East Sussex TN20 6TZ (e-mail mbugeja@sunspottours.com)

BUGGY, Niall Michael; s of Martin William Buggy (d 1985), of Ireland, and Kathleen Veronica, *née* Bourke (d 2004); *b* 3 October 1948; *Educ* Sandy Mount HS, Brendan Smith Acad, Abbey Theatre Sch; *Career* actor; joined Abbey Sch aged 15, various roles incl Trofimov in The Cherry Orchard, The Seagull; *Theatre incl* Crucible Theatre Sheffield: Stanley in The Birthday Party, Estragon in Waiting for Godot; RNT: Lucius O'Trigger in The Rivals, Scandal in Love for Love, Gal in Rough Crossing; other roles incl: Christie Mahon in Playboy of The Western World (Actor of the Year Award), Seamus Shields in Shadow of A Gunman (Young Vic, nominated for Helen Hayes Award), Memoir (Dublin and London), Spokesong (King's Head, Plays and Players' Award for Best Newcomer 1978), Baron Tusenbach in Three Sisters (Harvey Award), Major General in Pirates of Penzance (Best Supporting Actor Award), Casimir in Aristocrats (winner Clarence Derwent, Time Out and Obie Awards), Bluntschli in Arms and the Man, Player King in Hamlet, Captain Boyle in Juno and the Paycock (TMA Regional Theatre Best Actor Award), Dead Funny (Vaudeville, Olivier Award for Best Comedy Performance 1995), Song at Sunset (one man show, Hampstead 1996, NY 1997), The Misanthrope (Young Vic), No Man's Land (Gate, Dublin), Give Me Your Answer Do (Hampstead), Uncle Vanya (Gate Dublin and NY, Best Actor Irish Theatre Awards), The Weir (Royal Court, Broadway, Perth and Sydney), The Beckett Festival (Barbican), Snogging Ken (Almeida), The Importance of Being Oscar (one man show, NY 2001), John Bull's Other Island (Tricycle), Mr Nobody (Soho), An Inspector Calls (Playhouse Theatre), Guys and Dolls (Piccadilly), The Gigli Concert (Finborough Theatre), A Kind of Alaska (Gate Notting Hill); *Television* incl: Once in a Lifetime, The Gathering Seed, The Citadel, Red Roses for Me, The Promise, The Little Mother, Chinese Whispers, The Full Wax, 99–1, Little Napoleon, Agony Again, Upwardly Mobile, Father Ted, Lucy Sullivan is Getting Married, Grease Monkeys, Cruise of the Gods, Family Affairs, Malice Aforethought; *Films* incl: Zardoz, Portrait of the Artist as a Young Man, Alien 3, Playboys, King David, Close My Eyes, Anna Karenina, The Butcher Boy, Sweeney Todd, That Time, Spin the Bottle, Morality Play, The Libertine; *Style*— Niall Buggy, Esq; ✉ c/o ICM, Oxford House, 76 Oxford Street, London W1D 1BS

BUITER, Prof Willem Hendrik; CBE (2000); s of Harm Geert Buiter, of Groningen, Netherlands, and Hendrien, *née* van Schooten; *b* 26 September 1949; *Educ* European Sch Brussels, Univ of Amsterdam, Emmanuel Coll Cambridge (BA), Yale Univ (MA, MPhil, PhD); *Family* 1 s (David Michael Alejandro b 22 Feb 1991), 1 da (Elizabeth Lorca b 6 August 1993); m 2, 5 June 1998, Anne, da of Edwin Luther Sibert; *Career* asst prof of public and int affrs Princeton Univ 1975–76 and 1977–79, lectr in economics LSE 1976–77, prof of economics Univ of Bristol 1980–82, Cassel prof of economics with special reference to money and banking LSE 1982–85, Juan T Trippe prof of economics Yale Univ 1990–94 (prof of economics 1985–89), appointed prof of int macroeconomics Univ of Cambridge 1994, appointed prof of political economy Univ of Amsterdam 2000, prof of European political economy LSE 2005–; chief economist European Bank for Reconstruction and Devpt 2000–05; memb Monetary Policy Ctee Bank of England 1997–2000; research assoc Nat Bureau of Economic Research 1979, research fell Centre for Economic Policy Research 1983–, Irving Fisher visiting prof Yale Univ 1983–88, visiting prof Univ of Groningen June-July 1986 and June 1988, visiting prof LSE 1987–88; specialist advsr House of Commons Select Ctee on the Treasy and Civil Serv 1980; advsr Goldman Sachs Int 2005–; conslt: AT&T 1976, Oxford Analytica Ltd 1977, IMF 1985–, World Bank 1986–, Inter-American Devpt Bank 1992–, EBRD 1994–; assoc ed: World Politics 1978, Economic Jl 1980–85; jt winner Sanwa Monograph on Int Financial Markets Award 1993, Dr Hendrik Muller Prize (Netherlands prize for Social Sciences) 1995, N G Person Medal for contributions to economics 2000; corresponding memb Royal Netherlands Acad of Sciences 1989, memb Int Inst of Public Finance 1993, memb Cncl Royal Economic Soc 1997; FBA 1998; *Books* Temporary and Long-Run Equilibrium (1979), Budgetary Policy, International and Intertemporal Trade in the Global Economy (1989), Macroeconomic Theory and Stabilization Policy (1989), Principles of Budgetary and Financial Policy (1990), International Macroeconomics (1990), Financial Markets and European Monetary Cooperation - The Lessons of the 92–93 ERM Crisis (with G Corsetti and P Pesenti, 1997); author of numerous articles in learned jls and also of book reviews, comments and discussions; *Recreations* tennis, science fiction and phantasy, poetry; *Style*— Prof Willem Buiter, CBE, FBA; ✉ European Institute, London School of Econmics and Political Science, Houghton Street, London WC2A 2AE (tel 020 7955 6959, fax 020 7955 7546, e-mail w.buiter@lse.ac.uk)

BUKHT, Michael John; OBE (1996); s of Mirza Jawan Bukht (d 1971), and Lilian Ray, *née* Oaten (d 2006); *b* 10 September 1941; *Educ* Haberdashers' Aske's, KCL (BA, winner NUS Drama Award as director); *m* 11 Sept 1964, Jennie Mary, *née* Jones; 3 da (Annabel Kate b 12 Nov 1965, Susannah Jane b 9 May 1971, Lucy Taliesin b 1 Nov 1979), 1 s (Mirza Jonathan William b 16 May 1968); *Career* joined BBC as gen trainee 1963, worked on Tonight and 24 Hours 1964–67, prog controller Jamaica Broadcasting Corporation 1967–69, ed 24 Hours then ed special projects (incl supervising ed Gen Election 1970) BBC 1969–72, prog controller Capital Radio 1972–76, prog controller Radio 604 1979–80, princ Nat Broadcasting Sch 1980–85, md Invicta Radio 1985–88, prog controller GWR Group 1988–92, prog controller Classic FM 1992–97 (conslt 1997–); Classic FM awarded Nat Station of the Year Sony Radio Awards 1993 and 1997; food journalist (as Michael Barry) Food and Drink Prog (BBC2); chm: Kentish Fare, Canterbury Ethnic and Minorities Cncl; author of 29 books; govr St Edmunds Sch Canterbury 1997–2006; Hon DCL Univ of Kent 2002; fell Radio Acad; FRSA; *Recreations* dance, theatre, military history, sailing, cooking, travel; *Style*— Michael Bukht, Esq, OBE; ✉ 6 Chantry Hall, Canterbury, Kent CT1 2QS

BULFIELD, Prof Grahame John; CBE (2001); s of Frederick Robert Bulfield (d 1956), of Cheshire, and Madge, *née* Jones (d 1968); *b* 12 June 1941; *Educ* King's Sch Macclesfield, Univ of Leeds (BSc), Univ of Edinburgh (Dip Animal Genetics, PhD); *Career* Fulbright fell and NIH postdoctoral fell Dept of Genetics Univ of Calif 1968–70, research assoc Inst of Animal Genetics Univ of Edinburgh 1971–76 (SRC resettlement fell 1970–71), lectr and convenor of med genetics Dept of Genetics Univ of Leicester 1976–81, head of genetics gp AFRC Poultry Res Centre 1981–86, head of station and assoc dir Edinburgh Res Station Inst of Animal Physiology and Genetic Res 1988–93 (head of gene expression gp 1986–88), dir and chief exec Roslin Inst 1993–2002; Univ of Edinburgh: hon fell Dept of Genetics 1981–90, hon prof Div of Biological Science Univ of Edinburgh 1990–2002, vice-princ, head Coll of Sci and Engrg and prof of animal genetics 2002–; non-exec dir: BKU Ltd 2000–, Edinburgh Research and Innovation Ltd 2002–; memb: Genetical Soc 1971– (memb Ctee 1980–83 and 1986–90), Advsy Ctee on Genetic Modification 1990–96, Advsy Bd Partnerships UK 2002–03; fndr ed Genes and Development 1987–90; memb: Home Office Animal Proceedures Ctee 1998–2006, Research and Knowledge Transfer Ctee Scottish Funding Cncl 2002–07; author of research papers and book chapters on biochemical and molecular genetics; Hon DSc: Univ of Edinburgh 2000, Univ of Abertay 2003; FRSE 1992, CBiol, FIBiol 1995, Hon FRASE 1999, FRSA 2001; *Recreations* fell walking and cricket; *Style*— Prof Grahame Bulfield, CBE, FRSE; ✉ The University of Edinburgh, Weir Building, The King's Buildings, West Mains Road, Edinburgh EH9 3JY (tel 0131 650 5754, fax 0131 650 5738, e-mail grahame.bulfield@ed.ac.uk)

BULKELEY, *see:* Williams-Bulkeley

BULKIN, Dr Bernard J; s of Jacob Bulkin (d 1992), and Beatrice, *née* Kotkofsky (d 1990); *b* 9 March 1942, Trenton, NJ, USA; *Educ* Poly Inst of Brooklyn (BS), Purdue Univ (PhD); *m* 14 July 2002, Vivien, *née* Rose; 1 da (Anna b 31 Aug 1970), 2 s (Noah b 31 May 1977, David b 21 July 1979); *Career* postdoctoral fell Eidgenössische Technische Hochschule Zürich 1966–67, prof City Univ of NY 1967–75; Poly Inst of NY: dean of arts and sciences 1975–81, vice-pres 1981–85; Standard Oil of Ohio: dir analytical and environmental science 1985–87, dir R&D Sohio Oil 1987–88; BP plc: head Products Div 1989–92, R&D dir BP Oil 1992–97, dir manufacturing and supply 1993–97, vice-pres environmental affrs 1997–2000, chief scientist 2000–03; professorial fell New Hall Cambridge 2004–, ptnr Vantage Point 2004–, chm AEA Technology plc 2005–, non-exec dir Severn Trent plc 2006–, chm Chemrec AB 2007–; memb: Cncl Royal Instn, Cncl Scripps Inst of Oceanography; author of more than 125 papers and two books; Oscar Foster Award 1973, Coblentz Award 1975, Soc for Applied Spectroscopy Gold Medal 1978; FRSC 1989, FRSA 1995, FEI 1998; *Recreations* horseback riding; *Clubs* Reform; *Style*— Dr Bernard Bulkin; ✉ AEA Technology plc, Central House, Upper Woburn Place, London WC1H 0JN (tel 0870 190 5534, e-mail bernard.bulkin@aeat.com)

BULL, Christopher Robert Howard; s of Robert Golden Bull (d 1994), and Audrey, *née* Ineson; *b* 14 May 1942; *Educ* Christ's Hosp, CCC Cambridge (MA); *m* 1 April 1967, Rosemary Anne, da of Frank Coltman (d 1979); 2 s (Jeremy b 1969, Andrew b 1972), 1 da (Stephanie b 1976); *Career* Whinney Murray & Co 1964–68, Centre for Interfirm Comparison 1968–71, industrial gas div controller Air Products Ltd 1971–75, head of gp fin analysis BICC plc 1975–80, fin dir BICC Technologies Ltd 1981–84, corp treas BT 1984–88; fin dir: BTR plc 1988–91, Rio Tinto plc (formerly RTZ Corporation plc) 1991– (dir Rio Tinto Ltd Dec 1995–); non-exec dir Blue Circle Industries plc 1996–2001; govr Univ of Greenwich 1996–; FCA 1968; *Recreations* music, sailing; *Style*— Christopher Bull, Esq; ✉ Rio Tinto plc, 6 St James's Square, London SW1Y 4LD (tel 020 7930 2399, fax 020 7930 3249, e-mail crhbull@hotmail.com)

BULL, David; s of J W Bull; *Educ* Univ of Reading (BA, MA); *Career* various positions at academic and science publishers incl: Routledge, Thomson, Chapman & Hall, Taylor & Francis; dir of journals Palgrave (formerly Macmillan Press); *Publications* Marketing Explained (1997); author of numerous articles for industry publications; *Recreations* my children, writing, reading, music; *Style*— David Bull, Esq; ✉ Macmillan Publishers Ltd, Houndmills, Basingstoke RG21 6XS (tel 01256 329242, e-mail d.bull@palgrave.com)

BULL, David Neill; s of Denis Albert Bull (d 1986), of Grays, Essex, and Doreen Lilian, *née* Durham; *b* 21 June 1951; *Educ* Palmer's Sch for Boys Grays, Univ of Sussex (BA), Univ of Bath (MSc); *m* 1978, Claire, da of Peter Grenger; 1 da (Kate b 1984); *Career* public affrs offr Oxfam 1979–84, exec dir Environment Liaison Centre (Kenya) 1984–87, gen sec World University Service (WUS) UK 1987–90, dir Amnesty International UK 1990–99, exec dir UK Ctee for UNICEF 1999–; memb: Exec Ctee (vol) The Refugee Cncl 1987–90, Bd (vol) PAN UK 1987–99, Exec Ctee ACEVO 1994–98; *Books* A Growing Problem: Pesticides and the Third World Poor (1982), The Poverty of Diplomacy: Kampuchea and the Outside World (1983); *Style*— David Bull, Esq; ✉ UNICEF UK, Africa House, 64–78 Kingsway, London WC2B 6NB (tel 020 7405 5592, fax 020 7405 2332)

BULL, Deborah Clare; CBE (1999); da of Rev (Michael) John Bull, of London, and Doreen Audrey, *née* Plumb; *b* 22 March 1963; *Educ* The Royal Ballet Sch, Academie de Danse Classique de Monte Carlo; *Career* Royal Ballet 1981–2001 (soloist 1986, princ 1992), creative dir ROH2 2002–; major dance roles incl: Rite of Spring, La Bayadère, Sleeping Beauty, Agon, Steptext, Giselle, Song of the Earth, Don Quixote, In the Middle, Somewhat Elevated, Swan Lake; created major roles in: Still Life at the Penguin Café, Pursuit, Piano, Fearful Symmetries; memb cast: In the Middle, Somewhat Elevated (Laurence Olivier Award 1993); guest performances: Italy, Canada, Japan, N America; organised and performed in An Evening of British Ballet at The Sintra Festival 1994 and 1995; addressed Oxford Union 1996, delivered Arts Cncl Annual Lectr 1996, dir Artists' Devpt Initiative at ROH, columnist The Daily Telegraph, writer/presenter Dance Ballerina, Dance (BBC2) 1998; presenter: Travels with My Tutu (four part series, BBC2) 2000, Breaking the Law (5 part series, BBC Radio 4) 2001, Law in Order (5 part series BBC Radio 4) 2002, The Dancer's Body (three part series, BBC2) 2002, Saved for the Nation, Artsworld 2006; regular presenter live broadcasts BBC1 and BBC2; memb: Bd South Bank Centre 1997–2003, Arts Cncl of England 1998–2005, Bd of Govrs BBC 2003–06; winner Prix de Lausanne 1980, voted one of the Dancers of the Year by readers of Dance and Dancers 1991 and 1992, Olivier Award nomination for Outstanding Achievement in Dance (for Steptext at ROH) 1996; patron Nat Osteoporosis Soc; Hon Dr: Univ of Derby 1998, Sheffield Hallam Univ 2001, Open Univ 2005; *Books* The Vitality Plan (1998), Dancing Away - A Covent Garden Diary (1998), The Faber Guide to Classical Ballets (2004); *Recreations* literature, music, food, wine, dancing and mountain air; *Style*— Miss Deborah Bull, CBE

BULL, Sir George Jeffrey; kt (1998); s of Michael Herbert Perkins Bull (d 1965), and Hon Noreen Madeleine Hennessy, da of 1 Baron Windlesham; *b* 16 July 1936; *Educ* Ampleforth; *m* 7 Jan 1960, Fleur Thérèse (Tessa), da of Patrick Freeland (d 1977); 4 s (Sebastian b 1960, Rupert b 1963, Justin b 1964, Cassian b 1966), 1 da (Tamsin b 1972); *Career* Lt Coldstream Gds 1954–57, served in Ger and UK; chm and chief exec IDV Ltd 1984–1992; chm Grand Metropolitan plc 1996–97 (chief exec 1994–96), jt chm Diageo plc 1997–98, chm J Sainsbury plc 1998–2004; dir: Br Overseas Trading Bd 1990–95, BNP Paribas UK Holdings 2001–04, The Maersk Co Ltd 2001–06; memb Advsy Bd Marakon Assocs 2002–06; memb: President's Ctee CBI 1993–1996, BACC Advsy Bd 1994–98, Ctee Westminster Cathederal Centenary Appeal 1995–96; chm: MENCAP Jubilee Appeal Ctee 1995–98, Wine and Spirit Assoc of GB 1975–76, Ampleforth Bi-centenary Appeal 1999–2004, Wine & Spirit Benevolent Soc 2000–01; dir US Adv Educ Fndn 1994–98, founding dir The Mktg Cncl 1995–2000; pres Advtg Assoc (AA) 1996–2000, vice-pres CIM 1994; vice-pres Mencap 2000–; chm Old Codgers Assoc 2004–; Mktg Hall of Fame 1998; patron Keepers of the Quaich 1996–2005 (Grand Master 1995–96); Freeman City of London 1995, memb Worshipful Co of Distillers 1995–; FRSA 1992–98, Hon FCIM 1995, hon fell Mktg Soc 1997 (memb 1997); Chevalier de la Legion d'Honneur 1994; *Recreations* golf, shooting, photography; *Clubs* The Pilgrims, Cavalry and Guards', Royal Worlington Golf; *Style*— Sir George Bull; ✉ The Old Vicarage, Arkesden, Saffron Walden, Essex (tel 01799 550445)

BULL, Prof (Roger) John; CBE (2002); *b* 31 March 1940; *Educ* Churcher's Coll Petersfield, LSE (BSc); *m* 1964, Margaret Evelyn, *née* Clifton; 1 s, 1 da; *Career* student accountant then systems accountant Ford Motor Co 1958–62, lectr II in accounting NE London Poly 1965–66, res fell Dept of Educn and Science/ICAEW 1966–67, sr lectr in accounting NE London Poly 1967–68, princ lectr in accounting Trent Poly 1968–72, head Sch of Accounting and Applied Economics Leeds Poly 1972–84, vice-chllr and chief exec Univ of Plymouth 1989–2002 (dep 1985–89); chm LSC Devon and Cornwall 2002–, chm Plymouth Hosps NHS Tst 2002–; chm Dartington Coll of Arts 2003–; dep chm Universities Superannuation Scheme (USS) Ltd 2004–; author of pubns in accounting and academic mgmnt; FCCA 1976 (ACCA 1962); *Recreations* walking, music; *Style*— Prof John Bull, CBE; ✉ 3 Westmoor Park, Tavistock, Devon PL19 9AA

BULL, His Hon John Michael; QC (1983), DL (Surrey 1996); s of John Godfrey Bull (d 1969), and Eleanor, *née* Nicholson (d 1994); *b* 31 January 1934; *Educ* Norwich Sch, CCC Cambridge (Parker exhibitioner, State scholar, MA, LLM); *m* 20 Dec 1959, Sonia Maureen, da of Frank Edward Woodcock, of Norwich; 3 da (Caroline Elisabeth b 15 Dec 1961, Rachel Clare b 26 Feb 1963, Francesca Margaret b 23 Nov 1964), 1 s ((John) Michael Curties b 14 March 1968); *Career* called to the Bar Gray's Inn 1960; dep circuit judge 1972, standing counsel to Inland Revenue Western Circuit 1973–83, recorder of the Crown Court 1980–91, circuit judge (SE Circuit) 1991–2006 (dep circuit judge 2006–), dep High Court judge (Queen's Bench Div) 1991–2000, additional judge of Employment Appeal Tbnl 1991–2000, resident judge of the Crown Court at Guildford 1992–2000; hon recorder of Guildford 1998–; hon visiting prof of law Univ of Surrey 1999–2005; *Recreations* music and punting; *Style*— His Hon John Bull, QC, DL

BULL, Sir Simeon George; 4 Bt (UK 1922), of Hammersmith, Co London; s of Sir George Bull, 3 Bt (d 1987), and Gabrielle Muriel, *née* Jackson (d 1989); *b* 1 August 1934; *Educ* Eton, Innsbruck (Law Faculty), Ecole de Notariat Paris; *m* 17 June 1961, Annick Elisabeth Geneviève Renée (d 2000), yr da of late Louis Bresson (d 1960), of Château des Masselins, Chandai, Orne, France; 2 da (Jacqueline-Hester b 15 Oct 1964, Sophia Ann b 2 March 1971), 1 s (Stephen Louis b 5 April 1966); *Heir* s, Stephen Bull; *Career* admitted slr 1959; formerly sr ptnr legal firm of Bull & Bull; Cdre London Corinthian Sailing Club 1968–71, fndr hon sec Assoc of Thames Valley Sailing Clubs 1972–78, memb Cncl Royal Yachting Assoc 1977–79; Freeman City of London 1955, Liveryman Worshipful Co of Fishmongers; *Recreations* sailing, foreign travel, gardening, carpentry, reading; *Clubs* Royal Thames Yacht, MCC; *Style*— Sir Simeon Bull, Bt; ✉ Beech Hanger, Beech Road, Merstham, Surrey RH1 3AE

BULL, Tony Raymond; s of Henry Albert Bull (d 1963), and Phyllis Rosalie, *née* Webber; *b* 21 December 1934; *Educ* Monkton Combe Sch, London Hosp Med Coll; *m* June 1959, Jill Rosemary Beresford, da of Air Vice Marshal Albert Frederick Cook, CBE; 2 da (Amanda b 1960, Karen b 1962), 1 s (Antony b 1965); *Career* hon consIt surgn Charing Cross Hosp; consIt surgn: Royal Nat Throat Nose & Ear Hosp, King Edward VII's Hosp for Officers; Liveryman Worshipful Soc of Apothecaries; FRCS; *Recreations* tennis (Somerset County), hockey (Essex County); *Clubs* MCC, Queen's, Hurlingham, Savile; *Style*— Tony Bull, Esq; ✉ 107 Harley Street, London W1 (tel 020 7935 3171)

BULLEN, James Edward; s of Albert Edward Bullen (d 1977), and Doris Josephine, *née* McHale (d 1976); *b* 26 March 1943; *Educ* Univ of London (LLB); *m* 1, 1973 (m dis 1984); m 2, 27 Sept 1985, Mary, da of late Patrick Keane; 1 s (William James b 1986); *Career* called to the Bar Gray's Inn 1966, memb Senate of Inns of Ct and Bar 1979–82, recorder (Western Circuit) 1997–; *Recreations* music, reading, walking, horse riding; *Clubs* Garrick, RAC; *Style*— James Bullen, Esq; ✉ 1 Paper Buildings, Temple, London EC4Y 7EP

BULLIMORE, His Hon Judge John Wallace MacGregor; s of James Wallace Bullimore (d 1981), and Phyllis Violet Emily, *née* Brandt (d 1998); *b* 4 December 1945; *Educ* Queen Elizabeth GS Wakefield, Univ of Bristol (LLB); *m* 20 Dec 1975, Rev Christine Elizabeth Bullimore, da of late Valentine Sidney Charles Kinch; 2 s (Matthew James b 16 Dec 1977, Andrew Charles b 14 Oct 1981), 1 da decd; *Career* called to the Bar Inner Temple 1968, in practice 1968–91, circuit judge (NE Circuit) 1991–; chllr Diocese of: Derby 1981, Blackburn 1990; memb Gen Synod of the C of E 1970–; *Style*— His Hon Judge Bullimore; ✉ c/o NE Circuit Office, West Riding Street, Albion Street, Leeds LS1 5AA (tel 0113 244 1841)

BULLMORE, Prof Edward Thomas; s of Jeremy Bullmore, CBE, *qv*, of London, and Pamela Audrey, *née* Green; *b* 27 September 1960; *Educ* Westminster, ChCh Oxford (MA, Ida Mary Henderson scholar), Univ of London (MB BS, PhD); *m* 13 Dec 1992, Mary, da of Arthur Pitt; 3 s (Alfred b 1993, Sidney b 1996, Ferdinand b 2001); *Career* house offr Bart's and Hackney Hosps 1985–86, lectr in med Univ of Hong Kong 1987–88, SHO in psychiatry St George's Hosp London 1989–90, registrar, hon sr registrar then consIt psychiatrist Bethlem Royal & Maudsley Hosp London 1990–99, consIt psychiatrist Cambs and Peterborough Mental Health NHS Tst and Addenbrooke's Hosp Cambridge 1999–; Wellcome Tst advanced research trg fell Inst of Psychiatry 1996–99 (Wellcome Tst research trg fell and hon lectr 1993–96); Univ of Cambridge: prof of psychiatry 1999–, dir of fMRI Wolfson Brain Imaging Centre 2000–05, professorial fell Wolfson Coll 2002–, clinical dir MRC Behavioral & Clinical Neurosciences Centre 2005–; vice-pres experimental medicine and head Clinical Unit Cambridge and clinical pharm medicine GlaxoSmithKline 2005–; hon research assoc Inst of Neurology London 1994–96, visiting research fell Nat Inst on Aging (NIH) 1997, visiting prof Inst of Psychiatry KCL 1999–; memb MRC Neurosciences and Mental Health Bd 2002–06; memb Editorial Bd Psychological Medicine 2001, assoc ed Human Brain Mapping 2003; author of articles on brain mapping, statistics and psychiatry; Denis Hill Prize Inst of Psychiatry 1992, Br Neuropsychiatry Prize 1994; MRCP 1989, MRCPsych 1992; *Style*— Prof Ed Bullmore; ✉ University of Cambridge, Brain Mapping Unit, Department of Psychiatry, Addenbrooke's Hospital, Cambridge CB2 2QQ (tel 01223 336583, fax 01223 336581, e-mail etb23@cam.ac.uk)

BULLMORE, (John) Jeremy David; CBE (1985); s of Francis Edward Bullmore, and Adeline Gabrielle, *née* Roscow; *b* 21 November 1929; *Educ* Harrow, ChCh Oxford; *m* 1958, Pamela Audrey Green; 2 s (one of whom Prof Edward Thomas Bullmore, *qv*), 1 da; *Career* J Walter Thompson: joined 1954, dir 1964, dep chm 1975, chm 1976–87; dir J Walter Thompson (USA) 1980–87; non-exec dir: Guardian Media Group plc 1988–2001, WPP Group plc 1988–2004; chm Advertising Assoc 1981–87, memb Nat Ctee for Electoral Reform 1978–, pres NABS 1998–2001, pres The Market Research Soc 2004–; reg columnist: Management Today, Market Leader, Campaign; *Publications* Behind the Scenes in Advertising, Another Bad Day at the Office?, Ask Jeremy; *Clubs* Arts; *Style*— Jeremy Bullmore, Esq, CBE

BULLOCH, Gordon Campbell; s of Jim Bulloch; *b* 26 March 1975, Glasgow; *Educ* Hutchesons' GS Glasgow; *Career* rugby union player (hooker); clubs: W of Scotland RFC, Glasgow RFC; Scotland: 75 full caps (9 as capt), debut v South Africa 1997, winners Five Nations Championship 1999, memb squad World Cup Aust 2003; memb squad Br & I Lions tour Aust 2001 and NZ 2005; memb World XV v Argentina 1999; *Style*— Gordon Bulloch, Esq; ✉ The Scottish Rugby Union, Murrayfield, Edinburgh EH12 5PJ

BULLOCK, Prof Frederick William; s of Frederick Bullock (d 1936), of Bramshott, Hants, and Elizabeth May, *née* Kent (d 1979); *b* 24 April 1932; *Educ* UCL (BSc, PhD); *m* 1; 1 s (Ross b 7 July 1958); m 2, 30 Oct 1964, Margaret Ann, da of Robert Francis Tully (d 1973), of Dunstable, Beds; 2 s (Iain Robert b 22 Feb 1966, Andrew b 20 May 1967); *Career* UCL: research asst 1958–63, lectr 1963–74, reader in physics 1978–88, dean Faculty of Mathematical and Physical Sciences 1989–92, prof 1988–98, vice-provost 1992–98, prof emeritus 1998–; chm: Particle Physics Grants Sub-Ctee of the SERC 1986–90; memb: Particle Physics Ctee of the SERC 1985–90, Nuclear Physics Bd of the SERC 1986–90; chm Laser Fndn 2001–03; chm London and S Eastern Region Library Serv 1997–2001; FInstP, CPhys; *Recreations* golf, walking, family history research; *Style*— Prof Frederick Bullock; ✉ 37 Cranbrook Drive, St Albans, Hertfordshire AL4 0SR (tel 01727 767851, e-mail fwbullock@lineone.net)

BULLOCK, Gareth Richard; s of George Haydn Bullock, of Richmond, Surrey, and Veronica, *née* Jackson; *b* 20 November 1953; *Educ* Marling Sch Stroud, St Catharine's Coll Cambridge (MA); *m* 3 Sept 1983, Juliet Lucy Emma, da of Maj Cyril Vivian Eagleson Gordon, MC, of Winterbourne Gunner, Wilts; 3 s (Joshua b 1985, Marcus b 1987, Caspar b 1992); *Career* vice pres Citibank NA London 1984 (joined 1977), exec dir Swiss Bank Corp Investment Banking Ltd 1984–90, dep md UBS Phillips & Drew 1990–92, head of corporate banking Société Générale 1993–96; Standard Chartered Bank: joined 1996, formerly ceo Africa and gp chief info offr, currently dir and gp head of strategy; non-exec dir Spirax-Sarco Engineering plc 2005–; memb: Ctee St Catharine's Coll Soc, RSPB; *Publications* Euronotes and Euro-Commercial Paper (1987); *Recreations* second-hand book collecting, ornithology; *Style*— Gareth Bullock, Esq

BULLOCK, Hazel Isabel; da of Henry MacNaughton-Jones, MD (d 1950), and Isabel Jessie, *née* Pownceby (d 1929); *b* 12 June 1919; *Educ* Kingsley Sch Hampstead, RADA, St Martin's Sch of Art, Sir John Cass Coll of Art; *m* 1, 8 March 1945 (m dis 1950), Vernon Kelso (d 1959); m 2, 13 Feb 1951, Ernest Edgar Bullock (d 2002), s of Ernest Peter Bullock (d 1962); *Career* actress and painter (stage name Hazel Lawrence); BBC TV and London Stage 1943–51; solo exhibitions in London: Loggia Gallery 1973, Judd St Gallery 1985, Phoenix Gallery 1989; group exhibitions in London: Browse and D'Arby, Whitechapel Art Gallery, Nat Soc, RBA, HAC, FPS; memb Free Painters and Sculptors Soc DFN Gallery NY 2000–; *Recreations* travel; *Clubs* Arts; *Style*— Mrs Hazel Bullock; ✉ 32 Devonshire Place, London W1G 6JL (tel 020 7935 6409); Las Cancelas, La Herradura, Granada, Spain

BULLOCK, Hon Matthew Peter Dominic; yst s of Baron Bullock (Life Peer); *b* 9 September 1949; *Educ* Magdalen Coll Sch Oxford, Peterhouse Cambridge; *m* 1970, Anna-Lena Margareta, da of Sven Hansson, of Uppsala, Sweden; 1 s, 2 da; *Career* banker; dir of risk mgmnt Banking Div Barclays Bank plc 1993–94 (joined 1974); BZW Ltd: dir of debt capital mkts 1994–96, md Investment Banking Div 1996–97; md Treasy Relationship Mgmnt Barclays Capital Group 1997–99, chief exec Norwich and Peterborough Building Society 1999–, chm Building Societies Assoc, memb Financial Services Practitioner Panel 2001–07; *Recreations* gardening, reading, walking; *Clubs* Oxford and Cambridge; *Style*— The Hon Matthew Bullock; ✉ Easby House, High Street, Great Chesterford, Saffron Waldon, Essex CB10 1PL

BULLOCK, Peter Bradley; s of William H Bradley Bullock, of Benson, Oxon; *b* 9 June 1934; *Educ* Dudley GS, QMC London (BSc); *m* 1958, Joyce Frances Muriel, da of Horace Rea (d 1957); 2 da (Claire Elizabeth Bradley (Mrs Locke), Penelope Jane Bradley (Mrs Hembrow)); *Career* md Flymo Ltd (memb of Electrolux Group Sweden), jt md Electrolux Group UK until 1983; chief exec: James Neill Holdings plc 1983–89, Spear & Jackson Int plc 1985–89; chm: London & Geneva Securities Ltd 1990–2001, The Paterson Photax Gp Ltd 1992–94, James Dickie plc 1993–98, Scala Collections Ltd (Artigiano) 1997–2006; non-exec dir: 600 Gp plc 1989–2004, Wetherby Consultants Ltd 1990–96, Syltone plc 1990–99, Bison Bede Ltd 1997–98; Queen's Award: for Export 1966 and 1982, for Technol 1979 and 1983; CEng, MInstE, MCIM; *Recreations* France; *Clubs* Leander, Phyllis Court; *Style*— Peter Bullock, Esq; ✉ 5 Old Brewery Lane, Henley-on-Thames RG9 2DE (e-mail genelond1@aol.com)

BULLOCK, Susan Margaret; da of John Robert Bullock (d 1994), of Cheadle Hulme, Cheshire, and Mair, *née* Jones (d 2000); *b* 9 December 1958; *Educ* Cheadle Hulme Sch, Royal Northern Coll of Music (Jr Sch), Royal Holloway Coll London (BMus), Royal Acad of Music (LRAM), National Opera Studio; *m* Lawrence Archer Wallington, singer, s of Rev Christopher Wallington (d 1988); *Career* soprano; memb Glyndebourne Festival Chorus 1983–84, princ soprano English National Opera 1985–89; has performed with numerous major orchs incl: London Philharmonic, Royal Philharmonic, Royal Liverpool Philharmonic, BBC Nat Orch of Wales, BBC Scottish Symphony, Bournemouth Symphony, London Mozart Players, CBSO, Philharmonia, Hallé, Manchester Camerata, BBC Philharmonic, Czech Philharmonic, Sydney Symphony, Melbourne Symphony, Tokyo Philharmonic, BBC Symphony, NHK Tokyo, Hong Kong Philharmonic; regularly performs at overseas festivals incl Beaune, Istanbul, Aix-en-Provence, Prague Spring Festival; broadcasts regularly at the Proms and with BBC Concert Orch; hon fell Royal Holloway Univ of London; FRAM; *Roles* with ENO incl: Pamina in Die Zauberflöte, Gilda in Rigoletto, Tatyana in Eugene Onegin, Ellen Orford in Peter Grimes, title role in Madam Butterfly, Alice Ford in Falstaff, Yum Yum in The Mikado, Micaela in Carmen, Donna Anna in Don Giovanni, title role in Jenufa, Princess Natalie in The Prince of Homburg, Desdemona in Otello, the Mother in The Prisoner, Isolde; others incl: Marie in Wozzeck (Royal Opera Covent Garden), Jenufa (Glyndebourne, New Israeli Opera, Spoleto Festival Charleston USA), title role in Katya Kabanova (Glyndebourne), Hecuba in King Priam (Flanders Opera), Andromache in King Priam (Batignano Festival), Gilda in Rigoletto (Bergen Festival), Marguerite in Faust (New Israeli Opera), Lisa in The Queen of Spades (Glyndebourne), Madama Butterfly (New Israeli Opera, Portland Opera, Bonn, Houston Grand Opera, Teatro Colon Buenos Aires, NYC Opera), Tosca (Portland Opera and the Royal Albert Hall), Magda Sorel in The Consul (Spoleto Festival Italy, Teatro Colon Buenos Aires), Georgetta in Il Tabarro, title role in Suor Angelica (both Spoleto Festival), Isolde (Opera North, Rouen, Frankfurt and Bochumer Symphoniker), Brünnhilde in Ring Cycle (Tokyo), Brünnhilde in Götterdämmerung (Perth Festival), Els in Der Schatzgräber (Frankfurt), title role in Elektra (La Scala Milan, Stuttgart, Dresden, Rouen, Brussels and Frankfurt), Lady Macbeth (Vienna), Female Chorus in The Rape of Lucretia (Bayerische Staatsoper and Seville); *Recordings* incl: The Mikado (with ENO under Peter Robinson) 1988, Street Scene (with ENO under Carl Davis) 1989, Mahler's 8th Symphony (with London Philharmonic under Klaus Tennstedt) 1990, La Traviata/Acting (BBC TV, directed by Jonathan Miller), The Little Sweep (Thames TV), The Mikado (Thames TV), solo album 1994, Songs (La Nouvelle Musique Consonante) 1995, A Little Water Music 1997, Hindemith Sancta Susanna and Songs (with BBC Philharmonic under Yan Pascal Tortelier) 1998, Magda Sorel in The Consul, Lady Billows in Albert Herring 2002, Requiem Daffyd Bullock 2002; *Awards* Royal Over-Seas League Singers Award, Decca/Kathleen Ferrier Prize, Worshipful Co of Musicians' Silver Medal, Premio Pegaso Spoleto Festival Italy; *Recreations* theatre, films, playing the piano, cooking, reading, jazz; *Style*— Ms Susan Bullock; ✉ c/o Harrison Parrott Ltd, 12 Penzance Place, London W11 4PA (tel 020 7229 9166, fax 020 7221 5042, e-mail info@harrisonparrott.co.uk)

BULMER, (James) Esmond; er s of Edward Bulmer, and Margaret, *née* Roberts; *b* 19 May 1935; *Educ* Rugby, King's Coll Cambridge; *m* 1, 1959 (m dis 1990), Morella Kearton; 3 s, 1 da; m 2, 1990, Susan Bower; *Career* cmmnd Scots Gds 1954; H P Bulmer Holdings: dir 1962–2003, dep chm 1980–82, chm 1982–2000; dir W Midlands and Wales Regnl Bd National Westminster Bank plc 1982–92, chm Fleming High Income Investment Trust plc; MP (Cons): Kidderminster Feb 1974–83, Wyre Forest 1983–87; memb Exec Ctee National Tst 1977–87, chm Herefords Health Authy 1987–94; *Clubs* Boodle's, Beefsteak; *Style*— Esmond Bulmer, Esq

BULMER-THOMAS, Prof Victor Gerald; CMG (2007), OBE (1998); s of Ivor Bulmer-Thomas, CBE (d 1993), and Joan, *née* Bulmer; *b* 23 March 1948; *Educ* Univ of Oxford; *m* 7 Sept 1970, Barbara Ann, da of James Swasey; 2 s (Hadrian b 30 Nov 1972, Rupert b 3 May 1978), 1 da (Bianca b 11 Sept 1979); *Career* res fell Strathclyde Univ; Univ of London: lectr QMC 1978–, reader Queen Mary & Westfield Coll 1988–90, prof of econ Queen Mary & Westfield Coll 1990–98 (emeritus prof 1998–), dir Inst of Latin American Studies 1992–98 (hon res fell 1998–); dir Chatham House (RIIA) 2001–06; visiting prof Florida Int Univ Miami 2007–; non-exec dir New India Investment Tst; sometime conslt to: EC, US Agency for Int Devpt, Inter-American Devpt Bank; *Publications* incl: Input-Output Analysis: Sources, Methods and Applications for Developing Countries (1982), The Political Economy of Central America Since 1920 (1987), Studies in the Economics of Central America (1988), Latin America in Perspective (1991), The Economic History of Latin America Since Independence (1994, 2 edn 2004), Reflexiones sobre la Integración Centroamericana (1997); as ed incl: Britain and Latin America: A Changing Relationship (1989), Central American Integration, Report for the Commission of the European Community (and co-author,1992), Mexico and the North American Agreement: Who will Benefit? (co-ed, 1994), Growth and Development in Brazil: Cardoso's Real Challenge (co-ed, 1995), Rebuilding the State: Mexico After Salinas (co-ed, 1996), The New Economic Model in Latin America and its Impact on Income Distribution and Poverty (1996), Thirty Years of Latin American Studies in the United Kingdom (1997), Integración Regional en Centroamérica, San José (1998), The United States and Latin America: the New Agenda (co-ed, 1999), Regional Integration in Latin America and the Caribbean: the Political Economy of Open Regionalism (2001), The Cambridge Economic History of Latin America (2 vols, co-ed, 2006); *Clubs* Athenaeum; *Style*— Prof Victor Bulmer-Thomas, CMG, OBE; ✉ The Royal Institute of International Affairs, Chatham House, 10 St James's Square, London SW1Y 4LE

BULSON, Dr Philip Stanley; CBE (1986); s of Herbert Stanley Bulson (d 1978), and Sarah, *née* Churchill (d 1968); *b* 21 April 1925; *Educ* Yeovil Sch, Dolcoath Tech Sch, Plymouth and Devonport Tech Coll, Univ of London (BSc(Eng), DSc(Eng)), Univ of Bristol (PhD); *Career* engrg cadet (Army) and cmmn Royal Engrs until 1948; MOD: sr and princ scientific offr (military engrg, design and research) 1953–65, sr princ and dep chief scientific offr (individual merit) 1965–74; head Military Vehicles and Engrg Establishment Christchurch (formerly Military Engrg Experimental Establishment (MEXE)) 1974–85, dir Special Servs Div Mott Hay and Anderson 1986–88, conslt (specialising in the effects of explosions on structures) Mott MacDonald Gp 1988–2000; visiting prof Univ of Southampton 1983; chm Int Study on Military Bridging 1974–85, chm Br Standard Code of Practice Ctee on Structural Aluminium 1980–; Liveryman Worshipful Co of Engrs; FIStructE 1967, FIMechE 1970, FICE 1986, FREng 1985; *Books* The Stability of Flat Plates (1970), Background to Buckling (co-author, 1980), Engineering Structures (co-ed and contrib, 1983), Buried Structures (1985), Structures under Shock and Impact (ed and contrib, edns 1989, 1992 and 1994), The Future of Structural Testing (ed and contrib, 1990), Rapidly Assembled Structures (ed and contrib, 1991), Aluminium Structural Analysis (ed and contrib, 1992), Explosive Loading of Engineering Structures (1997); author of several chapters in books, numerous papers and articles in professional jls, and research reports and studies for the MOD; *Recreations* landscape artist, cocktail lounge pianist, writing, local and family history research, gardening; *Clubs* Athenaeum; *Style*— Dr Philip Bulson, CBE

BULSTRODE, Prof Christopher John Kent; s of John Christopher Bulstrode (d 1994), and Jacqueline Mary Bulstrode; *b* 5 January 1951; *Educ* Radley, UC Oxford (open scholar, MA), Univ of Cambridge (MA), Univ of Oxford (BM BCh, Pathology Research Prize, Pathology Prize, Medicine Prize, MCh); *Partner* Dr Victoria Louise Hunt, *née* Ashley-Taylor; 2 s (Harry b 1982, John-James b 1985), 1 da (Jennifer Jane b 1988); 3 step s (James, Glynn, Adam), 1 step da (Eloise); *Career* MO Ethiopian refugee prog Sudan 1977, lectr in human anatomy Univ of Dar es Salaam 1978, GP Kenya 1978, SHO Westminster Hosp London and Edinburgh Royal Infirmary 1979, The London Hosp 1980–86, Royal Nat Orthopaedic Hosp London 1984, Black Notley and Colchester Hosps Essex 1985; Univ of Oxford: clinical reader and prof of trauma and orthopaedics 1988–, assoc postgraduate dean 1996–99; visiting prof Montpellier Univ 1986; memb Editorial Bd: Jl of Bone and Joint Surgery 1994–98, Surgery 2003–; memb Cncl: RCSEd 2000– (dir of educn 2000–), RCS 2003–, GMC 2004–; examiner: FRCS and MRCS 1993–99, Intercollegiate Bd of Examiners Orthopaedics 1994–, FRCSEd 2001–; instr Advanced Trauma Life Support course 1994–98, co-ordinator and designer Pan-European Fellowship Exam in Orthopaedics; jt course designer and teacher: Examining Conslts 1995, Educating Conslts 1995–, Changing the Culture 1997–, Dental Trainers 1997–, Appointments Ctee 1998, Preparing to be a Conslt 1998–, Univ Teachers 1998–; Royal Army Medical Corps 2007–; Sir Robert Menzies travelling fell 1981, Sir Herbert Seddon Orthopaedic Research Prize 1984, BOA European travelling fell 1986, Cutler's Prize for surgical instrument design 1986, Pres's medal Br Orthopaedic Research Soc 1987, ABC travelling fell 1988, AO travelling fell in trauma 1993; Hunterian prof RCS 1995; FRCS 1982, FRCSEd 1982, FRCS in Orthopaedics (FRCSOrth) 1992; *Publications* Oxford Textbook of Trauma and Orthopaedics (ed-in-chief, 2002), Bailey & Love Textbook of Surgery (sr co-ed, 25 edn 2006), Orthopaedics at a Glance (2007); *Recreations* sailing, gardening, ornithology, family activities; *Style*— Prof Christopher Bulstrode; ✉ Stream House, Mill Street, Stanton St John, Oxford OX33 1HQ (tel 01865 358554); John Radcliffe Hospital, Headington, Oxford OX3 9DU (tel 01865 220233, e-mail cjkb@gwmail.jr2.ox.ac.uk)

BUNBURY, *see also:* Richardson-Bunbury

BUNBURY, Sir Michael William; 13 Bt (E 1681), of Stanney Hall, Cheshire; KCVO (2005), DL (Suffolk 2004); s of Sir (John) William Napier Bunbury, 12 Bt (d 1985), and late Margaret Pamela, *née* Sutton; *b* 29 December 1946; *Educ* Eton, Trinity Coll Cambridge (MA); *m* 1976, Caroline Anne, da of Col Anthony Derek Swift Mangnall, OBE; 1 da (Katherine Rosemary b 1978), 2 s (Henry Michael Napier b 1980, Edward Peter b 1986); *Heir* s, Henry Bunbury; *Career* landowner and farmer (1100 acres), fin advsr; conslt Smith & Williamson 1997– (ptnr 1974–97, chm 1986–93); chm Duchy of Lancaster 2000–05 (memb Cncl 1993–2005); dir: Fleming High Income Investment Tst plc 1995–97, JP Morgan Fleming Claverhouse Investment Tst plc 1996– (chm 2005–), Foreign and Colonial Investment Tst plc 1998–; memb Exec Ctee CLA 1992–97 and 1999–2004; chm Taxation Ctee 1999–2003 (chm Suffolk Branch Ctee 1995–97); tstee Calthorpe Edgbaston Estate; pres Suffolk Agric Assoc 2000–02; High Sheriff Suffolk 2006–07; *Recreations* shooting; *Clubs* Boodle's; *Style*— Sir Michael Bunbury, Bt, KCVO, DL; ✉ Naunton Hall, Rendlesham, Woodbridge, Suffolk IP12 2RD (tel 01394 460235); 25 Moorgate, London EC2R 6AY (tel 020 7131 4000)

BUNCE, Charlie; s of Michael Bunce, of London, and Tina, *née* Sims; *b* 26 December 1962; *m* 1994, Corinne, *née* D'Souza; 2 da; *Career* tv prodr; *Television* incl: Esther, Holiday, That's Life!; series prodr: Watchdog, Weekend Watchdog, Mysteries, Living Dangerously; exec prodr This Morning 2001–02, exec ed The Granada Academy 2002–03, series ed Property Ladder 2003, exec prodr Grand Designs 2004, ed factual progs 2004; *Radio* prodn credits incl: Loose Ends, Midweek, Desert Island Discs, Woman's Hour; *Style*— Charlie Bunce, Esq; ✉ TalkbackThames, 77 Woodside Road, Amersham, Buckinghamshire HP6 6AA (e-mail charlie.bunce@talkbackthames.tv)

BUNCE, Michael John; OBE (2001); er s of Roland John Bunce, ARIBA (d 1977), and Dorie, *née* Woods (d 1992); *b* 24 April 1935; *Educ* St Paul's, Kingston Coll; *m* 1 April 1961, Tina, *née* Sims; 2 s (Charles b 1962, Rupert b 1966 d 1990), 2 da (Miranda b 1968, Arabella b 1970); *Career* Nat Serv RAF; joined BBC as engr, subsequently studio mangr; prodr: People and Politics (World Service), A Man Apart - The Murderer (BBC1), Minorities in Britain (BBC1), The Younger Generation (BBC1), Italy and the Italians (BBC1); dir Gallery; ed: The Money Programme (BBC2) 1968–70, Nationwide (BBC1) 1970–75; BBC TV: chief asst Current Affrs 1976–78 (also ed Tonight), head Information Servs TV 1978–82, head Information Div 1982–83, controller Information Servs 1983–91; exec dir RTS 1991–2000; dir IBC Ltd 1997–; memb Comité d'Honneur Int TV Symposium and Tech Exhbn Montreux 1995–99; memb: Francis Ctee 1977, EBU Working Pty Direct Elections 1978, Advsy Bd Centre for Media Performance and Communications UC Salford; chm Nat Industries PR Offrs 1991–92, chm Int Broadcasting Convention Bd 1999– (dir 1997–99); tstee Elizabeth R Fund; Shell International TV award 1969; Marshall Fund fell USA 1975; FRTS 1989; *Recreations* gardening, visiting interesting buildings, fishing; *Clubs* Century; *Style*— Michael Bunce, Esq, OBE; ✉ IBC, International Press Centre, 76 Shoe Lane, London EC4A 3JB (e-mail show@ibc.org)

BUNCE, Dr Ross John; s of Ross Frederick Bunce, DFC, of Gerrards Cross, Bucks, and Gwendoline Janet, *née* Fox; *b* 28 March 1948; *Educ* Kingsbury County GS, UCL (BSc, PhD); *m* 29 Dec 1972, Monique Irene, da of Pierre Roy; 2 s (Philippe Ross b 27 Oct 1978, John Marc Alexander b 26 April 1980); *Career* asst vice-pres Investment Management Bankers Trust Co London 1974–81; Merrill Lynch Investment Mangers (formerly Mercury Asset Management): dep chm 1989–2002, md 1998–2002; dir: Mercury Asset Management Holdings 1987, Mercury Asset Management plc 1987 (vice-chm 1991), Mercury Int Tst Ltd 1995; non-exec dir: INCAT plc, Rontech Ltd; AIIMR; *Recreations* squash, tennis, golf; *Clubs* Southgate Squash, Porters Park Golf, Hadley Wood Tennis, Hadley Wood Golf; *Style*— Dr Ross Bunce

BUNCH, Anthony William Samson; s of Dennis John Bunch (d 1989), of Ramsgate, Kent, and Francisca, *née* Schwam; *b* 8 February 1953; *Educ* Chatham House GS Ramsgate, Univ of Nottingham (BA); *m* June 1980, Alison Jane, da of Ralph Cordell; 2 da (Naomi Leah Rebecca b 21 Sept 1983, Sarah Marie b 25 June 1985), 2 s (Adam Samuel b 29 June 1987, Simon Daniel b 1 Oct 1991); *Career* Masons (now Pinsent Masons): articled 1976–78, admitted slr 1978, salaried ptnr 1978, equity ptnr 1982–, admitted slr Hong Kong 1985, sr resident ptnr Hong Kong Office 1985–90, fndr Alternative Dispute

Resolution (ADR) Unit 1990, managing ptnr 1991–97, world-wide managing ptnr 1997–2002, bd memb, ptnr Int and Energy Dept; rep various professional bodies in dispute resolution; accreditied mediator CEDR; memb: ADR Ctee Chartered Inst of Arbitrators, Departmental Advsy Ctee on New Arbitration Act, Int Advsy Bd Arbitration Inst of Stockholm C of C; MACIArb; *Publications* National Report on Hong Kong in International Handbook on Commercial Arbitration (co-author), Handbook of Arbitration Practice (co-author); *Recreations* antiques, playing saxophone, theatre and the arts; *Style*— Anthony Bunch, Esq; ✉ Pinsent Masons, 30 Aylesbury Street, London EC1R 0ER (tel 020 7490 4000, fax 020 7490 2545, direct tel 020 7490 6216, direct fax 020 7490 6201)

BUNDY, Prof Alan Richard; s of Stanley Alfred Bundy (d 1994), and Joan Margaret Bundy; *b* 18 May 1947; *Educ* Heston Secdy Modern, Springgrove GS, Univ of Leicester (BSc, PhD); *m* 23 Sept 1967, Josephine, da of John Maule; 1 da (Rachel b 26 Nov 1970); *Career* tutorial asst Univ of Leicester 1970–71; Univ of Edinburgh: research fell 1971–74, lectr 1974–84, reader 1984–87, professorial fell 1987–90, prof 1990–, head of Div of Informatics 1998–2001; SPL Insight Award 1986; IJCAI Distinguished Service Award 2003, IJCAI Research Excellence Award 2007, CADE Herbrand Award 2007; fell American Assoc for Artificial Intelligence 1990, fell Artificial Intelligence and Simulation of Behaviour 1997–, fell European Coordinating Ctee for Artificial Intelligence 1999, FRSE 1996, FBCS 2002, FIEE 2005; *Books* Artificial Intelligence: An Introductory Course (1978), The Computer Modelling of Mathematical Reasoning (1983), The Catalogue of Artificial Intelligence (1984), Eco-Logic: Logic based approaches to ecological modelling (1991), Rippling: Meta-Level Guidance for Mathematical Reasoning (jtly, 2005); *Recreations* beer making, valley walking; *Style*— Prof Alan Bundy, FRSE; ✉ School of Informatics, University of Edinburgh, Appleton Tower, Edinburgh EH8 9LE (tel 0131 650 2716, fax 0131 650 6513, e-mail a.bundy@ed.ac.uk)

BUNDY, Christopher; *b* 7 October 1945; *Educ* Cheshunt GS; *m* 8 Aug 1970, Wendy Constance; 1 s (Dominic b 1973), 2 da (Phillipa b 1975, Prudence b 1979); *Career* CA; gp fin accountant Caravans Int Ltd, fin dir Subsidiary Lex Service Group plc; chm: E J Arnold and Sons Ltd, GRUK Ltd; md: Waterstones Glassware Ltd, Nice-Pak Int Ltd; dir: Hollis Bros & ESA Ltd, Pergammon Pres Ltd; currently freelance co doctor; *Recreations* wine, computers; *Style*— Christopher Bundy, Esq; ✉ e-mail christopher@bundy.co.uk

BUNKER, Prof Christopher Barry; s of Dr Nigel Vincent Delahunty Bunker, MBE (d 1967), and Joy, *née* Bolsover; *b* 22 November 1956; *Educ* Wycliffe Coll (top scholar), St Catharine's Coll Cambridge (Kitchener scholar, MA, MD, Sir Walter Langdon Brown Prize), Westminster Med Sch London (Kitchener scholar, MB BS); *m* 1991, Anna Christina, yst da of Dr J Kurowski, of Hull; 2 da (Minette b 1992, Matilda b 1995); *Career* currently: consIt dermatologist Chelsea & Westminster Hosp, Royal Marsden Hosp, St Luke's Hosp for the Clergy and King Edward VII Hosp for Officers, prof Imperial Coll Sch of Med London; Sir Jules Thorn res fell 1988–90, Gold Award American Acad of Dermatology (Historical Poster section) 1991, Bristol Cup Br Assoc of Dermatologists 1998, John Thornton Ingram Lecture RCP 2001; MRCS, FRCP; *Publications* author of numerous original papers and articles; *Style*— Prof Christopher Bunker; ✉ King Edward VII Hospital, Beaumont Street, London W1G 6AA (tel 020 7794 5943)

BUNKER, Christopher Jonathan; s of Jonathan William Bunker, and Beryl Kathleen Rose, *née* Wood; *b* 16 December 1946; *Educ* Ilford County HS, KCL; *m* 9 Sept 1972, Julia Doris, da of Arthur James Seymour Russell (d 1954); 2 da (Jennifer b 1978, Elizabeth b 1982); *Career* accountant; fin dir Westland Group plc 1987–96, gp fin dir Tarmac plc 1996–2000, gp fin dir Thames Water plc (latterly Water Div RWE AG) 2000–04; non-exec dir: DS Smith plc 2003–, Travis Perkins plc 2004–, Xansa plc 2006–; formerly non-exec dir: Mowlem plc, Baltimore Technologies plc; *Style*— Christopher Bunker, Esq

BUNKER, Very Rev Michael; *b* 22 July 1937; *Educ* Benjamin Adlard Sch Gainsborough, Acton and Brunel Colls London, Oak Hill Theol Coll Southgate; *m* Mary Helena, *née* Poulten; *Career* asst curate: St James's Alperton Middx 1963–66, St Helens Parish Church St Helens Merseyside (curate-in-charge daughter church St Andrew's) 1966–70; vicar: St Matthew's Muswell Hill London 1970–78, St James's Muswell Hill 1978–92; area dean W Haringey 1985–90, preb St Paul's Cathedral London 1990–92, dean of Peterborough Cathedral 1992–2006 (dean emeritus 2006–); memb: Edmonton Area Synod 1982–92, Diocesan (London) Synod 1985–91, Area Bishop's Cncl 1985–91, C of E Evangelical Cncl 1991–92, Diocesan (London) Fin Ctee 1992; chm Edmonton Area Evangelical Fellowship 1989–91, chm Diocesan (Peterborough) Cncl for Evangelism 1995–96; chm Peterborough Tourism 1996–98; chm Govrs: St James's CE Primary Sch 1978–92, King's Sch Peterborough 1992–97 (vice-chm 1997–); govr St David & St Katharine's C of E Comp Sch 1985–90; tstee: Oakham Sch 1992–2006, Uppingham Sch 1992–2006, Habitat for Humanity GB 1999–2002 (chm), Nat Kidney Research Fund 1999–2002; fundraising conslt 2006–; *Publications* The Church on the Hill (St James's Church, 1988), Ten Growing Churches (contrib); *Recreations* fly fishing; *Style*— The Very Rev Michael Bunker; ✉ Haffan Ddiogel, 69 Puffin Way, Broad Haven, Pembrokeshire SA62 3HP (e-mail mandmbbythesea@btinternet.com)

BUNNEY, John Herrick; OBE (1997); *b* 2 June 1945; *m* Pamela Anne Simcock; 1 s (b 1973), 1 da (b 1976); *Career* second sec FCO 1971–73, MECAS 1971–73, first sec Damascus 1974–78, FCO 1978–80, dep head of mission and consul Sana'a 1981–83, FCO 1983–87, first sec (political) Tunis 1987–90, FCO 1990–93, cnsllr Riyadh 1993–97, FCO 1997–2000, advsr Dept of Safeguards IAEA Vienna 2000–03, co dir 2004–; *Clubs* Savile, Royal Blackheath Golf; *Style*— John H Bunney, Esq, OBE

BUNTON, Christopher John; s of John Bunton, and Marion Helen, *née* Gotobed; *b* 22 February 1948; *Educ* Charterhouse, Trinity Coll Cambridge (MA), London Grad Sch of Business Studies (MBA); *m* 10 May 1975, Jane Melanie, da of Anthony J S Cartmell; 2 s (Anthony, Michael); *Career* with Gulf Oil Corp 1973–1985, gp treas Cordiant plc (previously Saatchi & Saatchi plc) 1986–97, dir Westcape Corporate Finance 1998–; tstee and treas Ataxia UK; vice-pres ACT 2001; *Recreations* music; *Clubs* Hawks' (Cambridge); *Style*— Christopher Bunton, Esq; ✉ Westcape Corporate Finance, 12 The Chowns, West Common, Harpenden, Hertfordshire AL5 2BN (tel 01582 769543, e-mail cbunton@westcape.co.uk)

BUONAGUIDI, David Mervyn; s of Gianfranco Buonaguidi, of Esher, Surrey, and Karen, *née* Petersen; *b* 13 August 1964; *Educ* City of London Freemans' Sch Ashtead Surrey, Epsom Sch of Art and Design Epsom Surrey (DATEC graphics); *Career* advtg art dir: TBWA 1984–85, Wight Collins Rutherford Scott 1985–88, Howell Henry Chaldecott Lury 1988–91, J Walter Thompson 1991–92, Howell Henry Chaldecott Lury 1992–93; jt creative dir St Luke's (formerly Chiat/Day) 1993–98, creative dir Channel Four TV Corporation 1998–2000, co-fndr and creative dir Karmarama Ltd 2000–; *Style*— David Buonaguidi, Esq

BURBECK, John; QPM (1999); *Educ* Devonport HS Plymouth, Univ of Leeds (BSc); *m* 1992, Karie; 3 s (Matthew, William, James), 1 da (Katherine); *Career* PC Met Police 1972; W Mercia Constabulary: Asst Chief Constable 1994–98, Dep Chief Constable 1998–2000; Chief Constable Warks Police 2000–06; ACPO: head of criminal justice systems business area 2001–05, head of criminal justice system IT portfolio 2002–06; business conslt 2006–; chair Police Sailing Section, skipper Force Sailing Team, treas Police Sport UK; FCMI (FIMgt) 1995; *Recreations* skiing; *Clubs* VSCC; *Style*— John Burbeck, Esq, QPM; ✉ tel 07747 766028, e-mail john@burbeck.biz

BURCH, Geoff; *Career* 'alternative business guru', conslt, business speaker, lectr and advsr to top companies on business issues and practices; devised tailor-made business trg progs to suit individual needs of companies and products; worked with wide range of staff from banks and multi-nationals to small and medium enterprises; *Books* Resistance is Useless - The Art of Business Persuasion (1995), Go it Alone! (1997), Writing on the Wall (2002), The Way of the Dog: The Art of Making Success Inevitable (2005); *Style*— Geoff Burch, Esq; ✉ c/o Speakers for Business, 1–2 Pudding Lane, London EC3R 8AB (tel 020 7929 5559, fax 020 7929 5558, e-mail geoff.burch@sfb.com, website www.sfb.com)

BURCHELL, Andrew; s of Joseph Fredrick Burchell, of Carshalton, Surrey, and Myrtle Miriam, *née* Bown; *b* 26 March 1955; *Educ* Wallington Co GS for Boys, LSE (BSc(Econ), MSc); *m* 1974, Susan Margaret, *née* Hewing; 1 da (Emma Elizabeth b 1980), 1 s (Matthew Thomas b 1982); *Career* economist DHSS 1976–82, econ advsr NAO 1982–84, various posts Dept of Health 1984–90; Dept of Tport: head Railways Econ Div 1990–96, dir Strategy and Analysis 1996–97, head of profession for Dept's economists 1995–97, memb Bd Central Tport Gp 1996–97; dir Tport Strategy DETR 1997–98, dir Environmental Protection Strategy DETR 1998–; author various articles on application of econ to health policy issues; *Recreations* music, watching football, playing golf; *Style*— Andrew Burchell, Esq

BURCHELL, Prof Brian; s of Kenneth and Grace Burchell; *b* 1 October 1946; *Educ* Univ of St Andrews (BSc), Univ of Dundee (PhD); *m* 1973, Ann, *née* Kinsella; 1 s (Colin James b 1978), 1 da (Karen Jane b 1982); *Career* post doctoral research fell Univ of Dundee 1972–74, lectr in biochemistry Loughborough Univ 1974–75; Univ of Dundee: lectr in biochemistry 1976–78, Wellcome Tst research leave fell 1978–80, Wellcome Tst sr lectr in biochemistry 1980–88, head of biomedical medicine 1988–96, prof of med biochemistry 1988–, head of molecular and cellular pathology 1999–; Ninewells Hosp Dundee: clinical dir of biochemical med 1990–96, dir human genetics 1996–; hon prof of biochemistry Univ of St Andrews 1991–; Morton J Rodman distinguished lectr in pharmacology Rutgers Univ USA 1994; ACB Fndn Award 1997; chm Int Scientific Advsy Ctee ISSX 1997; pres Euro Soc of Biochemical Pharmacology 2000–; FRCPath 1997, FRSE 1997; *Publications* author of more than 200 papers and reviews in learned jls; *Recreations* golf; *Clubs* Scots Craig GC; *Style*— Prof Brian Burchell, FRSE; ✉ Department of Molecular & Cellular Pathology, Ninewells Medical School, Dundee University, Dundee DD1 9SY (tel 01382 632164, fax 01382 633952, e-mail b.burchell@dundee.ac.uk)

BURDEN, Sir Anthony Thomas; kt (2002), QPM (1995); s of Thomas Edward Burden (d 1996), of Salisbury, Wilts, and Nora, *née* Dowding (d 2003); *b* 28 January 1950; *Educ* St Thomas Sch Salisbury, Open Univ (BSc); *m* 30 Aug 1971, Beryl Myra, *née* Hill; 2 da (Sharon Ann b 26 March 1973, Suzanne Louise b 14 Feb 1982), 1 s (Paul Anthony b 5 Aug 1975); *Career* Constable rising to Detective Chief Supt Wilts Constabulary 1969–89, Asst Chief Constable and Dep Chief Constable W Mercia Constabulary 1989–94, Chief Constable Gwent Police 1994–96, Chief Constable S Wales Police 1996–2003, ret; panel memb Morris Enquiry 2004; non-exec dep chm Reliance Secure Task Mgmnt 2005–, non-exec dep chm Reliance Security Services Ltd 2005–, non-exec dir Reliance Scotland Ltd 2006–; pres ACPO 2000–01, former vice-pres Police Mutual Assurance Soc, former co-dir Police Extended Interviews; life vice-pres Police Sport UK (former chm Police Athletic Assoc), memb Visiting Panel of Experts Police Assistance Mission of EC to Albania (PAMECA) 2005–; tstee Br Police Symphony Orch; Hon Dr Glamorgan Univ 2004; CCMI 2002; SBStJ 1998; *Recreations* cycling, walking, gardening; *Style*— Sir Anthony Burden, QPM; ✉ c/o South Wales Police, Police Headquarters, Cowbridge Road, Bridgend CF31 3SU (tel 01656 869200, fax 01656 869209, e-mail swp.execsupport@boltblue.com)

BURDEN, Richard; MP; s of late Kenneth Burden, and late Pauline Burden; *b* 1 September 1954; *Educ* Wallasey Tech GS, Bramhall Comp Sch, St John's Coll of FE Manchester, Univ of York (BA), Univ of Warwick (MA); *m* Jane Slowey; 2 step da, 1 step s; *Career* pres York Univ Students' Union 1976–77, dist offr W Midlands Dist NALGO 1981–92 (branch organiser N Yorks branch 1979–81); Parly candidate (Lab) Meriden 1987, MP (Lab) Birmingham Northfield 1992–, PPS to Jeff Rooker, MP, as Food Safety min then Pensions min 1997–2001, advsr on motorsport to min of state for Sport (Richard Caborn, MP) 2002–; memb House of Commons Euro Standing Ctee 1996–97, chm All-Pty Parly Gp on Electoral Reform 1997–, chm All-Pty Parly Motor Gp 1998–; chair Br-Palestine All-Pty Gp 2001–; sec: All-Pty Parly Water Gp 1994–97, PLP Trade and Indust Ctee 1996–97 (vice-chm 1995–96); chair Lab Campaign for Electoral Reform 1996–98 (vice-chair 1998–); fndr sec Jt Action on Water Services (JAWS) to oppose water privatisation 1985–90; chm Birmingham Gp of Lab MPs, vice-chair Lab Middle East Cncl 1995–96, fndr memb Bedale Lab Pty 1980; memb: W Midlands Regnl Assembly, Trade and Industry Select Ctee 2001–05, Int Devpt Select Ctee 2005–, Socialist Environment and Resources Assoc, Socialist Health Assoc, Lab Housing Gp, Fabian Soc, Co-op Pty, Electoral Reform Soc; *Recreations* motor racing, travel, cinema, reading, food; *Clubs* Kingshurst Lab, Austin Sports and Social, Austin Branch British Legion, 750 Motor; *Style*— Richard Burden, Esq, MP; ✉ House of Commons, London SW1A 0AA (tel 020 7219 2318, fax 020 7219 2170, constituency office 0121 475 9295, fax 0121 476 2400, e-mail burdenr@parliament.uk, website www.richardburden.com)

BURDEN, Roger Francis; s of Henry Burden (d 1974), of Bristol, and Rosalind, *née* Wiggins (d 1992); *b* 3 June 1946; *Educ* Cheltenham Tech HS; *m* 19 Sept 1970, Julie Ann, da of James Hopkins; 2 s (Stephen Paul b 22 June 1974, Peter David b 19 Jan 1977); *Career* Martins Bank Ltd 1963–67; Dowty Rotol Ltd 1967–69; Cheltenham & Gloucester plc (formerly Cheltenham & Gloucester Building Soc): various appts 1969–89, exec dir 1989–96, md 1997–2003, chm 2003–05; chm Cncl of Mortgage Lenders 2000–01, dir Lawyers Inc; memb Cncl Football Assoc, govr Bournside Comp Sch and Sixth Form Centre; Hon PhD Univ of Glos 2003; MBCS 1975, FCBSI 1987 (ACBSI 1982), FCIB 1993; *Recreations* football (chm Glos FA); *Style*— Roger Burden, Esq

BURDETT, Sir Savile Aylmer; 11 Bt (E 1665), of Burthwaite, Yorks; s of Sir Henry Aylmer Burdett, 10 Bt, MC (d 1943); *b* 24 September 1931; *Educ* Wellington, Imperial Coll London; *m* 1962, June Elizabeth Campbell, o da of late Dr James Mackay Rutherford, of Knowl Hill, Surrey; 1 da (Felicity Susan b 1963), 1 s (Crispin Peter b 8 Feb 1967); *Heir* s, Crispin Burdett; *Career* late temporary Sub-Lt RNVR; md Rapaway Energy Ltd 1977–99, ret; *Style*— Sir Savile Burdett, Bt; ✉ 2 Knapp Cottages, Gore Lane, Kilmington, Devon EX13 7NU (tel 0129 734200, e-mail savileburdett@tiscali.co.uk)

BURDON, (Gerald) Desmond Patrick; s of Dr David Joseph Burdon (d 1987), and Kathrine, *née* O'Reilly (d 1986); *b* 12 June 1956; *Educ* Notre Dame Int Sch Rome, Poly of NE London; *m* 28 Dec 2001, Pauline, *née* McCoy; *Career* photographer; numerous int clients; memb Assoc of Photographers (former chm Awards Ctee 1984–89 and vice-chm Cncl); *Awards* Ilford Advtg Photographer of the Year, Kodak Calendar Award, AOP awards 1997, 1999, 2000 and 2001; *Style*— Desmond Burdon; ✉ website www.desmondburdon.com

BURDON, Prof Roy Hunter; s of Ian Murray Burdon (d 1956), and Rose Carnegie Burdon (d 1962); *b* 27 April 1938; *Educ* Glasgow Acad, Univ of St Andrews (BSc), Univ of Glasgow (PhD); *m* 4 Sept 1962, Margery Grace; 2 s (Ian J, Keith A); *Career* Univ of Glasgow: asst lectr 1959–63, lectr 1964–68, sr lectr 1968–74, reader in biochemistry 1974–77, titular prof in biochemistry 1977–89; post doctorate and res fell Univ of NY 1963–64, guest prof of microbiology Polytechnical Univ of Denmark Copenhagen 1977–78, prof of molecular biology Univ of Strathclyde 1985–97 (chm Dept of Bioscience and Biotechnology 1986–88, prof emeritus 1997–); chm: Br Coordinating Ctee Biotechnol 1991–93, Scientific Advsy Ctee European Fedn of Biotechnology 1991; The Biochemical Soc: hon meetings sec 1981–85, hon gen sec 1985–89, chm 1989–92; treas European Soc for Free Radical Research 1994–97; govr W of Scotland Coll of Agric; FIBiol 1987, FRSE

1975; *Books* RNA Biosynthesis (1976), Molecular Biology of DNA Methylation (1985), Free Radical Damage and its Control (1994), Genes and the Environment (1999), The Suffering Gene (2003), Menace sur nos Gènes (2005); *Recreations* painting (group and one-person exhbns), golf, clarinet/saxophone playing in local orchestras (memb Strathendrick Singers); *Style*— Prof Roy Burdon, FRSE; ✉ 28 Station Road, Killearn G63 9NY (tel 01360 551726)

BURDON-COOPER, Alan Ruthven; s of Sqdn-Ldr Ruthven Hayne Burdon-Cooper (d 1970), of Radlett, Herts, and Anna (Nan) Kathleen Beverley, *née* Farquharson (d 1992); *b* 27 June 1942; *Educ* Oundle, Emmanuel Coll Cambridge (MA, LLB); *m* 2 Sept 1967, Virginia Louise, da of Archibald George Mobsby (d 1989), of Radlett, Herts; 1 s (John Ruthven b 1968 d 1993), 1 da (Sarah b 1970); *Career* admitted slr 1968; ptnr Collyer-Bristow (sr ptnr 1985–94); life memb Cambridge Union; govr Rose Bruford Coll 1992–; Liveryman Worshipful Co of Dyers; memb Law Soc 1968; *Recreations* sport, music, gardening, philately; *Style*— Alan Burdon-Cooper, Esq; ✉ Nettleden Farm, Nettleden, Hemel Hempstead, Hertfordshire HP1 3DQ (tel 01442 872072); Collyer-Bristow Solicitors, 4 Bedford Row, London WC1R 4DF (tel 020 7468 7209, fax 020 7405 0555, e-mail alan.burdon-cooper@collyerbristow.com, website www.collyerbristow.com)

BURDUS, (Julia) Ann; CBE (2003); da of Gladstone Beaty (d 1966), of Alnwick, Northumberland, and Julia Wilhamena Charlton, *née* Booth (d 1988); *b* 4 September 1933; *Educ* Univ of Durham (BA); *m* 1, 1956 (m dis 1961), William Ramsay Burdus; m 2, 11 June 1981, Ian Buchanan Robertson (d 1996); *Career* clinical psychologist 1956–60, research exec Mather & Crowther 1961–67, research dir Garland Compton (later Compton Partners) 1967–71, research dir McCann Erickson 1971–75, vice-chm McCann UK 1975–77, sr vice-pres McCann International 1977–79, chm McCann & Co 1979–81, dir strategic planning Interpublic Group of Cos 1981–83, dir AGB Research plc 1983–89, sr vice-pres mktg and communications Olympia & York Canary Wharf Ltd 1989–92; pt/t dir: Civil Aviation Authy 1992–96, Dawson International plc 1992–98; dir: Next plc 1993–, BEM Ltd 1992–95, Safeway plc 1993–99, Prudential Corporation plc 1996–2003; chm Advertising Assoc 1980–81; memb: NEDC 1984–88, Top Salaries Review Bd 1990–94, Ctee Automobile Association 1995–99, Cncl IOD 1995–2002; *Recreations* home building; *Style*— Miss Ann Burdus, CBE

BURFORD, Earl of; Charles Francis Topham de Vere Beauclerk; does not use courtesy title; s and h of 14 Duke of St Albans, *qv*; *b* 22 February 1965; *Educ* Sherborne, Hertford Coll Oxford; *m* 29 Dec 1994 (m dis 2001), Louise Ann Beatrice Fiona, eldest da of Col Malcolm Vernon Robey; 1 s (James Malcolm Aubrey Edward de Vere (does not use courtesy title) b 2 Aug 1995); *Career* pres and fndr De Vere Soc; tstee: Shakespearian Authorship Tst, Stringer Lawrence Meml Tst; appointed vice-chm (jt) The Royal Stuart Soc 1989; pres Shakespeare Oxford Soc 1995–97; Parly candidate (Democratic Party) Kensington & Chelsea by-election 1999; Liveryman Worshipful Co of Drapers; *Publications* Nell Gwyn: A Biography (2005); *Style*— Charles Beauclerk; ✉ e-mail charlesbeauclerk@aol.com

BURFORD, Dr Robert John; s of Robert John Burford, of Welham Green, Herts, and Grace Violet, *née* Piacentini; *b* 29 January 1941; *Educ* East Barnet GS, King's Coll London (BSc, PhD); *m* 2 March 1968, (Stephanie) Kaye, da of Ernest James Woodley, of Rugby, Warks; 1 da (Tracey b 1969), 2 s (David b 1970, Paul b 1972); *Career* OR analyst NCB 1965–66, conslt GPS Sciences Ltd 1966–71, divnl dir Software Sciences Ltd 1980–82 (princ conslt 1971–80), dir ASYST Systems Consultants Ltd 1982–83, sr mangr Perkin-Elmer Data Systems 1983–85, tech dir Data Logic Ltd 1985–96, princ conslt OSI Group 1997–2001, exec conslt Xansa 2001–06, managing conslt Vega 2006–07; MBCS 1974, MORS 1968, CEng 1991; *Recreations* American square dancing, travelling; *Style*— Dr Robert J Burford; ✉ 8 Winding Wood Drive, Camberley, Surrey GU15 1ER (tel 01276 28397, e-mail robert.burford@gmail.com)

BURGE, Prof Ronald Edgar; s of John Henry Burge, and Edith Beatrice, *née* Thompson; *b* 3 October 1932; *Educ* Canton HS Cardiff, KCL (BSc, PhD, FKC), Univ of London (DSc); *m* 1953, Janet Mary, *née* Pitts; 2 s; *Career* KCL: asst lectr in physics 1954–58, lectr in physics 1958–62, reader in biophysics 1962–63, prof of physics and head Dept of Physics 1984–92 (prof of physics and head Dept of Physics Queen Elizabeth Coll 1963–84), dean Faculty of Mathematics and Physical Sci 1985–87, Wheatstone prof of physics 1989–2001; dir of research in x-ray imaging (Leverhulme Tst grant) Univ of Cambridge 1994–98; Nanyang prof of electrical engrg Nanyang Technological Univ Singapore 2000–01; life memb Clare Hall Cambridge 1993 (visiting fell 1992); memb: Bd of Mgmnt Univ of London Computer Centre 1968–74, Planning Sub-Ctee and Univ Central Coordinating (Computing) 1968–90, Starlink Ctee SERC 1978–82, Computer Bd for Univs and Res Cncls (invited by Min of State for Educn and Sci) 1978–82, Swinnerton-Dyer Ctee 1979–82, Synchrotron Radiation Ctee SERC 1982–86, Computer Policy Ctee Univ of London (chm Networking Sub-Ctee) 1987–90, Cncl King's Coll (vice-princ 1987–91), King's Coll Fin and Gen Purposes Ctee 1987–91; chm: Coll Computing Ctee 1968–93, Computer Users Ctee Univ of London 1968–73, Computer Planning Sub-Ctee Univ of London 1974–78; chm Bd of Examiners for DSc in Physics Univ of London 1990–2000; author of papers in sci jls on theory of scattering (electrons, x-rays and radar) and devpt in electron microscopy and x-ray microscopy Rodman Medal RPS 1993, Daiwa Award for X-Ray Lasers 1994; MRI 1988; CPhys, FInstP, fell Microscopical Soc; *Style*— Prof Ronald Burge; ✉ 5 Toft Lane, Great Wilbraham, Cambridge CB1 5JH (tel 01223 881378)

BURGE, Prof (Peter) Sherwood; OBE (2005); s of Graham Mowbray Burge (d 1974), and Anne Elizabeth, *née* Batt; *b* 8 July 1944; *Educ* Lancing, Royal Free Hosp Sch of Med, London Sch of Hygiene & Tropical Med (MB BS, MSc, MD); *m* 18 Aug 1968, Dr Anne Willard, da of Canon James Stanley Willard (d 1988), Essex; 2 s (Cedd b 1974, Chad b 1977); *Career* lectr in Dept of Clinical Immunology Cardiothoracic Inst London 1976–80, conslt physician Solihull Hosp 1980–93, conslt chest physician Birmingham Heartlands Hosp 1980–, dir Occupational Lung Disease Unit Birmingham 1980–; prof of occupational med Univ of Birmingham; chm of Sci Ctee on ISOLDE trial in COPD; numerous sci pubns on: occupational lung diseases, indoor air quality and sick building syndrome, asthma and bronchitis; temporary advsr to WHO, NATO and EEC on indoor air quality and occupational lung disease; memb Acad of Indoor Air Science 1997; MRCS 1969, MFOM 1984, FRCP 1985, FFOM 1991, FRCPEd 2002; *Recreations* punt racing, skiing, brass rubbing, playing the recorder; *Style*— Prof Sherwood Burge, OBE; ✉ Birmingham Heartlands Hospital, Bordesley Green East, Birmingham B9 5SS (tel 0121 424 2000, fax 0121 772 0292, e-mail sherwood.burge@heartofengland.nhs.uk)

BURGESS, (Thomas Lionel) Ashley; s of Harry Severs Burgess (d 1953), and Marjorie, *née* Raines (d 1982); *b* 24 May 1933, Thornton-le-Dale, N Yorks; *Educ* Shrewsbury; *m* 19 April 1958, Margaret Gillian, *née* Naylor; 2 da (Victoria Jane b 30 July 1959, Sara Gillian b 22 Feb 1961); *Career* Nat Serv cmmnd RNVR Seatime HMS Indefatigable, HMS Leeds Castle; dir Criddle-Burgess Feeds Ltd 1969–1987, dir Whitegate Leisure plc, fndr and chm Burgess Group plc; former memb Nat Cncl and NE chm UK Agricultural Trade Assoc; memb Scarborough Hosps Ctee 1960–69, vice-chm N Yorks HA 1992–95, chm Scarborough and NE Yorks NHS Tst 1995–97; pres Royal Soc of St George 1979–85, govr Merchant Adventurers City of York 1989–99, memb Ct Univ of York 2000–; chm Macmillan Nurse Appeal Scarborough and Ryedale; benefactor: RNLI (Walmer Lifeboat "James Burgess"), Univ of York (James Burgess scholarships); tstee Ocean Youth Tst NE, memb Campaign Bd Rotunda Museum 2005–06; pres Ryedale Cons Assoc 2003–07 (chm 1990–93), memb Yorks Cons Business Cncl; *Recreations* sailing, shooting, tennis, golf, reading heavyweight books; *Clubs* Farmers, Ganton Golf, Royal Naval Sailing Assoc; *Style*— Ashley Burgess, Esq

BURGESS, James Christopher Appleyard; s of Christopher Gerald Burgess, of Suffolk, and Bridget Vaughan, *née* Parry-Jones; *b* 7 July 1957, Colchester, Essex; *Educ* Radley, Coll of Law Lancaster Gate; *m* 6 June 1980, Penelope, *née* Jacobs; 2 s (Benjamin, Toby (triplets) b 24 Sept 1987), 1 da (Tabitha (triplet) b 24 Sept 1987); *Career* admitted slr 1981; Bolton and Lowe 1977–81, Plummer & Co 1981–85, Plummer Gilsey & Ptnrs 1985–89, Burgess Cheves & Ptnrs 1985–87, Pitmans 1989–; memb Law Soc; *Recreations* shooting, tennis, skiing; *Clubs* Leander; *Style*— James Burgess, Esq; ✉ Magpie Farm, Yattendon, Berkshire RG18 8XX (tel 01635 200440); Pitmans, 47 Castle Street, Reading, Berkshire RG1 7SR (tel 0118 958 0224, fax 0118 958 5997, e-mail jburgess@pitmans.com)

BURGESS, Rear Adm John; CB (1987), LVO (1975); s of Albert Burgess (d 1957), of Coventry, Warks, and Winifred, *née* Evans; *b* 13 July 1929; *Educ* RNEC, RNC Greenwich (advanced engrg); *m* 21 June 1952, Avis, da of William Johnson-Morgan (d 1953), of Coventry, Warks; 2 da (Sara b 14 Jan 1958, Jenny (Mrs Andersson) b 6 Aug 1960); *Career* RN Serv 1945–; HMS: Aisne, Maidstone, Theseus, Implacable, Cumberland, Caprice; cmmnd 1952, lectr in Thermodynamics RNEC 1962–65, HMS Victorious, appt Cdr 1968, nuclear design and manufacture Rolls Royce 1968–70, naval staff Washington DC 1970–72, Royal Yacht Britannia 1972–75, head Forward Design Gp Ship Dept 1975–77, appt Capt 1976, naval asst to Controller Navy 1977–79, OC HMS Defiance 1979–81, OC HMS Sultan 1981–83, appt Adm 1983, md HM Docky Rosyth 1984–87; dir: Rolls Royce 1987– (special projects, business devpt), Rolls Royce Nuclear Ltd, Rolls Royce and Associates Ltd; contrib various papers for professional socs and periodicals; memb: naval charities, local church socs, conservation socs; Hon Freeman New Orleans 1974; CEng, FIMechE, FIMarE; *Recreations* sailing, golf, music, theatre; *Clubs* Cawsand Bay Sailing (pres), Rame Gig (vice-pres); *Style*— Rear Adm John Burgess, CB, LVO; ✉ Bay House, Combe Park Close, Cawsand, Cornwall PL10 1PW

BURGESS, Keith; OBE (2004); s of W H (Bert) Burgess, of Bargoed, Rhymney Valley; *b* 1 September 1946; *Educ* Lewis Sch for Boys Pengam, Univ of Bristol (BSc, PhD, LLD); *m* Dr Pat Burgess; 2 da (b 1972 and 1976); *Career* Andersen Consulting: joined 1971, managing ptnr UK and Ireland 1989–94, worldwide managing ptnr 1994–99, sr UK ptnr 2000; exec chm QA plc 2000–05 (chm 2005–06), chm Bearing Point Europe 2006–; vice-chm HM Treasury Public Services Productivity Panel 2000–06; pres Mgmnt Consultancies Assoc 1994–95; past chm Corporate Action for the Homeless, patron Univ of Bristol Campaign for Resources 1991–2001; Master Guild of Mgmnt Consultants 1998–99, Liveryman Worshipful Co of Info Technologists; FIMC; *Clubs* Reform; *Style*— Keith Burgess, Esq, OBE

BURGESS, Melvin; s of Chris Burgess, of Haworth, and Helen Burgess; *b* 25 April 1954; *Children* 1 s (Oliver b 26 April 1989), 1 da (Pearl b 15 June 1991); *Career* children's writer; various jobs incl: bus conductor, brick layer, fndr own business (marbling onto fabric for fashion indust); memb Soc of Authors 1991; *Books* Cry of the Wolf (1990), Burning Issy (1992), An Angel for May (1992), The Baby and Fly Pie (1993), Loving April (1994), The Earth Giant (1994), Tiger, Tiger (1996), Junk (1996, Guardian Award for Children's Fiction 1996, Library Assoc Carnegie Medal 1997, shortlisted Whitbread Children's Book Award 1997), Kite (1997), The Copper Treasure (1998), Bloodtide (1999), Old Bag (1999), The Ghost Behind the Wall (2000), Billy Elliot (2001, novelisation of the film), Lady (2001), Doing It (2003); *Recreations* walking, nature, cooking; *Style*— Melvin Burgess

BURGESS, Michael John Clement; s of David Clement Burgess (d 1966), and Dr Ethne Nannette Moira Barnwall, *née* Ryan (d 2002), of Kingston upon Thames; *b* 31 March 1946; *Educ* Beaumont Coll, KCL; *m* 31 July 1971, Catherine Vivian, da of late Vivian John Du Veluz Gout, of Mulhausen, Germany; 2 da (Alexandra b 1974, Nicola b 1976), 1 s (Peter b 1980); *Career* admitted slr 1970; conslt McNamara Ryan Weybridge 1986– (ptnr 1972–86), coroner Surrey 1986– (asst dep coroner 1979–86), coroner of the Royal Household 2002– (dep coroner 1991–2002); sec Coroners Soc of England and Wales 1993–2003 (asst sec 1991–93), pres SE England Coroners Soc 1990–91; pres West Surrey Law Soc 1985–86 (hon treas 1979–84), memb Catholic Union 1974–, chm Fin Ctee and memb Parish Cncl St Francis de Sales RC Church Hampton 1974–, helper (formerly gp ldr and regnl chm) Handicapped Children's Pilgrimage Tst, advsr to several local charities and trusts; Freeman: City of London, Worshipful Co of Feltmakers 1967; memb: Law Soc 1970, Coroners' Soc; *Recreations* reading, art, music, gardening; *Clubs* Surrey Law; *Style*— Michael Burgess, Esq; ✉ c/o McNamara Ryan, Ashburton House, 3 Monument Green, Weybridge, Surrey KT13 8QR (tel 01932 846041, fax 01932 857709)

BURGESS, (David) Patrick Henry; MBE (2002); s of David Clement Burgess (d 1966), and Dr Ethne Nanette Burgess, *née* Ryan (d 2002); *b* 31 October 1944, Cheam, Surrey; *Educ* Beaumont Coll, Gonville & Caius Coll Cambridge (MA); *m* 1994, Margaret Ann, *née* Mosey; by previous m, 2 s (Barnaby b 1971, Edmund b 1973), 1 da (Elizabeth b 1976); *Career* admitted slr 1972; with Gouldens 1972–2003 (sr ptnr 1997–2003), ptnr Jones Day 2003–04; non-exec dir: Strand Partners Ltd 1994–, First Technology plc 1997–2006 (sr dir), Liberty Int plc 2000– (sr dir), Standard Bank London Ltd 2000–; memb Law Soc; chm Thrombosis Research Inst, sometime regnl chm Handicapped Children's Pilgrimage Tst, chm Caius House Battersea, memb Advsy Cncl Chichester Cathedral Devpt Tst, memb Cncl St John Ambulance, supporter Friends of Arundel Cathedral; Past Master Worshipful Co of Feltmakers, Liveryman City of London Slrs Co; Knight of the Holy Sepulchre 2000, OStJ 2003; *Publications* incl Unlocking Growth: a venture capital study (2001); *Recreations* rowing, sailing, shooting, history, poetry, architecture; *Clubs* Boodle's, Leander, Royal Thames Yacht; *Style*— Patrick Burgess, Esq, MBE; ✉ Flat 9, 100 Piccadilly, London W1J 7NH; Shopwyke Hall, Chichester, West Sussex PO20 2AA; Jones Day, 21 Tudor Street, London EC4Y 0DJ (tel 020 7039 5459, fax 020 7039 5500, e-mail pburgess@jonesday.com)

BURGESS, Prof Robert George; s of George Burgess, and Olive, *née* Andrews; *b* 23 April 1947; *Educ* Bede Coll Durham (CertEd), Univ of Durham (BA), Univ of Warwick (PhD); *m* 1974, Hilary, da of Rev H R Joyce; *Career* Univ of Warwick: lectr 1974–84, sr lectr 1984–88, dept chair 1985–88, dir Centre for Educnl Devpt Appraisal and Research (CEDAR) 1987–99, prof of sociology 1988–99, chm Faculty of Social Sciences 1988–91, fndr chm Grad Sch 1991–95, sr pro-vice-chllr 1995–99; vice-chllr Univ of Leicester 1999–; ESRC: memb Research Resources Bd 1991–96, memb Cncl 1996–2000, chm Postgrad Trg Bd 1997–2000 (memb 1989–93, vice-chm 1996–97); fndr chm UK Cncl for Grad Educn 1993–99; pres: Br Sociological Assoc 1989–91, Assoc for the Teaching of the Soc Sciences 1991–99; chair: HEFCE Quality Assessment Ctee 2001–03, E Midlands Univs Assoc 2001–04, ESRC Funding Cncls Teaching and Learning Research Prog 2003–, Research Information Network 2004–, UCAS 2005– (memb Bd 2001–), HE Acad Bd 2007– (memb Bd 2003–); memb: HEFCE review of postgrad educn 1995–96, CVCP review of clinical academic careers 1996–97, HEFCE Research Libraries Strategy Gp 2001–02, Jt Equality Steering Gp 2001–03, Br Library Bd 2003–, Ctee HEFCE Quality Assurance Learning and Teaching 2003–07, Quality Assurance Agency (QAA) Implementation Gp on Postgrad Educn; Hon DLitt Staffordshire Univ 1998, Hon DUniv Northampton 2007; memb BERA; AcSS 2000; *Books* Experiencing Comprehensive Education (1983), In the Field (1984), Education, Schools and Schooling (1985), Sociology, Education and Schools (1986), Implementing In-Service Education (jtly, 1993), Research Methods (1993); also ed of 20 books on methodology and education; *Recreations* walking, listening to music and some gardening; *Style*— Prof Robert Burgess; ✉ Vice-Chancellor's Office, University of Leicester, Leicester LE1 7RH (tel 0116 252 2322, fax 0116 255 8691, e-mail vc@le.ac.uk)

BURGESS, Robert Lawie Frederick (Robin); s of Sir John Burgess (d 1987), of Carlisle, and Lady Burgess, *née* Gilleron; *b* 31 January 1951; *Educ* Trinity Coll Glenalmond; *m* 20 Sept 1986, Alexandra Rosemary, da of W A Twiston-Davies, of Herefords; 1 s (James), 3 da (Rose, Catherine, Rachel); *Career* 2 Lt The King's Own Royal Border Regt 1969–72; chief exec C N Group Ltd (formerly Cumbrian Newspapers Group Ltd) 1985–; pres Newspaper Soc 1996–97; dir: Cumberland and Westmorland Herald Ltd 1985–, Border TV plc 1987–2000; High Sheriff Cumbria 2006–07; *Clubs* Garrick, Army and Navy; *Style*— R L F Burgess, Esq; ✉ C N Group Ltd, Dalston Road, Carlisle, Cumbria CA2 5UA

BURGESS, Sally; *Career* opera and concert singer; mezzo-soprano; *Roles* with ENO incl: Carmen (debut, subsequently performed role at Bregenz Festival, Zürich, Berlin, NZ, Met Opera NY, Paris Bastille), Judith in Bluebeard's Castle, Charlotte in Werther, Octavian in Der Rosenkavalier, Mrs Begbick in Mahagonny, Herodias in Salome, Dulinée in Don Quixote, Azucena in Trovatore, Mistress Quickly in Sir John in Love 2006; other operatic roles incl: Fricka in Die Walküre (Scottish Opera), Amneris in Aida (Scottish Opera), Dido in The Trojans (Opera North), Laura in La Gioconda (Opera North), Azucena in Il Trovatore (Opera North), Margareta in Genoveva (Opera North), Ottavia in The Coronation of Poppea (WNO, also BBC), Eboli in Don Carlos 1998, Kabanicha in Katya Kabanova (Munich Staatsoper) 1999, Fricka in Das Rheingold (Geneva Opera) 1999, Mere Marie in Dialogue of the Carmelites by Poulenc (WNO) 1999, Die Walküre 2000, Baba the Turk, Rake's Progress 2002, Fortunata in Satyricon (Opera Nancy and Vlaamse Opera) 2004, Hanna Glawari in Merry Widow (Met Opera NY) 2004, Judith in Duke Bluebeard's Castle (Houston and Opera North) 2005, Carmen (Christchurch NZ) 2005, Fricka in Die Walkure (Marseille) 2007, Kabanicka in Katya Kabanova (Opera North) 2007; other performances incl: Liverpool Oratorio (world and American première, recorded with EMI), The Voyage by Philip Glass, Sorceress in Dido and Aeneas (recorded with Chandos and broadcast BBC TV), Showboat with Opera North and RSC (nominated Best Actress in a Musical Olivier Awards), Sally Burgess's Women (one woman jazz show, Lyric Theatre Hammersmith), Amelia in Mark-Anthony Turnage's Twice Through the Heart, Pierrot Lunaire (Almeida Theatre London) 2006; *Recordings* incl: Showboat, West Side Story, The King & I, works of Howard Ferguson, works of Delius, Sally Burgess sings Jazz (with husband Neal Thornton), The Other Me (jazz), Happy Talk: the Life and Works of Richard Rodgers, Bartok's Duke Bluebeard's Castle; *Style*— Ms Sally Burgess; ✉ c/o Jenny Rose, AOR Management, 6910 Roosevelt Way NE, PMB 221, Seattle, WA 98115, USA (tel 00 1 206 729 6160, fax 00 1 206 985 8499, e-mail jennyrose@aormanagementuk.com)

BURGESS, Sir (Joseph) Stuart; kt (1994), CBE (1984); *b* 20 March 1929; *Educ* Barnsley Holgate GS, UCL (BSc, PhD); *m* 1955, Valerie Ann, *née* Street; 1 da (Jacqueline Ann b 23 March 1959), 1 s (Timothy Stuart b 6 Oct 1961); *Career* The Radiochemical Centre Ltd 1953–61, UKAEA Risley 1961–62, Amersham International plc 1962–89, pres Amersham Corp USA 1975–77 (chief exec 1979–89), conslt Immuno International AG Vienna 1990–96; chm: Immuno UK Ltd 1993–96, Oxford RHA 1990–94, Anglia & Oxford RHA 1994–98, Finsbury Worldwide Pharmaceutical Tst plc 1995–2004, Haemonetics Corp USA 1998–2003, Chartered Mgmnt Inst Bd of Companions 1999–2002; dir Anagen plc UK 1993–97; vice-chm Asthma UK 2000–; fell UCL 1994; FRSC 1960, CIMgt 1986; *Recreations* golf, theatre, music, travel; *Clubs* RSM; *Style*— Sir Stuart Burgess, CBE

BURGESS, Rev Dr Stuart John; s of Frederick John Burgess (d 1993), and Winifred May, *née* Gowan (d 2002); *b* 18 March 1940, Birmingham; *Educ* Moseley GS Birmingham, St Peter's Coll, Wesley Coll Leeds, Univ of London (BD), Univ of Nottingham (MEd, MTh); *m* 17 July 1965, Elisabeth, *née* Fowler; 2 da (Alison Jane b 13 Sept 1968, Kathryn Elisabeth b 13 May 1970); *Career* chaplain Univ of Nottingham 1970–81, chaplain Univ of Birmingham 1981–89, chair York and Hull Methodist Dist 1989–2004, pres Methodist Church of GB 1999–2000; rural advocate; chair: Countryside Agency 2004–06, Cmmn for Rural Communities 2005–; memb: Ethics Ctee Dept of Work Pensions, Patient Liaison Gp BMA, Ct Univ of Nottingham; Hon MA Univ of Birmingham 1989; Hon DD: Univ of Hull 2001, Lambeth and Oxford 2003; Hon DUniv Birmingham 2006; *Publications* Spiritual Journey of John Wesley (1980), Reflections on the Stations of the Cross (1991), Coming of Age: Challenges and Opportunities for the 21st Century (1999); *Recreations* music, tennis, travel; *Clubs* Liberal; *Style*— The Rev Dr Stuart Burgess; ✉ Commission for Rural Communities, John Dower House, Crescent Place, Cheltenham, Gloucestershire GL50 3RA (tel 01242 521381, fax 01242 533290)

BURGH, 8 Baron (E 1529) Alexander Gregory Disney Leith; s of 7 Baron Burgh (d 2001); *b* 16 March 1958; *m* 1984 (m dis 1998), Catharine Mary, da of David Parkes; 2 s (Hon Alexander James Strachan b 1986, Hon Benjamin David Willoughby b 1988), 1 da (Hon Hannah Elizabeth Rose b 1990); m 2, 1999, Emma Jane, da of Martin Burdick; 1 s (Hon Peter Martin Vincent b 2002), 1 da (Hon Charlotte Alice Romi b 2004); *Heir* s, Hon Alexander James Leith; *Style*— The Rt Hon the Lord Burgh

BURGH, Anita, Lady; Anita Lorna Leith; da of Frederick Clements Eldridge (d 1973), and Alice Milner (d 1989); *b* 9 June 1937; *Educ* Chatham GS; *m* 29 Aug 1957 (m dis 1982), 7 Baron Burgh (d 2001); 2 s, 1 da; partner, William Westall Jackson; 1 da (Kate Rosalind Scarlett b 25 March 1971); *Career* novelist 1987–; columnist Country Gentlemen's Assoc; memb: Romantic Novelists' Assoc 1987, Soc of Authors 1990, The Historical Novelists Assoc; *Novels* as Anita Burgh: Distinctions of Class (1987), Love the Bright Foreigner (1988), The Azure Bowl (1989), The Golden Butterfly (1990), The Stone Mistress (1991), Advances (1992), Overtures (1993), Avarice (1994), Lottery (1995), Breeders (1996), The Cult (1997), On Call (1998), The Family (1999), Clare's War (2000), Exiles (2001), The House at Harcourt (2002), The Visitor (2003), The Broken Gate (2004), Heart's Citadel (2005); as Annie Leith: Tales From Sarson Magna: Molly's Flashings (1991), Hector's Hobbies (1994); *Recreations* bulldogs and nattering; *Style*— Anita Burgh; ✉ c/o The Mic Cheetham Agency, 11–12 Dover Street, London W1X 3PH (tel 020 7495 2002, fax 020 7495 5777, e-mail miccheetham@compuserve.com, website www.anitaburgh.com)

BURGHES, Prof David Noel; s of Edmund Noel Burghes (d 1944), and Lilian Mary, *née* Luckhurst; *b* 21 March 1944; *Educ* Christ's Coll Finchley, Univ of Sheffield (BSc, PhD); *m* 21 Sept 1968, Jennifer Jean, da of Dr Donald Harry Smith (d 1971); 4 s (Andrew b 1970, Christopher b 1972, Jamie b 1974, Timothy b 1975); *Career* asst lectr Dept of Applied Mathematics Univ of Sheffield 1970–71 (jr res fell 1968–70), lectr Sch of Mathematics Univ of Newcastle 1972–75, dir Cranfield Centre for Teacher Servs Cranfield Inst of Technol 1980–81 (lectr 1975–79); Univ of Exeter: prof of educn 1981, dir Centre for Innovation in Mathematics Teaching 1986, dir Kassel Project (int comparative study in sch mathematics) 1994–99, dir Mathematics Enhancement Project 1996, dir Int Project in Maths Attainment (IPMA) 1998; Univ of Plymouth: prof of educn 2005, seconded as dir Nat Centre for Excellence in the Teaching of Mathematics 2005–06, dir Int Comparative Study in Maths Teacher Training 2007–; memb Govt Numeracy Task Force 1997–98; author and co-author of over twenty books on mathematics and educn mathematics dir Spode Group 1980–; chm Indust and Educn Maths Ctee DTI 1985–88, founding ed jl Teaching Mathematics and its Applications 1985–; FIMA 1970; *Recreations* reading train timetables, travelling; *Style*— Prof David Burghes

BURGIN, Prof Victor; s of Samuel Burgin (d 1991), of Sheffield, S Yorks, and Gwendolyn Ann, *née* Crowther (d 1973); *b* 24 July 1941; *Educ* Firth Park GS for Boys Sheffield, Sheffield Coll of Art (NDD), RCA (ARCA), Yale Univ (MFA); *m* 1, 1964 (m dis), Hazel Patricia, da of Louis Rowbotham; 2 s (Julian Alexander b 1967, Gaius Louis b 1970); m 2, 1988, Francette Marie-Anne, da of Guy Edouard Pacteau; *Career* lectr: Sch of Fine Art Trent Poly 1965–73, Sch of Communication Central London Poly 1973–88, Bd of Studies in Art History Univ of Calif Santa Cruz 1988–95, Bd of Studies in History of Consciousness Univ of Calif Santa Cruz 1995–2001; prof emeritus of history of consciousness 2001–; Millard prof of fine art Goldsmiths Coll London 2001–; US/UK Bicentennial Arts Exchange fell NY 1976–77, Deutsche Akademische Austausdienst fell Berlin 1978–79; Hon DUniv Sheffield Hallam 2005; *Solo Exhibitions* incl: ICA London 1976, Stedelijk van Abbemuseum Eindhoven 1977, MOMA Oxford 1978, DAAD Gallery Berlin 1979, Musée de la Ville de Calais 1981, Zwiczek Polskich Artsow Fotografickow Warsaw 1981, Impressions Gallery of Photography York 1984, Renaissance Soc at the Univ of Chicago 1986, Albert and Vera List Visual Arts Centre Cambridge MA 1986, Orchard Gallery Derry 1986, Kettles Yard Cambridge 1986, ICA London 1986, Nat Gallery of Aust Canberra 1988, Film in the Cities St Paul 1989, Musée d'Art Moderne Villeneuve d'Ascq 1991, Centre for Research in Contemporary Art Univ of Texas at Arlington 1993, Univ at Buffalo Art Gallery/Research Centre in Art + Culture 1995, Mücsarnok Museum Budapest 1997, Galerie Fotohof Salzburg 1998, Yerba Buena Centre for the Arts San Francisco 1998–99, Weimar 99 Cultural Festival 1999, Architectural Assoc London 2000, Fundació Antoni Tàpies Barcelona 2001, Arnolfini Bristol 2002, LisboaPhoto Lisbon 2003, Cornerhouse Manchester 2003; *Group Exhibitions* incl: When Attitudes Become Form (ICA London) 1969, Information (MOMA NY) 1970, Guggenheim Int Exhbn (Solomon R Guggenheim Museum NY) 1971, The British Avant-Garde (NY Cultural Center) 1971, 36 Biennale de Venezia 1972, Documenta 5 (Museum Fredericianum and Neue Galerie Kassel) 1972, The New Art (Hayward Gallery London) 1972, Contemporanea (Parcheggio di Villa Borghese Rome) 1973, Art and Politics (Gallerie Bochum) 1974, Victor Burgin/ Art and Language (Musée d'Art er d'Industrie Saint-Etienne) 1975, Arte Inglese Oggi 1960–76 (Palazzo Reale Milan) 1976, Hayward Annual (Hayward Gallery London) 1977, Europe in the Seventies (Art Inst of Chicago) 1977, Kunst im Sozialen Kontext (Badische Kunstverein Karlsruhe) 1980, The Third Biennale of Sydney (Art Gallery of New South Wales) 1980, Three Perspectives in Photography (Hayward Gallery London) 1980, Photographic Image in Contemporary Art (Nat MOMA Tokyo) 1984, The Turner Prize (Tate Gallery London) 1987, Photography and Art (LA Co Museum and touring) 1987, Écran Politiques (Musee d'Art Contempoarain de Montreal) 1987, Berlinart 1961–1987 (MOMA NY) 1987, The British Edge (ICA Boston) 1987, British Art in the Twentieth Century (Royal Acad of Arts London) 1987, Difference: On Sexuality and Representation (New Museum of Contemporary Art NY) 1987, The Future of the Metropolis (Triennale di Milano) 1988; *Publications* The Art of Photography: 1839–1989 (Museum of Fine Arts Houston and touring) 1989, On the Art of Fixing a Shadow: One Hundred and Fifty Years of Photography (Art Inst of Chicago and touring) 1989, L'art conceptuel, une perspective (Musée d'Art Moderne de la Ville de Paris) 1989, 1965–75: Reconsidering the Object of Art (The Museum of Contemporary Art LA) 1995–96, 3e Biennale de Lyon 1995–96, Hall of Mirrors: Art and Film Since 1945 (The Museum of Contemporary Art LA) 1996, Photography after Photography (Kunsthalle München and touring) 1996, Text & Image (Frankfurter Kunstverein and MOMA Bolzano) 1996, Face á l'Histoire 1933–66 (Centre Georges Pompidou Paris) 1996–97, The Impossible Document: Photography and British Conceptual Art 1967–76 (Camerawork Gallery London) 1997, Notorious: Art and Cinema (MOMA Oxford and touring) 1999, Blast to Freeze (Kunstmuseum Wolfsburg) 2002, Sans commune mesure, Image et texte dans l'art actuel (Musee d'Art Moderne Lille) 2002, I Promise It's Political (Museum Ludwig Cologne) 2002, Rapture: art's seduction by fashion since 1970 (Barbican London) 2002–03, L'Art au Futur Anterieur (Musée de Grenoble) 2004, The Last Picture Show:Artists Using Photography 1960–1982 (Walker Art Centre Minneapolis) 2004, Eblouissement (Jeu de Paume Paris) 2004, Artists' Choice (ICA London) 2004; *Work in Public Collections* incl: MOMA NY, New York Public Library, LA Co Museum of Art LA, Museum of Contemporary Art LA, Walker Art Centre Minneapolis, Tate Gallery London, V&A London, Arts Cncl Collection London, Centre Georges Pompidou Paris; *Books* Work and Commentary (1973), Thinking Photography (1982), Between (1986), The End of Art Theory (1986), Passages (1991), In/Different Spaces (1996), Some Cities (1996), Venise (1997), Shadowed (2000), Victor Burgin (2001), Relocating (2002), The Remembered Film (2004); *Style*— Prof Victor Burgin

BURGON, Colin; MP; *Career* MP (Lab) Elmet 1997–; *Style*— Colin Burgon, Esq, MP; ✉ House of Commons, London SW1A 0AA (tel 020 7219 3000)

BURGON, Geoffrey Alan; s of Alan Wybert Burgon (d 1983), and Ada Vera Isom; Huguenot descent; *b* 15 July 1941; *Educ* Pewley Sch Guildford, Guildhall Sch of Music and Drama; *m* 1, 1963 (m dis), Janice Elizabeth, da of Frank Garwood; 1 da (Hannah b 1965), 1 s (Matthew b 1967); m 2, Jacqueline Louise, da of David Krofchak; 1 s (Daniel Milo b 1994); *Career* composer and conductor; dramatic works include: Joan of Arc 1970, Orpheus 1982, Hard Times 1990; orchestral music includes: Concerto for String Orchestra 1963, Gending 1968, Trumpet Concerto 1993, Piano Concerto 1997, A Distant Dawn 1999, Industrial Dreams 2006; orchestral music with voices includes: Requiem 1976, The World Again 1983, Revelations 1984, Mass 1984, Title Divine 1986, A Vision 1990, City Adventures (world premiere BBC Proms) 1996, Merciless Beauty 1996, Alleluia Psallat 2003, Three Mysteries 2003; ballet music includes: The Golden Fish 1964, Running Figures 1975, Songs Lamentations and Praises 1979, The Trials of Prometheus 1988; choral music includes: Three Elegies 1964, Short Mass 1965, Two Hymns to Mary 1967, Mai Hamama 1970, A Prayer to the Trinity 1972, The Fire of Heaven 1973, Noche Oscura 1974, Dos Coros 1975, This World From 1974, Nunc dimittis 1979, Laudate Dominum 1980, But Have Been Found Again 1983, The Song of the Creatures 1987, Four Sacred Pieces 1999, Magic Words 2000, Shirtless Stephen 2003, Of Flowers and Emeralds Sheen 2004, Death be not Proud 2005, Come let us pity Death 2005; chamber music includes: Gloria 1973, Six Studies 1980; chamber music with voices includes: Five Sonnets of John Donne 1967, Worldes Blissé 1971, Lunar Beauty 1986, Clarinet Quintet 1998, String Quartet 1999, Heavenly Things 2000, At Trafalgar 2005; film and tv scores include: The Changeling 1973, Dr Who and the Terror of the Zygons 1975, Monty Python's Life of Brian 1979, Tinker Tailor Soldier Spy 1979, The Dogs of War 1980, Brideshead Revisited 1981, Turtle Diary 1985, The Death of the Heart 1985, Bleak House 1986, The Chronicles of Narnia 1988, Children of the North 1990, Robin Hood 1991, The Agency 1991, Martin Chuzzlewit 1994, Silent Witness 1996, Turning World 1997, Cider with Rosie 1998, When Trumpets Fade 1998, Longitude 1999, Labrynth 2001, The Forsyte Saga 2002, Island at War 2004, Love Lies Bleeding 2006; *Recreations* cricket, jazz, wasting money on Bristol cars; *Style*— Geoffrey Burgon, Esq; ✉ c/o Chester Music, 14–15 Berners Street, London W1T 3LJ (tel 020 7612 7400)

BURKE, Cordell Aguilla; s of Ickford Aguilla Burke (d 1999), and Geraldine Margaret, *née* Crump; *b* 20 September 1957, Leicester; *Educ* Gateway Sch Leicester, Loughborough Coll of Art, Wimbledon Sch of Art; *m* 2 June 1984, Julie Ann, *née* Mitchell; 1 da (Christella Marie b 7 Jan 1985), 1 s (Lewis John b 9 June 1987); *Career* art dir: Latham Braley Cowan 1980–83, Benton & Bowles 1983–85, Lowe Howard-Spink 1985–86, BMP Business 1986–89; jt creative dir Ash Gupta Communications London 1989–91, dep creative dir/head of art Saatchi & Saatchi Direct 1991–93, freelance 1993–94; sr art dir Ogilvy & Mather Direct 1994–97; OgilvyOne Worldwide: dep creative dir/bd dir 1997–98, creative dir 1998–2003, exec creative dir/managing ptnr 2003–06, gp creative ptnr Ogilvy Gp UK 2006; exec creative dir Tequila London 2006–; DMA: memb Creative Cncl 1998–, memb Awards Ctee 2006–; chm Campaign Direct Awards Judges 2006; Creative Circle Silver 1988, 6 DMA Golds and 7 DMA Silvers 1997–2006, Campaign Direct Silver 2000, Cannes Lion 2002, DMA Echo Silver 2005; MIDM 2003; *Books* Shared Beliefs (contrib, 2002);

Recreations football; *Style*— Cordell Burke, Esq; ✉ Tequila London, 82 Dean Street, London W1D 3HA (tel 020 7440 1224, fax 020 7440 1101, e-mail cordell.burke@tequila-uk.com)

BURKE, David Patrick; s of Patrick Burke (d 1965), and Mary, *née* Welsh (d 1980); *b* 25 May 1934; *Educ* St Francis Xavier's Coll Liverpool, CCC Oxford, RADA; *m* 20 March 1971, Anna, da of Arthur Calder-Marshall; 1 s (Tom b 30 June 1981); *Career* actor; *Theatre* RSC 1986–87: Hector in Troilus and Cressida, Bessemenow in Philistines, Melons; NT 1988–91: William Goodchild in The Strangeness of Others, Zeal-of-the-Land Busy in Bartholomew Fair, Ghost and First Gravedigger in Hamlet, Mr Voysey in The Voysey Inheritance, Reverend John Hale in The Crucible, Watch on the Rhine; Birmingham Rep: Measure for Measure, The Devil is an Ass; Hampstead Theatre (and West End): Bodies, Rocket to the Moon; other credits incl: Othello (Young Vic), A Flea in her Ear (Thorndike), Slow Dance on the Killing Ground (Greenwich) 1991, Claudius and Ghost in Hamlet (Riverside Studios) 1992, The Colonel in States of Shock (Salisbury Playhouse) 1993, Simonides in Pericles (RNT) 1994, New England (RSC) 1994, The Woman In Black (Fortune) 1995, Kent in King Lear (RNT) 1997, Copenhagen (RNT) 1998–99, Old Gaunt in Richard II (Almeida) 2000, Further than the Furthest Thing (Tricycle Theatre) 2001, The Wind in the Willows (narrator, ROH) 2002–03, The Three Sisters (West End) 2003, The Rivals (Bristol Old Vic) 2004, Mary Stuart (Donmar) 2005, John Gabriel Borkman (Donmar) 2007; *Television* Dr Watson in The Mysteries of Sherlock Holmes, Ron Fisher in Casualty, James Maybrick in The James Maybrick Case, Crown Court, Holly and Inheritance, Sir John Crowborough in The House of Eliott, Sir Arthur Stanley in Hickory Dickory Dock, Oedipus in An A-Z of Greek Democracy, Kipling, Two Days in the Love of Michael Reagan, Barlowe at Large, Love School, Fair Trading on the Dance Ground, Esther Waters, Pope Pius XII, The Murder Machine, The Comedians, A Winter's Tale, Nannie, Henry VI Parts 1 and 2, Richard III, Dreams, Secrets, Beautiful Lies, Run for the Life Boat, Taking Liberties, The Woodlanders, Hotel in Amsterdam, Hine and Crimes of Passion, Rooms, Hammer and Sickle, Quiet as a Nun, The Guardian, Villain, Bertie and Elizabeth, Waking the Dead, Casualty, Inspector Lynley, Secret Histories; De Vauzesnes in Mesmer (film) 1993, King Lear (film) 1998, The Regicides 2004, Cathedral 2004, Dalziel and Pascoe 2004, Boy Soldiers 2004, Ghost Story 2005; *Books* Celia's Secret (with Michael Frayn, 2000); *Recreations* gardening, walking; *Style*— David Burke; ✉ c/o Scott Marshall Management

BURKE, David Thomas (Tom); CBE (1997); s of Jeremiah Vincent Burke, DSM (d 1990), and Mary, *née* Bradley (d 1998); *b* 5 January 1947; *Educ* St Boniface's Coll Plymouth, Univ of Liverpool (BA); *Career* lectr: Carlett Park Coll 1970–71, Old Swan Tech Coll 1971–73; Friends of the Earth: local gps co-ordinator 1973–75, exec dir 1975–79, dir special projects 1979–80, vice-chm 1980–81; dir The Green Alliance 1982–91 (memb Exec Ctee 1979–82), special advsr to Sec of State for the Environment 1991–97; environmental advsr: BP plc 1997–2001, Rio Tinto plc 1997–; advsr Central Policy Gp Office of the Dep PM 2002; non-exec dir Earth Resources Res 1975–88; memb: Waste Mgmnt Advsy Cncl 1976–80, Packaging Cncl 1978–82, Exec Ctee NCVO (also chm Planning and Environment Gp) 1984–89, UK Nat Ctee Euro Year of the Environment 1986–88, Exec Ctee Euro Environmental Bureau 1988–91 (policy advsr 1978–88), Co-operative Insurance Servs Environment Tst Advsy Ctee 1990–92, Cncl RSA 1990–92 (memb Environment Ctee 1989–96), Exec Bd World Energy Cncl Cmmn 1990–93, Cncl English Nature 1999–2005; chm Review of Environmental Governance in NI 2006–; founding dir E3Q 2004–; visiting prof Imperial Coll London 1997–, hon prof Faculty of Law UCL 2003–; chm Editorial Bd Environmental Data Services (ENDS) 2005–; hon visiting fell Manchester Business Sch 1984–86, visiting fell Cranfield Sch of Mgmnt 1990–94; tstee Borough Market Tstees 1999–2001; numerous radio and TV broadcasts, scriptwriter Crumbling Britain (BBC Radio 4) 1983; Parly candidate (SDP): Brighton Kemptown 1983, Surbiton 1987; Royal Humane Soc Testimonial on Parchment 1969 (on Vellum 1966); UNEP Global 500 laureate; FRSA 1987; *Books* incl: Europe Environment (1981), Pressure Groups in the Global System (1982), Ecology 2000 (co-author and picture ed, 1984), The Gaia Atlas of Planetary Management (contrib, 1984), The Green Capitalists (with John Elkington, 1987), Green Pages (with John Elkington and Julia Hales, 1988), Ethics, Environment and the Company (with Julie Hill, 1990); *Recreations* birdwatching, landscape photography, military history, walking; *Clubs* Reform; *Style*— Tom Burke, Esq, CBE; ✉ Studio 2, Clink Wharf Studios, Clink Street, London SE1 9DG (tel 020 7357 9146); 6 St James' Square, London (tel 020 7735 2374, fax 020 7735 2288, e-mail tom.burke@riotinto.co.uk and tom.burke2@btinternet.com)

BURKE, Prof Derek Clissold; CBE (1994), DL (Norfolk 1992); s of Harold Burke (d 1973), and Ivy Ruby, *née* Clissold (d 1973); *b* 13 February 1930; *Educ* Bishop Vesey's GS Sutton Coldfield, Univ of Birmingham (BSc, PhD); *m* 21 May 1955, Mary Elizabeth, da of Theodore Tiner Dukeshire; 3 da (Elizabeth Anne b 1957, Rosemary Margaret b 1962 d 2004, Virginia Ruth b 1964), 1 s (Stephen Dukeshire b 1959); *Career* res fell in chemistry Yale Univ 1953–55, scientist Nat Inst for Medical Res London 1955–60, lectr and sr lectr Dept of Biological Chem Univ of Aberdeen 1960–69, prof of biological scis Univ of Warwick 1969–82, Eleanor Roosevelt fell Univ of Colorado 1975–76, vice-pres and scientific dir Allelix Inc Toronto 1982–87, vice-chllr UEA 1987–95; chm Advsy Ctee on Novel Foods and Processes 1988–97, dir Cancer Res Campaign 1989–97, chm Cncl Paterson Inst of Cancer Res 1992–97; memb: Advsy Ctee on Genetic Modification 1987–95, Technol Foresight Steering Gp Office of Sci and Technol 1993–95, Sci and Engrg Bd and Technol Interaction Bd BBSRC 1994–97, Sci, Med and Technol Ctee C of E 1995–2000, Nuffield Cncl on Bioethics' Working Pty on Genetically Modified Crops 1997–99 and 2003–04; chm: Bd Genome Research Ltd 1997–98, Archbishops' Med Ethics Advsy Gp 1997–2006; dir: Inst for Food Research 1994–2002, Babraham Inst 1995–99; specialist advsr: House of Commons Sci and Technol Ctee 1995–2003, Euro Life Sciences Gp 2000–04; memb Editorial Bd Jl of General Virology 1969–92, ed in chief Jl of General Virology 1978–82, chair Cambridge Templeton Consortium 2004–; tstee Norfolk and Norwich Festival 1988–98, memb Bd Wingfield Arts Tst 1996–98; Hon LLD Univ of Aberdeen 1982, Hon ScD UEA 1995; hon fell St Edmund's Coll Cambridge 1997; memb EMBO; hon memb Soc for Gen Microbiology 2000 (pres 1987–90), Hon FIBiol; *Publications* Creation and Evolution (1985), Strategic Church Leadership (with Robin Gill, 1996), Cybernauts Awake! (1999); numerous scientific and popular articles on interferon and viruses and on plant genetic engrg; *Recreations* music, opera, walking; *Clubs* Norfolk; *Style*— Prof Derek Burke, CBE, DL; ✉ 12 Cringleford Chase, Norwich, Norfolk NR4 7RS (tel and fax 01603 503071, e-mail dcb27@cam.ac.uk); Sea-Green Cottage, Walberswick, Suffolk IP18 6TU (tel and fax 01502 723607)

BURKE, Frank Desmond; *b* 23 March 1944; *Educ* Newcastle (MB BS); *m* Linda Margaret; 2 s (Richard b 1972, Timothy b 1979), 1 da (Sarah b 1975); *Career* fell in hand surgery: Louisville Kentucky 1976, Iowa City 1977; conslt hand surgn Derbyshire Royal Infirmary 1981–; visiting prof of hand surgery Med Scis Dept Univ of Derby; sec Br Soc for Surgery of the Hand 1989 (pres 1997), pres Br Assoc of Hand Therapists 1989, memb American Soc of Surgery of The Hand 1989; FRCS 1972; *Books* Principles of Hand Surgery (with D A McGrougher and P J Smith, 1990); *Style*— Frank Burke, Esq; ✉ The Hand Unit, Derbyshire Royal Infirmary NHS Trust, London Road, Derby (tel 01332 347141 ext 4751)

BURKE, Gregory; s of Brian Joseph Burke, of Dunfermline, and Elizabeth, *née* Innes; *b* 2 August 1968; *Educ* Bayside Comp Gibraltar, St Columba's HS Dunfermline, Univ of Stirling; *Partner* Lorraine Ann Forbes; *Career* writer; early career fulfilling variety of roles in minimum wage economy; *Plays* Gagarin Way (performed Traverse Theatre Edinburgh, RNT, Arts Theatre London and worldwide) 2001 (First of the Fringe Firsts Edinburgh Festival 2001, Critics Circle Awards Most Promising Playwright 2002, Barclays/TMA Awards Best New Play 2002, Meyer-Whitworth Award Best New Play 2002), The Straits (Paines Plough Theatre Co) 2003, Debt (NT) 2004, On Tour (Royal Court Upstairs) 2005, Black Watch (Traverse Theatre Edinburgh) 2006; *Recreations* absorbing culture in all its guises; *Clubs* Dunfermline Athletic FC; *Style*— Gregory Burke, Esq

BURKE, (Michael) Ian; s of Ron Burke, of Morecambe, Lancs, and Rosemary, *née* Gannor; *b* 2 June 1956, Liverpool; *Educ* Imperial Coll London (BSc), London Business Sch (MSc); *m* 22 Sept 1979, Jane, *née* McGuinness; 1 da (Jennie b 27 Dec 1983), 1 s (Paul b 4 Feb 1987); *Career* various roles Bass plc 1991–98 (incl: md Holiday Inn, md Gala Clubs); ceo: Thistles Hotels plc 1998–2003, Holmes Place Health Clubs 2003–06, Rank Gp plc 2006–; dir Business in Sport and Leisure; ACMA; *Recreations* fell walking, cycling, philosophy; *Style*— Ian Burke, Esq; ✉ Rank Group plc, Statesman House, Stafferton Way, Maidenhead, Berkshire SL6 1AY (tel 01628 504000, fax 01628 504042, e-mail ian_burke@rank.com)

BURKE, Sir James Stanley Gilbert; 9 Bt (I 1797), of Marble Hill, Galway; s of Sir Thomas Stanley Burke, 8 Bt (d 1989), and Susanne Margaretha, *née* Salvisberg (d 1983); *b* 1 July 1956; *m* 1980, Laura, da of Domingo Branzuela, of Catmon, Cebu, Philippines; 1 s (Martin James b 1980), 1 da (Catherine Elizabeth b 1982); *Heir* s, Martin Burke; *Style*— Sir James Burke, Bt; ✉ Bleierstrasse 14, 8942 Oberrieden, Switzerland

BURKE, His Hon Judge Jeffrey Peter; QC (1984); s of Samuel Burke, of London, and Gertrude Burke; *b* 15 December 1941; *Educ* Shrewsbury, Brasenose Coll Oxford (open exhibitioner, BA); *m* Joanna Mary Heal; 1 s (Patrick Samuel b 1996), 1 da (Anna Natalya b 1998); 2 s and 1 da by previous m (Jason Daniel b 1970, Adam Francis b 1972, Sonya Clare b 1977); *Career* called to the Bar Inner Temple 1964; recorder of the Crown Court 1982–, dep judge of the High Court 1998, nominated Judge of Employment Appeal Tbnl 2000, circuit judge (SE Circuit) 2002–; memb Mental Health Review Tbnl 1993–; *Recreations* soccer, cricket, wine, singing, reading, removing brambles; *Clubs* Economicals AFC, Flamstead Cricket, De Todeni; *Style*— His Hon Judge Burke, QC; ✉ Luton Crown Court, 7 George Street, Luton LU1 2AA (tel 01582 522000)

BURKE, His Hon John Kenneth; QC (1985); s of Kenneth Burke (d 1960), of Stockport, and Madeline Lorina, *née* Eastwood; *b* 4 August 1939; *Educ* Stockport GS; *m* 30 March 1962, Margaret Anne, da of Frank Scattergood, of Nottingham; 3 da (Virginia b 1963, Joanna b 1967, Geraldine b 1969); *Career* Nat Serv with Cheshire Regt in Far E 1958–60, Capt 12/13 Bn The Parachute Regt (TA) 1962–67, Capt/Actg Maj 4 Bn The Parachute Regt (TAVR) 1974; called to the Bar Middle Temple 1965 (bencher 1992); recorder of the Crown Court 1980–95, circuit judge (Northern Circuit) 1995–2005; *Recreations* walking, drawing, painting; *Style*— His Hon John Burke, QC

BURKE, Prof (Ulick) Peter; s of John Patrick Burke (d 1993), and Jennie, *née* Colin (d 1994); *b* 16 August 1937; *Educ* St Ignatius's Coll Stamford Hill London, St John's Coll Oxford (open scholar), St Antony's Coll Oxford (senior scholar); *m* 1, 1972 (m dis 1983), Susan, *née* Dell; *m* 2, 1989, Maria-Lúcia, da of Francisco Garcia Pallares; *Career* Univ of Sussex: asst lectr in history School of European Studies 1962–65, lectr in history 1965–73, reader in intellectual history 1973–79; Univ of Cambridge: fell Emmanuel Coll 1979–, lectr 1979–88, personal readership in cultural history 1988, personal chair 1996; Herodotus fell Inst for Advanced Study Princeton 1967, visiting fell Humanities Research Centre ANU Canberra 1978 and 1983, dir Etudes Associé Ecole des Hautes Etudes Paris 1979 and 1991; visiting prof: Univ of State of São Paulo (UNESP) 1989, Instituto para Estudos Avançados Univ of São Paulo 1994–95, Vrije Universiteit Brussel (VUB) Brussels 2002; fell Wissenschaftskolleg Berlin 1989–90, holder of Charlemagne chair Univ of Nijmegen 1992–93, holder of Vonhoff chair Univ of Groningen 1998–99, Gadamer prof Univ of Heidelberg 2002, Royal Library fell Netherlands Inst for Advanced Studies 2005; Br rep Int Cmmn for the History of Historiography 1985– (memb of Bureau 1990–); memb Academia Europea; memb of jury: to select members Institut Universitaire de France 1995–96, for Prix Européen de l'histoire 1996–97, premio Casa de las Americas 1998; awarded Erasmus Medal 1998; Hon PhD Univ of Lund; FRHistS, FBA; *Books* The Renaissance Sense of the Past (1969), Culture and Society in Renaissance Italy (1972), Venice and Amsterdam: A Study of Seventeenth-Century Elites (1974), Popular Culture in Early Modern Europe (1978), Sociology and History (1980, rewritten as History and Social Theory 1992), Montaigne (1981), Vico (1985), Historical Anthropology of Early Modern Italy: Essays on Perception and Communication (1987), The Renaissance (1987), The French Historical Revolution: The Annales School 1929–89 (1990), The Fabrication of Louis XIV (1992), The Art of Conversation (1993), The Fortunes of the Courtier: The European Reception of Castiglione's Cortegiano (1995), Varieties of Cultural History (1997), The European Renaissance (1998), A Social History of Knowledge (2000), Eyewitnessing (2001), A Social History of the Media (with Asa Briggs, 2002), Languages and Communities in Early Modern Europe (2004); written more than a hundred articles in numerous learned journals; *Recreations* travel; *Style*— Prof Peter Burke, FBA; ✉ Emmanuel College, Cambridge CB2 3AP (tel 01223 334272, fax 01223 334426)

BURKE, Prof Philip George; CBE (1993); s of Henry Burke (d 1969), of South Woodford, London, and Frances Mary, *née* Sprague (d 1980); *b* 18 October 1932; *Educ* Wanstead Co HS London, UC Exeter (BSc London), UCL (Granville studentship, PhD); *m* 29 Aug 1959, Valerie Mona, da of Harold William Martin (d 1987), of Eastbourne, E Sussex; 4 da (Helen Frances b 1961, Susan Valerie b 1963, Pamela Jean b 1964, Alice Charlotte b 1973); *Career* research asst UCL 1956–57, asst lectr Computer Unit Univ of London 1957–59; research assoc Lawrence Radiation Lab Univ of Calif Berkeley: Alvarez Bubble Chamber Gp 1959–61, Theory Gp 1961–62; successively research fell, princ sci offr then sr princ sci offr Theoretical Physics Div UK Atomic Energy Authy Harwell 1962–67; Queen's Univ Belfast: prof of mathematical physics 1967–98 (prof emeritus 1998–), head Dept of Applied Mathematics and Theoretical Physics 1974–77, dir Sch of Mathematics and Physics 1988–90; head of Theory and Computational Sci Div Daresbury Lab (jt appt) 1977–82; many pubns in learned jls; founding ed Computer Physics Communications 1969–79 (hon ed 1979–), series ed (with H Kleinpoppen) Physics of Atoms and Molecules 1974–2004, series ed Springer Series on Atomic Optical and Plasma Physics 2005–; memb: Physics Ctee SRC 1967–71, Synchrotron Radiation Research Ctee SRC 1971–75, Atlas Computer Ctee SRC 1973–76, Jt Policy Ctee on Advanced Res Computing 1988–90, Cncl SERC 1989–94, Cncl Royal Soc 1990–92, Nuclear Research Advsy Cncl MOD 1997–2007; chm: Synchrotron Radiation Panel SRC 1969–71, Comput Physics Gp Euro Physics Soc 1976–78, Sci Bd Computer Ctee SRC 1976–77 and 1984–86, Computer Bd Computer Conslt Cncl 1983–85, Atomic, Molecular and Optical Physics Div Inst of Physics 1987–90, Allocations and Resources Panel Jt Research Cncls Advanced Research Computing Ctee 1988–89, SERC Scientific Computing Advsy Panel 1989–94, SERC Supercomputing Mgmnt Ctee 1991–94 (memb Advsy Bd for Res Cncls Supercomputing Sub-Ctee 1991–94), Jt Research Cncls High Performance Computing Mgmnt Ctee 1996–98; Guthrie Medal and Prize Inst of Physics 1994, Sir David Bates Prize Inst of Physics 2000; Hon DSc: Univ of Exeter 1981, Queen's Univ Belfast 1999; fell UCL 1986; FInstP 1970, fell American Physical Soc 1970, MRIA 1974, FRS 1978; *Books* Atomic Processes and Applications (jtly, 1976), Potential Scattering in Atomic Physics (1977), Atoms in Astrophysics (jtly, 1983), Electron Molecule Scattering and Photoionisation (jtly, 1988), Atomic and Molecular Processes: An R-Matrix Approach (jtly, 1993), Theory of Electron-Atom Collisions: Part I - Potential Scattering (jtly, 1995),

Photon and Electron Collisions with Atoms and Molecules (jtly, 1997); author of many papers in learned jls; *Recreations* walking, reading, listening to music; *Style*— Prof Philip Burke, CBE, FRS, MRIA; ✉ Brook House, Norley Lane, Crowton, Northwich, Cheshire CW8 2RR (tel 01928 788301); Department of Applied Mathematics and Theoretical Physics, Queen's University, Belfast BT7 1NN (tel 028 9097 5047, fax 028 9023 9182, e-mail p.burke@qub.ac.uk)

BURKE, Richard Sylvester; s of David Burke (d 1948), and Elizabeth, *née* Kelly (d 1987); chieftain of Burke, Bourke and de Burgh clan 1990–92 (hon life pres 1992–); *b* 29 March 1932; *Educ* Christian Brothers Sch Thurles and Dublin, Nat Univ of Ireland (BA, MA, HDipEd); *m* 1961, Mary Josephine, da of John J Freeley (d 1934); 3 s (Joseph (d 1962), David Joseph b 1964, Richard Anthony b 1969), 3 da (Mary Carmel b 1963, Audrey Elisabeth b 1966, Avila Therese b 1971); *Career* teacher: St Mary's Place 1950–53, Presentation Coll 1953–55, Blackrock Coll 1955–72; govr UC Dublin 1967–70; memb Dublin CC 1967–73 (chm 1972–73); barr-at-law King's Inns 1973–; TD 1969–77 and 1981–82, opposition chief whip and spokesman on Posts and Telegraphs 1969–73, Min for Educn 1973–76; memb and vice-pres Cmmn of Euro Communities 1977–81 and 1982–85; chm Player and Wills 1981–82; dir: Abbey Life 1981–82, Sedgwick Europe BV 1985–86; special advsr Euro Community Office Ernst and Young 1985–95, pres and ceo Canon Fndn in Europe 1988–98; memb Conseil d'Administration FIDEPS UNESCO Paris 1990–98, memb Devpt Cncl Eurasia Inst HEC Paris 1990–; pres: Harvard Club of Ireland 2005, Arts for Peace Fndn 2006; memb Academia Scientiarum et Artium Europaea Salzburg 1996–; assoc fell Harvard Univ Center for Int Affairs 1980–81; FRSA; Pro Merito Europa medal European Parliament 1980, Order of Leopold II (Grand-Cross) Belgium 1981, Order of Phoenix (Grand-Cross) Greece 1983; *Books* Anthology of Prose (ed, 1967); *Recreations* golf, music, travel; *Clubs* Royal Golf De Belgique (Brussels), Portmarnock Golf (Dublin), Galway Bay Golf, Connemara Golf, Elm Park Golf, The European, L'Association Royale de Golfeurs Seniors de Belgique, Golf des Communautes Europeennes; *Style*— Richard Burke, Esq; ✉ 13 Iris Grove, Mount Merrion, Blackrock, Co Dublin, Ireland (tel 00 353 1 210 9830, e-mail rsburke@eircom.net)

BURKE, Simon; s of Vincent Paul Burke (d 1989), and Beryl Mary, *née* Cregan; *b* 25 August 1958, Dublin; *Educ* St Mary's Coll Dublin; *Career* trainee accountant Binder Hamlyn 1976–82, various positions from supervisor to sr mangr Coopers & Lybrand 1982–87, corp fin mangr Virgin Gp plc 1987–88, md Virgin Retail Ltd 1988–94, chief exec Virgin Our Price 1994–96, chief exec Virgin Entertainment Gp 1996–99, chief exec and subsequently chm Hamleys plc 1999–2003; chm: Majestic Wine plc 2005– (non-exec dir 2000–), Superquinn (Ireland) 2005–; tstee Nat Gallery 2003–, chm Nat Gallery Co; FCA (Ireland); *Recreations* 17th Century Dutch art, flying (pilot's licence), history; *Style*— Simon Burke, Esq; ✉ 35 Chepstow Place, London W2 4TT (mobile 07802 323172, e-mail simon.burke@virgin.net)

BURKHARDT, Prof (George) Hugh; s of Dr (George) Norman Burkhardt (d 1991), of Manchester, and Caroline Mary, *née* Bell; *b* 4 April 1935; *Educ* Manchester Grammar, Balliol Coll Oxford (BA), Univ of Birmingham (PhD); *m* 21 Dec 1955 (m dis 1995), Diana Jeanette, da of Stapley Farmer (d 1970); 2 s (Roger b 1960, Ian b 1963), 1 da (Jan b 1962); *Career* res fell: Columbia Univ 1958–59, Caltech 1959–60; lectr then sr lectr in mathematical physics Univ of Birmingham 1960–76, prof of mathematical educn Univ of Nottingham 1976–92; dir Shell Centre for Mathematical Educn 1976–92, dir Balanced Assessment for the Mathematics Curriculum and other int projects 1992–; chm International Society for Design and Development in Educn 1999– visiting prof: UCLA 1968–69, CERN 1964–66 and 1973–74, UC Berkeley 1992–95, Michigan State Univ 1997–; memb: Jt Mathematical Cncl of the UK 1979–85 (treas 1982–85), Nat Curriculum Mathematical Working Gp 1987–88; nat memb Int Cmmn on Mathematics Instruction 1980–88; *Books* Dispersion Relation Dynamics (1969), The Real World and Mathematics (1981), Problem Solving - A World View (1988), Curriculum - towards the Year 2000; *Recreations* oboe, theatre, dance; *Style*— Prof Hugh Burkhardt; ✉ e-mail hugh.burkhardt@nottingham.ac.uk

BURLAND, James Alan; s of James Glyn Burland, and Elizabeth Beresford, *née* Thompson (d 1978); *b* 25 September 1954; *Educ* King Henry VIII Sch Coventry, Univ of Bath (BSc, BArch); *Career* architect; Arup Assocs 1978–86, Philip Cox Richardson Taylor and Partners Sydney 1986–90, dir and princ architect Arup Assocs 1996– (re-joined 1990), fndr BURLAND TM; projects incl: Stockley Park Heathrow, Bedford HS Jr Sch, Durham New Coll, Manchester Olympic and Nat Stadium, Johannesburg Athletics Stadium, Glasgow Nat Arena, Plantation House London; private cmmns The Body Shop Bath, Liverpool and Brighton 1982–83; current projects incl: Ealing Studios, Providence Row Refuge and Convent Devpt, Pinewood and Shepperton Film Studios, World One Sports Arena, Falcon Wharf Thameside apartments, Bermondsey St Market, conslt Manchester Cwlth Games Stadium; external tutor Univ of Sydney 1987–88; memb Nat Tst; RIBA 1983; *Recreations* racing bicycles, watercolouring, guitar, theatre; *Clubs* Chelsea Arts; *Style*— James Burland, Esq; ✉ BURLANDTM, 43–45 Charlotte Street, London W1T 1RS (tel 020 7255 2070, fax 020 7255 2071, e-mail jb@burlandtm.com)

BURLAND, Prof John Boscawen; CBE (2005); s of John Whitmore Burland (d 1994), and Margaret Irene, *née* Boscawen (d 1986); *b* 4 March 1936; *Educ* Parktown Boys' HS Johannesburg, Univ of the Witwatersrand (BSc, MSc, DSc), Emmanuel Coll Cambridge (PhD); *m* 30 March 1963, Gillian Margaret, da of John Kenneth Miller (d 1981); 2 s (David 1965, Timothy 1967), 1 da (Tamsin 1969); *Career* engr Ove Arup and Ptnrs London 1961–63; Building Res Estab: SSO, PSO 1966–72, SPSO head Geotechnics Div 1972–79, asst dir DCSO 1979–80; visiting prof Univ of Strathclyde 1973–82; ICSTM: prof of soil mechanics 1980–2001, sr research investigator 2001–, emeritus prof of soil mechanics 2001–, fell 2004–; vice-pres ICE 2002–05, memb Cncl Royal Acad of Engrg 1994–97; commendatore Ordine della Stella di Solidarieta' Italiana 2003, memb Academia Europea; Hon DEng Heriot-Watt Univ 1994, Hon DSc Univ of Nottingham 1998, Hon DEng Univ of Glasgow 2001, Hon DSc Univ of Warwick 2003; hon fell: Emmanuel Coll Cambridge 2004, Univ of Cardiff 2005; FIStructE 2001 (MIStructE 1976), FREng 1981, FICE 1982 (MICE 1969), FRS 1997, FCGI 1997; *Recreations* golf, sailing, painting; *Style*— Prof John Burland, CBE, FRS, FREng; ✉ Department of Civil Engineering, Imperial College London, South Kensington Campus, London SW7 2AZ (tel 020 7594 6079, fax 020 7225 2716)

BURLEY, Prof Jeffery; CBE (1991); s of Jack Burley (d 1978), and Eliza Nellie Victoria, *née* Creese (d 1949); *b* 16 October 1936; *Educ* Portsmouth GS, Univ of Oxford (MA, Basketball blue), Yale Univ (MF, PhD); *m* 26 Aug 1961, Jean Shirley, da of Douglas MacDonald Palmer (d 1989); 2 s (Jeremy Andrew b 1963, Timothy John b 1966); *Career* Lt Royal Signals short serv cmmn 1954–57; UNESCO expert offr i/c Forest Genetics Res Laboratory Agric Res Cncl of Central Africa 1965–68, sr res offr Cwlth Forestry Inst Oxford 1968–76, lectr in forestry Univ of Oxford 1976–83, head Dept of Forestry and dir Cwlth Forestry Inst 1983–84, dir Oxford Forestry Inst 1985–2002, devpt fell Green Coll Oxford 2002– (professorial fell 1985–2002, vice-warden 1996–2002); emeritus fell Public Understanding of Forest Sci Leverhulme Tst 2002–04; forty consultancies with int devpt agencies; chm C-Questor plc 2006–; advsr, sponsor, patron or memb Ctee: Earthwatch (UK), Tree Aid, Cwlth Forestry Assoc, Br Cncl, Int Soc of Tropical Foresters; chm Cwlth Forestry Assoc 2002–05; past pres Int Union of Forestry Research Organizations; tstee Tropical Forest Tst 1999–2006, patron Speedwell and WellBeing Tst 2003–; hon memb: Royal Swedish Acad of Agric Forest Sciences, Nat Acad of Forest Sciences Italy, Soc of American Foresters; hon research prof Chinese Acad of Forestry; hon fell Inst of Chartered Foresters; *Books* Tropical Trees: variation, breeding and conservation (ed with B T Styles, 1976), A Tree for all Reasons (with P J Wood), Managing Global Genetic Resources: forest trees (jtly, 1991), Elsevier Encyclopaedia of Forest Sciences (ed, with J Evans and J A Youngquist, 2004); *Style*— Prof Jeffery Burley, CBE; ✉ Woodside, Frilford Heath, Abingdon, Oxfordshire OX13 5QG (tel 01865 390754); Green College, Woodstock Road, Oxford OX2 6HG (tel 01865 274770, e-mail jeff.burley@plants.ox.ac.uk)

B

BURLEY, Jessica Jane; da of Anthony Douglas Wiseman (d 1997), and Jean Shirley Darby, *née* Evernden; *b* 24 January 1966, Lympstone, Devon; *Educ* Bristol Poly (BA), CAM cert; *m* 24 July 1994, Mark David Burley; *Career* publishing dir Gruner + Jahr 1997–99, gp publishing dir Financial Times Business 1999–2000; exec gp publishing dir: Future Publishing 2000–01, National Magazine Co 2001–; *Style*— Mrs Jessica Burley; ✉ The National Magazine Company, 72 Broadwick Street, London W1F 9EP (tel 020 7312 4103, e-mail jessica.burley@natmags.co.uk)

BURLEY, Philip George; s of Victor George Burley (d 1989), and Blanche Clara, *née* Coleman (d 1962); *b* 31 December 1943; *Educ* Whitgift Sch Croydon, London Coll of Printing; *m* 8 June 1974, Christine Elizabeth, da of Istvan Komaromy, of Shirley, Surrey; 3 da (Victoria b 1976, Elisabeth b 1979, Georgina b 1981); *Career* musician 1961–63, md Joint Marketing and Publishing Services Ltd 1970 (graphic designer 1963–69), fndr ptnr Design Counsellors and Incentive Counsellors 1971, fndr ptnr and creative dir The Incentive Group 1972, chm The Quadrant Group 1982, chm and chief exec Excelsior Group Productions Ltd 1989–, exec prodr The Darling Buds of May 1990–, exec prodr A Touch of Frost 1992–, exec prodr and prodr Pride of Africa 1997, exec prodr My Uncle Silas 2001; composer of music for theatre and TV incl title music for The Darling Buds of May 1990 (Ivor Novello Award for Best TV Theme Music 1991); festival dir Polesden Lacey Festival 1999–2002; chief barker Variety Club of GB 1999; govr Guildford Sch of Acting 2002–; *Recreations* music, theatre, art, reading, golf; *Clubs* Foxhills Golf and Country, Kingswood Golf and Country; *Style*— Philip Burley, Esq; ✉ Excelsior Group Productions Limited, Heathwoods, Dorking Road, Walton-on-the-Hill, Tadworth, Surrey KT20 7TJ (tel 01737 812673, fax 01737 813163)

BURMAN, Peter Ashley Thomas Insull; MBE (1991); s of Thomas Bayliss Insull Burman (d 1975), and Eileen Patricia Winifred, *née* King-Morgan; *b* 15 September 1944; *Educ* Tudor Grange GS, King's Coll Cambridge (exhibitioner, BA); *Career* successively asst sec, dep sec and sec C of E Cncl for the Care of Churches and Cathedrals Advsy Cmmn for England 1968–99, dir Centre for Conservation Dept of Archaeology Univ of York 1990–2002, dir of conservation and property servs Nat Tst for Scot 2003–; Esher Award for Outstanding Services to Conservation Soc for the Protection of Ancient Buildings 2003; chm: Fabric Advsy Ctee St Paul's Cathedral; Dr (hc) State Univ of Brandenburg Cottbus 2003; FSA; *Books* Chapels and Churches: Who Cares (with Marcus Binney, 1977), Change and Decay: The Future of our Churches (1977), St Paul's Cathedral (1989), Treasures on Earth (ed and contrib, 1993), Thomas Gambier Parry Catalogue (contrib, 1993), Economic Aspects of Architectural Conservation (ed and contrib, 1995), Conserving the Railway Heritage (ed and contrib, 1996), Heritage and Renewal: European Cathedrals in the late Twentieth Century (ed and contrib, 1996), Structure and Style (contrib, 1997), Architecture 1900 (ed and contrib, 1998), From William Morris: Building Conservation and the Arts & Crafts Cult of Authenticity 1877–1939 (contrib, 2005), St Paul's: The Cathedral Church of London 604–2004 (contrib, 2005), Architectural Heritage XVII (contrib, 2006), Stone Conservation, Principles & Practice (contrib, 2006, Sir Robert McAlpine International Book Award for Construction); *Recreations* playing the piano, mountain biking, travelling; *Style*— Dr Peter Burman, MBE; ✉ 39 (1F) Drummond Place, Edinburgh EH3 6NR (tel 0131 556 3876); The National Trust for Scotland, Wemyss House, 28 Charlotte Square, Edinburgh EH2 4ET (tel 0131 243 9439, e-mail pburman@nts.org.uk)

BURN, (Bryan) Adrian Falconer; s of Reginald Falconer Burn (d 1981), and Kathleen Ruth, *née* Davis (d 2002); *b* 23 May 1945; *Educ* Abingdon Sch; *m* 1968, Jeanette Carol; 4 c (Clare b 1976, Victoria b 1979, Katharine b 1983, James b 1985); *Career* chartered accountant Whinney Murray 1968–72 (articled clerk 1964–68); Binder Hamlyn: joined 1973, ptnr 1977, managing ptnr 1988–97; ptnr Arthur Andersen (following merger) 1994–99; chm: Atlas Group Holdings Ltd 1999–2002, Search Holdings Ltd 2000–06; non-exec dir: Brent International plc 1994–99, Era Group plc 1999–2001, Wolff Olins 1999–2001, G E Capital Bank Ltd 1999–, Richards Butler 1999–2006, Strutt and Parker 1999–2006, Pinewood Shepperton plc 2000–, Smart and Cook Hldgs 2004–07, Acertec plc 2006–; treas and tstee NSPCC 1999–; FCA (ACA 1968); *Style*— Adrian Burn, Esq; ✉ mobile 07770 581513, e-mail ab@adrianburn.fsnet.co.uk

BURN, Prof Edward Hector; s of Edward Burn, MBE (d 1982), and Bertha Maud, *née* Hector (d 1976); *b* 20 November 1922; *Educ* St Edward's Sch Oxford, Wadham Coll Oxford (MA, BCL); *m* 1, 21 Dec 1948, Helen Joyce (d 2000), da of Maj Merrick Hugh McConnel, RHA (ka 1917); m 2, 17 May 2001, Marilyn Kennedy-McGregor; *Career* cmmnd 1 Bucks Bn, Oxford Bucks, Capt GSO 3 1 Airborne Corps, Maj GSO 2 26 Indian Div (despatches Normandy 1944 and Sumatra 1946); called to the Bar Lincoln's Inn 1951 (hon bencher 1980); student and tutor in jurisprudence Christ Church Oxford 1954–90, Censor of Christ Church 1959–64, lectr in law Inns of Court 1965–80, prof City Univ 1990– (visiting prof 1983–90), lectr in law St Hugh's Coll Oxford 1990–2001; cmmr of Inland Revenue 1975–98, memb Tst Law Ctee; former govr: St Edward's Sch Oxford, Rossall Sch; Hon DCL: City Univ 1990, King's Univ Halifax Nova Scotia 1991; *Books* Maudsley and Burn Trusts and Trustees (edns 1–7), Maudsley and Burn Land Law (edns 1–8), Cheshire and Burn Modern Law of Real Property (edns 11–17); *Clubs* Athenaeum, MCC; *Style*— Prof Edward Burn; ✉ 52 Cumberland Terrace, London NW1 4HJ

BURN, Dr Geoffrey Robert Hale; s of George Robert Burn (d 1974), and Grace, *née* Downs; *b* 19 November 1945; *Educ* St Peter's Coll, RMA, Univ of Brighton (PhD, postgrad Dip); *m* 29 Dec 1985, Judith Irene, da of John William Palmieri, of Windsor; 1 s (Hale, decd), 2 da (Sacha b 1987, Vita b 1990); *Career* Lt RA 1967–71; sales exec Prentice Hall 1971–72, managing ed McGraw Hill 1971–72, publishing and mktg dir Methuen Publications 1975–82, pres Butterworth Canada 1982–87, md Butterworth Sci 1987–90; exec dir of publishing BMA 1990–95, chief exec Thomson Science and Professional 1995–98, chief exec Brooks/Cole 1998–2000, md Stanford Univ Press 2000–; faculty memb publishing courses and prog dir academic and professional publishing Banff Sch of Fine Arts 1986–87, faculty memb and course advsr Stanford Professional Publishing Courses 2001–; dir: Canadian Book Publishers' Cncl 1977–82, Academic and Professional Gp Publishers' Assoc 1988–90; memb Canadian Law Info Cncl 1982–87; lay min Hosp Chaplaincy, lay Eucharistic min; Liveryman Worshipful Soc of Apothecaries; FCMI, FInstD; Order of Polonia Restituta; *Recreations* gardening, reading, skiing, mountain biking; *Clubs* Athenaeum; *Style*— Dr Geoffrey R H Burn; ✉ Stanford University Press, 1450 Page Mill Road, Palo Alto, CA 94304, USA

BURN, Gordon; s of James Edward Burn, and Joyce, *née* Fisher; *b* 16 January 1948; *Educ* Rutherford GS Newcastle upon Tyne, Univ of London (BA); *Partner* since 1971, Carol Gorner, painter; *Career* writer; freelance writer and author 1969–, writer Sunday Times 1974–82; reg contrib to The Observer, TLS, The Guardian, Modern Painters; Columnist of the Year Award Magazine Publishing Awards 1991 (for column in Esquire); Hon DLitt Univ of Plymouth 1993; Sargant fell in critical and caratorial studies Br Sch at Rome 2008; *Books* Somebody's Husband, Somebody's Son - The Story of the Yorkshire

Ripper (1984, shortlisted Silver Dagger Award CWA of GB 1984, shortlisted Edgar Allen Poe Award CWA of USA 1985), Pocket Money (1986), Alma Cogan (1991, Best First Novel Whitbread Prize 1991), Fullalove (1995), Happy Like Murderers (1998), On the Way to Work (with Damien Hirst, 2001), The North of England Home Service (2003), Best and Edwards (2006), Sex and Violence, Death and Silence (2008); *Recreations* idling in pubs, reading, music, walking, drinking; *Clubs* Chelsea Arts; *Style*— Gordon Burn, Esq; ✉ c/o Gillon Aitken, Gillon Aitken Associates, 18–21 Cavaye Place, London SW10 9PT (tel 020 7373 8672, fax 020 7373 6002, e-mail gordonburn@aol.com)

BURN, (John) Ian; s of Cecil Walter Burn (d 1983), and Margaret Hannah, *née* Cawthorne (d 1988); *b* 19 February 1927; *Educ* Taunton Sch, Bart's Med Coll London (MB BS, capt athletics team and United Hosps cross-country team), Univ of Manchester (BA); *m* 1951, Fiona May, da of late Alexander Allan; 2 s (Alastair James b 1952, Jonathan Mark b 1964), 2 da (Hilary Kathryn (Mrs Arnell) b 1954, Lindsay Margaret (Dr O'Kelly) b 1958); *Career* RAF Med Serv 1952–54; Anatomy Dept Univ of Cambridge 1954–55, training posts in surgery Bart's and Hammersmith Hosp 1955–65, cancer res scholarship USA 1961–62; conslt surgn: Hammersmith Hosp 1965–73, Charing Cross Hosp 1973–87 (hon consltg surgn 1987–), Harley St Clinic 1973–91; visiting conslt surgn King Edward VII Hosp Midhurst 1988–97 (med dir 1993–95, emeritus consult 1997–); specialist in malignant disease (surgical oncology); Hunterian prof RCS 1967; pres: Br Assoc of Surgical Oncology 1980–83 (fndr memb 1973), Euro Soc of Surgical Oncology 1987–90 (fndr memb 1983), World Fedn of Surgical Oncology Socs 1992–95 (fndr memb 1992); vice-pres RSM 1989–91 (hon sec 1981–87), chm Treatment of Cancer Project Ctee Int Union Against Cancer 1989–94 (Roll of Honour 1996); Freeman City of London 1986, Liveryman Worshipful Co of Barbers 1986; hon memb Finnish Surgical Soc 1986, hon assoc memb Belgian Royal Soc for Surgery 1987; FRCS 1956, memb Assoc of Surgeons of GB 1963; *Books* Systematic Surgery (1965), Understanding Cancer (co-ed, 1977), Surgical Oncology (co-ed, 1989), Breast Cancer (co-ed, 1989), Operative Cancer Surgery (co-ed, 1992), The Company of Barbers and Surgeons (ed, 2000), Journey of a Cancer Surgeon (memoirs, 2007); author of numerous chapters and articles on cancer; *Recreations* opera, visiting islands, history of medicine; *Clubs* MCC, Petworth Park Cricket (life memb), Rother Valley Croquet (capt); *Style*— Ian Burn; ✉ Coleherne Cottage, 18A Sea Avenue, Rustington, West Sussex BN16 2DG

BURN, Prof John; s of Henry Burn, of West Auckland, Co Durham, and Margaret, *née* Wilkinson; *b* 6 February 1952; *Educ* Barnard Castle GS, Univ of Newcastle upon Tyne (BMedSci, MB BS, MD); *m* 5 Aug 1972, Linda Marjorie, da of Charles Frederick Wilson, of Winston, Darlington, Co Durham; 1 da (Danielle Louise b 17 Aug 1977), 1 s (James Richard David b 20 Sept 1981); *Career* jr med trg Newcastle teaching hosps 1976–80, hon sr registrar in clinical genetics Gt Ormond St Hosp 1981–84, conslt clinical geneticist Royal Victoria Infirmary Newcastle 1984–91; Univ of Newcastle upon Tyne: clinical lectr 1984–91, prof of clinical genetics 1991–, head Div of Human Genetics 1992–98; exec dir Northern Genetics Knowledge Park, med dir and head Inst of Human Genetics; chm UK Cancer Family Study Gp 1996–2002; memb: gen sec Clinical Genetics Soc of GB 1989–95, Ctee on Clinical Genetics RCP 1991–93, Bd Euro Soc of Human Genetics 1995–99, Human Genetics Cmmn 1999–2005; chair Int Soc for Gastrointestinal Hereditary Tumours (InSIGHT), pres European Soc of Human Genetics 2006–07; FRCP 1989 (MRCP 1978), FRCPCH 1997, FRCOG 1998, FMedSci 2000, FRCPEd 2003; *Recreations* running, golf, playing drums; *Style*— Prof John Burn; ✉ Institute of Human Genetics, Central Parkway, Newcastle upon Tyne NE1 3BZ

BURN, (Adrian) Lachlan; *Educ* Univ of Bristol; *Career* slr; Linklaters: articled clerk 1974–76, slr 1976–82, ptnr 1982– (Paris office 1982–87, capital markets 1987–); legal advsr Int Primary Markets Assoc; memb: Legal Risk Review Ctee Bank of England 1991–92, Financial Markets Law Ctee 2002–06, Advsy Ctee Listing Authy, Primary Markets Gp London Stock Exchange; gen ed Capital Markets Law Jl 2006–; *Recreations* music, literature, travel; *Style*— Lachlan Burn, Esq; ✉ Linklaters, One Silk Street, London EC2Y 8HQ (tel 020 7456 4614, fax 020 7456 2222, e-mail lburn@linklaters.com)

BURNE, Dr Yvonne Anne; da of Archie Ford (d 2004), and Florence Louise, *née* Knott (d 1986); *b* 29 August 1947; *Educ* Redland HS Bristol, Westfield Coll London (BA, PhD); *m* Aug 1968, Dr Anthony Burne, s of Reginald Burne; 1 da (Anna Claire Louise b June 1977), 1 s (Daniel Robert Charles b April 1980); *Career* teacher of French and German Harrow Co GS for Girls 1971–74, head of German and careers Lowlands Sixth Form Coll Harrow 1974–77, writer and educnl ed Educational Challenges Inc 1978–82, commissioning ed Mary Glasgow and Heinemann 1983–84, head of modern foreign languages and careers Northwood Coll 1984–87, headmistress St Helen's Sch Northwood 1987–95, headmistress City of London Sch for Girls 1995–2007; modern languages conslt John Murray Ltd 1984–89; GSA: chair London Region 2002–, chm London Branch 2003–06 (sec 2002); memb: ctee to estab N London Ind Girls' Schs' Consortium 1990–96, Centre for British Teachers (CfBT)/ISC 1997–99, Europe Ctee ISC 1998–, London and SE Regnl Ctee ISC 2002–; tstee Mitchell City of London Charity and Educnl Fndn 1995–; tstee Westfield Coll, govr Reigate GS 2002–, govr Berkhamsted Collegiate Sch; memb and non-exec dir Hillingdon Family Health Servs Authy 1990–96; memb Bd Int Inst for Object Relations Therapy (IORT) Washington DC; fndr memb Guild of Educators 2001 (memb Ct 2001–); *Publications* Tomorrow's News (short story, 1979), The Circus Comes to Town (1981); contrib to Zaner-Blosser Spelling Series (USA) and author of various magazine articles incl contribs to National Geographic World magazine (USA); *Recreations* theatre and arts, reading, entertaining, social bridge, swimming, walking; *Clubs* Univ Women's; *Style*— Dr Yvonne Burne; ✉ City of London School for Girls, St Giles' Terrace, Barbican, London EC2Y 8BB

BURNELL-NUGENT, Adm Sir James Michael; KCB (2004), CBE (1999); *Educ* CCC Cambridge (MA); *m* Mary *née* Woods; 1 da (Henrietta), 3 s (Anthony, Rupert, Tom); *Career* RN: joined 1971, Capt HMS Olympus (submarine) 1978, Capt HMS Conqueror (submarine) 1984–86, Capt 1990, Capt Second Frigate Sqdn and Capt HMS Brilliant 1992–93 (Bosnia), Cdre 1994, Capt HMS Invincible 1997–99 (Gulf, Kosovo), Rear Adm 1999, Asst Chief of Naval Staff 1999–2001, memb Admiralty Bd 1999–2001 and 2003–, Cdr UK Maritime Forces and ASW Striking Force 2001–02 (Operation Enduring Freedom), Vice Adm 2003–, Second Sea Lord and C-in-C Naval Home Command 2003–; Queen's Gold Medal, Max Horton Prize; yr bro Trinity House 2004; Freeman City of London 1999; hon fell CCC Cambridge; *Recreations* living in the country; *Style*— Adm Sir James Burnell-Nugent, KCB, CBE; ✉ The Naval Secretary, Victory Building, HM Naval Base, Portsmouth PO1 3NH

BURNETT, Alexander John (Sandy); s of George David Burnett (d 2000), and Margaret Marion Elizabeth, *née* Miller; *b* 29 October 1964; *Educ* Glasgow Acad, St Catharine's Coll Cambridge (MA); *m* 29 Oct 1994, Clare Elizabeth, *née* Gibbons; 1 s (Robbie b 5 July 1995), 1 da (Anna b 18 April 1997); *Career* freelance musical dir for regnl theatres, RSC, RNT (incl world tour of Richard III) and West End (incl Carousel) 1987–94; radio presenter: BBC Radio 3 1994– (incl: Proms 1996–, Edinburgh Int Festival morning concerts 2000–05, Morning on 3 2003–07), Lyric FM RTÉ 1999– (incl Calling the Tune 1999–2002), Grace Notes BBC Radio Scotland 2001–02; conductor: Bach cantata cycle St Michael and All Angels Church London 1997–, BWV Chamber Baroque, Pegasus Choir and Amici; jazz double bassist; *Style*— Sandy Burnett, Esq; ✉ sb@sandyburnett.com

BURNETT, (Ronald) Bruce Owen; s of Lt Col Ronald John Burnett, OBE, of Bentworth, Hants, and Stella Ruth, *née* Cundy; *b* 17 April 1959; *Educ* Denstone Coll, Univ of London (BA); *m* 1, 2 Nov 1991 (m dis 2002), Pippa Lesley, da of Sqdn Ldr Leslie Sands; m 2, 22 May 2004, Fiona Jane, da of John Sutherland; 1 da (Sienna Isabella Phoebe b 11 Oct 2004); *Career* Rowntree Mackintosh: sales rep 1981–82, nat accounts exec 1982–83, trade devpt exec 1983–84, trade mktg/sales promotion mangr 1984–85, asst nat sales mangr 1985–86, brand mangr 1986–87, sr brand mangr 1987–89, gp mktg mangr 1989–91; Trebor Bassett (subsid of Cadbury Schweppes): mktg mangr 1991–92, mktg gen mangr 1992–93, mktg dir 1993–97; gp commercial dir Communication Innovation Group; md: Creative Concept Development Ltd, Origin8 International Sourcing Ltd, Global Sponsorship Management Ltd 1997–2000; ceo i2i Face to Face Marketing Ltd 2001–; *Recreations* dressage, polo, mountaineering, photography, art and architecture, antiques; *Clubs* Cowdray Park Polo, Cirencester Park Polo; *Style*— Bruce Burnett, Esq

BURNETT, Sir Charles David; 4 Bt (UK 1913), of Selborne House, Co Borough of Croydon; s of Sir David Burnett, 3 Bt, MBE, TD (d 2002); *b* 18 May 1951; *Educ* Harrow, Lincoln Coll Oxford; *m* 21 Oct 1989 (m dis), Victoria Joan, er da of James Simpson, of Rye, E Sussex; 1 da (Roberta Elizabeth b 24 July 1992); m 2, 2 Sept 1998, Kay Rosemary, *née* Naylor; 1 da (Isabel Louise b 23 Jan 2004); *Career* international insurance broker; *Recreations* wine, fishing, travel, shooting; *Clubs* Brooks's, Turf, 106; *Style*— Sir Charles Burnett, Bt; ✉ 25 Marloes Road, London W8 6LG (tel 020 7975 2546, fax 020 7975 2840)

BURNETT, Charles John; s of Charles Alexander Urquhart Burnett (d 1977), of Fraserburgh, Aberdeenshire, and Agnes, *née* Watt; *b* 6 November 1940; *Educ* Fraserburgh Acad, Gray's Sch of Art Aberdeen (DA), Aberdeen Coll of Educn, Univ of Edinburgh (MLitt, 1992); *m* 29 April 1967, Aileen Elizabeth, da of Alexander Robb McIntyre (d 1982), of Portsoy, Banffshire; 1 da (Sara b 1969), 2 s (Sandy b 1972, John b 1976); *Career* Advertising Dept House of Fraser 1963–64, Exhibitions Div Central Office of Information 1964–68, asst curator Letchworth Museum and Art Gallery 1968–71, head of design Nat Museum of Antiquities of Scotland 1971–85, curator of fine art Scot United Servs Museum Edinburgh Castle 1985–96, chamberlain Duff House Banff 1997–2004; heraldic advsr Girl Guide Assoc Scotland 1978–, vice-patron Genealogical Soc of Queensland Aust 1986–, vice-pres Soc of Antiquaries of Scot 1992–95 (memb Cncl 1986–88), memb Advsy Bd Heraldry Soc of Ireland 1986–90, pres Heraldry Soc of Scot 2003– (vice-pres 1987–2003); librarian Priory of the Order of St John in Scot 1987–98; tstee St Andrews Fund for Socts Heraldry 2001–, chm Banff Preservation and Heritage Soc 2002–, advsr Pitsligo Castle Tst 2003–; pres 27th Int Congress for Genealogical and Heraldic Sciences 2006; numerous pubns on Scottish history and heraldry; HM Offr of Arms: Dingwall Pursuivant 1983, Ross Herald 1988–; tstee Bield Retirement Housing Tst 1992–96; first hon memb Dorothy Dunnett Readers' Assoc 2006; hon citizen State of Oklahoma USA 1989; convenor Companions of the Order of Malta 1991–94; FSA Scot 1964, AMA 1972, FHS Scot 1989; KStJ 1991 (CStJ 1982, OStJ 1974, SBStJ 1972); Knight of the Order of St Maurice and St Lazarus 1999, Knight of the Order of Francis I 2002; *Books* The Honours of Scotland (jtly, 1993), Scotland's Heraldic Heritage (jtly, 1997), The Order of St John in Scotland (jtly, 2000), Stall Plates of the Most Ancient and Most Noble Order of the Thistle in the Chapel of the Order within St Giles' Cathedral, The High Kirk of Edinburgh (jtly, 2001); *Recreations* reading, visiting places of historic interest; *Clubs* Banff Town and County; *Style*— Charles J Burnett, Esq; ✉ Seaview House, Portsoy, Banffshire AB45 2RS; Court of the Lord Lyon, HM New Register House, Edinburgh EH1 3YT (tel 0131 556 7255)

BURNETT, Prof Charles Stuart Freeman; s of Donald Stuart Burnett, and Joan, *née* Freeman; *b* 26 September 1951; *Educ* Manchester Grammar, St John's Coll Cambridge (BA, PhD), LGSM; *m* 1, 1985 (m dis 1991), Mitsuru Kamachi; m 2, 1995, Tamae Nakamura; 2 s (Ken Stuart b 21 Sept 1995, Miki Jo b 30 Dec 1997); *Career* jr research fell St John's Coll Cambridge 1975–79, sr research fell Warburg Inst London 1979–82, Leverhulme research fell Dept of History Univ of Sheffield 1982–84 and 1985, prof Warburg Inst London 1999– (lectr 1985–99); distinguished visiting prof Univ of Calif Berkeley 2003; FBA 1998; *Publications* Jesuit Plays on Japan and English Recusancy (with M Takenaka, 1995), Magic and Divination in the Middle Ages: Texts and Techniques in the Islamic and Christian Worlds (1996), The Introduction of Arabic Learning into England (1997); also author of over 100 articles in learned jls; *Style*— Prof Charles Burnett, FBA; ✉ Warburg Institute, Woburn Square, London WC1H 0AB (tel 020 7862 8949, e-mail charles.burnett@sas.ac.uk)

BURNETT, David Henry; s of George Dawson Burnett, CBE, TD, of Surrey, and Ferdinanda Anna; *Educ* Tonbridge, Churchill Coll Cambridge (MA); *Career* head of global research HSBC Bank plc; *Style*— David H Burnett, Esq; ✉ Faircroft, Vale of Health, London NW3 1AN; HSBC Bank plc, 8 Canada Square, London E14 5HQ

BURNETT, David John Stuart; s of John Edward Burnett (d 1989), and Margaret Kathleen (*née* Cole); *b* 6 February 1958; *Educ* Oundle, Peterhouse Cambridge; *m* 1988, Anne, da of C J C Humfrey (d 1993); 1 s (Joe Alexander Stuart b 9 Aug 1990), 1 da (Laura Frances Kathleen b 16 June 1992); *Career* Rowe & Pitman 1979–86 (ptnr 1985–86); dir S G Warburg Securities Ltd 1986–95, md SBC Warburg 1995–98; TT International: managing ptnr 1998–2005, ptnr 2005–; chm Smart & Cook Hldgs 2006–, dir BMS Finance 2006–; *Style*— David Burnett, Esq; ✉ Hall Farm, Wigsthorpe, Northamptonshire PE8 5SE (tel 01832 720488, fax 01832 720588); 49 Montagu Mansions, London W1U 6LG (tel 020 7935 1372); TT International, Moor House, 120 London Wall, London EC2Y 5ET (tel 020 7509 1230)

BURNETT, Ian Duncan; QC (1998); s of David John Burnett (d 1990); and Maureen Burnett, *née* O'Brien; *b* 28 February 1958; *Educ* St John's Coll Southsea, Pembroke Coll Oxford (MA); *m* 2 November 1991, Caroline Ruth Monks; 1 s (Robert Andrew b 4 Feb 1998), 1 da (Helen Alexandra b 12 June 2003); *Career* called to the Bar Middle Temple 1980 (Astbury scholar, bencher 2001), jr counsel to the Crown (common law) 1992–98, recorder 2000– (asst recorder 1998–2000), head of chambers 2003–; *Recreations* history, silver, music, wine; *Clubs* Carlton; *Style*— Ian Burnett, Esq, QC; ✉ 1 Temple Gardens, Temple, London EC4Y 9BB (tel 020 7583 1315, fax 020 7353 3969, e-mail ianburnett@1templegardens.co.uk)

BURNETT, Sir John Harrison; kt (1987); s of Rev T Harrison Burnett, of Paisley; *b* 21 January 1922; *Educ* Kingswood Sch Bath, Merton Coll Oxford; *m* 1945, Enid Margaret, er da of Rev Dr Edgar W Bishop; 2 s; *Career* served WWII Lt RNVR (despatches) Atlantic, Channel, Mediterranean; fell Magdalen Coll Oxford 1949–54; prof of botany: Univ of St Andrews 1955–60, Univ of Newcastle upon Tyne 1960–68; regius prof of botany Univ of Glasgow 1968–70, Sibthorpian prof of rural economy and fellow St John's Coll Oxford 1970–79, princ and vice-chllr Univ of Edinburgh 1979–87; exec sec World Cncl for the Biosphere 1987–93; chm: Co-ordinating Cmmn for Biological Recording 1988–2004, Int Orgn for Plant Info 1991–96, Nat Biodiversity Network Tst 1998–2005; hon research prof Open Univ 1996–2000; Hon DSc: Univ of Buckingham 1981, Univ of Pennsylvania 1983; Hon LLD: Univ of Dundee 1982, Univ of Strathclyde 1983, Univ of Glasgow 1987; Dr (hc) Univ of Edinburgh 1988; hon fell: Green Coll Oxford 1987, Merton Coll Oxford 1997; FRSE 1957, FIBiol 1969, Hon FRCSEd 1983; Commendatore Order of Merit Republic of Italy 1990; *Books* Vegetation of Scotland (1964), Fundamentals of Mycology (1968, 1976), Mycogenetics (1975), Fungal Walls and Hyphal Growth (with A J P Trinci, 1979), Edinburgh University Portraits II (1985), Speciation in Fungi (1988), Maintenance of the Biosphere (with N Polunin, 1990), Surviving with the Biosphere (with N Polunin, 1993), Biological Recording in the United Kingdom (jtly, 1995), Fungal Populations and Species (2003); *Recreations* writing, walking, gardening; *Clubs* Athenaeum, Royal Over-Seas League; *Style*— Sir John Burnett; ✉ 13 Field House Drive, Oxford OX2 7NT

BURNETT, Baron (Life Peer 2006), of Whitchurch in the County of Devon; John Patrick Aubone Burnett; *Educ* Ampleforth, Commando Trg Centre Royal Marines, Britannia Royal Naval Coll Dartmouth, Coll of Law London; *m* 1971, Elizabeth (Billie); 2 s, 2 da; *Career* Royal Marines 1964–70: troop cdr 42 Commando RM Borneo 1965–66, troop cdr and second in command company 40 Commando RM Far East and Middle East 1967–69, ret as Lt; qualified as slr 1975, ptnr then sr ptnr Burd Pearse Slrs Okehampton 1976–97; farmer 1976–98: memb cncl Devon Cattle Breeders' Soc 1985–97, winner Devon Cattle Breeders Soc Nat Herd Competition 1989; MP (Lib Dem) Devon W and Torridge 1997–2005; Lib Dem spokesman on legal affairs 1997–2002, memb Finance Bill Ctee 1998–2005, Lib Dem shadow Attorney General 2002–05; conslt Stephens & Scown 2005–; memb: Revenue Law Ctee Law Soc 1984–96, Royal Marines Assoc (N Devon Branch), Royal Br Legion; *Style*— The Rt Hon the Lord Burnett; ✉ Stephens & Scown, Curzon House, Southernhay West, Exeter EX1 1RS (tel 01392 210700, fax 01392 274010, e-mail commerce.exeter@stephens-scown.co.uk)

BURNETT, Richard Leslie; s of Sir Leslie T Burnett, Bt, CBE (d 1955), of Godstone, Surrey, and Joan, *née* Humphery; *b* 23 June 1932; *Educ* Eton, RCM, King's Coll Cambridge; *m* Katrina Eveline, *née* Hendrey; *Career* concert pianist, specialising in fortepianos (early pianos) 1970–; fndr and dir Finchcocks Museum; *Recordings* incl: Schubert's Die Schöne Müllerin (with Nigel Rogers) and Die Winterreise, Haydn's Sonatas, The Romantic Fortepiano, Clementi's Fortepiano Works, Beethoven's Violin Sonatas and Songs, Hummel's Violin and Piano Works, Mozart Piano Quartets, Mendelssohn's Clarinet Works, Brahms' Clarinet Trio; *Style*— Richard Burnett, Esq; ✉ Finchcocks, Goudhurst, Kent TN17 1HH (tel 01580 211702, fax 01580 211007)

BURNETT, Dr Rodney Alister; s of Ronald Andrew Burnett (d 1961), of Congleton, Cheshire, and Agnes Shirlaw, *née* McGauchie (d 1988); *b* 6 June 1947; *Educ* Sandbach Sch Cheshire, Univ of St Andrews (MB ChB); *m* 1974, Maureen Elizabeth, da of William Patrick Dunn (d 1982), of Burnside, Glasgow; 2 da (Claire Marie b 15 April 1975, Katharine Victoria b 2 June 1981); *Career* lectr in pathology Univ of Glasgow 1974–79, conslt pathologist and head admin Dept of Pathology Stobhill Hosp Glasgow 1979–85, lead clincian in pathology Univ Dept of Pathology Western Infirmary Glasgow 1985–; vice-pres ACP 2001–03 (pres Caledonian Branch 2001–04 (sec 1987–94)); FRCPath, FRIPH 1992 (memb Cncl 1992–97, chm Bd of Educn and Examination for Anatomical Pathology Technicians), FRCPGlas 1994; *Recreations* golf; *Style*— Dr Rodney Burnett; ✉ Department of Pathology, Western Infirmary, Glasgow (tel 0141 211 2000 ext 2343)

BURNETT, Timothy Adrian John; s of late Lt-Col Maurice John Brownless Burnett, DSO, DL, of Dalton, N Yorks, and late Crystal Henrietta Deschamps, *née* Chamier; *b* 12 April 1937; *Educ* Eton, Trinity Coll Cambridge (BA); *m* 15 July 1961, (Catherine Barbara) Jean, da of Dr Julius Harald Beilby (d 1978), of Bedale, N Yorks; 1 da (Henrietta b 1962), 1 s (James b 1964); *Career* 2 Lt Coldstream Gds 1956–58; asst keeper Dept of Manuscripts Br Museum 1961, manuscripts librarian Br Library 1986–97, conslt Robert Holden Ltd Fine Art Agents 1997–; memb Cncl Leather Conservation Tst; owner Dunsa Manor Estate, tstee Kiplin Hall Tst; FSA 2005; *Books* The Rise and Fall of a Regency Dandy, The Life and Times of Scrope Berdmore Davies (1981), Byron, Childe Harold Canto III (1988), Browning, The Ring and The Book (1998, 2000, 2004); *Recreations* architectural history, travel, sailing, shooting, fishing; *Clubs* Beefsteak, Pratt's, Royal Yacht Sqdn; *Style*— Timothy Burnett, Esq, FSA; ✉ 11 Highbury Place, London N5 1QZ (tel 020 7226 6234, e-mail tajburnett@aol.com); Dunsa Manor, Dalton, Richmond, North Yorkshire DL11 7HE; Robert Holden Fine Art Agents, 15 Savile Row, London W1X 1AE (tel 020 7437 6010, fax 020 7437 1733)

BURNETT-HALL, Richard Hamilton; s of Basil Burnett-Hall (d 1982), and Kathleen Ruth, *née* Wilson (d 1992); *b* 5 August 1935; *Educ* Marlborough, Trinity Hall Cambridge (MA); *m* 25 April 1964, Judith Diana (Judy), da of Robert Newton, CMG (d 1983); 1 da (Louisa b 1965), 2 s (John b 1967, Graham b 1970); *Career* Nat Serv RCS 1954–56, 2 Lt 1955; Carpmaels & Ransford 1960–68, Int Synthetic Rubber Co Ltd 1968–71; McKenna & Co Slrs: joined 1971, admitted slr 1974, ptnr 1974–94; head of Environmental Gp Bristows Slrs 1995–2000 (conslt 1998–); chm Bio Convertors plc, co sec Vertal Ltd; Freeman Berwick-upon-Tweed 1965; FCIPA 1965, FRSA; *Books* Environmental Law (1995); *Recreations* music; *Style*— Richard Burnett-Hall, Esq; ✉ Bristows, 3 Lincoln's Inn Fields, London WC2A 3AA (tel 020 7400 8000, fax 020 7400 8050, e-mail rh@b-hall.co.uk)

BURNETT-HITCHCOCK, (Basil) James; *b* 3 December 1943; *Educ* Eton, St Edmund Hall Oxford (BA); *m* 1, March 1973 (m dis 1997), Elizabeth Jane, *née* Samuel; 2 da (Gemma b 13 June 1977, Laura b 8 July 1980), 1 s (Tom b 25 Aug 1982); m 2, March 1998, Dawn Alison, *née* Perkins; *Career* admitted slr 1971; ptnr: Oswald Hickson Collier & Co 1972–78, Cameron Kenn Nordon 1978–80, Cameron Markby 1980–88, Cameron Markby Hewitt 1988–97 (head Litigation Dept 1990–96), CMS Cameron McKenna 1997–99 (conslt 1999–); visiting prof Coll of Law 1999–; qualified mediator CEDR/ADR Gp; memb Civil Litigation Ctee Law Soc 1993–2000, memb Law Soc Working Party on Lord Woolf's reforms; former pres London Slrs' Litigation Assoc; memb: Law Soc 1971, City Slrs' Co; *Recreations* sailing, boat-building, music, reading, gardening; *Clubs* Helford River Sailing; *Style*— James Burnett-Hitchcock, Esq; ✉ Three Chimneys, Cousley Wood, Wadhurst, East Sussex TN5 6QU

BURNEY, Sir Nigel Dennistoun; 4 Bt (UK 1921), of Preston House, Preston Candover, Co Southampton; s of Sir Cecil Dennistoun Burney, 3 Bt (d 2002); *b* 6 September 1959; *Educ* Eton, Trinity Coll Cambridge; *m* 1992, Lucy Vanessa, yst da of Bobby Brooks, of Chelsea; 2 s (Max Dennistoun b 15 Sept 1994, Otto James Cecil b 1 Dec 1995), 2 da (India Rose b 20 July 1999, Zara Louise b 21 May 2003); *Heir* s, Max Burney; *Clubs* Annabel's, White's; *Style*— Sir Nigel Burney, Bt; ✉ North Heath House, Chieveley, Newbury, Berkshire RG20 8UD (e-mail nigel@nigelburney.com)

BURNHAM, (Robert) Alan; s of Francis Bertram Burnham (d 1999), and Mabel, *née* Smith; *b* 9 October 1950; *Educ* Quarry Bank HS Liverpool, Univ of Liverpool (MA); *m* 1973, Valerie Ann, da of Richard Bolingbroke Cooper; 1 da (Laura Jane b 12 June 1980), 1 s (Michael Richard b 5 June 1986); *Career* joined Civil Service 1969, actg chief exec War Pensions Agency 2001 (dir of ops 1998–2001), chief exec Veterans Agency 2002–06; MIMgt 1995, memb Inst of Welfare 1996, MInstD 1999; *Recreations* foreign travel, music, film, poetry, 40 year association with Everton FC; *Style*— Alan Burnham, Esq

BURNHAM, Rt Rev Andrew; *see:* Ebbsfleet, Bishop of

BURNHAM, Rt Hon Andrew (Andy); PC (2007), MP; *b* 7 January 1970; *Educ* Fitzwilliam Coll Cambridge (MA); *m* 2000, Marie-France van Heel; 1 s, 2 da; *Career* researcher to Tessa Jowell, MP 1994–97, Parly offr NHS Confedn 1997, advsr to Football Task Force 1997–98, special advsr to Rt Hon Chris Smith, MP 1998–2001, MP (Lab) Leigh 2001–; memb Health Select Ctee 2001–03, formerly PPS to Rt Hon David Blunkett, MP, Parly sec Home Office 2005–06, min of state Dept of Health 2006–07, chief sec to the Treasy 2007–; chair Supporters Direct 2002–05; memb Co-op Pty, affliated to Unison and TGWU; *Recreations* football, rugby league, cricket; *Clubs* Everton FC; *Style*— The Rt Hon Andy Burnham, MP; ✉ House of Commons, London SW1A 0AA

BURNHAM, Eleanor; AM; da of Meirion Roberts (d 2003), and Emily Ellen, *née* White; *b* 17 April 1951, Wrexham; *Educ* Radbrook Coll Shrewsbury (HND), Manchester Met Univ 1993 (BSc), Yale Coll Wrexham; *m* (m dis 2005); 1 da (Delia Lavinia Elise b 6 July 1980), 1 s (Edward William Lawrence b 6 May 1983); *Career* teacher of underachieving 14–16 yr olds and lectr in aromatherapy 1998–2001; memb Nat Assembly for Wales (Lib Dem) N Wales 2001–; JP 1992–2001; Llangollen Int Eisteddfod Soprano Prizewinner 1990; *Recreations* gardening, singing, swimming, cycling; *Style*— Ms Eleanor Burnham, AM; ✉ Constituency Office (Rear Office), Kenmar, Chester Road, Rossett, Wrexham, North Wales LL12 0HW (tel 01244 571918); National Assembly for Wales, Cardiff Bay, Cardiff CF10 1NA (tel 029 2089 8345, fax 029 2089 8344, e-mail eleanorburnham@wales.gov.uk)

BURNHAM, 7 Baron (UK 1903); Harry Frederick Alan Lawson; 7 Bt (UK 1892); s of 6 Baron Burnham (d 2005), and Hilary Margaret, *née* Hunter; *b* 22 February 1968, London; *Educ* Eton; *Career* with Evening Standard 1988–95, investment mangr Williams de Broë plc 1996–2000, investment mgmnt dir Brewin Dolphin Securities Ltd 2000– (gp fund dir 2002–); pres Salt Hill Soc, tstee Prostate Cancer Research Centre; Liveryman Worshipful Co of Gunmakers; MSI; *Recreations* shooting, stalking, oenology, tobogganing, horse and greyhound racing, golf; *Clubs* Turf, Pratt's, St Moritz Toboggan, City Livery, Burnham Beeches Golf; *Style*— The Rt Hon the Lord Burnham; ✉ Brewin Dolphin Securities Ltd, 12 Smithfield Street, London EC1A 9BD (tel 0845 213 3387, fax 0845 213 3603, e-mail harry.burnham@brewin.co.uk)

BURNINGHAM, John Mackintosh; *b* 27 April 1936; *Educ* Summerhill Sch Leiston, Central Sch of Art London (Dip); *m* 1964; *Career* children's author and illustrator; *Books* Borka (1963, Kate Greenaway Medal), Trubloff (1964), Chitty Chitty Bang Bang (illustrator, 1964), John Burningham's ABC (1964), Humbert (1965), Cannonball Simp (1966), Harquin (1967), The Extraordinary Tug-of-War (1968), Mr Gumpy's Outing (1970, Kate Greenaway Award), Around the World in Eighty Days (1972), Mr Gumpy's Motor Car (1973), The Adventures of Humbert, Simp and Harquin (1976), Come Away from the Water, Shirley (1977, New York Times Best Illustrated Book Award 1977), Time to Get Out of the Bath, Shirley (1978), Would You Rather (1978), The Shopping Basket (1980), Avocado Baby (1982), The Wind In the Willows (illustrator, 1983), First Words (1984), Granpa (1984, Emil/Kurt Maschler Award, New York Times Best Illustrated Book Award), Oi! Get Off Our Train (1989), Aldo (1991), England (1992), Harvey Slumfenburger (1993, W H Smith Book Award), Courtney (1994), Cloudland (1996), France (1998), Whadyamean (1999), Husherbye (2000), The Time of Your Life: Getting On with Getting On (2002), The Magic Bed (2003), When We Were Young (2004); Wall Friezes: Birdland, Lionland, Storyland (1966), Jungleland, Wonderland (1968), Seasons (1969), Around the World (1972); Little Book series: The Baby, The Rabbit, The School, The Snow (1974), The Blanket, The Cupboard, The Dog, The Friend (1975), Play and Learn Books: abc, 123, Opposites, Colours (1985), Where's Julius? (1986), John Patrick Norman McHennessy - the Boy Who Was Always Late (1987); John Burningham's: Alphabet Book, Numbers Book, Colours Book, Opposites Book (1987); *Style*— John Burningham, Esq; ✉ c/o Random House UK Ltd, Random House, 20 Vauxhall Bridge Road, London SW1V 2FA

BURNLEY, Bishop of 2000–; Rt Rev John William Goddard; s of Rev William Goddard, and Anna-Elizabeth, *née* Notley; *Educ* Wells Cathedral Sch, St Chad's Coll Durham (BA, DipTh); *m* Vivienne, *née* Selby, 2 s (Michael 1976, Gareth 1979); *Career* ordained: deacon 1970, priest 1971; curate Southbank 1970–74, curate Cayton with Eastfield 1974–75, vicar Ascension Middlesbrough 1975–82, rural dean of Middlesbrough 1981–87, vicar All Saints Middlesbrough 1982–88, canon and prebend of York 1987–88, vice-princ Edinburgh Theol Coll 1988–92, team rector of Ribbleton 1992–2000; race and justice cmmr Churches Together 2002; memb Task Force Burnley '01; *Recreations* restoring old house and canal narrow boat, gardening, socialising, swimming, golf; *Style*— The Rt Rev the Bishop of Burnley; ✉ Dean House, 449 Padiham Road, Burnley BB12 6TE (tel 01282 470360, fax 01282 470361, e-mail bishop.burnley@ntlworld.com)

BURNS, Alan Robert; s of James Burns (d 1986), of Dunfermline, Fife, and Bella, *née* Lloyd (d 1988); *b* 12 July 1950; *Educ* Dunfermline HS, Univ of Edinburgh (MA); *m* 29 May 1976, Pamela Joan, da of Blair Thompson; 1 da (Jennifer Lyn b 6 Jan 1987), 1 s (Graeme James b 18 Jan 1991); *Career* mangr Adelaide Hosp Dublin 1978–85, dist gen mangr Peterborough HA 1985–92; chief exec: NW Anglia HA 1992–99, Cambs HA 1999–2001, Trent Strategic HA 2002–; chm NHS Service Delivery and Orgn R&D Bd 1999–; memb: NHS Central R&D Ctee 1994–2000, NHS Primary Care Policy Bd 2002–, NHS Info Mgmnt and Technol (IM&T) Policy Bd 2002–; NHS Confedn: memb Cncl 1996–, vice-chm 2003–; chm of govrs Nassington Sch 1996–; memb ICSA 1977; *Recreations* golf, diving, sailing holidays; *Style*— Alan Burns, Esq; ✉ Walnut House, 20 Church Street, Nassington, Peterborough, Cambridgeshire PE8 6QG (tel and fax 01780 783056, mobile 07785 907574); Trent Strategic Health Authority, Bostock's Lane, Sandiacre, Nottingham NG10 5QG (tel 0115 968 4430, fax 0115 968 4400, e-mail alan.burns@tsha.nhs.uk)

BURNS, Sir (Robert) Andrew; KCMG (1997, CMG 1992); s of Robert Burns, CB, CMG (d 1971), and Mary, *née* Goodland; *b* 21 July 1943; *Educ* Highgate Sch, Trinity Coll Cambridge (MA); *m* 19 July 1973, Sarah, da of Peter Cadogan (d 1962), and Joan, *née* Banbury (d 1979); 2 s ((Robert) Duncan b 29 May 1975, Thomas Alexander Luckwell b 15 March 1977), 1 step da (Ella Jane Kenion b 23 Nov 1968); *Career* HM Dip Serv: third sec UK Mission to UN 1965, second sec New Delhi 1967–71, first sec FCO and UK delg Conf on Security and Co-operation in Europe 1971–75, first sec and head of Chancery Bucharest 1976–78, private sec to Perm Under Sec FCO 1979–82, cnsllr (info) Washington 1983–86, head of British info services NY 1983–86, head S Asian Dept FCO 1986–88, head News Dept FCO 1988–90, asst under sec of state (Asia) FCO 1990–92, ambass to Israel 1992–95, dep under sec of state (non-Europe and trade) FCO 1995–97, consul-gen to Hong Kong Special Admin Regn and Macao 1997–2000, high cmmr to Canada 2000–03; dir JP Morgan Chinese Investment Tst 2003–; hon pres Canada-UK Colloquia 2004–, memb Br N American Ctee 2004–; chm Cncl Royal Holloway Univ of London 2004–, tstee UK Fndn of Univ of Br Columbia 2005–, dep chm Ctee of Univ Chairmen 2007–; chm Exec Ctee Anglo-Israel Assoc 2004–05, int govr BBC 2005–06, tstee Int Polar Fndn UK 2006–; chm: Hestercombe Gardens Tst 2005–, Advsy Cncl Br Expertise 2006– (memb 2003–06); fell Center for Int Affairs Harvard Univ 1982–83, Portland fell 2004–; FRSA; *Books* Diplomacy, War and Parliamentary Democracy (1985); *Recreations* music, theatre, walking; *Clubs* Garrick, RAC, Hong Kong; *Style*— Sir Andrew Burns, KCMG; ✉ Walland Farm, Wheddon Cross, Minehead, Somerset TA24 7EE

BURNS, Graham Gordon; s of Gordon Burns, of Bebington, Merseyside, and Freda, *née* Bayley; *b* 9 August 1958; *Educ* King's Sch Chester, Univ of Durham (BA); *Career* admitted slr 1983; Stephenson Harwood: articled clerk 1981–83, asst slr 1983–88, ptnr 1988–2001, conslt 2002–; Freeman City of London Slrs Co 1989; memb Law Soc 1983; *Books* Shipping Finance (ed, 1991, 2 edn 1995); *Recreations* yoga, skiing, cricket, walking; *Style*— Graham Burns, Esq; ✉ Stephenson Harwood, One St Paul's Churchyard, London EC4M 8SH (tel 020 7329 4422, fax 020 7606 0822, telex 886789 SHSPC G)

BURNS, Iain Keatings; *b* 6 April 1948; *Educ* Univ of Glasgow (BSc); *m* Adrienne, *née* Kelly; 2 s, 2 da; *Career* South of Scotland Electricity Bd 1970–73, Collins Publishers 1973–82, fin dir International Thomson Publishing Ltd 1982–85, gp fin dir Octopus Publishing Group plc 1985–87, chief exec Abaco Investments plc 1988–90 (gp fin dir 1987–88), dir British-Commonwealth Holdings plc 1988–90, gp md Macmillan Ltd 1993–95 (non-exec dir 1990–93), gp chief exec Aspen Group plc 1996–98, chief exec The Stationery Office 2001–03, chief exec KYP (Hldgs) plc 2004–05, fndr and chm Homepage Ventures Ltd 2006–; non-exec dir Nat Acad of Writing 2000–; ACMA 1973; *Recreations* music, opera; *Style*— Iain K Burns, Esq

BURNS, Julian Delisle (Jules); *b* 18 September 1949; *Career* Granada TV: joined as mangr Regnl Programmes 1976, head Programme Servs 1987–88, dir Business Affrs 1988–93 (also co sec and responsible for Personnel 1993), dir (Main Bd) Programme and Mgmnt Servs and md Granada Enterprises Dec 1993–94, jt md Granada TV and md Divnl Ops 1995, jt md Granada Productions 1996–2000, md ops Granada Media 2000–02; chief operating offr ALL3MEDIA 2003–; non-exec dir Liverpool FC; *Style—* Jules Burns, Esq; ✉ mobile 07768 725116, e-mail jules.burns@blueyonder.co.uk

BURNS, Simon Hugh McGuigan; MP; s of late Maj Brian Stanley Burns, MC, of Wilts, and Shelagh Mary Nash; *b* 6 September 1952; *Educ* Christ the King Sch Accra Ghana, Stamford Sch, Worcester Coll Oxford (BA); *m* 1982 (m dis); 1 da (Amelia b 1987), 1 s (Bobby b 1991); *Career* political asst to Rt Hon Mrs Sally Oppenheim, MP 1975–81, dir What to Buy Ltd 1981–83, conf organiser IOD 1983–87; MP (Cons): Chelmsford 1987–97, Chelmsford W 1997–; PPS to: Rt Hon Tim Eggar, MP 1989–93, Rt Hon Mrs Gillian Shephard, MP 1993–94; asst Govt whip 1994–95, a Lord Cmmr to HM Treasy (Govt whip) 1995–96, Parly under sec of state Dept of Health 1996–97; oppn spokesman on: social security 1997–98, environment 1998–99, health 2001–; *Recreations* photography, travelling, swimming; *Clubs* Chelmsford Conservatives (patron), The Essex; *Style—* Simon Burns, Esq, MP; ✉ House of Commons, London SW1 (tel 020 7219 3000)

BURNS, Baron (Life Peer UK 1998), of Pitshanger in the London Borough of Ealing; Sir Terence Burns; GCB (1995), kt (1983); s of Patrick Owen Burns, and Doris Burns; *b* 13 March 1944; *Educ* Houghton-le-Spring GS, Univ of Manchester (BA), London Business Sch; *m* 1969, Anne Elizabeth Powell; 1 s, 2 da; *Career* chief econ advsr to Treasy and head Govt Econ Serv 1980–91, perm sec to Treasy 1991–98; chm: Financial Services and Markets Jt Cmmn 1999, Ctee of Inquiry into Hunting with Dogs 2000, Nat Lottery Cmmn 2000–01; ind advsr on the Govt's BBC Charter Review 2003–, head Football Assoc structural review 2005; chm: Glas Cymru (Welsh Water) 2001–, Abbey National plc 2002–, Marks and Spencer plc 2006– (dep chm 2005); non-exec dir: Legal and General 1999–2001 (chm Audit Ctee 2000–01), Pearson plc 1999–, The British Land Co plc 2000–05, Banco Santander Central Hispano SA 2004–; dir Queens Park Rangers FC 1996–2001; pres: Royal Economic Soc 1992–, Soc of Business Economists 1999–(vice-pres 1985–99), NIESR 2003– (govr 1998–2003); memb Bd of Mgmnt Manchester Business Sch 1993–98; chair Governing Body Royal Acad of Music 2002– (memb 1998–), chm of tstees Monteverdi Choir and Orchestra; fell London Business Sch 1989–, visiting fell Nuffield Coll Oxford 1991–97; CIMgt 1992; *Recreations* soccer (spectator), golf, music; *Clubs* Reform; *Style—* The Rt Hon the Lord Burns, GCB; ✉ House of Lords, London SW1A 0PW (tel 020 7219 0312, e-mail burnst@parliament.uk)

BURNS, Rt Rev Thomas Matthew (Tom); s of William James Burns (d 1998), and Louisa Mary, *née* McGarry (d 1998); *b* 3 June 1944; *Educ* St Mary's Coll Blackburn, Winslade Sch Clyst St Mary, The Monastery Paignton, Heythrop Coll London (BD), Coll of Commerce & Technol Hull (Dip Business Studies), Open Univ (BA); *Career* ordained RC priest Soc of Mary (Marist Fathers) 1971 (ordinand 1965–71), curate St Anne's Parish Whitechapel London 1973–74, head of economics St Mary's GS Sidcup 1974–78, head of economics and social scis St Mary's Sixth Form Coll Blackburn 1979–86, chaplain Royal Navy 1986–92, bursar gen Soc of Mary (Marist Fathers) Rome 1992–93; Royal Navy: initial sea trg chaplain 1994–95, establishment co-ordinating chaplain HMS Nelson and HM Naval Base Portsmouth 1995–96, RN dir Armed Forces' Chaplaincy Centre Amport House 1996–98, princ RC Chaplain to the RN and Vicar Gen 1998–2002, dir Naval Chaplaincy Serv (Trg & Progs) 1998–2000, dir Naval Chaplaincy Serv (Manning) 2000–02, Bishop of the Forces 2002–; Queen's Honorary Chaplain (QHC) 1998–2002; dir RN Handicapped Children's Pilgrimage Tst 1998–2002, bishop promotor (dir and tstee) Apostleship of the Seas 2002, dir and tstee St Luke's Centre Manchester 2006; MIMgt; *Publications* Index of Laws of the Game of Rugby Football (ed and compiler); *Recreations* rugby assessor/advisor; *Style—* The Rt Rev Tom Burns, SM; ✉ RC Bishopric of the Forces, AGPDO, Middle Hill, Aldershot, Hampshire GU11 1PP (tel 01252 349004, e-mail office@rcforcesbishop.co.uk)

BURNS, Prof Thomas (Tom); CBE (2006); *Educ* Univ of Cambridge (MB BChir, MD), Univ of London (DSc); *Career* fndn prof of social and community psychiatry St George's Hosp Med Sch Tooting until 2003, prof of social psychiatry Univ of Oxford 2003–, fell Kellogg Coll Oxford 2003–; past chm Social and Community Section RCPsych; FRCPsych; *Books* Psychological Management of the Physically Ill (ed with J Hubert Lacey, 1989), Assertive Outreach in Mental Health: A Manual for Practitioners (with Mike Firn, 2002), Community Mental Health: A Guide to Current Practices (2004), Psychiatry: A very short introduction (2006); *Style—* Prof Tom Burns, CBE; ✉ Department of Psychiatry, University of Oxford, Warneford Hospital, Oxford OX3 7JX

BURNS, Prof (Duncan) Thorburn; s of James Thorburn Burns (d 1953), and Olive Mary Constance, *née* Waugh (d 1987); *b* 30 May 1934; *Educ* Whitcliffe Mount Sch, Univ of Leeds (BSc, PhD), Loughborough Univ (DSc), Queen's Univ Belfast (MA); *m* 1, 16 Dec 1961 (m dis 1994), Valerie Mary, *née* Vinten; 2 da (Mary Jane Thorburn b 1963, Susan Jean Thorburn b 1967), 1 s (James Fredrick Thorburn b 1979); m 2, 28 May 1994, Celia Mary Thorburn-Burns; *Career* lectr in physical chemistry Medway Coll of Technol 1959–63 (asst lectr 1958–59), sr lectr in analytical chemistry Woolwich Poly 1965–66, reader Loughborough Univ of Technol 1971–75 (sr lectr 1966–71), prof of analytical chemistry Queen's Univ Belfast 1975–99 (emeritus prof 1999–); author of numerous papers, books and reviews; chm Cmmn V/I IUPAC 1987–89, pres Analytical Div RSC 1988–90; memb: Cncl Pharmaceutical Soc of NI 1989–2000, Poisons Bd of NI 1989–; Theophilus Redwood Lecture RSC 1982, Analytical Reactions and Reagents Medal and Award RSC 1984, Boyle-Higgins Gold Medal Inst of Chemistry of Ireland 1990, AnalaR Gold Medal and Lecture BDH/RSC 1990, Erhen Gold Nadel Analytical Inst Tech Univ Vienna 1990, SAC Gold Medal RSC 1993, Pregl Medal Austrian Chem Soc 1993, Tertiary Chem Educnl Medal and Award RSC 1995, Sigillium Magnum Universitatis Univ of Bologna 1996, Analytical Chemistry Tribute of EUCheMS 2005; FRSC 1976, MRIA 1984, FRSE 1984, Hon MPS (NI) 2001; *Recreations* history of chemistry, walking; *Clubs* Savage, Ulster Reform; *Style—* Prof Thorburn Burns, FRSE; ✉ Department of Chemistry, Queen's University, Belfast BT9 5AG (tel 028 9066 8567, fax 028 9066 8567, e-mail profburns@chemistry.fsbusiness.co.uk)

BURNSIDE, David Wilson Boyd; MLA; s of John (Jack) Templeton (d 1990), and Elizabeth Joan (Betty) Carter; *b* 24 August 1951; *Educ* Coleraine Academical Inst, Queen's Univ Belfast (BA); *m* 1; 2 da (Anna b 1990, Agnes b 2004); m 2, 1999, Fiona; *Career* teacher 1973–74, press offr Vanguard Unionist Pty 1974–76, PR dir IOD 1979–84, public affrs dir British Airways plc 1984–93; chm: DBA Ltd 1993–, NCH Ltd 1995–; MP (UUP) Antrim S 2000–05, MLA (UUP) S Antrim 2003–; Campaign Service Medal (NI, for serving in the Ulster Defence Regt); Freeman City of London; *Recreations* fishing, shooting, motorcycling; *Clubs* Carlton, Royal British Legion (Antrim), Portballintrae Boat, Coleraine and District Motor; *Style—* David Burnside, Esq, MLA

BURNSIDE, Graham Mathieson; WS (1984); s of John Young Burnside, of Newtongrange, Midlothian, and (Mary) Ishbel, *née* Sim; *b* 23 March 1954, Edinburgh; *Educ* George Heriot's Sch Edinburgh, Univ of Edinburgh (Muirhead prize, LLB), LTCL; *Career* admitted slr 1978; trainee slr Dundas & Wilson 1976–78, slr Nat Coal Bd/CIN Properties Ltd 1978–82; Tods Murray LLP (formerly Tods Murray WS): slr 1983–84, ptnr 1984–, head Banking Dept 1999–; author of articles in professional jls on Scots law and on aspects of securitisation and of Islamic finance; hon sec and govr St Columba's Hospice, dir New Town Concerts Soc; *Recreations* opera, organ playing, hill walking; *Clubs* Scottish Arts; *Style—* Graham Burnside, Esq, WS; ✉ Tods Murray LLP, Edinburgh Quay, 133 Fountainbridge, Edinburgh EH3 9AG (tel 0131 656 2000, fax 0131 656 2024, e-mail graham.burnside@todsmurray.com)

BURNSTOCK, Dr Aviva Ruth; da of Prof Geoffrey Burnstock, of London, and Nomi, *née* Hirschfeld; *b* 1 September 1959; *Educ* King Alfred Sch Hampstead, Univ of Sussex (BSc), Courtauld Inst of Art (Dip Conservation, PhD); *m* 1988, Hugh, s of Dr Stephen Sebag-Montefiore; 3 c (Abraham, Esther, Sam); *Career* paintings conservator Art Gall of NSW Sydney 1984–85, scientist National Gallery London 1986–92, currently head Dept of Conservation and Technol Courtauld Inst of Art; memb Int Inst of Conservation 1981–; *Style—* Dr Aviva Burnstock; ✉ Department of Conservation and Technology, The Courtauld Institute of Art, Somerset House, Strand, London WC2R 0RN (tel 020 7848 2192, e-mail aviva.burnstock@courtauld.ac.uk)

BURNSTOCK, Prof Geoffrey; s of James Burnstock (d 1947), and Nancy, *née* Green (d 1978); *b* 10 May 1929; *Educ* Greenford Co GS, KCL (BSc), KCL and UCL (PhD), Univ of Melbourne (DSc); *m* 9 April 1957, Nomi, da of Sigmund Hirschfeld (d 1988); 3 da (Aviva b 1959, Tamara b 1960, Dina b 1964); *Career* Nat Serv 1947–48; Nat Inst for Med Res London 1956–57, Dept of Pharmacology Univ of Oxford 1957–59, Dept of Physiology Univ of Illinois (Rockefeller travelling fellowship) 1959; Univ of Melbourne Aust: sr lectr Dept of Zoology 1959–62, reader in physiological zoology 1962–64, prof of zoology and chm of dept 1964–75, assoc dean of biological sci 1969–72; visiting prof Dept of Pharmacology UCLA 1970; UCL: prof of anatomy 1975–, head Dept of Anatomy and Developmental Biology 1975–97, convener Centre for Neuroscience 1979–, vice-dean Faculty of Med Sci 1980–83; visiting prof RSM Fndn New York 1988; Autonomic Neuroscience Inst Royal Free and Univ Coll Med Sch UCL: dir 997–2004, emeritus prof 2004–, pres 2004–; author of over 1000 pubns in scientific and med jls and books; chm Scientific Advsy Bd Eisai London Ltd 1990–97, vice-pres Anatomical Society of Great Britain and Ireland 1990, memb Gt Barrier Reef Ctee, fndr memb Int Cncl for Scientific Devpt, Int Acad of Sci and Acad Med Sci; memb Cncl: The Bayliss and Starling Soc 1986–96, Royal Postgrad Med Sch 1989–97, Br Assoc (Medical) 1998; memb: Int Cncl Neurovegetative Res, Bd MRC, MRC Inst for Molecular Cell Biology, Br Physiological Soc, Aust Physiological and Pharmacological Soc, Int Soc for Biochemical Pharmacology, Br Pharmacological Soc, Br Anatomical Soc, Euro Artery Club, Int Brain Res Orgn, Int Soc for Devptal Neuroscience, Euro Neuroscience Assoc, Clinical Autonomic Res Soc, Euro Neuropeptide Club, Neurogastroenterology Soc, Academia Europaea 1992; foreign memb Russian Soc of Neuropathology 1993; Otto Krayer lecture Harvard 1976, Synthelabo lecture Paris 1979, British Physiological Soc Review lecture Birmingham 1979, Cummings Meml lecture 1980, Schueler Distinguished lecture in pharmacology Tulane Inst New Orleans 1982, First Ulf von Euler lecture in physiology Stockholm 1985, First John T Shepherd lecture Mayo Clinic Rochester 1986, Harold Lamport lecture in physiology Seattle 1986, Oliver-Sharpey lecture RCP 1987, Ariëns lecture Utrecht 1987, Heymans memorial lecture Gent 1990, Knight visiting prof lecture Miami 1993, Charnock Bradley lecture Edinburgh 1994, C Ladd Prosser lectr Illinois 1995, Ludwig R Müller Meml lecture European Fedn of Autonomic Socs Erlangen 2001, Horace Davenport Distinguished Lectureship American Physiological Soc Orlando 2001, Sherrington Lecture Liverpool 2001, IUPHAR Plenary Lecture San Francisco 2002, Stevenson Meml Lecture London and Ontario 2003, First Annual Burnstock Lecture Chapel Hill USA 2004; ed-in-chief: Autonomic Neuroscience: Basic and Clinical, Purinergic Signalling; series ed The Autonomic Nervous System Vols 1–14 1992–99; memb Editorial Bd of over 30 other jls incl: Jl of Anatomy, Jl of Vascular Research, Int Jl of Developmental Neuroscience, Autonomic Neuroscience (ed-in-chief); memb int advsy bd NeuroReport, conslt to Euro Jl of Pharmacology; Royal Medal Royal Soc 2000, The Janssen Award in Gastroenterology for lifetime achievement in digestive science 2000, corr academician Real Academia Nacinal de Farmacia Spain; hon memb Physiological Soc 2003; Hon MSc 1962, Hon MRCP 1987, Hon FRCS 1999, Hon FRCP 2000; FAA 1971, FRS 1986, FMedSci 1998, FRPharmS 2004; *Books* How Cells Work (1972), Adrenergic Neurons: Their Organisation, Function and Development in the Peripheral Nervous System (jtly, 1975); An Atlas of the Fine Structure of Muscle and its Innervation (jtly, 1976), Vascular Neuroeffector Mechanisms (jt ed, 1976), Purinergic Receptors (ed, 1981), Somatic and Autonomic Nerve-Muscle Interactions (jt ed, 1983), Nonadrenergic Innervation of Blood Vessels (jt ed, 1988), Peptides - A Target for New Drug Development (jt ed, 1991), Neural Endothelial Interactions in the Control of Vascular Tone (jt author, 1993), Nitric Oxide in Health and Disease (jtly, 1997), Cardiovascular Biology of Purines (jt ed, 1998); *Recreations* wood sculpture and tennis; *Style—* Prof Geoffrey Burnstock, FRS; ✉ Autonomic Neuroscience Institute, Royal Free and University College Medical School, Royal Free Campus, Rowland Hill Street, London NW3 2PF (tel 020 7830 2948, fax 020 7830 2949, e-mail g.burnstock@ucl.ac.uk)

BURNTON, Hon Mr Justice; Sir Stanley Jeffrey; kt (2000); s of Harry Burnton, of London, and Fay, *née* Levy; *b* 25 October 1942; *Educ* Hackney Downs GS, St Edmund Hall Oxford (MA); *m* 26 Feb 1971, Gwenyth, da of Frank Castle, of Aust; 2 da (Abigail b 1972, Rebecca b 1976), 1 s (Simon b 1974); *Career* called to the Bar Middle Temple 1965 (bencher 1991); QC 1982, recorder of the Crown Court 1994–2000, dep High Court judge (Chancery Division) 1995–2000, judge of the High Court of Justice (Queen's Bench Div) 2000–; FSALS; *Recreations* classical music, theatre, travel, reading; *Style—* The Hon Mr Justice Stanley Burnton; ✉ Royal Courts of Justice, Strand, London WC2A 2LL (tel 020 7947 6000)

BURR, Martin John; s of Bertram John Burr, and Margaret, *née* Mapleson; *b* 19 February 1953; *Educ* Berkhamsted Sch, Pembroke Coll Oxford (MA, Dip Comp Phil); *Career* called to the Bar Middle Temple 1978; joined: Lincoln's Inn 1980, Inner Temple 1988; head of chambers 1993– (joint head 1989–93); memb: Sion Coll, Henry Sweet Soc, Int Arthurian Soc, Seldon Soc, Philological Soc, Br Archeological Assoc, Cncl Henry Bradshaw Soc, Soc of Trusts and Estates Practitoners, Anglican and Eastern Churches Assoc, Ecclesiastical Law Soc; sec Guild Church Cncl St Dunstan-in-the-West Fleet St; Freeman City of London; ACIArb 1990 *Oratorios Composed* incl: Vita Sci Bonifati, Vita Sci Justi, Vita Sci Cuthberti, Vita Sci Ceddis, Vita Sci Dunstani, Vita Sci Edwardi, Confessoris et Regis, Vita Sci Bedae, Vita Moysis, Vita Eliae, Vita Sci Iohannis Baptistae, Vita Sci Pirani, Vita Abrahami, Vita Sci Petroci, Vita Isaiae, Vita Sci Brendani, Vita Job, Vita Sci Davidis, Vita Sci Jospehi, Vita Sci Patrici, Vita Adae, Vita Sci Maudeti, Vita Noe, Vita Sci Erci, Vita Danielis, Vita Sci Salomonis, Vita Sci Josephi de Arimathia, Vita Sci Sancreoti, Vita Christi, Vita Brevis Arturi Regius, Vita Sci Martini Papae et Martyris, Vita Sci Maderni, Vita Sci Georgi, Vita Brevis Sci Aldhelmi, Vita Sci Martini de Tours, Vita Sci Martini in Meneage, Vita Sci Judae, Vita Sci Sennani, Vita Sci Ruperti, Vita Sci Merdoci; *Publications* incl: The Law and Health Visitors (1982), Chancery Practice (1991 and 1997), Taxation: Recent Development (1999); numerous papers and various poems published; *Recreations* theology, liturgiology, opera, plainsong, singing, composing music, neumology, philology, writing poetry, railways; *Style—* Martin Burr, Esq; ✉ 1st Floor, Temple Chambers, Temple Avenue, London EC4Y 0DA (tel 020 7353 4636, fax 020 7353 4637)

BURR, His Hon Judge Michael Rodney; s of Frank Edward Burr, of Swansea, and Aileen Maud, *née* May; *b* 31 August 1941; *Educ* Brecon Boys GS, King Edward VI Sch Chelmsford; *m* 30 March 1963, Rhoda, da of Ernest Rule, of Aberdare; 4 s (David b 1964, Richard b 1965, Andrew b 1967, Edwin b 1973), 1 da (Elizabeth b 1970); *Career* admitted slr 1964; asst slr Hilliard and Ward Chelmsford 1964–69, sr ptnr Peter Williams and Co Swansea 1972–92, recorder 1988–92, circuit judge (Wales & Chester Circuit) 1992–; sec Inc Law Soc of Swansea and Dist 1980–83; memb Law Soc; non cncl memb of Law Soc ctees: Professional Purposes Ctee 1985–86, Adjudication Ctee 1986–89; *Recreations* flying; *Style—* His Hon Judge Burr

BURRAGE, Kenneth Walter; *b* 27 April 1939; *Educ* Churcher's Coll Petersfield, Guildford and Wimbledon Tech Coll (ONC, HNC); *m*; 3 c; *Career* British Railways Bd: signal engrg Southern Region 1956–77, regnl signal engr Western Region 1977–81, chief signal and telecommunications engr London Midland Region 1981–88, dir of signal and telecommunications engrg Bd HQ 1989–92 (dep dir 1988–89), dir of engrg standards Bd HQ 1992–94, memb BRT Bd 1993–94, controller Safety Standards Railtrack plc 1994–95; dir Westinghouse Signals Ltd 1995–99 (dep md 1998–99), chief exec Inst of Railway Signal Engineers 1999–2006; memb Cncl Engrg Cncl 1992–96 (memb Working Party on Unification of Engrg profession, chm Implementation Panel for Risk Code), memb Cncl IEE 1994–97; CEng, FIEE, FIRSE; *Recreations* music, motorsport, walking, ornithology; *Style—* Kenneth Burrage, Esq; ✉ Institution of Railway Signal Engineers, Floor 4, 1 Birdcage Walk, London SW1H 9JJ (tel 020 7808 1180, fax 020 7808 1196)

BURRAGE, Timothy Robert (Tim); s of Dennis Bradshaw Burrage (d 1962), and late Barbara, *née* Davies; *b* 8 May 1949, Chalfont St Giles, Bucks; *Educ* Berkhamsted Sch, Coll of Estate Mgmnt Reading; *m* (m dis), Elspeth, *née* Loudon; 1 da (Alice Caroline b 30 Jan 1979), 1 s (James Richard b 29 Jan 1981); partner, Charlotte Grayson, *née* Hallett; *Career* chartered surveyor; John D Wood & Co 1969–71, Lane Fox & Ptnrs 1971–78, Stags 1979– (currently sr ptnr); RICS 1970; *Recreations* skiing, sailing, shooting, fishing, tennis; *Style—* Tim Burrage, Esq; ✉ Stags, 19 Bampton Street, Tiverton, Devon EX16 6AA

BURRARD-LUCAS, Stephen Charles; *Educ* Christ's Hosp, Univ of Oxford (BA); *m*; 3 c; *Career* chartered accountant; in practice City of London 1978–83, various positions Shell Int Petroleum Co London, Hong Kong and E Africa 1983–94, fin dir Exploration and Production Div Br Gas 1994–98 (responsible for Int Downstream Business 1996–98), treas BG plc 1998–2000, fin dir Lattice Gp plc (following demerger from BG Gp) 2000–02, gp fin dir National Grid Transco (following merger) 2002–; chm Oil Industry Accounting Ctee 1996–98; careers cnsllr Sevenoaks Sch 1996–99; *Recreations* walking, rugby, travel; *Style—* Stephen Lucas, Esq; ✉ National Grid Transco plc, 1–3 Strand, London WC2N 5EH

BURRELL, Denis James; CBE (1982), DL (Bucks 1995); s of Edwin Charles Merrick Burrell (d 1950); *b* 25 May 1930; *Educ* Rugby, Clare Coll Cambridge (MA); *m* 1, 1977, Susan (d 1998), da of Eric Alwyn Ingham (d 1978); 1 s (Charles); m 2, 2000, Jennifer, da of Edward Noël Macmeekan (d 1970); *Career* Martin Baker Aircraft Co Ltd (mfr of ejection seats for use in mil aircraft): chm and md 1981–95, chm 1995–2004; Queen's Award for Export 1982, 1986 and 1997, Queen's Award for Technol 1993; High Sheriff Bucks 1997–98; Liveryman Worshipful Co of Coachmakers & Coach Harness Makers (Master 1991–92, memb Ct of Assts), Liveryman Guild of Air Pilots and Air Navigators; Hon DTech Brunel Univ, Hon DSc Univ of Buckingham; Hon FRAeS; *Recreations* gardens; *Clubs* Boodle's; *Style—* Denis Burrell, Esq, CBE, DL; ✉ Denham Mount, Denham, Buckinghamshire UB9 4HW

BURRELL, (Francis) Gary; QC (1996); *b* 7 August 1953; *Educ* Belfast Boys' Model, Univ of Exeter (LLB); *Career* called to the Bar Inner Temple 1977 (bencher 2002), recorder of the Crown Ct 1996– (asst recorder 1992), dep High Court judge 2001; specialist in personal injury, crime, and clinical negligence litigation; memb Bar Cncl; *Publications* author of various articles in periodicals; *Recreations* sailing, fishing; *Style—* Gary Burrell, Esq, QC; ✉ Paradise Chambers, 26 Paradise Square, Sheffield S1 2DE (tel 0114 273 8951, e-mail burrell@paradise-sq.co.uk); Chambers of John Foy QC, 9 Gough Square, London EC4A 3DE (tel 020 7353 5371)

BURRELL, Mark William; DL (W Sussex 2004); yr s of Sir Walter Burrell, 8 Bt, CBE, TD, DL (d 1985); *b* 9 April 1937; *Educ* Eton, Pembroke Coll Cambridge (BA); *m* 1966, Margot Rosemary, yr da of Westray Pearce, of Killara, NSW, Aust; 2 s (William, Anthony), 1 da (Sophia); *Career* dir Lazard Bros & Co Ltd 1974–86 (joined corp fin dept 1970), development dir Pearson plc 1986–97; chm Millbank Financial Serivces 1986–, chm Merlin Communications International Ltd 1997–2002, formerly non-exec chm Royal Doulton Ltd; non-exec dir RM plc 1997–2002; govr Northbrook Coll Sussex 2004–; memb Ct Univ of Sussex 1997–; High Sheriff W Sussex 2002–03; *Clubs* White's, Boodle's, Sussex; *Style—* Mark Burrell, Esq, DL; ✉ Bakers House, Shipley, Horsham, West Sussex RH13 8GJ (tel 01403 741215)

BURRELL, Michael Ian; s of Sydney Burrell, of Haslemere, Surrey, and Mary, *née* Smith; *b* 25 June 1950; *Educ* Godalming Co GS, St Peter's Coll Oxford (MA); *Career* journalist Durham Advertiser 1971–72, local govt corr Evening Argus Brighton 1972–73, lobby corr Westminster Press 1973–83, Profile PR 1983–86; chm Grayling Political Strategy Brussels 1990–2002, chm Westminster Strategy 2000–02 (md 1986–2000), vice-chm The Grayling Group 2000–02 (chief exec 1991–2000), European chm Public Affairs Edelman 2002–04, vice-chm Edelman Europe 2004–; chm Assoc of Professional Political Consultants 1999–2002, dep chm European Centre for Public Affairs 2005–; *Publications* Lobbying and the Media: Working with Politicians and Journalists; various articles on lobbying Westminster, Whitehall and the European Union; *Recreations* doing nothing in the sunshine; *Style—* Michael Burrell, Esq; ✉ Edelman, Haymarket House, 1st Floor, 28–29 Haymarket, London SW1Y 4SP (tel 020 7344 1289, fax 020 7344 1500, e-mail michael.burrell@edelman.com)

BURRELL, Sir (John) Raymond; 9 Bt (GB 1774), of Valentine House, Essex; s of Lt-Col Sir Walter Raymond Burrell, 8 Bt, CBE, TD, DL (d 1985), and Hon Anne Judith, OBE, da of 3 Baron Denman, GCMG, KCVO, PC, JP; *b* 20 February 1934; *Educ* Eton; *m* 1, 1959 (m dis 1971), Rowena Frances, da of Michael H Pearce; 1 s (Charles Raymond b 1962); m 2, 1971, Margot Lucy, da of F E Thatcher, of Sydney; 1 s (Andrew John b 1974), 1 da (Catherine Anne Lucy b 1977); *Heir* s, Charles Burrell; *Style—* Sir Raymond Burrell, Bt; ✉ 14 Rosemont Avenue, Woollahra, Sydney, NSW 2025, Australia

BURRIDGE, Rev Dr Richard Alan; s of Alan Burridge (d 2000), of Exmouth, Devon, and Iris Joyce, *née* Coates (d 1994); *b* 11 June 1955; *Educ* Bristol Cathedral Sch (County scholar), UC Oxford (MA), Univ of Nottingham (CertEd, DipTh, PhD); *m* 1 Sept 1979, Susan Burridge, *née* Morgan; 2 da (Rebecca b 5 Aug 1986, Sarah b 1 March 1988); *Career* classics master and house tutor Sevenoaks Sch 1978–82, curate St Peter and St Paul Bromley Parish Church 1985–87, Lazenby chaplain and pt/t lectr Depts of Theology and Classics and Ancient History Univ of Exeter 1987–94, dean and hon lectr Dept of Theology and Religious Studies KCL 1994–; lecture tour to American univs and seminaries 1993, St Matthiastide Lecture Bristol 1994, Boundy Meml Lectures Univ of Exeter 1993, preacher Univ Sermon Univ of Oxford 1994, inaugural lecture KCL 1995, commissary for Bishop of the High Veld Church of the Province of Southern Africa 1997–; memb: Cncl of Mgmnt St John's Coll Nottingham Ltd 1986–99, Cncl of Reference Monarch Publications 1992–2000, Gen Synod C of E 1994–, Studiorum Novi Testamenti Societas (SNTS) 1995–, Soc for the Study of Theology (SST) 1995–, Soc of Biblical Literature (SBL) 1995–; gen ed People's Bible Commentary Series 1997–; chm Eric Symes Abbot Meml Fund 1994–, chm Christian Evidence Soc 2000– (tstee 1994–), external examiner to SW Ministry Trg Course 1995–99, theological advsr for the film Miracle Maker 1995–2000, chm C of E's Educnl Validation Panel 1996–2004, Gen Synod rep Ptnrs in Mission Consultation for the Province of W Africa at Accra 1998, tstee King George VI and Queen Elizabeth Fndn of St Catherine's Cumberland Lodge 1998–, advsr and writer New Millennium Experience Co Greenwich Dome 1998–2000 lectr tour South African univs, seminaries and chuches 1998; reg contrib BBC TV and radio, World Serv and ITV; *Publications* Sex Therapy: Some Ethical Considerations (1985), What are the Gospels? A Comparison with Graeco-Roman Biography (1992, paperback reprint 1995, revised edn 2004), Four Gospels, One Jesus? (1994, reprinted in USA 1996 and 1999, reprinted in UK 1997 and 2000, revised edn 2005), Where Shall We Find God? (1998), John (1998), Faith Odyssey (2001, 2 edn 2003), Jesus Now and Then (2004); *Recreations* golf, swimming, music, cycling, being with my family; *Style—* The Rev Dr Richard Burridge; ✉ The Dean's Office, King's College London, Strand, London WC2R 2LS (tel 020 7848 2333, fax 020 7848 2344, e-mail dean@kcl.ac.uk, website www.kcl.ac.uk/dean/)

BURRIDGE, Simon St Paul; s of James Dugdale Burridge, of Ab Kettleby, Leics, and Anne Henrietta-Maria St Paul, *née* Butler; *b* 20 March 1956; *Educ* Sherborne, The Queen's Coll Oxford; *m* 13 Sept 1986, Camilla Rose, da of Bryan Rogerson Barkes; 3 da (Felicity Rose St Paul b 3 May 1989, Laura St Paul b 5 Sept 1991, Katie Victoria St Paul b 12 May 1994); *Career* advertising exec; grad trainee Ayer Barker Hegemann 1979, account exec Minden Luby & Associates 1979–1981; Dewe Rogerson: account exec 1981–82, account dir 1982–84, dir 1984–87; dir: J Walter Thompson 1988–93 (sr assoc dir 1987–88), Abbott Mead Vickers BBDO 1994–96, J Walter Thompson 1996 (managing ptnr 1997), co-ordinator People's Lottery bid 2000, chm HHCL 2001–; *Recreations* horse racing (family owns Desert Orchid), literature; *Style—* Simon Burridge, Esq

BURRILL, Timothy Peckover; yr s of Lyonel Peckover Burrill, OBE (d 1983), and Marjorie Sybil, *née* Hurlbutt (d 1976); *b* 8 June 1931; *Educ* Eton, Sorbonne; *m* 1, 1959 (m dis 1966), Philippa, o da of Maurice Hare; 1 da (Rebecca Nina b 1961); m 2, 1968 (m dis 1989), Santa, er da of John Raymond; 2 da (Jemima Lucy b 1970, Tabitha Sara b 1974), 1 s (Joshua Hal Peckover b 1973); *Career* film prodr; served Grenadier Gds 1949–52; jr mgmnt Cayzer Irvine & Co 1952–56; entered film indust 1956, joined Brookfield Productions 1965, md Burrill Productions 1966–, dir World Film Services 1967–69, first prodn admin Nat Film and TV Sch 1972; md: Allied Stars (responsible for Chariots of Fire) 1980–81, Pathé Productions Ltd 1994–99; dir: Artistry Ltd (responsible for Superman and Supergirl films) 1982, Central Casting 1988–92; conslt: Nat Film Devpt Fund 1980–81, The Really Useful Gp 1989–90; UK film industry rep on Eurimages 1994–96; chm: BAFTA 1980–83 (vice-chm 1979–81), Film Asset Development plc 1987–94, First Film Fndn 1989–98, Prodn Trg Fund 1993–2001; vice-chm The Producers' Assoc (PACT) 1993–94 (memb Exec Ctee 1990–2001); dir Br Film Cmmn 1997–99; prodr memb: Cinematograph Films Cncl 1980–83, Gen Cncl ACTT 1975–76, Exec Ctee Br Film and TV Prodrs' Assoc 1981–90; memb: UK Govt's Middleton Ctee on Film Finance 1996, Le Club des Producteurs Européens 1996–98, Bd Int Fedn of Film Prodrs Assoc 1997–2001, UK Govt's Film Policy Review 1997–98, European Film Acad 1997–; govr: Nat Film and TV Sch 1981–92, Royal Nat Theatre 1982–88; films inc: Fourth Protocol, Supergirl, Tess, Oliver twist, La Vie en Rose; *Recreations* gardening, theatre; *Style—* Timothy Burrill, Esq; ✉ 19 Cranbury Road, London SW6 2NS (tel 020 7736 8673, fax 020 7731 3921, mobile 07785 298680, e-mail timothy@timothyburrill.co.uk)

BURROUGHS, Prof Andrew Kenneth; s of Kenneth Douglas Burroughs, of Pineto, Italy, and Vidia, *née* Sfredda; *b* 26 May 1953; *Educ* Kent Coll Canterbury, Univ of Liverpool (MB ChB); *m* 1, 19 Aug 1979 (m dis 1991), Rajesvarie, da of Govindarajoloo Kamalason Nulliah, of Lydiate, Liverpool; 1 da (Natasha b 1983); m 2, 27 Nov 1993, Clare, da of James Davey, of Box, Wilts; 1 s (James b 1994), 1 da (Helena b 1996); *Career* registrar in gen med and gastroenterology Royal Free Hosp London 1979–81, hon clinical lectr Royal Free Hosp Sch of Med (now Royal Free and UC Med Sch) 1981–83; Royal Free Hosp/Royal Free and UC Med Sch: lectr in med and hon sr registrar 1983–87, sr lectr and hon conslt physician 1988–93, conslt physician and hepatologist 1993–, prof of hepatology Univ of London 2002–; chm Liver Section Br Soc of Gastroenterology 2004–; memb: Cncl Br Soc of Gastroenterology 1993–96 and 2004–, Ctee Euro Assoc for the Study of the Liver 1996–2000 (sec 1997–99), Cncl United Euro Gastroenterology Fedn 1999–2002, Cncl Int Assoc for the Study of the Liver 1999–2002, Cncl Int Liver Transplant Soc 2003–; FRCP 1991 (MRCP 1978), fell Euro Bd of Gastroenterology (FEBG) 1999; Cavaliere Ufficiale al Ordine del Merito della Repubblica Italiana 1989; *Recreations* philately, tourism; *Style—* Prof Andrew Burroughs; ✉ Liver Transplantation and Hepato-biliary Medicine, Royal Free and University College Medical School, Pond Street, Hampstead, London NW3 2QG (tel 020 7794 0500 ext 3978, fax 020 7472 6226, e-mail andrew.burroughs@royalfree.nhs.uk)

BURROUGHS, Andrew St John Wolfe; s of Peter Noel Gore Burroughs (d 2003), of Sudbury, Suffolk, and Jenifer Katherine Wolfe, *née* Potter; *b* 5 April 1958; *Educ* Bedford Sch, St Catharine's Coll Cambridge (exhibitioner, MA), Guildhall Sch of Music and Drama; *m* 1980 (m dis 1992), Jacqueline Margaret, da of Anthony Wylson; 1 da (Ellen Lora b August 1984), 1 s (Toby Walter Wolfe b Dec 1987); *Career* news trainee Westminster Press 1979–82, with Far East Broadcasting Seychelles 1982–84; BBC: with BBC World Serv 1984–85, BBC Radio 4 1985–86, prodr BBC TV News and Current Affrs 1986–88, religion, arts and community affrs corr Social Affrs Unit BBC TV 1988–94, social affrs corr and videojournalist (features) Social Affairs Unit BBC TV 1994–98, videojournalism features corr BBC News 1998–2001, videojournalism features corr BBC Europe Direct 2001–04, TV news corr BBC News 24 and BBC World 2001–; highly commended BP Arts Journalism Award 1991, TV Award Race in the Media 1994; *Books* BBC Review of the Year 1990 and 1991 (contrib); *Recreations* composer and performer of contemporary blues songs; *Clubs* Wolfe Soc (rep of descendant family Gen James Wolfe); *Style—* Andrew Burroughs; ✉ BBC Room 1630 Stage VI, Television Centre, Wood Lane, London W12 7RJ (tel 020 8624 9108, fax 020 8624 8570, mobile 07860 533828, e-mail andrew.burroughs@bbc.co.uk)

BURROUGHS, Philip Anthony; s of Anthony John Burroughs, of Berkhamsted, Herts, and Brenda Mabel, *née* Downing; *b* 2 October 1955; *Educ* Hemel Hempstead GS, Univ of Bristol (LLB); *m* 23 July 1977, Katharine Mary, da of Douglas Campbell Doughty, of Tring, Herts; 1 da (Rebecca b 1982), 1 s (Alastair b 1984); *Career* admitted slr 1980; asst slr Freshfields 1980–83; ptnr: Lawrence Graham 1985–93 (asst slr 1983–85), Coudert Brothers 1993–2000, McGrigors London (formerly KLegal) 2000–; chm Langleys Round Table 1988–89 (memb 1984); Freeman Worshipful Co of Solicitors; memb: Law Soc, City of London Law Soc, City Property Assoc; *Recreations* travel, Isles of Scilly, Barbados, sports cars, fine dining, 60s and 70s popular music, jukebox, reading, wine, gardening, family, golden retrievers; *Style—* Philip Burroughs, Esq; ✉ McGrigors London, 5 Old Bailey, London EC4M 7BA (tel 020 7054 2605, fax 020 7054 2501)

BURROW, Dr Charles Thomas; s of Richard Burrow, of Lancaster, and Ivy Reta, *née* Coates; *b* 22 September 1945; *Educ* Lancaster Royal GS, Univ of Liverpool (MB ChB); *m* Ann Jane, da of William George Frederick Gunstone (d 1977); 1 s (Michael b 1987), 2 da (Katharine b 1976, Lucy b 1977); *Career* lectr Univ of Liverpool 1975–77, conslt pathologist Univ Hosp Aintree (formerly Walton Hosp) Liverpool 1978–; FRCPath 1988 (MRCPath 1976); *Style—* Dr Charles Burrow; ✉ University Hospital Aintree, Lower Lane, Liverpool L9 7AL (tel 0151 525 5980)

BURROW, Prof John Wyon; s of Charles Wyon Burrow, of Exeter, and Amy Alice, *née* Vosper; *b* 4 June 1935; *Educ* Exeter Sch, Christ's Coll Cambridge (MA, PhD); *m* 11 Oct 1958, Diane Margaret, da of Harold William Dunnington (d 1983), of Cambridge; 1 s (Laurence b 1961), 1 da (Francesca b 1968); *Career* res fell Christ's Coll Cambridge 1959–62, fell Downing Coll Cambridge 1962–65, lectr UEA 1965–69; prof of intellectual history Univ of Sussex 1982–95 (reader in history 1969–82), prof of European thought Univ of Oxford 1995–2000, fell Balliol Coll Oxford 1995–2000 (emeritus prof 2000–); Dr in Scienze Politiche Univ of Bologna 1988; FRHistS, FBA; *Books* Evolution and Society (1966), A Liberal Descent (1981), Gibbon (1985), Whigs and Liberals (1988), The Crisis of Reason (2000); *Style—* Prof John Burrow, FBA; ✉ Balliol College, Oxford OX1 3BJ

BURROW, Robert Philip; s of Robert F Burrow, and Rosalind, *née* Hughes; *b* 24 March 1951; *Educ* St George's Coll Weybridge, Fitzwilliam Coll Cambridge (MA); *m* 21 July 1984, Angela Mary, da of Henry Cornelius Bourne Hill; 2 s (Matthew Robert Henry b 5 June 1985, Simon Richard Philip b 20 July 1987), 1 da (Julia Rosamund Mary b 28 June 1991); *Career* admitted slr 1975; slr: Clifford Turner 1975–76 (articled clerk 1973–75), Linklaters & Paines 1976–78; dir RIT Management Ltd 1979; md: J Rothschild & Co 1981–85, Transcontinental Service Group NV 1983–88; ptnr: SJ Berwin & Co 1985–2007, Chelsfield Ptnrs LLP 2007–; non-exec dir: Control Components Ltd 1983, Marylebone Warwick Balfour Group plc 2005–; memb Law Soc; *Style*— Robert P Burrow, Esq; ✉ Chelsfield Partners LLP, 67 Brook Street, London W1K 4NJ (tel 020 7290 2388)

BURROWES, David John Barrington; MP; s of John Burrowes (d 1986), and Mary Burrowes; *b* 12 June 1969, Barnet; *Educ* Highgate Sch, Univ of Exeter (LLB), Coll of Law London; *m* 1997, Janet, *née* Coekin; 4 s (Barnaby (twin) b 27 Aug 1997, Dougal b 1 May 1999, Noah b 24 Sept 2004, Toby b 15 April 2007), 2 da (Harriet (twin) b 27 Aug 1997, Dorothy b 21 Feb 2001); *Career* admitted slr 1994; trainee slr Turner and Debenhams 1991–93, slr Shepherd Harris and Co 1994–2005 (conslt 2005–), MP (Cons) Enfield Southgate 2005– (Parly candidate (Cons) Edmonton 2001); cncllr (Cons) Enfield BC 1994–2006; vice-pres Edmonton Cons Assoc, tstee and co-fndr Cons Christian Fellowship; memb Law Soc; *Publications* Moral Basis of Conservatism (1991), Such a Thing as Society: Maggie's Children (2006), Were you up for Twigg? (2006), Forgotten: The children of addicts (2006); *Recreations* sport enthusiast (football and cricket); *Style*— David Burrowes, Esq, MP; ✉ 1C Chaseville Parade, Chaseville Park Road, London N21 1PG (tel 020 8360 0234, e-mail david@davidburrowes.com, website www.davidburrowes.com); House of Commons, London SW1A 0AA (tel 020 7219 8144, fax 020 7219 5289)

BURROWS, Prof Clifford Robert; OBE (2005); s of Edward Stephen Burrows (d 1969), and Edith Mable, *née* Aspland; *b* 20 July 1937; *Educ* West Cliff HS for Boys, Univ of Wales (BSc), Univ of London (PhD, DSc); *m* 8 July 1961, Margaret Evelyn, da of Harry Percy Mathews (d 1983); 3 s (Stephen Peter b 1 Jan 1963, Paul Robert b 8 March 1965, John Alastair b 11 March 1967), 1 da (Rachael Elizabeth b 8 June 1974); *Career* reader Univ of Sussex 1980–82 (lectr 1969), prof of dynamics and control Univ of Strathclyde 1982–87; Univ of Bath: prof of systems engrg and dir Fluid Power Centre 1987–98, head Sch of Mech Engrg 1990–95, dean Faculty of Engrg and Design 1996–2002, dir Engrg Design Centre in Fluid Power Systems 1992–2001, dir Centre for Power Transmission and Motion Control 1998–2005; author of over 200 res papers; Joseph Bramah medal IMechE 1993, 83rd Thomas Hawksley lectr IMechE; non-stipendiary priest C of E 1977; Hon Dr Ing Aachen 2000, Hon DSc Aston Univ 2001; FIMechE 1982, FREng 1998; *Books* Fluid Power Control (1972); *Recreations* rugby football; *Style*— Prof Clifford Burrows, OBE, FREng; ✉ Centre for Power Transmission and Motion Control, University of Bath, Claverton Down, Bath BA2 7AY (tel 01225 826935, fax 01225 826928)

BURROWS, Prof Desmond David; *b* 11 July 1930; *Educ* Queen's Univ Belfast (MB BCh, BAO, MD); *m* 17 Dec 1958, Marie, *née* Madden; *Career* house offr Royal Victoria Infirmary 1953–54, asst lectr Dept of Pathology Queen's Univ Belfast 1954–56, sr registrar in dermatology Royal Victoria Hosp 1958–60 (registrar in dermatology 1956–58), MRC research fell Inst of Dermatology London 1960–61, conslt dermatologist Royal Victoria Hosp 1961– (chm Med Div 1981–83); Queen's Univ Belfast: memb Faculty of Med 1981–, hon lectr in dermatology 1985–, hon prof Clinical Med Sch 1990–; memb: Central Conslts and Hosp Specialities Ctee BMA 1980–82, Scientific Advsy Ctee Gen (Internal) Med and Related Specialities DHSS 1986; chm: Med Exec Ctee Royal Gp of Hosps 1984–86, Med Specialities Ctee Postgraduate Cncl NI 1989–; sec: Irish Dermatological Soc 1965–71, Euro Soc for Contact Dermatitis 1986–90 (memb Cncl 1987); pres: Irish Assoc of Dermatologists 1975–77, Euro Soc of Contact Dermatology 1990–92, Br Assoc of Dermatologists 1991–92 (memb Cncl 1975–77 and 1980–86); chm Br Contact Dermatitis Gp 1983–86 (memb Exec Ctee 1981–89); memb Cncl: Ulster Medical/Legal Soc 1976–78, Int League of Dermatological Socs 1981–88, Euro Environmental and Contact Dermatitis Gp 1985–96, BMA 1986–87, RCPEd; memb Editorial Bd: Contact Dermatitis - Environmental and Occupational Dermatitis 1985–99, Jl of the American Acad of Dermatology 1990–97, Jl of the Euro Acad of Dermatology and Venereology, Bollettino di Dermatologia Allergologia e Professionale; hon memb: Finnish Soc of Dermatology 1986, Swedish Dermatological Soc 1986, American Dermatology Assoc 1987, Academia Espanola de Dermatologia 1988, N American Clinical Dermatology Soc 1993, Br Assoc of Dermatologists 1993, Norwegian Dermatological Soc (corresponding memb); memb: Ulster Med Soc, Dowling Dermatological Soc, St John's Hosp Dermatological Soc; FRCPEd 1969 (MRCPEd), FRCP Dublin 1982, FRCP 1986; *Books* Chromium: Metabolism and Toxicity (1983); author of various book chapters and numerous published papers; *Recreations* golf; *Clubs* Corrigan; *Style*— Prof Desmond Burrows; ✉ Apartments 66/67, Stranmillis Wharf, Lockview Road, Belfast BT9 5GN (tel 028 9038 1669, mobile 07785 250521, e-mail desmond.burrows1@ntlworld.com)

BURROWS, Prof Malcolm; s of William Roy Burrows, and Jean Jones, *née* Brincklow; *b* 28 May 1943; *Educ* Jesus Coll Cambridge, Gatty Marine Lab Univ of St Andrews; *m* 1 Jan 1966, Christine Joan Ellis; 1 s (Mark Callum b 2 Sept 1969), 1 da (Gwynne Ruth b 23 July 1971); *Career* visiting asst prof and research fell Dept of Biology Univ of Oregon 1967–70, SRC fell and then Beit fell Dept of Zoology Univ of Oxford 1970–74; Univ of Cambridge: successively Balfour student, lectr, reader, then prof Dept of Neuroscience 1974–96, prof of zoology and head Dept of Zoology 1996–; visiting fell: Dept of Neurobiology ANU 1972, Univ of Regensburg 1980; visiting prof Univ of Konstanz1987, Wiersma visiting prof Caltech 1991, distinguished visiting prof Univ of Calif Davis 1992, Alexander von Humboldt Preisträger Freie Universitat Berlin 1993; ed Jl of Experimental Biology 1995–2005; memb Editorial Bd: European Jl of Neuroscience 1987–, Trends in Neuroscience 1993–2004; scientific medal Zoological Soc of London 1980, Frink medal Zoological Soc of London 2004, professorial fell Wolfson Coll Cambridge 1991–; memb: Academia Europaea 1992, Bavarian Acad Munich 1996; FRS 1985; *Books* Nervous Systems and Behaviour (jtly, 1995), The Neurobiology of an Insect Brain (1996); *Style*— Prof Malcolm Burrows, FRS; ✉ Department of Zoology, Downing Street, Cambridge CB2 3EJ (tel 01223 336628, fax 01223 336676, e-mail mb135@hermes.cam.ac.uk)

BURROWS, Peter Malcolm Grant; s of late John Grant Burrows, of Holywell, N Wales, and Elizabeth Eleanor, *née* Fryte; *b* 14 December 1952; *Educ* Holywell GS, Univ of Aberystwyth; *m* 26 Sept 1981, Louise Elizabeth, da of Dr W G Wenley; 1 da (Clare Elizabeth b 1 March 1984); *Career* articled clerk Philip Jones Hillyer & Jackson Chester 1975–77, slr Winter Wilkinson St Neots & St Ives 1977–87; Norton Rose: joined 1987, ptnr 1989–, mangr Commercial Property and Planning Dept 1994–2000, mangr London real estate team 2003–; Freeman: City of London, City of London Slrs' Co 1987; memb Law Soc 1977; *Recreations* cycling, polishing my car; *Style*— Peter Burrows, Esq; ✉ Norton Rose, Kempson House, Camomile Street, London EC3A 7AN (tel 020 7283 6000, direct tel 020 7444 3714, fax 020 7283 6500, e-mail burrowspmg@nortonrose.com)

BURROWS, Prof Philip Nicholas; s of Nicholas Charles Ernest Burrows, of Chorley, Lancs, and Winefred Grace Hart, *née* Coyle (d 2003); *b* 22 July 1964, Chorley, Lancs; *Educ* Oriel Coll Oxford (MA, DPhil); *Career* research scientist MIT 1989–98, PPARC advanced fell Univ of Oxford 1998–2002, sr lectr, reader and prof of physics Queen Mary Univ of London 2002–05, prof of accelerator physics John Adams Inst Univ of Oxford 2006–; sr research fell Jesus Coll Oxford; visiting scholar Stanford Univ; memb CPhys 1990, CSci 2003, FInstP 2004; *Recreations* music, the arts, travel, photography; *Style*— Prof Philip Burrows; ✉ John Adams Institute, Particle Physics, Keble Road, Oxford OX1 3RH (tel 01865 273451, fax 01865 273417, e-mail p.burrows@physics.ox.ac.uk)

BURROWS, (Anthony) Richard Brocas; s of Lt-Gen Montagu Brocas Burrows (d 1966), and Molly Rose, *née* Le Bas (d 1996); *b* 27 January 1939; *Educ* Eton; *m* 6 Oct 1966, Angela Margaret, da of John Vincent Sheffield; 3 da (Carey (Mrs Rupert English) b 1968, Joanna (Mrs Charles Cunningham-Reid) b 1969, Petra (Mrs Edward Walker) b 1972), 1 s (Brocas b 1975); *Career* chm Tex Holdings; Liveryman Worshipful Co of Grocers; *Recreations* golf, tennis, travel; *Clubs* White's; *Style*— Richard Burrows, Esq; ✉ Tex Holdings plc, Claydon Business Park, Gipping Road, Great Blakenham, Ipswich, Suffolk IP6 0NL

BURSELL, His Hon Judge Rupert David Hingston; QC (1986); s of Rev Henry Bursell (d 1983), and Cicely Mary, *née* Pawson (d 1977); *b* 10 November 1942; *Educ* St John's Sch Leatherhead, Univ of Exeter (LLB), St Edmund Hall Oxford (MA, DPhil), St Stephen House Oxford; *m* 1 July 1967, Joanna Ruth, da of Maj Robert Peter Davies Gibb (d 1999); 2 s (Michael Hingston b 1970, James David Hingston b 1972), 1 da (Polly Joanna Hingston b 1976); *Career* called to the Bar Lincoln's Inn 1968, circuit judge (Western Circuit) 1988–2003, official referee, judge of the Technol and Construction Ct 1992–, designated civil judge 1998–, sr circuit judge 2003–; ordained: deacon 1968, priest 1969; hon curate: St Marylebone 1968–69, St Mary The Virgin Almondsbury 1969–71, St Francis Bedminster 1971–83, Christ Church, St Stephen Bristol 1983–88, St Mary The Virgin Cheddar 1993–; chllr, vicar gen and official princ: Dio of Durham 1989–, Dio of Bath & Wells 1992–93, Dio of St Albans 1992–2002, Dio of Oxford 2002–; dep chllr: Dio of York 1994–, Dio of St Albans 2003–; hon chaplain 3 Vol Mil Intelligence Bn 1996–2001; *Books* Atkins Court Forms (contrib Ecclesiastical Law), Halsbury's Laws of England: Cremation and Burial and Ecclesiastical Law (contrib), Principles of Dermatitis Legislation (contrib), Crown Court Practice (jtly), Liturgy, Order and the Law; *Recreations* church music, military history, archaeology of Greece, Turkey and the Holy Land; *Clubs* MCC, Army and Navy; *Style*— His Hon Judge Bursell, QC; ✉ The Law Courts, Small Street, Bristol BS1 2HL (tel 0117 976 3030)

BURSTEIN, Joan; CBE (2006); da of Ashley Harvey Jotner (d 1956), and Mary, *née* Pleeth (d 1956); *b* 21 February 1926; *Educ* Henrietta Barnet Sch, Hampstead Garden Suburb; *m* Sidney Burstein, s of Barnet Burstein; 1 da (Caroline b 1949), 1 s (Simon b 1951); *Career* opened Browns: South Molton St 1970, Sloane St 1976; introduced many designers to London, Donna Karan, Giorgio Armani, Ralph Lauren, Calvin Klein, Romeo Gigli; V&A Award for Outstanding Achievement in Fashion 2006; Hon Dr Univ of the Arts London 2007; *Style*— Mrs Joan Burstein, CBE; ✉ Browns, 27 South Molton Street, London W1K 5RD (tel 020 7514 0000, fax 020 7408 1281, e-mail buyingoffice@brownsfashion.com)

BURSTIN, Nicholas Ernest; s of Capt Oswald Burstin, of London, and Lydia, *née* Hammerschmid; *b* 29 April 1957; *Educ* UCS London, Jesus Coll Cambridge, Harvard Business Sch; *Children* 1 da (Sophie Alexandra), 1 s (Dominic Hugo); *Career* dir J Walter Thompson Co Ltd 1989–; *Recreations* sailing, music; *Style*— Nicholas Burstin, Esq

BURSTOW, Paul Kenneth; MP; s of Brian Seymour Burstow, and Sheila, *née* Edmonds; *b* 13 May 1962; *Educ* Glastonbury HS for Boys Carshalton, Carshalton Coll, South Bank Univ (BA); *m* 11 Nov 1995, Mary; 3 c; *Career* Assoc of Lib Dem Cncls: cncllrs' offr 1989–92, campaigns offr 1992–96, acting political sec 1996–97; MP (Lib Dem) Sutton and Cheam 1997–; Lib Dem spokesman on disabled people 1997–98, chief spokesman on local government 1997–99, Lib Dem shadow min for older people 1999–2003, chief spokesman on health 2003–05, chief whip 2006–; chm All-Pty Parly Gp on Back Pain, co-chm All-Pty Parly Gp on Older People, vice-chm All-Pty Disablement Gp, vice-chm All-Pty Gp on ME, vice-chm All-Pty Gp on Business Services, memb All-Pty Parly Gp on Personal Soc Servs Panel; dep ldr London Borough of Sutton 1994–97 (cncllr 1986–2002); *Recreations* walking, cooking, working out in gym; *Clubs* National Liberal; *Style*— Paul Burstow, Esq, MP; ✉ Constituency Office, Epsom House, 312–314 High Street, Sutton, Surrey SM1 1PR (tel 020 8288 6555, fax 020 8288 6550, website www.paulburstow.com)

BURT, Prof Alastair David; s of George Hoggan Burt, of Glasgow, and Iris Helen Forrest Burt; *b* 9 March 1957; *Educ* Hummersknott GS Darlington, Eastwood HS Glasgow, Univ of Glasgow (BSc, MB ChB, MD); *m* 29 Dec 1980, Alison Carol, *née* Tweedlie; 1 da (Jennifer Alison b 24 Oct 1984), 1 s (Stuart Alastair b 20 Aug 1988); *Career* jr house offr in gen med Western Infirmary Glasgow 1981–82, jr house offr in gen surgery Royal Infirmary Glasgow 1982, SHO and registrar in pathology Western Infirmary Glasgow 1982–85, Peel travelling research fell Lab for Cell Biology and Histology Free Univ of Brussels 1985–86, registrar and sr registrar in pathology Western Infirmary Glasgow 1986–89; Univ of Newcastle upon Tyne: sr lectr in pathology 1989–95, personal professorship in hepatopathology 1995–98, prof of pathology and head Sch of Clinical and Lab Sciences 1998–2005; Newcastle upon Tyne Hosps NHS Tst: head of clinical service Dept of Cellular Pathology 1999–2005, dean of clinical medicine 2005–; visiting prof Univ of Otago 1993; ed Basic Sciences Section Hepatogastroenterology 1994–97, ed-in-chief Liver 1998–2002; memb: Editorial Bd Jl of Hepatology 1995–97, Editorial Bd Jl of Gastroenterology and Hepatology 1996–2005, Ctee on Pubn Ethics 1999–2002, Int Advsy Bd Med Electron Microscopy 2002–, Advsy Bd Clinical Science 2002–, Editorial Advsy Bd Jl of Pathology 2006– (reviews ed 1994–97); memb: Int Hepatopathology Gp 1995–, Scientific Ctee Children's Liver Disease Fndn, Research Assessment Exercise 2008 Panel A Subpanel 5; treas and tstee Pathological Soc of GB and I; memb: Br Assoc for the Study of the Liver 1990–, Int Assoc for the Study of the Liver 1990–, European Assoc for the Study of the Liver 1991–, American Assoc for the Society of Liver Diseases 1992–, Caledonian Soc Gastroenterology 1993–, NY Acad of Sciences 1995–97, Assoc of Profs of Pathology 1996–, Laennac Soc 1999–, Br Soc of Gastroenterology 2003–, Int Acad of Pathologists (Br Div); corresponding memb Hans Popper Hepatopathology Soc 1991–, perm memb Int Gastro-Surgical Club 1993–, hon memb Cuban Soc of Pathology 1997, fndr memb European Club for Liver Cell Biology 2000–, hon life memb Glasgow Univ Medico-Chirurgical Soc; Bellahouston Medal Univ of Glasgow 1992, C L Oakley lectr Pathological Soc of GB and I 1993, Ishak meml lectr 2005, Vincent McGovern meml lectr 2007; FIBiol 1996 (MIBiol 1991), FRCPath 1997 (MRCPath 1988); *Books* Pathology of the Liver (jtly, 3 edn 1994, 4 edn 2001, First Prize/Highly Commended Medical Book Awards, ed-in-chief 5 edn 2007), Multiple Choice Questions in Clinical Pathology (jtly, 1995), Liver Inflammation and Fibrogenesis (1996); *Recreations* music (baroque and contemporary classic), cooking; *Style*— Prof Alastair D Burt; ✉ Dean of Clinical Medicine's Office, Peacock Hall, Royal Victoria Infirmary, Newcastle upon Tyne NE1 4LP (tel 0191 282 0700, fax 0191 282 0702, e-mail a.d.burt@ncl.ac.uk)

BURT, Alistair James Hendrie; MP; s of James Hendrie Burt and Mina Christie Robertson; *b* 25 May 1955; *Educ* Bury GS, St John's Coll Oxford, Chester Coll of Law; *m* 1983, Eve Alexandra Twite; 1 s, 1 da; *Career* slr; memb London Borough of Haringey 1982–84; MP (Cons): Bury North 1983–97, Beds NE 2001–; PPS to Rt Hon Kenneth Baker MP 1985–90, Parly under-sec of state for Social Security 1992–95, min of state DSS 1995–97, shadow min for Educn and Skills 2001–02, PPS to Iain Duncan Smith 2002–03, PPS to Michael Howard 2003–05, shadow min for communities and regeneration 2005–07, shadow min for local govt and regeneration 2007–; sponsor min for Manchester and Salford 1994–97; sr search conslt Whitehead Mann GKR plc 1997–2001; vice-pres Tory Reform Gp; *Recreations* family, modern art, music, sport, church and religious affairs; *Style*— Alistair Burt, Esq, MP; ✉ House of Commons, London SW1A 0AA (tel 020 7219 8132, e-mail burta@parliament.uk)

BURT, David Jeffery; OBE (1985); *b* 24 March 1935; *Career* personnel dir Bowthorpe Holdings, chief exec Deutsch Ltd 1985–; chm: TBG Education/Training Gp, Consumer Complains Service (OCCS), General Optical Cncl 1988–99; former chm: CBI (Sussex), Dental Rate Study Gp; memb: Advsy Ctee on Conscientious Objectors House of Lords 1991–, Civil Service Arbitration Tbnl 1993–; Liveryman Worshipful Co of Spectacle Makers 1993, Freeman City of London; FIPM, FRSA; *Recreations* sculptor (exhibited at RA Summer Exhbn), Morgan Classic rally driver, farmer, squash player; *Style*— David Burt, Esq, OBE; ✉ Deutsch Ltd, St Leonards-on-Sea, East Sussex TN38 9RF (tel 01424 857102, e-mail d.burt@deutsch.co.uk)

BURT, Lorely; MP; *b* 10 September 1954; *Educ* High Arcal GS, Univ of Swansea, Open Univ (MBA); *m* Richard; 1 da, 1 step s; *Career* sometime asst govr HM Prison Service, personnel trg mangr, business conslt and md of small business in adult trg, mktg and financial servs; Parly candidate (Lib Dem) Dudley S 1991, MP (Lib Dem) Solihull 2005–; former cncllr (Lib Dem) Dudley MBC; former memb: Lib Dem Fed Policy Ctee, W Midlands Regional Exec; fell Institute of Sales and Mktg Mgmnt (ISMM); *Style*— Ms Lorely Burt, MP; ✉ House of Commons, London SW1A 0AA (e-mail burtl@parliament.uk, website www.solihull-libdems.org.uk)

BURT, Sir Peter Alexander; kt (2003); s of Robert Wallace Burt (d 1970), of Longniddry, E Lothian, and May Henderson, *née* Rodger (d 1991); *b* 6 March 1944; *Educ* Merchiston Castle Sch Edinburgh, Univ of St Andrews (MA), Univ of Pennsylvania (Thouron scholar, MBA); *m* 23 April 1971, Alison Mackintosh, da of John M Turner, OBE (d 1991), of Kilmarnock; 3 s (Michael Wallace b 1975, Hamish Jonathan b 1978, Angus Moncrieff b 1984); *Career* Hewlett Packard Co Palo Alto Calif 1968–70, Conversational Software Ltd Edinburgh 1970–74, Edward Bates & Sons Edinburgh 1974; Bank of Scotland: joined 1975, asst gen mangr Int Div 1979–84, divnl gen mangr Int Div 1984–85, jt gen mangr Int Div 1985–88, treas and chief gen mangr 1988–96, appointed main bd dir 1995, chief exec 1996–2001; chm Gleacher Shacklock UK Ltd 2000–05, chm Gleacher Shacklock LLP 2004–, non-exec chm ITV plc 2004–07, dep chm HBOS plc 2001–03; non-exec dir: Shell Transport eTrading 2002–05, Royal Dutch Shell 2004–06; dir Templeton Emerging Markets Investment Trust plc 2004–; FCIB (Scotland), FRSE; *Recreations* golf, tennis, skiing, reading; *Clubs* Royal & Ancient, Hon Co of Edinburgh Golfers, Gullane Golf; *Style*— Sir Peter Burt; ✉ Gleacher Shacklock LLP, Cleveland House, 33 King Street, London SW1Y 6RJ

BURTCH, Mervyn Arthur; MBE (2003); s of Walter James Powell Burtch (d 1956), and Mary Ann, *née* Jones (d 1992); *b* 7 November 1929; *Educ* Lewis Sch Pengam, UC Cardiff; *Career* composer; operas incl: Alice in Wonderland, Canterville Ghost, Coyote and the Winter that Never Ends, Wizard Things, The Raven King, Casablanca, Jason and Hanna, On Christmas Eve, Twm Sion Cati; various smaller operas; other works incl: I Saw a Child for choir and orch 1985, 13 String Quartets (number 1 1985, 2 1986, 3 1987, 4 1992, 5, 6 and 7 1994, 9 and 10 1995, 11 1996, 12 1998, 13 1999); concerto for: piano and brass band, cor anglais and strings, piano and strings, clarinet and strings, piano and orch, violin and orch, viola and orch, oboe and strings, bassoon and strings, trumpet and strings; also large number of smaller chamber, vocal and choral works; founded Kids-op to produce opera for children worldwide with librettist Mark Morris 1996; *Style*— Mervyn Burtch, Esq, MBE; ✉ Hillcroft, Park Lane, Tredomen, Ystrad Mynach, Mid Glamorgan CF82 7BX (tel 01443 812218, e-mail rsj@hillcroft70.fsnet.co.uk, website www.kidsop.com)

BURTON, Amanda; *b* 10 October 1956; *Educ* Ballougry Primary Sch, Londonderry HS, Manchester Poly Sch of Theatre; *m* (m dis); 2 da (Phoebe Marie, Brid Irina); *Career* actress; Hon DLitt Univ of Ulster; FRSA; *Theatre* incl: Playhouse Theatre Lancaster, Octagon Theatre Bolton; *Television* incl: Brookside (Channel Four) 1982–86, Boon (Central) 1988, Inspector Morse (Zenith), A Casualty of War 1990, The Greek Myths - Theseus and the Minotaur (Jim Henson Organisation) 1990, Stay Lucky (Yorkshire), Lovejoy (BBC), Minder (Thames), Medics (Granada), Peak Practice (Central) 1993–95, Silent Witness (BBC) 1996–, The Precious Blood (Screen 2) 1996, The Gift (Screen 1) 1998, Forgotten (LWT) 1999, Little Bird (Granada) 2000, The Whistle Blower (BBC) 2001, Bears in Idaho (BBC documentary), Helen West (ITV) 2002, Pollyanna (ITV) 2003, The Commander 2003, 2004 and 2007, Miss Marple 2006; *Awards* Nat TV Awards 1998, 1999 and 2001, Festival of TV Monte Carlo 1999, Woman of the Year Irish Tatler 2004; *Clubs* Groucho; *Style*— Ms Amanda Burton

BURTON, Amanda Jane; da of Michael Charles Pearson Burton, of N Yorks, and Ann Margaret Burton, of Suffolk; *b* 3 January 1959; *Educ* Queen Ethelburga's Harrogate, Bradford Girls' GS, Univ of Durham (BA), Coll of Law Guildford; *Career* slr Slaughter and May 1982–86, asst co sec Tiphook plc 1986–90, co sec Ratners Gp plc 1990–92; Meyer International plc: co sec 1992–97, legal and corp servs dir 1997–2000; Clifford Chance: regnl chief operating offr 2000–07, dir of global business servs 2006–; non-exec dir: Fresca Gp Ltd 1998–, UCM Timber plc 2002–03, Galliford Try plc 2005–; memb Law Soc; *Recreations* piano, interior design, theatre, swimming; *Clubs* Annabel's; *Style*— Miss Amanda Burton; ✉ Clifford Chance, 10 Upper Bank Street, London E14 5JJ (tel 020 7006 1000)

BURTON, Anthony George Graham; s of Donald Graham Burton (d 1960), and Irene, *née* Trotter (d 1992); *b* 24 December 1934; *Educ* King James's GS Knaresborough, Univ of Leeds; *m* 28 March 1959, Pip, da of Walter Sharman (d 1961); 2 s (Jonathan b 1961, Nicholas b 1964), 1 da (Jenny b 1963); *Career* freelance writer and broadcaster; *Books* incl: A Programmed Guide to Office Warfare (1969), The Jones Report (1970), The Canal Builders (1972, 4 edn 2005), The Reluctant Musketeer (1973), Canals in Colour (1974), Remains of a Revolution (1975, 2 edn 2001), The Master Idol (1975), The Navigators (1976), The Miners (1976), Josiah Wedgwood (1976), Canal (with Derek Pratt, 1976), Industrial Archaeological Sites of Britain (1977), A Place to Stand (1977), Back Door Britain (1977), The Green Bag Travellers (with Pip Burton, 1978), The Past at Work (1980), The Rainhill Story (1980), The Past Afloat (1982), The Shell Book of Curious Britain (1982), The Changing River (1982), The Waterways of Britain (1983), The National Trust Guide to Our Industrial Past (1983), The Rise and Fall of King Cotton (1984), Walking the Line (1985), Wilderness Britain (1985), Britain's Light Railways (jtly, 1985), Britain Revisited (1986), The Shell Book of Undiscovered Britain and Ireland (1986), Landscape Detective (jtly, 1986), Opening Time (1987), Steaming Through Britain (1987), Walking Through History (1988), Walk the South Downs (1988), The Yorkshire Dales and York (1989), The Great Days of the Canals (1989), Astonishing Britain (1990), Cityscapes (1990), Slow Roads (1991), The Railway Builders (1992), Canal Mania (1993), The Grand Union Canal Walk (with Neil Curtis, 1993), The Railway Empire (1994), The Rise and Fall of British Shipbuilding (1994), The Dales Way (1995), The Cotswold Way (1995), The West Highland Way (1996), The Southern Upland Way (1997), William Cobbett: Englishman (1997), The Wye Valley Walk (1998), The Caledonian Canal (1998), Best Foot Forward (1998), The Cumbria Way (1999), The Wessex Ridgeway (1999), Thomas Telford (1999), Weekend Walks Dartmoor and Exmoor (2000), Weekend Walks The Yorkshire Dales (2000), Traction Engines (2000), Richard Trevithick (2000), Weekend Walks in the Peak District (2001), The Orient Express (2001), The Anatomy of Canals: The Early Years (2001), The Daily Telegraph Guide to Britain's Working Past (2002), The Anatomy of Canals: the Mania Years (2002), The Daily Telegraph Guide to Britain's Maritime Past (2003), Hadrian's Wall Walk (2003), The Anatomy of Canals: Decline and Renewal (2003), On the Rails (2004), The Ridgeway (2005), The Cotswold Way (2007); *Recreations* steam engines, boats, walking, beer; *Style*— Anthony Burton, Esq; ✉ c/o Sara Menguc, 58 Thorkhill Road, Thames Ditton, Surrey KT7 0UG (tel 020 8398 7992, e-mail saramenguc@aol.com)

BURTON, Anthony Philip; s of Frank Burton (d 1975), and Lottie, *née* Lax (d 1996); *b* 25 October 1942; *Educ* The King's Sch Macclesfield, Wadham Coll Oxford (MA, BLitt); *m* 21 Sept 1985, Carol Deborah, da of Adrian Hilary Baker; *Career* asst keeper in the directorate V&A 1979–81 (asst keeper of the library 1968–79), head Bethnal Green Museum of Childhood 1981–97, research fell Research Dept V&A 1997–2002, chm of tstees Charles Dickens Museum 2003–05; *Books* Vision and Accident: The Story of the Victoria and Albert Museum (1999), The Great Exhibitor: the Life and Work of Henry Cole (with Elizabeth Bonython, 2003); *Style*— Anthony Burton, Esq; ✉ 59 Arlington Avenue, London N1 7BA (tel 020 7226 0394)

BURTON, Charles Philip Henry; s of Sir George Vernon Kennedy Burton, CBE, DL, *qv*, of Hadleigh, Suffolk, and Sarah Katherine, *née* Tcherniavsky; *b* 6 December 1952; *Educ* Charterhouse, Univ of Exeter (BA); *m* 2 Nov 1985, Susanna Louise, da of Peter Henry Buller; 2 da (Sophie Mary, Rose Elizabeth (twins) b 7 July 1993); *Career* economist Beecham Pharmaceuticals Ltd 1974–75; CBI 1975–85: head industrial trends and economic forecasting, dep dir Economic Directorate; business devpt mangr Wharton Econometric Forecasting Assocs Ltd 1985–88, chief exec Business Strategies Ltd 1996–2003 (jt md 1988–96), md Micromarketing Div Experian Ltd 2003–; memb Soc of Business Economists (memb Cncl 1996–, hon treas 1997–), memb Econ Advsy Ctee Univ of Strathclyde 1996–; FRSA; *Books* Competition and Markets (1990); *Recreations* music, history, photography; *Clubs* RAC; *Style*— Charles Burton, Esq; ✉ Experian Ltd, Nightingale House, 65 Curzon Street, London W1S 8PE (tel 0870 196 8201, fax 0870 196 8277)

BURTON, (Anthony) David; CBE (1992); s of Leslie Mitchell Burton (d 1967), and Marion, *née* Marsh (d 1976); *b* 2 April 1937; *Educ* Arnold Sch Blackpool; *m* 30 May 1964, Valerie, da of Harry Swire, of Burnley, Lancs; 2 da (Judith Alison b 1966, Anne Louise b 1968), 1 s (Michael John b 1971); *Career* Nat Serv RAPC 1955–57; chief dealer Bank of America NT & SA 1967–72, exec dir S G Warburg & Co Ltd 1979–92; LIFFE: fndr memb Working Party 1979, dir 1980–94, chm Membership & Rules Ctee 1982–88, dep chm 1985–88, chm 1988–92; chm: S G Warburg Futures & Options Ltd 1988–92, Marshalls Finance Ltd (int money brokers) 1989–98, Ludgate 181 Ltd 1999–2002, Ludgate 181 (Jersey) Ltd 2002–, Ludgate Investments Ltd 2004–, Beechwood House Finance Ltd 2004–, Ashley House plc 2004–07, Ashley House Properties Ltd 2005–07; fndr memb Assoc of Futures Brokers and Dealers 1986–88; memb: Br Invisible Exports Cncl 1988–90, Euro Ctee Br Invisibles 1990–92; dir: British Invisibles 1992–93, The Securities Inst 1992–93; non-exec dir Car Crash Line Gp plc 2003–05; memb Governing Bd City Res Project 1991–94; Freeman City of London 1984, Liveryman Worshipful Co of Glass Sellers 1984; FCIB, FCT; *Books* collector, lectr and writer on: early English glass c 1600–1800, English blackjacks and leather bottles c 1550–1700, early German Rhenish pottery c 1500–1650; *Recreations* fine wine, travel, sport, music, opera; *Style*— David Burton, Esq, CBE; ✉ e-mail david@burton1.com

BURTON, David Gowan; s of Reginald Frank Burton (d 1967), of Woodford Green, Essex, and Nellie Erwin, *née* Biggs; *b* 3 April 1943; *Educ* McEntree Tech Sch; *m* 8 Aug 1970, Hilary Kathleen, da of Canon Robert Smith; 2 s (Matthew Edward Gowan b 21 Oct 1972, Simon James Gowan b 19 May 1983), 1 da (Emma Claire b 8 Sept 1975); *Career* articles with Keens Shay Keens & Co 1960–65, Thomson McLintock 1965–73 (latterly sr mangr), sr mangr Neville Russell & Co (now Mazars) 1973–75; Touche Ross & Co: sr mangr 1975–79, ptnr 1979–93, seconded from London to IOM 1983–91, estab Green Field office IOM 1985, ptnr Cambridge office 1991–93; estab private consultancy and corp fin practice 1993; dir: IDEM Holdings Ltd 1999–2002, City Life Ltd 1999–2002, SigmaQC Ltd 2001–; chm: Ossys Holdings Ltd 1999–2004, Globaltech Solutions Ltd 2002–, Aon Alexander and Alexander UK Pensions Tstees Ltd 2006– (dir 2001–), Aon UK Pension Scheme 2006–, Hirco plc 2006–; founding ptnr Argyll Assocs 2004–; memb Advsy Bd Campbell Lutyens & Co Ltd (Corp Fin Boutique) 1993–2003; tstee Combined Britons Pension Plan 2006; memb Bd of Mgmnt Springboard Housing Assoc 1993–99; chm of tstees: Jubilee Centre, Relationships Fndn 1996–2002; treas Church Army 1995–2000; govr Chigwell Sch 1992–2002; Liveryman Worshipful Co of CAs in England and Wales; FCA 1976 (ACA 1965), FRSA 1993; *Recreations* family, golf, walking, gardening, farming; *Clubs* New (Edinburgh) Chigwell Golf; *Style*— David Burton, Esq; ✉ 3 The Green, Woodford Green, Essex IG8 0NF (tel 020 8505 5402)

BURTON, Diane Elizabeth (Di); da of Victor St Clair Yates, of Durban, South Africa, and Betty, *née* Woolliscroft; *b* 26 July 1954; *Educ* Univ of the Witwatersrand (BA), Huddersfield Poly (PGCE), Damelin Mgmnt Sch Johannesburg (DipPR); *m* 1979, Andrew Thomas Guy Burton; 1 da (Sarah St Clair b 1980), 1 s (Rupert Thomas b 1982); *Career* emigrated to UK 1985, dir Moss International Ltd 1988–89, md Cicada PR Ltd 2002–; sr lectr Leeds Business Sch 1992–94, Faculty of Media Univ of Leeds 1994–2001, conslt fell Univ of Leeds 1998–; memb Mktg Standards Lead Body for Dept for Educn and Employment NVQ Devpt; memb Cncl IPR 1998–2003; Business Personality of the Year Ackrill Media Gp Business Awards 2005; hon fell Trinity and All Saints Univ of Leeds; MInstD 1989 (chm Export Award Scheme), MIPD 1994, FRSA 2001, FCIPR (FIPR 1995), FCIPD; *Publications* Promoting the Product or Service in Financing Growth (for Leeds Poly, 1989), Management and Strategy Module (for CAM Distance Learning Prog, 1994), Masters in Corporate Direction Programme (contrib); *Recreations* tennis, horse riding, gardening; *Style*— Mrs Di Burton, FCIPR, FCIPD; ✉ Cicada Public Relations Ltd, 101 Station Parade, Harrogate HG1 1HB (tel 01423 567111, fax 01423 565660, e-mail di@cicada-pr.com, website www.cicada-pr.com)

BURTON, Frances Rosemary; da of Maj Richard Francis Heveningham Pughe, DFC, ERD (d 1990), of Ridlington, Norfolk, and Pamela Margaret, *née* Coates (d 1978); *b* 19 June 1941; *Educ* St Mary's Convent Bishop's Stortford, Tortington Park Arundel, Lady Margaret House Cambridge, St Anne's Coll Oxford, Univ of London (LLB), Univ of Leicester (LLM) (MA 1999); *m* 1, 26 Oct 1963 (m dis 1973), Robert Scott Alexander (later Baron Alexander of Weedon, QC (Life Peer), d 2005), s of Samuel James Alexander (d 1965), of Fleet, Hants; 2 s (David Robert James b 1964, William Richard Scott b 1969), 1 da (Mary Frances Anne b 1966); m 2, 28 Nov 1975 (m dis 1991), David Michael Burton (d 2000), s of Frank Raymond Burton (d 1965), of Wellington, Salop; 2 da (Jane Richenda Frances b 1979, Charlotte Alice Octavia b 1981); *Career* called to the Bar Middle Temple 1970 (ad eundem Lincoln's Inn 1972); in practice Chancery Bar 1973–75 and 1989–, tutor for Bar and Law Soc examinations, lectr and tutor Dept of Law and Faculty of Business City of London Poly 1989–93, dir of Bar courses BPP Law Sch 1992–93 (memb Advsy Bd 1993–2000), sr lectr in Law London Guildhall Univ 1993–2001, lectr Coll of Law of England and Wales 2001–02; princ lectr Univ of West of England 2002–; dep traffic cmmr S Eastern and Metropolitan Eastern and Western Traffic Areas 1996–2002, judicial chm Tport Tbnl 2002–; vice-pres Assoc of Women Barristers 2003– (memb Ctee 1996–, hon treas 1998–99, vice-chair 1999–2001, chair 2001–03), legal chm Residential Property Tbnl Service (formerly London Rent Assessment Panel) 1997–; author of legal text books; govr Westminster Coll 1969–73; numerous fundraising activities incl: Justice Br Section Int Cmmn of Jurists 1963–2000, Peckham Settlement 1973–85, Jubilee Sailing Tst 1985–, Cancer Res Campaign 1986–87, Duke of Edinburgh's Award Scheme 1987; chm Ctee Justice Ball 1983 and 1985, memb Exec Ctee Big Bang City Ball 1986; *Books* Family Law Textbook (1988, revised edn 1990), Bar Final General Paper Textbook (1990), Family Law - Documents, Forms and Precedents (1992), Criminal Litigation (jtly, 1994, 3 edn

1997), Family Law and Practice (1996), Guide to the Family Law Act 1996 (1996), Teaching Family Law (jtly, 1999), Family Law (2003, 2 edn 2006), ILEX Family Law Manual (2004), Core Statutes on Family Law (2005, 3 edn 2007); *Recreations* opera, history, archaeology; *Clubs* Oxford and Cambridge; *Style—* Mrs Frances Burton; ✉ 10 Old Square, Lincoln's Inn, London WC2A 3SU (tel 020 7405 0758, fax 020 7831 8237, mobile 07775 655088, e-mail frb@frburton.com)

BURTON, Frank Patrick; QC (1998); s of Robert Burton; *b* 19 June 1950; *Educ* Salesian Coll Farnborough, Univ of Kent (BA), LSE (PhD), City Univ (Dip Law); *m* 1983, Caroline Reid; 3 c (Daniel b 1 July 1984, Thomas b 8 Jan 1986, Tamar b 8 Sept 1987); *Career* lectr 1976–82, called to the Bar 1982 (bencher 2004), recorder 2000– (asst recorder 1999); chm Law Reform Ctee Bar Cncl 2003–, chm Personal Injury Bar Assoc 2004– (exec memb 1996–, vice-chm 2002–04); *Publications* The Politics of Legitimacy, Official Discourse (with P Carlen), Personal Injury Limitation Law (1994), Medical Negligence (1995); *Recreations* reading, sport, Suffolk; *Style—* Frank Burton, Esq, QC; ✉ 12 King's Bench Walk, Temple, London EC4Y 7EL (tel 020 7583 0811, fax 020 7583 7228, e-mail burton@12kbw.co.uk)

BURTON, Sir George Vernon Kennedy; kt (1977), CBE (1972, MBE 1945), DL (Suffolk) 1980; s of George Ethelbert Earnshaw Burton, and Francesca, *née* Holden-White; *b* 21 April 1916; *Educ* Charterhouse, Weimar Univ; *m* 1, 1945 (m dis), Sarah Katherine Tcherniavsky; 2 s; m 2, 1975, Priscilla Margaret Burton, MBE, da of Cecil Harmsworth King, and formerly w of St John Gore; *Career* formerly Capt RA WW II; chm Fisons 1973–86; dir: Barclays Bank International 1976–82, Thomas Tilling 1976–82, Rolls-Royce 1976–83; memb Cncl CBI 1970–84, chm CBI Overseas Ctee 1975–83; memb: BOTB 1972–82, NEDC 1975–79, Assoc Br Sponsorship of the Arts 1978–84; Br Nat Ctee of Int C of C 1979–86, govr Suttons Hosp in Charterhouse 1979–92; Cdr Order of Ouissam Alaouite Morroco 1968, Cdr Order of Leopold II Belgium 1974; FRSA; *Recreations* music; *Clubs* Farmers', Oriental; *Style—* Sir George Burton, CBE, DL; ✉ Aldham Mill, Hadleigh, Suffolk IP7 6LE

BURTON, Gerald; s of Edward Neville Burton (d 1985), of Kelsall, Cheshire, and Mary Elizabeth, *née* Bull (d 1977); *b* 12 August 1938; *Educ* Liverpool Collegiate GS; *m* 1, 1963 (m dis 2000), Gillian Margaret, da of John Dean Wilson (d 1986), of West Kirby, Cheshire; 3 s (John, James, Andrew), 1 da (Deborah); m 2, 2000, Carol Jane, da of Tom Moody (d 2001), of Driffield, E Yorks; *Career* Kidsons Impey (now Baker Tilly) chartered accountants: joined 1961, ptnr 1965, sr ptnr 1989–92; ptnr Cozumel Management Services 1993–2004; chief exec WRVS 1992–2002; dir: Regent House Properties Ltd 1993–, Bellerive Ltd 2007–; non-exec dir: Bradford and Bingley Building Soc London region 1994–97, Bethlem Maudsley NHS Tst 1994–99, Oxfordshire HA 2000–02; Freeman City of London 1980, Hon Asst and Liveryman Worshipful Co of Basketmakers 1982; FCA; *Recreations* golf, music, wine; *Clubs* City Livery; *Style—* Gerald Burton, Esq; ✉ Le Village, Cazaril-Tambourès, 31580, France (tel 00 33 5 62 00 78 48, e-mail gerry.burton1@wanadoo.fr)

BURTON, Sir Graham Stuart; KCMG (1999, CMG 1987); s of Cyril Stanley Richard Burton (d 1982), and Jessie Blythe Burton (d 1992); *b* 8 April 1941; *Educ* Sir William Borlase's Sch Marlow; *m* 30 Jan 1965, Julia Margaret Lappin; 1 da (b 1966), 1 s (b 1967); *Career* HM Dip Serv; FO 1961, Abu Dhabi 1964, ME Centre for Arabic Studies 1967, Kuwait 1969, FCO 1972, Tunis 1975, UK Mission to UN 1978, cnsllr Tripoli 1981, FCO 1984–87, consul-gen San Francisco 1987–90; ambass to: UAE 1990–94, Indonesia 1994–97; high cmmr to Nigeria and non-resident ambass to Benin 1997–2001; dir Magadi Soda Co 2001–, advsr Control Risks Gp 2001–, dir W Africa Business Assoc 2004–; tstee Sightsavers Int 2005–; *Recreations* golf, watching all sports, opera; *Clubs* MCC; *Style—* Sir Graham Burton, KCMG; ✉ e-mail burtongsjm@aol.com

BURTON, Humphrey McGuire; CBE (2000); s of Harry Burton (d 1980), and Kathleen Alice, *née* Henwood (d 1982); *b* 25 March 1931; *Educ* Long Dene Sch Chiddingstone, Judd Sch Tonbridge, Univ of Cambridge (BA); *m* 1, 1957 (m dis), Gretel, *née* Davis; 1 s (Matthew), 1 da (Clare); m 2, 1970, Christina, da of Svante Hellstedt; 1 s (Lukas), 1 da (Helena); *Career* head Music and Arts BBC TV 1965–67 and 1975–81; ed/host Aquarius LWT 1970–75; TV presenter: BBC Young Musician of the Year 1978–92, Cardiff Singer of the World 1991; broadcaster Classic FM's: Life of Leonard Bernstein (17 progs) 1994, Menuhin - Master Musician (20 progs) 1996, William Walton (7 progs) 2002; Artist in Focus BBC Radio 3 1999–2003; compere: Yehudi Menuhin 80th birthday tribute Buckingham Palace 1996, Mstislav Rostropovich 75th birthday tribute Buckingham Palace 2002; TV dir operas and concerts worldwide, artistic advsr Barbican Centre 1988–91, artistic dir The Scandinavian Arts Festival (Barbican Centre) 1992; chm TV Music Working Pty EBU 1976–85; columnist Classic FM magazine 1995–98, BBC Music Magazine 1998–99; lectr and host P&O Cruises Prospect Tours 2001–; conducting debut Verdi's Requiem (Royal Albert Hall) 2001; hon fell: CSD 1991, Fitzwilliam Coll Cambridge 1997; Chevalier de l'Ordre des Arts et des Lettres (France); *Books* Leonard Bernstein (1994), Menuhin (2000), William Walton, The Romantic Loner (2002); *Recreations* music, tennis, travel; *Style—* Humphrey Burton, Esq, CBE; ✉ 13 Linden Road, Aldeburgh, Suffolk IP15 5JQ

BURTON, Ian Richard; s of Jack Burton (d 1971), of Manchester, and Faie Burton (d 2002); *Educ* Whittingeham Coll Brighton; *m* 1973, Sarah Ruth, da of Reginald Ashbrook; 1 da (Lissa Rachel b 1975), 1 s (Jack David b 1978); *Career* admitted slr 1971; ptnr Nigel Copeland Glickman 1971–82, fndr and sr ptnr Burton Copeland Manchester 1982–2001, fndr and sr ptnr BCL Burton Copeland London 1991–; memb: Law Soc 1971, London Criminal Courts Slrs Assoc (LCCSA), Int Bar Assoc; *Recreations* family, opera; *Clubs* RAC, Mark's; *Style—* Ian Burton, Esq; ✉ BCL Burton Copeland, 51 Lincoln's Inn Fields, London WC2A 3LZ (tel 020 7430 2277, fax 020 7430 1101, e-mail ianburton@burtoncopeland.co.uk)

BURTON, (Sara) Jocelyn Margarita Elissa; da of Wing Cdr Roland Louis Ernest Burton, AFC (ret), of Correze, France, and Sian Joan, *née* Gwilliam Evans (d 1980); *b* 10 January 1946; *Educ* St Clare's Sch Devon, Lady Margaret House Cambridge, Sir John Cass Coll Central Sch of Art; *Career* Diamonds Int award 1968, first solo exhibition Archer Gallery Dover St 1971, modern silver collection for Jean Renet Bond St 1970–75; pieces in many public and private collections throughout world; works incl: silver table fountain for Worshipful Co of Fishmongers 1975, Fitzwilliam Cup 1984, centrepiece for Sir Roy Strong V&A; Prince Phillip City and Guilds Gold Medal for Services to Silversmithing 2003; Freeman: City of London 1974, Worshipful Co of Goldsmiths; *Recreations* playing harpsichord, travel, reading; *Clubs* Blacks, Academy; *Style—* Miss Jocelyn Burton; ✉ 50C Red Lion Street, Holborn, London WC1R 4PF (tel 020 7405 3042, fax 020 7831 9324, e-mail jocelynburton@hotmail.com)

BURTON, John Michael; s of Gerald Victor Burton, of Northampton, and Kathleen Blodwyn, *née* Harper; *b* 21 May 1945; *Educ* Oxford Sch of Architecture, DipArch; *m* 11 Sept 1971, Sally, da of Norman Donaby Bason (d 1987), of Northampton; 1 da (Amy Victoria b 17 Jan 1975), 1 s (Thomas Donaby b 19 April 1977); *Career* architect; sr ptnr Purcell Miller Tritton, Architects; conservation of: Wingfield Coll 1972–74, Lavenham Guildhall 1973–94, Holy Trinity Church Long Melford 1974–, Melford Hall 1975–96, Flatford Mill for Nat Tst 1979–85, Colchester Castle 1980–90, Newnham Coll Cambridge 1984–94, St Mary's Thaxted 1988–, Manor House Bury St Edmunds 1990–94, Hunsdon House Herts 1990–96; conservation advsr to the Crown Urban Estate; Surveyor to the Fabric of Canterbury Cathedral 1991–, Surveyor of the Fabric of Westminster Abbey 1999–, cmmr Cathedral Fabric Cmmn for England 1996–2006; pres Cathedral Architects Assoc 1996–99, chm Redundant Churches Uses Ctee Chelmsford; memb Diocesan Advsy Ctee: Chelmsford 1975–, St Edmundsbury & Ipswich 1987–98; govr Kent Inst of Art & Design 1993–2000; memb: Inst of Historic Building Conservation, Church Cmmrs Redundant Churches Ctee, English Heritage Places of Worship Panel, Historic Built Environment Advsy Ctee 1998–2002, Cncl Nat Tst 2007–; chm Colchester Arts Centre 1985–90, dir Mercury Theatre Bd Colchester 1998–2005; Freeman City of London, Liveryman and memb Ct of Assts Worshipful Co of Masons, Liveryman Worshipful Co of Carpenters 2007; memb IHBC, RIBA, AABC; *Recreations* skiing, woodwork, archaeology; *Clubs* Trinity Rotary; *Style—* John M Burton, Esq; ✉ Westminster Abbey, 2B Little Cloister, London SW1P 3PA (tel 020 7654 4807, mobile 07970 097415)

BURTON, 3 Baron (UK 1897); Michael Evan Victor Baillie; s of Brig Hon George Evan Michael Baillie, MC, TD (s of Baroness Burton, to whom Barony passed from 1 Baron by special remainder, and her 1 husband, Col James Baillie, MVO, JP, DL, MP Inverness-shire 1895–1900), by his w, Lady Maud, *née* Cavendish, CBE, JP, widow of Capt Angus Mackintosh, RHG, and da of 9 Duke of Devonshire, KG; suc grandmother 1962; *b* 27 June 1924; *Educ* Eton; *m* 1, 1948 (m dis 1977), (Elizabeth) Ursula (d 1993), da of late Capt Anthony Wise; 2 s, 4 da; m 2, 1978, Coralie, da of late Claude Cliffe; *Heir* s, Hon Evan Baillie; *Career* sat as Cons in House of Lords; formerly Lt Scots Gds and Lovat Scouts; landowner; memb: Inverness CC 1948–75, Inverness DC 1984–92; JP 1961–75, DL 1963–65; Grand Master Mason 1993–99; *Recreations* stalking, shooting, fishing, hunting; *Clubs* Cavalry and Guards', Pratt's, New (Edinburgh); *Style—* The Rt Hon the Lord Burton; ✉ Dochgarroch Lodge, Inverness IV3 8JG (tel 01463 861252, fax 01463 861366, office 01463 861377)

BURTON, Hon Mr Justice; Sir Michael John Burton; kt (1998); s of Henry Burton, QC (d 1952), and Hilda, *née* Shaffer (d 1986); *b* 12 November 1946; *Educ* Eton (King's scholar), Balliol Coll Oxford (MA); *m* 17 Dec 1972, Corinne Ruth (d 1992), da of Dr Jack Cowan (d 1999), MC, of Putney; 4 da (Josephine b 1977, Isabel b 1979, Genevieve b 1982, Henrietta b 1986); *Career* called to the Bar Gray's Inn 1970 (bencher 1993), QC 1984, recorder of the Crown Ct 1989–98, head Littleton Chambers 1991–98, dep judge of the High Ct 1993–98, judge of High Ct of Justice (Queen's Bench Div) 1998–, judge of Employment Appeal Tbnl 2000– (pres 2002–05); chm Central Arbitration Ctee 2000–, pres Interception of Communications Tbnl 2000–01, vice-pres Investigatory Powers Tbnl 2000–, memb Bar Cncl Legal Servs Cmmn 1995; lectr in law Balliol Coll Oxford 1970–73; candidate (Lab) Kensington Cncl 1971, Parly candidate (Lab) Stratford-on-Avon 1974, candidate (Social Democrat) GLC Putney 1981; hon fell Goldsmiths' Coll London 1999–, fell Eton Coll 2004–; *Publications* Civil Appeals (ed, 2002); *Recreations* amateur theatricals, lyric writing, singing, bridge; *Style—* The Hon Mr Justice Burton; ✉ Royal Courts of Justice, Strand, London WC2A 2LL

BURTON, Richard St John Vladimir; CBE (1996); s of Percy Basil Harmsworth Burton, and Vera, *née* Poliakoff; *b* 3 November 1933; *Educ* Bryanston, AA Sch of Architecture (AADipl); *m* 3 April 1956, Mireille, da of Joseph Dernbach-Mayen; 3 s (Mark b 24 April 1957, David b 25 Oct 1958, Jonathan b 2 Jan 1960), 1 da (Catherine b 7 Jan 1962); *Career* ptnr & dir Ahrends Burton & Koralek Architects 1961–2002 (conslt 2002–03, ret 2004); princ works incl: Chichester Theol Coll Gillett House 1965, Trinity Coll Dublin Library 1967, Chalvedon & Northlands Housing Basildon 1968 and 1980, Templeton Coll Oxford 1969–, Nebenzahl House 1972, Burton House 1987, British Embassy Moscow 1988–2000, Hooke Park Coll 1990, St Mary's Isle of Wight 'Low Energy' Hosp 1991; chm: Percent for Art Steering Gp Arts Cncl of GB 1989, RIBA Steering Gp on Educn 1991, Architecture Advsy Panel Arts Cncl of England 1994–98, 20–20 Vision: Future Healthcare Environments 2000–01, design advsr to NHS Estates 2003–06; RIBA 1957, FRSA 1980; *Recreations* painting, writing; *Style—* Richard Burton, Esq, CBE; ✉ 1B Lady Margaret Road, London NW5 4NE (tel and fax 020 7267 1198, mobile 07703 547731, e-mail rsvb@blueyonder.co.uk)

BURTON, Simon; s of Peter Burton, of London, and Sheila, *née* Hardy; *b* 22 June 1964; *Educ* Emanuel Sch London, Merton Coll Oxford; *Partner* Lesley Bainsfair; 2 c (Tom b 10 Dec 2000, Perdita (Purdey) b 3 Jan 2003); *Career* House of Lords: clerk 1988– (successively clerk in the Jl Office, Public Bill Office and Ctee Office), seconded to Cabinet Office as private sec to Chief Whip 1996–99, currently responsible for EU Ctee and e-delivery of servs; *Style—* Simon Burton, Esq; ✉ House of Lords, London SW1A 0PW (tel 020 7219 6083, fax 020 7219 6715)

BURTON-CHADWICK, *see:* Chadwick

BURTON-PAGE, Piers John; s of John Garrard Burton-Page, and Audrey Ruth Burton-Page (d 1989); *b* 25 July 1947; *Educ* Harrow, Wadham Coll Oxford (MA), Univ of Sussex (MA); *m* 1976, Patricia Margaret, da of Howard Cornish, OBE; 2 s (Andrew Patrick Bedeir b 1973 (adopted 1981), Thomas Andrew b 1977); *Career* teacher St John's Sch Northwood 1965–66, pt/t tutor Open Univ 1972–73; BBC: studio mangr 1971–75, newsreader and announcer Radio 4 1975–77, prodr Gramophone Dept Radio 3 1977–82, seconded as sr asst Management Unit BBC Secretariat 1981–82, music organiser BBC External Servs 1982–85, presentation ed Radio 3 1985–90, sr prodr and presenter Radio 3 1990–97, exec prodr Radio Classical Music 1997–2002; freelance writer and broadcaster 2002–; Ohio State Award for The Elements of Music 1986; *Publications* Philharmonic Concerto - The Life and Music of Sir Malcolm Arnold (1994), The Allegri at 50 (2003); *Recreations* theatre, cricket, travel, languages, philosophy, tennis, reading; *Clubs* Bushmen; *Style—* Piers Burton-Page

BURTON-RACE, John William; s of Denys Arthur Race, and Shirley, *née* Manning; *b* 1 May 1957; *Educ* St Mary's Coll Southampton, Highbury Tech Coll (City & Guilds 706/1, 706/2), Portsmouth Poly (HCITB Cert of Apprenticeship), Westminster Coll; *Children* 1 s (Charles Tobias), 1 da (Amelia); *Career* apprentice Wessex Hotel Winchester 1973–75, commis Quaglino's Hotel Meurice London 1975–76, first commis Chewton Glen Hotel 1976–78, chef Olivers Midhurst 1978–79, chef tournant La Sorbonne Oxford 1979–82, private chef MacKenzie-Hill Property Development International 1982–83, sous chef Les Quat'Saisons Oxford 1983–84, head chef and mangr Le Petit Blanc Oxford 1984–86, chef, md and chm L'Ortolan Shinfield 1986–2000, chef John Burton-Race at Landmark Hotel London 2000–02, in France (French Leave) 2002–03, prop The New Angel Dartmouth 2004–; memb: Chambre Syndicate de Haute Cuisine Française, Restaurateurs' Assoc of GB; *Awards* Mumm prizewinner 1987, Acorn Award Caterer and Hotelkeeper Magazine, Best in Britain Award Ackerman Guide, five stars AA, three stars Egon Ronay, Restaurant of the Year Egon Ronay 1991, included in Relais Gourmand, five out of five Good Food Guide 1990–94, four and a half out of five Good Food Guide 1995–97, eighteen out of twenty and three red toques Gault Millau Guide, two Michelin stars 1991–96, 1999 and 2001 (one star 1987–90), Personalité de l'Année Chef Lauréat Paris 1991, one Silver and two Gold medals Madrid Euro Olympics 1992, Grand Prix de l'Art de la Cuisine Int Acad of Gastronomy 1994, Chef of the Year Caterer and Hotelkeeper Magazine 1995, 8 out of 10 Good Food Guide 1999, one Michelin star 2005, AA Restaurant of the Year (England) 2005–06; *Television* series advsr and conslt to Chef (starring Lenny Henry, *qv*, BBC1); contrib: Best Fish, Best Game, Best Chocolate series 1987, Master Chefs of Europe 1988, Great British Chefs 1989, Great European Chefs 1990, French Leave 2003; *Books* Recipes from an English Masterchef (1994), French Leave (2003); *Recreations* Jaguar motor sports, fishing, shooting; *Clubs* 190 Queen's Gate, Acorn; *Style—* John Burton-Race, Esq; ✉ The New Angel, 2 South Embankment, Dartmouth, Devon TQ6 9BH

BURWELL, Prof (Richard) Geoffrey; s of Capt Arthur Reginald Burwell (d 1960), from Leeds, and Mabel Walker, *née* Robinson (d 1988); *b* 1 July 1928; *Educ* Leeds GS, Harrogate GS,

Univ of Leeds (BSc, MB ChB, MD); *m* 19 Jan 1963, Helen Mary, *née* Petty, da of Capt Frank Petty (d 1952); 1 s (Matthew b 30 Dec 1963), 1 da (Jane b 8 Dec 1965); *Career* Capt RAMC jr surgical specialist Gibraltar Hosps 1955–57; orthopaedic registrar Gen Infirmary Leeds 1957–58 (house surgn 1952), lectr in surgery Univ of Leeds 1963–65 (lectr in anatomy 1958–63), sr registrar in traumatic and orthopaedic surgery Robert Jones and Agnes Hunt Orthopaedic Hosp Oswestry 1965–68, prof of orthopaedics Univ of London 1968–72, prof of human morphology and experimental orthopaedics Univ of Nottingham 1974–93 (emeritus prof 1993); former hon conslt in orthopaedics Nottingham HA, hon conslt Centre for Spinal Studies and Surgery Univ Hosp Nottingham 1995–; pt/t med member Appeals Serv (Eastern Region) Lord Chllr's Dept 1985–2003; pres: Br Orthopaedic Res Soc 1982–84, Br Scoliosis Soc 1989–90; FRCS 1955; *Recreations* family, history, travel, archaeology; *Clubs* Old Oswestrians (pres 1990–91); *Style*— Prof Geoffrey Burwell; ✉ 34 Dovedale Road, West Bridgford, Nottingham NG2 6JA (tel 0115 923 2745, fax 0115 923 2272, e-mail burwell@bun.com)

BURY, John Edward; DL (1989); s of Col John Bury, OBE (d 1969), of Berden, Herts, and Ruth Alice, *née* Le Marchant (d 1982), eld da of Brig Gen Sir E T Le Marchant (4 Bt) KCB, CBE, JP, DL; *b* 26 September 1927; *Educ* Prince of Wales Sch Nairobi, Exeter Coll Oxford (MA); *m* 28 June 1961, Diana Mary, eld da of Lt-Col Godfrey Sturdy Incledon-Webber, TD, DL (d 1986), of Braunton, Devon; 1 s (Henry b 5 May 1962), 5 da (Mary Helen (Mrs Cumberlege) b 1964, Anne (Mrs Lucey) b 1965, Eleanor (Mrs MacDonald-Smith) b 1967, Jane b 1971, Clare b 1972); *Career* London Stock Exchange 1952–80, ptnr Pidgeon de Smitt and predecessor firms; chm: Croyde Bay Holidays Ltd 1986–88 (md 1981–86), Incledon Estates Ltd 1988–89, Lobb Fields Ltd 1991–99; NFU: memb Devon Cncl 1983–91, memb Devon Exec Cncl 1992–99, memb SW Regnl Cereals Ctee 1993–97, chm Barnstaple Branch 1995–96 (vice-chm 1993–94); dir Br Holiday and Home Park Association Ltd 1983–89, and 1999–2003; pres: Braunton and Dist Museum 1988–98, Great Torrington Hort Soc 1988–; dep pres Devon Branch BRCS 1985–97 (Badge of Honour 1991), vice-pres Devon Agric Assoc 1984–, life vice-pres North Devon Conservative Assoc 2003 (vice-pres 1999, pres 2000–03); chm N Devon and W Somerset Relief Fund 1990–, vice-chm Grenville Coll Bideford 1995–98 (govr 1989–98); memb: Exec Ctee W Country Tourist Bd 1985–88, TAVRA W Wessex 1986–2000, Agric Land Tbnl SW Area 1987–98, Ctee Devon Branch CLA 1987–96, Ctee N Devon C of C and Indust 1996– (hon memb for life 2004); assoc memb Wessex Reserve Forces and Cadets Assoc 2002– (memb 2000–02); fell Woodard Schs (Western Div) 1991–98; Banksian Bronze Medal RHS 1976; Freeman City of London 1964, Liveryman Worshipful Co of Clothworkers 1966; *Recreations* gardening; *Clubs* Army and Navy; *Style*— John Bury, Esq, DL; ✉ Buckland Manor, Braunton, Devon EX33 1HN (tel 01271 812016)

BURY, Very Rev Nicholas; s of John (Bill) Bury, and Joan, *née* Bacon; *Educ* King's Sch Canterbury, Queens' Coll Cambridge (MA), Cuddesdon Theol Coll (MA); *m* Jennifer, da of Dr John Loudon; 3 c (Barny b 1973, Sam b 1975, Corinne b 1984); *Career* curate Liverpool Parish Church 1968–71, chaplain ChCh Oxford 1971–75, vicar St Mary's Shephall Stevenage 1975–84, vicar St Peter's Broadstairs 1984–97, Dean of Gloucester 1997–; *Recreations* watercolourist, golf; *Style*— The Very Rev the Dean of Gloucester; ✉ The Deanery, Gloucester GL1 2BP (tel 01452 524167 or 01452 508217, e-mail thedean@gloucestercathedral.org.uk)

BURY, Dr Robert Frederick (Bob); s of William George Bury, and Evelyn Winifred, *née* Liggins; *b* 10 August 1948; *Educ* Kettering GS, Univ of London (BSc), Middx Hosp Med Sch (MB BS); *m* 18 Nov 1972, Linda Joyce, da of Samuel Hart; 3 s (Nicholas b 1974, Mathew b 1977, Tom b 1984), 1 da (Kate b 1976); *Career* MO RAF Med Branch 1971–88: med cadetship 1971–73, surgn PMRAF Hosp 1974–79 (55 Field Surgical Team 1976–77), radiologist 1979–88; conslt radiologist nuclear med 1988–, dir of radiology Leeds Teaching Hosps Tst 1996–99; ed: RCR Newsletter 1992–2004, Clinical Radiology 2006– (asst ed 1990–95, dep ed 1995–2006); FRCS 1978, FRCR 1983; *Books* Radiology: A Practical Guide (1988), Imaging Strategy: A guide for clinicians (with Dr Richard Fowler, 1992); *Recreations* hill walking, fishing, writing; *Style*— Dr Bob Bury; ✉ Department of Nuclear Medicine, Leeds General Infirmary, Great George Street, Leeds LS1 3EX (tel 0113 392 6471, fax 0113 392 2598, e-mail bobbury@gmail.com)

BUSBY, Richard Anthony; s of Ronald Arthur Busby (d 1991), of Bromley, Kent, and Sheila Annora, *née* Fitzherbert (d 1998); *b* 4 June 1950; *Educ* St Dunstan's Coll, Univ of Essex (BA); *m* 1, 24 July 1977 (m dis 1983), Karen, da of Ian Barr, of Edinburgh; *m* 2, 5 July 1985 (m dis 2006), Kathleen, da of Daniel Henebury (d 1984); 1 s (Lucas b 2006), 2 step s (Rhys b 1997, Brandon b 1997); *Career* articled clerk Touche Ross 1968–69, asst prodn mangr Hodder & Stoughton 1973–76, mktg mangr Futura Publications 1976–77, md C & C Communications 1977–85, chm and ceo Strategic Sponsorship Ltd 1985–93, ceo BDS Sponsorship Ltd 1993–, dir Andrew Mummery Gall; memb Variety Club of Great Britain; involved with various environmental and charitable orgns; *Publications* Measuring Successful Sponsorship (report); *Recreations* reading, current affairs, art, theatre, opera, sport, jazz and cinema; *Style*— Richard Busby, Esq; ✉ BDS Sponsorship Ltd, 19 Waterside, 44–48 Wharf Road, London N1 7UX (tel 020 7689 3333, fax 020 7689 3344)

BUSCALL, Robert Edmond; JP (Norfolk 1971), DL (Norfolk 1989); o s of Lt-Col Victor Henley Buscall (d 1979), of Carbrooke Hall, Thetford, Norfolk, and Gwendolene Mary Angela, *née* Mahony (d 1991); *b* 2 April 1935; *Educ* Downside, RAC Cirencester (MRAC); *m* 7 Oct 1961, Livia, da of Sir Stephen Lycett Green, 4 Bt, CBE (d 1996), of Snettisham, Norfolk; 2 s (Harry Charles b 1963, Patrick Edward b 1965); *Career* Lt Irish Guards 1953–56; farmer; cncllr Breckland DC 1983–91, gen cmmr of income tax 1983–91; memb: Agric Land Tbnl (E Area) 1983, Bd of Visitors Wayland Prison 1984–87; High Sheriff Norfolk 1993–94; *Recreations* country pursuits, gardening; *Clubs* White's, Allsorts (Norfolk); *Style*— Robert Buscall, Esq, DL; ✉ Carbrooke Hall, Thetford, Norfolk IP25 6TG (tel 01953 881274)

BUSCOMBE, Dr John Richard; s of Richard John Buscombe, MBE, of South Mundham, W Sussex, and Jacqueline Doreen, *née* Beet; *b* 7 December 1959; *Educ* Price's GS Fareham, London Hosp Med Coll (MB BS), UCL (MSc, MD); *m* 25 July 1981, Jacqueline Ann, da of Dr Ronald Phillip Smith; 1 da (Ruth Hazel b 21 Dec 1989), 1 s (Peter Leonard b 18 Oct 1992); *Career* registrar and lectr in nuclear med Middlesex Hosp 1988–92, conslt in nuclear med Royal Free Hosp 1994–; scientific advsr Int Atomic Energy Authy, memb Europa Donna, memb CancerKin, chair of tstees Care for St Anne's; memb Worshipful Co of Parish Clerks; FRCPEd 1998, FRCP 1999; *Recreations* travel, teaching, eating then dieting; *Style*— Dr John Buscombe; ✉ Royal Free Hospital, London NW3 2QG (tel 020 7830 2470, fax 020 7830 2469, e-mail j.buscombe@medsch.ucl.ac.uk)

BUSH, Catherine (Kate); *b* 30 July 1958; *Career* singer and songwriter; debut single Wuthering Heights (1978, UK no 1); albums: The Kick Inside (1978, reached UK no 3), Lionheart (1978, UK no 6), Never For Ever (1980, UK no 1), The Dreaming (1982, UK no 3), Hounds of Love (1985, UK no 1), The Whole Story (compilation, 1986, UK no 1), The Sensual World (1989, UK no 2), This Woman's Work (box set, 1990), The Red Shoes (1993), Hounds of Love (1998), Aerial (2005); Ivor Novello Award 1978–79, Best British Female Artist BRIT Awards 1987; film The Line, The Cross and The Curve (premiered London Film Festival) Nov 1993; *Style*— Miss Kate Bush; ✉ PO Box 120, Welling, Kent DA16 3DA

BUSH, Charles Martin Peter; s of Dr J P Bush (d 1993), and E M Bush, *née* Farnsworth; *b* 28 June 1952; *Educ* Melbourne GS, Univ of Melbourne, Trinity Coll Oxford (MA); *m* April 1977, Mary, *née* Nevin, da of R W Nevin; 3 s (Michael b 1979, Andrew b 1981, Paddy b 1984); *Career* teacher Aylesbury GS 1975–78 (head of pure mathematics

1977–78), head of mathematics Abingdon Sch 1978–82; Marlborough Coll: head of mathematics 1982–89, boarding housemaster 1988–93; headmaster Eastbourne Coll 1993–2005, headmaster Oundle Sch 2005–; memb HMC 1993–; *Publications* co-author SMP Revised Advanced Mathematics (1989–90); *Recreations* cricket, golf, reading, fell-walking; *Clubs* MCC (Marylebone and Melbourne), East India, Lansdowne; *Style*— Charles Bush, Esq; ✉ Oundle School, The Great Hall, Oundle, Peterborough PE8 4EH (tel 01832 277120, e-mail headmaster@oundleschool.org.uk)

BUSH, Janet Elizabeth; da of late Arthur William Henry Bush, and Mary Elizabeth, *née* Mitchell; *Educ* Berkhamsted Sch for Girls, Somerville Coll Oxford (MA), Centre for Journalism Studies Cardiff; *partner* Nick de Cent; 1 da (Eleanor b 28 April 1997); *Career* Reuters (London and Frankfurt) 1982–86; FT: dep econ corr 1986–87, NY corr 1987–90; presenter econ documentaries BBC2 Money Prog 1990–92; The Times: econ corr 1992–97, econ ed 1997–99; dir New Europe 1999–2003, co-dir No Campaign 2000–03, dir Advocacy Int Ltd 2004–, sr ed McKinsey Global Inst 2006–; Harold Wincott Young Fin Journalist of the Year 1987, finalist Br Press Awards Fin Journalist of the Year 1999; *Publications* The Economic Case Against the Euro (ed, 2001), In or Out? The case for and against UK membership of the Euro (with Larry Elliott, 2002), The Real World Economic Outlook (editorial conslt, 2003); various pamphlets for New Europe, Uniformity or Diversity? The Future of European Consumer Policy (2007); *Recreations* politics, family life, finding time to relax; *Style*— Ms Janet Bush; ✉ Blackacre, Colyton, Devon EX24 6SF (tel 01404 871672, fax 01404 871663, e-mail janet@janet-bush.com)

BUSH, Paul Anthony; OBE (2007); s of Anthony Clive Bush (d 1998), and Beatrice Catherine Bush (d 1997); *b* 11 June 1958; *Educ* South Wigston HS, Gateway Boys' Sch Leicester, Borough Road Coll of Physical Educn, Dunfermline Coll of Physical Educn Edinburgh (Dip Sports Coaching); *m* 15 April 1989, Katriona Christine, da of late James Edward Bayley; *Career* accounts clerk Gen Accident Life Assurance Co 1978–79, trainee surveyor Dist Valuer's Office Leicester 1979–81, chief coach Leics Amateur Swimming Assoc 1979–81, swimming devpt offr/chief coach City of Bradford Met Cncl 1982–84, chief coach City of Leicester Swimming Club 1984–87, swimming devpt offr Leeds Leisure Servs 1987–92, gen sec Br Swimming Coaches Assoc 1986–92, chm Br Swimming Grand Prix 1987–88 (sec 1987–90), sr team mangr England Swimming Team 1989–98, gen mangr England Swimming Team Cwlth Games Auckland 1990, GB Swimming Team mangr Olympic Games Barcelona 1992, dir of swimming Amateur Swimming Assoc 1992–96, dir of swimming Cwlth Games Victoria Canada 1994, asst head of development Sports Cncl 1996–97, dir of swimming Olympic Games Atlanta 1996, ptnr Sporting Initiatives 1997–, chief exec Scottish Swimming 1998–2004, gen team mangr Scottish Cwlth Games team 2000–02, chef de mission Scottish Cwlth Games Team 2003–06; GB Swimming Team mangr: European Championships Seville 1997 and World Championships Perth 1998; European Youth Olympics: dep chef de mission BOA Holland 1993, chef de mission BOA Bath 1995; conslt Gezira Sporting Club Egypt 1982 and 1983, tech dir Euro Jr Swimming and Diving Championships 1989 and 1992; dir of aquatics Universiade Sheffield 1991 (rep FISU Tech Ctee 1991); bd dir World Swimming Coaches Assoc 1994–98; memb: Exec Ctee and Swimming Ctee Yorks Amateur Swimming Assoc 1991–92, Swimming Ctee North Eastern Counties Amateur Swimming Assoc 1990–92, Swimming Ctee Amateur Swimming Assoc 1991–96; event dir Leeds Cycling Events (incl World Cyclo Cross Championships 1992) 1991–92, dep chief exec Event Scotland 2005– (int sports event mangr 2004–05), chair E of Scotland Inst of Sport 2006–; govr Gateway Boys' Sch 1996–99; memb: Br Inst of Sports Coaches 1987–, Inst of Swimming Teachers and Coaches 1980–, Br Swimming Coaches Assoc 1981– (hon life fell 1992), Inst of Leisure and Amenity Mgmnt 1992–; fell Br Inst of Sports Administrators; *Books* Take up Swimming (jtly, 1989), author of numerous articles in Swimming Times; *Recreations* most sports (especially golf, swimming, squash and running), travel, theatre, gardening; *Style*— Paul Bush, Esq, OBE; ✉ Ochil Paddocks, Burntfoot, Glendon, Dollar, Perthshire FK14 7JY (tel 0131 472 2308, fax 0131 472 2310, e-mail pbush@bshsport.demon.co.uk)

BUSH, Prof Ronald; s of Raymond Bush (d 1988), and Esther, *née* Schneyer (d 1979); *b* 16 June 1946; *Educ* Univ of Pennsylvania (BA), Univ of Cambridge (BA), Princeton Univ (MA, PhD); *m* 14 Dec 1969, Marilyn; 1 s (Charles b 26 May 1979); *Career* assoc prof of English Harvard Univ 1979–82 (asst prof 1974–79), prof of English Caltech 1985–97 (assoc prof 1982–85), Drue Heinz prof of American literature Univ of Oxford 1997–; NEH fellowship 1977–78 and 1992–93, fell Exeter Coll Oxford 1994–95, fell American Civilization Harvard 2004; *Books* The Genesis of Ezra Pound's Cantos (1976), T S Eliot: A Study in Character and Style (1983), T S Eliot: The Modernist in History (1991), Prehistories of the Future (1995), Claiming the Stones (2002); *Recreations* tennis, travel; *Style*— Prof Ronald Bush; ✉ St John's College, Oxford OX1 3JP (tel 01865 277300, e-mail ron.bush@ell.ox.ac.uk)

BUSH, Prof Stephen Frederick; s of Albert Edward Bush (d 1982), and Winifred May, *née* Maltby (d 1995); *b* 6 May 1939; *Educ* Isleworth GS, Trinity Coll Cambridge (MA, PhD, res scholar), MIT (MSc); *m* 26 Oct 1963, Gillian Mary, da of Reginald Charles Layton (d 2001), of Thorpe Bay, Essex; 1 s (James Henry b 1970), 1 da (Jane Elizabeth b 1972); *Career* gp mangr of chem engrg ICI Corporate Laboratory 1969–72, mangr Systems Technol Dept ICI Europa Ltd 1972–79; UMIST (now Univ of Manchester): prof of polymer engrg 1979–2004, head Polymer Engrg Div 1980–2000, chm Dept of Mech Engrg 1982–83 and 1985–87, dir Centre for Manufacture 2000–, emeritus prof of process manufacture 2006– (prof 2004–2005); md Prosyma Research Ltd 1987–, chm and co-fndr N of England Plastics Processors Consortium 1990–2000, int rep Polymer Processing Soc 1993–2001, memb Editorial Bd Int Industrial and Systems Engrg 2005–; dir SME Process Manufacture Centre 1996–2006; chm Applied Mechanics Ctee SERC 1985–87, vice-chm Campaign for Ind Britain 1991–98, memb Schs Examination and Assessment Ctee for Technol 1992–94; chm NEPPCO Ltd 2000–06 (dir 2006–07), co-fndr and dir Surgiplas Ltd 2001, co-fndr and dir Technomica 2004–; holder of 20 granted patents on polymer composites, chemical processes and healthcare products 1976–; Sir George Nelson Prize 1960, NATO research scholar MIT 1960–61, Moulton Medal 1969, Sir George Beilby Medal and Prize 1979; FIMechE (memb Cncl 1978–81), FIChemE; FPRI (memb Cncl 1985–87), FIMMM, FRSA 1998; *Technical Publications* Prediction of Chemical Oscillations (1969), Determination of Chemical Kinetics Mechanisms (with P Dyer, 1976), Macromolecular Chemistry (contrib, 1980), Polymer Engineering (contrib, 1984), Biological and Synthetic Networks (contrib, 1986), New Processes for Production of Polymer Composites (1990), Systems Concepts and Technological Change (1994), Long Glass Fibre Reinforcement of Thermoplastics (1997), Scale Order and Complexity in Polymer Processing (2000), New Processes for Smart Materials (with D R Blackburn, 2003), Technoeconomic Models for New Products and Processes (2005), and over 180 other scientific pubns and int conference presentations on mathematical modelling, economics of manufacture, and polymer and chemical engrg; *Political Publications* Britain's Future: Independence or Extinction - No Middle Way (1989), Models for 16–19 Education: More Matter less Art (1990),, The Meaning of the Maastricht Treaty (with G M Bush, 1992), Business, Industry and a New Relationship with the European Union (1998), The Importance of Manufacture to the Economy (2000),University Admissions and Fees (2004), and over 80 articles and letters in the nat press on political, industrial and educational matters; *Recreations* mountain walking, British imperial and military history, music, tennis; *Clubs* Manchester Statistical Soc (memb Cncl 2001–07), Royal

Economic Soc; *Style—* Prof Stephen Bush; ✉ Technomica, PO Box 599, Thurston, Bury St Edmunds IP31 3TS (tel 01359 271704, fax 01359 271852)

BUSHELL, Garry Llewellyn; s of George Frederick Henry Bushell, BEM (d 1996), and Evelyn May Mary, *née* Barker (d 1987); *b* 13 May 1955; *Educ* Colfe's GS, NE London Poly (BA), London Coll of Printing (NCTJ); *Children* 2 s (Danny John b 25 Aug 1980, Robert Llewellyn b 1 April 1988), 3 da (Julie Ann b 23 Nov 1978, Jenna Evelyn Vegas b 10 May 1999, Ciara Victoria b 24 Feb 2002); *Career* TV and radio broadcaster; TV critic: The Sun, Daily Star, Sunday People; presenter: The National Alf (Channel 4) 1994, Bushell on the Box (Carlton/Central for ITV) 1996–, Garry Bushell Reveals All (Granada Men and Motors) 2000; resident judge The Big Big Talent Show (LWT for ITV) 1997–, compere The Big Big Variety Show 1998–, resident TV critic The Big Breakfast (Channel 4) 2001–02; md Red Robin Productions 1998–, vice-pres Dave Lee's Happy Holidays Charity 1994–; freelance writer; rock singer The Gonads 1976–, rock writer 1977–86, mangr The Cockney Rejects 1979–80, conceived and organised No 1 single Let it Be (by Ferry Aid) 1986; *Books* Running Free (1985), The Face (2001), The Best of Bushell on the Box (2002), The Punk and Ska Years (2002); *Recreations* curry, Quasar, comedy; *Clubs* Charlton Athletic FC; *Style—* Garry Bushell, Esq; ✉ The Sunday People, 1 Canada Square, London E14 5AP (e-mail garry.bushell@people.co.uk, website www.garry-bushell.co.uk)

BUSHILL-MATTHEWS, Philip; MEP; *b* 1943, Droitwich; *Educ* Malvern Coll, UC Oxford (MA), Harvard Business Sch (Advanced Mgmnt Program); *m* Angela; 3 c; *Career* joined Unilever 1965, seconded to Thomas Lipton Inc USA 1976, nat accounts dir Birds Eye Sales Ltd 1977–80, md Iglo Portugal 1980–81, sales dir Birds Eye Walls Ltd 1981–88, dir Van den Bergh & Jurgens Ltd 1988–91, md Red Mill Snack Foods Ltd Wednesbury and Red Mill Co BV Netherlands 1991–99; MEP (Cons) West Midlands 1999–; FInstD; *Publications* The Gravy Train (2003), Who Rules Britannia? (2005); *Recreations* theatre, reading, enjoying the countryside; *Clubs* Harbury Working Men's; *Style—* Philip Bushill-Matthews, Esq, MEP; ✉ The European Parliament, ASP 14E 217, Rue Wiertz, B-1047 Brussels (tel 00 322 284 5114, fax 00 322 284 9114, e-mail pbushill@europarl.eu.int)

BUSS, Nicola Sian (Nicky); da of Dr David Buss, and Heather, *née* Parr; *b* 14 October 1967; *Educ* Farnborough Hill Convent Coll, Magdalen Coll Oxford (entrance scholar, Demy scholar, MA Philosophy & Psychology, Alec Varley Psychology Prize); *Career* Booz Allen & Hamilton/OC & C Strategy Consulting 1988–90, bd dir Planning Dept Saatchi & Saatchi Advertising 1991–94 (APG Gold Creative Planning Award for British Airways Club World, first prize AMSO Research Effectiveness Award), vice-pres Strategy and Planning MTV Europe 1994–96, exec planning dir and managing ptnr Ammirati Puris Lintas London 1996–99; memb: MRS 1991, Account Planning Gp 1991, Media Research Gp 1995; *Publications* AMSO Research Works (1992), Greener Communications (1993), Creative Planning, Outstanding Advertising (1994); *Recreations* sailing, music, fashion; *Clubs* Harbour; *Style—* Ms Nicky Buss

BUSSELL, Darcey Andrea; CBE (2006, OBE 1995); da of Philip Michael Bussell, and Andrea Pemberton, *née* Williams; *b* 27 April 1969; *Educ* Arts Educnl Sch, Royal Ballet Sch; *m* 1997, Angus Forbes; 2 da (Phoebe Olivia b 2001, Zoe Sophia b 2004); *Career* ballerina; appeared in 1986 and 1987 Royal Ballet Sch performances, joined Sadler's Wells Royal Ballet (now Birmingham Royal Ballet) 1987; Royal Ballet: joined as soloist 1988, first soloist 1989, princ 1989–2006, princ guest artist 2006–07; also international guest performances with various other cos, subject of Omnibus (BBC) 1998; *Performances* first professional leading role Myrthe in Giselle; classical repertory incl: Odette/Odile in Swan Lake, Princess Aurora in The Sleeping Beauty, Sugar Plum Fairy in The Nutcracker, Nikiya and Gamzatti in La Bayadère, title role in Giselle, Raymonda in Raymonda Act III; Sir Kenneth MacMillan ballets: cr role of Princess Rose in The Prince of the Pagodas, cr role of Masha in Winter Dreams 1991 (Farewell pas de deux created in advance for her and Irek Mukhamedov and performed at the HM Queen Elizabeth the Queen Mother's 90th Birthday Tribute and Royal Opera House 1990, also televised), title role in Manon, Juliet in Romeo and Juliet, leading role in Song of the Earth, leading role in Elite Syncopations, Agnus Dei role in Requiem, Mitzi Caspar in Mayerling; Balanchine ballets incl: appeared in Royal Ballet's first performances of Rubies and Stravinsky Violin Concerto, princ roles in Agon, Symphony in C, Tchaikovsky pas de deux, Duo Concertant, Serenade and Ballet Imperial, Terpsichore in Apollo, Siren in Prodigal Son; leading roles in other major ballets incl: Sir Frederick Ashton's Cinderella, Monotones II, Les Illuminations (role of Sacred Love), William Forsythe's In the Middle Somewhat Elevated 1992 and Hermann Schmerman 1993, first Royal Ballet performance of Glen Tetley's La Ronde (role of Prostitute), Dame Ninette de Valois' Checkmate (role of Black Queen), Galanteries, David Bintley's The Spirit of Fugue (cr leading role), Enigma Variations (role of Lady Mary), Ashley Page's Bloodlines (cr leading role), Twyla Tharp's Mr Worldly Wise (cr role of Mistress Truth-on-Toe) 1995, and Push Comes to Shove, Dances with Death (cr role) 1996, ...now languorous, now wild..., Pavane pour une infante défunte (cr role), Amores (cr role), Towards Poetry (cr role), Anastasia (role of Kschessinska) 1996, Push Comes to Shove 1997, La Bayadere (Kirov Ballet and Australian Ballet) 1998, Towards Poetry 1999, Serenade 1999, Lento 1999, Barber Violin Concerto 2000, Les Rendezvous 2000, The Concert 2000, There where she loves 2000, Dance Variations 2000, Lilac Garden (role of Caroline) 2000, Beyond Bach 2002, In the middle, somwhat elevated (role of Sylvie) 2002, Tryst 2002, Gong 2002, Sylvia (title role) 2004, A Month in the Country (role of Natalia Petrovna) 2005, La Fete Étrange (role of Bride) 2005, Tanglewood 2005, Le Jeune Homme et lat Mort 2006, Homage to The Queen (role of Queen of the Air) 2006, The Four Temperaments 2006, DGV 2006, Kiss 2006, Theme and Variations 2007; guest performances with NYC Ballet and Tokyo Ballet; *Awards* Prix de Lausanne 1986, Dancer of the Year Dance and Dancers magazine 1990, Most Promising Artiste of 1990 Variety Club of GB, Evening Standard Award 1991, Olivier Award (for In the Middle Somewhat Elevated) 1992; *Style—* Miss Darcey Bussell, CBE; ✉ The Royal Ballet, Royal Opera House, Covent Garden, London WC2E 9DD (tel 020 7240 1200)

BUSTANI, HE José Mauricio; s of Mauricio José Bustani, and Guajá, *née* de Figueiredo; *b* 5 June 1945, Porto Velho, Brazil; *Educ* Pontifícia Universidade Católica Rio de Janeiro (LLB), Rio Branco Inst Brazilian Dip Acad; *m* 1971, Janine-Monique, *née* Lázaro; 2 s, 1 da; *Career* Brazilian diplomat; Moscow 1970–73, Vienna 1973–77, UN NY 1977–84, Montevideo 1984–87, Montreal 1987–92, DG Dept for Int Orgns 1993–97, ambass 1995–, DG Orgn for Prohibition of Chemical Weapons 1997–2002, ambass to Ct of St James's 2003–; delg to int negotiations incl: 3rd UN Conf on Law of the Sea 1974–82, UN Gen Assembly 1977–83 and 1993–96, 1st and 2nd Special Sessions of UN Gen Assembly (Disarmament Affrs) 1978 and 1982, Montreal Protocol on Substances that Deplete the Ozone Layer 1989–92 (ldr), Multilateral Fund for Implementation of Montreal Protocol 1990–91, 13th and 15th Sessions of Prep Cmmn for Orgn for Prohibition of Chemical Weapons 1996–97 (ldr); *Recreations* classical music; *Style—* HE Mr José Mauricio Bustani; ✉ Embassy of Brazil, 32 Green Street, Mayfair, London W1K 7AT (tel 020 7399 9007, fax 020 7399 9101, e-mail bustani@brazil.org.uk)

BUSUTTIL, Prof Anthony; OBE; s of Anthony Busuttil (d 1973), of Malta, and Maria, *née* Vassallo (d 1978); *b* 30 December 1945; *Educ* St Aloysius' Coll Malta; *m* 31 Aug 1969, Angela, da of Angelo Bonello (d 1979), of Gozo; 3 s (Godwin b 1970, Christopher b 1973, Joseph b 1978); *Career* lectr in pathology Univ of Glasgow 1971–76, conslt pathologist Lothian Health Bd 1976–87, currently emeritus regius prof of forensic med Univ of Edinburgh (sr lectr in pathology 1976–87), contrib to several chapters on gastroenterology, genitourinary and forensic pathology; Euro Cncl for Legal Med; memb: BMA, Assoc of Clinical Pathology; DMJ(Path); fell Br Assoc of Forensic Med, FRCPath, FRCPE, FRCPGlas, FRSSA, FRCSEd, FFFLM; memb Order of Merit (Malta) 1998; *Recreations* classical music, reading; *Clubs* RSM; *Style—* Prof Anthony Busuttil, OBE; ✉ 78 Hillpark Avenue, Edinburgh EH4 7AL (tel 0131 336 3241); Forensic Medicine Section, Medical School, University of Edinburgh, Teviot Place, Edinburgh EH8 9AG (tel 0131 650 3281, fax 0131 651 1345, e-mail professor.busuttil@ed.ac.uk)

BUTCHARD, Timothy Robin (Tim); s of Capt John Bryan Butchard, RN (ret), of Wylye, Wilts, and Patricia Deidre Broke, *née* Tonks (niece of painter and Slade prof Henry Tonks); *b* 24 December 1944; *Educ* Shrewsbury, CCC Cambridge (MA), Univ of Exeter (PGCE); *Career* VSO India 1968–69, asst master Fettes Coll Edinburgh 1969–71; Br Cncl: VSO field offr Kenya 1971–75, dir Documentary Exhbns London 1975–79, dep dir Thailand 1979–83, first sec (cultural) Br Embassy Beijing and Shanghai 1984–87, dir Courses Dept London 1988–92, dir Drama and Dance Dept London 1992–96, dir Netherlands 1996–2000, dir São Paulo Brazil 2000–04; *Recreations* tennis, travel, the arts, the Orient; *Clubs* Travellers; *Style—* Tim Butchard; ✉ 4 Dorville Crescent, London W6 0HJ (tel 020 8741 0836, e-mail timbutchard@yahoo.co.uk)

BUTCHER, Ian George; s of George Wilfred Robert Butcher, of Winchmore Hill, London, and Joyce Patricia, *née* Payne; *b* 13 April 1950; *Educ* Winchmore Sch, City of London Coll; *m* 1, 15 Sept 1978 (m dis 2001), Sarah Jane, da of Donald Percy Jeffery, of Halton, Bucks; 2 da (Emma b 1981, Kellie b 1984), 1 s (Harry b 1987); m 2, 7 April 2001, Elizabeth Dundee Jones, *née* Davis; *Career* Touche Ross & Co (chartered accountants) 1969–74, exec dir County Bank Ltd 1974–84, fin dir Addison Page plc 1984–86, corp devpt dir Addison Conslt Group plc 1986–87, gp fin dir Charles Barker plc 1987–89, chm Lefax Publishing Ltd 1984–88, dir Whitehead Mann Group plc 1989–2002, chief fin offr Cambridge Disply Technol Ltd 2002–04, ptnr MWM Consulting Ltd 2004–; FCA; *Recreations* cricket, tennis, music, reading; *Clubs* MCC, RAC; *Style—* Ian G Butcher, Esq; ✉ 2502 El Greco Cove, Austin, Texas 78703, USA

BUTCHER, Mark Alan; s of Alan Raymond Butcher, the Surrey and England cricketer; *b* 15 August 1972, Croydon, Surrey; *Educ* Trinity Sch Croydon; *m* 1996 (m dis 2000), Judy, da of Micky Stewart, the former England cricketer and coach, and sis of Alec Stewart, the England cricketer; *Career* cricketer (batsman); Surrey CCC: joined 1989, first class debut 1992, capt 2005–, more than 200 first class appearances, winners Benson and Hedges Cup (one day) 1997 and 2001, County Championship 1999, 2000 and 2002, Sunday League (one day) 2000 (Div 2) and 2003, Twenty20 Cup (one day) 2003; England: 71 test caps (1 as capt), debut v Aust Edgbaston 1997, scored over 4000 runs (highest score 173 not out v Aust Headingley 2001); *Recreations* music, playing guitar; *Style—* Mr Mark Butcher; ✉ Surrey County Cricket Club, The Oval, Kennington SE11 5SS

BUTCHER, Stephen James; s of Geoffrey Cecil Butcher (d 2006), and Audrey Ray, *née* Vince (d 1985); *b* 25 February 1952; *Educ* Stonyhurst, St John's Coll Oxford (BA); *m* 11 Nov 1989, Jane Mary, da of Dr Toby Thorne; 2 da (Catherine Mary b 18 April 1992, Eleanor Margaret b 16 Dec 1995), 1 s (John Geoffrey b 1 April 1998); *Career* md Academic Div Cassell 1995–98, gen mangr Unitary Business Edexcel 1998–2002, chief exec Eduserv 2002–; *Style—* Stephen Butcher, Esq; ✉ Eduserv, Queen Anne House, 11 Charlotte Street, Bath BA1 2NE (tel 01225 474348, e-mail stephen.butcher@eduserv.org.uk)

BUTE, 7 Marquess of (GB 1796); Sir John Colum Crichton-Stuart; 12 Bt (S 1627); also Lord Crichton (S 1488), Earl of Dumfries, Viscount of Air, Lord Crichton of Sanquhar and Cumnock (S 1633), Earl of Bute, Viscount Kingarth, Lord Mountstuart, Cumra(e) and Inchmarnock (S 1703), Baron Mountstuart of Wortley (GB 1761), Baron Cardiff of Cardiff Castle (GB 1776), Earl of Windsor and Viscount Mountjoy (GB 1796); Hereditary Sheriff and Coroner of Co Bute, Hereditary Keeper of Rothesay Castle; patron of 9 livings; s of 6 Marquess of Bute, KBE (d 1993), and his 1 w, (Beatrice) Nicola Grace, *née* Weld-Forester; *b* 26 April 1958; *m* 1 (m dis 1993), Carolyn, da of Bryson Waddell (d 1975); 2 da (Lady Caroline b 1984, Lady Cathleen b 1986), 1 s (John Bryson, Earl of Dumfries b 21 Dec 1989); m 2, Serena Solitaire Wendell, da of Jac Wendell Maxwell-Hyslop; 1 da (Lady Lola Affrica b 23 June 1999); *Heir* s, Earl of Dumfries; *Career* motor racing driver (as Johnny Dumfries) 1980–91; British Formula Three champion 1984, runner-up FIA European Formula Three Championship 1984, contracted to Ferrari Formula One team as test driver 1985, number two driver for John Player Special Team Lotus 1986, works driver for World Champion Sports Prototype Team Silk Cut Jaguar 1988 (jt winner Le Mans 1988), lead driver for Toyota GB World Sports Prototype Championship 1989 and 1990; *Style—* Johnny C Bute; ✉ Mount Stuart, Rothesay, Isle of Bute PA20 9LR (tel 01700 503877)

BUTLER, Alan Edward; s of Albert Frederick Butler (d 1978), of Clacton on Sea, Essex, and Lillian Elizabeth, *née* Carlson (d 1969); *b* 6 December 1940; *Educ* Raine's Fndn GS, UCL (BSc); *m* 27 Nov 1981, Gail Katharine; 2 s (Richard b 1984, James b 1990); *Career* md: Carl Byoir and Associates Ltd 1975–85 (dir 1970), Communications Strategy Ltd 1985–86, Countrywide Communications Ltd 1987–93; managing ptnr Kudos Communications 1993–, conslt Kudos Consulting Dubai 1994–2000, dir YTJ Pacific Singapore 1994–; chm Wentworth Gate Management Co Ltd 1999–; former chm: Strangers Gallery NW Surrey House of Commons Dining Club, PRCA; Freeman City of London, Liveryman Worshipful Co of Marketors 1988–; memb Mktg Soc; MBCS, MIPRA, FIPR, FInstD; *Recreations* most sports; *Clubs* Wig & Pen; *Style—* Alan Butler, Esq

BUTLER, Dr Anthony David (Tony); s of Bernard Reuben Butler (d 1975), and Ethel Elizabeth, *née* Butter; *b* 7 April 1945; *Educ* Soham GS, Univ of Leicester (BSc), UC Wales Aberystwyth (MSc), Univ of Kent (PhD); *m* 14 April 1971, Rosemary Jane, da of Samuel Leight Medlar; *Career* workforce planner Civil Service Dept 1969–75, OECD conslt Athens 1971–72, statistician Dept of Environment 1975–82, head of Traffic Census Unit Dept of Transport 1982–88; Dept of Environment: project mangr for water privatisation 1988–90, head of business devpt and procurement 1990–93; dir of corp affrs HM Inspectorate of Pollution 1993–96, head of mgmnt services CPS 1996–98, dep DG Advertising Standards Authority and sec Ctee of Advertising Practice 1998–2001; chm Advtg Bodies Tstees Ltd 2001–, memb Mktg Codes Interpretation Panel Int C of C 2001–03, non-exec memb Bd Nat Patient Safety Agency 2001–07; lay memb: HM Inspectorate of Probation 2001–02, Preliminary Investigation Ctee RCVS 2001–; life memb: RSPB, British Museum, National Trust, WWF, Greenwich Soc; CStat RSS; *Recreations* swimming, choral singing, theatre, foreign travel, bird watching, gardening; *Style—* Dr Tony Butler; ✉ 19 Maidenstone Hill, Greenwich, London SE10 8SY (tel 020 8692 7845, e-mail anthony.butler1@virgin.net)

BUTLER, Anthony John (Tony); s of late Martin Edward Butler, of Folkestone, Kent, and Freda Alice, *née* Matson; *b* 30 January 1945; *Educ* Maidstone GS, UC Oxford (exhibitioner, MA), Trinity Hall Cambridge and Inst of Criminology Cambridge (Dip Criminology), Columbia Univ Law Sch; *m* Margaret Ann, da of George Randon; 1 da (Catherine b 19 July 1968), 1 s (James b 21 July 1971); *Career* Home Office 1969–96: successively asst princ Police and Criminal Depts, private sec to Min of State, princ Gen Dept, Sex Discrimination Legislation Unit, Race Relations Legislation Unit and Broadcasting Dept, private sec to Home Sec, asst sec Broadcasting Dept, Fin Dept and Prison Dept, asst under sec of state, seconded as dir Inner Cities DOE, princ fin offr, dir Personnel, Fin and Servs HM Prison Serv until 1996; fell New Coll Oxford 1996–2006 (emeritus fell 2006–); dir Oxford Univ Careers Serv 1996–2006; pres Assoc of Grad Careers Advsy

Servs 2004–06; FCIPD; *Recreations* music, gardening; *Style—* Tony Butler; ✉ e-mail tbutler@13rich.freeserve.co.uk

BUTLER, Prof (Ian) Christopher; s of Edward Martin Butler (d 1976), and Gladys Ruth, *née* Tilley; *b* 4 December 1940; *Educ* Brentwood Sch Essex, BNC Oxford (MA); *m* 1966, Gillian, da of Col C P Dawnay (d 1989); 2 da (Sophie b 1968, Josephine b 1970); *Career* Univ of Oxford: sr Hulme research scholar BNC 1962–64, jr research fell and teaching lectr ChCh 1964–70, fell (official student) and tutor in Eng lit ChCh 1970– (jr then sr censor 1972–77, curator of pictures 1988–95), sr proctor 1982–83, currently prof of Eng language and lit; Brown visiting fell Univ of the South Sewanee 1979, Hearst visiting scholar Univ of Baltimore 1995, int Vilas fell Center for Twentieth Century Studies Univ of Wisconsin Milwaukee 1987; memb Cncl of Mgmnt MOMA Oxford 1972–88 (memb Exec Ctee 1976–86), visitor Ashmolean Museum 1985–2002; OUP: delg 1987–2002, memb Fin Ctee 1988–2002; sometime external examiner: Univ of Southampton, Hatfield Poly, Univ of Warwick, Open Univ, Univ of Reading, UCL, KCL, Birkbeck Coll London, Sorbonne; chm: Ctee of Inquiry into the Future of the University Theatre 1984–85, Univ of Oxford Ctee on the Relationship of the Univ with Schs 1984–91; CNAA: memb Eng Subject Ctee 1974–86, memb Ctee for the Arts and Humanities 1986–88; govr Brentwood Sch 1980–2000, chm Ruskin Sch Ctee 1995–2005; *Books* Number Symbolism (1970), Topics in Criticism: an Ordered Set of Positions in Literary Theory (jtly, 1971), After the Wake: an Essay on the Contemporary Avant Garde (1980), Interpretation, Deconstruction and Ideology (1984), Early Modernism: Literature, Music and Painting in Europe 1900–1916 (1994), Postmodernism: A Very Short Introduction (2002), Pleasure and the Arts (2004); author of numerous articles and contribs to books; *Recreations* music, pictures, wine, photography, reading, walking, talking; *Style—* Prof Christopher Butler; ✉ Christ Church, Oxford OX1 1DP (tel 01865 276189, e-mail chris.butler@chch.ox.ac.uk)

BUTLER, Christopher John; s of late Dr John Lynn Butler, of Cardiff, and late Eileen Patricia Butler; *b* 12 August 1950; *Educ* Cardiff HS, Emmanuel Coll Cambridge (MA); *m* 25 March 1989, Jacqueline Clair, *née* Harper; 1 s (David John Robert b 29 Jan 1994); *Career* market res conslt 1972–77, Cons Res Dept 1977–80, Political Office 10 Downing St 1980–83, special advsr to Sec of State for Wales 1983–85, market res conslt 1985–86, special advsr to Min for Arts 1986–87, MP (Cons) Warrington S 1987–92, political conslt 1992–, dir Butler Kelly Ltd 1998–; fell Industry and Parly Tst; *Publications* Cardiff Mysteries; *Recreations* writing, tennis, collecting books, deltiology; *Style—* Christopher J Butler, Esq; ✉ e-mail chrisb@butlerkellyltd.co.uk

BUTLER, Dr David Edgeworth; CBE (1991); s of Prof Harold Edgeworth Butler (d 1951), and Margaret Lucy, *née* Pollard (d 1982); *b* 17 October 1924; *Educ* St Paul's, New Coll Oxford, Princeton Univ, Nuffield Coll Oxford (BA, MA, DPhil); *m* 1962, Dr Marilyn Speers Butler, FRSL, *qv*, da of Sir Trevor Evans (d 1981); 3 s (Daniel b 1963, Gareth b 1965, Edmund b 1967); *Career* Lt Staffs Yeo 1943–45; fell Nuffield Coll Oxford 1951–, PA to HM Ambass Washington 1955–56; Hon DUniv: Paris 1978, Essex 1993; Hon DSSc Univ of Belfast 1985; FBA 1994; *Books* British General Election Studies (1951–2005), Political Change in Britain (1974), British Political Facts 1900–2005 (2005); *Style—* Dr David Butler, CBE, FBA; ✉ 151 Woodstock Road, Oxford OX2 7NA (tel 01865 558323)

BUTLER, David John; s of John Carrol Butler (d 1979), of Sunderland, and Doris, *née* Stockdale; *b* 28 September 1952; *Educ* Bede Sch Sunderland, Sunderland Coll of Art; *Career* painter, printmaker, publisher and art conslt 1985; ed: Making Ways 1985, 1987 and 1992, Artists Newsletter 1985–95; devpt dir AN Publications 1995–99; freelance writer and ed 1985–; dir 'Round Midnight - an Inquiry into the State of the Visual Arts in the UK 1996, co-dir Interrupt Symposia: the role of artists in socially engaged art symposia 2003; coordinator Life Work Art Univ of Newcastle Sch of Art and Culture 2003; *Books* Live Art (jt ed, 1991), Across Europe (1992), Art of Negotiation (jt ed, 2007); *Style—* David Butler; ✉ Fine Art Department, School of Arts and Cultures, University of Newcastle upon Tyne, The Quadrangle, Newcastle upon Tyne NE2 1HQ (tel 0191 222 6052, e-mail david.butler@ncl.ac.uk)

BUTLER, Dawn; MP; *b* 1969, Forest Gate, London; *Educ* Waltham Forest Coll of FE (Dip); *Career* early career as systems analyst Johnson Matthey, exec Employment Serv and recruitment offr Public Service Union, nat race and equality min GMB 1995–2005; MP (Lab) Brent South 2005–, PPS to Jane Kennedy MP (as Min for Health) 2005–, memb Ctee for Modernisation of the House of Commons, chair All Pty Parly Gp on Youth Affrs; hon pres Br Youth Cncl; *Recreations* salsa dancing, spending time with family; *Style—* Ms Dawn Butler, MP; ✉ House of Commons, London SW1A 0AA

BUTLER, Dr Eamonn Francis; s of Richard Henry Bland Butler (d 1977), of Shrewsbury, and Janet Provan, *née* MacDonald (d 2001); *b* 3 January 1952; *Educ* Univ of Aberdeen, Univ of St Andrews (MA, MA Hons, PhD); *m* 1986, Christine Anna, da of Giuseppe Pieroni; 2 s (Richard Cosmo b 1988, Joseph Felix b 1990); *Career* economist; res assoc US House of Representatives 1976–77; dir Adam Smith Inst 1978–; asst prof of philosophy Hillsdale Coll Michigan 1977–78; ed The Broker 1979–87; memb Mont Pelerin Soc 1984–, govr Netherhall Sch Cambridge 2001–06; *Publications* Forty Centuries of Wage and Price Controls (jtly, 1979), Hayek: His Contribution to the Social and Economic Thought of Our Time (1983), Milton Friedman: A Guide to His Economic Thought (1985), Ludwig von Mises: Fountainhead of the Modern Microeconomics Revolution (1989), Adam Smith: A Primer (2007); with Madsen Pirie: Test Your IQ (1983), Boost Your IQ (1990), The Sherlock Holmes IQ Book (1995), IQ Puzzlers (1995); articles published in various newspapers and jls; *Recreations* archaeology, antiquarian books and prints; *Style—* Dr Eamonn Butler; ✉ The Adam Smith Institute, 23 Great Smith Street, London SW1P 3BL (e-mail info@adamsmith.org.uk)

BUTLER, Georgina Susan; da of late Alfred Norman Butler (d 1979), of Torquay, Devon, and Joan Mary, *née* Harrington; *b* 30 November 1945; *Educ* Torquay GS for Girls, UCL (LLB); *m* 1, 1970 (m dis 2000), Stephen John Leadbetter Wright, s of late John Harry Wright; 1 da (Charlotte Louisa b 27 June 1977), 1 s (James Nicholas b 31 Jan 1979); m 2, 2003, Robert Kelly, s of late Cecil Duncan Kelly; *Career* entered Dip Serv 1968, third sec Br Embassy Paris 1969–70, second then first sec Southern Euro Dept FCO 1971–75, UN Secretariat NY 1975–77, Directorate Gen for Devpt Euro Cmmn Brussels 1982–84, dep head Info Dept FCO 1985–87, conf organiser Forum Europe 1993–96, info corr Euro Cmmn London 1996–97, dep head Latin America and Caribbean Dept FCO 1999–2001, ambass to Costa Rica and Nicaragua 2002–06; fell UCL 2003; *Recreations* travel, riding, watersports, bird watching; *Clubs* Lansdowne, Bentham, UCL Dining; *Style—* Ms Georgina Butler; ✉ c/o FCO Association, Old Admiralty Building, London SW1A 2PA

BUTLER, Gwendoline; *Educ* Haberdashers' Aske's, Lady Margaret Hall Oxford (BA); *m* Dr Lionel Butler (decd), historian and author; 1 da (Lucilla b 1955); *Career* crime writer and novelist, lectr and broadcaster; author of over 70 books, series characters detectives Sir John Coffin, Charmian Daniels, Maj Mearns and Sgt Denny, also writes under pseudonym Jennie Melville; historical crime reviewer Crime Time magazine 1999–2002; memb Ctee and chm of judges of Gold Dagger Awards Crime Writers' Assoc, judge Ellis Peters Historical Crime Competition 2000; Silver Dagger Award Crime Writers' Assoc (for Coffin for Pandora) 1974, Romantic Novelists' Award (for The Red Staircase) 1981, Ellery Queen Short Story Award; sec Detection Club 1992–95; *Style—* Mrs Gwendoline Butler

BUTLER, Ian John; s of Donald Butler, and Eileen, *née* Green; *b* 26 February 1954; *Educ* Mexborough GS, Central Sch of Art & Design (BA Sculpture), Univ of Liverpool (BA Architecture), Poly of Central London (DipArch); *m* 1980, Theresa Mary, da of Patrick Tomlins; 3 s (David George b 1989, Peter John b 1991, George Patrick b 1997); *Career* architect; Powell Moya & Partners 1980, Llewelyn-Davies Weeks 1982–84, RMJM London Ltd 1985–91, RMJM Hong Kong Ltd 1991–2005 (latterly md), managing ptnr Northern Office Sheppard Robson 2005–; project architect several large complex building projects in Kong Kong and London; RIBA 1984; memb: ARBUK 1983, Hong Kong Inst of Architects 1993, Hong Kong Architects Registration Bd 1993; *Recreations* photography, golf; *Style—* Ian Butler, Esq

BUTLER, Sir (Percy) James; kt (2001), CBE (1981), DL (1995); s of Percy Ernest Butler (d 1942), of The Hill, Batheaston, Bath, and Phyllis Mary Butler (d 1950); *b* 15 March 1929; *Educ* Marlborough, Clare Coll Cambridge (MA); *m* 26 June 1954, Margaret Prudence, da of Percy Copland (d 1968); 2 da (Elizabeth Anne b 1957, Susan Margaret b 1958), 1 s (David James b 1961); *Career* Nat Serv 1947–49, 2 Lt RA; KPMG Peat Marwick: joined 1952, ptnr 1967, managing ptnr 1980–85, dep sr ptnr 1985, sr ptnr 1986–93, memb Exec Ctee and Cncl KPMG 1987–93, memb Euro Bd KPMG 1989–93, chm KPMG Int 1991–93; dir: Camelot plc 1994–2002 (dep chm 1995–2002), Royal Opera House 1994–97, Tomkins plc 1994, Wadworth & Co Ltd 1994–, Nicholson Graham & Jones Solicitors (non-exec) 1994–2004; pt/t memb BR Bd 1994–96, dir Eurostar (UK) Ltd 1994–99 (chm 1994–96), chm Union Railways 1995–96; tstee Winchester Cathedral Tst 1991–; chm: Cncl Marlborough Coll 1992–2001, Winchester Cathedral Appeal 1991–95, Brendoncare Fndn Appeal 1998–2004, Winchester Festival of Music 1999–2007; memb Indust & Commerce Gp and Cncl Save the Children Fund 1990–2000, dep chm The Royal Opera House Tst 1996–99 (chm 1992–96); dep chm Mersey Docks & Harbour Co (and govt dir) 1972–90, memb Govt Ctee on British Rail Fin, memb Financial Aspects of Corporate Governance Ctee, memb Prince of Wales Tst Advsy Gp; Master Worshipful Co of Cutlers 1995–96 (also memb Ct of Assts 1985–), memb Worshipful Co of Chartered Accountants; FCA (ACA 1955); *Recreations* farming, bridge, opera, ballet, shooting; *Clubs* Boodle's; *Style—* Sir James Butler, CBE, DL; ✉ Littleton House, Crawley, Winchester, Hampshire SO21 2QF (tel 01962 880206, fax 01962 886177)

BUTLER, James Walter; s of Walter Arthur Butler (d 1942), and Rosina Harriet, *née* Kingman (d 1967); *b* 25 July 1931; *Educ* Maidstone GS, Maidstone Sch of Art, St Martin's Sch of Art; *m* 1 (m dis); 1 da (Kate b 12 Dec 1966); m 2, 1975, Angela Elizabeth, da of Col Roger Berry; 4 da (Rosie b 23 Aug 1975, Saskia b 12 April 1977, Candida b 24 April 1979, Aurelia b 11 Aug 1983); *Career* sculptor; tutor of sculpture and drawing City and Guilds London Art Sch 1960–75; works in public places: portrait statue Pres Kenyatta Nairobi 1973, Monument to Freedom Fighters of Zambia Lusaka 1975, sculpture of Burton Cooper Staffs 1977, Meml to King Richard III Leicester 1980, portrait statue Field Marshal Earl Alexander of Tunis Wellington Barracks London 1985, bronze sculpture Skipping Girl Harrow 1985, Dolphin Fountain Dolphin Sq London 1987, portrait statue Sir John Moore and Figures of Rifleman and Bugler Sir John Moore Barracks Winchester 1986, portrait statue John Wilkes New Fetter Lane London, Wilkes Univ Pennsylvania 1988, bronze sculpture The Leicester Seamstress Leicester 1990, portrait head Sir Hugh Wontner Savoy Hotel London 1990, War Memorial to Royal Electrical and Mechanical Engineers Arborfield 1992, portrait statue Thomas Cook Leicester 1994, bronze sculpture The Stratford Jester Stratford-upon-Avon 1994, portrait statue James Henry Greathead Cornhill London 1994, meml statue Reg Harris (sprint cycling champion) 1995, portrait statue Billy Wright, CBE Molineux Wolverhampton 1996, D Day Memorial to Green Howard Regt Crepon Normandy 1996, portrait bust of Sir Nicholas Bacon St Albans Sch 1996, portrait statue of James Brindley canal engineer Coventry Canal Basin 1998, Fountain, Child and Whale KK Women's and Children's Hosp Singapore, portrait statue of Duncan Edwards Dudley, portrait bust of Robert Beldam, CBE CCC Cambridge 2000, Fleet Air Arm Memorial Victoria Embankment Gardens London 2000, portrait bust of R J Mitchell RAF Club London, portrait bust of Roy Chadwick RAF Club London, portrait statue of Jack Walker Blackburn Rovers FC, portrait statue of Stan Cullis Wolverhampton Wanderers FC, Great Seal of the Realm 2001; RA 1972 (ARA 1964), RWA, FRBS; *Recreations* golf, astronomy; *Clubs* The Arts; *Style—* James Butler, Esq, RA; ✉ Valley Farm, Radway, Warwickshire CV35 0UJ (tel 01926 641938, fax 01926 640624)

BUTLER, Prof Marilyn Speers; da of Sir Trevor Maldwyn Evans, CBE (d 1981), of Kingston upon Thames, Surrey, and Margaret Speers, *née* Gribbin; *b* 11 February 1937; *Educ* Wimbledon HS, St Hilda's Coll Oxford (MA, DPhil); *m* 3 March 1962, Dr David Edgeworth Butler, CBE, FBA, *qv*, s of Harold Edgeworth Butler (d 1951); 3 s (Daniel b 1963, Gareth b 1965, Edmund b 1967); *Career* trainee and talks producer BBC 1960–62; Univ of Oxford: research and teaching 1962–70, jr research fell St Hilda's Coll 1970–73, fell and tutor St Hugh's Coll 1973–86; King Edward VII prof of English literature Univ of Cambridge 1986–93; fell King's Coll Cambridge 1988–93; rector Exeter Coll Oxford 1994–2004; FRSL, FRSA, FBA 2002; *Books* Maria Edgeworth, a Literary Biography (1972), Jane Austen and the War of Ideas (1975), Peacock Displayed (1979), Romantics Rebels and Reactionaries (1981, 1985), Burke Paine Godwin and the Revolution Controversy (1984), The Works of Mary Wollstonecraft (ed, 1989), Maria Edgeworth - Castle Rackrent and Ennui (ed, 1992), Mary Shelley - Frankenstein (ed, 1993), Jane Austen - Northanger Abbey (ed, 1995), The Works of Maria Edgeworth (ed, 1999); *Style—* Prof Marilyn Butler; ✉ 151 Woodstock Road, Oxford OX2 7NA (tel 01865 558323)

BUTLER, (Kathleen) Mary; da of late Robert McPhail, and Kathleen, *née* Hartop; *b* 14 October 1943, Hitchin, Herts; *Educ* Queen Anne's Sch Caversham (scholar), St Hugh's Coll Oxford (BA); *m* 1969, David Dalrymple Butler (d 2006); 2 da (Alexandra Katrina b 26 Jan 1975, Miranda Henrietta b 31 May 1977); *Career* prodr's asst BBC Overseas Regnl Serv 1966–67, Euroscan Film Productions 1967, rights asst Secker & Warburg Publishers 1968–69, int rights dir Paul Elek Publishers 1969–80, md Trade Div Unwin Hyman (formerly Bell & Hyman Publishers) 1980–91, publishing dir (Tolkien) Harper Collins 1991–94, head of pubns V&A Pubns 1995–; memb: Nat Tst, Woodland Tst; friend: Almeida Theatre, RSC, Tate; FRSA 1995; *Recreations* theatre, film, horticulture; *Clubs* Highgate Soc, Highgate Scientific & Literary Inst; *Style—* Mrs Mary Butler; ✉ V&A Publications, V&A Museum, Cromwell Road, London SW7 2RL (tel 020 7942 2964, e-mail m.butler@vam.ac.uk)

BUTLER, Sir Michael Dacres; GCMG (1984, KCMG 1979, CMG 1975); s of T D Butler, of Almer, Dorset, and Beryl May, *née* Lambert; *b* 27 February 1927; *Educ* Winchester, Trinity Coll Oxford; *m* 1951, (Margaret) Ann, da of Rt Hon Lord Clyde (d 1975, MP (Cons) N Edinburgh 1950–54, Lord Justice Gen of Scotland 1954–72); 2 s, 2 da; *Career* HM Dip Serv: entered 1950, under sec in charge of EEC affairs FCO 1974–76, dep under sec of state FCO 1976–79, UK perm rep to EC Brussels 1979–85, ret; chm City of London Euro Ctee 1988–93, Lab Pty's special envoy on Euro enlargement 1996–97, advsr to Rt Hon Robin Cook, MP, as Foreign Sec 1997–98; chm Sr Experts Gp Br in Europe 2000–; dir: Hambros Bank 1986–97, Wellcome Fndn 1986–94; chm: European Strategy Bd ICL 1988–2001, European Unification Bd Hercules Europe 1989–94, Oriental Art Magazine 1988–94, Business Link Dorset 1994–2000, ICL Pathway Ltd 1995–2000, Guidephone Ltd 1998–2002, Homeport 2000–06; dep chm Bd of Tstees V&A 1985–97, pro-provost and chm Cncl RCA 1991–96; *Books* Europe More Than a Continent (1986), Seventeenth Century Chinese Porcelain from the Butler Family Collection (1990), Shunzhi Porcelain (2002), 17th Century Jingdezhen Porcelain from the Shanghai Museum and the Butler Collections (2005); *Recreations* collecting Chinese porcelain; *Clubs* Brooks's; *Style—* Sir Michael Butler, GCMG

BUTLER, Prof Michael Gregory; s of Maurice Gregory Butler (d 1973), and Winifred May, *née* Barker; *b* 1 November 1935; *Educ* High Pavement Sch Nottingham, Fitzwilliam Coll Cambridge (MA, LittD), Trinity Coll Oxford (DipEd), CNAA (PhD); *m* 31 Dec 1960, Jean

Mary, da of William John Griffith (d 1966); 1 s (Julian Michael b 1964), 1 da (Emma Catherine b 1967); *Career* asst master: King's Sch Worcester 1958–61, Reuchlin Gymnasium Pforzheim FRG 1961–62; head of German Ipswich Sch 1962–70; Univ of Birmingham: lectr 1970, sr lectr 1980–86, head Dept of German Studies 1984–2001, prof of modern German literature 1986–, head Sch of Modern Languages 1988–93; public orator 1997–2005; professorial fell Inst for German Studies 1997–, fell Inst for Advanced Research in Arts and Social Sciences 2003–; visiting fell Humanities Res Centre ANU 1979; pres Conf of Univ Teachers of German in GB and I (CUTG) 1996–99 (vice-pres 1994–96); ed Samphire 1968–81, gen ed New Perspectives in German Studies 2000–; govr Abbey HS Redditch 1971–88; FIL 1967; Knight's Cross of the Order of Merit (Federal Repub of Germany) 1999; *Publications* The Novels of Max Frisch (1975), Englische Lyrik der Gegenwart (ed, 1981), The Plays of Max Frisch (1985), Frisch - Andorra (1985), Rejection and Emancipation - Writing in German-speaking Switzerland 1945–91 (ed, 1991), The Narrative Fiction of Heinrich Böll (ed, 1994), The Challenge of German Culture (ed, 2000), The Making of Modern Switzerland, 1848–1998 (ed, 2000), Marks of Honour (2007); many contribs to edited books and learned jls, regular reviewer for TLS; *Recreations* avoiding retirement; *Style*— Prof Michael Butler; ✉ 45 Westfields, Catshill, Bromsgrove, Worcestershire B61 9HJ (tel 01527 874189); Department of German Studies, University of Birmingham, Edgbaston, Birmingham B15 2TT (tel 0121 414 6173, e-mail m.g.butler@bham.ac.uk)

BUTLER, Sir (Reginald) Michael Thomas; 3 Bt (UK 1922), of Old Park, Devizes, Wilts; QC (Can 1967); s of Sir (Reginald) Thomas Butler, 2 Bt (d 1959); *b* 22 April 1928; *Educ* Brentwood Coll Victoria, Univ of Br Columbia (BA), Osgoode Hall Sch of Law Toronto; *m* 1, 1952 (m dis 1967), Marja Margaret Elizabeth, o da of late Ewen H McLean, of Toronto; 3 s ((Reginald) Richard Michael b 1953, Geoffrey MacLean b 1956, Thomas David b 1960); m 2, 1968 (m dis 1974), Mrs Barbara Anne Hogan, da of late Kevin Cahill, of Dublin; 1 step and adopted s (Patrick Colman b 1958); partner, Judith Ann, da of late Harold Blackwell, of London, Ontario; *Heir* s, Richard Butler; *Career* barr and slr Ontario 1954 and BC 1967, ret ptnr Messrs Butler Angus (Victoria BC); dir Teck Corporation and other companies; *Style*— Sir Michael Butler, Bt, QC; ✉ Old Park Cottage, 634 Avalon Street, Victoria, BC V8V 1N7, Canada (e-mail blackbart@telus.net)

BUTLER, (John) Nicholas (Nick); OBE (1988); s of William Butler (d 1974), of Normanton, W Yorks, and Mabel Annie Butler (d 1974); *b* 21 March 1942; *Educ* Sch of Industrial Design Leeds Coll of Art (NDD), Dept of Industrial Design RCA (DesRCA); *m* 1, 1967 (m dis 1999), Kari Anne, da of George Morrison; 2 s (Finn b 24 June 1969, Liam b 22 July 1971); m 2, 2001, Mary Thompson; *Career* chartered designer; IBM fellowship to USA 1965–66, project ldr GLC Industrialised Building Systems 1966–67, currently chm and md BIB Design Consultants (fndr 1967), chief exec Design Gp and memb Bd BAA plc 1992–; Design Cncl: memb Awards Judging Panel 1975–, memb Industrial Advsy Ctee 1978–, memb Exec Ctee 1990–, shadow design dir 1994–; cmmr Royal Fine Arts Cmmn 1998–; chm: Br Design Export Group 1980–81, Br Design Awards Scheme (consumer and contract goods) 1988–; memb: Design Bd RSA 1986, Design Cncl 1988; presented two papers at ICSID World Design Conf Washington USA 1985, keynote speaker DTI Design Commitment Conf London 1986, main speaker Int Design Conf World Trade Centre NY 1986, visiting speaker Warren Centre Univ of Sydney 1987, design address Aust Govt Canberra 1987, visiting prof Faculty of Design RCA 1987, judge Br Design in Japan competition Tokyo 1987, opened Drawn from Britain (British Designers Work Overseas) exhbn Design Cncl 1988, external assessor Massey Univ NZ 1993–, chm Industrial Advsy Bd and visiting prof Univ of Central Lancashire 2001–; FCSD 1975 (hon treas 1978–80 and 1980–82), RDI 1981 (Master 1995–97), FRSA 1983; *Style*— Nick Butler, Esq, OBE, RDI

BUTLER, Norman John Terence (Terry); CBE (1993); s of Arthur Reginald Butler, and Lucy Mary Butler; *b* 18 February 1946; *Educ* Peveril Bilateral Sch Nottingham, Trent Poly Nottingham, Nat Inst of Social Work London, Brunel Univ (MA); *Family* 2 da; *Career* mental welfare offr Nottingham 1965–71, sr social worker Nottingham 1971–73, area mangr Haringey 1974–81, asst dir of social services Royal Borough of Kingston upon Thames 1981–83, dep dir of social services E Sussex 1983–88, dir of social services Hants 1988–, seconded as co-ldr Community Care Support Force Dept of Health 1992–93; memb: Govt Firth Ctee 1987, Ed Bd Community Care Management and Planning Jl, Home Office Advsy Bd on Restricted Patients 1995–2001, Data Protection Tbnl Bd; vice-pres Relatives' Assoc; hon treas Assoc of Dirs of Social Servs; author of articles in various jls incl Social Work Today, Insight and Community Care; *Recreations* tennis, soccer, entertaining, being entertained; *Clubs* Kingsgate Tennis; *Style*— Terry Butler, Esq, CBE; ✉ Edgar House, 17 Lansdowne Avenue, St Cross, Winchester, Hampshire SO23 9TU (tel 01962 856489); Hampshire County Council, Trafalgar House, The Castle, Winchester, Hampshire SO23 8UQ (tel 01962 841841, fax 01962 847159)

BUTLER, Dr Paul; s of Frank William Butler (d 1966), and Elizabeth, *née* Wright (d 1993); *b* 4 June 1952; *Educ* Cotham GS, UCL (BSc), Westminster Med Sch (MB BS); *m* 28 Jan 1978, Janet Ann Butler, da of Percival Jack Barber, of Sawbridgeworth, Herts; 1 da (Claire b 19 Dec 1980), 1 s (David b 20 Oct 1982); *Career* med registrar rotation Leicester AHA 1979, trainee in radiodiagnosis Manchester RHA 1983, sr registrar neuroradiology Manchester Royal Infirmary, currently conslt neuroradiologist Bart's and London NHS Tst; conslt neuroradiologist: London Ind Hosp, London Clinic, King Edward VII's Sister Agnes Hosp; Freeman City of London, Liveryman Worshipful Soc of Apothecaries; memb Br Soc of Neuroradiologists, MRCP 1979, DMRD 1983, FRCR 1983; *Publications* Imaging of the Nervous System (ed, 1990), Applied Radiological Anatomy (ed, 1999), Endovascular Neurosurgery (ed, 1999); *Recreations* classical music, opera; *Style*— Dr Paul Butler; ✉ Department of Neuroradiology, The Royal London Hospital, Whitechapel, London E1 1BB (tel 020 7377 7165, fax 01279 871791, e-mail paul.butler26@btopenworld.com)

BUTLER, (James) Pearse; s of James Butler, of Liverpool, and Nancy, *née* McManus; *b* 27 January 1957; *Educ* St Mary's Coll Crosby, Keble Coll Oxford (BA); *m* 11 Aug 1979, Deborah Veronica, *née* Downing; 1 s (Daniel John b 28 July 1985), 1 da (Alison Patricia b 26 Nov 1987); *Career* community worker Liverpool Cncl for Voluntary Serv 1979–80, hosp admin S Birmingham HA 1980–83, dep admin then admin Bolton Gen Hosp 1983–85, mgmnt conslt HAY-MSL Management Consultants 1985–86, gen mangr Obstetric and Gynaecology Serv Liverpool HA 1986–88, dist gen mangr Chester HA 1988–89; chief exec: Royal Liverpool Children's NHS Tst 1989–93, Wirral Health 1993–97, Wigan & Leigh Health Servs NHS Tst 1997–99, Royal Liverpool Univ Hosp 1999–2002, chief exec Cumbria and Lancashire SHA 2002–06, interim chief exec East of England SHA May-Nov 2006; *Recreations* sport, family, opera; *Clubs* West Lancs Golf, Campion Lawn Tennis; *Style*— Pearse Butler, Esq

BUTLER, Peter Robert; *b* 17 May 1949; *Educ* Southend HS, Univ of Bristol (BSc); *m* Linley; 1 s (Simon b 1980), 1 da (Rachel b 1984); *Career* articled clerk and accountant Touche Ross & Co 1970–75; BOC Gp plc: investigations accountant BOC Ltd London 1975–77, fin dir/fin mangr BOC Ltd Far East Singapore 1977–79, fin controller Oilfield Servs 1980, mangr Corp Fin (Welding) 1980–83, gp commercial mangr (Welding) 1983–84; British Sugar plc and Berisford International plc: joined as gp ops controller 1984–86, assoc dir Fin S & W Berisford 1987–88, fin dir British Sugar plc and Bristar Food and Agribusiness Div 1988–90, chief fin offr and exec dir Berisford International plc 1991–93; gp fin dir Hi-Tec Sports plc 1993–95; corp focus dir Hermes Pensions Management Ltd 1996–2004, chief exec Hermes Focus Asset Management Ltd 1998–2004, fndr ptnr and ceo Governance for Owners LLP 2004–; chm Essex and Southend Sports Tst 2002–, chm Southend Cricket Festival Ctee 2003–, Gen Ctee Essex CCC; MInstD, FCA 1979 (ACA 1973); *Recreations* cricket, football (Southend United FC, player/manager Old Southendians FC Veterans XI), France; *Clubs* MCC, Essex CCC, Southend United FC; *Style*— Peter Butler, Esq

BUTLER, Hon Sir Richard Clive; kt (1981), DL (Essex 1972); s of late Baron Butler of Saffron Walden, KG, CH, PC (Life Peer), by his 1 w, Sydney, da of Samuel Courtauld; *b* 12 January 1929; *Educ* Eton, Pembroke Coll Cambridge; *m* 1952, Susan Anne Maud, da of Maj Patrick Walker, MBE (s of Sir James Walker, 3 Bt); 2 s, 1 da; *Career* 2 Lt RHG BAOR 1948–49; farmer; md Sir Richard & Lady Butler's Farms Ltd 1985–; memb Cncl NFU 1962– (pres 1979–86); dir: NFU Mutual Insurance Soc 1985–96, NatWest Bank plc (formerly National Westminster)1986–96, NatWest Investment Bank Ltd 1989–92; chm: Ferruzzi Trading (UK) Ltd 1986–94, NatWest Investment Management Ltd 1989–96, Agroceres & Co Ltd 1994–97; tstee The Butler Tst, chm The Kennedy Inst of Rheumatology Tst; Master: Worshipful Co of Skinners 1994–95, Worshipful Co of Farmers 1997–98; *Recreations* hunting, shooting, DIY; *Clubs* Farmers'; *Style*— The Hon Sir Richard Butler, DL; ✉ Gladfen Hall, Halstead, Essex CO9 1RN (tel 01787 472828, fax 01787 478571)

BUTLER, Robin Noël Holman; s of George Noël Butler (d 1969), of Honiton, and Marjorie Blanche, *née* Dunn (d 1993); *b* 26 April 1943; *Educ* Allhallows Sch; *m* 17 Feb 1995 (m dis 1997), Wendy, da of Arthur Knott; m 2, 31 July 2003, Carol Zenia, da of Francis James Hunter; *Career* schoolmaster 1961–63, family antiques business 1963–, memb Br Antique Dealers' Assoc 1970–2000 (cncl 1984–87); *Books* Arthur Negus Guide to English Furniture (1978), Book of Wine Antiques (1986), The Albert Collection - 500 Years of British & European Silver (2004); *Recreations* photography, cooking, snooker and golf; *Clubs* Clifton, Flempton Golf; *Style*— Robin Butler, Esq; ✉ The School, Foxearth, Suffolk CO10 7JG

BUTLER, Rosemary Janet Mair; AM; da of Godfrey McGrath, of Llangibby, Monmouthshire, and Gwyneth, *née* Jones (d 1997); *b* 21 January 1943; *Educ* St Julian's HS S Wales; *m* 18 Dec 1966, Derek Richard Butler; 2 da (Kate Rebecca b 1968, Helen Alice b 1970); *Career* qualified chiropodist; cncllr (Lab) Newport BC and County BC 1973–99; memb Nat Assembly for Wales (Lab) Newport West 1999–; min for educn and children Nat Assembly for Wales 1999–2000, memb Ctee of the Regions of the EU 2001–, chair Culture, Welsh Language and Sport Ctee 2003–, elected dep presiding offr of Nat Assembly for Wales 2007–; dir Tourism S and W Wales 1993–99, chair leisure services Newport Cncl 1983–98, memb Museums and Galleries Cmmn 1996–2000, exec memb Cncl for Museums in Wales, memb Broadcasting Cncl for Wales 1997–99, chair Bd Nat Industrial and Maritime Museum Swansea 2001–; fndr and chair Newport Int Competition for Young Pianists 1979–; memb: GMB, Lab Pty, Sports Cncl of Wales 1993–99; mayor of Newport 1989–90; chair and fndr Newport-Kutaisi Twinning Assoc, hon citizen of Kutaisi Rep of Georgia 1997; hon fell Univ of Wales Newport 2000; *Style*— Rosemary Butler, AM; ✉ National Assembly for Wales, Cardiff Bay, Cardiff CF99 1NA (tel 02920 898470, fax 02920 898527); Constituency Office: 1 Transport House, Cardiff Road, Newport NP20 2EH (tel 01633 222523, fax 01633 221981)

BUTLER, (Stanley) Roy; s of Harry Butler (d 1950) of Epsom, Surrey, and Emily, *née* Whiteing (d 1950); *b* 16 February 1923; *m* 14 July 1951, Jessie, da of Edward James Fletcher (d 1966), of Brixton, London; 1 da (Deborah b 1958), 1 s (Glenn b 1961); *Career* departmental head Hawker Aircraft 1940–42, RA Ordnance Corps 1942–47, serv ME 1943–46; sr ptnr Wallis & Wallis The Militaria Arms and Armour auctioneers 1962– (auctioned gun that killed Jesse James 1993), dir Arms Fairs Ltd 1967–2002; fndr The Military Heritage Museum Lewes 1977; TV appearances: Going for a Song 1973, arms and militaria specialist Antiques Roadshow (BBC) 1977–2006, Heirlooms (ITV) 1987–88, Heirs and Graces (BBC) 1988, Going Live (BBC) 1991–92, Antiques Roadshow The Next Generation (BBC) 1992–93, 1996–2004; info advsr Antiques Inspectors (BBC) 1997; guest John Dunn Show 1993 and 1996, Down Your Way (Brian Johnston) 1988, conslt ed Miller's Annual Antiques Guide, guest lectr P&O Cruises, Fred Olsen Lines, Page and Moy Cruises, Victoria Travel, Cunard, and MyTravel Cruises, pres St John Ambulance (Lewes Div) 1981–, benefactor and life memb Soc of Friends of RN Museum, life memb HMS Warrior Assoc; memb: Rotary Club of Lewes 1968– (pres 1999–2000), 1805 Club and Nelson Soc, Military Historical Soc, Victorian Military Soc, Crimean War Soc, Army Historical Res Soc, Orders & Medals Soc, Arms & Armour Soc, Historical Breechloading Smallarms Assoc; Freeman City of London 1981, Liveryman Worshipful Co of Tobacco Pipe Makers 1979; FInstD; *Recreations* swimming, snooker, gardening; *Style*— Roy Butler, Esq; ✉ Wallis & Wallis, West Street, Auction Galleries, Lewes, East Sussex BN7 2NJ (tel 01273 480208, fax 01273 476562, e-mail auctions@wallisandwallis.co.uk)

BUTLER, Rt Rev Dr Thomas Frederick; *see:* Southwark, Bishop of

BUTLER, Vincent Frederick; *b* 27 October 1933; *Educ* Edinburgh Coll of Art (DA), Acad of Fine Art Milan; *m* 21 Aug 1961, Camilla Luisa, da of Cavaliere Giuseppe Meazza (d 1971), of Milan; 2 s (Angus, Adam); *Career* figurative sculptor; RSA 1971, RGI 1989; *Recreations* travel; *Style*— Vincent Butler, Esq; ✉ 17 Deanpark Crescent, Edinburgh EH4 1PH (tel 0131 332 5884, e-mail vincent.butler@talktalk.net)

BUTLER, Prof William Elliott; s of William Elliott Butler (d 1996), of Black Mountain, N Carolina, and Maxine Swan Elmberg; *b* 20 October 1939; *Educ* American Univ Washington DC (BA), Johns Hopkins Univ Baltimore (MA), Harvard Law Sch (JD), Sch of Law Inst of State and Law Russian Acad of Sciences (LLM), Johns Hopkins Univ (PhD), Univ of London (LLD); *m* 1, 2 Sept 1961, Darlene Mae Johnson (d 1989); 2 s (William Elliott III, Bradley Newman); m 2, 6 Dec 1991, Maryann Elizabeth Gashi; *Career* research asst Washington Centre of Foreign Policy Research Johns Hopkins Univ 1966–68, research assoc in law Harvard Law Sch and Assoc Russian Research Centre Harvard 1968–70; Univ of London: reader in comparative law 1970–76, prof of comparative law 1976–2005, emeritus prof 2005–, dean Faculty of Laws UCL 1977–79, dean Faculty of Laws Univ of London 1988–90; John Edward Fowler Distinguished Prof of Law Dickinson Sch of Law Pennsylvania State Univ 2005–; counsel Clifford Chance 1992–94, ptnr White & Case 1994–96, ptnr CIS Law Firm PricewaterhouseCoopers 1997–2001, ptnr Phoenix Law Associates CIS 2002–; visiting scholar: Moscow State Univ 1972 and 1980, USSR Acad of Sci 1976, 1981, 1983, 1984, and 1988, Mongolian State Univ 1979; memb Cncl SSEES 1973–88 and 1989–93 (vice-chm 1983–88); Speranskii prof of int and comparative law and dean 1994–2004, Faculty of Law Moscow Sch of Social and Econ Sci 1994–; visiting prof: NY Univ Law Sch 1978, Ritsumeikan Univ 1985, Harvard Law Sch 1986–87, Washington and Lee Law Sch 2005; memb Faculty Governing Cncl Sch of Int Affrs Penn State 2007–; coordinator UCL-USSR Acad of Sci Protocol on Co-operation in Social Sci 1981–, dir The Vinogradoff Inst UCL 1982–, lectr Hague Acad of Int Law 1985, memb Ctee of Mgmnt Inst of Advanced Legal Studies Univ of London 1985–88, govr City of London Poly 1985–89, visiting fell Research Centre for Int Law Univ of Cambridge 1991–92, Leverhulme Research Grant 1991–92; ed East European and Russian Yearbook of International and Comparative Law 2007–, author of more than 100 books, 900 articles, reviews, and translations on int and comparative law, especially Soviet and Russian law and other CIS legal systems, bookplates, and bibliography; awarded GI Tunkin Medal Russian Int Law Assoc 2003; sec The Bookplate Soc 1978–86 (foreign sec 1988–94), fndr ed: The Bookplate Jl 1983–92 (co-ed 1989–92), Bookplate International 1994–, Sudebnik 1996–, Russian Law 2004–; VP Fed Int des Sociétés d'Amateurs d'Ex-Libris 1984–86 (exec sec 1988–); memb: Dist of Columbia Bar,

Bar of US Court of Appeals for Dist of Columbia, Bar of US Supreme Court, Cncl Cole Corette and Abrutyn (London and Moscow) 1989–92, Russian Acad of Nat Sciences (section Russian Encyclopaedia) 1992–, EC Jt Task Force for Law Reform in the CIS 1992–93, Nat Acad of Sciences Ukraine 1992–, Russian Court of Int Commercial Arbitration 1995–, Bar of Uzbekistan 1996–, Bar of Russia 1997–, Russian Acad of Legal Sciences 1999–, Learned Cncl 2004–; special counsel USSR Cncl of Ministers Cmmn for Econ Reform 1989–91; tstee Hakluyt Soc 2004–; hon memb: All Union Soc of the Book (USSR) 1989, Soviet Maritime Law Assoc (USSR) 1990, USSR Union of Jurists 1990; memb Associé Int Acad of Comparative Law 1983–; FRSA 1986, FSA 1989; *Recreations* book collecting, bookplate collecting; *Clubs* Cosmos, Grolier; *Style*— Prof William Butler, FSA; ✉ e-mail webakademik@aol.com or web15@psu.edu

BUTLER OF BROCKWELL, Baron (Life Peer UK 1998), of Herne Hill in the London Borough of Lambeth; Sir (Frederick Edward) Robin Butler; KG (2003), GCB (1992, KCB 1988), CVO (1986), PC (2004); s of Bernard Daft Butler, and Nora, *née* Jones, of St Annes on Sea, Lancs; *b* 3 January 1938; *Educ* Harrow, UC Oxford (MA); *m* 1962, Gillian Lois, da of Dr Robert Galley, of Teddington, Middx; 2 da (Hon Sophie b 1964, Hon Nell b 1967), 1 s (Hon Andrew b 1968); *Career* private sec to: Rt Hon Edward Heath 1972–74, Rt Hon Harold Wilson 1974–75; princ private sec to Rt Hon Margaret Thatcher 1982–85, second perm sec HM Treasy 1985–87, Sec of the Cabinet and Head of the Home Civil Service 1988–98; master UC Oxford 1998–; memb Royal Cmmn on Reform of House of Lords 1999, chm Review of Intelligence on Weapons of Mass Destruction 2004; non-exec dir: ICI plc 1998–, HSBC Holdings plc 1998–; chm of govrs: Harrow Sch 1987–91, Dulwich Coll 1997–2003; hon memb Worshipful Co of Salters; *Recreations* competitive games, opera; *Clubs* Anglo-Belgian, Athenaeum, Brooks's, Beefsteak; *Style*— The Rt Hon Lord Butler of Brockwell, KG, GCB, CVO, PC; ✉ The Master's Lodgings, University College, Oxford OX1 4BH

BUTLER-SLOSS, Baroness (Life Peer 2006), of Marsh Green in the County of Devon; Rt Hon Dame (Ann) Elizabeth Oldfield Butler-Sloss; GBE (2005, DBE 1979), PC (1987); da of Hon Mr Justice Cecil Havers (d 1977), High Court judge (Queen's Bench Div), and Enid, *née* Snelling (d 1956), and sister of Baron Havers, PC, QC (d 1992); *b* 10 August 1933; *Educ* Wycombe Abbey; *m* 1958, Joseph William Alexander Sloss (later Butler-Sloss); 2 s, 1 da; *Career* called to the Bar Inner Temple 1955 (reader 1997, treas 1998), registrar Principal Registry, Probate Div (subsequently Family Div) 1970–79, judge of the High Court of Justice (Family Div) 1979–88, a Lord Justice of Appeal 1988–99, pres Family Div 1999–2005; Parly candidate (Cons) Lambeth Vauxhall 1959; sometime vice-pres Medico-Legal Soc, memb Judicial Studies Bd 1985–89, chm Cleveland Child Abuse Inquiry 1987–88; past pres Cwlth and English Bar Assoc; chm Security Cmmn; vice-chm Cncl KCL 1992–97, memb Cncl Wycombe Abbey Sch 1992–1997, chllr UWE 1993–; chm cmmn appointing the Archbishop of Canterbury 2002; chm Advsy Cncl St Paul's Cathedral; visitor St Hilda's Coll Oxford, fell Sarum Coll 2004; hon fell: St Hilda's Coll Oxford, Peterhouse Cambridge 2007; Hon DLitt Loughborough Univ 1992; Hon LLD: Univ of Hull 1989, Keele Univ 1991, Univ of Bristol 1991, Univ of Exeter 1992, Brunel Univ 1992, Univ of Central England 1994, Univ of Manchester 1995, Univ of Greenwich 1999, Univ of Cambridge 2000, UAE 2001, Univ of Liverpool 2001, Univ of Ulster 2004, Open Univ, Univ of London 2004, Buckingham Univ 2006; hon memb Merchant Taylors Co 2003; hon memb American Law Inst; FKC 1991; Hon FRCP 1992, Hon FRCPsych 1992, Hon FRCPCH, Hon FRSM 1997; *Style*— The Rt Hon the Lady Butler-Sloss, GBE, PC

BUTLER-WHEELHOUSE, Keith Oliver; s of Kenneth Butler-Wheelhouse (d 1998), and May, *née* Page (d 1981); *b* 29 March 1946, Walsall; *Educ* Queen Mary's GS Walsall, Grey HS Port Elizabeth, Port Elizabeth Univ, Witwatersrand Univ Johannesburg (BCom), Grad Sch of Business Univ of Cape Town; *m* 15 Dec 1973, Pamela Anne; 2 s (Duncan b 4 April 1981, Andrew b 3 Feb 1985); *Career* various assignments in product devpt, finance and sales and mktg Ford Motor Co 1965–86, led MBO of General Motor's South African business, chm and chief exec Delta Motor Corporation South Africa 1987–92, chief exec and worldwide pres Saab Automobile Sweden 1992–96, chief exec Smiths Gp plc UK 1996–; Citizen of the Year Port Elizabeth 1988; *Recreations* tennis, swimming, surfing, golf; *Clubs* Johannesburg Country, Fancourt (South Africa), St Francis Bay (South Africa), Moor Park, Wentworth; *Style*— Keith Butler-Wheelhouse, Esq; ✉ Smiths Group plc, 765 Finchley Road, London NW11 8DS (tel 020 8457 8272, fax 020 8458 8412)

BUTLIN, Martin Richard Fletcher; CBE (1990); s of Kenneth Rupert Butlin (d 1965), and Helen Mary, *née* Fletcher, MBE (d 1998); *b* 7 June 1929; *Educ* Rendcomb Coll, Trinity Coll Cambridge (MA), Courtauld Inst of Art Univ of London (DLit); *m* 31 Jan 1969, Frances Caroline, da of Michael Anthony Chodzko (d 1997); *Career* Nat Serv RAMC; asst keeper Tate Gallery 1955–67, keeper Historic Br Collection Tate Gallery 1967–89, conslt Christie's 1989–; involved in selection and cataloguing of exhibitions on Blake and Turner, author of numerous articles and reviews for magazines; FBA 1984; *Publications* incl: A Catalogue of the Works of William Blake in the Tate Gallery (1957, 3 edn 1990), Samuel Palmer's Sketchbook of 1824 (1962, 2 edn 2005), Turner Watercolours (1962), Turner (with Sir John Rothenstein, 1964), Tate Gallery Catalogues, The Modern British Paintings, Drawings and Sculpture (with Mary Chamot and Dennis Farr, 1964), The Later Works of JMW Turner (1965), William Blake (1966), The Blake-Varley Sketchbook of 1819 (1969), The Paintings of JMW Turner (with Evelyn Joll, 1977, 2 edn 1984, Mitchell Prize 1978), The Paintings and Drawings of William Blake (1981), Aspects of British Painting 1550–1800 from the collection of the Sarah Campbell Blaffer Foundation (1988), William Blake in the collection of the National Gallery of Victoria (with Tedd Gott, 1989), Turner at Petworth (with Mollie Luther and Ian Warrell, 1989), The Oxford Companion to J M W Turner (ed with Evelyn Joll and Luke Herrmann, 2001); *Recreations* opera, ballet, travel; *Style*— Martin Butlin, Esq, CBE, FBA; ✉ 74C Eccleston Square, London SW1V 1PJ

BUTT, Prof John; s of Wilfrid Roger Butt, of Stratford-upon-Avon, Warks, and Patricia Doreen Butt; *b* 17 November 1960, Solihull, W Midlands; *Educ* Solihull Sch, King's Coll Cambridge (MA, MPhil, PhD); *m* 22 July 1989, Sally Ann, *née* Cantlay; 4 s (Christopher Andrew b 26 March 1992, James Arthur b 23 June 1994, Angus Alastair b 6 April 1999, Fergus Alexander b 2 June 2004), 1 da (Victoria Ailidh b 11 Sept 1996); *Career* temp lectr Univ of Aberdeen 1986–87, research fell Magdalene Coll Cambridge 1987–89, assoc prof of music and univ organist Univ of Calif Berkeley 1989–97, univ lectr in music Univ of Cambridge 1997–2001 (fell King's Coll), Gardiner prof of music Univ of Glasgow 2001–; recorded 11 CDs for Harmonia Mundi on organ and harpsichord, other recordings with Koch, Centaur, Delphian and Linn; W H Scheide Award American Bach Soc 1992, Dent Medal RMA 2003; FRCO 1977, FRSE 2003, FBA 2006; *Books* Bach Interpretation (1990), Bach Mass in B Minor (1991), Music Education in the German Baroque (1994), Cambridge Companion to Bach (1997), Playing with History (2002); *Recreations* reading, hill walking; *Style*— Prof John Butt; ✉ Music Department, University of Glasgow, 14 University Gardens, Glasgow G12 8QQ (tel 0141 330 4571, mobile 07970 632685, e-mail j.butt@music.gla.ac.uk)

BUTT, Michael Acton; s of Leslie Acton Kingsford Butt and Mina Gascoigne Butt; *b* 25 May 1942; *Educ* Rugby, Magdalen Coll Oxford, INSEAD France (MBA); *m* 1, 1964 (m dis 1986), Diana Lorraine, *née* Brook; 2 s; m 2, 1986, Zoé Benson; *Career* joined Bland Welch Group 1964, dir Bland Payne Holdings 1970, chm Sedgwick Ltd 1983–87, dep chm Sedgwick Group plc 1985–87, chm and chief exec Eagle Star Holdings plc 1987–91, dir BAT Industries plc 1987–91, chm and chief exec Eagle Star Insurance Co 1987–91; dir: Marceau Investissements SA (France) 1987–95, Mid Ocean Ltd (pres and chief exec) 1992–98, Phoenix Securities Ltd 1992–95, Bank of NT Butterfield Bermuda 1996–2002, XL Capital Ltd 1998–2002; chm AXIS Capital Holdings Ltd 2002–; tstee: Monte Verdi Tst London 1989–2000, Bermuda Biological Station for Research 1996–; dep chm Exec Ctee Bermuda Underwater Exploration Inst 1997–2001; memb: Bd INSEAD France, Instituto Nazionale delle Assicurazioni (INA) Rome 1994–99; Liveryman Worshipful Co of Insurers; *Recreations* tennis, opera, reading, family, the European Movement; *Clubs* Travellers, Mid Ocean (Bermuda), Royal Bermuda Yacht (Bermuda), Coral Beach and Tennis (Bermuda); *Style*— Michael Butt, Esq; ✉ Leamington House, 50 Harrington Sound Road, Hamilton Parish CR04, Bermuda (tel 00 441 293 1378, fax 00 441 293 8511); AXIS Speciality Limited, PO Box HM 1254, Hamilton HM FX, Bermuda (tel 00 441 496 2600, fax 00 441 405 2720, e-mail michael.butt@axis.bm)

B

BUTTERFIELD, Leslie Paul; CBE (2007); s of Leslie John Butterfield (d 1983), and Ruth, *née* Andräs; *b* 31 August 1952; *Educ* NE London Poly (BA), Lancaster Univ (MA); *m* 14 May 1988, Judy Mary Tombleson; 1 da (Alexa); *Career* advertising exec and branding conslt; account planner and assoc dir Boase Massimi Pollitt Ltd 1975–80, planning dir Abbott Mead Vickers Ltd 1980–87, chm Partners BDDH (formerly Butterfield Day Devito Hockney) 1987–2001, ceo Butterfield8 2001–03, managing ptnr Ingram 2003–; IPA Effectiveness Award 1984 and 2000; FIPA 1988; *Books* Excellence in Advertising (1997, 2 edn 1999), Understanding the Financial Value of Brands (1998), AdValue (2003), Enduring Passion: The story of the Mercedes-Benz brand (2005); *Style*— Leslie Butterfield, Esq, CBE; ✉ Ingram, 7–10 Beaumont Mews, London W1G 6EB (tel 020 7317 2916, e-mail lesliebutterfield@theingrampartnership.com)

BUTTERFIELD, Hon Sarah Harriet Anne (Hon Mrs Willetts); da of Baron Butterfield, OBE (d 2000), and Isabel Ann Foster, *née* Kennedy; *b* 28 August 1953; *Educ* Sherborne Sch for Girls, Univ of Edinburgh (BA), Ruskin Sch of Fine Art and Drawing Univ of Oxford, Univ of Bristol (DipArch); *m* 19 April 1986, David Lindsay Willetts, MP, *qv*, s of John Roland Willetts, of Birmingham; 1 da, 1 s; *Career* architect 1978–86: California, Bristol, London; illustrator for Experimental Psychology Dept Cambridge Univ 1976–78, art critic Oxford Mail 1978; currently working as an artist; art reviewer Art and Entertainment Prog LBC 1999–2002; exhibitions incl: RCA 1978, Mall Galleries 1980, 1984, 1986 and 1988, Young Contemporaries Agnews 1988, Richmond Gallery London 1990, Roy Miles Gallery London 1991 and 1994, one-man shows Cadogan Contemporary London 1991, 1994 and 1997, Discerning Eye 1997, group show dfn Gallery NY 2000, one-man show 27 Cork St London 2001, group show The View - an Exhibition about Richmond Hill Orleans House Gallery Twickenham 2003, gp show Albemarle Gallery London 2004, one-man show Albemarle Gallery London 2005, official artist on Royal tour by HRH The Prince of Wales and HRH The Duchess of Cornwall on their visit to Egypt, Saudi Arabia and India 2006; paintings on permanent view at: British Airways Terminal 4 Heathrow Airport, Gatwick Airport, Wimbledon Lawn Tennis Museum, The Prudential, Trust House Forte Hotels (Exeter and Yorks); Egerton Coghill Landscape Award 1976, Windor & Newton Award 1978, finalist Hunting Gp Art Competition 1987, commended Spector Three Cities Competition 1988; actress: Joan Fielding in Catherine Cookson's Tillie Trotter (ITV) 1999, appearances in Stop, Look, Listen (Channel 4); memb: Equity, ARB; *Books* Word Order Comprehension Test (with Dr Gillian Fenn); *Clubs* Hurlingham, Emsworth Sailing; *Style*— The Hon Sarah Butterfield

BUTTERFILL, Sir John Valentine; kt (2004), MP; s of George Thomas Butterfill (d 1980), and Elsie Amelia, *née* Watts (d 1974); *b* 14 February 1941; *Educ* Caterham Sch, Coll of Estate Mgmnt London; *m* 1965, Pamela Ross, da of Frederick Ross-Symons; 3 da (Natasha (Mrs Toby Rougier) b 1969, Samara (Mrs Roger Jones) b 1974, Jemima (Mrs Darsh Dhillon) b 1976), 1 s (James b 1975); *Career* chartered surveyor; valuer Jones Lang Wootton 1962–64, sr exec Hammerson Gp 1964–69, dir Audley Properties Ltd (Bovis Gp) 1969–71, md St Paul's Securities Gp 1971–76, dir Micro Business Systems Ltd 1977–79, sr ptnr Curchod & Co Chartered Surveyors 1977–92, dir Pavilion Services Group Ltd 1992–94, conslt Curchod & Co 1992–, chm Conservation Investments Group, pres European Properties Associates; MP (Cons) Bournemouth W 1983– (Euro Parly candidate London S Inner 1979, Parly candidate Croydon NW by-election 1981); vice-chm Backbench Tourism Ctee 1985–88 (sec 1983–85), sec Backbench Trade and Industry Ctee 1987–88 and 1990; PPS to: Sec of State for Energy 1988–89, Sec of State for Tport 1989–90, Min of State for NI 1991–92; memb: Trade and Industry Select Ctee 1992–2001, Chm's Panel 1997–, Ct of Referees 1997–; vice-chm: Fin Ctee 1992–2000, Euro Affrs Ctee 1992–97; chm All-Pty Gp on Occupational Pensions 1992–; dep chm Euro Democrat Forum 1981–87, vice-chm Foreign Affairs Forum 1983–92, chm Cons Gp for Europe 1989–92; Parly conslt to BIIBA 1992–97, Parly advsr to BVCA 1994–2001; memb Cncl of Mgmnt PDSA 1990–; memb Ct Univs of Reading, Southampton and Exeter; memb Cncl of Mgmnt People's Dispensary for Sick Animals; FRICS 1974; *Recreations* skiing, tennis, bridge, music; *Style*— Sir John Butterfill, MP; ✉ House of Commons, London SW1A 0AA

BUTTERWORTH, Arthur Eckersley; MBE (1995); s of Harold Butterworth (d 1945), and Maria, *née* Nelson (d 1935); *b* 4 August 1923; *Educ* N Manchester GS, Royal Manchester Coll of Music; *m* 12 July 1952, Diana, da of Charles Stewart, OBE (d 1967); 2 da (Nicola Diana b 1960, Carolin Ann b 1962); *Career* RE attached 51 Highland Div 1942–47; composer: Symphony No 1 op 15 Cheltenham Festival 1957 and BBC Proms 1958, Symphony No 2 op 25 Bradford 1965, Organ Concerto 1973, Violin Concerto 1978, Symphony No 3 op 52 Manchester 1979, Piano Trio Cheltenham Festival Cmmn 1983, Symphony No 4 op 72 Manchester 1986, Odin Symphony for Brass op 76 London 1989, Northern Light op 88 Leeds 1991, Concerto alla Veneziana op 93 York 1992, Viola Concerto op 82 Manchester 1993, 'Cello Concerto op 98 Huddersfield 1994, Mancunians op 96 Hallé Orch Cmmn Manchester 1995, Viola Sonata Op 78 1996, Guitar Concerto op 109 Leeds 2000, Symphony No 5 op 115 Manchester 2003, Piano Trio No 2 Op 121 2004, Symphony No 6 Op 124 2006; conductor Huddersfield Philharmonic Soc 1964–93, various guest conductor appearances 1965–; *Recreations* country living, animal welfare, oil and water colour painting; *Style*— Arthur Butterworth, Esq, MBE; ✉ Pohjola, Dales Avenue, Embsay, Skipton, North Yorkshire BD23 6PE (tel 01756 792968)

BUTTERWORTH, David; s of John Butterworth (d 1971), and Annie May, *née* Claughton; *b* 24 October 1943; *Educ* Audenshaw GS, UCL (BSc(Eng)); *m* 2 Aug 1966, Pauline Patricia, da of Leonard Morgan; 1 s (Richard David b 9 Feb 1968); *Career* AEA Technology Harwell: res scientist/engr 1965–69, section ldr 1969–76, gp ldr 1977–89, md Heat Transfer and Fluid Flow Serv 1989–95 (sr conslt 1995–); visiting engr MIT 1976–77; visiting prof: Univ of Bristol 1993–, Cranfield Univ 1995–2002; Royal Acad of Engrg visiting prof Aston Univ 1996–2001; gen sec Aluminium Plate-Fin Heat Exchanger Mfrs' Assoc 1995–; D Q Kern Award for industrial application of heat transfer technol American Inst of Chem Engrs 1986; chm Heat Transfer Steering Gp Engrg Sciences Data Unit 1986–94, pres UK Heat Transfer Soc 1988–89; memb: Cncl and Engrg Practice Ctee Inst of Chem Engrs 1989–92 (also hon librarian), Scientific Cncl Int Centre for Heat and Mass Transfer 1990–2006, Int Ctee Royal Acad of Engrg 1993–96, UK Nat Ctee for Heat Transfer 1996–, Cncl Herb Soc UK 2004–; CEng 1969, FIChemE 1985, FREng 1991, Eur Ing 1991, FRSA 1993, CSci 2005; *Books* Introduction to Heat Transfer (1977), Two Phase Flow and Heat Transfer (jt ed, 1977, 1978 and 1979, also published in Russian 1980), Design and Operation of Heat Exchangers (jt ed, 1992); *Recreations* painting, cooking, website design; *Style*— David Butterworth, FREng; ✉ 29 Clevelands, Abingdon, Oxfordshire OX14 2EQ (tel 01235 525955)

BUTTERWORTH, Prof Ian; CBE (1984); s of Harry Butterworth, and Beatrice, *née* Worsley; *b* 3 December 1930; *Educ* Bolton Co GS, Univ of Manchester (BSc, PhD); *m* 9 May 1964, Mary Therese Gough (d 2007); 1 da (Jody); *Career* scientific offr and sr scientific offr UKAEA AERE Harwell 1954–58; Imperial Coll London: lectr 1958, sr lectr 1965, head of High Energy Nuclear Physics Gp 1971, head Dept of Physics 1980, hon fell 1988, sr res fell 1991–; prof of physics Univ of London 1971–91 (prof emeritus 1991–), princ QMC London 1986–91; visiting physicist Lawrence Berkeley Laboratory Univ of Calif 1964–65, gp leader Bubble Chamber Res Gp Rutherford Laboratory as sr princ scientific offr 1968–71, vice-pres Academia Europaea 1997–2003; visiting prof Univ of Calif Riverside 1970, res dir CERN 1983–86; author of numerous papers in learned jls; fell American Physical Soc; FRS, FInstP; *Recreations* reading, art history; *Style*— Prof Ian Butterworth, CBE, FRS; ✉ The Blackett Laboratory, Imperial College, Prince Consort Road, London SW7 2BZ (tel 020 7594 7525, fax 020 7823 8830, e-mail i.butterworth@imperial.ac.uk)

BUTTERWORTH, Nicholas Gerald; s of Gerald Leonard Butterworth, and Margaret, *née* Cooke; *b* 28 January 1958, Wimbledon; *Educ* Worth Sch, Poly of the South Bank (BSc); *m* 9 Sept 1983, Geraldine Serena, *née* Ruiz; 1 s (Robert Gerald b 11 Dec 1987), 1 da (Serena Catherine b 24 May 1989); *Career* dir DTZ Debenham Tie Leung 1989–2001, ceo Jackson-Stops & Staff 2001–; chm Worth Old Boys' Soc; Liveryman Worshipful Co of Founders 1996, Freeman City of London 1997; MRICS 1983; *Recreations* historic houses, shooting, motoring; *Clubs* East India; *Style*— Nicholas Butterworth, Esq; ✉ Whitmoor Court, Whitmoor Lane, Sutton Green, Guildford, Surrey GU4 7QB (tel 01483 562534); Jackson-Stops & Staff, 17C Curzon Street, London W1J 5HU (tel 020 7664 6644, fax 020 7664 6645, e-mail nbutterworth@jackson-stops.com)

BUTTON, Jenson; *b* 19 January 1980, Frome, Somerset; *Career* motor racing driver; winner Br Kart Super Prix 1989, winner Br Cadet Kart Series 1990, winner Br Open and Br Cadet Kart Series 1991, winner Br Open and Br Jr TKM Kart Series 1992, winner Br Open Kart Series 1993, fourth place Br Jr Kart Series 1994, winner races in Jr Intercontinental A Euro Series and Jr Intercontinental A Italian Winter Kart Series 1994, winner Sr ICA Italian Kart Series 1995, youngest ever runner-up World Formula A Kart Series 1995, third place World Cup 1996, third place American Kart Series 1996, winner Euro Supercup A Kart Series 1997, winner Ayrton Senna Meml Cup Suzuka 1997, winner Br Formula Ford Series 1998 (also winner Formula Ford Festival), second place Euro Formula Ford Series (Haywood Racing) 1998, third place Br Formula 3 Series 1999 (top rookie driver); Formula One: Williams 2000 (Grand Prix debut, best qualifying position third place, eighth place in Driver's Championship), Benetton 2001 (2 points), Renault F1 2002 (seventh place Driver's Championship, 14 points), Lucky Strike BAR Honda 2003; *Recreations* jet-skiing, cycling; *Style*— Jenson Button, Esq; ✉ c/o Essentially Sport, Heron House, l'Avenue de la Commune, St Peter, Jersey JE3 7BY (e-mail infor@essentiallygroup.com); website www.jensonbutton.com

BUTTREY, Prof Theodore Vern; s of Theodore Vern Buttrey (d 1982), and Ruth Jeanette, *née* Scoutt (d 2002); *b* 29 December 1929; *Educ* Phillips Exeter Acad, Princeton Univ (BA, Stinnecke prize, PhD); *m* 1954 (m dis 1967), Marisa, *née* Macina; 1 da (Stephanie b 1955), 3 s (James b 1956, Claude b 1959, Samuel b 1961); *m* 2, 1967 (m dis 1980), Ann Elizabeth, *née* Johnston; *Career* asst prof Dept of Classics Yale Univ 1958–64 (instr 1954–58); Dept of Classics Univ of Michigan: assoc prof 1964–68, prof of Greek and Latin 1968–85, dept chm 1968–71 and 1983–84, prof emeritus 1985–; dir Kelsey Museum of Archaeology 1969–71, keeper Dept of Coins and Medals Fitzwilliam Museum Cambridge 1988–91; chm Regnl Ctee (Europe) Mellon Fellowships in the Humanities 1984–92, life memb Clare Hall Cambridge 1972– (visiting fell 1971–72), pres Royal Numismatic Soc 1989–94 (medal 1983, life fell), hon sec UK Numismatic Tst 1989–98; Huntington medal American Numismatic Soc 1996; life memb American Philological Assoc, life memb Archaeological Inst of America, corresponding memb Royal Danish Acad of Scis and Letters; FSA; *Publications* numerous articles on Greek literature and ancient and modern numismatics; *Recreations* Ernest Bramah, P G Wodehouse; *Style*— Prof T V Buttrey, FSA; ✉ 6 de Freville Avenue, Cambridge CB4 1HR (tel and fax 01223 351156, e-mail tvb1@cam.ac.uk)

BUXTON, Andrew Robert Fowell; CMG (2003); s of Capt Joseph Gurney Fowell Buxton, Grenadier Gds (ka 1943, gggs of Sir Thomas Buxton, 1 Bt), and Elizabeth (da of late Maj Robert Barbour, of Bolesworth Castle, Tattenhall, Chester) who m subsequently Alexander Grant; *b* 5 April 1939; *Educ* Winchester, Pembroke Coll Oxford; *m* 1965, Jane Margery, da of Lt-Col Ian (John Peter) Grant, MBE, of Rothiemurchus, and Lady Katherine Grant; 2 da; *Career* 2 Lt Grenadier Gds; Barclays Bank plc: dir 1984–, gp md 1988–92, chief exec 1992–93, chm 1993–99; interim chm Xansa plc 2003 (dep chm 1999–), chm Cygnet Property and Leisure plc 2005–; ind dir United Bank of Kuwait 1999–2003, dir Capitaland Ltd Singapore 2003–, dir DBS (Devpt Bank of Singapore) 2006–; non-exec dir: SmithKline Beecham plc 1989–97, Bank of England 1997–2001; advsr Akbank 1999–; chm Heart of the City 2000–05; pres BBA 1997–2002; *Style*— Andrew Buxton, Esq, CMG

BUXTON, David Wavel; s of Ronald Buxton (d 1990), and Margret, *née* Austin (d 2005); *b* 23 May 1944, Caterham, Surrey; *Educ* Redhill Tech Coll, Brixton Sch of Building; *m* 1968, Jennifer *née* Mortimer; 1 s (Steven Wavel b 1970), 2 da (Madeline b 1971, Gillian Sue b 1974); *Career* Cubits Construction Co 1960–62, Holloway Construction Co 1962–65, Atherton Structural Engineer 1965–70, W & R Buxton Ltd 1970–2005; *Recreations* walking, golf, travel; *Clubs* RAC; *Style*— David Buxton, Esq; ✉ The Dene, Hole Hill, Westcott, Surrey RH4 3LS (tel 01306 743795, fax 01306 743131, e-mail david.buxton@biscituk.com); The Buxton Group, Cedar House, High Street, Caterham, Surrey CR3 5UH (tel 01883 348921, fax 01883 348238)

BUXTON, Henry Alexander Fowell; DL (Herts 1993); s of John Fowell Buxton (d 1970), of Wareside, Herts, and Katherine, *née* Bacon; *b* 21 May 1937; *Educ* Maidwell Hall, Eton; *m* 10 Oct 1964, Victoria, da of Ronald Bennett, of Bibury, Glos; 2 s (Nicholas Fowell b 17 March 1966, Anthony John b 3 April 1968), 1 da (Katharine Louise b 27 May 1971); *Career* farmer and landowner; Nat Serv 16th/5th The Queen's Royal Lancers; chm Herts Country Landowners' Assoc 1978–79; dir: Truman Hanbury Buxton 1961–72, Camgrain Ltd; govr: Abingdon Sch, Baesh Almshouses, Mico Coll Kingston Jamaica; High Sheriff Herts 1992; Liveryman Worshipful Co of Mercers; *Recreations* fishing, shooting; *Clubs* Brooks's; *Style*— Henry Buxton, Esq, DL; ✉ Mardocks Mill, Wareside, Ware, Hertfordshire SG12 7QN (tel 01920 463673, fax 01920 486331)

BUXTON, James Anthony Fowell; s of Robert James Buxton (d 1968), of Yeovil, Somerset, and Lilla Mary Alyson, *née* Pumphrey (d 1979); *Educ* Harrow, Trinity Coll Cambridge (MA); *m* 4 Nov 1975, Margaret Elizabeth, da of Adm the Hon Sir Guy Russell, GBE, KCB, DSO; 2 da (Harriet b 1976, Meriel b 1980), 2 s (Edward b 1978, Charles b 1986); *Career* called to the Bar 1971, in Chambers of late Joseph Jackson QC 1972–78, Chambers of Sir David Calcutt QC 1978–82; admitted slr 1984, ptnr Burges Salmon Bristol 1984–; memb: Law Soc, Agricultural Law Assoc; *Books* contrib: Law of Agricultural Holdings (1989), Halsburys Laws of England, Butterworths Forms and Precedents Agriculture Volume; *Recreations* shooting, fishing, tennis, walking, skiing; *Clubs* Brooks's, St James's; *Style*— James Buxton, Esq; ✉ Galhampton Manor, Yeovil, Somerset BA22 7AL (tel 01963 440297); Narrow Quay House, Narrow Quay, Bristol BS1 4AH (tel 0117 939 2000, telex 44736, fax 0117 902 4400, car 07970 772918)

BUXTON, Hon (Aubrey) James Francis; yr s of Baron Buxton of Alsa, *qv*; *b* 20 March 1956; *Educ* Ampleforth, RAC Cirencester; *m* 1981, Melinda, da of Peter Henry Samuelson, of Clare, Suffolk; 2 da (Emma Lucie Maria b 1984, Olivia Louise b 1986), 1 s (Henry James Aubrey b 19 May 1988); *Career* sr ptnr Bidwells Property Consultants Cambridge; *Recreations* shooting, painting, vintage cars, music; *Clubs* White's, Norfolk (Norwich); *Style*— The Hon James Buxton; ✉ Church Farm, Carlton, Newmarket, Suffolk CB8 9LD (tel 01223 290511); Bidwells Property Consultants, Trumpington Road, Cambridge CB2 2LD (tel 01223 841841, fax 01223 559194, e-mail jbuxton@bidwells.co.uk)

BUXTON, Sir Jocelyn Charles Roden; 7 Bt (UK 1840), of Belfield, Dorset; VRD; s of Capt Roden Henry Victor Buxton, CBE, RN (d 1970), and his 1 w, Dorothy Alina. *née* St John (d 1956); suc kinsman, Sir Thomas Fowell Victor Buxton, 6 Bt (d 1996); *b* 8 August 1924; *m* 1960, Ann Frances, JP, da of Frank Smitherman, MBE; 3 da (Frances Dorothy (Mrs Henry Jones-Davies) b 1960, Harriet Lucy (Hon Mrs Michael Dalrymple) b 1962, Caroline Sarah (Mrs Nicholas Jarrett) b 1964); *Heir* bro, Gerard Buxton; *Career* WWII (despatches) Korea Lt Cdr RNVR; *Style*— Sir Jocelyn Buxton, Bt, VRD; ✉ Rodwell House, Loddon, Norwich, Norfolk

BUXTON, Hon Lucinda Catherine; 2 da of Baron Buxton of Alsa, KCVO, MC, DL (Life Peer), *qv*, and Pamela Mary, *née* Birkin; *b* 21 August 1950; *Educ* New Hall Sch Chelmsford; *Career* wildlife cinematographer/dir; has made 18 TV films for Survival Wildlife series and 3 TV films for Partridge Films Ltd; sr prodr Z-Axis Corporation 1997–, European conslt; vice-pres Concept 2 1999, ceo C2 Imaginations 2000–; tstee Falkland Islands Appeal; vice-pres: Falkland Islands Fndn, United Kingdom Falkland Islands Ctee; Media Award 1982, Cherry Kearton Award RGS 1983; FRGS; *Books* Survival in the Wild (1980), Survival - South Atlantic (1983); *Recreations* tennis, gardening; *Style*— The Hon Lucinda Buxton; ✉ 7 Vicarage Crescent, London SW11 3LP (tel 020 7350 1241, fax 020 7350 1243, mobile 07952 884249, e-mail cindy.buxton@zaxis.com)

BUXTON OF ALSA, Baron (Life Peer UK 1978), of Stiffkey in the County of Norfolk; Aubrey Leland Oakes Buxton; KCVO (1997), MC (1943), DL (Essex 1975); s of late Leland William Wilberforce Buxton, s of Sir Thomas Fowell Buxton, 3 Bt, GCMG, JP, DL; *b* 15 July 1918; *Educ* Ampleforth, Trinity Coll Cambridge; *m* 1946, Pamela Mary (d 1983), da of Sir Henry Ralph Stanley Birkin, 3 Bt, and widow of Maj Samuel Luckyn Buxton, MC, 17/21 Lancers; 2 s, 4 da; m 2, 16 July 1988, Mrs Kathleen Peterson, of Maine, USA; *Career* Maj Supplementary Reserves; chief exec Anglia TV Group (dir 1955–88, chm 1986–88), chm ITN 1981–86; pres RTS 1973–77, treas London Zoological Soc 1977–83, chm Survival Anglia 1986–92; memb: Countryside Cmmn, Royal Cmmn on Pollution, Nature Conservancy Cncl 1988–90; exec prodr of wildlife films; Queen's Award for Industry 1974; vice-pres Wildfowl and Wetlands Tst, WWF, RSPB; Extra Equerry to HRH The Duke of Edinburgh 1964–, High Sheriff Essex 1972; *Style*— The Rt Hon the Lord Buxton, KCVO, MC, DL; ✉ Old Hall Farm, Stiffkey, Wells-next-the-Sea, Norfolk NR23 1QJ (tel 01328 830351, fax 01328 830781)

BUZAN, Prof Barry Gordon; s of Gordon Buzan, and Jean, *née* Burn; *b* 28 April 1946; *Educ* Univ of Br Columbia (BA), LSE (PhD); *m* 1973, Deborah Skinner; *Career* computer trainee Honeywell UK 1970, research fell Inst of Int Rels Univ of Br Columbia 1973–75; Univ of Warwick: lectr 1976–83, sr lectr 1983–88, reader 1988–90, prof 1990–95; prof of int studies Univ of Westminster 1995–2002, prof of int rels LSE 2002–; visiting prof Grad Sch of Int Rels Int Univ of Japan 1995, Olof Palme visiting prof Sweden 1997–98, hon prof Univ of Copenhagen 2005–; British Int Studies Assoc: ed Newsletter 1980–83, vice-chm 1986–87, chm 1988–90; int vice-pres Int Studies Assoc 1993–94; project dir Copenhagen Peace Research Inst 1988–2003; memb: Editorial Ctee Review of Int Studies 1982–92, Int Advsy Bd Jl of Peace Research 1986–, Editorial Ctee Int Organization 1988–94, Int Advsy Bd Euro Jl of Int Relations 1994–2000, Int Advsy Bd Co-operation and Conflict 1997–; ed Millennium 1971–72, co-ed The New Int Relations 1991–2005, ed Euro Jl of Int Relations 2004–; Francis Deak Prize American Jl of Int Law 1982; FBA 1998, AcSS 2001; *Books* Seabed Politics (1976), Change and Study of International Relations: the Evaded Dimension (ed with R J Barry Jones, 1981), People States and Fear: the National Security Problem in International Relations (1983, revised edn 1991), South Asian Insecurity and the Great Powers (jtly, 1986), An Introduction to Strategic Studies: Military Technology and International Relations (1987), The International Politics of Deterrence (ed, 1987), The European Security Order Recast: Scenarios for the Post-Cold War Era (jtly, 1990), The Logic of Anarchy: Neorealism to Structural Realism (with Charles Jones and Richard Little, 1993), Identity, Migration and the New Security Agenda in Europe (jtly, 1993), The Mind Map Book (with Tony Buzan, 1993), Security: A New Framework for Analysis (jtly, 1998), Anticipating the Future: Twenty Millennia of Human Progress (with Gerald Segal, 1998), The Arms Dynamic in World Politics (with Eric Herring, 1998), International Systems in World History: Remaking the Study of International Relations (with Richard Little, 2000), Regions and Powers: The Structure of International Security (with Ole Waever, 2003), From International to World Society? English School Theory and the Social Structure of Globalization (2004), The United States and the Great Powers: World Politics in the Twenty-First Century (2004); also author of numerous articles, pamphlets and book chapters; *Recreations* chess, motorcycle touring, gardening; *Style*— Prof Barry Buzan, FBA, AcSS; ✉ Department of International Relations, London School of Economics and Political Science, Houghton Street, London WC2A 2AE (tel 020 7955 6176, fax 020 7955 7446, e-mail b.g.buzan@lse.ac.uk)

BUZZARD, Sir Anthony Farquhar; 3 Bt (UK 1929), of Munstead Grange, Godalming, Surrey; s of Rear Adm Sir Anthony Wass Buzzard, 2 Bt, CB, DSO, OBE (d 1972), and Margaret (d 1989), da of Sir Arthur Knapp, KCIE, CSI, CBE; *b* 28 June 1935; *Educ* Charterhouse, ChCh Oxford (MA), Ambassador Coll Pasadena (BA), Bethany Theological Coll (MA Th); *m* 1970, Barbara Jean, da of Gordon Arnold, of Michigan; 3 da (Sarah Jane b 1971, Claire Judith b 1974, Heather Elizabeth b 1988); *Heir* bro, Timothy Buzzard; *Career* modern languages teacher at American School in London 1974–81, lectr in theology Atlanta Bible Coll Morrow Georgia (formerly Oregon Bible Coll Illinois) 1982–; articles on Christology & Eschatology in various theological journals, fndr of Restoration Fellowship; speaker Focus on the Kingdom (radio worldwide); *Books* The Coming Kingdom of the Messiah: A Solution to the Riddle of the New Testament (1987), The Doctrine of the Trinity: Christianity's Self-Inflicted Wound (1994), Our Fathers Who Aren't in Heaven: The Forgotten Christianity of Jesus the Jew (1995), The Law, The Sabbath and New Testament Christianity (2005), The Amazing Aims and Claims of Jesus: What You Didn't Learn in Church (2006), Jesus was not a Trinitarian: Recovering the Creed of Jesus (2007); *Recreations* music, tennis; *Style*— Sir Anthony Buzzard, Bt; ✉ 175 West Lake Drive, Fayetteville, GA 30214, USA (tel 00 1 770 964 1571, fax 00 1 770 964 1571, e-mail anthonybuzzard@mindspring.com, website www.restorationfellowship.org)

BYATT, Andrew Keir Campbell; *b* 1 October 1959; *Educ* Wellington, Univ of Bristol (BSc), UCL (MSc), CNAA; *Career* BBC: prodr The Swarm (part of Wildlife on One series) 1992–93 (festival winner Semina Internacional de Cine Cientifico Palme D'Or Antibes Underwater Film Festival 1994), prodr Really Wild Guide to Britain 1994, prodr Besieged (part of Wildlife on One series) 1994–95 (Wildscreen Best Series 1998), prodr Incredible Journeys 1995–96, prodr The Humpback - Seiner of the Sea (part of Wildlife on One Specials series) 1995–97, prodr The Blue Planet 1998–2001 (Best Documentary Series BPG TV Awards 2002, Best TV Prog Radio and TV Viewers Choice 2002, Documentary Prog of the Year TRIC Awards 2002, Diver of the Year Diver Magazine 2002), series prodr Monsters We Met 2001–02, co-dir Deep Blue (cinematic release of The Blue Planet) 2002–03, series prodr Amazon Abyss 2005, prodr Ocean Deep (part of Planet Earth series) 2006; head of dive team BBC Natural History Unit 1995–; FGS; *Publications* The Blue Planet (WHSmith Illustrated Book of the Year 2002, Best Educnl Book Br Book Awards 2002, Pubn of the Year Diver Magazine 2002); *Recreations* diving, sailing, skiing and ski mountaineering, photography; *Style*— Andrew Byatt, Esq

BYATT, Dame Antonia Susan (A S Byatt); DBE (1999, CBE 1990); da of His Hon Judge John Frederick Drabble, QC (d 1983), and Kathleen Marie Bloor (d 1984); *b* 24 August 1936; *m* 1, 1959 (m dis 1969), Sir Ian Byatt, *qv*; 1 da (Antonia b 1960), 1 s (Charles b 1961 d 1972); m 2, 1969, Peter John Duffy; 2 da (Isabel b 1970, Miranda b 1973); *Career* teacher: Westminster Tutors 1962–65, Extra-mural Dept Univ of London 1962–71; pt/t lectr Dept of Lib Studies Central Sch of Art and Design 1965–69, lectr Dept of English UCL 1972–81, tutor for admissions Dept of English UCL 1980–82 (asst tutor 1977–80), sr lectr Dept of English UCL 1981–83; full-time writer 1983–; regular reviewer and contrib to press, radio and TV; external assessor in lit Central Sch of Art and Design, external examiner UEA; judge Booker Prize 1974; chm Ctee of Mgmnt Soc of Authors 1984–88 (chair 1986–88); memb: Panel of Judges Hawthornden Prize, BBC's Social Effects of TV Advsy Gp 1974–77, Communications and Cultural Studies Bd CNAA 1978–84, Creative and Performing Arts Bd 1985–87, Kingman Ctee on English Language 1987–88, Advsy Bd Harold Hyam Wingate Fellowship 1988–92, Lit Advsy Panel Br Cncl 1990–98, London Library Ctee 1990–, Bd Br Cncl 1993–98; assoc Newnham Coll Cambridge 1977–82; Premio Malaparte Award Capri 1995, Mythopoeic Fantasy Award for Adult Literature (for The Djinn in the Nightingale's Eye) 1998, Toepfer Fndn Shakespeare Prize for contributions to British Culture 2002; Hon DLitt: Univ of Bradford 1987, Univ of Durham 1991, Univ of York 1991, Univ of Nottingham 1992, Univ of Liverpool 1993, Univ of Portsmouth 1994, Univ of London 1995, Univ of Cambridge 1999, Univ of Sheffield 2000; hon fell: Newnham Coll Cambridge 1999, London Inst 2000, UCL 2004, Univ of Kent 2004; fell English Assoc 2004, FRSL; Chevalier de l'Ordre des Arts et des Lettres (France) 2003; *Books* as A S Byatt: The Shadow of the Sun (1964, reisssued 1991), Degrees of Freedom (1965, reissued 1994), The Game (1967), Wordsworth and Coleridge in their Time (1970, reissued as Unruly Times 1989), The Virgin in the Garden (1978), Still Life (1985, PEN Macmillan Silver Pen of Fiction), Sugar and Other Stories (1987), Possession: A Romance (1990, Booker Prize, Irish Times/Aer Lingus Int Fiction Prize, filmed 2002), George Eliot: The Mill on the Floss (ed), George Eliot: Selected Essays and Other Writings (ed, 1990), Passions of The Mind (essays, 1991), Angels and Insects (1992, filmed 1996), The Matisse Stories (1993), The Djinn in the Nightingale's Eye: Five Fairy Stories (1994), Imagining Characters (with Ignês Sodré, 1995), Babel Tower (1996), The Oxford Book of English Short Stories (ed, 1998), Elementals: Stories of Fire and Ice (1998), The Biographer's Tale (2000), On Histories and Stories (2000), Ovid Metamorphosed (contrib, 2000), Portraits in Fiction (2001), The Bird Hand Book (jtly, 2001), A Whistling Woman (2002), Little Black Book of Stories (short stories, 2003), O Henry Prize Stories (contrib short story The Thing in the Forest, 2003); author of varied literary criticism, articles, prefaces, reviews and broadcasts; *Style*— Dame Antonia Byatt, DBE, FRSL; ✉ c/o Rogers, Coleridge and White, 20 Powis Mews, London W11 1JN

BYATT, Sir Ian Charles Rayner; kt (2000); s of Charles Rayner Byatt (d 1944), and Enid Marjorie Annie, *née* Howat (d 1977); *b* 11 March 1932; *Educ* Kirkham GS, St Edmund Hall Oxford, Nuffield Coll Oxford (BA, DPhil), Harvard Univ; *m* 1, 4 July 1959 (m dis 1969), Antonia Susan (Dame Antonia Byatt, DBE, FRSL, *qv*), da of His Hon Judge J F Drabble, QC (d 1982); 1 da ((Helen) Antonia b 1960), 1 s (Charles Nicholas John b 1961, d 1972); m 2, 12 Dec 1997, Prof Deirdre Kelly, da of Francis Kelly (d 1998); 2 step s (Eoin Matthew Parker b 1978, Lochlinn Francis Parker b 1980); *Career* serv RAF 1950–52; lectr in economics Univ of Durham 1958–62, economic conslt HM Treasy 1962–64, lectr LSE 1964–67, sr economic advsr DES 1967–69, dir of economics and statistics Miny of Housing (later DOE) 1969–72, dep chief economic advsr HM Treasy 1978–89 (head of public sector 1972–78), DG of Water Servs 1989–2000, co sec-gen Fndn for Int Studies on Social Security 2001–02; sr assoc Frontier Economics 2000–; memb Productivity Panel HM Treasy 2000–06; vice-pres Strategic Planning Soc 1993–; chm Water Industry Cmmn for Scotland 2005–; memb: Cncl of Mgmnt NIESR 1996–2002, Bd of Advsrs St Edmund Hall Oxford 1998–2003, Bd of Mgmnt Int Inst of Public Fin 2000–06, Cncl Regulatory Policy Inst 2001–07, Advsy Panel to Water Industry Cmmr for Scot 2002–04, Advsy Panel on Reform of Water Servs in NI 2003–06; govr Birkbeck Coll London 1997–2005, pres Human City Inst Birmingham 1999–2002, tstee Acad of Youth 2001–05; chm Friends of Birmingham Cathedral 1999–, memb Cncl Birmingham Cathedral 2003–; memb Holy Cross Centre Tst 1983–2002 (patron 2006–); Freeman City of London; fell Birkbeck Coll London; Hon DUniv: Brunel, Central England; Hon DSc: Aston Univ, Univ of Birmingham; memb Royal Econ Soc, CIMgt, Hon FIWEM; *Books* British Electrical Industry 1875–1914 (1979); *Recreations* painting and married life; *Clubs* Oxford and Cambridge; *Style*— Sir Ian Byatt; ✉ 34 Frederick Road, Birmingham B15 1JN (tel 0121 689 7946, fax 0121 454 6438, e-mail ianbyatt@blueyonder.co.uk); Water Industry Commission for Scotland, Ochil House, Spring Kerse Business Park, Stirling FK7 7XE (tel 01786 430200, fax 01786 430180, e-mail ian.byatt@watercommission.co.uk); Frontier Economics, 71 High Holborn, London WC1V 6DA (tel 020 7031 7067, fax 020 7031 7001, e-mail ian.byatt@frontier-economics.com)

BYERS, His Hon Judge the Hon Charles William; o s of Baron Byers, OBE, PC, DL (Life Peer, d 1984), and Joan (Lady Byers, d 1998); *b* 24 March 1949; *Educ* Westminster, ChCh Oxford; *m* 1, 8 July 1972 (m dis 1995), Suzan Mary, o da of Aubrey Kefford Stone (d 1980); 2 s (Jonathan Charles b 11 April 1975, George William b 19 Nov 1977); m 2, 10 Feb 2002, Mary Louise Elizabeth Ilett, da of John Ilett, of Hyde, Cheshire; *Career* called to the Bar Gray's Inn 1973; recorder of the Crown Court 1993–99, circuit judge (SE Circuit) 1999–; *Recreations* craft, the countryside, sailing, water skiing; *Style*— His Hon Judge the Hon Charles Byers; ✉ Blackfriars Crown Court, Pocock Street, London SE1 0BS

BYERS, Stephen John; PC (1998), MP; s of late Robert Byers; *b* 13 April 1953; *Educ* Chester City GS, Chester Coll of FE, Liverpool Poly (LLB); *Career* sr lectr in law Newcastle Poly 1977–92; Parly candidate (Lab) Hexham 1983, MP (Lab): Wallsend 1992–97, Tyneside N 1997– chm PLP Home Affairs Ctee 1992–94, oppn whip 1994–95, oppn spokesman on Educn and Employment 1995–97, min of State Dept for Educn and Employment (school standards) 1997–98, chief sec to the Treasy 1998, sec of state for Trade and Industry 1998–2001, sec of state for Tport, Local Govt and the Regions 2001–02; N Tyneside MBC: cncllr 1980–92, chm Educn Cee 1982–85, dep ldr 1985–92; chm Educn Ctee Assoc of Met Authorities 1990–92, ldr Cncl of Local Educn Authorities 1990–92, chm Nat Employers' Orgn for Teachers 1990–92, ldr Mgmnt Panel Nat Jt Cncl for FE 1990–92; memb: NATFHE 1975–84, NUPE 1984–; FRSA; *Recreations* cinema, travel, theatre, walking; *Style*— The Rt Hon Stephen Byers, MP; ✉ House of Commons, London SW1A 0AA (tel 020 7219 4085)

BYFIELD, Stephen Keith; s of Keith James Byfield, of Richmond, N Yorks, and Patricia Betty, *née* Smith; *b* 29 April 1963; *Educ* Richmond Sch, Univ of Leeds (BA); *m* 3 Aug 1991, Valérie Amparro Lucienne, da of Robert Legras; 2 da (Sophie b 1987, Heloïse b 1995), 1 s (Christopher b 1996); *Career* political researcher 1983; with Ian Greer Associates 1985–87, dir Profile Political Relations Ltd 1987–90, fndr and md PPS Group Ltd 1990–; *Recreations* exercise and sports; *Clubs* RAC; *Style*— Stephen Byfield, Esq; ✉ PPS Group, 69 Grosvenor Street, London W1K 3JW (tel 020 7529 1700, fax 020 7629 7514, mobile 07836 611503, e-mail stephen.byfield@ppsgroup.co.uk)

BYFIELD, Trevor Mills (Zig); s of Col Charles William Byfield, and Kathleen Florence, *née* Duggins; *b* 20 October 1943; *Educ* Preston GS; *m* 5 March 1966, Janet Yvonne, da of Richard Douglas Offor; 2 s (Dean Trevor b 20 March 1967, Adam Trevor b 12 June 1970); *Career* actor; mktg conslt for Neways; *Theatre* incl: Hair (West End), Jesus Christ Superstar, Mother Earth (Round House), The Rocky Horror Show; *Television* incl: Cats Eyes, Minder, The Professionals, The Gentle Touch, Dempsey and Makepeace, Metal Mickey, New Scotland Yard, The Lotus Eaters, Bust, The Manageress, The Bill, El CID, A Wanted Man, Birds of a Feather, The Chief, Lovejoy, Inspector Morse, Only Fools and Horses, Chancer, Rides, One Foot in the Grave, So Haunt Me, Fool's Gold, Bermuda Grace, Boon, Between the Lines, Casualty, Pale Horse, Crocodile Shoes, Thieftakers, The Knock, Taggart, Junk; *Films* incl: Who Dares Wins, Shock Treatment, Riding High, Slayground, Crime in the City, Wolves of Willoughby Chase, Pleasure, Goldeneye; *Albums* incl: Running, Yesterday's Dreams; composer Virgin Warrior; *Recreations* gardening, cooking, raising the awareness and credibility of the network marketing industry; *Style*— Zig Byfield, Esq; ✉ c/o Richard Ireson, The Narrow Road Company, 182 Bright Road, Coulsdon, Surrey CR5 2NF (tel 020 8763 9895, e-mail richardireson@narrowroad.co.uk)

B

BYFORD, Baroness (Life Peer UK 1996), of Rothley in the County of Leicestershire; Hazel Byford; DBE (1994); da of Sir Cyril Osborne MP, and Lady Osborne; *Educ* St Leonard's Sch St Andrews, Moulton Agric Coll Northampton; *m* 1962, C Barrie Byford; 1 da, 1 s (decd); *Career* former farmer; Cons shadow minister for food, farming and rural affrs House of Lords 1998–2007 (shadow minister for environment 1998–2003); *Recreations* golf, reading, bridge; *Clubs* Farmers'; *Style*— The Rt Hon the Baroness Byford, DBE; ✉ House of Lords, London SW1A 0PW (tel 020 7219 3095, e-mail byfordh@parliament.uk)

BYFORD, Mark; s of Sir Lawrence Byford, CBE, QPM, DL, and Muriel, *née* Massey; *b* 13 June 1958; *Educ* Lincoln Christ's Hosp Sch, Univ of Leeds (LLB); *m* Hilary Bleiker; 2 s (Sam b 1986, Harry b 1994), 3 da (Molly b 1988, Flora b 1992, Lily b 1996); *Career* regnl journalist BBC North 1979–82, asst news ed BBC South 1982–87, news ed BBC West 1987–88, home news ed BBC News and Current Affrs 1988–89, head of centre Leeds BBC North 1989–90; BBC Regnl Broadcasting: asst controller 1990–91, controller 1991–94, dep md 1994–96, dir of regnl broadcasting BBC Broadcast 1996–98; dir BBC World Service 1998–2002, dir BBC World Serv and Global News 2002–04, dep DG BBC 2004–; memb RTS, fell Radio Acad 2000; *Recreations* family life, entertaining close friends, football (esp Leeds United FC and Southampton FC), cricket (esp Yorks CCC), rock music, tennis, swimming, fell walking, cinema, theatre, visiting cathedrals, collecting rock memorabilia; *Clubs* Yorks CCC; *Style*— Mark Byford, Esq; ✉ Bolberry House, 1 Clifton Hill, Winchester SO22 5BL (tel 01962 860197, fax 01962 860944); BBC, Room MC4 A1, Media Centre, Media Village, 201 Wood Lane, London W12 7TQ (tel 020 8008 5900, fax 020 8008 5906, e-mail mark.byford@bbc.co.uk)

BYGRAVE, Clifford; s of Fred Bygrave (d 1993), of Caddington, Beds, and Beatrice Rose Bygrave (d 2006); *b* 24 May 1934; *Educ* Luton GS; *m* 15 July 1961, Jean Elizabeth, da of Edward Neale (d 1986); 3 da (Angela Joy b 1964, Paula Jane b 1968, Heather Alison b 1972); *Career* RNVR 1955–59; chartered accountant; ptnr: Hillier Hills Frary & Co 1962–81, Arthur Young (now Ernst & Young) 1981–96, sole practitioner 1996–; memb: Mgmnt Ctee Beds, Bucks and Herts Soc of Chartered Accountants 1971– (pres 1975–76, 1993–94, 2005–06 and 2006–07), Cncl ICAEW 1980–2003; non-exec dir Luton and Dunstable Hosp NHS Tst, and other companies; tstee of a number of local charitable tsts; Freeman City of London, Clerk Worshipful Co of Chartered Accountants; FCA 1958, ATII 1964; *Recreations* golf, soccer; *Clubs* Farmers', Dunstable Downs Rotary, Ashridge Golf; *Style*— Clifford Bygrave, Esq; ✉ The Rustlings, Valley Close, Studham, Dunstable, Bedfordshire LU6 2QN (tel 01582 872070, fax 01582 872070, e-mail clerk@wccaew.org.uk)

BYLES, David Warner; s of Charles Humphrey Gilbert Byles (d 1970), of Kemsing, Kent, and Pamela Beatrice Byles; *b* 6 April 1954; *Educ* Sevenoaks Sch, Univ of Kent (BA); *m* 1981, Susan Jane, da of Edward Fowles; 1 da (Jennifer Mary b 1985), 1 s (Thomas Edward b 1988); *Career* advtg exec; asst to Co Sec HP Drewry (Shipping Consultants) Ltd 1976–77; Benton & Bowles: graduate trainee 1977–78, media exec 1978–79, media gp head 1979–81; J Walter Thompson: dep media gp mangr 1981–82, media gp mangr 1982–83, asst media dir 1983–87, bd dir media 1987–89, media dir 1989–95, media dir Latin America (Mexico) and worldwide media dir working on Kellogg's account 1995–; accounts handled for JWT incl: Nestlé Rowntree, NatWest, Thomson Holidays, St Ivel, Kellogg; RAF Special Flying award 1970–71; memb RSPB 1985, MIPA 1988; *Recreations* ornithology, motorcycling, scuba diving; *Clubs* RAC; *Style*— David Byles, Esq

BYLLAM-BARNES, Joseph Charles Felix Byllam; s of Cyril Charles Byllam-Barnes (d 1976), of Ashtead, Surrey, and Barbara Isabel Mary, *née* Walls (d 2003); *b* 30 August 1928; *Educ* The Modern Sch Streatham, Shaftesbury, City of London Freemen's Sch; *m* 1 April 1978, Maureen Margaret Mary, da of Maj Claude Montague Castle, MC (d 1940), of Hampstead, London; *Career* RAMC 1946–49, i/c Mil and Public Health Servs Eritrea 1948–49; with Barclays Bank plc 1945–92 (Head Office inspr 1976–92); banking law conslt 1992–2000; elected memb Ct of Common Cncl City of London 1997–2004; govr City of London Freemen's Sch 1999–2004; vice-pres and hon sec Royal Soc of St George City of London Branch (chm 1994–95); pres: Farringdon Ward Club 1990–91, United Wards Club of the City of London 2002–03, Ward of Cheap Club 2003–04, City Livery Club 2005–06 (hon sec 1996–98); vice-chm London Rivers Assoc 2001–04; memb: Bluebell Railway Preservation Soc, Brighton Atlantic Project Ctee 2000–, Castle Baynards Ward Club, HAC, RUSI, IOD; Oblate Quarr Abbey 1963; Freeman City of London 1983, Master Guild of Freemen of the City of London 2000–01 (memb Ct of Assts 1990); Liveryman: Worshipful Co of Upholders 1984 (treas 1985, memb Ct of Assts 1986, Master 1993–94), Worshipful Co of Fletchers 1995; Freeman Guild of Int Bankers 2001; FCIB, FFA, FRSA; *Recreations* music, opera, study of law and theology; *Clubs* Carlton, Guards Polo, City Livery Yacht (ctee memb), Surrey CCC; *Style*— Joseph Byllam-Barnes, Esq; ✉ Walsingham House, Oldfield Gardens, Ashtead, Surrey KT21 2NA (tel 01372 277667, fax 01372 271533, e-mail byllambarnes@waitrose.com)

BYNOE, Ian Kellman; s of Harold Gore Bynoe (d 1970), and Sheila Mary, *née* Hay (d 2007); *b* 6 March 1953, Leamington Spa, Warks; *Educ* Monkton Combe Sch, Univ of Durham (BA), Coll of Law Guildford; *m* 22 April 1995, Denise, *née* Stevens; *Career* admitted slr 1977; slr Small Heath Community Law Centre Birmingham 1977–81, asst slr then ptnr David Gray & Co Slrs 1981–87, slr Springfield Advice and Law Centre Springfield Psychiatric Hosp London 1988, legal offr then legal dir and head Legal Dept MIND (Nat Assoc for Mental Health) 1988–94, self-employed public policy researcher (incl for IPPR), legal and practice trainer and conslt, and pt/t slr Scott Moncrieff, Harbour and Sinclair 1994–98; Police Complaints Authy: memb 1998–2001, second dep chm 2001–02, first dep chm 2002–04; cmmr Ind Police Complaints Cmmn 2004–; memb: Mental Health and Disability Sub-Ctee Law Soc 1989–94, BMA Working Party on the Health Needs of Remand Prisoners 1989–91, Legal and Parly Ctee Royal Assoc for Disability and Rehabilitation 1990–93, Ctee of Patrons (formerly Bd of Dirs) Revolving Doors Agency 1991–, Mentally Disordered Offender Sub-Ctee Mental Health Fndn 1992–94, Nat Advsy Ctee on Mentally Disordered Offenders Home Office/Dept of Health 1993–94, Working Party on Code of Practice on Advocacy with Older People Centre for Policy on Ageing 1994–95, Ind Ctee on the Role and Responsibilities of the Police Policy Studies Inst/Police Fndn 1993–96, Ctee on Reform of Coroners' Servs Liberty/Inquest 2002, Home Office Review of Misconduct Action Against Ethnic Minority Police Offrs 2002–03; memb: Legal Action Gp 1974, Law Soc 1977; FRSA 1993; *Publications* Equal Rights for Disabled People: The case for a new law (jtly, 1991), Treatment, Care and Security: Waiting for change (1992), Beyond the Citizen's Charter: New directions in social rights (1996), How to Comply with the Disability Discrimination Act 1995: An essential guide for solicitors (1997), Rights to Fair Treatment (1997), A Human Rights Commission: The options for

Britain and Northern Ireland (jtly, 1998), Mainstreaming Human Rights in Whitehall and Westminster (jtly, 1999); contrib of chapters to books and author of articles in jls and professional and nat press; *Recreations* cycling, walking, classical music; *Style*— Ian Bynoe, Esq; ✉ Brook House, Prestleigh Lane, Prestleigh, Shepton Mallet, Somerset BA4 4NG (tel 01749 830810); Independent Police Complaints Commission, Eastern Business Park, Wern Fawr Lane, St Mellons, Cardiff CF3 5EA (tel 029 2024 5403, fax 020 7166 3822, e-mail ian.bynoe@ipcc.gsi.gov.uk)

BYRNE, Anthony John; s of Benjamin James Byrne, of Dublin, and Ruby Anne, *née* O'Brien (d 1975); *b* 9 August 1947; *Educ* Oakham Sch, Lancaster Univ, Univ of Colorado, Sidney Sussex Coll Cambridge; *m* 5 Sept 1971, Kathy, da of Carl Strain, of Denver, Colorado; 2 da (Rachel, Jenny); *Career* PA to gen mangr Central Lancs Devpt Corp 1973–77, Inst of Advanced Architectural Studies Univ of York 1977–78, dir Bicentenary of the Iron Bridge Ironbridge Gorge Museum Tst 1978, project dir Watershed Media Centre Bristol 1980–83, dir Bristol Mktg Bd 1983–87, dir BAFTA 1987–94, dir of devpt CCC Cambridge 1994–2000, exec dir of devpt Sea Cadets 2001–; chm Sci-Tech Film and TV Festivals 1987 and 1989; tstee Brunel Tst Temple Meads Bristol; Parly candidate (Lab) Rutland and Stamford 1972–74; *Style*— Anthony Byrne, Esq

BYRNE, John Edward Thomas; s of John Byrne (d 1979), and Violet Mary, *née* Harris (d 1999); *b* 16 February 1935; *Educ* Kilkenny Coll, Mountjoy Sch Dublin, Trinity Coll Dublin (BA, MB BCh, BAO); *m* 23 Nov 1963, Margaret Elizabeth Ross, da of William Albert Wilson (d 1975); 2 da (Katharine b 1969, Johanna b 1971); *Career* house surgn and house physician Dr Steeven's Hosp Dublin 1961–62, fell in otology Wayne State Univ Detroit 1973, conslt in otolaryngology Belfast City Hosp 1974–2000, civilian conslt in otolaryngology HM Forces NI 1974–; external examiner to constituent colls Nat Univ of Ireland, examiner RCSI (otolaryngology), author of various pubns on blast injury to ears; memb: ORS, Irish Otolaryngological Soc (hon ed Proceedings 1974–93, pres 1994), Ulster Med Soc, Br Cochlear Implant Gp, TCD Assoc, RSM; FRCSI 1970; *Books* Scott/Brown's Otolaryngology (contrib, 1997); *Recreations* sailing, maritime history, gardening, theatre; *Clubs* Kildare St and Univ, Strangford Lough Yacht; *Style*— John Byrne, Esq; ✉ Mulroy Lodge, Ballymenoch Park, Holywood BT18 0LP (tel 028 9042 3374, e-mail jetb@btinternet.com)

BYRNE, Liam; MP; *b* 2 October 1970; *Educ* Univ of Manchester, Harvard Business Sch (Fulbright Scholar); *m* Sarah; 3 c (Alex, John, Elizabeth); *Career* joined Lab Pty 1985; began career at Andersen Consulting, moving to NM Rothschilds, co-fndr EGS Gp 2000; advsr Lab Pty 1996–97; MP (Lab) Birmingham Hodge Hill 2004– (by-election), Parly under sec of state for care services 2005–06, min of state Home Office 2006–; memb: Amicus, Fabian Soc, Co-op Soc; assoc fell Social Market Fndn; *Style*— Liam Byrne, Esq, MP; ✉ House of Commons, London SW1A 0AA

BYRNE, Lisa; da of Narinder Palta, of York, and Philomena, *née* Fleming (d 2001); *b* 12 April 1970, Shrewsbury, Salop; *Educ* Bar Convent Sch York, Goldsmiths Coll London; *m* 18 March 2006, David Byrne; *Career* OK! magazine: feature writer 1998–, dep ed 2002–04, ed 2004–; freelance writer: Mail on Sunday, Sunday Mirror, Sunday People, Chat; fundraiser for Children with Leukaemia; *Recreations* walking the dog (cocker spaniel called Diggerley), social events, theatre; *Style*— Mrs Lisa Byrne; ✉ The Northern & Shell Building, Number 10 Lower Thames Street, London EC3R 6EN (tel 0871 520 7066, fax 0871 434 7305, email lisa.byrne@express.co.uk)

BYRNE, His Hon Judge Michael David; s of late Gerard Robert Byrne, and Margaret Doreen, *née* Charlton; *b* 7 December 1945; *Educ* St Edward's Coll Liverpool, Univ of Liverpool (BA, LLB); *m* 1985, Felicity Jane, *née* Davies; *Career* called to the Bar 1971; barr 1971–2002, recorder 1992–2002 (asst recorder 1989–92), circuit judge (Northern Circuit) 2002–; non-exec dir Ashworth Special Hosp 1996–97 (chm Mangrs Advsy Ctee 1989–98), vice-chm Ashworth Special HA 1997–98; chm of govrs St Edward's Coll Liverpool 1995– (govr 1993–); *Recreations* music, literature, theatre, travel; *Style*— His Hon Judge Byrne; ✉ Preston Combined Court Centre, The Law Courts, Ring Way, Preston PR1 2LL

BYRNE, (James) Shane; s of Arthur Patrick Byrne, of Aughrim, Co Wicklow, and Elizabeth Christine, *née* Hanlon; *b* 18 July 1971, Dublin; *Educ* Blackrock Coll Dublin, Dundalk Inst of Technol, Dublin Inst of Technol; *m* 8 June 2001, Caroline, *née* Patterson; 2 da (Alex Josephine, Kerry Elizabeth (twins) b 4 Oct 2002); *Career* professional rugby player (hooker) 1996–; clubs: Blackrock Coll RFC 1990–92, Leinster 1991–2005 (over 130 appearances, most capped player), Saracens RFC 2005–; Ireland: 41 caps, debut v Romania 2001, memb squad World Cup 1995 and SA 2003, winners Triple Crown 2004; Barbarians 4 caps; memb British and Irish Lions touring squad NZ 2005 (3 test caps); dir: Arklow Waste Disposal 2001–, Pride Sports & Leisure 2003–; ptnr Focus Int

Property 2006–; *Recreations* golf; *Style*— Mr Shane Byrne; ✉ Cedar Lodge, Redbourn Lane, Harpenden, Herts AL5 2NA (tel 07725 142222, fax 01582 764884, e-mail shanebyrne2@eircom.net); c/o Saracens, Rigby House, 34 The Parade, High Street, Watford WD17 1EA

BYROM, Peter John; s of John Byrom (d 1988), and Mary, *née* Hinch (d 2004); *b* 23 June 1944; *Educ* Perse Sch, Univ of Southampton (BSc); *m* 2 June 1987, Melanie Signe, da of John Palmer; 3 da (Nicola Christa b 20 June 1987, Olivia Signe b 31 March 1989, Serena Melanie b 1 Oct 1993); *Career* Arthur Andersen & Co 1966–72; chm: Leeds Life Assurance Ltd 1994–96, Domino Printing Sciences plc 1996–, Molins plc 1999–; dep chm T&N plc 1989–96; dir: N M Rothschild & Sons Ltd 1972–96, Peter Black Holdings plc 1984–2001, Adwest Group plc 1989–94, China Investment Trust plc 1995–98, Rolls-Royce plc 1997–, Wilson Bowden plc 1998–2007, Amec plc 2005–; tstee Southampton Univ Devpt Tst 1998–; Freeman City of London 1989, Liveryman Worshipful Co of Goldsmiths 1993; FCA, FRAeS 1999; *Clubs* Bosham Sailing, Kandahar Ski; *Style*— Peter Byrom, Esq; ✉ Chalton Priory, Chalton, Hampshire PO8 0BG (tel 023 9257 0700, fax 023 9259 6591)

BYROM, Richard John; s of Richard Byrom (d 1961), of Bury, and Bessie, *née* Jardin; *b* 12 October 1939; *Educ* Denstone Coll, Univ of Manchester (BA, MPhil); *m* 4 April 1964, Susan Hope, da of Richard Clegg (d 1984), of Gwydir; 2 s (Peter b 1965, David b 1967), 1 da (Joy b 1968); *Career* private architectural practice 1964–, Byrom Clark Roberts Architects Surveyors and Consulting Engrs Manchester 1989–; chm RIBA Register Architects Accredited in Building Conservation 2003–; practising arbitrator; ISVA: chm Building Surveying Ctee 1986–90, chm Manchester and Dist Branch 1995; JP 1973–2000; reader Hawkshaw Parish Church 1964–; memb: Manchester Soc of Architects, Soc of Construction Law, Towpath Action Gp; govr Bolton Sch 1997–; RIBA 1965 (chm President's Ctee on Arbitration 1999–2002), FCIArb 1977 (chm NW Branch CIArb 1998–2000), FSVA 1976, FRICS 2000; *Recreations* industrial archaeology, antiquarian books; *Clubs* St James's (Manchester); *Style*— Richard J Byrom, Esq; ✉ Byrom Clark Roberts Ltd, Washbrook House, Old Trafford, Manchester M32 0FP (tel 0161 875 0600)

BYRON, 13 Baron (E 1643); Robert James Byron; 2 (but only surviving) s of 12 Baron Byron (d 1989), and his 2 w, Dorigen Margaret, *née* Esdaile (d 1985); *b* 5 April 1950; *Educ* Wellington, Trinity Coll Cambridge; *m* 1979, Robyn Margaret, da of John McLean, of Hamilton, NZ; 3 da (Hon Caroline b 1981, Hon Emily b 1984, Hon Sophie b 1986), 1 s (Hon Charles Richard Gordon b 1990); *Heir* s, Hon Charles Byron; *Career* barr 1974; admitted slr 1978; ptnr Holman Fenwick & Willan 1984–; *Style*— The Rt Hon the Lord Byron; ✉ Holman Fenwick & Willan, Marlow House, Lloyds Avenue, London EC3N 3AL

BYWATER, Isabella; da of Tom Stacey, of London, and Caroline, *née* Clay; *b* 6 October 1957; *Educ* Tunbridge Wells Girls GS, Godolphin & Latymer Sch, Cambridge Coll of Arts and Technol, Motley Sch of Theatre Design; *m* 1 (m dis), Michael Bywater, s of Dr Keith Bywater; 1 da (Benedicta May b 12 July 1984); *m* 2, Christopher Simon Sykes, s of late Sir Richard Sykes; *Career* opera and theatre designer; former: prop maker, scene painter; *Theatre* designs incl: Titus Andronicus 1987, A Midsummer Night's Dream 1992, A Doll's House 1992, Of Mice and Men 1992, The Tempest 1993, All My Sons 1993, School for Wives 1993, Twelfth Night 1994, Hedda Gabler 1996, The Cherry Orchard (Crucible Theatre Sheffield) 2007; *Opera* UK prodns incl: The Barber of Seville 1982, Nabucco 1982, Il Tabarro 1983, Soeur Angelica 1983, Gianni Schicci 1983, The Turn of The Screw 1983, Eugene Onegin 1984, Andrea Chenier 1984, The Flying Dutchman 1987, Belshazzar 1987, The Duenna 1991, Madama Butterfly 1992, La Finta Giardinera 1994, King Arthur 1995, The Marriage of Figaro 1996, The Elixir of Love 1996, The Emperor of Atlantis 1997, The Dictator 1997, Il Re Pastore 1999, Snegourochka 2001; overseas prodns incl: Cavalleria Rusticana (Stockholm Royal Opera) 1991, Pagliacci (Stockholm Royal Opera) 1991, The Elixir of Love (W Aust Opera, Qland Opera and Victoria State Opera) 1995, Ezio (Theatre des Champs Elysees Paris) 1995, La Traviata (Opera NI Belfast) 1996, Fidelio (Opera NI Belfast) 1996, The Masked Ball (Opera Monte Carlo) 1998, Nabucco (Zurich Opera) 1998, I Puritani (Bayerischer Staatsoper Munich) 2000, Ermione (Santa Fe Opera) 2000, Don Pasquale (Teatro Maggio Musicale di Firenze) 2001, Eugene Onegin (Santa Fe Opera) 2002, The Makropulos Case (Stockholm Royal Opera) 2003, Die Entführung aus dem Serail (Zurich Opera) 2003, L'Elisir D'Amore (Stockholm Royal Opera) 2003, Falstaff (New Nat Theatre Tokyo) 2004, Don Pasquale (Covent Garden Opera) 2004, Clemenza di Tito (Zurich Opera) 2005, Entführung aus dem Serail (Ancona) 2005, Jenufa (Glimmerglass USA) 2006, L'Elisir d'Amore (NYC Opera) 2006, Der Rosenkavalier (New Nat Theatre Tokyo) 2007, Fidelio (Aarhus) 2007; *Recreations* portrait sculpture, philosophy, gardening; *Style*— Ms Isabella Bywater; ✉ c/o Judy Daish, 2 St Charles Place, London W10 6EG (tel 020 8964 8811)

C

CABEZAS, HE Eduardo; *m* Berta; *Career* diplomat; ambass to the Ct of St James's 2003–; *Style—* HE Mr Eduardo Cabezas; ✉ Embassy of Ecuador, Flat 3B, 3 Hans Crescent, London SW1X 0LS

CABLE, Dr (John) Vincent (Vince); MP; s of (John) Leonard Cable (d 1981), and Edith, *née* Pinkney; *b* 9 May 1943, York; *Educ* Nunthorpe GS York, Univ of Cambridge (BA, pres Cambridge Union), Univ of Glasgow (PhD); *m* 1 Maria Olympia, *née* Rebelo (d 2001); 2 s (Paul, Hugo), 1 da (Aida); m 2, 2004, Rachel *née* Wenban Smith; *Career* fin offr Kenya Treasy (ODI/Nuffield fell) 1966–68, lectr in econs Univ of Glasgow 1968–74, first sec Diplomatic Serv 1974–76, dep dir Overseas Devpt Inst 1976–83, special advsr to late Rt Hon John Smith, MP as Sec of State for Trade 1979, special advsr (dir) Cwlth Secretariat 1983–90, advsr to Brundtland Cmmn on environment and devpt 1986, head Socio-Economic Studies Gp Planning Shell 1990–93, head Econs Prog Chatham House 1993–95, chief economist Shell (International) 1995–97, MP (Lib Dem) Twickenham 1997–; memb Treasy Select Ctee 1999, trade and industry spokesman Lib Dems 1999–2003, Lib Dem shadow Chllr of the Exchequer 2004–, dep ldr 2006–, dep chair All Pty Police Gp, chair All Pty Victims of Crime Gp; cncllr (Lab) Glasgow City Cncl 1971–74; contested: Glasgow Hillhead (Lab) 1970, York (Lib Dem) 1983 and 1987, Twickenham (Lib Dem) 1992; visiting fell: Nuffield Coll Oxford, LSE; *Publications* Protectionism and Industrial Decline (1983), Private Foreign Investment and Development (jtly, 1987), Trade Blocs (jtly, 1994), The World's New Fissures, The Politics of Identity (Demos, 1994), Global Superhighways (1995), China and India, The Emerging Giants (1995), Globalisation and Global Governance (1999), Multiple Identity (2005); *Clubs* British Legion (Twickenham); *Style—* Vincent Cable, MP; ✉ 102 Whitton Road, Twickenham, Middlesex TW1 1BS; House of Commons, London SW1A 0AA (tel 020 7219 1106); Constituency Office (tel 020 8892 0215, e-mail cablev@parliament.uk, website www.vincentcable.org.uk)

CABLE-ALEXANDER, Lt-Col Sir Patrick Desmond William; 8 Bt (UK 1809), of the City of Dublin; s of Sir Desmond William Lionel Cable-Alexander, 7 Bt (d 1988), and his 1 w Mary Jane, *née* O'Brien; *b* 19 April 1936; *Educ* Downside, RMA Sandhurst; *m* 1, 1961 (m dis 1976), Diana Frances, eldest da of late Col Paul Heberden Rogers, of Bushey, Herts; 2 da (Melanie Jane b 1963, Louise Fenella b 1967); m 2, 1976, Jane Mary, da of Dr Anthony Arthur Gough Lewis, MD, of Budleigh Salterton, Devon; 1 s (Fergus William Antony b 1981); *Heir* s, Fergus Cable-Alexander; *Career* former Lt-Col Royal Scots Dragoon Guards (Carabiniers and Greys), cmmnd 1956, serv BAOR, UK and Aden, Army Staff Coll 1967, asst mil attaché Saigon 1968–70, BAOR, MOD, Nat Def Coll 1975–76, cmd Duke of Lancaster's Own Yeo 1978–80, COS HQ NW Dist 1981–83, ret 1984; bursar and clerk Cncl Lancing Coll 1984–98; chief exec Inst of Optometry 1999–2006; *Recreations* the arts, painting, gardening, cricket, reading; *Style—* Lt-Col Sir Patrick Cable-Alexander, Bt; ✉ 15 Cambridge Road, Worthing, West Sussex BN11 1XD (tel 01903 233166, e-mail cable.alexander@btinternet.com)

CABORN, Rt Hon Richard George; MP; s of George and Mary Caborn; *b* 6 October 1943; *Educ* Hurlfield Comp Sch, Granville Coll of FE, Sheffield Poly; *m* 1966, Margaret; 1 s, 1 da; *Career* engineer; convenor of shop stewards Firth Brown Ltd 1967–79; MEP (Lab) Sheffield 1979–84, MP (Lab) Sheffield Central 1983–, chm Trade and Industry Select Ctee 1992–95; min of state: (regions, regeneration and planning) DETR 1997–99, Trade DTI 1999–2001, min of state for Sport 2001–; non-exec dir Sheffield United FC 1997–; *Style—* The Rt Hon Richard Caborn, MP; ✉ 29 Quarry Vale Road, Sheffield (tel 0114 239 3802); office: Barkers Pool House, Burgess Street, Sheffield S1 2HF (tel 0114 273 7947)

CADBURY, Sir (George) Adrian Hayhurst; kt (1977), DL (W Midlands 1995); s of Laurence John Cadbury, OBE (d 1982), and Joyce, *née* Mathews (d 1988), OBE; *b* 15 April 1929; *Educ* Eton, King's Coll Cambridge (MA); *m* 1, 1956, Gillian Mary (d 1992), da of Edmund Drane Skepper (d 1962), of Neuilly-sur-Seine, France; 2 s (Benedict, Matthew), 1 da (Caroline); m 2, 1994, Susan Jacqueline, da of David Bowie Sinclair (d 1945); *Career* chm: Cadbury Group 1965–69, Cadbury Schweppes plc 1975–89 (dep chm and md 1969–74); dir: Bank of England 1970–94, IBM (UK) Ltd 1975–94; chm: W Midlands Econ Planning Ctee 1967–70, CBI Econ and Financial Policy Ctee 1974–80, Food and Drink Industries Cncl 1981–83, PRO NED (orgn for promotion of non-exec dirs) 1984–95, Ctee on Financial Aspects of Corporate Governance (Cadbury Ctee) 1991–95; memb Covent Garden Market Authy 1974–89, chllr Aston Univ 1979–2004, pres Birmingham Chamber of Industry and Commerce 1988–89; Int Corp Governance Network Award 2001, Corporate Governance Laureate Medal 2005; High Sheriff W Midlands 1994–95; Hon DSc: Aston Univ 1973, Cranfield Inst 1985, Univ of Birmingham 1996; Hon LLD: Univ of Bristol 1986, Univ of Birmingham 1989, Lancaster Univ 1993, Univ of Cambridge 1994; Hon Dr: Univ of Gent 2003, Univ of Leuven 2003, UCE 2004; Hon DLitt Aston Univ 2005; RSA Albert Medal 1995; Freeman City of Birmingham 1982, Liveryman Worshipful Co of Grocers; CIMgt, FIPM, Hon FInstM, Hon FCGI; *Publications* Corporate Governance and Chairmanship (2002); *Clubs* Boodle's, Hawks' (Cambridge), Leander; *Style—* Sir Adrian Cadbury; fax 01564 771130

CADBURY, Sir (Nicholas) Dominic; kt (1997); *Career* Cadbury Schweppes plc: joined 1964, memb Bd 1975, gp chief exec 1983–93, chm 1993–2000; chm: The Economist 1993–2003, Wellcome Tst 2000–06, Misys plc 2005– (non-exec dir 2000–); jt dep chm EMI Gp plc 1999–2004 (non-exec dir 1998–2004), non-exec dep chm New Star Asset Mgmnt Gp plc 2005–; chllr Univ of Birmingham 2002–; *Style—* Sir Dominic Cadbury

CADBURY, Peter Hugh George; 3 s of (John) Christopher Cadbury, of Rednal, Birmingham, by his 1 w, Honor Mary, *née* Milward (d 1957); *b* 8 June 1943; *Educ* Rugby; *m* 1969, Sally, er da of Peter Frederick Strouvelle, of Cape Town, South Africa; 1 da (Eleanor (Duchess of Argyll) b 1973), 1 s (Simon b 1975); *Career* admitted slr, with Linklaters & Paines 1965–70, with Morgan Grenfell 1970–97 (dir 1977–97, dep chm 1992–97); chm: Henderson Smaller Companies Investment Trust plc 1989–2003, Close Brothers Corporate Finance Ltd 1997–99, Peter Cadbury & Co 1999–, DT2 Corporate Finance Ltd 2002–; dir: SMG plc 1998–2001, Celltech plc 2003–; *Clubs* Boodle's, Lansdowne; *Style—* Peter Cadbury, Esq

CADDY, David Henry Arnold Courtenay; s of Colonel John Caddy, of Highgate Village, London, and Elizabeth, *née* Day; *b* 22 June 1944; *Educ* Eton; *m* 1, 24 July 1971 (m dis 2000), Valerie Elizabeth Margaret, da of Dr Kelly Swanston, of Helmsley, N Yorks; 1 s (Julian b 1972), 1 da (Henrietta b 1978); m 2, 15 Sept 2000, Susan Lougher Jermine, da of Gwynne Lougher Porter, of Cyncoed, Glamorgan; *Career* articled to Layton Bennett Billingham and Co London 1962–68, qualified chartered accountant 1968; PricewaterhouseCoopers (formerly Coopers & Lybrand before merger) 1968–2000: ptnr Liberia 1974, managing ptnr Liberia 1974–77, ptnr UK 1977–2000, regnl chm UK South and East 1993–98; memb Ctee: London Soc of Chartered Accountants 1980, Cncl of Ptnrs Coopers & Lybrand 1989–97, Bd of Coopers & Lybrand 1994–97; fin dir Numasters.com 2000–; govr Reed's Sch 2006–; ICAEW 1968, ICA (Ghana) 1983, ICA (Nigeria) 1983; *Recreations* horse racing (owner), art, golf, swimming, walking, reading, opera, theatre; *Clubs* Boodle's, Leander; *Style—* David Caddy, Esq; ✉ Three The Dell, Bishopsgate Road, Englefield Green, Surrey TW20 0XP (tel 01784 477115); 104/392A Toorak Road, Toorak, Victoria 3142, Australia; Numasters.com Ltd, 29 Palace Street, London SW1E 5HW (tel 020 7592 0880)

CADMAN, 3 Baron (1937 UK); John Anthony Cadman; s of 2 Baron Cadman (d 1966); *b* 3 July 1938; *Educ* Harrow, Selwyn Coll Cambridge, RAC Cirencester; *m* 1975, Janet, da of Arthur Hayes, of Morecambe; 2 s (Hon Nicholas Anthony James b 18 Nov 1977, Hon Giles Oliver Richard b 5 Feb 1979); *Heir* s, Hon Nicholas Cadman; *Career* farmer and restaurateur; *Style—* The Lord Cadman; ✉ 32 Chemin de Labade, 11300 Pieusse, France (tel 00 33 468 20 90 66)

CADOGAN, 8 Earl (GB 1800) Charles Gerald John Cadogan; DL (Gtr London 1996); also Baron Cadogan of Oakley (GB 1718), Viscount Chelsea (GB 1800), and Baron Oakley of Caversham (UK 1831); s of 7 Earl Cadogan (d 1997); *b* 24 March 1937; *Educ* Eton; *m* 1, 1963, Lady Philippa Dorothy Bluett Wallop (d 1984), 2 da of 9 Earl of Portsmouth (d 1984); 1 da (Hon Anna-Karina b 1964), 2 s (Edward, Viscount Chelsea b 1966, Hon William b 1973); m 2, 1989 (m dis 1994), Jennifer Jane Greig, da of (J E) Keith Rae, and Mrs S Z de Ferranti; m 3, 1994, Dorothy Ann, MVO, yr da of late Dr W E Shipsey; *Heir* s, Viscount Chelsea; *Career* chm: Cadogan Gp, Leukaemia Research Fund; Freeman City of London, Liveryman Guild of Air Pilots and Air Navigators; hon fell: RVC, ISVA; *Style—* The Rt Hon the Earl Cadogan, DL; ✉ The Cadogan Office, 18 Cadogan Gardens, London SW3 2RP (tel 020 7730 4567, fax 020 7823 5514)

CAHILL, (Paul) Jeremy; QC (2002); s of late Dr Tim Cahill, and late Mary O'Mahony; *b* 28 January 1952, Birmingham; *Educ* Ratcliffe Coll Leicester, Univ of Liverpool; *Partner* Bettina Lugge; 2 da (Jenni Rachel b 6 Dec 1985, Eleanor Felicity b 12 April 1989); *Career* called to the Bar Middle Temple 1975 (Blackstone exhibitioner); practising barr No5 Chambers; memb: Planning and Environmental Bar Assoc, Compulsory Purchase Assoc; memb Grand Order of the Badgers; *Recreations* conversation, West Cork; *Clubs* Copt Heath Golf, RAC; *Style—* Jeremy Cahill, Esq, QC; ✉ No5 Chambers (Birmingham, London and Bristol) (tel 0870 203 5555, e-mail jc@no5.com)

CAHILL, Kevin; CBE (2007); *Career* head of educn RNT 1982–91; Comic Relief: dir of educn and info 1991, dir of communications 1992, dep dir (creative) 1993, dir 1994, chief exec 1997; bd pres Charity Projects Entertainment Fund 2007; former chair Trinity Coll London; memb: Bd Gate Theatre 1988– (currently chair), Cncl Drama Centre 1989–1992, Advsy Ctee ACU; former memb Bd Young Vic, former tstee Int Broadcasting Tst; *Style—* Kevin Cahill, Esq, CBE; ✉ Comic Relief UK, 5th Floor, 89 Albert Embankment, London SE1 7TP (tel 020 7820 5564, fax 020 7820 5508)

CAHILL, Teresa Mary; da of Henry Daniel Cahill (d 1948), of Rotherhithe, London, and Florence, *née* Dallimore (d 1964); *b* 30 July 1944; *Educ* Notre Dame HS Southwark, Guildhall Sch of Music & Drama, London Opera Centre; *m* 1, 1971 (m dis 1978), John Anthony Kiernander; m 2, 11 Nov 2005, Dr Robert Saxton, *qv*; *Career* opera and concert singer; Glyndebourne debut 1969, Covent Garden debut 1970, La Scala Milan 1976, Philadelphia Opera 1981, Liceo Barcelona 1991, specialising in Mozart & Strauss; concerts: all the London orchestras, Boston Symphony Orch, Chicago Symphony Orch, Vienna Festival 1983, Berlin Festival 1987, Bath Festival 2000, Rotterdam Philharmonic 1984, Hamburg Philharmonic 1985, West Deutscher Rundfunk Cologne 1985; promenade concerts BBC Radio & TV; recordings incl Elgar, Mozart, Strauss and Mahler for all major cos; recitals and concerts throughout Europe, USA and the Far East; examiner and vocal adjudicator Masterclasses, external examiner Univ of Reading 1992–95, masterclasses Univ of Oxford 1995–, artistic advsr Nat Mozart Competition 1997–2002, masterclasses and memb Int Jury S'Hertogenbosch Vocal Concours 1998 and 2000, masterclass Peabody Inst Baltimore USA 1999, adjudicator Live Music Now 1988– (music advsr 2000–), jury memb Kathleen Ferrier Competition 1988, adjudicator YCAT 1989–, adjudicator the Royal Overseas League Competition 1985–89, 1992, 1995 and 2000; prof of singing Trinity Coll of Music; govr Royal Soc of Musicians 2000–05 and 2006–; Silver medal Worshipful Co of Musicians, John Christie award 1970; AGSM, LRAM; *Recreations* cinema, theatre, travel, reading, collecting things, sales from car boots to Sotheby's, photography; *Clubs* Royal Over-Seas League (hon memb); *Style—* Ms Teresa Cahill; ✉ 65 Leyland Road, London SE12 8DW

CAHN, Sir Albert Jonas; 2 Bt (UK 1934), of Stanford-upon-Soar, Co Nottingham; s of Sir Julien Cahn, 1 Bt (d 1944); *b* 27 June 1924; *Educ* Harrow; *m* 1948, Malka (decd), da of Reuben Bluestone (d 1961); 2 da (Madeleine Jane (Mrs Smith) b 1949, Valerie Janet (Mrs Perry Crosthwaite) b 1954), 2 s (Julien Michael b 1951, Edward John b 1959); *Heir* s, Julien Cahn; *Career* former clinical dir The Elm Therapy Centre New Malden; *Style—* Sir Albert Cahn, Bt

CAHN, Andrew Thomas; CMG (2001); s of Robert Wolfgang Cahn, of Cambridge, and Patricia Lois, *née* Hanson; *b* 1 April 1951; *Educ* Bedales, Trinity Coll Cambridge (BA); *m* 1976, Virginia, da of David Fordyce Beardshaw; 1 da (Jessica b 1983), 2 s (Thomas b 1986, Laurence b 1994); *Career* civil servant; MAFF 1973–76, FCO 1976–77, MAFF 1977–81 (private sec to Perm Sec 1977–78), first sec perm rep to EC (FCO) 1982–84, Cabinet of Lord Cockfield (as vice-pres of EC) 1985–88, MAFF 1988–92; princ private sec: to chllr of Duchy of Lancaster 1992–94, to min for Agric Fisheries and Food 1994–95; under-sec Cabinet Office 1995–97, chef de cabinet to Rt Hon Neil Kinnock as cmmr for Tport then vice-pres and cmmr for Admin Reform 1997–2000; dir of govt and industry affrs BA 2000–06, chief exec UK Trade and Investment 2006–; non-exec dir Cadbury Ltd 1990–92; govr Bedales Sch 1993–98, tstee Gatsby Fndn 1996–, tstee Royal Botanic Gardens Kew 2002–; FRSA 1979; *Recreations* family, mountains, reading; *Clubs* RAC, Hampstead Golf, St Cyr Golf; *Style—* A T Cahn, Esq, CMG; ✉ UK Trade and Investment, Kingsgate House, 66–74 Victoria Street, London SW1E 6SW (tel 020 7215 4300, e-mail chief.executive@uktradeinvest.gov.uk)

CAIE, Prof Graham; *Educ* Univ of Aberdeen (MA), McMaster Univ (MA, PhD); *Career* Univ of Copenhagen until 1990, prof of English language Univ of Glasgow 1990–; memb: English Panel AHRC, Literature Ctee Scottish Arts Cncl, Cncl Dictionary of the Older Scottish Tongue, Bd Scottish Language Dictionaries; panelist Research Assessment Exercise, vice-pres Scottish Text Soc, vice-chair Bd and tstee Nat Library of Scotland, sec European Soc for the Study of English; founding fell English Assoc 1999, FRSE 2004, FRSA; *Books* incl: The Judgement Day Theme in Old English Poetry (1976), Bibliography of Junius XI Manuscript (1976), The Old English Poem: Judgement Day II (2000), The European Sun: Proceedings of the 7th International Conference on Medieval and Renaissance Scottish Language and Literature. (co-ed, 2001), Medieval Texts in Manuscript Context (co-ed, 2007); *Style*— Prof Graham Caie; ✉ Department of English Language, 12 University Gardens, University of Glasgow, Glasgow G12 8QQ

CAINE, Jeffrey; *Career* writer for film and TV; film: GoldenEye 1995, Inside I'm Dancing 2004, The Constant Gardener 2005; TV incl Dempsey & Makepeace 1985; creator: The Chief 1990, BodyGuards 1996; *Novels* The Cold Room (1976), Heathcliff (1977); *Style*— Jeffrey Caine, Esq

CAINE, Sir Michael (né Maurice Joseph Micklewhite); kt (2000), CBE (1992); s of late Maurice Micklewhite, and Ellen Frances Marie Micklewhite; *b* 14 March 1933; *Educ* Wilson's GS Peckham; *m* 1, 1955 (m dis), Patricia Haines; 1 da; m 2, 1973, Shakira Baksh; 1 da; *Career* actor; served Army Berlin and Korea 1951–53; asst stage mangr Westminster Repertory Horsham Sussex 1953, actor Lowestoft Repertory 1953–55, Theatre Workshop London 1955, numerous TV appearances 1957–63; awarded Special Award for Contribution to British Film Evening Standard British Film Awards 1999; *Films* incl: A Hill in Korea 1956, How to Murder a Rich Uncle 1958, Zulu 1964, The Ipcress File 1965, Alfie 1966, The Wrong Box 1966, Gambit 1966, Hurry Sundown 1967, Woman Times Seven 1967, Deadfall 1967, The Magus 1968, Battle of Britain 1968, Play Dirty 1968, The Italian Job 1969, Too Late the Hero 1970, The Last Valley 1971, Get Carter 1971, Zee & Co 1972, Kidnapped 1972, Pulp 1972, Sleuth 1973, The Black Windmill 1974, Marseilles Contract 1974, The Wilby Conspiracy 1974, Fat Chance 1975, The Romantic Englishwoman 1975, The Man who would be King 1975, Harry and Walter Go to New York 1975, The Eagle Has Landed 1976, A Bridge Too Far 1976, Silver Bears 1976, The Swarm 1977, California Suite 1978, Ashanti 1979, Beyond The Poseidon Adventure 1979, The Island 1979, Dressed to Kill 1979, Escape to Victory 1980, Death Trap 1981, Jigsaw Man 1982, Educating Rita 1982, The Honorary Consul 1982, Blame it on Rio 1984, Water 1985, The Holcroft Covenant 1985, Hannah and Her Sisters 1986, Mona Lisa 1986, The Fourth Protocol 1987, The Whistle Blower 1987, Surrender 1987, Jaws The Revenge 1987, Without a Clue 1988, Dirty Rotten Scoundrels 1988, Bullseye 1989, Mr Destiny 1990, A Shock to the System 1990, Noises Off 1992, Blue Ice 1992, The Muppets Christmas Carol 1992, On Deadly Ground 1994, Bullet to Beijing 1994, Blood and Wine 1995, 20,000 Leagues under the Sea 1996, Curtain Call 1997, Shadowrun 1997, Little Voice 1997, The Debtor 1998, The Cider House Rules 1998, Quills 1999, Shiner 2000, Miss Congeniality 2000, Last Orders 2000, Quick Sands 2000, The Quiet American 2001, Austin Powers - Gold Member 2002, The Actors 2002, Second-Hand Lions 2003, The Statement 2003, Around the Bend 2004, The Weather Man 2004, Batman Begins 2005, Bewitched 2005, Prestige 2006, Flawless 2006, Children of Men 2006, Sleuth 2007; films for TV: Jack The Ripper 1988, Jekyll and Hyde 1989, World War II: When Lions Roared 1994, Mandela and De Klerk 1996; *Awards* incl: Best Supporting Actor Oscar (for Hannah and her Sisters) 1987, Best Actor BAFTA (for Educating Rita) 1987, Golden Globe (for Little Voice) 1999, Eros Special Award British Film Awards 1999, Best Supporting Actor Oscar (for Cider House Rules) 2000, Best Supporting Actor Golden Globe (for Cider House Rules) 2000; *Books* Not Many People Know That (1985), Not Many People Know This Either (1986), Moving Picture Show (1988), Acting In Film (1990), What's It All About? (autobiography, 1992); *Recreations* cinema, theatre, travel, gardening; *Style*— Sir Michael Caine, CBE; ✉ c/o Duncan Heath, ICM Ltd, Oxford House, 76 Oxford Street, London W1D 1BS (tel 020 7636 6565, fax 020 7323 0101)

CAINE, Seth Fargher; s of Edwin Seth Caine (d 1964), and Anne, *née* Fargher; *b* 3 June 1956, Brighton, Sussex; *Educ* King William's Coll Castletown, Univ of Nottingham (LLB), Coll of Law Chester; *m* 28 Aug 1997, Joanne, *née* Sayle; 1 da (Georgia Blaa b 20 Nov 1998); *Career* slr; articled clerk Stanley Evans, Oates & Co slrs 1980–82, asst slr Metropolitan Police London 1983–85, head of branch Post Office Slr's Dept 1985–90; Cains Advocates: advocate 1990–94, ptnr 1994–, head of litigation 2000–; memb Editorial Advsy Bd Insolvency Intelligence Jl; memb Cncl IOM Law Soc 2005–, memb Assoc of Contentious Tst and Probate Specialists, memb Human Rights Inst; *Publications* International Commercial Fraud (contrib, 2002); *Recreations* rugby, music, reading; *Clubs* Ronnie Scott's; *Style*— Seth Caine, Esq; ✉ Cains Advocates, 15–19 Athol Street, Douglas, Isle of Man IM1 1LB (tel 01624 638356, fax 01624 638333, e-mail seth.caine@cains.com)

CAINES, Michael Andrew; MBE (2006); s of Peter Anthony Caines, and Patricia Caines (d 1995); *b* 3 January 1969; *Career* chef; Ninety Park Lane 1987–89, Le Manoir aux Quat'Saisons 1989–91, La Côte-d'Or France 1992–93, Joël Robuchon France 1993–94, exec chef Gidleigh Park Devon 1994–, md Michael Caines Restaurants (formed to run The Food and Beverage at Michael Caines at The Royal Clarence Hotel) 1999; Chef of the Year The Independent 1994, Relais Gourmand 1998, Michelin star 1998, 2 Michelin stars 1999, 5 out of 5 AA Rosettes 1998, 9 out of 10 Good Food Guide 1998, 8 out of 10 Good Food Guide 1999, Traditions and Qualite 2000 entry for Gidleigh Park, Hotel and Caterer Chef of the Year 2001; Hon LLD St Loye's Sch of Health and Sciences 2004; *Style*— Michael Caines, Esq, MBE; ✉ Gidleigh Park Hotel, Chagford, Devon TQ13 8HH (tel and fax 01647 433578, e-mail info@michaelcaines.com)

CAIRD, Rt Rev Donald Arthur Richard; s of George Robert Caird (d 1966), and Emily Florence, *née* Dreaper (d 1961); *b* 11 December 1925, Dublin; *Educ* privately, Wesley Coll Dublin, TCD (sr exhibitioner, scholar of the house, MA, DD, HDipEd, Semitic Languages prize, Kyle prize, Mental and Moral Sci prize, Lilian Mary Luce prize for Berkelian Philosophy); *m* 12 Jan 1963, Nancy Ballantyne, o da of Prof William Sharpe, MD, and Gwendoline Wolfe, of NY; 2 da (Ann Ballantyne b 18 Feb 1967, Helen Charlotte b 24 Jan 1972), 1 s (John Dudley Dreaper b 17 April 1968); *Career* ordained: deacon 1950, priest 1951, bishop 1970; curate St Mark's Belfast 1950–53, asst master and chaplain Portora Royal Sch Enniskillen 1953–57, lectr in philosophy St David's UC Lampeter 1957, rector Rathmichael PC Dublin 1960, asst master St Columba's Coll Dublin 1960–67, lectr in philosophy of religion Theol Coll Dublin 1962–69, asst lectr in philosophy TCD 1962–63, dean of Ossory 1969–70, bishop of Limerick, Ardfert and Aghadoe 1970–76, bishop of Meath and Kildare 1976–85, archbishop of Dublin, bishop of Glendalough and primate of Ireland and Metropolitan 1985–96, ret; visiting prof of Anglican studies The Gen Theol Seminary NY 1997; chm: Mgmnt Ctee Church of Ireland Theol Coll, Clergy Daughters' Sch Tst, Cmmn for the Care of the Elderly, Bd of Tstees and Govrs Marsh's Library, Church of Ireland Youth Cncl 1971–81, Cncl Alexandra Coll, Bd Church of Ireland Coll of Educn; patron: Nat Fedn of Youth Clubs, Moun Temple Comp Sch, E Glendalough Sch, Newpark Comp Sch; memb Bd: Thomond Coll Limerick, Siamsa Tire (The Irish Nat Theatre), Bord na Gaeilge (Govt Bd for Promotion of Irish Language), St Patrick's Hosp Dublin, Rotunda Hosp, Kings' Hosp Sch, Wilson's Hosp Sch; mangr Colaiste Moibhi (Irish Speaking Coll); memb RTE Review Ctee 1971–74; fell Columba's Coll Dublin 1972; Hon DD TCD 1988; Hon LLD: Nat Cncl for Educn Awards 1993, Nat Univ of Ireland 1995; Hon PhD Pontifical Univ of Maynooth 2002; life memb Royal Dublin Soc 1996; *Books* Directions (1970); *Recreations* reading, walking, swimming, cycling, painting; *Clubs* Kildare Street and University; *Style*— The Rt Rev D A R Caird; ✉ 3 Crofton Avenue, Dunlaoghaire, Co Dublin (tel 00 353 1 280 7869, fax 00 353 1 230 1053)

CAIRD, George; s of George Bradford Caird (d 1984), and Viola Mary, *née* Newport; *b* 30 August 1950; *Educ* Magdalen Coll Sch Oxford, Royal Acad of Music (LRAM, ARCM), Nordwestdeutsche Musikakademie Detmold, Peterhouse Cambridge (MA); *m* 1, 1974 (m dis), Sarah Verney; 3 s (Adam Benjamin b 23 April 1977, Oliver Ralph b 22 June 1978, Edmund George b 4 July 1989), 1 da (Iona Katharine Mary b 10 July 1991); m 2, 2001, Jane Amanda Salmon; 1 da (Elizabeth Jane b 7 May 2004); *Career* freelance oboist 1972–, memb Albion Ensemble 1976–, memb Acad of St Martin-in-the-Fields 1984–92; Royal Acad of Music: prof 1984–93, head Woodwind 1987–93, head Instrumental Studies 1990–93; princ Birmingham Conservatoire Univ of Central England 1993–; sec Fedn of Br Conservatoires (formerly Ctee of Princs of Conservatoires) 1998–2003, pres Incorporated Soc of Musicians 2004–05; chm: Music Educn Cncl 2001–04, MEC 2001–04; tstee: Symphony Hall Birmingham, Youth Music 2004–; memb: Ctee Br Double Reed Soc, Exec Ctee Music Educn Cncl 1997–, Regnl Ctee Arts Cncl W Midlands 2002–; memb and tstee Nat Youth Orch, chair Nat Assoc of Youth Orchs 2005–; memb: Royal Soc of Musicians, Incorporated Soc of Musicians (chm Birmingham Centre 1996–99, pres 2003–04), W Midlands Arts Bd 1999–2002; FRAM 1989 (ARAM 1985), FRSA 1993, Hon FLCM 1999, FRCM 1999, FRNCM 2004; *Recordings* incl: Mozart and Beethoven Quintets (Albion Ensemble) 1981, Kenneth Leighton Veris Gratia 1986, Mozart Serenade K361 (Albion Ensemble) 1989, Beethoven and Hummel Octets 1999, 20th Century English Music for Oboe and Piano 1999, An English Renaissance for Oboe and Strings 2004; *Recreations* reading, theatre, languages, travel, sport, walking; *Style*— Professor George Caird; ✉ Birmingham Conservatoire, Paradise Place, Birmingham B3 3HG (tel 0121 331 5910, fax 0121 331 7201, e-mail george.caird@uce.ac.uk)

CAIRD, John Newport; s of late Rev George Bradford Caird and Viola Mary, *née* Newport; *b* 22 September 1948; *Educ* Selwyn House Sch Montreal, Magdalen Coll Sch Oxford, Bristol Old Vic Theatre Sch; *m* 1, 1972 (m dis 1982), Helen Frances Brammer; m 2, 1982 (m dis 1990), Ann Dorzynski; 1 da (Joanna b 29 Jan 1983), 2 s (Benjamin b 10 Oct 1984, Samuel b 8 July 1987); m 3, 1990, Frances Ruffelle (m dis 1994); 1 da (Eliza b 18 April 1988), 1 s (Nathaniel b 17 June 1990); m 4, 1998, Maoko Imai; 1 s (Yoji b 19 Oct 1998), 2 da (Miyako b 18 Jan 2000, Yayako b 14 March 2002); *Career* director, writer and producer of plays, opera, musicals and film; hon assoc dir RSC 1990–, fndr and dir Caird Co 2001–05; chm Facing the Music (6th Birmingham Theatre Conference at Univ of Birmingham) 1995; govr dir Mountview Theatre Sch; tstee dir Friends of Highgate Cemetery; fell Welsh Coll of Music and Drama, fell Mansfield Coll Oxford; *Theatre* assoc dir Contact Theatre Manchester 1974–76: Look Back in Anger, Downright Hooligan, Krapp's Last Tape, Twelfth Night; fndr (with Steven Barlow and others) Circle of Muses touring music theatre gp; dir The Changeling (Univ of Ottawa) 1975, Last Resort (Sidewalk Theatre Co) 1976, Regina v Stephens (Avon Touring Co) 1976; resident dir RSC 1977–82: Dance of Death 1977, Savage Amusement 1978, Look Out Here Comes Trouble 1978, Caucasian Chalk Circle 1979, Nicholas Nickleby (co-dir with Trevor Nunn in London, NY and LA) 1980, 1982 and 1986, Naked Robots 1981, Twin Rivals 1981, Our Friends in the North 1982, Peter Pan (co-dir with Trevor Nunn) 1982–84; assoc dir RSC 1982–90: Twelfth Night 1983, Romeo and Juliet 1983, The Merchant of Venice 1984, Red Star 1984, Philistines 1985, Les Miserables (co-dir with Trevor Nunn in London, NY, Tokyo, Sydney and worldwide) 1985–, Every Man in His Humour 1986, Misalliance 1986, A Question of Geography 1987, The New Inn 1987, As You Like it 1989, A Midsummer Night's Dream 1989, The Beggar's Opera 1992, Columbus and the Discovery of Japan 1992, Antony and Cleopatra 1992; dir: Song and Dance (London) 1982, As You Like It (Stockholm, for TV 1985) 1984, Siegfried & Roy Spectacular (Las Vegas) 1989, Zaïde (Batignamo) 1991, The Beggar's Opera (RSC, Barbican) 1993, Trelawny of the Wells (RNT) 1993, Life Sentences (Second Stage Theatre NY) 1993, The Seagull (RNT) 1994, Watch your Step (Her Majesty's Theatre) 1995, Henry IV (also adaptor for BBC) 1995, The Millionairess (UK tour) 1995, Stanley (RNT and Broadway) 1996, (worldwide) 1998–2001, Money (RNT) 1999, Jane Eyre (Broadway) 2000, Hamlet (RNT and World tour) 2000, A Midsummer Night's Dream (Royal Dramatic Theatre Stockholm) 2000, Humbleboy (RNT, West End) 2001 (NY) 2003, Twelfth Night (Royal Dramatic Theatre Stockholm) 2002, What the Night is For (Comedy Theatre) 2002, Rattle of a Simple Man (Comedy Theatre) 2004, Becket (Theatre Royal Haymarket), Macbeth (Almeida Theatre)2005, Don Carlos (WNO) 2005; staged for Worldwide Fund for Nature: Religion and Nature Interfaith Ceremony (Assisi) 1986, Sacred Gifts for a Living Planet (Bhaktapur, Nepal) 2000; as prodr: new writing festivals 2001–02 (Gatehouse Theatre 2001, Jerwood Space 2002 and 2003, Pleasance Theatre 2002, Soho Theatre 2002), Robin Hood (RNT) 2002–03, Theatre Cafe (Arcola Theatre) 2004, Arab-Israeli Cookbook (Gate Theatre) 2004, New Directions (Theatre Royal Haymarket) 2004, The Lemon Princess (West Yorkshire Playhouse) 2005; writer and dir: Beethoven The Kingdom of the Spirit (a concert for actor and string quartet) 1986, Children of Eden (with music and lyrics by Stephen Schwartz, London and worldwide) 1991, Jane Eyre (with lyrics and music by Paul Gordon, Toronto, La Jolla and Broadway) 1996, Candide (with music by Leonard Berstein, RNT) 1999, Daddy Longlegs (with lyrics and music by Paul Gordon) 2002; writer Twin Spirits (ROH); *Awards* SWET Award 1980, Tony Award for Best Dir 1982 (both for Nicholas Nickleby), Tony Award for Best Dir 1986 and 1987 (for Les Miserables), Lawrence Olivier Award for Most Outstanding Musical (for Candide) 2000, Critics Outer Circle Award (for Stanley); *Publications* Peter Pan (1993, 2 edn, 1998), Children of Eden (1997), The Beggar's Opera (with Ilona Sekacz, 1999), Jane Eyre (2003), Candide (2003); *Style*— John Caird, Esq; ✉ Church House, 10 South Grove, Highgate, London N6 6BS (tel 020 8348 1996, fax 020 8340 5030)

CAIRD, Richard Francis; s of Prof Francis Irvine Caird, of Oxford, and Angela Margaret Alsop (d 1983); *b* 20 January 1958; *Educ* Glasgow Acad, New Coll Oxford (BA), Coll of Law Guildford; *m* 1985, Helen Vanessa, da of Anthony Simpson; 1 da (Julia Margaret b 1 July 1989), 1 s (James Francis b 27 Jan 1992); *Career* articled clerk Radcliffes & Co 1980–82; Wilde Sapte: asst slr 1983–87, ptnr 1987–98, head Litigation Dept 1994–98; head of legal and compliance Commerzbank Global Equities 1998–2005, ptnr Denton Wilde Sapte 2005–; memb Law Soc; *Recreations* sport, theatre, reading; *Style*— Richard Caird, Esq; ✉ Denton Wilde Sapte, 5 Chancery Lane, Clifford's Inn, London EC4A 1BU

CAIRNCROSS, Frances Anne; *see:* McRae, Frances Anne

CAIRNES, (Simon) Paul Steven; s of Edward Michael Hornby Cairnes, and Audrey Mary, *née* Stevens; *b* 19 December 1957; *Educ* Christ Coll Brecon, UCW Aberystwyth (LLB); *Career* barr; called to the Bar Gray's Inn 1980 (NSW Aust 1989); memb: Barrs Euro Gp 1989–, Personal Injury Bar Assoc 2000–, Planning and Environmental Bar Assoc 2005–; *Recreations* sailing, skiing, music, travelling; *Style*— Paul Cairnes, Esq; ✉ 3 Paper Buildings, Temple, London EC4Y 7EU (tel 020 7353 8192, fax 020 7353 6271, e-mail paul.cairnes@3paper.co.uk)

CAIRNS, Alun Hugh; AM; s of Hewitt John Cairns, and Margaret, of Clydach, Swansea; *b* 30 July 1970; *Educ* Ysgol Gyfun Ddwyieithog Ystalyfera, Univ of Wales; *m* 1996, Emma Elizabeth, da of Martin Graham Turner; *Career* Business Devpt Conslt Lloyds Bank Gp, Lloyds TSB South Wales Compliance Conslt; Cons Pty: memb Swansea West Assoc 1987–, Mid and West Wales Euro-Constituency Cncl rep for Swansea West 1990, Assoc dep treas 1993, memb Wales Area Cncl 1994, dep chm Wales Area Young Cons 1995, chm Policy Advsy Gp 1996–97, Parly candidate Gower 1997, Economic Spokesman for Wales 1997, memb Nat Assembly for Wales (Cons) South Wales West 1999–; radio panel memb and commentator; *Style*— Alun Cairns, Esq, AM; ✉ National Assembly for Wales, Cardiff Bay, Cardiff CF99 1NA (tel 029 2089 8733, fax 029 2089 8332, e-mail alun.cairns@wales.gov.uk)

CAIRNS, Christine Wilson; da of late Thomas Cairns, of Saltcoats, Scotland, and late Christine Dawson Galloway, *née* Wilson; *b* 11 February 1959; *Educ* Ardrossan Acad, RSAMD; *m* 13 July 1991, John David Peter Lubbock, *qv*, s of late Michael Ronald Lubbock and late Diana Lubbock *née* Crawley; 2 s (Adam Thomas b 28 Nov 1991, Alexander Michael b 30 June 1993); *Career* mezzo-soprano; performed with orchs incl: Berlin Philharmonic, LA Philharmonic, London Philharmonic, Royal Philharmonic, LSO, Vienna Philharmonic, BBC Scottish, Cleveland and Philadelphia Orchs, Euro Community Youth Orch; worked with conductors incl: Sir Colin Davis, André Previn, Vladimir Ashkenazy, Yuri Temirkanov, Simon Rattle, Christoph von Dohnányi, John Lubbock; currently giving concerts to raise money for autism, recorded fund-raising CD Songs for Alexander (2002), chm and fndr Music for Autism; teacher (singing) Birmingham Conservatoire 2000–; *Recordings* incl: Mendelssohn's Midsummer Night's Dream (with André Previn and the Vienna Philharmonic) 1986, Prokofiev's Alexander Nevsky (with André Previn and the LA Philharmonic) 1986, Mendelssohn's Die Erste Walpurgisnacht (with Christoph von Dohnányi and the Cleveland Orch) 1988; *Style*— Ms Christine Cairns; ✉ c/o Helen Sykes Artists Management, 100 Telsham Road, London SW15 (tel 020 8780 0060); website www.musicforautism.org.uk

CAIRNS, David; MP; *b* 1966, Inverclyde; *Educ* Gregorian Univ Rome, Franciscan Study Centre Canterbury; *Career* Catholic priest 1991–94, dir Christian Socialist Movement 1994–97, sec Lab Socialist Socs 1994–97, research asst to Siobhain McDonagh MP 1997–2001, cnclr Merton BC 1997–2001; MP (Lab): Greenock and Inverclyde 2001–05, Inverclyde 2005–; PPS to Malcolm Wicks, MP (Min of State Dept for Work and Pensions) 2003–06, Parly under sec of state Scotland Office 2005–, Parly under sec of state NI Office 2006–; *Style*— David Cairns, Esq, MP; ✉ House of Commons, London SW1A 0AA

CAIRNS, David Howard; OBE (1995); s of David Lauder Cairns, of Birmingham, and Edith, *née* Rose; *b* 4 June 1946; *Educ* Cheadle Hulme Sch, LSE (MSc); *m* 1 May 1980, Stella Jane, da of Stanley Cecil Askew, DSO, DFC (d 1996); *Career* chartered accountant; Pannell Kerr Forster 1964–71, Carlsberg Brewery Ltd 1971–72, Black & Decker Ltd 1972–75, ptnr Stoy Hayward 1975–85, sec gen Int Accounting Standards Ctee 1985–94, dir Int Fin Reporting 1995–; LSE: PD Leake fell 1973–75, visiting fell 1995–2004, visiting prof 2004–; memb: Financial Reporting Review Panel 2006–, Conseil National de la Comptabilité (France); pres Thames Valley Soc of Chartered Accountants 1979–80; FCA 1974 (ACA), FRSA 1996; *Books* Current Cost Accounting after Sandilands (1976), Financial Times Survey of 100 Major European Companies Reports and Accounts (1979), Financial Times World Survey of Annual Reports (1980), Survey of Accounts and Accountants (1983–84), Applying International Accounting Standards (2002), FT International Accounting Standards Survey (1999), The Convergence Handbook (2000), The International Accounting Standards Survey (2001); *Recreations* cricket, collecting contemporary British paintings, music; *Clubs* Turville Park Cricket, Henley Rugby; *Style*— David Cairns, Esq, OBE; ✉ Bramblewood, Turville Heath, Henley-on-Thames, Oxfordshire RG9 6JY (tel and fax 01491 638296, e-mail david@cairns.co.uk); International Financial Reporting, North Lea House, 66 Northfield End, Henley-on-Thames, Oxfordshire RG9 2JN (tel 01491 412444, fax 01491 411811, e-mail david@cairns.co.uk, website www.cairns.co.uk)

CAIRNS, The Hon Mrs Andrew Cairns; (Cecilia) Elizabeth Mary; da of Lt-Col Francis Cecil Leonard Bell, DSO, MC, TD, of Cross Glades, Chiddingfold, Surrey, and Mary Wynne, *née* Jacob; *b* 14 September 1943; *Educ* Priors Field Godalming Surrey, Trinity Coll Dublin (BA, LLB); *m* 22 Oct 1966, Hon (Hugh) Andrew David, s of Rear Adm The Earl Cairns, GCVO, CB (d 1989); 1 s (Bertie b 28 Jan 1972), 1 da (Katherine b 27 June 1974); *Career* Charity Commission 1972–78; ptnr Jaques and Lewis 1984–90, specialist legal practice in charity law 1990–2004, conslt Thomson, Snell & Passmore 2004–; chair ISP Children's Fndn; tstee Kent Gardens Tst, sec Garden History Soc; *Books* Charities: Law and Practice (1988), Fundraising for Charity (1996); *Recreations* gardening, fishing; *Style*— The Hon Mrs Andrew Cairns; ✉ Knowle Hill Farm, Ulcombe, Maidstone, Kent ME17 1ES (tel 01622 850240); Thomson Snell & Passmore, 3 Lonsdale Gardens, Tunbridge Wells TN1 1NX

CAIRNS, Joyce Winifred; da of Lt-Col Robert William Cairns, MBE, TD, (d 1972), and Marjorie Helen, *née* Dickson (d 1983); *b* 21 March 1947; *Educ* Mary Erskine Sch for Girls Edinburgh, Gray Sch of Art Aberdeen (dip and post dip), RCA (MA), Goldsmiths Coll London (ATC); *m* 1, 1975, Christopher George Dowland; m 2, 1980, Arthur James Watson; m 3, 1989, Capt Robert Kemp Hamilton Cunningham; *Career* artist and lectr; lectr Grays Sch of Art Aberdeen 1976–2004; visiting lectr: Glasgow Sch of Art, Duncan of Jordanston Coll of Art Dundee; fell Glos Coll of Art & Design; Scottish Arts Cncl: memb Art Ctee 1986–89, memb Awards Panel 1981–83 and 1987–90; memb: Aberdeen Artists Soc 1978 (first woman pres), Royal Scottish Soc of Painters in Watercolours 1979; ARSA 1985, RSA 1998; *Solo Exhibitions* Compass Gallery Glasgow 1980, ESU Edinburgh 1981, Peacock Printmakers Aberdeen 1981, Art Space Galleries Aberdeen 1984, Perth Museum and Art Gallery 1986, 369 Gallery Edinburgh 1986, The Third Eye Gallery Glasgow 1987, Talbot Rice Gallery Univ of Edinburgh 1991, Peacock Gallery Aberdeen 1991, Odette Gilbert Gallery London 1991, Kirkcaldy Art Gallery & Museum 1992, An Lanntair Stornoway 1992, Lamont Gallery 1993, Elektra Fine Art Toronto, Roger Billcliffe Gallery Glasgow 1995, Rendezvous Gallery Aberdeen 1998, The Weem Gallery Pittenweem 2003, Peacock Visual Arts Aberdeen 2003, The Rendezvous Gallery Aberdeen 2004, Aberdeen Art Gallery and Museum 2006; *Work in Public Collections* Aberdeen Art Gallery, Scottish Arts Cncl, Univ of Aberdeen, Fife Regnl Cncl, Graves Art Gallery & Museum Sheffield, Edinburgh City Arts Centre, Lanarkshire CC, Univ of Strathclyde, The Contemporary Arts Soc, BBC, Glasgow Art Gallery & Museum, Perth City Art Gallery and Museums, Glasgow MOMA, Flemings Bank, McMaster Museum Hamilton Ontario Canada, The Royal Scottish Academy, Nat Museums of Scotland, Aberdeen Asset Mgmnt, Grays Sch of Art Robert Gordon Univ, Nat Museums of Scotland (War Museum, Edinburgh Castle); *Awards* incl: Carnegie Travelling Scholarship, First Prize Arbroath Art Competition, ESU Scholarship to USA, Latimer Award RSA, bursary Scottish Arts Cncl, First Prize Morrison Portrait Competition 1989, May Marshall Brown Award RSW, W P J Burness Award RSA, First Prize Shell Expro, Sir William Gillies Travel Bursary 1997, second prize Shell Expo 2002, Mausde Gemmell Hutchison Award RSA 2006; *Publications* Joyce Cairns: War Tourist (illustrated anthology, 2006); *Recreations* eating and carousing; *Style*— Ms Joyce Cairns; ✉ 5 New Pier Road, Footdee, Aberdeen AB11 5DR (tel 01224 575331, e-mail joycewcairns@waitrose.com)

CAIRNS, Peter Granville; er s of late Maj Hugh William Cairns, MC (gs of 1 Earl Cairns), and Diana Katherine, *née* Soames (d 1997); *b* 3 September 1940; *Educ* Eton; *m* 10 May 1991, Mrs Ann Camilla Carlton, da of late J B Leworthy, of Beacon Hill, Westerham, Kent; *Career* Lt Royal Scots Greys, ret; banker; dir: Cater Ryder 1976–81, Cater Allen 1981–98; conslt Gerrard & National 1998–; *Recreations* fox-hunting; *Clubs* Turf, White's; *Style*— Peter Cairns, Esq

CAIRNS, Dr Roger John Russell; s of Arthur John Cairns (d 1982), and Edith Anne, *née* Russell (d 1979); *b* 8 March 1943; *Educ* Ranelagh Sch, Univ of Durham (BSc), Univ of Bristol (MSc, PhD); *m* 20 July 1966, Zara Corry, da of Herbert Bolton (d 1970); 2 s (Nigel b 1969, Alistair b 1973), 1 da (Kirsten b 1975); *Career* oilfield water mgmnt BP 1978–81, planner Qatar General Petroleum Corp 1981–83; md: Trafalgar House Oil and Gas Ltd (tech and commercial dir 1983–89), Hardy Oil and Gas plc 1989–97; chm and ceo CEDAR International plc (conslt 1997–); non-exec dir Sodra Petroleum AB 1998–2001; memb Cncl IP 1999–2003, chm EI Discussion Gp Ctee 1998–2005; Enhanced Recovery Systems Ltd: sr technical advsr 2000–06, md 2006–; non-exec dir Technip 2003–07; pres NSPCC Bucks (chm NSPCC Full Stop Campaign Ctee in Berks and Bucks 1998–2002); memb: SPE, IOD (educn liaison offr Bucks Ctee 2001–06); FRSC, EurChem, CChem, FInstPet, life fell Royal Instn of GB; *Recreations* theatre and music, wine, tennis, reading, chess; *Clubs* RAC; *Style*— Dr Roger Cairns; ✉ High Larch, Lewis Lane, Chalfont Heights, Gerrard's Cross, Buckinghamshire SL9 9TS (e-mail cairoilcon@aol.com)

CAIRNS, 6 Earl (UK 1878); Simon Dallas Cairns; CVO (2000), CBE (1992); also Baron Cairns (UK 1867) and Viscount Garmoyle (UK 1878); s of 5 Earl Cairns, GCVO, CB (d 1989); *b* 27 May 1939; *Educ* Eton, Trinity Coll Cambridge; *m* 4 Feb 1964, Amanda Mary, o da of late Maj Edgar Fitzgerald Heathcoat-Amory, RA; 3 s (Hugh Sebastian, Viscount Garmoyle b 1965, Hon (David) Patrick b 1967, Hon Alistair Benedict b 1969); *Heir* s, Viscount Garmoyle, *qv*; *Career* formerly with J A Scrimgeour; S G Warburg Gp plc: md 1979–85, dir 1985–95, vice-chm 1985–87, jt chm 1987–91, chief exec and dep chm 1991–95; chm: BAT Industries plc 1996–98 (dir 1990–), Allied Zurich 1998–2000 (also vice-chm Zurich Financial Services and Zurich Allied AG); dep chm Celtel Int BV 2004–; chm: VSO 1981–92, ODI 1994–2002, Commonwealth Development Corp (latterly CDC Group plc then Actis) 1995–2005, Commonwealth Business Cncl 1997–2002, Charities Aid Fndn 2003–; tstee Diana Princess of Wales Meml Fund 1998–2006; curator Univ of Oxford Chest 1995–2000; receiver gen Duchy of Cornwall 1990–2000; memb Ct of Assts Worshipful Co of Fishmongers; *Clubs* Turf; *Style*— The Rt Hon Earl Cairns, CVO, CBE

CAITHNESS, 20 Earl of (S 1455); Malcolm Ian Sinclair; 15 Bt (S 1631), PC (1990); also Lord Berriedale (S 1592); s of 19 Earl of Caithness (d 1965), and his 2 w Madeleine Gabrielle, *née* de Pury (d 1990); *b* 3 November 1948; *Educ* Marlborough, RAC Cirencester; *m* 1975, Diana Caroline (d 1994), da of Maj Richard Coke, DSO, MC, DL (gs of 2 Earl of Leicester); 1 da (Lady Iona b 1978), 1 s (Alexander James Richard, Lord Berriedale b 1981); *Heir* s, Lord Berriedale; *Career* Savills 1972–78, Brown and Mumford 1978–80, dir of various companies 1980–84; a Lord in Waiting and Government Whip 1984–85, under sec for transport 1985–86; min of state: Home Office 1986–88, Dept of the Environment 1988–89, HM Treasy 1989–90 (Paymaster Gen), FCO 1990–92, Dept of Tport 1992–94; conslt to and non-exec dir of various companies 1994–; conslt Victoria Soames Ltd (former dir), md Clan Sinclair Tst 1999–; tstee Queen Elizabeth Castle of May Tst (and various other trusts); FRICS; *Style*— The Rt Hon the Earl of Caithness, PC; ✉ House of Lords, London SW1A 0PW

CALAM, Prof Derek Harold; OBE (1997); s of Richard Hellyer Calam (d 1993), of Northwood, and Winifred Ella, *née* Nortier (d 1986); *b* 11 May 1936; *Educ* Christ's Hosp, Wadham Coll Oxford (MA, DPhil); *m* 15 Sept 1965, Claudia, da of Gerald Marcus Summers (d 1967); 2 s (Duncan b 1969, Douglas b 1973), 1 da (Josephine b 1971); *Career* Nat Serv 2 Lt RA 1954–56; Nat Inst for Med Res 1962–66 and 1969–72, Rothamsted Experimental Station 1966–69, Euro co-ordinator Nat Inst for Biological Standards and Control 1994–2001 (joined 1972, head Chemistry Div 1975–94), author of numerous pubns in jls; memb: Br Pharmacopoeia Cmmn 1982–2005 (vice-chm 1995–98, chm 1998–2005), Euro Pharmacopoeia Cmmn 1988–2005 (first vice-chm 1995–98, chm 1998–2001), Cmmn on Human Medicines 2005–; visiting prof Univ of Strathclyde 1998–; expert advsr WHO 1984–; hon memb Br Inst of Regulatory Affairs 1999; Hon DSc Univ of Strathclyde 2003; CChem, FRSC 1977, Hon MRPharmS 1992, FRSA 2000; *Recreations* walking, travel; *Style*— Professor Derek Calam, OBE; ✉ The Mill House, Honeystreet, Pewsey, Wiltshire SN9 5PS

CALDECOTE, 3 Viscount (UK 1939) Piers James Hampden Inskip; s of 2 Viscount Caldecote, KBE, DSC (d 1999); *b* 20 May 1947; *Educ* Eton, Magdalene Coll Cambridge; *m* 1, 1970 (m dis 1981), Susan Bridget, da of late W P Mellen, of Great Sampford, Essex; m 2, 1984, Kristine Elizabeth, da of late Harvey Holbrooke-Jackson, of Ramsey, Cambs; 1 s (Hon Thomas James b 22 March 1985); *Heir* s, Hon Thomas Inskip; *Career* exec dir Carlton Communications; *Recreations* golf, tennis; *Style*— The Rt Hon the Viscount Caldecote

CALDECOTT, Andrew Hilary; QC (1994); s of Andrew Caldecott, CBE (d 1990), and Zita, *née* Belloc; *b* 22 June 1952; *Educ* Eton, New Coll Oxford (BA); *m* 1977, Rosamond Ashton, *née* Shuttleworth; 2 s (Harry b 1981, Edmund b 1985), 2 da (Zita b 1983, Xanthe 1991); *Career* called to the Bar Inner Temple 1975 (bencher 2004); play Higher than Babel staged at Bridewell Theatre 1999; *Style*— Andrew Caldecott, Esq, QC; ✉ 1 Brick Court, Temple, London EC4Y 8BY (tel 020 7353 8845)

CALDER, Dr Angus Lindsay Ritchie; s of Ritchie Calder (d 1982), and Mabel Jane Forbes, *née* McKail, of Edinburgh; *b* 5 February 1942; *Educ* Wallington Co GS for Boys, King's Coll Cambridge (MA), Univ of Sussex (DPhil); *m* 1, 1 Oct 1963, Jennifer Rachel, da of David Daiches; 2 da (Rachel b 21 Aug 1965, Gowan b 29 May 1967), 1 s (Gideon b 10 April 1971); m 2, 19 Dec 1987, Catherine Janet Kyle, da of William Young; 1 s (Douglas b 28 May 1989); *Career* writer; lectr in literature Univ of Nairobi 1968–71, visiting lectr Univ of Malawi Zomba 1978, staff tutor in arts and reader in cultural studies Open Univ in Scotland 1979–93, visiting prof of English Univ of Zimbabwe Harare 1992; co-ed Jl of Commonwealth Literature 1981–87; founding convener Scottish Poetry Library 1982–88, convener Cwlth Writers Conf Edinburgh 1986, convener Writing Together Glasgow 1989–90; memb Bd: Royal Lyceum Theatre Edinburgh 1984–96 (also chair Artistic Policy Review Sub-Ctee), Fruitmarket Gallery Edinburgh 1984–92, 7:84 Theatre Co 1986–92, Wasafiri (magazine) 1997–, 2000 and 3 Estaitis 1998–2004; memb panel of judges Saltire Soc Scottish Book of the Year Award 1983–97, judge Eurasian Section Cwlth Writers Prize 1996; Eric Gregory Award 1967, John Llewelyn Rhys Meml Prize 1970, Scottish Arts Cncl Book Awards 1981 and 1994, Scottish Arts Cncl Writer's Bursary 2001; *Books* The People's War - Britain 1939–45 (1969), Russia Discovered (1976) Revolutionary Empire - The Rise of the English Speaking Empires from the 15th Century to the 1780's (1981), T S Eliot (1987), Byron (1987), The Myth of the Blitz (1991), Revolving Culture (1994), Waking in Waikato (poems, 1997), Wars (anthology, 1999), Horace in Tollcross (poems, 2000), Scotlands of the Mind (2002), Colours of Grief (poems, 2002), Gods, Mongrels and Demons 101 Brief But Essential Lives (2003), Dipa's Bowl (poems, 2004), Disasters and Heroes: On War, Memory and Representation (2004), Sun Behind the Castle: Edinburgh Poems (2004); ed and co-ed of numerous books; contrib reviews and articles to jls and newspapers; *Recreations* curling, cooking, cricket, listening to music; *Clubs* 37 Curling; *Style*— Dr Angus Calder; ✉ Luath Press, 543/2 Castlehill, The Royal Mile, Edinburgh EH1 2ND

CALDER, Dr John Forbes; s of Alexander Beattie Calder, of Glasgow, and Annie Scott, *née* Milne; *b* 13 May 1942; *Educ* The HS of Glasgow, Univ of Glasgow (MB ChB); *m* 28 March 1967, Marion, da of John Anderson Miller (d 1964), of Kirkintilloch; 1 s (Nicholas b 1972), 1 da (Lorna b 1975); *Career* govt MO Malawi 1968–70, sr registrar in radiology Glasgow 1973–76 (registrar in radiology 1971–73); sr lectr in radiology: Univ of Nairobi 1976–80, Univ of Aberdeen 1980–86; conslt radiologist Victoria Infirmary Glasgow 1986–2007, ret; elder Church of Scotland, memb Scottish Radiological Soc (pres 1997–99); FRCR (memb RCR 1975), memb RCPSG 1993, FRCP 1995; *Books* The History of Radiology in Scotland 1896–2000 (2001); *Recreations* music, hill walking, soccer; *Clubs*

Cwlth; *Style*— Dr John Calder; ✉ 145 Clober Road, Milngavie, Glasgow G62 7LS (tel 0141 956 3535)

CALDER, John Mackenzie; s of James Calder, of Ardargie, Forgandenny, Perthshire, and Lucianne Wilson; *b* 25 January 1927; *Educ* McGill Univ Montreal, Sir George Williams Coll, Univ of Zürich; *m* 1, 1949, Mary Ann Simmonds; 1 da; m 2, 1960 (m dis 1975), Bettina Jonic; 1 da; *Career* publisher, ed, author; fndr and md: John Calder (Publishers) Ltd 1950–91, Calder Publications Ltd 1991–; dir of other associated publishing cos; co-fndr Def of Lit and the Arts Soc, chm Fedn of Scot Theatres 1972–74; memb and administrator Godot Co; contested (Lib): Kinross and W Perthshire 1970, Hamilton 1974, Central Scot (European election) 1979; Chevalier de l'Ordre des Arts et des Lettres (France), Officer and Chevalier Ordre de Mérite Nat; dr (hc) Univ of Edinburgh; FRSA; *Books* The Defence of Literature (1994), The Philosophy of Samuel Beckett (1995), What's Wrong What's Right (poems, 2000), Pursuit (autobiography, 2001), The Garden of Eros (2003); ed: A Samuel Beckett Reader, Beckett at 60, The Nouveau Roman Reader, Gambit International Drama Review, William Burroughs Reader, Henry Miller Reader, As No Other Dare Fail - For Samuel Beckett on his 80th Birthday; author of fiction and plays; *Clubs* Caledonian, Scottish Arts; *Style*— John Calder, Esq; ✉ Calder Publications Ltd, 51 The Cut, London SE1 8LF (tel 020 7633 0599, fax 020 7928 5930, e-mail info@calderpublications.com, website www.calderpublications.com)

CALDER, Prof Muffy; da of Carmen Van Thomas (d 1996), and Lois, *née* Hallen; *b* Shawinigan, Canada; *Educ* Univ of Stirling (BSc), Univ of St Andrews (PhD); *m* 1998, David Calder; *Career* research appointments at Univ of Edinburgh and Univ of Stirling; Univ of Glasgow: prof 1988–, head Dept of Computing Science 2003–; memb Scottish Science Advsy Ctee (SSAC); author of over 50 scientific pubns; FRSE 2003, FIEE 2003; *Recreations* long-distance, hill running; *Clubs* Westerlands Cross Country; *Style*— Prof Muffy Calder; ✉ Department of Computing Science, University of Glasgow, Glasgow G12 8QQ (tel 0141 330 4969, e-mail muffy@dcs.gla.ac.uk)

CALDER, (Hon) Nigel David Ritchie; eldest s of Baron Ritchie-Calder, CBE (Life Peer, d 1982); *b* 2 December 1931; *Educ* Merchant Taylors', Sidney Sussex Coll Cambridge (MA); *m* 1954, Elisabeth, da of Alfred James Palmer; 2 s, 3 da; *Career* writer New Scientist 1956–66 (ed 1962–66); freelance author and TV scriptwriter 1966–; fell AAAS, FRAS; *Books* incl: Einstein's Universe (1979), Nuclear Nightmares (1979), The Comet is Coming (1980), Timescale (1983), The English Channel (1986), Spaceship Earth (1991), Giotto to the Comets (1992), The Manic Sun (1997), Magic Universe: The Oxford Guide to Modern Science (2003), The Chilling Stars (co-author, 2007); *Recreations* boating, painting; *Style*— Nigel Calder, Esq; ✉ 26 Boundary Road, Northgate, Crawley, West Sussex RH10 8BT (tel 01293 549969, e-mail nc@windstream.demon.co.uk)

CALDER, Rachel Elisabeth; da of Richard Calder, of USA, and Elisabeth, *née* Baber; *b* 25 January 1961, Derby; *Educ* Fyling Hall Sch Whitby, Univ of Hull (BA); *m* 30 March 1996, Daniel Kunkle; 2 s (Jack b 19 April 1995, Milo b 14 Jan 1998), 1 da (Matilda b 8 Oct 2001); *Career* Andre Deutsch 1982–83; literary agent: Curtis Brown Gp 1987–91, The Sayle Literary Agency (formerly Tessa Sayle Agency) 1991–; *Style*— Ms Rachel Calder; ✉ The Sayle Literary Agency, 1 Petersfield, Cambridge CB1 1BB (tel 01223 303035, fax 01223 301638, e-mail rachel@sayleliteraryagency.com)

CALDERWOOD, James William; OBE (1998); s of Rev James W Calderwood (d 1971), of Bready, Co Tyrone, and Kathleen Calderwood; *b* 3 December 1936; *Educ* Foyle Coll Londonderry, Queen's Univ Belfast (MB BCh, BAO); *m* 29 Aug 1967, Dr (Catherine) Lesley Crozier, da of George Crozier, of Enniskillen (d 1963); 2 da (Catherine, Claire); *Career* conslt orthopaedic surgn Belfast City and Musgrave Park Hosp 1975–2001, Royal Victoria Hosp 1977–2001; chm of med staff Musgrave Park Hosp 1998–2001; examiner of RCSEd 1986–2002; memb Editorial Bd Jl of Hand Surgery 1996–2000; pres Ulster Medical Soc 1997–98; memb: Br Soc for Surgery of the Hand 1980, Ulster Surgns Travelling Club 1990–; fell Br Orthopaedic Assoc (memb Cncl 1995–97); FRCS 1970, FRSM 1986; *Recreations* skiing, golf; *Style*— James Calderwood, Esq, OBE; ✉ 8 Broomhill Park, Belfast BT9 5JB (tel and fax 028 9066 6940)

CALDERWOOD, Robert; *b* 11 October 1953; *Educ* Camphill Sr Secdy Sch, Glasgow Coll of Technol (HND in Business Studies), Inst of Health Serv Mangrs (DipHSM), Univ of Aberdeen (Cert in Health Economics); *m*; 1 s; *Career* admin trainee NHS 1971–74, various admin posts Argyll and Clyde Health Bd 1974–85; Gtr Glasgow Health Bd: hosp admin Western Infirmary 1985–87, unit admin Western Gartnavel Hosp Group 1987–88, dir of property and strategic planning 1988–91, unit gen mangr Southern Gen Hosp Unit 1991–93; chief exec: Southern Gen Hosp NHS Tst 1993–97, Southern Gen Hosp/Victoria Inf NHS Tsts 1997–99, South Glasgow Univ Hosps NHS Tst 1999–2004, GGHB South Glasgow Univ Hosps Div 2004–06; chief operating off NHS Gtr Glasgow and Clyde Acute Servs Div 2006–; MHSM; *Recreations* golf; *Style*— Robert Calderwood, Esq; ✉ Divisional Management Office, Southern General Hospital, 1345 Govan Road, Glasgow G51 4TF (tel 0141 201 1207, fax 0141 201 1351, e-mail robert.calderwood@sgh.scot.nhs.uk)

CALDICOTT, Dame Fiona; DBE (1996); da of Joseph Maurice Soesan (d 1999), of Coventry, Warks, and Elizabeth Jane, *née* Ransley (d 2007); *b* 12 January 1941; *Educ* City of London Sch for Girls, St Hilda's Coll Oxford (MA, BM BCh); *m* 5 June 1965, Robert Gordon Woodruff Caldicott, s of Capt Gordon Ezra Woodruff (d 1941), of Louisville, KY; 1 da (Lucy Woodruff b 1968), 1 s (Richard Woodruff b 1971 d 1990); *Career* conslt psychiatrist Univ of Warwick 1979–85, conslt psychotherapist Uffculme Clinic 1979–96, sr clinical lectr in psychotherapy Univ of Birmingham 1982–96, unit gen mangr Mental Health Unit Central Birmingham HA 1989–91, dir Adult Psychiatric and Psychotherapy Services S Birmingham HA 1991–94, med dir S Birmingham Mental Health NHS Tst 1994–96; princ Somerville Coll Oxford 1996–, memb Cncl Univ of Oxford 1998–, pro-vice-chllr Univ of Oxford 2001– (chm Conf of Colls 2003–05); chm Section of Psychiatry Union of Euro Med Specialists 1996–99; memb: Conf (now Acad) of Med Royal Colls and their Faculties in UK 1993–96 (chm 1995–96), Central Manpower Ctee BMA 1977–89 and 1996–97, Med Workforce Advsy Ctee 1991–2001, Nat Advsy Ctee on Mentally Disordered Offenders 1993–96, Standing Ctee on Postgrad Med Educn 1993–99, Broadcasting Standards Cmmn 1996–2001; conslt advsr to Cmmrs for High Security Psychiatric Care 1996–2000; RCPsych: chm Manpower Ctee 1981–89, sub dean 1987–90, dean 1990–93, pres 1993–96; pres Guild of Health Writers 1996–99; chm Bd Med Ed BMA 1996–2000, chm Mgmnt Ctee Nat Counselling Service for Sick Doctors 1999–; pres Br Assoc of Counselling Psychotherapy 2000–06; tstee Nuffield Tst 1998–; elected memb GMC 1999–2003; non-exec dir: Coventry Building Soc 1997–2001, Oxford Radcliffe Hospitals NHS Tst 2002–; govr: Univ of Oxford, Cheltenham Coll 2000–, Rugby Sch 2005–; memb Czech Psychiatric Soc 1994; hon conslt psychiatrist S Birmingham Mental Health NHS Tst 1996; hon fell St Hilda's Coll Oxford 1996, Hon DSc Univ of Warwick 1996, Hon MD Univ of Birmingham 1997; FRCPsych 1985, FRSM 1990, fell Acad of Med Singapore 1994, FRCP 1995, FRCPI 1996, FRCGP 1996, FMedSci 1998; *Clubs* Reform; *Style*— Dame Fiona Caldicott, DBE; ✉ Somerville College, Oxford OX2 6HD (tel 01865 270630, fax 01865 280623, e-mail fiona.caldicott@somerville.ox.ac.uk)

CALDWELL, Sir Edward George; KCB (2002, CB 1990), QC (2002); s of late Prof A F Caldwell, and Olive Gertrude, *née* Riddle; *b* 21 August 1941; *Educ* St Andrew's Singapore, Clifton, Worcester Coll Oxford; *m* 1992, Helen, da of Mrs M D Burtenshaw, *née* Rose; *Career* slr Fisher Dowson & Wasbrough 1966, Law Cmmn 1967, 1974–76, 1987–88 and 2002–06, Parly counsel 1981–99, first Parly counsel 1999–2002 (joined Office of Parly Counsel 1969); *Style*— Sir Edward Caldwell, KCB, QC

CALDWELL, Prof John; s of Gilbert Reginald Caldwell (d 1990), and Marian Elizabeth Caldwell (1992); *b* 4 April 1947; *Educ* Chelsea Coll London (BPharm), St Mary's Hosp Med Sch London (PhD), Univ of London (DSc); *m* 13 Sept 1969, Rev Jill Caldwell, *née* Gregory; 2 s (David George Mawdsley b 2 June 1975, James Alexander Gregory b 17 Nov 1979); *Career* Imperial Coll Faculty of Med (St Mary's Hosp Med Sch until merger 1997): lectr in biochemistry 1972–74, lectr in biochemical pharmacology 1974–78, sr lectr in biochemical pharmacology 1978–82, reader in drug metabolism 1982–88, prof of biochemical toxicology 1988–2002, head Dept of Pharmacology and Toxicology 1992–97, dean Imperial Sch of Med at St Mary's 1995–97, head Div of Biomedical Sciences 1997–2002, head of undergraduate med 2000–02; dean Faculty of Med Univ of Liverpool 2002–, pro-vice chllr Univ of Liverpool 2007–; chair: Scientific Ctee N W Cancer Res Fund 2003–, European Fedn for Pharmaceutical Sciences Pharmacogenetics Leadership Gp 2005–; non-exec dir: St Mary's Hosp NHS Tst 1995–98, Huntingdon Life Sciences plc 1997–2003, Cheshire and Merseyside Strategic HA 2003–06, North West Strategic HA 2006–, Eden Biopharma Group Ltd 2004; fndr and dir Amedis Pharmaceuticals Ltd 2000–02; memb: WHO Task Gp on principles for the safety assessment of food additives and contaminants in food 1987, Int Expert Advsy Ctee Centre for Bio-Pharmaceutical Sciences Univ of Leiden 1989, MAFF Steering Gp for Food Surveillance 1993–96, Scientific Advsy Bd Merlin Venture Fund 1996–2004, Ctee on Safety of Meds 1999–2005, Nuffield Cncl for Bioethics Working Pty on Pharmacogenetics 2001–03; scientific advsr on peroxisomal proliferation Dijon Groupement d'Interet Scientifique Universite-Industrielle (appointed by French Miny of HE and Research) 1988–93, conslt for evaluation of chemicals for their carcinogenicity to humans Int Agency for Res on Cancer Lyon 1997–2000; Sterling-Winthrop distinguished prof Univ of Michigan 1995; prestige lectr Univ of Bradford 1996; author of numerous pubns on drug metabolism incl papers, invited contribs and 10 edited books; European ed and fndr Chirality 1989– (Assoc of American Publishers Award for Best New Jl in Science, Technol and Med 1991); past or present memb 17 editorial bds; membership of learned socs incl: Int Soc for the Study of Xenobiotics (memb Cncl 1986–90, pres 1994–95, hon life memb 2001–), Br Pharmacological Soc; tstee: Edgar Lawley Fndn 1997–2002, Francis Holland Educnl Tst 1998–2002, Westlakes Research Inst Cumbria 2003–05; hon memb Canadian Soc for Pharmaceutical Scis 2002–; Hon MRCP 1998; CBiol, FIBiol 1992; *Recreations* reader St Marylebone PC 1997–2002, travel, music (especially choral singing), military history, food and wine; *Clubs* Athenaeum, Liverpool Med Instn; *Style*— Prof John Caldwell; ✉ Dean's Office, Faculty of Medicine, University of Liverpool, Duncan Building, Daulby Street, Liverpool L69 3GA (tel 0151 706 4261)

CALDWELL, Dr Neil Edward; s of Robert Aldridge Caldwell (d 1999), of Barrow-in-Furness, Cumbria, and Kathleen Constance, *née* Barnard; *b* 17 April 1952; *Educ* Dr Challoner's GS Amersham, UCW Aberystwyth (BSc), Poly of Wales (PhD); *m* 1977, Betsan Charles, *née* Jones; 1 da (Catrin Lowri Iorwerth b 1978), 1 s (Owain Rhys Iorwerth b 1980); *Career* vice-pres Aberystwyth Guild of Students 1973–74, pres NUS Wales 1975–77, res student Poly of Wales (now Univ of Glamorgan) 1977–82; National Trust warden: for Llŷn 1982–85, for Gower 1985–88; dir: Campaign for the Protection of Rural Wales 1988–94, Prince of Wales' Ctee 1994–96, The Prince's Trust - Bro 1996–99, exec dir The Prince's Tst Cymru 1999–2000, ind community regeneration conslt; former ed Rural Wales Magazine; memb: European Environmental Bureau 1988–2000, Bd ENTRUST 1996–2002, SW Wales Economic Forum 1999–2004, Bd Wales Cncl for Voluntary Action 2000–, Aggregates Levy Sustainability Fund for Wales; chair Participation Cymru; former memb Welsh Language Bd; vice-chair Wales Wildlife and Countryside Link 1991–99; FRSA; *Books* Discovering Welshness (contrib, 1992), Environment of Wales (contrib, 1993), An Icon for Modern Wales: Realising the Benefits of the National Botanic Garden (2001); *Recreations* walking, cycling, reading, travelling; *Style*— Dr Neil Caldwell; ✉ Neil Caldwell Associates Ltd, Cwmau Uchaf, St Peters, Carmarthen SA33 5DS (tel and fax 01267 234529, e-mail neil@cwmau.fsnet.co.uk)

CALDWELL, Wilfrid Moores (Bill); s of Col Wilfrid Caldwell (d 1935), and Mabel Gertrude, *née* Moores (d 1997); *b* 14 October 1935; *Educ* Marlborough, Magdalene Coll Cambridge (MA); *m* 8 April 1972, Linda Louise, da of Robert Ian Hamish Sievwright (d 1978); 1 da (Fiona b 1976), 2 s (William b 1978, James b 1981); *Career* Nat Serv 2 Lt RA 1954–56, Lt (TA) 1956–59; CA, ptnr Price Waterhouse 1970–92 (joined 1959); non-exec chm: H Young Holdings plc 1993–2001, Jupiter Enhanced Income Investment Tst plc 1999–2004; dir: Powerscreen Int plc 1994–99, Korea Liberalisation Fund Ltd 1995–2000, Br Mediterranean Airways Ltd 1997–2007, Jupiter Second Enhanced Income Tst plc 2004–, Prinicple Capital Investment Tst plc 2005–; chm of govrs: Redcliffe Sch Fulham 1979–89, Arundale Sch Pulborough 1985–95; FCA 1963; *Recreations* golf, skiing, bridge, philately; *Clubs* Carlton; *Style*— Bill Caldwell, Esq; ✉ The Grange, Hesworth Lane, Fittleworth, Pulborough, West Sussex RH20 1EW (tel 01798 865384)

CALEB, Ruth Irene; OBE (2004); da of Emilio Caleb (d 1963), and Edith, *née* Pordes (d 1983); *b* 13 May 1942; *Educ* Church HS Newcastle upon Tyne, Bristol Old Vic Theatre Sch; *m* 1978, Martin Landy; 1 da (Francesca b 1979), 1 s (Jonathan b 1983); *Career* actress 1962–65; BBC: asst floor mangr 1965–67, prodn mangr 1967–72, assoc prodr 1972–79, prodr 1979–89, exec prodr 1989–, head of Drama Wales 1992–96, acting head of Drama Gp 1997, currently exec prodr BBC TV Drama Gp; memb: RTS, BAFTA; FRSA; Alan Clarke Award for outstanding creative contribution to TV 2001, Columbia Tristar Award for Women in Film 2001; *Television* Bread or Blood 1980, Month of the Doctors 1981, The Mountain and the Molehill 1982, Night on the Tyne 1983, Out of Love 1984, Stanley Spencer 1984, The Burston Rebellion 1986 (ACE Award LA, Samuel G Engel Award, Reims Award), Sweet As You Are 1988 (Silver Hugo Chicago, ACE Award LA, BANFF, RTS Writer Award), Ms Rymney Valley 1988, Can You Hear Me Thinking? 1988, Testimony of a Child 1990, Morphine & Dolly Mixtures 1990, Count of Solar 1991, Keeping Tom Nice 1991, Close Relations 1992 (Reims Award, ACE nomination), Black & Blue 1992, Civvies 1992, The Lost Language of Cranes 1992 (Sodom to Hollywood Award Turin, Golden Gate Award, BAFTA nomination), Friday on my Mind 1993, The Old Devils 1993 (Golden Gate Award, BAFTA Cymru Award), The Cormorant 1993, Selected Exits 1994, Pat & Margaret 1995 (Nymph D'Or Monte Carlo, Critics Award Monte Carlo, Reims Award), Street Life 1996, Trip Trap 1996, Bravo 2 Zero 1998, Big Cat 1998, Nice Girl 2000, Last Resort 2001 (Michael Powell Award for Best New Br Film Edinburgh Int Film Festival, Best Feature Thessalonica Film Festival, Best Feature Film Gijon Film Festival), Care 2001 (Best Single Drama BAFTA, Golden Rembrandt, Prix Italia for Single Drama), When I Was 12 2002 (Best Single Drama BAFTA), Tomorrow La Scala! 2002 (Best Made for TV Movie Award BANFF TV Festival, Best Single Drama Independent Award), Out of Control 2002 (Michael Powell Award for Best New Br Film Edinburgh Int Film Festival, Best Single Drama RTS, Best One Off Drama Broadcast Awards, Signis Prize Monte Carlo TV Festival), The Other Boleyn Girl 2003, Rehab 2003, Bullet Boy 2004, Red Dust 2004, England Expects 2004, Love and Hate 2004, Judge John Deed 2004 and 2005, Shooting Dogs 2005, Four Last Songs 2006, Shiny Shiny Bright New Hole in My Heart 2006, London 2006; *Style*— Ms Ruth Caleb, OBE; ✉ BBC Films/Drama Serials, BBC Television Centre, 80 Wood Lane, London W12 7RJ (fax 020 8225 78212)

CALEDON, 7 Earl of (I 1800); Nicholas James Alexander; JP; Baron Caledon (I 1790), Viscount (I 1797); s of 6 Earl of Caledon (d 1980), by his 2 w, Baroness Anne (d 1963), da of Baron Nicolai de Graevenitz (Grand Duchy of Mecklenburg-Schwerin 1847, Russia (Tsar Nicholas I) 1851); *b* 6 May 1955; *Educ* Gordonstoun; *m* 1, 1979 (m dis 1985), Wendy

Catherine, da of Spiro Nicholas Coumantaros, of Athens; m 2, 19 Dec 1989, Henrietta Mary Alison, er da of John Newman, of Compton Park, Compton Chamberlayne, Wilts; 1 s (Frederick James, Viscount Alexander b 15 Oct 1990), 1 da (Lady Leonora Jane b 26 May 1993); *Heir* s, Viscount Alexander; *Career* HM Lord Lieutenant for Co Armagh 1989–; chm Caledon Estates; *Recreations* travel, skiing, flying; *Clubs* Corviglia Ski, Helicopter Club of Ireland; *Style*— The Rt Hon the Earl of Caledon; ✉ Caledon Castle, Caledon, Co Tyrone (tel 028 90568 232)

CALIGARI, Prof Peter Douglas Savaria; s of Flt Lt Kenneth Vane Savaria Caligari, DFM (d 2003), of Worcester, and Mary Annetta, *née* Rock; *b* 10 November 1949; *Educ* Hereford Cathedral Sch, Univ of Birmingham (BSc, PhD, DSc); *m* 23 June 1973 (m dis); 2 da (Louise b 13 Jan 1978, Helena b 26 Sept 1980); *Career* res fell Univ of Birmingham 1974–81 (res asst 1971–74), princ scientific offr Scottish Crop Res Inst 1984–86 (sr scientific offr 1981–84), prof of agric botany Univ of Reading 1986–2006 (head Dept of Agric Botany 1987–98), prof titular Inst of Biology Univ of Talca Chile 2002– (dir 2004–); md: BioHybrids Gp; author of numerous scientific articles and reports; sr ed Heredity 1988–91 (jr ed 1985–88), memb Editorial Bd Euphytica 1991–, chm Pubns Ctee XVIIth Int Genetics Congress (1993) 1991–93; vice-pres Inst of Biology, chm Science Policy Bd 1999–2002; memb: Conf of Agric Profs 1986–2002, Governing Body Plant Science Research Ltd 1991–94, Governing Cncl John Innes Centre 1994–99, European Cncl for the Volcani Centre 1999–2002, Assoc of Applied Biologists, EUCARPIA (Euro Assoc for Res in Plant Breeding), Euro Assoc for Potato Res, Genetical Soc of GB (ex officio ctee memb 1985–91), Int Assoc for Plant Tissue Culture (IAPTC), Sociedad de Genética de Chile, Int Lupin Assoc, La Associación para la Cooperación en Investigaciones Bananeras en el Caribe y en América Tropical (ACORBAT); FRSA 1990, FIBiol 1998 (CIBiol); *Books* Selection Methods in Plant Breeding (with I Bos, 1995, 2 edn 2007), Compositae Vol II Biology and Utilisation (ed with N Hind, 1996), Cashew and Coconuts: Trees for Life (ed with C P Topper et al, 1999), Wheat Taxonomy: the legacy of John Percival (ed with P E Brandham, 2001), Introduction to Plant Breeding (with J Brown, 2007); *Style*— Prof Peter Caligari; ✉ Instituto de Biologia Vegetal y Biotechnologia, Universidad de Talca, 2 Norte 685, Talca, Chile (tel 00 56 71 200 280, fax 00 56 71 200 276, e-mail pcaligari@utalca.cl)

CALLADINE, Prof Christopher Reuben; s of Reuben Calladine (d 1968), of Stapleford, Nottingham, and Mabel, *née* Boam (d 1963); *b* 19 January 1935; *Educ* Nottingham HS, Peterhouse Cambridge (BA), MIT (SM), Univ of Cambridge (ScD); *m* 4 Jan 1964, Mary Ruth Howard, da of Alan Howard Webb (d 1990), of Bengeo, Hertford, and Constance, *née* Askham (d 1978); 2 s (Robert James b 1964, Daniel Edward b 1967), 1 da (Rachel Margaret b 1966); *Career* devpt engr English Electric Co 1958–60; Univ of Cambridge: univ demonstrator 1960–63, univ lectr 1963–78, reader in structural mechanics 1978–86, prof of structural mechanics 1986–2002 (now emeritus); emeritus fell Peterhouse (fell 1960–92, sr fell 1992–2002); memb Gen Bd Univ of Cambridge 1984–88; memb Cncl The Royal Soc 2000–02, former fndn govr Cherry Hinton Infants Sch, former govr Richard Hale Sch Hertford; tstee EMF Biological Research Tst 2005–; Hon DEng Univ of Technol Malaysia 2002; FRS 1984, FICE 1992 (James Alfred Ewing medal 1998), FREng 1994; *Publications* Engineering Plasticity (1969), Theory of Shell Structures (1983), Understanding DNA (with H R Drew, 1992, 3 edn 2004); numerous papers in engineering and scientific jls; *Style*— Prof Christopher Calladine, FREng, FRS; ✉ Peterhouse, Cambridge CB2 1RD (tel 01223 338200, e-mail crc@eng.cam.ac.uk)

CALLAGHAN, Rev Brendan Alphonsus; SJ; s of Dr Alphonsus Callaghan (d 1975), and Dr Kathleen Callaghan, *née* Kavanagh (d 1997); *b* 29 July 1948; *Educ* Stonyhurst, Heythrop Coll, Campion Hall Oxford (MA), Univ of Glasgow (MPhil), Heythrop Coll London (MTh); *Career* voluntary serv teacher Zimbabwe 1966–67; Soc of Jesus: joined 1967, ordained priest 1978, memb Formation Cmmn 1990–, formation asst to provincial 2002–07; superior: Merrivale Community KwaZulu-Natal 1997–98, Brixton Jesuit Community 1993–94, Wimbledon Jesuit Community 1998–2005, Clapham Jesuit Community 2007–; clinical psychologist: Glasgow Southern Gen Hosp 1974–76, Middx Hosp 1976–79; conslt various orders and dioceses 1975–, conslt Catholic Marriage Advsy Cncl 1981–; Heythrop Coll London: lectr in psychology 1980– (also Allen Hall Chelsea 1981–87), sr lectr 2007–, memb Academic Bd 1982–97, memb Governing Body 1982–97, princ 1985–97 (actg princ 1998–99); Univ of London: chm Bd of Examiners Theology and Religious Studies 1987–89, memb Schs Examination Bd 1987–97, memb Collegiate Cncl and Senate 1989–94, memb Cncl 1994–97 and 1997–98; memb Governing Body: Inst of Med Ethics 1989–2002 (hon asst then assoc dir 1976–89, gen sec 1998–2002), Syon House Angmering 1985–97, Campion Hall Univ of Oxford 1985–95; memb: Academic Advsy Ctee Jews Coll 1993–97, Ctee for People in Higher Educn RC Bishop's Conf of Eng and Wales 1985–97, Centre for the Study of Communication and Culture Univ of Santa Clara (chm) 1990–2000, Inst of St Anselm 1991–98, Family Res Tst 1991–2000, Ctee Bishop John Robinson Fellowship 1993–2002, Ethics Ctee Westminster Pastoral Fndn 1994–2002, Local Research Ethics Ctee St Thomas' Hospital 1989–2002 (dep chm 1989–97); visiting lectr: St Joseph's Inst of Theology Kwazulu-Natal 1987 and 1997–98, Imperial Coll London 1990–, KCL 1991–94; visiting prof Fordham Univ NY 1990, visiting scholar Weston Sch of Theology Cambridge Mass 1992; chm Govrs Digby Stuart Coll Roehampton Univ of Surrey (formerly Roehampton Inst London) 1998–2002; patron Inst of Ecumenical Studies Prague Czech Republic 1995–; memb: Br Psychological Soc (assoc fell), Royal African Soc, American Psychological Assoc (int affiliate), Catholic Inst for Int Rels, CND, Amnesty Int, Greenpeace, Centre for the Study of Theology Univ of Essex, Br and Irish Assoc for Practical Theology, Br Assoc for the Study of Religions; Hon FCP; FRSM, AFBPsS, CPsychol; *Publications* Life Before Birth (co-author, 1986); author of various articles, book reviews and poetry in jls; *Recreations* photography, long distance walking, poetry; *Style*— The Rev Brendan Callaghan, SJ; ✉ c/o Heythrop College, Kensington Square, London W8 5HQ (tel 020 7795 4224, fax 020 7795 4200, e-mail b.callaghan@heythrop.ac.uk)

CALLAGHAN, Dr (Thomas) Stanley; s of Thomas Callaghan, of Wyncroft, Killane Rd, Limavady, NI, and Marion, *née* Whyte; *b* 11 February 1948; *Educ* Limavady GS NI, Queen's Univ Belfast (MB BCh, MD), Univ of Abertay Dundee (MSc(HRM)); *m* 12 July 1973, Irene Helen Callaghan, MBE, da of R Bowie, of Stenhouse, Edinburgh; 1 da (Rhona b 29 Jan 1975), 1 s (Gavin b 29 March 1979); *Career* resident Royal Victoria Hosp Belfast 1972–73, registrar in med, cardiology and metabolic med, sr registrar in med and cardiology Royal Victoria Hosp Belfast and Belfast City Hosp, conslt cardiologist NHS Tayside; hon sr lectr in med Dundee Univ and Ninewells Hosp Sch of Med; memb: MRS, Br Hyperlipidaemia Soc, Aberdeen Medico-Chirological Soc, Scottish Soc of Physicians, Forfarshire Med Soc, Scottish Cardiac Soc, Br Cardiac Soc; MRCP, FRCPEd, fell Ulster Soc of Internal Med, FRSM; *Recreations* walking, shooting, photography, music; *Clubs* Edinburgh Angus, Royal and Northern Univ (Aberdeen); *Style*— Dr Stanley Callaghan; ✉ Department of Cardiology, Ninewells Hospital, Dundee (e-mail tscallaghan@aol.com)

CALLAHAN, J Loughlin (Lough); s of John G P Callahan, Lt-Col US Air Force (d 1992), of Dayton, Ohio, and Marie, *née* Loughlin (d 1995); *b* 18 January 1948; *Educ* Holy Cross Coll Worcester Massachusetts (BA), Harvard Law Sch (Juris Dr, cum laude); *m* 5 May 1973, Mary, da of Vincent Reilly (d 1969), of Tinton Falls, New Jersey; 1 s (Christopher b 1974), 1 da (Denise b 1976 d 1996); *Career* law Davis Polk & Wardwell NY 1972–80; investment banking dir: S G Warburg & Co Ltd 1983–86, S G Warburg Securities 1986–92; investment mgmnt dir Mercury Asset Mgmnt Ltd 1992–99, investment mgmnt conslt 1999–; pres: The Europe Fund Inc 1996–99, The United Kingdom Fund Inc 1996–99; dir: International Primary Market Assoc 1986–91 (vice-chm 1988–91), Euroclear Clearance System Société Cooperative 1991–93, Tribune Tst plc 1999–; chm The European Technology and Income Co Ltd 2000–02; conslt Fin Services Office Ernst & Young 1999–; dir Assoc of Investment Tst Companies 2001–; *Recreations* art, music, theatre and tennis; *Clubs* Chelsea Arts; *Style*— Lough Callahan, Esq; ✉ 7 Spencer Hill, London SW19 4PA (tel 020 8947 7726, fax 020 8947 1772, e-mail lough@maryandlough.com)

CALLANAN, Martin; MEP; *b* 8 August 1961; *Educ* Heathfield Sr HS, Newcastle Poly (BSc); *m* 1997, Jayne, *née* Burton; 1 s (Joseph b 1995); *Career* MEP (Cons) NE England 1999–; cncllr Tyne & Wear CC 1983–86, cncllr Gateshead MBC 1987–96; project engrg mangr Scottish & Newcastle Breweries 1986–98; *Style*— Martin Callanan, Esq, MEP

CALLAWAY-FITTALL, Betty Daphne; MBE (1984); da of William Arthur Roberts (d 1965), and Elizabeth Theobald, *née* Hayward (d 1972); *b* 22 March 1928; *Educ* St Paul's Convent, Graycoat Sch London; *m* 1, 1949, E Roy Callaway; m 2, 1978, late Capt William Percival Fittall; m 3, 2003 (remarried), E Roy Callaway; *Career* ice skating trainer; nat trainer W Germany 1969–72; pupils include: Angelika and Erich Buck (Euro Champions and second in World Championships 1972), Chrisztina Regoczy and Andras Sally (Hungarian and World Champions and Olympic Silver medallists 1980), Jayne Torvill and Christopher Dean (World and Euro Champions 1981, 1982, 1983–84, Olympic Champions 1984, Olympic Bronze medallists 1994); hon citizen Ravensburg Germany 1972, Gold medal Nat Skating Assoc 1955, Hungarian Olympic medal 1980, hon life memb Br Ice Teachers Assoc 1994, master coach Br Ice Teachers Assoc 1994, Coach of the Year Nat Coaching Fndn 1995, inducted Nat Coaching Fndn 'Hall of Fame' 1999; *Recreations* water skiing, music, gardening; *Style*— Betty Callaway-Fittall, MBE; ✉ 35 Long Grove, Seer Green, Beaconsfield, Buckinghamshire (tel 01494 67 6370)

CALLCUTT, John; CBE (2006); s of Roy Cyril Callcutt, of Englefield Green, Surrey, and Winifred Elizabeth, formerly Newton; *b* 15 January 1947; *Educ* Salesian Coll Chertsey Surrey, Brooklands Tech Coll, Coll of Law Guildford; *m* 3 June 1973, Claudie Jeanette, da of Bernard Le Coursonnois; 1 s (Marc Roy b 16 Nov 1979), 1 da (Nadine Elizabeth b 18 Sept 1982); *Career* articled clerk Lovegrove & Durant slrs Windsor, legal asst Stephenson Harwood & Tatham slrs until 1974; Crest Homes plc: legal asst 1974–77 (admitted slr 1977), regnl chief exec Westerham Kent 1977–79, company slr 1979, legal dir 1980–82, md 1982; Crest Nicholson plc (parent co of Crest Homes): main bd dir 1985–2006, chm subsids Crest Homes plc and Pearce Construction plc 1988, md ops 1989–91, chief exec 1991–2005, dep chm 2005–06; chief exec English Partnerships 2006–; memb Law Soc 1977; *Recreations* reading fiction, cooking, music, art; *Style*— John Callcutt, Esq, CBE; ✉ English Partnerships, 110 Buckingham Palace Road, London SW1W 9SA

CALLERY, Simon Laurence Christopher; s of Christopher Thomas Callery, and Shirley Fay, *née* Tennant; *Educ* Bloxham Sch, Campion Sch Athens, Berkshire Coll of Art & Design, S Glamorgan Inst of Higher Educn (BA); *Children* 2 s, by Paola Piccato; (Andreas Alessandro Christopher b Sept 1995, Lewis Ettore b May 2000); *Career* artist; *Solo Exhibitions* E14 SE10 (Free Trade Wharf London) 1991, Simon Callery (Anderson O'Day Gallery London) 1993 and 1994, Galleria Christian Stein Turin 1994–, Anthony Wilkinson Fine Art London 1996, Oxford Univ Museum of Nat History 1997, Pitt Rivers Museum Oxford 1997, Art Now 19 (Tate Gallery London, Kohn Turner Gallery LA) 1999, Philippe Casini Gallery Paris 2001, Philippe Casini Gall Paris 2001 and 2002, Segsbury Project Dover Castle 2003; *Group Exhibitions* incl: New Contemporaries (ICA London) 1983, National Eisteddfod (S Wales, prizewinner) 1986, Strictly Painting (Cubitt St Gallery London) 1993, John Moores 18 (Walker Art Gallery Liverpool, prizewinner) 1993, Young British Artists III (Saatchi Gallery) 1994, Landscapes (Ex-Lanificio Bona Torino) 1994, About Vision (MOMA Oxford) 1996–97, Khoj (Br Cncl New Delhi India) 1997, Sensation (touring Royal Acad of Art exbn) 1997–99, Fact & Value (Charlottenborg Copenhagen) 2000, Paper Assets (British Museum) 2001, Colour White (De La War Pavillion Bexhill), Multiples Object de Desir (Musee des Beaux-Arts Nantes); *Awards* Arts Cncl Young Artists grant 1983 and 1984, Gold Medal Nat Eisteddfod S Wales; *Style*— Simon Callery, Esq

CALLMAN, His Hon Clive Vernon Callman; o s of Dr Felix Callman, and Edith Callman; *b* 21 June 1927; *Educ* Ottershaw Coll, St George's Coll Weybridge, LSE (BSc); *m* 1967, Judith Helen, o da of Gus Hines, OBE, JP, of Adelaide, S Aust; 1 s, 1 da; *Career* called to the Bar Middle Temple 1951, in practice London and Norwich 1951–73, dep circuit judge in Civil and Criminal Jurisdiction 1971–73 and 2000–02, circuit judge (SE Circuit) and dep High Court judge 1973–2000; sitting: Royal Courts of Justice, Family Div, Mayor's and City of London Court, Central London County Court, Crown Courts; memb: Standing Ctee of Convocation 1958–79, Cncl Anglo-Jewish Assoc 1956–, Careers Advsy Bd 1979–, Advsy Ctee for Magistrates Courses 1979–, Statute 32 Ctee 1994–; legal assessor GMC and GDC; memb Editorial Bd: Professional Negligence, Child and Family Law Quarterly; dir Frank Cass & Co Ltd 2001–03, dir Vallentine Mitchell and Co Ltd Publishers; Univ of London: memb Senate 1978–94, memb Governing Cncl 1994–2001; govr: LSE, Hebrew Univ of Jerusalem; former memb Court City Univ, fell Birbeck Coll London (govr 1982–2000); *Recreations* the arts, travel, reading; *Clubs* Bar Yacht, Garrick; *Style*— His Hon Clive Callman; ✉ 11 Constable Close, London NW11 6UA (tel 020 8458 3010)

CALLOW, Simon; CBE (1999); *b* 15 June 1949; *Career* actor, director and writer; govr London Inst 2000, tstee Theatres Tst 2004; Hon DLL Queen's Univ Belfast 1999, Hon DLL Univ of Birmingham 2000; *Theatre* roles incl: The Resistable Rise of Arturo Ui (Half Moon) 1978, Titus Andronicus (Bristol Old Vic), Mary Barnes (Royal Court) 1978, Plumbers Progress (Prince of Wales), As You Like It (NT) 1979, title role in Amadeus (NT) 1979, Sisterly Feelings (NT), Verlaine in Total Eclipse (Lyric Hammersmith), Lord Are in Restoration (Royal Court) 1981, Beastly Beatitudes (Duke of York's) 1981, Lord Foppington in The Relapse (Lyric Hammersmith) 1983, On The Spot (Watford and West End) 1984, Melancholy Jacques (Traverse and Bush), Kiss of the Spiderwoman (Bush) 1985, Faust (Lyric Hammersmith) 1988, Single Spies (NT and Queens' Theatre) 1988 and 1989, The Destiny of Me (also dir, Haymarket Leicester) 1993, The Alchemist (Birmingham and RNT) 1996, The Importance of Being Oscar (Savoy) 1997, Chimes at Midnight 1998, The Mystery of Charles Dickens (West End, Broadway and world tour), Through the Leaves (Southwark Playhouse and West End) 2003, The Holy Terror (West End and tour) 2004, Woman in White (West End) 2006, Aladdin (Richmond) 2006, Present Laughter 2006, Merry Wives the Musical 2006; *as director* incl: Loving Reno (Bush) 1984, The Passport (Offstage) 1985, Amadeus (Clwyd) 1986, The Infernal Machine (Lyric Hammersmith) 1986, Cosi fan Tutte (Luzern, Switzerland) 1987, Shirley Valentine (West End/Broadway) 1988, Die Fledermaus (Scottish Opera) 1988–89, Carmen Jones (Old Vic) 1991, Shades (West End) 1992, My Fair Lady (nat tour) 1992, Il Trittico (Broomhill) 1995, La Calisto, Glimmerglass (NY) 1996, Les Enfant du Paradis (RSC) 1996, Il Turco in Italia (Broomhill) 1997, HRH (Playhouse) 1997, The Pajama Game (Birmingham Rep, Princess of Wales Toronto, West End) 1999, The Consul (Holland Park Opera) 1999, Jus' Like That (West End) 2003, Everyman (Norwich Festival) 2003, Le Roi Malgré Lui (Grange Park) 2003; *Television* BBC incl: Instant Enlightenment Inc VAT, Man of Destiny, Juvenilia, La Ronde, All the World's a Stage, Deadhead, David Copperfield (serial) 1986, Cariani and the Courtesan 1987, Old Flames 1989, Patriot Witness, Trials of Oz, Femmes Fatale, Crime and Punishment, Woman in White 1997, An Audience with Charles Dickens 1996 and A Christmas Dickens 1997; other credits incl: Wings of Song (Granada), Bye Bye Columbus (Greenpoint), Chance in a Million (Thames) 1983 and 1985–86, Scarecrow and Mrs King (Warner Bros), Handel (film, Channel 4), The Christmas Tree (YTV), Inspector Morse (Central), Trials, Retribution, Hans Christian Anderson 2001, Galileo's Daughter 2002, Miss Marple 2005, Dr Who 2005, Roman Mysteries 2006; *Radio* incl documentaries on: Charles Laughton (1987), Michéal macLiammóir (1992), Orson Welles (1999); dir Tomorrow Week (1999), The Man Who Came to Dinner (2000), The Judas Kiss (2000), I'll Be George (2001), Third Soldier 2004, Put Money in Thy Purse 2005, Single Spies 2006; *Film* Amadeus 1983, A Room with a View 1986, The Good Father 1986, Maurice 1987, Manifesto 1988, Mr and Mrs Bridge 1991, Crucifer of Blood, Postcards from the Edge 1991, Soft Top Hard Shoulder 1992, Four Weddings and a Funeral 1994, Jefferson in Paris 1995, Le Passager Clandestin 1995, When Nature Calls 1995, England My England 1995, Victory 1995, Bedrooms and Hallways 1998, Shakespeare in Love 1998, No Man's Land 2000, A Christmas Carol 2000, Thunderpants 2001, The Civilisation of Maxwell Bright 2003, Bright Young Things 2003, The Phantom of the Opera 2004, Bob the Butler 2005, Surveillance 2006, Arn the Warrior 2007; also dir: The Ballad of the Sad Café 1991; *Books* Being an Actor (1984, 2 edn 2003), A Difficult Actor: Charles Laughton (1987), Shooting the Actor (1990, 2 edn 2003), Acting in Restoration Comedy (1991), Orson Welles: The Road to Xanadu (1995), The National (1997), Love is Where it Falls (1999), Oscar Wilde and His Circle (2000), Charles Laughton's Night of the Hunter (2000), Henry IV Part One (2002), Henry IV Part Two (2003), Dickens's Christmas (2003), Hello America (2006); *Audio* incl: Shooting the Actor (1992), Fairy Tales (by Oscar Wilde, 1995), Handful of Dust (1995), Dance to the Music of Time (1995), Swann's Way (1996), The Road to Xanadu (1996), The Witches (1997), The Twits (1998), The Plato Papers (1999), London: A Biography (2000), What Ho Jeeves (2000), English Passengers (2001), Jeeves (series, 2003), Death in Venice (2004), Shakespeare (2005), The Aeneid (2006); *Style*— Simon Callow, Esq, CBE; ✉ c/o John Wood, Sally Hope Associates, 108 St Leonard Street, London EC2A 4XS

CALMAN, Prof Sir Kenneth Charles; KCB (1996); s of Arthur MacIntosh Calman (d 1951), and Grace Douglas, *née* Don; *b* 25 December 1941; *Educ* Allan Glens Sch Glasgow, Univ of Glasgow (BSc, MB ChB, PhD, MD); *m* 8 July 1967, Ann, *née* Wilkie; 1 s (Andrew John b 5 Feb 1970), 2 da (Lynn Ann b 16 Nov 1971, Susan Grace b 6 Nov 1974); *Career* lectr in surgery Univ of Glasgow 1968–74, res fell Chester Beatty Inst London 1972–74, prof of oncology Univ of Glasgow 1974–84, dean of postgrad med 1984–89, chief med offr England Dept of Health 1991–1998 (chief med offr Scotland 1989–91); vice-chllr and warden Univ of Durham 1998–2007, chllr Univ of Glasgow 2006–; memb Bd Macmillan Cancer Relief 1999–; Hon DUniv: Stirling 1991, Open Univ 1996, Paisley 1997; Hon DSc: Univ of Strathclyde 1993, Univ of Westminster 1995, Glasgow Caledonian Univ 1995, Univ of Glasgow 1996; Hon MD: Univ of Nottingham 1994, Univ of Birmingham 1996; FRCS, FRCP, FRCGP, FRCPATH, FRCR, FFPHM, FFPM, FRCOG, FRCSI, FRSM, FMedSci, FRSE 1979; *Books* Healthy Respect (with RS Downie, 2 edn 1994), The Potential for Health (1998), A Study of Story Telling, Humour and Learning in Medicine (2000), Medical Education: Past, present and future (2006); *Recreations* gardening, golf, cartoons; *Clubs* Reform, New (Edinburgh); *Style*— Prof Sir Kenneth Calman, KCB, FRSE; ✉ University of Glasgow, Glasgow G12 8QQ (tel 0141 330 4250)

CALNE, Sir Roy Yorke; kt (1986); s of Joseph Robert Calne (d 1984), and Eileen Calne (d 1989); *b* 30 December 1930; *Educ* Lancing, Guy's Hosp Med Sch; *m* 2 March 1956, Patricia Doreen; 4 da (Jane b 1958, Sarah b 1959, Deborah b 1962, Suzanne b 1963), 2 s (Russell b 1964, Richard b 1970); *Career* Nat Serv RAMC BMH Singapore RMO to KEO 2 Gurkhas 1954–56; conslt and sr lectr (surgery) Westminster Hosp London 1962–65, prof of surgery Univ of Cambridge 1965–98 (emeritus prof 1998–), conslt surgn Cambridge HA 1965–98, fell Trinity Hall Cambridge 1965; currently visiting prof of surgery Nat Univ of Singapore; pres Transplantation Soc 1992–94; King Faisal Int Award for Medicine Saudi Arabia 2001, Prince Mahidol Prize for Medicine Thailand 2002; Hon MD: Oslo Univ, Karachi Univ, Hanover Univ; Hon DSc Univ of Edinburgh; hon fell UMDS 1995; hon fell Royal Coll of Surgns of Thailand 1992; Hon FRCSEd 1993; *Books* Renal Transplantation (1963), Lecture Notes in Surgery (with H Ellis, 1965, updated 2005), A Gift of Life (1970), Clinical Organ Transplantation (ed 1971), Organ Grafts (1974), Liver Transplantation (ed & contrib 1983), A Colour Atlas of Transplantation (Renal (1984), Pancreas (1985), Liver (1985)), Transplant Immunology (ed & contrib 1984), Living Surgical Anatomy of the Abdomen (1988), Operative Surgery (ed with S Pollard, 1991), Too Many People (1994), Art, Surgery and Transplantation (1996), The Ultimate Gift (1998); *Recreations* squash, tennis, painting, sculpture; *Style*— Sir Roy Calne; ✉ 22 Barrow Road, Cambridge (tel 01223 359831); private office (tel 01223 361467, fax 01223 301601, e-mail ryc1000@cam.ac.uk)

CALTHORPE, *see:* Anstruther-Gough-Calthorpe

CALVER, Giles Christian; s of Peter Edwin Calver (d 2003), and Patricia Rosemary Calver; *b* 5 December 1958, Gibraltar; *Educ* St Joseph's Coll Ipswich, Gilberd Sch Colchester, Whitelands Coll London (BA), Univ of Western Ontario (MA); *m* (sep); 2 s (Rory Christian b 8 Dec 1991, Jake Harry b 8 July 1994); *Career* account mangr rising to account supervisor Ogilvy & Mather Direct 1985–87, account supervisor DMB&B Direct 1987–89, account dir Pearson Paul Haworth Nolan 1989–90, co-fndr Lippa Pearce Design 1990–2006 (also md); memb Bd Design Business Assoc, memb Parly Gp for Design and Innovation; author of numerous jl articles; MInstD 1994, memb Mktg Soc 2003, memb Communications in Business 2003; *Publications* Retail Graphics (2001), What is Packaging Design? (2004); *Recreations* reading, film, the arts, swimming, cycling; *Style*— Giles Calver, Esq; ✉ Giles Calver Consulting, 8A High Street, Hampton, TW12 2SJ (tel 020 8979 9147, e-mail gilescalver@hotmail.com)

CALVERLEY, 3 Baron (UK 1945); Charles Rodney Muff; s of 2 Baron Calverley (d 1971); *b* 2 October 1946; *Educ* Moravian Boys' Sch Fulneck; *m* 1972 (m dis 2000), Barbara Ann, da of Jonathan Brown, of Colne, Lancs; 2 s (Hon Jonathan Edward b 1975, Hon Andrew Raymond b 1978); *Heir* s, Hon Jonathan Muff; *Career* formerly with City of Bradford Police, memb W Yorkshire Police 1963–1996, seconded to RUC; took seat (Lib Dem) in House of Lords 1997; *Clubs* Parliamentary Sports and Social (hon life memb); *Style*— The Rt Hon the Lord Calverley; ✉ 8 Holden Road, Wibsey, Bradford, West Yorkshire BD6 1TF (tel 01274 679730)

CALVERLEY, Prof Peter Martin Anthony; s of Peter Calverley, and Jennifer, *née* Taylor; *b* 27 November 1949; *Educ* Queen Elizabeth GS Blackburn, Univ of Edinburgh (MB ChB); *m* 28 June 1973, Margaret Elizabeth, da of William Tatam, of Grantham, Lincs; 4 s (Adam Richard, James Iain (twins) b 1977, Robert Andrew b 1979, Thomas Peter b 1981); *Career* house offr Edinburgh 1973–74, SHO Dept of Med Leicester 1975–76, clinical fell MRC 1977–79, sr registrar Dept of Med Univ of Edinburgh 1979–85, MRC (Can) travelling fell McGill Univ Montreal 1982–83; currently: hon conslt physician Aintree Hosps Liverpool, prof of med (pulmonary rehabilitation) Univ of Liverpool; assoc ed Thorax until 1995, assoc ed Euro Respiratory Jl 2000–; chm Br Sleep Soc 2000–02; memb WHO/NHLBI Steering Ctee for Global Initiative in Obstructive Lung Disease; memb: American Thoracic Soc, Assoc of Physicians of GB and Ireland; FRCP, FRCPE, FCCP; *Recreations* travel, skiing and talking; *Style*— Prof Peter Calverley; ✉ University Clinical Department, University Hospital, Longmoor Lane, Aintree, Liverpool L9 7AL (tel 0151 529 5886, fax 0151 529 5888)

CALVERT, Prof (Alan) Hilary; *b* 18 February 1947; *Educ* Univ of Cambridge (BA), UCH London (MB BChir), Chelsea Coll London (MSc), MD; *m*; 3 c; *Career* house physician St Charles' Hosp London 1972–73, house surgn Northwick Park Hosp Harrow Middx 1973, SHO Renal Unit Royal Free Hosp London 1973–74, SHO in med Royal Marsden Hosp London 1974, locum registrar Renal Unit Royal Free Hosp Oct-Dec 1974; Royal Marsden Hosp: research fell 1975–77, hon sr registrar 1977–80, hon conslt in med Div of Med 1980–85, hon conslt Div of Med 1985–89; Inst of Cancer Research: lectr 1977–80, sr lectr 1980–85, reader in clinical pharmacology and team leader Clinical Pharmacology Team Drug Devpt Section 1985–89; Univ of Newcastle upon Tyne: prof of clinical oncology and dir Cancer Research Unit 1989–, head Dept of Oncology 1990–; formerly memb: SW Thames Head and Neck Co-operative Gp, MRC Bladder Cancer Chemotherapy Sub-gp, Advsy Panel Beatson Laboratories, Scientific Ctee Leukaemia Research Fund; currently memb: Phase I Clinical Trials Ctee Cancer Research Campaign, Drug Devpt Ctee and Pharmacokinetics and Metabolism Gp Euro Orgn for Research on Treatment of Cancer (memb Advsy Panel 1979); memb: Int Agency for Research on Cancer Working Gp on the Evaluation of the Carcinogenic Risk of Chemicals to Humans 1980, EORTC/Nat Cancer Inst (USA) Liaison Ctee 1988, EORTC/NCI/CRC Coordinating Ctee; author of numerous pubns and abstracts in learned jls; ed-in-chief Cancer Chemotherapy and Pharmacology, assoc ed Cancer Surveys; memb Editorial Bd: Anticancer Drug Design, Cancer Topics, Biochemical Pharmacology; numerous invited lectures in Europe, USA, Canada and NZ; memb: Br Assoc for Cancer Research, American Assoc for Cancer Research, Assoc of Cancer Physicians, American Soc of Clinical Oncology, Euro Soc of Med Oncology (invited memb), NY Acad of Scis (invited memb); FRCP 1988 (MRCP, accreditation in med oncology 1987); *Style*— Prof Hilary Calvert; ✉ Department of Oncology, Newcastle General Hospital, Westgate Road, Newcastle upon Tyne NE4 6BE (tel 0191 273 8811 ext 22617, fax 0191 273 4867, e-mail hilary.calvert@newcastle.ac.uk)

CALVERT, Margaret Ada Tomsett; JP; da of Donald Arthur Hodge (d 1997), of Seaford, E Sussex, and Ada Constance Janette, *née* Tomsett (d 1973); *b* 8 January 1924; *Educ* Haberdashers' Aske's, UCL (BA); *m* 4 July 1953, Dr Jack Maxwell Calvert, s of Albert Henry Calvert (d 1978), of Selby, N Yorks; 4 s (David b 1955, Ian b 1956, Jonathan b 1958, Alastair b 1967); *Career* WWII WRNS 1942–46; chartered accountant; princ accountant (first woman) Univ of Oxford 1952–53, in public practice as int tax specialist 1954–2002; memb: VAT Tbnls 1973–99, Nat Insurance Tbnl; lectr in comparative taxation Univ of Manchester 1958–88; memb: Taxation Advsy Panel ICAEW 1984–89, Consumer Panel Personal Investment Authy 1993–96; pres Br Fedn of Univ Women 1987–90, memb Women's Nat Cmmn 1990–93, treas Br Fedn of Women Graduates 1992–95 (govr and tstee BFWG Charitable Fndn for Postgrad Awards 1998–2002); former treas: Int Fedn Univ Women, World Assoc of Girl Guides and Girl Scouts; cmmr and memb Cncl Girl Guides Assoc, memb (former divnl pres) Cheshire Branch Br Red Cross; memb Community Health Cncl; FCA 1959; *Recreations* travel, photography; *Style*— Mrs Margaret Calvert; ✉ 3 Chyngton Place, Seaford, East Sussex BN25 4HQ (tel and fax 01323 490685, e-mail mcalvert@talk21.com)

CALVERT, Prof Peter Anthony Richard; s of Raymond Calvert (d 1959), of Helen's Bay, Co Down, and Irene Calvert, MP, *née* Earls (d 2000); *b* 19 November 1936; *Educ* Campbell Coll Belfast, Queens' Coll Cambridge (MA, PhD), Univ of Michigan (AM); *m* 1, 1962 (m dis 1987); 2 c; m 2, 1987, Susan Ann, da of Leonard John Milbank, of Slough, Berks; 2 s; *Career* Regular Army (NI Enlistment) 1955–57; teaching fell Univ of Michigan 1960–61; Univ of Southampton: lectr 1964–71, sr lectr 1971–74, reader in politics 1974–83, prof of comparative and international politics 1984–2002, emeritus prof 2002; visiting lectr Univ of Calif Santa Barbara 1966, res fell Charles Warren Center for Studies in American History Harvard Univ 1969–70, visiting prof Dept of Politics and Sociology Birkbeck Coll London 1984–85; memb Cambridge City Cncl 1962–64, co-opted memb Dorset Educn Ctee 1984–89; FRHistS 1972; *Books* The Mexican Revolution 1910–1914: The Diplomacy of Anglo American Conflict (1968), Latin America: Internal Conflict and International Peace (1969), A Study of Revolution (1970), Revolution (Key Concepts in Political Science) (1970), Mexico (1973), The Mexicans: How They Live and Work (1975), The Concept of Class (1982), The Falklands Crisis: The Rights and the Wrongs (1982), Politics Power and Revolution: An Introduction to Comparative Politics (1983), Revolution and International Politics (1984, 2 edn 1996), Guatemala, A Nation in Turmoil (1985), The Foreign Policy of New States (1986), The Process of Political Succession (ed, 1987), The Central American Security System: North-South or East-West? (ed, 1988), Argentina: Political Culture and Instability (jtly, 1989), Latin America in the Twentieth Century (jtly, 1990, 2 edn 1993), Revolution and Counter-Revolution (1990), Political and Economic Encyclopaedia of South America and the Caribbean (ed, 1991), Sociology Today (jtly, 1992), An Introduction to Comparative Politics (1993), The International Politics of Latin America (1994), Politics and Society in the Third World (jtly, 1995), The Resilience of Democracy (ed jtly, 1999), The South, the North and the Environment (jtly, 1999, 2 edn 2001), Comparative Politics: An Introduction (2002), Border and Territorial Disputes of the World (ed, 2004), A Political and Economic Dictionary of Latin America (2004), Civil Society in Democratization (jt ed, 2004), Politics and Society in the Developing World (jtly, 2007); *Recreations* non-jarring exercise; *Style*— Prof Peter Calvert; ✉ 19 Queens Road, Chandlers Ford, Eastleigh SO53 5AH (tel 023 8025 4130); School of Social Sciences, Politics and International Relations, University of Southampton, Highfield, Southampton SO17 1BJ (tel 023 8059 2577, fax 023 8059 3276, e-mail pcpol@socsci.soton.ac.uk)

CALVERT-SMITH, Hon Mr Justice; Sir David Calvert-Smith; kt (2002); s of Arthur Eustace Calvert-Smith (d 2002), and Stella Margaret, *née* Tilling (d 1995); *b* 6 April 1945; *Educ* Eton, King's Coll Cambridge (MA); *m* 4 Dec 1971, Marianthe; 1 s (Richard b 1972), 1 da (Stella b 1975); *Career* called to the Bar 1969; recorder of the Crown Court 1986–98, first sr Treasy Counsel 1995–97 (jr Treasy counsel 1986–91, sr Treasy counsel 1991–95), QC 1997, DPP 1998–2003, judge of the High Court of Justice (Queen's Bench Div) 2005–; *Style*— The Hon Mr Justice Calvert-Smith; ✉ c/o Royal Courts of Justice, Strand, London WC2A 2LL

CALVIN, Michael; s of Charles Calvin, of Watford, and Margaret, *née* Platts; *b* 3 August 1957; *Educ* Watford GS; *m* Lynn-Marie, da of Oliver Frank Goss; 3 s (Nicholas b 17 April 1987, Aaron b 15 April 1989, William b 20 Jan 1995), 1 da (Lydia Joy b 27 July 1997); *Career* Watford Observer 1974–77, Hayters Sports Agency 1977–79, chief sports writer Westminster Press Newspapers 1979–83, sports reporter Thames TV 1983–84; Daily Telegraph: gen sports feature writer 1984–86, chief sports feature writer 1986–96; sr sports writer The Times 1997–98, chief sports feature writer Mail on Sunday 1998–2002; md Calvin Communications (sports consultancy) 1996–2002, dep dir Eng Inst of Sport 2002–; memb winning British team Camel Trophy off-road rally around Amazon basin 1989, finished third on yacht Hofbrau Lager in British Steel Challenge round the world yacht race 1992–93; winner Seagrave Medal for Outstanding Achievement 1990; ldr Daily Telegraph sports writing team Newspaper of the Year in Sport for Disabled Media Awards 1991, 1992, 1993 and 1994; Sports Reporter of the Year 1992, Sports Journalist of the Year 1992, special award for services to yachting journalism 1994, Sports Reporter of the Year (highly commended) 1998, Sports Reporter of the Year 1999, Sports Story of the Year 2000; memb Sport Writers Assoc; *Books* Cricket Captaincy (1978), Only Wind and Water (1997); *Recreations* innocent adventure; *Clubs* Cape Horners', Royal Ocean Racing; *Style*— Michael Calvin, Esq; ✉ Broomwood, Higher Rads End, Eversholt, Bedfordshire MK17 9ED (tel 01525 280300, fax 01525 280182); The English Institute of Sport, Level 4, 2 Tavistock Place, London WC1H 9RA (tel 0870 759 0411, fac 0870 759 1811)

CALVIN-THOMAS, Joseph Wyndham (known as Wyn Calvin); MBE (1989); s of John Calvin-Thomas (d 1959), and Ethel Mary, *née* Griffiths (d 1974); *b* 28 August 1927; *Educ*

Canton HS Cardiff; *m* 1975, Carole Tarvin-Jones; *Career* served RASC 1944–45; non-stop theatre and broadcasting 1945–; memb Ctee Entertainment Artistes Benevolent Fund 1960–, chm Wales Ctee Variety Club of GB 1980–82, 1984–86 and 1993– (Silver Heart Award 1990); pres Cor Meibion de Cymru (Massed Male Choir of S Wales); vice-pres: London-Welsh Male Choir, Br Music Hall Soc; vice-chm SOS (Soc of Stars); hon prodr Wales Festival of Remembrance (Royal Br Legion); awarded Gold medal for services to tourism in Wales 1983; barker Variety Club of GB 1963–, "King" Grand Order of Water Rats 1990–91, Freeman City of London 1992, memb Welsh Livery Guild 2003; fell Royal Welsh Coll of Music and Drama 1994; OStJ 2000; *Recreations* writing, reading, world-wandering; *Style*— Wyn Calvin, Esq, MBE, OStJ; ✉ 121 Cathedral Road, Cardiff CF11 9PH (tel 029 2023 2777)

CALVOCORESSI, Peter John Ambrose; s of Pandia John Calvocoressi (d 1965), of London, and Irene, *née* Ralli; *b* 17 November 1912, Karachi; *Educ* Eton, Balliol Coll Oxford; *m* 1, 1938, Hon Barbara Dorothy Eden (d 2005), da of late 6 Baron Henley; 2 s; m 2, 2006, Rachel Scott; *Career* serv WWII Wing Cdr RAFVR (Air Intelligence); called to the Bar Inner Temple 1935; author; dir Chatto & Windus Ltd and The Hogarth Press Ltd 1954–65; reader in Int Relations Univ of Sussex 1966–71, editorial dir and chief exec Penguin Books 1972–76; chm: The Africa Bureau 1963–72, The London Library 1966–72, Open Univ Educnl Enterprises 1979–89; memb UN Sub-Ctee on Discrimination and Minorities 1962–71; memb Cncl: Royal Inst of Int Affairs, Inst of Strategic Studies; Hon Dr Open Univ; *Books* Nuremberg - The Facts, the Law and the Consequences (1947), Surveys of International Affairs (5 vols, 1947–54), Middle East Crisis (with Guy Wint, 1957), South Africa and World Opinion (1961), World Order and New States (1962), World Politics Since 1945 (1968, World Politics 1945–2000 8 edn 2001), Total War (with Guy Wint, 1972, 2 edn 1989), The British Experience 1945–75 (1978), Top Secret Ultra (1980), Independent Africa and the World (1985), A Time for Peace (1987), Who's Who in the Bible (1987), Resilient Europe 1870–2000 (1991), Threading my Way (1994), Fall Out (1997); *Clubs* Garrick; *Style*— Peter Calvocoressi, Esq

CAMBER, Richard Monash; s of Maurice Camber (d 1991), of Glasgow, and Libby Camber (d 1981); *b* 22 July 1944; *Educ* Glasgow HS, Univ of Edinburgh (MA), Univ of Paris, Univ of London; *m* 26 Oct 1970, Hon Angela Felicity, da of Baroness Birk (Life Peer), by her husband Ellis Birk; 2 da (Alice b 1974, Chloe b 1980), 1 s (Thomas b 1980); *Career* asst keeper Dept of Medieval and Later Antiquities Br Museum 1970–78; dir: Sotheby's London 1983–87, Sotheby's, Sotheby's International; conslt Euro Works of Art 1988–; FSA; *Recreations* reading, listening to music (particularly opera); *Style*— Richard Camber, Esq, FSA

CAMBRIDGE, Archdeacon of; *see:* Beer, Ven John

CAMDEN, 6 Marquess (UK 1812); David George Edward Henry Pratt; also Baron Camden (GB 1765), Earl Camden and Viscount Bayham (GB 1786), and Earl of Brecknock (UK 1812); s of 5 Marquess Camden, JP, DL (d 1983), and his 1 w, Marjorie Minna, DBE (d 1989), da of late Col Atherton Edward Jenkins; *b* 13 August 1930; *Educ* Eton; *m* 1961 (m dis 1985), Virginia Ann, only da of late Francis Harry Hume Finlaison, of Windsor; 2 s (1 decd), 1 da; *Heir* s, Earl of Brecknock; *Career* late 2 Lt Scots Gds; *Style*— The Most Hon the Marquess Camden; ✉ Wherwell House, Andover, Hampshire SP11 7JP (tel 01264 860020, fax 01264 860123)

CAMERON, (John) Alastair; *see:* Abernethy, Hon Lord

CAMERON, Alexander; s of Alexander Cameron, and Joan, *née* Campbell; *Career* graphic designer; art dir LM magazine 1995–2000, co-head of design CScape 2000–01, dir Cameron Sedley Assocs 2001–; memb Editorial Bd Design Agenda; friend Inst of Ideas; *Publications* Becoming Designers (contrib chapter Ethical Design: The End of Graphic Design?, 1999); *Recreations* five-a-side football (champions N London New Media League 2002), typography, design history; *Style*— Alexander Cameron, Esq; ✉ 51 Kenworthy Road, London E9 5RB (tel 020 8510 0943, mobile 07855 521650); Cameron Sedley Associates, 4 Pear Tree Court, London EC1R 0DS (tel 020 7689 8817, fax 020 7689 8801)

CAMERON, (Allan) Alexander; QC (2003); s of Ian Donald Cameron, and Mary Fleur, *née* Mount; *b* 27 August 1963, London; *Educ* Eton, Univ of Bristol (LLB); *m* 19 May 1990, Sarah Louise, *née* Fearnley-Whittingstall; 1 da (Imogen Clare b 3 Oct 2002), 1 s (Angus Ewan b 8 Oct 2004); *Career* called to the Bar 1986; practising barr, currently memb of chambers 3 Raymond Buildings; memb: Criminal Bar Assoc, Int Bar Assoc; *Recreations* various; *Clubs* White's, Queen's, MCC; *Style*— Alexander Cameron, Esq, QC; ✉ 3 Raymond Buildings, Gray's Inn, London WC1R 5BH

CAMERON, Prof Dame Averil Millicent; DBE (2006, CBE 1999); *b* 8 February 1940; *Educ* Westwood Hall Girls' HS Leek, Somerville Coll Oxford (exhibitioner, Passmore Edwards scholar, Rosa Hovey scholar, state student, MA), UCL (PhD); *m* 1962 (m dis 1980), Alan Douglas Edward Cameron; 1 s, 1 da; *Career* KCL: asst lectr in classics 1965–68, lectr in classics 1968–70, reader in ancient history 1970–78, prof of ancient history 1978–89, memb Cncl 1982–85, head Dept of Classics 1985–89, fell 1987–, prof of late antique and Byzantine studies 1989–94, dir Centre for Hellenic Studies 1989–94, chair Humanities Res Centres 1992–94; warden Keble Coll Oxford 1994–; pro-vice-chllr Univ of Oxford 2001–; chair: British Nat Byzantine Ctee 1983–89, Roman Soc Schs Ctee 1986–88, Classics Sub-Ctee Univ of London Arts Review 1987, Univ of London Byzantine Library Subject Sub-Ctee 1990–94; pres London Assoc of Classical Teachers 1988–90; memb: Cncl British Acad 1983–86, JACT Ancient History Ctee 1985–89, Ctee of Mgmnt and Fin Ctee Warburg Inst 1986–93; business mangr Dialogos Hellenic Studies Review 1994, memb Bd of Mgmnt Inst of Classical Studies 1990–94; ed Jl of Roman Studies 1985–90; visiting asst prof Columbia Univ NYC 1967–68, visiting memb Inst of Advanced Study Princeton 1977–78, Sather prof of classical literature Univ of Calif Berkeley 1986, visiting prof Collège de France 1987, distinguished visitor Inst of Advanced Study Princeton 1992, Lansdowne lectr Univ of Victoria 1992; chm Prosopography of the Byzantine Empire 1997–2005, co-dir Late Antiquity and Early Islam Project 1989–2004; pres Soc for the Promotion of Roman Studies 1995–98, Cncl for Br Research in the Levant 2004–, Ecclesiastical History Soc 2005; chm: Cathedrals Fabric Cmmn 1999– (vice-chm 1996–99), Review Gp on the Royal Peculiars 1999–2000, Inst of Classical Studies 2002–05; Hon DLitt: Univ of Warwick 1996, Univ of St Andrews 1998, Queen's Univ Belfast 2000, Lund Univ 2001, Univ of Aberdeen 2003, Univ of London 2005; corresponding memb Akademie der Wissenschaften zu Göttingen 2006; FBA 1981, FSA 1981; *Books* Procopius (abridged trans, 1967), Agathias (1970), Corippus In Laudem Iustini minoris libri quattuor (1976), Continuity and Change in Sixth-Century Byzantium (collected articles, 1981), Images of Women in Antiquity (ed with Amelie Kuhrt, 1983, revd 1993), Constantinople in the Eighth Century: the Parastaseis Syntomoi Chronikai (ed with Judith Herrin et al, 1984), Procopius and the Sixth Century (1985), The Greek Renaissance in the Roman Empire (ed with Susan Walker, 1989), History as Text (ed, 1989), Christianity and the Rhetoric of Empire (Sather lectr, 1991), The Byzantine and Early Islamic Near East I: Problems in the Literary Sources (ed with Lawrence I Conrad, 1992), Storia dell'età tardoantica/L'antiquité tardive (1992), The Later Roman Empire: Fontana History of the Ancient World (1993), The Mediterranean World in Late Antiquity AD 395–600: Routledge History of Classical Civilization (1993), The Byzantine and Early Islamic Near East II: Land Use and Settlement Patterns (ed with Geoffrey King, 1994), The Byzantine and Early Islamic Near East III: States, Resources and Armies (ed, 1995), Changing Cultures in Early Byzantium (1996), Cambridge Ancient History vol XIII (ed with Peter Garnsey, 1997), Eusebius, Life of Constantine (with S G Hall, 1999), Cambridge Ancient History vol XIV (ed with Michael Whitby and Bryan Ward-Perkins, 2000), Fifty Years of Prosopography (ed, 2003), Cambridge Ancient History vol XII (ed with Alan Bowman and Peter Garnsey, 2006), The Byzantines (2006); author of many articles in jls, etc; *Style*— Prof Dame Averil Cameron, DBE, FBA, FSA; ✉ Keble College, Oxford OX1 3PG (tel 01865 272700, fax 01865 272785)

CAMERON, Rt Rev (Andrew) Bruce; s of Andrew Cameron (d 1975), of Dunoon, Argyll, and Helen, *née* Adam McKechnie (d 1989); *b* 2 May 1941; *Educ* Eastwood Secdy Sch, Edinburgh Theol Coll (Luscombe scholar), New Coll Univ of Edinburgh (Cert Pastoral Studies), Urban Theol Unit Sheffield (Dip Theol and Mission); *m* 1974, Elaine; 2 s (Ewan b 1979, Dermot b 1981); *Career* ordained: deacon 1964, priest 1965; curate: St Michael and All Angels Helensburgh 1964–67, Holy Cross Church Edinburgh 1967–70; chaplain St Mary's Cathedral Edinburgh and diocesan and provincial youth chaplain 1970–75, rector St Mary's Church Dalmahoy and Anglican chaplain Heriot-Watt Univ 1975–82, team priest and churches devpt offr Livingston Ecumenical Parish Livingston New Town 1982–88, rector St John's Church Perth 1988–92, bishop of Aberdeen and Orkney 1992–2006, Primus of Scottish Episcopal Church 2000–06; convenor Scottish Episcopal Church's Mission Bd 1988–92; *Recreations* sport (golf and swimming), music, theatre, reading; *Clubs* Rotary; *Style*— The Rt Rev Bruce Cameron; ✉ 2 Newbigging Grange, Coupar Angus, Perthshire PH13 9GA

CAMERON, David William Duncan; PC (2005), MP; s of Ian Donald Cameron, and Mary Fleur Cameron; *b* 9 October 1966; *Educ* Eton, BNC Oxford (BA); *m* 1 June 1996, Samantha Gwendoline, *qv*, da of Sir Reginald Sheffield, Bt, DL, *qv*; 2 s (Ivan Reginald Ian b 8 April 2002, Arthur Elwen b 14 Feb 2006), 1 da (Nancy Gwendoline Barbara b 19 Jan 2004); *Career* with Cons Research Dept 1988–92, special advsr HM Treasy, then with Home Office, then head of corp affrs Carlton Communications plc; MP (Cons) Witney 2001–; shadow dep ldr of the house 2003–04, shadow local govt min and head of policy co-ordination 2004–05, shadow educn sec 2005, ldr Cons Pty and HM Oppn 2005–; memb Home Affrs Select Ctee 2001–; dir Urbium; *Style*— The Rt Hon David Cameron, MP; ✉ House of Commons, London SW1A 0AA

CAMERON, Dr Douglas; s of Dr Robert Cameron (d 1949), of Cambridge, and Louise Patricia, *née* Smith (d 1991); *b* 2 August 1943; *Educ* The Leys Sch Cambridge, Univ of Glasgow (BSc, MD); *m* 5 July 1969, Catherine Love, da of William Leslie Bews (d 1971), of Glasgow; 2 da (Esther b 1970, Sarah b 1972); *Career* conslt psychiatrist specialising in alcohol problems Leics Health Authy 1976–91; Univ of Leicester: sr lectr in substance misuse 1991–2000, fell 2001–; fndr Leics Community Alcohol and Drugs Servs 1978, interim then full exec memb Alcohol Concern 1983–87; fndr memb New Directions in the Study of Alcohol Gp 1976– (chair 1990–92); inaugural chair The Addictions Forum 1992–95; FRCPsych 1988 (MRCPsych 1974); *Publications* papers incl: Lessons from an Out-Patient Controlled Drinking Group (Journal of Alcoholism, with M T Spence, 1976), Teenage Drinking in South West Scotland (British Journal of Addiction, with R J McKechnie, I A Cameron and J Drewery, 1977), Intoxicated across Europe: In search of Meaning (Addiction Research 2000); contrib: The Misuse of Alcohol - Crucial Issues in Dependence, Treatment and Prevention (ed, N Heather, I Robertson and P Davies, 1985), Alcohol, Minimising the Harm: What Works (1997), Liberating Solutions to Alcohol Problems (1995), The Alcohol Report (with M Plant and D Cameron, 2000); assoc ed Addiction Research 1992–; *Recreations* participant observation of public house culture!; *Style*— Dr Douglas Cameron; ✉ Drury House, 50 Leicester Road, Narborough, Leicestershire LE9 5DF (tel 0116 225 6350, fax 0116 225 6370)

CAMERON, Prof Dugald; OBE (2000); s of late Andrew Cameron, and late May Irene, *née* Jamieson; *b* 4 October 1939; *Educ* HS of Glasgow, Glasgow Sch of Art (DA, Postgrad Dip); *m* Aug 1972, Nancy Cowan, da of late George and late Jean Inglis; *Career* freelance industrial designer and aviation artist 1962–; Glasgow Sch of Art: visiting lectr 1963–70, sr lectr in product design 1970–99, chm of furniture/interior/product design 1975–, govr 1976–82, head of design 1982–, dir (princ) 1991–99; visiting prof: Univ of Strathclyde 1999, Univ of Glasgow 2000; memb: Engrg Advsy Ctee Scottish Ctee Cncl of Industrial Design 1966–, Industrial Design (Engrg) Panel CNAA 1978–, 3D Design Bd CNAA 1978–, Scottish Ctee on Higher Educn Design Cncl 1985–; Lord Provost of Glasgow's Gold Medal for Educn 1998; fndr Squadron Prints Ltd 1977; chm: Skelmorlie Community Cncl 1987, Prestwick Airport Consultative Ctee 2004–; Deacon Incorporation of Weavers 2001–02 (memb Master Ct 1987); hon prof Univ of Glasgow 1993, DSc (hc) Univ of Strathclyde 2002; FCSD 1974, CRAeS 1996; *Books* Glasgow's Own: A History of 602 Sqdn Royal Aux Air Force (1987), Glasgow's Airport (1989), Eagles in the Sky: A Celebration of the RAF on its 75th Birthday (jtly, 1993), A Sense of Place: Glasgow Airport at the Millennium (2000), From Pilcher to the Planets (2003), Glasgow Central: Central to Glasgow (compiler, 2006); author of numerous articles on design and aviation; *Recreations* flying, railways, drawing; *Clubs* Glasgow Art; *Style*— Prof Dugald Cameron, OBE, DSc

CAMERON, Prof Iain Thomas; s of Maj James David Cameron (d 1993), of Preston, and Stella, *née* Turner (d 1999); *b* 21 February 1956; *Educ* Hutton GS, Univ of Edinburgh (BSc, MB ChB, MD), Univ of Cambridge (MA); *m* 1, 1983 (m dis); 2 da (Sarah b 22 Aug 1985, Fiona b 6 Jan 1988); m 2, 1992, Heidi, da of Dr Alan Francis Wade (d 1995); 1 s (James b 7 April 1993), 1 da (Mhairi b 13 July 1995); *Career* clinical and scientific training posts in Edinburgh, Melbourne and Cambridge 1980–92; regius prof of obstetrics and gynaecology Univ of Glasgow 1993–99; Univ of Southampton: prof of obstetrics and gynaecology 1999–, head Sch of Med 2004–, Univ Cncl 2004–07, memb Policy and Resources Ctee 2006–07; chm: Part 1 MRCOG MCQ Sub-Ctee RCOG 1996–99, Meetings Ctee RCOG 2000–03 (also convenor of postgraduate meetings), Jt RCOG/WellBeing Res Advsy Ctee 2003–08; specialist advsr menorrhagia Nat Inst for Clinical Effectiveness (NICE) 2000; memb: Soc for Reproduction and Fertility 1983 (meetings convenor 1997–2000), Blair Bell Research Soc RCOG 1985 (chm 1999–2002), British Fertility Soc 1991 (memb Scientific Meetings Sub-Ctee 1997–2001), American Soc for Reproductive Medicine 1992, Endocrine Soc 1992, Gynaecological Visiting Soc 1993, Soc for Gynecologic Investigation 1996, The 1942 Club 1998, Soc for Endocrinology 1999, Human Fertilisation and Embryology Authy 2001–06, Expert Advsy Network Health Technol Assessment Prog 2004–, MRC Coll of Experts 2005–, Exec Ctee Medical Schs Cncl 2006–; ed-in-chief Reproductive Medicine Review 1999–2002; FRCOG, MRANZCOG, ILTM; *Publications* numerous books and articles on reproductive medicine, menstrual disorders and the endometrium; *Style*— Prof Iain T Cameron; ✉ School of Medicine, South Academic Block, Southampton General Hospital, Tremona Road, Southampton SO16 5YD (tel 023 8079 6581, fax 023 8079 4160, e-mail itc@soton.ac.uk)

CAMERON, Prof Ian Rennell; CBE (1999); s of James Cameron (d 1985), of London, and Frances Mary, *née* Little (d 1959); *b* 20 May 1936; *Educ* Westminster, CCC Oxford (MA), St Thomas' Hosp Med Sch (BM BCh, DM); *m* 1, 1 Feb 1964, Jayne Heather, da of Lt-Col Frank Bustard, OBE (d 1974), of Haslemere, Surrey; 1 s (Hugh Nicholas b 1968), 1 da (Lucinda Emma b 1970); m 2, 24 Dec 1980, Jennifer Jane, da of George Stewart Cowin (d 1978), of IOM; *Career* St Thomas' Hosp Med Sch: med registrar and lectr 1963–68, sr lectr 1969–75, reader in med 1975–79, prof of med 1979–94, dean 1986–89; res fell Cedars-Sinai Med Center LA, asst prof Dept of Physiology UCLA 1968–69; provost and vice-chllr Univ of Wales Coll of Med 1994–2001; princ UMDS 1989–92, dir R&D SE Thames RHA 1993–94; non-exec dir S Glamorgan HA 1995–99; cmmr Cmmn for Health Improvement 1999–2004; chm Mgmnt Team W Lambeth DHA 1982–83, memb Medway HA 1981–86, memb Cncl KCL 1993–98 (hon fell 1998); chm UK Centre for Advancement of Inter Professional Educn (CAIPE) 1998–99; Freeman City of London 1984, Liveryman

Worshipful Soc of Apothecaries 1985 (Yeoman 1976); hon fell CCC Oxford 2000; Hon LLD Univ of Wales 2001, Hon DSc Univ of Glamorgan 2001, Hon PhD Tokyo Women's Med Univ 2001, Hon PhD Kobe-Gakuin Univ 2001, hon fell Cardiff Univ 2002; memb: CVCP 1994–2001, GMC 1994–2001 (treas 1997–2001); FRCP 1976, FMedSci 1998; *Books* Respiratory Disorders (with N T Bateman, 1983); *Recreations* collecting books, china, paintings; *Clubs* Athenaeum; *Style*— Prof Ian Cameron, CBE

CAMERON, Ivy; *b* 25 January 1948; *Educ* Rolle Coll of Educn Exmouth (CertEd), LSE (Dip Industrial Relations and Trade Union Studies); *Career* English teacher Bristol LEA and TEFL Lérida Spain 1969–72; Banking Insurance and Finance Union: area organiser W Midlands, negotiating offr Int Banks, asst sec, nat negotiator 1972–90; ptnr Cameron Woods Assocs 1990–93; memb: Trade Union Congress Women's Ctee 1984–90, EEC's IRIS Training Network; England rep to European Women's Lobby; German Marshall Fund fell Cornel Univ NY 1980, visiting fell Industrial Relations Pembroke Coll Oxford 1989; FRSA 1993; author of numerous articles in a variety of nat newspapers and int TU and mgmnt magazines; *Recreations* singing, dancing, reading, walking, cross-country skiing; *Style*— Ms Ivy Cameron; ✉ Cameron Woods Associates Ltd, Prospect House, 5 Hill Road, Clevedon BS21 7NE (tel 01275 342660, fax 01275 342661, e-mail directors@cameron-woods.co.uk)

CAMERON, John Alastair Nigel (Johnny); s of Col Sir Donald Cameron of Lochiel, KT, CVO, TD, 26 Chief of Clan (d 2004), and Margaret, née Gathorne-Hardy (d 2006); bro of Donald Cameron of Lochiel, *qv*; *b* 24 June 1954, Inverness; *Educ* Harrow, ChCh Oxford (BA), MIT (MSc); *m* 27 May 1982, Julia Rosemary, *née* Wurtzburg; 2 s (Hamish b 1985, Robert b 1991), 1 da (Kirsty b 1987); *Career* Jardine Matheson & Co 1976–80, McKinsey & Co 1981–83, County NatWest 1983–88, Dresdner Kleinwort Benson 1988–98, chief exec corporate banking and financial markets Royal Bank of Scotland 1998– (memb Bd 2006–), dir Citizens Bank USA 2004–; fell Inst of Scottish Bankers; *Recreations* golf, tennis, shooting; *Clubs* Pratt's, New (Edinburgh); *Style*— Johnny Cameron, Esq; ✉ Micheldever House, Micheldever, Hampshire SO21 3DF (tel 01962 774254); Royal Bank of Scotland, 135 Bishopsgate, London (tel 020 7334 1478, e-mail john.cameron@rbos.com)

CAMERON, John Bell; CBE; s of Capt John Archibald, MC (d 1960), and Margaret (d 1974); *b* 14 June 1939; *Educ* Dollar Acad; *m* 24 July 1964, Margaret, da of James Clapperton, OBE (d 1977); *Career* pres NFU of Scotland 1979–84 (first long term pres); chm: EEC Sheepmeat Ctee 1983–90, World Meats Gp 1983–93, UK Sheep Consultative Ctee 1984–86, BR (Scotland) Bd 1988–95, United Auctions Ltd 1988–92, Scottish Beef Cncl 1997–2001, chm Livestock Standards Ctee 2004–; pres: UK Hereford Cattle Soc 2003–04, Scottish Beef Cattle Assoc 2005–; memb BR Bd 1988–95; memb Bd: SW Trains 1995–, Island Line 1995–; chm Bd of Govrs Dollar Acad; Hon Dr of Technol (Railway) 1998; FRAgS, fell Scottish Agric Coll (FSAC); *Recreations* flying, shooting, swimming; *Style*— John Cameron, Esq, CBE; ✉ Balbuthie Farm, Leven, Fife (tel 01333 730210)

CAMERON, Prof Keith Colwyn; s of Leonard George Cameron (d 1969), and Ethel Cameron (d 1999); *b* 1 April 1939; *Educ* Jones' West Monmouth Sch, Univ of Exeter (BA), Univ of Cambridge (CertEd), Université de Rennes (LèsL, Docteur de l'univ); *m* 4 Aug 1962, Marie-Edith Françoise, da of Francis Marie-Joseph Briens (d 1978), of I et V, France; 3 da (Anne b 1963, Cécilia, b 1964, Virginia b 1968); *Career* asst lectr Univ of Aberdeen 1964–66; Univ of Exeter: lectr 1966–76, sr lectr 1976–88, reader 1988–94, dean Faculty of Arts 1991–94 and 1997–98, prof of French and Renaissance studies 1994–2001, prof emeritus 2001–; gen ed: Exeter Textes littéraires 1970–2001, CALL 1990–2001 (hon asst ed 2001–), European Studies 1993–, Europa 1994–; dir: Exeter Tapes 1972–, Elm Bank Pubns 1972–; vice-pres Societe Française d'Etude du Seizieme Siecle; hon vice-pres Euro Movement Devon Branch; FRHistS; Chevalier dans l'Ordre des Palmes Académiques; *Books* Montaigne et l'humour (1966), Agrippa d'Aubigné (1977), Henri III - a Maligned or Malignant King? (1978), Montaigne and his Age (1981), René Maran (1985), B Palissy, Recepte véritable (1988), Concordance de Du Bellay (1988), Computer Assisted Language Learning (1989), From Valois to Bourbon (1989), Louise Labé: Renaissance Poet and Feminist (1990), Humour and History (1993), The Nation: Myth or Reality? (1994), The Literary Portrayal of Passion through the Ages: An Interdisciplinary View (1996), Multimedia CALL: Theory and Practice (1998), National Identity (1999), CALL: Media, Design and Applications (1999), Concordance de Ph. Desportes (2000), CALL: The Challenge of Change (2001), The Changing Face of Montaigne (2003), Jean Boucher: La Vie et Faits Notables de Henry de Valois (2003), P Le Loyer: La Néphélococugie (2004); *Recreations* theatre, walking, travel; *Style*— Prof Keith Cameron; ✉ Villa Effra, 13 avenue Maréchal de Lattre de Tassigny, 06130 Grasse, France (tel 00 33 4 93 40 80 22, e-mail k.c.cameron@exeter.ac.uk)

CAMERON, Prof Robert Andrew Duncan; s of late George Duncan Cameron, of Chichester, W Sussex, and Margaret Mary, *née* Walker; *b* 7 April 1943; *Educ* Marlborough, St John's Coll Oxford (BA), Univ of Manchester (PhD); *m* 12 April 1969, Margaret, da of Romilly Ingram Redfern, of Ipswich; 1 s (Alexander b 1974), 1 da (Harriet b 1976); *Career* res fell and lectr Portsmouth Poly 1967–73; Univ of Birmingham: lectr in zoology 1973–80, sr lectr 1980–86, dep head of the Sch of Continuing Studies 1984–94, reader in ecological genetics 1986–89, prof of evolutionary biology 1989–94; Univ of Sheffield: dir Div of Adult Continuing Educn 1994–98, hon prof of evolutionary biology Dept of Animal and Plant Sciences 1998–; hon res assoc Natural History Museum 1998–; memb: Lib Dems, Br Ecological Soc, The Conchological Soc of GB and Ireland; pres Malacological Soc of London 2000–; Hon Univ Open Univ 2001; FLS 1969, FIBiol, CBiol; *Books* British Land Snails (with M Redfern, 1976), A Field Guide to the Land Snails of Britain and NW Europe (with M P Kerney, 1979); *Recreations* reading, photography, politics; *Style*— Prof Robert Cameron; ✉ 2 Victoria Road, Sheffield S10 2DL (tel 0114 268 6675, e-mail r.cameron@sheffield.ac.uk)

CAMERON, Samantha Gwendoline; da of Sir Reginald Adrian Berkeley Sheffield, Bt, DL, *qv*, and Annabel Astor, *née* Jones; *b* 18 April 1971, London; *Educ* Sch of St Helen and St Katherine Abingdon, Marlborough, Camberwell Coll of Arts, Bristol Poly (BA); *m* 1 June 1996, Rt Hon David William Duncan Cameron, MP, *qv*; 2 s (Ivan Reginald Ian b 8 April 2002, (Arthur) Elwen b 14 Feb 2006), 1 da (Nancy Gwendoline Barbara b 19 Jan 2004); *Career* creative dir Smythson of Bond St 1997–; *Style*— Mrs Samantha Cameron; ✉ Smythson of Bond Street, 40 New Bond Street, London W1S 2DE (tel 020 7629 8558, e-mail samanthacameron@smythson.com)

CAMERON, Sheila Morag Clark; CBE (2004), QC (1983); da of Sir James Clark Cameron, CBE, TD (d 1991), and Lady Irene Maud, *née* Ferguson (d 1986); *b* 22 March 1934; *Educ* Commonweal Lodge Sch Purley Surrey, St Hugh's Coll Oxford (MA); *m* 3 Dec 1960, Gerard Charles Ryan; 2 s (Andrew b 21 Aug 1965, Nicholas b 6 Dec 1967); *Career* called to the Bar Middle Temple 1957, Harmsworth law scholar 1958, pt/t lectr in law Univ of Southampton 1960–64, pt/t tutor Cncl of Legal Educn, recorder of the Crown Court 1985–99, bencher Middle Temple 1988; memb: Bar Cncl 1967–70, Cncl on Tbnls 1986–90, Boundary Cmmn for England 1989–96; chllr: Diocese of Chelmsford 1969–2001, Diocese of London 1992–2001; memb: Cncl Wycombe Abbey Sch 1972–86, Legal Advsy Cmmn Gen Synod of C of E 1975–; Vicar Gen Province of Canterbury 1983–2005, Dean of the Arches and Auditor 2001–, DCL (Lambeth) 2002; *Clubs* Caledonian; *Style*— Sheila Cameron, CBE, QC, DCL; ✉ Bayleaves, Bepton, Midhurst, West Sussex GU29 9RB

CAMERON, Susan Ruth; da of James Norval Cameron, and Ruth Scott Doig, *née* Nicolson; *Educ* Wycombe Abbey (head of sch), Westfield Coll London (exhibitioner, BA, pres Students' Union); *Career* teacher; VSO Oguta Nigeria, teacher and dep head Woodford House NZ; housemistress: Queenswood Sch 1977–78, Sherborne Sch for Girls 1978–84; headmistress: Cobham Hall 1985–89, Downe House 1989–96, North Foreland Lodge 1996–2002; govr: Queen Margaret's Sch York, Farlington Sch Horsham, Repton Sch, Gordonstoun Sch, The Maynard Sch Exeter, Bearwood Coll Wokingham, Marchant-Holliday Sch; pres Wycombe Abbey Srs' Assoc 1996–2004 (currently vice-pres), sec Sherborne Abbey Festival Ctee; *Recreations* music, reading, creative thinking, walking; *Style*— Miss Susan Cameron; ✉ 5 Minterne House, Minterne Magna, Dorchester, Dorset DT2 7AX (tel 01300 341616, fax 01300 341235, e-mail susan.cameron@tiscali.co.uk)

CAMERON, Thomas Anthony (Tony); s of late Thomas Alexander Cameron, and late Olive Cameron; *b* 3 February 1947; *Educ* Stranraer HS; *m* 1970, Elizabeth Christine, *née* Sutherland; 2 s; *Career* Dept of Agric and Fisheries for Scotland 1966–72; Scottish Office: private sec to dep under sec of state 1972–73, private sec to perm under sec of state 1973–74; Dept of Agric and Fisheries for Scotland: higher exec offr (A) 1974–77, princ 1977–82, asst sec 1982–87; Scottish Office: Finance Dept 1987–92, head of agric and food 1992–99; chief exec Scottish Prison Service 1999–2007; memb Duke of Edinburgh's Sixth Commonwealth Study Conf Aust 1986; *Recreations* reading, mountaineering, cycling; *Style*— Tony Cameron, Esq

CAMERON OF DILLINGTON, Baron (Life Peer UK 2004), of Dillington in the County of Somerset; Sir Ewen James Hanning Cameron; kt (2003), DL (Somerset 1989); s of Maj Allan Cameron, MBE, JP, DL, of Munlochy, Ross-shire, and Mary Elisabeth, *née* Vaughan-Lee; *b* 24 November 1949; *Educ* Harrow, Univ of Oxford (MA); *m* 1975, Caroline Anne, da of H D Ripley (d 1967), sometime chm of Willis Faber & Dumas insurance brokers; 3 s (Hon Ewen Allan Hanning b 10 July 1977, Hon James Alexander Hanning 14 May 1979, Hon Angus Derek Hanning b 19 March 1983), 1 da (Hon Flora Elisabeth Patricia b 13 Oct 1986); *Career* cross-bench memb House of Lords; owner and mangr Dillington Estate Somerset; fndr and chm Orchard Media Ltd (commercial radio stations) 1989–99; chm: Lets Go Travel Ltd 1998–2006, Airports Direct Travel Ltd 2006–; nat pres CLA 1995–97, chm Countryside Agency 1999–2004, UK Govt rural advocate 2000–04, memb UK Round Table for Sustainable Devpt 1997–2000; pres Somerset Fedn of Young Farmers' Clubs 1990–91, chm Somerset Strategic Partnership 2004–; High Sheriff Somerset 1986–87; Hon LLD Univ of Exeter 2004; FRICS 1992, FRAgS 1996, FRSA 1996; *Recreations* golf, windsurfing, shooting; *Style*— The Rt Hon the Lord Cameron of Dillington, DL; ✉ Dillington Estate, Ilminster, Somerset TA19 9EG (tel 01460 54614)

CAMERON OF LOCHBROOM, Baron (Life Peer UK 1984), of Lochbroom in the District of Ross and Cromarty; Kenneth John Cameron; PC (1984), QC (1972); s of Hon Lord (John) Cameron, KT, DSC (d 1996), and his 1 w, Eileen Dorothea, *née* Burrell (d 1943); *b* 11 June 1931; *Educ* Edinburgh Acad, Univ of Oxford (MA), Univ of Edinburgh (LLB); *m* 1964, Jean Pamela, da of late Col Granville Murray; 2 da (Hon Victoria Christian (Hon Mrs Fraser) b 1965, Hon Camilla Louise b 1967); *Career* served RN 1950–52; advocate 1958, Lord Advocate of Scotland 1984–89, senator Coll of Justice 1989–2003; chm Industrial Tbnls Scotland 1966–81, pres Pensions Appeal Tbnl Scotland 1976–84 (chm 1975), chm Ctee for Investigation in Scotland of Agric Mktg Schemes 1980–84; chm Royal Fine Art Cmmn for Scotland 1995–2005; chllr's assessor Univ of Edinburgh; Hon FRIAS 1994, FRSE 1990, Hon RSA 2004; *Clubs* New (Edinburgh); *Style*— The Rt Hon the Lord Cameron of Lochbroom, PC, QC, FRSE; ✉ House of Lords, London SW1A 0PW

CAMERON OF LOCHIEL, Donald Angus; 27 Chief of the Clan Cameron; s of Col Sir Donald Cameron of Lochiel, KT, CVO, TD, 26 Chief of Clan (d 2004), and Margaret, *née* Gathorne-Hardy (d 2006); bro of Johnny Cameron, *qv*; *b* 2 August 1946; *Educ* Harrow, ChCh Oxford (MA); *m* 1 June 1974, Lady Cecil Nennella Therese Kerr, da of 12 Marquess of Lothian, KCVO (d 2004); 3 da (Catherine Mary b 1 March 1975, a bridesmaid to HRH The Princess of Wales, Lucy Margot Therese b 5 July 1980, Emily Frances b 18 Jan 1986), 1 s (Donald Andrew John b 26 Nov 1976); *Heir* s, Donald Cameron, yr of Lochiel; *Career* 2 Lt 4/5 Queen's Own Cameron Highlanders (TA) 1966–68; dir J Henry Schroder & Co Ltd 1984–99; pres Highland Soc of London 1994–97; HM Lord-Lt Inverness; FCA 1971; *Style*— Donald Cameron of Lochiel; ✉ Achnacarry, Spean Bridge, Inverness-shire PH34 4EJ (tel 01397 712708)

CAMERON WATT, Prof Donald; s of Robert Cameron Watt (d 1982), and Barbara, *née* Bidwell (d 1977); *b* 17 May 1928; *Educ* Rugby, Oriel Coll Oxford (MA, DLitt); *m* 1, 1951, Marianne Ruth, *née* Grau (d 1962); 1 s (Ewen Cameron Watt, *qv* b 24 June 1956); m 2, 1962, Felicia Cobb Stanley, *née* Cobb (d 1997); 1 step da (Cathy); *Career* Nat Serv Sgt BTA 1946–48; FO Res Dept 1951–54, Rockefeller res fell Washington Centre for Policy Res 1960–61; LSE: asst lectr 1954–56, lectr 1956–62, sr lectr 1962–65, reader 1966–71, titular prof of int history 1972–82, Stevenson prof of int history 1982–93 (emeritus 1993); official historian Cabinet Office 1977–93; sec and chm Assoc of Contemporary Historians 1966–75, chm Greenwich Forum 1974–84, sec and treas Int Cmmn for the History of Int Rels 1982–95; ed: Survey of International Affairs (RIIA) 1962–75, Newsletter of the European Association of American Studies 1962–65; memb Editorial Bd: Political Quarterly 1965–2000, Review International Studies, Intelligence and National Security; corresponding memb Polish Acad of Sciences; hon fell Oriel Coll Oxford 1998; FBA, FRHistS; *Books* Oxford Poetry (1950, 1951), Britain and the Suez Canal (1956), Britain Looks to Germany (1965), Personalities and Policies (1965), Survey of International Affairs 1961–63 (ed, 1965–71), A History of the World in the Twentieth Century Part 1 (1967), Contemporary History in Europe (ed, 1969), Hitler's Mein Kampf (ed, 1969, 1992), Current British Foreign Policy (annual vols, 1970–72), Too Serious a Business (1975, 1991), British Foreign Policy: Selections from the Confidential Print, 1850–1939 (jt ed-in-chief, 1983–96), Succeeding John Bull - America in Britain's Place 1900–1975 (1984), How War Came (1989, 1999), Argentina Between the Powers (ed, 1991); *Recreations* cats, opera; *Style*— Prof Donald Cameron Watt; ✉ c/o London School of Economics and Political Science, London WC2A 2AE (tel 020 7405 7686, fax 020 7955 6800, telex 24655 B)

CAMERON WATT, Ewen; s of Prof Donald Cameron Watt, *qv*, and Marianne Ruth Grau; *b* 24 June 1956; *Educ* St Paul's, Oriel Coll Oxford (BA); *m* 8 Jan 1983, Penelope Ann Cameron Watt, *qv*, da of Robert Henry Weldon, of Stone, Bucks; 2 da (Heather Frances b 31 Dec 1991, Flora Imogen b 4 Sept 1995); *Career* ptnr E B Savory Milln 1979–85, divnl dir SG Warburg Securities (formerly Rowe & Pitman) 1986–90, dir SG Warburg Securities 1990–; *Recreations* walking, travel, Scottish watercolours; *Clubs* Vincent's (Oxford); *Style*— Ewen Cameron Watt, Esq; ✉ House 12, Redhill Park, 12 Pak Pat Shan Road, Tai Tam, Hong Kong; SG Warburg Securities Far East Ltd, 25th Floor, Alexander House, 16–20 Chater Road, Central Hong Kong (tel 01852 5246113, fax 01852 8452075)

CAMERON WATT, Penelope Ann; da of Robert Henry Weldon, and Brenda Marianne, *née* Jones; *b* 10 May 1959; *Educ* Clifton HS Bristol, St Hugh's Coll Oxford (BA); *m* 8 Jan 1983, Ewen Cameron Watt, *qv*, s of Prof Donald Cameron Watt, *qv*, of London; 2 da (Heather Frances b 31 Dec 1991, Flora Imogen b 4 Sept 1995); *Career* EB Savory Milln 1980–82, Wico Galloway and Pearson 1982–84, Kleinwort Benson 1984–87, investment mangr Robert Fleming 1987, dir Indosuez Asia Investment Services 1990–; *Recreations* travel, walking, Japanese language; *Style*— Mrs Ewen Cameron Watt; ✉ Indosuez Asia Investment Services, Suite 2606/2608, One Exchange Square, Central Hong Kong (tel 00 852 5214231, fax 00 852 8681447)

CAMI, Aziz; s of Viktor Cami, of Vienna, and Francesca Cami; *b* 1 November 1950; *Educ* Ravenswood Sch for Boys, Camberwell Sch of Art, London Coll of Printing; *m* 15 June

1991, Jean, *née* Hedley; *Career* graphic designer; asst: Moura George Briggs 1973, Ken Briggs and Associates 1974; dir PIC Design 1976; fndr: C S & S Design 1978, The Partners 1983 (part of WPP Gp); clients incl: 3i, Anglo American, Harrods, Patek Philippe, Boots, Rexam, Wedgwood, Jaguar, Ford (North America), Vertu, Natwest, Diageo, Nestle, DeBeers LV; pres D&AD 1992–93; memb Exec Cncl Design Business Assoc 1992–93; winner of more than 120 creative awards incl D&AD Yellow Pencils, DBA Design Effectiveness Awards, Art Dir's Club of NY and Communication Arts; Hon Dr of Design Univ of Wolverhampton; FCSD, FRSA; *Recreations* music, art, photography; *Clubs* Mosimann's; *Style*— Aziz Cami; ✉ The Partners, Albion Courtyard, Greenhill Rents, Smithfield, London EC1M 6PQ (tel 020 7608 0051, fax 020 7689 4574, e-mail ac@thepartners.co.uk)

CAMM, Prof (Alan) John; s of John Donald Camm, and Joan Camm; *b* 11 January 1947; *Educ* Guy's Hosp Med Sch London (BSc, MB BS, MD); *m* 1987, Joy-Maria, *née* Frappell; 1 s, 1 da; *Career* Guy's Hosp London: house surgn 1971, house physician 1971–72, jr registrar 1972, jr lectr in med 1972–73, registrar in cardiology 1973–74; clinical fell in cardiology Univ of Vermont 1974–75; Bart's London: Br Heart Fndn res registrar 1975–76, sr registrar 1977–79, Wellcome sr lectr and hon conslt cardiologist 1979–83, Sir Ronald Bodley Scott prof of cardiovascular med 1983–86; Prudential prof of clinical cardiology St George's Hosp Med Sch London 1986– (head Div of Cardiology); ed Europace; pres Arrhythmia Alliance, chm Jt Cardiology Ctee RCP; past memb Cncl: RCP, Br Cardiac Soc (past pres); tstee American Coll of Cardiology, past tstee N American Soc of Pacing and Electrophysiology; Freeman City of London, Liveryman Worshipful Soc of Apothecaries; MRSM, MRCS 1971, FACC 1981, FRCP 1984 (LRCP), FESC 1988, fell Cncl of Geriatric Cardiology (FAGC) 2000, fell American Heart Assoc (FAHA) 2001, FRCPEd; CStJ 1990, fell Heart Rhythm Soc; *Publications* First Aid - Step by Step (1978), Pacing for Tachycardia Control (1983), Heart Disease in the Elderly (1984 and 1994), Clinical Electrophysiology of the Heart (1987), Heart Disease in Old Age (1988 and 1990), Clinical Aspects of Arrhythmias (1988), Diseases of the Heart (1989 and 1995), Atrial Fibrillation for the Clinician (1995), Evidence Based Cardiology (1998 and 2003), Drug-Induced Long QT Syndrome (2003), Acquired Long QT Syndrome (2004), Clinical Electrophysiology of the Heart (2004), Dynamic Electrocardiography (2004), European Society of Cardiology Textbook on Cardiovascular Medicine (2006); approx 1000 papers in major jls; *Recreations* collector of prints, watercolours and antiques, model railway enthusiast; *Clubs* Oriental, RSM; *Style*— Prof A John Camm; ✉ St George's University of London, Cranmer Terrace, Tooting, London SW17 0RE (e-mail jcamm@sgul.ac.uk)

CAMOYS, 7 Baron (E 1264; called out of abeyance 1839); (Ralph) Thomas Campion George Sherman Stonor; GCVO (1998), PC (1997), DL (Oxon 1994); s of 6 Baron Camoys (d 1976), and Mary Jeanne, *née* Stourton (d 1987); the Stonors inherited the Barony through a Mary Biddulph who m Thomas Stonor 1732, descended from an earlier Thomas Stonor and Jeanne, da of John de la Pole, Duke of Suffolk, thus descending from Geoffrey Chaucer, the poet; *b* 16 April 1940; *Educ* Eton, Balliol Coll Oxford; *m* 11 June 1966, Elisabeth Mary Hyde, o da of Sir William Hyde Parker, 11 Bt; 3 da (Hon Alina (Hon Mrs Barrowcliff) b 1967, Hon Emily (Countess of Stair) b 1969, Hon Sophia (Baroness Moritz von Hirsch) b 1971), 1 s (Hon (Ralph) William Robert Thomas b 10 Sept 1974); *Heir* s, Hon William Stonor; *Career* md Rothschild Intercontinental Bank Ltd 1969–75, with Amex Bank Ltd 1975–78, md Barclays Merchant Bank 1978–84, dir Barclays Bank plc 1984–94, chief exec Barclays de Zoete Wedd Holdings Ltd 1986–87 (dep chm 1987–98), dep chm Barclays Capital 1997–98; dir 3i Group 1991–2002, dep chm Sotheby's Holdings Inc 1994–97, dir Perpetual plc 1994–2000, dir Brit Grolux Ltd 1994–; Lord Chamberlain of The Queen's Household 1998–2000 (Permanent Lord in Waiting to HM The Queen 2000, Lord in Waiting 1992–98); cmmr Eng Heritage 1984–87, memb Royal Cmmn on Historical MSS 1987–94; consultor Extraordinary Section of the Administration of the Patrimony of the Holy See 1991–2006; memb Court of Assts Fishmongers' Co (Prime Warden 1992–93); Hon DLitt Univ of Sheffield 2001; 1 class Order of Gorkha Dakshina Bahu (Nepal) 1980, GCSG 2006; *Recreations* the arts, family; *Clubs* Boodle's, Leander, Pilgrims; *Style*— The Rt Hon the Lord Camoys, GCVO, PC, DL; ✉ Stonor Park, Henley-on-Thames, Oxfordshire RG9 6HF (tel 01491 638644)

CAMP, Jeffery Bruce; s of George Camp, and Caroline Camp; *b* 17 April 1923; *Educ* Lowestoft and Ipswich Art Schs, Edinburgh Coll of Art; *m* 1963, Laetitia, *née* Yhap; *Career* artist; pt/t lectr Slade Sch of Fine Art Univ of London; public collections incl: Arts Cncl of GB, City Art Gallery Bradford, Br Cncl, Contemporary Arts Soc, DOE, Fermoy Art Gallery King's Lynn, Univ of London, Manchester Educn Dept, Norwich Castle Museum, The Nuffield Orgn, Tate Gallery, Towner Art Gallery Eastbourne, Harris Museum and Art Gallery Preston, RA; *Solo Exhibitions* Edinburgh Festival 1950, Galerie de Seine London 1958, Beaux Arts Gallery London 1959, 1961 and 1963, New Art Centre London 1968, Fermoy Art Gallery King's Lynn 1970, South London Art Gallery (Retrospective) 1973, Royal Shakespeare Theatre Stratford 1974, Serpentine Gallery (Arts Cncl) 1978, Bradford City Art Gallery 1979, Browse & Darby 1984, The 29 Aldeburgh Festival in assoc with the Arts Cncl of GB 1986, Nigel Greenwood Gallery 1986–87 and 1990, The Library Gallery Univ of Surrey 1988, Royal Albert Museum Exeter (Retrospective) 1988, Royal Acad of Arts London 1988, Manchester City Art Gallery 1988, Laing Art Gallery Newcastle 1988, Browse & Darby 1993, 1997 and 2001, Art Space Gallery 2002, Love In The Friends' Room at the Royal Academy 2003; *Group Exhibitions* incl: Aldeburgh Festival 1958, 1961 and 1963, Cafe Royal Centenary 1965, Marlborough Gallery London 1968, Br Painting 1974, Hayward Gallery London 1974, Br Painting 1952–77, Royal Acad Drawings at Burlington House 1977, Drawing and Watercolours for China (Edinburgh, Br Cncl Touring) 1982, Br Cncl Exhibition Delhi and Bombay 1985, Proud and Prejudiced Twining Gallery NY 1985, The Self Portrait A Modern View Artsite Gallery Bath and tour 1987, Small is Beautiful Angela Flowers Gallery London 1988, Picturing People - Figurative Painting from Britain 1945–89 (Br exhbn, Kuala Lumpur) 1988–89, Salute to Turner (Thos Agnew & Sons) London 1989, Images of Paradise Harewood House 1989, Nine Contemporary Painters Bristol Art Gallery 1990, For a Wider World (Br Cncl), RA Summer Exhbn 1990, Coastlines (Br Cncl) 1993, Nat Tst Exhbn Christies 1994; RA 1984 (ARA 1974); *Books* Draw (1981), Paint (1996); *Style*— Jeffery Camp, Esq, RA; ✉ 27 Stirling Road, London SW9 9EF

CAMPBELL, Alan; MP; *Career* MP (Lab) Tynemouth 1997–; PPS to: Rt Hon Lord MacDonald of Tradeston, CBE, PC, *qv* 2001–03, Rt Hon Adam Ingram, MP, *qv* 2003–05, asst Govt whip 2005–06, a Lord Cmmr of HM Treasy (Govt whip) 2006–; *Style*— Alan Campbell, Esq, MP; ✉ House of Commons, London SW1A 0AA (tel 020 7219 3000)

CAMPBELL, Alastair John; s of Donald Campbell, of Embsay, N Yorks, and Elizabeth Howie, *née* Caldwell; *b* 25 May 1957; *Educ* City of Leicester Boys' Sch, Gonville & Caius Coll Cambridge (MA); *Partner* Fiona Millar; 2 s (Rory b 23 Oct 1987, Calum b 29 July 1989), 1 da (Grace b 30 April 1994); *Career* trainee reporter Tavistock Times and Sunday Independent Truro Mirror Group Training Scheme 1980–82, freelance reporter London 1982–83, reporter Daily Mirror 1983–85, news ed Sunday Today 1985–86, reporter Daily Mirror 1986; Sunday Mirror: political corr 1986–87, political ed 1987–89, columnist 1989–92; Daily Mirror: political ed 1989–93, columnist 1992–93; presenter Week in Westminster (BBC) 1992–94, asst ed (politics) and columnist Today 1993–94, columnist Tribune 1993–, political commentator LBC 1993–94; press sec to Tony Blair as Ldr Lab Pty 1994–97, chief press sec Tony Blair as PM 1997–2003, PM's dir of communication and strategy 2001–03; *Recreations* bagpipes, Burnley FC; *Style*— Mr Alastair Campbell

CAMPBELL, Prof Alexander George Macpherson (Alex); s of Alexander McCorkindale Campbell, DSO, OBE, TD (d 1998), and Isabel Catherine, *née* Macpherson (d 1990); *b* 3 February 1931; *Educ* Dollar Acad, Univ of Glasgow (MB ChB); *m* 19 Sept 1959, Sheila Mary, da of Sir Peter George Macdonald (d 1983), of Edinburgh; 2 da (Fiona Ann b 1960, Patricia Mary b 1963), 1 s (Andrew Alexander Macdonald b 1965); *Career* Nat Serv Parachute Field Ambulance 16 Ind Parachute Bde 1956–58; registrar paediatrics Royal Hosp for Sick Children Edinburgh 1959–61, res house offr Gt Ormond St Hosp 1961–62, asst chief resident physician Children's Hosp of Philadelphia 1962–63; fell: paediatric cardiology Hosp for Sick Children Toronto 1963–64, perinatal physiology Nuffield Inst for Med Research Oxford 1964–66; lectr in child health Univ of St Andrews 1966–67, asst (later assoc prof) paediatrics Yale Univ Sch of Med 1967–73, prof of child health Univ of Aberdeen 1973–92; chm Jt Ctee for Vaccination and Immunisation Dept of Health 1989–96; Hon FRCPCH, FRCPE; *Books* Forfar & Arneil's Textbook of Paediatrics (co-ed, 1998); *Style*— Prof Alex Campbell; ✉ 34 Woodburn Crescent, Aberdeen AB15 8JX (tel 01224 319152, e-mail acamp55052@aol.com)

CAMPBELL, Her Hon Judge Ann Rosemary; DL (Oxfordshire 1998); da of Sqdn Ldr Richard Henry Beeching, and Gladys Maud, *née* Trussler; *b* 13 December 1948; *Educ* Lady Eleanor Holles Sch, New Hall Cambridge (MA); *m* His Hon Judge (John) Quentin Campbell, *qv*; 1 da (Arabella b 27 June 1977), 1 s (Frederick b 28 June 1982); *Career* slr in private practice 1972–92, formerly ptnr Henmans Oxford, district judge 1992–2004, recorder 1999–2004 (asst recorder 1995–99), circuit judge (South Eastern Circuit) 2004–; chm of govrs Oxford HS 1998–2004, memb Ct Oxford Brookes Univ 2001–, tstee Oxford Preservation Tst 2005–; *Style*— Her Hon Judge Ann Campbell, DL

CAMPBELL, The Rt Hon Lord Justice; Rt Hon Sir (William) Anthony; kt (1988), PC (1998); s of Harold Ernest Campbell, CBE (d 1980), of Rockmore, Newcastle, Co Down, and Marion Fordyce, *née* Wheeler (d 1996); *b* 30 October 1936; *Educ* Campbell Coll Belfast, Queens' Coll Cambridge (BA); *m* 8 July 1960, (Isobel Rosemary) Gail, da of Frederick Malcolm McKibbin, JP, of Holywood, Co Down; 3 da (Fiona (Mrs Chamberlain) b 1961, Nicola (Mrs Vernon-Powell) b 1963, Susan (Mrs Haig) b 1964); *Career* called to the Bar Gray's Inn 1960, hon bencher 1995; Inn of Court NI 1960, bencher 1983; QC 1974, sr crown counsel NI 1984–88, judge of the High Court of Justice NI 1988–98, a Lord Justice of Appeal NI 1998–; chm: Cncl of Legal Educn NI, Judicial Studies Bd for NI; chllr Diocese of Down & Dromore, memb Cncl St Leonards Sch St Andrews 1985–94, govr Campbell Coll Belfast 1976–98; *Recreations* hill walking, sailing; *Clubs* Royal Ulster Yacht, New (Edinburgh); *Style*— The Rt Hon Lord Justice Campbell; ✉ Royal Courts of Justice, Belfast BT1 3JY (tel 028 9023 5111)

CAMPBELL, Archibald Greig (Archie); s of William Greig Campbell (d 1986), and Isabel Hamilton, *née* Gordon (d 1961); *b* 17 March 1934; *Educ* Kelvinside Acad (capped for Scotland in rugby), Univ of Glasgow; *m* 1, 1960 (m dis 1986), Madge Eileen, *née* Baillie; 3 da (Deborah Elaine b 1963, Angela Gillian b 1965, Claire Patricia b 1967); m 2, 1986, Teresa Lois, *née* Kingsbury; *Career* Touche Ross (latterly Deloitte & Touche): joined 1958, regnl ptnr Asia Pacific Region Singapore 1975–78, dir Int Servs New York 1978–81, regnl ptnr Europe 1981–90, dep regnl dir Special Projects Europe 1990–92, dep ceo Central/Eastern Europe 1992–94; sr ptnr Campbell Fin Conslts 1992–; MICAS 1958, ACA 1977, ICA Hong Kong 1978, ICA Malaysia 1978, ICA Singapore 1978; *Recreations* golf, tennis; *Clubs* Loch Lomond Golf, St George's Hill Golf, Castle Royal Golf, Oaks Country (FL); *Style*— Archie Campbell, Esq; ✉ Water's Edge, Loddon Drive, Wargrave, Berkshire RG10 8HL; 362 MacEwen Drive, Osprey, Florida 34220, USA

CAMPBELL, (Mary Lorimer) Beatrix; da of James William Barnes, of Carlisle, Cumbria, and Catharina Johana, *née* Lorier; *b* 3 February 1947; *Educ* Harraby Secdy Modern Sch, Carlisle HS, AA; *m* 28 Oct 1968 (m dis 1978), Bobby Campbell (d 1997); *Career* journalist: Morning Star 1967–76, Time Out 1979, City Limits 1981–87; freelance reporter: New Statesman, The Guardian, The Observer, Marxism Today; columnist: The Independent 1993–95, The Guardian 1995–; broadcaster: I Shot My Husband and No One Asked Me Why (documentary, Channel 4), Listening to the Children (documentary, Channel 4), Vice and Virtue (Radio 4); memb: Women's Liberation Movement, Communist Party; *Books* Sweet Freedom (with Anna Coote, 1981), Wigan Pier Revisited (1984, winner of Cheltenham Literary Festival), The Iron Ladies - Why Women Vote Tory (1987, winner of Fawcett Prize), Unofficial Secrets - The Cleveland Child Sex Abuse Case (1988, new edn 1998), Goliath - Britain's Dangerous Places (1993), Diana, Princess of Wales - How Sexual Politics Shook the Monarchy (1998), And All the Children Cried (with Judith Jones, commissioned by West Yorkshire Playhouse, 2002); *Style*— Ms Beatrix Campbell; ✉ mobile 07866 370769, e-mail beatrixcampbell@yahoo.com

CAMPBELL, Bryn; s of Brinley Campbell (d 1990), and Dorothy Irene, *née* Hughes (d 2000); *b* 20 May 1933; *Educ* Mountain Ash GS (Viscount Hall travel scholarship), Univ of Manchester; *m* 1960, Audrey Campbell, da of late Thomas Idris Berryman; *Career* Nat Serv photographer RAF 1951–53, industrial photographer London 1956–57, agency photographer Fleet St 1957–58, asst ed Practical Photography and Photo News Weekly 1959–60, ed Cameras 1960–61, assoc ed British Journal of Photography 1962–63, redesigned and picture edited BJ Annual 1964, picture ed The Observer (helped to launch The Observer Colour Magazine) 1964–66, freelance photographer (retained by The Observer) 1966–72, official photographer Br Headless Valley Expedition (which carried out first ever N-S transnavigation of Canada by water) 1972, nominee photographer Magnum Photos 1972–73, external examiner in photography to eight polys and art colls 1974–80, first foreign photographer to lecture to Guild of Finnish Photographers Univ of Vaasa Finland 1974, hon assoc lectr PCL 1974–77, photographed final stages of Vietnam War 1975, travelled widely on assignment for maj magazines 1975–77, writer and presenter BBC TV series and book Exploring Photography 1978, official photographer Transglobe Expedition (which carried out first ever transnavigation of the world's surface on its polar axis) 1979–82, ed World Photography (UK, USA and Japan) 1981; conslt picture ed: Sunday Express Magazine 1984–85, The Illustrated London News 1985–87 and 1989–93, Daily Telegraph Magazine 1987–88; occasional appearances Saturday Review BBC TV 1985–86; memb: Photography Bd CNAA 1977–78, Arts Panel Arts Cncl of GB 1980–83 (memb Photography Ctee 1978–80); chm Sports Pictures of the Year Judging Panel 1984–88; Br judge: World Press Photo competition 1985, Int Center for Photography annual awards NY 1989, Humanity Photo Award Beijing 1998 and 2000; editorial conslt Photographers International magazine 1995–; judge 2006 Macao Visual Arts Exhbn; tstee The Photographers' Gallery London 1974–84, patron Herefordshire Photography Festival 1998–2003; solo exhibitions incl: Reports and Rumours (The Photographers' Gallery London and tour) 1973, Village School (Chichester 900 festival Sussex and tour) 1975, Caring and Concern (Kodak Gallery London) 1976, Sports View (Watford and tour) 1977, retrospective (Salzburg Coll Austria) 1978, Antarctic Expedition (Olympus Gallery London) 1980, colour retrospective (The Photographers' Gallery London then tour) 1981; gp exhibitions incl: The Camera and the Craftsman (Crafts Centre London) 1975, Personal View (Br Cncl London and tour) 1977, European Colour Photography (The Photographers' Gallery London) 1978, Kindness: The Keflex Collection (Hamiltons Gallery London) 1982, The Other Britain (Nat Theatre London) 1983; author of numerous books on photography; FBIPP 1969, Hon FRPS 1996 (FRPS 1971); *Awards* 1st Prize (News) Br Press Pictures of the Year 1969, Kodak Bursary 1973, Fenton Medal RPS 2002; *Books* Village School (1995), The Imprecise Image (1995), Reports and Rumours (2001, all books of own photographs); *Style*— Bryn Campbell, Esq;

✉ Stonehaven, Charterhouse Road, Godalming, Surrey GU7 2AT (tel 01483 424915, e-mail bryn.campbell@btopenworld.com)

CAMPBELL, Christopher Robert James (Chris); s of late Kenneth James Campbell, and Barbara Muir Kirkness Campbell; *b* 1 December 1958; *Educ* Daniel Stewart's and Melville Coll Edinburgh, Univ of Edinburgh (LLB); *m* 10 Sept 1983, Katharine Mairi, da of Archibald Macdonald; 1 s (Andrew Archibald Kenneth b 16 Nov 1988), 1 da (Victoria Barbara Dorothy b 8 April 1991); *Career* Dundas & Wilson CS: apprentice 1980–82, asst 1982–87, ptnr 1987–, ptnr i/c Glasgow office 1991–96, dep managing ptnr 1995–96, managing ptnr 1996–; *Recreations* golf, cycling, football, photography; *Clubs* Murrayfield Golf (Edinburgh), Royal Scottish Automobile; *Style—* Chris Campbell, Esq; ✉ Dundas & Wilson, Saltire Court, 20 Castle Terrace, Edinburgh EH1 2EN (tel 0131 228 8000, fax 0131 228 8888)

CAMPBELL, Colin A; *b* 6 January 1947; *Career* insurance clerk Sun Alliance Insurance Co; admitted as a slr 1973; Culross Lipkin Slrs: articled clerk, asst slr 1967–73; Associated Communications Corporation plc 1974–81, gp dir of Legal Affairs and co sec Central Independent Television plc 1981–94, head of rights gp BBC Network Television 1994–96, head of business affairs BBC Broadcasting 1996–97, dir of legal and business affairs Channel Five 1997–; memb: Law Soc, Fleet Street Lawyers Assoc; *Recreations* family pursuits, the Arts generally, most sports (currently playing golf and hockey), fine food and wine; *Style—* Colin Campbell, Esq; ✉ Channel 5 Broadcasting, 22 Long Acre, London WC2E 9LY (tel 020 7550 5506 and 01372 892155, e-mail colin.campbell@five.tv)

CAMPBELL, Prof Sir Colin Murray; kt (1994), DL (Notts 1996); s of late Donald Campbell, and late Isobel Campbell; *b* 26 December 1944; *Educ* Robert Gordon's Coll Aberdeen, Univ of Aberdeen (LLD); *m* 15 Aug 1974 (m dis 1999), Elaine, da of Roger Carlisle; 1 da (Victoria Louise b 1979), 1 s (Andrew William Roger b 1982); m 2, 12 Feb 2002, Maria Day; *Career* lectr: Faculty of Law Univ of Dundee 1967–69, Dept of Public Law Univ of Edinburgh 1969–73; Queen's Univ Belfast: prof of jurisprudence 1974–88, dean Faculty of Law 1977–80, pro-vice-chllr 1983–87; vice-chllr Univ of Nottingham 1988–; dir HEFCE E Univ Holding Co 2001–; chm: Qubis Ltd 1983–88, Lace Market Development Co 1989–97, Zeton Ltd 1990; dir Swiss Re 1999–2005; memb: Cncl Soc for Computers and Law 1973–88, Standing Advsy Cmmn on Human Rights for NI 1977–80, Legal Aid Advsy Ctee NI 1978–82, Mental Health Legislation Review Ctee NI 1978–82, UGC 1987–88, Nottingham Devpt Enterprise 1988–91, UFC Scottish Ctee 1989–93; chm: Ind Advice Gp on Consumer Protection in NI 1984, NI Econ Cncl 1987–94, Human Fertilization and Embryology Authy 1990–94, Med Workforce Standing Advsy Ctee 1991–2001, Food Advsy Ctee 1994–2001, Human Genetics Advsy Cmmn 1996–99; memb: HEFCE 1992–97, Inquiry into Police Responsibilities and Rewards 1992–93, Trent RHA 1992–96; vice-chm CVCP 1992–93; HM First Cmmr for Judicial Appts 2001–06; Hon LLD Shanghai Jiao Tong 2006; *Books* Law & Society (co-ed, 1979), Do We Need a Bill of Rights? (ed, 1980), Data Processing and the Law (ed, 1984); contrib numerous articles in books and periodicals; *Recreations* sport, walking, music, reading; *Style—* Prof Sir Colin Campbell, DL; ✉ University of Nottingham, University Park, Nottingham NG7 2RD (tel 0115 951 3001, fax 0115 951 3005, e-mail colin.campbell@nottingham.ac.uk)

CAMPBELL, Darren; MBE (2005); *b* 1975; *Career* athlete; memb Sale Harriers; achievements at 100m: Gold medal European Junior Championships 1991, Silver medal World Junior Championships 1992, semi-finalist World Championships Athens 1997, winner National Championships 1998, Gold medal European Championships Budapest 1998, Bronze medal European Championships Munich 2002, Bronze medal World Championships Paris 2003; achievements at 4x100m: Gold medal European Junior Championships 1991, Gold medal World Junior Championships 1992, Bronze medal World Championships Athens 1997, Gold medal European Championships Budapest 1998, Gold medal Cwlth Games Kuala Lumpur 1998, Silver medal World Championships Seville 1999, Gold medal Cwlth Games Manchester 2002, Gold medal European Championships Munich 2002, Gold medal Olympic Games Athens 2004, Gold medal European Championships Copenhagen 2006; achievements at 200m: Gold medal European Junior Championships 1991, Silver medal World Junior Championships 1992, Silver medal Olympic Games Sydney 2000, Bronze medal Cwlth Games Manchester 2002; former footballer with Newport FC; *Style—* Darren Campbell, MBE; ✉ c/o Sue Barrett, Nuff Respect, The Coach House, 107 Sherland Road, Twickenham, Middlesex TW1 4HB (tel 020 8891 4145, fax 020 8891 4140, website www.nuff-respect.co.uk)

CAMPBELL, David Allan; s of James Campbell, and Jean Campbell; *b* 9 December 1959, Ayr, Scotland; *Educ* William Hulme's GS Manchester, Univ of Bristol (LLB); *m* 8 June 1991, Susan, *née* Jenkins; 1 s (Ewan James b 14 March 1994), 1 da (Isabella Grace Caitlin b 2 Feb 2001); *Career* slr; ptnr Sansbury Campbell, chm SW Regnl Duty Slr Ctee 1995–, chief assessor Law Soc criminal litigation accreditation scheme 2001–06; memb Law Soc 1985; *Style—* David Campbell, Esq; ✉ Sansbury Campbell, 6 Unity Street, Bristol BS1 5HH (tel 0117 926 5341, fax 0117 922 5625, e-mail dcampbell@sansburycampbell.co.uk)

CAMPBELL, David Lachlan; *b* 4 September 1959, Glasgow; *Educ* Washington Univ St Louis MO (AB, MBA); *m* 15 July 1995, Tracey Helen, *née* Adams; 3 s, 1 da; *Career* General Mills US until 1982, Pepsi-Cola NY and London 1982–86, joined Virgin Entertainment Group 1986, i/c Virgin's Euro TV post prodn cos until 1992, chief exec Virgin Radio 1993–2000 (dir 1992–2000), chief exec Ginger Media 1997–2000, vice-chm Ministry of Sound 2001–02, chief exec Visit London 2003–05, pres and chief exec Anschutz Entertainment Group UK 2005–; Freeman City of Glasgow, memb Guild of Hammermen of Glasgow; memb: Mktg Soc 1984, Radio Acad 1992; *Recreations* flying (licensed helicopter pilot), travelling and live music; *Clubs* Soho House; *Style—* David Campbell, Esq

CAMPBELL, Donald Angus; s of William Alexander Campbell, of Elgin, Moray, and Williamina Scott, *née* Allan; *b* 10 April 1948; *Educ* Elgin Acad, Univ of Edinburgh (BSc, MB ChB); *m* 9 Sept 1972, Görrel Anna Kristina, da of (Stig Ture) Olof Sahlberg, of Sweden; 1 s (Alasdair Olof b 7 Oct 1981); *Career* neurosurgn: Karolinska Sjukhuset 1972, Royal Infirmary of Edinburgh 1972–73 and 1978; surgn: Köpings Lasarett 1973–76, King's Coll London 1976–77, Royal Marsden Hosp 1977–78; neurosurgn Walton Hosp Liverpool 1981–84, conslt neurosurgn to W Midlands RHA 1984–96, in full time private practice 1996–; med supt Svenska Londondoktorer 15 Harley Street; res papers on: chronic pain, epilepsy, head injury, meningiomas, stereotactic surgery; hon pres Headway Staffs; FRCS 1977, FRCSEd 1977, FRSM 1977; *Recreations* model aircraft engineering, parachuting, private pilot, photography; *Clubs* Soc of Model Aeronautical Engrs; *Style—* Donald Campbell, Esq; ✉ c/o Susan Thayer-Lewis, 48 Willow Road, Charlton Kings, Cheltenham GL53 8PQ (tel 01242 526836); 15 Harley Street, London W1N 1DA (tel 020 7636 7780); Sussex Nuffield Hospital, Woodingdean, East Sussex BN2 6DX (tel 01273 624488, e-mail bellerophon@msn.com)

CAMPBELL, Emily Jane; da of (Alfred) Graham Hayes, of Ince Blundell, Merseyside, and Sheila Frances, *née* Pemberton (d 2001); *Educ* Merchant Taylors' Crosby, Westminster, Clare Coll Cambridge (BA), London Coll of Fashion (Dip Clothing Technol), Yale Univ Sch of Art (MFA); *m* 31 May 1997, Edward Shanklin Campbell, s of Thomas Philip Campbell (d 1996), and Anne Campbell; 2 s (Arthur Shanklin b 29 Nov 1998, Edward Graham b 15 July 2001); *Career* pattern cutter Jean Muir 1989–91, graphic designer Pentagram Design NY 1993–96, head of design and architecture Br Cncl Arts Gp 1996–; *Style—* Ms Emily Campbell; ✉ British Council, 10 Spring Gardens, London SW1A 2BN (tel 020 7389 3153, fax 020 7389 3164, e-mail emily.campbell@britishcouncil.org)

CAMPBELL, HE Francis Martin; s of Daniel Campbell, of Warrenpoint, Co Down, and Brigid, *née* Cosgrove (d 1995); *b* 20 April 1970, Newry, Co Down; *Educ* Queen's Univ Belfast (BA), TCD, Katholieke Univ of Leuven Belgium (MA), Jagieollian Univ Krakow, Univ of Pensylvania (Thouron fell, MA); *Career* EU enlargement desk FCO 1997 and 1998–99, UN Security Cncl NY 1997–98, policy advsr PM's Policy Unit 1999–2001, private sec to the PM 2001–03, first sec (external) Br Embassy Rome 2003–05, sr dir of policy Amnesty Int 2005, ambass to the Holy See Rome 2005–; *Publications* Federalism Doomed (contrib chapter, 2002); *Recreations* reading, walking, travelling; *Style—* HE Mr Francis Campbell; ✉ British Embassy to Holy See, Via XX Settembre, 80A, Roma 00187, Italy (tel 00 39 06 4220 4000, fax 00 39 06 4220 4205, e-mail holysee@fco.gov.uk)

CAMPBELL, Gordon Arden; CBE (2006); s of Hugh Eric Campbell (d 1991), and Jessie, *née* Arden; *b* 16 October 1946; *Educ* Oldershaw GS, Churchill Coll Cambridge (MA); *m* Jennifer, *née* Vaughan; 2 da (Shona Alison b 1978, Claire Eleanor b 1983); *Career* Courtaulds plc: joined Courtaulds res 1968, jr prodn mangr Courtaulds Acetate 1970–71, yarn salesman 1972, mgmnt accountant 1973–74, gen mangr Rocel Ltd 1974–76, prodn dir Courtaulds Acetate 1976–80, dep md Courtaulds Acetate 1980–81, chief exec Courtaulds Acetate 1982–85, main bd dir 1987–99, chief exec 1996–99; md Saiccor (Pty) Ltd 1985; dir Usutu 1987; chm: IPT Ltd 1999–2001, Wade Potteries Ltd 1999–2002, Babcock Int Gp plc 2000–, British Nuclear Fuels plc 2004– (non-exec dir 2000–), Jupiter Second Split Capital Tst plc; non-exec dir: Argos plc 1997–98, Senior plc 2004–06; pres Comité International de Rayonne et Fibres Synthetiques 1995–98; pres IChemE 1998, non-exec memb UKAEA 1994–97; memb: Cncl Cranfield Univ, Cncl Br Heart Fndn 1999–2005; CIMgt, FREng 1992 (vice-pres 2000–04); *Recreations* golf, rugby, skiing; *Style—* Gordon Campbell, Esq, CBE, FREng; ✉ Babcock International Group plc, 2 Cavendish Square, London W1E 0PX (tel 020 7291 5010)

CAMPBELL, Gregory; MP, MLA; *b* 15 February 1953; *m* Frances; 1 s, 3 da; *Career* MP (DUP) Londonderry E 2001–; MLA (DUP) Londonderry E 1998–; min for regnl devpt until 2001 (resigned); *Style—* Gregory Campbell, Esq, MP, MLA; ✉ House of Commons, London SW1A 0AA; Northern Ireland Assembly, Parliament Buildings, Stormont Estate, Belfast BT4 3XX; Constituency Office, 25 Bushmills Road, Coleraine BT52 2BP (tel 028 7032 7327, fax 028 7032 7328); Constituency Office, 6–8 Catherine Street, Limavady BT49 9DB (tel 028 7776 6060, fax 028 7776 9531, e-mail wilkinsonh@parliament.uk)

CAMPBELL, Hugh Hall; QC (Scot 1983); s of William Wright Campbell (d 1992), of Cambuslang, Lanarkshire, and Marianne Doris Stewart, *née* Hutchison (d 1988); *b* 18 February 1944; *Educ* Glasgow Acad, Glenalmond Coll, Exeter Coll Oxford (BA), Univ of Edinburgh (LLB); *m* 1969, Eleanor Jane, da of Sydney Charles Hare (d 1990), of Stoke Poges; 3 s (Benjamin b 1972, Timothy b 1975, Thomas b 1978); *Career* advocate Scottish Bar 1969, standing jr counsel to Admty 1976; FCIArb 1986; *Recreations* carnival, wine, music; *Clubs* Hon Co of Edinburgh Golfers; *Style—* H H Campbell, Esq, QC; ✉ 12 Ainslie Place, Edinburgh EH3 6AS (tel 0131 225 2067)

CAMPBELL, Ian James; OBE (2001); s of James Patrick Campbell (d 1983), of Hythe, Kent, and Phyllis Eileen, *née* Hammond (d 1993); *b* 27 August 1947; *Educ* Ashford GS, Univ of Newcastle upon Tyne (BA); *m* 4 April 1970, Janette Elizabeth, da of Wilfred Johnston Bradley; 2 s (Christian James b 2 Oct 1976, Simon John b 13 Oct 1978); *Career* graduate trainee then relief station mangr British Overseas Airways Corporation 1969–73; Berol Corporation: export exec 1973–74, export mangr 1974–75, regnl mangr Africa/ME 1975–77; Caffrey Saunders Group of Companies: sales and mktg dir and latterly dep md Caffrey Saunders & Co Ltd 1977–84, md Caffrey Saunders & Co Ltd 1984–88, md Caffrey Saunders Services Ltd 1988–91; DG and sec Inst of Export 1992–2001; ind int trade advsr and writer 2001–; served on Govt's Export Forum 1997; chm British Exporters' Assoc 1987–90, memb Advsy Ctee Br Trade Int Export Clubs 1992–, memb Br Trade Int Regns Gp 1998–; regular contrib to nat and int seminars and confs on trade related issues, author of numerous articles and commentaries on int trade in professional jls; Int Export Assoc Award for Services to Export 1975; Freeman Worshipful Co of World Traders 1996 (memb 1992), Freeman City of London 1998; MIMgt 1981, FRSA 1992, FIEx 1995 (MIEx 1981), FICPD 1998, Hon FIL 2001; *Recreations* sailing, theatre, food and wine; *Clubs* Caledonian, Royal Yachting Assoc; *Style—* Ian Campbell, Esq, OBE; ✉ 30 City Harbour, Selsden Way, London E14 9GR (tel 020 7987 0622, fax 020 7897 6660)

CAMPBELL, Prof Ian William; s of William Campbell (d 1991), of Fife, and Janet Campbell (d 1991); *b* 23 November 1945; *Educ* Buckhaven HS, Univ of Edinburgh (BSc, MB ChB); *m* 1970, Catherine McEwan, *née* Burgess; 2 da (Lorna Jane b 3 April 1975, Christina Kate b 13 Dec 1980), 1 s (Alastair John b 17 Jan 1978); *Career* conslt physician Victoria Hosp Kirkcaldy 1978–, hon sr lectr in med Univ of Edinburgh 1978–, hon prof of biological and med sci Univ of St Andrews 1995–; chm: Scot Ctee Br Diabetic Assoc 1991–95, Scot Study Gp for the Care of the Young Diabetic 1993–97; memb Cncl RCPEd; presented papers and invited lectures (principally in field of diabetes mellitus) worldwide; 3rd Croom Lecture RCPEd 1977, J K Bekaert Meml Lecture Univ of Antwerp 1990, John Mathewson Shaw Endowed Lecture Belfast 1994; FRCPEd, FRCPGlas; *Books* Diagnosis and Management of Endocrine Diseases (jtly, 1981), Complications in Diabetes: Diabetic Retinopathy (jtly, 1992), Fast Facts: Diabetes Mellitus (jtly, 1996); also author of 200 papers in scientific jls and textbooks; *Recreations* squash, golf, classical music; *Clubs* Lundin Sports; *Style—* Prof Ian Campbell; ✉ Strathearn, 19 Victoria Road, Lundin Links, Fife KY8 6AZ (tel 01333 320533); Victoria Hospital, Hayfield Road, Kirkcaldy, Fife KY2 5AH (tel 01592 643355, fax 01592 647069)

CAMPBELL, Sir James Alexander Moffat Bain; 9 Bt (NS *ca* 1668), of Aberuchill, Perthshire; s of Sir Colin Moffat Campbell, 8 Bt, MC (d 1997); *b* 23 September 1956; *Educ* Stowe; *m* 6 Feb 1993, Carola Jane, yr da of George Denman, of Stratton House, Stoney Stratton, Somerset; 2 da (b 10 Nov 1994 and 16 May 1996), 1 s (b 1999); *Heir* s, Colin Campbell; *Career* Capt Scots Gds ret 1983, Capt London Scottish 1/51 Highlanders 1984–87; insurance broker 1983–2001 and 2007– (insurance conslt 2001–05); farmer 2001–; *Recreations* motorcycling, trees; *Style—* Sir James Campbell, Bt; ✉ Kilbryde Castle, Dunblane, Perthshire (tel 01786 824897)

CAMPBELL, James Farquhar Robin; s of Robin John Ronald Campbell, of Invernesshire, and Alison Barbara Rose, *née* Cave-Browne; *b* 26 November 1958; *m* 30 March 1985, Marina Caroline Vere, *née* Norton; 2 da (Ishbel b 30 Nov 1988, Isla b 16 Sept 1997), 2 s (Guy b 17 March 1991, Hugh (twin) b 16 Sept 1997); *Career* served 1 Bn Queen's Own Highlanders 1977–87 (ret as Capt); with: Towry Law & Co 1987–88, MIM Britannia 1988, Perpetual 1989–94; md: Jupiter Unit Trust 1994–98, ABN AMRO Fund Managers 1998–99, Artemis Unit Tst Mangrs 1999–; dir: Perpetual Unit Trust Managers 1989–94, Jupiter Asset Management 1994–98, ABN AMRO Asset Management 1998–99, Union Jack (Trading) Ltd; memb Queen's Body Guard for Scotland (Royal Co of Archers); *Recreations* bagpipes, farming, golf, field sports; *Style—* James Campbell, Esq; ✉ Artemis Unit Trust Managers, 42 Melville Street, Edinburgh EH3 7HA

CAMPBELL, Prof John; OBE (1993); s of Clarence Preston Campbell (d 1979), and Catherine Mary, *née* Crossley (d 2007); *b* 2 December 1938; *Educ* Gateway Sch Leicester, Fitzwilliam Coll Cambridge (MA), Univ of Sheffield (MMet), Univ of Birmingham (PhD, DEng); *m* 1, Jacqueline Pamela, *née* Harrison; 1 da (Zoe Elizabeth); m 2, Sheila Margaret, *née* Taylor; step s, Richard Bacon, MP; *Career* graduate trainee Tube Investments Ltd 1963–64, British Iron and Steel Research Assoc 1967–70, Fulmer Research Inst 1970–78; UNIDO: Cairo 1973, Lahore 1976, tech dir Cosworth R&D Ltd 1978–85, tech dir Cosworth Castings Ltd 1984–85; Triplex Alloys Ltd: tech dir 1985–89, R&D dir 1989–91; dir

Campbell Technology 1988–; non-exec dir: Cast Metals Development Ltd 1992–96, Alfer Ltd 1994–95, Alloy Technologies Ltd 1996–2000, Westley Group 1997–2004; Univ of Birmingham: visiting prof 1989–92, prof of casting technology 1992–2004, emeritus prof 2004–; chm VK Educnl Foundry Trust 1989–; ACTA Metallurgica lectr 1992–94; memb Editorial Bd: Cast Metals jl 1988–, Materials Science & Technology jl 1991–2002; hon dir Light Metals Founders Assoc R&D Ltd 1987–94; fell Inst of Cast Metal Engrs 1985; memb American Foundry Soc 1990; Sir Jonathan North Gold Metal 1957–58, Wilkinson Medal Staffs Iron and Steel Inst 1990, AFS Hall/Heroult Award 1997, IBF MM Hallett Medal 1999, AFS Howard F Taylor Award 2000, Merton C Flemings Award 2003; Liveryman Worshipful Co of Founders; FREng 1991; *Books* Castings (1991, 2 edn 2003), Castings Practice (2004); *Recreations* music, walking, writing; *Style*— Prof John Campbell, OBE, FREng; ✉ 6 Old Market Court, Ledbury HR8 2GE (tel 01531 636077, e-mail jc@campbelltech.co.uk); Department of Metallurgy and Materials, The University of Birmingham, Birmingham B15 2TT (e-mail j.campbell.met@bham.ac.uk)

CAMPBELL, John Donington; s of Maj John Donington Campbell (d 2001), of Heathfield, E Sussex, and Edith Jean, *née* Crick; *b* 23 April 1959; *Educ* Harrow, RMA Sandhurst; *m* 4 June 1988, Catriona Helen Cecelia, da of John Spence Swan (d 2004), of Letham, Fife; 1 da (Iona Helen b 18 Feb 1996), 2 s (Charles John b 9 Dec 2000, James Donington b 18 July 2002); *Career* cmmnd Royal Scots Dragoon Guards 1979, ADC to General Offr Cmd Scot 1985–87; Phoenix Burners Ltd 1977–79, Ivory and Sime plc 1987–89; md: Instate plc 1989–91, Framlington Pensions Management 1991–93, Latchly Management Ltd 1996–2000, State Street Corporation 2000–; dir: Cursitor Management Ltd 1993–98, Scottish Financial Enterprise 2001– (chm 2004–); memb Financial Services Strategy Gp 2003–05, dep chm Financial Services Advsy Bd 2005–, memb EU Advsy Gp City of London Corp 2005–; tstee Inst of Business Ethics 1995–, memb Advsy Bd Univ of Edinburgh Mgmnt Sch 2004–; hon vice-pres Border Bothie Assoc 2002–; FRSA 2006; *Recreations* country pursuits, tobogganing, exercise; *Clubs* New (Edinburgh), St Moritz Tobogganing; *Style*— John Campbell, Esq; ✉ State Street Corporation, 525 Ferry Road, Edinburgh EH5 2AN

CAMPBELL, Prof John Joseph; *b* 2 November 1956, Glasgow; *Educ* Univ of Stirling (BA), Univ of Calgary (MA), The Queen's Coll Oxford, Wolfson Coll Oxford (BPhil, John Locke prize), BNC Oxford, ChCh Oxford (DPhil); *Career* Univ of Oxford: research lectr ChCh 1983–86, fell and tutor New Coll 1986–2001, reader in philosophy 1997–2001, fell CCC 2001–, Wilde prof of mental philosophy 2001–, memb Editorial Ctee Oxford Philosophical Monographs 1993–, chm Search Ctee Faculty of Philosophy 2001– (memb 1989–95), chm Philosophy, Psychology and Physiology Ctee Faculty of Philosophy 2002– (memb 2001–), Willis S and Marion Slusser prof of philosophy Univ of California at Berkeley 2004–; visiting assoc prof UCLA 1988, visiting fell King's Coll Research Centre Cambridge 1990 and 1991, visiting fell Research Sch of Social Sciences ANU 1991–92, Br Acad research reader 1995–97, distinguished visitor in cognitive science Univ of Calif Berkeley 1996, fell Center for Advanced Study in the Behavioural Sciences Stanford Univ 2003–04; memb Steering Ctee Leverhulme Project on Consciousness and Self-Consciousness 1996–; European Soc for Philosophy and Psychology: memb Steering Ctee 1995–98, prog chair 1996–98, memb Bd 1999–, pres 2003–; *Publications* Past, Space and Self (1994), Reference and Consciousness (2002); author of numerous articles in learned jls; *Style*— Prof John Campbell; ✉ Department of Philosophy, 314 Moses Hall #2390, University of California, Berkeley, CA 94720–2390, USA

CAMPBELL, Dr John Malcolm; s of Malcolm Rider Campbell (d 1991), of London and latterly Wiltshire, and Sheila Stuart, *née* Robertson (d 1979); *b* 2 September 1947; *Educ* Charterhouse, Univ of Edinburgh (MA, PhD); *m* 1972, Alison Elizabeth, da of Thomas Archibald McCracken, and Olive Minnie, *née* Blackman, of Hawkhurst, Kent; 1 da (Robin Alexandra b 1981), 1 s (Patrick McCracken b 1983); *Career* freelance historian/biographer; memb Soc of Authors; author of book reviews for The Times, TLS, Independent, Sunday Telegraph, etc; FRHistS; *Books* Lloyd George: The Goat in the Wilderness (1977, second prize Yorkshire Post Award for Best First Book), F E Smith, First Earl of Birkenhead (1983), Roy Jenkins: A Biography (1983), Nye Bevan and the Mirage of British Socialism (1987), The Experience of World War II (ed, 1989), Makers of the Twentieth Century (series ed, 1990–91), Edward Heath: A Biography (1993, NCR Award for Non-Fiction 1994), Margaret Thatcher, Vol 1: The Grocer's Daughter (2000), Margaret Thatcher, Vol 2: The Iron Lady (2003), If Love Were All...: The Story of Frances Stevenson and David Lloyd George (2006); *Recreations* tennis, golf, theatre, music, amateur dramatics/directing; *Style*— Dr John Campbell; ✉ 2 Lansdowne Crescent, London W11 2NH (tel 020 7727 1920, e-mail johncampbell_@hotmail.com)

CAMPBELL, John Park; OBE (2000); s of Keith Campbell (d 1950), and Joan, *née* Park (d 1985); *b* 1 April 1934, Gourock, Glasgow; *Educ* Strathallan Sch Perthshire; *m* 3 Apr 1957, Catherine, *née* Kent; 1 da (Karen b 31 March 1958), 3 s (Ian b 26 Dec 1960, Keith 12 July 1963, Colin 14 Oct 1974); *Career* farmer 1950–, owner 10,000 acre farm, largest egg prodr in Scotland, largest free-range egg prodr in UK; former vice-pres Royal Highland and Agricultural Soc Scotland; convenor Tweeddale DC 1979–88, candidate Scottish Parl 1999; UK Farm Business of the Year 2004, category winner Entrepreneur of the Year 2004; former JP; *Clubs* Farmers; *Style*— John Campbell, Esq, OBE; ✉ Glenrath, Peebles EH45 9JW (tel 01721 740221, fax 01968 676957)

CAMPBELL, (Alastair) John Wilson; s of Wilson William Campbell (d 1975), and Pearl Gray, *née* Ackrill (d 2005); *b* 18 February 1947; *Educ* King's Sch Canterbury, Sidney Sussex Coll Cambridge (MA); *m* 25 Feb 1972, Sarah Jane, da of Patrick Philip Shellard (d 1982); 2 s (Milo b 1974, Rollo b 1978), 1 da (Coco b 1976); *Career* exec NM Rothschild & Sons Ltd 1969–72, dir Noble Grossart Ltd 1973–88, md McLeod Russel plc 1979–82, sr ptnr and co-fndr Campbell Lutyens & Co Ltd 1988–; *Clubs* Reform, New (Edinburgh); *Style*— John Campbell, Esq; ✉ 10 Campden Hill Gate, Duchess of Bedford's Walk, London W8 7QH (tel 020 7995 6445); Campbell Lutyens & Co Ltd, 3 Burlington Gardens, London W1S 3EP (tel 020 7439 7191, fax 020 7432 3749)

CAMPBELL, Ken; s of late Antony Colin Campbell, and Elsie, *née* Handley; *b* 10 December 1941; *Educ* Gearies Sch Barkingside, Chigwell Sch, RADA; *m* 1978, Prunella, *née* Gee; 1 da (Daisy Eris 1978); *Career* actor, director and writer; Ken Campbell's Roadshow 1969, fndr and dir Science Fiction Theatre of Liverpool 1976, artistic dir Everyman Theatre Liverpool 1980, presenter: Reality on the Rocks (Channel 4), Brainspotting, 6 Experiments which Changed the World; Theatre Stories (RNT) 1997, prof of ventriloquism RADA 1999–; Total Theatre Lifetime Achievement Award 1999; *Plays* Old King Cole, Skungpoomery, Jack Sheppard, School for Clowns, You See the Thing is This, One Night I Danced with Mr Dalton, Clowns on a School Outing, Madness Museum, Bendigo, Walking Like Geoffrey, The Recollections of a Furtive Nudist, Pigspurt (Time Out Award for One Man Show 1992), Jamais Vu (Evening Standard Best Comedy Award 1993, Best Entertainment and Best Comedy Performance Olivier Awards nomination 1994), Mystery Bruises, Knocked Sideways, Violin Time, Theatre Stories, History of Comedy Part One: Ventriloquism, Let Me Out; *Recreations* pursuit of the weird; *Style*— Ken Campbell, Esq; ✉ c/o PFD, Drury House, 34–43 Russell Street, London WC2B 5HA (tel 020 7344 1010)

CAMPBELL, Sir Lachlan Philip Kemeys; 6 Bt (UK 1815); er s of Col Sir Guy Theophilus Halswell Campbell, 5 Bt, OBE, MC (d 1993), and Elizabeth (stage name Lizbeth Webb), da of Alfred Rich Wills-Webber (d 1958) (*see* Campbell, Elizabeth, Lady); *b* 9 October 1958; *Educ* Lycée Français, Temple Grove, Eton, RMA Sandhurst; *m* 1986, Harriet Jane Sarah, o da of late Frank Edward Jex Girling; 2 s (Archibald Edward FitzGerald b 13 June 1990, Ivo David Orlando b 28 Sept 1997), 1 da (Georgia Charlotte Clementine b 10 May 1995); *Heir* s, Archibald Campbell; *Career* The Royal Green Jackets, served in N Ireland (short service cmmn), Queen Victoria's Rifles (TA); *Recreations* painting, rugby, cricket, golf; *Clubs* Army and Navy, MCC, London Scottish; *Style*— Sir Lachlan Campbell, Bt

CAMPBELL, Lucy B; da of James Allen Barnett (d 1999), of Portland, OR, and Jane, *née* Dodge (d 1952); *b* 26 January 1940; *Educ* Nightingale Bamford Sch NYC, The Garland Coll Boston MA; *m* 1, 1959 (m dis 1963), Clifford Smith, Jr, s of Clifford Smith (d 1961), of Rockport, Maine; 2 s (Clifford Allen b 24 Aug 1960, Grafton Dodge b 3 Dec 1961); m 2, 1965 (m dis 1981), Colin Guy Napier Campbell, s of Archibald Campbell (d 1975), of London; 2 da (Georgina Dorothy b 24 Jan 1969, Tessa Sylvia b 3 April 1971); *Career* fine art dealer; proprietor Lucy B Campbell Fine Art London (founded 1984) and Lucy B Campbell Ltd New York; exhibitions: The Fine Art and Antiques Fair Olympia London 1995–2003, The British Antique Dealers' Fair Duke of York's HQ London May 1995, The San Francisco Fall Antiques Show 1987–94, Art London 2004–07; memb: British Antique Dealers Assoc, The Pilgrims, Le Confédération Internationale des Négociants en Oeuvres d'Art (CINOA); *Style*— Mrs Lucy B Campbell; ✉ Lucy B Campbell Fine Art, 123 Kensington Church Street, London W8 7LP (tel 020 7727 2205, fax 020 7229 4252, e-mail lucy@lucybcampbell.co.uk)

CAMPBELL, Maggie; *b* 11 November 1950; *Educ* Haverstock Sch Chalk Farm London; *m* 3 Nov 1984, Joseph Washington Morton Campbell III; 1 da (Melissa Poppy b 7 Oct 1986); *Career* TV prodr/assoc dir Boase Massimi Pollitt Advertising 1973–88, sr prodr/assoc dir J Walter Thompson Advertising 1988–91, head of TV/dir Publicis Advertising 1991–94, freelance prodr 1994–; memb D&AD, MIPA; *Recreations* cooking (qualified London Cordon Bleu School); *Clubs* East Sussex National Golf; *Style*— Mrs Maggie Campbell; ✉ Town House Farm, Sloop Lane, Scaynes Hill, West Sussex RH17 7NP

CAMPBELL, Malcolm; s of Malcolm Brown Campbell (d 1940), and Helen Munro, *née* Carruthers (d 1992); *b* 3 January 1934; *Educ* Glenalmond Coll; *m* 1, 25 Sept 1960 (m dis 1977), Fiona, *née* McLaren; 3 s (Colin b 30 Sept 1961, David b 19 April 1963, Graham b 6 March 1967); m 2, 18 Feb 1983, Susan Elizabeth Patten, da of Sydney David (d 1965), of Mid Glamorgan; 1 s (James b 29 June 1984), 1 step da (Elizabeth b 7 Oct 1975); *Career* Nat Serv RA 1953–55; chm Malcolm Campbell Ltd 1969– (joined 1955, sales mangr 1959, sales dir 1961, md 1966); dir and pres Glasgow C of C 1995, memb Cncl Br Chambers of Commerce 1995–96; winner Scottish Special Free Enterprise Award by Aims of Indust 1988; memb: Bd of Govrs Queen's Coll Glasgow 1989–93, Court Glasgow Caledonian Univ 1993–98 (chm 1996–98); dir The Merchants House of Glasgow 1998–; Freeman City of London 1978, Liveryman Worshipful Co of Fruiterers 1978; *Recreations* golf (Western Gailes capt 1974), sailing; *Clubs* Royal and Ancient (St Andrews), Prestwick, Western; *Style*— Malcolm Campbell, Esq; ✉ e-mail malcolmcampbelltd@btinternet.com

CAMPBELL, Margaret Jane (Mrs Margaret Bain); da of Dr Colin Campbell, of Wendover, Bucks, and Daphne E M, *née* Robbins; *b* 15 June 1957; *Educ* Aylesbury HS, Royal Coll of Music; *m* 22 Dec 1990, Christopher Bain; 3 s, 1 da; *Career* princ flute: City of Birmingham Symphony Orchestra 1977–86, Orchestra of the Royal Opera House Covent Garden 1986; Nat Fedn of Music Socs Award for Young Concert Artists 1981; ARCM; *Style*— Ms Margaret Campbell; ✉ 90 Haven Lane, Ealing, London W5 2HY (tel 020 8998 6246, e-mail margaret@campbellbain.co.uk)

CAMPBELL, Rt Hon Sir (Walter) Menzies; kt (2004), CBE (1987), PC (1999), QC (Scot 1982), MP; s of George Alexander Campbell, and Elizabeth Jean Adam, *née* Phillips; *b* 22 May 1941; *Educ* Hillhead HS Glasgow, Univ of Glasgow (MA, LLB), Stanford Univ; *m* 1970, Elspeth Mary Grant-Suttie, da of Maj-Gen R E Urquhart, CB, DSO; *Career* admitted advocate 1968, advocate depute 1977–80, standing jr counsel to the Army in Scotland 1980–82; pt/t chm: VAT Tbnl 1984–87, Med Appeal Tbnl 1985–87; memb: Legal Aid Central Ctee 1983–86, Broadcasting Cncl for Scotland 1984–87, Scottish Legal Aid Bd 1986–87; Parly candidate (Lib): Greenock and Port Glasgow 1974 (both Gen Elections), E Fife 1979, NE Fife 1983; MP (Lib 1987–88, Lib Dem 1988–) Fife NE 1987–; Lib then Lib Dem spokesman on sport 1987–; Lib Dem spokesman on: defence 1988–95, foreign affairs and defence 1995–, foreign affairs, defence and Europe 1997–; Lib Dem shadow foreign sec, ldr Lib Dems 2006– (dep ldr 2003–06); memb House of Commons: Trade and Industry Select Ctee 1990–92, Defence Select Ctee 1992–99; capt UK athletics team 1965 and 1966, competed in Olympic Games Tokyo 1964 and Cwlth Games 1966, UK 100 metres record holder 1967–74; *Clubs* Reform; *Style*— The Rt Hon Sir Menzies Campbell, CBE, QC, MP; ✉ House of Commons, London SW1A 0AA (tel 020 7219 5090)

CAMPBELL, Michael David Colin Craven; DL (Hants 1994); s of Bruce Colin Campbell (d 1980), and Doris, *née* Craven-Ellis (d 2006); *b* 12 December 1942; *Educ* Radley; *m* 6 April 1967, Linda Frances, da of Charles Brownrigg (d 1982); 2 da (Alexandra Jane (Mrs James Andrew) b 1968, Laura Grace b 1977), 1 s (Jamie Loudoun Craven b 1970); *Career* Ellis Campbell Group: md 1977–, chm 1987–; memb and tstee Small Business Bureau 1999–2004 (patron 1983–98); memb Hants CC 1983–87; chm of govrs Treloar Sch and Coll 1993–98; chm: Whitchurch Silk Mill Tst 1986–98, Treloar Tst 1993–2002, Hants Community Fndn 2006–; tstee: Hants Building Preservation Tst 1984–2007, Hants Garden Tst 1986–, Hants Bobby Tst 1999–; *Recreations* shooting, sailing, escaping to Scotland; *Clubs* Boodle's, Royal Yacht Squadron (Vice Cdre 1998–2003), Highland Soc of London; *Style*— Michael Campbell, Esq, DL; ✉ Shalden Park House, Shalden, Alton, Hampshire GU34 4DS (tel 01256 381821, fax 01256 381921)

CAMPBELL, (Henrietta) Nina Sylvia; da of John Archibald Campbell (d 1974), and Elizabeth, *née* Pearth (d 1996); *b* 9 May 1945; *Educ* Heathfield Sch Ascot; *m* 1 (m dis 1978), Andrew Guy Louis De Chappuis Konig; 1 da (Henrietta Lucy Elizabeth b 1973), 1 s (Maximillian John b 1976); m 2 (m dis 1991), John Henry Deen; 1 da (Alice Nina b 1982); *Career* interior decorator; apprenticeship with John Fowler of Colefax & Fowler; own interior decoration business and shop 1974–; cmmns for many private residences in UK and abroad incl: Sunninghill Park (for Duke and Duchess of York), new sales rooms Christie's London, Hotel de Vigny Paris, Mark's Club London, Hotel Balzac Paris, Parc Victor Hugo Paris; former tstee V&A; patron Museum of Design and Domestic Architecture (MODA); govr Heathfield Sch; Women Who Most Influenced Style Internationally Award Night of Stars 1990 (Fashion Gp Int), Waterford Wedgwood Hospitality Award 2000, runner-up Best of the Best Award 2001 (for the Loire Silk Collection) London Design Week 2001; Hon DUniv Middlesex; FBIDA, FRSA; *Books* Elsie de Wolfe - A Decorative Life (1992), Nina Campbell on Decoration (1996), Decorating Secrets (2000); *Style*— Miss Nina Campbell; ✉ Nina Campbell Ltd, Bridge Studios, 318–326 Wandsworth Bridge Road, London SW6 2TZ (tel 020 7471 4270, fax 020 7471 4299, e-mail info@ninacampbell.com, website www.ninacampbell.com)

CAMPBELL, Paddy (Patricia Ann); da of Tom Webster (Daily Mail cartoonist, d 1963), and Ida Shelley, *née* Michael (d 1991); *b* 10 July 1940; *Educ* La Sainte Union des Sacrées Coeurs Highgate, RADA; *m* 1 Jan 1965, John Charles Middleton Campbell, s of Lord Campbell of Eskan; 3 da; *Career* fashion designer; began career as actress, entered fashion industry 1974, estab own business and opened first shop St Christopher's Place 1979, opened second shop Beauchamp Place 1984, signed licensing deal with Japanese co 1985, wholesaling since 1990; patron (former vice-pres) The Women of the Year Lunch (raising money for Gtr London Fund for the Blind, former chm); FRSA 1996; *Style*— Mrs Paddy Campbell; ✉ 8 Gees Court, St Christopher's Place, London W1M 5HQ (tel 020 7493 5646)

CAMPBELL, Cdr Peter Colin Drummond; LVO (1960), OBE (1996), DL (Antrim 1984); s of Maj-Gen Sir (Alexander) Douglas Campbell, KBE, CB, DSO, MC (d 1980), and Patience Loveday, *née* Carlyon (d 1996); *b* 24 October 1927; *Educ* Cheltenham Coll, RNC Dartmouth; *m* 1966, Lady Moyra Kathleen Campbell, CVO, da of 4 Duke of Abercorn (d 1979); 2 s; *Career* late Cdr RN; equerry to HM the Queen 1957–60; Ireland rep Irish Soc 1974–96; dir Bann System Ltd 1997–2002, dir Bann Partnership 2004–; life vice-pres RN Assoc 1979–; High Sheriff Co Antrim 1985; Freeman City of London 1975; *Recreations* boating and being trained by my Labrador; *Clubs* Army and Navy; *Style—* Cdr Peter Campbell, LVO, OBE, DL; ✉ Hollybrook House, Randalstown, Co Antrim BT41 2PB (tel 02894 472224, fax 02894 479486, e-mail peter@hollybrook1.fsnet.co.uk); Rathlin Island, Co Antrim BT54 6RT (tel 02820 763911)

CAMPBELL, Dr Philip; *Educ* Univ of Bristol, QMC London, Univ of Leicester (PhD); *Career* postdoctoral research asst Dept of Physics Univ of Leicester 1977–79, physical sciences ed Nature 1982–88 (asst ed 1979–82), founding ed Physics World 1988–95, ed-in-chief Nature and Nature Pubns 1995–, memb Bd of Dirs Nature Publishing Gp; tstee Cancer Research UK; Hon DSc Univ of Leicester 1999; FRAS, FInstP; *Style—* Dr Philip Campbell; ✉ Nature, The Macmillan Building, 4–6 Crinan Street, London N1 9XW

CAMPBELL, His Hon Judge (John) Quentin; s of John McKnight Campbell, OBE, MC (d 1949), and Katherine Margaret, *née* Grant (d 1983); *b* 5 March 1939; *Educ* Loretto, Wadham Coll Oxford (MA); *m* 1, 1960, Penelope Jane Redman; 3 s (James Alistair b 1962, John Marcus b 1964, Matthew b 1967), 1 da (Jessica Louise b 1970); m 2, 1977, Ann Rosemary (Her Hon Judge Campbell), *qv*, da of Sqdn Ldr Richard Henry Beeching (d 2000); 1 da (Arabella b 27 June 1977), 1 s (Frederick b 28 June 1982); *Career* admitted slr 1965, met stipendiary magistrate 1981–96, recorder of the Crown Court 1989–96, circuit judge (SE Circuit) 1996–; memb Mental Health Review Tbnl; judicial memb Parole Bd; chm of Govrs Bessels Leigh Sch Oxford 1977–96; *Clubs* Travellers, Frewen (Oxford); *Style—* His Hon Judge Quentin Campbell; ✉ The Crown Court, Inner London Sessions House, Newington Causeway, London SE1 6AZ

CAMPBELL, Rachel; da of William James Campbell, of Yorks, and Mary Frances, *née* Alder; *b* 5 February 1969, Newcastle upon Tyne; *Educ* St John Fisher RC HS, Univ of Durham (BA); *m* 19 Sept 1998, Mark Baillache; 1 da (Isabelle Kate b 17 Aug 2005); *Career* KPMG: joined 1989, ptnr 2000, UK head of people mgmnt 2004, memb UK Bd 2005; Business in the Community: memb Bd Race for Opportunity, memb leadership team ProHelp; FCA 2004 (ACA 1993); *Recreations* sport, music (oboe), theatre, relaxing with friends and family; *Style—* Ms Rachel Campbell; ✉ KPMG, 8 Salisbury Square, London, EC4Y 8BB (tel 020 7311 1000, e-mail rachel.campbell@kpmg.co.uk)

CAMPBELL, (Alistair) Robert Macbrair; s of Dr Bruce Campbell, OBE, and Margaret Campbell; *b* 9 May 1946; *Educ* Marlborough, Univ of Aberdeen (BSc); *m* 7 Sept 1968, Frances Rosemary, *née* Kirkwood; 1 s (Tomas b 11 Aug 1971), 2 da (Chloe b 5 July 1973, Nancy b 15 May 1977); *Career* md Blackwell Science Ltd 1987–2000, pres Blackwell Publishing 2000–07, sr publisher Wiley-Blackwell 2007–; chm: STM Assoc 1998–2000, INASP 2004–, Publishing Res Consortium, Forest of Oxford; Hon DUniv Oxford Brookes 2005; FIBiol 2007; *Books* A Guide to the Birds of the Coast (1976), Microform Publishing (1979), Journal Publishing (1997), Journal Production (1992); *Recreations* fly fishing, writing, Scottish history, tree planting; *Style—* Robert Campbell, Esq; ✉ Wiley-Blackwell, 9600 Garsington Road, Oxford OX4 2DQ (tel 01865 476117, fax 01865 476774, e-mail robert.campbell@oxon.blackwellpublishing.com)

CAMPBELL, Sir Robin Auchinbreck; 15 Bt (NS 1628), of Auchinbreck; s of Sir Louis Hamilton Campbell, 14 Bt (d 1970), and Margaret Elizabeth Patricia (d 1985), da of Patrick Campbell; *b* 7 June 1922; *Educ* Eton; *m* 1, 1948, Rosemary (Sally) (d 1978), da of Ashley Dean, of Christchurch, NZ; 1 s (Louis Auchinbreck b 1953), 2 da (Rosemary Fiona b 1955, Sophia Louise b 1960); m 2, 1978, Elizabeth Mary, da of Sir Arthur Colegate, MP, and formerly w of Richard Wellesley Gunston; *Heir* s, Louis Campbell; *Career* formerly Lt (A) RNVR; sheep farmer; *Clubs* Bembridge Sailing, Christchurch; *Style—* Sir Robin Campbell, Bt; ✉ 287A Waikawa Road, Picton, New Zealand

CAMPBELL, Ronnie; MP; s of Ronald Campbell, and Edna, *née* Howes; *b* 14 August 1943; *Educ* Ridley HS; *m* 17 July 1967, Deirdre, da of Edward McHale (d 1976); 5 s (Edward b 1968, Barry b 1971, Shaun b 1973, Brendan b 1973, Aiden b 1977), 1 da (Sharon b 1969); *Career* former miner, chm Bates NUM; MP (Lab) Blyth Valley 1987–; memb Public Admin Ctee 1997–; cncllr: Blyth Borough Cncl 1969–74, Blyth Valley DC 1974–88; *Style—* Ronnie Campbell, MP; ✉ House of Commons, London SW1A 0AA

CAMPBELL, Dr Simon Fraser; CBE (2006); s of William Fraser Campbell (d 1953), and Ellen Mary, *née* Casey (d 1998); *b* 27 March 1941; *Educ* Univ of Birmingham (BSc, PhD); *m* 1966, Jill, *née* Lewis; 2 s (Duncan John b 1970, Douglas Simon b 1973); *Career* res fell and visiting lectr Universidade de São Paulo Brazil 1970–72; Pfizer Central Research: staff chemist 1972–78, mangr Discovery Chem 1978–83, dir Discovery Chem 1983–92, gp dir Medicinals Discovery 1992–93, vice-pres Medicinals Discovery 1993–96, sr vice-pres Worldwide Discovery and Medicinals R&D Europe 1996–98, dir and memb Bd Pfizer; co-ed Current Opinion in Drug Discovery and Devpt 1998–2004; visiting prof Univ of Leeds 1996–99; memb: SERC Organic Chem Sub-Ctee 1988–91, SERC Sci Bd 1992–94, R&D Ctee Assoc of Br Pharmaceutical Industry 1994–96, Academic Advsy Bd for Chem Univ of Kent 1994–96, Review Panel for Wellcome SHOWCASE Awards 1997, Editorial Bd Perspectives in Drug Discovery and Design 1995–98, Industrial Advsy Bd Dept of Chem Univ of Bristol 1998–2001, Advsy Cncl Save Br Sci 1998–, Cncl Univ of Kent 1999–2007, RSC Steering and Co-ordinating Ctee 1999–2001, BP Technol Advsy Cncl 2000–04; chair MMV Expert Scientific Advsy Ctee for Malaria 1999–2003; RSC Award for Medicinal Chem 1989, E B Hershberg Award for Important Discoveries in Medicinally Active Substances ACS 1997, Industrial Research Inst (US) Achievement Award 1997, CIA Individual Achievement Award 2006, Salen Medal 2007; Hon DSc: Univ of Kent 1999, Univ of Birmingham 2004; ACS, FRSC 1985 (pres 2004–06), FRS 1999, FMedSci 2002; *Publications* over 110 scientific publications and patents; *Style—* Dr Simon Campbell, CBE, FRS

CAMPBELL, Sulzeer (Sol); s of Sewell Campbell (d 2003), and Wilhelmina Campbell; *b* 18 September 1974; *Career* professional footballer (defender); Tottenham Hotspur FC 1992–2001, Arsenal FC 2001–06 (winners Premier League 2002 and 2004, FA Cup 2002, 2003 and 2005, finalists UEFA Champions League 2006), Portsmouth FC 2006–; England: 69 caps (2 as capt), memb squad European Championships 1996, 2000 and 2004, memb squad World Cup 1998, 2002 and 2006; vice-patron Forest YMCA of E London; *Style—* Sol Campbell, Esq

CAMPBELL GARRATT, Jane Louise; da of Thomas Tertius Campbell Garratt (d 1973), and Patricia Marjorie, *née* Cobb, of Stoke d'Abernon, Surrey; *b* 6 July 1948; *Educ* Brooklands Sch, Claremont Sch; *m* 25 June 1988, Patrick Antony Stuart Rucker; *Career* account exec S H Benson advtg 1970–71 (joined 1966); Ogilvy & Mather: joined 1971, bd dir 1986–, mgmnt supervisor 1989–90, dir of recruitment and trg 1990–93, vice-chm 1993–97; advtg and HR conslt Results Business Consultancy 1998–2002; ed Now and Then magazine 1998–, advsr Bd of British Alpaca Fine Fibre Co 1999–2000; recipient Francis Ogilvy Award; *Recreations* gardening, antiques, French literature, farming alpacas; *Clubs* 2 Brydges Place; *Style—* Jane Campbell Garratt

CAMPBELL OF AIRDS, Alastair Lorne; er s of Brig Lorne Campbell of Airds, VC, DSO, OBE, TD (d 1991), and (Amy) Muriel Jordan, *née* Campbell (d 1950); *b* 11 July 1937; *Educ* Eton, Sandhurst; *m* 1960, Mary Ann, da of Lt-Col (George) Patrick Campbell-Preston, MBE; 4 c; *Career* Argyll and Sutherland Highlanders 1957–63, Royal Green Jackets TA 1964–69; md Waverley Vintners Ltd 1977–83; chm Christopher and Co Ltd 1975–83, chief exec Clan Campbell 1984–; HM Unicorn Pursuivant of Arms, memb Ct of the Lord Lyon 1987–, memb Queen's Body Guard for Scotland (Royal Co of Archers); memb Priory Chapter Scotland (Order of St John of Jerusalem) 1996; memb Cncl Nat Tst for Scotland 1996–2001; hon res fell Univ of Aberdeen 1996–2001; *Publications* History of Clan Campbell (3 vols), Two Hundred Years - The History of the Highland Society of London, History of the Queen's Body Guard for Scotland - The Royal Company of Archers (co-author); *Style—* Alastair Campbell of Airds

CAMPBELL OF ALLOWAY, Baron (Life Peer UK 1981), of Ayr in the District of Kyle and Carrick; Alan Robertson Campbell; ERD, QC (1965); s of late John Kenneth Campbell; *b* 24 May 1917; *Educ* Aldenham, Trinity Hall Cambridge, Ecole des Sciences Politiques Paris; *m* 1957, Vivien, yr da of late Cdr A H de Kantzow, DSO, RN; *Career* sits as Cons Peer in House of Lords; cmmnd 2 Lt RA supp reserve 1939, served in BEF France and Belgium 1939–40 (POW 1940–45); called to the Bar Inner Temple 1939 (bencher 1972); Western Circuit, recorder Crown Court 1976–89, head of chambers; conslt to Sub-Ctee of Legal Ctee of Cncl of Europe on Industrial Espionage 1965–74, chm Legal Res Ctee Soc of Cons Lawyers 1968–80; memb: Law Advsy Ctee Br Cncl 1974–80, Mgmnt Ctee Assoc for European Law 1975–90, Old Carlton Club Political Ctee 1967–79; co-patron Inns of Court Sch of Law Conservatives 1996–2000; pres Colditz Assoc 1998–; memb House of Lords Select Ctee on: Murder and Life Imprisonment 1988–89, Privileges 1982–2000, Personal Bills 1987–88, Joint Consolidation Bills 2000; memb: House of Lords Ecclesiastical Ctee, Jt Ctee on Human Rights until 2003, All-Pty Ctees on Defence and Children; *Clubs* Carlton, Pratt's, Beefsteak; *Style—* The Rt Hon Lord Campbell of Alloway, ERD, QC; ✉ House of Lords, London SW1A 0PW (tel 020 7219 3147)

CAMPBELL OF STRACHUR, David Niall MacArthur; s of (Ian) Niall MacArthur Campbell, of Strachur, 24th chief of the MacArthur Campbells of Strachur (d 2000); *b* 15 April 1948; *Educ* Eton, Exeter Coll Oxford; *m* 1974, Alexandra Wiggin, Marquesa de Muros, da of Sir Charles Wiggin, KCMG, DFC, AFC, Marques de Muros (d 1977); 1 s (Charles Alexander, yr of Strachur, b 26 May 1977), 1 da (Iona Margot (Mrs Geoffrey Hemphill) b 15 Jan 1979); *Career* int publishing dir of Hachette (Paris) 1983–90, md éditions du Chêne 1986–90, publisher Everyman's Library 1990–, chm Scala Publishers 1998–; Chevalier de la Legion d'Honneur 2007; *Clubs* Beefsteak, Groucho, Pratt's, White's; *Style—* David Campbell of Strachur; ✉ 51 Northumberland Place, London W2 5AS; Barbreck House, By Lochgilphead, Argyll PA31 8QW

CAMPBELL OF SUCCOTH, Sir Ilay Mark; 7 Bt (UK 1808), of Succoth, Dunbartonshire; s of Capt Sir George Ilay Campbell, 6 Bt, JP, DL (d 1967), and Clematis Elizabeth Denys, *née* Waring (d 1986); *b* 29 May 1927; *Educ* Eton, ChCh Oxford (MA); *m* 22 July 1961, (Margaret Minette) Rohais, da of (James) Alasdair Anderson of Tullichewan (d 1982); 2 da (Cecilia Margaret Lucy (Cecilia, Lady MacGregor of MacGregor) b 1963, Candida Harriett Rohais (Mrs Gerrard Rafferty) b 1964); *Heir* none; *Career* Christie's: Scottish agent 1968, jt Scottish agent 1973–92, chm Christie's Scotland 1978–96; pres Assoc for the Protection of Rural Scotland 1978–90, convener Church of Scotland Ctee for Artistic Matters 1987–91, hon vice-pres Scotland's Garden Scheme 1983–, Scottish rep Nat Art Collections Fund 1972–83; dir High Craigton Farming Co; tstee Tree Register of the British Isles 1988–2006; memb: Historic Buildings Cncl for Scotland 1989–98, Gardens Ctee Nat Tst for Scotland 1994–2001; chm Church Building Renewal Tst (Glasgow) 1995–98; FRSA 1986; *Recreations* heraldry, family history, collecting heraldic bookplates; *Clubs* Turf; *Style—* Sir Ilay Campbell of Succoth, Bt; ✉ Crarae Lodge, Inveraray, Argyll PA32 8YA (tel 01546 86274, fax 01546 86262)

CAMPBELL OF SURBITON, Baroness (Life Peer UK 2007), of Surbiton in the Royal Borough of Kingston upon Thames; Dame Jane Susan Campbell; DBE (2006, MBE 2000), PC (2007); da of Ronald James Capmbell (d 1987), and Jessie Mary, *née* Ball; *b* 19 April 1959, Kingston Hill, Surrey; *Educ* Hatfield Poly (BA), Univ of Sussex (MA); *m* 1, 27 Jun 1987 (husb d 1993); m 2, 17 Sept 2000, Roger Symes; *Career* equal opportunities liaison offr GLC 1984–86, disability trg devpt offr London Boroughs Disability Resource Team 1986–87, princ disability advsr London Borough of Hounslow 1987–88, dir of trg London Boroughs Disability Resource Team 1988–94, ind conslt Direct Payments 1994–96, co-dir Nat Centre for Ind Living 1996–2000 (now tstee), chair Social Care Inst for Excellence 2001–05; cmmr: Disability Rights Cmmn 2000–, Cmmn of Equality and Human Rights 2007– (chair Disability Ctee 2007–); chair Ind Living Review Expert Panel Office of Disability Issues 2006; sits in House of Lords as crossbench peer 2007–; memb Editorial Bd Br Jl of Social Work; Mayor's Community Award Kingston-upon-Thames 1994; Hon LLD Univ of Bristol 2002, Hon DUniv Sheffield Hallam Univ 2003; *Publications* Disability Equality Training (jtly, 1991), Disability Politics (jtly, 1996); *Recreations* theatre, cinema, gardening, family and friends; *Style—* The Rt Hon the Baroness Campbell of Surbiton, DBE; ✉ House of Lords, London SW1A 0PW (tel 020 7219 3000); website www.livingwithdignity.info

CAMPBELL-ORDE, Sir John Alexander; 6 Bt (GB 1790), of Morpeth, Northumberland; s of Maj Sir Simon Arthur Campbell-Orde, 5 Bt, TD (d 1969), and Eleanor Hyde, *née* Watts (d 1996); *b* 11 May 1943; *Educ* Gordonstoun; *m* 1973 (m dis 1991), Lacy Ralls, o da of T Grady Gallant, of Nashville, TN; 3 da (Alexandra Louise b 1974, Alice Theodora b 1976, Octavia Maie b 1978), 1 s (John Simon Arthur b 1981); *Heir* s, John Campbell-Orde; *Career* art dealer; *Style—* Sir John Campbell-Orde, Bt; ✉ PO Box 22974, Nashville, TN 37202, USA

CAMPBELL-SAVOURS, Baron (Life Peer UK 2001), of Allerdale in the County of Cumbria; Dale Norman Campbell-Savours; s of John Lawrence, and Cynthia Lorraine Campbell-Savours; *b* 23 August 1943; *Educ* Keswick Sch, Sorbonne Paris; *m* 1970, Gudrun Kristin Runolfsdottir; 3 s; *Career* formerly co dir; Parly candidate (Lab) Darwen Feb and Oct 1974, MP (Lab) Workington 1979–2001 (also contested by-election 1976); front bench spokesman: overseas devpt 1991–92, agriculture 1992–94, ret; memb: Public Accounts Ctee 1980–91, Procedure Ctee 1983–91, Member's Interests Select Ctee 1983–92, Agriculture Select Ctee 1994–96, Standards and Privileges Ctee 1996–2001, Intelligence and Security Ctee 1997–2001; memb UNISON 1970–; *Publications* The case for the Supplementary Vote (1990), The case for the University of the Lakes (1995); *Style—* The Rt Hon the Lord Campbell-Savours

CAMPION, David Bardsley (Barry); s of Norman Campion (d 1987), and Enid Mary, *née* Bardsley; *b* 20 March 1938; *Educ* Shrewsbury; *m* 1, 1962 (m dis 1972), Victoria Wild; 1 s (Mark), 1 da (Sarah); m 2, 1979, Sally, da of Frank Walter Manning Arkle; *Career* dir Wheatsheaf Distribution and Trading 1968–78, dir Linfood Holdings 1978–81, chm Food Div CWS Ltd 1982–87, chief exec Monarchy Foods Ltd 1987–90: chm: BAF Securities Ltd (dir 1972–), Meridian Foods Ltd 1990–97, Wilsons of Holyhead 1991–98, Burgess Supafeeds 1996–2004, Gott Foods Ltd 1996–2001, Gold Star (Natural Fruit Juices) Ltd 1997–98, Opus Europe Ltd 1999–2001, Wholebake Foods Ltd 2001–; dep chm Gold Crown Foods Ltd 1993–94; dir: Snackhouse plc 1990–2001, West Trust plc 1991–93, Sutton Hoo Produce Ltd 1995–98, Freshers Foods Ltd 2005–; MInstD 1972, FIGD 1983; *Recreations* golf, cricket, sailing; *Clubs* MCC, Delamere Forest Golf, Royal Birkdale Golf, Holyhead Golf, Trearddur Bay Sailing, Farmers'; *Style—* Barry Campion, Esq; ✉ Monarchy Hall Farm, Utkinton, Tarporley, Cheshire CW6 0JZ (tel 01829 752064, fax 01829 752075)

CAMPION, Prof Peter David; s of John Neville Campion, and Dorothy Mabel, *née* Shave (d 1968); *b* 14 April 1946; *Educ* Southend HS for Boys, Pembroke Coll Oxford (open exhibitioner, BA), London Hosp Med Coll (BM BCh), DCCH (Edinburgh), Univ of

Liverpool (PhD); *m* Jan 1971, Janet Elizabeth, *née* Davison; 4 c; *Career* house surgn (gen surgery and ENT) then house physician London Hosp 1971, jr lectr in morbid anatomy London Hosp Med Coll 1972, SHO in paediatrics Queen Elizabeth Hosp for Children 1973, princ in gen practice Brentwood 1974–80, lectr in gen practice Univ of Dundee and memb Med Sch Teaching Practice 1980–85, sr lectr in gen practice Univ of Liverpool 1985–96 (head Dept of Primary Care 1991–96), prof of primary care med Univ of Hull 1996–, ptnr Drs Jary, Rawcliffe, Kapur, Greene and Campion 1996–2001; memb Course Co-ordinating Ctee Faculty of Med 1988–92, jt chair Core Curriculum Working Gp 1992–94; external examiner Sultan Qaboos Univ Oman 1993–96; RCGP: memb Panel of Examiners 1988–2004, convenor Video Assessment Module 2002–04; memb Examination Bd DCH (RCP) 1992–95; referee Br Med Jl and Br Jl of Gen Practice 1985–; ordained elder Church of Scotland Dundee, reader C of E; MRCP, FRCGP 1990 (MRCGP); *Videos incl* Problems in Doctor-Patient Encounters (series, RSM, 1986), Turning from Alcohol and Reflections on Alcohol (both Univ of Liverpool TV Serv, A1991); *Books* Teaching General Practice to Undergraduates (with Prof M Roland and Prof C Whitehouse, 1995); also author of numerous refereed and review articles; *Recreations* playing the organ and piano, my family; *Style*— Prof Peter Campion; ✉ 8 North View, Little Weighton, Cottingham, East Yorkshire HU20 3UL (tel 01482 842035); tel 01482 464395, fax 01482 464174, e-mail p.d.campion@hull.ac.uk

CAMPION-SMITH, (William) Nigel; s of H R A Campion-Smith, of Gerrards Cross, Bucks, and Moyra, *née* Campion (d 2001); *b* 10 July 1954; *Educ* King George V Sch Southport, Royal GS High Wycombe, St John's Coll Cambridge (MA); *m* 31 July 1976, Andrea Jean, da of Edward Willacy, of Hale Barns, Cheshire; 1 da (Dr Joanna b 1983), 2 s (Jonathan b 1985, Timothy b 1990); *Career* admitted slr 1978; ptnr Travers Smith Braithwaite 1982–97, ptnr Latham & Watkins 2000–; Law Soc 1978; *Style*— Nigel Campion-Smith, Esq; ✉ tel 020 7710 1070, fax 020 7374 4460

CAMPLIN, Jamie Robert; *b* 27 April 1947; *Educ* Bishop's Stortford Coll, CCC Cambridge (MA); *Career* Thames & Hudson: editorial dir 1979–2005, md 2005–; *Books* The Rise of the Plutocrats - Wealth and Power in Edwardian England (London 1978, NY 1979); *Style*— Jamie Camplin, Esq; ✉ 10 Church Lane, London SW19 3PD (tel 020 8542 7015); Thames & Hudson Ltd, 181A High Holborn, London WC1V 7QX (tel 020 7845 5066, fax 020 7845 5051, e-mail j.camplin@thameshudson.co.uk)

CAMROSE, 4 Viscount (UK 1941); Sir Adrian Michael Berry; 4 Bt (UK 1921); s of Baron Hartwell, MBE, TD (Life Peer, d 2001); *b* 15 June 1937; *Educ* Eton, ChCh Oxford; *m* 1967, Marina Beatrice, da of Cyrus Sulzberger, of Paris; 1 s (Hon Jonathan William), 1 da (Hon Jessica Margaret); *Heir* s, Hon Jonathan Berry; *Career* sci corr Daily Telegraph 1977–96, consulting ed (science) Daily Telegraph 1996–; FRAS, FRGS, FBIS; *Publications* The Next Ten Thousand Years (1974), The Iron Sun (1977), From Apes to Astronauts (1980), High Skies and Yellow Rain (1983), The Super-Intelligent Machine (1983), Ice With Your Evolution (1986), Koyama's Diamond (fiction, 1984), Labyrinth of Lies (fiction, 1986), Harrap's Book of Scientific Anecdotes (1989), Eureka: The Book of Scientific Anecdotes (1993), The Next 500 Years (1995), Galileo and the Dolphins (1996), The Giant Leap (1999); *Style*— The Viscount Camrose; ✉ 11 Cottesmore Gardens, London W8 5PR

CAMSEY, Granville Thomas Bateman; s of Thomas Camsey (d 1970), and May, *née* Bradley (d 1966); *b* 1 March 1936; *Educ* Univ of Salford, Univ of Birmingham (MSc), Manchester Business Sch; *m* Maureen; 1 s (Jonathan Bickerstaff b 22 March 1964), 1 da (Megan Elizabeth b 10 April 1967); *Career* CEGB: joined as trainee N Western Region 1952, subsequently various appts at Trawsfynydd and Oldbury Nuclear Power Stations, dep station mangr Heysham 1 AGR nuclear station 1972–76, station mangr Rugeley A and B power stations 1976–80, various managerial posts London becoming dir of prodn S Eastern Region until 1987; md designate China Light and Power Co Hong Kong 1987–88, rejoined CEGB as chief exec designate Nat Power Div (Thermal) 1988, exec dir National Power plc 1990–96, md Gp Technol National Power plc 1993–96; advsr to Mgmnt Engrs Düsseldorf Germany; non-exec dir Stone & Webster Engineering Ltd 1996, professional assoc Gemini Consulting Ltd 1996; memb Cncl (now Senate) Engrg Cncl; memb Cncl Royal Acad of Engrg; Freeman City of London, Liveryman Worshipful Co of Engrs; CIMgt, FInstD, FInstE, FIMechE, FREng 1992; *Recreations* golf, wood-carving; *Style*— Granville T B Camsey, FREng; ✉ (tel and fax 01753 890819)

CANADY, Diane Elizabeth; da of late Jimmy Roger Canady, of High Wycombe, Bucks, and Kathleen Ann, *née* Knight; *b* 22 May 1954; *Educ* USAF Central HS USA, High Wycombe Tech Coll, Univ of Essex (BA, MA); *m* 2 Dec 1977, Brian Armistead, s of Douglas Armistead; 1 s (Benjamin James b 25 May 1981); *Career* grad trainee McCann Erickson advtg 1977–81, account supr Royds Advertising 1981–82, account dir NCK Advertising 1982–83, gp product mangr Levi Strauss 1983–84, bd dir Geers Gross 1984–91, client servs dir and exec bd dir rising to managing ptnr Publicis 1991–97, md Publicis Dialogue 1997–; lectr in advtg for CAM course Coll of Distributive Trades; memb: Bd Cosmetic Exec Women, WACL and Fragrance Fndn; patron Women of the Year Luncheon; *Recreations* music, interior decorating, reading, cooking; *Style*— Ms Diane Canady; ✉ Publicis Dialogue, 82 Baker Street, London W1M 2AE (tel 020 7935 4426, fax 020 7830 3290, mobile 07860 702140)

CANAVAN, Dennis Andrew; MSP; s of Thomas Canavan (d 1974), and Agnes Canavan; *b* 8 August 1942; *Educ* St Columba's HS Cowdenbeath, Univ of Edinburgh (BSc, DipEd); *Career* princ teacher Maths Dept St Modan's HS Stirling 1970–74, asst head Holy Rood HS Edinburgh 1974; cncllr Stirling DC 1973–74 (Lab Gp leader 1974); MP (Lab): West Stirlingshire 1974–83, Falkirk W 1983–2000; MSP (Falkirk W) Falkirk W 1999–; special interests: foreign affrs, health service, education, Br-Irish relations, arms control, sport; Scottish Parly Lab Gp: chm 1980–81, chm PLP NI Ctee 1989–97; memb Foreign Affrs Select Ctee 1982–97, memb British-Irish Inter-Parly Body 1992–2000, memb Int Devpt Select Ctee 1997–99; fndr and convener All-Pty Parly Scottish Sports Gp 1987–2000, convener Cross-Pty Parly Scottish Sports Gp 1999–; memb Euro and External Relations Ctee Scottish Parl 1999–; *Recreations* hill climbing, swimming, horse riding, angling, football spectating (former Scottish Univs' football internationalist); *Clubs* Camelon Labour, Bannockburn Miners' Welfare; *Style*— Dennis Canavan, MSP; ✉ Constituency Office, 37 Church Walk, Denny, Stirlingshire FK6 6DF (tel 01324 825922); The Scottish Parliament, Edinburgh EH99 1SP (tel 0131 348 5630)

CANBY, Michael William; s of Clarence Canby (d 2004), and Mary Frances, *née* Drake; *b* 11 January 1955; *Educ* Buckhurst Hill County HS, Univ of Cambridge (MA, LLB); *m* 6 Sept 1980, Sarah, da of John Houghton Masters (d 1965), and Mary, *née* Dymond; 1 s (Philip Charles Houghton b 1988), 1 da (Harriet Georgina Mary b 1991); *Career* admitted slr 1980; Linklaters: New York office 1982–84, ptnr 1986–, Paris office 1989–95; memb Law Soc; *Style*— Michael Canby, Esq; ✉ c/o Linklaters, One Silk Street, London EC2Y 8HQ (tel 020 7456 2000, fax 020 7456 2222, e-mail michael.canby@linklaters.com)

CANDY, Lorraine; da of Anthony Butler, and Vivienne Butler; *b* 8 July 1968; *Educ* NCTJ Proficiency Test 1988; *Career* journalist; The Cornish Times 1990, reporter The Sun Showbiz section 1990, feature writer The Daily Mirror 1990–93, women's ed The Sun Feb-Aug 1993, women's ed Today Newspaper 1993–95, dep ed Marie Claire 1995–97, dep ed Saturday Magazine The Times 1997–98, ed B Magazine 1998–99, features ed The Times 1999–2000, ed Cosmopolitan 2000–04, ed Elle 2004–; *Recreations* family; *Style*— Mrs Lorraine Candy

CANE, Alison; da of Ronald Cane, of Hutton Mount, Essex, and Jeanne, *née* Snow; *b* 18 August 1960; *Educ* Ongar Comp Sch Essex, Loughton Coll of Further Educn Essex, St Martin's Sch of Art; *Career* freelance designer 1982, designer Michael Peters plc 1982–86, asst creative dir Coley Porter Bell 1986–93, sr design dir Landor Associates until 1997; clients incl: Prestige, Corgi Toys, Marks and Spencer, Jacksons of Piccadilly, Bryant & May, Terrys of York, A&P-USA, Cadburys, Sainsbury's, Reuters, Philips, Yardley of London; various D&AD and Clio nominations, winner Design Effectiveness Award (food packaging) 1990, Clio winner (best packaging dairy) 1991, highly commended Int Design Annual Awards 1990, winner Best of Show (for Masterpiece Range) Int Brand Packaging Awards 1993; *Style*— Ms Alison Cane

CANN, (John William) Anthony; s of Dr John Cann (d 1991), and Enid Grace, *née* Long (d 2003); *b* 21 July 1947; *Educ* Old Malthouse Sch Swanage, Shrewsbury, Univ of Southampton (LLB); *m* 6 Jan 1973, Anne, da of Harold Thorswald Clausen (d 1994), of Johannesburg; 2 s (John Harold b 25 Nov 1973, Robert Charles b 13 Aug 1984), 1 da (Sally Elizabeth b 10 Jan 1978); *Career* admitted slr 1972; Linklaters 1970–2006: asst slr 1972–78, NY office 1975–82, ptnr 1978–2006, head Corp Dept 1995–2000, sr ptnr 2001–06; co-head M&A and Corp Practice Gp of Linklaters & Alliance 1998–2001; memb Advsy Ctee CAB Battersea 1973–75, non-exec dir and chm Remuneration Ctee Smiths News plc 2006–, chm Changing Faces, tstee Adventure Capital Fund, govr Haberdashers' Aske's Fedn; Freeman City of London Slrs Co 1978; memb Law Soc; *Books* Mergers & Acquisitions Handbook (Part D), Mergers and Acquisitions in Europe (United Kingdom); *Recreations* travel, photography, sports; *Clubs* Athenaeum, MCC, Trojans; *Style*— Anthony Cann, Esq; ✉ Langrick, 13 Murray Road, Wimbledon, London SW19 4PD (tel 020 8946 6731, e-mail anthony.cann@yahoo.com)

CANN, Prof Johnson Robin (Joe); s of late Johnson Ralph Cann, and Ethel Mary, *née* Northmore; *b* 18 October 1937; *Educ* St Alban's Sch, St John's Coll Cambridge (BA, MA, PhD, ScD); *m* 1, 10 Aug 1963, Janet Mary Teresa (d 1994), da of Prof Charles John Hamson (d 1987), of Trinity Coll Cambridge; 2 s (John b 1964, David b 1966); 2, 12 May 2001, Helen Dunham, former w of Prof Ansel Dunham; *Career* res fell St John's Coll Cambridge 1962–65, post doctoral res Cambridge 1962–66, Br Museum (Natural History) 1966–68, lectr then reader Sch of Environmental Sciences UEA 1968–77, J B Simpson prof of geology Univ of Newcastle upon Tyne 1977–89, adjunct scientist Woods Hole Oceanographic Instn 1987–, prof of earth sciences Univ of Leeds 1989–; Murchison Medal Geological Soc London 1990; FGS, FRS 1995; *Style*— Prof Joe Cann; ✉ Department of Earth Sciences, University of Leeds, Leeds LS2 9JT (tel 0113 233 5204, fax 0113 233 5259, e-mail j.cann@earth.leeds.ac.uk)

CANNADINE, Prof David Nicholas; *b* 7 September 1950; *Educ* King Edward's Five Ways Sch Birmingham, Clare Coll Cambridge (MA, Robbins prize), St John's Coll Oxford (DPhil); *Career* res fell St John's Coll Cambridge 1975–77, asst lectr in history Univ of Cambridge 1976–80 (lectr 1980–88, memb Faculty Bd of History 1983–85), fell and Coll lectr in history Christ's Coll Cambridge 1977–88 (dir of studies in history 1977–83, tutor 1979–81, memb Coll Cncl 1979–88, fell steward 1981–88), visiting memb Sch of Historical Studies Inst for Advanced Study Princeton 1980–81, assoc fell Berkeley Coll Yale Univ 1985–, prof of history Columbia Univ 1988–98 (memb Univ Senate 1989–90, chm Dept Personnel Ctee 1991–92, memb Governing Body Soc of Fellows 1992–98, Moore collegiate prof 1992–98); Inst of Historical Research Univ of London: dir 1998–2003, Queen Elizabeth the Queen Mother prof of Br history 2003–; a cmmr English Heritage 2001–; visiting prof Birkbeck Coll London 1995–97, visiting fell Whitney Humanities Center Yale Univ 1995–98; gen ed: Studies in Modern History 1979–, Penguin History of Britain 1989–, Penguin History of Europe 1991–; advsy ed Complete Edition of the Works of W S Gilbert 1988–, ed Historical Research 1998–2003; memb Editorial Bd: Urban History Yearbook 1979–83, Past and Present 1983–, Midland History 1985–88, Rural History 1995–, Prospect 1995–, Library History 1998–; tstee: Parliament History 1998–, London Jl 1998–; fell J P Morgan Library NY 1992–98; chm John Ben Snow Prize Ctee Conf on Br Studies 1993; memb: Cncl Urban History Gp 1980–88, Advsy Cncl Centre for the Study of Soc and Politics Kingston Univ 1997, Advsy Cncl Warburg Inst 1998–2003, Advsy Bd Inst of Contemporary Br History 1998–2003, Advsy Cncl PRO 1999–, Advsy Cncl Inst of US Studies 1999–2004, Advsy Cncl Inst of English Studies 2000–, Advsy Cncl Inst of Latin American Studies 2000–04, Eastern Regnl Ctee Nat Tst 2001–, Advsy Cncl Inst for Study of the Americas 2004–; vice-pres Br Record Soc 1998–, vice-pres Royal Historical Soc 1998–2003, pres Worcestershire Historical Soc 1999–, tstee Kennedy Memorial Tst 2000–, tstee Nat Portrait Gallery 2001–, tstee Br Empire and Cwlth Museum 2003–; govr Ipswich Sch 1982–88; T S Ashton Prize in Economic History 1977, Agricultural History Silver Jubilee Prize 1977, Lionel Trilling Prize 1991, Governors' Award 1991, Dean's Distinguished Award in the Humanities Columbia Univ 1996; Hon DLitt: UEA 2001, South Bank Univ 2001, Univ of Birmingham 2002; FRHistS 1981, FRSA 1998, FRSL 1999, FBA 1999; *Books* Lords and Landlords: The Aristocracy and the Towns 1774–1967 (1980), Patricians, Power and Politics in Nineteenth Century Towns (ed, 1982), Exploring the Urban Past: Essays in Urban History by H J Dyos (co-ed, 1982), Rituals of Royalty: Power and Ceremonial in Traditional Societies (co-ed, 1987), The Pleasures of the Past (1989), Blood, Toil, Tears and Sweat: Winston Churchill's Famous Speeches (ed, 1989), The First Modern Society: Essays in English History in Honour of Lawrence Stone (co-ed, 1989), The Decline and Fall of the British Aristocracy (1990), G M Trevelyan: A Life in History (1992), Aspects of Aristocracy: Grandeur and Decline in Modern Britain, (1994), History and Biography: Essays in Honour of Derek Beales (co-ed, 1996), Class in Britain (1998), History in Our Time (1998), Making History Now (1999), Ornamentalism: How the British saw their Empire (2001), In Churchill's Shadow: Confronting the past in modern Britain (2002), What is History Now? (ed, 2002), History and the Media (ed, 2004), Mellon: An American Life (2006), The National Portrait Gallery: A Brief Outline History (2007), Empire, The Sea and Global History: Britain's Maritime World 1763–1833 (ed and contrib, 2007); also author of numerous book chapters and articles in learned jls; *Style*— Prof David Cannadine; ✉ Institute of Historical Research, University of London, Senate House, Malet Street, London WC1E 7HU (tel 020 7664 4893, fax 020 7664 4894)

CANNING, Alison Mary; da of Dr William Carbis Canning, of Knowle, W Midlands, and Bertha Sheila, *née* McGill; *b* 15 April 1959; *Educ* Marlborough, PCL (BA), City Univ Business Sch (MBA); *m* 23 Sept 1994 (m dis 1997), Richard Albert Moore; *Career* Burson-Marsteller PR: graduate trainee rising to account exec London 1983–85, account supr rising to vice-pres/client servs mangr NY 1986–88, bd dir London 1988–89; sr vice-pres/md Cohn & Wolfe PR London 1989–94 (Best New Consultancy 1990 and 1991, numerous other UK and int awards), ceo Burson-Marsteller UK 1994–96, fndr md First & 42nd (mgmnt consultancy) 1997–2001, pres int ops Edelman Worldwide 2001–03; non-exec dir: Tulchan Communications, All About Brands plc; memb: Forum UK, RCA, IOD; *Recreations* diving, fishing, sailing, opera; *Style*— Ms Alison Canning

CANNING, Prof Elizabeth Ursula; da of Maj Miles Howell Canning MC, TD (d 1950), and Winifred, *née* Jenkins (d 1980); *b* 29 September 1928; *Educ* Truro HS, Imperial Coll London (BSc, DSc), London Sch of Hygiene and Tropical Med (PhD); *m* 15 Aug 1953, Christopher Maynard Wilson (d 1997), s of George Henry Cyril Wilson (d 1973); 2 da (Victoria Jane (Mrs M J Harvey) b 16 March 1958, Catherine Alexandra (Mrs J P Williams) b 3 March 1960), 1 s (Miles Richard Guy b 29 April 1966); *Career* Imperial Coll London: lectr 1951–70, sr lectr 1970–71, reader 1971–81, prof of protozoology 1981–93, sr research fell 1993–95, sr research investigator 1995–; former vice-pres Int Soc of Protozoologists (hon life memb 1993), former pres, vice-pres and sec Br Section Soc of Protozoologists (hon life memb 1999), memb Royal Soc of Tropical Med and Hygiene, hon life memb Br Soc of Parasitology 1997; Purkyne Medal Acad of Science Czech Republic 2004, Gold

Medal Faculty of Science Charles Univ Czech Republic 2004, Emile Brumpt Prize Paris 2005, Fndrs Prize Soc for Invertebrates Pathology 2005; Hon Dr Univ Blaise Pascal Clerment Ferrand; ARCS, FIBiol; *Books* The Microsporidia of Vertebrates (1986); *Recreations* golf, crossword puzzles, bridge; *Style*— Prof Elizabeth Canning; ✉ Tiles Cottage, Forest Road, Winkfield Row, Bracknell, Berkshire RG42 7NR; Imperial College at Silwood Park, Garden Wood Laboratories (West), Ascot, Berkshire SL5 7PY (tel 020 7594 2244, fax 020 7594 2339, e-mail e.canning@ic.ac.uk)

CANNING, Hugh Donaldson; s of David Donaldson Canning, of Whissendine, Leics, and Olga Mary, *née* Simms; *b* 28 May 1954; *Educ* Oakham Sch, Pembroke Coll Oxford (BA), UC Cardiff (Dip Theatre Studies); *Career* regular contrib The Western Mail 1977–82, freelance writer 1979 (Music & Musicians, Opera, Times Higher Educn Supplement), freelance contrib on music The Guardian 1983–87, music critic London Daily News 1987, music critic and feature writer (contract) The Guardian 1987–89, chief music critic Sunday Times 1989–; contrib and memb Editorial Bd Opera magazine; opera critic The Listener (until closure); Critic of the Year 1994 (Br Press Awards) 1995; memb Critics' Circle; *Recreations* theatre, music, eating out, watching tennis, gossip; *Style*— Hugh Canning; ✉ The Sunday Times, 1 Pennington Street, London E1 9XN

CANNING, HE Mark; *b* 15 December 1954; *Educ* Downside Sch, Univ of London (MBA); *m* 2004, Cecilia Kenny; 1 da (b 2004); *Career* entered HM Diplomatic Serv 1973, Freetown 1975–77, Georgetown 1982–86, Chicago 1986–88, Jakarta 1993–97, Kuala Lumpur 2001–06, ambass to Burma 2006–; cnsllr FCO 2000; *Style*— HE Mr Mark Canning; ✉ c/o Foreign and Commonwealth Office (Rangoon), King Charles Street, London SW1A 2AH

CANNINGS, Della Mary; QPM (2006); da of Frank Arthur Cannings (d 1971), and Yvonne Barbara Mary, *née* Oddy (d 1995); *b* 27 August 1952, Exeter; *Educ* Bishop Blackall GS Exeter, Univ of Bath (BSc); *m* 1977, Michael Baker; *Career* Devon and Cornwall Constabulary 1975–2000 (latterly Chief Supt), Asst Chief Constable then actg Dep Chief Constable Cleveland Police 2000–02, Chief Constable North Yorkshire Police 2002–; sr police advsr Home Office Police Research Gp 1993–95; memb ACPO 2000–; chm North Yorkshire Bd Prince's Tst; MInstD 2000; *Recreations* gardening, bird watching, walking, photography; *Style*— Ms Della Cannings, QPM; ✉ North Yorkshire Police Headquarters, Newby Wiske, Northallerton, North Yorkshire DL7 9HA (tel 01609 789000, fax 01609 789025)

CANNON, Fiona; da of John Cannon (d 2002), and Joan, *née* Henvey; *b* 7 January 1964, London; *Educ* Bishop Thomas Grant Sch London, Univ of Leeds (BA); *Partner* David Langan; 1 s (Joseph b 8 April 2000), 1 da (Jessica b 14 Dec 2001); *Career* Pepperell Unit Industrial Soc (now Work Fndn) 1987–89, freelance conslt 1989–90, head of equality and diversity Lloyds TSB Gp 1990–; cmmr Equal Opportunities Cmmn 2000– (dep chair 2006–); chair Practitioners Gp Taskforce on Racial Equality IPPR 2003–04; chm and fndr memb Employers for Childcare 1992–99, fndr memb Employers for Work-Life Balance 2000–03 (chm Steering Gp); fndr memb Race for Opportunity Campaign 1995; memb: Equal Opportunities Panel CBI, Ministerial Advsy Gp on Work-Life Balance 2001–02, Work and Parents Taskforce 2001–; *Recreations* reading, travelling; *Style*— Ms Fiona Cannon; ✉ Lloyds TSB Group plc, PO Box 112, Canons House, Canons Way, Bristol BS99 7LB (tel 020 7522 5666, fax 0117 943 3945, e-mail fiona.cannon2@lloydstsb.co.uk)

CANNON, Prof John Ashton; CBE (1985); s of George Ashton Cannon, and Gladys Violet Cannon; *b* 8 October 1926; *Educ* Hertford GS, Peterhouse Cambridge (MA), Univ of Bristol (PhD); *m* 1, 1948 (m dis 1953), Audrey Elizabeth, da of G R Caple, of Bristol; 1 s (Marcus b 1948), 1 da (Hilary b 1952); m 2, 1953, Minna Sofie, da of Frederick Pedersen, of Denmark; 1 s (Martin b 1966), 2 da (Susan b 1955, Annelise b 1962); *Career* RAF Flt Lt 1947–49 and 1952–55; reader Univ of Bristol 1970–75 (lectr 1961–67, sr lectr 1967–69), pro-vice-chllr Univ of Newcastle upon Tyne 1983–86 (prof of modern history 1976–92, dean Faculty of Arts 1979–82), chm Radio Bristol 1970–74; memb Univ Grants Ctee 1983–89 (vice-chm 1986–89, chm Arts Sub-Ctee 1983–89); FRHistS, FRSA; *Books* The Fox-North Coalition (1970), Parliamentary Reform (1973), The Letters of Junius (ed 1978), The Historian at Work (1980), The Whig Ascendancy (1981), Aristocratic Century (1984), Dictionary of Historians (ed 1988), Oxford Illustrated History of The Monarchy (with R Griffiths, 1988), Samuel Johnson and the politics of Hanoverian England (1994), Oxford Companion to British History (ed, 1997), Oxford Dictionary of British History (2001), The Kings and Queens of Britain (2001); *Recreations* music, sailing, tennis; *Style*— Prof John Cannon, CBE; ✉ 35a Osborne Road, Jesmond, Newcastle upon Tyne NE2 2AH (tel 0191 281 4096); Alma House, Grosmont, Gwent (tel 01981 240902); Department of History, University of Newcastle upon Tyne (tel 0191 232 8511, ext 6694)

CANNON, Prof Paul Stephen; s of John James Peter (d 2004), and Betty, *née* Carter (d 1996); *b* 28 October 1953; *Educ* Edmonton County GS, Univ of Southampton (BSc, MSc, PhD); *m* 14 May 1976, Vivian Avis Cannon, da of James Frederick Goodwin; 1 da (Ruth Avis b 27 Sept 1981), 1 s (Thomas James b 23 Oct 1984); *Career* engr; with RAE 1981–93, fndr Radio Science and Propagation Gp (later Centre for Propagation and Atmospheric Research) 1993, individual merit and fell DERA (Defence Evaluation and Research Agency) 1993–2002; QinetiQ: tech dir Communications Dept 2000–02, sr fell 2002, chief scientist Communications Div 2004–, univs partnership dir 2004–05; visiting prof Center for Atmospheric Research Univ of Massachusetts 1989–90, pt/t chair Communications and Atmospheric Sciences Univ of Bath 1998–, visiting chair in engrg Univ of Birmingham 2007–; NATO-AGARD (Advsy Gp for Aerospace Research and Devpt): nat rep Electromagnetic Propagation Panel and Sensors and Propagation Panel 1993–97, vice-chair and chair designate Sensors and Propagation Panel 1996–97; chair: UK-Canada-Norway-Sweden Doppler and Multipath Sounding Network (DAMSON) Project 1993–2000, Nat Facilities Funding Ctee PPARC 2000–2002; co-chair US/UK Memorandum of Understanding (MOU) on Effects of the Ionosphere on C3I Systems 1996–2001, chair URSI Commn G Ionospheric Radio Propagation 2005– (vice-chair 2002–05); national rep URSI Commn G 1993–99, assoc ed URSI Radio Science Bulletin 2002–04; IEE: memb Cncl 2003–06, member Antennas and Propagation Professional Network Exec 2003–04; FREng, FIET, CEng, MAGU (American Geophysical Union); *Publications* author of numerous articles in jls; *Recreations* photography, travelling, American presidential history; *Style*— Prof Paul Cannon; ✉ QinetiQ, St Andrews Road, Malvern, Worcestershire WR14 3PS (tel 01684 896468, fax 01684 894657, e-mail pcannon@qinetiq.com)

CANNON, (Jack) Philip; s of William George Cannon (d 1973), of Perranporth, Cornwall, and Charlotte Loraine, *née* Renoir (d 1984); *b* 21 December 1929; *Educ* Falmouth GS, Dartington Hall, Royal Coll of Music; *m* 1, 15 July 1950, Jacqueline Playfair Laidlaw (d 1984), da of Hugh Alexander Lyon Laidlaw; 1 da (Virginia Shona Playfair b 29 June 1953); m 2, 5 Nov 1997, Jane, Baroness Buijs van Schouwenburg, da of Stanley Dyson; *Career* composer; dep prof Royal Coll of Music 1953–59, lectr in music Univ of Sydney 1959–60, prof of composition Royal Coll of Music 1960–95; author of many articles for music jls; compositions incl: Morvoren (opera) 1964, String Quartet (winner of Grand Prix and Prix de la Critique Paris) 1965, Oraison Funèbre de L'Ame Humaine (symphony cmmnd by ORTF) 1971, Lacrimae Mundi (cmmnd by Gulbenkian Fndn for Music Gp of London) 1972, Son of Man (symphony cmmnd by BBC to mark Britain's entry to the EC) 1973, The Temple (cmmnd by The Three Choirs Festival) 1974, Te Deum (cmmnd by HM The Queen for St George's Day) 1975, Logos (clarinet quintet cmmnd by BBC for Silver Jubilee) 1977, Lord of Light Requiem (cmmnd by The Three Choirs Festival) 1980, Cinq Supplications sur une Bénédiction (cmmnd by RF) 1983, Dr Jekyll and Mr Hyde (cmmnd by BBC TV), A Ralegh Triptych (cmmnd by The Three Choirs Festival) 1992, Septain (in memoriam John Ogdon) 1993, Piano Quintet (for John Lill and the Medici String Quartet) 1994, Symphony (for BBC Philharmonic) 1996, Symphony for the Millennium 2000; memb: Royal Philharmonic Soc, ISM, Br Acad of Composers and Songwriters; Bard of Gorsedd Kernow 1997; FRCM 1971; *Recreations* exploring comparative philosophies, travel; *Clubs* Savile, Chelsea Arts; *Style*— Philip Cannon, Esq; ✉ Elmdale Cottage, Marsh, Aylesbury, Buckinghamshire HP17 8SP (tel 01296 613157)

CANNON, Prof Thomas; s of Albert Edward Cannon (d 1986), and Bridget, *née* Ryan (d 1996); *b* 20 November 1945; *Educ* St Francis Xavier's GS, South Bank Poly; *m* Frances, da of Bernard Constable; 1 da (Rowan), 1 s (Robin); *Career* res assoc Univ of Warwick 1968–71, lectr Enfield Coll of Technol 1971–72, brand mangr Imperial Group 1973–76, lectr Univ of Durham 1973–81, prof Univ of Stirling 1981–89, dir Manchester Business Sch 1989–92; chief exec: MDE Services 1973–2004, Mgmnt Charter Initiative 1995–2000, Respect London 2000–03, Ideopolis International Ltd; Mercers' Sch Memorial prof of commerce Gresham Coll 1996–2000; visiting prof: of business admin Kingston Univ, Univ of Bradford 1997–, Middlesex Univ 1997–; fell: Inst of Physical Distribution Mgmnt, Inst of Export; CIMgt, FInstM, FRSA; *Books* Advertising Research (1972), Distribution Research (1973), Advertising: The Economic Implications (1975), How to Win Profitable Business (1984), How to Win Business Overseas (1985), Small Business Development (1987), Enterprise (1991), Basic Marketing (1991, 4 edn 1996), The World of Business (1991), Women as Entrepreneurs (1991), Corporate Responsibility (1992), How to get Ahead in Business (1994), Guinness Book of Business Records (1996), Welcome to the Revolution (1996), The Good Sales Managers' Guide (1999), The Ultimate Book of Business Breakthroughs (2000); *Recreations* supporting Everton, computing; *Style*— Prof Thomas Cannon; ✉ 68 Rodney Street, Liverpoool L1 9AF (tel 07850 188035, e-mail tom@ideopolis.info)

CANNON-BROOKES, Dr Peter; s of Victor Montgomery (Joe) Cannon Brookes (d 2004), and Nancy Margaret, *née* Markham Carter (d 1994); *b* 23 August 1938; *Educ* Bryanston, Trinity Hall Cambridge (MA), Courtauld Inst of Art Univ of London (PhD); *m* 13 April 1966, Caroline Aylmer, da of Lt Col John Aylmer Christie-Miller, CBE, TD, DL, of Manor House, Bourton-on-the-Hill, Glos; 1 s (Stephen William Aylmer b 1966), 1 da (Emma Wilbraham Montgomery b 1968); *Career* keeper Dept of Art: City Museum and Art Gallery Birmingham 1965–78, Nat Museum of Wales 1978–86; fndr ed International Journal of Museum Management and Curatorship 2003– (ed 1981–2003), dir museum servs Stipple Database Services Ltd 1986–89, conslt curator The Tabley House Collection Univ of Manchester 1988–, int museum conslt 1990–; Int Cncl of Museums: memb Exec Bd UK Ctee 1973–81, pres Int Art Exhibitions Ctee 1977–79 (Exec Bd 1975–81), vice-pres Conservation Ctee 1978–81 (Exec Bd 1975–81); memb: Welsh Arts Cncl 1979–84 (memb Craft Ctee 1983–87, memb Art Ctee 1979–85), Projects and Orgns Ctee Crafts Cncl 1985–87; pres: Welsh Fedn of Museums 1980–82, S Wales Art Soc 1980–87; memb: Town Twinning Ctee Birmingham Int Cncl 1968–78, Birmingham Dio Synod 1970–78, Birmingham Dio Advsy Ctee for Care of Churches 1972–78, Edgbaston Deanery Synod 1970–78 (lay jt chm 1975–78), Abingdon Deanery Synod 1999–2007, Oxford Diocesan Synod 2003–07, Oxford Diocesan Bd of Educn 2004–07; JP: Birmingham 1973–78, Cardiff 1978–82; Liveryman Worshipful Co of Goldsmiths 1974 (Freeman 1969); FMA, Fell Int Inst of Conservation (FIIC), FRSA; *Books* European Sculpture (with H D Molesworth, 1964), Baroque Churches (with C A Cannon-Brookes, 1969), Lombard Painting (1974), After Gulbenkian (1976), The Cornbury Park Bellini (1977), Michael Ayrton (1978), Emile Antoine Bourdelle (1983), Ivor Roberts-Jones (1983), Czech Sculpture 1800–1938 (1983), Paintings from Tabley (1989), The Painted Word (1991), William Redgrave (1998), The Godolphin Arabian (2005); *Recreations* cooking, growing vegetables, photography; *Clubs* Athenaeum; *Style*— Dr Peter Cannon-Brookes; ✉ Thrupp Farm, Abingdon, Oxfordshire OX14 3NE (tel 01235 520595, fax 01235 534817)

CANOSA MONTORO, Francisco Octavio (Frank); s of Dr Francisco Canosa Lorenzo, and Elisa, *née* Montoro de la Torre; *b* 28 May 1951; *Educ* Columbia Univ NY (BA), Fordham Univ NY (JD); *m* 1, Dec 1972 (m dis 1975), Gloria de Aragón; m 2, 15 Sept 1979, Belinda Mary, da of Lt-Col Charles Reginald Clayton Albrecht, OBE, TA, of Pulborough, W Sussex; 2 da (Alexandra Elisa b 12 Jan 1983, Isabel Christina b 20 June 1985); *Career* asst to pres Bank of America NY 1975, asst vice-pres Manufacturers Hanover Trust Co NY 1978; Bank of America International Ltd London: vice-pres 1980, exec dir 1985, head corp fin UK and Europe 1987–89; vice-pres and sr mktg offr Bankers Trust Co 1989–92, first vice-pres and head of private banking Banca della Svizzera Italiana 1992–95, sr vice-pres and head of the branch and of private banking Bank Julius Baer & Co Ltd 1995–2000, md Julius Baer International Ltd 2000–04, conslt ABN Amro Bank NV Private Banking 2005–; chm Private Banking Ctee BBA 1996–2003; memb: Finances Ctee CAFOD 2001–06, Fin Advsy Gp Douai Abbey Tst 2001–, Advsy Panel PricewaterhouseCooper 2005–; visiting prof Univ of Buckingham 2005–; various broadcasts on private banking and various aspects relating to Cuba for the BBC, writer and presenter of series Cuba!Cuba! (Radio 4) 2000; memb: Advsy Cncl Philharmonia Orchestra 2001–, Public Membs Assoc of the Foreign Serv (Washington DC) 2006–; fell Securities and Investment Inst 2006–, FRSA 2006–; *Clubs* RAC, Nuevo, Madrid; *Style*— Frank Canosa Montoro, Esq

CANTER, Prof David Victor; s of Chaim Yizchak (Harry) Canter (d 1959), and Coralie Lilian, *née* Hyam (d 1970); *b* 5 January 1944; *Educ* Liverpool Collegiate GS, Univ of Liverpool (BA, PhD); *m* 10 Nov 1967, Sandra Lorraine, da of late Alfred Smith; 2 da (Hana b 1970, Lily Rebecca b 1979), 1 s (Daniel b 1972); *Career* visiting lectr Birmingham Sch of Architecture 1967–70, visiting res fell Tokyo Univ 1970–71, lectr Univ of Strathclyde 1970–71 (res fell Building Performance Res Unit 1965–70); Univ of Surrey: lectr 1972–78, reader 1978–83, personal chair in applied psychology 1983–87, chair of psychology 1987–94, head of dept 1987–91, academic head of dept 1991–94; prof of psychology Univ of Liverpool 1994–, dir Centre for Investigative Psychology Univ of Liverpool 1998–; managing ed Jl of Environmental Psychology 1981–, series ed Ethnoscopes: Current Challenges in the Environmental Social Sciences 1988–; numerous contribs to jls, TV and radio; writer, prodr and presenter Mapping Murder (six part TV documentary); chm Psychologists for Peace 1985–88; memb: Res Cncl for Complementary Med, London Advsy Bd Salvation Army, CND; Golden Dagger Award for non-fiction 1994, Anthony Award for non-fiction 1995; Freeman City of Quito 1985; Hon MD 1987, hon memb Japanese Inst of Architects 1970; FBPsS 1975, FAPA 1985, FIMgt 1985, CPsychol 1988, AcSS; *Books* Architectural Psychology (1970), Psychology for Architects (1974), Psychology and the Built Environment (1974), Environmental Interaction (1975), The Psychology of Place (1977), Designing for Therapeutic Environments (1979), Fires and Human Behaviour (1980, revised 1990), Psychology in Practice (with S Canter, 1982), Facet Theory: Approaches to Social Research (1985), The Research Interview: Uses and Approaches (1985), Environmental Social Psychology (1986), Environmental Perspectives (1988), Environmental Policy Assessment and Communication (1988), New Directions in Environmental Participation (1988), Periballontike Psychologia (in Greek, 1988), Football In Its Place (with M Comber and D Uzzell, 1989), Empirical Approaches to Social Representations (with G Breakwell, 1993), Criminal Shadows (1994), The Faces of Homelessness (1995), Psychology in Action (1996), Criminal Detection and the Psychology of Crime (with L Alison, 1997), Interviewing and Deception (with L Alison, 2000), The Social Psychology of Crime (with L Alison, 1999), Profiling in Policy and Practice (with L Alison, 1999), Profiling Property Crimes (with L Alison, 2000), Mapping Murder (2003), Becoming an Author (with G Fairbairn, 2006), Origins and Principles of

Geographical Offender Profiling (with D Youngs, 2007), Applications of Geographical Offender Profiling (with D Youngs, 2007); *Recreations* musical composition; *Style*— Prof David Canter; ✉ Department of Psychology, Eleanor Rathbone Building, The University of Liverpool, Liverpool L69 7ZA (tel 0151 794 3910, fax 0151 794 3938, e-mail dcanter@liv.ac.uk, website www.i-psy.com)

CANTERBURY, Archdeacon of; *see:* Evans, Ven Patrick Alexander Sidney

CANTERBURY, Dean of; *see:* Willis, Very Rev Robert Andrew

CANTERBURY, 104 Archbishop of 2002–; Most Rev and Rt Hon Dr Rowan Douglas Williams; PC (2002); *b* 1950; *Educ* Dynevor Sch Swansea, Christ's Coll Cambridge; *m* Jane; 2 c (Rhiannon, Pip); *Career* lectr in theology Coll of the Resurrection Mirfield 1975–77; ordained priest 1978; dean Clare Coll Cambridge and lectr in theology Univ of Cambridge 1984–86, Lady Margaret prof of divinity Univ of Oxford 1986–92, bishop of Monmouth 1992–2002, archbishop of Wales 1999–2002; FBA 1990, FRSL 2003; *Books* The Wound of Knowledge (1979), Resurrection (1982), The Truce of God (1983), Beginning Now: Peacemaking Theology (with Mark Collier, 1984), Arius, Heresy and Tradition (1987, 2 edn 2001), The Making of Orthodoxy (ed, 1989), Teresa of Avila (1991), Open to Judgement (sermons, 1994), Sergii Bulgakov: Towards a Russian Political Theology (1998), On Christian Theology (essays, 2000), Lost Icons: Reflections on Cultural Bereavement (2000), Christ on Trial (2000), Newman's Arians of the Fourth Century (ed, 2001), Love's Redeeming Work (ed, 2001), Poems of Rowan Williams (poetry, 2001), Ponder These Things (2002), Writing in the Dust (2002), Silence and Honey Cakes (2003), Anglican Identities (2004), Grace and Necessity (2005), Why Study the Past? (2005), Tokens of Trust (2007), Wrestling with Angels (2007); *Recreations* music, fiction; *Style*— The Most Rev and Rt Hon the Lord Archbishop of Canterbury

CANTLAY, Charles Peter Thrale; s of Peter Allen Cantlay, and Elizabeth Ann Cantlay; *b* 4 February 1954; *Educ* Radley, Oriel Coll Oxford (BA); *m* 1985, Sandra Jane; *Career* Alexander Howden Reinsurance Brokers Ltd: joined 1976, dir Marine Div 1983–86, md Marine Div 1986–92; ceo 1992–97; AON Group Ltd: chm Marine and Energy Reinsurance Div 2000– (dep chm 1997–2000), dep chm AON Reinsurance UK, head ReSpecialty; Liveryman Worshipful Co of Haberdashers; *Recreations* golf, hockey, skiing; *Clubs* Tandridge Golf, Oxted Hockey; *Style*— Charles P T Cantlay, Esq; ✉ AON Group Ltd, 8 Devonshire Square, London EC2M 4PL (tel 020 7623 5500, fax 020 7216 3211)

CANTOR, HE Anthony John James (Tony); s of John Stanley Frank Cantor (d 1980), and Olive Mary, *née* McCartney (d 2005); *b* 1 February 1946; *Educ* Bournemouth GS; *m* 3 Aug 1968, Patricia Elizabeth, da of Patrick Christopher Naughton; 2 da (Susan Jane b 26 May 1969, Sarah Louise b 23 Nov 1972), 1 s (Thomas James b 16 Sept 1980); *Career* joined FCO 1965, Fin Dept FCO 1966–68, third sec Rangoon 1968–71; lang trg: Univ of Sheffield 1971, Kamakura Japan 1972; third later second sec (commercial) Tokyo 1973–76, second sec (consular) Accra 1977–80, Aid Policy Dept FCO 1980–82, W Indian and Atlantic Dept FCO 1982, consul (commercial) Osaka 1983–89, dep head of mission Hanoi 1990–92, dep dir Invest (UK) DTI 1992–94, first sec (commercial) Tokyo 1994, dep consul-gen Osaka 1995–98, EU Dept (Bilateral) FCO 1998–2000, dep cmmr-gen UK Pavilion Expo 2000 Hanover 2000, head Expo Section Public Diplomacy Dept FCO 2001, ambass to Paraguay 2001–05, ambass to Armenia 2006–; *Recreations* travel, languages, riding, World War II in Asia; *Clubs* Royal Commonwealth Soc, Kobe (Japan), Britain-Burma Assoc; *Style*— HE Mr Anthony Cantor; ✉ c/o Foreign & Commonwealth Office (Yerevan), King Charles Street, London SW1A 2AH (e-mail tony.cantor@fco.gov.uk)

CANTOR, (Prof) Brian; *b* 11 January 1948; *Educ* Manchester Grammar, Christ's Coll Cambridge (MA, PhD), Univ of Oxford (MA); *m* 1, 1967 (m dis 1979), m 2, 1981 (widowed 1993); 2 s; *Career* research fell/lectr in materials science Sch of Engrg Univ of Sussex 1972–81; Dept of Materials Univ of Oxford: lectr in metallurgy 1981–91, reader in materials processing 1991–95, Cookson prof of materials and head of dept 1995–2000, head Div of Mathematical and Physical Sciences 2000–02; lectr then sr research fell Jesus Coll Oxford 1985–95, professorial fell St Catherine's Coll Oxford 1995–2002, vice-chllr Univ of York 2002–; dir Oxford Centre for Advanced Materials and Composites Univ of Oxford 1990–95; univ visiting fell Dept of Mechanical Engrg Northeastern Univ Boston USA 1976, Br Cncl fell Dept of Metallurgy Banaras Hindu Univ India 1980, industrial fell GE Research Labs Schenectady USA 1982; memb Bd: Isis Innovation Ltd 2000–02, Amaethon Ltd 2004–06; conslt: Alcan Int Research Labs 1986–94, Rolls-Royce plc 1996–; ed advsr/series ed: Inst of Physics Publications 1983–2006, Taylor & Francis 2006–; ed Progress in Materials Science; memb Bd: Worldwide Universities Network 2002–, Yorks Univs 2002–, White Rose 2002–, Nat Early Music Centre 2002–, York Science Park (Innovation Centre) Ltd 2004–06, Nat Science Learning Centre 2004–, Yorks Science 2004–; memb World Technol Forum 2002–; Rosenhain Medal Inst of Materials 1993, Ismanam prize 1998, Platinum Medal Inst of Materials 2002; hon prof: Northeastern Univ Shenyang PRC 1996–, Nat Inst of Metals, Chinese Acad of Sciences 1998–, Zhejiang Univ Hangjiao 2003–; memb: American Inst of Mining and Metallurgical Engrs 1980, Academia Europea 1999; CEng 1979, FIM 1989 (MIM 1970), FRMS 1993, FREng 1998, FInstP 1999; *Books* Rapidly Quenched Metals III (ed, 1978), A Tribute to J W Christian (ed jtly, 1992), Thermal Analysis of Advanced Materials (ed jtly, 1994), Stability of Microstructure in Metals and Alloys (jtly, 2 edn, 1996), Aerospace Materials (jt ed, 2001), Solidification and Casting (jt ed, 2002), Metal and Ceramic Matrix Composites (jt ed, 2003), Rapidly Quenched Metals 11 (jt ed, 2004), Novel Nanocrystalline Alloys and Magnetic Nanomaterials (jt ed, 2004); also author of numerous articles in learned jls; *Style*— Brian Cantor; ✉ Heslington Hall, University of York, York YO10 5DD (tel 01904 432001)

CANTY, Brian George John; CBE (1993, OBE 1988); s of George Robert Canty (d 1971), of Chingford, London, and Phoebe Charlotte, *née* Cobb (d 1984); *b* 23 October 1931; *Educ* SW Essex Tech Coll, Univ of London (external); *m* 4 Sept 1954, Maureen Kathleen (Kenny), da of William George Kenny (d 1982), of IOW; 1 da (Elaine b 1957), 1 s (Nigel b 1959); *Career* RN 1950–57; Civil Serv: Air Miny 1957, Fin Advsr's Office Cyprus 1960, Air Force Dept MOD 1963, RAF Staff Coll Bracknell 1970; Dip Serv: joined 1971, Br Embassy Oslo 1973, Br High Cmmn Kingston 1977, consul Vienna 1979, FCO London 1984, dep govr Bermuda 1986, govr Anguilla 1989–92, ret 1992; dir: A S Trust Ltd 1994–2005, St Helena Transhipment Servs Ltd 2002–2005; JP Bermuda 1986; *Recreations* travelling, tennis, writing (pen name Byron Casey); *Style*— Mr Brian Canty, CBE; ✉ e-mail canty@btinternet.com, website www.byroncasey.com

CAPALDI, Dr Michael John; *b* 22 May 1958; *Educ* Bedford Sch, UEA (BSc), Univ of Manchester (PhD); *m* 1 April 1989, Bryony Elizabeth, *née* Pearce; 2 s (Benjamin b 16 April 1991, Duncan b 8 June 1993); *Career* sr research offr (paediatrics and neonatal med) Royal Postgrad Med Sch Hammersmith Hosp 1983–84, section ldr Advanced Drug Delivery Research (ADDR) Unit Ciba Geigy Pharmaceuticals 1984–87, sales rep rising to sr project mangr Smith Kline and French (later SmithKline Beecham Pharmaceuticals) 1987–92, gp and European mangr Drug Devpt Services (DDS) Amersham International plc 1992–93, sales and mktg dir (N America) DDS Amersham Life Sciences Inc 1993–96, head of gp mktg Cell Biology/DDS Amersham International plc 1996, business devpt dir Core Group plc 1996–98, exec vice-pres strategic mktg Nycomed Amersham plc 1998–2000, commercial dir Oxford Asymmetry International plc 2000; ceo: Synaptica Ltd 2000–03, Scancell Ltd 2004–06, Hunter-Fleming Ltd 2006–; chm: BrainBoost Ltd, Mindweavers Ltd; memb UK Pharmaceutical Licensing Gp; former ed Pharmaceutical Forum: International Topics in Drug Devpt; MInstD, MRI, FRMS; *Publications* author of over 10 pubns in scientific jls and books 1982–86; *Recreations* golf, skiing, squash, walking, family; *Style*— Dr Michael Capaldi

CAPELLINO, Ally (aka Alison Lloyd); *b* 1956; *Educ* Middx Poly (BA); *Career* fashion designer; Courtaulds Central Design Studio 1978–79, estab Ally Capellino 'Little Hat' (initially selling accessories) 1979, developed clothing and sold Ally Capellino label internationally (Italy, USA, Japan) 1980–86, introduced menswear collection 1986, first showed London (mens and womenswear) 1986, opened first store Soho 1988, launched diffusion sportswear collection 'Hearts of Oak' 1990, launched diffusion collection 'ao' 1996, opened Ally Capellino shop in Sloane Avenue London 1997, formed Capellino Design Ltd 1999, redesigned Guides uniform 2000, launched Ally Capellino womenswear leather accessories collection 2000, launched 'A for Ally Capellino' womenswear collection for Debenhams 2001, redesigned Brownies uniform 2002, developed menswear accessories collection 2002, opened showroom and design studio Shoreditch 2002; *Style*— Ms Alison Lloyd

CAPIE, Prof Forrest Hunter; s of Daniel Forrest Capie (d 1975), and Isabella Ferguson, *née* Doughty (d 1996); *b* 1 December 1940; *Educ* Nelson Coll NZ, Univ of Auckland NZ (BA), LSE (MSc, PhD); *m* 11 Feb 1967, Dianna Dix, da of William John Harvey, of Auckland, NZ; *Career* economics tutor LSE 1970–72; lectr: Dept of Economics Univ of Warwick 1972–74, Sch of Economics Univ of Leeds 1974–79; Centre for Banking and Int Fin City Univ: lectr 1979–82, sr lectr 1982–83, reader 1983–86, prof of economic history 1986–2004, head of dept 1988–92, official historian (on secondment) Bank of England 2004–; ed Economic History Review 1993–99; memb: Economic History Soc 1970 (memb Cncl 1986–), Cliometric Soc 1986; FRSA; *Books* The British Economy Between the Wars (with M Collins, 1983), Depression and Protectionism, Britain Between the Wars (1983), Monetary History of the United Kingdom 1870–1970: Data Sources and Methods (with A Webber, 1985), Financial Crises and the World Banking System (ed with G E Wood, 1986), Monetary Economics in the 1980s: Some Themes from Henry Thornton (ed with G E Wood, 1988), A Directory of Economic Institutions (ed, 1990), Major Inflations in History (ed, 1991), Have the Banks Failed British Industry? (1992), Protectionism in World Economy (1992), Monetary Regimes in Transition (1993), The Future of Central Banking (with Charles Goodhart, 1994), Monetary Economics in the 1990s (with G E Wood, 1996), Asset Prices and the Real Economy (with G E Wood, 1997); *Recreations* golf, music, theatre; *Clubs* Travellers, Political Economy, Hampstead Golf, Middx Cricket; *Style*— Prof Forrest Capie; ✉ 2 Fitzroy Road, Primrose Hill, London NW1 8TZ (tel 020 7722 7456); Faculty of Finance, Cass Business School, 106 Bunhill Row, London EC1Y 8TZ (tel 020 7040 8730, e-mail f.h.capie@city.ac.uk)

CAPLAN, Jonathan Michael; QC (1991); s of Malcolm Denis Caplan, and Jean Hilary, *née* Winroope (d 1984); *b* 11 January 1951; *Educ* St Paul's, Downing Coll Cambridge (Harris open scholar); *m* Selena Anne, *née* Peskin; 2 s, 1 da; *Career* called to the Bar Gray's Inn 1973 (Holker scholar, bencher 2000); recorder of the Crown Court 1995– (asst recorder 1990–95); chm Bar Cncl Ctee on Televising the Courts 1989, chm Public Affrs Ctee Bar Cncl 1990–92; memb Editorial Bd Jl of Criminal Law; chm BAFTA Management Ltd; FRSA 1991, MCIArb 2003; *Books* The Confait Confessions (1977), The Bar on Trial (1978), Disabling Professions (1979); *Recreations* tennis, Thai and Khmer art, collecting manuscripts and historical newspapers, reading, writing, music, horseracing (flat); *Clubs* Queen's; *Style*— Jonathan Caplan, Esq, QC; ✉ 1st Floor, 5 Paper Buildings, Temple, London EC4Y 7HB (tel 020 7583 6117, fax 020 7353 0075)

CAPLAN, Simon Anthony; s of late Malcolm Denis Caplan and Jean Hilary, *née* Winroope; *b* 13 December 1946; *Educ* Carmel Coll; *m* 6 Sept 1970, Yolande Anne, da of Simon Albert (d 1978); 1 da (Amanda b 1971), 1 s (Benjamin b 1974); *Career* Touche Ross 1965–70; jt fndr Fin Advice Panels (within CAB); fndr Caplan Montagu Assoc Chartered Accountants, chm and md of Stagestruck Gp of Cos, chm and chief exec Transmedia Pictures and Transmedia Int Releasing; JP 1986 (ret); former Gen Cmmr of Income Tax; Barker of the Variety Club of GB; memb: BAFTA, RTS; Freeman City of London 1980; FTII, FCCA (FAPA); *Recreations* art and antique collecting, cinema; *Clubs* Savage, Soho House, Naval and Military; *Style*— Simon A Caplan, Esq; ✉ Stowe March, Barnet Lane, Elstree, Borehamwood, Hertfordshire WD6 3RQ (e-mail simon.caplan@virgin.net)

CAPLEHORN, Peter Leslie; s of Leslie Gilbert George Caplehorn (d 1994), and Glades, *née* Rankin (d 1986); *b* 23 October 1951; *m* 13 Sept 1991, Sally Anne, *née* Hare; 1 da (Katie b 10 May 1996); *Career* architect; worked in Winchester and Isle of Wight and own practice until 1980; Scott Brownrigg + Turner: joined 1980, assoc dir 1988–, divnl dir 1996–, tech dir 2000–, currently responsible for tech standards, specification and health and safety; projects incl: Concept 2000 Farnborough 1986 (Civic Tst Award 1987), Manchester Airport Y2 1990–93, new HQ Eastern Electricity 1996–98; ARB 1978, RIBA 1978; *Recreations* sailing, skiing, photography; *Clubs* Brightlingsea Yacht; *Style*— Peter Caplehorn, Esq; ✉ 12 Glyncastle, Caversham, Reading, Berkshire RG4 7XF; Scott Brownrigg + Turner, 46–48 Portsmouth Road, Guildford, Surrey GU2 4DU (tel 01483 568686, fax 01483 575830, mobile 07801 050404, e-mail p.caplehorn@sbtguildford.com)

CAPNER, Gareth Roger John; s of John Hammond Capner (d 1973), and Clarice May, *née* Gibbins (d 1971); *b* 14 May 1947; *Educ* Taunton Sch, Univ of Sheffield (BA, MA); *m* 2 Jan 1971, Susan Mary, da of Arthur Snell, of Lincs (d 1994); *Career* princ planning offr Berkshire CC 1973–79; Barton Willmore Partnership: assoc 1979–81, ptnr 1981–85, sr planning ptnr 1985–96, sr ptnr 1996–; MIMgt 1978, FRTPI 1983 (MRTPI 1974); *Recreations* boating, shooting, watching rugby, gourmet dining; *Style*— Gareth Capner, Esq; ✉ Dunley House, Dunley, Whitchurch, Hampshire RG28 7PU; Trafalgar Place, Lymington, Hampshire SO41 9BN; Barton Willmore, Theale Court, 11–13 High Street, Theale, Berkshire RG7 5AH (tel 0118 930 7444, fax 0118 930 7445, mobile 07850 491320,e-mail gareth.capner@bartonwillmore.co.uk)

CAPON, Timothy Wills Hugh; s of Rev Martin Gedge Capon (d 1998), and Mary Wills Hamlyn (d 1978); *b* 26 October 1940; *Educ* Prince of Wales Sch Nairobi, Magdalene Coll Cambridge (BA, LLB); *m* 3 Sept 1966, Elizabeth Fleming, da of Henry Campbell McAusland, OBE; 2 da (Sarah Elizabeth b 19 March 1969 d 1995, Lucy Jane b 10 July 1972), 1 s (Oliver Fleming b 1 Aug 1970); *Career* admitted slr 1965; res ptnr NY office Linklaters and Paines 1974–77 (ptnr 1970), exec dir The Diamond Trading Co (Pty) Ltd 1977–2000; dir: Bank Leumi UK plc 1987–2003, De Beers Consolidated Mines Ltd 1991–2001, De Beers Centenary AG 1991–2001; *Clubs* Boodle's; *Style*— Timothy Capon, Esq; ✉ 17 Charterhouse Street, London EC1N 6RA (tel 020 7404 4444, fax 020 7430 8939)

CAPPE, Mel; s of David Cappe, of Toronto, Canada, and Patty, *née* Wise; *b* 3 December 1948; *Educ* Univ of Toronto (BA), Univ of Western Ontario (MA); *m* 1971, Marni, *née* Pliskin; 1 s (Daniel b 30 June 1976), 1 da (Emily b 23 Oct 1978); *Career* Canadian diplomat; offr Treasy Bd 1975–85, asst dep min for Consumer and Corporate Affrs 1986, dep sec Treasy Bd Secretariat 1990, dep min of the Environment 1994, dep min HR Devpt Canada 1996, clerk of Privy Council and sec to Cabinet 1999, high cmmr to UK 2002–06, pres and ceo Inst for Research on Public Policy 2006–; chair: United Way of Ottawa, United Jewish Appeal Ottawa; Hon PhD Univ of Western Ontario; *Recreations* travel, reading, hiking, cooking; *Style*— Mel Cappe, Esq; ✉ IRPP, 1470 Peel Street, Suite 200, Montreal, Quebec, H3A 1T1 (tel 514 985 2461, fax 514 985 2559, e-mail mcappe@irpp.org)

CARAYOL, René; MBE (2004); *Career* entrepreneur, bd dir, business advsr, author and speaker; past clients incl: World Economic Forum, McKinseys, Barclays Bank, Tesco, PM's Delivery Unit; former bd dir IPC Magazines and PEPSI UK, md IPC Electric; e-chm e-photomail.com; non-exec dir Inland Revenue, chief exec Carayol Ltd; lectr and speaker worldwide; contrib to TV and radio documentaries and business news: BBC TV, Channel 4 and Sky, BBC Radio 4, BBC Radio 5 Live; columnist Observer; *Style*— René Carayol, Esq, MBE; ✉ c/o Jill Thorn, 3 Victoria Rise, Hilgrove Road, London NW6 4TH (tel 01707 646 731, fax 01707 851 259, e-mail rene@carayol.com, website www.carayol.com)

CARBERRY, Kay; CBE (2007); da of Sean Carberry (d 2000), and Sheila, *née* McCormack; *b* 19 October 1950, Dublin; *Educ* Royal Naval Sch Malta, Univ of Sussex (BA); *Family* 1 s (Joe b 17 July 1983); *Career* secdy sch teacher 1973–76, research asst NUT 1976–78; TUC: policy offr 1978–83, sr policy offr 1983–88, head of equal rights 1988–2003, asst gen sec 2003–; cmmr: Equal Opportunities Cmmn 1999–2007, Cmmn for Equality and Human Rights 2006–; tstee: One Parent Families, People's History Museum,Work Fndn; memb Franco-British Cncl; *Recreations* theatre, arts, swimming; *Style*— Ms Kay Carberry, CBE; ✉ Trades Union Congress, Congress House, Great Russell Street, London WC1B 3LS (tel 020 7467 1266, fax 020 7467 1277, e-mail kcarberry@tuc.org.uk)

CARBERY, 11 Baron (I 1715); Sir Peter Ralfe Harrington Evans-Freke; 7 Bt (I 1768); s of Maj the Hon Ralfe Evans-Freke, MBE (d 1969), 2 s of 9 Baron; suc unc, 10 Baron, 1970; *b* 20 March 1920; *Educ* Downside; *m* 1941, Joyzelle Mary, o da of late Herbert Binnie, of Sydney, NSW; 3 s (Hon Michael Peter b 11 Oct 1942, Hon John Anthony b 9 May 1949, Hon Stephen Ralfe b 2 March 1952), 2 da (Hon Maura Clare (Hon Mrs Fanshawe) b 1946, Hon Angela Mary (Hon Mrs Tomlins) b 1954); *Heir* s, Hon Michael Evans-Freke; *Career* served WWII 1939–45 as Capt RE in India and Burma; former memb London Stock Exchange; author of novels, plays and poetry; MICE; *Style*— The Rt Hon the Lord Carbery; ✉ 2 Hayes Court, Sunnyside, Wimbledon, London SW19 4SH (tel 020 8946 6615)

CARDALE, David Michael; s of Brig W J Cardale, OBE (d 1986), of Bury St Edmunds, Suffolk, and Audrey Vere, *née* Parry-Crooke (d 1996); *b* 26 December 1947; *Educ* Eton, Univ of Essex (BA), INSEAD (MBA); *m* 31 Aug 1985, Fionna, *née* MacCormick; 1 s (Hugo William b 7 March 1989), 2 da (Natasha Lucy Vere b 19 Dec 1990, Alicia Daisy Catherine b 11 May 1993); *Career* dir County NatWest 1983–90 (N American rep 1981–83), dir NatWest Ventures 1990–95; chm Oxford Community Internet Holdings plc 1999–2001 (non-exec dir 1997–99); co-fndr and chm Global Investor Relations Ltd 1999–; non-exec dir: Sphere Investment Trust plc 1988–96, The Emerging Markets Country Investment Trust plc 1994–2000, Toolex International NV (Sweden) 1995–2001, City of London Investment Gp plc 2006–; *Recreations* skiing, trail hunting, tennis, walking; *Style*— David Cardale, Esq; ✉ Lower Cranmore, Shipton Moyne, Tetbury GL8 8PU (tel 01666 880349, e-mail db@snow.co.uk)

CARDALE, William Tyndale; s of Brig W J Cardale, OBE, ADC (d 1986), and Vere Audrey, *née* Parry-Crooke (d 1996); *b* 10 December 1945; *Educ* Eton; *m* 13 Aug 1988, Lynn Meriel, da of Alan Thomas Brown, CBE, DL; 1 s (Thomas William b 24 Feb 1990); *Career* CA; Pricewaterhouse Coopers: UK dir of trust and accounting servs 1994–97, head Private Client Dept Midlands Region 1997–2005, ret; lectr in taxation at various professional bodies' courses; memb Fin Mgmnt Ctee Diocese of Birmingham 1997–2005, pres Birmingham and West Midlands Branch Securities Inst 1999–2001; tstee of several landed estates 2005–; trg for lay reader ministry Dio of St Edmundsbury and Ipswich 2006–; FCA; *Recreations* riding (hunter trials and events), tennis; *Style*— William T Cardale, Esq; ✉ West Lodge, Bradfield St George, Bury St Edmunds, Suffolk IP30 0DL (tel 01284 386327)

CARDEN, Sir John Craven; 7 Bt (I 1787), of Templemore, Tipperary; s of Capt Sir John Valentine Carden, 6 Bt, MBE (d 1935), and his 2 w, Dorothy Mary, *née* McKinnon; *b* 11 March 1926; *Educ* Eton; *m* 1947, Isabel Georgette, yst da of late Robert de Hart; 1 da (Isabel Mary b 1952); *Heir* kinsman, John Craven Carden b 17 Nov 1953; *Clubs* White's; *Style*— Sir John Carden, Bt

CARDEW, Anthony John; s of Lt-Col Martin Philip Cardew, of Rookley, IOW, and Anne Elizabeth, *née* Foster (decd); *b* 8 September 1949; *Educ* Bishop Wordsworth's Sch Salisbury, Marlborough; *m* 10 Dec 1971, Janice Frances, da of Alec Anthony Smallwood (d 1985); 1 s (James), 1 da (Sarah); *Career* chief reporter Surrey Mirror 1968–70, news reporter UPI 1970–71, fin corr Reuters 1972–74, dir then head of fin PR Charles Barker Ltd 1974–83, chm Grandfield Rork Collins 1985–91 (dir 1983–91), chm Cardew Group 1991–; *Recreations* book collecting, walking, shooting; *Clubs* Reform, London Library; *Style*— Anthony Cardew, Esq; ✉ Cardew Group, 12 Suffolk Street, London SW1Y 4HG (tel 020 7930 0777, fax 020 7925 0647)

CARDIFF, Archbishop of (RC) 2001–; Most Rev Peter David Smith; *b* 21 October 1943; *Educ* Clapham Coll, Univ of Exeter (LLB), St John's Seminary, Pontifical Univ of St Thomas Aquinas Rome; *Career* asst regnl mangr (Wales and SW) NACRO 1986–89, equal opportunities advsr Cardiff City Cncl 1989–92, head Equality Unit NHS Wales 1992–99, dir of HR and organisational devpt Bro Taf HA 1999–2003, dir NHS Centre for Equality and Human Rights 2003–05, dir Public Service Mgmnt Wales 2005–; equal opportunities cmmr for Wales Equal Opportunities Cmmn 2002–07, Wales cmmr Cmmn for Equality and Human Rights (CEHR) 2006–; non-exec dir: Chwarae Teg Wales Ltd 1996– (chair 2001), SE Wales Race Equality Cncl 1997–; co-chair Stonewall Cymru 2001–, memb Bd Stonewall UK 2002–, tstee and memb Bd Nat AIDS Tst 2002– (chair All-Wales HIV Reference Gp 1999–2003); vice-chair Welsh Food Alliance 1999–2003, memb Bd Health Living Centre New Opportunities Fund; govr Dyffryn Comp Sch Newport 1997–2003; hon fell: St Edmund's Coll Cambridge, Univ of Wales 2004, Univ of Cardiff 2006; fell Nat Centre for Public Policy, FCIPD; *Style*— His Grace the Archbishop of Cardiff

CARDIGAN, Earl of; David Michael James Brudenell-Bruce; s and h of 8 Marquess of Ailesbury; *b* 12 November 1952; *Educ* Eton, Rannoch, RAC Cirencester; *m* 1980, Rosamond Jane, er da of Capt W R M Winkley, of Bruton, Somerset, and Mrs Jane Winkley, of Pewsey, Wilts; 1 s (Thomas, Viscount Savernake b 1982), 1 da (Lady Catherine b 1984); *Heir* s, Viscount Savernake; *Career* 31 Hereditary Warden of Savernake Forest (position created in 1067) 1987–, owner mangr Savernake Forest; sec Marlborough Conservatives; memb exec Devizes Constituency Conservative Assoc; *Style*— Earl of Cardigan; ✉ Savernake Lodge, Savernake Forest, Marlborough, Wiltshire (tel 07802 270200, e-mail savernakeestate@hotmail.com)

CARDINAL, His Hon Judge Martin John; s of Ralph William Cardinal, of Sutton Coldfield, W Midlands, and Ella Winifred, *née* Austin; *b* 10 June 1952, Birmingham; *Educ* Magdalene Coll Cambridge (exhibitioner, Dame Rebecca Flower Squire scholar, MA, Magdalene Coll Law Prize); *m* 22 Oct 1977, Janet Dorothy, *née* Allnutt; 1 s (Stephen James b 20 Dec 1980), 1 da (Deborah Jane b 10 Dec 1984); *Career* admitted slr 1977; ptnr: Wood Amphlet Wild & Co 1978–85, Anthony Collins 1985–94, dist judge 1994–2004 (dep dist judge 1992–94), recorder 2000–04 (asst recorder 1997–2000), circuit judge (Midlands Circuit) 2004–; legal memb Mental Health Review Tbnl 1987–94; chllr Dio of Birmingham; *Books* Matrimonial Costs (2000); *Recreations* walking, swimming, gardening, lay reader; *Style*— His Hon Judge Cardinal; ✉ Brimingham County Court, 33 Bull Street, Birmingham B4 6DS (tel 0121 250 6392)

CARDOZO, Prof Linda Dolores; da of Felix Elia Cardozo (d 1971), of London, and Olga Annette, *née* Watts (d 1992); *b* 15 September 1950; *Educ* Haberdashers' Aske's, Acton Tech Coll, Univ of Liverpool (MB ChB, MD); *m* 13 July 1974, Stuart Ian Hutcheson, s of Ian Steen Hutcheson (d 1994); 2 da (Melissa b 27 Feb 1989, Juliet b 27 July 1990), 1 s (Marius (twin) b 27 July 1990); *Career* house offr and SHO in obstetrics and gynaecology Liverpool, res registrar in urodynamics St George's Hosp London 1976–78, conslt obstetrician and gynaecologist specialising in female urinary incontinence King's Coll Hosp 1985– (registrar then sr registrar 1979–85), prof of urogynaecology KCL 1994–; ed Br Jl of Obstetrics and Gynaecology 1995–2000, memb Editorial Bd of several other jls; pres ACPWH 1995–; chm: Continence Fndn UK 1998–2006, Br Menopause Soc 2001–03, Br Soc of Urogynaecology 2001–06 (founding chm); int fells rep Cncl RCOG 2001–07; memb: RSM (pres Section of Obstetrics and Gynaecology 2001–02), BMA, Int Urogynaecology Assoc (pres 1999–2000), Int Continence Soc (chm Educn Ctee 2002–08, exec offr and memb Advsy Bd); FRCOG 1991 (MRCOG 1980); *Publications* author of 13 books incl: Basic Urogynaecology (1993), Urogynaecology (1997), Urinary Incontinence in Primary Care (2000), Textbook of Female Urology and Urogynaecology (2001, 2 edn 2006); author of more than 400 publications relating to urogynaecology; *Recreations* theatre, bridge, gardening, scuba diving, skiing, water skiing; *Style*— Prof Linda Cardozo; ✉ The Sloes, Potter Street Hill, Pinner, Middlesex HA5 3YH (tel 020 8866 0291, fax 020 8866 0129, e-mail lcardozo@compuserve.com); King's College Hospital, Denmark Hill, London SE5 9RS (tel 020 7737 4000); 8 Devonshire Place, London W1G 6HP (tel 020 7935 2357, fax 020 7224 2797)

CARDWELL, Paul; s of Charles Alexander Cardwell, and Irene Julia-Ann, *née* Moodie; *b* 10 June 1952; *m* May 1984, Christina Hughes, da of Fergus Hughes Boyter; 2 da (Rebecca Caterina Madelaine Macdonald b 15 March 1986, Amelia Iona Francis b 29 Aug 1988); *Career* with advtg agencies: Foote Cone & Belding 1978–79, Young & Rubicam 1979–85, Publicis 1985–87; bd dir Leo Burnett 1987–89, joint chm and creative dir GGK London 1993–95 (creative dir 1989–93), creative dir Doner Cardwell Hawkins 1995–; contrib Horizon (BBC) and Channel 4 as freelance documentary writer through Brand X Ltd; winner (1991): Gold Medal The One Show NY, Lion D'Or Cannes Advtg Festival, Gold Award Art Dirs' Club of Europe, ITV Award, Gold and Silver Br TV Advtg Awards, Silver D&AD Award; memb: D&AD 1979, Royal Photographic Soc 1990, The Photographers Gallery 1991; *Books* The Race Against Time - The Story of Sport Aid (1988); *Recreations* theatre, travel, reading, photography; *Style*— Paul Cardwell, Esq

CARDWELL, Prof Richard Andrew; s of Lt Cdr Albert Cardwell RN (d 1995), of Helston, Cornwall, and Mary Margarethe, *née* Knight; *b* 16 July 1938; *Educ* Helston GS, Univ of Southampton (BA, DipEd), Univ of Nottingham (PhD); *m* 29 July 1961, Oithona Shaguine (Bunty), da of Edgar Treadwell (d 1968); *Career* lectr UCW Aberystwyth 1965–67 (asst lectr 1964–65); Univ of Nottingham: lectr 1967–74, sr lectr 1974–78, reader 1978–83, prof of modern Spanish lit and head Dept of Hispanic Studies 1983–96, emeritus prof 2003–; visiting prof Johns Hopkins Univ 1992; author of over 100 articles and 22 books and editions; memb: Assoc of Br Hispanists, Anglo-Catalan Soc; corresponding memb Real Academia Sevillana de Buenas Letras Seville Spain; Boy Scouts' Assoc Silver Cross for Gallantry and Royal Humane Soc Testimonial on Vellum for Gallantry 1958; *Books* Blasco Ibáñez's La Barraca (1972 and 1995), Juan Ramón Jiménez: The Modernist Apprenticeship (1977), Espronceda (1981), Gabriel García Márquez: New Readings (1987), Virgil: Essays for the Bimillennium (1987), Literature and Language (1989); Espronceda: Student of Salamanca (1990), Qué es el Modernismo? (1992), Zorrilla: Centennial Readings (1994), Sánchez Rodríguez (1996), Lord Byron the European (1997), ed Reception of British Authors in Europe: Byron Volume (2004); also edns of Juan Ramón Jiménez; *Recreations* writing, research, conversation with intelligent women; *Style*— Prof Richard A Cardwell; ✉ The Yews, 6 Town Street, Sandiacre, Nottingham NG10 5DP (tel 0115 939 7316, e-mail drrcardwell@aol.com); Department of Hispanic Studies, University of Nottingham, University Park, Nottingham NG7 2RD (tel 0115 951 5796/5800, fax 0115 951 5814)

CARDY, Peter John Stubbings; s of Gordon Douglas Stubbings, of Gosport, Hants, and Eva, *née* Walker; assumed the surname of Cardy by deed 1987; *b* 4 April 1947, Gosport, Hants; *Educ* Price's Sch, UC Durham (BA), Cranfield Inst of Technol (MSc); *m* 5 Sept 1987, Christine Mary, da of Ronald Edward Francis Doyle, of Manchester; *Career* dist sec WEA N of Scotland 1971–77, dep chief exec Volunteer Centre UK 1977–87, chief exec: Motor Neurone Disease Assoc 1987–94, MS Soc of GB and NI 1994–2001, Macmillan Cancer Support 2001–07, Maritime and Coastguard Agency 2007–; memb: Carnegy Ctee Community Educn in Scotland 1976–77, Conseil de Rédaction Aménagement et Nature Paris 1979–84, Morrison Ctee Broadcasting and Voluntary Action 1986–87, World Fed of Neurology Ctee on Motor Neurone Disease 1993–94, NHS R&D Ctee Consumers in Health Research 1998–2002, HTA Pharmaceutical Panel 2002–04; visiting lectr Australian Red Cross Soc 1981, treas Volonteurope 1981–84, Socio de Honor Assoc Geriatrica Valenciana Spain 1983, res assoc Policy Studies Inst 1984, dep chm Ctee Local Devpt Agencies Fund 1985–89, chm: Nat Assoc Volunteer Bureaux 1988–91, Regent's Bridge Gardens Ltd 2006–; pt/t conslt Charities Effectiveness Review Tst 1990–93, advsr: Migraine Tst 1991–92, London Cancer Centre 2002; admin tstee Fund For People in Need 1991–93, pt/t sec-gen Int Alliance of MND/ALS Assocs 1991–94, non-exec dir Northampton NHS Community Health Tst 1993–97, Medicines cmmr 1998–2003, chair: The Neurological Alliance 1998–2001, OST Foresight Healthcare Panel 1999–2000, Brain and Spine Fndn 2005–, Disability Benefits Consortium 2006, The Health Hotel 2006; bd memb Nat Cancer Res Inst (chair Lung Cancer Strategic Planning Gp) 2003–06, columnist Third Sector magazine 2005–, visiting fell Cass Business Sch City Univ 2006–, patron The Cancer Resource Centre 2007–, vice-pres Macmillan Cancer Support 2007–; Charcot Medal 2001; *Recreations* sailing, conversation, travel, drawing, Georgian glass; *Clubs* Reform; *Style*— Peter Cardy, Esq

CAREW, 7 Baron (I 1834 and UK 1838); Patrick Thomas Conolly-Carew; s of 6 Baron Carew, CBE (d 1994), and Lady Sylvia Gwendoline Eva Maitland (d 1991), da of 15 Earl of Lauderdale; *b* 6 March 1938; *Educ* Harrow, RMA Sandhurst; *m* 30 April 1962, Celia Mary, da of Col Hon (Charles) Guy Cubitt, CBE, DSO, TD; 3 da (Hon Virginia Mary (Hon Mrs McGrath) b 1965, Hon Nicola Rosamond (Hon Mrs de Montfort) b 1966, Hon Camilla Sylvia b 1969), 1 s (Hon William Patrick b 1973); *Heir* s, Hon William Conolly-Carew; *Career* late Capt Royal Horse Guards (The Blues), former int show jumping rider; memb Irish Olympic Three Day Event team: Mexico 1968, Munich 1972, Montreal 1976; pres: Equestrian Fedn of Ireland 1979–84 (vice-pres 1985–), Ground Jury Three Day Event Olympic Games Barcelona 1992 and Olympic Games Atlanta 1996, Irish Horse Trials Soc 1998–; chm Three Day Event Ctee FEI (memb Bureau) 1989–97 (hon memb Bureau 1997), memb Cncl and tstee Int League for the Protection of Horses; FEI Gold Medal for Three Day Eventing; *Recreations* all equestrian sports, shooting, cricket, bridge; *Clubs* Kildare St and Univ (Dublin); *Style*— The Rt Hon the Lord Carew; ✉ The Garden House, Donadea, Naas, Co Kildare, Ireland (tel 00 353 458 68204, fax 00 353 458 61105)

CAREW, Sir Rivers Verain; 11 Bt (E 1661), of Haccombe, Devon; s of Sir Thomas Palk Carew, 10 Bt (d 1976), and his 2 wife, Phyllis Evelyn, *née* Mayman; *b* 17 October 1935; *Educ* St Columba's Coll, Univ of Dublin (MA, BAgrSc Hort); *m* 1, 1968 (m dis 1991), Susan Babington, yr da of late Harold Babington Hill, of London; 3 da (Marcella Tamsin b 1970, Marina Lys b 1972, Miranda Rose b 1973), 1 s (Gerald de Redvers b 1975) and 1 s decd; m 2, 1992 (m dis 2003), Siobhán, da of late Criostóir Seán Mac Cárthaigh, of Cork; *Heir* s, Gerald Carew; *Career* ed, journalist and author; asst ed Ireland of The Welcomes (Irish Tourist Bd magazine) 1964–67, jt ed The Dublin Magazine 1964–69, journalist Irish TV 1967–87, BBC World Serv 1987–93; *Books* Figures out of Mist (poems with T Brownlow, 1966); *Recreations* reading, music, reflection; *Style*— Sir Rivers Carew, Bt; ✉ Cherry Bounds, 37 Hicks Lane, Girton, Cambridge CB3 0JS

CAREW POLE, Sir (John) Richard Walter Reginald; 13 Bt (E 1628), of Shute House, Devonshire; OBE (2000), DL (Cornwall 1988); s of Col Sir John Gawen Carew Pole, 12

Bt, DSO, TD (d 1993), and Cynthia Mary Burns, OBE (d 1977); *b* 2 December 1938; *Educ* Eton, RAC Cirencester; *Heir* s, Tremayne Carew Pole; *Career* late Coldstream Gds; memb Devon and Cornwall Ctee Nat Tst 1978–83, pres Surf Life Saving Assoc of GB 1978–87; High Sheriff Cornwall 1979; pt/t dir SW Electricity Bd 1981–90, regnl dir Portman Building Society 1989–91; pres Royal Cornwall Agric Show 1981, chm Devon and Cornwall Police Authy 1985–87; pres RHS 2001–06 (memb Cncl 1999–2006), vice-pres Garden History Soc 1999–; govr: Seale Hayne Agric Coll 1979–89, Plymouth Coll 1981–96; dir Theatre Royal Plymouth 1985–97; Cornwall CC: cncllr 1973–93, chm Planning and Employment Ctee 1980–84, chm Finance Cmmn 1985–89, chm Property Ctee 1989–93; tstee: Nat Heritage Memorial Fund 1991–2000, Tate Gallery 1993–2003, Eden Project 1996–, Tst House Charitable Fndn 1999–, Pilgrim Tst 2000–; pres Devon & Cornwall Record Soc 1999–2000; chm Combined Universities in Cornwall Steering Ctee 2000–03; memb Countryside Cmmn 1991–96; Liveryman Worshipful Co of Fishmongers (memb Ct of Assts 1993–, Prime Warden 2006–07); ARICS 1969; *Recreations* walking, contemporary pictures, gardening; *Style*— Sir Richard Carew Pole, Bt, OBE, DL; ✉ Antony House, Torpoint, Cornwall PL11 2QA (tel and fax 01752 814914)

CAREY, Sir de Vic Graham; kt (2002); s of Michael Carey (d 1964), of Guernsey, and Jean, *née* Bullen (d 1975); *b* 15 June 1940; *Educ* Bryanston, Trinity Hall Cambridge (MA), Caen Univ; *m* 22 June 1968, Bridget, da of Maj John Lindsay Smith (ka 1943); 2 s (Perrin b 1971, Julius b 1980), 2 da (Jenette b 1974, Henrietta b 1979); *Career* slr Supreme Court of Judicature 1965, advocate Royal Court of Guernsey 1966, in private practice 1966–76, people's dep States of Guernsey April-Dec 1976; Guernsey: HM Slr-Gen 1977–82, HM Attorney-Gen 1982–92, HM Receiver-Gen 1985–92, Dep Bailiff 1992–99, Bailiff 1999–2005, Lt Bailiff of the Royal Court 2005–, judge Court of Appeal 2005–; Jersey: judge of the Court of Appeal 2000–05, Cmmr of the Royal Court 2006–; QC 1989; memb Gen Synod C of E 1982–98, chm House of Laity Winchester Diocesan Synod 1993–97; *Style*— Sir de Vic Carey; ✉ Les Padins, St Saviour, Guernsey GY7 9JJ (tel 01481 264587, fax 01481 263687)

CAREY, Godfrey Mohun Cecil; QC (1991); s of Dr Godfrey Fraser Carey, LVO (d 1972), and Prudence Loveday, *née* Webb (d 1977); *b* 31 October 1941; *Educ* Eton; *m* 1, 1965 (m dis 1975), Caroline Jane; 1 da (Miranda b 1967), 2 s (Sebastian Fraser b 1969, d 1971, Hugo b 1972); m 2, 1978 (m dis 1985), Dorothy; 1 da (Lucy b 1978); *Career* legal asst Rolls Royce 1966–70; called to the Bar Inner Temple 1969 (bencher 2000); recorder of the Crown Court 1986–, memb Mental Health Review Tribunal 2000–; *Recreations* tennis, jazz, Aztec culture; *Clubs* Boodle's; *Style*— Godfrey Carey, Esq, QC; ✉ 5 Paper Buildings, Temple, London EC4Y 7HB (tel 020 7583 6117, fax 020 7353 0075, e-mail clerks@5pb.co.uk)

CAREY, Prof John; s of Charles William Carey (d 1965), and Winifred Ethel, *née* Cook (d 1967); *b* 5 April 1934; *Educ* Richmond and East Sheen County GS, St John's Coll Oxford (MA, DPhil); *m* 1960, Gillian Mary Florence, da of Reginald Booth (d 1968); 2 s (Leo b 1974, Thomas b 1977); *Career* 2 Lt E Surrey Regt 1953–54; Harmsworth sr scholar Merton Coll Oxford 1957–58, lectr ChCh Oxford 1958–59, Andrew Bradley jr res fell Balliol Oxford 1959–60; tutorial fell: Keble Coll Oxford 1960–64, St John's Coll Oxford 1964–75; Merton prof of English literature Univ of Oxford 1975–2001; princ book reviewer Sunday Times 1977–, author of articles in Modern Language Review, Review of English Studies etc; chm of judges: Booker Prize 1982 and 2003, WHSmith Literary Prize 1996–2003, Man Booker Int Prize 2005; hon fell: St John's Coll Oxford 1991, Balliol Coll Oxford 1992; FRSL, FBA 1996; *Books* The Poems of John Milton (ed with Alastair Fowler, 1968, 2 edn 1997), Milton (1969), The Private Memoirs and Confessions of a Justified Sinner (ed, 1970), The Violent Effigy: a Study of Dickens' Imagination (1973, 2 edn 1991), Thackeray: Prodigal Genius (1977), John Donne: Life, Mind and Art (1981, 2 edn 1990), Original Copy: Selected Reviews and Journalism 1969–1986 (1987), The Faber Book of Reportage (ed, 1987), The Intellectuals and the Masses (1992), The Faber Book of Science (ed, 1995), The Faber Book of Utopias (ed, 1999), Pure Pleasure: A Guide to the 20th Century's Most Enjoyable Books (2000), What Good are the Arts? (2005); *Recreations* swimming, gardening, beekeeping; *Style*— Prof John Carey, FBA; ✉ Brasenose Cottage, Lyneham, Oxfordshire OX7 6QL; 57 Stapleton Road, Headington, Oxford OX3 7LX (tel 01865 764304); Merton College, Oxford OX1 4JD (tel 01865 281266)

CAREY, Peter Philip; s of Percival Stanley Carey (d 1984), and Helen Jean Carey (d 1991); *b* 7 May 1943; *Educ* Geelong GS Aust; *m* 1 (m dis), Leigh Weetman; m 2, 16 March 1985, Alison Margaret, da of Stanley Newnham Summers (d 1987); 2 s (Sam Summers Carey b 1986, Charley Carey Summers b 1990); *Career* writer; teacher Princeton and NY Univs; Hon DLitt Univ of Queensland 1989, Hon DHL New Sch NY 1998, Hon DLitt Monash Univ 2000; FRSL; *Awards* NSW Premier Award for Lit 1979 and 1980, Miles Franklin Award 1980, 1989 and 1998, Nat Book Cncl Award 1980 and 1985, Victorian Premier Award 1985, Age Book of the Year Award 1985, Booker Prize 1988 and 2001, Cwlth Prize 1998 and 2001; *Books* The Fat Man in History (1979), Bliss (1980), Illywhacker (1985), Oscar and Lucinda (1988), The Tax Inspector (1991), The Unusual Life of Tristan Smith (1994), Jack Maggs (1997), True History of the Kelly Gang (2000), My Life as a Fake (2003), Wrong About Japan (2005), Theft: A Love Story (2006); *Recreations* swimming; *Style*— Peter Carey, Esq

CAREY OF CLIFTON, Baron (Life Peer UK 2002), of Clifton in the City and County of Bristol; George Leonard Carey; PC (1991); s of George Thomas Carey, and Ruby Catherine, *née* Gurney; *b* 13 November 1935; *Educ* Bifrons Secdy Modern Sch, London Coll of Divinity, KCL (ALCD, BD, MTh, PhD); *m* 25 June 1960, Eileen Harmsworth, da of Douglas Cunningham Hood; 2 da (Hon Rachel Helen b 30 May 1963, Hon Elizabeth Ruth b 26 Oct 1971), 2 s (Hon Mark Jonathan b 28 Feb 1965, Hon Andrew Stephen b 18 Feb 1966); *Career* Nat Serv 1954–56, served Egypt, Shaibah Iraq; curate St Mary's Islington 1962–66; lectr: Oakhill Theol Coll London 1966–70, St John's Theol Coll Notts 1970–75; vicar St Nicholas's Church Durham 1975–82, princ Trinity Coll Bristol 1982–87; bishop of Bath and Wells 1987–91, archbishop of Canterbury 1991–2002; memb House of Lords 1991–; presentation fell KCL 1996; memb Cncl Bath Int Art Festival, patron and pres of many organizations; Freeman: City of Wells 1990, City of Canterbury 1992, City of London 1997; Hon DD: Univ of Kent, Univ of Durham, Univ of Bath, Univ of Nottingham, Open Univ, City Univ, Notre Dame Univ USA, Sewanee Univ USA, Southwest Univ USA; distinguished fell Library of Congress Washington DC; *Books* I Believe in Man (1975), God Incarnate (1976), The Great Acquittal (1980), The Church in The Market Place (1984), The Meeting of The Waters (1985), The Gate of Glory (1986, updated and reissued 1992), The Message of the Bible (1986), The Great God Robbery (1989), I Believe (1991), Sharing a Vision (1993), Spiritual Journey (1994), My Journey, Your Journey (1996), Canterbury Letters to the Future (1998), Jesus (2000), Know the Truth (autobiography, 2004); *Recreations* walking, reading, music, family life; *Style*— The Rt Rev and Rt Hon the Lord Carey of Clifton, PC

CARGEEG, Joyce; da of J T Olds, and Irene Olds; *b* 17 August 1927; *Educ* Camborne Tech Coll; *m* 14 Sept 1949, E D Cargeeg, s of W F Cargeeg; 5 c; *Career* prop Botallack Manor; listed: Which? Hotel Guide 1996, Good Bed and Breakfast Guide 1996; Brilliant Bed and Breakfast Award Which? Hotel Guide 2002; pres St Just and Pendeen Cons Assoc, cmmr Girl Guides, youth club ldr, sch govr; *Recreations* gardening, decorating home, travel, going to the theatre, enjoying fine wine; *Style*— Mrs Joyce Cargeeg; ✉ Botallack Manor, Botallack, St Just, Penzance, Cornwall TR19 7QG (tel 01736 788525)

CARINGTON, Hon Rupert Francis John; DL (Bucks 2002); s and h of 6 Baron Carrington, *qv*; *b* 2 December 1948; *Educ* Eton, Univ of Bristol; *m* 12 Sept 1989, Daniela, da of Flavio Diotallevi; 1 s (Robert b 7 Dec 1990), 2 da (Francesca b 24 July 1993, Isabella Iona b 19 May 1995); *Career* dir: Morgan Grenfell International 1983–87, Hartwell plc 1990–2000, JP Morgan Fleming Smaller Companies Investment Trust (formerly The Fleming Smaller Companies Investment Trust plc) 1990–2004, Morgan Shipley Ltd 2001–, Sete Technical Services SA 2002–; chm: Korea Asia Fund Limited 1990–2000, Schroder Asia Pacific Fund plc 1995–, Schroder Emerging Countries Fund plc 1996–2003; memb Dubai UK Trade and Economic Ctee 1997–; chm Bucks CLA 2002–05, chm Bucks Strategic Partnership 2002–, memb Cncl Univ of Buckingham 2003–06; High Sheriff Bucks 2002–03; *Clubs* White's, Pratt's; *Style*— The Hon Rupert Carington, DL; ✉ Manor Farm, Church End, Bledlow, Buckinghamshire HP27 9PD (tel 01844 274461)

C

CARLILE OF BERRIEW, Baron (Life Peer UK 1999), of Berriew in the Co of Powys Alexander Charles Carlile (Alex); QC; *b* 12 February 1948; *Educ* Epsom Coll Surrey, KCL (LLB), Inns of Court Sch of Law; *m* 1968 (sep), Frances, da of Michael Soley; 3 da; *Career* Parly candidate (Lib) Flintshire E Feb 1974 and 1979, chm Welsh Lib Pty 1980–82, MP (Lib then Lib Dem) Montgomery 1983–97, former ldr Welsh Lib Dems and spokesman on Welsh Affrs, Justice and Home Affairs; a recorder of the Crown Court, hon recorder of the City of Hereford, bencher Gray's Inn, dep judge of the High Court; Ind Reviewer of Terrorism Legislation 2001–; pres Howard League for Penal Reform, pt/t chm Competition Appeal Tbnl; non-exec dir Wynnstay and Clwyd Farmers plc; fell Industry and Parliament Tst; FKC; *Style*— The Lord Carlile of Berriew, QC; ✉ House of Lords, London SW1A 1PW (tel 020 7219 3000, fax 020 7404 1405, e-mail carlileqc@aol.com)

CARLISLE, Anthony Edwin Charles Glen; s of George Geddes Glen Carlisle (d 1980), and Dorothy Louise, *née* Pickering; *b* 10 March 1947; *Educ* Charterhouse, Univ of Sussex (BA); *m* Nancy Susan, *née* Hayward; *Career* Lintas Advertising 1968–70; Dewe Rogerson Ltd: joined 1970, chief exec and dep chm 1986–95, exec chm 1995–98; exec dir Incepta Gp plc (and dir Citigate Dewe Rogerson) 1998–; non-exec dir CSR plc 2005–; Freeman City of London, Liveryman Worshipful Co of Glovers; MIPA, memb PRCA; *Recreations* travel, books, music, wine; *Style*— Anthony Carlisle, Esq

CARLISLE, 13 Earl of (E 1661); George William Beaumont Howard; Master of Ruthven; also Viscount Howard of Morpeth, Baron Dacre of Gillesland (both E 1661) and 13 Lord Ruthven of Freeland (S 1651); s of 12 Earl of Carlisle, MC, DL (d 1994), and Hon Ela Hilda Aline Beaumont (d 2002), da of 2 Viscount Allendale, KG, CB, CBE, MC; *b* 15 February 1949; *Educ* Eton, Balliol Coll Oxford (MA); *Heir* bro, Hon Philip Howard; *Career* joined 9/12 Royal Lancers 1967, Lt 1970, Capt 1974, Maj (Prince of Wales, Royal Armoured Corps) 1981–87; Parly candidate (Lib) Easington Co Durham 1987, Euro Parly candidate Northumbria 1989, Parly candidate (Lib Dem) Leeds W 1992; sec British-Estonian All-Pty Parly Gp 1997–, memb House of Lords All-Pty Defence Gp; Order of Marjamaa (1 class) Estonia 1998; *Clubs* Beefsteak; *Style*— The Rt Hon the Earl of Carlisle

CARLISLE, Bishop of 2000–; Rt Rev (Geoffrey) Graham Dow; s of Ronald Graham Dow (d 1983), of Harpenden, Herts, and Dorothy May, *née* Christie (d 1995); *b* 4 July 1942; *Educ* St Albans Sch, The Queen's Coll Oxford (BA, BSc, MA), Univ of Birmingham (Dip Pastoral Studies), Univ of Nottingham (MPhil); *m* 23 July 1966, Molly Patricia, da of Roland Eric Sturges; 3 s (Alastair Graham b 8 Dec 1968, James Peter Graham (Jamie) b 12 Dec 1970, Michael Graham b 10 Jan 1975), 1 da (Lindsay Patricia b 26 April 1972); *Career* ordained (Rochester): deacon 1967, priest 1968; asst curate Tonbridge Parish Church 1967–72, chaplain student St John's Coll Oxford 1972–75 (acting chaplain 1974–75), lectr in Christian doctrine St John's Coll Nottingham 1975–81, supr Univ of Nottingham 1975–81, vicar Holy Trinity Coventry 1981–92, canon theologian Coventry Cathedral 1988, bishop of Willesden 1992–2000; Coventry Dio: memb Bishop's Cncl for Miny 1981–87, memb Bishop's Cncl 1982–85, memb Deanery and Diocesan Synods 1982–, chm Coventry Christian Trg Project 1982–88 (dir Christian Trg Prog 1988–92), tstee Church Patronage Tst 1985; chm Bd of Social Responsibility London Dio 1992–97; chaplain Coventry Branch Owen Owen plc 1981–92, govr Blue Coat Sch Coventry 1981–92 (tstee 1981–87); *Publications* incl: The Local Church's Political Responsibility (1980), Whose Hand on the Tiller? (1983), Those Tiresome Intruders (1990), Christian Renewal in Europe (1992), Explaining Deliverance (1991), A Christian Understanding of Daily Work (1994), Pathways of Prayer (1996); *Recreations* steam and model railways, travel, music; *Style*— The Rt Rev the Bishop of Carlisle; ✉ Rose Castle, Dalston, Cumbria CA5 7BZ (tel 01697 476274, fax 01697 476550, mobile 07774 421678, e-mail bishop.carlisle@carlislediocese.org.uk)

CARLISLE, Hugh Bernard Harwood; QC (1978); s of William Harwood Carlisle (d 1979), and Joyce Carlisle; *b* 14 March 1937; *Educ* Oundle, Downing Coll Cambridge (MA); *m* 1964, Veronica Marjorie, da of George Arthur Worth, MBE, DL (d 1994), of Manton, Rutland; 1 s, 1 da; *Career* Nat Serv 2 Lt RA; called to the Bar Middle Temple 1961 (bencher 1985), jr treasy counsel (personal injuries cases) 1975–78, inspr Dept of Trade Inquiry into Bryanston Finance Ltd 1978–87, memb Criminal Injuries Bd 1982–, recorder of the Crown Court 1983–, inspr Dept of Trade Inquiry into Milbury plc 1985–87, head of chambers 1988–2001; pres Tport Tnbl 1997–; *Recreations* fishing, croquet; *Clubs* Garrick, Hurlingham (chm 1982–85); *Style*— Hugh Carlisle Esq, QC; ✉ 1 Temple Gardens, London EC4Y 9BB (tel 020 7583 1315, fax 020 7353 3969)

CARLISLE, Sir Kenneth Melville; kt (1994); s of Maj Kenneth Ralph Malcolm (Peter) Carlisle, TD (d 1983), and Hon Elizabeth Mary McLaren (d 1991), er da of 2 Baron Aberconway, CBE; *b* 25 March 1941; *Educ* Harrow, Magdalen Coll Oxford; *m* July 1986, Carla, da of A W Heffner, of Maryland USA; 1 s (Sam Fenimore Cooper b 28 Jan 1989); *Career* called to the Bar 1965; with Brooke Bond Liebig 1966–74; farmer; MP (Cons) Lincoln 1979–97, an asst Govt whip 1987–88, a Lord Cmmr of the Treasy (Govt whip) 1988–90; Parly under sec: Miny of Defence 1990–92, Miny of Transport 1992–93; memb Public Accounts Ctee 1995; memb Cncl: RSPB 1985–97, RHS 1996–2006; *Style*— Sir Kenneth Carlisle

CARLOWAY, Hon Lord Colin John MacLean Sutherland; s of Eric Alexander Cruickshank Sutherland, and Mary, *née* Macaulay; *b* 20 May 1954; *Educ* Edinburgh Acad, Univ of Edinburgh (LLB); *m* 1988, Jane Alexander Turnbull; 2 s; *Career* admitted to Faculty of Advocates 1977, advocate depute 1986–89, QC (Scot) 1990, treas Faculty of Advocates 1994–2000, senator of the Coll of Justice 2000–; *Clubs* Scottish Arts (Edinburgh); *Style*— The Hon Lord Carloway; ✉ Supreme Courts, Parliament House, Edinburgh EH1 1RQ (tel 0131 225 2595, fax 0131 225 8213)

CARLOWE, Melvyn Ian; OBE (2000); s of Harold Carlowe (d 1975), and Ann, *née* Brenner; *b* 13 April 1941; *Educ* Hackney Downs GS, Univ of Birmingham (BSoc Sci); *m* 15 Dec 1963, Jacqueline, da of Jacob Pressman; 2 da (Michaela Sally b 1965, Joanna Laura b 1968); *Career* schoolteacher Hockley Birmingham 1963–64; Jewish Welfare Bd: social worker 1964–67, chief social worker 1967–71, exec dir 1971–89; chief exec Jewish Care 1990–2000; tstee: NCVO 1996–2002, Inst for Jewish Policy Research 2000–03, Jewish Community Ombudsman 2000–, Jewish Chronicle Tst 2000–; panel memb Beacon Cncls DETR 2000–03; tstee N London Hospice 1986–2004; *Recreations* swimming, travel; *Style*— Melvyn Carlowe, Esq, OBE; ✉ 9 Rowanwood Mews, Enfield, Middlesex EN2 8QU (e-mail karlatsky@aol.com)

CARLSSON, HE Staffan; *m* Marie Thofte; *Career* Swedish diplomat; ambass to the Ct of St James's 2004–; *Style*— HE Staffan Carlsson; ✉ Embassy of Sweden, 11 Montagu Place, London W1H 2AL

CARLTON, Vivienne Margaret; da of John Carlton, and Phyllis Florence Kaye, *née* Minchin; *b* 28 September 1947; *Educ* Herts & Essex HS Bishop's Stortford, Trent Park Coll, Univ of London; *m* 1985 (m dis 2001), Julian Charles Bray, *qv*; 1 s (William Charles b 18 Aug 1989); *Career* account dir: Biss Lancaster plc 1980–82, Opus PR Ltd 1982–84; dir: Osca plc 1985–86, Leadenhall Associates Ltd 1986–91, NTN Television News Ltd 1988–90; princ Carlton Consulting 1991–; non-exec dir Queen Victoria Hosp NHS Tst 1999–2004; MIPR, FInstD (chm Central London IOD 1999–2004), MIMgt; *Recreations* theatre, interior design; *Style—* Ms Vivienne Carlton

CARLTON-PORTER, Robert William; s of Francis William Porter, of Derbys, and Cyrilla, *née* Carlton; *b* 29 November 1944; *Educ* St Helens Derby; *m* 9 Oct 1987, Angela, da of William Jenkins, of Hereford; 1 s (Alexander William b 8 Aug 1988); *Career* fin dir Hoechst UK Ltd 1973–83, fin dir English China Clays plc 1983–92, dir of a number of unlisted cos; non-exec dir: Newport Holdings plc (former chm), Rok property solutions plc (former chm), Michelmersh Brick Holdings plc, Hawtin plc (chm); former chm Assoc of Corp Treasurers, former memb Stock Exchange Pre-emption Ctee; former govr and treas Kingswood Sch Bath; former external examiner Univ of Exeter; ACIB 1968, MCInstM 1973, FIMgt 1976, FCT 1979 (fndn fell); *Recreations* antiques, philately, gardening, charity work; *Style—* Robert Carlton-Porter, Esq; ✉ 4 Laggan House, College Road, Bath BA1 5RU (tel 01225 484220)

CARLUCCIO, Antonio Mario Gaetano; s of Giovanni Carluccio (d 1978), and Maria, *née* Trivellone (d 1992); *b* 19 April 1937, Vietri Sul Mare, Italy; *Educ* Roland Matura Schule Vienna; *m* 22 Dec 1981, Priscilla Marion, da of Gerard Rupert Conran; *Career* restaurateur, food writer and broadcaster; former corr Gazzetta del Popolo and La Stampa Turin, resident in Germany 1963–75, wine merchant England 1975–81; restaurateur Neal Street Restaurant 1981–, proprietor (with wife) Carluccio's food retailers 1992–; memb Guild of Food Writers; hon assoc Altagamma Int Hon Cncl 2005; Commendatore Omri 1998; *Television* Antonio Carluccio's Italian Feasts (six part series, BBC 2, winner World Food Media Award 1997) 1996, Antonio Carluccio's Southern Italian Feast (six part series, BBC 2) 1998; co-winner James Beard Award for Best National Television Food Journalism Program USA 1999; *Books* An Invitation to Italian Cooking (1986), A Passion for Mushrooms (1989), A Passion for Pasta (1993), Antonio Carluccio's Italian Food (book of TV series, 1996, winner BBC Good Food Best Book Award 1997), Carluccio's Complete Italian Feast (1997), Carluccio's Complete Italian Food (1997), Southern Italian Feast (1998), Antonio Carluccio's Vegetables (2000), Antonio Carluccio Goes Wild (2001), An Invitiation to Italian Cooking (2002), Antonio Carluccio's Complete Mushroom Book (2003), Antonio Carluccio's Italia (2005); *Style—* Antonio Carluccio, Esq; ✉ The Neal Street Restaurant, 26 Neal Street, London WC2H 9QW (tel 020 7836 8368, fax 020 7240 3964); Carluccio's Italian Food Shop, 28A Neal Street, London WC2H 9PS (tel 020 7240 1487, fax 020 7497 1361)

CARLYLE, Robert; OBE; *b* 14 April 1961, Glasgow; *Educ* Glasgow Arts Centre; *m* 28 Dec 1997, Anastasia Shirley; 1 da (Ava b 4 July 2002); *Career* actor; fndr memb Rain Dog Theatre Co; *Television* incl: The Part of Valour 1981, The Bill 1984, Cracker 1993, Hamish Macbeth 1995, Looking After Jo Jo 1998, Hitler: The Rise of Evil 2003, Gunpowder, Treason & Plot 2003; *Films* Silent Scream 1990, Riff-Raff 1990, Safe 1993, Being Human 1993, Priest 1994, Go Now 1995, Trainspotting 1996, Carla's Song 1996, Face 1997, The Full Monty 1997, Ravenous 1999, Angela's Ashes 1999, Plunkett & Macleane 1999, The World is Not Enough 1999, The Beach 2000, To End All Wars 2000, The 51st State 2000, Once Upon a Time in the Midlands 2001, Black and White 2001, Dead Fish 2003, Marilyn Hotchkiss' Dance School 2004, In Like Flynn 2004; *Style—* Robert Carlyle, Esq, OBE; ✉ c/o Claire Maroussas, ICM Ltd, Oxford House, 76 Oxford Street, London W1N 0AX (tel 020 7636 6565, fax 020 7323 0101)

CARMAN, Charlotte Nina Hermione (Charlie); da of George Carman (d 2001), and Jacqueline Storm, *née* Wild (d 2001); *b* 3 March 1970; *Educ* James Allen's Girls' Sch, Pembroke Coll Cambridge (MA); *Career* Longman Publishers: sales and mktg co-ordinator 1991–92, ed 1992–94, commissioning ed 1994–95; Boxtree: commissioning ed 1995–97, sr ed 1997–98; ed Channel 4 Books 1998–2000, ed dir FilmFour Books 1999–2000, publisher Channel 4 and FilmFour Books 2000–, memb Mgmnt Bd Pan Macmillan Gp; *Books* The FilmFour Book of Film Quotes (2000); *Clubs* Soho House; *Style—* Ms Charlie Carman; ✉ Macmillan, 20 New Wharf Road, London N1 9RR (tel 020 7014 6000, fax 020 7014 6023)

CARMICHAEL, Alexander Morrison (Alistair); MP; s of Alexander Calder Carmichael, and Mina Neil, *née* McKay; *b* 15 July 1965; *Educ* Islay HS, Univ of Aberdeen (LLB, DipLP); *m* 19 Sept 1987 Kathryn Jane, da of Prof J Frederick Eastham; 2 s (Alexander Frederick Bethune b 31 March 1997, Simon Robin Calder 23 March 2001); *Career* hotel mangr 1984–89, dep procurator fiscal 1993–96, slr private practice 1996–2001; MP (Lib Dem) Orkney and Shetland 2001–; elder Church of Scot; memb Law Soc of Scot 1995–; *Recreations* music, theatre; *Style—* Alistair Carmichael, Esq, MP; ✉ House of Commons, London SW1A 0AA (e-mail carmichaela@parliament.uk); Torshavn, Finstown, Orkney

CARMICHAEL, Andrew James; s of James Horsfall Elliott Carmichael, MD, FRCR, DMRD, of Liverpool, and Maureen Catherine Carmichael, JP, *née* McGowan; *b* 8 August 1957; *Educ* St Edward's Coll Liverpool, Downing Coll Cambridge (MA); *Career* Linklaters: articled clerk 1979–81, slr 1981, ptnr 1987–; *Recreations* art, theatre; *Style—* Andrew Carmichael, Esq; ✉ Linklaters, One Silk Street, London EC2Y 8HQ (tel 020 7456 2000, fax 020 7456 2222)

CARMICHAEL, Keith Stanley; CBE (1981); s of Stanley Carmichael (d 1949), of Bristol, and Ruby Dorothy, *née* Fox (d 1980); *b* 5 October 1929; *Educ* Charlton House Sch, Bristol GS; *m* 1958, Cynthia Mary, da of John David Robert Jones (d 1971); 1 s (Richard John Carmichael b 1968); *Career* qualified CA 1951, ptnr Wilson Bigg and Co 1957–69; dir: H Foulks Lynch & Co Ltd 1957–69, Radio Rentals Ltd 1967–69; sole practitioner 1968–81 and 1990–, managing ptnr Longcrofts 1981–90; memb Monopolies and Mergers Cmmn 1983–92, Lloyd's underwriter 1979–90; memb Editorial Bd Simons Taxes 1970–82; pres Hertsmere Cons Assoc; chm Bd of Govrs and Tstees of The Royal Masonic Sch for Girls; fndr memb Soc of Share and Business Valuers; pres Gen Bd Grand Lodge of Mark Masons in England and Wales; memb Ct of Assts Worshipful Co of Chartered Accountants until 1996; FCA, FInstD, FTII, TEP; CStJ 2001; *Books* Spicer and Peglers Income Tax (1965), Ranking Spicer and Peglers Executorship Law and Accounts (ed, 1965–87), Corporation Tax (1966), Capital Gains Tax (1966), Taxation of Lloyd's Underwriters (with P Wolstenholme, 1988), Strategic Tax Planning (contrib, 1991); *Recreations* gardening, reading, golf; *Clubs* Carlton (dep chm 1989–95, tstee 1999–), MCC, Lord's Taverners; *Style—* Keith Carmichael, Esq, CBE; ✉ 117 Newberries Avenue, Radlett, Hertfordshire WD7 7EN (tel 01923 855098, fax 01923 855654); Flat 1, Princess Court, Bryanston Place, London W1H 7FP (tel 020 7258 1577, fax 020 7258 1578)

CARNAC, *see:* Rivett-Carnac

CARNARVON, 8 Earl of (GB 1793); George (Geordie) Reginald Oliver Molyneux Herbert; s of 7 Earl of Carnarvon (d 2001); *b* 10 November 1956; *Educ* Eton, St John's Coll Oxford (BA); *m* 1, 16 Dec 1989 (m dis 1997), Jayne M, eldest da of K A Wilby, of Cheshire, and Princess Frances Colonna di Stigliano, of Ashford, Co Wicklow; 1 da (Lady Saoirse b 2 June 1991), 1 s (George, Lord Porchester b 13 Oct 1992); m 2, 18 Feb 1999, Fiona Aitken, da of Ronnie Aitken (decd) and Frances Aitken (decd); 1 s (Hon Edward b 10 Oct 1999); *Heir* s, Lord Porchester; *Career* a page of honour to HM The Queen 1969–73; PA to Hon Peter Morrison, MP 1986–87, computer conslt/estate mgmnt 1976–92; founder shareholder: Telecom Express Ltd 1992–96, Digital People Ltd 1996–98; former dir Azur plc; *Clubs* White's; *Style—* The Rt Hon the Earl of Carnarvon; ✉ e-mail lordcarnarvon@highclerecastle.co.uk

CARNE, Dr Christopher Alan; s of Colin Ewing Carne, of London, and Philippa, *née* Trouton; *b* 31 October 1953; *Educ* Bryanston, Middx Hosp Med Sch (MB BS), Univ of London (MD), Univ of Cambridge (MA); *m* 1992, Julia Warnes; 1 s (Daniel b 1993), 1 da (Tulla b 2002); *Career* lectr genito-urinary med Middx Hosp Medical Sch 1984–87, conslt genito-urinary med Addenbrooke's Hosp Cambridge 1987–, assoc lectr Faculty Clinical Med Cambridge 1988–; former asst ed Genito-Urinary Medicine, former assoc ed Sexually Transmitted Infections; chm British Cooperative Clinical Gp 1999–2006 (sec 1993–99), hon sec Nat Audit Gp Br Assoc for Sexual Health and HIV (BASHH) 2004–; memb: STD Advsy Gp HEA 1990–92, Working Pty on HIV/AIDS Funding Dept of Health 1991, HIV and AIDS Clinical Trials Working Pty MRC 1991–94, Cncl MSSVD 1992–95 and 1999–2002, Working Pty on Koerner Coding in Genito-urinary Med Dept of Health 1994, Steering Gp UK Register of HIV Seroconverters 1994–, Specialist Advsy Ctee in Genito-urinary Med 1998–2002; memb BMA 1978, MSSVD 1983; FRCP; *Books* Aids (1987, 3 edn 1989); *Recreations* tennis, bridge; *Style—* Dr Christopher Carne; ✉ Clinic, 1A Addenbrooke's Hospital, Hills Road, Cambridge CB2 2QQ (tel 01223 217774, fax 01223 217807, e-mail christopher.carne@addenbrookes.nhs.uk)

CARNEGY, Christopher Roy; s of Julian Roy Carnegy, of New Malden, Surrey, and Vivien, *née* Kay-Menzies; *b* 9 December 1961; *Educ* Kingston GS, Univ of Southampton; *Career* presenter Radio Victory Portsmouth 1984–86, prog controller Ocean Sound Southampton 1986–92, md Spire FM Salisbury 1992–96, chief exec The Local Radio Co 1996–2000, md SouthCity FM Southampton 2000–04, broadcaster BBC World Service 2002–; sometime freelance broadcaster LBC, IRN and TVS; nominated for Best Local Radio Prog Sony Radio Awards 1986, winner Sony Radio Award Best Local Radio Station 1994, winner One World Broadcasting Award 1999, winner Andrew Cross Awards 1999; FRSA; *Recreations* boating; *Clubs* Royal Southampton Yacht; *Style—* Christopher Carnegy, Esq; ✉ BBC World Service, Bush House, Strand, London WC2B 4PH (tel 020 7557 2422, fax 020 7240 9745, e-mail chris.carnegy@bbc.co.uk)

CARNEGY, Patrick Charles; s of Canon Patrick Charles Alexander Carnegy (d 1969), and Joyce Eleanor, *née* Townsley (d 1995); hp of 14 Earl of Northesk, *qv*; *b* 23 September 1940; *Educ* Trinity Hall Cambridge (MA); *Career* writer, lectr, broadcaster on music, theatre and lit; journalist TES 1964–69, asst ed TLS 1969–78, ed music books Faber and Faber Ltd 1978–88, dir Faber Music Ltd 1979–88, dramaturg Royal Opera House 1988–92, Leverhulme research fell 1994–96; broadcasting incl contribs to BBC Radio 4's arts magazine Kaleidoscope; documentaries on: Kafka, Thomas Mann, Wagner's Ring; Stratford theatre critic The Spectator 1998; founding memb Bayreuth Int Arts Centre; memb: BBC Central Music Advsy Ctee 1986–89, BBC Gen Advsy Cncl 1990–96; *Books* Faust as Musician: A Study of Thomas Mann's novel 'Doctor Faustus' (1973), Christianity Revalued (ed, 1974), Wagner and the Art of the Theatre (2006, Royal Philharmonic Soc Award, George Greedley Special Jury Prize Award); *Recreations* mountains, model engineering, gardening; *Style—* Patrick Carnegy, Esq; ✉ patrick.carnegy@btopenworld.com

CARNEGY-ARBUTHNOTT, Bt-Col David; TD (1969); s of Lt-Col Wilmot Boys Carnegy-Arbuthnott (d 1973), and Enid Carnegy-Arbuthnott (d 1986), thirteenth of Balnamoon and thirteenth of Findowrie; Alexander Carnegy, 5 of Balnamoon, took part in 1715 rebellion, captured, imprisoned, pardoned 1721, estates forfeited, repurchased 1728; James Carnegy, subsequently 6 of Balnamoon, took part in 1745 rebellion, captured, tried but not convicted, because of misnomer - he had married Margaret Arbuthnott who became 5 of Findowrie and added her name to his; *b* 17 July 1925; *Educ* Stowe; *m* 1949, Helen Adamson (d 2000), da of Capt David Collier Lyell, MC (d 1970); 2 s (James, Hugh), 2 da (Sarah, Bridget); *Career* emergency cmmn Black Watch 1944–47, TA 1955–69, Bt-Col 1969, Hon Col First Bn 51 Highland Volunteers (TA) 1980–89; CA 1953, in practice Dundee 1956–89; landowner through family cos (3500 acres); pres Dundee C of C 1971–72, memb Ct Univ of Dundee 1977–85, govr Dundee Coll of Educn 1985–87 and Northern Coll of Educn 1987–91, convener Standing Ctee of the Scottish Episcopal Church 1987–92, tstee Scottish Episcopal Church 1992–2004; memb Queen's Body Guard for Scotland (Royal Co of Archers) 1959–; DL: Co of City of Dundee 1973–89, Co of Angus 1989–2001; Hon LLD Univ of Dundee 1982; *Recreations* shooting, country pursuits; *Clubs* New (Edinburgh), Army and Navy; *Style—* Bt-Col David Carnegy-Arbuthnott of Balnamoon, TD, DL; ✉ Meadowburn, Balnamoon, Brechin, Angus DD9 7RH (tel 01356 660273)

CARNEGY OF LOUR, Baroness (Life Peer UK 1982), of Lour in the District of Angus; Elizabeth Patricia Carnegy of Lour; DL (Angus 1988); eld da of Lt-Col Ughtred Elliott Carnegy of Lour, 12 of Lour, DSO, MC, JP, DL (d 1973), and Violet, MBE, *née* Henderson (d 1965); *b* 28 April 1925; *Educ* Downham Sch; *Career* worked in Cavendish Laboratory Cambridge 1943–46; Girl Guide Assoc: joined 1947, co cmmr Angus 1956–63, trg advsr Scotland 1958–62, trg advsr Cwlth HQ 1963–65, pres Angus 1971–84, pres Scotland 1979–89; co-opted onto Angus CC Educn Ctee 1967–75; chm: Working Pty on Professional Trg for Community Educn in Scotland 1975–77, MSC for Scotland 1981–83, Scottish Cncl Community Educn 1981–88 (memb 1978–88), Tayside Ctee on Med Res Ethics 1990–93; memb: Cncl Tertiary Educn Scotland 1979–83, MSC 1979–82, Scottish Econ Cncl 1981–93, Cncl Open Univ 1984–96, Admin Cncl Royal Jubilee Tsts 1984–88, Ct Univ of St Andrews 1991–96; cncllr Tayside Regnl Cncl 1974–82 (convener Recreation and Tourism 1974–76 and Educn Ctee 1977–81); memb various European legislation scrutiny ctees 1982–2000, memb Select Ctee on Delegated Legislation and Regulatory Reform 2001–05; Hon Sheriff 1969–84; hon memb Scottish Library Assoc 1989–; Hon LLD: Univ of Dundee 1991, Univ of St Andrews 1997; Hon DUniv Open Univ 1998; hon fell Scottish Cncl for Community Education; FRSA; *Clubs* Lansdowne, New Edinburgh; *Style—* The Rt Hon the Lady Carnegy of Lour, DL; ✉ Lour, Forfar, Angus DD8 2LR (tel 01307 820237); House of Lords, London SW1A 0PW

CARNOCK, 4 Baron (UK 1916); Sir David Henry Arthur Nicolson; 14 Bt (NS 1637), of Carnock, Co Stirling; recognised by Lord Lyon 1984 as holder of the Baronetcy of Lasswade (NS 1629) and as chief of the Clan Nicolson and Nicolson of that Ilk; s of Captain 3 Baron Carnock, DSO, JP, RN (d 1982), by his w, Hon Katharine Lopes (d 1968), da of 1 Baron Roborough; *b* 10 July 1920; *Educ* Winchester, Balliol Coll Oxford; *Career* served 1940–46 Royal Devon Yeo and Staff, DAQMG HQ Land Forces Hong Kong, Maj 1945; admitted slr 1949, ptnr Clifford-Turner Slrs 1955–86; Liveryman Worshipful Co of Scriveners; *Recreations* shooting, fishing, gardening, foreign travel; *Clubs* Travellers, Beefsteak; *Style—* The Rt Hon the Lord Carnock; ✉ 90 Whitehall Court, London SW1A 2EL (tel 020 7839 5544); Ermewood House, Harford, Ivybridge, Devon PL21 0JE (tel 01752 892519)

CARNWATH, Alison Jane; *Educ* Howells Sch Denbigh, Univ of Reading (BA), Univ of Munich; *Career* CA; KPMG 1975–80, Lloyds Bank International 1980–83, J Henry Schroder & Co 1983–93, Phoenix Securities 1993–97, md Donaldson Lufkin Jenrette 1997–2000; chm: Vitec Gp plc 1999–2004, Mgmnt Bd ISIS Equity Ptnrs LLP 2005–, MF Global 2007–; non-exec dir: Dwr Cymru 2001–, Man Gp plc 2001–, Friends Provident plc 2002–, Gallaher Gp plc 2003–05, Land Securities plc 2004–; memb Advsy Bd Xfi Centre for Finance and Investment Univ of Exeter 2004–; ACA 1980, FRSA 1989; *Recreations* tennis, skiing, music; *Style—* Mrs Alison Carnwath; ✉ The Old Dairy, Sidbury, East Devon EX10 0QR

CARNWATH, Francis Anthony Armstrong; CBE (1997); s of Sir Andrew Hunter Carnwath, KCVO, DL (d 1995), and Kathleen Marianne, *née* Armstrong (d 1968); bro of Rt Hon Lord Justice Carnwath, CVO, *qv*; *b* 26 May 1940; *Educ* Eton (Oppidan scholar), Trinity Coll Cambridge; *m* 1 March 1975, Penelope Clare, da of Sir Charles Henry Rose, 3 Bt (d 1965), of Hardwick House, Whitchurch-on-Thames, Oxon; 2 da (Flora Helen b 1976, Catriona Rose b 1978 d 1985), 1 s (Alexander Patrick b 1980); *Career* dir Baring Bros and Co Ltd 1979–89, chm Ravensbourne Registration Services Ltd 1981–89, dep dir The Tate Gallery 1990–94, advsr National Heritage Memorial Fund 1995–97 (actg dir 1995); dir: Foreign Anglican Church and Educational Assoc Ltd 1973–96 (co sec 1973–85), Greenwich Fndn for the Royal Naval Coll 1997–2002; tstee and treas Shelter Nat Campaign for the Homeless 1968–76 (dep chm 1973–76); treas: VSO 1979–84, Friends of Tate Gallery 1985–90; tstee: Phillimore Estates 1982–, Whitechapel Art Gallery 1994–2000, Musgrave-Kinley Outsider Arts Tst 1994– (chm 1999–), Royal Armouries 2000–07; chm: Henley Soc (Civic Amenity Tst Soc) 1984–88, Spitalfields Historic Bldg Tst 1984–2000, Commemorative Plaques Panel English Heritage 1995–2002, Yorkshire Sculpture Park 2004, Nat Tst Architectural Panel 2004–; memb: London Advsy Ctee English Heritage 1990–99, Bd Spitalfields Festival 2002–; Master Worshipful Co of Musicians 1995–96; Hon FTCL 2002, Hon RCM 2004; *Recreations* music, the arts, gardening, walking; *Clubs* Garrick, Beefsteak; *Style*— Francis Carnwath, Esq, CBE; ✉ 26 Lansdowne Gardens, London SW8 2EG (tel 020 7627 2158)

CARNWATH, Rt Hon Lord Justice; Rt Hon Sir Robert John Anderson; kt (1994), CVO (1995), PC (2002); s of Sir Andrew Hunter Carnwath, KCVO, DL (d 1995), and Kathleen Marianne, *née* Armstrong (d 1968); bro of Francis Carnwath, *qv*; *b* 15 March 1945; *Educ* Eton, Trinity Coll Cambridge (MA, LLB); *m* 18 May 1974, Bambina, da of G D'Adda, of Bergamo, Italy; *Career* called to the Bar 1969; jr counsel to Revenue 1980–85, QC 1985–94, attorney-gen to HRH The Prince of Wales 1988–94, judge of the High Court of Justice (Chancery Div) 1994–2002, a Lord Justice of Appeal 2002–; chm Law Cmmn 1999–2002, sr pres designate of tbnls 2004–; author of various legal pubns; chm Britten - Pears Fndn 2001– (tstee 1996–); Freeman Worshipful Co of Musicians; Hon FRAM 1994; *Recreations* violin, singing, tennis, golf; *Style*— The Rt Hon Lord Justice Carnwath, CVO; ✉ Royal Courts of Justice, Strand, London WC2

CAROLIN, Dr Brian; s of Lawrence Carolin, of Ellington, Northumberland, and Hazel, *née* Charlton; *b* 2 July 1956; *Educ* Ashington GS, Univ of Newcastle upon Tyne (BA), LSE (PhD); *m* 20 Sept 1975, Diane; 1 da (Sarah Carolin b 8 June 1987); *Career* graduate trainee Ford Motor Co Ltd 1980–84; Nissan 1984–: various positions incl personnel mangr, gen mangr Product Control and gen mangr Purchasing Nissan Motor Manufacturing (UK) Ltd Sunderland 1984–92, various positions incl gen mangr Corp Support and gen mangr Product Mktg Nissan Europe NV Holland 1992–95, md Nissan Motor (GB) Ltd 1998–2004 (mktg dir 1996–98), vice-pres (sales ops) Nissan Europe 2004–; *Recreations* cycling, reading; *Style*— Dr Brian Carolin

CARPANINI, Prof David Lawrence; s of Lorenzo Carpanini (d 2004), of Abergwynfi, W Glamorgan, and Gwenllian, *née* Thomas (d 1990); *b* 22 October 1946; *Educ* Glan Afan GS Port Talbot, Gloucestershire Coll of Art and Design (DipAD), RCA (MA), Univ of Reading (Art Teacher's Cert); *m* 1972, Jane Carpanini, *qv*; 1 s (Noel Dominic b 22 Aug 1977); *Career* artist and teacher; dir of art Kingham Hill Sch 1972–79, dir of art Oundle Sch 1979–86, sr lectr in art and design W Midlands Coll of HE 1986–89, head Dept of Art and Design Sch of Educn Univ of Wolverhampton (formerly Wolverhampton Poly) 1989–2000, prof of art Univ of Wolverhampton 1992–2000; pres Royal Soc of Painter-Printmakers 1995–2003, vice-pres Royal Soc of Br Artists 1982–86; subject of documentaries: Every One a Special Kind of Artist (Channel 4) 1984, David Carpanini (HTV) 1987, Elinor-Glamorgan (HTV) 1988, Zoom pm (WDR Cologne) 1989, Artist of Wales (Lifestyle Prodns Ltd (Cable TV)) 1991, A Word In Your Eye (HTV) 1997, A Visit to the Eisteddfod (HTV) 1998; de Lazlo Medal RBA 1980; Hon RWS 1996, Hon RBSA 2002; RBA 1976, RWA 1977, RE 1979, NEAC 1983, RCA 1992; *Solo Exhibitions* incl: Paintings, Etchings, Drawings (John Hansard Gallery Univ of Southampton) 1972, Paintings and Drawings at the John Nevill Gallery 1973, Paintings (Bristol Arts Centre) 1975, Etchings (The Arts Club London) 1982, Paintings and Drawings (Tegfryn Gallery) 1982, Etchings (Park Gallery Cheltenham) 1982, Paintings and Etchings (Ceri Richards Gallery Taliesin Art Centre UC Swansea) 1983, Paintings and Etchings (Business Art Galleries at the Royal Acad) 1984, permanent display of combined GLC and ASTMS (now MSF) collection of David Carpanini works at MSF HQ London and mgmnt coll Bishop's Stortford 1984–, Paintings and Etchings (East Gate Gallery Warwick) 1986, Paintings and Etchings (Mostyn Gallery Llandudno) 1988, Paintings and Etchings (Rhondda Heritage Park) 1989, Paintings 1968–88 (Walsall Museum and Art Gallery) 1989, David Carpanini Paintings and Prints (Attic Gallery Swansea) 1994 and 1998, The Royal Cambrian Acad Conwy 1998, 'Welsh Impressions' Etchings (St David's Hall Cardiff) 1999, New Drawings and Etchings (Taliesin Art Centre) 1999, Etchings and Drawings (Pam Schomberg Gallery) 2000, Paintings and Prints (Attic Gallery Swansea) 2001, Paintings, Etchings, Drawings (Attic Gallery Swansea) 2002, New Etchings (APW Gallery Melbourne) 2004, Attic Gallery Swansea 2005, Recent Paintings, Drawings and Etchings (Attic Gallery Swansea) 2008; *Two Person Exhibitions* with Jane Carpanini: Yarrow Gallery Oundle 1979, David and Jane Carpanini Paintings 1968–80 (Welsh Arts Council Exhbn) 1980, Paintings, Etchings and Watercolours (Queen Elizabeth Theatre Gallery Oakham) 1987, Paintings, Etchings and Drawings (Albany Gallery Cardiff) 1991, Rhondda Heritage Park Gallery 1994; also Paintings and Etchings with Richard Bawden RE (Royal Exchange Theatre Gallery Manchester) 1993, Print Noir with Peter Freeth and John Duffin (Bankside Gallery London) 2001; *Group Exhibitions* incl: Royal Acad Summer Exhbn 1973–, Royal W of England Acad Annual Exhbn 1973–, Royal Soc of Br Artists Annual Exhbn 1975–, Industrial Soc exhbn London 1974, The Artist in Society (Whitechapel Gallery London and Ulster Museum Belfast) 1978, Twelve Regular RA Exhibitors (Patricia Wells Gallery) 1979, Royal Soc of Painter-Etchers and Engravers Annual Exhbn 1979–, Six Welsh Artists: A View of Wales (Ceri Richards Gallery Swansea as part of National Eisteddfod) 1982, NEAC Annual Exhbn 1983–, Tradition and Innovation in Printmaking Today (national touring) 1985–86, Int Contemporary Art Fair (Olympia and Bath, with Bankside Gallery) 1985–, Contemporary Printmakers (Cadogan Fine Arts London) 1986–, Glynn Vivian Art Gallery Swansea 1986, Reflections of Summer (Bankside Gallery London) 1987, Contemporary Art Soc for Wales Collection (National Museum of Wales Cardiff) 1987, The Face of Wales (seven artists, tour of Wales) 1987–88, 20th Century Br Art Fair (with Fosse Gallery) 1988, Bristol Open Printmaking Exhbn (Royal W of England Acad) 1988, various exhbns of gallery artists Fosse Gallery (John Lindsey Fine Art) 1988–, British Printmaking Today (Br Cncl touring former Soviet Union) 1989–91, Wales Art Fair (Cardiff, with Albany Gallery) 1990 and (also with Attic Gallery) 1991, Art 90 Fair (Olympia, with Fosse Gallery) 1990, Albany Gallery 25th Anniversary Exhbn of Gallery Artists 1990, Past and Present RAs and RA Exhibitors (John Noott 20th Century Broadway) 1991, Welsh Coalmining - The End of an Era (New Gallery Swansea as part of Swansea Festival) 1991, Invited Members of the RE and RWS (Gorstella Gallery Chester) 1991, The NEAC in Wales (Albany Gallery Cardiff) 1992, Invited Members of the RE (Shell International London) 1992, RWS Open Exhbn (Bankside Gallery) 1993, Invited Members and Guests Royal Cambrian Acad 1993, Fedn of Br Artists National Print Exhbn (Mall Galleries) 1994–2003, Paintings, Drawings and Prints by Invited Artists (Gorstella Gallery Chester) 1994, Labour Intensive (City Gallery Leicester) 2000, What Makes Wales (Nat Museum of Wales Cardiff) 2001, Wrexham Print International 2001, Urban Perspectives (New Ashgate Gallery) 2001; *Work in Collections* incl: Ashmolean Museum Oxford, Fitzwilliam Museum Cambridge, Nat Museum of Wales, Nat Library of Wales, Newport Museum and Art Gallery, Glynn Vivian Art Gallery Swansea, Contemporary Art Soc for Wales, UC Swansea, Coleg Harlech, National Coal Board, Britoil, British Steel plc, Rank Xerox, Redpath Mining Corp Ontario, ASTMS (now MSF), Dept of the Environment, Royal Coll of Art, GLC, HM The Queen Windsor, numerous private collections in Europe, N America, Australia and Saudi Arabia; *Awards* Royal Instn Annual Scholarship for Engraving 1969, Catto Gallery Award RWS Open Exhbn 1993, first prize Daler Rowney Award RWS Open Exhbn 1995; *Recreations* opera, travel; *Style*— Prof David Carpanini; ✉ Fernlea, 145 Rugby Road, Milverton, Leamington Spa, Warwickshire CV32 6DJ (tel 01926 430658); c/o The Bankside Gallery, 48 Hopton Street, Blackfriars, London SE1 9JH (tel 020 7928 7521, fax 020 7928 2820); c/o The Attic Gallery, 14 Cambrian Place, Swansea SA1 1RG (tel 01792 653387)

CARPANINI, Jane; da of Derrick Stanley Allen (d 2004), of Streatley, Beds, and Joan, *née* Collins; *b* 13 October 1949; *Educ* Bedford HS, Luton Coll of Technol Sch of Art, Faculty of Art & Design Brighton Poly (DipAD), Sch of Education Univ of Reading (Art Teacher's Cert); *m* 1972, Prof David Lawrence Carpanini, *qv*, s of Lorenzo Carpanini (d 2004); 1 s (Noel Dominic b 22 Aug 1977); *Career* artist; art teacher: The High Sch Bedford 1972–73, Bishops Cleeve Comp 1973–76, Oundle Sch 1980–86 (pt/t); head of art and design King's HS for Girls Warwick 1987–97; hon treas Royal Watercolour Soc 1998–2003 (hon treas 1983–86, vice-pres 1992–93); RWA 1977, RWS 1978, RBA 1978, RCA 1992; *Television Documentaries* A Word in Your Eye (HTV) 1997; *Solo exhibitions* Watercolours and Drawings (Bristol Art Centre) 1975, Watercolours (Patricia Wells Gallery Thornbury Bristol) 1976, Watercolours and Drawings (Tegfryn Gallery) 1982, Watercolours (Ceri Richards Gallery Univ Coll Swansea) 1983, Watercolours of Wales (Nat Museum of Wales) 1984, Watercolours by Jane Carpanini (Warwick Museum) 1990, Watercolours (Albany Gallery Cardiff) 1991, Attic Gallery 2007; *Exhibitions with David Carpanini* David and Jane Carpanini Paintings 1968–80 (Welsh Arts Council Exhbn) 1980, Yarrow Gallery Oundle 1979, Rhondda Heritage Park Gallery 1994; *Group exhibitions* incl: Royal W of England Acad Summer Exhbn annually 1973–, RA Summer Exhbn 1974–80, Royal Soc of Br Artists Exhbn annually 1975–, Royal Soc of Painters in Watercolours annual London and tourning exhbns 1978–, Twelve Regular RA Exhibitors (Patricia Wells Gallery Thornbury) 1979, The Native Land (Welsh Arts Cncl Exhbn Mostyn Gallery Llandudno) 1980, Mason Watts Fine Art Warwick 1990 and 1993, Royal Cambrian Academy Annual Exhbn 1993, invited members of the RWS exhbn Gorstella Gallery Chester 1994; *Work in collections* incl: Nat Library of Wales, Nat Museum of Wales, Br Nat Oil Museum, Dixons Photographic, Diploma Collection of RWS, Burnley Building Society, Coleg Harlech, HM The Queen Windsor, numerous private collections; commissions: numerous paintings of independent schools and Oxford and Cambridge Colleges for Contemporary Watercolours Ltd; *Awards* Hunting Group Prize for watercolour of the year by a Br artist 1983; *Recreations* opera, travel; *Style*— Mrs Jane Carpanini; ✉ Fernlea, 145 Rugby Road, Milverton, Leamington Spa, Warwickshire CV32 6DJ (tel 01926 430658); c/o The Bankside Gallery, 48 Hopton Street, Blackfriars, London SE1 9JH (tel 020 7928 7521, fax 020 7928 2820); c/o The Attic Gallery, 14 Cambrian Place, Swansea SA1 1RG (tel 01792 653387)

CARPENTER, Prof (Mary) Christine; da of Kemball Johnston (d 1987), and Gertrud (Trude), *née* Porges (d 1991); *b* 7 December 1946, Oxford; *Educ* Perse Sch for Girls Cambridge (govrs scholar), Newnham Coll Cambridge (MA, PhD); *m* 8 Aug 1969, Roger Carpenter; 1 s (James b 31 July 1976), 1 da (Alison b 8 March 1979); *Career* Univ of Cambridge: freelance tutor and lectr various colls and Faculty of History 1976–79, fell and coll lectr New Hall 1979–2005, univ asst lectr 1983–88, univ lectr 1988–95, reader in medieval English history 1995–2005, prof of medieval English history 2005–, professorial fell New Hall 2005–; assoc ed Oxford DNB 1994–2002; James Ford special lectr Univ of Oxford 1996, guest lectr Moscow State Univ 2006; memb Editorial Bd The Fifteenth Century, memb Medieval Sources Advsy Panel TNA; co-ed Cambridge Univ Press Studies in Medieval Life and Thought; Royal Historical Soc Whitfield Prize 1992; Br Acad Leverhulme sr research fell 2002–03; AHRC maj research grants 1999–2008; memb: Governing Body Perse Sch, Cncl Francis Holland Schs; FRHistS (1982); *Publications* Locality and Polity: a study of Warwickshire landed society 1401–1499 (1992), Kingsford's Stonor Letters and Papers 1290–1483 (ed,1996), The Wars of the Roses: politics and the constitution in England c1437–1509 (1997 and repeat edns), The Armburgh Papers (ed, 1998), Calendars of Inquisitions Post Mortem XXII and XXIII (gen ed and dir of project, 2003 and 2004), Political Culture in Late Medieval Britain (ed with L Clark, 2004), various articles, reviews and chapters in books; *Recreations* music (concerts and opera), theatre, film, visiting art galleries, exhibitions and buildings and places of historical and artistic interest, reading, watching football, walking; *Style*— Prof Christine Carpenter; ✉ New Hall, Cambridge CB3 0DF (tel 01223 762262, e-mail mcc1000@cam.ac.uk)

CARPENTER, David Iain; RD (1994); s of Jeffrey Frank Carpenter, of Romsey, Hants, and Joyce Cumming, *née* Mitchell; *b* 14 October 1951; *Educ* Sutton GS, BRNC Dartmouth, Heriot-Watt Sch of Architecture Edinburgh (DipArch); *m* 20 Jan 1979, Anne Richmond, da of Dr Norman John McQueen, of Appin, Argyll; 4 s (Angus b 1980, Edward b 1981, Alexander b and d 1983, Simon b 1984); *Career* offr RN 1974–78, RNR 1979–2006 (memb Public Affrs Branch since 1992, head Public Affrs Branch 1996–98, Cdr 1998); architect J & F Johnston & Partners 1982–88 (assoc dir 1987), in own practice David Carpenter Architect Edinburgh 1988–; architect Northwood Devpt Team 1996–2004, chief ops support Multi-National Div SE Iraq (MND (SE)) Basrah 2004–05, Project Neptune Faslane 2005–; *Recreations* sailing, sketching, reading; *Clubs* Army and Navy, Langstone Sailing; *Style*— David Carpenter, Esq; ✉ David Carpenter Architect, 3 Argyle Park Terrace, Edinburgh EH9 1JY (tel 0131 229 1383, e-mail dcarchitect@tiscali.co.uk)

CARPENTER, Dr (George) Iain; s of George Anthony Carpenter (d 1967), of Horsmonden, Kent, and Dr Annie Pack MacKinnon; *b* 2 June 1950; *Educ* Christ's Hosp, Univ of Edinburgh (BSc, MD); *m* 1, 22 Feb 1970 (m dis 1982), (Marie) Catrine, da of Gaston Bauer, of Anglet, France; 1 da (Violaine b 1 May 1976), 1 s (Edward b 24 May 1979); m 2, 11 June 1983, Bridget Mary, da of Robert Charles Combley, of Headington, Oxford; 1 da (Annie b 18 Aug 1984), 1 s (James b 30 Jan 1986); *Career* sr registrar in geriatric med: Brighton Gen Hosp 1978–80, Bolingbroke 1980–81, St George's Hosp 1980–81; conslt geriatrician Royal Hampshire Co Hosp and St Paul's Hosp Winchester 1981–95 (also conslt in rehabilitation med 1990–95); regnl med advsr and dir of screening Beaumont Med Serv 1986–89, dir ICS Med Ltd 1989–91, sr lectr in health care of the elderly King's Coll Sch of Med and Dentistry 1995–, assoc dir and reader (older people) Centre for Health Services Studies Univ of Kent 2001–; memb: Br Geriatric Soc, BMA; FRCP 1993, FRCPEd 1994; *Books* All of Us - Strategies for Health Promotion for Old People (jtly, 1989), Housing, Care and Frailty (jtly, 1990), Assessment in Continuing Care Homes: Towards a National Standard Instrument (jtly, 1996), RAI Home Care (RAI-HC) Assessment Manual (jtly, 1996), Care of Older People - A Comparison of Systems in North America, Europe and Japan (jtly, 1999); *Recreations* walking, swimming, scuba diving, windsurfing, radio controlled model aircraft; *Style*— Dr Iain Carpenter; ✉ Centre for Health Service Studies, George Allen Wing, The University of Kent at Canterbury, Kent CT2 7NF (tel 01227 827760)

CARPENTER, Leslie Arthur; s of William and Rose Carpenter; *b* 26 June 1927; *Educ* Hackney Tech Coll; *m* 1, 1952, Stella Louise Bozza; 1 da; *m* 2, 1989, Louise Botting, CBE, *qv*; *Career* dir: Country Life 1965, George Newnes 1966; md Odhams Press Ltd 1968, dir International Publishing Corporation 1972, chm and chief exec IPC Ltd 1974; Reed International plc: dir 1974–, chief exec 1982–86, chm 1985–87; non-exec dir Watmough (Holdings) plc 1988–99; *Recreations* racing, gardening; *Style*— Leslie Carpenter, Esq

CARPENTER, Michael Alan; s of Walter Carpenter, and Kathleen Carpenter; *b* 24 March 1947, London; *Educ* Univ of Nottingham (BSc), Harvard Business Sch (MBA); *Career* with ICI 1968–71, conslt then vice-pres and dir Boston Consulting Gp 1973–83; General Electric Co: vice-pres of corporate business devpt and planning 1983–86, exec vice-pres GE Capital Corporation 1986–89, chm, pres and ceo Kidder, Peabody Gp Inc 1989–94; chm and ceo: Travelers Life & Annuity (also vice-chm Travelers Gp Inc) 1994–98, Citigroup Global Corporate & Investment Bank (also i/c Salomon Smith Barney Inc) 1998–2002, Citigroup Global Investments 2002–06, Southgate Holdings LLC 2006–; memb Bd: NYC Investment Fund, Mikronite Technologies Inc; Hon LLD Univ of Nottingham; *Style*— Mr Michael A Carpenter; ✉ Southgate Holdings LLC, 14th Floor - Suite 1404, 717 Fifth Avenue, New York, NY 10022, USA

CARPENTER, Michael Stephen Evans; s of Ernest Henry Carpenter (d 1974), and Eugenie, *née* Evans (d 1945); *b* 7 October 1942; *Educ* Eastbourne Coll, Univ of Bristol (LLB); *m* Gabriel Marie Lucie, da of Wing Cdr and Mrs Jack Brain; 1 da (Emma Lucie b 25 Aug 1970), 1 s (John Gerard b 6 Feb 1975); *Career* Slaughter and May: admitted slr 1967, ptnr 1974–94; Withers: ptnr 1994–96, conslt 1997; sec Garfield Weston Fndn 1997, legal cmmr Charity Cmmn 1998–2002, ind charity conslt 2003–; dep chair Charity Tstee Networks 2004–; chair Alpha Common Investment Fund for Income and Reserves 2005–; tstee: Chellington Project 2005–, Alpha Common Investment Fund for Endowments 2006–, Interactive Christian Extension Studies 2007–; memb Law Soc; *Recreations* hill walking, golf, the church; *Style*— Michael Carpenter, Esq; ✉ c/o Charles Russell, 8–10 New Fetter Lane, London EC4A 1RS (tel 01438 833754, e-mail michael.carpenter4@btinternet.com)

CARPENTER, Dr Percival Benjamin; s of Harold Percival Carpenter (d 2002), of Walsall, West Midlands, and Ida, *née* Baker (d 1997); *b* 4 August 1932; *Educ* Queen Mary's GS Walsall, Univ of Birmingham (MB ChB); *m* 8 Sept 1956, Janet Elizabeth, da of late Arthur James Bourne; 2 s (David Bryan b 15 Jan 1958, Michael Anthony b 7 Sept 1960), 2 da (Gillian b 1 Oct 1962, Petra Jane b 12 Jan 1969); *Career* Nat Serv Capt RAMC 1958–60; house offr St Chad's Hosp Birmingham 1957–58, sr registrar in radiology United Birmingham and other Birmingham Hosps 1963–65 (registrar 1960–63); conslt radiologist: West Birmingham Hosps 1966–85, Walsall Hosps 1975–; unit gen mangr Acute Services Walsall Hosp 1985–90 (chm Med Exec Ctee 1982–85), med dir Walsall Hosps NHS Trust 1990–97 (med advsr 1997–); FRCR 1965; *Recreations* model engineering, DIY, music; *Style*— Dr Percival Carpenter; ✉ 6 Sandra Close, Aldridge, West Midlands (tel 01922 453214, e-mail pcsandra@globalnet.co.uk); Manor Hospital, Moat Road, Walsall, West Midlands

CARR, Her Hon Judge (Elizabeth) Annabel; QC (1997); da of William John Denys Carr (d 1991), and Norah Betty, *née* Boot; *b* 14 November 1954; *Educ* Queenswood Sch Hatfield, Univ of Sheffield (LLB); *Children* 1 da (Hannah Betty), 1 s (Marcus John); *Career* called to the Bar Gray's Inn 1976, recorder 1996–2001, circuit judge 2001–; *Recreations* family, travelling, theatre; *Style*— Her Hon Judge Carr, QC; ✉ Sheffield Combined Court Centre, 50 West Bar, Sheffield S3 8PH

CARR, David Hugh; s of Tom Carr, and Katherine Mary, *née* Bull; *b* 11 October 1960, Northallerton, N Yorks; *Educ* Richmond Sch, Oriel Coll Oxford (exhibitioner, BA); *m* 14 May 1994, Julia May, *née* Dodd; 3 s (Robert James b 22 Nov 1994, Oliver Ben b 23 Aug 1999, Jonathan Adam b 2 Jan 2001); *Career* trainee then actuary Friends' Provident 1982–86, corporate pensions advsr The Wyatt Co 1986–87, property analyst Hillier Parker 1987–88; co-fndr and dir: Hazell Carr Training 1988–, Hazell Carr plc 1997–; Entrepreneur of the Year (Southern Region) 2003; supporter: London Chorus, Oxfam, Action Aid, Br Humanist Assoc; memb Co of Mercers, Grocers and Haberdashers Richmond; FIA 1988; *Recreations* singing (memb London Chorus), playing piano (Dip London Coll of Music), Concept 2 rowing, mountain biking, wine; *Style*— David Carr, Esq; ✉ Hazell Carr, Kings Reach, 38–50 Kings Road, Reading RG1 3AA (tel 0118 951 3700, fax 0870 762 7281, e-mail david.carr@hazellcarr.com)

CARR, Francis Christopher (Fred); s of Allan Eric John Carr (d 2002), of San Francisco, and Elizabeth Constance, *née* Hope-Jones (d 1989); *b* 6 March 1945; *Educ* Eton, Keble Coll Oxford (BA); *m* 7 May 1983, Corinna Elizabeth, da of Lt Cdr Cedric Wake-Walker, of Rogate, Hants; 2 da (Polly b 1985, Matilda b 1987); *Career* memb London Stock Exchange 1971, ptnr Smith Rice and Hill 1973, dir Capel-Cure Myers 1979–89; chief exec: W I Carr (Investments) Ltd 1991–93, Carr Sheppards Crosthwaite Ltd 1993–2004; chm: M & G High Income Investment Trust plc 1997–, The City of Oxford Geared Income Tst plc 1998–2005; dir: Investec Capital Accumulator Tst plc 2005–, SVM UK Active Fund plc 2006–; FSI 2005; *Recreations* fishing, shooting, aquatics, cooking; *Clubs* White's, Pratt's, Chelsea Arts, Leander, Vincent's (Oxford), City of London; *Style*— Fred Carr, Esq; ✉ 49 Moore Park Road, London SW6 2HP (tel 020 7731 2724)

CARR, Henry James; QC (1998); s of Malcolm Lester Carr (d 1984), of Liverpool, and Dr Sara Carr, *née* Leigh; *b* 31 March 1958; *Educ* King David Sch Liverpool, Hertford Coll Oxford (BA), Univ of British Columbia (LLM); *m* 22 Sept 1988, Jan Mary, da of Maj Richard Alfred Dawson, of Harrogate; 3 s (Oliver b 1989, Harry b 1991, Charlie b 1994); 1 da (Lily b 1997); *Career* called to the Bar Gray's Inn 1982; memb Cncl and Bd Intellectual Property Inst; *Books* Protection of Computer Software in the United Kingdom (1986, co-author 2 edn with R Arnold, 1992); *Recreations* tennis, swimming, skiing; *Clubs* RAC, Harbour, Hurlingham; *Style*— Henry Carr, Esq; ✉ 11 South Square, Gray's Inn, London WC1R 5EY (tel 020 7405 1222, fax 020 7242 4282)

CARR, Ian Henry Randell; s of Thomas Randell Carr (d 1979), of Gosforth, Newcastle upon Tyne, and Phyllis Harriet Carr (d 1985); *b* 21 April 1933; *Educ* Barnard Castle Sch, King's Coll Newcastle upon Tyne (BA, DipEd); *m* 1, 28 June 1963, Margaret Blackburn (d 1967), da of John Lowery Bell (missing presumed dead 1943), of Annfield Plain, Co Durham; 1 da (Selina b 29 July 1967); *m* 2, 9 Dec 1972 (m dis 1989), Sandra Louise, *née* Major; *Career* Nat Serv 2 Lt Royal Northumberland Fusiliers 1956–58, served NI and W Germany; jazz trumpeter; performer: Emcee Five Quintet 1960–62, Rendell-Carr Quintet 1963–69, Ian Carr's Nucleus 1969–89, The United Jazz and Rock Ensemble 1975– (worldwide tours); composed: Solar Plexus 1970, Labyrinth 1973, Will's Birthday Suite (for the Globe Theatre Tst) 1974, Out of the Long Dark 1978, Northumbrian Sketches 1988; assoc prof Guildhall Sch of Music and Drama; many presentations BBC Radio 3; memb: Greater London Arts Assoc 1975–80, Central Music Advsy Ctee BBC Radio and TV 1987–89; patron: Live Theatre Co Newcastle upon Tyne 1985–, Art at the Whittington Hosp Appeal Islington; Italian Calabria award 1982; memb: Royal Soc of Musicians of GB 1982, Assoc of Professional Composers 1983; PRS 1970; *Books* Music Outside (1973), Miles Davis: A Critical Biography (1982), Keith Jarrett: The Man and his Music (1991), Rough Guide to Jazz (jtly, 1995), Miles Davis: The Definitive Biography (1998); *Recreations* music, the visual arts, world literature, travel; *Style*— Ian Carr, Esq

CARR, Jimmy; s of Nora Mary Carr, *née* Lawlor (d 2001); *b* 15 September 1972, London; *Educ* Burnham GS, Royal GS High Wycombe, Gonville & Caius Coll Cambridge; *Partner* Karoline Copping; *Career* comedian; memb: Equity 2002, BAFTA 2004; *Performances* stand up incl: The Royal Variety Show 2002, Edinburgh Fringe Festival, Kilkenny Comedy Festival, Montreal Comedy Festival, Aspen Comedy Festival, Late Night with Conan O'Brien 2003, 2004, 2005 and 2006, The Tonight Show with Jay Leno 2003–05, Comedy Central Special 2004; *Television* Your Face or Mine (2 series) 2003, Distraction (UK 2 series, US 2 series) 2003–04, guest on Parkinson 2004, guest host Have I Got News for You 2004, panellist Question Time 2004, guest on Friday Night with Jonathan Ross 2004, 2005, 2006 and 2007; *Films* Confetti 2006, Stormbreaker 2006, Alien Autopsy 2006, I Want Candy 2007; *Awards* nominee Perrier Award 2002, Billy Marsh Award 2003, Best Stand Up Time Out Comedy Award 2003, Best On Screen Newcomer RTS Award 2003, Best Gameshow Silver Rose (for Your Face or Mine) 2003, nominee Best Presenter Golden Rose of Montreux (for Distraction) 2004, Best Stand-up Br Comedy Award 2006; *Recreations* tennis, enjoying all the trappings c-list celebrity life brings (attending parties, premieres and the like); *Clubs* Groucho; *Style*— Jimmy Carr, Esq; ✉ c/o Hannah Chambers, Chambers Management, 23 Long Lane, London EC1A 9HL (tel 020 7796 3588, fax 020 7796 3676, mobile 07803 126177, e-mail hannah@chambersmgt.co.uk)

CARR, Joanne (Jo); da of Ian Carr, of Andover, Hants, and Beryl, *née* Messenger; *b* 27 September 1968; *Educ* Harrow Way Comp Sch Andover, Univ of Birmingham (BA); *Career* teacher Kyoto 1990–92, conslt Corporate Communications Ltd Hong Kong 1992–95, PR conslt QBO (now QBO Bell Pottinger) 1995–2005 (dep md 2003–05), dir Teamspirit PR 2006–; *Style*— Ms Jo Carr; ✉ Teamspirit, 21 Tower Street, London WC2H 9NS (tel 020 7438 9400, e-mail jcarr@teamspirit.uk.com)

CARR, Jonathan Dodgson; s of Stephen Dodgson Carr (d 1970), and Lorna, *née* Smail; *b* 13 April 1939, Edinburgh; *Educ* Rugby, Emmanuel Coll Cambridge (MA); *m* 22 May 1965, Daphne Mary Robertson, *née* Davies; 1 s (James Andrew b 1966), 1 da (Candia Alexandra b 1968); *Career* Phillips and Drew 1962–67, L Messel & Co 1967–87, Bell Lawrie White 1990–93, S G Warburg 1993–99; tstee Barnwood House Tst, memb Finance Ctee Cheltenham Festivals Ltd; High Sheriff Glos 2007–08; memb London Stock Exchange 1970, MSI 1986; *Recreations* shooting, music; *Clubs* Boodle's, Brooks's, City of London, Isle of Harris Golf; *Style*— Jonathan Carr, Esq; ✉ Withington Court, Withington, Gloucestershire GL54 4BE (tel and fax 01242 890287, e-mail jondaf.carr@virgin.net)

CARR, Sir Peter Derek; kt (2007), CBE (1989), DL (Durham 1997); s of George William Carr (d 1972), and Marjorie, *née* Tailby; *b* 12 July 1930; *Educ* Fircroft Coll Birmingham, Ruskin Coll Oxford, Garnett Coll London; *m* 12 April 1958, Geraldine Pamela, da of Alexander Quarrier Ward, of Babbacombe, Devon; 1 s (Steven John b 1959), 1 da (Alyce b 1963); *Career* Nat Serv Mountain Rescue Serv RAF 1951–53; site mangr construction industry 1944–60, sr lectr in mgmnt Thurrock Coll 1964–69, advsr Nat Bd for Prices and Incomes 1967–69, dir Cmmn on Industrial Rels 1969–74, section dir ACAS 1974–78, Dip Serv cnsllr Br Embassy Washington DC 1978–83, regnl dir DOE (Northern) and ldr Govt City Action Team 1983–89; chm: Northern Screen Cmmn 1989–2002, Northern RHA 1990–94, Co Durham Devpt Co 1990–2001, NHS Supra Regnl Services Advsy Gp 1993–94, Durham County Waste Management Co 1993–, Premier Waste Management 1996–99, Occupational Pensions Bd 1994–97, Newcastle & North Tyne HA 1998–2002, Northumberland, Tyne & Wear SHA 2002–06, NE Regnl SHA 2006–; chm: Northern Regnl Awards Ctee NHS 2002–03, NE Health Forum 2003–, Northern Ctee on Clinical Excellence Awards 2004–; visiting fell Univ of Durham 1990–; memb Ct Univ of Newcastle upon Tyne 2005–; *Books* Worker Participation and Collective Bargaining in Europe, Industrial Relations in the National Newspaper Industry, It Occurred to Me; *Recreations* cabinet making, cycling, cooking, grandchildren, the history of the United States; *Clubs* Royal Over-Seas League; *Style*— Sir Peter D Carr, CBE, DL; ✉ Corchester Towers, Corbridge, Northumberland NE45 5NP (tel 01434 632841, e-mail petercarr@aol.com)

CARR, Sir (Albert) Raymond Maillard; kt (1987); s of Reginald Maillard Carr, of Bath; *b* 11 April 1919; *Educ* Brockenhurst Sch, ChCh Oxford; *m* 1950, Sara, da of Algernon Strickland, of Apperley, Glos; 3 s, 1 da; *Career* former fell All Souls' and New Coll Oxford, prof of Latin American history Univ of Oxford 1967–68, warden St Antony's Coll Oxford 1968–87; author; DLitt Univ of Oxford, Hon Dr Univ of Madrid; FBA, FRSL; *Recreations* foxhunting; *Style*— Sir Raymond Carr, FBA

CARR, Rodney Paul (Rod); OBE (2005); s of Capt George Paul Carr, of Whatton-in-the-Vale, Nottingham (d 2004), and Alma, *née* Walker (d 1960); *b* 10 March 1950; *Educ* Carlton Le Willows GS Nottingham, Univ of Birmingham (BSc); *m* 21 July 1971, Lynne Alison, da of Charles Wilfred Ashwell; 1 da (Joanne b 17 Oct 1979), 1 s (David b 15 Feb 1982); *Career* yachtsman; instr London Borough of Haringey 1972–75, chief instr and dep dir Nat Sailing Centre Cowes IOW 1979–81 (instr 1975–79), memb winning Br Admirals Cup team 1981, chief racing coach (yachting) Royal Yachting Assoc 1984– (olympic coach 1981–92), olympic team mangr 1992–97; coach to: J Richards and P Allam Flying Dutchman Class Bronze medal Olympic Games LA 1984, M McIntyre and B Vaile Star Class Gold medal Olympic Games Seoul 1988; mangr of: Ben Ainslie, John Merricks and Ian Walker (Silver medallists Olympic Games Atlanta 1996); dep chef de mission GB Olympic Team Sydney 2000; chief exec Royal Yachting Assoc 2000– (racing mangr 1987–2000); memb Bd UK Sport 2005–; yr bro Trinity House 2006; Hon MBA Southampton Inst 2002; *Recreations* sailing, music; *Style*— Rod Carr, Esq, OBE; ✉ 14 Spring Way, Alresford, Hampshire SO24 9LN (tel 01962 734148); Royal Yachting Association, RYA House, Ensign Way, Hamble, Southampton SO31 4YA (tel 023 8060 4100, fax 023 8060 4299, e-mail rod.carr@rya.org.uk)

CARR, Roger Martyn; *b* 22 December 1946; *Educ* Nottingham HS, Nottingham Poly; *m* Stephanie; 1 da; *Career* various appts Honeywell, gen mgmnt appts various engrg cos until 1982; Williams plc: gp md 1988–94, chief exec 1994–2000; chm: Thames Water plc 1999–2000, Chubb plc 2000–02, Mitchells & Butlers plc 2003–, Centrica plc 2004–; dep chm Cadbury Schweppes plc 2003– (non-exec dir 2001–), sr advsr Kohlberg Kravis Roberts Co Ltd; non-exec dir Bank of England 2007–; CIMgt, FRSA; *Style*— Roger Carr, Esq; ✉ Centrica plc, Millstream, Maidenhead Road, Windsor, Berkshire SL4 5GD

CARR, Sue; QC (2003); *Educ* Trinity Coll Cambridge (MA); *Career* called to the Bar 1987, master of the Inner Temple; practising barr specialising in professional liability; vice-chm: Professional Negligence Bar Assoc 2006–07, Conduct Ctee of the Bar Council; memb Chancery and Commercial Bar Assoc; accredited mediator; *Publications* Jackson & Powell: Professional Liability Precedents (gen ed and contrib author, 2000), Where There's a Will There's a Damages Claim (2001); *Style*— Ms Sue Carr, QC; ✉ 4 New Square, Lincoln's Inn, London WC2A 3RJ

CARR, Very Rev Dr (Arthur) Wesley; KCVO; s of Arthur Eugene Carr, and Irene Alice, *née* Cummins; *b* 26 July 1941; *Educ* Dulwich Coll, Jesus Coll Oxford (MA), Jesus Coll Cambridge (MA), Ridley Hall Cambridge, Sch of Ecumenical Studies Geneva, Univ of Sheffield (PhD); *m* 20 April 1967, Natalie Gay, da of Norman Robert Gill; 1 da (Helga b 1973); *Career* curate Luton Parish Church 1967–71, tutor Ridley Hall 1970–71 (chaplain 1971–72), Sir Henry Stephenson fell in biblical studies Univ of Sheffield 1972–74, hon curate Ranmoor Parish Church Sheffield 1972–74, chaplain Chelmsford Cathedral 1974–78 (canon residentiary 1978–87), dep dir and programme dir Chelmsford Cathedral Centre for Research and Trg 1974–82, Bishop of Chelmsford's dir of trg 1976–84, examining chaplain to Bishop of Chelmsford 1976–86, dean of Bristol 1987–97, dean of Westminster 1997–2006, Erikson scholar Austen Riggs 2006; memb Advsy Bd The Erikson Inst 1997–; hon fell Dept of Christian Ethics and Applied Theology New Coll Edinburgh 1986–94, Hon DLitt UWE 1996, Hon DLitt Sheffield 2003; *Books* Angels and Principalities (1981), 'Angels' and 'The Devil' in A Dictionary of Christian Spirituality

(1983), The Priestlike Task (1985), Brief Encounters, Pastoral Ministry through the Occasional Offices (1985), The Pastor as Theologian (1989), Lost in Familiar Places (with E R Shapiro, 1991), Manifold Wisdom (1991), A Handbook of Pastoral Studies (1997), A New Dictionary of Pastoral Studies (ed, 2002); articles in various jls; *Recreations* reading, writing, music, gardening; *Style*— The Very Rev Dr Wesley Carr, KCVO

CARR-ELLISON, Col Sir Ralph Harry; KCVO (1999), kt (1973), TD (1962), ED (TAVR 1974), DL (2001); s of Maj John Campbell Carr-Ellison (d 1956), of Hedgeley Hall, and his 1 wife, Daphne Hermione Indica, *née* Cradock (m dis 1946, d 1984); *b* 8 December 1925; *Educ* Eton; *m* 1, 1951, Mary Clare McMorrough (d 1996), da of Maj Arthur Thomas McMorrough Kavanagh, MC (d 1953), of Borris House, Co Carlow; 3 s, 1 da; m 2, 1998, Mrs Louise Gay, *née* Walsh, wid of Simon Dyer, CBE (d 1996); *Career* served: RGH CMF 1945–46, The Royal Dragoons BAOR 1946–49, TA and TAVR 1949–73; Lt-Col cmdg Northumberland Hussars 1966–69, Territorial Col (TAVR) 1969–73, Hon Col Northumbrian Univs OTC 1982–86, Northumberland Hussar Sqdns 1986–88, Queen's Own Yeo 1988–90, Col Cmdt The Yeo 1990–94, ADC (TAVR) to HM The Queen 1970–75; dir: Newcastle and Gateshead Water Co 1964–73, Trident Television 1972–81 (dep chm 1976–81); chm: Northumbrian Water Authy 1973–82, Tyne Tees Television Ltd 1974–97 (dir 1966–97); dir Yorkshire-Tyne Tees Holdings plc 1992–97 (dep chm 1992–93); chm: N Tyne Area Manpower Bd MSC 1983–84, N of England Territorial Assoc 1976–80 (pres 1987–90, vice-pres 1990–2000), Univ of Newcastle Devpt Tst 1979–81 (tstee 1992–98); vice-pres Automobile Assoc 1995–99 (vice-chm 1985–86, chm 1986–95); pres Northern Area Cons Cncl 1974–78 (treas 1961–66, chm 1966–69), pres Berwick and Tweed Constituency Cons Assoc 1973–77 (chm 1959–62), vice-chm Nat Union of Cons and Unionist Assoc 1969–71, govr Swinton Cons Coll 1967–81; memb Cncl Scout Assoc 1982–2000 (co cmmr Northumberland 1958–68, pres 1989–2000); pres: Hunter Improvement Soc 1995, Peterborough Royal Foxhound Show Soc 1998; dep govr Hunt Servants' Benefit Soc 1989–96; memb Ct Univ of Newcastle upon Tyne 1979–2002; former JP Northumberland, High Sheriff 1972, DL 1981–85, Vice Lord-Lt Northumberland 1984, HM Lord-Lt Tyne & Wear 1984–2000; Hon DCL Univ of Newcastle upon Tyne1989, Hon LLD Univ of Sunderland 1998; FRSA 1983; KStJ 1984; *Recreations* jt master West Percy Foxhounds 1950–90; *Clubs* Cavalry and Guards', Pratt's, White's, Northern Counties (Newcastle), MCC; *Style*— Sir Ralph Carr-Ellison, KCVO, TD, ED, DL; ✉ Beanley Hall, Beanley, Alnwick, Northumberland NE66 2DX (tel 01665 578273, fax 01665 578080)

CARR-LOCKE, Andrew Charles Philip; s of Lionel Charles Carr-Locke (d 1998), and Elsie Marjorie, *née* Wright; *b* 2 June 1953; *Educ* Whitgift Sch Croydon, Univ of Warwick (BSc); *m* 18 Aug 1979, Elizabeth Clare, *née* Hall; 2 da (Katherine Elizabeth b 1 April 1984, Sarah Ann b 20 Feb 1986); *Career* Europe finance dir consumer business Eastman Kodak 1974–85, finance dir Bowater Scott/Scott Ltd 1985–95, European finance dir United Distillers 1996–98, gp finance dir Courtaulds Textiles plc 1998–2000, gp finance dir George Wimpey plc 2001–07; non-exec dir AWG plc 2003–07; memb 100 Gp; FCMA 2006 (ACMA 1974); *Recreations* golf, tennis, travel; *Clubs* RAC, Limpsfield Chart Golf; *Style*— Andrew Carr-Locke, Esq

CARR-LOCKE, Prof David Leslie; s of Dennis Charlton Carr-Locke, of Melksham, Wilts, and Ruby Marjorie, *née* Gibbs; *b* 19 August 1948; *Educ* Hardenhuish GS Chippenham, Gonville & Caius Coll Cambridge (MA, MB BChir); *m* Sandra Anne Cialfi; 2 s (Alexander Charles Scott b 26 Nov 1974, Giles David b 10 March 1997), 2 da (Antonia Louise Papworth b 26 Nov 1974, Gemma Elizabeth b 16 Oct 1999); *Career* med and surgical house offr Kettering Gen Hosp 1972–73; sr house offr: obstetrics and gynaecology Orsett Hosp Essex 1973–74, med specialities Leicester Gp of Hosps 1974–75; lectr in med (gastroenterology) Univ of Leicester 1975–83, res fell in gastroenterology New England and Baptist Hosp Boston USA 1978–79, conslt physician Royal Infirmary 1983–89, dir of endoscopy Brigham and Women's Hosp 1989–, assoc prof of med Harvard Med Sch 1989–; pres Int Hepato-Pancreato-Biliary Assoc 1994–96, pres American Soc for Gastrointestinal Endoscopy 2002–; FRCP 1988; *Books* Hepatobiliary and Pancreatic Disease (1995), Pancreas (1997), ERCP in Children (1997); *Recreations* music, tennis, skiing, travel; *Clubs* Harvard (Boston USA); *Style*— Prof David Carr-Locke; ✉ Division of Gastroenterology, Brigham and Women's Hospital, 75 Francis Street, Boston, MA 02115, USA (tel 00 1 617 732 7414, fax 00 1 617 264 5171, e-mail dcarrlocke@partners.org)

CARR OF HADLEY, Baron (Life Peer UK 1975), of Hadley in Greater London; (Leonard) Robert Carr; PC (1963); s of late Ralph Edward Carr, and Katie Elizabeth Carr, of Totteridge, Herts; *b* 11 November 1916; *Educ* Westminster, Gonville & Caius Coll Cambridge; *m* 1943, Joan Kathleen, da of Dr E W Twining, of Cheadle, Cheshire; 1 s (decd), 2 da (Hon Susan Elizabeth (Hon Mrs Rhodri Bradley-Jones), Hon Virginia Sarah (Hon Mrs Michael Fox)); *Career* MP (Cons) Mitcham 1950–74, Sutton (Carshalton) 1974–75; PPS to Sir Anthony Eden 1951–55; Parly sec to Min of Lab and Nat Serv 1955–59, sec for Tech Co-operation 1963–64, sec of state for Employment 1970–72, Lord Pres of the Cncl and ldr of the House of Commons 1972, sec of state for Home Affairs 1972–74; chm John Dale Ltd 1958–63 (dir 1948–55); former dir: Metal Closures Ltd 1959–63 and 1964–70, Prudential Corp plc (chm 1980–85), Prudential Assurance Co Ltd (chm 1980–85), Securicor Ltd 1961–63, 1965–70 and 1974–85, SGB Group Ltd 1974–86, Cadbury Schweppes Gp plc 1979–87; chm Business in the Community 1984–87, former govr and dep chm of governing body Imperial Coll of Science and Technol (fell 1985), fell Gonville & Caius Coll Cambridge 2001; *Recreations* tennis, music, gardening; *Clubs* Brooks's, MCC, Surrey CCC (pres 1985–86), All England Lawn Tennis and Croquet (vice-pres 1990–); *Style*— The Rt Hon the Lord Carr of Hadley, PC; ✉ 14 North Court, Great Peter Street, London SW1

CARR-SMITH, Maj Gen Stephen R; *b* 3 December 1941; *Educ* RMA Sandhurst, Open Univ (BA 1992); *m*; 2 s, 1 da; *Career* cmmnd Royal Corps of Signals 1962, various staff and regtl appts UK, Germany, Aden and Libya, RMCS 1971, psc 1972, instr RMA Sandhurst, CO Armd Div Signals Regt 1979–82; instr Army Staff Coll Camberley (as Lt Col) 1982–84, promoted Col 1984, chief exec Tech Trg Coll Harrogate 1984–86, head of private office to chief exec Equipment Procurement (Army) MOD London 1986–88, promoted Brig 1988, dir Communications and Info Systems Plans and Policy Branch SHAPE 1988–91, promoted Maj Gen 1991, Dep DG NATO Communications and Info Systems Agency (NACISA) Brussels 1992–95; dir of special projects Defence Systems Ltd, sr mil advsr CORDA/BAeSEMA 1995–99, ombudsman for estate agents 1999–, chm Applied Systems Int plc 1999–2001, Hon Col FANY (Princess Royal's Volunteer Corps) 1996–, Col Cmdt Royal Signals 1996–; pres Stragglers of Asia CC 2002, former pres and chm Army and Combined Servs Cricket and Hockey Assocs; FIMgt 1990; *Recreations* politics and international affairs, bridge, golf, theatre, most sports; *Style*— Maj Gen S R Carr-Smith; ✉ c/o Cox's and King's, 7 Pall Mall, London SW1Y 5NA

CARRAGHER, Jamie; s of Philly Carragher, of Liverpool, and Paula Carragher; *b* 28 January 1978, Liverpool; *m* 1 July 2005, Nicola; 1 s (James b 11 Nov 2002), 1 da (Mia b 14 May 2004); *Career* footballer; Liverpool FC: debut v Middlesbrough 1996, over 350 appearances, winners FA Youth Cup 1996, League Cup 2001 and 2003, FA Cup 2001, UEFA Cup 2001, European Super Cup 2001 and UEFA Champions League 2005 (finalists 2007); England: 17 caps (also 27 Under 21 caps), debut v Hungary 1999, memb squad European Championship 2004; *Style*— Mr Jamie Carragher; ✉ c/o Liverpool Football Club, Anfield Road, Anfield, Liverpool L4 0TH

CARRAGHER, Patrick Matthew; s of Thomas A Carragher (d 1977), and Eileen M Carragher; *b* 21 September 1957; *Educ* St Catharine's Coll Cambridge (BA); *m* 1990, Alexandra; 2 da (Charlotte Maeve and Maria); *Career* gen sec Br Assoc of Colliery Mgmnt 1996– (full time offr 1981–); involved in a number of coal industry orgns incl Coal Soc, Coal Industry Social Welfare Orgn among others; *Recreations* squash, cinema, music; *Style*— Patrick Carragher, Esq; ✉ BACM-TEAM, Danum House, 6A South Parade, Doncaster, South Yorkshire DN1 2DY (tel 01302 815551, fax 01302 815552, e-mail gs@bacmteam.org.uk)

CARRELL, Prof Robin Wayne; s of Ruane George Carrell, of Christchurch, NZ, and Constance Gwendoline, *née* Rowe; *b* 5 April 1936; *Educ* Christchurch Boys' HS NZ, Univ of Otago (MB ChB), Univ of Canterbury (BSc), Univ of Cambridge (MA, PhD, ScD); *m* 27 Jan 1962, Susan Wyatt, da of John Leonard Rogers (d 1975), Christchurch, NZ; 2 da (Sarah Anne b 1963, Rebecca Susan b 1964), 2 s (Thomas Wyatt George b 1968, Edward Robin William b 1970); *Career* MRC Abnormal Haemoglobin Unit Cambridge 1965–68, dir clinical Biochemistry Christchurch NZ 1968–75, lectr and consIt Addenbrooke's Hosp and Univ of Cambridge 1976–78, prof of pathology Christchurch Clinical Sch Univ of Otago 1978–86, prof of haematology Univ of Cambridge 1986–2003, ret; Cwlth fell St John's Coll Cambridge 1985–86, fell Trinity Coll Cambridge 1987–; memb Gen Bd Univ of Cambridge 1989–92; govr Imperial Coll London 1997–98 (memb Ct 1999–2006); memb Spongiform Encephalopathy Advsy Ctee 2001–04; FRACP 1973, FRCPath 1976, FRSNZ 1980, FRCP 1990, FRS 2002; *Recreations* gardening, walking; *Clubs* Athenaeum; *Style*— Prof Robin Carrell; ✉ 19 Madingley Road, Cambridge CB3 0EG (tel 01223 312970); University of Cambridge, Cambridge Institute for Medical Research, Hills Road, Cambridge CB2 2XY (tel 01223 312970, fax 01223 336827, e-mail rwc1000@cam.ac.uk)

CARRICK, 10 Earl of (I 1748); David James Theobald Somerset Butler; also Viscount Ikerrin (I 1629) and (sits as) Baron Butler of Mount Juliet (UK 1912); s of 9 Earl of Carrick (d 1992), and his 1 w, (Mary) Belinda (d 1993), da of Maj David Constable-Maxwell, TD; *b* 9 January 1953; *Educ* Downside; *m* 1975, Philippa Janice Victoria, da of Wing Cdr Leonard Victor Craxton, RAF (ret), of Milford on Sea, Hants; 3 s ((Arion) Thomas Piers Hamilton, Viscount Ikerrin b 1975, Hon Piers Edmund Theobald Lismalyn, Hon Lindsay Simon Turville Somerset (twins) b 1979); *Heir* s, Viscount Ikerrin; *Style*— The Earl of Carrick

CARRICK, Michael; *b* 28 July 1981, Wallsend, Tyneside; *Career* professional footballer; clubs: West Ham United 1997–2004 (winners FA Youth Cup Final 1999, first team debut 1999, loaned to Swindon Town 1999 and Birmingham City 2000), Tottenham Hotspur 2004–06, Manchester United 2006– (winners FA Premiership 2007); England: 14 caps, debut v Mexico 2001, memb squad World Cup 2006; *Style*— Michael Carrick, Esq; ✉ c/o Manchester United FC, Old Trafford, Manchester M16 0RA

CARRINGTON, Prof Alan; CBE (1999); s of Albert Carrington (d 1971), of Chandler's Ford, Hants, and Constance, *née* Nelson (d 2004); *b* 6 January 1934; *Educ* Colfe's GS, Univ of Southampton (BSc, PhD); *m* 7 Nov 1959, (Noreen) Hilary, da of Patrick Ferraby Taylor (d 1981); 2 da (Sarah Elizabeth b 1962, Rebecca Anne b 1964), 1 s (Simon Francis b 1966); *Career* res fell Univ of Minnesota 1957–58, asst dir res and official fell Downing Coll Cambridge 1963–67 (GEC res fell 1959–60, asst res and res fell Downing Coll 1960–63), Royal Soc res prof Univ of Southampton 1979–84 and 1987–99 (prof of chemistry 1967–76, SERC sr res fell 1976–79), Royal Soc res prof and professorial fell Jesus Coll Oxford 1984–87, Leverhulme emeritus fell 1999; pres Faraday Div Royal Soc of Chemistry 1997–98; Harrison Meml Medal and Prize Chem Soc 1962, Meldola Medal Royal Inst of Chemistry 1963, Marlow Medal Faraday Soc 1966, Corday-Morgan Medal and Prize Chem Soc 1967, Award and Medal for Structural Chemistry Chem Soc 1970, Tilden Medal and lectureship Chem Soc 1972, Faraday Medal Royal Soc of Chemistry 1985, Davy Medal Royal Soc 1992, Longstaffe Medal Royal Soc of Chemistry 2005; hon fell Downing Coll Cambridge 1999, Hon DSc Univ of Southampton 1985; foreign hon memb American Acad of Arts and Scis 1987, foreign assoc US Nat Acad of Scis 1994; FRS 1971, FRSC 1989, CChem 1989, FInstP, CPhys 1993, FRSA 1999; *Books* Introduction to Magnetic Resonance (with A D McLachlan, 1967), Microwave Spectroscopy of Free Radicals (1974), Rotational Spectroscopy of Diatomic Molecules (with J M Brown, 2003); *Recreations* music; *Style*— Prof Alan Carrington, CBE, FRS; ✉ 46 Lakewood Road, Chandler's Ford, Hampshire SO53 1EX (tel 023 8026 5092, e-mail ac@soton.ac.uk)

CARRINGTON, Matthew Hadrian Marshall; s of late Walter Hadrian Marshall Carrington, of London, and Dilys Mary Gwyneth Carrington; *b* 19 October 1947; *Educ* French Lycée London, Imperial Coll London (BSc), London Business Sch (MSc); *m* 29 March 1975, Mary Lou, da of late Robert Darrow, of Columbus, OH; 1 da (Victoria b 11 June 1981); *Career* prodn foreman GKN Sankey 1969–72; banker: First National Bank of Chicago 1974–78, Saudi International Bank 1978–87; MP (Cons) Fulham 1987–97, PPS to Rt Hon John Patten MP as sec of state for Educn 1992–94, memb Treasy and Civil Serv Select Ctee 1994–96, chm Treasy Select Ctee 1996, asst Govt whip 1996–97; chm Outdoor Advertising Assoc 1998–2002, chief exec Retail Motor Industry Fedn 2002–06; *Recreations* cooking, political history; *Style*— Matthew Carrington, Esq; ✉ 34 Ladbroke Square, London W11 3NB

CARRINGTON, Nigel Martyn; s of Thomas Ronald Carrington, and Vera Carrington; *b* 1 May 1956; *Educ* Brighton Coll, St John's Coll Oxford (BA, pres Oxford Univ Law Soc); *m* 2 Jan 1988, Elisabeth Buchanan; 1 s, 2 da; *Career* Baker & McKenzie: articled clerk 1979–81, assoc 1981–87, ptnr 1987–2000, managing ptnr 1994–98, memb Int Exec Ctee 1998–2000; McLaren Gp Ltd: md 2000–05, dep chm 2005–; non-exec dir UCL Hosps NHS Fndn Tst 2005–; memb LSO Advsy Cncl 1998–2006; tstee: Crisis UK 2005– (also treas), The English Concert 2005– (chm 2006–), Jeans for Genes 2006– (chm), Independent Opera 2007–, Dreamchasing 2007–; *Books* Acquiring Companies and Businesses in Europe (1994); *Recreations* swimming, skiing, music, wine; *Clubs* RAC; *Style*— Nigel Carrington, Esq; ✉ McLaren Group Ltd, McLaren Technology Centre, Chertsey Road, Woking, Surrey GU21 4YH (tel 01483 261300, fax 01483 261301)

CARRINGTON, 6 Baron (I 1796, GB 1797); Peter Alexander Rupert Carington; KG (1985), GCMG (1988, KCMG 1958), CH (1983), MC (1945), PC (1959); sits as Baron Carington of Upton (Life Peer UK 1999), of Upton, Co Nottinghamshire; s of 5 Baron Carington, JP, DL (d 1938, n of 3 Baron, KG, GCMG, PC, JP, DL, sometime MP High Wycombe, and also 1 and last Marquess of Lincolnshire, govr of New South Wales, Lord Great Chamberlain of England and Lord Privy Seal) by his w, Hon Sybil, da of 2 Viscount Colville of Culross; *b* 6 June 1919; *Educ* Eton, RMC Sandhurst; *m* 1942, Iona, yr da of Sir Francis Kennedy McClean, AFC (d 1955); 1 s (Hon Rupert), 2 da (Hon Mrs de Bunsen, Hon Virginia); *Heir* s, Hon Rupert Carington, *qv*; *Career* served as Maj Grenadier Gds NW Europe; Parly sec Miny of Agric and Fisheries 1951–54, MOD 1954–56, high cmmr to Australia 1956–59, First Lord of Admiralty 1959–63, min without portfolio and ldr of House of Lords 1963–64, ldr of oppn House of Lords 1964–70 and 1974–79; sec of state: for defence 1970–74, Dept of Energy 1974; min of aviation supply 1971–74; sec of state for foreign and Cwlth affrs and min of overseas devpt 1979–82; chm Cons Party 1972–74, sec gen NATO 1984–88, chm EC Peace Conf on Yugoslavia 1991–92; chm GEC 1983–84 (dir 1982–84); dir: Christie's International plc 1988–98 (chm 1988–93), The Telegraph plc 1990–; non-exec dir: Chime Communications 1993–99, Christie's Fine Art Ltd 1998–; JP Bucks 1948, DL 1951; fell Eton 1966–81; memb Int Bd United World Colls 1982–84, chm Bd of Tstees V&A 1983–88; chllr: Order of St Michael and St George 1984–94, Univ of Reading 1992–, Order of the Garter 1994–; pres: Pilgrims 1983–2002, VSO 1993–98; hon fell St Antony's Coll Oxford 1982, hon bencher Middle Temple 1983, hon elder Brother Trinity House 1984; Hon LLD Univs of: Leeds 1981, Cambridge 1981, Philippines 1982, S Carolina 1983, Aberdeen 1985, Harvard 1986, Sussex 1989, Reading 1989, Buckingham 1989, Nottingham 1993, Birmingham 1993; Hon DCL: Univ of Newcastle upon Tyne

1998, Univ of Oxford 2003; Hon DSc Cranfield 1983, Hon DUniv Essex; Liveryman Worshipful Co of Clothworkers; *Books* Reflect on Things Past - The Memoirs of Lord Carrington (1988); *Clubs* Pratt's, White's; *Style*— The Rt Hon the Lord Carrington, KG, GCMG, CH, MC, PC; ✉ 32A Ovington Square, London SW3 1LR (tel 020 7584 1476); The Manor House, Bledlow, Princes Risborough, Buckinghamshire HP27 9PB (tel 01844 343499)

CARRINGTON, Prof Simon Robert; s of Robert Carrington (d 1996), of Suffolk, and Jean, *née* Hill (d 1991), of Wilts; *b* 23 October 1942; *Educ* ChCh Cathedral Choir Sch Oxford, The King's Sch Canterbury, King's Coll Cambridge, New Coll Oxford; *m* 2 Aug 1969, Hilary Elizabeth, da of Leslie Stott (d 1964); 1 da (Rebecca b 1971), 1 s (Jamie b 1973); *Career* dir The King's Singers 1968–93; freelance double bass player, teacher and adjudicator; dir Choral Summer Sch Marlborough Coll and Berwang Austria; with The King's Singers: 72 CDs for EMI and BMG, tours worldwide, concerts, workshops and master classes; regular TV appearances worldwide incl: Live at the Boston Pops 1983, BBC TV Series The King's Singers Madrigal History Tour 1984, ABC TV (USA) The Sound of Christmas from Salzburg 1987, 8 appearances on the Johnny Carson Tonight Show (NBC TV, USA) 1983–90; festival dir Barbican Summer in the City Festivals 1988–89, 20 Anniversary Concerts Worldwide 1988, Grammy nomination USA 1986; prof, dir of choral activities and artist in residence Univ of Kansas 1994–2001, dir of choral activities New England Conservatory Boston USA 2001–03, prof and choral dir Yale Univ Inst of Sacred Music and Sch of Music 2003–; choral conductor, clinician and memb int juries: German Nat Music Competition 1994, 1996 and 2002, Florilège Vocal de Tours, Int Choral Festival Arnhem Holland; FRSA; *Books* The King's Singers - a Self Portrait (1981); choral arrangements for publication; *Recreations* vintage cars, inland waterways, gardens, trees, walking, jogging; *Clubs* Royal Soc of Musicians, Inc Soc of Musicians; *Style*— Prof Simon Carrington; ✉ Yale University Institute of Sacred Music and School of Music, 409 Prospect Street, New Haven, Connecticut 06511, USA (tel 203 432 5180, fax 203 432 5296, e-mail sc@simoncarrington.com); Puy Calvel, 46240 Lamothe Cassel, France (tel 00 33 5 65 36 81 25)

CARROLL, Ben; s of Joseph Carroll, of Harrow, Middx, and Margaret, *née* O'Carroll; *b* 5 May 1945; *Educ* London Oratory; *m* 13 May 1967, Rosemary-Anne, da of Morris Tucker; *Career* Scottish Widows Fund & Life Assurance Soc 1964–66, Keith Shipton (Life & Pensions) Ltd 1966–68; Noble Lowndes & Partners Ltd 1968–93: md Noble Lowndes International Ltd 1986, md Employee Benefits 1988, md Personal Fin Servs 1990–93 (author of papers on behalf of firm); chief exec Bain Hogg Financial Services Ltd 1994, chm Bain Hogg Asset Management Ltd 1994, md Towry Law Financial Planning Ltd 1995, sales dir Corp Pensions Prudential 1998–2000, sr ptnr Carroll Consulting 2000–; head of qualifications Securities Inst 2001–02, dir of membership Securities Inst 2002–03; chm Syndaxi Financial Planning 2004–; dir: Towry Law plc, IFA Promotion Ltd 1993–96, IFA Assoc Ltd 1994, The Ideas Lab 2002–, Network Exams 2004–05, Dalbar Europe 2004–; chm Soc of Fin Advsrs 1993–95 (dir 1992–98); memb Memb Ctee PIA 1994–97, memb Disciplinary Tbnl Panel for Actuarial Profession 2005–; MSI, FPMI (pres 1987–89), FCII, assoc Personal Finance Soc (APFS); *Recreations* golf, travel, opera, theatre, modern films, walking; *Clubs* Croham Hurst Golf; *Style*— Ben Carroll, Esq; ✉ Springhurst Close, Shirley, Surrey CR0 5AT

CARROLL, Gerald John Howard; s of John Robert Carroll, and Catherine Florence, *née* Howard; lineal descendant of ancient Sept O'Carroll, Princes of Ely, Barons of Ely O'Carroll, Co Offaly, Ireland; *b* 9 October 1951; *Educ* Herrington House, Ipswich Sch; *Career* tstee Carroll Foundation 1972–, chm The Carroll Corporation and associated worldwide cos 1972–, chief exec Farnborough Aerospace Group Ltd 1985–; dir: Solid State Securities Ltd 1973–, Dukes Park Industrial Estates Ltd 1974–75, Culver Developments 1980–, Automated Machine Industries Ltd 1980–, Strategic R&D Corporation Ltd 1985–, Carroll Aircraft Corporation Ltd 1985–, The Manchester Canal and Business Park Development Corporation Ltd 1986–, Anglo Soviet Development Corporation Ltd 1988–, Carroll Anglo American Corporation 1989–, Carroll Australia Corporation Pty Ltd 1989–, Carroll Global Corporation plc 1989–, PYBT Development Fund (Northern) Ltd 1989–, Imperial Trading Corporation 1992–, Carroll Estate Corporation 1992–; tstee: Carroll Institute, Carroll Art Collection 1990–; memb: Br Helicopter Advsy Bd 1985–, Royal United Servs Inst 1988–, Chllr's Court of Benefactors Univ of Oxford 1990–, Capitol Historical Soc Washington DC; hon benefactor The Armoury Museum Kremlin Moscow; *Recreations* racing, sailing, shooting; *Clubs* Royal Thames Yacht, Old Ipswichian, Cavalry and Guards' (hon memb); *Style*— Gerald Carroll, Esq

CARROLL, John; s of Sean Carroll, of Bentley, nr Doncaster, and Norah, *née* Coombes; *b* 15 April 1964; *Educ* St Peter's HS Doncaster; *m* 17 Nov 1989, Tracy, da of John Hunter; 2 da (Danielle b 29 Oct 1990, Lauren b 4 Jan 1994); *Career* flat race jockey 1981–, best season 94 winners 1993; achievements: winner of Molecomb Stakes Group Three Goodwood 1988, winner of Cocked Hat of the North 1991, runner up Heinz 57 Group One Phoenix Park, winner Flying Childers Stakes Group Two on Paris House 1991, winner Newbury Sales Super Sprint Trophy on Paris House 1991, winner King George V Handicap on Learmont (Royal Ascot) 1993; winner Palace House Stakes Group Three: on Paris House 1993, on Mind Games 1995; winner Temple Stakes Group Two: on Paris House 1993, on Mind Games 1995; winner Norfolk Stakes Group Three on Mind Games; two winners inaugural Dubai World Cup Meeting 1996, winner 1000 Guineas Dubai 2002, winner Stanley Leisure Sprint Cup (Group I) on Invincible Spirit 2002; *Recreations* shooting, fishing, playing football, golf; *Style*— John Carroll, Esq; ✉ The Paddocks, 279 Park Lane, Preesall, Blackpool, Lancashire FY6 0LT (tel 01253 812299, mobile 07889 860797)

CARROLL, Prof John Edward; s of Sidney Wentworth Carroll (d 1959), and May Doris, *née* Brand; *b* 15 February 1934; *Educ* Oundle, Queens' Coll Cambridge (BA, MA, PhD, ScD); *m* Vera Mary, *née* Jordan; *Career* princ scientific offr Servs Electronic Res Laboratory 1961–67; Univ of Cambridge Engrg Dept: lectr 1967–76, reader 1976–83, prof 1983–2001 (emeritus prof 2001–), head of Electrical Div 1992–99; chm Cncl School of Technology Univ of Cambridge 1996–99; fell Queens' Coll Cambridge 1967–; FIEE 1965, FREng 1985; *Books* Hot Electron Microwave Generators (1970), Semiconductor Devices (1974), Rate Equations in Semiconductor Electronics (1985), Distributed Feedback Semiconductor Lasers (1998); *Recreations* carpentry, walking, reading; *Style*— Prof John Carroll, FREng; ✉ Department of Engineering, University of Cambridge, Trumpington Street, Cambridge CB2 1PZ (tel 01223 332829, fax 01223 332616, e-mail jec1000@cam.ac.uk)

CARROLL, His Hon Judge Michael John; s of Matthew Carroll, of Holbrook, Suffolk, and Gladys, *née* Hensman; *b* 26 December 1948; *Educ* Shebbear Coll, City of London Business Sch (BA), Cncl of Legal Educn; *m* 24 Aug 1974, Stella, da of Thomas Reilly; 3 da (Lisa, Erin, Joanna (decd), 2 s (Matthew, Padraig); *Career* called to the Bar Gray's Inn 1973; recorder 1994–96 (asst recorder 1990), circuit judge (SE Circuit) 1996–; *Recreations* reading, football; *Style*— His Hon Judge Carroll; ✉ Woolwich Crown Court, 2 Belmarsh Road, London SE28 0EY (tel 020 8312 7000, fax 020 8312 7078)

CARRUTHERS, (Philip) Anthony (Tony); s of Donald Carruthers (d 1983), and Beatrice Ada, *née* Tremain (d 1987); *b* 29 November 1934; *Educ* Homelands Tech HS Torquay, S Devon Tech Coll Torquay; *m* 4 April 1964, Sheila Mary, da of Rowdon Atkins (d 1956), and Kathleen Atkins, *née* Mooney (d 1971), of Torquay, Devon; 1 da (Anne-Marie Carole (Mrs Andrew Adams, JP) b 1966); *Career* RN 1951–54, RNR 1954–59; dir: Charles Moxham & Co Ltd 1960–68 (joined 1954), Moxhams of Torquay Ltd (Barlow Gp) 1968–72, Thos

Barlow Motors Ltd 1970–72, Barlow Handling Ltd 1972–94 (co sec 1975–94), Barlow Handling (Properties) Ltd 1973–94, Barlow Handling Gp Ltd 1975–94, Thos Barlow (Holdings) Ltd (Materials Handling Div of J Bibby & Sons plc) 1985–94, Barlow Pension Tst Ltd 1986–2005, DD Lamson plc 1990–94; memb Employment Tbnls England and Wales 1992–2005, memb and voluntary advsr Pension Advsy Serv (OPAS) London 1994–2004; memb Henley Royal Regatta 1976–, friend of Henley Festival of Music and Art 1990–, memb Fleet Air Arm Officers Assoc, memb NADFAS; Freeman City of London, Liveryman Worshipful Co of Gold and Silver Wyre Drawers; FInstD 1968; *Recreations* home computers, gardening, theatre, looking after two Bedlington terriers, music, opera, Probus, eating out, wine, enjoying retirement; *Clubs* Leander, Phyllis Court, Henley, IOD; *Style*— Tony Carruthers, Esq; ✉ St Marymead, Beverley Gardens, Wargrave, Berkshire RG10 8ED (tel 0118 940 2693, fax 0118 940 6208, e-mail tonycarr@globalnet.co.uk)

CARRUTHERS, Dr (George) Barry; s of George Harry Carruthers, CBE (d 1979), and Mary, *née* Barry (d 1990); *b* 22 December 1924; *Educ* St Paul's, Middx Hosp London (MD, MB BS); *m* 1; 4 s (Graeme David Barry b 2 June 1956, Stephen Robert b 3 Jan 1958, Richard Barry b 7 Jan 1965, Simon b 13 May 1967), 1 da (Nicola Jane Mary b 8 April 1971); *m* 2, 9 June 1990, Lesley Anne Connolly; *Career* med offr RAF 1949–57; med offr: Bank of England Printing Works 1956–71, Nat Heart Hosp 1960–, Royal Northern Hosp 1966–83; conslt in male infertility and dir of laboratories Royal Northern Hosp 1968–83, hon conslt Dept of Urology St Thomas' Hosp 1971–, med dir Wimpole St Med Centre 1981–; memb RSM 1971; *Books* Virility Diet (1973), Infertility (1981), Love Me, Love My Dog (1994), A History of Britain's Hospitals (with Lesley Anne Carruthers, 2005); *Recreations* antiquarian books and prints; *Style*— Dr Barry Carruthers; ✉ 55 Wimpole Street, London W1G 8YL

CARSBERG, Sir Bryan Victor; kt (1989); s of Alfred Victor Carsberg (d 2002), of Chesham Bois, Bucks, and Maryllia Cicely, *née* Collins (d 1996); *b* 3 January 1939; *Educ* Berkhamsted, LSE (MSc); *m* 1960, Margaret Linda, da of Capt Neil McKenzie Graham (d 1966); 2 da (Debbie, Sarah); *Career* in sole practice as chartered accountant 1962–64, lectr in accounting LSE 1964–68, visiting lectr Grad Sch of Business Univ of Chicago 1968–69, prof of accounting Univ of Manchester 1969–81 (dean Faculty of Econ and Social Studies 1977–78), visiting prof of business admin Univ of Calif Berkeley 1974, asst dir of res and technical activities Financial Accounting Standards Bd USA 1978–81, Arthur Andersen prof of accounting LSE 1981–87, dir of research (pt/t) ICAEW 1981–87, visiting prof of accounting LSE 1987–89, pt/t prof of accounting London Business Sch 1995–98; DG of telecommunications OFTEL 1984–92, DG Office of Fair Trading 1992–95, sec gen International Accounting Standards Ctee 1995–2001, chm Pensions Compensation Bd 2001–; memb Cncl ICAEW 1975–79, dep chm Accounting Standards Bd 1990–92 (memb 1990–94); dir: Economists Advsy Gp 1976–84, Economist Bookshop 1981–91, Philip Allan Publishers 1981–92 and 1995–, Nynex CableComms 1996–97, Cable and Wireless Communications 1997–2000, MLL Telecoms 1999–2002, RM plc 2002–, SvB Hldgs plc 2003–, Inmarsat 2005–; memb: Bd Radiocommunications Agency 1990–92, Cncl Univ of Surrey 1990–92, Cncl Loughborough Univ 1999– (chm 2001–); CAs Founding Society's Centenary award 1988, Sempier Award IFAC 2002 (hon MA Univ of Manchester 1973, hon fell LSE 1990; Hon ScD UEA 1992, Hon DLitt Loughborough Univ 1994, Hon DUniv Essex 1995, Hon LLD Univ of Bath 1996; Hon FIA 2000; FCA 1970; *Books* An Introduction to Mathematical Programming for Accountants (1969), Modern Financial Management (with H C Edey, 1969), Analysis for Investment Decisions (1974), Indexation and Inflation (with E V Morgan and M Parkin, 1975), Economics of Business Decisions (1975), Investment Decisions under Inflation (with A Hope, 1976), Current Issues in Accountancy (with A Hope, 1977), Topics in Management Accounting (with J Arnold and R Scapens, 1980), Current Cost Accounting (with M Page, 1983), Small Company Financial Reporting (with M Page and others, 1985); *Recreations* road running, theatre, opera, music; *Style*— Sir Bryan Carsberg

CARSLAKE, Hugh Bampfield; s of John Carslake, DL (d 1991), and Dorothea Jeanne, *née* Nesbitt; *b* 15 November 1946; *Educ* West House Sch Birmingham, Rugby, Trinity Coll Dublin (BA, LLB), Coll of Law; *m* 10 Oct 1970, June Helen, da of George Pratt McVitty; 6 c; *Career* slr; articled clerk Freshfields 1970–72, ptnr Martineau Johnson (formerly Ryland Martineau) Birmingham 1974– (sr ptnr 2004–07), NP 1981; tstee Worcester Cathedral Appeal 1988–, chm The Barber Inst of Fine Arts Univ of Birmingham 1989–, memb Cncl Univ of Birmingham 1991–2000; registrar Dio of Birmingham 1992–; govr King's Sch Worcester 2001–; memb: Law Soc, Ecclesiastical Law Soc; pres City of Birmingham Choir 2003–; *Recreations* music and family; *Style*— Hugh Carslake, Esq; ✉ Martineau Johnson, No1 Colmore Square, Birmingham B4 6AA (tel 0870 763 1486, fax 0870 763 1886)

CARSLAW, Debbie Patricia; da of John Murray Carslaw, of Gloucester, and Patricia Emily, *née* Smith; *b* 26 August 1961, Gloucester; *Educ* Ribston Hall GS for Girls Gloucester, Univ of Leeds (Margaret Harrison Simpson prize, LLB); *Career* slr; ptnr: Wilde Sapte 1996–98, Denton Wilde Sapte 1998–2002, Sidley Austin Brown & Wood 2003–; cases incl the acquisition of Canary Wharf Gp plc and the construction of the BBC Building in Portland Place London; memb Law Soc; supporter Terrence Higgins Tst; *Recreations* contemporary art (owner Madderrose Gallery), walking, cycling, music, dance; *Style*— Miss Debbie Carslaw; ✉ Sidley Austin, Woolgate Exchange, 25 Basinghall Street, London EC2V 5HA (tel 020 7360 3608, fax 020 7626 7937, e-mail dcarslaw@sidley.com)

CARSON, Ciaran Gerard; s of William Carson, of Belfast, and Mary Ellen, *née* Maginn; *b* 9 October 1948; *Educ* St Mary's Christian Brothers' Sch, Queen's Univ Belfast (BA); *m* 16 Oct 1982, Deirdre, da of Patrick Shannon; 2 s (Manus b 5 April 1986, Gerard 29 Oct 1987), 1 da (Mary Ellen b 3 Oct 1990); *Career* poet and prose writer; traditional arts offr Arts Cncl of NI 1975–98; Gregory Award 1976, Alice Hunt Bartlett Award 1988, Irish Times/Aer Lingus Award 1990, T S Eliot Poetry Prize 1993; *Books* poetry: The New Estate (1976), The Irish For No (1987, Alice Hunt Bartlett Award), Belfast Confetti (1989, Irish Times Irish Literature Prize for Poetry), First Language (1993, T S Eliot Prize), Opera Et Cetera (1996), The Alexandrine Plan (1998), The Twelfth of Never (1998), Breaking News (2003); non-fiction: The Pocket Guide to Irish Traditional Music (1986), Last Night's Fun (1996), The Star Factory (1997, Yorkshire Post Book Award), Shamrock Tea (2001), Dante Alighieri: The Inferno (translator, 2002); *Recreations* playing traditional music; *Style*— Ciaran Carson, Esq

CARSON, Hugh Christopher Kingsford; s of Col James Kingsford Carson (d 1995), and Elsie, *née* Cockersell; *b* 29 December 1945; *Educ* Tonbridge, RMA Sandhurst, Univ of London (BA), Univ of Reading (PGCE); *m* April 1972, Dr Penelope S E Carson, *née* Hollingbury; *Career* headmaster; cmmnd RTR 1967; 5 RTR 1967–69, 4 RTR 1970–71; adj The Royal Yeomanry 1971–73, instr RMA Sandhurst 1974–76; Epsom Coll: history/politics master 1980–90, careers master/house tutor 1980–85, housemaster 1985–90; headmaster: Denstone Coll 1990–96, Malvern Coll 1997–2006; memb: HMC 1990, SHA 1990, warden Worshipful Co of Skinners; *Recreations* historical research, photography, hill walking; *Style*— Hugh Carson, Esq; ✉ Hillside Farm, Back of Ecton, Wetton, Ashbourne, Derbyshire DE6 2AH (tel 01298 84544)

CARSON, Neil Andrew Patrick; s of Patrick Carson, and Sheila Margaret Rose Carson; *b* 15 April 1957, London; *Educ* Emanuel Sch, Coventry Univ (BSc); *m* 1988, Helen Barbara; 2 s (Peter Charles b 23 Dec 1992, Philip Robert b 5 May 1994), 1 da (Hannah Constance b 9 Oct 1997); *Career* Johnson Matthey plc: dir Catalytic Systems Div 1997, exec dir Catalysts Div 1999, exec dir Catalysts and Precious Metals Div 2003, chief exec

2004–; *Recreations* watching rugby, skiing, family; *Style*— Neil Carson, Esq; ✉ Johnson Matthey plc, 40–42 Hatton Garden, London EC1N 8EE (tel 020 7269 8400, fax 020 7269 8491, e-mail carson@matthey.com)

CARSON, (Thomas) Richard; s of Johnston Carson (d 1961), of Co Fermanagh, and Rebecca, *née* Farrell (d 1958); *Educ* Portora Royal Sch (Seale open scholar), Queen's Univ Belfast (Sullivan open scholar, BSc, PhD); *m* 1971, Ursula Margaret Mary, *née* Davies; 1 s (David Richard b 1973); *Career* theoretical physicist/astrophysicist; lectr Dept of Natural Philosophy Univ of Glasgow, sr scientific offr AWRE Aldermaston, currently hon reader in astrophysics Univ of St Andrews; sometime: conslt Atomic Weapons Research Establishment Aldermaston, visiting fell and prof Univ of Colorado, sr res assoc NASA Inst for Space Studies NY, visiting staff memb Los Alamos Nat Laboratory Univ of Calif, visiting prof Aust Nat Univ Canberra; memb: Int Astronomical Union 1966, American Astronomical Soc 1968, NY Acad of Sciences 1989; fndr memb Euro Astronomical Soc 1991; FRAS 1959; former: jr and sr 1 mile champion ATC (NI Cmd), co-holder NI and All Ireland 4 x 440 yards relay record; *Books* Atoms and Molecules in Astrophysics (ed with M J Roberts, 1972), also author of numerous research papers, reviews and articles in scientific literature; *Recreations* skiing, tennis, swimming, reading French prose and German verse, listening to Lieder and classical music; *Style*— Richard Carson, Esq; ✉ School of Physics and Astronomy, University of St Andrews, North Haugh, St Andrews KY16 9SS

CARSON, Scott Paul; *b* 3 September 1985, Whitehaven, Cumbria; *partner* Aimee Barton; 1 c; *Career* professional footballer; clubs: Leeds United 2002–05; Liverpool 2005– (UEFA champions League 2005), Sheffield Wednesday (on loan) 2006; memb squad World Cup 2006; *Style*— Scott Carson, Esq; ✉ c/o Liverpool Football Club, Anfield Stadium, Anfield Road, Liverpool L4 0TH

CARSON, William Hunter Fisher (Willie); OBE (1983); s of Thomas Whelan Carson, and Mary Hay; *b* 16 November 1942; *Educ* Riverside Sch Stirling; *m* 1, 1963 (m dis 1979), Carole Jane Sutton; 3 s (Antony Thomas, Neil John, Ross William); m 2, 5 May 1982, Elaine, da of John B Williams; *Career* former racehorse jockey (ret 1997); currently racing mangr to Prince Ahmed Bin Salman 1997–; apprentice to: Capt G Armstrong 1957–63 (first winner Catterick 1962), Fred Armstrong 1963–66; first jockey to: Lord Derby 1967, Dick Hern 1977–97; appointed Royal jockey 1977; major races won: 2000 Guineas 4 times (High Top 1972, Known Fact 1980, Don't Forget Me 1987, Nashwan 1989), Oaks 4 times (Dunfermline 1977 for HM The Queen, Bireme 1980, Sun Princess 1983, Salsabil 1990), Derby 4 times (Troy 1979, Henbit 1980, Nashwan 1989, Erhaab 1994), King George VI and Queen Elizabeth Diamond Stakes 4 times (Troy 1979, Ela-Mana-Mou 1980, Petoski 1985, Nashwan 1989), St Léger 3 times (Dunfermline 1977 for HM The Queen, Sun Princess 1983, Minster Son 1988), the Eclipse twice (Nashwan 1989, Elmaamul 1990), Ascot Gold Cup 1983 (Little Wolf), 1000 Guineas 1990 (Salsabil); champion jockey 1972, 1973, 1978, 1980, 1983; has ridden over 100 winners every season since 1972 (except 1984 when injured), became third most successful Br jockey with 3,882 wins Aug 1990 (incl over 100 group one races), only jockey to ride and breed Classic winner (Minster Son, St Leger 1988); Swindon Town FC: dir 1997–, head of PR 1997–, chm 2001–; racing pundit BBC 1997–; Hon Dr Univ of Stirling 1998; *Style*— Willie Carson, Esq, OBE; ✉ Minster House, Barnsley, Cirencester, Gloucestershire

CARSS-FRISK, Monica; QC (2001); *Educ* Univ of London (LLB), Univ of Oxford (BCL); *Career* called to the Bar Gray's Inn 1985; practising barr specialising in administrative and public law, employment law and human rights 1986–; currently memb Blackstone Chambers; pt/t tutor in law UCL 1984–87, memb Treasy Slrs Supplementary Common Law Panel 1997–99, jr counsel to the Crown (A Panel); memb Cncl of Justice; frequent participant in conferences on public law, human rights and employment law; *Publications* contrib: Halsbury's Laws of England: Constitutional Law and Human Rights (vol 8, 2 edn 1996), Butterworth's Human Rights Law and Practice (1999 and 2004), European Employment Law in the UK (2001); *Style*— Ms Monica Carss-Frisk, QC; ✉ Blackstone Chambers, Blackstone House, Temple, London EC4Y 9BW (tel 020 7583 1770, fax 020 7822 7350, e-mail clerks@blackstonechambers.com)

CARSTAIRS, Ian Andrew; s of Alexander Gordon Carstairs, of Leics, and Dorothy Mary, *née* Carr; *b* 13 February 1951; *Educ* Hinckley GS (now John Cleveland Coll), St John's Coll Cambridge (MA); *m* 1973, Kay, da of Keith Reginald Muggleton, of Leics; 3 s (Thomas Andrew b 1979, Benjamin James b 1980, Joseph William b 1983); *Career* Sun Life Assurance Society Ltd 1972–80, J Rothschild Investment Management Ltd 1980–84, Target Investment Management Ltd 1984–89, Mercury Asset Management Ltd 1989–92, global ptnr AMVESCAP plc 1992–; *Recreations* golf, tennis, squash, swimming, food and wine, crosswords; *Style*— Ian Carstairs, Esq

CARSWELL, Douglas; MP; s of John Wilson Carswell, OBE, FRCS, and Margaret, *née* Clark; *b* 3 May 1971, London; *Educ* Charterhouse, UEA, KCL; *Career* with Invesco Asset Mgmnt 1999–2003, memb Cons Party Policy Unit 2004–05, MP (Cons) Harwich 2005– (Parly candidate (Cons) Sedgefield 2001); *Publications* Paying for Localism (2003), Direct Democracy: an agenda for a new model party (2005), The Localist Papers (2007); *Clubs* Clacton Cons; *Style*— Douglas Carswell, Esq, MP; ✉ House of Commons, London SW1A 0AA (e-mail carswelld@parliament.uk); Constituency Office tel 01255 423112

CARSWELL, Baron (Life Peer UK 2004), of Killeen in the County of Down; Sir Robert Douglas Carswell; kt (1988), PC (1993); s of Alan Edward Carswell (d 1972), of Belfast, and Nance Eileen, *née* Corlett (d 2000); *b* 28 June 1934; *Educ* Royal Belfast Academical Inst, Pembroke Coll Oxford (MA), Univ of Chicago Law Sch; *m* 1961, Romayne Winifred, *qv*, da of James Ferris, JP, of Co Down; 2 da (Catherine, Patricia); *Career* called to the Bar NI 1957, English Bar (Gray's Inn) 1972, counsel to Attorney Gen for NI 1970–71, QC 1971, sr Crown counsel in NI 1979–84, judge of the High Court of NI 1984–93, Lord Justice of Appeal NI 1993–97, Lord Chief Justice of NI 1997–2004, a Lord of Appeal in Ordinary 2004–; bencher Inn of Court of NI 1979; hon bencher: Gray's Inn 1993, King's Inns Dublin 1997; chm Law Reform Advsy Ctee NI 1989–97; pro-chllr and chm Cncl Univ of Ulster 1984–94, chllr Dioceses of Armagh and of Down and Dromore 1990–97; *Recreations* golf; *Clubs* Ulster Reform (Belfast); *Style*— The Rt Hon the Lord Carswell, PC

CARSWELL, Lady; Romayne Winifred Carswell; OBE (1988), JP (2000); da of James Ferris, JP (d 1960), of Greyabbey, Co Down, and Eileen, *née* Johnston; *Educ* Victoria Coll Belfast, Queen's Univ Belfast; *m* 11 July 1961, Baron Carswell, PC (Life Peer), *qv*; 2 da (Catherine b 5 March 1963, Patricia b 2 Dec 1967); *Career* former memb NI Civil Serv; dep chm Police Complaints Bd for NI (subsequently Ind Cmmn for Police Complaints) 1983–94 (memb 1977–83); pt/t memb: Standing Advsy Cmmn on Human Rights 1984–86, Industrial Tbnls 1987–97; pres Friends of the Ulster Museum 1996–, tstee Ulster Historical Fndn 1992–2003 (dep chm 1997–2000), tstee Winston Churchill Meml Tst 2002–, convener Project Ctee Ulster Architectural Heritage Soc 1991–2000; memb: Bd of Govrs Victoria Coll Belfast 1979–99 (dep chm 1995–99), Ards Historical Soc, Ulster Soc for the Preservation of the Countryside, Ulster Wildlife Tst; HM Lord-Lt Co Borough of Belfast 2000– (DL 1997–2000); Hon Capt Royal Navy Reserve 2005; CStJ 2000; *Style*— Lady Carswell, OBE

CARTE, Brian Addison; TD (1976); s of late James Carte; *b* 7 August 1943; *Educ* St Lawrence Coll Ramsgate, Wharton Business Sch Univ of Pennsylvania; *m* 1969, Shirley Anne, da of Lt-Col W H Brinkley; 2 da; *Career* Co Cdr Queen's Regt TA, Maj GSO II HQ London Dist, asst project offr DTA and C, RARO 1987; dir County Bank Ltd 1976–85, md National Westminster Insurance Services Ltd 1985–89, chief exec Lombard North Central plc 1989–96 (dir 1996–97); chm Motability Finance Ltd 1992–95, dep chm First National Bank plc 1998–2003, chm Caffyns plc 2003– (non-exec dir 1996–2003); non-exec dir: PPP Ltd 1996–99, Fletcher King plc 1997–2002, Royal Automobile Club Ltd 1998–99; former pres Assoc of Corp Treasurers; memb Cncl Order of St John Surrey; Freeman and Liveryman Worshipful Co of Scriveners; FCIB, FCT, FRSA, FIMI; *Recreations* golf, shooting, opera; *Clubs* New Zealand Golf, RAC; *Style*— Brian Carte, Esq, TD; ✉ Fairfield Lodge, Hardwick Close, Knott Park, Oxshott, Surrey KT22 0HZ; Caffyns plc, Meads Road, Eastbourne, East Sussex BN20 7DR (tel 07850 887839)

CARTER, His Hon (Frederick) Brian; QC (1980); s of late Arthur Carter, and late Minnie Carter; *b* 11 May 1933; *Educ* Stretford GS, KCL (LLB); *m* 1960, Elizabeth Hughes, JP, da of late W B Hughes; 1 s (and 1 s decd), 3 da; *Career* called to the Bar Gray's Inn 1955; practised Northern Circuit 1957–85, prosecuting counsel for Inland Revenue Northern Circuit 1973–80, recorder of the Crown Court 1978–85, circuit judge (Northern Circuit) 1985–2001 (dep circuit judge 2001–), actg deemster 2001–03; *Recreations* golf, travel; *Clubs* Chorlton-cum-Hardy Golf, Big Four (Manchester); *Style*— His Hon Brian Carter, QC

CARTER, Sir David Craig; kt (1996); s of Horace Ramsay Carter, and Mary Florence, *née* Lister; *b* 1 September 1940; *Educ* Univ of St Andrews (MB ChB), Univ of Dundee (MD); *m* 23 Sept 1967, Ilske Ursula, da of Wolfgang August Luth (d 1945), of Riga, Latvia; 2 s (Adrian b 5 Jan 1969, Ben b 3 Nov 1970); *Career* St Mungo prof of surgery Univ of Glasgow 1979–88, regius prof of clinical surgery Univ of Edinburgh 1988–96; surgn to HM The Queen in Scotland 1993–97, CMO for Scotland 1996–2000; former memb: Biomedical Research Ctee Scottish Home and Health Dept, Br Broadcasting Cncl Scotland, Cncl RCSEd, Int Surgical Gp; chm: Scottish Fndn for Surgery in Nepal 1987–, Scottish Cncl for Postgrad Med Educn 1990–96, Bd of Science BMA 2002–05, Queens Nursing Inst Scot 2002–, Health Fndn 2003–, Bd for Academic Medicine 2004–; pres: Int Hepato-Biliary and Pancreatic Assoc 1988–89, Surgical Research Soc 1996–97, Assoc of Surgns of GB and I 1996–97, BMA 2001–02, Bd for Academic Medicine 2005–; vice-princ Univ of Edinburgh 2000–02, chm Scientific Advsy Ctee Cancer Research Campaign 2000–02, pres BMA 2001–02, vice-pres Royal Soc Edinburgh 2000–03, govr PPP Healthcare Fndn 2001–03, memb Sci Exec Bd Cancer Research UK 2002–04, tstee and vice-chm Cancer Research UK 2004–; overseas assoc Inst of Medicine USA 1998–; Hon DSc: Univ of St Andrews, Queen Margaret UC Edinburgh, Univ of Aberdeen, Univ of Edinburgh; hon sec: Br Jl of Surgery 1991–95, James IV Assoc of Surgns 1990–96; Hon LLD Univ of Dundee; Hon FRCSI, Hon FACS, Hon FRACS, Hon FRCGP, Hon FRCPS (Glas), Hon CSHK 2003, Hon FRCP 2005; FRCSEd, FRCPEd, FRCSGlas, FRCS (Eng), FFPHM 1998, fell Acad Med Sci 1998; fell American Surgical Assoc 2000, FRSE; awarded Gorka Dakshim Bahu (Nepal, 1999); *Books* Peptic Ulcer (1983), Principles and Practice of Surgery (1985, 2 edn 1989), Atlas of General Surgery (1986, 2 edn 1996), British Journal of Surgery (co-ed, 1986–91), Perioperative Care (1988), Pancreatitis (1989), Surgery of the Pancreas (1993 and 1997), Rob & Smith's Operative Surgery series (co-ed); *Recreations* gardening, philately, music; *Clubs* New (Edinburgh), Luffness New; *Style*— Sir David Carter, FRSE; ✉ 19 Buckingham Terrace, Edinburgh EH4 3AD (tel 0131 332 5554)

CARTER, Elliott Cook; *b* 11 December 1908; *Educ* Harvard Univ (MA), Longy Sch of Music, Ecole Normale de Musique Paris; *Career* composer; studied under: Gustav Holst 1930–32, Nadia Boulanger 1932–35; music dir George Balanchine's Ballet Caravan 1937–39, prof Yale Univ 1960, Ford Fndn composer-in-residence Berlin 1964, composer-in-residence American Acad Rome 1968; subject of several int retrospectives and television documentaries (incl LWT); compositions incl: Pocahontas (ballet) 1939, Symphony No 1 1942, Holiday Overture 1944, Piano Sonata 1946, The Minotaur (1947), Cello Sonata 1948, Eight Études and a Fantasy for woodwind quartet 1949, String Quartet No 1 (first prize Concours Internationale de Quatuors a Cordes 1953) 1951, Sonata for Harpsichord, Flute, Oboe and Cello (Naumburg Prize) 1952, Variations for Orchestra 1955, String Quartet No 2 (Pulitzer Prize 1960) 1959, Double Concerto 1961, Piano Concerto 1967, Concerto for Orchestra 1969, String Quartet No 3 (Pulitzer Prize 1973) 1973, Duo for Violin and Piano 1974, A Mirror on Which to Dwell 1976, A Symphony of Three Orchestras 1976, Syringa 1978, Night Fantasies 1980, In Sleep, In Thunder 1982, Triple Duo 1983, Penthode 1985, String Quartet No 4 1986, Oboe Concerto 1988, Three Occasions for orchestra 1986–89, Violin Concerto 1990, Quintet for piano and winds 1991, Scrivo in Vento for solo flute 1991, Trilogy for harp and oboe 1992, Partita for orch 1994, Of Challenge and Of Love for soprano and piano 1994, Adagio Tenebroso for orch (cmmnd BBC, world premiere BBC Proms 1995) 1995, Esprit Rude/Esprit Doux II for flute clarinet and marimba 1995, String Quartet No 5 1996, Clarinet Concerto 1996, Allegro scorrevole (Euro premiere BBC Proms 1997), Symphonia: Sum Fluxae Pretium Spei 1997, Luimen 1997, What Next? (opera) 1998, Quintet for Piano and Strings 1998, Tempo E Tempi 1999, Oboe Quartet 2000, Cello Concerto 2001, Hyoku 2001, Boston Concerto 2002, Au Quai 2002, Dialogues 2003, Micomicón 2002; Prix de Rome 1953, Gold Medal for Eminence in Music Nat Inst of Arts & Letters 1971, Ernst Von Siemens Music Prize 1985, Nat Medal of Arts (awarded by Pres of USA) 1985, Commandeur de l'Ordre des Arts et des Lettres (France) 1987, Commendatore Order of Merit of Italy 1991, Prince Rainier Foundation Prize 1998; Hon PhD: Princeton Univ 1967, Harvard Univ 1970, Yale Univ 1970, Univ of Cambridge 1983; *Recordings* incl: Night Fantasies, Variations for Orchestra, Cello Sonata, A Mirror on Which to Dwell, Four String Quartets (winner Grammy Award and Grand Prix du Disque), Syringa, In Sleep In Thunder, Triple Duo; *Style*— Elliott Carter, Esq

CARTER, (William) George Key; CBE, DL (W Midlands 1996); s of Lt-Col William Tom Carter, OBE, JP (d 1956), and Georgina Margaret, *née* Key (d 1986); *b* 29 January 1934; *Educ* Warwick Sch; *m* 30 June 1965, Anne Rosalie Mary, da of Trevor Acheson-Williams Flanagan (d 1987); 1 da (Louisa Mary-Anne b 1968), 1 s (Alexander Corfield Key b 1971); *Career* 2 Lt 16/5 The Queen's Royal Lancers 1958–60 (asst Adj 1959); qualified CA 1957; Price Waterhouse: joined 1956, mangr 1963, ptnr 1966, sr ptnr (W Midlands) 1982–94; pres: Birmingham C of C and Industry 1993–94, Worcs Branch ESU 1998–2003; chm: W Midlands Devpt Agency 1989–95, Black Country Development Corp 1994–98; vice-chm: Birmingham Mktg Partnership 1993–95, Birmingham Children's Hosp NHS Tst 1996–2003; dir Birmingham Economic Devpt Partnership 1991–95; memb: Ferrous Foundry Industry Advsy Ctee 1974–80, Pharmacist Review Bd 1980–97, Cncl W Midlands CBI 1988–98, Advsy Bd Univ of Birmingham Business Sch 1993–2000, N Worcs HA 1994–96, Cncl Aston Univ 1995–98; feoffee and govr Old Swinford Hosp Sch 1986–2000; chm: Cncl Order of St John W Midlands 1994–2001, Lunar Soc 1996–99 (vice-chm 1999–2001); High Sheriff W Midlands 1998–99; FCA 1957, FRSA 1993; *Books* The Work of the Investigating Accountant; *Recreations* golf, shooting, sailing, gardening; *Clubs* Cavalry and Guards'; *Style*— George Carter, Esq, CBE, DL, CStJ, FCA; ✉ The Old Rectory, Elmley Lovett, Droitwich, Worcestershire WR9 0PS (tel 01299 851251, fax 01299 851458, e-mail wgkcarter@aol.com)

CARTER, Gillian; *Career* journalist; former ed Family Circle, ed BBC Good Food 2004– (dep ed 2003–04); *Style*— Ms Gillian Carter; ✉ BBC Good Food, Woodlands, 80 Wood Lane, London W12 0TT

CARTER, John; s of Eric Gordon Carter (d 1991), and Mercia Gertrude, *née* Edmonds; *b* 3 March 1942; *Educ* Twickenham Sch of Art, Kingston Sch of Art, British Sch in Rome; *m* 11 July 1986, Belinda Juliet, da of Alan Cadbury; *Career* artist; *Solo Exhibitions* incl: Redfern Gallery 1968, 1971, 1974 and 1977, Univ of Reading 1979, Nicola Jacobs Gallery 1980, 1983, 1987 and 1990, Retrospective 1965–83 1983, Warwick Arts Tst 1983, Moris

C

Gallery Tokyo 1987 and 1989, Gallery Yamaguchi Osaka 1989, Sumi Gallery Okayama 1989, Galerie Hoffmann Friedberg 1990, Knoedler Gallery London 1991, Galerie Wack Kaiserslautern 1991, 2002 and 2007, Museum Moderner Kunst Landkreis Cuxhaven 1994, Belloc Lowndes Fine Art Chicago 1995, Gudrun Spielvogel Galerie Munich 1995 and 1999, Ecole Superiere des Arts Visuels de la Cambre Brussels 1995, Francis Graham-Dixon Gallery London 1996, Galerie Lattemann Darmstadt 1996 and 2003, Galerie St Johann Saarbrucken 1998, Slade Gallery UCL 2002, Espace Fanal Basle 2002, Gallery Benoot Knokke-Zoute 2003, Artmark Galerie, Spital am Pyhrn, The Blue Gallery London 2004, Konstruktiv Tendens Stockholm 2005, Galerie Konkret Martin Wörn 2006, De Vierde Dimensie Plasmolen 2007; *Group Exhibitions* incl: New Generation Whitechapel Gallery 1966, New British Painting and Sculpture UCLA Art Galleries LA and USA tour, British Painting Hayward Gallery 1974, British Art Show Mappin Art Gallery Sheffield and tour 1979, The British Cncl Collection Serpentine Gallery 1980, British Art 1940–80 The Arts Cncl Collection Hayward Gallery 1981, British Art Show Birmingham Museum and tour 1984, New Works on Paper Br Cncl and world tour 1984, Die Ecke Galerie Hoffmann Friedberg 1986, Britannica - 30 ans de Sculpture Musée André Malraux Le Havre 1988, The Presence of Painting Aspects of British Abstraction 1957–88 Mappin Art Gallery and tour 1988, Britse Sculptuur 1960–88 Museum van Hedendaagse Kunst Antwerp 1989, Arte Constructivo y Sistematico Centro Cultural de la Villa Madrid 1989, 1000 Kubikzentimeter Geom Minituren Wilhem-Hack-Museum Ludwigshafen 1990, Universal Progression Manege Moscow 1990, Piccolo Formato Arte Struktura Milan 1990, Geometrisk Abstraktion X Konstruktiv Tendens Stockholm 1991, Royal Acad of Arts Summer Exhbn 1992, 2002, 2003, 2004 and 2005, Aspects de la Mouvance Construite Internationale Musée des Beaux Arts Verviers 1993, Skulptur und Architektur: Ein Diskurs T H Lichtwiese Darmstadt 1993, Interférences Musée des Beaux-Arts Mons, Blick über den Armelkanal Pfalzgalerie Kaiserslautern 1994, Kunstmuseum Thun 1996, Mondiale Echo's Mondriaanhuis Amersfoort 2000, Das Entgrenzte Wilhelm-Hack-Museum Ludwigshafen 2002, Mesures Art International (Musée Matisse Le Cateu-Cambresis); *Awards* Leverhulme travelling scholarship to Italy 1963, Peter Stuyvesant Fndn travel bursary to USA 1966, Arts Cncl awards 1977 and 1979; *Style*— John Carter, Esq; ✉ 71A Westbourne Park Road, London W2 5QH; c/o Edition & Galerie Hoffmann, Görbel Heimer Mühle, D-61169 Friedberg, Germany (tel 00 49 6031 2443)

CARTER, Sir John Gordon Thomas; kt (1998); *Career* Commercial Union plc: i/c UK ops 1984–87, dir 1987–98, chief exec 1994–98, chm Commercial Union Assurance Company plc (princ operating subsid) 1994–98 (memb UK Bd until 2000); chm: ABI 1995–97, NHBC (Nat House-Building Cncl) 2003– (dir 1999–); advsr to Bd HSBC Investment Bank plc 1998–2002; non-exec dir Canary Wharf plc until 2004; chair Policy Protection Bd HM Treasy; chm: Cncl London Met Univ, Ctee of Univ Chairmen; Liveryman Worshipful Co of Insurers; FIA; *Style*— Sir John Carter

CARTER, Dr Mary Elizabeth (Mrs B H Neville); *Educ* St Mary's Hosp Med Sch Univ of London (women's entrance scholar, MB BS, MD); *Career* house physician Med Unit and Dept of Psychiatry St Mary's Hosp London then house surgn in gen and orthopaedic surgery Paddington Gen Hosp London 1954, house physician in gen med, cardiology and neurology King Edward Meml Hosp Ealing 1955, house physician St Mary's Hosp London 1956; MRC Rheumatism Research Unit Canadian Red Cross Meml Hosp Taplow: registrar 1957–59 and 1960–62, Empire Rheumatism Cncl research fell 1959–60; sr registrar in gen med St Mary's Hosp London 1963–65, hon research rheumatologist St Mary's Hosp 1965–70, med advsr to Medicovision (closed circuit colour TV progs for int postgrad centres) 1970–71, hon clinical sr lectr and conslt physician in rheumatology and rehabilitation St Mary's Hosp (first woman conslt clinician and fndr first Dept of Rheumatology and Rehabilitation) 1971–91, sr research fell in clinical rheumatology Dept of Biological and Med Systems Imperial Coll and hon consulting physician St Mary's Hosp 1991–2003; pres Paddington Branch Arthritis Care 1974–94; chm: Disability Action Westminster 1985–2003, Ctee for Employment of Disabled People NE London 1986–91; memb: Exec Ctee Gtr London Assoc for Disabled People 1986–91, Cncl and Distribution Ctee London Catalyst 1989–2006 (formerly Metropolitan Hosp Sunday Fund); RCPEd: regnl advsr for Gtr London and NW Thames 1982–99, rep Central Conslts and Specialists Ctee 1983–97, memb Cncl 1993–96, rep Lister Inst of Preventive Med 1994–99; advsy memb Social and Community Agencies Standing Ctee Euro League Against Rheumatism 1975–97, memb Exec Ctee Br Soc for Rehabilitation Med 1987–90; memb: Br Soc for Rheumatology (formerly Heberden Soc) 1958– (elected fell 2005), Soc for Back Pain Research 1987–97; FRSM 1960–, FRCPEd (MRCPEd); *Publications* author of various book chapters and numerous scientific and socio-medical papers; fndr chief ed Excerpta Medica: Rheumatology Abstracts; *Recreations* opera, theatre, stage and costume design, fine art, music, gardening, travel; *Clubs* RSM; *Style*— Dr Mary Carter, MD, FRCPEd; ✉ The Spinney, 16 Woodlands Road, Ashurst, Hampshire SO40 7AD

CARTER, Peter; QC (1995); s of Tom Carter, and Winifred Carter, of Huddersfield, W Yorks; *b* 8 August 1952; *Educ* King James' GS Huddersfield, UCL (LLB); *m* 1973, Caroline Ann, da of Leslie Hugh Adams; 1 s (Jonathan Edwin b 3 Nov 1988); *Career* called to the Bar Gray's Inn 1974 (bencher 2003); chair Bar Human Rights Ctee, govr Br Inst of Human Rights, memb Legal Section Amnesty; memb: Criminal Bar Assoc (sec 1985–89), Inst of Advanced Legal Studies; *Books* Offences of Violence; *Recreations* poetry, sport, walking; *Style*— Peter Carter, Esq, QC; ✉ 18 Red Lion Court, London EC4A 3EB; Park Court Chambers, 16 Park Place Leeds LS1 2SJ

CARTER, Dr Peter John; OBE (2006); s of Reginald John Carter (d 1982), and Mary Doreen Carter; *Educ* Univ of Birmingham (MBA, PhD), RMN, RGN; *m* Lilian; 2 da (Catherine b 13 March 1971, Elizabeth b 22 Jan 1973); *Career* head of personnel SW Herts HA 1980–83, commissioning mangr S Beds HA 1990–92 (dir of ops 1986–90); chief exec: NW London Mental Health NHS Tst 1995–98 (dir of ops 1993–95), Brent Kensington Chelsea and Westminster Mental Health NHS Tst 1998–99, Central and NW London Mental Health NHS Tst 1999–2007, RCN 2007–; memb various ctees incl Review Panel examining prescribing practice in the UK, expert witness in health related litigation; memb RCN, MIPD; *Recreations* rugby, scuba diving and most other sports, music, opera, cycling, gardening, ballet; *Clubs* Cricketers of London, Harpenden RFC, National Liberal; *Style*— Dr Peter Carter, OBE; ✉ Royal College of Nursing, 20 Cavendish Square, London W1G 0RN (tel 020 7647 3781)

CARTER, Sir Philip David; kt (1991), CBE (1981); s of Percival Carter and Isobell, *née* Stirrup; *b* 8 May 1927; *Educ* Waterloo GS Liverpool; *m* 1946, Harriet Rita, *née* Evans; *Career* Fleet Air Arm 1945; Littlewoods Orgn 1944–83 (chief exec 1976–83), ret; chm: Mail Order Traders of GB 1979–83, Man Made Fibre Working Pty 1980, Liverpool Cons Assoc 1985–95, Merseyside Tourism Bd 1986–92, Empire Trust 1986–, Empire Theatre Trust 1987–, Forminster plc 1995–; pres: Euro Mail Order Traders Assoc 1983, Football League 1986–88; life pres Everton FC 2004 (dir 1975–2004, chm 1977–91 and 1998–2004); memb: Jt Textile Ctee NEDO 1979, Distributive Trades EDC 1980, Merseyside Devpt Corp 1981– (chm 1987–91), Manchester Olympic Bid Ctee 1989; chm John Moores Univ Trust 1993– (dep chm of govrs 1994–97, chm of govrs 1997); John Moores Univ Liverpool: pro-chllr 1994–, chm Ct 1997–; chm Roy Castle Lung Cancer Fndn 1998; *Recreations* private flying, music, theatre, football; *Style*— Sir Philip Carter, CBE; ✉ Oak Cottage, Noctorum Road, Noctorum, Wirral, Cheshire CH43 9UQ

CARTER, Philip Mark (Phil); s of Brian Carter, of Norwich, Norfolk, and Barbara Mary, *née* Herod; *b* 26 September 1955; *Educ* Thorpe GS Norwich, Great Yarmouth Coll of Art, Norwich Sch of Art (BA), RCA (MA); *m* 1984, Deborah, da of David Catford; 1 s (Joseph b 1985), 1 da (Caitlin b 1989); *Career* designer Minale Tattersfield & Partners 1980–83, fndr ptnr/creative dir Carter Wong Tomlin 1984–; work featured in various pubns incl: D&AD Annual 1983, 1985, 1988, 1989, 1990, 1994, 1995, 1999, 2000, 2001, 2002, 2003, 2004 and 2005, Graphis Annual 1996; D&AD Silver Award (Heal's Corp Identity) 1983, Media Natura Award (Marine Conservation Identity) 1988, DBA Design Effectiveness Awards winner 1999, D&AD Silver Award nomination 2002 and 2003, Design Week Award 2003, DBA Design Effectiveness Awards winner 2004; external assessor: Bath Coll of HE 1991–96, Kingston Univ 1994–97, Dept of Communication Art and Design RCA; memb: Exec Ctee D&AD 1992–94, D&AD Jury 2000, 2002, 2003, 2004 and 2005, DBA, SCR RCA; *Recreations* swimming, cycling, tennis; *Style*— Phil Carter; ✉ Carter Wong, 29 Brook Mews North, London W2 3BW (tel 020 7569 0000, fax 020 7569 0001, e-mail p.carter@carterwongtomlin.com)

CARTER, Ronald (Ron); OBE (1999); s of Harry Victor (d 1969), of Rednal, and Ruth, *née* Allensen (d 1976); *b* 3 June 1926, Edgbaston, Birmingham; *Educ* Birmingham Coll of Art and Design (NDD, Louisa Anne Ryland Scholarship), RCA (DesRCA (Furniture), Silver Medal, Corning Scholarship USA); *m* 1985, Ann, *née* Willingale; 3 da from previous m (Michele b 1956, Carol b 1958, Ruth b 1960); *Career* designer; work with consultancies 1954–80: Lupton Morton Furniture, Stag, Consort, Peak, Collins & Hayes, Gordon Russell; fndr: Miles Carter 1980, Ron Carter Design Ltd 1998; other work incl: Interna Chicago USA 1995, Opus Magnum 1996, BeZone Japan 1997; sr fell RCA 1994 (hon fell 1974); FCSD 1961, FRSA 1973, RDI 1974; *Commercial and Public Commissions* incl: BBC, Br Airports Authy, FCO, Design Cncl, Design Cncl Edinburgh, Lord Chllr's Office, V&A, IOD, Law Soc, Standard Chartered Bank, Nat Gall, Clore Gall Tate, Harvard Univ, JP Morgan, Br Library, Br Pavillion Expo 92 Seville, Hinxton Hall Wellcome Tst, Mead Gall Univ of Warwick, HM The Queen, 2 Temple Gdns, Brick Ct Chambers, New Nature Museum Chicago, St Catherine's Coll Oxford; *Style*— Ron Carter, Esq, OBE, RDI, DesRCA, FCSD

CARTER, Stephen Andrew; CBE (2007); s of Mr and Mrs G R Carter, of Pitlochry; *b* 12 February 1964; *Educ* Univ of Aberdeen (LLB), Harvard Business Sch (AMP); *m* Anna Maria, da of Kevin and Joan Gorman; 1 s (Max Gorman Alexander b 11 Oct 1996), 1 da (Ellie Gorman Imogen b 7 Feb 1999); *Career* md/ceo JWT UK Gp Ltd 1995–2000; md and chief operating offr NTL UK and Ireland 2000–03, chief exec Ofcom 2003–06, gp chief exec Brunswick Gp 2007–; non-exec dir Travis Perkins, non-exec dir Royal Mail 2007–; chm Mktg Gp of GB 2005–06; vice-pres Unicef, chm elect Ashridge Tst; *Style*— Stephen Carter, Esq, CBE; ✉ Brunswick Group LLP, 16 Lincoln's Inn Fields, London WC2A 3ED

CARTER, Will; *b* 30 November 1956, Madras, India; *Educ* Malvern, Jesus Coll Oxford (BA); *m*; 1 c; *Career* United Biscuits (UK) Ltd: mktg trainee/asst product mangr 1979–81, product mangr/sr product mangr 1981–84, brand gp mangr/sr brand gp mangr 1984–86, mktg controller McVities 1986–89, mktg dir Terry's Group 1989–93 (business devpt dir April-Oct 1989), UK mktg dir KP Foods Group 1993–96 (mktg devpt dir July-Oct 1993), dir of snacks KP Foods 1996–98, mktg dir McVitie's UK 1998–99, md KP Foods Group 1999–2001, md Snacks Category 2001–03, md UBUK 2003–04; *Recreations* family, motorcycles, skiing, hill walking; *Style*— Will Carter, Esq

CARTER, Prof Yvonne Helen; OBE (2000); da of Percival Anthony Daniel Carter (decd), and Ellen, *née* Bore (decd); *b* 16 April 1959; *Educ* St Mary's Hosp Med Sch London (BSc, MB BS), DRCOG, DCH, MD (London); *m* 21 May 1988, Dr Michael Joseph Bannon, s of Christopher Bannon (decd); 1 s (Christopher Anthony Michael b 30 Dec 1989); *Career* jr hosp appts St Charles' Hosp London, Warrington Dist Gen Hosp and Walton & Fazakerley Hosps Liverpool, GP trainee Maghull Health Centre Merseyside 1986–87; parity princ in shared gen practice: Stoneycroft Liverpool 1987–90, Newcastle-under-Lyme Staffs 1990–93; hon research fell Centre of Epidemiology, Public Health Med and Primary Health Care Keele Univ 1990–92, sr lectr Dept of Gen Practice Univ of Birmingham 1992–96, pt/t med advsr Staffs then Walsall FHSA 1992–94, pt/t clinical asst Bellevue Surgery Edgbaston 1993–96, pt/t GP tutor Queen Elizabeth Postgrad Med Centre Edgbaston 1994–96, prof and head Dept of Gen Practice and Primary Care Barts and the London Queen Mary's Sch of Med and Dentistry Univ of London 1996–2003, pt/t princ in shared practice Chrisp Street Health Centre E London 1997–2003, head of Div Community Sciences, Barts and the London Queen Mary's Sch of Med and Dentistry Univ of London 2001–03, vice-dean Leicester Warwick Med Schs 2003–06, academic GP and hon conslt in primary care Coventry Primary Care Tst 2003–, dean Warwick Med Sch Univ of Warwick 2004–, non-exec dir Univ Hosps of Coventry and Warwickshire NHS Tst 2004–; RCGP: memb Cncl 1994–2004, memb Cncl Exec Ctee 1996–2000, chair of research 1996–2000, dir of Meds Surveillance Orgn 1996–2000, memb Scientific Fndn Bd 1997–99; govr Health Fndn 1999–2007, memb Cncl Acad of Med Sciences 2007–; author of papers in academic and professional jls; memb Editorial Bd: Medical Education Review 1996–99, Palliative Medicine 1997–; hon fell Queen Mary's Sch Univ of London 2004; FRSA 1996, FRSM 1997, fndr FMedSci 1998, FRCGP; *Books* Research Methods in Primary Care (jt ed, 1996), Handbook of Sexual Health in Primary Care (jtly, 1996, 2 edn 2006), Handbook of Palliative Care (jtly, 1997, 2 edn 2005), Practical Peadiatric Problems in Primary Care (jt ed, 2007); also contrib to edited works; *Style*— Prof Yvonne H Carter, OBE; ✉ Warwick Medical School, The University of Warwick, Coventry CV4 7AL (tel 024 7657 3080, fax 024 7657 3079, e-mail yvonne.carter@warwick.ac.uk)

CARTER-MEGGS, Jonathan Charles; s of John Anthony Carter-Meggs (d 1996), of East Dereham, Norfolk, and June Dorothy, *née* Carter; *b* 24 August 1960; *Educ* Univ of Bristol (BSc); *m* 28 July 1984, Claire Louise, *née* Hutley; 2 da (Camilla Louise b 29 Jan 1990, Sophia Fleur b 9 March 1993); *Career* with Anderson Consulting 1981–85, dir Chase Manhattan Bank Private Equity 1985–96, sr ptnr and gp head JP Morgan Partners 1996–2006; dir: Life Assurance Holding Corp 1994–2006 (chm), Mobifon SA 1998–2006, TIW Czech NV 1999–2006, M&H Plastics Ltd 2003–06, Siteco Finanzierungs GmBH 2003–06; involved with Prince's Tst Business Mentor Prog; FRSA; *Recreations* golf, scuba, tennis, flying; *Clubs* Home House, Chinawhite, Wisley Golf; *Style*— Jonathan Carter-Meggs, Esq, FRSA; ✉ tel 07710 019262, e-mail jonathan@carter-meggs.com

CARTER-STEPHENSON, George Anthony; QC (1998); s of Raymond M Stephenson, and Brenda S Carter; *b* 10 July 1952; *Educ* Arnold Sch Blackpool, Univ of Leeds (LLB); *m* 1974, Christine Maria; 1 s (Christian James b 31 Jan 1977), 1 da (Sarah Louise b 22 April 1981); *Career* called to the Bar Inner Temple 1975; *Recreations* motorcycling, theatre, cinema, music; *Style*— George Carter-Stephenson, Esq, QC; ✉ 25 Bedford Row, London WC1R 4HD (tel 020 7067 1500, fax 020 7067 1507)

CARTHY, Eliza Amy Forbes; da of Martin Carthy, MBE, of Robin Hood's Bay, N Yorks, and Norma Waterson, MBE; *b* 23 August 1975, Scarborough, N Yorks; *Educ* Fylinghall Sch, Scarborough Sixth Form Coll; *Partner* Benedict Ivitsky Molleson; *Career* self-employed musician 1993–; concerts incl: Getty Museum LA, Royal Albert Hall, St Paul's Cathedral, tours of Europe, America, Australia, Hong Kong and Japan, concerts for Br Cncl in Bolivia, Peru and Spain, concerts for Unison, Reclaim the Streets, Folkworks and Cuba Solidarity Campaign; memb: Lab Pty, Greenpeace, Musicians' Union; ambass Vagina Monolgues' V-Day; *Albums* with Nancy Kerr: Eliza Carthy & Nancy Kerr 1993, Shape of Scrape 1995; with Waterson:Carthy (with Martin Carthy, MBE, and Norma Waterson, MBE): Waterson:Carthy 1994, Common Tongue 1996, Broken Ground 1998, A Dark Light 2000, Fishes & Fine Yellow Sand 2004; solo albums:

Heat, Light & Sound 1996, Red Rice 1998, Angels & Cigarettes 2000, Anglicana 2002; appeared on Billy Bragg/Wilco album Mermaid Avenue 1998 (nominated Grammy Award); *Awards* nominated Mercury Music Prize (for Red Rice) 1998 and (for Anglicana) 2002, Track of the Year 1999, Best Group and Best Album BBC2 Folk Awards 2001, Best Folk Singer of the Year, Best Album (for Angelicana) and Best Traditional Track Award BBC Radio 2 Folk Awards 2003, Album of the Year Classic Rock Soc 2003; *Style*— Miss Eliza Carthy; ✉ c/o The Stables, Westwood House, Main Street, North Dalton, East Yorkshire YO25 9XA (tel 01377 217815, e-mail nigel@adastey.demon.co.uk)

CARTLEDGE, Graham Stanley; s of Thomas S Cartledge (d 1967), and Doris B Cartledge (d 1991); *b* 7 January 1947; *Educ* Magnus Boys GS Newark, Leics Sch of Architecture (DipArch); *m* 31 July 1972, Jo, da of J W Booth; 2 s (Ben b 17 March 1978, Tom b 15 June 1979), 1 da (Amy b 21 July 1984); *Career* architect; sr ptnr Gordon Benoy & Partners 1975–88 (merged with Fitch & Co 1992); chm and md Benoy, responsible for buildings in UK, Hong Kong, Spain, Portugal, Holland, Sweden and Greece; maj fund-raiser for Cancer Research, supporter of local hospice Save The Children Fund; RIBA 1972, FCSD 1990; *Recreations* golf, cricket, football; *Clubs* Nottingham Forest FC (life vice-pres); *Style*— Graham Cartledge, Esq; ✉ Benoy Ltd, 210 High Holborn, London WC1V 7DL (tel 020 7404 7666, fax 020 7404 7980, e-mail graham.cartledge@benoy.co.uk)

CARTLEDGE, Prof Paul Anthony; s of Marcus Raymond Cartledge (d 1990), and Margaret Christobel Cartledge (d 2000); *b* 24 March 1947; *Educ* St Paul's (fndn scholar), New Coll Oxford (Ella Stephens open scholar, MA, DPhil); *Career* Craven fell Univ of Oxford 1969–70, Salvesen jr res fell Univ Coll Oxford 1970–72, lectr in classics New Univ of Ulster 1972–73, lectr in classics Trinity Coll Dublin 1973–78, lectr in classical civilization Univ of Warwick 1978–79; Univ of Cambridge: lectr in classics 1979–93, fell Clare Coll 1981– (professorial fell 1999–), reader in Greek history 1993–99, prof of Greek history 1999–, chm Faculty of Classics 2001–02; Hellenic Parl global distinguished prof NYU 2006–; invited speaker at numerous int confs and symposia; pres Cambridge Philological Soc 1994–96, memb Br Ctee for the Reunification of the Parthenon Marbles; awarded Leverhulme Tst research grant 1982; FSA 1980; Golden Cross of Honour (Greece) 2002, Hon Citizen of Sparta Greece 2005; *Books* Sparta and Lakonia: a regional history 1300–362 BC (1979, 2 edn 2001), CRUX: Essays in Greek History presented to G E M de Ste Croix on his 75th birthday (co-ed and contrib, 1985), Agesilaos and the Crisis of Sparta (1987), Hellenistic and Roman Sparta: a tale of two cities (jtly, 1989, revised edn 2001), Aristophanes and his Theatre of the Absurd (1990, revised edn 1999), NOMOS: Essays in Athenian Law, Politics and Society (co-ed and contrib, 1990), L Bruit Zaidman & P Schmitt-Pantel: Religion in the Ancient Greek City (ed and trans, 1992), The Greeks. A Portrait of Self and Others (1993, 2 edn 2002), Hellenistic Constructs: Essays in culture, history, and historiography (co-ed and contrib, 1997), The Cambridge Illustrated History of Ancient Greece (creator, ed and contrib, 1997), Xenophon: Hiero the Tyrant and Other Treatises (jtly, 1997, revised edn 2006), KOSMOS: Essays in Athenian Order, Conflict and Community (co-ed and contrib, 1998), Democritus and Atomistic Politics (1998), The Greeks: Crucible of Civilization (2000), Spartan Reflections (2001), Money, Labour and Land. Approaches to the economies of ancient Greece (co-ed and contrib, 2001), The Spartans: An Epic History (2002, 2 edn 2003), Alexander the Great: The hunt for a new past (2004), Thermopylae: The Battle That Changed the World (2006); *Recreations* theatre, ballet, opera; *Style*— Prof Paul Cartledge; ✉ Clare College, Cambridge CB2 1TL (tel 01223 333265, fax 01223 845808, e-mail pac1001@cam.ac.uk); Faculty of Classics, Sidgwick Avenue, Cambridge CB3 9DA (fax 01223 335409)

CARTWRIGHT, Jim; s of Jim Cartwright, of Farnworth, Lancs, and Edna, *née* Main; *b* 27 June 1958; *Educ* Harper Green Secdy Sch Farnworth; *m* Angela Louise, da of Samuel Jones; 2 s (James Lewis b 22 Oct 1984, Samuel Aaron b 2 May 1998), 2 da (Georgina Lucy b 12 June 1996, Charlotte Emily (twin) b 2 May 1998); *Career* writer; *Plays* Road (performed Royal Court Theatre 1986–87, adapted for BBC TV 1987), Baths (radio, 1987), Vroom (film on Channel 4, 1988), Bed (RNT 1989), TWO (Octagon Bolton and Young Vic London 1989–90), June (BBC TV 1990), Wedded (BBC TV 1990), The Rise and Fall of Little Voice (RNT then Aldwych 1992), I Licked a Slag's Deodorant (Royal Court at the Ambassadors 1996), Prize Night (Royal Exchange 1999), Hard Fruit (Royal Court 2000), Strumpet (BBC 2002), Vacuuming Completely Nude In Paradise (BBC 2002); *Awards* for Road: Samuel Beckett Award, Drama Magazine Award, jt winner George Devine Award and Plays and Players Award, Golden Nymph Award for Best Film at Monte Carlo TV and Film Festival; for TWO: Manchester Evening News Theatre Award for Best New Play; for The Rise and Fall of Little Voice: Best Comedy Evening Standard Drama Awards 1992, Best Comedy Laurence Olivier Awards 1993; *Style*— Jim Cartwright, Esq; ✉ AJ Associates, Department C, Higher Healey House, Higher House Lane, White Coppice, Chorley, Lancashire PR6 9BT

CARTWRIGHT, John Wallace; s of Reginald Cartwright (d 1982), of Cambridge, and Iris Marion, *née* Dear (d 1992); *b* 10 March 1946; *Educ* Bedford Sch, Cranfield Mgmnt Sch (MBA); *m* 1973, Christine Elise, da of Jack Whitaker, of Newbury; 1 s (Timothy b 1975), 2 da (Genevieve b 1978, Bethany b 1980); *Career* emerging mkts, banking and investment mgmnt; former marketing dir Ashmore Invest Mgmnt (formerly ANZ Emerging Mkts Fund Mgmnt)ır: ANZ Invest Bank Ltd 1989, Grindlay Brandts Ltd 1985, ANZ Grindlays 3i Invest services Ltd 1989, Second India Invest Fund Ltd 1990, Matlock Bank Ltd 2002; FCIB; *Recreations* gardening, golf and travel; *Style*— John Cartwright, Esq; ✉ 16 Millfield, Berkhamsted HP4 2PB (tel 01442 864984)

CARTWRIGHT, Prof Nancy Delaney; *b* 24 June 1944; *Educ* Univ of Pittsburgh (BS), Univ of Illinois (Carnegie fell, Danforth fell, Woodrow Wilson fell, PhD); *Career* asst prof of philosophy Univ of Maryland 1971–73; Stanford Univ: asst prof of philosophy 1973–77, assoc prof 1977–83, prof 1983–91, chair Philosophy Dept 1988–90; LSE: prof of philosophy, logic and scientific method 1991–, dir Centre for Philosophy of Nat and Social Science 1993–; prof of philosophy Univ of Calif San Diego 1997–; visiting lectr Univ of Cambridge 1974, visiting asst prof UCLA 1976, visiting assoc prof Princeton Univ 1978, visiting prof Univ of Pittsburgh 1984, short term visiting prof Univ of Oslo 1993 and 1994; fell: Center for Interdisciplinary Research (ZiF) Bielefeld Germany 1976–77 (memb Advsy Bd 1993–), Philosophy of Science Center Univ of Pittsburgh 1982–83 and 1984, Wissenschaftskolleg Berlin 1987–88 (memb Advsy Bd 1991–96); pres: Soc for Exact Philosophy 1985, American Assoc of Univ Profs Stanford Chapter 1986–87; MacArthur Fndn Award 1993; memb Deutsche Akademie der Naturforscher Leopoldina 1999–; Old Dominion fell Princeton Univ 1996; memb: American Acad of Arts and Scis 2001, American Philosophical Soc 2004; FBA 1996; *Books* How the Laws of Physics Lie (1983), Nature's Capacities and their Measurement (1989), Otto Neurath: Philosophy between Science and Politics (jtly, 1995), The Dappled World - A Study of the Boundaries of Science (1999), Measuring Causes: Invariance, Modularity and Causal Markov Condition (2000); also author of numerous articles in learned jls; *Style*— Prof Nancy Cartwright, FBA; ✉ Department of Philosophy, Logic, and Scientific Method, London School of Economics and Political Science, Houghton Street, London WC2A 2AE (tel 020 7955 7341/7901, fax 020 7955 6845)

CARTWRIGHT, Rt Rev Richard Fox; s of Rev George Frederick Cartwright (vicar of Plumstead, d 1938), and Constance Margaret, *née* Clark (d 1975); *b* 10 November 1913; *Educ* The King's Sch Canterbury, Pembroke Coll Cambridge (MA), Cuddesdon Theol Coll; *m* 6 Sept 1947, Rosemary Magdalen (d 2003), da of Francis Evelyn Bray (d 1973), of Woodham Grange, Surrey; 1 s (Andrew Martin b 1948), 3 da (Rosemary Jane (Mrs Turner) b 1951, Mary Katharine (Mrs Bradley) b 1953, Susan Margaret (Mrs Meikle) b 1958); *Career* curate St Anselm Kennington Cross 1936–40, princ Lower Kingswood 1940–45; vicar: St Andrew Surbiton 1945–52, St Mary Redcliffe Bristol 1952–72 (with Temple 1956–72 and St John Bedminster 1965–72); hon canon Bristol 1960–72, suffragan bishop of Plymouth 1972–81; asst bishop: Diocese of Truro 1982–91, Diocese of Exeter 1988–; proctor in convocation 1950–52, memb Gen Synod C of E 1976–80; dir: Ecclesiastical Insurance Gp 1964–85, All Churches Tst 1985–91; chm of govrs Kelly Coll Tavistock 1973–88, govr Summerfields Sch Oxford 1964–88; Grand Chaplain United Grand Lodge of England 1973–75; Hon DD Univ of the South Tennessee 1969; OStJ 1957; *Recreations* fly fishing, gardening, water colour painting; *Clubs* Army and Navy; *Style*— The Rt Rev Richard Cartwright; ✉ 5 Old Vicarage Close, Ide, Devon EX2 9RE (tel 01392 211270)

CARTWRIGHT, Sally Amanda; OBE (2001); da of Dennis Cartwright (d 1990), and Eileen Sergeant Cartwright (d 1979); *b* 8 May 1944; *Educ* Merton House Sch Keymer; *m* 1, 23 Feb 1973, John William Robinson; m 2, 29 Feb 1980, John Brian Hutchings; *Career* sec 1961–69; IPC Magazines: merchandising exec 1970, promotions exec 1971–76, publicity mangr 1976–79, asst publisher 1979–82, publisher 1983–86; md: Capital Magazine 1987, Harmsworth Publications (pt of Assoc Newspapers) 1988–90; publishing dir Hello! magazine 1990–; pres Women's Advtg Club of London 1992–93, assoc Women of the Year Luncheon; chm: PPA 1998–2000, Environmental Ctee Int Fedn of the Periodical Press (FIPP); memb Cncl Advtg Standards Authy 2007–; *Recreations* reading, embroidery, skiing, swimming, opera, theatre; *Clubs* Ski Club of GB (chm and pres 2001–05); *Style*— Ms Sally Cartwright, OBE; ✉ Hello! Ltd, Wellington House, 69/71 Upper Ground, London SE1 9PQ (tel 020 7667 8751, fax 020 7667 8742)

CARTY, Dr Austin Timothy; s of Dr Thomas James Augustine (Gus) Carty (d 1975), of Glasnevin, Dublin, and Dr Catherine Anne Carty, *née* Quinn (d 1981); *b* 22 June 1941; *Educ* Belvedere Coll Dublin, UCD (MB BCh, BAO); *m* 23 Sept 1967, Prof Helen Carty, DL, *qv*, da of Roland Moloney (d 1971), of Dun Laoghaire, Co Dublin and Dungarvan, Co Waterford; 1 s (Timothy b 1968), 2 da (Jennifer b 1970, Sarah b 1973); *Career* conslt radiologist Liverpool HA 1974–2004 (ret), clinical sub-dean Univ of Liverpool at Royal Liverpool Hosp 1987–90, chm Dist Med Advsy Ctee Liverpool HA 1989–90, med dir Royal Liverpool Univ Hosp NHS Tst 1991–95; Liverpool Med Inst: pres 1990–91, ed Transactions 1991–97, hon librarian 1995–99, appeal dir 1996–97; memb Advsy Ctee Marie Curie Centre Liverpool 2000–03; hon staff pres Liverpool Med Students' Soc 1999–2000; FRCR, FRCPI; *Recreations* dinghy sailing, opera, wine, salmon fishing; *Clubs* Athenaeum, Twenty (Liverpool) (pres 1990–91), Innominate (Liverpool), Artists (Liverpool) (pres 1996–97, hon wine steward 2000–, hon sec 2001–); *Style*— Dr Austin Carty; ✉ 6 Grosvenor Road, Cressington Park, Liverpool L19 0PL (tel 0151 427 6727, fax 0151 494 9182, e-mail austincarty@btinternet.com)

CARTY, Prof Helen; DL (Merseyside 2005); da of Roland Moloney (d 1971), of Dublin, and Honor, *née* Frame (d 1982); *b* 12 May 1944; *Educ* St Mary's Arklow Co Wicklow, UCD (MB BCh, BAO); *m* 23 Sept 1967, Dr Austin Carty, *qv*, s of Dr Thomas J A Carty (d 1975), of Dublin; 1 s (Timothy Mark b 13 Oct 1968), 2 da (Jennifer Ann b 29 Aug 1970, Sarah Lucy b 7 Feb 1973); *Career* house offr and med registrar Mater Hosp Dublin 1967–71, registrar in radiology St Thomas' Hosp London 1971–74, sr registrar Broadgreen Hosp Liverpool 1974–75, clinical dir radiology Alder Hey Hosp Liverpool 1977–2001 (conslt radiologist 1975–2004); prof of paediatric radiology Univ of Liverpool 1996–2004; chm Intercollegiate Standing Ctee on Nuclear Med London 1989–95; pres Liverpool Med Instn 1993–94; RCR: sometime memb Bd of Faculty, Cncl and Educn Bd, examiner Final Fellowship 1988–91; memb Steering Ctee for monitoring Nat Breast Screening Prog Dept of Health 1987–96, warden RCR 1998–2002, pres Euro Congress of Radiology 2003–04 (chm Exec Bd 2004–05); *Books* Imaging Children: A Textbook of Paediatric Radiology (jt ed and author of several chapters, 1994; 2 edn, ed-in-chief and author of chapters, 2004), Emergency Paediatric Radiology (1999), Paediatric Ultrasound (ed, 2000), The Encyclopedia of Medical Imaging - Vol VII: Paediatrics (2001); *Recreations* birdwatching, theatre, cooking; *Style*— Prof Helen Carty, DL; ✉ 6 Grosvenor Road, Cressington Park, Liverpool L19 0PL (tel 0151 427 6727, fax 0151 494 9182)

CARTY, Hilary; da of Solomon Carty, of London, and Catherine, *née* Bailey; *b* 26 May 1962; *Educ* Waverley Girls Sch, Leicester Poly (BA), Cultural Trg Centre Jamaica (Cert Dance Educn), Univ of Westminster (MBA); *Career* community arts devpt offr Leicester Expressive Arts 1984–86, dance and mime offr E Midlands Arts 1986–90, gen mangr Adzido 1990–94, Arts Cncl of England: dir of dance 1994–2003, dir of performing arts 2003–04, seconded as dir of culture and educn London 2012 (Olympic Bid) 2004–05, dir London Arts 2005–06; dir Cultural Leadership Prog 2006–; Hon Dr of Arts De Montfort Univ 2001; FRSA 1996; *Books* Folk Dances of Jamaica (1988); *Style*— Ms Hilary Carty; ✉ Cultural Leadership Programme, Lafone House, The Leathermarket, Weston Street, London SE1 3HN

CARUS, Louis Revell; s of Lt-Col Martin MacDowall Carus-Wilson, RAEC (d 1969), and Enid Madeleine Thaxter, *née* Revell (d 1973); *b* 22 October 1927; *Educ* Rugby, Brussels Conservatoire of Music, Peabody Conservatory of Music (USA); *m* 11 July 1951, Nancy Reade, da of Percival Edward Noell (d 1981), of Durham, N Carolina, USA; 2 s (Kenneth Edward b 20 Feb 1953, Colin Martin b 4 Sept 1956), 1 da (Alison Noell (Mrs L J Du Cane) b 29 May 1955); *Career* violinist, teacher and administrator; memb Scot Nat Orch 1950–55, head of strings Royal Scot Acad of Music and Drama 1955–75, princ of Faculty Birmingham Sch of Music (now Birmingham Conservatoire) 1975–87, artistic dir Int String Quartet Week 1985–, conslt Benslow Tst Musical Instrument Loan Scheme 1987–; former pres ISM, former chm Euro String Teachers' Assoc (Br Branch), hon fell Univ of Central England; FRCM, FRSAMD, FBSM, Hon RAM; *Recreations* gardening, walking, travel, voluntary work; *Clubs* Rotary Int; *Style*— Louis Carus, Esq

CARUSO, Adam; *Educ* McGill Univ Montreal; *Career* architect; early career with Florian Beigel and Arup Assocs; co-fndr (with Peter St John) Caruso St John Architects 1990–; major projects: New Art Gallery Walsall, Brick House London, Stortorget Sweden, Gagosian Gallery London, Museum of Childhood London; prof of architecture Univ of Bath 2002–04; teacher: Univ of N London 1990–2000, Grad Sch of Design Harvard Univ 2005; visiting prof: Acad of Architecture Mendrisio Switzerland 1999–2001, LSE 2005–08, ETH Zürich 2007–09; *Style*— Adam Caruso, Esq; ✉ Caruso St John Architects, 1 Coate Street, London E2 9AG (tel 020 7613 3161, fax 020 7729 6188)

CARVELL, John Edward; s of Robert Charles Carvell (d 1984), and Ivy, *née* Dutch (d 1987); *b* 30 May 1946; *Educ* Perth Acad, Univ of St Andrews (MB ChB), Univ of Dundee (MMSc); *m* 22 July 1972, Carol, da of Gilbert D Ritchie, of Broughty Ferry, Dundee; 1 da (Claire b 1976), 1 s (Robin b 1979); *Career* registrar in orthopaedics Royal United Hosps Bath 1976–77, sr registrar in orthopaedics Nuffield Orthopaedic Centre Oxford and John Radcliffe Hosp Oxford 1978–83, conslt orthopaedic and trauma surgn Salisbury Dist Hosp 1983–2001 (emeritus conslt spinal and orthopaedic surgn 2001–), hon visiting conslt Royal United Hospital Bath 2002–07; sr MO Larkhill Point-to-Point Racecourse 2001–06; BMA: chm Wessex Regnl Conslts and Specialists Ctee 1997–2001 (hon sec 1994–97), memb CCSC 2001–, chm Orthopaedic Sub-Ctee CCSC 2003– (rep 1995–99 and 2001–2002), memb Private Practice Ctee, dep Medico-Legal Ctee; Br Orthopaedic Assoc: memb Cncl 2002–04, memb Medico-Legal Ctee 2004– (memb 2003–04), memb Professional Practice Ctee; memb Nat Orthopaedic Project Team DHS, gov Salisbury Dist Hosp Fndn Tst 2006–; tutor RCS 1996–2000; dist pres Arthritis Research Campaign; memb Int Soc of Arthroscopy Knee Surgery and Orthopaedic Sports Med; FRCSEd 1976, FRCS (ad eundem) 1997, FBOA 1983, fell Br Scoliosis Soc 1988; *Recreations* music, gardening, tennis; *Style—* John Carvell, Esq; ✉ Newstead, 143 Bouverie Avenue South, Salisbury, Wiltshire SP2 8EB (tel 01722 330519); New Hall Hospital, The Lodge, Bodenham, Salisbury SP5 4EY (tel 01722 435168)

CARVER, (James) John; s of James Carver, and Jean Mary, *née* Kerry; *b* 28 September 1957; *Educ* Dulwich Coll, Canterbury Coll of Art; *m* 1, 1987; m 2 1997; *Career* md designate J Carver & Co 1977–79, account exec International Marketing & Promotions (pt of the Masius Gp) 1979–81, creative exec Promotional Marketing Limited (pt of O & M) 1981–82, freelance art dir and writer 1982–85, creative dir and fndr ptnr The Leisure Process 1985–97, fndr Harry Monk creative consultancy and Cunning Stunts media co 1997–; winner various advtg prizes and awards from the music indust and mktg/advtg sector 1985–91; *Books* Duran Duran (1985), Michael Jackson (1985); *Recreations* marlin fishing, hot air ballooning, historic car racing, classic car collecting, carp fishing, aerobics, Thai boxing, travel, origami, Ntse Tui and wakebayne (mental arts), natural healing, skydiving, running marathons; *Style—* John Carver

CARVER, Wyndham Houssemayne; s of Capt Edmund Squarey Carver, DSC, RN (d 2001), and Freda Wilmot Houssemayne, *née* Du Boulay (d 1970); *b* 4 May 1943; *Educ* Malvern Coll, Harvard Business Sch (PMD); *m* 1 (m dis), Jocelyn Mary Anne, da of Graham Rogers, of Hyde, Hants; m 2, Shona Leslie, da of Maj Ian McKillop, of East Cholderton, Hants; 1 da (Tamsin b 7 Sept 1985); *Career* International Distillers & Vintners (subsid of Grand Metropolitan) 1965–97, Hunters and Frankau Ltd 1997–2001, business assoc 2001–; *Recreations* tennis, golf, forestry, shooting, travel; *Clubs* Boodle's, IoD; *Style—* Wyndham Carver, Esq; ✉ Rondle Wood House, Milland, Liphook, Hampshire GU30 7LA (tel 01730 821397, fax 01730 821136, e-mail wyndhamcarver@carverw.com)

CARVILLE, Fiona Mary; da of Cdr David Leslie Gordon (d 1984), and Anne Josephine, *née* Haywood (d 1999); *b* 2 June 1951; *Educ* Hurst Lodge Sunningdale, Beechlawn Tutorial Coll Oxford; *Career* dir: Brook-Hart Advertising Ltd 1980–85, Hewland Consultants International Ltd 1980–85; md First Public Relations Ltd 1985–; MCIPR, MIPA; *Clubs* Morton's, Teatro; *Style—* Mrs Fiona Carville; ✉ First Public Relations Ltd, Molasses House, Clove Hitch Quay, Plantation Wharf, London SW11 3TN (tel 020 7978 5233, fax 020 7924 3134, e-mail fiona@firstpr.co.uk)

CARWARDINE, Prof Richard John; s of John Francis Carwardine (d 2005), and Beryl, *née* Jones (d 2001); *b* 12 January 1947, Cardiff; *Educ* Monmouth Sch, CCC Oxford (William Jones exhibitioner, MA), The Queen's Coll Oxford (Ochs-Oakes sr scholar, DPhil), Univ of Calif Berkeley; *m* 17 May 1975, Dr Linda Margaret Kirk; *Career* historian; Univ of Sheffield: lectr, sr lectr then reader in American history 1971–94, prof of history 1994–2002, dean Faculty of Arts 1999–2001; Rhodes prof of American history Univ of Oxford 2002–, fell St Catherine's Coll Oxford 2002–; visiting asst prof Syracuse Univ NY 1974–75, visiting fell Univ of N Carolina at Chapel Hill 1989; Birkbeck lectr Trinity Coll Cambridge 2004, Stenton lectr Univ of Reading 2004; Arthur Miller American Studies Prize 1997, Lincoln Prize 2004; Leverhulme Tst Res Fellowship 2001–04; FRHistS 1983, FBA 2006; *Publications* Transatlantic Revivalism: Popular Evangelicalism in Britain and America 1790–1865 (1978), Evangelicals and Politics in Antebellum America (1993), Lincoln (2003, revised edn 2006); author of numerous articles in learned jls; *Recreations* acting, theatre-going, walking; *Style—* Prof Richard Carwardine, FBA; ✉ St Catherine's College, Oxford OX1 3UJ (tel 01865 271798, e-mail richard.carwardine@history.ox.ac.uk)

CARWOOD, Andrew; s of Thomas George Carwood (d 1973), and Daisy Ninnes (d 1991); *b* 30 April 1965; *Educ* John Lyon Sch Harrow, St John's Coll Cambridge (choral scholar); *Career* singer and conductor; artistic dir Edington Music Festival 1991–97, memb Cncl Plainsong and Medieval Music Soc 1997–2001; winner Gramophone Early Music Award 1995; hon fell Acad of St Cecilia; assoc RSCM; *Singer* lay clerk: Christ Church Oxford 1987–90, Westminster Cathedral 1990–95; solo and consort work with: The Tallis Scholars, The Sixteen, The English Concert, The King's Concert, Finzi Singers, Oxford Camerata, Parley of Instruments, Collegium Musicum 90, City of London Sinfonia, Orch of the Age of Enlightenment, The Monteverdi Choir, Choeur de la Chapelle Royale, Pro Cantione Antiqua, Gabrieli Consort, Acad of Ancient Music, The Schütz Choir; *Conducting* dir of music The London Oratory 1995–2000; dir: The Cardinall's Musick 1989–, The Edington Schola Cantorum 1998–; *Recordings* as singer: works by Hans Leo Hassler, Antonio Vivaldi, Henry Purcell, Franz Josef Haydn, Peter Warlock, Herbert Howells, Leoš Janáček, Christopher Headington; as conductor: works of Nicholas Ludford, Robert Fayrfax, William Cornysh, William Byrd, Thomas Tallis, Giovanni Pierluigi da Palestrina, Tomas Luis de Victoria, Orlandus Lassus, John Merbecke, Sir William Harris; *Recreations* theatre, British comedy, wine; *Style—* Andrew Carwood, Esq; ✉ e-mail a.carwood@cardinallsmusick.com

CARY, HE Anthony Joyce; CMG (1997); s of Sir Michael Cary, GCB, and Lady (Isabel) Cary; *b* 1 July 1951, London; *Educ* Eton, Trinity Coll Oxford (MA), Stanford Business Sch (Harkness fell, MBA); *m* 1975, Clare, *née* Elworthy; 3 s (Sam b 1978, Tom b 1980, Arthur b 1983), 1 da (Harriet b 1985); *Career* entered HM Dip Serv 1973; served: Br Military Government Berlin 1974–77, Policy Planning Staff FCO 1978–80, EC Dept FCO 1982–84; private sec to min of state FCO 1984–86, head of Chancery Kuala Lumpur 1986–88, on loan to Cabinet of Sir Leon Brittan (now Baron Brittan of Spennithorne, PC, QC, DL (Life Peer), *qv*) European Cmmn 1989–82, head EU Dept FCO 1993–96, cnsllr Washington DC 1997–99, on loan as chef de cabinet to Rt Hon Chris Patten, CH (now The Rt Hon the Lord Patten of Barnes, CH, PC, *qv*), European Cmmn 1999–2003, ambass to Sweden 2003–07, high cmmr to Canada 2007–; *Style—* HE Mr Anthony Cary, CMG; ✉ c/o Foreign & Commonwealth Office (Ottawa), King Charles Street, London SW1A 2AH (e-mail anthony.cary@fco.gov.uk)

CARY, Sir Roger Hugh; 2 Bt (UK 1955); s of Sir Robert Archibald Cary, 1 Bt (d 1979), sometime MP for Eccles and Manchester (Withington), PPS to Capt Harry Crookshank 1951–55; *b* 8 January 1926; *Educ* Eton, New Coll Oxford (BA); *m* 1, 1948 (m dis 1951), Marilda (d 1996), da of Maj Philip Pearson-Gregory, MC; 1 da (Marcia Susan (Hon Mrs Robin Gibson-Watt) b 1949); m 2, 1953, Ann Helen Katharine, eldest da of Hugh Blair Brenan, OBE; 2 s (Nicolas Robert Hugh b 1955, Dr (Roger) Nathaniel Blair b 1957), 1 da (Charlotte Rhoda Rosamond (Mrs David Mayou) b 1960); *Heir* s, Nicolas Cary; *Career* served Grenadier Gds 1944–47 (Signals Offr Gds' Trg Bn 1946–47); former sub ed and leader writer The Times and dep ed The Listener, sr asst then special asst (public affairs) BBC 1972–77, special asst to md BBC TV 1977–82, chief asst to dir of programming BBC TV 1983–86, conslt to DG BBC 1996–2002; tstee Kedleston 1989–2002; *Recreations* looking at pictures; *Clubs* Pratt's, First Guards', Travellers; *Style—* Sir Roger Cary, Bt

CARY-ELWES, Charles Gervase Rundle; s of Lt-Col Oswald Aloysius Joseph Cary-Elwes (d 1994), and (Elisabeth) Pamela Rundle, *née* Brendon (d 1996); *b* 8 November 1939; *Educ* Ampleforth, Sorbonne, Trinity Coll Oxford (MA); *m* 2 April 1972, Angela Jean, da of Maj Eric Rowland, TD, TA (d 1960); 1 da (Lucy b 1974), 1 s (James b 1976); *Career* stockjobber Durlacher Oldham Mordaunt Godson 1962–65, in film prodn 1965–74, Peat Marwick Mitchell & Co Chartered Accountants 1975–79, corporate finance exec Grieveson Grant & Co 1980–83, Exco International plc 1983–85; chm Br America's Cup Challenge plc 1984; dir: British & Commonwealth Holdings plc 1986–89, Leopold Joseph & Sons Ltd 1991–93, Woolton Elwes Ltd 1993–2004, Orion Publishing Group Ltd 1994–2003, Fiduciary Corp Ltd 1997–, Open Annuities Ltd 2001–; Research, Recommendations and Electronic Voting plc (RREV) 2003–05; hon treas Keats Shelley Memorial Assoc; FCA, CIT; *Recreations* golf, music, theatre, travel; *Clubs* Athenaeum, Rye Golf; *Style—* Charles Cary-Elwes, Esq

CASE, Her Hon Judge Janet Ruth; da of James Anthony Simpson (d 1997), and Cathleen, *née* King; *b* 29 June 1943; *Educ* Univ of Durham (LLB); *m* 1965 (m dis 1982), Jeremy David Michael Case, s of Glyn Pryce (d 1980), of Gunley; 1 da (Charlotte b 1966), 1 s (Edwin b 1969); *Career* called to the Bar Inner Temple 1975, Wales & Chester Circuit 1975; chm Med Appeals Tbnl 1988–97, recorder of the Crown Court 1995–2001, circuit judge (Wales & Chester Circuit) 2001–, designated family judge 2001–05; *Recreations* gardening, opera; *Clubs* Lansdowne; *Style—* Her Hon Judge Case; ✉ The Law Courts, Legh Street, Warrington, Cheshire WA1 1UR

CASE, Prof (Richard) Maynard; s of John (Jack) Case (d 1985), of Stockport, Cheshire, and Joycelyn Mary, *née* Ashcroft (d 2001); *b* 23 July 1943; *Educ* Stockport GS, King's Coll Durham (BSc), Univ of Newcastle upon Tyne (MRC scholar, PhD); *m* 1, 22 Dec 1967, Gillian Mary (d 1997), da of John Guy; m 2, 2 April 2001, Miriam Diane, da of Frank Basil Shaftoe; 1 s (Samuel Thomas b 17 Dec 2004); *Career* Dept of Physiology Univ of Newcastle upon Tyne: lectr 1967–75, sr lectr 1975–76, reader 1976–79; Univ of Manchester: prof of physiology 1979–, head Dept of Physiology 1980–86, head Dept of Physiological Scis 1986–90, dean Sch of Biological Scis 1990–94 and 2001–04, assoc vice-pres 2006–; lectr Inst of Physiology Aarhus Univ 1970–71, Northern regnl tutor Open Univ 1973–75, lectr Dept of Physiology Univ of Sydney 1976–77; res leave fell Wellcome Tst 1994–97; memb: Animal Scis and Psychology Sub-Ctee Biological Scis Ctee SERC 1981–84, Res and Med Advsy Ctee Cystic Fibrosis Res Tst 1982–87, Grants Ctee A Cell Bd MRC 1983–87, Scientific and Res Awards Ctee Br Digestive Fndn 1989–93, Biochemistry and Cell Biology Ctee BBSRC 1994–96; managing ed Cell Calcium 1978–99; memb Editorial Bd: Gut 1984–87, Yonsei Med Jl 1986–, Pancreas 1986–92; Br Soc of Gastroenterology: Res Medal 1981, chm Basic Scis Section 1986–88, memb Res Ctee 1991–93; chm Gastrointestinal Cmmn Int Union of Physiological Scis 1993–2002; Daiwa Prize Daiwa Anglo-Japanese Fndn 1994; memb: Physiological Soc (memb Ctee 1996–2000), Biochemical Soc, Soc for Experimental Biology, Br Biophysical Soc, Br Soc for Cell Biology, Euro Pancreatic Club (memb Cncl 1983–85 and 1992–95, pres 1985); *Books* Stimulus-Secretion Coupling in the Gastrointestinal Tract (co-ed, 1976), Electrolyte and Water Transport across Gastrointestinal Epithelia (co-ed, 1982), Secretion: Mechanisms and Control (co-ed, 1984), Variations in Human Physiology (ed, 1985), EPC - European Pancreatic Club Extracts (ed, 1985), The Exocrine Pancreas (ed, 1990), Human Physiology: Age, Stress and the Environment (2 edn of Variations in Human Physiology, co-ed, 1994); author of over 150 articles in learned scientific journals; *Recreations* Italy, gardening, classical music; *Style—* Prof Maynard Case; ✉ Faculty of Life Sciences, University of Manchester, Floor 2, Core Technology Facility, 46 Grafton Street, Manchester M13 9NT (tel 0161 275 5406, fax 0161 275 5600, e-mail maynard.case@manchester.ac.uk)

CASE, Richard Ian; CBE (2002); *b* 14 June 1945; *Educ* Cranfield Inst of Technol (MSc); *m*; 2 c; *Career* Westland Helicopters Ltd: joined as apprentice 1961, various positions 1969–78, tech mangr Arab British Helicopters (Egypt) 1978, chief designer 1982, divnl dir (engrg) and chief designer 1985, engrg dir 1985, EH101 project dir and engrg dir 1988, md Westland Helicopters Ltd 1992–95; dir Westland Group plc 1993–95, chief exec GKN Westland Helicopters 1995–2001, md AgustaWestland and chm Westland Helicopters Ltd 2001–04; non-exec dir: FKI plc 2006–, Aerosystems International; memb Cncl: RAeS, SBAC; FRAeS 1985 (MRAeS 1982), FREng 1993; *Recreations* opera, theatre, golf, travel; *Style—* Richard Case, Esq, CBE, FREng

CASEMENT, Ann D Elizabeth; *Educ* Sorbonne Univ Paris (Dip French), LSE (BSc), Westminster Fndn (Dip), Univ of London; *Career* NY State licensed pyschoanalyst; psychiatric placement St Mary Abbotts Hosp London 1979–82, Jungian analyst Assoc of Jungian Analysts London 1982–; chair UK Cncl for Psychotherapy 1998–2001; lectr and teacher in Jungian psychoanalysis & psychotherapy and anthropology; asst ed Jl of Analytical Psychology; memb: Int Assoc of Analytical Psychology Zurich 1985 (chair Organizing Ctee for their Int Conf in Cambridge 2001, memb Exec Ctee), Programme Ctee Int Congress Int Assoc of Analytical Psychology, House of Lords Working Pty on Statutory Regulation of Psychotherapy, Br Psychological Soc, Int Neuro-Psychoanalytic Soc, Nat Assoc for the Advancement of Psychoanalysis USA; FRAI 1976, FRSM 2005; *Books* Post-Jungians Today (ed), Carl Gustav Jung; chapters in: Psicologica Analytica Contemporanea, Handbook of Individual Therapy, When a Princess Dies, Globalized Psychotherapy, The Handbook of Jungian Psychology (contrib), Who Owns Psychoanalysis? (ed, 2004), The Idea of the Numinous (2006), Who Owns Jung (2007); articles and book reviews for The Economist and others; *Clubs* Analytical Psychology; *Style—* Mrs Ann Casement; ✉ 3D Hans Crescent, London SW1X 0LN (e-mail case@easynet.co.uk)

CASEWELL, Prof Mark William; s of William John Ivor Casewell (d 1951), of Hants, and Phyllis Rebecca, *née* Raymond (d 1976); *b* 17 August 1940; *Educ* Royal Masonic Sch, Univ of London (BSc, MB BS, MD); *m* 1, 8 July 1967 (m dis 1972), Carolle Anne, da of Richard Eaton, of Portsmouth, Hants; m 2, 9 Dec 1995, Rosa Coello, da of Alfredo Coello of Orense, Spain; *Career* house physician St Bartholomew's Hosp 1965–66, asst pathologist Univ of Cambridge 1967–70, sr lectr and hon conslt in microbiology (former lectr) St Thomas' Hosp 1971–81, reader and hon conslt in microbiology The London Hosp 1982–84, prof and head of Dulwich Public Health Laboratory and Med Microbiology King's Coll Sch of Med and Dentistry 1984–97, emeritus prof Univ of London 1997–; ind conslt on use of antibiotics in food animals 1997–; memb AIDS Advsy Gp King's Healthcare 1985–97; memb Editorial Bd: Jl of Hosp Infection, Jl of Antimicrobial Chemotherapy; chm Hosp Infection Soc 1987–91 (fndr memb 1979, scientific sec 1979–85); MRCS 1965, LRCP 1965, FRCPath 1986 (MRCPath 1975), Hon FRCP 1999 (Hon MRCP 1994); *Books* Hospital Infection Control: Policies and Practical Procedures (jtly with J Philpott-Howard, 1994); chapters in: Skin Microbiology: Relevance to Clinical Infection (1981), Recent Advances in Infection (1982), Quality Assurance Principles and Practice in the Microbiology Laboratory (1999), Antibiotic and Chemotherapy (2001); *Publications* numerous contribs incl: BMJ, Jl of Clinical Pathology, Jl of Hospital Infection, Jl of Antimicrobial Chemotherapy; *Recreations* cooking, Spain, very fast cars; *Clubs* Porsche GB, Fountain (Barts), Real Madrid FC, Tate Modern; *Style—* Prof Mark Casewell; ✉ 43 Primrose Gardens, London NW3 4UL (tel 020 7586 3181, fax 020 7722 1957, e-mail mark@casewell.co.uk); Department of Infectious Diseases, Guy's, King's and St Thomas' School of Medicine, Bessemer Road, London SE5 9RS (fax 020 7346 3404)

CASEY, Gavin Frank; *b* 18 October 1946; *Career* chartered accountant Harmood Banner & Co 1965–69, Cooper Brothers & Co 1970–71, various appts rising to dep chief exec County Natwest Ltd 1972–89, fin dir and chief operating offr Smith New Court plc 1989–95, chief admin offr int equities Merrill Lynch International Ltd (following takeover of Smith New Court) 1995–96, chief exec London Stock Exchange plc 1996–2000; chm: Tragus Holdings 2002–, Corporate Synergy 2003–; dir: Kinetic Info System Servs Ltd 2001–03, Lawrence plc 2002–, Abingdon Capital 2004–, Tellings Golden Miller Group plc; dep chm Corp Fin Advsy Bd PricewaterhouseCoopers LLP 2001–; Freeman City of London, memb Worshipful Co of Chartered Accountants in England and Wales; FCA 1970; *Recreations* horse racing, shooting, theatre; *Clubs* City of London, Turf; *Style—* Gavin Casey, Esq

CASEY, Prof Patricia Rosarie; da of James Casey (d 1991), of Co Cork, and Margaret Casey; *b* 27 October 1952; *Educ* Presentation Convent Fermoy, UC Cork (MD); *m* John McGuiggan, barr-at-law; 2 s (James b 29 Nov 1987, Gavan b 19 Aug 1991); *Career* MRC research fell MRC Unit for Epidemiological Studies in Psychiatry Royal Edinburgh Hosp 1982–84, statuatory lectr in psychiatry Regnl Hosp Cork 1984–91, prof of psychiatry Univ Coll Dublin/Mater Hosp Dublin 1991–; ed Psychiatric Bulletin 2008–; elected memb: Irish Med Cncl 1994–, Cncl Royal Coll of Psychiatrists 1995–; FRCP, FRCPsych, fell Irish Coll of Physicians; *Publications* A Guide to Psychiatry in Primary Care (1990, 2 edn 1996), Social Function: the hidden axis of psychiatric diagnosis (1990), Psychiatry and the Law (with K Craven, 1999); contrib to 20 books; *Recreations* listening to classical music, cooking, writing for newspapers; *Style*— Prof Patricia Casey; ✉ Department of Psychiatry, Mater Hospital, Eccles Street, Dublin 7, Ireland (tel 00 353 1 803 2176, fax 00353 1 830 9323, e-mail apsych@mater.ie)

CASH, Prof John David; CBE (1998); s of John Henry Cash (d 1982), and May Annie, *née* Taylor (d 1986); *b* 3 April 1936; *Educ* Ashville Coll, Univ of Edinburgh (BSc, PhD, MB ChB); *m* 22 Sept 1962, Angela Mary, da of Robert David Thomson (d 1980); 1 s (Michael Peter b 1965), 1 da (Julie Suzanna b 1967); *Career* dir Regnl Blood Transfusion Serv Edinburgh and S E Scotland 1974–79, nat med dir Scot Nat Blood Transfusion Serv 1979–90, nat med and science dir Scottish Nat Blood Transfusion Serv 1990–97; pres Royal Coll of Physicians of Edinburgh 1994–97; memb Bd Nat Inst for Biological Standards and Control 1996–2004; hon prof Univ of Edinburgh 1986–97; FRCPE, FRCPath, FRCPGlas, FRCSEd, FRCP; *Recreations* fishing, gardening; *Style*— Prof John Cash, CBE

CASH, William Nigel Paul (Bill); MP; s of Capt Paul Trevor Cash, MC (ka Normandy 1944), and Moyra Margaret Elizabeth, *née* Morrison; *b* 10 May 1940; *Educ* Stonyhurst, Lincoln Coll Oxford (MA); *m* 1965, Bridget Mary, da of James Rupert Lee; 2 s (William, Samuel), 1 da (Laetitia); *Career* slr William Cash and Co; MP (Cons): Stafford 1984–97, Stone 1997–; shadow attorney gen 2001–03, shadow sec of state constitutional affairs 2003; memb Select Ctee on Euro Legislation 1985–; chm All-Pty Parly Ctee: on E Africa 1988–2000, on Complementary and Alternative Medicine 1991–97, on Uganda 1997–, on Malaysia 2006–; chm Cons Backbench Ctee Euro Affrs 1989–91; chm All-Pty Jubilee Campaign for Reduction of Third World Debt 1998–; fndr and chm: European Fndn, European Jl; *Books* A Democratic Way to European Unity, Arguments against Federalsim (1990), Against a Federal Europe - The Battle for Britain (1991), Europe - The Crunch (1992), Vision of Europe (contrib, 1993), Are We Really Winning on Europe? (1995), Response to Chancellor Kohl (1996), The Blue Paper (1996), British and German National Interests (1998), Britain and Europe, Challenging Questions for Tony Blair, Kenneth Clarke and Michael Heseltine (1999), Associated but not Absorbed (2000), The European Constitution: A Political Timebomb (2003), The Strangulation of Britain and British Business (2004); monthly editorials Euro Jl 1993–; *Recreations* cricket, tennis, jazz, heritage, cutting lawns, cutting red tape; *Clubs* Beefsteak, Carlton, Vincent's (Oxford), Garrick; *Style*— Bill Cash, Esq, MP; ✉ Upton Cressett Hall, Bridgnorth, Shropshire WV16 6HH (tel 01746 714307); House of Commons, London SW1A 0AA (tel 020 7219 6330)

CASHMAN, Michael Maurice; MEP (Lab) West Midlands; s of John Cashman, of London, and Mary Alvena, *née* Clayton; *b* 17 December 1950; *Educ* Cardinal Griffin Secdy Modern, Gladys Dare's Sch; *Partner* Paul Cottingham (civil partnership 11 March 2006); *Career* actor in theatre, musical theatre, TV, films and radio 1963–99, first role in Oliver 1963, other roles incl Colin in EastEnders (BBC), Horst in RNT prodn of Bent, Noises Off (Mobil Touring Theatre) 1995 and Prospero in The Tempest (Shared Experience Theatre) 1997; MEP (Lab) W Midlands 1999–; memb Lab Pty 1975–, memb Lab Pty NEC 1998–, auditor European PLP 1999–; cncllr and hon treas Br Actors' Equity 1994–98, memb Bd Shared Experience Theatre 1998–2000; founding dir Stonewall Gp (chm 1988–96); patron: European Policy Network, SPACE (AIDS counselling), Gibraltar Gay Rights, Malta Gay Rights Movement, Friends and Families for Lesbians and Gays, Volunteering England, Volunteering Europe, Hereford and Worcester Lesbian and Gay Switchboard (HWLGS), Nat Secular Soc; tstee Evelyn Norris Tst; Hon Doctorate Univ of Staffordshire 2007; special serv award from American Assoc of Physicians for Human Rights 1998, nominated EV50 most influential actors 2002, nominated EV50 politician of the year, named as one of 20 most influential gays in the UK by The Observer; FRSA 1996; *Recreations* travel, photography; *Style*— Michael Cashman, Esq, MEP

CASHMORE, Prof Roger John; CMG (2004); s of Cyril John Charles Cashmore, of Dudley, Worcs, and Elsie May, *née* Jones; *b* 22 August 1944; *Educ* Dudley GS, St John's Coll Cambridge (MA), Balliol Coll and UC Oxford (DPhil, Weir jr res fell, 1851 res fell); *m* 6 Aug 1971, Elizabeth Ann, da of Rev S J C Lindsay; 1 s (Christopher John Hrothgar Lindsay-Cashmore b 1976); *Career* res assoc Stanford Linear Accelerator Centre Calif 1969–74; Univ of Oxford: res offr 1974–78, lectr ChCh 1976–78, sr res fell Merton Coll 1977–79, tutorial fell Balliol Coll and univ lectr in physics 1979–90, reader in experimental physics 1990–91, prof of experimental physics 1991–2003; dep DG and dir of research CERN Geneva 1999–2003, princ BNC Oxford 2003–; SERC sr res fell 1982–87, guest scientist Fermilab Chicago 1986–87, visiting prof Vrije Univ Brussels 1982; chm: Scientific Ctee of Laboratorie Nazional de Gran Sasso 2004, NRAC 2005; CV Boys Prize Inst of Physics 1983, Alexander Von Humboldt Fndn Humboldt Research Award 1995–96; memb Academia Europa 1992; FInstP 1985, FRSA 1996, FRS 1998; *Recreations* sports, wine; *Style*— Prof Roger Cashmore, CMG, FRS; ✉ Brasenose College, Oxford OX1 4AJ (tel 01865 277821, fax 01865 277514, e-mail roger.cashmore@physics.ox.ac.uk)

CASKEN, Prof John; *b* 15 July 1949; *Educ* Barnsley and Dist Holgate GS, Univ of Birmingham (BMus, MA), Univ of Durham (DMus), Acad of Music Warsaw; *Career* lectr in music Univ of Birmingham 1973–79, fell in composition Huddersfield Poly 1980–81, lectr in music Univ of Durham 1981–92, prof of music Univ of Manchester 1992–; compositions incl: Tableaux des Trois Ages 1976–77, Orion Over Farne 1984, Maharal Dreaming 1989, Darting the Skiff 1992–93, Sortilège 1996, Symphony (Broken Consort) 2004, Rest-ringing for string quartet and orchestra 2005; concertos: Masque 1982, Erin 1982–83, Cello Concerto 1990–91, Violin Concerto 1994–95, Distant Variations 1997; opera: Golem (chamber opera) 1986–88, God's Liar 1996–2000; vocal: Ia Orana, Gauguin 1978, Firewhirl 1979–80, To Fields We Do Not Know 1983–84, Still Mine 1991–92, Farness (three poems of Carol Ann Duffy) 2006, Chansons de Verlaine 2006; instrumental and ensemble: Kagura 1972–73, Music for the Crabbing Sun 1974, Thymehaze 1976, Amarantos 1977–78, String Quartet No 1 1981–82, Vaganza 1985, Salamandra 1986, Piano Quartet 1989–90, String Quartet No 2 1993, Infanta Marina 1993–94, Après un silence 1997–98, Piano Trio 2000–02, Blue Medusa 2002; recordings on: NMC Ancora, Metier Sound and Vision; first Britten Award for Golem 1990, Northern Electric Performing Arts Award 1990, Gramophone Award for Golem (recording) 1991, Fondation Prince Pierre de Monaco Prize for Still Mine 1993; FRNCM; *Style*— John Casken; ✉ c/o Sally Groves, Schott & Co Ltd, 48 Great Marlborough Street, London W1V 2BN (tel 020 7494 1487, fax 020 7287 1529, e-mail john.casken@manchester.ac.uk, website www.schott-music.com)

CASS, Sir Geoffrey Arthur; kt (1992); s of Arthur Cass (d 1982), of Darlington and Oxford, and Jessie, *née* Simpson (d 1967); *b* 11 August 1932; *Educ* Queen Elizabeth GS Darlington, Jesus Coll Oxford (MA), Dept of Social and Administrative Studies Oxford, Nuffield Coll Oxford, Jesus Coll Cambridge (MA), Clare Hall Cambridge; *m* 1957, Olwen Mary, JP, DL, da of late William Leslie Richards, of Brecon; 4 da (Fiona (Mrs Patrick Allen), Karen (Mrs Gavin Clunie), Miranda (Mrs John Hosking), Fleur (Mrs Philip Clegg)); *Career* cmmnd PO RAFVR (Oxford Univ Air Sqdn) 1954, Nat Serv PO 1958, Flying Offr 1960, Air Min Directorate Work Study RAF 1958–60; conslt PA Mgmnt Conslts 1960–65;

private mgmnt conslt: British Communications Corp, Controls and Communications Ltd 1965; md George Allen & Unwin 1967–71 (dir 1965–67); dir: Controls and Communications Ltd 1966–69, Chicago Univ Press (UK) Ltd 1971–86; chief exec Cambridge Univ Press 1972–92 (sec the Press Syndicate 1974–92, Univ Printer 1982–83 and 1991–92, conslt 1992–); dir Weidenfeld Publishers Ltd 1972–74; dir: Newcastle Theatre Royal Tst 1984–89, American Friends Royal Shakespeare Theatre 1985–2000, Cambridge Theatre Co 1986–95, Theatres Tst 1991–2000, Marc Sinden Productions 2000–02; memb Restoration Appeal Ctee Theatre Royal Bury St Edmunds 2002–; The All England LTC (Wimbledon) Ltd 1997–99, The All England Lawn Tennis Ground plc 1997–99, fndr memb Inigo Productions 1996–, tstee and guardian Shakespeare Birthplace Tst 1982– (life tstee 1994–); chm: RSC 1985–2000 (govr 1975–, dep pres 2000–), Royal Shakespeare Theatre Tst 1983– (fndr dir 1967–); Lawn Tennis Assoc of GB: memb Cncl 1976–, memb Mgmnt Bd 1985–90 and 1993–2000, chm Nat Ranking Ctee 1990–99, memb Int Events Ctee 1991–93, memb Nat Trg and Int Match Ctee 1982–90 and 1992–93 (chm 1985–90), memb Reorganisation Working Pty 1984–85 and 1994–99 (chm), dep pres 1994–96, pres and chm Cncl 1997–99; Wimbledon Championships: memb Ctee of Mgmnt 1990–2002, memb Jt Fin Ctee 1993–2002 (chm 1997–99), Jt Fin Bd 1989–93; govr Perse Sch for Girls Cambridge 1997–98 (chm Bd of Govrs 1978–88); memb: Governing Syndicate Fitzwilliam Museum Cambridge 1977–78, Univ of Cambridge Ctee and Exec Sub-Ctee of Mgmnt of Fenners 1976–, Exec Ctee Univ of Cambridge Careers Service Syndicate 1982–2002 (memb 1977–2002); pres Macmillan Cancer Relief Cambridgeshire 1998–, chm Univ of Cambridge ADC Theatre Appeal 2000–, chm Univ of Cambridge Sports Centre Appeal 2001–, patron Cambridge Rowing Tst 2001–, tstee Univ of Cambridge Fndn 1998–; Oxford tennis blue 1953, 1954 and 1955 (sec 1955), Oxford badminton blue 1951 and 1952 (capt 1952); chm Cambridge Univ Lawn Tennis Club 1977–, pres Cambridgeshire Lawn Tennis Assoc 1980–82; played Wimbledon Championships: 1954, 1955, 1956, 1959; played in inter-county lawn tennis championships for Durham Co (singles champion 1951) then for Cambridgeshire (singles champion 1976) 1952–82, represented RAF 1958–59; Br Veterans Singles (45 and over) champion Wimbledon 1978; memb Br Veterans Int Championships Dubler Cup Team: Barcelona 1978, Milano Marittima 1979 (Capt); hon Cambridge tennis blue 1980; fell Clare Hall Cambridge 1979; hon fell Jesus Coll Oxford 1998; life FInstD 1968, FIIM (formerly FIWM) 1979, CCMI (CIMgt 1980), FRSA 1991; Chevalier de l'Ordre des Arts et des Lettres (France) 1982; *Recreations* lawn tennis, theatre; *Clubs* All England Lawn Tennis and Croquet (hon memb 2000), Hurlingham, Queen's (hon memb 1997), Hawks' (Cambridge; hon memb), IOD, Int Lawn Tennis of GB, The 45 (hon memb), Cambridge Univ Lawn Tennis, West Hants LTC (hon memb 2000–), Veterans Lawn Tennis GB; *Style*— Sir Geoffrey Cass; ✉ Middlefield, Huntingdon Road, Girton, Cambridge CB3 0LH

CASS, Marilyn Lal Ross; da of Garrett Taylor Lionel Maurice Graham, of Bath, and Lal Elizabeth Joan, *née* Norton; *b* 26 February 1954, Trowbridge, Wilts; *Educ* Royal Sch Bath, Univ of Exeter (BA, PGCE), Univ of Bath (MA); *m* 6 Aug 1977, Geoffrey Philip Cass; 2 s (Philip Tristan b 12 Sept 1980, David Alexander b 25 Sept 1982); *Career* cmmnd Army 1973, travel and various posts incl hotel mgmnt, libraries and voluntary work 1979–89, geography teacher, housemistress and head of modern studies Royal Sch Bath 1992–97, dep head Redland HS Bristol 1997–2000, headmistress Shrewsbury HS 2000–; memb GSA (memb HMC/GSA Professional Devpt Ctee); memb Cncl Univ of Birmingham; memb Drapers Co Shrewsbury; *Recreations* skiing, travel, walking, reading; *Clubs* Lansdown, Univ Women's; *Style*— Mrs Marilyn Cass; ✉ Shrewsbury High School, 32 Town Walls, Shrewsbury SY1 1TN

CASS, Richard Martin; s of Edward Charles Cass, of Cheshire, and Hazel Rosemary; *b* 25 May 1946; *Educ* High Wycombe GS, Sheffield Univ (BArch, MA); *m* 1977, Judith Claire, da of Dr Linton Morris Snaith, of Newcastle upon Tyne; 2 s (Simon b 1983, Alexander b 1986); *Career* architect and landscape architect; dir Brian Clouston and Ptnrs 1979–82; Cass Assocs: princ 1982–, sr partner 1989–; enabler Cmmn for Architectue and the Built Environment 2001–, dir Cass Projects Ltd 2001–; *Recreations* music, theatre, gardening, sailing, reading; *Style*— Richard M Cass, Esq; ✉ Osborne House, Fulwood Park, Liverpool (tel 0151 727 7614); Cass Associates, Studio 104, The Tea Factory, 82 Wood Street, Liverpool L1 4DQ (tel 0151 707 0110, fax 0151 707 0332)

CASSEL, Sir Timothy Felix Harold; 4 Bt (UK 1920), of Lincoln's Inn, City of London, QC (1988); s of His Hon Sir Harold Cassel, 3 Bt, TD, QC (d 2001); *b* 30 April 1942; *Educ* Eton; *m* 1, 1971 (m dis 1975), Mrs Jenifer Samuel, da of Kenneth Bridge Puckle; 1 da (Natalia Hermione b 1972), 1 s (Alexander James Felix b 25 May 1974); *m* 2, 1979, Ann, (Baroness Mallalieu, QC (Life Peer), *qv*, only da of Sir William Mallalieu; 2 da (Hon Bathsheba Anna b 1981, Hon Cosima b 1984); *Heir* s, Alexander Cassel; *Career* called to the Bar Lincoln's Inn 1965 (bencher 1994); jr prosecutor for the Crown of the Central Criminal Court 1978, asst boundary cmmr 1979, sr prosecutor for the Crown 1986; *Recreations* country sports, opera, skiing; *Clubs* Garrick, Turf; *Style*— Sir Timothy Cassel, Bt, QC; ✉ 5 Paper Buildings, Temple, London EC4

CASSELTON, Prof Lorna Ann (Mrs Tollett); da of William Charles Henry Smith (d 1980), and Cecille, *née* Bowman (d 1999); *b* 18 July 1938; *Educ* Southend HS, UCL (BSc, PhD), Univ of London (DSc), Univ of Oxford (MA); *m* 1961 (m dis); *m* 2, 1981, William Joseph Dennis Tollett, s of William Alfred Herbert Tollett; *Career* Univ of London: sr student Royal Cmmn for the Exhibition of 1851 1963–65, temp asst lectr Royal Holloway Coll 1966–67, lectr Queen Mary Coll 1967–76, reader Queen Mary Coll 1976–89, prof Queen Mary & Westfield Coll 1989–91, visiting prof 1997–; Univ of Oxford: AFRC/BBSRC postdoctoral research fell 1991–95, BBSRC sr research fell 1995–2001, hon research lectr 1993, prof of fungal genetics 1997–2003, fell St Cross Coll 1993–2003, hon fell St Hilda's Coll 2000–; Leverhulme emeritus fell 2003–05; foreign sec and vice-pres Royal Soc 2006–; memb: Genetics Soc, Soc for Gen Microbiology 1974; hon memb Br Mycological Soc 2003–; FRS 1999; *Publications* over 50 research articles; over 20 review articles; *Recreations* music, theatre, dancing, walking; *Style*— Prof Lorna Casselton, FRS; ✉ Department of Plant Sciences, University of Oxford, South Parks Road, Oxford OX1 3RB (tel 01865 275100, fax 01865 275074, e-mail lorna.casselton@plants.ox.ac.uk)

CASSIDY, Bryan Michael Deece; s of William Francis Deece Cassidy (d 1986), and Kathleen Selina Patricia, *née* Geraghty (d 1989); *Educ* Ratcliffe Coll Leicester, Sidney Sussex Coll Cambridge (MA); *m* 27 Aug 1960, Gillian Mary, da of Austen Patrick Bohane (d 1988); 2 da (Katherine b 1961, Siobhan b 1962), 1 s (Dominic b 1964); *Career* cmmnd RA 1955–57 (Malta and Libya), HAC 1957–62; with Ever Ready, Beechams and Reed Int; memb Cncl CBI 1981–84, dir gen Cosmetic Toiletry and Perfumery Assoc 1981–84; Parly candidate Wandsworth Central 1966, memb GLC (Hendon N) 1977–85 (oppn spokesman on industry and employment 1983–84); MEP (Cons): Dorset E and Hampshire W 1984–94, Dorset and E Devon 1994–99; former Cons spokesman on Legal Affairs and Citizens' Rights Ctee; memb Econ & Monetary Affrs & Industrial Policy Ctee, memb European Economic and Social Ctee 2002–; vice-pres Euro Parly delgn to USA; fndr Cassidy and Associates 1999–; memb Advsy Bd Euro Performance Inst Brussels 1999–2002; assignments for BESO: Estonia 2000, Mongolia 2002; dir Studies for Hawksmere Brussels Briefings; Woodrow Wilson fell at various USA Univs; currently writer, lectr and conslt on the EU, vice-chm Single Market Observatory European Economic and Social Ctee; *Publications* Hawksmere European Lobbying Guide; *Recreations* country pursuits; *Clubs* Carlton; *Style*— Bryan Cassidy, Esq; ✉ 11 Esmond Court, Thackeray Street, London W8 5HB (tel 020 7937 3558, fax 020 7937 3789, e-mail cassidy@europundit.co.uk and bmdcassidy@aol.com, website www.europundit.co.uk)

CASSIDY, Denis Patrick; *b* 2 February 1933; *Career* former chm: The Boddington Group plc, Ferguson International plc (formerly Ferguson International Holdings plc), The Oliver Group plc, Kingsbury Group plc, Liberty plc, Newcastle United plc; currently non-exec dir: Compass Group plc, Forever Broadcasting plc; *Style*— Denis Cassidy, Esq

CASSIDY, Rt Rev George Henry; *see:* Southwell and Nottingham, Bishop of

CASSIDY, Michael John; CBE (2004); s of Francis Cassidy, and Vera Rosina, *née* Valler; *b* 14 January 1947; *Educ* Downing Coll Cambridge (BA), City Univ Business Sch (MBA); *m* 1, 7 Sept 1974 (m dis 1988), Amanda Fitzgerald; 2 da (Kate b 1977, Annabel b 1979), 1 s (Thomas b 1981); m 2, 7 June 1997, Amelia, da of George Simpson (d 1985); 2 da (Georgia Rose b 30 Sept 1997, Netanya Sylvie b 16 Sept 2002); *Career* ptnr: Maxwell Batley Slrs 1971–2002 (sr ptnr 1991–2002), DJ Freeman Slrs 2002–03, Hammonds 2003–05; conslt: Olswang Slrs 2003–04, DLA Piper Slrs 2005–, Armstrong Bonham-Carter 2007–; chm: Askonas Holt Ltd 2002–, Hemingway Properties Ltd 2003–06, Bulgarian Land Devpt plc 2006–07, Trinity Capital plc 2006–; dir British Land Co plc 1996–2007, non-exec dir UBS Ltd; memb: Bd Int Financial Servs London (IFSL) 2007–, London Pension Fund Authy 2007–; memb Corp of London Cncl 1980– (chm Planning and Communications Ctee 1986–89, chm Policy and Resources Ctee 1992–97), estates ctee chm London Inst 1999–2005, chm Barbican Arts Centre 2000–03, memb Development Bd City Univ 2000–05, pres London C of C and Industry 2005– (memb Bd 2004), chm Museum of London 2005–; Master Worshipful Co of Slrs; Hon Degree: City Univ 1996, South Bank Univ 1996; hon fell London Business Sch; memb Law Soc 1971; FRSA, Hon FRIBA; *Recreations* boating; *Style*— Michael Cassidy, Esq, CBE; ✉ 3 Noble Street, London EC2V 7EE (tel 020 7796 6887)

CASSIDY, Nigel Peter; s of Rev Albert Cassidy (d 1970), and Hilda May, *née* Newport (d 1996); *b* 26 December 1954; *Educ* Thames Valley GS, Univ of Portsmouth, London Coll of Printing; *m* Ann, da of Donald Clark (d 1995); 2 da (Ruth, Claire); *Career* Dimbleby Newspapers 1972–74; BBC: Radio Sussex 1974–77, Radio London 1978–86, Current Affrs Dept BBC TV 1986–87, Radio News 1987–88, Parly Unit 1988–89, business presenter and TV reporter 1989–, business correspondent Today programme 1995–2002, author and business writer 2004–; chair: (deviser and co-writer) The Board Game 1992–2001 (New York Radio Festival Medal), Newstalk 1996–98, Workplace 1994, Shelf Lives 1994–, Tricks of the Trade 1998, Workers Without Frontiers 2002, Paying for Old Age 2004, The Global Sell Off 2005, The Climate Change Challenge 2007; *Publications* Starting Out: How to Choose a Career (2004), Jumpstart Your Career (2006); *Recreations* family, writing, food, travel, cutting things out of newspapers; *Style*— Nigel Cassidy, Esq; ✉ BBC News Centre, Wood Lane, London W12 7RJ (tel 020 8743 8000, e-mail nigel.cassidy@bbc.co.uk)

CASSIDY, Dr Sheila Anne; da of Air Vice Marshal John Reginald Cassidy, CBE (d 1974), and Barbara Margaret, *née* Drew; *b* 18 August 1937; *Educ* Our Lady of Mercy Coll Parramatta, Univ of Sydney, Univ of Oxford (MA, BM BCh); *Career* Radcliffe Infirmary 1963–68, Leicester Royal Infirmary 1968–71, went to Santiago Chile to work in Assistencia Publica in emergency hosp and church clinic 1971, detained for 2 months for treating wounded revolutionary, tortured and expelled 1975, writer and human rights worker 1975–77, student Ampleforth Abbey 1977–78, novice St Bernard's Convent Slough 1978–80, SHO Dept of Radiotherapy Plymouth Gen Hosp 1980–82, med dir St Lukes Hospice Plymouth 1982–93; Plymouth Gen Hosp: specialist in palliative care 1993–96, specialist in psychosocial oncology 1996–2002, psychotherapist; UKCncl for Psychotherapy (UKCP) registered psychotherapist; regular writer, broadcaster and preacher, lectr on med and religious issues throughout UK and abroad; Valiant for Truth Media Award Order of Christian Unity, Templeton Prize for Religion 1995; Freedom City of Plymouth 1998; Hon DSc Univ of Exeter 1991, Hon DLitt Cheltenham and Glos Coll of HE (via CNNA), Hon DM Univ of Plymouth 2001; memb Br Psychosocial Oncology Soc; *Books* Audacity to Believe (1977), Prayer for Pilgrims (1979), Sharing the Darkness (1989), Good Friday People (1991, special award Collins Religious Book Award), Light from The Dark Valley (1994), The Loneliest Journey (1995), The Creation Story (1996), Made for Laughter (2006); *Recreations* writing, sewing, painting, entertaining, TV; *Style*— Dr Sheila Cassidy; ✉ 7 The Esplanade, The Hoe, Plymouth PL1 2PJ

CASSIDY, (Michael) Stuart; s of John Michael Cassidy, of Tunbridge Wells, Kent, and Jacqueline Eleanor, *née* Allison; *b* 26 September 1968; *Educ* White Lodge, Royal Ballet Sch; *m* 1993, Nicola Jane, *née* Searchfield; 2 s (Sean William b 1998, Alexander Michael b 2001); *Career* principal dancer; Royal Ballet: Siegfried in Swan Lake, Romeo in Romeo and Juliet, Prince in Sleeping Beauty, Prince of The Pagodas, Nutcracker and Cinderella, Solor in La Bayadère, Lescaut in Manon, Basilio in Don Quixote, Colas in La Fille Mal Gardée, Jean de Brienne in Raymonda, Gloria, Song of the Earth, Galanteries, Persuit, Pas de Six, Elite Syncopations; cr roles in David Bintley's Spirit of Fugue and Ashley Page's Piano; Ashton's Pas de Deux in the opera Die Fledermaus (BBC2) 1990; fndr memb K Ballet Co (touring Japan and Europe) 1999–; Nora Roche Award 1984, Prix de Lausanne Professional Prize 1987; *Recreations* classic cars, music (all types), computers, food; *Style*— Stuart Cassidy, Esq; ✉ 23 Devonshire Road, Chiswick, London W4 2EX

CASSON, Prof Mark Christopher; s of Rev Stanley Christopher Casson (d 1988), and Dorothy Nowell, *née* Barlow (d 1974); *b* 17 December 1945; *Educ* Manchester Grammar, Univ of Bristol, Churchill Coll Cambridge; *m* 26 July 1975, Janet Penelope, da of William Louis Close (d 1961); 1 da (Catherine Mary b 1984); *Career* Dept of Economics Univ of Reading: lectr 1969–77, reader 1977–81, prof 1981–, head of dept 1987–94; chm Business Enterprise Heritage Tst 2000–; memb Cncl Royal Economic Soc 1985–90; pres Assoc of Business Historians 2007–08; fell Acad of Int Business 1993, FRSA 1996; *Books* Introduction to Mathematical Economics (1973), The Future of the Multinational Enterprise (1976), Alternatives to the Multinational Enterprise (1979), Youth Unemployment (1979), Unemployment: A Disequilibrium Approach (1981), The Entrepreneur: An Economic Theory (1982), Economics of Unemployment: An Historical Perspective (1983), Growth of International Business (1983), Economic Theory of the Multinational Enterprise: Selected Papers (1985), Multinationals and World Trade (1986), The Firm and the Market: Studies in Multinational Enterprise and the Scope of the Firm (1987), Enterprise and Competitiveness: A Systems View of International Business (1990), Multinational Corporations (1990), Entrepreneurship (1990), Economics of Business Culture: Game Theory, Transaction Costs and Economic Performance (1991), Global Research Strategy and International Competitiveness (1991), International Business and Global Integration (1992), Multinational Enterprises in the World Economy (1992), Industrial Concentration and Economic Inequality (1993), Entrepreneurship and Business Culture (1995), The Organization of International Business (1995), Theory of the Firm (1996), Information and Organization: A New Perspective on the Theory of the Firm (1997), Culture, Social Norms and Economics (1997), Institutions and the Evolution of Modern Enterprise (1998), Economics of Marketing (1998), Economics of International Business (2000), Enterprise and Leadership (2000), Cultural Factors in Economic Growth (2000), Oxford Handbook of Entrepreneurship (2005); *Recreations* book collecting; *Style*— Prof Mark Casson; ✉ 6 Wayside Green, Woodcote, Reading RG8 0QJ (tel 01491 681483); Department of Economics, University of Reading, Box 218, Reading RG6 2AA (tel 0118 931 8227, fax 0118 975 0236, telex 847813, e-mail m.c.casson@reading.ac.uk)

CASSONI, Maria Luisa (Marisa); da of Nicola Ugo Dante Cassoni, of London, and Leonita Greco Cassoni; *b* 27 December 1951; *Educ* Sacred Heart Convent London, St Benedict's Sch Ealing, Imperial Coll London (BSc); *Career* early career as hosp physicist, teacher, market researcher, cashier and sales asst; Deloitte Haskins & Sells: trainee accountant then accountant-in-charge London 1975–79, audit sr then sr mangr Milan 1979–84, corp fin mangr 1984–86; Prudential Gp: fin ops mangr then fin controller Prudential Property Services Ltd 1986–91, fin controller then fin dir Prudential Home Service Div 1991–94, fin dir Prudential UK Div 1994–98; gp fin dir Britannic Assurance plc 1998–2001, gp fin dir Royal Mail Gp plc 2001–05, finance dir John Lewis Partnership 2006–; non-exec dir: Severn Trent plc 2001–, WSP Gp plc 2006–; memb Accounting Standards Bd; govr Peabody Tst; ARCS, ACA 1979; *Recreations* travel, skiing, theatre, opera; *Style*— Ms Marisa Cassoni

CASTELL, Sir William Martin (Bill); kt (2000), LVO (2004); s of William Gummer Castell, and Gladys Castell, *née* Doe; *b* 10 April 1947; *Educ* St Dunstan's Coll, City of London Coll (BA); *m* 1971, Renice, *née* Mendelson; 2 da, 1 s; *Career* chartered accountant Spicer & Pegler 1971–75; Wellcome plc: fin controller Europe 1976–79, controller fin and admin continental Europe Africa and Asia 1979–81, md Wellcome Biotech 1982–84, commercial dir 1984–89; chief exec Amersham plc 1990–2004, ceo and pres GE Healthcare (formerly Amersham plc) 2004–06, vice-chm General Electric Co 2004–06 (dir 2006–), chm Wellcome Tst 2006–; non-exec dir: Marconi plc (formerly General Electric Co plc) 1997–2002, British Petroleum 2006–; visiting fell Green Coll Oxford 1993–; memb: MRC 2001–04, Bd Inst of Life Sciences Univ of Michigan 2003–; chm: Design Dimension Educnl Tst 1994–99, Regeneration Through Heritage 1997–2000, The Prince's Tst 1998–2003; tstee Natural History Museum 2004–; Outstanding Achievement Award ICAEW 2004; Hon DCL Univ of Oxford 2005; hon memb Academia Europea Assoc in support of Russian Science and Educn 1996; FCA 1980 (ACA 1974); *Recreations* int affairs, shooting, golf, skiing, tennis; *Clubs* Athenaeum, RAC; *Style*— Sir William Castell, LVO; ✉ Wellcome Trust, 215 Euston Road, London NW1 2BE (tel 020 7611 8888, fax 020 7611 8545)

CASTLE, Rt Rev Brian Colin; *see:* Tonbridge, Bishop of

CASTLE STEWART, 8 Earl (I 1800) Arthur Patrick Avondale Stuart; 15 Bt (S 1628); also Baron Castle Stuart (I 1619), and Viscount Castle Stuart (I 1793); s of 7 Earl Castle Stewart, MC (d 1961), and Eleanor May (d 1992), da of Solomon R Guggenheim, of New York; *b* 18 August 1928; *Educ* Eton, Trinity Coll Cambridge; *m* 1952, Edna (d 2003), da of William Edward Fowler; 1 s, 1 da; m 2, 2004, Gillian Fitzwilliams, da of Frederick William Savill of Blaby, Leics; *Heir* s, Viscount Stuart; *Career* late Lt Scots Gds; farmer; memb Advsy Bd Peggy Guggenheim Museum Venice; FIMgt; *Clubs* Carlton; *Style*— The Rt Hon the Earl Castle Stewart; ✉ Stuart Hall, Stewartstown, Co Tyrone, BT71 5AE (tel 028 8773 8208); Willoughby House, Barbican, London EC2Y 8BN

CASTLEDEN, Prof (Christopher) Mark; s of Dr Leslie Ivan Mark Castleden (d 1984), and Joan, *née* Smith; *b* 22 July 1944; *Educ* UCS, Bart's and Univ of London (MB BS, MD); *m* Julie Dawn; 3 da (Emily Jayne b 1972, Lorraine b 1974, Caroline b 1975), 1 s (Luke b 1991); *Career* RCP: memb 1972, memb Geriatrics Ctee 1979–85, fell 1984, prof 1987–98, prof emeritus 1998; chm: Advsy Sub-Ctee Geriatrics Med Tst 1981, Regl Educn Ctee on Geriatric Med 1994–96; dir of CME/CPD Br Geriatrics Soc 1998–2003 (chm Scientific Ctee 1994–97); memb: Ctee Safety of Meds 1984–86, Advsy Ctee on NHS Drugs 1991–99; *Recreations* sailing, gardening, antiques, reading; *Style*— Prof Mark Castleden; ✉ 2 Clinton Terrace, Budleigh Salterton, Devon EX9 6RX (e-mail c.castleden@doctors.org.uk)

CASTLEMAINE, 8 Baron (I 1812); Roland Thomas John Handcock; MBE; s of late 7 Baron (1973); *b* 22 April 1943; *Educ* Campbell Coll Belfast; *m* 1988, Lynne Christine, eldest da of Maj J M Gurney, RAEC; 1 s (Hon Ronan Michael Edward b 27 March 1989); *Heir* s, Hon Ronan Handcock; *Career* Lt-Col Army Air Corps, ret; aviation conslt; *Style*— The Rt Hon the Lord Castlemaine

CASTRO, Dr John Edward; s of Edward George Castro, of Norfolk, and Ivy Leuze Castro; *b* 10 August 1940; *Educ* Barnet GS, UCL (scholar, BSc, Suckling Prize for anatomy), UCH Med Sch (Fanny Magrath scholar in surgery, MRCS, LRCP, MB BS, MS, PhD, Sir Frances Walshe Prize in neurology, Erichson Prize for practical surgery); *m* 1 (m dis), Sylvia Rosemary Barber; 1 s (Ashley John b 1967), 2 da (Naomi Jane b 1970, Rebecca Elizabeth b 1973); m 2, Pamela Elizabeth, da of Rev Preb John Clifford Dale; *Career* house surgn UCH July-Dec 1965 (house physician Jan-June 1965), GP 1966; sr house surgn: Accident Service Luton and Dunstable Hosp Jan-June 1967, Hammersmith Hosp July-Dec 1967; res fell and hon urological registrar RPMS 1968–69, rotating surgical registrar Norfolk and Norwich Hosp 1969–71, scientific worker 1971–73 (Nat Inst for Med Res Mill Hill and Clinical Res Centre Harrow), res grant Cancer Res Campaign 1975, Arris-Gale lectr RCS 1975, hon conslt urologist Hammersmith Hosp 1975–79 (sr surgical registrar urology 1973–75), sr lectr in urology RPMS 1975–79 (tutor in surgery and lectr in immunology 1973–75), conslt urologist and transplant surgn 1979–; Patey Prize Surgical Res Soc 1973 and 1975, Univ Medal Univ of Hiroshima 1975, Ethicon Travel fellowship 1977; memb: Int Transplant Soc, BMA, Br Assoc of Urological Surgeons, European Dialysis and Transplantation Assoc, Euro Assoc of Urology; fndr memb Br Transplantation Soc, FRSM, FRCS (Edinburgh) 1968, FRCS (Eng) 1970; *Books* Treatment of Benign Prostate Hypertrophy and Neoplasia (1974), Immunology for Surgeons (1976), Immunological Aspects of Cancer (1978), Treatment of Renal Failure (1980); *Recreations* gardening, cooking, collecting card cases; *Clubs* Chelsea Clinical Soc; *Style*— Dr John Castro; ✉ The Old Vicarage, Fressingfield, Eye, Suffolk IP21 5PE (tel 01379 586537)

CATCHPOLE, Andrew; s of David John Catchpole, of Bath, and Jennifer Susan, *née* Roskruge; *b* 1 October 1966, Devon; *Educ* King's Coll Taunton, Goldsmiths Coll London (BA), London Inst (Dip Publishing); *m* 1 Dec 2001, Miranda, *née* Mather; *Career* early work with Oddbins and Bloomsbury Publishing; wine ed Channel 11 1996–97, dep ed Harpers Wine and Spirit Weekly 1997–99, food and drink ed Ampersand Magazine 2000–01, ed Hot Magazine 1999–2002, wine corr Daily Telegraph 2001–05; freelance food, wine, travel and restaurant writer, lectr and broadcaster 2000–; memb Circle of Wine Writers 1998–; *Recreations* cooking, literature, sailing, photography; *Style*— Andrew Catchpole, Esq; ✉ c/o Miranda Mather (tel 020 7697 8628, mobile 07949 078614); e-mail andrew.catchpole@virgin.net

CATCHPOLE, Prof David Ridley; s of Rev Cyril Walter John Catchpole (d 1973), and Winifred Patricia Mary, *née* Critchell (d 2003); *b* 1 May 1938; *Educ* Cheltenham GS, The Queen's Coll Oxford (MA), Pembroke Coll Cambridge (PhD); *m* 21 Aug 1963, Dorothy Ann, da of Lt-Col Charles Alexander Scott (d 1960); 2 da (Helen Margaret b 1966, Catherine Ailsa b 1970); *Career* tutor Clifton Theol Coll Bristol 1966–69, lectr and sr lectr Dept of Religious Studies Lancaster Univ 1969–84, prof of theological studies Univ of Exeter 1984–98 (univ fell 1998–, emeritus prof 2002–), currently scholar in residence Sarum Coll Salisbury; memb Gen Synod C of E 1970–75 (reader C of E 1970–), sec Soc for New Testament Study 1983–88; *Books* The Trial of Jesus (1971), The Quest for Q (1993), Resurrection People (2000), Jesus People (2006); *Recreations* gardening, cricket, theatre; *Style*— Prof David Catchpole; ✉ Binstead House, 15 Uplowman Road, Tiverton, Devon EX16 4LU (tel 01884 252100, e-mail anndavid@catchpole.fslife.co.uk); Sarum College, 19 The Close, Salisbury SP1 2EE (tel 01722 424800)

CATES, Armel Conyers; s of Conyers Seely Cates (d 1965), of Guildford, Surrey, and Jacqueline Maude, *née* Geoffroy (d 1988); *b* 3 May 1943; *Educ* Charterhouse, Univ of Southampton (LLB); *m* 8 July 1967, Pamela Susan, da of Colin Huson Walker, of Barrington, Cambs; 2 s (Tom b 1974, Sam b 1978), 1 da (Ilaria b 1980); *Career* articled to Theodore Goddard (London) and Vinters (Cambridge) 1967–69, admitted slr 1969; asst slr Coward Chance 1970–72, Clifford-Turner 1972–75, ptnr Clifford Chance 1975–2002; non-exec dir The Law Debenture Corp plc 2001–; former editorial advsr International Financial Law Review; tstee Charterhouse in Southwark; memb: Law Soc 1969, Int Bar

Assoc; Liveryman Worshipful Co of Slrs; *Recreations* golf, tennis, photography; *Style*— Armel Cates, Esq; ✉ Graves Farm, Catmere End, Saffron Walden, Essex CB11 4XG

CATFORD, Gordon Vivian; s of Harry George Bascombe (d 1984), of Weston-super-Mare, and Gladys Annie, *née* Horton (d 1951); *b* 23 November 1927; *Educ* Clifton, Univ of Bristol (MB ChB); *m* 10 June 1955, June Crichton, da of Robert Baxter (d 1983), of Edinburgh; 2 s (Gordon Baxter b 1958, Paul Nicholas b 1961); *Career* Nat Serv, Sqdn Ldr RAF Med Br CME 1954–56; house appts: Bristol Royal Infirmary 1951–52, Bristol Eye Hosp 1952–54; chief clinical asst Moorfields Eye Hosp 1960–64 (house appt 1958–60); conslt ophthalmic surgn: St George's Hosp London 1963–88 (first asst 1961–63), Royal London Homoeopathic Hosp 1969–88, Royal Masonic Hosp London 1973–98, St Luke's Hosp for the Clergy 1988–98; ophthalmologist: Linden Lodge Sch for the Blind 1978–89, Greenmead Sch for Multiple Handicapped 1978–89, John Aird Sch 1978–93; tutor Univ of London 1964–88, clinical teacher London Missionary Sch of Med 1975–89; examiner DipOphth Exam Bd of England 1967–73, memb Ct of Examiners RCS 1975– (chm Ophth 1979–81), external examiner RCS(Ed) 1984–88; ed British Ophthalmic Tapes 1966–76; memb Med Appeals Tbnl London South 1988–99, MAT 1988–99, founder memb UKISCRS (formerly UK Implant Soc) 1977–2002, advsr Br Orthoptic Soc; govr: Linden Lodge Sch 1978–89, Clifton Coll 1982– (memb Cncl 1982–93); Freeman City of London 1963, Liveryman Worshipful Soc of Apothecaries 1963; hon fell of orthoptics Br Orthoptic Soc 1988; memb BMA 1952, FRSM 1961, FRCS 1961, FRCOphth 1988 (hon archivist 1988–2002); *Recreations* gardening, freemasonry; *Style*— Gordon Catford, Esq; ✉ 9 St Johns Wood Park, London NW8 6QP

CATFORD, Sir (John) Robin; KCVO (1993), CBE (1990); er s of Adrian Leslie Catford (d 1979), and Ethel Augusta, *née* Rolfe (d 1988); *b* 11 January 1923; *Educ* Hampton GS, Univ of St Andrews (BSc), St John's Coll Cambridge (DipAg); *m* 21 Aug 1948, Daphne Georgina (d 2005), da of Col John Francis Darby, CBE, TD (d 1951); 3 s (John Charles b 1949, Simon Leslie b 1956, Francis James Robin b 1959), 1 da (Lucy Georgina b 1952); *Career* Sudan CS Dept of Agric and Forests 1946–55; commercial appts in UK 1955–66; MAFF 1966–82 (princ 1966, asst sec 1972, under sec 1979); transferred to PM's office 1982, sec for appts to PM and ecclesiastical sec to Lord Chllr 1982–93; crafts advsr Radcliffe Tst 1993–; *Recreations* sailing, travel, theatre, arts; *Clubs* Oxford and Cambridge; *Style*— Sir Robin Catford, KCVO, CBE; ✉ Priory Cottage, Priory Road, Chichester, West Sussex PO19 1NS (tel 01243 783197)

CATHCART, 7 Earl (UK 1814); Charles Alan Andrew Cathcart; also 16 Lord Cathcart (S *circa* 1447), Baron Greenock and Viscount Cathcart (both UK 1807); s of 6 Earl Cathcart, CB, DSO, MC (d 1999); *b* 30 November 1952; *Educ* Eton; *m* 1981, Vivien Clare, o da of Francis Desmond McInnes Skinner, of Snetterton, Norfolk; 1 da (Lady Laura Rosemary b 11 June 1984), 1 s (Alan George, Lord Greenock b 16 March 1986); *Heir* s, Lord Greenock; *Career* cmmnd Scots Gds 1972–75; CA Ernst and Whinney 1976–83, Hogg Robinson plc 1983, dir Gardner Mountain and Capel-Cure Agencies Ltd 1987–94, Murray Lawrence Holdings Ltd 1995–96; currently dir: RGA Holdings Ltd, RGA Capital Ltd, Vivien Greenock Ltd; cncllr for Breckland DC 1998–2007; memb Queen's Body Guard for Scotland (Royal Co of Archers); ACA; *Clubs* Pratt's; *Style*— The Rt Hon the Earl Cathcart; ✉ Gateley Hall, Dereham, Norfolk NR20 5EF

CATHERWOOD, Andrea Catherine; da of H R C Catherwood, and Adrienne Catherwood; *Educ* Strathearn Sch Belfast, Univ of Manchester (LLB); *m* 28 Sept 2002, Gray Smith; 3 s (Finn, Jago, Ruari); *Career* reporter UTV (Ulster Television) 1990–93, SE Asia corr NBC Asia Hong Kong 1994–98 (also anchor CNBC Asia), newscaster and reporter ITN 1998–99, anchor Channel 5 News 2000, newscaster and int corr ITV News 2001–; NI Young Presenter of the Year 1984 (pt/t work for BBC NI while at sch); *Recreations* sailing, diving, travel; *Clubs* Royal North of Ireland Yacht, Foreign Correspondents' (Hong Kong), Home House, Electric; *Style*— Ms Andrea Catherwood

CATHERWOOD, Sir (Henry) Frederick Ross (Fred); kt (1971); s of late Harold Matthew Stuart, and late Jean Catherwood, of Co Londonderry; *b* 30 January 1925; *Educ* Shrewsbury, Clare Coll Cambridge; *m* 1954, Elizabeth, er da of Rev Dr D Martyn Lloyd-Jones, of Westminster Chapel, London; 2 s (Christopher b 1955, Jonathan b 1961), 1 da (Bethan b 1958); *Career* articled clerk Price Waterhouse, qualified CA 1951; sec Laws Stores Ltd Gateshead 1952–54, chief exec Richard Costain Ltd 1955–60 (sec and controller 1954–55), md British Aluminium Co 1962–64 (asst md 1960–62), chief industrial advsr DEA 1964–66, dir gen NEDC 1966–71 (memb Cncl 1964–71), md and chief exec John Laing & Son Ltd 1972–74; chm Br Overseas Trade Bd 1975–79; MEP (EDG) Cambridge and North Bedfordshire 1979–94; Euro Parl: chm Ctee on External Economic Relations 1979–84, a vice-pres 1989–92, vice-pres Foreign Rels Ctee 1992–94; Br Inst of Mgmnt: memb Cncl 1961–66 and 1969–79, vice-chm 1972, chm 1974–76, vice-pres 1976–; pres: Fellowship of Ind Evangelical Churches 1977 (vice-pres 1976), Univs and Colls Christian Fellowship 1983–84 (chm Cncl 1971–77), Evangelical Alliance 1992–2001; vice-pres Int Fellowship of Evangelical Students 1995–2003 (treasurer 1979–91); memb Central Religious Advsy Ctee to BBC and IBA 1975–79; Hon DSc Aston Univ 1972, Hon DSc (Econ) Queen's Univ Belfast 1973, Hon DUniv Surrey 1979; hon fell Clare Coll 1992; *Books* The Christian in Industrial Society (1964), Britain with the Brakes Off (1966), The Christian Citizen (1969), A Better Way (1976), First Things First (1979), God's Time God's Money (1987), Pro Europe? (1991), David - Poet, Warrior, King (1993), At the Cutting Edge (memoirs, 1995), Jobs & Justice, Homes & Hope (1997), It Can be Done (2000), The Creation of Wealth (2002); *Recreations* music, gardening, reading; *Clubs* Oxford and Cambridge; *Style*— Sir Frederick Catherwood; ✉ Sutton Hall, Balsham, Cambridgeshire CB1 6DX (fax 01223 894032)

CATLIN, John Anthony; CB (2004); s of John Vincent Catlin (d 1961), and Kathleen Glover Brand (d 1982); *b* 25 November 1947; *Educ* Ampleforth, Univ of Birmingham (LLB); *m* 25 Aug 1974, Caroline Jane, *née* Goodman; 1 s, 2 da; *Career* Gregory Rowcliffe & Co: articled clerk 1970–72, admitted slr 1972, asst slr 1972–75; Civil Serv: joined as legal asst Treasy Slrs' Dept 1975 (sr legal asst 1978), transferred to Dept of Environment as asst slr 1984–89, appointed dep slr (under sec (legal)) Dept of Environment 1989, seconded 1996 and transferred to DSS 1998, dir Legal Servs (social security) 1996–2004, dir Legal Servs (health) 2004–; memb Law Soc 1972; *Recreations* music, history, computers; *Style*—John Catlin, Esq, CB; ✉ Office of the Solicitor, Department for Work and Pensions, Room 455, New Court, 48 Carey Street, London WC2A 2LS (tel 020 7412 1229)

CATLING, Prof Brian David; s of Leonard Frederick Catling, of London, and Lilian Alice Catling; *b* 23 October 1948; *Educ* NE London Poly, RCA; *m* 1; 1 s (Jack Ishmael b 19 Dec 1983); m 2; 1 da (Florence Pike b 13 April 1989), 1 s (Finn Bell b 23 Nov 1990); *Career* artist and poet; visiting lectr: Jan Van Eyck Akademie Maastricht Netherlands 1980–84, Chelsea Sch of Art, Royal Acad, Vestlandets Kunsteakademi Bergen Norway, Kunsteakademi Trondheim Norway; Henry Moore fell in sculpture Norwich Sch of Art 1982–85, tutor in sculpture RCA 1983–90, princ lectr in sculpture Brighton Poly, head of sculpture Ruskin Sch of Drawing and Fine Art 1991–, fell Linacre Coll Oxford 1991, prof of fine art Univ of Oxford; winner Paul Hamlyn Fndn Award for Visual Art 2001; hon fell Dartington Sch of Arts; *Solo Exhibitions* incl: Air Gallery London 1977, Camden Arts Centre London 1979, Arnolfini Gallery Bristol 1980, Norwich Sch of Art Gallery 1982–84, Atlantis Gallery London 1984, South Hill Park Arts Centre Berkshire 1984, Liefsgade 22 Copenhagen 1986, Hordaland Kunstnercentrum Bergen 1987, Matt's Gallery London 1987, Neue Gallerie Sammlung Ludwig Aachen 1988, MOMA Oxford 1989, At the Lighthouse (Matt's Gallery London) 1991, Gallerie Satellite Paris 1993, TEN Gallery Fukuoka Japan 1993, The Blindings (Serpentine Gallery London), A Conceptual Telescope for Bergen (cmmnd public sculptures over five sites) 1994, Window (installed sculpture for Br Embassy Dublin) 1995, Cyclops (video installation, Galerie Satellite Paris, South London Gallery, Museet for Samtidskunst Oslo, Project Gallery Leipzig) 1995–97, Vanished! a video seance (with Tony Grisoni, Ikon Gallery Birmingham and South London Gallery) 1999, Palermo Apport Tables (Bluecoat Arts Centre Liverpool) 2000, Cyclops (Inst Friedrichsbau Bühl) 2002, Trans-Art Trondheim 2002; *Group Exhibitions* incl: Albion Island Vortex (Whitechapel Gallery London) 1974, Imagination is the Venom (Ikon Gallery London) 1981, Art and the Sea (Arnolfini Gallery Bristol and ICA London) 1982, Nordic Winter Symposium (Geilo) 1982, Bookworks (V&A Museum London) 1988, MOBSHOP IV (Viborg and Malmö Kunsthaller Sweden) 1989, Upturned Art (Pitt Rivers Museum Oxford) 1990, Nylistasfnid (The Living Art Museum Reykjavik) 1990, 3 Artists from Oxford (St Catherine's Coll Oxford and Kobe Japan) 1993, Oak Repels Lightning (Science Museum London) 1998, Small Acts at the Millennium 2000; *Performance Works* incl: Miltonian Ghost Dance (Whitechapel Gallery London) 1980, Spogelsemasse (Leifscade 22 Copenhagen) 1986, five performances (cmmnd by MOMA Oxford) 1989, Two Works for Trondheim (Trondelac Arts Centre Trondheim Norway) 1990, Refined White (Tate Gallery London) 1993, Augenlied (Schloss Plüschow Art Centre Mecklenburg) 1993, Sunflint (Artifact Gallery Tel Aviv) 1993, Hidden Cities (bus tour, Laboratory Gallery Oxford) 1995, Clepsydra (South London Gallery) 1996, Freiwild Festival (Halle) 1996, Madrid Festival 1997, One Night Stands (Norwich Gallery) 1997, Hush (Slaughter House Gallery) 1997, Night of the Living Tongues (Cambridge) 1997, Flylkingen (Stockholm) 1997, Science Museum London 1997, Bergen Performance Festival 1997, Stadt Gallerie Berne 1998, Virus (Freiwild Festival Halle) 1998, Nat Review of Live Art (Glasgow) 2000–02, Steder: More Places For Ever (Lillehammer) 2002, The Boulavards (Den Bosch) 2002, Acts of Faith and Generosity (La Bisbal) 2002, The Wolf (Greenland tour) 2003; *Publications* The First Electron Heresy (1977), Vorticegargen (1979), Pleides in Nine (1981), Vox Humana (1984), Das Kranke Tier (1984), The Tulpa Index (1986), Lair (1987), Boschlog (1988 and 1989), The Stumbling Block (1990), Future Exiles (1991), The First London Halo (1994), Thyhand (1994), The Blindings (1995), Large Ghost (2001), Late Harping (2001), Thyhand (2001); poem The Stumbling incl in OUP Anthology of 20th Century British and Irish Poetry (2001); subject of Tending the Vortex: the Works of B Catling (by Simon Perrill, 2001); *Style*— Prof Brian Catling; ✉ Ruskin School of Drawing & Fine Art, 74 High Street, Oxford OX1 4BG (tel 01865 276940, e-mail brian.catling@ruskin-school.ox.ac.uk)

CATO, Andy; *née* Andrew Coecup; *b* Yorkshire; *Career* musician: former DJ and fndr record label Skinnymalinky; memb Groove Armada (with Tom Findlay, *qv*); top 20 singles incl: At The River (re-release) 1999, I See You Baby 1999, Superstylin' 2001, I See You Baby (re-issue) 2004; albums: Northern Star 1998, Vertigo 1999, Back to Mine 2000, The Remixes 2000, Goodbye Country (Hello Nightclub) 2001, Another Late Night: Groove Armada 2002, Lovebox 2002, Doin' It After Dark 2004, The Best Of 2004; collaborations incl album Pursuit of Happiness (Weekend Players) 2002; Young Jazz Musician of the Year 1995; *Style*— Andy Cato, Esq; ✉ c/o Liz Gould, Sanctuary Management, The Sanctuary Group plc, Sanctuary House, 45–53 Sinclair Road, London W14 0NS (tel 020 7602 6351)

CATON, Brian; *b* 28 July 1950; *Career* trade unionist; joined Prison Service 1977; Prison Offrs Assoc (POA, now Professional Trades Union for Prison Correctional and Secure Psychiatric Workers): memb Branch Ctee HMP Wakefield 1979 and 1994 (health and safety rep 1979, branch sec 1980–89), memb NEC 1989 (vice-chair 1990–94), asst sec 1996–2000, gen sec 2000– (also ed Gatelodge magazine, sec to various POA ctees, memb Cncl of Civil Service Unions Superannuation Sub-Ctee, memb Review of Pensions Jt Working Gp); TUC: press offr Wakefield 1983, vice-pres and political offr Wakefield 1984, pres Wakefield 1986–89, gen sec Wakefield 2000–, currently memb Gen Cncl, memb Lesbian and Gay, Bisexual and Transsexual Ctee, memb Nat Trades Cncl TUC Ctee; currently exec memb Cncl European Fedn of Employees in Public Serv (also pres Justice Gp); memb Lab Pty; *Style*— Brian Caton, Esq; ✉ POA, Cronin House, 245 Church Street, Edmonton, Middlesex N9 9HW (tel 020 8803 0255, fax 020 8803 1761, e-mail gs@poauk.org.uk)

CATON, Martin; MP; *Career* MP (Lab) Gower 1997–; *Style*— Martin Caton, Esq, MP; ✉ House of Commons, London SW1A 0AA (tel 020 7219 5111/2078); constituency office: 9 Pontardulais Road, Gorseinon, Swansea (tel 01792 892100, fax 01792 892375)

CATON, HE Dr Valerie; da of Robert Caton (d 1996), and Florence Amy, *née* Aspden; *b* 12 May 1952, Darwen, Lancs; *Educ* Blackburn HS for Girls, Univ of Bristol (BA, PhD), Reading Grad Sch (MA); *m* 5 Sept 1987, David Mark Harrison; 1 da (Isobel b 29 May 1992), 1 s (Thomas b 5 Nov 1994); *Career* diplomat; tutor in French Univ of Exeter 1978–80; joined FCO 1980, with UK Perm Representation to the EU Brussels then second then first sec (EC affrs) Brussels 1982–84, desk offr Southern Africa Dept FCO 1984–86, dep head policy planners FCO 1986–88, first sec (political) Paris 1988–92, dep head of mission and consul-gen Stockholm 1993–96, cnsllr (financial and economic) Paris 1997–2001, sr assoc memb St Antony's Coll Oxford 2001–02, head Environment Policy Dept FCO 2002–04, head Climate Change and Energy Gp FCO 2004–06, ambass to Finland 2006–; *Publications* France and the Politics of EMU (2002); author of articles on Raymond Queneau; *Recreations* walking, riding, theatre, collecting first editions by P G Wodehouse and Mark Twain; *Style*— HE Dr Valerie Caton; ✉ c/o FCO (Helsinki), King Charles Street, London SW1A 2AH (tel 00 358 2286 5222, fax 00 358 2286 5284, e-mail valerie.caton@fco.gov.uk)

CATOR, Albemarle John; s of John Cator, of Woodbastwick, Norfolk, and Elizabeth Jane, *née* Kerrison; *b* 23 August 1953; *Educ* Harrow; *m* 1, 29 Nov 1980 (m dis 1992), Fiona Mary, da of Robert Edgar Atheling Drummond; 2 s (John b 1983, Robert Henry b 1985); m 2, 17 May 1995, Victoria Katherine, da of Maj-Gen David Pank, CB; 2 s (Christian David b 22 Sept 1996, Sebastian Edward b 20 Feb 1999); *Career* Lt Scots Guards 1971–74; with Samuel Montagu 1975–84, exec dir Chemical Bank International Ltd 1984–88, exec dir Chemical Securities Ltd 1988–91, vice-pres Chemical Bank 1988–91; NatWest Capital Markets Ltd: exec dir 1991–95, md 1995–97; chm AC European Finance Ltd 1997–2003, dir ECU Gp plc 2004–, dir Longleat Enterprises Ltd 2004–; *Recreations* sailing, shooting, skiing; *Clubs* RYS, Pratt's; *Style*— Albemarle Cator, Esq; ✉ Woodbastwick Hall, Woodbastwick, Norwich, Norfolk NR13 6HL

CATOR, Charles; s of Peter Cator (d 2006), and Katharine, *née* Coke; *b* 1 October 1952, London; *Educ* Eton, Univ of Bristol; *Career* joined Christie's 1973, dep chm Christie's Europe 1995–2000, co-chm Christie's Int UK Ltd 2001–06, dep chm Christie's Int 2007–; *Publications* contrib on subject of furniture to: Jl of the Furniture History Society, Apollo, Dictionary of English Furniture Makers 1660–1840, Country Life; *Recreations* gardening, opera, architecture and design; *Clubs* White's, Brooks's; *Style*— Charles Cator, Esq; ✉ Christie's, 8 King Street, London SW1Y 6QT (tel 020 7389 2355, fax 020 7389 2501, e-mail ccator@christies.com)

CATT, Michael John (Mike); MBE (2004); s of James Ernest Catt, of Port Elizabeth, South Africa, and Anne Gillian, *née* Crowther; *b* 17 September 1971; *Educ* Grey HS Port Elizabeth; *m* Dec 2001, Allison Hastie; *Career* rugby union back; club: Bath 1993–2004 (Courage League Champions 1996, winners Pilkington Cup 1996, winners Heineken European Cup 1998), London Irish 2004–; England: 71 caps, debut v Wales 1994, memb squad World Cup 1995, 2003 (champions) and 2007, winners Grand Slam 1995 and Six Nations Championship 2000 and 2001; memb Br Lions tour to SA 1997 and Aust 2001;

Bath Player of the Year 1994, Most Promising Player of the Year Award 1995; *Recreations* socialising, golf; *Style*— Mike Catt, Esq, MBE

CATTANEO, Peter; *Educ* RCA; *Career* director; attached to Paul Weiland Film Co to direct commercials 1991; *Television* Diary of a Teenage Health Freak II (Limelight/Channel Four) 1992, The Bill (Thames Television) 1992, The Full Wax (BBC) 1992–93; *Film* True or False - The Big Easy 1989, Two 12 Minute Films 1990, Dear Rosie 1990, Say Hello to the Real Dr Snide 1990, Loved Up 1995, The Full Monty 1997, Lucky Break 2001; *Style*— Peter Cattaneo, Esq

CATTERALL, John Stewart; s of John Bernard Catterall (d 1965), and Eliza, *née* Whitiker; *b* 13 January 1939; *Educ* Blackpool Tech Coll Sch of Art; *m* 18 Sept 1965, (Ann) Beryl, da of Edgar Watkin Hughes; 2 s (Andrew b 4 Aug 1969, Stewart b 3 Feb 1971); *Career* Nat Serv band memb 12 Royal Lancers 1958–60; dep auditor Preston CBC 1966–68, sr accountant Derby CBC 1968–70, mgmnt and chief accountant Cambs and Isle of Ely CC 1970–73, asst co treas Cambs CC 1973–76, dist treas Southampton & SW Hants HA 1976–78, area treas Hants AHA 1978–82, regnl treas NE Thames RHA 1982–85; dep dir fin mgmnt Dept of Health and head Health Serv 1985–88, dir consultancy for health 1988–89; md and chief exec C International Ltd 1989–92, dir Healthcare Consultancy Capita plc 1992–93, md C & T Ltd 1993–2001, dir Agenda Planning and Research 2002–; memb CIPFA; *Recreations* golf, tennis; *Style*— John Catterall, Esq; ✉ Le Moulin, Stock Lane, Landford Wood, Wiltshire SP5 2ER (mobile 07900 261551, e-mail johncatterall@btconnect.com)

CATTERSON, Her Hon Judge Marie Thérèse; da of James Joseph Catterson, and Rosemary, *née* McCarthy; *b* 14 October 1948; *Educ* Wyggeston Girls' GS Leicester, UCL (LLB); *m* 4 Aug 1984; 2 da; *Career* called to the Bar Gray's Inn 1972; recorder of the Crown Court 1996–2001, circuit judge (SE Circuit) 2001–; *Style*— Her Hon Judge Catterson; ✉ The Crown Court at St Albans, Bricket Road, St Albans, Hertfordshire AL1 3JW (tel 01727 753220, fax 01727 753221)

CATTO, Hon Alexander Gordon; 2 s (by 1 m) of 2 Baron Catto; *b* 22 June 1952; *Educ* Westminster, Trinity Coll Cambridge; *m* 1981, Elizabeth Scott, da of late Maj T P Boyes, MC, of Whitford, Devon; 2 s (Thomas Innes Gordon b 1983, Alastair Gordon b 1986), 1 da (Charlotte Gordon b 1988); *Career* vice-pres Morgan Guaranty Trust Co of New York 1980–85; dir: Yule Catto & Co plc 1981–, Morgan Grenfell & Co Ltd 1986–88; md: Lazard Bros & Co 1988–94, CairnSea Investments Ltd, other private and public cos; *Style*— The Hon Alexander Catto; ✉ Yule Catto & Co plc, Temple Fields, Harlow, Essex CM20 2BH (tel 01279 442791)

CATTO, Prof Sir Graeme Robertson Dawson; kt (2002); s of Dr William Dawson Catto, of Aberdeen, and Dora Elizabeth, *née* Spiby (d 1978); *b* 24 April 1945; *Educ* Robert Gordon's Coll Aberdeen, Univ of Aberdeen (MB ChB, MD, DSc), Harvard Univ; *m* 14 July 1967, Joan, da of James Alexander Sievewright (d 1958), of Aberdeen; 1 da (Sarah b 1970), 1 s (Simon b 1972); *Career* house offr Aberdeen Royal Infirmary 1969–70, Harkness fell in med Harvard Med Sch 1975–77; Univ of Aberdeen: lectr in med 1970–75, sr lectr in med 1977–88, prof of med and therapeutics 1988–2000, dean Faculty of Clinical Med 1992–95, vice-princ and dean Faculty of Med & Med Sciences 1995–98, vice-princ 1998–2000; hon conslt physician and nephrologist Grampian Health Bd 1977–2000, co-ordinator of clinical services Acute Services Unit Grampian Health Bd 1988–92, vice-chm Aberdeen Royal Hosps NHS Tst 1992–99, hon physician Guy's and St Thomas' Hosp NHS Tst 2000–05; vice-princ King's Coll London 2000–05 (fell 2005–), dean GKT 2000–05, pro-vice-chllr Univ of London 2003–05, prof of medicine Univ of Aberdeen 2005–, hon conslt physician and nephrologist NHS Grampian 2005–; govr: PPP Healthcare Med Tst 2001–02, Qatar Science Technol Park 2003–; pres GMC 2002– (chm Educn Ctee 1999–2002), memb Scottish Higher Educn Funding Cncl 1996–2002, chief scientist NHS Scotland 1997–2000, treas Acad of Med Scis 1998–2001; memb: SE London Strategic HA 2002–05, Cncl for the Regulation of Healthcare Professionals 2003–, Assoc of Physicians of GB and I; chm Robert Gordon's Coll Aberdeen 1995–2005; Burgess of Guild City of Aberdeen; Hon LLD Univ of Aberdeen 2002, Hon DSc Univ of St Andrews 2003, Hon MD Univ of Southampton 2004, Hon DSc Robert Gordon Univ 2004, Hon DSc Univ of Kent 2007, Hon DSc South Bank Univ; Hon FRCGP, Hon FRCSE; FRCP, FRCPEd, FRCPGlas, FMedSci, FRSE; *Books* Clinical Nephrology (1988), Transplant Immunology (1993); *Recreations* hill walking; *Clubs* Royal Northern and University, Athenaeum; *Style*— Prof Sir Graeme Catto, FRSE; ✉ Maryfield, Glenbuchat, Strathdon, Aberdeenshire AB36 8TS (tel 01975 631317); General Medical Council, 350 Euston Road, London NW1 3JN (tel 020 7189 5012)

CATTO, 3 Baron (UK 1936); Sir Innes Gordon Catto; 3 Bt (UK 1921); s (by 1 m) of 2 Baron Catto (d 2001); *b* 7 August 1950; *Educ* Grenville Coll, Shuttleworth Agric Coll; *Career* dir Caledonian Opera Co; *Style*— The Rt Hon the Lord Catto; ✉ Flat 17, Centre Point Flats, St Giles High Street, London WC2H 8LW

CATTRALL, Peter Jeremy; s of late Ralph W Cattrall, of Margate, Kent, and Sally Cattrall; *b* 8 January 1947; *Educ* King's Sch Canterbury, Trinity Coll Oxford (MA); *m* 26 April 1975, Amanda Jane Maria, da of Maj Gen W N J Withall, CB, and Pamela Withall, of Wiltshire; 1 s (Charles David b 1 March 1980), 1 da (Sarah Louise b 21 Sept 1982); *Career* former sch master Holmewood House Kent; admitted slr 1974, asst slr Knocker and Foskett Kent 1974–77, slr to Esso UK plc / Exxon Corp 1977–2000; slr and legal advsr to EMC Ltd and Saipem UK 2001–03, conslt to Carroll & Ptnrs Ltd 2000–, also conslt to Mitsui and various other cos; memb: Oxford Union, Law Soc; memb Kent Co squash team 1970–78; MEI; *Recreations* golf, swimming, squash doubles, watching sport, travel, reading, music, current affairs; *Clubs* Oxford and Cambridge, MCC, Rye Golf, Free Foresters, I Zingari, Stragglers of Asia, Arabs, Jesters, Band of Brothers, Harlequins, Vincent's (Oxford), Beckenham Cricket; *Style*— Peter Cattrall, Esq; ✉ 21 Whitmore Road, Beckenham, Kent (home tel 020 8658 7265, e-mail petercattrall@hotmail.com); office tel 020 7623 2228

CAUTE, (John) David; JP (1993); *b* 16 December 1936; *Educ* Edinburgh Acad, Wellington, Wadham Coll Oxford; *m* 1, 1961 (m dis 1970), Catherine Shuckburgh; 2 s; m 2, 1973, Martha Bates; 2 da; *Career* served Army Gold Coast 1955–56; novelist and historian; Henry fell Harvard Univ 1960–61, fell All Souls Oxford 1959–65, visiting prof NY and Colombia Univs 1966–67, reader in social and political theory Brunel Univ 1967–70, Regent's lectr Univ of Calif 1974, visiting prof Univ of Bristol 1985; literary ed New Statesman 1979–80, co-chm Writers' Guild 1981–82; FRSL 1998; *Novels* At Fever Pitch (1959, Authors' Club Award, John Llewelyn Rhys Prize), Comrade Jacob (1961), The Decline of the West (1966), The Occupation (1971), The Baby-Sitters (as John Salisbury, 1978), Moscow Gold (as John Salisbury, 1980), The K-Factor (1983), News From Nowhere (1986), Veronica or the Two Nations (1988), The Women's Hour (1991), Dr Orwell and Mr Blair (1994), Fatima's Scarf (1998); *Plays* Songs for an Autumn Rifle (1961), The Demonstration (1969), The Fourth World (1973); *Radio Plays* Fallout (1972), The Zimbabwe Tapes (1983), Henry and the Dogs (1986), Sanctions (1988), Animal Fun Park (1995); *Non-Fiction* Communism and the French Intellectuals 1914–1960 (1964), The Left in Europe Since 1789 (1966), Essential Writings of Karl Marx (ed, 1967), Fanon (1970), The Illusion (1971), The Fellow-Travellers (1973, revised edn 1988), Cuba, Yes ? (1974), Collisions - Essays and Reviews (1974), The Great Fear - The Anti-Communist Purge under Truman and Eisenhower (1978), Under the Skin - The Death of White Rhodesia (1983), The Espionage of the Saints (1986), Sixty-Eight - The Year of the Barricades (1988), Joseph Losey: A Revenge on Life (1994), The Dancer Defects - The Struggle for Cultural Supremacy During the Cold War (2003); *Style*— David Caute, Esq; ✉ 41 Westcroft Square, London W6 0TA

CAVALIER, David John; s of John Richard Cavalier, of Bloxwich, Birmingham, and Jackie Orama, *née* Wheatley; *b* 12 February 1962; *Educ* Mandeville County Secdy Sch, Aylesbury Coll of Further Educn (City and Guilds Certs, Cert of Royal Inst of Health and Hygiene), Ealing Coll of Higher Educn (City and Guilds Cert); *m* 2 Feb 1985, Susan Caroline, da of Ronald Dorsett; 2 da (Jennifer b 22 Oct 1988, Alexandra b 24 Oct 1995), m 2, 1 June 2000, Jo-Anne Karen, da of Sidney Bibby; 2 da (Françoise Molly-Anna b 30 Jan 2002, Beatrice Millie Helena b 19 Dec 2006); *Career* commis chef Royal Garden Hotel 1979–81, first commis chef Grosvenor House Hotel 1981–82, chef de partie Dorchester Hotel 1982–84, sous chef Auberge du Mail France 1984, first sous chef Berkeley Hotel 1984–85; chef and proprietor: Pebbles Restaurant 1985–87, Cavalier's Restaurant 1987–; head chef: The Bell Inn Aston Clinton 1992–93, L'Escargot 1993–95; jt proprietor Chapter One 1996–, proprietor Memo restaurant 1996–, exec chef Mosimanns 1999–2000, High Holborn 2000–01, food innovation dir Charlton House 2001–; winner: Gold medal (potato work) Hotel Olympia, Gold medal for best exhibit in jr class, finalist Young Chef of the Year competition 1987; awarded: 4 rosette AA Guide, 2 star Michelin Guide, black clover Ackerman Guide, 1 star Egon Ronay; memb Restaurant Assoc GB 1985; *Recreations* classic cars, fishing; *Style*— David Cavalier, Esq; ✉ 1 Minall Close, Tring, Hertfordshire HP23 5BH

CAVALIER, Stephen; s of Kenneth Cavalier, and Marion, *née* Hussey; *b* 26 February 1962, St Albans, Herts; *Educ* Univ of Oxford (BA); *partner* Claire Sullivan; 2 s (Cameron b 22 Nov 1990, Keir b 8 Oct 1992); *Career* slr; Thompsons: joined as slr 1987, head Employment Rights Unit 1996, client dir 2003, ceo 2007–; former chair Industrial Law Soc; memb Lab Pty 1979–; *Publications* Transfer of Undertakings (1997 and 2006); *Recreations* politics, football; *Clubs* Tottenham Hotspur FC; *Style*— Stephen Cavalier, Esq; ✉ Thompsons, Congress House, Great Russell Street, London WC1B 3LW (tel 020 7290 0007, e-mail stephencavalier@thompsons.law.co.uk)

CAVALIER, Stephen Ronald (Steve); s of Ronald Ernest Cavalier, of Romford, Essex, and Jean, *née* Chinery; *b* 25 June 1952; *Educ* Harold Hill GS Essex, Colchester Sch of Art; *m* 1 Sept 1979, Christine, da of William Alfred Guerrier; 1 da (Clare Jean b 31 Aug 1982), 1 s (James William b 11 Feb 1985); *Career* photographer; asst with advertising photographers London 1971–77, fndr Steve Cavalier Studios 1977– (Central London then moving to St John's Wood); Gold and Silver Awards Design and Art Directors' Assoc, Gold and Silver Campaign Press Awards, Gold Award The One Show NY, commendation Benson & Hedges Gold Award 1990, Silver Award Campaign Poster Awards 1995; memb: Assoc of Photographers (formerly Assoc of Fashion, Advertising and Editorial Photographers), D&AD; *Style*— Steve Cavalier, Esq; ✉ Steve Cavalier Studios, 19 Chippenham Mews, London W9 2AN (tel 020 7286 9700, e-mail steve@stevecavalier.co.uk, website www.stevecavalier.co.uk)

CAVALIER-SMITH, Prof Thomas (Tom); s of Alan Cavalier-Smith (d 1976), and Mary Cavalier-Smith (d 2006); *b* 21 October 1942, London; *Educ* Gonville & Caius Coll Cambridge (maj open scholar, MA) KCL (PhD), Open Univ (BA); *m* 1, 1967, Gillian; m 2, Ema, *née* Chao; 2 da (Jane b 1964, Rose Mary b 1994), 1 s (Neal b 1966); *Career* guest investigator Rockefeller Univ 1967–69; KCL: lectr 1969–82, reader in biophysics 1982–89; prof of botany Univ of British Columbia 1989–99; Univ of Oxford: research prof NERC 1999–, prof of evolutionary biology 2000–; Int Prize for Biology 2004, Linnean Medal for Zoology 2007; FRSC 1997, FRS 1998, fell Canadian Inst for Advanced Research 1998, FRSA, FLS, FIBiol; *Publications* Biology, Society and Choice (ed with J P Hudson. 1982), The Evolution of Genome Size (ed, 1985); author of nearly 200 scientific articles and book chapters; *Recreations* reading, natural history; *Style*— Prof Thomas Cavalier-Smith; ✉ Department of Zoology, University of Oxford, South Parks Road, Oxford OX1 3PS (e-mail tom.cavalier-smith@zoo.ox.ac.uk)

CAVALIERO, Dr Glen; s of Clarence John Cavaliero (d 1958), and Mildred Osborne Cavaliero, *née* Tilburn (d 1950); *b* 7 June 1927, Eastbourne, E Sussex; *Educ* Tonbridge, Magdalen Coll Oxford (MA), St Catharine's Coll Cambridge (MA, PhD); *Career* poet; staff memb Lincoln Theol Coll 1956–61; St Catharine's Coll Cambridge: research fell 1967–71, fell commoner 1986; pres The Powys Soc; FRSL 1986; *Publications* incl: The Ancient People (poems, 1973), John Cowper Powys: Novelist (1973), Paradise Stairway (poems, 1977), The Rural Tradition in the English Novel (1977), A Reading of E M Forster (1979), Elegy for St Anne's (poems, 1982), Charles Williams: Poet of Theology (1983), The Supernatural and English Fiction (1995), Steeple on a Hill (poems, 1997), The Alchemy of Laughter (2000), Ancestral Haunt (poems, 2002), The Justice of the Night (poems, 2007); *Style*— Dr Glen Cavaliero; ✉ St Catharine's College, Cambridge CB2 1RL

CAVAN, 13 Earl of (I 1647); Roger Cavan Lambart; has not yet established claim; also Viscount Kilcoursie (I 1647) and Lord Lambart, Baron of Cavan (I 1617); o s of Frederick Cavan Lambart (d 1963), and Audrey May, *née* Dunham (d 2002); suc kinsman, 12 Earl of Cavan, TD, 1988; *b* 1 September 1944; *Educ* Wilson's Sch Wallington, KCL, St Clare's Oxford; *Heir* kinsman, Cavan Lambart (presumed heir); *Style*— The Rt Hon the Earl of Cavan

CAVANAGH, John Eric; s of Charles Cavanagh, and Jean Burns Cavanagh; *b* 27 December 1964; *Career* broadcaster, musician and writer; presenter BBC Radio 1990–, wide range of material across the BBC network incl the Radio One Rock Show and Music Machine (Radio 3) and shows on BBC Scotland and World Service; memb Electroscope (over 100 titles released) 1996–2000; Phosphene (music project) 2000– (albums: Long Meadow Felt Company 2001, Projection 2003, The Plum, the Orange and the Matchbox 2005, Phoenix Trees 2007); collaborations incl work with: Mount Vernon Arts Lab, Hefner, Isobel Campbell, Lol Coxhill, Bridget St John, Bill Wells, Nalle, Aube (Japanese performance artist), Colleen, Colour Match by Simon Patterson Tate Modern; *Publications* The Piper at the Gates of Dawn (2003); *Recreations* vintage analogue sound instruments and recording, travel, wine, cinema; *Clubs* BBC, Pastelism, Joe Meek Appreciation Soc; *Style*— John Cavanagh, Esq; ✉ BBC Radio One, Glasgow G12 8DG (e-mail john.cavanagh@bbc.co.uk and phosphene@debrett.net, website www.phosphene.debrett.net)

CAVANAGH, John Patrick; QC (2001); s of Dr Gerry Cavanagh (decd), of Welford-on-Avon, Warks, and Anne, *née* Kennedy; *b* 17 June 1960, Belfast; *Educ* Warwick Sch, New Coll Oxford (open scholar, MA), Clare Coll Cambridge (LLM), Univ of Illinois Coll of Law; *m* 6 May 1989, Suzanne Fiona (Suzie), da of Harry Tolley; 3 da (Sophie Marie b 1 Oct 1990, Emma Rosanne b 19 March 1992, Isabelle Grace b 29 Dec 1996), 1 s (John Patrick b 27 Sept 1994); *Career* called to the Bar Middle Temple 1985; Treasy counsel (B Panel) 1997–2001; pt/t lectr New Coll Oxford 1984–86; memb editorial team: Tolley's Employment Handbook 1998–2005 (jt ed), Harvey on Industrial Relations and Employment Law 2000–04, Butterworth's Local Government Law; frequent speaker and writer on employment law and public law issues; chair Employment Law Bar Assoc 2005–; memb: Administrative Law Bar Assoc, Commercial Bar Assoc; *Recreations* family, reading, music, football; *Style*— John Cavanagh, Esq, QC; ✉ 11 King's Bench Walk, Temple, London EC4Y 7EQ (tel 020 7632 8500, fax 020 7583 9123, e-mail cavanagh@11kbw.com)

CAVE, *see:* Haddon-Cave

CAVE, Sir John Charles; 5 Bt (UK 1896), of Cleve Hill, Mangotsfield, Co Gloucester, Sidbury Manor, Sidbury, Co Devon, and Stoneleigh House, Clifton, Bristol; DL (Devon 2001); o s of Sir Charles Edward Coleridge Cave, 4 Bt (d 1997); *b* 8 September 1958; *Educ* Eton,

RAC Cirencester; *m* 1984, Carey Diana, er da of John Lloyd, of Coombeland, Cadeleigh, Tiverton, Devon; 2 s (George Charles b 8 Sept 1987, William Alexander b 7 May 1992), 1 da (Alice Elizabeth b 28 June 1989); *Heir* s, George Cave; *Career* High Sheriff Devon 2005, Vice-Lord Lt Devon 2007; *Style*— Sir John Cave, Bt, DL; ✉ Sidbury Manor, Sidmouth, Devon EX10 0QE

CAVE, Prof Terence Christopher; s of Alfred Cyril Cave (d 1979), and Sylvia Norah, *née* Norman (d 1989); *b* 1 December 1938; *Educ* Winchester, Gonville & Caius Coll Cambridge (MA, DPhil); *m* 31 July 1965 (m dis 1990), Helen Elizabeth; 1 s (Christopher b 1969), 1 da (Hilary b 1970); *Career* lectr Univ of St Andrews 1963–65 (asst lectr 1962–63), sr lectr Univ of Warwick 1970–72 (lectr 1965–70), fell and tutor St John's Coll Oxford 1972–2001 (emeritus res fell 2001–), prof of French literature Univ of Oxford 1989–2001 (emeritus prof 2001–); visiting posts: Cornell Univ 1967–68, Univ of Calif Santa Barbara 1976, Univ of Virginia 1979, Princeton Univ 1984, Univ of Trondheim 1991, Univ of Alberta Edmonton 1992, Univ of Paris 7 1995 and 2002, UCLA 1997, NYU 2003, Univ of Oslo 2006; visiting fell All Souls Coll Oxford 1971; hon sr res fell Inst of Romance Studies London, memb Royal Norwegian Soc of Sciences and Letters; hon fell Gonville & Caius Coll Cambridge; memb Academia Europaea; FBA; Chevalier dans l'Ordre National du Mérite (France); Hon DLit Univ of London 2007; *Books* Devotional Poetry in France (1969), The Cornucopian Text (1979), Recognitions (1988), Pré-histoires (1999), Pré-histoires II (2001), How to Read Montaigne (2007); *Style*— Prof Terence Cave, FBA; ✉ St John's College, Oxford OX1 3JP (tel 01865 280176, fax 01865 277435, e-mail terence.cave@sjc.ox.ac.uk)

CAVE-BROWNE-CAVE, Sir Robert; 16 Bt (E 1641), of Stanford, Northamptonshire; s of Sir Clement Charles Cave-Browne-Cave, 15 Bt (d 1945), and Dorothea Plewman, *née* Dwen; *b* 8 June 1929; *Educ* St George's Sch Vancouver, Univ Sch Victoria, British Columbia Univ; *m* 1, 1954 (m dis 1975), Lois Shirley, da of John Chalmers Huggard, of Winnipeg, Canada; 1 da (Lisé Irene b 1955), 1 s (John Robert Charles b 1957); m 2, 1977, Joan Shirley, da of Dr Kenneth Ashe Peacock, of W Vancouver, BC; *Heir* s, John Cave-Brown-Cave; *Career* pres Cave and Co Ltd, Seabord Chemicals Ltd; *Style*— Sir Robert Cave-Browne-Cave, Bt; ✉ 20901–83 Avenue, RR11, Langley, British Columbia V3A 6Y3, Canada

CAVENAGH-MAINWARING, Charles Rafe Gordon; s of Capt Maurice Kildare Cavenagh-Mainwaring, DSO, RN, and Iris Mary, *née* Denaro; *Educ* Downside; *m* 20 Oct 1973 (m dis), Rosemary Lee, da of Capt Thomas Lee Reay Hardy (d 1982), of London; 1 s (Rupert William b 1976); *Career* Lt RM Reserve 1964–67, Lt HAC (RHA) 1967–73, transferred to RARO 1974; dir Hinton Hill Underwriting Agents Ltd 1987–89, conslt Allied Dunbar 1990–96, fin advsr Eggar Forrester 1996–97; social researcher Nat Centre for Social Research (NatCen) 2002–; memb Bd Atlantic Cncl (NATO Support Gp) 1997–, memb Insurance Brokers Registration Cncl 1997–2000; govr Salesian Coll; Knight of Justice in Simple Vows Sovereign Mil Order of Malta (memb Cncl Grand Priory of England), Knight of Justice of the Sacred Mil Order of Constantine of St George; *Recreations* shooting, skiing, watching rugby union football, tennis; *Clubs* Hurlingham, Harlequins RFC; *Style*— Charles Cavenagh-Mainwaring, Esq

CAVENDISH, Lucy; da of Edward Patrick James Cavendish (d 2000), and Pamela, *née* Iles; *b* 16 December 1966; *Children* 1 s (Raymond Stanley Ellison b 1996); *Career* journalist; ed Observer Food Monthly until 2002, interviewer and features writer Evening Standard 2002–; *Style*— Ms Lucy Cavendish

CAVENDISH OF FURNESS, Baron (Life Peer UK 1990), of Cartmel in the County of Cumbria; Richard Hugh Cavendish; DL (Cumbria 1988); s of late Capt Richard Edward Osborne Cavendish, DL; *b* 2 November 1941; *Educ* Eton; *m* 1970, Grania Mary, da of Brig Toby St George Caulfeild, CBE; 1 s, 2 da; *Career* int merchanting and banking London 1961–71, chm Holker Estate Gp of Cos 1971–, dir UK Nirex Ltd 1993–99; High Sheriff of Cumbria 1978, cncllr Cumbria CC 1985–90; a Lord in Waiting (Govt whip) 1990–92; memb: Select Ctee on Croydon Tramlink Bill 1992–93, EU Sub-Ctee B (Energy, Indust and Tport) 2001–04, House of Lords Select Ctee on the EU 2001–, Assoc of Cons Peers; cmmnr Historic Buildings and Monuments Cmmn (English Heritage) 1992–98; chm Morecambe and Lonsdale Cons Assoc 1975–78, chm of govrs St Anne's Sch Windermere 1983–89, chm Lancs and Cumbria Fndn for Med Res 1994–96, co-fndr St Mary's Hospice Ulverston (chm 2003–); Liveryman Worshipful Co of Fishmongers; FRSA 1988; *Recreations* gardening, National Hunt racing, shooting, fishing, reading, travel; *Clubs* Brooks's, White's, Pratt's, Beefsteak; *Style*— The Lord Cavendish of Furness, DL; ✉ Holker Hall, Cark-in-Cartmel, Cumbria LA11 7PL (tel 01539 558220, office 01539 558123, fax 01539 558776, e-mail cavendish@holker.co.uk)

CAWDOR, 7 Earl (UK 1827); Colin Robert Vaughan Campbell; also Baron Cawdor of Castlemartin (GB 1796) and Viscount Emlyn (UK 1827); the full designation of the Earldom in its patent of 1827 was Earl Cawdor of Castlemartin; s of 6 Earl Cawdor (d 1993), and his 1 w, Cathryn, *née* Hinde; *b* 30 June 1962; *Educ* Eton, St Peter's Coll Oxford; *m* 21 Oct 1994, Lady Isabella Rachel Stanhope, da of 11 Earl of Harrington; 1 s (James Chester, Viscount Emlyn b 8 July 1998); *Heir* s, Viscount Emlyn; *Style*— The Rt Hon the Earl Cawdor

CAWDRON, Peter Edward Blackburn; *m* 1968, Diana Anderson; 2 s (Nicholas, Benjamin), 1 da (Emily); *Career* with: Peat Marwick Mitchell 1961–70, S G Warburg & Co Ltd 1970–77, D'Arcy MacManus & Masius (advtg agency) 1977–83; Grand Metropolitan plc: joined 1983, gp planning dir 1983–87, gp strategy development dir 1987–97, main bd dir 1993–97; non-exec chm: Capital Radio plc 2002–05, GCap 2005–, Punch Taverns plc 2007– (non-exec dir 2003–); dep chm and sr non-exec dir Compass Group plc (formerly non-exec dir) 1999–; non-exec dir: Capita Group 1997–, Johnston Press 1998–, ARM Hldgs plc 1998–, Christian Salvesen plc 1997–, Arla Foods UK plc 2000–06; *Style*— Peter Cawdron, Esq

CAWKWELL, Paul G J; s of Geoffrey Cawkwell, and Louise, *née* Langan; *b* 3 October 1969, Dagenham, Essex; *Educ* Campion Sch Hornchurch, Havering Coll of FE; *m* 29 Oct 1994, Tina, *née* Evans; 2 da (Grace b 23 Dec 1995, Lily b 30 Sept 1998); *Career* Coutts & Co 1986–91, Hambros Bank Ltd 1991–93, joined HM Prison Service 1993, dep govr HM Prison Norwich 2004–06, govr HM Prison Blundeston 2006–; *Style*— Paul Cawkwell, Esq; ✉ HM Prison Blundeston, Lowestoft, Suffolk NR32 5BG

CAWLEY, 4 Baron (UK 1918); Sir John Francis Cawley; 4 Bt (UK 1906); s of 3 Baron Cawley (d 2001); *b* 28 September 1946; *Educ* Eton; *m* 1979, Regina Sarabia, da of late Marqués de Hazas (cr of 1873 by King Amadeo I), of Madrid; 1 da (Hon Susan Mary b 1980), 3 s (Hon William Robert Harold b 1981, Hon Thomas Frederick José-Luis b 1982, Hon Andrew David b 1988); *Heir* s, Hon William Cawley; *Style*— The Rt Hon the Lord Cawley; ✉ Castle Ground, Ashton, Leominster, Herefordshire HR6 0DN (tel 01584 711209, e-mail john.cawley@farmline.com)

CAWLEY, Dr Michael Ian David; RD; s of late William Miller Seddon Cawley, CBE, of Bexhill, E Sussex, and late Edith Mary, *née* Setchell; *b* 14 October 1935; *Educ* Caterham Sch, Bart's Med Coll Univ of London (MB BS, MD); *m* 1997, Alison Lindsey, *née* Chapman; 2 da; *Career* Nat Serv Lt and Capt RAMC 1960–62, surgn Lt Cdr RNR 1970–90; house offr 1959–60: Norwich, Bournemouth, Bart's; med registrar 1962–68: Bart's, Lewisham Hosp London; Aylwen res fell Bart's 1965–66, sr registrar and tutor in med Bristol Royal Hosp 1968–70, ARC visiting res fell Univ of Texas at Dallas 1971–72, lectr in rheumatology Univ of Manchester 1970–73; conslt physician rheumatology: Wrightington Hosp 1973–74, Southampton Univ Hosps 1974– (clinical tutor 1979–82, hon sr lectr 1990–); civilian conslt to RN 1989–, visiting conslt Princess Elizabeth Hosp Guernsey 1997–; author of papers and chapters on rheumatic diseases; memb: Ctee on Rheumatology RCP 1983–89 (dist tutor 1987–93), Cncl Br Soc of Rheumatology 1986–88, Central Conslts and Specialists Ctee BMA 1986–93, Cncl BMA 1996–98, Cncl RCP 1998–2001; vice-pres Rheumatology Section RSM; Heberden Roundsman Br Soc for Rheumatology 1992; pres S Wales S West and Wessex Rheumatology Club 1986–89; memb: American Coll of Rheumatology, Br Soc for Rheumatology, Br Soc for Immunology, Bone and Tooth Soc; Liveryman Worshipful Soc of Apothecaries 1990 (Freeman 1982, memb Livery Ctee 2004–); FRCP 1979 (MRCP), FRSM; *Recreations* classical music, sailing, skiing; *Clubs* Royal Lymington Yacht, Royal Naval Sailing Association, Royal Southampton Yacht, Ski Club of Great Britain; *Style*— Dr Michael Cawley; ✉ Paddock Cottage, Bramshaw, Lyndhurst, Hampshire SO43 7JN (tel 01794 390934, secretary tel and fax 02380 476386)

CAWSEY, Ian; MP; *m* Linda; 2 da (Hannah, Lydia), 1 s (Jacob); *Career* MP (Lab) Brigg and Goole 1997–; PPS to Rt Hon Lord Williams of Mostyn, PC, QC 2001–02, PPS to Rt Hon David Miliband, MP 2002–05, Govt whip 2005–; memb Home Affrs Select Ctee 1997–2001; chm PLP Home Affrs Ctee 1997–2001, chm Assoc Parly Gp on Animal Welfare 1998–2005; ldr N Lincs Cncl 1995–97, chm Humberside Police Authy 1993–97; *Style*— Ian Cawsey, MP; ✉ House of Commons, London SW1A 0AA (tel 020 7219 5237, e-mail cawseyi@parliament.uk); Constituency Offices, 7 Market Place, Brigg, North Lincolnshire DN20 8HA (tel 01652 651327, e-mail waudbya@parliament.uk), The Courtyard, Boothferry Road, Goole, East Yorkshire DN14 6AE (tel 01405 767744, e-mail pattersonr@parliament.uk)

CAWTHRA, David Wilkinson; CBE (1997); s of Jack Cawthra (d 1974), and Dorothy, *née* Wilkinson; *b* 5 March 1943; *Educ* Heath GS Halifax, Univ of Birmingham (BSc); *m* Maureen Mabel, da of late Eric Arthur Williamson; 1 s (Richard Giles b 18 Oct 1969), 1 da (Caroline Eleanor b 30 Jan 1974); *Career* Mitchell Construction Co Ltd: jr engr 1964, site agent 1967, contracts mangr 1970; divnl dir Tarmac Construction Ltd 1976–79 (contracts mangr 1973–76), gen mangr Balfour Beatty Ltd 1981 (divnl dir 1979); md: Balfour Beatty Construction Ltd 1985, Balfour Beatty Ltd 1988; chief exec: Balfour Beatty Ltd 1990–91, Miller Group Ltd 1991–94; mgmnt conslt Cawthra & Co 1995–2005, ret; vice-pres ICE 1996–99, chm Nat Rail Contractors Gp 1999–2005; Freeman City of London; FICE 1980, FREng 1990; *Recreations* hill walking, geneology, American history; *Style*— David Cawthra, Esq, CBE, FREng; ✉ Willow House, Riverside Close, Oundle, Peterborough PE8 4DN (tel 01832 273439, fax 01832 273159, e-mail cawthraco@clara.co.uk)

CAYLEY, Dr (Arthur) Charles Digby; s of Dr Forde Everard de Wend Cayley, MBE, of Thames Ditton, Surrey, and Eileen Lillian, *née* Dalton; *b* 8 November 1946; *Educ* Middx Hosp Med Sch London (MB BS); *m* 1 Nov 1969, Jeanette Ann, da of George Richard Avery (d 1968), of Plymouth, Devon; 3 s (George b 1971, Adam b 1975, Seth b 1980); *Career* sr registrar in geriatric med and hon lectr Middx Hosp 1974–76, conslt physician in med of the elderly NW London Hosps NHS Tst and Brent PCT 1976– (clinical dir med and care of the elderly 2001–, assoc med dir 2002–); recognised teacher Univ of London, hon clinical sr lectr ICSTM London; *Books* Hospital Geriatric Medicine (1987); *Recreations* walking, listening to classical music; *Style*— Dr Charles Cayley; ✉ Department of Medicine for the Elderly, Central Middlesex Hospital, Acton Lane, London NW10 7NS (tel 020 8453 2184, fax 020 8961 1827, e-mail charles.cayley@nwlh.nhs.uk)

CAYLEY, Sir Digby William David; 11 Bt (E 1661), of Brompton, Yorkshire; o s of William Arthur Seton Cayley (d 1964; ggs of 7 Bt), and Natalie Maud, *née* Grey (d 1994); suc his kinsman Maj Sir Kenelm Henry Ernest Cayley, 10 Bt, 1967; *b* 3 June 1944; *Educ* Malvern, Downing Coll Cambridge (MA); *m* 1, 19 July 1969 (m dis 1987), Christine Mary, o da of late Derek Francis Gaunt, of Ilkley; 2 da (Emma Jane b 1974, Catherine Mary b 1975); m 2, 1993, Cathryn M, elder da of Brian Russell, of Gosport, Hants; 2 s (Thomas Theodore William b 17 Feb 1997, George Edward Digby b 22 June 1999); *Heir* s, Thomas Cayley; *Career* asst classics master: Portsmouth GS 1968–73, Stonyhurst Coll 1973–81; antique dealer 1981–89; asst classics master: Marlborough Coll 1989–90 and 1994–97, Abingdon Sch 1990–94; master i/c shooting Marlborough Coll 1994–2000; *Recreations* target rifle shooting, bridge; *Style*— Sir Digby Cayley, Bt

CAYTON, William Henry Rymer (Harry); OBE (2001); s of Dr H Rymer Cayton (d 1989), and Mrs Marion Cayton (d 1999); *b* 27 March 1950; *Educ* Bristol Cathedral Sch, New Univ of Ulster (BA), Univ of Durham (Dip), Univ of Newcastle upon Tyne (BPhil); *Career* teacher: King's Sch Rochester 1972–73, Dame Allan's Sch Newcastle upon Tyne 1973–76, Northern Counties Sch for the Deaf 1976–80; National Deaf Children's Soc: educn offr 1980–82, dir 1982–91; elected hon life memb European Fed of Deaf Children's Assocs 1991, chief exec Alzheimer's Soc 1991–2003, dir Patients and Public Dept of Health 2003–07, chief exec Cncl for Healthcare Regulatory Excellence 2007; vice-chair Consumers in NHS Research and Devpt 1998–2003; social care advsr Macmillan Cancer Support 2003–; tstee: Hearing Research Tst 1985–2005, Comic Relief 2005–; memb: Alzheimer Europe 1998–2002, Central R&D Ctee NHS 1999, NHS Modernisation Bd 2000–03; fell Faculty of Public Health 2007; Distinguished Grad Award Univ of Ulster 2003, Alzheimer Europe Award 2004, Lifetime Achievement Award RCPsych 2007; Canadian Cwlth fell 1982, FRSA 1996; *Publications* Alzheimers and other Dementias (2002); author of numerous essays and articles; *Recreations* modern British art, music, cooking and eating; *Clubs* Athenaeum; *Style*— Harry Cayton, Esq, OBE; ✉ 24 Barlby Gardens, North Kensington, London W10 5LW; CHRE, 11 Strand, London WC2N 5HR (tel 020 7389 8030)

CAYZER, Hon Charles William; s of 2 Baron Rotherwick (d 1996); *b* 26 April 1957; *Educ* Harrow; *m* 1985, Amanda Cosbie Sara, 2 da of John Squire, of Marbella, Spain; 1 da (Victoria Amanda b 22 June 1989), 1 s ((Charles) William b 14 July 1991); *Career* late The Life Guards; dir: Caledonia Investments plc, The Cayzer Trust Company Ltd, The Sloane Club Group Ltd; *Style*— The Hon Charles Cayzer; ✉ Brize Lodge, Leafield, Oxfordshire OX7 3DD

CAYZER, Sir James Arthur; 5 Bt (UK 1904), of Gartmore, Co Perth; s of Sir Charles William Cayzer, 3 Bt, MP (d 1940), and Eileen (Lady Cayzer, OBE) (d 1981), da of James Meakin (d 1912), and Emma Beatrice (d 1935), later wife of 3 Earl Sondes; suc his bro, Sir Nigel John Cayzer, 4 Bt, 1943; *b* 15 November 1931; *Educ* Eton; *Heir* Robin Cayzer, 3 Baron Rotherwick, *qv*; *Career* dir: Caledonia Investments 1958–88, Cayzer Trust Co 1988–2001; Liveryman Worshipful Co of Clockmakers; *Clubs* Carlton; *Style*— Sir James Cayzer, Bt; ✉ Kinpurnie Castle, Newtyle, Angus PH12 8TW (tel 01828 650207)

CAYZER-COLVIN, Jamie Michael Beale; s of Michael Keith Beale Colvin MP (d 2000), and Nichola, *née* Cayzer (d 2000); *b* 1 April 1965, London; *Educ* Gordonstoun, RMA Sandhurst, Henley Mgmnt Coll (MBA); *m* 31 Oct 1992, Esther Anne Mary, *née* Tree; 2 da (Molly Isabella Elizabeth b 30 Sept 1995, Lily Georgia Daphanne b 8 April 1999); *Career* Lt Grenadier Gds 1985–89, Close Bros plc 1989–90, Whitbread Beer Co 1991–92, Amber Ind Holdings plc 1992–95, exec dir Caledonia Investments plc 1995–; non-exec dir: Polar Capital Ptnrs 2000–, Rathbone Bros plc 2002–, Eddington Capital Mgmnt 2003–, Indian Capital Growth Fund plc 2005–, Ermitage Ltd 2006–; chm of tstees Children's Fire and Burns Tst; *Recreations* family, country and gardens; *Clubs* Boodles; *Style*— Jamie Cayzer-Colvin, Esq; ✉ Caledonia Investments plc, Cayzer House, 30 Buckingham Gate, London SW1E 6NN (tel 020 7802 8080)

CAZALET, Hon Lady (Camilla Jane); da of 6 Viscount Gage, KCVO, by his 1 w, Hon Imogen Grenfell; *b* 12 July 1937; *Educ* Benenden; *m* 24 April 1965, Sir Edward Stephen Cazalet,

C

DL, *qv*; 2 s, 1 da; *Career* dir Lumley Cazalet 1967–2002; tstee Glyndebourne Arts Tst 1978–2004; memb Cncl: Friends of Covent Garden 1977–2005 (memb Mgmnt Ctee 1994–2000), RNT 1997– (memb Bd 1991–97); govr Royal Ballet 2000–; *Recreations* visual and performing arts, music, tennis; *Style*— The Hon Lady Cazalet; ✉ Shaw Farm, Plumpton Green, East Sussex BN7 3DG (tel 01273 890207, fax 01273 890358); Flat 10, 41 Stanhope Gardens, London SW7 5QY (tel 020 7244 6182, fax 020 7341 4496)

CAZALET, Sir Edward Stephen; kt (1988), DL (E Sussex 1989); s of Peter Victor Ferdinand Cazalet, JP, DL (d 1973), the race horse trainer, and his 1 w, Leonora, *née* Rowley, step da of Sir P G Wodehouse; *b* 26 April 1936; *Educ* Eton, ChCh Oxford; *m* 24 April 1965, Hon Camilla Jane (Hon Lady Cazalet, *qv*), da of 7 Viscount Gage, KCVO (d 1982); 2 s (David b 1967, Hal b 1969), 1 da (Lara b 1973); *Career* subaltern Welsh Guards 1954–56; called to the Bar Inner Temple 1960 (bencher 1985); QC 1980, recorder of the Crown Court 1985–88, judge of the High Court of Justice (Family Div) 1988–2000; chm: Horse Race Betting Levy Appeal Tbnl 1979–88, CAB Royal Courts of Justice 1993–97, Br Agencies for Adoption and Fostering 2000–05, Jockey Club Appeal Bd 2001–05, Injured Jockeys Fund; tstee Winston Churchill Meml Tst 2005–; fell Eton Coll 1989–2004; *Recreations* riding, ball games, chess; *Clubs* Garrick; *Style*— Sir Edward Cazalet, DL; ✉ Shaw Farm, Plumpton Green, Lewes, East Sussex BN7 3DG

CAZALET, (Charles) Julian; s of Vice Adm Sir Peter Grenville Lyon Cazalet, KBE, CB, DSO, DSC (d 1982), of Newick, E Sussex, and Lady Beatrice Elise, *née* Winterbotham; *b* 29 November 1947; *Educ* Uppingham, Magdalene Coll Cambridge (MA); *m* 29 Nov 1986, Jennifer Clare, da of Maurice Nelson Little (d 1985), of Laverton, Glos; 1 s (Charles b 1987), 1 da (Fleur b 1989); *Career* ptnr Cazenove & Co Investment Bankers 1978–2001, md corp fin Cazenove & Co Ltd 2001–05, md corp fin JP Morgan Cazenove 2005–07; memb Cncl White Ensign Assoc Ltd 2003–; govr Cothill House Sch 2005–; FCA 1977; *Recreations* golf, sailing, skiing, stalking; *Clubs* City Univ (chm 1994–), Wisley Golf; *Style*— Julian Cazalet, Esq; ✉ 38 Norland Square, London W11 4PZ (tel 020 7727 1756, fax 020 7792 2358, e-mail wwbcazalet@aol.com)

CAZENOVE, Bernard Michael de Lerisson; TD; s of David Michael de Lerisson Cazenove (d 1988), and Euphemia, *née* Maclean (d 1997); *b* 14 June 1947; *Educ* Radley, RMA Sandhurst; *m* 19 Dec 1971, Caroline June, da of Richard Moore (d 1963), of Wellington, NZ; 2 s (Richard b 1974, George b 1977), 1 da (Edwina b 1984); *Career* cmmnd Coldstream Guards 1967, ADC to HE Govr Gen of NZ 1970, transferred Parachute Regt (TA) 1973, Hon Col 4 Bn Parachute Regt 1999–2006; ptnr Cazenove & Co 1982–2001 (joined 1973), md Cazenove Gp 2001–2004; memb Ct of Patrons RCS (Royal Coll of Surgns of Eng) 2004; govr Forest Sch; hon fell Darwin Coll Cambridge 2005; Liveryman Worshipful Co of Dyers; *Clubs* White's, Pratt's, Rock Sailing, Flyfishers, Kandahar Ski; *Style*— Bernard Cazenove, Esq, TD; ✉ Brocas, Ellisfield, Basingstoke, Hampshire RG24 2QS

CAZENOVE, Christopher de Lerisson; s of Brig Arnold de Lerisson Cazenove, CBE, DSO, MVO (d 1969; descended from Arnaud de Cazenove, Seigneur de Lerisson, of Guienne, France who m 1, 1578, Anne de Bruil, and m 2, 1596, Marie de Laumond), and Elizabeth Laura (d 1994), 3 da of late Sir Eustace Gurney, JP, of Walsingham Abbey, Norfolk; *b* 17 December 1943; *Educ* Eton, Bristol Old Vic Theatre Sch; *m* 12 Sept 1973 (m dis 1993), Angharad Mary Rees, *qv*, da of Prof Linford Rees, CBE (d 2004); 2 s (Linford b 20 July 1974 d 1999, Rhys William b 12 Dec 1976); *Career* actor; *Theatre* incl: The Lionel Touch 1969, My Darling Daisy 1970, The Winslow Boy 1970, Joking Apart 1979, Goodbye Fidel (Broadway) 1980, The Sound of Music 1992, Peter Pan (Aust) 1996, An Ideal Husband 1998, Private Lives (Hong Kong) 1999, The Turn of the Screw 1999, Brief Encounter 2000, Art 2003, Dracula 2005, My Fair Lady (UK tour) 2005–06 and (US tour) 2007–08, Side by Side by Sondheim (West End) 2007; *Television* incl: The Regiment 1971–72, The British Hero, The Pathfinders, K is for Killer 1973, The Duchess of Duke Street 1976–77, Jenny's War, Lace II, Dynasty 1986–87, Ticket to Ride 1988–89, To Be the Best 1990, The Way to Dusty Death 1994, Judge John Deed 2001, Johnson County War 2001, La Femme Musketeer 2002; *Film* incl: Royal Flash 1975, East of Elephant Rock 1976, Zulu Dawn 1979, Eye of the Needle 1980, From A Far Country 1980, Heat and Dust 1982, Until September 1984, The Fantasist 1985, Souvenir 1987, Tears in the Rain 1987, Hold my Hand I'm Dying 1988, Three Men And a Little Lady 1990, Aces 1991, The Proprietor 1995, Shadow Run 1997, A Knight's Tale 2000, Trance 2001, Alexander the Great 2004; *Style*— Christopher Cazenove, Esq; ✉ c/o Diamond Management, 31 Percy Street, London W1T 2DD (tel 020 7631 0400, fax 020 7631 0500, e-mail agents@diman.co.uk)

CECIL, Desmond Hugh; CMG (1995); s of Dr Rupert Cecil, DFC, and Rosemary, *née* Luker; *b* 19 October 1941; *Educ* Magdalen Coll Sch Oxford, The Queen's Coll Oxford (MA); *m* 1964, Ruth Elizabeth, *née* Sachs; 3 s, 1 da; *Career* studied violin, viola and oboe with Profs Max Rostal in Berne and Joy Boughton in London, subsequently violinist and oboist in Switzerland (leader Neuchâtel Chamber Orch 1965–70); HM Dip Serv 1970–95: second sec London 1970–73, first sec Bonn 1973–74, FCO 1974–76, press offr Mission to UN Geneva 1976–80, FCO 1980–85, cnsllr and chargé d'Affaires Vienna 1985–89, FCO 1989–92, on secondment with Bd of P&O European Ferries 1992, under sec FCO 1992–95; sr advsr to: BT 1996–97, British Nuclear Fuels plc 1996–2006, Marconi 1998–2001; chm Arena Pal Ltd 2002–03, UK rep AREVA 2006–; antiquarian book dealer 1997–; dir and tstee Jupiter Orch London 1996–2002; Royal Philharmonic Soc: memb Cncl 1995–2005, chm Sponsorship Ctee, hon co-treas; memb Cncl Britain-Russia Centre 1998–2000; advsr Menuhin Festival Gstaad 2001–; memb Cncl and tstee Voices for Hospices 2000–04, advsr Russia Arts Help Charity Moscow 2000–; tstee: Norbert Brainin Fndn Asolo 2004–, London Philharmonic Orchestra 2005–; memb: Mensa 1968–, Sherlock Holmes Soc of London 1970–, Kingston Chamber Music Soc 1990–, Panel 2000 Germany Project Bd 1999–2000, Br-German Assoc 2001–05, Bd Int Mendelssohn Fndn Leipzig 2001–, Appeal Ctee The Queen's Coll Oxford 2005–; *Recreations* playing music and cricket, downhill skiing, chess, antiquarian travel books; *Clubs* Athenaeum (chm Wine Ctee 1999–2002, chm Gen Ctee 2003–), MCC (European cricket advsr 1998–2002), Claygate Cricket (life vice-pres); *Style*— Desmond Cecil, Esq, CMG; ✉ 38 Palace Road, East Molesey, Surrey KT8 9DL (tel 020 8783 1998, e-mail desmondcecil@dial.pipex.com)

CECIL, Henry Richard Amherst; 4 s (twin) of Hon Henry Kerr Auchmuty Cecil (ka 1942), and Elizabeth Rohays Mary, *née* Burnett of Leys (later Lady Boyd-Rochfort); *b* 11 January 1943; *Educ* Canford, RAC Cirencester; *m* 1, 18 Oct 1966 (m dis), Julia, da of Sir (Charles Francis) Noel Murless (d 1987); 1 s (Noel b 3 Feb 1973), 1 da (Katrina b 17 June 1971); m 2, 15 Feb 1992 (m dis 2002), Natalie, da of Richard Payne; 1 s (Jake Henry Richard Amherst b 22 Feb 1994); *Career* champion racehorse trainer on the flat (10 times); trained four Derby winners, seven Oaks winners, two 2000 Guineas winners, six 1000 Guineas winners, and four St Léger winners; *Books* On The Level; *Recreations* gardening, shooting; *Style*— Henry Cecil, Esq; ✉ Warren Place, Newmarket, Suffolk CB8 8QQ (tel 01638 662387); office tel 01638 662192, fax 01638 669005)

CECIL, Jonathan Hugh; s of Lord Edward Christian David Gascoyne Cecil, CH (d 1986), of Cranbourne, and Rachel Mary Veronica, *née* MacCarthy (d 1982); *b* 22 February 1939; *Educ* Eton, New Coll Oxford (BA), LAMDA; *m* 1, 1963, Vivien Sarah Frances, da of David Granville Heilbron (d 1993), of Glasgow; m 2, 3 Nov 1976, Anna, da of William Sharkey, of Glasgow; *Career* actor and writer; contrib to: The Independent, The Spectator, TLS, The Oldie, Daily Mail, Daily Telegraph; former regular book reviewer for The Evening Standard; memb Cncl of Mgmnt Actor's Church Union 1993–2007, Br Equity cncllr 2006; *Theatre* incl: A Heritage and its History 1965, Halfway Up the Tree 1967, The Ruling Class 1969, Lulu 1971, Cowardy Custard 1972, The Bed Before Yesterday 1976, The Orchestra 1981, Good Morning Bill 1987, Uncle Vanya 1988, Poor Nanny 1989, The Dressmaker 1990, The Family Reunion 1992, Twelfth Night 1992, The Taming of the Shrew 1993, The Incomparable Max (one man show) 1994, 1995 and 1996, The Seagull 1995, The Importance of Being Earnest 1995, Pride and Prejudice 1996, The Incomparable Max (Br and Middle Eastern tours) 1997, As You Like It 1998, A Mad World My Masters 1998, Plum Sauce 1998, The Importance of Being Earnest 1999, The Jermyn Street Revue 2000, Plum Sauce 2000, The Incomparable Max 2000, Plum Sauce 2001 and 2002, The Incomparable Max 2001, Emma 2001 and 2002, Plum Sauce 2003, Othello 2004, The Sneeze 2004, one man show 2005, John Betjeman Gala 2006, Elling 2007; *Television* incl: Maggie 1964, Love's Labour's Lost 1975, Gulliver in Lilliput 1981, The Puppet Man 1984, 13 at Dinner 1985, Murder in 3 Acts 1987, The Sign of Command 1989, F.L.I.P. 1991, Beethoven Is Not Dead 1992, The Rector's Wife 1993, Late Flowering Lust 1993, Murder Most Horrid 1993, Madawiad Arthur 1994, Just William 1994, The Entertainers 1995, One Foot in the Grave 2000, Victoria and Albert 2000, Heroes of Comedy 2002, The Worst Week of My Life 2005; has also starred in numerous comedy series; *Films* incl: The Great St Trinian's Train Robbery 1965, Otley 1968, Catch Me a Spy 1971, Barry Lyndon 1973, Joseph Andrews 1976, History of the World Part 1 1980, E la Nave Va (Fellini) 1983, The Fool 1990, Tchin Tchin 1990, Kleptophilia 1992, As You Like It 1992, RPM 1995, Day Release 1997, Fakes 2003, The Cinema of Comic Illusion 2003, Revenge 2003, Inside 2005, Van Wilder 2 2006; *Audio* recorded many P G Wodehouse novels and others for BBC Audio Books 1984–2007 (Earphones Award 1996); *Recreations* reading, music, history of theatre and music hall; *Clubs* Garrick; *Style*— Jonathan Cecil, Esq; ✉ Gardner-Herrity, 24 Conway Street, London W1T 6BG

CEENEY, Natalie Anna; da of Anthony Ceeney, of Bath, and Jacqueline Ceeney; *b* 22 August 1971, Harlow, Essex; *Educ* Newnham Coll Cambridge (MA, Jemima Clough Prize); *partner* Simon Chaplin; *Career* pres Univ of Cambridge Students' Union 1990–91, business mangr Northwick Park Hosp 1992–94, contracts mangr Herts HA 1994–96, directorate mangr medicine Gt Ormond St Hosp 1996–98, engagement mangr McKinsey & Co 1998–2001, dir ops and servs Br Library 2001–05, chief exec Nat Archives (keeper of the public records and historic manuscripts cmmr) 2005–; *Recreations* theatre, film, literature; *Style*— Ms Natalie Ceeney; ✉ The National Archives, Ruskin Avenue, Kew, Richmond TW9 4DU (tel 020 8392 5220, fax 020 8487 9207, e-mail natalie.ceeney@nationalarchives.gov.uk)

CELLAN-JONES, (Nicholas) Rory; s of James Cellan-Jones, of Kew, Surrey, and Sylvia, *née* Parish; *b* 17 January 1958; *Educ* Dulwich Coll, Jesus Coll Cambridge (BA); *m* 7 April 1990, Diane Coyle, *qv*; 2 s (Adam Joseph b 13 Sept 1990, Rufus Gareth b 11 July 1998); *Career* BBC TV: researcher Look North BBC Leeds 1981–83, sub ed TV News London, asst prodr Newsnight, prodr TV News Special Projects 1983–85, reporter BBC Wales Cardiff 1986–88, reporter Breakfast Time 1988, business reporter TV News and Money Programme 1989–, internet corr BBC TV News 1999– (business corr 1994–); *Style*— Rory Cellan-Jones, Esq; ✉ BBC TV, Wood Lane, London W12 7RJ (tel 020 8624 8992)

CHADLINGTON, Baron (Life Peer UK 1996), of Dean in the County of Oxfordshire; Peter Selwyn Gummer; s of Rev Canon Selwyn Gummer (d 1999), and (Margaret) Sybille Vera, *née* Mason (d 1993); bro of Rt Hon John Selwyn Gummer, MP, *qv*; *b* 24 August 1942; *Educ* King's Sch Rochester, Selwyn Coll Cambridge (MA); *m* 23 Oct 1982, Lucy Rachel, da of Antony Ponsonby Dudley-Hill (d 1969), of Fordingbridge, Hants; 3 da (Hon Naomi b 10 Jan 1984, Hon Chloe b 17 Nov 1985, Hon Eleanor b 5 Aug 1988), 1 s (Hon James b 4 Aug 1990); *Career* Portsmouth and Sunderland Newspaper Gp 1964–65, Viyella Int 1965–66, Hodgkinson & Partners 1966–67, Industrial & Commercial Fin Corp 1967–74; chief exec and dir Huntsworth plc 2000–; chm: Understanding Industry Tst 1991–96, Shandwick Int plc 1994–2000 (founder, chair and chief exec 1974–94), ROH 1996–97, Internat PR 1998–2000, Chadlington Consultancy 1999–, Oxford Resources 1999–2002, Black Box Music Ltd 1999–2001, guideforlife.com 2000–02, Action on Addiction 2000– (tstee 1999–2000), Hotcourses 2000–04; dir: Walbrook Club Ltd 199–2004, CLC Services Ltd 2000–03, CLC Properties (Cheltenham) Ltd 2000–03, Hill Hay Saddle Ltd 2002–; non-exec dir: CIA Group plc (now Tempus plc) 1990–94, Halifax Building Society (now Halifax plc) 1994–2001 (non-exec dir London Bd 1990–94), Oxford Resources plc 1999–2002, hotcourses.com 2000–04; non-exec memb: Arts Cncl of GB 1991–94, NHS Policy Bd 1991–95, Arts Cncl of England 1994–96 (chm Arts Cncl Lottery Bd until 1996); memb: Cncl Cheltenham Ladies' College 1998–2003, Bd of Tstees American Univ 1999–2001, Select Ctee on EU Sub-Ctee B (Energy, Industry and Tport) House of Lords 2000–03; hon fell Bournemouth Univ 1999; tstee Atlantic Partnership 1999–; FRSA, FInstD, FIPR, FInstM; *Recreations* opera, cricket, rugby; *Clubs* White's, Garrick, MCC, Carlton, Walbrook (dir 1999–); *Style*— The Lord Chadlington; ✉ Huntsworth plc, 15–17 Huntsworth Mews, London NW1 6DD

CHADWICK, Prof David William; s of Harold Chadwick (d 1979), of Rochdale, and Elsie, *née* Mills (d 1983); *b* 14 December 1946; *Educ* Bolton Sch, St Catherine's Coll Oxford (MA, DM); *m* 30 July 1969, Vivienne Ruth, da of Richard Jones (d 1979), of St Helens; 1 s (Benjamin b 1975), 1 da (Ellen b 1977); *Career* lectr in neurology Univ Dept of Neurology Inst of Psychiatry London 1974–76, first asst in neurology Univ of Newcastle upon Tyne 1978–79, conslt neurologist Mersey RHA 1979–92, prof of neurology Univ of Liverpool 1993–; sec Br Branch Int League Against Epilepsy 1984–88; FRCP 1984; *Books* Living With Epilepsy (1987), Medical Neurology (1989); *Style*— Prof David Chadwick; ✉ Department of Medicine and Surgical Neurology, Walton Hospital, Lower Lane, Liverpool L9 7LJ (tel 0151 525 3611 ext 4348)

CHADWICK, Dr Derek James; s of Dennis Edmund Chadwick (d 1955), and Ida Chadwick (d 1979); *b* 9 February 1948; *Educ* St Joseph's Coll Blackpool, Keble Coll Oxford (Pfizer industrial scholar, open scholar, sr scholar, BA, BSc, MA, DPhil); *m* 20 Dec 1980, Susan (d 2002), da of Dr (Hugh) Alastair Reid, OBE (d 1983); 2 s (Andrew John b 1984, (Frederick) Mark b 1986); *Career* ICI fell Univ of Cambridge 1972–73, Prize fell Magdalen Coll Oxford 1973–77, Royal Soc European exchange fell ETH-Zürich 1975–77, lectr, sr lectr then reader Univ of Liverpool 1977–88, dir The Novartis Fndn (formerly The Ciba Fndn) London 1988–; Emilio Noelting visiting prof École Nationale Supérieur Mulhouse 1988, visiting prof Univ of Trondheim 1995–; vice-chm Assoc of Medical Research Charities 1994–2000; cncl memb Cncl for the Central Lab of the Research Cncls 2002–07; memb: Steering Ctee Media Resource Serv Scientists' Inst for Public Information NY 1989–96, Scientific Ctee Louis Jeantet Fndn Geneva 1989–98; sec Hague Club of Directors of Euro Fndns 1993–97; Liveryman Worshipful Soc of Apothecaries 1990; FRSC 1982; *Books* contrib to: Aromatic & Heteroaromatic Chemistry (1979), Comprehensive Heterocyclic Chemistry (1984), The Research and Academic Users' Guide to the IBMPC (1988), Physical and Theoretical Aspects of 1H-Pyrroles (1990); author of over 100 pubns incl papers in learned jls, book chapters and computer progs; *Recreations* gardening, music, skiing; *Style*— Dr Derek Chadwick; ✉ 4 Bromley Avenue, Bromley, Kent BR1 4BQ (tel 020 8460 3332); The Novartis Foundation, 41 Portland Place, London W1B 1BN (tel 020 7636 9456, fax 020 7436 2840, e-mail dchadwick@novartisfound.org.uk)

CHADWICK, Rt Hon Sir John Murray Chadwick; kt (1991), PC (1997), ED (1979); s of Capt Hector George Chadwick, (ka 1942), and Margaret Corry, *née* Laing (d 1977); *b* 20 January 1941; *Educ* Rugby, Magdalene Coll Cambridge (MA); *m* 5 Dec 1975, Diana Mary, da of Charles Marshall Blunt, DL (d 1986), of March, Cambs; 2 da (Jane b 1976, Elizabeth b 1978); *Career* called to the Bar Inner Temple 1966 (bencher 1986, treas 2004); jr counsel Dept of Trade 1974–80, QC 1980, judge of the Courts of Appeal of Guernsey and Jersey 1986–93, recorder of the Crown Court 1990–91, judge of the High Court of Justice (Chancery Division) 1991–97, Chancery supervising judge Birmingham, Bristol and

Cardiff 1995–97, a Lord Justice of Appeal 1997–2007; memb Gen Cncl of the Bar 1989–91; dir United Services Tstee Ltd; Maj (TAVR) 4 Bn Royal Green Jackets 1973–76; memb Wine Standards Bd Vintners' Co 1983–90; vice-pres Corp of the Sons of the Clergy; *Recreations* sailing; *Clubs* Athenaeum, Beefsteak, Royal Yacht Squadron; *Style*— The Rt Hon Sir John Chadwick; ✉ Royal Courts of Justice, Strand, London WC2A 2LL

CHADWICK, Sir Joshua Kenneth Burton; 3 Bt (UK 1935), of Bidston, Co Palatine of Chester; s of Sir Robert Burton-Chadwick, 2 Bt (d 1983), and his 2 w (Beryl) Joan, *née* Brailsford; *b* 1 February 1954; *Heir* none; *Style*— Sir Joshua Burton-Chadwick, Bt

CHADWICK, Julian William Mark; s of Douglas Herbert Chadwick, of London, and Elizabeth Mary, *née* Evans (d 1994); *b* 3 January 1957; *Educ* Royal GS High Wycombe, ChCh Oxford (MA); *Career* admitted slr 1982; ptnr: Gamlens 1985–90, Penningtons 1990– (managing ptnr Newbury Office); former: jt master West Welsh Foot Beagles, sr master Christ Church and Farley Hill Beagles; currently hunt chm Palmer Marlborough Beagles; sec and hon slr Newbury Spring Festival; chm Latin Mass Soc; tstee: ACN(UK), CIEL(UK), SSCS; memb: Law Soc, Assoc of Masters of Beagles and Harriers; Liveryman Worshipful Co of Glass Sellers, Freeman City of London; Knight of Magistral Grace SMOM; *Recreations* field sports; *Clubs* Travellers; *Style*— Julian Chadwick, Esq; ✉ Penningtons Solicitors LLP, Newbury House, 20 Kings Road West, Newbury, Berkshire RH14 5XR (tel 01635 571000, e-mail chadwickjw@penningtons.co.uk); Bryntawel, Drefach, Llanbydder, Ceredigion SA40 9SY (tel 01570 480267)

CHADWICK, Peter; s of Kenneth Fred Chadwick (d 1985), and Grace Jean, *née* Holden (d 1991); *b* 19 August 1946; *Educ* St Paul's, Churchill Coll Cambridge (MA); *m* 27 Oct 1971, Diana Kathryn Lillian, da of Frank Richard Stanford Kellett (d 2004); 1 da (Lindsey Nicola b 1974); *Career* princ Dept of Indust 1977–79; KPMG: ptnr 1982–2006, managing ptnr Kent 1983–91; FCA 1979 (ACA 1970); *Recreations* art, travel; *Clubs* Arts; *Style*— Peter Chadwick, Esq; ✉ Charles Street, Mayfair, London W1J 5EX

CHADWICK, Dr Priscilla; da of Prof Sir Henry Chadwick; *b* 7 November 1947; *Educ* Oxford HS, Clarendon Sch N Wales, Girton Coll Cambridge (BA), Univ of Oxford (PGCE), Univ of London (MA, PhD); *Career* head of RE: St Helen's Sch Northwood 1971–73, Putney HS 1973–78, St Bede's C of E/RC Comp Redhill 1979–82; dep head Twyford C of E HS Acton 1982–85, headteacher Bishop Ramsey C of E Sch Ruislip 1986–91, dean of educnl devpt South Bank Univ 1992–96, princ Berkhamsted Collegiate Sch 1996–; chm HMC 2005; memb: Eng Anglican/RC Ctee 1981–, BBC/ITC Central Religious Advsy Ctee 1983–93, Youth Crime Ctee NACRO 1988–94, Cncl Goldsmiths Coll London 1991–97; govr: King's Sch Canterbury 1990–97, Westminster Sch 1998–; Hon DEd Univ of Hertfordshire 2006; FRSA 1992; *Publications* Schools of Reconciliation (1994), Shifting Alliances: the partnership of Church and State in English education (1997); author of articles in various educnl jls; *Recreations* music, the arts, world travel; *Clubs* East India; *Style*— Dr Priscilla Chadwick; ✉ Berkhamsted Collegiate School, Castle Street, Berkhamsted, Hertfordshire HP4 2BB (tel 01442 358002, fax 01442 358003, e-mail info@bcschool.org)

CHADWYCK-HEALEY, Sir Charles Edward; 5 Bt (UK 1919), of Wyphurst, Cranleigh, Co Surrey, and New Place, Luccombe, Somerset; DL (Cambs); s of Sir Charles Arthur Chadwyck-Healey, 4 Bt, OBE, TD (d 1986), and Viola, *née* Lubbock (d 1995); *b* 13 May 1940; *Educ* Eton, Trinity Coll Oxford (MA); *m* 16 Sept 1967, Angela Mary, eldest da of late John Metson, of Little Dunmow, Essex; 2 da (Catherine b 1970, Faith b 1977), 1 s (Edward Alexander b 1972); *Heir* s, Edward Chadwyck-Healey; *Career* publisher and investor; dir Open Democracy Ltd 2001–; vice-chm Wildlife Tsts for Beds, Cambs, Northants and Peterborough 2004–; memb Centre for Contemporary Br History 2005–; chm Cambs Police Shrievalty Tst 2005–; High Sheriff Cambs 2004–05, dep-lt Cambs 2004–; hon fell Trinity Coll Oxford 2005; Liveryman: Worshipful Co of Fishmongers, Worshipful Co of Stationers & Newspaper Makers; FRGS; *Clubs* Brooks's, Athenaeum; *Style*— Sir Charles Chadwyck-Healey, Bt, DL; ✉ Manor Farm, Bassingbourn, Cambridgeshire SG8 5NX (tel 01763 242447)

CHAIN, Julia; *Educ* Univ of Cambridge; *Career* slr; Shearman and Sterling NY 1982–84, Herbert Smith 1984–93, managing ptnr Garretts 1994–98 (joined 1993), gen counsel Bd T-Mobile UK 1998–2003, strategic conslt Jomati Conslts 2003–; cmmr Cmmn for Racial Equality, memb Academic Cncl BPP plc, tstee Jewish Assoc for Business Ethics, memb Bd Jewish Chronicle, memb Bd of Mgmnt Golders Green Synagogue, tstee Norwood Ravenswood; *Style*— Ms Julia Chain; ✉ Jomati Ltd, 3 Amen Lodge, Warwick Lane, London EC4M 7BY (tel 020 7248 1045)

CHAITOW, Christopher John Adam; s of Boris Reuben Chaitow (d 1995), and of Elizabeth, *née* Rice (d 1980); *b* 19 January 1943; *Educ* Worthing HS; *m* 18 May 1974, Susan Patricia, da of George Joseph Foley, of Cardiff; 1 da (Ella b 1983), 1 s (Daniel b 1984); *Career* research/institutional sales Northcote & Co 1964–70, ptnr Beamish & Co 1970–75, returned to institutional sales Northcote & Co 1975–79; technical analyst: Simon & Coates 1979–86, Chase Manhattan Securities 1986, Morgan Grenfell Securities 1986–88; dir Value and Momentum Research and Chartroom UK 1989–92, technical analyst Credit Lyonnais Laing 1992–94, dir and head of technical analysis Robert Fleming Securities 1995–99, technical analyst Collins Stewart 1999–; fell STA, MSI; *Recreations* music, golf; *Style*— Christopher Chaitow, Esq; ✉ Caroline House, 29–30 Alwyne Road, London N1 2HW (tel 020 7226 4471)

CHAKRABARTI, Shami; CBE (2007); da of Syamalendou Chakrabarti, and Shyamali, *née* Chattergee; *b* 16 June 1969, London; *Educ* Bentley Wood HS Harrow, LSE; *m* 22 July 1995, Martyn John Hopper; 1 s; *Career* called to the Bar Middle Temple 1994; Legal Advsr's Branch Home Office 1996–2001; Liberty: in-house counsel 2001–03, dir 2003–; memb: Ct of Govrs LSE, Cncl Tate; govr BFI; *Recreations* cinema, family; *Style*— Ms Shami Chakrabarti, CBE; ✉ Liberty, 21 Tabard Street, London SE1 4LA (tel 020 7403 3888, e-mail info@liberty-human-rights.org.uk)

CHAKRABARTI, Sir Sumantra (Suma); KCB (2006); s of Hirendranath Chakrabarti, and Gayatri, *née* Rudra; *Educ* City of London Sch, New Coll Oxford (BA), Univ of Sussex (MA); *Career* economist Govt of Botswana 1981–83, official Overseas Devpt Admin 1984–96, leader Treasy team 1997–98, dep dir budget and public fin Treasy 1998, dir Performance and Innovation Unit Cabinet Office 1998–99, head Economic and Domestic Secretariat (EDS) Cabinet Office 2000–01, subsequently DG Regnl Progs DFID, perm sec DFID 2002–; *Recreations* Indian history, soul music, football; *Style*— Sir Suma Chakrabarti, KCB

CHALAYAN, Hussein; MBE (2006); *Educ* Central St Martins (BA); *Career* fashion designer; designer TSE NY 1998–2000, appointed creative dir Asprey 2001; costume design: Current/See Michael Clark Co 1998, Handel's Messiah (John Jay Coll Theater NY) 1999; work featured in numerous exhibitions and shows incl: The Tangent Flows (final year collection, Browns boutique London) 1993, Cartesia (first solo collection, West Soho Galleries London) 1994, Temporary Interface (Tokyo and Kobe) 1994, Nothing/Interscope (winner inaugural Absolut Vodka Absolut Creation Award) 1995, Jam - Style + Music + Media (Barbican Art Gallery) 1996, The Cutting Edge Exhibition (V&A) 1997, Addressing the Century: 100 Years of Art & Fashion (Hayward Gallery) 1998–99, Visions of the Body: Fashion or Invisible Corset (Kyoto Costume Inst) 1999, Echoform Exhibition (Fast Forward San Francisco, Atlantis Gallery London, Festival des Jeunes Createurs Hyeres, Exposing Meaning in Fashion Through Presentation NY and Fast Forward Vienna) 1999, Airmail Clothing (Musee de la Mode Palais du Louvre) 1999, La Beauté (installation, Avignon) 2000, Century City (installation, Tate Modern) 2001, Egofugal (7th Int Istanbul Biennial and Tokyo Opera City) 2001, Great Expectations (Design Cncl installation, Grand Central Terminal NY) 2001, London Designers (Museum at FIT NY) 2001, Radical Fashion (V&A) 2001; Designer of the Year Br Fashion Awards 1999 and 2000; nominated: Lloyds Designer of the Year Award 1995, 1996 and 1997, Avant Garde Designer Award VH1 Fashion Awards 1998; *Style*— Hussein Chalayan, Esq, MBE; ✉ 109–123 Clifton Street, London EC2A 4LD (tel 020 7613 5494, fax 020 7613 3741)

CHALDECOTT, Axel James; s of John James Chaldecott, of Beltinge, Kent, and Alix Mathilde, *née* Von Kauffmann (d 2001); *b* 11 December 1954; *Educ* Charterhouse, Canterbury Coll of Art (BA); *m* 14 Feb 1987, Claire, da of Kenneth Evans; *Career* art dir: Ogilvy & Mather 1977–80, Crawfords 1980–81, Gold Greenlees Trott 1981–85; creative gp head Wight Collins Rutherford Scott 1985–87, co-fndr and creative ptnr HHCL and Partners 1987–2003 (awards incl Agency of the Decade Campaign magazine 2001), co-fndr SMLXL 2003–; JWT: global creative chief HSBC account 2005–; *Style*— Axel Chaldecott, Esq

CHALFONT, Baron (Life Peer UK 1964), of Llantarnam in the County of Monmouthshire; Alun Arthur Gwynne Jones; OBE (1961), MC (1957), PC (1964); s of Arthur Gwynne Jones (d 1982), and Eliza Alice, *née* Hardman (d 1975); *b* 5 December 1919; *Educ* West Monmouth Sch, SSEES Univ of London; *m* 1948, Mona, da of late Harry Douglas Mitchell, of Grimsby; 1 c decd; *Career* sits as Independent in House of Lords, pres Lords All-Pty Defence Gp; Col (ret) S Wales Borderers (Reg Army Offr 1940–61, served Burma, Ethiopia, Malaya, Cyprus, Egypt); former defence and mil correspondent The Times; min of state FO 1964–70, Br perm rep to WEU 1969–70; foreign ed New Statesman 1970–71; dir: IBM UK Holdings Ltd, IBM UK Ltd 1973–90; former dep chm IBA; non-exec dir: Lazard Bros 1981–90, Shandwick plc, The Television Corporation 1996–2001 (dep chm 1997–2001); pres Nottingham Building Soc 1983–90; chm: VSEL plc 1987–95, The Radio Authy 1990–95, Marlborough Stirling Gp 1994–99, Euro Atlantic Gp, Exec Ctee Pilgrims Soc, Southern Mining Corp 1997–99; pres RNID until 1990; Liveryman Worshipful Co of Paviors; *Books* The Sword and the Spirit (1963), The Great Commanders (1973), Montgomery of Alamein (1976), Waterloo - Story of Three Armies (1979), Star Wars - Suicide or Survival (1985), By God's Will - a portrait of the Sultan of Brunei (1989), The Shadow of My Hand (2000); *Recreations* music, theatre; *Clubs* Garrick; *Style*— The Rt Hon the Lord Chalfont, OBE, MC, PC; ✉ House of Lords, London SW1A 0PW

CHALK, Clive Andrew; s of Herbert Chalk (d 1981), of Chelsfield, Kent, and Gertrude Edith Chalk (d 1992); *b* 2 November 1946; *Educ* St Dunstan's Coll, Univ of Exeter (LLB), Harvard Business Sch (AMP); *m* 1, 7 March 1970 (m dis), Judith Rosamond, da of Dr Samuel Dudley Sawyer; 2 da (Harriet Rosamond Louise b 17 Oct 1975, Olivia Emma Jane b 8 March 1977); m 2, 20 Dec 1985, Iris Marita, da of Lars Hjelt; 2 s (Nicholas Gyles Edward b 24 Sept 1986, Jonathan Clive Alexander b 20 Jan 1989); *Career* Coopers & Lybrand 1968–73, Williams & Glyn's Bank 1973–77, dir Samuel Montagu & Co Ltd 1982–96 (joined 1977); dir: corp fin and advsy HSBC Investment Bank plc (formerly HSBC Samuel Montagu) 1996–99, Industrial Control Services Gp plc 1999–2000, English Tst Co Ltd 1999–2001; md Insinger English Tst (M&A) 2001–03, advsy dir Insinger de Beaufort 2003–04, chm Sixty Knightsbridge Ltd 2006– (dir 2003–2006); memb Corp Fin Ctee London Investment Bankers Assoc (LIBA) 1992–95, FCA 1972; *Recreations* sailing, skiing, golf, opera, ballet; *Clubs* Royal Thames Yacht (Rear Cdre 2002–03), Harvard Business Sch of London, Royal Wimbledon Golf; *Style*— Clive Chalk, Esq; ✉ 12 Rydon Mews, London SW19 4RP (tel 020 8947 1626, fax 020 8947 0659, e-mail c_a_chalk@msn.com)

CHALK, Gilbert John; s of Ronald Arthur Chalk (d 1993), of Chorleywood, Herts, and Elizabeth, *née* Talbot; *b* 21 September 1947; *Educ* Lancing, Univ of Southampton (BSc), Lancaster Univ (MA), Columbia Univ NY (MBA); *m* 12 April 1975 (m dis 1999), Gillian Frances Audrey, da of Sir Gervase Blois, 10 Bt (d 1967); 2 s (Alexander John Gervase b 1976, Christopher Harry Gilbert b 1985), 1 da (Nicola Elizabeth b 1978); m 2, 26 Jan 2001, Verena Elizabeth Burrowes; *Career* dir: Centaur Communications Ltd 1981–98, Hambros Bank Ltd 1984–94, Hambro Gp Investments 1988–94; md Hambro European Ventures Ltd 1987–94, sr advsr ECI Ventures Ltd 1994–95, sr advsr ABSA Bank Ltd 1998–99 (head of corp fin 1995–98), ptnr Baring Private Equity Partners 1999–2005, chm Baring English Growth Fund 2000–, chm Parkside Int Ltd 2000–04, dir Secure Mail Services Ltd 2002–06, dir Constantine Holdings Ltd 2004–; Parly candidate (Cons) Strangford 1997; *Recreations* tennis, riding, skiing; *Clubs* City, Queen's, Turf, Berkshire Golf; *Style*— Gilbert Chalk, Esq; ✉ 103 Elgin Crescent, London W11 2JF (tel 020 7727 1981)

CHALKE, Rev Stephen John (Steve); MBE (2004); s of Victor Joseph Chalke (d 1993), and Ada Elizabeth, *née* Wroth; *b* 17 November 1955; *Educ* Spurgeon's Coll London; *m* 23 Aug 1980, Cornelia Marta, da of Otto Reeves (d 1996); 2 da (Emily Louise b 5 July 1982, Abigail Lucy b 9 June 1986), 2 s (Daniel John b 5 Feb 1984, Joshua Thomas b 12 May 1988); *Career* writer and television/radio broadcaster, charity founder; minister of Tonbridge Baptist Church 1981–85 (ordained 1981); founding dir Oasis Tst 1985, chm Oasis Media Communications Ltd, chm exalt Ltd, fndr Faithworks, sr minister church.co.uk Waterloo 2003–; vice-pres Bible Soc; pres Crusaders; patron: Arts Centre Group, The Viva Network, Habitat for Humanity, Deaf Link, Leeds Faith in Schools, Network Youth Schools; presenter Changing Places BBC Radio 4; individual Templeton UK Award 1997 (for contrib made in the field of the advancement of spiritual values); hon fell Sarum Coll Salisbury 2005; *Television* appearances on Sunday Morning (ITV Networked), GMTV, The Time The Place, First Light, Songs of Praise; numerous commentaries on charity, social action, poverty and homelessness; nat charity projects incl: Christmas Cracker, Get Up and Give & Motivation Weekend (in assoc with GMTV); *Publications* Making A Team Work (1995), More Than Meets the Eye (1995), I Believe in Taking Action (1995), The Truth About Suffering (1996), Sex Matters (1996), How to Succeed as a Parent (1997), Get Up And Give (1998), Managing Your Time (1998), Parent Talk (2000), Faithworks (2001), Faithworks Stories of Hope (2001), Faithworks Unpacked (2002), Intimacy and Involvement (2003), The Lost Message of Jesus (2003); The Parentalk Guide series ed: The Parentalk Guide to the Childhood Years (1999), The Parentalk Guide to the Teenage Years (1999), The Parentalk Guide to the Toddler Years (1999), The Parentalk Guide to your Child and Sex (2000), The Parentalk Guide to Great Days Out (2001), The Parentalk Guide to Working Parents (2002), Trust: A Radical Manifesto (2004), Intelligent Church: A Journey Towards Christ-Centered Community; also regular contrib to newspapers and magazines incl: The Mail on Sunday, The Guardian, Hello, Woman's Weekly, The Sun; *Recreations* gym, swimming, running (Guinness World Record for Most Money Raised by a Marathon Runner 2005); *Style*— The Rev Steve Chalke, MBE; ✉ Oasis, 115 Southwark Bridge Road, London SE1 0AX (tel 020 7633 2098, fax 020 7620 1944)

CHALKER OF WALLASEY, Baroness (Life Peer UK 1992), of Leigh-on-Sea in the County of Essex; Lynda Chalker; PC (1987); da of late Sidney Henry James Bates, and late Marjorie Kathleen Randell; *b* 29 April 1942; *Educ* Roedean, Univ of Heidelberg, Westfield Coll London, Central London Poly; *m* 1, 1967 (m dis 1973), Eric Robert Chalker (chm Greater London Young Conservatives 1966–67); m 2, 1981 (m ds 2003), Clive Landa (chm Tory Reform Gp 1979–82 and chm Young Cons 1972–74); *Career* statistician Research Bureau Ltd (Unilever subsid) 1963–69, market researcher Shell Mex & BP Ltd 1969–72, chief exec Int Div Louis Harris International 1972–74; chm Gtr London Young Cons 1969–70, nat vice-chm Young Cons 1970–71; MP (Cons) Wallasey 1974–92; memb BBC Gen Advsy Ctee 1975–79, oppn spokesman for Social Servs 1976–79; Parly under sec of state: DHSS 1979–82, Tport 1982–83; min of state: Tport 1983–86, FCO 1986–97, for Overseas Devpt 1989–97; ind conslt on Africa and Devpt to business and public sector 1997–; chm:

LSHTM 1998–2006, Africa Matters Ltd 1998–, Medicines for Malaria 2006–; non-exec dir: Capital Shopping Centres plc 1997–2000, Freeplay Energy Holdings 1997–2007, Landell Mills Ltd 1999–2003, Ashanti Goldfields Co 2000–04, Group Five Ltd 2001–, DCI 2002–03, Unilever plc 2004–07 (advsy dir 1998–2004), Equator Exploration Ltd 2005–; memb Int Advsy Bd: Lafarge & Cie 2004–, Merchant Bridge & Co 2006–, Merchant Int Gp (MIG) 2007–; memb Panel 2000; hon fell: Liverpool John Moores Univ, Queen Mary & Westfield Coll London, Univ of East London, Univ of Liverpool; Hon Dr: Univ of Westminster, Cranfield Univ, Univ of Bradford, Univ of Warwick; hon memb RGS, Hon FRSS, Hon FIHT; *Recreations* theatre, driving; *Style*— The Rt Hon Baroness Chalker of Wallasey; ✉ House of Lords, London SW1A 0PW (tel 020 7976 6850, fax 020 7976 4999, e-mail lchalker@africamatters.com)

CHALLACOMBE, Prof Stephen James; s of Kenneth Vivian Challacombe, of Sudbury, Suffolk, and Caryl Graydon, *née* Poore (d 1986); *b* 5 April 1946, London; *Educ* Culford Sch, Guy's Hosp Dental Sch (state scholar, Malleson Prize for Student Research, BDS), Univ of London (PhD); *m* 2 Aug 1969, Tina, da of Bishop Frank Cocks, and Barbara Cocks; 1 s (Benjamin James b 8 June 1973), 1 da (Fiona Lucy b 8 May 1976); *Career* Dept of Oral Immunology and Microbiology Guy's Hosp Med and Dental Schs: research fell 1971–72, lectr 1972–76, sr lectr 1976–85; reader in oral immunology Univ of London 1985–88, prof of oral med Univ of London 1988–; UMDS (GKT since 1998): sub dean of dental studies Guy's Hosp Med and Dental Schs 1983–87, head Dept of Oral Med and Pathology 1986–2005, postgrad sub dean (dental) 1992–2002, dir of postgrad studies 1998–2003, chm Div of Oral Med, Pathology, Microbiology and Immunology GKT Dental Inst 1998–2005, dir of external relations KCL Dental Inst 2004–; sr research fell and asst prof Dept of Immunology Mayo Clinic Rochester MN 1978–79 (Edward C Kendall Research Fellowship), external conslt Specialised Caries Research Centre Dows Inst of Dental Research Coll of Dentistry Univ of Iowa 1984–91, visiting prof Dept of Oral Biology Univ of Calif San Francisco 1995; hon conslt in oral immunology and microbiology Guy's Hosp 1982–, control of infection offr Guy's Dental Hosp 1984–2000, conslt in diagnostic microbiology, cytology and immunology Lewisham and N Southwark HA (now Guy's and St Thomas' Hosp NHS Tst) 1984–, dir Centre for the Study of Oral Manifestations of HIV Infection Guy's Hosp 1990–2000; hon conslt in oral med to UK Armed Forces 1998–; memb Clinical Dentistry Research Assessment Exercise Panels HEFCE 1996–97 and 1999–2001 (also vice-chm), memb Cncl Br Sjogren's Syndrome Assoc; pres: Br Soc for Oral Med 1995–97, Br Soc for Dental Research (Br Div IADR) 2000–02 (treas 1993–2001), Odontological Section RSM 1996–97 (treas 1992–95), Metropolitan Branch BDA 1999, IADR 2003–04 (pres Experimental Pathology Gp 1998–99, vice-pres 2001, pres-elect 2002); memb: Br Soc for Immunology, RSM, Br Soc for Oral Pathology, Int Assoc for Oral Pathology, Br Soc of Oral Med, European Assoc for Oral Med (treas 1997–2005), Int Soc for Mucosal Immunology; author or co-author of 7 books, over 200 peer-reviewed scientific pubns and 150 other pubns; Colgate Research Prize Br Div IADR 1977, Newland-Pedley Travelling Scholarship Guy's Hosp Med and Dental Schs 1978, Basic Research in Oral Science Award IADR 1981, Cwlth Travelling Scholarship 1990, Distinguished Scientist Award for Experimental Pathology IADR 1997; pres: Guy's Hosp (now GKT) Swimming and Water Polo Club 1985–2005, Guy's Hosp RFC (now Guy's, King's and St Thomas' Hosps RFC) 1991–2001; LDSRCS 1968, FRCPath 1992 (MRCPath 1981), FDSRCSE 1994, FMedSci 1998, FDSRCS 2005; *Recreations* golf, tennis, rugby, sailing, swimming; *Clubs* MCC, Savage, Nobody's Friends, Royal Blackheath Golf, Felixstowe Ferry Golf, Hunterian Soc (pres 2006–07); *Style*— Prof Stephen Challacombe; ✉ 101 Mycenae Road, Blackheath, London SE3 7RX (tel 020 8858 7933); Guy's, King's and St Thomas' Dental Institute, King's College London, Guy's Hospital, London SE1 9RT (tel 020 7188 4374, fax 020 7188 1159, e-mail stephen.challacombe@kcl.ac.uk)

CHALLEN, Colin; MP; *b* 12 June 1953, Scarborough; *Educ* Norton Secdy Modern, Malton GS, Open Univ, Univ of Hull (BA); *Career* RAF 1971–74, PO 1974–78, self-employed printer and publisher 1982–94, mktg advsr to co-op businesses Humberside Co-op Dept Agency (CDA) 1992–93 (fndr memb CDA 1982), Lab Pty organiser 1994–2000, self-employed writer and researcher 2000–01; MP (Lab) Morley and Rothwell 2001–; chair All Party Parly Climate Change Gp 2005–; Lab Pty: joined 1984, chr N Hull Constituency 1986–87, agent Humberside Constituency Euro elections 1989, Parly candidate Beverley 1992, agent Leeds NE Parly election 1997, sec Morley S Branch 1998–2001; sec Leeds Soc Co-op Pty 2000–03; Hull City Cncl: cncllr 1986–94, sec Lab Gp 1991–94, chair Performance Review Ctee 1992–94; ed Labour Organiser 1997–2001; memb: League Against Cruel Sports 1976–, Socialist Environment Resources Assoc (SERA); former memb: Hull Cncl For Voluntary Serv, Humberside Area Manpower Bd; *Publications* The Quarrelsome Quill: Hull's Radical Press from 1832 (1984), In Defence of the Party: The Secret State, the Conservative Party and dirty tricks (with Mike Hughes, 1996), The Price of Power: the secret funding of the Conservative Party (1998), Save As You Travel: New directions in mutual ownership (1999); *Style*— Colin Challen, MP; ✉ House of Commons, London SW1A 0AA; Constituency Office, 2 Commercial Street, Morley, Leeds LS27 8HY

CHALLIS, Dr Christine Joyce; OBE (2003); da of Bernard Arthur Black (d 1995), of Nottingham, and Nora Alice, *née* Willoughby (d 1985); *b* 24 February 1940; *Educ* Queen Ethelburga's Sch Harrogate, Nottingham HS for Girls, Bedford Coll London (BA), QMC London (PhD); *m* 4 Jan 1967, Christopher Edgar Challis, *qv*, s of Edgar Challis; *Career* pt/t tutor in history Univ of London, public relations offr Castlefield Textiles 1964–69; Univ of Leeds: admin asst 1969–72, asst sec 1972–74, dep sec 1974–83; pt/t CVCP admin trg offr for UK univs 1980–83, sec LSE 1983– (dir of admin 2001–); dir: Enterprise LSE, LSE LETS, VELSE, Southern Universities Management Services, Univs Superannuation Scheme Ltd 1989–97 (dir Audit Ctee), LSE Fndn Inc; chm: UK Organising Gp for UK/Swedish Univ Registrars and Secretaries Link, Univs Superannuation Scheme Ltd Audit Ctee 1999– (ind memb 1997–); UK and Ireland rep Heads of Univs Mgmnt and Admin in Europe 1997–; memb: South Bank Univ Human Resources Ctee, South Bank Univ Hon Fells Ctee, South Bank Univ Renumeration Ctee, Careers Advsy Bd Univ of London 1991–96, Trg and Mgmnt Ctee Univ of London 1991–96, South Bank Univ Audit Ctee 1992–96, Euro Round Table for Sr Univ Administrators in Europe, Steering Ctee Assoc of Heads of Univ Administrators 1989–94, SAUL Negotiating Ctee, Frank Knox Fellowship Selection Panel, Advsy Cncl Civil Serv Coll 1986–89; contrib to historical and univ jls and publications; govr: Fulneck Girls' Sch Pudsey W Yorks 1973–83, South Bank Univ 1995–; FRSA; *Recreations* music, vernacular architecture; *Clubs* Athenaeum; *Style*— Dr Christine Challis, OBE; ✉ London School of Economics and Political Science, Houghton Street, London WC2A 2AE (tel 020 7955 7009, fax 020 7852 3646)

CHALLIS, Dr Christopher Edgar; s of Edgar Challis (d 1957), of Leeds, and Hilda May, *née* Elsworth (d 1989); *b* 5 February 1939; *Educ* Cockburn HS Leeds, Univ of Bristol (BA, CertEd, PhD); *m* 4 Jan 1967, Dr Christine Joyce Challis, OBE, *qv*, da of Bernard Arthur Black, of Nottingham; *Career* Univ of Leeds: asst lectr 1964–67, lectr 1967–78, sr lectr 1978–82, reader 1982–2001, chm of the sch 1988–91; ed Br Numismatic Journal 1980–89; vice-pres Br Numismatic Soc 1995– (pres 1988–93), tstee UK Numismatic Tst 1988– (pres 2000–); memb Royal Mint Advsy Ctee on the Design of Coins, Medals, Seals and Decorations 1991–98; John Sanford Saltus Gold Medal of Br Numismatic Soc 1992; FRHistS 1970, FSA 1987, FRSA 1991; *Books* The Tudor Coinage (1978), A New History of the Royal Mint (ed, 1992); *Recreations* walking; *Style*— Dr Christopher Challis, FSA; ✉ Old Manor House, Nether Silton, Thirsk, North Yorkshire YO7 2JZ (tel 01609 883375)

CHALLIS, George Hubert; CBE (1991); s of Hubert William Challis (d 1969); *b* 26 May 1921; *Educ* King Edward VI Sch Stourbridge; *m* 1946, Margaret Beatrice, da of Reginald Percy Bonner (d 1965); 1 s, 1 da; *Career* served 1940–46 1/9 Gurkha Rifles (despatches twice); banker and co dir; with Lloyds Bank plc 1938–81 (head of Premises Div 1974–81); dir: Lloyds Bank Property Co 1974–81, Towco Group Ltd 1982–84, Westminster Property Group plc 1983–84; memb: Ct of Common Cncl City of London 1978–2000, Cncl London C of C and Industry 1979–89, Thames Water Authy 1982–83; dep govr The Hon Irish Soc 1983–84; chm: Port and City of London Health and Social Servs Ctee 1988–90, City Lands and Bridge House Estates Ctee 1990 and 1991; memb Benefices Ctee Corp of London 2000–; pres 9 Gurkha Rifles UK Regtl Assoc 2000–; Master Worshipful Co of Tobacco Pipe Makers and Tobacco Blenders 1992–93, Hon Liveryman Worshipful Co of Chartered Secretaries and Administrators (Hon Clerk 1984–94); Cdr of the Order of Merit (Federal Republic of Germany) 1986, Commendatore Order of Merit (Republic of Italy) 1990; *Recreations* travel, reading, music; *Clubs* RAC, MCC, Guildhall, City Livery; *Style*— George Challis, Esq, CBE; ✉ 77 West Hill Avenue, Epsom, Surrey KT19 8JX (tel 01372 721705)

CHALLIS, Prof Richard; *Educ* Imperial Coll London (BSc, PhD); *Career* clinical engr Guy's Hosp London 1975–78, professor visitante Federal Univ of Rio de Janeiro 1978–80, appointed lectr in bioengineering and physiology Univ of London 1980, prof of engineering physics Keele Univ until 1998, head Sch of Electrical and Electronic Engrg Univ of Nottingham 1998–2003, head Applied Ultrasonics Lab (AUL) Univ of Nottingham 1998–; sometime sec Physical Acoustics Gp Inst of Physics; Roy Sharp Prize for Research British Inst of Non-Destructive Testing; CEng, CPhys, fell British Inst of Non-Destructive Testing (FBINDT), FIEE, FInstP, FREng; *Style*— Prof Richard Challis; ✉ School of Electrical and Electronic Engineering, University of Nottingham, University Park, Nottingham NG7 2RD

CHALMERS, Ian Pender; CMG (1993), OBE (1980); s of John William Pender Chalmers (d 1977), and Beatrice Miriam, *née* Emery (d 1973); *b* 30 January 1939; *Educ* Harrow, TCD; *m* 1962, Lisa Christine, da of Prof John D Hay; 2 s (James William Pender b 27 July 1964, Nicholas John Pender b 4 May 1971), 3 da (Sara Pender b 8 Sept 1965 (decd), Lisa Francesca Pender b 1 Oct 1968, Charlotte Anne Pender b 8 March 1976); *Career* entered HM Dip Serv 1963, second sec Beirut 1966–68, FCO 1968–70, first sec Warsaw 1970–72, FCO 1972–76, first sec Paris 1976–80, FCO 1980–84, cnsllr UK Mission to UN Geneva 1984–87, cnsllr FCO 1987–94; *Recreations* golf, reading, watching sport, dogs; *Clubs* Huntercombe Golf, Army and Navy; *Style*— Ian Chalmers, Esq, CMG, OBE; ✉ The Croft, Packhorse Lane, Marcham, Oxfordshire OX13 6NT

CHALMERS, Judith; OBE (1994); da of David Norman Chalmers, FRICS (d 1953), and Millie Locke, *née* Broadhurst; *b* 10 October 1937; *Educ* Withington Girls' Sch Manchester, LAMDA; *m* 3 Jan 1964, Neil Durden-Smith, OBE, *qv*, s of Anthony James Durden-Smith, FRCS (d 1963); 1 da (Emma (Mrs Gordon Dawson) b 4 March 1967), 1 s (Mark b 1 Oct 1968); *Career* began broadcasting in Manchester BBC Children's Hour at age of 13 (while still at school); interviewer/presenter many radio and TV programmes in North and then London from 1960 with BBC; joined Thames TV with own afternoon programme 1972; first series of travel programme Wish You Were Here...? 1973–2004; developed own idea for home interest programme Hot Property; joined Radio 2 to host own daily programme 1990; reporter Castle in the Country (BBC 2) 2005, contrib Breakfast BBC TV; commentator for many royal and state occasions; travel ed Woman's Realm; past memb Nat Consumer Cncl; memb Peacock Ctee on Broadcasting; conslt: BAA, Holiday Property Bond; pres emeritus Lady Taverners; vice-pres Holiday Care Service; memb British Guild of Travel Writers; Freeman City of London; *Books* Wish You Were Here ...?: 50 of the Best Holidays (1987), At Home and away with Judith Chalmers (2001, 2002, 2003, 2004 and 2005); *Recreations* watching rugby and cricket; *Clubs* Mosimann's; *Style*— Miss Judith Chalmers, OBE; ✉ c/o Julie Ivelaw-Chapman, The Chase, Chaseside Close, Cheddington, Bedfordshire LU7 0SA (tel 01296 662441)

CHALMERS, Sir Neil Robert; kt (2001); s of William King Chalmers, and Irene Margaret, *née* Pemberton; *b* 19 June 1942, London; *Educ* KCS Wimbledon, Magdalen Coll Oxford (MA), St John's Coll Cambridge (PhD); *m* 28 Feb 1970, Monica Elizabeth Byanjeru, *née* Rusoke; 2 da (Emily Anne Nsemere b 5 Dec 1970, Louise Jane Kobuyenje b 11 Oct 1977); *Career* lectr in zoology Makerere UC Kampala Uganda 1966–69, scientific dir Nat Primate Res Centre Nairobi Kenya 1969–70; Open Univ: lectr, sr lectr then reader in biology 1970–85, dean of sci 1985–88; dir Natural History Museum (previously Br Museum (Natural History)) 1988–2004, warden Wadham Coll Oxford 2004–; pres: Assoc for the Study of Animal Behaviour 1989–92, Marine Biology Assoc UK 2002–07, Inst of Biology 2004–06; chair Nat Biodiversity Network Tst 2005–; tstee St Andrews Prize for the Environment 2002–; hon fell: Birkbeck Coll London 2002, KCS Wimbledon 2003; Hon DSc Univ of Plymouth 2004; FZS, FLS, FIBiol, FRSA 1988; *Books* Social Behaviour in Primates (1979), contrib numerous papers on animal behaviour to various jls; *Recreations* music, golf; *Clubs* Oxford and Cambridge, Athenaeum; *Style*— Sir Neil Chalmers; ✉ Wadham College, Oxford OX1 3PN (tel 01865 277931, fax 01865 277964)

CHALMERS, Dr Robert James Guille; s of James Alexander Chalmers (d 1998), of Oxford, and Lois Guille, *née* Taudevin (d 1980); *b* 18 November 1950; *Educ* St Edward's Sch Oxford, Middx Hosp Med Sch (MB BS); *m* 1 Oct 1988, Elizabeth Joyce, da of Leonard Cater (d 1980), of Balwest, Cornwall; *Career* conslt dermatologist 1983–: Salford Royal Hospitals NHS Trust, Royal Bolton Hospitals NHS Trust, Manchester Royal Infirmary; FRCP; *Recreations* travelling, playing the bassoon; *Clubs* Royal Society of Medicine; *Style*— Dr Robert Chalmers; ✉ The Dermatology Centre, Hope Hospital, Stott Lane, Salford, Manchester M6 8HD (tel 0161 206 1016, fax 0161 206 1018, e-mail r.chalmers@man.ac.uk)

CHALONER, Nicholas Joseph (Nick); s of John Seymour Chaloner, of London, and Katharine Joan, *née* Horton (d 2001); *b* 19 July 1955; *Educ* Kingston GS, UC Cardiff (BA), RMA Sandhurst; *m* 16 Dec 1978, Jane Philippa, da of late John Schwerdt; 2 da (Emma Katharine b 12 Jan 1985, Alice Caroline b 28 Feb 1990); *Career* Capt QOH 1978–82, awarded GSM NI 1979; assoc dir Burson-Marsteller 1982–88, exec vice-pres Hill & Knowlton 1988–97, dir of corp affrs Abbey National plc 1997–2000, head of communications Brightstation plc 2000–01, dir of communications SABMiller plc 2001–05, chief exec 48 Fitzroy Ltd 2005–; Hill & Knowlton PR Man of the Year 1997; MIPR 1982; *Recreations* sailing, skiing, reading; *Style*— Nick Chaloner, Esq

CHAMBERLAIN, Andrew Michael John; s of Alan Chamberlain (d 2000), and Patricia, *née* Stevens; *b* 14 February 1963, Lytham, Lancs; *Educ* King Edward VII Sch Lytham, Univ of Nottingham (BA), Trent Poly; *m* 28 Aug 1999, Cathy, *née* Wienholdt; 1 s (James (twin) b 16 Sept 2005), 1 da (Anna (twin) b 16 Sept 2005); *Career* slr; articled clerk then slr Freshfields 1986–92, DLA 1993–95 (ptnr 1994), ptnr Addleshaw Goddard 1995– (head of employment gp 2003–); memb Law Soc; *Recreations* golf, music, family, watching all major sports; *Clubs* Royal Automobile, Royal Lytham & St Anne's Golf, Royal Liverpool Golf; *Style*— Andrew Chamberlain, Esq; ✉ Addleshaw Goddard, 100 Barbirolli Square, Manchester M2 3AB (tel 0161 934 6444, e-mail andrew.chamberlain@addleshawgoddard.com)

CHAMBERLAIN, Arthur; s of Lt-Col Arthur Chamberlain, MC, TD (d 1986), of Edgbaston, Birmingham, and Elizabeth Susan, *née* Edwards (d 1986); *b* 20 February 1952; *Educ* Milton Abbey, Oxford Brookes Univ; *m* 1, 18 June 1988 (m dis 1993), Dominique Jane Patricia; 1 da (b 17 Oct 1991); m 2, 6 Dec 1997, Vivien Elizabeth, *née* Visser, of Cape Town, South Africa; 2 s (Arthur b 2 Oct 1998, William Louis b 19 July 2000); *Career*

Bank of London and South America Ecuador 1975–76, Bank of London and Montreal Guatemala 1976–77, Lloyds Bank International London 1977–79, dir Banco La Guaira International Venezuela 1979–82, md Lloyds Bank Nigeria Ltd 1982–84, sr corp mangr Lloyds Bank plc London 1984–2000, relationship dir Corporate Banking Lloyds TSB 2001–03; dir Barton Advisory Services Ltd, investment dir Beer and Partners Ltd; Freeman City of London; Liveryman: Worshipful Co of Gunmakers, Worshipful Co of Cordwainers; MInstD; *Recreations* shooting, fishing, travel, photography; *Clubs* Shikar, Hurlingham; *Style*— Arthur Chamberlain, Esq; ✉ e-mail chamberlain@bartonadvisory.com

CHAMBERLAIN, Colin Ellis; s of Ellis Robert Chamberlain (d 1988), and Edith Elisabeth, *née* Spencer (d 1989); *b* 5 March 1951, London; *Educ* Felsted Sch, Univ of Sussex; *m* 30 May 1981, Annabel; 2 da (Harriet b 2 Sept 1986, Florence b 10 Oct 1988); *Career* admitted slr 1977; Herbert Smith 1974–85, CC&P 1985–89, ptnr Herbert Smith 1989–; memb Law Soc; *Publications* Tolley's Practical Guide to Employees' Share Schemes (4 edn 2003); *Recreations* reading history, golf, sailing, tennis; *Clubs* Broadgate, Aldeburgh Golf; *Style*— Colin Chamberlain, Esq; ✉ 99 Barnsbury Street, London N1 1EP (tel 020 7607 0480, fax 020 7700 5938); Herbert Smith, Exchange House, Primrose Street, London EC2A 2HS (tel 020 7374 8000, fax 020 7374 0888, e-mail colin.chamberlain@herbertsmith.com)

CHAMBERLAIN, Prof Geoffrey Victor Price; RD (1974); s of Albert Victor Chamberlain, MBE (d 1978), and Irene May Chamberlain, MBE, *née* Price (d 1996, aged 102); *b* 21 April 1930; *Educ* Llandaff Cathedral Sch, Cowbridge GS, UCL, UCH Med Sch (MB BS, MD); *m* 23 June 1956, Prof Jocelyn Olivia Peter Chamberlain, da of Sir Peter Kerley, KCVO (d 1979), of Putney, London; 3 s (Christopher b 1957, Mark b 1959, Patrick b 1962), 2 da (Hilary (Mrs H Sarsfield) b 1961, Virginia (Mrs James F Puzey) b 1966); *Career* RNVR 1955–57, RNR 1957–74, Surgn Lt 1955, Surgn Lt Cmdr 1961, Surgn Cdr 1970–74; prosector in anatomy Royal Univ of Malta 1956–57, resident Royal Postgraduate Med Sch, Hosp for Sick Children Great Ormond Street, and others 1958–62, registrar then sr registrar King's Coll Hosp 1962–69, Fulbright fell George Washington Univ USA 1966–67, conslt obstetrician and gynaecologist Queen Charlotte's Hosp for Women 1970–82, prof and head Dept of Obstetrics and Gynaecology St George's Hosp Med Sch 1982–95, emeritus conslt obstetrician Singleton Hosp Swansea 1995–2000; tutor in history of med Coll of Med Cardiff and Soc of Apothecaries and lectr in history of med Clincial Med Sch Univ of Wales Swansea; pres RCOG 1993–94; ed-in-chief Contemporary Reviews in Obstetrics and Gynaecology 1988–2000, ed-in-chief Br Jl of Obstetrics and Gynaecology 1992–94; visiting prof: USA 1984, Hong Kong 1985, Brisbane 1987, South Africa 1988, Peshawar 1993, Chicago 1995; med examiner: Univ of London 1972–2000, Univ of Liverpool 1973–75 and 1991–94, Univ of Manchester 1979–83, Univ of Birmingham 1979–82, Univ of Cambridge 1981–86, Univ of Glasgow 1985–87, Univ of Kuala Lumpur 1986–87, Univ of Nottingham 1987–90, Univ of Wales 1988–90, Univ of Malta 1988–91, Univ of Columbo Sri Lanka 1993–94; examiner RCOG 1972–94, chm Scientific Ctee Nat Birthday Tst, chm Assoc of Profs in Obstetrics and Gynaecology; pres: Blair Bell Res Soc (former chm), Sci Ctee Birthright Charity 1993–95, Victor Bonney Soc 1993–95; hon gynaecologist Br Airways, fell UCL, treas RSM, inspr of Nullity; Freeman of the City of London 1982, Liveryman Worshipful Soc of Apothecaries; FRCS 1960, MRCOG 1963, FRCOG 1978, FACOG (Hon) 1992, Hon FSLCOG (Sri Lankan Coll of Obstetrics and Gynaecology) 1993, Hon FFFP (Faculty of Family Planning RCOG) 1996; *Books* Lecture Notes in Obstetrics (1984, 1992, 1996, 1999), Practice of Obstetrics and Gynaecology (1985, 1990, 2000), Pregnancy Survival Manual (1986), Birthplace (1987), Lecture Notes in Gynaecology (1988, 1989, 1995, 1999), Manual of Obstetrics (1988), Obstetrics (with Alec Turnbull, 1989), Ten Teachers in Obstetrics and Gynaecology (1990 and 1995); Preparing for Parenthood (1990), Illustrated Textbook of Obstetrics (1991), ABC of Antenatal Care (1992, 1994, 1996, 2001), Pregnacy Care in the 1990s (1992), Pain and its Relief in Childbirth (1993), Homebirths (1996), Clinical Physiology in Obstetrics (1980, 1991, 1998), ABC Labour Care (1999), Victor Bonney (2000), William Nixon (2003), A History of British Obstetrics and Gynaecology (2005); *Recreations* opera, writing, Egyptology; *Clubs* Perinatal, Blair Bell Soc, McDonald; *Style*— Prof Geoffrey Chamberlain; ✉ Sycamores, Llanmadoc, Gower, Swansea SA3 1DB (tel 01792 386325)

CHAMBERLAIN, Kevin John; CMG (1992); s of Arthur James Chamberlain, of Purley, Surrey, and Gladys Mary, *née* Harris; *b* 31 January 1942; *Educ* Wimbledon Coll, King's Coll London (LLB); *m* 23 Sept 1967, Pia Rosita, da of Jean Frauenlob, of Geneva, Switzerland; 1 da (Georgina b 26 Aug 1975); *Career* called to the Bar Inner Temple 1965; FCO: asst legal advsr 1965–73, legal advsr Br Mil Govt Berlin 1973–76, first sec (legal advsr) HM Embassy Bonn 1976–78, legal cnsllr 1979–83, cnsllr (legal advsr) Office of the UK Perm Rep to the EC 1983–87, legal cnsllr 1987–90, dep legal advsr 1990–99; barr; CEDR accredited mediator; memb NATO Appeals Bd; *Recreations* opera, choral singing, tennis; *Style*— Kevin Chamberlain, Esq, CMG; ✉ Fairfield, Warren Drive, Kingswood, Tadworth, Surrey KT20 6PY (tel 01737 832003, e-mail chamberlain@kt206py.fsnet.co.uk); York Chambers, 14 Toft Green, York YO1 6JT (tel 01904 620048, fax 01904 610056)

CHAMBERLAIN, Rev (George Ford) Leo; OSB; s of late Brig Noel Chamberlain, CBE, and late Sally, *née* Ford; *b* 13 August 1940; *Educ* Ampleforth, UC Oxford (open scholar, MA); *Career* Ampleforth Abbey: novitiate 1961, solemn profession 1964, ordained priest 1968; Ampleforth Coll: history, politics and religious studies teacher 1968, housemaster St Dunstan's House 1972–92, sr history master 1975–92, actg headmaster 1992–93, headmaster 1993–2003; master St Benet's Hall Univ of Oxford 2004–07; memb: HMC, Cncl of Mgmnt Keston Inst, Catholic Bishops' Advsy Ctee on Europe 1985–2001, Catholic Independent Schs Conference Ctee 1993–2000; govr St Gregory the Great Catholic Secdy Sch Oxford 2005–; *Recreations* engaged in the support of Eastern European Christians since 1970; *Clubs* Oxford and Cambridge; *Style*— The Rev Leo Chamberlain, OSB; ✉ Ampleforth Abbey, York YO62 4EN

CHAMBERLAIN, Dr Michael Albert John; s of Frederick Chamberlain (d 1980), and Mary, *née* O'Hare (d 1975); *b* 9 May 1948, Liverpool; *Educ* Univ of Manchester (BA, MA), Florida State Univ (PhD); *m* 1, 16 June 1973 (m dis 1978), Jane Margaret, *née* Pickering; m 2, 2 June 1978, Noreen, *née* Laurie; 2 da (Laura Mary b 14 Nov 1978, Dr Charlotte Ann b 16 June 1980); *Career* specialist writer on econ affairs and economist ITN 1973–76, ed Campaign magazine 1976–78, fndr ed/publisher Marketing Week and md Centaur Business Publishing 1978–89, head of new media United Newspapers plc 1994–96, dir Informed Sources Int 1996–97, vice-pres and head of media Arthur D Little 1998–2000, ptnr and industry ldr IBM Business Consltg Servs EMEA 2001–04, chm BMJ Publishing Gp Ltd and dir BMA 2004–; non-exec dir Alphameric plc; tstee: Breathlessness Res Charitable Tst 2000–, MedFASH 2006–; *Publications* Interactive Marketing (contrib, 1996), Mad Cow Crisis: Health and the Public Good (contrib, 1998); *Recreations* clay shooting; *Clubs* London Sporting Targets; *Style*— Dr Michael Chamberlain; ✉ No 1 Denmark Avenue, Wimbledon, London SW19 4HF (tel 020 8946 3136, e-mail michaelcham1@aol.com)

CHAMBERLAIN, (Leslie) Neville; CBE (1990); s of Leslie Chamberlain (d 1970), and Doris Anne, *née* Thompson; *b* 3 October 1939; *Educ* King James GS Bishop Auckland, King's Coll Durham; *m* 13 April 1971, Joy Rachel, da of Capt William Wellings (d 1979); 3 da (Louise b 1972, Elizabeth b 1974, Christina b 1981), 1 s (Andrew b 1984); *Career* UKAEA: mgmnt trainee 1962–64, health physicist Springfields 1964–67, res scientist Capenhurst 1967–71; mangr URENCO 1971–77; BNFL: works mangr Springfields 1977–81, enrichment business mangr Risley 1981–84, dir Enrichment Div Risley 1984–86; British Nuclear Fuels plc Risley: chief exec 1986–96, dep chm 1995–99; chm: Br Energy Assoc 1998–2001, TEC Nat Cncl 1999–2001, Manufacturing Inst 2002–, URENCO Ltd 2002–05, Cheshire and Warrington Economic Alliance 2005– Northern Way 2006–; non-exec dir AMEC Nuclear 2005–; memb Int Nuclear Energy Acad (chm 2001–03); hon fell: Inst of Nuclear Engrg, Euro Nuclear Soc; Freeman City of London; CIMgt, FInstP, FInstE, FRSA; *Recreations* racing, swimming, music, fell walking; *Clubs* Athenaeum; *Style*— Neville Chamberlain, Esq, CBE; ✉ Oaklands, 2 The Paddock, Hinderton Road, Neston, South Wirral, Cheshire CH64 9PH (tel 0151 353 1980, fax 0151 353 1981)

CHAMBERLAIN, Rt Rev Neville; *see:* Brechin, Bishop of

CHAMBERLAIN, Peter Edwin; s of late Dr Eric Alfred Charles Chamberlain, OBE, and Susan Winifred Louise, *née* Bone; *b* 25 July 1939; *Educ* Royal HS, Univ of Edinburgh (BSc), RNC Manadon, RNC Greenwich, RCDS; *m* 27 July 1963, Irene May, *née* Frew; 2 s (Mark b 1964, Paul b 1965), 1 da (Louise b 1970); *Career* MOD 1963–92: asst constructor ship and submarine design ME and Bath 1963–68, constructor 1968–69, submarine construction Birkenhead 1969–72, ship structures R&D Dunfermline 1972–74, mgmnt of Postgrad Progs of Naval Architecture UCL 1974–77, Ship Design Bath 1977–78, chief constructor and head of Secretariat to DG Ships 1978–80, Surface Ship Forward Design Bath 1980–82, asst sec head of Secretariat to MGO London 1984–85, under sec dir gen Future Material Programmes 1985–87, dep controller Warship Equipment 1987–88, chief Underwater Systems Exec 1988–89, head Def Res Agency Improvement Team 1989–92; BAe Systems: engrg dir Systems and Services 1992–99, dir ANZAC WIP (Weapons Improvement Prog) BAe Land and Sea Systems 1999, dir of engrg Sea Systems Gp 2002; dir Timely Solutions Ltd 2000–06, dir Pal Faena SRL 2002–; memb Royal Acad of Engrg Ctees: Programmes 1991–94, International 2001–04; memb Int Cncl on Systems Engrg (INCOSE) 1994–; RCNC 1960, FRINA 1986, FREng 1988; *Recreations* enjoying Italy, visual arts, poetry, recreational computing; *Style*— Peter Chamberlain, FREng; ✉ Coste Faena 112, 06057 Monte Castello di Vibio (PG), Italy (e-mail peter_e_chamberlain@compuserve.com)

CHAMBERLAIN, (Richard) Sebastian Endicott; s of late Lawrence Endicott Chamberlain, of Tonerspuddle, Dorchester, and Anne Zacyntha, *née* Eastwood (d 1969); *b* 13 April 1942; *Educ* Radley; *m* 1 Oct 1966, Lady Catherine Laura Chetwynd-Talbot, da of late 21 Earl of Shrewsbury and Waterford; 2 da (Sophie b 1968, Amy b 1971), 1 s (Tom b 1973); *Career* London Div RNR 1961–70, demobbed as Lt; Maguire Roy Marshall (formerly Maguire Kingsmill): joined 1960, ptnr 1974; W Greenwell & Co 1986; dir: Greenwell Montagu Stockbrokers 1987–92, Allied Provincial Securities 1993–95; div dir Brewin Dolphin 1995–; memb New Forest Dist Cncl 1973–79; Freeman City of London 1963, Liveryman Worshipful Co of Cordwainers 1963 (memb Ct of Assts 1999–, Second Warden 2002–03, Sr Warden 2003–04, Master 2004–05); memb London Stock Exchange 1964; MSI; *Recreations* sailing, fly fishing; *Clubs* Royal Lymington Yacht; *Style*— Sebastian Chamberlain, Esq; ✉ Stocks Farm, Burley Street, Ringwood, Hampshire BH24 4BZ (tel 01425 403313); Brewin Dolphin, 98 High Street, Lymington, Hampshire, SO41 9AP (tel 01590 674288)

CHAMBERLAYNE-MACDONALD, Major Nigel Donald Peter; CVO (1997, LVO 1960), OBE (1980), DL (1975); s of Sir Geoffrey Bosville Macdonald of the Isles, 15 Bt, MBE (d 1951), and Hon Rachael Audrey, *née* Campbell (d 1978); *b* 10 June 1927; *Educ* Radley; *m* 15 April 1958, Penelope Mary Alexandra, da of Tankerville Chamberlayne; 2 s (Alexander Nigel Bosville b 1959, Thomas Somerled b 1969), 2 da (Diana Mary (Countess of Lindsay) b 1961, Frances Penelope b 1965 d 1985); *Career* cmmnd Scots Gds 1946, served Italy 1946–47 and Malaya 1950–51, Canal Zone 1952–53; equerry to HRH The Duke of Gloucester 1954–55, asst private sec 1958–60; High Sheriff Hants 1974–75; a Gentleman Usher to HM The Queen 1979–97, Extra Gentleman Usher to HM The Queen 1997–; memb Queen's Body Guard for Scotland (Royal Co of Archers); chm Hants Assoc of Boys' Clubs 1967–82, a vice-chm Nat Assoc of Boys' Clubs 1969–90; pres: The Coaching Club 1982–90, Eastleigh and Chandlers Ford Boy Scouts Assoc 1962–2002; OStJ 1958; *Recreations* coaching, shooting, stalking; *Clubs* White's, Brooks's, Pratt's, Royal Yacht Squadron; *Style*— Major Nigel Chamberlayne-Macdonald, CVO, OBE, DL; ✉ Cranbury Park, Winchester, Hampshire SO21 2HL (tel 023 8025 2617); 17 William Mews, London SW1X 9HF (tel 020 7235 5867)

CHAMBERLEN, Nicholas Hugh; s of Rev Leonard Saunders Chamberlen, MC (d 1987), of Heathfield, E Sussex, and Lillian Margaret, *née* Webley (d 1996); *b* 18 April 1939; *Educ* Sherborne, Lincoln Coll Oxford (BA); *m* 1, 18 Sept 1962, Jane Mary (d 1998), da of Paul Lindo (d 1970); 3 s (Julian b 1964, Mark b 1965, Alexander b 1970), 1 da (Camilla b 1967); m 2, 9 Aug 2001, Christine Mary Lacy; *Career* Nat Serv RN 1957–59, Lt RNR, with NCR 1962–67; Clive Discount Co Ltd 1967– (dir 1969, chm 1977–93); chm: London Discount Market Assoc 1985–87, European Corporate Finance Prudential-Bache Securities (UK) Inc 1990–92, dir Imperial Group Pension Trust Ltd 1993–; *Recreations* shooting, golf, cricket; *Clubs* Turf, R&A; *Style*— Nicholas Chamberlen, Esq; ✉ Lampool, Fairwarp, East Sussex TN22 3DS (tel 01825 712636); 10 Rawlings Street, London SW3 2LS (tel 020 7584 1155)

CHAMBERLIN, Richard Alexander; s of John Alexander Chamberlin, MC, of Lenham, Kent, and Kathleen Mary, *née* Fraser (d 1990); *b* 1 July 1951; *Educ* The King's Sch Canterbury, Jesus Coll Cambridge (BA); *m* 1977, Mary-Angela, da of Norman William Stoakes Franks, of Folkestone, Kent; 2 da (Zoe b 1977, Naomi b 1979); *Career* articled Clerk Wedlake Bell 1973–75, admitted slr 1975, ptnr Freshfields 1981– (joined 1976); memb Worshipful Co of Solicitors; memb Law Soc; *Recreations* archaeology, sailing; *Clubs* Leander, Kent Archaeological Soc, Cambridge Soc (Kent Branch); *Style*— Richard Chamberlin, Esq; ✉ Freshfields, 65 Fleet Street, London EC4Y 1HS

CHAMBERS, Andrew David; s of (Lewis) Harold Chambers (d 1963), of Brundall, Norfolk, and Florence Lilian, *née* Barton (d 1979); *b* 7 April 1943; *Educ* St Albans Sch, Hatfield Coll Durham (BA); *m* 1, 1969 (m dis 1984), Mary Elizabeth Ann Kilbey; 2 s (Gregory b 1976, Thomas b 1979); m 2, 2 Oct 1987, Celia Barrington, da of Rev Hugh Pruen, of Old Bolingbroke, Lincs; 2 da (Chloë b 1988, Phoebe b 1992), 2 s (Theo b 1990, Cosmo b 1992), 1 step s (Henry b 1985); *Career* audit sr Arthur Andersen & Co 1965–69, admin exec Barker & Dobson 1969–70, systems gp mangr fin United Biscuits 1970–71; City Univ Business Sch: lectr computer applications in accountancy 1971–74, Leverhulme sr res fell internal auditing 1974–78, sr lectr audit and mgmnt control 1978–83, prof of internal auditing 1983–93, admin sub-dean 1983–86, dean 1986–91 (acting dean 1985–86), emeritus prof 1993–; prof of audit and control Univ of Hull 1994–98; non-exec chm Harlequin IT Services 1998–1999; dir: National Home Loans plc (now Paragon Group of Companies plc) 1991–2003, National Mortgage Bank 1991–92, Management Audit Ltd 1991–, Pilgrim Health NHS Tst 1996–2000, FTMS Online 1999–2002; visiting prof in computer auditing Univ of Leuven Belgium 1980–81 and 1991–92, Deloittes Prof of Int Auditing (pt/t) London South Bank Univ 2004–; warden Northampton Hall City Univ 1983–86 (dep warden 1972–76); memb: Cncl BCS 1979–82, Educn Training & Technol Transfer Ctee Br Malaysian Soc 1987–91, Corp Govt Ctee ICAEW 2004–; ed: International Jl of Auditing 1997–2003, Internal Control Newsletter 1997–, Corporate Governance Newsletter 1998–; govr Islington Green Sch 1989–91; Liveryman Worshipful Co of Loriners; CEng, FBCS, FCCA, FCA, FIIA, FRSA; *Books* Keeping Computers Under Control (with O J Hanson, 1975), Internal Auditing (1981), Computer Auditing (1981), Effective Internal Audits (1992), Auditing the IT Environment (with G Rand, 1994), Auditing Contracts (with G Rand, 1994), Internal Auditing (ed, 1996), The Operational

Auditing Handbook - Auditing Business Processes (with G Rand, 1997), Leading Edge Internal Auditing (with J Ridley, 1998), The Tolley Corporate Governance Handbook (2002, 2 edn 2003); *Recreations* family, conservation; *Clubs* Reform, Travellers; *Style*— Prof Andrew Chambers; ✉ Management Audit Ltd, 6 Market Street, Sleaford, Lincolnshire NG34 7SF (tel 01529 413344, fax 01529 413355, e-mail email@management-audit.com)

CHAMBERS, Christopher Michael; s of Walter Michael Chambers (d 1996), of Glos, and Marlis, *née* Stiefel (d 1978); *b* 28 June 1961, Warks; *m* 19 May 1990, Alexa Adderley, da of Sir Michael Hodson, Bt, *qv*; 3 da (Lara Adderley *b* 25 June 1992, Gemma Marlis *b* 8 April 1994, Anna Isabel *b* 5 March 1998); *Career* dir BZW Securities until 1997, dir de Zoete and Bevan Ltd until 1997, md and head European Equity Capital Markets Credit Suisse First Boston (Europe) Ltd until 2002, ceo Man Investments 2002–05, dir Man Gp plc 2003–05; govr Kensington Prep Sch for Girls, policy advsr to HRH The Prince of Wales' Charities Office; FRSA; *Recreations* skiing; *Clubs* Turf, Hurlingham; *Style*— Christopher Chambers, Esq; ✉ 1 Napier Avenue, London SW6 3PS

CHAMBERS, Daniel (Dan); s of Michael Chambers, *qv*, and Florence Ruth, *née* Cooper; *b* 13 September 1968; *Educ* William Ellis Sch, UC Sch, BNC Oxford (BA); *Partner* Rebecca Cotton; *Career* journalist Evening Standard 1991–92, researcher/asst prodr Panorama, Dispatches and Equinox 1992–96, dir Equinox Sun Storm 1996, dir Equinox Russian Roulette 1997; Sci Dept Channel 4: dep commissioning ed 1998–99, ed Channel 4 1999–2001; Channel 5 (now Five): controller of factual progs 2001–03 (devised History Strand Revealed (2002 RTS Best History for Dambusters), cmmnd World War I in Colour, Kings & Queens), dir of programmes 2003–06; govr London Int Film Sch 2006–; author of play Selling Out (dir by Sir Alan Ayckbourn, CBE, *qv*); *Recreations* photography, scuba diving, television watching; *Clubs* Ski-Slovenia (fndr memb); *Style*— Dan Chambers, Esq

CHAMBERS, David Phillip; s of Joseph Christopher Chambers (d 1994), and Bernadette Mary, *née* Costello (d 1978); *b* 2 August 1953; *Educ* Beaufoy Sch Lambeth, Slough Coll of Further Educn (City and Guilds Basic Cookery), Ealing Coll of Further Educn (City and Guilds Chefs Dip), Westminster Coll of Further Educn; *m* 7 March 1987, Helena, da of Branko Nikola Jovicich; 2 da (Zoe Anne *b* 17 April 1975, Amy Louise *b* 21 Aug 1978), 1 s (Liam Christie *b* 12 Nov 1992); *Career* apprentice chef: Piccadilly Hotel 1969–70, St Ermins Hotel 1970–71; chef tournant St Ermins Hotel 1971–72, chef saucier East Indian Sports and Public Schools Club 1972, Claridges Hotel 1973–74 (commis poissonier, commis saucier), chef gardemanger St Ermins Hotel 1974; sous chef: Mullard House 1974–75, Army and Navy Club 1975–76, Carlton Tower Hotel 1976–78; executive chef Portman Intercontinental 1980–81 (sous chef rising to first sous chef 1978–80), exec chef Le Restaurant Dolphin Square 1981, first sous chef Hyatt Carlton Tower 1981–82, chef de cuisine Dukes Hotel 1982–85; exec head chef: Le Meridien Piccadilly 1985–94, London Hilton on Park Lane 1994–97, chef and dir Rules (London's oldest restaurant) 1997–2004, exec chef Mount Wolseley Hotel Tullow 2004–; various TV appearances; awards for the Oak Room Restaurant: one Michelin Star, three AA rosettes, one Star Egon Ronay, 4/5 Good Food Guide, 17/20 and three Toques Gault Millau; awards for Windows Roof Restaurant: three AA rosettes, 3/5 Good Food Guide, 16/20 and two Toques Gault Millau, voted Best Game Restaurant 1999 Quantum Publications Ltd; Rules voted British Restaurant of the Year Tio Pepe Carlton London Awards 2003; sr academician mentor Acad of Culinary Arts; memb: Conseil Culinaire Français (Palmes Culinaires), Guilde des Fromagers Compagnon de Saint-Uguzon; Maitrise Escoffier; *Recreations* cooking, reading, shooting; *Style*— David Chambers, Esq

CHAMBERS, Guy; s of Colin Chambers, of Oxon, and Pat Carroll; *b* 12 January 1963, Hammersmith, London; *Educ* King Edward's Liverpool, Guildhall Sch of Music; *m* 6 Aug 1999, Emma; 2 da (Isis *b* 19 May 2000, Gala *b* 8 Dec 2003), 1 s (Marley *b* 11 Oct 2002); *Career* songwriter, prodr and musician; early career as keyboard player with artists incl Julian Cope and The Waterboys, joined World Party 1986, formed The Lemon Trees 1993–95; co-writer, co-prodr and musical dir with Robbie Williams, *qv* 1997–, albums incl Life Thru A Lens, I've Been Expecting You (Best Produced Album Int Managers Forum Award 1998), Sing When You're Winning, Swing When You're Winning and Escapology, numerous singles incl Angels, Millennium, Strong, No Regrets, Let Me Entertain You, She's the One/It's Only Us and Rock DJ; prodr and songwriter for numerous artists incl: Andrea Bocelli, Annie Lennox, BBMak, Beverley Knight, Brian McFadden, Busted, Cathy Dennis, Charlotte Church, Delta Goodrem, Diana Ross, Hilary Duff, James Blunt, Jamie Cullum, Jessica Simpson, Jewel, The Isis Project, Kylie Minogue, Mel C, Natasha Bedingfield, Rachel Stevens, Ross Copperman, Ryan Cabrera, Skin, Texas, Tom Jones, Will Young; Ivor Novello Awards 1998 (three) and 1999, 3 Brit Awards; *Clubs* Century, Soho House, RAC, Groucho; *Style*— Guy Chambers, Esq; ✉ c/o Sleeper Music, Sleeper Studios, Block 2, 6 Erskine Road, London NW3 3AJ (tel 020 7586 3995, fax 020 7900 6244, e-mail dylan@sleepermusic.co.uk)

CHAMBERS, Dr John Boyd; s of Dr Kenneth Boyd Chambers, and Taissia, *née* Petrova; *b* 28 December 1954; *Educ* Tonbridge (entrance scholar), Pembroke Coll Cambridge (entrance scholar, MA, MD), KCH London (MB BChir); *m* 1983 (m dis 1990), Ann Millward; *Career* house physician Kent and Sussex Hosp 1979–80, house surgn Farnborough Hosp 1980; SHO: A&E Bromley Hosp 1980–81, gen med Worthing Hosp 1981, gastroenterology St James' Hosp Balham 1981–82, neurology Atkinson Morley's Hosp 1982–83; registrar in gen med St Peter's Hosp 1983–84, registrar in cardiology St George's Hosp Tooting 1984–85 (SHO in cardiology 1982), Br Heart Fndn jr fell KCH London 1985–89, lectr and hon sr registrar Guy's Hosp 1989–91, sr lectr and hon conslt in cardiology Guy's and UMDS then Guy's and St Thomas' NHS Tst and KCL 1991–, conslt cardiologist Maidstone Hosp 1994–2002, cardiac tutor St Thomas' Hosp 1998–; Guy's and St Thomas' Hosp: estab clinical echocardiographic res 1991, fndr Valve Study Gp 1998, fndr Core Lab 1998, head of non-invasive cardiology 2001–, reader in cardiology 2001–; estab Dept of Echocardiography Guy's Hosp; examiner for MD examination Univ of London 1992, 1994, 1998 and 2001; lead clinician regnl cardiology audit 1998–2000; Br Soc of Echocardiography: memb Cncl 1993–98 and 2000–, pres 2003–05, chief examiner 1995–98, chm Educn Ctee 1996–98, memb Trg and Res Ctees; memb: Br Med Ultrasound Res Liaison Ctee, Int Panel Canadian Guidelines on Valve Surgery, Nucleus Working Gp on Valve Disease Euro Soc of Cardiology, Ctee on Prosthetic Heart Valves BSI 1991–, Ctee on Prosthetic Heart Valves ISO 2001–; fndr memb Soc for Valve Disease (chm Working Gp on Echocardiography); reviewer: Br Heart Fndn, Wellcome Tst, Scot Office, Mental Health Fndn, Irish Health Res Bd, NHS R&D Prog; memb Editorial Bd Br Jl of Clinical Practice 1991–, ed Jl of Heart Valve Disease 1995–2004 (memb Editorial Bd 1994–); UK ed echocardiographic section American Coll of Cardiology educn CD; session chm and invited speaker: Br Soc of Echocardiography 1994–, Br Cardiac Soc 1994–, EuroEcho 1998–, European Soc of Cardiology 1998–, American Coll of Cardiology 2002; invited speaker and lectr at confs and symposia worldwide; fell Euro Soc of Cardiology 1997, fell American Coll of Cardiology 1997; FRCP 1996 (MRCP 1982); *Publications* Acute Medicine: a Practical Guide to Medical Emergencies (jtly, 1990, 3 edn 2001), Echocardiography: an International Review (jt ed, 1993), Clinical Echocardiography (1995), Echocardiography in Primary Care (1996), A Slide Atlas of Echocardiography (1997), Echocardiography: Guidelines for Reporting (jtly, 1998); numerous case reports, chapters, reviews and invited articles; *Recreations* studio ceramics; *Style*— Dr John Chambers; ✉ Cardiothoracic Centre, St Thomas' Hospital, London SE1 7EH (tel 020 7188 1047, fax 020 7188 1011, e-mail jboydchambers@aol.com)

CHAMBERS, Lt-Col John Craven; s of Ernest Chambers (d 1996), of Seaton, Devon, and Margaret Joyce, *née* Batty; *b* 17 March 1947; *Educ* Latymer Upper Sch, RMA Sandhurst (Agar Meml Prize), RMCS (BSc), Cranfield Univ (MSc), Army Staff Course (Div 1), RAF Advanced Staff Course; *m* 1, 4 Sept 1971 (m dis 2002), Sandra, da of Herbert William Raby (d 1996); 1 da (Kathryn Jay *b* 11 August 1973), 1 s (Daniel John *b* 1 March 1975); *m* 2, 18 March 2005, Fiona Kersti Henrietta, da of Edward Malise Wynter Wagstaff; *Career* cmmnd Royal Corps of Signals 1967, served various staff and field appts MOD and res estab in Germany, Cyprus and the Falkland Islands until 1993; sec/chief exec Royal Masonic Tst for Girls and Boys 1993–2005; Freeman City of London 1994, Liveryman Worshipful Co of Wax Chandlers 1998 (memb Ct of Assts 2005); *Recreations* music (organ playing and singing), sailing, bridge, Freemasonry; *Clubs* Little Ship Club; *Style*— Lt-Col John Chambers; ✉ Wyckham House, Anstey Lane, Alton, Hampshire GU34 2NB (tel 01420 88980)

CHAMBERS, Lucinda Anne; da of Michael and Anne Chambers; *b* 17 December 1959; *Educ* Convent of the Sacred Heart Woldingham; *m* 1991, Simon Crow; 2 s (Theo *b* 4 Feb 1993, Gabriel *b* 1 March 2004); 1 other s (Toby Knott *b* 23 Feb 1988); *Career* sr fashion ed Elle Magazine UK 1986–88, fashion dir Vogue Magazine 1992– (former exec fashion ed); *Style*— Miss Lucinda Chambers; ✉ Vogue Magazine, Vogue House, Hanover Square, London W1S 1JU

CHAMBERS, Michael; s of Jack Chambers (d 1987), and Gerda, *née* Eisler (d 2001); *b* 30 November 1941; *Educ* William Ellis GS, LSE (BSc); *m* 1967 (m dis 1999), Florence; 2 s (Daniel, *qv*, b 1968, Jesse *b* 1973), 1 da (Hannah *b* 1976); *Career* lectr in sociology Univ of Ife Ibadan Nigeria; called to the Bar Lincoln's Inn 1966; practising barr 1966–69, head Legal Dept Monsanto UK 1972–73; chief exec: Orbach & Chambers Ltd (book and magazine publishers) 1969–, Chambers & Partners (recruitment agency) 1973–; producer Orbach & Chambers Records Ltd 1977–79; ed: Chambers Legal Directories 1989–, Commercial Lawyer (jl) 1995–, The Chambers Gallery 2003–; *Books* London: the Secret City (1973), There was a Young Lady... A Book of Limericks (1978); *Recreations* jazz trumpet; *Style*— Michael Chambers, Esq; ✉ Chambers & Partners, Saville House, 23 Long Lane, London EC1A 9HL (tel 020 7606 1300, fax 020 7606 0906, website www.chambersandpartners.com)

CHAMBERS, Nicholas Mordaunt; QC (1985); s of Marcus Mordaunt Bertrand Chambers, and Lona Margit, *née* Gross (d 1987); *b* 25 February 1944; *Educ* King's Sch Worcester, Hertford Coll Oxford; *m* 1966, Sarah Elizabeth, da of Thomas Herbert Fothergill Banks; 2 s, 1 da; *Career* called to the Bar Gray's Inn 1966 (bencher 1994), recorder of the Crown Court 1987–99, dep High Court judge 1994–99, circuit judge (Wales & Chester Circuit) 1999–; chm Inc Cncl of Law Reporting 2001–; *Recreations* sketching; *Clubs* Garrick, Lansdowne; *Style*— Nicholas Chambers, Esq, QC; ✉ The Mercantile Court for Wales, The Civil Justice Centre, 2 Park Street, Cardiff CF10 1ET (tel 02920 376400, fax 02920 376475)

CHAMBERS, Prof Richard Dickinson; *b* 16 March 1935; *Educ* Stanley GS, Univ of Durham (PhD, DSc); *m* 17 Aug 1959, Anne, *née* Boyd; 1 s (Mark *b* 1963), 1 da (Louise *b* 1965); *Career* res fell Univ of Br Columbia 1959–60, visiting lectr Fulbright fell Case Western Reserve Univ Cleveland Ohio 1966–67, fndn fell Univ of Durham 1988–89 (lectr 1960, reader 1968, prof 1976–2000, head of dept 1983–86, emeritus res prof 2000–), Tarrant visiting prof Univ of Florida 1999; non-exec dir F2 Chemicals Ltd 1995–2000; American Chem Soc Award for creative work in fluorine chemistry 1991, Prix Moissan 2003; memb: Royal Soc of Chem, American Chem Soc; FRS 1997; *Books* Fluorine in Organic Chemistry (1973); *Recreations* opera, golf, soccer, jogging; *Style*— Prof Richard Chambers, FRS; ✉ 5 Aykley Green, Whitesmocks, Durham DH1 4LN (tel 0191 386 5791); Department of Chemistry, University Science Laboratories, South Road, Durham DH1 3LE (tel 0191 334 2020, fax 0191 384 4737, e-mail r.d.chambers@durham.ac.uk)

CHAMBERS, Robert George; s of Peter Bertram Chambers, of Thetford, Norfolk, and Wendy, *née* Randall; *b* 30 May 1954; *Educ* Oundle, Univ of Hull (BSc); *m* 16 May 1987, (Christine) Belinda, da of Roy Johnson, of Littlington, Herts; 2 s (Nicholas *b* 6 Dec 1989, Charles Robert *b* 10 Aug 1993), 1 da (Serena *b* 13 Dec 1990); *Career* ptnr Wedd Durlacher Mordaunt and Co 1985–86; dir: Barclays de Zoete Wedd 1986–89, ABN AMRO Hoare Govett 1989–2001; exec dir UBS 2001–; MSI 1988 (memb Stock Exchange 1980); *Recreations* shooting, fishing, cricket (level II cricket coach), golf, powerboating; *Clubs* MCC, Royal Worlington Golf, Jockey Club Rooms (Newmarket); *Style*— Robert Chambers, Esq; ✉ UBS, 1 Finsbury Avenue, London EC2M 2PP (tel 020 7568 8870, e-mail robert.chambers@ubs.com)

CHAMBERS, Prof Robert John Haylock; OBE (1995); *b* 1 May 1932; *m* Jennifer; 3 c; *Career* res assoc IDS Univ of Sussex 1997– (fell 1972–97); memb visiting faculty Admin Staff Coll Hyderabad India 1989–91; varied experience incl rural field res India, Kenya and Sri Lanka and participatory rural appraisal devpt and trg; formerly: evaluation offr UNHCR Geneva, lectr Univ of Glasgow, prog offfr Ford Fndn New Delhi, memb Band Aid/Live Aid Project Ctee; tstee Action Aid 1993–2000 and 2002–; sometime conslt: Aga Khan Fndn, Asian Devpt Bank, Br Cncl, FAO, Ford Fndn, Consultative Gp for Int Agric Res, House of Commons, Int Inst for Environment and Devpt, ILO, INTRAC, League of Red Cross and Red Crescent Socs, Swedish Int Devpt Agency, Swiss Devpt Cooperation, ODA, World Bank; Hon DLitt UEA, Hon DSocS Univ of Edinburgh, Hon DLitt Univ of Sussex; *Books* incl: Settlement Schemes in Tropical Africa (1969), Managing Rural Development - Ideas and Experience from East Africa (1974), Seasonal Dimensions to Rural Poverty (jt ed, 1981), Rural Development - Putting the Last First (1983), Managing Canal Irrigation - Practical Analysis from South Asia (1988), To the Hands of the Poor - Water and Trees (jtly, 1989), Farmer First - Farmer Innovation and Agricultural Research (jt ed, 1989), Challenging the Professions: frontiers for rural development (1993), Whose Reality Counts? Putting the first last (1997), Voices of the Poor: Crying Out for Change (jtly, 2000), Participatory Workshops: a Source Book of 21 Sets of Ideas and Activities (2002), Ideas for Development (2005); *Recreations* mountaineering, long distance running; *Style*— Robert Chambers; ✉ Institute of Development Studies, University of Sussex, Brighton BN1 9RE (tel 01273 606261, fax 01273 621202/691647)

CHAMBERS, Sarah; *Career* former head Automotive Unit DTI, former dir of licensing Oftel, chief exec Postal Services Cmmn (Postcomm) 2004–; *Style*— Ms Sarah Chambers; ✉ The Postal Services Commission, Hercules House, Hercules Road, London SE1 7DB (tel 020 7593 2110, e-mail sarah.chambers@psc.gov.uk)

CHAMBERS, Stuart John; s of Reginald Chambers, and Eileen Chambers; *b* 25 May 1956; *Educ* Friends Sch Great Ayton, UCL (BSc); *m* 1984, Nicolette, *née* Horrocks; 1 s, 2 da; *Career* with Shell 1977–88, with Mars Corp 1988–96; Pilkington plc: gp vice-pres (mktg) Bldg Products 1996–97, gen mangr Pilkington UK Ltd 1997–98, md Primary Products Europe 1998–2000, pres Bldg Products Worldwide 2000, gp chief exec 2002–06; chief exec Pilkington Gp Ltd 2006–, dir Nippon Sheet Glass Co 2006–; non-exec dir: Associated British Ports (Hldgs) plc 2002–06, Smiths Gp plc 2006–; dir NW Business Leadership Team 1997– (chm 2006–); *Recreations* sailing, tennis; *Style*— Mr Stuart Chambers; ✉ Pilkington Group Limited, Prescot Road, St Helens WA10 3TT (tel 01744 28882, fax 01744 20038)

CHAMBERS, Dr Timothy Lachlan; JP (Bristol 1993); b Seamus Rory Dorrington, s of late Mary Theresa, of Moate, Co Westmeath; adopted s of Victor Lachlan Chambers (d 1970), of Purley, Surrey, and Elsie Ruth, *née* Reynolds (d 2002); *b* 11 February 1946; *Educ* Wallington Co GS, King's Coll London and King's Coll Hosp Univ of London (LRCP, MRCS, MB BS); *m* 9 Oct 1971, (Elizabeth) Joanna, da of John Carrington Ward (d 1989), of Barnstone, Notts; 2 da (Catherine Louise (Mrs P J M Chapman) b 1973 (d 2007), Rachel Elizabeth b 1976), 1 s (Oliver Lachlan Dorrington b 1978); *Career* consulting paediatrician and nephrologist Bristol and Weston-super-Mare 1979–; Univ of Bristol: sr clinical lectr in child health 1979–, a clinical dean 1983–90, memb Governing Bd Inst of Child Health 1987–97, memb Ct 1994–99; conslt in paediatrics to MOD 1985–, civilian conslt in paediatrics to RN 1993–; Lt Col RAMC (V) 1997– (cmmnd 1984), Regtl MO Somerset Cadet Bn LI (ACF) 2002–, clinical dir 243 (The Wessex) Field Hosp 2006–; dep med dir Southmead Health Servs NHS Tst 1994–96; pres: Union of Nat Euro Paediatric Socs and Assocs 1990–94, Paediatric Section RSM 1994–95, Bristol Medico-Chirurgical Soc 1996–97, Bristol Div BMA 1999–2000, United Services Section RSM 2000–03, SW Paediatric Club 2004–06, Bristol Medico-Legal Soc 2007–; RCP: past censor, cncllr; RCPCH: hon sec (BPA) 1984–89, hon sec Int Bd 1998–2000; regnl advsr RCPEd (SW England) 1996–2001; sec of state's appointee: Hosps for Sick Children (London) Special HA 1993–94, Ctee on Safety of Meds 1999–2005 (memb Paediatric Meds Working Gp 2000–05); chm Advsy Bd for the Registration of Homoeopathic Products 2003– (memb 2000–); present and past examiner to UK and int diploma and degree awarding bodies; sometime memb and chm sundry professional advsy ctees at home and abroad; tstee: Royal Med Benevolent Fund 1998–2004, Education and Resources for Improving Childhood Continence (ERIC) 2006–; reader and eucharistic min RC Cathedral Church of SS Peter and Paul Clifton, master Bristol branch Guild of Catholic Doctors 2006–; memb: Euro Soc for Paediatric Nephrology 1978–, Philosophical Soc Oxford 1990–; membre correspondant de la Sociétié Française de Pédiatrie 1994; memb: Bristol Savages, St Vincent Lodge, No 1404; Freeman City of London 1983, Liveryman Worshipful Soc of Apothecaries 1984 (memb Ct of Assts 2000–, chm Academic and Resources Ctee 2003–), Freeman Worshipful Co of Barbers 2004; FRSM 1979 (hon ed 1997–2001, vice-pres 2001–03), FRCP 1983, FRCPEd 1985, FRCPI 1995, FRCPCH 1997, Hon FSLCPaed 2002; *Publications* Fluid Therapy in Childhood (1987), Clinical Paediatric Nephrology (chapter, 1986 and 1994), author of contribs to scientific and lay literature; *Recreations* l'ampleur; *Clubs* Athenaeum, Army & Navy, MCC (assoc), Clifton (Bristol), The Galle Face Hotel (Colombo); *Style*— Dr Timothy Chambers; ✉ 4 Clyde Park, Bristol BS6 6RR (tel 01179 742814); Consulting Rooms: 2 Clifton Park, Bristol BS8 3BS (tel 01179 064209)

CHAMPION, Dr Audrey Elizabeth; da of Robert George Champion, of Alveston, S Glos, and Muriel Madge, *née* Matthews; *b* 13 July 1951; *Educ* Thornbury GS, Univ of Sheffield (MB ChB); *m* 8 Oct 1977, John Robert Glover Rogerson, s of Benjamin Rogerson, of Morley, Leeds (d 1955); 1 da (Kathryn b 1987), 1 s (Alastair b 1989); *Career* visiting conslt: Doncaster HA 1984–92, Rotherham HA 1992–97; conslt in clinical oncology Weston Park Hosp NHS Tst Sheffield 1984–97, dir North Wales Cancer Centre 1997–; memb BMA; FRCR 1981 (memb Cncl), FRCP 1996 (MRCP 1977); *Style*— Dr Audrey Champion; ✉ North Wales Cancer Treatment Centre (tel 01745 445151, fax 01745 445212, e-mail dr.audrey.champion@cd-tr.wales.nhs.uk)

CHAMPION, Jonathan Martin (Jon); s of David Yeo Champion, of York, and Maureen Ray, *née* Wilby; *b* 23 May 1965; *Educ* Archbishop Holgate's GS York, Trinity and All Saints' Coll Leeds (BA); *m* 1 Oct 1994, Anna Clare, *née* Clarke; 1 da (Emily Susannah b 6 July 1995), 3 s (Benjamin Henry b 2 Feb 1998, Harry George b 20 Oct 1999, William James b 7 Sept 2002); *Career* sports broadcaster; sports reporter BBC Radio Leeds 1988–89, presenter BBC Night Network 1989, presenter/commentator BBC Radio Sport 1990–96 (incl: occasional presenter Sports Report, presenter Champion Sport Radio 5, worked at World Cups 1990, 1994 and 1998 and Olympic Games 1992, 1996 and 2000); football commentator Match of the Day BBC TV 1995–2001 (incl World Cup 1998 and Olympic Games Sydney 2000), cricket commentator Test Match Special Radio 4, football commentator ITV 2001– (incl World Cup 2002 and 2006, also princ commentator Rugby World Cup 2007); *Recreations* music (piano and violin player), fell walking, cycling, cricket, golf; *Clubs* Worcs CC; *Style*— Jon Champion, Esq; ✉ c/o CSS Stellar Management Ltd, Drury House, 34–43 Russell Street, London WC2B 5HA (tel 020 7078 1457)

CHAMPION, Robert (Bob); MBE; s of Bob Champion (d 1987), and Phyllis Doreen Champion, of Guisborough, N Yorks; *b* 4 June 1948; *Educ* Earl Haig Sch Guisborough; *m* 1, Oct 1982 (m dis 1985); 1 s (Michael Robert b 1983); m 2, Oct 1987 (m dis 1998); 1 da (Henrietta Camilla b 1988); *Career* jockey and racehorse trainer; one of the four top jockeys of the 1970s, recovered from cancer to win 1981 Grand National on Aldaniti (portrayed by John Hurt in film Champions 1984); fndr Bob Champion Cancer Tst; Hon DCL UEA 2004, Hon LLD Univ of Teesside 2005; *Books* Champion Story; *Recreations* riding; *Style*— Bob Champion, MBE; ✉ e-mail bob@bobchampion.com and bob@bobchampion.co.uk, website www.bobchampion.com

CHANCE, Alan Derek; s of Derek Arthur Chance (d 1997), of Funtington, W Sussex, and Kay, *née* Renshaw (d 1988); *b* 12 April 1951; *Educ* Eton, Merton Coll Oxford (MA); *m* 30 May 1981, Sarah Elizabeth, da of (William) Denis Delany, of Funtington, W Sussex; 2 s (Benjamin b 1984, Thomas b 1987); *Career* dir Streets Financial Ltd 1979–83, chm Chance Plastics Ltd 1978–87; md: Money Marketing Ltd 1983–86, The Moorgate Group plc 1988–89 (dir 1986); ptnr Chance Jarosz 1990–93; dir: Allison Mitchell Ltd 1992–, Lawpack Publishing Ltd 2003–; *Recreations* skiing, backgammon, croquet; *Clubs* Hurlingham; *Style*— Alan Chance, Esq; ✉ Allison Mitchell Ltd, Bucklersbury House, 11 Walbrook, London EC4N 8EL (tel 020 7248 7200)

CHANCE, Sir (George) Jeremy ffolliott; 4 Bt (UK 1900), of Grand Avenue, Hove, Co Sussex; s of Sir Roger James Ferguson Chance, 3 Bt, MC (d 1987), and Mary Georgina, *née* Rowney (d 1984); *b* 24 February 1926; *Educ* Gordonstoun, ChCh Oxford (MA); *m* 4 March 1950, his cousin, Cecilia Mary Elizabeth, 2 da of Sir (William) Hugh Stobart Chance, CBE (d 1981); 2 da (Victoria Katharine Elizabeth b 1952, Helena Mary ffolliott b 1957), 2 s ((John) Sebastian b 1954, Roger William Tobias (Toby) b 1960); *Heir* s, Sebastian Chance; *Career* late Lt RNVR, former dir Massey-Ferguson Ltd Coventry; *Recreations* choral singing, painting; *Style*— Sir Jeremy Chance, Bt; ✉ Ty'n y Berllan, Lôn Ednyfed, Criccieth, Gwynedd LL52 0AH

CHANCE, Michael Edward Ferguson; s of John Wybergh Chance (d 1984), of London, and Wendy Muriel Chance (d 1970); *b* 7 March 1955; *Educ* Eton, King's Coll Cambridge (MA); *Career* opera and concert singer; princ singer Kent Opera 1984–88, BBC Promenade Concerts 1985–; appearances/debuts incl: Lincoln Centre NY 1985, La Scala Milan 1985, Lyon Opera 1985 (Andronico in Tamerlano), Paris Opera 1988 (Ptolomeo in Giulio Cesar), Glyndebourne Festival 1989 (Oberon in A Midsummer Night's Dream), Netherlands Opera 1990 (Anfinomo in Il Ritorno D'Ulisse), Sao Carlo Lisbon 1991 (Gofredo in Rinaldo), Royal Opera House Covent Garden 1992 (Apollo in Death in Venice), ENO 1992 (Anfinomo in Return of Ulysses), Scottish Opera 1992 (title role in Julius Caesar), Australian Opera Sydney 1993 (Oberon in A Midsummer Night's Dream); has made over 50 recordings; *Style*— Michael Chance, Esq; ✉ c/o Ingpen and Williams Ltd, Ingpen & Williams, 7 St George's Court, 131 Putney Bridge Road, London SW15 2PA

CHANCELLOR, Alexander Surtees; s of Sir Christopher John Chancellor, CMG (d 1989), and Sylvia Mary, OBE (d 1996), eld da of Sir Richard Paget, 2 Bt, and his 1 w, Lady Muriel Finch-Hatton, CBE, only da of 12 Earl of Winchilsea and Nottingham; *b* 4 January 1940; *Educ* Eton, Trinity Hall Cambridge; *m* 1964, Susanna, da of Martin Debenham, JP (3 s of Sir Ernest Debenham, 1 Bt, JP, and Cecily, niece of Rt Hon Joseph Chamberlain); 2 da; *Career* Reuters News Agency 1964–74, ed The Spectator 1975–84, asst ed The Sunday Telegraph 1984–86; dep ed The Sunday Telegraph 1986, US ed The Independent 1986–88, ed The Independent Magazine 1988–92, writer The New Yorker 1992–93, assoc ed The Sunday Telegraph 1994–95, ed The Sunday Telegraph Magazine 1995, currently freelance columnist Saturday Guardian; *Style*— Alexander Chancellor, Esq

CHANDE, Manish; *Career* co-fndr and chief exec Trillium Gp 1997–2000, memb Bd Land Securities plc 2000–02, co-fndr and chief exec Mountgrange Capital plc 2002–; non-exec dir: National Car Parks Ltd 2002–05 (chm), Property Fund Management plc 2002–04, Mitie Gp 2002–06; cmmr English Heritage 2003–; tstee Windsor Leadership Tst 2005–; *Style*— Manish Chande, Esq; ✉ Mountgrange Capital plc, 13 Albemarle Street, Mayfair, London W1S 4HJ

CHANDLER, Charles Henry; s of late Charles Chandler; *b* 6 March 1940; *Educ* Highgate Sch; *m* 1965, Christine Elizabeth, *née* Dunn; 1 s (Stephen), 1 da (Dani); *Career* chm Walthamstow Stadium Ltd 1976–; dir: Greyhound Racing Association Ltd 1965–99, British Greyhound Racing Board 1992–, British Greyhound Racing Fund 1993–; chm NGRC Racecourse Promoters Ltd 1992–; *Style*— Charles Chandler, Esq; ✉ Mymfield, Kentish Lane, Brookmans Park, Hatfield, Hertfordshire AL9 6NQ (tel 01707 652478, fax 01707 653414, e-mail chc@mymfield.fsnet.co.uk); office (tel and fax 01707 644288)

CHANDLER, Sir Colin Michael; kt (1988); s of Henry John Chandler, and Mary Martha, *née* Bowles; *b* 7 October 1939; *Educ* St Joseph's Acad Blackheath, Hatfield Poly; *m* 8 Aug 1964, Jennifer Mary Crawford; 1 s (Jamie), 1 da (Pippa); *Career* commercial apprentice de Havilland Aircraft Co 1956–61, contracts offr Hawker Siddeley Aviation Hatfield 1962–66; Hawker Siddeley Aviation Kingston: commercial mangr 1967–72, commercial dir 1973–76, dir and gen mangr 1977; gp mktg dir British Aerospace 1983–85 (divnl md Kingston-Brough Div 1978–82), seconded to MoD as Head of Defence Export Servs 1985–89; Vickers plc: md 1990–92, chief exec 1992–98, chm 1998–99; chm and ceo Racal Electronics 1999–2000, non-exec chm Easyjet plc 2003– (dep chm 2002–03), Automotive Technik Holdings 2003–; dep chm Smiths Gp plc 2000–05; non-exec dir: TI Group plc 1992–2000, Guardian Royal Exchange plc 1995–99, Clarity Commerce Solutions plc 2007–; pro-chllr Cranfield Univ, govr Reigate GS; Cdr Order of the Lion of Finland 1982; FRAeS, FCMA; *Recreations* tennis, gardening, theatre; *Clubs* Reform, Mark's, Queen's; *Style*— Sir Colin Chandler

CHANDLER, Godfrey John; *b* 4 July 1925; *Educ* Clarks Coll London; *m* 1948, Audrey Haydee, *née* Pilon; 1 da (Susan b 1949), 3 s (Timothy b 1952, Graham b 1953, Henry b 1960); *Career* ptnr Cazenove & Co 1957–85; dir: Globe Investment Tst plc 1980–90, Halifax Building Soc (London Bd) 1981–87, Strata Investment Tst plc 1985–90, Stratton Investment Tst plc 1986–90, Lloyds Devpt Capital Ltd 1986–90; dep chm W H Smith Gp 1982–88; govr Jawaharlal Nehru Meml Tst 1986–95; hon fell Darwin Coll Cambridge; *Recreations* gardening, chess; *Clubs* City of London; *Style*— Godfrey Chandler, Esq; ✉ Stormont Court, Godden Green, Sevenoaks, Kent TN15 0JS (tel 01732 761505)

CHANDLER, Air Cdre John Edgar; CBE (1998, OBE 1991); s of Thomas Edgar Chandler, and Jessie Chandler; *Educ* Romford Royal Liberty GS, RAF Coll Cranwell; *Career* OC Engineering Supply Wing RAF Brüggen 1988–91, Base Support Cdr RAF Detachment Bahrain 1990, MOD project duties Saudi Arabia 1991–94, Station Cdr RAF Scaland 1994–97, appointments in Africa and Far East 1997–98, Air Cdre Logistics HQ Strike Command 1998–2001, MOD project duties Saudi Arabia 2001–04; memb Parole Bd 2005–; FRAeS 1995; *Recreations* rowing, travel, hill walking; *Clubs* RAF; *Style*— Air Cdre John Chandler, CBE; ✉ tel 01480 462053

CHANDLER, Prof Richard John; s of John Harris Chandler (d 1987), of Stamford, Lincs, and Agnes Mary Chandler (d 1961); *b* 20 September 1939; *Educ* Stamford Sch, Loughborough Univ of Technol (BSc), Univ of Birmingham (MSc, PhD); *m* 19 Oct 1963, Eunice, da of Bertie Thomas Howes; 2 s (Simon John b 19 June 1966, Mark Richard b 20 April 1969); *Career* res fell Univ of Birmingham 1965–68; Imperial Coll London: lectr 1969–81, reader in soil mechanics 1981–90, prof of geotechnical engrg 1990–2003, emeritus prof of geotechnical engrg 2003–; chm Tstees and Editorial Bd Br Birds Jl; DSc(Eng) Univ of London 1990; FGS 1965, FICE 1989, FREng 2001; *Publications* North Atlantic Shorebirds (1989); author of many papers on engrg, especially soil mechanics, and many articles on field ornithology; *Recreations* ornithology, climbing; *Clubs* Fell and Rock Climbing Club of the English Lake District, British Ornithologists; *Style*— Prof Richard Chandler; ✉ 4 Kings Road, Oundle, Northamptonshire PE8 4AX

CHANDOS, 3 Viscount (1954 UK); Thomas Orlando Lyttelton; sits as Baron Lyttelton of Aldershot (Life Peer UK 2000), of Aldershot, Co Hampshire; s of 2 Viscount Chandos (d 1980, himself ggs of 4 Baron Cobham) and Caroline (da of Sir Alan Lascelles, who was in his turn gs of 4 Earl of Harewood); *b* 12 February 1953; *Educ* Eton, Worcester Coll Oxford; *m* 19 Oct 1985, Arabella Sarah Lucy, da of Adrian Bailey; 2 s (Hon Oliver Antony b 21 Feb 1986, Hon Benedict b 30 April 1988), 1 da (Hon Rosanna Mary b 19 March 1990); *Heir* s, Hon Oliver Lyttelton; *Career* corp fin dir Kleinwort Benson 1985–93, exec dir Botts & Co 1994–; chm: Capital and Regional Properties plc 2000– (non-exec dir 1993–), The Television Corporation 2004–06; non-exec dir: Lopex 1993–, Chrysalis Group plc 1994–96; dir Social Market Fndn; formerly: govr Nat Film and TV Sch, memb Gen Advsy Cncl IBA; *Style*— The Viscount Chandos

CHANG, Dr Jung; *née* Er-Hong; da of Shou-Yu Chang (d 1975), of Yibin, China, and De-Hong Xia, *née* Bao-Qin Xue; *b* 25 March 1952; *Educ* No 4 Middle Sch Chengdu (oldest state sch in China, founded 141 BC), Sichuan Univ (BA), Ealing Coll of HE, Univ of York (PhD, first person from Communist China to receive PhD from British instn); *m* 26 July 1991, Jon Arthur George Halliday; *Career* author; Hon DLit Univ of Buckingham 1996; Hon Dr: Univ of York 1997, Univ of Warwick 1997, Open Univ 1998, Bowdoin Coll 2005; *Books* Wild Swans - Three Daughters of China (1992, NCR Book Award 1992, Writers' Guild of GB Best Non-Fiction Award 1992, Fawcett Soc Book Award 1992, Book of the Year 1993, Humo's Gouden Bladwijzer Belgium 1993 and 1994, Bjørnsonordenen Den Norske Orden for Lit Norway 1995), Mao: the Unkown Story (with Jon Halliday, 2005); *Recreations* reading, travelling, swimming, gardening; *Style*— Dr Jung Chang; ✉ c/o Gillon Aitken Associates, 18–21 Cavaye Place, London SW10 9PT (tel 020 7373 8672, fax 020 7373 6002, e-mail gillon@gillonaitken.co.uk)

CHANG, Yat Sen; *Educ* Cuba Nat Ballet Sch; *Career* ballet dancer; Nat Ballet of Cuba (under Alicia Alonso) 1989–92, touring in Brazil, Colombia, Argentina, Mexico, Peru and Bulgaria; took part in Int Dance Festival of La Baule France 1992, 1993 and 1996; Jeune Ballet de France 1992–93 performing in Poland, Mongolia, China, Vietnam, The Philippines, Singapore, Hong Kong and Thailand; princ English National Ballet 1993–; roles incl: Bluebird in The Sleeping Beauty, Gopak in The Nutcracker, Paquita, Dances from Napoli, Franz in Hynd's Coppélia, Mercutio in Nureyev's Romeo and Juliet, Mauro Bigonzetti's X N Tricities, White Rabbit in Alice in Wonderland; *Awards* Best Partner Varna 1990, Gold Medal Chicloyo Peru, reached finals Contemporary Dance Competition Paris 1993; *Style*— Yat Sen Chang, Esq; ✉ English National Ballet, Markova House, 39 Jay Mews, London SW7 2ES (tel and fax 020 7602 1536, website www.yschang.co.uk)

CHANNER, Jill; da of Eric David Kerr, MC, of Oxford, and Betty, *née* Knight; *b* 2 July 1949; *Educ* Univ of York (BA, MA); *m* 14 Feb 1998, Donal Gilbert O'Connell Channer, s of Anthony Mosley Channer, TD, MBE (d 1978); *Career* Dept of MSS and Early Printed Books Trinity Coll Dublin 1971–72, Photo-Archives Courtauld Inst Univ of London 1973–75, Canterbury Cathedral (estab system for recording the restoration of the stained glass) 1975, Radcliffe Tst Scheme for the Crafts 1974–75, sec Corpus Vitrearum Medii Aevi GB (Br Acad) 1975–84; English Heritage: inspr 1984–88, head Western Region Historic Bldgs Div 1988–91, head SW Region (Cons) 1991–98, project dir 1998–2002; dir The Prince of Wales' Phoenix Tst (UK Historic Building Preservation Tst) 2002–; author of various contribs to specialist lit; tstee Ancient Monuments Soc 2002–; memb: Br Soc of Master Glass Painters 1969–86 (memb Cncl and hon jt ed of jl 1983–86), Br Archaeological Assoc 1972–85 (memb Cncl 1981–85), Assoc for Studies in the Conservation of Historic Bldgs 1984– (visits sec 1988–2002, memb Ctee 1990–2002), Stained Glass Advsy Ctee Cncl for the Care of Churches of the C of E 1984–91, Inst of Historic Buildings Conservation (IoHBC) 1997–; hon sec to the Tstees Ely Stained Glass Museum 1978–84; Freeman City of London 1984, Liveryman Worshipful Co of Glaziers Painters and Stainers of Glass; FRSA 2002, FSA 2003; *Recreations* flyfishing, talking, gardening; *Style*— Mrs Jill Channer

CHANNON, Prof Keith Michael; *b* Lincoln; *Career* prof of cardiovascular med Univ of Oxford, hon conslt cardiologist John Radcliffe Hosp Oxford; chm Br Atherosclerosis Soc, assoc ed Heart Journal; *Style*— Prof Keith Channon; ✉ Department of Cardiovascular Medicine, John Radcliffe Hospital, Oxford OX3 9DU (tel 01865 851085, fax 01865 222077, e-mail keith.channon@cardiov.ox.ac.uk)

CHANON, Charles; s of Ben Shimon Shimon (d 1974), and Behar Zelda (d 1989); *b* 16 May 1934; *Educ* École Alliance Française Baghdad, Shamash Sch Baghdad, Technion Israel Inst of Technol Haifa (BSc); *m* 22 July 1964 (m dis 1986), Nepomiachty Marina, da of Leonid (d 1962); 1 s (Robert b 7 Oct 1965), 2 da (Sophie b 23 May 1967, Nathalie b 6 May 1975); *Career* design engr Schwartz Hautmont Paris 1957–60, head Contol Dept OTH Paris 1960–64, assoc ptnr Lowe Rodin & OTH London 1969–71 (chief engr 1964–69), md OTH UK London 1971–73, pres Charles Chanon & Partners London 1973–, main bd dir Finotel plc London 1984–99; memb Cncl French C of C London 1991–; contrib numerous articles to professional jls; MInstM 1972, FIMgt (MIMgt 1973), CEng 1975, MICE 1975, Eur Ing 1995, FInstD 1996, ACE 2001; *Books* Construction in the Common Market (1974), The Business of Building in France (jtly, 1993); *Recreations* swimming, shooting, golf, music; *Style*— Charles Chanon, Esq; ✉ 12 Admiral Court, Chelsea Harbour, London SW10 0UU (tel 020 7823 3159); Charles Chanon & Partners, 9 Belgrave Road, London SW1V 1QB (tel 020 7828 7570/5470, fax 020 7233 6024, e-mail ccp@clara.net)

CHANT, (Elizabeth) Ann; CB (1997); da of Capt Harry Charles Chant (d 1945), and Gertrude, *née* Poel (d 1998); *b* 16 August 1945; *Educ* Blackpool Collegiate Sch; *Career* Nat Assistance Bd Lincoln 1963–66, Miny of Social Security Lincoln 1966–70, NHS Whitley Cncl DHSS London 1970–72, DHSS Lincoln 1972–74, DHSS Regnl Office Nottingham 1974–82, mangr DHSS Sutton-in-Ashfield 1982–83, DHSS HQ London 1983–85, princ private sec to perm sec DHSS 1985–87, head Records Branch DSS Newcastle upon Tyne 1987–89, head Contributions Unit DSS 1990–91, chief exec Contributions Agency DSS 1991–94, chief exec Child Support Agency DSS 1994–97; Reviews of Public Tst Office and Legal Services ombudsman Lord Chancellor's Dept 1999, chm Inland Revenue 2004 (dep chm 2000–04), DG HM Revenue and Customs 2005, dep dir of charities The Office of HRH The Prince of Wales 2005–; md Business in the Community 1997–99, exec memb Bd Industry Soc 1993–2000; lay govr London South Bank Univ 2000–; FRSA 1991; *Recreations* friends, music (especially opera), theatre; *Clubs* Royal Cwlth Soc, Athenaeum; *Style*— Miss Ann Chant, CB; ✉ The Office of HRH The Prince of Wales, Clarence House, London SW1A 1BA

CHANT, Anthony; s of Percival James Chant, and Ethel Eleanor, *née* Quick (d 1987); *b* 21 February 1938; *Educ* Hitchin GS, Univ of London (BSc, MB BS, MS); *m* 21 March 1959, Ann Nadia, da of Edwin Venning (d 1940); 3 s (Ben b 1963, Harvey b 1964, Thomas b 1966); *Career* conslt vascular surgn and sr lectr, Hunterian prof Royal Coll of Surgns, hon dir British Vascular Fndn, ret; author of works on vascular physiology, vascular and gen surgery, med mgmnt and ethics; FRCS; *Recreations* fishing; *Style*— Anthony Chant, Esq; ✉ Vascular Foundation, Royal College of Surgeons, Lincoln's Inn Fields, London WC2A 3PE

CHANTER, Rev Canon Anthony R; s of Charles Harry Chanter (d 1989), of Jersey, CI, and Eva Marjorie, *née* Le Cornu (d 1966); *b* 24 October 1937; *Educ* Hautlieu Sch Jersey, Salisbury Theol Coll, Open Univ (BA), Univ of London (MA); *m* 10 Sept 1966, Yvonne, da of Flt Lt William Reid (ka 1944); 2 da (Fiona b 31 May 1968, Alison b 15 May 1975); *Career* priest vicar Lincoln Cathedral 1970–73; headmaster: Bishop King Sch Lincoln 1970–73, Grey Court Sch Ham Richmond upon Thames 1973–77, Bishop Reindorp Sch Guildford 1977–84; dir of educn Dio of Guildford 1984–2001, hon canon Guildford Cathedral 1984–2001 (canon emeritus 2002–); memb Educn Ctee Surrey CC 1984–2001, dir Guildford Diocesan Bd of Fin; memb Nat Assoc of Headteachers; *Books* Student Profiling (co-author 1980); *Recreations* golf, cricket, country skiing, iconography, music, opera; *Clubs* Sion Coll, Worplesdon Golf, MCC, Ham Manor Golf; *Style*— The Rev Canon Anthony Chanter; ✉ Thalassa, 62 Sea Avenue, Rustington, West Sussex BN16 2DJ (tel 01903 774288, e-mail tonychanter@hotmail.com)

CHANTLER, Sir Cyril; kt (1996); s of Fred Chantler (d 1957), of Blackpool, and Marjorie, *née* Clark; *b* 12 May 1939; *Educ* Wrekin Coll, St Catharine's Coll Cambridge (BA), Guy's Hosp Med Sch London (MB BChir), Univ of Cambridge (MD); *m* 1963, Shireen M Saleh; 2 s (Paul Frederick b 29 July 1965, Jonathan Mark b 22 June 1967), 1 da (Nariane Emma b 24 May 1970); *Career* Guy's Hosp: sr lectr in paediatrics and conslt paediatrician 1971–2000, chm Mgmnt Bd and unit gen mangr 1985–88; prof of paediatric nephrology Guy's Hosp Med Sch 1980–2000 (emeritus prof 2001–), princ UMDS 1992–98 (clinical dean 1989–92), dean GKT 1998–2000, vice-princ KCL 1998–2000; pro-vice-chllr for med Univ of London 1997–2000, chm Cncl Heads of UK Med Schs 1998–99; MRC: memb external staff 1967, clinical research fell 1967–69, travelling fell Univ of Calif 1971; co-ed Paediatric Nephrology 1986–96, memb Editorial Bd Jl of the American Medical Assoc 2002–; chair: Scientific Advsy Ctee Fndn for the Study of Infant Deaths 1987–90, Great Ormond St Hosp for Sick Children 2001–, Beit Meml Fellowships for Med Research 2004–, King's Fund London 2004–, Shared Medical Record Ctee NHS Connecting for Health 2005–06; memb: Registration Ctee Euro Dialysis and Transplant Assoc 1975–80, Cncl Euro Soc for Paediatric Nephrology 1978–81, Academic Bd Br Paediatric Assoc 1983–86, NHS Policy Bd 1989–95, Cncl Renal Assoc 1981, Grants Cncl Br Kidney Patients' Assoc 1985–, GMC 1994–2003 (chm Standards Ctee 1997–2003), Public Sector Advsy Panel Doctors.net.uk 2007–; med advsr Children Nationwide Med Research Fund 1986–2005; RCP: fell 1977, lectr 1987, pro-censor 1989, censor 1990, Harveian orator 2002; pres Br Assoc of Med Mangrs 1991–97; James Spence medallist RCPCH 2005; memb: Cncl Southwark Cathedral 2000–, Bd of Govrs London South Bank Univ 2002–05; non-exec dir By the Bridge 2006–; tstee: Dunhill Medical Tst 2001–, Media Standards Tst 2006–; Hon DUniv: Lille 1998, South Bank 1999, London 2005; hon memb American Paediatric Soc 1991, foreign assoc memb Inst of Med Nat Acad of Sci USA 1999; FRCP 1977, FRCPCH 1996, FKC 1998, FMedSci 1999; *Publications* jt author of reports for Br Assoc of Paediatric Nephrology: Future Care of Children with Renal Failure (1975), Siting of Units to Care for Children with Chronic Renal Failure (1980); contrib to scientific literature on paediatrics, kidney disease and management in the NHS; *Recreations* golf, walking, reading, opera; *Clubs* Athenaeum; *Style*— Sir Cyril Chantler; ✉ 22 Benbow House, New Globe Walk, London SE1 9DS (tel 020 7401 3246)

CHANTLER, Paul Anthony; s of Peter Victor Chantler, of Tunbridge Wells, Kent, and Joy Edith, *née* Austin; *b* 12 October 1959; *Educ* Skinners' Sch Tunbridge Wells; *Career* trainee reporter Kent & Sussex Courier 1978–82, reporter Kent Messenger 1982–83, sr reporter Kent Evening Post 1983–84, journalist and presenter Invicta Radio 1984–88, news ed Southern Sound 1988–89, breakfast show presenter BBC Wiltshire Sound 1989; Chiltern Radio Network: head of news 1989–90, prog controller 1990–92, gp prog dir 1992–95; md Network News 1991–95, chief exec Galaxy Radio 1994–96, gp prog dir Essex Radio Gp 1996–2000, prog dir Talksport 2000, gp prog dir Wireless Gp 2000–01, radio prog conslt (GMG Radio, EMAP Radio, Century FM, Metro Radio, Hallam FM, Newstalk Ireland) 2002–, sr ptnr United radio Conslts 2006–; UK Commercial Radio Programmer of the Year 1997; *Books* Local Radio Journalism (1992 and 1997), Basic Radio Journalism (2003); *Recreations* pop music, reading, travel, wine and food, driving; *Clubs* Radio Acad; *Style*— Paul Chantler, Esq; ✉ 1 Candle Cottages, Stoney Lane, Hailsham, East Sussex BN27 2AP (tel 01323 440026, e-mail chantler@aol.com, website paulchantler.com)

CHAPMAN, Prof Antony John; s of Arthur Charles Chapman (d 1997), of London, and Joan Muriel, *née* Brown (d 1997), of Canterbury; *b* 21 April 1947; *Educ* Milford Haven GS, Bexley GS, Univ of Leicester (BSc, PhD); *m* 1 June 1985, Siriol Sophia Jones, da of Cledan David, of Llanddowror; 2 s (David Charles Luke b 1987, Luke Christopher David b 1989), 2 da (Harriet Emily Siriol b 1991, Madeleine Sophie Elizabeth b 1993); *Career* sr lectr UWIST Cardiff 1978–83 (lectr 1971–78); Univ of Leeds: prof 1983–98, head Dept of Psychology 1983–91, dir Centre for Applied Psychological Studies 1987–90, dean of science 1992–94, pro-vice-chllr 1994–98, visiting prof 1998–2003, pt/t secondment to CVCP Academic Audit Unit 1990–94; DETR-DTLR-DFT Child Pedestrian Safety conslt 1993–2004; prof Univ of Wales 1998–; vice-chllr/princ and chief exec Univ of Wales Inst Cardiff 1998–, sr vice-chllr Univ of Wales 2004–07; dir BPS Communications Ltd 1979–, fndr dir Sound Alert Ltd 1994; Prince of Wales Award for Industry 1997, Design Cncl Millennium Product Awards for Sound Localizer (emergency vehicles) and Localizer Beacon (fire egress); dir: Quality Assurance Agency for HE 2000–, Cardiff Business Technol Centre 2000–, Univs and Colls Employers Assoc 2002–06, Leadership Foundation for HE 2004–; chm: Br Psychological Soc Qualifying Examination 1986–90, Assoc of UK Heads of Psychology Depts 1990–92, UK Deans of Science Ctee 1993–94, ESRC Research Studentships Open Competition 1993–95, ESRC Research Recognition Exercise 1993–96, ESRC Psychology Area Panel 1996–2001, HE Wales 2002–04, HE Wales Tst 2002–04, Quality Assurance Agency Access Recognition and Licensing Ctee 2003–06, Quality Assurance Agency Advsy Ctee for Wales 2004–06; assoc ed Br Jl of Devpt Psychology 1983–88, co-ed Current Psychology 1984–, ed Br Jl of Psychology 1989–95; pres: Br Psychological Soc 1988–89, Psychology Section BAAS 1993–94, Assoc Learned Socs in the Social Sciences 1995–98; vice-pres Univs UK 2002–04; vice-chm ESRC Trg Bd 1995–96; memb: Exec Bd Int Soc for Research in Humor 1993–98, Bd NEAB 1994–98, HEFCE Psychology Advsy Gp 1997–2000 (memb Research Assessment Panel (Psychology) 1992 and 1996), Royal Soc Scientific Unions Ctee 1999–2002, Cncl CBI Wales 1999–, Cncl Industry and HE 2003–, Bd Univs UK 2004–, Cncl Cardiff C of C 2004–, Cncl All-Party Univ Gp 2004–; Founder AcSS 1999; CPsychol 1989, FRSA 1994, Hon FBPsS 1999 (FBPsS 1978); *Publications* 15 jt books incl: Humour and Laughter: Theory, Research and Applications (1976, 2 edn 1995), Models of Man (1980), Friendship and Social Relations in Children (1980, 2 edn 1995), Road Safety: Research and Practice (1981), Pedestrian Accidents (1982), Noise and Society (1984), Cognitive Processes in the Perception of Art (1984), Psychology and Social Problems (1984), Elements of Applied Psychology (1994), Psychology and Law (1994), Cognitive Science, Vols I, II and III (1995), Biographical Dictionary of Psychology (1997); co-ed 11 special issues of journals and 3 book series, Psychology for Professional Groups, Psychology in Action, International Library of Critical Writings in Psychology; author of articles in books and learned jls; *Style*— Prof Antony J Chapman; ✉ Office of the Vice-Chancellor, UWIC, PO Box 377, Western Avenue, Cardiff CF5 2SG (tel 029 2041 6101, fax 029 2041 6910, e-mail ajchapman@uwic.ac.uk)

CHAPMAN, Christine; AM; da of late John Price, and Jean Price, of Rhondda; *b* 7 April 1956; *Educ* Porth County Girls' Sch, Univ of Wales Aberystwyth (BA), South Bank Poly (Dip), Univ of Wales Cardiff (MScEcon, MPhil), Univ of Swansea (PGCE); *m* 1981, Dr Michael Chapman, s of late Don Chapman, and Mai Chapman; 1 da (Rhiannon b 3 June 1983), 1 s (Stephen b 1 Oct 1985); *Career* Mid Glamorgan: Community Services Agency 1979–80, Careers (careers advsr) 1980–92, Educn Business Partnership 1992–93; teacher trg 1993–94, conslt 1995–96, co-ordinator Torfaen Educn Business Partnership 1996–99; secdy sch teacher, pt/t tutor; memb Nat Assembly for Wales (Lab Co-op) Cynon Valley 1999–, dep min for educn and lifelong learning and finance, local govt and public servs 2005–; chair Objective One Prog Monitoring Ctee 2000–05; memb: Inst of Careers Guidance (memb Nat Cncl 1992–94), Co-operative Pty; *Recreations* womens history and gender issues, gym, pt/t study; *Style*— Ms Christine Chapman, AM; ✉ Cynon Valley Constituency Office, Bank Chambers, 28A Oxford Street, Mountain Ash, Rhondda Cynon Taff CF45 3EU (tel 01443 478098, fax 01443 478 311); National Assembly for Wales, Cardiff Bay, Cardiff CF99 1NA (tel 029 2089 8364, fax 029 2089 8365, e-mail christine.chapman@wales.gov.uk)

CHAPMAN, Christopher Henry George (Kit); MBE (1989); s of Peter Francis Chapman (d 1997), of Taunton, Somerset, and Georgette (Etty), *née* Rosi (d 2004); *b* 10 March 1947; *Educ* Taunton Sch, Univ of Surrey (BSc, pres Food and Wine Soc); *m* 1971, (Marie) Louise Anne, da of late Peter Edward Guiver; 2 s (Dominic Alexander Pierre b 1973, Nicholas Mark Christopher b 1975); *Career* in advertising 1969–76 (latterly with Benton and Bowles Ltd); prop The Castle Hotel Taunton 1980–; creator and fndr: BRAZZ 1998 (ceo 2002–), The English Brasserie Co plc 1999–2002, BRAZZ plc 2002–; chm Prestige Hotels 1985–87, dir Orchard Media Ltd 1992–99; columnist Caterer and Hotelkeeper 1983–88; writer and presenter: Simply the Best: A Celebration of British Food (12 films for ITV and Channel 4) 1991 and 1993, Of Madeleines and Other Masterpieces (arts prog, BBC Radio 2) 1994, Diary of an Innkeeper (6 part documentary series for Carlton TV, inspired by book An Innkeeper's Diary) 2003; chm Commercial Membs' Gp West Country Tourist Bd 1980–86; ministerial appointee Exmoor Nat Park Ctee 1979–81; memb: Leisure Industries Econ Devpt Ctee NEDC 1987–89, Bd Somerset TEC 1989–94; visiting sr fell Sch of Mgmnt Studies Univ of Surrey 1999; Freeman City of London 1984; *Awards* Ward Cavendish Trophy for the Small Business Award 1980 and 1981, British Airways and BTA Award for Overseas Mktg 1981, Caterer and Hotelkeeper Awards (CATEYS) Tourism Award 1987, Good Hotel Guide César Award for Best Town Hotel 1987, Guild of Food Writers Michael Smith Award 1996, CATEYS Best Ind Mktg Campaign for BRAZZ 1999, Best Out-of-Town Restaurant for The Castle Tatler Restaurant Awards 2002; *Books* Great British Chefs (1989, shortlisted André Simon Book Award 1990), Great British Chefs 2 (1995), An Innkeeper's Diary (1999); *Recreations* good food and wine, walking the Quantocks with the dogs, reading, keeping a journal; *Clubs* Garrick; *Style*— Kit Chapman, Esq, MBE; ✉ The Castle Hotel, Taunton, Somerset TA1 1NF (tel 01823 272671, fax 01823 336066, e-mail chapman@the-castle-hotel.com)

CHAPMAN, Prof Christopher Hugh; s of John Harold Chapman (d 1999), of Milton-under-Wychwood, Oxon, and Margaret Joan, *née* Weeks (d 2001); *b* 5 May 1945; *Educ* Latymer Upper Sch, Christ's Coll Cambridge (MA, PhD); *m* 1 June 1974, Lillian, da of Michael Tarapaski, of Redwater, Canada; 1 s (Timothy b 26 May 1978), 1 da (Heather b 24 June 1981); *Career* asst prof Dept of Geology and Geophysics Univ Calif Berkeley 1972–73, assoc prof Dept of Physics Univ of Alberta 1973–74 (asst prof 1969–72), Green scholar Univ of Calif San Diego 1978–79, prof Dept of Physics Univ of Toronto 1980–84 and 1988–90 (assoc prof 1974–80), prof of geophysics Dept of Earth Sciences Univ of Cambridge 1984–88, scientific advsr Schlumberger Cambridge Research 1991–2005 (conslt 2005–); hon prof of theoretical seismology Dept of Earth Sciences Univ of Cambridge 2006–; memb SEG, FRAS, FAGU; *Recreations* sailing, photography; *Style*— Prof Christopher Chapman; ✉ 7 Spinney Drive, Great Shelford, Cambridge CB22 5LY (tel 01223 845007); Schlumberger Cambridge Research, High Cross, Madingley Road, Cambridge CB3 0EL (tel 01223 325434)

CHAPMAN, Prof David John; s of late John Chapman, and Anthea Chapman, of Woodhouse, Sheffield; *b* 29 April 1936; *Educ* Eckington GS, Sheffield Coll of Technol (Electrical Engrg), Sheffield City Poly (Dip Mgmnt Studies, Atcheson Prize, MSc); *m* 1 (m dis); m 2, 1994, Dr Maria Angyalova, of Kosice, Slovakia; *Career* initially involved in R&D and design of electrical and electronic equipment, subsequently in mktg and gen mgmnt in capital electronic equipment and in consultancy relating to business aspects of new technol; various posts incl assoc head Sheffield Business Sch 1986–2001; visiting prof Sheffield Hallam Univ; assoc: Univ of Lincoln, Leon Kosminsky Univ Warsaw; dir: Adams Chapman Consultants Ltd 1981, (specialising in industrial mktg and Central Europe) Mktg Cncl 1999; tstee: RoSPA 1999–2003, Medicalert 2004–06; nat chm CIM 1997–98 (vice-chm 1994–97); Pres's Award CIM 1993; Freeman City of London 1996, Liveryman Worshipful Co of Marketors 1996; Chartered Marketer 1998, FRSA 1998, Hon FCIM 1999 (MCIM 1972, FCIM 1988); *Books* contrib: Make Ready for Success (1982), Measures for Success (1985), Profit from Marketing (1986), Pricing for Profit (1987), The Power of Value Added (with Barrie Hill, 1993), Gower Handbook of Marketing (contrib, 4 edn 1995), New Public Sector Marketing (with T P Cowdell, 1998), Books and Public Services Management (contrib); *Recreations* car restoration, electronic design, travel, music; *Style*— Prof David Chapman; ✉ Adams Chapman Consultants Ltd, 16 Endcliffe Vale Road, Sheffield S10 3EQ (tel 0797 001 5985, e-mail d.j.chapman@btinternet.com)

CHAPMAN, Sir David Robert Macgowan; 3 Bt (UK 1958), of Cleadon, Tyne & Wear; DL; s of Col Sir Robert (Robin) Chapman, 2 Bt, CBE, TD, JP, DL (d 1987), and Barbara May, *née* Tonks; bro of Peter Stuart Chapman, *qv*; *b* 16 December 1941; *Educ* Marlborough, Grenoble Univ, McGill Univ Montreal (BCom); *m* 19 June 1965, Maria Elizabeth de Gosztonyi-Zsolnay, da of Dr Nicholas de Mattyasovszky-Zsolnay, of Ottawa, Canada; 1 s (Michael Nicholas b 1969), 1 da (Christina Elisabeth b 1970); *Heir* s, Michael Chapman; *Career* stockbroker; chm Stock Exchange NE Region Advsy Gp 1991–98; first vice-pres Merrill Lynch Int Bank Ltd 1999–2002; chm Northern Enterprise (General Partner) Ltd 2000–; dir: Wise Speke Ltd 1987–99 (ptnr Wise Speke & Co 1971–87), Breathe North Ltd 1988–95, British Lung Fndn 1989–94, Team General Partner (chm) 1993–, Montfort Press Ltd 1994–95, Northern Rock plc (formerly Northern Rock Building Society) 1996–2004, Sunderland City Radio Ltd 1997–98, Gordon Durham Holdings Ltd 1997–98, High Gosforth Park Ltd 1999–2004, NES General Partner Ltd 1999–, Zytronic plc 2000–, NE Regional Investment Fund Two Ltd 2001–, CNE General Partner Ltd 2001–; conslt UBS Wealth Management Ltd 2002–; chm CBI NE Region 000–02 (dep chm 2003–05); memb Cncl: The Stock Exchange 1979–88, Univ of Durham (chm Ustinov Coll (grad soc) 2001–04); memb: The Greenbury Ctee 1995, Northern Regnl Cncl CBI 1996–2006, NE Regnl Investment Fund Ltd 1999–, NE Regnl Investment Fund Three Ltd 2004–, Northern Business Forum Ltd 2003–05; chm Northumbria Coalition against Crime 1995–2000; High Sheriff Tyne & Wear 1993–94; *Recreations* travel, tennis, reading; *Clubs* Northern Counties (Newcastle); *Style*— Sir David Chapman, Bt, DL; ✉ The Hawthorns, Marsden Road, Cleadon, Sunderland, Tyne & Wear SR6 7RA (tel 0191 536 7887); UBS Wealth Management, 2 St James' Gate, Newcastle upon Tyne NE4 7JH (tel 0191 211 1004, fax 0191 211 1001)

CHAPMAN, Dinos; *b* 1962, London; *Educ* Ravensbourne Coll of Art (BA), RCA (MA); *Career* artist, in partnership with brother Jake Chapman, *qv*, fndr Chapman FineART London, curated Some of My Best Friends are Geniuses (Ind Art Space London) 1996; shortlisted Turner Prize 2003; *Selected Two-Person Exhibitions* We Are Artists (Hales Gallery London and Bluecoat Gallery Liverpool) 1992, The Disasters of War (Victoria Miro Gallery London) 1993, Mummy & Daddy (Galeria Franco Toselli Milan) 1994, Great Deeds Against the Dead (Victoria Miro Gallery London) 1994, Five Easy Pissers (Andréhn-Schiptjenko Gallery Stockholm) 1995, Bring Me the Head of Franco Toselli! (Ridinghouse Editions London) 1995, Zygotic acceleration, biogenetic, de-sublimated libidinal model (enlarged x 1000) (Victoria Miro Gallery London) 1995, Gavin Brown's Enterprise NY 1995, Chapmanworld (ICA London) 1996, Zero Principle (Giò Marconi Milan) 1996, P-House Tokyo 1996, Chapmanworld (Grazer Kunstverein Graz) 1997, Six Feet Under (Gagosian Gallery NY) 1997, Galerie Daniel Templon Paris 1998, Disasters of War (White Cube London) 1999, Jake & Dinos Chapman (Fig 1 London) 1999, Jake & Dinos Chapman GCSE Art Exam (The Art Ginza Space Tokyo) 2000, Jake & Dinos Chapman (Kunst Werke Berlin) 2000, Jackie & Denise Chapwoman. New Work (Modern Art London) 2001, Jake and Dinos Chapman (Groninger Museum) 2002, Work from the Chapman Family Collection (White Cube London) 2002, Jake & Dinos Chapman (Museum Kunst Palast Düsseldorf) 2003, The Rape of Creativity (Modern Art Oxford) 2003, Jake & Dinos Chapman (Saatchi Gallery London) 2003, The Marriage of Reason and Squalor (Centro de Arte Contemporáneo Malaga and Dunkers Kulturhaus Sweden) 2004, Insult to Injury (Kunst Sammlungen der Veste Coburg) 2004, The New and Improved Andrex Works (Thomas Olbricht Collection Essen) 2004, Explaining Christians to Dinosaurs (Kunsthaus Bregenz) 2005, Bad Art for Bad People (Tate Liverpool) 2006, When Humans Walked the Earth (Tate Britain) 2007; *Selected Group Exhibitions* Great Deeds Against the Dead (Andrea Rosen Gallery NY) 1994, Liar (Hoxton Square London) 1994, The Institute of Cultural Anxiety: Works from the Collection (ICA London) 1995, General Release: Young British Artists (Venice Biennale Scuola di San Pasquale Venice) 1995, Brilliant! New Art from London (Walker Art Center Minneapolis and Museum of Contemporary Art Houston) 1995, Young British Artists (Roslyn Oxley Gallery Sydney) 1996, Florence Biennale 1996, Gothic (ICA Boston) 1997, Minor Sensation (Victoria Miro Gallery London) 1997, Body (Art Gallery of NSW Sydney) 1997, Sensation: Young British Artists from the Saatchi Collection (Royal Acad of Arts London) 1997, Future, Present, Past (Venice Biennale) 1997, Wounds: Between Democracy and Redemption in Contemporary Art (Moderna Museet Stockholm) 1998, Heaven: An Exhbn that will break your heart (Kunsthalle Düsseldorf and Tate Gallery Liverpool) 1999, Sex and the British - Slap and Tickle (Galerie Thaddeaus Ropac Salzburg and Galerie Thaddaeus Ropac Paris) 2000, Ant Noises II (Saatchi Gallery London) 2000, Out There (White Cube London) 2000, The Pölstar Art Programme (Leicester Square London) 2000, Apocalypse: Beauty and Horror in Contemporary Art (Royal Acad of Arts London) 2000, Nervous Kingdom (Bluecoat Gallery Liverpool) 2000, ManMoMa. A Thick Bloke Kicking a Dog to Death (International 3 Summer Fête Fairfield Manchester) 2000, Jake & Dinos Chapman and Francisco Goya y Lucientes (The Power Plant Toronto) 2000, Disasters of War. Francisco de Goya, Henry Darger and Jake and Dinos Chapman (PS1 Contemporary Art Center NY) 2000, Paper Assets: Collecting Prints and Drawings 1996–2001 (British Museum London) 2001, Francisco Goya and Jake and Dinos Chapman: The Disasters of War (Musée des Beaux-Arts de Montréal) 2001, Art Crazy Nation Show (Milton Keynes Gallery) 2002, Rapture: Art's Seduction by Fashion since 1970 (Barbican Gallery London) 2002, Fran el Greco till Dali (Nationalmuseum Sweden Stockholm) 2003, Mars. Art and War (Neue Galerie am Landesmuseum Joanneum Graz) 2003, Summer Exhbn (Royal Acad of Arts London) 2003 (Charles Wollaston Award), The Turner Prize (Tate Britain London) 2003, Gewalt (Loushy Art & Editions Tel Aviv) 2004, Mike Kelley: The Uncanny (Tate Liverpool) 2004, At War (Centre de Cultura Contemporània de Barcelona) 2004, After Images (Neues Museum Weserburg Bremen) 2004, Deliver Us From Evil (Matthew Marks Gallery NY) 2004, The Charged Image (Joseloff Gallery CT) 2004, Paper Democracy: Contemporary Art in Editions on Paper (Edificio Cultura Inglesa Sao Paulo) 2004, The Christmas Exhibition (Edinburgh Printmakers) 2004, Critic's Choice (FACT Liverpool) 2005, Mixed-up Childhood: An Exhibition for Grown-ups (Auckland Art Gallery) 2005, Glasgow International Festival of Contemporary Visual Art (Glasgow Print Studio) 2005, Body: New Art from the UK (Vancouver Art Gallery) 2005, Bidibidobidiboo: La Collezione Sandretto Re Rebaudengo (Turin) 2005; *Work in Public Collections* Deste Fndn Athens, Rubell Family Collection, Saatchi Collection, Walker Art Centre Minneapolis, British Museum, Simmons & Simmons London, The Israel Museum Jerusalem, Groninger Museum, Museum Kunst Palast Düsseldorf, MOMA NY; *Style*— Dinos Chapman, Esq; ✉ c/o White Cube, 48 Hoxton Square, London N1 6PB

CHAPMAN, His Hon Judge Frank Arthur; s of Dennis Arthur Chapman, of Culcheth, Warrington, Cheshire, and Joan, *née* Dickinson; *b* 28 May 1946; *Educ* Newton-le-Willows GS, UCL (LLB, LLM, Brigid Cotter Prize 1994); *m* 27 July 1968, Mary Kathleen, da of late Edwin Keith Jones, and Marion Jones, of Pontypool, Gwent; 1 da (Rachel Lynn (now Mrs D Heron) b 12 March 1971), 1 s (Thomas William Lawson b 21 Oct 1973); *Career* called to the Bar 1968, practised Midland & Oxford Circuit 1969–91, asst recorder 1982–86, recorder 1986–92, circuit judge (Midland & Oxford Circuit) 1992–97, res judge Wolverhampton Court 1997–2007, sr circuit judge 2002–, resident judge Birmingham Crown Court 2007–; memb Bar Cncl 1989–91; *Recreations* mountaineering, angling, travel; *Style*— His Hon Judge Chapman; ✉ Midland & Oxford Circuit, 2 Newton Street, Birmingham B4 7LU

CHAPMAN, Frank Watson; s of Thomas Chapman (d 1965), of Bournemouth, Dorset, and Beatrice, *née* Padgett (d 1976); *b* 7 November 1929; *Educ* Swindon Coll, Marine Sch of South Shields; *m* 18 March 1955, Wendy Joanna, da of Roger Philip Holly (d 1972), of Switzerland; 1 da (Susie b 1956), 1 s (Thomas b 1963); *Career* cadet MN 1946; deck offr: Union Steamship Co NZ 1951–54, Royal Mail Lines 1954–58, Cunard Steamship Co 1958–62; salesman Telephone Rentals 1962; fndr and md 1964: Bahamas Properties Ltd, Sovereign Travel Ltd; purchased Loch Rannoch and Forest Hills Hotels Scotland 1974, fndr Multi-Ownership & Hotels Ltd 1975 (thereby becoming fndr of Timeshare in UK), 2 devpts in Wales 1978, 3 devpts Forest Hills Hotel 1980, sold co to Barratt Devpts plc 1982 (md until 1988); fndr and chm Sovereign Travel & Leisure Gp plc 1988–, chm The Timeshare Cncl 1995–, dir Orgn for Timeshare in Europe (OTE); *Recreations* travel, gardening, reading, swimming; *Style*— Frank Chapman, Esq; ✉ Moulsey House, 11 Wolsey Road, East Molesey, Surrey KT8 9EL (tel 020 8783 9437); Sovereign Travel & Leisure Group plc, 74 High Street, Wimbledon Village, London SW19 5EG (tel 020 8879 7199)

CHAPMAN, Honor Mary Ruth; CBE (1997); da of Alan Harry Woodland (d 1993), and Frances Evelyn Woodland, *née* Ball (d 1988); *b* 29 July 1942; *Educ* Convent of St Marie Auxiliatrice, Leeds Girls HS, Coll of Estate Mgmnt Univ of London (BSc), UCL (MPhil), London Business Sch (Sloan Fellow); *m* 1966, David Edwin Harold Chapman (m dis 1997); *Career* surveyor Valuation Dept LCC 1963–64, planner Nathaniel Lichfield and Partners 1966–76 (ptnr 1971), freelance conslt 1976–79, ptnr Jones Lang Wootton 1979–99, chief exec London First Centre (secondment) 1993–95, int dir and chm of global consulting Jones Lang Lasalle 1999–2002, conslt Jones Lang Lasalle 2002–03, chm London Devpt Agency 2003– (dep chm 2000–03); memb bd English Estates 1984–92, memb bd Cardiff Bay Devpt Corp 1987–94, govr and memb exec Centre for Economic Policy Research 1988–96, non-exec dir Legal & General plc 1993–2001, cmmr Crown Estate 1997–2003, chm Burlington Gardens Ctee Royal Acad 2002–; Freeman City of London, Liveryman Worshipful Co of Goldsmiths 1985; hon fell Soc of Property Researchers 1998; FRTPI 1971, FRICS 1979, FRSA 1992; *Recreations* dairy farming, watching people do things well; *Clubs* University Womens; *Style*— Ms Honor Chapman, CBE; ✉ The London Development Agency, Devon House, 58–60 St Katharine's Way, London E1W 1JX (tel 020 7954 4615)

CHAPMAN, (Francis) Ian; CBE (1988); s of Rev Peter Chapman (d 1962), of Glasgow, and Frances Maud, *née* Burdett; *b* 26 October 1925; *Educ* Shawlands Acad Glasgow, Ommer Sch of Music Glasgow; *m* 1953, Marjory Stewart, *née* Swinton; 1 s, 1 da; *Career* aircrew cadet RAF 1943–44, Nat Serv coal mines 1945–47; William Collins Sons & Co Ltd: joined as mgmnt trainee 1947, NY Branch 1950–51, gen sales mangr London 1955, gp sales dir 1959; jt md William Collins (Holdings) Ltd 1967 (dep chm 1976); dir: Hatchards Ltd 1961, Pan Books Ltd 1962–84, Ancient House Bookshop (Ipswich) Ltd 1972–89, Scottish Opera Theatre Royal Ltd 1974–79, Book Tokens Ltd 1981–95, IRN Ltd 1983–85, Stanley Botes Ltd 1985–89, United Distillers plc 1987–91; chm: Scottish Radio Holdings plc 1972–96 (pres 1996–2001), Hatchards Ltd 1976–89, Harvill Press Ltd 1976–89, William Collins Publishers Ltd 1979, The Listener Publications 1988–93, Radiotrust plc 1997–2001, Nat Acad of Writing 1999–2003 (vice-pres 2003–); chm and gp chief exec William Collins Holdings plc 1981–89, non-exec dir Guinness plc 1986–91, jt chm Harper and Row NY 1987–89, chm and md Chapmans Publishers 1989–94, chm Guinness Publishing 1992–97 (dep chm 1997–99), gp dep chm The Orion Publishing Group 1993–94; directeur gen de la SAS Guinness Media Paris 1996–99; The Publishers' Assoc: memb Cncl 1962–77, vice-pres 1978 and 1981, pres 1979, tstee 1992–98; memb Bd Book Devpt Cncl 1967–73, tstee Book Trade Benevolent Soc 1982–2003, memb Governing Cncl SCOTBIC 1983, chm Advsy Bd Univ of Strathclyde Business School 1985–88; Scot Free Enterprise Award 1985; Hon DLitt Univ of Strathclyde 1990; CIMgt 1982, FRSA 1985; *Recreations* music, golf, reading, grandchildren; *Clubs* Garrick, Royal Wimbledon Golf, MCC, Walton Heath Golf; *Style*— Ian Chapman, Esq, CBE; ✉ Kenmore, 46 The Avenue, Cheam, Sutton, Surrey SM2 7QE (tel 020 8642 1820, fax 020 8770 0225, e-mail fic@onetel.com)

CHAPMAN, Ian Stewart; s of Francis Ian Chapman, of Cheam, Surrey, and Marjory Stewart, *née* Swinton; *b* 15 January 1955; *Educ* Cranleigh Sch, Univ of Durham (BA, 1 XI Cricket); *m* Maria, da of late Daniel Samper; 1 s (Gabriel Ian Daniel b 22 July 1983), 2 da (Sabrina Stewart Burdett b 11 Nov 1986, Natalya Alexa Campbell b 5 Nov 1990); *Career* publisher; started as asst on shop floor W H Smith Paris 1974–75; trainee: Doubleday & Co Inc NY 1980–81, Berkley Publishers The Putnam Group NY May-Nov 1981; editorial asst William Morrow & Co Inc NY 1981–82, ed rising to editorial dir Hodder & Stoughton Ltd London 1983–87, publishing dir Pan Books Ltd rising to gp publisher Pan Macmillan Ltd 1987–94, md Macmillan General Books 1994–99, md and ceo Simon & Schuster 2000–; *Recreations* cricket, golf, walking, skiing; *Clubs* Garrick, Rye Golf; *Style*— Ian S Chapman, Esq; ✉ Benedict House, Staplecross Road, Northiam, East Sussex TN31 6JJ (tel 01580 830222, fax 01580 830027); Simon & Schuster UK Ltd, Africa House, 64–78 Kingsway, London WC2B 6AH (tel 020 7316 1910, fax 020 7316 0331, e-mail ian.chapman@simonandschuster.co.uk)

CHAPMAN, Jake; s of Red Rum, and Barbie; *b* Cheltenham, 1966; *Educ* Grange Hill Comp, Hastings Sch of Art, Poly of London (BA), RCA (MA), London Marathon 1991; *Career* artist, in partnership with brother Dinos Chapman, *qv*; fndr Chapman FineART London; curated Some of My Best Friends are Geniuses (Ind Art Space London) 1996; shortlisted Turner Prize 2003; memb: Secret Police, CIA, FBI, MI5, MFI; professorship (mail-order); professional bodies: arms, legs, feet back (bad), etc; key to Hastings; *Selected Two-Person Exhibitions* We Are Artists (Hales Gallery London and Bluecoat Gallery Liverpool) 1992, The Disasters of War (Victoria Miro Gallery London) 1993, Mummy & Daddy (Galeria Franco Toselli Milan) 1994, Great Deeds Against the Dead (Victoria Miro Gallery London) 1994, Five Easy Pissers (Andréhn-Schiptjenko Gallery Stockholm) 1995, Bring Me the Head of Franco Toselli! (Ridinghouse Editions London) 1995, Zygotic acceleration, biogenetic, de-sublimated libidinal model (enlarged x 1000) (Victoria Miro Gallery London) 1995, Gavin Brown's Enterprise NY 1995, Chapmanworld (ICA London) 1996,

Zero Principle (Giò Marconi Milan) 1996, P-House Tokyo 1996, Chapmanworld (Grazer Kunstverein Graz) 1997, Six Feet Under (Gagosian Gallery NY) 1997, Galerie Daniel Templon Paris 1998, Disasters of War (White Cube London) 1999, Jake & Dinos Chapman (Fig 1 London) 1999, Jake & Dinos Chapman GCSE Art Exam (The Art Ginza Space Tokyo) 2000, Jake & Dinos Chapman (Kunst Werke Berlin) 2000, Jackie & Denise Chapwoman. New Work (Modern Art London) 2001, Jake and Dinos Chapman (Groninger Museum) 2002, Work from the Chapman Family Collection (White Cube London) 2002, Jake & Dinos Chapman (Museum Kunst Palast Düsseldorf) 2003, The Rape of Creativity (Modern Art Oxford) 2003, Jake & Dinos Chapman (Saatchi Gallery London) 2003, The Marriage of Reason and Squalor (Centro de Arte Contemporáneo Malaga and Dunkers Kulturhaus Sweden) 2004, Insult to Injury (Kunst Sammlungen der Veste Coburg) 2004, The New and Improved Andrex Works (Thomas Olbricht Collection Essen) 2004, Explaining Christians to Dinosaurs (Kunsthaus Bregenz) 2005, Bad Art for Bad People (Tate Liverpool) 2006, When Humans Walked the Earth (Tate Britain) 2007; *Selected Group Exhibitions* Great Deeds Against the Dead (Andrea Rosen Gallery NY) 1994, Liar (Hoxton Square London) 1994, The Institute of Cultural Anxiety: Works from the Collection (ICA London) 1995, General Release: Young British Artists (Venice Biennale Scuola di San Pasquale Venice) 1995, Brilliant! New Art from London (Walker Art Center Minneapolis and Museum of Contemporary Art Houston) 1995, Young British Artists (Roslyn Oxley Gallery Sydney) 1996, Florence Biennale 1996, Gothic (ICA Boston) 1997, Minor Sensation (Victoria Miro Gallery London) 1997, Body (Art Gallery of NSW Sydney) 1997, Sensation: Young British Artists from the Saatchi Collection (Royal Acad of Arts London) 1997, Future, Present, Past (Venice Biennale) 1997, Wounds: Between Democracy and Redemption in Contemporary Art (Moderna Museet Stockholm) 1998, Heaven: An Exhbn that will break your heart (Kunsthalle Düsseldorf and Tate Gallery Liverpool) 1999, Sex and the British - Slap and Tickle (Galerie Thaddeaus Ropac Salzburg and Galerie Thaddaeus Ropac Paris) 2000, Ant Noises II (Saatchi Gallery London) 2000, Out There (White Cube London) 2000, The Pölstar Art Programme (Leicester Square London) 2000, Apocalypse: Beauty and Horror in Contemporary Art (Royal Acad of Arts London) 2000, Nervous Kingdom (Bluecoat Gallery Liverpool) 2000, ManMoMa. A Thick Bloke Kicking a Dog to Death (International 3 Summer Fête Fairfield Manchester) 2000, Jake & Dinos Chapman and Francisco Goya y Lucientes (The Power Plant Toronto) 2000, Disasters of War. Francisco de Goya, Henry Darger and Jake and Dinos Chapman (PS1 Contemporary Art Center NY) 2000, Paper Assets: Collecting Prints and Drawings 1996–2001 (British Museum London) 2001, Francisco Goya and Jake and Dinos Chapman: The Disasters of War (Musée des Beaux-Arts de Montréal) 2001, Art Crazy Nation Show (Milton Keynes Gallery) 2002, Rapture: Art's Seduction by Fashion since 1970 (Barbican Gallery London) 2002, Fran el Greco till Dali (Nationalmuseum Sweden Stockholm) 2003, Mars. Art and War (Neue Galerie am Landesmuseum Joanneum Graz) 2003, Summer Exhbn (Royal Acad of arts London) 2003 (Charles Wollaston Award), The Turner Prize (Tate Britain London) 2003, Gewalt (Loushy Art & Editions Tel Aviv) 2004, Mike Kelley: The Uncanny (Tate Liverpool 2004), At War (Centre de Cultura Contemporània de Barcelona) 2004, After Images (Neues Museum Weserburg Bremen) 2004, Deliver Us From Evil (Matthew Marks Gallery NY) 2004, The Charged Image (Joseloff Gallery CT) 2004, Paper Democracy: Contemporary Art in Editions on Paper (Edificio Cultura Inglesa Sao Paulo) 2004, The Christmas Exhibition (Edinburgh Printmakers) 2004, Critic's Choice (FACT Liverpool) 2005, Mixed-up Childhood: An Exhibition for Grown-ups (Auckland Art Gallery) 2005, Glasgow International Festival of Contemporary Visual Art (Glasgow Print Studio) 2005, Body: New Art from the UK (Vancouver Art Gallery) 2005, Bidibidobidiboo: La Collezione Sandretto Re Rebaudengo (Turin) 2005; *Work in Public Collections* Deste Fndn Athens, Rubell Family Collection, Saatchi Collection, Walker Art Centre Minneapolis, British Museum, Simmons & Simmons London, The Israel Museum Jerusalem, Groninger Museum, Museum Kunst Palast Düsseldorf, MOMA NY; *Publications* Razzle; *Recreations* drugs, fast cars, molecular biology; *Clubs* Water Mark, Harpo, Variety, Seal; *Style—* Prof Jake Chapman; ✉ c/o White Cube, 48 Hoxton Square, London N1 6PB

CHAPMAN, James Keith (Ben); MP; s of John Hartley Chapman (d 1983), of Kirkby Stephen, Cumbria, and Elsie Vera, *née* Bousfield (d 1978); *b* 8 July 1940; *Educ* Appleby GS Cumbria; *m* 1, 1970 (m dis 1984), Jane Deirdre, da of Norman Roffe, of Morecambe, Lancs; 3 da (Bridget b 1971, Charlotte b 1973, Clare b 1975); m 2, 1999, Maureen Ann Kelly; *Career* PO RAFVR (T) 1959–61; Miny of Pensions and Nat Insurance 1958–62, Miny of Aviation/BAA 1962–67, Rochdale Ctee of Inquiry into Shipping 1967–70, BOT 1970–74, first sec (commercial) Dar es Salaam 1974–78, first sec (econ) Accra 1978–81, asst sec DTI 1981–87, commercial cnsllr Br Embassy Beijing 1987–90, DTI dep regnl dir NW and DTI dir Merseyside 1991–93, DTI regnl dir NW 1993–94, dir Trade and Industry in the Government Office for the NW 1994–95; fndr Ben Chapman Associates 1995–97, ptnr The Pacific Practice 1996–97, MP (Lab) Wirral S (by-election and then gen election) 1997–; PPS to Rt Hon Richard Caborn, MP 1997–2005; memb DCMS Backbench Ctee 2001–05, memb Intelligence and Security Ctee 2005–, memb Environmental Ctee 2005–; memb Lab Pty Departmental Ctees for: Environment, Tport and the Regions 1997–2001, Foreign and Cwlth Affrs 1997–2001, Trade and Industry 1997–2001; memb Exec Ctee Cwlth Parly Assoc 2005–; former chm UNCTAD Econ Ctee and Buffer Stock Int Natural Rubber Agreement, former DG Int Wool Study Gp, former chm Int Cotton Advsy Conf; dir Heswall Soc 1996–97; dir Wirral C of C 1996–97, hon vice-pres Wirral Investment Network, Int Friend of the Wirral 1995–; hon ambass for Cumbria and Merseyside; memb Exec Ctee GB-China Centre; former memb: Chemicals EDC (chm Forward Assessment Gp), Tyre EDC, Plastics Processing EDC, Business Link Implementation Strategy Gp, Business Devpt Panel BBC Philharmonic Orchestra, Advsy Cncl Liverpool Business Sch; former vice-pres Int Students Advsy Cncl for Merseyside; patron: Claire House Appeal 2003–, Clatterbridge Hosp League of Friends 2003–; chm Rural Challenge Cumbria, memb Cncl Lake District Summer Music; fell 48 Group Club 2005– (memb 1994); *Recreations* opera, theatre, music, walking; *Style—* Ben Chapman, Esq, MP; ✉ House of Commons, London SW1A 0AA (tel 020 7219 1143, e-mail chapmanb@parliament.uk)

CHAPMAN, Jennifer Mary; da of Peter Norman Johnson (d 2007), of Royston, Herts, and Agnes Mabel, *née* Taylor (d 1989); *b* 19 February 1950; *Educ* St Albans HS; *m* 1, 1971 (m dis 1979), Paul Robin Moncrieff Westoby; 2 da (Frances b 1974, Anna b 1976); m 2, 1980, Geoffrey Richard Chapman; 1 da (Quinta b 1990); *Career* NCTJ apprenticeship Westminster Press 1968–72, Heart of England Newspapers 1972–73, Coventry Evening Telegraph 1974, Mid-Anglia Newspapers 1976–80, fndr Multi Media PR consultancy 1980–; co-fndr Chapman and Vincent Literary Agents (formerly Media House) 1995–; currently business ed Cambridge Evening News; Midlands Journalist of the Year 1974, Business and Financial Journalist of the Year UK Regnl Press Awards 2005; memb: Soc of Authors 1982, English PEN 1993; MIPR 1986; *Books* The Geneva Touch (thriller, as Lydia Hitchcock, 1982), The Long Weekend (novel, 1984), Mysterious Ways (novel, 1985), Not Playing the Game (novel, 1986), Regretting It (novel, 1987), The Last Bastion - the case for and against women priests (1989), Barnardo's Today (foreword by HRH the Princess of Wales, 1991), Victor Ludorum (novel, 1991), Made in Heaven (1993), Jeremy's Baby (novel, 2001); *Clubs* Groucho; *Style—* Mrs Jennifer Chapman; ✉ The Mount, Sun Hill, Royston, Hertfordshire SG8 9AT

CHAPMAN, Dr John Clifford; s of James Clifford Crossley Chapman (d 1983), and Marion, *née* Harrison (d 1992); *b* 21 February 1923; *Educ* Ilford HS, Imperial Coll London (BSc, PhD); *m* 18 Oct 1947, Roberta Blanche, da of Robert Broughton Gingell; 1 da (Sarah b 1953), 1 s (Andrew b 1958); *Career* Capt RE 1942–46; res fell and reader in structural engrg Imperial Coll 1950–71, dir Constructional Steel R&D Orgn 1971–73, gp tech dir George Wimpey plc 1973–81, dir Chapman Associates (formerly Chapman Dowling Associates Ltd) consulting engrs 1981–, visiting prof ICSTM London 1991–2005; winner 12 awards; FREng 1979, FCGI 1987, FICE, FRINA, FIStructE; *Publications* many papers on structural engrg in professional jls; *Recreations* tennis, squash, mountain walking, music; *Style—* Dr John C Chapman, FREng; ✉ 41 Oathall Road, Haywards Heath, West Sussex RH16 3EG

CHAPMAN, Prof John Newton; s of John Avi Chapman (d 1978), and Nora, *née* Newton (d 1982); *b* 21 November 1947, Sheffield; *Educ* King Edward VII Sch Sheffield, St John's Coll Cambridge (exhibitioner, scholar, Wright Prize, MA), Fitzwilliam Coll Cambridge (PhD); *m* 23 Sept 1972, Judith Margaret, *née* Brown; 1 da (Catherine Helen b 2 Dec 1977), 1 s (Christopher John b 26 March 1980); *Career* research fell Fitzwilliam Coll Cambridge 1971–74; Univ of Glasgow: lectr Dept of Natural Philosophy 1974–84, reader Dept of Natural Philosophy 1984–88, prof Dept of Physics and Astronomy 1988–, head of dept 2001–06; assoc ed Jl of Physics D, Applied Physics 1993–2002 (memb Editorial Bd 1989–93); memb Editorial Bd: Jl of Microscopy 1987–93, Jl of Magnetism and Magnetic Materials 1990–; EPSRC: memb 2003–, memb Coll (previously Functional Materials Coll then Physics Coll), memb Magnetism and Quantum Fluids Review Panel 1997, chm Advanced Magnetics Prog Mgmnt Panel 1998–2000 (memb 1997–98), memb Audit Ctee 2003–; chm: Electron Microscopy and Analysis Gp Inst of Physics 1982–83 (memb 1977–79, hon sec 1981–83), UK Magnetics Chapter IEEE 1992–94; memb: Magnetism Gp Inst of Physics 1990–94, Technical Ctee Magnetism Soc IEEE 1991–95, Mgmnt Gp UK Magnetics Soc 1995–2001, Mgmnt Ctee UK Info Storage Consortium 1996–2001, Scientific Ctee European Materials Research Soc 1996–, Advsy Bd Max Planck Inst fur Mikrostrukturphysik 1998–, IT, Electronics and Communications Task Force DTI 1999–2000, LINK Evaluation Panel on Storage and Displays DTI 2001–, Magnetic Soc Adcom IEEE 2005–; coordinator Magnetism and Magnetic Materials Initiative SERC 1990–94; distinguished visitor Univ of Western Aust 1995, distinguished lectr IEEE Magnetics Soc 2003; MIEEE (sr memb), FRSE 1991, FInstP; *Publications* 275 scientific papers; *Recreations* tennis, hill walking, photography, music; *Style—* Prof John N Chapman; ✉ Department of Physics and Astronomy, University of Glasgow, Glasgow G12 8QQ (tel 0141 330 4462, fax 0141 330 4484, e-mail j.chapman@physics.gla.ac.uk)

CHAPMAN, Prof (Stephen) Jonathan; s of Stephen Cyril Chapman, of N Yorks, and Pauline Mary Chapman; *b* 31 August 1968, Keighley, W Yorks; *Educ* South Craven Sch Crosshills, Merton Coll Oxford (BA), St Catherine's Coll Oxford (DPhil); *m* 1 Dec 1996, Aarti; 1 s (Tarun Stephen b 11 Aug 2000), 1 da (Maya Yasmin b 19 April 2002); *Career* postdoctoral research fell Stanford Univ 1992, Nuclear Electric research fell St Catherine's Coll Oxford 1993–95, Royal Soc univ research fell St Catherine's Coll Oxford 1995–99, prof of mathematics and its applications Mansfield Coll Oxford 1999–; author of pubns in learned jls; Richard C Diprima Prize Soc for Industrial and Applied Maths (SIAM) 1994, Whitehead Prize London Mathematical Soc 1998, Julian Cole Prize SIAM 2002; *Recreations* bridge, golf; *Style—* Prof Jonathan Chapman; ✉ Mathematical Institute, 24–29 St Giles', Oxford OX1 3LB (tel 01865 270507, fax 01865 250515, e-mail chapman@maths.ox.ac.uk)

CHAPMAN, Kenneth James; s of Kenneth Roland Chapman, of Lincoln, and Marie Louise, *née* Robinson; *b* 14 September 1950; *Educ* Hornchurch GS, The Sweyne Sch Rayleigh, Univ of Wales (BSc, DipTP); *m* 31 Aug 1970, Pamela Margaret, da of Alan Henry Sertin, of Midsomer Norton, Avon; 2 s (Mark b 1974, Daniel b 1979), 1 da (Kelly b and d 1977); *Career* Glamorgan CC 1972–73, Mid Glamorgan CC 1974–75, Monmouth BC 1975–79, Edwin H Bradley & Sons Ltd 1979–81, managing ptnr Chapman Warren 1981–2000; dir: RPS Group plc 2000–04, iCP Commercial Ltd 2004–, Meadfleet Ltd 2004–, Sports Solutions GB Ltd 2006–, Futureland Asset Mgmnt Ltd 2007–; chm Swindon Town FC 1990–91, dir Cirencester Town FC; memb Cncl Swindon C of C and Industry; govr Wootton Bassett Sch; MRTPI 1978, MIMgt 1979, FRSA 2000; *Recreations* professional and non-league football, commemorative china and Dinky car collecting; *Style—* Kenneth Chapman, Esq; ✉ Woodbridge Lodge, Stoppers Hill, Brinkworth, Wiltshire SN15 5DW (tel 01666 510137)

CHAPMAN, Baroness (Life Peer UK 2004), of Leeds in the County of West Yorkshire; Nicola Jane Chapman; da of Peter Chapman, and Marlene, *née* Heath; *b* 3 August 1961; *Educ* John Jamieson Sch for Physically Disabled Children, Park Lane Coll Leeds, Trinity and All Saints Coll Leeds; *Career* vol tutor Apex Trust 1985–86, fin clerk Leeds City Cncl 1986–92, IT tutor E Leeds Women's Workshops 1992–93; chair: Leeds United Disabled Orgn 1997–, Leeds Centre for Integrated Living 2004–; Hon DBA Leeds Met Univ 2006; *Recreations* football (Leeds Utd); *Style—* The Rt Hon the Baroness Chapman; ✉ House of Lords, London SW1A 0PW (tel 020 7219 6756, e-mail chapmann@parliament.uk)

CHAPMAN, Nigel; *m*; 2 c; *Career* BBC: trainee 1977, former prodr Nationwide, Newsnight and Breakfast News, ed Public Eye 1989–92, head of centre SE Elstree 1992–94, head of broadcasting Midlands and E 1994–96, controller BBC English Regions 1996–99, dir BBC Online 1999–2000, dir BBC World Service 2004– (dep dir 2000–04), chair World Service Tst; chair Plan (UK); *Style—* Nigel Chapman, Esq; ✉ BBC World Service, Bush House, London WC2B 4PH

CHAPMAN, Nigel Peter; s of Lt Col Sidney Rex Chapman, MC, of Lincs, and Joan Mary, *née* Bates; *b* 31 January 1950; *Educ* Kimbolton Sch; *m* 26 Sept 1981, Heather Elizabeth, da of James Lindsay, of London; 3 s (Nicolas b 1982, Daniel b 1984, Cullan b 1999), 2 da (Jennifer b 1987, Clare b 1990); *Career* CA; md: LHM plc 1991–, Four Winds Resorts plc 2003–, Luxury Family Hotels plc 2004–; *Recreations* tennis, cricket; *Clubs* Reform; *Style—* Nigel P Chapman, Esq; ✉ Fairfields House, Murrells End, Hartpury, Gloucestershire GL19 3DF (mobile 07710 504804, e-mail nigel.chapman@fourwindsresorts.com)

CHAPMAN, Peter Richard; s of Lt Ernest Richard Chapman, RNVR (d 1974) and Edith Winifred, *née* Softly; *b* 1 April 1942; *Educ* St Paul's Cathedral Choir Sch, St John's Sch Leatherhead; *m* 1 June 1974, Stephanie Daynel, da of Kenneth Paul Alexander Watson; 2 s (Richard b 1975, Philip b 1978); *Career* CA 1964; Ogden Parsons & Co: joined 1959, ptnr 1970–71; ptnr: Harmood Banner & Co 1972–73, Deloitte Haskins & Sells 1974–90, PricewaterhouseCoopers (formerly Coopers & Lybrand before merger 1998) 1990–98 (chm Int Banking Industry Gp); sr banking advsr FSA 1997–2006, sr advsr IMF 1999; chm DH&S Banking Industry Gp 1983–89; memb Church Urban Fund 1988–94, memb Ct of Advsrs St Paul's Cathedral 1981–99, chapter and lay canon St Paul's Cathedral 2000–, govr St Paul's Cathedral Sch 2004–, vice-chm St Pauls Cathedral Fndn 2000, treas St Paul's Cathedral Sch Fndn; tstee Monteverdi Choir and Orchestra; memb Guild of Int Bankers; FCA, CMI; *Recreations* music, golf; *Clubs* Athenaeum, Walton Heath Golf, RAC; *Style—* Peter Chapman, Esq; ✉ Rydens, 3 Downs Way, Tadworth, Surrey KT20 5DH (tel and fax 01737 813073)

CHAPMAN, Peter Stuart; s of Sir Robin Chapman, Bt (d 1987), and Lady (Barbara) Chapman; bro of Sir David Chapman, Bt, DL, *qv*; *b* 24 August 1944; *Educ* Trinity Coll Cambridge (MA), LSE (MSc); *m* 4 Aug 1972, Joan; 1 s, 3 da; *Career* research assoc Centre for Urban and Regnl Studies Univ of Birmingham 1967–69, asst research offr Sociological Research Section Miny of Housing and Local Govt 1969–70, asst ed Built Environment The Builder Gp 1970–72, devpt asst Peabody Tst 1972–73, housing and social planning conslt Llewelyn-Davies, Weeks, Forestier-Walker & Bor 1973–75, princ housing offr

Admin & Resource Control London Borough of Hammersmith and Fulham 1975–79, asst dir of housing and property servs (devpt) RBK&C 1979–85, princ conslt Urban Renewal Consultancy KMG Thomson McLintock 1985–87, dir of housing and urban renewal consultancy CIPFA Services Ltd 1987–88; dir: Chapman Hendy Assocs Ltd 1988–2000, HACAS Chapman Hendy Ltd, HACAS Gp Ltd and Tribal HCH 2000–06, Assettrust Housing Ltd 2003–, Trafford Trading Ltd; princ Peter S Chapman Consltg 2007–, chm National Communities Resource Centre; special advsr House of Commons Environment, Tport and Regnl Affrs Ctee; memb Cranfield Mgmnt Assoc; MInstD, fell Chartered Inst of Housing; *Publications* Local Housing Companies Implementation Manual (co-ed); *Recreations* tennis, walking, theatre, cinema; *Style*— Peter Chapman, Esq; ✉ Peter S Chapman Consulting (tel 020 7937 6579, e-mail peterschapman@chapmanlondon.com)

CHAPMAN, Hon Mrs (Rhiannon Elizabeth); *née* Philipps; da (by 1 m) of 2 Viscount St Davids (d 1991); *b* 21 September 1946; *Educ* Tormead Sch, King's Coll London (LLB, AKC); *m* 1974 (m dis 1991), Donald Hudson Chapman, s of late Francis Robert Chapman; 2 step s; *Career* dir of personnel London Stock Exchange 1980–90; chief exec: The Industrial Society 1991–93, National Australia Group CIF Trustee Ltd 1994–96, S R Gent plc 1994–97, Welsh Devpt Agency 1994–98, Plaudit 1994–; chm Fleming Managed Growth plc 1999–2002, dir Bibby Financial Services Ltd 2002–03; external reviewer of complaints Teacher Training Agency 1998–2004, advsr on people and skills Soc of British Aerospace Companies 2005–07; memb Bd Accountancy Nat Training Agency 2000–01; dir SW of England Urban Regeneration Fund 2003–; memb Employment Appeal Tbnl; FCIPD, FRSA, CIMgt; *Recreations* opera and theatre, travel, handcrafts, keeping fit; *Style*— The Hon Mrs Chapman; ✉ 3 Church Green, Great Wymondley, Hitchin, Hertfordshire SG4 7HA (tel 01438 759102)

CHAPMAN, Dr Roger William Gibson; s of Lt-Col Roy Chapman, OBE, of Pantmawr, Whitchurch, S Wales, and Margaret Gibson, *née* Abraham; *b* 16 February 1949; *Educ* Whitchurch GS Cardiff, Bart's Med Sch London (BSc, MD, MB BS); *m* 24 April 1972, Gillian Patricia, da of Dr James C Prestwich (d 1969), of Portsmouth; 3 s (James b 1977, Andrew b 1979, George b 1983), 1 da (Emily b 1987); *Career* house physician Bart's 1974–76, med registrar Southampton 1976–78, med lectr Liver Unit Royal Free Hosp 1978–81, conslt gastroenterologist and hepatologist John Radcliff Hosp Oxford 1987– (sr registrar 1981–87); sec Br Assoc for the Study of the Liver 1990–93; FRCP; *Books* Topics in Gastroenterology (co-ed and written with Dr D P Jewell, 1985), Drugs for the Gut (1997), Hepatobiliary Medicine (2003); *Recreations* tennis, golf, skiing, cinema; *Style*— Dr Roger Chapman; ✉ Department of Gastroenterology, John Radcliffe Hospital, Headington, Oxford OX3 9DU (tel 01865 220618, fax 01865 751100, e-mail roger.chapman@ndm.ox.ac.uk)

CHAPMAN, Stuart James; s of Geoffrey Gordon Chapman (d 2005), and Margaret, *née* Bennett; *b* 15 August 1965, Grimsby; *Educ* Whitgift Comp Sch Grimsby, Univ of Nottingham (BA); *m* 21 July 1990, Fiona Jane, *née* Clague; 2 da (Kate Graihagh b 11 Oct 1996, Sophie Cara b 21 Oct 2000), 1 s (Edward Orry b 9 March 1998); *Career* admitted slr 1991; Linklaters 1989–94, Eversheds 1994–98, Pinsent Masons 1998–; *Recreations* sport, reading, family; *Style*— Stuart Chapman, Esq; ✉ Pinsent Masons, 1 Park Row, Leeds, LS1 5AB (tel 0113 225 5455, fax 0113 244 8000, e-mail stuart.chapman@pinsentmasons.com)

CHAPMAN, Sir Sydney Brookes; s of W Dobson Chapman (d 1965), and Edith Laura, *née* Wadge (d 1978); *b* 17 October 1935; *Educ* Rugby, Univ of Manchester; *m* 1, 1976 (m dis 1987), Claire Lesley, *née* Davies; 2 s, 1 da; m 2, 2005, Teresa Munoz Ernest; *Career* memb Exec Ctee Nat Union of Cons and Unionist Assocs 1961–70, nat chm Young Cons 1964–66, contested (Cons) Stalybridge and Hyde 1964; MP (Cons): Birmingham Handsworth 1970–74, Chipping Barnet 1979–2005; PPS: to Sec of State for Tport 1979–81, to Sec of State for Social Servs 1981–83; memb Select Ctees on: Environment 1983–87, House of Commons Services 1983–87; chm Accommodation and Works Select Ctee 1997–2001; memb 1922 Exec Ctee 1997–2001; asst Govt whip 1988–90, a Lord Cmmr of the Treasy (Govt whip) 1990–92, Vice-Chamberlain of HM Household 1992–95; memb: Cncl of Europe Assembly 1997–2005, WEU 1997–2005, Public Administration Select Ctee 2002–05; chm Cncl of Europe Sustainable Devpt Ctee 2001–04; non-practising chartered architect and chartered town and country planner; vice-pres Cncl RIBA 1974–76 (memb 1972–76); instigator Nat Tree Planting Year 1973, vice-pres Tree Cncl; pres: Arboricultural Assoc 1983–89, London Green Belt Cncl 1986–89; Queen's Silver Jubilee medal 1977; RIBA, FRTPI, Hon MLI, Hon FFB, Hon FBEng, Hon FSVA, FRSA, Hon FASI, Hon RICS, hon memb Br Vet Assoc; *Clubs* United and Cecil (vice-chm 1982–2003); *Style*— Sir Sydney Chapman

CHAPPATTE, Philippe Paul; s of Joseph Chappatte (d 1998), and Sallie van Zwanen Berg; *b* 6 October 1956; *Educ* Bryanston, Univ of Oxford (MA), Université Libre de Bruxelles (Licencie Spéciale en Droit Européen); *m* 22 June 1985, Sarah Jane; 3 c (Sam b 29 Dec 1986, Jessica b 23 March 1989, Hannah b 26 April 1997); *Career* slr; with Slaughter and May 1980–; specialises in competition law; pres and co-fndr European Competition Lawyers Forum; *Recreations* skiing; *Style*— Philippe Chappatte, Esq; ✉ Slaughter and May, 1 Bunhill Row, London EC1Y 8YY (tel 020 7090 4424, fax 020 7090 5000, e-mail philippe.chappatte@slaughterandmay.com)

CHAPPIN, Andrew Darryl; s of Dennis John Chappin, and Margaret Violet, *née* Howell; *b* 9 July 1954; *Educ* St Albans Sch, Brighton Poly Faculty of Art & Design (BA); *Career* designer Granada Publishing 1977–78, asst art ed New Scientist 1978–79, sr designer Now! magazine 1979–81, art ed Eagle Moss Publications April-Nov 1981, designer The Times 1981–82, art ed Sunday Express Magazine 1982–86, art dir London Daily News 1986–87, art dir FT 1987–; Soc of Newspaper Design USA: award of excellence 1988, 1990, 1991 and 1993, Silver award 1990; NDA/Linotype Awards (with David Case): Best Designed Newspaper 1990, Best News Pages 1990; memb: D&AD Assoc 1988, Soc of Newspaper Design USA 1987, Typographic Circle 1994; jt fndr (former chm) Euro Soc for News Design; *Recreations* playing rugby, skiing, scuba diving and golf, watching football, cinema, reading; *Clubs* Old Albanian; *Style*— Andrew Chappin, Esq; ✉ Financial Times, Number One, Southwark Bridge, London SE1 9HL (tel 020 7873 3328, fax 020 7407 5700)

CHAPPLE, Brian John; s of Capt John Ernest Chapple (d 1977), and Mildred, *née* Fairbrother (d 1988); *b* 24 March 1945; *Educ* Highgate Sch, RAM (GRSM, LRAM, ARAM); *m* 20 Dec 1973, Janet Mary, *née* Whittaker-Coldron; 1 da (Rosalind Bailey); *Career* composer; compositions incl: Trees Revisited 1970, Hallelujahs 1971, Scherzos 1970 (premiered Proms Royal Albert Hall 1976), 5 Blake Songs, Praeludiana 1973 (premiered Royal Festival Hall), Green and Pleasant 1973 (BBC Monarchy 1000 Prize), Veni Sancte Spiritus 1974, In Ecclesiis 1976, Piano Concerto 1977, Cantica 1978 (cmmnd Highgate Choral Soc), Venus Fly Trap 1979 (cmmnd London Sinfonietta), Little Symphony 1982 (cmmnd Haydn Society), Lamentations of Jeremiah 1984, Piano Sonata 1986 (cmmnd Dartington Int Summer Sch), Magnificat 1987 (cmmnd Highgate Choral Soc), Confitebor 1989, In Memoriam 1989, Tribute I and II 1989 and 1990, Requies 1991, Missa Brevis 1991 (cmmnd St Paul's Cathedral), Three Motets 1992, Songs of Innocence 1993 (cmmnd Finchley Children's Music Gp), Ecce Lignum Crucis 1993, Holy Communion Service in E 1993 (cmmnd St John the Baptist, Chipping Barnet), Ebony and Ivory 1994, A Bit of a Blow 1996, Magnificat and Nunc Dimittis The St Paul's Service 1996 (tercentenary celebrations cmmnd St Paul's Cathedral), Tribute for Jo Klein 1997, Songs of Experience 1998 (cmmnd Finchley Children's Music Gp), Klein Tribute Quartet, The Cloud-Capped Towers 2000, Burlesque 2000, A Birthday Suite for John 2002, Viola Suite 2004, Tribute for JMC 2004, Bagatelles Diverses 2005, God's Love Come Among Us 2005, Two Dances and Lullaby 2005, Swing's the Thing 2007, Three Sacred Pieces 2007, anthems and canticles for New Coll Oxford, Canterbury Cathedral and St Paul's Cathedral, children's songs, piano and instrumental music; PRS, MCPS; *Style*— Brian Chapple, Esq; ✉ c/o Chester Music, 8–9 Frith Street, London W1V 5TZ

CHAPPLE, Prof (Alfred) John Victor; s of Alfred Edward Chapple (d 1942), and Frances Lilian, *née* Taylor (d 1972); *b* 25 April 1928; *Educ* St Boniface's Coll Plymouth, UCL (BA, MA); *m* 6 Aug 1955, Kathleen, da of James Sheridan Bolton (d 1979); 4 s (Andrew b 1958, John b 1960, James b 1964, Christopher b 1967), 1 da (Clare b 1962); *Career* Nat Serv RA 1946–49: 2 Lt 1947, short serv cmmn as Lt; res asst Yale Univ 1955–58, asst Univ of Aberdeen 1958–59, asst lectr, lectr then sr lectr Univ of Manchester 1959–71 (hon prof of English 1998–2000), prof of English Univ of Hull 1971–92 (dean of Arts 1980–82, pro-vice-chllr 1985–88), visiting fell Corpus Christi Coll Cambridge 1992; memb Int Assoc of Profs of English 1986–, pres Gaskell Soc 1998– (chm 1990–97); *Books* The Letters of Mrs Gaskell (ed with Arthur Pollard, 1966, new issue 1997), Documentary and Imaginative Literature 1880–1920 (1970), Elizabeth Gaskell: A Portrait In Letters (1980), Science and Literature in the Nineteenth Century (1986), Private Voices: the Diaries of Elizabeth Gaskell and Sophia Holland (ed with Anita Wilson, 1996), Elizabeth Gaskell: the Early Years (1997), Further Letters of Mrs Gaskell (ed with Alan Shelston, 2000, new issue 2003); *Recreations* music, wine, gardening, calligraphy; *Style*— Prof John Chapple; ✉ 8 Lomax Close, Lichfield (tel 01543 251964, e-mail javckc@dsl.pipex.com)

CHAPPLE, His Hon Judge Roger Graham; s of Robert William Chapple (d 1997), and Elsie Mary, *née* Hubbard (d 1995); *b* 28 August 1951, London; *Educ* Univ of Leeds (LLB), Inns of Court Sch of Law; *Career* called to the Bar Gray's Inn 1974; barr specialising in gen common law Francis Taylor Bldg Temple 1974–94, dep judge advocate 1994–95, asst judge advocate gen 1995–2004, recorder 2000–04 (asst recorder 1999–2000), circuit judge (South Eastern Circuit) 2004–, resident judge Middx Guildhall Crown Court 2005–07; *Recreations* all types of music (especially opera), travel; *Style*— His Hon Judge Chapple; ✉ c/o Judicial Secretariat for the London & South East Regions, Rose Court, 2 Southwark Bridge, London SE1 9HS (e-mail hhjudge.chapple@judiciary.gsi.gov.uk)

CHAPPLE, Sean; s of Brian Edward William John Chapple, and Valerie Ann, *née* Giles; *Educ* Harwich Secdy Comp; *Career* RM 1984–2006 (completed Commando trg 1985, received Offr Cmm to rank of Lt 2002); explorer: ldr Erukenya Expdn 1987 (lightweight mountaineering climb Mt Kenya), equipment mangr Karakoram Expdn 1991 (lightweight mountaineering climb Yazghill Sar, Pakistan), expdn ldr Grand Canyon Ironman Challenge 1992 (270 mile cycle over San Francisco mountains, 40 mile trek through Grand Canyon, 106 mile run through Painted Desert, 4 mile swim at Flagstaff), ldr Northern Trail Expdn 1994 (ski crossing of Rondane NP Norway), ldr Icelandic 500 Expdn 1995 (first ski crossing of Iceland from W to E), ldr Frozen Fields expdn 1996 (ski expdn to Beechy Is to pay tribute to last resting place of RM William Braine of the ill-fated 1875 Franklin Expdn), ldr Polar Connection Expdn 1997, ldr Polar North Expdn 1998 (first RM attempt to ski unaided to geographical N Pole), ldr Polar Quest Expdn 2006–07 (ski to magnetic N Pole and geographical S Pole unsupported); Keeling Trophy for outstanding achievements for expdn ldrship and planning; FRGS; *Publications* No Ordinary Tourist (1996); *Recreations* hill walking, Polar history, genealogy, painting; *Style*— Sean Chapple, Esq; ✉ e-mail enquire@seanchapple.co.uk, website www.seanchapple.co.uk

CHAPPLE-HYAM, Peter William; s of William Henry Chapple-Hyam, of Itchington, Warwicks, and Mary Constance, *née* Mann; *b* 2 April 1963; *Educ* Princethorpe Coll; *m* 24 June 1990, Jane Fiona, da of Andrew Sharpe Peacock; *Career* racehorse trainer; Young Trainer of the Year 1991 and 1992; trained winner of: The Derby, 2,000 Guineas and Irish 2000 Guineas (all 1992), Italian Derby 1993, Irish 2000 Guineas 1994 and 1995, Hong King Cup 2002 (based in Hong Kong 1999–2003); *Recreations* soccer, cricket, tennis; *Style*— Peter Chapple-Hyam, Esq; ✉ website www.peterchapplehyam.com

CHARAP, Prof John Michael; s of Samuel Lewis Charap (d 1995), and Irene, *née* Shaw (d 1984); *b* 1 January 1935; *Educ* City of London Sch, Trinity Coll Cambridge (MA, PhD); *m* 11 June 1961, Ellen Elfrieda, da of Eric Kuhn (d 1986); 1 s (David b 1965); *Career* res assoc: Univ of Chicago 1959–60, Univ of Calif Berkeley 1960–62; memb Inst for Advanced Study Princeton 1962–63, lectr in physics Imperial Coll London 1964–65 (sr scientific offr 1963–64); Queen Mary Univ of London: reader in theoretical physics 1965–78, prof of theoretical physics 1978–, head Dept of Physics 1980–85, dean Faculty of Science 1982–85, pro princ 1987–89, vice-princ 1989–90; Univ of London: chm Bd of Studies in Physics 1976–80, memb Senate 1981–94, memb Ct 1989–94, memb Cncl 1994–2000; memb: American Physical Soc 1960, European Physical Soc 1980; FInstP 1979, CPhys 1988; *Publications* Explaining the Universe: The New Age of Physics (2002); *Recreations* walking, talking; *Style*— Prof John Charap; ✉ 33 Langbourne Avenue, London N6 6PS (tel 020 8340 3599, fax 020 8347 9960, e-mail j.m.charap@qmul.ac.uk)

CHARING, Rabbi Douglas Stephen; *b* 1945, London; *Educ* Leo Baeck Coll London; *m* Oct 1972, Eve; 1 s (Benjamin); *Career* ordained rabbi 1970; former: rabbi to progressive synagogues in N and W London and Leeds, visiting rabbi Bristol & The West Progressive Synagogue, pt/t dir Jewish Information Serv, pt/t lectr Theol and Religious Studies Dept Univ of Leeds and Gtr Manchester Police Coll, specialist advsr Theol and Religious Studies Bd CNAA, memb Planning Ctee Centre for the Study of Judaism and Jewish/Christian Rels, pt/t dir Concord Multi-Faith Resources Centre, visiting rabbi Sha'arei Shalom Synagogue Manchester, conslt Int Consultancy on Religion, Educn and Culture; currently: dir Jewish Educn Bureau (fndr), tutor Greenwich Univ, specialist assessor Higher Educn Funding Cncl for Wales, visiting rabbi Bradford Synagogue, accredited lectr Potchefstroom Univ of Christian Higher Educn SA, hon sec Leeds Living Heritage Centre, visiting lectr Northern Ordination Coll; memb: Inter-European Cmmn on Church and Sch, Cncl of Christians and Jews, World Congress of Faiths, Inter-Faith Network, Cncl of Reform and Liberal Rabbis, Advsy Ctee Nat Community Folktale Centre, Christian-Jewish Consultation of the United Reformed Church, Bd of Dirs Anne Frank Educnl Tst UK, Exec Cncl for Religious Educn, Professional Cncl for Religious Educn, Assoc of Religious Educn Insprs, Advsr & Conslts (AREIAC), Soc for Storytelling, Network of Biblical Storytellers; *Publications* incl: Comparative Religions (jtly, 1982, reprinted 1984 and 1991, renamed as Six World Faiths, 1996), The Jewish World (1983, reprinted 1985, 1992, 1995 and 1996), Visiting a Synagogue (1984, reprinted 1988), The Torah (1993), Religion in Leeds (contrib, 1994), Renewing the Vision (contrib, 1996), Judaism (2003); writer of Rabbinic stories for children on BBC TV; *Style*— Rabbi Douglas Charing; ✉ 8 Westcombe Avenue, Leeds LS8 2BS (tel 0870 730 0532, fax 0870 800 8533, e-mail rabbi@jewisheducationbureau.co.uk)

CHARING CROSS, Archdeacon of; *see:* Jacob, Ven Dr William Mungo

CHARKIN, Richard Denis Paul; s of Frank Charkin (d 1963), and Mabel Doreen, *née* Rosen; *b* 17 June 1949; *Educ* Haileybury and ISC, Trinity Coll Cambridge (MA); *m* 7 Aug 1972, Susan Mary, da of Sidney William Poole; 2 da (Emily b 1973, Boo b 1977), 1 s (Toby b 1975); *Career* Oxford University Press: med ed 1974–76, head of Sci and Med Div 1976–80, head of Reference Div 1980–84, md Academic Div 1984–88; exec dir Octopus Publishing Group 1988–; chief exec: Reed Consumer Books 1990–94, Reed International Books 1994–95 (formerly with Reed Elsevier (UK) Ltd), Current Science Group 1995–96, Macmillan Ltd 1997–; chair Common Purpose; *Recreations* cricket, music, art; *Style*— Richard Charkin, Esq; ✉ Macmillan Ltd, 4 Crinan Street, London N1 9XW (tel 020 7843 3600)

CHARLES, Caroline (Mrs Malcolm Valentine); OBE (2002); *b* 18 May 1942; *Educ* Sacred Heart Convent Woldingham, Swindon Coll of Art; *m* 8 Jan 1966, Malcolm Valentine; 2 c (Kate, Alex); *Career* fashion designer; apprentice to Michael Sherard British Couture Curzon St London 1960, worked for Mary Quant London 1961, estab Caroline Charles London 1963; exhibitor V&A Summer Exhbn 1989; memb British Colour & Textile Group; Yardley Young Designer Award NY 1964, Evening Standard Design Award 1978; *Books* Weekend Wardrobe; *Recreations* travel, theatre, tennis; *Style*— Ms Caroline Charles, OBE; ✉ 56–57 Beauchamp Place, London SW3 1NY (tel 020 7225 3197, fax 020 7589 4029, website www.carolinecharles.co.uk)

CHARLES, Jonathan; s of Henry Simon Charles, of Nottingham, and Diane Betty, *née* Lewis; *b* 9 July 1964; *Educ* Nottingham Boys' HS, Oriel Coll Oxford; *Career* editorial trainee ITN 1986–87; BBC: joined as reporter 1987, New York corr 1988, Europe reporter Paris 1989–90, Europe business corr Brussels 1990–94, Europe corr Frankfurt 1995–; *Recreations* reading, music (classical and popular), skiing, cookery, impressionist and modern art; *Clubs* Frontline; *Style*— Jonathan Charles, Esq; ✉ BBC News, Frankfurt Bureau, Friedrichstrasse 40, 60323 Frankfurt, Germany (tel 00 49 172 660 0361, e-mail jonathan.charles@bbc.co.uk)

CHARLES, Susan Jane; da of Alfred Norman Harris, of Solihull, and Esme Joyce, *née* Skey; *b* 2 January 1959; *Educ* Tudor Grange Girls' GS, Solihull Sixth Form Coll, St Catherine's Coll Oxford (MA, Swimming half blue), Cranfield Sch of Management (PR Week scholar, MBA), Chartered Inst of Marketing (DipM); *m* 1 Sept 1992, Prof Ian George Charles; *Career* pre-doctoral res asst Univ of Leicester 1981–84 (res demonstrator 1984–85); Kempsters Communications Gp: tech conslt 1984–85, PR tech writer 1985, PR account exec 1985–87, PR dir 1987–89, gp business dir 1989–91; md and chm De Facto Consultants Ltd 1991–98 (managed PR launch of Dolly the sheep), princ conslt Charles Consultants 1991–2004, chief exec HCC De Facto Gp plc 1997–2001, fndr and ceo Northbank Communications Ltd 2002–; non-exec chm Bang Communications Ltd 1991–99; dir: Genus Communications Ltd 1994–97, BioScape Ltd 1994–97, Int Career Alternatives for Scientists 2001–03, Axia Therapeutics Ltd 2002–04; MCIM, MCIPR; *Style*— Mrs Susan Charles; ✉ Northbank Communications, 85 Tottenham Court Road, London W1T 4TQ

CHARLES, Hon Mr Justice; Sir (Arthur) William Hessin Charles; kt (1998); s of Arthur Attwood Sinclair Charles (d 2001), and Dr May Davies Charles, *née* Westerman (d 2005), of Frith Common, Worcs; *b* 25 March 1948; *Educ* Malvern Coll, Christ's Coll Cambridge (MA); *m* 22 June 1974, Lydia Margaret, da of John Barlow Ainscow, of Ambleside, Cumbria; 1 s (Simon b 1980), 1 da (Florence b 1983); *Career* called to the Bar Lincoln's Inn 1971; jr counsel to the Crown Chancery 1986–89, first jr counsel to the Treasy in Chancery matters 1989–98, judge of the High Court of Justice (Family Div) 1998–; *Recreations* golf, tennis; *Clubs* Hawks' (Cambridge), Denham Golf; *Style*— The Hon Mr Justice Charles; ✉ c/o Royal Courts of Justice, The Strand, London WC2A 2LL

CHARLESWORTH, David Anthony; s of David Harold Charlesworth, MBE (d 1970), and Jessie Vilma, *née* Waldron (d 1970); *b* 19 July 1936; *Educ* Haileybury and ISC; *m* 1970 (m dis 1975), Carol Ann, *née* Green; partner Charles David Micklewright FRSA (civil partnership, 2005); *Career* Capt RAPC; dir and sec: Sika Contracts Group of Cos 1965–76, Surban Trading Co Ltd 1968–; dir: SGB Group 1973–76, Johnson and Avon Ltd 1977–82, Michael Ashby Fine Art Ltd 1978–84, NHM Agency Holdings Ltd 1982–91, Michael Watson (Management) Ltd 1983–87, P J Dewey (Agencies) Co 1983–91, Shaftesbury Mews Co Ltd 1984–97 and 2006–, Nelson Hurst & Marsh Agencies Ltd 1985–90, Jardine (Lloyd's Agencies) 1990–91, Rimmer Properties Limited 1990–92, Glenrand Marsh Ltd 1992–95, Andrew Wallas & Marsh Ltd 1994–98; underwriting memb of Lloyd's 1975–2002; memb Eurotunnel Shareholder Ctee 2002–06; tstee Mickworth Charitable Tst 2004–; *Recreations* listening to Mozart, motorcycling, reading biographies; *Clubs* IOD; *Style*— David Charlesworth, Esq; ✉ 1 Shaftesbury Mews, Stratford Road, London W8 6QR (tel 020 7937 3550)

CHARLTON, (Richard Wingate) Edward; s of Col Wingate Charlton, OBE, DL, of Great Canfield Park, Takeley, Essex, and Angela Margot, *née* Windle; *b* 3 May 1948; *Educ* Eton, Univ of Neuchâtel; *m* 1 Feb 1979, Claudine Marie Germaine, da of Maître Hubert Maringe (d 1988), of Champlin, Premery, Nievre, France; 1 s (Andrew b 9 Nov 1981), 2 da (Emma b 29 Sept 1985, Jessica b 28 April 1989); *Career* Frere Cholmeley & Co Slrs 1968–73, Swales & Co Slrs 1974–76, Hambros Bank 1977–81, exec dir Banque Paribas London 1981–88, md Banque Internationale à Luxembourg London 1988–; various co directorships; slr of the Supreme Court 1976; Freeman City of London, memb Ct of Assts Worshipful Co of Merchant Taylors; MInstD; *Recreations* various active sports, cinema and family pursuits; *Clubs* White's, Turf, City of London; *Style*— Edward Charlton, Esq

CHARLTON, (William Wingate) Hugo; s of Lt Col D R W G Collins-Charlton, OBE, MBE, DL, and Angela Margot, *née* Windle; *b* 23 September 1951; *Educ* Eton, Univ of York (BA); *m* 1, 21 Oct 1978 (m dis 1984); m 2, 21 July 1994, Jane Louise, da of Donald Frank Sidnell; 2 da (Lavinia Sophie b 1 May 1997, Isabella Alice b 16 June 1999); *Career* called to the Bar Gray's Inn 1978; Distillers Co 1977–84, in practice as barrister 1986–; Inns of Court and City Yeomanry 1987–94; Green Pty: law offr 1991–97, home affairs spokesman 1998–2005, chair 2003–05; dir Social, Ethical and Environmental Fndn (SEEF) 2000–; memb: Criminal Bar Assoc, Environmental Law Fndn; govr of the Royal Humane Society; Freeman: City of London, Worshipful Co of Merchant Taylors; *Publications* A Guide to Council Tax Appeals; *Recreations* riding, skiing, scuba, hermetism; *Style*— Hugo Charlton, Esq; ✉ 1 Gray's Inn Square, London WC1R 5AA (tel 020 7405 8946, e-mail hugo@gn.apc.org)

CHARLTON, Louise; da of John Charlton, and Patricia Mary Crawford, *née* Hulme; *b* 25 May 1960; *m* 1985, Andrew, s of David Durant; 2 s (Sam b 10 Sept 1991, Jack b 14 Feb 1996), 1 da (Olivia b 16 Aug 1993); *Career* Broadstreet Associates 1984–87, founding ptnr Brunswick Group Ltd 1987– (sr ptnr 2004–); *Recreations* family; *Style*— Ms Louise Charlton; ✉ Brunswick Group Ltd, 15–17 Lincoln's Inn Fields, London WC2A 3ED (tel 020 7404 5959, fax 020 7831 2823)

CHARLTON, Mervyn; s of Rowland Charlton (d 1986), of Warwick, and Madge Louise, *née* Eaton; *b* 2 July 1945; *Educ* Loughton Coll of FE (Art Fndn Course), Nottingham Art Coll; *m* 1982, Ann, da of John James Hewitson; 1 s (Conrad Alexander b 1 March 1986); *Career* artist-in-residence: Holly Head Jr Sch (South Hill Park Artist in Schs Project) 1981, Guildford House 1983, Hammond Middle Sch Surrey (in conjunction with SE Arts) 1994, Windlesham Village Infant Sch (sponsored by SE Arts)1996, Long Cross Sch Slough 1996, ATD Fourth World Charity (workshops and exhbn) 1998–99, St Catherine's Sch Bramley 2001, BBC Big Arts Week Thames Ditton Junior Sch 2002; Gulbenkian Printmaker award 1983; *Solo Exhibitions* Moira Kelly Fine Art 1981 and 1982, Festival Gallery Bath 1983, Sally Hunter/Patrick Seale Fine Art 1985, Anne Berthoud Gallery 1988, Sally Hunter Fine Art 1989, South Hill Park Arts Centre Bracknell 1991, Boundary Art Gallery London 1992, The Economist London 1994, The Yehudi Menuhin Sch 1994, Lewis Elton Gallery Univ of Surrey Guildford 2004; *Group Exhibitions* incl: Metro Show (Docklands Art Gallery) 1980, London Summer Show (Whitechapel Art Gallery) 1980, Third and Fourth Nat Exhibition Tours (Tolly Cobbald) 1981 and 1983, Subjective Eye Midland Gp (Nottingham and tour) 1981–82, Leicestershire Schs Exhibition 1982, Whitechapel Open (Whitechapel Gallery) 1982, 1983 and 1984, The London Gp (Camden Arts Centre and tour) 1982, Eight in the Eighties (NY) 1983, Touring Exhibition of Hosps (City Gallery Milton Keynes, funded by Arts Cncl) 1983–84, Art for Schs (Gainsborough's House 1983 and Sackhouse Gallery Norwich 1984), Royal Academy Summer Exhibition 1984, Guildford House Summer Show Guildford 1984, London Group Show (RCA) 1984, Bath Festival Show 1984 and 1987, Curwen Gallery 1984, Open House (City Gallery Arts Tst Milton Keynes) 1984, Quintin Green Gallery London 1985, Side By Side (Nat Art Gallery Kuala Lumpur and Br Cncl tour) 1986, Vorpal Gallery (NY) 1987, The Circus Comes to Town (Northern Centre for Contemporary Art Sutherland and tour) 1987, Mixed Summer Show (Thumb Gallery) 1987–90, CAS Art Market (Smith's Gallery) 1990–91 and 1992, Boxes and Totems (England & Co) 1990, Ikon Gallery Group Touring Exhibition 1991, Leleco Art Gallery London 1991, 1st Reading Arts Festival 1992, Touch of Red (Boundary Gallery London) 1992, Art for Sale (Whiteleys, in conjunction with The Guardian) 1992–93, Contemporary Art Fair London 1993, Royal Acad Summer Exhibition London 1993, The New Ashgate Gallery 1993, Interiors (Open Show Towner Art Gallery Eastbourne) 1993, Christmas Show (Boundary Gallery) 1993, East West Gallery London 1993, New Collectables (Stormont Studio Rye) 1994, CAS Festival Hall London 1994, FARA Romanian Appeal Bonhams London 1994, The Colour Blue Boundary Gallery London 1995, ojects of obsession (Boundary Gallery) 1996, Strange Encounters (Sally Hunter Fine Art London) 1996, Working Images (Archiutti and Cable & Wireless London), Manifestation - Borderlands & Two By Four Studios Surrey 1998, Christmas Show Boundary Gallery London 1998, Art Fair Business Design Centre Boundary Gallery 1998–2000, 50over50 (Univ of Brighton) 2006, Brian Sinfield Gallery Burford 2006, Plumbline Gallery St Ives 2006; *Work in Collections* incl: BP, Unilever, Euro Parl Luxembourg, Leics Schs, Blond Fine Art, Guildford House, Nat Art Gallery Kuala Lumpur, South East Arts, Halton Roy Productions/Howard Guard Productions, England & Co Art Gallery, Electra Management Trust Ltd, Lady Antonia Fraser, Lady Patricia Gibberd, Tim Sayer, Nancy Balfour, Coopers & Lybrand, Boundary Gallery, The Economist Building London, John Allen, Peter Dicks, Avia Willment, Standerwick Court, Freshfields Bruckhaus Deringer; *Publications* subject of articles in publications incl Apollo, London Portrait, Artscribe, Arts Review and Art Monthly; *Recreations* interest in non-western belief systems and their religious expressions and in exotic art in general, walking, travel, reading; *Style*— Mervyn Charlton, Esq; ✉ 1 Rose Cottages, Downside Bridge Road, Cobham, Surrey KT11 3EJ (tel 01932 864899)

CHARLTON, Peter John; s of J V Charlton (d 2001), and S M Charlton; *b* 16 December 1955; *Educ* Royal GS Newcastle upon Tyne, UCL (LLB), Coll of Law; *m* 1980, Rosemary, *née* Markham; 2 s (Christopher b June 1983, John b Oct 1984), 1 da (Elizabeth b Aug 1987); *Career* Clifford Chance LLP (formerly Coward Chance): articled clerk 1979, corp fin ptnr 1986, managing ptnr corp London 1993, managing ptnr London region 2000–05, global head of corporate practice 2005–; winner Ptnr of the Year The Lawyer Awards 2001; involved with numerous orgns incl London First and Br Chilean C of C; memb Law Soc 1979; *Recreations* golf, travel; *Style*— Peter Charlton, Esq; ✉ Clifford Chance, 10 Upper Bank Street, London E14 5JJ (tel 020 7006 1217, fax 020 7600 5555, e-mail peter.charlton@cliffordchance.com)

CHARLTON, Philip; OBE (1987); s of late George Charlton, of Chester, and Lottie, *née* Little (d 1976); *b* 31 July 1930; *Educ* City GS Chester; *m* 27 June 1953, Jessie, da of Joseph Boulton (d 1966), of Chester; 1 da (Margaret b 1959), 1 s (Philip John b 1962); *Career* Nat Serv RN 1947–49; gen mangr: Chester Savings Bank 1966–75, TSB Wales and Border Counties 1975–81; chief gen mangr Central Bd Trustee Savings Bank 1982–83 (dep chief gen mangr 1981–82); dir: TSB Computer Services (Wythenshawe) Ltd 1976–81, TSB Trust Co Ltd 1979–82, TSB Holdings Ltd 1982–86, TSB Group Computer Services Ltd 1981–84, Central Trustee Savings Bank 1982–86; chief gen mangr TSB England and Wales 1983–85, dir TSB England and Wales 1985–87, gp chief exec TSB Group plc 1986–89 (non-exec dep chm 1990–91), chm Philip Charlton Associates Ltd 1991–96; vice-pres Inst of Bankers 1991– (memb Cncl 1982–, dep chm 1988–89, pres 1990–91); memb Bd of Admin: Int Savings Banks Inst Geneva 1985–91 (vice-pres 1985–91), Euro Savings Bank Gp Brussels 1989–91; FCIB, CIMgt, FRSA; *Clubs* Chester City, RAC; *Style*— Philip Charlton, Esq, OBE; ✉ 62 Quinta Drive, Arkley, Hertfordshire EN5 3BE (tel 020 8440 4477)

CHARLTON, Susannah Karen; da of Bryan Michael Charlton, and Valerie, *née* Henderson; *Educ* Fairfield GS Bristol, Sorbonne, UCL (BA), Birkbeck Coll London (Cert), Bartlett Sch of Architecture UCL (MSc); *Career* editorial asst rising to sr ed QPD (first UK paperback book club) then managing ed World Books Book Club Assocs 1982–96, publisher Telegraph Books 1997–2002, mangr guidebooks English Heritage 2002–04, publisher (books and RHS online) Royal Horticultural Soc 2004–; dir Twentieth Century Soc; memb Nat Tst; memb Soc of Bookmen 2000; *Recreations* travel, history of art and architecture, swimming, walking, theatre, gardening, reading; *Clubs* Union; *Style*— Ms Susannah Charlton; ✉ Royal Horticultural Society, 80 Vincent Square, London SW1P 2PE

CHARMLEY, John Denis; s of John Charmley (d 1977), and Doris, *née* Halliwell (d 1990); *b* 9 November 1955; *Educ* Rock Ferry HS, Pembroke Coll Oxford (open scholar, MA, A M P Read scholar, DPhil); *m* 1, 1977 (m dis 1992), Ann Dorothea; 3 s (Gervase Nicholas Edward, Gerard Timothy John (twins) b 8 Jan 1980, Christian Francis Robin (Kit) b 14 June 1989); m 2, 1992 (m dis 2003), Lorraine, da of K G Charles, MBE; *Career* UEA: lectr 1979–93, sr lectr 1993–96, reader in English history 1996–98, prof of modern history 1998–, dean Sch of History 2002–; visiting fell Churchill Coll Cambridge 1985, Fulbright prof Westminster Coll Fulton MO 1992–93; scriptwriter Peace In Our Time (Channel 4) 1989; pres Norfolk and Norwich Historical Assoc, chm Mid Norfolk Cons Assoc, vice-chair Cons History Gp 2003–; FRHistS 1986; *Books* Duff Cooper (1986, Yorkshire Post Best First Book Prize 1986), Lord Lloyd and the Decline of the British Empire (1987), Chamberlain and the Lost Peace (1989), Churchill - The End of Glory (1993), Churchill's Grand Alliance (1995), A History of Conservative Politics 1900–1996 (1996), Splendid Isolation? (1999); *Recreations* reading, writing letters, dining out; *Clubs* Norfolk; *Style*— Prof John Charmley; ✉ c/o Felicity Bryan, 2A North Parade, Oxford OX2 6PE (tel 01865 513816)

CHARNLEY, William Francis; s of Louis Charnley, and Pauline Mary Charnley; *b* 21 August 1960; *Educ* Rivington and Blackrod GS, Bolton Inst of Technol (HND), Sheffield City Poly (Postgrad Dip Co Admin), Lancaster Univ (LLB), Manchester Poly (Law Soc Finals), Univ of Cambridge (MA); *m* 1999, Kathryn Patricia, da of James Mylrea, of Toronto, Canada; 1 s (Piers Augustus William b 21 Sept 1999), 1 da (Henrietta Blythe Venetia b 14 June 2001); *Career* articled clerk Slater Heelis 1985–87, corp fin ptnr Booth & Co Leeds 1989–94 (slr 1987–89), corp fin ptnr Corp Dept Simmons & Simmons 1994–98, ptnr London office McDermott Will & Emery 1998–; dir C D Bramall plc 2000–04; city fell Hughes Hall Cambridge 2003–; chm External Devpt Bd Lancaster Univ 2002–; tstee Children's Heart Surgery Fund (charity) 1992–2001; memb Appeals Ctee Canine Partners, memb Advsy Bd Grange Park Opera; memb Assoc of Lancastrians in London; memb Guild of Int Bankers; Freeman City of London; Liveryman: Worshipful Co of Drapers, Worshipful Co of Slrs, Worshipful Co of Chartered Secretaries and Administrators; memb Law Soc 1987, FCIS; *Recreations* Scottish Impressionist art, keeping fit, country pursuits, music, food, wine; *Clubs* City of London, Brooks's, Pingus, Jockey Club Rooms; *Style*— William Charnley, Esq; ✉ McDermott Will & Emery UK LLP, 7 Bishopsgate, London EC2N 1AR (tel 020 7577 6910, fax 020 7577 6950 e-mail wcharnley@europe.mwe.com)

CHARNOCK, (Frederick) Mark Luckhoff; s of Frederick Niven Charnock, of Cape Town, South Africa, and Alta Anna, *née* Luckhoff; *b* 20 June 1945; *Educ* Diocesan Coll Cape Town, Univ of Cape Town (MB ChB); *m* 8 April 1970, Margaret Isobel, da of Frances Neale Murray, of Cape Town, South Africa; 1 da (Annabel b 1982), 1 s (Alasdair b 1984); *Career* house offr: Queen Charlotte's Hosp 1971, Samaritan Hosp 1975–76; registrar and sr registrar Bart's 1977–80; currently: conslt obstetrician and gynaecologist Radcliffe and Churchill Hosp Oxford, hon sr lectr Univ of Oxford; examiner: RCOGS, RCS, Univs of Oxford, Cambridge, and London; memb and cncllr: RCOG 1983–89, RCS; sec: Section O & G RSM 1989–90, Br Gynaecological Cancer Soc 1999–; Liveryman Worshipful Soc of Apothecaries 1989, Freeman City of London 1985; FRCS (Eng), FRCS(Ed), FRCOG; *Recreations* tennis, skiing, reading, opera, art; *Style—* Mark Charnock, Esq; ✉ Manor Farm House, Bletchingdon, Oxfordshire OX5 3DP (tel 01869 350149); The Manor Hospital, Beech Road, Headington, Oxford OX3 7RP (tel 01869 350451, fax 01869 350728)

CHARTER, HE Joseph Stephen; s of late Vivian Charter, and late Daphne, *née* Baptiste; *b* 26 December 1943, Grenada; *Educ* Univ of London (BEd); *m* 30 July 1968, Aileen Valerie, *née* Cox; 3 s (Mervyn b 8 June 1969, Jason b 27 May 1975, Stephen b 8 June 1983), 1 da (Gillian b 5 March 1971); *Career* Grenadian diplomat; HM Forces (Royal Signals) 1966–70; teacher: Edith Cavell Sch, Haverstock Sch Business & Enterprise Coll; dep princ Alleyne Sch Barbados 1979–80, chief of educn Grenada 1980, ambass to Libya 1982–84, perm sec Ministries of Health, Social Servs, Foreign Affrs and Educn 1995–2004, high cmmr to UK 2005–; lectr in Caribbean studies St George's Univ Grenada 2003–05; chm Nat Insurance Scheme Grenada; vice-pres Grenada Chamber of Industry and Commerce 1991–95; *Recreations* music, sport; *Clubs* Rotary; *Style—* HE Mr Joseph Charter; ✉ 93 Dale Wood Road, Petts Wood BR6 0BY (tel 01689 822632); Grenada High Commission, The Chapel, Archel Road, West Kensington, London W14 9QH (tel 020 7385 4415, fax 020 7381 4807, e-mail grenada@high-commission.demon.co.uk)

CHARTRES, Rt Rev Richard John Carew; *see:* London, Bishop of

CHARVIS, Colin Lloyd; s of Lloyd Charvis, and Lynné Charvis; *b* 27 December 1972, Sutton Coldfield; *Educ* Queen Mary's GS for Boys Birmingham; *Career* rugby union player; memb: London Welsh RFC 1991–95, Swansea RFC 1995–2003, Tarbes France 2003–04, Newcastle Falcons 2004–06, Newport-Gwent Dragons 2006–; Wales: under 21s 1994, Wales A (2 caps), Wales 7s 1994–97, nat team 1996– (84 caps, memb squad World Cup 1999 (scored opening try of tournament v Argentina), capt tour South Africa, memb squad World Cup Aust 2003, winners Six Nations Championship 2005); memb Br Lions tour Aust 2001 (2 caps); *Recreations* mountain biking, scuba diving (PADI qualified), water skiing, hill walking, Bilbo (5 year old German Shepherd); *Style—* Mr Colin Charvis

CHASE, Prof Howard Allaker; s of Peter Howard Chase, and Phoebe Farrar Chase; *b* 17 November 1954; *Educ* Westminster, Magdalene Coll Cambridge (exhibitioner, Bundy scholarship, Mynors Bright prize, MA, PhD), Univ of Cambridge (ScD); *Career* with Gen Electric Co 1971–72; Univ of Cambridge: postdoctoral res asst Dept of Biochemistry 1978–81, res fell St John's Coll 1978–82, res assoc Dept of Chemical Engrg 1982–83, lectr in chemical engrg 1986–96 (asst lectr 1984–86), reader in biochemical engrg 1996–2000, head Dept of Chemical Engrg 1998–2006, prof of biochemical engrg 2000– (personal professorship); Magdalene Coll Cambridge: bye-fell 1977–78, fell 1984–, dir of studies in chemical engrg and lectr in natural sciences 1984–, tutor for grad students 1987–93, sr tutor 1993–96, tutor 1996–98; Dept of Chemical and Biochemical Engrg UCL: visiting prof 1991–92, hon res fell 1993–; external examiner: Dept of Chemical Engrg Univ of Bradford 2001–05, Sch of Chemical Engrg and Advanced Materials Univ of Newcastle upon Tyne 2003–05; memb Engrg and Biological Systems Directorate Network Gp BBSRC, memb EPSRC assessment panels; memb Editorial Bd: Biotechnology and Bioengineering, Jl of Bioscience and Bioengineering; conslt to firms with interests in biochemical engrg; SERC Advanced Fellowship 1983 (not taken up), Royal Soc 1983 Univ Res Fellowship 1983–84 (at Dept of Chemical Engrg Univ of Cambridge), Sir George Beilby Medal and Prize Soc of Chemical Industry, RSC and Inst of Metals 1993, BOC Environmental Award IChemE Awards 2001; fell Philosophical Soc Cambridge; CEng, CChem, CSci, MRSC 1987, MIBiol 1991, FIChemE 1998, FREng 2005; *Publications* author of numerous articles published in learned jls; *Recreations* food and drink, travel; *Clubs* The Pickprops (Cambridge); *Style—* Prof Howard Chase; ✉ Magdalene College, Cambridge CB3 0AG (tel 01223 332128); Department of Chemical Engineering, University of Cambridge, Pembroke Street, Cambridge CB2 3RA (tel 01223 334799, fax 01223 334796, e-mail hac1000@cam.ac.uk)

CHASE, Robert Henry Armitage; s of Philip Martin Chase (d 1987), of Foxley, Norfolk, and Jean Alison, *née* Barr (d 1976); *b* 10 March 1945; *Educ* Ipswich Sch; *m* 1972, Moya, da of Dr William Jones (d 1985), of Shotley Bridge, Co Durham; 2 s (Patrick William Armitage b 1975, Thomas Martin b 1986), 1 da (Ella Kathleen b 1977); *Career* chartered accountant; Voluntary Serv Nigeria 1963; articled clerk Lovewell Blake & Co Norwich 1964–69, with Cooper Brothers London and Kenya 1969–76, fin dir Mackenzie (Kenya) Ltd 1976, asst md GEC Hong Kong 1982–86 (fin dir 1981–82), chief fin offr Orient Overseas (Holdings) Ltd 1986–89, dir Furness Withy & Co Ltd 1987–90, gp md and memb Ctee Automobile Assoc 1990–97, non-exec dir London Transport 1996–99; ceo Albert Abela Gp 2002–03; chm Intelligent Processing Solutions Ltd 2007–; chm International Assoc of Financial Executives Insts 1995; Liveryman Worshipful Co of Information Technologists 1990, Freeman City of London 1991; FCA 1969, MCT 1984; *Recreations* golf, shooting, vintage automobiles; *Clubs* Hong Kong; *Style—* Robert Chase, Esq; ✉ Garden Cottage, Upper Farringdon, Alton, Hampshire GU34 3DT (e-mail bob.chase@btopenworld.com)

CHASE, Rodney Frank; CBE (2000); *m* Diana; 2 s; *Career* BP plc: joined 1964, various appts with BP Shipping, Refining & Marketing, Distribution, Oil Trading, Gas, Finance and Strategic Planning, chief exec BP Finance and gp treas (incl t/o of Standard Oil and Britoil), chief exec Western Hemisphere BP Exploration Inc and exec vice-pres/chief financial offr BP America Inc until 1992, an md The BP Co plc 1992–98 (i/c Western Hemisphere region and chief exec BP Exploration/Production), dep gp chief exec 1998–2003; chm Petrofac 2005–, dep chm Tesco plc 2004– (non-exec dir 2002–); non-exec dir: Diageo plc 1999, Computer Sciences Corp 2001; sr advsr Lehman Bros; FCT; *Recreations* golf, downhill skiing; *Style—* Rodney Chase, Esq, CBE

CHASSAY, Tchaik; s of Arthur Arcade Chassay (d 1970), and Margot Epstein; *b* 14 September 1942; *m* 1975, Melissa North; 1 s (Clancy), 1 da (Dixie); *Career* architect; year out (AA) Ram Karmi Associates Tel Aviv; Edward Cullinan Architects 1969–81 (latterly sr ptnr), fndr Tchaik Chassay Architects 1982, co-fndr (with Malcolm Last) Chassay + Last Architects 1997; co-fndr: Zanzibar Club (1975), 192 Restaurant (1982), The Groucho Club (1984); vice-pres AA 1986–; former lectr and visiting tutor: Faculty of Architecture Univ of Cambridge, Bristol and Hull Univs, Oxford and Thames Polys, AA; former external examiner Dept of Architecture and Interior Design RCA, currently external examiner Univ of Central England Birmingham; assessor Civic Tst Awards 1981 and 1983; *Recreations* travel, tennis; *Clubs* Groucho; *Style—* Mr Tchaik Chassay; ✉ Chassay + Last Architects, Berkeley Works, Berkley Grove, London NW1 8XY (tel 020 7483 7700)

CHASSELS, (James) David Simpson; s of Robert Brown Chassels, and Frances Amelia, *née* Simpson; *b* 2 April 1947; *Educ* Rannoch Sch; *m* 21 May 1976, Angela Elizabeth, da of James Nicol Martin Bulloch; 2 s (Ross b 30 Nov 1977, Scott b 29 March 1980), 1 da (Nicola b 28 Feb 1983); *Career* articled clerk then chartered accountant French & Cowan Glasgow 1965–70, Arthur Young Edinburgh 1970–74, investment exec 3i (formerly ICFC) Glasgow & Edinburgh 1974–81, dir 3i Corporate Finance 1981–93, ptnr BDO Binder Hamlyn CAs Glasgow 1993–95; fndr Procession plc 1994 (initially chm, now ceo and dep chm); memb Cncl ICAS 1993–97; govr Rannoch Sch 1972–2000, memb Polmont Borstal Visiting Ctee 1978–83; former Deacon Incorporation of Barbers Trades House of Glasgow 1985–86; MICAS 1973; *Recreations* sailing, skiing; *Clubs* RSAC, CCC (hon treas 1993–97); *Style—* David Chassels, Esq; ✉ 10 Duart Drive, Newton Mearns, Glasgow G77 5DS (tel 0141 639 3914, e-mail david.chassels@btinternet.com)

CHASTNEY, John Garner; s of Alec Richardson Chastney (d 1981), and Constance May, *née* Edwards (d 1983); *b* 5 January 1947; *Educ* Henry Mellish GS Nottingham, Lancaster Univ (MA); *m* 4 Aug 1973, Susan Thirza, da of Norman Dunkerley; 1 da (Catherine Jane b 1978), 2 s (Martin Richard b 1980, David Paul b 1982); *Career* CA; princ lectr Sheffield Hallam Univ 1974–79, currently ptnr Mazars (sr nat trg mangr 1979–83, devpt ptnr 1983–88, head Consultancy Div 1990–94), on secondment as under sec DTI/dir Industrial Devpt Unit 1988–90; former memb Bd of Funding Agency for Schs, sometime external examiner London Met Univ, advised Sec of State on sale of The Independent newspaper, advsr to Ofgem on price control review of Transco plc, memb London Weighting Advsy Panel; prize essayist; chm of govrs secdy sch London Borough of Tower Hamlets; FCA 1973; *Books* True and Fair View (1974), European Financial Reporting: The Netherlands (with J H Beeny, 1976); *Recreations* people, building, design, gardening; *Style—* John Chastney, Esq; ✉ Mazars, 24 Bevis Marks, London EC3A 7NR (tel 020 7220 3337, fax 020 7220 3437, e-mail john.chastney@mazars.co.uk)

CHATAWAY, Mark Denys; s of Rt Hon Sir Christopher Chataway, and Anna Maria, *née* Lett; *b* 21 March 1960; *Educ* Troy State Univ Alabama (BSc), NY Univ (MSc); *Career* programme dir WRNG Atlanta USA 1980–82, exec prodr WMCA NY 1982–83, dir of communications GMHC (the AIDS Serv and Educn Fndn USA) 1983–84, vice-pres heading Med Info Div Van Vechten and Associates NY 1984–87; Hill and Knowlton (UK): dir Special Servs Div 1987–89, md Mktg Communications Div 1990, md Eurosciences Communications Div 1991–93; princ Interscience Communications 1993–2000, chm Baird's Communication Mgmnt Conslts Ltd 2002–, advsr Int AIDS Vaccine Initiative 1996–, memb Scientific Advsy Gp Population Scis Div Rockefeller Fndn NY 1997–2001, sr cnsllr Edelman Health Europe 2000–, Bd of Ambassadors Nat AIDS Tst 2001–, conslt World Vision Int 2002–, advsr Population Programme Hewlett Fndn 2003–, memb Govt of SA Review Panel on Vaccines 2007; former freelance TV journalist for Turner Broadcasting/CNN (US) and TV-AM, former freelance radio assignments for BBC, Ind Radio News (UK), CBS and Capital Radio (South Africa); author of feature or news articles for various UK and US publications; memb Sardis Chapel Ynysddu; memb Chartered Inst of Journalists; *Recreations* physical fitness, languages, running, church activities; *Clubs* Frontline, Royal Over-Seas League; *Style—* Mark Chataway, Esq; ✉ Baird's Communication Management Consultants Ltd, 34 Heol Maindee, Cwmfelinfach, Ynysddu, Casnewydd NP11 7HR (tel 01495 200321)

CHATER, Keith Frederick; s of Frederick Ernest Chater (d 1987), of Croydon, Surrey, and Marjorie Inez, *née* Palmer; *b* 23 April 1944; *Educ* Trinity Sch of John Whitgift, Univ of Birmingham (BSc, PhD); *m* 1966, Jean, da of Frederick Arthur Wallbridge, and Ellen, *née* Bennett (d 1998); 1 da (Alison Clare b 23 April 1970), 3 s (Simon Frederick b 24 Sept 1972, Julian David b 17 July 1978, Timothy Felix b 8 Aug 1980); *Career* John Innes Centre (formerly John Innes Inst): scientist 1969–, dep head 1989–98, head Genetics Dept 1998–2001, head Molecular Microbiology Dept 2001–04, emeritus fell 2004–; hon prof: UEA 1988, Chinese Acad of Sciences Inst of Microbiology 1998, Huazhong Agric Univ 2000, Newcastle Univ 2006; Fulbright scholar Harvard Univ 1983, Fred Griffith Review Lecture (Soc for Gen Microbiology) 1997, Leeuwenhoek Lecture (Royal Soc) 2005; memb: Soc for Gen Microbiology 1975, CND, Norfolk and Norwich Naturalists Assoc, Norfolk Contemporary Art Soc, RSPB, Nat Tst, Friends of the Royal Academy; FRS 1995; *Books* Genetic Manipulation of Streptomyces (one of 10 co-authors, 1985), Genetics of Bacterial Diversity (jt ed with Prof Sir D A Hopwood, *qv*, 1989), Practical Streptomyces Genetics (one of five co-authors, 2000); *Recreations* bird-watching, art, gardening, cooking; *Style—* Prof Keith Chater, FRS; ✉ 6 Coach House Court, Norwich NR4 7QR (tel 01603 506145); John Innes Centre, Norwich Research Park, Colney, Norwich NR4 7UH (tel 01603 450297, fax 01603 450778, e-mail keith.chater@bbsrc.ac.uk)

CHATER, Stephen Paul; s of John Charles Chater, of Northallerton, N Yorks, and Patricia Norby, *née* Oakes; *b* 2 March 1956; *Educ* Hartlepool GS, ChCh Oxford (MA); *m* 10 Sept 1988, Susan Frances Margaret, da of late Charles Harborne Stuart, of Combe, Oxon; 1 s (Anthony Charles Thomas b 10 Aug 1996); *Career* slr; ptnr: Allen & Overy 1989–2003 (articled 1979–81, asst slr 1981–88), Addleshaw Goddard 2006– (conslt 2003–06); memb: Law Soc, Soc of Genealogists, Durham CCC; *Recreations* music, genealogy, cricket; *Style—* Stephen Chater, Esq; ✉ Addleshaw Goddard LLP, 150 Aldersgate Street, London EC1A 4EJ (tel 020 7606 8855, fax 020 7606 4390)

CHATFIELD, 2 Baron (1937 UK); Ernle David Lewis Chatfield; s of 1 Baron Chatfield, GCB, OM, KCMG, CVO, PC (Admiral of the Fleet, d 1967); *b* 2 January 1917; *Educ* Dartmouth, Trinity Coll Cambridge; *m* 16 May 1969, (Felicia Mary) Elizabeth, da of late Dr John Roderick Bulman, of Hereford; *Career* ADC to Govr-Gen of Canada 1940–44; *Style—* The Rt Hon the Lord Chatfield

CHATTERJEE, Mira; da of Dr Haradlan Chatterjee (Capt IMS/IAMC SEAC, Burma Star), of Chigwell, Essex, and Kamala, *née* Banerjee; *b* 19 April 1948; *Educ* City of London Sch for Girls; *m* 19 April 1980, Dr Gautam Chaudhuri, s of Dr Punendu Chandhuri, of Calcutta; 1 da (Sarada b 28 Jan 1981); *Career* called to the Bar Middle Temple 1973, in practice SE circuit; chm Eastwards Tst; memb Guild of Scholars; FRSA; *Recreations* reading, philosophy; *Clubs* Wig and Pen, Chigwell Rotary; *Style—* Miss Mira Chatterjee; ✉ 4 Brick Court, Middle Temple, London EC4Y 9AD (tel 020 7797 8910, fax 020 7797 8929)

CHATTERTON DICKSON, HE Robert Maurice French; *b* 1 February 1962; *m* 1995, Teresa Bargielska Albor; 2 da, 1 step da, 1 step s; *Career* diplomat; former investment analyst and portfolio mangr Morgan Grenfell Asset Management Ltd, entered HM Dip Serv 1990, Security Policy Dept FCO 1990–91, second sec (Chancery and info) Manila 1991–94, SE Asian Dept FCO 1994–95, UN Dept FCO 1995–96, first sec (press and public affrs) Washington 1997–98, private sec to HM Ambass Washington 1998–2000, Security Policy Dept FCO 2000–03, Iraq Policy Unit FCO 2003, ambass to Macedonia 2004–; *Style—* HE Mr Robert Chatterton Dickson; ✉ c/o Foreign & Commonwealth Office (Skopje), King Charles Street, London SW1A 2AH

CHATTINGTON, Barry John; s of John William Chattington (d 1967), of Kent, and Rose Amelia, *née* Darlington; *b* 24 April 1947; *Educ* Dartford Tech High Sch; *Career* film ed 1963–66, film dir 1972–; md: Goldcrest Facilities Ltd 1988, Elstree Studios, Roger Cherrill Ltd, Cherry Video Ltd 1991; chm: Renaissance Productions Ltd, Money Spark Ltd; works incl: numerous long and short films for Paul McCartney, Pink Floyd and others, drama series for US TV, major documentary for Kuwait TV, charity films with the Prince of Wales and the Princess Royal; memb Br Kinematograph Sound & TV Soc 1963; chm: Directors' Guild of GB 1985–86, Producers' and Directors' Section ACTT 1985–86; Br delegate on Federation Européene des Industries Techniques de l'Image et du Son; *Awards* 4 Golden Halos from S Calif Motion Picture Cncl, Silver award NY Int Film and TV Festival 1982, numerous D&AD commendations, nomination Best Design BAFTA Interactive 1999; *Publications* David Lean: An Intimate Portrait (2001); *Clubs* Groucho, Variety, Reform, Chelsea Arts; *Style—* Barry Chattington, Esq; ✉ mobile 07831 570516, e-mail barry_chattington@hotmail.com

CHATTO, Lady Sarah Frances Elizabeth; *née* Armstrong-Jones; *see: Royal Family Section*

CHAUDHURI, Amit Prakash; s of Nages Chandra Chaudhuri, and Bijoya, *née* Nandi Majumdar; *b* 15 May 1962; *Educ* Cathedral and John Connon Sch Bombay, UCL (BA), Balliol Coll Oxford (Dervorguilla scholar, DPhil); *m* 12 Dec 1991, Rosinka Shubhasree, da of Shiva Ranjan Khastgir; *Career* writer; Harper-Wood studentship for English poetry and literature St John's Coll Cambridge 1992–93, Creative Arts fell Wolfson Coll Oxford 1992–95, Leverhulme special research fell Faculty of English Univ of Cambridge 1997–99; fiction and poetry have appeared in London Review of Books, The Observer, London Magazine and Oxford Poetry; contrib articles and reviews to TLS, London Review of Books, The Guardian, The Observer, The Spectator, Vogue, The New Yorker, Granta and other jls; bursary Kathleen Blundell Trust; Arts Cncl Writers Award 1994; trained singer N Indian classical tradition (released albums on HMV 1992 and 1994); *Books* A Strange and Sublime Address (1991, Betty Trask Award Soc of Authors, runner-up Guardian Fiction Award, Cwlth Writer's Prize for Best First Book (Eurasia)), Noon in Calcutta (contrib, anthology, 1992), New Writing 2 (contrib, British Cncl anthology, eds Malcolm Bradbury and Andrew Motion, 1993), Afternoon Raag (1993, Encore Award Soc of Authors 1994, Southern Arts Lit Prize 1994, runner-up Guardian Fiction Award 1993), Vintage Book of Indian Writing: 1947–97 (ed with Salman Rushdie and Elizabeth West, 1997), Freedom Song (1998), Freedom Song: Three Novels (1999, Los Angeles Times Book Award for Fiction 2000), A New World (2000, Sahitya Akademi Award Govt of India 2002), Picador Book of Modern Indian Literature (ed, 2001), Real Time (short stories, 2002), D H Lawrence and Difference (2003); *Style*— Amit Chaudhuri, Esq; ✉ c/o Peter Straus, Rogers, Coleridge and White Ltd, 20 Powis Mews, London W11 1JN

CHAWLA, Dr Shanti Lal; s of Puran Chand Chawla, of Delhi, India, and Indra Wati Chawla; *b* 26 October 1936; *Educ* Univ of Delhi (BSc), Punjab Univ (LSMF, MB BS), Univ of London (DMRT), Dublin (FFRRCSI); *m* 12 May 1967, Mrs Kamlesh, da of Chuni Lal Monga, of New Delhi, India; 2 da (Sangita b 21 Feb 1971, Rita b 26 May 1972); *Career* house surgn Dayanand Med Hosp 1963–64, asst surgn Govt Dispensary Gurgoan 1964, res MO in med and surgery Tirath Ram Hosp Delhi 1966–67, asst surgn Govt Dispensary Delhi 1967–69, registrar in radiotherapy Cookridge Hosp Leeds 1971–72 (SHO 1969–71), sr registrar Catterbridge Hosp 1974–80 (registrar in radiotherapy 1972–74); S Cleveland Hosp: conslt in radiotherapy and oncology 1980–2001, head of dept 1980–91, clinical dir 1991–94; hon clinical lectr in radiotherapy Univ of Newcastle upon Tyne 1980–, hon conslt James Cork Univ Hosp Middlesbrough 2002, pt/t locum clinical conslt in clinical oncology Beetson Oncology Centre 2002–04; Stockton sec and md Teeside Health Care 1996–2003; Gold Award Northern RHA Newcastle upon Tyne 1990, Bronze Medallion ABI Medical Community Award Newcastle upon Tyne 1991; numerous pubns in jls; pres: Indian Assoc of Cleveland 1991 (pres 1987–89, vice-pres 1990), Indian Doctors of Cleveland 1993–98 (treas 1985–91, memb Exec Ctee 1998–); chm Local Negotiating Ctee SCH 1996–2001; treas Hindu Cultural Soc 1990– (sec 1985–89), memb various orgns of Middlesbrough Cncl; memb BMA, accredited memb LNC; MRCR, FRSM 2006; *Style*— Dr Shanti Chawla; ✉ 1 West Moor Close, Yarm, Cleveland TS15 9RG (tel 01642 786465)

CHAYTOR, David; MP; *Career* MP (Lab) Bury N 1997–; *Style*— David Chaytor, Esq, MP; ✉ House of Commons, London SW1A 0AA (tel 020 7219 3000)

CHEAL, (Martin) Jonathan (Cedric); s of Wilfrid Cheal (d 1987), of Sussex, and Barbara, *née* Ledgard; *b* 30 June 1950, Crawley, W Sussex; *Educ* Gt Walstead Sch Lindfield, St Lawrence Coll Ramsgate, L'École des Roches Verneuil, Coll of Law Chester and Guildford; *m* 11 July 1986, Miriam Diana, *née* Mead; 2 da (Diana Juliet b 28 June 1988, Hermione Claudia b 20 June 1990), 1 s (Henry Hugh Ogden b 2 July 1993); *Career* admitted slr 1976; slr specialising in agricultural property with particular interest in rights of way cases; slr Hong Kong 1976–82, legal advsr CLA 1983–87, ptnr Thring Townsend 1987– (currently head of agric); memb Ctee CLA, panel slr NFU; tstee Somerset Military Museum Tst, lay chm Lullington and Orchardleigh PCC; memb: Prayer Book Soc, Royal Soc of St George, Freedom Assoc, Campaign for Ind Britain, Democracy Movt; memb: Agric Law Assoc, Law Soc; *Books* as Pelham Witherspoon: The Drink-Spotty Book (1984), The High-Spotty Book (1985); *Recreations* stage, books, music, topography, military history, cricket; *Style*— Jonathan Cheal, Esq; ✉ Thring Townsend Solicitors, Midland Bridge, Bath, Somerset BA1 2HQ (tel 01225 340060, fax 01225 319735, e-mail jcheal@ttuk.com)

CHECKLAND, Sir Michael; kt (1992); s of Leslie Checkland, and Ivy Florence, *née* Bemand; *b* 13 March 1936; *Educ* King Edward's GS Fiveways Birmingham, Wadham Coll Oxford; *m* 1, 25 March 1960 (m dis 1983), Shirley Frances Corbett; 2 s (Philip Michael b 1962, Richard Bruce b 1965), 1 da (Helen Julia b 1968); m 2, 23 Oct 1987, Susan, da of Ernest Harold Walker, ISO; *Career* auditor Parkinson Cowan Ltd 1959–62, accountant Thorn Electronics 1962–64; BBC: sr cost accountant 1964–67, head of Central Finance Unit 1969–71, chief accountant Central Finance Services 1969–71, chief accountant TV 1971–76, fin controller 1976–77, controller planning and resource mgmnt TV 1977–82, dir of resources TV 1982–85, chm BBC Enterprises 1986–87 (dir 1979–92), DG BBC 1987–92 (dep DG 1985–87); dir: Visnews 1980–85, Nynex Cable Communications Ltd 1995–97; vice-pres RTS 1985–94, pres Cwlth Broadcasting Assoc 1987–88, memb ITC 1997–2003; dir: National Youth Music Theatre 1992–2002, Wales Millenium Centre 2003–; chm: NCH Action for Children 1991–2001, Brighton Festival 1993–2002, CBSO 1995–2001 (dir 1993–95), Higher Educn Funding Cncl for England 1997–2001; tstee Reuters 1994–; govr: Westminster Coll Oxford 1993–97, Birkbeck Coll London 1993–97, Univ of Brighton 1996–97 and 2001–07 (chm 2002–06); hon fell Wadham Coll Oxford 1989; FCMA, FRTS, CIMgt; *Recreations* music, theatre, travel; *Style*— Sir Michael Checkland; ✉ Orchard Cottage, Park Lane, Maplehurst, West Sussex RH13 6LL

CHECKLAND, Prof Peter Bernard; s of Norman Checkland (d 1983), and Doris, *née* Hiscox (d 1976); *b* 18 December 1930; *Educ* George Dixons GS Birmingham, St John's Coll Oxford (BSc); *m* 29 July 1955, Glenys Margaret (d 1990), da of Leonard George Partridge (d 1936); 2 da (Kristina b 13 May 1959, Katherine b 22 July 1961); *Career* Nat Serv RAF Sgt-instr 1948–49; tech offr, section ldr, assoc res mangr ICI Fibres Ltd 1955–69, prof of systems Lancaster Univ 1969–98 (emeritus prof of systems and mgmnt sci 1998–), hon conslt prof Northwestern Poly Univ Xi'an China 1987–; visiting prof: Univ of New England Aust 1990–, Univ of Central Lancashire 1995–97; former memb: UK Nat Ctee for Int Inst for Applied Systems Analysis, DTI Ctee for Terotechnol; memb: Operational Res Soc, Int Soc for the Systems Sciences (pres 1986–87); Hon DSc City Univ 1991; Hon Dr: Open Univ 1996, Erasmus Univ Rotterdam 1998, Prague Univ of Economics 2004; Most Distinguished and Outstanding Contributor Award Br Computer Soc 1994, Outstanding Contributions to Systems Thinking Award UK Systems Soc 1997, Leverhulme Emeritus Fellowship Award 1998; *Books* Systems Thinking, Systems Practice (1981), Soft Systems Methodology in Action (with J Scholes, 1990), Information, Systems and Information Systems (with Sue Holwell, 1998), Soft Systems Methodology: a 30–year retrospective (1999), Learning for Action (with J Poulter, 2006); *Recreations* rock climbing, studying the evolution of the jazz idiom; *Style*— Prof Peter Checkland; ✉ Management School, University of Lancaster, Bailrigg, Lancaster LA1 4YX (tel 01524 65201, fax 01524 844885 or 01524 822256)

CHECKLEY, Prof Stuart Arthur; s of Arthur William George Checkley, of Eastbridge, Suffolk, and Hilda Dorothy, *née* Chapman; *b* 15 December 1945; *Educ* St Albans Sch, Brasenose Coll Oxford (BA, BM, BCh); *m* 1 Aug 1971, Marilyn Jane, da of Dr Percy Cyril Connick Evans, of Hampton, Middx; 1 da (Anna Mary b 2 July 1974), 1 s (Andrew John b 15 March 1977); *Career* ret conslt psychiatrist Maudsley Hosp, emeritus prof of psychoneuroendocrinology and former dean Inst of Psychiatry; currently asst principal King's College London; numerous articles in jls on depression; FRCPsych, FRCP, FKC; *Recreations* bird watching; *Style*— Prof Stuart Checkley

CHEESMAN, Prof Anthony David (Tony); s of Leslie Charles Cheesman (d 1968), of Shoreham-by-Sea, W Sussex, and Eileen, *née* Griggs (d 1994); *b* 14 November 1939; *Educ* Steyning GS, Charing Cross Hosp Medical Sch, Univ of London (BSc, MB BS); *m* 24 Sept 1966, Janet, da of Eric James Bristow, of Haywards Heath, W Sussex; 2 s (David b 1969, James b 1972), 1 da (Katherine b 1974); *Career* conslt surgn; ENT surgn Univ Hosp of W Indies Jamaica 1972–74; otolaryngologist head and neck surgn: Charing Cross Hosp, Royal Nat Throat Nose and Ear Hosp 1974–2000, Nat Hosp for Neurology and Neurosurgery 2000–03, visiting prof Bart's and The London (Queen Mary's Sch of Med and Dentistry) 2001–; Hunterian professorship RCS 1994–95; memb: RSM (pres Section of Laryngology & Rhinology 1994–95), Ct of Examiners RCS; pres Br Skull Base Soc 1996–97, sec World Fedn of Skull Base Socs 1996–2004; fell Royal Coll of Speech and Language Therapists 1996; FRCS; *Books* numerous papers and chapters on otolaryngology; *Recreations* yachting, skiing, flying; *Clubs* Sussex Yacht, Politzer Soc, Little Ship; *Style*— Prof Tony Cheesman; ✉ 323 Cromwell Tower, Barbican, London EC2Y 8NB (tel 020 7638 1998, e-mail drtonycheesman@aol.com)

CHEESMAN, Dr Clive Edwin Alexander; s of Wilfrid Henry Cheesman (d 1994), and Elizabeth Amelia, *née* Hughes (d 1993); *b* 21 February 1968, London; *Educ* Latymer Upper Sch, Oriel Coll Oxford (MA), Scuola Superiore di Studi Storici Università di San Marino (PhD), City Univ (Dip Law); *m* 8 April 2002, Roberta, *née* Suzzi Valli; *Career* called to the Bar Middle Temple 1996 (Harmsworth maj exhibitioner and Astbury scholar); special asst and curator Dept of Coins and Medals Br Museum 1990–2000, Rouge Dragon Pursuivant Coll of Arms 1998–, lectr in ancient history Birkbeck Coll London 2002–03; jt ed The Coat of Arms 2004–; visiting fell Oriel Coll Oxford 2007–; memb Cncl Friends of the Nat Archives 2001–, advsr Portable Antiquities Scheme DCMS 2004–; tstee Oriel Coll Devpt Tst 2006–; *Books* Rebels, Pretenders and Impostors (jtly, 2000), The Armorial of Haiti (ed, 2007); *Style*— Dr Clive Cheesman; ✉ The College of Arms, Queen Victoria Street, London EC4V 4BT (tel 020 7236 2191, fax 020 7248 6448, e-mail rougedragon@college-of-arms.gov.uk)

CHEETHAM, Anthony John Valerian; s of Sir Nicolas John Alexander Cheetham, KCMG (d 2002), of London, and Jean Evison, *née* Corfe; *b* 12 April 1943; *Educ* Eton, Balliol Coll Oxford (BA); *m* 1, 1969 (m dis), Julia Rollason; 2 s (Nicolas b 1971, Oliver b 1973), 1 da (Flavia b 1976); m 2, 1979 (m dis 1996), Rosemary de Courcy; 2 da (Emma b 1981, Rebecca b 1983); m 3, 1997, Georgina Capel; *Career* editorial dir Sphere Books 1968; md: Futura Publications 1973, Macdonald Futura 1979, Century Hutchinson 1985–89; fndr and chm Century Publishing 1982–85, chm and chief exec Random Century Group 1989–91, fndr and ceo The Orion Publishing Group 1991–2003, exec chm Quercus Publishing plc 2006– (non-exec chm 2005–06); *Books* Richard III (1972); *Recreations* walking, tennis, gardening; *Style*— Anthony Cheetham, Esq; ✉ Quercus Publishing plc, 21 Bloomsbury Square, London WC1A 2QA

CHEETHAM, Prof Juliet; OBE (1995); da of Col Harold Neville Blair (d 1989), of London, and Isabel, *née* Sanders (d 1988); *b* 12 October 1939; *Educ* Univ of St Andrews (MA), Univ of Oxford; *m* 26 April 1965, (Christopher) Paul Cheetham, s of Robert Cheetham, of Wallasey; 1 s (Matthew b 1969), 2 da (Rebecca b 1972, Sophie b 1983); *Career* probation offr 1959–65, lectr in applied social studies and fell Green Coll Oxford 1965–85, prof and dir Social Work Research Centre Univ of Stirling 1986–95 (prof emeritus 1995–); co-ordinator Scottish Higher Educn Funding Cncl 1996–97, social work cmmr Mental Welfare Cmmn for Scotland 1998–2005, memb Mental Health Tbnl for Scotland 2005–, inspr Social Work Inspection Agency 2006–; memb: Ctee of Enquiry into the Working of the Abortion Act 1971–74, Cmmn for Racial Equality 1977–84, Social Security Advsy Ctee 1983–84; *Books* Social Work with Immigrants (1972), Unwanted Pregnancy and Counselling (1977), Social Work and Ethnicity (1982), Social Work with Black Children and their Families (1986), Evaluating Social Work Effectiveness (1992), The Working of Social Work (1997); *Recreations* canal boats; *Style*— Prof Juliet Cheetham, OBE; ✉ Peffermill House, 91 Peffermill Road, Edinburgh EH16 5UX (tel and fax 0131 661 0948)

CHEETHAM, Rt Rev Dr Richard Ian; *see:* Kingston, Bishop of

CHEEVERS, Anthony William (Tony); s of Thomas Joseph Cheevers (d 1984), and Jessie, *née* Strahan; *b* 1 May 1956; *Educ* Finchley GS, Royal Holloway Coll, Univ of London (BMus); *Career* joined BBC 1978; Music Dept BBC Radio 3: prodr 1984–90, ed Speech and Music 1991–93, ed Music Talks and Documentaries 1993–95; head of radio Mentorn Radio 1995–2001, freelance prodr 2001–02, ed BBC Radio 3 2002–; memb Opera Panel Olivier Awards 2006–07; *Recreations* tennis, opera, music, cinema; *Style*— Tony Cheevers, Esq; ✉ Room 3015, BBC Broadcasting House, London W1A 1AA (tel 020 7765 4404, e-mail tony.cheevers@bbc.co.uk)

CHEFFINS, Prof Brian Robert; s of Ronald Cheffins, and Sylvia, *née* Green; *b* 21 January 1961; *Educ* Univ of Victoria BC Canada (BA, LLB), Univ of Cambridge (LLM); *m* 10 Oct 1992, Joanna Hilary, *née* Thurstans; 2 da (Hannah Victoria b 24 May 1998, Lucy Sylvia b 9 Feb 2002); *Career* memb Bar of Br Columbia 1985–; Univ of Br Columbia Canada: asst prof 1986–91, assoc prof 1991–97, prof 1997; SJ Berwin prof of corp law Univ of Cambridge and professorial fell Trinity Hall Cambridge 1998–, fell European Corp Governance Inst 2005–; visiting prof Harvard Law School 2002; visiting fell: Wolfson Coll/Centre for Socio-Legal Studies Univ of Oxford 1992–93, Duke Law Sch/Duke Global Markets Center 2000, Stanford Law School 2003; John S Guggenheim Meml Fellowship 2002–03; *Books* Company Law: Theory, Structure & Operation (1997), The Trajectory of (Corporate Law) Scholarship (2004); *Style*— Prof Brian Cheffins; ✉ Faculty of Law, University of Cambridge, 10 West Road, Cambridge CB3 9DZ (tel 01223 330084, e-mail brc21@cam.ac.uk)

CHEFFINS, John Patrick; CBE (2007); s of Edward Michael Cheffins (d 2003), and Sheila Marion, *née* Doolin (d 2004); *b* Redhill, Surrey; *Educ* Perse Sch Cambridge, UMIST (BSc), Tuck Business Sch Dartmouth Coll NH; *m* 1980, Janet Marie, *née* Dessertine; 2 s (Patrick b 1981, Martin b 1983); *Career* joined as undergrad apprentice Rolls-Royce Ltd 1967; Rolls-Royce (Canada) Ltd: prodn control mangr 1975–80, vice-pres ops 1980–86, vice-pres mktg 1986–89, pres 1989–91; pres and ceo Rolls-Royce Industries Canada Inc 1991–93; Rolls-Royce plc: dir civil engine business 1993–98, pres civil aerospace 1998–2001, chief operating offr 2001–; memb Cncl Soc of Br Aerospace Cos (SBAC); Francois-Xavier Bagnould Prize for Aerospace 2001; FRAeS, FREng; *Recreations* skiing, shooting, fly fishing; *Style*— John Cheffins, Esq, CBE; ✉ Rolls-Royce plc, 65 Buckingham Gate, London SW1E 6AT (tel 020 7227 9195, fax 020 7227 9120, e-mail john.cheffins@rolls-royce.com)

CHELL, Edward B; s of Charles Robert Chell, and June Beryl, *née* Silversides; *Educ* Hipperholm Boys' GS, Univ of Newcastle upon Tyne (BA), RCA (MA); *Career* artist; work in numerous private collections; Lloyds Printmaker Award 1987, Hunting Group Award First Prize Winner 1988, Br Inst Fund Award 1988; *Solo Exhibitions* exhibitions incl: Newcastle Poly Gallery 1989, Blason Gallery London 1990, Anthony Wilkinson Fine Art London 1995, Galerie Thieme + Pohl Darmstadt 1996, Galerie Bugdahn und Kaimer Düsseldorf 1997 and 2000, Anthony Wilkinson Gallery London 2001; *Group Exhibitions* incl: Promenade des Anglais (Galerie Ralph Debarrn Nice) 1994–95, Lead & Follow (Atlantis Gallery London and tour) 1994–95, 7th Open Exhibition (Oriel Mostyn Gallery Llandudno) 1995, John Moores 19 (Walker Art Gallery Liverpool) 1995, White Out (Curwen Gallery London) 1995, Hunting Group Prize Winners Exhibition (RCA) 1997, East 96 (Norwich Gallery) 1997, Black, Grey & White (Galerie Bugdahn und Kaimer Düsseldorf) 1997, Whitechapel Open (Delfina Gallery London) 1997, Foil (Bedford Hill

Gallery London) 1997, Shuttle (Anthony Wilkinson Fine Art London) 1997, John Moores 20 (Walker Art Gallery Liverpool) 1997, Host (Tramway Gallery Glasgow) 1998, Whitechapel Open (Whitechapel Art Gallery London) 1998, Tech (Jason & Rhodes Gallery London) 1998, Foil (Stanley Picker Gallery Kingston) 1998, Tech (Galerie EOF Paris) 1998, Near (MOMA Sharjar UAE) 1998, The Vauxhall Gardens (Norwich Gallery) 1998, Zwischenraum #1 (Galerie Bugdahn und Kaimer Düsseldorf) 1999, Zwischenraum #2 (Galerie Bugdahn und Kaimer Düsseldorf) 1999, Now Showing (Houldsworth Fine Art London) 1999, Chora (Underwood Street Gallery London, Abbott Hall Gallery Kendal, Bracknell Gallery and Hot Bath Gallery Bath) 1999–2000, The Wreck of Hope (Nunnery Gallery London, also jt curator) 2000, FOIL (Gallery Westland Place London, Falmouth Sch of Art Gallery and Herbert Read Gallery KIAD Canterbury) 2001, Record Collection (VTO Gallery London and Euro tour) 2001, British Abstract Painting 2001 (Flowers East Gallery London) 2001, Paradise Valley (LUSAD) 2001, Yes. I am a long way from home (Wolverhampton Art Gallery, The Nunnery London, Northern Gallery for Contemporary Art and Herbert Read Gallery Canterbury) 2003, Will and Compulsion (Broadbent Fine Art London) 2004, John Moores 23 (Walker Art Gallery Liverpool) 2004; *Work in Public Collections* Arts Cncl of GB, Arthur Andersen & Co London, Northern Arts Assoc, Northumberland County Libraries, Grizedale Forrest Soc, Bede Gallery Jarrow, People's Theatre Newcastle upon Tyne, British Telecom, Laing Art Gallery Newcastle upon Tyne, American Express London, RCA, Newcastle Poly Gallery, TI Group London; *Solo Catalogues* Parmenides Dilemma (1990), Vanishing Point (2000); *Recreations* mycology, cultural history, packaging and graphics, natural sciences; *Style*— Edward Chell, Esq; ✉ Anthony Wilkinson Gallery, 242 Cambridge Heath Road, London E2 9DA (tel 020 8980 2662, fax 0870 128 6531, e-mail info@anthonywilkinsongallery.com); Galerie Bugdahn und Kaimer, Düsseldorfer Strasse 6, 40545 Düsseldorf, Germany (tel 0049 211 329140, fax 0049 211 329147, e-mail bugdahn.kaimer@t-online.de)

CHELMSFORD, Dean of; *see:* Judd, Very Rev Peter Somerset Margesson

CHELMSFORD, 4 Viscount (UK 1921) Frederic Corin Piers (Kim) Thesiger; s of 3 Viscount (d 1999); *b* 6 March 1962; *Career* early career as TV prodr; fndr Webcast Ltd 1996, co-fndr Gossiptel 2003; currently md TTL; former conslt: Virgin Management, idesk plc, Chyron Corporation, Dentsu, NTT, Fuji Television; memb Advsy Bd XConnect; fndr memb Internet Telephony Service Providers Assoc 2004– (currently vice-chair); *Style*— The Rt Hon the Viscount Chelmsford

CHELMSFORD, Bishop of 2003–; Rt Rev John Warren Gladwin; s of Thomas Valentine Gladwin (d 1991), and Muriel Joan, *née* Warren (d 1988); *b* 30 May 1942; *Educ* Hertford GS, Churchill Coll Cambridge (MA), St John's Coll Durham (DipTh); *m* 5 Sept 1981, Lydia Elizabeth, da of William Adam (d 1966), and Ivy Adam (d 1962); *Career* asst curate St John the Baptist Church Kirkheaton 1967–71, tutor St John's Coll Durham 1971–77, dir Shaftesbury Project 1977–82, sec Bd for Social Responsibility Gen Synod C of E 1982–88, provost of Sheffield 1988–94, bishop of Guildford 1994–2003; pres St John's Coll Durham, memb Gen Synod C of E; memb House of Lords 1999–; *Books* God's People in God's World (1978), Dropping the Bomb (ed, 1983), The Good of the People (1987), Love and Liberty (1998); *Recreations* gardening, music, theatre, bee keeping, supporter of Tottenham Hotspur FC; *Style*— The Rt Rev the Lord Bishop of Chelmsford

CHELSOM, Peter Anthony; s of Reginald Chelsom (d 1970), and Catherine Chelsom (d 1977); *b* 20 April 1956; *Educ* Wrekin Coll, Central Sch of Drama; *Career* actor; leading roles: RSC, NT, Royal Court; TV incl: Sorrell and Son, Woman of Substance, Christmas Present; writer and dir of films incl: Treacle (BAFTA nomination), Hear My Song 1992 (Best Newcomer Evening Standard Film Awards), Funny Bones 1994 (The Peter Sellers Award for Comedy Evening Standard Awards 1995), The Mighty 1997, Town and Country 1999, Serendipity 2001, Shall We Dance 2004; dir of commercials; memb: BAFTA, DGA, WGA, American Acad of Motion Pictures Arts and Sciences; *Clubs* RAC; *Style*— Peter Chelsom, Esq

CHELTENHAM, Archdeacon of; *see:* Ringrose, Ven Hedley Sidney

CHENERY, Peter James; s of Dudley James Chenery, and Brenda Dorothy, *née* Redford; *b* 24 October 1946; *Educ* Forest Sch, ChCh Oxford (MA, hon sec ChCh Boat Club, chm OU Tory Reform Gp), SOAS Univ of London (Cert Arabic and Islamic Studies); *m* 1979, (Alice) Blanche, *née* Faulder; 3 da (Athena b 1980, Elizabeth b 1983, Victoria b 1987); *Career* teacher Ghana Teaching Serv 1967–70; British Cncl: joined 1970, Amman 1971–73, Middle East Dept 1973–77, Freetown Sierra Leone 1978–80, dir Jedda Saudi Arabia 1981–84, dir Sana'a Yemen 1984–88, dir Munich 1988–90, sec of the Cncl and head of public affairs 1990–97, dir Greece 1997–2000, dir Canada and cultural cnsllr Br High Cmmn 2000–06; gen mangr Royal Anniversary Tst 2007–; memb Cncl and treas Canada-UK Colloquia; Bronze medals of Univs of Sana'a, Ulm and Ioannina, and of the municipality of Missolonghi Greece; memb SCR St Antony's Coll Oxford; FRSA; *Publications* The International Encyclopaedia of Cheese (contrib); *Recreations* books, art, old coins; *Clubs* Leander, Int Lawrence Durrell Soc; *Style*— Peter Chenery, Esq; ✉ Walton Cottage, 25 Bromley Common, Bromley, Kent BR2 9LS

CHENEVIX-TRENCH, Jonathan Charles Stewart; s of Anthony Chenevix-Trench (d 1979), and Elisabeth, *née* Spicer (d 1992); *b* 24 March 1961, Bradfield; *Educ* Eton, Merton Coll Oxford (BA); *m* 30 May 1998, Lucy, *née* Ward; 2 da (May Lygon Gillespie, Evie Laura), 1 s (Jack Ward Lygon); *Career* Morgan Stanley Int: joined 1984, vice-pres financial engrg 1990, exec dir and overall risk mangr for European derivative products 1992, md 1994, head of fixed income in Europe 1999–2004, global head of interest rates and foreign exchange 2000–05, chm 2006–; tstee Chelsea Physic Garden; *Recreations* reading, outdoor activities, gardening; *Clubs* Pratts, Walbrook; *Style*— Jonathan Chenevix-Trench, Esq; ✉ 4 Albert Place, London W8 5PD (tel 020 7376 1193, fax 020 7376 1196); Morgan Stanley International, 25 Cabot Square, Canary Wharf, London E14 4QA (tel 020 7677 7830, fax 020 7425 5471, e-mail jonathan.chenevix-trench@morganstanley.com)

CHENEY, Donald Harvey; s of Arthur Stanley Cheney (d 1975), and Jessie Cheney (d 1986); *b* 16 January 1931; *Educ* Eggars GS Alton, Harrow Weald Co GS, Regent St Poly Sch of Architecture (DipArch); *m* 13 Feb 1956, Gillian Evelyn Florence Frances Cheney, JP, da of Guy Holman Tatum (d 1969); 3 da (Frances b 1956, Fiona (Mrs Ford) b 1960, Claire b 1968); *Career* qualified as architect 1955, in practice NZ 1956–62, in practice S Coast of England 1963–96, ptnr Cheney & Thorpe architects (joined 1970), ret; cncl memb RIBA 1983, external examiner Canterbury Sch of Architecture 1982–87, memb Franco-Br Union of Architects 1977; Freeman City of London 1983; Liveryman Worshipful Co of Arbitrators 1983; RIBA 1956, assoc memb NZ Inst of Architects 1956, FCIArb 1981 (ACIArb 1976); *Recreations* sailing, photography; *Clubs* Royal Cinque Ports Yacht, Naval; *Style*— Donald Cheney, Esq; ✉ Crosstrees, North Road, Hythe, Kent (tel 01303 268720); La Lande Du Burgos, Guehenno 56, France

CHERNS, Penelope Ann (Penny); da of Albert Bernard Cherns (d 1987), and Barbara Simone, *née* Brotman (d 2003); *b* 21 May 1948; *Educ* N London Collegiate Sch, Univ of Kent (BA), Drama Centre London (Dip Directing), LSE (MSc); *Career* director; numerous teaching appts incl: LAMDA, RADA Drama Centre, WSCAD, Royal Coll of Music, Trent Poly, Loughborough Univ, Oslo, Univ of Iowa, Juilliard Sch NY, Guildhall Sch of Drama, Nat Film Sch, Cultura Inglesa Sao Paolo Brazil, Anglo Inst Montevideo Uruguay, Amsterdam Int Theatre Workshop, Institut del Teatr Barcelona, Brandeis Univ USA, Yale Univ USA, Central Sch of Speech and Drama; Theatre and Conflict workshop, fndr Dramatic Solutions 1997; script conslt: Channel 4 1987, Warner Sisters (Hothouse Warner Sisters 1989), Family Pride (Channel 4) 1993; *Theatre* Hello and Goodbye Pal Joey 1974, Stop The World 1975, My Fair Lady 1975, West Side Story 1976 (all Northcott Theatre Exeter), Smile for Jesus (ICA and Sheffield Crucible Studio) 1976, A Winter's Tale 1977, Guys and Dolls 1977, Cabaret 1977 (all Gateway Theatre Chester), Queen Christina (RSC) 1977, School for Clowns (Haymarket Leicester) 1977, Dusa, Fish, Stas and Vi (Bristol Old Vic) 1977, Wreckers (7:84) 1977, Prodigal Father (Soho Poly) 1978, Kiss Me Kate 1978, Beaux Stratagem 1978, Alice 1978 (all Nottingham Playhouse), You Never Can Tell 1978, Side By Side By Sondheim 1979 (both Palace Theatre Watford), Julius Caesar 1979, Teeth 'n' Smiles 1979 (both Nottingham Playhouse), Trees in the Wind (7:84) 1979, Heroes 1979, Statements (Bristol Old Vic) 1980, Letters Home 1980, Strangers 1981 (all New End), Chicago 1981, Pinocchio 1981 (both Newcastle Playhouse), Mourning Pictures (Monstrous Regiment) 1981, The Boyfriend (Churchill Theatre Bromley) 1982, Duet for One (Br Cncl India Tour) 1983, A Day In The Death of Joe Egg (Haymarket Leicester) 1984, Vigilantes (Asian Co-op Theatre) 1985, Alarms (Monstrous Regiment 1986, Riverside Studios 1987) Panorama (The King's Head) 1988, The Millionairess (Greenwich) 1988, Iranian Nights (Royal Court) 1989, Revelations (Traverse Edinburgh) 1992, Tant Per Tant Shakespeare (Barcelona) 1995, The Odd Couple (York Theatre Royal) 1997, Birth of Pleasure (Rosemary Bransch) 1997, A Doll's House (Harrogate) 1998, The Wolf Road (Gate Theatre) 1998–99, Perfect Day (Haymarket Basingstoke) 2000; *Television and Film* for Channel 4: Letters Home 1982, The Inner Eye (asst prodr only) 1986, Iranian Nights 1989, Bite the Ball 1989, Mixing It 1990; for BBC: Prisoners of Incest (Horizon) 1983, Battered Baby (Horizon) 1985, Home Front 1988, And The Cow Jumped Over The Moon 1990; other credits incl: Clients and Professionals and Managing Change (Melrose Film Productions) 1990; *Recreations* travel, languages, swimming; *Style*— Ms Penny Cherns; ✉ e-mail penelope.cherns@virgin.net

CHERRY, Alan Herbert; CBE (2003, MBE 1985), DL; *Career* chm Countryside Properties plc, memb Bd MEPC Ltd; fndr ptnr and former md Bairstow Eves, former chm Workspace Gp plc; chm Kent Thames Economic Bd, memb Manchester Salford Pathfinder Partnership, memb Medway Renaissance Bd; former chm: Sustainable Devpt Round Table for the East of England, Anglia Poly Univ, New Homes Mktg Bd; past nat pres House Builders' Fedn (former memb Housing Policy Ctee); former dir Invest East of England; former memb: Govt's Urban Task Force, East of England Devpt Agency, Nat Cncl CBI, Thames Gateway S Essex Partnership, Bank of England Property Forum, Teesside Devpt Corp, City and West End Advsy Gp National Westminster Bank, Duke of Edinburgh's Inquiry into Br Housing, Inner City Cmmn, New Homes Environmental Study Gp, Joseph Rowntree Fndn Inquiry into Planning for Housing; Hon Dr Anglia Poly Univ 2002; Freeman City of London, memb Worshipful Co of Blacksmiths; FRICS, Hon MRTPI 1991; *Style*— Alan Cherry, Esq, CBE, DL; ✉ Countryside Properties plc, Countryside House, The Drive, Brentwood, Essex CM13 3AT (tel 01277 260000, fax 01277 690629)

CHERRY, John Mitchell; QC (1988); s of John William (Jack) Cherry (d 1967), of Cheshunt, Herts, and Dorothy Mary, *née* Maybury (d 1975); *b* 10 September 1937; *Educ* Cheshunt GS; *m* 7 Oct 1972, Eunice Ann; 2 s (Troy Alexander b 10 July 1968 d 1995, Matthew John b 13 April 1971), 2 da (Suzanne Marie, Katherine Ann (twins) b 3 Jan 1970); *Career* called to the Bar Gray's Inn 1961; recorder of the Crown Court 1987–2003 (asst recorder 1984–87); memb: Criminal Injuries Compensation Bd 1989–2002, Mental Health Review Tbnl 2002–; *Recreations* cricket, rugby, food, wine; *Style*— John Cherry, Esq, QC; ✉ Winterton, Turkey Street, Bulls Cross, Enfield, Middlesex EN1 4RJ (tel 01992 719018); Lamb Chambers, Lamb Building, Temple, London EC4Y 7AS (tel 020 7797 8300, fax 020 7797 8308)

CHERRY, Richard John; s of John Cherry, and Rosina Florence, *née* Walker; *b* 3 February 1944; *Educ* Enfield GS, London Hosp Med Coll (MB BS); *m* 1 (m dis); m 2, 16 April 2005, Helen, da of Arthur Whewell; *Career* sr lectr in orthopaedic surgery Univ of Warwick 1995–; memb: Christian Med Fellowship, BMA; FRCS 1972, FIMgt 1980; *Recreations* music, photography, sailing, skiing; *Clubs* Naughton Dunn, Olton Mere, Birmingham Medico-Legal Soc; *Style*— Richard Cherry, Esq; ✉ 13 Fentham Court, Ulverley Crescent, Solihull B92 8BD (e-mail richard.cherry@doctors.org.uk and richard.cherry@rjcherry.co.uk); Coventry and Warwickshire Hospital, Stoney Stanton Road, Coventry (tel 024 7622 4055)

CHERRY, Prof Richard John; s of Leslie George Cherry (d 1970), and Dorothy Emily, *née* Tasker (d 1969); *b* 3 January 1939; *Educ* Hitchin Boys GS, St John's Coll Oxford (BA), Univ of Sheffield (PhD); *m* 23 June 1962, Georgine Mary, da of George Walter Ansell; 2 s (Simon Richard b 1965, Matthew James b 1972); *Career* scientific offr SERL 1960–64, scientist Unilever Res 1964–70, res fell Dept of Chemistry Univ of Sheffield 1970–73, privat dozent Dept of Biochemistry ETH Zürich 1973–82, prof of biological chemistry Univ of Essex 1982–2004 (emeritus prof 2004–); memb Editorial Bd: Biochemical Journal 1984–91, European Journal of Biophysics 1984–91, Progress in Lipid Research 1990–97; co-ordinator SERC Membranes Initiative 1989–93; memb: Molecular and Cell Panel Wellcome Tst 1988–91, Biochemistry and Cell Biology Ctee BBSRC 1994–96; Ruzicka prize for chem Switzerland 1981; memb: Biochemical Soc 1971, Biophysical Soc 1973; ARPS 2007; *Books* Techniques for the Analysis of Membrane Proteins (with C I Ragan, 1986), New Techniques of Optical Microscopy and Microspectroscopy (1991), Structural and Dynamic Properties of Lipids and Membranes (with P J Quinn, 1992); *Recreations* photography, gardening, music; *Style*— Prof Richard Cherry; ✉ Department of Biological Sciences, University of Essex, Colchester CO4 3SQ (tel 01206 872244, fax 01206 873598)

CHERRYMAN, John Richard; QC (1982); s of Albert James Cherryman (d 1963), and Mabel, *née* Faggetter; *b* 7 December 1932; *Educ* Farnham GS, LSE (LLB), Harvard Law Sch; *m* 18 Sept 1963, Anna, da of Edward Greenleaf Collis; 3 s (Oliver b 1964, Nicholas b 1966, Rupert b 1968), 1 da (Louise b 1971); *Career* called to the Bar Gray's Inn 1955 (bencher 1989); property litigation specialist; memb: Chancery Bar Assoc, Property Bar Assoc; *Recreations* restoring property in France, gardening, trying to play the piano; *Style*— John Cherryman, Esq, QC

CHESHAM, 6 Baron (UK 1858); Nicholas Charles Cavendish; er s of 5 Baron Chesham, PC, TD (d 1989); *b* 7 November 1941; *Educ* Eton; *m* 1, 4 Nov 1965 (m dis 1969), Susan Donne, eldest da of late Frederick Guy Beauchamp, of London; m 2, 1973, Suzanne Adrienne, eldest da of late Alan Gray Byrne, of Sydney; 2 s (Hon Charles Gray Compton b 11 Nov 1974, Hon William George Gray b 13 April 1980); *Heir* s, Hon Charles Cavendish; *Career* chartered accountant; investment advsr; Capt of the Queen's Body Guard of the Yeoman of the Guard (dep chief whip House of Lords) 1995–97, a dep chm of Ctees House of Lords 1997–99, dep speaker House of Lords 1998–99; *Recreations* tennis, skiing, shooting; *Clubs* Pratt's, Australian (Sydney), Royal Sydney Golf; *Style*— The Rt Hon the Lord Chesham; ✉ The Old Post House, Church Street, Ropley, Alresford, Hampshire SO24 0DR

CHESHER, Prof Andrew Douglas; s of Douglas George Chesher (d 1980), of Croydon, Surrey, and Eileen Jessie, *née* Arnott; *b* 21 December 1948; *Educ* Whitgift Sch, Univ of Birmingham (G Henry Wright Prize, Birmingham C of C Prize); *m* 1, 1971 (m dis), Janice Margaret Elizabeth, *née* Duffield; 2 s (James Richard b 21 July 1976, Thomas Andrew b 27 Dec 1978); m 2, 2000, Valérie Marie Rose Jeanne, da of Claude Pierre Lechene; 2 da (Jacqueline Rose b 1 July 2004, Joséphine Hannah b 5 Jan 2006); *Career* res assoc Acton Soc 1970–71, lectr in econometrics Univ of Birmingham 1971–83; Univ of Bristol: prof of econometrics 1984–99, head Dept of Economics 1987–90 and 1996–98; prof of economics UCL 1999–; chair Res Grants Bd ESRC 2001–05; dir Centre for Microdata Methods and Practice 2001–, govr NIESR 2002–; memb: Nat Food Survey Ctee 1987–,

Cncl Royal Econ Soc 1998–2004, ESRC 2001–05; co-ed Econometric Soc Monographs 2001–; assoc ed: Econometric Reviews 1986–87, Econometric Theory 1990–93, Econometrica 1990–96 and 2000–03, Jl of Econometrics 1995–2003, Economics Jl 1997–2000, Jl of the Royal Statistical Soc A 1999–2001; referee for numerous learned jls; involved in numerous nat and int seminars and confs; md Survey Information Systems Ltd; fell Econometric Soc 1999, FBA 2001; *Publications* Vehicle Operating Costs: Evidence from Developing Countries (jtly, 1987); articles, working papers and reports; *Style—* Prof Andrew Chesher; ✉ Woodcroft, Foxcombe Lane, Boars Hill, Oxford OX1 5DH; Department of Economics, University College London, Gower Street, London WC1E 6BT (tel 020 7679 5857, e-mail andrew.chesher@ucl.ac.uk)

CHESHIRE, Lt-Col Colin Charles Chance; OBE (1993); s of Air Chief Marshal Sir Walter Graemes Cheshire, GBE, KCB, ADC (d 1978), and Mary Cheshire, DL (d 1992); *b* 23 August 1941; *Educ* Worksop; *m* 1, 8 Aug 1968, Cherida Evelyn, da of Air Chief Marshal Sir Wallace Kyle, GCB, KCVO, CBE, DSO, DFC; 1 da (Philippa b 1969), 1 s (Christopher b 1971); m 2, 2 Oct 1976, Angela Mary, da of D Fulcher, of Bury St Edmunds, Suffolk; 2 step da (Sarah Linnington b 1968, Emma Graham b 1970); *Career* Lt-Col RTR (ret 1981); served: Aden, Borneo, Singapore, Malaysia, BAOR, NI, UK, Armour Sch Bovington Camp 1968 (tt), RMC of Sci 1972–73 and Staff Coll Camberley 1974 (psc+); sales and marketing mangr: def equipment Vickers Instruments Ltd York 1981–83, army systems Ferranti Computer Systems Ltd Cwmbran 1983–85; gp sales and mktg dir Wallop Group (md Walloptronics Ltd) Andover 1985–87; bursar Oundle Sch 1987–95, memb Exec Ctee Ind Schools' Bursar Assoc 1992–95; National Rifle Assoc: vice-chm Exec Ctee 1990–92, memb Cncl 1990–95, vice-chm 1992–95, chief exec 1995–2002; sec-gen Int Confedn of Fullbore Rifle Assoc (ICFRA) 2003–; chm GB Target Shooting Fedn 1994–97; rifle shooting (int full bore); rep: England 1970–, GB 1970– (vice-capt 1982, 1989, 1998 and 1999, adj 1988, capt 1991, 1992, 1994 and 1995), Army 1967–81, Yorks, Hereford Worcs and Hants (capt 1987–89); cmdt Br Cadet Athelings Rifle Team 1990; Middle Warden and memb Ct of Assts Guild of Sports Internationalists 1998–2001; FIMgt; *Recreations* full bore target rifle shooting, golf; *Clubs* HAC; *Style—* Lt-Col Colin Cheshire, OBE; ✉ Santa Marina No 22, PO Box 91, 7743 Psematismenos Village, Larnaca, Cyprus (tel 00357 24 333380, e-mail c4@cytanet.com.cy)

CHESHIRE, Ian Michael; s of Don Cheshire, and Pamela, *née* Wilson; *b* 6 August 1959, Miri, Malaysia; *Educ* King's Sch Canterbury, Christ's Coll Cambridge (BA, economics scholar); *m* 1 Sept 1984, Kate, *née* Atherton; 2 s (Thomas b 28 July 1987, George b 5 Nov 1988), 1 da (Alice b 13 Aug 1991); *Career* formerly with: Boston Consulting Gp, Guinness plc, Healthworks plc, Pied à Terre, Piper Trust, Sepals plc; exec dir Kingfisher plc 2000–, chief exec B&Q plc 2005–; non-exec dir: HIT plc 1998–2000, Bradford & Bingley plc 2004–; chm of tstees MediCinema, chair of govrs Ernest Bevin Coll; FRSA, MInstD; *Recreations* family, books, music, sailing (badly); *Clubs* Reform, Bembridge Sailing; *Style—* Ian Cheshire, Esq; ✉ B&Q plc, 1 Hampshire Corporate Park, Eastleigh, Hampshire SO53 3YX (e-mail ian.cheshire@b-and-q.co.uk)

CHESHIRE, Prof Jenny; *Educ* LSE (BA), Univ of Reading (PhD); *Career* lectr rising to sr lectr Birkbeck Coll London 1983–91, prof of English linguistics Univ of Fribourg and Univ of Neuchâtel Switzerland 1991–96, prof of linguistics Queen Mary & Westfield Coll London (now Queen Mary Univ of London) 1996–; Erskine visiting fell Univ of Canterbury Christchurch NZ 1995 and 2001; memb Editorial Bd: English WorldWide, Int Jl of Applied Linguistics, Jl of Multilingual and Multicultural Devpt, Jl of Sociolinguistics, Language in Society, Multilingua, Te Reo; *Books* Variation in an English Dialect: A Sociolinguistic Study (1982), Describing Language (jtly, 1986, 2 edn 1994), Dialect in Education: Some European Perspectives (jtly, 1989), Dialect and School in the European Countries (jtly, 1989), English around the World: Sociolinguistic Perspectives (ed, 1991), Taming the Vernacular: From Dialect to Written Standard Language (co-ed, 1997), A Reader in Sociolinguistics Volume 1: Multilingualism and Variation (co-ed, 1998), A Reader in Sociolinguistics Volume 2: Gender and Discourse (co-ed,1998), Social Dialectology (co-ed, 2003); *Style—* Prof Jenny Cheshire; ✉ Department of Linguistics, School of Modern Languages, Queen Mary, University of London, Mile End Road, London E1 4NS

CHESHIRE, Dr (Christopher) Michael; s of Gordon Sydney (d 1983), of Birmingham, and Vera, *née* Hepburn; *b* 18 July 1946; *Educ* West Bromwich GS, Univ of Manchester (BSc, MB ChB); *m* 1 Aug 1970, Jane Mary, da of Claude Cordle, of Norwich; 1 da (Amy Tamsin b 1 April 1977), 1 s (Jonathan Christopher b 5 Nov 1980); *Career* house offr Manchester Royal Infirmary and Hope Hosp Salford 1976–77 (pharmacist 1969–71), SHO Central and S Manchester Hosps 1976–79, lectr in geriatric med Univ of Manchester 1979–83, conslt physician in gen and geriatric med Manchester Royal Infirmary and Barnes Hosp 1983, dean of clinical studies Manchester Med Sch 1991–93; Central Manchester Health Care Tst: med dir 1993–97, dir of educn 1997–, dir of postgrad med educn 2000–05; head of intermediate care Central Manchester PCT 2005–07; censor Royal Coll of Physicians London 2005–07, clinical vice-pres Royal Coll of Physicians London 2007–; memb: Br Geriatrics Soc (chm NW branch), British Assoc of Med Mangrs; FRCP 1990; *Recreations* gardening, swimming; *Style—* Dr Michael Cheshire; ✉ 38 The Crescent, Davenport, Stockport, Cheshire SK3 8SN (tel 0161 483 2972); The Royal Infirmary, Oxford Road, Manchester (tel 0161 276 3517, e-mail mike.cheshire@cmmc.nhs.uk)

CHESNEY, Dr Margaret; da of Ernest Hamer (d 1961), and Edith Hamer (d 1981); *b* 23 August 1946, Delph, Gtr Manchester; *Educ* Univ of Huddersfield (BSc), Univ of Surrey (MSc), Univ of Sheffield (PhD), Bolton Univ (Dip), Univ of Manchester (CertEd); *m* 1 May 1965, Harry Roy Chesney (d 2003); 2 da (Carol Ann b 6 Feb 1966, Kris Tina b 11 Jan 1973); *Career* EN 1976, registered nurse 1979, registered midwife 1981; Birch Hill Hosp Rochdale: burns unit 1977, staff nurse intensive care 1977–79, staff midwife 1981, community midwifery sis 1981–85, midwife teacher 1985–89, midwifery mangr 1989–91; midwife teacher Northern Coll 1995–96; Univ of Salford: lectr in midwifery 1996–97, sr lectr 1997–, currently dir of midwifery; memb Rochdale Met Cncl Twinning Gp; Silver medal Best Student Nurse 1979; 9 field trips to work in Sahiwal Pakistan; memb Royal Coll of Midwives 1981 (memb Cncl); author of numerous refereed conf proceedings, chapters and articles in professional jls incl Br Jl of Midwifery, Nurse Researcher, Nursing Times, The Midwifery Database and Midwives; *Recreations* writing, walking, reading; *Style—* Dr Margaret Chesney; ✉ Haugh Cottage, 7 Haugh Fold, Newhey, Rochdale OL16 3RF (tel 01706 841520, e-mail margaret@chesney999.fsnet.co.uk); University of Salford, Allerton Building, Frederick Road, Salford M6 6PU (tel 0161 295 2513, fax 0161 295 2501, e-mail m.chesney@salford.ac.uk)

CHESSHYRE, (David) Hubert Boothby; CVO (2004, LVO 1988); s of Col Hubert Layard Chesshyre (d 1981), and (Katharine) Anne, *née* Boothby (d 1995); *b* 22 June 1940; *Educ* King's Sch Canterbury, Trinity Coll Cambridge (MA), ChCh Oxford (DipEd); *Career* former vintner and language teacher; green staff offr at Investiture of Prince of Wales 1969, Rouge Croix Pursuivant 1970–78, on staff of Sir Anthony Wagner as Garter King of Arms 1971–78, Chester Herald of Arms 1978–95, Norroy and Ulster King of Arms 1995–97, Clarenceux King of Arms 1997–; Registrar Coll of Arms 1992–2000; lay clerk Southwark Cathedral 1971–2003, lately lectr for NADFAS and Speaker Finders; memb: Westminster Abbey Architectural Advsy Panel 1985–98, Fabric Commission 1998–2003; hon genealogist Royal Victorian Order 1987, sec of the Order of the Garter 1988–2003; memb: HAC 1964–65, Soc of Genealogists 1968–, Bach Choir 1979–93, Madrigal Soc 1980–, London Docklands Singers 2002; Freeman City of London 1975, Liveryman Worshipful Co of Musicians 1995 (Freeman 1994); fell Heraldry Soc 1990 (memb Cncl 1973–85), FSA 1977; *Books* Heraldry of the World (ed, 1973), The Identification of Coats of Arms on British Silver (1978), The Green, A History of the Heart of Bethnal Green (with A J Robinson, 1978), Heralds of Today (with Adrian Ailes 1986, new edn 2001), Dictionary of British Arms Medieval Ordinary Vol I (jt ed with T Woodcock, 1992), Garter Banners of the Nineties (1998), The Most Noble Order of the Garter, 650 Years (with P J Begent, 1999); *Recreations* singing, gardening, motorcycling; *Style—* Hubert Chesshyre, Esq, CVO, FSA, Clarenceux King of Arms; ✉ Hawthorn Cottage, 1 Flamborough Walk, London E14 7LY (tel 020 7790 7923); College of Arms, Queen Victoria Street, London EC4V 4BT (tel 020 7248 1137)

CHESTER, Bishop of 1996–; Rt Rev Peter Robert Forster; s of Thomas Forster (d 1991), of Birmingham, and Edna, *née* Russell; *b* 16 March 1950; *Educ* Tudor Grange GS for Boys Solihull, Merton Coll Oxford (MA), Univ of Edinburgh (BD, PhD), Edinburgh Theol Coll; *m* 1978, Elisabeth Anne, da of Rev Dr Eric Stevenson; 2 da (Inge b 1979, Helen b 1985), 2 s (Thomas b 1981, Douglas b 1993); *Career* curate Mossley Hill Parish Church Liverpool 1980–82, sr tutor St John's Coll Durham 1983–91, vicar Beverley Minster 1991–96; memb House of Lords 2001–; *Recreations* tennis, woodwork, family life, gardening; *Style—* The Rt Rev the Lord Bishop of Chester; ✉ Bishop's House, Abbey Square, Chester CH1 2JD (tel 01244 350864, fax 01244 314187)

CHESTER, Richard Waugh; MBE (1999); s of Cyril Waugh Chester (d 1999), of Great Broughton, N Yorks, and Margaret, *née* Dally; *b* 19 April 1943; *Educ* Friends' Sch Great Ayton, Huddersfield Coll of Technol (ARCM), Royal Acad of Music (FRAM, GRSM); *m* 12 Dec 1970, Sarah, da of Thomas Arthur Leopold Chapman-Mortimer (d 1979); 1 s (Matthew b 1973), 2 da (Lucy b 1976, Emily b 1979); *Career* flautist; fndr memb Nash Ensemble 1964; BBC NI 1965–67; princ flautist and soloist; Scottish Nat Orchestra 1967–87; fndr memb Cantilena, dir Nat Youth Orchestras of Scotland 1987–2007; fndr memb and past pres European Fedn of Nat Youth Orchestras, chm Glasgow Festival Strings, fndr ctee memb World Youth Orchestra Conference, vice-chm World Fedn of Amateur Orchestras, former memb Scottish Arts Cncl; former chm St Mary's Music Sch Edinburgh; tstee: Nat Youth Choir of Scotland, Lochaber Music Sch, Acting for Charities Tst, Scottish Schools Orch Tst, Cantilena Festival on Islay; conductor, adjudicator and examiner; FRSA, FRAM; *Recreations* walking, reading; *Style—* Richard Chester, Esq, MBE; ✉ Milton of Cardross, Port of Menteith, Stirling (tel 01877 385634); 13 Somerset Place, Glasgow (tel 0141 332 8311, fax 0141 332 3915, e-mail info@nyos.co.uk)

CHESTERFIELD, Archdeacon of; *see:* Garnett, Ven David Christopher

CHESTERS, Prof Graham; s of Thomas Leslie Chesters (d 1972), and Nellie, *née* Tortington (d 1995); *b* 10 October 1944; *Educ* Crewe Co GS, UC Swansea (BA, MA); *m* 26 Oct 1968, Veronica Anne; 1 s (Tim b 1976), 1 da (Anna b 1982); *Career* lectr in French Queen's Univ Belfast 1970–72; Univ of Hull: lectr in French 1972–80, sr lectr 1980–88, prof 1988, dean Sch of Euro Languages and Cultures 1988–91, pro-vice-chllr 1991–96, dir Computers in Teaching Initiative Centre for Modern Languages 1989–2000, dir Inst for Learning 1997–2005, univ advsr (educnl partnerships) 2005; *Books* Some Functions of Sound-Repetition (1975), Anthology of Modern French Poetry (1976), The Appreciation of Modern French Poetry (1976), Baudelaire and the Poetics of Craft (1988), Baudelaire: Les Fleurs du Mal (1995); *Recreations* chess, gardening; *Style—* Prof Graham Chesters; ✉ University of Hull, Hull HU6 7RX (tel 01482 465447, fax 01482 466546, e-mail g.chesters@hull.ac.uk)

CHESTERTON, Fiona Mary; da of Clarence Herbert Chesterton (d 1977), of Leicester, and Mary Biddulph; *b* 19 May 1952; *Educ* Wyggeston Girls' GS Leicester, Lady Margaret Hall Oxford (BA); *m* 1 Jan 1980, Howard Anderson; 2 da (Sarah Elizabeth b 26 June 1984, Rachel Clare b 22 April 1987); *Career* BBC: news trainee 1975–77, TV news scriptwriter 1977–79, prodr TV current affairs esp Nationwide 1979–87, ed London Plus 1987–89, ed Newsroom South East 1989–91, ed Bi-Media South East 1991–92; commissioning ed Daytime Ch4 TV 1996–98 (dep commissioning ed news & current affrs 1992–96), commissioning ed for adult educn BBC 1998, controller Adult Learning BBC 2000–03; dir TV Skillset 2006–; vice-chair Broadcasting Support Services 1998–2006; educn and trg memb Cncl RTS 2007– (memb 2000–04); non-exec dir Cambs & Peterborough Mental Health NHS Tst 2004–06, tstee Nat Extension Coll, memb E of England Ctee Heritage Lottery Fund; FRSA; *Recreations* swimming, gardening, tennis; *Style—* Ms Fiona Chesterton; ✉ e-mail fchesterton@hotmail.com

CHETWODE, 2 Baron (UK 1945); Sir Philip Chetwode; 8 Bt (E 1700); s (by 1 m) of Capt Roger Charles George Chetwode (d 1940, s of 1 Baron), and Hon (Molly) Patricia, *née* Berry (d 1995), da of 1 Viscount Camrose; suc grandfather 1950; *b* 26 March 1937; *Educ* Eton; *m* 1, 10 Aug 1967 (m dis 1979), Susan Janet, da of Capt Voltelin James Howard Van der Byl, DSC, RN (ret), and formerly wife of Alwyn Richard Dudley Smith; 2 s (Hon Roger b 1968, Hon Alexander b 1969), 1 da (Hon Miranda b 1974); m 2, 12 July 1990, Mrs Fiona Holt, da of late Christos Tsintsaris, of Thessaloniki, Greece; *Heir* s, Hon Roger Chetwode; *Career* Capt (ret) Royal Horse Guards; dir NCL Investments 1986–95; *Clubs* White's; *Style—* The Rt Hon the Lord Chetwode; ✉ 72 Eaton Place, London SW1X 8AU

CHETWYND, 10 Viscount (I 1717); Adam Richard John Casson; also 10 Baron Rathdown (I 1717); s of 9 Viscount (d 1965); *b* 2 February 1935; *Educ* Eton; *m* 1, 19 Feb 1966 (m dis 1974), Celia Grace, er da of Cdr Alexander Robert Ramsay, DSC, RNVR; 1 da (Hon Emma Grace b 5 May 1967), 2 s (Hon Adam Douglas, Hon Robert Duncan (twins) b 26 Feb 1969); m 2, 15 Aug 1975, Angela May, o da of Jack Payne McCarthy (d 1982), of Nottingham; *Heir* s, Hon Adam Chetwynd; *Career* Lt Queen's Own Cameron Highlanders (the 79th); life assurance agent Prudential Assurance Co of SA Ltd 1978 (until merger with Liberty Life Association of Africa 1986), exec conslt Liberty Life 1986–; life and qualifying memb (18 years) Million Dollar Round Table 1979– (10 times memb Top of the Table 1985–); certified financial planner (CFP); fellow Inst of Life and Pension Advsrs (FILPA) 1982 (by examination); Liveryman Guild of Air Pilots and Air Navigators 1996 (Freeman 1965); *Recreations* travel, astronomy; *Clubs* Rotary (Morningside), Madison Avenue Sports Car Driving and Chowder Eating Society (Johannesburg Chapter, vice-pres); *Style—* The Viscount Chetwynd; ✉ PO Box 69062, Bryanston 2021, South Africa (e-mail chetwynd@pixie.co.za)

CHEVALIER, Tracy; *b* 1962; *Educ* Oberlin Coll OH (BA), UEA (MA); *m*; 1 s; *Career* writer; former reference book ed; *Books* The Virgin Blue (1997), Girl with a Pearl Earring (1999, film adaptation 2003), Falling Angels (2001), The Lady and the Unicorn (2003); *Style—* Ms Tracy Chevalier; ✉ c/o Jonny Geller, Curtis Brown, Haymarket House, 28–29 Haymarket, London SW1Y 4SP (tel 020 7393 4400, e-mail hello@tchevalier.com)

CHEVALLIER, Andrew Bretland; s of Lt Cdr John Bretland Chevallier, RN (d 1995), of Barnston, Wirral, Merseyside, and Rosemary Catherine, *née* Wylie; *b* 20 February 1953; *Educ* Tonbridge, Univ of Warwick (BA), NE London Poly (postgrad cert in educn), Sch of Phytotherapy Hailsham Sussex (cert of herbal med); *m* 1985, Maria Mercedes, *née* Uribe; 1 s by prev m (Leon b 26 Aug 1978), 1 step da (Tamara Davidson-Uribe b 6 Aug 1980); *Career* in private practice as conslt med herbalist 1985–, tutor and examiner in pharmacology Sch of Phytotherapy 1987–93 (tutor and supervisor Sch Trg Clinic 1988–93), lectr in herbal med Middlesex Univ 1994–95, sr lectr in herbal med and professional advsr BSc in herbal med Middx Univ 2000– (sr lectr in herbal med and prog ldr 1995–2000); med herbalist memb Multi Disciplinary Complementary Health Practice St Leonard's Hosp London 1990–95; Nat Inst of Med Herbalists: a dir and student liaison offr 1989–91, vice-pres and dir of educn 1991–, pres 1994–96, chm Nat Inst of Med Herbalists Educnl Fndn 1996–; memb Cncl Natural Med Soc 1993–96, chm Cncl for Complementary and Alternative Med 1996–98 (memb 1991–), vice-chm Euro

Herbal Practitioners Assoc 2001–; fell Nat Inst of Med Herbalists 1997 (memb 1985); *Publications* Herbal First Aid (1993), Herbal Teas: A Guide for Home Use (1994), Encyclopaedia of Medicinal Plants (1996, revised edn 2001), Fifty Vital Herbs (1998), Hypericum - The Natural Anti-Depressant and More (1999); *Style—* Andrew Chevallier, Esq; ✉ 154 Stoke Newington Church Street, London N16 0JU (tel 020 7249 2990)

CHEVALLIER GUILD, John Marjoribanks; s of Cyril Harrower Guild (d 1978), and Perronelle Mary, *née* Chevallier; *b* 23 August 1933; *Educ* BRNC Dartmouth; *m* 18 Dec 1965, Jennifer Isobel, da of Col Brian Sherlock Gooch, DSO, TD, DL, JP; 2 s (John Barrington b 1967 (m 1997, Dale Kerry Hosking; 1 da (Olivia Sophie b 1999), 1 s (Edward Charles Temple b 1999)), Henry b 1968); *Career* Lt Cdr RN serv at sea 1951–63, HM Yacht Britannia 1959, Staff Coll Camberley 1964, cmd HM Ships Badminton, Upton, Bronington 1965–67, served BRNC Dartmouth 1967–69; ret RN to take over family owned cyder, apple juice and cyder vinegar business Aspall Cyder (estab 1728); *Recreations* travel, good food; *Clubs* Army and Navy; *Style—* John Chevallier Guild, Esq; ✉ Aspall Hall, Stowmarket, Suffolk IP14 6PD (tel 01728 860492); Aspall Cyder, Aspall Hall, Stowmarket, Suffolk IP14 6PD (tel 01728 860510, fax 01728 861031)

CHEVSKA, Maria Elizabeth; da of Klemens Skwarczewski (d 1985), and Susan Skwarczewska (d 2007); *b* 30 October 1948; *Educ* Our Lady's Convent Abingdon, Oxford Poly, Byam Shaw Sch of Art London; *Career* artist; prof of fine art Ruskin Sch of Fine Art Univ of Oxford (fell Brasenose Coll); *Solo Exhibitions* incl: Air Gallery London 1982, Midland Group Nottingham 1985, Chapter Gallery Cardiff 1986, Bernard Jacobson Gallery London 1987, Anderson O'Day Gallery London 1989, 1990, 1992 and 1994, Warehouse Gallery Amsterdam 1993, Angel Row Gallery Nottingham 1994, Andrew Mummery Gallery London 1996, 1990, 2001, 2004 and 2006, Kunstmuseum Heidenheim 1997, Galerie Awangarda BWA Wroctaw 1997, Museum Goch 1997, Abott Hall Art Gallery and Museum Cumbria 1999, Wateroven Galerie Vlissingen 2000, Galerie Philippe Casini Paris 2000, 2002 and 2006, Maze Galerie Turin 2000, Maison de la Culture Amiens 2002 (also Caen and Bagneux 2003), Wetterling Stockholm 2002, Kunst Punkt Berlin 2003, Moca London 2005, Slought Fndn PA 2005, Musée Clamecy France 2006; *Group Exhibitions* incl: Art and the Sea (John Hansard Gallery Univ of Southampton, ICA London) 1981, British Drawing (Hayward Annual London) 1982, Whitechapel Open (Whitechapel Gallery London) 1983–92, Gulbenkian Fndn Award Winners' Prints (touring GB and Ireland) 1983, New Blood on Paper (MOMA Oxford) 1983, Landscape Memory and Desire (Serpentine Gallery London) 1984, XXII Int Festival of Painting (Chateau Musée Music Grimaldi) 1990, Crossover (Anderson O'Day Gallery) 1993, British Painting (Arts Cncl Collection, Royal Festival Hall) 1993, Museo Pigorini Rome 1994, New Painting (touring Darlington, Newcastle and Norwich) 1994, Permission to Speak (Worcester City Museum and Art Gallery, touring Derby and Peterborough) 1994, White Out (Curwen Gallery London) 1995, Museum of Art Bacau 1998, Presencing (Eagle Gallery London) 1998, Chora (London and touring) 1999, Marianne Hollenbach Gallery Stuttgart 2001, STOFF (Stadtische Galerie Albstadt) 2002, Independence (South London Gallery) 2003, Translator's Notes (London) 2003, Lekker (APT London) 2005, Weiss (Rokunstbau Sacrow Palace Berlin) 2007; *Work in Public Collections* Arts Cncl of GB, Bolton City Art Gallery, Gulbenkian Fndn, Br Cncl, World Bank, Contemporary Art Soc, New Hall Coll Cambridge, NatWest Art Collection, Oldham Gallery, Heidenheim Museum, Bachau Museum; *Awards* Arts Cncl of GB Award 1977 and 2005, Gtr London Arts Assoc Award 1979 and 1984, Gulbenkian Fndn Printmakers' Award 1982, Austin Abbey Award British Sch Rome 1994, Br Cncl 2002 and 2005, Arts Cncl of England 2004; *Publications* subject of mongraph Vera's Room: The Art of Maria Chevska (2005); *Style—* Ms Maria Chevska; ✉ c/o Mummery & Schnelle Gallery, 83 Great Titchfield Street, London W1W 6RH (e-mail maria.chevska@ruskin-school.ox.ac.uk)

CHEW, (Gaik) Khuan; *b* 10 October 1956; *Educ* Roedean, Bath HS GPDST, Univ of London (BMus), RAM, Trinity Coll of Music, London Coll of Furniture, Inchbald Sch of Design (Dip Interior Design); *Career* interior designer (construction and bldg indust); design dir David Hicks International plc 1986–88, in practice Khuan Chew and Associates (London, Dubai, Nicosia) 1988–; int projects incl: Hilton Int Hotel Cardiff, PortemilioAll-SuiteHotel Beirut, Bayan Bay Marina Clubhouse Penang, Nusa Dua Beach Hotel Bali, Okura Hotel Tokyo, Jumeirah Beach Resort Hotel Dubai (Condé Nast Hotel of the Year 1999), Burj Al Arab Tower Hotel Dubai, Madinat Jumeirah Dubai, Jumeirah Beach Club (refurbishment) Dubai, Dubai Int Airport, Ghantoot Royal Palace Abu Dhabi, Sheraton Hotel Taba Golden Coast Resort Egypt, Corporate Head Office Nicosia, Hilton Int Hotel Budapest (voted Best Architecture Design), Castillo Son Vida Majorca, Arabian Ranches Dubai, Abdul Aziz Yacht, Private Royal Palace Riyadh, Four Seasons Hotel Hongkong; FCSD, FRSA; *Style—* Miss Khuan Chew; ✉ KCA International Designers Ltd, 111 Westminster Business Square, Durham Street, London SE11 5JH (tel 020 7582 8898, fax 020 7582 8860)

CHEYNE, David Watson; s of Brig William Watson Cheyne, DSO, OBE (d 1970), and Laurel Audrey, *née* Hutchison; *b* 30 December 1948; *Educ* Stowe, Trinity Coll Cambridge (BA); *m* 22 April 1978, (Judith) Gay McAuslane, da of late David Anstruther Passey; 3 s (Alexander William David b 25 Nov 1980, Rory Alistair Watson b 22 Aug 1984, Rupert Valentine Hutchison b 20 Feb 1989); *Career* Linklaters & Paines: articled clerk 1972–74, asst slr 1974–80, ptnr 1980–, head Corporate Dept 2000–05, sr corporate ptnr 2005–06, sr ptnr 2006–; memb: City of London Slrs' Co 1980, Law Soc; *Recreations* shooting, fishing, collecting antiques; *Style—* David Cheyne, Esq; ✉ 19 Ladbroke Gardens, London W11 2PT (tel 020 7908 1901); Linklaters, One Silk Street, London EC2Y 8HQ (tel 020 7456 2000, fax 020 7456 2222)

CHICHESTER, Dean of; *see:* Frayling, Very Rev Nicholas Arthur

CHICHESTER, Dermot Michael Claud; s of Lord Desmond Chichester, MC, of Hitchin, Herts, and Felicity Stella, *née* Harrison; *b* 22 November 1953; *Educ* Harrow; *m* 1, 26 April 1975 (m dis 1979), Frances Jane Berners, da of Michael Edward Ranulph Allsopp, of Faringdon, Oxon; m 2, 14 July 1982 (m dis 1999), Shan, da of Alastair Ros McIndoe (d 1984); 1 s (Rory b 1985), 2 da (Ottilie b 1988, Sapphira b 1990); m 3, 4 Sept 1999, Catherine Julie Paule, da of Erik De Clercq, of Vosselaar, Belgium; 2 s (George b 1997, Maximilian b 2000); *Career* Christie's (formerly Christie, Manson & Woods Ltd): joined 1974, chm Christie's International Motor Cars Ltd 1997–, chm Christie's Int (UK) Ltd 2001–; *Recreations* cricket, golf, shooting, fishing, skiing; *Clubs* White's, Pratt's; *Style—* Dermot Chichester, Esq; ✉ Christie's, 8 King Street, London SW1Y 6QT (tel 020 7839 9060, fax 020 7389 2065)

CHICHESTER, Giles; MEP; s of Sir Francis Charles Chichester KBE (d 1972), and Sheila Mary, *née* Craven (d 1989); *b* 29 July 1946; *Educ* Westminster, ChCh Oxford (MA); *m* 1979, Virginia; 2 s (George b 1981, Charles b 1990), 1 da (Jessica b 1984); *Career* trainee Univ of London Press and Hodder & Stoughton 1968–69, mangr family business Francis Chichester Ltd 1969–; contested: ILEA election Fulham Parly constituency 1986, Hammersmith and Fulham BC election 1986; PA to chm Cons Pty Orgn (Lord Tebbit) gen election campaign 1987; campaign asst to Sir Gerard Vaughan MP 1992; MEP (Cons): Devon and E Plymouth 1994–99, SW England 1999–2004, SW England and Gibraltar 2004–; chm: St James's Place Assoc (conservation/environment) 1980–, St James's Ward Ctee Westminster 1982–84 (memb 1975–88 and 1989–96), Westminster Branch Small Business Bureau (fndr) 1983–88, Hammersmith Cons Assoc 1984–87, London W European Constituency Cncl 1987–88, Foreign Affairs Forum 1987–90 (hon treas 1985–87), Dr Edwards' and Bishop King's Estate Charity 1990–93, Political Ctee Carlton Club 1992–95 (hon sec 1988–92), Industry Research and Energy Ctee European Parl 2004–07; pres European Energy Forum (formerly European Energy Fndn) 2004– (vice-pres 1995–2004); memb: Advsy Ctee Gtr London CPC 1984–91 (GP Ctee 1989–91), Nat Advsy CPC (co-opted) 1987–90 and 1994–97, Exec Ctee Cons Nat Union 1988–90 and 1997–98, Gen Cncl Cons Gp for Europe 1991–95, Exec Cncl Parly Gp for Energy Studies 1994–; tstee: United Charities of St James's Church Piccadilly 1977–97, 6s & 7s Club 1980–, Hammersmith United Charities (caring for the elderly) 1985–95; primary sch govr: Tower Hamlets 1983–86, Hammersmith 1983–2000; memb Cncl Air League 1995–2000; sporting career: rowed for sch, coll and England VIIIs (jr trials medal in VIIIs for Oxford), capt and navigator across N Atlantic 1978, 1979 and 1981, and S Indian Ocean 1979; MRIN, FRGS 1972; *Recreations* rowing, sailing, snooker, vegetarian cooking; *Clubs* London Rowing, Pratt's, Royal Western Yacht of England, Royal Yacht Sqdn, United and Cecil; *Style—* Giles Chichester, Esq, MEP; ✉ Longridge, West Hill, Ottery St Mary, Devon EX11 1UX (e-mail giles@gileschichestermep.org.uk, website www.gileschichestermep.org.uk); Francis Chichester Ltd, 9 St James's Place, London SW1A 1PE (tel 020 7493 0932, fax 020 7409 1830)

CHICHESTER, 9 Earl of (UK 1801); Sir John Nicholas Pelham; 14 Bt (E 1611); also Baron Pelham of Stanmer (GB 1762); s of 8 Earl of Chichester (ka 1944), and Ursula (d 1989), da of Walter de Pannwitz, of Benebroek, Holland; *b* 14 April 1944, (posthumously); *Educ* Stanbridge Earls Sch, Mozarteum Salzburg; *m* 1975, Mrs June Marijke Hall, da of Gp-Capt E D Wells, DSO, DFC, of Marbella; 1 da (Lady Eliza b 12 May 1983); *Heir* kinsman, Richard Pelham; *Career* farmer; *Recreations* music, theatre; *Style—* The Rt Hon the Earl of Chichester; ✉ 53 Shawfield Street, London SW3 4BA (tel 020 7352 1516); Little Durnford Manor, Salisbury, Wiltshire SP4 6AH

CHICHESTER, Bishop of 2001–; Rt Rev John William Hind; s of Harold Hind (d 1997), and Joan Mary, *née* Kemp (d 1976); *b* 19 June 1945; *Educ* Watford GS, Univ of Leeds (BA); *m* 16 April 1966, Janet Helen, da of David Hamilton Burns McLintock; 3 s (Dominic b 1967, Jonathan b 1969, Philip b 1971); *Career* asst master Leeds Modern Sch 1966–69, asst lectr King Alfred's Coll Winchester 1969–70, student Cuddesdon Theol Coll Oxford 1970–72, asst curate St John the Baptist Catford 1972–76, vicar Christ Church Forest Hill 1976–82, priest i/c St Paul's Forest Hill 1981–82, princ Chichester Theol Coll 1982–91, Bursalis prebendary and residentiary canon Chichester Cathedral 1982–91, bishop of Horsham 1991–93, bishop of Gibraltar in Europe 1993–2001; chm: Faith and Order Advsy Gp 1991–, Chichester Dio Ctee for Social Responsibility 1991–93; memb Faith and Order Cmmn WCC 1998–; *Books* contrib to: Church, Kingdom, World (1986), Working for the Kingdom (1986), Stepping Stones (1987), Leuenberg, Meissen and Porvoo (1996), Community, Union, Communion (1998), Anglicanism - A Global Communion (1998), Petrine Ministry and the Unity of the Church (1999), Apostolicity and Unity (2002); *Style—* The Rt Rev the Bishop of Chichester; ✉ The Palace, Chichester, West Sussex PO19 1PY (tel 01243 782161, fax 01243 531332, e-mail bishchichester@diochi.org.uk)

CHICHESTER, Julian Edward; o s of Cdr Michael Guy Chichester, RN, and Eleanor Sarah, *née* Riddell-Blount (d 2004); *b* 16 October 1949; *Educ* Bedales, Univ of Sussex; *Career* called to the Bar Inner Temple 1977; practising barrister 1979–; *Recreations* photography, modelmaking, skiing, scuba diving, travel; *Clubs* Groucho; *Style—* Julian Chichester, Esq; ✉ 4/5 Gray's Inn Square, Gray's Inn, London WC1R 5JP (tel 020 7404 5252, fax 020 7242 7803, e-mail jules@blount.demon.co.uk)

CHICHESTER-CLARK, Sir Robert (Robin); kt (1974); s of Capt James Jackson Lenox-Conyngham Chichester-Clark, DSO (and Bar), DL, MP, and Marion Caroline Dehra, *née* Chichester (later Mrs Charles Edward Brackenbury); bro of Penelope Hobhouse, *qv*; *b* 10 January 1928; *Educ* Magdalene Coll Cambridge (BA); *m* 1, 6 Nov 1953 (m dis 1972), Jane Helen, o da of Air Marshal Sir (Robert) Victor Goddard, KCB; 1 s, 2 da; m 2, 1974, Caroline, o child of Col Anthony Bull, CBE, RE, of London; 2 s; *Career* MP (UU) Londonderry City and Co 1955–74, PPS to Financial Sec to HM Treasy 1958–59, Lord Cmmr of the Treasy 1960–61, comptroller of HM Household 1961–64; chief oppn spokesman on: NI 1964–70, Public Bldg and Works 1965–70, The Arts 1965–68; min of state Dept of Employment 1972–74; memb Cncl of Europe 1959–91, delg WEU 1959–61; mgmnt conslt; dir: Alfred Booth and Co 1975–86, Welbeck Group Ltd; chm: Restoration of Appearance and Function Tst 1988–2000, Arvon Fndn 1997– (chm 1997–2001, jt pres 2001–); tstee: RPO Development Tst 1993–95, Quentin Blake Gall of Illustration 2002–; Hon FIIM (formerly FIWM), FIPM; *Clubs* Brooks's; *Style—* Sir Robin Chichester-Clark

CHICK, Dr Jonathan Dale; s of Cdr William E Chick, DSC, of Darlington, and Vonda Hope, *née* Dale; *b* 23 April 1945; *Educ* Queen Elizabeth GS Darlington, Corpus Christi Coll Cambridge (MA), Univ of Edinburgh (MB ChB, MPhil); *Children* 2 s (Greg b 8 Sept 1976, Aylwin b 24 Nov 1978); *Career* med posts Edinburgh teaching hosps 1971–76, memb scientific staff MRC 1976–79, conslt psychiatrist and pt/t sr lectr in psychiatry Univ of Edinburgh 1979–, over 50 contribs to scientific books and jls; visiting lectr on occupational aspects of mental health; advsr WHO; memb: Alcohol Educn and Res Cncl 2000–, Cncl European Soc for Biomedical Research on Alcohol 2002–; MRCP 1973, FRCPsych 1988, FRCPE 1990; *Books* Drinking Problems (1984, 2 edn 1992), Seminars in Alcohol and Drug Misuse (1994), Understanding Alcohol and Drinking Problems (1997, 4 edn 2003); *Style—* Dr Jonathan Chick; ✉ Royal Edinburgh Hospital, Edinburgh EH10 5DX (tel 0131 537 6557, fax 0131 537 6866, e-mail jonathan.chick@gmail.com)

CHIDDICK, Prof David Martin; s of Derek Chiddick (d 2001), and Jeanette, *née* Curtis; *b* 26 October 1948, Norwich; *Educ* Paston Sch North Walsham, Poly of Central London, Cranfield Inst of Technol (MSc); *m* 21 April 1973, Jane Elizabeth, *née* Sills; 2 da (Lucy Jane b 17 Sept 1977, Sally Helen b 16 Jan 1981), 1 s (Thomas Harry b 3 Aug 1986); *Career* sr planning offr Herts until 1979, prof of land economy Leicester Poly until 1985 (sr dean until 1987), dep dir then pro-vice-chllr De Montfort Univ until 2000, currently vice-chllr Lincoln Univ; founding ed Jl of Property Mgmnt, author of numerous articles on planning and land economy; chair Lincoln Strategic Partnership, dir Lincoln Enterprise, memb Bd Govt Office for the E Midlands (GOEM); Liveryman Worshipful Co of Merchant Taylors; MRICS 1974, MRTPI 1979; *Recreations* watching rugby, travelling; *Style—* Prof David Chiddick; ✉ Lincoln University, Brayford Pool, Lincoln LN6 7TS (tel 01522 886100, fax 01522 886200, mobile 07775 810880)

CHIDGEY, Baron (Life Peer UK 2005), of Hamble-le-Rice in the County of Hampshire; David William George Chidgey; s of late Cyril Cecil Chidgey, of Bruton, Somerset, and Winifred Hilda Doris, *née* Weston; *b* 9 July 1942; *Educ* Brune Park Sch, Royal Naval Coll Portsmouth, Portsmouth Poly (Dip Civil Engrg); *m* 1964, April Carolyn, da of Glyn Idris-Jones; 1 s (Hon David Ryan b 1965), 2 da (Hon Joanna Louise b 1969, Hon Caitlin Victoria b 1971); *Career* grad mech and aeronautical engr The Admiralty 1958–64, sr highways and civil engr motorway design and construction Hants CC 1965–72; Brian Colquhoun and Partners Consltg Engrs 1973–94: princ engr traffic mgmnt studies 1973–78, dir Ireland and chief tech advsr Dept of Tport and Dublin Tport Authy integrated tport planning 1978–88, assoc ptnr (projects totalling over £200m) Repub of Guinea 1979–85, assoc ptnr and dir responsible for Central and Southern England (incl facilities mgmnt of 13 military bases for MOD) 1988–94; MP (Lib Dem) Eastleigh 1994–2005; Lib Dem spokesman on: Employment and Training 1995, Transport 1995–97, DTI 1997–99; memb: Speaker's Chm's Panel 2001–06, Foreign Affrs Ctee 1999–06, jt Ctee on Human Rights 2003–06; memb Assoc of Consulting Engrs of Ireland 1993; CEng 1971, MCIT 1983, FIHT 1990, FIEI 1990, FICE 1993; *Recreations* golf, reading; *Clubs* National Liberal; *Style—* The Rt Hon the Lord Chidgey; ✉ House of Lords, London SW1A 0PW (tel 020 7219 6944, fax 020 7219 2810)

CHIGNELL, Anthony Hugh; s of Thomas Hugh Chignell (d 1965), and Phyllis Una, *née* Green; *b* 14 April 1939; *Educ* Downside, St Thomas' Hosp London (MB BS, DO, FRCS); *m* 16 June 1962, Phillippa Price, da of Rear Adm F B P Brayne-Nicholls, CB, DSC, RN, of London; 2 da (Caroline Paula b 1963, Georgina Natalie b 1966), 1 s (Christopher Damien b 1965); *Career* conslt ophthalmic surgn St Thomas' Hosp 1973–99, civilian conslt in ophthalmology to Army 1983–99, conslt surgn King Edward VII Hosp for Offrs 1985–, advsr in ophthalmology to Met Police 1987–99; author of numerous papers on retinal detachment surgery; govr Royal Nat Coll for the Blind 1987–97, memb Cncl Guide Dogs for the Blind 1989–; memb Club Jules Gonin; memb Ct of Assts Worshipful Co Spectacle Makers 1987 (Renter Warden 1997–98, Upper Warden 1998–99, Master 1999–2000); OStJ; *Books* Retinal Detachment Surgery (2 edns), Management of Vitreo-Retinal Disease - A Surgical Option (1998); *Recreations* fly fishing, golf, the country; *Clubs* MCC, Anglo-Belgian; *Style*— Anthony Chignell, Esq

CHILD, Graham Derek; s of Albert Edward Child (d 1992), of Aldridge, Staffs, and Phyllis, *née* Wooldridge (d 1973); *b* 24 June 1943; *Educ* Bedford Sch, Worcester Coll Oxford (MA); *Career* Slaughter and May: asst slr 1968–75, ptnr 1976–95, resident ptnr Frankfurt 1993–95, Slaughter and May visiting fell in Euro competition law Lincoln Coll Oxford 1995–2002, visiting prof Faculté de droit Univ of Paris II 2000–02; *Books* Common Market Law of Competition (with C W Bellamy QC, 1978); *Recreations* travel, walking; *Clubs* Reform, Hurlingham, Highgate Golf, Soc of Cons Lawyers; *Style*— Graham Child, Esq

CHILD, Sir (Coles John) Jeremy; 3 Bt (UK 1919), of Bromley Palace, Bromley, Kent; s of Sir (Coles) John Child, 2 Bt (d 1971), and Sheila, *née* Mathewson (d 1964); *b* 20 September 1944; *Educ* Eton, Poitiers Univ (Dip); *m* 1, 1971 (m dis 1976), Deborah Jane, da of Henry Percival Snelling; 1 da ((Honor) Melissa b 1973); m 2, 1978 (m dis 1987), Jan Todd, yst da of Bernard Todd, of Kingston upon Thames, Surrey; 1 da (Leonora b 25 July 1980), 1 s ((Coles John) Alexander b 10 May 1982); m 3, 1987, Elizabeth, yst da of Rev Grenville Morgan, of Canterbury, Kent; 1 da (Eliza Caroline b 29 Jan 1989), 1 s (Patrick Grenville b 3 Jan 1991); *Heir* s, Alexander Child; *Career* actor; trained Bristol Old Vic Theatre Sch; memb Cncl Shakespeare's Globe Theatre; *Theatre* 3 plays Royal Court, Misalliance (Mermaid), Scenes from an Execution (with Glenda Jackson, Almeida), Dr Richard Warren in The Madness of George III (RNT); West End: Conduct Unbecoming (Queen's), Donkey's Years (Globe), Oh Kay and An Ideal Husband (Westminster), Plenty (Albery), Ying Tong (New Ambassadors) 2005; Out of Order (Far East tour) 1995, The Deep Blue Sea (Royal Theatre Northampton), The Seduction of Ann Boleyn (Nuffield Southampton), Pride and Prejudice (tour), Denial (Bristol Old Vic) 2000, The Circle 2002; *Television* incl Father Dear Father, Wings, Glittering Prizes, Edward and Mrs Simpson, The Jewel in the Crown, Edge of Darkness, Fairly Secret Army, First Among Equals, Game Set and Match, Fools Gold, Harnessing Peacocks, Demob, Sharpe's Enemy, Frank Stubbs, Dance to the Music of Time, Love in a Cold Climate, A Touch of Frost, Doc Martin, Midsomer Murders, Falklands Play, Casualty, Judge John Deed, Amnesia, Eastenders; *Films* incl: High Road to China 1982, Give My Regards to Broad Street 1984, Taffin 1987, A Fish Called Wanda 1988, The Madness of George III 1994, Regeneration 1996, Whatever Happened to Harold Smith? 1995, Don't Go Breaking My Heart 1997, Lagaan (Bollywood) 2000, Laisser Passez 2000, South Kensington 2001, Wimbledon 2004, Separate Lies 2004; *Recreations* travel, gardening; *Clubs* Garrick; *Style*— Sir Jeremy Child, Bt

CHILD, Prof John; s of Clifton Child (d 1994), and Hilde, *née* Hurwitz (d 1999); *b* 10 November 1940; *Educ* Purley GS (state scholar), St John's Coll Cambridge (scholar, MA, PhD, ScD); *m* 1965, Dr Elizabeth Anne Mitchiner, da of Geoffrey Mitchiner; 1 s (Martin Edmund b 12 Jan 1970), 1 da (Caroline Marianne b 10 April 1973); *Career* personnel offr and systems analyst Rolls Royce Ltd 1965–66, research fell Aston Univ 1966–68, sr research offr London Business Sch 1968–73, prof of organizational behaviour Aston Univ 1973–91, dean Aston Business Sch 1986–89, Guinness prof (later Diageo prof) of mgmnt studies Univ of Cambridge 1991–2000; fell St John's Coll Cambridge 1991–2000; chair of commerce Univ of Birmingham 2000–; visiting prof Euro Inst for Advanced Studies in Mgmnt 1971–75; dean and dir China-Euro Community Mgmnt Inst Beijing China 1989–90, dir Judge Inst of Mgmnt Studies Univ of Cambridge 1992–93, dir Centre for Int Business and Mgmnt 1995–98; ed-in-chief Organization Studies 1992–96; memb Mgmnt and Industrial Relations Ctee SSRC 1978–82; memb: Br Sociological Assoc 1962, Acad of Int Business 1993; Acad of Mgmnt: memb 1977, distinguished lectr 1980, 1991 and 2000, fell 2002; Hon Dr Helsinki Sch of Economics 1996; fell Br Acad of Mgmnt 2002 (fndr memb 1987), FBA 2006; *Publications* author of 18 books incl: Management in China (1994), Strategies of Co-operation (jtly, 1998), The Management of International Acquisitions (jtly, 2001), Organization (2005), Co-operative Strategy (jtly, 2005), Corporate Co-evolution (jtly, 2007); also author of numerous articles; *Recreations* dinghy sailing, mountain walking, bridge; *Clubs* Earlswood Lakes Sailing; *Style*— Prof John Child; ✉ Tudor Croft, Tanners Green Lane, Earlswood, Solihull, West Midlands B94 5JT (e-mail j.child@bham.ac.uk)

CHILD, John Frederick; s of Frederick George Child (d 1980), and Doris Frances, *née* Henley; *b* 18 April 1942; *Educ* King Edward's Sch Bath, Univ of Southampton (BA), Sidney Sussex Coll Cambridge (scholar, LLB (now LLM)), Univ of Columbia Leiden (Dip American Law); *m* 2 Sept 1972, Dr Jean Alexander, da of Dr Albert Alexander Cunningham, of Esher, Surrey; 2 s (Andrew b 25 May 1974, Jeremy b 11 May 1977); *Career* called to the Bar Lincoln's Inn 1966 (Droop scholar and Tancred common law student); Chancery barr; memb Hon Soc of Lincoln's Inn, supervisor in law Sidney Sussex Coll Cambridge 1966–78; memb: Chancery Bar Assoc, Revenue Bar Assoc; *Books* Vol 19 (Sale of Land) Encyclopaedia of Forms and Precedents (main contrib 4 edn), Accumulation and Maintenance Settlements, Encyclopaedia of Forms and Precedents, Vol 40(3) (2006); *Recreations* walking, foreign travel; *Style*— John Child, Esq; ✉ Wilberforce Chambers, 8 New Square, Lincoln's Inn, London WC2A 3QP (tel 020 7306 0102, fax 020 7306 0095, e-mail jchild@wilberforce.co.uk, website www.wilberforce.co.uk/child.html)

CHILD, Prof Mark Sheard; *b* 17 August 1937; *Educ* Pocklington Sch, Clare Coll Cambridge (BA, PhD); *m*; 3 c; *Career* lectr in theoretical chemistry Univ of Glasgow 1963–66; Univ of Oxford: lectr in theoretical chemistry 1966–89, Aldrichian praelector in chemistry 1989–92, prof of chemical dynamics 1992–94, Coulson prof of theoretical chemistry 1994–2004; sr research fell Univ Coll Oxford 2004– (professorial fell 1994–2004), emeritus fell St Edmund Hall Oxford 1994– (tutorial fell 1966–94); FRS 1989; *Style*— Prof Mark Child, FRS; ✉ Physical and Theoretical Chemistry Laboratory, South Parks Road, Oxford OX1 3QZ

CHILDS, Edward Samuel (Ted); OBE (1997); s of Samuel Walter Childs (d 1980), of London, and Helena Elizabeth, *née* Flynn; *b* 26 December 1934; *Educ* St Bonaventure's Sch London, Univ of Nottingham (BA); *m* 1963, Kathleen Anne, da of Denis Houlihan; 2 da (Anne-Marie b 28 Aug 1965, Madeleine b 21 June 1968); *Career* Nat Serv cmmnd Pilot Offr RAF 1958, Flying Offr 1959; ABC Television Ltd: joined as trainee prog dir 1960, documentary prodr 1967–73 (progs incl This Week and The World at War); television drama prodr Euston Films Ltd 1973–78 (progs incl The Sweeney, Van Der Valk and Quatermass), freelance writer, prodr and dir 1978–84; Central Independent Television plc: head of drama 1984–87, md Central Films 1987–95, exec prodr various series incl Inspector Morse, Cadfael, Soldier Soldier, Kavanagh QC, Goodnight, Mr Tom, The Brief, Making Waves and Lewis; dir: Yorkshire Programme Gp Ltd 1997–98, Griffin Films Ltd 1997–98, Childscreen Ltd 1997–; tstee BAFTA 1999 (chm 1993/94); Cyril Bennett Award RTS 1995, RTS Baird Medal 1995, Alan Clarke Award for Outstanding Creative Contribution BAFTA 1998, Broadcasting Press Guild Harvey Lee Award for Outstanding Contribution to Broadcasting 2001; FRTS 1991; *Recreations* sailing, walking, theatre, cinema; *Clubs* RAC, Garrick; *Style*— Ted Childs, Esq, OBE; ✉ c/o PFD, Drury House, 34–43 Russell Street, London WC2B 5HA (tel 020 7344 1043)

CHILDS, Robert Simon; s of Walter Childs (d 1991), and Patricia Rose, *née* Carton; *b* 21 June 1951; *Educ* St Joseph's Coll Ipswich, Bedford Coll London (BA); *m* 5 Aug 1997, Mary, *née* James; 2 s (Benjamin Joseph James b 19 Nov 1980, Joshua William James b 31 Oct 1983), 1 da (Alexandra Mary b 20 Sept 1987); *Career* Hiscox Group: joined as dep underwriter 1986, underwriter Syndicate 33 1993–2001, dir of underwriting 2001, currently gp chief underwriting offr and memb Exec Gp and exec dir and princ Hiscox Ltd, ceo Hiscox Bermuda, chm Hiscox Inc (USA); chm Lloyd's Market Assoc 2003–05, formerly chm War, Civil War and Financial Guarantee Sub-Ctee, memb Worldwide Markets Bd and memb Authorisation Ctee Lloyd's of London; chm Advsy Bd Sch of Mgmnt Royal Holloway Univ; *Recreations* tennis, sailing; *Clubs* Travellers, Royal Bermuda Yacht; *Style*— Robert Childs, Esq; ✉ Hiscox, 1 Great St Helens, London EC3A 6HX (tel 020 7448 6006, fax 020 7448 6599)

CHILSTON, 4 Viscount (UK 1911); Alastair George Akers-Douglas; s of late Capt Ian Stanley Akers-Douglas (gs of 1 Viscount Chilston), by his 2 w, Phyllis Rosemary; suc kinsman, 3 Viscount Chilston, 1982; *b* 5 September 1946; *Educ* Ashdown House, Eton; *m* 1971, Juliet Anne, da of late Lt-Col Nigel Lovett, of The Old Rectory, Inwardleigh, Okehampton, Devon; 3 s (Hon Oliver Ian b 1973, Hon Alexander Hugh b 1975, Hon Dominic b 1979); *Heir* s, Hon Oliver Akers-Douglas; *Career* film producer; *Style*— The Rt Hon the Viscount Chilston; ✉ Tichborne Cottage, Tichborne, Arlesford, Hampshire SO24 0NA (tel 01962 734010, fax 01962 734409, e-mail alastair@littlescreen.com)

CHILTON, John James; s of Thomas William Chilton (d 1943), and Eileen Florence, *née* Burke (d 1967); *b* 16 July 1932; *m* 1963, Teresa, da of Thomas McDonald; 1 da (Jennifer b 1963), 2 s (Martin b 1964, Barnaby b 1971); *Career* jazz musician, writer, composer; worked in advertising agency then nat newspaper; professional jazz trumpeter 1957–; ldr own band 1958, memb Bruce Turner's Jump Band 1958–63, memb various big bands led by Mike Daniels and Alex Welsh 1960s, ldr own band and backing musician for Buck Clayton, Ben Webster, Bill Coleman, Charlie Shavers, Roy Eldridge 1963–69, musical dir for George Melly 1972–2002, ldr Feetwarmers 1972– (jt ldr with Wally Fawkes 1969–72); hon citizen New Orleans 1997; *Awards* Grammy for best album notes 1983, ARSC Award USA for best researched jazz and blues book 1992, Br Jazz Award for Jazz Writer of the Year 2000; *Books* Who's Who of Jazz (1970), Billie's Blues (1974), McKinney's Music (1978), Teach Yourself Jazz (1979), A Jazz Nursery (1980), Stomp Off Let's Go (1983), Sidney Bechet - The Wizard of Jazz (1987), The Song of the Hawk (1990), Let The Good Times Roll (1992), Ride, Red, Ride - The Life of Henry 'Red' Allen (1999), Roy Eldridge - Little Jazz Giant (2002), Who's Who of British Jazz (2004); *Style*— John Chilton, Esq

CHILTON, (Frederick) Paul; s of Charles Frederick Chilton, of Rochester, Kent, and Elizabeth, *née* Docherty; *b* 28 July 1946; *Educ* St Stephens Roman Catholic Sch, NW Kent Coll of Technol, Harvard Business Sch (Advanced Mgmnt Prog); *m* 1991, Moira, *née* Seaward; *Career* conslt Aon Ltd; *Recreations* shooting, fishing, equestrian sports; *Style*— Paul Chilton, Esq; ✉ Aon Ltd, 8 Devonshire Square, London EC2M 4PL (tel 020 7623 5500, fax 020 7216 3760)

CHILTON, Dr Robert (Bob); OBE (2007); *Career* dir Local Govt Studies Audit Cmmn 1989–2001, former cmmr for transport Transport for London; chief exec: Local Govt Cmmn 1995–96, Gtr London Authy 1999–2001; non-exec dir Waste & Resources Action Prog (WRAP), vice-chair Bd Nat Consumer Cncl (chair E Thames Gp), ind memb Bd Office of Information Cmmn, ind memb Home Office Audit Ctee, memb Bd Central Police Trg and Devpt Authy; *Style*— Dr Bob Chilton, OBE; ✉ National Consumer Council, 20 Grosvenor Gardens, London SW1W 0DH (tel 020 7730 3469, fax 020 7730 0191)

CHILVER, Baron (Life Peer UK 1987), of Cranfield in the County of Bedfordshire; Sir (Amos) Henry Chilver; kt (1978); e s of Amos Henry Chilver, of Southend-on-Sea, Essex, and A E Chilver, *née* Mack; *b* 30 October 1926; *Educ* Southend HS, Univ of Bristol; *m* 1959, Claudia Mary Beverley, o da of Sir Wilfrid Vernon Grigson, CSI (d 1948), of Pelynt, Cornwall; 2 da (Hon Helen (Hon Mrs Prentice) b 1960, Hon Sarah (Hon Mrs Vaughan) b 1962), 3 s (Hon John b 1964, Hon Mark b 1965, Hon Paul b 1967); *Career* prof of civil engrg Univ of London 1961–69, vice-chllr Cranfield Inst of Technol 1970–89; chm: Milton Keynes Devpt Corp 1983–92, English China Clays plc 1989–95, RJB Mining plc 1992–97, Chiroscience plc 1995–98, Plymouth Devpt Corp 1996–98; dir: ICI plc 1990–93, Zeneca plc 1993–95; pres: Inst of Mgmnt Servs 1982–95, Inst of Logistics 1993–95; Hon DSc: Univ of Leeds 1982, Univ of Bristol 1983, Univ of Salford 1983, Univ of Strathclyde 1986, Univ of Bath 1986, Cranfield Inst of Technol 1989, Univ of Buckingham 1990, Univ of Compiègne (France) 1990; hon fell CCC Cambridge 1981; CIMgt, FRS 1982, FREng 1977; *Clubs* Athenaeum, Oxford and Cambridge; *Style*— The Rt Hon Lord Chilver, FRS, FREng

CHILVERS, Prof Edwin Roy; s of Derek John Chilvers, of Ipswich, Suffolk, and Marjorie Grace, *née* Bugg; *b* 17 March 1959; *Educ* Deben HS Felixstowe, Univ of Nottingham Med Sch (BMedSci, BM BS), Univ of London (PhD), Univ of Leicester, Univ of Edinburgh, Univ of Cambridge (MA); *m* 26 June 1982, Rowena Joy, *née* Tyssen; 1 da (Caroline b 30 May 1985), 2 s (Timothy b 15 May 1987, Alastair b 27 Dec 1992); *Career* Wellcome Tst sr clinical fell, hon sr lectr then reader Univ of Edinburgh 1992–98, prof of respiratory med Univ of Cambridge 1998–, hon conslt physician Addenbrooke's and Papworth Hosps 1998–, fell St Edmund's Coll Cambridge 1999–; non-exec dir Papworth Hosp NHS Tst 2003–07; FRCPEd 1995, FRCP 1999 (MRCP 1985), FHEA 2007, FMedSci 2007; *Publications* Davidson's Principles and Practice of Medicine (ed, 17 edn 1995, 18 edn 1999, 19 edn 2002); author of papers on neutrophil cell biology and cell signalling; *Recreations* reading, gardening, music; *Style*— Prof Edwin Chilvers; ✉ Department of Medicine, University of Cambridge School of Clinial Medicine, Box 157, Addenbrooke's Hospital, Cambridge CB2 2QQ (tel and fax 01223 762007, e-mail erc24@cam.ac.uk)

CHIN, Dr Lincoln Li-Jen; s of Pun-Jian Chin, and Grace Chin, *née* Sun; *b* 2 November 1942; *Educ* Christ's Coll Cambridge, MIT (ScD); *m* 21 Jan 1971, Lillian Chen Ming, da of Wen Hsiung Chu; 1 s (Nicholas b 1973), 1 da (Tamara b 1975); *Career* chm Chindwell Co Ltd; memb Forest Stewardship Cncl; *Recreations* Chinese art, travelling, music; *Clubs* Oxford and Cambridge; *Style*— Dr Lincoln Chin; ✉ Chindwell Co Ltd, Hyde House, The Hyde, London NW9 6JT (tel 020 8205 6171, fax 020 8205 8800, e-mail lincoln@chindwell.com)

CHINN, James (Jimmie); s of Edith Chinn (d 1985); *b* 30 March 1940; *Educ* Durnford Street Secdy Modern Middleton Manchester, RADA, Whitelands Coll Putney; *Career* teacher in Southall, full time playwright 1984–; memb Writers' Guild of GB; *Stage Plays* Our Linda, Our Carol and Freda, To The Island, Albert Make Us Laugh, After September, Straight and Narrow (Writers' Guild Macallan Award nomination for Best West End Play 1992), Sylvia's Wedding, Whatever Happened to Kathy Kirby?, Home Before Dark, Finishing Touches, Farewell Performances, The Garden Party (with Hazel Wyld); *Television* Emmerdale (Yorks TV), A Different Way Home, Whatever Happened to Kathy Kirby (since retitled to Something to Remember You By); *Radio* From Here to the Library, Too Long An Autumn, A Woman Who Does, In Room Five Hundred and Four, A Different Way Home, Where Evening Gathers, Mr Twilfit is Dead, Pity About Kitty, Looks Like Rain, Looks Like Rain Again, Perfect Timing; *Screenplays* In By The Half, Farewell Performance; *Publications* From Here to the Library, A Respectable Funeral,

Take Away the Lady, Too Long An Autumn, In Room Five Hundred and Four, But Yesterday, Pity About Kitty, Interior Designs, Straight and Narrow, In By the Half, After September, Home Before Dark, Sylvia's Wedding, Something to Remember You By, Albert Make Us Laugh, The Garden Party, A Different Way Home; *Recreations* reading, walking, listening to radio; *Style*— Jimmie Chinn, Esq; ✉ c/o Richard Hatton Ltd, 29 Roehampton Gate, London SW15 5JR (tel 020 8876 6699, fax 020 8876 8278)

CHINUBHAI, Sir Udayan; 3 Bt (UK 1913), of Shahpur, Ahmedabad, India; original name of baronetcy Runchorelal; s of Sir Chinubhai Madhowlal Runchorelal, 2 Bt (d 1990), and Tanumati Zaverilal (d 1970), da of Zaverilal Bulakhiram Mehta, of Ahmedabad; *b* 25 July 1929; *m* 1953, Muneera Khodadad, da of Khodadad Mancherjee Fozdar, of Bombay; 1 s, 3 da; *Heir* s, Prashant Chinubhai; *Career* nat pres India Jr Chamber 1961–62, currently a Jaycee senator; represented Gujarat in Ranji Trophy in Cricket and played the combined Univ XI against Pakistan; represented India in int events in target shooting on 4 occasions; awarded Arjun award for target shooting 1972–73; *Recreations* cricket, target shooting; *Style*— Sir Udayan Chinubhai, Bt

CHIODINI, Prof Peter Leslie; s of Leslie Chiodini (d 1990), of London, and Catherine Beatrice, *née* Coleman (d 2001); *b* 27 October 1948; *Educ* Dunstable GS, KCH Med Sch (BSc, PhD, MB BS); *m* 5 Sept 1981, Jane Heather, da of Alan Edgar Bennett; 2 s (James Peter b 13 Jan 1986, Jonathan Peter b 19 Aug 1988); *Career* house physician KCH 1978, house surgn Royal Sussex Co Hosp 1979; SHO: St James's Hosp 1979–80, Royal Marsden Hosp 1980; med registrar: St George's Hosp 1981, Broadgreen Hosp 1981–82; sr registrar East Birmingham Hosp 1982–85, conslt parasitologist Hosp for Tropical Diseases 1985–, dir HPA Malaria Reference Lab 2003–; hon prof LSHTM; Stephen Whittaker prize West Midlands Physicians' Assoc 1984, Medicine-Gillilland travelling fell 1985; fell Linnean Soc 2005–; MRCS, FRSTM&H 1970 (memb Cncl 1987–90 and 2002–05), FRCP 1992 (LRCP, MRCP), FRCPath 1996, FFTM RCPS(Glas) 2006; *Recreations* cathedrals, running; *Style*— Prof Peter Chiodini; ✉ 9 Lavenham Drive, Biddenham, Bedford MK40 4QR; Department of Clinical Parasitology, Hospital for Tropical Diseases, Mortimer Market, London WC1E 6JB (tel 020 7387 4411 ext 5418, fax 020 7383 0041, e-mail peter.chiodini@uclh.nhs.uk)

CHIPMAN, Dr John Miguel Warwick; CMG 1999; s of Lawrence Carroll Chipman (decd), and Maria Isobel, *née* Prados (decd); *b* 10 February 1957; *Educ* Westmount HS Montreal, Harvard Univ (BA), LSE (MA), Balliol Coll Oxford (MPhil, DPhil); *m* 28 June 1997, Lady Theresa Manners, da of 10 Duke of Rutland (d 1999); 2 s (Ivor, Warwick (twins) b 24 Dec 2000); *Career* res assoc: IISS 1983–84, Atlantic Inst for Int Affrs Paris 1985–87; IISS: asst dir 1987–90, dir of studies 1990–93, chief exec 1993–; fell NATO 1983; *Books* NATO's Southern Allies (1988), French Power and Africa (1989); numerous chapters in books, scholarly articles and newspaper editorial pieces; *Recreations* tennis, skiing, riding; *Clubs* White's, Brooks's, Beefsteak, Garrick, Harvard (NY); *Style*— Dr John Chipman, CMG; ✉ IISS, Arundel House, 13–15 Arundel Street, Temple Place, London WC2R 3DX (tel 020 7395 9101, fax 020 7395 9186, e-mail chipman@iiss.org)

CHIPPERFIELD, David Alan; CBE (2004); s of Alan John Chipperfield, and Peggy, *née* Singleton; *b* 18 December 1953; *Educ* Wellington Sch, Architectural Association (AADipl); *Partner*, Dr Evelyn Stern; 3 s (Chester, Gabriel, Raphael), 1 da (Celeste); *Career* architect; princ David Chipperfield Architects 1984–; visiting prof: Harvard Univ 1987–88 (visiting lectr 1986–87), Univ of Naples 1992, Univ of Graz 1992, École Polytechnique Fédérale de Lausanne 1993–94, London Inst 1997–; Staatliche Akademie der Bildenden Künste Stuttgart 1995–2001; Mies van der Rohe Chair Escola Tècnica 2001; fndr and dir 9H Gallery London 1985; tstee Architectural Fndn London 1992–97; projects incl: private museum Tokyo 1989, Tak Design Centre Kyoto Japan 1989, River and Rowing Museum Henley-on-Thames 1996–98, Neues Museum Berlin 1997, Ernstings Service Centre Münster Germany 1998, Museum Island Masterplan Berlin 1998, San Michele Cemetery Venice 1998, Palace of Justice Salerno Italy 1999, Figge Art Museum Iowa USA 1999, Ansaldo 'City of Cultures' Milan 2000, Anthony Gormley Studio London 2003, Des Moines Public Library US 2006, America's Cup Building Valencia 2006, Museum of Modern Literature Marbach 2006, the Hepworth Wakefield 2006, Freshfields Bruckhaus Deringer office building Amsterdam 2007, Liangzhu Culture Museum China 2007, Empire Riverside Hotel Hamburg 2007, Gallery Hinter dem Giesshaus 1 Berlin 2007; current projects: Neues Museum Berlin, Museum Island Masterplan Berlin, San Michele Cemetery Venice, Palace of Justice Salerno, City of Justice Barcelona, Turner Contemporary Margate, The Hepworth Wakefield; hon fell AIA 2007; RIBA; *Awards* Andrea Palladio Prize 1993, RIBA Regnl Award 1996 and 1998, RIBA Commercial Architecture Award 1998, Civic Trust Award 1999, Tessenow Gold Medal Award 1999, Royal Fine Art Cmmn Tst/Br Sky Broadcasting Best Building (England) 1999, RIBA Category Award Architecture in Arts and Leisure Award 1999, RIBA Award 2003 and 2004, Leaf Award 2006, AIA Regnl Awards 2006, RIBA European and International Awards 2007; *Books* Theoretical Practice (1994), David Chipperfield: Architectural Works 1990–2002 (2003), Elcroquis: David Chipperfield, Architectural Works 1998–2004 (2004), David Chipperfield: Idea e Realta (2005); *Style*— David Chipperfield, Esq, CBE; ✉ David Chipperfield Architects, 1A Cobham Mews, Agar Grove, London NW1 9SB (tel 020 7267 9422, fax 020 7267 9347, website www.davidchipperfield.com)

CHIPPINDALE, Christopher Ralph; s of Keith Chippindale, and Ruth Chippindale; *b* 13 October 1951; *Educ* Sedbergh, St John's Coll Cambridge (BA), Girton Coll Cambridge (PhD); *m* 1976, Anne, *née* Lowe; 2 s, 2 da; *Career* ed: Penguin Books, Hutchinson Publishing Group 1974–82, Antiquity 1987–97; res fell in archaeology Girton Coll Cambridge 1985–87, asst curator Cambridge Univ Museum of Archaeology and Anthropology 1987–, reader in archaeology Univ of Cambridge 2001–; *Books* Stonehenge Complete (1983, 1994 and 2004), Who Owns Stonehenge? (1990), The Archaeology of Rock Art (1998); *Recreations* archaeology, worrying; *Style*— Christopher Chippindale, Esq; ✉ 46 High Street, Chesterton, Cambridge CB4 1NG (e-mail cc43@cam.ac.uk)

CHISHOLM, Sir John Alexander Raymond; kt (1999); *b* 27 August 1946; *Educ* Univ of Cambridge (MA); *m*; 2 c; *Career* apprentice Vauxhall Motors Luton 1964–69; Scicon Ltd: analyst and programmer London 1969–74, managing conslt and fndr memb Milton Keynes Branch 1974–76, gp mangr 1976–79; CAP Scientific: fndr 1979–81, md 1981–86, memb Bd Cap Group plc 1986–88, md UK 1988–91; Sema Gp plc; chief exec Defence Evaluation and Res Agency 1991–2001; QinetiQGroup plc: chief exec 2001–05, chm 2005–06, non-exec chm 2006–; chm MRC 2006–; non-exec dir: Exprolnt plc 1994–2003, Bespak plc 1999–2006; pres IET 2005–06; CEng, FIEE, FREng 1996, FRAeS, FIP; *Style*— Sir John Chisholm, FREng; ✉ QinetiQ, Ively Road, Farnborough, Hampshire GU14 0LX (tel 01252 394500, fax 01252 394777)

CHISHOLM, Malcolm; MSP; *b* 7 March 1949; *Educ* Univ of Edinburgh (MA, DipEd); *m*; 3 c; *Career* former teacher of English Castlebrae HS and Broughton HS; MP (Lab): Edinburgh Leith 1992–97, Edinburgh N and Leith 1997–2001; Parly under-sec of state Scottish Office 1997 (resigned); MSP Edinburgh N and Leith 1999–; dep min for Health and Community Care 1999–2001, min for Health and Community Care 2001–04, min for Communities 2004–06; memb Educnl Inst of Scotland; *Style*— Malcolm Chisholm, Esq, MSP; ✉ The Scottish Parliament, Edinburgh EH99 1SP

CHISHOLM, Paul William; *Career* various mgmnt positions in New England Telephone & Telegraph Co and AT&T Corp 1974–85, vice-pres Shawmut Bank Boston 1985–88, vice-pres and gen mangr Teleport Communications Boston Inc 1988–92, md COLT Telecommunications 1992–95, pres and ceo COLT Telecom Group plc 1996–; first chm Other Licensed Operators Gp 1993–95; *Style*— Paul Chisholm, Esq

CHITNIS, Baron (Life Peer UK 1977), of Ryedale in the County of North Yorkshire; Pratap Chidamber Chitnis; s of late Chidamber N Chitnis, and Lucia Mallik; *b* 1 May 1936; *Educ* Penryn Sch, Stonyhurst, Univ of Birmingham, Univ of Kansas; *m* 1964, Anne, da of Frank Mansell Brand; 1 s (decd); *Career* sits as ind peer in House of Lords, head of Liberal Pty Orgn 1966–69; chief exec Rowntree Social Serv Tst 1974 (dir 1975–88); memb Community Relations Cmmn 1970–77; chm Br Refugee Cncl 1986–; author of ind reports on the elections in Zimbabwe 1979 and 1980, Guyana 1980, El Salvador 1982, 1984 and 1988 and Nicaragua 1984; *Style*— The Lord Chitnis

CHITTENDEN, Rear Adm Timothy Clive (Tim); s of Frederick William John Chittenden (d 1993), and Pauline Beryl, *née* Cockle (d 1978); *b* 25 May 1951; *Educ* Chatham House GS, Churchill Coll Cambridge (MA, Shooting half blue), RN Engrg Coll (MSc), RNC Greenwich (Dip Nuclear Engrg); *m* 2 Feb 1974, Clare Anne, da of David Style; 3 da (Sarah b 1975, Victoria b 1977, Alice b 1982); *Career* Marine Engr Offr HMS Warspite 1982–85, Marine Engr Offr HMS Talent 1988–90, asst dir Nuclear Safety MOD (PE) 1990–93, production manager Clyde Submarine Base Faslane 1993–94, Capt 1994, conducted MOD Dual Nuclear Regulation Study 1994–95, asst dir Business and Safety Chief Strategic Systems Directorate MOD 1995–97, asst dir S&T Update MOD 1997–99, dir in Service Submarines Ship Support Agency MOD DLO 1999–2000, ldr Submarine Support IPT Warship Support Agency 2000–03, Rear Adm 2003, COS (Support) to CINCFLEET 2003–05; astute prog dir BAESYSTEMS Submarines 2005–; Inst Nuclear Engineers Prize 1975; Freeman Worshipful Company of Carmen 2004; FINucE 2005 (MINucE 1982), FIMechE 2001 (MIMechE 1988), CEng 1988; *Recreations* sailing and dinghy racing (RYA coastal skipper), hill walking, 0.22 target rifle shooting, reading, listening to music; *Clubs* Bassenthwaite Sailing, Hawks' (Cambridge), RN and RM Rifle; *Style*— Rear Adm Tim Chittenden; ✉ BAESYSTEMS Submarines, Barrow-in-Furness, Cumbria LA14 1AF (tel 01229 874048)

CHITTOCK, John Dudley; OBE (1982); s of James Hiram Chittock (d 1973), of Leytonstone, and Phyllis Lucy Milner (d 1985); *b* 29 May 1928; *Educ* Oxford and Elson House, Forestdene, SW Essex Tech Coll; *m* 1, 1947, Joyce Kate (d 2001), da of Roy Ayrton Winter (d 1969), of Kent; m 2, 2005, Margaret Rose Robinson; *Career* writer, film prodr, publisher; exec ed Focal Press 1954–58, sr ptnr Films of Indust 1958–61, film and video columnist The Financial Times 1963–87, chm Screen Digest 1974–96 (fndr 1971); dir National Video Corporation Ltd 1981–86, non-exec chm NVC Cable Ltd 1983–86; chm: Br Fedn of Film Socs 1969–78 (vice-pres 1978–), The Grierson Meml Tst 1989–2000 (fndr 1974, patron 2006–), Kraszna-Krausz Fndn (media book prize and grants) 1996–2003 (tstee 1985–2003); dep chm Br Screen Advsy Cncl 1986–90; tstee Kraszna-Krausz Will Tst 2003–; conslt ed Royal TV Soc Journal 1978–82; chm of various film and TV indust ctees and numerous media confs, prodr and dir of over 30 documentary films, author of numerous articles, papers and books on film, TV and video; Hood Medal Royal Photographic Soc 1973, Queen's Silver Jubilee Medal 1977, Presidential Award Incorporated Inst of Photographers 1983, Video Writer of the Year Award 1983, Br Kinematograph, Sound and TV Soc (BKSTS) Cncl's Award for servs to the soc 1997, Charles Roebuck Cup for servs to film socs; FRPS, FRTS, FBKSTS; *Recreations* the human condition, period home and antiques, cooking, gardening, work, the arts; *Clubs* RAC; *Style*— John Chittock, Esq, OBE; ✉ The Old Vicarage, Wickhambrook, Suffolk CB8 8XH; 37 Gower Street, London WC1E 6HH (tel 020 7580 1502, fax 020 7580 1504)

CHITTY, Alison Jill; OBE (2004); da of Ernest Hedley Chitty, and Irene Joan Waldron; *b* 16 October 1948; *Educ* King Alfred Sch London, St Martin's Sch of Art, Central Sch of Art and Design, Arts Cncl scholar; *Career* theatre designer; dir Motley Theatre Design course; Victoria Theatre Stoke-on-Trent 1970–79 (designed over 40 prodns, head of design 4 years); dir Motley Theatre Design Course 2000– (co-dir 1992–2000); Hon Doctorate Univ of Staffordshire 2005; Mischa Black Award 2007; *Theatre* RNT incl: A Month in the Country, Don Juan, Much Ado About Nothing, The Prince of Homburg, Danton's Death, Major Barbara, Kick for Touch, Tales from Hollywood, Antigone, Martine, Venice Preserv'd, Fool for Love, Neaptide, Antony and Cleopatra, The Tempest, The Winter's Tale, Cymbeline, Cardiff East, Two Thousand Years, The Voysey Inheritance 2006; RSC incl: Tartuffe, Volpone, Breaking the Silence, Romeo and Juliet, Orpheus Descending (Haymarket), The Rose Tattoo (Playhouse), Hamlet; other prodns incl: Old King Cole (Theatre Royal Stratford East), Ecstasy and Uncle Vanya (Hampstead Theatre Club), Measure for Measure and Julius Caesar (Riverside Studios), The Way South (Bush), Carmen Jones and Lennon (Crucible Sheffield), Rememberance of Things Past (RNT) 2000 (Olivier Award 2001), Hamlet (RSC) 2001, Luther (RNT) 2001, Scenes from the Big Picture (RNT) 2003, The Merchant of Venice (Chichester) 2003, The Seagull (Chichester) 2003, A Midsummer Night's Dream (Chichester) 2004, The Master and Margerita (Chichester) 2004, Days of Wine and Roses (Donmar Warehouse) 2005, King Lear (Chichester) 2005; Best Costume Designer Lawrence Olivier Award 2007; *Opera* The Marriage of Figaro (Opera North), New Year (Houston Grand Opera), BowDown/Down by the Green Wood Side (Southbank), The Siege of Calais (Wexford), The Vanishing Bridegroom (St Louis Opera Theatre), Gawain (ROH), Falstaff (Gothenburg Music Theatre), Jenufa (Dallas Opera) 1994, Billy Budd (Grand Theatre Geneva) 1994, Blond Eckbert (Santa Fé Opera) 1994, Khovanshchina (ENO) 1994, Billy Budd (ROH) 1995, Modern Painters (Santa Fé Opera) 1995, Arianna (ROH) 1995, Billy Budd (Bastille Opera Paris) 1996, The Mask of Orpheus (Royal Festival Hall) 1996, Die Meistersinger von Nürnberg (Danish Royal Opera Copenhagen) 1996, Misper (Glyndebourne) 1997, Turandot (Bastille Opera Paris) 1997, Billy Budd (Dallas Opera and Houston Grand Opera) 1997–98, The Flying Dutchman (Bordeaux Opera) 1998, Tristan and Isolde (Seattle Opera) 1998, The Bartered Bride (ROH at Sadlers Wells) 1998, Julius Caesar (Bordeaux Opera) 1999, Otello (Bavarian Opera Munich) 1999, Dialogues of the Carmelites (Santa Fé Opera) 1999, Aida (Grand Theatre Geneva) 1999, Tristan and Isolde (Lyric Opera Chicago) 2000, The Last Supper (Staats Oper Berlin and Glyndebourne) 2000, Ion (Aldeburgh Festival and Almeida Opera) 2000, Billy Budd (Seattle and Tel Aviv), Jenufa (San Francisco), La Vestale (ENO) 2002, Bacchai (RNT) 202, Original Sin (Crucible Sheffield) 2002, Cavalleria Rusticana (Royal Albert Hall) 2002, Pagliacci (Royal Albert Hall) 2002, Khovanshchina (ENO) 2003, L'Enfant et les Sorlileges (Maastricht) 2003, Cosi Fan Tutti (ENO) 2003, The Flying Dutchman (Vilnius) 2004, The Io Passion (Aldeburgh Festival, Almeida Opera, Bregenz and UK tour) 2004, Billy Budd (Washington) 2004, Jenufa (Dallas Opera) 2004, Tangier Tattoo (Glyndebourne) 2005, Midsummer Marriage (Chicago Lyric Opera) 2005, Carmen (Greek Nat Opera) 2007; *Film* Blue Jean, Aria, Life is Sweet, Black Poppies (BBC), Naked, Secrets and Lies (Palm d'Or Cannes), The Turn of the Screw (BBC); *Style*— Ms Alison Chitty, OBE; ✉ c/o Allied Artists, 42 Montpellier Square, London SW7 1JZ (tel 020 7589 6243, fax 020 7622 1720)

CHITTY, Air Cdre Jon; OBE (1991); *Educ* King Edward VII GS Sheffield, Imperial Coll London (RAF scholarship), RAF Coll Cranwell; *m* Judith; 2 s (Jordan, Jack); *Career* OC Armament Servicing Flight RAF Kinloss, posted RAF Gütersloh and RAF Wattisham, instr Dept of Specialist Ground Trg RAF Coll Cranwell, cmd Armament Engrg Sqdn RAF Coningsby, tours RAF Stanley, HQ Strike Command and RAF Wattisham, promoted Wing Cdr 1989, ldr Tornado Role Office HQ Strike Command 1989, Advanced Staff Course, OC Engrg and Supply Wing RAF Brüggen, promoted Gp Capt, Dep Dir Weapons (RAF) RAF Wyton, ldr Air Strike Div Ordnance Bd 1999, Comdt Air Cadets RAF Coll Cranwell 2003–; chm: RAF Sub Aqua Assoc, Jt Services Sub Aqua Assoc, RAF Martial Arts Assoc; ret 2005; involvement with: Royal Aeronautical Soc, Farnborough International Airshow 2006, SBAC and DTI for Enterprise Week 2006;

C

formed Jon Chitty Consultancy 2005, dir Venture Diving; *Recreations* diving, martial arts (black belt Shotokan karate), skiing, travel; *Style*— Air Cdre Jon Chitty, OBE; ✉ JC Consultancy Ltd, 3 Riddiford Crescent, Brompton, Cambridgeshire PE28 4YH (tel 01480 437977, mobile 07875 890760, e-mail jonchitty@venturediving.com)

CHITTY, Sir Thomas Willes; 3 Bt (UK 1924), of The Temple; s of Sir (Thomas) Henry Willes Chitty, 2 Bt (d 1955); *b* 2 March 1926; *Educ* Winchester, UC Oxford; *m* 23 Aug 1951, Susan, da of Rudolph Glossop (d 1993), and Antonia White, FRSL (d 1980); 1 s (Andrew Edward Willes b 1953), 3 da (Cordelia Anne b 1955, Miranda Jane b 1967, Jessica Susan b 1971); *Heir* s, Andrew Chitty; *Career* served RN 1944–47; Granada Arts fell Univ of York 1964–65, visiting prof Boston Univ 1969–70; novelist, biographer (pen name: Thomas Hinde); *Style*— Sir Thomas Chitty, Bt; ✉ Bow Cottage, West Hoathly, West Sussex RH19 4QF (tel 01342 810269, e-mail thomas.chitty@ukgateway.net); c/o Andrew Hewson, John Johnson, 45–47 Clerkenwell Green, London EC1R 0HT (tel 020 7251 0125)

CHIVERS, Christopher John Adrian (Kit); s of Reginald Chivers, of Cardiff, and Dorothy Nicholson, *née* Jenkins; *b* 8 March 1945; *Educ* Bradford GS, Solihull Sch, Glasgow HS, Univ of Glasgow (MA), Trinity Coll Oxford (MA); *m* 22 July 1969, Geertje Bouwes; 1 da (Guinevere Beatrice Joanna b 24 Nov 1972), 1 s (Gregory Richard Reginald b 30 March 1976); *Career* HM Treasy: asst princ Expenditure and Taxation Divs 1968–71, asst private sec to Chancellor of the Exchequer 1971–73, princ Overseas Fin Gp 1973–76; first sec (fin) Br Embassy Washington 1976–78; HM Treasy: princ Defence Div 1978–81, asst sec and head Treasy Expenditure Div 1981–84; DOE 1984, grade 5 Efficiency Unit PM's Office 1984–86; HM Treasy: head Pay Div 1986–90, head Specialist Support Gp 1990–93, head privatisation of Forward Civil Service Catering (sub-dept of HM Treasy) 1993–94, Fundamental Expenditure Review of Treasy 1994; Dept of Nat Savings: dir of resources 1994–95, dep dir 1994–95, actg dir of savings 1995–96, dep chief exec 1996–98; HM chief inspr of the Magistrates' Courts Serv 1998–2003, chief inspr of criminal justice in NI 2003–; hon sec Brixton Cncl of Churches, treas Brixton Methodist Circuit; *Recreations* swimming, golf; *Style*— Kit Chivers, Esq; ✉ Criminal Justice Inspectorate, 14 Great Victoria Street, Belfast BT2 7BA

CHO, HE Dr Yoon-Je; *b* 22 February 1952; *Educ* Seoul Nat Univ Korea (BA), Stanford Univ USA (MA, PhD); *m*; 1 s, 2 da; *Career* Korean diplomat; served in Korean Air Force 1976–77; economist: World Bank 1984–89, IMF 1989–92; adjunct prof Georgetown Univ USA 1990, sr economist World Bank 1992–93; Korea Inst of Pub Fin: sr fell and dir of res 1993–94, vice pres 1995–96; sr cnsllr to the Dep PM and Min of Fin and Economy 1996–97, prof of economics Grad Sch of Int Studies Sogang Univ Seoul 1997–2003, chief economic advsr to the Pres 2003–05, ambass of the Republic of Korea to the Court of St James's 2005–; *Style*— HE Dr Yoon-Je Cho; ✉ Embassy of the Republic of Korea, 60 Buckingham Gate, London SW1E 6AJ

CHOAT, Jonathan Martin Cameron; *Educ* Dulwich Coll, Univ of London (BA); *Career* former mktg positions: Lever Bros, Texaco, J Lyons, Burmah Oil; currently fndr and chm Nexus Communications Gp, chm The Justin de Blank Co (restaurateurs); Freeman City of London, Liveryman Worshipful Co of Fruiterers; FRSA; *Style*— Jonathan Choat, Esq; ✉ Comberton House, Comberton, Ludlow, Shropshire SY8 4HE; Nexus Communications Group, 1 Chelsea Manor Gardens, London SW3 5PN (tel 020 7808 9712, fax 020 7808 9838)

CHODEL, Peter; s of Stanislaw Chodel (d 1978), of Mirfield, W Yorks, and Helena, *née* Naczenko; *b* 15 April 1956; *Educ* Mirfield Secdy Modern, Batley Art Sch, Central Sch of Art and Design (BA); *m* 1 Aug 1981, Vanessa, da of James Fredrick Lowery King, OBE; 1 s (Fredrick Stanislaw b 9 Feb 1988), 1 da (Molly Irena b 15 Feb 1990); *Career* freelance designer Mitchell Beazley Books 1979; designer: Observer Magazine 1979 (summer vacation placement 1978), Stadden Hughes Ltd 1980–84; design dir Michael Peters Group plc (Annual Reports Ltd, Right Angle, Michael Peters Corporate Literature, Michael Peters Literature) 1984–91, creative dir Addison Design Company Ltd 1991–; judge D&AD Awards 1994 and 2000; *Awards* D&AD award (for Yorkshire TV Good Companions Brochure 1981), MEAD Annual Report Show awards (for Michael Peters Group 1984 annual report 1985 and for Prestwich Holdings plc 1986 annual report 1987), Business Magazine/Price Waterhouse Annual Report of the Year award (for Tesco plc 1990); *Recreations* home and family, things Medieval; *Style*— Peter Chodel, Esq; ✉ 20 Finsen Road, Camberwell, London SE5 9AX (tel 020 7274 3848); Addison Corporate Marketing Ltd, 2 Cathedral Street, London SE1 9DE (tel 020 7403 7444, fax 020 7403 1243, e-mail peter.chodel@addison.co.uk)

CHOI, Christopher (Chris); s of Denis Choi, and Gloria, *née* Stephenson; *Educ* Univ of Nottingham (LLB); *Career* broadcaster; prodr That's Life (BBC1) 1991–93, presenter/reporter Watchdog (BBC 1) 1993–97, reporter Holiday (BBC 1) 1993–98, presenter You and Yours (Radio 4) 1997–98, presenter Radio Five Live 1997–99, consumer ed ITV News 1999–; *Recreations* argument, social drinking, country activities; *Style*— Chris Choi, Esq; ✉ ITN, 200 Gray's Inn Road, London WC1X 8XZ (tel 020 7833 3000, fax 020 7430 4302, e-mail chris.choi@itn.co.uk)

CHOLMONDELEY, 7 Marquess of (UK 1815); David George Philip Cholmondeley; KCVO (2007); also Viscount Cholmondeley of Kells (I 1661), Baron Cholmondeley of Namptwich (E 1689), Viscount Malpas and Earl of Cholmondeley (GB 1706), Baron Newborough (I 1715), Baron Newburgh (GB 1716), and Earl of Rocksavage (UK 1815); o s of 6 Marquess of Cholmondeley, GCVO, MC (d 1990); *b* 27 June 1960; *Educ* Eton, La Sorbonne Paris; *Heir* cous, Charles Cholmondeley; *Career* a page of honour to HM The Queen 1974–76; jt Hereditary Lord Great Chamberlain of England 1990–; *Style*— The Most Hon the Marquess of Cholmondeley; ✉ Cholmondeley Castle, Malpas, Cheshire (tel 01829 22202); Houghton Hall, King's Lynn, Norfolk

CHOLMONDELEY CLARKE, Marshal Butler; s of Maj Cecil Cholmondeley Clarke (d 1924), of Holycross, Co Tipperary, and late Fanny Ethel Carter; *b* 14 July 1919; *Educ* Aldenham; *m* 1947, Joan Roberta (d 2004), da of late John Kyle Stephens, JP, of Holywood, Co Down; 2 s (Edward, Robert); *Career* slr 1943; master of the Supreme Court of Judicature (Chancery Div) 1973–92; ed The Supreme Court Practice 1987–92; chm: Family Law Ctee 1970–72, Legal Aid Ctee 1972, Chancery Procedure Ctee 1968–72; memb Cncl Law Soc 1966–72; pres City of Westminster Law Soc 1971–72; *Books* Sweet & Maxwell's High Court Litigation Manual (conslt ed); *Recreations* reading, genealogy; *Clubs* Turf; *Style*— Marshal Cholmondeley Clarke, Esq; ✉ 44 Pelham Court, 145 Fulham Road, London SW3 6SH

CHOO, Jimmy; Hon OBE (2003); s of Kee-Yin Choo, of Penang, Malaysia, and Ah-Yin Moo Choo, of Penang, Malaysia; *b* 15 November 1952; *Educ* Cordwainer Coll; *Career* shoe designer; started own label 1988; has designed for the Royal Shakespeare Co and for the films Goldeneye (featuring character James Bond) and French Kiss; clients incl: royalty, film stars, pop stars and many other celebrities; visiting prof London Inst 2001–; Best Accessories Award Bridal Awards 1989, Accessory Designer of the Year Br Fashion Awards 2000 (nominated 6 times 1989–94), Gold Award Assoc of Colls 2000; Hon Dato given by Sultan of Pahang for contribution to Malaysia; Hon Liveryman Worshipful Co of Cordwainers 2004; *Style*— Jimmy Choo, Esq, OBE; ✉ Jimmy Choo Couture, 18 Connaught Street, London W2 2AF (tel 020 7262 6888)

CHOPE, Christopher Robert; OBE (1983), MP; s of His Hon Judge Robert Charles Chope (d 1988), and Pamela, *née* Durell (d 2004); *b* 19 May 1947; *Educ* Marlborough, Univ of St Andrews (LLB); *m* Christine, *née* Hutchinson; 1 s (Philip Robert), 1 da (Antonia); *Career* called to the Bar 1972; ldr Wandsworth BC 1979–83 (memb 1974–83); MP (Cons): Southampton Itchen 1983–92, Christchurch 1997–; Parly under sec of state: DOE 1986–90, Dept of Transport 1990–92; oppn frontbench spokesman on: tport, housing and construction 1997–98, trade and industry 1998–99, Treasy 2001–02, tport 2002–05; a vice-chm Cons Pty 1997–98, chm Cons Way Forward 2002–, memb 1922 Exec Ctee 2005–; memb: Health and Safety Cmmn 1993–97, Local Govt Cmmn 1994–95, House of Commons Trade and Industry Ctee 1999–, Speaker's Panel of Chm 2005–, Select Ctee on Procedure 2005–, UK delgn to Cncl of Europe 2005–; conslt Ernst & Young 1992–98; *Style*— Christopher Chope, Esq, OBE, MP; ✉ House of Commons, London SW1A 0AA (tel 020 7219 3000)

CHOPE, Dr John Norman; JP (Devon); s of William Pearse Chope, and Kathleen Mary, *née* Calvert (d 1955); *b* 27 June 1948; *Educ* Waverley GS Birmingham (awarded Reserved Cadetship Dartmouth RNC), Univ of Bristol (Associated Dental Co scholar, BSc, BDS, MRC Award, L E Attenborough Medal, George Fawn Prize), LDS RCS Eng, MFDGP (UK); *m* 1970, Susan Mary, da of Clinton and Kathleen Le Page; 1 da (Jenny Kathleen b 28 Sept 1976); *Career* trainee dental technician 1965, dental pathology res technician Univ of Birmingham 1966; neurophysiologist USA and subsequently Sudan (helped found Khartoum Dental Sch) 1969 and 1973, SHO (oral surgery) United Bristol Hosps 1973; assoc dental surgn: Backwell Somerset 1973, Stockwood Bristol and Shepton Mallet Somerset 1973–74; princ dental surgn and dental practice owner: Holsworthy Devon 1974–, Hartland Devon 1975–, Bude Cornwall 1981–90, Okehampton Devon 1983–98; hypnotherapist 1977–; conslt to Veterinary Drug Co plc 1996–98; conf lectr on practice mgmnt, business skills, communication, marketing dental health, the dental team and training; ed: Code of Practice (dental business quarterly) 1995–2004, CODE business advice sheets (series) 1995–2004; memb Editorial Bd: Dentistry 2000, t-dental.com 2000–; formerly: memb N Devon Dist and SW Regnl Dental Advsy Ctees, chm N Devon BDA, memb N Devon Dental Postgrad Ctee, chm Confedn of Dental Employers 1995–2004; currently: fndr memb, bd memb and treas SW Div Faculty of Gen Dental Practitioners (UK) RCS Eng, fndr memb and memb Ctee N Devon Independent Dental Practitioners' Gp; elected memb GDC 1996–, chm GDC Standards Ctee 2005–; expert lay panel memb Family Health Servs Appeal Authy 2001–; memb numerous professional socs incl: BDA, RSM, DPA, FGDP (UK), RCS, FDI, AOG; farmer/landowner 1976–, proprietor small specialist bldg co 1976–; chm: Speke Valley Services Ltd 1979– (t/a Firmadenta 1993–96 dental wholesalers and mktg co), Codental Products Ltd (dental service co for voluntary soc) 1995–2001, The Penroses Consultancy Ltd (business and mgmnt consultancy) 1997–2000; columnist for Dentistry 2002–; memb: CLA, Magistrates' Assoc, Cwlth Magistrates' and Judges' Assoc; *Publications* numerous publications on neurophysiology of taste receptors, therapeutic lasers, dental bodies corporate, dental health marketing, dental business management; *Recreations* architecture, building, structural design, writing, sketching, drawing, natural history, animal husbandry, gardening, swimming, walking, skiing, theatre; *Style*— Dr John Chope; ✉ Delivery 1, Hartland, Devon EX39 6DZ

CHORLEY, 2 Baron (UK 1945); Roger Richard Edward Chorley; s of 1 Baron Chorley, QC (d 1978); *b* 14 August 1930; *Educ* Stowe, Gonville & Caius Coll Cambridge (BA); *m* 31 Oct 1964, Ann Elizabeth, yr da of late Archibald Scott Debenham, of Ingatestone, Essex; 2 s (Hon Nicholas Rupert Debenham b 1966, Hon Christopher Robert Hopkinson b 1968); *Heir* s, Hon Nicholas Chorley; *Career* memb (elected hereditary peer) House of Lords 2001–; ptnr Coopers & Lybrand (CA) 1967–89; chm Ordnance Survey Advsy Bd 1982–85, chm Nat Tst 1991–96, hon vice-pres Royal Geographical Soc 1993– (pres 1987–90), pres Assoc for Geographic Information 1995–, vice-pres Cncl for Nat Parks 1996–; memb: Royal Cmmn on the Press 1975–78, Bd Nat Theatre 1980–90, Bd British Cncl 1981–99 (vice-chm 1991–99), NERC 1988–94; patron Br Mountaineering Cncl 1996–; Hon DSc: Reading 1990, Kingston 1992; Hon LLB Lancaster 1995; hon fell Univ of Central Lancashire 1994; Hon FRICS, FCA; *Style*— The Rt Hon the Lord Chorley; ✉ 50 Kensington Place, London W8 7PW

CHOUDHURY, HE Anwar Bokth; s of Afruz Bokth Choudhury, and Ashrafun Nessa Choudhury; *b* 15 June 1959, Sylhet, Bangladesh; *Educ* Univ of Salford (BSc), Univ of Durham (MBA); *m* Jan 2001, Momina; 2 c (Umar, Amani); *Career* diplomat; princ engr Siemens Plessey 1985–89, strategist and consltt RAF 1990–94, asst dir MOD 1995–99, dir Cabinet Office 2000–03, high cmmr to Bangladesh FCO 2004–; memb RIIA; *Recreations* bridge, cricket, cinema; *Style*— HE Mr Anwar Choudhury; ✉ c/o Foreign & Commonwealth Office (Dhaka), King Charles Street, London SW1A 2AH; British High Commission, United Nations Road, Bori Dara, Dhaka, Bangladesh (tel 00 88 02 882 2705, fax 00 88 02 882 3437, e-mail anwar.choudhary@fco.gov.uk)

CHOW, Sir C K; kt (2000); *b* 9 September 1950; *Educ* Univ of Wisconsin (BS), Univ of Calif (MS), Chinese Univ of Hong Kong (MBA), Harvard Business Sch (AMP); *Career* research engr Climax Chemical Co New Mexico 1974–76, process engr Sybron Asia Ltd Hong Kong 1976–77; The BOC Gp plc: various sr positions in Hong Kong and Australia 1977–86, pres BOC Japan 1986–89, gp mangr England and USA Gases Business Devpt 1989–91, regnl dir North Pacific 1991–93, chief exec Gases 1993–96, md 1994–97; chief exec GKN plc 1997–2001, ceo Brambles Industries plc 2001–03, ceo MTR Corp Ltd 2003–; non-exec dir Standard Chartered Bank (Hong Kong) Ltd 1997–; pres Soc of Br Aerospace Companies Ltd 1999; Hon DEng; Hon FHKIE, FREng, FIChemE, FCGI, FCILT, Fell Hong Kong Acad of Engrg Science; *Style*— Sir C K Chow

CHOW-STUART, Alexander; *see:* Stuart, Alexander Charles

CHOWDHURY, Ajay; s of Manindra Narayan Chowdhury, of New Delhi, India, and Indira, *née* Kumar; *b* 29 April 1962, Delhi, India; *Educ* Sydenham Coll of Economics Bombay (BComm), Wharton Sch Univ of Pennsylvania (MBA), Central Sch of Speech and Drama London (Dip); *m* 1 July 1995, Elizabeth McDonnell; 2 da (Layla Catriona b 4 April 1997, Eva Maya b 13 Oct 2000); *Career* mgmnt trainee IBM 1983–84, conslt then mangr Bain & Co 1986–91, successively gp devpt mangr, md United Interactive, dir United Broadcasting & Entertainment and ceo LineOne United News & Media 1991–99, pres and ceo NBC Internet Europe 2000, co-fndr and managing ptnr IDG Ventures Europe 2000–06, gen ptnr Acacia Capital Ptnrs 2006–07, ceo ENQII plc 2007–; chm Shazam Entertainment 2002–, non-exec dir Virtual Internet plc until 2002, dir Empower Interactive 2003–06, dir Lionhead 2004–06; artistic dir Rented Space Theatre Co, dir Museums, Libraries and Archives Cncl 2000–06, dir BSAC, tstee 24 Hour Museum 2003–06; *Recreations* music, diving, books, theatre, film; *Style*— Ajay Chowdhury, Esq; ✉ 16 Harman Drive, London NW2 2EB (tel 020 8452 2234, e-mail ajay@ajaychowdhury.com)

CHOY, Dr Ernest Ho Sing; s of Kim Hung Choy, of Hong Kong, and Foo Chun Fok Choy; *b* 15 June 1961; *Educ* Sutton Valence, Univ of Wales Coll of Med (MB BCh, MD); *m* 30 July 1999, Christina Bik Fun Mok; 1 da (Catrina b 2 Oct 2000); *Career* house physician Merthyr Tydfil Hosp 1985–86, house surgn Wrexham Maelor Hosp 1986, SHO (A&E) Walsall Gen Hosp 1986–87, SHO (Gen Med) Wrexham Maelor Hosp 1987–88, med registrar Maidstone Hosp 1989, registrar in rheumatology Rheumatology Unit Guy's and Lewisham Hosps 1989–90, research fell Rheumatology Unit UMDS Guy's Hosp 1990–93, lectr in clinical and academic rheumatology King's Coll Sch of Med and Dentistry (KCSMD) and UMDS 1993–98, conslt sr lectr in rheumatology and head of therapeutic rheumatology Academic Dept of Rheumatology Guy's, King's and St Thomas Hosps Sch of Med 1998–; chm Arthritis Research Campaign Clinical Trial Collaboration, expert advsr NICE, memb Standing Ctee Rheumatology and Rehabilitation section RSM 1992–95; memb: Br Soc for Rheumatology, Br Soc of Immunology, American Coll of Rheumatology; hon memb Hong Kong Soc of Rheumatology; FRCP 2002 (MRCP 1988);

Publications author of numerous articles and book chapters; *Recreations* classical music, visiting galleries and exhibitions of early 20th century art, tennis, golf; *Style—* Dr Ernest Choy; ✉ Academic Department of Rheumatology, Guy's, King's and St Thomas Hospitals School of Medicine, King's College London, King's College Hospital, Denmark Hill, London SE5 9RS (tel 020 7346 1732, fax 020 7346 1734 e-mail ernest.choy@kcl.ac.uk)

CHRISFIELD, Lawrence John (Larry); s of Sydney George Chrisfield (d 1977), and Minnie, *née* Underwood (d 1999); *b* 31 March 1938; *Educ* St Olave's and St Savior's GS; *m* Patricia Maureen, *née* Scoble; 4 c (Cindy Jane b 1961, Susan Melinda b 1962, Carol Ann b 1964, David Alexander b 1967); *Career* articled clerk, accountant Merrett Son and Street 1955–63, tax sr, mangr Arthur Young McClelland Moores & Co 1963–72, UK tax mangr Unilever plc 1972–74, ptnr Ernst & Young (formerly Arthur Young) 1975–97 (mangr 1974–75); currently ind tax conslt; chm Br Film Advsy Gp; dir: PACT Finance Ctee, Nat Film and Television Soc Fin Ctee, Redbus Gp Ltd, Coolabi plc, Hammer Entertainment Ltd, Rainmaker Films Ltd; memb Br Screen Advsy Cncl; FCA 1963, CTA 1963; *Recreations* theatre, photography; *Style—* Larry Chrisfield, Esq; ✉ St Paul's Parochial Room, Royal Hill, Greenwich, London SE10 8SS (tel and fax 020 8469 0799)

CHRISTENSEN, Poul Adrian; CBE (1994); s of Arnold Christensen (d 2004), and May Christensen (d 2002); *b* 10 January 1944, Liverpool; *Educ* East Grintead Co GS, RAC Cirencester (Dip Agric); *m* Margaret; 3 s (David Andrew, Simon Poul, Toby James), 1 da (Katie Joanne); *Career* jt fndr Tenant Farmers' Assoc 1981, sr ptnr Kingston Hill Farm Oxon; pres Fedn of Agric Co-operatives 1998–2003; chair: UK Fedn of Milk Gps 1998–2000, LINK Sustainable Livestock Prog DEFRA 2004–, Rural Devpt Service 2005–; memb: BBC Rural Affrs Advsy Ctee 1992–95, Bd Milk Marque 1994–2000 (chair Milk Marque and Axis Milk 1997–2000), Min of Agric's CAP Reform Gp 1994–95, Bd SE England Devpt Agency (SEEDA) 2002–, Bd Agric Central Trading; non-exec dir ADAS 1986–94; chm of govrs John Blandy Primary Sch 1976–80, govr Witney Coll 1993–96, memb Sch of Agric Advsy Ctee RAC Cirencester 1994–97; *Recreations* sailing, golf; *Style—* Poul Christensen, Esq, CBE

CHRISTIAN, Dominic Gerard; s of Denis Ambrose Christian, and Marie Stephenson, *née* Falconer; *b* 12 October 1960, York; *Educ* Ratcliffe Coll Silby, St Joseph's Coll Ipswich, UEA (BA); *m* August 1993, Catherine (Kate), *née* Birch; 1 s (Joey b 11 Nov 1994), 1 da (Julia b 10 July 1997); *Career* J K Buckenham 1984–89, Greig Fester Ltd 1989–97 (dir 1995); Benfield Gp: head of retro 1997–2002, head of specialty 2002–04, memb Bd 2004, ceo Int Div 2005–, ceo Benfield Ltd 2005–; dir Juvenile Diabetes Research Fndn, memb Norfolk Churches Tst; MInstD; *Recreations* football, Norfolk, history, church architecture, family; *Clubs* Nat Lib; *Style—* Dominic Christian, Esq; ✉ Benfield Limited, 55 Bishopsgate, London EC2N 3BD (tel 020 7578 7000, fax 020 7578 7002, e-mail dominic.christian@benfieldgroup.com)

CHRISTIAN, Louise; *Career* admitted slr 1978; specialises in personal injury, clinical negligence and public law; with Lovell White and King Slrs until 1979, slr Plumstead Community Law Centre 1979–81, advsr to GLC Police Ctee 1981–84, co-fndr and ptnr Christian Khan Slrs (formerly Christian Fisher Slrs) 1985–; has represented victims of the Marchioness disaster and of the Paddington, Southall and Potters Bar rail crashes and British detainees in Guantanamo Bay; sr fell Coll of Personal Injury Law; chair INQUEST, memb Cncl Liberty, memb Bd Centre for Corporate Accountability, memb Personal Injury and Clinical Negligence Panel Law Soc; tstee Article 19; Hon Dr Staffordshire Univ 2003; Legal Aid Personality of the Year LAPG/Independent Lawyer 2004, Liberty/Law Soc/Justice Human Rights Award 2004 for outstanding contribution to defending the rule of law; *Publications* Inquests: a Practitioners Guide (co-author, 2002); *Style—* Ms Louise Christian; ✉ Christian Khan, 42 Museum Street, London WC1A 1LY (tel 020 7831 1750, e-mail louisec@christiankhan.co.uk)

CHRISTIAN, Prof Reginald Frank; s of Herbert Alexander Christian (d 1965), of Liverpool, and Jessie Gower, *née* Scott (d 1969); *b* 9 August 1924; *Educ* Liverpool Inst, The Queen's Coll Oxford (MA); *m* 29 March 1952, Rosalind Iris, da of Capt Malcolm Napier (d 1973), of Brockenhurst, Hants; 1 da (Jessica Ilott b 1953), 1 s (Giles Nicholas b 1955); *Career* WWII Flying Offr 231 Sqdn and Atlantic Ferry Unit RAF 1943–46; FO Br Embassy Moscow 1949–50, lectr in Russian Univ of Liverpool 1951–55, prof of Russian and head of dept Univ of Birmingham 1955–66, assoc dir Centre for Russian and E European Studies 1963–66, prof of Russian and head of dept Univ of St Andrews 1966–92 (dean Faculty of Arts 1975–78, prof emeritus 1992–); visiting prof: McGill Univ Montreal 1961–62, Moscow 1964–65; Br memb Int Ctee of Slavists; pres Br Univs Assoc of Slavists 1975–78; *Books* Korolenko's Siberia (1954), Russian Syntax (1959), Tolstoy's War and Peace (1961), Russian Prose Composition (1962), Tolstoy - A Critical Introduction (1969), Tolstoy's Letters (ed and trans, 1978), Tolstoy's Diaries (ed and trans, 1985, revised and abridged edn, 1994), Alexis Aladin. The Tragedy of Exile (1999); *Recreations* violin, reading; *Style—* Prof Reginald Christian; ✉ Culgrianach, 48 Lade Braes, St Andrews, Fife KY16 9DA (tel 01334 474407); 7 Knockard Road, Pitlochry, Perthshire PH16 5HJ (tel 01796 472993)

CHRISTIANS, Sharon Jane; da of John Hlywka (d 1982), and Rose Theresa, *née* Yastrzhembsky (d 1990); *b* 6 October 1951; *Educ* Notre Dame Coll Sch Canada, Carleton Univ of Ottawa Canada (BA); *m* 18 Aug 1988, Ian Douglas Christians, s of Douglas Tamplin Christians, of Swansea, Wales; *Career* researcher and speech writer House of Commons Ottawa 1972–75, dir Ontario Youth Secretariat 1975–76, fed affrs analyst Canadian Inst of CA 1976–78; dir of public affrs: Northern Pipeline Agency Alaska Highway Gas Pipeline Project Canada 1978–80, Ontario Energy Corporation 1980–82; mangr International Communications General Electric USA 1982–88; dir of corporate affrs: THORN EMI plc 1988–90, Stanhope Properties plc 1990–91; dir of corporate affrs and sec to the Bd Amersham International plc 1991–93, exec vice-pres of corp affrs EMI Group plc (formerly THORN EMI) 1994–8, dir Client Communications McKinsey and Co Incorporated UK 1998–; non-exec dir: Ashford Hosp NHS Tst Middx 1992–94, HMV Group Ltd 1997–98; FRSA 1990, memb Investor Rels Soc 1994; *Recreations* music, tennis, languages; *Style—* Mrs Sharon Christians; ✉ McKinsey and Co Incorporated UK, 1 Jermyn Street, London SW1 4UH (tel 020 7839 8040, e-mail sharon_christians@mckinsey.com)

CHRISTIANSEN, Rupert Elliott Niels; s of Michael Robin Christiansen (d 1983), and Kathleen Gertrude, *née* Lyon (d 2004); *b* 6 September 1954; *Educ* Millfield, King's Coll Cambridge (MA, MLitt), Columbia Univ (Fulbright Scholar); *Career* arts ed Harpers & Queen 1988–95, dep arts ed The Observer 1990–93; opera critic: The Spectator 1989–96, Daily Telegraph 1996–; dance critic Mail on Sunday 1996–; Somerset Maugham Prize 1989; dir Gate Theatre 1995–; memb Ctee London Library 1989–92 and 1995–; tstee Charleston Tst 1999–; FRSL 1997; *Books* Prima Donna (1984), Romantic Affinities (1988), The Grand Obsession (ed, 1988), Tales of the New Babylon (1994), Cambridge Arts Theatre (ed, 1997), The Visitors: Culture Shock in 19th Century Britain (2000), Arthur Hugh Clough: The Voice of Victorian Sex (2001), Pocket Guide to Opera (2002), Who Was William Shakespeare? (2003), The Complete Book of Aunts (2006); *Recreations* swimming, skiing, walking; *Clubs* Two Brydges Place; *Style—* Rupert Christiansen, Esq, FRSL; ✉ c/o PFD, Drury House, 34–43 Russell Street, London WC2B 5HA (tel 020 7344 1000, fax 020 7836 9541)

CHRISTIE, Dr Campbell; CBE (1997); s of Thomas Christie (d 1944), and Johnina, *née* Rolling (d 1965); *b* 23 August 1937; *Educ* Albert Senior Secdy Sch Glasgow, Langside Coll Glasgow, Woolwich Poly London; *m* 2 Feb 1963, Elizabeth Brown, da of Alexander Cameron (d 1968); 2 s (Andrew Cameron b 1963, Douglas Campbell b 1965); *Career* RN 1956–58; Civil Serv: Admiralty 1954–59, DHSS 1959– 72; Soc of Civil and Public Servants 1972–85 (dep gen sec 1975–85), gen sec Scottish TUC 1986–98; pres Scottish Civic Forum 1997–; vice-chair British Waterways 2004– (memb Bd 1998–, chair Scotland Gp 2001–); non-exec dir Forth Valley NHS Bd, chm Falkirk FC; memb Bd: South West Trains Ltd, Scottish Enterprise 1998–2005, Scottish Futures Forum 2005–; Hon DLit: Napier Univ, Queen Margaret Univ Edinburgh, Univ of Stirling, Univ of St Andrews; Hon LLD Glasgow Caledonian Univ; FScotvec, FEIS; *Recreations* golf; *Clubs* Glenbervie Golf; *Style—* Dr Campbell Christie, CBE; ✉ 31 Dumyat Drive, Falkirk FK1 5PA (tel 01324 624555, e-mail christiec@globalnet.co.uk)

CHRISTIE, Gus; s of George Christie, of Ringmer, E Sussex, and Mary, *née* Nicholson; *b* 4 December 1963, Lewes, Sussex; *Educ* St Aubyns Rottingdean, Eton, KCL; *m* (m dis); 4 s (Jackson, Romulus (twins) b 17 Jul 1996, Alexander b 30 Jan 2000, Ivo b 29 Apr 2001); *Career* early career in wildlife filmmaking, trg with Partridge Films, freelance cameraman 1992, films incl Buffalo, The African Boss, Red Monkeys of Zanzibar and New Fox in Town; exec chm Glyndebourne Productions Ltd 2000–; dir South-East Arts; awards for Glyndebourne: Royal Philharmonic Soc Audience Devpt Award (Zoe, Last Supper, La Boheme, Don Giovanni) 2000, Opera Award (Fidelio) 2001 South Bank Show Opera Award (Pelleas et Melisande) 2000 and (Giulio Cesare) 2005, Theatrical Mgmnt Assoc Award Outstanding Achievement in Opera (Tristan und Isolde) 2003; *Recreations* sport, music, nature; *Style—* Gus Christie, Esq; ✉ Glyndebourne, Lewes, East Sussex BN8 5UU (tel 01273 812321, fax 01273 814391, e-mail gus.christie@glyndebourne.com)

CHRISTIE, Linford; OBE (1998, MBE 1990); *b* 2 April 1960; *Career* athlete; full UK int (over 50 appearances); achievements at 100m: UK champion 1985, 1987, 1990, 1991, 1992 and 1993, AAA champion 1986, 1988, 1989, 1991, 1992 and 1993, Gold medal Euro Championships 1986, 1990 and 1994, Gold medal Cwlth Games 1990 and 1994 (Silver medal 1986), Gold medal Dinner Europa Cup 1987, 1989, 1991 and 1993, Gold medal World Cup 1989 and 1992, Gold medal Olympic Games 1992 (Silver 1988), Gold medal World Championships 1993 (Silver medal 1991), Gold medal World Cup 1994; achievements at 200m: AAA indoor champion 1981, 1982, 1987, 1988, 1989 and 1991, UK champion 1985 and 1988, AAA champion 1988, Gold medal Euro Indoor Championships 1986 (Bronze 1988), winner Europa Cup 1987, Bronze medal Euro Championships 1990, Silver medal World Cup 1992; achievements at 60m: Gold medal Euro Indoor Championships 1988 and 1990, AAA indoor champion 1989, 1990 and 1991; also winner various 4 x 100m relay medals; record holder: UK, Euro and Cwlth 60m and 100m, UK and Cwlth 4 x 100m relay; only person to win both 60m and 200m at AAA Indoor Championships (twice, 1989 and 1991); Male Athlete of the Year - Br Athletics Writers' Assoc 1988 and 1992, Panasonic Sports Personality of the Year 1992, BBC Sports Personality of the Year 1993; involved with various charities incl: Westminster Drugs Project, Sportability, Br Assoc of Sport for Disabled; BBC TV athletics pundit, presenter Linford's Record Breakers (BBC1); Freeman Borough of Hammersmith and Fulham 1988; *Books* Linford Christie - An Autobiography (1989), A Year in the Life Of, To Be Honest With You; *Style—* Linford Christie, OBE; ✉ c/o Susan Barrett, Nuff Respect, The Coach House, 107 Sherland Road, Twickenham, Middlesex TW1 4XJ (tel 020 8891 4145, website www.nuff-respect.co.uk)

CHRISTIE, Nan Stevenson; da of James Cowan Christie, of Ayr, and Henrietta, *née* Rock (d 1988); *b* 6 March 1948; *Educ* Ayr Acad, RSAMD, London Opera Centre; *m* 16 June 1972, Andrew S Hendrie, s of William Hendrie; 1 s (Ross b 2 July 1983); *Career* soprano; operatic debut as Fiametta in The Gondoliers (Scottish Opera), Covent Garden debut as First Esquire in Parsifal; toured in Switzerland, Portugal, Germany, Poland and Japan, princ guest artist Frankfurt Opera; worked with conductors incl: Claudio Abbado, André Previn, Sir John Pritchard, Sir Bernard Haitink, Sir Simon Rattle, Sir Alexander Gibson, John Mauceri, Michael Gielen; prof of singing and head of classical voice Goldsmiths Coll London; James Caird travelling scholarship, Peter Stuyvesant scholarship, Countess of Munster scholarship, Peter Styvesant scholarship, James Caird travelling scholarship, Countss of Munster scholarship; *Roles* incl: Pamina in The Magic Flute (Eng Music Theatre, Opera de Nancy), Sophie in Tom Jones (Eng Music Theatre), Xenia in Boris Godunov (Scot Opera), Flora in The Turn of the Screw (Scot Opera), Galla in The Cataline Conspiracy (Scot Opera), Tytania in A Midsummer Night's Dream (Scot Opera, Opera North), Susanna in The Marriage of Figaro (Scot Opera, Frankfurt Opera), Despina in Cosi fan Tutte (Scot Opera, Netherlands Opera, Glyndebourne), Frasquita in Carmen (Edinburgh Festival, Earls Court, Japan), Oscar in Un Ballo in Maschera (Frankfurt Opera), Marie in Die Soldaten (Frankfurt Opera), Euridice in Orpheus in the Underworld (ENO), Countess Adele in Count Ory (ENO), Adele in Die Fledermaus (ENO), Queen of Night in The Magic Flute (Scot Opera, Marseille, ENO), Arbace in Mitridate (La Fenice Venice, Italian debut), Blonde in Mozart's Die Entführung aus dem Serail (Scot Opera, Frankfurt Opera), Oscar in Verdi's Un Ballo in Maschera (Bonn Opera), Peter Maxwell Davies' Dr of Myddfai (WNO, World Première) William Bolcom's Songs of Innocence & Experience (Royal Festival Hall, Eurp Première), Madame Herz in Ser Schauspieldirektor (BBC), Cunegonde in Candide (London Symphony Orchestra), Frasquita in Carmen (Edinburgh Festival), Despina in Cosi Fan Tutte (Glyndebourne), Carlotta in The Phantom of the Opera (HM Theatre Haymarket); *Recordings* audio incl: La Vita Nuova (with the Nash Ensemble and Nicholas Maw), Anthology of Italian Opera, Gli Orazie ed i Curiazi, Melancholia (by Dusapin, with Orchestra de Lyon), Dr of Myddfai (by Peter Maxwell Davies, with WNO); video incl: various Gilbert and Sullivan, Gianetta in The Gondoliers, Aline in The Sorcerer, title role in Princess Ida; *Recreations* painting, reading, gardening; *Style—* Ms Nan Christie; ✉ e-mail nanchristie@hotmail.co.uk

CHRISTIE, Stuart; DL (Merseyside 2005); s of Samuel Albert Christie (d 1977), and Alice Duncan, *née* Fellows (d 1999); *b* 26 November 1934; *Educ* Liverpool Inst HS, Univ of Liverpool (LLB); *m* 1972, Her Hon Judge Elizabeth Mary Steel, DL, *qv*, da of late His Hon Edward Steel; 2 c (Elspeth Victoria b 19 Nov 1976, Iain Duncan b 17 Feb 1978); *Career* Nat Serv RA 1959–61; Alsop Stevens & Co (now DLA): articled clerk 1954–58, asst slr 1958–59 and 1961–63, ptnr 1963–91, conslt 1992–; memb: The Liverpool Law Soc, The Notaries Soc; hon memb Royal Liverpool Philharmonic Soc; Freeman City of London (by purchase), memb City of London Slrs' Co; High Sheriff Merseyside 2004–05; hon German consul for Merseyside, ret; Cross of the Order of Merit (Germany) 2000; *Recreations* choral singing (Royal Liverpool Philharmonic Choir); *Clubs* Athenaeum (Liverpool, pres 1992–93), Lancs CCC, Artists (Liverpool); *Style—* Stuart Christie, Esq, DL; ✉ 70 Knowsley Road, Cressington Park, Liverpool L19 0PG (tel 0151 427 3760)

CHRISTIE-BROWN, Jeremy Robin Warrington; s of Robson Christie-Brown (d 1971), and Mildred, *née* Warrington (d 1970); *b* 15 July 1936; *Educ* Harrow, Univ of Oxford (MA, BM BCh), UCH Med Sch, DPM; *m* 3 Nov 1962, Margaret Elizabeth, da of Frederick Stafford (d 1979); 2 s (Dominic b 9 Oct 1963, Jonathan b 15 Nov 1964), 1 da (Sarah b 3 May 1968); *Career* conslt psychiatrist UCH and Friern Hosp 1971–76, conslt psychiatrist The Maudsley Hosp 1976–1995 (conslt emeritus 1995); FRCP, FRCPsych; *Style—* Dr Jeremy Christie-Brown; ✉ 127 Harley Street, London W1G 6AZ (tel 020 7486 3631)

CHRISTIE-MILLER, Andrew William Michael; DL (Wilts 1993); o s of Maj Samuel Vandeleur Christie-Miller, CBE (d 1968), of Clarendon Park, Wilts, and Esmée Antoinette Fraser, *née* Hutcheson; *b* 22 September 1950; *Educ* Eton, RAC Cirencester (Dip Rural Estate Mgmnt, Dip Advanced Farm Mgmnt); *m* 6 Feb 1976, Barbara, da of Maj Charles Alexander Neil (d 1959), of London; 2 da (Rebecca Claire b 1976, Victoria Phoebe b 1978), 1 s (Alexander William Henry b 1982); *Career* Spicer & Pegler 1970–73, Savills 1978–82; chm Grainfarmers Ltd; memb Wilts CC 1985–93; chm Game Conservancy Tst 2000–06;

High Sheriff Wilts 1996–97; ARICS 1979; *Recreations* shooting, travel, conservation; *Clubs* White's; *Style*— Andrew Christie-Miller, Esq, DL; ✉ Elvaston Cottage, 22a Elvaston Place, London SW7 5QE (tel 020 3155 0039, e-mail andrew@christiemiller.co.uk); Podere Torrione, Strada per Pienza 58, 53026 Pienza, Siena, Italy (tel 0039 0578 757802)

CHRISTMAS, Colin Adrian; s of R F Christmas, and M Haskey; *b* 11 December 1938; *Educ* Forest Sch, architectural colls Essex and London; *m* 31 March 1962, Elisa Curling, da of H H Curling Hope; 1 da (Laura b 14 Oct 1966), 1 s (Paul b 7 Feb 1968); *Career* with Sir Giles Gilbert Scott Son and Partner 1959–63; work on: Liverpool Cathedral, Bankside Power Station; Fitzroy Robinson Partnership: designer/planner 1963, ptnr 1987–92, conslt 1992–; architectural and historic conslt Covent Garden Market and Royal Exchange 1997–; designs for shopping, office, residential and industrial complexes in UK and abroad; responsible for design and implementation of extension and refurbishment of Royal Exchange London 1983–91 and Pinners Hall City of London; Civic Tst commendation for Watling Court, Design Award Chancery House Sutton, Stone Fedn commendation and City Heritage Award for Royal Exchange; *Books* The Caliphs Design (conslt, ed by Paul Edwards, 1986), The Royal Exchange (contrib, 1997); *Recreations* east coast sailing, music, travel, art; *Style*— Colin Christmas, Esq; ✉ 33 The Drive, North Chingford, London E4 7AJ (tel and fax 020 8529 0925); Kevin Dash Architects, 67 Shelton Street, Covent Garden, London WC2H 9HE (tel 020 7379 1920, fax 020 7379 3202)

CHRISTMAS, Timothy John; s of Leslie George Christmas, of Poole, Dorset, and Lydia Valerie, *née* Brown; *b* 2 February 1956; *Educ* Bournemouth, Middx Hosp Med Sch London (Simmonds' scholar, MB BS, MD, Univ of London laurels 1979); *m* 2003, Dr Ethna Mannion; *Career* house surgn Middx Hosp 1980, demonstrator in anatomy Univ of Cambridge 1981, SHO rotation Addenbrooke's Hosp Cambridge 1982–83, SHO/registrar surgical rotation Univ Hosps Nottingham 1983–85; surgical registrar: Addenbrooke's Hosp 1985, Royal London Hosp 1985–87; research fell UC and Middx Sch of Med 1987–90, sr registrar Bart's 1990–92, research fell Norris Cancer Hosp Univ of Southern Calif LA 1992, RCS Ethicon travelling scholar 1992, Shackman travelling scholar 1992, William Cook scholar 1996, conslt urological surgn Charing Cross Hosp 1992–, conslt urological surgn Chelsea and Westminster Hosp 1992–2000, Royal Marsden Hosp 2000–; memb: Br Assoc of Urological Surgns 1992, Br Assoc of Surgical Oncology 1995; FRCS 1984, FRCS(Urol) 1991, FEBU 1992, FRSM 1990; *Books* Urodynamics Made Easy (jtly, 1989), Benign Prostatic Hyperplasia (jtly, 1993), Benign Prostatic Hyperplasia: a colour guide (jtly, 1994), Prostate Cancer (jtly, 1995), Disease of the Testis (jtly, 1999); *Recreations* travel, ornithology, photography, skiing, warm-hearted abuse; *Style*— Timothy Christmas, Esq; ✉ Private Patients Wing, 15th Floor, Charing Cross Hospital, Fulham Palace Road, London W6 8RF

CHRISTOPHER, (Phyllis) Ann; da of William Christopher (d 1986), of Rickmansworth, Herts, and Phyllis, *née* Vennall (d 2005); *b* 4 December 1947; *Educ* Watford Girls GS, Harrow Sch of Art, W of Eng Coll of Art (Dip AD); *m* 19 July 1969, Kenneth Harold Cook, s of Harold Gilbert Cook (d 2005), of Oldland Common, nr Bristol; *Career* sculptor; numerous gp and solo exhibitions 1969–; works in public collections incl: Bristol City Art Gallery, Univ of Bristol, Glynn Vivian Art Gallery Swansea, Royal W of Eng Acad, Chantrey Bequest Royal Acad, Harrison Weir Collection London; commissions incl: Corten Sculpture (4.9m) Marsh Mills Plymouth 1996, Bronze Sculpture (2.4m) Linklaters & Paines London 1997, Bronze Sculpture (3m) private garden Great Barrington USA 1998, Corten Sculpture (5.5m) Port Marine Bristol 2001, Bronze Sculpture (2.2m) private garden Albi France 2002; RWA 1983 (assoc 1972), RA 1989 (assoc 1980), FRBS 1992; *Recreations* cinema, travel, architecture; *Style*— Miss Ann Christopher, RA

CHRISTOPHER, Baron (Life Peer UK 1998), of Leckhampton in the County of Gloucestershire; Anthony Martin Grosvenor (Tony) Christopher; CBE (1984); s of George Russell Christopher (d 1951), and Helen Kathleen Milford, *née* Rowley (d 1971); *b* 25 April 1925; *Educ* Cheltenham GS, Westminster Coll of Commerce; *m* 1962, Adela Joy Thompson; *Career* chm Trades Union Unit Trust Mangrs Ltd 1983; political and PR conslt 1989–; Inland Revenue Staff Fedn: asst sec 1957–60, asst gen sec 1960–74, jt gen sec 1975, gen sec 1976–88; chm Civil Serv Bldg Soc 1958–87, pres TUC Gen Cncl 1988–89 (memb 1976–89); memb: Bd Civil Serv Housing Assoc 1958–96 (vice-chm 1988–96), Cncl of Nat Assoc for Care and Resettlement of Offenders 1956–98 (chm 1973–98), Home Sec's Advsy Cncl for Probation and After-Care Ctee 1966–79, Home Sec's Working Party on Treatment of Habitual Drunken Offenders 1969–71, Cncl of Policy Studies Inst, Cncl Inst of Manpower Studies, Econ Social Res Cncl 1985–88, TUC Gen Cncl 1976–89, TUC Econ Ctee 1977–89, TUC Educn Ctee 1977–85, TUC Employment Policy and Orgn Ctee 1979–89, TUC Int Ctee 1982–89, TUC Media Working Group 1979–89 (chm 1985–89), TUC Fin Gen Purposes Ctee 1984–89, TUC Educn and Trg Ctee 1985–86, Tax Consultative Ctee 1974–88, Royal Cmmn on Distribution of Income and Wealth 1979–80, IBA 1978–83, Broadcasting Complaints Cmmn 1989–96, Audit Cmmn 1989–95, GMC 1989–94, Ind Inquiry into Rover Cowley Works Closure Proposals 1990; tstee Inst for Public Policy Res (treas 1991–94); chm: NEDO Tyre Ind Econ Devpt Ctee 1983–84, Alcoholics Recovery Project 1970–76; FRSA 1989; *Books* Policy for Poverty (jtly, 1970), The Wealth Report (jtly, 1979); *Recreations* gardening, reading, music; *Clubs* Beefsteak, Wig & Pen, RAC; *Style*— The Lord Christopher, CBE; ✉ c/o T U Fund Managers Ltd, Congress House, Great Russell Street, London WC1B 3LQ; House of Lords, London SW1A 0PW

CHRISTOPHERS, Richard Henry Tudor (Harry); s of Richard Henry Christophers (d 1991), of Canterbury, Kent, and Constance Clavering, *née* Thorp (d 1987); *b* 26 December 1953; *Educ* Canterbury Cathedral Choir Sch, King's Sch Canterbury, Magdalen Coll Oxford; *m* 2 June 1979, Veronica Mary, da of Francis Vincent Hayward; 2 da (Antonia Lucy Mary b 30 Nov 1984, Cecilia Mary b 1 March 1991), 2 s (Dominic James b 18 March 1987, Sebastian John b 14 April 1989); *Career* conductor; South Bank debut 1983, Salzburg Festival debut 1989, Proms debut 1990, Opera debut (Lisbon Opera) 1994, Musikverein debut 1998, Concertgebiuw Amsterdam debut 1999, ENO debut 2000; conductor and fndr: The Sixteen (choir), The Symphony of Harmony and Invention (orchestra); orchs conducted incl: Tapiola Sinfonietta, Avanti!, Scot Chamber Orch, Deutsche Kammerphilharmonie, Royal Concertgebouw Chamber Orch, Lahti Symphony Orch, Stavanger Symphony Orch, St Louis Symphony Orch, Helsinki Philharmonic, Orch of the Age of Enlightenment, City of London Sinfonia, BBC Nat Orch of Wales, English Chamber Orch, Northern Sinfonia, Bergen Philharmonic, BBC Philharmonic, London Symphony Orch, Hallé Orch, Academy of St Martin-in-the-Fields, Royal Liverpool Philharmonic, San Francisco Symphony Orchestra; *Recordings* numerous recordings with The Sixteen (The Symphony of Harmony and Invention) incl: Taverner's Festal Masses Vols I-VI (1984–93) and Missa Gloria Tibi Trinitas (1989, Grand Prix du Disque), Monteverdi's Masses (1987) and Vespers (1988), Handel's Messiah (1989, Grand Prix du Disque), Byrd's Mass à 5 (1989) and Mass à 4 (1990), Poulenc's Figure Humaine (1990), Bach's St John Passion (1990), Palestrina's Missa Papae Marcelli (1990), 20 Century Christmas Collection (1990), Eton Choirbook Vols 1–5 (1991–95, Vol 1 winner Gramophone Award 1992), Handel's Alexander's Feast (1991, Deutschen Schallplatten, 1992), Purcell's Fairy Queen (1991), Sheppard's Sacred Music Vols 1–4 (1990–92), 20 Century American Collection (1991), Britten's Choral Music Vols 1–3 (1992–93, Vol 2 Deutschen Schauplatten, 1993), Bach's Christmas Oratorio (1993), Handel's Israel in Egypt (1993), Bach's B Minor Mass (1994), Stravinsky's Symphony of Psalms with the BBC Philharmonic (1995, Diapason d'Or 1995), Handel's Esther (1996), Messiaen's Cinq Rechants (1996), Handel's Samson (1997), Scarlatti's Stabat Mater (1997), Victoria's Sacred Music Vols 1–3 (1997–98), Buxtehude's Membra Jesu Nostri (2001), Renaissance (2004, Classical Brit Award 2005); video Handel's Messiah in Dublin (1992); *Recreations* cooking, Kent CCC, Arsenal FC; *Style*— Harry Christophers, Esq; ✉ c/o The Sixteen Limited, Raine House, Raine Street, Wapping, London E1W 3RJ (tel 01865 793999, fax 01865 793274, e-mail info@thesixteen.org.uk, website www.thesixteen.com)

CHRISTOU, Dr Alex; *b* 24 February 1963; *Educ* Oxford Sch, Imperial Coll London (BSc, ARCS), Trinity Coll Oxford (DPhil); *m* 8 Dec 2001, Tracy Moore; *Career* jr res fell St John's Coll Oxford 1987; Accenture: mgmnt conslt 1987, ptnr 2000–, md 2003–, memb UK & I Bd 2005–; *Recreations* sailing, skiing, riding, tennis, football; *Clubs* RAC, Arsenal FC; *Style*— Dr Alex Christou; ✉ Accenture, 20 Old Bailey, London EC4M 7AN (tel 020 7844 4766, e-mail alex.christou@accenture.com)

CHRUSZCZ, Charles Francis; QC (1992); s of Jan Franciszek Chruszcz, of Cheadle, Cheshire, and Kathleen Whitehurst; *b* 19 November 1950; *Educ* Brookway HS, QMC London (LLB); *m* Margaret Olivia, da of John Chapman; 3 s (Alexander John b 30 Aug 1977, Edward Charles b 26 March 1979, Thomas Robert b 20 May 1981); *Career* called to the Bar Middle Temple 1971, entered chambers at Peters St Manchester 1973, recorder of the Crown Court 1991– (asst recorder 1986–91); *Recreations* keen interest in lacrosse, rugby, reading, music, politics and the outdoors; *Style*— Charles Chruszcz, Esq, QC; ✉ Exchange Chambers, 7 Ralli Court, Westriverside, Manchester M3 5FT (tel 0161 833 2722)

CHRYSTAL, Prof (Kenneth) Alexander (Alec); s of Kenneth Hugh Chrystal (d 1945), and Dorothy Bell, *née* Anderson (d 2003); *b* 21 January 1946; *Educ* Oldershaw GS Wallasey, Univ of Exeter (BA), Univ of Essex (MA, PhD); *m* 1, 4 April 1972 (m dis 1978); 1 s (Mark Kenneth James b 1972); m 2, 29 July 1995, Alison Anne Wigley; *Career* lectr: Univ of Manchester 1971–72, Civil Serv Coll 1972–75; econ advsr HM Treasy 1975–76, lectr Univ of Essex 1976–84, visiting prof Univ of Calif Davis 1979–80, visiting scholar Federal Reserve Bank of St Louis 1983–84, prof of economics Univ of Sheffield 1984–88, prof of monetary economics City Univ Business Sch 1988–99 (head Dept of Banking Fin 1996–97), sr advsr Bank of England 1997–2001, prof of money and banking City Univ Business Sch (now Sir John Cass Business Sch) 2001–; FSS 1967, FRSA 1995; *Books* Controversies in Macroeconomics (1979), Political Economics (with J Alt, 1983), Exchange Rates and the Open Economy (ed with R Sedgwick, 1987), Introduction to Positive Economics (with R G Lipsey, 1995), Economics for Business and Management (with R G Lipsey, 1997), Principles of Economics (with R G Lipsey, 1999), Economics (with R G Lipsey, 2004); *Recreations* music, travel, economics; *Clubs* Athenaeum; *Style*— Prof Alec Chrystal; ✉ 34 Liberia Road, London N5 1JR (tel 020 7704 0144); Sir John Cass Business School, City of London, 106 Bunhill Row, London EC1Y 8TZ (tel 020 7040 0159, e-mail a.chrystal@city.ac.uk)

CHRYSTIE, Dr Kenneth George; s of Gordon Buchanan Chrystie (d 1993), and Winifrede Mary Chrystie (d 1993); *b* 24 November 1946, Glasgow; *Educ* Univ of Glasgow (LLB, PhD), Univ of Virginia; *m* 11 June 1975, Mary Harrison Chrystie, *née* Kirkpatrick; 1 s (Patrick William Gordon b 19 Nov 1978), 2 da (Kate Helen b 18 June 1980, Lindsay Elizabeth b 21 July 1983); *Career* lawyer; sr ptnr McClure Naismith; non-exec dir Murgitroyd plc; chm Discipline Ctee ICAS; memb Law Soc of Scotland; past pres Royal Glasgow Inst of the Fine Arts; chm: Hugh Fraser Fndn, Emily Fraser Tst; dir: Glasgow Culture and Leisure, Glasgow Science Centre; FRSA; *Publications* Encyclopaedia of Scots Law (contrib, 1988), International Handbook on Contracts of Employment (contrib, 1988); *Recreations* golf, tennis, curling; *Clubs* Prestwick Golf, Glasgow Art, Glasgow Golf; *Style*— Dr Kenneth Chrystie; ✉ McClure Naismith, 292 St Vincent Street, Glasgow G2 5TQ (tel 0141 204 2700, fax 0141 248 3998, e-mail kchrystie@mcclurenaismith.com)

CHU, Dr Anthony Christopher; s of Yu-Chang Chu, of Bexley, Kent, and Frances Nelly Chu; *b* 13 May 1951; *Educ* Alleyn's Sch Dulwich, Guy's Hosp Med Sch (BSc, MB BS); *m* 11 March 1978 (m dis 1987), Sian Meryl, da of John Daniel Griffths, of Hailey, Oxon; 2 da (Jessica Louise b 1979, Alexandra Mary b 1980); m 2, 30 Dec 1989, Jenny Frances, da of Robert Morris, of Haughley Green, Suffolk; 2 da (Natasha Victoria and Caroline Frances b 1999), 1 s (James Andrew Portman b 1999); *Career* various posts NHS 1975–80, sr staff assoc coll of physicians and surgns Columbia Presbyterian Hosp New York 1980–81, sr registrar St John's Hosp for Skin Diseases 1981–82; sr lectr (also conslt dermatologist and Wellcome sr res fell): Royal Post Grad Med Sch Hammersmith Hosp, St John's Hosp for Skin Diseases 1982–89; sr lectr and conslt dermatologist Imperial Coll Sch of Med at Hammersmith Hosp (Royal Postgrad Med Sch until merger) and Ealing Hosp 1989–2005, conslt dermatologist, hon sr lectr and head of dermatology Hammersmith Hosps Tst and Ealing Hosp 2005–; memb and sec: Int Histiocyte Soc, Br Assoc of Univ Teachers of Dermatology; chm Acne Support Gp; Freeman City of London 1991, Liveryman Worshipful Soc of Apothecaries 1989; FRCP 1993 (MRCP 1978); *Recreations* horticulture, painting; *Style*— Dr Anthony Chu; ✉ Unit of Dermatology, Imperial College School of Medicine, Hammersmith Hospital, Du Cane Road, London W12 0NN (tel 020 8383 3264, e-mail a.chu@imperial.ac.uk)

CHUNG, Dan; s of Thiam Chung, of Costock, Leics, and Pearl, *née* Yeo; *b* 29 May 1971, Loughborough, Leics; *Educ* Univ of Plymouth (BSc), Sheffield Coll (NCTJ); *Partner* Tania Anin Branigan; *Career* photographer: Derby Evening Telegraph 1994–95, Newsteam Int 1995–97, Reuters Ltd 1997–2003, The Guardian 2003–; memb Br Press Photographers' Assoc; Nikon Press Photographer of the Year 2002, Photographer of the Year Picture Eds Award 2004, What The Papers Say Photographer of the Year 2004 and 2005, Nikon Celebrity Photographer 2005, James Cameron Meml Special Award 2006; *Publications* contrib: The Art of Sport (2002), Guardian Yearbook (2003), The State of the World (2006), Photojournalism: The World's Top Photographers (2006); *Recreations* music, travel; *Style*— Dan Chung, Esq; ✉ The Guardian, 119 Farringdon Road, London EC1R 3ER (tel 020 7713 4161, fax 020 7239 9951, e-mail dan.chung@guardian.co.uk)

CHUNG, Prof (Kian) Fan; s of Young Cheong Chung (d 1991), and Ah-Lime Cheung Kam Cheong; *b* 12 February 1951; *Educ* Royal Coll Curepipe Mauritius (Gold Medal Chamber of Agric, Govt Mauritius scholar), Middx Hosp Med Sch Univ of London (Thomas Meyerstein scholar, Harold Boldero scholar, MB BS, MD, DSc), MRC (Dorothy Temple Cross scholar); *m* 9 July 1977, Soop-Chin Claire, da of Ng Kee Kwong; 3 da (Joanne b 20 April 1982, Katie b 16 Feb 1991, Annabelle b 1 March 1996); *Career* house offr Hammersmith & Middlesex Hosp and Radcliffe Infirmary Oxford 1975–78, chief resident Hosp Cantonal Geneva 1978–79, sr registrar Charing Cross Hosp 1979–83, visiting sci Univ of Calif 1983–85, currently prof of respiratory med Nat Heart and Lung Inst ICSTM (sr lectr and reader in respiratory med 1987–96); hon conslt physician Royal Brompton and Harefield NHS Tst; visiting prof: Changgung Univ Hosp Taiwan 1997, Univ of Natal SA 1998, Univ of WA 1999; memb Editorial Bd: Euro Respiratory Jl 1995–99, American Jl of Respiratory and Critical Care Med 1996–2003, Jl of Euro Soc of Allergy and Clinical Immunology 1999–2005, Euro Jl of Clinical Pharmacology 2000–, Therapy in Respiratory Disease 2001–; res awards: Wellcome Tst 1995–, MRC 1999–, Nat Inst of Health 2001–; memb: Br Thoracic Soc 1986–, American Thoracic Soc 1986–, Euro Respiratory Soc 1987– (memb: Exec 1998–, Sci Ctee 2001–, Prog Ctee Annual Congress 1999–), Br Pharmacological Soc 1987–, American Coll of Chest Physicians 1989–, Prog Ctee World Asthma Meeting Chicago 2001, Br Guidelines on Asthma Mgmnt Nat Asthma Campaign 2001; co-chm Euro Asthma Congress Moscow 2001; FRCP 1992; *Publications* Therapeutics of Respiratory Disease (co-author, 1994), Asthma: Mechanisms and Protocols (co-ed, 2000), Clinicians' Guide to Asthma (2002), Cough: Causes, Mechanisms and Treatment (co-ed, 2003); author of 400 scientific pubns; *Recreations* table tennis, travel, history; *Style*— Prof Fan Chung; ✉ National Heart and Lung Institute, Imperial College, Dovehouse Street, London SW3 6LY (tel 020 7351 8995, fax 020 7351 8126, e-mail f.chung@imperial.ac.uk)

CHUNN, Louise; da of Jeremiah Alfred Chunn, of Auckland, NZ, and Yvonne Chunn; *b* 24 July 1956; *Educ* St Joseph's Convent Otahuhu, Baradene Coll Remuera, Univ of Aukland (BA); *m* 1, Aug 1981 (m dis), Dominic Anthony Free; 1 s (Charlie b 11 March 1986), 1 da (Alice b 23 June 1988); m 2, April 2001, Andrew John Anthony; 1 da (Isabel b 14 June 2000); *Career* ed Just Seventeen 1985–86, dep ed Elle 1986–89; The Guardian: ed Women's Page 1989–94, ed Madame Figaro 1993–95, assoc features ed 1994–95; Vogue: assoc ed 1995–96, features dir 1996–97, dep ed 1997–98; ed: ES Magazine 1998–2000, InStyle magazine 2002–06 (dep ed 2001–02), Good Housekeeping 2006–; fndr memb Women in Journalism; *Style*— Ms Louise Chunn

CHURCH, Jonathan; s of Tony Church, of Nottingham, and Marielaine, *née* Douglas; *b* 4 March 1967; *Educ* Frank Weldon Comp Nottingham, Clarendon Coll of FE Nottingham; *m* 1998, Veronica Dorsey; *Career* theatre director; asst electrician Dukes Playhouse Lancaster and Crucible Theatre Sheffield 1987–89, stage mangr Crucible Sheffield, Metro Theatre Co, Hull Truck and Roundabout TIE Nottingham 1989–90, asst dir Nottingham Playhouse 1990–91 (asst prodr 1992), artistic dir Triptych Theatre Co 1993–97, assoc dir Derby Playhouse 1994–95, artistic dir Salisbury Playhouse 1995–99, assoc dir Hampstead Theatre 1999–2001, artistic dir Birmingham Rep 2001–06, artistic dir Chichester Festival Theatre 2006–; tutor: Nottingham Trent Univ Design Course 1995, Rose Bruford Design Course 1999; external course monitor: Welsh Coll of Music & Drama 2002, Royal Scot Acad 2003; assessor Arts Cncl 1998–2001; *Theatre* The Ballad of Reading Gaol (Crucible Theatre Sheffield) 1988, The Bear (Crucible Theatre Sheffield) 1988, Saint Oscar (Nottingham Playhouse) 1992, Mirror of the Moon (Man in the Moon) 1992, In Lambeth (Ensemble Theatre Vienna) 1992 and (Lyric Hammersmith) 1993, Frankie & Johnny (Derby Playhouse) 1993, Magnetic North (W Yorks Playhouse) 1993, Two (Derby Playhouse) 1993, Someone Who'll Watch Over Me (Derby Playhouse) 1994, The Broken Heart (Lyric Hammersmith) 1994, Absurd Person Singular (Derby Playhouse) 1994, Importance of Being Earnest (Derby Playhouse) 1994, Oleanna (Derby Playhouse) 1995, Derby 100 (Derby Playhouse) 1995, The Crucible (Birmingham Old Rep) 1995, Comic Cuts (Salisbury Playhouse) 1995, The Rover & The Banished Cavaliers (Salisbury Playhouse) 1995, The Merchant of Venice (Salisbury Playhouse) 1996, Oleanna & Educating Rita (Chichester Festival Theatre) 1996, Time & The Conways (Salisbury Playhouse and Colchester Mercury) 1997, The Rehearsal & The Double Inconstancy (Salisbury Playhouse) 1997, Disappearances (Salisbury Playhouse) 1997, The Cherry Orchard & Racing Demon (Salisbury Playhouse) 1997, Romeo and Juliet (Salisbury Playhouse and nat tour) 1998, Angels Rave On (Nottingham Playhouse) 1998, The Alchemical Wedding (Salisbury Playhouse) 1998, Top Girls (Salisbury Playhouse and Plymouth Theatre Royal) 1998, Just Between Ourselves (Salisbury Playhouse) 1999, Colombe (Salisbury Playhouse) 1998, You Be Ted and I'll Be Sylvia (Hampstead Theatre) 1999, A Busy Day (Bristol Old Vic and Lyric Shaftesbury Ave) 2000, Red Velvet (Hampstead Theatre) 2000, God and Stephen Hawking (Bath Theatre Royal and tour) 2000, The Diary of Anne Frank (touring consortium) 2000, Private Lives & Closer (Birmingham Rep) 2001, Of Mice and Men (Birmingham Rep) 2001 and (Liverpool and tour) 2003, Peter Pan (Birmingham Rep) 2002, Hobson's Choice (Plymouth Theatre Royal and touring consortium) 2002, Elizabeth Rex (Birmingham Rep) 2002, Murmuring Judges (Birmingham Rep) 2003, Absence of War (Birmingham Rep) 2003, Racing Demon (Birmingham Rep) 2003; *Awards* Wall to Wall Award (for Comic Cuts)1995, Salisbury C of C Award for significant contribution to the community 1996, nominee TMA Theatre of the Year 1998, Peter Brook Empty Space Award for Special Regnl Achievement 1998; *Style*— Jonathan Church, Esq; ✉ c/o Conway van Gelder, 3rd Floor, 18–21 Jermyn Street, London SW1Y 6HP (tel 020 7287 0077)

CHURCH, Prof Roy Anthony; s of William Alfred Church (d 1973), of Kettering, and Lillian Gertrude Church (d 1990); *b* 21 February 1935; *Educ* Kettering GS, Univ of Nottingham (BA, PhD); *m* 10 Oct 1959, Gwenllian Elizabeth, da of James Whyte Martin (d 1984), of Kettering; 3 s (Benjamin b 1964, Joseph b 1969, Thomas b 1970), 1 da (Naomi b 1980); *Career* economic historian; BBC 1958–60, Purdue Univ Indiana USA 1960–61, Univ of Washington Seattle USA 1961–62, Univ of Br Columbia Vancouver Canada 1962–63, Univ of Birmingham 1963–72; UEA: prof of economic and social history 1972–, pro-vice-chllr 1986–89, dean Sch of History 1997–1999; visiting research fell Univ of Canberra 1998, Wellcome special research fell 1999–2003; pres Assoc of Business Historians; memb: Cncl of Econ History Soc, Econ and Social Research Cncl; govr History of Advertising Trust; FRHistS 1972; ed Economic History Review 1982–90; *Books* Economic and Social Change in a Midland Town 1815–1900: Victorian Nottingham (1966), Kenricks in Hardware: A Family Business, 1790–1965 (1969), The Great Victorian Boom (1975), Herbert Austin: The British Motor Car Industry to 1941 (1979), The Dynamics of Victorian Business (ed, 1980), The History of the British Coal Industry, Volume 3: 1830–1913, Victorian Pre-eminence (1986, Wadsworth Prize), The Rise and Decline of the British Motor Industry (1994), Strikes and Solidarity: Coalfield Conflict in Britain 1889–1966 (with C E Outram, 1999); *Recreations* tennis, badminton, fell walking, theatre; *Style*— Prof Roy Church; ✉ School of History, University of East Anglia, Norwich (tel 01603 456161)

CHURCH, William Henry; s of Henry Albion Church (d 1981), and Iris Edith, *née* Duddy (d 1986); *b* 23 July 1946; *Educ* St Joseph's Coll Ipswich, King's Coll, Univ of London (MB BS); *m* 6 Jan 1973, Jane Ann, da of Hugh Parry, of Aberdaron, Gwynedd; 3 s (Edward b 1974, James b 1976, Martin b 1977), 1 da (Sarah b 1981); *Career* sr registrar in ophthalmology Royal Victoria Infirmary Newcastle upon Tyne 1984–88, consult ophthalmologist Aberdeen Royal Infirmary 1988–; mountaineering achievements: first solo ascent N Face Mount Kenya 1969, first ascent N face Koh-i-Mondi Afghanistan with P Boardman, M Wragg and C Fitzhugh 1972, first ascent Chong Kumdan I (7,071m) E Karakoram India with D Wilkinson, N McAdie and J Porter 1992, 11 first ascents in Eastern Greenland Alps with David Wilkinson and Brian Davison 2004; MRCP 1975, FRCS 1983, FRCOphth 1991; *Recreations* mountaineering, rock climbing, skiing, fly fishing; *Clubs* Alpine; *Style*— William Church, Esq; ✉ Aberdeen Royal Infirmary, Foresthill, Aberdeen AB9 2ZB (tel 01224 681818, ext 52422)

CHURCHER, Neville John (Nev); MBE (1996); s of Nigel Churcher, of Gosport, and Eileen Helen, *née* Ryman; *b* 22 May 1945; *Educ* Portsmouth GS, Portsmouth Sch of Architecture; *m* 1970, Marilyn Jean (Maz), da of Anthony John Stapleton; 2 c (Joe b 1972, Eppie b 1976); *Career* architect specialising in early years and primary educn and one-off houses on small and difficult sites; with Hampshire CC 1978–; awards assessor, pt/t educator; RIBA 1980, FCSD 1996, FRSA 1996; *Awards* for Jamaica Cottage 1975; for Woodlea Sch: The Educn Award 1992, RIBA President's Building of the Year Award 1993, BBC Design Awards Arch and Environment and Designer of the Year Awards 1994; for offices and gardens Old Churcher's Coll at Petersfield: Civic Tst Award 1996, BDA Public Building Award 1998; for Whiteley Primary School: RIBA Award 2002; Civic Tst Award 2003, BDA Sustainability Award 2003; *Recreations* old competition cars, wooden gliders and boats, classical, jazz and world music, photography; *Clubs* VSCC, Midland Automobile; *Style*— Nev Churcher, Esq, MBE; ✉ Jamaica Cottage, Jamaica Place, Gosport, Hampshire PO12 1LX (tel 023 9252 7202)

CHURCHILL, Caryl Lesley; da of Robert Churchill, and Jan, *née* Brown; *b* 3 September 1938; *Educ* Trafalgar Montreal Canada, LMH Oxford; *m* David Richard Harter; 3 s (Joe b 1963, Paul b 1964, Rick b 1969); *Career* playwright; wrote: one-act play Downstairs (produced by Oriel Coll Oxford) 1958, Having A Wonderful Time (Questors Theatre) 1960, Easy Death (Oxford Playhouse) 1962; BBC radio plays incl: The Ants (Third Prog) 1962, Lovesick 1967, Identical Twins 1968, Abortive 1971, Not..Not..Not..Not Enough Oxygen 1971, Schreber's Nervous Illness 1972 (subsequently adapted for stage, King's Head Theatre Islington), Henry's Past 1972, Perfect Happiness 1973; BBC TV plays incl: The Judge's Wife 1972, Turkish Delight 1974, The After Dinner Joke 1978, Crimes 1982; other stage plays incl: Owners (Theatre Upstairs, Royal Court) 1972, Objections To Sex And Violence (Royal Court) 1975, Light Shining in Buckinghamshire (Joint Stock UK tour, Theatre Upstairs, Royal Court) 1976, Vinegar Tom (Monstrous Regt UK tour, ICA Theatre) 1976, Traps (Theatre Upstairs, Royal Court) 1977, Cloud 9 (Joint Stock UK tour, Royal Court 1978 and 1980, 2 years Off-Broadway), Three More Sleepless Nights (Soho Poly and Theatre Upstairs, Royal Court) 1980, Top Girls (Royal Court, New York Shakespeare Festival Theatre) 1982–83, Fen (Joint Stock UK tour, Almeida Theatre, New York Shakespeare Festival Theatre) 1983–84, Softcops (RSC, The Barbican) 1984, A Mouthful of Birds (with David Lan, Joint Stock UK tour, Royal Court) 1986, Serious Money (Royal Court, Wyndhams Theatre, New York Shakespeare Festival then Broadway) 1987–88, Ice Cream (Royal Court) 1989, Ice Cream with Hot Fudge (Public Theatre) 1989, Mad Forest (Central Sch of Speech and Drama London, Nat Theatre Bucharest, Royal Court) 1990, Lives of the Great Poisoners (with Orlando Gough and Ian Spink, Second Strike UK tour, Riverside Studios) 1991, The Skriker (RNT) 1994, Thyestes (trans, Royal Court Theatre Upstairs) 1994, Hotel (Second Stride, The Place) 1997, This is a Chair (Royal Court) 1997, Blue Heart (Out of Joint, Royal Court and tour) 1997, Far Away (Royal Court, Albery) 2000, A Number (Royal Court) 2002, Drunk Enough to Say I Love You? (Royal Court) 2006; *Awards* incl: Obie for Cloud 9 1982, Obie for Top Girls 1983, Hollywood Dramalogue Critics Award for Cloud 9, Susan Blackburn Award 1984 and 1987, Best Play Olivier Award, Best Comedy Evening Standard Award and the Plays and Players Award all for Serious Money 1987; *Style*— Ms Caryl Churchill; ✉ Casarotto Ramsay Ltd, National House, 60–66 Wardour Street, London W1V 3HP (tel 020 7287 4450, fax 020 7287 9128)

CHURCHILL, Jane (Lady Charles Spencer-Churchill); da of Hon Mark Wyndham, and Hon Mrs Wyndham, *née* Winn; *b* 17 January 1948; *m* 9 Dec 1970, Lord Charles Spencer-Churchill; 3 s (Rupert b 26 Nov 1971, Dominic b 15 Dec 1979, Alexander b 9 June 1983); *Career* interior designer; began at Colefax & Fowler, fndr and owner gift shop Treasure Island until 1982, fndr fabric and wallpaper shop Jane Churchill Design 1982 (sold to Colefax & Fowler 1989); fndr Jane Churchill Interiors Ltd (projects incl interiors in UK, Europe, USA, Aust and Caribbean); with Annie Charlton: presenter TV series Finishing Touches (Granada) and author of accompanying book, home furnishings conslt to Next plc and Hunters of Brora, designer Simplicity Patterns 1994–, designer Pimlico Road (for cos incl Drexel Heritage, Frederick Cooper and Tynedale, Sherrill Furniture and NDI); TV guest: Elsa Klensh Style (CNN), Dream Home (GMTV); *Style*— Jane Churchill; ✉ Jane Churchill Interiors Ltd, 81 Pimlico Road, London SW1W 8PH (tel 020 7730 8564, fax 020 7823 6421, e-mail jchurchill@janechurchillinteriors.co.uk, website www.janechurchillinteriors.com)

CHURCHILL, Dr Kenneth Geoffrey; OBE (1995); s of Edward John Churchill (d 1976), and Florence Ruby, *née* Adams; *b* 28 June 1947; *Educ* Weymouth GS, Judd Sch Tonbridge, Clare Coll Cambridge (MA, PhD); *m* 15 Jan 1972, Paulette Marie, *née* Leveque; 1 da (Caroline Sarah b 15 Jan 1975), 1 s (Andrew Edward Paul b 13 Jan 1976); *Career* British Council: asst dir Madras 1973–75, asst dir Rome 1975–77, Literature Dept 1977–80, dep dir Accra 1980–83, Literature Dept 1983–85, dep dir Cologne 1985, dep dir Paris 1985–89, dir Dublin 1989–94, dir Belgium and Luxembourg 1994–99, Y2K mangr 1999, temporary duty Argentina and Tunisia 2000, dir Lebanon 2000–05, dir Palestinian Territories 2005–; *Books* Italy and English Literature (1980); *Recreations* travel, reading; *Style*— Dr Kenneth Churchill, OBE; ✉ The British Council, 31 Nablus Road, PO Box 19136, Jerusalem 97200, Palestinian Territories (e-mail ken.churchill@ps.britishcouncil.org)

CHURCHILL, Lawrence; s of Austin Churchill (d 1969), and Kathleen, *née* Keating (d 1993); *b* 5 August 1946, Birkenhead; *Educ* Birkenhead Sch, St John's Coll Oxford (MA); *m* 7 Sept 1991, Karen, da of Arnold Darcy, and Mary Darcy; 2 da (Charlotte Mary Kathleen, Sophie Janet Tonia (twins) b 16 March 2000); by previous m, 1 s (Andrew Mark b 23 Aug 1973), 1 da (Emma Jane b 3 May 1975); *Career* systems analyst Procter & Gamble Ltd 1969–73, systems analyst rising to exec dir Allied Dunbar Assurance plc 1973–91 (memb Bd 1985–91), joined National Westminster Bank plc 1991 (held several internal directorships 1992–98), fndr chief exec NatWest Life 1992–96, md NatWest Life & Investments 1995–98, chm and md UNUM Ltd 1998–2002, chief exec UK, Irish and int life Zurich Fin Services 2002–04, chair Pensions Protection Fund 2004–; non-exec dir: Monkton plc 2004–, Huntswood 2005–06, The Children's Mutual 2005–; dir PIA 1994–97, dir ABI 1996–98 (memb Life Insurance Cncl 1994–96 and 2000–04), non-exec dir Fin Ombudsman Serv 2002–05, memb Bd for Actuarial Standards 2006–; memb Ministerial Advsy Gp Incapacity Benefit Reform 2003–05, memb Disability Advsy Gp Nat Employment Panel, vice-pres Employment Opportunities, advsr Int Longevity Centre; tstee Royal Soc of Arts 2000–02; memb Chartered Inst of Technol Professionals, MBCS, MCMI, FInstD, FRSA; *Recreations* rugby, bridge, opera, gardening; *Style*— Lawrence Churchill, Esq; ✉ Pension Protection Fund, Knolly's House, 17 Addiscombe Road, Croydon, Surrey CR0 6SR (tel 020 8633 4985, fax 020 8633 4903); e-mail lawrence.churchill@tiscali.co.uk

CHURCHILL, 3 Viscount (UK 1902); Victor George Spencer; OBE (2001); also 5 Baron Churchill of Wychwood (UK 1815); s of 1 Viscount Churchill, GCVO (d 1934), by his 2 w Christine Sinclair (Lady Oliphant); suc half-bro 1973; *b* 31 July 1934; *Educ* Eton, New Coll Oxford (MA); *Heir* (to Barony only) kinsman, (Richard) Harry Spencer; *Career* Lt Scots Gds 1953–55; Morgan Grenfell and Co Ltd 1958–74; investment mangr: The Central Bd of the Church of England 1974–99, The Charities Official Investment Fund 1974–95; dir: Local Authorities' Mutual Investment Tst 1978–98, CCLA Investment Management Ltd 1987–99, Charter European Investment Tst plc 1992–2002, Schroder Split Fund plc 1993–2001, Allchurches Tst Ltd 1994–99, F&C Income Growth Investment Tst plc 1994–2005; church cmmr 2001–04; *Style*— The Viscount Churchill, OBE; ✉ 6 Cumberland Mansions, George Street, London W1H 5TE (tel 020 7262 6223)

CHURCHILL, Winston Spencer; s of Hon Randolph Frederick Edward Spencer Churchill, MBE (d 1968) (s of Sir Winston Churchill, KG, OM, CH, FRS) by his 1 w, Hon Pamela Harriman (US ambass to France 1992–97, d 1997), da of 11 Baron Digby, KG, DSO, MC, TD; *b* 10 October 1940; *Educ* Eton, ChCh Oxford (MA, capt Univ of Oxford ski team 1961); *m* 1, 1964 (m dis 1997), Mary Caroline (Minnie) d'Erlanger; 2 s, 2 da; m 2, 1997, Luce Engelen; *Career* circumnavigated Africa in single-engined aircraft 1962–63; author, journalist and war corr 1962–70 (incl Vietnam 1966, Middle E 1967 and Biafra 1969), BBC presenter 1964–65, roving foreign corr The Times 1969–70; Parly candidate (Cons) Manchester Gorton 1967, MP (Cons) Stretford 1970–83, MP (Cons) Davyhulme 1983–97; PPS: to Min of Housing and Construction 1970–72, to Min of State FCO 1972–73; Cons spokesman on defence 1976–78, vice-chm Cons Pty Defence Ctee 1979–83, memb Exec 1922 Ctee 1979–83, treas 1922 Ctee 1987–88, Cons Pty co-ordinator for Defence and Disarmament and chm Campaign for Defence and Multilateral Disarmament 1982–84; memb Select Ctee on Defence 1984–97; sponsored: Motor Vehicles (Passenger Insurance)

Act 1972, Crown Proceedings (Armed Forces) Act 1987; pres: Trafford Park Industrial Cncl (TRAFIC) 1971–97, Friends of Airborne Forces 1996–2002, War Memls Tst 2004– (chm 1997–2004); tstee: Winston Churchill Meml Tst 1968– (chm 2002–), Nat Benevolent Fund for the Aged 1974– (chm 1995–), Sandy Gall's Afghanistan Appeal 1995–; govr English Speaking Union 1975–80; memb Cncl: The Air League 1982–96, Consumers' Assoc 1990–93, Br Kidney Patients' Assoc 1990–2004; memb and vol pilot St John's Ambulance Air Wing 1975–93; Commercial Pilot's Licence (UK) 1982, Airline Tport Pilot's Licence (USA) 1982; hon fell: Churchill Coll Cambridge 1969, Soc of Engrs 1988; Hon LLD Westminster Coll Fulton Missouri 1972, Hon DSc Technion - Israel Inst of Technol 1997; *Books* First Journey (1964), The Six Day War (1967), Defending the West (1980), Memories and Adventures (1989), His Father's Son (1996), The Great Republic (1999), Never Give In! The Best of Winston Churchill's Speeches (2003); *Clubs* Buck's, White's, Air Sqdn, St Moritz Tobogganing; *Style*— Winston S Churchill, Esq; ✉ c/o White's Club, 37 St James's Street, London SW1A 1JG

CHURCHMAN, Michael Anthony; s of Richard John Churchman (d 1978), of Islington, London, and Mary, *née* Bradley (d 2001); *b* 6 February 1952; *Educ* St Ignatius Coll London, Worcester Coll Oxford (MA); *m* 1974, Christine Elizabeth, da of Bryan Bernard George Dyer, of Lowestoft, Suffolk; 3 s (Anthony Laurence b 4 Aug 1979, Christopher Michael b 28 July 1981, Alexander Richard b 19 Nov 1986); *Career* account exec Young and Rubicam 1973–75, account mangr Benton and Bowles 1975–77, account supervisor Lintas 1977–79, account dir Wasey Campbell Ewald 1979–83; bd dir: AAP Ketchum 1983–87, Grey Ltd 1987–89; md PML Creative Strategy 1990–91, fndr Churchmans Marketing Communications Ltd 1991–; memb: Advertising Advsy Ctee ITC, Cncl of Nat Advertising Benevolent Soc 1975–, Oxford Business Alumni 2000–; FIPA 1989 (MIPA 1982), FInstD (dip in co mgmnt 1988); *Recreations* travel, reading, book collecting, classical music, theatre-going; *Clubs* IOD; *Style*— Michael Churchman, Esq; ✉ 20 Rutland Place, Maidenhead, Berkshire SL6 4JA (tel 01628 639404, fax 01628 418677, e-mail mike@churchmans.com)

CHURSTON, 5 Baron (UK 1858), of Churston Ferrers and Lupton, Devon; Sir John Francis Yarde-Buller; 6 Bt (GB 1790); o s of 4 Baron Churston, VRD (d 1991), and his 1 w, Elizabeth Mary, *née* Du Pre (d 1951); *b* 29 December 1934; *Educ* Eton; *m* 1973, Alexandra Joanna, o da of Anthony Contomichalos; 1 s (Hon Benjamin Francis Anthony b 1974), 2 da (Hon Katherine Marina b 1975, Hon Francesca Elizabeth b 1980); *Heir* s, Hon Benjamin Yarde-Buller; *Career* late 2 Lt RHG; *Recreations* freemasonry; *Clubs* Buck's, White's; *Style*— The Rt Hon the Lord Churston; ✉ Yowlestone House, Puddington, Tiverton, Devon EX16 8LN

CHYNOWETH, David Boyd; s of Ernest Chynoweth (d 1982), and Blodwen, *née* Griffiths; *b* 26 December 1940; *Educ* Simon Langton Sch Canterbury, Univ of Nottingham (BA); *m* 15 June 1968, Margaret, da of Thomas Slater, of Edensor, Derbys; 2 da (Susan b 1971, Claire b 1974), 1 s (Richard b 1981); *Career* dep co treas W Suffolk CC 1969–73, co treas S Yorks CC 1973–85, dir of fin Lothian Regnl Cncl 1985–94, chief exec Universities Superannuation Scheme Ltd 1994–2003; pres CIPFA 1992–93 (vice-pres 1991–92, Cncl 1983–99); dir: CIPFA Holdings Ltd 1985–89, CSL Ltd 1985–89, Fndn for IT in Local Government Ltd 1987–90, Fndn for the Regulation of the Accountancy Profession 1999–2004; vice-chm: American Property Trust 1981–85, UK American Properties Inc 1981–86; memb: Investment Ctee Nat Assoc of Pension Funds (NAPF) 1977–80, 1982–86 and 1999–2004 (memb Cncl 1998–2003), Ctee Lazard Small Companies Exempt Unit Tst 1979–95, UK Steering Ctee on Local Govt Superannuation 1988–94, Sec of State for Scotland's Scottish Valuation Advsy Cncl 1989–94, Consultative Cncl of Accountancy Bodies 1991–93, Auditing Practices Bd 1991–94; *Recreations* walking, photography; *Clubs* Royal Over-Seas League; *Style*— David Chynoweth, Esq; ✉ 27 Whitehall Road, Rhos-on-Sea, Colwyn Bay LL28 4HW (tel 01492 545867)

CICLITIRA, Prof Paul Jonathan; s of Dennis J Ciclitira, and Grace, *née* Cooksley (d 2003); *b* 7 July 1948; *Educ* Wycliffe Coll, Bart's Med Sch (MB BS), Univ of Cambridge (MD, PhD); *m* Dr Diane Watson; 1 da (Katherine Anne b 1989), 1 s (James Alexander b 1992); *Career* SHO in gen med: Rochford Hosp 1972–73 (house offr 1971), Bart's 1973–74 (house offr in gen surgery 1971), Royal Marsden Hosp 1975; hon sr registrar Addenbrooke's Hosps 1977–80 (med registrar 1975–77), trg fell MRC Lab of Molecular Biology Cambridge 1980–83 (Drummond nutrition fell 1977–80), hon sr registrar Guy's Hosp 1980–83; UMDS Guy's and St Thomas' Hosp Tst: sr res fell Wellcome Tst 1983–89, sr lectr and hon conslt physician 1983–, prof of gastroenterology 1994–, head of Research Unit The Rayne Inst; memb: Darwin Coll Cambridge, Editorial Bd Clinical and Experimental Immunology; Br Soc of Gastroenterology Res Medal 1986, Br and Eire Socs of Gastroenterology and Lilly Res Award 1988, Euro Soc of Gastroenterology and Lilly Res Award 1989; memb: Assoc of Physicians of the UK, Biochemical Soc, Br Soc of Gastroenterology (memb Nutrition Ctee), Br Soc of Immunology, Euro Soc of Clinical Investigation, Med Res Soc of GB, Soc of Cell Biology; FRSM, FRCP 1991 (MRCP); *Publications* author of various pubns in learned jls particularly on coeliac disease; *Recreations* squash, swimming, theatre, cooking, wine tasting; *Clubs* Athenaeum, Chelsea Arts, Groucho; *Style*— Prof Paul J Ciclitira; ✉ Gastroenterology Unit, UMDS, The Rayne Institute, St Thomas' Hospital, London SE1 7EH (tel 020 7928 9292 ext 3063, fax 020 7620 2597)

CIECHANOWIECKI, Count Andrew Stanislaus; s of Count George Ciechanowiecki (d 1930), Polish diplomat and landowner, and Matylda, *née* Countess Osiecimska-Hutten-Czapska (d 1991), Dame of Honour and Devotion SMOM, Dame Grand Cross of Justice Constantinian Order of St George, Dame Cdr Order of SS Mauritius and Lazarus; *b* 28 September 1924, Warsaw; *Educ* Lycée S Batory Warsaw, Higher Sch of Economic Studies Kraków (BA), Jagiellonian Univ Kraków (MA), Karl Eberhard Univ Tübingen (PhD); *Career* anti-Nazi resistance in Poland 1941–45 (Lt Home Army, Polish war decorations); cnsllr Polish FO in Govt of National Unity and chef de protocole Miny of Foreign Trade 1945–46; political prisoner 1950–56; former lectr Jagiellonian Univ Kraków, sometime museum curator in Poland; md: Mallett at Bourdon House (London) 1961–65, Heim Gallery (London) Ltd 1965–86, Old Masters Gallery (London) Ltd 1986–93; fndr Ciechanowiecki Family Fndn Royal Castle Warsaw 1986; sometime memb Presidential Advsy Bd for Culture in Poland, tstee various Polish charities in Poland and elsewhere abroad; memb and hon memb numerous learned Polish and foreign bodies; hon prof Acad of Fine Arts Warsaw; Hon PhD: Univ of Warsaw, Univ of Minsk, Univ of New Mexico; memb Polish Acad of Sciences; FSA; Knight Order of the White Eagle (Poland), Knight Grand Cross Order of Polonia Restituta, Knight Grand Cross Order of St Gregory the Great (Holy See), Knight Cdr Order of Merit (Italy), Cdr Grosses Silbernes Ehrenzeichen (Austria), Cdr Order of Merit (Senegal), Cdr Order of the Polar Star (Sweden), Bundesverdienstkreuz First Class (Germany), Chevalier Légion d'Honneur (France), Order of F Skaryna (Belarus), Bailiff, Knight Grand Cross of Honour and Devotion and Knight Grand Cross of Merit SMOM, chm of fndn Polish Assoc of SMOM in Britain, Knight Order of St Januarius, Bailiff Grand Cross of Justice Constantinian Order of St George (decorated with the Collar), Knight Grand Cross Order of Francis I (Royal House of Naples), Knight Grand Cross Order of St Joseph (Tuscany), Knight Grand Cross Orders of SS Andrew, Alexander and Anne of Russia (dynastic), Knight Grand Cross Order of SS Mauritius and Lazarus, Knight Grand Cross Order of Civil Merit of Savoy, Offr of the Doorward Guard of the Lord High Constable of Scotland; Merentibus Medal Jagiellonian Univ Kraków, hon citizen towns of Ciechanowiec and Zaslaw; *Books* author of several books and numerous articles in the field of art and history of culture; *Recreations* reading, genealogy, travelling; *Clubs* Brooks's, Polish Hearth; *Style*— Count Andrew Ciechanowiecki, FSA; ✉ Flat 2, 92 Mount Street, London W1K 2SX (tel 020 7491 1967, fax 020 7629 9774)

CIERACH, Lindka Rosalind Wanda; da of Edek (Edward) Cierach, MBE (d 1992), and Diana Rosemary, *née* Wilson; f mapped large tracts of Africa, decorated for Battle of Monte Cassino with highest Order of Virtuti Military, Kirzyz Walecznych, Star medal 1939–44, Star Italian Campaign, Star of Monte Cassino, Star Defense MBE; *b* June 1952; *Educ* Uganda, Convent of the Holy Child Jesus St Leonards and Mayfield, London Coll of Fashion; *Career* fashion designer; worked for Vogue magazine, established couture house 1984, designed wedding dress for Duchess of York's wedding on 23 July 1986, launched ready-to-wear collection 1987, currently designs couture for int client base; contrib to gala fashion shows for charities incl: Unicef, Leukaemia Research, Martletts Hosp; appearances in TV series incl Ladette to Lady (ITV) 2006, designer for TV specials incl Lesley Garrett Tonight (BBC 2) 1998; patron Full of Life; Designer of the Year Award 1987; *Recreations* music, films, reading, walking, boating, safari, meditation; *Style*— Lindka Cierach; ✉ The Studio, 1c Clareville Grove, London SW7 5AU (tel 020 7373 3131, fax 020 7373 1675, e-mail lindka@lindka-cierach.co.uk, website www.lindka-cierach.co.uk)

CINA, Colin; s of Louis Cina of Glasgow, and Ettie, *née* Barkofsky; *b* 24 April 1943; *Educ* Glasgow Sch of Art, Central Sch of Art (DipAD); *m* 1962, Gill, *née* Nicholas; 2 da (Jane b 1972, Chloe b 1976); *Career* artist and fine art teacher; visiting fell in fine art Univ of Newcastle upon Tyne 1971–72; pt/t teaching: Manchester Sch of Art (fine art) 1967–71, Central Sch of Art 1968–75; princ lectr in charge of painting Wimbledon Sch of Art 1975–80 (acting head of fine art 1975–76), head of fine art Chelsea Sch of Art 1988 (head of Painting Dept 1980), dean Sch of Art Chelsea Coll of Art and Design 1989–99, head Chelsea Coll of Art & Design 1998–; fine art and fndn external examiner for various colls and univs, author of various articles and catalogues; govr London Inst 1986–89 (memb of various Ctees); coll govr: Canterbury Coll of Art 1982–86; CNAA Fine Art Panel: specialist advsr 1982–, memb of Panel 1985–87, specialist register 1987–; memb CNAA Ctee for Art and Design 1989–91; memb Architects and Artists Action Gp 1983–84, chm Nat Assoc for Fine Art Educn 1989–90 (vice-chm 1988–89); ELIA (The European League of Insts of the Arts): memb Founding Ctee 1989–90, elected memb Bd 1996–98; memb French Miny of Culture Ctee for Reformation of Art Schools 1997–99; conslt for various orgns incl: BBC, Dept of Tport, Kent Inst of Art and Design, RNIB, European Union, Ontario Coll of Art; specialist reviewer Art & Design Quality Assurance Agency UK 1998–2000; *Solo Exhibitions* incl: Serpentine Gallery 1980, Library Gallery Univ of Surrey 1983, Angela Flowers London 1984; *Group Exhibitions* incl: Redhill Street Open Studios London 1987, 21st Anniversary Exhibition of Richard Demarco Gallery (Smiths Gallery) London 1988, Scottish Art Since 1900 (Gallery of Modern Art Edinburgh Festival 1989–90), Barbican Art Gallery London 1989/90, Master Class (London Inst Gallery) 1991, Small is Beautiful (Flowers East Gallery) 1992, 1998 and 1999; *Public Collections* incl: Arts Cncl of GB, City Art Gallery Bristol, Contemporary Arts Soc, CNAA, National Gallery Budapest Hungary, Scot Arts Cncl, Scot Nat Gallery of Modern Art Edinburgh, Nat Gallery of Iceland, V&A, Allende Museum Chile; *Style*— Colin Cina, Esq; ✉ c.cina@chelsea.linst.ac.uk

CINNAMOND, Prof Michael James; s of James Herbert Cinnamond (d 1977), and Mary Elizabeth, *née* Stewart; *b* 16 September 1943; *Educ* The Methodist Coll Belfast, The Queen's Univ Belfast (MB BCh, BAO); *m* 18 Dec 1965, Judith Patricia, da of William Edmund Guthrie, of Newcastle, Co Down; 2 s (Michael b 8 Nov 1966, Neil b 31 March 1971), 1 da (Adrienne b 7 Nov 1972); *Career* conslt otolaryngologist 1976–79: Royal Belfast Hosp for Sick Children, Royal Victoria Hosp, Belfast City Hosp; sr lectr otorhinolaryngology Queen's Univ Belfast 1979–81; conslt paediatric otolaryngologist 1979–81 and 1981–: Royal Belfast Hosp for Sick Children, Belfast City Hosp; prof of otorhinolaryngology Queen's Univ Belfast 1981–; memb: Industrial Injuries Advsy Cncl, Speciality Advsy Ctee in Otolaryngology to Jt Ctee Higher Surgical Trg; FRCS Ed 1974, FRCSI ad eundem 1987; *Books* Scott-Brown's Otolaryngology (5 edn, contrib, 1987), Accident and Emergency Medicine (2 edn, contrib, 1989); *Style*— Prof Michael Cinnamond; ✉ A Floor, Tower Block, Belfast City Hospital, Belfast BT9 7AB (tel 028 9032 9241 ext 2356)

CIPOLLA, Prof Roberto; s of Salvatore Cipolla, of Agrigento, Italy, and Concetta, *née* Criminisi; *b* 3 May 1963, Solihull; *Educ* Solihull Sixth Form Coll, Queens' Coll Cambridge (fndn scholar, BA), Univ of Pennsylvania (MSE), Osaka Univ of Foreign Studies (Dip Japanese), Univ of Electrocommunications Tokyo (Monbusho scholar, MEng), Balliol Coll Oxford (IBM research studentship, DPhil); *m* 9 Sept 2000, Maria Cristina Bordin, da of Oreste Bordin; 1 da (Francesca Sofia b 1 Aug 2002); *Career* research asst Valley Forge Research Center PA, visiting researcher Electrotechnical Lab Tsukuba Japan, Lady Wolfson research fell St Hugh's Coll Oxford 1990–92, Toshiba fell Toshiba R&D Centre Kawasaki 1991–92; Univ of Cambridge: lectr in engrg 1992–97, reader of info engrg 1997–2000, prof of info engrg 2000–; Jesus Coll Cambridge: fell 1992–, actg praelector 1994 and 1996, fell steward 1998–99, currently dir of studies, organiser Sculpture in the Close exhbn 1994, curator of works of art 1998; scientific advsr: Sci and Technol Agency Japan 1996, Nanyang Technological Univ Singapore (distinguished visitor 1994 and 1999), Univ of Bologna 2003–; external examiner UCL; MIEE, MIEEE; *Publications* incl: Active visual inference of surface shape (1995), Computer vision for human-machine interaction (1998), Visual motion of curves and surfaces (2000), Mathematics of surfaces (2000); more than 200 contribs to int jls and confs; *Recreations* photography (Seeking Gandhara exhbn Tokyo 1992), wine, Japanese language and culture, tennis, cycling; *Style*— Prof Roberto Cipolla; ✉ Jesus College, Cambridge CB5 8BL; Department of Engineering, University of Cambridge, Cambridge CB2 1PZ (tel 01223 332849, fax 01223 332662, e-mail cipolla@eng.cam.ac.uk)

CITRON, Dr Kenneth Michael; s of Cosman Citron (d 1984), and Muriel, *née* Bourne (d 1975); *b* 2 April 1925, Southend-on-Sea, Essex; *Educ* Taunton Sch, Guys Hosp Medical Sch (MB BS, MD); *m* 1, 1963 (m dis 1976), Mary, *née* Burge; 1 s (Peter b 17 Dec 1969); m 2, 1979, Susan, *née* Hudson; *Career* conslt physician in respiratory medicine and hon sr lectr Cardiothoracic Inst Royal Brompton Hosp 1959–90; advsr in respiratory med and tuberculosis to Dept of Health 1976–86, chm BCG Vaccination Ctee Dept of Health 1986–96; chm or co-ordinator of research projects concerned with tuberculosis in UK and developing countries 1960–90; author of over 100 papers and contributions to textbooks on medical topics incl tuberculosis, also author of surveys of tuberculosis in homeless people in London for Crisis; pres: Br Soc for Allergy and Clinical Immunology 1972–75, Br Thoracic Soc 1985–87; tstee Cncl Royal Soc of Medicine, fndr tstee TB Alert; Weber Parkes Medal RCP 1987; FRCP 1968; *Recreations* sailing, indoor rowing, reading; *Clubs* RSM; *Style*— Dr Kenneth Citron; ✉ 4 Riverside Drive, Esher, Surrey KT10 8PG (tel 01372 464696, e-mail kencitron@beeb.net)

CIULLI, Dr Franco; s of Antonio Ciulli, of Verona, Italy and Sydney, Aust, and Gabriella Ciulli (d 1981); *b* 19 August 1960; *Educ* St Ignatius Coll Sydney, Univ of Verona (MD); *Career* transplant surgn Papworth Hosp 1991, sr registrar Glasgow Royal Infirmary 1993, sr transplant fell St Vincent's Hosp Sydney 1994, conslt cardiothoracic surgn Sheffield 1995, conslt cardiothoracic surgn Bristol 1999, clinical dir Cardiothoracic Surgery Bristol Royal Infirmary 2000–; memb: Soc of Cardiothoracic Surgns of GB and I 1998, European Soc of Cardiothoracic Surgns 1998; memb RYA 2001; *Publications* Essentials of Thoracic and Cardiac Surgery (jt ed, 2003); *Recreations* sailing, tennis, general aviation; *Clubs* Bristol Lawn Tennis and Squash; *Style—* Dr Franco Ciulli; ✉ Dolphin House, Department of Cardiothoracic Surgery, Bristol Royal Infirmary, Bristol BS2 8UW (tel 0117 042 0494, fax 0117 042 0496, e-mail franco.ciulli@ubht.swest.nhs.uk)

CLAGUE, Andrew Charlesworth; s of John Charlesworth Clague, of Canterbury, Kent, and Margaret Elsie, *née* Musgrave; *b* 15 May 1951; *Educ* St Edmund's Sch Canterbury, Kent Inst of Design (DipArch); *m* 1 (m dis 1991); 2 s (James Charlesworth, Nicholas Charlesworth), 2 da (Anna Genevieve, Isabel Lucy); m 2 April 2005, Philippa Louise Johnson, da of Lt-Col W R P Adams; *Career* sr ptnr Clague (architects, urban designers, historic buildings consultants and interior designers) Canterbury (HQ) and Ashford Kent, fndr and dir Countryman Properties Ltd 1986–; vice-pres Practice RIBA 1998–99; RIBA: chm Canterbury and Dist 1989–91, memb Cncl 1995–2001, chm SE Region 1996–98; memb Rotary Club (Canterbury), pres Round Table (Canterbury and Dist) 1997–98 (chm 1990–91); govr Kent Inst of Art and Design 2000–05; pres St Edmund's Soc 2002–03; *Recreations* yachting, music; *Clubs* Kent and Canterbury; *Style—* Andrew Clague, Esq, RIBA; ✉ 14 Westgate Grove, Canterbury, Kent CT2 8AA; Clague, 62 Burgate, Canterbury, Kent CT1 2BJ (tel 01227 762060, fax 01227 762149, e-mail andrewclague@clague.co.uk)

CLAGUE, Dr Roy Bridson; s of William Alan Clague, of Douglas, IOM, and Doris, *née* Bridson; *b* 16 January 1948; *Educ* Douglas HS for Boys, Univ of Newcastle upon Tyne (MB BS, MD); *m* 16 Jan 1971, Helen da of John de Legh, of Manchester; 3 da (Bethany b 1971, Emma b 1973, Joanna b 1978); *Career* registrar in gen med 1973–76, sr registrar in rheumatology 1976–80, trg fell MRC 1976–79, conslt rheumatologist Withington Hosp Manchester and Devonshire Royal Hosp Derbys 1980–91, conslt physician rheumatologist Noble's Hosp IOM 1991–; memb Rheumatology Cmmn RP 1988–93, pres IOM Medical Soc 2006–07, pres local branch Arthritis Research Campaign IOM; FRCP 1989 (MRCP 1974); *Recreations* golf, previously dinghy sailing; *Style—* Dr Roy Clague; ✉ Noble's Hospital, Strang, Isle of Man IM4 4RJ (tel 01624 650000)

CLANCARTY, 9 Earl of (I 1803); Nicholas Power Richard Le Poer Trench; also Viscount Clancarty (UK 1823), Baron Kilconnel (I 1797), Viscount Dunlo (I 1801), Baron Trench (UK 1815), Marquis of Heusden in the Kingdom of the Netherlands (1818); s of Hon Power Edward Ford Le Poer Trench (yst s of 5 Earl; d 1975), and Jocelyn Louise, *née* Courtney (d 1962); suc uncle, 8 Earl of Clancarty 1995; *b* 1 May 1952; *Educ* Westminster, Ashford GS, Plymouth Polytechnic, Univ of Colorado; *Career* artist/film-maker; *Style—* The Rt Hon the Earl of Clancarty; ✉ e-mail clancarty@hotmail.com

CLANMORRIS, 8 Baron (I 1800) Simon John Ward Bingham; s of 7 Baron Clanmorris (d 1988), and Madeleine Mary, da of Clement Ebel; *b* 25 October 1937; *Educ* Downside, Queens' Coll Cambridge (MA); *m* 1971, Gizella Maria, da of Sandor Zverko, of Budapest (d 1979); 1 da (Lucy Katherine Gizella); *Heir* kinsman, Derek Bingham; *Career* 13/18 Royal Hussars (QMO) 1956–58; CA; FCA 1975; *Recreations* skiing, sailing; *Style—* The Lord Clanmorris; ✉ c/o Child & Co, 1 Fleet Street, London EC4Y 1BD

CLANWILLIAM, 7 Earl of (I 1776); Sir John Herbert Meade; 9 Bt (I 1703); also Baron Clanwilliam (UK 1828), Viscount Clanwilliam and Baron Gillford (I 1766); yr s of Adm the Hon Sir Herbert Meade-Fetherstonhaugh, GCVO, CB, DSO, s of 4 Earl of Clanwilliam; suc cous, 6 Earl of Clanwilliam, 1989; *b* 27 September 1919; *Educ* RNC Dartmouth; *m* 1956, Maxine (d 2004), o da of late James Adrian Hayden Scott, and former w of Michael John Willson Levien; 2 da (Lady Rowena Katherine (Lady Rowena Crichton-Stewart) b 1957, Lady Tania Frances (Lady Tania Compton) b 1963), 1 s (Patrick James, Lord Gillford b 1960); *Heir* s, Lord Gillford, *qv*; *Clubs* Turf; *Style—* The Rt Hon the Earl of Clanwilliam; ✉ Blundells House, Tisbury, Salisbury SP3 6JP (e-mail cl@nwilliam.co.uk)

CLAPHAM, Adam John; s of Sir Michael John Sinclair Clapham, KBE (d 2002), and Hon Elisabeth Russell Rea (d 1994), yr da of 1 Baron Rea of Eskdale, PC; *b* 8 April 1940; *Educ* Bryanston, Univ of Grenoble; *Career* Anglia TV 1960–63, scriptwriter ABC TV 1963; BBC TV: prodr Man Alive 1965–69, ed Braden's Week 1969–71, ed Man Alive 1972–75, exec prodr documentary features 1975–82; chief exec Griffin Productions 1982–97, dir Gryphon Films 1998–2005; dir British Pathé News Ltd 1991–92; Imperial Relations Tst Bursary 1971, Leverhulme fell Sri Lanka 1979; Freeman City of London 1976; *Books* As Nature Intended (1982), Beware Falling Coconuts (2007); *Clubs* Oriental, Mangalore; *Style—* Adam Clapham, Esq; ✉ 254 Alexandra Park Road, London N22 7BG (tel 020 8889 9035, fax 020 8374 5165, e-mail adamclapham@rediffmail.com)

CLAPHAM, Prof Christopher S; s of Anthony Clapham (d 1973), and Veronica Mary, *née* Lake; *b* 20 March 1941; *Educ* Bryanston, Keble Coll Oxford (MA, DPhil); *m* 1 Nov 1975, Caroline Margaret, da of Brig John J S Tutton, CBE, of Awre, Glos; 1 da (Phoebe b 1977), 1 s (Thomas b 1979); *Career* lectr in law Univ of Addis Ababa 1966–67, res fell Univ of Manchester 1968–71, prof of politics and int rels Lancaster Univ 1989–2002 (lectr 1971–74, sr lectr 1974–89); memb Cncl: Br Tst for Ornithology 1976–79, African Studies Assoc of the UK 1981–84 and 1989–94 (pres 1992–94); ed, Journal of Modern African Studies 1998–; Liveryman Worshipful Co of Ironmongers 1968; *Books* Haile-Selassie's Government (1969), Liberia and Sierra Leone (1976), Third World Politics (1985), Transformation and Continuity in Revolutionary Ethiopia (1988), Africa and the International System (1996), African Guerrillas (1998); *Recreations* ornithology; *Style—* Prof Christopher Clapham; ✉ Centre of African Studies, University of Cambridge, Cambridge CB2 3RQ (e-mail csc34@cam.ac.uk)

CLAPHAM, Michael; MP; *b* 15 May 1943; *Educ* Barnsley Tech Coll, Leeds Poly London Ex (BSc), Univ of Leeds (PGCE), Univ of Bradford (MPhil); *m*; 1 s, 1 da; *Career* miner 1958–70, lectr 1974–77, dep head Compensation Dept NUM 1977–83, head Industrial Relations Dept NUM 1983–92, MP (Lab, UCATT sponsored) Barnsley W and Penistone 1992–; memb Select Ctee Trade and Industry 1992–97 and 2003–; PPS to Min of State for Health 1997 (resigned), vice-chm backbench Trade and Industry Ctee 1995–96, chm All-Pty Gp on Occupational Safety and Health 1996, chm All-Pty Coalfields Community Gp 1997, chm Fire Safety All-Pty Gp 2000; memb NATO Assembly 2000, chair of civil dimensions of security NATO; chm Barnsley Crime Prevention Partnership 1995, chm Barnsley Multi Agency Panel 1997; memb: Lab Pty 1979–, Co-operative Pty, NUM, UCATT; hon vice-pres Inst of Occupational Health and Safety (IOSH) 2003–; *Style—* Michael Clapham, Esq, MP; ✉ House of Commons, London SW1A 0AA (tel 020 7219 2907, fax 020 7219 5015, e-mail claphamm@parliament.uk); constituency office: 18 Regent Street, Barnsley S70 2HG (tel 01226 731244, fax 01226 731259)

CLAPP, Peter Michael; s of Percival Dennis Clapp (d 1994), of Exmouth, Devon, and Lily, *née* Duck (d 1988); *b* 12 March 1943; *Educ* Exeter Sch, Dept of Architecture Hammersmith Coll of Art and Building (DipArch, RIBA Sir Bannister Fletcher Silver Medal); *m* 26 Sept 1964, Ann; 2 s (Giles Benedict b 25 Dec 1966, Adam Julian b 10 Oct 1968); *Career* architect and designer; own practice and RIBA res award 1964–67, assoc ptnr in various practices incl Whinney McKay Lewis and Louis de Soissons 1968–74, Architect's Dept London Borough of Camden 1975–80; W H Smith: responsible for Do-it-All building prog 1981–82, dep chief architect 1983–86, design mangr 1987–92 (with overall responsibility for all design, architecture, advtg, art purchasing and corp identity); chief architect Sport England 1996–2001 (princ architect 1992–96) (responsible for multi-disciplinary team advising on buildings, funded by the Sport England Lottery Fund); design conslt 2001–; 2 Civic Tst Awards 1981, DOE Good Design in Housing Award 1982; Civic Tst assessor 1982–; visiting lectr: London Business Sch, RCA, Templeton Coll Oxford; ARIBA 1966 (memb Cncl 1972–75), FCSD 1991; *Recreations* landscape photography, theatre, music, walking; *Style—* Peter Clapp, Esq; ✉ 12 Jeffrey's Place, London NW1 9PP (tel 020 7267 2445, e-mail peterclapp@ukonline.co.uk)

CLAPPERTON, (Alexander) Wallace Ford; s of Alexander Clapperton (d 1943), of Edinburgh, and Kathleen Nora, *née* Ford (d 1991); *b* 22 July 1934; *Educ* Charterhouse; *m* 27 March 1965, Catherine Anne, da of Sir Henry Horsman, MC (d 1966), of Bermuda; 1 da (Alison Nicola b 1967), 1 s (Graeme Alexander Ford b 1969); *Career* Nat Serv RCS 1957–59; ptnr de Zoete and Bevan stockbrokers (formerly de Zoete and Gorton) 1963–86, dir Barclays de Zoete Wedd Securities Ltd 1986–92; non-exec chm Scantronic Holdings 1992–95, non-exec dir Henderson TR Pacific Investment Trust 1992–2003; MICAS; *Recreations* golf, skiing; *Clubs* Hon Co of Edinburgh Golfers, Denham Golf, Woburn Golf, City of London; *Style—* Wallace Clapperton, Esq; ✉ Broomfield House, Broomfield Hill, Great Missenden, Buckinghamshire HP16 9PD (tel 01494 862559, fax 01494 890732)

CLAPPISON, James; MP; s of late Leonard Clappison, and late Dorothy Clappison; *b* 14 September 1956; *Educ* St Peter's Sch York, The Queen's Coll Oxford (scholar); *m* 6 July 1984, Helen Margherita, *née* Carter; 1 s, 3 da; *Career* called to the Bar 1981; MP (Cons) Hertsmere 1992– (Parly candidate Barnsley E 1987, Euro Parly candidate Yorks S 1989 Parly candidate Bootle May and Nov 1990 (by-elections)); PPS to min of state Home Office 1994–95, Parly under-sec of state Dept of the Environment 1995–97; oppn front bench spokesman: on home affrs (crime, immigration and asylums) 1997–99, for educn 1999–2000, for treasy 2000–01; shadow min for work 2001–02, shadow min for Treasy 2002–03; *Clubs* Carlton; *Style—* James Clappison, Esq, MP; ✉ House of Commons, London SW1A 0AA

CLAPTON, Eric Patrick; CBE (2004, OBE 1995); *b* 30 March 1945; *Educ* St Bede's Sch Surrey, Kingston Coll of Art; *m* 1, 1979 (m dis 1988), Patti Harrison; 2 c by subseq ptnr (Conor b 1987 d 1991, Ruth b 1985); m 2, 2002, Melia McEnery; 1 da (Julie Rose); *Career* guitarist and singer; has worked with Howlin' Wolf, Steve Winwood, The Beatles, The Rolling Stones, Pete Townshend, Elton John, Phil Collins and others; joined Yardbirds as lead guitarist 1963, recorded album Five Little Yardbirds (live, 1964), joined John Mayall's Bluesbreakers 1965; albums with John Mayall: Lonely Years (1965), Blues Breakers (1966, reached UK no 6); formed Cream 1966; albums with Cream: Fresh Cream (1967, UK no 6), Disraeli Gears (1967, UK no 5), Wheels Of Fire (1968, UK no 3), Goodbye (1969, UK no 1), The Best Of Cream (compilation, 1969, UK no 6), Live Cream (live, 1970, UK no 4), Live Cream - Vol 2 (live, 1972, UK no 15); formed Blind Faith 1969, recorded album Blind Faith (1969, UK no 1); started solo career 1970, formed Derek & The Dominoes 1970, recorded albums Layla And Other Love Songs (1970, US no 16), Derek & The Dominoes In Concert (live, 1973, UK no 36); solo albums: Eric Clapton (1970, UK no 17), History Of Eric Clapton (1972, UK no 20), Eric Clapton's Rainbow Concert (live, 1973, UK no 19), 461 Ocean Boulevard (1974, UK no 3), There's One In Every Crowd (1975, UK no 15), E C Was Here (live, 1975, UK no 14), No Reason To Cry (1976, UK no 8), Slowhand (1977, UK no 23), Backless (1978, UK no 18), Just One Night (1980, UK no 3), Another Ticket (1981, UK no 18), Time Pieces - The Best Of Eric Clapton (1982, UK no 20), Money And Cigarettes (1983, UK no 13), Backtrackin' (compilation, 1984, UK no 29), Behind The Sun (1985, UK no 8), August (1986, UK no 3), The Cream Of Eric Clapton (compilation, UK no 3), Crossroads (box set, 1988), Journeyman (1989, UK no 2), 24 Nights (live, 1992), Unplugged (1992, UK no 3), Stages (1993), From the Cradle (1994), Crossroads 2: Live in the 70s (1996), Pilgrim (1998), Riding with the King (2000), Reptile (2001), Eric Clapton Live (2002), The Road to Escondido (with JJ Cale, 2006); has worked on numerous film soundtracks incl: Tommy, The Colour Of Money, Lethal Weapon, Rush; *Awards* incl: winner Grammy award for Best Male Rock Vocal (for Bad Love) 1991, Variety Club Best Recording Artist of 1992, six Grammy awards 1993, winner Grammy award for Best Traditional Blues Recording (for From the Cradle) 1995, winner Grammy awards for Record of the Year and Best Male Pop Vocalist (for Change the World) 1997, winner Grammy award for Best Male Pop Vocal (for My Father's Eyes) 1999; *Style—* Eric Clapton, CBE

CLARE, Prof Anthony Ward; s of Bernard J Clare (d 1995), of Ranelagh, Dublin 6, and Mary Agnes, *née* Dunne (d 1993); *b* 24 December 1942; *Educ* Gonzaga Coll Dublin, UCD (MB BCh, BAO, MD), Univ of London (MPhil); *m* 4 Oct 1966, Jane Carmel, da of Gabriel Sarsfield Hogan (d 1989), of Dublin; 3 s (Simon John b 1970, Peter Tobias b 1975, Sebastian Patrick b 1985), 4 da (Rachel Judith b 1967, Eleanor Ruth b 1971, Sophie Carolyn b 1978, Justine Chiara b 1982); *Career* intern St Joseph Hosp Syracuse NY 1966–67; registrar: St Patrick's Hosp Dublin 1967–69, Bethlem Royal and Maudsley Hosps London 1970–72; dep dir Gen Practice Res Unit Inst of Psychiatry 1979–82 (sr registrar and res worker 1973–78), prof and head Dept of Psychological Med St Bartholomew's Hosp Med Coll 1982–88, med dir St Patrick's Hosp Dublin and prof of clinical psychiatry Trinity Coll Dublin 1989–95; chm The Prince of Wales Advsy Gp on Disability 1989–97; numerous broadcasts incl: Let's Talk About Me, In The Psychiatrist's Chair (BBC 1982–), Stop The Week; FRCPI 1983, FRCPsych 1986 (vice-pres); *Books* Psychiatry in Dissent (1976, 2 edn 1980), Let's Talk About Me (1981), In the Psychiatrist's Chair (1984), Lovelaw (1986), In the Psychiatrist's Chair (1992), Depression and How to Survive It (with Spike Milligan, 1993), In the Psychiatrist's Chair II (1995), In the Psychiatrist's Chair III (1998); *Recreations* tennis, opera, family life; *Style—* Prof Anthony W Clare; ✉ c/o St Edmundsbury Hospital, Lucan, Co.Dublin, Republic of Ireland

CLARE, John Charles; CBE (2004); s of Sidney Charles Clare (d 1990), of Great Yarmouth, and Joan Mildred, *née* Hall (d 1997); *b* 2 August 1950, Great Yarmouth; *Educ* Great Yarmouth GS, Univ of Edinburgh (BSc); *m* 22 June 1974, Anne, *née* Ross; 2 s (Tony Charles b 20 July 1976, Andy James b 12 Nov 1981); *Career* various sales and mktg roles Mars Ltd 1972–82, mktg dir Ladbrokes Racing Div 1982–85, md Dixons Ltd 1986 (mktg dir 1985), md Dixons Stores Gp Ltd and dir Dixons Gp plc 1988, chief exec Dixons Gp plc (now DSG Int plc) 1994–2007; dir Hammersons plc; memb Devpt Bd Univ of Edinburgh, memb Nat Employment Panel, pres ISBA; *Recreations* boating, sports, music; *Style—* John Clare, Esq, CBE

CLARE, Jonathan; s of John Clare, and Sheila, *née* Crush; *b* 25 July 1954; *Educ* Windsor GS, Lancaster Univ (BA); *Partner* Celeste Warner; *Career* business and fin journalist 1975–86 (Morgan Grampian, Investors Chronicle, Birmingham Post, The Times, Daily Mail), Streets Financial 1986–88, fndr and dep md Citigate Communications Group 1988–98, md Citigate Dewe Rogerson (following merger) 1998–; memb: Int Spinal Research Tst, Cruising Assoc, RNLI, RHS, RYA, MIPR; *Recreations* mountain walking, sailing, skiing, reading; *Style—* Jonathan Clare, Esq; ✉ Citigate Dewe Rogerson, 3 London Wall Buildings, London EC2M 5SY

CLARE, Mark Sydney; *b* 10 August 1957; *m* 26 July 1980, Alison; 1 s (David), 2 da (Nicola, Emily); *Career* fin mangr GEC-Marconi 1985–88; STC plc: gp fin mangr 1989–90, fin controller Telecoms System Div 1990, asst fin dir STC Telecommunications 1990–91; fin controller Telecoms Systems Gp Nortel 1991–92, fin dir STC Submarine Systems Nortel 1992–94, gp fin controller British Gas plc 1994–97, gp fin dir Centrica plc 1997–2000, dep chief exec Centrica plc 2000–06, md British Gas Residential Energy 2002–06, gp chief exec Barratt Developments plc 2006–; non-exec dir BAA plc until 2006; FCMA; *Recreations* squash, tennis, fast cars; *Style—* Mark Clare, Esq; ✉ Barratt Developments plc, Rotterdam House, 116 Quayside, Newcastle upon Tyne NE1 3DA

CLARE, Michael George; s of Thomas Clare (d 1967), of Beaconsfield, Bucks, and Betty, *née* Jeffries (d 2000); *b* 8 February 1955; *Educ* High Wycombe Coll; *m* 27 Oct 1979, Carol, *née* Ballingall; 2 s (Thomas b 31 Dec 1984, Edward b 2 April 1986), 2 da (Rebecca b 13 Aug 1991, Hannah b 13 Oct 1992); *Career* branch mangr Williams Furniture 1976–78, area mangr Hardys Furniture 1978–80, area mangr Perrings Furniture 1980–84, sales dir W H Deanes Furniture 1984–86, chief exec Dreams plc 1987–; pres Furniture Trade Benevolent Assoc, bd dir Br Retail Consortium; tstee Buckinghamshire Fndn, govr Buckinghamshire Chiltern UC; patron Retail Tst; Freeman City of London 2002; Ernst & Young Regnl Entrepreneur of the Year 2002; FInstD; *Recreations* travelling the world, making dreams a reality; *Clubs* Beaconsfield 41, Cliveden; *Style*— Michael Clare, Esq; ✉ Dreams plc, Knaves Beech, High Wycombe, Bucks HP10 9YU (tel 01628 535363, fax 01628 522122, e-mail mikeclare@dreams.co.uk)

CLARE, Pauline Ann; CBE (2002), QPM (1996), DL (Lancs 1998); *b* 26 July 1947; *Educ* Open Univ (BA); *m*; 2 step da; *Career* joined Lancs Constabulary 1966, various positions Southport and Kirkby until 1974, Police Staff Coll Bramshill 1974, inspr Merseyside Police 1974–83, Jr Cmd Course Police Staff Coll 1983, chief inspr Liverpool City Centre and Community Affrs Dept 1983–87, sub-divnl cdr Southport 1988–89, Intermediate Cmd Course 1989, chief supt 1991, Sr Cmd Course 1991, divnl cdr Bootle 1991–92; Merseyside Police: asst chief constable (Crime) 1992–94, asst chief constable (Ops) 1994; dep chief constable Cheshire Constabulary 1994–95, chief constable Lancs Constabulary 1995–2002; Hon Col Lancs ACF (Queen's Lancs Regt) 1996–2002, vice-pres Lancs Assoc of Clubs for Young People (pres 1995–2002), memb Cncl St John Ambulance Assoc in Lancs, memb NW Bd Princess Royal Tst for Carers 2000; Hon Dr Open Univ 1999; hon fell Univ of Central Lancs 1994; CIMgt 1996; SSStJ 1995, FRSA 2002; *Awards* Lancashire Woman of the Year 1993, North West Woman of the Year 1995; *Recreations* gardening, preparing and hosting dinner parties, horse riding, reading, attending the theatre; *Style*— Mrs P A Clare, CBE, QPM, DL; ✉ e-mail pauline.clare@paulineclare.com

CLARE, (Rear Adm) Roy Alexander George; CBE (2007); s of John Arnold Clare (d 1978), and Ludmilla, *née* Nossoff (d 2002); *b* 30 September 1950; *Educ* St George's GS Cape Town, BRNC Dartmouth, RN Staff Coll, RCDS; *m* 1, 1979, Leonie (Mimi), *née* Hutchings (d 1979); m 2, 1981, Sarah Catherine Jane, da of Anthony Parkin; 1 s (Oliver Christopher George b 16 June 1984), 2 da (Philippa Anne Elizabeth b 16 Sept 1986, Louisa Jane Natasha b 1 Feb 1990); *Career* jr seaman 1966, midshipman 1970; chief mate yacht 'Adventure' Whitbread Round the World Yacht Race 1973–74; co: HMS Bronington 1980–81 (second in command 1975–77), HMS Birmingham 1987–89, HMS York and 3 Destroyer Sqdn 1991–92, HMS Invincible 1996–97, BRNC 1998–99 (led opening of BRNC to paying visitors 1998); Rear Adm (NATO appt) 1999–2000, dir Nat Maritime Museum 2000–07; memb Bd Creative and Cultural Skills Sector Skills Cncl 2005–07; chief exec Museums and Libraries and Archives Cncl 2007– (memb Bd 2006–07); vice-pres Bronington Tst 1999–2002 (tstee 1989–99), pres Midland Naval Offrs Assoc 2000–02; fndr Britannia Museum, tstee Naval Review 1999–, tstee Britannia Assoc 2001–04; memb Assembly Univ of Greenwich 2001–07, memb Greenwich Forum 2001–07; Hon DLitt Univ of Greenwich 2007; Sword of Honour 1972, Queen's Silver Jubilee Medal 1977, GSM 1977 and 1989; Freeman: City of London 2001, Worshipful Co of Shipwrights 2002, Worshipful Co of Clockmakers 2004; CCMI 2001, FRSA 2005; *Books* Bronington - The Last of Britain's Wooden Walls (ed, 1996); *Recreations* family, sailing, walking; *Clubs* Anchorites, RN Sailing Assoc, RN of 1765 and 1785, Royal Yacht Sqdn (naval memb); *Style*— Roy Clare, CBE; ✉ Museums, Libraries and Archives Council, Victoria House, Southampton Row, London WC1B 4EA (tel 020 7273 1476, mobile 07779 947483, fax 020 7273 1404, e-mail r.clare@virgin.net)

CLARENDON, 7 Earl of (GB 1776); George Frederick Laurence Hyde Villiers; also Baron Hyde (GB 1756); s of late Lord Hyde and late Hon Marion, *née* Glyn, da of 4 Baron Wolverton; suc gf 1955; *b* 2 February 1933; *Educ* Eton, Univ of Madrid; *m* 1974, Jane Diana, da of Edward William Dawson (d 1979), of Idmiston, Wilts; 1 s (George Edward Laurence, Lord Hyde b 12 Feb 1976), 1 da (Lady Sarah Katherine Jane Villiers b 1977); *Heir* s, Lord Hyde; *Career* page of honour to HM King George VI 1948–49; Lt RHG 1951–53; Glyn Mills and Co 1955–60, Seccombe Marshall and Campion 1960–93 (md 1962, chm 1985–93); memb Ct of Assts Worshipful Co of Fishmongers (Prime Warden 1999–2000); *Style*— The Rt Hon the Earl of Clarendon; ✉ Holywell House, Swanmore, Hampshire SO32 2QE (tel 01489 896090, fax 01489 892353)

CLARIDGE, Prof Michael Frederick; s of Frederick William Claridge (d 1965), of Rugby, Warks, and Eva Alice, *née* Jeffery (d 1969); *b* 2 June 1934; *Educ* Lawrence Sheriff Sch Rugby, Keble Coll Oxford (MA, DPhil); *m* 30 Sept 1967, (Lindsey) Clare, da of Gilbert Hellings (d 1973), of Shipton-under-Wychwood, Oxon; 2 s (John, Robert), 1 da (Elin); *Career* UC Cardiff: lectr in zoology 1959–76, reader in entomology 1977–83, personal chair in entomology 1983–89, acting head of zoology 1987–88; Univ of Wales Cardiff: head Sch of Pure and Applied Biology 1989–94, prof of entomology 1989–2000, emeritus prof of entomology 2001–; pres: Linnean Soc of London 1988–91 (memb Cncl 1984–91), Systematics Assoc 1991–94 (memb Cncl 1984–87); editorial offr Royal Entomological Soc 2002– (memb Cncl 1971–74 and 1998–2002, pres 2000–2002); memb British Ecological Soc (memb Cncl 1976–79); Linnean Medal for Zoology 2000; FLS, FRES, FIBiol; *Books* The Leafhoppers and Planthoppers (contrib, 1985), The Organization of Communities, Past and Present (contrib, 1987), Prospects in Systematics (contrib, 1988), Handbook for the Identification of Leafhoppers and Planthoppers of Rice (jtly, 1991), Evolutionary Patterns and Processes (contrib, 1993), Planthoppers: Their Ecology and Management (contrib, 1993), Species the Units of Biodiversity (ed and contrib, 1997), Insect Sounds and Communication (ed and contrib, 2005); *Recreations* cricket, music, natural history; *Clubs* The Entomological; *Style*— Prof Michael Claridge; ✉ 84 The Hollies, Quakers Yard, Treharris, Mid Glamorgan CF46 5PP (e-mail claridge@cardiff.ac.uk)

CLARK, *see also:* Chichester-Clark, Stewart-Clark

CLARK, Adrian; *b* 20 May 1957; *Educ* King Edward VI GS Retford, Peterhouse Cambridge (exhibitioner), Coll of Law; *Career* slr; Slaughter and May 1981–86; Ashurst: joined 1986, seconded to Panel on Takeovers and Mergers 1988–90, ptnr 1990–, head Corp Dept 2004–; *Clubs* MCC; *Style*— Adrian Clark, Esq; ✉ Ashurst, Broadwalk House, 5 Appold Street, London EC2A 2HA

CLARK, (Thomas) Alastair; s of Andrew Clark (d 1998), and Freda Clark (d 2004); *b* 27 February 1949; *Educ* Stockport GS, Emmanuel Coll Cambridge (open scholar, sr scholar, MA), LSE (MSc), Stanford Univ (Exec Prog); *m* 1986, Shirley Anne, *née* Barker; 1 da (Joanna b 1987 d 1995), 1 s (Andrew b 1989); *Career* Bank of England: Economics Div 1971–80, PA to dep govr 1980–81, Internatinal Div 1981–83, UK alternate exec dir IMF 1983–85, Gilt-Edged Div 1985–87, UK alternate dir EIB 1986–88, head Fin Mkts and Instns Div 1987–93, head Europe Div 1993–94, dep dir Fin Structure 1994–97, exec dir Fin Stability 1997–2003, advsr to the govr 2003–07; dir International Financial Services London (formerly British Invisibles) 1997–2007; non-exec memb Mgmnt Bd Rolls Royce Cars 1991–94; govr Kings Coll Sch Wimbledon, mem Advsy Cncl Assoc of Corporate Treasurers, memb Advsy Bd City Univ; *Recreations* hill walking, joinery; *Style*— Alastair Clark, Esq; ✉ 54 Forest Road, Richmond, Surrey TW9 3BZ (e-mail t.alastair.clark@btinternet.com)

CLARK, Anthony Richard; s of Noel Edmund Clark, and Marianne Edith, *née* Sayres; *b* 4 April 1958; *Educ* Downside, Univ of Manchester (BA Drama, Dip Playwriting); *m* 1984, Delia Mary, da of John Goddard; 4 c (Anna Magdalene, Gabriel James, Eleanor Pearl, Crispin Lee); *Career* director and writer; dir Orange Tree Theatre Richmond 1981–83, artistic dir Contact Theatre Manchester 1984–89, assoc artistic dir Birmingham Rep Theatre Co 1990–2001, artistic dir Hampstead Theatre 2003–; *Theatre* Contact Theatre prodns incl: Face Value, Two Wheel Tricycle, McAlpine's Fusiliers, Green, Homeland, Mother Courage and her Children, Blood Wedding, A Midsummer Night's Dream, The Duchess of Malfi, To Kill a Mockingbird (European Premiere), Oedipus Rex; Birmingham Rep incl: The Seagull, Macbeth, Of Mice and Men, Saturday Sunday Monday, Cider with Rosie (nat tour), The Threepenny Opera, The Pied Piper, My Mother Said I Never Should, The Grapes of Wrath, The Atheist's Tragedy, The Playboy of the Western World, Peter Pan, Pygmalion, The Red Balloon, The Entertainer, Gentlemen Prefer Blonds, Julius Caesar, St Joan; new plays incl: Belonging, The Slight Witch, My Best Friend, Silence, All That Trouble That We Had, Home Truths, True Brit, Rough, Playing by the Rules, Nervous Women, Syme (co-prodn with RNT studio), Paddies, Confidence; Hampstead Theatre prodns incl: The Maths Tutor, Revelations, When the Night Begins, Osama the Hero, A Single Act, Nathan the Wise; freelance dir incl: Dr Faustus (Young Vic), To Kill a Mockingbird (Greenwich), The Snowman (Leicester Haymarket), The Red Balloon (Bristol Old Vic and RNT), The Day After Tomorrow (RNT), Mother Courage and her Children (RNT), The Wood Demon (Playhouse), Loveplay (RSC), Tender (Hampstead Theatre), Edward III (RSC); as writer plays incl: Hand it to Them, Wake, The Power of Darkness (Orange Tree), Tidemark (RSC Thoughtcrimes Festival), A Matter of Life and Death (RNT), Green; as writer musical adapts incl: The Snowman, The Little Prince, The Red Balloon, (all Contact Theatre Manchester), The Pied Piper, Pinocchio (both Birmingham Rep), Winnie the Witch; *Awards* RSC Buzz Award 1979, Manchester Evening News Best Prodn Award (for To Kill a Mockingbird) 1984, TMA/Martini Award for Best Dir (for The Atheist's Tragedy) 1994, TMA/Martina Award for Best Show for Children and Young People (for The Red Balloon) 1995, Mentorn First Night Prodn Award (for Playing by the Rules); *Publications* The Power of Darkness (trans Tolstoy, 1987), The Red Balloon (1997), Winnie the Witch (2002), The Pied Piper (2003); *Style*— Anthony Clark, Esq; ✉ c/o Catherine King, ICM, Oxford House, 76 Oxford Street, London W1N 0AX (tel 020 7636 6565)

CLARK, Antony Roy; s of Roger Maule Clark, of Cape Town, South Africa, and Betty Nadine, *née* Davies; *b* 7 November 1956; *Educ* St Andrew's Coll Grahamstown, Rhodes Univ (BA, HDE), Downing Coll Cambridge (Douglas Smith scholarship, MA); *m* 12 Dec 1981, Brigitte, *née* Lang; 1 s (Andrew b 12 June 1989), 2 da (Frances 14 April 1992, Katherine b 10 Dec 1996); *Career* teacher Westerford HS Cape Town 1984–90, investment business 1990–91; headmaster: St Joseph's Marist Coll Cape Town 1992–93, St Andrew's Coll Grahamstown 1994–2002, Gresham's Sch Holt 2002–; *Recreations* cricket, squash, tennis, hiking, chess; *Clubs* Hawks' (Cambridge), East India, Lansdowne; *Style*— Antony Clark, Esq; ✉ Gresham's School, Cromer Road, Holt, Norfolk NE25 6EA (tel 01263 714511, fax 01263 712028, e-mail headmaster@greshams.com)

CLARK, Brian Robert; *b* 3 June 1932; *Career* playwright; *TV* credits incl: Achilles Heel, Operation Magic Carpet, Parole, Easy Go, The Saturday Party, The Country Party, There's No Place, Happy Returns, Telford's Change (10 part series, BBC) 1979, Late Starter (BBC) 1985; *Theatre* Post Mortem, Campion's Interview (Soho Poly Theatre), Whose Life is it Anyway? (Mermaid, Savoy and Broadway) 1978–80 (film 1982), Can You Hear Me at the Back? (Piccadilly Theatre) 1979, Kipling (Mermaid) 1984 (later televised Channel 4), The Petition (Broadway, National Theatre and West End) 1986–87, Hopping to Byzantium (co-wrote with Kathy Levin, premiered Osnabruck West Germany) 1990, In Pursuit of Eve (King's Head Threatre) 2001; *Awards* for Whose Life is it Anyway?: Best Play Society of West End Theatre Awards 1978, Most Promising Playwright Evening Standard Drama Awards 1978, Best Play Plays and Players Award 1978; BAFTA Shell International TV Award (for Telford's Change) 1979; *Style*— Brian Clark, Esq, FRSL; ✉ Judy Daish Associates Ltd, 2 St Charles Place, London W10 6EG (tel 020 8964 8811, fax 020 8964 8966)

CLARK, Brian Stephen; s of Stephen Wilfred Clark (d 1974), and Florence Sybil Elizabeth, *née* Webb; *b* 11 August 1936; *Educ* Willesden Co GS, LSE (LLB); *m* 17 Feb 1962, Rita, *née* Jones; 2 s (Stephen Nicholas b 2 Oct 1963, Andrew Simon b 26 July 1966); *Career* admitted slr 1961; Goodman Derrick & Co 1958–69 (articled clerk, asst slr, ptnr), exec International Management Group (IMG) London 1969–71, sr corp ptnr Nabarro Nathanson 1988–93 (ptnr 1971–93), dir of European legal affrs IMG 1993–2000 (conslt to IMG 2000–), Catella Financial Office Ltd 2006–; memb Law Soc; *Recreations* golf, photography, opera; *Style*— Brian Clark, Esq; ✉ Catella Financial Office Limited, Chiswick Gate 598–608, Chiswick High Road, London W4 5RT (tel 020 8104 1000, fax 020 8994 0993, e-mail b.s.clark@btinternet.com)

CLARK, Prof Charles Victor; s of Dennis Clark, and Margaret, *née* Slowther; *b* 11 August 1956; *Educ* George Heriot's Sch Edinburgh, Univ of Edinburgh (BSc, MB ChB, MD, ChM, DSc, LLM); *m* 15 Dec 1983, Maureen, da of James Corr (d 1978); *Career* sr surgical registrar Moorfields Eye Hosp London 1986–88, conslt ophthalmic surgn Royal Infirmary of Edinburgh and sr lectr in ophthalmology Univ of Edinburgh 1988–91, prof of ophthalmology and dir Glaucoma Servs Univ of Queensland 1991–94, prof of educn Griffith Univ Queensland 1995–; md: Charles V Clark Med Pty Ltd 1991–02, Orion Eye Centre 2003–; conslt ophthalmic surgeon London Diabetes and Lipid Centre 2003–, conslt ophthalmic surgeon London 2005–; specialist in glaucoma and diabetic eye disease and nutrition; author of 6 books and over 60 scientific papers; memb: Assoc for Eye Res, Oxford Ophthalmological Congress, Clinical Autonomic Res Soc; fell RMS 1979, FRCSEd 1985, FRCOphth 1988, CBiol, FIBiol 1991, fell Royal Aust Coll of Ophthalmologists 1991, fell Royal Aust Coll of Surgns 1992, fell American Acad of Opthalmology 1992, fell Aust Inst of Biology 1994, FSA Scot 2000; *Recreations* photography, music, theatre, rugby football; *Style*— Prof Charles Clark

CLARK, His Hon Judge Christopher Harvey; QC (1989); s of Harvey Frederick Beckford Clark, of Winchester, Hants, and Winifred Julia, *née* Caesar; *b* 20 December 1946; *Educ* Taunton's Sch Southampton, The Queen's Coll Oxford (MA); *m* 25 March 1972 (m dis 2004), Gillian Elizabeth Ann, da of Anthony Mullen; 1 s (Patrick Harvey b 1974), 2 da (Melanie Julia b 1976, Lucy Elizabeth b 1980); m 2, 5 June 2004, Wendy Gaye Keith, da of Harvey Hepworth; *Career* called to the Bar Gray's Inn 1969 (bencher 2000); memb Western Circuit 1970–, asst recorder 1982–86, recorder of the Crown Court 1986–2005, head Pump Court Chambers 2001–05, circuit judge 2005–; memb Wine Ctee Western Circuit 1985–90, chm Fees and Legal Aid Ctee Western Circuit 1989; chllr Dio of Winchester 1993–, dep chllr Dio of Chichester 1995–2006, dep chllr Dio of Salisbury 1997–, chllr Dio of Portsmouth 2003– (dep chllr 1994–2003); hon legal advsr to the Hampshire Assoc of Parish and Town Cncls 1996–99, memb Ecclesiastical Judges Assoc Standing Ctee 1996–2004, memb Legal Advsy Cmmn Gen Synod 1996–2001; chm Stockbridge Dramatic Soc 1977–, memb Longstock Parish Cncl 1979–2002, youth club organiser (The Longstock Tadpoles) 1981–90; licensed reader C of E 1998–; *Recreations* amateur dramatics, golf, fishing, swimming, gardening, walking, skiing, reading; *Clubs* Athenaeum, Flyfishers; *Style*— His Hon Judge Christopher Harvey Clark, QC; ✉ 3 Pump Court, Temple, London EC4Y 7AJ (tel 020 7353 0711)

CLARK, Christopher Richard Nigel; s of Rev Vivian George Clark (d 1996), of Plympton St Maurice, and Aileen Myfanwy, *née* Thompson; *b* 29 January 1942, St Austell, Cornwall; *Educ* Marlborough, Trinity Coll Cambridge, Brunel Coll (LIM), Sir John Cass Coll (MIM); *m* 20 March 1964, Catherine Ann, *née* Mather; 3 s (James Michael Christopher b 8 Oct 1964 d 1973, Jeremy Richard Anthony b 29 Jan 1969, Hugo Benedict James b 1 Oct 1974), 1 da (Joanna Catherine Lucy b 24 Sept 1966); *Career* Johnson Matthey: joined 1962, product mangr Johnson Matthey Metals 1969–75, product gp mangr 1975–79, mktg mangr Metal Products Div USA 1979–84, gen mangr noble metals fabrication business 1984–87, head Platinum Mktg 1987–88, head Catalytic Systems Div 1988–90, head Colour and Print Div 1990, exec dir 1990, head Materials Technol Div 1991, chm Cookson

Matthey Ceramics plc 1994–98 (chief exec 1994), gp md Electronic Materials 1995–96, chief operating offr 1996–98, chief exec 1998–2004; non-exec chm: Associated British Ports 2004–, Wagon plc 2005–, Urenco Ltd 2006–, JSC Severstal 2007–; dep chm Rexam plc 2003–06; non-exec dir: Trinity Hldgs plc 1992–97, FKI plc 2000–06; Centenary Medal Soc of Chemical Industries 2002, Distinguished Achievement Award Int Precious Metals Inst 2004; Freeman: City of London, Worshipful Co of Goldsmiths; Liveryman Worshipful Co of Gold and Silver Wire Drawers; MIM, MinstD 1990, MCMI (MIMgt 2001); *Recreations* shooting, golf, opera, ballet, watching rugby, cricket; *Clubs* Travellers, Jesters; *Style*— Christopher Clark, Esq; ✉ 30 Marryat Road, London SW19 5BD (tel 020 8946 5887); Associated British Ports, 150 Holborn, London EC1N 2LR (tel 020 7430 6824)

CLARK, Dr David Findlay; OBE (1990), DL (Banffshire 1992); s of Rev Dr David Findlay Clark (d 1966), and Annie, *née* McKenzie (d 1963); *b* 30 May 1930; *Educ* Banff Acad, Univ of Aberdeen (MA, PhD); *m* 9 Oct 1954, Janet Anne, da of Gavin M Stephen, of Brechin, Angus; 2 da (Morag Anne (Mrs Baptie) b 1955, Linda Jane (Mrs Wimble) b 1958); *Career* Flying Offr RAF 1951–53, RAFVR 1953–57; psychologist Leicester Industrial Rehabilitation Unit 1953–56, princ clinical psychologist Leicester Area Clinical Psychology Serv 1960–66 (sr clinical psychologist 1956–60), dir and top grade clinical psychologist Grampian Health Bd 1966–90, clinical sr lectr Dept of Mental Health Univ of Aberdeen 1966–, conslt clinical psychologist in private practice 1990–96; former: chm Div of Clinical Psychology Br Psychological Soc (memb Cncl), memb Health Serv Planning Cncl, town and co cncllr Banff and Banffshire, Safeguarder (under terms of SWK Scotland Act) 1985–2001; Hon Sheriff Grampian and Highlands and Islands at Banff 1979–; FBPsS 1969, ARPS 1991; *Books* Help, Hospitals and the Handicapped (1984), One Boy's War (1997), Stand by Your Beds (2001), Remember Who You Are! (2007); contrib to major textbooks and author of numerous jl articles; *Recreations* golf, photography, painting, guitar, piano, travel, writing; *Clubs* Duff House Royal Golf, Banff Rotary (past pres); *Style*— Dr David Clark, OBE, DL; ✉ Glendeveron, 8 Deveron Terrace, Banff AB45 1BB (tel 01261 812624, e-mail drdavidfindlayclark@btinternet.com)

CLARK, His Hon Denis; s of John Clark, of Tranmere, Birkenhead, and Mary Elizabeth, *née* Kenna; *b* 2 August 1943; *Educ* St Anselm's Coll Birkenhead, Univ of Sheffield (LLB); *m* 7 Jan 1967, Frances Mary Corcoran; 4 da (Rebecca b 19 Aug 1967, Rachel 25 Jan 1969, Catherine b 7 Jan 1971, Judith b 28 Jan 1972); *Career* called to the Bar Inner Temple 1966, in practice Northern Circuit 1966–88, recorder 1984–88, circuit judge (Northern Circuit) 1988–2007; *Recreations* Medieval history, theatre, cricket; *Style*— His Hon Denis Clark

CLARK, Derek Roland; MEP; s of Horace William Alfred (d 1984), and Doris Alice, *née* Beer (d 1984); *b* 10 October 1933, Bristol; *Educ* Bristol Cathedral Sch, Redland Trg Coll (Cert), St Luke's Coll Univ of Exeter (Cert, Dip); *m* 26 May 1973. Rosemary Jane, *née* Purser; *Career* teacher of sci Air Balloon Hill Secdy Modern Bristol 1954–62, head Sci Dept Cherry Orchard Secdy Sch Northampton 1962–74 (tutor exam courses 1968–74, sr master 1970–74), sr head of house Lings Upper Sch Northampton 1974–85, sr teacher Falcon Manor Sch Towcester 1985–93; MEP (UK Independence) E Midlands 2004–, memb Ctee on Employment and Social Affrs European Parl; UK Independence Party: chm Northants Branch 1995–2004, chm E Midlands Regnl Ctee 1996–2003, memb NEC 2001–04, party sec 2002–04; assoc Coll of Preceptors 1971; memb (non-singing) World Festival Choir; *Recreations* rugby (union) and cricket (but past playing days), travel, gardening; *Clubs* Northampton Saints RFC; *Style*— Derek Clark, Esq, MEP; ✉ 31 Tall Trees Close, Northampton NN4 9XZ (tel 01604 766064, e-mail derekrclark@hotmail.co.uk); Rowan House, 23 Billing Road, Northampton NN1 5AT (tel 01604 620064, fax 01604 636002, e-mail mep_eastmids@hotmail.com)

CLARK, Dingle Charles; s of Dr Charles Clark (d 1995), of Eltham, London, and Marcelle Pamela, *née* Marrable; *b* 7 June 1959; *Educ* Eltham Coll, Univ of Southampton (BSc), Central London Poly (Dip Law); *m* 15 April 1989, Caroline, da of John Patrick Hough, of Blackheath; 1 da (Charlotte Annabel Felicity b 18 Jan 1991), 3 s (Angus Lorne b 27 March 1993, Hugo Charles Alexander b 24 Sept 1995, James Archie b 15 Oct 1997); *Career* called to the Bar Middle Temple 1981, asst dep coroner (Essex) 1993–96; pt/t lectr: Cncl of Legal Educn 1987–, City Univ (Inns of Ct Sch of Law) 2002–; cncllr London Borough of Greenwich 1982–90 (Cons chief whip 1985–90); dir Original Holloway Friendly Soc Gloucester 1991–94; govr Woolwich Coll 1990–92; *Recreations* golf, football (Charlton Athletic supporter); *Clubs* Royal Blackheath Golf, Frinton Golf, Frinton Meml; *Style*— Dingle Clark, Esq; ✉ Goldsmith Building, Temple, London EC4Y 7AX (tel 020 7353 9328, fax 020 7583 5255)

CLARK, Eric; s of Horace Ernest Clark (d 1978), of Weston-super-Mare, Somerset, and Hilda Dorothy, *née* Mitchley (d 1996); *b* 29 July 1937; *Educ* Handsworth GS; *m* 1, 2 Aug 1958 (m dis 1972), Frances Grant; m 2, 12 April 1972, Marcelle, da of Jacob Bernstein (d 1956), of Manchester; 2 da (Rachael b 1975, Charlotte b 1978), 1 s (Daniel b 1980); *Career* staff reporter The Daily Mail 1962–64, staff writer The Guardian 1964–66, various appts The Observer 1966–72; articles published in foreign newspapers incl Melbourne Age and Washington Post; writer of fiction and non fiction 1972–; memb: Soc of Authors, Author's Guild, Mystery Writers of America, NUJ, Int Fedn of Journalists, Int Thriller Writers Inc; Fell Eng Centre Int PEN; *Books* Corps Diplomatique (1973), Black Gambit (1978), The Sleeper (1979), Send in The Lions (1981), Chinese Burn (1984), The Want Makers: The World of Advertising, How They Make You Buy (1988), Hide and Seek (1994), The Real Toy Story (2007); *Recreations* cinema, opera, jazz; *Clubs* Savile; *Style*— Eric Clark, Esq; ✉ c/o Agent, Bill Hamilton, A M Heath & Co Ltd, 6 Warwick Court, London WC1R 5DJ; c/o Child & Co, 1 Fleet Street, London EC4Y 1BD

CLARK, Sir Francis Drake; 5 Bt (UK 1886), of Melville Crescent, Edinburgh; s of Sir Thomas Clark, 3 Bt, DL, FRSE (d 1977); suc bro, Sir John Douglas Clark, 4 Bt, 1991; *b* 16 July 1924; *Educ* Edinburgh Acad; *m* 14 Aug 1958, Mary (d 1994), yr da of late John Alban Andrews, MC, FRCS; 1 s (Edward Drake b 27 April 1966); *Heir* s, Edward Clark; *Career* RN 1943–46; dir Clark Travel Service Ltd 1948–78; *Style*— Sir Francis Clark, Bt; ✉ Woodend Cottages, Burgh-next-Aylsham, Norfolk NR11 6TS

CLARK, Prof Frank; CBE (1991); *b* 17 October 1946; *m*; 2 da; *Career* clerical trainee Bd of Mgmnt Royal Cornhill and Associated Hosps 1965–67, higher clerical offr Kingseat Hosp 1967–69, hosp sec Canniesburn and Schaw Hosps 1970–71 (dep hosp sec 1969–70), admin Glasgow Royal Infirmary 1974–77 (dep hosp sec Glasgow Royal Infirmary and Sub-Gp 1971–74), dist gen admin Gtr Glasgow Health Bd Eastern Dist 1981–83 (asst dist admin 1977–81); dir Appeal Ctee West of Scotland Postgrad Dental Educn Centre 1981–83; Lanarkshire Health Bd: dist admin Hamilton and E Kilbride Unit 1983–84, dir of admin servs Hamilton and East Kilbride Unit June-Sept 1984, sec to the Bd 1984–85, gen mangr 1985–96; gen mangr Lothian Health Bd May-Dec 1990; dir Strathcarron Hospice 1996–; non-exec dir: VAMW Homes Ltd, VAMW Training Ltd 1996–; hon prof Dept of Nursing and Midwifery Univ of Stirling 1997–; memb: Working Pty on the Introduction of General Mgmnt at Unit Level 1984–85, Advsy Gp on New Devpts in Health Care 1984–90, Nat Specialist Servs Advsy Ctee (NSSAC) 1985–90, Scottish Health Mgmnt Efficiency Gp 1985–91, Univ Grants Ctee (Scottish Sub-Ctee) 1987–89, Working Pty on Community Med in Scotland (The Robertson Report) 1988–89, Working Pty on the Future of Dental Educn in Scotland (The McCallum Report) 1988–89 (Sec of State appt to 3 Memb Working Pty), Univs Funding Cncl (Scottish Ctee) 1989–91, Chief Scientists Health Serv Res Ctee 1989–93, Scottish Health Serv Advsy Cncl (Sec of State appt) 1990–93, Scottish Health Bd Gen Managers Gp 1990– (vice-chm 1990–93 and 1995, chm 1993–95) Advsy Gp on Acute Serv (successor body to NSSAC) 1990–93, Nat Nursing Strategy Gp 1990–93, West of Scotland Dental Educnl Tst Distance Learning Unit Appeal Ctee 1992–93, Scottish Overseas Health Support Policy Bd 1990–96, Jt Working Gp on Purchasing 1992–96, Bd New Lanarkshire Ltd 1992–97, Scottish Implementation Gp Jr Doctors' and Dentists' Hours of Work 1992–96, Scottish Cncl for Postgraduate Med and Dental Educn 1993–96, Editorial Advsy Bd Health Bulletin 1993–96, Scottish Health Services Mgmnt Centre Implementation Gp 1993–95, Strategy Gp R&D Strategy for NHS in Scotland 1994–96, Cncl of Mgmnt Scottish Partnership Agency 1998–2001 (dep chm 1999), Ind Hospices Rep Ctee Help the Hospices 1999–2001, Ministerial Advsy Panel on the Strategic Devpt of Mgmnt and Decision Making in NHS Scotland 2002; chm: Working Pty on Introduction of Hay Grading System to the NHS in Scotland 1989–90, Jt Mgmnt Exec/Gen Mangrs Manpower Gp 1990–93, West of Scotland Health Service Res Network 1990–95, Lanarkshire Drugs Action Team 1995–96, Scottish Hospices Forum 1998–2001, Central Scotland Health Care NHS Tst 1999, Forth Valley Primary Care NHS Tst 1999, Forth Valley NHS Bd 2002–03, Scottish Partnership for Palliative Care 2003– (hon treas 2001–03), Delivery Gp Scottish Acad for Health Policy and Mgmnt; head of Ministerial Taskforce Tayside Health Bd 2000; vice-chm of govrs Queen's Coll Glasgow 1988–93; memb Glasgow Dental Alumnus Assoc 1983; MHSM DipHSM 1974; *Clubs* Rotary of Cumbernauld; *Style*— Prof Frank Clark, CBE; ✉ Strathcarron Hospice, Randolph Hill, Denny, Stirlingshire FK6 5HJ (tel 01324 826222, fax 01324 824576)

CLARK, Gerald Edmondson; CMG (1989); s of Edward John Clark, and Irene Elizabeth Ada, *née* Edmondson; *b* 26 December 1935; *Educ* Johnston GS Durham, New Coll Oxford (MA); *m* 1967, Mary Rose Organ; 2 da; *Career* joined FO 1960, Hong Kong 1961, Peking 1962–63, FO 1964–68, Moscow 1968–70, FCO 1970–73, head of Chancery Lisbon 1973–77, Cabinet Office 1977–79, seconded to Barclays Bank International 1979–81, commercial cnsllr Peking 1981–83, FCO 1984–87, UK ambass to IAEA and other international orgns in Vienna 1987–92, sr civilian dir RCDS 1993, sec-gen Uranium Inst 1994–2000; gen sec Energy Strategists Consultancy Ltd 2001–, sec Int Nuclear Energy Acad (INEA) 2001–; ptnr KMT Ptnrs, energy advsr 33 St James's 2004–; fell Energy Inst 1998–; *Recreations* architecture, gardening, conversation; *Clubs* Athenaeum; *Style*— Gerald Clark, Esq, CMG; ✉ Lew Hollow, Beer Hill, Seaton, Devon EX12 2PY (tel 01297 22001, e-mail geraldeclark@aol.com)

CLARK, Gillian Margaret Rose; da of Cyril Geoffrey Gunning Lockwood (d 1981), and Vera Irene Lockwood, *née* Marchant (d 1991); *b* 15 January 1949; *Educ* Varndean GS for Girls, Ashridge Mgmnt Coll (City Univ) (MBA); *m* 16 Oct 1982, Philip Stephen Clark; 1 da (Juliette Annabelle b 11 March 1984); *Career* chartered insurer 1989; Eagle Star (now Zurich Financial Services): joined as accident underwriting clerk 1968, head clerk Chatham branch 1972–74, accident underwriting superintendent Maidstone 1974–81, underwriting superintendent UK 1981–82, asst planning mangr 1982–83, asst mktg mangr 1983–86, mktg servs mangr 1986–88, mktg mangr UK Gen Div 1988–90, business devpt mangr 1990–91, divnl dir 1991–98, dir of Implementation and Integration Zurich Financial Services 1998–99, e-commerce coordination dir 1999–2001, non-exec dir Prophit Share Ltd 1999–2004, conslt Zurich Financial Services 2001–03, exec mentor and mgmnt conslt 2003–; FCII 1974, AIPM 1979, MCIM 1986, memb Soc of Fellows London 1987, DipMktg, MInstM; *Recreations* golf; *Clubs* Sherdons Golf; *Style*— Mrs Gillian Clark; ✉ Hill Barn, Cowley, Gloucestershire GL53 9NJ (tel 01242 870555)

CLARK, Prof Gordon Leslie; *b* 10 September 1950; *Educ* Monash Univ Melbourne (BEcon, MA), McMaster Univ Hamilton (Benefactors scholar, PhD), Univ of Oxford (MA, DSc); *Career* Ford fell in urban studies McMaster Univ 1976–78, asst prof John F Kennedy Sch of Govt and Grad Sch of Design Harvard Univ 1978–83, assoc prof Dept of Geography Center for Urban Studies and Center for Organisation Studies Univ of Chicago 1983–85, prof Heinz Sch of Public Policy and Management Center for Labor Studies and Center for Economic Devpt Carnegie Mellon Univ Pittsburgh 1985–91; Monash Univ Melbourne 1989–95: prof and head Dept of Geography and Environmental Science and Grad Sch of Environmental Science, dir Inst of Ethics and Public Policy Grad Sch of Govt, head Faculty of Arts 1993, memb Advsy Bd Nat Key Center in Industrial Relations Grad Sch of Management; Univ of Oxford: fell St Peter's Coll 1995–, Halford Mackinder prof of geography 1995–, head of sch 2003–, fell Saïd Business Sch; academician Learned Socs for the Social Sciences 2000–; memb Academic Panel Nat Assoc of Pension Funds 2001–, govr Pensions Policy Inst 2002–; fell Lincoln Land Inst Cambridge MA 1981–82, Andrew Mellon fell Nat Acad of Scis 1981–82, fell Acad of Soc Scis Australia 1993–; Distinguished Alumni Award McMaster Univ 1998, Conference Medal Royal Australian Inst of Planners 1988, Chllr's Medal Univ of Calif 2000; FBA 2005; *Books* Interregional Migration, National Policy and Social Justice (1983), State Apparatus: Structures and Language of Legitimacy (jtly, 1984), Judges and the Cities: Interpreting Local Autonomy (1985), Regional Dynamics: Studies in Adjustment Theory (jtly, 1986), Unions and Communities Under Siege: American Communities and the Crisis of Organized Labor (1989), Multiculturalism, Difference and Postmodernism: Image and Representation in Australia (co-ed, 1993), Pensions and Corporate Restructuring in American Industry: A Crisis of Regulation (1993), Management Ethics: Theories, Cases and Materials (co-ed, 1995), Asian Newly Industrialized Economies in the Global Economy: Corporate Strategy and Industrial Restructuring in the 1990s (jtly, 1995), Accountability and Corruption (co-ed, 1997), Pension Fund Capitalism (2000), The Oxford Handbook of Economic Geography (co-ed, 2000), European Pensions & Global Finance (2003), Global Competitiveness and Innovation (jtly, 2004), The Oxford Handbook of Pensions and Retirement Income (co-ed, 2006), The Geography of Finance (jtly, 2007); also author of numerous papers and articles in learned jls; *Style*— Prof Gordon L Clark; ✉ Oxford University Centre for the Environment, South Parks Road, Oxford OX1 3QY (tel 01865 285072, e-mail gordon.clark@ouce.oxford.ac.uk)

CLARK, Graham Ronald; s of Ronald Edward Clark (d 2003), of Preston, Lancs, and Annie, *née* Eckersley (d 1984); *b* 10 November 1941; *Educ* Kirkham GS, Loughborough Coll of Educn (DLC), Loughborough Univ (MSc); *m* 1, 9 April 1966 (m dis 1975), Susan, da of late Walter George Fenn, of Oxford; m 2, 31 March 1979, Joan Barbara, da of Albert Frederick Lawrence (d 1955), of Dunstable, Beds; 1 step da (Sarah Elisabeth b 8 Oct 1965); *Career* tenor; teacher and dir of PE 1964–69; sr regnl offr The Sports Cncl 1971–75; princ Scottish Opera 1975–77, debut London Bomarzo (Ginastera) 1976, princ ENO 1978–85 plus guest appearances (19 princ roles); freelance 1985–; int venues 1976– incl: Bayreuther Festspiele Germany (over 100 performances as Mime and Loge in The Ring (two prodns), David in Die Meistersinger, Steuermann in Der Fliegende Holländer, Melot and Seemann in Tristan and Isolde) 1981–92 and 2001–04, The Metropolitan Opera NY (Herodes in Salome, Steva in Jenufa, Vere in Billy Budd, Bégearss in the Ghosts of Versailles (world première), Hauptmann in Wozzeck (two prodns), Gregor in Makropulos Case, Loge and Mime in The Ring, Prinz/Marquis in Lulu, Tanzmeister in Ariadne auf Naxos) 1985–2006, ROH, WNO, Vienna Staatsoper, Milan La Scala, Aix en Provence, Amsterdam, Barcelona, Berlin (Deutsche Staatsoper, Deutsche Oper), Bilbao, Bonn, Chicago, Cologne, Copenhagen, Dallas, Geneva, Hamburg, Madrid (Real, Zarzuela), Matsumoto, Munich, Nice, Paris (Bastille, Châtelet, Champs Élysées, Palais Garnier), Rome Catania, Salzburg, San Francisco, Stockholm, Tokyo, Toronto, Toulouse, Turin, Vancouver, Washington, Yokohama, Zurich; festivals incl: Proms, Amsterdam, Antwerp, Bamberg, Berlin, Brussels, Canaries, Edinburgh, Lucerne, Milan, Paris, Rome, Tel Aviv; recordings with: Decca, Sony, Philips, Erato, EMI, BBC, Teldec, BMG, Chandos, Euroarts, The Met, Opus Arte, WDR, Opera Rara; videos incl: The Ghosts of Versailles (Met Opera

NY), The Ring (Bayreuther Festspiele), Der Fliegende Hollander (Bayreuther Festspiele), Die Meistersinger (Bayreuther Festspiele), The Ring (Gran Teatre del Liceu Barcelona), The Ring (De Nederlandse Opera Amsterdam), Lady Macbeth of Mtensk (Gran Teatre del Liceu Barcelona), The Makropulos Case (Canadian Opera Toronto), Ariadne auf Naxos (Opéra National de Paris), Wozzeck (Deutsche Staatsoper Berlin), Wozzeck (Met Opera NY); over 350 Wagner performances incl over 250 performances of De Ring des Nibelungen; Laurence Olivier Award for Mephistopheles in Busoni's Dr Faust 1986, 3 nominations for Outstanding Individual Achievement in Opera incl EMMY for Bégearss in The Ghosts of Versailles at The Met; Hon DLitt Loughborough Univ 1999; *Recreations* sports; *Clubs* Garrick; *Style*— Graham Clark, Esq; ✉ c/o Ingpen & Williams Ltd, 7 St George's Court, 131 Putney Bridge Road, London SW15 2PA (tel 020 8874 3222, fax 020 8877 3113)

CLARK, Greg; MP; *b* 1967, Middlesbrough; *Educ* Univ of Cambridge, LSE (PhD); *m* Helen; 2 da; *Career* Boston Consulting Gp, chief advsr commercial policy BBC, special advsr to Ian Lang MP (Sec of State for Trade and Industry) 1996–97, dir of policy Cons Pty 2001–05; MP (Cons) Tunbridge Wells 2005–; *Style*— Greg Clark, MP; ✉ House of Commons, London SW1A 0AA (e-mail greg@gregclarkmp.org)

CLARK, Gregor Munro; CB (2006); s of Ian Munro Clark (d 1995), of Keills, Isle of Jura, and Norah Isobel, *née* Joss (d 1998); *b* 18 April 1946; *Educ* Queen's Park Sr Secdy Sch Glasgow, Univ of St Andrews (LLB); *m* 1, 30 March 1974, Jane Maralyn (d 1999), da of Leslie John Palmer (d 1972); 1 s (Aidan Benedikt b 1979), 2 da (Flora Daisy Louise b 1982, Madeleine Alexandra Rose b 1984); m 2, 21 Feb 2000, Alexandra Groves, da of Duncan McIntyre Miller; *Career* admitted Faculty of Advocates 1972, in practice 1972–74; Lord Advocate's Dept: joined 1974, asst parly draftsman then dep parly draftsman 1974–79, Scottish parly counsel and asst legal sec 1979–99, counsel to the Scottish Law Cmmn 1995–2000 and 2006–, Scottish parly counsel to the Scottish Exec 1999–2002 and 2005–06, Scottish parly counsel to UK Govt 2002–05; *Recreations* music, Scandinavian languages and literature, walking; *Style*— Gregor Clark, Esq, CB; ✉ 18 Rocheid Park, Inverleith, Edinburgh EH4 1RU(tel 0131 315 4634); Scottish Law Commission, 140 Causewayside, Edinburgh EH9 1PR (tel 0131 6625219)

CLARK, Guy Wyndham Nial Hamilton; JP (1981), DL (Renfrewshire 1987); s of Capt George Hubert Wyndham Clark (d 1978), and Lavinia Maraquita Smith, *née* Shaw Stewart (d 1971); *b* 28 March 1944; *Educ* Eton, Mons OCS; *m* 28 Jan 1968, Brighid Lovell, da of Maj Lovell Greene, of SA; 2 s (Charles Guy Lovell Wyndham, Thomas Houston Marcus Wyndham), 1 da (Nicola Fiona Vivienne); *Career* cmmnd Coldstream Gds 1962–67; investment mangr Murray Johnstone Ltd Glasgow 1973–77, ptnr RC Greig & Co (stockbrokers) Glasgow 1977–86, dir Greig Middleton & Co Ltd (stockbrokers) 1986–97, md Murray Johnstone Private Investors Ltd 1997–2001, dir Aberdeen Private Investors Ltd 2001–06, divnl dir Bell Lawrie Investment Mgmnt 2006–; vice-chm JP Advsy Ctee for Inverclyde 1990–2001; memb Exec Ctee Erskine Hosp for Ex-Servicemen 1983–87; Lord-Lt Renfrewshire 2007– (Vice Lord-Lt 2002–07); memb Int Stock Exchange 1983, FSI 2005 (MSI 1992); *Recreations* country sports, gardening; *Clubs* Turf, Western, MCC; *Style*— Guy Clark, Esq, DL; ✉ Braeton House, Inverkip, Renfrewshire, PA16 0DU (tel 01475 520619); Bell Lawrie, 48 St Vincent Street, Glasgow G2 5TS (tel 0141 314 8129, fax 0141 314 8142, e-mail guy.clark@bell-lawrie.co.uk)

CLARK, Prof Ian; s of Alexander Buchanan Clark (d 1984), and Amanda, *née* Vangsnes (d 1995); *b* 14 March 1949; *Educ* Hamilton Acad (Dux Gold Medal), Univ of Glasgow (MA), Australian Nat Univ (PhD); *m* 1970, Janice, *née* Cochrane; 1 da (Paula), 1 s (Steven); *Career* lectr Univ of Western Australia 1974–81 (sr lectr 1981–84); Univ of Cambridge: fell Selwyn Coll Cambridge 1985–97 (hon fell 2000), teaching fell Defence Studies 1984–88, asst dir Studies in Int Relations 1988–97, dep dir Centre of Int Studies 1993–97; prof of int politics Univ of Wales Aberystwyth 1998–; memb Br Int Studies Assoc 1980–, memb IISS 1990–; Leverhulme major res fell 2001, ESRC professorial fell 2007–; FBA 1999 (memb Cncl 2001–04, chair political studies 2005–08); *Publications* Waging War (1988), Nuclear Diplomacy and the Special Relationship (1994), Globalization and Fragmentation (1997), Globalization and International Relations Theory (1999), The Post-Cold War Order (2001), Legitimacy in International Society (2005), International Legitimacy and World Society (2007); *Recreations* hill walking in N Wales, being a grandfather; *Style*— Prof Ian Clark; ✉ Department of International Politics, University of Wales, Penglais, Aberystwyth SY23 3FE (tel 01970 621767, fax 01970 622709, e-mail iic@aber.ac.uk)

CLARK, HE James; *b* 12 March 1963; *Partner* Anthony Stewart; *Career* diplomat; entered HM Dip Serv 1988, Mexico and Central America Dept FCO 1988–90, language trg Cairo 1990–91, second sec (external relations) UKREP Brussels 1991–93, Republic of Ireland Dept FCO 1993–94, Economic Relations Dept FCO 1994–95, Press Office FCO 1995–97, on secondment German Foreign Miny 1997–98, first sec (EU) Bonn 1998–99, head Conf and Visits Gp FCO 1999–2003, commercial dir FCO Services 2003–04, ambass to Luxembourg 2004–07, consul-gen Chicago 2007–; *Style*— HE Mr James Clark; ✉ c/o Foreign & Commonwealth Office, King Charles Street, London SW1A 2AH

CLARK, Prof John Benjamin; s of Percy Benjamin Clark (d 1976), of Rayleigh, Essex, and Joan Ellen, *née* Smith (d 2004); *b* 30 January 1941; *Educ* Southend HS for Boys, UCL (BSc, PhD), Univ of London (DSc); *m* 18 Sept 1965, Joan, *née* Gibbons; 2 s (Philip b 11 Jan 1969, Anthony b 5 June 1971), 1 da (Jacqueline b 19 Oct 1973); *Career* Bart's Med Coll London: lectr, sr lectr then reader in biochemistry 1965–86, prof of cell biochemistry 1986–90; prof of neurochemistry and chm Miriam Marks Dept of Neurochemistry Inst of Neurology London 1990–2006 (prof emeritus 2006–, academic vice-dean 1996–2002), hon consIt neurochemist Nat Hosp London 1990–2006; memb: MRC Neurosciences Grants Ctee and Bd 1984–93, Action Research Scientific Advsy Bd 1988–92; MRC travelling fell Johnson Research Fndn Univ of Pennsylvania 1969–70; author of numerous articles in various academic jls and book chapters on the role of mitochondria in health and disease; memb: Biochemical Soc 1965 (memb Cncl 2005–), American Soc of Biochemistry and Molecular Biology 1996, American Soc of Neurochemistry 1997, Int Soc of Neurochemistry (memb Cncl 1997–2001, co sec 2003–), European Soc of Neurochemistry (memb Cncl 2001–); *Recreations* walking, fine wines, reading; *Clubs* RSM; *Style*— Prof John Clark; ✉ Neurochemistry, Institute of Neurology, University College London, Queen Square, London WC1N 3BG (e-mail jclark@ion.ucl.ac.uk)

CLARK, Sir Jonathan George; 5 Bt (UK 1917), of Dunlambert, City of Belfast; s of Sir Colin Douglas Clark, 4 Bt, MC (d 1995), and Margaret Coleman, *née* Spinks; *b* 9 October 1947; *Educ* Eton; *m* 1971, Susan Joy, da of Brig Thomas Ian Gordon Gray; 2 da (Polly Caroline b 1973, Tessa Louise b 1978), 1 s (George Simon Gray b 1975); *Heir* s, George Clark; *Career* late Capt Royal Green Jackets, md DC Training and Recruitment Solutions Ltd; *Recreations* horse trials; *Style*— Sir Jonathan Clark, Bt; ✉ Somerset House, Threapwood, Malpas, Cheshire SY14 7AW (tel 01948 770205, fax 01948 770305, e-mail jonathan@dcsolutions.biz)

CLARK, Katy; MP; *b* 3 July 1967; *Career* solicitor then head of memb legal servs Unison; MP (Lab) Ayrshire N and Arran 2005–; *Style*— Ms Katy Clark, MP; ✉ House of Commons, London SW1A 0AA

CLARK, Keith; s of Douglas William Clark (d 1967), of Chichester, W Sussex, and Evelyn Lucy, *née* Longlands; *b* 25 October 1944; *Educ* Chichester HS for Boys, St Catherine's Coll Oxford (MA); *m* 1 (m dis); 1 s (Nicholas Howard Douglas b 1980), 1 da (Katherine Sara Amy b 1984); m 2, 15 Dec 2001, Helen Patricia, da of James Paterson, of Kent; *Career* slr; Clifford Chance: joined 1971, ptnr 1977–, sr ptnr 1993–2001, various mgmnt appts; int gen counsel Morgan Stanley 2002–; memb: Law Soc 1971, Slrs' Benevolent Soc, Int Bar Assoc; *Recreations* hiking, family, modern art, modern jazz; *Style*— Keith Clark, Esq; ✉ Morgan Stanley, 25 Cabot Square, Canary Wharf, London E14 4QA

CLARK, Lance; s of Tony Clark (d 1994), and Eileen Clark (d 1999); *b* 30 April 1936; *Educ* Univ of Oxford (BA), Harvard Univ, INSEAD; *m* 6 Dec 2003, Ying; 1 c (Yoyi b 12 June 2004); *Career* md: Clarks Ltd, Clarks Ireland, Clarks Australia, Padmore & Barnes, Barkers; chm: Edward Green, Terra Plana; mangr Soul of Africa; Drapers Award for contribution to industry 2005; *Recreations* painting, art, tennis, swimming, skiing; *Clubs* Lansdowne; *Style*— Lance Clark, Esq; ✉ Unit 14, 2 Archie Street, London SE1 3JT (fax 020 7357 8565, e-mail lancelotclark@yahoo.co.uk); Terra Plana, 124 Bermondsey Street, London SE1 3TX (tel 020 7407 3758)

CLARK, Prof Leslie Arthur; OBE (2001); s of Arthur George Clark, of Chadwell Heath, Essex, and Lilian Rosina, *née* Procter; *b* 3 May 1944; *Educ* Ilford Co HS for Boys, Univ of Sheffield (Cicely Courtauld scholar, BEng, PhD, Mappin medal); *m* 29 Dec 1973, Helen Rose, da of William Ireson Tripp; 2 da (Laura Jane b 18 March 1977, Georgina Ann b 2 Dec 1980); *Career* res engr in design Cement and Concrete Assoc 1968–78; Sch of Civil Engrg Univ of Birmingham: lectr 1978–86, sr lectr 1986–91, prof of structural engrg 1991–, pro-vice-chllr (estates and infrastructure) 2005–; pres IStructE 1998–99; FIStructE 1986 (MIStructE 1975), FREng 1994, FICE 1995 (MICE 1973), Hon FICT 2001; *Books* Concrete Bridge Design (1983), Concrete Slabs: Analysis and Design (1984); *Recreations* cricket, football, jazz music; *Clubs* MCC; *Style*— Prof Leslie Clark, OBE, FREng; ✉ Pro-Vice-Chancellor's Office, University of Birmingham, Edgbaston, Birmingham B15 2TT (tel 0121 414 5939, fax 0121 414 4534, e-mail l.a.clark@bham.ac.uk)

CLARK, Dr Michael; s of late Mervyn Clark, and Sybilla Norma, *née* Winscott; *b* 8 August 1935; *Educ* King Edward VI GS Retford, KCL, Univ of Minnesota, St John's Coll Cambridge; *m* 1958, Valerie Ethel, da of C S Harbord; 1 s, 1 da; *Career* mgmnt conslt and industrial chemist; with ICI 1960–66, Smiths Industries 1966–69, PA Consulting Gp 1969–93; chm Cambridgeshire Cons Assoc 1980–83 (treas 1975–78, vice-chm 1978–80); Parly candidate (Cons) Ilkeston 1979; MP (Cons): Rochford 1983–97, Rayleigh 1997–2001; hon sec: Parly and Scientific Ctee 1985–90, Anglo-Nepalese All-Pty Gp 1985–90, All-Pty Gp for the Chem Industry 1985–90 (vice-chm 1990–94, chm 1994–97); hon treas: Br-Malawi All-Pty Gp 1987–2001, Exec Ctee Inter Pty Union 1987 (chm 1990–93), All-Pty Space Ctee 1988–90; chm: All-Pty Gp for Energy Studies 1992–97, Parly Office of Science and Technol 1993–98, Br-Russia All-Pty Gp 1993–2001, Br-Venezuela All-Pty Gp 1995–2001, House of Commons Select Ctee for Sci and Technol 1997–2001; memb: House of Commons Select Ctee for Energy 1983–92 (chm 1989–92), Trade and Industry Select Ctee 1992–94, Exec 1922 Ctee 1997–2001, Speakers' Panel of Chm 1997–2001; exec chm MAT Tport Gp 2002–04; FKC 1987, FRSC 1988; *Books* The History of Rochford Hall (1990), Clark of the House (2005); *Recreations* golf, gadding about, grandchildren; *Style*— Dr Michael Clark

CLARK, Dr Michael Llewellyn; *b* 17 June 1935; *Educ* W Monmouth GS Pontypool Monmouthshire, KCL, St George's Hosp Med Sch Univ of London (LRCP, MB BS, MD); *m* 2 c; *Career* house physician: Neurological Unit Atkinson Morley's Hosp London 1959–60, Brompton Hosp London 1960; jr med specialist HM Forces QAMH Millbank London 1960–63; St George's Hosp London: house physician 1958, house surgn Surgical Unit 1958–59, med registrar 1963–66, clinical res registrar Med Unit 1964–66, sr registrar in med 1968; fell in gastroenterology Philadelphia Gen Hosp Univ of Pennsylvania 1966–68; Bart's London: clinical res asst and hon lectr in med 1969–70, sr lectr in med Bart's Med Coll 1970–93, postgrad sub-dean Bart's Med Coll 1974–80, head Gastroenterology Dept 1986–91; City & Hackney Health Dist: conslt physician 1970–93, unit gen mangr Hackney Unit 1985–88, unit gen mangr City Unit 1988–90, dir of res and clinical devpt 1990–92; conslt physician: St Leonards Hosp 1970–84, Hackney Hosp 1984–85, Princess Grace Hosp 1990–; postgrad educnl co-ordinator Royal Hosps Tst 1994–2003, reg teacher for MRCP examination; author of numerous published articles in learned jls; MRCS, FRCP 1975 (MRCP); *Books* Clinical Medicine (jtly, 1987, 1990, 1994, 1998, 2002 and 2005); *Style*— Dr Michael Clark; ✉ 7 Sherwood Park Road, Sutton, Surrey SM1 2SQ (tel 020 8642 5993, e-mail michaelclark467@hotmail.com)

CLARK, Paul Evans; s of Harry Frederick Clark, of Derby, and Joyce Evelyn, *née* Margetts; *b* 18 March 1946; *Educ* Bemrose GS Derby, Univ of Manchester (LLB); *m* 25 July 1970 (dis), Jane Mary, da of Edmund Patrick Flowers; 2 s (Guy Edmund b 22 Feb 1977, Ben Thomas b 28 July 1980), 2 da (Nina Jane b 13 Dec 1972, Lucy Anna b 25 March 1975); m 2, 26 May 2000, Susan Roxana, da of Frederick White; *Career* admitted slr 1970; asst slr Rubinstein Nash & Co 1970–72 (articled clerk 1968–70), asst slr Property Dept Linklaters & Paines 1972–83, D J Freeman 1984–2003 (joined 1984, ptnr 1985, head of property 1990–2000), conslt Cripps Harries Hall LLP 2003–; UK rep Clarity; memb Law Soc 1970; *Recreations* pianist, music, church membership, reading; *Style*— Paul Clark, Esq; ✉ Cripps Harries Hall LLP, Wallside House, 12 Mount Ephraim Road, Tunbridge Wells, Kent TN1 1EG (tel 01892 515121, fax 01892 544878, e-mail paul.clark@crippslaw.com)

CLARK, Paul Gordon; MP; s of Gordon Thomas Clark, and Sheila Gladys, *née* Warner; *b* 29 April 1957; *Educ* Gillingham GS, Keele Univ (BA), Univ of Derby (Dip Mgmnt Studies); *m* 29 Nov 1980, Julie, da of Thomas Hendrick; 1 da (Rachel Julie b 2 May 1990), 1 s (James Paul b 29 April 1993); *Career* Amalgamated Engineering Union: successively researcher, president's researcher then educn administrator 1980–86; centre mangr TUC Nat Educn Centre London 1986–97; MP (Lab) Gillingham 1997–; PPS Lord Chancellor's Dept 1999–2001, PPS to Rt Hon Lord Falconer of Thoroton, QC, *qv* 2001–03, asst govt whip 2003–05, PPS to Rt Hon John Prescott, MP (as Dep PM), *qv*, 2005–07; sec All-Pty Parly Thames Gateway Gp 1997–, sec All-Pty Regeneration Gp; memb: Lab Pty 1975–, Thames Gateway Kent Partnership Bd 2000–, Groundwork Medway/Swale Bd 2001–; *Recreations* genealogy, politics, family; *Clubs* Old Anchorians; *Style*— Paul Clark, Esq, MP; ✉ House of Commons, London SW1A 0AA (tel 020 7219 5207, fax 020 7219 2545, e-mail clarkp@parliament.uk, website www.paulclarkmp.com)

CLARK, Paul Richard; s of Henry Clark (d 1981), and Daphne, *née* Andreazzi; *b* 7 November 1962, London; *Educ* Univ of Reading (BA, MPhil); *m* July 2003, Tracey, *née* Adamson; 1 s (Harry b 1 March 1996), 1 da (Eleanor b 24 May 1999); *Career* Prudential Investment Management (PIM) 1986–89, sr surveyor Donaldsons 1990, assoc dir DTZ Debenham Tie Leung 1990–99, dir Hemingway Properties Ltd 1999–2001, dir ISG Occupancy Ltd (now Dunlop Haywards) 2001–03, chief surveyor Church Commissioners for England 2003–; dir Real Service Ltd; memb Investors Property Forum, memb Residential Ctee Br Property Fedn; MRICS 1989; *Recreations* cricket, golf, theatre, cinema; *Style*— Paul Clark, Esq; ✉ Church House, Great Smith Street, London SW1P 3AZ (tel 020 7898 1634, fax 020 7898 1153)

CLARK, Dr Peter John Alleguen; OBE (1993); s of Dr Kenneth Clark (d 1971), and Kitty Matilda, *née* Ruffle (d 1990); *b* 17 May 1939; *Educ* Loughborough GS, Southend HS for Boys, Keele Univ (BA), Downing Coll Cambridge, Univ of Leicester (PhD); *m* 1, 1968 (m dis 1980), Isobel, *née* Rankin; 1 s (John Paul Jeremy b 1972); m 2, 1980, Theresa Mary Philomena Brown, *née* Alleguen; 1 step da (Kate Philomena b 1968), 2 s (Gabriel Edwin Alleguen b 1981, Nathaniel Luke Alleguen b 1983); *Career* mathematics teacher Ankara Coll and teacher of English British Council 1962–63, tutorial asst Dept of History Univ of Leicester 1964–66, lectr in general studies Duncan of Jordanstone Coll of Art 1966–67; British Council: trg 1967–68, Jordan 1968–70, MECAS 1970–71, Sudan 1971–77, London 1977–80, Yemen 1980–84, Tunisia 1984–88, UAE 1988–92, dir Syria 1992–97, advsr

Middle East and North Africa Dept 1997–99, dir Middle East Cultural Advsy Services 1999–; memb Middle East Studies Assoc 1993; conslt ed Banipal; chair Advsy Panel Br Centre for Literary Translation 2000–02; tstee Karim Rida Said Fndn 1999–2004; conslt AMAR Int Charitable Fndn 2000–01 (ceo 2002–04); FRGS 1982, FIL 1993; *Books* Three Sudanese Battles (1977), Karari (trans, 1980), Henry Hallam (1982), Marmaduke Pickthall British Muslim (1986), Dubai Tales (trans, 1991), Thesiger's Return (1992), A Balcony Over Fakihani (trans, 1993), Sabriya (trans, 1995), Grandfather's Tale (trans, 1998), Arabic Literature Unveiled: Challenges of Translation (2000), Pearl-Fishing in the Gulf: A Kuwaiti Memoir (trans, 2000), The Iraqi Marshlands - A Human and Environmental Study (co-ed with Emma Nicholson, 2002), Memory of the Flesh (trans, 2003), Sardines and Oranges (ed, 2005), The Woman of the Flask (trans, 2005), The Lefties' Guide to Britain (ed); *Recreations* writing book reviews, grandfatherhood, walking in hills; *Style—* Dr Peter Clark, OBE; ✉ 71 Nunney Road, Frome, Somerset BA11 4LF (tel 01373 300310, e-mail mecas@blueyonder.co.uk)

CLARK, Sir Robert Anthony; kt (1976), DSC (1944); yr s of John Clark, and Gladys, *née* Dyer; *b* 6 January 1924; *Educ* Highgate Sch, King's Coll Cambridge; *m* 1949, Andolyn Marjorie Beynon Lewis; 2 s, 1 da; *Career* ptnr Slaughter and May slrs 1953–61; dir: Alfred McAlpine plc 1957–96, Hill Samuel Bank Ltd 1961–91 (chm 1974–87), Bank of England 1976–85, Eagle Star Holdings Ltd 1976–87, Rover Group plc 1977–88, Shell Transport and Trading Co plc 1982–94, Vodafone Group plc 1988–98; chm: Hill Samuel Group plc 1980–88 (chief exec 1976–80), IMI plc 1981–89, Marley plc 1985–89, Mirror Group plc 1991–98, Rauscher Pierce & Clark 1992–, Fenchurch Lambert Group Ltd 1995–98 (dep chm 1992–95); vice-chm SmithKline Beecham plc 1987–95, dep chm TSB Group plc 1989–91 (dir 1987–91); chm: Doctors' and Dentists' Review Body 1979–86, Charing Cross and Westminster Hosp Med Sch 1981–95; Hon DSc Cranfield Inst of Technol 1982; *Recreations* reading, music, collecting antiquarian books; *Clubs* Pratt's; *Style—* Sir Robert Clark, DSC; ✉ Munstead Wood, Godalming, Surrey GU7 1UN (tel 01483 417867); RP&C International, 31A St James's Square, London SW1Y 4JR (tel 020 7766 7000)

CLARK, Robin Douglas; *b* 15 November 1956; *Educ* Eastbourne Coll, Univ of Southampton, Harvard Business Sch; *m* 25 April 1981, Sonia Margaret, *née* Glover; 1 s (Christopher b 24 March 1985), 2 da (Stephanie b 23 May 1988, Jennifer b 10 July 1991); *Career* chartered accountant Deloitte Haskins & Sells 1982–83 (articled clerk 1979–82), exec positions ICAEW and Accounting Standards Ctee 1983–85, Lloyd's of London 1986; Investment Mgmnt Regulatory Orgn (IMRO): mangr membership 1987–89, asst dir investigations 1990, dir monitoring 1991–95, dir regulatory relations 1995–96; dir regulation and controls Threadneedle Asset Mgmnt 1997–98; AXA Investment Managers: global head of regulatory affrs 1998–, gp co sec 2002–05, head of int audit 2004–05; co sec AXA Framlington Gp 2005; sec Forum of European Asset Mangrs 2005–06; memb: Regulation and Taxation Ctee Fund Managers Assoc 1998–2002, General Regulations Ctee Investment Mgmnt Assoc 2002–03, HM Treasury Moneylaundering Advsy Ctee 2002–03, Int Strategy Ctee Investment Mgmnt Assoc 2003–; actg sec-gen European Asset Mgmnt Assoc 2002–04; ACA 1982; *Recreations* motor racing; *Style—* Robin Clark, Esq; ✉ AXA Investment Managers, 7 Newgate Street, London EC1A 7NX (tel 020 7003 1000, fax 020 7575 8657, e-mail robin.clark@axa-im.com)

CLARK, Prof Robin Jon Hawes; CNZM (2004); s of Reginald Hawes Clark, JP (BCom), of Christchurch, NZ, and Marjorie Alice, *née* Thomas; *b* 16 February 1935; *Educ* Christ's Coll Christchurch, Canterbury UC Univ of NZ (BSc, MSc), UCL (PhD, DSc); *m* 30 May 1964, Beatrice Rawdin Clark, JP, da of Ellis Rawdin Brown (d 1978); 1 da (Victoria b 23 June 1967), 1 s (Matthew b 14 Dec 1971); *Career* UCL: asst lectr 1962, lectr 1963–71, reader 1972–81, prof 1982–88, dean of sci 1988–89, head Dept of Chem 1989–99, Sir William Ramsay prof 1989–, memb Cncl 1991–94, fell 1992; senator Univ of London 1988–93; chm: 11th Int Conf on Raman Spectroscopy London 1988, Advsy Ctee Ramsay Meml Fellowships Tst 1989–, Steering Ctee Int Confs on Raman Spectroscopy 1990–92; memb Cncl Royal Soc 1993–94; sec Royal Inst of GB 1998–2004; visiting prof: Columbia 1965, Padua 1967, Western Ontario 1968, Texas A and M 1978, Bern 1979, Fribourg 1979, Auckland 1981, Odense 1982, Sydney 1985, Bordeaux 1988, Pretoria 1991, Würzburg 1997, Indiana 1998, Thessaloniki 1999; Royal Soc of Chemistry lectr: Tilden 1983–84, Nyholm 1989–90, Thomas Graham 1991, Harry Hallam 1993 and 2000, Liversidge 2003–04; Kresge-Hooker lectr Wayne State Univ 1965, Frontiers in Chemistry lectr Case-Western Reserve Univ 1978, John van Geuns lectr Univ of Amsterdam 1979, Firth lectr Univ of Sheffield 1991, Carman lectr SA Chemical Inst 1994, Moissan lectr ENSC Paris 1998, Leermakers lectr Wesleyan Univ 2000, Hassel lectr Univ of Oslo 2000, Royal Soc UK-Canada Rutherford lectr 2000, Ralph Anderson lectr Worshipful Co of Horners 2003, Royal Soc Bakerian lectr 2008; tstee: Ramsay Meml Fellowships Tst 1994– (vice-chm 2006–), Univ of Canterbury NZ Tst 2004– (chm 2005–); govr Haberdashers' Aske's Sch 1995–98; Joannes Marcus Marci Medal (Czech Spectroscopy Soc) 1998; T K Sidey Medal (Royal Soc NZ) 2001; Hon DSc Canterbury Univ NZ 2001; memb Academia Europaea 1990; Hon FRSNZ 1989, FRSC 1969, FRS 1990, FRSA 1992, Hon FRI 2004; *Books* The Chemistry of Titanium and Vanadium (1968), The Chemistry of Titanium Zirconium and Hafnium (1973), The Chemistry of Vanadium Niobium and Tantalum (1973), Advances in Spectroscopy Vols 1–26 (co ed, 1975–98), Raman Spectroscopy (co ed, 1988); also author of about 500 scientific papers; *Recreations* golf, bridge, music, theatre, travel; *Clubs* Athenaeum, Porters Park; *Style—* Prof Robin Clark, CNZM, FRS; ✉ 3a Loom Lane, Radlett, Hertfordshire WD7 8AA (tel 01923 857899); Christopher Ingold Laboratories, University College London, 20 Gordon Street, London WC1H 0AJ (tel 020 7679 7457, fax 020 7679 7463, e-mail r.j.h.clark@ucl.ac.uk)

CLARK, Rodney; OBE (2001); *b* 7 September 1944; *Educ* Andover GS, UCL; *m*; *Career* mangr family furniture removals business 1965–67, gen asst Welfare Dept Hampshire CC 1967–68, Israeli Kibbutz 1968–69, admin asst Welfare Dept London Borough of Camden 1969–71; London Borough of Islington then Camden and Islington AHA: administrator Personal Health Servs 1971–72, opened and managed Highbury Grange Health Centre 1972–74, sr administrator Islington Sch Health Serv 1974–77, capital projects mangr Islington Health Dist 1977–78; projects administrator RNID 1978–81, chief exec Sense (Nat Deafblind and Rubella Assoc) 1981–2001; chm: SIGN (Nat Soc for Mental Health and Deafness) 1994–, Christopher Brock Charitable Tst 1994–, Br Dyslexia Assoc 2002–05, Parents Autism Campaign for Educn (PACE) 2003–05, Woodford Fndn 2003–; vice-chm Hearing Conservation Cncl 2001–, sec Deafblind International 1987–2001; treas: European Deafblind Network 1989–2001, UK Cncl on Deafness 1995–2003; tstee: Whitefields Devpt Tst 1996–2005, KIDS 1997–2005, Royal Sch for Deaf Children Margate 2005–06, Richmond Charitable Tst 2005–; conslt in mgmnt and devpt to the voluntary sector 2001–; mgmnt speaker at seminars and confs for voluntary organisations; *Recreations* choral singing, tennis, swimming, walking, theatre, opera and concerts; *Style—* Rodney Clark, Esq, OBE; ✉ 31 Sutton Road, Shrewsbury, Shropshire SY2 6DL (tel 01743 358998, e-mail rod.clark@virgin.net)

CLARK, Prof Stephen Richard Lyster; s of David Allen Richard Clark (d 1986), and Mary Kathleen, *née* Finney (d 1992); *b* 30 October 1945; *Educ* Nottingham HS, Balliol and All Souls Colls Oxford (MA, DPhil); *m* 1 July 1972 (Edith) Gillian, da of Prof John Callan James Metford, of Bristol; 1 s (Samuel b 1974), 2 da (Alexandra b 1976, Verity b 1985); *Career* fell All Souls Coll Oxford 1968–74, lectr in moral philosophy Univ of Glasgow 1974–83 (Gifford lectr 1982); Univ of Liverpool: prof of philosophy 1984–, dean Faculty of Arts 1995–98; Stanton lectr Univ of Cambridge 1987–89, Wilde lectr Univ of Oxford 1990, Scott Holland lectr 1992, Read Tuckwell lectr Univ of Bristol 1994, Alan Richardson fell Univ of Durham 1999; Leverhulme major research fellowship 2003–06; memb: Farm Animal Welfare Cncl 1997–2002, Animal Procedures Ctee 1998–2006; ed Jl of Applied Philosophy 1990–2001; *Books* Aristotle's Man (1975), The Moral Status of Animals (1977), The Nature of the Beast (1982), From Athens to Jerusalem (1984), The Mysteries of Religion (1986), La Naturaleza De La Bestia (1987), Money, Obedience and Affection (ed, 1989), Civil Peace and Sacred Order (1989), A Parliament of Souls (1990), God's World and the Great Awakening (1991), How to Think about the Earth (1993), How to Live Forever (1995), Animals and their Moral Standing (1997), God, Religion and Reality (1998), The Political Animal (1999), Biology and Christian Ethics (2000), G K Chesterton: Thinking Backwards, Looking Forwards (2006); *Recreations* science fiction, computers; *Style—* Prof Stephen R L Clark; ✉ 1 Arnside Road, Oxton, Prenton CH43 2JU (tel 0151 653 4908); Department of Philosophy, University of Liverpool, Liverpool L69 3BX (tel 0151 794 2788, fax 0151 794 2789, e-mail srlclark@liv.ac.uk)

CLARK, Sir Terence Joseph; KBE (1990), CMG (1985), CVO (1978); s of Joseph Henry Clark (d 1971), of London, and Mary Ann Matilda Clark (d 2003); *b* 19 June 1934; *Educ* Parmiter's Foundation Sch London, Univ of Grenoble, Univ of Cambridge, Univ of London, Univ of Freiburg; *m* 1960, Lieselotte Rosa Marie, da of Lt Cdr Erich Ernst Müller, of Kiel; 2 s (Adrian, Martin), 1 da (Sonja); *Career* Pilot Offr RAF VR 1955, entered HM Foreign Serv 1955, ME Centre of Arab Studies Lebanon 1956–57; third sec Bahrain 1957–58, Amman 1958–60, vice-consul Casablanca 1960–62, FO 1962–65, asst political agent Dubai Trucial States 1965–68, first sec (info) Belgrade 1969–71, head of Chancery and consul Muscat 1972–73, asst head ME Dept FCO 1974–75, cnsllr (info) Bonn 1976–79, cnsllr Belgrade 1979–82, dep ldr of UK Delgn to Conf on Security and Cooperation in Europe (Madrid) 1982–83, head Info Dept FCO 1983–85, ambass to Repub of Iraq 1985–89, ambass to Sultanate of Oman 1990–94, ret; sr conslt Middle East Conslts 1995–, dir Int Crisis Gp Bosnia Project Sarajevo 1996, dir Middle East Assoc 1998–2005; vice-pres Anglo-Omani Soc 2004– (chm 1995–2004); memb: Cncl Soc of Arabian Studies 1994–2001, Royal Soc for Int Affrs, Br Museum Soc, Cncl RSAA 2001–07, Cncl Br Sch of Archaeology in Iraq 2003– (hon vice-pres 1985–89); FRGS; *Books* The Saluqi: Coursing hound of the East (maj contrib, 1995), Unfolding the Orient (contrib, 2001), Al-Mansur's Book on Hunting (trans, 2001), Dogs in Antiquity (contrib, 2001), Oman in Time (contrib, 2001), Underground to Overseas: the Story of Petroleum Development Oman (2007); *Recreations* salukis, walking; *Clubs* Hurlingham; *Style—* Sir Terence Clark, KBE, CMG, CVO; ✉ 29 Westleigh Avenue, London SW15 6RQ (e-mail sirterenceclark@aol.com)

CLARK, Terrence Michael; s of Douglas Gordon Clark, of Littlehampton, W Sussex, and Doris, *née* Landymore; *b* 5 May 1946; *m* 29 May 1976, Sally-Marie, da of Ronald Strange, of Ripley, Surrey; 2 s (Paul b 1967, Tobias b 1989), 1 da (Rebecca b 1983); *Career* artist craftsman in metals; ed Br Blacksmith Magazine 1980–84 and 1999–; vice-chm Br Artist Blacksmiths' Assoc 1992–94; organiser and chm The Int Blacksmithing Conf 1985; first artsmith to have a gate accepted by the Royal Acad Ctee under sculpture 1986; toured Missouri, Kansas and Texas lecturing and demonstrating blacksmiths skills 2002; Environmental Project Award for Sculptural Railings Runnymede Cncl 1997 and 2001, Godalming Tst Civic Design Award 1998, winner Waverley Design Awards 1999; Freeman City of London 1997, fell Worshipful Co of Blacksmiths (Silver medal) 1995; *Exhibitions* incl: Towards a New Iron Age V&A 1982, New York Craft Centre 1982, Br Artist Blacksmiths' Assoc Exhibitions 1983–92, Int Metalwork and Sculpture Exhibition Friedrichshafen W Germany 1987, Fe - an exploration of iron through the senses 1995–96; won Addy Taylor Cup awarded by Worshipful Co of Blacksmiths 1983, Hot Metal 1998; *Commissions* HH Sheik Mohammed Bin Rashid Al Maktoum 1984–95, Guildford Cathedral 1985, public sculpture Horsham Cncl 1994, 50m x 4m public cmmn High St Godalming 1995, external and internal work Grace Barrand Studio Nutfield 1995, 3 pairs of gates Dorneywood 1995, gates and railings Brasenose Coll Oxford 1996, Restoration Work Chancellor's residence Dorneywood 1997, gates Town Hall Chester 1998, gates and screens Geffrye Museum London 1998, stainless steel entrance Chelsea Flower Show 1998, 7 metre high sculpture Staines 1998, 3 public art sculptures Leatherhead 1999, public art sculpture Staines 1999, public art sculpture Guildford 1999, gates Jesus Coll Oxford 2000, sculpture Regents Coll London 2000; *Books* Towards a New Iron Age (1982), Schmeidearbeiten von Heute (1986), Art From The Fire (1986), Art for Architecture (1987), Metal-Handwerk & Technik (1987); *Recreations* holder of pilot's licence, skiing, golf; *Style—* Terrence Clark, Esq; ✉ Wildfields Farm, Woodstreet Village, Guildford, Surrey GU3 3BP (tel 01483 235244, fax 01483 236456, e-mail terrence@artsmith.co.uk, website www.artsmith.co.uk)

CLARK, Prof Timothy John Hayes (Tim); *b* 18 October 1935; *Educ* Christ's Hosp, Guy's Hosp Med Sch London (BSc, MRCS, LRCP, MB BS, MD); *m*; 4 c; *Career* house offr: Guy's Hosp 1961, Brompton Hosp 1961–62, Hammersmith Hosp 1962–63, Nat Hosp for Nervous Diseases London 1963; fell in med Johns Hopkins Hosp Baltimore 1963–64, registrar Hammersmith Hosp 1964–66; Guy's Hosp: sr lectr Depts of Med and Physiology 1966–68, hon sr registrar 1966–68, conslt physician 1968–90, prof of thoracic med UMDS 1977–90; specialist advsr to Social Servs Ctee House of Commons 1980–81 and 1984–85, conslt in thoracic med to the CMO Dept of Health 1985–90; Royal Brompton Hosp: conslt physician 1990–98 (pt/t 1970–90), prof of pulmonary med Nat Heart and Lung Inst 1990–; dean: Guy's Campus 1984–86, United Dental and Med Schs 1986–89 (govr 1982–90), Nat Heart and Lung Inst 1990–97; pro-rector Imperial Coll and dep princ Imperial Coll Sch of Med 1995–97, pro-rector (educational quality) Imperial Coll 1997–2000, provost Imperial Coll at Wye 2000–2001, pro-rector (admissions) 2001–02; pro-vice-chllr for med and dentistry Univ of London 1987–89; special tstee Guy's Hosp 1982–89; pres Br Thoracic Soc 1990–91; memb: Lambeth Southwark and Lewisham AHA 1978–82, Lewisham and N Southwark HA 1982–85, SE Thames RHA 1985–87, Systems Bd MRC 1985–88, Royal Brompton Hospital NHS Tst 1993–98; fell: City and Guilds Inst, King's Coll London; hon prof Xian Med Coll Xian China 1985–; FRCP 1973; *Publications* author of over 200 textbooks, articles and papers on respiratory; *Style—* Prof Tim Clark; ✉ 8 Lawrence Court, London NW7 3QP (tel 020 8959 4411)

CLARK, Timothy Nicholas (Tim); s of Sir Robert Clark, of Godalming, Surrey, and Andolyn Marjorie Beynon, *née* Lewis; *b* 9 January 1951; *Educ* Sherborne, Pembroke Coll Cambridge (MA); *m* 24 Aug 1974, Caroline, *née* Moffat; 2 s (Nicholas b 1979, Richard b 1984); *Career* Slaughter and May: joined 1974, ptnr 1983, sr ptnr 2001–; govr Bradfield Sch, tstee Geoffrey de Havilland Flying Fndn, memb Nat Gallery Devpt Ctee, memb governing body ICC UK; memb Law Soc 1976; *Recreations* flying, Italy, history, theatre, football, cricket; *Clubs* Air Sqdn, Lowtonians; *Style—* Tim Clark, Esq; ✉ Slaughter and May, 1 Bunhill Row, London EC1Y 8YY (tel 020 7600 1200, fax 020 7090 5000, e-mail tim.clark@slaughterandmay.com)

CLARK, William James; s of William Clark, of Glencarse, Scotland, and Elizabeth Shanks Clark; *b* 3 May 1950; *Educ* Dundee HS, Univ of Edinburgh (BSc), Univ of W Ontario Canada (MBA); *m* 28 Aug 1981, Karen Neergaard, da of HE Jorgen Holm; 2 da; *Career* Chemical Bank: mktg offr 1974–79, regnl mktg mangr Singapore 1979–80, gen mangr Singapore 1980–83, regnl mangr (energy and minerals) London 1984–87, regnl mangr (origination and corp fin) London 1987–91; chief operating offr Pricoa Capital Group Ltd 1995–99 (dir 1991–99), md Leveraged Fin Royal Bank of Scotland 1999–; represented GB at athletics 1973–75, UK triple jump champion 1974, Scot triple jump champion 1975 and 1977–78; *Recreations* sport, farming; *Clubs* RAC; *Style—* William J Clark, Esq; ✉ Royal Bank of Scotland, 135 Bishopsgate, London EC2M 3UR (tel 020 7085 8293)

CLARK OF CALTON, Baroness (Life Peer UK 2005), of Calton in the City of Edinburgh; Dr Lynda Margaret Clark; QC (Scot 1989); *Educ* Univ of St Andrews (LLB), Univ of Edinburgh (PhD); *Career* lectr in law Univ of Dundee 1973–76, called to the Scottish Bar 1977, called to the Bar Inner Temple 1990; Bd Memb Scottish Legal Aid Bd 1990–93; Parly candidate (Lab) NE Fife 1992, MP (Lab) Edinburgh Pentlands 1997–2005, advocate-gen for Scotland 1999–, memb Select Ctee on Pub Admin 1997–; memb Ct Univ of Edinburgh 1995–97; *Style*— The Rt Hon the Lady Clark of Calton, QC; ✉ House of Lords, London SW1A 0PW

CLARK OF WINDERMERE, Baron (Life Peer UK 2001), of Windermere in the County of Cumbria; David George Clark; PC (1997), DL (Cumbria 2007); s of George Clark, and Janet, of Askham, Cumbria; *b* 19 October 1939; *Educ* Windermere GS, Univ of Manchester (BA, MSc), Univ of Sheffield (PhD); *m* 1970, Christine, da of Ronald Kirkby, of Grasmere, Cumbria; 1 da; *Career* former forester, lab asst, student teacher, univ lectr; Parly candidate (Lab) Manchester Withington 1966; MP (Lab): Colne Valley 1970–74 (also contested Oct 1974), South Shields 1979–2001; oppn spokesman on agric and food 1973–74, oppn spokesman on defence 1980–81, oppn front bench spokesman on the environment 1981–87, memb Shadow Cabinet 1986–97; chief oppn spokesman on: agric and rural affairs 1987–92, defence, disarmament and arms control 1992–97; chllr of the Duchy of Lancaster 1997–98; ldr UK delgn to NATO; dir: Homeowners Friendly Soc 1989–97 and 1999–, Thales plc 1999–, Carlisle United (1921) Ltd; chm Forestry Cmmn 2001–; *Books* Industrial Manager (1966), Radicalism to Socialism (1981), Victor Grayson (1985), We Do Not Want the Earth (1992); *Style*— The Rt Hon the Lord Clark of Windermere, PC, DL

CLARKE, Alison Jane; da of Leonard William Clarke, of Cheltenham, Glos, and Florence, *née* Pitt; *b* 17 October 1960; *Educ* Pate's GS for Girls, Bulmershe Coll of HE (BA); *m* 6 May 1995, Nigel Andrew Mogridge, s of Ralph John Mogridge; *Career* graduate trainee Pedigree Petfoods; Welbeck Golin/Harris Communications (Shandwick Welbeck from May 1998): account exec 1985–90, bd dir 1990–, dep md 1993–96, md 1996–97, chief exec 1997–99; chief exec Weber Shandwick Asia Pacific 2000–02, gp business dir Huntsworth plc 2003–; FCIPR 1999 (MCIPR 1989, pres 2000–); *Recreations* theatre, opera; *Style*— Ms Alison Clarke; ✉ Huntsworth plc, 15–17 Huntsworth Mews, London NW1 6DD (tel 020 7298 6520, fax 020 7493 3048, e-mail alison.clarke@huntsworth.com)

CLARKE, Andrew Bertram; QC (1997); s of Arthur Bertram Clarke, and Violet Doris, *née* Lewis; *b* 23 August 1956; *Educ* Crewe Co GS, KCL (LLB, AKC), Lincoln Coll Oxford (BCL); *m* 1 Aug 1981, Victoria Clare, da of Kelsey Thomas; 1 s (Christopher Harding b 1985), 2 da (Judith Ellen b 1987, Alexandra Clare b 1990); *Career* called to the Bar Middle Temple 1980; head Littleton Chambers 2006–; *Recreations* football, cricket, gardening and wine; *Clubs* Gloucestershire CCC; *Style*— Andrew Clarke, Esq, QC; ✉ Littleton Chambers, 3 King's Bench Walk North, Temple, London EC4Y 7HR (tel 020 7797 8600, fax 020 7797 8699)

CLARKE, Prof Angus John; *b* 20 December 1954, London; *Educ* King's Coll Cambridge (BA), Univ of Oxford (BM, BCh, DM); *Career* house offr John Radcliffe Hosp 1979–80, SHO general medicine Peterborough Dist Gen Hosp 1980–81, SHO in paediatrics S Manchester Hosps 1981–82, SHO in neonatal medicine Bristol Maternity Hosp 1982–83, registrar in general and neonatal paediatrics S Glamorgan HA 1983–85, research assoc Section of Medical Genetics Univ of Wales Coll of Medicine and registrar in paediatrics S Glamorgan Hosps 1985–86, research assoc and (hon) sr registrar in Depts of Human Genetics and Child Health Univ of Newcastle upon Tyne 1987–89; Univ of Wales Coll of Medicine: clinical sr lectr and hon conslt clinical geneticist Dept of Medical Genetics 1989–, reader 1996–2000, prof 2000–; chm Medical Advsy Bd Ectodermal Dysplasia Soc 1998–, CMO rep for Wales on Human Genetics Cmmn 2004–; memb: Research Advsy Bd Wellbeing of Women 2003–06, Editorial Bd Communication & Medicine 2003–, Medical Advsy Panel Rett Syndrome Assoc UK; FRCP 1994 (MRCP 1982), FRCPCH 1997; *Publications* Genetic Counselling: practice and principles (ed, 1994), Culture, Kinship and Genes (jt ed, 1997), Genetics, Society and Clinical Practice (jtly, 1997), The Genetic Testing of Children (ed 1998), Risky Relations. Family and Kinship in the Era of New Genetics (jtly, 2006), Living with the Genome (jt ed, 2006); articles in professional jls; *Style*— Prof Angus Clarke; ✉ Institute of Medical Genetics, University Hospital of Wales, Cardiff CF14 4XN

CLARKE, Rt Hon Sir Anthony Peter; kt (1993), PC (1998); s of Harry Alston Clarke (d 1979), and Isobel, *née* Kay; *b* 13 May 1943; *Educ* Oakham Sch, King's Coll Cambridge; *m* 7 Sept 1968, Rosemary, da of K W Adam, of Barnham, W Sussex; 2 s (Ben b 7 Jan 1972, Thomas b 20 June 1973), 1 da (Sally b 3 June 1977); *Career* called to the Bar Middle Temple 1965 (bencher 1987); QC 1979, recorder of the Crown Court 1985–92, judge of the High Court of Justice 1993–98, a Lord Justice of Appeal 1998–2005, Master of the Rolls 2005–; conducted: Thames Safety Inquiry 1999, Marchioness and Bowbelle Inquiries 2000; arbitrator Lloyd's and ICC, wreck cmmr and memb Chambre Arbitrale Maritime until 1992; *Recreations* tennis, golf, holidays; *Style*— The Rt Hon Sir Anthony Clarke; ✉ Royal Courts of Justice, Strand, London WC2A 2LL

CLARKE, Sir Arthur C(harles); kt (1998), CBE (1989); s of Charles Wright Clarke, and Nora Mary, *née* Willis; *b* 16 December 1917, Minehead, Somerset; *Educ* Huish's GS Taunton, KCL (BSc); *m* 1953 (m dis 1964), Marilyn Mayfield; *Career* science and science fiction writer; auditor HM Exchequer and Audit Dept 1936–41; Royal Air Force: cmmnd Flt Lt 1941, instr No 9 Radio Sch Yatesbury, i/c prototype Ground Controlled Approach (GCA) Radar MIT Radiation Lab until 1946, developed theory of communication satellite 1945; undergraduate KCL 1946–48, asst ed Physics Abstracts IEE 1948–50, chm Br Interplanetary Soc 1946–47 and 1950–53, underwater explorer Great Barrier Reef 1954, emigrated Sri Lanka 1956, lectr in US 1957–70 (also covered Apollo Space Missions for CBS TV), now full-time writer; writer and presenter of Yorkshire Television series: Arthur C Clarke's Mysterious World 1980, Arthur C Clarke's World of Strange Powers 1984, Arthur C Clarke's Mysterious Universe 1994; Vikram Sarabhai prof Physical Research Labs Ahmedabad India 1980, Nehru Meml Lecture New Delhi 1986, Alistair Cooke Lecture 1992; chllr: Univ of Moratuwa Sri Lanka 1979–2002, Int Space Univ 1989–2002; master Richard Huish Coll Taunton; hon chm Soc of Satellite Professionals, pres Br Science Fiction Assoc, hon vice-pres H G Wells Soc, hon life pres UN Assoc of Sri Lanka, life memb Assoc of Br Science Writers, memb Cncl Soc of Authors, tstee Inst of Integral Educn; patron: Arthur Clarke Inst for Modern Technols Sri Lanka, Sri Lanka Assoc for the Advancement of Sci, Sri Lanka Astronomical Assoc, Sri Lanka Animal Welfare Assoc, Science Fiction Fndn, Br Sub-Aqua Club, Nat Inst for Paraplegics Sri Lanka; memb Advsy Cncl: Fauna International Sri Lanka, Earth Tst; memb Bd: Nat Space Soc USA, Space Generation Fndn USA, IAU (SETI) Cmmn 51, Planetary Soc USA, Lindbergh Award Nominations Ctee USA; dir: Rocket Publishing Co UK, Underwater Safaris Sri Lanka; hon fell: Br Interplanetary Soc, American Astronautical Assoc, Int Acad of Astronautics, AIAA, Instn of Engrs Sri Lanka 1983, Ceylon Coll of Physicians 1991; fell: Franklin Inst 1971, KCL 1977, Inst of Robotics Carnegie-Mellon Univ 1981, Int Aerospace Hall of Fame San Diego CA 1989, Int Space Hall of Fame Alamagordo New Mexico 1989; academician World Acad of Art and Science, foreign assoc Nat Acad of Engrg USA 1986, assoc fell Third World Acad of Sciences 1987; memb: Royal Asiatic Soc, Br Astronomical Assoc, Science Fiction Writers of America, Astronomical Soc of the Pacific; Hon DSc Beaver Coll Pennsylvania 1971, Hon DSc Univ of Moratuwa 1979, Hon DLitt Univ of Bath 1988; Freeman Town of Minehead 1992; FRAS, FRSA; *Awards* non-literary awards incl: Stuart Ballantine Gold Medal Franklin Inst 1963, Aerospace Communications Award AIAA 1974, Bradford Washburn Award Boston Museum of Science 1977, Engrg Award Acad of TV Arts and Sciences 1981, Marconi International Fellowship 1982, Centennial Medal IEEE 1984, Vidya Jyothi Medal (Sri Lankan Presidential Science Award) 1986, Charles A Lindbergh Award 1987, Hall of Fame Soc of Satellite Professionals 1987, Special Achievement Award Space Explorers' Assoc Riyadh 1989, Robert A Heinlein Meml Award Nat Space Soc USA 1990, Int Science Policy Fndn Medal 1992, Lord Perry Award 1992, nominated for Nobel Peace Prize 1994, Hon DLitt Univ of Liverpool (via satellite) 1995, NASA Distinguished Public Serv Medal 1995, BIS Space Achievement Medal and Trophy 1995, Hon DLit Baptist Univ of Hong Kong 1996, Mohamed Sahabdeen Award for Sci 1996, von Kármán Award Int Acad of Astronautics 1996; literary awards incl: International Fantasy Award 1952, Hugo award World Science Fiction Convention 1956, 1974 and 1980, Nebula award SF Writers of America 1973, 1974 and 1979, Kalinga Prize UNESCO 1961, Robert Ball Award Aviation/Space Writers' Assoc 1965, Westinghouse Science Writing Prize AAAS 1969, Playboy Editorial Award 1971 and 1982, John W Campbell Award 1974, Galaxy Award 1979, E M Emme Astronautical Literature Award AAS 1984, Grand Master SF Writers of America 1986; *Books* author of over 100 books, 500 articles and numerous short stories; non-fiction incl: Arthur C Clarke's Mysterious World (with Simon Welfare and John Fairley, 1980), Arthur C Clarke's World of Strange Powers (with Simon Welfare and John Fairley, 1984), Ascent to Orbit (1984), How the World Was One (1992), The Snows of Olympus: A Garden on Mars (1994), Greetings, Carbon-based Bipeds! (1999); fiction incl: Childhood's End (1953), 2001 - A Space Odyssey (1968, also co-author of screenplay with Stanley Kubrick, Oscar nominated for best screenplay), 2010 - Odyssey II (1982, filmed 1984), The Songs of Distant Earth (1986), 2061 - Odyssey III, The Ghost from the Grand Banks (1990), 3001: The Final Odyssey (1997); *Recreations* table tennis, computers, observing Equatorial skies through telescope; *Style*— Sir Arthur C Clarke, CBE; ✉ Leslie's House, 25 Barnes Place, Colombo 7, Sri Lanka (tel 00 94 11 2699757/2694255, fax 00 94 11 2698730); Rocket Publishing Co, Dene Court, Bishops Lydeard, Somerset TA4 3LT (tel 01823 432671); c/o David Higham Associates, 5–8 Lower John Street, Golden Square, London W1R 4HA

CLARKE, Barry James; s of Robert Clarke, of Olney, Bucks, and Carol, *née* Lodge; *b* 10 May 1970, Derby; *Educ* Redborne Sch Ampthill, Univ of Manchester (BA, Bradford scholar, TF Tout Prize), Coll of Law Chester (CPE, LSFE), LSE (MSc Econ); *m* 22 Aug 1992, Dr Kathryn Walters; 2 da (Elena b 13 Jan 1997, Manon b 15 Jan 2004), 1 s (Daniel b 12 Sept 2000); *Career* admitted slr 1996; articled clerk Frere Cholmeley; Russell Jones & Walker: joined 2000, ptnr 2002–, currently head Employment Law Dept; chm of employment tbnls 2005–, immigration judge 2006–, nat chm Employment Lawyers' Assoc 2006–, arbitrator ACAS 2007–; tstee Cardiff Law Centre, guest lectr Univ of Cardiff; Wig and Pen Prize 1996, commended Asst Slr of the Year The Lawyer Awards 2002; *Books* Challenging Racism (ed, 2002); *Recreations* music, guitar playing, cycling, keep fit, history and mythology; *Style*— Barry Clarke, Esq; ✉ Russell Jones & Walker, 51 Charles Street, Cardiff CF10 2GD (tel 029 2026 2867, fax 029 2026 2828, e-mail b.j.clarke@rjw.co.uk)

CLARKE, Brian; s of Edward Ord Clarke, (d 1979), and Lilian, *née* Whitehead; *b* 2 July 1953; *Educ* Clarksfield Sch Oldham, Oldham Sch of Arts and Crafts (jr scholarship), Burnley Sch of Art, N Devon Coll of Art and Design (DipAD); *m* Elizabeth Cecila, da of Rev John Finch; 1 s (Daniel John Finch b 11 Feb 1989); *Career* artist; memb Cncl Winston Churchill Meml Tst 1985–, tstee and memb Ctee Robert Fraser Fndn 1990–, tstee The Ely Stained Glass Museum; visiting prof of architectural art UCL 1993, executor the estate of Francis Bacon 1998; memb Ctee DRC Cmmn for Architecture and the Built Environment 1999, tstee The Lowe Educational Charitable Fndn 2001; FRSA 1988, Hon FRIBA 1993; *Selected Major Exhibitions* Glass/Light Exhibition (Festival of the City of London with John Piper and Marc Chagall) 1979, New Paintings Constructions and Prints (RIBA) 1981, Paintings (Robert Fraser Gallery Cork Street) 1983, 1976–86 (Seibu Museum of Art Tokyo) 1987, Malerei und Farbfenster 1977–88 (Hessiches Landesmuseum) 1988, Intimations of Mortality (Galerie Karsten Greve Köln Germany), Paintings (Indar Pasricha Gallery New Delhi) 1989, Into and Out of Architecture (Mayor Gallery London) 1990, Architecture and Stained Glass (Sezon Museum of Art Tokyo) 1990, Architecture and Light (Ingolstadt Germany, in assoc with Future Systems) 1992, Designs on Architecture (Oldham Art Gallery) 1993, New Paintings (The Mayor Gallery London) 1993, Paintings and Stained Glass Works in Architecture (The Tony Shafrazi Gallery NY), Paintings and Stained Glass Works in Architecture (The Tony Shafrazi Gallery NY) 1995, Brian Clarke Linda McCartney (Musée Suisse du Vitrail au Château de Romont and the German Museum for Stained Glass) 1997–98, 80 Artistes autour du Mondial (Galerie Enrico Navarra Paris) 1998, Fleurs de Lys, exhibition of new paintings (Faggionato Fine Arts London) 1999, Flowers for New York - a tribute to New York in stained glass and painting on canvas (The Corning Gallery Steuben NY) 2002, Transillumination (Tony Shafrazi Gallery NY) 2003, Lamina (Gagosian Gallery London) 2005; *Selected Major Works* St Gabriel's Church Blackburn 1976, All Saints Church Habergham 1976, Queen's Medical Centre Nottingham 1978, Olympus Optical Europa GmbH Headquarters Building Hamburg 1981, King Kahled Int Airport Riyadh 1982, The Buxton Thermal Baths 1987, The Lake Sagami Country Club Yamanishi (in assoc with Arata Isozaki) 1988, The New Synagogue Darmstadt 1988, Victoria Quarter Leeds 1989, stage designs for Paul McCartney World Tour 1989, Cibreo Restaurant Tokyo 1990, Glaxo Pharmaceuticals Stockley Park Uxbridge 1990, Stansted Airport (in assoc with Sir Norman Foster) 1991, The Spindles Shopping Centre Oldham 1991–93, España Telefonica Barcelona 1991, The Carmelite London 1992, 100 New Bridge St London 1992, façade of Hotel de Ville des Bouches-du-Rhones Marseille (with Will Alsop) 1992–94, The Glass Dune - Hamburg (with Future Systems) 1992, EAM Building Kassel 1992–93, design of stadia sets for Paul McCartney New World Tour 1993, design of stage sets for The Ruins of Time (a ballet in tribute to Rudolph Nureyev by the Dutch National Ballet) 1993, The New Synagogue Heidelberg 1993, SMS Lowe The Grace Building NY 1994, Crossrail Paddington London (design) 1994, Schadow Arkaden Düsseldorf 1994, Norte Shopping Rio de Janeiro 1995, Rye Hosp Sussex (with Linda McCartney) 1995, Valentino Village Noci 1996, Kinderhaus Regensburg 1996, Centre Villa-Lobos São Paulo (design) 1997, Willis Corroon Building Ipswich 1997, RWE Essen (refurbishment of lobby) 1997, Offenbach Synagogue (curved glass wall and thorah shrine) 1997, Heidelberg Cathedral (design) 1997, Obersalbach 1997, Pfizer Pharmaceuticals NY 1997, Chicago Sinai 1997, Warburg Dillon Read Stamford CT (stained glass cone) 1998, Al Faisaliah Centre Riyadh (in assoc with Lord Foster of Thames Bank) 2000, Olympus Optical Europa GmbH (new HQ building) Hamburg 2000, Pfizer Pharmaceuticals NY 2001, West Winter Garden Heron Quays London (design) 2001, Hotel and Thalassotherapy Centre Nova Yardinia 2002, Pfizer Pharmaceuticals NY 2003, Ascot Racecourse 2003, Pyramid of Peace Astana Kazakhstan (design with Lord Foster of Thames Bank) 2005; *Awards* Churchill fellowship in architectural art 1974, Art and Work award special commendation 1989, Europa Nostra award 1990, The Leeds Award for Architecture Special Award for Stained Glass 1990, The Euro Shopping Centre Award 1995, BDA Auszeichnung guter Bauten Heidelberg 1996; *Recreations* reading, hoarding; *Style*— Brian Clarke, Esq; ✉ c/o Eastman & Eastman, 39 West 54th Street, New York, NY 10019, USA (tel 00 1 212 246 5757, fax 00 1 212 977 8408); website www.brianclarke.co.uk

CLARKE, Prof Bryan Campbell; s of Robert Campbell Clarke (d 1941), of Sywell, Northants, and Gladys Mary, *née* Carter (d 1987); *b* 24 June 1932; *Educ* Fay Sch Southborough Mass, Magdalen Coll Sch Oxford, Magdalen Coll Oxford (MA, DPhil); *m* 20 Aug 1960, Dr Ann Gillian, da of Prof John Jewkes, CBE (d 1988), of Boar's Hill, Oxford; 1 s (Peter b 1971), 1 da (Alexandra b 1975); *Career* PO RAF 1951–52; Univ of Edinburgh: asst in zoology 1959–63, lectr in zoology, reader in zoology 1969–71; Univ of Nottingham: prof of genetics 1971–, research prof 1994– (emeritus 1997); SERC sr res fell 1976–81; vice-pres: Genetical Soc 1981, Linnean Soc 1983–85, Soc for the Study of Evolution (USA) 1990, Zoological Soc of London 1998; scientific expeditions to: Morocco 1955, Polynesia 1962, 1967, 1968, 1980, 1982, 1986, 1991, 1994 and 2000; chm: Biological Sciences Panel HEFCE 1992–98, Cncl Royal Soc 1994–96; hon res fell Nat History Museum 1993–; chm of tstees Charles Darwin Tst 2000–06; ed: Heredity 1977–84, Proceedings of the Royal Soc Series B 1989–93; Linnean Medal for Zoology 2003; foreign memb American Philosophical Soc 2003, hon foreign memb American Acad of Arts and Scis 2004; FRS 1982; *Books* Berber Village (1959), The Evolution of DNA Sequences (ed, 1986), Frequency-Dependent Selection (ed, 1988); *Recreations* painting, archaeology; *Clubs* RAF; *Style*— Prof Bryan Clarke, FRS; ✉ Linden Cottage, School Lane, Colston Bassett, Nottingham NG12 3FD (tel 01949 81243); Institute of Genetics, Queen's Medical Centre, Clifton Boulevard, Nottingham NG7 2UH (tel 0115 970 9397, e-mail bryan.clarke@nottingham.ac.uk)

CLARKE, Catherine; *Career* former trade publishing dir OUP, agent and dir The Felicity Bryan Agency; *Style*— Ms Catherine Clarke; ✉ The Felicity Bryan Agency, 2A North Parade, Oxford OX2 6LX

CLARKE, Dr Charles Richard Astley; s of Prof Sir Cyril Astley Clarke, KBE, FRS (d 2000), and Frieda Margaret Mary, *née* Hart (d 1998); *b* 12 February 1944; *Educ* Rugby, Gonville & Caius Coll Cambridge (MA, MB); *m* 23 March 1971, Dr Ruth Seifert, *qv*, da of Sigmund Seifert (d 1978), of London; 2 da (Rebecca Astley b 1973, Naomi Astley b 1976); *Career* conslt neurologist: Bart's 1979–96, Whipps Cross Hosp London 1983–2006, Nat Hosp for Neurology and Neurosurgery 1996–2006; chm Dept of Neurology and Neurosurgery London Bridge Hosp 1989–95, clinical dir Dept of Clinical Neurosciences Bart's 1990–94; Br Mountaineering Cncl: hon med offr 1981–, pres 2006–; chm Mount Everest Fndn 1990–92 and 2002–04, vice-pres Alpine Club 1990–92; dir The Second Step Mountaineering Bookshop Islington London; The Robert Atkins prize for Contribution to Sports Med 1991; Freeman: City of London 1984, Worshipful Soc of Apothecaries; FRCP (memb Cncl 2002–04 and 2005–); *Books* Everest - The Unclimbed Ridge (1983), Tibet's Secret Mountain, The Triumph of Sepu Kangri (1999) (all with Sir Christian Bonington, *qv*); *Recreations* mountaineering, exploration, sailing, model yacht racing; *Clubs* Alpine, RGS, Athenaeum; *Style*— Dr Charles Clarke; ✉ 152 Harley Street, London W1G 7LH (tel and fax 020 7359 6412)

CLARKE, Rt Hon Charles Rodway; PC (2001), MP; s of Sir Richard Clarke, KCB, OBE (d 1975), and Brenda, *née* Skinner; *b* 21 September 1950; *Educ* Highgate Sch (fndn scholar), King's Coll Cambridge (BA, pres Students' Union); *m* 1984, Carol, da of Ken and Linda Pearson; 2 s (Christopher b 25 Jan 1987, Matthew b 22 Aug 1990); *Career* pres NUS 1975–77, with World Youth Festival 1977–78, community offr Hackney People in Partnership 1978–80, cncllr London Borough of Hackney 1980–86 (vice-chm Econ Devpt Ctee 1981–82, chm Housing Ctee 1982–84), political advsr to Neil Kinnock, MP as shadow Educn Sec 1981–83, head of Neil Kinnock's office 1983–92, chief exec Quality Public Affairs 1992–97; MP (Lab) Norwich S 1997–; Parly under sec Dept for Educn and Employment 1998–99, min of state Home Office 1999–2001, min without portfolio and chm Lab Pty 2001–02, sec of state for educn 2002–04, sec of state Home Office 2004–06; *Recreations* chess, reading, walking; *Clubs* Norwich Labour; *Style*— The Rt Hon Charles Clarke, MP; ✉ House of Commons, London SW1A 0AA (tel 020 7219 1194)

CLARKE, Christopher Alan; s of Harry Alston Clarke (d 1979), and Isobel Corsan, *née* Kay; *b* 14 May 1945, Edinburgh; *Educ* Oakham, Selwyn Coll Cambridge (MA), London Business Sch (MSc (now known as MBA)); *m* 9 Dec 1978, Charlotte, *née* Jenkins; 1 da (Katherine b 1981), 1 s (Henry b 1984); *Career* Shell Int Petroleum 1967–73, IDJ Ltd 1973–74, Arbuthnot Latham & Co Ltd 1974–82 (dir 1978–82), md Arbuthnot Latham Asia Ltd 1979–82; dir: Samuel Montagu & Co 1982–96, HSBC Investment Banking 1996–98; non-exec dir: The Weir Gp plc 1999–, Omega Underwriting Holdings plc 2005–06, Omega Insurance Holdings Ltd 2006–; dep chm Competition Cmmn 2004– (memb 2001–); *Recreations* golf, fishing, books; *Clubs* Berkshire Golf; *Style*— Christopher Clarke, Esq; ✉ Competition Commission, Victoria House, Southampton Row, London WC1B 4AD (tel 020 7271 0100, fax 020 7271 0203, e-mail christopher.clarke@cc.gsi.gov.uk)

CLARKE, Christopher George; s of Philip George Clarke (d 1991), and José Margaret Clarke (d 1979); *b* 18 September 1944; *Educ* Radley; *m* 1 June 1968, Jane, *née* Ellis; 2 da (Natasha Jane b 12 June 1970, Vanessa Clare b 5 April 1973); *Career* articled clerk Hodgson Morris & Co Chartered Accountants 1963–67 (qualified 1967), investment mangr Wm Brandts 1968–72, investment mangr JH Vavasseur London 1972–74; Henderson Investors: joined 1974, dir Henderson Administration Ltd 1976–, dir Henderson Administration Gp plc 1983–1998; dir Witan Investment Co plc 1993–2006 (md 1993–2000); non-exec dir Rensburg Sheppards plc (formerly BWD Securities) 1999– (chm 2003); memb Cncl Radley Coll (vice-chm 2004); *Style*— Christopher Clarke, Esq; ✉ e-mail cgclarke@onetel.net

CLARKE, Christopher John David; s of Maj John Herbert Thomson Clarke (d 1983), and Hazel, *née* Chapman (d 1988); *b* 21 March 1950; *Educ* Fettes, Coll of Law London; *m* 4 April 1992, Catherine, *née* Shuttlewood; 1 da (Lucy b 9 Dec 1992), 1 s (Rory b 22 Feb 1994); *Career* admitted slr England and Hong Kong 1974; Denton Hall: ptnr Hong Kong 1978–84, ptnr London 1984–92, sr ptnr Asia 1992–99; sr and managing ptnr Asia CMS Cameron McKenna 1999–2003, sr commercial litigation ptnr Asia DLA Piper 2003–; dir: Arnhold Holdings Ltd, Baltrans Holdings Ltd; memb: Int Bar Assoc, Law Assoc; *Recreations* travel, food, family; *Clubs* Hong Kong, China; *Style*— Christopher J D Clarke, Esq

CLARKE, Hon Mr Justice; Sir Christopher Simon Courtenay Stephenson; kt (2005); yr s of Rev John Stephenson Clarke (d 1982), and Enid Courtenay, *née* Manico; *b* 14 March 1947; *Educ* Marlborough, Gonville & Caius Coll Cambridge (MA); *m* 14 Sept 1974, Caroline Anne, da of Prof Charles Montague Fletcher, CBE; 2 da (Henrietta b 16 Aug 1977, Louisa b 21 June 1979), 1 s (Edward b 31 May 1981); *Career* called to the Bar Middle Temple 1969 (bencher 1991); advocate of the Supreme Court of the Turks and Caicos Is 1975, QC 1984, head of chambers Brick Court Chambers 1990–2005, recorder of the Crown Court 1990–2005, judge Court of Appeal of Jersey and Guernsey 1998–, judge of the High Court of Justice (Queen's Bench Div) 2005– (dep judge 1993–2005); counsel to Bloody Sunday Inquiry 1998–2004; chm Ctee of Inquiry of States of Guernsey into Barnett Christie (Fin) Ltd 1985–87; cncllr Int Bar Assoc 1988–91, chm Commercial Law Bar Assoc 1993–95, memb Bar Cncl 1993–99; FRSA 1994; *Clubs* Brooks's, Hurlingham; *Style*— The Hon Mr Justice Christopher Clarke; ✉ c/o Royal Courts of Justice, Strand, London WC2A 2LL

CLARKE, Prof Colin Graham; *b* 21 October 1938, Worcester; *Educ* Jesus Coll Oxford (Collins exhibitioner, MA), Univ of Oxford (DPhil, DLitt); *m*; 2 c; *Career* research assoc Research Inst for the Study of Man NY 1963–64; Univ of Liverpool: Leverhulme research fell in geography 1964–66, lectr Dept of Geography and Centre for Latin American Studies 1966–74, sr lectr 1974–77, chm Bd of Geographical Studies 1975–76, reader in geography and Latin American studies 1977–81, memb Senate and Academic Planning Ctee 1979–81; Univ of Oxford: lectr in urban and social geography 1981–97, chm Anthropology and Geography Faculty Bd 1991–93 (vice-chm 1989–91), prof of urban and social geography 1997–2003, head of dept Sch of Geography and the Environment 1998–2001, emeritus prof of geography 2003; official fell Jesus Coll Oxford 1981 (sr research fell 2003); visiting asst prof Dept of Geography Univ of Toronto 1967–68, visiting lectr Dept of Geography Univ of Leeds 1970–71, visiting prof Instituto de Geográfia Universidad Nacional Autonóma de México 1982, visiting prof Facultad de Humanidades Universidad Central Caracas 1988; assoc fell Centre for Caribbean Studies Univ of Warwick 1983–93; memb: Latin American Field Ctee Oxfam 1971–77, Co-ordinating Cncl for Area Studies Assocs 1980–84 and 1993–95, Comité Scientifique Centre d'Etude de Geographie Tropicale (CNRS) Bordeaux 1990–92, Area Studies Panel for Coursework Awards ESRC 1993, Latin American Studies Panel HEFCE Research Assessment Exercise 1996; pres d'honneur Assoc for European Research on Central America and the Caribbean 1988– (memb Exec Ctee 1985–86), pres Soc for Latin American Studies 1993–95 (memb Ctee 1990–93), life memb Soc for Caribbean Studies 2004 (sec 1977–79 and 1983–84, chm 1979–81), memb Inst of Br Geographers 1961– (sec Population Study Gp 1968–71); ed Liverpool Centre for Latin American Studies monograph series 1970–73 and 1976–81, ed Bulletin of Latin American Research 1992–97 (memb Editorial Bd 1981–92); memb: Editorial Advsy Bd Jl of Latin American Studies 1977–89, Comision Dictaminadora Editorial del Instituto de Geogràfia Universidad Nacional Autonóma de México 1982–92, Conseil Scientifique Cahiers d'Outre-mer 1988–, Conseil Scientifique Iles et Archipels 1988–, Editorial Bd European Review of Latin American and Caribbean Studies 1990–2001, Int Advsy Bd Third World Planning Review 1991–2001; Gold Medal RSGS 1999; *Publications* Jamaica in Maps (1974), Kingston, Jamaica: Urban Development and Social Change, 1692–1962 (1975), Caribbean Social Relations (ed, 1978), A Geography of the Third World (jtly, 1983, 2 edn 1996), Georaphy and Ethnic Pluralism (jt ed, 1984), East Indians in a West Indian Town: San Fernando Trinidad 1930–1970 (1986), Cambio Social y Económico en Latinoamerica: Perspectivas Geográficas (jt ed, 1986), Politics, Security and Development in Small States (jt ed, 1987), South Asians Overseas: Migration and Ethnicity (jt ed, 1990), Society and Politics in the Caribbean (ed, 1991), Class, Ethnicity and Community in Southern Mexico: Oaxaca's Peasantries (2000); also author of book contribs and papers and articles published in learned jls; *Style*— Prof Colin Clarke; ✉ Jesus College, Oxford OX1 3DW

CLARKE, David; s of Dennis Percy Clarke, of Himbleton, Worcs, and Vera, *née* Timpson; *b* 19 March 1954; *Educ* Sevenoaks Sch, Bromsgrove Sch, Univ of Bristol Sch of Architecture (BA(Arch), DipArch); *m* 21 May 1983, Victoria, da of late Peter Kysylicia; 1 s (Jonathan David b 1987); *Career* architect; Watkins Gray Woodgate International 1977–79, Peterborough Devpt Corp 1979–82; Building Design Partnership (BDP) Sheffield office: joined 1986, assoc 1988–97, architect dir 1997–; projects incl White Rose Centre Leeds (Br Cncl of Shopping Centres New Shopping Centre Award 1997 and Int Cncl of Shopping Centres commendation New Centre Category 1998); memb ARCUK, RIBA; *Recreations* windsurfing, motor cars, cycling; *Style*— David Clarke, Esq; ✉ Building Design Partnership, Blackhall Green, Dublin 7, Eire

CLARKE, Hon Mr Justice; Sir David Clive Clarke; kt (2003); s of Philip George Clarke (d 1991), and José Margaret, *née* Fletcher (d 1979); *b* 16 July 1942; *Educ* Winchester, Magdalene Coll Cambridge (MA); *m* 2 Aug 1969, Alison Claire, da of Rt Rev (Percy) James Brazier (d 1989); 3 s (Andrew b 1970 d 1993, Jonathan b 1972, Edward b 1975); *Career* called to the Bar Inner Temple 1965; in practice Northern Circuit until 1993 (treas 1988–92), QC 1983, recorder of the Crown Court 1981–93, circuit judge (Northern Circuit) 1993–1997, sr circuit judge and hon recorder of Liverpool 1997–2003, judge of the High Court of Justice (Queen's Bench Div) 2003–, presiding judge Northern Circuit 2006–; memb Criminal Justice Consultative Cncl 1999–2003; Hon LLD Univ of Liverpool, hon fell Liverpool John Moores Univ 2007; *Recreations* canals, sailing, swimming; *Style*— The Hon Mr Justice David Clarke; ✉ Royal Courts of Justice, Strand, London WC2A 2LL

CLARKE, David Edwin; s of Ernest Wilfred Clarke (d 1972), and Irene Elisabeth, *née* Bennett (d 1974); *b* 7 March 1953; *Educ* Solihull Sch, Abington PA USA; *m* 10 Sept 1977, Nicola Jayne, da of John Frank Cordwell; 2 da (Hannah Jayne b 10 Jan 1982, Caroline May b 18 Aug 1984); *Career* reporter Birmingham Post & Mail Group 1974–78, PRO Midlands Electricity Bd 1978–79, exec Priority PR 1979–80, md Graham Rote & Co Ltd 1983–86 (dir 1981–83), md Clarke Associates UK Ltd 1986–, chm Edelman Public Relations Network (UK) 1994–98; nat hon treas IPR 1986–89; chm Birmingham Forward 2000–02 (dir 1997–); dir Birmingham Settlement 1992–2001, chm Birmingham Business Breakfast Club 1994–99, dir Marketing Birmingham 2001–; Barker Variety Club of Great Britain 1998–; chm of Judges Midlands Business Awards 2001–; FCIPR (FIPR 1991, MIPR 1973); *Books* The Rabbit Guide to Birmingham (2004); *Recreations* walking, travel, keep fit, Birmingham Baltis; *Style*— David Clarke, Esq; ✉ Pinley Cottage, Pinley, Claverdon, Warwickshire CV35 8NA (tel 01926 84 2266); Clarke Associates UK Ltd, Centre Court, 1301 Stratford Road, Birmingham B28 9AP (tel 0121 702 2525, fax 0121 702 2085, e-mail david-c@clarke-associates.co.uk)

CLARKE, Hon Mr Justice Frank; s of Ben Clarke (d 1963), of Walkinstown, Dublin, and Sheila, *née* Bailey (d 1996); *b* 10 October 1951, Dublin; *Educ* Drimnagh Castle Christian Bros Sch, NUI Dublin (UCD) (BA), King's Inns Sch of Law; *m* 29 Dec 1977, Dr Jacqueline Hayden; 1 s (Ben b 13 July 1986), 1 da (Charlotte b 14 Sept 1988); *Career* called to the Bar King's Inns Dublin 1973 (bencher 1995); sr counsel 1985, judge of the High Court of Ireland 2004–; twice appointed by Supreme Court as counsel to argue Article 26 references; memb: Bar Cncl of Ireland 1977–85 and 1987–95 (vice-chair 1992, chair 1993–95), Cncl Int Bar Assoc 1996–2004 (co-chair Forum for Barrs and Advocates 1999–2003), Cncl of King's Inns 1997–2004 (chair 1999–2004); hon memb: Canadian Bar Assoc 1994, Australian Bar Assoc 2003; memb Bd Leopardstown Racecourse 1995– (chair 2003–05), memb Turf Club and Irish Nat Hunt Steeplechase Ctee 1999– (dep sr steward 2003–05), memb Bd of Horse Racing Ireland 2003–05; *Recreations* horse racing, music; *Clubs* Turf (Dublin), Kildare St and Univ (Dublin); *Style*— The Hon Mr Justice Frank Clarke; ✉ The High Court, Fourt Courts, Dublin 7, Ireland (tel 00 353 1 888 6000, fax 00 353 1 872 5669, e-mail fclarke@courts.ie)

CLARKE, Geoffrey; s of John Moulding Clarke, and Janet, *née* Petts; *b* 28 November 1924, Darley Dale, Derbys; *Educ* RCA; *m*; 2 s; *Career* artist and sculptor; RA 1975 (ARA 1970); *Exhibitions* Gimpel Fils Gallery 1952 and 1955, Redfern Gallery 1965, Taranman Gallery 1975, 1976 and 1982, Yorkshire Sculpture Park 1994, Friends Room RA 1994, Christchurch Mansion Ipswich (retrospective, tour) 1994, Fine Art Soc 2000 and 2006; *Commissions* incl: iron sculpture Time Life Building New Bond Street London, mosaics Univ of Liverpool Physics Block and stained glass windows Treasury Lincoln Cathedral, bronze sculpture Thorn Electric Building Upper St Martin's Lane London, three stained glass windows, high altar, cross and candlesticks and the flying cross and crown of thorns Coventry Cathedral, screens in Royal Military Chapel Birdcage Walk; *Works in Public Collections* V&A, British Museum, Tate Gallery, Arts Cncl, MOMA NY; prizes for engraving: Triennial 1951, London 1953, Tokyo 1957; RA 1976; *Style*— Geoffrey Clarke, Esq, RA; ✉ Stowe Hill, Hartest, Bury St Edmunds, Suffolk IP29 4EQ (tel 01284 830319, fax 01284 830126)

CLARKE, Gillian; da of John Penri Williams (d 1957), and Ceinwen, *née* Evans (d 1997); *b* 8 June 1937; *Educ* UC Cardiff (BA); *m* 2, David Thomas; 3 c from previous m: 1 da (Catrin b 1961), 2 s (Owain b 1963, Dylan b 1966); *Career* writer, lectr and broadcaster; res asst News Information Dept BBC London 1958–60, pt/t lectr in English and liberal studies

C

Reardon Smith Nautical Coll Cardiff 1965–75, pt/t lectr and poet-in-residence Dept of Art History and Cultural Studies Newport Coll of Art Gwent 1975–84, Welsh Arts Cncl creative writing fell St David's UC Lampeter 1984–85, Lampeter Writers Workshop 1984–, tutor MPhil in creative writing Univ of Glamorgan 1993–; ed The Anglo-Welsh Review 1976–84 (reviews ed 1971–76); chm: English Language Section Academi Gymreig 1988–93, Ty Newydd 1990– (life pres); memb: Literature Ctee Welsh Arts Cncl 1976–82 and 1987–93, Gen Advsy Cnl BBC 1992–95, Bd ARTS 2000 Year of Literature 1992–96; Glyndwr Award 1999; hon fell: UC Cardiff 1985, Univ of Wales Swansea 1995, Univ of Wales Lampeter 2000; Hon MA Univ of Wales 2001; FRSL 2000; *Books* One Moonlit Night (stories for children, trans from Welsh, 1991); *Poems* Snow on the Mountain (1971), The Sundial (1978), Letter from a Far Country (1982), Selected Poems (1985), Letting in the Rumour (1989, Poetry Book Soc recommendation), The King of Britain's Daughter (1993, Poetry Book Soc recommendation), Collected Poems (1997), Five Fields (1998, Poetry Book Soc recommendation), The Animal Wall and Other Poems (for children, 1999), Owain Glyn Dwr (2000), Nine Green Gardens (2000), Making the Beds for the Dead (2004); *Radio* Talking in the Dark (1978), Letter from a Far Country (1981), Bridgewater (1997); *TV* Imagine This (BBC 2, 1991); *Anthologies* The Poetry Society Anthology (ed, 1987–88), I Can Move The Sea: Poems by Children (ed, 1995), The Whispering Room: Anthology of Haunted Poems for Children (ed, 1996); *Drama* The Time of the Wolf (for Theatr Powys, 1996), Rhiannon (for Sherman Theatre), Talking to Wordsworth (Sherman and BBC Radio), The Blue Man (for BBC Radio 4) 2000, Honey (BBC Radio 4) 2002, Letter From a Far Country (dramatised from poem) 2004, Shopping for Happiness 2004, A Field of Hay (2006); *Recordings* Poems read by Gillian Clarke (cassette) 1999, 20 Poems (CD) 2003; *Recreations* gardening, farming and conserving 17 acres of hills woodland; *Style*— Ms Gillian Clarke; ✉ Blaen Cwrt, Talgarreg, Llandysul, Ceredigion SA44 4EU (tel 01545 590311)

CLARKE, Graham Neil; s of Henry Charles Owen Clarke, MVO (d 1996), and Doris May, *née* Morgan (d 2002); *b* 23 July 1956; *Educ* Rutherford Sch London, RHS, Sch of Horticulture Wisley; *m* 2 Feb 1980, Denise Carole, da of Robert Fraser Anderson; 2 da (Rebecca Sarah b 1990, Helena Charlotte b 1994); *Career* gardener: Buckingham Palace 1975–76, Royal Parks Nursery 1976; Amateur Gardening: sub-ed 1976–79, chief sub-ed 1979–81, dep ed 1981–86; ed: Home Plus Magazine 1985, Amateur Gardening 1986–98; ed IPC Gardening Magazines (gp ed 1993–95): Amateur Gardening, Your Garden, The Gardener, special projects ed 1995–98, ed at large 1998–99; GMC Publications: devpt ed 1999–2000, editorial mangr 2000–2002; freelance publishing and horticultural conslt 2002–04, ed Horticulture Week 2004–05, conslt 2005–06 chm Hamdene Horticultural Publishing Servs Ltd 2006–; memb Exec Ctee: RHS Garden Club 1975–82, Garden Writers' Guild 2005–, Commercial Horticulture Assoc 2005–, Royal Parks Guild 2006–; prodr and presenter Hosp Radio London and Bournemouth 1976–89; FLS, MIHort; *Books* Step-By-Step Pruning (1984), A-Z of Garden Plants (1985), Autumn/Winter Colour in the Garden (1986), Your Gardening Questions Answered (1987), The Complete Book of Plant Propagation (1990), The Ultimate House Plant Handbook (1996), Beginner's Guide to Water Gardening (2002), Collins Practical Gardener: Water Gardening (2004), Collins Practical Gardener: Pruning (2005), Success with Roses (2007), Success with Shade-Loving Plants (2007), Success with Sun-Loving Plants (2007), Success with Water Gardens (2007); *Recreations* gardening, writing, genealogy; *Style*— Graham Clarke, Esq; ✉ Hamdene House, 127 Magna Road, Bearwood, Bournemouth, Dorset BH11 9NE (e-mail gra.clarke@virgin.net)

CLARKE, Graham Staward; TD (1971); s of Douglas Staward Clarke (d 1949), and Beatrice, *née* Auld (d 1988); *b* 16 March 1937; *Educ* St Bees Sch Cumberland, Emmanuel Coll Cambridge (MA); *m* 1964, Rita Elisabeth Karoline, da of Oskar Becker (d 1961); 1 da (Tessa b 1965), 1 s (Douglas b 1968); *Career* Maj RA, Euro theatre; gp fin dir: Telex Computers Ltd 1972–75, Coles Cranes Ltd 1976–81, Fairey Holdings Ltd 1981–84; md Energy and Military Engrg Div Fairey Holdings Ltd 1984–86; chm: Fairey Engineering Ltd 1984–86, Elequip Ltd 1984–86, Bourn Management Consultants Ltd 1985–2000; dir: Fairey Holdings Ltd 1981–86, Fairey Developments Ltd 1981–86, Fairey Construction Ltd 1984–86, Mathews and Yates Ltd 1984–86, Fairey Nuclear Ltd 1984–86, Begley Engineering Ltd 1984–91, Nightingale Secretariat plc 1991–95; chm and md: Bourn Developments 1986–, Bourn Properties Ltd 1997–2000, Bourn Investments Ltd 1999–; prop Bourn Estates 1980–; chm Fedn of Oxshott Residents and Associations (memb Mgmnt Ctee 1988–); involved with town planning, community, environment and green belt issues in Surrey 1993–98; FCA, FRSA; *Recreations* bridge, travel, geo-politics, business management; *Clubs* RAC, IOD; *Style*— Graham S Clarke Esq, TD; ✉ Bourn Investments Ltd, Bourn Reach, 9 Montrose Gardens, Oxshott, Surrey KT22 0UU (tel 01372 843445, fax 01372 842216, e-mail graham9mg@aol.com)

CLARKE, Greg; *Career* ceo: Cable & Wireless Communications plc 1999–2000, ICO-Teledesic Global 2000–; *Style*— Greg Clarke, Esq; ✉ ICO-Teledesic Global, The Mill House, Loudwater Road, Loudwater, High Wycombe, Buckinghamshire HP10 9QN

CLARKE, Henry Benwell; s of Stephen Lampard Clarke (d 1984), of Hastings, and Elinor Wade, *née* Benwell (d 1974); *b* 30 January 1950; *Educ* St John's Sch Leatherhead, South Bank Poly (BSc), Imperial Coll London (MSc, DIC, British Airways prize for MSc); *m* 18 Aug 1973, Verena Angela, da of late Dennis Howard Lodge; 1 da (Jessamy Anne b 1976), 4 s (Samuel John b 1977, Timothy Michael b 1980, Philip Andrew b 1982, Jonathan Peter b 1992); *Career* British Rail Property Bd: S Region 1972–78, NW Region 1978–82, E Region 1982–85, regnl estate surveyor and mangr Midland Region 1985–86, chief estate surveyor HQ 1986–87, nat devpt mangr 1987–88; The Crown Estate Cmmn: dep chief exec 1988–92, actg chief exec and accounting offr 1989; jt md People and Places International 1993–2004, md People and Places Property Consultants Ltd 1993–2004; conslt Anthony Green and Spencer 1993–, princ Henry Clarke Associates 2004–; memb Bd: The Rail Estate Consultancy Ltd 1998–, Crowmead Properties Ltd 1998–, Telecom Property Ltd 1999–, Crystal Palace Devpt Co 2000–04, Kings Yard Devpts Ltd 2004, Intelligent Business Space Ltd 2004–, C-Space Ltd 2005–, Jackson Green Ltd 2006–; memb: Cncl Christian Union for Estate Profession 1983–88, Gen Cncl Br Property Fedn 1989–92, Bd Youth With a Mission (Eng) 1990–, Br Cncl of Shopping Centres 1990–92, British Urban Regeneration Assoc 1992–, Urban Village Group 1992–, Bd Mercy Ships UK 1997–; tstee: Moggerhanger House Preservation Tst 1998–2005, The Railway Children 2002–, Lindow Mission Tst 2003–, BCF Harpenden Tst 2004–; MIMgt 1975, ACIArb 1979, FRICS 1986 (ARICS 1973), MInstD 1993; *Publications* author of various articles in periodicals; *Recreations* reading, walking, classic public transport, architecture, church; *Style*— Henry Clarke, Esq; ✉ Rail Estate, 12 Bridge Wharf, 156 Caledonian Road, London N1 9UU (tel 020 7837 1114, fax 020 7713 0328, e-mail henryclarke@railestate.co.uk)

CLARKE, Jane; da of Michael David Hilborne-Clarke, and Margaret, *née* Lythell; *Educ* Norwich HS for Girls, UCL (Campbell Clarke Scholarship Sessional Prize, BA), Slade Film Unit Slade Sch of Fine Art (postgrad research); *Children* 1 da (Amelia Frances Clarke Trevette b 6 Sept 1986); *Career* journalist Time Out magazine and freelance and lectr RCA Sch of Film and TV 1978–80, film programmer BFI 1980–82, freelance film programmer Barbican Arts Centre Cinema 1982; TV-am 1982–88: ed Henry Kelly Saturday Show 1984–85, features ed Good Morning Britain 1985–86, ed After Nine 1987–88; series ed Children First Granada Television 1989, prodr The Other Side of Christmas Thames Television 1989, series ed New Living and dep ed Living Now New Era Television Ltd 1990, controller features Westcountry Television 1991–95, dep dir BFI 1995–97 (actg dir Oct-Dec 1997), chief exec Bafta 1998, head TV and Radio Section FCO Public Diplomacy Dept 1999–2002, head FCO Strategy and Programmes Public Diplomacy Policy Dept 2002–04, head Public Diplomacy Team FCO 2004–06, head of communications Sport England 2006–; *Books* Move Over Misconceptions - Doris Day Re-appraised (BFI Dossier, with Diana Simmonds, 1980); *Recreations* literature, football (Tottenham Hotspur FC), air rifle shooting; *Style*— Miss Jane Clarke; ✉ e-mail jane.clarke@sportengland.org

CLARKE, Jane Mary; *b* 2 August 1959; *Educ* Holy Trinity Convent Bromley; *m* 16 July 1988, Andrew Sizer; 1 da (Mary Natasha b 28 Feb 1991), 1 s (William James b 5 Feb 1996); *Career* tax asst Smith & Williamson CAs 1977–80, advertisement asst Daily Mail 1981–82, sr account exec (sponsorship) Charles Barker Lyons 1982–87, account gp head Karen Earl Ltd 1987–90, client servs dir Strategic Sponsorship Ltd 1990–93, sabbatical Boston MA 1993–94, devpt dir CSD 1994–97, md Allies Ltd (sponsorship conslts) 1997–2005, legacy dir Business in the Community 2005–; FRSA; *Recreations* running, cycling, travel; *Clubs* Bedford Harriers; *Style*— Ms Jane Clarke; ✉ Business in the Community, 137 Shepherdess Walk, London N1 7RG (tel 020 7566 8718, e-mail jane.clarke@bitc.org.uk)

CLARKE, Prof John; s of Victor Patrick Clarke (d 1995), of Cambridge, and Ethel May, *née* Blowers (d 1978); *b* 10 February 1942; *Educ* Perse Sch for Boys Cambridge, Univ of Cambridge (BA, MA, PhD, ScD); *m* 15 Sept 1979, Grethe, da of Hartwig Fog Pedersen (d 1990), of Copenhagen; 1 da (Elizabeth Jane b 1980); *Career* postdoctoral fell Univ of Calif 1968–69, princ investigator Materials Sciences Div Lawrence Berkeley Laboratory 1969–; Univ of Calif Berkeley: asst prof 1969–71, assoc prof 1971–73, prof of physics 1973–, Luis W Alvarez meml chair for experimental physics 1994–; visiting appts: Cavendish Laboratory Cambridge 1972 and 1979, HC Orsted Inst Copenhagen 1972, 1979 and 1985, Univ of Karlsruhe Germany 1978, CEN Saclay France 1986, visiting fell Clare Hall Cambridge 1989; faculty research lectr Univ of California Berkeley 2005; by-fell Churchill Coll Cambridge 1998; Alfred P Sloan Fndn Fellowship 1970–72, Adolph C and Mary Sprague Miller Res Professorship 1975–76 and 1994–95, John Simon Guggenheim Fellowship 1977–78; Charles Vernon Boys Prize Br Inst Physics 1977, Soc of Exploration Geophysics Award for best paper in geophysics (with T D Gamble and W M Goubau) 1979, Technology Magazine Technology 100 Award (with Gamble and Goubau) 1981, Distinguished Teaching Award Univ of Calif Berkeley 1983, Award for Sustained Outstanding Res in Solid State Physics in Dept of Energy's 1986 Materials Sciences Res Competition, Calif Scientist of the Year 1987, Fritz London Meml Award for Low Temperature Physics 1987, Federal Laboratory Consortium Award for Excellence in Technol Transfer 1992, Dept of Energy Div of Materials Sciences Award for Solid State Physics - Significant Implications for DOE Related Technols 1992, Electrotechnology Transfer Award Inst of Electrical and Electronic Engrs Activities Bd 1995, Joseph F Keithley Award for Advances in Measurement Sci The American Physical Society 1998, Comstock Prize in Physics Nat Acad of Sci 1999, IEEE Cncl on Superconductivity Award for Significant and Continuing Contributions to Applied Superconductivity 2002, The Scientific American 50 Award 2002, Olli V Lounasmaa Prize Finnish Acad of Arts and Scis 2004, Hughes Medal Royal Society 2004; hon fell Christ's Coll Cambridge 1997; fell: AAAS 1982, American Physical Society 1985; FRS 1986, FInstP 1999; *Style*— Prof John Clarke, FRS; ✉ Department of Physics, 366 Leconte Hall, University of California, Berkeley, CA 94720-7300, USA (tel 00 1 510 642 3069, fax 00 1 510 642 1304)

CLARKE, Dr John Charles; s of Percy Charles Clarke, of Brackley, Northants, and Gladys May, *née* Gibbard (d 1967); *b* 18 January 1947; *Educ* Magdalen Coll Sch Brackley, Wadham Coll Oxford (minor scholar, MA, DPhil); *m* 1976, Celia Imogen, da of Cecil Ralph Wathen (d 1976); *Career* fell All Souls Coll Oxford 1967–1976, 1979–86, 1995–, sr lectr in history Univ Coll at Buckingham 1976–84, lectr in history Wadham Coll Oxford 1979–86, dean of humanities Univ of Buckingham 1994– (reader in history 1984–); *Books* George III (1972), The Age of Cobbett (1976), The Book of Buckingham (1984), British Diplomacy and Foreign Policy (1989), The Book of Brackley (1987), Yesterday's Brackley (1990); *Recreations* railways; *Style*— Dr John Clarke; ✉ Dean Faculty of Humanities, University of Buckingham, Yeomanry House, Hunter Street, Buckingham MK18 1EG (tel 01280 820294)

CLARKE, Prof John Frederick; s of Frederick William Clarke (d 1974), and Clara Auguste Antonie, *née* Nauen (d 1975); *b* 1 May 1927; *Educ* Warwick Sch, QMC (BSc, PhD); *m* 19 Dec 1953, Jean Ruth, da of Joseph Alfred Hector Roberts Gentle (d 1960), 2 da (Jenny b 1956, Julie b 1957); *Career* pupil pilot Naval Aviation RN 1946–48; aerodynamicist English Electric Co Ltd 1956–57, lectr Coll of Aeronautics Cranfield 1958–65, Fulbright scholar and visiting assoc prof of Stanford Univ 1961–62, reader Cranfield Inst of Technol 1965–72 (prof theoretical gas dynamics 1972–91, emeritus prof 1992–), fell Queen Mary & Westfield Coll London 1993–; visiting prof at various UK, Euro, Aust and US univs, memb various ctees for science, author of various contribs to learned jls; first G C Steward visiting fell Gonville & Caius Coll Cambridge 1992; FIMA 1965, FRAeS 1969, FRS 1987, FInstP 1999; *Books* The Dynamics of Real Gases (with M McChesney, 1964), Dynamics of Relaxing Gases (with M McChesney, 1976); *Recreations* Sunday painter; *Style*— Prof John F Clarke, FRS; ✉ Field House, Green Lane, Aspley Guise, Milton Keynes MK17 8EN (tel 01908 582234, e-mail john.clarke@eidosnet.co.uk)

CLARKE, Prof John Innes; OBE (2003), DL (Co Durham 1990); s of late Bernard Griffith Clarke, of Bournemouth, Dorset, and Edith Louie, *née* Mott; *b* 7 January 1929; *Educ* Bournemouth Sch, Univ of Aberdeen (MA, PhD), Univ of Paris; *m* 2 April 1955, Dorothy Anne, da of late George May Watkinson, of Ashbourne, Derbys; 3 da (Gemma b 1956, Anna b 1959, Lucy b 1969); *Career* Nat Serv FO RAF 1952–54; asst lectr in geography Univ of Aberdeen 1954–55, lectr in geography Univ of Durham 1955–63, prof of geography UC of Sierra Leone 1963–65; Univ of Durham: reader 1965–68, prof of geography 1968–90, pro-vice-chllr and sub warden 1984–90, Leverhulme emeritus fell 1990–92, emeritus prof 1990–; chm: Exec Ctee HESIN 1987–89, Durham HA 1990–92, N Durham HA 1992–96, NE Regnl Awards Ctee National Lottery Charities Bd 1997–2002; non-exec memb County Durham Fndn; FRSA, FRGS (Victoria Medal 1991, vice-pres 1991–95); *Books* Population Geography (1965), Population Geography and Developing Countries (1971), The Future of Population (1997), The Human Dichotomy (2000); ed: An Advanced Geography of Africa (1975), Geography and Population (1984); co-ed: Population & Development Projects in Africa (1985), Population & Disaster (1989), Mountain Population Pressure (1990), Environment and Population Change (1994); *Recreations* hill walking, family history, travel; *Style*— Prof John Clarke, OBE, DL; ✉ Tower Cottage, The Avenue, Durham DH1 4EB (tel 0191 384 8350, e-mail johniclarke@msn.com)

CLARKE, Very Rev John Martin; s of Roland Clarke (d 1993), and Edna, *née* Hay; *b* 20 February 1952; *Educ* West Buckland Sch, Hertford Coll Oxford (MA), New Coll Edinburgh (BD), Edinburgh Theol Coll; *m* 1985, Cressida, da of Norman Nash; 2 s (Benedict b 1989, Edmund b 1992), 1 da (Esther b 1993); *Career* asst curate The Ascension Kenton 1976–79, precentor St Ninian's Cathedral Perth 1979–82, info offr and communications advsr to the Gen Synod Scottish Episcopal Church 1982–87, Philip Usher Meml scholar Greece 1987–88, vicar St Mary's Battersea 1989–96, princ Ripon Coll Cuddesdon 1997–2004, canon and prebendary Lincoln 2000–2004, dean of Wells 2004–; *Recreations* walking, reading, music; *Style*— The Very Rev the Dean of Wells; ✉ The Dean's Lodgings, 25 The Liberty, Wells, Somerset BA5 2SZ

C

CLARKE, Rear Adm John Patrick; CB (1996), LVO, MBE; s of Frank Clarke (d 1965), and Christine Margaret, *née* Sendell (d 1996); *b* 12 December 1944; *Educ* Epsom Coll, BRNC Dartmouth; *m* 1, 1969 (m dis), Ann, da of Bishop A G Parham; 1 s (b 1971), 2 da (b 1973, b 1977); m 2, 1998, Mrs J J Salt; *Career* Capt HMS Finwhale 1976, Capt HMS Oberon 1977, Capt HMS Dreadnought 1979–81, cmdg offr Submarine COs Qualifying Course 1981–83, Exec Offr HM Yacht Britannia 1985–86, Capt Submarine Sea Trg 1986–89, Capt 7 Frigate Sqdn and HMS Argonaut 1989–90, Asst Dir Naval Staff Duties 1990–91, Dir Naval Warfare 1992, Dir Naval Mgmnt and CIS 1993–94, Flag Offr Trg and Recruiting 1994–96, Hydrographer of the Navy and chief exec UK Hydrographic Office 1996–2001, chief exec Br Marine Fedn 2001–; hon RICS, FBIM; *Recreations* golf, sailing; *Clubs* Lansdowne, Liphook Golf, Royal Yacht Sqdn, RNSA, Yeovil Golf; *Style*— Rear Adm John Clarke, CB, LVO, MBE, FBIM; ✉ BMF, Marine House, Thorpe Lea Road, Egham, Surrey TW20 8BF (tel 01784 223608)

CLARKE, Keith Edward; s of Albert Clarke, and Eileen Clarke; *b* 1940, London; *Educ* Alleyne's GS, Univ of Bradford (BEng), Imperial Coll London (Dip Computing Sci, MPhil); *m* 1965, Barbara; 1 s (Vaughan), 1 da (Julie); *Career* Miny of Technol 1969–70, various research posts rising to dir BT Laboratories 1970–92, sr vice-pres Engrg BT N America San José CA 1992, various dir-level posts on technol strategy for BT plc 1992–2000; BABT: exec dir 2000, conslt 2001–; dir: Cellnet 1989–92, BT (CBP) Ltd 1989–95, Br Approvals Bd for Telecommunications 1992–2000, BABT Inc 2000, Hermont (Hldgs) Ltd 2001–03; memb: DTI Advsy Ctee on Flat Screen Displays Technol 1985–87, Editorial Advsy Bd Telematics and Informatics Jl 1989–98, various IEE ctees incl Standards Policy Ctee 1992–93, EC Parly Gp for Engrg Devpt 1996–2000, Gen Engrg Ctee Royal Acad of Engry 1997–2000, EU ACTS Res Monitoring Panel 1998–99, Bd Fedn of Electronic Industries 1998–2000; chm: Industrial Advsy Bd Univ of Bradford 1992–97, EU High Level Strategy Gp for IT Standards 1998; author of numerous articles in professional jls, sometime lectr various educnl estabs, occasional broadcaster; winner Charles Babbage Premium Instn of Electronic and Radio Engrs 1983; Freeman City of London (memb Guild of Freemen), Freeman Worshipful Co of Engrs, Liveryman Worshipful Co of Info Technologists (sec IT Industry Panel 2003–05); FIEE, FBCS, FIMgt, FREng 1995, FRSA 2003; *Recreations* cruising, theatre-going; *Clubs* Little Ship, City Livery Yacht, Windsor Yacht (past Cdre); *Style*— Keith Clarke, Esq, FREng; ✉ e-mail kclarke@totalonline.net

CLARKE, Rt Hon Kenneth Harry; PC (1984), QC (1980), MP; s of Kenneth Clarke, of Nottingham; *b* 2 July 1940; *Educ* Nottingham HS, Gonville & Caius Coll Cambridge (pres Cambridge Union); *m* 1963, Gillian Mary, da of Bruce Edwards, of Sidcup, Kent; 1 s, 1 da; *Career* called to the Bar Gray's Inn 1963 (bencher 1989); MP (Cons) Rushcliffe 1970–; oppn spokesman: on social servs 1974–76, on industry 1976–79; Parly under sec Dept of Tport 1979–82, min of state (health) DHSS 1982–85, HM paymaster-gen and min for employment 1985–87, chllr of the Duchy of Lancaster and min for trade and industry 1987–88, sec of state for health 1988–90, sec of state for education and science 1990–92, home sec 1992–93, chllr of the Exchequer 1993–97; Cons Pty leadership challenger 1997, 2001 and 2005; chm Cons Pty Democracy Task Force 2005–; dep chm British American Tobacco plc 1998–, dir Independent News and Media (UK) 1999–; *Recreations* modern jazz, bird watching, watching football (Nottingham Forest FC), cricket and motor racing; *Style*— The Rt Hon Kenneth Clarke, QC, MP; ✉ House of Commons, London SW1A 0AA (tel 020 7219 3000)

CLARKE, Prof Kieran; da of Kevin James O'Leary (d 1992), and Barbara Christophers Scott; *b* 15 May 1951, Adelaide, Australia; *Educ* Flinders Univ S Australia (BSc), Univ of Queensland (PhD); *partner* 10 April 1971, Warwick John Clarke; *Career* clinical biochemist Repatriation Gen Hosp S Australia 1974–76, res asst Griffith Univ Queensland and Univ of Queensland 1978–86, lectr in physiology and pharmacology Sch of Sci Griffith Univ 1987, sr res fell in med and tutor in medical physiology Harvard Med Sch USA 1988–89 (visiting fell 1985), adjunct prof Dept of Physiology Univ of Ottawa 1990–92, assoc res offr and gp ldr Biomedical NMR Nat Res Cncl Canada 1990–91; Univ of Oxford: Br Heart Fndn sr research fell 1992, assoc dir Br Heart Fndn Gp 1996, sr departmental teaching assoc Dept of Biochemistry 1996–2003, dir Magnetic Resonance Lab 1998–, Br Heart Fndn princ scienist 2001–, dir Cardiac Metabolism Research Gp Univ Lab of Physiology 2003–, currently prof of physiological biochemistry; memb: Int Soc for Heart Res 1981, Int Soc for Magnetic Resonance in Med 1987 (memb Dynamic NMR Spectroscopy Study Gp), Basic Sci Cncl American Heart Assoc 1987, Br Soc for Cardiovascular Res 1991, Biochemical Soc 1994, Biophysical Soc 1998, Soc for Cardiovascular Magnetic Resonance 1998, Working Gp on Cardiovascular MR European Soc of Cardiology 1999, American Diabetes Assoc 2003; memb: Project Grants Ctee Br Heart Fndn 2002–05, External Advsy Bd NIH Roadmap Interdisciplinary Res Center Washington Univ, Oxford branch Br Heart Fndn; conslt: Argose, Br Technol Gp EMX Biochip Inc/N-vu Ltd, GlaxoSmithKline, A* Star; dir TdeltaS 2005–; holder of various European and US patents; referee for scientific and med jls; grant reviewer for int bodies; numerous res articles in professional jls and book contribs; American Heart Assoc Howard B Sprague fell 1989; *Style*— Prof Kieran Clarke; ✉ Department of Physiology, Anatomy & Genetics, University of Oxford, Parks Road, Oxford OX1 3PT (tel 01865 282248, fax 01865 282272, e-mail kieran.clarke@dpag.ox.ac.uk)

CLARKE, (Victor) Lindsay; s of Victor Metcalfe Clarke (d 1972), of Halifax, W Yorks, and Clara, *née* Bell; *b* 14 August 1939; *Educ* Heath GS Halifax, King's Coll Cambridge (BA); *m* 1, 1961 (m dis 1972), Carolyn Pattinson; 1 da (Madeleine Sara b 1966); m 2, 1980, Phoebe Clare Mackmin, *née* Harris; *Career* novelist; sr master ODA Secdy Sch Ghana 1962–65, lectr Great Yarmouth Coll of Further Educn 1965–67, co-ordinator of Liberal Studies Norwich City Coll 1967–70, co-dir Euro Centre Friends World Coll 1970–79, currently assoc lectr Univ of Wales (writer in residence 1995); memb PEN Int 1989; *Radio Dramas* Cathal of the Woods (1994), A Stone from Heaven (1995); *Books* Sunday Whiteman (1987), The Chymical Wedding (Whitbread award for fiction, 1989), Alice's Masque (1994), Essential Celtic Mythology (1997), Parzival and the Stone from Heaven (2001), The War at Troy (2004), The Return from Troy (2005); *Recreations* life drawing, divination, shooting pool; *Style*— Lindsay Clarke, Esq; ✉ c/o PFD, Drury House, 34–43 Russell Street, London WC2B 5HA (tel 020 7344 1000)

CLARKE, Lorna; da of Lincoln and Norma Gayle; *b* 8 March 1962; *Career* news reporter: Radio Humberside 1986, Metro Radio 1986, BBC Radio Cornwall 1987; prodr: Radio London, Everyman BBC TV 1987, Caribbean Service BBC World Service 1988, GLR 1989; prog dir: Kiss 100 1990–97, EMAP Radio SA 1997–98; BBC: successively ed Music Entertainment, head of mainstream music and head of daytime programming BBC Radio One, currently head BBC Talent; current memb Radio Academy; memb Ctee Shelter; Commercial Radio Programmer of the Year 1996; *Style*— Miss Lorna Clarke; ✉ e-mail lorna.clarke@bbc.co.uk

CLARKE, Prof Malcolm Alistair; s of Kenneth Alfred William Clarke (d 1973), and Marion, *née* Rich (d 1967); *b* 1 April 1943; *Educ* Kingswood Sch Bath, St John's Coll Cambridge (MA, LLB, PhD); *m* 1968, Eva, *née* Nathan; 2 s (Timothy b 1972, Nicholas b 1975); *Career* asst Inst De Droit Comparé Paris 1965–6, res fell Fitzwilliam Coll Cambridge 1966–68, lectr Univ of Singapore 1968–70, fell St John's Coll Cambridge 1970–, lectr Univ of Cambridge 1970–97, reader Univ of Cambridge 1997–99; memb: Br Maritime Law Assoc, Br Insurance Law Assoc; memb Great St Mary's Church Cambridge; *Books* Aspects of the Hague Rules (1976), Shipbuilding Contracts (ed and contrib, 2 edn 1992), Contracts for the Carriage of Goods (contrib, 1993), International Encyclopedia of Comparative Law (contrib, vol 3 1996), Policies and Perceptions of Insurance (1997), The Law of Insurance Contracts (2006), Contracts of Carriage by Air (2002), The International Carriage of Goods by Road: CMR (2003), The Law of Contract, Part 4: Vitiating Factors (contrib, 2003, Butterworths series), Contracts of Carriage by Land and Air (jtly, 2004), Policies and Perceptions of Insurance in the Twenty-First Century (2005); *Recreations* cycling, walking, photography, music; *Style*— Prof Malcolm Clarke; ✉ St John's College, Cambridge CB2 1TP (tel 01223 338600)

CLARKE, Martin Courtenay; s of Douglas Archibald Clarke (d 1992), of London, and Marjorie, *née* Blinkhorn (d 1987); *b* 7 January 1941; *Educ* Winchester, Trinity Coll Cambridge (MA); *m* 5 Sept 1974, Esmee Frances, da of Col J F Cottrell, OBE, MC (d 1972), of Exmouth; *Career* ptnr Deloitte & Touche 1973–96; exec chm Heathcroft Properties plc 1998–2004, chm Norland Nursery Training College Ltd; memb Auditing Practices Ctee Consultative Ctee of Accounting Bodies 1982–88; De Montfort Univ: chm Bd of Govrs 1997–, sr fell, pro-chllr; govr Merchant Taylors' Sch 1991–; chm: City of London Outward Bound Assoc 1999–, Bassishaw Ward Club 1997; churchwarden St Lawrence Jewry next Guildhall; Freeman City of London; Liveryman: Worshipful Co of Merchant Taylors 1970 (memb Ct of Assts 1991, Master 1997), Worshipful Co of Loriners 1983, memb City Livery Ctee 1998–2000; Sheriff of the City of London 2002–03; FCA, FRSA; OStJ; *Recreations* sailing, gardening, skiing, opera, reading; *Clubs* City of London, Royal Yacht Sqdn, Royal Southampton Yacht, City Livery; *Style*— Martin Clarke, Esq; ✉ 91 Bedford Gardens, Kensington, London W8 7EQ

CLARKE, Martin Peter; *b* 26 August 1964; *Educ* Univ of Bristol; *m* Veronica; *Career* various positions with Daily Mail 1986–95, news ed The Mirror 1995; ed: The Scottish Daily Mail 1995–97, The Scotsman 1997–98; ed-in-chief: Scottish Daily Record & Sunday Mail Ltd 1998–2000, Ireland on Sunday 2001–; *Recreations* football, newspapers; *Style*— Martin Clarke, Esq

CLARKE, Mary; da of late Frederick Clarke, and Ethel Kate, *née* Reynolds (d 1984); *b* 23 August 1923; *Educ* Mary Datchelor Girls' Sch; *Career* ed The Dancing Times London 1963–, ballet critic The Guardian 1977–94, ret; author; memb Grand Cncl The Royal Acad of Dance; Queen Elizabeth II Coronation Award Royal Acad of Dancing 1990; tstee: Dance Teachers' Benevolent Fund, Gordon Edwards Charitable Tst; Knight of the Order of Dannebrog 1992; Nijinsky Medal Poland 1995; *Books* The Sadler's Wells Ballet: A History and an Appreciation (1955), Dancers of Mercury: the Story of Ballet Rambert (1962), Design for Ballet (with Clement Crisp, 1978), The History of Dance (with Clement Crisp, 1981), Ballet: an Illustrated History (with Clement Crisp, new edn 1992); contrib to Encyclopedia Britannica (1974), contrib to New Dictionary of National Biography; *Recreations* watching dancing, travel, reading; *Clubs* Gautier; *Style*— Miss Mary Clarke; ✉ 54 Ripplevale Grove, Islington, London N1 1HT; The Dancing Times, 45–47 Clerkenwell Green, London EC1R 0EB (tel 020 7250 3006, fax 020 7253 6679, e-mail marydt@dancing-times.co.uk)

CLARKE, Hon Lord Matthew Gerard; QC (Scot 1989); s of Thomas Clarke (d 1978), and Ann, *née* Duddy (d 1984); *Educ* Holy Cross HS Hamilton, Univ of Glasgow (Francis Hunter scholar, Chartered Inst of Secretaries scholar, Cunninghame bursar, LLB, MA); *Career* admitted slr Scotland 1972, admitted memb Faculty of Advocates 1978; lectr Faculty of Law Univ of Edinburgh 1972, standing jr counsel Scot Home and Health Dept 1983–89, Senator Coll of Justice 2000; pt/t chm Industrial Tbnls 1987–2000; chm Br Cncl's Law and Governance Ctee (Scotland) 2001–; judge Court of Appeals Jersey and Guernsey 1996–2000; memb: Consumer Credit Licensing Appeal Tbnl 1976–2000, Estate Agents Tbnls 1980–2000, UK Delgn Cncl of Euro Bars and Law Socs 1989–99 (ldr 1993–96), Trademarks Appeal Tbnl 1996; hon fell Faculty of Law Univ of Edinburgh 1995–; *Books* The Unfair Contract Terms Act 1977 (1978), Sweet & Maxwell Encyclopaedia of Consumer Law (Scottish ed, 1978–85), Company Law: The European Dimension (contrib, 1991), EC Legal Systems (contrib, 1992), Green's Guide to European Law in Scotland (contrib, 1996), McPhail's Sheriff Court Practice (contrib, 1999), Court of Session Practice (contrib, 2005); *Recreations* travel, opera, chamber music, the music of Schubert; *Style*— The Hon Lord Clarke, QC; ✉ Parliament House, Edinburgh EH1

CLARKE, (Christopher) Michael; s of Patrick Reginald Rudland Clarke, of Helmsley, N Yorks, and Margaret Catherine, *née* Waugh; *b* 29 August 1952; *Educ* Felsted, Univ of Manchester (BA); *m* 1 July 1978, Deborah Clare, da of Paul Wilfred Cowling; 2 s (Oliver Paul b 29 June 1984, Alexander Patrick b 19 April 1986), 1 da (Emily Louisa b 15 Sept 1992); *Career* art asst York Art Gallery 1973–76, res asst Br Museum 1976–78, asst keeper i/c prints Whitworth Art Gallery Univ of Manchester 1978–84; Nat Gallery of Scotland: asst keeper 1984–87, keeper 1987–2000, dir 2001–; visiting fell Paul Mellon Center for Studies in Br Art Yale Univ 1985; FRSA 1996; *Books* The Tempting Prospect: A Social History of English Watercolours (1981), The Arrogant Connoisseur: Richard Payne Knight (co ed with Nicholas Penny, 1982), The Draughtsman's Art: Master Drawings in the Whitworth Art Gallery (1982), Lighting Up The Landscape: French Impressionism And Its Origins (1986), Corot And The Art Of Landscape (1991), Eyewitness Art: Watercolour (1993), Corot, Courbet und die Maler von Barbizon (co ed with Christoph Heilmann and John Sillevis, 1996), The Concise Oxford Dictionary of Art Terms (2001), Monet: The Seine and the Sea (with Richard Thomson, 2003); *Recreations* golf, music; *Style*— Michael Clarke, Esq; ✉ National Gallery of Scotland, The Mound, Edinburgh EH2 2EL (tel 0131 624 6511, fax 0131 220 0917)

CLARKE, Prof Michael Gilbert; CBE (2000), DL (Worcs 2000); s of Canon Reginald Gilbert (Rex) Clarke (d 1993), of Kirkby Lonsdale, Cumbria, and Marjorie Kathleen, *née* Haslegrave (d 1991); *b* 21 May 1944; *Educ* Queen Elizabeth GS Wakefield, Univ of Sussex (BA, MA); *m* 1 July 1967, Angela Mary, da of John Bowen Cook (d 1988), of Easingwold, N Yorks; 2 da (Joanna Mary (Mrs Gavin Hill) b 1970, Lucy Elizabeth (Mrs Mark Mathieson) b 1972), 1 s (Thomas John Kempe b 1980); *Career* teaching asst Univ of Essex 1967–78, lectr and dir of studies in politics Univ of Edinburgh 1969–75, dep dir policy planning Lothian Regnl Cncl 1977–81 (asst dir 1975–77), chief exec Local Govt Trg Bd 1981–90, chief exec The Local Govt Mgmnt Bd 1990–93; Univ of Birmingham: head Sch of Public Policy 1993–98, pro-vice-chllr 1998–, vice-princ 2003–; memb W Midlands Regnl Assembly 1999–; pres: Worcester Civic Soc 1999–, Herefordshire and Worcestershire Community First 2005–; chair: Worcestershire Partnership Bd 2002–, Central Techology Belt 2003–, VisitWorcester 2006–; dir: Birmingham Research Park, Malvern Hills Science Park; memb Gen Synod C of E 1990–93 and 1995–; lay canon Worcester Cathedral 2001–; govr: Queens Coll Birmingham 1996–, Univ Hosp Birmingham 2004–, The King's Sch Worcester 2006–, Univ of Worcester 2007–; FRSA 1992; *Publications* books, academic jls and press contributions on local and national govt; *Recreations* gardening, history, grandchildren; *Clubs* Reform; *Style*— Canon Prof Michael Clarke, CBE, DL; ✉ Millington House, 15 Lansdowne Crescent, Worcester WR3 8JE (tel 01905 617634); University of Birmingham, Birmingham B15 2TT (tel 0121 414 4538, fax 0121 414 4534)

CLARKE, (John) Neil; s of George Philip Clarke (d 1969); *b* 7 August 1934; *Educ* Rugby, King's Coll London (LLB); *m* 1958, Sonia Heather, *née* Beckett; 3 s; *Career* dep chm Charter Consolidated plc 1982–88 (chief exec 1980–88); chm: Johnson Matthey plc 1984–89, Molins plc 1989–91, Genchem Holdings Ltd 1989–2006, British Coal Corporation 1991–97; dir Travis Perkins plc 1990–2002; chm European Sch of Mgmnt 1986–2006; FCA; Chevalier Ordre Nationale du Mérite (France) 2002; *Clubs* MCC, Royal W Norfolk Golf, Addington Golf; *Style*— J Neil Clarke, Esq; ✉ High Willows, 18 Park Avenue, Farnborough Park, Orpington, Kent BR6 8LL (tel 01689 851651); Willow Cottage, Hall Lane, Thornham, Norfolk PE36 6NB

CLARKE, Nicky; OBE (2007); s of William Clarke, of London, and Irene, *née* Lignu; *b* 17 June 1958; *Educ* Archbishop Tenisons GS; *m* Lesley, *née* Gale; 1 s (Harrison b 13 May 1986), 1 da (Tellisa b 25 Oct 1988); *Career* hairdresser; Leonard of Mayfair 1974–76, Stafford and Frieda 1976–80, John Frieda 1980–90, Nicky Clarke 1990–; *Awards* incl: Br Hairdresser of the Year (three times), Session Hairdresser of the Year (twice), Br Hairdresser of the Year (twice), World Master Award Art and Fash Gp USA, Most Newsworthy Hairdresser Worldwide Int Beauty Show NY, Hairdresser of the Year Fellowship of Br Hairdressing, Image of the Year (twice), Golden Scissors Award Fellowship of Br Hairdressing; *Publications* Hair Power (1999); *Recreations* skiing (water and snow), indoor rock climbing, tennis, squash, keep fit, scuba diving; *Style—* Nicky Clarke, Esq, OBE; ✉ 130 Mount Street, Mayfair, London W1K 3NY (tel 020 7491 8334, fax 020 7491 9564, mobile 07979 646253, e-mail vicky@nickyclarke.com)

CLARKE, Oz; *Educ* Canterbury Choir Sch, King's Sch Canterbury, Pembroke Coll Oxford (MA); *Career* wine writer and broadcaster; co-presenter Food & Drink BBC TV; drinks correspondent The Daily Telegraph; *Books* Oz Clarke's Wine Guide, Oz Clarke's New Classic Wines, Oz Clarke's Wine Atlas, Microsoft Wine Guide, Grapes and Wines, Oz Clarke's Pocket Wine Book: 2003; *Recreations* any sport, virtually any music; *Style—* Oz Clarke, Esq; ✉ c/o Limelight, 33 Newman Street, London W1P 3PD (tel 020 7637 2529)

CLARKE, Prof Peter Bernard; s of Peter James Clarke (d 1979), and Anne Elizabeth, *née* Agar (d 2002); *b* 25 October 1940; *Educ* St Mary's Coll Grange-over-Sands, Univ of Oxford (MA), KCL (MPhil, PhD); *m* (sep); 1 s (Andrew David b 1974); *Career* assoc prof of history Univ of Ibadan Nigeria 1974–78, lectr KCL 1978–94, prof of the history and sociology of religion KCL 1994–2003 (prof emeritus 2003–), professorial memb Faculty of Theology Univ of Oxford 2003–; fndr and ed Jl of Contemporary Religion; memb Int Advsy Bd Netherlands Orgn for Scientific Research 2003–05; hon prof Univ of Birmingham 2001; *Publications* Encyclepedia of New Religious Movements (2005), New Religions in Global Perspective (2006); author and ed of over 20 other books and 100 articles on subjects incl Islamic history and society, and African and Asian (particularly Japanese) religions; *Recreations* music, walking, learning about other cultures; *Style—* Prof Peter Clarke; ✉ e-mail peter.clarke@wolfson.oxford.ac.uk

CLARKE, Prof Peter Frederick; s of John William Clarke (d 1987), and Winifred, *née* Hadfield (d 2000); *b* 21 July 1942; *Educ* Eastbourne GS, St John's Coll Cambridge (BA, MA, PhD, LittD); *m* 1, 29 March 1969 (m dis 1990), Dillon, *née* Cheetham; 2 da (Emily Jane, Liberty Lucy (twins) b 4 July 1974); m 2, 20 July 1991, Dr Maria Tippett, FRS (Canada), of Victoria, BC; *Career* reader in modern history UCL 1978–80 (asst lectr then lectr in history 1966–78); Univ of Cambridge: lectr in history 1980–87, fell St John's Coll 1980–2000, tutor St John's Coll 1982–87, reader in modern history 1987–91, prof of modern British history 1991–2004, master Trinity Hall 2000–04; chm: Cambs Area Pty of SDP 1981–82, Editorial Bd Twentieth Century British History 1988–98; hon fell Trinity Hall Cambridge 2005; FBA 1989; *Books* Lancashire and the New Liberalism (1971), Liberals and Social Democrats (1978), The Keynesian Revolution in the Making (1988), A Question of Leadership: from Gladstone to Thatcher (1991, 2 edn 1999 (renamed From Gladstone to Blair)), Hope and Glory: Britain 1900–1990 (1996, 2nd edn, 2004 (renamed Hope and Glory: Britain 1900–2000)), Understanding Decline: perceptions and realities of British economic performance (jt ed, 1997), The Keynesian Revolution and its Economic Consequences (1998), The Cripps Version: The Life of Sir Stafford Cripps (2002), The Last Thousand Days of the British Empire (2007); *Style—* Prof Peter Clarke, FBA; ✉ Brick Cottage, Kettlebaston, Suffolk IP7 7QA; PO Box 100, South Pender Island, British Columbia, Canada V0N 2M0

CLARKE, Peter Lawrence; s of George David Clarke, of Bramshill, Berks, and June, *née* Bray; *b* 28 October 1954, Hitchin, Herts; *Educ* Culford Sch Bury St Edmunds, Queen's Coll Cambridge; *m* 12 June 1993, Prunella, *née* Townsend-Green; 1 da (Tabitha Laura Alice b 21 Jan 1995), 1 s (Barnaby George Oliver b 30 Oct 1996); *Career* admitted slr 1985; Slaughter and May 1985–86, Morgan Grenfell & Co Ltd 1986–88, Citicorp Investment Bank 1988–91, head of M&A Nikko Securities 1991–93; Man Gp plc: head of corporate finance 1993–2000, memb Bd 1997–, gp finance dir 2000–07, dep ceo 2005–07, ceo 2007–; *Recreations* tennis, country sports; *Style—* Peter Clarke, Esq; ✉ Man Group plc, Sugar Quay, Lower Thames Street, London EC3R 6DU

CLARKE, Peter Lovat; JP (1970); s of Harold Clarke (d 1945), of Warrington, and Alice Taylor (d 1992); *Educ* Ellesmere; *m* 1956, Audrey Christine, da of Walter Jonathan Elston, of Cheshire; 3 s (John b 1956, Simon and Timothy (twins) b 1964), 1 da (Denise b 1959); *Career* dir: The Greenalls Group plc (chm Drinks and Leisure Div), The Greenalls Group Pension Trustees Ltd; non-exec dir: Communicado/SPA Group, Quellyn Roberts Ltd; former chm North and Mid-Cheshire TEC Ltd, dir Warrington Community Health Care (NHS) Tst until 1996; Liveryman Worshipful Co of Distillers 1979; CCMI, FCIMA, ACIS; *Recreations* golf, music, reading, swimming; *Clubs* Knutsford Golf, Wine and Spirit Over 40, Punt, Old Codgers, Majority, Walton Investment; *Style—* Peter Clarke, Esq; ✉ Brook House, Cann Lane South, Appleton, Warrington, Cheshire WA4 5NJ (tel 01925 261660)

CLARKE, Peter William; QC (1997); s of Judge Edward Clarke, QC (d 1989), and Dorothy May, *née* Leask (d 1996); *b* 29 May 1950; *Educ* Sherborne, Inns of Court Sch of Law; *m* 9 Sept 1978; Victoria Mary, da of Michael Francis Gilbert, CBE, TD (d 2006); 2 c (Edward Benedict, Jessica Alice); *Career* called to the Bar Lincoln's Inn 1973 (bencher 2003); recorder to the Crown Court 1991– (asst recorder 1987); specialising in criminal law; memb: Criminal Bar Assoc, South Eastern Circuit; *Recreations* losing at tennis to my children, skiing, golf (winner Bar Golf Tournament 1985), photography, enjoying my wife's paintings; *Clubs* Garrick; *Style—* Peter Clarke, Esq, QC; ✉ Queen Elizabeth Building, 3rd Floor, Temple, London EC4Y 9BS (tel 020 7583 5766, fax 020 7583 5156)

CLARKE, Richard Allen; s of Allen Lee Clarke, of London, and Anne Clarke; *b* 19 August 1942; *Educ* Aldenham, The Architectural Assoc Sch (AADipl); *m* 11 May 1968, Mary Mildred Irene, da of Dr James Francis Hanratty, OBE, of London; 2 s (Jason b 1970, Dominic b 1979), 2 da (Antonia b 1973, Louisa b 1976); *Career* architect; ptnr Clifford Tee & Gale 1977– (joined 1974); Freeman City of London 1964; RIBA; *Recreations* shooting, gardening; *Style—* Richard Clarke, Esq; ✉ Clifford Tee & Gale, 5 Eccleston Street, London SW1W 9LY

CLARKE, Richard Ian; s of Sidney Clarke, of Market Harborough, Leics, and Florence Joan, *née* Broadbent (d 1999); *b* 7 September 1955; *m* 1, Oct 1978 (m dis), Anne, *née* Menzies; 1 s (James b 16 Nov 1984); m 2, Nov 1993, Sheenagh Marie, *née* O'Connor; 2 s (Dante b 18 March 1995, Joe b 14 May 1997), 1 da (Eleanor b 16 Nov 2000); *Career* joined Dip Serv 1977, third later second sec Caracas 1978–83, second later first sec FCO 1983–87, first sec Washington 1987–91, asst head of planning staff FCO 1991–93, dep head UN Dept FCO 1993–96, cnsllr and dep head of mission Dublin 1996–98, head of policy planning staff FCO 1998–2000, high cmmr to Tanzania 2001–03; *Recreations* Leicester City FC, reading, Wars of the Roses, American Civil War, crisps, early 20th Century art; *Style—* Richard Clarke, Esq; ✉ c/o Foreign & Commonwealth Office, King Charles Street, London SW1A 2AH

CLARKE, Most Rev Richard Lionel; *see:* Meath and Kildare, Bishop of

CLARKE, Robert Sandifer; s of Robert Arthur Clarke (d 1988), of Abinger Manor, Abinger Common, Surrey, and Agnes Joyce, *née* Coventry (d 1987); *b* 9 May 1934; *Educ* Westminster, ChCh Oxford (MA), Coll of Law; *m* 12 Sept 1964, Cherry June Leslie, da of William Attwood Waudby, of Mombasa, Kenya; 2 da (Vanessa-Jane b 4 Sept 1965, Georgina Ann b 25 Aug 1973), 1 s (Damian Rupert b 4 Jan 1968); *Career* Nat Serv RN 1952; cmmnd RNVR: Midshipman 1952, Sub Lt 1953, Lt RNR 1955, ret 1960; slr 1962, conslt Vizards Tweedie; UK ed Droit Et Affaires France 1968–75; chm: Fedn Field Sports Assocs (UK) of EEC 1978–83, Br Delgn to Int Cncl of Hunting and Conservation of Game UK 1983–90; vice-pres and fell Game Conservancy Fordingbridge; Freeman City of London 1975, Liveryman Worshipful Co of Gunmakers 1975; memb Law Soc 1962; *Recreations* sailing, shooting, skiing, tennis, travel; *Clubs* Turf, Oxford and Cambridge, Shikar, RNSA; *Style—* Robert Clarke, Esq; ✉ Vizards Tweedie, Barnards Inn, 86 Fetter Lane, London EC4A 1AD

CLARKE, Prof Roger Howard; CBE (2005); *b* 22 August 1943; *Educ* King Edward VI Sch Stourbridge, Univ of Birmingham (BSc, MSc), Univ of Westminster (PhD); *m* 15 Oct 1966, Sandra Ann; 1 s, 1 da; *Career* res offr CEGB 1965–77; National Radiological Protection Bd: head of nuclear power assessments 1978–82, Bd sec 1983–87, dir 1987–2003; visiting prof Centre for Environmental Technology ICSTM London 1991–2002, visiting prof in radiation and environmental protection Dept of Physics Univ of Surrey 1993–; chm Int Cmmn on Radiological Protection 1993–2005; memb: CEC Gp of Experts in Basic Safety Standards for Radiation Protection 1987–2003; UK delg to UN Sci Ctee on Effects of Atomic Radiation 1990–2003; US Health Physics Soc William Morgan Award 1994, RSM Ellison-Cliffe Medal 1996, Hanns-Lagendorff Medal, Deutscher Strahlenschutzärtze 2002, medal of the French Assembly 2005; hon vice-pres Instn of Nuclear Engrs 2002, hon fell Soc of Radiological Protection; Hon DUniv Surrey 2004; Hon FRCR; *Publications* Carcinogenesis and Radiation Risk: A Biomathematical Reconnaissance (with W V Mayneord, 1977); author of numerous papers in scientific lit; *Recreations* theatre, gardening, travel; *Style—* Prof Roger Clarke, CBE; ✉ Corner Cottage, Woolton Hill, Newbury, Berkshire RG20 9XJ (tel 01635 253957, e-mail clarke.rogerh@btopenworld.com)

CLARKE, Sally Vanessa; da of Brian Trent Clarke, of Surrey, and Sheila Margaret, *née* Coomber; *b* 6 January 1954; *Educ* Guildford HS, Croydon Tech Coll (Dip Hotel and Catering Ops); *Career* studied and worked in Paris (Cordon Bleu Advanced Cert) 1974–75, asst cook Leiths Good Food Catering Co 1976–77, head teacher and demonstrator Leiths Sch of Food and Wine 1977–79, moved to Los Angeles to work with Michael McCarty and helped set up Michaels Santa Monica 1979, asst cook and asst night mangr Michaels Santa Monica Calif and West Beach Cafe Venice Calif 1980–83; opened: Clarke's in London 1984, & Clarke's 1988, & Clarke's Bread 1989; *Books* Sally Clarke's Book, Recipes from a Restaurant, Shop and Bakery (1999, Glenfiddich Food Book of the Year 2000); *Recreations* cooking, eating, drinking good wine, opera; *Style—* Miss Sally Clarke; ✉ Clarke's, 124 Kensington Church Street, London W8 4BH (tel 020 7221 9225, fax 020 7229 4564, e-mail restaurant@sallyclarke.com)

CLARKE, Simone Louise; da of Alfred Clarke, of Leeds, and Janet, *née* Gibbins; *b* 5 April 1970, Leeds; *Educ* Royal Ballet Sch (Nora Roche Award 1987, Arnold Haskel Award 1987, Markova Bagrit Award 1988, Paul Clarke Award 1988); *partner* Yat-Sen Chang; 1 da (Olivia Lucy b 9 Nov 2002); *Career* ballerina; Birmingham Royal Ballet (formerly Sadlers Wells Royal Ballet) 1988–98 (soloist 1992, sr soloist 1997), English Nat Ballet 1998– (princ dancer 2003); *Style—* Miss Simone Clarke; ✉ c/o English National Ballet, Markova House, 39 Jay Mews, London SW7 2ES

CLARKE, His Hon Judge Stephen Patrick; s of Leslie Clarke (d 1998), and Anne Mary, *née* Jones (d 1981); *b* 23 March 1948; *Educ* Rostrevor Coll Adelaide S Australia, Univ of Hull (LLB); *m* 6 July 1974, Margaret Roberta, da of Robert Millar, of Buckna, Co Antrim, N Ireland; 2 s (Christopher James b 1975, Andrew Paul b 1977); *Career* called to the Bar Inner Temple 1971; memb Wales & Chester Circuit (jr 1988–89), recorder of the Crown Court 1992–95 (asst recorder 1988–92), circuit judge (Wales & Chester Circuit) 1995–, liaison judge for Chester and Vale Royal magistrates; asst Parly boundary cmmr for Wales; memb: Courts Bd for Cheshire, Probation Bd for Chester, Cncl of HM Circuit Judges; *Recreations* golf, cricket, theatre; *Clubs* City (Chester), Upton-by-Chester Golf, Lancs CCC; *Style—* His Hon Judge Stephen Clarke; ✉ Seven Gables, 26A Linksway, Upton, Chester CH2 1EA (tel 01244 380293); The Crown Court, The Castle, Chester CH1 2AN (tel 01244 317606)

CLARKE, Susanna; *b* 1959, Nottingham; *Educ* St Hilda's Coll Oxford; *Career* writer; previously worked in non-fiction publishing incl Gordon Fraser and Quarto; taught English in Turin and Bilbao; ed cookery list Simon and Schuster 1993–2003; *Books* Jonathan Strange and Mr Norrell (2004, Best Novel Hugo Award 2005, World Fantasy Award 2005, shortlisted Whitbread First Novel, shortlisted Guardian First Book Award), The Ladies of Grace Adieu and Other Stories (2006); *Style—* Ms Susanna Clarke

CLARKE, Thomas Sydney (Tom); s of Thomas William Clarke (d 1991), and Evelyn Elizabeth, *née* Hodge (d 1962); *b* 29 April 1939; *Educ* Isleworth GS; *m* 12 Sept 1961, Margaret Jean, da of Archibald Morgan (d 1953); 2 da (Heather b 1964, Donna b 1966), 1 s (Morgan b 1968); *Career* journalist: Hayes Chronicle, Herts Advertiser St Albans, The Chronicle Bulawayo Southern Rhodesia, Daily and Sunday Nation Nairobi Kenya, Daily Express London, Queen Magazine, Evening Standard; sports ed: Evening Standard 1972–74, Daily Mail 1975–86, The Times 1986–93; ed The Sporting Life 1993–98; chm Nat Jt Pitch Cncl 2001–07; memb PCC 1995–98; *Recreations* watching sport (particularly racing), playing golf, touring France; *Clubs* Thorndon Park Golf, Hardelot Golf, Sloane, Lord's Taverners, Army & Navy; *Style—* Tom Clarke, Esq; ✉ The Coach House, Horseman Side, Navestock, Brentwood, Essex CM14 5ST (tel 01277 375386, fax 01277 375387, e-mail tom.clarke@tcom.co.uk)

CLARKE, Rt Hon Thomas (Tom); PC (1997), CBE (1980), JP (Lanark 1972), MP; s of James Clarke, and Mary, *née* Gordon; *b* 10 January 1941; *Educ* Columba HS, Coatbridge and Scottish Coll of Commerce; *Career* former asst dir Scottish Film Cncl; memb Coatbridge Cncl 1964–74, provost Monklands DC 1974–82, pres Convention of Scottish Local Authorities 1978–80 (vice-pres 1976–78); MP (Lab): Coatbridge and Airdrie 1982–83, Monklands W 1983–97, Coatbridge and Chryston 1997–; sponsor Disabled Persons' Act 1986, memb Shadow Cabinet 1992–97; chief oppn spokesman: on Scottish affrs 1992–93, on devpt and co-operation 1993–94, on disabled people's rights 1994–97; min for film and tourism Dept for Culture, Media and Sport 1997–98; govr BFI; *Books* Managing Third World Debt (co-author); *Style—* The Rt Hon Tom Clarke, CBE, MP; ✉ House of Commons, London SW1A 0AA

CLARKE, (George) Timothy Horace De Courquetaine; s of late Denis Horace Hilary Clarke, of Powick, Worcs, and Louise Marie, *née* Schlincker; *b* 20 April 1949; *Educ* Oundle, St John's Coll Cambridge (MA); *m* 2 Sept 1989, Henrietta Barbara, da of Alexander Neilson Strachan Walker, CMG (d 1980); 1 s (Matthew Alexander Henry b 24 April 1994), 1 da (Veronica Julia b 31 July 1996); *Career* admitted slr 1974; ptnr Linklaters 1982–; *Recreations* gardening, reading, France; *Style—* Timothy Clarke, Esq; ✉ Linklaters, One Silk Street, London EC2Y 8HQ (tel 020 7456 2000, fax 020 7456 2222)

CLARKE, Sir (Charles Mansfield) Tobias; 6 Bt (UK 1831), of Dunham Lodge, Norfolk; adopted name Tobias 1962; s of Sir Humphrey Orme Clarke, 5 Bt (d 1973), and Elisabeth, *née* Cook (d 1967); *b* 8 September 1939; *Educ* Eton, ChCh Oxford (MA), Univ of Paris, New York Univ Graduate Business Sch; *m* 1, 1971 (m dis 1979), Charlotte, da of Roderick Walter; m 2, 1984, Teresa Lorraine Aphrodite, da of Somerset Struben de Chair, of St Osyth's Priory, Essex; 2 da (Theodora Roosevelt b 4 Aug 1985, Augusta Elfrida b 25 April 1987), 1 s ((Charles) Lawrence Somerset b 1990); *Heir* s, Lawrence Clarke; *Career* vice pres London Branch of Bankers Tst Co New York 1974–80 (joined 1963); assoc dir Swiss Bank Corp London 1992–94; memb Standing Cncl of the Baronetage 1980– (hon treas 1980–92, vice-chm 1990–92, chm 1993–96, vice-pres 2002–); ed and originator The Baronets' Journal 1987–; tstee Baronets' Tst 1989– (chm 1996–2002); Lord of the Manor of Bibury; *Recreations* accidental happenings, gardening, photography, stimulating conversation; *Clubs* Boodle's, White's, Pratt's, Beefsteak, Pilgrims, Jockey (Paris), The Brook, Racquet and Tennis (NY), MCC; *Style*— Sir Tobias Clarke, Bt; ✉ The Church House, Bibury, Cirencester, Gloucestershire GL7 5NR (tel 01285 740225)

CLARKE, William Oliver; s of late Charles Frederick Orme (Toby) Clarke, of Switzerland, and Silvia Vera, *née* Kaelin; *b* 17 August 1943; *Educ* Gordonstoun, Trinity Coll Dublin (MA), Camberwell Sch of Art (Cert in Archive Preservation); *m* 1981, Elizabeth, da of John William Linnell Ivimy; 3 s (Frederick William Michael b 9 July 1982, Percival John Theodore b 29 Oct 1983, Maximilian Tobias Ivimy b 13 Oct 1986); *Career* Morgan Grenfell & Co Ltd 1968–71, asst conservation offr Oriental Antiquities Dept Br Museum 1974–76, paper conservator Area Museum Serv for SE Eng (AMSSEE) Fitzwilliam Museum 1976–78, paper conservator (head of conservation) Courtauld Inst of Art 1978–; memb Cncl Queen Alexandra's House 1997–; govr Bute House Girls' Prep Sch 1990– (chm 2000); memb Worshipful Co of Mercers (Master 1995–96); memb Inst of Paper Conservation 1976; *Publications* The Spooner Collection of British Watercolours (with Michael Broughton and Joanna Selborne, 2005); *Recreations* country pursuits, painting in watercolours; *Clubs* Boodle's, Hurlingham, Chelsea Arts, Bembridge Sailing; *Style*— W O Clarke, Esq; ✉ 13 Pembridge Gardens, London W2 4EA (tel 020 7229 8518); Courtauld Gallery, Somerset House, Strand, London WC2R 0RN (tel 020 7848 2567, fax 020 7848 2589, e-mail william.clarke@courtauld.ac.uk)

CLARKE OF HAMPSTEAD, Baron (Life Peer UK 1998), of Hampstead in the London Borough of Camden; Anthony James (Tony) Clarke; CBE (1998); *b* 17 April 1932; *Educ* Hampstead, New End & St Dominic's RC Sch Kentish Town, Ruskin Coll Oxford (by correspondence); *Career* Nat Serv Royal Signals 1950–52; Post Office: successively telegraph boy, postman then sorter until 1979; CWU (formerly Union of Post Office Workers): memb Ctee Hampstead 1953–62, branch sec 1962–69, memb District Cncl (London) Ctee 1964–68, memb Exec Ctee London District Cncl 1965–79, district orgnr 1968–70, sec (London all grades) 1972–79 (dep sec 1970–72), memb Exec Cncl 1975, nat ed UPW Jl 1979–82, dep gen-sec 1982–93; Lab Pty: chm 1992–93, memb NEC, chm Int Ctee 1986–93; Cnclr London Borough of Camden 1971–78, Parly candidate Hampstead Feb and Oct 1974; memb: London Trades Cncl 1965–69, TUC Disputes Panel 1972–93, TUC SE Regl Cncl 1974–79; tstee Post Office Pension Funds 1991–97; tstee RAF Museum Hendon 2001–; KStG 1994; *Style*— The Lord Clarke of Hampstead, CBE; ✉ House of Lords, London SW1A 0PW (tel 020 7219 1379)

CLARKSON, Prof Euan Neilson Kerr; s of Dr Alexander Clarkson (d 1946), of Newcastle upon Tyne, and Helen, *née* Griffin (d 1977); *b* 9 May 1937; *Educ* Shrewsbury, Univ of Cambridge (MA, PhD), Univ of Edinburgh (DSc); *m* 31 Aug 1962, Cynthia Margaret, da of Eric Cowie (d 1979), of Kirkbymoorside, N Yorks; 4 s (John Alexander Joseph b 21 Nov 1965, Peter Bruce Mark b 21 Jan 1967, Thomas Hamish Martin b 29 Jan 1971, Matthew Dougal Charles b 10 March 1973); *Career* Nat Serv 1955–57; Univ of Edinburgh: asst lectr 1963–65, lectr 1965–78, dir of studies 1967–73 and 1995–2001, assoc dean Sci Faculty 1978–81, sr lectr 1978–81, reader 1981–98, prof of palaeontology 1998–2002 (currently emeritus prof), ret; author of 110 sci articles in learned jls; memb Edinburgh Geological Soc (pres 1985–87), tstee Natural History Museum 1987–92, pres Palaeontological Assoc 1998–2000; FRSE 1984; *Books* Invertebrate Palaeontology and Evolution (1979, 4 edn 1998), Edinburgh Rock: The Geology of Lothian (jtly, 2006); *Recreations* classical music, fell walking, story writing, history, travel; *Style*— Prof Euan Clarkson, FRSE; ✉ 4 Cluny Place, Edinburgh EH10 4RL (tel 0131 447 2248); School of Geosciences, University of Edinburgh, King's Buildings, West Mains Road, Edinburgh EH9 3JW (tel 0131 650 8514, e-mail euan.clarkson@ed.ac.uk)

CLARKSON, Jeremy Charles Robert; s of Edward Grenville Clarkson, of Doncaster, and Shirley Gabrielle, *née* Ward; *b* 11 April 1960; *Educ* Repton; *m* Frances Catherine, da of Maj Robert H Cain, VC; 2 da (Emily Harriet b 21 July 1994, Katya Helena b 24 Nov 1998), 1 s (Finlo Robert Edward b 14 March 1996); *Career* trainee journalist Rotherham Advertiser 1978–83, fndr Motoring Press Agency 1983; presenter: Top Gear (BBC) 1989–99 and 2002–, Jeremy Clarkson's Motorworld (BBC) 1995 and 1996, Extreme Machines (BBC) 1998, Robot Wars (BBC), Clarkson (BBC) 1998, 1999 and 2000, Clarkson's Car Years (BBC) 2000, Speed (BBC) 2001, Meet The Neighbours (BBC) 2002, Great Britons: Brunel (BBC) 2003, For Valour (BBC) 2003; fndr BBC Top Gear Magazine 1993; columnist: The Sunday Times 1993–, The Sun 1995–; *Style*— Jeremy Clarkson, Esq

CLARKSON, Prof (Peter) John; s of Alan Geoffrey Clarkson, and Monica Ruth, *née* Lightborne; *b* 11 November 1961, Oswestry, Salop; *Educ* Trinity Hall Cambridge (BA, Rex Moir Prize, Baker Prize, Charles Lamb Prize, PhD); *m* 13 Aug 1988, Mary Susan Joan, *née* Moore; 2 da (Alice Mary b 6 June 1989, Hannah Miriam b 13 June 1991), 2 s (David John b 19 Oct 1994, Patrick Edward b 1 Jan 2001); *Career* gp ldr PA Consulting Gp 1988–95; Univ of Cambridge: lectr in engrg design 1995–2001, dir Cambridge Engrg Design Centre 1997–, reader in engrg design 2001–04, prof of engrg design 2004–; fell Trinity Hall Cambridge 1995–; Pres's Medal Ergonomics Soc 2005; memb: Design Soc 2001, ASME 2002; FIET 2004; *Books* Countering Design Exclusion: An Introduction to Inclusive Design (jtly, 2003), Inclusive Design: Design for the Whole Population (jt ed, 2003), Design Process Improvement: A Review of Current Practice (jt ed, 2005); *Recreations* music; *Style*— Prof P John Clarkson; ✉ Department of Engineering, University of Cambridge, Trumpington Street, Cambridge CB2 1PZ (tel 01223 748246, fax 01223 332662, e-mail pjc10@eng.cam.ac.uk)

CLARKSON, Patrick Robert James; QC (1991); s of Cdr Robert Anthony Clarkson, LVO, of Crudwell House, Wiltshire, and Sheila Clarissa, *née* Neale; *b* 1 August 1949; *Educ* Winchester; *m* 26 July 1975, Bridget Cecilia Doyne, da of Col Robert Harry Doyne (d 1965), of Barrow Court, Galhampton, Somerset; 2 s (Benjamin Robin b 1978, William Patrick b 1985), 1 da (Georgia Emily b 1980); *Career* called to the Bar Lincoln's Inn 1972, recorder of the Crown Court 1996; memb Hon Soc of Lincoln's Inn and Inner Temple; *Recreations* cutting grass; *Clubs* Boodle's, MCC; *Style*— Patrick Clarkson, Esq, QC; ✉ Landmark Chambers, 180 Fleet Street, London EC4A 2H6 (tel 020 7430 1221)

CLARKSON, Dr Peter David; s of Maurice Roland Clarkson (d 1992), and Jessie *née* Baker; *b* 19 June 1945; *Educ* Epsom Coll, Univ of Durham (BSc), Univ of Birmingham (PhD); *m* 1974, Rita Margaret, *née* Skinner; 1 da; *Career* geologist with British Antarctic Survey 1967–89: wintered in Halley Bay Antarctica 1968 and 1969, base cdr 1969, Antarctic field seasons in Shackleton Range (ldr 3 times) 1968–78, in S Shetland Islands 1974–75, ldr in Antarctic Peninsula 1985–86; exec sec Scientific Ctee on Antarctic Research 1989–; articles on Antarctic geology; UK advsr to PROANTAR Brazil 1982; hon sec Trans-Antarctic Assoc 1980–95 (tstee 1995–); Polar Medal 1976, FGS 1980; *Publications* Natural Wonders of the World (with J Baxter, E Cruwys and B Riffenburgh, 1995), Volcanoes (2000); *Recreations* walking, woodworking, photography, music, all matters Antarctic; *Clubs* Antarctic; *Style*— Dr Peter Clarkson; ✉ Scientific Committee on Antarctic Research, Scott Polar Research Institute, Lensfield Road, Cambridge CB2 1ER (tel 01223 362061, fax 01223 336550, e-mail pdc3@cam.ac.uk)

CLARRICOATS, Prof Peter John Bell; CBE (1996); s of John Clarricoats, OBE (d 1969), of London, and Alice Cecilia, *née* Bell (d 1982); *b* 6 April 1932; *Educ* Minchenden GS, Imperial Coll London (BSc, PhD, DSc); *m* 1, 6 Aug 1955 (m dis 1963), (Mary) Gillian Stephenson, da of George Gerald Hall (d 1971), of Leeds; 1 s (Michael b 1960), 1 da (Alison b 1962); m 2, 19 Oct 1968, Phyllis Joan, da of Reginald Blackburn Lloyd (d 1989), of Newton Abbot; 2 da (Angela b 1969, Caroline b 1969); *Career* scientific staff GEC 1953–59; lectr: Queen's Univ of Belfast 1959–62, Univ of Sheffield 1962–63; prof Univ of Leeds 1963–67; Queen Mary Univ of London 1968–: dean of engrg 1977–80, head of electronic engrg 1979–96, govr 1976–79 and 1987–90; chm: IEE Electronics Div 1979, Br Nat Ctee for Radio Sci 1985–89, numerous conferences on microwaves and antenna; distinguished lectr IEEE Antenna and Propagation Soc 1986–88; Coopers Hill Meml Prize (IEE) 1964, Measurement Prize (IEE) 1989, JJ Thomson Medal (IEE) 1989, European Microwave Prize 1989, Millennium Medal (IEEE) 2000, Distinguished Achievement Award (IEEE) 2001, European Microwave Medal 2005; Hon DSc: Univ of Kent 1993, Aston Univ 1995; vice-pres: IEE 1989 (hon fell 1993), International Union of Radio Science 1993; FInstP 1964, FIEE 1968, FIEEE 1968, FCGI 1980, FREng 1983, FRS 1990; *Books* Microwave Ferrites (1960), Corrugated Horns for Microwave Antennas (1984), Microwave Horns and Feeds (1994); *Recreations* classical music; *Style*— Prof Peter Clarricoats, CBE, FRS, FREng; ✉ The Red House, Grange Meadows, Elmswell, Suffolk IP30 9GE (tel 01359 240585, fax 01359 242 665); Department of Electronic Engineering, Queen Mary, University of London, Mile End Road, London E1 4NS (tel 020 7882 5330, fax 020 7882 7997, e-mail p.j.b.clarricoats@elec.qmul.ac.uk)

CLARY, Prof David Charles; s of Cecil Raymond Clary (d 1979), and Mary Mildred, *née* Hill; *b* 14 January 1953; *Educ* Colchester Royal GS, Univ of Sussex (BSc), CCC Cambridge (PhD), Magdalene Coll Cambridge (ScD); *m* 1975, Heather Ann, da of Trevor Vinson; 3 s (James b 1979, Simon b 1981, Nicholas b 1984); *Career* IBM World-Trade postdoctoral fell San José 1977–78, postdoctoral fell Univ of Manchester 1978–80, res lectr in chemistry UMIST 1980–83; Dept of Chemistry Univ of Cambridge: demonstrator 1983–87, lectr 1987–93, reader in theoretical chemistry 1993–96; Magdalene Coll Cambridge: fell 1983–96, dir of studies in natural scis 1988–96, sr tutor 1989–93; UCL: prof of chemistry 1996–2002, dir of Centre for Theoretical and Computational Chemistry; Univ of Oxford: head of division of mathematical and physical sciences 2002–05, prof of chemistry 2002–, fell St John's Coll 2002–05, pres Magdalen Coll 2005–; visiting fell: Univ of Colorado, Canterbury Univ NZ, Hebrew Univ Jerusalem, Univ of Sydney, Université de Paris Sud, Univ of Calif Berkeley, National Univ of Singapore; George B Kistiakowsky Lectr Harvard Univ 2002, Kenneth Pitzer lectr Univ of Calif Berkeley 2004; Royal Soc of Chemistry: Meldola Medal 1981, Marlow Medal Faraday Div 1986, Corday-Morgan Medal 1989, Tilden lectr 1998, Prize for Chemical Dynamics 1998, Polanyi Medal 2004; memb Int Acad of Quantum Molecular Scis 1998 (Annual Medal 1989); hon fell Magdalene Coll Cambridge 2005; FRSC 1997 (pres Faraday Div 2005– (vice-pres 1997–2000, memb Cncl 1990–93 and 1994–2001)), FInstP 1997, FRS 1997 (memb Cncl 2003–05), fell APS 2003, foreign hon memb American Acad of Arts and Scis 2003, fell AAAS 2003; FRSA 2005; *Publications* ed Chemical Physics Letters; author of papers in scientific jls on chemical physics and theoretical chemistry; *Recreations* family, football, foreign travel; *Style*— Prof David Clary, FRS; ✉ Magdalen College, Oxford OX1 4AU

CLARY, Julian Peter McDonald; s of Peter John Clary, and Brenda, *née* McDonald; *b* 25 May 1959; *Educ* St Benedict's Sch Ealing, Goldsmiths Coll London (BA); *Career* comedian and entertainer; *Theatre* Bravo in Splendid's (Lyric) 1995; numerous tours and live shows; *Television* shows/appearances for LWT incl: Saturday Night Live, Trick or Treat; for Channel Four incl: Sticky Moments with Julian Clary, Sticky Moments on Tour with Julian Clary, Desperately Seeking Roger, Terry & Julian, Brace Yourself Sydney; for BBC incl: Wogan, Open Air, Paramount City, All Rise for Julian Clary, Brassen Hussies (Screen Two), It's Only TV But I Like It 1999, Who Do You Think You Are? (BBC 1) 2005, National Lottery (BBC 1) 2006, The Underdog Show (BBC 2) 2007; for Sky TV incl: Prickly Heat 1999; *Radio* Big Fun Show (Radio 4), Intimate Contact with Julian Clary (Radio 1), With Great Pleasure (Radio 4), Just a Minute (Radio 4); *Film* Carry on Columbus 1992, Baby Juice Express 2002; *Recordings* Leader of the Pack (10 Records/Virgin) 1988, Wandrin' Star (Wonderdog Records Ltd) 1990; *Video* Julian Clary aka The Joan Collins Fan Club - The Mincing Machine 1989, The Best of Sticky Moments, My Glittering Passage 1993; *Books* My Life with Fanny the Wonder Dog, How to be a Real Man (1992), A Young Man's Passage (2005), Murder Most Fab (2007); *Recreations* housework; *Style*— Julian Clary, Esq; ✉ c/o International Artistes Drama, 4th Floor, 197 High Holborn, London, London WC1V 7BD (tel 020 7025 0600)

CLASPER, Michael; CBE (1995); s of Douglas Clasper (d 1992), and Hilda Clasper; *b* 21 April 1953; *Educ* Bede Sch Sunderland, St John's Coll Cambridge (MA); *m* 6 Sept 1975, Susan Rosemary; 1 da (Jacqueline Sarah b 21 July 1983), 2 s (Matthew Dennis Owen b 16 Jan 1986, Christopher Duncan b 28 Feb 1989); *Career* BR 1974–78; Procter & Gamble Ltd: joined as brand asst 1978, subsequently various posts in advtg then advtg dir 1985–88, gen mangr Holland 1988–91, md UK 1991, md and vice-pres UK 1991–95, regnl vice-pres laundry Europe 1995–98, pres global home care and Europe fabric and home care 1998–99; chief exec BAA plc 2003–06 (dep chief exec 2001–03); non-exec dir ITV plc 2006–; memb Advsy Bd Judge Inst Univ of Cambridge; memb HRH The Prince of Wales' Business and the Environment prog; *Recreations* swimming, cycling, skiing, tennis, golf; *Style*— Michael Clasper, Esq, CBE

CLATWORTHY, Robert Ernest; s of Ernest William Clatworthy (d 1985), of Bridgwater, Somerset, and Gladys, *née* Tugela; *b* 31 January 1928; *Educ* Dr Morgan's GS Bridgwater, W of England Coll of Art, Chelsea Sch of Art, Slade Sch of Fine Art; *m* 1954 (m dis 1966), Pamela, *née* Gordon; 2 s (Benn b 1955, Thomas b 1959), 1 da (Sarah Alexandra b 1957); *Career* Nat Serv head Fine Art Wing E Formation Coll 1949; lectr W of England Coll of Art 1967–71, visiting tutor RCA 1960–72, memb Fine Art Panel Nat Cncl for Dips in Art and Design 1961–72, govr St Martin's Sch of Art 1970–71, head Dept of Fine Art Central Sch of Art and Design 1971–75; works in the collections of: Arts Cncl, Contemporary Art Soc, Tate Gallery, V&A, GLC, Nat Portrait Gallery, Monumental Horse and Rider; RA 1973 (ARA 1968); *Exhibitions* Hanover Gallery, Waddington Galleries, Holland Park Open Air Sculpture, Battersea Park Open Air Sculpture, Br Sculpture in the Sixties Tate Gallery, Br Sculptors Burlington House 1972, Basil Jacobs Fine Art Ltd, Diploma Galleries Burlington House, Photographer's Gallery, Quinton Green Gallery, Keith Chapman Gallery 1988, 1990, 1992, 1994 and 1996, Austin/Desmond Fine Art 1990 and 1998, Thompson's Gallery 2003, Keith Chapman Fine Art 2008; *Recreations* music; *Clubs* Chelsea Arts; *Style*— Robert Clatworthy, Esq, RA; ✉ Moelfre, Cynghordy, Llandovery, Carmarthenshire SA20 0UW (tel 01550 720201, e-mail robertclatworthy@hotmail.com)

CLAUGHTON, John Alan; s of Ronald Kirby Claughton, of Southampton, and Patricia May, *née* Dobell (d 2003); *b* 17 September 1956, Leeds; *Educ* Bradford GS (govrs' scholar), King Edward's Sch Birmingham (fndn scholar, King Edward's scholar), Merton Coll Oxford (postmastership, BA, Cricket blue, capt Oxford Univ CC); *m* 13 April 1993, Alexandra Mary Benbow, *née* Dyer; 3 s (James Ian b 23 March 1994, Thomas Hugh b 24 Jan 1996, Samuel John Benbow b 24 Sept 2000); *Career* professional cricketer Warks CCC 1979–80, corporate finance advsr N M Rothschild & Sons 1980–82, schoolmaster Bradfield Coll 1982–84, Eton Coll 1984–2001 (master i/c cricket 1985–96, house master 1997–2001), headmaster Solihull Sch 2001–05, chief master King Edward's Sch Birmingham 2006–; memb HMC; *Publications* Herodotus and the Persian Wars (2008); *Recreations* travel (to Italy), ballet, classical literature, sport; *Clubs* Warks CCC (chm Cricket Ctee), Lunar Soc; *Style*— John Claughton, Esq; ✉ Vince House, 341 Bristol Road, Edgbaston, Birmingham B5 7SW (tel 0121 472 0652); King Edward's School, Edgbaston Park Road, Birmingham B15 2UA (tel 0121 472 1672, e-mail claughtonj@kes.bham.sch.uk)

CLAVELL-BATE, Michael; s of Frederick Clavell-Bate, and Barbara, *née* Dean; *b* 25 March 1966; *Educ* Fishermore Catholic Sch, Univ of Newcastle upon Tyne (LLB), Chester Coll of Law; *m* 2 Sept 1989, Judith, *née* Sharples; 2 da (Hannah b 25 May 1995, Elia b 25 Jan 1998); *Career* admitted slr 1990; Eversheds: joined 1988, ptnr 1997, currently head of commercial litigation Manchester; memb Cncl Law Soc, pres Manchester Law Soc 2001–02; *Recreations* AC Cobra owner and enthusiast, tennis, northern soul music; *Style*— Michael Clavell-Bate, Esq; ✉ Eversheds, Eversheds House, 70 Great Bridgewater Street, Manchester M1 5ES (tel 0161 831 8000)

CLAXTON, Prof Guy; s of Eric Lennox Claxton (d 1990), and Ruby Mary, *née* Pinnock (d 1997); *b* 20 June 1947, London; *Educ* King's Sch Worcester, Trinity Hall Cambridge (scholar, MA), Magdalen Coll Oxford (DPhil); *Career* lectr in educn: Inst of Educn Univ of London 1974–79, Chelsea Coll London 1979–86; sr lectr in educn KCL 1986–90, founding faculty Schumacher Coll Dartington 1990–93, prof Univ of Bristol 1993–; FBPsS 1986; *Books* Hare Brain, Tortoise Mind (1997), Wise Up (1999), The Wayward Mind (2005); *Style*— Prof Guy Claxton; ✉ University of Bristol Graduate School of Education, 35 Berkeley Square, Bristol BS8 1JA (tel 0117 928 7043, e-mail guy.claxton@bristol.ac.uk)

CLAY, David Nicholas; s of late John Clay, and late Edith Mary Clay; *b* 18 January 1944; *Educ* Ellesmere Coll, KCL (LLB), Liverpool John Moores Univ (LLM); *Career* slr; sr ptnr Dodds Ashcroft Liverpool 1986 (articled clerk 1966), merged with Davies Wallis Foyster 1988; *Style*— David Clay, Esq; ✉ DWF, 5 Castle Street, Liverpool, L2 4XE (tel 0151 907 3000, fax 0151 907 3030, e-mail david.clay@dwf.co.uk)

CLAY, Sir Edward; KCMG (2005, CMG); *b* 21 July 1945; *m* 1969, Anne, *née* Stroud; 3 da; *Career* HM Dip Serv: desk offr N and E African Dept FCO 1968–70, third later second sec (Chancery) Nairobi 1970–72, second later first sec (Chancery) Sofia 1973–75, desk offr Defence Dept FCO 1975–78, first sec (commercial) Budapest 1979–82, area offr later asst Personnel Ops Dept FCO 1982–85, dep high cmmr Nicosia 1985–89, head Personnel Ops Dept subsequently Personnel Mgmnt Dept 1989–93, high cmmr to Uganda 1993–97 (non-resident ambass to Repub of Rwanda 1994–95 and to Repub of Burundi 1994–96), dir Public Servs 1997–99, high cmmr to Cyprus 1999–2001, high cmmr to Kenya 2001–05 (concurrently UK perm rep to the UN Centre for Human Settlements (HABITAT) and to the UN Environment Prog), ret; tstee of charities incl Leonard Cheshire; *Style*— Sir Edward Clay, KCMG

CLAY, John Gerald Robert; s of Eric Clay (d 1983), and Joe Kirby (d 1982); *b* 24 March 1939, London; *Educ* Downside, Trinity Hall Cambridge (exhibitioner, MA), Brunel Univ (MA); *m* 21 June 1969, Catrine, da of Eustace Beresford-Huey; 3 c (Yasmin b 12 Dec 1971, Farida b 10 Aug 1973, Asif b 18 Nov 1975); *Career* asst to dep sec-gen WEU London 1964–66, dir of studies Leith Hill Place 1966–70, head of educn Peper Harow 1970–75, author and Jungian analyst 1982–; memb Br Assoc of Psychotherapists; FRSL 2000; *Publications* Culbertson (1985), Men at Midlife (1989), John Masters - A Regimented Life (1992), R D Laing - A Divided Self (1996), Tales from the Bridge Table (1998), Maconochie's Experiment (2001); *Clubs* Academy; *Style*— John Clay, Esq; ✉ 4A Drayton Court, Drayton Gardens, London SW10 9RQ (tel 020 7244 7705, e-mail johnclay@msn.com)

CLAY, John Peter; s of Harold Peter Clay, FIA (d 1970), and Mary Dansie Clay (d 1974); *b* 26 June 1934; *Educ* St Paul's, The Queen's Coll Oxford (MA); *m* 1972, Jennifer Mary Ellen, da of Dr William Ernest Coutts (d 1992); 3 da (Teresa, Lalage, Xanthe); *Career* investment mangr; Vickers da Costa Ltd: joined 1957, dep chm 1976–81; chm Clay Finlay Ltd 1981–; memb Cncl Stock Exchange 1974–77; fndr and publisher Clay Sanskrit Library; hon fell The Queen's Coll Oxford; *Recreations* flying; *Clubs* City, Queen's; *Style*— John Clay, Esq; ✉ e-mail jclay@clayfinlay.com; website www.claysanskritlibrary.org

CLAY, Lindsey; da of Michael John Clay (d 2000), of Distington, Cumbria, and Patricia Anne, *née* Dunn; *b* 28 November 1965, Workington, Cumbria; *Educ* St Bees Sch Cumbria, Jesus Coll Cambridge (MA); *m* 29 Dec 2000, Matthew White; 2 da (Lydia Esme b 25 July 2000, Xanthe Olivia b 30 Sept 2003); *Career* Clarke Hooper Consulting 1989–92, gp account dir McCann Communications 1992–94, bd account dir McCann Erickson 1994–97; JWT (J Walter Thompson): bd account dir 1997–99, managing ptnr 1999–2001, dir of account mgmnt 2001–06, dep md 2005–06, chief talent offr 2006–; memb: IPA, Exec Ctee WACL; *Style*— Ms Lindsey Clay; ✉ JWT, 1 Knightsbridge Green, London SW1X 7NW (tel 020 7656 7516, e-mail lindsey.clay@jwt.com)

CLAY, Sir Richard Henry; 7 Bt (UK 1841), of Fulwell Lodge, Middlesex; s of Sir Henry Felix Clay, 6 Bt (d 1985), and Phyllis Mary, *née* Paramore (d 1997); *b* 2 June 1940; *Educ* Eton; *m* 14 Sept 1963, Alison Mary, o da of Dr James Gordon Fife (d 1998); 2 da (Virginia Rachel (Mrs Robin P Taylor) b 9 July 1964, Catherine Victoria b 9 June 1971), 3 s (Charles Richard b 18 Dec 1965, Thomas Henry b 28 July 1967, James Felix b 13 April 1969); *Heir* s, Charles Clay; *Career* FCA 1966; *Recreations* sailing; *Style*— Sir Richard Clay, Bt; ✉ The Copse, Shiplate Road, Bleadon BS24 ONX (tel 01934 815203)

CLAYDEN, Dr Graham Stuart; s of Colin Stewart Clayden (d 1985), of Bournemouth, and Amy Joyce, *née* Burrough; *b* 8 January 1947; *Educ* Bournemouth Sch, Univ of London (MD); *m* 15 Aug 1970, Christine, da of Reginald Thomas Steele (d 1980); 1 s (Jonathan Stuart b 1972), 1 da (Anna Francesca b 1974); *Career* sr registrar in paediatrics Hosp for Sick Children Gt Ormond St 1977, sr lectr and hon conslt in paediatrics St Thomas' Hosp 1977–89, reader in paediatrics and hon conslt GKT (formerly UMDS) 1989–; procensor RCP, memb Exec Ctee Royal Coll of Paediatrics and Child Health; founding govr Br Paediatric Computer and Info Gp; FRCP 1984 (MRCP 1972); *Books* Treatment and Prognosis in Paediatrics (1988), Catechism in Paediatrics (1987), Constipation in Childhood (1991), Illustrated Paediatrics (1996); *Recreations* choral singing, bassoon; *Style*— Dr Graham Clayden; ✉ Paediatric Unit, GKT Medical School, Lambeth Palace Road, London SE1 7EH (tel 020 7928 9292, ext 3046)

CLAYDEN, Phillippa; da of Alan John Clayden, of Truro, Cornwall, and Pauline Vivien, *née* Dye; *b* 4 August 1955; *Educ* Creighton Comp, Hackney Stoke Newington Coll of Further Educn, Central Sch of Art & Design (BA), Royal Acad of Art (Post Grad Dip); *Career* artist; study of drawing with Cecil Collins 1977–83, fndr tutor and curator Young Visions: An Extravaganza of Extraordinary Art 1979–, freelance lectr in univs, corporations and art orgns around Britain 1982–, dir of art Islington Arts Factory 1989–, adult painting and life drawing The Sternberg Centre 2005–; *Exhibitions* incl: New Contemporaries 1977, solo show Camden Art Centre 1978, Premiums Show RA Dipl Gallery 1981 and 1982 (winner Landseer prize and Dorothy Morgan prize), RA Summer Show 1982–90 and 2001, solo show Southampton City Art Gallery 1988, Berkeley Square Gallery 1988, Blim Sanat Gallery Istanbul 1995, solo show Boundary Gallery 1993, 1995, 1997 and 2002, Plymouth Museum Gallery 2000–04, Penwith Soc of Artists Cornwall 2005, A Brush with Words (Martins Gallery, Burlington Arcade) 2006; memb: Royal Acad Schs Alumni, Penwith Soc of Artists, Plymouth Soc of Artists; *Recreations* walking, gardening; *Style*— Ms Phillippa Clayden; ✉ 68 Woodland Rise, Muswell Hill, London N10 3UJ (tel 020 8883 7985, mobile 07900 317874, e-mail phillippa-c@hotmail.co.uk)

CLAYDON, Geoffrey Bernard; CB (1990); s of Bernard Claydon (d 1978), and Edith Mary, *née* Lucas (d 1991); *b* 14 September 1930; *Educ* Leeds Modern, King Edward's Birmingham, Univ of Birmingham (LLB); *Career* articled clerk Pinsent & Co Birmingham 1950, slr of the Supreme Court 1954, sr legal asst Treasy Slr's Dept 1965 (legal asst 1959), asst slr DTI 1973, asst Treasy slr 1974, princ asst Treasy slr and legal advsr Dept of Energy 1980–90, review of private legislative procedures Dept of Tport 1990–95; pres Tramway and Light Railway Soc 1996–2001 (chm 1967–93, vice-pres 1993–96), pres Nat Tramway Museum 2005–06 (sec 1958–84, vice-chm 1969–99, vice-pres 1998–2005), chm Consultative Panel for the Preservation of Br Tport Relics 1982–; vice-pres Light Rail Transit Assoc 1968– (chm 1963–68), dir Heritage Railway Assoc 2003– (chm Legal Services Ctee 2002–); memb: Fixed Track Section Confederation of Passenger Transport UK 1995–, Editorial Bd Jl of Energy and Natural Resources Law 1983–90; memb Inst of Tport Admin 1972, MCIT 1997, MILT 1999; *Publications* Halsbury's Laws of England (contrib Tramways, 2000), British Tramway Accidents (ed, 2006); *Recreations* rail transport, travel; *Clubs* RAC; *Style*— Geoffrey Claydon, Esq, CB; ✉ 23 Baron's Keep, London W14 9AT (tel 020 7603 6400, fax 020 7603 6405)

CLAYTON, Adam; s of Brian Clayton, and Josephine (Joe) Clayton; *b* 13 March 1960; *Educ* Castle Park Sch Dalkey, St Columba's Coll Rathfarnham; *Career* bass guitarist and fndr memb U2 1978– (with Bono, The Edge, and Larry Mullen, Jr, *qqv*); first U2 release U23 (EP) 1979; *Albums* Boy 1980, October 1981, War 1983 (entered UK chart at no 1), Under A Blood Red Sky 1983 (live album), The Unforgettable Fire 1984 (entered UK charts at no 1), Wide Awake in America 1985, The Joshua Tree 1987 (entered UK charts at no 1, fastest selling album ever in UK, Album of the Year Grammy Awards 1987), The Joshua Tree Singles 1988, Rattle & Hum 1988 (entered UK charts at no 1), Achtung Baby 1991, Zooropa 1993 (no 1 in 18 countries, Best Alternative Album Grammy Awards 1993), Pop 1997 (no 1), The Best of 1980–1990 1998, All That You Can't Leave Behind 2000 (no 1, Best Rock Album Grammy Awards 2002), The Best of 1990–2000 2002, How To Dismantle An Atomic Bomb 2004 (Album of the Year and Best Rock Album Grammy Awards 2006); *Singles* incl: Fire 1981, New Year's Day (first UK Top Ten hit) 1983, Pride (In the Name of Love) 1984, Unforgettable Fire 1985, With or Without You 1987, I Still Haven't Found What I'm Looking For 1987, Where The Streets Have No Name 1987 (Best Video Grammy Awards 1989), Desire (first UK no 1 single) 1988 (Best Rock Performance Grammy Awards 1989), Angel of Harlem 1988, When Love Comes to Town 1989, All I Want Is You 1989, Night & Day (for AIDS benefit LP Red Hot & Blue) 1990, The Fly (UK no 1) 1991, Stay 1993, Discotheque (UK no 1) 1997, Staring at the Sun 1997, Sweetest Thing 1998, Beautiful Day (UK no 1) 2000 (Record of the Year, Song of the Year and Best Rock Performance by a Duo or Group with Vocal Grammy Awards 2001), Stuck in a Moment You Can't Get Out Of 2001 (Best Song by a Pop Duo or Group Grammy Awards 2002), Elevation 2001 (Best Rock Performance by a Duo or Group with Vocal Grammy Awards 2002), Walk On 2001 (Record of the Year Grammy Awards 2002), Electrical Storm 2002, Vertigo (UK no 1) 2004 (Best Rock Performance by a Duo or Group with Vocal, Best Rock Song and Best Short Form Music Video Grammy Awards 2005), Sometimes You Can't Make It On Your Own (UK no 1) 2005 (Song of the Year, Best Rock Duo or Group Vocal and Best Rock Song Grammy Awards 2006); *Film* Rattle & Hum 1988; *Tours* incl: UK, US, Belgium and Holland 1980, UK, US, Ireland and Europe 1981–83, Aust, NZ and Europe 1984, A Conspiracy of Hope (Amnesty International Tour) 1986, Joshua Tree tour 1987, Rattle & Hum tour 1988, Zoo TV tour (played to 5 million people) 1992–93, Popmart Tour 1997–98, Elevation 2001 tour 2001, Vertigo tour 2005; also appeared at: Live Aid 1985 (Best Live Aid Performance Rolling Stone Readers' Poll 1986), Self Aid Dublin, Smile Jamaica (Dominion Theatre, in aid of hurricane disaster relief) 1988, New Year's Eve concert Dublin (broadcast live to Europe and USSR) 1989; performed at venues incl: Wembley Stadium, Madison Square Garden NY, Longest Day Festival Milton Keynes Bowl, Croke Park Dublin, Sun Devil Stadium AZ; *Awards* Best Band Rolling Stone Readers' Poll 1986 (also jt winner Critics' Poll), Band of the Year Rolling Stone Writers' Poll 1984, Best International Act BPI Awards 1989 and 1990, Best Live Act BPI Awards 1993, Best International Group Brit Awards 2001, Outstanding Contribution to the Music Industry Brit Awards 2001, Outstanding Song Collection Ivor Novello Awards 2003, Golden Globe Award (for Hands that Built America) 2003, Oscar nomination (for Hands that Built America) 2003; *Style*— Adam Clayton, Esq

CLAYTON, Charles; s of late Charles Harry Clayton, of Overstrand, Norfolk, and Elizabeth, *née* Appleyard-Entwisle (d 1999); *b* 27 January 1947; *Educ* The Royal Sch Armagh, Queen Elizabeth GS Middleton, Moseley Hall GS Cheadle, Loughborough Univ (BSc), Westminster Theological Seminary Philadelphia (MA); *m* 17 Oct 1970, Anne, da of late Frank Wharton; 2 da (Rachel Fiona b 2 March 1973, Victoria Elizabeth b 9 Oct 1975); *Career* civil engr City Engineers' Dept Glasgow 1970–72, Scottish area dir The Navigators 1980–84 (area rep 1972–80), sabbatical study USA 1984–86, southern regnl leader The Navigators 1986–89, exec dir World Vision UK 1989–2003, gp chief exec Shaftesbury Housing Gp 2003–04, nat dir World Vision Jerusalem/West Bank/Gaza 2004–; MCMI 1993, FInstD 1995, FRSA 1995; *Recreations* walking, sailing, church activities; *Style*— Charles Clayton, Esq; ✉ c/o World Vision International, PO Box 51399, Jerusalem 91513, Israel (tel +972 2 628 1793, e-mail charles_clayton@wvi.org)

CLAYTON, Sir David Robert; 12 Bt (GB 1732), of Marden Park, Surrey; s of Sir Arthur Harold Clayton, 11 Bt, DSC (d 1985), and his 2 w, Alexandra, *née* Andreevsky; *b* 12 December 1936; *Educ* HMS Conway, Sir John Cass Coll London; *m* 1971, Julia Louise, da of Charles Henry Redfearn (d 1969); 2 s (Robert Philip b 1975, John Richard b 1978); *Heir* s, Robert Clayton; *Career* Capt Merchant Navy; *Recreations* shooting, sailing; *Clubs* Royal Dart Yacht, Penarth Yacht (hon memb); *Style*— Sir David Clayton, Bt; ✉ Rock House, Kingswear, Dartmouth, Devon TQ6 0BX

CLAYTON, John Reginald William; *b* 3 December 1950; *Educ* King Edward VI Camp Hill Sch, Downing Coll Cambridge (MA, Rugby blue); *Career* co sec and gp sr counsel Invensys plc, previously co sec and dir Legal Secretariat Guardian Royal Exchange plc; admitted slr 1976; *Clubs* East India, Hawks' (Cambridge); *Style*— John Clayton, Esq; ✉ Invensys plc, Portland House, London SW1E 5BF (tel 020 7821 3723, e-mail john.clayton@invensys.com)

CLAYTON, Michael Aylwin; s of Aylwin Goff Clayton (d 1995), of Bournemouth, Dorset, and Norah Kathleen Joan, *née* Banfield (d 1978); *b* 20 November 1934; *Educ* Bournemouth GS; *m* 1988, Marilyn Crowhurst, da of Ernest George John Orrin; *Career* journalist, author, broadcaster; news corr BBC radio and TV 1965–73, ed Horse and Hound 1973–94; ed-in-chief 1994–97: Horse and Hound, Country Life, Shooting Times, The Field, Eventing; main bd dir IPC Magazines plc 1994–97; chm: Br Horse Soc 1998–2001, Br Horse Industry Confedn 1999–2004, chm Countryside Alliance Midlands 2005–07; *Recreations* fox hunting; *Style*— Michael Clayton, Esq; ✉ Melville House, Morcott, Rutland LE15 9DY (e-mail maclayton1@aol.com)

CLAYTON, Richard Anthony; QC (2002); s of Dennis Lloyd Clayton (d 1969), of London, and Patricia Estelle, *née* Morris; *b* 25 May 1954; *Educ* Westminster, New Coll Oxford; *m* 1 (m dis 1987); 2 s (Benjamin Daniel, Jack James); *m* 2, 27 April 1994, Anne Bernadette Burns; *Career* called to the Bar Middle Temple 1977; S Islington Law Centre 1980–82, Osler Hoskin & Harcourt Toronto Canada 1983; visiting fell Centre for Public Law Univ of Cambridge 2001–; memb Ctee Legal Action Gp 1985–; *Books* Practise and Procedure at Industrial Tribunals (1986), Civil Actions Against the Police (2 edn, 1992), A Judicial Review Procedure (2 edn, 1996), Police Actions; a practical guide (2 edn, 1996), Law of Human Rights (2000); *Recreations* reading, theatre, cinema, travel; *Style*— Richard Clayton, Esq, QC; ✉ 39 Essex Street, London WC2R 3AT (tel 020 7832 1111, fax 020 7353 3978, e-mail richard.clayton@39essex.com)

CLAYTON, Robert; s of Colin Clayton, and Rose Ann Clayton; *b* 23 July 1970; *Educ* Wintringham Sch Grimsby, Grimsby Coll of Technol (BTEC); *m* 18 Sept 1999, Sara Louise, *née* Wilson; 2 da (Imogen Olive b 8 May 2001, Liberty Molly Clayton b 15 August 2004); *Career* commis chef Menage à Trois Restaurant 1988–89, demi chef Heath Lodge Hotel 1989–90, demi chef Chez Nico 1990–91, head chef Hunstrete House Hotel 1991–97, Priory Hotel Bath 1997–, Merchant Inns plc 2005–; *Awards* finalist Chef of the Year 1994 and 1995, second place Roux Scholarship 1996 (finalist 1994), AA 3 Rosettes 1995 and 1996, Michelin Star 1996 and 1999–; *Recreations* jogging, fly fishing, shooting, watercolours; *Style—* Robert Clayton, Esq; ✉ 4 & 6 Pen Hill Road, Weston, Bath BA1 4ED (tel 01225 311017, e-mail claystarmk1@aol.com)

CLAYTON-SMITH, David Charles; s of late John Anthony Clayton-Smith, of Lichfield, Staffs, and Winifred Mary, *née* Elvy; *b* 5 November 1953; *Educ* Malvern Coll, Kingston Poly (BA), Dip Accounting and Fin; *m* 7 Nov 1987, Katharine Clare, da of Dr Owen Jones; 3 da (Philippa Clare b 11 July 1989, Eleanor Jane b 23 Dec 1990, Joanna Mary b 13 March 1997); *Career* Courage Ltd: joined as grad trainee 1977, dir of mktg (Take Home Trade) 1985–87, md (Take Home Trade) 1987–88, regnl sales dir E Region 1988–89, exec dir sales and mktg 1989–91, exec dir and gen mangr E Trading Region 1991–92, gp exec dir mktg 1992–93; mktg and merchandise dir Do it All Ltd 1993–98, dir of special projects Boots the Chemist (incl co's sponsorship of the Millennium Dome) 1998–99, dir of mktg Boots the Chemist 1999–2000, mktg and merchandise dir Halfords Ltd 2000–03; dir: Handbag.com 1999–, The Foundation 2004–06; dir: Advtg Standards Bd of Fin (ASBOF) 1998–2004, Imagesound plc 2006–, Andrum Ltd 2007–; memb: Exec Ctee Advtg Assoc 1989–90, Retail Ctee Brewers' Soc 1989–90, CBI Mktg Forum 1989–93, Advtg Advsy Ctee ITC; chm Ctee of Advtg Practice CAP 1996–98; memb Nat Cycling Strategy Bd 2002–03; Freeman: Worshipful Co of Brewers 1990, City of London 1992; fell Industry and Parl Tst 1998; memb: Marketing Gp GB, Mktg Soc; FInstD 1991; *Recreations* family, gardening, motor racing; *Style—* David Clayton-Smith, Esq; ✉ Andrum Consulting, New Broad Street House, New Broad Street, London EC2M 1NH (tel 020 7100 9776)

CLAYTON-WELCH, Anthony Roy (Tony); s of Flt Lt Roy Hector Welch, AFC, AE, of Flamstead, Herts, and Barbara Joan, *née* Clayton; *b* 5 September 1942; *Educ* St Albans Abbey Sch, Poly of Central London (DipArch), Carpenters Sch (scholarship); *m* 4 Feb 1967, Kathleen Margaret, da of Henry Samuel Norman, of Wembley Park, Middx; 1 s (Bruno b 20 Oct 1975), 1 da (Sophie b 27 Sept 1977); *Career* architect; TA Offr Trg Corps 1962–64; London ptnr Melich & Welch Florida USA 1970–74, fndn ptnr Renton Welch Partnership 1974–96; appointed church architect Diocesan Advsy Cncl (DAC) 1996–; adjudicator and ctee memb Royal Jubilee Tst and Prince's Tst; awards incl: Carpenters Award 1965, Civic Design Award 1987, 2002, 2003, 2004 and 2005, Educational Award 1988, Environment and Access Awards 1991, Heritage Trust Awards 2001, 2002, 2003, 2004 and 2006; educnl bldg advsr: DfEE, DOW, RBKC; vice-chm Local Bd Sch Govrs St John's Sch Stanmore; RIBA 1966, FInstD 1995; *Books* 3-D Structural Model Analysis of Space Frames (1967), Rationalised Constructions (1970), Herts CC Educational Building - An Appraisal 1942–70 (1986); *Recreations* chess, sub-tropical plant cultivation and landscaping, voice-overs; *Clubs* The Arts, Morton's, RAF, St Stephens; *Style—* Tony Clayton-Welch, Esq, RIBA; ✉ Brousings, The Grove, 23 Warren Lane, Stanmore Common, Middlesex HA7 4LD (tel 020 8954 4625); Tony Welch Associates, Chartered Architects, Grove Studios, Stanmore Common, Middlesex HA7 4LD (tel 020 8385 7624, fax 020 8385 7625, e-mail twa@arcwelch.demon.co.uk)

CLEAL, Adam Anthony; s of Anthony Frederick Graham Cleal (d 1982), of Chelsea, and Yvonne Dallas, *née* Eskell; *b* 10 March 1956; *Educ* Allhallows Sch, Univ of Leeds (LLB); *m* 11 Aug 1984, Noreen, da of George Monger; 2 s (Charles Anthony b 16 Aug 1986, George Hugo b 22 Aug 1992), 1 da (Harriet Catherine b 14 March 1989); *Career* articled clerk 1979–81, slr 1982–91, ptnr Allen & Overy 1991–; Freeman City of London; *Recreations* music, opera, fine wine, running, scuba diving, cycling; *Clubs* Reform, MCC; *Style—* Adam Cleal, Esq; ✉ Allen & Overy, One Bishops Square, London E1 6AO (tel 020 3088 0000, fax 020 3088 0088)

CLEAVE, Brian Elseley; CB (1994), Hon QC (1999); s of Walter Edward Cleave (d 1986), and Hilda Lillian, *née* Newman (d 1974); *b* 3 September 1939; *Educ* Eastbourne Coll (Duke of Devonshire's scholar), Univ of Exeter (LLB, Lloyd Parry prize, Bracton prize), Kansas Univ, Univ of Manchester; *m* 10 Feb 1979, Celia Valentine, da of Maurice Lovel Burton Williams, MBE, and Patricia Cawood Williams; *Career* articled clerk Wilkinson, Howlett & Moorhouse 1963–66, student Coll of Law 1965–66, admitted slr 1966, asst slr Wilkinson, Howlett & Durham 1966–67; Solicitor's Office Inland Revenue: legal asst 1967–72, sr legal asst 1972–78, asst slr 1978–86, princ asst slr 1986–90, slr of Inland Revenue 1990–99; called to the Bar Gray's Inn 1999; sr legal advsr EU-Tacis Taxation Reform Project Moscow Phase 1 2000–02 and Phase 2 2003–05, sr legal advsr EU-Tacis Assistance to Tax Administrator of Ukraine Project Kiev 2006–07; memb Inst for Fiscal Studies; memb Int Fiscal Assoc; FRSA 1995; *Recreations* travel, music, photography, theatre; *Style—* Brian Cleave, Esq, CB, QC; ✉ Gray's Inn Tax Chambers, Third Floor, Gray's Inn Chambers, London WC1R 5JA (tel 020 7262 2642, fax 020 7831 9017)

CLEAVER, Sir Anthony Brian; kt (1992); s of William Brian Cleaver (d 1969), and Dorothea Early Cleaver (d 1989); *b* 10 April 1938; *Educ* Berkhamsted Sch, Trinity Coll Oxford (MA); *m* 1, 1962, Mary Teresa, *née* Cotter (d 1999); 1 s (Paul Anthony b 31 Aug 1972), 1 da (Caroline b 14 Nov 1977); m 2, 2000, Jennifer Guise Lloyd Graham; *Career* IBM United Kingdom Ltd: trainee instr 1962, conslt systems engr 1968, branch mangr 1969; asst to vice-pres (devpt) IBM World Trade Corporation USA 1973–74; IBM UK: dist mangr 1974–76, sales dir 1976–77, divnl dir 1977–80; IBM Europe: gp dir 1980, vice-pres (mktg and servs) 1981–82; IBM UK: gen mangr 1982–86, chief exec 1986–92, chm 1990–94; chm: UK Atomic Energy Authy 1993–96, General Cable plc 1995–98 (non-exec dir 1994–95), AEA Technology plc 1996–99 (non-exec chm 1999–2001), The Strategic Partnership Ltd 1996–2000, MRC 1998–2006, The Baxi Partnership Ltd 1999–2000, IX Europe plc 1999–, SThree 2000–, UK eUniversities Worldwide Ltd 2001–04, Working Links (Employment) Ltd 2003–, Nuclear Decommissioning Authy 2004–07; non-exec dir: General Accident Fire and Life Assurance Corporation plc 1988–98, Smith & Nephew plc 1993–2002, The Cable Corporation 1995–97, Lockheed Martin Tactical Systems UK Ltd 1995–99, Lockheed Martin UK Ltd 1999–; dir Nat Computing Centre 1977–80; memb Univ of Oxford Devpt Prog Advsy Bd 1999–; memb Cncl: Templeton Coll Oxford 1982–93, Policy Studies Inst 1985–89, RIPA 1986–89; memb Bd: Centre for Econ & Environmental Devpt 1985–98 (dep chm 1989–98), Assoc for Business Sponsorship of the Arts 1986–98, American C of C 1987–90, ENO 1988–2000 (dep chm 1998–2000), Royal Coll of Music 1998–2007 (chm 1999–2007); chm Business in the Environment 1989–99, dep chm Business in the Community 1992–2000 (memb Pres's Ctee 1986–92); memb: BOTB 1988–91, Presidents' Ctee CBI 1988–92, Nat Trg Task Force 1989–92, ACBE 1991–93, NACETT 1994–98, Ctee on Standards in Public Life 1997–2003, Govt Panel for Sustainable Devpt 1998–2000, Singapore Br Business Cncl 1999–2000 and 2003–04; chm: RSA Inquiry into Tomorrow's Company 1992–95, Industrial Devpt Advsy Bd 1993–99, Independent Assessors of TECs 1994–98, Cncl for Excellence in Mgmnt and Leadership 2000–02, Asia Pacific Advsrs (Trade Ptnrs UK) 2000–03; pres: Classical Assoc 1995–96, Involvement and Participation Assoc 1997–2002, Inst of Mgmnt 1999–2000, Business Commitment to the Environment 2000–; chm of govrs Birkbeck Coll London 1989–98; UN Environment Prog Global 500 Roll of Honour 1989; Hon LLD: Univ of Nottingham 1991, Univ of Portsmouth 1996, Univ of Hull 2002; Hon DSc: Cranfield Univ 1995, Univ of Hull 2002, City Univ 2002; Hon DTech London Met Univ 2003, Hon DUniv Middlesex Univ 2003; hon fell Trinity Coll Oxford 1989, hon fell Birkbeck Coll London 1999, fell City and Guilds Inst 2004, hon fell Univ of Central Lancs 2007; FBCS 1976, FCIM (currently vice-pres), Hon FCIPS 1996; *Recreations* music, opera, cricket, golf, skiing, reading; *Clubs* RAC, MCC, Lord's Taverners, Serpentine Swimmers; *Style—* Sir Anthony Cleaver

CLEESE, John Marwood; s of Reginald Cleese (né Cheese), and Muriel Cleese; *b* 27 October 1939; *Educ* Downing Coll Cambridge (MA); *m* 1, 1968 (m dis 1978), Connie Booth; 1 da (Cynthia); m 2, 1981 (m dis 1990), Barbara Trentham; 1 da (Camilla); m 3, 1992, Alyce Faye Eichelberger, *qv*, formerly w of David Eichelberger; 2 step s; *Career* comedian, writer and actor; started making jokes professionally 1963, started on British TV 1966; fndr and former dir Video Arts Ltd; Hon LLD Univ of St Andrews, A D White prof-at-large Cornell Univ 1999–; *Television* series incl: The Frost Report 1966, At Last the 1948 Show 1967, Monty Python's Flying Circus 1969–73, Fawlty Towers 1975, Look at the State We're In! (BBC) 1995, The Human Face 2001; *Films* incl: Interlude 1968, The Magic Christian 1969, And Now For Something Completely Different 1971, Romance with a Double Bass 1974, Monty Python and the Holy Grail 1975, Life of Brian 1979, Privates on Parade 1982, The Meaning of Life 1983, Silverado 1985, Clockwise 1986, A Fish Called Wanda 1988, Erik the Viking, Frankenstein 1993, Jungle Book 1994, The Wind In The Willows 1996, Fierce Creatures 1997, George Of The Jungle 1997, Parting Shots 1998, The Out-of-Towners 1999, The World is Not Enough 1999, Isn't She Great 2000, Harry Potter and the Philosopher's Stone 2001, Rat Race 2001, Die Another Day 2002, Harry Potter and the Chamber of Secrets 2002; *Books* Families and How to Survive Them (with Dr Robin Skynner, 1983), The Golden Skits of Wing Commander Muriel Volestrangler FRHS and Bar (1984), The Complete Fawlty Towers (with Connie Booth, 1989), Life and How to Survive It (with Dr Robin Skynner, 1993), The Human Face (with Brian Bates, 2001); *Recreations* gluttony and sloth; *Style—* John Cleese, Esq; ✉ c/o David Wilkinson Associates, 115 Hazlebury Road, London SW6 2LX (tel 020 7371 5188, fax 020 7371 5161)

C

CLEGG, Jeremy Paul Jermyn; s of Maj Benjamin Beattie Clegg, MC* (d 1993), of Ridgeway, nr Sheffield, and Rosemary Anne, *née* Coles (d 1955); *b* 11 July 1948; *Educ* St Anselms Bakewell, Fettes, Univ of Sussex (BSc); *m* 24 March 1973, Marilyn Anne, da of Edward Towndrow, of Barnet, Herts; 1 da (Anna-Louise b 6 March 1978), 1 s (Oliver b 14 Feb 1980); *Career* Commercial Union 1970–74, Leslie & Godwin 1974–82, MPA Ltd 1982–86; dir: Baring Investment Management (Baring Brothers & Co) 1986–90, Henderson Pension Fund Management (Henderson Administration plc) 1990–95; J P Morgan Fleming Asset Management 1995–2001, dir AIG Global Investment Corp (Europe) Ltd 2001–; *Recreations* golf, tennis, dry flyfishing, photography; *Style—* Jeremy Clegg, Esq; ✉ The Old Cottage, Church Street, Crondall, Farnham, Surrey GU10 5QQ (tel 01252 850229, fax 01252 852032, e-mail j@jbear.co.uk)

CLEGG, Nicholas William Peter (Nick); MP; s of Nicholas P Clegg, and Hermance Eulalie, *née* Van den Wall Bake; *b* 7 January 1967; *Educ* Westminster, Robinson Coll Cambridge (MA), Univ of Minnesota, Coll of Euro Bruges (MA); *m* Sept 2000, Miriam, *née* Gonzalez-Durantez; 2 s; *Career* trainee journalist The Nation magazine NY 1990, conslt GJW Govt Relations London 1992–93, EC official Relations with New Independent States 1994–96, memb EC Cabinet Office of Lord Brittan of Spennithorne 1996–99, MEP (Lib Dem) E Midlands 1999–2004, MP (Lib Dem) Sheffield Hallam 2005–; Lib Dem spokesperson for: FCO 2005–06, home affrs 2006–; David Thomas Prize FT 1993; *Recreations* skiing, theatre; *Style—* Nick Clegg, Esq, MP; ✉ House of Commons, London SW1A 0AA

CLEGG, His Hon Judge Philip Charles; s of Charles Ward, and Patricia Doreen Clegg, of Thornton-Cleveleys, Lancs; *b* 17 October 1942; *Educ* Rossall Sch Fleetwood, Univ of Bristol (LLB, memb Vintage Austin Trans-Africa Expdn 1963); *m* 1, 11 Sept 1965 (m dis 1996), Caroline Frances, da of Oscar Madley Peall; 2 da (Olivia Doreen b 31 March 1967, Madeleine Flora b 28 July 1973), 1 s (Francis Philip Henry Peall b 22 April 1970); m 2, 11 January 1997, Fiona Cameron, da of Bruce Cameron; *Career* called to the Bar Middle Temple 1966; practised in Manchester on Northern Circuit 1966–87, recorder 1980–87, circuit judge (Northern Circuit) 1987–90, circuit judge (SE Circuit) 1990–, resident judge Basildon Combined Court 1996–; memb Sentencing Advsy Panel 2005–; *Recreations* vintage cars and sailing; *Style—* His Hon Judge Clegg; ✉ Basildon Combined Court, The Gore, Basildon, Essex SS14 2EU

CLEGG, Simon Paul; CBE (2006, OBE 2001); s of Peter Vernon Clegg, and Patricia Anne Clegg; *Educ* Stowe, RMA Sandhurst; *Career* army offr RHA 1981–89; dep gen sec BOA 1989–97, chef de mission European Youth Olympic Games (Bath) 1995, chief exec BOA 1997–; non-exec dir: London Olympic Bid Co 2003–05, London Olympic Games Organising Ctee 2005–; mangr Br Biathlon Team 1984–87; Olympic and Olympic Winter Games: team official 1988, dep chef de mission 1992, 1994 and 1996, chef de mission 1998, 2000, 2002, 2004 and 2006; *Recreations* skiing, golf; *Clubs* Cavalry and Guards'; *Style—* Simon Clegg, Esq, CBE; ✉ British Olympic Association, 1 Wandsworth Plain, London SW1B 1EH (tel 020 8871 2677, fax 020 8871 9104)

CLEGG, William; QC (1991); s of Peter Hepworth Clegg, and Sheila, *née* Needham; *b* 5 September 1949; *Educ* St Thomas Moore HS for Boys, Univ of Bristol (LLB); *m* 5 Oct 1974 (m dis 2002), Wendy Doreen, da of George Chard; 1 s (Peter William Christopher), 1 da (Joanna Sheila); *Career* called to the Bar Gray's Inn 1972, in practice SE Circuit, memb SE Circuit Ctee 1990–, recorder of the Crown Court 1992–, head of chambers 1995–, chm Essex Bar Mess 1998–2001; *Recreations* squash, cricket; *Clubs* Sudbury Racquets, Garrick, Our Society, MCC; *Style—* William Clegg, Esq, QC; ✉ 2 Bedford Row, London WC1R 4BU (tel 020 7440 8888, fax 020 7242 1738)

CLEGG LITTLER, Hon Mrs (Sarah Victoria); known as Sarah Long; da of 4 Viscount Long; *b* 1958; *m* 19 May 1990, George G Clegg Littler, *qv*, er s of George Clegg Littler, and Mrs Frithjof Meidell-Andersen; 1 s (Alexander George Richard b 17 Jan 1996), 1 da (Xenia Charlotte Marina b 15 April 1999); *Career* gallery owner and art conslt; dir Long & Ryle Ltd; *Recreations* gardening, reading, music, visiting galleries and museums; *Clubs* Chelsea Arts; *Style—* Sarah Long; ✉ Long & Ryle, 4 John Islip Street, London SW1P 4PX (tel 020 7834 1434)

CLEGG LITTLER, George Gordon Vysokovsky; s of late George Clegg Littler, OBE, TD, of Ibiza, Spain, and Barbara Noble Meidell-Andersen, *née* Gordon, of Bergen, Norway; *b* 1 May 1950; *Educ* Bradfield, Coll of Law; *m* 1, 25 April 1981 (m dis 1986), Emma, da of Sir John Greville Stanley Beith, KCMG; m 2, 19 May 1990, Hon Sarah, *qv*, da of Viscount Long; 1 s (Alexander George Richard b 17 Jan 1996), 1 da (Xenia Charlotte Marina b 15 April 1999); *Career* slr; ptnr Simmons & Simmons 1985– (joined 1981); memb Law Soc; *Recreations* contemporary art, association football, my garden; *Clubs* Brooks's; *Style—* George Littler, Esq; ✉ 20 Oakley Gardens, London SW3 5QG (tel 020 7352 3555)

CLEGHORN, Bruce Elliot; CMG (2001); *b* 19 November 1946; *Educ* Sutton Valence, St John's Coll Cambridge; *m* 1976, Sally Ann, *née* Robinson; 3 s; *Career* diplomat; entered HM Dip Serv 1974, first sec UK delgn to NATO Brussels 1976, first sec New Delhi 1980–83, cnsllr UK delgn to Conf on Security and Co-operation in Europe Vienna 1987–89, dep head UK delgn to Conf on Conventional Forces in Europe Vienna 1989–92, cnsllr and dep high cmmr Kuala Lumpur 1992–95, head Non-Proliferation Dept FCO 1995–97, min and dep perm rep UK delgn to NATO Brussels 1997–2001, high cmmr to Malaysia 2001–06; *Style—* Bruce Cleghorn, Esq, CMG

CLELAND, Helen Isabel; da of John Douglas Cleland (d 1996), and Hilda Malvina Cleland (d 2006); *b* 3 July 1950; *Educ* King Edward VI HS for Girls Birmingham, Univ of Exeter (BA), Homerton Coll Cambridge (PGCE); *m* 1973, Dr Robin Hoult (d 2001); 1 s (William Ben b 4 Sept 1980), 1 da (Sophie Clare b 3 June 1983); *Career* English teacher Dame Alice Owen's Sch London 1972–76, sr teacher and head of sixth form Haverstock Sch London 1979–86 (English teacher 1976–79), dep head Edmonton Sch 1986–91, headteacher Woodford Co HS 1991–; *Recreations* walking, travel, reading, theatre, gardening; *Style—* Miss Helen Cleland; ✉ Woodford County High School, High Road, Woodford Green, Essex IG8 9LA (tel 020 8504 0611, fax 020 8506 1880)

CLELLAND, David Gordon; MP; s of Archibald (Clem) Clelland, of Gateshead, Tyne & Wear, and Ellen, *née* Butchart; *b* 27 June 1943; *Educ* Kelvin Grove Boys Sch Gateshead, Gateshead and Hebburn Tech Coll; *m* 1, 31 March 1965 (m dis); 2 da (Jillian, Vicki); m 2 Brenda, da of Frank Sumner; *Career* apprentice electrical fitter 1959–64, electrical tester 1964–81; shop steward AEU 1965–79, memb Works Ctee, sec Combine Ctee, sec Health and Safety Ctee; memb Lab Party 1970–, Parly candidate Gateshead W 1983, MP (Lab) Tyne Bridge 1985–; govt whip 1997–2001; Lord Cmmr to HM's Treasy 2001; memb Gateshead Cncl 1972–86 (chm Parks and Recreation Ctee 1976–84, ldr 1984–86); nat sec Assoc of Cncllrs 1981–86; *Recreations* golf, music, reading; *Style*— David Clelland, Esq, MP; ✉ House of Commons, London SW1A 0AA (e-mail davidclellandmp@aol.com)

CLEMENCE, John Alistair; CBE (1996), TD (1972); s of L A Clemence (d 1978), of Bexhill-on-Sea, E Sussex, and Helen, *née* Gillies (d 1982); *b* 17 May 1937; *Educ* Tonbridge, Cutlers' Co Capt Boot scholar; *m* 8 April 1967, Heather May Kerr, da of Canon C J Offer (d 1964), of Ightham, Kent; 3 s (William b 1969, James b 1970, Jonathan b 1973); *Career* Nat Serv Seaforth Highlanders 1956–58, cmmnd 1957; London Scottish Regt TA 1959–67, Regtl Col 1989–95; 51 Highland Volunteers 1967–72, Maj 1970, Dep Hon Col 1 Bn 1989–93, Dep Hon Col The London Regt 1993–95, Hon Col S E London Sector ACF 1999–2006; ptnr BDO Stoy Hayward (and predecessor firms) 1966–2001; conslt to Gilbert Allen Chartered Accountants 2001–; Liveryman Worshipful Co of Skinners 1969; FCA, FInstD, FIMgt, FRSA; *Recreations* gardening; *Style*— J A Clemence, Esq, CBE, TD, FCA; ✉ Bassetts, Mill Lane, Hildenborough, Kent TN11 9LX (tel 01732 833338, fax 01732 834284)

CLEMENCE, Raymond Neal (Ray); MBE; s of William Percy Clemence, and Muriel May, *née* Scott; *b* 5 August 1948; *Educ* Lumley Secdy Modern Skegness; *m* Veronica Mary, da of Donald Gillespie; 2 da (Sarah Jayne b 19 Nov 1973, Julie Maria b 17 Dec 1974), 1 s (Stephen Neal b 31 March 1978); *Career* former professional footballer (goalkeeper), football mangr and currently coach; player: Scunthorpe United 1965–67, Liverpool FC 1967–81, Tottenham Hotspur FC 1981–88; over 1,200 first team appearances in total; hons with Liverpool: 5 League Championships, 3 European Cups, 2 UEFA Cups, 1 FA Cup, 1 League Cup; hons with Tottenham Hotspur: 1 FA Cup, 1 UEFA Cup; 61 full caps (4 under-23 caps); first team coach Tottenham Hotspur until 1993, mangr Barnet FC 1994–96, memb England coaching staff (goalkeeping) 1996–; *Recreations* golf, badminton; *Style*— Ray Clemence, Esq, MBE; ✉ The Football Association, 25 Soho Square, London

CLEMENS, Prof Michael J (Mike); s of Thomas Truscott Clemens, of Camborne, Cornwall, and Doris Edith, *née* Osborne; *b* 25 May 1947; *Educ* Truro Sch, Univ of Bristol (BSc, Albert Fry meml prize for sci), Sch of Biological Scis Univ of Sussex (DPhil); *m* 17 Oct 1970, Virginia Marion, da of late Victor James Pain; *Career* Beit meml research fell Nat Inst for Med Research London 1970–73, research assoc and Fulbright-Hays travel scholar Dept of Biology MIT 1973–74, Royal Soc Mr and Mrs John Jaffé fell Div of Biochemistry Nat Inst for Med Research London 1974–76; St George's Hosp Med Sch: lectr Dept of Biochemistry 1976–78, sr lectr 1978–87, reader 1987–89, prof of biochemistry Div of Biochemistry Dept of Cellular and Molecular Scis 1990–91, prof of biochemistry and immunology 1991–96 and 1997–2007, visiting prof 2007–; research prof in biochemistry Sch of Life Scis Univ of Sussex 2007–; scientific sec MRC Working Pty on Interferon in Cancer Therapy 1975–80; external examiner (2 MB course) Univ of Cambridge 1998–2001, PhD examiner numerous UK univs, assessor Aust Research Cncl; memb Editorial Bd: Int Jl of Biochemistry and Cell Biology 1995–2005, Jl of Interferon and Cytokine Research 1996–; managing ed Euro Jl of Biochemistry 1988–97; Cancer Research Campaign Career Devpt Award 1980–86; chm Brighton Early Music Festival; memb: Biochemical Soc, American Soc for Microbiology, American Assoc for Cancer Research, Int Soc for Interferon and Cytokine Research, Greenpeace, WWF, Sussex Wildlife Tst; *Books* Cytokines (Medical Perspective Series) (eds A P Rea and T Brown, 1991), Protein Phosphorylation in Cell Growth Regulation (ed, 1996); also author of over 130 published scientific papers and review articles in learned jls; *Recreations* performing vocal and instrumental music of the Renaissance and Early Baroque (memb Brighton Consort and E Sussex Bach Choir), photography, gardening, walking; *Style*— Prof Mike Clemens; ✉ School of Life Sciences, University of Sussex, Falmer, Brighton BN1 9QG (tel 01273 678554); e-mail m.clemens@sgul.ac.uk

CLEMENT, Barrie John; s of William George Clement (d 1983), and Amy Enid, *née* Parry (d 1986); *b* 21 September 1947; *Educ* Neath GS S Wales, Aston Univ (BSc), Cardiff Univ (Dip Journalism); *m* Dec 1973, Susan Margaret, da of Alexander James Lane; 3 s (Matthew b 16 Nov 1977, Gareth b 8 Jan 1980, Jonathan b 18 Aug 1984); *Career* Kent Messenger Group 1972–75: gen news reporter then sub-ed Kent Messenger, gen news reporter then sub-ed Kent Evening Post; chief City sub-ed and feature writer Sunday Telegraph 1975–82; The Times 1982–86: dep business features ed, City reporter, labour reporter; freelance journalist Jan-July 1986; The Independent Aug 1986–: labour reporter, labour corr, currently: labour ed, transport ed; memb NUJ; *Recreations* reading, classical music and jazz, rugby, eating hot curries; *Style*— Barrie Clement, Esq; ✉ The Independent, Independent House, 191 Marsh Wall, London E14 9RS (tel 020 7005 2004, fax 020 7005 2047 or 020 7005 2051)

CLEMENT, John; s of Frederick Clement, and Alice Eleanor Clement; *b* 18 May 1932; *Educ* Bishop's Stortford Coll; *m* 1956, Elisabeth Anne, *née* Emery; 1 da (Anne Catherine Bloomfield b 4 June 1957), 2 s (John Emery b 6 April 1959, Richard Frederick b 10 Dec 1965); *Career* Howard Dairies Westcliff on Sea 1949–64, United Dairies London Ltd 1964–69, asst md Rank Leisure Services Ltd 1969–73, chm and chief exec Unigate plc 1976–91; chm: The Littlewoods Organisation plc 1982–90, Culpho Consultants 1991–, Tuddenham Hall Foods 1991–, Anglo American Insurance Co Ltd 1993–94 (dir 1991–94), Ransomes plc 1993–98, King's Coll Cambridge (business expansion scheme) 1993–98, Nat Car Auctions 1995–98, Dresdner RCM Second Endowment Policy Tst plc 1998– (dir 1993–); dir: Eagle Star Holdings 1981–84, NV Verenigde Bedrijven Nutricia 1981–92, Jarvis Hotels Ltd 1994–2004; chm: Children's Liver Disease Fndn 1982–95, Br Liver Tst 1992–99; chm of govrs Framlingham Coll 1991–2001 (govr 1982–2001); High Sheriff Suffolk 2000–01; FIGD 1979; *Recreations* shooting, sailing, bridge, rugby, tennis; *Clubs* Farmers', Cumberland Lawn Tennis, Royal Harwich Yacht; *Style*— John Clement, Esq; ✉ Tuddenham Hall, Tuddenham, Ipswich, Suffolk IP6 9DD (tel 01473 785099, e-mail johnclement@keme.co.uk)

CLEMENT, Dr Michele Ingrid; da of Maj Joseph Cyril Clement (d 1984), and Joyce Mona Clement; *b* 18 September 1951; *Educ* Queenswood Sch, UCL (BSc), UCH (MB BS); *Family* 2 s (Edward Harry Clement Corn b 1983, Charles Joseph Clement Corn b 1985); *Career* med qualifications and house post UCH; jr med posts: King's Coll Hosp 1977–78, UCH 1978–79; dermatology trg: St John's Hosp 1980, King's Coll Hosp 1980–87; conslt dermatologist Bromley Hosps NHS Tst 1987–; FRCP 1994 (MRCP 1978); *Books* Topical Steroids for Skin Disorders (1987); *Style*— Dr Michele Clement; ✉ Dermatology Department, Orpington Hospital, Sevenoaks Road, Orpington, Kent BR6 9JU (tel 01689 865261)

CLEMENT-JONES, Baron (Life Peer UK 1998), of Clapham in the London Borough of Lambeth; Timothy Francis Clement-Jones; CBE (1988); s of Maurice Llewelyn Clement-Jones (d 1988), of Haywards Heath, W Sussex, and Margaret Jean, *née* Hudson; *b* 26 October 1949; *Educ* Haileybury, Trinity Coll Cambridge (MA); *m* 1, 14 June 1973, Dr Vicky Veronica Clement-Jones (d 1987), fndr of Cancer BACUP, da of Teddy Yip, of Hong Kong; m 2, 15 July 1994, Jean Roberta Whiteside; 1 s (Harry Alexander b 1 March 1998); *Career* slr; articled clerk Coward Chance 1972–74, assoc Joynson-Hicks & Co 1974–76, corp lawyer Letraset International Ltd 1976–80, asst head (later head) Legal Servs LWT Ltd 1980–83, legal dir retailing div Grand Met plc 1984–86, gp co sec and legal advsr Kingfisher plc 1986–95; dir Political Context Ltd 1996–99, chm Environmental Context Ltd 1997–; ptnr Independent Corporate Mentoring (ICM) 1996–99, co-chm global govt relations practice DLA Piper (int law firm) 1999–; vice-pres Eurocommerce (Euro Retail Fedn) 1992–95; chm: Assoc of Lib Lawyers 1982–86, Lib Pty 1986–88; Liberal Democrats: chm Fed Fin Ctee 1991–98, dir Euro Election Campaign 1992–94, vice-chm Gen Election Group 1994–97, chm Lib Dem London Mayoral Assembly Campaign 2000 and 2004, federal treas 2005–; House of Lords: Lib Dem spokesman on Health 1998–2004, currently Lib Dem spokesman on culture, media and sport, vice-chm All-Pty Autism Gp 2000–, vice-chm All-Pty China Gp 2005–; chm Crime Concern Advsy Bd 1981–95, chm Lambeth Crime Prevention Tst 2004–; memb Advsy Bd Br American Business Int (BABi); chm of tstees Treehouse (sch and centre of excellence for children with autism) 2000–, tstee Cancer BACUP; memb: Law Soc, RSA; *Recreations* walking, riding, travelling, reading, eating, talking, diving; *Style*— Lord Clement-Jones, CBE; ✉ House of Lords, London SW1A 0PW (tel 020 7219 3660, e-mail clementjonest@parliament.uk)

CLEMENTI, Sir David Cecil; kt (2004); s of Air Vice Marshal Cresswell Montagu Clementi, CB, CBE, and Susan, da of late Sir (Edward) Henry Pelham, KCB; gs of Sir Cecil Clementi, GCMG (d 1947); *b* 25 February 1949; *Educ* Winchester, Univ of Oxford (MA), Harvard Business Sch (MBA); *m* 23 Sept 1972, Sarah Louise (Sally), da of Dr Anthony Beach Cowley; 1 da (Anna b 26 Nov 1976), 1 s (Tom b 17 April 1979); *Career* with Arthur Andersen & Co 1970–73; qualified as CA 1973; Kleinwort Benson Ltd: joined 1975, dir 1981, chief exec 1994–97, vice-chm 1997; dep govr Bank of England 1997–2002, chm Prudential plc 2002–; non-exec dir: Thames Water plc 1997, Rio Tinto plc 2003–, Rio Tinto Ltd 2003–; tstee ROH 2006–; memb Worshipful Co of Mercers; FCA; *Recreations* sailing, ballet; *Clubs* Royal Yacht Sqdn, Royal Ocean Racing; *Style*— Sir David Clementi; ✉ Prudential plc, Laurence Pountney Hill, London EC4R 0HH

CLEMENTS, Judi; *b* 27 June 1953; *Educ* Nelson Tomlinson Sch Wigton, Univ of Birmingham (LLB), Brunel Univ (MA), Inst of Housing (Dip), London Business Sch (Exec Programme Cert), Civil Serv/Cabinet Office (Top Mgmnt Prog); *m* 10 Oct 1998, Rex Hewitt; *Career* London Borough of Camden: estate mangr 1974–76, sr estate mangr 1976–78, sabbatical (masters degree, sponsored) 1978–79, tenancy servs offr and actg dep dist housing offr 1979–81, business systems analyst 1981–82, asst dir of housing (Estate Mgmnt) 1982–87; dep and actg borough housing mangr Brighton BC 1987–91, head of mgmnt practice Local Govt Mgmnt Bd 1991–92, chief exec/nat dir Mind (Nat Assoc for Mental Health) 1992–2001; currently ind conslt and coach; dir Healthcare Nat Trg Org 1998–2000; memb Bd Univ of Brighton 2001–; patron Revolving Doors 2000–; fndr memb Women in Local Govt Network 1987; memb: London Business Sch Alumni, Bd UCL 1998–2001, Bd Mentality 2002–03, UK Grants Ctee Comic Relief 2003–; Dr of Social Sciences (hc) Brunel Univ 1997; FRSA; *Style*— Ms Judi Clements; ✉ Studio One, Limehouse Cut, Morris Road, London E14 6NQ (tel 020 7987 9487, fax 020 7515 2942, e-mail judi@studione.info)

CLEMENTS, Nicholas David Beckwith (Nick); s of Desmond Lyle Clements (d 2000), of Wells, Somerset, and Rosemary Jill, *née* Beckwith; *b* 11 November 1958; *Educ* Rossall Sch, Liverpool John Moores Univ; *m* 7 Sept 1996, Michaela, *née* Rosner; 1 s (Luke Beckwith b 2001); *Career* buyer Transocean Gp 1979–81, media planner/buyer Tony Rowse Media 1981–85, sr account mangr Foote Cone and Belding 1985–87, client servs dir/int business dir S P Lintas 1987–95, int bd account dir Bates Dorland 1995–99, ceo Atlas Advertising Ltd 1999–; tstee CRISIS; MIPA, memb Mktg Soc, memb D&AD; *Recreations* cricket, golf, riding; *Clubs* Buck's, MCC; *Style*— Nick Clements, Esq; ✉ Atlas Advertising Ltd, 10 Welbeck Street, London W2 1LA (tel 020 7467 3140, e-mail nclements@atlasadvertising.co.uk)

CLEMENTS, Paul Michael; s of Stanley Clements, and Edna, *née* Garber; *b* 29 April 1953; *Educ* Haberdashers' Aske's, Univ of Birmingham (LLB); *m* 1, 4 June 1983 (m dis 1995), Pamela Anne, da of Robert David Poulton Hughes; 1 s (Simon Lewis b 11 June 1985); m 2, 1 June 1996 (m dis 1999), Melinda, da of John Pinfold; m 3, 7 May 2005, Elaine, da of George Scribens; *Career* admitted slr 1977; litigation asst Bird & Bird 1977–79; RadcliffesLeBrasseur (and predecessor firms): litigation asst 1979–80, salaried ptnr 1980–84, equity ptnr 1985–2004, head Litigation Dept 1988–89 and 1991–2004, managing ptnr 1989–91, head Commercial Dispute Resolution Dept 2002–04; head of dispute resolution Rooks Rider 2004–; recorder SE Circuit 1997– (asst recorder 1992–97); memb: Law Soc, London Slrs' Litigation Assoc; Liveryman Worshipful Co of Broderers; *Recreations* amateur drama participant, rugby, opera, classical music; *Style*— Paul M Clements, Esq; ✉ Rooks Rider, Challoner House, 19 Clerkenwell Close, London EC1R 0RR

CLEMENTS, Roger Varley; s of Harold William Clements (d 1993), of Harpole, Northants, and Rose Maud, *née* Smith (d 1978); *b* 26 February 1936; *Educ* St Lawrence Coll Ramsgate, CCC Oxford (MA, BM BCh), UCH London; *m* 1, 10 Sept 1959 (m dis 1967), Clemency Mary Holme, da of Thomas Fox; m 2, 1971, Charlotte Susan, da of Maj Charles Robins (d 1995), of Leasowe, Wirral; 1 s (Charles Maxwell b 29 March 1974), 1 da ((Esther) Lucy b 27 Feb 1976); *Career* conslt obstetrician and gynaecologist N Middx Hosp London 1973–94 (clinical dir 1988–91), hon gynaecologist Hammersmith Hosp London and hon lectr in obstetrics and gynaecology Royal Free Hosp Sch of Med London 1990–94, chm Dist Med Advsy Ctee Haringey HA 1988–91, med exec dir N Middx NHS Tst 1991–94; clinical risk mgmnt conslt QRM Health Care Ltd 1994–, ed-in-chief Clinical Risk 1994–; asst prof UK Faculty St George's Med Sch Grenada WI; author of papers on central venous pressure monitoring in obstetrics, infertility, high risk pregnancy, osteomalacia in pregnancy, medical negligence and risk mgmnt; examiner: Central Midwives Bd, Conjoint Bd, RCOG, Univ of London (Royal Free), Univ of Ibadan Nigeria, W African Coll of Surgns, Post Grad Coll of Nigeria; fndr govr Expert Witness Inst; Freeman City of London 1984; Liveryman: Worshipful Soc of Apothecaries 1983, Worshipful Co of Barbers 1986; memb BMA; FRSM, FRCSEd, FRCOG, FAE; *Books* First Baby After 30 (1985), Safe Practice in Obstetrics and Gynaecology: A Medico-Legal Handbook (1994), Medical Evidence (2001), Risk Management and Litigation in Obstetrics and Gynaecology (2001); *Recreations* cricket, opera; *Clubs* MCC, Savile; *Style*— Roger V Clements, Esq; ✉ 111 Harley Street, London W1G 6AW (tel 020 7486 1781 or 020 7637 0701, fax 020 7224 3852, mobile 07702 719923, e-mail roger.clements@dial.pipex.com)

CLEMINSON, Sir James Arnold Stacey; KBE (1990), kt (1982), MC (1945), DL (Norfolk 1983); s of late Arnold Russel Cleminson, JP, himself sometime chm Reckitt and Colman, and Florence, da of James Stacey, of New Zealand; *b* 31 August 1921; *Educ* Rugby; *m* 1950, Helen Juliet Measor; 1 s, 2 da; *Career* served WWII Para Regt; Reckitt and Colman Ltd: joined 1946, dir overseas co 1957, chief exec 1973–80, chm 1977–86; chm Jeyes Hygiene plc 1985–89; vice-chm: Norwich Union Life Insurance Society Ltd 1983–92 (dir 1979–92), Norwich Union Fire Insurance Society Ltd, Scottish Union & National Insurance Co (subsids of Norwich Union Life Insurance); non-exec dir: United Biscuits (Holdings) plc 1982–89, Eastern Counties Newspaper Group 1986–93, Fenners plc 1989–97 (dep chm 1993–97), Riggs National Corp 1991–93, Riggs AP Bank Ltd 1985–2002 (non-exec chm 1986–91); pres Food Mfrs Fedn 1980–82, vice-pres Endeavour Trg 1997– (pres 1984–97); chm: Food and Drink Industries Cncl 1983–84, BOTB 1986–90, Nurses Pay Bd 1986–90; memb CBI Cncl 1978– (pres 1984–86); pro-chllr Univ of Hull 1985–94, chm Theatre Royal Norwich Tst 1991–98; pres Norfolk Branch SSAFA - Forces Help 1994–2000; hon fell RCGP, Hon LLD Univ of Hull 1985; *Recreations* field sports, golf; *Clubs* Norfolk; *Style*— Sir James Cleminson, KBE, MC, DL; ✉ Loddon Hall, Hales, Norfolk NR14 6TB (tel 01508 520717, fax 01508 528557)

CLEMMOW, Richard Gordon Menzies; s of David Clemmow, and Frances Clemmow, of Cambs; *b* 25 June 1955; *Educ* Sevenoaks Sch, Jesus Coll Cambridge (BA); *m* 19 December 1995, Jana Bennett, *qv*, da of late Gordon Bennett; 2 c (Alexandra b 1 August 1991, Skomer b 26 May 1994); *Career* researcher House of Commons 1981–82, offr London Borough of Islington 1982–83; BBC: general trainee 1983–85, with News and Current Affrs Dept (responsibilities incl This Week Next Week, Newsnight, Panorama) 1985–86; with ITN (script writer, chief sub-ed and prog ed Channel 4 News) 1986–92; BBC 1992–2002: dep ed Newsnight, ed daily parly progs, ed Live Budget/Conference coverage, dep head Political Progs Dept, managing ed News Progs Dept, head of News Progs Dept; dir of factual programmes Carlton 2002–; winner of Best Topical Feature RTS Awards 1989; *Recreations* mountain climbing, cycling, cooking; *Style*— Richard Clemmow, Esq

CLEMMOW, Simon Phillip; s of Phillip Charles Clemmow, of Cambridge, and Joan Alicia, *née* Watkins; *b* 30 June 1956, Cambridge; *Educ* Perse Sch Cambridge, Univ of Reading (BA); *m* 1987, Elizabeth Danuta, *née* Kaminska; 1 s (Nicholas Kazik b 1989), 1 step da (Eva Charlotte b 1972); *Career* account planner GGT 1983–88, co-fndr Simons Palmer Denton Clemmow & Johnson 1988 (co sold to Omnicom 1997), exec planning dir TBWA GGT Simons Palmer (later TBWA\London) 1997–99, ceo TBWA\London 1999–2001 (also memb TBWA\Worldwide Bd), co-fndr Clemmow Hornby Inge 2001; *Recreations* books, records, golf, skiing; *Clubs* The Union, Home House, Brocket Hall; *Style*— Simon Clemmow, Esq; ✉ Clemmow Hornby Inge, 7–9 Rathbone Street, London W1T 1LY (tel 020 7462 8500, fax 020 7462 8501, mobile 07764 199666, e-mail simon.clemmow@chiadvertising.com)

CLEOBURY, Nicholas Randall; s of Dr John Frank Cleobury, of Chartham, Kent, and Brenda Julie, *née* Randall; bro of Stephen Cleobury, *qv*; *b* 23 June 1950; *Educ* King's Sch Worcester, Worcester Coll Oxford (MA); *m* 4 Nov 1978, Heather Noelle, da of Noel Kay (d 1981), of Upper Poppleton, York; 1 s (Simon Randall b 23 Oct 1979), 1 da (Sophie Noelle b 12 Dec 1981); *Career* asst organist: Chichester Cathedral 1971–72, Christ Church Oxford 1972–76; chorus master Glyndebourne Opera 1977–79, asst dir BBC Singers 1978–80, princ conductor of opera RAM 1981–87, dir Aquarius 1983–92, artistic dir Cambridge Festival 1992, music dir Broomhill 1990–94; 1980–: int conductor working throughout UK, Europe, Scandinavia, USA, Canada, Australia and Singapore, regular TV and BBC Radio and Prom and Classic FM appearances, numerous commercial recordings; princ guest conductor Gävle Orch (Sweden) 1989–91, princ conductor Britten Sinfonia 1991–2004, guest conductor Zurich Opera House 1992–, music dir Oxford Bach Choir 1998–, artistic advsr Berkshire Choral Festival 2002–, artistic dir Mozar Ways (Canterbury) 2003–07, assoc dir Orchestra of the Swan 2004–, fndr princ conductor Sounds New 2007– (artistic dir 1997–2007); FRCO 1968; Hon RAM 1985; *Recreations* theatre, cricket, reading, walking, food, wine; *Clubs* Savage, Lord's Taverners, MCC; *Style*— Nicholas Cleobury, Esq; ✉ Barcheston House, North Side, Steeple Aston, Oxon OX25 4SE (tel 01869 340439, e-mail nicholascleobury@btinternet.com)

CLEOBURY, Stephen John; s of Dr John Frank Cleobury, of Chartham, Canterbury, and Brenda Julie, *née* Randall; bro of Nicholas Cleobury, *qv*; *b* 31 December 1948; *Educ* King's Sch Worcester, St John's Coll Cambridge (MA, MusB); *Children* 3 da (Suzannah Helen b 1973, Laura Elizabeth b 1976, Olivia Eleanor b 2003); *Career* organist St Matthew's Church Northampton, dir of Music Northampton GS 1971–74, sub-organist Westminster Abbey 1974–78, master of music Westminster Cathedral 1979–82, fell, organist and dir of music King's Coll Cambridge 1982–, conductor Cambridge Univ Musical Soc 1983–, chief conductor BBC Singers 1995–2006 (conductor laureate 2006–); also works in Europe, America and Australasia, regular TV and radio performances; recordings with EMI, Decca Records, Signum, Columns Classics and Collins Classics; pres: Inc Assoc of Organists 1985–87, Cathedral Organists' Assoc 1988–90, Royal Coll of Organists 1990–92 and 2008– (hon sec 1981–90); Hon DMus Anglia Ruskin Univ; memb Advsy Bd Royal Sch of Church Music 1981–2007; memb ISM, FRCO 1968, FRCM; *Recreations* reading; *Style*— Stephen Cleobury, Esq; ✉ King's College, Cambridge CB2 1ST (tel 01223 331224, fax 01223 331890, e-mail choir@kings.cam.ac.uk)

CLEREY, (Christopher) Kevin Nelson; s of Colin Charlton Clerey (d 1996), of Guernsey, CI, and Margaret Elizabeth, *née* Nelson (d 2006); *b* 2 February 1957; *Educ* Sedbergh (Capt running VIII), Bristol Poly; *m* 3 Oct 1981, Amanda Jean, da of Ronald Charles Houslip; 2 s (Duncan Christopher Houslip b 18 May 1983, David Alasdair b 16 Sept 1985), 1 da (Helen Jean Alice b 19 July 1990); *Career* Coopers & Lybrand 1976–77, EDG (Europe) Ltd 1977–78; Credit Suisse Trust Ltd Guernsey: joined 1981, dir 1985–, md 1990–94, chm and ceo 1997–; md: Credit Suisse Trust Switzerland 1994–, Credit Suisse Trust Holdings Ltd 1994–; dir: Credit Suisse Fund Administration 1988–2005, Credit Suisse Trust Ltd IOM 1988–, Credit Suisse Trust Ltd Gibraltar 1991–97, Inreska Insurance 1992–2000, Credit Suisse Trust Ltd Bahamas 1999–, Credit Suisse Trust Singapore 2001–; co sec Guernsey Colour Laboratories 1981–97; sec: Guernsey Branch Inst of Chartered Secs 1981–85, Old Sedberghians Club (CI Branch) 1992–94; FCIS 1983, MInstD 1991, TEP 1998; *Recreations* fell and alpine walking, tennis, video editing, genealogy, skiing; *Clubs* Old Sedberghians; *Style*— Kevin Clerey, Esq; ✉ Bergwiesenstrasse 8, 8123 Ebmatingen, Switzerland (tel and fax 00 41 4 980 5207, e-mail kevin@clerey.com); Credit Suisse Trust, PO Box 122, Helvetia Court, South Esplanade, St Peter Port, Guernsey (tel 01481 719000, fax 01481 715210, e-mail kevin.clerey@credit-suisse.com)

CLERK OF PENICUIK, Sir Robert Maxwell; 11 Bt (NS 1679), of Penicuik, Edinburgh; OBE (1995), DL (1995); s of Sir John Dutton Clerk, 10 Bt, CBE, VRD (d 2002), and Evelyn Elizabeth, *née* Robertson; *b* 3 April 1945; *Educ* Winchester, Univ of London (BSc); *m* 1970, Felicity Faye, yr da of George Collins, of Bampton, Oxon; 1 da (Julia Elizabeth b 1973), 2 s (George Napier b 1975, Edward James b 1986); *Career* ptnr Smiths Gore chartered surveyors; vice-pres Assoc of Salmon Fishery Bds, chm Atlantic Salmon Tst; Brig Queen's Body Guard for Scotland (Royal Co of Archers); FRICS; *Recreations* field sports, landscape gardening, beekeeping; *Clubs* New (Edinburgh); *Style*— Sir Robert M Clerk, Bt, OBE, DL

CLERKE, Sir John Edward Longueville; 12 Bt (E 1660), of Hitcham, Buckinghamshire; s of Francis William Talbot Clerke (ka 1916), s of 11 Bt; suc gf, Sir William Francis Clerke, 11 Bt, 1930; *b* 29 October 1913; *Educ* Eton, Magdalene Coll Cambridge (MA); *m* 1948 (m dis 1986), Mary (d 1999), da of Lt-Col Ivor Reginald Beviss Bond, OBE, MC (d 1967); 2 da (Albinia Jennifer b 1949, Teresa Mary (Mrs M C Waller-Bridge) b 1951), 1 s (Francis Ludlow Longueville b 1953); *Heir* s, Francis Clerke; *Career* Capt Royal Wilts Yeo (TA); FCA 1948, ret; *Recreations* lawn tennis, fishing; *Style*— Sir John Clerke, Bt

CLEUGH, Christopher Joseph (Chris); JP (Wirral 2000–01, Ealing 2002); s of Leslie Major Cleugh, of Crosby, Liverpool, and Frances Mary, *née* Ferguson; *b* 15 May 1952; *Educ* St Mary's Coll Crosby, Univ of Hull (MSc); *m* 29 June 1974, Christina Linda (Tina), da of late Christy Dorman, of Castleknock, Dublin; 2 s (Damien Paul b 18 Nov 1976, Gerard Norman b 23 July 1979), 2 da (Francesca Margaret b 11 April 1978, Carmel Linda b 8 June 1981); *Career* asst sci teacher St Kevin's RC Comp Kirkby 1975–76; St Mary's Coll Crosby: chemistry and maths teacher 1976–86, head of sixth form and dep headmaster 1986–93, actg headmaster 1991; headmaster: St Anselm's Coll Birkenhead 1993–2001, St Benedict's Sch Ealing 2002–; memb: SHA 1989, HMC 1993; dep chm of tstees St Mary's Coll Crosby; memb St Vincent de Paul Soc; BP International Chemicals Prize 1972; *Recreations* cycling, reading, walking; *Style*— Chris Cleugh, Esq; ✉ St Benedict's School, 54 Eaton Rise, Ealing, London W5 2ES (tel 020 8862 2010, fax 020 8862 2007, e-mail ccleugh@stbenedicts.org.uk)

CLEUGH, Grae; s of late John Cleugh, and Marion Cleugh; *Educ* Bellahouston Acad Glasgow (sch capt), Univ of Glasgow (LLB, DipLP), RSAMD (BA); *Career* actor and writer; *Plays* as writer: Eight, Nine, Ten, Out (1998, shortlisted Westminster Prize Soho Theatre 1998), F***ing Games (Royal Court, Most Promising Playwright Olivier Awards 2002) 2001; *Recreations* cinema, theatre, gym; *Style*— Grae Cleugh, Esq; ✉ c/o Dolina Logan, Pat Lovett Associates, 43 Chandos Place, London WC2N 4HS (tel 020 7379 9111)

CLEVERDON, Julia Charity; CVO (2003), CBE (1996); (Mrs John Garnett); da of Douglas Cleverdon (d 1987), of London, and Elinor Nest Lewis (d 2003); *b* 19 April 1950; *Educ* Camden Sch for Girls, Newnham Coll Cambridge (BA); *m* 1, 30 June 1973 (m dis), Martin Ollard; m 2, 3 April 1985, (William) John Poulton Maxwell Garnett, CBE (d 1997), s of Maxwell Garnett (d 1960); 2 da (Charity b 1982, Victoria b 1985); *Career* dir of educn The Industrial Soc 1981–87, chief exec Business in the Community 1992– (md 1988–); dir In Kind Direct; ambass WWF, tstee 300 Gp, chair Teachfirst; fndn govr Camden Sch for Girls, govr Channing Sch; assoc Newnham Coll Roll, memb Ct Henley Mgmnt Coll; *Recreations* gardening, cooking, junk shops; *Style*— Ms Julia C Cleverdon, CVO, CBE; ✉ 8 Alwyne Road, London N1 2HH; Business in the Community, 137 Shepherdess Walk, London N1 7RQ

CLEWS, Michael Graham; s of late Reginald Alan Frederick Clews, of Bristol, and Alwine Annie, *née* Adams; *b* 11 October 1944; *Educ* Kingswood GS, Oxford Sch of Architecture (DipArch); *m* 24 July 1971, Heather Jane, da of late Douglas Charles Sharratt, of Coventry; 2 da (Camilla b 1976, Helena b 1985), 2 s (Charles b 1978, Jonathan b 1983 d 1984); *Career* architect; fndr ptnr Clews Architectural Partnership 1972–; works incl historic buildings: Champneys, Sulgrave Manor Visitors' Centre; conslt to DOE on historic buildings 1984–87 (historic buildings survey Oxfordshire, Warwickshire and Northamptonshire); pilot project for computerisation of historic building records for English Heritage; Oxford diocesian surveyor; architect to Llandaff and Coventry Cathedrals; ARIBA; *Recreations* sailing, golf; *Style*— Michael Clews, Esq

CLIBBORN, John Donovan Nelson dalla Rosa; CMG (1997); s of Donovan Harold Clibborn, CMG (d 1996), and his 1 w Margaret Mercedes Edwige, *née* Nelson (d 1966); *b* 24 November 1941; *Educ* Downside, Oriel Coll Oxford (MA); *m* 11 May 1968, Juliet Elizabeth, da of John Brian Dermer Pagden (d 1980); 2 da (Imogen Margaret Elizabeth b 14 April 1969, Araminta Joan b 29 Jan 1981), 1 s (Benedict John Nelson dalla Rosa b 17 Aug 1971); *Career* HM Dip Serv: FCO 1965–67, third later second sec (devpt aid) Nicosia 1967–69, FCO 1969–72, first sec (economic) Bonn 1972–75, first sec (scientific) UK Rep to Cmmn of EEC Brussels 1975–78, on secondment to Jt Res Centre EEC 1978–81, FCO 1981–88, cnsllr Washington 1988–91, FCO 1991–92, cnsllr Washington 1992–95, FCO 1995–; memb: Soc for the Promotion of Roman Studies 1966, Soc for the Promotion of Hellenic Studies 1967; *Recreations* classical literature and history; *Clubs* Athenaeum; *Style*— John Clibborn, Esq, CMG; ✉ c/o Foreign & Commonwealth Office, King Charles Street, London SW1A 2AH

CLIFF, Prof Andrew David; s of Alfred Cliff (d 1965), and Annabel, *née* McQuade (d 1975); *b* 26 October 1943; *Educ* Grimsby Wintringham Boys' GS, King's Coll London (state scholar, BA), Northwestern Univ Illinois (MA), Univ of Bristol (PhD, DSc 1982); *m* 1964, Margaret, da of Arthur Blyton; 3 s (Ross Andrew b 6 Sept 1966, Michael Peter b 28 July 1968, Timothy Edward b 12 April 1972); *Career* Northwestern Univ: Fulbright scholar, teaching asst in geography 1964–65, head teaching asst in geography 1965–66; lectr in geography Univ of Bristol 1969–72 (research assoc 1968–69), prof of theoretical geography Univ of Cambridge 1997– (univ lectr in geography 1973–91, MA 1973, reader in theoretical geography 1991–97), head of dept 1999–2001, chair Sch of Physical Scis 2001–03, pro-vice-chllr 2004–; Christ's Coll Cambridge: dir of studies and Coll lectr 1973–, fell 1974–; visiting scholar: WHO 1989, 1990, 1994 and 1995, Epidemiology Program Office US Centres for Disease Control and Prevention Atlanta GA 1990, 1991 and 1993; memb Academia Europaea 2002; FSS 1968, FBA 1996, CGeog 2002; *Books* Spatial Autocorrelation (with J K Ord, 1973), Elements of Spatial Structure: A Quantitative Approach (jtly, 1975), Locational Analysis in Human Geography (with P Haggett and A E Frey, Locational Models and Locational Methods both form pts I and II of this book, 1977), Spatial Processes: Models and Applications (with J K Ord, 1981), Spatial Diffusion: An Historical Geography of Epidemics in an Island Community (jtly, 1981), Spatial Components in the Transmission of Epidemic Waves through Island Communities: the spread of Measles in Fiji and the Pacific (with P Haggett, 1985), Spatial Aspects of Influenza Epidemics (with P Haggett and J K Ord, 1986), Atlas of Disease Distributions: Analytic Approaches to Epidemiological Data (with P Haggett, 1988, 2 edn, 1992), London International Atlas of AIDS (with M R Smallman-Raynor and P Haggett, 1992), Measles: an Historical Geography of a Major Human Viral Disease from Global Expansion to Local Retreat, 1840–1990 (with P Haggett and M R Smallman-Raynor, 1993), Diffusing Geography (ed jtly, 1995), Deciphering Epidemics (with P Haggett and M R Smallman-Raynor, 1998), Island Epidemics (with P Haggett and M R Smallman-Raynor, 2000), War Epidemics (with M R Smallman-Rayner, 2004), World Atlas of Epidemic Diseases (with P Haggett and M R Smallman-Rayner, 2004), Poliomyelitis: A World Geography (with M R Smallman-Raynor and P Haggett); also author of numerous related papers; *Recreations* watching Grimsby Town FC, old roses, theatre; *Style*— Prof Andrew Cliff, FBA; ✉ Vice-Chancellor's Office, University of Cambridge, The Old Schools, Trinity Lane, Cambridge CB2 1TN (tel 01223 339655, fax 01223 765693, e-mail adc2@hermes.cam.ac.uk)

CLIFF, HE Ian Cameron; OBE (1991); s of Gerald Shaw Cliff (d 1970), of Wakefield, and Dorothy, *née* Cameron (d 1999); *b* 11 September 1952; *Educ* Hampton GS, Magdalen Coll Oxford; *m* 2 July 1988, Caroline Mary, da of Noel Redman; 1 s (Richard b 27 March 1989), 2 da (Louise b 24 Dec 1993, Julia b 14 May 2001); *Career* history master Dr Challoner's GS Amersham 1975–79; joined FCO 1979, first sec Khartoum 1982–85, FCO 1985–89, first sec UK mission New York 1989–93, dir exports to Middle East DTI 1993–96, dep head of mission Vienna 1996–2001, ambass to Bosnia and Herzegovina 2001–05, ambass to Sudan 2005–07, UK perm rep to Orgn for Security and Co-operation in Europe (OSCE) Vienna 2007–; *Recreations* railways, music, theatre, philately; *Style*— HE Mr Ian Cliff, OBE; ✉ c/o Foreign & Commonwealth Office, King Charles Street, London SW1A 2AH

CLIFFORD, Brian David; s of Lt W D Clifford (d 1978), and Doris Septima, *née* Magnay (d 1997); *b* 15 July 1942; *Educ* Downhills Central Sch London; *m* 1, 5 Nov 1965 (m dis), Jenny Margaret, da of Morgan Goronwy Rees (d 1980); 2 s (Samuel William (Sam), *qv*, b 29 May 1966, Benjamin Luke b 24 Oct 1968); m 2, 22 Oct 1977, Linda Mary, *née* Stearns; *Career* newsroom copy messenger Daily Mirror 1957–59, photographs asst Daily Mirror 1959–60, picture ed Woman's Mirror Magazine 1961–62, dep picture ed Sunday Mirror 1962–65, exec picture ed The Sun 1965–66, night picture ed Daily Mail 1966–67, prodr Yorkshire TV 1968; info advsr EC 1969–73; BBC TV: script writer TV news 1969, stills mangr 1969–73, sales mangr photographs 1973–79, ed picture publicity 1979–86, chief asst Info Div 1986–87, dep head Info Div 1987–88, head of info servs 1988–92, head of corporate promotions 1992–94; assoc dir Creative Audio Visual 1994, md Creative Corporate Communications 1995–; corp affrs advsr: CAB 1997–, Prince's Youth Business Tst 1997–, Mid Kent Water 1997, Eclipse Scientific Gp 1998–, Arrow Yacht & Aviation Monaco 1998, Gaming Insight plc; mktg conslt Kent River Walk 1998; website dir/publisher Racing Network.co.uk 1999–, chm Sissinghurst Millennium Festival 1998–;

head chorister St Philip's Church 1955–57; footballer Tottenham Schoolboys 1956–57, rugby coach Cranbrook RFC 1979, memb Mgmnt Ctee Biddenden CC 1980; parish cncllr Cranbrook Parish 1999–; memb: NUJ, RTS; MInstD 2002–; FRSA; *Awards* Dunkin Gold Award 1990, BPME Gold Medallion 1992, RTS Television Commercials Award 1993, co-winner New York Radio Festival 1993; *Recreations* horse racing, directing charity stage shows; *Style*— Brian Clifford, Esq; ✉ Mount House, Sissinghurst Castle, Sissinghurst, Kent TN17 2AB (tel 01580 713668, e-mail brian@brianclifford.net)

CLIFFORD, Daniel; s of Tony Clifford, and Denise, *née* Wynn; *b* 6 August 1973, Canterbury, Kent; *Educ* Canterbury HS; *m* Valerie, *née* Arnou; 3 da (Shannon b 29 May 1999, Fay b 18 Oct 2000, Saffron b 28 Sept 2003); *Career* commis chef Howfield Manor Hotel and Restaurant Canterbury 1989–92, first commis chef The Bell Inn Aston Clinton 1992, demi-chef de partie The Box Tree Ilkley 1992–93, chef de partie Millers Harrogate 1993, sous chef Provence Restaurant Hordle 1993–95, chef de partie Jean Bardet Restaurant Tours 1995–96, sr sous chef Rascasse Leeds 1996–98, head chef Midsummer House Restaurant Cambridge 1998– (2 Michelin Stars, Egon Ronay 2 Stars, AA Guide 4 Rosettes (Best Wine List of the Year runner-up 2003–05), Good Food Guide County Restaurant of the Year 2005, Square Meal BMW Award Best Out of Town Restaurant 2005, Cambridge Local Secrets Best Fine Dining Restaurant 2004 and 2005, Harpers & Queen Best Outside London Restaurant Award 2005 (Chef of the Year nomination 2005), Tatler Restaurant Awards Best Restaurant Outside London 2006, Best Overall Restaurant Local Secrets Restaurant Awards 2006); *Style*— Daniel Clifford, Esq; ✉ Midsummer House, Midsummer Common, Cambridge CB4 1HA (tel 01223 369299, fax 01223 302672)

CLIFFORD, David Robert; s of Mark Clifford, of Puriton, Somerset, and Dorothy Emily, *née* Lee; *b* 14 September 1952; *Educ* Dr Morgan's GS Bridgwater, Univ of Wales Inst of Science and Technol (BSc); *m* 13 Sept 1975 (m dis 2001), Audrey Elizabeth, *née* Potter; 1 s (John David b 14 May 1980), 1 da (Rachel Elizabeth b 23 Dec 1983); *Career* vice-pres compensation and benefits Bank of America NT & SA 1978–86, personnel dir Citicorp Scrimgeour Vickers Ltd 1986–88, personnel dir Citicorp Investment Bank Ltd 1988–92, ptnr KPMG 1992–99, gp HR dir Robert Fleming & Co Ltd 2000, ptnr Ernst & Young 2000–04, exec vice-pres global reward ABN Amro NV 2005–; memb Chartered Inst of Personnel Mgmnt; *Recreations* skiing, family activities; *Style*— David Clifford, Esq

CLIFFORD, Max; s of Frank and Lilian Clifford, of London; *b* 1943; *m* Elizabeth (d 2003); 1 da (Louise); *Career* PR consultant; left school aged 15; successively: on staff local department store (until sacked), jr reporter Merton and Morden News, Press Office staff EMI (promoting then unknown Liverpool band The Beatles), asst to Syd Gillingham (ex-chief press officer EMI) in new PR company promoting pop stars incl Tom Jones, Jimi Hendrix, the Bee Gees and Cream; fndr proprietor Max Clifford Associates Press and Public Relations Consultants ca 1968–; official/unofficial private clients have included Frank Sinatra, Mohammed Ali, Diana Ross, David Copperfield, Geoffrey Boycott and OJ Simpson, corp clients incl Laing Homes; other clients and stories incl: Jeffrey Archer, the Blair baby and Gary Glitter; subject of various TV and radio progs incl documentary for BBC TV, Is This Your Life? (Channel 4) and Sixty Minutes (American TV), subject of numerous newspaper and magazine articles worldwide; speaker at univs throughout Britain incl Univs of Oxford and Cambridge; *Style*— Max Clifford, Esq; ✉ Max Clifford Associates Ltd, 49/50 New Bond Street, London W1Y 11A (tel 020 7408 2350, fax 020 7409 2294)

CLIFFORD, Neil; *m* ; 2 c; *Career* various roles incl head of merchandising and distribution Champion Sport Div Burton Gp 1985–93, head of retail Premium Shoe Div British Shoe Corporation Sears Gp 1993–95; Kurt Geiger Ltd: successively sales and mktg dir buying dir, dep md then md 1995–2002, ceo 2003–, led MBO 2005; vice-pres of global sales and memb Exec Ctee Bally Gp 2002–04; *Recreations* owning too many cars and shoes; *Style*— Neil Clifford, Esq; ✉ Kurt Geiger, 75 Bermondsey Street, London SE1 3XF

CLIFFORD, Nigel Richard; s of John Clifford (d 1995), of Emsworth, Hants, and Barbara Dorothy Clifford; *b* 22 June 1959; *Educ* Downing Coll Cambridge (MA), Univ of Strathclyde (MBA), DipM, DipCAM; *m* 1989, Jeanette, *née* Floyd; 2 s (Aidan b 1990, Brendan b 1992), 1 da (Caitlin b 1995); *Career* British Telecommunications plc 1981–92: commercial mangr 1981–84, product mangr 1984–85, gp product mangr 1985–87, gen mangr BT International Operator Servs 1987–90, sr strategist 1990, head of business strategy BT Mobile 1990–92; chief exec Glasgow Royal Infirmary Univ NHS Tst 1992–98, sr vice-pres Cable & Wireless Communications Ltd 1998–2000, ceo Tertio Hldgs Ltd 2000–; fndr tstee Herald Fndn for Women's Health; FIMgt, FRSA; *Recreations* running, walking; *Clubs* Morpeth Comrades Club and Institute Union; *Style*— Nigel Clifford, Esq

CLIFFORD, Sir Roger Joseph Gerrard; 7 Bt (UK 1887), of Flaxbourne, Marlborough, New Zealand; s (twin, by 1 m) of Sir Roger Charles Joseph Clifford, 6 Bt (d 1982); *b* 5 June 1936; *Educ* Beaumont Coll; *m* 19 April 1968, Joanna Theresa, da of Cyril James Ward, of Christchurch, New Zealand, and gda of Sir Cyril Rupert Joseph Ward, 2 Bt; 2 da (Angela Mary Jane b 1971, Annabel Mary Louise b 1973); *Heir* bro, Charles Clifford; *Career* vice-pres Stonyhurst Centenaries Appeal; *Clubs* Christchurch, Christchurch Golf (capt); *Style*— Sir Roger Clifford, Bt

CLIFFORD, Samuel William; *b* 29 May 1966; *Educ* Latymer Upper Sch, Coll d'Enseignement Secondaire St Sauveur Le Vicomte France, Cranbrook Sch; *m* 26 June 1996, Natalie Odile Eddison, da of Prof Keith Roberts; 2 da (Molly Maritza b 26 June 1993, Krysta Margaret b 19 March 1999), 1 s (Joshua Rees b 3 May 1995); *Career* apprentice Trinity Club London 1983–85, commis chef rising to chef de partie RSJ London 1985–86, head chef Brasted's Restaurant Norwich 1986–87, head chef Brasserie l'Abri Norwich 1988–89, stagiaire for Christain Bourrillot, Brasserie Le Nord and Larivoire au Lord du Rhone (all in Lyon) Jan-Nov 1989, sous chef Adlard's Restaurant Norwich 1989–91, prop Sams Restaurant Norwich 1991–93, various positions (forced to give up due to ill health) 1993–96, head chef Adlard's 1996–97, self employed 1997–98 (mainly working for Rhubarb Food Design London and Lord Lloyd-Webber), chef and patron Tatlers 1998, currently employed by Lord Lloyd Webber; presenter Get Stuffed, guest judge Masterchef 2001; head boy Old Adlardians (Norfolk) Soc; memb HCIMA; *Awards* incl: Michelin Star (for Adlard's) 1996, Good Food Guide 4 out of 5 (for Adlard's) 1996, 2 AA Rosettes (Tatlers) 2002, 2 AA Rosettes 2003; *Recreations* fishing, sailing, cooking for friends, drinking fine wines; *Style*— Sam Clifford, Esq

CLIFFORD, Sir Timothy Peter Plint; kt (2002); s of late Derek Plint Clifford, of Sittingbourne, Kent, and Ann, *née* Pierson (d 1984); *b* 26 January 1946; *Educ* Sherborne, Courtauld Inst, Univ of London (BA), Museums Assoc (AMA); *m* 1968, Jane Olivia, yr da of Sir George Paterson, QC, OBE (d 1996), of Sherborne, Dorset; 1 da (Pandora b 1973); *Career* asst keeper: Dept of Paintings Manchester City Art Galleries 1968–72 (acting keeper 1972), Dept of Ceramics V&A 1972–76, Dept of Prints and Drawings British Museum (Historic Br Colls) 1976–78; dir Manchester City Art Galleries 1978–84; DG Nat Galleries of Scotland 2001–06 (dir 1984–2001); tstee Wallace Collection 2003–; pres NADFAS 1996– (vice-pres 1990–96); memb Ateneo Veneto Italy 1997–; BIM Special Award 1991; Freeman City of London, Freeman Worshipful Co of Goldsmiths; Hon LLD Univ of St Andrews 1996, Hon DLitt Univ of Glasgow 2001; FRSE, FSA Scot, FSA Scot, FRSE; Commendatore al Ordine nel Merito della Repubblica Italiana 1999 (Cavaliere 1988); *Recreations* birdwatching; *Clubs* Turf, Beefsteak, New (Edinburgh); *Style*— Sir Timothy Clifford, FRSE

CLIFFORD OF CHUDLEIGH, 14 Baron (E 1672) Thomas Hugh Clifford; DL; Count of the Holy Roman Empire; s of 13 Baron Clifford of Chudleigh (d 1988), and Katharine, Lady Clifford of Chudleigh (d 1999); *b* 17 March 1948; *Educ* Downside; *m* 1, 15 Dec 1980 (m dis 1993), (Muriel) Suzanne, yr da of Maj Campbell Austin; 1 da (Hon Georgina Apollonia b 1983), 2 s (Hon Alexander Thomas Hugh b 24 Sept 1985, Hon Edward George Hugh b 1988); m 2, 21 Nov 1994, Clarissa Anne, da of His Honour Anthony Charles Goodall, MC, DL (d 2001), of Moretonhampstead, Devon; *Heir* s, Hon Alexander Clifford; *Career* late Capt Coldstream Gds, served Norway, Turkey, Berlin, Ireland, British Honduras (Belize); mangr: The Clifford Estate Co, Ugbrooke Enterprises, Ugbrooke Reception Enterprise; KSOM; *Style*— Capt the Rt Hon the Lord Clifford of Chudleigh, DL; ✉ Ugbrooke Park, Chudleigh, South Devon TQ13 OAD (tel 01626 852179)

CLIFT, Prof Roland; CBE (2006, OBE 1994); s of Leslie William Clift, of Wallington, Surrey, and Ivy Florence Gertrude, *née* Wheeler; *b* 19 November 1942; *Educ* Trinity Sch of John Whitgift Croydon, Trinity Coll Cambridge, McGill Univ Montreal; *m* 1, 1968, Rosena Valory, da of Robert Bruce Davison; 1 da (Vanessa b 14 July 1972); m 2, 1979, Diana Helen, da of William Reginald Dermot Manning; 2 s (Julian William Dermot b 2 Oct 1979 d 1997, Adrian Manning b 3 July 1982); *Career* tech offr and chem engr ICI Ltd 1964–67; McGill Univ Montreal: lectr 1967–70, asst prof 1970–72, assoc prof 1972–75; lectr in chem engrg Imperial Coll London 1975–76; Univ of Cambridge: lectr in chem engrg 1976–81, fell Trinity Coll 1978–81, praelector 1980–81; Univ of Surrey: prof of chem engrg 1981–92, head Dept of Chem and Process Engrg 1981–91, prof of environmental technology and dir Centre for Environmental Strategy 1992–2005, distinguished prof 2002–; visiting prof Universitá di Napoli 1973–74, visiting prof Environmental System Analysis Chalmers Univ Sweden 1999–; ed-in-chief Powder Technology 1987–95; chm: Process Engrg Ctee SERC 1989–90, Clean Technol Unit SERC and AFRC 1990–94, Engrg Research Bd AFRC 1992–94; memb BBSRC 1994–96; dir: Clifmar Associates Ltd 1986–, Particle Consultants Ltd 1988–2005, Merrill Lynch New Energy Techologies 2000–, Industrial Ecology Solutions Ltd 2001–07; memb: UK Ecolabelling Bd 1992–99, Comité des Sages on LCA and Ecolabelling European Cmmn 1993–98, Tech Opportunities Panel EPSRC 1994–98, Royal Cmmn on Environmental Pollution 1996–2005, Science Advsy Cncl DEFRA 2006–; expert advsr Science and Technol Ctee House of Lords 2004–05; Henry Marion Howe Medal American Soc for Metals 1976, Moulton Medal Inst of Chem Engrs 1979, Sir Frank Whittle Medal Royal Acad of Engrg 2003; hon citizen Augusta GA 1987; FIChemE 1984 (MIChemE 1979), FREng 1986; *Books* Bubbles, Drops and Particles (with J R Grace and M E Weber, 1978, reprinted 2005), Fluidization (ed with J F Davidson and D Harrison, 1985), Slurry Transport using Centrifugal Pumps (with K C Wilson and G R Addie, 1992, 3 edn 2005), Gas Cleaning at High Temperatures (ed with J P K Seville, 1993), Processing of Particulate Solids (with J P K Seville and U Tüzün, 1997), Sustainable Development in Practice: Case Studies for Engineers and Scientists (ed with A Azapagic and S Perdan, 2004); *Recreations* thinking, arguing; *Clubs* Athenaeum; *Style*— Prof Roland Clift, CBE, FREng; ✉ 93 Peperharow Road, Godalming, Surrey GU7 2PN (tel 01483 417922); Centre for Environmental Strategy, University of Surrey, Guildford, Surrey GU2 7XH (tel 01483 689271, fax 01483 686671, e-mail r.clift@surrey.ac.uk)

CLIFTON, Bishop of (RC) 2001–; Rt Rev Declan Lang; *b* 15 April 1950, Cowes, IOW; *Educ* Ryde Sch, St Edmund's Coll Ware, Royal Holloway Coll London (BA); *Career* ordained priest 1975; asst priest St John's Cathedral Portsmouth 1975–79, chaplain St Edmund's Comp Sch Portsmouth 1975–79, chllr and sec to bishop of Portsmouth 1979–83, parish priest Our Lady, Queen of Apostles Bishop's Waltham 1983–87, parish priest Sacred Heart Bournemouth 1987–90, moderator of the Curia Diocese of Portsmouth 1990, admin St John's Cathedral Portsmouth 1990–96, a vicar gen Dio of Portsmouth 1996–2001, parish priest St Edmund Abingdon 1996–2001; adult religious educn advsr Religious Educn Cncl 1983–90 (co-prodr Parish Project), sometime chaplain Portsmouth Gp pilgrimage to Lourdes, former chair Working Pty on Clergy Appraisal Bishop's Conf/Nat Conf of Priests; *Style*— The Rt Rev the Bishop of Clifton; ✉ St Ambrose, North Road, Leigh Woods, Bristol BS8 3PW (tel 0117 973 3072, fax 0117 973 5913)

CLIFTON, His Hon Judge Gerald Michael; s of Frederick Maurice Clifton (d 1988), of Rainford, Lancs, and Jane, *née* Hayes (d 1986); *b* 3 July 1947; *Educ* Liverpool Coll, Brasenose Coll Oxford (open classical scholar, MA); *m* 21 July 1973, Rosemary Anne Vera, da of Reginald Edward Jackson, of Birkdale, Southport; 2 s (Gerald Rupert Edward b 1977, Giles Michael Charles b 1980); *Career* called to the Bar Middle Temple 1970 (bencher 2006), memb Manx Bar 1992; asst recorder of the Crown Court 1982–88, recorder Northern Circuit 1988–92, circuit judge (Northern Circuit) 1992–; pres Mental Health Review Tbnl (NW Region) 1997–2004, memb Parole Bd 2004–; fndn memb and vice-pres Liverpool Coll; *Recreations* sailing, tennis, walking, philately; *Clubs* Bar Yacht, Athenaeum (Liverpool); *Style*— His Hon Judge Clifton; ✉ c/o The Crown Court, Queen Elizabeth II Law Court, Derby Square, Liverpool L2 1XA

CLIFTON, Nigel John; OBE (2007); s of Henry Clifton, of Helensburgh, Dunbartonshire, and Pamela, *née* Damment; *b* 19 November 1951; *Educ* Wellingborough Sch, Univ of St Andrews (MA); *m* 1974, Elizabeth, *née* Dacre; 1 s (Andrew James b 1977); *Career* dep hosp admin Northern General Hosp Sheffield 1976–81, admin W Fife Hosps 1981–83; gen mangr: Community and Acute Servs Chesterfield Royal Hosp 1983–87, Univ Hosp Queens Med Centre Nottingham 1987–90; chief exec: Salisbury Health Authy 1990–92, N Nottinghamshire Health Authy 1992–97, Doncaster Royal & Montagu Hosp NHS Tst 1997–2001, Doncaster & Bassetlaw Hospitals NHS Tst 2001–04, Doncaster & Bassetlaw Hospitals NHS Fndn Tst 2004–; MHSM 1979; *Recreations* watching cricket, archery, cooking; *Style*— Nigel Clifton, Esq, OBE; ✉ Doncaster & Bassetlaw Hospitals NHS Foundation Trust, Armthorpe Road, Doncaster, South Yorkshire DN2 5LT (tel 01302 366666, fax 01302 792301)

CLIFTON, Rita Ann; da of Arthur Leonard Clifton (d 1970), of Marlow, Bucks, and Iris Mona, *née* Hill; *b* 30 January 1958; *Educ* High Wycombe HS, Newnham Coll Cambridge (MA); *Partner* Brian Martin Astley; 2 da; *Career* D'Arcy MacManus & Masius advtg agency 1979–81, Saatchi & Saatchi 1981–82, J Walter Thompson 1983–86; Saatchi & Saatchi: sr account planner 1986–89, bd dir 1989, gp planning dir 1990–92, dir of strategic planning 1992–95, vice-chm 1995–97; chief exec Interbrand brand consultancy 1997–, chm 2002–; non-exec dir: Dixons Gp plc 2003–, EMAP plc 2005–; non-exec chm Populus Ltd 2004–; visiting prof Henley Mgmnt Coll 2006–; memb: Bd of Advsrs Judge Business Sch Univ of Cambridge, Editorial Bd Jl of Brand Mgmnt, Sustainable Devpt Cmmn, Business Advsy Bd Duke of Edinburgh's Award; pres Women's Advertising Club of London 1997–98; memb: RSA, IPA, MRS, Account Planning Gp, Marketing Soc, Marketing Gp of GB; *Style*— Ms Rita Clifton; ✉ c/o Interbrand, 85 Strand, London WC2R 0DW (tel 020 7554 1000)

CLIFTON-BROWN, Geoffrey; MP; s of Robert Clifton-Brown, and Elizabeth Clifton-Brown (d 2006); *b* 23 March 1953; *Educ* Eton, RAC Cirencester; *m*; 1 s, 1 da; *Career* chartered surveyor PSA Dorchester 1975, investment surveyor Jones Lang Wootton 1975–79, md own farming business Norfolk 1979–; MP (Cons): Cirencester and Tewkesbury 1992–97, Cotswold 1997–; PPS to Rt Hon Douglas Hogg 1995–97; oppn whip DETR 1999–2001; oppn spokesman for: environment, food and rural affrs 2001, transport, local govt and the regions 2001–02, local govt and the regions 2002–04; oppn whip 2004–05, shadow min for trade and foreign affrs 2005–; memb: Environment Select Ctee 1992–95, Public Accounts Ctee 1997–99; chm All-Pty Gp on Population, Devpt and Reproductive Health 1995–97; chm N Norfolk Constituency Cons Assoc 1986–91, memb Exec Ctee and Agric

Ctee Eastern Area Cons Assoc 1986–91, vice-chm Cons Back Bench Ctee on European Affairs 1997; vice-chm: Charities Property Assoc 1993–2001, Small Business Bureau 1995–, Euro Atlantic Gp 1996–; Freeman City of London; Liveryman Worshipful Co of Farmers; FRICS (ARICS); *Publications* Privatising the State Pension - Secure Funded Provision for All (Bow Group); *Recreations* fishing, rural pursuits; *Clubs* Carlton, Farmers', Annabel's; *Style—* Geoffrey Clifton-Brown, Esq, MP, FRICS; ✉ House of Commons, London SW1A 0AA

CLIFTON-SAMUEL, Anthony David; s of David Clifton-Samuel (d 1960), of London, and Sarah Vera, *née* Cohen; *b* 25 June 1932; *Educ* Emscote Lawns Sch, Merchant Taylors', Univ Tutorial Coll, The Royal Dental Hosp of London Sch of Dental Surgery (BDS, LDS, RCS, The Parris prize, Robert Woodhouse prize); *m* 26 March 1961, Andrée Josephine, da of Alfred Falcke Fredericks; 1 da (Ruth Charlotte b 27 March 1965), 1 s (Jason Ian b 1 April 1967); *Career* Nat Serv Royal Army Dental Corps 1956–58 (Lt 1956, Capt 1957); OC Army Dental Centre Limassol 1956–57, Derna Cyrenaica 1957–58; in private practice 1958–60, own practice Kensington 1960–81, own practice Harley St 1965–2004; memb Kensington Chelsea & Westminster Local Dental Ctee 1964–, rep London Local Dental Ctee (later Fedn) 1966–88, former dental rep St Charles Hosp Med Soc; Gen Dental Practitioners Assoc: joined 1962, chm Southern Branch 1970–85, vice-chm Assoc 1978–79 and 1981–82, pres 1979–81 and 1993–May 1996, vice-pres 1987–92; memb BDA until 1970 (served on Rep Bd); *Recreations* motor boating, mechanical engineering, electronics, photography, DIY, reading; *Clubs* Kensington Rotary, Royal Yachting Assoc; *Style—* Mr Anthony D Clifton-Samuel; ✉ 6 Tiverton Road, London NW10 3HL

CLINCH, David John (Joe); OBE (1997); s of Thomas Charles Clinch (d 1995), and Madge Isobel, *née* Saker (d 1984); *b* 14 February 1937; *Educ* Nautical Coll Pangbourne, Univ of Durham (BA), Indiana Univ USA (MBA); *m* 1963, Hilary, da of John Herbert Jacques (d 1984), of Claxby, Lincs; 1 s (John), 1 da (Helen); *Career* Nat Serv 1955–57, RN Acting Sub-Lt; admin Univ of Sussex 1963–69, sec Open Univ 1981–98 (dep sec and registrar 1969–80), dir Milton Keynes City Orchestra 2001–, dir Countec 2005–; The Int Baccalaureate Orgn: treas Cncl Fndn 2000–05 (memb 1999–2005, sec 2003–05), hon memb 2005–; tstee Int Baccalaureate Fund USA, Canada and UK 2004–; Open Univ Students Assoc: hon vice-pres 2000–05, hon memb 2005–; memb Ct Univ of Surrey Roehampton 2000–03, conslt on HE Milton Keynes Economy and Learning Partnership 2000–; Hon DUniv Open; FRSA; *Recreations* music, walking; *Style—* Joe Clinch, Esq, OBE; ✉ 39 Tudor Gardens, Stony Stratford, Milton Keynes MK11 1HX (tel 01908 562475)

CLINTON, 22 Baron (E 1299); Gerard Neville Mark Fane Trefusis; JP (Bideford 1963), DL (Devon 1977); s of Capt Charles Fane (ka 1940), s of Hon Harriet Trefusis, herself da of 21 Baron Clinton (d 1957); assumed additional surname Trefusis by Deed Poll 1958 and suc to Barony 1965 on termination of abeyance; *b* 7 October 1934; *Educ* Gordonstoun; *m* 1959, Nicola Harriette, da of Maj Charles Robert Purdon Coote (d 1954); 2 da (Hon Caroline Harriet b 23 May 1960, Hon Henrietta Jane b 31 Jan 1964), 1 s (Hon Charles Patrick Rolle b 21 March 1962); *Heir* s, Hon Charles Fane Trefusis; *Career* memb Prince of Wales's Councils 1968–79; landowner; *Style—* The Rt Hon the Lord Clinton, DL; ✉ Heanton Satchville, Okehampton, North Devon EX20 3QE

CLINTON, Robert George; s of George Thomas Clinton, and Mary Josephine, *née* Harris; *b* 19 August 1948; *Educ* Beaumont Coll Windsor, BNC Oxford (MA); *m* 28 Aug 1981, Annita Louise, *née* Bennett; 1 s (Thomas Mark George), 1 da (Joanna Marika Alice); *Career* slr; sr ptnr Farrer & Co 2002–; memb Law Soc 1975; *Recreations* sailing, travel; *Clubs* Garrick; *Style—* Robert Clinton, Esq; ✉ Farrer & Co, 66 Lincoln's Inn Fields, London WC2A 3LH (tel 020 7242 2022, fax 020 7405 2296, e-mail rgc@farrer.co.uk)

CLINTON-DAVIS, Baron (Life Peer UK 1990), of Hackney in the London Borough of Hackney; Stanley Clinton Clinton-Davis; PC (1998); s of Sidney Davis; assumed the surname of Clinton-Davis by Deed Poll 1990; *b* 6 December 1928; *Educ* Hackney Downs Sch, Mercers Sch, KCL; *m* 1954, Frances Jane, *née* Lucas; 1 s, 3 da; *Career* Parly candidate: Portsmouth Langstone 1955, Yarmouth 1959 & 1964; cncllr (Hackney) 1959–71, Mayor Hackney 1968–69; MP (Lab) Hackney Central 1970–83, Parly under sec Trade 1974–79; oppn frontbench spokesman on: Trade 1979–81, Foreign and Cwlth Affrs 1981–83; memb Cmmn of Euro Communities (responsible for tport, environment and nuclear safety) 1985–89, princ spokesperson for the oppn on Tport in the House of Lords and supporting spokesman on trade and indust and on foreign affrs 1990–97, min for trade DTI 1997–98; slr 1953–; conslt on Euro and environmental law and affrs with SJ Berwin & Co slrs 1989–97 and 1998–; conslt: Euro Cockpit Assoc 1990–97, Soc of Lab Lawyers 1990–; vice-pres: Soc of Lab Lawyers 1987–, Chartered Inst of Environmental Health; hon memb Exec Cncl of Justice, exec memb Inst of Jewish Affairs 1993–97; memb UN Selection Ctee UNEP-Sasakawa Environment Award 1989– (chm 1999–); chm: Refugee Cncl 1989–96 (pres 1996–97), Advsy Ctee on protection of the sea 1989–97 and 1998–2001 (pres 2001–), Packaging Standards Cncl until 1996; memb: GMBH, Advsy Panel CIS Environ Tst until 1997; pres: Br Multiple Sclerosis Soc (Hackney Branch) until 1997, UK Pilots Assoc (Marine) until 1997, Assoc of Municipal Authorities until 1997, Inst of Travel Mgmnt until 1997, Br Airline Pilots Assoc until 1997 and 1998–, Aviation Environment Federation until 1997; tstee Int Shakespeare Globe Centre until 1997; memb Panel 2000; Grand Cross Order of Leopold II (Belgium) for servs to the EC 1990; Hon Dr Poly Univ of Bucharest; fell: Queen Mary & Westfield Coll London, KCL; fell Chartered Institution of Water and Environmental Management; *Books* Report of a British Parliamentary Delegation to Chile (jtly, 1982); contrib to books and jls on environment issues; *Recreations* reading political biographies, golf, watching assoc football; *Style—* The Rt Hon Lord Clinton-Davis, PC; ✉ House of Lords, London SW1A 0PW; DTI: (tel 020 7215 5501)

CLITHEROE, 2 Baron (UK 1955), also 3 Bt (UK 1945); Ralph John Assheton; DL (Lancs); s of 1 Baron Clitheroe, KCVO, PC (d 1984), and Hon Sylvia Benita Frances, *née* Hotham (d 1991), er da of 6 Baron Hotham; *b* 3 November 1929; *Educ* Eton, ChCh Oxford (MA); *m* 2 May 1961, Juliet, o da of Lt-Col Christopher Lionel Hanbury, MBE, TD; 2 s (Ralph Christopher, John Hotham), 1 da (Elizabeth Jane); *Heir* s, Hon Ralph Assheton, TD; *Career* late Life Guards; former dir: RTZ Corporation plc, First Interstate Bank of California, American Mining Congress, Halliburton Company; former chm: RTZ Borax, The Yorkshire Bank plc; former Vice Lord-Lt Lancs; Liveryman Worshipful Co of Skinners; *Clubs* Boodle's, RAC; *Style—* The Rt Hon Lord Clitheroe, DL; ✉ Downham Hall, Clitheroe, Lancashire BB7 4DN (tel 01200 441210)

CLIVAZ, Brian Melville Winrow-Campbell; s of Anthony Constant Clivaz, and Glynneth, *née* Williams; *b* 7 May 1960; *Educ* Woking Co GS, Ealing Tech Coll; *Career* entrepreneur; varied hotel experience 1976–81 (The Dorchester Hotel London, L'Hotel Plaza Athenee Paris, L'Hotel Meurice Paris, The Hyde Park Hotel London, Dubai International Hotel UAE); md: The Old Lodge Restaurant Ltd (Michelin Star, Egon Ronay Star, numerous other awards) 1981–88, ACA Catering Services 1986–88; gen mangr The Fourways Inn Bermuda 1988–90; md: Simpson's-in-the-Strand Ltd 1990–97, Berkeley Adam Ltd 1995–2005, Home House Ltd 1995–2005, Mayfair Valley Ltd 2000–, Scott's Restaurant Ltd 2002–2004, By Recommendation Ltd, The Arts Club (London) Ltd; hon memb Savoy Gastronomes, pres Reunion des Gastronomes 1997–99; co-organiser The Times World Chess Championship 1993, dir The World Memory Championships 1993–, vice-pres The Brain Tst 1993–; hon treas The Philidor Soc; co-fndr The Staunton Soc, chm The Whitebait Soc; memb: Br Hospitality Assoc (memb Club Panel), Restaurateurs Assoc of GB (past memb Nat Ctee), Academy of Culinary Arts, Les Arts de la Table, The Fountain Soc, The Chopin Soc; Freeman: City of London 1994, Worshipful Co of Cooks; FRSA, FHCIMA; Knight Order of Merit Royal House of Savoy, Knight of the Order of Francis I; *Recreations* gardening, collecting old cookery books, chess; *Clubs* Arts, Travellers, Home House; *Style—* Brian Clivaz, Esq; ✉ 40 Dover Street, London W1S 4NP (tel 020 7290 3550, e-mail brian@clivaz.com)

CLIVE, Prof Eric McCredie; CBE (1999); s of Robert M Clive (d 1971), and Mary, *née* McCredie (d 1976); *b* 24 July 1938; *Educ* Stranraer Acad, Stranraer HS, Univ of Edinburgh (MA, LLB), Univ of Michigan (LLM), Univ of Virginia (SJD); *m* 6 Sept 1962, Kay, da of Rev Alastair McLeman (d 1940); 4 c (Gael b 6 Sept 1963 d 1996, Alastair M M b 19 March 1965, Sally b 22 March 1968, Rachel b 9 Sept 1969); *Career* slr; Univ of Edinburgh: lectr 1962–69, sr lectr 1969–75, reader 1975–77, prof of Scots law 1977–81, visiting prof 1999–; memb Scottish Law Commission 1981–99; FRSE 1999; *Books* Law of Husband and Wife in Scotland (1974, 4 edn 1997), Scots Law for Journalists (jtly 1965, 5 edn 1988); *Style—* Prof Eric Clive, CBE, FRSE; ✉ School of Law, University of Edinburgh, Old College, South Bridge, Edinburgh (tel 0131 650 9588, e-mail eric.clive@ed.ac.uk)

CLOGHER, Bishop (RC) of 1979–; Most Rev Joseph Augustine Duffy; s of Edward Duffy (d 1956), and Brigid MacEntee (d 1963); *b* 3 February 1934; *Educ* Maynooth (BD), Nat Univ of Ireland (MA, HDipEd); *Career* St Macartan's Coll Monaghan 1960–72, St Michael's Parish Enniskillen 1972–79; *Books* Lough Derg Guide (1978), Monaghan Cathedral (1992), Patrick In His Own Words (2000); *Recreations* history, travel; *Style—* The Most Rev the Bishop of Clogher; ✉ Tigh an Easpaig, Monaghan, Ireland (tel 00 353 47 81019, fax 00 353 47 84773, e-mail cloghdiocoffmon@eircom.net)

CLOGHER, Bishop of 2002–; Rt Rev Dr Michael Geoffrey St Aubyn Jackson; s of Robert Stewart Jackson (d 2001), and Margaret Jane Frances, *née* Sloan; *b* 24 May 1956; *Educ* Portora Royal Sch Enniskillen, TCD (BA, Gold medal, MA), St John's Coll Cambridge (fndn scholar, MA, Nowell-Rostron prize, Bishop Lightfoot prize, Wordsworth scholar, PhD), Church of Ireland Theol Coll (Downes essay prize, Moncrieff-Cox sermon prize, Elrington theol prize); *m* 2 May 1987, Inez Elizabeth, *née* Cooke; 1 da (Camilla Elizabeth St Aubyn b 21 March 1990); *Career* ordained: deacon 1986, priest 1987; curate asst Zion parish Rathgar 1986–89, minor canon, treas's vicar and chllr's vicar St Patrick's Cathedral Dublin 1987–89, asst lectr Dept of Hebrew, Biblical and Theol Studies TCD and Church of Ireland Theol Coll 1987–89; Univ of Oxford: MA and DPhil (by incorporation) 1989, coll chaplain ChCh 1989–97 (student 1993–97), asst lectr Theology Faculty 1991–97, dir of studies in theology St Anne's Coll 1995–97; incumbent St Fin Barre's Union Cork and dean of Cork 1997–2002, chaplain UC Cork and Cork Inst of Technol 1997–2002, asst lectr Schs of Classics and Educn UC Cork 1997–2002, examining chaplain to bishop of Cork, Cloyne and Ross 1999–2002; chaplain: Vincents' Club 1992–97, Oxford Diocesan Branch C of E Guild of Vergers 1996–97; Travers Smith lectr St Bartholomew's Church 1997; author of articles and reviews published in: Classica et Mediaevalia, Studia Patristica, The Church Times, Search, Jl of Theol Studies, Hermathena, The Furrow, The Irish Theol Quarterly, Doctrine and Life, The Ecumenical Review; chm: Oxford Univ Chaplains' Mission Ctee 1991–92, St Fin Barre's Beyond 2000 1998–2002; chairperson Network for Inter-Faith Concerns in the Anglican Communion (NIFCON) 2004–; memb: Ethics Ctee Cork Univ Hosp 1999–2002, Int Anglican-Oriental Orthodox Cmmn 2002–; *Clubs* Kildare St and Univ (Dublin); *Style—* The Rt Rev the Bishop of Clogher; ✉ The See House, Fivemiletown, Co Tyrone BT75 0QP (tel and fax 028 8952 2475, e-mail bishop@clogher.anglican.org)

CLORE, Melanie Sarah Jane; da of Martin Clore, of London, and Cynthia Clore; *b* 28 January 1960; *Educ* Channing Sch Highgate, Univ of Manchester (BA); *m* 22 July 1994, Yaron Meshoulam; 1 s (Theo Felix Clore b 18 May 1996), 1 da (Martha Lily Clore b 27 June 1998); *Career* Sotheby's: graduate trainee 1981, jr cataloguer in Impressionist and Modern Art Dept 1982, auctioneer 1985–, dep dir 1986–88, dir 1988–91, sr dir 1991–, head of Impressionist and Modern Art Dept Europe 1992–, memb Bd Sotheby's Europe 1994– (dep chm 1997–), co-chm Worldwide Impressionist and Modern Art Dept 2001–; tstee: Whitechapel Art Gallery 1988–98, Tate 2004–; *Recreations* travel, cinema; *Style—* Ms Melanie Clore; ✉ Impressionist and Modern Art Department, Sotheby's, 34–35 New Bond Street, London W1A 2AA (tel 020 7293 5394, fax 020 7293 5932)

CLOSE, Prof Frank; OBE; *Educ* Univ of St Andrews, Magdalen Coll Oxford (DPhil); *m*; 2 da; *Career* postdoctoral fell Stanford Univ, research CERN Geneva 1973–75, research physicist rising to head Theoretical Physics Div Rutherford Appleton Lab 1975–2001, concurrently head of communication and public educn activities CERN Geneva 1997–2000, prof of physics Univ of Oxford 2001–, fell and tutor in physics Exeter Coll Oxford 2001–, prof of astronomy Gresham Coll London 2001–04; vice-pres BAAS; delivered Royal Instn Christmas Lectures 1993, Kelvin Medal Inst of Physics 1996; *Books* incl: An Introduction to Quarks and Partons (1979), The Cosmic Onion: Quarks and the Nature of the Universe (1983), The Particle Explosion (with Michael Marten and Christine Sutton, 1987), End: Cosmic Catastrophe and the Fate of the Universe (1988), Spectroscopy of Light and Heavy Quarks (ed with Ygo Gastaldi and Robert Klapisch, 1989), Too Hot to Handle: The Story of the Race for Cold Fusion (1990), Lucifer's Legacy: The Meaning of Asymmetry (2000), The Particle Odyssey: A Journey to the Heart of the Matter (with Michael Marten and Christine Sutton, 2002), Particle Physics: A Very Short Introduction (2004); *Recreations* playing squash and real tennis, writing, walking, singing, Peterborough United; *Style—* Prof Frank Close, OBE; ✉ Rudolf Peierls Centre for Theoretical Physics, 1 Keble Road, Oxford OX1 3RH

CLOSE, Seamus; OBE (1997); s of late James Close, of Lisburn, and Kathleen, *née* Murphy; *b* 12 August 1947; *Educ* St Malachy's Coll Belfast, Coll of Business Studies (Dip Business Studies); *m* 15 April 1978, Deirdre, da of late Barney McCann; 3 s (Christopher b 9 Feb 1979, Brian b 5 July 1981, Stephen b 13 Jan 1984), 1 da (Natasha b 27 July 1987); *Career* memb Lisburn BC 1973– (mayor 1993–94); Alliance Pty: chm 1981–82, dep ldr 1991–2001; memb NI Assembly 1982–86, MLA (Alliance) Lagan Valley 1998–2007; key negotiator: Brooke-Mayhew Talks 1991–92, Good Friday Agreement 1996–98; delg: Atkins Conf on NI 1980, NI Forum for Peace and Reconciliation 1994–95, NI Forum for Political Dialogue 1996; dir S D Bell & Co Ltd 1986–; *Recreations* sports, family, current affairs; *Style—* Seamus Close, Esq, OBE

CLOTHIER, Sir Cecil Montacute; KCB (1982), QC (1965); s of Hugh Montacute Clothier (d 1961), of Blundellsands, Liverpool; *b* 28 August 1919; *Educ* Stonyhurst, Lincoln Coll Oxford (BCL, MA); *m* 1, 1943, Mary Elizabeth (d 1984), da of Ernest Glover Bush (d 1962), of Aughton, Lancs; 1 s, 2 da; m 2, 7 Aug 1992, Mrs Diana Stevenson, da of Louis Durrant, lately of Richmond, Surrey; *Career* served WWII 51 Highland Div, Army Staff Washington DC, Hon Lt-Col Royal Signals; called to the Bar Inner Temple 1950 (bencher 1972); recorder Blackpool 1965–72, recorder of the Crown Court 1972–78, judge of Appeal IOM 1972–78, legal assessor to Gen Med and Gen Dental Cncls 1972–78; memb Royal Cmmn on NHS 1976–78, Parly cmmr for Admin and Health Service cmmr for England Wales and Scotland 1979–84; vice-pres Interception of Communications Tbnl 1986–96; chm: Police Complaints Authy 1985–89, Cncl on Tbnls 1989–92, The Allitt Inquiry 1994, Review Panel on Machinery of Govt Jersey 1999–2001, The Harefield Res Fndn 2001–03; hon pres Sir Magdi Yacoub Research Inst; conslt SSRB 1995–97 (memb 1989–95); Rock Carling fell 1988; memb Advsy Cncl British Library 1993–98; Hon LLD Univ of Hull 1983; hon fell Lincoln Coll Oxford 1984; hon memb Assoc of Anaesthetists 1987, Hon FRPharmS 1990, Hon FRCP 1998; *Clubs* Leander; *Style—* Sir Cecil Clothier, KCB, QC; ✉ 1 Temple Gardens, Temple, London EC4Y 9BB (tel 020 7353 3400)

CLOTHIER, Richard John; s of John Neil Clothier, of Montacute, Somerset, and Barbara Evelyn, *née* Rothwell; *b* 4 July 1945; *Educ* Peterhouse Sch Zimbabwe, Univ of Natal (BSc),

C

Harvard Univ (AMP); *m* 1, 1972, Ingrid Hafner (d 1994); 2 s (Ben Raoul b 21 November 1972, William Neil b 11 March 1976); m 2, 1995, Sarah Riley; *Career* Milk Mktg Bd 1971–77; Dalgety plc: with Dalgety Agriculture 1977–88, chief exec Pig Improvement Co 1988–92, exec main bd dir 1992–97, chief exec 1993–97; chief exec Plantation and General Investments plc 1998–, chm Robinson plc 2004–; non-exec dir Granada plc 1996–2004; *Recreations* competitive yachting; *Clubs* Royal Thames Yacht, Farmers; *Style—* Richard Clothier, Esq; ✉ 81 Carter Lane, London EC1V 5EP (tel 020 7236 0207)

CLOUGH, Dr Chris; s of George Clough (d 1996), of Knaresborough, and Daisy, *née* Elsdon-Howard; *b* 30 August 1953, London; *Educ* Univ of Manchester (MB, ChB); *m* 17 March 1979, Lyn, *née* Griffiths; 1 da (Sophie Laura b 18 March 1980), 2 s (Jonathan James b 5 Jan 1982, Joshua Edward b 25 May 1984); *Career* registrar Hull Royal Infirmary 1976–79, research fell Mount Sinai Med Centre NY 1980–81, sr registrar Midland Centre for Neurology and Neurosurgery Birmingham 1982–88, conslt neurologist Brook Regnl Neuroscience Centre 1989–95, dir King's Regnl Neuroscience Centre 1991–98, conslt neurologist KCH 1994– (med dir 1998–2003), chief med advsr SE London RHA 2003–, med dir RCP 2005–; memb: Doctors' Forum Dept of Health 2002, External Reference Gp Nat Serv Framework for Long-term Conditions Dept of Health 2002; Liversedge Prize 1982; FRCP 1992 (MRCP 1978); *Publications* Parkinson's Disease Fast Facts (2004), Training Tomorrow's Physicians (2005); author of papers on Parkinson's disease, restless legs and lumbar puncture 1977–; *Recreations* tennis, Spurs fan, walking, cinema; *Clubs* Fabian Soc, Labour Party; *Style—* Dr Chris Clough

CLOUGH, Mark Gerard; QC (1999); *b* 13 May 1953; *Educ* Ampleforth, Univ of St Andrews (MA); *m* Joanne Elizabeth, *née* Dishington; 2 s, 1 da; *Career* called to the Bar Gray's Inn 1978, slr advocate Supreme Court of England and Wales 1996; slr 1995– (specialising in: EC law, competition law and sectoral regulation, int trade law); ptnr Competition and Trade Gp Ashurst Morris Crisp (now Ashurst) 1995–2006, ptnr Addleshaw Goddard LLP 2006; chm Slr's Assoc of Higher Court Advocates (SAHCA) 2003–06, memb Advsy Bd Br Inst of Int and Comparative Law Competition Law Forum; dir Camden People's Theatre; memb IBA anti-trust and int trade law ctee, assoc memb American Bar Assoc; *Publications* books incl: Shipping And EC Competition Law (1990), EC Merger Regulation (1995) and Butterworth's European Community Law Service EC Anti-Dumping, Subsidies And Trade Barrier Regulation Sections (1997), Trade and Telecoms (2002); contributed articles to numerous journals and chapters to books; *Recreations* golf, tennis, theatre, poetry; *Clubs* Travellers; *Style—* Mark Clough, Esq, QC

CLOUGH, Peter; s of Michael Clough, of St Ives, Cornwall, and Stella, *née* Ripley (d 1989); *b* 3 March 1967, St Ives, Cornwall; *Educ* Humphry Davy Sch Cornwall, UC Cardiff (LLB); *m* 18 Nov 2005, Annie, *née* Walshe; 2 da (Lottie b 3 Aug 1997, Olivia b 31 Oct 1999), 1 s (Xavier b 23 Sept 2003); *Career* head of litigation and dispute resolution Osborne Clarke; slr specialising in technology, energy and natural resources and financial servs; *Recreations* veteran motorsport, sailing, scuba diving, tennis, travel; *Style—* Peter Clough, Esq; ✉ Osborne Clarke, 2 Temple Back East, Temple Quay, Bristol BS1 6EG (tel 0117 917 4060, fax 0117 917 4061, e-mail peter.clough@osborneclarke.com)

CLOVER, Charles Robert Harold; s of Harold Percy Clover (d 1973), and Diana Patricia, *née* Hutchinson Smith (d 1975); *b* 22 August 1958; *Educ* Westminster, Univ of York (BA); *m* Pamela Anne, da of Leonard C Roberts; 2 s (Duncan Harold Cairns, Thaddeus John Charles); *Career* asst ed The Spectator 1979; Daily Telegraph: reporter Peterborough Column 1982, rock critic 1983–86, TV critic and feature writer 1986–87, environment corr 1987–89, environment ed 1989–; nat journalist Media Nature's Br environment and media awards 1989, 1994 and 1996; *Books* Highgrove (with HRH The Prince of Wales, 1993), The End of the Line (2004, special award André Simon Meml Fund Book Awards 2004, Derek Cooper Award Guild of Food Writers 2005, Biosis Award for Communicating Zoology Zoological Soc of London); *Recreations* fly fishing; *Style—* Charles Clover, Esq; ✉ Daily Telegraph, 111 Buckingham Palace Road, London SW1W 0DT (tel 020 7931 2523, e-mail charles.clover@telegraph.co.uk)

CLUCKIE, Prof Ian David; *b* 20 July 1949; *Career* with W S Atkins Swansea 1966–72, with Central Water Planning Unit Reading 1974–76, lectr Univ of Birmingham 1976–88, prof of water resources Univ of Salford 1988–97 (chm Civil Engrg Dept 1991–96), academic dir Salford Civil Engrg Ltd 1989–97, dir Telford Research Inst 1993–94 and 1996–97, prof of hydrology and water mgmnt (dir of Water and Environmental Mgmnt Research Centre) Univ of Bristol 1997–; chm: Aquatic Atmospheric and Physical Sciences Ctee 1991–94 (memb Research Grants and Trg Awards Ctee 1988–91), EPSRC Flood Risk Mgmnt Research Consortium (FRMRC) 2003–; memb: NERC Ctee, Terrestrial and Freshwater Sciences Ctee, Marine Sciences Ctee, Atmospheric Sciences Ctee, various HE ctees 1991–94, European Environmental Research Orgns 1998–; pres elect Int Ctee on Remote Sensing 2007–; FRSA 1993, FREng 1997; *Books* Hydrological Applications of Weather Radar (co author with C G Collier, 1991); *Publications* author of various contributions to learned jls; *Recreations* sailing, hill walking; *Style—* Professor Cluckie, FREng; ✉ University of Bristol, Department of Civil Engineering, Lunsford House, Cantocks Close, Bristol BS8 1UP (tel 0117 928 9767, fax 0117 928 9770, e-mail i.d.cluckie@bristol.ac.uk)

CLUFF, John Gordon (Algy); s of Harold Cluff (d 1989), and Freda Cluff; *b* 19 April 1940; *Educ* Stowe; *m* 1993, Blondel, *née* Hodge; 3 s (Harry b 30 Dec 1993, Philip Randolph Macartney b 4 July 1996, Charles b 7 Feb 2002); *Career* Mil Serv: Lt Grenadier Gds 1959–62, Capt Gds Parachute Co 1962–64, serv W Africa, Cyprus, Malaysia; chm and chief exec Cluff Mining plc 1996–2004, chm Cluff Gold Ltd 2004–; chm: Apollo Magazine, The Spectator until 2004; Parly candidate (Cons) Ardwick Manchester 1966; chm Cmmn on the Cwlth 2001; tstee Anglo-Hong Kong Tst, a dir The Centre for Policy Studies, chm The War Memls Tst a govr Cwlth Inst, govr Stowe Sch; *Clubs* White's, Pratt's, Beefsteak, Royal Yacht Sqdn, The Brook (New York), Rand (Johannesburg), Special Forces; *Style—* J G Cluff, Esq

CLUGSTON, John Westland Antony; DL; s of Leonard Gordon Clugston, OBE, DL (d 1984), and Sybil Mary Bacon (d 1981); *b* 16 May 1938; *Educ* Sandroyd, Gordonstoun; *m* 1, Patricia, da of Gordon Columba Harvey (d 1994); 2 s (Alistair b 1970, David b 1972), 2 da (Linda b 1973, Christina b 1976); m 2, Jane Elizabeth Ann (d 1996), da of Charles Burtt Marfleet (d 1967); m 3, Fiona Margaret Yuill Baillie, da of Lt-Col James Yuill Ferguson, MBE, MC, and Margaret Ferguson; *Career* Lt Sherwood Rangers Yeo (TA); apprentice: at Huttenwerk Rheinhausen A G Iron and Steel Works Germany 1958–60, Lorraine Escaut Iron and Steel Works at Mont-St-Martin and Senelle France 1960–61; dir: Clugston Holdings Ltd 1964, Roadstone Div 1965–68 (dir for all subsidiary cos 1970), E Bacon & Co 1985; chm: Roadstone Div 1969, Reclamation Div and St Vincent Plant Ltd 1980; gp chm: Colvilles Clugston Shanks (Holdings) Ltd, Colvilles Clugston Shanks Ltd 1984, Clydesdale Excavating and Construction Co Ltd 1987–; dir: Appleby Gp Ltd 1983, Market Rasen Racecourse Ltd 1995–; chm and md: Clugston Holdings Ltd 1984 (gp vice-chm and md 1978), Clugston Gp Ltd 1991–; past pres Humberside branch Br Inst of Mgmnt, pres Lincolnshire Iron and Steel Inst 1989–90, pres Hull and Humber C of C and Shipping 2005–06; chm S Humberside Business Advice Centre, former memb Cncl British Aggregates Construction Materials Industry; pres Humberside Scout Cncl (formerly exec chm), chm Lincoln Cathedral Preservation Cncl, chm of govrs Brigg Prep Sch; High Sheriff Humberside 1992–93; Freeman City of London, Master Worshipful Co of Paviors 1996–97 (Liveryman 1965, memb Ct of Assts 1986, Upper Warden 1996); assoc Inst of Quarrying, MInstD, FIHT 1984; *Recreations* shooting, fishing, tennis, music; *Style—* J W A Clugston, Esq, DL; ✉ The Old Vicarage, Scawby, Brigg, Lincolnshire DN20 9LX (tel 01652 657100); Clugston Group Ltd, St Vincent House, Normanby Road, Scunthorpe, North Lincolnshire DN15 8QT (tel 01724 843491, fax 01724 282853, e-mail group@clugston.co.uk, website www.clugston.co.uk)

CLUTTERBUCK, Prof David; *b* 4 June 1947; *Educ* Christ's Coll Finchley, Westfield Coll London (BA); *m*; 4 s; *Career* Dept of Immigration Home Office 1968–69, ed Journal of the British Nuclear Energy Society (ICE) 1969–70, news ed (technol) New Scientist 1970–73, assoc ed rising to managing ed/ed-in-chief International Management 1973–83; fndr ed: Issues magazine 1984–90, Strategic Direction and Technology Strategies 1985–89, Marketing Business 1988–90; Euro ed On Achieving Excellence 1989–92; chm ITEM Group Ltd (communications project mgmnt co) 1982–, sr ptnr Clutterbuck Associates (mgmnt consultancy) 1983–; dir: The European Mentoring Centre 1991–, Mentoring Directors Ltd, Boardroom Effectiveness Ltd 1995–97, Clutterbuck, Palmer, Schneider 1996–98, Nothing Publishing Ltd 1999–; public sector clients incl: Benefits Agency, NHS, Dept of Employment, Inland Revenue, DTI, DSS, BR Systems, Cabinet Office; private sector clients incl: ASDA, British American Tobacco, Brooke Bond Foods, Shell, British Aerospace, Coates Viyella, Audit Cmmn, Kellogg, Whitbread; also leader various in-house research programmes; assoc prof Int Mgmnt Centres (IMCB), visiting prof Sheffield Hallam Univ 2000–, visiting prof Oxford Brookes Univ; Hon DLitt IMCB; memb Assoc of Mgmnt Educn and Devpt; MInstD, MIPD, MIMgt; *Publications* incl: How to be a Good Corporate Citizen (1981), The Tales of Gribble the Goblin (1983), New Patterns of Work (1985), Everyone Needs a Mentor (1985, 4 edn 2004), Clore: The Man and his Millions (1986), Businesswoman (1987), Turnaround (1988), The Makers of Management (1990), Making Customers Count (1991), Inspired Customer Service (1993), The Independent Board Director (with Peter Waine, *qv*, 1993), The Power of Empowerment (1994), Charity as a Business (1995), Mentoring in Action (1995), The Winning Streak Mark II (1997), Learning Alliances (1998), Learning Teams (1998), Mentoring Executives and Directors (1999), Doing it Different (1999), Mentoring and Diversity (2001), Implementing Mentoring Schemes (2001), Talking Business (2002), Managing Work-Life Balance (2003), The Situational Mentor (2004), Techniques for Coaching and Mentoring (2005), Making Coaching Work (2005), Coaching the Team at Work (2007); also author of numerous articles and papers; *Videos* Beyond the Winning Streak (1989), The Service Dimension (1991), Creating Tomorrow's Company Today (1993), The Mentor Dimension (1994); *Recreations* learning a new sport each year; *Style—* Prof David Clutterbuck; ✉ Clutterbuck Associates, Grenville Court, Britwell Road, Burnham, Buckinghamshire SL1 8DF (tel 01628 661667, fax 01628 661779, e-mail david@clutterbuckassociates.co.uk, website www.clutterbuckassociates.com)

CLUTTERBUCK, Jasper Meadows; s of late Hugh Meadows Clutterbuck; *b* 5 February 1935; *Educ* Eton; *m* 1958, Marguerite Susan, *née* Birnie; 1 s, 1 da; *Career* Lt Coldstream Gds 1953–56; dir Whitbread & Co 1975–88, chm Morland & Co plc 1993–96; *Style—* Jasper Clutterbuck, Esq; ✉ Mottisfont House, Mottisfont, Hampshire SO51 0LN (tel 01794 340475, fax 01794 341472)

CLUTTON, (Bernard Geoffrey) Owen; s of Maj Arthur Henry Clutton, MC (d 1979), and Joyce, *née* Worthington (d 2002); *b* 3 March 1951; *Educ* St Aidans Coll Grahamstown, Univ of the Witwatersrand (BA, LLB), Univ of Oxford (BCL); *m* 12 Oct 1979, Rosemary Elizabeth, da of Geoffrey Thomas Skett; 1 s (William Edward Henry b 28 March 1988), 1 da (Alice Elizabeth Katherine b 5 Aug 1990); *Career* admitted slr 1980; ptnr Macfarlanes 1984–; President's Certificate Nat Playing Fields Assoc; Liveryman Worshipful Co of Slrs; memb Law Soc; CTA, TEP (founding memb); *Style—* Owen Clutton, Esq; ✉ Macfarlanes, 10 Norwich Street, London EC4A 1BD (tel 020 7831 9222, fax 020 7831 9607, telex 296381, e-mail owen.clutton@macfarlanes.com)

CLUTTON, Rafe Henry; CBE (1992); s of Robin John Clutton (d 1978), and Rosalie Muriel, *née* Birch (d 1978); *b* 13 June 1929; *Educ* Tonbridge; *m* 1954, Jill Olwyn, da of John Albert Evans, of Haywards Heath, W Sussex; 4 s (Owen b 1958, Gareth b 1960, Jonathan b 1962, Niall b 1964), 1 da (Helen b 1968); *Career* chartered surveyor; ptnr Cluttons 1955–92 (sr ptnr 1982–92); dir: Legal and General Group Ltd 1972–93, Rodamco (UK) BV 1990–95; memb: Bd Royal Nat Theatre 1976–93, Salvation Army Housing Assoc 1987–95, Royal Cmmn for Exhbn of 1851 1988–99; govr Royal Fndn of Grey Coat Hosp 1967–2002 (chm 1981–2001); FRICS; *Publications* Take One Surveyor (2004); *Recreations* grandchildren, books, and admiring the view; *Clubs* Royal Thames Yacht; *Style—* Rafe Clutton, Esq, CBE; ✉ Providence Cottage, Church Road, Barcombe, East Sussex BN8 5TP (tel 01273 400763)

CLUTTON-BROCK, Prof Timothy Hugh (Tim); *b* 13 August 1946; *Educ* Rugby, Magdalene Coll Cambridge (MA, PhD, ScD); *Career* Game Dept Zambia 1964–65, researcher Sub-Dept of Animal Behaviour Madingley Cambridge (and field work in Tanzania and Uganda) 1969–70, NERC res fell Animal Behaviour Res Gp Univ of Oxford 1972–73, lectr in biology Sch of Biological Scis Univ of Sussex 1973–76, sr res fell in behavioural ecology Res Centre King's Coll Cambridge 1976–80; Dept of Zoology Univ of Cambridge: fndr Large Animal Res Gp 1980, SERC advanced res fell 1981–83, Royal Soc res fell in biology 1983–88, univ lectr 1987–91, reader in animal ecology 1991–, prof of animal ecology 1994–, Prince Phillip chair of ecology and evolutionary biology 2007–; co-fndr and dir Wildlife Consultants Ltd 1976–86, chm Deer Specialist Gp IUCN 1980–91; res projects incl: primate ecology, the evolution of mammalian breeding systems, natural and sexual selection, the evolution of sexual care, population regulation in ungulates, management of deer populations; memb Editorial Bd: Jl of Animal Ecology, Behavioural Ecology, Behavioural Ecology and Sociobiology; jt ed Princeton Univ Press Monograph series in behavioural ecology; contrib to various radio and TV progs (incl script for BBC Horizon prog on Rhum); Scientific Medal Zoological Soc of London 1984, C Hart Merriam Award American Soc of Mammalogists 1991, Frink Medal 1998, Marsh Award Br Ecological Soc 1998; FRS 1993; *Publications* Primate Ecology (ed, 1977), Current Problems in Sociobiology (ed, 1982), Red Deer - Behaviour and Ecology of Two Sexes (jtly, 1982, Wildlife Soc of America best book award), Rhum - the Natural History of an Island (ed jtly, 1987), Reproductive Success - Studies of Individual Variation in Contrasting Breeding Systems (ed, 1988), Red Deer in the Highlands (jtly, 1989), The Evolution of Parental Care (1991); author of around 300 articles in learned jls; popular articles in New Scientist, Nat Geographic, Natural History and The Field; *Style—* Prof Tim Clutton-Brock, FRS; ✉ Large Animal Research Group, Department of Zoology, Downing Street, Cambridge CB2 3EJ (tel 01223 336618)

CLWYD, Rt Hon Ann; PC (2004), MP; da of Gwilym Henri Lewis, and Elizabeth Ann Lewis; *b* 21 March 1937; *Educ* Holywell GS, The Queen's Sch Chester, UC Bangor; *m* 1963, Owen Dryhurst Roberts; *Career* former journalist The Guardian and The Observer, reporter BBC; Parly candidate (Lab) Denbigh 1970 and Gloucester Oct 1974, MEP (Lab) Mid and W Wales 1979–84, MP (Lab) Cynon Valley 1984–; oppn front spokesperson on educn and women's affrs 1987–88, memb Shadow Cabinet 1989–93, shadow sec on overseas devpt 1989–92, shadow Welsh sec 1992, shadow Nat Heritage sec 1992–93, oppn front bench spokesperson on employment 1993–94, oppn front bench spokesperson on foreign affrs 1994–95, dep to John Prescott 1994–95; memb Select Ctee on Int Devpt 1997–2005, chm All-Pty Gp on Human Rights 1997–, memb Select Ctee on Strategic Export Controls on Arms Sales 2000–05; vice-chair PLP 2001–, vice-chair Inter-Parly Union (UK branch) 2001–; chair International Campaign on Iraqi War Crimes (INDICT) 1997–, special envoy to the PM on human rights to Iraq 2003–; vice-chm Welsh Arts Cncl 1975–79; memb Royal Cmmn on NHS 1977–79, memb Lab NEC 1983–84; hon fell UCNW; *Style—* The

Rt Hon Ann Clwyd, MP; ✉ 6 Deans Court, Dean Street, Aberdare, Mid Glamorgan; House of Commons, London SW1A 0AA (tel 020 7219 3000, fax 020 7219 5943)

CLYDE, Baron (Life Peer UK 1996), of Briglands in Perthshire and Kinross; James John Clyde; PC (1996); s of Rt Hon Lord Clyde (d 1975), and Margaret Letitia Dubuisson (d 1974); *b* 29 January 1932; *Educ* Edinburgh Acad, Univ of Oxford (BA), Univ of Edinburgh (LLB); *m* 1963, Ann Clunie, da of Donald Robert Armstrong Hoblyn (d 1975); 2 s (Hon James b 1969, Hon Timothy b 1973); *Career* advocate Scotland 1959, QC (Scot) 1971, advocate depute 1973–74, chllr to Bishop of Argyll and the Isles 1972–85, memb Scottish Valuation Advsy Cncl 1972–96 (vice-chm 1980–87, chm 1987–96), ldr UK Delgn to the CCBE 1981–84, chm Med Appeal Tbnls 1974–85, judge in the Courts of Appeal for Jersey and Guernsey 1979–85, senator Coll of Justice 1985–96, a Lord of Appeal in Ordinary 1996–2001, Justice Oversight Cmmn NI 2003–06; pres: Scottish Young Lawyers' Assoc 1988–97, Scottish Univs Law Inst 1991–97; vice-pres The Royal Blind Asylum and Sch 1987–; tstee: Nat Library of Scotland 1977–94, St Mary's Music Sch 1978–93; dir Edinburgh Acad 1979–88, chm Cncl St George's Sch for Girls 1989–97, govr Napier Univ (formerly Napier Poly) 1989–93; Univ of Edinburgh: assessor to Chllr 1989–97, vice-chm of Court 1993–96, chm Europa Inst 1990–97; hon pres Dumfries Burns Club 1996–97, chm Children in Scotland 2003–; Hon DUniv: Heriot-Watt 1991, Edinburgh 1997; Hon DLitt Napier Univ 1995; hon bencher Middle Temple 1996, hon fell CCC Oxford 1996; *Recreations* music, gardening; *Clubs* New (Edinburgh); *Style—* The Rt Hon the Lord Clyde, PC; ✉ House of Lords, London SW1A 0PW

CLYDESMUIR, 3 Baron (UK 1948); David Ronald Colville; s 2 Baron Clydesmuir, KT, CB, MBE, TD (d 1996), and Joan Marguerita, *née* Booth; *b* 8 April 1949; *Educ* Charterhouse; *m* 1978, Aline Frances, da of Peter Merriam, of Holton Lodge, Holton St Mary, Suffolk; 2 s (Hon Richard b 1980, Hon Hamish b 1989), 2 da (Hon Rachel b 1983, Hon Harriet b 1985); *Heir* s, Hon Richard Colville; *Style—* The Rt Hon the Lord Clydesmuir; ✉ Langlees House, Biggar, Lanarkshire ML12 6NP

COAD, Jonathan George; *b* 2 February 1945; *Educ* Lancing, Keble Coll Oxford (BA); *m* 16 April 1976, Vivienne Jaques; 2 da (Jennifer b 1982, Felicity b 1986); *Career* historian, archaeologist; inspr of ancient monuments and historic bldgs; pres Royal Archaeological Inst 2006–; vice-pres Soc for Nautical Res; tstee Bermuda Maritime Museum; FSA; *Books* Historic Architecture of The Royal Navy (1983), The Royal Dockyards 1690–1850, Architecture and Engineering Works of the Sailing Navy (1989), Dover Castle (1995), The Portsmouth Block Mills (2005); *Recreations* reading, travel, woodworking; *Clubs* Eclectic; *Style—* Jonathan G Coad, Esq, FSA; ✉ Baileys Reed, Salehurst, East Sussex TN32 5SP

COADY, Chantal; da of Anthony Coady (d 1975), and Sybil, *née* Bateman; *b* 17 April 1959; *Educ* St Leonards-Mayfield Convent of the Holy Child Jesus, St Martin's Sch of Art, Camberwell Sch of Art (BA); *m* Nov 1992, James Booth; 1 s (William Fergus b 26 Feb 1997), 1 da (Emily Sybil Esther b 17 May 1999); *Career* opened Rococo Chocolates 1983, fndr Campaign for Real Chocolate 1986, fndr (with Nicola and Alan Porter) Chocolate Society 1990; treas Bonnington Square Garden Assoc, supporter Sense; fndr memb Acad of Chocolate 2005; Chocolate Oscar Award for Best Chocolate Book Eurochocolate Festival Perugia 1996, winner Best Chocolate Book Gourmand Awards 2003; *Books* Chocolate - Food of the Gods (1993), The Chocolate Companion (1995, revised 2006), Real Chocolate (2003); *Recreations* food, wine, music, photography, spending time with family in London and Provence; *Clubs* Bluebird; *Style—* Ms Chantal Coady; ✉ Michael Alcock, Johnson & Alcock Ltd, Clerkenwell House, 45–47 Clerkenwell Green, London EC1R 0HT (tel 020 7251 0125, fax 020 7251 2172, e-mail chantal@rococochocolates.com)

COAKER, Vernon; MP; *Career* MP (Lab) Gedling 1997–; formerly: PPS to Stephen Timms, MP, *qv*, PPS to Rt Hon Estelle Morris, MP, *qv*; asst whip 2003–05, Govt whip 2005–06, Parly under sec of state Home Office 2006–; *Style—* Vernon Coaker, Esq, MP; ✉ House of Commons, London SW1A 0AA (tel 020 7219 3000, fax 0115 920 4500, e-mail coakerv@parliament.uk, website www.vernon-coaker-mp.co.uk)

COAKHAM, Prof Hugh Beresford; s of William Coakham (d 1973), and Evelyn Grace, *née* Cale; *b* 17 September 1944; *Educ* Windsor GS, UCL (BSc), UCH (MB BS); *m* 1, 15 May 1972, Elspeth Margaret, da of Harold Macfarlane; 1 da (Simone b 29 May 1977), 2 s (Alexander b 22 Dec 1978, Jonathan b 24 April 1982); m 2, 11 Sept 1992, Janet James, da of George McKie; *Career* conslt neurosurgeon Frenchay Hosp and Bristol Royal Infirmary 1980–, dir Brain Tumour Res Laboratory 1980–86, clinical dir Imperial Cancer Res Fund Paediatric and Neuro-Oncology Group 1990–96, prof of neurosurgery Univ of Bristol 1993–; memb Editorial Bd: Br Jl of Neurosurgery 1991, Clinical Neurosurgery 1992, Pan-Arab Jl of Neurosurgery 1998, Neurosurgical Revue; memb: Soc of Br Neurological Surgns, Br Neuropathological Assoc, Br Neuro-Oncology Gp, Euro Assoc of Neurosurgical Soc; author of numerous published papers in int jls of neurosurgery and cancer research; Heart of Gold Award BBC TV 1988 (for NHS fundraising), ABI Medical Award 1991, Hunterian prof Royal Coll of Surgns 1993; FRCS 1974, FRCP 1991 (MRCP); *Books* Recent Advances in Neuropathology (contrib, 1985), Tumours of the Brain (contrib, 1986), Biology of Brain Tumours (contrib, 1986), Medulloblastoma:Clinical and Biological Aspects (contrib, 1986), Progress in Surgery - Vol 2 (contrib, 1987), Progress in Paediatric Surgery - Vol 22 (contrib, 1989), Cranial Base Surgery (ed, 2000); *Recreations* jazz saxophone; *Style—* Prof Hugh Coakham; ✉ Mansion House Stables, Litfield Road, Clifton, Bristol BS8 3LL (tel 0117 973 4963, e-mail hcoakham@aol.com, website www.coakham.com); Neurosurgical Clinic, BUPA Hospital Bristol, Redland Hill, Bristol BS6 6UT (tel 0117 980 4075, website www.facepain.co.uk)

COATES, *see also:* Milnes Coates

COATES, Anne Voase (Mrs Anne Hickox); OBE (2004); da of Maj Laurence Calvert Coates (d 1968), and Kathleen Voase, *née* Rank (d 1977); *b* 12 December 1925; *Educ* High Trees Sch Horley, Bartrum Gables Broadstairs; *m* 24 April 1958 (m dis), Douglas Arthur Hickox (d 1988), s of Horace Robert Hickox (d 1987); 2 s (Anthony Laurence Voase b 30 Jan 1959, James Douglas Rank b 20 June 1965), 1 da (Emma Elizabeth b 11 April 1964); *Career* film editor; memb: Acad of Motion Picture Arts and Sciences, BAFTA; work incl: Lawrence of Arabia 1961–62, Becket 1963, Tunes of Glory 1960, Murder on the Orient Express 1975, The Elephant Man 1980, Greystoke Lord of the Apes 1983, Ragtime 1984, I Love You to Death 1989–90, Chaplin 1991–92, In the Line of Fire 1992/93, Pontiac Moon 1993–94, Congo 1994–95, Striptease 1995–96, Out of Sight 1997–98, Passion of Mind 1998–99, Erin Brockovich 1999, Sweet November 2000, Unfaithful 2001–02, Taking Lives 2003, Catch and Release 2004–05, The Golden Compass 2006–07; prodr The Medusa Touch 1977; *Awards* three BAFTA nominations 1975, 1981 and 1993, Academy Award USA 1962 (also nominated 1964, 1981, 1993 and 1999), four ACE nominations USA 1962, 1964, 1993 and 1999, ACE Career Achievement Award 1995, Woman in Film Crystal Int Award 1997, Carlton Woman in Film Award 2000; fell Br Acad 2007; *Style—* Ms Anne Coates, OBE; ✉ 8455 Fountain Avenue (Apt 621), Los Angeles, CA 90069, USA (tel 00 1 213 654 7282)

COATES, Clive; s of John Alfred Henry Coates (d 1963), and Sonja, *née* van Blaaderen (d 1995); *b* 21 October 1941; *Educ* St Paul's Sch London, Westminster Hotel Sch (Student of the Year 1964); *m* 1, 1965 (m dis 1983), Rosalind, *née* Cohen; 1 da (Emma Jane b 1966), 1 s (Ben Jonathan b 1968); m 2, 1984 (m dis 1994), Juliet Trestini, eld da of David Burns, MW; *Career* promotions mangr IEC Wine Soc of Stevenage 1967–73, dir Genevieve Wine Cellars 1973–75, exec dir Wines Div British Transport Hotels 1975–81, dir Les Amis du Vin (UK) 1981–84, fndr ed The Vine (monthly fine wine magazine) 1985– (special commendation Wine Guild of GB 1992), concurrently ind writer on wine, lectr and conslt; Glenfiddich Trophy for Trade Wine Writer of the Year 1980, Ruffino/Cyril Ray Meml Prize for writing on Italian wine 1994, Rame D'Or for Services to French wine 1994, Lanson Wine Writer of the Year and Champagne Writer of the Year 1998; MW 1971 (chm Educn Ctee 1985, memb Cncl 1976–82 and 1990–93); Chevalier de l'Ordre du Mérite Agricole 1994; *Books* Claret (1982), The Wines of France (1990), Grands Vins, The Finest Châteaux of Bordeaux (1995), Côte D'Or - A Celebration of the Great Wines of Burgundy (1997, winner of André Simon, James Beard and Clicquot Awards for Best Book of the Year), The Wine Lover's Companion to Burgandy (1997), Encyclopaedia of the Wines and Domaines of France (2000); *Recreations* music, cooking, visiting old churches, watching athletics and cricket, lying by a pool in the south of France with a good book; *Style—* Clive Coates, Esq

C

COATES, Sir David Charlton Frederick; 3 Bt (UK 1921), of Haypark, City of Belfast; s of Brig Sir Frederick Gregory Lindsay Coates, 2 Bt (d 1994), and Joan Nugent, *née* Spinks (d 2005); *b* 16 February 1948; *Educ* Millfield; *m* 1973, Christine Helen, da of Lewis F Marshall, of Ely, Cambs; 2 s (James Gregory David b 12 March 1977, Robert Lewis Edward b 22 July 1980); *Heir* s, James Coates; *Style—* Sir David Coates, Bt; ✉ Launchfield House, Briants Puddle, Dorchester, Dorset DT2 7HN

COATES, David Randall; CB (2000); *b* 22 March 1942; *Educ* Leeds GS, The Queen's Coll Oxford (BA), LSE (MScEcon); *Career* research asst Univ of Manchester 1966–68, econ advsr Miny of Technol and DTI 1968–74; DTI: sr econ advsr 1974–82, asst sec 1982–89, grade 3 1989, chief econ advsr 1990–2002; chm NW Economic Forecasting Panel NW Devpt Agency 2003–; *Recreations* family, gardening, music; *Style—* David Coates, Esq, CB

COATES, James Richard; CB (1992); s of William Richard Coates (d 1974), and Doris Coral, *née* Richmond (d 1992); *b* 18 October 1935; *Educ* Nottingham HS, Clare Coll Cambridge (major scholar, MA); *m* 22 March 1969, (Helen) Rosamund, da of John William Rimington, MBE (d 1996); 1 s (Nicholas Benjamin b 14 Nov 1972), 1 da (Beatrice Emma b 28 May 1975); *Career* Miny of Tport: asst princ 1959–63, princ Road Safety and Channel Tunnel Divs 1963–69, private sec to Min 1969–71; DOE: asst sec 1972–77, Urban Tport Policy Div 1972–75, Directorate of Civil Accommodation (PSA) 1975–77, under sec 1977–83, dir of civil accommodation 1977–79, dir London Region (PSA) 1979–83; Dept of Tport: under sec 1983–, Highways Policy and Prog Directorate 1983–85, Railways Directorate 1985–91, Urban and Gen Directorate 1991–94, Urban and Local Tport Directorate 1994–95; independent conslt 1995–; FCIT 1996, FCILT 2004; *Recreations* reading, listening to music, looking at buildings; *Style—* James Coates, Esq, CB; ✉ 10 Alwyne Road, London N1 2HH (tel 020 7359 7827)

COATES, Prof John Henry; s of James Henry Coates (d 1970), of Australia, and Beryl Lilian, *née* Lee (d 1952); *b* 26 January 1945; *Educ* Australian Nat Univ (BSc), Ecole Normale Superieure Paris, Univ of Cambridge; *m* 8 Jan 1966, Julie Mildred, da of Henry Basil Turner (d 1988); 3 s (David b 3 Jan 1970, Stephen b 7 Nov 1971, Philip b 22 June 1973); *Career* asst prof Harvard Univ 1969–72, assoc prof Stanford Univ 1972–75, lectr Univ of Cambridge 1975–77; prof: Australian Nat Univ 1977–78, Université de Paris XI (Orsay) 1978–85; prof and dir of mathematics École Normale Superieure Paris 1985–86; Univ of Cambridge: fell Emmanuel Coll 1975–77 and 1986–, Sadleirian prof of mathematics 1986–, head Dept of Pure Mathematics and Mathematical Statistics 1991–97; pres London Mathematical Soc 1988–90, vice-pres Int Mathematical Union 1991–95; Dr (hc) École Normale Superieure Paris 1997; FRS 1985; *Style—* Prof John Coates, FRS; ✉ 104 Mawson Road, Cambridge CB1 2EA (tel 01223 360884); Department of Pure Mathematics and Mathematical Statistics, University of Cambridge, 16 Mill Lane, Cambridge CB2 1SB (tel 01223 337989, fax 01223 337920, e-mail j.h.coates@dpmms.cam.ac.uk)

COATES, His Hon Judge Marten Frank; s of Frank Herbert Coates (d 2000), of Henley-in-Arden, Warks, and Violet, *née* Livermore (d 2003); *b* 26 March 1947; *Educ* Pocklington Sch, Univ of Durham (BA); *m* 17 Feb 1973, Susan, da of Dr Derek Anton-Stephens, of Leighton Powys; 3 da (Laura Jane b 17 March 1977, Anna Louise, Mary Elizabeth (twins) b 10 Oct 1978); *Career* called to the Bar Inner Temple 1972, recorder of the Crown Court 1993–97, circuit judge (Midland & Oxford circuit) 1997–; chllr Lichfield Dio 2006–; *Style—* His Hon Judge Coates; ✉ The Priory Courts, 33 Bull Street, Birmingham B4 6DW

COATES, Michael Odiarne; s of Gordon Lionel Coates (d 1990), of Oxted, Surrey, and Dorothy Madeleine, *née* Nelson (d 2003); *b* 4 July 1938; *Educ* Haileybury and ISC; *m* 20 April 1963, Frances Ann, da of Harold P S Paish; 2 da (Annabel Frances b 29 March 1965, Rebecca Jane b 21 Jan 1967); *Career* qualified chartered quantity surveyor 1962, sr ptnr Gardiner and Theobald 1979–2000 (ptnr 1966–); memb Cncl Benenden Sch 1982–; Past Master Worshipful Co of Chartered Surveyors, memb Worshipful Co of Masons; FRICS 1971; *Recreations* wife and family, farming, sports; *Clubs* Boodle's; *Style—* Michael Coates, Esq; ✉ Great Shoesmiths Farm, White Gates Lane, Wadhurst, East Sussex TN5 6QG (tel 01892 782156)

COATES, Prof Nigel; s of Douglas Coates, of Great Malvern, Worcs, and Margaret Trigg, of Cambridge; *b* 2 March 1949; *Educ* Hanley Castle GS Malvern, Univ of Nottingham (BArch), Architectural Assoc London (AADipl, year prize, Italian Govt scholarship to Univ of Rome); *Career* architect and designer; unit master Architectural Assoc 1979–89, fndr memb Narrative Architecture Today (NATO) 1983–86, course master Bennington Coll Vermont USA 1980–81; fndr ptnr: Branson Coates Architecture (with Doug Branson) 1985–, Nigel Coates Designs 1987–; TV features incl: Building Sites (BBC 2) 1989, Omnibus (BBC 1) 1992; work featured in numerous int pubns and jls; lectr worldwide; prof of architectural design RCA 1995– (currently head Dept of Architecture); external examiner: Bartlett Sch of Architecture and Architectural Assoc 1993–94, Dept of Architecture Univ of Cambridge 2000–02; memb Advsy Bd ICA 1987–89, chm Architecture Ctee V&A 2003; columnist Independent on Sunday 2003–; tstee Architecture Fndn 2000–; memb Soc of Authors; *Projects* with Branson Coates: Arca di Noe Japan 1988, Katharine Hamnett Shop London 1988, Hotel Otaru Marittimo Japan 1989, Nishi Azabu Wall Tokyo 1990, Taxim Nightclub Istanbul 1991, Art Silo Building Tokyo 1993, La Forêt and Nautilus Restaurants Schiphol Airport Amsterdam 1993, shops for Jigsaw women and men's fashion in UK, Ireland and Japan, new depts for Liberty store Regent's Street, Bargo bar Glasgow 1996, gallery extention of Geffrye Museum London 1998, Nat Centre for Popular Music Sheffield 1999, Body Zone Millennium Dome Greenwich 2000, Inside Out (Br Cncl int travelling exhbn) 2001, Marketing Suite and Roman Amphitheatre display London 2002; Living Bridge Exhbn Royal Acad 1996, Erotic Design Exhbn Design Museum 1996, Br Exhbn Lisbon '98, Powerhouse::uk Horseguards Parade London 1998, House to Home Exhbn Houses of Parliament 2004; *Design Commissions* Metropole and Jazz furniture collections (for Rockstone) 1986, Noah collection (for SCP) 1988, Female, He-man and She-woman mannequins (for Omniate) 1988, Tongue chair (for SCP) 1989, carpet collection (for V'soske Joyce) 1990, Slipper chair (for Hitch Mylius) 1994, collection of mannequins (for Stockman London) 1994, David collection (for Liberty) 1995, glassware (for Simon Moore) 1997, Oyster Furniture Collection (for Lloyd Loom of Spalding) 1998–, OXO sofa system (for Hitch Mylius) 1998, Fiesolani glassware collection (for Salvati) 2002, Tête á Tête furniture and glassware collection (for Fornasetti) 2002, Dafne lamps (for Slamp) 2003, Shoom bowl (for Alessi) 2004; *Exhibitions* incl: Latent Utopias (Graz) 2002, Micro Utopias (Valencia Bienual) 2003, Vextacity (Fabbrica Europa Florence) 2003; work exhibited in London, Milan, NY, Paris and Tokyo and in the collections of V&A London and Cooper-Hewitt NY; *Awards* Inter-Design Award for contrib to Japanese cities through architectural work 1990; with Branson Coates: finalist

BBC Design Awards 1994, finalist invited competition for luxury highrise apartments Beirut 1995, invited competition for Millennium Markers Richmond 1995, winner of Concept House (Oyster House) 1998; *Publications* Guide to Ecstacity (2003), Collidoscope (2004); *Monographs* The City in Motion, Rick Poyner (1989), Nigel Coates: Body Buildings and City Scapes, Jonathan Glancey, Cutting Edge series (1999); *Recreations* contemporary art, video making, motorcycling, Italian language and culture; *Clubs* Groucho, Blacks; *Style*— Prof Nigel Coates

COATES, Prof Philip David; s of Frank Coates (d 1983), of Leeds, and Elsie, *née* Tyreman; *b* 20 September 1948; *Educ* Cockburn HS Leeds, Imperial Coll London (BSc), Univ of Leeds (MSc, PhD); *m* 3 July 1971, Jane Margaret, da of Robert (Sandy) McNab (d 1994); 3 da (Emma Caroline b 8 March 1975, Charlotte Ruth b 14 Nov 1977, Laura Jane b 2 Sept 1984), 1 s (John Philip b 6 Aug 1986); *Career* post-doctoral res fell in physics Univ of Leeds 1976–78; Univ of Bradford: lectr in manufacturing systems engrg 1978–81, lectr in mechanical engrg 1981–84, sr lectr in mechanical engrg 1984–89, reader 1989–90, prof of polymer engrg Dept of Mechanical and Medical Engrg/IRC in Polymer Sci and Technol Univ of Bradford 1990–, dir Polymer Insights 1994–, assoc dir IRC in Polymer Sci and Technol 1996–, pro-vice-chllr Research Innovation & Knowledge Transfer 2004–; conslt various cos 1979–, tech assessor DTI 1993–; memb: Plymers and Composites Ctee SERC 1989–92, Structural Composites Ctee DTI/SERC Link 1989–; chm Polymer Processing and Engrg Ctee Inst of Materials 1989– (memb cncl 2000–); ed Plastics, Rubber and Composites 1999–; organiser of eleven int confs in polymer field; FIM 1987, FIMechE 1990, FREng 1995; *Awards* Competitive Res Fellowship Sci Research Cncl 1976–78, Silver Medal Plastics and Rubber Inst 1982 and 1987, Personal Res Award Wolfson Fndn 1988, Thatcher Bros Prize IMechE 1995, Netlon Award Inst of Materials 1999; *Publications* Concise Encyclopedia of Polymer Processing (contrib, 1992), Encyclopedia of Advanced Materials (contrib, 1994), Reactive Processing of Polymers (contrib, 1994), Polymer Process Engineering (ed, 1997 and 1999), Solid Phase Processing of Polymers (ed, 2000); author of over 210 scientific pubns; *Recreations* family, playing various musical instruments, computers, gardening; *Style*— Prof Philip Coates, FREng; ✉ University of Bradford, Bradford BD7 1DP (tel 01274 234540, fax 01274 234505, e-mail p.d.coates@bradford.ac.uk)

COATS, Sir Alastair Francis Stuart; 4 Bt (UK 1905), of Auchendrane, Maybole, Co Ayr; s of Lt-Col Sir James Stuart Coats, 3 Bt, MC (d 1966), and Lady Amy Gordon-Lennox, er da of 8 Duke of Richmond (d 1975); *b* 18 November 1921; *Educ* Eton; *m* 6 Feb 1947, Lukyn, da of Capt Charles Gordon; 1 da (Sarah Mary (Mrs Sarah Lloyd) b 1948), 1 s (Alexander James b 1951); *Heir* s, Alexander Coats; *Career* Capt Coldstream Gds 1939–45; *Style*— Sir Alastair Coats, Bt; ✉ Birchwood House, Durford Wood, Petersfield, Hampshire GU31 5AW (tel 01730 892254)

COATS, Dr David Jervis; CBE (1984); s of Rev William Holms Coats, DD (d 1954), of Glasgow, and Muriel Gwendoline, *née* Fowler (d 1984); *b* 25 January 1924; *Educ* HS of Glasgow, Univ of Glasgow (BSc); *m* 24 March 1955, Hazel Bell, da of John Livingstone (d 1979), of Glasgow: 2 da (Gillian b 1956, Pamela b 1958), 1 s (Michael b 1960); *Career* REME 1943–47, Major cmdg Mobile Workshop Company in India 1947; Babtie Shaw and Morton: engr in design office and on sites 1947–61, ptnr 1962–78, sr ptnr 1979–87, sr conslt 1988–93; appointed memb all reservoirs panel of engrs under Reservoirs Act 1975 and its predecessors 1968–98; chm Assoc Consulting Engrs 1979–80; vice-pres: Int Cmmn on Large Dams 1983–86 (chm Br Section 1980–83), ICE 1987–89; convenor Glasgow Univ Business Ctee of Gen Cncl 1982–85; chm: Glasgow Univ Tst 1985–92, Scot Construction Indust Gp 1986–92; Hon DSc Univ of Glasgow 1984; FICE, FREng 1982, FRSE 1986, FRSA; *Publications* author of many papers published in learned jls (awarded Telford Medal ICE 1983); *Recreations* genealogy, family, TV and cinema, painting; *Style*— Dr David Coats, CBE, FREng, FRSE; ✉ 8/9 Rattray Drive, Edinburgh EH10 5TH (tel 0131 447 0223, e-mail david.coats2@btopenworld.com)

COATS, Percy Murray; s of Percy Murray Coats (d 1968), and Lizzie Burroughs Blance (d 1980); *b* 8 January 1941; *Educ* Highgate Sch, Bishop Vesey's GS Sutton Coldfield, Univ of London, St George's Hosp (MB BS, DCH); *m* 20 Sept 1975, Margaret Elisabeth Joan, da of Donald Clarence Ashley; 3 da (Louise b 1976, Caroline b 1978, Maria b 1981), 1 s (Edward b 1980); *Career* Surgn Lt RN 1966–72; Queen Charlotte's and Chelsea Hosp for Women 1973–74, King's Coll Hosp 1974–80, conslt obstetrician and gynaecologist SW Surrey Health Dist 1980–2001, dist tutor in obstetrics and gynaecology SW Surrey, med dir Surrey County Hosp NHS Tst 1995–97 (dir Obstetrics and Gynaecology Dept 1990–95), special professional interest ultrasound and subfertility; author of specialist medical papers; Liveryman Worshipful Soc of Apothecaries; memb: BMA, London Obstetrics and Gynaecological Soc; MRCP, FRCS 1974, FRCOG 1988; *Publications* specialist medical papers; *Recreations* fly fishing; *Clubs* Royal Soc of Med, Carlton; *Style*— Percy M Coats, Esq; ✉ Fairacre, Horsham Road, Bramley, Surrey GU5 0AW; Private Consulting Rooms, Nuffield Hospital, Guildford (tel 01483 555812, e-mail p.coats@btinternet.com)

COBB, John Martin; s of Richard Martin Cobb (d 1966), of Rochester, Kent, and Ursula Joan, *née* Abell (d 1990); *b* 28 September 1931; *Educ* Canford Sch; *m* 25 July 1959, Susan Mary Cochrane, yst da of Roderick Watson (d 1975), of London; 2 da (Mary b 1960, Philippa b 1962), 1 s (James b 1964); *Career* seaman offr RN 1949–69; served Far East, Aust, Med, W Indies and the Persian Gulf, cmd landing ship and anti-submarine frigate; def policy staff MOD 1966–69, ret as Cdr (RN) 1969; Private Clients Dept Sheppards Stockbrokers 1969–91 (ptnr and dir i/c 1982–89), currently chm London Pension Fund Bank Julius Baer; chm: Assoc of Private Client Investment Managers and Stockbrokers (APCIMS) 1990–97, City North Group plc 1998–; FSI; *Recreations* skiing, riding, gardening, music; *Style*— J M Cobb, Esq; ✉ c/o Bank Julius Baer Investments Ltd, Bevis Marks House, Bevis Marks, London EC3A 7NE (tel 020 7623 4211)

COBB, Stephen William Scott; QC (2003); s of Sir John Cobb (d 1977), of Harrogate, N Yorks, and Joan Mary, *née* Knapton; *b* 12 April 1962, Sheffield; *Educ* Winchester, Univ of Liverpool (LLB); *m* 16 Dec 1989, Samantha, *née* Cowling; 1 da (Isabel b 31 Jan 1992), 2 s (James b 2 Jan 1994, Edward b 4 March 1997); *Career* called to the Bar Inner Temple 1985; recorder 2004–; memb: Family Justice Cncl 2004–, Professional Advsy Gp Nat Youth Advocacy Serv, Ctee Family Law Bar Assoc; *Publications* Essential Family Practice (ed, 2000, 2001 and 2002), Clarke Hall and Morrison on Children (ed, 2006); *Recreations* sailing, family; *Clubs* Bembridge Sailing; *Style*— Stephen Cobb, Esq, QC; ✉ One Garden Court, Temple, London EC4Y 9BJ (tel 020 7797 7900, fax 020 7797 7929, e-mail cobb@1gc.com)

COBBE, Prof Stuart Malcolm; s of Brian Morton Cobbe, OBE (d 1991), and Catherine Mary, *née* Caddy (d 1985); *b* 2 May 1948; *Educ* Royal GS Guildford, Univ of Cambridge (MA, MD), St Thomas' Hosp Med Sch (MB BChir); *m* 11 Dec 1970, Patricia Frances, da of George Bertram Barrett, of London; 3 da (Lindsay Ann, Heather Jane (twins) b 21 Aug 1974, Sarah Caroline b 9 May 1977); *Career* gen med trg in Nottingham, Birmingham, Worthing and St Thomas' Hosp London 1972–76, registrar in cardiology Nat Heart Hosp London 1976–77, res fell in cardiology Cardiothoracic Inst London 1977–79, sr registrar in cardiology John Radcliffe Hosp London 1979–81, res fell Univ of Heidelberg Germany 1981–82, clinical reader John Radcliffe Hosp Oxford 1982–85, Walton prof of med cardiology Univ of Glasgow 1985–; author of over 200 scientific papers on cardiac metabolism, cardiac arrhythmias, coronary prevention and other cardiac topics; memb: Br Cardiac Soc, Assoc of Physicians of GB and I; FRCP, FRCPG, FMedSci, FRSE; *Recreations* walking; *Style*— Prof Stuart Cobbe; ✉ Department of Medical Cardiology, Royal Infirmary, 10 Alexandra Parade, Glasgow G31 2ER (tel 0141 211 4722, fax 0141 552 4683, e-mail stuart.cobbe@clinmed.gla.ac.uk)

COBBOLD, 2 Baron (UK 1960), of Knebworth, Co Hertford; David Antony Fromanteel Lytton Cobbold; DL (Herts 1993); er s of 1 Baron Cobbold, KG, GCVO, PC (d 1987); assumed by Deed Poll 1960 the additional surname of Lytton before his patronymic; *b* 14 July 1937; *Educ* Eton, Trinity Coll Cambridge (BA); *m* 7 Jan 1961, Christine Elizabeth, 3 da of Maj Sir Dennis Frederick Bankes Stucley, 5 Bt (d 1983); 3 s (Hon Henry Fromanteel b 1962, Hon Peter Guy Fromanteel b 1964, Hon Richard Stucley Fromanteel b 1968, a Page of Honour to HM The Queen 1980–82), 1 da (Hon Rosina Kim b 1971); *Heir* s, Hon Henry Lytton Cobbold; *Career* NATO flying in Canada, served in RAF 1955–57; Bank of London and S America 1962–72, Finance for Industry 1974–79, BP 1979–87, TSB England and Wales plc 1987–88; md Gaiacorp UK Ltd 1989–94; dir: 39 Production Co Ltd 1987–2000, Hill Samuel Bank Ltd 1988–89, Close Brothers Gp plc 1993–2000, Stevenage Leisure Ltd 1999–2002, English Sinfonia Ltd 1999–2002, Shuttleworth Tst 1999–2002; chm: Lytton Enterprises Ltd 1970–, Stevenage Community Tst 1990–2006; hon treas Historic Houses Assoc 1988–97, govr Union of Euro Historic Houses Assocs 1993–97; crossbench memb House of Lords; Univ of Herts: pres Devpt Ctee 1992–2005, memb Bd of Govrs 1993–2005, fell 2006; tstee: Pilgrim Tst 1993–, Knebworth House Educn and Preservation Tst 2001–; FACT 1983; *Style*— The Lord Cobbold, DL; ✉ Park Gate House, Knebworth, Hertfordshire SG3 6QD (tel and fax 01438 817455, website www.knebworthhouse.com); 2D Park Place Villas, London W2 1SP (tel 020 7724 3734)

COBBOLD, Hon Rowland John Fromanteel; yr s of 1 Baron Cobbold, KG, GCVO, PC; *b* 20 June 1944; *Educ* Eton, Trinity Coll Cambridge (MA); *m* 3 June 1969, Sophia Augusta, da of late B N White-Spunner; 1 s, 1 da; *Career* Lt Kent and Co of London Yeo (TA); with BOAC/Br Airways 1966–80, Swire Group 1980–94; chm Ecco Tours Ltd 1995–, dir Groundstar Ltd 1999–2004; Cathay Pacific Airways 1987–94, regnl dir (Europe) Hong Kong Tourist Assoc 1994–97, Air Partner plc 1996–2004; dir Swindon and Marlborough NHS Tst 2003–; *Clubs* White's, Hong Kong, Shek-O; *Style*— The Hon Rowland Cobbold; ✉ Hallam House, Ogbourne St George, Marlborough, Wiltshire SN8 1SG (tel 01672 841212)

COBDEN, Dr Irving; s of Manuel Cobden, of Newcastle upon Tyne, and Fay, *née* Alexander; *b* 18 May 1950; *Educ* Royal GS Newcastle upon Tyne, Univ of Newcastle Med Sch (MB BS, MD); *m* 1, 1972 (m dis 1991), Jennifer Deborah, da of Mark Gilbert; 3 da (Sarah b 1975, Gemma b 1977, Laura b 1982); m 2, 1992, Carolyn Michelle, da of Kenneth Collett; 2 da (Imogen b 1994, Josephine b 1996); *Career* conslt physician N Tyneside Health Centre 1985–, clinical tutor in postgrad med 1986–92, clinical lectr in med Univ of Newcastle upon Tyne 1992–, clinical dir of med North Tyneside Hospital 1994–98, med dir Northumbria Healthcare NHS Tst 1998–2002, sr med advsr Dept of Health 2002–, hon clinical reader Hull-York Med Sch 2004–, med dir Tees, E and N Yorks Ambulance Service 2004–; Wyeth USA travelling fell 1988; contrib many pubns on gastroenterology; hon fell Société Royale Belge de Gastro Enterologie; MRCP 1976, FRCP 1991; *Recreations* bridge, angling, travel, golf; *Style*— Dr Irving Cobden; ✉ North Tyneside Hospital, Rake Lane, North Shields, Tyne & Wear NE29 8NH (tel 0191 2932581, e-mail irving.cobden@northumbria-healthcare.nhs)

COBHAM, Viscountess Penelope; da of Roy Cooper (d 1980), and Dorothy, *née* Henshall (subsequently Mrs Turner, d 2006); *b* 2 January 1954, Manchester; *Educ* St James's Sch Malvern; *Career* prtnr Hagley Hall recreation 1979–1994, chm Triton Television Ltd 1989–92, dir Chrysalis Radio London Ltd 1994–2000, chm Chrysalis Radio Midlands Ltd 1993–2007; conslt Ernst & Young; dep chm Visit Britain 2005– (memb Bd 2003–); cmmr: English Heritage 1989–92, Countryside Cmmn 1991–92, Museums and Galleries Cmmn 1993–2000; special advsr to Sec of State for Nat Heritage 1992, tstee V&A 1993–2003; memb Bd: Historic Royal Palaces Bd 1990–98, LAPADA 1993–94, London Docklands Devpt Corporation 1993–99; chm of tstees: Civic Tst 1999–2003, Art Fund Prize for Museums & Galleries; chm Br Casino Assoc, dir Partridge Fine Art; memb Cncl: Nat Tst, Historic Houses Assoc; pres Midlands Woman of the Year; *Recreations* historic buildings, gardening; *Style*— Penelope, Viscountess Cobham; ✉ Canal House, 200 Hagley Road, Stourbridge, West Midlands DY8 2JN (e-mail canalhse@aol.com)

COCHAND, Charles Maclean (Chas); s of Louis Emile Cochand, and Morna Aldous, *née* Maclean; *b* 2 May 1951; *Educ* Aiglon Coll Chesieres Villars, Univ of Western Ontario (BA); *m* 6 July 1982, Judith Ann, da of John David Harrison, QC, OBE; 3 s (Nicholas John b 1984, Matthew Charles b 1986, Alexander Maclean b 1989); *Career* called to the Bar Middle Temple 1978; in criminal law practice Western Circuit; *Recreations* writing, sailing, skiing, scouting; *Clubs* Eagle Ski (Gstaad); *Style*— Chas M Cochand, Esq; ✉ Brook Farm, Blissford, Fordingbridge, Hampshire SP6 2JQ; De Grassi Pt, Lefroy, Ontario, Canada L0L 1W0; 18 Carlton Crescent, Southampton SO15 2ET (tel 023 8063 9001, fax 023 8033 9625)

COCHRANE, Dr Gordon McLellan (Mac); s of Robert Brown Cochrane, of Cheltenham, and Ivy, *née* Elvidge; *b* 24 February 1945; *Educ* Tudor Grange GS Solihull, Univ of London (BSc, MB BS); *m* 3 Sept 1966, Jill Lesley, da of Lt Sidney Herbert Castleton, of Solihull; 1 s (James b 15 April 1974), 1 da (Katie b 12 March 1979); *Career* sr house offr and registrar Brompton Hosp 1971–73, conslt physician Guy's 1977– (houseman 1969–70, lectr and registrar 1973–79), hon sr lectr in physicology UMDS, chm of confidential inquiry into the death of Ms S Bull for Greenwich Health Authy, SE Thames RHA and DHSS 1985–86; educnl film Understanding Asthma won BMA film competition Gold Award 1984, BLAT trophy 1985; Univ of London rep to Greenwich Health Authy 1983–, memb Editorial Bd Thorax 1984–, memb Cncl and chm Manpower Ctee Br Thoracic Soc 1989, memb Int Bd of Soc of Euro Pneumologists; FRCP 1985 (MRCP 1972), FRSM 1986; *Books* Bronchodilator Therapy (ed, 1984), Colour Atlas of Asthma (jtly, 1989); articles: Asthma Mortality (jtly Thorax, 1975), Management of Asthma in General Practice (jtly Respiratory Medicine, 1989), Compliance with Therapy in Asthmatics (European Respiratory Jl, 1993); *Recreations* skiing, walking, wine tasting, photography; *Style*— Dr Mac Cochrane

COCHRANE, Keith; *Career* CA; early career with Arthur Andersen, gp chief exec Stagecoach Holdings plc 1996–2002, dir of gp financial reporting Scottish Power 2003–06, gp finance dir The Weir Gp plc 2006–; *Style*— Keith Cochrane, Esq

COCHRANE, Sir (Henry) Marc Sursock; 4 Bt (UK 1903), of Woodbrook, Old Connaught, Bray, Co Wicklow, Lisgar Castle, Bailieborough, Co Cavan, and Kildare Street, City of Dublin; s of Sir Desmond Oriel Alastair George Weston Cochrane, 3 Bt (d 1979), and Yvonne, *née* Sursock; *b* 23 October 1946; *Educ* Eton, Trinity Coll Dublin (BBS, MA); *m* 28 June 1969, Hala, 2 da of Fouad Mahmoud Bey es-Said, of Beirut; 2 s (Alexander Desmond Sursock b 1973, Patrick Talal b 1976), 1 da (Faiza Maria Rosebud b 1971); *Heir* s, Alexander Cochrane; *Career* hon consul gen for Ireland in Lebanon 1979–84; dir: Hambros Bank Ltd 1979–85, GT Management plc/LGT Asset Mgmnt 1985–98, INVESCO 1998–99, Henderson Global Investors 2000–; tstee Chester Beatty Library and Gallery of Oriental Art Dublin; *Recreations* electronics, skiing, shooting; *Clubs* Annabel's, Ham & Petersham Rifle and pistol; *Style*— Sir Marc Cochrane, Bt; ✉ Woodbrook, Bray, Co Wicklow, Republic of Ireland (tel 00 3531 2821421); Palais Sursock, Beirut, Lebanon

COCHRANE, Prof Peter; OBE (1999); s of Colin Cochrane, of Sutton-in-Ashfield, Notts, and Gladys, *née* Keeton; *b* 11 July 1946; *Educ* Trent Poly (BSc, IEE Prize of the Year), Univ of Essex (MSc, PhD, DSc); *m* 2 May 1971, Brenda; 2 da (Catherine b 24 Sept 1973, Sarah b 16 Dec 1974), 2 s (Richard b 27 Nov 1981, Paul b 25 Aug 1987); *Career* student engr British PO 1969–73 (technician system maintenance 1962–69), head of gp British PO

Research Labs 1979–83 (exec engr 1973–79); British Telecom: head of section BTRL 1983–87, divnl mangr Optical Networks BTRL 1987–91, divnl mangr systems research BT Labs 1991–93, gen mangr BT Research Labs 1993–94, head of BT Labs Advanced Research 1994–99, chief technologist 1999–2001; co-fndr and dir Concept Labs California 1998–, dir Picosecond Pulse Labs Colorado 1999–2006, co-founding dir Knowledge Vector NC 2003–; non-exec dir iBookers 1999–2003; pt/t lectr People's Coll of Further Educn Nottingham 1972, visiting prof CNET Lannion Univ France 1978, visiting industrial prof Poly of East London 1980–90, scientific collaborator Univ of Liège 1981–91, industrial visiting fell UNCW at Bangor 1985–90; visiting prof: Univ of Essex 1988–2001, Opto-electronics Research Centre Univ of Southampton 1991–98, Telecommunications & IT Systems Centre UCL 1994–2000; hon prof of communication & electronics and memb Ct Univ of Kent 1991–99; Collier Chair for the Public Understanding of Science and Technology Univ of Bristol 1999–2001; external examiner: CNAA MSc in Info Systems Robert Gordon's Inst of Technol 1990–93, CNAA BSc in Electrical Engrg Nottingham Poly 1991–94; memb Computer Science Corporation Advsy Bd 1996–99; occasional lectr and presenter on telecommunication matters worldwide; author of over 700 scientific papers, patents, articles, edited books and chapters; Hon DUniv Essex 1996; Hon DTech: Staffordshire Univ 1996, Robert Gordon Univ 1999, Univ of Abertay Dundee 2004; Hon DEng: Nottingham Trent Univ 1999, Brunel Univ 2002; FIEE 1987 (MIEE 1977), FIEEE 1992 (MIEEE 1983, sr memb 1987), FREng 1994 (CEng 1977), memb NY Acad of Scis 1995; *Recreations* swimming, running, walking, music, reading, flyfishing; *Style*— Prof Peter Cochrane, OBE, FREng; ✉ Cochrane Associates, Suffolk (tel 07747 863013, e-mail peter@ca-global.org)

COCHRANE OF CULTS, 4 Baron (UK 1919); (Ralph Henry) Vere Cochrane; DL (Fife, 1976); 2 s of 2 Baron Cochrane of Cults, DSO (d 1968), and his 1 w, Hon Elin, *née* Douglas-Pennant (d 1934), yst da of 2 Baron Penrhyn; suc bro, 3 Baron 1990; *b* 20 September 1926; *Educ* Eton, King's Coll Cambridge (MA); *m* 18 Dec 1956, (Janet) Mary (Watson), da of Dr William Hunter Watson Cheyne, MB, MRCS, LRCP (d 1957); 2 s (Hon Thomas Hunter Vere b 7 Sept 1957, Capt Hon Michael Charles Nicholas, OBE, RN b 1959); *Heir* s, Hon Thomas Cochrane; *Career* Lt RE 1945–48; farmer 1951–; memb House of Lords 1990–99 (Private Members Bill enacted 1993), underwriting memb Lloyds 1965–96; tstee and vice-chm Cupar Fife TSB 1960–73, dir Tayside and Central TSB (Fife Area Bd) 1973–83, dir and chm Craigtoun Meadows Ltd 1972–; gen cmmr for Income Tax 1962–2001; cmmr Scout Assoc (incl serv at Scottish HQ and memb Cncl) 1952–73; memb Queen's Body Guard for Scotland (Royal Co of Archers) 1962–; *Recreations* travel, industrial archaeology, railways, racehorse owner; *Clubs* New (Edinburgh); *Style*— The Rt Hon Lord Cochrane of Cults

COCKAYNE, Prof David John Hugh; s of John Henry Cockayne (d 1992), and Ivy, *née* Hatton (d 1965); *b* 19 March 1942; *Educ* Geelong C of E GS, Trinity Coll Univ of Melbourne (BSc, MSc), Magdalen Coll Oxford (DPhil); *m* 28 July 1967, Jean Mary Kerr; 2 da (Sophie b 11 May 1973, Tamsin b 11 March 1975), 1 s (James b 10 Nov 1977); *Career* research fell Dept of Materials Univ of Oxford 1969–74, research lectr and jr research fell ChCh Oxford 1969–74; Univ of Sydney: dir Electron Microscope Unit 1974–2000, prof of physics 1992–2000; fell Linacre Coll Oxford 2000–, prof of the physical examination of materials Univ of Oxford 2000–; gen sec Asia-Pacific Socs for Electron Microscopy 1984–96, gen sec Int Fedn of Socs for Electron Microscopy 1995–2002, pres Int Fedn of Socs for Microscopy 2003–; hon prof: Univ of Science and Technol Beijing 2005–, Univ of Sydney, Lanzhou Univ; author of more than 190 published papers; FRS 1999, FInstP 1999, FAIP 1999; *Recreations* walking; *Style*— Prof David Cockayne; ✉ Department of Materials, University of Oxford, Parks Road, Oxford OX1 3PH (tel 01865 273654, e-mail david.cockayne@materials.ox.ac.uk)

COCKBURN, Charles Christopher; s and h of Sir John Elliot Cockburn, 12 Bt, *qv*, and Glory Patricia, *née* Mullings; *b* 19 November 1950; *Educ* Emanuel Sch, City of London Poly (BA), Garnett Coll London (CertEd); *m* 1, 1978, Beverly J (d 1999), o da of B Stangroom (d 1995), of Richmond, Surrey; m 2, 1985, Margaret Ruth, da of Samuel Esmond Bell (d 1999), of Bury Green, Herts; 2 s (Christopher Samuel Alexander b 24 March 1986, William James John b 26 Feb 1996), 1 da (Charlotte Elspeth Catherine (twin) b 24 March 1986); *Career* lectr; conslt in govt relations, ed Financial Regulation Review, chm Portcullis Research Ltd (govt relations conslts); MCIPR, MInstD; *Recreations* rowing, cycling, song writing, travelling; *Clubs* IOD, Twickenham Rowing; *Style*— Charles Cockburn, Esq; ✉ West Dene House, 84 Medstead Road, Beech, Alton, Hampshire GU34 4AE; Portcullis Research Limited, St James House, 13 Kensington Square, London W8 5HD (tel 020 7368 3100, e-mail info@portcullispublicaffairs.com)

COCKBURN, Prof Forrester; s of Forrester Cockburn, and Violet Elizabeth, *née* Bunce; *b* 13 October 1934; *Educ* Leith Acad, Univ of Edinburgh (MB ChB, MD); *m* 15 Jan 1960, Alison Fisher, da of Roger Allison Grieve; 2 s (David, John); *Career* Huntington - Hartford res fell Univ of Boston USA 1963–65, Nuffield sr res fell Univ of Oxford 1965–66, Wellcome sr res fell Univ of Edinburgh 1966–71, sr lectr Dept of Child Life and Health Univ of Edinburgh 1971–77, Samson Gemmell prof of child health Royal Hosp for Sick Children Glasgow 1977–96 (prof emeritus 1996–); chm: Yorkhill NHS Tst, Children's Hospice Assoc Scotland; FRCPGlas, FRCPEd, Hon FRCPCH, Hon FRCSEd, FRSE 1999; *Books* Neonatal Medicine (with Drillien, 1974), Practical Paediatric Problems (with Hutchison, 6 edn, 1986), Craig's Care of the Newly Born Infant (with Turner and Douglas, 1988), Fetal and Neonatal Growth (1988), Diseases of the Fetus and Newborn (jtly, 1995), Children's Medicine and Surgery (jtly, 1995); *Recreations* sailing; *Style*— Prof Forrester Cockburn, CBE, FRSE; ✉ 53 Hamilton Drive, Glasgow G12 8DP (tel 0141 339 2973); Department of Child Health, Royal Hospital for Sick Children, Yorkhill, Glasgow G3 8SJ (tel 0141 201 0236, fax 0141 201 0837)

COCKBURN, Sir John Elliot; 12 Bt of that Ilk (NS 1671); s of Lt-Col Sir John Brydges Cockburn, 11 Bt, DSO (d 1949), and Isabel Hunter, *née* McQueen (d 1978); *b* 7 December 1925; *Educ* RNC Dartmouth, RAC Cirencester; *m* 7 Sept 1949, Glory Patricia, er da of late Nigel Tudway Mullings, of Cirencester, Glos; 3 s (Charles Christopher b 1950, James Chandos b 1952, Jonathan McQueen b 1956), 2 da (Julia Georgina b 1954, Catherine Isabel (Mrs Stephen E Keal) (twin) b 1956); *Heir* s, Charles Cockburn, *qv*; *Career* served RAFVR 1943–48; wine broker; *Style*— Sir John Cockburn, Bt; ✉ 48 Frewin Road, London SW18 3LP

COCKBURN, William; CBE (1989), TD (1980); s of Edward Cockburn (d 1986), of Edinburgh, and Alice, *née* Brennan (d 1983); *b* 28 February 1943; *Educ* Holy Cross Acad Edinburgh (Dip); *m* 25 July 1970, Susan Elisabeth, da of Maj William Phillpots, MBE; 2 da (Rachel b 1974, Rebecca b 1977); *Career* TA Royal Logistic Corps Postal and Courier Serv 1968, Hon Col 1990, Hon Col Cmdt 1996–2007; PO: Glasgow 1961, PA to Chm 1971–73, asst dir of fin and planning 1973–77, dir of central planning 1977–78, dir postal fin 1978–79, dir London Postal Region 1979–82, memb PO Bd 1981, memb for Fin Counter Servs and Planning 1982–84, memb for Royal Mail Ops 1984–86; md Royal Mail 1986–92, chief exec The Post Office 1992–95, chm International Postal Corporation 1994–95; chief exec W H Smith Group plc 1996–97 (dir 1995–97), gp md British Telecommunications plc 1997–2001; non-exec chm Parity Group plc 2001–04, non-exec dep chm Business Post Group plc 2002–; non-exec dir: Watkins Holdings Ltd 1985–93, Lex Service plc 1993–2002, Whitbread plc 1995 (resigned Nov), Centrica plc 1996–99; dep chm AWG plc 2003–06; non-exec memb Bd Business in the Community 1990–2003, memb Cncl The Industrial Soc 1992–2002, govr Euro Fndn for Quality Mgmnt 1992–95, chm Sch Teachers' Review Body 2002–; Freeman City of London 1980; CIMgt 1995; FCIT 1991, FRSA 1992; *Style*— William Cockburn, Esq, CBE, TD

COCKBURN-CAMPBELL, Sir Alexander Thomas; 7 Bt (UK 1821), of Gartsford, Ross-shire; s of Sir Thomas Cockburn-Campbell, 6 Bt (d 1999), and (Josephine) Zoi, eldest da of Harold Douglas Forward, of Cunjardine, W Australia; *b* 16 March 1945; *m* 1969, Kerry Anne, eldest da of late Sgt K Johnson, of Mount Hawthorne, Western Australia; 1 s (Thomas Justin b 10 Feb 1974), 1 da (Felicity Ann b 9 June 1981); *Heir* s, Thomas Cockburn-Campbell; *Style*— Sir Alexander Cockburn-Campbell, Bt

COCKCROFT, Dr John Anthony Eric; s of Eric William Cockcroft, OBE and RFC Pilot (d 1979), of Todmorden, W Yorks, and Haidee Greenlees, *née* Sutcliffe (d 1980); *b* 9 August 1934; *Educ* Todmorden GS, Univ of Cambridge (tech state scholarship, MA), Univ of Aberdeen (MLitt), Univ of Manchester (PhD); *m* 5 Sept 1965, Victoria Mary, da of Frank Lawrence Hartley, of Castleford, W Yorks; 1 da (Vicki (Mrs Simon Foster) b 1967), 2 s (John b 1972, Alexander b 1974); *Career* RTR Germany and Air Despatch Nat Serv cmmn 1954–55 (Sword of Honour), TA cmmn Duke of Lancasters Own Yeomanry (14/20 King's Own Hussars) Manchester 1959–65; Ford Motor Co 1959, UK private industry 1960–64, OECD Paris sci and devpt fell Miny of Economic Coordination Athens 1965–67, UK private industry 1968–69, FCO and ODA advsr Inter Ministerial Investment Advsy Ctee Kabul 1970–72, UN expert Miny of Nat Economy Amman 1973, md Anglo W German Manufacturing Co 1974–78, fell NATO Brussels 1979–80, UN conslt Dar es Salaam 1980, fell Centre for Def Studies Univ of Aberdeen 1980, prof of economics and mgmnt Nigeria 1982, Killam fell Centre for Foreign Policy Studies Dalhousie Univ Canada 1982–84; ldr and mktg conslt Int Mgmnt Consultancy Team World Bank and Price Waterhouse Dhaka 1985, md Manchester UK 1986–89, Allied Textiles plc 1990–91, conslt Sekers Int-Stoddard Sekers plc 1991–94, ldr US Agency for Int Devpt (USAID) Washington DC (Adis Ababa Ethiopia) 1994, team leader/mgmt specialist for European Union Agri Project Dhaka Bangladesh 1994–97, conslt USAID Washington DC (Cairo Egypt) 1997, prof Adv Int Relations and lectr in Business Studies and Geography Queen's Univ Dhaka Bangladesh 1997–98, conslt and disaster relief fund-raiser Dhaka Bangladesh 1998, sr mgmnt conslt Helen Keller Int New York and Dhaka 1998–99; conslt: DFID, Adam Smith Inst, Public Enterprise Reform Prog Orissa India 2000, ITC/UNCTAD/WTO Geneva, Cotton Demand, Benin, Burkina Faso, Ghana, Uganda, Tanzania 2000, UNMIK/EU/EAR Kosovo, Public Enterprise Conversion 2000, Paris, EU Bid Drafting, Bosnia and Herzegovina Public Enterprise conversion 2001, Miny of Public Enterprise/State/Private transition Cairo 2001; actg team ldr EU Re-structuring Project Bosnia and Herzegovina Sarajevo 2002, ITC nominee World Bank-led Integrated Framework Diagnostic Trade Integration Study Malawi 2002, specialist Support for Economic Growth and Institutional Reform Kosovo USAID 2003, conslt Assessment of Potentials for Haiti Economic Recovery and Opportunity Act (HERO) USAID 2003, conslt Regnl Agricultural Trade Expansion Support (RATES) (Kenya, Mauritius, Malawi, Tanzania, Uganda, Zambia, Republic of South Africa) USAID 2003, advsr Regnl Activity to Promote Integration via Dialogue and Policy Implementation (RAPID) (Namibia, Mozambique, Botswana, Republic of South Africa) USAID 2003–04, trade conslt Paraguay Exports USAID 2004–, team leader African, Caribbean, Pacific (ACP) Textile and Clothing Sector EU 2004–, expert Southern Africa Global Competitiveness Hub USAID 2004–; hon res fell Centre for Defence Studies Univ of York 2000–03, hon research fell Defence Research Inst Univs of Lancaster and York 2000–03; author of Symphony in A(sia) Minor, Motor and private papers for govts and int orgns incl: Science and Development, The Pilot Teams Greece (OECD, jtly), Proposals for Industrial Development Order Kabul (ODA), Export Promotion Investment Attraction Amman (UN), Alliance Economic Co-operation & Military Assistance in South-East Flank (NATO), The Textile Sector Jordan (UN), The Textile Sector Afghanistan (ODA), Contemporary Soviet Strategy & Space Weapons (thesis, Univ of Manchester), Cotton Sector Assessment Ethiopia restructuring/privatisation prog (USAID), Textile Sector Orissa India (DFID/ASI), Cereal Seeds Bangladesh (EC), Privatisation Study Cairo, Egypt private sector devpt prog (USAID), Cotton Sector Demand Study Benin, Burkino Faso, Ghana, Uganda, Tanzania, ITC, Geneva 2000, Public Sector Conversion Kosovo, UNMIK/EAR Pristina 2000, Ballistic Missile Defence and Politics, BMD, NATO, Europe and UK 2000–, Integrated Economic Devpt (Section) Malawi World Bank 2002, Assessment of the Textile and Garment Sector USAID Kosovo 2002, Assessment of the Haiti Economic Recovery Opportunity Act (HERO) USAID Washington DC 2003, Export Team Assessment Namibia AGOA & WTO, USAID Botswana (jtly) 2003, Regional Market Assessment on Lint and Textiles AGOA Perspective USAID Nairobi 2003, Assessment of Textile & Garment Sector USAID Mozambique 2004, Study on the ACP Textile and Clothing Sector EU Brussels 2005; FInstD 1975, CText 1978; memb: RUSI 1979, IISS 1980, RIIA 1980; FTI 1986, MCSD 1990 (MSIAD 1975); *Recreations* music, pictures and prints, walking, tennis, supporting Manchester United, horse and motor racing; *Clubs* Cavalry and Guards'; *Style*— Dr John Cockcroft; ✉ The Old Vicarage, Ledsham, South Milford, Leeds LS25 5LT (tel 01977 683326, fax 01977 685476, e-mail cockcroftj@aol.com)

COCKCROFT, John Hoyle; s of late Lionel Fielden Cockcroft, of Todmorden, W Yorks, and late Jenny, *née* Hoyle; nephew of Sir John Cockcroft (d 1967), who was winner of Nobel prize for physics 1951 and first master of Churchill Coll Cambridge 1959; *b* 6 July 1934; *Educ* Oundle, St John's Coll Cambridge (sr maj scholar, MA); *m* 1971, Tessa Fay, da of Dr William Shepley (d 1968); 3 da (Lucia b 1972, Gemma b 1974, Eloise b 1978); *Career* Nat Serv 2 Lt RA 1953–55; feature writer Financial Times 1959–61, economist GKN 1962–67 (re-acquisitions 1962–65), seconded to Treasy Public Enterprises Tport Div 1965–66, econ leader writer Daily Telegraph 1967–74, leader writer Sunday Telegraph 1981–86; MP (Cons) Nantwich 1974–79; memb Select Ctee on: Nationalised Industries (tport) 1975–79, Co Secretaries Bill (private members) 1978–79; conslt: GKN 1971–76, Mail Users' Assoc 1976–79, Inst of Chartered Secs 1977–79, Cray Electronics 1982–84, Wedgwood 1983–84, Crystalate Holdings 1983–86, Dowty Group 1983–86, Commed Ltd (telecommunications co) 1983–93, Camden Associates (political PR) 1984–88, CCF Laurence Prust (stockbrokers) 1986–90, Raitt Orr (govt relations) 1992–95, MAP Securities (corp fin) 1992–95, Heathmere (UK) Ltd 1996–, ESL&N 2006–; advsr: NEI history archives 1980–85, GHN history 2002–; BR: conslt 1979–84, memb Bd (Eastern Region) 1984–89; dir International Conflict Resolution 1990–; memb Cncl: European Movement 1973–74 and 1983–84, Cons Gp for Europe 1980–87; memb Ctee: Assoc of Youth Clubs 1970–74, Cons Computer Forum 1983–90, PITCOM 1985–90; memb: RUSI Defence Studies, IOD, Eur-Atlantic Gp, Railway Devpt Soc, UNA; treas Cambridge Univ Cons Assoc 1958, pres Cambridge Union 1958; tstee Sanderson Tst (Oundle) 1992–; *Publications* Reforming the Constitution (jtly, 1968), Belgium Quarterly Review (EIU) (1969–71), Self-Help Reborn (jtly, 1969), Why England Sleeps (1971), Internal History of Guest Keen and Nettlefolds (jtly, 1976), Microtechnology in Banking (1984), Microelectronics (1982); contrib reviews, interviews and articles to Jl of Contemporary British History, The Scotsman, The European and Daily Telegraph 1979–; also columnist and contrib: Microscope 1982–85, Banking World 1984–87, Electronics Times 1985–90, Westminster Watch; *Recreations* reading, writing, walking, entertaining, the history of twentieth century Chelmsford (writing); *Style*— John Cockcroft, Esq; ✉ 315 Broomfield Road, Chelmsford CM1 4DU

COCKER, Victor; CBE (2000); s of Harold Nathan Cocker (d 2001), and Marjorie Cocker (d 1986); *b* 30 October 1940, Sheffield; *Educ* King Edward VII GS Sheffield, Univ of

Nottingham (BA); *m* 24 Aug 1963, Jennifer Muriel, *née* Nicholls; 2 da (Jane Andrea (Mrs Nutt) b 13 Nov 1965, Susan Frances (Mrs Williams) b 2 May 1967); *Career* Severn Trent Water Ltd: md 1991–95, chair 1995–2000; gp chief exec Severn Trent plc 1995–2000; chair: Waste and Resources Action Prog (WRAP) 2000–, Cncl WaterAid 2001–07 (tstee 1996–2007), Aga Foodservice Gp 2004– (non-exec dir 2000–); memb Cncl: RNLI, RSA 2004; Freeman City of London, Liveryman Worshipful Co of Water Conservators; Hon DUniv Central England 2006; Hon FCIWM 2004, FCIWEM, FCMI, FRSA; *Recreations* walking, national hunt racing, N Norfolk; *Clubs* RAC; *Style*— Victor Cocker, Esq, CBE; ✉ Tredington Manor, Tredington, Shipston on Stour, Warwickshire CV36 4NJ

COCKERAM, Eric Paul; s of John Winter Cockeram (d 1976), of Birkenhead, Cheshire, and Mildred Edith, *née* O'Neill (d 1977); *b* 4 July 1924; *Educ* The Leys Sch Cambridge; *m* 2 July 1949, Frances Gertrude, da of Herbert Irving (d 1979), of Birkenhead, Cheshire; 2 s (Howard b 1950, James b 1955), 2 da (Susan b 1952, Julia (twin) b 1955); *Career* Capt Gloucestershire Regt 1942–46, D-Day landings (wounded twice); MP (Cons): Bebington 1970–Feb 1974, Ludlow 1979–87; former PPS to: Chllr of the Exchequer, Min for Industry, Min for Posts and Telecommunications; chm Watson Prickard Ltd; memb Lloyd's; JP Liverpool 1960; Liveryman (and memb Ct of Assts) Worshipful Co of Glovers; Freeman: City of London, City of Springfield IL; *Recreations* shooting, golf, bridge; *Clubs* Carlton; *Style*— Eric Cockeram, Esq; ✉ Fairway Lodge, Caldy, Wirral CH48 1NB (tel 0151 625 1100)

COCKING, Prof Edward Charles Daniel; s of Charles Edward Cocking (d 1965), and Mary, *née* Murray (d 1994); *b* 26 September 1931; *Educ* Buckhurst Hill Co HS, Univ of Bristol (BSc, PhD, DSc); *m* 6 Aug 1960, Bernadette, da of Frank Keane (d 1948); 1 s (Sean Daniel b 1961), 1 da (Sarah Anne b 1966); *Career* Civil Serv Cmmn res fell 1956–59; Univ of Nottingham: lectr in plant physiology 1959–66, reader in botany 1966–69, prof of botany 1969– (emeritus 1997–), head Dept of Botany 1969–91; memb: Bd of Tstees Royal Botanic Gardens Kew 1983–93, Cncl Royal Soc 1986–88; memb Governing Body Rothamsted Experimental Station 1991– (chm 1999–2003, memb Lawes Agric Tst Ctee 1987–91), memb Lawes Agric Tst Co 1999–; Royal Soc assessor AFRC 1988–90, memb Cncl AFRC 1990–94 (chm Plants & Environment Res Ctee); tstee Uppingham Sch; Leverhulme Tst res fell 1995–97 (emeritus res fell 2000–02); Lifetime Achievement Award Univ of Toledo USA 2004; memb Academia Europaea 1993, hon memb Hungarian Acad of Scis 1995, fell Indian Acad Agric Sciences 2000, fell World Innovation Fndn 2003; FRS 1983; *Books* Introduction to the Principles of Plant Physiology (with W Stiles, 1969); *Recreations* walking, travelling by train, gothic architecture (A W N Pugin), occasional chess; *Style*— Prof Edward Cocking, FRS; ✉ Centre for Crop Nitrogen Fixation, Plant Science Division, Schools of Biology and Biosciences, University Park, University of Nottingham, Nottingham NG7 2RD (tel 0115 951 3056, fax 0115 951 3240, e-mail edward.cocking@nottingham.ac.uk)

COCKLE, Roger Anthony; s of Raymond John Cockle (d 1998), of Swansea, S Wales, and Beryl Winifred, *née* Hurden; *b* 3 July 1943; *Educ* Dynevor Sch Swansea, Univ of Manchester Sch of Architecture (BA, MA); *m* 1967, Jennifer Griffiths Evans; 1 s (Owen William David b 1971), 1 da (Anna Katherine b 1972); *Career* architect Lambert & Simm Ottawa Canada 1967–68, lectr Univ of Manchester Sch of Architecture 1968–72; Percy Thomas Partnership: assoc 1972–83, ptnr 1983–94, dir Percy Thomas Partnership (Architects) Ltd 1994–; wide range of commercial, industrial, govt and healthcare clients in the UK and abroad, research cmmns for various govt depts incl MOD, involved in large projects for automotive industry incl General Motors (Thailand) and Rover (Birmingham); lectr (and papers published) on architectural project mgmnt and CAD systems in the UK and abroad; chm E Midlands Regn RIBA 1992–93, external examiner Univ of Nottingham 1992–; ARIBA 1968; *Recreations* squash, golf; *Clubs* Nottingham Squash Rackets; *Style*— Roger Cockle, Esq

COCKRILL, Maurice Edwin; s of William Edwin Cockrill (d 1970), of Wrexham, Clwyd, and Edith, *née* Godfrey (d 1968), both originally from Hartlepool; *b* 8 October 1936, Hartlepool; *Educ* Grove Park GS Wrexham, Wrexham Sch of Art, Univ of Reading; *Family* 2 s (Steven Paul b 1958, Joel b 1964); partner, Helen Moslin; 1 s (William Alexander b 1989); *Career* artist; lectr Faculty of Art Liverpool Poly 1967–80; visiting tutor: St Martin's Sch of Art 1984–90, RCA 1988, Slade Sch of Art 1990, RA Schs 1993–98; prof of contemporary fine art Liverpool John Moores Univ 2005; keeper Royal Acad of Arts London 2004; *Solo Exhibitions* incl: Serpentine Gallery London 1971, Bluecoat Gallery Liverpool 1974, 1979, 1980 and 1982, Liverpool Acad Gallery 1976, Seven in Two (Lime Street Station Liverpool) 1979–80, Univ of Nottingham 1983, Edward Totah Gallery London 1984 and 1985, Kunstmuseum Düsseldorf 1985, Udo Bugdahn Gallery Düsseldorf 1986 and 1994, Bernard Jacobson Gallery London 1987–90 (and NY 1988), Acheus Fine Art London 2002, Galerie Vidal St Phalle Paris 2003, Galerie Bruno Mary Burgundy 2004, Hillsboro Fine Art Dublin 2005, Cheltenham Museum 2007; *Group Exhibitions* incl: Art in a City (ICA London) 1967, Spectrum North (Arts Cncl tour) 1971, John Moores Liverpool Exhbns 9 1974 (prizewinner), 10, 13 and 14, Arts Council Collection 1976–77 (Hayward Gallery London) 1977, British Drawing (Hayward Annual London) 1982, Hommage aux Femmes (ICC Berlin, Leverkusen Cologne) 1985, Athena Art Awards (Barbican) 1987; *Collections* work in several public and private collections incl: Kunstmuseum Düsseldorf, British Museum, Arts Cncl of GB, Contemporary Art Soc, Unilever, Deutsche Bank, Ulster Museum, Welsh Arts Cncl, Walker Art Gallery; *Awards* Arts Cncl of GB Maj Award 1977–78, Arts Cncl Award for Work of Art in Public Spaces (project at Lime Street Station Liverpool) 1978–79; elected to Royal Acad of Arts 1999; *Publications* subject of monograph on paintings since 1989 (2002); *Clubs* Chelsea Arts, Dover Street Arts, Lansdowne; *Style*— Maurice Cockrill, Esq; ✉ 78B Park Hall Road, London SE21 8DW, e-mail admin@cockrill.co.uk, website www.cockrill.co.uk)

COCKROFT, His Hon Judge (Peter) John; s of Walter Philip Barron Cockroft, of Birstwith, N Yorks, and Nora, *née* Collett; *b* 24 September 1947; *Educ* Queen Elizabeth I GS Darlington, Queens' Coll Cambridge (BA, LLB); *m* 3 April 1975, Maria Eugenia, *née* Coromina, 2 da of Carlos Coromina Margui, and Teresa Perandones Moreto; 2 da (Anna Maria b 9 Nov 1979, Isabel Maria b 6 April 1982), 1 s (Thomas Philip Carlos b 25 June 1986); *Career* called to the Bar Middle Temple 1970 (Astbury scholar), tenant at Pearl Chambers 22 E Parade Leeds 1971–93 (memb NE Circuit), recorder 1989–93 (asst recorder 1985–89), circuit judge assigned to Bradford and Leeds area (NE Circuit) 1993–; *Recreations* gardening, visiting Spain; *Clubs* Yorkshire CCC, Yorkshire RUFC; *Style*— His Hon Judge Cockroft

COCKS, David John; QC (1982); *Educ* Univ of Oxford (MA); *Career* called to the Bar Lincoln's Inn 1961, head of chambers 5 King's Bench Walk, recorder of the Crown Court; chm Criminal Bar Association 1985–88; *Style*— David Cocks, Esq, QC; ✉ 18 Red Lion Court, London EC4A 3EB (tel 020 7520 6000)

COCKS, Dr Leonard Robert Morrison (Robin); OBE (1999), TD (1979); s of Ralph Morrison Cocks (d 1970), and Lucille Mary, *née* Blackler (d 1996); *b* 17 June 1938; *Educ* Felsted, Hertford Coll Oxford (MA, DPhil, DSc); *m* 31 Aug 1963, Elaine Margaret, da of Canon J B Sturdy; 1 s (Mark b 1964), 2 da (Zoe b 1967, Julia b 1970); *Career* 2 Lt RA 1957–59, active serv Malaya; scientist Nat History Museum 1965– (Keeper of Palaeontology 1986–98), cmmr Int Cmmn on Zoological Nomenclature 1980–2000; visiting prof Imperial Coll London 1997–2001; sec Geological Soc 1985–89 (pres 1998–2000); visitor Oxford Univ Museum 1997–; pres: Palaeontological Assoc 1986–88, Palaeontographical Soc 1994–98, Geologists' Assoc 2004–06; CGeol, FGS; *Books* The Evolving Earth (1981), Encyclopedia of Geology (2005), contrib to over 160 articles in sci jls on geology and palaeontology; *Style*— Dr Robin Cocks, OBE, TD; ✉ Department of Palaeontology, Natural History Museum, Cromwell Road, London SW7 5BD (tel 020 7942 5140, fax 020 7942 5546, e-mail r.cocks@nhm.ac.uk)

COCKSHAW, Sir Alan; kt (1992); s of John Cockshaw (d 1986), and Maud, *née* Simpson (d 1996); *b* 14 July 1937; *Educ* Farnworth GS, Univ of Leeds (BSc); *m* 17 Dec 1960, Brenda, da of Fred Payne; 1 s (John Nigel b 1964), 3 da (Elizabeth Ann b 1967, Sally Louise b 1970, Catherine Helen b 1979); *Career* chief exec: Fairclough Civil Engineering Ltd 1978–85, Fairclough-Parkinson Mining Ltd 1982–85; AMEC plc: dir 1983–97, chief exec 1984–88, chm 1988–97; chm: Overseas Projects Bd 1992–95, Oil & Gas Projects & Supplies Office 1994–97, Manchester Millennium Ltd 1996–2003, Shawbridge Management Ltd 1996–, Roxboro Gp plc 1997–2005, English Partnerships 1998–2001, Commission for New Towns 1998–2001, Major Projects Assoc 1998–2004, New East Manchester Ltd 1999–2002, Cibitas Investments Ltd 2003–, HPR Hldgs Ltd 2003–; chm and dir Br Airways Regnl 1999–2003; non-exec dep chm NORWEB plc 1992–95, non-exec dir The New Millennium Experience Co Ltd 1997–2000, dir Pidemco/Capitaland Ltd Singapore 1999–2005; memb British Overseas Trade Bd 1992–95; life pres North West Business Leadership Team 1997–, pres ICE 1997–98 (sr vice-pres 1996–97); chm of Govrs Bolton Sch 1997–; Hon DEng UMIST 1997, Hon DSc Univ of Salford 1998; FREng 1986; *Recreations* rugby (both codes), cricket, walking, gardening; *Style*— Sir Alan Cockshaw, FREng; ✉ e-mail sac@shawbridge.co.uk

CODARIN, Judith; da of William Ernest Walker (d 1971), of Thornham, N Norfolk, and Mary Eileen Jacob; *b* 8 July 1946; *Educ* Kings Lynn HS for Girls, Norwich Sch of Art, Birmingham Coll of Art; *m* Armando Codarin, s of Venceslao Codarin; 1 da (Melanie Maria b 8 Dec 1973), 1 s (Pierre Daniel b 28 April 1980); *Career* design conslt; architectural asst Casson Conder & Partners 1968–72; freelance res and commercial illustrating, designing and concept presentation and development for cos incl: Conran Design Group, Fitch, McColl, Ryman, Rottenberg Associates 1972–76; working with: Franco Nadali Ltd 1973–, Baker Sayer 1984–88; practises as Codarin Associates Interior Designers & Design Management for nat and int clients 1988–; lectr in interior design: SE Essex Coll 1993–2000 (former govr for design industry), London Inst 2001–; author of numerous published articles and courses; CSD: fell 1998, past chm Interiors Gp; *Recreations* walking, swimming, looking at buildings, holidaying with the family; *Style*— Mrs Judith Codarin; ✉ Codarin Associates Interior Designers & Design Management, 14 Riviera Drive, Southend on Sea, Essex SS1 2RB

CODD, (Ronald) Geoffrey; s of Thomas Reuben Codd (d 1976), and Betty Leyster Justice, *née* Sturt; *b* 20 August 1932; *Educ* Cathedral Sch Llandaff, The Coll Llandovery, Presentation Coll Cobh; *m* 2 April 1960, Christine Ellen Leone, da of Flt Lt Reginald Arthur John Robertson, of Needham Market, Suffolk; 2 da (Louise b 11 May 1962, Emma b 19 July 1966), 1 s (Justin b 27 Oct 1968); *Career* RAF Tport Command 1952–57; Rolls-Royce 1957–58, International Computers 1958–61, Marconi Co 1961–70, J Bibby and Sons 1970–74, Weir Group 1974–80, Brooke Bond Group 1981–86, under sec and dir of Info and Risk Management ECGD 1986–90, managing ptnr InterChange Associates 1990–; dir Randolph Enterprise and RE-APM 1992–97; non-exec advsr Bd of Customs and Excise 1992–97, memb Nat Teleworking Advsy Cncl 1993–96; Freeman City of London, Liveryman Worshipful Co of Info Technologists; Certified IT Professional (CITP), CEng, FBCS, FIMgt, FInstD; *Publications* The Drowning Director; contrib to various business pubns; *Recreations* sailing, theatre, practical pastimes; *Clubs* Royal Dorset, City Livery; *Style*— Geoffrey Codd, Esq; ✉ The White House, Church Lane, Osmington, Dorset DT3 6EJ (tel and fax 01305 832247, e-mail geoff@interchange.eclipse.co.uk)

CODD, (Robin Hugh Ian Anthony) Patrick; TD (1978, 2 Bars); s of Lionel Hugh Codd (d 1979), of Oakford, N Devon, and Isabel Elma, *née* Berry (d 1985); *b* 11 November 1937; *Educ* Belmont Coll; *m* 1, Patricia, *née* Grant; 1 da (Antoinette Elizabeth Gaillies b May 1964); m 2, Susan Ann, *née* Turner; 1 da (Devona Holly Chelsea Elma b 16 Jan 1987); *Career* journalist/reporter: North Devon Journal Herald, Western Evening Herald, The Sun, Daily Mail, Daily Express; Daily Star: helped launch as feature writer Oct 1978, show business and TV news ed 1981, show business ed 1987–97; freelance showbusiness journalist; cncllr (Cons) Royal Borough of Kingston upon Thames 1994–; *Recreations* military clubs, cinema, Camra recommended pubs, Golden Age American comics; *Style*— Patrick Codd, Esq, TD; ✉ 2 Fairlawn Close, Kingston Hill, Kingston upon Thames, Surrey KT2 7JW (tel 020 8549 5760)

CODRON, Michael Victor; CBE (1989); s of I A Codron (d 1981), and Lily, *née* Morgenstern (d 1981); *b* 8 June 1930; *Educ* St Paul's, Worcester Coll Oxford (BA); *Career* theatrical producer and manager; dir: Hampstead Theatre, Aldwych Theatre, Theatre Mutual Insurance Co; Cameron Mackintosh visiting prof of contemporary theatre Univ of Oxford 1992–93; *Theatre* prodns incl: Share My Lettuce, Breath of Spring 1957, The Caretaker 1960, Loot 1965, The Killing of Sister George 1968, The Boyfriend (revival) 1967, Absurd Person Singular 1973, Funny Peculiar 1976, The Unvarnished Truth 1978, The Dresser 1980, Noises Off 1982, A View from A Bridge 1987, Uncle Vanya 1988, Henceforward 1988, Hapgood Re:Joyce! 1988, The Cherry Orchard 1989, Man of the Moment 1990, Hidden Laughter 1990, The Rise and Fall of Little Voice 1992, Time of My Life 1993, Dead Funny 1994, Arcadia 1994, The Sisters Rosensweig 1994, Tom and Clem 1997, Things We Do For Love 1998, Alarms & Excursions 1998, The Invention of Love 1998, Copenhagen 1999, Comic Potential 1999, Peggy for You 2000, Blue/Orange 2001, Bedroom Farce 2002, My Brilliant Divorce 2003, Dinner 2003, Democracy 2004; *Film* Clockwise 1986; *Recreations* collecting Carolinia (of Brunswick) memorabilia; *Clubs* Garrick; *Style*— Michael Codron, Esq, CBE; ✉ Aldwych Theatre Offices, Aldwych, London WC2B 4DF (tel 020 7240 8291, fax 020 7240 8467)

CODY, Sebastian; s of Stephen Cody (d 1990), and Maria Cody; *b* 6 October 1956; *Educ* King Alfred Sch Hampstead, Univ of Vienna, Univ of York (BA), Nat Film Sch (trained as dir); *m* 1997, Annabel, *née* Cole; 2 da (Elsa b 31 July 1999, Rosa b 23 Aug 2002), 1 s (Christopher b 30 May 2004); *Career* researcher BBC TV 1979–81; prodr and dir: Why Do I Believe You... 1983, Before His Very Eyes 1984; staff prodr Royal Opera House Covent Garden 1985, ed After Dark (Channel 4, BBC) 1987–2003; freelance writer and conslt 1979–; exec prodr Open Media 1987–; progs: The Secret Cabaret 1990–92, James Randi - Psychic Investigator 1991, Opinions 1993–94, Brave New World 1994, Is This Your Life? 1995–96, The Mediator 1995, Natural Causes 1996, Suez 1996, Secrets of the Psychics 1997, Mossad: The Spy Machine 1998, Danny Does Tricks 1998; fell 21st Century Tst 1996–; visiting fell Rothermere American Inst Univ of Oxford 2001–, sr assoc memb St Antony's Coll Oxford 2004, special advsr to the dir Int Inst for Applied Systems Analysis (IIASA) 2005–; *Clubs* Garrick; *Style*— Sebastian Cody, Esq; ✉ Open Media, The Mews Studio, 8 Addison Bridge Place, London W14 8XP (tel 020 7603 9029, fax 020 7603 9171, website www.openmedia.co.uk)

COE, Albert Henry (Harry); *b* 28 May 1944; *m*; 2 c; *Career* fin dir Granada Television 1981–88; Airtours plc: fin dir 1988–97, dep chief exec 1996–97, gp md 1997–99, non-exec dir 1999–2000; non-exec dir Britannia Building Soc 2000–03; non-exec chm: Travelsphere Holdings Ltd 2000–, Jaycare Holdings Ltd 2000–04, Leisure Ventures plc 2001–; *Recreations* cricket, tennis, golf, skiing; *Clubs* Alderley Edge Cricket, Wilmslow Golf, Manchester Ski; *Style*— Harry Coe, Esq

COE, Gerry; s of Jack Turland Saunders Coe, and Sarah Jane, *née* McCabe; *m* 17 Sept 1976, Lorna, *née* Mayne; 1 da (Emma Jane b 18 March 1981); *Career* photographer; only Irish winner of AGFA UK and Ireland Portrait Photographer of the Year Award, first triple fell in Ireland for pictorial/illustrative photography; FBIPP, FMPA, FRPS, FSWPP; *Publications* contributions to many articles and magazines; *Recreations* mostly photographic, walking, reading, computer studies; *Style*— Gerry Coe, Esq; ✉ Lasting Image, 667 Lisburn Road, Belfast BT9 7GT (tel 028 9066 8001, e-mail gerry@gerrycoe.co.uk, website www.gerrycoe.co.uk)

COE, Jonathan; s of Roger Frank Coe, of Birmingham, and Janet Mary Kay; *b* 19 August 1961; *Educ* King Edward's Sch Birmingham, Trinity Coll Cambridge (BA), Univ of Warwick (MA, PhD); *m* 1989, Janine McKeown; 2 da (Matilda b Sept 1997, Madeline b Nov 2000); *Career* writer; memb Soc of Authors 1995; *Awards* Mail on Sunday John Llewellyn Rhys Prize 1995, Prix du Meilleur Livre Etranger 1996, Writer's Guild Best Fiction Award 1997, Prix Médicis Etranger 1998, Bollinger Everyman Wodehouse Prize 2001, Premio Arzobispo San Clemente 2003; *Books* The Accidental Woman (1987), A Touch of Love (1989), The Dwarves of Death (1990), What A Carve Up! (1994), The House of Sleep (1997), The Rotters' Club (2001), Like a Fiery Elephant: The Story of B S Johnson (2004, Samuel Johnson Prize 2005), The Rain Before It Falls (2007); *Style*— Jonathan Coe, Esq; ✉ c/o Tony Peake, Peake Associates, 14 Grafton Crescent, London NW1 8SL (tel 020 7267 8033, fax 020 7284 1876)

COE, Baron (Life Peer UK 2000), of Ranmore in the County of Surrey; Sir Sebastian Newbold Coe; KBE (2006, OBE 1990, MBE 1981); s of Peter Coe, and Angela, *née* Lall (d 2005); *b* 29 September 1956; *Educ* Tapton Sch Sheffield, Loughborough Univ (BSc); *m* 23 Aug 1990, Nicola McIrvine; 2 da (Hon Madeleine Rose b 8 July 1992, Hon Alice India Violet b 25 Sept 1998), 2 s (Hon Harry Sebastian Newbold b 29 Sept 1994, Hon Peter Henry Christopher b 31 May 1996); *Career* former athlete; broke 12 world records incl 800m (holder until 1997), 1500m and 1 mile, Gold medal 1500m Olympic Games 1980 and 1984, Silver medal 800m Olympic Games 1980 and 1984, Gold medal 800m World Cup 1981, Gold medal 800m Euro Championships 1986, ret 1990; MP (Cons) Falmouth and Camborne 1992–97; PPS to Roger Freeman: as min of state for defence 1994–95, as Chllr of the Duchy of Lancaster 1995–96; PPS to Michael Heseltine as dep PM 1995–96, Govt whip 1996–97; chief of staff and private sec to Rt Hon William Hague, MP as Ldr of the Oppn 1997–2001; chm and pres London 2012 Olympic Games bid 2004–05 (vice-chm 2003–04), chm LOCOG (London Organising Ctee of the Olympic Games and Paralympic Games) 2005–; memb Sports Cncl of GB 1983– (vice-chm 1986), chm Sports Cncls Olympic Review 1985–86; memb: Health Educn Authy (formerly Health Educn Cncl) 1986–, Athletes Cmmn, Med Cmmn Int Olympic Ctee 1987–2002, Cncl Int Assoc of Athletics Fedns (IAAF) 2003–; assoc memb Académie Des Sports France 1982–; steward Br Boxing Bd of Control 1994–; global advsr Nike, columnist Daily Telegraph; pres Amateur Athletics Assoc of England until 2004, founding memb Laureus World Sports Acad; Kiphuth fell Yale Univ 1982, Hon DTech Loughborough Univ 1985, Hon DSc Univ of Hull 1988; *Books* Running Free, Running for Fitness with Peter Coe (1983), The Olympians (1984, 2 edn 1996); *Clubs* East India and Sportsman's; *Style*— The Lord Coe, KBE; ✉ House of Lords, London SW1A 0PW

COE, Stephen; s of Richard Gerald Coe (d 1964), of Brentwood, Essex, and Mary, *née* Fox (d 1961); *b* 6 Feb 1943, Khartoum; *Educ* Brentwood Sch, London Coll of Printing; *m* 1965 (m dis 1975); 1 s (Simon b 1966), 1 da (Elinor b 1976); *Career* photographer; freelance for Picture Agency until 1963, own studio 1963–93, freelance fine art photographer 1993–; current project African film and book: Dinesen & Finch Hatton; features incl: various cmmns in Vogue 1961–63, American 6 Fleet in Mediterranean, Cassius Clay (Muhammad Ali), covers for Queen and About Town magazines, posters of African landscapes for Athena; advtg campaigns incl: Heinz soup posters 1963–66, Tern Shirts, Remington, Volkswagen, Rolls Royce, COI, Samaritans, Red Cross, Microsoft 1996; exhbns incl: Little Squares of Hampstead 1987, NW3 and Beyond (London, Africa & Scandinavia) 1988, Spirit of Hampstead (Burgh House London) 1994, Awesome Tones & Moments (Burgh House London) 1997; work in private collections in London, Paris, Melbourne, Nairobi, Sweden and throughout USA; initial memb: Advtg Film and Video Prodrs Assoc (formerly Advtg Film Prodrs Assoc) 1967, Assoc of Photographers (formerly AFAEP) 1969 (vice-chm 1973–74); memb Pilgrims to Willoughby Res Assoc Heath & Old Hampstead; memb Players and Playwrights; *Awards* Master Photographers Assoc Shield, Layton Award (for Heinz campaign) 1963, various D&AD awards 1965–76, One Show Award (USA) 1966, Communication Art Award (USA) 1966, Venice Film Festival Award (Diploma) 1968, D&AD Silver Award, Creative Circle Award, Brit Press Award and two Grand Slam Awards for COI campaign Put Your Fingers over Headlights 1976; *Publications* Africa Adorned (with Angela Fisher, 1983), Lazy Afternoon (fine art print), Hampstead Memories (2000); articles in Br Jl of Photography; *Recreations* cinema, music, lighting design, memb local initiatives on restoration of Victorian street lighting, conservation and tree mgmnt etc, architectural woodwork, creative writing, hill and coastal walking, tennis, creative recycling, browsing, antiquarian books; *Clubs* White Elephant on the River, Club Rollei (Jersey); *Style*— Stephen Coe, Esq; ✉ e-mail stephencoe@telia.com

COELHO, George Arjun; s of George Victor Coelho (d 1999), of India, and Rani, *née* Krishnamachari (d 1997); *b* 8 June 1952; *Educ* American Univ (BS), George Washington Univ (MBA); *m* 20 April 1995, Margo, da of Robert O'Brien, of California, and Jo Ann, *née* Ulloa (d 1989); *Career* vice-pres: Bank of America Airlines and Aerospace Gp 1978–80, Union Bank of Switzerland 1980–86, Nomura Securities 1987–90; asst treas M&A and strategic investments Intel Corp 1990–95, vice-pres Intel International 1995–99, ptnr Benchmark Capital Europe 2000–; memb Bd TiE UK (charter memb), memb Bd of Advsrs Sch of Business George Washington Univ, life memb Ognisko Polskie; *Recreations* bass guitar, skiing, shooting, classic rallying; *Clubs* Home House, Chemistry, Century, Classic Rally Assoc; *Style*— George A Coelho; ✉ e-mail gacoelho@aol.com

COEY, Prof (John) Michael David; s of David Stuart Coey (d 1993), and Joan Elizabeth, *née* Newsam (d 2003); *b* 24 February 1945, Belfast; *Educ* Univ of Cambridge (BA), Univ of Manitoba (PhD), Institut Nat Polytechnique Grenoble (Diplôme d'Habilitation), Univ of Dublin (ScD); *m* 1 Sept 1973, Wong May; 2 s (James b 1978, Dominic b 1985); *Career* chargé de recherche CNRS Grenoble 1971–78, IBM Yorktown Heights 1976–77, successively lectr, assoc prof and prof of experimental physics Trinity Coll Dublin 1978–; visiting academic appts: IBM Yorktown Heights 1979, Inst of Physics Peking 1980, McGill Univ Montreal 1982, Univ of Bordeaux 1984, Centre d'Études Nucléiares (CEN) Grenoble 1985, Johns Hopkins Univ 1986, Univ of Paris VI 1992, Univ of Calif San Diego 1997, Florida State Univ 1998, Univ of Paris XI 1998, Le Mans Univ 1999, 2001 and 2003; advsy ed: Physical Review Letters, Jl of Magnetism and Magnetic Materials, Materials Science and Engrg B; fndr and dir Magnetic Solutions Ltd 1994; Charles Chree Medal and Prize Inst of Physics 1997, Fulbright fell 1997; fell Trinity Coll Dublin 1982, Dr (hc) Institut Nat Polytechnique Grenoble 1994; fell American Mineralogical Soc 1995, fell American Physical Soc 2000, foreign assoc Nat Acad of Sciences; FInstP 1984, MRIA 1987 (vice-pres 1989–90), FRS 2003; *Publications* Magnetic Glasses (with K Moorjani, 1984), Current Topics in Magnetism (1987), Structural and Magnetic Phase Transitions in Minerals (1988), Concerted European Action on Magnets (ed, 1989), Rare Earth Iron Permanent Magnets (1996), Permanent Magnetism (with R Skomski, 1999); also over 500 research and review papers in refereed jls; *Recreations* gardening; *Style*— Prof Michael Coey; ✉ tel 00 353 1 608 1470, fax 00 353 1 671 1759, e-mail jcoey@tcd.ie

COFFEY, Ann; MP; *b* 31 August 1946; *Educ* Nairn Acad, Bodmin GS, Bushey GS, South Bank Poly, Walsall Coll of Educn, Univ of Manchester (BSc, MSc); *m* 1 (m dis); m 2 Peter Saraga 1998; 1 da; *Career* social worker: Birmingham 1972–73, Gwynedd 1973–74, Wolverhampton 1974–75, Stockport 1977–82, Cheshire 1982–88; team ldr (fostering) Oldham Social Servs 1988–92; MP (Lab) Stockport 1992– (Parly candidate (Lab) Cheadle 1987); oppn whip 1995–96, oppn frontbench spokesperson on health (community care and social servs) 1996–97; PPS to: Rt Hon Tony Blair, MP, *qv*, 1997–98, Rt Hon Alistair Darling, MP, *qv*, 1998–; memb Select Ctee Modernisation; cncllr Stockport DC 1984–92 (ldr Lab gp 1988–92); memb USDAW; *Recreations* photography, drawing, cinema, swimming, reading; *Style*— Ann Coffey, MP; ✉ House of Commons, London SW1A 0AA

COGBILL, Alan; *b* 1 December 1952; *Educ* Exeter Coll Oxford; *m*; 1 s, 1 da; *Career* joined Civil Serv 1974, Home Office 1974–91, various positions rising to finance dir Lord Chllr's Dept (latterly DCA) 1992–2005, dir Wales Office 2005–; *Style*— Alan Cogbill, Esq; ✉ Wales Office, Gwydyr House, Whitehall, London SW1A 2ER (tel 020 7270 0558, fax 020 7270 0588, e-mail alan.cogbill@walesoffice.gsi.gov.uk)

COGDELL, Prof Richard John; s of Harry William Frank Cogdell (d 1991), and Evelyn, *née* Passmore; *b* 4 February 1949; *Educ* Royal GS Guildford, Univ of Bristol (BSc, PhD); *m*; 2 c; *Career* postdoctoral res Cornell Univ 1973–74, sr fell Dept of Biochemistry Univ of Washington 1974–75; Dept of Botany Univ of Glasgow: lectr in biochemistry 1975–86, sr lectr 1986, head of dept 1987–93, titular prof 1988, Hooker chair of botany 1993–; EMBO fell Univ of Göttingen 1977; visiting res fell: Univ of Calif 1979, Univ of Illinois 1980; visiting prof: Univ of Munich 1983, Univ of Calif 1986, Univ of Paris-Sud 2004; pres Int Soc for Carotenoid Research; memb: Biochemical Soc, Br Photobiology Soc, American Photobiology Soc, Scottish and Newcastle Bioenergetics Gp; memb bd govrs Scottish Crop Research Inst; dir Mylnefield Research Services Ltd, dir Mylnefield Holdings Ltd, tstee Mylnefield Tst; guest lectr award Max Planck Inst for Radiation Chemistry Germany 1997; Alexander von Humboldt Research Prize 1996, Diawa Adrian Prize Tokyo 2001; author of numerous scientific pubns; chm Glasgow McIntyre Begonia Tst 2002–; FRSE 1991; *Style*— Prof Richard Cogdell, FRSE; ✉ Division of Biochemistry and Molecular Biology, Institute of Biochemical and Life Sciences, University of Glasgow, Glasgow G12 8QQ (tel 0141 330 4232, fax 0141 330 4620, e-mail r.cogdell@bio.gla.ac.uk)

COGHILL, Sir Patrick Kendal Farley; 9 Bt (GB 1778) of Coghill, Yorkshire; s of late Sir Toby Coghill, 8 Bt; *b* 3 November 1960; *Heir* kinsman, John Coghill, OBE; *Career* audio visual conslt; *Recreations* skiing, windsurfing, paragliding; *Style*— Sir Patrick Coghill, Bt; ✉ 82 Woodbourne Avenue, London SW16 1UT (tel 020 8769 5372, e-mail patrick@innerspacesystems.co.uk)

COGHLAN, Terence Augustine; QC (1993); s of Austin Coghlan (d 1981), of Horsted Keynes, W Sussex, and Ruby, *née* Comrie; *b* 17 August 1945; *Educ* Downside, Perugia, Univ of Oxford (MA); *m* 11 Aug 1973, Angela, da of Rev F E Westmacott (d 1987), of Barsham, Suffolk; 1 s (Thomas Alexander b 1975), 2 da (Candida Mary b 1978, Anna Frances b 1988); *Career* RAFVR (Oxford Univ Air Sqdn) 1964–67; film extra 1967–68; called to the Bar Inner Temple 1968 (scholar, bencher 2005); in practice 1968–, recorder of the Crown Court 1989– (asst recorder 1985–89); memb Ct of Appeal Mediation Panel 1998–, pres Mental Health Review Tbnl 2000–; memb Inner Temple; chm St Endellion Festivals Tst; dir: City of London Sinfonia, Temple Music Fndn; MCIArb; *Recreations* music, birdwatching, cycling, windsurfing, cooking, skiing, wines; *Clubs* Omar Khayyam, Les Six, MCC; *Style*— Terence Coghlan, Esq, QC; ✉ 1 Crown Office Row, Temple, London EC4Y 7HH (tel 020 7797 7500, fax 020 7797 7540, e-mail terence.coghlan@1cor.com)

COGHLIN, Hon Mr Justice; Sir Patrick Coghlin; kt (1997); s of James Edwin Coghlin (d 1959), and Margaret van Hovenberg, *née* Brown (d 1977); *b* 7 November 1945; *Educ* Royal Belfast Academical Instn, Queen's Univ Belfast (LLB), Christ's Coll Cambridge (Dip Criminology); *m* 6 Aug 1971, Patricia Ann Elizabeth, da of Robert Young; 3 da (Jennifer Elaine b 9 April 1974, Caroline Laura b 28 Dec 1975, Sara Gail Rhodes b 6 March 1981), 1 s (Richard James b 1 Aug 1978); *Career* called to the Bar: NI 1970, England and Wales 1975, Republic of Ireland 1993, NSW 1993; jr crown counsel NI 1983–85, QC (NI) 1985, dep County Court judge 1983–94, sr crown counsel NI 1993–97, judge of the High Court of Justice NI 1997–; vice-chm Mental Health Review Tbnl NI 1986–97, memb Law Reform Advsy Ctee NI 1989–93, vice-pres VAT Tbnl NI 1990–93, chm Exec Cncl of the Bar NI 1991–93, pres Lands Tbnl NI 1999–, dep chm Boundary Cmmn for NI 1999–2002, memb Cncl Assoc of European Competition Law Judges 2002–; hon bencher Gray's Inn 2000; *Recreations* reading, travelling, rugby, squash; *Clubs* Royal Ulster Yacht, Bangor Rugby and Cricket, Ballyholme Bombers Football, Ulster Perennials Rugby; *Style*— The Hon Mr Justice Coghlin; ✉ The Royal Courts of Justice, Chichester Street, Belfast BT1 3JF (tel 028 902 35111)

COGILL, Julie Antoinette; da of Arthur Harold Berry (d 1971), of Blackburn, Lancs, and Mary Margaret, *née* Driscoll (d 1991); *b* 25 August 1945; *Educ* Notre Dame GS Blackburn, Univ of Liverpool (BSc), KCL (MA, EdD); *m* 1967, Stephen Richard Cogill, s of Joseph Cogill (d 1981), of Scarborough, N Yorks; 3 c (Adelene Mary b 1968, Eleanor Ruth b 1969, Geoffrey Owen b 1971); *Career* sr teacher and head of mathematics Tolworth Girl's Sch 1980–87, chief educn offr BBC 1991–2001 (educn offr 1987–88); currently educn media conslt; memb: Assoc of Teachers of Mathematics, Nat Assoc of Advsrs for Computers in Educn, Coll of Teachers, Educn Ctee Br Educnl Communications and Technol Agency (Becta); FRSA; *Recreations* walking, sailing, skiing; *Style*— Dr Julie Cogill; ✉ tel 020 8663 1501, e-mail juliecogill@hotmail.com

COHEN, *see also:* Waley-Cohen

COHEN, Dr Andrew Timothy; s of John Alan Cohen, of Leeds, and Audrey Pamela Cohen (d 1974); *b* 11 July 1952; *Educ* Leeds GS, Leeds Med Sch (MB ChB); *m* 1, 1977 (m dis 1991); m 2, 1997, Alison Jane, *née* Pittard; 2 da (Hannah b 9 Jan 1999, Rachel b 29 March 2000); *Career* lectr in anaesthesia Univ of Manchester 1980–83, instr anaesthesiology Univ of Michigan 1982–83; Leeds Teaching Hosps: conslt anaesthetist, clinical dir Intensive Care Unit 1983–96, div dir Cinical Support Servs 1996–98; hon sr lectr Univ of Leeds; memb: BMA, Intensive Care Soc, Med Protection Soc, Assoc Anaesthetists, Euro Soc of Intensive Care Medicine, Cncl Intensive Care Soc 1997–2004 (hon sec 2002–04); examiner: Royal Coll of Anaesthetists 1996–, European Dip in Intensive Care Medicine 2006–, UK Dip in Intensive Care Medicine 2007–; DRCOG 1977, FFARCS 1979; *Recreations* wine, horse riding, skiing, scuba diving, information technology; *Style*— Dr Andrew T Cohen; ✉ 3 Bluecoat Court, Collingham, Wetherby, West Yorkshire LS22 5NH (tel 01937 573695, e-mail atcohen@hotmail.com); St James's Hospital, Beckett Street, Leeds LS9 7TF (tel 0113 243 3144)

COHEN, Arnaldo; s of Eliazar Cohen (d 1985), of Brazil, and Rachel, *née* Ainbinder; *b* 22 April 1948; *Educ* Colegio Pedro II Rio de Janeiro, Sch of Music Fed Univ of Rio de Janeiro; *m* Ann Louise Strickland Cohen, da of William Strickland; 1 s (Gabriel b 12 Oct 1976), 1 step s (Rodrigo Strickland b 24 Feb 1978), 1 step da (Luiza Strickland b 30 Nov 1979); *Career* pianist, former memb Amadeus Piano Trio; performed with orchs incl: Philadelphia, Cleveland, Royal Philharmonic, Philharmonia, Bavarian Radio, Santa Cecilia, Suisse-Romande, City of Birmingham Symphony, Rotterdam Philharmonic; worked with conductors incl: Kurt Masur, Kurt Sanderling, Yehudi Menuhin, Klaus Tennstedt; appeared at venues incl: Royal Festival Hall, La Scala Milan, Champs-Elysées Paris, Concertgebouw Amsterdam, Musikverein Vienna; taught at Sch of Music Federal Univ of Rio de Janeiro and RNCM Manchester (fell 2000), given masterclasses in Italy, Switzerland, Brazil, USA, England and others, prof Royal Acad of Music 2002–; memb jury various int competitions incl: Busoni Competition, Liszt Competition, Chopin Competition (Warsaw); 1st prize: Beethoven Competition 1970, Busoni Competition 1972; *Recordings* incl: Chopin works (1978), Liszt works (1991 and 1997), Brahms works (1997),

Schumann works (1997); exclusive contract with Bis (Swedish recording co) 4 cd contract: Brasiliana (2002); *Style—* Arnaldo Cohen, Esq

COHEN, Arnold Judah; s of Samuel Cohen (d 1982), and Leah, *née* Sperling; *b* 17 December 1936; *Educ* Grocers' Co Sch, Gateshead Talmudical Coll; *m* 1, Ruth (d 1977), da of Leo Kremer, of Zurich; m 2, Sara, da of S D Kaminski, of Brussels; 4 s (Daniel b 25 May 1965, Joseph b 30 July 1968, Moshe Broner b 11 Oct 1970, Avigdor Broner b 13 Sept 1971), 1 da (Mrs Yudit Eytan b 7 Dec 1974); *Career* Cohen Arnold & Co Chartered Accountants: articled clerk 1958–62, ptnr 1962–75, sr ptnr 1975–; lectr in economics and accounting Westminster Coll 1968–72, lectr in Talmudics Hillel House 1968, lectr in Jewish civil law Hasmonean HS 1981–86; pres Fedn of Synagogues 1989–2001 (treas 1986–89); FCA 1967 (ACA 1962), ATII 1967, MInstD 1978–91; *Books* An Introduction to Jewish Civil Law (1990); monographs: The Rabbi who helped Columbus (1972), The Miracle Worker of London (1973); *Recreations* research into Jewish Civil Law, boating; *Style—* Arnold Cohen, Esq; ✉ 807 Finchley Road, London NW11 8DP (tel 020 8458 2720); Cohen Arnold & Co, 1075 Finchley Road, London NW11 0PU (tel 020 731 0777, fax 020 8731 0778)

COHEN, Ben Christopher; MBE (2004); n of George Cohen (memb England football World Cup team 1966); *b* 14 September 1978, Northampton; *Educ* Kingsthorpe Upper Sch Northampton; *Career* rugby union player (wing); currently with Northampton Saints RUFC (winners Heineken Cup 2000); England: 43 caps, 29 tries, scored two tries on debut v Ireland 2000, jt leading try scorer Six Nations Championship 2000, winners Six Nations Championship 2000, 2001 and 2003 (Grand Slam 2003), ranked no 1 team in world 2003, winners World Cup Aust 2003; memb squad Br Lions tour to Aust 2001; *Style—* Ben Cohen, Esq, MBE; ✉ c/o Rugby Football Union, Rugby House, Rugby Road, Twickenham, Middlesex TW1 1DS

COHEN, Ven Clive Ronald Franklin; s of Ronald Arthur Wilfred Cohen, MBE, and Janet Ruth Lindsay, *née* Macdonald; *Educ* Tonbridge, Salisbury and Wells Theol Coll; *m* June; 1 da, 4 s (1 s decd); *Career* asst master Edinburgh House Sch 1965–67, Midland Bank 1967–79; asst curate Esher 1981–85, rector of Winterslow 1985–2000, rural dean of Alderbury 1989–93, hon canon and prebend Salisbury Cathedral 1992–2000, archdeacon of Bodmin 2000–; ACIB 1971; *Books* Crying in the Wilderness (1994), So Great a Cloud (1995); *Style—* The Ven the Archdeacon of Bodmin; ✉ Archdeacon's House, Cardinham, Bodmin, Cornwall PL30 4BL (tel and fax 01208 821614)

COHEN, Dr (Johnson) David; CBE (2001); s of John Solomon Cohen (d 1974), and Golda, *née* Brenner (d 1968); *b* 6 January 1930; *Educ* Christ's Coll Finchley, Lincoln Coll Oxford (MA), Brandeis Univ USA (Fulbright Fell), KCL, Westminster Hosp Med Sch (MB BS, MRCS, LRCP); *m* 28 Aug 1962 (m dis 2002), Veronica, da of Felix Addison Salmon (d 1969), of London; 2 da (Imogen b 1964, Olivia b 1966); m 2, 2 Sept 2003, Jillian, da of David Barker, OBE; *Career* Nat Service 1948–50; GP 1969–2000; memb: Camden and Islington AHA 1973–78, Hampstead DHA 1983–87; govr Hosps for Sick Children Great Ormond St 1974–79, special tstee Royal Free Hosp 1984–88; chm: Camden and Islington Family Practitioner Ctee 1982–87, Camden and Islington Local Med Ctee 1983–86, John S Cohen Fndn 1974– (tstee 1965–), David Cohen Family Charitable Tst 1981–2002; govr Royal Ballet Schs 1978–93; memb: Int Bd of Govrs Hebrew Univ of Jerusalem 1975–91 (now hon govr), Exec Ctee Prison Reform Tst 1985–88, Bd Opera Factory 1986–96, Ballet Bd ROH 1987–93, Bd ENO 1988–2000, Cncl London Sinfonietta 1989–96; vice-pres London Int String Quartet Competition 1989–2000, chm English Touring Opera (formerly Opera 80) 1987–97; memb: Devpt Advsy Panel Cncl of Friends Courtauld Inst 1990–, Bd International Musicians Seminar 1991–94, Cncl Jewish Policy Research (JPR) 1992–, Bd Nat Opera Studio 1995–2004, Chllr's Ct of Benefactors Univ of Oxford 1994–, Cncl of Friends ROH 1995–2001, RNT Devpt Cncl 1998–2006 (now hon memb), Int Advsy Bd Modern Art Oxford 2000–, Cncl Br Museum Devpt Tst 2001–04, ENO Restoration Cncl 2001–04, Advsy Bd Wordsworth Tst 2002–, Leadership Gp Amnesty Int 2003–, Devpt Advsy Ctee Zoological Soc of London 2005–; tstee: ENO Benevolent Fund 1990–2002, ENO Tst 1993–, RPO Tst 1995–, Wiener Library Endowment Tst 1996–2007 (chm 1999–2007), Royal Free Hosp Cancer Research Tst 2003–07; patron: Proms at St Jude's 2003–, Bleddfa Tst 2003–, Arvon Fndn 2004–; fndr David Cohen Prize for Literature; hon life memb Balint Soc 1994; Freeman City of London 1982, Worshipful Co of Musicians; hon fell: Lincoln Coll Oxford 1986, Harris Manchester Coll Oxford 2004; fell Royal Free Hosp Sch of Med 1994; Hon GSM 1996; FRSM 1969, FRCGP 1979, FRSA 2005; *Recreations* friends, music, literature, history; *Style—* Dr David Cohen, CBE; ✉ PO Box 21277, London W9 2YH

COHEN, Prof Gerald Allan; s of Morrie Cohen (d 1985), of Montreal, and Bella, *née* Lipkin (d 1972); *b* 14 April 1941; *Educ* Strathcona Acad Montreal, McGill Univ Montreal (BA), Univ of Oxford (BPhil); *m* 1, 24 July 1965 (m dis 1996), Margaret Florence, da of Henry Aubrey Pearce, of Whitstable, Kent; 1 s (Gideon Patrick Edward b 22 Oct 1966), 2 da (Miriam Florence Laura b 20 Dec 1970, Sarah Judith Tamara b 6 Aug 1975); m 2, 12 July 1999, Michèle Jacottet-Perrenoud, da of Robert Henri Perrenoud, of La Chaux de Fonds, Switzerland; *Career* reader in philosophy UCL 1978–85 (lectr 1963–78), visiting asst prof McGill Univ Montreal 1965, visiting assoc prof Princeton Univ 1975, Chichele prof of social and political theory and fell All Souls Coll Oxford 1985–; FBA; *Books* Karl Marx's Theory of History (1978, expanded edn 2000), History Labour and Freedom (1988), Self-Ownership, Freedom, and Equality (1995), If You're an Egalitarian, How Come You're So Rich? (2000); *Recreations* Guardian crossword puzzles, looking at and reading about art and architecture, patience, travel; *Style—* Prof G A Cohen; ✉ All Souls College, Oxford OX1 4AL (tel 01865 279339, fax 01865 279299)

COHEN, Harry Michael; MP; *b* 10 December 1949; *m* 1978, Ellen, *née* Hussain; 1 step s, 1 step da; *Career* accountant; MP (Lab): Leyton 1983–97, Leyton and Wanstead 1997–; memb House of Commons Defence Select Ctee 1997–2001; chm Lab Backbench Def Ctee House of Commons 1987–92, chm Sub-Ctee for Econ Co-operation and Convergence with Eastern and Central Europe N Atlantic Assembly Econ Ctee 1994–2000, currently rapporteur; vice-chm PLP Backbench Ctee on Defence 1997–2001; sec All-Pty Gp Race and Community; cncllr Waltham Forest BC 1972–83 (chm Planning Ctee, sec Lab Gp); master of science, politics and admin Birkbeck Coll London 1994; hon vice-pres Royal Coll of Midwives; memb UNISON, former memb CIPFA; *Style—* Harry Cohen, MP; ✉ House of Commons, London SW1A 0AA (tel 020 7219 6376)

COHEN, Prof Jonathan; s of Dr Norman A Cohen, of London, and Ruth N, *née* Kimche; *b* 11 October 1949; *Educ* William Ellis GS, Univ of London (BSc, MB BS, MSc); *m* 6 Jan 1974, Dr Noemi Cohen, da of Richard Weingarten (d 1968), of India; 1 da (Joanna b 1979), 1 s (Richard b 1981); *Career* formerly prof and head Dept of Infectious Diseases Imperial Coll Sch of Med at Hammersmith Hosp (Royal Postgrad Med Sch until merger 1997) and hon conslt physician Hammersmith Hosp, dean Brighton and Sussex Med Sch 2002–; author of scientific papers and contribs to books on infection and infectious disease; FRCP, FRCPath, FRCPEd, FMedSci; *Recreations* skiing, photography; *Style—* Prof Jonathan Cohen; ✉ Brighton and Sussex Medical School, University of Sussex, Falmer BN1 9PX (tel 01273 877577, fax 01273 877576, e-mail j.cohen@bsms.ac.uk)

COHEN, Jonathan Lionel; QC (1997); s of Hon Leonard Cohen, OBE, and Eleanor Lucy, *née* Henriques; *b* 8 May 1951; *Educ* Eton, Univ of Kent at Canterbury (BA); *m* 1983, Bryony Frances, *née* Carfrae; 2 s, 1 da; *Career* called to the Bar Lincoln's Inn 1974 (bencher 2004–), recorder 1997–, dep judge of the High Court (Family Div) 2005–; memb Mental Health Review Tbnl 2000–; govr: Skinners' Sch for Girls 1994–2002, Judd Sch Tonbridge 2002–06, Tonbridge Sch 2006– (chm 2007–); memb Ct of Assts Worshipful Co of Skinners 2000– (Master 2005–06); *Recreations* cricket, golf; *Style—* Jonathan Cohen, QC; ✉ 4 Paper Buildings, Temple, London EC4Y 7EX (tel 020 7583 0816, fax 020 7353 4979)

COHEN, Lawrence Francis Richard; QC (1993); s of Harris Cohen of Willesden, and Sarah *née* Rich; *b* 4 November 1951; *Educ* Preston Manor Sch, Univ of Birmingham (LLB), Inns of Court Sch of Law; *m* 24 May 1986, Alison Jane, da of Dr Rowland Patrick Bradshaw of Cobham, Surrey; 1 da (Sophie 1987), 1 s (Leo b 1989); *Career* called to the Bar Gray's Inn 1974; recorder 1998– (asst recorder 1995–98); memb: Chancery Bar Association, Insolvency Lawyers Association, Commercial Bar Association (COMBAR); ACIA 1986; *Recreations* reading, cycling; *Style—* Lawrence F R Cohen, Esq, QC; ✉ 24 Old Buildings, Lincoln's Inn, London WC2A 3UP (tel 020 7404 0946, fax 020 7405 1360)

COHEN, Dr Martin; s of Prof Desmond Cohen, and Prof Brenda Almond; *Educ* Univ of Sussex (BA), Univ of Exeter (PhD); *Career* ed The Philosopher (Jl of the Philosophical Soc) 1995–; memb Quantificational Aesthetics Working Gp; first person to swim River Wharfe from Bolton Abbey to Ilkley 1996; *Books* 101 Philosophy Problems (1999), Political Philosophy: from Plato to Chairman Mao (2001), Adam Smith and the Wealth of Nations (2001); *Recreations* axioms of set theory, inverse-propositional logic, felicific calculus, scrabble (in Latin); *Style—* Dr Martin Cohen; ✉ Centre for Lifelong Learning, University of Newcastle upon Tyne, Newcastle upon Tyne NE1 7RU

COHEN, Michael Alan; s of Harris Cohen, of London, and Cissie, *née* Rich; *b* 30 July 1933; *Educ* Ilford Co HS, UCL (LLB); *m* 3 July 1955, Ann Cohen; 1 s (Julian Andrew b 1967), 1 da (Nicola Amanda b 1970); *Career* Flt Lt RAF 1955–58; called to the Bar; formerly: registered insurance broker and independent fin advsr, md Avery Rich Assocs Ltd, ptnr ARA Financial Services, dir ARA Life Assurance Services; currently practising arbitrator, mediator, dispute resolver, insurance expert and conslt, ptnr Michael Cohen Associates, dir ARA Conference Services, dir ADR Centre London; vice-pres: Br Insurance Law Assoc, EuroExpert (pres); emeritus chm Acad of Experts; memb: Disciplinary Tbnl Inst of Actuaries, Cncl Int Fedn of Commercial Arbitration Centre, Advsy Bd Center Analysis of Alternative Dispute Resolution Systems (CAADRS) Chicago, Ct of Appeal ADR Steering Gp, various ctees Chartered Inst of Arbitrators, Int Chambers of Commerce (Paris) Standing Ctee in Expertise; Freeman City of London; Liveryman Worshipful Cos of: Spectacle Makers, Insurers, Arbitrators; memb Hon Soc of Gray's Inn and of Lincoln's Inn; hon certified forensic expert; hon fell Br Assoc of Criminal Experts; hon memb: FNCEJ (French experts), BVS (German experts), ANPTJ (Spanish experts); QDR, FCIArb, FInstBA, FAE, FRSA; *Recreations* sailing, swimming, driving, collecting, yoga; *Clubs* Athenaeum, City Livery, Bar Yacht; *Style—* Michael Cohen, Esq; ✉ 3 Gray's Inn Square, Gray's Inn, London WC1R 5AH (tel 020 7430 0333, fax 020 7430 0666, e-mail mac@aracs.co.uk)

COHEN, Prof Morton Norton; s of Samuel Cohen (d 1956), of Massachusetts, and Zelda Jenny Miller (d 1946); *b* 27 February 1921; *Educ* Tufts Univ (AB), Columbia Univ (MA, PhD); *Career* instr in English W Virginia Univ 1950–51, lectr in English Rutgers Univ 1952–53; City Coll and Graduate Center CUNY: tutor rising to prof 1951–82, memb Doctoral Faculty 1964–82, dep exec offr PhD program in English 1976–78 and 1979–80, actg exec offr 1980–82, prof emeritus 1982–; visiting prof Syracuse Univ 1965–66 and 1967–68; chm: CCNY English Honors Ctee 1962–65, Electives Ctee 1972–73, Grad Sch Structure 1976–78; memb: Grad Cncl CUNY 1976–80, Faculty Policy Ctee CUNY Grad Sch 1978–80, Faculty Advsy Cncl CUNY Research Fndn 1976–80, Advsy Cncl American Tst for the Br Library 1980–; memb: Lewis Carroll Soc UK, Lewis Carroll Soc of N America; guest curator Lewis Carroll exhbn Pierpont Morgan Library NY 1982; author numerous chapters and articles 1958–; numerous appearances on television and radio progs in UK, Canada and USA; FRSL 1996; *Awards* Ford Fndn faculty fell 1951–52, Fulbright fell Univ of Leeds 1954–55, American Philosophical Soc grants 1962 and 1964, American Cncl of Learned Soc grant-in-aid 1963, Guggenheim fell 1966–67, sr fell Nat Endowment for the Humanitites 1970–71 and 1978–79, Fulbright Sr research fell ChCh Oxford 1974–75, research grant Nat Endowment for the Humanities 1974–75, Guggenheim Fndn Publication Grant 1979; *Books* Rider Haggard: His Life and Works (1960, 2 edn 1968), A Brief Guide to Better Writing (co-author, 1960), Rudyard Kipling to Rider Haggard: The Record of a Friendship (ed, 1965), The Russian Journal - II (ed, 1979), Lewis Carroll, Photographer of Children: Four Nude Studies (1979), Lewis Carroll and the Kitchins (ed, 1980), The Letters of Lewis Carroll (ed, 2 vols, 1979), Lewis Carroll and Alice 1832–1982 - A Celebration of Lewis Carroll's Hundred and Fiftieth Birthday (1982), The Selected Letters of Lewis Carroll (ed, 1982, 3 edn 1996), Lewis Carroll and the House of Macmillan (co-ed, 1987), Lewis Carroll: Interviews and Recollections (ed, 1989), Lewis Carroll: A Biography (1995, 2 edn 1996), Reflections in a Looking Glass: A Centennial Celebration of Lewis Carrol, Photographer (1998), Lewis Carroll and His Illustrations: Collaborations and Correspondence, 1865–1898 (co-ed, 2003); contrib: Cambridge Bibliography of English Literature, Dictionary of National Biography; *Recreations* travel, theatre, antiques, art; *Clubs* Century (NY), Athenaeum, Garrick, Reform, Arts (Edinburgh); *Style—* Prof Morton N Cohen, FRSL; ✉ 55 East 9th Street, Apt 10–D, New York, NY 10003, USA; c/o A P Watt, 20 John Street, London WC1N 2DR (tel 020 7405 6774, fax 020 7831 2154, e-mail watt@dial.pipex.com)

COHEN, Prof Sir Philip; kt (1998); s of Jacob D Cohen, of London, and Fanny, *née* Bragman; *b* 22 July 1945; *Educ* Hendon Co GS, UCL (BSc, PhD); *m* 17 Feb 1969, Patricia Townsend, da of Charles H T Wade, of Greenmount, Lancs; 1 da ((Suzanne) Emma b 1974), 1 s (Simon Daniel b 1977); *Career* SRC/NATO fell Univ of Washington Seattle 1969–71; Univ of Dundee: lectr in biochemistry 1971–78, reader in biochemistry 1978–81, prof of enzymology 1981–84, Royal Soc research prof 1984–, dir MRC Protein Phosphorylation Unit 1990–; dir Wellcome Trust Biocentre 1997–; fell UCL 1993; author of over 470 articles in learned jls; tstee Robert T Jones Jr Meml Tst 2000–; Hon DSc: Univ of Abertay 1998, Univ of Strathclyde 1999, Linkoping Univ Sweden 2004, Univ of Debrecen Hungary 2004, Univ of St Andrews 2005; hon pres Br Biochemical Soc 2006 (hon memb 2003); FRS 1984, FRSE 1984, Hon FRCPath 1998, FMedSci 1999; *Awards* Colworth Medal Br Biochemical Soc 1977, Anniversary Prize Fedn of Euro Biochemical Socs 1977, CIBA Medal Br Biochemical Soc 1991, Prix van Gysel Belgian Royal Acads of Med 1992, Bruce Preller Prize Royal Soc of Edinburgh 1993, Dundee City of Discovery Rosebowl Award 1993, Prix Louis Jeantet de Médecine (Geneva) 1997, Croonian Lecture Royal Soc 1998, Pfizer innovation award for Europe 1999, named by ISI as third most highly cited UK based scientist of 1990s), Sir Hans Krebs Medal Fedn of Euro Biochemical Societies 2001, Bristol Myers Squibb Distinguished Achievement Award in Metabolic Res 2002, World's Second Most Cited Scientist in Biology and Biochemistry 1992–2003, Debrecen Award for Molecular Medicine 2004, Royal Medal Royal Soc of Edinburgh 2004; *Books* Control of Enzyme Activity (1976, 2 edn 1983, trans into German, Italian, Russian and Malay), Molecular Aspects of Cellular Regulation (series ed); *Recreations* bridge, chess, golf, natural history; *Clubs* Downfield Golf (Dundee), Isle of Harris Golf; *Style—* Prof Sir Philip Cohen, FRS, FRSE; ✉ Inverbay II, Invergowrie, Dundee DD2 5DQ (tel 01382 562 328); School of Life Sciences, University of Dundee, Dundee (tel 01382 384238, fax 01382 223778)

COHEN, Robert; s of Raymond Cohen, and Anthya, *née* Rael; *b* 15 June 1959; *Educ* Purcell Sch, Guildhall Sch (Cert Advanced Solo Studies); *m* 1 Aug 1987, Rachel, *née* Smith; 4 s (Joshua b 4 Sept 1992, Isaac b 13 May 1994, Joseph b 15 May 1996, Louis b 16 July 1999); *Career* concert cellist and conductor; concerto debut Royal Festival Hall 1971; recital debuts: Wigmore Hall 1976, NY 1979, LA 1979, Washington DC 1979; many TV and radio appearances incl subject of documentary (Thames TV) 1979; gives master classes in: USA, Europe, Scandinavia, Australia, UK, NZ, Israel; visiting prof Royal Acad of Music 1998–, prof of advanced cello and chamber music Conservatorio Della Svizzera Italiana Lugano 2000–; patron Beauchamp Music Club, dir Charleston Manor Festival 1989–, fell Purcell Sch for Young Musicians; memb Inc Soc of Musicians; *Performances* major concerto tours since 1980: USA, Europe, Eastern Europe, Scandinavia, Israel, UK, NZ, Aust and Japan; orchs: all major Br orchs, Detroit Symphony, Minnesota Orch, Swiss Romande, Rotterdam Philharmonic, Helsinki Philharmonic, Leipzig Gewandhaus, Netherlands Philharmonic, Oslo Philharmonic, ECYO, Sydney Symphony, Sapporo Symphony; working with conductors incl: Abbado, Dorati, Jansons, Marriner, Masur, Muti, Otaka, Rattle, Sinopoli; conductor and directing guest of several European chamber orchs 1992– (symphony orchs 2000–); chamber ptnrs incl: Amadeus Quartet, Massimo Quarta, Peter Donohoe, Heini Kärkkäinen, Cohen Trio, Paul Ostrovsky; *Recordings* Elgar Cello Concerto (silver disc), Dvorák Cello Concerto, Tchaikovsky Rococo Variations, Grieg Sonata/Franck Sonata, Rodrigo Concerto En Modo Galante; virtuoso cello music: Locatelli Sonata, Chopin Intro and Polonaise Brillante, Dvorák Rondo, Popper 3 pieces, Beethoven Triple Concerto (with F P Zimmerman and W Manz), Dvorák Complete Piano Trios (with Cohen Trio), Schubert String Quintet (with Amadeus Quartet), Bach 6 Solo Suites, Howard Blake Diversions 1991, Elgar Concerto 1993, Bliss Concerto 1994, Walton Concerto 1995, Britten 3 Solo Suites 1997, Morton Feldman Concerto 1998, Britten Cello Symphony 1998, Sally Beamish Cello Concerto River 1999, H K Gruber Cello Concerto 2003, Tchaikovsky Souvenir de Florence (with the Endellion String Quartet); recording contract (7 years) with Decca/Argo 1992–; *Awards* Suggia prize 1967–71, Martin Tst award 1973–75, winner Young Concert Artists Int Competition NY 1978, Piatigorsky prize USA 1978, winner UNESCO Int Competition Czechoslovakia 1980; *Recreations* photography, alternative medicine, healing, philosophy; *Clubs* Inst of Advanced Motorists; *Style*— Robert Cohen, Esq; ✉ c/o Ms J Carpenter Music Management and PR (tel 020 7737 5994, fax 0870 912 5965, e-mail jo@jocarpenter.com); website www.robertcohen.info

COHEN, Prof Robert Donald; CBE (1997); *b* 11 October 1933; *Educ* Clifton, Trinity Coll Cambridge (MA, MD); *m* 14 Feb 1961, Barbara Joan, *née* Boucher; 1 da (Susan b 1963), 1 s (Martin b 1966); *Career* The London Hosp Med Coll Univ of London (St Bartholomew's and the Royal London Sch of Med and Dentistry since1995): prof of metabolic med 1974–82, prof of med 1982–99, emeritus prof of med 1999–; chm Editorial Bd Clinical Science 1973–75; chm: DHSS Computer R&D Ctee 1976–80, Special Advsy Ctee in Gen Internal Med of Jt Ctee on Higher Med Trg 1985–90, Br Diabetic Assoc Review Body 1990–95, Virucides Steering Ctee MRC 1993–2004, Cncl ICRF 1994–2003 (memb 1989–, vice-chm 1991–94); memb: GMC 1988–96 (memb Educn Ctee 1988–89 and 1990–95), Physiological Systems Bd MRC 1990–92, Health Servs Res Ctee MRC 1990–92, Physiological Med and Infections Bd MRC 1992–94 (dep chm), Health Servs and Public Health Bd MRC 1992–94, Cncl Nat Kidney Res Fund 1992–98, Jt Ctee on Higher Med Trg 1997–98, Cncl King Edward VII Hosp Midhurst 1997–2000, Cncl Cancer Res UK 2001–03, Acad Advsy Cncl Asian Inst of Med, Sci and Technol (Malaysia) 2002–, Academic Research Ctee Specialist Trg Authy of the Royal Colls; first vice-pres and sr censor RCP London 1991–93; hon fell QMC London 2001; FRCP 1971, FMedSci 1999; *Books* Clinical and Biochemical Aspects of Lactic Acidosis (with H F Woods, 1976), The Metabolic and Molecular Basis of Acquired Disease (ed with B Lewis, K G M M Alberti and A M Denman, 1990); scientific papers on metabolic disorders and liver metabolism; *Recreations* watercolour painting, walking; *Clubs* Athenaeum; *Style*— Prof Robert Cohen, CBE; ✉ Longmeadow, East Dean, Chichester, West Sussex PO18 0JB (tel 01243 811230, fax 01243 811924, e-mail rcohen@doctors.org.uk)

COHEN, Sir Ronald Mourad; kt (2001); s of Michael Mourad Cohen (d 1997), and Sonia Sophie, *née* Douek; *b* 1 August 1945; *Educ* Orange Hill GS London, Exeter Coll Oxford (MA, pres Oxford Union), Harvard Business Sch (MBA, Henry fellowship); *m* 1, Dec 1972 (m dis 1975), Carol Marylene, da of Gérard Belmont, of Geneva; m 2, Dec 1983 (m dis 1986), Claire Whitmore, da of Thomas Enders, of New York; m 3, 5 March 1987, Sharon Ruth, da of Joseph Harel, of Tel Aviv; 1 da (Tamara Jennifer Harel-Cohen b 7 Oct 1987), 1 s (Jonathan Michael Harel-Cohen b 3 June 1991); *Career* conslt McKinsey & Co (UK and Italy) 1969–71, chargé de mission Institut de Développement Industriel France 1971–72, fndr chm Apax Partners Worldwide LLP (formerly The MMG Patricof Group plc) 1972–2005; chm Bridges Community Ventures 2002–, fndr and chm The Portland Tst 2003–, chm Portland Capital LLP 2006–, chm Sterling Publishing Group plc until 1993; fndr dir: British Venture Capital Assoc (former chm) 1983, Euro Venture Capital Assoc 1985, City Gp for Smaller Cos (now Quoted Cos Alliance) 1992; dir NASDAQ Europe 2001–, fndr and vice-chm EASDAQ 1995–2001, chm Bridges Community Ventures Ltd 2002–; chm: DTI Tech Stars Steering Ctee 1997–99, Social Investment Task Force HM Treasy 2000–; memb: CBI Wider Share Ownership Ctee 1988–90, Stock Exchange Working Pty on Smaller Cos 1993, CBI City Advsy Gp 1993–99, Exec Ctee Centre for Economic Policy and Research 1996–99, Fin Ctee Inst for Social and Economic Policy in the Middle East Kennedy Sch Harvard Univ 1997–98, Franco-British Cncl 1997–99, Advsy Bd Fulbright Cmmn 1997–99, Advsy Cncl Fndn for Entrepreneurial Mgmnt London Business Sch 1997–99, DTI UK Competitiveness Ctee 1998, IMRO, SFA; tstee and memb Exec Ctee IISS 2004–; vice-chm Ben Gurion Univ 2002–; memb: Dean's Bd of Advsrs Harvard Business Sch 2003–, Chllr's Ct of Benefactors Univ of Oxford 2003–; advsr Inter-Action Group (charity); tstee Br Museum 2005–; Lib candidate Kensington North Gen Election 1974 and London West for Euro Parl 1979; hon fell Exeter Coll Oxford 2000; *Recreations* music, art, tennis, travel; *Clubs* Athenaeum, RAC, Queen's; *Style*— Sir Ronald Cohen; ✉ 42 Portland Place, London W1B 1NB (tel 020 7182 7801, fax 020 7182 7897)

COHEN, Shimon; s of Louis Cohen, of Stanmore, Middx, and Elaine, *née* Liss; *b* 24 May 1960; *Educ* Llanedeyrn HS Cardiff, Univ of Manchester; *m* 24 July 1994, Jessica Dana, da of Sydney Ann Blair, of New York; 1 da (Ava Siena b 7 March 2000); *Career* ceo Office of the Chief Rabbi 1983–90, sr conslt Bell Pottinger Consultants 1990–2000, ceo Bell Pottinger Public Relations 2000–; dir: Jewish Chronicle Newspaper Ltd 1994–2003, Inst for Jewish Policy Research 1995–, Totally 2004–; tstee Teaching Awards Tst 2001–; MIPR, FRSA; *Recreations* theatre, dining; *Style*— Shimon Cohen, Esq; ✉ Bell Pottinger Public Relations, 20–22 Stukeley Street, London WC2B 5LR (tel 020 7430 2276, fax 020 7831 7663, e-mail scohen@bell-pottinger.co.uk)

COHEN, Stanley Solomon; OBE; s of Emanuel Cohen (d 1967), and Hilda Cohen; *b* 22 July 1926, London; *Educ* W Hove Sch, Lauriston Sch Hackney; *m* 22 July 1952, Joy Audrey, *née* Curtis; 1 s (Andrew Lynton b 2 May 1953), 2 da (Susan Lorraine (Mrs Rubin) b 24 July 1957, Phillipa Rose (Mrs Hasenson) b 18 Sept 1965); *Career* Betterware plc 1972–96, Glenmore Ltd 1996–; chm Shield Ctee Duke of Edinburgh Awards; chm Scopus Jewish Educnl Tst; pres Maccabi GB; *Recreations* vintage cars, football, cricket, walking; *Style*— Stanley Cohen, Esq, OBE; ✉ Glenmore Commercial Estates, 52 Queen Anne Street, London W1G 8HL (tel 020 7935 0100, fax 020 7935 7787, e-mail stanley@glenmore-group.co.uk)

COHEN OF PIMLICO, Baroness (Life Peer UK 2000), of Pimlico in the City of Westminster; Janet Cohen; da of George Edric Neel (d 1952), and Mary Isabel, *née* Budge; *b* 4 July 1940; *Educ* South Hampstead HS, Newnham Coll Cambridge (BA); *m* 1 (m dis); m 2, 18 Dec 1971, James Lionel Cohen, s of Dr Richard Henry Lionel Cohen, CB, of Cambridge; 2 s (Henry b 1973, Richard b 1975), 1 da (Isobel b 1979); *Career* articled clerk Frere Cholmeley 1963–65, admitted slr 1965, ABT Assoc Cambridge MA 1965–67, John Laing Construction 1967–69, princ (later asst sec) DTI 1969–82; dir: Cafe Pelican Ltd 1983–90, Charterhouse Bank Ltd 1987–2000 (joined 1982); chm BPP Holdings plc 2002–06 (non-exec dir 1994–2006), non-exec dir and vice-chair Yorkshire Building Soc 1991–99; non-exec dir: John Waddington plc 1994–97, London and Manchester Corporation plc 1997–98, United Assurance Gp plc 1999–2000, Defence Logistics Organisation 1999–2005, London Stock Exchange plc 2001–; advsy dir HSBC Investment Bank 2000–02, MCG plc 2003–, TRL Electronics 2006–; memb Expert Panel on the Strategic Defence Review 1997–98; memb Bd of Govrs BBC 1994–99; pres Combustion Engrg Assoc 2006–; chm Parl Choir 2006–; writer; *Books* Deaths Bright Angel (as Janet Neel, 1988, John Creasey Award for Best First Crime Novel), Death on Site (1989), Death of a Partner (1991), The Highest Bidder (as Janet Cohen, 1992), Death Among the Dons (1993), Children of a Harsh Winter (as Janet Cohen, 1994), A Timely Death (1996), To Die For (1998), O Gentle Death (2000), Ticket to Ride (2005); *Recreations* writing, theatre; *Style*— Baroness Cohen of Pimlico; ✉ House of Lords, London SW1A 0PW

COHN, Prof Paul Moritz; s of late James Cohn, and late Julia Mathilde, *née* Cohen; *b* 8 January 1924; *Educ* Trinity Coll Cambridge (MA, PhD); *m* 27 March 1958, Deirdre Sonia Sharon, da of Arthur David Finkle (d 1968), of London; 2 da ((Susan) Juliet, (Ursula) Yael); *Career* Chargé de Recherches (CNRS) Univ of Nancy France 1951–52, lectr Univ of Manchester 1952–62, reader QMC London 1962–67, prof and head Dept of Maths Bedford Coll London 1967–84; UCL: prof 1984–86, Astor prof 1986–89, prof emeritus and hon research fell 1989; visiting prof: Yale Univ, Univ of Calif Berkeley, Univ of Chicago, SUNY Stonybrook, Rutgers Univ, Univ of Paris, Tulane Univ, Indian Inst of Technol Delhi, Univ of Alberta, Carleton Univ, Haifa Technion, Univ of Iowa, Univ of Bielefeld, Univ of Frankfurt, Univ of Hamburg (Wilhelm-Blaschke prof), Bar Ilan Univ, Univ d'Etat Mons; author and ed; memb Cncl SRC Maths 1977–79, chm Nat Ctee for Maths 1988–89, pres London Math Soc 1982–84 (memb 1957), IMU rep Int Rels Ctee Royal Soc 1990–93; L R Ford award Math Assoc of America 1972, Berwick prize London Math Soc 1974; FRS 1980 (memb Cncl 1985–87); *Books* incl: Lie Groups (1957), Universal Algebra (1965, 1981), Free Rings and Their Relations (1971, 1985), Algebra I (1974, 1982), Algebra II (1977, 1989), Algebra III (1990), Algebraic Numbers and Algebraic Functions (1991), Elements of Linear Algebra (1994), Skew Fields, Theory of General Division Rings (in Encyclopedia of Mathematics and its Applications, vol 57, 1995), Introduction to Ring Theory (2000), Classic Algebra (2000), Basic Algebra (2002), Further Algebra and Applications (2003), New Dictionary of National Biography (contrib, 2004), Free Ideal Rings and Localization in General Rings (2006); translations into Spanish, Italian, Russian and Chinese, contrib New DNB (2004); *Recreations* language in all its forms; *Style*— Prof P M Cohn, FRS; ✉ Department of Mathematics, University College London, Gower Street, London WC1E 6BT (tel 020 7679 4459, fax 020 7383 5519)

COHN-SHERBOK, Rabbi Prof Daniel Mark (Dan); s of Bernard Cohn-Sherbok, of Denver, Colorado, and Ruth Cohn-Sherbok; *b* 1 February 1945; *Educ* E Denver HS, Williams Coll MA (BA), Hebrew Union Coll Cincinnati (MA, DD), Wolfson Coll Cambridge (MLitt, PhD); *m* 19 Dec 1976, Lavinia Charlotte, da of late Graham Douglas Heath; *Career* ordained rabbi 1971; chaplain Colorado State House of Representatives 1971; lectr in theology Univ of Kent 1975–97 (dir Centre for the Study of Religion and Society 1982–90); visiting prof: Univ of Essex 1993–94, Univ of Wales Lampeter 1994–97 (currently prof of Judaism), Univ of Middx 1994–2001, Univ of Wales Bangor 1998, Univ of Vilnius 2000, Univ of Durham 2002; dir Centre for the Study of the World's Religions Univ of Wales Lampeter 2003–; fell Hebrew Union Coll 1972, corresponding fell Acad of Jewish Philosophy 1978, visiting fell: Wolfson Coll Cambridge 1991, Harris Manchester Coll 2002; visiting scholar: Mansfield Coll Oxford 1994, Oxford Centre for Postgrad Hebrew Studies 1994; memb London Soc for the Study of Religion 1981; finalist Times Preacher of the Year 2001; *Books* On Earth As It Is In Heaven (1987), The Jewish Heritage (1988), Holocaust Theology (1989), A Dictionary of Christianity and Judaism (1990), Rabbinic Perspectives on the New Testament (1990), Blackwell's Dictionary of Judaica (1991), Israel (1992), The Crucified Jew (1992), Atlas of Jewish History (1993), The Jewish Faith (1993), The American Jew (1994), Judaism and Other Faiths (1994), The Future of Judaism (1994), Jewish and Christian Mysticism (1994), Jewish Mysticism: An Anthology (1995), Modern Judaism (1996), The Hebrew Bible (1996), Biblical Hebrew For Beginners (1996), Mediaeval Jewish Philosophy (1996), Fifty Key Jewish Thinkers (1996), After Noah (1997), The Jewish Messiah (1997), Consice Encyclopedia of Judaism (1998), Understanding the Holocaust (1999), Messianic Judaism (2000), Holocaust Theology: A Reader (2001), Interfaith Theology: A Reader (2001), Anti-Semitism (2002), Judaism: History, Belief and Practice (2003), The Vision of Judaism: Wrestling with God (2004), Pursuing the Dream: A Jewish-Christian Conversation (2005), Dictionary of Jewish Biography (2005), An Encyclopedia of Judaism and Christianity (2005), The Paradox of Antisemitism (2006), The Politics of Apocalypse: The History and Influence of Christian Zionism (2006); *Recreations* keeping cats, walking; *Clubs* Athenaeum, Lansdowne, Williams (NY); *Style*— Rabbi Prof Dan Cohn-Sherbok; ✉ Department of Theology and Religious Studies, University of Wales, Lampeter, Ceredigion SA48 7ED (tel 01570 424968, fax 01570 423641)

COID, Dr Donald Routledge; s of Charles Routledge Coid, of Wheathampstead, Herts, and Marjory Macdonald Coid, *née* Keay; *b* 13 June 1953; *Educ* Bromley GS for Boys, Harrow Co Sch for Boys, Univ of Nottingham (BMedSci, BM BS), London Sch of Hygiene and Tropical Med (MSc), Univ of NSW; *m* 1985, Susan Kathleen Ramus, da of Clifford Roy Crocker; 1 da (Joanna Fleur Julia b 6 Dec 1987), 2 adopted da (Amber Ramus b 4 Feb 1976, Holly Ramus b 21 Sept 1978); *Career* house physician Univ Dept of Therapeutics Nottingham July 1976–77, house surgn Univ Dept of Surgery Nottingham 1977, SHO in gen med Brook Hosp London 1977–78, locum med offr Medic International Ltd London 1978–79, research asst (clinical epidemiology) Dept of Community Med Middx Hosp Med Sch 1979, field MO Eastern Goldfields Section Royal Flying Doctor Serv of Aust 1979–80, MO Community and Child Health Servs Kalgoorlie Western Aust 1981–82, regional dir of public health Eastern Goldfields Western Aust 1982–85 (med superintendent Kalgoorlie Regional Hosp 1984–85); Fife Health Bd: community med specialist 1985–89, conslt in public health 1990–92, asst gen mangr 1992–93; chief admin med offr, dir of public health and exec dir Tayside Health Bd 1994–98, conslt in health servs research Univ of Dundee 1998–2001, public health conslt Grampian Health Bd 1999–2001, dir of med servs Armadale Health Serv W Aust 2001–06, exec dir of med servs Wide Bay Health Serv Dist Queensland 2006–; hon sr lectr Univ of Dundee 1994–2001; author of pubns on various public health topics in learned jls; memb: Christian Church, Royal Aust Coll of Med Admins 1985, Br Schools' Exploring Soc, Aust Faculty of Public Health Med, Aust Med Assoc; FFPHM 1996, FRCPEd 1997, FRIPH 1997; *Recreations* public health theory, golf, cricket, piano and singing; *Clubs* Royal & Ancient Golf (St Andrews), New Golf (St Andrews), Lakelands Country (W Aust), Bargara Golf (Queensland); *Style*— Dr Donald R Coid; ✉ 5 Judith Street, Bargara, Queensland 4670, Australia (e-mail dcoid@internode.on.net)

COJOCARU, Alina; *b* Bucharest, Romania; *Educ* Ukrainian State Ballet Sch Kiev, Royal Ballet Sch (Prix de Lausanne scholarship); *Career* ballet dancer; formerly with Kiev Ballet, princ Royal Ballet 2001– (joined 1999); guest dancer: Kirov Ballet, American Ballet Theatre, Royal Danish Ballet, Hungarian Nat Ballet, Paris Opera Garnier, Romanian Nat Ballet, Bolshoi Ballet (debut La Sylphide); *Performances* with Kiev Ballet incl: Kitri, Aurora, Cinderella, Clara, Swanilda; with Royal Ballet incl: Sugar Plum Fairy, Nikiya,

Kitri, Juliet, Giselle, Odette, Odile, Mary Vetsera, Aurora, Tatiana, Olga in Onegin, Titania in The Dream, Manon, Raymonda, Cinderella, Vera in A Month in the Country, La Sylphide pas de deux, The Leaves are Fading, Scènes de ballet, Ondine, Symphonic Variations, The Veriginous Thrill of Exactitude, Symphony in C, This House Will Burn Down, Les Saisons; *Style—* Ms Alina Cojocaru; ✉ c/o The Royal Ballet, Royal Opera House, Covent Garden, London WC2E 9DD

COKE, Edward Peter; s of Lt Cdr John Hodson Coke, RN, of East Stour, Dorset, and Kathleen Mary, *née* Pennington (d 2000); *b* 12 October 1948; *Educ* St John's Coll Southsea, Univ of Warwick (LLB), Inns of Court Sch of Law; *m* 6 July 1968 (m dis 1994), Josephine Linette, da of Frederick Francis Kennard (d 1987); 1 s (Dominic Francis), 2 da (Sarah Marie, Jessica Mary); *Career* trainee mangr W Woolworth 1966–69, postman PO 1969–71, sr advsy offr Consumer Protection Dept W Midlands CC; called to the Bar Inner Temple 1976; tenant St Ive's Chambers 1977– (head of chambers 1990–2000 (re-elected 1997)), recorder of the Crown Court 2005–; memb: Midland Circuit, Criminal Bar Assoc; dir Conviction Pictures Ltd 2002; memb crew yacht Portsmouth Times Round the World Yacht Race 2000–01; *Recreations* theatre, cinema, walking, gardening; *Style—* Edward Coke, Esq; ✉ St Ive's Chambers, Whittal Street, Birmingham B4 6DH (tel 0121 236 0863, fax 0121 236 6961, e-mail eddiecoke@hotmail.com or edwardcoke@convictionpictures.com)

COLACICCHI, Clare Elizabeth Vivienne; da of Richard Clutterbuck, of Worcs, and Gillian, *née* Harding; *b* 3 August 1958, Leamington Spa, Warks; *Educ* Queens Gate Sch London, Somerville Coll Oxford; *m* June 1982, William Colacicchi; 3 da (Cecilia Mary Elizabeth b 18 April 1988, Lucy Anne Isabella b 17 Sept 1990, Caroline Daisy b 16 July 1993); *Career* admitted slr 1983; articled clerk then asst slr Macfarlanes 1981–89, partner Hewitsons 1990– (slr 1989); worldwide chm Soc of Tst and Estate Practitioners 2003–04; memb Law Soc 1983; *Recreations* theatre, gardening; *Style—* Mrs Clare Colacicchi; ✉ Hewitsons, 7 Spencer Parade, Northampton NN1 5AB (tel 01604 233233, fax 01604 627941, e-mail clarecolacicchi@hewitsons.com)

COLBOURNE, Christopher Richard Leslie (Chris); s of Robert Henry Colbourne, of Chichester, and Jane Freda, *née* Gardner; *b* 19 November 1947; *Educ* Lexington HS Mass, Boston Univ (BA), AA Sch of Architecture (AADip); *m* 1977, Anne Louise, da of James McElhatton; 1 s (Tom Robert b 25 Jan 1980), 1 da (Clare Rosina b 22 April 1987); *Career* Llewelyn-Davies Weeks: architect, planner and devpt dir 1974–78, assoc 1977; dir Tibbalds Monro (formerly Tibbalds Colbourne Partnership) 1978–96; Masterworks Devpt Corp: dir devpt Europe 1998–2001, vice-pres NY 2001–; RIBA: memb Cncl 1976–, chm London Region 1992–93, vice-pres Public Affairs 1994–96, dep DG 1996–98, dir RIBA Insurance Agency Ltd 1998–, dir Jt Contracts Tbnl Ltd 1998–; chm communications Cwlth Assoc of Architects 2000–; teacher Brunel Univ; external examiner: Kingston Univ, Bartlett Sch of Architecture UCL; Freeman City of London, Liveryman Worshipful Co of Chartered Architects; *Recreations* sailing, skiing; *Style—* Chris Colbourne, Esq; ✉ Masterworks Development Corporation, 7–12 Gracechurch Street, London EC1Y 0DR (tel 020 7666 1820, fax 020 7623 2469, e-mail ccolbourne@masterworksdev.com); Masterworks Development Corporation, 56 West 45th Street, 4th Floor, New York, NY 10036, USA

COLCHESTER, Prof Alan Charles Francis; s of John Sparrow Colchester (d 1981), of East Chiltington, E Sussex, and Norah Diana Taylor, *née* Pengelley; *b* 4 October 1947; *Educ* Haileybury, BNC Oxford (BA), UCH London (BM BCh), Univ of London (PhD), Univ of Oxford (MA); *m* 17 Aug 1974, Nicola Jane, da of Edward Rocksborough Smith (d 1989), of Briantspuddle, Dorset; 2 da (Nancy b 1979, Emily b 1981), 1 s (Rupert b 1984); *Career* research MO RAF Inst of Aerospace Med Farnborough 1978–81, registrar in neurology The London Hosp 1982–83, sr registrar in neurology Atkinson Morley's and St George's Hosps 1983–87, sr lectr UMDS 1987–96, conslt neurologist Guy's Hosp London and E Kent Hosps Tst 1987–, lead clinican for neurosciences E Kent Hosps 2002–05; prof of clinical neuroscience and med image computing and dir of research Kent Inst of Med and Health Scis (KIMHS) Univ of Kent at Canterbury 1999–; research and publications in med image computing, Creutzfeld-Jakob disease, BSE, stroke, and image guided surgery; chm XIIth Int Conf on Info Processing in Med Imaging 1991; chm Int Mgmnt Bd conference series and pres Int Soc Med Image Computing and Computer Assisted Intervention Cambridge 1999–2007; patron Human BSE Fndn; FRSM 1983, FRCP 1993; *Style—* Prof Alan Colchester; ✉ The Old Rectory, Stowting, Kent TN25 6BE; KIMHS, University of Kent, Canterbury CT2 7PD (tel 01227 827200, fax 01227 827205, e-mail a.colchester@kent.ac.uk)

COLCHESTER, Charles Meredith Hastings; s of Rev Halsey Sparrowe Colchester, CMG, OBE (d 1995), of Southrop House, Oxon, and Rozanne Felicity Hastings, *née* Medhurst; *b* 12 January 1950; *Educ* Dragon Sch Oxford, Radley, Magdalen Coll Oxford (BA); *m* 3 July 1976, Dr Serena Laura Peabody, da of Hon John M W North (d 1987), of Wickhambreaux, Kent; 3 s (Alexander North Peabody b 1981, Benjamin Medhurst Pawson b 1983, Zachary Wheatland Maynard b 1988), 3 da (Tamara Sarah Sparrowe b 1985, Talitha Chloë Jacob b 1991, Zoë Francesca Tatiana b 1995); *Career* dir: The Well Tst 1978, The Initiative Project Tst 1980, Well Marine Reinsurance Advisors Ltd 1986–94, Tear Fund 1989–94; Christian Action Res and Educn (CARE): chm of campaigns 1982, gen dir 1987–; gen dir CARE for the Family 1997–; chm: Centre for Bioethics and Public Policy 1998–2001, P & P Tst 1998–, Christian Inspiration Tst 2000–; pres: Reconciliation and Peace Fndn 2005–, Office of Int Diplomacy (US and Canada) 2005–, Care for Europe (AISBL) 1990–; dir: Riding Lights Tst 2004–, The Doha Int Inst for Family Studies and Devpt 2005–; chm of tstees Dolphin Sch Tst 1988–; tstee Swinfen Charitable Tst 1999–; church warden: Holy Trinity Church Brompton 1978–93, St Paul's Anglican Fellowship 1996–2000, St Mary's Bryanston Square 2000–; *Recreations* family, water colouring, travel, reading; *Clubs* Travellers; *Style—* Charles Colchester, Esq; ✉ CARE, 53 Romney Street, London SW1P 3RF (tel 020 7233 0455, fax 020 7233 0983, e-mail international.director@care.org.uk)

COLCLOUGH, Prof Christopher Louis; s of Frederick Colclough (d 2003), of Glossop, Derbys, and Margaret, *née* McMellon; *b* 10 July 1946, Glossop, Derbys; *Educ* Univ of Bristol (BA, Powesland Meml Prize in Economics), CCC Cambridge (Dip, PhD); *m* Sarah Elizabeth, *née* Butler; 1 s (Giles Louis b 15 Jan 1989); *Career* economic advsr Miny of Fin and Devpt Planning Govt of Botswana (appointed by Br Govt) 1971–75, fell Inst of Devpt Studies Univ of Sussex 1975–2004 (professorial fell 1994), dir Educn for All Global Monitoring Report UNESCO Paris 2002–04, prof of the economics of educn and dir Centre for Cwlth Educn Univ of Cambridge 2005–; managing ed economics Jl of Devpt Studies 1989–2004, memb Bd Int Jl of Educnl Devpt 1990–; delg Task Force 3 Millennium Devpt Project UNDP 2002–05, chair Educn Expert Gp Global Governance Initiative World Economic Forum Davos 2002–06; memb: Devpt Studies Panel HEFCE Research Assessment Exercise 2008 2004–08, Educn Advisory Ctee UK Nat Cmmn for UNESCO 2004–; dir: New Research Consortium on Improving Educational Outcomes for Pro-poor Devpt 2005–10, Gender and Primary Schooling in Africa; pres Br Assoc for Int and Comparative Educn 2004–05; *Publications* The Political Economy of Botswana: A Study of Growth and Distribution (co-author, 1980), States or Markets? Neo-Liberalism and the Development Policy Debate (co-ed, 1991), Educating All the Children: Strategies for Primary Schooling in the South (co-author, 1993), Public Sector Pay and Adjustment: Lessons from Five Countries (ed, 1997), Marketizing Education and Health in Developing Countries: Miracle or Mirage (ed, 1997), Achieving Schooling for All in Africa: Costs, Commitment and Gender (co-author, 2003); co-author of int reports incl: Gender and Education for All: The Leap to Equality (2003), Education for All: The Quality Imperative (2004); author of numerous articles in refereed books and jls incl: Jl of Educn Devpt, Jl of Int Devpt, World Devpt, Renewing Devpt in Sub-Saharan Africa, Prospects, Targeting Devpt: Critical Perspectives on the Millennium Devpt Goals; *Recreations* playing the piano and cello, opera, walking in the Pennines; *Clubs* Royal Cwlth Soc; *Style—* Prof Christopher Colclough; ✉ Centre for Commonwealth Education, Faculty of Education, University of Cambridge, 184 Hills Road, Cambridge CB2 2PQ (tel 01223 507133, fax 01223 767602, e-mail c.colclough@educ.cam.ac.uk); Little Hallands, Norton, Seaford, East Sussex BN25 2UN (tel 01323 896101)

COLCLOUGH, Rt Rev Michael John; *see:* Kensington, Bishop of

COLDMAN, (David) John; *b* 27 June 1947; *Educ* Selhurst GS Croydon; *m* 7 Sept 1979, Nicola Anne, *née* Teuten; 2 s (Charles William Edward b 18 June 1984, Thomas Frederick John b 11 May 1994), 1 da (Katharine Elizabeth Jayne b 27 January 1988); *Career* Greig Fester 1963–81, asst dir Alwen Hough Johnson Ltd 1981–84; Benfield Gp Ltd: dir 1985–86, md 1986–96, chm 1996–; chm Brit Insurance Holdings plc 1996–2000, dep chm Lloyd's of London 2001–06; non-exec dir Improvement Fndn Ltd 2006–; tstee Edenbridge and Westerham Citizens Advice Bureau; govr: Tonbridge Sch (chm Tonbridge Sch Fndn), New Beacon Sch Sevenoaks, Chiddingstone C of E (Volutary Controlled) Primary Sch; Liveryman Worshipful Co of Skinners; MInstD, CCMI 2002 (MIMgt 1995); *Recreations* country sports and reading; *Clubs* RAC, City of London, Naval and Military; *Style—* John Coldman, Esq; ✉ Benfield Group Ltd, 55 Bishopsgate, London EC2N 3BD (tel 020 7578 7027, fax 020 7578 7004, e-mail john.coldman@benfieldgroup.com)

COLDSTREAM, John Richard Francis; s of Gerald Coldstream, and Marian, *née* Gatehouse; *b* 19 December 1947; *Educ* Bradfield Coll, Univ of Nice, Univ of Sussex; *m* 1977, Susan Elizabeth, *née* Pealing; *Career* journalist Evening Echo 1971–74, Peterborough Column Daily Telegraph 1974–84; dep literary ed: Daily Telegraph 1984–91, Sunday Telegraph 1989–91; literary ed Daily Telegraph 1991–99; *Books* The Daily Telegraph Book of Contemporary Short Stories (ed, 1995), Dirk Bogarde: The Authorised Biography (2004); *Clubs* Garrick; *Style—* John Coldstream, Esq; ✉ e-mail jcoldstream@dial.pipex.com

COLE, Dr Anthony Paul; JP (1996); s of Bernard Joseph Cole, ISO (d 1948), and Mary Veronica, *née* Ryden (d 1987); *b* 23 January 1939; *Educ* St Boniface Coll, Univ of Bristol (MB ChB); *m* 24 July 1970, Elizabeth Mary, da of Leonard Vaughan-Shaw (d 1957); 2 da (Sarah b 27 July 1971, Alice b 11 May 1979), 2 s (Nicholas b 7 June 1973, Matthew b 24 Oct 1976); *Career* conslt paediatrician Worcester Royal Infirmary 1974, sr clinical tutor Univ of Birmingham 1986; govr St Richard Hospice; med dir Lejeune Clinic; fndr pres Worcestershire Medico Legal Soc; memb Br Paediatric Assoc 1974; chm Catholic Union of GB 2000–; Master Guild of Catholic Doctors 1994; FRCP 1983, FRCPCH 1997; KCHS 1991, KSG; *Publications* Looking for Answers, Ethics and Wisdom in Medicine (ed); *Recreations* music, sailing, golf; *Clubs* Catenians, Royal Commonwealth Soc; *Style—* Dr Anthony Cole; ✉ Downside, Battenhall Road, Worcester WR5 2BT (tel 01905 352967)

COLE, Ashley; *b* 20 December 1980, Stepney, London; *Career* footballer; with Arsenal FC 2000–06 (over 200 appearances, winners FA Premiership 2002 and 2004, FA Cup 2002, 2003 and 2005 (finalists 2001)), Chelsea 2006– (winners FA Cup 2007, Carling Cup 2007); England: 59 full caps, debut v Albania 2001, memb squad World Cup 2002 and 2006, memb squad European Championship 2004; *Publications* My Defence (autobiography, 2006); *Style—* Mr Ashley Cole

COLE, Graham; *b* 26 August 1946; *Educ* Hardye's Sch Dorchester, Univ of Exeter (BA); *Children* 2 c (Simon, Juliet (twins) b 6 Sept 1972); *Career* ptnr Deloitte Haskins & Sells (latterly Coopers & Lybrand) 1979–95, former dir of corp fin Beeson Gregory (stockbrokers) 1995–2002; non-exec dir Vantis plc 2002–; non-exec chm Stagecoach Theatre Arts plc 2002–; former memb Exec Ctee Quoted Co Alliance (formerly CISCO); Freeman City of London; FCA, MSI; *Recreations* shooting, collecting antiquarian maps; *Clubs* Marks, Harry's Bar, Annabel's, Les Ambassadeurs, The Clermont; *Style—* Graham Cole, Esq; ✉ 37 First Street, London SW3 2LB (tel 020 7584 0684, e-mail gc.consult@virgin.net)

COLE, Joe; *b* 8 November 1981, Islington, London; *Career* professional footballer; clubs: West Ham United 1999–2003, Chelsea 2003– (winners FA Premiership 2005 and 2006 (runners up 2004 and 2007), League Cup 2005 and 2007, FA Cup 2007); England: 42 caps, debut v Mexico 2001, memb squad World Cup 2002 and 2006, memb European Championship 2004; *Style—* Mr Joe Cole; ✉ c/o Chelsea Football Club, Fulham Road, London SW6 1HS

COLE, Maggie; da of Robert Lawrence Cole, of NY, and Cyrella, *née* Golden (d 1972); *b* 30 March 1952; *Educ* Nyack HS NY, Juilliard Sch, Lawrence Univ, Geneva Conservatory of Music; *m* 21 March 1982, Richard Paul Macphail, s of Maj David Lamont Macphail, of Chichester; *Career* harpsichordist; recordings made of Bach, Scarlatti and other seventeenth and eighteenth century composers for Hyperion, Amon Ra and Virgin; performed at a series of Bach concerts at the Wigmore Hall 1985, numerous recordings for BBC Radio 3 and concerts throughout Europe, USA, Poland and Russia; active in organising music in local primary schs in Notting Hill, fund raiser through charity concerts for London Lighthouse (the first hospice for AIDS sufferers in the UK); *Recreations* swimming, walking, reading, looking at paintings; *Style—* Miss Maggie Cole

COLE, Martina; *b* 30 March 1959; *Educ* Grays Convent; *Career* novelist; patron Chelmsford Women's Aid, memb Crime Writer's Assoc (CWA); *Books* Dangerous Lady (1992, TV adaptation 1995), The Ladykiller (1993), Goodnight Lady (1994), The Jump (1996, TV adaptation 1998), The Runaway (1998), Two Women (1999), Broken (2000), Faceless (2001), Maura's Game (2002), The Know (2003); *Clubs* Gerry's; *Style—* Martina Cole; ✉ c/o Darley Anderson Literary, TV and Film Agency, Estelle House, 11 Eustace Road, London SW6 1JB (tel 020 7385 6652, fax 020 7386 5571)

COLE, Simon; *Educ* Univ of Manchester; *Career* Manchester Piccadilly Radio: presenter and prodr 1983–86, head of progs 1986–87; fndr PPM Radiowaves (ind prodn sector of Manchester Piccadilly Radio) 1987–89, fndr ptnr The Unique Broadcasting Co 1989–2000, gp chief exec UBC Media Gp 2000–; fell Radio Acad 2001; *Style—* Simon Cole; ✉ UBC Media, 50 Lisson Street, London NW1 5DF

COLE-HAMILTON, Prof David John; s of Lt Cdr Anthony Mervyn Cole-Hamilton, of Stevenage, Herts, and Monica Mary, *née* Cartwright (d 1954); *b* 22 May 1948; *Educ* Haileybury, Univ of Edinburgh (BSc, PhD); *m* 25 Aug 1973, Elizabeth Ann, da of Bruce Lloyd Brown (d 2002), of Victoria, BC; 2 s (Alexander Geoffrey b 22 July 1977, Nicholas Anthony Michael b 23 May 1986), 2 da (Rose Monica Elizabeth b 17 June 1979, (Sian) Fiona Non (twin) b 23 May 1986); *Career* temp lectr Imperial Coll London 1975–78 (post doctoral fell 1974–75), sr lectr Univ of Liverpool 1983–85 (lectr 1978–83), Irvine prof of chemistry Univ of St Andrews 1985–; chm: Chemistry Sectional Ctee Royal Soc of Edinburgh 1994–95, Chemistry Section Br Assoc for the Advancement of Science 1995–96; 310 pubns on organometallic chemistry and homogeneous catalysis; RSC: Corday Morgan medallist 1983, Sir Edward Frankland fell 1984–85, Industry Award for Organometallic Chemistry 1998, Tilden Lectureship 2000–01, Sir Geoffrey Wilkinson Prize Lectureship 2005–06; runner-up Museums and Galleries Cmmn Award for Innovation in Conservation 1995, runner-up Acad Award IChemE 2001; FRSE 1988, FRSC; *Books* Reactions of Organometallic Compounds with Surfaces (ed, 1989), Catalyst Separation, Recovery and Recycling: Chemistry and Process Design (ed, 2006); *Style—* Prof David Cole-Hamilton, FRSE; ✉ School of Chemistry, University of St Andrews, St Andrews, Fife KY16 9ST (tel 01334 463805, fax 01334 463808, e-mail djc@st-and.ac.uk)

COLE-MORGAN, John Anthony; s of Ensor James Henry Cole-Morgan (d 1970), of Swansea, and Kathleen, *née* Thomas (d 2004); *b* 10 May 1937; *Educ* Swansea GS, Univ of Reading (BSc, Miller Mutal award), DipCAM; *m* 2 May 1964, Maria Tereza da Cunha, da of late Mateus Cardoso Peres; 2 da (Alexandra b 9 May 1965, Anna Marie b 21 Sept 1973), 2 s (Lawrence Ensor b 25 Dec 1966, Dominic Matthew b 15 Aug 1970); *Career* asst farm mangr Nickerson Farms 1960–61, asst PRO Spillers Ltd 1961–63, press and tech offr Agric Engineers Assoc 1963–65, account mangr Astral Public Relations 1965–67, PRO Fertilizer Div Fisons 1967–71, head of information ARC 1971–75, head of publicity BOTB 1975–79, dep head of information Dept of Trade 1979–81, dir of PR British Council 1981–84, PR conslt 1984–; memb Salisbury DC 1991, memb Bd Southern Arts 1998–2002, memb SW Regnl Arts Cncl 2002–05; memb Guild of Agric Journalists; FCIPR 1980; *Books* Visiting Craft Workshops in the English Countryside (ed, 1992); contrib to several pubns on PR; *Recreations* sailing and the arts; *Style*— John Cole-Morgan, Esq; ✉ Greenstone Byre, Charlton, Shaftesbury, Dorset SP7 0EN (tel 01747 828777)

COLEBROOK, Miles William Merrill; s of Peter Merrill Colebrook, MC, JP (d 1999), of Princes Gate, Ascot, and Joyce Hay, *née* Ruthven (d 1969); *b* 14 January 1948; *Educ* Shrewsbury, Ann Arbor Univ Michigan; *m* 1 Sept 1973 (m dis); 1 da (Lucy b 1977) 2 s (Thomas b 1978, George b 1987); m 2, 12 June 1997, Teresa Celdran, *née* Degano; *Career* J Walter Thompson: media exec 1966–70, account exec 1970–78, bd dir 1978–85, md 1985–88, pres and chief exec Europe 1988–96, int gp pres JWT Worldwide 1996, chm JWT Asia-Pacific; FIPA 1990; *Recreations* shooting, skiing, cooking; *Style*— Miles Colebrook, Esq

COLECLOUGH, Stephen Donald Gillings; s of Donald Derek Coleclough (d 1997), of Tamworth, Staffs, and Vera Rosemary Coleclough; *b* 6 April 1962; *Educ* King Edward VI Sch Lichfield, Univ of Sheffield (LLB), Coll of Law Chester (Willis Mills Prize); *m* 21 June 1997; *Career* slr Graham & Rosen Hull 1986 (articled clerk 1984–86); Simmons & Simmons: slr Corp Tax Dept 1987–91, ptnr 1991–96, head Corp and Indirect Taxes Gp 1995–96; ptnr Tax and Legal Servs PricewaterhouseCoopers (formerly Coopers & Lybrand before merger) 1997–; conslt HM Revenue & Customs Trg Bd 1996–; memb: Indirect Taxation Sub-Ctee Int Bar Assoc, Cncl Chartered Inst of Taxation 2000– (chm Tech Ctee 2005–, chm Indirect Taxes Sub-Ctee), Bd Confédération Fiscal Europèene 2005– (chm Indirect Tax Ctee 2001–05, chm Fiscal Ctee 2005–), VAT Sub-Ctee Br Property Fedn; regular speaker at confs UK and overseas; memb Mensa; Freeman City of London; Liveryman: City of London Slrs' Co, Worshipful Co of Tax Advsrs; memb: Law Soc 1986 (memb VAT Sub-Ctee Revenue Law Ctee 1991–96), Int Bar Assoc 1993–2005; ATII 1987, FTII 2000, FRSA, FCIPD; *Publications* Butterworths Company Law Service (tax conslt), Butterworths Encyclopaedia of Forms and Precedents (contrib), Longman's Knight on Private Company Acquisitions (contrib 4 and 5 edns), Tolley's Digest VAT on Property, Tolley's Digest VAT and Insolvency; also author of numerous articles in various professional jls; *Recreations* golf, heavy metal music and guitar playing, making preserves; *Clubs* Three Locks Golf, Stowe Golf; *Style*— Stephen Coleclough, Esq; ✉ PricewaterhouseCoopers LLP, Southwark Towers, 32 London Bridge Street, London SE1 9SY (tel 020 7212 4911, fax 020 7804 3911)

COLEGATE, Isabel Diana (Mrs Michael Briggs); da of Sir Arthur Colegate, sometime MP (d 1956), and Winifred Mary (d 1955), da of late Sir William Henry Arthington Worsley, 3 Bt; *b* 10 September 1931; *Educ* Runton Hill Sch; *m* 12 Sept 1953, Michael Briggs, s of Denis Briggs, CBE; 1 da (Emily (see Jonathan Azis, *qv*) b 1956), 2 s (Barnaby b 1964, Joshua b 1967); *Career* author; literary agent Anthony Blond (London) Ltd 1952–57; Hon MA Univ of Bath 1988; FRSL 1981; *Books* The Blackmailer (1958), A Man of Power (1960), The Great Occasion (1962), Statues in a Garden (1964), Orlando King (1968), Orlando at the Brazen Threshold (1971), Agatha (1973), News from the City of the Sun (1979), The Shooting Party (1980, W H Smith literary award, filmed 1985), A Glimpse of Sion's Glory (1985), Deceits of Time (1988), The Summer of the Royal Visit (1991), Winter Journey (1995), A Pelican in the Wilderness (2002); *Style*— Isabel Colegate; ✉ Midford Castle, Bath BA2 7BU

COLEMAN, Brenda Anne (Mrs Tarquin Gorst); da of late Gordon Barton Coleman, and Moira, *née* Vogt; *b* 28 September 1959; *Educ* Harrow Co GS, KCL (LLB, intermediate scholar in law, AKC), Coll of Law Lancaster Gate; *m* 7 Sept 1991, Tarquin Harold Gorst, s of Sir John Gorst, *qv*; 3 s (Thomas Barton b 18 Aug 1992, Charles William Eldon b 23 Feb 1994, Rupert Edward Lowndes b 17 July 1995); *Career* slr Slaughter and May 1984–89 (articles 1982–84); ptnr: Herbert Smith (Tax Dept) 1991–98, Allen & Overy (Tax Dept) 1998–; author various articles in jls; memb: City of London Slrs' Co, Law Soc; *Recreations* swimming, tennis, reading; *Style*— Ms Brenda Coleman; ✉ Allen & Overy (Solicitors), One New Change, London EC4M 9QQ (e-mail brenda.coleman@allenovery.com)

COLEMAN, Brian John; AM; s of John and Gladys Coleman; *b* 25 June 1961; *Educ* Queen Elizabeth's Boys Sch Barnet; *Career* London Borough of Barnet: cncllr 1998–, cabinet memb for environment 2002–04, Mayor's Escort 2002–03, dep mayor 2004–05, cabinet memb for community safety 2006–; GLA: memb London Assembly (Cons) Barnet and Camden 2000–, dep ldr Cons Gp 2002–, dep mayor's escort 2003–04, chm London Assembly 2004–05 and 2006–07 (dep chm 2005–06 and 2007–08); ldr Cons Gp and dep chm London Fire and Emergency Planning Authy 2000–; jt pres London Home and Water Safety Cncl 2001–, memb and Cons ldr N London Waste Authy 2002– (chm 2006–); dep chm Chipping Barnet Cons Assoc 1999–2002; columnist New Statesman website; govr: Christchurch Sch Finchley 1993–, Ravenscroft Sch 1996–; memb: Church Cncl Finchley Methodist Church 1981–2003, Ctee Friends of Finchley Meml Hosp 1981–, Hendon and Edgware District Scouts 2004–, Barnet CHC 1991–94; tstee Finchley Charities 2001–; Freeman City of London; FRSA; *Recreations* opera, theatre; *Clubs* Finchley Rotary; *Style*— Councillor Brian Coleman, AM, FRSA; ✉ 1 Essex Park, Finchley, London N3 1ND (tel 020 8349 2024, fax 020 8349 2024, e-mail cllr.b.coleman@barnet.gov.uk); London Assembly, City Hall, Queens Walk, Southwark, London SE1 2AA (tel 020 7983 4367, 020 7983 4419, e-mail brian.coleman@london.gov.uk)

COLEMAN, Brian Robert; OBE (1990); s of Edward Ernest Coleman, and Betty Coleman; *Educ* The Leys Sch Cambridge, Univ of London, UEA; *Career* teaching in universities and colleges 1968–77; civil servant MOD 1977–90, head Computing Div MOD 1990–92, cnsllr Br Embassy Washington DC 1992–95, dir Home Office Police Scientific Devpt Branch 1995–, memb Exec Panel Office of Sci and Technol US Dept of Justice 1998–; dir Musica Deo Sacra 1970–78; FRSA 1996; *Recreations* music; *Clubs* Special Forces; *Style*— Brian Coleman, Esq, OBE; ✉ Home Office, Police Scientific Development Branch, Sandridge, St Albans, Hertfordshire AL4 9HQ (tel 01727 816298, fax 01727 816320, e-mail brian.coleman@homeoffice.gsi.gov.uk)

COLEMAN, David; *see*: Firth, David

COLEMAN, Prof David Anwyll; s of Matthew Anthony Coleman (d 1961), and Mary Helena, *née* Anwyll (d 1984); *b* 26 June 1946; *Educ* St Benedict's Sch Ealing, The Queen's Coll Oxford (MA, Dip Human Biology), LSE (PhD); *m* 2 Aug 1974, Sarah Caroline, *née* Babington; 3 da (Caroline Jane b 26 Aug 1976, Margaret Clare b 4 June 1978, Katherine Mary Louise b 28 Dec 1979); *Career* VSO Nigeria 1968–69, lectr in physical anthropology UCL 1970–80; Univ of Oxford: lectr in demography 1980–, reader in demography 1996–, prof of demography 2002–, fell St John's Coll 2002–; special advsr Home Office and DoE 1987–87, conslt Home Office, conslt UN, hon advsr Migration Watch UK; dir Telford Housing Co 1997–; memb: Br Soc for Population Studies 1974, Int Union for the Scientific Study of Population 1981 (memb Cncl 1997–), Galton Inst 1990, Assoc des Demographies de Langue Française 1995, Population Assoc of America 2000; jt ed European Jl of Population 1992–2000; Parly candidate (Cons) Islington N 1983; FRSS 1998; *Publications* 8 books incl: The British Population: Patterns, Trends and Processes (with J Salt, 1992); author of approx 100 scientific papers; *Recreations* music, amateur astronomy, naval history; *Style*— Prof David Coleman; ✉ 13 Crick Road, Oxford OX2 6QL (tel 01865 558453); Department of Social Policy and Social Work, Barnett House, Wellington Square, Oxford OX1 2ER (tel 01865 270345, fax 01865 270324)

COLEMAN, David Frederick; QPM (2004); *b* 4 October 1952; *Educ* Univ of Manchester (BA); *Career* joined Derbyshire Constabulary 1975 (Divnl Cdr 1994–96), Asst Chief Constable Leicestershire Constabulary 1996–2000, Chief Constable Derbyshire Constabulary 2001–; *Style*— David Coleman, Esq, QPM; ✉ Derbyshire Constabulary HQ, Butterley Hall, Ripley, Derbyshire DE5 3RS

COLEMAN, John; s of Peter Coleman, of Sawbridgeworth, Herts, and Katherine Jane Drummond Bailey Napier; *b* 17 June 1952; *Educ* Hyndland Sr Secdy Sch, Univ of Glasgow (Bachelor of Accountancy, Arthur Young Medal); *m* 5 Oct 1974, Maureen Sheila Helen, da of David Venters (d 1989); 2 s (Euan Stuart b 24 Jan 1986, Neil Scott b 17 Aug 1988); *Career* various fin appts Procter & Gamble Ltd 1974–79, various fin appts Oil Tools International Ltd 1979–83; The Burton Group plc: dep fin dir 1983–86, md Top Shop Retail Ltd 1986–90, md Top Shop/Top Man 1990–91, md Dorothy Perkins Retail Ltd 1991–93; chief exec Texas Homecare 1993–95, main bd dir Ladbroke Group plc (parent co of Texas until 1995) 1993–95, chief exec House of Fraser plc 1996–2006; non-exec dir Travis Perkins 2005–; CIMA 1977; *Style*— John Coleman, Esq

COLEMAN, (Elisabeth) Kay (Mrs Rodney Graves); OBE (1994), DL (Gtr Manchester 2006); da of Harvey Wild (d 1999), of Prestbury, Cheshire, and Ann, *née* Sutcliffe (d 1977); *b* 28 December 1945; *Educ* Brentwood Girls' Sch; *m* 1, 1971 (m dis 1985); 1 s (Julian Graham b 1973), 1 da (Lisa-Kay b 1975); m 2, 1993, Rodney Michael Graves, s of Brian William Graves; *Career* mgmnt trainee Harveys & Co (Clothing) Ltd 1962–68, flight stewardess BOAC (Br Airways) 1968–73; Harveys & Co Ltd: chief exec 1985–2001, non-exec dir 2001–; non-exec dir British Regional Airlines Gp plc 1998–2001; vice-chm Cons Pty 2001–06; memb: Armed Forces Pay Review Body 1996–2002, Bd of Govrs Manchester Metropolitan Univ 1996–2002; *Recreations* opera, tennis, horse racing; *Style*— Mrs Kay Coleman, OBE, DL; ✉ Mere Hall, Mere, Cheshire WA16 0PY; Flat 27, 25 Cheyne Place, London SW3 4HJ; Harveys & Co Limited, Glodwick Road, Oldham OL4 1YU (tel 0161 624 9535, fax 0161 627 2028, e-mail kaycoleman@harveys.co.uk)

COLEMAN, Martin Andrew; s of Joseph Coleman (d 1990), and Betty, *née* Yarrow (d 1975); *b* 19 November 1952, London; *Educ* Preston Manor HS Wembley, Worcester Coll Oxford (BA, BCL); *m* 19 April 1991, Heather Ishbel, *née* MacLeod; 2 da (Olivia Betty b 20 July 1992, Kirsten Eilidh Miriam b 20 Feb 1998), 1 s (Alasdair Calum Joseph b 29 May 1996); *Career* lectr in law Brunel Univ 1979–89; Norton Rose: ptnr 1991, managing ptnr Brussels office 1991–96, global head of competition and regulation 1997–; memb: Law Soc 1979, Legal Services Consultative Panel 2006–; *Publications* The Competition Act 1998 (1999); *Recreations* travel, modern novels; *Style*— Martin Coleman, Esq; ✉ Norton Rose, 3 More London Riverside, London SE1 2AQ (tel 020 7283 6000, fax 020 7283 6500, e-mail martin.coleman@nortonrose.com)

COLEMAN, His Hon Judge Nicholas John; s of Leslie Earnest Coleman (d 1955), and Joyce Coleman (d 1990); *b* 12 August 1947; *Educ* Royal Pinner Sch, Univ of Liverpool (LLB); *m* April 1971, Her Hon Judge Isobel Plumstead; 1 s (Thomas George Bartholomew b 5 March 1978), 2 da (Victoria Alice Beatrice b 13 Feb 1982, Flora Nancy Joyce b 5 July 1985); *Career* called to the Bar Inner Temple 1970 (bencher 2005); lectr Inns of Court Sch of Law 1970–72; recorder 1989–98 (asst recorder 1986–89), circuit judge 1998–, resident judge Peterborough Crown Court 2001–; judicial memb Parole Bd for England and Wales 2004–; pres Cambs Magistrates Assoc 2007–; *Recreations* sport, reading, theatre, films; *Clubs* MCC, Hunstanton Golf, Hampstead and Westminster Hockey; *Style*— His Hon Judge Coleman; ✉ Peterborough Combined Court, Crown Buildings, Rivergate, Peterborough PE1 1EJ (tel 01733 349161)

COLEMAN, Peter John; *b* 9 June 1954, 1954; *Educ* Sch of Arch Brighton Poly (BA, DipArch, Crown Prize for Schs of Arch); *m*; 3 c; *Career* architect; formerly with: Phippen Randall and Parks, Chamberlain Powell and Bon, Manning & Clamp; dir Building Design Partnership 1989– (joined 1981, specializing in the design of various shopping environments); memb: Br Cncl of Shopping Centres (BCSC), ICSC (Int Cncl of Shopping Centres); speaker AJ Conf on Retail Regeneration 2006; jury memb BCSC Awards; Retail Architect of the Year 2004; RIBA; *Projects* incl: Brent Cross London, Westgate Oxford, Eden Quarter Kingston, urban regeneration of new retail quarter Sheffield, Chapelfield regeneration Norwich, masterplanning of waterfront city in Melbourne Aust, retail projects in Europe incl Tres Aguas Madrid; other completed retail devpt schemes incl: redevelopment New Cathedral Street Manchester, West Quay Southampton, upgrading and extending Brent Cross Shopping Centre, Via Catarina Oporto, Lancer Square Kensington Church Street, Tunsgate Square Guildford; experience of housing design incl housing for sale as part of mixed-use devpt schemes and free-standing residential devpt for private and public sector use; *Exhibitions* 21 New Architects (Design Centre) 1984; *Books* Shopping Environments: Evolution, Planning and Design (2006); *Recreations* tennis, cycling; *Style*— Peter Coleman, Esq; ✉ BDP, 16 Brewhouse Yard, Clerkenwell, London EC1V 4LJ (tel 020 7812 8081, fax 020 7812 8399, e-mail peter.coleman@bdp.co.uk)

COLEMAN, Sir Robert John; KCMG (2005); s of Lt Cdr Frederick Coleman, RN; *b* 8 September 1943; *Educ* Devonport HS for Boys Plymouth, Jesus Coll Oxford (MA), Univ of Chicago Law Sch (JD); *m* 23 Sept 1966, Malinda Tigay, da of Preston Skidmore Cutler; 2 da (Emily Ann b 1975, Laura Elizabeth b 1979); *Career* lectr in law Univ of Birmingham 1967–70, fndr memb Legal Aid and Advice Centre Birmingham Settlement 1968–70, called to the Bar 1969, barr-at-law in civil practice London 1970–73, memb Home Office Legal Advsrs Branch 1973; Euro Cmmn: admin later princ admin 1974–82, dep head of Div (Safeguard Measures and Removal of Non-Tariff Barriers) 1983, head of Div (Intellectual Property and Unfair Competition) 1984–87, dir (Public Procurement) 1987–90, dir (Approximation of Laws, Freedom of Establishment and Freedom to Provide Services, the Professions) 1990–91, DG (Transport) 1991–99, DG (Health and Consumer Protection) 1999–2004; *Publications* author of various articles on EU law and policy; *Recreations* fitness training, music; *Style*— Sir Robert Coleman, KCMG

COLEMAN, Prof Roger; s of Ronald Coleman, of Finchingfield, Essex, and Grace, *née* Thomas (d 1994); *b* 20 March 1943; *Educ* Ealing GS, Univ of Edinburgh (MA), Edinburgh Sch of Art (Andrew Grant scholar, Dip Art); *m* 1, 1964 (m dis), Alison Fell, *qv*; 1 s (Ivan b 1967); m 2, 1995, Sally Reilly; *Career* visiting lectr Dept of Liberal Studies Bradford Regional Coll of Art 1967–68, lectr Dept of Liberal Studies Leeds Sch of Art and Design 1967–70, sr lectr Dept of Humanities St Martin's Sch of Art and Design 1970–72; fndr memb: Community Press London (printing and publishing co-op) 1972–73, Pitsmoor Builders Sheffield (bldg/design co-op) 1973–75; joiner and wood-machinist John Brignell & Co Ltd Cambridge (specialist joinery and restoration) 1975–76, ptnr Coleman & Hollis Cambridge (furniture and joinery design) 1976–82, conslt and freelance designer 1982–85, dir and project mangr Community Construction & Design Ltd 1984–91, co-dir London Innovation Ltd (R&D co with expertise in design and devpt of socially and environmentally desirable products) 1985–2003; RCA: sr research fell and dir DesignAge prog and co-ordinator Euro Design for Ageing Network 1991–99, dir Helen Hamlyn Res Centre 1999–, prof of inclusive design 2003–; numerous invited conf papers and lectures at home and abroad incl Kelmscott Lectr 1992, contrib academic and professional jls; featured in Designers: Making Money or Making Sense (through work of London Innovation) BBC 2 1987; co-fndr, advsr and memb Bd Welfare State International 1968–2006, chair Jury RSA Student Design Awards 2002–06; Sir Misha Black Award for Innovation in Design Educn 2001; FRCA 1996, FRSA 1999; *Books* The Art of Work (1988), Designing for our Future Selves (ed, 1993), Design für die Zukunft (1997), The Methods Lab: User Research for Design (1999), Moving On: The Future of City Transport (jtly, 2000), Living Longer: The New Context for Design (2001), Inclusive Design: Design for the Whole Population (jtly, 2003), Design for Patient Safety: A System-Wide Design-Led Approach to Tackling Patient Safety in the NHS (jtly, 2004); *Style—* Prof Roger Coleman; ✉ Helen Hamlyn Centre, Royal College of Art, Kensington Gore, London SW7 2EU (tel 020 7590 4242, fax 020 7590 4244, e-mail roger.coleman@rca.ac.uk, website www.hhc.rca.ac.uk)

COLEMAN, Sylvia May; da of Capt Gordon Barton Coleman, of Harrow, Middx, and Marie Jessie Therese, *née* Vogt; *b* 10 December 1957; *Educ* Harrow Co GS for Girls, Univ of Birmingham (LLB), Coll of Law Lancaster Gate; *Career* admitted slr 1982; Stephenson Harwood 1980–85, co lawyer Gallaher Ltd 1985–86, dir of corp business affrs and co sec Sony Music Entertainment (UK) Ltd (formerly CBS Records) 1987–95, sr vice-pres business affrs Sony Music Entertainment Europe 1995–2005, sr vice-pres business affrs EMI Music 2005–; chm of tstees Chicken Shed Theatre Co; memb: Action Aid, Law Soc 1980; *Recreations* dance, music; *Clubs* Soho House; *Style—* Miss Sylvia Coleman; ✉ 19 Coulson Street, London SW3 3NA

COLEMAN, Terence Francis Frank (Terry); s of Jack Coleman (d 1978), of Poole, Dorset, and Doreen, *née* Grose; *b* 13 February 1931; *Educ* 14 schs, Univ of London (LLB); *m* 27 June 1981, Vivien Rosemary Lumsdaine Wallace, *qv*; 1 da (Eliza b 1983), 1 s (Jack b 1984); *Career* journalist: Poole Herald, Savoir Faire (ed), Sunday Mercury, Birmingham Post; reporter, arts corr, chief feature writer The Guardian 1961–74, special writer Daily Mail 1974–76; The Guardian: chief feature writer 1976–78, New York corr 1981, special corr 1982–89; assoc ed The Independent 1989–91; Feature Writer of the Year Br Press Awards 1983, Journalist of the Year Granada Awards 1987; FRSA; *Books* The Railway Navvies (1965, revised edn 2001, Yorkshire Post Prize for the Best Book of the Year), A Girl for the Afternoons (1965), Providence and Mr Hardy (with Lois Deacon, 1966), The Only True History (collected journalism, 1969), Passage to America (1972), The Liners (1976), An Indiscretion in the Life of an Heiress (ed 1976), The Scented Brawl (collected journalism, 1978), Southern Cross (1979), Thanksgiving (1981), Movers and Shakers (collected interviews, 1987), Thatcher's Britain (1987), Empire (1994), Nelson: Man and Legend (2001, shortlisted Marsh Biography Prize), Olivier: The Authorised Biography (2005); *Recreations* cricket, opera, circumnavigation; *Clubs* MCC; *Style—* Terry Coleman, Esq; ✉ 18 Clapham Common North Side, London SW4 0RQ (tel 020 7720 2651)

COLEMAN, Dr Vernon Edward; s of Edward Coleman, and late Kathleen Coleman; *b* 18 May 1946; *Educ* Univ of Birmingham (MB ChB); *m* 3 Dec 1999, Donna Antoinette Davidson; *Career* GP NHS 1972–83; ed Br Clinical Jl 1972–74, ed European Medical Jl 1984–; publisher: EMJ Books, Chilton Designs, Blue Books; TV presenter, columnist numerous nat magazines and newspapers; Hon DSc, hon prof holistic med and hon chllr Open Int Univ Sri Lanka; *Books* author of over 100 books incl fiction and non-fiction; *Recreations* books, cycling, golf, cricket, travel, sitting in cafés; *Clubs* MCC, National Liberal; *Style—* Dr Vernon Coleman; ✉ European Medical Journal, Publishing House, Trinity Place, Barnstaple, Devon EX32 9HG (tel 01271 328892, fax 01271 328768, e-mail vernon@vernoncoleman.com)

COLEMAN, Victor; s of Richard William Coleman, and Edna Grace Coleman; *b* 28 February 1952; *Educ* Greenford Co GS, Univ of Cambridge (MA), Aston Univ (Dip Occupational Safety and Hygiene); *m* 4 Jan 1978, Eleanor Jane, *née* Kirkwood; *Career* HM Inspr of Health and Safety 1973–, HM Dep Chief Inspr of Railways 1995–98, HM Chief Inspr of Railways 1998–2002, head of policy for hazardous industries 2002–03, head of finance and planning Health and Safety Exec 2004–07; memb Channel Tunnel Safety Authy 1995–98, chm Health and Safety Cmmn Railway Industry Advsy Ctee 1998–2001, memb EU Safety and Health Cmmn for Mining and Other Extractive Industries 2002–03; *Books* Transport Kills (1982), Ensuring Safety on Britain's Railways (1993); *Recreations* theatre, walking, photography; *Style—* Victor Coleman, Esq; ✉ c/o Health and Safety Executive, Rose Court, 2 Southwark Bridge, London SE1 9HS (tel 020 7717 6474, fax 020 7717 6679, e-mail vic.coleman@hse.gsi.gov.uk)

COLEMAN-SMITH, Ashton John (Ash); s of Richard Coleman-Smith, and Edna, *née* Roach; *Educ* Queen Elizabeth HS Northumberland, Univ of Newcastle upon Tyne (BA); *m* Pamela Anne, da of Hugh Griffith Davies; 1 s (Toby b 2 June 1992), 1 da (Hannah b 4 July 1994); *Career* PR exec; mktg exec Med Sickness Soc 1984–86, assoc dir Murray Evans Associates 1986–88, account dir Charles Barker 1988–92, former div md Hill & Knowlton (bd dir 1992–2000), md Edelman PR Worldwide 2000–02, md Cohn and Wolfe 2002–05, md EMEA Ogilvy PR 2005–; FRSA, IPR, ICCO; *Recreations* running, archaeology field research (papers published); *Style—* Ash Coleman-Smith; ✉ Ogilvy Public Relations Worldwide, 10 Cabot Square, Canary Wharf, London E14 4BA (tel 020 7309 1105, e-mail ash.colemansmith@ogilvy.com)

COLEMAN-SMITH, Brian Francis; s of Derek Gordon Coleman-Smith of Putney, London, and Patricia Edwina Cronin (d 1972); *b* 26 October 1944; *Educ* Emanuel Sch; *m* 19 Oct 1984, Frances Mary, da of John Alexander Gladstone; 1 step da (Alison Hysom b 13 June 1970), 2 step s (Douglas Croxford b 22 Jan 1973, Bruce Croxford b 21 Sept 1979); *Career* northern fin advertisement mangr The Guardian 1976–79, advertisement dir Financial Weekly 1979–81, fin sales dir The Guardian 1981–85; dir: Burson-Marsteller Financial 1985–91, Burson-Marsteller Ltd 1989–91; fndr md Smith Franklin Ltd 1991–94, dir Binns & Co Public Relations Ltd 1994–2002, exec vice-chm Beattie Financial 2002–05, currently ptnr Cubitt Consulting; *Recreations* sport, theatre, cinema, classical music; *Style—* Brian Coleman-Smith, Esq; ✉ Cubitt Consulting, 20 Coleman Street, London EC2R 5AL (tel 020 7367 5100, e-mail brian.colemansmith@cubitt.com)

COLERAINE, 2 Baron (UK 1954); (James) Martin Bonar Law; s of 1 Baron, PC (d 1980, himself s of Andrew Bonar Law, Prime Minister 1922–23); *b* 8 August 1931; *Educ* Eton, Trinity Coll Oxford; *m* 1, 30 April 1958 (m dis 1966), Emma Elizabeth, o da of late Nigel Richards; 2 da; m 2, 31 Aug 1966, (Anne) Patricia (d 1993), yr da of late Maj-Gen Ralph Henry Farrant, CB; 1 s, 2 da (1 decd); m 3, 12 Sept 1998, Marion Rohina (Bobbie) Smyth (da of late Sir Thomas and Lady Ferens, and wid of Peter Smyth); *Heir* s, Hon Peter Law; *Style—* The Rt Hon the Lord Coleraine; ✉ 3/5 Kensington Park Gardens, London W11 (tel 020 7221 4148)

COLERIDGE, David Ean; s of late Guy Cecil Richard Coleridge, MC, and Katherine Cicely Stewart Smith; *b* 7 June 1932; *Educ* Eton; *m* 1955, Susan, *née* Senior; 3 s (one of whom, Nicholas Coleridge, *qv*); *Career* Lloyd's underwriter; non-exec dir Highway Insurance Holdings plc (chm 1994–96); chm Lloyd's 1991–92 (dep chm 1985, 1988 and 1989); Liveryman Worshipful Co of Grocers; *Recreations* racing, golf, early English watercolours, family; *Style—* David Coleridge, Esq; ✉ 37 Egerton Terrace, London SW3 2BU (tel 020 7581 1756, fax 020 7591 0637); Spring Pond House, Wispers, Midhurst, West Sussex GU29 0QH (tel 01730 813277)

COLERIDGE, Geraldine Margaret (Gill) (Mrs David Leeming); da of Antony Duke Coleridge (d 2000), and June Marion, *née* Caswell; *b* 26 May 1948, Surrey; *Educ* Queen Anne's Sch Caversham, Marlborough Secretarial Coll Oxford; *m* 18 May 1974, David Roger Leeming; 2 s (Robert b 5 Oct 1978, Toby b 12 Aug 1981); *Career* sales and publicity mangr Sidgwick & Jackson 1968–70, publicity dir Chatto & Windus 1970, dir Anthony Sheil Associates 1973–87, literary agent and dir Rogers, Coleridge and White Ltd 1987–; memb Royal Literary Fund Ctee, past pres Assoc of Authors' Agents; *Recreations* reading, opera, gardening, travel; *Style—* Gill Coleridge; ✉ Rogers, Coleridge and White Limited, 20 Powis Mews, London W11 1JN (tel 020 7243 9501, fax 020 7229 9084, e-mail gill@rcwlitagency.com)

COLERIDGE, Nicholas David; s of David Ean Coleridge, *qv*, and Susan, *née* Senior; *b* 4 March 1957; *Educ* Eton, Trinity Coll Cambridge; *m* 22 July 1989, Georgia, eldest da of George Metcalfe and Mrs John Ungley; 3 s (Alexander James b 22 May 1991, Frederick Timothy b 14 Jan 1993, Thomas Maximillian b 22 Dec 1999), 1 da (Sophie Cecily b 14 March 1996); *Career* assoc ed Tatler 1980–82, columnist Evening Standard 1982–84, ed Harpers and Queen 1986–89 (assoc ed 1984–86), currently md Condé Nast Publications (editorial dir 1989); memb Cncl Royal Coll of Art 1995–2000; chm Br Fashion Cncl 2000–03, chm Fashion Rocks Prince's Tst 2003, chm Periodical Publishers Assoc 2004–06; Young Journalist of the Year 1984; Mark Boxer Award for Lifetime Achievement and Editorial Excellence 2001; *Books* Tunnel Vision (collected journalism, 1982), Shooting Stars (1984), Around the World in 78 Days (1984), The Fashion Conspiracy (1988), How I Met My Wife and Other Stories (1991), Paper Tigers (1993), With Friends Like These (1997), Streetsmart (1999), Godchildren (2002), A Much Married Man (2006); *Recreations* travel, shuttlecock; *Clubs* Harry's Bar, Mark's, George; *Style—* Nicholas Coleridge, Esq; ✉ Condé Nast, Vogue House, Hanover Square, London W1S 1JU (tel 020 7499 9080)

COLERIDGE, Hon Mr Justice; Sir Paul James Duke Coleridge; kt (2000); s of James Bernard Coleridge (d 1991), and Jane Evelina, *née* Giffard; *b* 30 May 1949; *Educ* Cranleigh, Coll of Law London; *m* 6 Jan 1973, Judith Elizabeth, da of Hugh Trenchard Rossiter; 1 da (Alice b 19 Sept 1974), 2 s (William b 7 July 1976, Edward b 22 Oct 1980); *Career* called to the Bar Middle Temple 1970, in practice at Queen Elizabeth Bldg 1970–85 and 1989–2000, QC 1993, judge of the High Court of Justice (Family Div) 2000–; int legal advsr Baron Hans Heinrich Thyssen-Bornemisza Lugano Switzerland 1985–89; *Recreations* Dorset, gardening, motorbikes; *Clubs* MCC; *Style—* The Hon Mr Justice Coleridge; ✉ Royal Courts of Justice, Strand, London WC2A 2LL

COLERIDGE, 5 Baron (UK 1873); William Duke Coleridge; er s of 4 Baron Coleridge, KBE, DL (d 1984; ggs of 1 Baron who was gn Samuel Taylor Coleridge, the poet), and (Cecilia) Rosamund, *née* Fisher (d 1991); *b* 18 June 1937; *Educ* Eton, RMA Sandhurst; *m* 1, 17 Feb 1962 (m dis 1977), Everild Tania, da of Lt-Col Beauchamp Hambrough, OBE; 2 da (Hon Tania Rosamund b 1966, Hon Sophia Tamsin b 1970), 1 s (Hon James Duke b 1967); m 2, 1977, Pamela, da of George William Baker, CBE (d 1996); 2 da (Hon Vanessa Layla b 1978, Hon Katharine Suzannah b 1981); *Heir* s, Hon James Coleridge; *Career* served King's African Rifles (pre Kenyan Independence) and Kenyan Army; Maj Coldstream Gds (ret 1977), commanded Guards Independent Parachute Co 1970–72; resident dir Abercrombie & Kent Riyadh 1977–83; dir 1984–90: Abercrombie & Kent, European Leisure Estates plc, Universal Energy Ltd; dir National Marine Aquarium 1990–; govr Royal West of England Sch for Deaf; patron: Colway Theatre Tst, Rhino Rescue, Nat Marine Aquarium, Friends of All Saints Babbacombe, Royal West of England Sch for Deaf (ret, 2000); *Recreations* golf; *Style—* The Rt Hon the Lord Coleridge; ✉ The Stables, The Chanter's House, Ottery St Mary, Devon EX11 1DQ (tel 0140 481 5589)

COLES, Adrian Michael; s of Kenneth Ernest Coles, and Constance Mary, *née* Sykes; *b* 19 April 1954; *Educ* Holly Lodge Smethwick, Univ of Nottingham (BA), Univ of Sheffield (MA); *m* 23 May 1981, Marion Alma, da of Joseph Henry Hoare; 1 s (David), 1 da (Verity); *Career* economist Electricity Cncl 1976–79; Building Societies Association: economist 1979–81, head of Economics and Statistics Dept 1981–86, head of External Relations Dept 1986–93, DG Cncl of Mortgage Lenders 1993–96, DG BSA 1993–; sec-gen Int Union for Housing Fin 2001–; examiner econ affrs CBSI 1984–87; dir: Ind Housing Ombudsman Ltd 2001–04, Housing Securities Ltd, Banking Code Standards Bd Ltd, Communicate Mutuality Ltd; tstee Money Advice Tst 1994–2004; sch govr (chm of Govrs 1991–93, 1997–99 and 2003–06), memb Bd Housing Assoc 1989–2000 (chm 1990–93); regular contrib: Mortgage Fin Gazette, Housing Fin Int, Bldg Soc Yearbook; *Recreations* family, gym, photography, reading history; *Style—* Adrian Coles, Esq; ✉ The Building Societies Association, 3 Savile Row, London W1S 3PB (tel 020 7437 0655, fax 020 7734 6416)

COLES, Ian Ronald; s of Ronald Frederick Coles, of Mexborough, S Yorks, and Rosena, *née* Haigh; *b* 12 September 1956; *Educ* Mexborough GS, Univ of Cambridge (BA), Harvard Univ (LLM); *m* 27 March 1988, Bethann, da of Bernard Firestone (d 1989); 2 da (Katharine Emma Mary b 15 Aug 1990, Hannah Elizabeth Jane b 20 Jan 1998), 1 s (Benjamin Charles Frederick b 16 Oct 1992); *Career* called to the Bar Lincoln's Inn 1979; attorney NY State Bar 1983; lectr in law City of London Poly 1978–80; Mayer Brown and Platt: assoc NY and London 1981–86, ptnr London 1986–99, ptnr-in-charge 1999–2002; fin gp head and memb London Exec Ctee Mayer Brown Rowe & Maw LLP 2002–; memb: Bar Assoc for Commerce, Fin and Industry 1979; *Recreations* music, wine, books, skiing, football; *Clubs* IOD; *Style—* Ian Coles, Esq; ✉ Mayer Brown Rowe & Maw LLP, 11 Pilgrim Street, London EC4V 6RW (tel 020 7246 6205, fax 020 7782 8774, e-mail icoles@mayerbrownrowe.com)

COLES, Joanna Louise; da of Michael Edward Coles, and Margaret Coles; *b* 20 April 1962; *Educ* Prince Henry's Comprehensive Sch Otley, UEA (BA); *m* Peter Godwin; 2 s; *Career* dep literary ed The Spectator 1986–89 (graduate trainee 1984–86), news/feature writer Daily Telegraph 1989; The Guardian: news/feature writer until 1991, arts corr 1991–93, columnist 1993–, weekly Guardian interview 1996–, head NY bureau The Times until 2001, features ed then articles ed New York magazine 2001–04, exec ed More 2004–06, ed-in-chief Marie Claire (US edition) 2006–; broadcaster 1993– (incl contrib ABC, CNN and MSNBC), launch presenter Radio 4 mediumwave 1993–95; founding memb American Friends of the Royal Court Theatre; *Publications* Three of Us (co-author); *Style—* Ms Joanna Coles

COLES, Sir (Arthur) John; GCMG (1997, KCMG 1989, CMG 1984); s of Arthur Strixton Coles, and Doris Gwendoline Coles; *b* 13 November 1937; *Educ* Magdalen Coll Sch Brackley, Magdalen Coll Oxford (MA); *m* 1965, Anne Mary Sutherland (MA, PhD), da of Christopher Graham, of Lymington, Hants; 2 s, 1 da; *Career* served HM Forces 1955–57; HM Dip Serv: Middle Eastern Centre for Arabic Studies Lebanon 1960–62, third sec Khartoum 1962–64, FO 1964–68, asst political agent Trucial States (Dubai) 1968–71, FCO 1971–75, head of Chancery Cairo 1975–77, cnsllr (developing countries) UK Perm Mission to EEC 1977–80, head S Asian Dept FCO 1980–81, private sec to the PM 1981–84, ambass to Jordan 1984–88, high cmmr to Australia 1988–91, dep under sec of state (Asia and the Americas) FCO 1991–93, perm under sec of state for foreign and Cwlth affrs and head Dip Serv 1994–97, ret; non-exec dir BG plc 1998–; visiting fell All Souls Coll Oxford 1998–99; govr Ditchley Fndn 1997–; chm Sight-Savers Int 2001–07, tstee Imperial War Museum 1999–2004; memb Cncl Atlantic Coll 2001–03, govr Charterhouse 2001–05; *Books* British Influence and the Euro (1999), Making Foreign Policy (2000), Blindness and the Visionary: The Life and Work of John Wilson (2006); *Style—* Sir John Coles, GCMG; ✉ Kelham, Dock Lane, Beaulieu, Hampshire SO42 7YH

COLES, Dr John Morton; s of John Langdon Coles (d 1986), and Alice Margaret, *née* Brown (d 1980); *b* 25 March 1930, Ontario, Canada; *Educ* Univ of Toronto (BA, Tennis blue), Univ of Cambridge (MA, ScD), Univ of Edinburgh (PhD); *m* 1, 1958 (m dis 1985), Mona McLellan, *née* Shiach; 2 da (Joanne Campbell, Alison Reid), 2 s (Steven Langdon, Chris Dalgleish); m 2, 1985, Bryony Jean Orme; *Career* scholar Carnegie Tst/res fell Univ of

Edinburgh 1959–60; Univ of Cambridge: univ asst lectr 1960–65, lectr 1965–76, reader 1976–80, prof of European prehistory 1980–86, chm Faculty of Archaeology & Anthropology 1982–84; fell Fitzwilliam Coll Cambridge 1963– (life fell 1986, hon fell 1987), fell McDonald Inst for Archaeological Res Univ of Cambridge 1991–95; hon prof Univ of Exeter 1993–2003 (res fell 1986–88); visiting Br Acad fell Royal Swedish Acad of Letters, History and Antiquities 1990, 1998 and 2002, visiting fell Japan Assoc for the Promotion of Science 1994–95, visiting prof Centre for Maritime Archaeology Nat Museum of Denmark 1994; co-dir Somerset Levels Project 1973–89; chm: The Fenland Project 1981–98, Inst of Field Archaeologists 1985, NW Wetlands Survey 1989–94, Humber Wetlands Project 1992–98; pres: The Prehistoric Soc 1978–82 (awarded Europa Prize for Prehistory 2000), Somerset Archaeological and Natural History Soc 1975; vice-pres: Soc of Antiquaries of London 1982–86 (Gold medal 2002), Cncl for Br Archaeology 1985–88, Glastonbury Antiquarian Soc 1988–; memb: President's Cncl Victoria Univ in Univ of Toronto 1988–93, Royal Cmmn on the Ancient and Historical Monuments of Scotland 1992–2002, Discovery Programme Directorate Ireland 2001–; ed: Proceedings of the Prehistoric Soc 1970–79, Somerset Levels Papers 1975–89, NewsWARP 1986–; Grahame Clark Medal for Prehistory Br Acad 1995, ICI Medal Br Archaeological Awards 1998, European Archaeological Heritage Prize 2006; Hon MIFA 1991, Hon PhD Univ of Uppsala 1997; corresponding memb Deutsches Archäologisches Institut; FSA 1963 (vice-pres 1982–86), FRSA, FBA 1978, memb Academia Europaea 1989, Hon MRIA 2005; *Books* The Archaeology of Early Man (with E S Higgs, 1969), Field Archaeology in Britain (1972), Archaeology by Experiment (1973), The Bronze Age in Europe (with A F Harding, 1979), Experimental Archaeology (1979), Prehistory of the Somerset Levels (with B J Orme, 1980), The Archaeology of Wetlands (1984), Sweet Track to Glastonbury (with B J Coles, 1986, Br Archaeological book award), Meare Village East (1987), People of the Wetlands (with B J Coles, 1989), Images of the Past (1990), From the Waters of Oblivion (1991), Arthur Bulleid and the Glastonbury Lake Village 1892–1992 (with A Goodall and S Minnitt, 1992), Fenland Survey (with D Hall, 1994), Rock Carvings of Uppland (1994), Industrious and fairly civilized: the Glastonbury Lake Village (with S Minnitt, 1995), Enlarging the Past: the contribution of wetland archaeology (Rhind Lectures 1995, with B Coles, 1996), The Lake Villages of Somerset (with S Minnitt, 1996), Changing Landscapes: the ancient Fenland (with D Hall, 1998), Patterns in a Rocky Land. Rock Carvings in South-West Uppland (2000), Shadows of a Northern Past: Rock Carvings of Bøhuslän and Østfold (2005); ed of numerous books and author of approx 250 papers on European prehistory, wetland archaeology, experimental archaeology, rock art and conservation; *Recreations* music, woodlands, wetlands; *Style*— Dr John Coles, FSA, FBA; ✉ Fursdon Mill Cottage, Thorverton, Devon EX5 5JS (tel 01392 860125)

COLES, Ronald John; s of late Reginald Herbert Coles, and late Mary McAlpine McLeish, *née* Leslie; *b* 18 July 1944; *Educ* Wellingborough GS, Sunderland Coll of Educn, Univ of Leeds; *m* 22 Nov 1969, Stefanie, da of late Richard Ewart Smith; 1 da (Melanie b 11 June 1973), 1 s (Toby b 4 Aug 1975); *Career* BBC Radio: prodr local and network radio 1969–75, trg instr radio prodn techniques 1975–76, prog organiser Nottingham 1976–78, mangr Sheffield 1978–80; md: Radio Trent Ltd 1980–89, Midlands Radio plc 1989–92; radio conslt 1992–; md: Investors In Radio Ltd 1996–98, Radio 106FM Ltd 1996–98; dir of radio Saga Gp 1999–2007; Assoc of Ind Radio Contractors: chm Labour Relations Ctee 1982–83, elected to Cncl 1982–92 (chm 1986–87), chm of finance 1988–92; chm Radio Academy 1995–98 (memb Cncl 1989–98, vice-chm 1994–95, fell 1998–); memb: Rare Breeds Survival Tst, Notts Beekeepers Assoc; ed The Beekeepers' Annual 1993–97; FRSA 2001; *Recreations* beekeeping, bearded collie dogs, broadcasting; *Style*— Ronald Coles, Esq; ✉ Manor Farm, Main Street, Upton, Newark, Nottinghamshire NG23 5ST (tel 01636 812289, e-mail ron@coles41.freeserve.co.uk)

COLES, Sadie; da of William Coles, and Judith Coles; *Educ* Middx Poly (BA); *Career* gallery owner; jr asst to Sir John Tooley Royal Opera House 1986–87, mktg asst NT 1987–89, asst dir Arnolfini Art Centre 1989–90, dir Anthony D'Offay Gallery 1990–96, prop Sadie Coles HQ 1997–; int art advsr Deutsche Bank Kunst 2001–; memb Bd ICA 1999–2001; tstee Whitechapel Art Chapel 2003–; *Recreations* art, travel; *Clubs* Groucho; *Style*— Ms Sadie Coles; ✉ Sadie Coles HQ, 35 Heddon Street, London W1B 4BP (tel 020 7434 2227, fax 020 7434 2228, e-mail sadie@sadiecoles.com)

COLEY, (Susan) Gaynor; da of Kenneth Matthews, of Usk, Gwent, and Eileen, *née* Wheeldon (d 2002); *b* 22 July 1958, Wales; *Educ* Croesyceiliog Sch Gwent, UCL (BSc Econ), Inst of Educn London (PGCE); *m* 3 Sept 1988, Nicholas Coley; *Career* Touche Ross & Co 1982–87, KPMG 1987–90, finance dir Horizon Farms 1990–92, dir of finance Univ of Plymouth 1992–97, md Eden Project 1997–; non-exec dir Atlantic Broadcasting 2005–; govr Cornwall Coll 1998–2003; Finance Team of the Year Accountancy Age 2001, Best All Rounder SW Region ICAEW 2005; ACA 1986; *Recreations* reading, gardening, interior design, walking the dog; *Style*— Mrs Gaynor Coley; ✉ Eden Project Limited, Foundation Building, Bodelva, Cornwall PL24 2SG (tel 01726 811953, e-mail gcoley@edenproject.com)

COLFOX, Sir (William) John; 2 Bt (UK 1939), of Symondsbury, Co Dorset, JP (Dorset 1962); s of Sir (William) Philip Colfox, 1 Bt, MC, DL (d 1966), and Mary Frances, *née* Symes-Bullen (d 1973); *b* 25 April 1924; *Educ* Eton; *m* 13 Jan 1962, Frederica Loveday, da of Adm Sir Victor Alexander Charles Crutchley, VC, KCB, DSC, DL, of Mappercombe Manor, Bridport, Dorset; 2 s (Philip John b 1962, Edward Timothy b 1969), 3 da (Victoria Mary (Mrs Fergus Byrne) b 1964, Charlotte Ismay Joan (Mrs James W H Daniel) b 1966, Constance Ruth (Mrs Edward Found) b 1971); *Heir* s, Philip Colfox; *Career* Lt RNVR 1939–45; land agent 1950, chm Land Settlement Assoc 1979–81, vice-chm Television South West plc 1981–92; past chm Agric Exec Ctee Sir John Colfox Sch Bridport (formerly Dorset Colfox Sch); High Sheriff Dorset 1969; *Style*— Sir John Colfox, Bt, DL; ✉ Symondsbury House, Bridport, Dorset DT6 6HB (tel 01308 424116)

COLGAN, Michael Anthony; s of James Colgan, and Josephine, *née* Geoghegan; *b* 17 July 1950, Dublin; *Educ* Trinity Coll Dublin (BA); *Career* theatre prodr and dir; dir Abbey Theatre Dublin 1974–78, co mangr Irish Theatre Co 1977–78; Dublin Theatre Festival: mangr 1978–81, artistic dir 1981–83, memb Bd of Dirs 1983–; artistic dir Gate Theatre Dublin 1984– (also memb Bd); exec dir Little Bird Films 1986–, fndr Belacqua Film Co 1998, co-fndr Blue Angel Film Co 1999 (prodrs The Beckett Film Project 2000 cmmnd by Channel 4 and RTÉ (Best Drama Award South Bank Show 2002, US Peabody Award 2003) and Celebration by Harold Pinter Channel 4 2006); artistic dir Parma Festival 1982; theatre prodns incl: faith Healer (Dublin and NY), I'll Go On, Juno and the Paycock, Salomé, 5 Beckett Festivals Dublin, NY and London (all 19 Samuel Beckett stage plays), 4 Pinter Festivals Dublin and NY; world premieres incl: Molly Sweeney, Afterplay, Shining City, The Home Place; prodr Two Lives (TV drama, RTÉ) 1986; chm St Patrick's Festival 1996–99; memb Bd: Millennium Festivals Ltd, Laura Pels Fndn NY; memb: Irish Arts Cncl 1989–94, Governing Authy Dublin City Univ; Sunday Independent Arts Award 1985 and 1987, Nat Entertainment Award 1996, People of the Year Award 1999; Dr of Laws (hc) Trinity Coll Dublin; Chevalier dans l'Ordre des Arts et des Lettres 2007; *Recreations* middle distance running, chamber music; *Clubs* Groucho; *Style*— Michael Colgan, Esq; ✉ The Gate Theatre, 1 Cavendish Row, Dublin 1, Ireland (tel 00 353 1 874 4369, fax 00 353 1 874 5373, e-mail info@gate-theatre.ie)

COLGAN, His Hon Judge Samuel Hezlett; s of Henry George Colgan (d 1989),of Coleraine, Co Londonderry, and Jane Swan, *née* Hezlett; *b* 10 June 1945; *Educ* Foyle Coll Londonderry, Trinity Coll Dublin (MA, LLB); *Career* called to the Bar Middle Temple 1969 in practice SE Circuit 1969–90, recorder 1987–90, circuit judge (SE Circuit) 1990–; *Recreations* travelling, the arts; *Style*— His Hon Judge Colgan; ✉ Isleworth Crown Court, 36 Ridgeway Road, Isleworth, Middlesex TW7 5LP

COLGRAIN, 3 Baron (UK 1946); David Colin Campbell; s of 2 Baron Colgrain, MC (d 1973), and Margaret Emily (Madge), *née* Carver (d 1989); *b* 24 April 1920; *Educ* Eton, Trinity Coll Cambridge; *m* 1, 20 June 1945 (m dis 1964), Veronica Margaret, da of late Lt-Col William Leckie Webster, RAMC; 1 s, 1 da; m 2, 1973, Mrs Sheila McLeod Hudson; *Heir* s, Hon Alastair Campbell; *Career* served WWII, Lt 9 Lancers, UK and ME (wounded Alamein 1942); exec Grindlays Bank: India and Pakistan 1945–48, London 1949; Antony Gibbs & Sons Ltd and successive cos 1949–83 (dir 1954–83, ret 1983); *Recreations* music, farming, forestry; *Clubs* Cavalry and Guards'; *Style*— The Rt Hon the Lord Colgrain; ✉ Bushes Farm, Weald, Sevenoaks, Kent TN14 6ND (tel 01732 463279)

COLIN, John Fitzmaurice; s of Bishop Gerald Fitzmaurice Colin (d 1995), of Louth, Lincs, and Iris Susan Stuart, *née* Weir; *b* 8 March 1942; *Educ* KCL (MB BS), Westminster Med Sch Univ of London (MS); *m* 20 July 1974, Christel Elizabeth, da of Franciskus Kern (d 1981), of Ziegenhain, W Germany; 3 da (Katharine b 1976, Alexandra b 1979, Anna b 1981); *Career* Westminster Hosp: house physician 1965–66, sr registrar 1975–79; conslt surgn United Norwich Hosps 1979–, tutor RCS 1983–89; memb: Cncl Assoc of Surgns of GB and I, Vascular Surgical Soc; memb and vice-chm SAC in General Surgery 1996–2001; LRCP, FRCS; *Recreations* fishing, tennis; *Clubs* Strangers (Elm Hill Norwich); *Style*— John Colin, Esq; ✉ Norfolk and Norwich University Hospital, Colney, Norwich NR4 7UZ (tel 01603 286442)

COLIN-THOMÉ, Prof David Geoffrey; OBE (1997); s of William James Charles Colin-Thomé (d 1987), and Pearl Erin Colin-Thomé; *b* 5 October 1943, Ceylon (now Sri Lanka); *Educ* Univ of Newcastle upon Tyne Med Sch (MB BS); *m* 7 June 1969, Christine Mary, da of Francis Bernard Simpson; 1 s (Antony Mark b 2 Jan 1970), 1 da (Nicola Jill b 18 March 1972); *Career* hosp serv NE Eng 1967–71: house offr in surgery and med, SHO in paediatrics and obstetrics and gynaecology, paediatric registrar Newcatle upon Tyne Teaching Hosp; GP Castlefields Health Centre Runcorn 1971– (pt/t 1994–, managing ptnr 1987–98); primary care advsr Mersey Regnl HA 1992–94, pt/t dir of primary care NW Regnl Office NHSE 1994–96 (primary care advsr 1998–2001), pt/t SMO Primary Care Directorate Scot Office 1997–98, dir of primary care London Regnl Office NHSE 1998–2001 (primary care advsr 2001–02), primary care advsr Dorset Community Tst and Dorset HA 1998–2001, nat clinical dir for primary care Dept of Health 2001–; hon prof: Manchester Centre for Public Policy and Mgmnt 2002– (hon fell 1988–2002), Sch of Health Univ of Durham 2003–; memb Editorial Advsy Bd: Jl of Mgmnt in Med, Employing Med and Dental Staff; former chm Mersey Faculty RCGP; former memb: Steering Gp Future Healthcare Workforce Bournemouth Univ (formerly Univ of Manchester), Abrams Ctee, Functions and Manpower Ctee, Steering Gp Nat Community Care Devpt Prog, Ctee Nat Assoc of Fundholding Practices, Steering Gp Nat Primary Care R&D Centre Working Pty on new roles for the healthcare workforce RCP; DRCOG, DCH 1971; FRCGP 1990 (MRCGP 1973), MHSM 1998, FFPHM 2002; *Publications* Fundholding Management Handbook (ed); author of articles, papers and contribs to books on subjects relating to primary care and on clinical resource mgmnt and clinical inappropriateness; *Recreations* travelling overseas, eclectic tastes in music, dance, theatre, films and books; *Style*— Prof David Colin-Thomé, OBE; ✉ Department of Health, Floor 11, New Kings Beam House, 22 Upper Ground, London SE1 9BW (tel 020 7633 4023, fax 020 7633 4054, e-mail david.colin-thome@dh.gsi.gov.uk)

COLKER, Richard Frank; s of Frank Colker (d 1986), of Grosse Pointe Woods, Michigan, USA, and Marjorie, *née* Humphrys (d 1993); *b* 5 October 1945; *Educ* Univ of Michigan State USA (BA); *m* 24 Nov 1979, Marie-Claude, da of Jean-Louis Fouché, of Carquefou, France; 3 da (Emilie b 1980, Jennifer b 1982, Stephanie b 1985); *Career* served US Army until 1968; Wells Fargo Bank San Francisco US 1969–72 (London 1973–75), vice-pres corp fin Banque de la Société Financière Européenne Paris 1976–83, md investment banking Kidder Peabody Int London 1983–90, managing ptnr Colker Gelardin & Co 1990–, interim chm and ceo Havas Paris 2005, currently memb Bd Havas SA Paris; *Recreations* golf, classical music, European history; *Clubs* Royal St George's Golf (Kent), White's (London), Sunningdale Golf (Berks), Union (New York); *Style*— Richard Colker, Esq; ✉ e-mail richardfcolker@aol.com

COLLACOTT, Peter Barrie; s of Dr Ralph Albert Collacott, of Great Glen, Leicester, and Ruby Hilda, *née* Nash; *b* 19 June 1944; *Educ* King's Sch Rochester; *m* 4 Sept 1971, Frances Rosamond, da of Lt Cdr Hibbard (d 1983), of Rochester, Kent; 2 s (Nicholas b 1973, Piers b 1978), 2 da (Esther b 1976, Hannah b 1985); *Career* CA; articled clerk Jackson Pixley 1963–68, audit sr Price Waterhouse 1968–71; accountant: Keyser Ullman Ltd 1971–75, N M Rothschild & Sons Ltd 1976–79; accountant/sec MOD 1977–79, auditor gen Govt of Tonga 1979–80, fin controller 1980–85; md fin and admin Rothschild Asset Management Ltd 1985–98; dir of product devpt State Street Global Advisors United Kingdom Ltd 1998–; non-exec dir: State Street Global Advisors Ireland Ltd, SSgA Cash Management Fund plc, International Biotechnology Trust plc; FICA; *Recreations* cricket, squash, tennis; *Style*— Peter B Collacott, Esq

COLLECOTT, HE Dr Peter Salmon; CMG (2001); s of George William Collecott (d 1983), and Nancie Alice Salmon (d 2006); *b* 8 October 1950, Chingford, Essex; *Educ* Chigwell Sch, St John's Coll Cambridge (BA, PhD), MIT (Kennedy scholar); *m* 31 July 1982, Judith Patricia, *née* Pead; *Career* diplomat; Royal Soc fell Max Planck Institut für Physik und Astrophysik Munich 1976–77; entered HM Dip Serv 1977, first sec Khartoum 1980, first sec (economic/commercial/agric) Canberra 1982, head Iran/Iraq Section FCO 1986, asst head EC Dept (External) FCO 1988, cnsllr then dep head of mission Jakarta 1989, cnsllr (EU and economic) Bonn 1994, dir of resources FCO 1999, chief clerk then DG corporate affrs FCO 2001, ambass to Brazil 2004–; *Style*— Dr Peter Collecott, CMG; ✉ c/o Foreign & Commonwealth Office (Brasilia), King Charles Street, London SW1A 2AH

COLLENDER, His Hon Judge Andrew Robert; QC (1991); s of John Talbot Collender (d 1966), and Kathleen Collender; *b* 11 August 1946; *Educ* Mount Pleasant Boys' HS Zimbabwe, Univ of Bristol (LLB); *m* 26 Oct 1974, Titia, da of Reinier Tybout, of Holland; 2 s (Guy b 1979, Paul b 1981); *Career* called to the Bar Lincoln's Inn 1969; recorder of the Crown Court 1993–2006, dep judge of the High Court 1998–, head of chambers 2002–05, circuit judge (SE Circuit) 2006–; *Recreations* violin, sailing; *Clubs* Bosham Sailing; *Style*— His Hon Judge Collender, QC; ✉ Snaresbrook Crown Court, 75 Hollybush Hill, London E11 1QW

COLLET, Robert Thomson (Robin); s of Robert Alan Collet (d 1979), of Epsom, and Jean Edith Isobel, *née* Thomson (d 1993); *b* 26 November 1939; *Educ* Malvern Coll, Pembroke Coll Cambridge (MA); *m* 6 May 1972, Olivia Diana Mary, da of Leonard Clough-Taylor; 1 da (Eloise b 1974), 1 s (Henry b 1977); *Career* chartered accountant; dir Tilhill Forestry Ltd 1979–92, gp fin dir Addis Ltd 1992–, dir PKG Holdings Ltd 1998–, dir Internet Digital Media Ltd; Freeman City of London 1964, memb Worshipful Co of Coopers 1964; FCA 1966, FInstD 1993, FRSA 1996; *Recreations* golf, skiing, walking; *Style*— Robin Collet, Esq; ✉ The School House, Wimble Hill, Crondall, Farnham, Surrey GU10 5KL (tel 01252 850824); Addis Ltd, Conbar House, Mead Lane, Hertford, Hertfordshire SG13 7AS (tel 01992 584221, fax 01992 553050, e-mail robin.collet@btopenworld.com)

COLLETT, Sir Ian Seymour; 3 Bt (UK 1934), of Bridge Ward in the City of London; s of David Seymour Collett (d 1962), by his w, now Lady Miskin (w of His Honour Judge Sir James Miskin, QC); suc gf, Sir Henry Seymour Collett, 2 Bt, 1971; *b* 5 October 1953; *Educ* Lancing; *m* 18 Sept 1982, Philippa, da of James R I Hawkins (d 2004), of Preston St

Mary, Suffolk; 1 s (Anthony Seymour b 1984), 1 da (Georgina b 1986); *Heir* s, Anthony Collett; *Recreations* fishing, shooting, cricket; *Clubs* MCC, Aldeburgh Golf, Aldeburgh Yacht; *Style*— Sir Ian Collett, Bt

COLLEY, Prof Linda Jane; *Educ* Univ of Bristol (BA, George Hare Leonard Prize in History), Girton Coll Cambridge (MA, PhD); *m* Prof David Cannadine; *Career* jt lectr King's Coll and Newnham Coll Cambridge 1978–79, fell and lectr in history Christ's Coll Cambridge 1979–82, dir of studies in history Christ's Coll Cambridge 1981–82; Yale Univ USA: asst prof of history 1982–85, tenured assoc prof of history 1985–90, sr faculty fell 1987, memb Humanities Advsy Ctee 1988–94, dir grad studies Dept of History 1988–90, dir Lewis Walpole Library 1988–96, prof of history 1990–92, memb Exec Ctee Dept of History 1991–93, Richard M Colgate prof of history 1992–98, memb Cncl on West European Studies 1993–97; Leverhulme res prof and sch prof in history LSE 1998–2003, Shelby MC Davis 1958 prof of history Princeton Univ 2003–; Eugenie Strong res fell Girton Coll Cambridge 1975, res fell Huntington Library California, Morse fell Yale Univ 1983, visiting fell St John's Coll Cambridge 1988, fell Whitney Humanities Center Yale Univ 1991, Hooker distinguished visiting prof McMaster Univ 1999; Trevelyan lectr Cambridge 1997, Wiles lectr Queen's Univ Belfast 1997, Ford Special lectr Oxford 1999, Prime Minister's Millennium lectr 10 Downing St 1999, Bateson lectr Oxford 2003, Nehru lectr LSE 2003, Chancellor Dunning Tst lectr Queen's Univ Kingston Ontario 2004, Byrn lectr Vanderbilt Univ 2005, annual lecture in in history LSE 2006, annual lecture in imperial and maritime studies Nat Maritime Museum 2007; sr fell Nat Humanities Center 2006; memb: Editorial Bd Jl of Modern History 1983–86, Editoral Br Eighteenth Century Studies 1987–90, Editoral Bd Jl of Br Studies 1990–, Cncl of North American Conf on Br Studies 1995–98, Advsy Cncl Paul Mellon Centre for Studies in Br Art 1998–2003, Cncl Tate Gallery 1999–2003, Br Library Bd 1999–2003; hon degrees: South Bank Univ 1999, Univ of Essex 2004, UEA 2005, Bristol 2006; FRHistS 1988, FBA 1999, FRSL 2005; *Publications* In Defiance of Oligarchy: The Tory Party 1714–1760 (1982), Namier (1989), Britons: Forging the Nation 1707–1837 (1992, Wolfson Prize 1993), Captives: Britain, Empire and the World 1600–1850 (2002), The Ordeal of Elizabeth Marsh: A Woman in World History (2007); also author of numerous essays, chapters, and articles; *Style*— Prof L Colley; ✉ Department of History, Princeton University, 129 Dickinson Hall, Princeton, NJ 08544–1017, USA (e-mail lcolley@princeton.edu)

COLLIE COUSINS, Philippa Jane Elizabeth Caroline; da of Alexis John Poole Cousins, and Jean, *née* Berry; *Educ* Our Lady's Convent Sch Cardiff, Univ of Warwick, Nat Film Sch Beaconsfield, Br Inst Florence, Univ of Westminster; *m* 8 May 1999, David Andrew Collie, s of Dr Bertie Harold Guy Collie; 1 da (Isabella b 29 Jan 2000), 1 s (Lucas b 26 April 2001); *Career* film writer and dir; dir: Celtic Prodns 1990–, Ruby Films 2001–; exec BBC Drama; dir of commercials for brands incl: Glenmorangie Whiskey, Tropicana Orange Juice, Time Out, Family Planning (Bronze Arrow Best Newcomer Br TV Awards); memb: Prodrs Alliance in Film and TV (PACT) 1992–, Nat Film and TV Grad Soc 1998–, Warwick Univ Grad Soc 1998–; patron: Tate, Demos, Plan Int; called to the Bar Lincoln's Inn 2006; *Film* Tom Jones: The Voice Made Flesh, Jazz on the Beacons, The Mask, The Enchanted Castle (writer and dir, nomination Best Documentary BAFTA Awards), Car Boot Sale, The Deadness of Dad (Best Short Film BAFTA Awards, Best New Dir Galway Film Festival, Best Short Film Celtic Film and TV Festival), Happy Now? (Best Feature Film Variety Critics Choice), Mansworld (exec prodr), Hereafter (exec prodr), Edwina Mountbatten (exec prodr); *Publications* incl: Battle of the Allies (Young Poet of the Year 1977), Kissing with Confidence (play, winner Silver Baird 1985), The Deadness of Dad (1998), Happy Now? (2002); *Recreations* tropical snorkelling, politics, poetry; *Clubs* Electric House, Notting Hill; *Style*— Mrs Philippa Collie Cousins; ✉ c/o Anthony Jones, PFD, Drury House, 34–43 Russell Street, London WC2B 5HA (tel 020 7344 1000, fax 020 7836 9543, e-mail ajones@pfd.co.uk)

COLLIER, Andrew John; CBE (1995); s of Francis George Collier (d 1976), and Margaret Nancy, *née* Nockles; *b* 29 October 1939; *Educ* UCS, St Johns Coll Cambridge (MA); *m* 25 July 1964, Gillian Ann, da of George Thomas Ernest Churchill (ka 1945); 2 da (Susan b 1965, Sarah b 1968); *Career* asst master Winchester Coll 1962–68, Hants CC Educn Dept 1968–71, sr asst educn offr Bucks 1971–77, chief educn offr Lancs 1980–96 (dep chief offr 1977–79), gen sec Soc of Educn Offrs 1996–99, schools adjudicator Dept for Educn and Employment 1999–2005; memb: Cncl Lancaster Univ 1981–86, 1988–93 and 1996–99, Visiting Ctee Open Univ 1982–88, Cncl for Accreditation of Teacher Educn 1984–89, Nat Trg Task Force 1989–92, Gen Synod Bd of Educn 1993–2001, Educn Ctee Royal Soc 1996–2000; advsr: Assoc of CC's, Cncl of LEA; govr: Myerscough Coll 1996–2003, St Martin's Coll Lancaster 2001–; pres: Lancs Young Farmers Clubs 1985–88, Soc of Educn Offrs 1990; Liveryman Worshipful Co of Wheelwrights 1972–2002; *Recreations* opera, walking, the greenhouse; *Clubs* Athenaeum, Leander, Salcombe Yacht; *Style*— Andrew Collier, Esq, CBE; ✉ Bullsnape Barn, Bullsnape Lane, Goosnargh, Preston, Lancashire PR3 2EF

COLLIER, David Gordon; s of John Collier, and Pat, *née* Healy; *b* 22 April 1955, Leicester; *Educ* Loughborough GS, Loughborough Univ (BSc); *m* 12 July 1980, Jennifer, *née* Pendleton; 1 da (Zoe b 8 Aug 1983), 2 s (Simon b 5 Nov 1984, Mark b 15 July 1988); *Career* dep mangr Adams Sports Centre Wem 1979–80, dep sec mangr Essex CCC 1980–83, chief exec Glos CCC 1983–86, mktg mangr Sema Gp plc 1986–88, sr vice-pres American Airlines/Sabre 1988–95, md Servisair plc 1995–97, chief exec Leics CCC 1997–99, chief exec Notts CCC 1999–2004, chief exec ECB 2005–; int hockey umpire; memb: Appts Ctee European Hockey Fedn, Exec Bd and Mktg Ctee Int Hockey Fedn; Sydney Friskin Award 2003; *Recreations* cricket, hockey, golf; *Style*— David Collier, Esq; ✉ The England and Wales Cricket Board, Lord's Cricket Ground, London NW8 8QZ (tel 020 7432 1200)

COLLIER, Air Vice Marshal James Andrew (Andy); CB (2005), CBE (1995); s of Charles Robert Collier (d 1952), and Cynthia, *née* Walsh, step s of Paul Scott (d 2002); *b* 6 July 1951; *Educ* Headlands Sch Swindon, Van Mildert Coll Durham (BSc); *m* 18 Nov 1972, Judith, *née* Arnold; 1 da (Ruth b 27 Oct 1978); *Career* cmmnd RAF 1972, Sqdn Ldr 1980, Wing Cdr 1987, Gp Capt 1991, Air Cdre 1998, Air Vice Marshal 2003; *Recreations* golf, cross-country skiing, watching sport (especially rugby), reading about science; *Style*— Air Vice Marshal Andy Collier, CB, CBE; ✉ e-mail collierandy@fsmail.net

COLLIER, John Spencer; s of James Bradburn Collier, of Bramhall, Cheshire, and Phyllis Mary Collier; *b* 4 March 1945; *Educ* Cheadle Hulme Sch, Trinity Coll Cambridge (BA); *m* 25 March 1972, Theresa Mary, da of Charles John Peers; 2 s (Barnaby James b 26 March 1973, Edward John b 19 Dec 1977), 1 da (Amy Louise b 16 Feb 1975); *Career* tutor in geography KCL 1967–69; Price Waterhouse: student, mangr then sr mangr London and Aust 1969–81, ptnr Aberdeen 1981–84, ptnr Newcastle upon Tyne 1984–92; chief exec: The Newcastle Initiative 1992–95, Lowes Gp plc 1995–96, sec gen ICAEW 1997–2002 (memb Cncl 1991–97 and 2003–), dir Clive & Stokes International 2004–; FCA (ACA 1972), MICAS 1981; *Recreations* mountains and marathons; *Clubs* Travellers; *Style*— John Collier, Esq; ✉ 147 Queens Road, Richmond, Surrey TW10 6HF (tel 020 7828 9900, mobile 07710 269795, e-mail johncollier@blueyonder.co.uk)

COLLIER, Peter Neville; QC (1992); s of Arthur Neville Collier (d 1990), of Hull, and Joan Audrey, *née* Brewer; *b* 1 June 1948; *Educ* Hymers Coll Hull, Selwyn Coll Cambridge (MA); *m* 1972, Susan Margaret, da of John Williamson; 2 s (Andrew James Neville b 6 Sept 1975, Richard John Stephen b 13 Sept 1978); *Career* called to the Bar Inner Temple 1970 (bencher 2002); in practice NE Circuit 1973– (ldr 2002–05), recorder of the Crown Court 1988–, dep High Court judge (Family Div) 1998–; chllr: Diocese of Wakefield 1992–, Diocese of Lincoln 1998–; lay canon York Minster 2001–, memb York Minster Cncl 2001– (chm 2005–); *Recreations* walking, reading, music; *Style*— Peter Collier, Esq, QC; ✉ Sovereign Chambers, 46 Park Place, Leeds LS1 2RY (tel 0113 245 1841, fax 0113 242 0194)

COLLIN, Jack; s of John Collin, and Amy Maud, *née* Burton; *b* 23 April 1945; *Educ* Consett GS, Univ of Newcastle upon Tyne (MB BS, MD), Mayo Clinic USA, Univ of Oxford (MA); *m* 17 July 1971, Christine Frances, da of Albert Proud (d 1973), of Durham; 1 da (Beth b 1974), 3 s (Neil b 1976, Graham b 1980, Ivan b 1985); *Career* registrar in surgery Newcastle 1971–80, research fell Mayo Clinic USA 1977, Arris and Gale lectr RCS 1976, European fell Surgical Research Soc 1979, Moynihan travelling fell Assoc of Surgeons 1980, reader in surgery Oxon 1980–, conslt surgn John Radcliffe Hosp, professorial fell Trinity Coll Oxford, Hunterian Prof RCS 1988–89; non-exec dir Nuffield Orthopaedic Centre NHS Tst 1990–93; David Dickson Research Prize 1973, Jacksonian prizewinner RCS 1979, Jobst Prize Vascular Surgical Soc 1990, James IV travelling fell 1993; Assoc of Surgeons of GB and I: memb Cncl 1999–, dir of educn 2001–; memb: Dist Research Ctee, Regnl Med Advsy Ctee, Bd of Faculty Clinical Medicine (chm 1990–92), Governing Body and Bursarial Ctee Trinity Coll, Gen Purposes Ctee Faculty of Clinical Med; examiner: in surgery Univ of Oxford, in anatomy RCS; memb: Vascular Surgical Soc 1982 (memb Cncl 1992–94), European Vascular Surgical Soc 1988, Int Soc of Surgeons 1994, European Surgical Assoc 1994; FRCS 1972; *Recreations* food, family, gardening; *Style*— Mr Jack Collin; ✉ Nuffield Department of Surgery, John Radcliffe Hospital, Oxford OX3 9DU (tel 01865 221 282/286, fax 01865 221117, e-mail jack.collin@nds.ox.ac.uk)

COLLIN, (John) Richard Olaf; s of Dr John Olaf Collin, MB, BChir (d 2000), of Forest Row, E Sussex, and late Ellen Vera, *née* Knudsen (d 2001); *b* 1 May 1943; *Educ* Charterhouse, Univ of Cambridge (MA, MB); *m* 1993, Dr Geraldine O'Sullivan; 2 da (Sophie b 1994, Olivia b 1996); *Career* ophthalmic surgeon with conslt appts to Moorfields Eye Hosp and Hosp for Sick Children Gt Ormond St 1981 and King Edward VII Hosp for Offrs 1993; special interest in eyelid surgery; Master Oxford Opthalmological Congress 1997–98; pres: Br Ocular Plastic Surgery Soc 2002–05, European Soc of Oculo Plastic and Reconstructive Surgery 2003–05; Liveryman: Worshipful Soc of Apothecaries, Worshipful Co of Coachmakers & Coach Harness Makers; FRCS, DO; *Books* publications on ophthalmic plastic surgery incl: A Manual of Systematic Eyelid Surgery (1983, 2 edn 1989, 3 edn 2006), Colour Atlas of Ophthalmic Plastic Surgery (1995, 2 edn 2001); *Recreations* sailing, shooting, tennis, hunting, opera; *Clubs* Royal Ocean Racing, Hurlingham; *Style*— Richard Collin, Esq; ✉ 67 Harley Street, London W1G 8QZ (tel 020 7486 2699, fax 020 7486 8626, e-mail richard.collin3@btopenworld.com)

COLLINGE, (Richard) Paul; s of Graham Collinge (d 1965), and Winifred Mary, *née* Farley (d 1969); *b* 26 June 1946; *Educ* (Architectural) Thames Poly (ATP); *m* (m dis 1991); 1 da (Emma b 23 Oct 1972), 2 s (Jake b 2 May 1974, Luke b 14 Sept 1976); *Career* princ Aldington Craig & Collinge 1986– (ptnr from 1979); external examiner N London Poly Sch of Architecture 1986–89, assessor RIBA awards 1988; selected in 1985 as one of the 40 under 40 young architects; design awards received: RIBA award 1987, 1991 (two awards) and 1995 (commendation 1978), DoE Good Housing award 1978, Civic Tst awards 1978, 1987 and 1988 (commendation 1992), Brick Devpt Assoc Biennial award 1979, 1991 and 1998 (commendation 1991), CSD Malcolm Dean award 1996, 1997 and 2000, highly commended RIBA Downland Prize 1998; RIBA 1972, MCSD 1984, memb Brick Devpt Assoc 1998, memb Assoc of Conslt Architects; *Recreations* wine, good food, cricket, golf; *Clubs* Dinton Cricket; *Style*— Paul Collinge, Esq; ✉ Aldington Craig & Collinge, The Byre Albury Court, Albury, Thame, Oxfordshire OX9 2LP (tel 01844 339911, fax 01844 339922, e-mail pc@aldingtoncraigandcollinge.co.uk)

COLLINGE, Roger Arnold; s of Arnold Roy Collinge (d 1971), of Burnley, Lancs, and Elsie, *née* Loftus (d 1989); *b* 18 December 1942; *Educ* Sedbergh; *m* 15 Oct 1966, Alison May, da of Squire Dent; 1 s (David Roger), 1 da (Jane Elizabeth); *Career* articled clerk J H Lord & Co Chartered Accountants Bacup 1961–66, fin planner Black & Decker then asst to fin dir Reliant Engineering until 1972; ptnr: J H Lord & Co 1972–82, BDO Binder Hamlyn 1982–94, BDO Stoy Hayward 1994–2002; chm: ELTEC 1997–2000, Business Link (East Lancashire) Ltd 1997–2001, Latham Jenkins Ltd 1996–99; non-exec dir Cumberland Building Soc 2006–07; pres NW Soc of Chartered Accountants 1990–91, chm Cumbria Branch IOD 2005; FCA 1971 (ACA 1966); *Recreations* gardening, classic cars, walking, reading; *Clubs* British Over-Seas League, Burnley Rugby; *Style*— Roger Collinge, Esq; ✉ Laneside, Hall Lane, Staveley, Kendal LA8 9QZ (tel 01539 822412, e-mail uncleroger5@btinternet.com)

COLLINGHAM, Christopher Eric; s of Harold Eric Collingham, of Carlton-in-Lindrick, Notts, and Olive, *née* Radcliffe; *b* 4 August 1952; *Educ* Henry Harland Sch Worksop, Granville Coll Sheffield; *m* 5 July 1975, Michele Kathleen, da of Eric Keep, of Carlton in Lindrick, Notts; *Career* BBC: communications engr 1971–78, mangr special projects 1978–82; chief engr TV-am plc 1983–89 (joined 1982), md Broadcast Projects Ltd 1989–, tech dir Channel S TV 1990–93, controller Engrg and Ops Channel 5 Broadcasting Ltd 1996–2001, dir of engrg Pearson TV 2001–02; currently vice-pres Technology and Facilities The Hospital Gp (joined as dir of facilities 2002); memb RTS; *Recreations* gliding, power flying; *Style*— Christopher Collingham, Esq; ✉ Pilgrims Landing, The Hamlet, Potten End, Berkhamstead, Hertfordshire HP4 2RD

COLLINGRIDGE, Prof Graham Leon; s of Cyril Leon Collingridge, and Marjorie May, *née* Caesar; *b* 1 February 1955; *Educ* Enfield GS, Univ of Bristol (BSc), Univ of London (PhD); *m* 1992, Catherine Rose; 1 s, 2 da; *Career* res fell Univ of British Columbia 1980–82, sr res offr Dept of Physiology and Pharmacology Univ of New South Wales 1983; reader Univ of Bristol 1990 (lectr 1983–90); prof and head Dept of Pharmacolgy Univ of Birmingham 1990–94; Univ of Bristol: prof of neuroscience 1994–, head Dept of Anatomy 1996–98, dir MRC Centre for Synaptic Plasticity 1999–; ed-in-chief Neuropharmacology 1993; memb Grant Panel: MRC, Wellcome Tst, Royal Soc; fndr Euro Dana Alliance for the Brain 1999; pres Br Neuroscience Assoc 2007–; CBiol, FIBiol 1997, FMedSci 1998, FRS 2001, fell Br Pharmacological Soc 2005; *Recreations* skiing, football, running; *Style*— Prof Graham Collingridge; ✉ Department of Anatomy, University of Bristol, Bristol BS8 1TD (tel 0117 928 7402, fax 0117 929 1687, e-mail g.l.collingridge@bristol.ac.uk)

COLLINGS, Dr Anthony Denis; s of Cyril John Collings, of Westcliff-on-Sea, Essex, and Mary Honora, *née* Fitzgerald; *b* 26 December 1946; *Educ* Westcliff HS for Boys, Univ of Newcastle upon Tyne (MB BS); *m* 6 Dec 1975 (m dis 1986), Melanie, da of Walter Robson (d 1979), of Colwell, Northumbria; 1 s (Simon b 1978), 1 da (Catherine b 1977); *Career* former cmmnd Capt RAMC (V) 1985, conslt physician to Army with rank of Actg Maj; conslt physician Southend Health Dist 1981– (specialising in med of old age, gastroenterology and neurology); acts as med expert witness for both crown and def in Crown and High Courts; former sec local branch BMA, chm local branch Physicians Ctee, former chm regnl advsy ctee on geriatric med; FRCP; memb: BMA, Br Geriatrics Soc, RSM, BATS Soc Newcastle upon Tyne; *Style*— Dr Anthony Collings; ✉ Southend General Hospital, Westcliff-on-Sea, Essex SS0 0RY

COLLINGS, Matthew; *b* 1955; *Educ* Finchden Manor Therapeutic Community, Byam Shaw Sch of Drawing and Painting, Goldsmiths Coll London; *Family* 1 da (Babette Semmer b 24 Aug 1989); m, 22 July 2000, Emma, da of Richard Biggs; *Career* artist, writer and television presenter; ed Artscribe Int 1983–87, prodr and presenter The Late Show (BBC) 1988–96, presenter The Turner Prize (Channel 4) 1997–; writer and presenter: This is Modern Art (Channel 4) 1999, Hello Culture (Channel 4) 2001, Matt's Old Masters

(Channel 4) 2003, Impressionism: Revenge of the Nice 2005, The Me Generation: Artists' Self Portraits 2005; *Books* Blimey! From Bohemia to Britpop: The London Artworld from Francis Bacon to Damien Hirst (1997), It Hurts: New York Art from Warhol to Now (1998), This is Modern Art (1999), Art Crazy Nation: The Post Blimey Art World (2001), British Abstract Painting (introduction, 2001), Sarah Lucas (2002), Matt's Old Masters: Titian, Rubens, Velàquez, Hogarth (2003); *Style*— Matthew Collings

COLLINGS, Very Rev Neil; s of James Philip Sanford Collings, of Paignton, Devon, and Edith Lilian, *née* Neill (d 1998); *b* 26 August 1946, Torquay, Devon; *Educ* Torquay GS, KCL (AKC), St Augustine's Coll Canterbury (BD); *Career* team vicar Littleham cum Exmouth 1972–74 (curate 1970–72), chaplain Westminster Abbey 1974–79, rector St Nicholas Hereford 1979–86, dir of ordinands and post-ordination training 1979–86, rector St Nicholas Harpenden 1986–99, canon residentiary and treas Exeter Cathedral 1999–2006 (also chaplain St John Devon and Devon and Cornwall Constabulary 1999–2006), dean of St Edmundsbury 2006–; *Recreations* reading, music, walking, swimming, travelling; *Clubs* National; *Style*— The Very Rev the Dean of St Edmundsbury; ✉ The Cathedral Office, Angel Hill, Bury St Edmunds IP33 1LS (tel 01284 754933, fax 01284 768655, e-mail dean@burycathedral.fsnet.co.uk)

COLLINGS, Peter Glydon; s of Alfred James Collings, of Poole, Dorset, and late Margot Lavinia, *née* Harper; *b* 4 November 1942; *Educ* Worksop Coll; *m* 1 Sept 1967, Rosemary Anne, da of Henry William Wesley-Harkcom (d 1966); 2 da (Sarah Jane b 1968, Emma Louise b 1970); *Career* asst regnl mangr Old Broad St Securities Ltd Birmingham 1970–75, regnl mangr Grindlays Industrial Finance Ltd Birmingham 1976–82, chief exec W Midlands Enterprise Ltd 1982–2000, princ Wellesley Consulting 2000–, head of corp fin W Midlands Haines Watts 2002–03, fin dir UK Biofuels (Midlands) Ltd 2003–04, gp fin dir Aston Manor Brewery Co Ltd; dir: Tangye Ltd 1986–87, Fairne Textile Holdings Ltd 1986–2000, Aston Manor Brewery Co Ltd 1986–, Raydyot Ltd 1987–2000, E R Hammersley & Co Ltd 1989–91, Jeenay plc 1990–97, D H Haden plc 1991–2000, G R Smithson & Co Ltd 1992–96, Somers Handling plc 1992–96, Airfield Estates Ltd 1992–2000, Butler Group plc 1994–2004, Excalibur Manufacturing Jewellers Ltd 1995–97, Clayton Holdings Ltd 1995–2002, Barker Ellis Silver Company Ltd 1996–97, Payton Pepper Ltd 1996–97, LAP Electrical Ltd 1996–98, Venetian Blind Manufacturing Company Ltd 1998–99, Vit-Tec Enamel Ltd 1998–2000, Hipkiss Holdings Ltd 1998–2002, A F Holdings Ltd 1998–2002, Precision Engineering (Worcester) Ltd 2000–02, Richardson Oseland Ltd 2000–02, Procam Tooling Ltd 2001–02, Knights Cider Ltd 2006–; Birmingham and W Midlands Soc of Chartered Accountants: hon sec 1997–99, vice-pres 1999–2000, dep pres 2000–01, pres 2001–02; memb: Br Venture Capital Assoc Regnl Ctee 1995–2001, Midlands Regn Electricity Consumers Ctee 1996–2001, Ctee Old Worksopian Soc 1996–2001, Corp Fin Faculty Exec Ctee 1998–2003; FCA 1966; *Recreations* rugby football, cricket, theatre, opera, jazz; *Clubs* Sutton Coldfield RFC (vice-pres), Warwickshire CCC; *Style*— Peter Collings, Esq; ✉ Squirrels Leap, 15 Oaklands Road, Four Oaks, Sutton Coldfield, West Midlands B74 2TB (tel 0121 308 5434, fax 0121 308 5188)

COLLINGWOOD, Charles Henry; s of Henry Ernest (Jack) Collingwood (d 1994), and Evelyn Mary (Molly), *née* Atherton (d 1999); *b* 30 May 1943; *Educ* Sherborne, RADA; *m* 13 Nov 1976, Judy Bennett; 1 da (Jane Molly b 4 June 1979), 2 step s (Toby Daniel Scott-Hughes b 20 March 1967, Barnaby William Scott-Hughes b 23 Jan 1969); *Career* radio and television actor; *Theatre* extensive repertory work in Guildford, Canterbury, Derby, Liverpool and Harrogate; roles incl: William Featherstone in How The Other Half Loves (Greenwich) 1973, Cocklebury-Smythe in Dirty Linen (Arts) 1979–80, Philip in Relatively Speaking (Globe Theatre Co: Hong Kong, Singapore, Bangkok) 1996, touring own show Laughter and Intrigue (with Judy Bennett); *Television* numerous shows incl: Undermanning (co-host with Bernard Manning), The Bretts, Hannay, Inspector Morse, For The Greater Good, Chief, Tonight at 8:30, Up The Garden Path, The Upper Hand, Hot Metal, Trouble in Mind, 10%ers, Telly Addicts, Call My Bluff, White Teeth, Midsomer Murders, Countdown; over 20 years continual work for BBC Sch TV as presenter, actor and commentator: 3 series of Castles Corner (with Roy Castle), 3 series with Harry Worth, 2 series with Jack Smethurst, 4 series of Stilgoes Around (with Richard Stilgoe); subject of This is Your Life 2003; *Radio* numerous leading roles in BBC Radio Drama notably Brian Aldridge in The Archers 1975–, Just a Minute, Quote, Unquote; *Books* The Book of the Archers (co-author, 1994); *Recreations* cricket, golf, fishing and gardening; *Clubs* MCC, Stage Cricket, Cryptics Cricket, Stage Golf Soc, Cross Arrows Cricket, RAC; *Style*— Charles Collingwood, Esq; ✉ c/o NSM, The Nightingale Centre, 8 Balham Hill, London SW12 9EA (tel 020 8772 0100)

COLLINGWOOD, Paul David; MBE (2006); *b* 26 May 1976, Shotley Bridge, Co Durham; *Career* cricketer (all-rounder); Durham CCC: one day debut 1995, first class debut 1996, more than 100 first class appearances; England: 27 test caps, 131 one-day appearances, 6 Twenty20 appearances, capt one-day team 2007–, one-day debut v Pakistan Edgbaston 2001, test debut v Sri Lanka Galle 2003, memb squad ICC World Cup South Africa 2003 and WI 2007, capt squad Twenty20 World Cup 2007; *Style*— Mr Paul Collingwood, MBE; ✉ Durham County Cricket Club, County Ground, Riverside, Chester-le-Street, County Durham DH3 3QR

COLLINS, Adrian John Reginald; s of John Reginald Mauldon Collins, MBE, and Jennifer Anne, *née* Wasey; *b* 29 May 1954; *Educ* Leys Sch Cambridge; *m* 2, 6 Aug 1984 (m dis); 1 s (Mark John Ford), 1 da (Seil Charlotte); m 3, 28 July 1994, Susan Margaret, *née* Greenwood; 2 s (Robert Jonathan Mauldon b 20 Nov 1994, Theodore Oliver Mauldon b 1 Nov 1996); *Career* chief exec: Gartmore Investment 1974–84, Royal Trust Asset Management Ltd 1985–90, Fincorp International Ltd 1984–, Lazard Investors Ltd 1994–96; formerly with Buchanan Capital Management Ltd; dep chm ITG Europe 1998–2000, dir Strand Partners Ltd 2003–; memb Bd: City Natural Resources High Yield Tst plc, Deutsche Land plc, Midas Capital Ptnrs Ltd, New City High Yield Tst plc, Raven Russia Ltd; *Clubs* City of London; *Style*— Adrian Collins, Esq; ✉ 4 Campden Hill Square, London W8 7LB (tel 020 7229 5100, e-mail collins@chsq.co.uk)

COLLINS, Aletta Rachel; da of Michael John Collins, of Lower Street, Cavendish, Suffolk, and Sonja Anne, *née* O'Hanlon; *b* 12 April 1967; *Educ* LCDT; *Career* choreographer; memb 4D Performance Group 1987–88, cmmnd Place Portfolio choreographer 1988, choreographer Phoenix Dance Co Leeds (Digital Dance award) 1988, res choreographer Place Theatre 1988–89, dancer LCDT 1990–; freelance choreography incl: Stand By Your Man (LCDT), Samson and Dalila (Bregenz Festival) 1988 and 1989, Carmen (Earls Court, Tokyo, Aust), The Aletta Collins Collection (Place Theatre), Beatrice and Benedict (ENO), Sunday in the Park with George (NT), It's Gonna Rain (LCDT), Gang of Five (Bonnie Bird award, Phoenix Dance Co) 1990, assoc dir and choreographer King Priam (Opera North) 1991, co-dir and choreographer La Bohème (Stuttgart Opera) 1991, co-dir and choreographer Don Giovanni (Scottish Opera) 1992, Shoes (London Contemporary Dance Theatre) 1993, Alistair Fish (BBC2/Arts Cncl short, dance film) 1993; *Awards* incl: first prize 2 Concorso Internazionale Di Citta Cagliari Italy 1987, major prize for Dance Theatre Twentieth Int Choreographic Meeting Bagnolet France 1990; *Style*— Ms Aletta Collins

COLLINS, Andrew John; s of John William Collins, and Christine, *née* Ward; *b* 4 March 1965; *Educ* Weston Favell Upper Sch Northampton, Nene Coll Northampton, Chelsea Sch of Art; *m* 3 Sept 1994, Julie, *née* Quirke; *Career* freelance illustrator 1987–88, features ed New Musical Express 1991–92 (asst art ed 1988–89, staff writer 1990–91), staff writer Vox magazine 1990–91; features ed: Select magazine Jan-Sept 1993, Q magazine Oct 1993–95; ed: Empire 1995, Q magazine 1995–97; film ed Radio Times 2001–; BBC: co-writer and performer Fantastic Voyage Radio 5 1993, weekly series Collins and Maconie's Hit Parade (with Stuart Maconie, Radio 1) 1994 (Sony Gold Radio Award 1995), presented (with Stuart Maconie) Mercury Music Prize and Brit Awards (Radio 1) 1994, 1995, 1996 and 1997, regular appearances on the Mark Radcliffe show (Radio 1); appeared in own weekly satire slot (with Stuart Maconie) for Naked City (C4) 1994; presenter: (with Stuart Maconie) Collins and Maconie's Movie Club (ITV) 1997–98, Back Row (BBC Radio 4) 2000–02, Teatime (6 Music) 2002–05, The Day the Music Died (BBC Radio 2) 2004–, Chart Show (BBC 6 Music) 2005–07, weekend shows (BBC 6 Music) 2005–07, Banter (BBC Radio 4) 2006–; writer: Family Affairs (Channel 5) 1997–99, Eastenders (BBC 1) 1999–2002, (with Lee Mack) Not Going Out (BBC 1, RTS Breakthrough Award 2007, Rose D'Or 2007); Thames TV Bursary 1986, nominated Writers' Guild of GB Award 1993; *Publications* Still Suitable for Miners: The Official Biography of Billy Bragg, Where Did It All Go Right? (memoir), Friends Reunited, Heaven Knows I'm Miserable Now (memoir), That's Me in the Corner (memoir); *Recreations* cats, music, film, cooking, trivia, military history, nutrition, bird watching; *Style*— Andrew Collins, Esq; ✉ c/o Amanda Howard Associates, 21 Berwick Street, London W1V 3RG (tel 020 7287 9277, fax 020 7287 7785, e-mail acol37@btinternet.com)

COLLINS, Andrew Seymour; TD (1977); s of Seymour John Collins, JP (d 1970), and Nancye Westray, *née* Yarwood; *b* 2 November 1944; *Educ* Radley, Coll of Law; *m* 1, 17 July 1971 (m dis 1985), Susan Lucretia, da of Cdr John Weston Chase, RN (d 1989); 3 s (Charles b 1972, James b 1975 d 1993, Giles b 1977), 1 da (Amelia b 1974); m 2, 26 Nov 1986 (m dis 1999), Virginia Mary Crisp, da of John Richard Craik-White, MC (d 1988); m 3, 4 Nov 1999, Caroline Elizabeth (d 2003), da of Patrick Forester Agar (d 2001); *Career* TA/TAVR 1964–87, Maj 1977, memb Ctee TA&VRA 1981–85; admitted slr 1969; ptnr: Walker Martineau 1986–94, Laytons 1995–; non-exec dir Red Bull Racing; gen cmmr of taxes 1983; memb Cncl London C of C and Trade 1993–98; chm Multilaw Eastern and Central Euro Gp 1992–94; cdre Old Radleian Sailing Assoc 2002–04, vice-cdre Inns of Court and City Yeo Yacht Sqdn 1991–; memb: Law Soc, Holborn Law Soc (memb Ctee 1990–94), City of London Law Soc; Liveryman Worshipful Co of Fanmakers 1970 (Master 1996–97); *Books* Negotiating International Business Acquisitions, The Business Website Manual; *Recreations* sailing, shooting; *Clubs* Royal Thames Yacht (Rear Cdre (Sailing) 2005–), Royal Corinthian Yacht, Real Club Nautico de Palma de Mallorca, Royal Solent Yacht, HAC; *Style*— Andrew Collins, Esq, TD; ✉ Carmelite, 50 Victoria Embankment, London EC4Y 0LS (tel 020 7842 8000, fax 020 7842 8080, e-mail andrew.collins@laytons.com)

COLLINS, Charles Douglas; s of Prof Douglas Henry Collins, OBE (d 1964), of Sheffield, and Jean, *née* Wright; *b* 18 March 1939; *Educ* St Edward's Sch Oxford, Queens' Coll Cambridge (MA, MB BChir), Univ of Sheffield (MB ChM); *m* 5 June 1965, Jhoann Temlett, da of Jack Marke (d 1977), of Huish Champflower, Somerset; 2 s (James b 8 Dec 1969, William b 15 July 1974), 1 da (Victoria b 11 Feb 1971); *Career* conslt surgn in Taunton 1973–2004, med dir Taunton and Somerset NHS Tst 1991–95; regnl advsr RCS 1990–97, med advsr WPA 1994–; memb: BMA 1963–, Cncl RCS (Eng) 1995–2003; memb Cncl Nat Tst 2003–; FRCS 1967, FRCSEd (ad hominem) 2001; *Recreations* equestrian pursuits; *Style*— Charles Collins, Esq; ✉ Crowcombe House, Crowcombe, Taunton, Somerset TA4 4AE (tel 01984 618266, e-mail charlesdcollins@hotmail.com); Taunton and Somerset Hospital, Musgrove Park, Taunton, Somerset (tel 01823 342100)

COLLINS, Christopher Douglas; *b* 19 January 1940; *Educ* Eton; *m* 1976, Susan Anne, *née* Lumb; 1 s, 1 da; *Career* Hanson plc: joined 1989, main bd dir 1991–, dir of corp devpt 1991–95, vice-chm 1995–98, chm 1998–; dir: The Go-Ahead Gp plc 1999–, Alfred McAlpine plc 2000–; chm: Forth Ports plc 2000–, Old Mutual plc 2005– (dir 1999–2005); articled clerk Peat Marwick Mitchell 1959–65, amateur steeplechase jockey 1965–75, md Goya Ltd 1968–75 (dir 1975–80), represented GB in 3-day equestrian events 1974–80, steward of Jockey Club 1980–81, memb Horse Race Betting Levy Bd 1982–84; chm: Br 3-Day Equestrian Team Selection Ctee 1981–84, Aintree Racecourse Ltd 1983–88, Nat Stud 1986–88; ACA 1965; *Recreations* riding, skiing; *Clubs* Jockey, White's; *Style*— Christopher Collins, Esq; ✉ Old Mutual plc, Old Mutual Place, 2 Lambeth Hill, London EC4V 4GG (tel 020 7002 7000)

COLLINS, David; s of John Edward Collins, and Helen, *née* Kennedy; *Educ* St Conleths Coll Dublin, Bolton Sch of Architecture (BArch), Trinity Coll Dublin; *Career* architect; qualified 1980; founded David Collins Associates 1985; designed restaurants incl: Mirabelle, Quo Vadis, Claridges Bar, J Sheekey, The Blue Bar at The Berkeley; memb bd Crusaid 1998–, memb Sargent Cancer Fund, patron Gilda's Club; ARIA 1986, DBA; *Books* The New Hotel (2001); *Recreations* travelling, writing, composing, collecting 20th century furniture, reading; *Style*— David Collins, Esq; ✉ David Collins Architecture & Design, 7 Chelsea Wharf, Lots Road, London SW10 0QJ

COLLINS, David Stuart; s of James Henry Collins, of Dalkeith, Midlothian, and Hilda, *née* Oldfield (d 1977); *b* 24 February 1945; *Educ* Fazakerley Comprehensive Liverpool, Liverpool Coll of Commerce; *m* 14 Oct 1967, Penelope Noël, da of Herbert Lancelot Charters, of Maghull, Liverpool; 1 s (Mark Stuart b 1977), 1 da (Nicola Caroline b 1980); *Career* Granada Publishing Ltd: mangr South Africa 1974–77, area sales mangr North Africa, ME, India and Pakistan 1977–81, trade mangr 1981–83; export sales mangr Harrap Ltd 1983–84 (sales dir 1984–91), Columbus Books Ltd 1986–91, md Verulam Publishing Ltd 1992–; *Recreations* travel, walking, reading, swimming, good conversation; *Style*— David Stuart Collins, Esq; ✉ 152A Park Street Lane, Park Street, St Albans, Hertfordshire AL2 2AU (tel 01727 872770, fax 01727 873866, e-mail verulampub@yahoo.co.uk)

COLLINS, (Andrew) Dominic John Bucke; s of Preb John Collins, and Diana, *née* Kimpton; *b* 26 December 1956, London; *Educ* Marlborough; *m* July 1993, Caroline, *née* Braine; 2 da (Cornelia b 2 May 1994, Cressida b 26 July 1996), 1 s (Benedict b 18 June 1999); *Career* joined Lloyd Thompson Ltd 1984 (dir 1995), dir Jardine Lloyd Thompson plc 1997–2006 (memb Gp Exec Ctee and chm JLT Risk Solutions), chm R K Harrison Ltd 2007–; non-exec dir Tribal Group plc 2002–05; *Style*— Dominic Collins, Esq

COLLINS, Mrs Michael; (Lesley) Elizabeth; *see:* Appleby, (Lesley) Elizabeth

COLLINS, Hannah; da of Clifford Collins, of Horsham, W Sussex, and Christine Collins; *b* 10 August 1956; *Educ* Lady Eleanor Holles Sch, Slade Sch of Fine Art UCL (Dip Fine Art) Fulbright-Hays scholar to USA; *partner* John Egan; 1 s (Echo Collins Egan b 29 Feb 1988); *Career* artist and photographer; lectr in fine art Chelsea Sch of Fine Art London, prof of art in photography and new media Univ of Calif Davis 2001–; shortlisted Turner Prize 1993; *Solo Exhibitions* incl: Film Stills (Matt's Gallery London) 1986, Heart and Soul (Ikon Gallery Birmingham) 1988, Viewpoints (Walker Art Centre Minneapolis) 1989, Stairway to Heaven (Hacienda Club Manchester) 1989, Stonefree (Tinglado II Tarragona) 1991, Signs of Life (3rd Istanbul Biennale) 1992, Signs of Life (Leo Castelli Gallery NY) 1994, Slow Time (Galeria Helga de Alvear Madrid) 1995, A Worldwide Case of Homesickness (Irish MOMA Dublin) 1996, Filming Things (Centre National de Photographie Paris) 1997, True Stories (Leo Castelli Gallery NY) 1998, Life on Film (Galeria Joan Prats Barcelona) 1999, Hotel of Being (Galeria Joan Prats Barcelona) 2002, La Mina / The Mind - The Gypsy Project (Nelson Gallery Davis CA and Printemps en Septiembre Toulouse) 2003, Another City Not My Own (Peer Fndn London) 2003; *Group Exhibitions* incl: Antidotes to Madness (Riverside Studios London) 1986, The British Edge (ICA Boston) 1987, Australian Biennale (Sydney and Melbourne) 1988, Aperto '88 (Venice Biennale Italy) 1988, Une Autre Objectivité (Centre Nationale des Arts Plastiques Paris) 1989, Polaroid Works (V&A Museum London) 1989, British Artists in Russia (Kiev and Moscow) 1990, Art and Photography (Modern Art Museum Kyoto and MOMA

C

Tokyo) 1990, Turner Prize Exhibition (Tate Gallery London) 1993, A Positive View (Saatchi Gallery London) 1994, Warworks (V&A Museum London and Canadian Center for Photography Toronto) 1995–96, Prospect 96 (Frankfurt) 1996, Surroundings (Tel Aviv Museum of Art) 1997, Contact (city poster project, Cardiff) 1998, Chime: Thinking Aloud (Kettles Yard Cambridge, Cornerhouse Manchester and Camden Arts Centre London) 1998, Invisible Museum (House Cairo) 1999, Opening Exhibition (Tate Modern London) 2000, New Works (Museo Reina Sofia Madrid) 2001, Acquired Works (Irish MOMA Dublin) 2002, Buscando la Vida (35mm feature film, Sitges Film Festival Barcelona) 2002, After the News (Centre de Cultura Contemprània Barcelona) 2003; *Work in Public Collections* EPolaroid Int, Arts Cncl of GB, Br Cncl, Walker Art Center Minneapolis, V&A Museum London, Fonds Régional d'Art Contemporain (FRAC) Rhone Alpes, Fonds Régional d'Art Contemporain (FRAC) Lyon, Fonds Régional d'Art Contemporain (FRAC) Bretagne, Fonds National d'Art Contemporain (FNAC), Museo Reina Sofia Madrid, Tate Gallery London; *Style—* Ms Hannah Collins; ✉ website www.hannahcollins.net

COLLINS, Jackie; da of Joseph William Collins (d 1988), and his 1 w, Elsa, *née* Bassant (d 1962); sis of Joan Collins, OBE, *qv*; *Educ* Francis Holland Sch; *m* Oscar Lerman; 2 da (Tiffany, Rory); *Career* writer; *Books* incl: The World is Full of Married Men (1968), The Stud (1969), The World is Full of Divorced Women (1975), Lovers and Gamblers (1977), Sinners (1981), Chances (1982), Hollywood Wives (1984), The Bitch (1985), Lucky (1985), Hollywood Husbands (1986), Rock Star (1988), The Love Killers (1989), Lady Boss (1990), American Star (1993), Hollywood Kids (1994), Vendetta - Lucky's Revenge (1996), LA Connections (1999), Dangerous Kiss (1999), Lethal Seduction (2001), Hollywood Wives - The New Generation (2001), Deadly Embrace (2002), Hollywood Divorces (2003), Lovers and Players (2005); *Style—* Ms Jackie Collins; ✉ c/o Andrew Nurnberg, Andrew Nurnberg Associates, Clerkenwell House, 54–74 Clerkenwell Green, London EC1R 0QX (tel 020 7417 8800, fax 020 7417 8812, website www.jackiecollins.com)

COLLINS, Joan Henrietta; OBE (1997); da of Joseph William Collins (d 1988), and his 1 w, Elsa, *née* Bessant (d 1962); sis of Ms Jackie Collins, *qv*; *b* 23 May 1933; *Educ* Francis Holland Sch, St Margaret's Middx, RADA; *m* 1, May 1954 (m dis 1957), Maxwell Reed, actor (d 1974); m 2, May 1963 (m dis), Anthony Newley, actor; 1 s (Alexander b 8 Sept 1965), 1 da (Tara b 12 Oct 1963); m 3, Feb 1972 (m dis 1983), Ron Kass, film prodr; 1 da (Katyana b 20 June 1972); m 4, Nov 1985 (m dis 1987), Peter Holm; m 5, Feb 2002, Percy Gibson; *Career* film and television actress since 1951; guest ed Christmas edn Marie Claire 1993; *Theatre* incl Last of Mrs Cheyne 1980, Private Lives (Aldwych Theatre and US tour/Broadway) 1990, Love Letters (US tour) 2000, Over the Moon (Old Vic London) 2002, Full Circle (UK nat tour) 2004, Legends (USA tour) 2006; *Television* Br TV incl: Tales of the Unexpected, The Persuaders; US TV incl: Star Trek 1975, Batman 1975, The Moneychangers 1976, Mission Impossible 1976, Police Woman 1976, Starsky and Hutch 1978, Space 1999 1979, Fantasy Island 1981, The Making of a Male Model 1983, My Life as a Man 1984, Dynasty 1981–89, Sins 1985, Monte Carlo 1986, Rosanne 1991, Mamas Back 1992, Annie - A Royal Adventure 1995, Hart to Hart (TV film) 1995, Pacific Pallisades (series) 1997, Will & Grace 2000, These Old Broads (TV film) 2000; *Films* Br films incl: The Road to Hong Kong 1962, Can Hieronymus Merkin Ever Forget Mercy Humppe and Find True Happiness 1969, Tales From the Crypt 1972, The Big Sleep 1977, The Stud 1978, The Bitch 1979, Decadence 1993, In the Bleak Mid-Winter 1995, The Clandestine Marriage 1998; US films incl: Land of the Pharaohs 1954, The Virgin Queen 1955, The Opposite Sex 1956, Rally Round the Flag Boys 1958, Esther and the King 1960, Joseph Amazing Technicolour Dreamcoat, The Flintstones: Viva Rock Vegas 1999, Ozzie 2001; *Awards* Hollywood Women's Press Club Golden Apple Award 1982, Golden Globe Best Actress in a TV Drama Award (Alexis in Dynasty) 1983, People's Choice Most Popular Actress Award 1983 and 1984, Golden Nymph Award Monte Carlo Television Festival 2001; *Books* Past Imperfect (1978), Joan Collins' Beauty Book (1982), Katy - A Fight for Life (1983), Prime Time (1988), Love and Desire and Hate (1990), My Secrets (1994), Too Damn Famous (1995), Second Act (1996), My Friends' Secrets (1999), Star Quality (2002), Joan's Way (2002), Misfortune's Daughters (2004); *Recreations* travelling, collecting 18 century antiques, writing; *Style—* Miss Joan Collins, OBE; ✉ c/o Paul Keylock, 16 Bulbecks Walk, South Woodham Ferrers, Essex CM3 5ZN (tel 01245 328367, fax 01245 328625)

COLLINS, Sir John Alexander; kt (1993); s of Maj John Constantine Collins, of Bodmin, Cornwall, and Nancy Isobel, *née* Mitchell; *b* 10 December 1941; *Educ* Campbell Coll Belfast, Univ of Reading (BSc); *m* 24 April 1965, Susan Mary, da of Robert Reid Hooper, of Wimborne, Dorset; 1 da (Helen b 18 June 1968), 1 s (Robert b 18 May 1970); *Career* joined Shell 1964, various appts Kenya, Nigeria and Colombia, chm and chief exec Shell UK Ltd 1990–93; chief exec Vestey Group Ltd 1993–2001; chm: Cantab Pharmaceuticals 1996–99, National Power plc 1998–2000 (non-exec dir 1996–2000), chm DSG int plc 2002– (dep chm 2001–02); non-exec dir: British Sky Broadcasting Group plc 1994–97, NM Rothschild & Sons Ltd 1995–2005, Peninsular and Oriental Steam Navigation Co 1998–2006, Stoll Moss Theatres Ltd 1999–2000, Rothschild Continuation Holdings AG 1999–; chm: Advsy Ctee on Business and the Environment 1991–93, DTI/DEFRA Sustainable Energy Policy Advsy Bd; pres The Energy Inst 2005–07; CIMgt; *Recreations* theatre, sailing, tennis, a love of the New Forest; *Clubs* Royal Southampton Yacht, Royal Yacht Squadron, Muthaiga Country (Kenya); *Style—* Sir John Collins; ✉ DSG international plc, Maylands Avenue, Hemel Hempstead, Hertfordshire HP2 7TG

COLLINS, John Joseph; s of Patrick Collins (d 1982), of Killiney, Dublin, and Mary Josephine, *née* O'Brien (d 1954); *b* 23 May 1944; *m* 1, 1970 (m dis 1998), (Eline) Mary, da of James Cullen (d 1978); 2 s (Patrick James, Paul Ivor), 1 da (Aisling Mary); m 2, 1998, Sophia, *née* Clooney (m dis 2003); 1 s (Glenn Michael); *Career* called to the Bar King's Inns Ireland 1967 (in practice 1967–71), called to the Bar Middle Temple 1971; fndr chambers at 11 South Square Gray's Inn 1980; fndr and head of chambers in: Lewes 1987, Hastings and Chichester 1996; called to the Aust Bar in Supreme Court of NSW 1989; memb Ctee Int Bar Assoc 1990–, chm Int Assoc of Irish Lawyers 1992–; *Recreations* reading, walking, swimming; *Style—* John Collins, Esq; ✉ Westgate Chambers, 64 High Street, Lewes, East Sussex BN7 1XJ (tel 01273 480510, fax 01273 483179, e-mail jcwestgate@aol.com, website www.westgate-chambers.co.uk)

COLLINS, John Morris; s of Emmanuel Cohen, MBE (d 1980), of Leeds, and Ruby Cohen (d 1988); *b* 25 June 1931; *Educ* Leeds GS, The Queen's Coll Oxford (MA); *m* 19 March 1968, Sheila, da of David Brummer (d 2005), of Hendon, London; 1 da (Simone Natalie (Mrs Baxter) b 1974); *Career* called to the Bar Middle Temple 1956, jt head of (Zenith) chambers 2001–02 (sole head of chambers 1966–2001), dep co ct judge 1970–71, asst recorder 1971, dep circuit judge 1972–80, recorder of the Crown Court 1980–98; *Recreations* walking, communal work; *Style—* John M Collins, Esq; ✉ 14 Sandhill Oval, Leeds LS17 8EA (tel 0113 268 6008); Zenith Chambers, 10 Park Square, Leeds LS1 2LH (tel 0113 245 5438, fax 0113 242 3515, website www.zenithchambers.co.uk)

COLLINS, Dr John Vincent; s of Thomas Ernest Collins (d 1987), of Denham, Bucks, and Zillah Phoebe, *née* Jessop (d 1997); *b* 16 July 1938; *Educ* Univ of London (BDS, MB BS, MD), Guy's Hosp, St Mary's Hosp, Westminster Hosp; *m* 1963, Helen Eluned, da of William Alan Cash; 1 s (Jonathan James b March 1972), 1 da (Philippa Helen b Sept 1977); *Career* house physician Guy's Hosp 1966–67, house surgn 1966–67, SHO in neurology St Mary's Hosp 1967, med registrar 1968–70, sr med registrar Westminster and Brompton Hosp 1970–72, sr lectr in med and conslt physician Bart's Med Coll 1973–76; conslt physician: Royal Brompton and National Heart Hosps (now Royal Brompton Hosp) 1976–, Riverside HA 1979–, Lister Hosp; med dir Chelsea and Westminster Hosp until 2003, conslt physician and med dir Benenden Hosp, sr med advsr Benenden Healthcare Soc, gp med advsr Smith and Nephew plc; *Recreations* tennis, drawing, painting; *Style—* Dr John Collins; ✉ Royal Brompton Hospital, Sydney Street, London SW3 6NP (tel 020 7351 8030, fax 020 7351 8937, e-mail john.collins@chelwest.nhs.uk)

COLLINS, Julian Peter; s of Edward Arthur Burnette Collins (d 1999), and Dorothy, *née* Wragg (d 1989); *b* 15 November 1942; *Educ* Nottingham HS, Gonville & Caius Coll Cambridge (MA, LLM); *Career* admitted slr 1967, head of Industrial Branch Legal Dept NCB 1973, legal advsr and slr Br Coal Corpn 1988–93, slr British Coal Pension Schemes 1993–97; chm Bd of Tstees Austin Knight Pension Scheme; memb: Law Soc (chm Commerce and Industry Gp 1993–94); JUSTICE: tstee and memb Exec Bd and Cncl, hon treas, chm Fin Ctee; companion Inst of Mining Engrs 1996; *Recreations* theatre, travel; *Style—* Julian Collins, Esq; ✉ 62 Fairacres, Roehampton Lane, London SW15 5LY (tel 020 8876 6347, e-mail julianpcollins@aol.com)

COLLINS, Sir Kenneth Darlingston; kt (2003); s of late Nicholas Collins and Ellen Williamson; *b* 12 August 1939; *Educ* St John's GS, Hamilton Acad, Univ of Glasgow (BSc), Univ of Strathclyde (MSc); *m* 1966, Georgina Frances, *née* Pollard; 1 s, 1 da; *Career* steelworks apprentice 1956–59, planning offr 1965–66, tutor-organiser WEA 1966–67; social geographer; lectr: Glasgow Coll of Bldg 1967–69, Paisley Coll of Technol 1969–79; memb: E Kilbride Town and DC 1973–79, Lanark CC 1973–75, E Kilbride Devpt Corp 1976–79; MEP (Lab) Strathclyde E 1979–99, dep ldr Labour Gp Euro Parl 1979–84, chm Environment Public Health and Consumer Protection Ctee 1979–84 and 1989–99 (vice-chm 1984–87), European Parl socialist spokesman on environment, public health, and consumer protection 1984–89; chm Scottish Environment Protection Agency 1999–; chm: Central Scotland Forest Tst 1998–2001, Tak Tent Cancer Support 1999–2002; memb: Advsy Bd ESRC Genomics Policy and Research Forum, Professional Practices Panel European Public Affrs Consultancies' Assoc (EPACA), EC's High Level Gp on Competitiveness, Energy and the Environment, Advsy Bd Jl of Water Law; former: memb Bd Inst for European Environmental Policy London, vice-pres Nat Soc for Clean Air, memb Bd Energy Action Scotland, memb Bd Central Scotland Forest Tst, memb Mgmnt Bd European Environment Agency, memb Br Waterways Scot Gp, memb Bd Forward Scot; hon pres Scottish Assoc of Geography Teachers 2003–06; hon vice-pres: Royal Environmental Health Inst of Scot, Int Fedn on Environmental Health, Town and Country Planning Assoc, Inst of Trading Standards Admin; Hon Dr Univ of Paisley; fell Industry and Parl Tst; hon memb Landscape Inst, Hon FCIWEM, Hon FCIWM, FRSGS; *Recreations* music, boxer dogs, gardening; *Style—* Sir Ken Collins; ✉ 11 Stuarton Park, East Kilbride, Lanarkshire G74 4LA (tel 01355 237282, fax 01355 237282)

COLLINS, Mark William Gerard; s of William Henry Collins, of Sheffield, S Yorks, and Oonagh Sheila Maria, *née* Lissenden; *b* 14 May 1953, Sheffield, S Yorks; *Educ* De La Salle Coll Sheffield; *m* 30 Oct 1985, Elisabeth Jayne, *née* Frith; 1 s (Alexander William James b 10 May 1987), 1 da (Emma Elisabeth Alexandra b 18 Oct 1988); *Career* Moore Fletcher & Co: articled clerk 1971–76, audit mangr 1977–80; Sheffield Insulation Ltd: joined 1980, gp financial controller 1985–87, dir 1987–90; finance dir and co sec Brooke Industrial Holdings plc 1990–96; Cattles plc: chief accountant 1996–99, finance dir 1999–2001, treasy and risk dir 2001–; memb Cncl CBI Yorkshire and Humber; FCA 1983 (ACA 1977); *Recreations* travel, golf, motor sport; *Clubs* Walbrook, Abbeydale Golf; *Style—* Mark Collins, Esq; ✉ Cattles plc, Kingston House, Woodhead Road, Birstall WF17 9TD (tel 01924 444466, fax 01924 448324, e-mail markcollins@cattles.co.uk)

COLLINS, (John) Martin; QC (1972); s of John Lissant Collins (d 1962), and Marjorie Mary, *née* Jefferson (d 1982); *b* 24 January 1929; *Educ* Uppingham, Univ of Manchester (Dauntsey prize int law); *m* Daphne Mary, da of George Swindells (d 1960), of Prestbury; 2 s (Benedict George, Toby Francis), 1 da (Arabella Jane); *Career* called to the Bar: Gray's Inn 1952 (bencher 1981, vice-treas 1998, treas 1999), Gibraltar 1990; dep chm Cumberland Quarter Sessions 1964–72, recorder of the Crown Court 1972–88, judge Court of Appeal Jersey 1984–99 (Guernsey 1984–2000), cmmr Royal Court Jersey 2000–02; memb: Senate of Inns of Court and Bar 1981–84, Gen Cncl of the Bar 1991; Liveryman Worshipful Co of Makers of Playing Cards 1982–2002; *Clubs* Athenaeum; *Style—* Martin Collins, Esq, QC; ✉ Les Grandes Masses, 50580 Denneville, Normandy, France (e-mail martin.collins@wanadoo.fr)

COLLINS, Michael Geoffrey; QC (1988); s of (Francis) Geoffrey Collins (d 1982), of Scottburgh, South Africa, and Margaret Isabelle, *née* Harper-Gow (d 1989); *b* 4 March 1948; *Educ* Peterhouse Marandellas Rhodesia, Univ of Exeter (LLB); *m* 13 April 1985, Bonnie Gayle Bird, da of John Wilbur Bird (d 1988), and Frances Ratliff Bird (d 1995), of New Albany, Indiana; *Career* called to the Bar Gray's Inn 1971 (bencher 1999); recorder of the Crown Court 1997–2001, special legal conslt Fulbright & Jaworski LLP Washington DC 2002–; *Books* Private International Litigation (contrib, 1988); *Recreations* golf, tennis, watercolour painting, amateur dramatics; *Clubs* Woking Golf; *Style—* Michael Collins, Esq, QC; ✉ Fulbright & Jaworski LLP, 801 Pennsylvania Avenue NW, Washington DC 20004–2623, USA (tel 1 202 662 4527, fax 1 202 662 4643, e-mail mcollins@fulbright.com); Essex Court Chambers, 24 Lincoln's Inn Fields, London WC2A 3EG (tel 020 7813 8000, fax 020 7813 8080)

COLLINS, Prof Michael John; s of Frederick Allenby Collins, and Gwendoline Violet, *née* Hersey-Walker; *b* 27 January 1962; *Educ* Royal Coll of Music (ARCM); *m* 1997, Isabelle van Keulen; 1 s (Simon John b 31 Jan 1999); *Career* clarinettist; with Nash Ensemble 1982–88; principal clarinet: London Sinfonietta 1982–, Philharmonia Orch 1988–95; prof: Royal Coll of Music 1985–, Royal Acad of Music 1996–; Carnegie Hall debut (with Philharmonia) 1992; soloist Last Night of the Proms 1995, soloist with Russian Nat Orch BBC Proms 1996; winner: BBC TV Young Musician of the Year 1978, Leeds Nat Competition for Musicians 1980, Int Rostrum of Young Performers UNESCO 1985, Worshipful Co of Musicians Medal 1980, Tagore Gold Medal Royal Coll of Music; awarded Hon RAM 1997; *Recreations* record collecting, walking, travel; *Style—* Prof Michael Collins; ✉ c/o Van Walsum Management, 4 Addison Bridge Place, London W14 8XP (tel 020 7371 4343, fax 020 7371 4344)

COLLINS, Dr Michael Lawrence; s of Sidney Collins, of Leeds, and Essie, *née* Gross; *b* 26 May 1943; *Educ* Roundhay Sch Leeds, Univ of Leeds Sch of Med (MB ChB); *m* 27 June 1971, Jackie, da of Theodore Hall, of Leeds; 1 s (Spencer b 1974), 1 da (Antonia (Mrs James Rubin) b 1977); *Career* house surgn and SHO United Leeds Hosps 1969–72, teaching fell Univ of Br Columbia 1972–73, registrar Leeds Maternity Hosp and Hosp for Women 1973–76, specialist in gynaecological endocrinology and infertility McMaster Univ Med Centre 1977–79, princ gen practice Middx 1980–84, specialist practice in gynaecological endocrinology 1980–, med advsr Well Woman Clinics 1980–, clinical dir Lynbrook Hosp 1992–94, lectr in med gynaecology; ed Gynaecology and Infertility Digest; memb: Hillingdon FPC 1980–84, Hillingdon Local Med Ctee 1980–84, Hillingdon Brunel Univ Liaison Ctee; MDU, Assoc of Profs in Gynecology and Obstetrics; memb: BMA, RSM; *Recreations* art, photography, writing, antiquarian books, croquet; *Clubs* Phyllis Court, Henley; *Style—* Dr Michael Collins; ✉ Melnick House, Ascot, Berkshire SL5 8TS; 144 Harley Street, London W1G 7LD (e-mail dr.collins@consultant.com)

COLLINS, Neil Adam; s of Clive Dinant Collins, and Joan Collins; *Educ* Uppingham, Selwyn Coll Cambridge; *m* 1, 1981 (m dis 1994), Vivien Goldsmith; 1 da (Alice Laura b 30 July 1982); m 2, 1999, Julia Barnes; 1 da (Fleur Joan), 1 s (Arthur Jeremy); *Career* journalist: Daily Mail 1974–79; city ed: Evening Standard 1979–84, The Sunday Times 1984–86, The Daily Telegraph 1986–2005; fly fishing corr The Spectator 2002–04, columnist

Evening Standard 2005–; dir: Templeton Emerging Markets Investment Tst 2006–, Dyson James Ltd 2006–; Fin Journalist of the Year 2002; *Style*— Neil Collins, Esq

COLLINS, Nicci Russell; *b* 9 September 1971; *Educ* Cheney Comp Sch Oxford, Trinity Coll Cambridge (BA); *Children* 1 da (Kitty b 10 Sept 2003); *Career* former cncllr (Lab) Westbourne Westminster CC; with Office of Rt Hon Margaret Beckett, MP, *qv*, 1994–98, special advsr to Pres of the Bd of Trade 1998, special advsr to Pres of the Cncl and Ldr of the House 1998–2001, special advsr to sec of state for Environment, Food and Rural Affrs 2001–; *Style*— Ms Nicci Collins; ✉ Department of Environment, Food and Rural Affairs, Nobel House, 17 Smith Square, London SW1P 3JR (tel 020 7238 5378, e-mail nicci.collins@defra.gsi.gov.uk)

COLLINS, Patrick Michael; s of Patrick John Collins (d 1990), of London, and Julia Ann, *née* Canty (d 1988); *b* 23 November 1943; *Educ* St Joseph's Acad Blackheath; *m* 1969, Julie Kathleen, da of Leslie Gordon Grundon; 3 s (Michael Patrick b 19 Sept 1970, Daniel Timothy b 7 Feb 1972, Patrick Joseph Gerard b 13 Jan 1983), 1 da (Mary Julie b 31 Dec 1974); *Career* sports writer; cub reporter Kentish Mercury 1962–65; sports writer: Sunday Citizen 1965–67, News of the World 1967–78; sports columnist: London Evening News 1978–80, London Evening Standard 1980–82; chief sports writer Mail on Sunday 1982–, sports columnist Punch 1990–92; memb English Sports Cncl 1999–2002; Br Sports Journalist of the Year 1989, 1990, 1997 and 2002; commendations: Br Press Awards 1978, 1987, 1988, 1991, 1993, 1996, 1998, 1999, 2001 and 2003, Sports Cncl Awards 1979, 1985, 1986, 1988, 1992, 1994, 1996, 1998, 2000, 2001, 2002, 2003, 2004 and 2006; Br Magazine Columnist of the Year 1990, Sports Feature Writer of the Year Br Sports Journalism Award 1993, 2002 and 2004, Sports Columnist of the Year Br Sports Journalism Award 1999, 2000, 2004 and 2006; former sports rep: Kent rugby union XV, London schs athletics team; *Books* The Sportswriter (1996); *Recreations* lunch, family; *Style*— Patrick Collins, Esq; ✉ Mail on Sunday, Northcliffe House, 2 Derry Street, London W8 5TS (tel 020 7938 6000, e-mail patrick.collins@mailonsunday.co.uk)

COLLINS, His Hon Judge Paul Howard; CBE (1999); s of Michael Collins, and Madie Collins; *b* 31 January 1944; *Educ* Orange Hill GS Edgware, St Catherine's Coll Oxford (MA); *m* 24 Oct 1987, Susan; 1 stepson (Daniel Fallows b 14 Nov 1973); *Career* called to the Bar 1966, asst recorder 1985–89, recorder 1989–92, circuit judge (SE Circuit) 1992–, sr circuit judge Central London Civil Justice Centre, designated civil judge London Gp of County Cts 2001–; dir of studies Judicial Studies Bd 1997–99; *Recreations* theatre, reading, the gym; *Clubs* The Questors; *Style*— His Hon Judge Paul Collins, CBE; ✉ Central London Civil Justice Centre, 26 Park Crescent, London W1B 4HT

COLLINS, Dr Peter Donald Bruce; s of Douglas Collins (d 1984), and Marjorie, *née* Reynolds; *b* 3 January 1939; *Educ* William Hulme's GS Manchester, Univ of Bristol (Lacrosse colours, BSc, PhD); *m* 1970, Margaret, *née* Purnell; 2 s (Andrew Richard Purnell b 1974, Nigel Antony Lawrence b 1976); *Career* research fell Univ of Calif Berkeley 1963–65; Univ of Durham: lectr in theoretical physics 1965–73, sr lectr 1973–83, reader 1983–98, dean Faculty of Science 1988–91, pro-vice-chllr 1991–97, sub warden 1994–97; chm Higher Edcn Support for Industry in the North (HESIN) 1993–97, chm Foresight North East 1997–2006; dir: Regnl Technol Centre (North) 1990–97, County Durham Development Co 1994–97, Durham Univ Investment Ltd and subsidiary cos 1994–2002, Northern Infomatics Applications Agency 1995–97, Gentoo Gp Ltd 2007–; chm Houghton and Hetton Housing Co Ltd 2001–06; chm of govrs Houghton Kepier Sch 1997–; vice-chm Sunderland Schools' Forum 2003–06; memb American Physical Soc 1964–; FRSA 1991, FInstP 1992; *Books* Regge Poles in Particle Physics (with E J Squires, 1967), Regge Theory and High Energy Physics (1976), Hadron Interactions (with A D Martin, 1984), Particle Physics and Cosmology (with A D Martin and E J Squires, 1989); *Recreations* cricket, gardening, house restoration, railway modelling; *Clubs* Durham CCC; *Style*— Dr Peter Collins

COLLINS, Richard Denis James; s of Patrick Joseph Collins (d 1993), and Kathleen, *née* O'Mahony (d 1992); *b* 15 February 1942, Co Cork, Ireland; *Educ* Bray Nat Boys Secdy Sch Co Dublin, Our Lady of Grace Secdy Sch Charlton London, SE London Tech Sch Deptford, Coll of Estate Mgmnt Reading and London; *m* Noreen, *née* O'Keeffe; 2 da (Catherine Marie b 31 Aug 1964, Amanda Jane b 5 Sept 1966), 1 s (Robert John b 4 March 1972); *Career* surveyor; Morden College Estates 1958–63, Purvis & Purvis Architects and Surveyors 1963–72, GLC/ILEA 1964–68, chief building surveyor London Borough of Bexley 1968–72, ptnr Kennedy & Partners 1972–2001 (sr ptnr 1982); currently dir and chm: Dunlop Haywards Ltd, Kennedy Properties Ltd, Haywards Property Services Ltd, Kennedy and Partners Ltd, Kennedy Haywards Ltd, Kennedy and Partners (UK) Ltd, Construction Consultants Consortium Ltd, Swan New Homes Ltd, Erinaceous (Ireland) Ltd; currently dir: Kennedy Woodward Allen Ltd; Charlton Athletic FC Ltd (also life pres and former chm), Charlton Athletic Hldgs Ltd, PDR Ventures Ltd, Sundridge Park Golf Club Ltd, Building Control Charity; RICS: former pres Building Surveyors Div, chm Construction Design and Economics Practice Panel, memb various ctees and panels; various appts as arbitrator; dir and former pres Bexley and Greenwich C of C; former memb London Rent Assessment Panel Leasehold Valuation Tbnl; conslt to FA of Ireland; Irish Businessman of the Year 2002; memb: Soc of Construction Law, Adjudication Soc; FRICS 1968, FCIArb 1971, FBEng 1974, MAE 1991, FInstD 1986; *Recreations* flying light aircraft (holds private pilot's licence), football, golf; *Style*— Richard Collins, Esq; ✉ 5 Kinnaird Avenue, Bromley, Kent BR1 4HG (tel home 020 8290 1779, business 020 8466 0500, fax 020 8313 9200, e-mail richard.collins@erinaceous.com)

COLLINS, Prof Rory Edwards; s of late Jack Collins, and Catherine, *née* Burke; *b* 3 January 1955, Hong Kong; *Educ* Dulwich Coll, George Washington Univ Washington DC (BSc), Univ of London (LMSSA), St Thomas' Hosp Med Sch London (MB BS), Univ of Oxford (MSc, MA); *m* Julie Elliott; *Career* Dept of Cardiovascular Med John Radcliffe Hosp Oxford: research asst (hon SHO, registrar then sr registrar) 1981–91, hon conslt in public health 1991–; Univ of Oxford: joined Clinical Trial Service Unit (CTSU) and Epidemiology Studies Unit Nuffield Dept of Clinical Med 1981, co-dir (with Prof Sir Richard Peto, *qv*) CTSU 1986–, Br Heart Fndn prof of med and epidemiology 1996–, fell Green Coll 1997–; co-dir MRC Directly Supported Team 1996–; chief exec UK Biobank 2005–; memb: Br Atherosclerosis Soc 1986–, Br Cardiac Soc 1986–, American Coll of Cardiology 1991–, Br Hypertension Soc 1993–, European Soc of Cardiology 1994–, Assoc of Physicians 1998–, American Heart Fndn 1999–; Hon Medal Polish Card Soc 1994, European Award for Excellence in Stroke Research (jtly) 1995, Prix Raymond Bourgine for Achievement in Cancer Research (jtly) 1996, Fothergill Medal Med Soc of London (jtly) 1998, Sr Aspirin Award 2000 (jtly), Queen's Anniversary Prize for Research 2005; FRCPEd 2002; *Style*— Rory Collins; ✉ 41 Southmoor Road, Oxford OX2 6RF (tel 01865 557636); Clinical Trial Service Unit and Epidemiological Studies Unit, University of Oxford, Richard Doll Building, Old Road Campus, Roosevelt Drive, Oxford OX3 7LF (tel 01865 743834, fax 01865 743985, e-mail secretary@ctsu.ox.ac.uk)

COLLINS, Prof Roy; s of Reginald George Collins (ka 1940), and Bertha Mary, *née* Smith; *b* 4 March 1937; *Educ* Southfield Sch Oxford, Univ of Bristol (Hele-Shaw Prize, Albert Fry Prize, BSc), Univ of London (PhD); *m* 1962, Elissa Kedward, da of Edwin John Parry; 2 s (Loel b 8 Oct 1965, Matthew b 20 Aug 1969); *Career* AERE Harwell 1959–61; UCL: lectr 1961–73, sr lectr 1973–85, reader 1985–92, prof of mechanical engrg 1992–2002, dean Faculty of Engrg 1995–97, head of dept Mechanical Engrg 2001–02; emeritus prof Univ of London 2002–; MIMechE; CEng 1972; *Publications* author of numerous papers in scientific jls incl: Proceedings of The Royal Society, Jl of Fluid Mechanics, Chemical Engineering Science; *Recreations* music, piano, cabinet making and joinery; *Style*— Prof Roy Collins; ✉ 131 Whiteknights Road, Reading, Berkshire RG6 7BB; Department of Mechanical Engineering, University College London, Torrington Place, London WC1E 7JE (tel 020 7679 3925, fax 020 7383 0831)

COLLINS, Roy William; s of Charles Albert Collins (d 1987), and Lilian Maud, *née* Williamson (d 1960); *b* 17 July 1948; *Educ* SE Essex Co Tech HS; *m* 1, 1971 (m dis 1975), Barbara Anne, *née* Askew; m 2, 1987, Sheila Anne, da of Leslie Arthur Love; 1 da (Lucy Elizabeth b 3 Jan 1987); *Career* gen reporter Barking Advertiser 1967, sports ed Express & Independent Walthamstow 1967–68, sports writer Essex & East London Newspapers 1968–69, sports columnist Evening Echo Southend 1969–74, freelance sports and news features journalist Fleet Street 1974–79, gen sports writer then columnist Sunday People 1979–83, freelance sports and gen journalist 1983–86, chief sports writer and columnist Today 1986–95 (following paper's closure), sports columnist The People 1996–2000, freelance writer The Guardian 2000–03, football corr Sunday Telegraph 2003–; memb: SWA, Football Writers' Assoc; *Recreations* tennis, running, chess, pubs, horse racing; *Clubs* Nothing Writers' Overseas Dining (treas), Coolhurst Tennis; *Style*— Roy Collins, Esq; ✉ 48 Rosebery Road, Muswell Hill, London N10 2LJ (tel 020 8883 6706, e-mail roycol@aol.com)

C

COLLINS, Sheila Mary; da of Peter Gilbert Stuart Dawson, of Ringwood, Hants, and Mary Violet, *née* Rabbetts (d 1992); *b* 10 March 1952; *Educ* Dorchester GS for Girls, UCL (LLB), Coll of Law Lanchester Gate London; *m* John Brook Collins; 1 da (Michelle Mary Elizabeth b 1984), 1 s (Dominic John Luke b 8 March 1986); *Career* admitted slr 1976; practice mangr Messrs Harold G Walker & Co Slrs Bournemouth 1996–; chair Royal Bournemouth & Christchurch Hosps NHS Tst 1997– (non-exec dir 1991–97); treas Young Slrs Gp Bournemouth 1981–85, hon sec Bournemouth and Dist Law Soc 1985–; independent lay visitor Hesley Gp of Schs 1992–95; memb: Law Soc of England and Wales 1976, Soc of Tst and Estate Practitioners 1996; *Recreations* horse riding, quiz team member, wine appreciation; *Style*— Mrs Sheila Collins; ✉ Royal Bournemouth & Christchurch Hospitals NHS Foundation Trust, Castle Lane East, Bournemouth, Dorset BH7 7DW

COLLINS, Thomas Brendan; OBE (2007); s of late Stephen Paul Collins, of Lurgan, Co Armagh, and Mary Ethna, *née* Breen; *b* 12 August 1959; *Educ* St Colman's Coll Co Down, New Univ of Ulster, City Univ London (BA); *m* Mary Christina, da of late James Dugan and late Anne Dugan; 1 s (Joshua Stephen James b 16 Oct 1998), 1 da (Eleanor Grace Ethna Anne b 18 June 2001); *Career* ed Carrickfergus Advertiser and E Antrim Gazette 1984–85 (reporter 1983–84), chief sub ed The Ulster News Letter 1988–90 (dep chief sub ed 1985–88), ed The Irish News 1993–99 (dep ed 1990–93); Queen's Univ Belfast: dir of communications 1999–2005, dir of mktg, recruitment and communications 2005–; memb Guild of Eds 1994–99; Regnl Newspaper Ed of the Year 1995; chm Ulster Orch; FRSA 2003; *Recreations* classical music, opera; *Style*— Tom Collins, Esq, OBE; ✉ Queen's University Belfast, Belfast BT7 1NN (tel 028 9097 3259, e-mail t.collins@qub.ac.uk)

COLLINS, Tim William George; CBE (1996); s of William Alfred Collins (d 1997), and Diana Mary Collins; *b* 7 May 1964; *Educ* Chigwell Sch, LSE (BSc(Econ)), King's Coll London (MA); *m* July 1997, Clare, da of Geoffrey Benson; 1 s (Christopher); *Career* special advsr: DOE 1989–90, Dept of Employment 1990–92; press sec to PM gen election 1992 and leadership election 1995, dir of communications Cons Pty 1992–95, business conslt WCT Live Communications Ltd 1995–97; MP (Cons) Westmorland and Lonsdale 1997–2005; oppn whip 1998–99, sr vice-chm Cons Pty 1999–2001, shadow min for the Cabinet Office 2001–02, shadow Tport sec 2002–03, shadow educn sec 2003–; memb Cons Pty Policy Bd 2001–02; *Recreations* theatre, cinema, reading; *Style*— Tim Collins, Esq, CBE; ✉ 112 Highgate, Kendal, Cumbria LA9 4HE (tel 01539 721010, e-mail listening@timcollins.co.uk)

COLLINS, Prof Vincent Peter; s of James Vincent Collins (d 1989), of Dublin, and Mary Ann, *née* Blanche; *b* 3 December 1947; *Educ* St Fintains HS Dublin, UCD (MB BCh, BAO), Karolinska Inst Stockholm (MD); *Career* jr hosp and research posts Regnl Hosp Limerick, Mater Hosp Dublin, Stockholm's Cancer Soc and Karolinska Inst Stockholm 1971–74, various med appts and research posts in pathology Karolinska Inst and Hosp Stockholm 1974–97; latter appts: prof of pathology (with particular responsibility for neuropathology) Univ of Gothenburg Sweden 1990–94, prof of tumour pathology Karolinska Inst Stockholm 1994–97, sr conslt pathologist and latterly chm Dept of Oncology-Pathology Karolinska Hosp Stockholm 1994–97, head of clinical research Ludwig Inst Stockholm 1986–98; current appts: prof of histopathology and morbid anatomy Univ of Cambridge 1997–, hon conslt in histopathology Addenbrooke's Hosp Cambridge 1997–; memb: Bd Stockholm Cancer Soc 1995–99, Scientific Bd Swedish Childhood Cancer Fund 1996–; Minerva Prize Minerva Fndn Stockholm 1987, Joanne Vandenberg Hill Award and William O Russell Lectureship in Anatomical Pathology Anderson Hosp and Tumor Inst Univ of Texas 1990, research fell Japan 1991, Lucien J Rubenstein Neuropathology Research Lectureship Virginia Neurological Inst Univ of Virginia 1994, Roll of Honour Int Union Against Cancer (UICC) 1996, Linse Bock Visiting Professorship in Neuro-Oncology Mayo Clinic Rochester Minnesota 1997, Takao Hoshino Lectureship Univ of Calif San Francisco 1998, Lucien J Rubenstein Neuropathology Lectureship Virginia Neurological Inst 2000; memb various professional orgns incl: Int Soc of Neuropathology, Br Neuropathological Soc, Euro Soc of Pathology, NY Acad of Scis; FRCPath 1996 (MRCPath 1988); *Publications* author of numerous pubns in learned jls; memb Editorial Bd: Cancer Letters, Brain Pathology, Jl of Neuropathology & Experimental Neurology, Neuropathology & Applied Neurobiology; memb Int Editorial Bd (Section on Pathology and Pathological Anatomy) Excerpta Medica; *Recreations* sailing, skiing; *Style*— Prof V Peter Collins; ✉ Department of Histopathology, Box 235, Addenbrooke's Hospital, Hills Road, Cambridge CB2 2QQ (tel 01223 336072, fax 01223 216980, e-mail vpc20@cam.ac.uk)

COLLINSON, Alicia Hester; da of His Hon Judge Richard Jeffreys Hampton Collinson (d 1983), and Gwendolen Hester, *née* Ward; *b* 12 August 1956; *Educ* Birkenhead HS, St Hugh's Coll Oxford (MA, MPhil); *m* 23 April 1988, Damian Howard Green, MP, *qv*, s of Howard Green, KSG; 2 da (Felicity b 1990, Verity b 1993); *Career* called to the Bar Middle Temple 1982 (Harmsworth scholar); memb Bar Cncl 1990–93; memb Ct of Common Cncl Corporation of London 1991–94; Freeman City of London; *Publications* Tough Love: A Critique of the Domestic Violence, Crime and Victims Bill 2003 (2004), Politics for Partners: How to live with a politican (2007); *Clubs* Oxford Union; *Style*— Miss Alicia Collinson; ✉ 2 Harcourt Buildings, Temple, London EC4Y 9DB (tel 020 7353 6961, fax 020 7353 6968); Harcourt Chambers, Churchill House, St Aldates Courtyard, 38 St Aldates, Oxford OX1 1BN (tel 01865 791559, fax 01865 791585, e-mail acollinson@harcourtchambers.law.co.uk)

COLLINSON, Leonard; DL (Merseyside 2002); s of Sidney Lupton Collinson (d 1987), and Jane, *née* Crooks (d 1999), of Immingham; *b* 30 March 1934; *Educ* Humberstone Fndn Sch Cleethorpes, Univ of Nottingham (Dip); *m* 17 Sept 1955, Shirley Grace, da of Ernest Frederick Funnell (d 1962); 2 s (Christopher b 1956, Andrew b 1962); *Career* Nat Serv RAF 1952–54; organiser Nat Cncl of Lab Colls 1954–58, personnel mangr rising to dep nat mangr Bakery Div Co-operative Gp 1958–66, dir manpower Plessey Telecommunications and Office Systems 1966–71, fndr and exec chm Collinson Grant Group 1971–96; chm: European Consortium of Mgmnt Consults 1991–97, Newsco Pubns 1994–99, Grosvenor Career Services 1996–98, Central Plastics 2000–04, Industry Northwest 2002–04; dir: Collinson Grant Gp 1971–, United Gas Industries 1975–82,

Wormald Int Holdings 1979–83, RAD Sheep Marketing 2006–; CBI: memb Smaller Firms Cncl 1980–86, memb NW Regnl Cncl 1987–93 and 1998–, memb Nat Cncl 1995–98; chm Private Sector Partners 2001–04, dir and chm Forum of Private Business 2004– (dir 1994–2001); dir: Manchester TEC 1989–92, Univs Superannuation Scheme 1989–2004; memb Ct Univ of Manchester 1994–, chm Manchester Diocesan Cncl for Church in the Economy 1994–99; dep chm NW Regnl Assembly 2001–02; tstee People's History Museum 1994–; hon prof Univ of Central Lancashire 2007 (hon fell 2005); FCIM 1967, FCIPD 1970, FCBC 1980, CCMI 1985, FRSA 1990; *Books* Employment Law Keynotes (with C M Hodkinson, 1985), Manual for Small Business (1983), The Line Manager's Employment Law (16 edns since 1978); *Recreations* Wales, politics; *Clubs* RAC, Portico; *Style*— Leonard Collinson, Esq, DL; ✉ Colgran House, 20 Worsley Road, Swinton, Manchester M27 5WW (tel 0161 794 9538, fax 0161 794 1594, e-mail lcollinson@colgranhouse.com)

COLLINSON, Prof Patrick; CBE (1993); s of William Cecil Collinson (d 1952), and Belle Hay, *née* Patrick (d 1972); *b* 10 August 1929; *Educ* King's Sch Ely, Pembroke Coll Cambridge (MA, coll prize), Univ of London (PhD); *m* Dec 1960, Elizabeth Albinia Susan, da of Geoffrey Selwyn (d 1934); 2 da (Helen Hay b 1962, Sarah Christina b 1965), 2 s (Andrew Cecil b 1963, Stephen Selwyn b 1968); *Career* Univ of London: postgrad student Royal Holloway Coll 1952–54, res fell Inst of Hist Res 1954–55, res asst UCL 1955–56; lectr in history Univ of Khartoum 1956–61, lectr in ecclesiastical history KCL 1962–69 (asst lectr 1961–62); prof of history: Univ of Sydney 1969–75, Univ of Kent at Canterbury 1976–84; prof of modern history Univ of Sheffield 1984–88, regius prof of modern history Univ of Cambridge 1988–96, Douglas S Freeman visiting prof Univ of Richmond VA 1999, assoc visiting prof Univ of Warwick 2000–03; visiting fell All Souls Coll Oxford 1981, Andrew W Mellon fell Huntington Library Calif 1984, fell Trinity Coll Cambridge 1988–; chm Advsy Editorial Bd Jl of Ecclesiastical History 1982–93; pres Ecclesiastical History Soc 1985–86, memb Cncl Br Acad 1986–89, memb Academia Europaea 1989, corresponding memb Massachusetts Historical Soc 1990; Hon DUniv York 1988; Hon DLitt: Univ of Kent at Canterbury 1989, Trinity Coll Dublin 1992, Univ of Sheffield 1995, Univ of Oxford 1997, Univ of Essex 2000, Univ of Warwick 2003; FRHistS 1967 (memb Cncl 1977–81, vice-pres 1983–87 and 1994–98, hon vice-pres 2001–), FBA 1982; *Books* The Elizabethan Puritan Movement (1967, USA 1967, reprinted 1982 and 1990), Archbishop Grindal 1519–1583 - The Struggle for a Reformed Church (1979, USA 1979), The Religion of Protestants - The Church in English Society 1559–1625 (Ford Lectures Univ of Oxford 1979 and 1982), Godly People - Essays on English Protestantism and Puritanism (1983), English Puritanism (1983), The Birthpangs of Protestant England - Religious and Cultural Change in the 16th and 17th Centuries (1988), Elizabethan Essays (1994), A History of Canterbury Cathedral (ed with N Ramsay and M Sparks, 1995), The Reformation in English Towns (ed with J Craig, 1998), A History of Emmanuel Coll Cambridge (with S Bendall and C N L Brooke 1999), Short Oxford History of the British Isles: The Sixteenth Century (ed, 2002), The Reformation (2003), Conferences and Combination Lectures of the Elizabethan Church: Dedham and Bury St Edmunds 1582–1590 (with J Craig and B Usher, 2003), The Cowbells of Kitale (2003), From Cranmer to Sancroft (2006), Elizabeth I (2007); articles and reviews in Historical Res, Eng Historical Review, Jl of Ecclesiastical History, Studies in Church History, TLS, London Review of Books; *Recreations* walking, music, grandchildren; *Style*— Prof Patrick Collinson, CBE, FBA; ✉ New House, Crown Square, Shaldon, Devon TQ14 0DS (tel 01626 871245); Trinity College, Cambridge CB2 1TQ (tel 01223 338400)

COLLIS, Pamela Caroline Neild; da of Michael Neild Collis, of Beds, and Ann, *née* Strong; *b* 9 March 1957; *Educ* Rosemead Sch for Girls Littlehampton Sussex, Univ of Bristol (LLB), Guildford Coll of Law; *m* 22 Dec 1987, Joseph Sinyor, s of Samuel Joseph Sinyor; 2 s (Joshua Samuel b 17 Nov 1988, Benjamin Jonathon b 30 June 1990); 1 da (Jessica Claire Rachael b 1 Jan 1994); *Career* asst slr Herbert Smith 1981–82 (articled clerk 1979–81); Kingsley Napley: joined 1982, ptnr 1985–99, head Family Law Dept 1989–99; conslt and head Family Law Dept Cawdery Kaye Fireman & Taylor 1999–; accredited memb: Family Law Panel Law Soc, Slrs' Family Law Assoc; fell Acad of Int Matrimonial Lawyers; *Recreations* tennis, cycling, reading; *Style*— Ms Pamela Collis; ✉ Cawdery Kaye Fireman & Taylor, 25–26 Hampstead High Street, London NW3 1QA (tel 020 7317 8720, fax 020 7317 8751, e-mail pcollis@ckft.com)

COLLIS, Peter George; CB (2005); s of Martin Arthur Collis, of Send, Surrey, and Margaret Sophie, *née* Luigs (d 1996); *b* 13 October 1953, Dorking, Surrey; *Educ* Woking Co GS for Boys, Univ of Aston Birmingham (BSc); *m* 1, 1978, Linda Jean, *née* Worssam; 1 s (David Anthony b 10 Aug 1983), 1 da (Alexa Jane b 19 April 1986); m 2, 2000, Jan Morgan; 1 step s (Christopher Kiel b 3 July 1986); *Career* admin trainee DTI and Dept of Prices and Consumer Protection 1975–78, higher exec offr DTI and (secondment) National Enterprise Bd 1978–80, princ Consumer Affairs Div DTI 1980–83, seconded as mktg exec Balfour Beatty Engrg Ltd 1983–85, princ Civil Aviation Policy Directorate Dept of Transport 1985–88; head: Driver Licensing Div DVLA 1988–91, Finance Exec Agencies Div Dept of Transport 1991–92, Highways Resource Mgmnt Div Dept of Transport 1992–94; memb Bd Highways Agency 1994–96 (strategy dir 1994–95, private finance dir 1995–96), dir of business devpt Dept of Transport 1997, finance and commercial policy dir Employment Serv 1997–99, chief land registrar and chief exec HM Land Registry 1999–; non-exec dir Swansea Futures Ltd 2006–; memb British German Assoc; hon memb RICS 2004 (currently memb Governing Cncl); *Recreations* family, travel, enjoying the coast and the countryside; *Style*— Peter Collis, Esq, CB; ✉ HM Land Registry, Room 106, 32 Lincoln's Inn Fields, London WC2A 3PH (tel 020 7166 4497, fax 020 7166 4339, e-mail peter.collis@landregistry.gsi.gov.uk)

COLLIS, Terrence Ivor; *b* 1 February 1954; *Educ* Laxton GS Oundle, Univ of Durham (BSc); *m* 21 Oct 1989, Sarah Lilian Anderson, CBE, da of Derek Anderson; 1 s (Benjamin Ivor b 7 May 1991), 1 da (Sophie Helena b 14 April 1993); *Career* press serv exec Nicholas Mendes & Associates 1975–76, press and PRO Barlow Handling Ltd 1976–78, press offr Lucas Group 1978–81, sr PR exec Hawker Siddeley Group 1981–85; Vickers plc: media rels mangr 1985–87, dep dir of public affrs 1988, dir of public affrs 1988–92; md Bell Pottinger Financial (formerly Lowe Bell Financial) 1992–97, dir of corp affrs and memb Exec Mgmnt Ctee National Westminster Bank plc 1997–2000, dir of gp corp communications Lloyds TSB Gp plc 2000–05; tstee Br Red Cross 2004–; FRSA 1993, FIPR 2002 (MIPR 1988); *Recreations* wicket-keeping, astronomy; *Clubs* Pimlico Astronomical Soc, Mortlake Casuals Cricket; *Style*— Terrence Collis, Esq

COLLIVER, Douglas John; s of Douglas John Colliver (d 1983), and Alice Emily, *née* White; *b* 22 March 1947; *Educ* The GS Farnborough, Univ of Bristol (LLB); *m* 27 Feb 1971, Lulu, da of Henry William Hayes (d 1983), of Camberley, Surrey; 3 s (Toby b 1972, Jasper b 1979, Giles b 1981), 1 da (Sophy b 1974); *Career* slr; articled clerk Durrant Cooper and Hambling 1969–71; ptnr: Norton Rose 1978–97 (joined 1973), Dewey Ballantine 1998–99, Garretts (Andersen Legal) 2000–02, Hammonds 2002–05, CMS Cameron McKenna LLP 2005–; memb Law Soc; *Recreations* reading, guitar; *Style*— Douglas Colliver, Esq

COLLS, Alan Howard Crawfurd; s of Maj Derek Archibald Colls, MBE (d 1991), of London, and Amy, *née* Christie-Crawfurd (d 1982); *b* 15 December 1941; *Educ* Harrow; *m* 20 March 1969, Janet Mary, da of Capt Michael Gillespie (d 1986); 1 da (Nina b 15 Jan 1970), 1 s (Toby b 19 Dec 1970); *Career* dir Stewart Wrightson Holdings plc 1981–87; chm: Stewart Wrightson Aviation Ltd 1975–86, Stewart Wrightson International Group 1981–85, Stewart Wrightson Ltd 1986–87, Nicholson Chamberlain Colls Ltd 1988–94, Nicholson Leslie Ltd 1994–97, AON Group Ltd 1997–98; dep chm Lloyd's Insurance Brokers' Ctee 1986–87 and 1989–90 (chm 1991–92), memb Lloyd's Market Bd 1992–94; ret; *Recreations* golf, travel; *Clubs* Annabel's; *Style*— Alan Colls, Esq; ✉ 23 Victoria Road, London W8 5RF (tel 020 7937 7226)

COLMAN, Sir Anthony Colman; kt (1992); s of Solomon Colman (d 1991), and Helen, *née* Weiss (d 1987); *b* 27 May 1938; *Educ* Harrogate GS, Trinity Hall Cambridge (BA, MA); *m* 23 Aug 1964, Angela Barbara, da of Hyman Glynn (d 1984), of London; 2 da (Deborah b 1967, Rosalind b 1971); *Career* Nat Serv Instr RAEC 1957–59; called to the Bar Gray's Inn 1962; in commercial practice 1963 (specialising in shipping, int trade and insur), QC 1977, chm ces of enquiry and disciplinary ctees at Lloyd's 1982–84, recorder of the Crown Court 1985, bencher Gray's Inn 1986, dep High Court judge 1987, judge of the High Court of Justice (Queen's Bench Div) 1992–2007, judge i/c Commercial List 1996–97; int commercial arbitrator 2007–; judge conducting investigation into loss of MV Derbyshire 1999–2000; advsr to Czech Republic on commercial litigation 2000–2001; accession advsr to European Cmmn: on Czech Republic 2002, on Slovakia 2003; memb Bar Cncl 1989–92; chm: Commercial Bar Assoc 1991–92 (treas 1989–91), The British-Bulgarian Law Assoc 1993–96; pres Trinity Hall Assoc 1998–99; hon pres Societate di Mediazone Rome 2003–, princ Faculty of Mediation and vice-pres Acad of Experts 2004–; FCIArb 1978; *Books* Mathew's Practice of the Commercial Court (2 edn 1965), The Practice and Procedure of the Commercial Court (1983, 2 edn 1986, 5 edn 2000), The Encyclopaedia of International Commercial Litigation (gen ed and contrib, 1 edn 1991); *Recreations* tennis, gardening, painting; *Style*— Sir Anthony Colman; ✉ c/o Royal Courts of Justice, Strand, London WC2A 2LL

COLMAN, Prof David Robert; OBE (2003); s of Colin Robert Colman, of London, and Jessica Ada, *née* Gregson (d 1972); *b* 14 May 1940; *Educ* Bury GS, Latymer Upper Sch, Wye Coll London (BSc), Univ of Illinois (MS), Univ of Manchester (PhD); *m* 9 Aug 1969, Susan, da of William Blundell (d 1952); 2 da (Lucy b 1974, Sophie b 1976); *Career* res asst Univ of Illinois 1963–65, tech advsr Govt of Malawi 1972–73, visiting prof Cornell Univ 1978–79; Univ of Manchester: lectr 1965–74, sr lectr 1974–79, prof 1979–, head Sch of Economic Studies 1994–97 and 1999–; chm Exec Agric Economics Soc 1980–83 and 1989–91 (pres 1994–95); pres-elect IAAE; memb: AES 1965, IAEA 1974 (AAEA 1968); *Books* The United Kingdom Cereals Market (1972), Principles of Agricultural Economics (1989), Economics of Change in Less-Developed Countries (3 edn, 1994); *Recreations* badminton, fishing, philately, theatre, food and drink; *Style*— Prof David Colman, OBE; ✉ 11 Brooklyn Crescent, Cheadle, Cheshire SK8 1DX; School of Economic Studies, University of Manchester, Manchester M13 9PL (tel 0161 275 4804, fax 0161 275 4929)

COLMAN, Jeremy Gye; s of Philip Colman, and Georgina Maude, *née* Gye; *b* 9 April 1948; *Educ* John Lyon Sch Harrow, Peterhouse Cambridge (MA), Imperial Coll London (MSc, DIC), Open Univ (PGDCCI); *m* 1, 1978 (m dis 1996), Patricia Ann Stewart; m 2, 1997, Gillian Margaret Carless; *Career* CS offr 1971–75, princ HM Treasy 1975–78, CS Dept 1978–81, private sec to Head of Home Civil Service 1980–81, princ HM Treasy 1981–84, private sec to Permanent Sec and Jt Head of Home Civil Service 1981–82, asst sec HM Treasy 1984–87; dir County NatWest Ltd 1988–90, ptnr Price Waterhouse 1991–93, dir National Audit Office 1993–98, asst auditor gen 1999–2005, auditor gen for Wales 2005–; Freeman of the City of London, Freeman Worshipful Co of Ironmongers; *Recreations* cookery, opera, furniture-making, wine; *Clubs* Oxford and Cambridge; *Style*— J G Colman, Esq; ✉ Wales Audit Office, 2–4 Park Grove, Cardiff CF10 3PA (tel 029 2026 0260, e-mail jeremy.colman@wao.gov.uk)

COLMAN, Sir Michael Jeremiah; 3 Bt (UK 1907), of Gatton Park, Gatton, Surrey; s of Sir Jeremiah Colman, 2 Bt (d 1961); *b* 7 July 1928; *Educ* Eton; *m* 29 Oct 1955, Judith Jean Wallop, da of late Vice Adm Sir Peveril Barton Reibey William-Powlett, KCB, KCMG, CBE, DSO; 3 da (Olivia Helena Judith (Mrs Patrick J Whitworth) b 1956, Victoria Rose (Mrs Matthew S Persson) b 1960, Alice Mary (Mrs Timothy A C Page) b 1965), 2 s (Jeremiah Michael Powlett b 1958, John Powlett b 1962); *Heir* s, Jeremiah Colman; *Career* chm Reckitt and Colman plc 1986–95; first church estates cmmr Church Commissioners 1993–99; dir Foreign & Colonial Ventures Advisors Ltd 1988–99 (dir Private Equity Tst 1995–2002); dir: UK Centre for Economic and Environmental Devpt 1985–1999 (chm 1996–99); chm Trade Affrs Bd 1982–84, memb Cncl Chemical Industries Assoc; memb Cncl: Royal Warrant Holders 1977– (pres 1984); Trinity House: assoc 1984–93, memb Lighthouse Bd 1984–93, Younger Brother 1994–; memb Gen Cncl and Finance Ctee King Edward's Hosp Fund for London 1978–2004, special tstee for St Mary's Hosp 1988–99; tstee The Royal Fndn Grey Coat Hosp 1989–2004; memb Cncl The Scouts' Assoc 1985–2000; memb Ct of Assts of Worshipful Co of Skinners 1985– (Master 1991); tstee Allchurches Tst Ltd 1994–; Hon LLD Univ of Hull 1993; awarded Archbishop of Canterbury's Cross of St Augustine; *Recreations* farming, forestry, golf, shooting; *Clubs* Cavalry and Guards'; *Style*— Sir Michael Colman, Bt; ✉ Malshanger, Basingstoke, Hampshire RG23 7EY (tel 01256 780252); Tarvie, Bridge of Cally, Blairgowrie, Perthshire PH10 7PJ (tel 01250 881264)

COLMAN, Dr Richard Douglas; s of Jack Douglas Colman, of Huby, N Yorks, and Muriel, *née* Longden; *b* 5 March 1949; *Educ* Ansdell County Secdy Modern Lytham St Annes, King Edward VII Lytham St Annes, Magdalene Coll Cambridge (MA, MB BChir), Bart's Med Coll, Univ of Hull (Cert Moral Philosophy); *m* 17 March 1979, Mary Janet van der Westhuizen, da of Dr Fiona Waugh; 3 da (Rose Mary Fiona b 10 Sept 1983, Bethany Ellen b 19 May 1985, Shannon Elizabeth b 31 May 1992), 2 s (Jack Pieter Dale b 24 Feb 1987, Rowan Richard Grant b 27 June 1989); *Career* vocational trg in gen practice, ind med practice 1985– (challenged UK law on restrictions on advtg, lost High Court judgement but appealed to European Court of Human Rights, subsequently accepted friendly settlement with Govt following GMC's removal of restrictions at insistence of DTI 1993), currently occupational physician NE; memb GMC 1994–99; DipRCOG, MRCGP, DOccMed; *Recreations* outdoor activities, practical self sufficiency, judo (coach); *Clubs* Hawks' (Cambridge); *Style*— Dr Richard Colman; ✉ Cowl House, Bransdale, Fadmoor, York YO62 7JW (tel 01751 432342, e-mail richardcol@doctors.org.uk)

COLMAN, Sir Timothy James Alan; KG (1996); 2 (but only surviving) s of late Capt Geoffrey Russell Rees Colman, of Norwich, and Lettice Elizabeth Evelyn Colman; *b* 19 September 1929; *Educ* RNC Dartmouth and Greenwich; *m* 1951, Lady Mary Cecilia, twin da of late Lt-Col the Hon Michael Claude Hamilton Bowes-Lyon, and Elizabeth Margaret Bowes-Lyon; 2 s, 3 da; *Career* Lt RN 1950 (ret 1953); chm Eastern Counties Newspapers Group Ltd 1969–96; dir: Reckitt & Colman plc 1978–89, Whitbread & Co plc 1980–86, Anglia Television Group plc 1987–94; life tstee Carnegie UK Tst 1966–2000 (chm 1982–87); pro-chllr UEA 1974–2000 (chm Cncl 1973–86); chm Royal Norfolk Agric Assoc 1985–96 (pres 1982 and 1997); chm of tstees: Norwich and Norfolk Festival 1974–2002, E Anglia Art Fund 1993–2005 (pres 2005–), Norwich Cathedral Tst 1998–; memb: Eastern Regnl Ctee Nat Tst 1967–71, Countryside Cmmn 1971–76, Water Space Amenity Cmmn 1973–76, Advsy Ctee for England Nature Conservancy Cncl 1974–80; pres: Friends of Norwich Museums 1978–, E Anglian TAVRA 1992–96; chm Norfolk Naturalists Tst 1962–78; JP 1958, High Sheriff Norfolk 1970, HM Lord-Lt Norfolk 1978–2004 (DL 1968); Hon DCL UEA 1973, Hon DUniv Anglia Poly 1999, hon fell UEA 2004; FRSA 1995; KStJ 1979; *Clubs* Turf, Pratt's, Norfolk (Norwich), Royal Yacht Squadron; *Style*— Sir Timothy Colman, KG; ✉ Bixley Manor, Norwich, Norfolk NR14 8SJ (tel 01603 626957 or 01603 625298)

COLMER, Ven Malcolm John; *b* 15 February 1945; *Educ* Royal GS Guildford, Univ of Sussex (BSc, MSc), St John's Coll Nottingham (BA); *m* Liz; 4 c; *Career* scientific offr Royal Aircraft Estab Bedford 1967–71; asst curate: St John's Egham 1973–76, Chadwell St

Mary 1976–79; vicar St Michael's South Malling Lewes 1979–85, team rector Hornsey Rise Whitehall Park London 1985–96, area dean of Islington 1990–95, archdeacon of Middx 1996–2005, archdeacon of Hereford 2005–; *Style*— The Ven the Archdeacon of Hereford; ✉ The Palace, Hereford HR4 9BL (tel 01432 373324, fax 01432 352952, e-mail archdeacon@hereford.anglican.org)

COLQUHOUN, Andrew John; s of Maj Kenneth James Colquhoun, MC (d 1990), and Christine Mary, *née* Morris; *b* 21 September 1949; *Educ* Tiffin Sch, Univ of Nottingham (BSc), Univ of Glasgow (PhD), City Univ (MBA); *m* 22 Feb 1975, Patricia, da of John Beardall; 1 s (Simon James b 1976), 1 da (Helen Elizabeth b 1978); *Career* FCO: joined 1974, served London and ME, seconded to Cabinet Office 1981–83, Planning Staff 1983–84; Shandwick Consultants 1984–86 (seconded to ICAEW), sec and chief exec ICAEW 1990–97 (dir of educn and trg 1987–90); sec Consultative Ctee of Accountancy Bodies 1990–97; DG RHS 1999–; chm Nat Horticultural Forum 2002–, memb Rail Passengers Ctee for Southern England 1998–2003; lay memb Univ of Nottingham Cncl 1999–; author of various articles on horticulture, accountancy, educn and recruitment; *Recreations* gardening, bird watching, reading, walking, country life; *Clubs* Reform; *Style*— Andrew Colquhoun, Esq; ✉ Radford, Haywards Heath Road, Balcombe, West Sussex RH17 6NJ (tel 01444 811367)

COLQUHOUN, Barry John (BJ); s of Alan John Colquhoun, and Elsie Vera, *née* Chinn; *Educ* St Crispin's Wokingham; *Career* photographer; dir art and advtg El Arenal Palma de Mallorca 1966–67, private art cmmns throughout the Caribbean and USA 1967–68, lectr on creative black and white photographic techniques 1970–75, freelance journalist, lectr and conslt on 100% digital imaging 1997–; past pres and memb cncl Lytham St Annes Photographic Soc; Distinction of the Photographic Alliance of GB (DPAGB) 2003; FRPS (ARPS), FBIPP; *Recreations* property repairs and maintenance; *Style*— BJ Colquhoun, Esq; ✉ ALBA Co (Digital Imaging), 154 St Andrews Road South, St Annes-on-Sea, Lancashire FY8 1YA (tel 01253 720217, e-mail bjc.albaco@btinternet.com and bjc@bjc100.co.uk)

COLQUHOUN, Prof David; *b* 19 July 1936; *Educ* Univ of Leeds (BSc), Univ of Edinburgh (PhD); *m* April 1976, Margaret Anne, *née* Boultwood; 1 s (Andrew Stuart b 24 Dec 1984); *Career* asst lectr Dept of Pharmacology Univ of Edinburgh 1962–64, visiting asst then assoc prof Dept of Pharmacology Yale Univ Sch of Med 1964–72, sr lectr Dept of Physiology and Biochemistry Univ of Southampton 1972–75 (acting head of dept 1974–75), sr lectr in pharmacology St George's Hosp Med Sch 1976–79; UCL: reader of pharmacology 1979–83, prof 1983–, A J Clark chair 1985–, dir Wellcome Laboratory for Molecular Pharmacology 1993–2004; visiting scientist Dept of Physiology and Biophysics Univ of Washington 1974, visiting prof Max Planck Institut für Medizinische 1990–91; memb: Editorial Bd Jl of Physiology 1974–81, Sir Ronald Fisher Meml Ctee 1975– (tstee Meml Fund), Sectional Ctee Royal Soc 1988–91 (chm 1990), Editorial Bd Royal Soc Pubns 1989, Academia Europaea 1992; J C Krantz prize lectr Univ of Maryland 1987, Alexander von Humboldt prize 1990; hon fell UCL 2004; FRS 1985; *Style*— Prof David Colquhoun, FRS; ✉ e-mail d.colquhoun@ucl.ac.uk

COLQUHOUN, (Ernest) Patrick; s of Wing Cdr Edgar Edmund Colquhoun, MBE (d 1953), and Elizabeth Colquhoun (d 1986); *b* 5 January 1937; *Educ* Shrewsbury, Univ of Cambridge; *m* 16 Jan 1964, Patricia Susan Alexandra, da of Baron and Baroness Frederick von Versen (d 1953); 3 s (James b 1966, Henry b 1969, Frederick b 1980); *Career* Lt Scots Gds 1955–57; banker; md Henderson Administration Ltd 1969–76, vice-pres Swiss Bank Corp 1983–88; dir: Rowan Investment Mangrs 1974–77, Electra Gp Services Ltd 1978–79, Cavendish Partners Ltd 1990–97, Right Cavendish Ltd 1997–98, Right Mgmnt Consultants 1999–2000; vice-pres Nat Tst for Scotland London Members Centre 2005– (chm 2002–05), dep chm Devpt Cncl Royal Acad of Dance 2001–07; memb: Advsy Cncl Brazilian Investments SA 1975–2007, Trading Ctee Royal Sch of Needlework 1988–89, Int Advsy Ctee Befrienders Int 1990–94; tstee: Royal Ballet Benevolent Fund 2002–, Dancers' Career Devpt 2006–; *Recreations* shooting, cricket, music, ballet, fine art; *Clubs* Boodle's, Pratt's, Puffins, MCC, Highland Society; *Style*— Patrick Colquhoun, Esq; ✉ 40 Markham Street, London SW3 3NR (tel 020 7352 8318, e-mail epclq@aol.com)

COLQUHOUN-DENVERS, Nicholas John Arthur; s of HE John Dalrymple Colquhoun-Denvers, Australian Consul-Gen, of Bombay, India, and Winifred May, *née* Mitchell; *b* 5 January 1949; *Educ* Christ Church Coll, Perth; *m* 20 May 1978, Anne Patricia, da of Maj Charles Walter Douglas Wellesley Alexander (d 1983), late of 3 Carabiniers and Royal Scots Dragoon Gds; *Career* sec to Chm Australian Public Service Bd Canberra 1966–69; offr RA served BAOR, Hong Kong, N Ireland Capt 1969–77, ret; with Adnan Khashoggi's Triad Corporation 1977–85; md: CLC 1985–87, Hurlingham (Management) Ltd 1987–; ceo FAL Energy (UK) Ltd; Gen Service Medal 1971; steward Hurlingham Polo Assoc; *Recreations* polo, shooting; *Clubs* Guards Polo, Ham Polo (chm 1995–); *Style*— Nicholas Colquhoun-Denvers, Esq; ✉ Dorchester Court, 77 Sloane Street, London SW1X 9SE (tel 020 7259 5654/6808); FAL Energy (UK) Limited, The Bridge, 334 Queenstown Road, London SW8 4NP (tel 020 7486 2600, fax 020 7486 2700, mobile 078 8055 5555, e-mail cd@fal.uk.com)

COLQUHOUN OF LUSS, Capt Sir Ivar Iain; 8 Bt (GB 1786), of Luss, Dumbarton, JP (Dunbartonshire 1951), DL (1952); Chief of the Clan Colquhoun; s of Lt-Col Sir Iain Colquhoun, 7 Bt, KT, DSO, LLD (d 1948); *b* 4 January 1916; *Educ* Eton; *m* 17 April 1943, Kathleen, 2 da of late Walter Atholl Duncan, of 53 Cadogan Square, SW1; 1 da (Iona Mary (Duchess of Argyll) b 1945), 1 s (Malcolm Rory, yr of Luss b 1947) (and 1 s decd); *Heir* s, Malcolm Colquhoun, yr of Luss; *Career* Capt Grenadier Gds; Hon Sheriff (former Hon Sheriff substitute); *Clubs* White's, Puffin's, Royal Ocean Racing, Sloane; *Style*— Capt Sir Ivar Colquhoun of Luss, Bt, DL; ✉ Camstraddan, Luss, Argyllshire G83 8NX (tel 0143 6860245)

COLSTON, His Hon Colin Charles; QC; yr s of Eric Lawrence Colston, JP (d 1975), of Bucks, and Catherine Colston (d 2000); *b* 2 October 1937; *Educ* Rugby, Trinity Hall Cambridge (MA); *m* 23 March 1963, Edith Helga, da of Dr Wilhelm Hille (d 1993), of Austria; 2 s (Martin b 1965, Dominic b 1968), 1 da (Helen-Jane b 1970); *Career* Nat Serv 1956–58, cmmnd RNR 1957–64, Lt RNR; called to the Bar Gray's Inn 1962; in practice Midland & Oxford Circuit (recorder Midland Circuit 1968–69); memb of the Senate of the Inns of Court and Bar 1977–80, recorder Crown Court 1978–83, circuit judge (SE Circuit) 1983–2003 (dep circuit judge 2003–), resident judge Crown Court at St Albans 1989–2000; memb: Criminal Ctee Judicial Studies Bd 1989–92, Parole Bd for Eng and Wales 2004–; lay judge Court of Arches for Province of Canterbury 1992–; chm St Albans Diocesan Bd of Patronage 1989–2000, hon canon of the Cathedral and Abbey Church of St Albans 2000–; *Recreations* shooting, travel; *Style*— His Hon Colin Colston, QC; ✉ The Crown Court, Bricket Road, St Albans, Hertfordshire AL1 3JW

COLT, Sir Edward William Dutton; 10 Bt (E 1694), of St James's-in-the-Fields Liberty of Westminster, Middlesex; s of Major John Rochfort Colt, N Staffs Regt (d 1944), half-bro of 9 Bt; suc unc Sir Henry Archer Colt, 9 Bt, DSO, MC (d 1951); *b* 22 September 1936; *Educ* Stoke House Seaford, Douai Sch, UCL (MB); *m* 1, 1966 (m dis 1972), Jane Caroline, da of James Histed Lewis; m 2, 1979, Suzanne Nelson, *née* Knickerbocker; 1 da (Angela Cecily b 1979), 1 s (Tristan Charles Edward b 1983 d 19 May 1992); *Heir* none; *Career* attending physician St Luke's Hosp New York, assoc clinical prof of med Columbia Univ; FACP, FRCP; *Style*— Sir Edward Colt, Bt; ✉ 444 Central Park West, Apt 5F, New York, NY 10025, USA

COLTART, Dr (Douglas) John; s of Frank Joseph John Coltart (d 1974), of Blandford, Dorset, and Hilda Kate, *née* Moore; *b* 7 October 1943; *Educ* Hardye's Sch Dorchester, Bart's Med Sch London (MD); *m* 7 May 1977 (m dis 2004), Linda Maitland, da of Stuart Douglas Luxon, of Riversdale, Bucks; 1 s (Rupert b 4 July 1978), 3 da (Cordelia b 7 Feb 1980, Clementine b 23 Sept 1982, Christianna b 19 June 1991); *Career* conslt physician and cardiologist Royal Masonic Hosp London 1974, conslt physician to St Luke's Hosp for The Clergy 1975 and St Dunstan's Hosp for the Blind 1980; currently: conslt physician and cardiologist Guy's and St Thomas' Hosps London, conslt cardiologist King Edward VII Hosp, clinical dir of cardiac servs Guy's and St Thomas' Hosp, conslt physician to Met Police, civilian conslt in cardiology to the Army; visiting prof: univs in Middle East and Far East, Stanford Univ USA; author of chapters in textbooks of med and over 250 scientific pubns; pres Cardiology Section RSM, sec Br Cardiac Soc, vice-pres Postgrad Fedn, memb Exec Bds Br Heart Fndn Coronary Prevention Gp; memb: Br Cardiac Soc, Med Defence Union; Buckston Browne Prize Harveian Soc; Liveryman Worshipful Soc of Apothecaries, Freeman City of London; FRCP, FACC, FESC; *Books* Cardio-vascular Pharmacology (textbook); *Recreations* athletics, tennis, keep fit; *Style*— Dr John Coltart; ✉ 47 Weymouth Street, London W1G 8NE (tel 020 74865787, fax 020 7486 5470, e-mail drcoltart@btconnect.com)

COLTART, His Hon Judge Simon Stewart; s of Gilbert McCallum Coltart, of Lindfield, W Sussex, and Mary Louise, *née* Kemp; *b* 3 September 1946; *Educ* Epsom Coll, Univ of Leeds (LLB); *m* 8 March 1973, Sarah Victoria, da of John Claude Birts; 3 s (Mark Cresswell, Edward John (twins) b 23 Nov 1974, William James b 3 June 1978); *Career* called to the Bar Lincoln's Inn (Eastham Sch) 1969; jr SE Circuit Bar Mess 1970–71, jr Sussex Bar Mess 1973–86, recorder SE Circuit Bar Mess 1987–90, recorder 1987–91, circuit judge (SE Circuit) 1991–; memb Parole Bd 1997–2003; govr: Stoke Brunswick Sch 1991–2006 (chm 2002–06), Oundle Sch 2003–; memb Ct of Assts Worshipful Co of Grocers 1991 (Freeman 1975, Liveryman 1984, Master 1999); *Recreations* sailing, golf, fishing shooting; *Clubs* Boodle's, Royal Yacht Sqdn, Bar Yacht, Rye Golf, Sussex; *Style*— His Hon Judge Coltart; ✉ Lewes Combined Court, High Street, Lewes, East Sussex BN7 1YB

COLTON, Prof Christopher Lewis; s of Lewis Henry Colton (d 1983), of Nottingham, and Florence Clarke, *née* Haynes (d 1992); *b* 9 September 1937; *Educ* Worksop Coll, St Thomas' Hosp Med Sch (MB BS); *m* 1, 16 Feb 1960 (m dis 1980), Verena Hilary, da of Anthony David Hunt (d 1980), of Chichester; 3 s (Mark Anthony b 1 Aug 1960, Carl Andrew b 5 July 1962, Douglas John b 14 Sept 1963), 1 da (Samantha Mary b 15 Dec 1964); m 2, 2 Dec 1980, Josephine Mary, da of Joseph Peacock, of Barnsley, S Yorks; *Career* Hon Lt-Col Nigerian Armed Forces Med Servs 1968; lectr in orthopaedic surgery Inst of Orthopaedics Univ of London 1970–73, sr surgical offr Royal Nat Orthopaedic Hosp London 1970–73, prof of trauma and orthopaedic surgery Nottingham Univ Hosp 1973–2001; pres: Br Orthopaedic Assoc 1994–95, AO Foundation 1996–98; LRCP, FRCS 1963, FBOA 1973, FRCSEd 1979; *Books* Orthopaedics (with Hughes and Benson, 1987), Frontiers in Fracture Management (with Bunker and Webb, 1988), Atlas of Orthopaedic Surgical Approaches (with Hall, 1991), AO/ASIF Instrumentation - A Technical Handbook (with Texhammer, 1993); *Recreations* running, scuba diving, computer graphics, public speaking; *Style*— Prof Christopher Colton; ✉ Post Box Cottage, Farmington, Cheltenham GL54 3ND (tel 01451 861553)

COLTON, Mary Winifred; da of James Colton (d 1952), and Winifred Alice, *née* Smith (d 1995); *b* 2 January 1933; *Educ* Kingsbury Co Sch, Univ of London (LLB); *Career* called to the Bar Middle Temple 1955, SE Circuit, recorder of the Crown Court 1989–99; *Style*— Miss Mary Colton; ✉ 9 Bedford Row, London WC1R 4AZ (tel 020 7489 2727, fax 020 7489 2828, e-mail clerks@9bedfordrow.co.uk)

COLTRANE, Robbie; OBE (2006); s of Dr Ian Baxter McMillan (d 1969), of Rutherglen, Glasgow, and Jean Ross, *née* Howie; *b* 31 March 1950; *Educ* Trinity Coll Glenalmond, Glasgow Sch of Art (Dip Drawing and Painting); *Children* 1 s, 1 da; *Career* actor; BAFTA Best Actor nomination for Tutti Frutti 1987, Evening Standard Peter Sellers Award for contribution to Br film comedy 1990; involved with: Lab Pty, Amnesty, Greenpeace, Friends of the Earth, CND; hon pres Heriot-Watt Univ; *Theatre* toured univs with the San Quentin Theatre Workshop 1974–75, John Byrne's Slab Boys and Threads (Traverse Theatre Edinburgh) 1975–79, Snobs and Yobs (Edinburgh Festival) 1980, Your Obedient Servant (one man show on Dr Samuel Johnson, Lyric Hammersmith) 1987, Mistero Buffo 1990; *Television* incl: Alfresco (2 series), A Kick Up the Eighties, The Lenny Henry Show, The Comic Strip Presents (various programmes), Laugh I Nearly Paid My Licence Fee, The Young Ones (several guest roles), Tutti Frutti (lead role), Blackadder III (guest role) and Blackadder Xmas Special, Robbie Coltrane Special, GLC and S Atlantic Raiders (Comic Strip Presents), Mistero Buffo 1990, Alive and Kicking 1991, Coltrane in a Cadillac (ITV) 1993, Cracker (Granada 1993–95, winner Broadcast Press Guild Best Actor Award 1994, BAFTA Best TV Actor Award 1994, 1995 and 1996, RTS Best Male Performance Award 1994, Cable Ace USA Award for Best Actor 1995), Silver Nymph (Best Performance TV Series, Monte Carlo 1994, FIPA Award for Best Actor Nice 1994), The Ebb Tide 1997, Coltrane's Planes and Automobiles 1997, Alice in Wonderland, The Plan Man 2002, Cracker (special episode) 2005; co-writer (with Morag Fullarton) and dir Jealousy (short film for BBC2); *Film* incl: Scrubbers 1982, The Supergrass (Comic Strip feature film) 1984, Defence of the Realm 1985, Revolution 1985, Caravaggio 1985, Absolute Beginners 1985, Mona Lisa 1985, Eat the Rich 1987, The Fruit Machine 1987, Danny Champion of the World 1988, Henry V (as Falstaff) 1988, Let It Ride 1988, Nuns on the Run 1989, Perfectly Normal 1989, The Pope Must Die 1990, Oh What a Night 1991, Huck Finn 1992, Goldeneye 1995, Buddy 1996, Montana 1997, Frogs For Snakes 1997, Message in a Bottle 1998, The World is Not Enough 1999, On the Nose 2000, From Hell 2000, Harry Potter and the Philosopher's Stone 2001, Harry Potter and the Chamber of Secrets 2002, Harry Potter and the Prisoner of Azkaban 2004, Ocean's Twelve 2005, Harry Potter and the Goblet of Fire 2005, Stormbreaker 2005, Provoked 2005, Harry Potter and the Order of the Phoenix 2006, The Brothers Bloom 2007; *Recreations* vintage cars, painting, sailing, clubs, playing piano; *Clubs* Groucho, Colony Room, Moscow, Glasgow Arts, Soho House; *Style*— Robbie Coltrane, Esq, OBE; ✉ c/o Caroline Dawson Associates, 125 Gloucester Road, London SW7 4TE (tel 020 7373 3323, fax 020 7373 1110)

COLVILL, Robert; *Career* dir Samuel Montagu & Co 1977–79 (joined 1968), vice-pres Chemical Bank 1979–85; Marks and Spencer plc: md Marks and Spencer Financial Services 1985, dir financial activities 1990, fin dir 1993–2002; non-exec dir: Witan Investment Company 1994–, Eldridge Pope and Co plc 2002–04; chm Money Advice Tst 1995–2004, tstee and treas RNLI 2006–; FCIS; *Style*— Robert Colvill, Esq

COLVILLE OF CULROSS, 4 Viscount (UK 1902); John Mark Alexander Colville; QC (1978); also 14 Lord Colville of Culross (S precedency 1609) and 4 Baron Colville of Culross (UK 1885); s of 3 Viscount (k on active service 1945); 1 cous of Lord Carrington and 1 cous once removed of late Sir John Colville; *b* 19 July 1933; *Educ* Rugby, New Coll Oxford (MA, hon fell 1997); *m* 1, 4 Oct 1958 (m dis 1973), Mary Elizabeth, da of Col Mostyn Hird Wheeler Webb-Bowen, RM; 4 s; m 2, 1974, Margaret Birgitta, LLB, JP (Inner London), barr 1985, da of Maj-Gen Cyril Henry Norton, CB, CBE, DSO, and former w of 2 Viscount Davidson; 1 s; *Heir* s, Master of Colville; *Career* sits as elected cross-bench Peer in Lords; Lt Grenadier Gds (Reserve); called to the Bar Lincoln's Inn (bencher 1986); recorder 1990–93, circuit judge (SE Circuit) 1993–99; min of state Home Office 1972–74, UK rep UN Human Rights Cmmn 1980–83, special rapporteur on Guatemala 1983–87; exec dir Br Electric Traction Co 1981–84 (and cos in gp 1968–84), dir Securities and Future Authy until 1993; chm: Mental Health Act Cmmn 1983–1987, Alcohol Educn and

C

Res Cncl 1984–90, Parole Bd for England and Wales 1988–92, House of Lords Select Ctee on Religious Offences 2002–03; memb UN Human Rights Ctee 1995–2000, asst surveillance cmmr 2001–; Queen's Body Guard for Scotland (Royal Co of Archers); Hon DCL UEA 1998; *Style*— His Hon The Viscount Colville of Culross, QC; ✉ The Manor House, West Lexham, King's Lynn, Norfolk PE32 2QN

COLVIN, Andrew James; s of Gilbert Russell Colvin, OBE, and Dr Beatrice Colvin; *b* 28 April 1947; *Educ* LLM; *m* 1971, Helen Mary, *née* Ryan; 3 da (Clare *b* June 1975, Fiona *b* March 1979, Sarah *b* March 1982), 1 s (Simon *b* May 1977); *Career* admitted as slr 1975; articled clerk then asst town clerk London Borough of Ealing 1971–82, dep town clerk and borough slr Royal Borough of Kensington and Chelsea 1982–89, the Comptroller and City Slr The Corp of London 1989–; Vice-Chamberlain of London; pres City of London Arizona Educnl Tst Inc; advsr: LBA 1985, AMA 1990, ALG 1996; govr: St Gregory's RC Sch 1989–92, Cardinal Wiseman RC Sch 1992–98; Freeman City of London 1989; *Recreations* sailing, cycling, music; *Style*— Andrew Colvin, Esq; ✉ The Comptroller and City Solicitor, The Corporation of London, PO Box 270, Guildhall, London EC2P 2EJ (tel 020 7606 3030 ext 1660)

COLVIN, Dr Brian Trevor; s of Clifford James Leslie Colvin (d 1990), of Sevenoaks, and Ivy Emmeline, *née* Goodchild (d 1996); *b* 17 January 1946; *Educ* Sevenoaks Sch, Clare Coll Cambridge (MA, MB BChir), London Hosp Med Coll; *m* 21 Aug 1971, Kathryn Frances, former HM ambass to The Holy See, da of Ernest Osborne (d 1966); *Career* sr lectr in haematology and conslt haematologist: St Peter's Hosp Gp and Inst of Urology 1977–86, Barts and the London NHS Tst; dir of postgrad med and dental educn Royal Hosps Tst 1996–99, dean Queen Mary's Sch of Medicine and Dentistry 1998–; dir Clinical Pathology Accreditation Ltd 1998–2004; memb: Standing Ctee of Membs RCP 1973–77, Ctee Br Soc for Haematology 1983–86, Med Advsy Ctee The Haemophilia Soc 1993–; chm: Haemostasis and Thrombosis Sub-Ctee BCSH 1991–94, Steering Ctee UK Nat External Quality Assurance Scheme (NEQAS) in Blood Coagulation 1992–96 and 2005–, UK Haemophilia Centre Dirs Orgn 1993–96, Panel of Examiners in Haematology RCPath 1994–99, Nat Quality Assurance Advsy Panel in Haematology 1996–98, Ethics Ctee RCPath 2004–; pres Cncl Pathology Section RSM 1996–98; Liveryman Worshipful Soc of Apothecaries; memb BMA; FRCPath 1988 (MRCPath 1976), FRCP 1990 (MRCP 1972), FRSM 1989; *Publications* author of various papers, articles and contrib to books incl Haematology Pocket Consultant (with A C Newland, 1988); *Recreations* foreign travel, opera, cricket; *Clubs* MCC; *Style*— Dr Brian Colvin; ✉ Department of Haematology, Royal London Hospital, Whitechapel Road, London E1 1BB (tel 020 7377 7455, fax 020 7377 7016, e-mail b.t.colvin@qmul.ac.uk)

COLVIN, Prof Calum Munro; OBE (2001); s of Dr David Colvin, CBE, of Edinburgh, and Elma; *b* 26 October 1961, Glasgow; *Educ* North Berwick HS, Duncan of Jordanstone Coll of Art Dundee (diploma in sculpture), RCA London (MA); *m* 11 Aug 1988, S J Colvin (*née* Moore); 1 da (Heather *b* 1992), 2 s (Robbie David Nichol *b* 1993, Finlay *b* 1998); *Career* artist; prof of fine art photography Univ of Dundee 2001; exhibited widely incl Orkney, LA and Ecuador; work in collections incl: Met MOMA NY, Museum of Fine Art Houston TX, V&A, Scottish Nat Portrait Gallery Edinburgh, Gallery of Modern Art Glasgow; awards incl: Photographers Gallery Brandt Award 1987, RPS gold medal 1989, 13th Higashikawa Overseas Photographer Prize 1997, Leverhulme scholarship 2000, Creative Scotland Award 2000, Leverhulme Tst Research Fellowship 2000, Carnegie Tst Award 2002, Critics Award for Theatre in Scotland (set design) 2003; *Publications* Constructed Narratives (1986), Calum Colvin (1990), The Seven Deadly Sins & the Four Last Things (1993), Sacred & Profane (1998), Ossian · Fragments of Ancient Poetry (2002); *Style*— Prof Calum Colvin, OBE; ✉ c/o Open Eye Gallery, 34 Abercromby Place, Edinburgh EH3 6QE (tel 0131 557 1020, mobile 07603 274694, website www.calumcolvin.com)

COLVIN, Marie Catherine; da of William Colvin, of Oyster Bay, NY, and Rosemarie Colvin; *Educ* Yale Univ (BA); *Career* Paris bureau chief UPI 1984–85; Sunday Times: Middle East corr 1986–95, foreign affrs corr 1995–; patron: Reporters Sans Frontieres, Child Hope; *Awards* Journalist of the Year Foreign Corr's Assoc 2000, Courage in Journalism USA 2000, Foreign Corr of the Year UK Press Awards 2001, Women of the Year UK 2002; *Recreations* sailing; *Clubs* Groucho; *Style*— Ms Marie Colvin; ✉ The Sunday Times, 1 Pennington Street, London E1 9XW (tel 020 7782 5692, fax 020 7782 5050)

COLWYN, 3 Baron (UK 1917); Sir (Ian) Anthony Hamilton-Smith; 3 Bt (UK 1912), CBE (1989); s of 2 Baron Colwyn (d 1966); *b* 1 January 1942; *Educ* Cheltenham Coll, Univ of London (BDS, LDS, RCS); *m* 1, 1964 (m dis 1977), Sonia Jane, er da of Peter Henry Geoffrey Morgan; 1 da (Hon Jacqueline *b* 5 March 1967), 1 s (Hon Craig Peter *b* 13 Oct 1968); *m* 2, 1977, Nicola Jeanne, da of Arthur Tyers; 2 da (Hon Kirsten *b* 17 Jan 1981, Hon Tanya *b* 14 Jan 1983); *Heir* s, Hon Craig Hamilton-Smith; *Career* dental surgeon 1966–; chm: Dental Protection Ltd 1995–2001, Project Hope 1997–2001, Action against Hunger 2000–01; elected Conservative in House of Lords, pres Parly All-Pty Gp on Alternative and Complementary Medicine 1989–; chm Offices Sub-Ctee on refreshment 1997–2002, chm Refreshment Select Ctee 2002–04, memb Select Ctee on EU Sub-Ctee G 2004–; memb Cncl Medical Protection Soc, memb Science and Technol Sub-Ctee III (complementary medicine 2000–01); pres: Natural Medicines Soc 1988–2005, Arterial Health Fndn 1993–2004, Soc for Advancement of Anaesthesia in Dentistry 1995–97; patron: Blackie Fndn, Res Cncl for Complementary Medicine; former patron Eastman Research Inst; musician, bandleader; FRSM; *Style*— The Rt Hon the Lord Colwyn, CBE; ✉ House of Lords, London SW1A 0PW (tel 020 7219 3000)

COLWYN-THOMAS, Anthony (Tony); s of Bertie Colwyn-Thomas, of Bridgend, and Brenda, *née* Kendrick; *b* 5 October 1956; *Educ* Ogmore GS, Univ of Southampton (BSc); *m* 1982, Janet, da of James Harries; 2 s (Owain *b* 19 Dec 1986, Trystan *b* 1 July 1988); *Career* qualified as chartered accountant KPMG 1978–82, internal auditor and fin accountant Bass plc 1982–85, gp fin accountant Trusthouse Forte plc 1985–87, co accountant Hamells (subsid of C & A) 1987–88, fin controller/co sec ACL (subsid of Standard Chartered Bank plc) 1988–93, mangr Business Planning and Risk Mgmnt Halifax Mortgage Services Ltd 1993–96, fin control conslt Pearl Assurance plc 1997, gp fin mangr HFC Bank plc (subsid of HSBC plc) 1998–2003, md Cetelem (UK) Ltd (subsid of BNP Paribas) 2004– (fin dir 2003–04); former chm Cardiff and Dist Soc of Chartered Accountants; former memb: Cncl ICAEW, Ctee S Wales Dist Soc of Chartered Accountants, Br Jr Chamber Cardiff; FCA 1991 (ACA 1981); *Recreations* local history, football, gardening, bringing up two sons; *Style*— Tony Colwyn-Thomas, Esq; ✉ Cetelem (UK) Ltd, Leo House, Station Approach, Wallington, Surrey SM6 0XX (tel 020 8254 7174)

COMBER, Darren Edwin; s of Gary Edwin Comber, of Maidstone, Kent, and Maree Rosalie, *née* Hickmott; *b* 14 August 1966; *Educ* W Kent Coll of FE, Univ of Plymouth (BA), UCL (DipArch); *m* 1996, Anja, *née* Hemstra; 3 s (Tias *b* 4 Oct 2000, Kaspar, Nicklaus (twins) *b* 23 Dec 2002); *Career* architect; joined Scott Brownrigg 1995 (appointed main bd dir 2002); Camden Soc of Architects Design Excellence Award, work commended Civic Tst Awards 2000; former violinist Maidstone Youth Orch; ARB 1992, RIBA 1992; *Recreations* skiing, golf, motorsport; *Clubs* Reform; *Style*— Darren Comber, Esq; ✉ Scott Brownrigg, Tower House, 10 Southampton Street, London WC2E 7HA

COMFORT, Nicholas Alfred Fenner; s of Dr Alex Comfort (d 2000), of Cranbrook, Kent, and Ruth Muriel, *née* Harris (d 2000); *b* 4 August 1946; *Educ* Highgate Sch, Trinity Coll Cambridge (exhibitioner, MA); *m* 1, 1970 (m dis 1988), Deborah Elliott; 1 da (Caroline Sarah *b* 1 June 1974), 1 s (John Miles *b* 23 July 1977); *m* 2, 1990 (sep), Corinne Reed; 1

s (Alexander Thomas Reed *b* 18 Aug 1994); *Career* municipal corr Morning Telegraph Sheffield 1968–74; Daily Telegraph: Midlands corr 1974–75, Washington bureau 1976–78, political staff writer 1978–87, ldr writer 1987–89; political ed Independent on Sunday 1989–90, political ed The European 1990–91, political ed Daily Record 1992–95, obiturist Daily Telegraph 1995–, conslt Politics International 1996–97, conslt European presentation DTI 2000–01, special advsr to sec of state for Scotland 2001–02, govt affrs advsr QinetiQ plc 2003–06; memb: Railway Study Assoc, Omnibus Soc; FRGS; *Publications* The Tunnel: The Channel and Beyond (co-author, 1987), Brewer's Politics: A Phrase and Fable Dictionary (1993), The Lost City of Dunwich (1994), The Mid-Suffolk Light Railway (1998), Politico's Guide to How to Handle the Media (2003), The Politics Book (2005), The Channel Tunnel and its High-Speed Links (2006); *Recreations* music, cricket; *Clubs* Athenaeum, Essex CCC; *Style*— Nicholas Comfort, Esq; ✉ Flat 2, 39 Egerton Gardens, London SW3 2DD (tel 07979 958753, e-mail nc65464@yahoo.com)

COMINS, David; s of Jack Comins (d 2002), of Scarborough, N Yorks, and (Mabel) Marjorie, *née* Rowbotham (d 1973); *b* 1 March 1948; *Educ* Scarborough HS for Boys (head boy, rugby capt), Downing Coll Cambridge (MA), Cambridge Inst (PGCE); *m* 22 July 1972, (Christine) Anne, da of Thomas Brian Speak (d 2003); 2 da (Laura *b* 4 Sept 1976, Amy *b* 20 April 1980), 1 s (Robert *b* 3 June 1978); *Career* asst maths teacher: Mill Hill Sch 1971–75, Strathallan Sch 1975–76; Glenalmond Coll: asst maths teacher 1976–80, head of maths 1980–85, dir of studies 1985–89; dep head Queen's Coll Taunton 1989–94 (head of maths 1991–94), rector Glasgow Acad 1994–2005; chm HMC Scottish Div 2001, memb Gen Teaching Cncl of Scotland 1974, memb HMC 1994; memb Tayside Expedition Panel (Duke of Edinburgh's Award); Winston Churchill fell 1981 (for expedition to Peruvian Andes); *Recreations* mountaineering, crosswords, ballet; *Clubs* East India, Alpine; *Style*— David Comins, Esq; ✉ Flat 6, Block 8, Kirklee Gate, Glasgow G12 0SZ (e-mail d.comins@hotmail.co.uk)

COMPSTON, Prof (David) Alastair Standish; s of Dr Nigel Dean Compston, CBE, MD, FRCP (d 1986), and Diana Mary, *née* Standish; *b* 23 January 1948; *Educ* Rugby, Middx Hosp Med Sch London (MB BS, PhD); *m* 21 July 1973, Juliet Elizabeth, da of Sir Denys Page (d 1978); 1 da (Polly Clare *b* 5 Nov 1981); *Career* various hosp appts 1971–82, conslt neurologist Univ Hosp of Wales Cardiff 1982–85; prof of neurology: Univ of Wales Coll of Med Cardiff 1987–88, Univ of Cambridge 1989–; professorial fell Jesus Coll Cambridge 1990–, hon conslt neurologist Addenbrooke's Hosp Cambridge 1989–, head Dept of Clinical Neurosciences 2004–; chm MRC Cambridge Centre for Brain Repair 1990–2000; ed: Jl of Neurology 1989–99, Brain 2004–; FRCP 1986, FRSA 1997, FMedSci 1998, FIBiol 2000; *Publications* McAlpine's Multiple Sclerosis (4 edn 2005); also author of articles in periodicals on human and experimental demyelinating disease; *Recreations* being outside, antiquarian books; *Clubs* Garrick; *Style*— Prof Alastair Compston; ✉ Pembroke House, Mill Lane, Linton, Cambridge CB1 6JY (tel 01223 893414); University of Cambridge Neurology Unit, Level 5, Addenbrooke's Hospital, Hills Road, Cambridge CB2 2QQ (tel 01223 217091, fax 01223 336941, e-mail alastair.compston@medschl.cam.ac.uk)

COMPSTON, His Hon Judge Christopher Dean; s of Vice Adm Sir Peter Maxwell Compston, KCB (d 2000), and Valerie Marjorie, *née* Bocquet; *b* 5 May 1940; *Educ* Epsom Coll, Magdalen Coll Oxford (MA); *m* 1, Bronwen, da of Martin Henniker Gotley, of Derwenlas, Powys; 2 s (Harry *b* 1969 (decd), Joshua Richard *b* 1970 (decd)), 1 da (Emily *b* 1972); *m* 2, Caroline Philippa, da of Paul Odgers, of Haddenham, Bucks; 1 da (Harriet *b* 1985), 2 s (Rupert *b* 1987, Benjamin *b* 1992); *Career* called to the Bar Middle Temple 1965 (bencher 2006); recorder of the Crown Court 1982–86, circuit judge (SE Circuit) 1986–; memb Senate Inns of Court 1983–86; *Recreations* the arts, writing, gardening; *Clubs* Seaview Yacht; *Style*— His Hon Judge Compston; ✉ Royal Courts of Justice, Strand, London WC2A 2LL

COMPSTON, David; CBE (1999); s of Denis Compston, of Sandside, Cumbria, and Nancy Morley; *b* 21 October 1938; *Educ* Mill Hill Sch, Manchester Coll of Science and Technol; *m* 1962, Helga Ann, da of Richard Postlethwaite; 1 s (James Richard *b* 4 June 1965); *Career* chm: Allott & Lomax 1989–98, Allott & Lomax (Holdings) Ltd 1989–98, Allott & Lomax (Hong Kong) Ltd 1989–98, Fairbairn Services Ltd 1989–98, Ceramic Industrial Projects Ltd 1989–98, Allott Projects Ltd 1989–98, INKOPLAN GmbH 1990–98, Manchester TEC 1992–99 (estab Business Link Manchester 1994), Cumbria Inward Investment Agency 2000–03, City of Salford Standards Ctee 2000–04; dir: Trafford Park Mfrg Inst 1994–97, Marketing Manchester 1996–98, TEC Nat Cncl Ltd 1997–99, Manchester Investment Devpt Agency Services Ltd 1997–2000, Manchester Commonwealth Games Ltd 1999–2002; memb: Construction Industry Sector Gp NEDO 1990–93, Personnel Standards Vocational Qualifications Lead Body (and its Advsy Forum) 1993–94, TEC Nat Cncl 1996–99 (chm Trg and Educn Policy Ctee 1997–2000), Trg Standards Cncl 1998–2001, Mgmnt Bd Govt Offices in the Regions 1999–2001; chm Cumbria Corp Bd NSPCC Full Stop Campaign 1999–2000; FICE 1973, FREng 1996; *Publications* Design and Construction of Buried Thin Walled Pipes (1978), Rihand Power Station Civil Works - An Indo-British Solution (1986); *Recreations* fly fishing, hill walking; *Clubs* Old Millhillians; *Style*— David G Compston, Esq, CBE, FREng; ✉ The Old Stables, Quinta, Oswestry, Shropshire SY10 7LW (tel 01691 778597)

COMPTON, Prof Richard Guy; s of Joseph Bennett Compton, and Doreen, *née* Broughton; *Educ* Frome GS, Univ of Oxford (BA, DPhil); *Career* lectr in physical chemistry Univ of Liverpool 1981–85; jr res fell The Queen's Coll Oxford 1980–81, lectr in physical chemistry Univ of Oxford 1985–96, titular prof of chemistry Univ of Oxford 1996–, fell St John's Coll Oxford 1985–; RSC award in electrochemistry 1994, RSC award in electroanalytical chemistry 1999, Research Medal Worshipful Co of Dyers 1998; Hon Dr Estonian Agric Univ 1998; memb ACS 1995, memb Electrochemical Soc 1997, FRSC 1999; *Books* Electrode Potentials (1996), Foundations of Physical Chemistry (1996), Foundations of Physical Chemistry: Worked Examples (1998); over 500 research papers and articles; *Recreations* watching soccer (Oxford United, Everton), travel; *Style*— Prof Richard Compton; ✉ 17 Blackhall Road, Oxford OX1 3QF (tel 01865 277432); Physical and Theoretical Chemistry Laboratory, South Parks Road, Oxford OX1 3QZ (tel 01865 275413, fax 01865 275410, e-mail compton@ermine.ox.ac.uk)

COMPTON, Robert Edward John (Robin); DL (N Yorks 1981); s of Maj Edward Robert Francis Compton, JP, DL (d 1977; s of Lord Alwyne Compton, DSO, DL, 3 s of 4 Marquess of Northampton), and his 1 w, Sylvia, *née* Farquharson (d 1950); *b* 11 July 1922; *Educ* Eton, Magdalen Coll Oxford; *m* 5 July 1951, (Ursula) Jane, 2 da of Maj Rodolph Kenyon-Slaney, JP, DL, and formerly w of (i) Lt-Col Peter Lindsay, DSO (d 1971), (ii) Sir Max Aitken, 2 Bt, DSO, DFC (d 1985), by whom she had 2 das; 2 s (James Alwyne *b* 30 May 1953, Richard Clephane *b* 18 April 1957); *Career* served WWII with Coldstream Gds 1941–46, military asst to British Ambass Vienna 1945–46; W S Crawford Ltd advtg 1951–54; Time Life International: joined 1954, dir Time Life International Ltd 1958– (chm 1979–90, md 1985–87), advtg dir Time UK 1958–62; chm CXL UK Ltd 1971–73; bd dir: Extel Corporation Chicago 1973–80, Transtel Communications Ltd 1974–83; pres Highline Financial Services SA 1985–94, vice-chm Yorks Ctee Nat Tst 1970–85; former pres: N of England Horticultural Soc 1984–86, Northern Horticultural Soc 1985–96, Yorks Agric Soc 1995–96; pres Nat Cncl for Conservation of Plants and Gardens 1994– (chm 1988–94), vice-pres RHS 1995 (VMH 1993), chm Castle Howard Arboretum Tst 1997–2002; High Sheriff North Yorkshire 1977; FInstD 1951–91; *Recreations* gardening, music; *Clubs* White's; *Style*— Robin Compton, Esq, DL; ✉ Newby Hall Estate Office,

Ripon, North Yorkshire HG4 5AE (tel 01423 322583, website www.newbyhall.com); The Manor House, Marton-le-Moor, Ripon, North Yorkshire HG4 5AT

COMPTON MILLER, Richard Maurice MacEwen; s of Sir John Compton Miller (d 1992), of Crown Office Row, London, and Mary Baird-Smith (d 1998), of Wheathampstead, Herts; *b* 18 March 1945, Brocket Hall, Hertfordshire; *Educ* Westminster, New Coll Oxford (MA, ed Cherwell); *Career* called to the Bar Inner Temple 1969; co-fndr Advise 1968, trainee property developer Star (GB) Hldgs 1970, journalist Daily Express, Daily Mail, Sunday Times, Harper's & Queen and Evening Standard 1972–78, diary writer William Hickey column Daily Express 1977, ed In Town column Evening News and Evening Standard 1978–82, freelance feature writer (incl ed People column Daily Express) 1982–85, ed William Hickey column, TV critic and sr feature writer Daily Express 1985–95, freelance feature writer Daily Mail, Daily Express, Independent and Sunday Express 1995–, art critic London Magazine 1998–2003, ed property column Evening Standard 2000–; ed Who's Really Who 1983–; chm and co-fndr Leonard Tst 1996–, memb Ctee Professional Hair and Beauty Benevolent 1996–, memb Ctee New Coll Soc 2006–; *Recreations* partying, dabbling with property, collecting antiques, listening to early rock'n'roll; *Clubs* Biographers'; *Style*— Richard Compton Miller, Esq; ✉ c/o Andrew Lownie Literary Agency, 36 Great Smith Street, London SW1P 3BU

COMYNS, District Judge Jacqueline Roberta; da of late Jack Fisher, and late Belle, *née* Offenbach (d 1994); *b* 27 April 1943; *Educ* Hendon Co GS, LSE (LLB); *m* 29 Aug 1963, Dr Malcolm John Comyns, s of Louis Comyns (d 1962); 1 s (David b 13 Aug 1975); *Career* called to the Bar Inner Temple 1969, in practice SE Circuit, district judge (Magistrates' Court) 1982–, recorder of the Crown Court 1991–2002; *Recreations* travel, theatre, swimming; *Style*— District Judge Comyns; ✉ Thames Magistrates Court, Bow Road, London E3 4DJ (tel 020 8271 1202)

CONANT, Sir John Ernest Michael; 2 Bt (UK 1954), of Lyndon, Co Rutland; s of Sir Roger John Edward Conant, 1 Bt, CVO (d 1973); *b* 24 April 1923; *Educ* Eton, Corpus Christi Coll Cambridge; *m* 1, 16 Sept 1950, Periwinkle Elizabeth (d 1985), er da of late Dudley Thorp, of Brothers House, Kimbolton, Hunts; 2 da (Fiona Elizabeth (Mrs Jonathan P N Driver) b 1955, Melanie Lucinda (Mrs Richard A Firmston-Williams) b 1961), 2 s ((Simon) Edward Christopher b 1958, William John Nathaniel b 1970) (and 1 s decd); m 2, 11 July 1992, Mrs (Mary) Clare Attwater, yr da of William E Madden, of Petersfield, Hants; *Heir* s, Edward Conant; *Career* farmer, High Sheriff Rutland 1960; *Style*— Sir John Conant, Bt; ✉ Periwinkle Cottage, Lyndon, Oakham, Rutland LE15 8TU (tel 01572 737275)

CONDON, Baron (Life Peer UK 2001), of Langton Green in the County of Kent; Sir Paul Condon; kt (1994), QPM (1989); *Educ* St Peter's Coll Oxford (MA); *m*; 1 da, 2 s; *Career* Metropolitan Police: joined 1967, served various stations in East End 1967–72, St Peter's Coll Oxford 1972–75, uniformed Inspr West End 1975–78, Chief Inspr Community Relations Branch 1978–81, Supt Bethnal Green 1981–82, staff offr to Sir David McNee as Cmmr 1982–84, Sr Cmd Course Police Staff Coll 1984; Asst Chief Constable Kent Constabulary 1984–87, Dep Asst Cmmr i/c W London then Asst Cmmr i/c personnel and trg Metropolitan Police 1987–89, Chief Constable Kent 1989–93, Cmmr Metropolitan Police 1993–2000; dir Int Cricket Cncl Anti-Corruption Unit 2000–; non-exec dir Securicor plc 2000–; hon fell St Peter's Coll Oxford; CIMgt 1992, FRSA 1992; *Recreations* swimming, horse riding, reading; *Style*— The Rt Hon the Lord Condon, QPM

CONGDON, Prof Timothy George (Tim); CBE (1997); s of Douglas George Congdon, of Colchester, Essex, and Olive Emma, *née* Good; *b* 28 April 1951; *Educ* Colchester Royal GS, St John's Coll Oxford (open scholar, BA), Nuffield Coll Oxford; *m* 18 June 1988, Dorianne, da of Percy Preston-Lowe; 1 da (Venetia Andrea Dorianne b 30 July 1991); *Career* economics staff The Times 1973–76, chief economist L Messel & Co 1976–87 (ptnr 1980–86), chief UK economist Shearson Lehman 1987–88; Lombard Street Research: md 1989–2001, chief economist 2001–05; non-exec chm SBW Insurance Research 1994–97; non-exec dir: Invesco Recovery Tst 1991–, Highland Timber 1997–2005; memb HM Treasy Panel of Ind Forecasters 1992–97; hon prof Cardiff Business Sch 1990–2006, visiting prof City Univ Business Sch 1997–2006, visiting research fell LSE 2005–; hon sec Political Economy Club; MSI, FRSA 1990, Hon FIA 2002; *Books* Monetarism: Essay in Definition (1978), Monetary Control in Britain (1982), The Debt Threat (1988), Monetarism Lost (1989), Reflections on Monetarism (1992), Money and Asset Prices in Boom and Bust (2005), Keynes, the Keynesians and Monetarism (2007); *Recreations* opera, chess, reading; *Clubs* RAC; *Style*— Prof Tim Congdon, CBE; ✉ Huntley Manor, Huntley, Gloucestershire GL19 3HQ

CONGLETON, 8 Baron (UK 1841); Sir Christopher Patrick Parnell; 11 Bt (I 1766); 3 s of 6 Baron Congleton (d 1932), and Hon Edith Mary Palmer Howard, MBE, da of late Baroness Strathcona and Mount Royal (in her own right) and R J B Howard; suc bro 1967; *b* 11 March 1930; *Educ* Eton, New Coll Oxford (MA); *m* 19 Nov 1955, Anna Hedvig, er da of Gustav Adolf Sommerfelt, of Oslo; 2 s, 3 da; *Heir* s, Hon John Parnell; *Career* Salisbury and Wilton RDC 1964–74 (chm 1971), chm Salisbury and S Wilts Museum 1972–77, memb Advsy Bd for Redundant Churches 1981–87; pres: Br Ski Fedn 1976–81, Ski Club of GB 1991–97; tstee: Sandroyd Sch Tst 1972–92 (chm 1980–84), Wessex Med Tst 1984–90 (chm 1997–2000), Univ of Southampton Devpt Tst 1986–95; Hon LLD Univ of Southampton 1990; *Recreations* music, fishing; *Style*— The Lord Congleton; ✉ West End Lodge, Ebbesbourne Wake, Salisbury, Wiltshire SP5 5JR

CONINGSBY, His Hon Thomas Arthur Charles; QC (1986); s of Francis Charles Coningsby, of Chipstead, Surrey, and Eilleen Rowena, *née* Monson; *b* 21 April 1933; *Educ* Epsom Coll, Queens' Coll Cambridge (MA); *m* 8 Aug 1959, Elaine Mary, da of Edwin Stanley Treacher (d 1983), of Sussex; 2 s (Andrew b 1960, James b 1964), 3 da (Sara b 1962, Elizabeth, Katharine (twins) b 1963); *Career* Nat Serv RA 1951–53, Capt City of London Field Regt (TA) and Aerial Photographic Interpretation (Intelligence Corps) 1953–67; called to the Bar Gray's Inn 1957; recorder of the Crown Court 1986–92, dep High Court judge (Family Div) 1989–2006 (also Queen's Bench Div 1996–2006), circuit judge (SE Circuit) 1992–2006, designated civil judge (Croydon Gp) 1999–2006; head of barrs' chambers 3 Dr Johnson's Bldgs Temple 1988–92; chllr Dio of York 1977–2006, vicar gen Province of York 1980–, chllr Dio of Peterborough 1989–2006; memb: Gen Synod of C of E 1970–, Legal Advsy Cmmn of Gen Synod 1976–; chm Chipstead Village Preservation Soc 1983–88, memb Matrimonial Causes Rule Ctee 1985–89, chm Family Law Bar Assoc 1988–90 (sec 1986–88); memb: Gen Cncl of the Bar 1988–90, Supreme Ct Procedure Ctee 1988–92; hon treas Bar Lawn Tennis Soc 1969–92; pres Chipstead Tennis Club 1985–2007 (chm 1981–85); *Recreations* lawn tennis; *Clubs* Athenaeum; *Style*— His Hon Thomas Coningsby, QC; ✉ Leyfields, Elmore Road, Chipstead, Surrey CR5 3SG (tel 01737 553304, e-mail tconingsby@btopenworld.com)

CONKLIN, Margery (Margi); da of Theodore E Conklin, of Gardiner, NY, and Susan Meadows Conklin; *b* 31 May 1972, Schenectady, NY; *Educ* Cobleskill Central HS NY, Medill Sch of Journalism Northwestern Univ IL (BSJ); *Partner* Christopher J Yates; *Career* journalist; early career as reporter on local newspapers and prodn asst on local TV USA, reporter The Journal Newcastle upon Tyne 1994–95, features writer rising to features ed Take A Break 1996–1998, features ed then asst ed New Woman 1998–2000, ed Celebrity Looks 2000–01 (shortlisted New Ed of the Year BSME Awards 2001), dep ed Elle 2001–03 (actg ed Jan-April 2002), dep ed InStyle 2003–04, ed New Woman 2004–05, actg ed Wedding 2006–; *Style*— Ms Margi Conklin; ✉ New Woman, Endeavour House, 189 Shaftesbury Avenue, London WC2H 8JG (tel 020 7208 3727, e-mail margi.conklin@emap.com)

CONLAN, John Oliver; s of Eugene J Conlan, of Dublin, Ireland, and Bridgid, *née* Hayes; *b* 13 July 1942; *Educ* Thurles Christian Brothers Sch Ireland; *m* 19 March 1968, Carolyn Sylvia, da of Raymond Ingram, of Luton, Beds; 3 da (Tara Louise b 1972, Amanda Carolyn (Mrs Richard Otley) b 1973, Alison Theresa b 1980); *Career* md: EMI Leisure 1980–81, Trust House Forte Leisure 1981–83; chief exec First Leisure Corporation plc 1988–97 (md 1983–88), chm Urbium plc (formerly Chorion plc) 1997–, chm Barracuda plc 2002–; dir: Blue Green SA, London Irish Holdings; *Recreations* golf; *Style*— John Conlan, Esq; ✉ Urbium plc, Vernon House, 40 Shaftesbury Avenue, London W1V 7DD (tel 020 7434 0030)

CONLON, James; *b* 1950, New York City; *Educ* Juilliard Sch; *Career* conductor; music dir Cincinnati May Festival 1979–, music dir Rotterdam Philharmonic 1983–91, chief conductor Cologne Opera 1989–98, music dir Gürzenich Orchestra Cologne 1989–2002, gen music dir City of Cologne, princ conductor Paris Nat Opera 1996–2004, music dir designate Ravinia Festival Chicago 2004–; worked with orchs incl: NY Philharmonic (debut 1974), Chicago Symphony, Boston Symphony, Philadelphia Orch, Cleveland Orch, Nat Symphony, Berlin Philharmonic, Staatskapelle Dresden, London Philharmonic, LSO, BBC Symphony, Orchestre de Paris, Orchestre National de France, Munich Philharmonic, RSO-Berlin, Orchestre de la Suisse Romande, Orchestra di Santa Cecilia, European Community Youth Orch, Orch of the Kirov Opera, Bayerische Rundfunk Orch; repertoire of over 70 operas and 200 symphonic works incl: Die Zauberflöte (Met Opera debut 1976 over 200 performances), Don Carlos (ROH Covent Garden debut 1979), I Pagliacci (Opéra de Paris debut 1982), La Forza del Destino (Chicago Lyric Opera debut 1988), Oberon (Milano La Scala debut 1992), Der Fliegende Holländer, Pelléas et Mélisande, Lady Macbeth of Mtzensk, Die Entführung aus dem Serail, Semiramide, Don Giovanni, Cosi fan Tutte, Le Nozze di Figaro, Lohengrin, Aida, La Bohème, Boris Godunov, Carmen, Jenufa, Khovanschina, Salomé, Tosca, La Traviata, Il Trovatore, Peter Grimes, Macbeth, Tristan und Isolde, Die Meistersinger, Tannhäuser, Das Rheingold, Die Walkyrie, Siegfried, Götterdämmerung, Parsifal, Wozzeck, Otello, Falstaff, Rigoletto, Luisa Miller, Il Trittico, Turandot, Madame Butterfly, Nabucco, Rosenkavalier, Elektra, Simon Boccanegra, Un Ballo in Maschera, Cavalleria Rusticana; Zemlinsky Prize 1999; Hon Dr Juillard Sch 2004; Commandeur de l'Ordre des Arts et des Lettres (France) 2004 (Officier 1996), Chevalier de la Légion d'Honneur (France) 2001; *Style*— James Conlon, Esq; ✉ c/o ICM Talent, 40 West 57th Street, New York, NY 10019, USA (tel 00 1 212 556 5600)

CONNAGHAN, John Gerard; s of John Connaghan (d 1984), and Mary, *née* Hendry; *b* 2 September 1954; *Educ* St Mungo's Acad, Glasgow Coll of Technol (BA), Univ of Strathclyde (DMS, MBA); *m* 1 Oct 1983, Evelyn Joyce, da of J W B Steven, of Flode, Dornoch; 3 s (Christopher b Oct 1986, James b Dec 1988, Paul b March 1990), 1 da (Ruth b 6 Feb 1994); *Career* various positions at following: Wm Collins & Sons Ltd 1977–79; Charles Letts (Scotland) Ltd Edinburgh 1979–87, Greater Glasgow Health Bd 1987–93; chief exec: Western General Hospitals NHS Tst 1994–99, Fife Acute Hospitals Tst 1999, currently dir of delivery Dept of Health Scottish Exec; dir: Opex Ltd, NWTU Scot Exec, Maggies Cancer Tst; memb bd Clinical Resources and Audit Gp (CRAG); *Recreations* hill walking, cycling, fine wines, golf, reading; *Style*— John Connaghan, Esq; ✉ e-mail jconnaghan@yahoo.com

CONNAL, (Robert) Craig; QC (2002); s of James Brownlee Connal (d 2000), and Jean Elizabeth, *née* Polley; *b* 7 July 1954, Brentwood, Essex; *Educ* Hamilton Acad, Univ of Glasgow (LLB); *m* 29 June 1976, Mary Ferguson, *née* Bowie; 2 da (Lindsay Chalmers b 18 Oct 1981, Gillian Melissa b 13 Nov 1984); *Career* admitted: slr 1977, slr-advocate (civil) 1996, slr-advocate (criminal) 2004, slr England and Wales 2006; ptnr McGrigor Donald 1980– (head of commercial litigation 2002–); memb Cncl Royal Faculty of Procurators in Glasgow 1995–98, memb Scottish Law Cmmn Working Party on Partnership Law 2000–03; author of articles in professional jls and general press; external examiner Univ of Aberdeen 2001–05; memb: Law Soc of Scotland (convenor Higher Rights Course), Law Soc of\england and Wales, Soc of Slrs in Supreme Court, Scottish Law Agents' Soc, R3; NP; *Publications* Stair Memorial Encyclopaedia of Scots Law (contrib, 1986); *Recreations* rugby referee, food and wine, gardens (not gardening); *Clubs* Whitecraigs Rugby; *Style*— R Craig Connal, Esq, QC; ✉ McGrigors, Pacific House, 70 Wellington Street, Glasgow G2 6SB (tel 0141 248 6677, fax 0141 221 5178, e-mail craig.connal@mcgrigors.com)

CONNARTY, Michael; MP; s of late Patrick Connarty, and Elizabeth, *née* Plunkett; *b* 3 September 1947; *Educ* St Patrick's HS Coatbridge, Univ of Stirling (BA(Econ)), Jordanhill Coll of Educn, Univ of Glasgow (DCE); *m* 9 Aug 1969, Margaret Doran; 1 s, 1 da; *Career* teacher of economics at secdy and special needs schs 1976–92, ldr Stirling DC 1980–90 (cncllr 1977–90), memb Lab Pty Scottish Exec Ctee 1981–92; MP (Lab): Falkirk E 1992–2005, Linlithgow and E Falkirk 2005–; PPS to Rt Hon Tom Clarke, CBE, JP, MP as Min of State for Film and Tourism 1997–98; memb: Euro Directives Ctee A (Agriculture, Environment, Health and Safety) 1992–97, Select Ctee on the Parly Cmmr for Administration 1994–97, Information Select Ctee 1997–2001, European Scrutiny Select Ctee 1998– (chm 2006–); memb Bd Parly Office of Sci and Technol 1997–; sec: PLP Science and Technol Ctee 1992–97, Parly Scottish Opera Gp 1996–97, Parly Gp for Haemophilia 2001–06; chair Parly Gp for Peru 2001, sec Offshore Oil and Gas Gp 2002–, sec Nuclear Energy Gp 2006–; memb Standing Ctees on: Bankruptcy (Scotland) Act 1993, Prisoners and Criminal Proceedings Act 1993, Local Govt Etc (Scotland) Act 1994, Children (Scotland) Bill 1995, Crime and Punishment (Scotland) Bill 1996; sec: CWU (Communication Workers Union) Parly Gp 2003–, Parly Gp for Iraqi Kurdistan 2004–; chair Parly Jazz Appreciation Gp 1998–; chm Scottish PLP Gp 1998–99 (chm Economy, Industry & Energy Sub-Ctee 1994–97); exec Labour Middle East Cncl 2001–; task force leader on skills and training in Scotland and Youth & Students Scottish co-ordinator Labour Crime & Drugs Campaign 1995–97; chm: Lab Pty Scottish Local Govt Ctee 1989–91, Stirlingshire Co-operative Pty 1990–92; vice-chm Lab Gp COSLA 1988–90; *Recreations* family, reading, music, hill walking; *Style*— Michael Connarty, Esq, MP; ✉ House of Commons, London SW1A 0AA (tel 020 7219 5071, fax 020 7219 2541, e-mail connartym@parliament.uk, website www.mconnartymp.org.uk)

CONNAUGHTON, Col Richard Michael; s of Thomas Connaughton (d 1981), of Huntingdon, and Joan Florence, *née* Lisher (d 1979); *b* 20 January 1942; *Educ* Duke of York's Royal Military Sch Dover, Univ of Cambridge (MPhil), Lancaster Univ (PhD); *m* 12 June 1971, (Annis Rosemary) Georgina, da of Capt George Frederic Matthew Best, OBE, RN (d 1994), and Rosemary Elizabeth, *née* Brooks, of Dorset; 1 s (Michael b 1972), 1 da (Emma b 1974); *Career* RMA Sandhurst 1960–61, III Co RASC (Guided Weapons) W Germany 1962–64, 28 Co Gurkha Army Serv Corps Hong Kong 1965–67, Jr Ldrs' RCT Taunton 1967–69, 28 Sqdn Gurkha Tport Regt Hong Kong 1969–71 (Adj 1971–73), student Army Staff Coll Camberley 1974, GSO 2 Co-ord MVEE Chertsey 1975–76, cmd 2 Sqdn RCT W Germany 1977–79, 2 i/c Logistic Support Gp Regt Aldershot 1979–81, cmd 1 Armd Div Tport Regt RCT W Germany 1982–84, memb Directing Staff Army Staff Coll Camberley and Australian Army Cmd and Staff Coll Fort Queenscliff Victoria 1984–86, Col Tport HQ BAOR W Germany 1987–89; def fellowship St John's Coll Cambridge 1989–90, Colonel Defence Studies 1990–92, exec dir National & International Consultancy 1992–; FIMgt 1981, FCIT 1989; *Books* The War of The Rising Sun and Tumbling Bear: The Russo-Japanese War 1904–05 (1989, revised edn 2003), The Republic of the Ushakovka (1990), Military Intervention in the 1990s: a New Logic of War (1992), To Loose the Bands of Wickedness (contrib, ed Nigel Rodley, 1992), The Changing Face of Armed Conflict: Today and Tomorrow (1994), Shrouded Secrets: Australia's Mainland

War with Japan 1942–44 (1994), The Nature of Future Conflict (1995), The Battle for Manila 1945 (with Drs Anderson and Pimlott, 1995), Celebration of Victory (1995), Descent into Chaos (1996), MacArthur and Defeat in the Philippines (2001), Military Intervention and Peacekeeping: The Reality (2001), Omai: The Prince Who Never Was (2003); *Recreations* writing, family tennis; *Style*— Col Richard Connaughton; ✉ Wallhayes, Nettlecombe, Bridport, Dorset DT6 3SX (tel 01308 485002, fax 01308 485446, e-mail richard.m.connaughton@lineone.net, website www.connaughton.org.uk)

CONNAUGHTON, Shane; s of Brian Connaughton (d 1983), and Elizabeth, *née* Moylett (d 1979); *b* 4 April 1941; *Educ* St Tiarnachs Clones, Bristol Old Vic Theatre Sch; *m* Ann-Marie, da of Paul Hammersley-Fenton; 1 da (Tara b 17 March 1974), 1 s (Tom b 10 March 1979); *Career* writer; actor in repertoire and Nat Theatre London and Abbey Theatre Dublin; Hennessy Award for Irish Fiction 1985, The Irish Post Award 1987; *Novels* A Border Station (1989, shortlist GPA Literary Award), The Run of the Country (1991); *Plays* Sir Is Winning (1977, NT), Weston Coyney Cowboy (1975, Stoke-on-Trent), George Davis is Innocent OK (1976, Half Moon), Divisions (1981, Dublin Theatre Festival), Lily (1984, The Irish Co); *Screenplays* Every Picture Tells A Story (Channel 4), Dollar Bottom (1981, Oscar Best Short Film), My Left Foot (1990, Oscar nomination Best Adapted Screenplay), The Playboys (1992), O Mary This London (1994), The Run of the Country (1995), Tara Road (2005), various others for BBC and ITV; *Recreations* smelling flowers, my wife; *Style*— Shane Connaughton, Esq

CONNELL, Douglas Andrew; *b* 18 May 1954, Callander, Perthshire; *Educ* McLaren HS Callander, Univ of Edinburgh (LLB); *m* 1 Oct 1983, Marjorie Elizabeth; 2 s (Richard Thomson b 28 Nov 1984, Nicholas Alastair b 19 June 1987); *Career* admitted slr 1976; ptnr Dundas & Wilson 1979–97, jt sr ptnr Turcan Connell (following de-merger from Dundas & Wilson) 1997–; gen cncl assessor Ct of Univ of Edinburgh 2007–; memb Political and Taxation Ctee and Scottish Ctee Historic Houses Assoc, tstee Historic Scotland Fndn, chm Significance Ctee Scottish Museums Cncl, chm Buildings of Scotland Tst; patron: Nat Galleries of Scotland, Nat Museums of Scotland; former chm Lottery Ctee Scottish Arts Cncl, former chm Edinburgh Book Festival; former memb Ct Univ of St Andrews; *Style*— Douglas Connell, Esq; ✉ Turcan Connell, Princes Exchange, 1 Earl Grey Street, Edinburgh EH3 9EE (tel 0131 228 8111, fax 0131 228 8118, e-mail dac@turcanconnell.com)

CONNELL, (Frances) Elizabeth; da of (Gordon) Raymond Connell (d 1968), and (Maud) Elizabeth, *née* Scott (d 1994); *b* 22 October 1946; *Educ* Springs Convent, Univ of the Witwatersrand, Johannesburg Coll of Educn, London Opera Centre; *Career* opera singer; debut: Wexford Festival 1972, Aust Opera 1973–75, ENO 1975–80, Covent Garden 1976, Bayreuth 1980, La Scala 1981, Salzburg 1983, Glyndebourne 1985, Metropolitan Opera 1985, Paris 1987; has sung with major orchs, opera houses, festivals and maestri throughout the world; recordings incl: duets with Sutherland and Pavarotti, I Due Foscari, Suor Angelica, Guglielmo Tell, Poliuto, Mahler No 8, Mendelssohn No 2, Schubert Lieder recital, Vaughan Williams Serenade to Music, Schoenberg Gurrelieder, Lohengrin, Verdi Requiem Mass, Schreker Die Gezeichneten; Maggie Teyte Prize 1972; *Style*— Ms Elizabeth Connell; ✉ c/o Askonas Holt, Lonsdale Chambers, 27 Chancery Lane, London WC2A 1PF (tel 020 7400 1700, fax 020 7400 1799)

CONNELL, Prof John Muir Cochrane; *b* 10 October 1954; *Educ* Univ of Glasgow (MB ChB, MD); *Career* registrar in gen med and endocrinology Univ Dept of Med Western Infirmary Glasgow 1980–83, clinical scientist MRC Blood Pressure Unit Western Infirmary Glasgow 1983–86, visiting research fell Howard Florey Inst for Experimental Physiology and Med Univ of Melbourne 1986–87, sr clinical scientist MRC Blood Pressure Unit Western Infirmary Glasgow 1987–95 (also hon conslt physician), hon prof of med Faculty of Med Univ of Glasgow 1993, prof of endocrinology Univ of Glasgow 1996–, currently hon conslt physician N Glasgow Hosps Univ NHS Tst; Div of Cardiovascular and Med Sciences Faculty of Med Univ of Glasgow sec Assoc of Physicians of GB and Ireland 2001–; author of over 200 peer-reviewed papers and over 20 book chapters in specialist endocrine and cardiovascular textbooks; R D Wright lectr High Blood Pressure Cncl of Aust 1994, Richard Underwood Meml Lecture Harvard Univ and Brigham & Women's Hosp 1999, Croonian Lecture RCP 2000; Soc Endocrinol Medal 2005; MRCP 1979, FRCPGlas 1990, FMedSci 1999, FRCPEd 2002, FRSE 2002; *Clubs* Glasgow Golf, New Golf (St Andrews); *Style*— Prof John Connell; ✉ 68 Newlands Road, Newlands, Glasgow G43 2JH; Division of Cardiovascular and Medical Sciences, Gardiner Institute, Western Infirmary, Glasgow G11 6NT (tel 0141 211 2108, fax 0141 211 1763, e-mail jmcc1m@clinmed.gla.ac.uk)

CONNELL, Margaret Mary; da of Leo Connell (d 1995), and Margaret Isobel, *née* Nelson (d 2002); *b* 3 January 1949; *Educ* St Mary's Coll Leeds, Lady Margaret Hall Oxford (MA), Univ of Leeds (PGCE); *Career* physics teacher Headington Sch Oxford 1970–76, mathematics teacher N London Collegiate Sch 1976–86, dep headmistress Bromley HS GPDST 1986–91, headmistress More House Sch 1991–99, princ Queen's Coll London 1999–; *Recreations* music, theatre, travel; *Clubs* Univ Women's; *Style*— Miss Margaret Connell; ✉ Queen's College, 43–49 Harley Street, London W1G 8BT (tel 020 7291 7000, fax 020 7291 7099, e-mail mconnell@qcl.org.uk)

CONNELLY, Kevin Aloysuis Scott; *b* 27 August 1957; *Educ* St Mary's Marist Fathers Coll Middlesbrough; *Career* mangr McCoys Restaurant Northallerton 1979–90; full time comedy writer and performer 1990–; appearances and contribs to radio and TV progs incl Dead Ringers BBC Radio 4 and BBC 2 (Best Radio Comedy Sony Awards 2001, Best Radio Comedy TV and Radio Comedy Awards 2002); after dinner speaker, supporter Comic Heritage Fndn; *Clubs* Lord's Taverners, Naval; *Style*— Kevin Connelly, Esq; ✉ c/o Jane Morgan Management, Thames Wharf Studios, Rainville Road, London W6 9HA (tel 020 7386 5345, fax 020 7386 0338, e-mail enquiries@janemorganmgt.com)

CONNER, Angela Mary (Mrs Bulmer); da of late Judge Cyril Conner, and Mary Stephanie, *née* Douglass; *Educ* spent much of childhood travelling; *m* John Frederick Bulmer; 1 da (Georgia Sophie McCullough Bulmer); *Career* sculptor; worked for Dame Barbara Hepworth UK then full-time painter and sculptor; researched and developed use of water, sun and wind for abstract mobile sculptures in contemporary art; FRSBS; *Solo Exhibitions* incl: Browse & Darby London, Istanbul Biennale, Lincoln Centre NY, UN, Jewish Art Museum NY, Lincoln Center NYC, Economist Plaza London, Hirschl Gall London; *Group Exhibitions* incl: Chicago Arts Fair, Gimpel Fils NY, Carnegie Museum Pittsburgh, Nat Portrait Gall London, Washington Museum, Royal Acad; *Important Public and Private Works* incl: centrepiece water mobile lent to Downing St for use of PM (cmmnd by Silver Trust), biggest mobile sculpture in Europe Dublin, large water mobile Chatsworth, entrance sculpture for Marquess of Salisbury, three works for Lincoln Center NY, Great Tipper Germany, large centrepiece for Horsham, Victims of Yalta Meml (Brompton Rd London), Quartet (water sculpture and co-designed Plaza) Heinz Hall Pittsburgh, water sculptures for King Fahid, 20ft water mobile Aston Univ, 30ft water mobile Economist Plaza St James's London, 20ft water mobile for Fidelity Investment HQ Kent, 14ft wind/water sculpture Madrid, 85ft mobile water arch Longleat, largest indoor mobile in Europe Lovells London; numerous private cmmns for Duke of Devonshire Collection, Gunter Sachs, Mrs Henry Ford II, President Chirac; *Portraits* incl: statues of de Gaulle, Sir Noel Coward (London, NY and Jamaica); busts: HRH The Prince of Wales, HM The Queen, HM Queen Elizabeth the Queen Mother, Lucien Freud, Lord Sainsbury, Drue Heniz, Duke of Devonshire, Harold Macmillan (Earl of Stockton), Sir John Betjeman, Sir John Tavener, Dame Janet Baker, Rab Butler (House of Commons), Paul Mellon, Sir Peter O'Sullevan, Sir Alec Douglas Home, Lord Rothschild, Sir Tom Stoppard; *Awards* incl: Honor Award of American Inst of Architects, Best Br Equestrian Sculptor Award Br Sporting Art Tst; winner various competitions incl: Lexington Airport Int Competition, Hereford City Nat Competition, W Midlands Arts Nat Competition for Aston Univ, Darlington Art Centre Competition; *Recreations* breeding and showing Morgan horses, co-founded the breed in Britain; *Style*— Angela Conner; ✉ George and Dragon Hall, Mary Place, London W11 4PL (tel 020 7221 4510, fax 020 7243 1167, e-mail angela.conner@which.net, website www.angelaconner.co.uk)

CONNER, Rt Rev David John; s of William Ernest Conner (d 1989), and Joan Millington, *née* Cheek (d 1994); *b* 6 April 1947; *Educ* Erith GS, Exeter Coll Oxford (Symes exhibitioner, MA), St Stephen's House Oxford; *m* 10 July 1969, Jayne Maria, da of Lt-Col George E Evans, OBE; 2 s (Andrew David b 1970, Jonathan Paul b 1972); *Career* chaplain St Edward's Sch Oxford 1973–80 (asst chaplain 1971–73), team vicar Wolvercote with Summertown Oxford 1976–80, sr chaplain Winchester Coll 1980–86, vicar St Mary the Great with St Michaels Cambridge 1987–94, rural dean of Cambridge 1989–94, bishop of Lynn 1994–98, dean of Windsor and register of the Most Noble Order of the Garter 1998–; bishop to The Forces 2001–, hon chaplain to Pilgrims 2002; hon fell Girton Coll Cambridge 1995; *Recreations* reading and friends; *Style*— The Rt Rev the Dean of Windsor; ✉ The Deanery, Windsor Castle, Berkshire SL4 1NJ (tel 01753 865561, fax 01753 819002)

CONNERADE, Prof Jean-Patrick; s of George Auguste Joseph Louis Connerade, and Marguerite Marie, *née* David; *b* 6 May 1943; *Educ* Lycée Français Charles De Gaulle, Imperial Coll London (BSc, PhD, DIC, DSc); *m* 19 Dec 1970, Jocelyne Charlette, da of Eugene Dubois, of Mareil-Marly, France (d 1988); 1 s (Florent b 1971), 1 da (Laetita b 1973); *Career* ESRO fell 1968–70, scientist Euro Space Res Inst Italy 1970–73, visiting prof École Normale Supérieure Paris 1979–80; Imperial Coll London: lectr 1973–79, reader 1980–85, prof of atomic and molecular physics 1985–98, Lockyer prof of physics 1998–; guest researcher Physikalisches Institut Univ of Bonn 1969–; pres Euroscience Assoc, memb Ampboard of Euro Physical Soc; FInstP, FRSC; *Books* Atomic and Molecular Physics in High Field (co-ed, 1982), Giant Resonances in Atoms Molecules and Solids (1986), Correlations in Clusters and Related Systems (ed, 1996), Highly Excited Atoms (1998); *Recreations* painting; *Style*— Prof Jean-Patrick Connerade; ✉ Blackett Laboratory, Imperial College of Science Technology and Medicine, Prince Consort Road, London SW7 2BW (tel 020 7594 7858, fax 020 7594 7714, e-mail j.connerade@ic.ac.uk, telex 929484 IMPCOLG)

CONNERY, Sir Sean Thomas; kt (2000); s of Joseph Connery, and Euphamia Connery; *b* 25 August 1930; *m* 1, 29 Nov 1962 (m dis 1974), Diane (who m 3, 1985, Anthony Shaffer, playwright), da of Sir Raphael West Cilento (d 1985), and former w of Andrea Volpt; 1 s (Jason Connery b 1963); *m* 2, Jan 1975, Micheline Roquebrune; *Career* actor, fell: Royal Scottish Academy of Music and Drama, BAFTA; Freeman City of Edinburgh 1991; Hon DLitt Heriot-Watt Univ 1981; Golden Globe Cecil B De Mille Lifetime Achievement Award 1996, Lifetime Achievement Award Palm Springs Int Film Festival 2001; films incl: Tarzan's Greatest Adventure 1959, The Longest Day 1962, Dr No 1963, From Russia With Love 1964, Goldfinger 1965, Thunderball 1965, A Fine Madness 1966, You Only Live Twice 1967, Shalako 1968, Diamonds are Forever 1971, Murder on the Orient Express 1974, The Man Who Would be King 1975, Outland 1981, Never Say Never Again 1983, Highlander 1986, The Name of the Rose 1986, The Untouchables 1987, The Presidio 1988, Indiana Jones - The Last Crusade 1989, The Hunt For Red October 1990, Family Business 1990, Highlander II 1991, Robin Hood Prince of Thieves 1991, The Russia House 1991, The Medicine Man 1992, Just Cause 1995, King Arthur in First Knight 1995, The Rock 1996, the voice of Draco in Dragonheart 1996, The Avengers 1998, Entrapment 1998, The James Bond Story 1999, Finding Forrester 2000, The League of Extraordinary Gentlemen 2003; *Style*— Sir Sean Connery

CONNOCK, Stephen Leslie; MBE (1999); s of Leslie Thomas Connock, of Peterborough, Cambs, and Gladys Edna, *née* Chappell; *b* 16 November 1949; *Educ* Univ of Sheffield (BA), LSE (MPhil); *m* 18 Aug 1973, Margaret Anne, da of Richard Bolger, of Palmers Green, London; 2 s (Adrian b 1981, Mark b 1985); *Career* Philips Electronics: industrial relations mangr 1979–85, mgmnt devpt mangr 1985–87; gen mangr human resources Pearl Assurance plc 1987–92, customer and corp affrs dir Eastern Group plc (formerly Eastern Electricity plc) 1992–97, chm Inst of Customer Service 1996–2001, chm The Garland Appeal (fndn in honour of Linda McCartney), managing partner Integrys Ltd, people dir easyJet plc 2003–05, dir of gp HR Aggreko plc 2006–; chm: Albion Opera Co, Albion Music Ltd, Albion Records, Braga Santos Fndn Lisbon; MIPD 1973; *Books* Industrial Relations Training for Managers (1981), Cost Effective Strategies in Industrial Relations (1985), H R Vision - Managing a Quality Workforce (1991), Ethical Leadership (1995), There was a Time - RVW in Photographs (ed, 2003), The Complete Poems of Ursula Vaughan Williams (ed, 2003); *Recreations* music (chm Ralph Vaughan Williams Soc), writing, football (Spurs), cricket (Surrey); *Clubs* Reform; *Style*— Stephen Connock, Esq, MBE

CONNOLLY, Amanda Jane; da of M F Connolly, of Burnley, Lancs, and S N Connolly, *née* Todd; *b* 10 July 1963; *Educ* Burnley Girls' HS, Lancaster Univ (BA); *m* 1992, Stewart Reed; *Career* brand mangr: Nestlé 1985–87, Burton's Biscuits 1987–88; Coley Porter Bell: account dir 1988–94, head of brands 1994–95, md 1995–; memb Mktg Soc, MInstD; *Recreations* aerobics, gym, tennis, opera, cooking, walking; *Style*— Ms Amanda Connolly

CONNOLLY, Billy; CBE (2003); *b* 24 November 1942; *m* 1990, Pamela Stephenson; 3 da (Daisy, Amy, Scarlett); from previous m; 1 s (Jamie), 1 da (Cara); *Career* comedian, actor, musician, playwright and presenter; started work as apprentice welder, began show business career with Gerry Rafferty and The Humblebums; as playwright The Red Runner (Edinburgh Fringe) 1979; *Theatre* The Great Northern Welly Boot Show (Palladium), The Beastly Beastitudes of Balthazar B (West End) 1982; *Television* Androcles and the Lion 1984, Return to Nose and Beak (Comic Relief), HBO special (with Whoopi Goldberg) 1990, South Bank Show Special (25th Anniversary commemoration) 1992, Down Among the Big Boys (BBC) 1993, Head of the Class, Billy, Billy Connolly's World Tour of Scotland (6 part documentary) 1994, The Big Picture (BBC) 1995, Billy Connolly's World Tour of Australia 1996, Gentleman's Relish 2000 (BBC), World Tour of England, Ireland and Wales 2002, World Tour of NZ 2004; *Films* incl: Absolution (with Richard Burton) 1979, Bullshot 1984, Water (with Michael Caine, *qv*) 1984, The Big Man (with Liam Neeson) 1989, Pocahontas (animation) 1995, Billy Big Bones in Treasure Island (Muppet Movie) 1996, William Brodie in Deacon Brodie (BBC Film) 1996, Ship of Fools 1997, Mrs Brown (with Judi Dench, *qv*) 1997, Still Crazy 1998, The Debt Collector 1999, Gabriel & Me 2001, Man Who Sued God 2002, Timeline 2003, The Last Samurai 2003, Lemony Snicket: A Series of Unfortunate Events 2004, Open Season 2006, Garfield - A Tail of Two Kitties 2006, Fido 2007, Good Sharma 2007; *Videos* numerous releases incl: Bite your Bum 1981 (Music Week and Record Business Award 1982), 25 BC, Billy and Albert, An Audience with Billy Connolly, Billy Connolly Live, Hand-Picked by Billy Connolly 1982, Live at Hammersmith 1991, Live' 94, World Tour of Scotland 1995, World Tour of Australia 1996, Two Night Stand 1997, Erect for 30 Years 1998, One Night Stand/Down Under (Live 99) 1999, Billy Connolly - The Greatest Hits 2001, World Tour of England, Ireland and Wales 2002, Billy Connolly Live 2002, Handpicked by Billy 2003, Bites Yer Bum 2003, Billy Connolly's World Tour of NZ 2004, Billy Connolly Live in NY 2006; *Albums* numerous releases incl: The Great Northern Welly Boot Show (incl no 1 hit DIVORCE), Pick of Billy Connolly (gold disc) 1982, Billy Connolly's Musical Tour of NZ 2004; *Books* Gullible's Travels (1982); *Style*— Billy

Connolly, Esq, CBE; ✉ c/o Tickety-boo Limited, 2 Triq Il-Barriera, Balzan BZN1200, Malta (tel 00 356 2155 6166, fax 00 356 2155 7316, e-mail tickety-boo@tickety-boo.com)

CONNOLLY, Denys E; OBE; *Career* with Peat Marwick Mitchell & Co CAs 1955–85 (sr ptnr Hong Kong 1978–85); non-exec dir: Hong Kong Bank 1985–1997, HSBC Holdings plc 1990–2001, Kowloon-Canton Railway Corp 1990–2002; chm Sheko Devpt Co Ltd 1994–; FCA; *Style*— Denys Connolly, Esq, OBE; ✉ 17 Sheko, Hong Kong (tel 00 8522 809 4476)

CONNOLLY, Prof Joseph Edward; s of Patrick Joseph Connolly (d 1985), and Kathryn Mary, *née* Mcnaney; *b* 15 June 1950; *Educ* Cornell Univ (AB), Harvard Univ (MBA); *Career* second vice-pres Continental Bank London 1975–81, gp head Bank of Boston London 1981–83, sr analyst Moody's Investors NY 1984–86, dir Euro Ratings Ltd London 1986–88, vice-pres and gp head Citibank London 1988–99, exec dir UBS-Warburg London and Zurich 1999–2004, ceo Connolly Associates (CH) 2004–; non-exec dir J M Huber Fin Servs Ltd 2000–04; dir Princeton Center for Economic Studies 1995–99, Willard Brown distinguished prof of global finance and Islamic finance American Univ in Cairo 2005–07, distinguished prof of corp finance Ecole Nationale des Ponts et Chauseés Paris 2007; US cmmr UK-US Bilateral Cmmn for Fulbrights 2005–; memb: Swiss Bankers Assoc 1999–2006, Advsy Bd Islamic Inst of Banking and Insurance in London 2006–, Advsy Bd Centre for Islamic Finance Swiss Banking Inst Univ of Zurich; dir Wealth Mgmnt Congress 2003–04; tstee Richmond The American Int Univ of London 2003–; MInstD; *Books* The International Data Communications Market; *Recreations* racing, looking at pictures, skiing; *Clubs* Harvard (NY, London, Zurich and Boston), Kildare St and Univ (Dublin); *Style*— Prof Joseph Connolly; ✉ 52A Eaton Place, London SW1X 8AL (tel 020 7245 1223, e-mail josconnolly@yahoo.com); 83 Montvale Avenue, Woburn, Massachusetts, USA

CONNOLLY, Dr (Charles) Kevin; TD (1981); s of Dr Charles Vincent Connolly (d 1961), of Rothwell, Northants, and Frances Elliott, *née* Turner; *b* 26 September 1936; *Educ* Ampleforth, Gonville & Caius Coll Cambridge, Middx Hosp Med Sch (MA, MB BChir); *m* 24 Oct 1970, Rachel Bronwen, da of Lewis Philip Jameson Evans (d 1972), of Bromsgrove, Worcs; 3 da (Kate b 1971, Celia b 1973, Clare b 1975); *Career* house physician Middx Hosp 1961, resident med offr Brompton Hosp 1963, sr med registrar St George's Hosp 1967, conslt physician Darlington and Northallerton Hosp 1970–2000 (hon physician 2000–), clinical tutor Northallerton Health Dist 1974–82, examiner Temporary Registration and Professional Linguistics Assessment Bd 1975–2000, hon clinical lectr Dept of Med Univ of Newcastle upon Tyne 1988–; vice-pres Nat Assoc of Clinical Tutors 1981–83, past memb various ctees RCP and Br Thoracic Soc; pres: Northallerton Div BMA 1974–76, Yorks Thoracic Soc 1982–84, Northern Thoracic Soc 1991–92; memb: Darlington HA 1981–90, Thoracic Soc, Med Res Soc, Exec Ctee Breathe North; memb Tbnal/Appeals Serv 1988– Liveryman Worshipful Soc of Apothecaries 1964; FRCP 1977 (MRCP 1964); *Recreations* tennis, skiing; *Clubs* Army and Navy; *Style*— Dr C K Connolly, TD; ✉ Aldbrough House, Aldbrough St John, Richmond, North Yorkshire DL11 7TP (tel 01325 374244, fax 01325 374759, e-mail drckconnolly@gmail.com)

CONNOLLY, Sarah Patricia; da of Gerald Joseph Connolly, DSO (d 1995), and Jane, *née* Widdowson; *b* 13 June 1963; *Educ* Queen Margaret's York, Clarendon Coll Nottingham, RCM (DipRCM (piano and voice), ARCM); *m* 1998, Carl Talbot; 1 da (Lily Jane Talbot b 6 May 2003); *Career* studied under David Mason and now with Gerald Martin Moore; former memb BBC Singers, joined Glyndebourne Festival Chorus 1992, winner second prize s'Hertogenbosch Int Concours Holland 1994, opera début Annina in Der Rosenkavalier (WNO) 1994, currently co princ ENO; appeared on My Night with Handel (Channel 4), numerous broadcasts BBC Radio; nominated Olivier Award for Outstanding Achievement in Opera 2006; FRSA; *Performances* opera roles: Messenger in Monteverdi's Orfeo (ENO), title role in Handel's Xerxes (ENO), title role in Handel's Ariodante (NY City Opera, Richard Gold Debut Award 2000, ENO, dir David Alden 2002), Ruggiero in Handel's Alcina (ENO), Susie in The Silver Tassie (world premiere by Mark Anthony Turnage, ENO, South Bank Show Award 2001), Nerone in L'Incoronazione di Poppea Monteverdi (Maggio Musicale, Florence), Ottavia in L'incoronazione di Poppea, Dido in Dido and Aeneas, Ino and Juno in Semele (San Francisco Opera), Romeo in I Capuleti ei Montecchi (NYC Opera) 2001, Lucretia in Britten's The Rape of Lucretia (Aldeburgh Festival, ENO, filmed for BBC, South Bank Show Award 2002), Sesto in Giulio Cesare (Paris Opera, with Minkowski), Juno in Handel's Semele (Theatre des Champs Elysées Paris) 2004, Lucretia (Bayerische Staatsoper Munich) 2004, title role in Giulio Cesare (Glyndebourne) 2005, Annio in Mozart's La Clemenza di Tito (Met Opera NY) 2005, title role in Purcell's Dido and Aneas (La Scala Milan) 2006, Octavia in Der Rosenkavalier (Scottish Opera) 2006, alto in Bach's St Matthew's Passion (Glyndebourne) 2007; concert roles: Mozart's Requiem (with Acad of St Martin's in the Field under Sir Neville Marriner), Bach's B minor Mass and Bach Cantatas (with Philippe Herreweghe and Berlin Philharmonie), Wigmore Hall Recital début (with Julius Drake) 1998, Bach Cantatas (with Collegium Vocale and Philippe Herreweghe in Concertgebouw, Amsterdam), Elgar's Dream of Gerontius (under Edo de Waart, Sydney, and Mark Elder with LPO), Mark Anthony Turnage's Twice Through the Heart (with London Sinfonietta under Markus Stenz), Queen of Sheba in Handel's Solomon (with Ivor Bolton at Maggio Musicale, Florence), Marguerite in Berlioz' Damnation of Faust (Perth Festival Aust), world premiere of Rime d'Amore ('Rhyme of Love', with Giuseppe Sinopoli, Rome), Berlioz's Les Nuits d'Été (Vienna Konzerthaus and Concertgebouw, with Acad of Ancient Music under Christopher Hogwood), Mahler's Kindertodenlieder (with Daniel Harding and Mahler Chamber Orchestra), St Matthew Passion (with Sir Colin Davis), Haydn Harmoniemesse (with Sir Simon Rattle), Mozart Dominicus Mass (Salzburg Festival debut) 2002, Mahler's Das Lied von der Erde (Concertgebouw under Daniel Harding) 2006, Mahler's Rucker Lieder (with Mark Elder and Hallé Orch) 2006, Elgar's The Kingdom (with Mark Elder and Hallé Orch) 2007; *Recordings* Bach Cantatas (with Philippe Herreweghe and Collegium Vocale, Grammy Nomination 1998), Rameau's Les Fêtes d'Hebe (with Les Art Florissants under William Christie, winner Gramophone Award for Early Opera 1998, Grammy Nominated), Vivaldi's Juditha Triumphans (with King's Consort under Robert King), Vaughan Williams Sir John in Love (with Richard Hickox), Schoenberg's Das buch der hängenden gärten (with Iain Burnside) 2002, Heroes and Heroines (Handel, with The Sixteen and Harry Christophers) 2004, Mahler's Des Knaben Wunderhorn (with Philippe Herreweghe and Orch des Champs Elysèes, Edison Award for Vocal Performance), The Exquisite Hour, Giulio Cesare at Glyndebounre 2005, vocal solist in film Children of Men 2006, Mozart's Mass in C Minor; *Recreations* animals, reading, jazz and classical piano playing, films, theatre; *Style*— Miss Sarah Connolly; ✉ c/o Askonas Holt, Lonsdale Chambers, 27 Chancery Lane, London WC2A 1PF

CONNOR, (Jill) Alexandra; da of John Connor, and Ella Crossley, *née* Worthington; *b* 23 April 1959; *m* (m dis); *Career* writer, artist and television presenter; one woman exhibitions: Marina Henderson Gallery, Richmond Gallery; work cmmnd by RSC and Aspreys; former presenter Past Masters on This Morning, featured in documentary 40 Minutes (BBC); subject of many articles in national newspapers and magazines, numerous appearances on TV, regular BBC radio slots; FRSA; *Books* non-fiction: The Wrong Side of the Canvas (1989), Rembrandt's Monkey (1991), Private View (2002); fiction: The Witch Mark (1986), Thomas (1987), The Hour of the Angel (1989), The Mask of Fortune (1990), The Well of Dreams (1992), The Green Bay Tree (1993), Winter Women: Midsummer Men (1994), The Moon is My Witness (1997), Midnight's Smiling (1998), Green Baize Road (1999), An Angel Passing Over (2000), Hunter's Moon (2001), The Sixpenny Winner (2002), A Face in the Locket (2003), The Turn of the Tide (2004), The Tailor's Wife (2005), The Lydgate Widow (2006); as Alexandra Hampton: The Experience Buyer (1994), The Deaf House (1995); medical thrillers: Bodily Harm (1998), Cipher (1999), The Watchman's Daughter (2007); *Recreations* collecting antiques and rare art books; *Style*— Alexandra Connor, FRSA; ✉ c/o Ed Victor Ltd, 6 Bayley Street, Bedford Square, London WC1B 3HB (tel 020 7304 4100)

C

CONNOR, Clare Joanne; OBE (2006, MBE 2004); da of Michael Connor, of Brighton and Hove, Sussex, and Norma, *née* Harwood; *b* 1 September 1976, Brighton; *Educ* Brighton Coll (academic scholar), Univ of Manchester (BA); *Career* cricketer; Sussex: capt 1996–, coach women's team and jr teams 2003–, winners County title 2003, 2004 and 2005; England: debut 1995, capt 2000–06, memb Ashes winning team 2005 (after 42 years held by Australia), ret from int cricket 2006; player Lashings World XI 2006 (first woman to sign professional terms); sports columnist for Observer, presenter and interviewer The Cricket Show (Channel 4), reporter Test Match Special (BBC Radio 4) 2003–05; currently English teacher and head of pr and mktg Brighton Coll; ambass: Women's Sports Fndn, Chance to Shine scheme ECB; Vodafone England Cricketer of the Year 2002, runner-up Sunday Times Sportswoman of the Year 2005; *Recreations* reading, travelling, theatre; *Style*— Ms Clare Connor, OBE; ✉ Brighton College, Eastern Road, Brighton BN2 0AL (tel 01273 704200, fax 01273 704204, e-mail cconnor@brightoncollege.net)

CONNOR, Howard Arthur; s of Arthur Albert William Connor (d 1969, Sgt RAF), of Chingford, London, and Winifred Edith, *née* Rugg (d 1983); *b* 31 January 1938; *Educ* Richmond House Sch Chingford, Chingford Co HS; *m* 23 July 1960, Dorothy Myrtle, da of Frederick Hobbs (d 1981), of Chingford, London; 2 da (Alison b 1964, Melinda b 1966); *Career* chartered accountant; princ G H Attenborough and Co; memb and former chm Broxbourne Parliamentary Cons Assoc Business Gp; chartered tax advsr; FCA, ATII; *Recreations* horse riding, bridge, golf, badminton; *Clubs* Rotary of Hoddesdon (former pres); *Style*— Howard Connor, Esq

CONNOR, Leslie John; s of William John Connor (d 1980), of Lancs, and Doris Eliza, *née* Neild (d 2000); *b* 23 April 1932; *Educ* St Mary's Coll Crosby, Univ of Liverpool (BA), Calif Univ of Advanced Studies (MBA); *m* 1951, Jean Margaret, da of Roger Pendleton, of Lancs; 2 da (Christine Lesley b 1964, Hilary Elaine b 1968); *Career* exec trainee C & A Modes 1956–58, Great Universal Stores 1958–63, Connor Finance Corporation Ltd 1963–, md Leisure and General Holdings Ltd 1970–73, fndr and chm First Castle Electronics plc 1973–86; dir: Connor Finance Corporation Ltd, W J Connor Properties Ltd; Br Show Pony Soc (BSPS): memb Cncl 1978–83, treas 1979–83, show pres 1994–; *Books* The Managed Growth of a Quoted British Public Company, The Working Hunter Pony (jtly); *Recreations* showing horses, farming, antiques, porcelain and painting, walking, writing, golf; *Clubs* Farmers'; *Style*— Leslie Connor, Esq; ✉ Greenacres, Bowker's Green Farm, Bowker's Green, Aughton, Lancashire L39 6TA; Connor Finance Corporation Ltd, Bowker's Green Court, Bowker's Green, Aughton, Lancashire L39 6TA (tel 01695 424200, fax 01695 424109)

CONNOR, Prof (James) Michael; s of James Connor (d 1981), of Grappenhall, Cheshire, and Mona, *née* Hall; *b* 18 June 1951; *Educ* Lymm GS, Univ of Liverpool (BSc, MB ChB, MD, DSc); *m* 6 Jan 1979, Rachel Alyson Clare, da of Donald Brooks, of Woodbridge, Suffolk; 2 da (Emily b 1986, Katherine b 1987); *Career* res fell Univ of Liverpool 1977–79, resident in internal med and instr in med genetics Johns Hopkins Univ Baltimore USA 1979–82, Wellcome Tst sr lectr Univ of Glasgow 1984–87, prof of med genetics, dir of the W of Scotland Regnl Genetics Serv and hon conslt Univ of Glasgow 1987–; memb: Assoc of Physicians, Br Soc of Human Genetics, American Soc of Human Genetics; FRCPGlas, FRCPEd; *Books* Essential Medical Genetics (5 edn, 1997), Prenatal Diagnosis in Obstetric Practice (2 edn, 1995), Emery and Rimoin's Principles and Practice of Medical Genetics (5 edn, 2006); *Recreations* sea kayaking, mountain biking; *Style*— Prof Michael Connor; ✉ Institute of Medical Genetics, Yorkhill, Glasgow G3 8SJ (tel 0141 201 0363/5, fax 0141 357 4277, e-mail j.m.connor@clinmed.gla.ac.uk)

CONNOR, His Hon Roger David; DL (Bucks 2005); s of Thomas Bernard Connor (d 1962), of Aisby, Lincs, and Susie Violet, *née* Spittlehouse (d 1964); *b* 8 June 1939; *Educ* Merchant Taylors, Brunel Coll of Advanced Sci and Technol; *m* 25 March 1967, Sandra, da of Eldred Rolef Holmes, of Bicester, Oxon; 2 s (Hugh b 1969, Rupert b 1970); *Career* admitted slr 1968; ptnr Messrs Hodders 1970–83, met stipendiary magistrate 1983, recorder of the Crown Court 1987, circuit judge (SE Circuit) 1991–2005; *Recreations* music, gardening, golf; *Style*— His Hon Roger Connor, DL; ✉ Bourn's Meadow, Little Missenden, Amersham, Buckinghamshire HP7 0RF

CONNOR, Vincent; s of Stanley Connor (d 2005), and Mary Patricia, *née* McAlindon (d 1973); *b* 17 April 1964, Glasgow; *Educ* Univ of Glasgow (LLB, DipLP); *m* 14 Sept 1996, Gillian Johnston; *Career* admitted slr 1989; trainee then asst slr Hughes Dowall 1987–90; ptnr: McGrigors 1995–98 (asst slr 1990–93, assoc 1993–95), Pinsent Masons 1998–; memb Law Soc of Scotland 1989; accredited construction law specialist and mediator Law Soc of Scotland; *Recreations* music, cinema, cycling; *Clubs* Western Baths (Glasgow); *Style*— Vincent Connor, Esq; ✉ Pinsent Masons, 123 St Vincent Street, Glasgow G2 5EA (tel 0141 249 5401, fax 0141 248 6655, e-mail vincent.connor@pinsentmasons.com)

CONNORS, Dr Steven George; s of Stanley George Connors, of Cardiff, and Jeanne, *née* White; *b* 10 September 1956, Cardiff; *Educ* Llanrumney HS Cardiff, UC Swansea (BA, PhD); *m* 22 Aug 1981, Elizabeth Anne, *née* Dawson; 2 s (Owain James, Cullen George Stuart); *Career* teacher of English Denstone Coll 1981–86, head of English Queen's Coll Taunton 1986–91, head of English, housemaster of the int centre and head of boarding Sevenoaks Sch 1991–2000, dep head Christ's Hosp Horsham 2000–05, headmaster Monmouth Sch 2005–; *Recreations* reading, theatre-going, hill walking; *Clubs* East India, Devonshire, Sports and Public Schools; *Style*— Dr Steven Connors; ✉ Monmouth School, Almshouse Street, Monmouth NP25 3XP (tel 01600 713143, fax 01600 772701, e-mail hm-sec@monmouthschool.org); Monnow Bank House, The Parade, Monmouth NP25 3PA

CONOLEY, Mary Patricia; da of Sir Jack Rampton (d 1994), of Tonbridge, Kent, and Lady Rampton, *née* Eileen Hart; *b* 7 September 1951; *Educ* Walthamstow Hall Sevenoaks, Univ of Birmingham (BA); *m* 1972, (m dis 1980), Christopher Conoley; *Career* PR offr (UK) The Dredging & Construction Co Ltd 1973–77, PR consultant UK and Aust 1977–81, sr public affairs offr Woodside Offshore Petroleum Pty Ltd 1981–84, gp PR exec The Littlewoods Organisation 1985–88, dir Shandwick Communications Ltd 1989–91, jt md Shandwick PR 1991, dir corp affrs Hawker Siddeley Group 1991, head of corp communications National Power plc 1992–96, PR conslt 1997–, lectr and conslt interior decoration 2001–; vice-chm Market and Coastal Towns Assoc; *Recreations* house renovation, cooking, gardening; *Style*— Mrs Mary Conoley; ✉ One Cross Street, Helston, Cornwall TR13 8NQ

CONQUEST, Dr (George) Robert Acworth; CMG (1996), OBE (1955); s of Robert Folger Westcott Conquest (d 1959), of Vence, Alpes Maritimes, and Rosamund Alys, *née* Acworth (d 1973); *b* 15 July 1917; *Educ* Winchester, Univ of Grenoble, Magdalen Coll Oxford (MA, DLitt); *m* 1, 1942 (m dis 1948), Joan, *née* Watkins; 2 s (John b 1943, Richard b 1945); m 2, 1948 (m dis 1962), Tatiana, *née* Mikhailova; m 3, 1964 (m dis 1978), Caroleen, *née* Macfarlane; m 4, 1979, Elizabeth, da of late Col Richard D Neece, USAF; *Career* writer; Capt Oxfordshire and Bucks LI 1939–46; HM Foreign Serv 1946–56: second sec Sofia, first sec UK Delgn to the UN, princ FO; fell LSE 1956–58, visiting poet Univ of Buffalo 1959–60, literary ed The Spectator 1962–63, sr fell Columbia Univ 1964–65, fell

The Woodrow Wilson Int Center 1976–77, sr res fell The Hoover Inst Stanford Univ 1977–79 and 1981–, visiting scholar The Heritage Fndn 1980–81, research assoc Harvard Univ 1983–; memb Soc for the Promotion of Roman Studies; FBIS 1968, FRSL 1972, FBA 1994; *Books* incl: Poems (1955), Power and Policy in the USSR (1961), Between Mars and Venus (1963), The Great Terror (1968), Lenin (1972), The Abomination of Moab (1979), Present Danger (1979), Forays (1979), The Harvest of Sorrow (1986), New and Collected Poems (1988), Stalin (1991), Reflections on a Ravaged Century (1999), Demons Don't (1999), The Dragons of Expectation (2005); *Clubs* Travellers; *Style—* Dr Robert Conquest, CMG, OBE, FBA, FRSL; ✉ 52 Peter Coutts Circle, Stanford, California 94305, USA; Hoover Institution, Stanford, California 94305, USA (tel 00 1 650 723 1647)

CONRAD, Alan David; QC (1999); s of Maurice Conrad (d 1990), and Peggy Rose Conrad; *b* 10 December 1953; *Educ* Bury GS, BNC Oxford (BA); *m* 1982 (m dis 1999), Andrea, *née* Williams; 1 s (Jonathan b 23 June 1988), 1 da (Anna b 1 Dec 1990); m 2, Julie, *née* Whittle; *Career* called to the Bar 1976, recorder 1997, practising barrister specialising in criminal law; memb Middle Temple Criminal Bar Assoc; *Recreations* reading, travel, food and drink, cricket; *Clubs* Lancashire CCC; *Style—* Alan Conrad, Esq, QC; ✉ Lincoln House Chambers, 5th Floor, Lincoln House, 1 Brazenose Street, Manchester M2 5EL

CONRAD, Henrietta; *Educ* Yale Univ; *Career* fndr and co-dir (with Sebastian Scott, *qv*) Princess Productions 1996–; prodns incl: Friday Night Project, The Search, The Wright Stuff, Get Me The Producer; *Style—* Ms Henrietta Conrad; ✉ Princess Productions, Third Floor, Whiteley's Centre, 151 Queensway, London W2 4SB

CONRAD, Peter John; s of Eric Conrad (d 1989), and Pearl Conrad (d 1999); *b* 11 February 1948, Hobart, Tasmania; *Educ* Hobart HS, Univ of Tasmania (BA), Univ of Oxford (MA); *Career* fell All Souls Coll Oxford 1970–73, tutor in English literature ChCh Oxford 1973–, reviewer and feature writer The Observer; Hon DLitt Univ of Tasmania 1993; FRSL 1974, hon fell Australian Acad of the Humanities 2004; *Publications* The Victorian Treasure House (1973), Shandyism (1977), Romantic Opera and Literary Form (1978), Imagining America (1980), Television: The Medium and 15 Manners (1982), The Art of the City (1984), Everyman History of English Literature (1985), A Song of Love and Death (1987), Down Home (1988), Where I Fell to Earth (1990), Underworld (1992), Feasting with Panthers (1994), To Be Continued (1996), Modern Times Modern Places (1998), The Hitchcock Murders (2000), Orson Welles (2003), At Home in Australia (2003), Tales of Two Hemispheres (2004), Creation: Artists, Gods and Origins (2007); *Style—* Peter Conrad, Esq; ✉ Christ Church, Oxford OX1 1DP (tel 01865 276194)

CONRAN, Jasper Alexander; s of Sir Terence Conran, *qv*, and Shirley Ida Conran, *qv*; *b* 12 December 1959; *Educ* Bryanston, Parsons Sch of Design NY; *Career* md and designer Jasper Conran Ltd 1978–; Fil d'Or (Int Linen award) 1982 and 1983, British Fashion Cncl Designer of the Year award 1986–87, Fashion Gp of America award 1987, Laurence Olivier Costume Designer of the Year award 1991 for Jean Anouilh's The Rehearsal (Almeida Theatre 1990, Garrick Theatre 1990–91), British Collections award British Fashion Awards 1991; *Style—* Jasper Conran Esq; ✉ Jasper Conran Ltd, 1–7 Rostrevor Mews, Fulham, London SW6 5AZ (tel 020 7384 0800, fax 020 7384 0801)

CONRAN, Shirley Ida; OBE (2004); da of W Thirlby Pearce, and Ida Pearce; *b* 21 September 1932; *Educ* St Paul's Girls' Sch; *m* 1955 (m dis 1962), as his 2 w, Terence Orby Conran (now Sir Terence), *qv*; 2 s (Sebastian Conran, Jasper Conran, *qv*); *Career* designer/writer; co fndr Conran Fabrics Ltd 1957, memb Selection Ctee Design Centre 1961, first woman ed Observer Colour Magazine 1964–69, woman ed Daily Mail 1968; fndr pres: Mothers in Mgmnt 1998–, Work-Life Balance Tst 2000–; *Books* Superwoman (1974), Superwoman Year Book (1975), Superwoman in Action (1977), Futures (with E Sidney), Lace (1982), The Magic Garden (1983), Lace 2 (1984), Savages (1987), The Amazing Umbrella Shop (1990), Down with Superwoman (Penguin, 1990), Crimson (1992), Tiger Eyes (1994), The Revenge (1997); *Style—* Ms Shirley Conran, OBE

CONRAN, Sir Terence Orby; kt (1983); *b* 4 October 1931; *Educ* Bryanston, Central Sch of Arts & Crafts; *m* 2, 1955 (m dis 1962), Shirley Ida Pearce (Shirley Conran, *qv*); 2 s (Jasper Conran, *qv*, Sebastian Conran); m 3, 1963 (m dis 1996), Caroline Herbert (the cookery writer Caroline Conran); 2 s, 1 da; m 4, 2000, Victoria Davis; *Career* designer, retailer, restaurateur; currently chm: The Conran Shop Ltd 1976–, Jasper Conran Ltd 1982–, Benchmark Ltd 1989–, Blue Print Café Ltd 1989–, Terence Conran Ltd 1990–, Conran Shop Holdings Ltd 1990– (shops in London, Paris, Tokyo, New York, Hamburg, Fukuoka, Berlin and Dusseldorf), Le Pont de la Tour Ltd 1991–, Quaglino's Restaurant Ltd 1991–, Butlers Wharf Chop House Ltd 1992–, Conran Shop SA 1992–,Conran & Partners Ltd (formerly CD Partnership Ltd) 1993–, Conran Holdings Ltd 1993–, Mezzo Ltd 1993–, The Bluebird Store Ltd 1994–, Conran Restaurants Ltd 1994–, Conran Shop (Marylebone) Ltd 1996–, Conran Shop (Germany) Ltd 1997–, Afterdecide Ltd 1997–, Guastavino's Inc 1997–, Conran Distribution SARL Ltd 1997–, Conran Collection Ltd 1997–, Conran Properties (Marylebone) Ltd 1997–, Coq d'Argent Ltd 1997–, Conran Shop (Manhattan) Inc 1997–, Great Eastern Hotel Co Ltd 1997–, Orrery Restaurant Ltd 1997–, Sartoria Restaurant Ltd 1997–, Zinc Bar & Grill Ltd 1997–, Atlantic Blue SNC 1998–, Conran Finance Ltd 1998–; currently dir: Conran Ink Ltd 1969–, Conran Roche Ltd 1980–, Conran Octopus Ltd 1983–, Bibendum Restaurant Ltd 1986–, Michelin House Devpt Co Ltd 1989–, Michelin House Investment Co Ltd 1989–; jt chm Ryman Conran Ltd 1968–71; Habitat/Storehouse group: fndr 1971, chm Habitat Group Ltd 1971–88, chm Habitat France SA 1973–88, chm J Hepworth and Son Ltd 1981–83 (dir 1979–83), chm Habitat Mothercare plc (following merger) 1982–88, chm Richard Shops Ltd 1983–87, chm Heal and Son Ltd 1983–87, chm and chief exec Storehouse plc (following merger of Habitat/Mothercare with British Home Stores) 1986–88 (chm only 1988–90, non-exec dir 1990), dir BhS plc 1986–88; also formerly dir: RSCG Conran Design (formerly Conran Design Group/Conran Associates) 1971–92, The Neal Street Restaurant 1972–89, Conran Stores Inc 1977–88, Electra Risk Capital Group plc 1981–84, Savacentre Ltd 1986–88; memb: Royal Cmmn on Environmental Pollution 1973–76, Cncl RCA 1978–81 and 1986–, Advsy Cncl V&A 1979–83, Bd of Tstees V&A 1984–90, Assoc for Business Sponsorship of the Arts; estab Conran Fndn for Design Educn and Res 1981; chm Design Museum 1992– (tstee 1989–), vice-pres FNAC 1985–89, pres D&AD Awards 1989, provost RCA; Commandeur de l'Ordre des Arts et des Lettres (France) 1991; Hon FRIBA 1984, FSIAD; *Awards* Daily Telegraph/Assoc for Business Sponsorship of the Arts Award to Habitat Mothercare 1982, SIAD Medal 1982, RSA Bicentenary Medal 1984, RSA Presidential Medal for Design Mgmnt to Conran Gp, RSA Presidential Award for Design Mgmnt to Habitat Designs 1975, Hon Doctorate RCA 1996; *Books* The House Book (1974), The Kitchen Book (1977), The Bedroom and Bathroom Book (1978), The Cook Book (with Caroline Conran, 1980), Terence Conran's New House Book (1985), Conran Directory of Design (1985), Plants at Home (1986), The Soft Furnishings Book (1986), Terence Conran's France (1987), Terence Conran's DIY By Design (1989), Terence Conran's Garden DIY (1991), Toys and Children's Furniture (1992), Terence Conran's Kitchen Book (1993), The Essential House Book (1994), Terence Conran on Design (1996), The Conran Cookbook (1997, rev edn of The Cook Book), The Essential Garden Book (with Dan Pearson, 1998), Easy Living (1999), Chef's Garden (1999), Terence Conran on Restaurants (2000), Terence Conran on London (2000), Small Spaces (2001); *Recreations* gardening, cooking; *Style—* Sir Terence Conran; ✉ Terence Conran Ltd, 22 Shad Thames, London SE1 2YU (tel 020 7378 1161, fax 020 7403 4309)

CONROY, Harry; *b* 6 April 1943; *m* Margaret; 3 c (Lynn, Stuart, Ewan); *Career* trainee laboratory technician Southern Gen Hosp 1961–62, night messenger (copy boy) Scottish Daily Express 1962–63, sub ed Scottish Daily Express 1963–64, reporter Scottish Daily Mail 1966–67, fin corr Daily Record 1969–85 (reporter 1964–66 and 1967–69); NUJ: memb 1963–, memb Nat Exec Cncl 1976–85, vice-pres 1980–81, pres 1981–82, gen sec 1985–90, elected memb of honour 2000; campaign dir Scottish Constitutional Convention 1990–92; business writer, author and PR conslt 1992–; managing ed Scottish Catholic Observer 2001–05 (ed 2000–); dir Consumer Credit Counselling Service (Glasgow) 1996–99; TUC delegate 1981, 1982 and 1983; STUC delegate 1981–85; assoc memb Gen and Municipal Boilermakers' Union 1984–85; *Books* Guilty by Suspicion (with James Allison, 1995), The Long March of the Market Men (with Allan Stewart, MP, 1996), Off The Record - a Lifetime in Journalism (1997), The People Say Yes (ed, author Kenyon Wright), They Rose Again (ed and contrib, 2002), Jim Callaghan (2006); *Recreations* stamp collecting, hill walking, supporting Glasgow Celtic FC; *Style—* Harry Conroy, Esq; ✉ Conroy Associates, 44 Redwood Crescent, Dumbagard, Cambuslang, Glasgow G72 7FZ (tel 0141 641 9071)

CONROY, Paul Martin; s of Dennis Conroy, and Muriel Conroy, of Wallingford, Oxon; *b* 14 June 1949; *Educ* John Fisher Sch Purley, Ewell Tech (social sec); *m*; 2 c; *Career* agent for bands incl: Caravan, Fortunes, Van Der Graf Generator, Genesis, Lindisfarne, Kokomo, Chilli Willi, Dr Feelgood; fndr Charisma Agency (with Tony Stratton Smith), mangr The Kursaal Flyers; gen mangr Stiff Records working with: Elvis Costello, Ian Dury, Nick Lowe, Lene Lovich, Madness; mktg dir then md (US Div) Warners working with: Madonna, ZZ Top, Prince, Simply Red; pres Chrysalis Records 1990–92 working with: Sinead O'Connor, Billy Idol, and others; md then pres Virgin Records UK Ltd 1992–2002; artists incl: The Rolling Stones, Blue, Lennie Kravitz, Janet Jackson, Meat Loaf, UB40, Placebo, Massive Attack, The Spice Girls, Richard Ashcroft, Embrace, The Chemical Brothers, Gomez, Billie; currently chief operating officer Adventure Records and Adventures In Music Mgmnt; chm The BRIT Awards 1998–2000, memb Bd of Dirs BPI, chm BPI PR Ctee 2000–02; winner of President's Award for work on Country Music (first non-American recipient); memb Country Music Assoc; *Recreations* sport and more sport, Chelsea FC, antique fairs, family; *Style—* Paul Conroy, Esq; ✉ e-mail paul@adventuresin-music.com

CONROY, Stephen Alexander; s of Stephen James Conroy (d 1993), of Renton, Dunbartonshire, and Elizabeth Ann, *née* Walker; *b* 2 March 1964; *Educ* St Patrick's HS Dunbarton, Glasgow Sch of Art (BA, Harry McLean Bequest, Jock McFie award, postgrad award); *Career* artist; solo exhibitions: Marlborough Fine Art London 1989, 1992 and 1999 (and tour 1989), Glasgow Art Gallery & Museum 1989, Whitworth Art Gallery Manchester 1989, Marlborough Gallery NY 1995 and 2003, Everard Read Gallery Johannesburg SA 1996, Marlborough Galleria Madrid 1997, Musée Granet Aix-en-Provence 1998, FIAC Paris 2000, Marlborough Graphics London 2003, Schloss Gottorf Schleswig Germany 2003; gp exhibitions incl: The Vigorous Imagination - New Scottish Art (Scottish Nat Gallery of Modern Art, Edinburgh) 1987, The New British Painting tour USA 1988, Scottish Art Since 1990 (Scottish Nat Gallery of Modern Art Edinburgh and The Barbican London) 1989, Glasgow's Great British Art Exhibition 1990, Through The Artists Glass (Marlborough Graphics London) 1991, Scottish Art since 1900 (Gallery of Modern Art Edinburgh) 1992, The Portrait Now (Nat Portrait Gallery London) 1993, The Line of Tradition (Royal Scot Acad Edinburgh) 1994, An American Passion (Glasgow Museum and Royal Coll of Art London) 1994, Su Carta - On Paper (Galleria D'Arte Il Gabbiano Rome) 1996, Mirror Image (National Gallery London) 1998, L'Ecole de Londres (Musée Maillol Paris) 1998; work in the collections of: Aberdeen Art Gallery, The British Cncl, Birmingham Art Gallery, Contemporary Art Soc, Metropolitan Museum of Art NY, RCS, Robert Fleming Holdings Ltd, Scottish Nat Gallery of Modern Art, Scottish Nat Portrait Gallery, Southampton Art Gallery, Nat Portrait Gallery; awarded Grand Prix de Monte Carlo International Painting Prize 1998; *Style—* Stephen Conroy, Esq; ✉ Marlborough Fine Art, 6 Albemarle Street, London W1X 4BY (tel 020 7629 5161, fax 020 7629 6338)

CONRY, Rt Rev Kieran Thomas; *see:* Arundel and Brighton, Bishop of (RC)

CONSTABLE, Prof (Charles) John; s of Charles Constable (d 1997), of Bedford, and Gladys May, *née* Morris (d 2003); *b* 20 January 1936; *Educ* Durham Sch, Univ of Cambridge (MA), Univ of London (BSc), Harvard Univ (DBA); *m* 9 April 1960, Elisabeth Mary, da of Ronald Light (d 1981); 1 da (Harriet b 1961), 3 s (Charles b 1962, Giles b 1965, Piers b 1970); *Career* mgmnt educator and conslt; Cranfield Sch of Mgmnt: prof of mgmnt 1971–82, dir 1982–85; DG Br Inst of Mgmnt 1985–86; currently prof emeritus Cranfield Univ; non-exec dir: Lodge Ceramics Ltd and SIMAC Ltd 1982–90, International Military Services Ltd 1984–91, Lloyds Abbey Life plc 1987–97, Sage Group plc 1996–2005, NMBZ Ltd 1997–2003; chm: Bright Tech Developments Ltd 1989–98, LTB Ltd 2001–03, Internetcamerasdirect Ltd 2001–04; tstee Pensions Tst 1996–2003; govr Harpur Tst 1979–2003 (chm 1994–2003); memb: NEDO Heavy Electrical Machinery EDC 1977–87, N Beds DHA 1987–90; *Books* Group Assessment Programmes (with D A Smith, 1966), Text and Cases in Operations Management (with C C New, 1976), Cases in Strategic Management (with J Stopford and D Channon, 1980), The Making of British Managers (with R McCormick, 1987); *Recreations* family, golf; *Clubs* Bedfordshire Golf, Minehead and W Somerset Golf; *Style—* Prof John Constable

CONSTABLE, Paule; da of Wing Cdr Paul Constable, RAF, AFC, of Saudi Arabia, and Evelyn Rose Hadley; *b* 9 November 1966; *Educ* Goldsmiths Coll London; *Partner* Ian Richards; 1 da (Morgan Jezebel Richards b 14 May 1996), 1 s (Bram Willoughby Moon Richards b 6 August 1998); *Career* lighting designer; appts as lighting electrician incl: Midnight Design Ltd 1988–1990, Opera 80 (dep) 1990, Edinburgh Int Theatre (chief for Churchill Theatre 1990, dep chief for Playhouse Theatre 1991), English Shakespeare Co (chief) 1990–91, Rose English's The Double Wedding (prodn, LIFT) 1991, Shared Experiences UK tour of Anna Karenina (prodn) 1991, Rosie Lee (prodn) 1992, Mayfest (chief) 1992; appts as prodn mangr incl: International Workshop Festival 1990, Theatre de Complicité's The Winters Tale (UK tour) 1992, Theatre de Complicité's The Street of Crocodiles (World tour) 1993–94; tstee Cmmn to Promote Ribald Discourse Amongst Lighting Designers; memb Assoc of Lighting Designers; *Theatre* prodns incl: The Resistable Rise of Arturo Ui (7:84 Scotland) 1991, Scotland Matters (7:84 Scotland) 1992, The Street of Crocodiles (Theatre de Complicité/RNT (Olivier Award nomination for Best Lighting Design 1993)) 1992, Billy Liar (RNT Mobil touring prodn) 1992, India Song (Theatr Clwyd) 1993, Bondagers (Traverse and Donmar Warehouse) 1993, The Three Lives of Lucie Cabrol (Theatre de Complicité) 1994, Omma, Oedipus and the Luck of Thebes (Young Vic) 1994, The Slab Boys Trilogy (Young Vic) 1994, Out of a House Walked a Man (Theatre de Complicité/RNT) 1994, Lucky (David Glass Mime Ensemble) 1995, Spring Awakening (RSC) 1995, Tartuffe (Royal Exchange) 1995, The Jungle Book (Young Vic) 1995, Henry IV (parts I & II, English Touring Theatre) 1996, A Christmas Carol (Lyric Hammersmith) 1996, The Mysteries (RSC) 1997, The Caucasian Chalk Circle (RNT) 1997, Beckett Shorts (RSC) 1997, The Weir (Royal Court Upstairs) 1997, Morebinyon Tales (Young Vic and Broadway) 1997, Uncle Vanya (RSC/Young Vic) 1998, Haram and the Sea of Stories (RNT) 1998, Amadeus (Old Vic) 1998; *Opera* Magic Flute (Opera North) 1994 and 1997, Death of the Carmelites (Guildhall School) 1995, Worthur (English Touring Opera) 1995, Life with an Idiot (ENO) 1995, Ines de Castro (Scottish Opera) 1996, Don Giovanni (WNO) 1996, Sweeny Todd (Opera North) 1998, Fidelio (Wellington Int Festival NZ) 1998; *Recreations* travel, cricket; *Style—* Ms Paule Constable; ✉ c/o Richard Haig, Performing Arts Management, 6 Windmill Street, London W1P 1HF (tel 020 7255 1362, fax 020 7631 4631)

CONSTANT, Richard Ashley Meyricke; MBE (1983); s of Maj Ashley Henry Constant (d 1985), and Mabel Catherine (Kate), *née* Meyricke (d 1972); *b* 25 November 1954; *Educ* King's Sch Canterbury, RMA Sandhurst, Univ of Durham (BA); *m* 1984, Melinda Jane, da of late H J Davies; 2 s (Llewelyn Ashley Meyricke b 1985, Tristam Ashley Meyricke b 1987), 2 da (Sophia, Rosanna (twins) b 1989); *Career* cmmnd Royal Green Jackets 1973, ret with the rank of Maj; merchant banker Robert Fleming & Co Ltd 1985–89; chief exec Gavin Anderson & Company UK Ltd 1999–, chief exec Gavin Anderson Worldwide 2000–; non-exec dir: Austin Reed Group plc 1992–2001, Fibrowatt Ltd; *Recreations* shooting, eventing, fishing; *Clubs* IOD, Royal Green Jackets, Wig and Pen; *Style—* Richard Constant, Esq, MBE; ✉ Gavin Anderson & Co Ltd, 85 Strand, London WC2R 0DW (tel 020 7554 1404)

CONSTANTINE, David John; s of William Bernard Constantine, of Deganwy, N Wales, and Bertha, *née* Gleave; *b* 4 March 1944; *Educ* Manchester Grammar, Wadham Coll Oxford (BA, DPhil); *m* 9 July 1966, Helen Frances, da of Richard Stanley Best; 1 da (Mary Ann b 27 Nov 1968), 1 s (Simon Martin b 1 Oct 1972); *Career* sr lectr in German Univ of Durham 1979–80 (lectr 1969–79), fell in German The Queen's Coll Oxford 1980–2000; fndr memb Durham Cyrenians charity for homeless (sec 1972–80); jt ed Modern Poetry in Translation; *Books* poetry: A Brightness to Cast Shadows (1980), Watching for Dolphins (1983, Alice Hunt Barlett Award), Madder (1987, Southern Arts Literature Prize), New and Selected Poems (1991), Caspar Hauser (1994), The Pelt of Wasps (1998), Something for the Ghosts (2002), Collected Poems (2004); fiction: Davies (1985), Back at the Spike (1994), Under the Dam (2005); trans: Selected Poems of Friedrich Hölderlin (1990, new edn 1996), Goethe's Elective Affinities (1994), Kleist: Selected Writings (1997), Hölderlin's Sophocles (2001), H M Enzensberger: Lighter than Air (2002), Goethe: Faust Part I (2005); biography: Fields of Fire, A Life of Sir William Hamilton (2001); academic works: Early Greek Travellers and the Hellenic Ideal (1984, Runciman Prize); Hölderlin (1988); *Recreations* walking; *Style—* David Constantine, Esq; ✉ 1 Hill Top Road, Oxford OX4 1PB

CONSTANTINIDES, Prof Anthony George; s of George Anthony Constantinides, and Paraskeve Constantinides Skaliondas; *b* 1 January 1943; *Educ* The Pancyprian Gymnasium, Univ of London (BSc, PhD); *m* 21 Dec 1968, Pamela Maureen, da of Anthony Robert Bowman (ka 1940); 1 s (George Anthony b 21 Oct 1975); *Career* sr research fell PO Research Dept 1968–70, prof in signal processing Imperial Coll of Science and Technol 1983– (lectr then reader 1970–83), hon visiting prof Inst of Archaeology UCL; author of six books and over 200 papers in learned jls on aspects of digital signal processing; FIEE 1985, FRSA 1986, FIEEE 1997 (MIEEE 1978), FREng 2004; Officier dans l'Ordre des Palmes Académiques (France); *Recreations* reading; *Style—* Prof Anthony Constantinides; ✉ Imperial College London, Department of Electrical and Electronic Engineering, Exhibition Road, London SW7 2BT (tel 020 7594 6233)

CONSTANTINOU, Achilleas; s of Nicos Constantinou (d 1971), of London, and Efthymia, *née* Cleanthous; *b* 21 April 1948; *Educ* Arnos Secdy Modern Sch Southgate, Waltham Forest Tech Coll, KCL (LLB); *m* Androulla, da of George Georgallides; 3 s (Alexander Nicholas b 21 June 1981, Nicholas George b 3 May 1982, Marcus Aristos b 18 July 1990), 1 da (Lana Marie b 4 Aug 1984); *Career* started fashion business Aristos of London with late bro Aristos at 45 Carnaby St in 1966, joined family co full time in 1971, by 1973 owned 6 retail outlets in Carnaby St and Oxford St, a wholesale showroom in Great Portland St and headquarters in Marylebone, subsequently added retail stores in Duke St, London, Lausanne, Switzerland, and a franchised store in Chicago USA; relocated showrooms to Mortimer St and subsequently to larger premises in Great Portland St; now focuses exclusively on designs and marketing wholesale from expansive headquarters in Wood Green; was honoured by a royal visit by Princess Anne in 1992 to celebrate co's 25th anniversary; chm and md Ariella Fashions Ltd & Group of Cos (winner of two Woman Fashion Awards for Best Cocktail Dress and Best Evening Dress 1985, winner of the Br Apparel Export Award 1996, winner of The Queen's Award for Export Achievement 1998); fndr Br Fashion & Design Protection Assoc 1974 (which succeeded in gaining copyright protection extended to cover original fashion garment designs in 1980), advsr to Govt on amendments to Design Copyright and Patents Act 1988, UK rep EEC meeting of Assoc Européene des Industries de L'Habillement, fndr memb Fashion Indust Action Gp (responsible for formation of Br Fashion Cncl (BFC)), fndr memb and dir Br Fashion Cncl, chm BFC Mainstream Ctee, former memb Advsy Bd London Fashion Exhibition, memb Bd of Management and former chm of the Women's Wear Exec Ctee Br Knitting and Clothing Export Cncl (BKCEC, now UK Fashion Exports); memb Gray's Inn; *Books* Memorandum on the Law of Copyright, Design Protection (contrib); *Style—* Achilleas Constantinou, Esq; ✉ Ariella Fashions Ltd, Zenth House, 69 Lawrence Road, London N15 4TG (tel 020 8800 5777, fax 020 8880 2882, e-mail ac@ariella.co.uk, website www.ariella.co.uk)

CONTE HELM, Marie; *b* 13 November 1949, New York City; *Educ* City Univ of NY (BA), East West Center Univ of Hawaii (MA); *Career* lectr art history Leeward Community Coll Hawaii 1973–74, cultural offr Japan Info Centre Embassy of Japan London 1975–79, lectr in art history Sunderland Poly 1979–86, head Japanese Studies Div and reader in Japanese studies Univ of Sunderland 1986–94, reader in Japanese studies Univ of Northumbria 1994–99; visiting prof Univ of Northumbria 1999–; The Daiwa Anglo-Japanese Fndn: dir 1999–2000, dir gen 2000–; memb: British Assoc for Japanese Studies (hon sec 1992–94), Royal Soc for the Encouragement of Arts, Manufacturers and Commerce; memb Cncl Japan Soc 1992–96, memb Educn Ctee Japan Festival 1991 1989–91 (N Regnl Ctee 1988–91), memb Ctee Japan Language Assoc 1990–94, Univ of Sunderland rep Anglo-Korean Network 1990–, chair Anglo-Japanese Women's Soc 1990–94; memb Culture and E Asian Working Gp of UK-Japan 2000 Gp 1992–; HEFCE subject assessor South and East Asian Studies 1996–99; *Books* Japan and the North East of England - From 1862 to the Present Day (1989, a Financial Times Book of the Year 1989, Japanese edn 1991), The Japanese and Europe: Economic and Cultural Encounters (1996); author of numerous articles and reviews; *Style—* Prof Marie Conte Helm; ✉ The Daiwa Anglo-Japanese Foundation, Daiwa Foundation Japan House, 13–14 Cornwall Terrace, London NW1 4QP (tel 020 7486 4348, fax 020 7486 2914, e-mail marie.conte-helm@dajf.org.uk)

CONTI, Most Rev Mario Joseph; *see:* Glasgow, Archbishop of (RC)

CONTI, Thomas A (Tom); s of Alfonso Conti (d 1961), of Paisley, Renfrewshire, and Mary McGoldrick (d 1979); *b* 22 November 1941; *Educ* Royal Scottish Acad of Music; *m* 1967, Katherine Drummond, da of Wilson George Drummond Tait, of Edinburgh; 1 da (Nina b 1973); *Career* actor, director and novelist; *Theatre* began 1960; London appearances incl: Savages (Royal Court and Comedy) 1973, The Devil's Disciple (RSC Aldwych) 1976, Whose Life Is It Anyway? (Mermaid and Savoy) 1978 (also NY 1979), They're Playing Our Song (Shaftesbury) 1980, Romantic Comedy (Apollo) 1983, Jeffrey Bernard Is Unwell (Lyric) 1990, The Ride Down Mount Morgan (Wyndhams) 1991, Present Laughter (also dir) 1993, Chapter Two (Gielgud) 1996, Jesus my Boy (Apollo)1998; as director: Last Licks (Broadway) 1979, Before the Party (Oxford Playhouse and Queen's) 1980, The Housekeeper (Apollo) 1982; *Television* incl: Madame Bovary, The Norman Conquests, The Glittering Prizes, The Quick and the Dead (TV film), The Beatte Klarsfeld Story (mini-series), Wright Verdicts (USA), Cinderella and Me, I Was a Rat, Donovan; *Film* incl: Galileo 1974, Flame 1974, Eclipse 1975, Full Circle 1977, The Duellists 1977, The Wall 1980, Merry Christmas Mr Lawrence 1983, Reuben Reuben 1983, American Dreamer 1984, Heavenly Pursuits 1985, Saving Grace 1985, Miracles 1986, Beyond Therapy 1987, Two Brothers Running 1988, That Summer of White Roses 1989, Shirley Valentine1989, Someone Else's America 1994, XSUB Down 1996, Something to Believe In 1996, Out of Control 1997, The Enemy 2000, Derailed 2004, Paid 2004, Beyond Friendship 2005; *Awards* for Whose Life Is It Anyway?: Best Actor in a New Play SWET 1978, Best Stage Actor Variety Club of GB 1978, Tony for Best Actor 1979; *Books* The Doctor (2004); *Clubs* Garrick; *Style—* Tom Conti Esq; ✉ c/o Finch & Partners, 4–8 Heddon Street, London, W1B 4BS

CONTRERAS, Prof Dame (Carmen) Marcela; DBE (2007); da of Dr Juan Eduardo Contreras (d 1993), of Coelemu, Chile, and Elena Mireya, *née* Arriagada; *b* 4 January 1942; *Educ* Dunalastair Br Sch for Girls Santiago Chile, Sch of Med Univ of Chile (clinical/immunology scholar, BSc, LMed, Medico-Cirujano, MD); *m* 1968 (m dis 1997); 1 s (Claudio b 10 Nov 1968), 1 da (Carolina b 1 May 1972); *Career* trg prog in internal med, immunology and immunohaematology (Univ of Chile) Univ Hosp J J Aguirre and Hosp San Juan de Dios Santiago 1968–72, lectr in immunology and immunohaematology Centre of Immunohaematology Univ Hosp J J Aguirre Santiago 1971–72, Br Cncl scholar Royal Postgraduate Med Sch and MRC Blood Gp Unit London 1972–74, head Immunohaematology Lab North London Blood Transfusion Centre Edgware 1974–78, sr registrar in haematology St Mary's Hosp London and Northwick Park Hosp Harrow 1978–80; North London Blood Transfusion Centre London: dep dir 1980–84, chief exec/med dir 1984–95; exec dir London and SE Zone Nat Blood Serv 1995–99, dir of diagnostics, development and research Nat Blood Serv 1999–; prof of transfusion med Royal Free and Univ Coll Hosp Med Sch 1998–, visiting prof Faculty of Applied Sciences Univ of the West of England 2004–; memb Cncl: Int Soc of Blood Transfusion (pres 1996–98), RCPath (chm Sub-Ctee on Transfusion Med 1994–95 and 1999–2001); pres Section of Pathology RSM 1992–94, pres Br Blood Transfusion Soc 2000–02; review ed Vox Sanguinis 1987–95 and 2003– (ed-in-chief 1996–2003), assoc ed Transfusion Alternatives In Transfusion Medicine 1989–96 and 1999–; memb Editorial Bd: Transfusion Medicine 1990–, Transfusion Medicine Reviews 1993–, Blood Reviews 1995–; hon sr lectr St Mary's Hosp London 1999–, hon memb MRC Blood Gp Unit; memb: bd of dirs NATA, Br Soc for Haematology, BMA, American Assoc of Blood Banks (AABB), Int Soc of Blood Transfusion (ISBT), Br Blood Transfusion Soc (BBTS), RSM (Sections of Pathology and Immunology), Euro Sch of Transfusion Med, Euro Cord Blood Banking Gp; hon academic Faculty of Medicine Univ of Buenos Aires 1989, Paul Harris fell Rotary Fndn of Rotary Int 1990, honoured guest lectr Hong Kong Red Cross Blood Transfusion Soc 1993; Zoutendyk Medal Univ of Johannesburg 1995, H R Nevanlinna Medal Helsinki 2002, ISBT Award for outstanding contrib to blood transfusion and transfusion medicine 2004, ACOBASMET & Gp CIAMT Transfusion Medicine Award 2004, AABB/BBTS/ISBT Int Women in Transfusion Award 2005; hon memb: Chilean Soc for Haematology 1990, Brazilian Soc for Haemotherapy 1993; FRCPEd 1992, FRCPath 1997 (MRCPath 1988), FRCP 1998, fell Acad Med Sci 2003; *Books* Blood Transfusion in Clinical Med (jtly, 8 edn 1987, 10 edn 1997), ABC of Transfusion (1990, 3 edn 1998), Blood Transfusion: The Impact of New Technologies (1990); author of over 300 pubns in the field of transfusion med; *Recreations* opera, theatre, walking, reading, training in developing countries, riding; *Clubs* International Medical, Haematology Travellers'; *Style—* Prof Dame Marcela Contreras, DBE

CONVERY, Francis; s of John Joseph Convery (d 1994), and Alice Agnes, *née* Burns (d 1992); *b* 12 February 1956; *Educ* St Mirins Acad Paisley, Edinburgh Coll of Art (BA, Dip); *m* Lyn Sneddon; 3 da (Eve b 12 June 1991, Blythe b 16 May 1994, Mirin b 5 Jan 2001); *Career* mech engr 1972–76; pt/t lectr Edinburgh Coll of Art 1984–86 (student 1979–83 and 1984), head of painting Gray's Sch of Art Aberdeen 1997– (lectr in drawing and painting 1987–97); pres Aberdeen Artists Soc; RSA 2005 (ARSA 1994); *Solo Exhibitions* Festival Club Univ of Edinburgh 1984, Mercury Gallery Edinburgh 1984, Andrew Grant Gallery Edinburgh Coll of Art 1988, The Scottish Gallery Edinburgh 1991 and 1995; *Group Exhibitions* incl: Stowells Exhibition (Royal Acad) 1983, Mall Galleries London 1983, Mercury Gallery Edinburgh 1983 and 1985, Akademie Der Bildenden Kunste Munich 1984, Mercury Gallery London 1984, 1986, 1988, 1989 and 1994, Compass Gallery Glasgow 1984, 1992 and 1993, Royal Scottish Acad Edinburgh 1984, 1991, 1992, 1993, 1994, 1995 and 1996, Contemporary Art (Bath Festival) 1985, Edinburgh/Dublin (Edinburgh Festival) 1985, Scottish Drawing (Paisley Art Galleries) 1985 and 1987, Int Art Fair Olympia 1986, Water Tower Art Fndn Louisville 1986, Selected Works (Edinburgh Festival) 1987, Day Book (Smiths' Gallery London) 1988, Fruit Market (touring) 1988, Fruit Market Open (Edinburgh) 1988, Morrison Portrait Exhibition (RSA Edinburgh) 1989, Scottish Myths (The Scottish Gallery Edinburgh) 1990, Largo Awards Exhibition (Loomshop Gallery Fife) 1991, 20th Century British Art (RCA London) 1991, The Scottish Gallery Edinburgh 1993 and 1994, Fosse Gallery Stow-on-the-Wold 1993, 1994 and 1995, Fresh Paint (City Art Centre Edinburgh) 1995, Networking (Edinburgh Int Festival) 1996, The Hunting Art Prizes (RCA London) 1997, The Hunterian Museum Glasgow 1997, Moby Dick (limited edn book of prints int tour) 1997–98, Paperwork (Loyola Univ New Orleans) 2001, Line Management (Hunter Coll NYC) 2001, Jewel Art Centre Boston 2003–04, York Coll NYC 2003–04, Painters in Parallel (Aberdeen Art Gallery) 2005; *Collections* Aberdeen City Art Gallery, Univ of Edinburgh, Edinburgh Coll of Art, Edinburgh Cncl, Edinburgh City Arts Centre, Fosse Gallery Stow-on-the-Wold, Mercury Gallery London, Paisley Art Gallery & Museums, Scottish Gallery Edinburgh, Royal Scotish Acad, Br Airways, various private collections in UK, USA and Europe; *Awards* first prize Rowney Competition for painting 1982, Carnegie travelling scholarship for painting 1983, RSA Keith Prize 1983, John Kinross travelling scholarship to Florence 1983, RSA Latimer Award for painting 1984, Largo Award for painting 1984, RSA Scottish Post Office Bd Award 1992, RSA Highland Soc of London Award 1994, Shell Expro Award 1995, highly commended Hunting Art Prizes 1997; *Style—* Francis Convery, Esq, RSA; ✉ Stracathro House, Stracathro, by Brechin, Angus DD9 7QF (tel 01356 649775, mobile 07793 214802); Gray's School of Art, Garthdee Road, Aberdeen (tel 01224 263633, fax 01224 263636)

CONVILLE, Clare Benedicta; da of David Conville, of Blandford Forum, Dorset, and Margaret, *née* Bury (d 1967); *b* 14 October 1959, London; *Educ* Cranborne Chase Sch, Westminster, Univ of Bristol; *m* 1, 26 Oct 1984 (m dis), Simon Pell; m 2, 4 Aug 1989 (sep), Jonathan Riley; 2 s (Thomas b 18 Aug 1988, Edward b 14 Sept 1991), 1 da (Mary b 4 Aug 1993); *Career* Random House Children's Books: publicity and mktg dir 1989–91, publishing dir 1991–93; agent A P Watt 1993–2000, fndr and dir Conville & Walsh Ltd 2000–; *Recreations* reading, listening to classical music, bikram yoga; *Clubs* Academy; *Style—* Miss Clare Conville; ✉ 30 Chelsham Road, London SW4 0NP (tel 020 7720 7618); Conville & Walsh Limited, 2 Ganton Street, London W1F 7QL (tel 020 7287 3030, fax 020 7287 4545, e-mail clare@convilleandwalsh.com)

CONWAY, Dr Ashley V; *b* 7 September 1956; *Educ* St Edward's Sch Oxford, Univ of Southampton (BSc), Univ of London (PhD); *m* 7 July 1984, Martine Louise, *née* Jeronimus; 2 da (Emily Louise b 29 Aug 1987, Catherine May b 25 April 1993), 1 s (Joseph Jeronimus b 15 March 1989); *Career* psychologist specialising in therapy for trauma, anxiety and stress-related illness; sec Univ Psychology Soc 1977–79, hon psychologist Charing Cross Hosp 1985–95, psychologist Devonshire Clinic London 1986–91, trauma conslt PPC UK Ltd 1993–98; pt/t med res examining mind/body interactions 1985–, memb Cncl Hypnosis and Psychosomatic Med RSM 1998–; author of numerous published papers on related subjects in med and psychological jls; FRSM 1998; *Style—* Dr A V Conway; ✉ 144

Harley Street, London W1G 7LD (tel 020 7935 0023, fax 020 7935 5972, e-mail aconway@easynet.co.uk)

CONWAY, Dr David Ian; s of Jack and Gita Conway, of Salford; *b* 21 April 1948; *Educ* Manchester Grammar, Univ of Manchester (MB ChB, MD), Open Univ (BA); *m* 23 Oct 1975, Pauline; 3 s (Jonathan b 1978, Benjamin b 1983, Duncan b 1988), 4 da (Rachel b 1979, Heather b 1981, Felicity b 1982, Rebecca b 1986); *Career* lectr obstetrics and gynaecology (specialising in infertility) Univ of Bristol 1980–84, hon sr lectr in obstetrics and gynaecology Univ of Glasgow; conslt; Monklands Dist Gen Hosp Airdrie 1984–; FRCOG 1992 (MRCOG 1977); *Recreations* my family; *Style*— Dr David Conway; ✉ 53 Kirkintilloch Road, Lenzie, Glasgow G66 4LB (tel 0141 776 1463); Monklands District General Hospital, Monkscourt Avenue, Airdrie, Lanarkshire ML6 0JS (tel 01236 712285); Glasgow Nuffield Hospital, Beaconsfield Road, Glasgow G12 0PJ (tel 0141 334 9441, fax 0141 339 1352, e-mail david.conway@lanarkshire.scot.nhs.uk)

CONWAY, Derek Leslie; TD, MP; s of Leslie Conway, and Florence Gwendoline, *née* Bailes; *b* 15 February 1953; *Educ* Beacon Hill Boys' Sch; *m* 1980, Colette Elizabeth Mary, da of Charles Lamb; 2 s (Henry b 1982, Fredrick b 1985), 1 da (Claudia b 6 March 1989); *Career* memb Cons Pty Nat Exec 1972–81, nat vice-chm Young Cons 1973–75; borough cncllr 1974–78, ldr Tyne & Wear Met CC 1979–82 (memb 1977–83); Parly candidate: (Cons) Durham Oct 1974, Newcastle upon Tyne E 1979; MP (Cons): Shrewsbury and Atcham 1983–97, Old Bexley and Sidcup 2001–; PPS: to min of state for Wales 1988–91, to min of state Dept of Employment 1992–93; asst Govt whip 1993–94; a Lord Cmmr HM Treasy (Govt whip) and memb Bd Treasy 1994–96, Vice-Chamberlain of HM Household (Govt whip) 1996–97; memb Select Ctees: on Agriculture, on Tport, on Armed Forces Discipline 1990–91, on Defence 2005–06; chm Accomodation and Works Ctee 2001–05, vice-chm Defence Ctee 1991–93; memb: Speaker's Panel of Chairmen 2001–, Liaison Ctee of Chairmen 2001–05, Admin Ctee 2005–; chief exec Cats Protection League 1998–; memb: Bd Washington Devpt Corpn 1979–83, Bd Newcastle Airport 1979–82; Maj 5 Bn The LI TA; *Style*— Derek Conway, Esq, TD, MP; ✉ House of Commons, London SW1A 0AA

CONWAY, Prof Sir Gordon Richard; KCMG (2005), DL (East Sussex 2006); s of Cyril Gordon Conway (d 1977), of Kingston, Surrey, and Thelma, *née* Goodwin (d 1992); *b* 6 July 1938; *Educ* Kingston GS, Kingston Tech Coll, Univ of Wales Bangor (BSc), Univ of Cambridge (DipAgSc), Univ of West Indies Trinidad (DTA), Univ of Calif Davis (PhD); *m* 20 March 1965, Susan Mary, da of Harold Mumford, of Winchester, Hants; 1 s (Simon Goodwin b 10 Feb 1967), 2 da (Katherine Ellen, Zoe Martha (twins) b 2 March 1973); *Career* entomologist State of Sabah Malaysia 1961–66, statistician Inst of Ecology Univ of Calif 1966–69; Univ of London: res fell and lectr Dept of Zoology & Applied Entomology Imperial Coll 1970–76, reader in environmental mgmnt 1976–80, prof of environmental technol 1980–88, chm Centre for Environmental Technol 1980–86 (dir 1977–80), dir Sustainable Agric Prog Int Inst for Environment and Devpt 1986–88; rep for India, Nepal and Sri Lanka The Ford Foundation New Delhi 1989–92, vice-chllr Univ of Sussex 1992–98, pres Rockefeller Fndn NY 1998–2004, chief scientific advsr DfID 2004–; visiting prof Imperial Coll London 1989–, emeritus prof Univ of Sussex; memb Royal Cmmn on Environmental Pollution 1984–88; pres RGS 2006–; chm: Bd IDS 1992–98, Runnymede Cmmn on British Muslims and Islamaphobia 1996–98; co-chm Living Cities 1999–2003; hon fell Univ of Wales Bangor, fell Imperial Coll London, Hon LLD Univ of Sussex, Hon DSc Univ of West Indies Trinidad, Hon DSc Univ of Brighton, Hon DUniv Open Univ; Hon FIBiol, FCGI, FAAAS, FRS; *Books* Pest and Pathogen Control (1980), After The Green Revolution (jtly, 1989), Unwelcome Harvest (jtly, 1991), The Doubly Green Revolution (1997); *Recreations* travel, music; *Clubs* Reform; *Style*— Prof Sir Gordon Conway, KCMG, DL, FRS; ✉ Imperial College, Exhibition Road, London SW7 2AY

CONWAY, Robert David; s of Walter Conway, of Guildford; *b* 11 December 1949; *Educ* Univ of London (LLB); *m* 17 Jan 1976, Patricia Lock; 2 da (Anna b 6 Oct 1978, Laura b 20 Sept 1980); *Career* tax offr 1969, DPP 1973, called to the Bar Inner Temple 1974, SE circuit, lectr in law and legal conslt to Legal Protection Insurance Co; writer and performer (as Walter Zerlin Jr); winner Edinburgh Festival Scotsman Award 1975 and 1980, own tv show on Granada, six plays published and performed worldwide; dir: Entertainment Machine Theatre Co, Coups De Theatre Ltd, Conway McGillivray Publishing House; legal advsr to A Fish Called Wanda, and Marlon Brando's A Dry White Season; *Books* Miss You've Dropped Your Briefs (cartoonist), The British Alternative Theatre Directory (ed yearly); *Recreations* art, music, swimming; *Style*— Robert Conway, Esq

CONYNGHAM, 7 Marquess (I 1816); Frederick William Henry Francis Conyngham; also (sits as) Baron Minster (UK 1821), Earl Conyngham (I 1781), Baron Conyngham (I 1781), Viscount Conyngham (I 1789), Viscount Mount Charles (I 1797), Earl of Mount Charles and Viscount Slane (I 1816); patron of one living; s of 6 Marquess Conyngham (d 1974), by his 2 wife Antoinette Winifred, *née* Thompson (d 1966); *b* 13 March 1924; *Educ* Eton; *m* 1, 1950 (m dis 1970), Eileen Wren, o da of Capt Clement Wren Newsam; 3 s; m 2, 1971, Elizabeth Ann, yr da of late Frederick Molyneux Hughes, and formerly w of David Sutherland Rudd; m 3, 1980, Daphne Georgina Adelaide (d 1986), eldest da of R C Armour, and formerly w of C P V Walker; m 4, 1987, (Emma Christianne) Annabelle, o da of (Denys) Martin Agnew; *Heir* s, Earl of Mount Charles; *Career* late Capt Irish Gds; *Recreations* fishing, shooting, golf, tennis; *Clubs* Royal St George Yacht; *Style*— The Most Hon the Marquess Conyngham; ✉ Myrtle Hill, Ramsey, Isle of Man IM8 3UA

COODE, Edward Robert (Ed); MBE (2005); s of Jonathan Coode, and Judy, *née* Hall; *b* 19 June 1975, Indian Queens, Cornwall; *Educ* Eton, Univ of Newcastle upon Tyne, Univ of Oxford (Rowing blue); *m* Clare Smales; *Career* amateur rower; memb Leander Club; achievements incl: Silver medal coxless fours World Junior Championships 1993, Silver medal coxed fours World Under 23 Championships 1996, Bronze medal coxed fours World Championships 1997, winner coxless fours World Cup 1999, Gold medal coxless fours World Championships 1999, fourth place coxless pairs Olympic Games Sydney 2000, Gold medal coxless fours World Championships 2001, Bronze medal eights World Championships 2003, Gold medal coxless fours Olympic Games Athens 2004; trainee slr Burges Salmon Bristol; *Recreations* diving, surfing; *Style*— Ed Coode, Esq, MBE; ✉ c/o Matt Jones, Benchmark Sport, Henrietta Street, London (tel 020 7240 7700, e-mail matt@benchmarksport.com)

COODE-ADAMS, (John) Giles Selby; OBE (1998), DL (Essex); s of Geoffery Coode-Adams (d 1986), and Cynthia Mildred, *née* Selby-Bigge (d 1998); *b* 30 August 1938; *Educ* Eton; *m* 30 April 1960, Sonia Elisabeth, da of Laurence Frederick York (d 1965); 1 da (Henrietta Guest b 5 Feb 1962), 1 s (Ben b 19 Aug 1965); *Career* 2 Lt 16/5 Queen's Royal Lancers 1956–58; ptnr L Messel 1967 (joined 1959, taken over by Shearson Lehman Hutton 1986), md then sr advsr Lehman Brothers 1986–99; dir: Guardian Media Gp plc 1999–, Rathbone Brothers plc 1999–, Trader Media Gp plc 2003–; chm Westonbirt and Bedgebury Advsy Ctee, treas RHS, former chief exec Royal Botanic Gardens Kew Fndn, former memb Gardens Ctee English Heritage, former memb Cncl Univ of Essex; High Sheriff Essex 2000–01; Freeman: City of London, Worshipful Co of Merchant Taylors; *Recreations* fishing, music, gardening; *Clubs* Boodle's; *Style*— Giles Coode-Adams, Esq, OBE, DL; ✉ Feeringbury Manor, Feering, Colchester, Essex CO5 9RB (tel 0137 656 1946)

COOGAN, Steve; *b* 14 October 1965, Manchester; *Educ* Manchester Poly; *Career* comedian, actor and writer; co-fndr Baby Cow Productions 1999; Showbusiness Personality of the Year Variety Club Awards 1999, Perrier Award 1992 *Television* incl: Spitting Image (various voices) 1984, Paul Calf's Video Diary 1993, The Day Today 1994, Knowing Me, Knowing You with Alan Partridge 1994, Paul Calf's Wedding Video (Three Fights, Two Weddings and a Funeral) 1994, Coogan's Run 1995, The Tony Ferrino Phenomenon 1997, I'm Alan Partridge 1998–2002, Dr Terrible's House of Horrible 2001, Paul and Pauline Calf's Cheese and Ham Sandwich 2003, The Private Life of Samuel Pepys 2003, The All Star Comedy Show 2004, I Am Not an Animal 2004, Saxondale 2005; *Radio* incl: On the Hour (BBC Radio 4) 1991–92 (Best Radio Comedy Br Comedy Awards 1992), Knowing Me, Knowing You with Alan Partridge (BBC Radio 4) 1992–93; *Film* incl: The Indian in the Cupboard 1995, The Wind in the Willows 1996, The Parole Officer (also writer) 2001, 24 Hour Party People 2002, Around the World in 80 Days 2004, A Cock and Bull Story 2005, Marie Antoinette 2006, Hot Fuzz 2007; *Style*— Steve Coogan; ✉ c/o Baby Cow Productions, 77 Oxford Street, London W1D 2ES (tel 020 7399 1267, fax 020 7399 1262, website www.babycow.co.uk)

COOK, Alan Ronald; CBE (2006); s of late Ronald Joseph Cook, and Dorothy, *née* Wills; *b* 23 September 1953, Wembley, Middx; *Educ* Ealing GS for Boys; *m* 20 Sept 1970, Anita, *née* Kelleher; 2 s (Christopher b 23 April 1978, Martin b 6 March 1986), 1 da (Jennifer b 10 April 1981); *Career* Prudential Assurance Co Ltd 1970–93, sr vice-pres Jackson National Life USA 1993–96; Prudential Assurance Co Ltd: acquisitions dir 1996–97, md gen insurance 1997–99, md retail insurance ops 1999–2000, chief exec insurance servs 2000–01, chief operating offr UK and Europe 2001–02; chief exec National Savings and Investments 2002–06, md Post Office Ltd 2006–; govr Inst of Financial Servs; memb Ct Univ of Bedfordshire; Freeman City of London, memb Worshipful Co of Insurers 2005; FCII 1975, FRSA 2000, FCIM 2005; *Recreations* family, fell walking, swimming; *Style*— Alan Cook, Esq, CBE; ✉ Post Office Limited, 80 Old Street, London EC1V 9NN (tel 020 7320 7400, fax 020 7320 7601, e-mail alan.cook@postoffice.co.uk)

COOK, Alastair Nathan; *b* 25 December 1984, Gloucester; *Educ* Bedford Sch; *Career* cricketer; Essex CCC 2003–; England: 21 Test caps, 11 one day int appearances, 2 Twenty20 appearances, Test debut v India Nagpur 2006, one day int debut v Sri Lanka Old Trafford 2006, capt under 19 team World Cup 2004; NBC Denis Compton Award 2003, 2004 and 2005, Cricket Writers' Club Young Cricketer of the Year 2005, Professional Cricketers Assoc Young Player of the Year 2005 and 2006; ✉ England and Wales Cricket Board, Lord's Cricket Ground, St John's Wood Road, London NW8 8QZ

COOK, Alistair Copland Campbell; s of George Arthur Campbell Cook (d 1978), of Edinburgh, and Margaret Maule, *née* McMurtrie (d 1987); *b* 3 July 1953; *Educ* Daniel Stewart's Coll Edinburgh, Univ of Aberdeen (BSc), Univ of Strathclyde; *m* 22 June 1979, Dr Glynis Elizabeth, da of Douglas Cruickshank Watson; 3 s (Stuart b 9 Dec 1982, Richard b 7 Dec 1984, Graeme b 19 June 1988); *Career* articled clerk Touche Ross & Co Edinburgh 1976–80, mangr Price Waterhouse Hong Kong 1980–84, sr mangr Price Waterhouse London 1984–87, fin dir and co sec D'Arcy Masius Benton & Bowles Ltd London 1987, chief fin offr DMB&B Holdings Ltd (UK, Ireland and Middle East) 1990–95, chief fin offr Ammirati Puris Lintas UK/Northern Europe 1996–2000; McCann-Erickson: sr vice-pres and regnl fin dir Central and Eastern Europe 2000–02, exec vice-pres and chief fin offr EMEA 2003–06; M&A advsr to various US and UK private equity partnerships 2006–; memb Fin Ctee EACA 1998–2006; tstee and hon treas Int Family Health 1996–2003; MICAS 1979, MIPA 1990, FRSA 2005; *Recreations* golf, motoring, travel, Scottish art, opera; *Clubs* RAC, Hever Golf, Hong Kong Cricket; *Style*— Alistair C C Cook, Esq; ✉ Tan House Farm, Toy's Hill, near Edenbridge, Kent TN8 6NX (tel 01732 750666, fax 01732 750129, e-mail alistaircc.cook@btinternet.com)

COOK, Allan Vincent Cannon; CBE (1999); s of Cyril Percy Cannon Cook (d 1957), and Jocelyne Marie Anne, *née* Cockell; *b* 28 February 1940; *Educ* Wimbledon Coll, LSE (BSc Econ); *Career* audit sr Knox Cropper & Co Chartered Accountants 1964–65 (articled clerk 1961–64); Unilever: accounting mangr then system analyst MacFisheries 1966–71, accountant Central Pensions Dept 1971–75, memb fin gp 1975–78, asst accounting principles offr 1978–79, seconded as sec International Accounting Standards Ctee (IASC) 1979–81; head of accounting res Shell International Petroleum Co 1982–90; chm Working Gp on Accounting Standards BIAC OECD; visiting prof Middlesex Univ 1997–; memb: Consultative Gp IASC, Accounting Standards Ctee 1987–90; tech dir Accounting Standards Bd 1990–2003, Technical Expert Gp of the European Financial Reporting Gp 2001–05, co-ordinator Int Financial Reporting Interpretations Ctee Int Accounting Standards Bd 2005–07; numerous contribs to learned jls; FCA 1974 (ACA 1964), FRSA; *Recreations* theatre, music, walking; *Style*— Allan Cook, Esq, CBE; ✉ c/o International Accounting Standards Board, 30 Cannon Street, London EC4M 6XH

COOK, Beryl Frances; OBE (1996); da of Adrian Stephen Barton Lansley, and Ella, *née* Farmer-Francis; *b* 10 September 1926; *Educ* Kendrick Girls' Sch Reading; *m* 2 Oct 1948, John Victor Cook, s of Victor Harry Cook (d 1980); 1 s (John Lansley b 24 May 1950); *Career* artist; exhbns incl: Plymouth Arts Centre 1975, Whitechapel Gallery London 1976, The Craft of Art (Walker Gallery Liverpool) 1979, Musée de Cahors 1981, Chelmsford Gallery Museum 1982, Portal Gallery London 1985, travelling retrospective exhbn (Plymouth Museum, Stoke-on-Trent, Preston, Nottingham and Edinburgh) 1988–89, Scunthorpe Museum and Art Gallery 1992, York City Art Gallery 1992, Portal Gallery 1993 and 1997, anniversary exhbtn Plymouth Arts Centre 1995, travelling exhibition (Blackpool, Durham, Hartlepool, Stoke-on-Trent) 1998, travelling exhbn (Durham Museum) 2003 and (Stoke-on-Trent) 2004; *Books* The Works (1978), Private View (1980), One Man Show (1981), Beryl Cook's New York (1985), Beryl Cook's London (1988), Bouncers (1991), Happy Days (1995), Cruising (2000), Beryl Cook: The Bumper Edition (2000); illustrated: Seven Years and a Day (1980), Bertie and the Big Red Ball (1982), My Granny (1983), Mr Norris Changes Trains (1990), The Loved One (1992), The Prime of Miss Jean Brodie (1998); *Recreations* reading, travel; *Clubs* Lansdowne; *Style*— Mrs Beryl Cook, OBE; ✉ Rogers Coleridge & White, 20 Powis Mews, London W11

COOK, Brian Francis; s of Harry Cook (d 1959), and Renia Maria, *née* Conlon (d 1962); *b* 13 February 1933; *Educ* St Bede's GS Bradford, Univ of Manchester (BA), Downing Coll and St Edmund's House Cambridge (MA), Br Sch at Athens; *m* 18 Aug 1962, Veronica Mary Teresa, da of Bernard Dewhirst (d 1974); *Career* Nat Serv 1956–58, 16/5 The Queen's Royal Lancers; Dept of Greek and Roman Art Metropolitan Museum of Art NY: curatorial asst 1960, asst curator 1961–65, assoc curator 1965–69; keeper of Greek and Roman antiquities Br Museum 1976–93 (asst keeper 1969–76); currently writer and lectr on archaeology; corresponding memb German Archaeological Inst 1977, FSA 1971; *Books* Inscribed Hadra Vases in The Metropolitan Museum of Art (1966), Greek and Roman Art in the British Museum (1976), The Elgin Marbles (1984, Spanish edn 2000, 2 edn 1997), The Townley Marbles (1985), Greek Inscriptions (1987, Dutch edn 1990, French edn 1994, Japanese edn 1996), The Rogozen Treasure (ed, 1989), Relief Sculpture of the Mausoleum at Halicarnassus (with B Ashmole and D Strong 2005); *Recreations* reading, gardening; *Style*— B F Cook, Esq, FSA; ✉ 4 Belmont Avenue, Barnet, Hertfordshire EN4 9LJ (tel 020 8440 6590)

COOK, Charles Stuart; s of Norman Charles Cook (d 1994), of Wells, Somerset, and Dorothy Ida, *née* Waters (d 1994); *b* 19 December 1936; *Educ* King Edward VI Sch Southampton, Alleyn's Sch Dulwich, St Catherine's Coll Oxford (MA); *m* 28 July 1962 (m dis 1986), Jennifer, da of George Henry Baugh (d 1988), of nr Cowbridge, S Glamorgan; 2 s (Adam b 1966, Edward b 1969); *Career* Nat Serv 2 Lt The Buffs, The Royal East Kent Regt 1956–58, Capt TA List B 1961–74; asst master St Dunstan's Coll London 1961–67; called to the Bar Lincoln's Inn 1966; Hardwicke scholar 1963, Sir Thomas More bursary 1966, in practice 1967–2002, chm Med Appeals Tbnl 1979–90, recorder to the Crown Court

1987–2002 (asst recorder 1981–87), jr of the Wales & Chester Circuit 1987–88; external examiner Cardiff Law Sch BVC (Bar Vocational Course) Univ of Wales 2002–06; memb Llandaff PCC 1978–82; memb Criminal Bar Assoc 1988–2002; *Recreations* fine wines, photography, travel; *Clubs* United Services Mess (Cardiff), Naval and Military (In & Out); *Style*— Charles Cook, Esq; ✉ 33 Park Place, Cardiff CF10 3TN (tel 029 2023 3313, fax 029 2022 8294)

COOK, Christopher Paul; s of Edward Peter Cook, of Great Broughton, N Yorks, and Joyce, *née* Layland; *b* 24 January 1959; *Educ* Barnard Castle Sch, Univ of Exeter (BA, combined arts prize, Gladys Hunkin poetry prize), RCA (MA, J Andrew Lloyd scholar, John Minton travel award), Accademia di Belle Arti Bologna (Italian Govt scholar); *m* Jennifer Jane, da of Edward John Mellings; 2 s (Matthew b 13 Jan 1983, Samuel b 3 Nov 1988); *Career* artist, poet; Univ of Plymouth: sr lectr 1992–, reader in painting 1997–; visiting lectr RCA 1990–99; guest artist Stadelschule Frankfurt-am-Main 1991, visiting artist Academie van Beeldende Kunsten Rotterdam 1992, visiting fell Ruskin Sch Univ of Oxford 1993, distinguished visiting artist Calif State Univ Long Beach 1994, visiting artist BHU Varanasi India 1995, Arts Cncl residency Eden Project Cornwall 2001, visiting artist Univ of Memphis 2004; *Solo Exhibitions* incl: Camden Arts Centre 1985, Br Cncl Amsterdam 1985, Spacex Gallery Exeter 1986, Galleria Maggiore Bologna 1987, Benjamin Rhodes Gallery 1988, 1990 and 1993, The Cleveland Gallery Middlesbrough 1989, Plymouth Arts Centre 1989, Stadelschule Frankfurt-am-Main 1991, Kasteel van Rhoon Rotterdam 1992, Darlington Arts Centre 1992, Oldham Museum 1992, Northern Centre for Contemporary Art Sunderland 1994, Collins Gallery Glasgow 1995, Angel Row Nottingham 1995, Plymouth City Museum 1995, Galerie Helmut Pabst Frankfurt 1995 and 1999, Jason & Rhodes Gallery 1996, Haugesund Kunstforening 1997, De Beyerd Breda 1999, Heidelberger Kunstverein 2000, Bundanon Tst North Nowra 2000, Hirschl Contemporary Art London 2000 and 2001, Ferens Hull 2001, Towner Eastbourne 2001, Koraalberg Gallery Antwerp 2002, EZG Galerie Frankfurt 2003, Art Museum Memphis 2004, Mary Ryan Gallery NY 2004 and 2007, Yokohama Museum 2005, Today Art Museum Beijing 2007, Eyestorm UK 2007; *Group Exhibitions* incl: The Sheffield Open (Mappin Gallery) 1985, The Camden Annual 1984 1985 (first prizewinner), Romantic Visions (Camden Arts Centre) 1988, Minories Colchester 1988, Figure 2 - A Personal Mythology (Welsh Arts Cncl tour) 1988, Met Museum of Art NY 1989, Eros in Albion (Casa Masaccio San Giovanni Valdarno) 1989, 3 Ways (Br Cncl/RCA tour to Eastern Europe) 1990–94, Modern Painters (Manchester City Art Gallery) 1990, Da Bacon a Oggi (Palazzo Vecchio Florence) 1991, EAST (The Norwich Gallery) 1991, Bristol City Museum 1992, Camouflage (Br Cncl tour) LA 1994, 27e Festival International de la Peinture Cagnes-sur-Mer 1995, European Union Artists (Univ of Bangkok) 1995, de Peus a Terra (Galeria 4RT Barcelona) 1996, John Moores XXI (Walker Art Gallery Liverpool) 1999 (prizewinner), West by South West (Kunstforening Stavanger) 1999, Kunstenkunst (Stade Museum Hamburg) 2001, East of Eden (Spacex Gallery Exeter) 2002, Crossing Borders (Morley Gallery London) 2003, Site and Situation (Univ of Southern Calif LA) 2003, Yale Center for British Art 2005, Leaded (Univ of Richmond touring exbhn USA) 2007; *Poetry* incl: New Nerves (1983), The Choosing and other Poems (1984), A Mythic Cycle (1989), A Lowdown Ecstasy (1991), Pilgrimage III (Into Night) (1992), Dust on the Mirror (1997), For and Against Nature (2000), A Thoroughbred Golden Calf (2003); *Style*— Christopher Cook, Esq; ✉ e-mail c1cook@blueyonder.co.uk

COOK, Christopher William Batstone; s of Cecil Batstone Cook (d 1965), and Penelope, *née* Mayall (d 2003); *b* 21 January 1951; *Educ* Eton; *m* 15 July 1978 (m dis 1991), Margaret Anne, da of Maj John Christopher Blackett Ord (d 1996), of Whitfield Hall, Northumberland; 1 da (Emma b 1980), 2 s (Edward b 1982, Benjamin b 1983); m 2, 11 April 1997, Emma Caroline Faber, *née* Miller-Stirling; *Career* Lloyd's broker; dir C T Bowring & Co (Insurance) Ltd 1980–91, md Marsh & McLennan Worldwide 1988–91, chief exec Johnson and Higgins (Aviation) 1991–98, md Aviation and Space J & H Marsh McLennan 1998–, md Marsh Aviation 1999–2004; *Recreations* shooting, stalking, fishing; *Style*— Christopher W B Cook, Esq; ✉ 45 Eland Road, London SW11 5JX (tel 020 7228 5937, fax 020 7350 2998, mobile 07889 829410, e-mail cwb.cook@freeserve.uk)

COOK, Sir Christopher Wymondham Rayner Herbert; 5 Bt (UK 1886), of Doughty House, Richmond, Surrey; s of Sir Francis Ferdinand Maurice Cook, 4 Bt (d 1978), and Joan Loraine, *née* Ashton-Case (d 1995); *b* 24 March 1938; *Educ* King's Sch Canterbury; *m* 1, 1958 (m dis 1975), Malina, da of Aster Gunasekera, and former w of Cyril Wettasinghe, of Ceylon; 1 s (Richard Herbert Aster Maurice b 1959), 1 da (Priscilla Melina b 1968); m 2, 1975, Margaret, da of late John Murray, and former w of Ronald Miller; 1 da (Caroline Emma b 1978), 1 s (Alexander James Frederick b 1980); *Heir* s, Richard Cook; *Career* dir Diamond Guarantees Ltd 1980–91; *Style*— Sir Christopher Cook, Bt; ✉ La Fosse Equierre, Bouillon Road, St Andrew's, Guernsey GY6 8YN

COOK, David Julian; s of Stanley Cook, and Dorothy Mary, *née* Daft; *b* 15 July 1962; *Educ* Colchester Royal GS, Merton Coll Oxford (MA), Coll of Law London; *m* 10 Sept 1988, Christine Margaret Alice, da of Keith Roy Barnard; 2 s (Jonathan William David b 13 May 1995, Matthew Henry David b 12 Dec 2001), 1 da (Katherine Sarah Elizabeth b 1 April 1999); *Career* articled clerk then slr Freshfields 1988–91; Office of the Parly Counsel: asst counsel 1991–95, sr asst counsel 1995–99, dep Parly counsel 1999–2003, Parly counsel 2003–; on secondment as head of drafting team Tax Law Rewrite Project Inland Revenue 2003–05; *Recreations* walking, archaeology, tennis, Victorian novels; *Style*— David Cook, Esq

COOK, David Kenneth; s of George Thomas Cook (d 2004), and Beatrice, *née* Jackson (d 1990); *b* 21 September 1940; *Educ* Rishton Secdy Modern Sch, RADA; *Career* formerly actor; worked in TV (hosted children's prog Rainbow 1972) and in repertory in Dundee, Bristol Old Vic, Watford and Windsor; writer; memb: PEN, Soc of Authors, Writers' Guild, Actors' Equity; *Books* Albert's Memorial (1972), Happy Endings (1974, E M Forster Award 1977), Walter (1978, Hawthornden Prize 1978), Winter Doves (1979, shortlisted Arts Cncl Fiction Prize 1980), Sunrising (1984, Southern Arts Fiction Prize), Missing Persons (1986), Crying Out Loud (1988, shortlisted Whitbread Novel of the Year), Second Best (1991, Odd Fellows Social Concern Book Award 1992); *Television Plays* Willy (1972), Why Here?, Jenny Can't Work Any Faster, Mary's Wife (1980), Couples (series), Walter (Channel 4, Special Jury Award Monte Carlo, runner-up Int Emmy award), Love Match (1986), Missing Persons (1990), Closing Numbers (1993, Special Jury Award Monte Carlo); *Film* Second Best (1994, Special Jury Award San Sebastian); *Style*— David Cook, Esq; ✉ c/o Deborah Rogers, Rogers Coleridge & White Ltd, 20 Powis Mews, London W11 1JN (tel 020 7221 3717)

COOK, David Ronald; JP (1989); s of Charles Henry Cook, of Bristol, and Myrtle Ovington, *née* Harwood (d 1989); *b* 9 November 1943; *Educ* Thornbury GS; *m* 1, Frances Ann, *née* Leigh (d 1972); 2 da (Vicky Frances Leigh (Mrs Moss) b 24 April 1965, Jennifer Elaine Leigh b 9 Sept 1966); m 2, 21 June 1974, Angela Susan, da of Cecil Robert Cogdell (d 1988); 1 s (Charles David b 14 Aug 1978); *Career* articled clerk Parker Leader and Co Bristol 1960–65, audit sr Ricketts Cooper and Co 1965–69; ptnr: Burkett James and Co 1969–81, Pannell Kerr Forster (Bristol) 1981–96 (chm and managing ptnr 1985–95), N M G W forensic accountants 1996–2000, dir forensic accounting Numerica plc 2000; treas Bristol Referees Soc (RFU); Law Soc approved Expert Witness, memb Soc Expert Witnesses; FCA 1972 (ACA 1966); *Recreations* rugby football, squash, boating; *Clubs* Clifton, Redwood Lodge (chm); *Style*— David Cook, Esq; ✉ Westway, School Lane, Barrow Gurney, Somerset BS48 3RZ (tel 01275 472 406)

COOK, Derek Edward; TD; *b* 7 December 1931; *Educ* Denstone Coll, CCC Oxford (MA), Univ of Salford, Univ of Bradford, Huddersfield Tech Coll; *m*; 2 c; *Career* Nat Serv 1950–52, cmmnd Z Battery BAOR, W Riding Artillery 1952–68; with Tootal Ltd 1955–61, with John Emsley Ltd 1961–63, md A & S Henry & Co Ltd (Bradford) 1963–70, md Fibreglass Pilkington Ltd Bombay 1971–75 (chm 1976–79), chm and md Hindustan Pilkington Glass Works Ltd Calcutta 1976–79, dir R H Windsor Ltd India 1976–79, dir Killick Halco Ltd India 1977–79, chief exec Pilkington Brothers South Africa Ltd 1979 (chm 1981–84), chief exec Armourplate Safety Glass South Africa Ltd 1979 (chm 1981–84), dir Fibreglass South Africa Ltd 1979–82, chm Pilkington Glass Zimbabwe Ltd 1981–84, dir Pilkington Glass Ltd 1982 (chm 1984–85), dir Pilkington plc 1984–92, dir Flachglas AG 1985–89, chm Pilkington Superannuation Scheme 1987–, dep chm Pilkington plc 1987–92 (gp md 1990–92); dir: Libbey-Owens-Ford Co (USA) 1987–92, D E Cook Consits 1992– (sr conslt 1992–), Minories Investment Tst plc 1993–96, Hobart Pension Tstee Ltd 1993–97, Littlewoods Pension Tst Ltd 1994–2001; non-exec dir: Rowntree plc 1987–88, Charter Consolidated plc 1988–93, Charter plc 1993–96, Powell Duffryn plc 1989–98, Leeds Permanent Building Society 1991–95, MFI (Furniture Gp) plc 1992–99, Littlewoods Organisation plc 1992–99, Kwik Save Group plc 1993–98, Halifax Building Soc 1995–97, Halifax plc 1996–98, Somerfield plc 1998–99; tstee: MFI Pension Plan 1994–99, Halifax plc (formerly Building Soc) Retirement Fund 1995–98, Kwik Save Retirement Fund 1997–2000 (chm 1998–2000); memb Ct Univ of Leeds, dir Univ of Leeds Fndn 1989–2002; dir Breach Candy Hospital Tst 1974–79; memb Cncl: Industry and Parl Tst 1987–92, CBI 1988–92, Textile Inst 1994–; memb Cook Soc 1985–2002, tstee W Riding Artillery Tst 2001–, govr The Cathedral Sch Bombay 1974–79; Holder of Royal Warrant of Appointment 1984–85; Freeman City of London, Liveryman Worshipful Co of Glass Sellers 1991–; FRSA, FSS, FTI, CText, CIMgt, FInstD; *Recreations* sailing, general sporting and country life interests; *Clubs* Oriental, New (Edinburgh), Cavalry and Guards, East India, RAC, Royal Ocean Racing, Royal Thames, Royal Yorkshire Yacht, Royal Bombay Yacht (Cdre 1977–78), Leander, Racquets (Manchester), Rand (Johannesburg), Country (Johannesburg); *Style*— Derek Cook, Esq, TD; ✉ 3 Abbey Mill, Prestbury, Cheshire SK10 4XY (tel 01625 827985)

COOK, Francis (Frank); MP; s of James Cook, and Elizabeth May Cook; *b* 3 November 1935; *Educ* Corby Sch Sunderland, De La Salle Manchester, Inst of Educn Leeds; *m* 1959 (m dis), Patricia, da of Thomas Lundrigan; 1 s, 3 da; *Career* MP (Lab) Stockton N 1983–, oppn whip 1987–91, dep speaker 1999–; memb Select Ctee on: Employment 1983–87, Procedure of the House 1988–92, Defence 1992–97; memb: OSCE Parly Assembly 1992–2001, N Atlantic Assembly 1988–2001 (vice-pres 1998–2000), NATO Parly Assembly 2005–; *Style*— Frank Cook, MP; ✉ House of Commons, London SW1A 0AA

COOK, Prof Gordon Charles; s of Charles Francis Cook (d 1983), of Petersfield, Hampshire, and Kate, *née* Grainger (d 1979); *b* 17 February 1932, Wimbledon; *Educ* Wellingborough GS, Kingston upon Thames GS, Raynes Park GS, Royal Free Hosp Sch of Med London (BSc, MB BS, LRCP, MD, DSc, Charlotte Brown prize, Cunning award, Legg award); *m* 1963, Elizabeth Jane, da of late Rev Stephen Noel Agg-Large, of Longparish, Hants; 3 da (Rosamund Elizabeth b 7 June 1967, Caroline Jane b 10 June 1969, Susanna Catherine b 23 July 1973), 1 s (David Charles Stephen (twin) b 10 June 1969); *Career* cmmnd RAMC (Capt), seconded Royal Nigerian Army 1960–62; various appts Royal Free, Hampstead Gen, Royal Northern, Brompton and St George's Hosps 1958–63, lectr Royal Free Hosp Sch of Med and Makerere UC Uganda 1963–69; prof of med and conslt physician: Univ of Zambia 1969–74, Univ of Riyadh 1974–75, Univ of Papua New Guinea 1978–81; sr MO MRC 1975–76, sr lectr in clinical scis London Sch of Hygiene and Tropical Med 1976–97; hon conslt physician: Hosp for Tropical Diseases and UCLH 1976–97, St Luke's Hosp for the Clergy 1988–; visiting prof UCL 2000– (hon sr lectr in tropical med and infectious diseases 1981–2000), hon lectr in clinical parasitology Bart's Med Coll 1992–; research assoc Wellcome Tst Centre for the History of Medicine 1997–2002; visiting prof Univs of Basrah, Mosul and Doha; memb Editorial Bd: Jl of Infection (ed 1995–97), Postgraduate Medical Jl; examiner RCP 1977–84; pres: Royal Soc of Tropical Med and Hygiene 1993–95, Osler Club of London 1993–95, Fellowship of Postgrad Med 2000– (memb Cncl 1989–, vice-pres 1996–2000), History of Med Section RSM 2003–04 (vice-pres 1994–96); chm Erasmus Darwin Fndn Lichfield 1994–; tstee Bookpower (formerly Educnl Low-Priced Sponsored Texts (ELST)) 1996–; hon archivist Seamen's Hosp Soc 2002–; research assoc Greenwich Maritime Inst Univ of Greenwich 2003–; memb Exec Ctee and examiner Faculty of History and Philosophy of Medicine and Pharmacy 1997–, memb Cncl Galton Inst 2005–; vice-chair Friends of the Florence Nightingale Museum 2005–; Frederick Murgatroyd meml prize RCP 1973; Hugh L'Etang Prize RSM 1999; Freeman City of London, Liveryman Worshipful Soc of Apothecaries 1981 (examiner Worshipful Soc of Apothecaries of London 1997–); memb various professional bodies incl: RSM 1962, MRS 1965, Br Soc of Gastroenterology 1968, Physiological Soc 1971, Assoc of Physicians of GB and I 1973, Med Soc of London 1976, Br Soc for the Study of Infection 1982, Soc of Authors 1985 (memb Cncl Med Writers' Gp 1995–, chm 1997–99), Harveian Soc, Hunterian Soc, JCHMT 1987–93; FRCP 1972, FRACP 1978, FLS 1989, FRCPE 2002, MRCS; *Books* Acute Renal Failure (jt ed, 1964), Tropical Gastroenterology (1980), 100 Clinical Problems in Tropical Medicine (jtly, 1987, 2 edn 1998), Communicable and Tropical Diseases (1988), Parasitic Disease in Clinical Practice (1990), From the Greenwich Hulks to Old St Pancras: a history of tropical disease in London (1992), Gastroenterological Problems from the Tropics (ed, 1995), Travel - Associated Disease (ed, 1995), Manson's Tropical Diseases (ed, 20 edn 1996, 21 edn 2003), Victorian Incurables: A History of the Royal Hospital for Neuro-Disability, Putney (2004), John MacAlister's Other Vision: A History of the Fellowship of Postgraduate Medicine (2005), The Incurable Movement: An Illustrated History of the British Home (2006), Tropical Medicine: An Illustrated History of the Pioneers (2007), Disease in the Merchant Navy: History of the Seamen's Hospital Society (2007); *Recreations* walking, cricket, baroque and classical music, history (medical and scientific), philately; *Clubs* Athenaeum, MCC, Baconian (St Albans; pres 1995–96); *Style*— Prof Gordon Cook; ✉ 11 Old London Road, St Albans, Hertfordshire AL1 1QE (tel 01727 869000); Fellowship of Postgraduate Medicine, 12 Chandos Street, London W1G 9DR (tel 020 7636 6334, fax 020 7436 2535)

COOK, James Robert; s of Robert James Cook (d 1961), of Hailsham, E Sussex, and Irene May Winsper, *née* Leyden (d 1997); *b* 7 December 1945; *Educ* Co GS for Boys Bexhill-on-Sea, Brighton Tech Coll, Univ of Oxford (Dip); *m* 1; 2 s (Andrew Paul b 15 Sept 1968, Stephen John b 21 April 1970); m 2, 7 April 1990, Suzanne Valerie; *Career* audit sr: Douglas Wells & Co 1964–66, Cooper Brothers & Co 1967–69; fin accountant Overseas Containers Ltd 1969–73, chief accountant Frampton Property Group 1973–74; Blue Circle Industries plc: mgmnt accountant 1974–85, gp pensions mangr 1984–95; dep md AshakaCem plc Nigeria 1996–2002; qualified first place (John C Latham prize) ACCA finals 1966, awarded Jt Dip in Mgmnt Accounting Servs 1981; ordinand Dio of Oxford 2005; FCCA 1973 (ACCA 1968); *Recreations* voluntary work, church, music, theatre, travel; *Style*— James Cook, Esq; ✉ The Wyld, Forge Hill, Hampstead Norreys, Thatcham, Berkshire RG18 0TE (tel 01635 200428, e-mail jamesrobertcook@aol.com)

COOK, Kandis; *b* 10 May 1950; *Educ* Nova Scotia Coll of Art and Design, Halifax Nova Scotia Canada (BA), ENO (design course); *Children* 1 s (Turner Moyse b 10 Oct 1987), 1 da (Kate Moyse b 29 May 1980); *Career* set and costume designer: Dr Faustus (Lyric Hammersmith and Fortune), Berenice (Lyric), Britannicus (Lyric), Faith Healer (Royal Court), Women Beware Women (Royal Court), Grace of Mary Traverse (Royal Court), Bite of the Night (RSC), Epicoene (RSC Swan), The Last Days of Don Juan (RSC), Orlando

C

(Wexford Opera Festival), Arden of Faversham (RSC), Hamlet (Donmar Warehouse and Piccadilly); costume designer The Relapse (Lyric Hammersmith); *Style—* Ms Kandis Cook

COOK, Leonard Warren (Len); CBE (2005); s of Archie Ellwood Cook (d 1990), of Dunedin, NZ, and Jean Margaret, *née* Paterson (d 2004); *b* 13 April 1949; *Educ* Bayfield HS Dunedin (Dux), Univ of Otago (BA); *Partner* Shirley Flora Vollweiler; *Career* govt statistician NZ 1992–2000 (dep govt statistician 1986–91), nat statistician and registrar-gen of England and Wales 2000–05; memb Royal Cmmn on Social Policy NZ 1987–88; budget advsr CAB 1988–99; visiting fell Nuffield Coll Oxford; CStat 1973; Companion Royal Soc of NZ (CRSNZ) 2005; *Recreations* fly fishing, travel, languages; *Style—* Len Cook, Esq, CBE; ✉ 59 Ponsonby Road, Karori, Wellington, New Zealand (tel 00 64 4 4767477, e-mail len_cook@xtra.co.nz)

COOK, Lindsay Mary; da of Francis John Cook (d 1972), and Elsie Mary, *née* Gilliatt; *b* 24 July 1951; *Educ* Havelock Comp Sch Grimsby, Open Univ (BA); *m* 1 May 1987, Tony Wilkinson, s of Ernest Wilkinson; 2 s (Rory b 14 Aug 1988, Gray b 27 Jan 1991); *Career* trainee journalist Grimsby Evening Telegraph 1969–74, reporter and consumer writer Morning Telegraph Sheffield 1974–76, freelance writer Sunday Times 1976–77, freelance contrib Money Mail (pt of Daily Mail) 1977–79, United Newspapers London 1977–86 (number 3 on newsdesk, features dept, dep London ed 1984), personal finance ed The Daily Telegraph 1986–89; The Times: money ed 1990–93, dep business ed 1993–94, business ed 1994–97; managing ed The Express 1997–98, gp managing ed and dir Express Newspapers 1998–2001 (editorial devpt dir 1998–2001), media conslt 2001–03, editorial dir CMP Information 2004–; Personal Finance Journalist of the Year 1987; *Books* The Money Diet, Three Months To Financial Fitness (1986), Working Mum: The Survival Guide (2000); *Recreations* food, theatre; *Style—* Miss Lindsay Cook; ✉ 10 Duncan Terrace, London N1 8BZ (mobile 07831 237030, fax 020 7837 4509, e-mail lindsay.cook@stop-press.co.uk)

COOK, Malcolm Roderick Grant; s of Harold Cook, of Warwickshire, and Brenda Eileen, *née* Moore; *b* 29 November 1955; *Educ* Univ of Bath (BSc Econ); *m* Ann Cook; 1 da (Victoria Ann b 12 March 1989); *Career* chartered accountant; Arthur Young Chartered Accountants 1977–84, gp accountant F H Thomkins plc 1984–86, business servs gp mangr Arthur Young 1986–87; Pannell Kerr Forster Birmingham: business servs gp mangr 1987–89, ptnr 1989–, managing ptnr 1991–; dir Birmingham Press Club Ltd; MInstD, ACA; *Style—* Malcolm Cook, Esq; ✉ Pannell Kerr Forster, New Guild House, 45 Great Charles Street, Queensway, Birmingham B3 2LX (tel 0121 212 2222, fax 0121 212 2300, mobile 078 3159 0025)

COOK, Martin Philip; s of Ian Cook, and Maureen Staniford, *née* Steele, of Maldon, Essex; step s of Leonard Staniford, of Maldon, Essex; *b* 4 August 1958, London; *Educ* Christ's Hosp, Univ of Exeter (BA); *m* 4 July 1987, Evelyn, *née* Child; 2 da (Katherine (Kate) b 20 June 1989, Alice b 3 April 1991), 1 s (Tobias (Toby) b 16 May 1994); *Career* civil servant Home Office 1982–93; Capgemini (formerly Capgemini Ernst & Young): joined Ernst & Young consltg 1993, ptnr 1999, head of public sector business 2002–, dir Working Links 2002–03, ceo Aspire 2004–06, global sales offr Capgemini Outsourcing 2006–; *Recreations* reading, music, learning to play the guitar; *Clubs* Reform; *Style—* Martin Cook, Esq; ✉ Capgemini UK plc, No 1 Forge End, Woking, Surrey GU21 6DB (tel 0870 238 8931, fax 020 7297 3900, e-mail martin.p.cook@capgemini.com)

COOK, His Hon Michael John; s of George Henry Cook (d 1947), and Nora Wilson, *née* Mackman; *b* 20 June 1930; *Educ* Leeds GS, Worksop Coll, Univ of Leeds; *m* 1, 1958, Anne Margaret Vaughan; 3 s, 1 da; m 2, 1974, Patricia Anne Sturdy; 1 da; *Career* Lt RA (Nat Serv Canal Zone); slr; sr ptnr Ward Bowie 1968–86, recorder Crown Court 1980–86, circuit judge (SE Circuit) 1986–2003 (dep circuit judge 2003–05), conslt Underwoods Slrs 2005–; author, lectr and former broadcaster; past pres London Slrs Litigation Assoc; past pres Assoc of Law Costs Draftsmen, memb Bd Royal Med Fndn; govr Epsom Coll; Freeman City of London; *Books* The Courts and You, Cook on Costs (annual), Butterworth's Costs Service (gen ed), The Litigation Letter (gen ed), Cordery on Solicitors (contrib); *Recreations* horse riding, tennis, cycling, walking, gardening, reading, theatre, travel; *Clubs* The Law Soc, St George's Hill Tennis; *Style—* His Hon Michael Cook

COOK, Prof Nicholas John; s of John Manuel Cook (d 1994), and Enid May, *née* Robertson (1976); *b* 5 June 1950, Athens, Greece; *Educ* Univ of Cambridge (BA, MA, PhD), Univ of Southampton (BA); *m* 14 Feb 1975, Louise Catherine Bridget, da of Harry Elgie; 1 da (Chloe b 1984), 1 s (Christopher b 1987); *Career* lectr Univ of Hong Kong 1982–90; Univ of Southampton: prof of music 1990–99, research prof 1999–2003; prof of music then professorial research fell Royal Holloway Univ of London 2004–, dir AHRC Research Centre for the History and Analysis of Recorded Music 2004–; FBA 2001; *Books* A Guide to Musical Analysis (1987), Musical Analysis and the Listener (1989), Music, Imagination and Culture (1990), Beethoven: Symphony No 9 (1993), Analysis Through Composition: Principles of the Classical Style (1996), Analysing Musical Multimedia (1998), Music: A Very Short Introduction (1998, revised edn 2000), The Schenker Project: Culture, Race and Music Theory in Fin-de-siècle Vienna (2007); co-edited and co-authored books and author of numerous articles; *Style—* Prof Nicholas Cook; ✉ Royal Holloway, University of London, Egham, Surrey TW20 0EX (tel 01784 443532, fax 01784 439441, e-mail nicholas.cook@rhul.ac.uk)

COOK, Patrick Donald; s of Donald George Herbert Cook (d 1992), of Henley-on-Thames, Oxon, and Doreen Elizabeth, *née* Simpson; *b* 11 July 1956; *Educ* Abingdon Sch, Pembroke Coll Oxford (MA); *m* 10 Oct 1981, Caroline Elizabeth, da of John Andrew Graves, of Barnstaple, Devon; 3 da (Megan Elizabeth b 25 April 1986, Florence Emma b 4 Oct 1989, Imogen Amy b 25 Nov 1994), 1 s (Charles Patrick (twin) b 25 Nov 1994); *Career* admitted slr 1981; ptnr Osborne Clarke 1986–, licensed insolvency practitioner 1989–; memb: Law Soc 1981, Insolvency Lawyers Assoc 1989, Insolvency Practitioners Assoc 1989, R3 Soc of Business Recovery Professionals 1989; *Recreations* sports (various), theatre, reading, gardening; *Style—* Patrick Cook, Esq; ✉ Osborne Clarke, One London Wall, London EC2Y 5EB

COOK, Prof Paul Derek; MBE (1985); s of James Walter Cook, and Florence, *née* Jefferay; *b* 12 March 1934; *Educ* QMC London (Sir John Johnson scholar, BSc, PhD); *m* 1954, Frances Ann, *née* James; 4 da; *Career* res scientist: MRC 1960–62, Middx Hosp Med Sch 1962–65; chm and md Scientifica-Cook Ltd 1962–; Brunel Univ: prof of laser technol 1986–97, prof of laser physics 1986–91, prof of environmental sci 1992–97; scientific advsr to: min for the Environment and Countryside DoE 1990–92, British Gas 1990–93; laser conslt BAe 1986–; responsible for design and devpt of numerous laser systems used in med and mil estab throughout world, originator and inventor of Laser Guidance Systems for weapon alignment in Tornados, contrib to Europe's first laser gyroscope, invented laser instrument that improves motor safety by detecting and correcting night myopia, established world's first Night Vision Clinic for treating night blindness disorders 1986, developed (and registered for patent) Reaction Time Exerciser Measurement Gauge (a means of registering and improving the response time of motor vehicle drivers and sports people) 2007; fndr and pres The Br Sci and Technol Tst (helping disabled children worldwide) 1985–96, originator Lena Appeal (sending med aid to sick children in Russia) 1991, fndr and pres Sci and Technol Tst (presenter Animal SciTech Awards) 2002; dep chm Conserve (Cons Govt Environmental Gp) 1990–92; envoy to Boris Yeltsin 1992; UK pres Japanese Zen Nippon Airinkai 1978–81; CEng, MIEE 1963; *Recreations* breeding and rearing exotic Japanese carp, inventing, experimenting with ideas, especially those related to improving safety on the roads, passion for early automobile number plates; *Style—* Prof Paul Cook, MBE; ✉ Carlton House, 78 Bollo Bridge Road, London W3 8AU

COOK, Prof Sir Peter Frederic Chester; kt (2007); s of Maj Frederick William Cook, and Ada, *née* Shaw (d 1986); *b* 22 October 1936; *Educ* Ipswich Sch, Bournemouth Sch, Bournemouth Coll of Art, AA Sch of Architecture (AADipl); *m* 1960 (m dis 1990), Hazel, *née* Fennell; m 2, 1990, Yael Reisner; 1 s (Alexander b 1990); *Career* architect and teacher; asst in various offices in London and Bournemouth 1956–63, Taylor Woodrow Design Gp 1962–64, fndr memb Archigram Gp 1963–76, ptnr Cook and Hawley Architects 1979, prof of architecture HBK Städelschule Frankfurt-am-Main 1984–2002, Bartlett prof of architecture UCL 1990– (chm Bartlett Sch of Architecture 1990–2004), design princ HOK International 2004–, jt prof of architecture Royal Acad 2005–; work featured in numerous worldwide exhbns; advsr numerous architectural schools worldwide; chief designer extension of the Municipality of Pinto Madrid 2003–; dir ICA 1970–72, fndr dir Art Net 1972–79; memb: Euro Acad of Sci and Art 1998; RIBA 1968, RSA 1970, RA 2003; Commandeur de l'Ordre des Arts et des Lettres (France) 2002; *Awards* winner first prize for: old people's housing 1963, Monaco centre 1970, solar housing 1980, museum in lower Australia 1996, Graz Kunsthaus (now under construction) 2000; Los Angeles Medal American Inst of Architecture 1989, Jean Tschumi Medal Int Union of Architects 1998, Royal Gold Medal RIBA 2002, Gustav Eiffel Prize Ecole Spéciale d'architecture Paris 2005; *Books* Architecture: Action and Plan (1966), Experimental Architecture (1972), New Spirit in Architecture (1991), Six Conversations (1995), Primer (1998), Power of Contemporary Architecture (1999), Paradox of Contemporary Architecture (2001); *Recreations* listening to music, restaurants, gossip, walking; *Style—* Prof Sir Peter Cook; ✉ HOK International Limited, 216 Oxford Street, London W1C 1DB

COOK, Dr Peter John; CBE (1996); s of late John and Rose Cook, of Sale, Cheshire; *b* 15 October 1938; *Educ* Chorlton GS, Univ of Durham (BSc, DSc), ANU Canberra (MSc), Univ of Colorado Boulder (PhD); *m* 1961, Norma Irene; 2 s (John b 24 Nov 1964, Julian b 20 July 1968); *Career* geologist: Univ of Cambridge Gornergletcher Glaciological Expedition 1959, Univ of Durham Spitsbergen Expedition (ldr) 1960, Oil Search Gp Aust Bureau of Mineral Resources (BMR) 1961–64, Aust Nat Antarctic Res Expedition 1964–65, Phosphate Section BMR 1966–69; sr geologist Phosphate and Marine Geology BMR 1969–76, sr res fell in econ geology Res Sch of Earth Sciences ANU 1976–82 (chm of Faculty 1978–79, visiting fell 1982–90 and 1995), visiting fell Resource Systems Inst East-West Center Univ of Hawaii 1979, chief scientist BMR Div Continental Geology 1982–89, assoc dir BMR 1989–90, dir British Geological Survey 1990–98, exec dir Aust Petroleum Co-op Res Centre 1998–2003, chief exec CO2CRC 2003–, chief exec Innovative Carbon Technologies Pty Ltd 2003–; dir PJC International 1998–, dir MineXchange Pty Ltd 2000–; conslt: Astrogeology Div US Geological Survey 1967, Le Nickel Exploration 1977, Agrico Chemical Co 1980, Esso Exploration 1981–82; prof Institut de Geologie Universite Louis Pasteur Strasbourg 1989; chm: ACT Div Geological Soc of Aust 1972–73, Consortium for Ocean Geosciences of Aust Univs 1980–82, Cwlth-state Hydrogeological Ctee 1983–87, Tech Prog Int Sedimentological Congress 1983–86; memb: Indian Ocean Working Gp Int Union of Geology and Geophysics 1974–78, Geosciences Delgn to China Aust Acad of Sciences 1978, Cncl Aust Inst of Marine Sciences 1979–85, Advsy Ctee Centre for Remote Sensing Univ of NSW 1985–90, Review Ctee Dept of Geology James Cook Univ 1987, Advsy Cncl Aust Nuclear Sci and Technol Orgn 1986–90, Advsy Bd Inst of Engrg Surveying and Space Geodesy Univ of Nottingham 1990–98, Geological Museum Advsy Panel Natural History Museum 1990–, Advsy Bd Univ of Manchester, Earth Sciences Ctee NERC 1991–98, Advsy Bd Global Sedimentary Geology Prog 1991–96, Bd Mineral Industry Research Orgn 1991–98, Bd of Patrons Earth Centre Edinburgh 1992–98, Earth Science and Technol Bd NERC 1994–98; Adrian fell Univ of Leicester 1992–98; chm: UNESCO/IOC Prog of Ocean Sci in Relation to Non-Living Resources 1985–2001, Forum of Dirs of Euro Geological Surveys 1997; pres: Aust Geoscience Cncl 1987–88, Euro Geo Surveys 1995–96 (vice-pres 1997); memb: American Assoc of Petroleum Geologists, Geological Soc London, Geological Soc of Aust (chm 1972–73), Int Rels Ctee Australian Acad of Technol, Sci and Engrg 2001–; Geological Soc of London Cope Medal 1997, Australian Public Service Medal 2001, Centenary Medal 2003, German Geological Soc Leopold von Buck Medal 2004, Aust Petroleum Exploration Assoc Lewis G Weeks Gold Medal 2004, French Order of Merit 2005; fell Australian Acad of Technol, Sci and Engrg (FTSE) 1998; *Publications* Sedimentology & Holocene History of a Tropical Estuary (1978), Phosphate Deposits of the World (1986), Australia: Evolution of a Continent (1990), Continental Shelf Limits: the scientific and legal interface (2000), IPCC Special Volume: Carbon Dioxide Capture and Storage (co-ordinator and lead author, 2005); author of 130 papers and articles in learned jls; *Recreations* skiing, walking, history, travel; *Clubs* Geological Soc, Commonwealth; *Style—* Dr Peter J Cook, CBE, FTSE; ✉ CO2CRC, GPO Box 463, Canberra ACT 2601, Australia (tel +61 261 201600, fax +61 262 737181, e-mail pjcook@co2crc.com.au)

COOK, Roger James; s of Alfred Herbert Owen Cook (d 1968), and Linda May, *née* Kirk (d 1994); *b* 6 April 1943; *Educ* Hurlstone Agric Coll, Univ of Sydney; *m* 1, 1966 (m dis 1974), Madeline Koh; m 2, 1982, Frances Alice Knox; 1 da (Belinda Claire b 1985); *Career* TV and radio reporter ABC Aust 1960–66, TV and radio dir Warnock Sandford Advertising Aust 1966–68, reporter World at One and World This Weekend (BBC Radio 4) 1968–76, freelance documentary dir 1968–72, creator and presenter Checkpoint (BBC Radio 4) 1973–85, presenter and reporter Time For Action/Reel Evidence (BBC Radio 4) and investigative reporter Nationwide/Newsnight (BBC TV) 1972–84, reporter and presenter The Cook Report (Central) 1985–97, with Yorkshire TV 1998, presenter Cook Report Specials (Carlton/ITV Network) 1999–2003, Cook Report Retrospective (ITV) 2007; visiting prof Centre for Broadcast Jouralism Nottingham Trent Univ 1997–; Hon DLitt Nottingham Trent Univ 2004; memb: NUJ 1968–; *Awards* BPG award for outstanding contrib to radio 1978, Pye (now Sony) Radio Personality of the Year 1979, Ross McWhirter fndn award for courage exhibited in the course of his work 1980, Valiant for Truth award 1980, TV and Radio Industries Club award ITV Prog of the Year (for the Cook Report) 1993, Genesis/Brigitte Bardot Int award for campaigning wildlife journalism 1997, Charleston Worldfest Gold Award for Investigative Journalism 1997, Special Award BAFTA for 25 years of outstanding quality investigative reporting 1997, TV and Radio Industries Club award for outstanding contrib to broadcasting 1998; *Books* What's Wrong With Your Rights? (with Tim Tate, 1988), Dangerous Ground (memoir, 1999), More Dangerous Ground (memoir, 2007); *Recreations* music, motor sport; *Style—* Roger Cook, Esq; ✉ c/o The Roseman Organisation, 51 Queen Anne Street, London W1G 9HS (tel 020 7486 4500, fax 020 7486 4600)

COOK, Stephanie Jayne; MBE (2001); da of Dr Paul Edward Rutledge Cook, and Valerie Pauline Cook; *b* 7 February 1972; *Educ* The HS Bedford, Perse Sch for Girls Cambridge, Peterhouse Cambridge (MA, Rowing and Athletics half blues), Lincoln Coll Oxford (BM BCh, Modern Pentathlon, Cross Country and Athletics blues, Fencing half blue); *m* 28 May 2005, Daniel Carroll; *Career* doctor and modern pentathlete; achievements incl: Univ of Oxford Varsity Match champion 1997, winner 2 Gold, 8 Silver and 1 Bronze medals at World and European Championships 1998–2000, individual Gold medal Olympic Games Sydney 2000, individual Gold medal, team Gold medal and team relay Bronze medal European Championships 2001, individual Gold medal, team Gold medal and team relay Gold medal World Championships 2001; memb England Cross Country running team 1997; Sports Writers Assoc Sports Woman of the Year 2001, Sunday Times Helen

Rollason Award for Inspiration 2001; house physician Poole Hosp NHS Tst 1997–98, house surgn John Radcliffe Hosp Oxford and Churchill Hosp Oxford 1998, res fell Dept of Vascular Surgery Royal Surrey Co Hosp Guildford 1998–99, SHO rotation Royal United Hosp Bath 2001–04, ENT SW rotation 2004–; vice-pres Royal United Hosp Forever Friends Appeal 2001–; Glaxo Wellcome Fellowship RSM 1998; memb: BMA, RSM, Women in Surgical Trg, Med Women's Fedn, Med Equestrian Assoc; patron: SportsAid, Helen Rollason Cancer Care Centre Appeal, Access Sport, Crimestoppers Tst; tstee Against Malaria; involved in fundraising activities for charities incl: CLIC, SPARKS, Merlin, Cystic Fibrosis Tst; Hon Freedom Borough of Bedford; MRCS; *Style*— Miss Stephanie Cook, MBE; ✉ c/o Bryn Vaile, Esq, MBE, Matchtight Ltd, PO Box 2729, Bath BA2 7YL (tel 01225 323518, fax 01225 323738, e-mail bryn@matchtight.co.uk)

COOK, Stephen Sands; s of John Stevenson Cook, and Elizabeth, *née* Brown; *b* 6 April 1960; *Educ* Duncanrig Sch East Kilbride, Univ of Aberdeen (LLB, Dip LP); *m* 8 Aug 1981, Andrina, da of Henry Alexander Waters; 1 da (Kirsty Andrina b 2 Aug 1989), 1 s (Simon Stephen b 6 March 1996); *Career* trainee Moncrieff Warren Patterson Glasgow 1982–84, asst McGrigor Donald 1984–87, ptnr Herbert Smith London 1991–93 (asst 1987–91), head Company Dept McGrigor Donald 1994–96, conslt Wiggin & Co 1998– (ptnr 1996–1998); dir Flextech plc 1998–; dir Telewest plc 2000–; memb: Law Soc of Scotland 1984, Law Soc of England and Wales 1989; *Recreations* medieval history, walking the dog, wine; *Style*— Stephen Cook, Esq

COOK, Susan Lorraine (Sue); da of William Arthur Thomas, of Ickenham, Middx, and Kathleen May, *née* Prow; *b* 30 March 1949; *Educ* Vyner's GS Hillingdon, Univ of Leicester (BA, DLitt); *m* 1, 20 May 1981 (m dis 1987), John Christopher Williams, s of Leonard Williams (d 1988), of The Monkey Sanctuary, Looe, Cornwall; 1 s (Alexander Charles (Charlie) b 12 Oct 1982); partner 1986–2001, William James Macqueen; 1 da (Megan Jane Emily b 30 March 1988); m 2, 27 Aug 2004, Ian Sharp, s of Frederick Sharp, of Clithene, Lancs; *Career* radio prodr and broadcaster Capital Radio 1974–76, radio presenter of You and Yours, Making History, documentaries and topical features for BBC Radio 4 and World Service, reporter and presenter for BBC TV's Nationwide 1979–83; presenter BBC TV: Pebble Mill at One, Breakfast Time, Out of Court, Holiday, Crimewatch UK (until 1995), Daytime Live, Having a Baby, Children in Need Appeal, That's the Way the Money Goes, Omnibus at the Proms, The Story of the London Sinfonietta, Maternity Hospital, The Children's Royal Variety Performance; presenter Collectors' Lot and Hampton Court Palace (Channel 4); patron: Rainbow Tst, Children's Liver Disease Fndn; ambass Prince's Tst; *Books* Accident Action (jtly, 1978), Crimewatch UK (jtly, 1987), The Crimewatch Guide to Home Security and Personal Safety (1988), On Dangerous Ground (fiction, 2006); *Recreations* tennis, singing, spending time at home with the family; *Style*— Miss Sue Cook; ✉ John Miles Organisation, Cadbury Camp Lane, Clapton-in-Gordano, Bristol BS20 7SB (tel 01275 854675, website www.suecook.com)

COOK, Thomas Roger Edward; o s of Lt-Col Sir Thomas Cook, MP, JP (d 1970), of Sennowe Park, and Gweneth, o da of Spencer Evan Jones (d 1999); gggs of Thomas Cook (d 1884); *b* 21 August 1936; *Educ* Eton, RAC Cirencester; *m* 1, Virginia (d 1978), yr da of Leslie Aked (d 1964), of Knaresborough, N Yorks; m 2, Carola, da of Capt Roger Harvey (d 1976), of Ramsbury, Wilts; *Career* Grenadier Gds 1954–56; farmer, forester and landowner; tstee Ernest Cook Tst; High Sheriff Norfolk 1991–92; *Recreations* country pursuits, flying; *Clubs* The Air Sqdn, White's, Pratt's, Norfolk, Allsorts (Norfolk); *Style*— Thomas R E Cook, Esq; ✉ Gateleyhill, Gateley, Norfolk NR20 5EJ (tel 01328 829122)

COOK, William (Bill); s of William James Cook, of Eltham, London, and Lillian Maud, *née* Avery; *b* 19 November 1955, London; *Educ* Colfe's GS; *m* 5 Nov 1988, Diana Helen (formerly Mrs Sangway); 1 da (Louise Sarah b 13 April 1980); *Career* Dept of Trade 1974–77, private sec to Stanley Clinton Davis MP 1977–79, private sec to Reginald Eyre MP 1979–80, DTI 1980–84, Cabinet Office 1984–87, HM Treasy 1987, Ernst & Young 1987–99 (ptnr 1994–99), variously head of public sector, dir of corp devpt, finance dir, commercial dir, finance dir and head of ops Capgemini 1999–; dir Working Links Ltd 2000–; *Recreations* golf, cricket, bridge; *Clubs* Brailes Golf, Long Compton Cricket, Old Colfeians Assoc; *Style*— Bill Cook, Esq; ✉ Capgemini UK, 76 Wardour Street, London W1F 0UU (tel 07891 158934, e-mail bill.cook@capgemini.com)

COOKE, Anthony Roderick Chichester Bancroft; yr twin s of Maj-Gen Ronald Basil Bowen Bancroft Cooke, CB, CBE, DSO (d 1971), and Joan (d 1989), da of late Maj Claude Chichester, of Tunworth Down House, Basingstoke; *b* 24 July 1941; *Educ* Ampleforth, London Business Sch (MSc); *m* 1972, Daryll, *née* Aird-Ross; 2 s, 1 da; *Career* chartered accountant 1964; chm and chief exec Ellerman Lines plc 1985–87 (dir 1976), chm and md Cunard Ellerman Ltd 1987–91, chief exec Andrew Weir & Co Ltd 1991–99, chm Baltic Exchange Ltd 2005–07, chm Devpts Div Oikos Storage Ltd 2007–; dir: James Fisher & Sons plc 2002–, West of England Mutual Insurance Assoc (Luxembourg) 2002–; pres Chamber of Shipping 1996–97, pres Inst of Chartered Shipbrokers 2002–04; High Sheriff Hants 2001–02; Liveryman Worshipful Co of Shipwrights; *Clubs* Boodle's; *Style*— Anthony Cooke, Esq; ✉ Poland Court, Odiham, Hampshire RG29 1JL (tel 01256 702060)

COOKE, Barry; *Career* FCA; Ernest & Whinney W Africa 1973, fin conslt to Liberian Min of Fin, Ernest & Whinney Paris 1976, Balfour Beatty Power Transmission Div, Cementation International 1978–84, Gammon Construction Hong Kong 1984–88, fin dir Foster and Partners 1988–; FCA; *Style*— Barry Cooke, Esq

COOKE, (Brian) Christopher; s of Samuel Burgess Ridgway Cooke (d 1978), and Diana, *née* Witherby; *b* 1 February 1951; *Educ* Westminster, Peterhouse Cambridge (MA); *Career* articled clerk then slr Bischoff & Co 1974–78, slr Bristows Cooke & Carpmael 1978–86, ptnr Linklaters 1989–2007 (slr 1986–89); *Style*— Christopher Cooke, Esq; ✉ 5 Provost Road, London NW3 4ST (tel 020 7722 6819)

COOKE, Christopher Edward Cobden; s of Reginald Garforth Cooke (d 1991), of Marlow, Bucks, and Phyllis Mary Blackburn, *née* Wilde (d 1992); *b* 18 April 1944; *Educ* King William's Coll IOM, Univ of Southampton (LLB); *m* 26 July 1969, (Greta) Yvonne, da of Raymond Vere Alberto (d 1979); 3 da (Lisa b 25 May 1971, Lucy b 11 March 1973, Lindy b 19 Jan 1977); *Career* slr; ptnr Rooks Rider (formerly Rooks & Co) London 1970– (currently sr ptnr); memb Int Ctee Soc of Tst and Estate Practitioners; memb: Law Soc 1969, Holborn Law Soc 1988, Int Tax Planning Assoc, Soc of Tst and Estate Practitioners; Freeman: City of London 1966, City of Monroe Louisiana 1986; Liveryman Worshipful Co of Makers of Playing Cards 1966; *Recreations* skiing; *Style*— Christopher Cooke, Esq; ✉ Rooks Rider, Challoner House, 19 Clerkenwell Close, London EC1R 0RR (tel 020 7689 7000, fax 020 7689 7001, mobile tel 077 8522 5196, e-mail ccooke@rooksrider.co.uk)

COOKE, David Charles; s of Frederick John Edward Cooke (d 1969), of Clitheroe, Lancs, and Hilda, *née* Hughes (d 1996); *b* 22 March 1938; *Educ* Accrington GS, Victoria Univ of Manchester (LLB); *Career* admitted slr 1961; asst slr: Hall Brydon & Co Manchester 1961–64, King & Partridge Madras India 1964–67; Pinsent Masons (formerly Pinsents): asst slr 1967–69, ptnr 1969–87, sr ptnr 1987–94, conslt 2002–; chm Med, Dental, Opthalmic, Pharmaceutic Disciplinary Ctee Birmingham and Black Country SHA 1996–2004; sec W Midlands Devpt Agency 1986–99; memb: Law Soc 1961–, Birmingham Law Soc 1967–, Cncl Birmingham C of C and Industry 1993–98, West Midlands Regnl Cncl CBI 1993–98, St John Cncl for the W Midlands 1997–2006; *Recreations* classical music, fell walking, fine arts, sheep; *Clubs* Oriental; *Style*— David C Cooke, Esq; ✉ Pinsent Masons, 3 Colmore Circus, Birmingham B4 6BH (tel 0121 200 1050, fax 0121 626 1040)

COOKE, David John; s of Matthew Peterson Cooke, of Rugby, and Margaret Rose; *b* 23 August 1956; *Educ* Lawrence Sheriff Sch Rugby, Trinity Coll Cambridge (MA); *m* 31 March 1979, Susan Margaret, da of Albert Arthur George, of Rugby; 1 s (Stephen b 1984), 1 da (Helen b 1986); *Career* slr; ptnr Pinsents (now Pinsent Masons) 1982–2001; district judge 2001–; memb: Law Soc; *Recreations* sailing, golf, competitive swimming; *Clubs* Olton Golf; *Style*— D J Cooke, Esq; ✉ Birmingham Civil Justice Centre, Bull Street, Birmingham B4 6DW

C

COOKE, Prof David John; s of John McKay Cooke (d 2001), of Glasgow, and Esther Doonan, *née* Burch (d 1982); *b* 13 July 1952; *Educ* Larbert HS, Univ of St Andrews (BSc), Univ of Newcastle upon Tyne (MSc), Univ of Glasgow (PhD); *m* 28 Sept 1979, Janet Ruth, da of Francis Salter; 2 da (Rachael Elizabeth b 2 Sept 1988, Esther Jane b 26 Feb 1991); *Career* basic grade clinical psychologist: Northumberland AHAs 1974–76, Greater Glasgow Health Bd 1976–78; sr clinical psychologist Gartnavel Royal Hosp Glasgow 1978–83; Douglas Inch Centre: princ clinical psychologist 1984, top grade clinical psychologist 1984– (with greater responsibility 1989–); prof of forensic psychology Dept of Psychology Glasgow Caledonian Univ 1992–; visiting prof: Univ of Glasgow 1997–2001, Univ of Bergen 2006–; Cropwood fell Inst of Criminology Univ of Cambridge 1986; Sr Award for outstanding lifetime contribution to forensic psychology Div of Forensic Psychology BPsS 2006; FBPsS 1986, FRSE 2004; *Books* Psychology in Prisons (with P Baldwin and J Howison, 1990), Treatment as an Alternative to Prosecution (1990), Psychological Disturbance in the Scottish Prison System: Prevalance, Precipitants and Policy (1994), Predicting Recidivism in a Scottish Prison Sample (with C Michie, 1997), International Perspectives on Psychopathy (with A Forth, J Newman and R Hare, 1997), Psychopathy: Theory, Research and Implications for Society (with A Forth and R Hare, 1998); *Recreations* sailing, cooking, opera; *Clubs* Loch Lomond Sailing; *Style*— Prof David Cooke; ✉ Douglas Inch Centre, 2 Woodside Terrace, Glasgow G3 7UY (tel 0141 211 8000, fax 0141 211 8005, e-mail djcooke@rgardens.vianw.co.uk)

COOKE, Col Sir David William Perceval; 12 Bt (E 1661), of Wheatley Hall, Yorkshire; s of Sir Charles Arthur John Cooke, 11 Bt (d 1978), of Fowey, Cornwall, and Diana, *née* Perceval (d 1989); *b* 28 April 1935; *Educ* Wellington, RMA Sandhurst, Open Univ (BA 1983); *m* 30 March 1959, Margaret Frances, da of Herbert Skinner (d 1984), of Knutsford, Cheshire; 3 da (Sara Elisabeth Mary b 1960, Louise Diana Margaret b 1962, Catherine Faith Maria b 1968); *Heir* kinsman, Edmund Cooke-Yarborough; *Career* 4/7 RDG 1955, RASC 1958, RCT 1965, ret 1990; dir Finance & Resources Bradford City Technology Coll 1990–91; conslt DC Research Consultancy 1992–; *Recreations* bird-watching, walking, social and local history, fishing; *Style*— Col Sir David Cooke, Bt; ✉ c/o Midland Bank, Knutsford, Cheshire WA16 6BZ

COOKE, Dominic; s of Malcolm Cooke, and Gloria Solomon, *née* Turower; *b* 1 February 1966, London; *Educ* Westminster City Sch, Univ of Warwick (BA); *Career* theatre dir; assoc dir Royal Court Theatre 1998–2002 (prodns incl: Plasticine, The People are Friendly, Fucking Games, Redundant, Spinning into Butter, Fireface, Other People), assoc dir RSC 2002–07 (prodns incl: The Malcontent, Cymbeline, Macbeth, As You Like It, Postcards from America, The Crucible (Best Dir Olivier Awards 2006), The Winter's Tale, Pericles), artistic dir Royal Court Theatre 2007– (prodns incl: Rhinocerus, The Pain and the Itch); other theatre incl: Autogeddon (Assembly Rooms Edinburgh, Fringe First Award 1991), Arabian Nights (Young Vic, UK and world tour, New Victory Theatre NY, TMA Award 2000), prodns at Wyndham Theatre, Gate Dublin, Donmar Warehouse, Theatr Clwyd, Bolton Octagon and Nottingham Playhouse; opera incl: The Marriage of Figaro (Manchester Evening News Award 1990), The Magic Flute (Welsh National Opera), I Capuleti e I Montecchi and La Bohème (both Grange Park Opera); *Publications* Arabian Nights (1998); *Style*— Dominic Cooke, Esq; ✉ Royal Court Theatre, Sloane Square, London SW1W 8AS (tel 020 7565 5050, fax 020 7565 5000, e-mail info@royalcourttheatre.com)

COOKE, (John) Howard; s of Capt Jack Cooke, MC, of Exeter, and Ellen Jean, *née* Passmore; *b* 7 January 1952; *Educ* Exeter Sch, QMC London (LLB); *m* 1, 22 July 1972 (m dis 1983), Sally-Anne, da of Sydney Evans; m 2, 25 March 1983, Dr (Jayne) Elizabeth Mann; 2 da (Elena b 1983, Lauren b 1986); *Career* admitted slr 1976; ptnr Frere Cholmeley Bischoff 1980–95 (conslt 1995–97), conslt Lawrence Tucketts 1997–2000 (now TLT Solicitors); dir Wildbrook Investments 1996–; memb Law Soc; *Recreations* country pursuits; *Style*— Howard Cooke, Esq; ✉ Cotleigh House, Elstone, Chulmleigh, North Devon EX18 7AQ (tel 01769 580538)

COOKE, Jean Esme Oregon; da of Arthur Oregon Cooke, and Dorothy Emily, *née* Cranefield (d 1981); *b* 18 February 1927; *Educ* Blackheath HS, Central Sch of Art and Crafts, Goldsmiths' Coll Sch of Art (Dip Art & Design), Camberwell Sch of Art, City and Guilds Coll of Arts, RCA (Royal scholar); *m* 2 April 1953, John Randal Bratby; 3 s (David Johnathon Fernando b 1955, Jason Sovereign b 1959, Dayan Edvardo Joachim Jesse b 1968), 1 da (Wendy Dolores Carmen Hirondell b 1970); *Career* artist; lectr: Oxford Sch of Art, Royal Coll of Art 1964–74; Chantrey Bequest Purchases 1969 and 1972; portraits: Dr Egon Wellesz, Dr Walter Oakshott for Lincoln Coll Oxford, Mrs Mary Bennett for St Hilda's Coll Oxford 1976, John Bratby for Royal Coll of Art Collection, John Bratby called Lilly Lilly on the Brow; self portrait: Tate Gallery, Royal Acad Collection, Usher Gallery Lincoln Collection, Royal Coll of Art Collection, HM Government Collection, The John Madejski Fine Rooms Royal Acadamy; pres Blackheath Arts Soc, former pres Friends of Woodlands Art Gallery; RA 1972 (memb Cncl 1983–85, 1992–94 and 2002–, sr hanger 1993 and 1994); *Recreations* Tai Chi, finding stones on the beach, riding a bike, swimming; *Clubs* Arts; *Style*— Miss Jean Cooke, RA

COOKE, Hon Mr Justice; Sir Jeremy Lionel Cooke; kt (2001); s of Eric Edwin Cooke, of Warlingham, Surrey, and Margaret Lilian, *née* Taylor; *b* 28 April 1949; *Educ* Whitgift Sch Croydon, St Edmund Hall Oxford (open exhibition, MA, Rugby blues 1968 and 1969); *m* 24 June 1972, Barbara Helen, da of Geoffrey Curtis Willey, of Wallington, Surrey; 2 da (Emily b 3 June 1978, Josie b 28 March 1980), 1 s (Samuel b 29 June 1984); *Career* admitted slr 1973, called to the Bar Lincolns' Inn 1976 (bencher 2001); slr Coward Chance 1973–76; QC 1990, recorder 1998–2001 (asst recorder 1994–98), head of chambers 2000–01, judge of the High Court of Justice (Queen's Bench Div Commercial Ct) 2001–, presiding judge South Eastern Circuit 2007–; vice-chm LICC Ltd 1999–; reader C of E 2001–, vice-pres Lawyers' Christian Fellowship 2003–; memb Harlequins RFC 1970–75; *Recreations* golf; *Clubs* National; *Style*— The Hon Mr Justice Cooke; ✉ Royal Courts of Justice, Strand, London WC2A 2LL

COOKE, John Arthur; s of Arthur Hafford Cooke, MBE (d 1987), Warden New Coll Oxford, and Ilse Cooke, *née* Sachs (d 1973); *b* 13 April 1943; *Educ* Dragon Sch Oxford, Magdalen Coll Sch Oxford, Univ of Heidelberg, King's Coll Cambridge (MA), LSE; *m* 21 Feb 1970, Tania Frances, da of Alexander Cochrane Crichton; 2 da (Olga b 1972, Beatrice b 1977), 1 s (Alexander b 1975); *Career* asst princ Bd of Trade 1966, second then first sec UK Delgn to Euro Communities 1969–73, DTI 1973–76, Office of UK Perm Rep to Euro Communities 1976–77, DTI 1977–80, asst sec DTI 1980–84, seconded as asst dir to Morgan Grenfell & Co 1984–85, DTI 1985–97, under sec Overseas Trade Div 2 DTI 1987–89, head Central Unit DTI 1989–92, dir Deregulation Unit 1990–92, head Int Trade Policy Div 1992–96, dir and advsr on trade policy DTI 1996–97; leader UK delgn to ninth UN conf on trade and devpt 1996, chm OECD Trade Ctee 1996–97; head of Int Relations Assoc of Br Insurers 1997–2003, int economic relations conslt 2003–; non-exec dir: RTZ Pillar Ltd 1990–93, West Middx Univ Hosp NHS Tst 1996–98; chm Liberalisation of Trade in Services (LOTIS) Ctee Int Financial Servs London 2006–,

European co-chm Financial Ldrs' Working Gp 2006–, dep chm SITPRO Ltd 2006–; memb: Editorial Bd International Trade Law Reports 1997–, Exec Bd Anglo-Irish Encounter 2004–, Advsy Cncl The Federal Tst 2004–; bd sec ENO 1996–, tstee ENO Benevolent Fund 2001–; St Luke's Community Tst: memb, tstee 1983–93 and 1996–2000, vice-chm 1991–93, patron 2000–; memb Cncl Marie Curie Cancer Care 1992–, memb Bd Marie Curie Trading 1999–2002; *Recreations* reading, travelling, looking at buildings; *Clubs* Oxford and Cambridge, Cambridge Union; *Style*— John Cooke, Esq; ✉ 29 The Avenue, Kew, Richmond, Surrey TW9 2AL (tel 020 8940 6712, fax 020 8332 7447)

COOKE, Cdre Jonathan Gervaise Fitzpatrick; OBE (1983); s of Rear Adm John Gervaise Beresford Cooke, CB (d 1976), and Helen Beatrice, *née* Cameron; *b* 26 March 1943; *Educ* Summerfields Oxford, Marlborough, RNC Dartmouth; *m* 9 April 1983, Henrietta Lorraine Deschamps, da of late Maj Saunders Edward Chamier, MC, of Wadhurst, E Sussex; 2 da (Arabella b 1984, Serena b 1985), 1 s (Hugo b 1987); *Career* joined RN 1961; cmd three submarines (HMS Rorqual 1974–76, HMS Churchill 1981–82, HMS Warspite 1980–84), Cdr submarine sea trg 1984–86, Capt 3 Submarine Sqdn 1986–89, Br Naval Attaché Paris 1990–92, RCDS 1993, Cdre MOD and ADC 1993–96; chief exec Leathersellers' Co 1996–, dir Anglo-Siberian Oil Co 1998–2003; Yr Bro Trinity House 1994; Cdr de l'Ordre Nationale de Mérite (France) 1992; *Recreations* tennis, golf, gardening; *Clubs* Naval and Military, Queen's; *Style*— Cdre Jonathan Cooke, OBE, RN; ✉ Downstead House, Morestead, Winchester, Hampshire SO21 1LF (tel 01962 777765); Leathersellers' Company, 15 St Helen's Place, London EC3A 6DQ (tel 020 7330 1444, e-mail jcooke@leathersellers.co.uk)

COOKE, Martin James Paul; s of Lt-Col Cedric Paul Cooke (d 1974), and Katharine Norah Blanche *née* Lowick (d 1998); *b* 25 January 1947; *Educ* Haileybury and ISC; *m* 1, 19 Oct 1974 (m dis 1983), Janet Elizabeth, da of Alan Byrne, of Llanderffel, N Wales; 1 da (Anna b 1976), 1 s (Nicholas b 1978); m 2, 4 Jan 1985, Frances Mary, da of John Peter Jackson (d 1985), of Croydon, Surrey; 3 s (Jonathan b 1986, Charles b 1988, Benedict b 1990), 1 da (Helena b 1994); *Career* chartered accountant; Touche Ross & Co 1969–72, ptnr Rensburg Stockbrokers 1976 (joined 1972), non-exec dir Radio City plc 1987–91, chm Northern Stock Exchange Conference 1988, dir BWD Rensburg Ltd 1988–2007; chm Chester Summer Music Festival 1979–81 (fin dir 1978–87), chm St Endellion Summer Festival 1990–2005; pres: Liverpool Soc of Chartered Accountants 1992–93, Cncl Liverpool Sch of Tropical Med 1999–; memb Stock Exchange 1973; FCA 1969, AIIMR 1973; *Recreations* sailing, music; *Clubs* City (Chester); *Style*— Martin Cooke, Esq; ✉ Lion House, Tattenhall Road, Tattenhall, Chester, Cheshire CH3 9QH; Rensburg Sheppards, 100 Old Hall Street, Liverpool L3 9AB (tel 0151 227 2030)

COOKE, Nicholas Huxley; s of Geoffrey Whitehall Cooke (d 1995), and Anne Heathorn, *née* Huxley (d 1989); *b* 6 May 1944; *Educ* Charterhouse, Worcester Coll Oxford (MA); *m* 27 June 1970, Anne, da of James Whittington Landon, DFC (d 1994); 3 da (Fenella (Mrs A S J Richmond) b 1973, Sophie b 1976, Caroline b 1978), 2 s (James b 1983, Toby b 1986); *Career* dir: (Scotland) British Tst for Conservation Volunteers 1978–84, Scottish Conservation Projects (formerly Scottish Conservation Projects Tst) 1984–99, CLEAR Services Ltd 2000–, Rockdust Ltd 2005–; chm Callander Youth Project Tst 2004–; memb: Scottish Ctee for European Year of the Environment 1987–88, Bd Scottish Cncl for Voluntary Orgns 1992–2002; chm: Youthlink Scotland 1996–99 (also memb Bd), Scottish Ctee Voluntary Sector Nat Trg Orgn 1997–2001, Gowanbank Historic Village Ltd 2001–04, Scottish Organic Prodrs Assoc 2002–04 (memb Bd 2004–05), Inc Glasgow and Stirlingshire Sons of the Rock Soc 2003–05; sec Scottish Sr Alliance for Volunteering in the Environment (SSAVE) 2001–03; pres Amateur Entomologists Soc 1975 (treas 1972–78); FRSA; *Recreations* field entomology, walking, photography, fly fishing; *Style*— Nicholas Cooke, Esq; ✉ Easter Stonefield, Port of Menteith, Stirling FK8 3RD (tel 01877 382411, fax 01877 382365, e-mail nhcooke@aol.com)

COOKE, Nicholas Orton; QC (1998); only surviving s of Mr B O Cooke, of Rogerstone, nr Newport, and Mrs V Cooke, *née* Price; *b* 1 July 1955; *Educ* King Edward's Sch Birmingham, UCW Aberystwyth (Sweet and Maxwell Prize); *m* 1979, Jean Ann, da of late Mr W H Tucker; *Career* called to the Bar Middle Temple 1977 (Blackstone entrance exhbn 1976); Wales & Chester Circuit 1978–, recorder 1997– (asst recorder 1994–97); dep pres Mental Health Review Tnbl for Wales 1999–; chm Bristol and Wales Chancery Bar Assoc, chm Wales Public Law and Human Rights Assoc; Church in Wales: memb Governing Body 1999–, judge of the Provincial Court 2004–, chllr Dio of St David's 2005–; *Recreations* hockey, theatre; *Style*— Nicholas Cooke, Esq, QC; ✉ 9 Park Place, Cardiff, South Glamorgan CF10 3DP (tel 029 2038 2731, fax 029 2022 2542)

COOKE, Nigel; *b* 17 July 1973, Manchester; *Educ* Nottingham Trent Univ (BA), RCA (MA), Goldsmiths Coll London (PhD); *Career* artist; *Solo Exhibitions* Chapman Fine Arts London 2000, Modern Art London 2002 and 2005, Art Now Tate Britain 2004, Andrea Rosen Gallery NY 2004, Blum and Poe LA 2005; *Group Exhibitions* Interesting Painting (City Racing London) 1997, New Contemporaries 98 (Camden Arts Centre and tour) 1998, Glory (Br Cncl Window Gallery Prague) 1999, Wooden Heart (Avco London) 2000, Homage to the Budokan (Foyles Gallery London) 2000, A Sport & a Pastime (Greene Naftali Inc NY) 2001, Tattoo Show (Modern Art London) 2001, Melodrama (Israel and Spain) 2002, Still Life (Br Cncl Chile, Venezuela, Argentina and Columbia) 2002–03, Exploring Landscape (Andrea Rosen Gallery NY) 2003, Dirty Pictures (The Approach London) 2003, I See a Darkness (Blum and Poe LA) 2003, Contemporary Drawing (Jack Hanley Gallery San Francisco) 2003, Painting (Gallery Somme Tel Aviv), Frass (122 Leadenhall St London), Gewalt (Loushy Art and Editions Tel Aviv); *Style*— Nigel Cooke, Esq; ✉ c/o Modern Art, 73 Redchurch Street, London E2 7DJ (tel 020 7739 2081, fax 020 7729 2017, e-mail modernart@easynet.co.uk, website www.modernartinc.com)

COOKE, (William) Peter; CBE (1997); s of Douglas Edgar Cooke, MC (Lt Durham LI, d 1964), of Gerrards Cross, Bucks, and Florence May, *née* Mills (d 1986); *b* 1 February 1932; *Educ* Kingswood Sch Bath, Merton Coll Oxford (MA); *m* 1, 22 April 1957, Maureen Elizabeth (d 1999), da of Dr E A Haslam-Fox (d 1975) of Holmes Chapel, Cheshire; 2 s (Nicholas b 1959, Andrew b 1964), 2 da (Caroline b 1960, Stephanie b 1970); m 2, 20 Aug 2005, Julia Mary Bain, *née* Warrack; *Career* Nat Serv RA 1951; joined Bank of England 1955; seconded: to Bank for International Settlements Basle Switzerland 1958–59, as PA to md IMF Washington DC 1961–65, as sec City Takeover Panel 1968–69; Bank of England: first dep chief cashier 1970–73, advsr to Govrs 1973–76, head Banking Supervision 1976–85, assoc dir 1982–88; chm: City EEC Ctee 1973–80, Ctee on Banking Regulations and Supervisory Practices Bank for International Settlements Basel Switzerland 1977–88, Price Waterhouse World Regulatory Advsy Practice 1989–97; dir: Safra Republic Holdings SA 1989–99, Alexander & Alexander Services Inc 1994–96, Financial Security Assurance (UK) Ltd 1994–, Bank of China International Holdings 1997–98, The Housing Finance Corporation 1997–2003, Bank of China International (UK) Ltd 1998–, State Street Bank (UK) Ltd 1998–2006, Bank of China Ltd 2004–07, Medicapital Holdings plc 2006–; advsr: PricewaterhouseCoopers 1997–2002, HSBC Republic Holdings 2000–02; chm Merton Soc 1979–95 (pres 1995–98); memb Bd: The Housing Corporation 1989–97 (chm 1996–97), Eng Churches Housing Gp 1977–93, Salzburg Seminar 1990–2004; memb Cncl RIIA 1992–2005 (dep chm 1998–2005); govr: Pangbourne Coll 1982–2002, Kingswood Sch 1990–2002; hon fell Merton Coll Oxford 1997; *Recreations* music, golf, travel; *Clubs* Reform, Denham Golf; *Style*— Peter Cooke, Esq, CBE; ✉ Oak Lodge, Maltmans Lane, Chalfont St Peter, Gerrards Cross, Buckinghamshire SL9 8RP (tel 01753 886236, fax 01753 886236, e-mail e-mail@petercooke.co.uk)

COOKE, Peter Stephen; s of Henry Peter Cooke (d 1988), and Patricia Jean Cooke, *née* Wearing; *b* 13 April 1948; *Educ* Guildford Royal GS, Univ of Southampton (BSc); *m* 1, 24 July 1971 (m dis 1989), Patricia Ann, da of Robert Frederick Meredith; 2 da (Alexander b 1978, Amy b 1979); m 2, 15 July 1989, Elizabeth Margaret, da of Glyndwr Thomas; 1 s (George Henry b 1991); *Career* slr; legal advsr to Engrg Employers' Fedn 1978–83, managing ptnr Theodore Goddard 1984– (currently head Employment and Employee Benefits Gp); memb Worshipful Co of Slrs 1989; memb Law Soc; *Books* Croners Employment Law (1980), Croners Industrial Relations Law (contrib 1989); *Recreations* music, cycling and sailing; *Style*— Peter Cooke, Esq; ✉ 302 Cromwell Tower, Barbican, London EC2Y 8DD; Theodore Goddard, 150 Aldersgate Street, London EC1A 4EJ (tel 020 7606 8855, telex 884678, fax 020 7606 4390)

COOKE, Richard Kennedy Gordon; s of Alfred Gordon Cooke (d 1992), and Mary Eluned, *née* Mason (d 2003); *b* 23 April 1950; *Educ* St Paul's Cathedral Choir Sch, Monkton Combe Sch, King's Coll Cambridge; *m* 31 May 1980 (m dis 2004), Alison Mary, da of Hon (Arthur) Maxwell Stamp (d 1984); 2 da (Florence Mary b 10 Sept 1982, Hannah Marian b 4 May 1984), 1 s (Maxwell Richard Gordon b 3 Nov 1985); partner, Christina Mariam Astin; 1 da (Emily Freya b 17 Oct 2004), 1 s (Wilfred Gregor b 14 Nov 2006); *Career* conductor; conductor Cambridge Univ Chamber Orch and asst conductor Cambridge Univ Music Soc 1972–73, dir of choral music Tiffin Sch Kingston upon Thames 1974–81, conductor London Philharmonic Choir 1982–91, chorus master Opéra de Lyon 1992–95, music dir Royal Choral Soc 1995–; other appointments incl: dir of music St Columb Festival 1969–90, asst conductor Gemini Opera 1974–80, conductor Univ of Essex Choir 1981–, conductor Canterbury Choral Soc 1984–, asst chorus master London Symphony Chorus 1976–82; various conducting in Europe and Scandinavia incl: Gothenburg Symphony Orchestra, Opéra de Lyon, Aix-en-Provence Festival; Hon Doctorate Univ of Essex 1996; *Recordings* as conductor incl: Orff Carmina Burana (with RPO and Royal Choral Soc) 1995, Last Night of the Proms (with RPO and Canterbury Choral Soc) 1996, Elgar The Apostles (Philharmonia and Canterbury Choral Soc) 2005; as chorus master incl: Brahms Requiem (LPO under Klaus Tennstedt) 1986, Mahler Symphony No 8 (with LPO under Tennstedt, Grammy nomination) 1987, Cherubini Mass (with LPO under Riccardo Muti) 1987, Vaughan Williams Sea Symphony (with LPO under Bernard Haitink) 1989; *Recreations* cricket, reading, surfing, politics; *Style*— Richard Cooke, Esq; ✉ 2A The Foreland, Canterbury CT1 3NT (tel 01227 472420, e-mail richardcooke@tiscali.co.uk)

COOKE, His Hon Roger Arnold; s of Stanley Gordon Cooke (d 1994), of Nether Alderley, Cheshire, and Frances Mabel, *née* Reading (d 2001); *b* 30 November 1939; *Educ* Repton, Magdalen Coll Oxford (MA); *m* 16 May 1970, Hilary, da of Eric Robertson (d 1993), of Shorwell, IOW; 2 s (James b 1972, Thomas b 1975), 2 da (Elizabeth (Mrs Lees) b 1973, Mary b 1979); *Career* called to the Bar Middle Temple 1962 (Astbury scholar), ad eundem Lincoln's Inn 1967 (bencher 1994); practised at the Chancery Bar 1963–89, head of Chambers 1985–88, jt head of Chambers 1988–89, recorder 1987–89 (asst recorder 1982–87), circuit judge (SE Circuit) 1989–2005; authorised to sit as judge of the High Court: Chancery Div 1992–, Queen's Bench Div 1994; pt/t students offr Lincoln's Inn 1976–80, hon sec Chancery Bar Assoc 1979–89; memb: Disciplinary Tbnls Bar 1988–89 and 1997, Inns of Court Advocacy Training Ctee 1995–2004, memb Advocacy Studies Bd 1996–2000; churchwarden: Little Berkhamsted 1979–94, St Mary Ashwell 2000–; memb Fin and Gen Purposes Ctee Broxbourne Cons Assoc 1986–89; govr The Pines Sch Hertford 1988–96 (chm 1990–95); Freeman (by purchase) City of London 1986; memb Inst Conveyancers 1983; *Recreations* gardening, photography, travel, history, old buildings, food; *Clubs* Athenaeum, Royal Inst of GB; *Style*— His Hon Roger Cooke

COOKE, Sir Ronald Urwick (Ron); kt (2002); s of Ernest Oswald Cooke (d 1948), of Maidstone, Kent, and Lilian, *née* Mount (d 1949); *b* 1 September 1941; *Educ* Ashford GS, UCL (BSc, MSc, PhD, DSc); *m* 4 Jan 1968, Barbara Anne, da of Albert Henry Baldwin (d 1969), of Petts Wood, Kent; 1 s (Graham Stephen b 1971), 1 da (Emma Louise b 1974); *Career* Dept of Geography UCL: lectr 1961–75, reader 1975, prof and head of dept 1981–91, dean of arts 1991–92, vice-provost 1991–93; vice-chllr Univ of York 1993–2002; Bedford Coll London: prof 1975–81, dean of sci 1978–80, vice-princ 1979–80; co-fndr, dir and chm Geomorphological Services Ltd 1980–90; cmmr US-UK Fulbright Cmmn 1995–2000; tstee Nat Sci Museum 2002–, chm Jt Info Systems Ctee 2004–; govr: Watford Boys' GS, Watford Girls' GS 1985–92; Hon Freeman City of York 2006; memb: Inst of Br Geographers (pres 1991–92), HEFCE 1997–2003, RGS (pres 2000–03), RSA; *Books* incl: Geomorphology in Deserts (with A Warren, 1973), Geomorphology in Environmental Management (with J C Doornkamp, 1974, 2 edn 1990), Arroyos and Environmental Change in the American Southwest (with R W Reeves, 1976), Environmental Hazards in Los Angeles (1984), Urban Geomorphology in Drylands (with D Brunsden, J C Doornkamp and DKC Jones, 1982), Desert Geomorphology (with A Warren and A S Goudie, 1993), Crumbling Heritage (with G Gibbs, 1993); *Clubs* Merchant Adventurers; *Style*— Sir Ron Cooke; ✉ c/o 92 Sandwich House, Sandwich Street, London WC1H 9PW

COOKE, Stephen Giles; s of late Basil Cooke, and Dora Cynthia, *née* Richards; *b* 30 July 1946; *Educ* Stamford Sch, Leicester Sch of Architecture; *m* Jane Lesley, da of late Cowper Fredrick Ide; 2 s (Henry Stephen b 1975, James Cowper b 1979); *Career* articled clerk Clay Allison & Clark Worksop Notts, admitted slr 1971, ptnr Withers 1973– (joined 1971); dir Ockenden International (refugee charity), tstee The Living Landscape Tst; chm London Handel Soc; *Books* Inheritance Tax and Lifetime Gifts (1987); *Recreations* music, the countryside, gardening; *Clubs* Garrick; *Style*— Stephen Cooke, Esq; ✉ The Pond House, Well, Hook, Hampshire RG29 1TL; Withers LLP, 16 Old Bailey, London EC4M 7EG (tel 020 7597 6000, fax 020 7597 6543)

COOKE, Stephen John; s of Robert Cooke (d 1995), and Barbara Cooke (d 2000); *b* 7 March 1959; *Educ* Lincoln Coll Oxford (MA); *Career* slr; Slaughter and May: joined 1982, NY office 1989–90, ptnr 1991–, head of M&A 2001–; *Publications* Takeovers (1997); *Clubs* Groucho, Blacks; *Style*— Stephen Cooke, Esq; ✉ Slaughter and May, 1 Bunhill Row, London EC1Y 8YY (tel 020 7090 3261, e-mail stephen.cooke@slaughterandmay.com)

COOKE, Prof Timothy; *b* 16 September 1947; *Career* house offr Royal Southern Hosp Liverpool 1973–74, demonstrator in anatomy Univ of Liverpool 1974–75, casualty offr Broadgreen Hosp Liverpool 1975–76 (SHO in orthopaedics 1975), registrar to Professorial Surgical Unit Liverpool Royal Infirmary 1976, registrar Wallasey Victoria Central 1976–77, registrar in paediatric surgery Alder Hey Children's Hosp 1977, research asst Dept of Surgery Liverpool Royal Infirmary 1978–79 (registrar to Professorial Surgical Unit 1977–78), registrar in surgery Professorial Unit Broadgreen Hosp 1979–80, lectr in surgery and hon sr registrar Univ of Southampton 1980–83; sr lectr in surgery and hon conslt surgn: Charing Cross and Westminster Med Sch 1983–86, Univ of Liverpool/Royal Liverpool and Broadgreen Hosps 1986–89; St Mungo prof of surgery and hon conslt surgn Royal Infirmary Glasgow 1989–; memb: Specialist Advsy Ctee in Gen Surgery, MRC Colorectal Cancer Ctee, UKCCCR Colorectal Cancer Ctee, Cncl Br Oncological Assoc, Exec Ctee Br Assoc of Cancer Research; author of numerous pubns in learned jls; memb Editorial Bd: Br Jl of Surgery (also memb Cncl), Br Jl of Cancer, Surgical Oncology, Current Practice in Surgery, GUT, Annals of the RCSEd; memb: Surgical Research Soc, Assoc of Surgns of GB and I, Br Breast Gp, RSM, Br Assoc for Cancer Research, Cell Kinetic Soc; *Style*— Prof Timothy Cooke

COOKE OF ISLANDREAGH, Baron (Life Peer 1992), of Islandreagh in the County of Antrim; Victor Alexander Cooke; OBE (1981), DL (Antrim 1970); s of (Norman) Victor Cooke, of Greenisland, Co Antrim; *b* 18 October 1920; *Educ* Marlborough, Trinity Coll

Cambridge (MA); *m* 1951, Alison Sheila, only da of late Maj-Gen Francis Casement, DSO; 2 s (Hon Michael John Alexander b 1955, Hon James Victor Francis b 1960), 1 da (Hon Victoria Sally (Hon Mrs Nicholas Yonge) b 1956); *Career* Lt RN 1940–46; chm: Henry R Ayton Ltd Belfast 1970–89 (with firm 1946–89), Springvale EPS (formerly Polyproducts) Ltd 1964–2000, Belfast Savings Bank 1963, Harland & Wolff Ltd 1980–81 (dir 1970–87); dir NI Airports 1970–85; memb: Senate NI Parly 1960–68, NI Economic Cncl 1974–78; cmmr Irish Lights 1983–95 (chm 1990–92); CEng, FIMechE; *Clubs* Naval; *Style—* The Rt Hon Lord Cooke of Islandreagh, OBE, DL; ✉ House of Lords, London SW1A 0PW

COOKE-PRIEST, Rear Adm Colin Herbert Dickinson; CB (1993); s of Dr William Hereward Dickinson Priest (d 1988), of Jersey, and Harriet Lesley Josephine, *née* Cooke (d 1998); *b* 17 March 1939; *Educ* Marlborough, BRNC Dartmouth; *m* 20 March 1965, Susan Mary Diana (Sue), da of Air Vice Marshal John Forde Hobler, CB, CBE, of Queensland, Australia; 2 da (Diana b 1966, Marina b 1974), 2 s (Nicholas b 1969, James b 1971); *Career* Cdr RN 1973, CO HMS Plymouth 1975, CO HMS Berwick 1976, Capt 1980, CO HMS Boxer 1983, dir Maritime Tactical Sch 1985, CO HMS Brilliant and Capt (F) Second Frigate Sqdn 1987, Cdr RN Task Force Gulf 1988, Rear Adm 1989, Dep Asst Chief of Staff (Ops) SHAPE Belgium and maritime advsr SACEUR 1989, Flag Offr Naval Aviation 1990–93; chief exec Trident Trust 1994–99; chm Fleet Air Arm Offrs' Assoc 1998–2005; gentleman usher to HM The Queen 1994; Freeman City of London 1986, Liveryman Worshipful Co of Coachmakers and Coach Harness Makers 1986, Liveryman Guild of Air Pilots and Air Navigators 1999 (Master Elect 2008); FRAeS 1992; *Clubs* Army and Navy; *Style—* Rear Adm Colin Cooke-Priest, CB

COOKSEY, Sir David James Scott; kt (1993), GBE (2007); s of late Dr Frank Sebastian Cooksey, CBE, of Suffolk, and Muriel Mary, *née* Scott; *b* 14 May 1940; *Educ* Westminster, St Edmund Hall Oxford (MA, hon fell 1995); *m* 1973 (m dis 2003), Janet Clouston Bewley, da of Dr Ian Aysgarth Bewley Cathie, of Glos; 1 s (Alexander b 1976), 1 da (Leanda b 1974); *Career* chm: Advent Venture Ptnrs 1987–2006 (md 1981–87), Bespak plc 1995–2004 (dir 1993–2004); a dir of the Bank of England 1994–2005 (chm non-exec dir ctee 2001–05); dir: British Venture Capital Association 1983–89 (chm 1983–84), William Baird plc 1995–2002, Establishment Investment Tst plc 2002–, Diamond Light Source Ltd 2002– (chm), Resolution plc 2004–, European Venture Capital Association 2004– (chm 2005–06); memb Innovation Advsy Bd DTI 1988–93; chm: Audit Cmmn for Local Govt and the NHS in England and Wales 1986–95, Local Govt Cmmn 1995–96, UK Clinical Research Collaboration Industry Reference Gp Dept of Health 2004–, State Honours Ctee 2005–, Cooksey Review of UK Health Research HM Treasury 2006–, London & Continental Railways 2006–; memb Cncl Univ of Southampton 1993–2003; govr Wellcome Tst 1995–99; tstee: Mary Rose Tst 1993–2001 (chm 1996–2001); Liveryman Worshipful Co of Info Technologists; Hon DBA Kingston Univ, hon fell Univ of Wales Cardiff; hon fell British Assoc; FRSA, Hon FMedSci; *Recreations* sailing, performing and visual arts; *Clubs* Boodle's, Royal Yacht Squadron, Royal Thames Yacht; *Style—* Sir David Cooksey, GBE; ✉ London & Continental Railways Ltd, 183 Eversholt Street, London NW1 1AY (tel 020 7391 4310)

COOKSON, Clive Michael; s of Richard Clive Cookson, and Ellen, *née* Fawwaz; *b* 13 February 1952; *Educ* Winchester, BNC Oxford (BA); *m* 8 April 1978, Caroline Davidson; 1 s (Robert b 9 Oct 1984), 1 da (Emma b 10 July 1986); *Career* sci journalist; trainee journalist Luton Evening Post (Thomson Regional Newspapers) 1974–76, American ed (in Washington) Times Higher Education Supplement 1977–81 (science corr 1976–77), technol corr The Times 1981–83, sci and med corr BBC Radio 1983–87, sci ed Financial Times 1991– (technol ed 1987–90); Feature Writer of the Year (UK Technol Press Awards) 1988 and 1989, Glaxo Sci Writer of the Year 1994 and 1998; *Style—* Clive Cookson, Esq; ✉ The Financial Times, 1 Southwark Bridge, London SE1 9HL (tel 020 7873 4950, fax 020 7873 4343, e-mail clive.cookson@ft.com)

COOKSON, Thomas Richard (Tommy); s of Dr Samuel Harold Cookson (d 1986), and Elizabeth Mary, *née* Mitchell (d 1994); *b* 7 July 1942, Bournemouth, Dorset; *Educ* Winchester, Balliol Coll Oxford; *m* 30 Dec 1972, Carol, *née* Hayley; 3 da (Harriet b 1974, Camilla b 1977, Elizabeth b 1980); *Career* Winchester Coll: head English Dept 1974–83, housemaster 1983–90; headmaster King Edward VI Sch Southampton 1990–96, headmaster Sevenoaks Sch 1996–2001, princ Br Sch Colombo Sri Lanka 2002, headmaster Winchester Coll 2003–05; memb Ctee HMC 1997–2000; *Books* Keats (1972), Bernard Shaw (1972); *Recreations* golf, theatre; *Clubs* Rye Golf; *Style—* Tommy Cookson, Esq

COOMBE, Donald Howard; MBE (1992), JP (1973); er s of Howard James Coombe (d 1988) and Rose May *née* Tate (d 1997); *b* 21 October 1927; *Educ* Northbrook C of E Sch Lee, Roan Sch Greenwich, Univ of the World (MA); *m* 5 June 1948, Betty Joyce, da of George William Adie (d 1938); 2 s (Richard Howard b 25 April 1953, David b 8 Oct 1958); *Career* RN 1942–47, hon cmmn to Adm Texas Navy 1976, hon cmmn to Gen Washington 2001; chm: RTC Ltd (Lloyd's Brokers) 1971–; fndr chm: Coombe Tst Fund, Coombe Holiday Tst Fund (both registered charities for Needy Children); life memb Royal Soc of St George; former cmmr Scouts Assoc; hon attorney-gen N Carolina, chm of bench 1982, cmmr Income Tax 1978–85; Grand Offr (Freemasons) United Grand Lodge of England, Grand Chamberlain Mediaeval Knights of London 2002; Freeman: City of London 1970, City of Dallas Texas 1976; Liveryman Worshipful Co of Poulters 1978; ACII; Order of St George (Sweden) 1974; *Books* The Geezer Wiv the Flahr; *Recreations* charity fundraising, social work, boxing; *Clubs* New Three Rooms, Naval and Military, Special Forces, St Stephens; *Style—* Donald H Coombe, Esq, MBE, JP; ✉ Sunarise, Beckenham Place Park, Kent BR3 5BN (tel 020 8658 2714); Pelican House, One Hundred Tooley Street, London SE1 2TH (tel 020 7407 6350)

COOMBE, John David; s of Sidney Coombe; *b* 17 March 1945; *Educ* Haberdashers' Aske's, Univ of London (BSc); *m* 1970, Gail Alicia, *née* Brazier; 3 da; *Career* CA; gp treas The Charterhouse Group plc 1976–84, mangr fin and treasy Charter Consolidated plc 1984–86, md fin and main bd dir Glaxo Holdings plc 1992–95 (fin controller 1986–92), fin dir Glaxo Wellcome plc 1995–2000, chief financial offr GlaxoSmithKline plc 2000–05, chm Hogg Robinson plc 2006–; dir: Supervisory Bd Siemens AG 2003–, HSBC Holdings plc 2005–, GUS plc 2005–06, Home Retail Gp plc 2006–; chm Hundred Gp of Fin Dirs 1999–2001; memb Accounting Standards Bd 1996–2003; tstee Royal Acad of Arts Tst; *Clubs* Carlton; *Style—* John Coombe, Esq; ✉ tel 07901 828741

COOMBE, His Hon Michael Ambrose Rew; s of John Rew Coombe (d 1985), of King's Langley, Herts, and Phyllis Mary (d 1980); *b* 17 June 1930; *Educ* Berkhamsted, New Coll Oxford (MA); *m* 7 Jan 1961, (Elizabeth) Anne (d 1998), da of Tom Hull (d 1957); 3 s (Nicholas b Dec 1961, Jonathan b and d 1966, Peter b 1970), 1 da (Juliet b 1967); *Career* Nat Serv RAF; called to the Bar Middle Temple 1957 (bencher 1984, autumn reader 2001); second prosecuting counsel to the Inland Revenue Central Criminal Court and 5 Courts of London Sessions 1971, second counsel to the Crown Inner London Sessions 1971–74, first counsel to the Crown Inner London Crown Court 1974, second jr prosecuting counsel to the Crown Central Criminal Court 1975–77 (fourth jr 1974–75), recorder of the Crown Court 1976–85, first jr prosecuting counsel to the Crown Central Criminal Court 1977–78, a sr prosecuting counsel to the Crown at the Central Criminal Court 1978–85, circuit judge (SE Circuit) 1985–2003, judge Central Criminal Court 1986–2003; Freeman City of London 1986, Liveryman Worshipful Co of Stationers 2002, Liveryman Worshipful Co of Fruiterers 2002; *Recreations* theatre, antiquity, art and architecture, printing; *Clubs* Garrick; *Style—* His Hon Michael Coombe; ✉ Central Criminal Court, Old Bailey, London EC4M 7EH

COOMBES, Prof (Raoul) Charles Dalmedo Stuart; s of Col R C Coombes, MC, of Aldbourne, Wilts, and Doreen Mary, *née* Ellis; *b* 20 April 1949; *Educ* Douai Sch, St George's Hosp Med Sch (MB BS), UCL (PhD, MD, BS); *m* 27 July 1984, Caroline Sarah, da of David Oakes, of St Helens, Merseyside; 2 s (Jack Raoul b 1985, Charles David b 1992), 2 da (Sophie Flora b 1987, Matilda Rose b 1989); *Career* house physican and SHO in med and surgery St George's and associated hosps London 1971–73, SHO Radiotherapy Dept and research registrar Endocrine Unit Hammersmith Hosp 1973–74, MRC clinical res fell Inst of Cancer Research and Endocrine Unit Hammersmith Hosp 1974–76; Royal Marsden Hosp: registrar then clinical scientist and sr registrar 1976–80, sr lectr and hon conslt physician 1980–87; sr clinical scientist Ludwig Inst for Cancer Res 1980–87, conslt physician, med oncologist and head Clinical Oncology Unit St George's Hosp and hon sr lectr St George's Hosp Med Sch 1987–90, prof of med oncology and head Dept of Medical Oncology 1990–97, dean of research Charing Cross and Westminster Med Sch 1993–97, co-dir Cancer Servs and Clinical Haematology Directorate Hammersmith Hosps Tst 1994–, head Dept of Cancer Medicine Imperial Coll Sch of Med 1997–, hon conslt med oncologist Hammersmith Hosps Tst 1999–, prof of med oncology and dir Cancer Research (UK) Labs Hammersmith Hosp 1999–; co-ordinator of nat and int trials for Int Collaborative Cancer Gp; memb: SW Thames Regnl Cancer Gp, Br Breast Gp 1988; memb: Br Assoc Cancer Res 1988, American Assoc Cancer Res 1988, Endocrine Soc of GB, NY Acad of Sciences, European Soc for Clinical Oncology, Assoc of Cancer Physicians, European of Medical Oncology, American Assoc for the Advancement Science; FRCP 1983 (MRCP 1973), FMedSci 2001; *Publications* Breast Cancer Management (jt ed, 1981), New Endocrinology of Cancer (jt ed, 1986), New Targets in Cancer Therapy (1994); author of more than 400 papers on breast cancer; *Recreations* painting; *Style—* Prof Charles Coombes; ✉ Imperial College School of Medicine at Hammersmith Hospital, Du Cane Road, London W12 (tel 020 8383 5828, fax 020 8383 5830, e-mail c.coombes@ic.ac.uk)

COOMBS, Anthony Michael Vincent; s of Clifford Keith Coombs, of Knowle, W Midlands, and Celia Mary Gostling, *née* Vincent; *b* 18 November 1952; *Educ* Charterhouse, Worcester Coll Oxford (MA); *m* 21 Sept 1984, Andrea Caroline, da of Daniel Pritchard, of Netherton Dudley, W Midlands; 1 s (Alexander Graham Daniel); *Career* fndr and md Grevayne Properties Ltd; MP (Cons) Wyre Forest 1987–97; PPS: to Rt Hon David Mellor 1989–92, to Rt Hon Gillian Shephard as sec of state for Educn and Employment 1995–96; asst govt whip 1996–97; memb Nat Heritage Select Ctee 1994–96; former vice-chm: Back Bench Educn Ctee, Parliamentary Friends of Cyprus, All-Pty Human Rights Gp; chm Businessforsale.com plc 1998–2002, md S & U plc 1999–; memb Advsy Bd PACT Management Consultants 1997–99; memb Nat Exec Consumer Credit Assoc 2001–; tstee: Nat Inst for Conductive Educn (chm of tstees 2004–), Midlands Bd Business for Sterling, Birmingham Royal Ballet 1999–; dir Schools Outreach, memb Devpt Ctee Worcester Coll Oxford 1996–98; *Recreations* tennis, golf, skiing, football, music; *Clubs* RAC, Annabel's, '92 Group; *Style—* Anthony M V Coombs, Esq

COOMBS, Derek Michael; s of Clifford Coombs (d 1975), and Elizabeth Mary, *née* Evans (d 1974); *b* 12 August 1937; *Educ* Bromsgrove Sch; *m* 2, 1986; Jennifer Sheila, *née* Lonsdale; 2 s; 1 s and 1 da by previous m; *Career* political journalist, active pro-European and specialist in economic affrs; MP (Cons) Yardley 1970–74, dir Metalrax Group plc 1975–2002; Prospect Publishing Ltd: chm 1995–, chief exec 1999–, chm Prospect magazine; non-exec chm S & U plc 1976–2007; govr Royal Hosp & Home for Incurables Putney; *Recreations* friends, art, chess, skiing and walking; *Style—* Derek Coombs, Esq

COOMBS, Prof Graham H; *b* 22 September 1947; *Educ* UCL (BSc, PhD); *Career* research fell Biological Lab Univ of Kent 1972–74; Dept of Zoology Univ of Glasgow: lectr 1974–86, sr lectr 1986–88, reader 1988–90, titular prof 1990–95, head of dept 1991–94; Inst of Biomedical and Life Sciences Univ of Glasgow: head Parasitology Lab Div of Molecular and Cellular Biology 1994–95, with Div of Infection & Immunity 1995–, personal professorship in biochemical parasitology 1995–, dep dir Glasgow Biomedical Research Centre 2005–; pres Br Section Soc of Protozoologists, UK rep Int Cmmn of Protozoology; MRC: memb Physiological Med and Infections Bd 1999–2003, memb Cross Bd Gp 2000–04; Seymour H Hutner Prize Soc of Protozoologists 1986; FRSE 1993; *Publications* incl: Trypanosomiasis and leishmaniasis: Biology and Control (jt ed, 1997), Evolutionary Relationships among Protozoa (jt ed, 1998); author of more than 170 papers, articles and reviews, particularly on subjects relating to protozoan parasites; *Style—* Prof Graham H Coombs; ✉ Division of Infection & Immunity, University of Glasgow, Glasgow Biomedical Research Centre, University Avenue, Glasgow G12 8TA (tel 0141 330 4777, fax 0141 330 3516, e-mail g.coombs@bio.gla.ac.uk)

COOMBS, Stephen Geoffrey; s of Geoffrey Samuel Coombs, of Meols, Wirral, and Joan Margaret, *née* Jones; *b* 11 July 1960; *Educ* Caldy Grange GS, Royal Northern Coll of Music, Royal Acad of Music; *Career* concert pianist; London debut Wigmore Hall 1975; performed at numerous festivals incl: Salisbury 1987, Henley 1988, Cheltenham 1988, Spoleto Italy 1988–90, Aldeburgh 1989–90, Radley 1990, Proms 1990, Three Choirs 1991, Bath 1993, Lichfield 1993 and 1995, Cardiff 1995, Sintra Portugal 1996, Newbury 1999; regular appearances throughout Europe; visiting lectr Univ of Central England 1994–96, dir of music Blackheath Conservatoire of Music and the Arts 2001–; fndr and artistic dir 'Pianoworks' Int Piano Festival London 1998–99; Gold medal Int Liszt Concourse Hungary 1977, Worshipful Co of Musicians/Maisie Lewis award 1986; ARAM 2002; *Recordings* incl: The Hussey Legacy 1988, Complete Two Piano Works of Debussy 1989, Ravel Works for Two Pianos 1990, Mendelssohn Two Double Piano Concertos 1992, Arensky Piano Concerto in F Minor and Fantasy on Russian Folk Songs 1992, Bortkiewicz Piano Concerto No 1 1992, Arensky Suites for Two Pianos 1994, Glazunov Complete Piano Works 4 Vols 1995, Glazunov Piano Concertos Nos 1 & 2 1996, Goedicke Concertstück 1996, Reynaldo Hahn Piano Concerto 1997, Massenet Piano Concerto 1997, Bortkiewicz Piano Works Vol 1 1997 and Vol 2 2000, Liadov Piano Works 1998, Milhaud Works for Two Pianos 1998, Arensky Piano Works 1998, Scriabin Early Piano Works 2001, Hahn Piano Quintet 2001, Vierne Piano Quintet 2001, Pierné Complete Works for Piano and Orchestra 2002; *Publications* Russian Romantic Repertoire Vols 1 & 2 (compiler and ed), French Romantic Repertoire Vols 1 & 2, American Romantic Repertoire Vols 1 & 2; *Recreations* genealogy, pubs, reading; *Style—* Stephen Coombs, Esq; ✉ c/o Wordplay, 35 Lizban Street, Blackheath, London SE3 8SS

COONEY, Raymond George Alfred (Ray); OBE (2005); s of Gerard Joseph (d 1987), of London, and Olive Harriet, *née* Clarke (d 1975); *b* 30 May 1932; *Educ* Alleyn's Sch Dulwich; *m* 8 Dec 1962, Linda Ann, da of Leonard Spencer Dixon (d 1985), of Epping; 2 s (Danny b 1964, Michael b 1966); *Career* actor, writer, producer, director; Nat Serv RASC 1950–52; acting debut Song of Norway (Palace Theatre) 1946; playwright: One For The Pot 1961, Chase Me Comrade 1964, Charlie Girl 1965, Not Now Darling 1967, Move Over Mrs Markham 1969, Why Not Stay for Breakfast? 1970, There Goes the Bride 1974, Elvis (musical) 1981, Run for your Wife 1983, Two into One 1984, Wife Begins at Forty 1985, It Runs In the Family 1989, Out of Order 1990 (Olivier Award for Best Comedy 1991), Funny Money 1993, Caught in the Net 2000 (nominated Olivier Award for Best New Comedy 2002), Tom, Dick & Harry 2003, Twice Upon a Time (musical) 2007; also dir and prodr many of own plays: One Good Turn 1997, Times Up 1998; also dir Pygmalion 1996 (revival), Chiltern Hundreds 1999 (revival), Caught in the Net (West Coast premiere LA); also prodr: Lloyd George Knew My Father 1972, Say Goodnight to Grandma 1973, At the End of the Day 1973, The Dame of Sark 1974, A Ghost on Tiptoe 1974, Bodies 1980, Whose Life Is It Anyway? 1980, They're Playing

Our Song 1980, Elvis 1981, Duet for One 1981, Children of a Lesser God 1982; as actor played leading role in many of his plays incl: Funny Money (London), Run For Your Wife (London and New York), It Runs in the Family (London), Caught in the Net (LA), Not Now Darling (film), Chase Me Comrade (film); fndr The Theatre of Comedy Co 1983 (artistic dir 1983–88); memb Actors' Equity, Dir Guild; *Recreations* tennis, swimming; *Style*— Ray Cooney, Esq, OBE

COOPER, *see also:* Astley-Cooper

COOPER, Alan Guthlac; s of late John Carr Cooper, of Harrogate, N Yorks, and late Veronica Dora, *née* Ludolf; *b* 23 August 1955; *Educ* Brentwood Sch, Univ of Durham (BA); *m* 17 July 1990, Carol, da of late Alexander Beattie; 2 s (Matthew Guthlac b 30 Sept 1991, Samuel Alexander b 3 July 1993), 2 da (Rebecca Aimi b 26 May 1995, Abigail Flora b 30 Jan 1997); *Career* British Market Research Bureau Ltd 1977–80, sr researcher rising to planning dir Leo Burnett Advertising Ltd 1980–84, sr planner rising to assoc dir Gold Greenlees Trott Ltd 1984–88, bd/planning dir DDB Needham Ltd 1988; Simons Palmer Clemmow Johnson Ltd: bd/planning dir 1989–97, head of planning 1993–97, chm Account Planning Gp 1996–98; planning dir TBWA Simons Palmer (following merger) 1997–98; md Brand Vitality Ltd 1999–; ptnr HPI Research Gp 2000–; Marketing Soc Brand of the Year Award 1993; IPA Advertising Effectiveness Award 1986 and 1994; memb MRS; *Books* Advertising Works (contrib Vol 4, 1987 and Vol 8, 1995), Understanding Brands (1996), How To Plan Advertising (ed, 1997), CBI Communications Handbook (contrib, 1997); *Recreations* running, playing the bodhran, horticulture, enjoying my family; *Clubs* Farmers', IOM TT Marshals Assoc; *Style*— Alan Cooper, Esq; ✉ Bramble Brae, Quarterbridge Road, Douglas, Isle of Man IM2 3RH (tel 01624 623220)

COOPER, Hon Alice Clare Antonia Opportune (Artemis); only da of 2 Viscount Norwich, CVO, *qv*; *b* 22 April 1953; *m* 1 Feb 1986, Antony Beevor, *qv*, s of John Grosvenor Beevor, OBE (d 1987); 1 da (Eleanor Allegra Lucie (Nella) b 19 Jan 1990), 1 s (Adam John Cosmo b 10 Feb 1993); *Career* writer; tstee: London Library 1994–2002, 999 Club 2004–; administrator Duff Cooper Prize 1993– Chevalier de l'Ordre des Arts et des Lettres (France) 1997; *Books* A Durable Fire: The Letters of Duff and Diana Cooper (ed, 1983), Cairo in The War 1939–45 (1989), Mr Wu and Mrs Stitch: The Letters of Evelyn Waugh and Diana Cooper (ed, 1991), Watching in the Dark - A Child's Fight for Life (1992), Paris after the Liberation 1944–49 (with Antony Beevor 1994), Writing at the Kitchen Table: The Authorised Biography of Elizabeth David (1999); *Style*— Ms Artemis Cooper; ✉ 54 St Maur Road, London SW6 4DP

COOPER, Dr Andrew Michael; s of Peter Cooper, of Blythe Bridge, Staffs, and Eileen Mildred, *née* Billings; *b* 31 October 1958; *Educ* Longton HS Stoke-on-Trent, City of Stoke-on-Trent Sixth Form Coll, Univ of Leeds Sch of Med (MB ChB, MRCGP, Dip RCGP); *m* 1 July 1989, Ann, da of Roy Rossington; 1 s (Michael David b 20 Jan 1992), 1 da (Bethan Sarah b 23 June 1997); *Career* house offr Leeds Gen Infirmary 1982–83, SHO A&E Cardiff Royal Infirmary 1983–84, SHO obstetrics and gynaecology Llandough Hosp Cardiff 1984–85, S Glamorgan Vocational Trg Scheme for Gen Practice 1985–87, ptnr Fairwater Health Centre Cardiff 1987–; clinical teacher Univ of Wales Coll of Med 1998; course organiser S Glamorgan Vocational Trg Scheme Univ of Wales Coll of Med Dept of Postgraduate Studies 1992–; RCGP: memb Welsh Cncl 1989–97, memb Central Cncl 1990–95, treas SE Wales Faculty 1991–94, chm SE Wales Faculty 1994–97, memb Patient Liaison Gp 1994–95, provost SE Wales Faculty 1997–2000; memb: RCP/RCPsych Working Pty on Care of Elderly Patients with Mental Illness 1994–95, UK Alcohol Forum 2000; memb BMA 1982, memb RSM 1989; FRCGP 1999 (MRCGP 1987); *Recreations* golf, cricket, skiing, travel, music; *Clubs* Radyr Golf; *Style*— Dr Andrew Cooper; ✉ Fairwater Health Centre, Plasmawr Road, Fairwater, Cardiff CF5 3JT (tel 029 2056 6291, fax 029 2057 8870, e-mail geirwen@mac.com)

COOPER, Dr Brian Thomas; s of Dr Andrew Matthew Cooper (d 1979), and Irene Elizabeth, *née* Roulston; *b* 20 May 1947; *Educ* Monkton Combe Sch Bath, Univ of Birmingham (BSc, MB ChB, MD); *m* 31 Aug 1973, Dr Griselda Mary Cooper, da of Dr Charles James Constantine Davey, of Box, Chippenham, Wiltshire; 1 da (Charlotte b 4 Aug 1987); *Career* lectr in med Univ of Bristol 1978–85, conslt physician Dunedin Hosp Dunedin NZ 1985–86, conslt physician City Hosp and Edgbaston Nuffield Hosp Birmingham, sr clinical lectr in med Univ of Birmingham 1987–; treas Br Soc of Gastroenterology 1998–2003; FRCP 1991 (censor 2003–05, cncllr 2006–); *Books* Manual of Gastroenterology (1987); *Recreations* military history, classical music and opera, skiing; *Style*— Dr Brian Cooper; ✉ 6 Lord Austin Drive, Marlbrook, Bromsgrove, Worcestershire B60 1RB (tel 0121 445 2727); Gastroenterology Unit, City Hospital, Dudley Road, Birmingham B18 7QH (tel 0121 507 4590, fax 0121 507 5665)

COOPER, Rt Rev Carl Norman; *see:* St Davids, Bishop of

COOPER, Prof Cary Lynn; CBE (2001); s of Harry Cooper, of LA, USA, and Caroline Lillian, *née* Greenberg; *b* 28 April 1940; *Educ* Fairfax Sch LA, Univ of Calif (BS, MBA), Univ of Manchester (MSc), Univ of Leeds (PhD); *m* 1, 1970 (m dis 1984), (Edna) June Taylor; 1 s (Hamish Scott b 1972), 1 da (Natasha Beth b 1974); m 2, 1984, Rachel Faith Davies; 2 da (Laura Anne b 1982, Sarah Kate b 1985); *Career* lectr in psychology Univ of Southampton 1967–73; UMIST: prof of mgmnt educn methods 1975–79, prof of organisational psychology 1979–98, pro-vice-chllr 1995–99, dep vice-chllr 2000–02; prof of organisational psychology and health BUPA 1998–2003; Lancaster Univ: prof of organisational psychology and health 2003–, pro-vice-chllr 2004–; temp advsr: WHO and ILO 1982–84, Home Office (on police stress) 1982–84; memb Bd of Tstees American Inst of Stress 1984–, pres Br Acad of Mgmnt 1986–90 and 1999–2004, treas Int Fedn of Scholarly Assoc of Mgmnt 1990–92; ed Jl of Organizational Behavior 1980–98, co-ed Stress Medicine 1992–; chm Business and Mgmnt RAE Panel HEFCE 1996 and 2001; pres: Inst of Welfare Officers 1999–, ISIS 2000, Br Assoc of Counselling and Psychotherapy 2006– (vice-pres 2000–05); ambass The Samaritans 2000–; dir Robertson Cooper Ltd; broadcaster; Myers Lecture Br Psychological Soc 1986; memb American Psychosomatic Assoc, fell American Acad of Mgmnt 1997 (Distinguished Service Award 1998, memb Bd of Govrs 2001–03); hon prof of psychology Univ of Manchester 1986–2003; Hon DLitt Heriot-Watt Univ 1998, Hon DBA Wolverhampton Univ 1999, Hon DSc Aston Univ 2002, Hon Dr Univ of Middlesex 2003; CIMgt 1997, FRSA, FBPsS, FRSM, FRSH, FBAM, AcSS 2000, Hon FFOM 2005, Hon FRCP 2006; *Books* incl: T-Groups (jtly, 1971), Theories of Group Processes (1976), Developing Social Skills in Managers (1976), Stress at Work (jtly, 1978), Executives Under Pressure (1978), Behavioural Problems in Organisations (1979), Learning From Others in Groups (1979), The Executive Gypsy (1979), Current Concerns in Occupational Stress (1980), The Stress Check (1980), Improving Interpersonal Relations (1981), Psychology and Management (jtly, 1982), Management Education (jtly, 1982), Stress Research (1983), Public Faces, Private Lives (jtly, 1984), Working Women (jtly, 1984), Psychology for Managers (jtly, 1984), Change Makers (jtly, 1985), Man and Accidents Offshore (jtly, 1986), International Review of Industrial and Organisational Psychology (jtly, 1986–2004), Pilots Under Stress (jtly, 1986), Women and Information Technology (jtly, 1987), Pressure Sensitive (jtly, 1988), High Flyers (jtly, 1988), Living with Stress (jtly, 1988), Early Retirement (jtly, 1989), Career Couples (jtly, 1989), Managing People at Work (jtly, 1989), Understanding Stress (jtly, 1990), Stress Survivors (jtly, 1991), Industrial and Organizational Psychology Vols 1 and 2 (1991), Stress and Cancer (1991), Accidents and Stress in the Offshore Oil and Gas Industry (jtly, 1991), Relax: Dealing with Stress (jtly, 1992), Shattering the Glass Ceiling (jtly, 1992), Total Quality and Human Resource Management (jtly, 1992), Women's Career Development (jtly, 1992), Stress in the Dealing Room (jtly, 1993), The Workplace Revolution (jtly, 1993), Business Elites (jtly, 1994), Creating Healthy Work Organizations (jtly, 1994), Trends in Organizational Behavior (jtly, 1994), Work Psychology (jtly, 1995), Managing Mergers, Acquistions and Strategic Alliances (jtly, 1996), Handbook of Stress, Medicine, and Health (1996), Managing Workplace Stress (jtly, 1997), Blackwell Encyclopaedia of Management (12 vols, 1997 and 2004), Balancing Your Career, Family and Life (jtly, 1998), Personality: Critical Concepts in Psychology (jtly, 4 volumes, 1998), Dealing with the New Russia (jtly, 1998), Concise Encyclopedia of Management (jtly, 1999), Stress and Strain (jtly, 1999, 2 edn 2003), Industrial and Organisational Psychology: Theory and Practice (jtly, 2000), Strategic Stress Management (jtly, 2000), Who's Who in the Management Sciences (2000), Classics in Management Thought (2 vols, 2000), Organizational Stress (jtly, 2001), Handbook of Organizational Culture and Climate (jtly, 2001), Managerial, Occupational and Organizational Stress Research (2001), FT Guide to Executive Health (jtly, 2002), Creating a Balance (jtly, 2003), The Employment Relationship (jtly, 2003), Managing the Risk of Workplace Stress (jtly, 2003), Shut Up and Listen (jtly, 2004), Leadership and Management in the 21st Century (2004), Handbook of Stress Medicine and Health (2004), Stress: A brief history (jtly, 2004), Work-Life Integration (jtly, 2005), Work (jtly, 3 vols, 2005), Research Companion for Occupational Health Psychology (jtly, 2005), Business and the Beautiful Game (jtly, 2005), Managing the Emotions in Mergers and Acquisitions (jtly, 2005), Managing Value Based Organizations (jtly, 2006), Happy Performing Managers (jtly, 2006), Inspiring Leaders (jtly, 2006), How to Deal with Stress (jtly, 2007), Positive Organizational Behavior (jtly, 2007); *Recreations* raising children, Russian literature, swimming, celebrating in Manchester City FC, following politics; *Clubs* St James's; *Style*— Prof C L Cooper, CBE; ✉ 25 Lostock Hall Road, Poynton, Cheshire (tel 01625 871 450); Lancaster University Management School, Lancaster University, Lancaster LA1 4YX (tel 01524 592080, e-mail c.cooper1@lancaster.ac.uk)

COOPER, David John; s of John Alec Cooper, of London, and Norma May, *née* Kennard; *b* 4 July 1951; *Educ* Green Sch, Univ of London (BEd); *Career* analyst Unilever plc 1967–71, chemistry master Barking Abbey 1974–75, business devpt and mktg exec Baxter Inc 1975–79, mktg exec Smith and Nephew Ltd 1979–82, business devpt and mktg exec LIG Int Ltd, dir Pfizer Inc 1984–87, corporate financier Robert Fleming 1987–88, fndr and md DCA (high technology business devpt consultancy) 1974–; memb Maritime Volunteer Service; Freeman City of London 1985, Liveryman Worshipful Co of Marketors 1985; confrerie des chevaliers du sacavin; FIMgt 1984, FInstD 1984, FCInstM 1984, MCInstB 1987, FRSA 1990, MIMC 1994, MSCI 1994; *Clubs* Athenaeum, Savage, Loophole (fndr), City Livery Yacht (Cdre); *Style*— David J Cooper, Esq; ✉ DCA, 52 Queen Anne Street, London W1G 8HL (tel 020 7935 7374, fax 020 7935 8372, e-mail davidcooper@dca-uk.com)

COOPER, Derek Anthony (Tony); s of Donald Cooper (d 1985), and Freda, *née* Sheridan (d 1991); *b* 11 December 1943; *Educ* Whitehaven GS, Univ of Edinburgh (BSc); *m* 23 Sept 1967, June, da of Thomas Iley; 2 da (Yvette b 23 March 1969, Nichola b 11 Feb 1971), 2 s (David b 4 Nov 1973, Edward Lois b 11 July 1989); *Career* forest offr Forestry Cmmn 1967–77; Inst of Professional Civil Servants: negotiations offr 1977–81, asst sec 1981–84, asst gen sec 1984–88, dep gen sec 1988–91; gen sec Engrs and Mangrs Assoc 1991–2001, jt gen sec Prospect 2001–02; non-exec cmmr: Postal Services Cmmn 2000–, Forestry Cmmn 2000–; chm Nuclear Industry Assoc (formerly Br Nuclear Industry Forum) 2002–04, chm Combined Nuclear Pension Plan Trustees Ltd 2006–, non-exec memb Nuclear Decommissioning Authority 2004–; DTI: memb Energy Advsy Panel 1993–2003, non-exec memb Strategy Bd 2002–04, memb Investment Ctee 2002–04; memb: Energy Consultative Ctee EU 1992–95, DETR/TU Sustainable Devpt Ctee 1995–2000, Gen Cncl TUC 1996–2000; chm PPP Consultancy Ltd; dir: Aid Transport Ltd 1993–2000, Way Ahead Training Ltd 1995–2000; *Recreations* sailing, hill walking; *Style*— Tony Cooper, Esq

COOPER, Edward James Oswald; s of Derek Cooper (d 2002), of Eynsford, Kent, and Julia, *née* Vinson; *b* 12 June 1959, London; *Educ* Tonbridge, Univ of Bristol (LLB), Guildford Law Coll; *m* 27 Nov 1992, Atinuke Olubunmi Alake (Bobbie), *née* Akinboro; 3 s (Oliver b 8 Feb 1996, Jonathan b 3 July 1998, Reuben b 24 July 2001); *Career* slr; Simmons & Simmons 1982–85 (joined as trainee), Russell Jones and Walker 1985– (ptnr and head Employment Dept 1988–); tstee and memb Mgmnt Ctee Richmond Gymnastics Assoc, govr Smallwood Primary Sch; jt winner Employment Team of the Year Lawyer Awards 2000, 2002 and 2006 (2nd place 2007); *Publications* Encyclopaedia of Forms and Precedents (Trade Union Section, 2005); *Recreations* jazz saxophone, family, tennis; *Clubs* MCC, Crocodiles Cricket (fndr memb and capt); *Style*— Edward Cooper, Esq; ✉ Russell Jones & Walker, 324 Gray's Inn Road, London WC1X 8DH (tel 020 7339 6435, fax 020 7713 1710, e-mail e.o.cooper@rjw.co.uk)

COOPER, Eileen; *b* 1953; *Educ* Goldsmiths Coll London, Royal Coll of Art; *m* Malcolm Southward; 2 s (b 1984 and 1986); *Career* artist; pt/t tutor Printmaking Dept Royal Coll of Art; artist in residence Dulwich Picture Gallery London 1998–99, AHRB Award for Ceramic Work 1999; RA 2001, RE 2001; *Solo Exhibitions* Air Gallery 1979, House Gallery 1981, Blond Fine Art 1982, 1983 and 1985, Artspace Gallery Aberdeen 1985, Castlefield Gallery Manchester 1986, Artsite Gallery Bath 1987, Benjamin Rhodes Gallery London 1988, 1989 (Works on Paper), 1990, 1992 and 1994, Lifelines (touring England) 1993–94, Sadlers Wells Theatre London 1994, Bohun Gallery Oxon 1995, Graphic Work (touring Darlington and Harrogate 1996, Benjamin Rhodes Gallery London 1997), Graphic Work (Bridport Arts Centre) 1998, Open Secrets 1998, Art First (Cork Street London) 1998, Second Skin (Wolverhampton Museum and touring and Nottingham & Towner Museum Eastbourne) 1999, Dulwich Picture Gallery (work made from collection) 2000, Art First (new paintings, London 2000), Passions: New Work on Paper (Art First NY and Art First London) 2002, Eileen Cooper 50 (new paintings and drawings; celebration of the artist's 50th birthday) 2003; *Group Exhibitions* numerous gp exhbns since 1974 incl: The Essential Myth (Philip Graham Contemporary Art London) 1994, Figuratively Speaking (Atkinson Gallery Somerset) 1995, Cabinet Art (Jason & Rhodes London) 1996, An American Passion (RCA London) 1995, Spirit on the Staircase (100 years of print publishing at RCA and V&A London) 1996–97, Down to Earth (Lamont Gallery London and The Body Politik Wolverhampton 1997), From the Interior, Chinese & British Artists touring show 1997–98, British Figurative Art Part 1 (Flavers East London) 1997, Monotypes (Art Space Gallery London) 1997, RA Summer Show 1998, Figure of Eight (New Arts Gallery Bantam Connecticut) 1999, Hand to Hand (new porceline ceramics, Shipley Art Gallery Gateshead) 1999, Mixing It (new ceramic work with Annie Turner, Midlands Arts Centre Birmingham and touring) 1999, AA First in Print (Art First London) 2001, RA Summer Show 2001, 10x10 (Art First London) 2001, Starting a Collection (Art First London) 2002, RA Summer Show 2002, From Little Acorns 2002; *Public Collections* incl: Open Univ, Imperial Coll London, British Cncl, Kunsthalle Nuremberg (Purchase prize), Arts Cncl of GB, Contemporary Arts Soc, Cleveland Gallery, V&A Museum, Whitworth Art Gallery Manchester, Towner Art Gallery Eastbourne, Unilever plc, TI Group plc, Br Museum Soc, Manchester City Art Galleries, Harvard USA; *Major Commissions* incl: Staircase Project (ICA London) 1982, The Art (tv prog BBC Educn) 1993, Inside Art (C4) 1994, cover and illustrations for Carol Anne Duffy's Meeting Midnight 1999; *Style*— Ms Eileen Cooper; ✉ c/o Art First, 9 Cork Street, London W1X 1PD (tel 020 7734 0386)

COOPER, Granville John; s of Joseph Cooper (d 2000), of Tibshelf, Derbys, and Edna May, *née* Slack (d 1989); *b* 1 May 1940; *Educ* Tupton Hall GS, Univ of N London (BSc); *Career*

microwave engr GEC Applied Electronics Laboratories 1963–67, dep engrg mangr NATO Phase II Satellite Terminal Project 1968–69, project mangr Scot Naval Satellite Communications (SATCOM) project 1971–73 (engrg mangr 1970–71), divnl mangr SATCOM Marconi Space and Defence Systems Ltd 1973–76, tech dir McMichael Ltd 1977–85 (joined 1976), md Vistek Electronics Ltd 1986–96, chm Vistek Group 1996–98, dir Deltatel Ltd; CPhys, CEng, FIEE, MInstP, FREng 1994; *Recreations* work, science, music, opera; *Style*— Granville Cooper, Esq, FREng; ✉ Springfield, 21 Lower Road, Higher Denham, Uxbridge UB9 5EB

COOPER, Dr Griselda Mary; OBE (2006); da of Dr Charles James Constantine Davey (d 2001), of Box, Wilts, and Dr Gwyneth June Davey, *née* Pearson; *b* 8 April 1949; *Educ* Bath HS, Univ of Birmingham (MB ChB); *m* 31 Aug 1973, Dr Brian Thomas Cooper, s of Dr Andrew Matthew Cooper (d 1979); 1 da (Charlotte b 1987); *Career* sr lectr in anaesthesia Univ of Bristol 1981–87, conslt anaesthetist Dunedin Public Hosp NZ 1985–86, sr lectr in anaesthesia Univ of Birmingham 1988–; FRCA (vice-pres 2004–05); *Recreations* walking, skiing, embroidery; *Style*— Dr Griselda Cooper, OBE; ✉ 6 Lord Austin Drive, Grange Park, Marlbrook, Bromsgrove, Worcestershire B60 1RB (tel 0121 445 2727); Birmingham Women's Hospital, Queen Elizabeth Medical Centre, Edgbaston, Birmingham B15 2TG (tel 0121 627 2060)

COOPER, Prof Helen; da of Sir Peter Kent, and Betty, *née* Hood; *b* 6 February 1947; *Educ* New Hall Cambridge (MA, PhD), Univ of Oxford (LittD); *m* 18 July 1970, Dr Michael Cooper; 2 da (Katy b 8 Jan 1973, Anne b 1 May 1976); *Career* tutorial fell in English UC Oxford 1978–2004 (first woman fell since Coll's fndn in 1249, tutor for admissions 1985–89, sr tutor 1997–2000), prof Univ of Oxford 1996–2004 (chair English Faculty 1990–93, chair Undergraduate Studies Ctee 1995–97), prof of Medieval and Renaissance English Univ of Cambridge 2004–, fell Magdalene Coll Cambridge 2004–; distinguished visiting mediaevalist Univ of Connecticut 1991; Br Acad res readership 2000–02; delivered lectures and papers at numerous univs and conferences in UK, Europe, USA, Japan and India; ed Old and Middle English language and literature Medium Aevum 1989–2001; pres New Chaucer Soc 2000–02; Hon DLitt Washington and Lee Univ 2001; FBA 2006; *Publications* Pastoral: Mediaeval into Renaissance (1978), The Structure of the Canterbury Tales (1983, reprinted 1992), Oxford Guides to Chaucer: The Canterbury Tales (1989, 2 edn 1996), The Long Fifteenth Century: Essays for Douglas Gray (co-ed with Sally Mapstone, 1997), Sir Thomas Malory: Le Morte Darthur (ed, 1998), The English Romance in Time (2004); numerous articles on Chaucer, Gower, the Gawain-poet, romance, Wyatt, Spenser, Shakespeare et al; numerous reviews incl articles in TLS and London Review of Books; *Style*— Prof Helen Cooper, FBA; ✉ University of Cambridge, Faculty of English, 9 West Road, Cambridge (tel 01223 335070, e-mail ehc31@cam.ac.uk); Magdalene College, Cambridge CB3 0AG

COOPER, Imogen; CBE (2007); da of Martin Cooper (d 1986), and Mary, *née* Stewart (d 1998); *b* 28 August 1949; *Educ* Paris Conservatoire (Premier Prix); *m* 1982 (m dis 2002), John Batten; *Career* pianist; regular performer at Proms since televised debut 1975, first UK pianist and first woman to appear in South Bank Piano Series 1975, regular performer with all major orchs; orchestral engagements with: Berlin Philharmonic, Vienna Philharmonic, Boston Symphony, New York and Los Angeles Philharmonic Orchs; int tours incl: Austria, Italy, Germany, Australasia, Holland, France, Scandinavia, Spain, USA, Japan; *Recordings* incl: six CDs of Schubert, the piano works of Schubert's last six years, Schumann, Haydn, Mozart and Beethoven with Wolfgang Holzmair, Mozart double and triple piano concertos with Alfred Brendel, Schubert Trios and Arpeggione with Raphaël Oleg and Sonia Wieder-Atherton, Imogen Cooper & Friends (solo, chamber and lieder works), Mozart Concertos with Northern Sinfonia (aria); *Recreations* hill walking, architecture, cooking; *Style*— Imogen Cooper, CBE

COOPER, Janet; *b* 18 May 1959; *Educ* Univ of Leeds (LLB), London Business Sch; *Career* slr; ptnr and head of global employee incentives Linklaters 1991–; dir: Employee Share Ownership Centre 1991, Global Equity Orgn 1999– (vice-chair 2003–); dir ifsProShare Faculty Bd 2005–; course dir ICSA Cert Employee Share Plans; memb: Law Soc 1984, Inst of Business Ethics; *Publications* Tolley's Directors Remuneration (1996); *Recreations* family and friends, opera and theatre, skiing and scuba diving; *Style*— Ms Janet Cooper; ✉ Linklaters, One Silk Street, London EC2Y 8HQ

COOPER, Hon Jason Charles Duff Bede; s and h of 2 Viscount Norwich; *b* 27 October 1959; *Educ* Eton, New Coll Oxford (BA), Oxford Brookes Univ (BA, Dip Arch); *Career* architect, designer, journalist; RIBA; *Recreations* piano, travel, skiing; *Style*— Jason Cooper; ✉ 14 Alexander Street, London W2 5NT (tel 020 7727 3104)

COOPER, Jilly; OBE (2004); da of Brig W B Sallitt, OBE (d 1982), and Mary Elaine, *née* Whincup (d 1997); *b* 21 February 1937; *Educ* Godolphin Sch Salisbury; *m* 7 Oct 1961, Leo Cooper, s of Leonard Cooper (d 1997), of Yorks; 1 s (Matthew Felix b 5 Sept 1968), 1 da (Emily Maud Lavinia b 13 June 1971); *Career* writer; former cub reporter Middlesex Independent Brentford 1955–57, followed by several jobs incl info offr, puppy fat model and switch board wrecker; newspaper columnist: Sunday Times 1969–82, Mail on Sunday 1982–87; winner of Lifetime Achievement Award British Book Awards 1998; *Books* author of 38 books incl: Class (1979), Animals in War (1983), The Common Years (1984), Riders (1985), Rivals (1988), Polo (1991), The Man Who Made Husbands Jealous (1993), Araminta's Wedding (1993), Appassionata (1996), Score! (1999), Pandora (2002), Wicked! (2006); *Recreations* wild flowers, reading, mongrels, merry making, music and rescued greyhounds; *Style*— Mrs Leo Cooper, OBE; ✉ c/o Vivienne Schuster, Curtis Brown, Haymarket House, 28–29 Haymarket, London SW1Y 4ST (tel 020 7396 6600)

COOPER, John; s of Kenneth Cooper, of Manchester, and Irene, *née* Wright; *b* 29 April 1955; *Educ* Manchester Grammar, Royal Coll of Music (ARCM), King's Coll Cambridge (MA); *m* 5 Oct 1983, Jane Mary, da of late Alan Arthur Kingshotte, of Strawberry Hill, Middx; 1 da (Charlotte b 28 Aug 1984), 1 s (Benedict b 26 April 1988); *Career* admitted slr 1979, avocat au barreau de Paris 1992; ptnr Lovell White & King 1985–88 (articled clerk 1977), ptnr Lovells (formerly Lovell White Durrant) 1988–; Freeman Worshipful Co of Slrs 1981; memb Law Soc; *Recreations* golf, horse racing, wine; *Style*— John Cooper, Esq; ✉ Lovells, 50 Holborn Viaduct, London EC1A 2DY (tel 020 7796 2000, fax 020 7296 2001)

COOPER, John Gordon; s of John Gordon Cooper, of Wolverhampton, and Mary, *née* Hallam (d 1992); *b* 15 September 1958; *Educ* Regis Comp Sch, Univ of Newcastle upon Tyne (LLB, Butterworth Prize, Badminton blue), Cncl of Legal Educn; *Career* writer, barrister and broadcaster (named in Bar Nat Directory as one of the most highly regarded and leading barristers in London (top 40), commended as Barrister of the Year Lawyer Awards 1998); called to the Bar Middle Temple 1983, called to the Aust Bar NSW 1989, lawyer Clifford Chance 1989 (defended in Leah Betts Ecstasy trial, employees rep BCCI litigation, Lord Ahmed vs Govt regarding privacy action, rep families in Deepcut Barracks case, Appeal advsr in Jill Dando case, Appeal Advsr in R vs Whitewind (infanticide) case, advised Law Cmmn on reform of the law of murder, Finsbury Park Mosque case), chief counsel to the Statute Law Revision Soc 2002–, sr prosecutor for Attorney-General 2003–; legal advsr to: Lab Pty 1994–, Treasy 1997–2003 (Shadow Treasy 1993–97), Louise Woodward Campaign, Manjit Basuta Campaign 1999, FO 2003–; judicial cmmr Children First Cmmn 2000–02; sec: Lab Media Ctee, Lab Criminal Justice Ctee, Lab Human Rights Ctee; writer: The Cure (Royal Court Theatre), Burning Point (Tricycle Theatre Kilburn), The Cured (Finborough Arms Theatre), The Law Lord (Screen Two film, BBC), The Advocates (3 part drama, Scottish TV), The Bill (contrib, Thames), Cutting Loose (LWT), Too Few to Mention (Channel 4), The Trial of Charles Stuart (Globe Theatre), Like Minds, To the Death (Bush Theatre); contrib: Legal Eagles (BBC Radio WM), Presenter (BBC Radio), The Talking Show (Channel 4), Street Legal (Channel 4), Talkback (Sky TV), The Moral Maze (Radio 4), Kangaroo Court (Endemol), Teens on Trial (Channel 4), Law in Action (BBC Radio 4), presenter Mindfield (BBC), The Trial of Dick Turpin (five); res diarist The Lawyer 1992–2002, various TV appearances as legal expert; assoc prodr Zenith North; memb: Bar Cncl (co-opted) 1981–84 and 2000–, Bar Human Rights Ctee 2002–, Bar Working Pty on Broadcasting in the Courtroom (co-author of paper); spokesperson Bar Cncl: Essex Bar Mess Ctee, Criminal Bar Assoc 2003–; contested (Lab): Surrey NW 1987, Amber Valley 1992; cnclr Watford 1990–94; advsr to Slovakian oppn in Gen Election; chm Nat Exec League Against Cruel Sports 1995– (memb 1992–); memb Civic Theatre Tst Palace Theatre Watford 1991; academic advsr UCL Jurisprudence Review 2007–; fndr creative writing course Poly of Central London (now Univ of Westminster) 1984, ed Criminal Bar Quarterly 1999–, memb Editorial Bd Wildlife Guardian (BBC Magazine of the Year 1998), memb Editorial Bd Catalyst (political think-tank) 1999–, ed Criminal Bar Newsletter 2003–, bi-weekly columnist Justis.com 1999–2004, columnist The Times 1999–, feature writer Sunday Express 2004–; *Publications* Planning and Environmental Law Bulletin (1991), Police and Criminal Evidence Act (2000), Judicial Review (2000), Cruelty - An Analysis of Article 3 (2000), The Courts Bill (2003), Domestic Violence, Crime and Victims (2004), Encyclopedia of Data Protection & Privacy (co-editor, 2004), Blair's Law: 10 Years of Criminal Legislation (2007); *Recreations* photography, working out, football, the English Civil War; *Clubs* Chelsea Arts, Groucho, Home House, Wolverhampton Wanderers FC; *Style*— John Cooper, Esq; ✉ Parsonage Farm, Dairy Way, Abbots Langley, Hertfordshire WD5 0QJ (tel and fax 01923 291264); 25 Bedford Row, London WC1R 4HD (tel 020 7067 1500, e-mail clerks@25bedfordrow.com); c/o ICM Ltd, 4–6 Soho Square, London W1D 3DZ (tel 020 7432 0800)

COOPER, John Kaye; s of Ernest James Cooper, of Swillington, W Yorks, and Doreen Annie, *née* Kaye (d 1990); *b* 20 May 1947; *Educ* Rothwell GS, RSAMD; *m* 1 (m dis); 1 da (Gemma Lys b 1 Oct 1970); m 2, 1979, Charlotte Nerys Anne, da of Rev Canon Stephen Jackson; 2 s (Adam b 27 Oct 1980, Simon b 15 June 1982); *Career* cameraman Scottish Television 1967, floor mangr Thames Television 1968–72, prodn mangr Yorkshire Television 1972–76, drama prodr Tyne Tees Television 1976–77, prodr/dir Entertainment Dept LWT 1977–83, prodr/dir Limehouse Television 1983–84, controller of entertainment TVS 1984–87, independent prodr and md John Kaye Cooper Productions 1988–90, controller of entertainment and comedy LWT 1990–95, md Talent Television 1995–2002, creative dir Talent TV 2002–; prodr Euro '96 Opening Ceremony Wembley Stadium; prodr numerous progs and series incl: Stanley Baxter Specials 1979–81, Stanley Baxter series 1982 (BAFTA Best Light Entertainment Prog 1982), Russ Abbot's Madhouse 1981–84, Save the Children with Michael Crawford 1988, Surgical Spirit (dir) 1988–89, That's Showbusiness 1990, BAFTA Craft Awards 1990, Cluedo 1990, Royal Variety Performance 1991, 1993 and 1995, Time After Time 1994–95, Audience with Alf Garnett 1997, 50th British Academy Film Awards 1998, British Academy TV Awards 1998, Alan Davies - Urban Trauma 1998, Our Vera 1999, The Villa 1999–2003, Making of Witches of Eastwick 2000, Bill Bailey - Bewilderness, TV Scrabble, Test the Nation; exec prodr 1990–95: Gladiators, Barrymore, The Brian Conley Show, Second Thoughts, Br Comedy Awards; memb: RTS, BAFTA; *Recreations* supporting Leeds United; *Style*— John Kaye Cooper, Esq; ✉ website www.talenttv.com

COOPER, Michael John; OBE (1997); s of Stanley Donald Cooper (d 1978), of Norwich, Norfolk, and Evelyn Joyce, *née* Norgate; *b* 5 April 1949; *Educ* Sutton HS, Univ of York (BA, PGCE); *m* 23 Aug 1975, Gillian Mary, *née* Isted; 2 s (David John b 11 June 1981, Simon John b 14 Jan 1983); *Career* VSO Chassa Secdy Sch Zambia 1972, dir of biology Mill Hill Sch London 1974–78 (teacher 1973–74), dep head upper sch Moulsham HS Chelmsford 1978–81, dep headteacher Valley Sch Worksop 1982–85, headteacher Hillcrest Sch Hastings 1985–90, princ Br Sch in the Netherlands 1990–99, headteacher Latymer Sch London 1999–; hon vice-pres Confedn of Br Schs in the European Communities, additional memb HMC; memb Bd of Govrs: Enfield Coll, Middlesex Univ; MIBiol 1971, FRSA 1990; *Recreations* walking, gardening, swimming, reading; *Clubs* East India; *Style*— Michael Cooper, Esq, OBE; ✉ The Latymer School, Haselbury Road, Edmonton, London N9 9TN (tel 020 8807 2470, e-mail cpr@latymer.co.uk)

COOPER, Natasha; *see:* Wright, (Idonea) Daphne

COOPER, Neil Hunter; s of Keith Hunter Cooper (d 1977), and Margaret Anne, *née* Golden (d 2002); *b* 30 June 1947; *m* Marion Louise, *née* Woodward; 1 s (Ewan Charles Hunter), 1 da (Louise Elizabeth Anne); *Career* Government Insolvency Service 1966–72, public practice 1972–97, ptnr Buchler Phillips (now Kroll Inc) 1997–; past pres Assoc Européenne de Practiciens des Procedures Collectives, pres Insol Int; conslt with World Bank, UNCITRAL, ADB, OECD, EBRD and Insol Int on int insolvency law reform; regular speaker at professional and commercial confs on insolvency law and practice; FCCA, FIPA, FSPI, FRSA; *Books* Tolley's European Insolvency Guide, Recognition and Enforcement of Cross-Border Insolvency; *Recreations* classical music, opera, fly fishing, mountaineering, bird watching, photography; *Clubs* Athenaeum; *Style*— Neil Cooper, Esq; ✉ Kroll, 10 Fleet Place, London EC4M 7RB (tel 020 7029 5211, fax 020 7029 5001, e-mail ncooper@kroll.com)

COOPER, Paul; *b* 30 July 1965; *Educ* Archbishop Holgate's GS York, York Coll of Arts and Technol; *Career* photographer; trainee serv engr rising to product mktg mangr Azlan plc (formerly ADT Ltd) 1984–94, fndr Bailey-Cooper Photography 1995; FBIPP, FMPA; *Awards* over 100 awards incl several BIPP Gold awards and UK Fuji Film Wedding & Portrait Awards; Master Photographers Assoc: UK Master Photographer of the Year 1999, UK Digital Photographer of the Year 2000, UK Commercial Photographer of the Year 2002, UK Fashion Photographer of the Year 2002, Awards of Excellence in Digital, Avant Garde Wedding and Under 5s categories, BIPP Peter Grugeon Award for Fellowship 2003, BIPP UK Commercial Photographer of the Year 2003, BIPP Photographer of the Year 2003; *Style*— Paul Cooper, Esq; ✉ Bailey-Cooper Photography, 4 Geldof Road, Huntington, North Yorkshire YO32 9JT (tel 01904 416684, fax 01904 421141, e-mail pc@baileycooper.co.uk)

COOPER, Paul Antony; s of Raymond Dennis Cooper, of Oxford, and Margaret, *née* Gingell; *b* 6 February 1953, Oxford; *Educ* The Oxford Sch, Selwyn Coll Cambridge (MA); *m* 2 Oct 1976, Nicola Francesca, *née* Jarvis; 3 s (Nicholas Guy David b 12 June 1981, Robert Antony Douglas b 1 April 1984, David Paul Edward b 22 Nov 1988); *Career* admitted slr 1977; trainee slr then slr Boodle Hatfield 1975–78, slr Norton Rose 1978–80, ptnr Bevan Ashford 1981–97 (slr 1980–81), ptnr Osborne Clarke 1997–; Corporate Lawyer of the Year Western Daily Press 2004, 2005 and 2006; memb Law Soc 1977; *Recreations* E-type Jaguar, running, wine; ✉ Osborne Clarke, 2 Temple Back East, Temple Quay, Bristol BS1 6HE (tel 0117 917 4252, fax 0117 917 4253, e-mail paul.cooper@osborneclarke.com)

COOPER, Philip Anthony Robert; s of Stanley Ernest Cooper, and Amy May, *née* Coleman; *b* 13 January 1950; *Educ* Felsted, Univ of Leeds (BSc), Univ of Cambridge (MA); *m* 17 July 1976, (Elizabeth) Jane, da of Dr Harold Leslie Keer Whitehouse; 1 s (Oliver Edward Keer b 1986), 2 da (Harriet Amy Jane b 1980, Emily Sarah Rose b 1982); *Career* lectr Sch of Architecture Univ of Cambridge 1974–78, engr Harris and Sutherland (London and Cambridge) 1978–, assoc and currently tech dir Cameron Taylor Bedford Civil and Structural Engineers, prof of structural design (first in UK) Univ of Leeds 1986–91; lectr: Architectural Assoc 1993–, Univ of Cambridge; visiting prof Bath Univ; engr to the

Royal Acad of Arts; memb Cathedrals Fabric Cmmn for Eng; FIStructE, FICE; *Recreations* tennis, music, windsurfing; *Style*— Philip Cooper, Esq; ✉ 2 Pound Hill, Cambridge, Cambridgeshire CB3 0AE (tel 01223 312055); Cameron Taylor Bedford, Michael Young Centre, Purbeck Road, Cambridge CB2 2QL (tel 01223 271820, fax 01223 271821)

COOPER, Philip Richard; s of Roy Cooper, of Weybridge, Surrey, and Sheila Horseman, *née* Royle; *b* 27 May 1966, Birmingham; *Educ* Brooklands Tech Coll; *m* 25 May 1997, Nina, da of John Poyiadgi; *Career* chef; formerly: chef de partie Claridge's, chef de partie Souffle Restaurant, sous chef QE2, chef Le Manoir aux Quat' Saisons, chef Waterside Inn; currently exec chef and chef de cuisine Mirabelle; *Recreations* golf, skiing, tennis, reading; *Style*— Philip Cooper, Esq; ✉ Mirabelle, 56 Curzon Street, London W1J 8PA (tel 020 7499 4636, fax 020 7499 5449)

COOPER, Prof Rachel Faith Davies; da of David Withers (d 1973), of Leicester, and Elizabeth, *née* Parkes (d 1982); *b* 26 November 1953, Derby; *Educ* Staffordshire Poly (BA), Manchester Poly (PhD); *m* 1, 1974 (m dis 1982); *m* 2, 1984, Cary Cooper; 2 da (Laura Ann *b* 1 Nov 1982, Sarah Kate *b* 2 March 1985); *Career* freelance designer and pt/t lectr in design 1976–91, research fell Manchester Poly 1978–82, prof Salford Univ 1995–2005 (research fell 1991–95), prof Lancaster Univ and dir Lancaster Inst for the Contemporary Arts 2006–; memb Cncl AHRC 2005–; strategic advsr EPSRC 2002–05; FRSA; *Publications* The Design Agenda (1995), The Design Experience (2003), The Design and Construction Process (2004); *Recreations* gardening; *Style*— Prof Rachel Cooper

COOPER, Prof Richard Anthony; s of Arthur Charles Cooper, and Joan Mary, *née* Cutter; *Educ* Manchester Grammar, New Coll Oxford (BA, DPhil, Lacrosse half blue); *m* 1973, Clara Maria Florio; 2 s (Edward *b* 1977, Alexander *b* 1981); *Career* lectr in French Lancaster Univ 1971; Univ of Oxford: fell BNC 1977, reader in French 1996, prof of French 1998; memb Académie des Sciences, Belles Lettres et Arts Lyon 1997, memb Institut des Sciences de l'Homme Lyon; Officier dans l'Ordre des Palmes Académiques 1996, Commendatore dell'Ordine al Merito della Repubblica Italiana 2003; *Publications* Rabelais et L'Italie (1991), Litterae in Tempore Belli (1997), The Entry of Henri II into Lyon, September 1548 (1997); *Recreations* sport, wine, gardening; *Clubs* Vincent's (Oxford); *Style*— Prof Richard Cooper; ✉ 26 Polstead Road, Oxford OX2 6TN (tel 01865 510030); Brasenose College, Oxford OX1 4AJ (tel 01865 277864, e-mail richard.cooper@bnc.ox.ac.uk)

COOPER, Richard Devereux Burcombe; s of late Alexander Burcombe Cooper, of Downleaze, Bristol, and late Alma Gwendoline, *née* Harris; *b* 10 April 1943; *Educ* Clifton, The Taft Sch Watertown CT, Trinity Coll Cambridge (MA); *m* 19 July 1975, Janet, da of late Lt-Col Archibald Michael Lyle, OBE, of Dunkeld, Perthshire, and late Hon Mrs Lyle; 3 da (Daisy *b* 17 Sept 1983, Hester *b* 21 Dec 1985, Tilly *b* 18 July 1988); *Career* ptnr Slaughter and May 1975–2004; former chm Int Bar Assoc (Legal Opinions); former memb Editorial Bd: The European Lawyer, Europaische Zeitschrift fur Wirtschftsrecht EuZW; sometime English int real tennis player; Cambridge blue: squash, real tennis; vice-pres PHAB, chm Tennis & Rackets Assoc Amateur Status Ctee; govr Clifton Coll 2001–; tstee Br Sch at Rome 2004–; Freeman Worshipful Co of Goldsmiths 1986–; *Recreations* music, tennis, shooting, riding, travel, Chinese paintings, languages; *Clubs* Boodle's, Pratt's, MCC, Queen's, Hawks' (Cambridge), Jesters', Hong Kong, China; *Style*— Richard Cooper, Esq; ✉ 9 Applegarth Road, London W14 0HY

COOPER, Dr Richard Michael; s of late Harry Cecil Cohen, of London, and Sadie, *née* Speier; *b* 25 November 1940; *Educ* Belmont, Mill Hill Sch, Charing Cross Hosp (Gynaecology Prize, Forensic Med Prize); *m* Dawne Cooper, JP, da of late Alfred Matlow, and Phoebe, *née* Levy; 1 s (Adam *b* 31 July 1968), 2 da (Louise *b* 6 May 1972, Gabrielle *b* 22 Nov 1972); *Career* house appts at Charing Cross Hosp and Mount Vernon Hosp; princ in gen practice: 74 Brooksby's Walk London 1966–70, 71 Amhurst Park London 1970–76; in private practice 17 Harley St London 1966–; med conslt WPP Advertising; med examiner numerous insurance cos, conslt med offr Vardon plc and Pinnacle Insurance Cos; memb Cncl Ind Doctors' Forum (also educn offr); fell: Assurance Med Soc (also sec), Hunterian Soc; FRSM 1969; *Recreations* family, broadcasting, fund raising and other communal activities, writing med articles, foreign travel; *Clubs* Old Millhillians, Knightsbridge Speakers'; *Style*— Dr Richard M Cooper; ✉ 35 West Hill Park, Highgate, London N6 6ND (tel 020 8342 8818); 17 Harley Street, London W1G 9QH (tel 020 7580 3324, 020 7636 3126, fax 020 7436 0661)

COOPER, Robert Francis; CMG (1997), MVO (1975); s of Norman Cooper (d 1966), and Frances Cooper (d 1999); *b* 28 August 1947; *Educ* Delamere Sch Nairobi, Worcester Coll Oxford (BA), Univ of Pennsylvania (MA); *Career* HM Dip Serv 1970, FCO 1970–71, Language Study 1971–73, Br Embassy Tokyo 1973–77, FCO 1979–82, seconded to Bank of England 1982–84, UK rep to EC Brussels 1984–87, head Far Eastern Dept FCO 1987–89, head of Policy Planning Staff 1989–92, British Embassy Bonn 1993–98, dir Asia Pacific FCO 1998–99, on loan to Cabinet Office 1999–2001, govt special rep on Afghanistan 2001–02, DG for external affrs EU Cncl Secretariat 2002–; Order of the Sacred Treasure (4 Class, Japan) 1975; *Publications* The Breaking of Nations (2003); *Recreations* bicycles, ballroom bridge and the Bard; *Style*— Robert Cooper, Esq

COOPER, Robert George; s of Alan Cooper, and Helen Cooper; *b* 8 September 1950; *Educ* Univ of Hull (BA); *Children* 2 da (Zoe *b* 1984, Emily *b* 1987); *Career* prodr of Alan Bleasdale's Scully series for Radio City Liverpool 1974–76, stage mangr Victoria Theatre Stoke-on-Trent 1977, radio drama prodr for BBC (incl radio plays by Anthony Minghella, Jimmy McGovern, Stewart Parker, William Trevor and Neil Jordan), head of drama BBC Northern Ireland 1989–2004, dir Great Meadow Prodns 2004–; prodr: Truly Madly Deeply 1990, Love Lies Bleeding 1993, The Precious Blood 1996, Divorcing Jack 1997, Rebel Heart 2000, As The Beast Sleeps 2002; exec prodr: Ballykissangel 1995–, The Hanging Gale 1995, Dance Lexie Dance 1997, Amongst Women 1998, Eureka Street 1999, Messiah 2001, Sinners 2002, Holy Cross 2003; *Awards* BAFTA nominations for: Truly Madly Deeply 1992, Breed of Heroes 1995, Ballykissangel 1997, Hanging Gale 1996, The Precious Blood 1997, Amongst Women 1999; Prix Italia radio award Hangup 1988, RTS award for Ballykissangel 1997, BANNF award Amongst Women 1999, FIPA awards for: The Hanging Gale 1996, Life After Life 1996; Emmy nomination The Precious Blood 1996, Oscar nomination for Dance Lexie Dance 1998; Monte Carlo TV Festival Awards for: Sinners 2002, Messiah 2002; Shanghai TV Festival Awards for: Sinners 2002, Holy Cross 2004; RTS nomination for Holy Cross 2004; *Recreations* cinema, theatre, sailing; *Style*— Robert Cooper, Esq; ✉ Great Meadow Ltd tel 020 7734 9988

COOPER, Prof Robin Hayes; s of Dennis Joffre Cooper, and Marjorie, *née* Wilding; *b* 23 December 1947; *Educ* Corpus Christi Coll Cambridge (MA), Univ of Massachusetts (PhD); *m* 14 June 1985, Elisabet Britt, da of Gunnar Engdahl; 2 da (Anna Julia *b* 12 May 1986, Maria Emily *b* 19 March 1991); *Career* lectr in English language Univ of Freiburg 1969–71; Univ of Massachusetts: teaching asst in linguistics and TEFL 1971–73, research asst in natural language semantics 1973–75; asst prof Dept of Linguistics Univ of Texas 1975–76, Univ of Massachusetts 1976–77; assoc prof Dept of Linguistics Univ of Wisconsin 1981–87 (asst prof 1977–81); docent Dept of Linguistics and Phonetics Lund Univ 1984–87; Univ of Edinburgh: reader Dept of Artificial Intelligence and Centre for Cognitive Science 1989–92 (lectr 1986–89), princ investigator Human Communication Research Centre 1989–96, reader Centre for Cognitive Science 1992–96; prof of computational linguistics Göteborg Univ 1995–, dir Swedish Nat Grad Sch of Language Technol 2001–; Stanford Univ: Mellon fell in linguistics and philosophy 1980–81, fell Center for Advanced Study in the Behavioural Sciences 1981–82; Guggenheim fell

1986–87; fil dr hc Uppsala 2006; FBA 1993, fell Royal Soc of Arts and Sciences Göteborg 1996; *Books* Quantification and Syntactic Theory (1983); *Recreations* yoga, music; *Style*— Prof Robin Cooper, FBA; ✉ Bigatan 1, S-431 39 Mölndal, Sweden (tel 00 46 31 82 94 38); Department of Linguistics, Göteborg University, Box 200, S-40530, Göteborg, Sweden (tel 00 46 31 786 2536, fax 00 46 31 786 4853, e-mail cooper@ling.gu.se)

COOPER, Dr Rosemary Anne; da of Dr William Francis Cooper (d 1950), and Eileen Beryl, *née* Hall (d 1976); *b* 6 April 1925; *Educ* Westonbirt Sch, Cheltenham Ladies' Coll, Girton Coll Cambridge, KCH Med Sch (MA, MB BChir); *m* 14 Jan 1956, Walter van't Hoff (d 2002), s of Robert van't Hoff (d 1979); 3 s (William *b* 1958, Hugh *b* 1960, Graham *b* 1961); *Career* med registrar: Westminster Hosp 1955–56, London Hosp 1959–62; Fulbright scholar 1956–57, res fell in paediatrics Harvard Univ at Children's Med Centre Boston 1956–57, conslt clinical neurophysiologist North Staffordshire Hosp Centre 1958–89, sr res fell in clinical neurophysiology Keele Univ 1980–89; memb: Jt Ctee on Higher Med Trg 1976–84, Hon Advsy Neurology Panel Dept of Tport 1988–98; pres: The Electroencephalographic Soc (now Br Soc for Clinical Neurophysiology) 1982–84, Assoc of Br Clinical Neurophysiologists 1984–87, Electrophysiological Technologists' Assoc 1987–92; memb: British Fulbright Scholars Assoc (BFSA), Medical Arts Soc; FRCP, FRSM; *Books* Sleep (ed, 1993); also author of papers in scientific jls; *Recreations* music, travel, painting; *Clubs* Trollope Soc; *Style*— Dr Rosemary Cooper; ✉ Granida, 9 East Street, Hambledon, Hampshire PO7 4RX (tel 023 9263 2382, fax 023 9263 2617, e-mail ra.vanthoff@btinternet.com)

COOPER, Rosie; MP; *b* 5 September 1950; *Career* Lord Mayor of Liverpool 1992–93; dir Merseyside Centre for Deaf People; MP (Lab) Lancashire W 2005– (Parly candidate (Lab) Liverpool Broadgreen 1992); *Style*— Ms Rosie Cooper, MP; ✉ House of Commons, London SW1A 0AA

COOPER, Prof Susan Catherine; *Career* prof of experimental physics Univ of Oxford 1995–; *Style*— Prof Susan Cooper; ✉ Department of Physics, University of Oxford, Keble Road, Oxford OX1 3RH (tel 01865 273355, fax 01865 273417, e-mail s.cooper@physics.ox.ac.uk)

COOPER, Prof Thomas Joshua; s of Duahne William Cooper (d 1993), of Yuma, Arizona, USA, and Nancy, *née* Roseman (d 1964); *b* 19 December 1946; *Educ* Humboldt State Univ Calif (BA, Secdy Teaching Credential, Community Coll Teaching Credential), Univ of New Mexico Alberquerque (MA); *m* 1993, Catherine Alice, da of James Patrick Mooney, of Voorschoten, The Netherlands; 2 da (Laura Indigo *b* 4 March 1995, Sophie Alice *b* 1 Nov 1997); *Career* visual artist 1969–; teacher of photography Arcata HS Calif 1969, instr in photography Coll of the Redwoods Community Coll Eureka Calif 1970, teacher Dana Elementary Sch Nipomo Calif 1971, visiting lectr in photography Inst of American Indian Art Santa Fe New Mexico 1973, course dir for photographic studies and sr lectr in photography and history of photography Trent Poly Nottingham 1973–76, visiting asst prof of art Humboldt State Univ 1978–80, visiting artist Univ of Tasmania Sch of Art 1982; conductor of annual workshops: The Photographers Place Bradbourne 1982–95, Salzburg Coll Salzburg Austria 1986–91, Inversnald Photography Workshop Scotland 1992–; founding head Dept of Photography Sch of Fine Art Glasgow Sch of Art 1982–2002, head of fine art Glasgow Sch of Art 2000–02; memb: Photography Advsy Panel Scottish Arts Cncl 1986, Photography Bd CNAA 1986–87, Art Ctee Scottish Arts Cncl 1989–93; work in numerous public collections throughout world and in maj private collections in America, Britain, Europe, Japan and Australia; hon prof Univ of Glasgow 1998; memb Soc for Photographic Educn 1969, fndr memb Scottish Soc for the History of Photography 1983, professional memb SSA 1984; *Major Exhibitions* incl: Images of our Mortality (Robert Self Gallery) 1977, A Quality of Dancing (Humboldt State Univ) 1984, American Photography: 1945–1980 (Barbican Art Gallery) 1985–86, The Hayward Annual (Hayward Gallery) 1985, John Weber Gallery NY 1988, 1990 and 1993, New North (Tate Gallery Liverpool) 1990, The Swelling of the Sea (Art Gallery and Museum Kelvingrove Glasgow) 1990, Kunst Europa (Heidelberg Kunstverein) 1991, Sojourn - Ten Years (Cairn Gallery and Mackintosh Gallery) 1992, Seashore (Galerie Stadpark Krems Austria) 1993, Eight Photographers of the 90's (Laura Carpenter Fine Art, Santa Fe) 1993, Simply Counting Waves - 25 Years of Photographic Picture-Making by Thomas Joshua Cooper (Gulbenkian Fndn Centre for Modern Art Lisbon) 1994, Site Santa Fe - Longing and Belonging - From the Faraway Nearby (Mexico Museum of Fine Art Santa Fe and Site Santa Fe) 1995, Two Artists - Thomas Joshua Cooper and Alfred Graf (Bregenz Austria) 1995, Light from the Darkroom - A Celebration of Scottish Photography (Edinburgh Festival Exhibition, Royal Scottish Acad and Nat Galleries of Scotland) 1995, Archipelago - Thomas Joshua Cooper and Alfred Graf (Kunstlerhaus Palais Thurn und Taxis Bregenz Austria) 1995, Rivers and Ritual - 1975/1995 1996, Where the Rivers Flow (Fruitmarket Gallery Edinburgh) 1997, River Works - America-Scotland 1998, Work from The New Found Land 1999, Moving West - Being West. New Photographs from the Atlantic Coasts (Sean Kelly Gallery NY) 2001, The Great River: Rio Grande River Crossings - From The Source to The Sea 1994–2000 (James Kelly Contemporary Santa Fe) 2001, From the Very Edges of the World (Tate Gallery St Ives) 2001, Settlement (Blains Fine Art London) 2002, Seashore: along Brandan's Path (Mount Stuart Isle of Bute) 2002, Running to Sea - a ten year retrospective of European Sea Pictures (Cesar Manrique Fndn Lanzarote Canary Islands, touring Spain), Some Rivers, Some Trees, Some Rocks, Some Seas (Galleria Il Prisma Cuneo) 2003, Point of No Return (Haunch of Venison) 2004; *Awards* John D Phelan Award in Art & Literature 1970, maj photography bursary Arts Cncl of GB 1976, photography fell Nat Endowment of the Arts USA 1978, artists major bursary Scottish Arts Cncl 1994, Lannan Fndn Major Artist's Award Santa Fe 1999–, Creative Scotland Award Scottish Arts Cncl 2005; *Publications* incl: Dialogue with Photography (1979, 2 edn 1992), Between Dark and Dark (1985), Dreaming the Gokstadt (1988), A Handful of Stones (1993), Simply Counting Waves - 25 Years of Photographic Picture-Making by Thomas Joshua Cooper (1994), Archipelago - Thomas Joshua Cooper and Alfred Graf (1995), Longing and Belonging - From Faraway Nearby - Site Santa Fe (1995), Tokyo Today (1996), Les Printemps de Cahore - Photographie and Arts Visuals (1996), Prospect 92 - Photographie in der GegenwartsKünst (1996), Photography at Princeton - Celebrating 25 Years of Collecting and Teaching the History of Photography (1998), The Promise of Photography - The D G Bank Collection (1998), Sea Change - A Review of the Seascape in Contemporary Photography (1998), An American Century of Photography - From Digital to Dry Plate - The Hallmark Photographic Collection (1999), Katalog, Kvartalstisskrift for Fotografi (1999), Eclipse (2000), Atoms of Delight (2000), Wild (2001), Some Rivers, Some Trees, Some Rocks, Some Seas (2003), Point of No Return (2004); *Recreations* cinema, reading, music (Renaissance, choral, country and western, operatic); athletics, barbecues, walking, wine; *Style*— Prof Thomas Joshua Cooper; ✉ c/o Glasgow School of Art, 167 Renfrew Street, Glasgow G3 6RQ (tel and fax 0141 353 4681)

COOPER, Sir William Daniel Charles; 6 Bt (UK 1863), of Woollahra, New South Wales; s of Sir Charles Eric Daniel Cooper, 5 Bt (d 1984), and his 2 w, Mary Elisabeth, *née* Graham-Clarke; *b* 5 March 1955; *m* 22 Aug 1988, Julia Nicholson; *Heir* bro, George Cooper; *Career* dir: The Gdn Maintenance Serv, GMS Vehicles; *Style*— Sir William D C Cooper, Bt

COOPER, Yvette; MP; da of Tony Cooper, and June, *née* Iley; *b* 20 March 1969; *Educ* Eggars Comp, Alton Sixth Form Coll, Balliol Coll Oxford (BA), Harvard Univ (MA, Kennedy Scholar), LSE (MSc); *m* 10 Jan 1998, Edward Balls, qv; 1 s, 2 da; *Career* economic researcher for late John Smith, MP as shadow Chllr of the Exchequer 1990–92, policy advsr to Bill Clinton presidential elections 1992, policy advsr to Lab Treasy team

1993–94, research assoc Centre for Economic Performance LSE 1994–95, econ columnist and ldr writer The Independent 1995–97, MP (Lab) Pontefract and Castleford 1997–, Parly under-sec of state and min for Public Health 1999–2002, Parly sec Lord Chllr's Dept 2002–03, Parly sec ODPM 2003–05, min for housing and planning ODPM 2005–06, min of state Dept for Communities and Local Govt 2006–07, min of state for Housing 2007–; *Recreations* swimming, watching The West Wing between Disney videos; *Style—* Ms Yvette Cooper, MP; ✉ House of Commons, London SW1A 0AA (tel 020 7219 5080, fax 020 7219 0912, e-mail coopery@parliament.uk, website www.yvettecooper.com)

COORAY, His Hon Judge (Bulathsinhalage) Anura (Siri); s of Vincent Cooray (d 1965), of Kotte, Sri Lanka, and Dolly, *née* Manchanayake (d 1983); *b* 20 January 1936; *Educ* Christian Coll Kotte Sri Lanka, Univ of London; *m* 20 March 1957, Manel Therese, da of George Arthur Perera; 3 da (Carmalika Battolla b 31 Oct 1957, Sita Persaud b 21 July 1959, Samantha b 7 Aug 1966), 2 s (Vincent b 8 Aug 1961, Marlon b 6 July 1973); *Career* RAF Locking 1952–55, Royal Ceylon Air Force 1955–60; called to the Bar Lincoln's Inn 1968, practised Common Law Chambers Middle Temple and later dep head of Chambers 1 Gray's Inn Square, prosecuting counsel SE Circuit 1969–82, dep stipendary magistrate 1978–82, metropolitan stipendiary magistrate (first non-white ever appointed) 1982, asst recorder 1985–88, recorder of the Crown Court 1988–90, memb Ctee of Magistrates 1990–91, circuit judge (SE Circuit) 1991–; *Recreations* wine making, playing with grandchildren; *Style—* His Hon Judge Anura Cooray; ✉ Kingsland, Etul Kotte, Sri Lanka (tel 00 941 869223)

COOTE, Sir Christopher John; 15 Bt (I 1621), of Castle Cuffe, Queen's County, Ireland; s of Rear Adm Sir John Ralph Coote, 14 Bt, CB, CBE, DSC (d 1978), and Noreen Una, *née* Tighe (d 1996); *b* 22 September 1928; *Educ* Winchester, Christ Church Oxford (MA); *m* 23 Aug 1952, Anne Georgiana, yr da of Lt-Col Donald James Handford, RA (d 1980), of Guyers, Corsham, Wilts; 1 s (Nicholas Patrick b 1953), 1 da (Vanessa Jean b 1955); *Heir* s, Nicholas Coote; *Career* late Lt 17/21 Lancers; coffee and tea merchant 1952–; *Style—* Sir Christopher Coote, Bt

COOTE, Prof John Haven; s of Albert Ernest Coote (d 1967), of Enfield, and Gladys Mary Elizabeth, *née* Noble; *b* 5 January 1937; *Educ* Enfield GS, Chelsea Coll, Royal Free Hosp Sch of Med, Univ of London (BSc, PhD), Univ of Birmingham (DSc), Jagiellonian Univ Kraców (Dip Faculty of Med); *m* 28 Dec 1974, Susan Mary, da of Dr William Hawkins Hylton (d 1989), of Clevedon; 1 s (Edward John b 1976), 2 da (Rachel Elizabeth b 1978, Naomi Caroline b 1981); *Career* Univ of Birmingham: lectr 1967, sr lectr 1970, reader 1977, prof of physiology and head of dept 1984–2003, Bowman prof of physiology 1985–2003, head Sch of Basic Med 1988–91, emeritus prof 2003–; hon lectr Royal Free Hosp Sch of Med 1966; visiting prof: Tokyo 1974, Chicago 1988, Shanghai 1989, Heidelberg 1992, in cardiology Glenfield Hosp Univ of Leicester 2003–, in biomedical scis Univ of Warwick 2003–, Univ of Nankai China 2004; chair Ed Bd Experimental Physiology; memb: Ctee Physiological Soc 1976–80, Soc for Experimental Biology 1976–, Ethics Ctee Defence Evaluation and Research Agency 1998–, Cncl British Heart Fndn 1998–, Physiologica Soc 2002–, Defence Science Advy Cncl 2003–; Carl Ludwig Distinguished Lecture Award American Physiological Soc 2003; hon memb Physiological Soc 2004–, civil conslt Applied Physiology RAF; FBiol 1988, CBiol 1988, memb NY Acad of Sciences 1991, FRGS 2004; *Recreations* running, mountaineering (Birmingham Med Res Expeditionary Soc); *Clubs* Univ of London Graduate Mountaineering; *Style—* Prof John Coote; ✉ Division of Neuroscience, The Medical School, University of Birmingham, Birmingham B15 2TJ (tel 0121 414 6916, fax 0121 414 6924)

COPE, Prof David Robert; s of Lawrence William Cope (d 1990), and Ethel Anne, *née* Harris (d 1980); *Educ* KCS Wimbledon, Univ of Cambridge (BA, MA), LSE (MSc); *m* 25 Aug 1992, Reiko, da of Junji Takashina (d 1989), of Higashi Fushimi, Japan; *Career* res offr UCL 1968–70, lectr Univ of Nottingham 1970–81, environmental team ldr Int Energy Agency 1981–86, exec dir UK Centre for Econ and Environmental Devpt 1986–97, prof of energy economics Doshisha Univ Kyoto Japan 1997–98, dir Parly Office of Science and Technology Houses of Parliament 1998–; memb: Depts of Environment and Trade and Indust Environmental Advsy Gp 1988–93, Caltex Green Fund research fell Univ of Hong Kong 1990, Cabinet Office Advsy Cncl on Sci and Technol Environment Ctee 1990–92, Dept of Environment Environmental Statistics Advsy Ctee and Academic Economists' Panel 1994–97, Cncl Nat Soc for Clean Air and Environmental Protection 1990–97, Packaging Standards Cncl 1994–96; external examiner Centre for Urban Planning and Environmental Mgmnt Univ of Hong Kong 1997–; chm Europe-Japan Experts Assoc 2001–07; tstee GB Sasakawa Fndn 2006–; memb Cncl Canada-UK Colloquium 2006–; DPhil (hc) Univ of N London; FSS 1979, FRGS 1997; *Books* Energy Policy and Land-Use Planning - an International Perspective (with P Hills and P James, 1984); *Recreations* hill walking, woodworking, classical music; *Style—* Prof David R Cope; ✉ Parliamentary Office of Science and Technology, 7 Millbank, London SW1P 3JA (tel 020 7219 2848, fax 020 7219 2849, e-mail coped@parliament.uk)

COPE, Jerry; s of Michael Ewart Cope, and Maureen Ann, *née* Casey; *b* 30 November 1951; *Educ* St Paul's, Jesus Coll Cambridge (MA), Univ of Warwick (MSc, MBA); *m* 19 Oct 1985, Dianne Elizabeth Gilmour; 1 s (Jonathan b 21 Nov 1989); *Career* Post Office: joined 1973, early roles in personnel and line mgmnt, gen mangr London 1988, dir gp strategy 1993, full time memb Bd 1996, gp md strategy and int 1998; md UK Royal Mail 2002–03; dir Camelot 2000–03, chair t-three Ltd (formerly HRS Ltd) 2004–; chair Prison Service Pay Review Body 2005–; chair Bd of Govrs Kingston Univ 2002–07, non-exec dir GCDA 2007–; *Recreations* supporting Fulham FC, bridge, arts, cooking, avoiding the gardening; *Clubs* Hurlingham; *Style—* Jerry Cope, Esq; ✉ 24 Auckland Road, London SE19 2DJ

COPE, Jonathan; CBE (2003); *b* 1963; *Educ* White Lodge Royal Ballet Sch; *m* Maria Almeida; 1 da (Anoushka), 1 s (Joseph); *Career* ballet dancer; princ Royal Ballet 1987–90 (joined 1982), business career 1990–92, returned to Royal Ballet 1992; leading roles (with Royal Ballet) incl: Prince in Swan Lake, The Sleeping Beauty and The Nutcracker, Solor in La Bayadère, Albrecht in Giselle, Romeo and Juliet, Le Baiser de la Fée, The Prince of the Pagodas, Cinderella, Palemon in Ondine, Serenade, Agon, Apollo, Opus 19/The Dreamer, The Sons of Horus, Young Apollo, Galanteries, The Planets, Still Life at the Penguin Café, The Spirit of Fugue, Concerto, Gloria, Requiem, Triad, A Broken Set of Rules, Pursuit, Piano, Grand Pas Classique, Monotones, Crown Prince Rudolph in Mayerling, Woyzeck in Different Drummer, Second Friend and Foreman in The Judas Tree, Anastasia, Beliaev in A Month in the Country, The Poet in Illuminations, Birthday Offering, La Valise, Air, Monotones II, Thaïs, Armand in Marguerite and Armand, Fox in Renard, Fearful Symmetries, ...now languorous, now wild..., Symphony in C (partnering Sylvie Guillem), Duo Concertant, Jean de Brienne in Raymonda Act III, Remanso, Seranade, The Firebird, Andantino Boy in Les Biches, The Lover in Lilac Garden, If This Is Still A Problem, Dances with Death, Pavane Pour une Infante Défunte, Sawdust and Tinsel, Words Apart, Tidelines, Cry Baby Kreisler, 3:4, The Crucible, Dance Variations, Tryst, There Where She Loves, Des Grieux in Manon, Beyond Bach, Por Vos Muero, Escamillo in Carmen; various TV perfomances with Royal Ballet; South Bank Show Dance Award 2003; *Style—* Jonathan Cope, Esq, CBE; ✉ The Royal Ballet, Royal Opera House, Covent Garden, London WC2E 9DD (tel 020 7240 1200, fax 020 7212 9121)

COPE, Wendy Mary; da of Fred Stanley Cope (d 1971), of Kent, and Alice Mary, *née* Hand (d 2004); *b* 21 July 1945; *Educ* Farringtons Sch Chislehurst, St Hilda's Coll Oxford (MA), Westminster Coll Oxford (DipEd); *Career* primary sch teacher: London Borough of Newham 1967–69, ILEA 1969–86 (seconded to Contact Newspaper as Arts and Reviews ed 1982–84, pt/t teacher 1984–86); freelance writer 1986–; Cholmondeley Award for Poetry 1987, Michael Braude Award American Acad of Arts and Letters 1995; Hon DLitt: King Alfred's Coll Winchester/Univ of Southampton 1999, Oxford Brookes Univ 2003; FRSL; *Books* Making Cocoa for Kingsley Amis (1986), Twiddling Your Thumbs (1988), The River Girl (1991), Is That The New Moon? Poems by Women Poets (ed, 1988), Serious Concerns (1992), The Orchard Book of Funny Poems (ed, 1993), The Funny Side (ed, 1998), The Faber Book of Bedtime Stories (ed, 2000), If I Don't Know (2001), Heaven on Earth: Happy Poems (ed, 2001), George Herbert: Verse and Prose (ed, 2002), Selected Poems (2008); *Recreations* playing the piano; *Style—* Ms Wendy Cope, FRSL; ✉ c/o Faber & Faber, 3 Queen Square, London WC1N 3AU (tel 020 7465 0045)

C

COPE OF BERKELEY, Baron (Life Peer UK 1997), of Berkeley in the County of Gloucestershire; Sir John Ambrose Cope; kt (1991), PC (1988); s of late George Arnold Cope, MC, FRIBA; *b* 13 May 1937; *Educ* Oakham; *m* 1969, Djemila, da of late Col P V Lovell Payne, and late Mrs Tanetta Blackden, of the American Colony of Jerusalem; 2 da; *Career* chartered accountant; Parly candidate (Cons) Woolwich E 1970; MP (Cons): S Glos 1974–83, Northavon 1983–97; asst Govt whip 1979–81, a Lord Cmmr of the Treasury 1981–83, dep chief whip and treas HM's Household 1983–87, min of state Dept of Employment and minister for Small Firms 1987–89, min of state Northern Ireland 1989–90, dep chm Cons Pty 1990–92, Paymaster Gen 1992–94; oppn spokesman on NI House of Lords 1997–98, oppn spokesman on Home Affrs House of Lords 1998–2001, oppn chief whip House of Lords 2001–07; FCA; *Clubs* Beefsteak, Pratt's, Carlton (chm), Tudor House Chipping Sodbury; *Style—* The Rt Hon Lord Cope of Berkeley, PC; ✉ House of Lords, London SW1A 0PW (e-mail copej@parliament.uk)

COPELAND, Prof John Richard Malcolm; s of Lorenzo Copeland (d 1982), and Kathleen Mary, *née* Hopkinson (d 1970); *b* 14 October 1932; *Educ* Newcastle under Lyme HS, Emmanuel Coll Cambridge (MA, MD, BChir), Univ of London (academic DPM); *m* 1963, Mary Bridget, da of Thomas O'Dwyer; 2 da (Caroline Mary Teresa b 1964, Veronica Anne Louise b 1965), 1 s (Andrew Thomas John b 1967); *Career* West End Hosp for Neurology and Neurosurgery London 1962–64, Maudsley Hosp 1964–76, lectr and sr lectr in psychiatry Inst of Psychiatry London 1969–76 (UK dir US/UK Diagnostic Project 1970–77), hon lectr Guy's Hosp 1970–76; Univ of Liverpool: prof and head Dept of Psychiatry 1976–97, founding dir Inst of Human Ageing 1981–97, hon conslt psychiatrist North Mersey Community Tst 1976–97; head: Collaborating Centre on Ageing, World Fedn for Mental Health, Inst of Human Ageing 1998–; Sandoz lectr Basle 1990, Maudsley Bequest lectr RCPsych, Hakone lectr Japan 1998; advsr WHO, advsr and visiting prof Univ of Garounis (Libya) 1980–90; chm Jt Ctee on Higher Psychiatric Trg in the Br Isles 1988–91, chair Mgmnt Ctee European Concerted Action on Depression in Older Age Eurodep 1993–; int chair World Mental Health Day 2003–05; memb: Advsy Bd on the Conferment of Titles Univ of London 1991–97, Sci Ctee Int Inst of Psychosocial and Social Economic Research Univ of Maastricht 1990–, Research Ctee Alzheimers Disease Soc UK 1990–99, chm Academic Old Age Psychiatry Assoc 1998–2006, Steering Ctee MRC Cognitive Function and Ageing Study, Mgmnt Ctee MRC AGENET Foresight Initiative 1996–2001; Gold medal Yonsei Univ Coll of Med (Korea); Lifetime Achievement Award Indian Neuroscience Gp 2003; memb: World Fedn for Mental Health (pres 2007, treas 1999–2003, chair Disaster Response Initiative 2005–), European Psychogeriatric Assoc; FRCPsych 1977, FRCP 1980, FRSM (memb Cncl Section on Geriatrics and Gerantology 1992–97); *Books* Psychiatric Diagnosis in New York and London (jtly, 1972), The Mind and Mood of Ageing: The Mental Health Problems of the Community Elderly in New York and London (jtly, 1983), Alzheimer's Disease: Potential Therapeutic Strategies (ed, 1992), Principles and Practice of Geriatric Psychiatry (sr ed, 2 edn 2002); *Recreations* porcelain, skiing, Victorian house maintenance; *Clubs* Oxford and Cambridge, Nat Ski Club of GB; *Style—* Emeritus Prof John Copeland; ✉ Liverpool University Department of Psychiatry, Section of Old Age Psychiatry, St Catherine's Hospital, Birkenhead, Wirral CH42 0LQ (tel 0151 604 7333, fax 0151 653 3441, e-mail jrmcop@btinternet.com)

COPELAND, Stephen Andrew; s of Derek Copeland, of Nantwich, Cheshire, and Peggy, *née* Strangward; *b* 7 May 1946; *Educ* Nantwich GS, St Bartholomew's Hosp Med Sch London (MB BS); *m* 3 April 1972, Jennifer Ann, da of Dr John Almeyda, KSG (d 1986); 1 da (Sara Clare b 26 Feb 1973), 1 s (Matthew Scott b 17 March 1976); *Career* sr registrar Bart's 1975–79, clinical lectr Royal Nat Orthopaedic Hosp 1978, conslt orthopaedic surgn Royal Berkshire Hosp Reading 1979–2002, dir Reading Shoulder Unit 2002–; pres Euro Shoulder and Elbow Surgery Soc, chm Int Bd of Shoulder and Elbow Surgeons; former: pres Br Shoulder and Elbow Soc, memb Cncl Orthopaedic Section RSM; memb Editorial Bd JBJS; developed own design of shoulder replacement; author of papers on shoulder surgery; hon memb American Shoulder Surgery Soc, ABC travelling fell; *Books* Surgical Reconstruction in Rheumatoid Disease (1993), Operative Shoulder Surgery (1995), Shoulder Surgery (1996), Stiffness in the Upper Limb (1997); *Recreations* cars, garden; *Style—* Stephen Copeland, Esq; ✉ Woodlands, Woodlands Road, Harpsden, Henley-on-Thames, Oxfordshire RG9 4AA (tel 0118 940 2114); Capio Hospital, Wensley Road, Coley Park, Reading, Berkshire (tel 0118 902 8063, e-mail stephen.copeland@btinternet.com)

COPEMAN, Dr Peter William Monckton; s of William Sydney Charles Copeman, CBE, TD, JP, MA, MD, FRCP (d 1970), and Helen, *née* Bourne (d 1980); head of the Copeman family, formerly of Sparham, Norfolk (*see* Burke's Landed Gentry, 18 edn, Vol III, 1972); *b* 9 April 1932; *Educ* Eton, CCC Cambridge (MA, MD, Copeman medal 1973), St Thomas' Hosp; *m* 19 May 1973, Lindsey Bridget, da of late David Vaughan Brims, of Heddon Hall, Northumberland; 3 da (Mary (Mrs Rose) b 1975, Louisa b 1977, Caroline b 1980), 1 s (Andrew b 1980); *Career* emeritus conslt physician for diseases of the skin i/c Dept of Dermatology Westminster and Westminster Children's Hosp; research fell Mayo Clinic USA 1968; Wellcome research fell 1969–73; clinician and researcher; hon conslt dermatologist St Luke's Hosp for the Clergy London; Willan librarian RCP; hon sr lectr Westminster Med Sch; former memb Gen and Exec Ctees The Game Conservancy (co-fndr Research Planning Ctee 1971), tstee Arthritis Research Campaign 1970–2004 (vice-pres 2004), The Soc of the Faith; co-patron (with A R C Copeman) Living of St James the Less Hadleigh Essex; co-patron and tstee St Mary's Bourne St London 1969– (churchwarden 1970–95); Liveryman Worshipful Soc of Apothecaries, Freeman City of London; fell or memb: Br Assoc of Dermatologists, Med Soc of London, Hunterian Soc, Osler Club, RSM, European Soc of Clinical Investigation, Soc for Investigative Dermatology Inc, American Fedn for Clinical Research; FRCP 1975; OStJ (memb Hosp Ctee 1972–99); *Publications* On Cutaneous Diseases: Robert Willan (book and CD-Rom, 1998); author of textbook chapters, and 150 papers in int jls on original research in gen med, dermatology and history of med; *Recreations* field sports, improving the landscape (Laurent Perrier Conservation Award finalist), enjoying the picturesque; *Clubs* Athenaeum (past chm Wine Ctee), Old Etonian Rifle; *Style—* Dr Peter Copeman; ✉ 20 Spencer Park, London SW18 2SZ (tel 020 8874 7549); Consulting Rooms, 82 Sloane Street, London SW1X 9PA (tel 020 7245 9333, fax 020 7245 9232); Abshiel Farm, Morpeth, Northumberland NE65 8QN (tel 01670 772268)

COPISAROW, Sir Alcon Charles; kt (1988); o s of late Dr Maurice Copisarow, of Manchester, and Eda Copisarow; *b* 25 June 1920; *Educ* Univ of Manchester, Imperial Coll London, Sorbonne (DUniv); *m* 1953, Diana Elissa, yr da of Maj Ellis James Castello, MC, TD (d 1983); 2 s, 2 da; *Career* serv WWII Lt RN; HM cnsllr (scientific) Br Embassy Paris 1954–60, dir Dept of Scientific and Industrial Res 1960–62, chief tech offr NEDC 1962–64, chief scientific offr Miny of Technol 1964–66, sr ptnr McKinsey and Co Inc 1966–76, former dir Br Leyland; memb: Br Nat Oil Corp, Touche Remnant Holdings, Press Cncl, Cncl Lloyd's; special advsr Ernst & Young; chm: Trinity Coll of Music London, Youth Business Initiative, ARINSO Int; first chm The Prince's Youth Business Tst, chm of tstees The Eden Project, dep chm Lloyd's Tercentenary Fndn (former chm), dep chm of Govrs ESU; dir Windsor Festival; tstee Duke of Edinburgh's Award, govr Benenden Sch; memb Admin Cncl Royal Jubilee Tsts; patron Conseil National des Ingénieurs et des Scientifiques de France; archives by-fell Churchill Coll Cambridge; Hon Freeman City of London, Liveryman Worshipful Co of Armourers and Brasiers; Hon FTCL; *Clubs* Athenaeum (sr tstee, past chm), Beefsteak; *Style*— Sir Alcon Copisarow; ✉ 7 Southwell Gardens, London SW7 4SB

COPLAND, Dr Geoffrey Malcolm; CBE (2007); s of Cyril Charles Copland (d 1984), and Jessie, *née* Ogden; *b* 28 June 1942; *Educ* Fitzmaurice GS Bradford-on-Avon, Merton Coll Oxford (open postmastership, Harmsworth sr scholar, MA, DPhil); *m* 1, 1967, Janet Mary Todd; 1 da (Heidi Louise b 1970), 1 s (Alistair Hugh b 1973); m 2, 1985, Dorothy Joy Harrison; *Career* postdoctoral research Yale Univ 1967–69; Univ of London: postdoctoral research Queen Mary Coll 1969–71, lectr in physics Queen Elizabeth Coll 1971–80, dean of studies Goldsmiths Coll 1981–87; Univ of Westminster (formerly Poly of Central London): dep rector 1987–95, rector and vice-chllr 1995–2007; govr Harrow Coll 1995–2003; chm Thomas Wall Tst; memb cncl Edexcel Fndn 1998–2003, tstee and memb Cncl CIHE (Cncl for Industry and Higher Educn) 1999–2007, chm Univs and Colleges Employers Assoc (UCEA) 2002–06; UUK (formerly CVCP): memb Cncl 1998–2007, vice-pres 2003–07, chm England and NI Cncl 2003–07; govr Int Student House 2002–, pres Assoc Sandwich Educn of Trg (ASET) 2006–; FInstP 2003 (MInstP 1974), FRSA 1990, FGCL 2000, Hon FTCL 2000; *Publications* author of research papers and review articles in various academic jls; *Recreations* walking, gardening, cricket; *Clubs* Oxford and Cambridge; *Style*— Dr Geoffrey Copland, CBE; ✉ 24 The Broadway, Wheathampstead, St Albans, Hertfordshire AL4 8LN (tel and fax 01438 833663, e-mail coplang494@aol.com)

COPLAND, (William) Michael Ainslie; s of William Oranmore Copland (d 1980), of Tarporley, Cheshire, and Ethel Ainslie, *née* Bond; *b* 17 April 1947; *Educ* Sedbergh, St Catherine's Coll Oxford (MA), DMS; *m* 9 May 1970, Elizabeth Proctor, da of Edgar Anthony Francis; 1 s (Christopher Ainslie b 31 Jan 1974), 1 da (Sarah Elizabeth b 19 July 1975); *Career* editorial asst FMT Editorial & Writing Services Ltd 1970–73, PR mangr Inst of Mktg 1973–75, gp communications exec Giltspur Ltd 1975–77, dir of advtg and PR Burroughs Machines Ltd 1979–83 (PR mangr 1977–79), media rels mangr STC plc 1983–86, md Brodeur A Plus (formerly A Plus Group Ltd PR) 1992–98 (dir 1986–), md Brodeur Worldwide EMEA 1998–; memb Bd of Mgmnt PRCA; MCIM 1991; *Recreations* tennis, walking, Amnesty International; *Style*— Michael Copland, Esq; ✉ Brodeur A Plus, New Tithe Court, 23 Datchet Road, Slough, Berkshire SL3 7PT (tel 01753 790700, fax 01753 790701)

COPLAND-GRIFFITHS, Dr Michael Charles; s of Lt Cdr (Frederick) Charles Brandling Copland-Griffiths, MBE, of Bramley Cottage, Trowle House, Wingfield, Trowbridge, Wilts, and Mary Esmah Elizabeth, *née* Fry; *b* 7 November 1946; *Educ* Bradfield Coll, Anglo-Euro Coll of Chiropractic (Dr of Chiropractic); *m* 1, 28 Aug 1976 (m dis 1980), (Lorna) Penelope, da of John Napthine, of Spondon, Derbys; m 2, 6 Dec 1980 (m dis 2005), Noelle Mary (Penny), da of Herbert Bexon Spencer (d 1989), of Horton, Dorset; m 3, 18 Nov 2006, Larysa, da of Vasyl Senyk, of Tryduby, Ukraine; *Career* chiropractor; memb Faculty Anglo-Euro Coll of Chiropractic 1977–81 (memb Cncl 1978–80); Br Chiropractic Assoc: memb Cncl 1979–91 and 1993–97, asst sec 1979–85, pres 1985–87, vice-pres 1993–94, Br rep Euro Chiropractors' Union 1986–87, memb Fin and Gen Purposes Ctee 1986–88 and 1993–94 (chm 1986–87), chm Parly Ctee 1987–90 and 1994–97 (memb 1987–97), President's Award for outstanding serv to the profession 1991, Western Provident Assoc Cup for servs to the chiropractic profession 1996; dir Chiropractic Registration Steering Group Ltd 1992–97 (chm 1994–97, memb Safe and Competent Practice Working Pty 1994–95); memb: Advsy Ctee and Educn Ctee Inst for Complementary Med 1982–85, Bd of Advsrs Jl of Alternative and Complementary Med 1986–99; vice-pres Anglo Euro Coll of Chiropractic Alumni Assoc 1982–91; Cncl for Complementary and Alternative Med: memb Ctee 1984–89, vice-chm 1986–89; Gen Chiropractic Cncl: chm Cncl 2002–06 (memb 1997–2007), chm Code of Practice Working Gp 1997–99, memb Standards of Proficiency Working Gp 1997–99, memb Professional Conduct Ctee 1999–2002 and 2006–07, memb Chiropractic Clinical Effectiveness Ctee 2000–02, memb Common Codes Virtual Gp 2000–02, memb Education Ctee 2002–06, memb Resource Mgmnt Ctee 2002–06, memb Communications Strategy Working Gp 2002–04, memb Health Ctee 2006–07; memb Cncl for the Regulation of Healthcare Professionals 2003–06; fell Coll of Chiropractors 1999, fell Br Chiropractic Assoc 2005; *Books* Dynamic Chiropractic Today - The Complete and Authoritative Guide (1991); *Recreations* archaeology, post-medieval country pottery, history, natural history, British heritage, organic gardening, contemporary ceramics; *Style*— Dr Michael Copland-Griffiths; ✉ Trowle House, Wingfield, Trowbridge, Wiltshire BA14 9LE (tel 01225 752199); Healthcare 2000 Clinics of Chiropractic and Complementary Medicine, Trowle House, Wingfield, Trowbridge, Wiltshire BA14 9LE (tel 01225 752199, fax 01225 769842, e-mail mccg@healthcare2k.co.uk)

COPLEY, Paul MacKriell; s of Harold Copley (d 1971), of Denby Dale, W Yorks, and Rene, *née* Hudson (d 1994); *b* 25 November 1944; *Educ* Penistone GS, Northern Counties Coll of Educn (Assoc Drama Bd Teachers' Cert); *m* 7 July 1972, (Primula) Natasha Mary Menzies, da of Lt-Col John Menzies Pyne (d 1965); *Career* actor and writer; *Theatre* incl: For King and Country 1976 (Olivier Award for Actor of the Year in a New Play, plays and Players Award for Most Promising Actor), Sisters 1978, Whose Life is it Anyway? 1979, Rita Sue And Bob Too 1982, Other Worlds 1983, Fool in King Lear 1987 (with Anthony Quayle as Lear), Twelfth Night (tour of Iraq, Pakistan, Ethiopia, Sudan and Zimbabwe) 1987–88, Prin 1989, The Awakening 1990, I Thought I Heard a Rustling 1991, The Mortal Ash 1994, The Servant (Martini TMA Regional Theatre Award for Best Actor in a Supporting Role) 1995, With Every Beat 1995, When we are Married 1996, Celaine 1999, The Mysteries (RNT) 2000, The Contractor 2001, Sing Yer Heart Out for the Lads (RNT) 2002, Got To Be Happy (Bush Theatre) 2003, Billy Liar (tour) 2004, Breathing Corpses (Royal Court) 2005, Ghosts (Gate Theatre London) 2007; *Television* incl: Days of Hope 1974, Chester Mystery Plays 1976, Treasure Island 1977, Travellers 1978, Cries from Watchtower 1979, Death of a Princess 1980, A Room for the Winter 1981, The Gathering Seed 1983, The Bird Fancier 1984, Dangerous Journey 1985, Oedipus at Colonus 1986, Gruey 1987, Young Charlie Chaplin 1988, Testimony of a Child 1989, Landmarks - Christopher Columbus 1990, Collision Course 1991, Stay Lucky 1991, Heartbeat 1992, Rides II 1992, Harry 1993, Cracker (series 1, 2, 3) 1993–95, A Pinch of Snuff 1993, Roughnecks 1994, Peak Practice (series 3) 1994, Sloggers 1995, This Life 1996, The Lakes 1997, Hornblower 1998–99, The Lakes II 1998, Queer as Folk 1999, Silent Witness 1999, In Deep 2001, Hornblower II 2001, Clocking Off II 2001, Nice Guy Eddie 2002, Dalziel & Pascoe 2002, Horn Blower III 2003, Burn It 2003, The Key 2003, How Clean is your House? 2003–05 (narrator), Born and Bred 2004, Inspector Lynley Mysteries 2004, New Tricks 2004, Messiah III 2004, Best Friends 2004, Dead Man Weds 2005, A Most Mysterious Murder 2005, Waking the Dead 2005, Life on Mars 2006, The Street 2006, Shadow in the North 2007; *Films* incl: Alfie Darling 1974, A Bridge Too Far 1976, Zulu Dawn 1979, Doll's Eye 1982, Ends and Means 1984, War and Remembrance 1987, The Pile Rats 1988, How's Business 1991, The Remains of the Day 1993, Jude 1996, Driven 1998, Blow Dry 2000; *Radio* incl: The Marshalling Yard 1986, The Pilgrim's Progess 1988, Jesus 1990, The Fight For Barbara 1991, Tolkien's Smith of Wooton Major 1992, Vlad the Impaler 1992, That Summer 1993, Sons and Lovers 1994, The Snow Queen 1995, King St Junior 2003 (12th Series), Markurell 1998, Ironhand 1999, Challenged 2000, Bad Weather 2000, Ernest's Tower 2001, Heart/Attack 2002, Saturday Night and Sunday Morning 2003, Serjeant Musgrave's Dance 2003, Selby - Death of a Coalfield 2004, Selby - Life After the Pits 2005; audio book: Adam Bede (Penguin), Sons and Lovers (Penguin); *Writing* incl: Hitch (1976), Pillion (1977), Viaduct (1979), Tapster (1981), Fire Eaters (1984), Calling (1986), On Mayday (1987), Shakespeare in Africa (1990), Sally's Tree (1992), Tipperary Smith (1993), King St Junior (1998), Words Alive! (1998), Odysseus and the Cyclops and Pardoner's Tale for Heinemann Educ Literacy Worlds - Plays (1999), Loki the Mischief Maker (2000), Jennifer Jenks (2000); *Recreations* swimming, motorcycling, travel, photography; *Style*— Paul Copley, Esq; ✉ c/o Amanda Howard Assoicates, 21 Berwick Street, London W1F 0PZ (tel 020 7287 9277, fax 020 7287 7785, e-mail mail@amandahowardassociates.co.uk); c/o Casarotto Ramsay Ltd, National House, 60–66 Wardour Street, London W1V 3HP (tel 020 7287 4450, fax 020 7287 9128)

COPLEY, His Hon Judge Peter Edward; s of Edward Thomas Copley (d 1975), of London, and Florence Hilda Copley (d 1971); *b* 15 February 1943; *Educ* Pinner County GS, Coll of Law; *m* 2, 1986, Janice Patricia, da of Edward George Webster; 1 da (Caroline b 12 September 1989); 2 c from previous m; 1 s (Lance b 22 August 1973), 1 da (Jane b 6 December 1975); *Career* articled clerk 1961–66, admitted slr 1966, recorder of the Crown Court 1993–95 (asst recorder 1989–93), circuit judge (SE Circuit) 1995–; *Recreations* sailing; *Style*— His Hon Judge Copley; ✉ South Eastern Circuit Office, 2nd Floor, Rose Court, 2 Southwark Bridge, London SE1 9HS

COPLEY, Robert Anthony; s of Anthony Copley, DL (d 2000), and Bridget Griselda Kemble, *née* Emmott; *b* 29 January 1960; *Educ* Sherborne; *m* 25 Oct 1986, Diana, da of Charles Talbot Rhys Wingfield, DL; 1 s (Jack Anthony Talbot b 6 Oct 1989), 1 da (Alice Florence Hastings b 2 Feb 1992); *Career* Christie's: head Furniture Dept 1995, dep chm 2000–, int head Furniture Dept 2007–; *Clubs* Brooks's; *Style*— Robert Copley, Esq; ✉ Christie's, 8 King Street, London SW1Y 6QT (tel 020 7389 2353, fax 020 7389 2225, e-mail rcopley@christies.com)

COPLIN, Prof John Frederick; CBE (1996); *b* 29 October 1934; *Educ* Bablake Sch Coventry, Imperial Coll London (BSc); *m* 1957, Jean Fowler; 3 s (Stephen b 1965, Richard b 1966, David b 1970); *Career* Rolls-Royce: joined as grad apprentice Derby 1956, grad of the year 1958, chief designer RB211 1968–77, asst engrg dir Aero-Div 1977, dir of technol 1978, dir of design 1983, dir of new products engrg Rolls-Royce plc 1987, md Rolls-Royce Business Ventures Ltd 1988–91; UK advsr to Indonesian min of state for Research and Technol Jakarta 1991–99, chm and chief exec Hiflux Ltd 2000–; Fellowship of Engrg: memb Cncl 1981–84, memb F & GP Ctee 1985–88; chm Aerospace Technol Bd MOD 1984–85 (memb 1980–83); memb: Advsy Cncl for Applied R&D 1983–86, Def Scientific Advsy Cncl MOD 1984–85; assoc fell Univ of Warwick, visiting prof of principles of engrg design Univ of Oxford 1989–91, visiting prof Imperial Coll London 1998–; Akroyd Stuart Award 1966 (with G L Wilde) and 1985, James Clayton Prize (with Frank Turner); FREng 1980, FCGI, FRAeS, FIMechE, FRSA; *Publications* author of numerous tech papers and articles worldwide; *Style*— Prof John Coplin, CBE, FREng; ✉ Cramond, Eaton Bank, Duffield, Belper, Derbyshire DE56 4BH (tel 01332 840532, fax 01332 843160, e-mail jcoplin@dsl.pipex.com)

COPPEL, Laurence Adrian; DL; s of Henry Coppel (d 1979), and Anne Coppel (d 1964); *b* 15 May 1939; *Educ* Belfast Royal Acad, Queen's Univ Belfast (BSc); *m* 28 Oct 1964, Geraldine Ann, da of David Morrison (d 1991); 2 s (Kenton Andrew b 1968, Mark Hugo b 1972); *Career* exec dir: Singer & Friedlander Ltd 1971–91, Singer & Friedlander Group plc 1987–91; dir Nottingham Building Society 1985–2004 (sometime chm); dir: British Polythene Industries plc 1989–2004, Jenner Fenton Slade Group Ltd 1991–95, Wade Furniture Group Ltd 1991–, SOL Construction Holdings Ltd 1991–95; chm Landmatch plc 1993–95; non-exec memb Queen's Med Centre Univ Hosp NHS Tst 1993–98; FCA; *Recreations* sailing, tennis, walking, music; *Style*— Laurence Coppel, Esq, DL

COPPEN, Dr Alec James; s of Herbert John Wardle Coppen (d 1974), of London, and Marguerite Mary Annie, *née* Henshaw (d 1971); *b* 29 January 1923; *Educ* Dulwich Coll, Univ of Bristol (MB ChB, MD, DSc), Maudsley Hosp, Univ of London (DPM); *m* 9 Aug 1952, Gunhild Margareta, da of Albert Andersson, of Bastad, Sweden; 1 s (Michael b 1953); *Career* Br Army 1942–46; registrar then sr registrar Maudsley Hosp 1954–59, MRC Neuropsychiatry Research Unit 1957–74, MRC External Staff 1974–88; conslt psychiatrist: St Ebba's Hosp 1959–64, West Park Hosp Epsom 1964–90 (emeritus 1990); hon conslt St George's Hosp 1965–70, head WHO designated Centre for Biological Psychiatry UK 1974–88, memb Special HA Bethlem Royal and Maudsley Hosp 1982–86; conslt WHO 1977–, examiner RCPsych 1973–77, Andrew Woods visiting prof Univ of Iowa 1981; lectr in: Europe, N and S America, Asia, Africa; memb Cncl and chm Research and Clinical Section RMPA 1965–70, chm Biology Psychiatry Section World Psychiatric Assoc 1972, pres Br Assoc Psychopharmacology 1975 (life time achievement award 1998); ECNP Eli Lilly Award for outstanding research in neuropsychopharmacology 1991, CINP Pioneer in Psychopharmacology award 2000; author of numerous scientific papers on mental health; Freeman City of London 1980, Liveryman Worshipful Soc of Apothecaries 1985 (memb 1980); memb: Collegium Internationale Neuropsychopharmacologicum 1960 (memb Cncl 1979, pres 1990), RSM 1960, Br Pharmacological Soc 1977; hon memb: Mexican Inst of Culture 1974, Swedish Psychiatric Assoc 1977; corr memb American Coll Neuropsychopharmacology 1977, FRCP 1980 (MRCP 1975), distinguished fell APA 1981, Hon FRCPsych 1995 (FRCPsych 1971); *Books* Recent Developments in Schizophrenia (1967), Recent Developments in Affective Disorders (1968), Biological Psychiatry (1968), Psychopharmacology of Affective Disorders (1979), Depressive Illness: Biological and Psychopharmacological Issues (1981), 5-Hydroxytryptamine in Psychiatry (1991); *Recreations* golf, opera, photography; *Clubs* Athenaeum, The Harveian Soc, RAC; *Style*— Dr Alec Coppen; ✉ 5 Walnut Close, Epsom, Surrey KT18 5JL (tel 01372 720800, fax 01372 742602, e-mail acoppen@globalnet.co.uk)

COPPEN, Luke Benjamin Edward; s of Canon Martin Coppen, and Christine, *née* Stevens; *b* 8 February 1976, Basingstoke, Hants; *Educ* Cricklade Tertiary Coll Andover, SOAS (BA), Univ of Wales Cardiff (Dip Journalism Studies); *m* 14 Aug 2004, Marlena, *née* Marciniszyn; 1 da (Grace Teresa b 4 Nov 2006); *Career* film ed The London Student 1996–97; The Catholic Herald: reporter 1998–2000, dep ed 2000–04, ed 2004–; Faith in Brief columnist The Times 2001–05; *Recreations* travel, food, film; *Style*— Luke Coppen, Esq; ✉ The Catholic Herald, Herald House, Lambs Passage, Bunhill Row, London EC1Y 8TQ (tel 020 7448 3606, fax 020 7256 9728, e-mail luke@catholicherald.co.uk)

COPPEN, Dr Michael James; s of Dr Alec James Coppen, of Epsom, Surrey, and Gunhild Margaretta, *née* Andersson; *b* 3 December 1953; *Educ* Epsom Coll, Royal Free Hosp Univ of London (MB BS); *m* 3 Sept 1983, Dr Regina Goh, da of Goh Choe Jim (d 1987); 1 da (Victoria Jade b 3 Sept 1991), 1 s (Daniel James Michael b 25 Nov 1993); *Career* sr house offr (later registrar) Guy's Hosp 1979–82, sr registrar UCH and Whittington Hosp 1982–87, conslt histopathologist Mayday Univ Hosp 1987–; FRCPath 1996 (MRCPath 1985); memb: Assoc Clinical Pathologists, British Soc of Clinical Cytology; *Articles* incl: Chrohn's Disease of the Appendix (1988), Coexistent Crone's Disease and Sigmoid Diverticulosis (1989), Giant Cell Arteritis Presenting as Limb Caudication (1989), Chronic Periaortitis Presenting As Common Bile Duct Obstruction (1991), Audit of Necropsies in a British District General Hospital (1992), Histoplasmosis of the Central Nervous System (1992), A Case of Warthin's Tumour with Co-existent Hodgkin's Disease (1993), Predication of the Histologic Grade of Breast Carcinoma by Fine Needle Aspiration Cytology (1994), Changes in Oestrogen Receptor, Progesterone Receptor and pS2 Expression in Tamoxifen-resistant Breast Cancer (1995), The Role of Thyroid Fine Needle Aspirate Cytology in a District General Hospital Setting (1995), Isolated Arteritis of the Uterine Cervix (1996), A Six-Year Follow up of Cervical Cytology in 329 Women from Croydon after Loop Excisional Biopsies (1997); pubns incl Evaluation of Buffy Coat Microscopy for the Early Diagnosis of Bacteraemia (1981); *Recreations* golf, reading, music; *Clubs* RAC, Hole in One; *Style*— Dr Michael Coppen; ✉ Department of Histopathology, Mayday Hospital, Mayday Road, Thornton Heath, Surrey (tel 020 8401 3000 ext 5014, e-mail mcoppen@doctors.org.uk)

COPPOCK, Lawrence Patrick; s of Eric Francis Coppock, of Harrogate, and Betty Winifred, *née* Wilson; *b* 27 January 1952; *Educ* Royal GS, King George V GS; *m* 1 May 1982, Gillian Mary, da of Richard Charles Darby, of Stratford-on-Avon; 2 da (Katherine b 1984, Victoria b 1987), 1 s (Richard b 1993); *Career* chartered accountant Coopers & Lybrand 1971–75, gp fin dir Heron Motor Group 1983–84, gp fin controller Heron Corporation plc 1985, fin and ops dir HP Bulmer Drinks Ltd 1986–88, fin dir B & Q plc 1988–94, gp fin dir Hunter Timber Group Ltd 1994–95, fin dir Sunsail International plc 1996–98, fin dir Haskins Group 1998–2000, dir Nicholas King Homes plc 2000–05; chm Broadreach Retail Services Ltd 1992–94, chm Girl Heaven Ltd 2000–01; dir Close Mgmnt Servs Ltd 2000–; govr Kings' Sch Winchester; FCA 1980; *Recreations* skiing, tennis, club motor racing; *Clubs* East India; *Style*— Lawrence Coppock, Esq

CORBEN, David Edward; s of Cyril Edward Corben, of Elmbridge, Surrey, and Florence Ethel Jessie, *née* Lewthwaite; *b* 5 March 1945; *Educ* St Paul's; *m* 1, 4 Jan 1969 (m dis), Fiona Elizabeth Macleod, da of Prof David Stern, of Teddington, Middx; 1 s (Mark b 1971), 1 da (Victoria b 1973); m 2, 7 May 1988 (m dis), Miranda Davies, da of David McCormick, of Salisbury, Wilts; *Career* Lloyd's broker; chm Jardine Lloyd Thompson Reinsurance Holdings Ltd (formerly Jardine Thompson Graham) 1986–99; dir: Matheson & Co 1984–2003, JIB Group plc 1990–97, JLT Group plc 1997–2000; chm: Macrobins plc 2000–03, Richmond Vikings Ltd 2000, Richmond Athletic Assoc 2000, Richmond Football Club Ltd 2004–; *Recreations* skiing, golf, sailing, motor racing, riding, rugby football; *Clubs* Travellers; *Style*— David Corben, Esq; ✉ 1 Sydney Road, Richmond, Surrey TW9 1UB (tel 020 8948 6641)

CORBET, Prof Philip Steven; s of Alexander Steven Corbet (d 1948), of Tilehurst, Berks, and Irene Trewavas (d 1989), of Newlyn, Cornwall; *b* 21 May 1929; *Educ* Nelson Boys' Coll NZ, Dauntsey's Sch West Lavington, Univ of Reading (BSc, DSc), Gonville & Caius Coll Cambridge (PhD, ScD); *Career* zoologist E African Freshwater Fisheries Res Orgn Jinja Uganda 1954–57, entomologist E African Virus Res Orgn Entebbe Uganda 1957–62, research scientist Entomology Research Inst Canada Dept of Agric Ottawa Canada 1962–67, dir Research Inst Canada Dept of Agric Belleville Canada 1967–71, prof and chm Dept of Biology Univ of Waterloo Canada 1971–74, prof and dir Jt Centre for Environmental Sciences Univ of Canterbury and Lincoln Coll Canterbury NZ 1974–78, prof Dept of Zoology Univ of Canterbury Christchurch NZ 1978–80, head Dept of Biological Sciences Univ of Dundee 1983–86 (prof of zoology 1980–90, prof emeritus 1990–); visiting Cwlth prof Dept of Applied Biology Univ of Cambridge 1979–80; hon prof Univ of Edinburgh 1996–; pres: Br Dragonfly Soc 1983–92 (hon memb 1991), Worldwide Dragonfly Assoc 2001–03; memb: NZ Govt Fact Finding Gp on Nuclear Energy 1975–77, NZ Environmental Cncl 1976–79, Ctee for Scot Nature Conservancy Cncl 1986–90, Cncl Scot Wildlife Tst 1995–96, Cncl Cornwall Wildlife Tst 1997–2004; hon memb: Int Odonatological Soc 1985, Soc Française Odonatologie 1997, Dragonfly Soc of the Americas 2000; Neill Prize RSE 2002; DSc Univ of Edinburgh 2003, DSc Univ of Dundee 2005; fell Entomological Soc of Canada 1977 (pres 1971–72, Gold Medal 1974); FRES 1950, FIBiol 1967, FRSTM&H 1985, FRSE 1987, FRSA 1991, EurBiol 1998, memb Inst of Ecology and Environmental Mgmnt (MIEEM) 2001; *Books* Dragonflies (with C Longfield and N W Moore, 1960), A Biology of Dragonflies (1962), The Odonata of Canada and Alaska vol 3 (with E M Walker, 1975), Dragonflies: Behaviour and Ecology of Odonata (1999); author of numerous scientific papers in learned jls; *Recreations* natural history, music; *Clubs* Arctic; *Style*— Prof Philip S Corbet, FRSE; ✉ Crean Mill, Crean, St Buryan, Cornwall TR19 6DH (tel 01736 810333, fax 01736 810056)

CORBETT, Gerald Michael Nolan; s of John Michael Nolan Corbett (d 1982), of Sedlescombe, E Sussex, and Pamela Muriel, *née* Gay; *b* 7 September 1951; *Educ* Tonbridge, Pembroke Coll Cambridge (fndn scholar, MA), London Business Sch (MSc), Harvard Business Sch (Exchange scholarship); *m* 19 April 1976, Virginia Moore, da of Neill Newsum, of Warham, Norfolk; 3 da (Sarah b 4 June 1979, Olivia b 13 Nov 1982, Josephine b 5 Oct 1984), 1 s (John b 20 Jan 1981); *Career* Boston Consulting Gp 1975–82; Dixons Gp plc: gp fin controller 1982–85, corporate fin dir 1985–87; gp fin dir Redland plc 1987–94, gp fin dir Grand Metropolitan plc 1994–97, chief exec Railtrack plc 1997–2000; chm: Woolworths Gp plc 2001–07, Holmes Place plc 2003–06, SSL International plc 2005–, Britvic plc 2005–; non-exec dir: MEPC plc 1995–98, Burmah Castrol plc 1998–2000, Greencore Gp plc 2004–; chm of govrs Abbot's Hill Sch 1997–2002, govr Univ of Luton 2002–04; *Recreations* country pursuits, golf; *Clubs* Downhill Only, MCC, Oxford and Cambridge, Aldeburgh Golf; *Style*— Gerald Corbett, Esq; ✉ Holtsmere End Farm, Redbourn, Hertfordshire AL3 7AW

CORBETT, Prof Greville G; *b* 23 December 1947; *Educ* Univ of Birmingham (BA, MA, PhD), Univ of Belgrade, Univ of Moscow; *m*; 3 c; *Career* Univ of Surrey: lectr Dept of Linguistic and International Studies 1974–85, reader in Russian 1985–88, prof of linguistics and of Russian language 1988–2000, fndn research prof of linguistics and of Russian language 2000–, distinguished prof 2002–; pres Linguistics Assoc of GB 1994–97 (sometime memb chair Linguistics RAE Panel), memb Cncl Philological Soc 1993–98, memb Research Grants Bd ESRC 1994–98; memb Bd of Consltg Eds: Linguistics (also memb Editorial Bd), Russian Linguistics, Yearbook of Morphology; author of numerous jl articles; univ research fellowship Univ of Melbourne 1980–81, ESRC research fellowship 2002–04; FBA 1997, AcSS 2000; *Books* Predicate Agreement in Russian (1979), Hierarchies, Targets and Controllers: Agreement Patterns in Slavic (1983), Computers, Language Learning and Language Teaching (jtly, 1985), Gender (1991), Heads in Grammatical Theory (jt ed, 1993), The Slavonic Languages (jt ed, 1993), Agreement (ed, 1999), Number (2000), Agreement (2006); *Style*— Prof Greville G Corbett; ✉ Surrey Morphology Group, Department of Culture, Media and Communication, University of Surrey, Guildford, Surrey GU2 7XH

CORBETT, James Patrick; QC (1999); s of Patrick Francis Corbett (d 1999), and Kathleen Mary Corbett, of Welford, Northants; *b* 10 May 1952; *Educ* Sloane Sch Chelsea, Univ of Exeter (LLB, LLM), Inns of Court Sch of Law (Duke of Edinburgh scholarship, Ashworth scholarship); *m* 1979, Barbara Janet, *née* Willett; 4 da (Anna b 1982, Alice b 1986, Katharine, Rose (twins) b 1988), 1 s (James b 1984); *Career* called to the Bar Inner Temple 1975; practising barrister 1977– (Midland & Oxford Circuit), recorder 2000 (asst recorder 1996); lectr in law Univ of Leicester 1975–77; Bar of Ireland 1981, Bar of Northern Ireland 1994, Bar of New South Wales 2002, Bar of Anguilla 2002, Bar of St Kitts and Nevis 2004, Bar of British Virgin Islands 2004; memb Lincoln's Inn (ad eundem) 1998; Parly candidate (SDP): Erewash 1983, Staffordshire Moorlands 1987; European Parly candidate Cheshire E 1984; former memb Gas Consumers Cncl and special advsr on competition and consumer affairs; chm Welford Parish Cncl 1988–92 and 1996–2001; Freeman City of London 2000; Liveryman: Worshipful Co of Arbitrators 2000, Worshipful Co of Bowyers 2003; FCIArb 1997, FHKIArb 2001, FSIArb 2002; *Recreations* jazz, cinema, rugby league; *Clubs* Athenaeum; *Style*— James Corbett, Esq, QC; ✉ Serle Court Chambers, 6 New Square, Lincoln's Inn, London WC2A 3QS (tel 020 7242 6105, fax 020 7405 4004)

CORBETT, (Richard) Panton; s of Richard William Corbett, TD (d 1987), and Doris Vaughan, *née* Kimber (d 1991); *b* 17 February 1938; *Educ* Sunningdale, Eton, Aix en Provence Univ; *m* 1, 28 April 1962 (m dis 1973), Leila Francis, *née* Wolsten-Croft; 1 s (Oliver b 1965); m 2, 11 July 1974, Dame Antoinette Sibley, DBE, *qv*, da of E G Sibley (d 1991), and W M Sibley (d 2002) of Birchington on Sea; 1 s (Isambard b 1980), 1 da (Eloise b 1975); *Career* 2 Lt Welsh Gds 1957; dir Singer and Friedlander Holdings plc 1973–98; dir: Interfinance and Investment Corporation 1974–80, First British American Corporation Ltd 1976–93, Saxon Oil plc 1980–86, Tex Holdings 1987–, Peninsula TV 1989–93, Haynes Publishing Group plc 1993–, South Staffordshire Gp plc 1993– (formerly South Staffordshire Water Holdings), SPG Media Gp plc 1995–2004; chm Alternative Investment Market (AIM) London Stock Exchange 1995–98; dir Royal Opera House Tst 1989–95, tstee Royal Ballet Benevolent Fund 1985–2002,memb Exec and chm Fin Ctee Royal Acad of Dance until 2005, currently memb Finance Ctee and tstee Dancers Career Devpt Tst; High Sheriff of Shropshire 2000–01; Freeman City of Shrewsbury 1979, Freeman City of London 2000; FRAD; *Recreations* tennis, shooting, opera, skiing, fishing; *Clubs* Boodle's, Queen's; *Style*— Panton Corbett, Esq; ✉ 24 Chapel Street, London SW1X 7BY (tel 020 7235 4506, fax 020 7235 9565); 2 Grove Farm, Longnor, Shrewsbury SY5 7PR (tel 01743 718370, fax 01743 718280, e-mail panton.corbett@btinternet.com)

CORBETT, Peter George; s of Dr John Hotchkins Corbett (d 1999), and Patricia Kathleen, *née* Hope (d 1998); *b* 13 April 1952; *Educ* Liverpool Coll, Liverpool Coll of Art and Design (fndn), Manchester Regnl Coll of Art and Design (BA); *Career* artist (oil on canvas); 1st XV hooker Waterloo RUFC Liverpool 1973–74; memb: Creative Minds Arts Gp Ctee 1978–81, New Age Festival Organising Ctee 1983 and 1984; lead singer and fndr memb rock band Aquarian 1983–85, composer and musical dir Dr F and The TV Kids (Unity Theatre Liverpool) 1985, fndr memb Merseyside Contemporary Artists Mgmnt Ctee (formerly Liverpool Acad of Arts) 1988, chm and fndr memb Merseyside Visual Arts Festival (Visionfest) 1989–90, originator Liverpool European Capital of Culture 2008 1996–97; American Biographical Inst Minister of Culture 2003; hon prof: Académie des Sciences Humaines Universelles Paris 1993, St Lukas Acad Memmelsdorf Germany 1998; life fell and hon prof of fine art Inst of Co-ordinated Research Victoria Aust 1994; memb: Nat Artists Assoc 1988–89 (chm Merseyside Branch), Maison Internationale des Intellectuels Paris 1994, Design and Artists Copyright Soc; former memb Abstract Artists Organisation London; fndr memb: Order of St Francis Liberal Catholic Church, American Order of Excellence in the Fields of Painting and Poetry American Biographical Inst 2003; Peter G Corbett Award Fndn 2007 estab by American Biographical Inst; ambass Liverpool European Capital of Culture 08 2006; numerous awards from American Biographical Inst; other awards incl: Cert of Merit Int Biographical Centre Cambridge1988, Purchase Prize Merseyside Contemporary Artists Exhbn Albert Dock Liverpool 1988, Dip winner Int Open Scottish Poetry Competition 1998, Outstanding Achievement Award Albert Einstein Int Acad Fndn 1998, Int German Art Prize, Van Gogh Award and Gold Medal, and Friedrich Hölderin Award and Gold Medal for Poetry St Lukas Acad Memmelsdorf Germany 2000, Int Poet of Merit Award Int Soc of Poets USA 2002, Int Peace Prize United Cultural Convention USA 2002, Int Soc of Poets' Poet of the Year 2003 (nominated 1997), Poet of the Year Int Soc of Poetry USA 2003, Best Poems and Best Poets of the Year Int Library of Poetry 2004; *Exhibitions* incl: Centre Gallery Liverpool 1979, Liverpool Playhouse 1982, Acorn Gallery Liverpool 1985, Major Merseyside Artists Exhibition (Port of Liverpool Building) 1988, Merseyside Contemporary Artists Exhibition (Albert Dock Liverpool) 1988, Surreal Objects Exhibition (Tate Gallery Liverpool) 1989, Unity Theatre Liverpool 1990, Royal Liver Building Liverpool (two person) 1991, Alternative 17 Exhibition (Merkmal Gallery Liverpool) 1991, Angelus Gallery Winchester (mixed) 1992, Senate House Gallery Liverpool Univ (one man) 1993, Acad of Arts Liverpool (two man) 1994, Vision Fest (open) 1994, Grosvenor Museum Exhibition Chester (open) 1995, Atkinson Gallery Southport (one man) 1995, The Three Month Gallery Liverpool (mixed) 1996, Liverpool Acad of Arts (mixed) 1997, Liverpool Acad of Arts 1998, Hanover Gallery Liverpool (two man) 1999, Liverpool Biennial of Contemporary Art (one man, independent) 1999, DFN Gallery NY (mixed) 2000, Influences and Innovations (Agora Gall NY, mixed) 2002, Paintings and Open Studio (Bluecoat Arts Centre Liverpool) 2002, Paintings 1987–2002 (one man retrospective, Senate House Gallery Univ of Liverpool, part of Liverpool Biennial of Contemporary Art, Independent) 2004, Lexmark European Art Prize (Air Gallery London, mixed, Northwest UK regnl winner Lexmark European Art Prize) 2004, Design and Artists Copyright Soc (DACS) 20th Anniversary Exhbn (Mall Galleries London) 2004, The Art Cell Gallery Barcelona (five person) 2005, The Cornerstone Gallery Hope Univ Liverpool 2005, Flowers East Gallery London 2006, Life and Image (Daily Post and Echo Building Liverpool) 2006, Artfinder Gallery Liverpool 2007, Loop Gallery Liverpool Hope Univ 2007, Florence Biennale of Contemporary Art 2007; *Work in Collections* paintings in public collections: Univ of Liverpool Art Collection, Atkinson Gallery Southport, Hope Univ Liverpool; paintings in private collections in USA, Netherlands, Aust, Germany, Britain; *Poetry Anthologies* included in: 'Voices of the Wind' and 'On the Other Side of the Mirror' (for Int Soc of Poets), The Best Poems of 1997 (1997, Editor's Award), The Star-Laden Sky (for Int Soc of Poets), The Sound of Poetry I & II (cassette), Honoured Poets of 1998 (1998), A Celebration of Poets (1999), Best Poems of 1998 (1999), Time and Tide (2000), Prominent Voices (2000), Parnassus of World Poets (2000), Memories of the Millennium: The Best Poems and Poets of the Twentieth Century (2000), Prominent Voices (2000), Santuary (2000), Poetry Now, Northern England (2001), Messages from Within (2001), Tales from Erewhon (Selected Poems 1980–2000) (full anthology of own work, 2001), The Best Poems and Poets of 2002 (2002), Yesterday's Tides (2002), Poetry Now, Northern England (2002), A Nation of Poets (2003), Pictured Visions (2003), A Crossroads In Time (2003), Unexpected Illusions (2003), The Pool of Life (full anthology of own work, 2003), Images of Life (2004); poem included on audio compilation The Sound of Poetry (2002, incl Int Library of Poetry USA); *Publications* contrib to numerous creative jls incl Poetry Now 2004–; *Recreations* musical composition, playing the piano, meditation, yoga, contemporary dance; *Style*— Peter Corbett, Esq; ✉ Flat 4, 7 Gambier Terrace, Hope Street, Liverpool L1 7BG (tel 0151 709 4045, website www.axisartists.org/artistid/petercorbett)

CORBETT, Richard; MEP (Lab) Yorks and Humber; *b* 6 January 1955, Southport; *Educ* Farnborough Rd Sch Southport, Int Sch Geneva, Trinity Coll Oxford (BA), Univ of Hull (PhD); *m* 1, 1984, Inge van Gaal; 1 s; m 2, 1989, Anne de Malshe; 2 da; *Career* worked in voluntary sector for youth orgns 1977–81, civil servant 1981–89, dep sec-gen Socialist Gp European Parl 1994–96 (policy advsr 1989–94), advsr to Elisabeth Gigou (European Parl rep at Amsterdam Treaty Inter-Governmental Conf); MEP (Lab): Merseyside West 1996–99, Yorks and Humber 1999–; European Parl: memb Environment and Consumer Protection Ctee 1997–99, memb Jt Parly Ctee with Bulgarian Parl 1997–99, memb Constitutional Ctee 1997– (vice-pres 1997–99, Socialist Gp spokesman 1999–), memb Econ and Monetary Affrs Ctee 1999–, memb Civil Liberties Ctee 2004–, memb delgn to SE Asia and Korea; Lab Pty: memb 1973–, memb Gen Mgmnt Ctee of CLP 1975–76, memb Regnl Exec Ctee NW Region 1997–98, memb Yorks and Humber Regnl Bd 1999–, memb

Nat Policy Forum 2001–03, dep ldr Lab MEPs 2006–, special liaison memb for Belgium and Luxembourg; pres Jeunesse Européenne Fédéraliste 1979–81, pres Links Europa 1998–03, vice-pres European Movement, vice-pres Local Govt Gp for Europe, memb Steering Gp Yorks and Humber in Europe; memb GMB (pres GMB MEPs); Silver Medal European Parl 1996; *Publications* A Socialist Policy for Europe (1985), The Treaty of Maastricht: From Conception to Ratification (1992), The European Parliament's Role in Closer EU Integration (1998), The European Parliament (7 edn 2007), Combating Mythology and Changing Reality: the debate on the future of Europe (pamphlet, 2001); numerous chapters in books and articles in newspapers and learned jls incl the annual review on institutional devpts for Jl of Common Market Studies 1992–98; *Style*— Richard Corbett, Esq, MEP; ✉ 2 Blenheim Terrace, Leeds LS2 9JG (tel 0113 245 8978, fax 0113 245 8992, e-mail richard@richardcorbett.org.uk, website www.richardcorbett.org.uk); European Parliament, rue Wiertz, Brussels, Belgium (tel 00 322 284 7504, fax 00 322 284 9504, e-mail richard.corbett@europarl.europa.eu)

CORBETT, Ronald Balfour (Ronnie); OBE; *b* 4 December 1930; *Career* television and stage comedian; memb The Two Ronnies (with Ronnie Barker); *Television* appearances incl: Crackerjack 1955, No That's Me Over Here! 1967, The Ronnie Barker Yearbook 1971, Ronnie Corbett in Bed 1971, The Two Ronnies 1971, Now Look Here 1971, All This and Corbett Too 1975, The Picnic 1975, Sorry! 1981, The Ronnie Corbett Show 1987, The Two Ronnies in Australia 1987, An Audience with Ronnie Corbett 1997, Timbuctoo 1998, Two Ronnies Night 1999, The Two Ronnies at the Movies 1999, A Shaggy Dog Story 1999, The Nearly Complete and Utter History of Everything 1999, 30 Years of Monty Python: A Revelation 1999, Cinderella 2000, Night of a Thousand Shows 2000; subject of This is Your Life 1970; *Films* appearances incl: You're Only Young Twice 1952, Fun at St Fanny's 1956, Rockets Galore! 1957, Casino Royale 1957, Some Will Some Won't 1969, No Sex Please - We're British 1973, Fierce Creatures 1997; *Style*— Ronnie Corbett, Esq, OBE; ✉ c/o International Artistes Ltd, 4th Floor, Holborn Hall, 193–197 High Holborn, London WC1V 7BD (tel 020 7025 0600, fax 020 7404 9865)

CORBETT OF CASTLE VALE, Baron (Life Peer UK 2001), of Erdington in the County of West Midlands; Robin Corbett; s of Thomas Corbett, of West Bromwich, Staffs, and Marguerite Adele Mainwaring; *b* 22 December 1933; *Educ* Holly Lodge GS Smethwick; *m* 1970, Val Hudson; 1 s, 2 da; *Career* journalist 1954–69, sr Lab advsr IPC Magazines Ltd 1969–74; Parly candidate (Lab): Hemel Hempstead 1966 and Feb 1974, West Derbyshire (by-election) 1967; MP (Lab): Hemel Hempstead Oct 1974–1979, Birmingham Erdington 1983–2001; communications conslt 1979–83; chm PLP Home Affairs Ctee 1983–85, jt sec Aust and NZ Parly Gp 1983–97 (chm 1997–2001), W Midlands Lab Whip 1984–85, memb Select Ctee on Home Affrs 1983–85; oppn front bench spokesman: on home affrs 1985–92, on broadcasting, media and national heritage 1992–94, on disabled rights 1994–95; dir Rehab UK; chm: All-Pty Multiple Sclerosis Gp 1997–2001, Parly Lab Peers' Gp; vice-chm: All-Pty Motor Gp 1987–, Friends of Cyprus 1987–2001 (chm 2001–), Indo-Br Parly Gp; treas Parly Renewable and Sustainable Energy Gp 2002–; memb: Agricultural Select Ctee 1996–97, Home Affairs Ctee 1997–2001; jt sec: All-Pty Film Industry Gp, Parly Human Rights Sub-Ctee on Iran; memb Cncl: RCVS 1989–92, Save The Children 1987–90; memb Wilton Park Academic Cncl 1996–2005; chm: Castle Vale Neighbourhood Mgmnt Bd 2001–05, Castle Vale Partnership Bd 2005–; *Recreations* walking, collecting bric-à-brac; *Style*— The Rt Hon the Lord Corbett of Castle Vale; ✉ House of Lords, London SW1A 0PW (tel 020 7219 3420)

CORBIN, Christopher John (Chris); s of Frederick Christopher Corbin (d 1959), of Bournemouth, Dorset, and Vera, *née* Copperwaite (d 1984); *b* 1 March 1952, Bournemouth, Dorset; *Educ* St Christopher's Sch Bournemouth, Kingsley Secdy Modern Bournemouth; *m* 1982, Francine, *née* Checinski; 2 c (James, Amy (twins) b 8 Nov 1988); *Career* restaurateur; mangr Langan's Brasserie London; dir and prop (with Jeremy King, *qv*): Caprice Holdings Ltd 1981–2003 (restaurants opened incl: Le Caprice 1981, The Ivy 1990, J Sheekey 1998), The Wolseley 2003–, St Alban 2006–; Caterer and Hotelkeeper Restaurateur of the Year 1993 (jtly); memb Ctee Leuka 1998–; *Recreations* eating, tennis, modern British art, life drawing, meditation; *Clubs* Queen's, RAC, Groucho; *Style*— Chris Corbin, Esq; ✉ 11 Crescent Grove, London SW4 7AF (tel 020 7978 2628, fax 020 7978 2629, e-mail chris@chriscorbin.co.uk)

CORBIN, Jane; da of Aubrey George Corbin (d 1989), and Olive May, *née* Amery; *b* 16 July 1954; *Educ* King's Coll London (BA); *m*; 2 c; *Career* television correspondent and presenter; early career with Granada TV and Thames TV, foreign corr Channel 4 News 1983–88; BBC Television News & Current Affrs 1988–; sr corr Panorama (BBC1) 1988–; presenter: Behind the Headlines (BBC2) 1991–93, The Money Programme (BBC2) 1995–96; corr Election Night Special 1992, occasional presenter BBC news bulletins; *Assignments* for Channel 4 News incl: US presidential election 1984, assassination of Indira Gandhi (last journalist to interview her) and subsequent election of Rajiv Gandhi 1984–85, return of Benazir Bhutto to Pakistan 1988; for Panorama incl: fall of the Berlin Wall 1989, environmental effect of Chernobyl disaster 1990, Red Army's quashing of Azerbaijani rebellion, Cambodia ten years after Year Zero 1988, Iraqi weapons of mass destruction progs 1989–93, newly liberated Kuwait 1991, Iranian nuclear weapons prog 1993, Bosnia 1993, Norwegian involvement in Israeli/Palestinian peace accord (The Norway Channel) 1993, return of Yasser Arafat to Gaza 1994, investigation of war crimes at Srebrenica Bosnia 1996, investigation of death of Diana Princess of Wales 1997, The Killing of Kosovo 1999; *Awards* four RTS TV Journalism Awards, Rainier Award Monte Carlo TV Festival (for The Poisoned Land, The Dying Sea) 1990, Emmy nomination for Best Investigative Journalist (for Saddam's Secret Arms Ring) 1992; *Books* The Norway Channel (1994); *Recreations* sleeping, gardening, cooking; *Style*— Ms Jane Corbin

CORBY, Sir (Frederick) Brian; kt (1989); s of Charles Walter Corby (d 1984), of Raunds, Northants, and Millicent, *née* Pentelow (d 1997); *b* 10 May 1929; *Educ* Kimbolton Sch, St John's Coll Cambridge (MA); *m* 1 Aug 1952, Elizabeth Mairi, da of Dr Archibald McInnes (d 1973); 2 da (Fiona b 1955, Jane b 1957), 1 s (Nicholas b 1960); *Career* chm: Prudential Corporation plc 1990–95 (gp chief exec 1982–90), Prudential Assurance Co Ltd 1982–90, Mercantile and General Reinsurance Co plc 1985–90; dir Bank of England 1985–93, pres CBI 1990–92, pres NIESR 1994–2003; chm South Bank Bd 1990–98; chllr Univ of Herts 1992–96; Hon DSc: City Univ London 1989, Univ of Herts 1996; Hon DLitt Cncl for Nat Academic Awards 1991; FIA; *Recreations* golf, gardening, reading; *Style*— Sir Brian Corby; ✉ Fairings, Church End, Albury, Ware, Hertfordshire SG11 2JG

CORBY, Peter John Siddons; s of John Siddons Corby (d 1955), and Helen Anna, *née* Ratray (d 1974); *b* 8 July 1924; *Educ* Taplow GS; *m* 1, 1950 (m dis 1959), Gail Susan Clifford-Marshall; 2 s (Mark b 1950, Michael b 1951); m 2, 1960, Ines Rosemary, da of Dr George Anderson Mandow (d 1991); 1 s (John b 1962); *Career* RAFVR 1942–48; created manufactured and marketed many products incl The Corby Electric Trouser Press (1961); non-exec dir various cos (plc and private) 1950–; memb Lloyd's 1974–; Freeman City of London 1977, Liveryman Worshipful Co of Marketors 1978; FInstD 1955; *Recreations* sailing, bridge; *Clubs* Ocean Cruising, Island Sailing, Yacht Club de France; *Style*— Peter Corby, Esq; ✉ The Sloop, 89 High Street, Cowes, Isle of Wight PO31 7AW (tel 01983 292188, fax 01983 291598, e-mail pjscorby@onwight.net)

CORBYN, Jeremy Bernard; MP; s of David Benjamin Corbyn, and Naomi Loveday, *née* Jocelyn; *b* 26 May 1949; *Educ* Adams GS Newport; *Career* memb Haringey Borough Cncl 1974–83, NUPE area offr 1975–83; MP (Lab) Islington N 1983–, memb Select Ctee on Social Security 1991–97; chm: London Gp of Lab MPs 1992–96, PLP Health and Social Security Ctee 1985–89, PLP Northern Ireland Ctee 1985–89 and 1990–96; memb All Party Parly Gp on: Angola (chair), Campaign for Nuclear Disarmament Parliamentary Gp (chair), Liberation, Human Rights (vice-chair), Latin America (vice-chair), Mexico (treas), Traveller Law Reform, Cycling; memb Parly Gp: RMT, PCS, CWU, RMT, Socialist Campaign; chair Parly Campaign for Nuclear Disarmament Gp, chair and memb Nat Cncl CND, memb Lab CND, chair Liberation, memb Steering Ctee Stop the War Coalition; tstee: Highbury Vale Blackstock Tst, Dalit Solidarity Campaign; patron Mitford Under Fives; *Recreations* running, gardening, reading; *Style*— Jeremy Corbyn, Esq, MP; ✉ House of Commons, London SW1A 0AA

CORDER, Simon; *b* 11 February 1960; *Career* lighting designer 1984–; clients incl: NT, RSC, ENO, Scottish Opera, WNO, Lumiere & Son, Cholmondeleys, Night Safari Singapore, La Scala Milan; Special Projects Award Lighting Design Awards 2006, nomination Olivier Awards 2004; memb Assoc of Lighting Designers; *Recreations* cycling, gadgets; *Clubs* London Cycling Campaign; *Style*— Simon Corder; ✉ 112 Blackstock Road, London N4 2DR (tel 020 7503 7102, fax 020 7691 9633, mobile 07973 552348, e-mail simon@simoncorder.com, website www.simoncorder.com)

CORDINGLEY, Maj Gen Patrick Anthony John; DSO (1991); s of Maj Gen John Edward Cordingley, and Ruth Pamela, *née* Boddam-Whetham; *b* 6 October 1944; *Educ* Sherborne, RMA Sandhurst; *m* 1968, Melissa, da of James Eric Crawley, OBE; 2 da (Antonia b 1972, Miranda b 1974); *Career* CO 5 Royal Inniskilling Dragoon Gds 1985–87 (cmmnd 1965), Bde Cdr 7 Armd Bde (Desert Rats) 1988–91, GOC 2nd Division 1992–96, Sr Br Loan Serv Offr Sultanate of Oman 1996–2000, Col Royal Dragoon Gds 2000–04, Hon Col Bristol Univ OTC 2000–05; Bronze Star (US) 1991, Order of Oman 2000; chm: MMI Res 2001–, Defence and Security Forum 2002–, Cavalry and Guards' Club 2002–04; govr Sherborne Sch 2001–; chm of tstees Gilbert White's House and the Oates Museum 2002–; Freeman: City of London, Worshipful Co of Ironmongers (memb Ct 2000–); DSc (hc) Univ of Hull 2007; OStJ 1992; FRGS; *Books* Captain Oates: Soldier and Explorer (1982), In the Eye of the Storm (1996); *Recreations* country pursuits, whale and dolphin watching; *Clubs* Cavalry and Guards'; *Style*— Maj Gen Patrick Cordingley, DSO, DSc; ✉ c/o Cavalry and Guards' Club, 127 Piccadilly, London W1J 7PX (e-mail pajc@onetel.com)

CORDINGLY, Dr David Michael Bradley; s of Rt Rev Eric William Bradley Cordingly, MBE (d 1976), and Mary Eileen, *née* Mathews; *b* 5 December 1938; *Educ* Christ's Hosp, Oriel Coll Oxford (MA), Univ of Sussex (DPhil); *m* 8 May 1971, Shirley Elizabeth, da of Ian Gibson Robin and Shelagh Marian, *née* Croft; 1 s (Matthew), 1 da (Rebecca); *Career* graphic designer and typographer 1960–66, teacher in Jamaica 1966–67, exhibition designer British Museum 1968–71, keeper of Art Gallery and Museum Brighton 1971–78, asst dir The Museum of London 1978–80; Nat Maritime Museum: asst keeper 1980–86, keeper of pictures 1986–89, head of exhibitions 1989–93; writer and exhibition organiser 1993–; contrib articles: Burlington Magazine, The Connoisseur, Apollo Magazine, History Today; FRSA 1974; Order of the White Rose (Finland) 1986; *Books* Marine Painting in England (1974), Painters of the Sea (1979), Nicholas Pocock (1986), Captain James Cook, Navigator (ed, 1988), Pirates, Fact and Fiction (1992), Life among the Pirates: the Romance and The Reality (1995), Pirates, an Illustrated History (1996), Ships and Seascapes, an Introduction to Maritime Prints, Drawings and Watercolours (1997), Heroines and Harlots: Women at Sea in the Great Age of Sail (2001), Billy Ruffian: The Bellerophon and the Downfall of Napoleon (2003); *Style*— Dr David Cordingly; ✉ 2 Vine Place, Brighton, East Sussex BN1 3HE

CORDREY, Peter Graham; s of Wing-Cdr Percival William George Cordrey (d 1997), and Marjorie Joan, *née* Strickland; *b* 1 June 1947; *Educ* Wellingborough Sch, City Univ (MSc); *m* 1972, Carol Anne, da of Peter Lawrence Ashworth (d 1996); 2 da (Joanne b 1979, Rowena b 1982); *Career* merchant banker and chartered accountant; Singer & Friedlander Ltd 1972–96 (dir Bank 1982, latterly head of banking); chm: Hampshire Trust plc 1997–2006, Potential Finance Gp 2006–, London Scottish Bank plc 2007–; non-exec dir Benchmark Group plc; *Recreations* tennis, golf, swimming; *Clubs* Royal Automobile; *Style*— Peter Cordrey, Esq

CORDY, Timothy Soames; s of John Knutt Cordy, and Margaret Winifred, *née* Sheward; *b* 17 May 1949; *Educ* Dragon Sch Oxford, Sherborne, Univ of Durham (BA), Univ of Glasgow (MPhil); *m* 1974, Dr Jill Margaret Tattersall; 2 c; *Career* asst city planning offr Leicester City Cncl 1980–85 (joined 1974), Communauté Urbaine de Strasbourg 1978–79, asst chief exec Bolton Municipal Borough Cncl 1985–87, chief exec Royal Soc for Nature Conservation 1987–94, dir Town and Country Planning Assoc 1994–96, dir Global to Local Ltd; author of articles on housing renewal, sustainable devpt and nature conservation; memb Bd: UK 2000, Volunteer Centre UK; MRTPI 1976, FRSA 1991; *Recreations* music, food, France; *Style*— Timothy Cordy, Esq

COREN, Alan; s of Samuel and Martha Coren; *b* 27 June 1938; *Educ* East Barnet GS, Wadham Coll Oxford, Yale Univ, Univ of Calif Berkeley; *m* 14 Oct 1963, Anne, da of Michael Kasriel (d 1981), of London; 1 s (Giles, *qv*, b 1969), 1 da (Victoria b 1972); *Career* writer/broadcaster; Punch: joined 1963, asst ed until 1966, literary ed 1966–69, dep ed 1969–77, ed 1978–87; TV critic The Times 1971–78, ed The Listener 1988–90; columnist: Daily Mail 1972–76, Mail on Sunday 1984–92, The Times 1988–, Sunday Express 1992–96; contribs incl: Sunday Times, TLS, Observer, Spectator, Tatler; rector Univ of St Andrews 1973–76; Hon DLitt Univ of Nottingham 1993; *TV series* The Losers 1978, Call My Bluff 1995–; *Radio Series* The News Quiz 1977–, Freedom Pass 2003–; *Books* The Dog It Was That Died (1965), All Except the Bastard (1969), The Sanity Inspector (1974), The Bulletins of Idi Amin (1974), Golfing for Cats (1974), The Further Bulletins of Idi Amin (1975), The Lady From Stalingrad Mansions (1977), The Peanut Papers (1977), The Rhinestone as Big as the Ritz (1979), The Pick of Punch (ed annual, 1979–89), Tissues for Men (1980), The Best of Alan Coren (1980), The Cricklewood Diet (1982), Present Laughter (1982), The Penguin Book of Modern Humour (ed, 1983), Bumf (1984), Something for the Weekend (1986), Bin Ends (1987), Seems Like Old Times (1989), More Like Old Times (1990), A Year in Cricklewood (1991), Toujours Cricklewood? (1993), Animal Passions (ed, 1994), A Bit on the Side (1995), The Alan Coren Omnibus (1996), The Cricklewood Dome (1998), The Cricklewood Tapestry (2000), Waiting for Jeffrey (2002); The Punch Book of Short Stories: Book 1 (ed, 1979), Book 2 (1980), Book 3 (1981); *Recreations* broadcasting, riding, bridge; *Style*— Alan Coren, Esq

COREN, Anne; da of Michael Maximilian Kasriel (d 1981), and Isabel, *née* Koss (d 1996); *Educ* North London Collegiate Sch, Royal Free Hosp Sch of Med Univ of London (MB BS); *m* 14 Oct 1963, Alan Coren, *qv*, s of Sam Coren (d 1989); 1 s (Giles, *qv*, b 1969), 1 da (Victoria b 1972); *Career* Nat Heart Hosp, Charing Cross Hosp, sr registrar Middx Hosp, conslt anaesthetist Moorfields Eye Hosp; memb: Assoc of Anaesthetists, RSM; fell Coll of Anaesthetists, FRCA; memb BMA; *Style*— Dr Anne Coren; ✉ >e-mail< anne.coren@btinternet.com

COREN, Giles Robin Patrick; s of Alan Coren, *qv*, and Dr Anne Coren, *qv*, *née* Kasriel; *b* 29 July 1969, London; *Educ* Westminster (capt Fives), Keble Coll Oxford (BA, Fives half blue); *Career* ed Tatler About Town 1998–2000; The Times: feature writer 1994–97, columnist 1999–, Parly sketch writer 2000, Diary ed 2000–01, restaurant critic 2001–; columnist GQ 2004–; Best Food and Drink Writer British Press Awards 2005; *Books* Against the Odds: An Autobiography (with James Dyson, *qv*, 1997), Winkler (novel, 2005); *Recreations* fives, cricket, writing; *Clubs* Queen's Park Rangers; *Style*— Giles Coren, Esq; ✉ The Times, 1 Pennington Street, London E98 1TT (tel 020 7782 5000, e-mail giles.coren@thetimes.co.uk)

CORFIELD, Corrie Kear; da of Bernard Corfield, and Molly Corfield; *b* 28 April 1961; *Educ* Stratford-upon-Avon GS for Girls, Goldsmiths Coll London (BA); *Career* studio mangr

BBC World Service 1984–87 (trainee studio mangr 1983–84), announcer and newsreader BBC World Service 1987–88, announcer and newsreader BBC Radio 4 1988–91 and 1995–; newsreader Radio 702 Johannesburg SA and prodr Canadian Broadcasting Co (based in SA) 1991–1995; *Recreations* skiing, gardening, cryptic crosswords, fine wines, reading; *Style*— Miss Corrie Corfield; ⌧ BBC Radio 4, Broadcasting House, London W1A 1AA (tel 020 7765 2821, e-mail corrie.corfield@bbc.co.uk)

CORK, Richard Graham; s of Hubert Henry Cork, of Bath, and Beatrice Hester, *née* Smale; *b* 25 March 1947; *Educ* Kingswood Sch Bath, Trinity Hall Cambridge (MA, PhD); *m* 1970, Vena, da of James Jackson; 2 s (Adam James b 1974, Joe John b 1980), 2 da (Polly Beatrice b 1975, Katy Anna b 1978); *Career* author, critic, historian, exhibition organiser and broadcaster; art critic: Evening Standard 1969–77 and 1980–83, The Listener 1984–90, The Times 1991–2002, New Statesman 2003–07; Lethaby lectr RCA 1974, ed Studio International 1975–79, Durning-Lawrence lectr UCL 1987, Slade prof of fine art Univ of Cambridge 1989–90, Henry Moore fell Courtauld Inst of Art 1992–95; John Llewelyn Rhys Meml Prize 1976, Sir Banister Fletcher Award 1985, Nat Art Collections Fund Award 1995; memb: Editorial Bd Tate - The Art Magazine, Advsy Ctee Hayward Gallery until 1996, Ctee Contemporary Art Soc until 1997, Fine Arts Advsy Ctee British Cncl until 1997, Trafalgar Square Vacant Plinth Advsy Gp 1999–2000, St Paul's Cathedral Font Selection Ctee 1999–2000, Paul Mellon Centre for Br Art Advsy Cncl 1999–2005, Diana Princess of Wales Memorial Fountain Design Ctee 2000–02, Syndic Fitzwilliam Museum Cambridge 2002–; chm Visual Arts Advsy Panel Arts Cncl 1995–98; tstee Public Art Devpt Tst until 1996; elector to Slade professorship of fine art Cambridge, selector Sunderland Gateway Cmmn 1999–2000, Watson Gordon lectr Univ of Edinburgh 2005; judge: Turner Prize 1988, Nat Art Collections Fund Awards 1994, Citibank Photography Prize 1997, NatWest Painting Prize 1998, John Moores Prize 1999, Charles Wollaston Award 1999, Times/Artangel Open 1999–2000, Art 2000 Commission 1999–2000, Jerwood Drawing Prize 2001, BBC Churchill Memorial 2003–04, Trafalgar Square Crib Sculpture 2005, Blind Art 2006, St Martin-in-the-Fields East Window 2006–07, Ronse Kent Public Art Award 2006–07; *Exhibitions* organiser of various exhbns incl: Critic's Choice (Tooth Gallery) 1973, Beyond Painting and Sculpture (Arts Cncl) 1973, Vorticism and Its Allies (Hayward Gallery) 1974, Sculpture Now: Dissolution or Redefinition? (RCA) 1974, Art for Whom? (Serpentine Gallery) 1978, David Bomberg Retrospective (Tate Gallery) 1988, The Last Days of Mankind (Altes Museum Berlin) 1994, A Bitter Truth (Barbican Art Gallery) 1994; co-organiser: Arte Inglese Oggi (Palazzo Reale Milan) 1976, Un Certain Art Anglais (Musée d'Art Moderne Paris) 1979, British Art in the Twentieth Century (Royal Acad) 1987, The British Art Show 4 (Manchester, Edinburgh and Cardiff) 1995–96; North Meadow Art Project (Millennium Dome) 2000; *Publications* Vorticism and Abstract Art in the First Machine Age (vol 1 1975, vol 2 1976), The Social Role of Art: Essays in Criticism for a Newspaper Public (1979), Art Beyond the Gallery in Early Twentieth Century England (1985), David Bomberg (1987), Architect's Choice: Art in Architecture in Great Britain since 1945 (with Eugene Rosenberg, 1992), A Bitter Truth: Avant-Garde Art and the Great War (1994), Bottle of Notes: Claes Oldenburg/Coosje van Bruggen (1997), Jacob Epstein (1999), Everything Seemed Possible: Art in the 1970s (2003), New Spirit, New Sculpture, New Money: Art in the 1980s (2003), Breaking Down the Barriers: Art in the 1990s (2003), Annus Mirabilis? Art in the Year 2000 (2003), Michael Craig-Martin (2006); contrib numerous essays to art magazines and exhbn catalogues; *Recreations* enjoying my family, looking at art, going to the cinema; *Style*— Richard Cork, Esq; ⌧ email richardcork@hotmail.com

CORK AND ORRERY, 15 Earl of (I 1620) and (I 1660) respectively; John Richard Boyle; also Baron Boyle of Marston (GB 1711), Baron Boyle of Youghal (I 1616), Viscount Dungarvan (I 1620), Viscount Boyle of Kinalmeaky, Baron of Bandon Bridge and Baron Boyle of Broghill (I 1628), Earl of Orrery (I 1660); s of 14 Earl d 2003); *b* 3 November 1945; *Educ* Harrow, BRNC Dartmouth; *m* 1973, Hon Rebecca Juliet Noble, yst da of Baron Glenkinglas (Life Peer; d 1984); 2 da (Lady Cara Mary Cecilia b 16 June 1976, Lady Davina Claire Theresa b 10 Dec 1978), 1 s (Rory Jonathan Courtenay, Viscount Dungarvan (twin) b 10 Dec 1978); *Heir* s, Viscount Dungarvan; *Career* Lt Cdr RN (ret); dir E D & F Man Sugar Ltd London, ret 2006; *Clubs* Boodle's, RYS; *Style*— The Rt Hon the Earl of Cork and Orrery; ⌧ Lickfold House, Petworth, West Sussex GU28 9EY

CORKERY, Michael; QC (1981); s of Charles Timothy Corkery (d 1968), of London, and Nellie Marie, *née* Royal; *b* 20 May 1926; *Educ* King's Sch Canterbury; *m* 29 July 1967, Juliet Shore, da of Harold Glyn Foulkes (d 1966), of Shrewsbury; 1 s (Nicholas b 8 June 1968), 1 da (Charlotte b 29 May 1970); *Career* Lt Welsh Gds 1945–48; called to the Bar Lincoln's Inn 1949, bencher 1973, treasurer 1992; jr treasury counsel 1959–70, sr treasury counsel 1970, first sr treasury counsel Central Criminal Ct 1979–81; *Recreations* fishing, shooting, sailing, music, gardening; *Clubs* Cavalry and Guards', Garrick, Hurlingham, Itchenor Sailing, Household Division Yacht, Friends of Arundel Castle Cricket; *Style*— Michael Corkery, Esq, QC; ⌧ 5 Paper Buildings, Temple, London EC4 (tel 020 7583 6117, fax 020 7353 0075)

CORKREY, Michael Christopher; s of Thomas Edward Lawrence Corkrey, of Moulsoe, Bucks, and Carole Martha, *née* Snape; *b* 24 November 1962; *Educ* Wootton Upper Sch, Bedford Coll of HE (DA), Leeds Poly (BA), Royal Acad Schs (post-dip painting, Henfield Award, Worshipful Co of Painter-Stainers' Prize, De Segonzac Travelling Scholarship); *Career* artist; *Solo exhibition* Seascapes (Sarah Myerscough Fine Art London) 2004; *Group exhibitions* John Player Portrait Award Exhbn (Nat Portrait Gall) 1986, 1987 and 1989, BP Portrait Award Exhbn (Nat Portrait Gall) 1990, 1991 and 1992, Three Young Painters (New Grafton Gall) 1990, Portrait Painters (Wyndham Fine Art) 1992, 1993 and 1994, Five (Atlantis Gall) 1993, Hunting/Observer Art Prizes Exhbn 1993, Hunting Group Art Prizes Exhbn 1994, 1995, 1997 and 1999, Figure it Out (Harrogate Art Gallery) 1996, Summer Show (Offer Waterman London) 1997, Line Up (gf2 London) 2001, S.O.A.P. Artists (Gallery Fine London) 2001, Wall to Wall (Sarah Myerscough Fine Art) 2002, Waterline (Sarah Myerscough Fine Art) 2002, To be Continued... (gf2) 2002, Art 2002 (gf2) 2002, London Art Fair (Sarah Myerscough Fine Art) 2003, 2005 and 2005, Art London (Sarah Myerscough Fine Art) 2003 and 2004, Miniatures (Sarah Myerscough Fine Art) 2003, Initmacy (Sarah Myerscough Fine Art) 2004; *Portraits* incl: Jeffrey Bernard 1992, Keith Miller 1993, The Earl Spencer 1993; *Awards* Elizabeth Greenshield Fndn Award 1990, First Prize Hunting Gp Art Prizes 1994; *Style*— Michael Corkrey, Esq

CORLEY, Paul; *b* 1950; *Educ* Bablake Sch Coventry, Worcester Coll Oxford (BA); *Career* graduate trainee journalist Westminster Press 1972–75, sr feature writer Thomson Newspapers Newcastle upon Tyne 1975, journalist Look North BBC North East 1976–78, regnl features prodr BBC North East 1978–80, current affrs prodr BBC TV London 1980–82, prodr The Tube live music magazine prog (winner various int awards incl TV Times special award for innovation) Tyne Tees TV Newcastle upon Tyne 1982–84, dir of progs and exec prodr of all network progs Border TV Carlisle 1984–91, dir of progs North East TV (bidding for NE franchise) 1991, controller of factual progs Carlton Television 1991–95, md Carlton Broadcasting 1995–96, controller of factual progs ITV Network 1996–97, chief exec Border TV 1998–2000, md GMTV 2001–07; *Style*— Paul Corley, Esq

CORLEY, Roger David; CBE (1993); s of Thomas Arthur Corley (d 1989), and Erica, *née* Trent (d 2003); *b* 13 April 1933; *Educ* Hymers Coll Kingston upon Hull, Univ of Manchester (BSc); *m* 14 May 1964, Dr Brigitte, da of Leo Hubert Anton Roeder (d 1977);

3 s (Martin b 1966, Kevin b 1969, Steffan b 1971); *Career* Nat Serv Sub Lt RNVR 1954–56; Clerical Medical and General Life Assurance Society: joined 1956, investment mangr 1961–72, actuary 1972–80, dir 1975–96, dep gen mangr 1980–82, gen mangr 1982, md 1991–95; chm: St Andrew's Group plc 1995–2003, Pharos SA 1995–2006; dir: Korea Asia Fund 1990–2000, Lands Improvement Hldgs plc 1994–1999, City of Westminster Arts Cncl 1994–2003, Br Heart Fndn 1995–2004, Med Defence Union Ltd 1996–2004, Fidelity Investments Life Insurance Ltd 1997–, RGA Reinsurance UK Ltd 1998–; memb Fin Services Cmmn (Gibraltar) 1995–2000; Inst of Actuaries: fell 1960, memb Cncl 1976–94, hon sec 1980–82, vice-pres 1985–88, pres 1988–90; memb Cncl Int Actuarial Assoc 1983–98 (vice-pres 1990–98); Freeman City of London 1979, memb Ct of Assts Worshipful Co of Actuaries 1985– (Liveryman 1979, Sr Warden 1991–92, Master 1992–93); FIA 1960, DGVM 1975, FRSA 1990; *Recreations* music, theatre, opera, visual arts, books, travel; *Clubs* Gallio, Actuaries; *Style*— Roger Corley, Esq, CBE; (fax 020 8731 7628, e-mail roger@corleys.org.uk)

CORMACK, Ian Donald; s of Andrew Gray Cormack (d 1993), of Falmouth, Cornwall, and Eliza Cormack; *b* 12 November 1947; *Educ* Falmouth GS, Pembroke Coll Oxford (MA, fndn fell); *m* 1, 14 Sept 1968, (Elizabeth) Susan (d 1994), da of Mark Tallack (d 1976), of Penryn, Cornwall; 1 s (James Mark Ian (Jamie) b 1975), 1 da (Sally Elizabeth b 1979); *m* 2, 12 Sept 1997, Caroline Castleman, of South Africa, da of Norman Westcott; *Career* Citibank NA: joined 1969, dir SCAM 1976–78, head of Euro Trg Centre 1979, personnel dir N Europe 1980–84, head Financial Instns Gp UK 1984–88, head Financial Instns Gp Europe 1989–95, country corp offr UK 1993–98, global industry head Investment Industry 1996–2000; chm Citicorp UK Pension Fund 1980–89; ceo Europe American Int Gp Inc 2000–02, with Cormack Tansey Partners (conslts) 2002–05, chm Entertaining Finance Ltd 2003–, memb Advsy Bd Millennium Associates AG 2003–06, chm Aberdeen Growth Opportunities VCT2 plc 2005–, chm Earth Fuel Resources Ltd 2006–, chm Bank Trg & Devpt Ltd 2006–; non-exec dir: Aspen Insurance Hldgs Bermuda 2003–, American Assocs of NT Inc 2003–, Klipmart Corp 2003–, Mphasis BFL Ltd 2004–05, Nat Angels Ltd 2004–, Pearl Gp Ltd 2005–, Qatar Financial Centre 2006–; Assoc of Payment Clearing Systems (APACS): memb Cncl 1985–96, chm Risk Steering Gp 1990–91, memb Settlement Risk Gp 1991–93; London Stock Exchange: memb Securities Settlement Bd 1990–92, chm TAURUS Monitoring Gp 1992–93, memb CREST Task Force 1993; chm: Woolnoth Soc City of London 1990–92, CHAPS 1993–96; memb: Bd Cedel SA Luxembourg 1985–96, Clearing House Formation Ctee (LSE) 1989–91, Cncl ABSAL 1993–96, Chllr's City Promotion Panel 1995–2001, Devpt Bd Oxford Business Sch 1999–2003, Devpt Cncl NT 2000–, Advsy Gp Pembroke Coll Oxford; *Recreations* skiing, golf, fly fishing, theatre; *Clubs* RAC; *Style*— Ian Cormack, Esq; ⌧ 24 Kensington Court Gardens, London W8 5QF (tel 020 7937 1407, fax 020 7795 6930); The Boat House, Restronguet Point, Truro, Cornwall TR3 6RB (tel 01872 862020); 14 Egret Lane, Steenberg, Constantia, South Africa; Cormack Tansey Partners (ctp), 7–10 Adam Street, The Strand, London WC2N 6AA (tel 020 7520 9230, e-mail ian.cormack@ctpartners.co.uk)

CORMACK, Dr John Francis; s of James E Cormack, of Chipping Norton, and Theresa, *née* Hill; *b* 27 April 1947; *Educ* St Joseph's Coll, London Hosp Med Coll, Corpus Christi Coll Cambridge; *m* 24 June 1978, Susan, *née* Hazelton; 1 da (Laura b 5 June 1980), 2 s (Ben b 13 Oct 1982, Marcus b 27 Nov 1987); *Career* sr ptnr in gen practice, med writer and broadcaster; hon press sec BMA; former memb GMC; *Style*— Dr John Cormack; ⌧ Dr Cormack, Greenwood Surgery, Tylers Ride, South Woodham Ferrers, Essex (tel 01245 426898, fax 01245 328233, e-mail greenwood.surgery@btinternet.com)

CORMACK, Sir Patrick Thomas; kt (1995), MP; s of Thomas Charles Cormack, of Grimsby, and Kathleen Mary Cormack; *b* 18 May 1939; *Educ* St James's Choir Sch Grimsby, Havelock Sch Grimsby, Univ of Hull; *m* 1967, Kathleen Mary, da of William Eric McDonald, of Aberdeen; 2 s; *Career* second master St James's Choir Sch Grimsby 1961–66, former English master and asst housemaster Wrekin Coll, head of History Dept Brewood GS Stafford; MP (Cons): Cannock 1970–74, Staffs S Feb 1974–; PPS to jt Parly Secs DHSS 1970–73; chm: All-Pty Ctee Widows and One Parent Families 1974, Cons Pty Arts and Heritage Ctee 1979–83, All-Pty Heritage Ctee 1979–, Br-Croatian Parly Gp 1992–97, Br-Bosnian Parly Gp 1992–97 and 2001–, Br-Finnish Parly Gp 1992–, NI Affrs Ctee 2005–; memb: Select Ctee Educn Science and Arts 1979–83, Speaker's Panel of Chm in the House of Commons 1983–98, Foreign Affrs Ctee 2001–03; chm: House of Commons Works of Art Ctee 1987–2000, Cons Party Arts and Heritage Advsy Ctee 1988–99; dep shadow ldr House of Commons 1997–2000; rector's warden St Margaret's Westminster 1978–90, Parly warden 1990–92; visiting Parly fell St Antony's Coll Oxford 1994, visiting sr scholar Univ of Hull 1995–; ed House Magazine 1981–2004 (life pres 2005–), int pres First Magazine 1994–; elected govr ESU 1999; vice-chm Heritage in Danger; memb: Historic Buildings Cncl 1979–85, Faculty Jurisdiction Cmmn 1981–84, Royal Cmmn on Historical Manuscripts 1981–2003, Cncl Winston Churchill Meml Tst 1983–93, House of Commons Cmmn 2002–05, Nat Archives Cncl 2003–, Cncl for Br Archaeology; pres: Staffs Historic Churches Tst 1998– Staffs Parks and Gardens Tst 2006–; tstee: Historic Churches Preservation Tst 1972–2005 (vice-pres 2005), History of Parliament Tst 1983– (chm 2001–); memb Gen Synod C of E 1995–2005; Freeman City of London, Liveryman Worshipful Co of Glaziers & Painters of Glass; FSA (vice-pres 1994–98); hon citizen of Texas; Cdr Order of the Lion of Finland 1998; *Books* Heritage in Danger (1976), Right Turn (1978), Westminster Palace and Parliament (1981), Castles of Britain (1982), Wilberforce the Nation's Conscience (1983), English Cathedrals (1984); *Recreations* visiting old churches, fighting philistines, not sitting on fences; *Clubs* Athenaeum; *Style*— Sir Patrick Cormack, MP, FSA

CORMACK, Prof Robert John; s of John Cormack (d 1979), and Christina, *née* Milne (d 1992); *b* 14 December 1946; *Educ* Montrose Acad, Univ of Aberdeen (MA); *m* 1973, Dr Elisabeth Charlotte Fischer, da of Ludwig Fischer; 2 da (Kelly Ann b 16 July 1976, Flutra b 1 Jan 2000 (adopted 2003)), 1 s (Nicholas John Ludwig b 17 May 1979); *Career* Brown Univ USA 1969–73 (Woodrow Wilson fell 1972–73); Queen's Univ Belfast: lectr in sociology 1973–87, sr lectr 1987–92, reader 1992–95, prof 1995–, dean Faculty of Economics and Social Sciences 1993–95, pro-vice-chllr 1995–2001; princ UHI Millennium Inst 2001–; conslt Fair Employment Cmmn Standing Advsy Cmmn on Human Rights, memb Cncl Soc for Research into HE; expert contrib confs on HE Cncl of Europe; chm Belfast CAB 1989–93; FRSA 1999; *Books* Religion, Education and Employment (co-ed, 1983), Education and Social Policy in Northern Ireland (co-ed, 1987), Discrimination and Public Policy in Northern Ireland (co-ed, 1991), After the Reforms (co-ed, 1993); *Recreations* relaxing in the Highlands of Scotland; *Style*— Prof Robert Cormack; ⌧ UHI Millennium Institute, Executive Office, Ness Walk, Inverness IV3 5SQ (tel 01463 279000, fax 01463 279001, e-mail robert.cormack@eo.uhi.ac.uk)

CORMAN, Charles; *b* 23 October 1934; *Educ* St Paul's Sch, UCL (BA, LLB), Univ of Calif Berkeley (Fulbright scholar, LLM); *Career* assoc Goldstein Judd & Gurfein NY (attorneys) 1960; Dechert (formerly Titmuss Sainer Dechert solicitors): articles 1955–58, asst slr 1959 and 1960–61, ptnr 1963–97, conslt 1997–; *Style*— Charles Corman, Esq; ⌧ Dechert LLP, 160 Queen Victoria Street, London EC4V 4QQ (tel 020 7184 7000, fax 020 7184 7001)

CORNELL, David; s of Henry Arthur Cornell (d 1949), of London, and Edith Rose, *née* Short (d 1989); *b* 18 September 1935; *Educ* Central Sch of Art, Harrow Sch of Art, Acad of Fine Art Univ of Pennsylvania; *m* 1 (m dis) 2 s (Darren b 1963, Simon b 1965); *m* 2, Geraldine Anne, *née* Condron; 2 s (Paul b 1983, Steven b 1985); *Career* sculptor and medallist; mil serv in 42 Commando Royal Marines; won Royal Mint nat selection and was appointed coin and medal engraver 1965, dir of sculpture John Pinches Ltd, int dir Franklin Mint; collaborations incl work with Henry Moore, Pablo Picasso, Salvador Dali, Marc Chagall and Sir John Betjeman; specialises in official portraits of the Royal Family; designs for int coinage incl: Bahamas, Bermuda, China, Falkland Islands, New Zealand, Turkey and UAE; commissions incl: portrait cameos of the children of the Dutch Royal Family, birthday portrait of HM Queen Elizabeth the Queen Mother, portrait of Diana Princess of Wales, retirement bronze of Lestor Piggott, Unicorn bronze for Wellcome Fndn HQ, set of sovereigns depicting the Kings and Queens of England and their coats of arms, life-size bronze of Sir Arthur Conan Doyle, life-size portraits of Leonardo Di Caprio and Kate Moss, 21st birthday portrait of HRH Prince William, works for Royal Doulton, Welsh Porcelain, Spink, Coalport, Franklin Mint, Wedgwood, Richard Borek and the Richmond Herald of Arms; formerly judge at Goldsmiths and Silversmiths Art Cncl Awards of GB; vice-pres Soc of Portrait Sculptors 1977–, FRSA, FRBS; *Selected Exhibitions* Royal Acad London 1967, San Diego USA 1969, Krakow 1970, 14th Int Medaille Cologne 1975–79, Soc of Portrait Sculptors Mall Galleries London 1979, Guildhall London 1980, Hall Place Kent 1982, Palk Walk Galleries London 1983, Plazzotta Studio London 1984, Cadogan Gall London 1985, Blackheath Gall London 1986 and 1991, Harrods Fine Art Gall London 1987, St Albans Arts Festival 1988, Llewellyn Alexander London 1989, Seymours Gardens Surrey 1990, Henry Brett Gall Paris 1992, Woodlands Gall 1993, RBS London 1994, London Contemporary Art 1995, Docklands Gall London 1996, Alwin Davis Tunbridge Wells 1997 and 1998, Sausmarez Manor Guernsey 1999; *Recreations* brown belt at judo, swimming, running; *Style—* David Cornell, Esq; ✉ e-mail davidcornell1@aol.com, website www.davidcornell.com

CORNELL, Jim Scott; s of James William Cornell (d 1976), and Annie, *née* Scott (d 1994); *b* 3 August 1939; *Educ* Thirsk GS, Bradford Inst of Technol; *m* 28 July 1962, Winifred Eileen, da of John Rayner (d 1974); *Career* British Rail: student civil engr 1959–64, asst divnl civil engr King's Cross 1974–76, divnl civil engr King's Cross 1976–78, divnl civil engr Newcastle 1978–81, asst regnl civil engr York 1981–83, regnl civil engr Scotland 1983–84, dep gen mangr Scotrail 1984–86, gen mangr Scotrail 1986–87, dir civil engrg 1988–92, md Regnl Railways 1992–93, md Infrastructure Servs 1993–96, exec dir Railway Heritage Tst 1996–, non-exec dir Network Rail 2002–; Webb Prize ICE; CEng, FREng, FICE, FCILT, FCMI, FPWI; *Recreations* tennis, gardening; *Style—* Jim Cornell, FREng; ✉ Railway Heritage Trust, 40 Melton Street, London NW1 2EE (tel 020 7557 8090, fax 020 7557 9700)

CORNELL, Peter Charles Edward; s of Sydney Page Cornell (d 1997), and Marjorie Joan, *née* Edwards (d 1998); *b* 5 October 1952, Tonbridge, Kent; *Educ* Tonbridge Sch, Univ of Exeter, Chester Coll of Law; *m* Bernadette, *née* Conway; 1 s (Tom b 22 Nov 1985), 3 da (Kate b 16 July 1987, Stephanie b 2 May 1989, Isabel b 25 Sept 1991); *Career* trainee Clifford Chance 1975–78; managing ptnr Clifford Chance: Singapore office 1983–85, Madrid office 1990–2000, Barcelona office 1993–2000, Europe 1995–2000; global managing ptnr Clifford Chance 2001–06; guest lectr: Harvard Business Sch, Madrid Business Sch; Lawyer of the Year Legal Business 2007; *Recreations* family, sport; *Clubs* Roehampton, La Moraleja (Madrid), Club de Campo (Madrid); *Style—* Peter Cornell, Esq; ✉ Cornell Institute, 71 Camino Ancho, Madrid 28109, Spain

CORNER, Timothy Frank; QC (2002); s of Frank Herbert Corner (d 1983), and June Ruby, *née* Benson; *b* 25 July 1958, Salford; *Educ* Bolton Sch, Magdalen Coll Oxford (Demy, MA, BCL); *Career* called to the Bar Gray's Inn 1981; recorder 2004–; chair Advsy Panel on Standards for the Planning Inspectorate 2006–, vice-chm Planning and Environment Bar Assoc 2004–; *Clubs* Athenaeum; *Style—* Timothy Corner, Esq, QC; ✉ 4–5 Gray's Inn Square, Gray's Inn, London WC1R 5AH (tel 020 7404 5252)

CORNES, John Addis; s of John Frederick Cornes; *b* 16 August 1944; *Educ* Eton, Univ of Oxford; *m* 1971, Veronica Mary Alicia; 2 c; *Career* dir UBS Wealth Mgmnt Ltd; dir West Downs School Ltd; chm: Gloucester 15 Ltd, Gloucester 13 Ltd; tstee: London Catalyst, Royal Coll of Music Investments; treas LEPRA; Liveryman Worshipful Co of Grocers; *Recreations* walking, watching sport; *Style—* John Cornes, Esq; ✉ 23 West End Terrace, Winchester, Hampshire SO22 5EN

CORNFORD, James Peters; s of John Cornford (d 1936), and Rachel Peters (d 1985); *b* 25 January 1935; *Educ* Winchester, Trinity Coll Cambridge (Earl of Derby student, sr scholar, MA); *m* 1960, Avery Amanda, da of late B R Goodfellow; 1 s (Thomas b 1964), 3 da (Frances b 1965, Emma b 1968, Sophie b 1970); *Career* fell Trinity Coll Cambridge 1960–64, Harkness fell Cwlth Fund 1961–62; research assoc Dept of Sociology Univ of Calif Berkeley 1961, attached to Dept of Political Science Univ of Chicago 1961–62; Univ of Edinburgh: lectr in politics 1964–68, prof of politics 1968–76, dir Outer Circle Policy Unit 1976–80, dir Nuffield Fndn 1980–88; dir: Inst for Public Policy Research 1989–94, The Paul Hamlyn Fndn 1994–97; chm Constitution Unit Faculty of Laws UCL 1995–97, special advsr to the Chllr of the Duchy of Lancaster 1997–98; literary ed The Political Quarterly 1977–93, chm Political Quarterly Publishing Co 1993–99; chm Job Ownership Ltd 1998–2002 (dir 1979–97), chm Cncl Campaign for Freedom of Info 1984–97 and 1998–; dep dir Inst of Community Studies 1998–2000, chm School for Social Entrepreneurs 2000–02; tstee and chm South African Advanced Educn Project 1987–98, tstee UnLtd The Fndn for Social Entrepreneurs 2001–05; chm Dartington Hall Tst 2001– (tstee 1998–), tstee The Young Fndn 2005–; author of numerous reports and articles on political and constitutional subjects; visiting fell All Souls Coll Oxford 1975–76; FRHistS 1970; *Style—* James Cornford, Esq; ✉ Osborne House, High Street, Stoke Ferry, Kings Lynn, Norfolk PE33 9SF (tel 01366 500808, e-mail j.cornford808@btinternet.com)

CORNICK, Roger Courtenay; s of William Charles Cornick (d 1968), of Singapore, and Cynthia Avisa Louise, *née* Courtenay; *b* 13 February 1944; *Educ* various army schs in Egypt, Queen Elizabeth's Sch Crediton Devon; *m* 8 July 1995, Susan Mary (Susie); 2 da (Kate Elizabeth b April 1979, Victoria Rose b Feb 1981); *Career* trainee Royal Insurance Group 1963–68, rep Abbey Life Assurance Co 1968–70, asst dir Hambro Life Assurance Ltd 1970–77, dir Crown Financial Management Ltd 1977–80, ptnr Courtenay Manning Partners 1980–83, dep chm and gp mktg dir Perpetual plc 1982–2000; non-exec dir Aberdeen Asset Management 2004–; tstee River and Rowing Museum; *Recreations* golf, tennis, skiing, theatre; *Clubs* Riverside, Royal Mid-Surrey Golf; *Style—* Roger Cornick, Esq

CORNISH, Alan Stewart; s of Alfred Stewart Cornish (d 1980), of Orpington, Kent, and Ann Selina, *née* Westgate (d 2000); *b* 27 April 1944; *Educ* Beckenham and Penge GS; *m* 8 March 1969, Daphne Elisabeth, da of Charles Gordon Saunders; 3 s (Nigel b 1972, Graham b 1975, Iain b 1982); *Career* gp fin controller Associated Communications Corporation plc 1975–82, vice-pres Euro regnl office RCA Records 1982–84, gp chief exec Good Relations Group plc 1984–86, gp md Lowe Bell Communications Ltd 1986–89, chm and chief exec Deal Holdings Ltd 1989–90, chm Cornish Ltd 1989–98, chief fin offr Hilton International 1992–95, gp chief exec Eurobell (Holdings) plc 1996–2000, chief exec Deutsche Telekom Ltd 1997–99, dir Cable Communications Assoc 1996–99, dep chm MORI 2000–04; chm: Management Team Ltd 2001–04, Unitel Communications Ltd 2001–02, Azzurri Communications Ltd 2003–, Local Press Ltd 2004–05, Telecity plc 2004–05; London Borough of Bromley: cncllr 1974–80, dep ldr 1976–78, dep mayor 1978–79; fndr memb Orpington Dist Guide Dogs for the Blind Assoc; FCMA 1976 (assoc 1971), FCMI 1978, FInstD 1986; *Recreations* sport; *Clubs* local golf; *Style—* Alan Cornish, Esq; ✉ Aspens, 42 Oxenden Wood Road, Chelsfield Park, Orpington, Kent BR6 6HP (tel 01689 856880, fax 01689 860091, e-mail ascanddec@aol.com)

CORNISH, Charles T (Charlie); s of Charlie Cornish, of Strathaven, Strathclyde, and late Isabel, *née* McEwan; *b* 30 November 1959, Hamilton, Strathclyde; *Educ* Univ of Strathclyde (BA), Inst of Personnel and Devpt (Dip); *m* Margo; 1 s (Calum), 3 da (Eilidh, Katie, Fiona); *Career* chief exec West of Scotland Water 2001 (customer services dir 1997); RWE Thames: global business performance dir 2001, chief operating offr UK 2003; md United Utilities NW and gp bd (P2C) exec dir United Utilities 2004–; dir Young Enterprise UK, chm Young Enterprise NW, memb Mersey Employment Coalition; *Recreations* golf, football; *Style—* Charlie Cornish, Esq; ✉ tel 01925 234000, fax 01925 233024, e-mail charlie.cornish@uuplc.co.uk

CORNISH, Prof William Rodolph; Hon QC (1997); s of Jack Rodolph Cornish (d 1978), and Elizabeth Ellen, *née* Reid; *b* 9 August 1937; *Educ* St Peter's Coll Adelaide, Univ of Adelaide (LLB), Univ of Oxford (BCL), Univ of Cambridge (LLD); *m* 25 July 1964, Lovedy Elizabeth, da of Edward Christopher Moule (d 1942); 1 s (Peter b 1968), 2 da (Anna b 1970, Cecilia b 1972); *Career* lectr in law LSE 1962–68, reader QMC London 1969–70, prof of English law LSE 1970–90, prof of law Univ of Cambridge 1990–95, dir Centre for Euro Legal Studies 1991–94, Herchel Smith prof of intellectual property law Univ of Cambridge 1995–2004, pres Magdalene Coll Cambridge 1998–2001; external academic memb Max Planck Inst for Patent Law Munich 1989–; bencher Gray's Inn 1998; FBA 1984; *Books* The Jury (2 edn, 1970), Law and Society in England 1750–1950 (1989), Intellectual Property: Patents, Copyright, Trade Marks and Allied Rights (5 edn, 2003); *Style—* Prof William Cornish, QC, FBA; ✉ Magdalene College, Cambridge CB3 0AG

CORNWALL-JONES, Mark Ralph; OBE (2004); s of Brig Arthur Thomas Cornwall-Jones, CMG, CBE (d 1980), and Marie Joan Evelyn, *née* Hammersley-Smith; *b* 14 February 1933; *Educ* Glenalmond Coll, Jesus Coll Cambridge (MA); *m* 1959, Priscilla, da of Col Harold E Yeo (d 1957); 1 da (Kate b 1961), 3 s (Adam b 1964, Matthew b 1967, Jason b 1969); *Career* investment mangr: The Debenture Corporation 1959–67, John Govett and Co Ltd 1967–90 (investment dir 1983–88); chm Allchurches Tst, dir Trades Union Fund Managers and other cos; treas The Corporation of the Church House; *Recreations* books, stalking, gardening, sailing, carpentry; *Clubs* Boodle's; *Style—* Mark Cornwall-Jones, Esq, OBE; ✉ Erin House, 3 Albert Bridge Road, Battersea SW11 4PX

CORNWALLIS, 3 Baron (UK 1927); Fiennes Neil Wykeham Cornwallis; OBE (1963), DL (Kent 1976); only s of 2 Baron Cornwallis, KBE, KCVO, MC, JP, DL (d 1982), by his 1 w, Cecily (d 1943), da of Sir James Heron Walker, 3 Bt; *b* 29 June 1921; *Educ* Eton; *m* 1, 17 Oct 1942 (m dis 1948), Judith, o da of Lt-Col Geoffrey Lacy Scott, TD; 1 s, 1 da (decd); m 2, 1 June 1951, Agnes Jean (d 2001), yr da of Capt Henderson Russell Landale; 1 s, 3 da; m 3, 6 April 2002, Stephanie, o da of Capt Reginald Phillips Minchin, OBE, RA, and wid of F Anthony H Coleman; *Heir* s (by 1 w), Hon Jeremy Cornwallis; *Career* served WWII Lt Coldstream Gds (1941–44, then invalided); pres: Br Agric Contractors' Assoc 1952–54, Nat Assoc of Agric Contractors 1957–63 and 1986–98; dir Planet Building Society 1968– (chm 1971–75); chm: Magnet and Planet Building Society 1975–79, Town and Country Building Society 1979–81 and 1990–92 (dir 1979–92), CBI Smaller Firms Cncl 1974–82 (chm 1979–82); pres English Apples and Pears Ltd 1993–97 (chm 1989–93); memb Bd of Tstees Chevening Estate 1979–98; rep of Horticultural Co-operatives in EEC 1975–86; vice-pres Fedn of Agric Co-operatives 1984–86; chm: FAC Fruit Forum 1972–89, Kingdom Quality Assurance Scheme 1986–89, All-Pty Parly Br Fruit Gp 1994–98; exec govr Cobham Hall Sch 1962–69, govr Sevenoaks Sch 1992–99; Pro Grand Master (Freemasons) United Grand Lodge 1982–91 (previously Dep Grand Master), Liveryman Worshipful Co of Fruiterers; FIHort, FRPSL; *Recreations* fishing, philately; *Clubs* Brooks's, Flyfishers'; *Style—* The Rt Hon the Lord Cornwallis, OBE, DL

CORNWELL, Bernard; OBE (2006); s of William Oughtred, of British Columbia, Canada, and Dorothy Cornwell; *b* 23 February 1944; *Educ* Monkton Combe Sch, Coll of St Mark and St John London (BA); *m* 1970 (m dis 1976), Lindsay Leworthy; 1 da (Antonia b 4 Oct 1971); m 2, 1980, Judy Cashdollar; *Career* prodr Current Affairs BBC TV 1971–76, head Current Affairs BBC Northern Ireland 1976–79, ed News Thames TV 1979–80; freelance writer 1981–; *Books* Sharpe's Eagle, Sharpe's Gold, Sharpe's Company, Sharpe's Sword, Sharpe's Enemy, Sharpe's Honour, Sharpe's Regiment, Sharpe's Siege, Sharpe's Rifles, Sharpe's Revenge, Sharpe's Waterloo, Sharpe's Devil, Sharpe's Battle, Sharpe's Tiger, Sharpe's Triumph, Sharpe's Fortress, Sharpe's Trafalgar, Sharpe's Prey, Sharpe's Havoc, Sharpe's Escape, Rebel, Copperhead, Battle Flag, The Bloody Ground, Redcoat, Wildtrack, Sea Lord, Crackdown, Stormchild, Scoundrel, The Winter King, Enemy of God, Excalibur, Stonehenge, Harlequin, Gallows Thief, Vagabond, Heretic, The Last Kingdom, The Pale Horseman, Lords of the North Country; *Recreations* sailing, scuba diving, swimming; *Style—* Bernard Cornwell, Esq, OBE; ✉ c/o Toby Eady Associates Ltd, 9 Orme Court, London W2 4RL (tel 020 7792 0092, fax 020 7792 0879, e-mail bc@bernardcornwell.net, website www.bernardcornwell.net)

CORNWELL, David John Moore; *see:* Le Carré, John

CORNWELL, Judy Valerie; da of Darcy Nigel Barry Cornwell (d 1967), of Australia, and Irene, *née* McCullen (d 1996); *b* 22 February 1940; *Educ* Convent of Mercy Australia, Lewes GS; *m* 18 Dec 1960, John Kelsall Parry, *qv*, s of Edward Parry (d 1983), of Loughborough; 1 s (Edward Dylan b 20 June 1965); *Career* actress and author; pres: Relate (Brighton) 1988–94, Nat Assoc of Deaf Children (E Sussex) 1984–97, Brighton and Hove Entertainment Mangrs' Assoc 1998–2000; chm Brighton Alcohol Recovery Shelter (BARS) 1983–95; memb: Bd West Pier Tst 1974–89, Cncl Equity 1982–85, Bd Inst of Alcohol Studies 1983–91; memb: Equity 1955, Soc of Authors 1986, PEN 1989, Royal Soc of Literature 1994; JP Brighton and Hove 1985–97; *Television* Younger Generation plays 1961 (nominated Tommorrow's Star Actress Daily Mirror 1961), Call Me Daddy (Emmy Award) 1967, Moody and Pegg 1974, Cakes and Ale 1974 (nominated Best Actress SFTA), The Good Companions 1980, Keeping Up Appearances 1990–95; *Radio* The Navy Lark 1962, The Scan 1999; *Theatre* Oh! What A Lovely War 1963, RSC season at Stratford-upon-Avon 1972, Bed Before Yesterday 1976, Rose (NZ tour) 1981, The Government Inspector 1988, The Cemetery Club 1993, Romeo and Juliet 1997; *Films* Wuthering Heights 1971, Santa Claus The Movie 1985, Persuasion 1994, David Copperfield 1999; *Books* Cow and Cowparsley (1985), Fishcakes at the Ritz (1989), Seventh Sunrise (1993), Fear and Favour (1996), Adventures of a Jellybaby (autobiography, 2005); *Recreations* travel, philosophy, reading; *Style—* Ms Judy Cornwell; ✉ c/o Ken McReddie Ltd, 36–40 Glasshouse Street, London W1B 5DL

CORNWELL, Prof Keith John; *b* 4 April 1942; *Educ* Rickmansworth GS, Watford Tech Coll, City Univ (BSc, PhD), Heriot-Watt Univ (DEng); m; 2 c; *Career* apprentice then engrg designer J G Slatter Ltd 1959–65, Electricity Cncl research fell and latterly lectr Middlesex Poly 1965–70, sr lectr Dept of Mechanical Engrg Heriot-Watt Univ 1979–82 (lectr 1970–79), md KC Heat Pumps Ltd and KC Products Ltd 1982–86; Dept of Mechanical and Chemical Engrg Heriot-Watt Univ: reader and dir Energy Technol Unit 1986–87, head of dept 1989–93 (dep head 1988–89), dean of engrg 1993–96, dir of quality 1996–2003; head Sch of Mathematical and Computing Sciences 2003–06, head Dubai Campus Herriot-Watt Univ 2006–; CEng, FIMechE; author of over 80 pubns; *Style—* Prof Keith Cornwell; ✉ Heriot-Watt University, Riccarton, Edinburgh EH14 4AS (tel 0131 451 3201, e-mail k.cornwell@hw.ac.uk)

CORNWELL, Rupert Howard; s of Ronald Cornwell (d 1975), of Maidenhead, and Jean Margaret Cornwell; *b* 22 February 1946; *Educ* Winchester, Magdalen Coll Oxford (BA); *m* 1, April 1972, Angela Doria; 1 s (Sean b Oct 1974); m 2, March 1988, Susan Jean, da of Samuel Smith, of Edwardsville, Illinois; *Career* journalist; Reuters: joined London 1968, Paris 1969, Brussels 1969–70, Paris 1970–72; Financial Times: joined 1972, Foreign Desk

1972, Paris Bureau 1973–76, lobby corr Westminster 1976–78, Rome corr 1978–83, Bonn corr 1983–86; The Independent: joined 1986, Moscow corr 1987–91, former Washington corr from 1991, currently with The Independent; Foreign Correspondent of the Year Granada 1988, David Holden prize 1989; *Books* God's Banker, The Life of Roberto Calvi (1983); *Recreations* foreign languages, cricket, travel; *Style*— Rupert Cornwell, Esq; ✉ The Independent, Independent House, 191 Marsh Wall, London E14 9RS (tel 020 7293 2000)

CORP, Rev Ronald Geoffrey; SSC; s of Geoffrey Charles Corp, and Elsie Grace, *née* Kinchin; *b* 4 January 1951; *Educ* Blue Sch Wells, ChCh Oxford (MA), Univ of Southampton (DipTheol); *Career* librarian, prodr and presenter BBC Radio 3 1973–87; composer: various choral works, And All the Trumpets Sounded (cantata) performed 1989, Laudamus (cantata) performed 1994, Four Elizabethan Lyrics 1994, Cornucopia 1997, Piano Concerto performed 1997, A New Song performed 1999, Mass 'Christ Our Future' 2001, Mary's Song 2001, Adonai Echad 2001, Kaleidoscope 2002, Missa San Marco 2002, Dover Beach 2003, Forever Child 2004, Guernsey Postcards 2004, Waters of Time 2006; conductor: Highgate Choral Soc 1984–, London Choral Soc 1985–, New London Orch 1988–, New London Children's Choir 1991–; dir of choir (Jr Dept) RCM 1993–95; dir New London Collegium 1994–96; various recordings with New London Orch and New London Children's Choir; involved with: BBC Singers, BBC Scottish Symphony Orch; tstee Musicians Benevolent Fund 2000– (chm Educn Ctee 2003–), vice-pres The Sullivan Soc; memb: Assoc of Br Choral Directors; non-stipendiary min St Mary's Kilburn with St James' West End Lane 1998–2002, non-stipendiary asst curate Christ Church Hendon 2002–07, asst priest St Alban's Holborn 2007–; Freeman Worshipful Co of Musicians 2007; *Books* The Choral Singer's Companion (1987 and 2000); *Recreations* reading; *Style*— The Rev Ronald Corp, SSC; ✉ 76 Brent Street, London NW4 2ES (e-mail ronald.corp@btconnect.com)

CORRALL, Dr Roger James Martin; s of Alfred James Corrall (d 1985), and Amy Adeline, *née* Martin; *b* 4 August 1944; *Educ* Univ of Edinburgh (BSc, MB ChB, MD); *m* 19 Feb 1972, Rhona Lockyer, da of Maxwell Cameron McIntosh; 1 s (Euan James b 4 April 1974), 1 da (Fiona Helen b 1 Jan 1976); *Career* registrar in gen med diabetes and metabolic disorders Royal Infirmary Edinburgh 1970–71, clinical res fell in endocrinology Case Western Reserve Univ Cleveland OH 1971–73, sr registrar Edinburgh Northern Gp of Hosps 1975, hon clinical tutor Dept of Med Univ of Edinburgh 1975, conslt physician specialising in diabetes and endocrinology Bristol Royal Infirmary 1979–; author of in excess of 200 scientific pubns on diabetes, clinical endocrinology and hypoglycaemia; memb: Br Diabetic Assoc, Autonomic Research Soc, Euro Assoc for the Study of Diabetes, Euro Soc for Clinical Investigation, MRS; MRCP 1970, FRCPEd 1984, FRCP 1985; *Recreations* music, theatre, the arts, wine, history, British countryside, dogs; *Style*— Dr Roger Corrall; ✉ 10 Elgin Park Road, Redland, Bristol BS6 6RU; Directorate of Medicine, Bristol Royal Infirmary, Bristol BS2 8HW (tel 0117 928 2768, fax 0117 928 4081, e-mail roger.corrall@googlemail.com)

CORRICK, Philip; s of Frank Corrick (d 1999), of Sidmouth, Devon, and Violet, *née* Willey (d 1991); *b* 30 March 1954; *Educ* Sidmouth Secdy Modern Sch, Exeter Coll (City & Guilds); *m* Karen, *née* Geddes; 1 s (Cameron b 16 Dec 1996), 1 da (Olivia b 20 Jan 1999); *Career* jr sous chef Claridges Hotel London 1979–80, sous chef The Berkeley Knightsbridge 1980–84, exec chef Westbury Hotel London 1984–87, exec chef (all restaurants) Grosvenor House Park Lane 1989–90, exec chef Royal Automobile Club 1990–; affiliate memb Académie Culinaire de France 1986, memb Assoc Culinaire Française 1995; Trusthouse Forte Chef of the Year 1988, finalist Meilleur Ouvrier de Grande Bretagne 1991, Maitrise Escoffier Award (Conseil Culinaire) 1998; *Recreations* music, swimming; *Clubs* Barnsdale Country; *Style*— Philip Corrick, Esq; ✉ 12 Westfield Way, Langtoft, Peterborough PE6 9RH (tel 01778 380269); The RAC, 89–91 Pall Mall, London SW1Y 5HS (tel 020 7747 3377, fax 020 7976 1086, e-mail chef@royalautomobileclub.co.uk)

CORRIE, His Hon Judge Thomas Graham Edgar Corrie; s of John Alexander Galloway Corrie, OBE, MC (d 1986), of Chobham, Surrey, and Barbara Phyllis, *née* Turner; *b* 18 December 1946; *Educ* Eton, BNC Oxford (MA); *m* 17 July 1971, Anna, da of John Logsdail; 2 da (Tamsin Laura b 12 Dec 1974, Alice Kate Marguerite b 6 Nov 1976), 1 s (Matthew John Galloway b 4 June 1981); *Career* called to the Bar Gray's Inn 1969; in practice 1971–94, circuit remembrancer 1988–94, recorder 1988–94, circuit judge (Midland & Oxford Circuit) 1994–; Freeman City of London; *Recreations* gardening, cycling, canal boating; *Clubs* Frewen (Oxford); *Style*— His Hon Judge Corrie; ✉ Oxford Combined Court Centre, St Aldates, Oxford OX1 1TL (tel 01865 264200)

CORRIGAN, Clare; da of Major J B Corrigan, and Frances Corrigan; *Educ* St Martin's Sch of Art (BA); *Career* fashion designer; knitwear designer Thierry Mugler Paris, knitwear designer Karl Lagerfeld Paris, ready-to-wear designer Liberty London; *Recreations* travelling, contemporary art, breeding daschunds; *Style*— Ms Clare Corrigan

CORRIGAN, Prof (Francis) Edward (Ed); s of Anthony Corrigan (d 1994), and Eileen, *née* Ryan; *b* 10 August 1946; *Educ* St Bede's Coll Manchester, Christ's Coll Cambridge (MA, PhD); *m* 18 July 1970, Jane Mary, *née* Halton; 2 da (Anna Louise b 16 July 1972, Laura Jane b 13 July 1982); 2 s (David Noel b 22 Dec 1974, Richard Francis b 11 July 1984); *Career* academic; Univ of Durham: Addison Wheeler Fell 1972–74, CERN Fell 1974–76, lectr in applied mathematics 1976, sr lectr 1982, Sir Derman Chistopherson Fndn fell 1983–84, reader 1987, prof of mathematics 1992–99, visiting prof in the Centre for Particle Theory 1999–2002; prof of mathematics and head of dept Univ of York 1999–; external examiner for universities incl: Cambridge, Imperial Coll, Edinburgh, Hull; awarded Daiwa-Adrian Prize 1998; memb numerous ctees Univ of Durham 1979–99; hon ed Jl of Physics A 1999–2003; memb: London Mathematical Soc 1989, IMA 1998; FRS 1995, FInstP 1999; *Publications* articles on mathematics and theoretical physics in numerous learned jls; *Recreations* squash, piano, walking; *Style*— Prof Edward Corrigan, FRS; ✉ University of York, Heslington, York YO10 5DD (tel 01904 433774, fax 01904 433071, ec9@york.ac.uk)

CORRIGAN, District Judge Peter William; s of William Corrigan, of Bristol, and Dorothy, *née* Bird (d 1993); *b* 28 March 1949; *Educ* Clifton, Univ of Leeds (LLB); *m* 26 Feb 1987, Meriel; 3 s (James, Edward, Christopher), 1 da (Sara); *Career* slr; articled clerk and asst slr Wansbrough Willey and Hargrave until 1976, ptnr Porter Dodsons 1976–99; district judge: Torquay and Plymouth 1999–2005, Weston-super-Mare, Taunton and Bristol 2005–; memb Law Soc; *Recreations* golf, tennis, cricket, rugby and soccer, current affairs, reading and theatre; *Clubs* Sportsman's, Taunton, Mendip Golf; *Style*— District Judge Corrigan

CORRIGAN, Richard; *b* 10 February 1964; *m* Maria; 1 da, 2 s; *Career* restaurateur and chef; trainee chef Kirwin Hotel Co Meath and Kylemore Hotel Co Cavan 1978–81, chef de partie various hotels in Holland 1981–85; head chef: The Meridien Hotel Picadilly 1985–86, Blandford St W1 1986–87, Mulligan's Mayfair, Bentleys W1, Fulham Road (Michelin star); launched Searcy's Barbican 1996 (formed partnership with Searcy's), prop and chef Lindsay House Soho 1997– (Michelin Star 1999–, Outstanding London Chef Carlton London Restaurant Awards 2000); conslt BA Culinary Cncl; *Books* From the Waters and the Wild (1999); *Recreations* reading; *Clubs* Groucho; *Style*— Richard Corrigan, Esq; ✉ Lindsay House, 21 Romilly Street, London W1D 5AF (tel 020 7439 0450, fax 020 7437 7349, e-mail richardcorrigan@lindsayhouse.co.uk)

CORRIGAN, Thomas Stephen; OBE (1999); s of Thomas Corrigan (d 1992), and Renée Victorine, *née* Chaborel (d 1994); *b* 2 July 1932; *Educ* Beulah Hill; *m* 1963, Sally Margaret, da of George Ernest Everitt (d 1980); 2 da (Caroline (Mrs Kenneth Clancy), Linda (Mrs Gerard Comyns)); *Career* chartered accountant; chm: Inveresk Group plc 1974–83 (md 1971–83), Havelock Europa plc 1983–89, Post Office Users' Nat Cncl 1984–94, Rex Stewart Group plc 1987–91, Rex Stewart Tst 1989–97, Direct Mail Accreditation and Recognition Centre 1995–97; also dir various other cos; pres Br Paper and Board Industry Fedn 1975–77, vice-pres European Confedn of Pulp, Paper and Packaging Industries 1981–82; chm 2change 2003–; memb ind judging panel Charter Mark Awards Cabinet Office 2001–03 (advsr and chief assessor 1994–2000); memb London Award Panel Prince's Tst 2001–; memb Investment Ctee Printers' Charitable Corporation 2005–; Master Worshipful Co of: Makers of Playing Cards 1978–79, Stationers and Newspaper Makers 1990–91, Marketors 1995; *Recreations* golf, tennis, bridge; *Clubs* MCC, R&A, Walton Heath Golf; *Style*— Thomas Corrigan, Esq, OBE; ✉ 57 Marsham Court, Marsham Street, London SW1P 4JZ (tel 020 7828 2078)

C

CORRIN, His Hon John William; CBE (1995); s of Evan Cain Corrin (d 1967), of IOM, and Dorothy Mildred, *née* Teare (d 1990); *b* 6 January 1932; *Educ* King William's Coll; *m* 1961, Dorothy Patricia Corrin, OBE, da of John Stanley Lace (d 1964), of IOM; 1 da (Jane b 1965); *Career* HM first deemster, clerk of the Rolls 1988–98, HM attorney gen for IOM 1974–80, HM second deemster 1980–88, dep govr IOM 1988–98; Freeman Borough of Douglas 1998; *Recreations* music, bridge, gardening; *Style*— His Hon J W Corrin, CBE; ✉ 28 Devonshire Road, Douglas, Isle of Man (tel 01624 621806)

CORRY, Dan; *Career* economist Dept of Employment 1984–86, economist Treasy 1986–89, advsr Lab Pty Front Bench economics team 1989–92, sr economist IPPR 1992–97, special advsr to Sec of State for Trade and Indust 1997–2001, special advsr to Sec of State for Transport, Local Govt and the Regions 2001–02, dir New Local Govt Network 2002–05, special advsr to Sec of State for Educn 2005–06, special advsr to Sec of State for Communities and Local Govt 2006–; fndr ed IPPR Jl New Economy; *Publications* author of numerous books on the regulation of utilities; numerous essays and articles on economic policy, political economy, and the role of the market in professional sport; several pamphlets on new localism and aspects of local govt; *Style*— Dan Corry, Esq

CORRY, Sir James Michael; 5 Bt (UK 1885), of Dunraven, Co Antrim; s of Lt Cdr Sir William Corry, 4 Bt (d 2000); *b* 3 October 1946; *Educ* Downside; *m* 1973, Sheridan Lorraine, da of Arthur Peter Ashbourne (d 2007); 3 s (William James Alexander b 1981, Robert Philip John b 1984, Christopher Myles Anthony b 1987); *Heir* s, William Corry; *Career* Shell-Mex and BP 1966–75, BP 1975–2001 (latterly ops mangr Gas Dept BP Nederland BV Amsterdam); *Style*— Sir James Corry, Bt; ✉ Chackeridge Cottage, Ashbrittle, Wellington, Somerset TA21 0LJ (tel 01823 672993, e-mail james.corry@btopenworld.com)

CORRY, Martin Edward; MBE (2004); s of David Corry, and Mary, *née* Davies; *b* 12 October 1973; *Educ* Tunbridge Wells GS, Univ of Northumbria (BA); *Career* rugby union player; formerly with: Tunbridge Wells RFC, Newcastle Gosforth RFC, Bristol RFC; with Leicester Tigers 1997– (capt 2005–, champions Premiership 1999, 2000, 2001 and 2002, winners European Cup 2001 and 2002); England: 58 caps, debut 1997, winners World Cup Aust 2003, memb squad World Cup France 2007; memb British and Irish Lions touring squad Aust 2001 and NZ 2005; Zurich Premiership Player of the Season 2005; *Style*— Martin Corry, Esq, MBE

CORSAR, Col Charles Herbert Kenneth; LVO (1989), OBE (1981), TD 1960, DL (Midlothian 1975); s of Capt Kenneth Charles Corsar (d 1967), of Midlothian, and Winifred Paton, *née* Herdman (d 1989); *b* 13 May 1926; *Educ* Merchiston Castle Sch Edinburgh, King's Coll Cambridge (MA); *m* 25 April 1953, Hon Mary Drummond Buchanan-Smith, da of Rt Hon Lord Balerno of Currie; 2 s (George b 1954, David b 1957), 3 da (Kathleen b and d 1960, Katharine b 1961, Mary b 1965); *Career* TA Col 1972–75, Hon ADC to HM The Queen 1977–81, Hon Col 1/52 Lowland Volunteers 1975–87, chm Lowland TA & VRA 1984–87; cncllr for Midlothian 1958–67, JP 1965, zone cmmr Home Def E Scotland 1972–75, pres Edinburgh Bn Boys' Bde 1969–87 (vice-pres UK 1970–91), chm Scottish Standing Conf of Voluntary Youth Orgns 1973–78, memb Scottish Sports Cncl 1972–75, chm Earl Haig Fund Scotland 1984–90; govr: Clifton Hall Sch 1965–90, Merchiston Castle Sch Edinburgh 1975–89; sec Royal Jubilee and Prince's Tsts (Lothians and Borders) 1977–93; sec for Scotland Duke of Edinburgh's Award Scheme 1966–87; Vice Lord-Lt Midlothian 1993–96; *Recreations* gardening; *Clubs* New (Edinburgh); *Style*— Col Charles H K Corsar, LVO, OBE, TD, DL; ✉ 8564 South Oswald Road, Edinburgh EH9 2HH (tel and fax 0131 662 0194)

CORSTON, Baroness (Life Peer UK 2005), of St George in the County and City of Bristol; Jean Ann Corston; PC (2003); da of late Charles (Laurie) Parkin, and late Eileen Parkin; *b* 5 May 1942; *Educ* Yeovil Girls' HS, LSE (LLB 1989), Inns of Court Sch of Law; *m* 1, 1961, Christopher Corston; 1 s, 1 da; m 2, 1985, Prof Peter Townsend, *qv*; *Career* called to the Bar Inner Temple 1990; organiser Taunton Lab Pty 1974–76, regnl organiser SW Regn Lab Pty 1981–85 (asst regnl organiser 1976–81), asst nat agent London 1985–86, sec Lab Pty Annual Conf arrangements 1985–86, MP (Lab) Bristol E 1992–2005; PPS to sec of state for Educn and Employment 1997–2000; memb Select Ctee on: Agric 1992–95, Home Affrs 1995–97; chair All-Pty Gp on Parenting, sec All-Pty Parly Child Support Agency Monitoring Gp 1993–97, chair Jt Ctee on Human Rights 2001–05; PLP: chair 2001–05, vice-chair 1997–98 and 1999–2000, co-chair PLP Women's Gp 1992–97, chair Children and the Family Gp 1995–97, chair Civil Liberties Gp 1997–2005; chair Cwlth Women Parliamentarians 2000; memb: TGWU, Co-op Party, Exec Ctee Cwlth Parly Assoc UK 1999–2005; *Recreations* gardening, reading, walking; *Style*— The Rt Hon the Lady Corston, PC

CORTAZZI, Sir (Henry Arthur) Hugh; GCMG (1984, KCMG 1980, CMG 1969); s of Frederick Edward Mervyn Cortazzi (d 1966), of Sedbergh, Cumbria, and Madge, *née* Miller (d 1945); *b* 2 May 1924; *Educ* Sedbergh, Univ of St Andrews, Univ of London; *m* 3 April 1956, Elizabeth Esther, da of George Henry Simon Montagu (d 1976), of London; 1 s (William b 1961), 2 da (Rosemary b 1964, Charlotte b 1967); *Career* served RAF 1943–47; joined FO 1949, former cnsllr (Commercial) Tokyo, RCDS 1971–72, min (Commercial) Washington 1972–75, dep under sec of state FCO 1975–80, ambass to Japan 1980–84; dir: Hill Samuel Bank Ltd 1984–91, F & C Pacific Investment Trust 1984–98 (non-exec), GT Japan Investment Trust 1984–99 (non-exec); non-exec chm Thornton Pacific Investment Fund (SICAV) 1986–2001; advsr to: Mitsukoshi Ltd 1984–, NEC Corp Japan 1992–98, Dai-ichi Kangyo Bank Japan 1992–99, Bank of Kyoto 1992–99, Wilde Sapte slrs London 1992–99, PIFC 1993–99, Matsuura Machinery Co Ltd 1996–2000 and 2004–; memb ESRC 1984–90, pres Asiatic Soc of Japan 1982 and 1983, chm Cncl Japan Soc London 1985–95 (hon chm 1995–96, hon vice-pres 1996–), memb Ct Univ of Sussex 1985–92; Hon DUniv Stirling 1988, Hon DLitt UEA 2006; hon fell Robinson Coll Cambridge 1988; Yamagata Banto Prize Osaka 1991; Grand Cordon Order of the Sacred Treasure (Japan) 1995; *Books* translations from Japanese: Genji Keita - The Ogre and other stories of Japanese Salarymen (1972), The Guardian God of Golf and other humorous stories (1972), both reprinted as The Lucky One (1980); Mary Crawford Fraser: A Diplomat's Wife in Japan - Sketches at the Turn of the Century (ed, 1982), Isles of Gold - Antique Maps of Japan (1983), Dr Willis in Japan - British Medical Pioneer 1862–1877 (1985), Mitford's Japan - The Memoirs and Recollections of the First Lord Redesdale (ed, 1986), A British Artist in Meiji Japan (ed, 1991), Britain and Japan - Themes and Personalities (ed with Gordon Daniels, 1991), Richard Henry Brunton - Building Japan 1868–1876 (ed, 1991); Victorians in Japan - In and around the Treaty Ports (1987), Kipling's Japan (ed with George Webb, 1988), The Japanese Achievement (1990), Modern Japan: A Concise Survey (1993), Caught in Time: Japan (jt ed, 1994),

Japan and Back and Places Elsewhere, a Memoir (1998), Japan Experiences: Fifty Years, One Hundred Views: Post-War Japan through British Eyes 1945–2000 (compiled and ed, 2000), Biographical Portraits of Anglo-Japanese Personalities Volume IV (ed, 2002), Biographical Portraits of Anglo-Japanese Personalities Volume V (ed, 2004), British Envoys in Japan (ed, 2004), The Thames and I (by the Crown Prince of Japan, translated, 2006); various books (written and edited) translated into Japanese and various articles on Japanese themes in English and Japanese publications; *Recreations* music, opera, gardening; *Clubs* RAF; *Style*— Sir Hugh Cortazzi, GCMG; ✉ Ballsocks, Ballsocks Lane, Vines Cross, Heathfield, East Sussex TN21 9ET

CORY, Charlotte; da of Charles Peveril Phillips (d 1981), and Hilda May Flax, *née* Battle (d 1976); *b* 23 September 1956; *Educ* N London Collegiate Sch, Univ of Bristol (BA), Univ of York (DPhil); *m* April 1988 (m dis), Robert William Cory; *Career* novelist, playwright, photographer and woodcut artist; radiophonic poet; fndr memb UMPTY (millenium project for the growing of monkey puzzle trees); exhbn Mercer Art Gallery Harrogate 2006; *Books* An ABC in Black & White (1987), The Unforgiving (1991), The Laughter of Fools (1993), The Guest (1996), The Visitors (All clichés conserved) (2007); *Plays* The Day I Finished Off Charlotte Brontë, The Wonderful World of Allaetitia, Mangosteen Mania, Something Sort Of, Don't Ask Me, The Brave New World of Allaetitia, Snap, The Great Snarling; *Recreations* dogs, toy theatre, cultivating monkey puzzles, travel; *Style*— Charlotte Cory; ✉ c/o David Godwin, David Godwin Associates, 55 Monmouth Street, London WC2H 9DG (tel 020 7240 9992); e-mail charlotte@charlottecory.com

CORY, Sir (Clinton Charles) Donald; 5 Bt (UK 1919), of Coryton, Whitchurch, Co Glamorgan; s of Sir Clinton James Donald Cory, 4 Bt (d 1991), and Mary, *née* Hunt (d 2001); *b* 13 September 1937; *Educ* Brighton Coll, abroad; *Heir* kinsman, (Douglas) Richard Campbell Perkins-Cory, b 5 May 1940; *Style*— Sir Donald Cory, Bt; ✉ 18 Cloisters Road, Letchworth Garden City, Hertfordshire SG6 3JS (tel 01462 677206); PO Box 167, Mpemba, Malawi

CORY-WRIGHT, Sir Richard Michael; 4 Bt (UK 1903), of Caen Wood Towers, Highgate, St Pancras, Co London and Hornsey, Middx; s of Capt (Anthony John) Julian Cory-Wright (ka 1944), and gs of Capt Sir Geoffrey Cory-Wright, 3 Bt (d 1969); *b* 17 January 1944; *Educ* Eton, Univ of Birmingham; *m* 1, 1976 (m dis 1994), Veronica Mary, o da of James Harold Lucas Bolton; 3 s; m 2, 11 Nov 1998, Helga Wright, da of George James Godfrey; *Heir* s, Roland Cory-Wright; *Style*— Sir Richard Cory-Wright, Bt

COSGROVE, Rt Hon Lady; Hazel Josephine Cosgrove; CBE (2004), PC (2003); da of Moses Aron Aronson (d 1978), of Glasgow, and Julia Tobias (d 1998); *b* 12 January 1946; *Educ* Glasgow HS for Girls, Univ of Glasgow (LLB); *m* 17 Dec 1967, John Allan Cosgrove, s of Rev Dr Isaac Kenneth Cosgrove, DL, JP (d 1973); 1 da (Jillian Abigail b 1970), 1 s (Nicholas Joseph b 1972); *Career* advocate The Scottish Bar 1968–79, standing jr counsel to Dept of Trade 1977–79, QC (Scot) 1991; Sheriff of: Glasgow and Strathkelvin 1979–83, Lothian and Borders at Edinburgh 1983–96; temp judge Court of Session and High Court of Justiciary 1992–96; Senator Coll of Justice 1996–2006; memb Parole Bd for Scotland 1988–91, chm Mental Welfare Cmmn for Scotland 1991–96, chm Expert Panel on Sex Offending 1998–2001, dep chm Boundaries Cmmn for Scotland 1996–2006; Hon LLD: Napier Univ 1997, Univ of Strathclyde 2002, Univ of Glasgow 2002, Univ of St Andrews 2003, Univ of Stirling 2004; hon fell Harris Manchester Coll Oxford 2001; *Recreations* swimming, opera, foreign travel; *Style*— The Rt Hon Lady Cosgrove, CBE; ✉ e-mail hazelcosgrove@blueyonder.co.uk

COSH, (Ethel Eleanor) Mary; da of Arthur Lionel Strode Cosh (d 1952), and Ellen, *née* Janisch (d 1931); *Educ* Clifton HS Bristol, St Anne's Coll Oxford (MA); *Career* freelance writer, historian, architectural historian and lectr; contrib to: The Times, TLS, Glasgow Herald, Country Life, Spectator, Highbury & Islington Express; memb all nat conservation orgns, former memb Ctee Soc of Architectural Historians of GB; vice-pres Islington Soc, vice-chm Islington Archaeology and History Soc (former chm); tstee Islington Museum; FSA 1987; *Books* The Real World (1961), Inveraray and the Dukes of Argyll (with late Ian Lindsay, 1973), A Historical Walk through Clerkenwell (2 edn, 1987), With Gurdjieff in St Petersburg and Paris (with late Anna Butkovsky, 1980), A Historical Walk through Barnsbury (1981, revised 2 edn 2001), The Squares of Islington (Part I 1990, Part II 1993), The New River (revised edn, 2001), Edinburgh: The Golden Age (2003), A History of Islington (2005), 53 Cross Street (jtly, 2007); *Recreations* architecture, opera, reading, historical research, travel; *Style*— Mary Cosh, FSA; ✉ 10 Albion Mews, London N1 1JX (tel 020 7607 9305)

COSH, Nicholas John; s of John Henry Cosh (d 1982); *b* 6 August 1946; *Educ* Dulwich Coll, Queens' Coll Cambridge; *m* 1973, Anne Rosemary, da of Lewis Nickolls, CBE (d 1970); 2 s; *Career* former professional cricketer Surrey CCC 1968–70; dir Charterhouse Japhet Ltd 1978–82 (joined 1972), fin dir MAI plc 1985–91, gp fin dir JIB Group plc 1991–1997; non-exec chm Fleming American Investment Trust plc 1997–2003 (non-exec dir 1983–2003), chm Kiln plc 2005–; non-exec dir: Bradford & Bingley plc 1999–, Hornby plc 1999–, Invesco Income Growth Tst plc 1997–2001, ICAP plc 2000–, Computacenter plc 2002–, Sportev Ltd 2000–; FCA; *Recreations* cricket (blue 1966–68), golf, bridge, rugby (blue 1966); *Clubs* MCC, Hawks' (Cambridge); *Style*— Nick Cosh, Esq

COSSLETT, Andrew; *b* 1955; *Educ* Victoria Univ of Manchester (BA, MA); *m*; 2 c; *Career* various mktg positions Unilever plc 1979–90, successively mktg dir Schweppes GB, chm Cadbury Schweppes Aust, ceo Asia Pacific (confectionery), md GB and Ireland and pres EMEA Cadbury Schweppes plc 1990–2005, chief exec InterContinental Hotels Gp plc 2005–; non-exec chm Duchy Originals Ltd; *Recreations* rugby, tennis, golf, music; *Style*— Andrew Cosslett, Esq; ✉ InterContinental Hotels Group, 67 Alma Road, Windsor, Berkshire SL6 3HD (tel 01753 410100)

COSSONS, Sir Neil; kt (1994), OBE (1982); s of Arthur Cossons (d 1963), of Beeston, Notts, and Evelyn Edith, *née* Bettle (d 1986); *b* 15 January 1939; *Educ* Henry Mellish GS Nottingham, Univ of Liverpool (BA, MA); *m* 7 Aug 1965, Veronica, da of Henry Edwards (d 1986), of Liverpool; 2 s (Nigel b 1966, Malcolm b 1972), 1 da (Elisabeth b 1967); *Career* curator of technology Bristol City Museum 1964–69, dep dir City of Liverpool Museums 1969–71; dir: Ironbridge Gorge Museum Tst 1971–83, Nat Maritime Museum 1983–86, Science Museum 1986–2000; Collier prof in public understanding of science Univ of Bristol 2001–02; cmmr Historic Bldgs and Monuments Cmmn (English Heritage) 1989–95 and 1999–2000 (memb Ancient Monuments Advsy Ctee 1984–98), chm Royal Cmmn on Historical Monuments of England (English Heritage) 2000–07; pres: Museums Assoc 1981–82, Assoc of Ind Museums 1983– (chm 1977–83), Assoc for Science Educn 1996, RGS Inst of Br Geographers 2003–06; memb: BBC Gen Advsy Cncl 1987–90, Design Cncl 1990–94, Cncl Fndn for Manufacturing and Industry 1993–97, Br Waterways Bd 1995–2001; pro-provost and chm Cncl RCA 2007– (govr 1989–), govr ICSTM 1989–93; tstee: Mary Rose Tst 1983–2000, Civic Tst 1987–93, HMS Warrior Tst 1988–99; Newcomen Soc: memb 1963–, pres 2002–03, Dickinson Meml Medal 2001; Freeman City of London 1983; memb Comité Scientifique Conservatoire National des Arts et Métiers 1991–2000; Norton Medlicott Medal Historical Assoc 1991, President's Medal Royal Acad of Engrg 1993, Maitland Medal IStructE 2002; Hon: DSocSc Univ of Birmingham 1979 (hon prof 1994–), DUniv Open Univ 1984, DLitt Univ of Liverpool 1989, DLitt Univ of Bradford 1991, DLitt Nottingham Trent Univ 1994, DUniv Sheffield Hallam Univ 1995, DLitt UWE 1995, DSc Univ of Leicester 1995, DLitt Univ of Bath 1997, DArts De Montfort Univ 1997, DUniv York 1998, DSc Univ of Nottingham 2000, DLitt Univ of Greenwich 2004; hon fell RCA; FSA 1968, FMA 1970, CIEE 1991, CIMgt 1996, Hon CRAeS 1996, FRGS 1997, Hon FRIBA 2002, Hon MSCI 2002, Hon FCIWEM 2002, hon fell BAAS 2007; *Books* Industrial Archaeology of the Bristol Region (with R A Buchanan, 1968), Industrial Archaeology (1975, 1987 and 1993), Ironbridge: Landscape of Industry (with H Sowden, 1977), The Iron Bridge: Symbol of the Industrial Revolution (with B S Trinder, 1979, 1989 and 2002), Management of Change in Museums (ed, 1985), Making of the Modern World (ed, 1992), Perspectives on Industrial Archaeology (ed, 2000), England's Landscape series (series ed, 2006); *Clubs* Athenaeum; *Style*— Sir Neil Cossons, OBE; ✉ The Old Rectory, Rushbury, Shropshire SY6 7EB (tel 01694 771603, fax 01694 771703)

COSTALL, Prof Brenda; da of John Costall, of Wellingore, Lincs, and Eileen Stella, *née* Austin; *b* 12 September 1947; *Educ* Kesteven and Grantham Girls' Sch, Univ of Bradford (BPharm, PhD, DSc); *m* 13 Dec 1969, Robert John Naylor, s of John Edwin Naylor; *Career* Univ of Bradford: research fell MRC 1972–73, lectr in pharmacology 1973–79, sr lectr in pharmacology 1979–83, reader in neuropharmacology 1983–85, prof of neuropharmacology 1985–, pro-vice-chllr (planning and resources) 1990–92, sr pro-vice-chllr (planning and resources) 1992–94, dep vice-chllr (with special responsibility for research, planning and resources) 1994–98, head Sch of Pharmacy 1998–2004; cnslt in educn and pharmaceutical devpts Marley Hall 2007–; memb: Br Pharmacological Soc (non-offr memb Ctee), Brain Research Assoc, Collegium Internationale Neuro-Psychopharmacologicum, Euro Neurosciences Assoc of Psychopharmacology, Euro Coll of Neuropsychopharmacology, New York Acad of Sciences; *Recreations* managing a large Jacobean property, collecting antique furniture and paintings, love of arts including fashion and theatre; *Style*— Prof Brenda Costall; ✉ Marley Hall, Marley, Bingley, West Yorkshire BD16 2DN (tel 01535 680419, mobile 07725 962160, e-mail b.costall@yahoo.co.uk)

COSTELLO, Dr John Francis; s of William Francis Costello (d 1987), of Dublin, and Sarah, *née* O'Donoghue (d 1968); *b* 22 September 1944; *Educ* Belvedere Coll Dublin, UCD, Mater Hosp Dublin (MB BCh, BAO, MD); *m* 1, 11 Nov 1972 (m dis 1986), Dr Christine White, da of Wilfred White, and Irene White; 3 s (Declan b 12 Aug 1973, Manus b 26 Feb 1976, Hugh b 5 July 1980); m 2, 5 July 1996, Susanna, da of late Nicholas Clarke; 2 s (William b 8 Jan 1997, Charlie b 4 April 1998); *Career* house staff Mater Hosp Dublin 1968–69, SHO St Stephen's Hosp, Royal Northern Hosp, Royal Postgrad Med Sch and Hammersmith Hosp 1970–72, registrar Brompton Hosp 1972–74, lectr Dept of Med Univ of Edinburgh and Royal Infirmary 1974–75, asst prof of med, attending physician and dir Pulmonary Function Laboratory San Francisco Gen Hosp and Univ of Calif 1975–77, conslt physician in gen med with special interest in respiratory disease King's Coll Hosp London 1978–2003 (med dir 1991–94), sr lectr in med GKT (previously King's Coll of Med and Dentistry) 1982–2003, clinical dir of acute servs Camberwell HA 1988–91 (chm of conslts 1989–91), clinical dir of med King's Healthcare Tst 1997–2003 (med dir and memb Bd 1991–94), dir Dept of Respiratory Med King's Coll Sch of Med 1982–98, clinical dir Sackler Inst for Pulmonary Pharmacology 1993–2003, medical dir Medicsight plc 2002–06 (memb bd 2003–); chm: Capital Hospitals Ltd (rebuilding Barts and the Royal London) 2006–, Bd of Tstees Ind Dirs' Forum Educnl Tst 2006–; author of numerous scientific papers, reviews, books and chapters on aspects of respiratory disease; FRCP, FRCPI, FRSM (fndr pres Respiratory Section 1991–93); *Recreations* scuba diving, golf, opera, reading; *Clubs* Royal Wimbledon Golf, Portmarnock Golf; *Style*— Dr John Costello; ✉ 12 Melville Avenue, London SW20 0NS (tel 020 8879 1309 and fax 020 8947 7090); Cromwell Hospital, Cromwell Road, London SW5 0TU (tel 020 7460 5795, fax 020 7580 6966, e-mail jfcostello@btinternet.com)

COSTELLOE, Paul; *b* Dublin; *Educ* Blackrock Coll Dublin, design coll Dublin, Chambre Syndical Paris; *m*; 7 c; *Career* fashion designer; design asst Jacquest Sterel Paris 1969–71, designer Marks & Spencer 1972, chief house designer A Rinascente Milan 1972–74, designer Anne Fogerty NY, Pennaco NY and Trimfit Philadelphia 1974–79, own design house 1979–; company currently sells in the UK, Ireland, Europe, Scandinavia and N America under Paul Costelloe Collection and Dressage labels, flagship store Beauchamp Place Knightsbridge; designer of new British Airways uniform 1994; memb London Designer Collection UK 1980–93; *Awards* Fil d'Or 1987, 1988 and 1989, nominee Br Designer of the Year 1989, Woman's Jl Designer of the Year 1990, Stazenbreau Designer of the Year 1991; *Style*— Paul Costelloe, Esq; ✉ Ladieswear: Signature House, 4 Fitzhardinge Street, London W1H 6EG (tel 020 7725 0700, fax 020 7725 0701); Menswear: 30 Westminster Palace Gardens, Artillery Row, London SW1P 1RR (tel 020 7233 2210, fax 020 7233 2230)

COSTELLOE BAKER, Linda; *Educ* Manchester Business Sch (MBA); *Career* mgmnt conslt; chm Advsy Ctee S Lanarkshire Children's Panel 1996–2000, Scottish Legal Services Ombudsman 2000–06; memb: Parole Bd for Scotland 1995–2000, Criminal Injuries Compensation Appeals Panel 1996–2000, Standards Cmmn for Scotland 2002–05; *Style*— Mrs Linda Costelloe Baker

COTIER, James Charles; s of James Charles Cotier (d 1992), of Southend-on-Sea, Essex, and Edna Roberts (d 1984); *b* 8 March 1949; *Educ* Wentworth Secdy Modern, Southend Art Coll; *m* 27 May 1987, Louise Roxane, da of David Hugh Jenkins; 2 da (Francesca Alice b 28 Dec 1987, Isabella Fleur 23 Nov 1990), 1 s (Louis Charles b 5 March 1994); *Career* advertising photographer 1974–; winner of: numerous D&AD awards, campaign press and poster awards, Creative Circle awards; exhibitor Hamilton's Gallery 1983; *Books* Nudes in Budapest (1991); *Recreations* photography, sky diving, cooking; *Style*— James Cotier, Esq

COTRAN, His Hon Prof Eugene; s of Michael Cotran (d 1985), former Chief Justice of Cameroon, and Hassiba, *née* Khouri; *b* 6 August 1938; *Educ* Victoria Coll Alexandria Egypt, Univ of Leeds (LLM), Trinity Hall Cambridge (Dip Int Law, LLD); *m* 6 Oct 1963, Christiane, da of Homer Avierino (d 1972); 3 s (Marc b 1964, Patrick b 1966, Paul b 1972), 1 da (Layla b 1980); *Career* called to the Bar Lincoln's Inn 1959; lectr SOAS Univ of London 1962–77, judge High Court Kenya 1977–82, practice in African Cwlth and int law; visiting prof in law (with ref to Africa and ME) and chm Centre for Islamic and ME Law SOAS Univ of London; recorder of the Crown Court until 1992, circuit judge (SE Circuit) 1992–2007; int arbitrator; FCIArb; *Books* Re-statement of African Law (Kenya 1963), Case Book on Kenya Customary Laws (1987), Butterworth's Immigration Law Service (gen ed, 1991), Yearbook of Islamic and Middle Eastern Law (gen ed, 1994–), Arbitration in Africa (ed with Austin Amissah, 1996), The Role of the Judiciary in the Protection of Human Rights (ed with Adel Omar Sherif, 1997), Democracy, the Rule of Law and Islam (ed with Adel Omar Sherif 1999), The Palestinian Exodus 1948–1998 (ed with Ghada Karmi), The Rule of Law in the Middle East and the Islamic World (ed with Dr Mai Yamani, 2000); also gen ed CIMEL book series; *Recreations* racing, swimming, bridge; *Style*— His Hon Prof Eugene Cotran; ✉ 32 Gloucester Road, London W3 8PD (tel 020 8992 0432, fax 020 8992 7228, e-mail chris.cotran@virgin.net)

COTTAM, Graeme Robin; s of late Desmond Augustine Herbert Cottam, and Rosella Fothergill, *née* Smith; *b* 6 June 1955; *Educ* Reed's Sch Cobham, Univ of Bristol (LLB), Coll of Law; *m* Gloriana Marks de Chabris; 1 da (Rosella Adèle Misia Fothergill b 17 Jan 2000); *Career* called to the Bar Middle Temple 1978, pupillage 1978–79, Price Waterhouse 1979–85, Arthur Andersen & Co 1985–86; Price Waterhouse: sr mangr London 1986–90, tax ptnr Eastern Europe 1990–91, tax ptnr New York 1991–94, tax ptnr London 1994–98; princ GR Cottam & Co (business conslts) 1998–; dir Leonard X Bosack and Bette M Kruger Fndn 2001–05; tstee: Southwark Festival 1995–99, Borough High Street Amenity Fndn 1997–2005, Chawton House Library 2000–04 (dir 2004–06); memb: Int Fiscal Assoc, American Bar Assoc; fell ICAEW 1993 (assoc 1983); FRSA 2005;

Publications contribs to tax jls and other technical publications; *Recreations* theatre, opera, cinema, travel; *Style*— Graeme Cottam, Esq; ✉ Parson's Farm, Warren Corner, Froxfield, Hampshire GU32 1BJ (tel 01730 827586, e-mail grcottam@hotmail.com)

COTTAM, Harold; s of Rev Canon Frank Cottam (d 1974), and Elizabeth, *née* Wilson (d 1982); *b* 12 October 1938; *Educ* Bedford Sch; *m* 1962, Lyn, *née* Minton; 2 da (Hilary Anne b 25 Jan 1965, Rachel Marjorie b 21 May 1966); *Career* head of corp planning SmithKline Beecham UK 1964–66, commercial dir for Spain Simon Engineering Group 1966–68; Ernst & Young (and preceding firms): ptnr 1968–92, managing ptnr UK 1986–92, chm Ernst & Young pan-European consultancy gp 1992–93, chm Ernst & Young CASE Services (International) Paris 1992–93; chm: Haden MacLellan Holdings plc 1992–97, Anglo United plc 1993–96, Rebus Group plc 1996–99, Britannic Gp plc 1996–2004; ptnr Investor Relations Devpt 2002–; dir Allied Colloids Group plc 1992–97; FCA (ACA 1960); *Recreations* music, tennis, farming; *Style*— Harold Cottam, Esq; ✉ Investor Relations Development LLP, 8a Burton Mews, London SW1W 9EP (tel 020 7730 5016)

COTTAM, Dr Hilary; da of Harold Cottam, and Malin Cottam; *b* 25 January 1965; *Educ* St Hugh's Coll Oxford (BA), Univ of Sussex (MPhil), Open Univ (DPhil); *m* 21 August 2004, Nigel Carter; 1 da (b 21 Dec 04); *Career* with REST (Ethiopia) Khartoum Sudan 1987–89, CARE Int Dominican Republic 1989–91, urban social policy specialist World Bank Washington DC USA 1993–95, fndr dir School Works Ltd 1998–2001, dir The Do Tank Ltd 1999–, dir Design Cncl 2001–06, founding dir Participle Ltd 2007–; visiting fell LSE 1998–99; Top 100 Int Creative Business Award BT/Henley Mgmnt Centre 2001; associate Demos, memb Cncl CARE Int; FRSA 2001; *Publications* author of articles in numerous newspapers, magazines and jls; *Recreations* my allotment, modern dance, architecture, film, walking; *Style*— Dr Hilary Cottam; ✉ 8A Burton Mews, London SW1W 9EP

COTTENHAM, 9 Earl of (UK 1850); Sir Mark John Henry Pepys; 12 and 11 Bt (GB 1784 and UK 1801); also Baron Cottenham (UK 1836) and Viscount Crowhurst (UK 1850); s of 8 Earl of Cottenham (d 2000), and Sarah, *née* Lombard-Hobson; *b* 11 October 1983; *Educ* Cothill, Eton, Collingham, Univ of Bristol; *Heir* bro, Hon Sam Pepys; *Recreations* cricket, golf, tennis, football, skiing; *Style*— The Rt Hon the Earl of Cottenham

COTTER, Baron (Life Peer 2006), of Congresbury in the County of Somerset; Brian Joseph Michael Cotter; *b* 24 August 1936; *Educ* Downside; *m* Eyleen; 2 s, 1 da; *Career* Nat Serv army; in business for 40 years latterly co md; MP (Lib Dem) Weston-super-Mare 1997–2005 (Parly candidate Weston-super-Mare 1992); House of Commons: memb Lib Dem Trade and Industry team (spokesman on small business) 1997–2005; former: vice-chm All-Pty Gp on Retail Industry, vice-chm All-Pty Gp on Small Business, vice-chm All-Pty China Gp, treas All-Pty Autism Gp; Lib Dem dist cncllr and chm Cncl Youth Ctee 1986–90; memb: Lib Dem Parly Candidates Assoc, Assoc of Lib Dem Cncllrs, Amnesty Int, Green Lib Dems, Ct Univ of Bristol, Consultative Ctee Weston Foyer; pres Weston Savoyards; patron Somewhere To Go Project, nat patron Surf (Rwandan widows charity); former memb Weston Community Health Cncl; *Style*— The Rt Hon the Lord Cotter; ✉ e-mail cotterb@parliament.uk

COTTER, Sir Patrick Laurence Delaval; 7 Bt (I 1763), of Rockforest, Cork; s of Laurence Stopford Llewelyn Cotter (ka 1943, yr s of 5 Bt), and Grace Mary, *née* Downing; suc unc, Sir Delaval Cotter, 6 Bt (d 2001); *b* 21 November 1941; *Educ* Blundell's, RAC Cirencester; *m* 1967, Janet, da of late George Potter, of Goldthorne, Barnstaple, N Devon; 1 s (Julius Laurence George b 1968), 2 da (Jemima Grace Mary b 1970, Jessica Lucy Kathleen b 1972); *Heir* s, Julius Cotter; *Career* antique dealer; *Style*— Sir Patrick Cotter, Bt

COTTERELL, Sir John Henry Geers; 6 Bt (UK 1805) of Garnons, Herefordshire; DL (Hereford and Worcester); s of Lt-Col Sir Richard Charles Geers Cotterell, 5 Bt, CBE (d 1978), and 1 w, Lady Lettice, *née* Lygon (d 1973), da of 7 Earl Beauchamp, KG, KCMG, TD, PC, and Lady Lettice Grosvenor, da of late Earl Grosvenor, s of 1 Duke of Westminster; *b* 8 May 1935; *Educ* Eton, RMA Sandhurst; *m* 7 Oct 1959, (Vanda) Alexandra Clare (d 2005), da of Maj Philip Alexander Clement Bridgewater; 3 s (Henry Richard Geers (Harry) b 1961, James Alexander Geers b 1964, David George Geers b 1968), 1 da (Camilla Jane (Mrs Mark Houldsworth) b 1963); *Heir* s, Harry Cotterell; *Career* offr Royal Horse Gds 1955–61; chm: Hereford and Worcs CC 1977–81, Radio Wyvern 1981–97, Herefordshire Community Health Tst 1991–97; currently chm: Hereford Mappa Mundi Tst, Rural Youth Tst; memb The Jockey Club, pres Nat Fedn of Young Farmers' Clubs 1986–91; *Style*— Sir John Cotterell, Bt, DL; ✉ Downshill House, Bishopstone, Hereford HR4 7JT (tel 01981 590232, fax 01981 590496, e-mail alicot@downshill99.fsnet.co.uk)

COTTERRELL, Prof Roger Brian Melvyn; s of Walter Leslie Cotterrell (d 1977), and Hilda Margaret, *née* Randle (d 1970); *b* 30 November 1946, Selly Oak, Birmingham; *Educ* King Edward VI Camp Hill Sch Birmingham, UCL (LLB, LLM), Birkbeck Coll Univ of London (MSc Soc), Univ of London (LLD); *m* 1969, Ann Zillah Poyner; 1 s (David Roger b 1974), 1 da (Linda Ann Margaret b 1975); *Career* lectr in law Univ of Leicester 1969–74; QMC (then Queen Mary and Westfield Coll Univ of London, now Queen Mary Univ of London): lectr in law 1974–78, sr lectr in law 1978–85, reader in legal theory 1985–90, acting head Dept of Law 1989–90, prof of legal theory 1990–2005, head Dept of Law 1990–91, dean Faculty of Laws 1993–96, anniversary prof of legal theory 2005–; visiting prof and Jay H Brown Centennial Faculty fell in law Univ of Texas 1989, George Lurcy lectr Amherst Coll Massachusetts 1989; visiting prof: Univ of Lund 1996, Katholiek Universeit Brussel and Facultés Universitaires Saint Louis Brussels 1996–97, Int Inst for the Sociology of Law Onati Spain 2003 and 2004; memb: Ctee of Heads of Univ Law Schs 1993–96, Ct of Govrs Univ of Leicester 2000–03, Res Assessment Exercise Law Panel and Sub-Panel 1999–2001 and 2005–, Law Assessment Ctee Flemish Interuniversity Cncl Belgium 2006–07; Law and Soc Assoc: tstee 1996–99, chair Articles Prize Ctee 1999–2000; FBA 2005; *Books* The Sociology of Law: An Introduction (1984, 2nd edn 1992), Law, Democracy and Social Justice (jt ed, 1988), The Politics of Jurisprudence: A Critical Introduction to Legal Philosophy (1989, 2nd edn 2003), Law and Society (ed, 1994), Process and Substance: Butterworth Lectures on Comparative Law (ed, 1994), Law's Community: Legal Theory in Sociological Perspective (1995), Emile Durkheim: Law in a Moral Domain (1999), Sociological Perspectives on Law (ed, 2 vols 2001), Bass Lines: A Life in Jazz (jt author, 2002), Law in Social Theory (ed, 2006), Law, Culture and Society: Legal Ideas in the Mirror of Social Theory (2006); *Recreations* listening to and writing about music, exploring cities, European cinema; *Style*— Prof Roger Cotterrell; ✉ Law School, Queen Mary, University of London, Mile End Road, London E1 4NS (tel 020 7882 5142, fax 020 8981 8733, e-mail r.b.m.cotterrell@qmul.ac.uk)

COTTESLOE, Cdr 5 Baron (UK 1874); Sir John Tapling Fremantle; 5 Bt (UK 1821), JP (Bucks 1984); Baron of the Austrian Empire (1816); s of Lt-Col 4 Baron Cottesloe, GBE, DL (d 1994), and his 1 w, Lady Elizabeth Harris (d 1983), da of 5 Earl of Malmesbury; *b* 22 January 1927; *Educ* Eton; *m* 26 April 1958, Elizabeth Ann, er da of Lt-Col Henry Shelley Barker, DSO (d 1970), of Rugby; 2 da (Elizabeth (Betsy) Wynne (Hon Mrs Duncan Smith) b 1959, Hon Frances (Fanny) Ann (Hon Mrs Stanley) b 1961), 1 s (Hon Thomas Francis Henry b 1966); *Heir* s, Hon Thomas Fremantle; *Career* joined RN 1944, Lt 1949, Lt Cdr 1957, Cdr 1962, ret 1966; chm Oxon-Bucks Div Royal Forestry Soc 1981–83; pres: Bucks County Show 1986 (chm 1977–82), Bucks Branch CLA until 1997 (chm 1976–79, vice-pres 1997–2001), HMS Concord Assoc, Bucks County Rifle Assoc, Bucks Assoc for the Blind, Bucks Farming and Wildlife Advsy Gp until 2000; dep pres RASE 1995–96; vice-pres: Hosp Saving Assoc until 2001, BASC (previously WAGBI), Royal Agric Soc of England, Bucks Co Agric Assoc, Radcliffe tstee (chm 1997); patron: Royal Naval Assoc (Aylesbury Branch), The Ferris Fndn; govr Stowe Sch 1983–89; High Sheriff of Bucks 1969–70, Lord Lieut 1984–97; Hon Dr Univ of Buckingham 1993; KStJ 1984; *Recreations* shooting, crosswords, Sherlock Holmes, steam railways; *Clubs* Travellers, RN and Royal Albert (Portsmouth); *Style*— Cdr the Rt Hon the Lord Cottesloe, RN (ret); ✉ The Estate Office, Home Farm, Swanbourne, Milton Keynes, Buckinghamshire MK17 0SW (tel and fax 01296 720256)

COTTINGHAM, Barrie; s of John Cottingham, of Sheffield, and Eleanor, *née* Price; *b* 5 October 1933; *Educ* Carfield Sch Sheffield; *m* 5 Oct 1957, Kathleen, da of John Ernest Morton (d 1945), of Sheffield; 1 s (Nigel David b 13 Dec 1964), 1 da (Michelle Jayne b 5 Aug 1962, d 1998); *Career* RAF 1955–57, cmmnd PO 1956; Coopers & Lybrand 1957–95: ptnr 1964, memb UK Bd 1974–93, exec ptnr i/c of the regions 1986–93; chm: SIG plc 1993–2004, Cattles plc 1995–; memb Bd: VP plc 1996–, Dew Pitchmastic plc 1997–; pres Sheffield and Dist Soc of CAs 1964; FCA 1955, ATII 1965; *Recreations* squash, golf, watching rugby and cricket, opera; *Clubs* Naval and Military; *Style*— Barrie Cottingham, Esq; ✉ Cattles plc, Kingston House, Centre 27, Business Park, Woodhead Road, Batley WF17 9TD (tel 01924 444466, fax 01924 448366)

COTTIS, Matthew; s of John Cottis, of Wantage, Oxon, and Janie, *née* Moon; *b* 13 May 1962, Epping, Essex; *Educ* King Alfred's Sch Wantage, Keble Coll Oxford (BA); *m* 5 May 2000, Ann Marie, *née* Arstall; 2 da (Joanna b 26 March 1993, Isabel b 27 Aug 1997); *Career* admitted slr 1987; Lovells: joined 1985, ptnr 1993–, head of acquisition finance 2000–; *Recreations* golf, walking, travel; *Clubs* Chislehurst Golf; *Style*— Matthew Cottis, Esq; ✉ Lovells, 50 Holborn Viaduct, London EC1A 2DY (tel 020 7296 5482, fax 020 7296 2000, e-mail matthew.cottis@lovells.com)

COTTLE, Gerry; s of Reginald Brookes Cottle (d 1975), of Highbury, London, and Joan Miriam, *née* Ward (d 1993), of Streatham, London; *b* 7 April 1945; *Educ* Rutlish Sch Wimbledon; *m* 7 Dec 1968, Betty, da of James Fossett (d 1972), of Henley-in-Arden; 3 da (Sarah b 1970, April b 1973, Juliette b 1976), 1 s (Gerry b 20 Jan 1981); *Career* ran away from school and joined a small circus becoming juggler and equestrian 1961, formed Gerry Cottle's Circus 1974; flew complete circus to Oman for Sultan's birthday 1976; overseas tours 1981–84: Bahrain, Iran, Shajah, Iceland, Hong Kong, Macáu, Singapore, Malaysia; currently world's most travelled circus, touring 46 weeks a year, touring Moscow State Circus in UK 1995–, touring Circus of Horrors in UK and overseas 1995, touring Cottle and Austen Combined Circus in UK 1999, touring Chinese State Circus in UK 2000–; prop Wookey Hole Caves Somerset 2004; memb: Variety Club of GB, Assoc of Circus Proprietors of GB 1973–; *Recreations* horse riding, collecting show business memorabilia; *Style*— Gerry Cottle, Esq; ✉ The Mill, Wookey Hole, Wells, Somerset BA5 1BB (tel 01749 672243, fax 01749 677749)

COTTO, Mario; *b* 4 May 1938; *Educ* Univ of Turin; *Career* gen mangr London Branch Istituto Bancario San Paolo di Torino 1988–92 (joined bank 1957), chm and chief exec IMI Sigeco (UK) Ltd 1992–; chm Foreign Banks and Securities Houses Assoc 1992, gen mangr Banca IMI SpA, currently md Sanpaolo IMI Mgmnt Ltd; *Clubs* RAC; *Style*— Mario Cotto, Esq

COTTON, Diana Rosemary (Mrs R B Allan); QC (1983); da of Arthur Frank Edward Cotton (d 1990), of Herts, and Muriel, *née* John (d 1986); *b* 30 November 1941; *Educ* Berkhamsted Sch for Girls, Lady Margaret Hall Oxford (exhibitioner, MA); *m* 1966, Richard Bellerby Allan, *qv*, s of John Bellerby Allan (d 1985), of Oxon; 2 s (Jonathan b 1972, Jeremy b 1974), 1 da (Joanna b 1977); *Career* called to the Bar Middle Temple 1964 (bencher 1990); memb Midland Circuit, recorder of the Crown Court 1982–; asst boundary commissioner 2000; memb: Criminal Injuries Compensation Bd 1989–2000, Criminal Injuries Compensation Appeals Panel 1996–, Bar Cncl 1997–99, Mental Health Ind Review Tbnl 1997–; *Recreations* family, sport; *Style*— Miss Diana Cotton, QC; ✉ Devereux Chambers, Devereux Court, Temple, London WC2R 3JH (tel 020 7353 7534)

COTTON, John Nicholas; s of Sir John Cotton, KCMG, OBE, and Mary Bridget, *née* Connors; *b* 6 August 1941; *Educ* Downside, Merton Coll Oxford (MA); *m* 1 (m dis 1976), Caroline, da of Michael Stoop, MC; 1 s (Tanguy b 1969); *m* 2, Martine, da of Roland du Roy de Blicquy; 1 da (Charlotte b 1981), 1 s (Edward b 1986); *Career* Samuel Montagu London 1963–65, Spencer Thornton Belgium 1965–68, vice-pres Loeb Rhoades Belgium 1968–72, exec dir Cogefon Belgium 1972–77; md: Edwin H Bradley Belgium 1977–80, Banque Belge Ltd London 1980–92, Merrill Lynch Investment Managers (formerly Mercury Asset Management plc) 1992–2003; chm Queensborough Steel Co Ltd 1989–97, ptnr Dalton Strategic Partnership LLP 2003–, memb Advsy Bd Close Trustees (Switzerland) LLP 2003–; vice-chm Anglo-Belgian C of C 1992; *Clubs* Boodle's, Eagle (Gstaad); *Style*— John Cotton, Esq; ✉ 19 Bourne Street, London SW1W 8JR (tel and fax 020 7730 1685, e-mail jncotton8@yahoo.co.uk)

COTTON, Oliver; s of Robert Cotton, of London, and Ester, *née* Bonessen; *b* 20 June 1944; *Educ* Chiswick Poly, Drama Centre London; *m* 1, Catherine, *née* Stevens; 1 da (Abigail b 1969); *m* 2, Irene, *née* Gorst; 1 da (Sophie b 1986); *Career* actor and writer; stage debut Off Broadway NY 1966, The National Theatre 1966–68, Royal Court 1966–75, repertory at Cheltenham and Watford 1969–72, RSC 1975, NT 1975–79, RSC 1988–89, RNT 1990–91; *Theatre* prodns incl: Teddy in The Homecoming (Garrick) 1978, James Leeds in Children of a Lesser God (Albery) 1982, David in Benefactors (Vaudeville) 1984, David in That Summer (Hampstead) 1987, Butterfly Kiss (world premiere, Almeida) 1994, Dr Ostermark in Strindberg's The Father (tour) 1995; Wet Weather Cover (writer only) 1994–95, Frank in Educating Rita (tour) 1996, lead role in King Lear (Southwark Playhouse) 1996, Tom Sergent in Skylight 1997, Jack Kent in Blast From the Past (W Yorkshire Playhouse) 1998, Robert Chiltern in An Ideal Husband (Haymarket Theatre) 1998, Agamemnon in Troilus and Cressida (RNT) 1999, Lord Glossmore in Money (RNT) 1999, Suslov in Summer folk (RNT) 1999, Wet Weather Cover (writer, Tiffany Theatre LA) 1999, Lockit in The Villains Opera (NT) 2000, Hubert in Life x 3 (NT and Old Vic) 2000–01, Malvolio in Twefth Night (Globe prodn at Middle Temple Hall) 2002, the Mayor in Brand (RSC Stratford and Theatre Royal Haymarket) 2003, Seth Lord in The Philadelphia Story (Old Vic) 2005, Northumberland in Richard II (Old Vic) 2005; as writer: Man Falling Down (Shakespeares' Globe) 2005, Valverde in Royal Hunt of the Sun (NT) 2006, Clifford in Piano Forte (Royal Court) 2006; *Television* incl: Cesare Borgia in The Borgias 1980, Ford in The Party 1987, Giles in Room at the Bottom 1988, Anderez in Boon 1989, Gregorie Rolf in Poirot 1989, Neville Nunn in Redemption 1991, Max Erstweiler in The Camomile Lawn 1991, Alan Cromer in Westbeach 1992 and 1993, Fireworks 1993, Space Cops 1994, Harry 1994, Sharpe's Battle 1994, The Story of Joseph 1994, Joseph Chamberlain in Rhodes 1995, Gregory Watling in Wokenwell 1996, Declan in The Preston Front 1997, Augelini in Innocents 2000, Maurice Phillips in Judge John Deed 2001, Dalziel and Pascoe 2002, Casualty 2003, Sir Charles Stewart in Waking the Dead 2003, Artoym Bia Toulos in Murder Investigation Team 2004, Midsomer Murders 2005, Sensitive Skin 2005–06, Mr Dovic in Hotel Babylon 2006, Donald in The Commander 2007, Aetius in Atilla 2007; *Radio* Jocylin in The Spire 2005; *Films* incl: John the Disciple in The Day Christ Died 1979, Monks in Oliver Twist 1981, Priabin in Firefox 1982, Katis in Eleni 1985, Landis in Hiding Out 1987, Roccafino in The Sicilian 1987, Harana in Columbus - The Discovery 1992, King Heroac in Son of Pink Panther 1992, Paulo Lusano in The Innocent Sleep 1994, Charles Elliot in The Opium Wars 1996, Hrothgar in Beowulf 1997, Merino in The Dancer Upstairs 2000, Ron Wood in Baby Blue 2000, Stein in Jimmy Figg 2001, Moshe in The Gisella Perl Story 2002, Jack the Ripper in Shanghai Knights 2002, Regulus in Bonehunter 2002, Metaclfe in Colour Me Kubrick 2004, Duke in Rain Dogs 2004; as writer: Singing for Stalin 1994–95, Daytona 2000, Deadtime 2005, Diamond Geezer 2006, 24 Hours from Tulse Hill 2006; *Recreations*

C

classical guitar, listening to music, talking, running, writing; *Style*— Oliver Cotton, Esq; ✉ c/o PFD, Drury House, 34–43 Russell Street, London WC2B 5HA (tel 020 7344 1010, e-mail oliver36@btopenworld.com)

COTTON, Richard Selkirk; s of A G Cotton, of Bicester, Oxon, and V M, *née* Woolley (d 1993); *b* 29 March 1947, Woodstock, Oxon; *Educ* Univ of London (BSc, Dip Farm Business Admin); *Partner* Penelope Rankin; *Career* chartered surveyor; Cluttons: resident ptnr Middle East 1977–87, managing ptnr 2001–03, sr ptnr 2003–; Master Worshipful Co of Chartered Surveyors; FRICS; *Recreations* theatre, travel, tennis, bridge; *Style*— Richard Cotton, Esq; ✉ 21c Sunderland Terrace, London W2 5PA (tel 020 7727 0313); Cluttons LLP, Portman House, 2 Portman Street, London W1H 6DU (tel 020 7647 7266, fax 020 7647 7076, e-mail richard.cotton@cluttons.com)

COTTON, Robert George (Bob); OBE (2003); s of A G Cotton, of Oxford, and V H Cotton, *née* Wholley (d 1993); *b* 26 August 1948, Woodstock, Oxon; *Educ* Colston's Sch Bristol, Univ of Surrey; *Career* with Trust House Forte and Gardner Merchant 1975–98 (latterly dir of corporate affrs, communications and strategic planning), tourism advsr to DCMS 1999–2000, chief exec Br Hospitality Assoc 2000–; chm Best Practice Forum DTI; memb Bd: Tourism Alliance, Tourism South East; pres Hospitality Action; tstee: Springboard UK, PM Tst; Master Innholder 2001, Special Catey Award Caterer & Hotelkeeper 2002, Arena Accolade 2003; hon fell Thames Valley Univ, visiting fell Bournemouth Univ; FHCIMA; *Style*— Bob Cotton, Esq, OBE; ✉ British Hospitality Association, Queens House, 55–56 Lincoln's Inn Fields, London WC2A 3BH (tel 0845 880 7744, fax 020 7404 7799)

COTTON, Sir William Frederick (Bill); kt (2001), CBE (1989, OBE 1976); s of William Edward (Billy) Cotton, and Mabel Hope; *b* 23 April 1928; *Educ* Ardingly; *m* 1, 1950, Bernadine Maud Sinclair; 3 da; m 2, 1965, Ann Corfield, *née* Bucknall; 1 step da; m 3, 1990, Kathryn Mary, *née* Ralphs; *Career* jt md Michael Reine Music Co 1952–56; BBC TV: prodr Light Entertainment Dept 1956–62, asst head of light entertainment 1962–67, head of variety 1967–70, head of Light Entertainment Gp 1970–77, controller BBC1 1977–81, dep md 1981–82, md DBS 1982–84, chm BBC Enterprises 1982–86 and 1987–88 (vice-chm 1986–87), md BBC Television 1984–88; chm Noel Gay TV and dir Noel Gay Organisation 1988–97, non-exec dir Alba plc 1988–, non-exec dir Billy Marsh Associates 1998–, non-exec chm Meridian Broadcasting Ltd 1996–2001 (non-exec dep chm 1991–96); pres RTS 1992–95; JP Richmond 1976–84; Hon Dr Arts Bournemouth Univ 2000; FRTS, fell BAFTA 1998; *Clubs* Royal Motor Yacht, Hurlingham, Royal & Ancient, Garrick; *Style*— Sir Bill Cotton, CBE

COTTRELL, David Vernon Swynfen; s of George Swinfen Cottrell (d 1960), of Bredon, Worcs, and Dorothy Mary Catherine, *née* Liddell (d 1957); *b* 15 November 1923; *Educ* Eton, Windsor, Trinity Coll Cambridge; *m* 6 June 1950, Leontine Mariette (Marylena), da of Capt James Allan Dyson Perrins, MC (d 1974), of Hartlebury, Worcs; 1 da (Sarah (Mrs Caulcutt) b 1953), 1 s (Mark b 1955), 1 step s (Rupert b 1945), 1 step da (Rozanna (Mrs Hammond) b 1946); *Career* RNVR 1942–46; admitted slr 1951, conslt practising Birmingham, ret 1990; chm and dir: S J Bishop & Son Ltd IOW 1955–63, Waterloo House (Birmingham) Ltd 1957–2002, Temple St (Birmingham) Ltd 1957–88; dir Dares Brewery Ltd Birmingham 1960–63, fndr and life dir Newater Investments Ltd Birmingham 1963–2002, chm Tewkesbury Marina Ltd 1969–2002 (md 1969–90); memb Cncl Assoc Brokers & Yacht Agents 1970–89, pres and chm Nat Yacht Harbour Assoc 1979–82 (memb Cncl 1972–91, vice-pres 1974–76, vice-chm 1984–90), chm Midlands Region Br Marine Industry Fedn 1988–90; High Sheriff Hereford & Worcs 1976; memb Cncl Lower Avon Navigation Tst 1951–2001, pres Gloucester Branch Inland Waterways Assoc 1976–2000 and 2001–06 (chm 1974–76, 1999–2001), chm The Stratford and Warwick Waterways Tst 2004–05; memb: Law Soc 1951–90, Yacht Brokers Designers and Surveyors Assoc 1975–2002 (hon fell 1995–); *Publications* Memories of an Unusual Able Seaman on Russian and East Coast Convoys in World War Two; *Recreations* yachting, landscape painting; *Clubs* Royal Yacht Sqdn (Cowes IOW), Royal Solent Yacht, Island Sailing; *Style*— David Cottrell, Esq; ✉ The Tewkesbury Marina Ltd, Bredon Road, Tewkesbury, Gloucestershire (tel 01684 293737)

COUCHMAN, Martin; OBE (2005); s of Frederick Alfred James Couchman (d 1970), of Halstead, Kent, and Pamela Mary, *née* Argent; *b* 28 September 1947; *Educ* Sutton Valence, Exeter Coll Oxford (MA); *m* 29 Oct 1983, Carolyn Mary Constance, da of Victor Frow Roberts (d 1987), of Childer Thornton, Cheshire; 3 s (Edmund Frederick Martin b 1985, William Thomas James b 1987, Nicholas Robert David b 1992), 1 da (Annie Elizabeth Constance b 1989); *Career* bldg industry 1970–77; Nat Econ Devpt Office: indust advsr 1977–84, head of admin 1984–87, on secondment as UK dir of Euro Year of the Environment 1987–88, sec to Nat Econ Devpt Cncl 1988–92; chm CBI Sectoral Employment Issues Ctee 2000–; dep chief exec British Hospitality Assoc 1993–, chm Social Affrs Euro Hotel and Restaurant Confedn (HOTREC) 2001– (memb Exec Ctee 1997–2000); memb Green Alliance 1988–; FRSA 1987; *Recreations* amateur dramatics, Anglo-Saxon history, armchair archaeology; *Clubs* St Julians; *Style*— Martin Couchman, Esq, OBE; ✉ The Old School, Halstead, Sevenoaks, Kent TN14 7HF

COULL, Ian D; *Career* held various sr mgmnt positions at Ladbrokes, Texas Homecare and Cavenham Foods, exec dir J Sainsbury plc 1988–2003, chief exec Slough Estates plc 2003–; non-exec dir House of Fraser 2003–06; memb Regnl Bd Royal & Sun Alliance; FRICS; *Style*— Ian Coull, Esq

COULSFIELD, Rt Hon Lord; John Taylor Cameron; PC (2000), QC (Scot, 1973); s of John Reid Cameron, MA (d 1958), former Dir of Educn, Dundee, and Annie Duncan, *née* Taylor (d 1982); *b* 24 April 1934; *Educ* Fettes, CCC Oxford (MA), Univ of Edinburgh (LLB); *m* 4 Sept 1964, Bridget Deirdre, da of Ian Caldwell Perston Sloan, The Black Watch (d 1940); *Career* admitted Faculty of Advocates 1960, lectr in public law Edinburgh Univ 1960–64, QC 1973, advocate-depute 1977–79, keeper of Advocates' Library 1977–87, judge Courts of Appeal of Jersey and Guernsey 1986–87, Senator of Coll of Justice with title of Lord Coulsfield 1987–2002; chm: Med Appeal Tbnls 1985–87, Scottish judge Employment Appeal Tbnl 1992–96, Ctee on Commercial Cause Procedure 1993, Working Pty on Ordinary Procedure 1997–98, Jt Standing Ctee on Legal Educn (Scotland) 1997–2003, Esmée Fairbairn Fndn Inquiry Alternatives to Custody 2003–05, Scottish Cncl for Int Arbitration 2003–; judge of appeal Botswana 2005–; consulting ed Scottish Law & Practice Quarterly 1996–2003; tstee Nat Library of Scotland 2000–; *Style*— The Rt Hon Lord Coulsfield, PC

COULSON, His Hon Judge Peter David William; QC (2001); s of David Coulson, and Pamela, *née* Shorter; *b* 31 March 1958, London; *Educ* The Pilgrims' Sch Winchester, Lord Wandsworth Coll Hants, Univ of Keele (BA); *m* 25 May 1985, Veronica, *née* Lachkovic; 1 s (Thomas David Peter b 30 July 1989), 2 da (Joanna Clare b 1 June 1991, Kate Mary b 28 Dec 1997); *Career* barr Keating Chambers 1984–2004, recorder 2002–04, sr circuit judge 2004–; Sir Malcolm Hilberry Award Gray's Inn 1982; ACIArb; *Publications* Lloyds Professional Negligence Law Reports (founding ed, 1999), Professional Negligence and Liability (chapter, 2000), The Technology and Construction Court (2006); *Recreations* comedy, British art (1750–1950), renovating a castle in France; *Clubs* Travellers, Santa Monica Flyers; *Style*— His Hon Judge Coulson, QC; ✉ Technology and Construction Court, St Dunstan's House, 133–137 Fetter Lane, London EC4A 1HD (tel 020 7947 6497, e-mail peter.coulson@hmcourts-service.gsi.gov.uk)

COULSON-THOMAS, Prof Colin Joseph; s of Joseph Coulson Thomas, of Mullion, Cornwall, and Elsie Coulson Thomas; *Educ* Helston GS, LSE (Trevennon exhibitioner), London Business Sch (MSc), Univ of London (DPA, MSc(Econ)), Univ of Southern Calif (AM), Univ of SA (MPA), Aston Univ (PhD), DipM, DipCAM; *m* (m dis 1992), Margaret Anne, *née* Grantham; 2 da (Yvette May b 1978, Vivien Jane b 1980); 1 s (Trystan Joseph b 1991); *Career* articled clerk Neville Hovey Gardner & Co 1970–73 (qualified CA 1973), student London Business Sch 1973–75, conslt Coopers and Lybrand Associates Ltd 1975–77, research exec IOD 1977–78; ed/publisher: Professional Administration (ICSA) 1978–81, Casebook & Director Casebook Publications Ltd 1979–80; head of pubns and PR ICSA 1980–81, publishing dir (Periodicals) Longman Group Ltd 1981–84; Rank Xerox UK Ltd: mangr corp affrs 1984–87, corp affrs counsel 1987–93; chm: Adaptation Ltd 1994– (chm and ceo 1987–94), Attitudes Skills and Knowledge Ltd 1994–2003, ASK Europe plc 1995–2003, ASK Multimedia Ltd 1995–98, Policy Publications Ltd 1995–, Cambridge Management Centres plc 1998–2003, Cotoco Ltd 1998–, Creative Database Projects Ltd 2000–01; corp affrs advsr BIM 1987–91, memb Home Office Partnership Advsy Bd 1993–94, leader and co-ordinator COBRA Project (EC) 1994–95, assoc dir The Chamberlain Partnership 2003–05; visiting research fell IT Inst Univ of Salford 1987–95, head of exec progs Univ of Southern Calif UK Prog 1987–88, dir of external affrs Euro Business Sch 1987–88, visiting fell Aston Business Sch 1988–93 (fndr dir Centre for the Professions 1988–89), sr visiting research fell City Univ Business Sch 1991–94, The Willmott Dixon prof of corp transformation Univ of Luton 1994–97 (dean Faculty of Mgmnt Univ of Luton 1994–97), visiting prof Univ of Luton 1998–2000, prof and head Centre for Competitiveness Univ of Luton 2000–06, prof of direction and leadership Univ of Lincoln 2005–, visiting prof Univ of Bedfordshire 2006–; ed The Learning Organisation 2005; sr assoc judge Inst Univ of Cambridge 1994–97, Hooker distinguished visiting prof McMaster Univ 1995, visiting prof East China Univ of Science and Technology Shanghai 1996, visiting prof Mgmnt Devpt Inst India 1997–; memb Advsy Bd NI Graduate Mgmnt Devpt Programme 1994–96; govr Moorfields Eye Hosp 1978–88, dep chm London Electricity Consultative Cncl 1980–86; memb: Cncl for Professions Supplementary to Med 1982–89, Nat Biological Standards Bd 1985–94; treas Central London Branch BIM 1977–79; chm: Crossbencher (Parly Liaison) Prog 1977–80, Public Affrs Ctee Inst of Mktg 1979–80; memb Ctee London Soc of Chartered Accountants 1979–81; pres Soc of Co and Commercial Accountants 1984–85 (memb Cncl 1978–86), vice-pres Soc of Conservative Accountants 1990– (sec 1978–83, chm 1983–90); memb Cncl IPR 1983–86 (chm Professional Practices Ctee 1985–86), memb Professional Standards Ctee and Chartered Accreditation Bd IoD 1997–, memb Bd of Examiners IoD 1998– (memb Professional Devpt Ctee 1989–97); memb Cncl Conflict Res Soc 1974–76, treas The Beauchamp Lodge Settlement 1976–77, cncllr London Borough of Greenwich 1977–82, memb Greenwich Community Health Cncl 1977–80, govr Eltham Green, Kidbrooke, Roan and Charlton Schs 1977–81, memb Cncl Anglo-Brasilian Soc 1978–81; chm: Bow Group and Bow Publications 1982–83, Focus Group 1981–82 (pres 1983–86); memb Cncl: Royal Cwlth Soc 1981–85, Parly Info Technol Ctee 1987–96 and 1997–2002, Fndn for Sci and Technol 1987–92; tstee Community Network 1989–; memb Advsy Panel Forum for Technol and Trg 1993–95, memb Nat Trade and Indust Forum 1993–2002; judge: Sword of Excellence Awards 1990–92, BT Award for Innovation in Electronic Trading 1993–99 (chm 1995–99), eBusiness Innovations Awards 2000– (chm 2000–); Freeman City of London 1978; memb Worshipful Co of: Chartered Secs and Administrators 1978, Bakers 1984; FCA 1979, FCIS 1984, FSCA 1978, FCCA 1980, FMS 1984, FITD 1989, FIPR 1990, FIPM 1991, Hon FAIA 2003, FCIM 2006, FRGS, FRSA; *Publications* A Guide to Business Schools (1975), Company Administration Made Simple (1975), Public Relations: A Practical Guide (1979), Public Relations is Your Business (1981), Marketing Communications (1983), The 'New Professionals' (BIM, 1988), The Responsive Organisation, People Management, the challenge of the 1990s (with Richard Brown, BIM, 1989), Too Old at 40? (BIM, 1989), Beyond Quality: Managing the Relationship with the Customer (with Richard Brown, BIM, 1990), The Complete Spokesperson (with Peter Bartram, 1990), The Flat Organisation: Philosophy and Practice (with Trudy Coe, BIM, 1991), Creating the Global Company - Successful Internationalisation (1992), Transforming the Company (1992, w edn 2002), Creating Excellence in the Boardroom: A Guide to Shaping Directorial Competence and Board Effectiveness (1993), Developing Directors: Building An Effective Boardroom Team (1993, 2 edn 2007), Business Restructuring and Teleworking (ed, 1994), Business Process Re-engineering: Myths and Realities (ed, 1994), The Responsive Organisation: Re-engineering new patterns of work (gen ed, 3 vols, 1995), The Competitive Network (exec ed, 1996), The Future of the Organization (1997), Winning Major Bids - The Critical Success Factors (exec ed, 1997), Developing Strategic Customers and Key Accounts (exec ed, 1998), Individuals and Enterprise (1999), Winning Business Series of Reports (exec ed, 1999–2001), Developing a Corporate Learning Strategy (1999), The Information Entrepreneur (2000), Shaping Things to Come (2001), Pricing for Profit (2002), Winning New Business: the critical success factors (jt author, 2003), The Knowledge Entrepreneur (2003), How to Make Your Case to the Media (jtly, 2006), Winning Companies, Winning People (2007); *Recreations* country life, boating, the music of the Rolling Stones; *Clubs* Carlton, City Livery; *Style*— Prof Colin Coulson-Thomas; ✉ Adaptation Ltd, Mill Reach, Mill Lane, Water Newton, Cambridgeshire PE8 6LY (tel 01733 361149, fax 01733 361459, e-mail colinct@tiscali.co.uk)

COULTER, Michael Daley; s of Thomas Coulter (d 1976), of Glasgow, and Elizabeth, *née* Daley (d 1991); *b* 29 August 1952; *Educ* Holy Cross HS Hamilton; *Children* 2 s (Luke b 21 Jan 1981, Eliot b 18 Feb 1987), 2 da (Ruth b 8 April 1983, Sophie b 23 May 1985); *Career* dir of photography 1985–; winner BAFTA Scotland Award for outstanding contribution to film and TV 1997; memb: BSC 1988, Acad of Motion Picture Arts and Sciences 1995; supporter Amnesty Int; *Film* incl: No Surrender 1985, The Good Father 1985, Housekeeping 1987, The Dressmaker 1988, Where Angels Fear To Tread 1991, The Long Day Closes 1992, Being Human 1993, Four Weddings and a Funeral 1993 (BSC nomination), Neon Bible 1995, Sense and Sensibility 1996 (Oscar, BAFTA and BSC nominations 1997), Eskimo Day (for TV) 1996, Fairy Tale: A True Story 1997, Notting Hill 1998, Mansfield Park 1999, Love Actually 2003; *Recreations* cinema, movies, walking, reading, watching football; *Clubs* Groucho; *Style*— Michael Coulter, Esq; ✉ c/o McKinney Macartney Management Ltd, The Barley Mow Centre, 10 Barley Mow Passage, London W4 4PH (tel 020 8995 4747, fax 020 8995 2414)

COULTHARD, David; *b* 27 March 1971; *Career* motor racing driver; achievements incl: Scottish Jr Kart champion 1983, 1984 and 1985, Scottish Open and Br Super 1 Kart champion 1986 and 1987, Scottish Open Kart champion 1988, first Formula Ford 1600 Championship 1989, fourth Br Vauxhall Lotus Challenge 1990, fifth GM Lotus Euroseries 1990, first Grand Prix (Silverstone) 1990, second Br Formula Three Championship 1991, winner Macáu Grand Prix 1991, winner Marlboro Masters of Europe Race 1991, ninth European Formula 3000 Championship 1992, third Formula 3000 Championship 1993; Williams test driver 1993 and 1994, Formula One debut 1994, drove for Williams-Renault team 1994, signed for Williams-Renault for 1995 season, signed for McLaren International Ltd (now McLaren-Mercedes) 1996, 1997, 1998 (3rd Drivers' Championship), 1999, 2000 (3rd Drivers' Championship), 2001 (2nd Drivers' Championship), 2002 and 2003 seasons; Formula One career: 13 Grand Prix wins (incl Br Grand Prix 1999 and 2000), 12 pole positions; McLaren Autosport Young Driver of the Year 1990, ITV/Panasonic Young Sports Personality of the Year 1994, Daily Express Scottish Sports Personality of the Year 1994; *Style*— David Coulthard, Esq

COUNT, Dr Brian Morrison; s of Douglas John Count, of Suffolk, and Ethel Sarah, *née* Goodwin; *b* 18 February 1951; *Educ* Bungay GS, King's Coll Cambridge (BA), Univ of

Exeter (PhD); *m* 1975, Jane Elizabeth, *née* Hudson; 3 s (Michael Andrew b 8 May 1978, David Brian b 3 January 1981, Jonathan Peter b 22 October 1985); *Career* CEGB: research offr 1974–84, with Corp Planning Dept 1984–86, planning mangr 1986–90; National Power plc: dir of projects 1990–93, dir of power generation 1993–96, dir of ops and technol 1996–99, memb Bd 1996–2000, md of UK business 1999–2000; Innogy plc: chief operating offr 2000–01, ceo 2001–03; ceo RWE Trading 2003–; memb Industrial Devpt Advsy Bd DTI 2004–; FRSA 1980, FInstP 1997, CEng 1997; *Recreations* rugby, fly fishing, golf; *Clubs* Newbury Rugby, Sandford Springs Golf; *Style*— Dr Brian Count; ✉ RWE Trading GmbH, Huyssenalle 2, 45128 Essen, Germany (tel 0049 201 12 17800, fax 0049 201 12 17802, e-mail brian.count@rwe.com)

COUPE, Barry Desmond; s of Harold Desmond Coupe (d 1992), and Alice, *née* Roberts; *b* 4 June 1951; *Educ* Canford Sch, Leeds Sch of Architecture (BA, Dip Arch); *m* 6 May 1978, Shan Patricia, da of James Ninian Reid Wilson, of Westbourne, Poole; 2 s (Matthew b 6 Sept 1981, Benjamin b 11 Feb 1985); *Career* architect; Fitzroy Robinson & Ptnrs 1977–80, fndr ptnr Forum Architects 1980–2004; works incl: Nobelight Bldg 1983, leisure complex Whittaker House 1984, offrs' club RAF Mildenhall 1986, Bow Housing 1989, HQ Bldg Domino plc Cambridge 1987, The Quorum Development 1991, Wolverhampton Nuffield Hosp, Animal Hosp Animal Health Tst 1995, Animal Hosp Univ of Edinburgh 1996, Large Animal Hosp Royal Veterinary Coll 1998, Nat Call Centre 2004, Dogs Tst Harefield 2005; Usafe Design award 1986, 1987, 1988 and 1989, Usafe Worldwide award 1986, Civic Tst award, commendation 1987, Jersey Design Award 1998; dir Agora Mgmnt; chm Dyslexia Action; govr Canford Sch; RIBA 1979, ARB; *Recreations* classic cars, photography, real tennis; *Clubs* Cambridge Univ Real Tennis, Newmarket Real Tennis, Old Canfordian Soc (pres); *Style*— Barry Coupe, Esq; ✉ Glebe Barn, 6 Manor Farm Close, Pimperne, Dorset DT11 8XL (tel 07887 931513); Porthenor, Old Town, St Mary's, Isles of Scilly (tel 01720 423664)

COUPER, Dr Heather Anita; CBE (2007); da of George Couper Elder Couper (d 1998), and Anita, *née* Taylor (d 1984); *b* 2 June 1949; *Educ* St Mary's GS, Univ of Leicester (BSc), Univ of Oxford; *Career* mgmnt trainee Peter Robinson Ltd 1967–69, res asst Cambridge Observatories 1969–70, lectr Greenwich Planetarium 1977–83, broadcaster and writer on astronomy and sci 1983–, Gresham prof of astronomy 1993–96; cmmr Millenium Cmmn 1994–2007; dir Pioneer Film and TV Productions 1988–99; astronomy columnist: The Independent, BBC Focus Magazine; presenter of and contrib to many radio programmes incl Seeing Stars (BBC World Serv); pres: Br Astronomical Assoc 1984–86, Jr Astronomical Soc 1987–89; Hon DLitt Loughborough Univ 1991, Hon DSc Univ of Hertfordshire 1994, Hon DSc Univ of Leicester 1997; FRAS 1970, FInstP 1998, CPhys 1998; *Television* Channel 4: The Planets 1985, The Stars 1988, Avalanche 1995, Raging Planet 1998, Killer Earth 1998, Stormforce 1998, Universe 1999, Space Shuttle: Human Time Bomb 2003; Horizon Special: A Close Encounter of the Second Kind (BBC 2) 1992; Pioneer Productions: The Neptune Encounter (ITV) 1989, ET Please Phone Earth 1992, Space Shuttle Discovery 1993, Electric Skies 1994, Arthur C Clarke: The Visionary (Discovery Channel Europe) 1995, Wonders of Weather (Discovery Channel Europe and Learning Channel USA) 1995, On Jupiter (Discovery Channel America and Channel 4) 1995, Black Holes (Discovery Channel USA, ABC Aust, Channel 4) 1997, Stephen Hawking: Profile (BBC) 2002; *Radio* presenter and scriptwriter Red Planet (BBC Radio 4) 2003, Worlds Beyond (BBC Radio 4) 2005, Arthur C Clarke: The Science and the Fiction (BBC Radio 4) 2005, A History of British Rocketry (BBC Radio 4) 2007; *Books* 33 pubns incl: The Space Scientist series, The Universe, The Restless Universe, The Stars, The Planets, The Space Atlas, How the Universe Works, Guide to the Galaxy, Black Holes, Big Bang, Is Anybody Out There?, To the Ends of the Universe, Universe, Mars: The Inside Story, Extreme Universe, Philips Stargazing (annual series), Out of this World; *Recreations* travel, the English countryside, wine, food, music; *Clubs* Groucho; *Style*— Dr Heather Couper, CBE; ✉ David Higham Associates, 5–8 Lower John Street, Golden Square, London W1R 4HA (tel 020 7437 7888)

COUPLAND, (William) James; s of late William Arthur Coupland, and Patricia Anne, *née* Martin; *b* 25 May 1957; *Educ* KCS Wimbledon; *m* 13 Sept 1980, Helen Jane, da of late Charles Alfred Everett; 3 s (Christopher Everett, Benjamin Jake b 1981, Joshua James b 1987); *Career* dir Shearson American Express Ltd 1982–92, md Shearson Lehman Metals Ltd 1985–93, dir Shearson Lehman Hutton Commodities Tokyo Ltd, sr vice-pres Shearson Lehman Hutton Inc 1986–93, chm Shearson Lehman Hutton Commodities (now Lehman Brothers Commodities Ltd) 1987–93; dir The London Metal Exchange Ltd 1992–93, sr vice-pres Kidder Peabody International Ltd 1993–94, dir Deutsche Sharps Pixley Metals Ltd 1994–95, md and head of metals Standard Bank London Ltd 1995–, dir Standard Resources China Ltd; dir LME Hldgs Ltd and London Metal Exchange 2005–; FRSA; *Recreations* tennis, golf, painting; *Style*— James Coupland, Esq; ✉ 5 Durrington Park, Wimbledon, London SW20 8NU (e-mail james.coupland@standardbank.com)

COURT, Pamela Mary (Pam); da of Thomas Richardson (d 2004), of Gosforth, Newcastle upon Tyne, and Kathleen, *née* Carroll; *b* 10 November 1954; *Educ* Gosforth Grammar, Dorset House Coll of Occupational Therapy (Dip Occupational Therapy), PCL (BSc), City Univ (MHM); *m* 17 Sept 1977, David Court, s of James Court (d 1990), of Moreton Morrell, Warks; 2 da (Rebecca b 4 Nov 1985, Kathryn b 15 Nov 1988); *Career* occupational therapist: Spinal Injuries Unit Hexam Hosp, Stroke Unit St Pancras Hosp, Camden Rehabilitation Centre (head occupational therapist); Waltham Forest HA: head occupational therapist Whipps Cross Hosp until 1986, dist occupational therapist 1986–91, therapy servs mangr 1991–93; Forest Healthcare NHS Tst: dir Women and Children's Servs and Learning Disabilities and Mental Health and Med Care Gp 1993–98, dep dir of ops Primary and Community and Mental Health Servs 1996–98, serv dir Women and Children's Servs 1996–98, actg operational dir Primary and Community Servs, Community and Primary Care Servs, Learning Disabilities and Women's and Children's Servs 1998–2000, dir of ops Primary, Community Women and Children and Mental Health Servs 2000–01; project dir Chingford (estab Wanstead and Woodford PCT) 2000–01, chief exec Harlow PCT 2001–06, actg chief exec Uttlesford PCT 2004, chief exec SW Essex PCT 2006–; memb Essex and E of England Leadership Devpt (NHS); vice-chair Harlow 2020 Local Strategic Partnership; *Recreations* walking, reading, cooking, gardening; *Clubs* Lansdowne; *Style*— Mrs Pam Court; ✉ South West Essex Primary Care Trust, Phoenix Court, Christopher Martin Road, Basildon, Essex SS14 3HG (tel 01268 705000, e-mail pam.court@swessexpct.nhs.uk)

COURT-BROWN, Charles Michael; s of William Michael Court-Brown, OBE (d 1968), and Caroline Gordon Stephen, *née* Thom; *b* 3 February 1948; *Educ* George Watson's Coll Edinburgh, Univ of Aberdeen (BSc), Univ of Edinburgh (MD, MB ChB); *m* 6 July 1974, Jacqueline Yek Quen, da of To Leong Mok; 1 s (Michael b 1988), 1 da (Johanna b 1979); *Career* conslt orthopaedic surgn 1985–, pt/t sr lectr Dept of Orthopaedic Surgery Univ of Edinburgh 1985, conslt orthopaedic surgn Lothian Health Bd 1992–; chm Scottish Orthopaedic Research Tst; fndr memb Br Trauma Soc; fell BOA, FRCS 1979, BORS 1983, FRCSEd (Orth) 1984; *Books* External Skeletal Fixation (1984), Atlas of Intramedullary Nailing of the Tibia and Femur (1991), Management of Open Fractures (1996), Tibia and Fibula (1997), Mastercases in Orthopaedic Surgery (1999); *Recreations* house building, cooking; *Style*— Charles Court-Brown, Esq

COURTENAY, Sir Thomas Daniel (Tom); kt (2001); s of Thomas Henry Courtenay (d 1984), of Hull, and Annie Eliza, *née* Quest (d 1962); *b* 25 February 1937, Hull; *m* Isabel; *Career* actor; *Theatre* numerous performances from 1960–; venues incl The Old Vic Theatre, Royal Exchange Theatre, various locations in the West End and Broadway; *Television* incl: The Old Curiosity Shop 1994, Young Indiana Jones 1995, Pretending To Be Me 2003; *Films* incl: Private Potter 1962, The Loneliness of the Long Distance Runner 1962 (BAFTA winner), Billy Liar 1963 (BAFTA nomination), King and Country 1964 (BAFTA nomination), Operation Crossbow 1965, Doctor Zhivago 1965 (Oscar nomination), King Rat 1965, Night of the Generals 1967, The Day the Fish Came Out 1967, A Dandy in Aspic 1968, Otley 1969, One Day in the Life of Ivan Denisovich 1970, To Catch a Spy 1971, Keep Your Fingers Crossed 1971, I Heard the Owl Call my Name 1973, The Dresser 1983 (Oscar nomination, BAFTA nomination, Golden Globe winner), Me and the Girls 1985, Absent Friends 1985, Leonard Part 6 1987, Happy New Year 1987, The Last Butterfly 1990, Let Him Have It 1991, Redemption 1991, The Boy from Mercury 1996, A Rather English Marriage 1998, Whatever Happened to Harold Smith? 1999, Last Orders 2001, Nicholas Nickleby 2003; *Books* Dear Tom (2000); *Style*— Sir Tom Courtenay; ✉ c/o Jonathan Altaras Associates, 11 Garrick Street, London WC2E 9AR

C

COURTENAY-LUCK, Dr Nigel Stephen; s of Gerald Harold Courtenay-Luck (d 1969), and Margaret Elizabeth Mary, *née* Bishop (d 1983); *b* 2 December 1952; *Educ* Kingsway-Princeton Coll, St George's Hosp and Chelsea Coll London (BSc), Royal Post Grad Med Sch Univ of London (PhD); *m* 27 July 1975, Maria, *née* Lombardi; 1 s (Giovanni Gerald b 3 Aug 1979), 2 da (Santina Rosa b 23 June 1986, Francesca Aurora b 9 March 1992); *Career* researcher ICRF 1981–84; Hammersmith Hosp London: sr researcher 1984–87 (Unilever research scholar), lectr in immunology 1987–99; co-fndr Antisoma (now Antisoma plc) 1991, chief scientific offr Antisoma Research Ltd 2003– (tech dir 1991–2003); sr lectr Imperial Coll Sch of Med London 2001; PhD examiner Univ of London 2004–; co-ordinator European Sch of Oncology 1989, scientific advsr Bio-Industry Assoc 1993–98; author of more than 30 papers in oncology and immunology jls and of 8 chapters in books; more than 50 invited lectures in UK and abroad; Eureka Award DTI 1993, Smart Award DTI 1998; memb: Inst of Biology 1980–, Br Soc of Immunology 1991–, American Soc of Clinical Oncology 2004–; FRSM 1999; *Recreations* walking, travelling, skiing, ski-jetting, family activities; *Clubs* Courtenay Soc, Powderham Castle (Devon), David Lloyd's; *Style*— Dr Nigel Courtenay-Luck; ✉ Antisoma Research Ltd, Hanger Lane, London W5 3QR (tel 020 8799 8200, fax 020 8799 8201)

COURTENAY-STAMP, (David) Jeremy; s of David Courtenay-Stamp, and Helen Annette, *née* Smith; *b* 25 April 1962; *Educ* Blundell's (scholar), LSE (LLB); *m* Elizabeth Ann, *née* Crawford; 2 da (Georgina Louise b 31 March 1993, Alexandra Isobelle b 22 April 1995); *Career* ptnr Macfarlanes 1992– (joined 1984, currently head Commercial Section); memb: Worshipful Co of Dyers, City of London Solicitors Co, Law Soc; ACA 1986; *Recreations* golf, scuba, skiing, sailing, tennis, squash; *Clubs* Chelsea Harbour; *Style*— Jeremy Courtenay-Stamp, Esq; ✉ Macfarlanes, 10 Norwich Street, London EC4A 1BD (tel 020 7831 9222, fax 020 7831 9607)

COURTIS, John; s of Thomas Courtis (d 1976), of Stock, Essex, and Marjorie May, *née* Dodson (m 2 Massey); *b* 14 July 1937; *Educ* Westminster; *m* 1, 15 Jan 1966 (m dis 1995), Jane Margaret, da of William McCall-Smith (d 1970), of Stradishall, Suffolk; 1 da (Claudia Janet b 1969), 1 s (Neil Thomas b 1970); m 2, 12 July 1996, Dorothy Mary, *née* Miller; *Career* cmmnd RAF 1960–63; Ford Motor Co 1963–67; dir: Reed Executive 1967–71, Executive Appointments Ltd 1971–74; sr ptnr Courtis & Partners Ltd 1974–; chm: DEEKO plc 1981–88, FRES 1986–87, Recruitment Soc 1991–93; FCA 1959; *Books* Bluffer's Guide to Management (1986), Marketing Services (1987), Bluffer's Guide to Accountancy (1987), Interviews - Skills and Strategy (1988), Bluffer's Guide to Photography (1989), 44 Management Mistakes (1989), Recruiting for Profit (1990), Getting A Better Job (1992), Recruitment Advertising: Right First Time (1994); *Recreations* writing, cooking; *Clubs* VSCC, RAF; *Style*— John Courtis, Esq; ✉ Ryde Villa, Mount Pleasant, Reydon, Southwold, Suffolk IP18 6QQ

COURTNEY, Diana Jean; da of Albert John Courtney, of Chiswick, London, and Sophia, *née* Fogg; *b* 20 March 1939; *Educ* Lourdes Mount Convent; *m* 1966 (m dis 1985), Edward John Charles, s of Edward George; 2 da (Nicola Diana b 9 Aug 1971, Antonia Jane b 17 April 1975); *Career* articled clerk Rexworthy Bonsor & Simons 1955–60; ptnr: Herbert Openheimer Nathan & Vandyk 1966–88 (slr 1961–66), Denton Hall 1988–99; non-exec dir Bradford & Bingley Building Society; memb: Law Soc 1960, Anglo American Real Property Inst; FRSA; *Recreations* horse racing, gardening, opera, theatre; *Style*— Ms Diana Courtney; ✉ tel 020 7221 5567

COURTNEY, Prof James McNiven; s of George Courtney (d 1972), of Glasgow, and Margaret, *née* McNiven (d 1980); *b* 25 March 1940; *Educ* Whitehall Sr Secdy Sch Glasgow, Univ of Glasgow (BSc), Univ of Strathclyde (PhD), Univ of Rostock (Dr sc nat); *m* 26 June 1965, Ellen Miller, da of James Copeland; 1 da (Margaret Ellen Louise b 28 March 1966), 2 s (James George b 28 June 1969, David William b 3 Aug 1975); *Career* rubber technologist: Maclellan Rubber Ltd 1962–65, Uniroyal Ltd 1965–66; Univ of Strathclyde: postgrad student 1966–69, lectr Bioengineering Unit 1969–81, sr lectr 1981–85, reader 1986–89, prof 1989–; Int Soc for Artificial Organs (sec treas 1994), Int Faculty for Artificial Organs 1995 (tenured prof 1992); Rudolf Virchow prize 1986, Univ of Rostock prize of honour 1987; EurChem 1994; FRSC 1977, FIM 1993; *Books* Artificial Organs (ed, 1977), Biomaterials in Artificial Organs (ed, 1984), Progress in Bioengineering (ed, 1989); *Recreations* football supporter (Glasgow Rangers); *Style*— Prof James M Courtney

COURTNEY, Keith; s of Raymond Courtney, of Newtownabbey, NI, and Margaret Faulkner, *née* McClelland; *b* 16 May 1966; *Educ* Boys' Model Sch, Univ of Ulster (BA); *m* 21 May 1994, Katherine Jane, da of Francis Allen Charles Barnard; *Career* art dir: GGT Advertising 1988–91 (accounts incl Cadbury's, Holstein Pils, Toshiba and Daily Mirror), Simons Palmer Denton Clemmow & Johnson 1991–93 (accounts incl Nike, BT and Greenpeace); sr art dir WCRS 1993–94 (accounts incl Carling, Radio Rentals, BMW and Canon), bd art dir Lowe Howard-Spink 1994–95 (accounts incl Stella, Heineken, Vauxhall and Reebok), creative dir K Advertising 1995–97 (accounts incl Pentax, Carlesberg, Cheltenham & Gloucester and Commercial Union); memb: Creative Directors' Forum, Soc for the Protection of Ancient Buildings, creative dir Leagas Shafron Davis 1997–98; *Awards* D&AD Silver Award (Nike) and Silver nominations (Toshiba and Nike), British TV Gold Award (Toshiba) and Silver Award (BT), Campaign Press Silver Awards (Nike and Stella Artois), Creative Circle Silver Awards (Toshiba, Carling, Nike and Cadbury), Campaign Poster Silver Award (Nike); *Books* The Oldie Book of Cartoons (contrib, 1994); *Recreations* contemporary dance, collecting memorabilia; *Clubs* Michael's Piano Bar, Groucho, Soho House, Colony Rooms; *Style*— Keith Courtney, Esq

COURTNEY, Rohan Richard; s of Arthur Richard Courtney (d 2002), of Chingford, London, and Cecelia, *née* Harrington (d 2006); *b* 28 January 1948; *Educ* William Morris GS London; *m* 12 Jan 1974 (m dis 2004), Marilyn, da of Ernest Arthur Charles Goward (d 1972), of Waltham Cross, Herts; 1 s (Liam b 1975), 1 da (Siân b 1977); *Career* banker and co director; National Provincial Bank London 1965–68; mangr: Rothschild Intercontinental Bank Ltd London 1968–75, Amex Bank Ltd London 1975–76; asst dir Amex Bancom Ltd Hong Kong 1976–78, md Euro Asian Fin (Hong Kong) Ltd Hong Kong 1978–80, sr mangr Creditanstalt Bankverein London 1980–82, gen mangr State Bank of NSW London 1982–90, md Rohan Courtney & Partners Ltd 1990–96, gp chief exec Robert Fraser & Co Ltd 1991–92, dir and co-fndr UCG Partnership Ltd 2005–, dir UCG Engrg Ltd 2007–; chm: Associated Australian Banks in London 1988, Br Overseas Cwealth Banks Assoc 1990, Sterling Trust plc 1992–94 (dir 1991–94), Swaine Adeney Brigg Ltd 1993–94, International Pacific Securities plc 1993–96, West 175 Media Gp 1996–2001, Sanctuary Music Productions plc 1997–98, Chartfield Fund Management plc 1997–98, Project

Leaders Int Ltd 1998–2001, Corporate Consulting Community Ltd 2002–, Creative Realisation Ltd 2002–03, Britain-Australia Soc 2003–05 (dep chm 2001–03); dep chm: Galleon Holdings plc 2001–03 (non-exec 1999–2001); chief exec Turnbulls Group Ltd 2002–03; non-exec dir: Tullow Oil plc 1993–, Boisdale plc 1993–2005, Inn Business Group plc 1995–97, London Chamber of Commerce and Industry Commercial Educn Tst 2002–03, Education Development International plc 2002–03, Stockval plc 2007–; memb The Cook Soc 1989– (chm 2000); tstee: Sir Robert Menzies Educational Tst 1999–, Brit-Oz E-Pals Tst 2005– (chm tstees); Freeman City of London, Liveryman Worshipful Co of Woolmen; *Recreations* country pursuits; *Clubs* Royal Over-Seas League, Hong Kong CC; *Style*— Rohan Courtney, Esq; ✉ 9 Vale Farm Road, Woking, Surrey GU21 6DE (mobile 07879 498544, e-mail rohan.courtney@ucgp.com)

COURTOWN, 9 Earl of (I 1762); James Patrick Montagu Burgoyne Winthrop Stopford; also (sits as) Baron Saltersford (GB 1796), Baron Courtown (I 1758), Viscount Stopford (I 1762); s of 8 Earl of Courtown, OBE, TD, DL (d 1975); *b* 19 March 1954; *Educ* Eton, Berkshire Agric Coll, RAC Cirencester; *m* 6 July 1985, Elisabeth Dorothy, yr da of Ian Rodger Dunnett, of Pinders, Broad Campden, Glos; 2 da (Lady Rosanna Elisabeth Alice b 13 Sept 1986, Lady Poppy Patricia Lilly b 19 Oct 2000), 1 s (James Richard Ian Montagu, Viscount Stopford b 30 March 1988); *Heir* s, Viscount Stopford; *Career* land agent; ARICS; Lord in Waiting (Govt whip) 1995–97, oppn whip 1997–2000; former govt spokesman for Home Office Scotland and Transport; *Style*— The Rt Hon the Earl of Courtown; ✉ House of Lords, London SW1A 0PW

COUSINS, James Mackay (Jim); MP; *b* 23 February 1944; *Educ* New Coll Oxford (scholar), LSE; *Career* contract researcher and lectr in steel shipbuilding and inner city job markets for trade unions, Cmmn on Industrial Rels and Depts of Employment and the Environment; MP (Lab) Newcastle upon Tyne Central 1987–; memb Treasury Select Ctee 1997–; memb: Wallsend Borough Cncl 1969–73, Tyne & Wear CC 1973–86 (dep ldr 1981–86), CND, MSF; *Style*— Jim Cousins, Esq, MP; ✉ 21 Portland Terrace, Newcastle upon Tyne NE2 1QQ (tel 0191 2819888, fax 0191 2813383, e-mail cousinsj@parliament.uk); House of Commons, London SW1A 0AA

COUSINS, Jeremy Vincent; QC (1999); s of Eric Cousins of Headington, and Joyce, *née* Gurl; *b* 25 February 1955; *Educ* Oxford Sch, Univ of Warwick (LLB); *m* 27 July 1993, Jane, da of Dr John Owens, FRCPsych, of Sutton Coldfield; 2 s, 1 da; *Career* called to the Bar Middle Temple 1977, asst recorder 1996, recorder 2000; chm: Midland Bar Assoc 2002–, Commercial Gp St Philip's Chambers 2003–; sidesman and memb Parochial Church Cncl St Anne's Moseley; *Recreations* wine, France and Italy; *Style*— Jeremy Cousins, Esq, QC; ✉ St Philip's Chambers, 55 Temple Row, Birmingham B2 5LS (tel 0121 246 7000, fax 0121 246 7001)

COUSINS, John Stewart; s of L R Cousins (d 1976), and Margaret Betty Kate, *née* Fry (d 2001); *b* 31 July 1940; *Educ* Brentwood Sch, Britannia RNC Dartmouth, Jesus Coll Cambridge (MA); *m* 1, 26 Oct 1970 (m dis 1979), Anne Elizabeth, da of Patrick O'Leary (d 1976); 1 da (Charlotte b 1973); m 2, 28 Dec 1979, Geraldine Anne, da of Col Thomas Ivan Bowers, CBE, DSO, MC* (d 1980); *Career* RN 1958–62, Sub Lt 1960, served Far East in HMS Belfast and HMS Maryton; Kleinwort Benson Ltd: joined 1966, Far East rep Tokyo 1970–73, md Hong Kong 1973–78; fin advsr to chm Porodisa Gp Indonesia 1979–80, ptnr de Zoete and Bevan 1980–85, dir Barclays de Zoete Wedd Securities 1985–92, md Barclays de Zoete Wedd Equities Ltd, chief exec BZW Puget Mahé SA Paris; currently conslt and non-exec dir: Corney & Barrow Group Ltd, Baring Emerging Europe plc; memb Int Equities Ctee London Stock Exchange 1990–92; ASIP, MSI; *Recreations* racing, rugby, cricket, field sports; *Clubs* Brooks's, Caledonian; *Style*— John Cousins, Esq; ✉ 73 Redcliffe Gardens, London SW10 9JJ (tel and fax 020 7373 1919); Lamarie, 46140 Luzech, France (tel 00 33 5 65 20 11 95, fax 00 33 5 65 36 79 96)

COUSINS, Eur Ing Raymond John Randal; s of Henry George Cousins (d 1983), and Freda Isabella, *née* Roberts; *b* 14 July 1938; *Educ* Alleyn's Sch Dulwich, King's Coll London (BSc); *m* 28 Dec 1963, Ruth Imogen, da of William Charles Vigurs (d 1982); 2 da (Fiona Mary b 4 Oct 1967, Kirstie Ann b 6 Oct 1969); *Career* civil engr; sr ptnr Cyril Blumfield and Ptnrs 1988– (ptnr 1973–); chm Assoc of Consltg Engrs 1997–98; govr: Dulwich Coll 1991–95, Alleyn's Sch 1991– (chm 2002–); tstee Dulwich Estate 1989–2004 (chm 1997–98); Master Worshipful Co of Woolmen 1993–94 (Liveryman 1973, clerk 1975–87, memb Court of Assts 1986–), Master Worshipful Co of Engrs 2002–03 (Liveryman and memb Ct of Assts 1983–, Asst Clerk 1983–98; CEng, FICE, FIStructE, FConsE; *Recreations* golf, ornithology, hill walking; *Clubs* Athenaeum, Dulwich and Sydenham Hill Golf; *Style*— Eur Ing Raymond J R Cousins; ✉ 33 Hitherwood Drive, London SE19 1XA (tel 020 8670 4673, e-mail randr.cousins@btclick.com); Cyril Blumfield & Partners (tel and fax 020 8761 0072, e-mail cyril.blumfield@btinternet.com)

COUSSINS, Baroness (Life Peer UK 2007), of Whitehall Park in the London Borough of Islington; Jean Elizabeth Coussins; PC (2007); da of Walter Leonard Coussins (d 1973), and Jessica, *née* Hughes (d 1996); *b* 26 October 1950, London; *Educ* Godolphin & Latymer Sch, Newnham Coll Cambridge (MA); *Children* 2 da (Anna b 1978, Claudia b 1988), 1 s (Matthew b 1981); *Career* UNA 1973–75, NCCL 1975–80, dep dir Child Poverty Action Gp 1980–83, sr educn offr ILEA 1983–88; Cmmn for Racial Equality: dir Social Policy 1988–94, dir Equality Assurance 1994–96; ceo The Portman Gp 1996–2006; memb: Crime Prevention Panel DTI 1999, Scottish Ministerial Advsy Gp on Alcohol Problems 2001–06, BBFC 2002–05, ASA 2003–, PM's Strategy Unit Advsy Gp 2003–04, Dept of Health Taskforce on Consumers and Markets 2004, Alcohol Educn & Research Cncl 2004–07, Better Regulation Cmmn 2004–07; ind conslt on corporate responsibility 2006–; fndr memb and chair Maternity Alliance 1980s; assoc fell and memb Governing Body Newnham Coll Cambridge 2002–05; author of numerous pamphlets, articles and chapters in books; FRSA 1994; *Books* Taking Liberties (1977), Shattering Illusions (co-author, 1986); *Recreations* family, travel, food, swimming; *Clubs* Fulham FC; *Style*— The Rt Hon the Baroness Coussins

COUTTS, Anne Jane; da of Rev Alistair Sutherland, of Watlington, Oxfordshire, and Mysie, *née* Dunn; *b* 19 April 1956, Watford, Herts; *Educ* Univ of Warwick (BSc, PGCE, MEd); *m* 2 Sept 1978, Ian Alexander Coutts; 2 da (Amy b 22 Aug 1983, Rachael b 22 April 1985); *Career* dep head Edgbaston C of E Coll 1989–92; headteacher: Eothen Sch Caterham 1992–95, Sutton HS (GDST) 1995–2003, Headington Sch Oxford 2003–; memb: HMC, ISI Inspectorate, QCA Ctee Advsy Gp on Research into Assessment and Qualifications (AGRAQ); *Recreations* photography, saxophone, cooking, reading, choral singing; *Clubs* Lansdowne; *Style*— Mrs Anne Coutts; ✉ Headington School, Oxford OX3 7TD (tel 01865 759100, fax 01865 760268, e-mail acoutts@headington.org)

COUTTS, Derek James; s of Donald James Coutts, and Margaret Joan Coutts; *Educ* William Morris Sch London, Colchester Art Sch, Royal Coll of Art London (ARCA); *Children* 2 s (Jonathan James, Julien Mignonac); *Career* freelance photographer 1966–75, commercials dir 1975–; recipient of numerous advertising awards from D&AD, Cannes, etc; *Clubs* Groucho; *Style*— Derek Coutts

COUTTS, (Thomas) Gordon; QC (Scot 1973); s of Thomas Coutts (d 1976), and Evelyn Gordon Coutts; *b* 5 July 1933; *Educ* Aberdeen GS, Univ of Aberdeen (MA, LLB); *m* 1 Aug 1959, Winifred Katherine, da of William Alexander Scott (d 1982); 1 s (Julian b 1962), 1 da (Charlotte b 1964); *Career* passed Advocate 1959, standing jr counsel to Dept of Agric and Fisheries (Scot) 1965–73; chm: Industrial Tbnls 1972–2003, Med Appeal Tbnls 1984–2006, VAT Tbnls 1990–96, Financial Services and Markets Tbnl 2001–; temp judge Court of Session Scot 1991–2004, vice-pres (Scot) VAT and Duties Tbnls 1996–; called to the Bar Lincoln's Inn 1995; FCIArb; chm Faculty Services Ltd 1989–93 (exec dir 1974–84); *Recreations* historical studies, travel, stamp collecting; *Clubs* New (Edinburgh), Bruntsfield Links Golf (Edinburgh); *Style*— T Gordon Coutts, Esq, QC; ✉ 6 Heriot Row, Edinburgh EH3 6HU (tel 0131 556 3042, fax 0131 556 5947)

COUTTS, Herbert; s of late Herbert Coutts, and Agnes, *née* Boyle; *b* 9 March 1944; *Educ* Morgan Acad Dundee; *m* 24 Dec 1970, Angela Elizabeth Mason, da of late Henry Smith; 1 s (Christopher b 10 Feb 1976), 3 da (Antonia b 17 Nov 1971, Naomi b 12 April 1977, Lydia b 31 Dec 1980); *Career* keeper of antiquities and bygones Dundee Museum 1968–71 (asst keeper 1965–68), supt of Edinburgh City Museums 1971–73, city curator Edinburgh City Museums and Galleries 1973–94; City of Edinburgh Cncl: head of museums and galleries 1994–97, head of heritage and arts 1997–98, acting dir of recreation 1998–99, dir of recreation 1999–2001, dir of culture and leisure 2001–07; major projects: City of Edinburgh Art Centre 1980, Museum of Childhood Extension 1986, The People's Story Museum 1989, City of Edinburgh Art Centre Extension 1992, Newhaven Heritage Museum 1994, Makars' Court (Scotland's Poets Corner) 1998, Scott Monument Restoration 1999, Usher Hall Restoration 1999; vice-pres Museum Assts Gp 1967–70; memb: Govt Ctee on Future of Scotland's National Museums and Galleries 1978–80 (report published 1981), Cncl of Museums Assoc 1977–78 and 1986–88, Bd of Scottish Museums Cncl 1971–74 and 1986–88, Registration Ctee Museums and Galleries Cmmn 1989–2000, Bd Museums Training Inst 1995–98, Bd Cultural Heritage NTO 1998–2005; museums advsr to Convention of Scottish Local Authorities 1986–90; tstee: Paxton House 1988–2002, E Lothian Community Devpt Tst 1989–2007, East Lothian Leisure 2007–; external examiner Univ of St Andrews 1993–97; contested (Lab) S Angus 1970; SBStJ 1977, AMA 1970, FSA Scot 1965, FMA 1976; *Publications* Ancient Monuments of Tayside (1970), Tayside Before History (1971), Edinburgh - An Illustrated History (1975), Huntly House (1980), Lady Stair's House (1980), The Pharoah's Gold Mask (1998); exhibition catalogues incl: Edinburgh Crafts (with R A Hill, 1973), Aince a Bailie Aye a Bailie (1974), Gold of The Pharaohs (ed, 1988), Dinosaurs Alive (ed, 1990), Sweat of the Sun - Gold of Peru (ed, 1990), Dinosaurs Alive (ed, 1990), Golden Warriors of the Ukranian Steppes (ed, 1993), Star Trek - The Exhibition (ed, 1995), Quest for a Pirate (ed, 1996), Gateway to the Silk Road: Cultural Relics from the Han to the Tang Dynasties from Xi'an, China (ed, 1996), Faster, Higher, Stronger: An Exhibition about the Olympic Dream (ed, 1997); author of professional and academic papers and popular articles; *Recreations* gardening, swimming, music, family; *Style*— Herbert Coutts, Esq; ✉ Kirkhill House, Queen's Road, Dunbar, East Lothian, EH42 1LN (tel 01368 863113)

COUZENS, Air Vice-Marshal David Cyril; s of Cyril Couzens (d 1982), and Joyce, *née* Walker (d 2000); *b* 15 October 1949; *Educ* Ecclesbourne Sch, Churchill Coll Cambridge (MA), RAF Coll Cranwell, Loughborough Univ (Dip), Open Univ Business Sch (MBA); *m* 1977, Deborah, *née* Cawse; 1 s, 1 da; *Career* RAF: initial trg 1968–72, practical aircraft and weaponry appts 1972–88, personnel mgmnt 1988–89, Superintendent of Armament 1990–91, MOD Support Policy (Operational Requirements) 1991–94, Air Cdre 1995, CIS HQ Strike Command 1995–97, Dir Logistics Information Strategy 1997–98, Air Vice-Marshal 1998, Air Offr Logistics Information and Indust Interface Study 1998–99, DG Defence Logistics (CIS) 1999–2000, DG Defence Logistics (IS) 2000–01, DG Capability (DLO) 2001–02, COS Surgn Gen 2002–03, SDS (Air) RCDS 2003–; pres Combined Servs and RAF Rugby League; CEng 1979, FIMechE 1991, memb RCDS 1994, FRAeS 1995, FCMI 2002; *Recreations* hill walking, gardening, music; *Clubs* RAF; *Style*— Air Vice-Marshal David Couzens; ✉ Seaford House, 37 Belgrave Square, London SW1X 8NS (tel 020 7915 4841)

COVENEY, Prof James; s of James Coveney (d 1973), and Mary, *née* Sims (d 1976); *b* 4 April 1920; *Educ* St Ignatius Coll, Univ of Reading (BA), Univ of Strasbourg (Dr de l'Univ de Strasbourg); *m* 17 Sept 1955, Patricia Yvonne *née* Townsend; 2 s (Patrick John b 1956, Prof Peter Vivian Coveney, *qv*, b 1958); *Career* served WWII: Welch Regt, Royal West Kent Regt, RAF Flt Lt (Pilot); Univ of Strasbourg: French Govt res scholar 1950–51, lectr 1951–53; lectr in medieval French Univ of Hull 1953–58, asst dir Civil Serv Cmmn 1958–59, UN Secretariat NY 1959–61, NATO Secretariat 1961–64; Univ of Bath: sr lectr and head of modern languages 1964–68, jt dir Centre for European Industrial Studies 1969–75, prof of French 1969–85, emeritus prof 1985; visiting prof: École Nationale d'Administration Paris 1974–85, Univ of Buckingham 1974–86 (memb Academic Advsy Cncl 1974–83), Bethlehem Univ 1985; language trg advsr McKinsey & Co 1967–73; conslt: Univ of Macau 1988, International Communications Inc Tokyo 1991–94; tstee Friends of Birzeit Univ 1991–2004; memb: Br-French Cultural Cmmn 1973–79, Bd of Govrs Br Inst in Paris 1975–79, Euro League for Econ Co-operation 1997; confrère de Saint-Etienne Alsace 1998; corresponding memb Académie des Sciences Agriculture Arts et Belles-Lettres Aix-en-Provence 1975; Chevalier Ordre des Palmes Académiques (France) 1978, Officier Ordre National du Mérite (France) 1986; *Books* incl: La Légende de l'Empereur Constant (1955), Glossary of French and English Management Terms (with S Moore, 1972), Le Français pour l'Ingénieur (with J Grosjean, 1974), Guide to French Institutions (with S Kempa, 1978), French Business Management Dictionary (with S Moore, 1993); *Clubs* Travellers; *Style*— Prof James Coveney; ✉ 2 Campions Court, Graemesdyke Road, Berkhamsted, Hertfordshire HP4 3PD (tel 01442 865657)

COVENEY, Michael William; s of William Coveney, and Violet Amy, *née* Perry; *b* 24 July 1948; *Educ* St Ignatius Coll, Worcester Coll Oxford; *m* Susan Monica Hyman; 1 s (Thomas Geoffrey b 16 Dec 1977); *Career* ed Plays and Players 1975–78 (asst ed 1973–75), theatre critic and dep arts ed Financial Times 1981–89 (contrib 1972–80), theatre critic The Observer 1990–97, theatre critic Daily Mail 1997–2004; *Books* The Citz (1990), Maggie Smith (1992), The Aisle is Full of Noises (1994), Knight Errant (with Robert Stephens, 1995), The World According to Mike Leigh (1996), Cats on a Chandelier (1999); *Recreations* music, travel, running; *Style*— Michael Coveney, Esq; ✉ 11 Shirlock Road, London NW3 2HR (tel 020 7485 0709, e-mail michaelcoveney@btinternet.com)

COVENEY, Prof Peter Vivian; s of Prof James Coveney, *qv*, of Bath, and Patricia Yvonne, *née* Townsend; *b* 30 October 1958; *Educ* Beechen Cliff Sch Bath, Lincoln Coll Oxford (BA), Princeton Univ (Jane Eliza Procter fell), Merton Coll Oxford (sr scholar, MA), Keble Coll Oxford (Sir Edward P Abraham jr res fell, DPhil); *m* 9 May 1987, Samia Antonios Néhmé, da of Antonios Néhmé; 1 da (Elena b 22 Oct 1993), 1 s (Christopher b 12 March 1999); *Career* Wiener-Anspach fell Free Univ of Brussels 1985–86, sr coll lectr in physical chemistry Keble Coll Oxford 1987–88, lectr in physical chemistry Univ of Wales Bangor 1987–90; Schlumberger Cambridge Res Cambridge: prog ldr 1990–93, sr scientist 1993–98; prof and head of physical chemistry and dir Centre for Computational Science Queen Mary Univ of London 1999–2002, prof of physical chemistry and dir Centre for Computational Science UCL 2002–, co-dir UCL e-Science Centre of Excellence; special invited lectr Dept of Applied Mathematics and Theoretical Physics Queen's Univ Belfast 1989–90, scholar in residence Inst for Science, Engrg and Public Policy Portland OR 1993, visiting fell in theoretical physics Wolfson Coll Oxford 1996–2000, visiting sr res fell UMIST 1997–2000, visiting scholar Dept of Mathematics Tufts Univ USA 2005–06; chair: UK Collaborative Computational Projects Steering Panel, UK High-End Computing Strategy Ctee Working Gp on HEC Strategic Framework Review 2005–06; memb: Scientific Steering Ctee Isaac Newton Inst Univ of Cambridge, JISC Ctee for Support of Research; ed Computer Physics Communications, author and ed of articles in books and scientific jls; holder of 7 patents for technical inventions; memb: American Physical Soc (USA) 1985, Soc of Petroleum Engrs 1993; assoc memb Center for Advanced Mathematical Sciences American Univ of Beirut 1999–; CChem 1988, CPhys 1988, FRSC, FInstP; *Books* The Arrow of Time (with Roger Highfield, 1990), Frontiers of Complexity (with Roger Highfield, 1995); *Recreations* soccer, squash, swimming; *Style*— Prof Peter Coveney; ✉ Centre for Computational Science, Department of Chemistry, University College London, 20 Gordon Street, London WC1H 0AJ (tel 020 7679 4560, fax 020 7679 7463, e-mail p.v.coveney@ucl.ac.uk, websites www.chem.ucl.ac.uk/ccs and www.realitygrid.org)

COVENTRY, Bishop of 1998–; Rt Rev Colin James Bennetts; s of James Thomas Bennetts, of Lymington, Hants, and Winifred Florence, *née* Couldrey; *b* 9 September 1940; *Educ* Battersea GS, Jesus Coll Cambridge (open exhibitioner, MA), Ridley Hall Cambridge; *m* Oct 1966, Veronica Jane, da of Norman Leat; 2 s (Duncan James b 1967, Jonathan Mark b 1971), 2 da (Katharine Louise b 1970, Anna Jane b 1973); *Career* ordained (Rochester Cathedral): deacon 1965, priest 1966; asst curate: St Stephen Tonbridge 1965–68, St Aldate Oxford 1969–72 (concurrently chaplain to the Oxford Pastorate); chaplain Jesus Coll Oxford 1975–79 (asst chaplain 1973–75), vicar St Andrew Oxford 1979–90, rural dean of Oxford 1984–89, canon residentiary Chester Cathedral and diocesan dir of ordinands 1990–94, select preacher before the Univ of Oxford 1994, bishop of Buckingham 1994–98; *Recreations* DIY, Medieval and Renaissance music, woodcutting; *Style*— The Rt Rev the Bishop of Coventry; ✉ Bishop's House, 23 Davenport Road, Coventry CV5 6PW (tel 024 7667 2244, fax 024 7671 3271, e-mail bishcov@btconnect.com)

COVENTRY, Dean of; *see:* Irvine, Very Rev John

COVILLE, Air Marshal Sir Christopher Charles Cotton; KCB (2000, CB 1995); *Educ* RAF Coll Cranwell, Open Univ (BA), RAF Staff Coll Bracknell, RCDS; *m* Irene; 1 s, 2 da; *Career* joined RAF 1964; pilot (Lightning) 5 Sqdn, instr Operational Conversion Unit, pilot (Phantom) 43 Sqdn 1973, served Phantom Operational Conversion Unit RAF Coningsby, fighter specialist Central Tactics and Trials Org 1977, PSO to UKMILREP NATO HQ Brussels, OC Ops Wing RAF Stanley Falkland Islands, Cdr 111 (Fighter) Sqdn RAF Leuchars 1983–85, Gp Capt Air HQ 11 Gp Strike Command, Cdr RAF Coningsby, Air Cdre Flying Trg HQ Support Command, promoted Air Vice-Marshal 1992, AOC Trg Units 1992–94, AOC Trg Gp Personnel and Trg Command 1994, Asst Chief of Defence Staff Operational Requirements (Air Systems) 1994–98, Dep C-in-C Allied Forces Central Europe (re-titled Allied Forces N Europe 2000) 1998–2001, Air Memb for Personnel and C-in-C Personnel and Trg Command 2001–03; defence advsr to BT (Defence) 2003–; chm Westland Helicopters 2005–; chm C4 Defence and Aerospace Ltd 2003–; FCIPD, FRAeS; *Recreations* flying, shooting, mountaineering; *Style*— Air Marshal Sir Christopher Coville, KCB; ✉ Royal Air Force Club, 128 Piccadilly, London W1J 7PY

COWAN, Dr David Lockhart; s of Dr James Lockhart Cowan, JP, TD (d 1970), and Meryl Lockhart, *née* Cook; *b* 30 June 1941; *Educ* George Watson's Coll Edinburgh, Trinity Coll Glenalmond, Univ of Edinburgh (MB ChB); *m* 16 Sept 1966, Eileen May, da of Rev John William Gordon Masterton, of Edinburgh; 3 s (Christopher b 26 July 1967, Richard b 14 Oct 1969, Douglas b 31 May 1973), 1 da (Lindsey b 7 Jan 1971); *Career* chief resident prof Bryce Gen Hosp Toronto 1968–69; conslt otolaryngologist 1972–: City Hosp, Western Gen Hosp, Royal Hosp for Sick Children Edinburgh; hon sr lectr Univ of Edinburgh, hon sec Laryngology Section RSM; FRCSEd 1988; *Books* Paediatric Otolaryngology (1982), Logan Turner's Diseases of the Ear Nose and Throat (jtly, 1980), Coping with Ear Problems (1985); *Recreations* golf, sailing, all sports; *Clubs* Honourable Co of Edinburgh Golfers (Muirfield), Royal & Ancient (St Andrews), Seniors Golfing Soc, Elie Golf House; *Style*— Dr David Cowan; ✉ Kellerstane House, Gogar Station Road, Edinburgh EH12 9BS (tel 0131 339 0293)

COWAN, David Neville; s of Roy Neville Cowan (d 1987), of Heyshott, W Sussex, and Dorne Margaret, *née* Burgoyne-Johnson (d 1998); *b* 21 May 1950; *Educ* Marlborough, Univ of Bath (BSc, BArch); *m* 23 Aug 1975, Gillian Judith, da of David Hay Davidson, OBE (d 1983), of Lymington, Hants; 2 s (Jonathan b 1979, Christopher b 1988); *Career* architect 1975–; dir: Cowan Architects (formerly David Cowan Associates) 1989– (formed 1983), Charterfield Group of Cos 1985–; memb: SPAB, Panel of Architects Chichester Dio; author of papers on designing for the elderly and disabled, expert witness to the Courts on disability housing; dir Nat Conservation Conf 1999–2005, tstee Sussex Heritage Tst 2005; RIBA 1976, FRSA 2006; *Recreations* skiing, sailing, golf, shooting; *Style*— David N Cowan, Esq; ✉ Oak Tree Cottage, Nursery Lane, Maresfield, East Sussex (e-mail davidcowan@btconnect.com); Cowan Architects, 9–10 Old Stone Link, Ship Street, East Grinstead, West Sussex (tel 01342 410242)

COWAN, Prof Edward James (Ted); s of William Cowan (d 1987), and Margaret, *née* MacBryde (d 1997); *b* 15 February 1944, Edinburgh; *Educ* Univ of Edinburgh (MA); *m* 1, 14 Dec 1963; 2 da (Karen b 26 April 1964, Morna b 1 Dec 1965), 1 s (David b 18 Oct 1966); m 2, 15 Jan 2004, Lizanne Frances, *née* Henderson; *Career* lectr in Scot history Univ of Edinburgh 1967–79, prof of history and chair of Scot studies Univ of Guelph Ontario 1979–93, prof of Scot history Univ of Glasgow 1993– (dir Crichton Campus Dumfries 2005–); Scot Arts Cncl Award 1978; FRSE 2004; *Publications* Montrose for Covenant and King (1977), The Ballad in Scottish History (2000), Alba: Celtic Scotland in the Medieval Era (2000), Scottish History: The Power of the Past (2002), For Freedom Alone: The Declaration of Arbroath 1320 (2004); *Recreations* hill walking, bird watching, folk music; *Style*— Prof Ted Cowan; ✉ Dalarran House, Balmaclellan, Castle Douglas DG7 3PP (tel 01644 420839); University of Glasgow, Crichton Campus, Bankend Road, Dumfries DG1 4ZL (tel 01387 702042, fax 01387 702043, e-mail ted.cowan@crichton.gla.ac.uk)

COWAN, Fay; da of Hamilton C McMillan, of Stranraer, and Janet, *née* Dalrymple; *b* 5 July 1966, Stranraer; *Educ* St Denis and Cranley Sch Edinburgh, Strathclyde Univ (BA), Wine and Spirit Educn Tst (Dip); *m* 12 Sept 1992,Graham Kerr Cowan, *qv*; 2 s (Kerr McMillan b 25 April 1996, Ruadhan McKinlay b 30 Sept 1997); *Career* working career with McMillan Hotels (family business); AA Hotel of the Year for Scotland and NI 2005–06, Hotel Review Scotland Luxury Hotel of the Year 2005, Castle Hotel of the Year 2006; memb Acad of Food and Wine Serv 1996; *Style*— Mrs Fay Cowan; ✉ Glenapp Castle, Ballantrae, Ayrshire KA26 0NZ (tel 01465 831212, fax 01465 831000, e-mail thecowans@glenappcastle.com)

COWAN, Graham Kerr; s of Robert Kerr Cowan, and Agnes Una, *née* McKinlay; *b* 30 January 1964, Edinburgh; *Educ* George Watson's Coll Edinburgh, Univ of Edinburgh (BVMS, MRCVS); *m* 12 Sept 1992, Fay Cowan, *qv*; 2 s (Kerr McMillan b 25 April 1996, Ruadhan McKinlay b 30 Sept 1997); *Career* vet surgn 1986–94, hotelier Glenapp Castle 1994–; AA Hotel of the Year for Scot & NI 2005–06, Luxury Hotel of the Year Hotel Review Scot 2005, Castle Hotel of the Year Hotel Review Scot 2006; *Style*— Graham Cowan, Esq; ✉ Glenapp Castle, Ballantrae, Ayrshire KA26 0NZ (tel 01465 831212, fax 01465 831000, e-mail thecowans@glenappcastle.com)

COWAN, Matthew Alexander; s of Ian Alexander Cowan, of Bristol, and Jacqueline, *née* Matthews; *b* 31 March 1967, Bristol; *Educ* Bristol GS, Univ of Exeter (BSc, BA), Coll of Law Guildford; *m* 2 Oct 1993, Shammima Bibi, *née* Golaup; 1 da (Hannah Bibi b 3 Sept 1997), 1 s (Adam Ali Alexander b 21 Dec 2001); *Career* slr; ptnr: Olswang 1998–2003 (joined 1993), Clyde & Co 2004–; memb Law Soc; *Recreations* reading, gardening, classic cars; *Style*— Matthew Cowan, Esq; ✉ Clyde & Co, Beaufort House, Chertsey Street, Guildford GU1 4HA

COWAN, Michael John Julian; s of Kenneth Christopher Armstrong Cowan (d 1955), and Flora Muriel, *née* Stewart; *b* 24 June 1952; *Educ* Midhurst GS Sussex, Churchill Coll Cambridge (MA); *m* 26 Sept 1981, Hilary Jane, da of Albert Edward Slade (d 1987); 2 da (Eleanor Josephine, Philippa Rose), 1 s (Christopher David Andrew); *Career* investment advsr NM Rothschild & Sons Ltd 1973–78, investment dir Lazard Bros & Co Ltd 1979–87, princ Morgan Stanley International 1987–95, pres Silchester International Investors 1995–; *Recreations* golf, tennis, DIY; *Style*— Michael Cowan, Esq, FSI; ✉ Sendholme, Send, Surrey GU23 7JH; Silchester International Investors, Time & Life Building, 1 Bruton Street, London W1J 6TL (tel 020 7518 7102, fax 020 7491 7495)

COWAN, Paul Adrian Dallas; s of E Cowan (d 1988), and Peggy Dallas, *née* Johnston; *b* 5 August 1951; *Educ* Oxted GS, London Coll of Printing and Design, Univ of Surrey (MSc); *m* Jan 1979, Rosemary, *née* Nimmo; 3 da (Jo b 17 Sept 1980, Patty, Chrissy (twins) b 30 Nov 1983); *Career* tracing servs for detective agency 1970, messenger rising to account exec Ogilvy & Mather advtg agency 1971–73, sr account exec CPV Advertising 1973–74, account supr Ogilvy & Mather 1975–78; Saatchi & Saatchi: account supervisor 1978, account dir 1979–84, bd account dir 1984–86, gp account dir 1986–90; fndr md: Cowan Kemsley Taylor 1990–97, RPM3 (following merger with Butler Lutos Sutton Wilkinson) 1997–2000, fndr and md (e=) 2000–, fndr Client Relationship Consultancy; tstee Candid Arts; MIPA, MInstM; *Recreations* flying, sailing, cooking, family, advertising; *Style*— Paul Cowan, Esq; ✉ (e=), 6 Pensioners Court, The Charterhouse, London EC1M 6AU (tel 020 7251 3330, fax 087 0056 7404)

COWAN, Robert Charles (Rob); s of Maurice Bernard Cowan, of Finchley, London, and Vera, *née* Zec; *b* 14 April 1948; *Educ* Lees House Sch London; *m* 30 July 1971, Georgina, *née* Gilmour; 2 da (Francesca Sara b 26 Dec 1977, Victoria Leah b 8 Nov 1980); *Career* archivist Boosey and Hawkes Music Publishers 1978–89; ed CD Review magazine 1990–92, ed Classics (published by Gramophone magazine) 1992–93, contributing ed Gramophone magazine 1999, classical record critic The Independent 1999–; presenter: Classic Verdict (Classic FM) 1993–96, CD Choice (Classic FM) 1999–2001, CD Masters (BBC Radio 3) 2001–07, The Cowan Collection (BBC Radio 3) 2003–07, Breakfast (BBC Radio 3) 2007–; memb Judging Panel: Gramophone Awards, Classical Brit Awards, Classic Record Collector Awards; Best Historical Album Grammy Award Heifetz Collection 1995; *Publications* Guinness Classical 1000 (1998); *Recreations* reading, walking; *Style*— Rob Cowan, Esq

COWARD, Maj Gen Gary Robert; OBE (1996); s of Lt-Col R V Coward (d 2002), and Marion Avril Coward; *b* 26 August 1955; *Educ* Duke of York's Royal Mil Sch, RMA Sandhurst, RMCS Shrivenham; *m* 30 Dec 1978, Chrissie, *née* Hamerton; 1 s (Ben b 24 Sept 1982); *Career* Troop Cdr 2 Field Regt RA 1975–79, Flight Cdr 3 Regt AAC 1979–82, second-in-command and Flight Cdr 660 Sqdn AAC 1983–84, Adj 7 Regt AAC 1985–87, Div 2 ASC 1987–89, staff offr BAS Washington 1989–91, Cmd 656 Sqdn AAC 1991–93, SO1 HQ DAAVN 1993–94, UN mil spokesman Bosnia 1994–95, CO 1 Regt AAC 1996–98, Sec COS Ctee MOD 1998–2000, Dep Cdr JHC (Jt Helicopter Cmd) 2000–03, DEC (ALM) MOD 2003–05, Cmd JHC 2005–; vice-pres 656 Sqdn Assoc; CGIA; *Recreations* wine tasting, cycling, skiing; *Style*— Maj Gen Gary Coward, OBE; ✉ Headquarters, Joint Helicopter Command, Erskine Barracks, Wilton, Salisbury SP2 0AG

COWARD, (John) Stephen; QC (1984); s of Frank Coward (d 1980), of Huddersfield, W Yorks, and Kathleen, *née* Bell; *b* 15 November 1937; *Educ* King James's GS Huddersfield, UCL (LLB); *m* 4 March 1967, Ann Lesley, da of Frederick Leslie Pye, of Leighton Buzzard, Beds; 4 da (Victoria b 1969, Sarah b 1971, Laura b 1974, Sophie b 1976); *Career* served RAF 1957–59; lectr in law and constitutional history UCL and Police Coll Bramshill 1962–64; called to the Bar Inner Temple 1964 (bencher 2002); recorder of the Crown Court 1980–2003, former head of chambers; memb: Scaldwell Chamber Choir, Northampton Philharmonic Choir; *Recreations* wine, gardening, singing; *Clubs* Scaldwell; *Style*— Stephen Coward, Esq, QC; ✉ The Grange, Scaldwell, Northampton NN6 9JP (tel 01604 880255, fax 01604 881997)

COWDEN, Stephen (Steve); *b* 13 July 1952; *Educ* Allan Glen's Sch Glasgow, Univ of Edinburgh (LLB); *m* 1985; 1 s; *Career* slr Biggart Baillie & Gifford Glasgow 1974–77, Beecham Group plc 1977–90, Glaxo Wellcome plc 1991–2001, gen counsel and co sec Reed Elsevier plc 2001–; memb Gen Counsel 100 Gp; memb Law Soc of Scotland 1976, memb Internatinal Bar Assoc; *Recreations* golf; *Style*— Stephen J Cowden, Esq; ✉ Reed Elsevier plc, 1–3 Strand, London WC2N 5JR (tel 020 7166 5681, e-mail steve.cowden@reedelsevier.com)

COWDRAY, Christopher Charles Blanshard; s of Charles George Blanshard Cowdray, of Johannesburg, and Maureen, *née* Neil; *b* 4 November 1955; *Educ* Falcon Coll Essexvale Zimbabwe, Grad Sch of Business Columbia Univ NY, Tech Coll Bulawayo (HND); *m* 10 Jan 1981, Christine Anne, da of John Stewart Ian McIntosh; 1 s (Andrew Chris Blanshard b 17 Feb 1987), 1 da (Emma Rose b 8 Jan 1994); *Career* articled clerk Pulbrook, Wright & Underwood Harare 1977–79; asst front of house mange Selson Park Hotel S Croyden 1979–80; food and beverage mangr Oasis Motel Harare 1980, rooms div mangr then dep gen mangr Jameson Hotel Harare 1981–82, gen mangr Churchill Arms Hotel Bulawayo 1982–83, dep mangr Peterborough Moat House 1983–84; exec asst mangr: Eastern Province Palaces Saudi Arabia 1984–85, Riyadh Conf Palace 1985–86, Pavilion Inter-Continental Singapore 1986–88; resident mangr Hotel Inter-Continental Sydney 1988–91, gen mangr Al Bustan Palace Hotel Muscat Oman 1991–92, gen mangr Muscat Inter-Continental and regnl dir of ops Oman 1992–93, gen mangr Churchill Inter-Continental Hotel London 1993–98, md Claridge's London 1998–2004, gen mangr The Dorchester 2004–; memb London Ctee Br Hospitality Assoc (chm 1999–2000); chm Bond St Assoc, memb West One Gen Mangrs' Assoc (chm 1998); govr Eng Nat Ballet; Master Innholder; Freeman City of London; FHCIMA; *Recreations* photography, sailing, travel, outdoor pursuits, sport (especially tennis and squash); *Style*— Christopher Cowdray, Esq; ✉ The Dorchester, Park Lane, London W1A 2HJ (tel 020 7629 0114)

COWDRAY, 4 Viscount (UK 1917); Sir Michael Orlando Weetman Pearson; 4 Bt (UK 1894), DL (West Sussex 1996); also Baron Cowdray (UK 1910); s of 3 Viscount Cowdray, TD, DL (d 1995), and his 1 w, Lady Anne Cowdray *née* Bridgeman, da of 5 Earl of Bradford; *b* 17 June 1944; *Educ* Gordonstoun; *m* 1, 1977 (m dis 1984), Ellen (Fritzi), da of late Hermann Erhardt, of Munich; m 2, 1 July 1987, Marina Rose, 2 da of John Howard Cordle, of Malmesbury House, Salisbury, and Mrs Venetia Caroline Ross Skinner, *née* Maynard; 3 da (Hon Eliza Anne Venetia b 31 May 1988, Hon Emily Jane Marina b 13 Dec 1989, Hon Catrina Sophie Lavinia b 13 March 1991), 2 s (Hon Peregrine John Dickinson b 27 Oct 1994, Montague Orlando William b 17 May 1997); also by Barbara Page; 1 s (Sebastian William Orlando b 1970); *Heir* s, Hon Peregrine Pearson; *Clubs* White's; *Style*— The Rt Hon Viscount Cowdray, DL; ✉ Cowdray Park, Midhurst, West Sussex GU29 0AY

COWELL, His Hon Judge Peter Reginald; s of Reginald Ernest Cowell, CBE (d 1982), of Lowmoor, Craddock, Devon, and Philippa Eleanor Frances Anne, *née* Prettejohn (d 1993); *b* 9 March 1942; *Educ* Bedford Sch, Gonville & Caius Coll Cambridge (MA); *m* 4 Aug 1975, Penelope Jane, da of Andrew John Presgrave Bowring (d 1987), of New Romney, Kent; 2 s (Nicholas b 1976, William b 1980), 1 da (Sarah b 1980); *Career* called to the Bar Middle Temple 1964 (bencher 1997), recorder of the Crown Court 1992–96, circuit judge (SE Circuit) 1996–; memb Senate Inns of Court 1975–78; occasional memb Ctee: Thames Hare and Hounds Club, The Old Stagers; *Books* Cowell, A Genealogy (1986); *Recreations* sculling, acting, genealogy; *Clubs* Garrick; *Style*— His Hon Judge Cowell; ✉ Central London Civil Trial Centre, 26–29 Park Crescent, London W1B 1HT

COWELL, Prof Raymond (Ray); CBE (2004), DL (Notts 1996); s of Cecil Cowell (d 1970), and Susan, *née* Green (d 2003); *b* 3 September 1937; *Educ* St Aidan's GS Sunderland, Univ of Bristol (state scholarship, state studentship, BA, PhD), Univ of Cambridge

(PGCE, annual essay prize Educn Dept); *m* 14 Aug 1963, Sheila, da of George Bolton (d 1970); 1 s (Simon Jonathan b 1965), 1 da (Emma Victoria b 1968); *Career* asst English master Royal GS Newcastle upon Tyne 1962–66, sr lectr Trinity and All Saints Coll Leeds 1966–70, head of English Dept Nottingham Coll of Educn 1970–73, dep rector Sunderland Poly 1981–87 (dean 1974–81), dir and chief exec Nottingham Poly 1988–92, vice-chllr Nottingham Trent Univ 1992–2003; chm Univs' and Colls' Staff Devpt Agency 1993–98 (memb Cncl 1992–93); memb: CNAA 1974–77 and 1981–85, Unit for Devpt of Adult and Continuing Educn 1986–90, Mgmnt Ctee of Dirs of Polys 1989–91, Directing Gp OECD Prog on the Mgmnt of Higher Educn 1990–97, Br Cncl Ctee for Int Co-operation in Higher Educn 1990–2000, Cncl NCVQ 1991–97; chm: Ctee of Vice-Chllrs and Princs (CVCP) Working Gp on Vocational Higher Educn 1993–96, Staff and Educnl Devpt Assoc (SEDA) 1993–99; memb Bd: Greater Nottingham Trg and Enterprise Cncl 1990–93 (chm Strategic Forum), Nottingham City Challenge 1991–93, Cncl of Mgmnt Higher Educn Int 1991–94, Arts Cncl of England 1996–98, Opera North 2000–, Nottingham Building Soc 2003– (vice-chm 2005–), Viva: The Orchestra of the E Midlands 2005– (chm), Djanogly City Acad Nottingham 2005–; chm: E Midlands Arts Bd 1995–2001, E Midlands Business Leadership Team (Business in the Community) 2001–03; Midlander of the Year (for Arts Leadership) Carlton TV 2002; FRSA 1996; *Recreations* music, theatre, golf; *Clubs* RAC; *Style*— Prof Ray Cowell, CBE, DL

COWELL, Robert Douglas; s of Douglas Walter Cowell, of Newport, Gwent, and Gladys, *née* Williams; *b* 9 February 1947; *Educ* Newport GS Gwent, Balliol Coll Oxford (MA, DPhil); *m* 1, 18 Oct 1969 (m dis 1984), Janice Carol; 2 da (Elizabeth Sarah b 1978, Julia Mary b 1980); m 2, 24 July 1986, Elizabeth Henrietta, da of Timothy Patrick Neligan, of Petworth, West Sussex; *Career* night shift foreman Turner & Newall Ltd 1972, investment analyst Hoare Govett Ltd 1972–77, UK corporate devpt mangr Hanson Trust plc 1977–80, md Hoare Govett Securities (Hoare Govett) 1980–89, fndr ptnr Makinson Cowell 1989–; *Recreations* horse racing, golf; *Style*— Robert Cowell, Esq; ✉ Makinson Cowell Ltd, Cheapside House, 138 Cheapside, London EC2V 6LQ (tel 020 7670 2500, fax 020 7670 2501)

COWELL, Simon; s of Eric P Cowell (d 1999), of London, and Julie Cowell; *b* 7 October 1959; *Educ* Dover Coll, St Columba's Coll St Albans; *Career* with EMI Music Publishing 1977–82 (started as post boy), fndr and co-owner Fanfare Records 1982–89, joined as A&R conslt BMG Records (now BMG Sony) 1989 (artists incl Curiosity Killed the Cat, Sonia, 5ive and Westlife, artists sold over 150 million records and more than 70 number one singles in UK and US), fndr and co-owner S Records 2001–, fndr Syco Entertainment, fndr Syco Music 2002; judge: Pop Idol (ITV) 2001–02, American Idol (Fox) 2002–07; exec prodr and judge X-Factor (ITV) 2004–06 (Best Entertainment Prog BAFTA Awards 2006 and 2007), creator and judge Britain's Got Talent (ITV) 2007; creator and exec prodr: American Inventor 2006–07, America's Got Talent 2006–07, Celebrity Duets 2006; appearances on numerous other TV shows; Record Exec of the Year 1998 and 1999, A&R Man of the Year 1999, included in Top Entertainers of the Year Entertainment Weekly 2004, UK Personality of the Year Variety 2006, ranked 29th Forbes Celebrity 100 Power List 2006; *Publications* I Don't Mean to Be Rude But... (2003); *Recreations* motor racing; *Style*— Simon Cowell, Esq; ✉ S Records, Bedford House, 69–79 Fulham High Street, London SW6 3JW (tel 020 7384 7707, fax 020 7973 0332, e-mail simon.cowell@bmg.com)

COWEN, (Alan) Geoffrey Yale (Geoff); s of Alan Cowen (d 1975), and Agnes, *née* Yale (d 1960); *b* 24 September 1937; *Educ* St Edward's Coll Liverpool; *m* 22 Sept 1962, Eileen Frances, da of Reginald Altoft Johnston (d 2002), of Henleaze, Bristol; 2 da (Sian b 18 March 1965, Sara b 17 May 1966); *Career* Nat Serv Sgt RAEC 1959–61; various appts in publishing 1962–, appointed md Phaidon Press 1987, chief exec Windsor Books International 1991–, chm WRTH Publications Ltd 1998–, chm Meyer and Meyer Sport UK Ltd 2000–, chm Star Book Sales 2005–, pres Roundhouse Publishing Gp 2006–; vice-pres World Sports Publishers Assoc 2003–; *Recreations* rugby; *Clubs* Maidenhead Rugby; *Style*— Geoff Cowen, Esq; ✉ Egerton Cottage, 31 Furze Platt Road, Maidenhead, Berkshire SL6 7NE (tel 01628 29237); Windsor Books Limited, 5 Castle End Park, Castle End Road, Ruscombe, Berkshire RG10 9XQ (tel 0118 934 6367, fax 0118 934 6368)

COWEN, Joseph; s of Denis Joseph Cowen (d 1986), and Hylda Yvette, *née* Burletson (d 2000); *b* 30 April 1941; *Educ* Eton, RAC Cirencester; *m* 12 Sept 1970, Victoria Sarah, da of Brig Mark Stuart Ker Maunsell (d 1980) and Ruth Hunter Maunsell; 2 s (Philip Edward b 8 March 1972, Andrew Joseph b 7 Oct 1976); *Career* chartered surveyor and land agent; asst Davis & Bowring Kirkby Lonsdale 1963–65, Ingham & Yorke Clitheroe 1965–66; Fisher & Co (now Fisher German): Evesham 1966–70, ptnr head office Market Harborough 1974–2004 (joined 1970); RICS: chm Leics & Northants Branch 1984–85, memb Div Exec of Rural Practice Div 1988–93; MFH Fernie 1972–, chm MFHA Disciplinary Ctee 2000–04, hon treas MFHA and CHA 2005–; High Sheriff Leics 1995–96; FRICS (ARICS 1967); *Recreations* foxhunting, farming, all countryside matters, racing; *Clubs* Farmers', Turf, Land Surveyors; *Style*— Joseph Cowen, Esq; ✉ Laughton Manor Farm, Laughton Hills, Lutterworth, Leicestershire LE17 6QA (tel and fax 01858 880441, mobile 07860 230346)

COWEY, Prof Alan; s of Harry Cowey, and Mary, *née* Boyle; *b* 28 April 1935; *Educ* Bede Sch Sunderland, Emmanuel Coll Cambridge (MA, PhD, Athletics half blue); *m* 4 April 1959, Patricia, da of John Leckonby; 3 da (Lesley b 22 April 1963, Lisa b 16 June 1965, Jill b 19 April 1970); *Career* Rockefeller Fndn fell Univ of Rochester NY 1961–62, demonstrator in experimental psychology Univ of Cambridge 1962–66, Fulbright fell Harvard Univ 1966–67; Univ of Oxford: sr res offr 1967–68, Henry Head res fell of Royal Soc 1968–73, reader in experimental psychology 1973–81, prof of physiological psychology 1981–2003, emeritus prof 2003–; fell: Emmanuel Coll Cambridge 1964–67, Lincoln Coll Oxford 1968–2002 (emeritus fell 2002–); MRC: chm Neurosciences Grants Ctee 1979–81 (memb 1974–77), chm Neurosciences Bd 1981–83 (memb 1979–83), memb Cncl 1981–85, dir Brain and Behaviour Res Centre 1990–96, non-clinical res prof 1996–2002; pres: Euro Brain and Behaviour Soc 1986–88, Experimental Psychology Soc 1990–92; Spearman medal Br Psychological Soc 1967, Ferrier Medal Royal Soc 2004; Hon DSc Univ of Durham 2000; FRS 1988, FMedSci 1998; *Recreations* swimming, running, reading; *Style*— Prof Alan Cowey, FRS; ✉ Department of Experimental Psychology, University of Oxford, South Parks Road, Oxford OX1 3UD (tel 01865 271352, fax 01865 310447, e-mail alan.cowey@psy.ox.ac.uk)

COWGILL, Brig Anthony Wilson; MBE (1945); s of Harold Wilson Cowgill (d 1965), and Hilda, *née* Garritt (d 1933); *b* 7 November 1915; *Educ* Bradford GS, Manchester Grammar, Univ of Birmingham (BSc), RMCS; *m* 2 April 1949, Joan Noel Mary (d 2005), da of Peter James Stewart (d 1960); 1 da (Patricia Anne b 1951), 1 s (Andrew Anthony b 1957); *Career* cmmnd 1939, Def HQ Ottawa 1943–44, NW Europe 1944–45, GHQ India 1947, AHQ Pakistan 1948, Cwlth Div Korea 1953–54, MOD 1962–68, ret as Brig 1969; chief industrial engr Rolls-Royce Ltd 1969–77, dir Br Mgmnt Data Fndn 1979–; headed Br Mgmnt Advanced Tech study teams to US, Japan and Europe 1980–92, chm Klagenfurt Conspiracy inquiry which cleared Harold Macmillan (late Earl of Stockton) and senior army officers of war crimes charges 1986–90; FIMechE, FIET, FCMI, Hon FMS, int fell American Soc for Advancement of Engrg (Int Technol Transfer Award 1987); *Books* Management of Automation (1982), The Repatriations from Austria in 1945 (with Lord Brimelow and Christopher Booker, 1990), The Maastricht Treaty in Perspective (1992), The Treaty of Amsterdam in Perspective (with Andrew Cowgill, 1998), The Treaty of Nice in Perspective (with Andrew Cowgill, 2001), An Analysis of the Draft Treaty Establishing a Constitution for Europe (with Andrew Cowgill, 2003), The European Constitution in Perspective (with Andrew Cowgill, 2004); *Recreations* reading; *Clubs* Army and Navy, Beefsteak, RAC; *Style*— Brig Anthony Cowgill, MBE; ✉ Highfield, Longridge, Sheepscombe, Stroud, Gloucestershire GL6 7QU (tel 01452 813211, fax 01452 812527, e-mail bmdfstroud@aol.com)

COWIE, Alfred George Adam; s of Dr Alfred Cowie, DSO, TD (d 1987), of Aberdeen, and Edith Aileen Meldrum; *b* 22 August 1937; *Educ* Aberdeen GS, Leeds GS, Gonville & Caius Coll Cambridge (BA, MA), UCH (MB BChir); *m* 1 Aug 1959, Barbara Jean, da of Victor Henry Kelly (d 1979), of Brighton, E Sussex; 2 da (Fiona b 30 March 1963, Alison (Mrs Marshall) b 13 Feb 1965); *Career* conslt surgn Eastbourne District Hosp Tst 1995, emeritus conslt surgn UCHL (incl Middx Hosp and Hosp for Tropical Diseases) 1995, hon conslt surgn St Luke's Hosp for the Clergy 1984, ret; chm Regnl Trg Ctee NE Thames RHA, memb Ctee Bloomsbury HA London; memb: BMA 1962, RSM 1984; FRCS 1984, FICS; *Recreations* hill walking, vintage cars, DIY; *Style*— Alfred Cowie, Esq; ✉ 7 Chesterfield Road, Eastbourne BN20 7NT; Eastbourne District General Hospital, King's Drive, Eastbourne, East Sussex BN21 2UD (tel 01323 417400)

COWIE, Prof John McKenzie Grant; s of George Cowie (d 1985), and Helen Taylor, *née* Smith (d 1985); *b* 31 May 1933; *Educ* Royal HS, Univ of Edinburgh (BSc, PhD, DSc); *m* 6 Sept 1958, Agnes (Ann), da of James Campbell, of Edinburgh; 2 s (Graeme b 1969, Christian b 1970); *Career* asst lectr Univ of Edinburgh 1956–58, assoc res offr Nat Res Cncl of Canada 1958–67, lectr Univ of Essex 1967–69, prof of chemistry Univ of Stirling 1973–88 (sr lectr 1969–73), fndn prof of chemistry of materials Heriot-Watt Univ 1988–98 (prof emeritus 1998–); chm: Scottish Spinal Cord Injury Assoc, Br High Polymer Res Gp 1990–98, Macro Group UK 1994–98; vice-chm Scottish Cncl for Disability; hon pres: Stirling Assoc of Voluntary Orgns (formerly Cncl for Social Servs Stirling), Cncl for Disability Stirling; Macrogroup-UK medallist 2001; Hon DSc Heriot Watt Univ 2005; FRSE 1977, FRSC; *Books* Polymers: Chemistry and Physics of Modern Materials (1973, 2 edn 1991), Alternating Copolymers (1985); *Recreations* painting, reading, music; *Style*— Prof John Cowie, FRSE; ✉ Traquair, 50 Back Road, Dollar, Clackmannanshire FK14 7EA (tel 01259 742031); Department of Chemistry, Heriot-Watt University, Edinburgh EH14 4AS (tel 0131 451 3106, fax 0131 451 3180, e-mail j.m.g.cowie@hw.ac.uk)

COWIE, Sir Thomas (Tom); kt (1992), OBE (1982); s of Thomas Stephenson Knowles Cowie (d 1960), and Florence, *née* Russell (d 1984); *b* 9 September 1922; *Educ* Bede GS Sunderland; *m* 1, 1948, Lillas Roberts, *née* Hunnam (decd); 1 s (Thomas Andrew b 1950), 4 da (Elizabeth b 1951, Susan b 1953, Sarah b 1959, Emma b 1962); m 2, 1975, Mrs Diana Carole Wentworth Evans; 3 da (Alexandra b 1975, Charlotte b 1978, Victoria b 1982), 1 step s (Steven b 1964), 1 step da (Catherine b 1965); *Career* life pres Arriva plc (formerly T Cowie plc, fndr chm, chief exec until 1993); chm and owner: Sir Tom Cowie Hldgs Ltd (incorporating North European Marine Services Ltd, NEMS Singapore PTE Ltd, Penguin Metals Ltd, Gainmanor Ltd), Puffin Properties (Durham) Ltd, Murton Grange Ltd; landowner (4092 acres); *Recreations* music, game shooting, walking; *Style*— Sir Tom Cowie, OBE; ✉ Broadwood Hall, Lanchester, Co Durham (tel 01207 520 464)

COWING, Malcolm; s of Cyril Cowing (d 1992), of Doncaster, S Yorks, and Irene Cowing; *b* 7 August 1949; *m* 9 Sept 1988, Laura Madelaine, da of Henry Sutcliffe; 1 step da (Lucy Barwick-Ward b 12 Aug 1980); *Career* head of PR Union Carbide UK Ltd 1979–84, PR dir Borodin Communications 1984–89, managing ptnr Brahm Ltd 1989–; winner IPR Sword of Excellence 1994 and 1998; FCIM 2004 (MInstM 1979), MIPR 1979, MInstD 1984; *Recreations* horse racing, skiing, opera; *Style*— Malcolm Cowing, Esq; ✉ Brahm Ltd, Alma Road, Leeds LS6 2AH (tel 0113 230 4000, fax 0113 230 2332, mobile 07770 512266, e-mail m.cowing@brahm.com)

COWLEY, Caroline; *b* 19 November 1967; *Educ* Kingston Univ (LLB), Coll of Law Guildford; *Career* admitted slr 1992; Owen White: joined as trainee slr 1990, ptnr 2000–, ldr social housing team; legal advsr Chartered Inst of Housing; founding memb Social Housing Law Assoc (SHLA); *Style*— Ms Caroline Cowley; ✉ Owen White, Senate House, 62–70 Bath Road, Slough SL1 3SR (tel 01753 876800, fax 01753 876876, e-mail caroline.cowley@owenwhite.com)

COWLEY, 7 Earl (UK 1857); Garret Graham Wellesley; also Baron Cowley of Wellesley (UK 1828), Viscount Dangan (UK 1857); s of 4 Earl Cowley (d 1962), by his 2 w, Mary Elsie May; suc half n, 6 Earl, 1975; *b* 30 July 1934; *Educ* Univ of S Calif (BS), Harvard Univ (MBA); *m* 1, 1961 (m dis 1966), Elizabeth Susanne, da of late Haynes Lennon; 1 s, 1 da; m 2, 1968, Isabelle O'Bready; m 3, 1981, Paige Deming; *Heir* s, Viscount Dangan, *qv*; *Career* gp vice-pres Bank of America NT and SA London; Int Investment Management Service 1980–85; dir Bank of America Int (London) 1978–85, dir various Bank of America Tst Cos; chm Cowley & Co financial and business conslts 1985–90, investment ptnr Thomas R Miller & Son (Bermuda) 1990–2000; dir: Duncan Laurie (Isle of Man) Ltd 1994–2002, Scottish Provident Int Ltd 1998–; chm L-R Global Fund 2003–; dir Kazimir Russia, Ukraine and Caspian Funds 2006–; Lloyds Register: memb Investment Ctee 2004–, memb Gen Ctee 2006–, memb Audit Ctee 2006–; memb Assoc of Cons Peers; *Clubs* Brooks's, Philippics, The Pilgrims; *Style*— The Rt Hon the Earl Cowley

COWLEY, John Henry Stewart; s of Kenneth Cyril Cowley (d 1983), of Douglas, IOM, and Daphne, *née* Leake; *b* 20 February 1947; *Educ* King William's Coll; *m* 1, 12 May 1971, Mary, da of late Geoffrey Whitehead, of Manchester; 1 da (Joanne Jane Caroline b 1973), 1 s (George Edward Douglas b 1976); m 2, 20 March 1986, Carolyn, da of Barry Walter Golding Thompson, of Tunbridge Wells; 1 s (Daniel Kenneth Gordon b 1986), 1 da (Charlotte Mary Frances b 1989); m 3, 28 Dec 1995, Gillian, da of John Arthur Holland (d 2001), formerly of Southport and of IOM; *Career* Heron and Brearley Ltd (became Isle of Man Breweries, reverted to Heron and Brearley 1996): dir 1972, chm and md 1983–92, non-exec dir 1992–, vice-chm 1996–99; dir: Okell and Son Ltd (brewers) 1972–, Marsh (IOM) Ltd 1984–2000, Castletown Brewery Ltd 1986–; memb Cncl IOM C of C 1985 (chm 1981–83, pres 1983–85); *Recreations* game shooting, sailing; *Style*— John Cowley, Esq; ✉ Rock Villa, Strathallan Road, Onchan, Isle of Man IM3 1NN (tel 01624 671808, fax 01624 671809); Heron and Brearley Ltd, Kewaigue, Douglas, Isle of Man IM2 1QG (tel 01624 699400, fax 01624 699475)

COWLEY, Prof Roger Arthur; s of Cecil Arthur Cowley (d 1964), of Romford, Essex, and Mildred Sarah, *née* Nash (d 1991); *b* 24 February 1939; *Educ* Brentwood Sch, Univ of Cambridge (BA, PhD); *m* 4 April 1964, Sheila Joyce, da of Charles Wells (d 1970), of Romford, Essex, and Phoebe Florence, *née* England (d 1989); 1 da (Sandra Elizabeth b 1966), 1 s (Kevin David b 1969); *Career* res fell Trinity Hall Cambridge 1963–64, res offr Atomic Energy Canada Ltd 1964–70, prof of physics Univ of Edinburgh 1970–88, Dr Lees prof of experimental philosophy Univ of Oxford 1988– (chm of physics 1993–96 and 1999–2002); FRSE 1971, FRS 1978, FRSC 2001; *Books* Structural Phase Transitions (1981); *Style*— Prof Roger Cowley, FRS, FRSC, FRSE; ✉ Tredinnock, Harcourt Hill, Oxford OX2 9AS (tel 01865 247 570); Department of Physics, Clarendon Laboratory, Parks Road, Oxford OX1 3PU (tel 01865 272224, e-mail r.cowley@physics.ox.ac.uk)

COWLING, (Thomas) Gareth; s of Clifford Cowling (d 1987), and Beryl Elizabeth, *née* Thomas (d 2002); *b* 12 November 1944; *Educ* Eastbourne Coll; *m* 6 June 1970, Jill Ann, da of late Francis Neville Stephens; 1 s (Rupert b 13 Dec 1973), 1 da (Camilla b 16 March 1976); *Career* admitted slr 1969; asst Slrs Dept New Scotland Yard 1969–72, called to the Bar Middle Temple 1972, ad eundem Western Circuit 1972; district judge (Magistrates Court): Metropolitan Area 1988–89, Hampshire 1989; recorder of the Crown Court 1998–, circuit judge (Western Circuit) 2004–; *Style*— His Hon Judge Cowling; ✉ The Courts of Justice, Winston Churchill Avenue, Portsmouth, Hampshire (tel 023 9289 3000)

COWLING, Peter John; s of Harry Clifford Cowling, and Irene Charlotte, *née* Phillips; *b* 11 November 1944; *Educ* Bletchley GS, BRNC Dartmouth (Robert Roxburgh Meml Prize, Ronald McGraw Meml Prize, Graham Naval History Prize, Queen's Gold Medal); *m* 1979, Sara Anne, da of Alexander Fox; 2 da (Lucie Charlotte b 14 Jan 1981, Olivia Elizabeth Mary b 17 Dec 1983 d 2006); *Career* served RN 1963–94; Capt HMS Naiad 1979–81, Capt 3 Destroyer Sqdn 1988–90, Capt RN Presentation Team 1990–91, Sr Naval Offr Middle East 1991, Dir Naval Ops 1991–94; dir RSA 1994–96, dir of corp rels ProShare (UK) Ltd 1997–98, dir Nat Maritime Museum Cornwall 1998–2003, dir Falmouth Quay Conslts 2003–; project dir Leach Pottery Restoration Project 2005–; chm: Friends of the Benjamin Franklin House 1996, SSAFA Cornwall 2005; younger bro Trinity House 1982, memb Pilgrims Soc 1995–; *Recreations* gardening, sailing; *Style*— Peter Cowling, Esq; ✉ Parc Vean, Mylor Churchtown, Falmouth, Cornwall TR11 5UD (e-mail peter@falmouthqc.co.uk)

COWPE, William Arthur; s of Allan Cowpe (d 1974), and Margery Cowpe (d 2004), of Worsley, Manchester; *b* 8 November 1945; *Educ* Hollings Coll Manchester (Dip Hotel & Catering); *m* 5 Aug 1972, Pauline Elizabeth, da of Frederick Trevor Holt; 2 da (Charlotte Elizabeth, Hannah Louise (twins) b 21 Feb 1976), 1 s (Richard William Allan b 12 May 1979); *Career* commis de cuisine: The Savoy London 1964–67, Hotel Chateau d'Ouchy Lausanne 1967–68, Hotel Baur au Lac Zurich 1968; chef de partie Kur Hotel Bad Neuenahr 1968–69; The Goring Hotel London: jr asst mangr 1969–70, sr asst mangr 1970–74, mangr 1974–78, gen mangr 1978–89, dir 1989–2002, md 2002–; chm Mgmnt Ctee St John's Church Waterloo; memb: Considerate Hoteliers City of Westminster, Union Soc of Westminster, Lord's Taverners; hon memb Acad of Food and Wine Service 1989, memb Euro Hotel Mangrs Assoc, memb Reunion des Gastronomes (memb Ctee 1981); Master Innholder 1995, Freeman City of London 1995; FHCIMA 1995; *Recreations* golf, cricket, tennis; *Clubs* Woking Golf, Wentworth Golf, MCC; *Style*— William Cowpe, Esq; ✉ The Goring, Beeston Place, Grosvenor Gardens, London SW1W 0JW (tel 020 7396 9000, fax 020 7834 4393, e-mail wcowpe@goringhotel.co.uk)

COWPER-COLES, HE Sir Sherard Louis; KCMG (2004, CMG 1997), LVO (1991); s of Sherard Hamilton Cowper-Coles (d 1968), of Sevenoaks, Kent, and Dorothy, *née* Short; *b* 8 January 1955; *Educ* Freston Lodge, New Beacon, Tonbridge (scholar), Hertford Coll Oxford (scholar); *m* 1982, Bridget Mary, da of Neil Emerson Elliott; 5 c (Henry Sherard b 27 Nov 1982, Rupert Neil b 16 Aug 1984, Minna Louise b 18 Feb 1986, Frederick Peter b 20 May 1987, Myles Philip b 21 March 1990); *Career* Foreign Office London 1977–78, Arabic language trg 1978–80, third then second sec Cairo 1980–83, first sec Planning Staff FCO 1983–85, private sec to Perm Under Sec 1985–87, first sec Washington 1987–91, asst Security Policy Dept FCO 1991–93, efficiency scrutineer FCO 1993, res assoc Int Inst for Strategic Studies 1993–94, head Hong Kong Dept FCO 1994–97, political cnsllr Paris 1997–99, princ private sec to Sec of State for Foreign and Commonwealth Affairs 1999–2001, ambass to Israel 2001–03, ambass to Saudi Arabia 2003–07; Liveryman Worshipful Co of Skinners 1988; hon fell Hertford Coll Oxford; *Style*— HE Sir Sherard Cowper-Coles, KCMG, LVO; ✉ c/o Foreign & Commonwealth Office, King Charles Street, London SW1A 2AH (e-mail sherard.cowper-coles@fco.gov.uk)

COX, Alex; s of Jack Cox, of the Wirral, and Moyna Reese, *née* Hinton; *b* 15 December 1954; *Educ* Wirral GS, Worcester Coll Oxford (MA), Univ of Bristol, UCLA (Fulbright fell, MFA); *m* 14 Dec 1989, Cecilia Luzmila Montiel Ginocchio, da of late Mañuel Fernando Montiel Ruiz; *Career* film director: Sleep Is For Sissies 1980, Repo Man 1983, Sid and Nancy 1985, Straight To Hell 1986, Walker 1987, El Patrullero 1991, Death and the Compass (TV movie) 1992, The Winner 1996, Three Businessmen 1998, Kurosawa - The Last Emperor 1999, A Hard Look (TV movie) 2000; formerly presenter Moviedrome series (BBC2); hon citizen Tucson Arizona 1988; memb: BECTU (UK film union) 1985, STIC (Mexican film union) 1990; *Recreations* the desert; *Style*— Alex Cox, Esq

COX, Alistair Richard; s of Gerald Cox, of Leeds, and Jean, *née* Townsend; *b* 25 February 1961, Leeds; *Educ* Univ of Salford (BSc, Dip), Stanford Grad Sch of Business (MBA); *m* 30 Jan 1988, Merete, *née* Oftedahl; 2 s (Henrik Thomas b 21 Oct 1995, Carl George b 30 July 1997); *Career* Br Aerospace 1978–82, Schlumberger 1983–90, McKinsey &Co 1990–94, Blue Circle Industries 1994–2002, chief exec Xansa plc 2002–07, chief exec Hays plc 2007–; *Recreations* skiing, scuba diving, wakeboarding, sailing; *Style*— Alistair Cox, Esq; ✉ Hays plc, Hays, 141 Moorgate, London EC2M 6TX

COX, Antonia Mary; da of Dr Edgar Joseph Feuchtwanger, of Sparsholt, Hants, and Primrose Mary, *née* Essame; *b* 12 November 1963; *Educ* St Swithun's Sch Winchester, Jesus Coll Cambridge (exhibitioner, MA, Fencing half blue); *m* 24 June 1989, Simon Cox, s of Prof Antony Dawson Cox; 3 s; *Career* graduate trainee Morgan Grenfell 1985–87, corporate fin analyst C J Lawrence Morgan Grenfell Inc (NY) 1987–89, banking corr Daily Telegraph 1989–94 (city reporter 1989), freelance 1994–96, city columnist then capital markets corr Evening Standard 1997–2000, asst ed BreakingViews 2000–01, leader writer Evening Standard 2001–; Cons Pty Approved Candidates' List 2006–; LEA-appointed govr QEII Jubilee Sch London; *Publications* The Best Kit: Why Britain's defence doesn't need an all-British defence industry (2004); *Style*— Mrs Antonia Cox; ✉ c/o Evening Standard, Northcliffe House, Derry Street, London W8 5EE (tel 020 7938 7677, fax 020 7937 9306, e-mail antonia.feuchtwanger@standard.co.uk)

COX, Barry Geoffrey; *b* 25 May 1942; *Educ* Tiffin Sch Kingston upon Thames, Magdalen Coll Oxford (BA); *Children* 2 s, 2 da; *Career* journalist with: The Scotsman 1965–67, Sunday Telegraph 1967–70; reporter and prodr Granada TV 1970–74; London Weekend Television: ed 1974–77, head of current affrs 1977–81, controller of features and current affrs 1981–87, dir of corp affrs 1987–94, special advsr to chief exec 1994–95; dir ITV Assoc 1995–98, dep chm Channel 4 1999–2006; chm: Digital TV Stakeholders Gp 2002–04, Digital UK (formerly SwitchCo Ltd) 2005– (chm SwitchCo working gp 2004–05); conslt to: United Broadcasting & Entertainment (UBE) 1998–2001, ITN 1998–; memb Cncl Inst of Educn 2000–, govr Euro Inst for the Media 1999–2001, chm Oval House 2001–07; visiting prof of broadcast media Univ of Oxford 2003; FRTS; *Books* Civil Liberties In Britain (1975), The Fall of Scotland Yard (jtly, 1977), Free for All? (2004); *Style*— Barry Cox; ✉ e-mail barry.cox3@btopenworld.com

COX, Brian Denis; CBE (2003); s of Charles Cox, and Mary Ann Guillerline McCann; *b* 1 June 1946; *Educ* London Acad of Music and Dramatic Arts; *m* 1, 1967 (m dis), Caroline Burt; 1 s (Alan), 1 da (Margaret); *m* 2, 2001, Nicole Elisabeth Ansari; 2 s (Orson, Torin); *Career* actor and director; LLD (hc) Univ of Dundee 1994; *Theatre* Orlando in As You Like It (Birmingham and Vaudeville (London debut)) 1967, title role in Peer Gynt (Birmingham Rep) 1967, Ulfhejm in When We Dead Awaken (Assembly Hall Edinburgh) 1968, Steven in In Celebration (Royal Court) 1969, Gregers Werle in The Wild Duck (Edinburgh Festival) 1969, Alan in The Big Romance (Royal Court) 1970, Norman in Don't Start Without Me (Garrick) 1971, Knight of Riprafatta in Mirandolina (Gardner Centre Brighton) 1971, Brian Lowther in Getting On (Queen's) 1971, Gustav in The Creditors (Open Space Theatre) 1972, Eilert Lovborg in Hedda Gabler (Royal Court) 1972, Berowne in Love's Labour's Lost (Playhouse Nottingham) 1972, title role in Brand (Playhouse) 1972, Sergeant Match in What The Butler Saw (Playhouse) 1972, D'Artagnan in The Three Musketeers (Playhouse) 1972, Proctor in Cromwell (Royal Court) 1973, Sergius in Arms and the Man (Royal Exchange Manchester) 1974, Sir Henry Harcourt Reilly in The Cocktail Party (Royal Exchange) 1975, Emigres (Nat Theatre Co, Young Vic) 1976, Theridamas in Tamburlaine the Great (NT) 1976, Brutus in Julius Caesar (NT) 1977, De Flores in The Changeling (Riverside Studios) 1978, title role in Herod (NT) 1978, Ireton in The Putney Debates (NT) 1978, Mickey in On Top (Royal Court) 1979, Vicomte Robert de Trivelin in Have You Anything to Declare? (Royal Exchange then Round House) 1981, title role in Danton's Death (NT) 1982, Edmund Darrell in Strange Interlude (Duke of York 1984, Nederlander Theatre NY 1985), DI Nelson in Rat in the Skull (Royal Court 1984, Public Theatre NY 1985), Paul Cash in Fashion (RSC, The Pit) 1988, title role in Titus Andronicus (Swan Theatre Stratford-upon-Avon and on tour in Madrid, Paris and Copenhagen) 1988, The Taming of the Shrew (RSC, Theatre Royal), Johnny in Frankie and Johnny in the Clair-de-Lune (Comedy Theatre) 1989, title role in King Lear (NT, toured E and W Europe, Cairo and Tokyo) 1990–91, Richard III (RNT), Harold Hill in The Music Man (Open Air Theatre) 1995; as director prodns incl: The Man with a Flower in His Mouth (Edinburgh Festival) 1973, The Stronger (Edinburgh Festival) 1973, I Love My Love (Orange Tree) 1983, Mrs Warren's Profession (Orange Tree) 1989, The Crucible (Moscow Art Theatre, Riverside and Edinburgh) 1988–89, The Philanderer (Hampstead) 1991, The Master Builder (Royal Lyceum Edinburgh and Riverside) 1993–94, Richard III (Regent's Park) 1995, St Nicholas (London, Dublin, NY) 1997, St Nicholas off Broadway (Primary Stages, winner of The Lucille Lortel Award) 1998, Art (Broadway, The Royale Theatre) 1998, Dublin Carol (Royal Court) 1999, St Nicholas (Nice Drama Festival 1999), Uncle Varrick (Royal Lyceum Edinburgh) 2004, Ride Down Mount Morgan (LA) 2005, Rock'n'Roll (West End) 2006; *Television* Laurent in Therese Raquin, Jemima Shore, Rat in the Skull, Alas Smith and Jones, Perfect Scoundrels, The Cloning of Joanna May, Lost Language of the Cranes, Van der Valk, Redfox, The Big Battalions, Six Characters in Search of an Author, Inspector Morse, Sharpe's, Grushko 1994, The Negotiator 1994, Food for Ravens 1997, Herman Goering in Nuremberg, Longitude, Morality Play, The Court, The Rookie, Frasier, Adaptation, Blue/Orange, The Strange Case of Sherlock Holmes and Arthur Conan Doyle; *Radio* James McLevy (series) 2001–03; *Film* Trotsky in Nicholas and Alexandra 1971, Steven Shaw in In Celebration 1975, Father Gora in Pope John Paul II (movie CBS) 1984, Dr McGrigor in Florence Nightingale (movie NBC) 1985, Dr Lektor in Manhunter 1986, Duffy in Shoot for the Sun 1986, Peter Kerrigan in Hidden Agenda 1990, Iron Will, Argyle in Braveheart 1994, Killearn in Rob Roy 1994, Chain Reaction 1996, The Glimmer Man 1996, Long Kiss Goodnight 1996, Kiss the Girl 1996, Desperate Measures 1996, Good Vibrations 1996, The Corruptor 1998, Mad About Mambo 1998, The Minus Man 1998, Rushmore 1998, For The Love of The Game 1999, Complicity 1999, Saltwater 1999, The Cup 1999, Nuremberg 1999, Strictly Sinatra 1999, Oz 2000, Supertroopers 2000, The Biographer 2000, L.I.E. 2000, Affair of the Necklace 2000, The Ring 2002, The 25th Hour 2002, The Bourne Identity 2002, X-Men 2 2003, Troy 2004, The Ringer 2004, The Bourne Supremacy 2004, The Reckoning 2004, Match Point 2005, A Woman in Winter 2005, Red Eye 2005, Running with Scissors 2005; *Awards* Olivier Award Best Actor (for Rat in the Skull) 1985, Drama Magazine Best Actor Award (for Rat in the Skull) 1985, Olivier Award Best Actor in a Revival (for Titus Andronicus) 1988, Drama Magazine Award (for work in the RSC 1987–88 season) 1988, International Theatre Institute Award 1989, Emmy Award (for Nuremberg) 2001, Gemini Award (for Nuremberg) 2001, Boston Critics Award (for L.I.E.) 2002, Golden Satellite Award (for L.I.E.) 2002; *Publications* Salem to Moscow - An Actor's Odyssey (1991), The Lear Diaries (1993); *Recreations* keeping fit; *Style*— Brian Cox, Esq, CBE; ✉ c/o Conway van Gelder Ltd, 18–21 Jermyn Street, London SW1Y 6HP (tel 020 7287 0077, fax 020 7287 1940)

COX, Baroness (Life Peer UK 1983), of Queensbury in Greater London; Caroline Anne Cox; da of Robert John McNeill Love, MS, FRCS (d 1974), of Brickendon, Herts, and Dorothy Ida, *née* Borland; *b* 7 July 1937; *Educ* Channing Sch, Univ of London (BSc, MSc); *m* 1959, Murray Newell Cox, FRCPsych (d 1997), s of Rev Roland Lee Cox, of London (d 1988); 2 s (Hon Robin Michael b 1959, Hon Jonathan Murray b 1962), 1 da (Hon Philippa Ruth Dorothy b 1965); *Career* head Dept of Sociology N London Poly 1974–77, dir Nursing Educn Research Unit Chelsea Coll London 1977–83; sits as crossbench peer in House of Lords (dep speaker 1986–2005), baroness-in-waiting and Govt whip 1985; chllr: Bournemouth Univ 1991–2001, Liverpool Hope Univ 2006–; vice-pres: Royal Coll of Nursing, Liverpool Sch of Tropical Med; chm Int Islamic Christian Orgn (IICORR), ceo Humanitarian Aid Relief Tst (HART); non-exec dir Andrei Sakharov Fndn; pres: Tushinskaya Children's Hosp Tst, Standing Conf of Women's Orgns, London Sch of Theology, Dean Close Sch Cheltenham; tstee Siberian Med Univ; patron: Med Aid for Poland Fund, Youth With a Mission, Physicians for Human Rights UK, Premier Radio; memb Trusthouse Charitable Fndn; William Wilberforce Award 1995, Medal from Fridtjof Nanen Int Fndn Moscow 2003; hon fell Univ of Westminster; Hon PhD Polish Univ in London 1988, Hon DH Univ of Utah, Hon LLD CNAA, Hon DSc City Univ, Hon DSc Univ of Wolverhampton, Hon DSS Queen's Univ Belfast, hon degree Eastern Coll USA, LLD (hc) Univ of Dundee; Hon Doctorate: Univ of Yerevan, Armenia, Univ of Nagorno Karabekh; Hon FRCS, Hon FCGI; Cdr Cross of the Order of Merit Republic of Poland 1990, Mkhitar Gosh Medal (Armenia) 2005; *Books* The Right to Learn (jtly, 1982), Sociology: An Introduction for Nurses, Midwives and Health Visitors (1983), Trajectories of Despair: Misdiagnosis and Maltreatment of Soviet Orphans (1991), Ethnic Cleansing in Progress: War in Nagorno Karabakh (jtly, 1993), Made to Care: The Case for Residential and Village Communities for People with a Mental Handicap (jtly, 1995), Remorse and Reparation (contrib, 1999), The 'West', Islam and Islamism: Is Ideological Islam Compatible with Liberal Democracy? (jtly, 2003, 2 edn 2006), Cox's Book of Modern Saints and Martyrs (jtly, 2006), This Immoral Trade: Slavery in the 21st Century (jtly, 2006); *Recreations* tennis, campanology, hill walking; *Clubs* Royal Over-Seas League, Cumberland Lawn Tennis; *Style*— The Rt Hon Lady Cox; ✉ House of Lords, London SW1A 0PW (tel 020 8204 7336, fax 020 8204 5661, e-mail ccox@ertnet.demon.co.uk)

COX, Charles; s of Harry Cox (d 1996), and Myra Emily, *née* Brooking; *b* 25 September 1949; *Educ* Stratford GS London; *m* 12 April 1975, Sandra Carol, da of Victor Anthony Willis Taylor (d 1974); 1 da (Helen b 1976), 1 s (Peter b 1978); *Career* CA; Turquands Barton Mayhew 1968–79, ptnr PKF (UK) LLP (Pannell Kerr Forster) 1984– (joined 1979); chm and non-exec dir HBV Enterprise; tstee Hornchurch Dist Scout Cncl; Liveryman Worshipful Co of Gardeners; FCA 1972, FRSA 1998; *Recreations* hill walking, reading, Scout leader; *Clubs* RAC, MCC; *Style*— Charles Cox, Esq; ✉ PKF (UK) LLP, Farringdon Place, 20 Farringdon Road, London EC1M 3AP (tel 020 7065 0000, fax 020 7065 0650, e-mail charles.cox@uk.pkf.com)

COX, Christopher Charles Arthur; s of Col Harold Bernard Cox (d 1990), of Farnham, Surrey, and Ivie Vera, *née* Warren (d 1981); *b* 21 July 1944; *Educ* St Edward's Sch Oxford, Hertford Coll Oxford (MA, BCL); *m* 5 May 1984, Kathleen Susan Anne May, da of James Buist Mackenzie (d 1976), of Madrid, Spain; 2 da (Andrea b 1986, Georgina b 1987); *Career* admitted slr 1970; Coward Chance 1968–77, Spicer & Oppenheim 1981–84, ptnr Nabarro Nathanson 1986–97 (slr 1984–86), ptnr: Beachcroft Stanleys 1997–99, Beachcroft Wansbroughs 1999–2006, Beachcroft LLP 2006–; memb: Int Fiscal Assoc, VAT Practitioners' Gp; Freeman City of London 1986; *Books* Partnership Taxation (jtly, 1979), Capital Gains Tax on Businesses (jtly, 1992); *Recreations* politics, mountain walking, music, theatre; *Style*— Christopher Cox, Esq; ✉ Beachcroft LLP, 100 Fetter Lane, London EC4A 1BN (tel 020 7242 1011, fax 020 7894 6550, e-mail ccox@beachcroft.co.uk)

COX, Dennis William; s of Albert Frederick Cox (d 1978), and Margot, *née* Auerbach; *b* 27 February 1957; *Educ* Hornchurch GS, Westfield Coll London (exhibitioner, BSc); *m* 31 Aug 1996, Lisette Mermod; 2 step da (Natalie b Nov 1981, Candace b Nov 1983); *Career* various positions rising to sr mangr banking and fin Arthur Young (now Ernst &

Young) 1978–88, sr mangr banking and fin BDO Binder Hamlyn 1988–90, audit mangr Midland Bank rising to sr audit mangr (Compliance) HSBC Holdings plc 1991–97; dir: risk mgmnt Prudential Portfolio Managers 1997–2000, operational risk HSBC Operational Risk Consultantcy Div 2000–01; ceo: Risk Reward Ltd 2002–, Complysmart Ltd 2004–07, Europa-ICS Ltd 2005–, Legal Eagles 2006–; ICAEW: memb Cncl 1995–, memb Ctee Workplace 2000 1996–99, chm Quality and Practice Review Task Force 1998–2001, dep chm Fin Servs Authorisation Ctee 1998–2002 (memb 1996–2002), memb Remuneration Ctee 1998–2004, chm Pensions Task Force 1999–2000, chm Pensions Review Task Force 1999–2004, memb Professional Standards Bd 2001–07; fndr memb Securities Inst: Compliance Forum 1996–, Risk Forum 2002–; chairperson Risk Forum Securities Inst 2002–; lectr on risk mgmnt for: ICAEW, Securities Inst, Inst of Internal Auditors and others; memb: Editorial Bd Securities and Investment Review 1998–2007, Working Gp on the Liberalization of Capital Markets Inst of Int Fin 1999–2001, Main Ctee LSCA 2001–, Fin Planning Ctee LSCA 2001– (dep chm 2002–05, chm 2005–), Professional Risk Mangrs' Int Assoc (PRMIA), Global Assoc of Risk Professionals (GARP); ind memb: Fin Authorisation Ctee Inst of Actuaries 1999–. Designated Professional Body Inst of Actuaries 2002–; pres S Essex Soc of Chartered Accountants 1994–95 (memb Main Ctee 1983–, chm Educn and Trg 1983–93); MIB 1988, FCA 1991 (ACA 1981), FSI 2006 (MSI 1992); *Publications* Banks: Accounts, Audit and Practice (1993), The Mathematics of Banking and Finance (2006), Frontiers of Risk Management (ed, 2007); also author of various articles in Internal Auditing, Securities & Investment Review, Butterworths Jl of Banking and Finance, True and Fair and others; *Recreations* hockey, travel, music, art; *Clubs* Upminster Hockey; *Style—* Dennis Cox, Esq; ✉ Risk Reward Ltd, 46 Moorgate, London EC2R 6EH (tel 020 7638 559, mobile 07968 164793, e-mail dwc@riskrewardlimited.com)

COX, Geoffrey; QC (2003), MP; *b* 30 April 1960, Devon; *Educ* Kings Coll Taunton, Downing Coll Cambridge; *m* Jeanie; 1 da, 2 s; *Career* barrister, co-fndr Thomas More Chambers 1992, standing counsel Govt of Mauritius 1996; MP (Cons) Devon W and Torridge 2005– (also contested 2001); memb Criminal Bar Assoc, Br Inst International and Comparative Law; *Style—* Geoffrey Cox, Esq, QC, MP; ✉ House of Commons, London SW1A 0AA (e-mail tellgeoffrey@geoffreycox.co.uk, website www.geoffreycox.co.uk)

COX, Sir George Edwin; kt (2005); s of George Herbert Cox (d 1986), and Beatrice May, *née* Lillywhite (d 1981); *b* 28 May 1940; *Educ* QMC London (BSc); *m* 1, 1963 (m dis), Gillian Mary, *née* Mannings; 2 s (Russell Edwin b 24 Aug 1963, Paul Daniel James b 18 Aug 1966); m 2, 1996, Lorna Janet, *née* Moon; 2 da (Louise Beatrice b 3 Oct 1994, Eve Elizabeth b 29 Nov 1996); *Career* engr Flight Test Dept Vickers-Armstrong (later British Aircraft Corp) 1962–64, mgmnt trainee rising to mfrg admin mangr Molins Machine Co 1964–68, mgmnt consit Urwick Orr & Ptnrs 1968–73, dir of UK ops Diebold 1973–77, md Butler Cox (later Butler Cox plc) 1977–92, chm and chief exec P-E International plc 1992–94; Unisys Corp: chief exec Unisys Ltd 1995, chief exec Information Services Europe 1996–98, chm Unisys Ltd 1996–99; DG IOD 1999–2004, chair Design Cncl 2004–; non-exec memb Mgmnt Bd Inland Revenue1996–99; memb Bd: LIFFE 1995–2002 (sr ind dir), Bradford & Bingley 2000–07 (sr ind dir and chm Renumeration Ctee 2003–), Shorts 2000–; memb: Supervisory Bd Euronext 2002–07, Bd NYSE-Euronext 2007–; author Cox Review for HM Govt 2005; pres Mgmnt Consultancies Assoc 1991; visiting prof Royal Holloway Coll London, chair Advsy Bd Warwick Business Sch; speaker at conferences on mgmnt-related topics worldwide; chm Bd of Tstees Merlin (Med Emergency Relief Int) 2001–07, tstee VSO 2005–; pres Royal Coll of Speech and Language Therapists 2004–; chief coach Univ of London BC 1976–78, occasional coach OUBC, Br team coach and chm of selectors Br Men's Rowing 1978–80; Freeman City of London, memb Worshipful Co of Information Technologists, Master Guild of Mgmnt Conslts 1997; hon fell Queen Mary Univ of London; Hon Dr: Middx Univ, Univ of Wolverhampton, Northumbria Univ, De Montfort Univ; CIMgt, FInstD, FIMC, FRSA; *Recreations* rowing, gliding, theatre, history of aviation; *Clubs* Leander; *Style—* Sir George Cox

COX, Gilbert Kirkwood; MBE; s of William Cox (d 1972), and Mary, *née* Bryce (d 1995); *b* 24 August 1935; *Educ* Airdrie Acad, Glasgow Royal Tech Coll (ARTC); *m* 11 July 1959, Marjory, *née* Taylor; 2 s (Alan Bryce b 5 Nov 1961, Ian Taylor b 20 Feb 1967), 1 da (Jill Ann b 29 Jan 1968); *Career* surveyor Nat Coal Bd 1953–63, sales dir David A McPhail & Son Ltd 1963–68, gp sales dir Monteith Holdings 1968–71, dir Associated Perforators & Weavers Ltd 1971–97; dir tstee Airdrie Savings Bank (pres 1995–97); bench serving magistrate N Lanarkshire; chair: N Lanarks JP Advsy Ctee, S Lanarkshire JP Advsy Ctee; lay assessor: GMC Fitness to Practice Directorate, Royal Coll GPs Scotland; Hon Sheriff 2003, HM Lord-Lt Lanarkshire 2000– (DL 1989); memb Bd: Lanarkshire Prince's Tst Scotland, New Lanarkshire-Supercounty; past pres Monklands Rotary Club, past chm Bd of Mgmnt Coatbridge Coll; past chair: Monklands Festival Ctee, Airdrie 300 Ctee, Royal Nat Mod 1993; Paul Harris fell 1998; *Recreations* grandchildren, golf, gardening, travel; *Style—* Gilbert K Cox, Esq, MBE; ✉ Bedford House, Commonhead Street, Airdrie, North Lanarkshire ML6 6NS (tel 01236 763331, e-mail coxgk@fsmail.net); Lieutenancy Office, Civic Centre, PO Box 14, Motherwell, North Lanarkshire ML1 1TW (tel 01698 302252, fax 01698 230265, e-mail chief.executive@northlan.gov.uk)

COX, Dr James (Jim); OBE (2003), DL (Cumbria 2004); s of Dr Michael Ievers Cox, and Betty, *née* Firth; *Educ* Keswick Sch, Univ of Newcastle upon Tyne (MB BS, MD); *m* 1 Feb 1975, Fiona Mary, *née* Rolland; 1 da (Tamsin b 30 Oct 1978), 1 s (Charles b 8 July 1982); *Career* asst prof Dept of Family Practice Southern Illinois Univ Sch of Med 1976–78; GP: Morpeth Northumberland 1978–80, Caldbeck Cumbria 1980–2002; assoc advsr in gen practice Univ of Newcastle upon Tyne 1988–97, assoc dir Nat Clinical Assessment Authy 2002–05, med dir Cumbria Ambulance Service NHS Tst 2005–07; memb Bd Cmmn for Rural Communities; jt master Blencathra Foxhounds 1997–2005; FRCGP 1991 (memb Cncl 1990–2003), FRCPEd 1997; *Books* A-Z of the Human Body (conslt ed, 1987), The Good Health Fact Book (conslt ed, 1995), Rural Healthcare (1998), Understanding Doctors' Performance (2005); *Recreations* fell walking; *Clubs* Athenaeum, Farmers; *Style—* Dr Jim Cox, OBE; ✉ The Barn, Caldbeck, Wigton, Cumbria CA7 8DP (tel 01697 478730, e-mail jim.cox@btconnect.com)

COX, John Colin Leslie; CBE (1994); s of Dr Leslie Reginald Cox, OBE, FRS (d 1965), and Hilda Cecilia Cox (d 1991); *b* 23 October 1933; *Educ* UCS London, Queens' Coll Cambridge (BA); *m* 16 April 1983, Avril Joyce, da of H A G Butt (d 1975), of Sibford Gower, Oxon; 1 da (Victoria b 13 Dec 1983), 1 s (Charles b 16 March 1987); *Career* Nat Serv 2 Lt 2/10 Princess Mary's Own Gurkha Rifles 1956–58, GSM Malaya 1958; Shell Gp: joined 1958, exec posts Shell Ghana 1962–65 and London 1966–67, personnel dir Shell Chemicals UK 1978–81; dir: business devpt and chm subsid companies 1981–86, Public Health Laboratory Service 1997–; DG Chem Ind Assoc 1987–95; chm: governing body Westminster Adult Educn Service 1998–, London Europe Gateway Ltd 1997–, UK Centre for Economic and Environmental Devpt 1999– (memb bd 1996–); chief exec: London First Centre 1995–96, Pensions Protection and Investment Accreditation Bd 2000–; memb: Public Standards Bd, Edexcel Fndn 1997–, Edexcel Cncl 2001–; elected memb for Knightsbridge Westminster City Cncl 1998–; FRSA 1989; *Recreations* sailing, antiques, country pursuits, photography; *Clubs* Army and Navy, Hurlingham, Leander, Royal Solent Yacht (IOW); *Style—* John C L Cox, Esq, CBE

COX, John Edward; OBE (1993); s of Edward Ralph Cox (d 2006), of Sutton-on-Sea, Lincs, and Evelyn Lavinia Mary, *née* Pawley; *b* 18 October 1946; *Educ* The GS Brigg, BNC Oxford (BA); *m* 17 Jan 1974, Diane, da of Bernard Sutcliffe (d 1985), of Hemingford Grey, Cambs; 1 da (Laura b 29 Jan 1976); *Career* called to the Bar Middle Temple; sales mangr: International Book Information Services Ltd 1968–71, The Open Univ 1971–76; md Open Univ Educational Enterprises Ltd 1976–81, mktg dir telepublishing Butterworth and Co Ltd 1981–83; md: Scholastic Publications Ltd 1983–90, B H Blackwell Ltd 1990–94, Carfax Publishing Ltd 1994–98; md John Cox Associates 2003– (ptnr 1998–2003); memb Air Travel Trust Ctee, chm Air Tport Users' Ctee until 1992; chm Air Travel Insolvency Protection Advsy Ctee 2000–; FInstD 1991; *Recreations* theatre, conversation; *Style—* John Cox, Esq, OBE; ✉ Rookwood, Bradden, Towcester, Northamptonshire NN12 8ED (tel 01327 861193, fax 020 8043 1053, e-mail john.e.cox@btinternet.com)

COX, Prof John Lee; *b* 9 October 1939; *Educ* Univ of Oxford (MA, BM BCh, DM), The London Hosp; *m*; 3 c; *Career* house surgn The London Hosp 1966, house physician then SHO in chest and gen med St Charles' Hosp London 1966–68, SHO in gen med St Leonard's Hosp London 1968–69, locum registrar Paddington Chest Clinic Feb-April 1969, registrar Univ Dept of Psychiatry The London Hosp Dec 1969–72 (SHO April-Dec 1969), lectr Dept of Psychiatry Makerere Univ Kampala Uganda, hon lectr The London Hosp and hon conslt Butabika Hosp Kampala 1972–74, lectr Dept of Psychiatry The London Hosp 1974–75, sr lectr Dept of Psychiatry Univ of Edinburgh and hon conslt Royal Edinburgh Hosp and Western Gen Hosp 1975–86, prof of psychiatry Keele Univ 1986–2002 (head of dept Sch of Postgraduate Med 1986–94), conslt psychiatrist City Gen Hosp Combined Health Care NHS Tst 1986–; sec gen World Psychiatric Assoc 2002–; RCPsych: former chm Gen Psychiatry Specialist Ctee, dean 1993–98, pres 1999–2002; formerly WHO conslt Botswana and Br Cncl conslt Zimbabwe; fndr memb and past pres Marcé Soc (int soc for the prevention and mgmnt of postnatal mental illness), Marcé Medal 1996; DPM, FRCPEd 1985, FRCPsych 1986 (pres 1999–); *Books* Postnatal Depression: A Guide for Health Professionals (1986), Transcultural Psychiatry (ed and contrib, 1986), Racial Discrimination and the Health Service (jt ed, 1989), Current Approaches: Childbirth as a Life Event (jt ed, 1989), Prevention of Postnatal Depression: uses and misuses of the Edinburgh Postnatal Depression Scale (jt ed); author of various book chapers and numerous academic pubns; *Style—* Prof John L Cox

COX, (Edward) John Machell; s of Sqdn Ldr Edward Machell Cox (d 1992), and late Joan Edith, *née* Hewlett; *b* 18 September 1934; *Educ* Charterhouse, St Peter's Hall Oxford (MA); *m* Elizabeth Jean, da of Maj Anthony Frederick Halliday Godfrey (ka France 1939); 1 s (Charles Mark Machell), 1 da (Victoria Rachel Machell); *Career* Nat Serv Lt RASC 1953–55; CA; ptnr: Brown Peet & Tilly 1969–71, Howard Tilly 1971–88, Baker Tilly 1988–91; interim DG Euro Script Fund 1992–93; Royal Borough of Kensington and Chelsea: cncllr 1974–, mayor 1986–87, chm Planning Ctee 1979–81, chm Housing and Social Servs Ctee 1988–93, memb Policy and Resources Ctee 1988–2001, memb Cabinet for Finance and Property 2001–04, chm Investment Ctee 2001–, chm Overview & Scrutiny Ctee for Children and Family Servs 2006–, vice-chm Planning Servs Ctee 2006–, vice-chm Maj Planning Devpts Ctee 2006–; dir: Kensington & Chelsea Tenant Mgmnt Orgn 1998–, Grand Union Homes Ltd 2005–, London Pension Fund Authy 2007–; non-exec dir: NW London Mental Health NHS Tst 1993–99 (chm 1997–99), W London Mental Health NHS Tst 2000– (chm Audit Ctee 2000–); chm: North Kensington City Challenge Co Ltd 1994–99, Fighting Unemployment in North Kensington 1999–2003; memb Mgmnt and Fin Ctees Octavia Housing and Care 1995–2004; Freeman City of London, Liveryman Worshipful Co of Fruiterers; FCA; *Clubs* Hurlingham; *Style—* E J M Cox, Esq; ✉ 13 St Ann's Villas, London W11 4RT (tel 020 7603 9828, fax 020 7371 6200, e-mail johncox909@aol.com)

COX, Ven John Stuart; s of Arthur Francis William Cox (d 1988), and Clarice Mildred, *née* Dadswell (d 1992); *b* 13 September 1940; *Educ* Judd Sch Tonbridge, Fitzwilliam House Cambridge (MA), UC Rhodesia and Nyasaland (Rotary Int fellowship), Wycliffe Hall/Linacre Coll Oxford (BA), Univ of Birmingham (DPS); *m* 1 Feb 1964, Mary Diane, da of Jack Henry Watson Williams; 1 s (David John b 20 June 1969), 1 da (Elizabeth Diane b 13 Feb 1972); *Career* asst curate: St Mary Prescot Lancs 1968–71, St George Newtown Birmingham 1971–73; rector St George Newtown Birmingham 1973–78, selection sec Advsy Cncl for Church Miny 1978–83, canon residentiary Southwark Cathedral 1983–91, dir of ordinands and post-ordination trg Southwark 1983–91, vicar Roehampton Ecumenical Parish 1991–95, archdeacon of Sudbury 1995–2006, moderator Southwark OLM Trg Scheme 2001–; memb Gen Synod 1990–95 and 2000–05; sr inspector House of Bishops Inspections 1998–2006; tstee Anglican Gp Educnl Tst; memb Cncl Missions to Seafarers; *Books* Religion and Medicine Vol 1 (contrib, 1970), Say One for Me (contrib, 1992); *Recreations* reading, music, golf, gardening, theatre; *Style—* The Ven John Cox; ✉ 2 Bullen Close, Bury St Edmunds IP33 3JP (tel 01284 766796, fax 01284 766796, e-mail archdeacon.john@stedmundsbury.anglican.org)

COX, Jonson; s of Peter Cox, and Bobbie, *née* Sutton; *b* 11 October 1956; *Educ* King Edward VI Sch Totnes, Clare Coll Cambridge (BA); *partner* Barbara Wight; 1 s, 2 da; *Career* business mgmnt roles with Royal Dutch/Shell Gp 1979–92, chm and md Yorkshire Environmental Ltd 1993–96, md Kelda Gp plc 1994–2000, md Yorkshire Water 1996–2000, chief operating offr Railtrack plc 2000–01; chief exec: Valpak 2002–03, Anglian Water Gp plc 2004–, NED Wincanton plc; non-exec dir Wincanton plc 2005–; fndr dir Right to Read; *Recreations* skiing and outdoor activities; *Style—* Jonson Cox, Esq; ✉ Anglian Water Group plc, Ambury Road, Huntingdon, Cambridgeshire PE29 3NZ

COX, Josephine; da of Bernard Brindle, and Mary Jane Brindle; *b* 15 July 1940; *m* Kenneth George Cox; 2 s (Spencer John, Wayne Kenneth); *Career* writer; former jobs incl: clerk to Milton Keynes Devpt Cncl, various secretarial positions, ptnr family landscaping co, teacher for 14 years, sociology/history lectr Bletchley Coll Milton Keynes; 34 novels as Josephine Cox, 4 novels as Jane Brindle; Superwoman of GB 1980; *Books* Her Father's Sins, Let Loose the Tigers, Angels Cry Sometimes, Take This Woman, Outcast, Whistledown Woman, Alley Urchin, Vagabonds, Don't Cry Alone, Jessica's Girl, Nobody's Darling, Born to Serve, More Than Riches, A Little Badness, Living a Lie, The Devil You Know, A Time for Us, Cradle of Thorns, Bad Boy Jack, Lovers and Liars, Beachcomber, The Woman Who Left, Jonne, Live the Dream, The Journey, Journeys End, The Loner; as Jane Brindle: Scarlet, No Mercy, The Tallow Image, No Heaven No Hell, The Seeker; *Recreations* swimming, walking, reading, creating board games; *Style—* Mrs Josephine Cox

COX, Hon Mrs Justice; Dame Laura Mary; DBE (2002); da of John Arthur Bryant (d 1972), of Wolverhampton, and Mary Eileen, *née* Clarke; *b* 8 November 1951; *Educ* Wolverhampton HS for Girls, Queen Mary Coll London (LLB, LLM); *m* 1970, David John Cox, s of Harry Cox; 3 s (Jonathan James b 25 April 1980, Leo John b 7 June 1983, Benjamin David b 19 May 1993); *Career* called to the Bar Inner Temple 1975 (bencher 2000), QC 1994, recorder of the Crown Court 1995–2002, head of chambers 1996–2002, judge of the High Court of Justice (Queen's Bench Division) 2002–; judge Employment Appeal Tbnl 2000–; chm Sex Discrimination Ctee Bar Cncl 1996–2000, memb Cncl of Justice 1998–2002, chm Equal Opportunities Ctee Bar Cncl 2000–02; Br memb ILO Ctee of Experts 1998–, pres Assoc of Women Barrs 2005–, memb Ctee UK Assoc of Women Judges 2005–; hon fell Queen Mary Univ of London 2005; *Recreations* music, theatre, cinema, football, good food and wine; *Style—* The Hon Mrs Justice Cox, DBE; ✉ Royal Courts of Justice, Strand, London WC2

COX, Neil Derek; s of Clifford Walter Ernest, and Meryl Rita, *née* Holland; *b* 1 August 1955; *Educ* King Edward VI GS Stafford, Glasgow Caledonian Univ (BSc); *m* 23 March 1981, Averin Moira, da of Philip Anthony Donovan; 2 da (Katy b 1984, Jocelyn b 1990), 1 s (Andrew b 1986); *Career* sr optometrist Moorfields and KCH London, private contact lens practice London; lectured widely and published papers on clinical applications of contact lenses; tstee Fight for Sight; vice-pres Warlingham RFC; Liveryman Worshipful Co of Spectaclemakers; FCOptom (FBCO 1978), FAAO 1991; *Recreations* wine, food, photography; *Style—* Neil D Cox, Esq; ✉ 11 Milford House, 7 Queen Anne Street, London W1G 9HN (tel 020 7631 1046, fax 020 7436 0564)

COX, Patrick Lathbridge; s of Terry Brian Cox, of Victoria, BC, Canada, and Maureen Patricia, *née* Clarke; *b* 19 March 1963; *Educ* Cordwainer's Coll Hackney (DATech); *Career* footwear designer; work included in collections of: Vivienne Westwood, John Galliano, Richard James, Alistair Blair, Lanvin, John Flett & Katherine Hamnett London and Paris 1985–92; exhibited in: Aust Nat Gallery, V&A; Accessory Designer of the Year Br Fashion Awards 1994 and 1995; *Style—* Patrick Cox, Esq

COX, Paul William; s of Oliver Jasper Cox, CBE, of London, and Jean Denise, *née* Cooper; *b* 31 July 1957; *Educ* Port Regis Sch, Stanbridge Earls Sch, Camberwell Sch of Art And Crafts (BA), RCA (MA); *m* 28 Nov 1987, Julia Claire, da of Capt Peter Dale Nichol, RN, (d 1997), of Hayling Island, Hants; 1 da (Harriet Claire b 16 Aug 1991), 1 s (Jack William b 22 July 1994); *Career* freelance artist and illustrator 1982–; contrib: The Times, Telegraph, Independent, Spectator, Punch, Sunday Times, Observer, Sunday Express, Daily Express, Radio Times, The Guardian, New Yorker, Vanity Fair, Town and Country, Wall Street Jl, Traditional Home, Chatelaine, Business Week, House Beautiful; visiting lectr in illustration Camberwell Sch of Art and Crafts 1982–90, reportage illustrations for Blueprint 1984–89; watercolour drawings exhibitions: Workshop Gallery 1984, Illustrators' Gallery 1985, Chris Beetle's Gallery 1989, 1993, 2001 and 2006, Scandinavian Contemporary Art Gallery 1993, Molesworth Gall (Dublin) 2001, Durrell Wildlife Conservation Tst 2006; designed commemorative stamps for 600th anniversary of The Lord Mayor's Show 1989, historical images for Drama & Debate exhbn Hampton Ct Palace 2004, designed Mural for Eleanor Davies Colley Lecture Theatre Royal Coll of Surgns 2004, designed and painted sets for 50th anniversary prodn of Salad Days 2005 and 2006, 15 paintings for St Charles Hosp 2007; hon memb Soc of Architect Artists 1993; *Books* illustrated: Experiences of an Irish RM (1984), The Common Years (1984), A Varied Life (1984), The Outing (1985), The Character of Cricket (1986), Romantic Gardens (1988), Evacuee (1988), Rebuilding The Globe (1989), Dear Boy (1989), Leave it to Psmith (1989), Three Men in a Boat (1989), The Cricket Match (1991), Honourable Estates (1992), Favourite Songs of Denmark (1993), Wind in the Willows (1993), The Russian Tea Room (1993), Rumpole (1994), Look Out London (1995), Jeeves and Wooster (1996), The Plums of PG Wodehouse (1997), Three Men on the Bummel (1998), Tinkerbill (1999), Jeeves Two (2000), Best After-Dinner Stories (2003), The Giver (2003), The Train to Glasgow (2003), The Best of Blandings (2004), The Folio Book of Comic Short Stories (2005), My Family and other Animals (2006); *Clubs* Chelsea Arts, Bembridge Sailing; *Style—* Paul Cox, Esq; ✉ Twytten House, Wilmington, East Sussex BN26 5SN (tel 01323 871264, fax 01323 871265, e-mail paulwcox@gmail.com)

COX, Dr Robin Anthony Frederick; s of Ronald Frederick Cox (d 1986), of Sheringham, Norfolk, and Hilda Mary, *née* Johnson (d 1990); *b* 29 November 1935; *Educ* Ashby-de-la-Zouch GS, Gonville & Caius Coll Cambridge (MA, MB BChir), Guy's Hosp; *m* 8 Sept 1962, Maureen Jennifer, da of William Jackson Moore (d 1969), of North Walsham, Norfolk; 1 da (Fiona b 1964), 1 s (Andrew b 1967); *Career* conslt occupational physician, ret; princ in med practice Gorleston on Sea Norfolk 1964–76, dir North Sea Med Centre 1972–76, med dir Phillips Petroleum Co Europe and Africa 1976–86; CMO: CEGB 1986–90, National Power 1990–92; previously: med advsr Prudential Insurance Co, Wellcome Tst, BUPA, Nomura International and Goldman Sachs; previously pres Int Assoc Physicians for Overseas Serv, vice-dean Faculty of Occupational Med; pres Cambridge Bird Club (former chm), former pres Gorleston Rotary Club, chm Diving Med Advsy Ctee, memb Cncl Br Tst for Ornithology; Bronze medallist Royal Humane Soc 1974, Freeman City of London 1978, Liveryman Worshipful Soc of Apothecaries; FRCP, FFOM, DDAM; *Books* Offshore Medicine (1982), Fitness for Work (2000); *Recreations* ornithology, fly fishing, gardening, photography, walking; *Clubs* RSM, British Ornithologists'; *Style—* Dr Robin Cox; ✉ Linden House, Long Lane, Fowlmere, Cambridgeshire SG8 7TG (tel 01763 208636, fax 01763 208549, e-mail erithacus@uwclub.net)

COX, Simon Foster Trenchard; s of Foster Trenchard Cox (d 1996), and Madeleine Winifred Needham, *née* Cooper (d 1989); *b* 17 January 1956; *Educ* Eton, Trinity Coll Oxford (MA); *m* 1 Feb 1992, Hania Katherine, da of Jan and Sophie Mier Jedrzejowicz; *Career* HAC 1980–88, cmmnd 1985; admitted slr 1980; Norton Rose: articled clerk 1978–80, slr 1980–88, ptnr 1988–; chm and hon treas Br Polish Legal Assoc 2000–; tstee: Needham Cooper Charitable Tst 1990–, Peter Kirk Meml Fund 1997–; Freeman City of London Slrs Co; memb Law Soc 1980; MSI 1992; *Recreations* water sports, running; *Clubs* HAC, Ognisko Polskie; *Style—* Simon Cox, Esq; ✉ Norton Rose, 3 More London Riverside, London SE1 2AQ (tel 020 7283 6000, fax 020 7283 6500, e-mail simon.ft.cox@nortonrose.com)

COX, Stephen James; CVO (1997); *b* 5 December 1946; *Educ* Univ of Birmingham (BA), Univ of Leeds (Dip ESL), Univ of Sussex (MA); *m* 1970, Pauline Victoria, *née* Greenwood; 1 s (David), 1 da (Rachel); *Career* English teacher Bolivia (VSO) 1965–66, Br Cncl 1969–84 (incl postings Warsaw, Accra and London), educn attaché Br Embassy Washington DC 1984–85, asst sec for int affrs Royal Soc 1985–91, DG Commonwealth Inst 1991–97, chief exec Westminster Fndn for Democracy 1995–97, exec sec Royal Soc 1997–; chair Br Cncl Whitley Cncl Trades Union Side 1981–84, chair Bd Cwlth Round Table 2002–06 (memb 1994–); memb: Exec Ctee GB-E Europe Centre 1988–91, educn and field work ctees Royal Geographical Soc 1995–; memb Cncl: Parly and Scientific Ctee 1997– (vice-pres 2004–2007), BAAS 1997–, Fndn for Sci and Technol 1997–; tstee: Cncl for Assisting Refugee Academics 1997–, Int Polar Fndn 2006–; Kingston Univ: memb Bd 2002–, chair Audit Ctee 2004–; chair Duke of Edinburgh Award Forum Richmond; Hon DSc Lancaster Univ 2003; FRGS; *Recreations* cricket, visiting galleries; *Clubs* Royal Over-Seas League, Geographical; *Style—* Stephen Cox, Esq, CVO; ✉ Royal Society, 6 Carlton House Terrace, London SW1Y 5AG (tel 020 7451 2506, fax 020 7451 2691, e-mail stephen.cox@royalsoc.ac.uk)

COX, Stephen Joseph; s of Leonard John Cox (d 1984), of Bristol, and Ethel Minnie May McGill (d 1980); *b* 16 September 1946; *Educ* St Mary Redcliffe Sch Bristol, Central Sch of Art and Design; *m* 1 June 1970, Judith, da of John Douglas Atkins, of Well Court Farm, Tyler Hill, nr Canterbury, Kent; 2 da (Pelé Delaney, Georgia Easterly); *Career* sculptor; Arts Cncl major awards 1978 and 1980, Br Cncl bursaries 1978 and 1979, Hakone Open Air Museum prize Japan 1985, Indian Triennale Gold medal 1986, Goldhill Sculpture prize Royal Acad 1988, Capital and Counties Art and Work award 1991; subject of book by Henry Moore Fndn, The Sculpture of Stephen Cox 1995; sr research fell Wimbledon Sch of Art 1995–96; *Solo Exhibitions* Tate Gallery, Lisson Gallery, Nigel Greenwood Gallery, 25 Festival dei Due Mondi Spoleto 1982, Bath Festival Artsite 1988, Arnolfini Gallery Bristol 1985 (touring to MOMA Oxford, Midland Group Gallery Nottingham), also Amsterdam, Milan, Rome, Gothenberg, Bari, Florence, Geneva, Basle, Paris, New Delhi (Br rep Indian Triennale 1986)), Museum of Egyptian Modern Art Cairo 1995, Stephen Cox: Surfaces and Stones of Egypt Henry Moore Inst 1995, Sight of Kephren Michael Hue-Williams Fine Art 1995, Royal Botanic Gardens Kew 1995–96, An Indian Decade 3 exhibitions - Art Today Gallery, Indian Cncl for Cultural Rels (ICCR) Ajanta Gallery and Jamali Kamali Gardens, Michael Hugh-Williams Fine Art 1996, Dulwich Picture Gallery 1997, Glyndebourne Opera House 1998, Michael Hue-Williams

Fine Art 1998–99, Interior Space (Santa Maria Della Scala) Siena 1999, Fasti (Museum Archeologico Aosta Italy) 2000, Organs of Action (Culture Gallery) NY 2001, Eyestorm Gallery London 2004, Mappa Mundi (Hereford Cathedral and Meadow Gallery Burford) 2004, Shrewsbury Museum 2005, San Fracesco Della Scarpa Bari 2005, Stephen Cox: Sculptor, origins and influences (Bristol City Museum and Art Gallery) 2006; *Group Exhibitions* Paris Biennale 1977, British Sculpture in the Twentieth Century (Whitechapel Art Gallery) 1981, Venice Biennale 1982 and 1984, New Art Tate Gallery 1983, Int Garden Festival Liverpool 1984, Int Survey of Painting and Sculpture (MOMA NY) 1984, 40 Years of Modern Art 1945–85 (Tate Gallery), British Art in the 1980's (Brussels) MOMA, New Displays (Tate Gallery) 1992, Sculptors Drawings (Tate Gallery) 1994, Time Machine (British Museum) 1994–95 (travelling to Museo Egizio Torino), Hathill Fndn Goodwood, Centenary Display (Tate Gallery) 1997, British Sculpture (Schloss Ambrass Innsbruck), Jesus Coll Cambridge 1999, Kamakura Mie Sapporo (Japanese tour), Encounters: New Art from Old (Nat Gallery), Sculpture and the Divine (Winchester Cathedral) 2000, Sculpture in the Park (Mile End Park) 2001, Thinking Big: Exhibition of British sculpture (Guggenheim Venice) 2002, Lingam of a 1000 Lingams (Cass Sculpture Fndn) 2002, BLOK: Festival of Sculpture (Canterbury) 2003, Sculpture: A Spectator Sport (Bryanston plc Dorset) 2003, Summer Exhibition (Burghley House Lince) 2003, Akeley Heads Art and Landscape Project (Durham) 2003; *Collections* Tate Gallery, V&A, Br Museum, Br Cncl, Arts Cncl, Walker Art Gallery Liverpool, Henry Moore Centre for Sculpture, Hunterian Art Gallery, Groningen Museum Netherlands, Peter Ludwig Collection FRG, Fogg Museum USA, Hakone Open Air Museum Japan, Gori Collection Celle Pistoia Italy; *Commissions* Tondo: Ascension (Royal Festival Hall) 1983, Cairo Opera House (FCO cmmn) 1988–89, Ganapathi & Devi (Broadgate London) 1989, Osirisisis (Stockley Park London) 1991, Hymn (Univ of Kent Canterbury) 1991, Mantra (Br Cncl building New Delhi) 1992, Echo (Fleet Place Ludgate), Reredos, altar, font and stations of the cross (Church of St Paul Haringey), Rajiv Gandhi Samadhi New Delhi (central feature) 1995–97, Adam and Eve vessels St Luke's Chelsea 1996, Eucharist Cathedral Church of St Nicholas Newcastle upon Tyne 1997, Br High Cmmn Canberra Aust (Tribute Sculpture, FCO cmmn) 1997, faceted column Finsbury pavement London 1999, altar St Anselm's Chapel Canterbury Cathedral consecrated 2006; *Clubs* Chelsea Arts; *Style—* Stephen Cox, Esq; ✉ Lower House Farm, Coreley, Ludlow, Shropshire SY8 3AS (tel 01584 891532, fax 01584 891674, e-mail coxstepstone@aol.com)

COX, Prof Timothy Martin; s of late William Neville Cox, of Leics, and late Joan Désirée, *née* Ward; *b* 10 May 1948; *Educ* Oundle, London Hosp Med Coll (MSc, MD), Univ of Cambridge (MA, MD); *m* 1975, Susan Ruth, da of late Harry Philips Mason, of Builth Wells, Powys; 3 s, 1 da; *Career* house physician and surgn Professorial Units The London Hosp 1971–72, jr lectr in morbid anatomy Bernard Baron Inst 1972–74, jr clinical posts United Oxford Hosp 1974–75, Wellcome Tst sr clinical fell 1979–85; Imperial Coll of Med London (formerly Royal Post Grad Med Sch): jr clinical posts 1974, registrar, hon sr registrar and MRC res fell 1975–79, sr lectr 1985–87, sr lectr in haematology and conslt Dept of Med 1987–89; prof of med Univ of Cambridge and fell Sidney Sussex Coll 1989–; visiting scientist Dept of Biology MIT 1983–84, visiting prof Univ of Manchester 1994, Schorstein Meml lectr London Hosp Med Coll 1994, Bradshaw lectr RCP 1996, McFadzean Meml lectr Hong Kong Univ 1990, Flynn lectr RCPath 2001; external examiner in med: Hong Kong Univ 1990, Univ of London 1992–97, Royal Coll of Surgeons Ireland 1994–97, Chinese Univ Hong Kong 2001, Univ of Oxford 2001–; memb Exec Ctee Assoc of Physicians of GB and Ireland 1995–97 (memb 1984), pres Cambridge Philosophical Soc 2002–03 (vice-pres 1998–2000), memb syndicate CUP 1998–, tstee Croucher Fndn Hong Kong 2001–, fell Galton Inst 2006–; FRCP 1984, FMedSci 1998, FRSA 2000; *Books* Molecular Biology in Medicine (co-ed, 1997, Spanish trans 1998, Chinese trans 2000, Serbo-croat trans 2001), Oxford Textbook of Medicine (ed, 4 edn 2003); *Publications* numerous articles on inborn errors and metabolic diseases; *Recreations* music, making cider; *Style—* Prof Timothy Cox; ✉ Department of Medicine, University of Cambridge School of Clinical Medicine, Addenbrooke's Hospital, Hills Road, Cambridge CB2 2QQ (tel 01223 336864, fax 01233 336846, e-mail jbg20@medschl.cam.ac.uk)

COXON, Richard; *Educ* Royal Northern Coll of Music; *Career* tenor; studies with John Mitchinson; princ Scottish Opera 1993–96, freelance 1996–; performances with Scottish Opera incl: Alfredo in La Traviata, Trabuco in La Forza del Destino, Sailor in Tristan und Isolde, Jacquino in Fidelio, Nemorino in L'Elisir d'Amore, Narraboth in Salome, Flavio in Norma, Barbarigo in I due Foscari, Jiri in The Jacobin, Don Ottavio in Don Giovanni, Brighella in Ariadne, Alfred in Die Fledermaus, Kudrias in Katya Kabanova; other credits: Nemorino (Opera Northern Ireland and Opera Zuid Maastricht), Ralph Rackstraw in HMS Pinafore (National Operetta Company), Die Freunde von Salamanka (Edinburgh Int Festival and Aix-en-Provence Festival), Steuerman in Flying Dutchman (Opera Ireland), Messiah (Royal Albert Hall), Alfredo in La Traviata (Opera Northern Ireland), Brighella in Ariadne auf Naxos (ENO), Young Convict in House of the Dead (ENO), Fenton in Falstaff (ENO), Painter in Lulu (ENO), Nick in Handmaiden's Tale (ENO), Mr By-Ends in The Pilgrims Progress (Royal Opera, also recorded for Chandos), Gaston in La Traviata (Royal Opera), Squeak in Billy Budd (Royal Opera, also recorded for Chandos), Iego in The Bird of Nigh (Royal Opera) Tom Rakewell in The Rake's Progress (New Israel Opera), Major Domo and Lieutenant Bonnet in War and Peace (Spoleto Festival, also recorded for Chandos), Bill in Flight (Nat Reiss Opera and Glyndebourne Festival Opera, recorded for Chandos), Italian singer in Der Rosenkavalier (Opera North, Spoleto Festival), Kudryash in Katya Kabanova (Florida Grand Opera and Opéra de Montréal), Edoardo in Un Giorno di Regno (Buxton Festival Opera), Piquillo in La Péricole (Buxton Festival Opera), Troilus in Troilus and Cressida, Gastone (Nat Reiss Opera and Opera North), Voice from the Forge (Opera North and Greek Nat Opera), Flute in Midsummer Night's Dream (La Monnaie Brussels), Monostatos in Magic Flute (Florida Grand Opera); oratorio and solo recitals with: Hallé Orchestra, Royal Scottish Nat Orchestra, Bergen Philharmonic Orchestra, Royal Liverpool Philharmonic, BBC Scottish Symphony Orchestra, London Pops Orchestra, London Musici (world premiere of A Live Flame), City of London Sinfonia, Scottish Chamber Orchestra, Scottish Opera Orchestra, Vara Radio Orchestra, BBC Symphony Orchestra, Israel Camerata; London Symphony Orch; recorded Kurt Weill under Sir Andrew Davis Royal Place; filmed role of Edgardo at Toronto Festival, filmed role of Fox in The Cunning Little Vixen under Kent Nagano for DVD; Van Man in The Little Prince recorded for Sony Classical and DVD; Webster Booth/Esso Award, Clonter Opera Prize, Ricordi Opera Prize, Peter Moores Foundation Award, Wolfson Tst Award; *Style—* Richard Coxon, Esq; ✉ c/o Helen Sykes Artists' Management, 100 Felsham Road, Putney, London SW15 1DQ (tel 020 8780 0060, fax 020 8780 8772)

COXWELL-ROGERS, Col Richard Annesley; DL (Gloucestershire); s of Maj-Gen Norman Annesley Coxwell-Rogers, CB, CBE, DSO (d 1985), of Cheltenham, and Diana Mary, *née* Coston (d 1995); *b* 26 April 1932; *Educ* Eton, Sandhurst; *m* 1, 21 Sept 1965, Martha Felicity (d 1998), da of Col G T Hurrell, OBE (d 1989); 2 s (James b 1969, Edward b 1973); *m* 2, 5 July 2003, Louisa, *née* Clowes, wid of David Wagg (d 2000); *Career* served 15/19 The King's Royal Hussars 1952–82 (CO Regt 1973–75): Malaya, Germany, UK; Col 15/19 Hussars 1988–92; area appeals organiser Avon, Glos and Wilts Cancer Research Campaign 1982–93; Vice Lord-Lt Glos 1993–, High Sheriff Glos 1994–95; *Recreations* golf, country sports; *Clubs* Cavalry and Guards', MCC; *Style—* Col Richard A

Coxwell-Rogers, DL; ✉ Hookash View, Foxcote, Andoversford, Cheltenham, Gloucestershire GL54 4LP (tel 01242 821410)

COYLE, Diane; *b* 12 February 1961; *Educ* BNC Oxford (exhibitioner, MA, Gibbs prize), Harvard Univ (MA, PhD); *m* 7 April 1990, Rory Cellan-Jones, *qv*; 2 s (Adam Joseph b 13 Sept 1990, Rufus Gareth b 11 July 1998); *Career* Sumner Slichter fell Harvard Univ and research asst Nat Bureau of Econ Research Cambridge MA 1981–85, sr econ asst HM Treasy 1985–86, sr economist DRI Europe 1986–88, intern The Economist 1988–89, Euro ed Investors Chronicle 1989–93 (actg features ed 1993), econ corr and reporter City and Business section then econ ed The Independent 1993–2001 (Wincott Award for Sr Financial Journalist 2000), currently ind economics conslt and md Enlightenment Economics; visiting prof Inst for Political and Economic Governance (IPEG) Univ of Manchester; memb Competition Cmmn 2001–; memb Advsy Bd: ING Direct UK, EDF Energy; memb: Exec Ctee Centre for Econ Policy Research, Advsy Panel Centre for the Study of Globalisation Univ of Warwick; memb BBC Tst 2006–; sometime broadcaster BBC Radio 4; fell Br-American Project 1995– (treas 1996); memb: Royal Econ Soc (memb Ctee for Women in Economics), Soc of Business Economists, American Econ Assoc; FRSA; *Publications* incl: Britain and EMU: The Case for Joining (1997), The Weightless World (1997), Britain's Urban Boom: the new economics of cities (working paper, 1998), Social Inclusion: Possibilities and Tensions (contrib, 2000), Governing the World Economy (2000), Understanding Economic Forecasts (contrib, 2001), Paradoxes of Prosperity (2001), Getting the Measure of the New Economy (jtly, 2002), Sex, Drugs and Economics (2002), Making Sense of Globalization: A Guide to the Economic Issues (jtly, 2002), The Consequences of Saying No (jtly, 2003), New Wealth for Old Nations: Scotland's Economic Prospects (jt ed, 2005), The Soulful Science (2007); *Style—* Ms Diane Coyle

COYLE, Michael Thomas Patrick; s of Michael Coyle (d 1985), and Mary Elizabeth, *née* Skelly; *b* 21 January 1955; *Educ* Finchley Catholic GS, UEA (BA), Lancaster Gate Coll of Law; *Career* advertising exec; trainee rising to account mangr Young & Rubicam 1979–83, account mangr rising to account dir Saatchi & Saatchi 1983–88, Ogilvy & Mather 1988–89 (dir (Australia), client service dir, dep md), int bd dir Bates (formerly BSB Dorland) 1989–; regnl dir and european client dir Bates Europe 1996–, vice-chm Bates Pan Gulf until 2000, exec vice-pres Bates Europe 2000–; *Recreations* reading, music, travelling, tennis, cricket, football, bobsleigh; *Clubs* Albanian Assoc, Queen's, Annabel's; *Style—* Michael Coyle, Esq; ✉ Bates Europe, 121–141 Westbourne Terrace, London W2 6JR (tel 020 7262 5077, fax 020 7258 3757)

COYNE, Gary; s of Brian Coyne, of Galway, Ireland, and Ann; *b* 29 March 1965; *m* 4 Jan 1994, Sandra; *Career* restaurant mangr; hotel training in Germany and Ireland 1984–88, Heathrow Penta Hotel 1989–90, asst restaurant mangr The Churchill London 1990–91, restaurant mangr Hanbury Manor Herts 1991–92, dep gen mangr Quaglinos 1992–95, gen mangr Vong Restaurant London 1995–97, gen mangr/dir Itsu 1998–; *Style—* Gary Coyne, Esq

CRABB, Stephen; MP; *b* 1973; *Educ* Tasker Milward Sch, Univ of Bristol, London Business Sch; *Career* Parly affrs offr Nat Cncl for Voluntary Youth Servs 1996–98, election monitor OSCE (Bosnia Herzegovina) 1998, policy mangr London C of C 1998–2002; MP (Cons) Preseli Pembrokeshire 2005– (Parly candidate (Cons) Preseli Pembrokeshire 2001); chm N Southwark and Bermondsey Cons Assoc 1998–2000; *Style—* Stephen Crabb, Esq, MP; ✉ House of Commons, London SW1A 0AA (website www.stephencrabb.com)

CRACKNELL, Prof Arthur Philip; s of Christopher Theodore Cracknell (d 1969), of Ilford, Essex, and Phyllis Mary, *née* Staines (d 1985); *b* 18 May 1940; *Educ* Chigwell Sch, Pembroke Coll Cambridge (MA), The Queen's Coll Oxford (DPhil), Univ of Singapore (MSc); *m* 13 April 1966, Margaret Florence, da of James Grant (d 1972), of Gateshead, Tyne & Wear; 1 s (Christopher Paul b 15 April 1967), 2 da (Anne Patricia b 3 March 1972, Andrée Jacqueline b 30 Nov 1975); *Career* lectr in physics: Univ of Singapore 1964–67, Univ of Essex 1967–70; Univ of Dundee: sr lectr 1970–74, reader 1974–78, prof of theoretical physics 1978–2002, emeritus prof 2002–; ed International Journal of Remote Sensing 1983; former chm Remote Sensing Soc; FInstP 1970, FRSE 1976, FRSA 1992, FRSPSoc 1995; *Books* Applied Group Theory (1968), The Fermi Surfaces of Metals (jtly, 1971), Ultrasonics (1980), Computer Programs for Image Processing of Remote Sensing Data (ed, 1982), Magnetism in Solids - Some Current Topics (ed jtly, 1982), Remote Sensing Applications in Marine Science and Technology (ed, 1983), Introduction to Remote Sensing (jtly, 1991), The Advanced Very High Resolution Radiometer (1997, 2 edn 2007), Visible Infrared Imager Radiometer Suite: A New Operational Cloud Imager (jtly, 2006); author of numerous scientific res papers in scientific journals; *Recreations* reading, hill walking, gardening; *Style—* Prof Arthur P Cracknell, FRSE; ✉ Flat 8, 97 East London Street, Edinburgh EH7 4BF; Division of Electronic Engineering and Physics, School of Engineering and Physical Sciences, University of Dundee, Dundee DD1 4HN (tel 01382 344549, fax 01382 345415, e-mail a.p.cracknell@dundee.ac.uk)

CRACKNELL, David John; s of David Lewis Cracknell, of Woodford Green, Essex, and Norma Rose, *née* Beasley; *Educ* Forest Sch, Univ of Southampton (LLB), Pembroke Coll Oxford (BCL); *m* 9 May 1998, Rachel Annie Laurent; 2 da (Poppy Natasha b 24 July 1999, Freya Sophie b 11 April 2001), 1 s (Laurent Patrick David b 18 Feb 2004); *Career* journalist; reporter Coventry Evening Telegraph 1993–95, political corr Press Assoc 1995–98, political ed Sunday Business 1998–99, dep political ed Sunday Telegraph 1999–2001, political ed Sunday Times 2001–; *Style—* David Cracknell, Esq; ✉ The Sunday Times, 1 Pennington Street, London E98 7ST (tel 020 7782 5746, fax 020 7782 5237, e-mail david.cracknell@sunday-times.co.uk)

CRACKNELL, James Edward; OBE (2005, MBE 2001); *Educ* Kingston GS, Univ of Reading (BSc), Inst of Educn Univ of London (PGCE), Brunel Univ (MSc); *m* 2002, Beverley Turner; 1 s (Croyde b 2003); *Career* amateur rower; memb Br rowing team 1991–; achievements incl: Gold medal World Jr Championships, Gold medal coxless fours World Championships 1997, 1998 and 1999, Gold medal coxless fours Olympic Games Sydney 2000, Gold medal coxed pairs and Gold medal coxless pairs World Championships 2001, Gold medal coxless pairs World Championships 2002, Gold medal coxless fours Olympic Games Athens 2004, Atlantic rowing race completed 2006; winner Team of the Year BBC Sports Personality of the Year Awards 2004 (with Matthew Pinsent, Ed Coode and Steve Williams); contrib Daily Telegraph 1998–, TV presenter for ITV and Channel 4; patron: SPARKS, Sports Aid, Access Sport; Hon Degree Brunel Univ; *Books* The Crossing (2006); *Recreations* surfing, motorbikes, travelling, reading, concerts, music; *Clubs* Leander; *Style—* James Cracknell, Esq, OBE; ✉ c/o Jonathan Marks, MTC, 20 York Street, London W1U 6PU (tel 020 7935 8000, fax 020 7935 8066)

CRACKNELL, His Hon Judge (Malcolm) Thomas; s of Percy Thomas Cracknell (d 1988), and Doris Louise Cracknell (d 1997); *b* 12 December 1943; *Educ* Royal Liberty Sch Romford, Univ of Hull (LLB), KCL (LLM); *m* 1, 1968 (m dis 1980) Ann; 1 s (Simon Anthony b 1970), 1 da (Rebecca Judith b 1972); m 2, 30 July 1988, Felicity Anne, da of Prof David M Davies, of Boston Spa; 1 da (Alexandra Flora Louise b 1990), 2 s (William David Thomas b 1992, Oliver George Thomas b 1994); *Career* lectr in law Univ of Hull 1968–74, barr 1970–89, asst rec 1984, recorder of the Crown Ct 1988, circuit judge (NE Circuit) 1989–, designated family judge Hull Combined Court Centre 1994–; *Recreations* golf, cricket, gardening, reading; *Style—* His Hon Judge Cracknell

CRACROFT-ELEY, Bridget Katharine; JP; da of Lt-Col Sir Weston Cracroft-Amcotts, MC, DL (d 1975), of Hackthorn Hall, Lincoln, and Rhona, *née* Clifton-Brown, DL (d 1997); *b* 29 October 1933; *Educ* Lincoln Girls' HS, Crofton Grange Sch Buntingford; *m* 31 Oct 1959, Robert Peel Charles (Robin) Cracroft-Eley, DL (d 1996) (who assumed the additional surname of Cracroft), s of Charles Ryves Maxwell Eley, OBE (d 1983), of East Bergholt Place, Suffolk; 1 da (Annabel b 1961), 1 s (William b 1963); *Career* worked for charities and voluntary orgns; parish cncllr and sch govr; High Sheriff Lincs 1989–90, HM Lord-Lt Lincs 1995–; Hon LLD: De Montfort Univ 1999, Lincoln Univ 2002; *Recreations* gardening, upholstery; *Style—* Mrs Robin Cracroft-Eley; ✉ The Little House, Hackthorn, Lincoln LN2 3PQ (e-mail bcracrofteley@hackthorn.com)

CRADDOCK, Malcolm Gordon; s of Gilbert Craddock, and Evelyn Marion, *née* Gordon; *b* 2 August 1938; *Educ* St Albans Sch, Queens' Coll Cambridge (MA); *m* 1, 29 May 1965, Jenni, da of David Maclay; 2 s (Sam, Ben), 1 da (Emily); m 2, 12 June 1999, Rachel, da of Peter and Jennifer Glaister; 1 s (Archie), 1 da (Lily); *Career* entered film industry 1962; asst dir to Joseph Losey 1964–66 (Accident, Modesty Blaise); dir: Mr Lewis 1965, The Beach 1967; film dir of TV commercials (Sunday Times awards) 1966–89, founding ptnr and dir Picture Palace Prodns Ltd 1970–; prodr TV drama 1984–: Tandoori Nights (Channel 4) 1985–87, Ping Pong (Venice Int Film Festival) 1986, twenty one short films, 4 Minutes (winner Gold Award for Drama NY 1986), Firing the Bullets, Hunting the Squirrel and Pushed (Channel 4 and ECA) 1989–90, When Love Dies (Channel 4) 1990, The Orchid House (series, Channel 4) 1991, Sharpe's Rifles and Sharpe's Eagle (ITV) 1993, Little Napoleons (Channel 4) 1994, Sharpe's Company, Sharpe's Enemy and Sharpe's Honour (ITV) 1994 (nominated BAFTA Award Best TV Drama Series), Karaoke Love Affair (NHK Tokyo) 1994, Sharpe's Sword, Sharpe's Gold and Sharpe's Battle (ITV) 1995, Sharpe's Regiment, Sharpe's Siege and Sharpe's Mission (ITV) 1996, Sharpe's Revenge, Sharpe's Justice and Sharpe's Waterloo (ITV) 1997, A Life for A Life - The True Story of Stefan Kiszko (ITV) 1998 (winner Royal TV Soc Best Writer and Best Newcomer, nominated BAFTA Award Best Single Drama), Extremely Dangerous (ITV) 1999, Rebel Heart (BBC1) 2001, Frances Tuesday (ITV) 2004, Sharpe's Challenge (ITV) 2004; *Recreations* tennis, watching Tottenham Hotspur FC; *Clubs* Groucho; *Style—* Malcolm Craddock, Esq; ✉ 13 Egbert Street, London NW1 8LJ (tel 020 7722 2745); Picture Palace Films Ltd (tel 020 7586 8763, website www.picturepalace.com)

CRAFT, Prof Sir Alan William; kt (2004); *b* 6 July 1946; *Educ* Rutherford GS Newcastle upon Tyne, Univ of Newcastle upon Tyne (MB BS, MD); *Career* postgrad trg in Newcastle upon Tyne Hosps, MRC trg fell Royal Marsden Hosp London 1976–77; conslt paediatrician: N Tyneside and Newcastle upon Tyne 1978–86, Royal Victoria Infirmary Newcastle upon Tyne 1986–91; James Spence prof of child health Univ of Newcastle upon Tyne 1993– (prof of paediatric oncology 1991–93); pres: Int Paediatric Oncology Soc (SIOP) 2001–04 (memb 1980, sec gen 1993–99), Assoc for Care of Terminally Ill Children (ACT) 2002–, RCPCH 2003–06 (vice-pres 1998–2002); chm Acad of Medical Royal Colls 2004–; FMedSci, FRCPCH, FRCP, FRCPE, FRCA, FRCR, FFPHM, FMedSci, FRCPI, FAAP, FIAP; *Style—* Prof Sir Alan Craft; ✉ 1 The Villas, Embleton, Northumberland NE66 3XG (tel 01665 576619); Department of Child Health, Royal Victoria Infirmary, Newcastle upon Tyne NE1 4LP (tel 0191 202 3010, fax 0191 202 3022, e-mail a.w.craft@ncl.ac.uk)

CRAFT, Prof Ian Logan; s of Reginald Thomas Craft, of Essex, and Mary Lois, *née* Logan; *b* 11 July 1937; *Educ* Owen Sch London, Univ of London, Westminster Hosp Med Sch (MB BS); *m* 19 Dec 1959 (m dis 1998), Jacqueline Rivers, da of John James Symmons (d 1985), of London; 2 s (Simon b 4 Sept 1964, Adrian b 1 Sept 1968); *Career* house offr Radiotherapy Dept and Dept of Obstetrics and Gynaecology Westminster Hosp 1961–62, SHO (later house surgn and house physician) St James Hosp Balham 1962–63, house surgn Hammersmith Hosp 1965, SHO (later surgical registrar) Professional Unit Westminster Hosp 1965–66, res MO Queen Charlotte's Hosp London 1967, gynaecological registrar (later res registrar) Inst of Obstetrics and Gynaecology Chelsea Hosp for Women 1968–69, res MO Gen Lying-In Hosp London 1969, registrar Queen Mary's Hosp Roehampton 1970, sr registrar Westminster Hosp London 1970, rotational sr registrar Kingston Hosp 1971–72, sr lectr and hon conslt Queen Charlotte's Hosp and Chelsea Hosp for Women 1972–76, prof of obstetrics and gynaecology Royal Free Hosp Sch of Med 1976–82, dir of gynaecology Cromwell Hosp London 1982–85, dir of fertility and obstetrics studies Humana Hosp Wellington London 1985–90, dir London Fertility Centre 1990–; visiting prof UCL; frequent lectr and prolific contrib to med literature; life memb: Zoological Soc, Nat Tst, English Heritage, RNLI, Friends of St Paul's Cathedral, Friends of Durham Cathedral, Byron Soc, Turner Soc, Walpole Soc; memb: RSM, Br Fertility Soc, Harveian Soc (London), Med Soc of London; FRCS 1966, FRCOG 1986 (MRCOG 1970); *Recreations* art, ceramics, sculpture, music, opera, theatre, most sports, antiquities; *Clubs* Heritage, Natural Pursuits, Ornithology; *Style—* Prof Ian Craft; ✉ London Fertility Centre, Cozens House, 112A Harley Street, London W1G 7JH (tel 020 7224 0707, fax 020 7224 3120, e-mail info@lfc.org.uk); PA tel 020 7486 5071, fax 020 7486 5073, e-mail prof@lft.org.uk

CRAFTS, Prof Nicholas Francis Robert; s of Alfred Hedley Crafts, of Sutton-in-Ashfield, Notts, and Flora Geraldine Mary Crafts (d 1992); *b* 9 March 1949; *Educ* Brunts GS Mansfield, Trinity Coll Cambridge (Wrenbury scholar, MA); *m* 29 March 1969, Barbara, da of Arthur Daynes (d 1992); 2 da (Rachel b 22 Oct 1969, Helen b 13 Aug 1971), 1 s (Adam b 26 Sept 1973); *Career* lectr in economic history Univ of Exeter 1971–72, lectr in economics Univ of Warwick 1972–77, fell and praelector in economics UC Oxford 1977–86; prof of economic history: Univ of Leeds 1987–88, Univ of Warwick 1988–95, LSE 1995–2005, Univ of Warwick 2006–; visiting asst prof of economics Univ of Calif Berkeley 1974–76, visiting prof of economics Stanford Univ 1982–83; memb Cncl: Royal Econ Soc 1991–93, Econ History Soc 1992–; FBA 1992; *Books* British Economic Growth During the Industrial Revolution (1985), Britain's Relative Economic Performance 1870–1999 (2002); *Recreations* horse-racing; *Style—* Prof Nicholas Crafts, FBA; ✉ Department of Economics, University of Warwick, Coventry CV4 7AL

CRAGG, Anthony Douglas (Tony); CBE (2002); s of late Douglas Roland Cragg, and late Audrey May, *née* Rutter; *b* 9 April 1949, Liverpool; *Educ* Glos Coll of Art Cheltenham, Wimbledon Sch of Art (BA), RCA (MA); *m* 1 (m dis), Ute Oberste-Lehn; 2 s (Daniel Anthony b 1979, Thomas Douglas b 1981); m 2, Tatjana Verhasselt; 1 s (John Eric b 1987), 1 da (Catharina Eve May b 1989); *Career* sculptor; lab technician Nat Rubber Prodrs Research Assoc 1966–68, art college 1969–77, prof L'Ecole des Beaux Arts de Metz 1976; Düsseldorf Kunstakademie: tutor 1978–88, prof 1988–2001, vice-chllr 1988–2001; prof Universität der Künste Berlin 2001–06, prof Kunstakademie Düsseldorf 2006–; visiting prof Univ of the Arts London 2005; Von der Heydt prize 1988, Turner Prize 1988, Shakespeare Prize 2001, Piepenbrock Prize 2002, Best Sculpture Prize Beijing Biennale 2005; memb Akademie der Künste Berlin 2001; hon prof Budapest Univ 1996, Hon Dr Univ of Surrey 2001, hon fell John Moores Univ Liverpool 2001; Chevalier de l'Ordre des Arts et des Lettres (France); RA 1994; *Solo Exhibitions* incl: Lisson Gallery London 1979, 1980, 1982, 1985, 1988, 1991, 1992, 1997, 1998, 2001 and 2006, Galerie Konrad Fischer Düsseldorf 1979, 1980, 1982, 1986, 1989, 1990 and 1999, Arnolfini Gallery Bristol 1980, Whitechapel Art Gallery London 1981, Nouveau Musée Lyon 1981 and 1982, Musée d'Art et d'Industrie St Etienne 1981, Schellmann & Klüser München 1981, 1982 and 1984, Rijksmuseum Kröller-Müller Otterloo 1982, Marian Goodman NYC 1982, 1983, 1984, 1986, 1987, 1989, 1991, 1994, 1998, 2000, 2003 and 2007, Badischer Kunstverein Karlsruhe 1982, Kanransha Gallery Tokyo 1982, 1984, 1987, 1989 and 1990, Kunsthalle Bern 1983, Thomas Cohn Rio de Janeiro 1983 and 1989 and Sao Paulo 1992, 2001, 2003 and 2006, Galerie Buchmann St Gallen 1983, Basel 1986, 1988, 1990, 1992, 1993 and 1995, Köln 1996, 1999, 2002 and 2004 and Berlin 2006, Louisiana MOMA 1984,

Humlebaek Denmark 1984, Kölnischer Kunstverein Köln 1984, Galerie Bernd Klüser München 1985, 1988, 1990, 1991, 1994, 1997, 2000, 2003 and 2005, Palais des Beaux-Arts Brussels 1985, ARC Musée d'Art Moderne de la Ville de Paris 1985, Kestner-Gesellschaft Hannover 1985, Staatsgalerie Moderner Kunst Munich 1985, The Brooklyn Museum NYC 1986, Hayward Gallery London 1987, Corner House Manchester 1987, Gallerie Tucci Russo Turin 1987, 1990 and 1992, Venice Biennale 1988, Galerie Crousel-Robelin Paris 1988, 1991 and 1994, Stedelijk Van Abbemuseum Eindhoven 1989 and 1991, Kunstsammlung Nordrhein-Westfalen Düsseldorf 1989, Tate Gallery London 1989, Newport Harbour Art Museum Newport Beach Calif 1990, Corcoran Gallery of Art Washington DC 1991, Power Plant Toronto 1991, Houston Contemporary Art Museum 1991, IVAM Valencia 1992, Tramway Glasgow 1992, CCA Glasgow 1992, Musée des Beaux Arts Nantes 1994, Stadtgalerie Saarbrücken 1994, Museo Nacional Centro de Arte Reina Sofia Madrid 1995, Nationalgalerie Prag 1995, Centre Georges Pompidou Paris 1996, Henry Moore Fndn Halifax 1996, Galerie Karsten Greve Paris 1996, 1998 and 2000 and Milan 1996, Whitechapel Art Gallery 1997, Nationalgalerie Skopje 1997, Nationalgalerie Sofia 1997, Nationalgalerie Bratislava 1997, Nationalgalerie Warschau 1997, Gallerie Maeye-Ellinger Frankfurt 1997, National Museum of Contemporary Art Seoul 1997, Toyota Municipal Museum of Art 1997, Galerie Seitz Berlin 1998, 2001 and 2003, Kenji Taki Gallery Nagoya 1998, 1999, 2004 and 2006, Galerie Chantal Crousel Paris 1999 and 2003, Galerie Stefan Andersson Umea 1999, 2001 and 2006, Summer Exbhn (Royal Acad) 1999, Tate Gallery Liverpool 2000, Glyndebourne 2000, Malmö Konsthall 2001, Somerset House London 2001, Galerie Carles Taché Barcelona 2002 and 2005, Kunst und Auststellungshalle der Bundesrepublik Deutschland Bonn 2003, Macro Museum of Contemporary Art Rome 2003, Museu Serralves Porto 2004, Central House of Artists Moscow 2005, Neues Museum Nürnberg 2005, Galerie Catherine Putnam Paris 2005, Museum der Wahrnehmung Graz 2005, Galerie Thaddaeus Ropac Paris 2005, Cass Sculpture Fndn Goodwood 2005, Gow Langsford Gallery Auckland 2005, Jiri Svestka Gallery Prag 2006, Künstlerverein Malkasten Düsseldorf 2006, Krefelder Kunstverein 2006, Das Potential der Dinge (Akademie der Künste Berlin 2006 and (Lehmbruck Museum Duisburg) 2007, Tony Cragg Exposición (Argentina) 2006, Haunch of Venison Zürich 2007, Tony Cragg 1995–2006 (Museo de Arte de Lima Peru) 2007, Galleria Sculptor Helsinki 2007, Tony Cragg Exposición (MAVI Chile) 2007; *Group Exhibitions* incl: Aperto '80 Venice Biennale 1980, Venice Biennale 1986, Dokumenta 8 Kassel 1987, Venice Biennale 1993, Recent British Sculpture from the Arts Cncl Collection (South Bank Centre London) 1993, Museum of Contemporary Art Madrid 1994, Museum of Modern Art Dublin 1995, Museum Folkwang Essen 1996, Hayward Gallery London 1997, MAC Marseille 1998, Le Champs de la Skultur Paris 1999, Sprengel Museum Hannover 2000, Guggenheim Museum Venice 2002, Nasher Sculpture Center Dallas 2003, Tehran Museum of Contemporary Art Tehran 2004, 'Intersezoni' Catanzaro 2005, 'Contemporary Voices' at MOMA NY 2005, Kunstmuseum Wolfsburg 2006; *Major Projects and Commissions* 'World Events' High Museum of Modern Art Atlanta USA 1996, 'Wave Forms' Battery Park City Authy NYC 1996, 'Dancing Columns' Br Embassy Berlin 2000, 'Think Thing' Stockholm Univ 2001, 'Changing Minds' The Hobby Center for Performing Arts, Houston USA 2002, 'First Appearances, Second Thoughts' APO Bank Düsseldorf 2003, 'Constant Change' Barclay's Bank London 2005, 'Points of View' 2006 Winter Olympics Turin Italy 2005; *Style*— Tony Cragg, Esq, CBE, RA; ✉ website www.tony-cragg.com

CRAGG, Anthony John; CMG (2000), JP (2005); s of Samuel Arthur Leslie Cragg (d 2000), and Gwendolen Mary, *née* Pevler (d 1991); *b* 16 May 1943; *Educ* Hastings GS, Lincoln Coll Oxford (open scholar, BA); *m* 4 Sept 1971, Jeanette Ann, da of Alfred Richard Rix; 2 da (Alexandra Frances Helen b 14 Feb 1977, Susannah Rose b 14 April 1982); *Career* MOD: asst princ 1966, asst private sec to Perm Under Sec 1968–70, princ 1971, asst private sec to Sec of State for Defence 1974–76, seconded to FCO 1977–79, asst sec 1979, head of Naval Resource Planning Secretariat 1980–83, chief offr UK Sovereign Base Areas Cyprus 1983–85, RCDS 1988, under sec 1990, chm Defence Orgn Planning Team 1991–92; asst sec gen for Defence, Planning & Operations NATO Brussels 1993–99, MOD 1999–2003; sr assoc res fell Centre for Defence Studies KCL, assoc fell RUSI 2003–; lay memb Asylum and Immigration Tbnl 2003–; visiting lectr: NATO Defence Coll 2003–, Geneva Centre for Security Policy 2005–; numerous articles and papers on int defence and security issues; *Recreations* swimming, walking, music, reading; *Style*— Anthony Cragg, Esq, CMG; ✉ c/o Royal United Services Institute, Whitehall, London SW1A 2ET

CRAGG, Bernard Anthony; *Career* finance dir Carlton Communications plc 1987–2001 (co sec 1985–87); non-exec chm: Datamonitor plc, i-mate; non-exec dir: Mothercare plc, Workspace Group plc, Astro All Asia Networks plc, Bristol & West Investments plc; ACA; *Style*— Bernard Cragg, Esq

CRAIG, Amanda Pauline; da of Dennis Bathurst Craig, of Rome, and Zelda Rose Craig; *b* 22 September 1959; *Educ* Bedales, Clare Coll Cambridge (exhibitioner); *m* 1988, Robin John Cohen, s of L Jonathan Cohen; 1 da (Leonora Rose), 1 s (William Alexander); *Career* novelist; freelance journalist 1984–; Young Journalist of the Year Award 1985, Catherine Pakenham Award 1987; memb Soc of Authors; *Books* Foreign Bodies (1990), A Private Place (1991), A Vicious Circle (1996), In a Dark Wood (2000), Love in Idleness (2003); *Recreations* reading, gardening, music, children; *Style*— Ms Amanda Craig; ✉ c/o Antony Harwood Agency, 103 Walton Street, Oxford OX2 6EB (tel 01865 559615); website www.amandacraig.com

CRAIG, Dr Brian George; s of Very Rev Dr William Magee Craig, of Moira Co Down, and Maud, *née* Macrory; *b* 6 September 1953; *Educ* Portadown Coll, Queen's Univ Belfast (MD, BCh, BAO); *m* Jennifer, da of Albert Mawhinney; 2 s (Adam b 1984, Matthew b 1986); *Career* sr registrar: cardiology Royal Victoria Hosp 1982–83, Hosp for Sick Children Toronto Canada (clinical fell in paediatric cardiology) 1983–85, paediatrics Royal Belfast Hosp for Sick Children 1985–86; conslt in paediatric cardiology Royal Belfast Hosp for Sick Children 1986–; author of numerous publications in learned jls; memb: Ulster Paediatric Soc 1979–, Br Paediatric Cardiac Assoc 1987–, Br Paediatric Assoc 1988–, Irish Cardiac Soc 1988–, Br Cardiac Soc 1990, Assoc of Euro Paediatric Cardiologists 1994, Boys Bde; elder Presbyterian Church; FRCP, FRCPCH; *Recreations* gardening, family, tennis; *Style*— Dr Brian Craig; ✉ 10 Plantation Avenue, Lisburn, Co Antrim BT27 5BL (tel 028 9267 1587); Royal Belfast Hospital for Sick Children, 180–184 Falls Road, Belfast BT12 6BE (tel 028 9063 2397, e-mail brian.craig@royalhospitals.n-i.nhs.uk)

CRAIG, Colin David; s of Joseph Craig, of Glasgow, and Phyllis, *née* Merrilees; *b* 15 January 1962; *Educ* Douglas Acad, Bell Coll Hamilton, Univ of Strathclyde (BSc); *Partner* Lesley Crosfield , *qv*; *Career* restaurateur; previous jobs incl: lumberjack, auxiliary nurse, lifeguard, electronic engr, itinerant folk singer, mountaineer, fish farmer; chef and co-prop Albannach Hotel 1990– (Michelin BIB Gourmand 1997, Award for McAllan Overall Excellence 1998, Award for McAllan Best Restaurant with Rooms 1998, Good Food Guide W Coast Newcomer of the Year 2000, Scotland the Best! Award for Excellence 2000, Which? Hotel Guide Hotels of the Year category 2002, 2 AA Rosettes 2002, Scottish Hotel Bedroom of the Year Hotel Review Scotland 2007); tenant crofter; memb Assynt Mountain Rescue Team 1991–96, memb SNP (social convenor Milngavie); RYA, Br Motorcycle Fedn, Small Business Fedn; *Books* Scotland on a Plate (2001); *Recreations* mountaineering, subaqua diving, sailing, motorcycling, Scotland, all things French (particularly those that can be eaten or drunk); *Clubs* Scottish SubAqua, Malt Whisky Soc, Triumph Owners Motorcycle, MG Owners; *Style*— Colin Craig, Esq; ✉ The Albannach, Baddidarroch, Lochinver, Sutherland IV27 4LP (tel 01571 844407, fax 01571 844285, e-mail the.albannach@virgin.net, website www.thealbannach.co.uk)

CRAIG, Colin Fetherston; s of Rev Cuthbert Leslie Craig (d 1982), of Weardale, and Muriel, *née* Cole; *b* 29 August 1947; *Educ* Kent Coll Canterbury, Kingston Coll of Art; *m* 4 July 1989, Linda Jayne, da of Edward Howard; *Career* creative dir: Cogent Elliott Ltd 1975–78, Doyle Dane Bernbach Ltd 1978–79, Grierson Cockman Craig & Druiff Ltd 1979–86, Grey Ltd 1986–87; planning creative dir TBWA (formerly Holmes Knight Ritchie then TBWA Holmes Knight Ritchie) 1987–93; writer of music for TV and radio 1968–, lectr in TV technique, writer of screenplays for TV and cinema, writer of party political broadcasts for the Lib Dem Party, winner of over 60 nat and int TV awards, multi-instrumentalist, singer, conductor; memb: D & AD 1969, Songwriters' Guild 1978, PRS 1977; *Recreations* music, horticulture, cinema, church, dalmatians; *Clubs* Lansdowne; *Style*— Colin Craig, Esq; ✉ The Consulting Room, 6 Brewer Street, London W1R 3FP (tel 020 7734 0031, fax 020 7734 0036)

CRAIG, Daniel; s of Tim Craig, and Olivia Craig; *b* 2 March 1968, Chester; *Educ* Br Nat Youth Theatre, Guildhall Sch of Music and Drama; *Career* actor; *Theatre* The Rover (Women's Playhouse Trust), Angels in America (RNT), No Remission (Lyric Studio Hammersmith), Hurly Burly (Old Vic), A Number (RNT); *Television* incl: Charing Cross, Anglo Saxon Attitudes, Genghis Cohn, Our Friends in the North, Moll Flanders, Kiss and Tell, The Icehouse, The Visitor, Sword of Honour, Copenhagen; *Film* incl: The Power of One 1992, Obsession 1997, Love is the Devil 1998, Elizabeth 1998, Love and Rage 1998, The Trench 1999, I Dreamed of Africa 2000, Hotel Splendide 2000, Some Voices 2000, Tomb Raider 2001, The Road to Perdition 2002, The Mother 2003, Sylvia 2003, Enduring Love 2004, Layer Cake 2004, The Jacket 2005, Munich 2005, Casino Royale 2006 (Best Actor Evening Standard British Film Awards 2007), Infamous 2007; *Style*— Daniel Craig; ✉ c/o ICM, Oxford House, 76 Oxford Street, London W1N 0AX (tel 020 7636 6565, fax 020 7323 0101)

CRAIG, Prof Edward John; s of Charles William Craig (d 1989), and Annie, *née* Taylor (d 1983); *b* 26 March 1942; *Educ* Charterhouse, Trinity Coll Cambridge (BA, PhD, Cricket blue); *m* 1, 1973 (m dis 1986), Isabel Nina, *née* Barnard; 2 da (Ellen Elizabeth b 23 June 1980, Claire Madeleine b 8 Aug 1982); m 2, 1987, Gillian Helen Elizabeth Edwards; *Career* Univ of Cambridge: res scholar Trinity Coll 1963–66 (sr scholar 1962–63), fell Churchill Coll 1966–, asst lectr in philosophy 1966–71, lectr 1971–92, reader in modern philosophy 1992–98, Knightbridge prof of philosophy 1998–2005; visiting lectr Univ of Melbourne 1974, guest prof Univ of Heidelberg 1981; visiting prof: Univ of Hamburg 1977–78, Indian Inst of Advanced Study Shimla 1996; ed Ratio 1987–92; gen ed: Routledge Encyclopedia of Philosophy 1991–98, Routledge Encyclopedia of Philosophy Online 2000–; FBA 1993; *Books* David Hume: Eine Einführung in seine Philosophie (1979), The Mind of God and the Works of Man (1987), Knowledge and the State of Nature (1990), Was Wir Wissen Können (1993), Hume on Religion (1997), Philosophy: A Very Short Introduction (2002); *Recreations* music, golf; *Style*— Prof Edward Craig, FBA; ✉ Churchill College, Cambridge CB3 ODS

CRAIG, George Charles Graham; s of George Craig (d 1970), and Elizabeth Strachan, *née* Milne; *b* 8 May 1946; *Educ* Univ of Nottingham (BA); *m* 9 March 1968, (Ethne) Marian, da of Herbert Henry Asquith Gallagher (d 1989); 2 s (Andrew b 9 June 1971, Robert b 13 July 1974), 1 da (Emily b 5 June 1978); *Career* asst princ Miny of Tport 1967; Welsh Office: private sec to min of state 1971, princ 1973, princ private sec to Sec of State 1978, asst sec 1980, under sec 1986, princ establishment offr until 1994, head Tport Planning and Environment Gp 1994–98, dir Social Affrs 1999–; *Style*— George Craig, Esq

CRAIG, Ian Alexander (Alec); s of Andrew Craig (d 1991), and Sarah Craig; *b* 28 September 1957; *Educ* Univ of Sheffield (BA); *m* 10 Feb 1992, Sally, *née* Bowen; 3 s (Alexander Richard b 17 Nov 1991, James William Blair b 27 Oct 1993, Thomas Patrick b 12 March 1995); *Career* admitted slr 1983; Halliwells: ptnr 1990–, sr ptnr 2001–; dir of several public and private cos; memb Law Soc; sec Snowsport GB 2001–; MSI 1990; *Recreations* soccer, skiing, ornithology; *Clubs* RAC; *Style*— Alec Craig, Esq; ✉ Halliwells LLP, St James's Court, Brown Street, Manchester M2 2JF (tel 0161 831 2691, fax 0161 831 2641, e-mail alec.craig@halliwells.com)

CRAIG, Prof Ian Watson; s of Gordon Craig, and Olive, *née* Watson; *b* 21 August 1943; *Educ* Univ of Liverpool (BSc, PhD); *m* 17 Sept 1966; 3 s (Robert James b 25 June 1972, Gavin Michael b 1 Sept 1973, Stuart Gordon b 28 Feb 1977 d 2002); *Career* NATO postdoctoral research fell Univ of Calif Santa Barbara 1968–1970 (sabbatical visitor 1979); Univ of Oxford: demonstrator 1970, lectr 1972, prof of genetics 1996–; St Catherine's Coll Oxford: fell 1972–, sr tutor 1983–87, domestic bursar; visiting fell Birth Defects Research Unit Melbourne 1986; head of Molecular Genetics Gp SGDP Research Centre Inst of Psychiatry London 1997–; Human Genome Organisation (HUGO): memb 1989–, sr genome database ed 1993–, elected to Cncl 1999; co-chm Chromosome 12/13 Ctee Human Gene Mapping Genome Database (GDB) 1988–89, chm Chromosome 12 Human Gene Mapping 1989–, ed Chromosome 12 for GDB, sr genome database ed Chromosome Co-ordinating Ctee 1993–; co-author of numerous articles in learned jls; *Recreations* sailing, skiing, gardening; *Style*— Prof Ian Craig; ✉ St Catherine's College, Oxford OX1 3UJ (tel 01865 271727, e-mail i.craig@iop.kcl.ac.uk)

CRAIG, Sir (Albert) James Macqueen; GCMG (1984, KCMG 1981, CMG 1975); s of James Craig (d 1954), of Scone by Perth, and Florence, *née* Morris; *b* 13 July 1924; *Educ* Liverpool Inst HS, The Queen's Coll Oxford, Magdalen Coll Oxford, Univ of Cairo; *m* 1, 1952, Margaret Hutchinson (d 2001); 3 s, 1 da; m 2, 2002, Bernadette Hartley Lane; *Career* former lectr in Arabic Univ of Durham; HM Dip Serv: entered 1956, ambass Syria 1976–79, ambass Saudi Arabia 1979–84; visiting prof in Arabic Univ of Oxford 1985–91, lectr Pembroke Coll Oxford, sr assoc memb St Antony's Coll Oxford 1992 (fell 1970–71); DG Middle East Assoc 1985–93 (pres 1993–), pres British Soc for Middle East Studies 1987–94, vice-chm Middle East International 1990–2005, chm Anglo-Arab Assoc 2000–03; chm Roxby Engineering International Ltd 1988–98; dir: Saudi-British Bank 1985–94, Egyptian-British Bank 1987–94 (advsr 1994–2000); advsr Hong Kong and Shanghai Bank 1985–92; tstee Karim Rida Said Fndn 1985–99; hon fell Centre for Middle Eastern and Islamic Studies Univ of Durham 1986, hon fell Queen's Coll Oxford 2007; OStJ 1984 (memb Cncl 1984–90); *Publications* Shemlan: A History of the Middle East Centre for Arab Studies (1998), The Arabists of Shemlan (ed, 2006); *Clubs* Travellers; *Style*— Sir James Craig, GCMG

CRAIG, Keren; da of Adam Craig (d 2001), and Bobbie Spargo; *b* 27 February 1976, Switzerland; *Educ* Brighton Art Coll (BA); *Partner* Piers North; *Career* freelance designer creating one-off pieces for fashion houses 2001–04, fndr and creative dir Marchesa 2004–; *Style*— Ms Keren Craig

CRAIG, Stuart; OBE (2003); s of Norman Craig, and Kate, *née* Ralph; *Educ* RCA; *Career* film prodn designer 1978–; *Films* credits incl: The Elephant Man (BAFTA Award), Gandhi (Acad Award 1981), Greystoke, Cal, The Mission, Cry Freedom, Memphis Belle, Chaplin, The Secret Garden (Evening Standard Film Award), Dangerous Liaisons (Acad Award 1988), Shadowlands, Mary Reilly, In Love and War, The English Patient (Acad Award 1996), The Avengers, The Legend of Bagger Vance, Harry Potter and the Philosopher's Stone (Evening Standard Film Award), Harry Potter and the Chamber of Secrets, Harry Potter and the Prisoner of Azkaban, Harry Potter and the Goblet of Fire; *Style*— Stuart Craig, Esq, OBE; ✉ Steve Kenis & Co, Royalty House, 72–74 Dean Street, London W1D 3SG (tel 020 7434 9055, fax 020 7287 6328); The Skouras Agency, 631

Wiltshire Boulevard, 2nd Floor Suite C, Santa Monica, CA 90401, USA (tel 001 310 395 9550, fax 001 310 395 4295)

CRAIG, Ted; s of Hugh Hoad Craig, and Hazel Ethel Craig; *Educ* Caulfield GS Melbourne; *Career* artistic dir: Lyceum Theatre Crewe 1968–71, Connaught Theatre Worthing 1971–73; assoc dir Old Tote Theatre Co Sydney 1973–75, dir of prods Drama Theatre Sydney Opera House 1977–78, freelance dir 1978–86, artistic dir and chief exec Warehouse Theatre Co 1986–; FRSA; *Recreations* wine appreciation, cinema, gardening; *Style*— Ted Craig, FRSA; ✉ 87 Great Titchfield Street, London W1W 6RL (tel 020 7580 1000, mobile 07951 152002, e-mail tedcraig@hotmail.com); Warehouse Theatre Company, Dingwall Road, Croydon CR0 2NF (tel 020 8681 1257, fax 020 8688 6699, e-mail ted@warehousetheatre.co.uk)

CRAIG, (Anne Gwendoline) Wendy; da of George Dixon Craig (d 1968), and Anne Lindsay (d 1998); *b* 20 June 1934; *Educ* Durham HS for Girls, Darlington HS, Yarm GS, Central Sch of Speech Training and Dramatic Art; *m* 30 Sept 1955, John Alexander (Jack) Bentley (d 1994), s of John Bentley (d 1944); 2 s (Alastair b 5 April 1957, Ross b 10 Nov 1961); *Career* actress; vice-pres The Leprosy Mission 1993–; Hon MA Teesside Univ 1994; *Theatre* incl: Ipswich Repertory Theatre 1953, Epitaph For George Dillon (Royal Court and Broadway) 1957, The Wrong Side of the Park 1960, The Gingerman, Ride A Cock Horse, I Love You Mrs Patterson, Finishing Touches, Peter Pan 1968, Breezeblock Park 1975, Beyond Reasonable Doubt (Queen's) 1987, Matters Matrimonial 1996–98, Easy Virtue (Chichester Festival) 1999, The Rivals (RSC) 2000, The Circle 2002, The Importance of Being Earnest (tour) 2004; various pantomimes; *Television* incl: Not In Front Of The Children, And Mother Makes Three, And Mother Makes Five, Nanny, Butterflies, Laura and Disorder, Brighton Belles, The Forsyte Saga 2002, Midsomer Murders 2002, The Royal 2002–07; *Films* incl: The Mindbenders, The Servant (British Academy nomination), The Nanny, Just Like A Woman, I'll Never Forget What's-Is-Name, Joseph Andrews; *Recordings* incl: Tales of Beatrix Potter (gold disc), Show Me The Way 1988, I'm Growing 1990; *Awards* incl: BAFTA Award Best Actress 1968, BBC Personality of the Year 1969 (ITV 1973); *Books* Happy Endings (1972), The Busy Mums Cook Book (1983), Busy Mums Baking Book (1986), Kid's Stuff (1988), Guideposts for Living (1999), Show Me the Way (2006); *Recreations* walking, gardening, classical music; *Style*— Miss Wendy Craig; ✉ c/o Daphne Waring, 22 Grafton Street, London W1S 4EX (tel 020 7491 2666, fax 020 7409 7932)

CRAIG-COOPER, Sir (Frederick Howard) Michael; kt (1991), CBE (1982), TD (3 bars), DL (Gtr London 1986); s of Frederick William Valentine Craig-Cooper (d 1975), and Elizabeth Oliver-Thompson Craig-Cooper, *née* Macdonald (later Mrs Carroll-Leahy); *b* 28 January 1936; *Educ* Horris Hill, Stowe, Coll of Law London; *m* 8 March 1968, Elizabeth Snagge, MVO, da of Leonard William Snagge (d 1971), and Eleanor Randolf Snagge (d 1983); 1 s (Peter b 3 March 1972); *Career* Nat Serv RA served combined ops UK Malta and Cyprus 1954–56, TA 1956–88 (cmd NGLO Unit 29 Commando Regt RA 1972–75); articled slr (to Sir Arthur Driver) Jaques & Co 1956–61, slr Allen & Overy 1962–64; Inco Ltd 1964–85: dir of cos in UK, Europe, Africa, ME and India 1972–84, conslt and non-exec dir UK and ME 1984–85; md: Craig Lloyd Ltd 1968–, Paul Ray International 1984–91 (also non-exec dir), Carré Orban & Partners Ltd 1989–93, Tichborne Enterprises Ltd 1993–, National Bank of Kuwait (International) plc 1993– (also non-exec dir), Whichford International Ltd 1994–96, Ely Place Holdings Ltd 1994–, Craigmyle and Company Ltd 1995–, Westminster Forum Ltd 1996–; memb Cncl Mining Assoc of UK 1977–82, chm Disciplinary Appeal Ctee Chartered Inst of Mgmnt Accountants 1994–2005; chm Employers' Support Ctee TAVRA Gtr London 1987–90; Cons Party: Parly candidate (Cons) Houghton-le-Spring 1966 and 1970, chm Chelsea Cons Assoc 1974–77 (pres 1983–95), pres Kensington and Chelsea Cons Assoc 1995–2005, treas Gtr London Area Nat Union of Cons and Unionist Assocs 1975–84 (memb 1975–91), chm Cons Nat Property Advsy Ctee 1986–93 (memb 1986–); Royal Borough of Kensington & Chelsea: cncllr 1968–74, memb Cncl 1968–78, Cons chief whip 1971–74, chm Fin Ctee 1972–74, memb Investment Ctee 1973–, Alderman 1974–78, Rep Lt Kensington and Chelsea 1987–2006; chm Order of St John for London 1990–94 (memb Chapter-Gen 1993–99); tstee: Copper Devpt Tst Fund 1974–85, Order of Malta Homes Tst 1980–2003, The Orders of St John Care Tst 1988–2003; Cmmr Royal Hosp Chelsea 1998–2005; pres Boys' Bde (London Dist) 2002–2005; vice Lord-Lt Gtr London 2005–; Freeman City of London 1964, master Worshipful Co of Drapers 1997–98 (Liveryman 1970, memb Ct of Assts 1987–); memb Law Soc 1962–; FCIArb 1992– (MCIArb 1983); Offr Order of Merit with Swords SMOM 1986, KStJ 1990 (OStJ 1978), Cdr of Merit in the Order Pro Merito Melitensi SMOM 2001; *Books* Management Audit: How to Create an Effective Management Team (with Philippe De Backer, 1993), Maw on Corporate Governance (with Prof N N Graham Maw and Lord Lane of Horsell, 1994), Maximum Leadership: The World's Top Business Leaders Discuss How They Add Value to Their Companies (with Charles Farkas, Philippe De Backer and Lord Sheppard of Didgemere, 1995, 3 edn 2000); *Recreations* admiring wife's gardening; *Clubs* Beefsteak, Pratt's, White's; *Style*— Sir Michael Craig-Cooper, CBE, TD, DL

CRAIG-MARTIN, Michael; CBE (2001); s of Paul F Craig-Martin, of Dublin, and Rhona, *née* Gargan; *b* 28 August 1941; *Educ* The Priory Sch Washington DC, Fordham Univ NYC, Yale Univ (BA, BFA, MFA); *m* 25 May 1963 (sep), Janice Lucia, da of Franklin Hashey; 1 da (Jessica Clodagh b 10 dec 1963); *Career* artist; various teaching appts NY and England 1965–: artist in residence King's Coll Cambridge 1970–72, Goldsmiths Coll London 1974–, Millard prof of fine art 1994–; tstee Tate Gallery 1989–94; *Solo Exhibitions* incl: Rowan Gallery London 1969–80, Inst of Modern Art Brisbane and touring in Australia 1978, Galeria Foksal Warsaw 1979 and 1994, Galerie Bama Paris 1980, Fifth Triennale India New Delhi 1982, Waddington Galleries London 1982, 1985, 1988, 1992 and 1993, A Retrospective 1968–89 (Whitechapel Gallery London) 1989, Galerie Claudine Papillon Paris 1990 and 1993, Projects 27 (MOMA NY) 1991, Musée des Beaux Arts Le Havre 1991, Pompidou Centre Paris 1994, Museum Sztuki Lódź Poland 1994, Museum of Contemporary Art Chicago 1995; *Group Exhibitions* incl: 7 Exhibitions (Tate Gallery) 1972, The New Art (Hayward Gallery) 1972, Idea and Image in Recent Art (Art Inst of Chicago) 1974, Art as Thought Process (Serpentine Gallery London) 1974, IX Biennale des Jeunes Artistes (Paris) 1975, Sydney Biennale (Art Gallery of New S Wales) 1976 and 1990, Documenta VI (Kassel FDR) 1977, Un Certain Art Anglais (Paris) 1979, Aspects of British Art Today (Met Art Museum Tokyo and touring in Japan) 1982, Between Object and Image - Contemporary British Sculpture (Palacio de Velazquez Madrid and touring in Spain) 1986, Starlit Waters: British Sculpture, an International Art 1968–88 (Tate Liverpool) 1988, Wall to Wall (Serpentine) 1994, The Adventure of Painting (Kunstverein Düsseldorf and Stuttgart) 1995; *Public Collections* incl: Tate Gallery, MOMA NY, Australian Nat Gallery Canberra, V&A, Musée des Beaux Arts Andre Malraux Le Havre, Haags Gemeentemuseum Netherlands, British Cncl, Arts Cncl of GB; *Commissions* incl: Midland Bank NY, Hasbro-Bradley UK Ltd London, Rosehaugh Stanhope Investments plc for Broadgate London, Morgan-Stanley International Canary Wharf London public collections, New Tokyo Exhibition Center, Jigsaw New Bond Street; *Publications* incl: Michael Craig-Martin: A Retrospective Exhibition 1968–89 (catalogue, Whitechapel Gallery, 1989), Michael Craig-Martin (catalogue, Musee des Beaux Arts Andre Malraux Le Havre, 1991); *Style*— Michael Craig-Martin, Esq, CBE; ✉ c/o Alan Cristea Gallery, 31 Cork Street, London W1X 2NU (tel 020 7439 1866, fax 020 7734 1549); School of Visual Arts, Goldsmiths' College, London SE14 6NW (tel 020 7919 7671)

CRAIG OF RADLEY, Marshal of the RAF Baron (Life Peer UK 1991), of Helhoughton in the County of Norfolk; Sir David Brownrigg Craig; GCB (1984, KCB 1981, CB 1978), OBE (1967); s of Maj Francis Brownrigg Craig (d 1943), of Dublin, and Olive Craig (d 1958); *b* 17 September 1929; *Educ* Radley, Lincoln Coll Oxford; *m* 1955, Elisabeth June, da of Charles James Derenburg (d 1976), of West Byfleet, Surrey; 1 s (Hon Christopher Charles Bronwrigg b 28 March 1957), 1 da (Hon Susan Elisabeth b 26 April 1960); *Career* cmmnd RAF 1951, AOC No 1 Gp RAF Strike Cmd 1978–80, VCAS 1980–82, AOC-in-C Strike Cmd and C-in-C UKAF 1982–85, CAS 1985–88, CDS 1988–91, Marshal of the RAF 1988; memb House of Lords Select Ctee on Science and Technology 1993–99, convenor of the Crossbench Peers 1999–2004; chm Cncl King Edward VII's Hosp Sister Agnes 1998–2004; FRAeS; *Clubs* RAF (pres 2002–); *Style*— Marshal of the RAF the Lord Craig of Radley, GCB, OBE; ✉ House of Lords, London SW1A 0PW (e-mail craigd@parliament.uk)

CRAIGAVON, 3 Viscount (UK 1927); Sir Janric Fraser Craig; 3 Bt (UK 1918); s of 2 Viscount Craigavon (d 1974); *b* 9 June 1944; *Educ* Eton, Univ of London (BA, BSc); *Heir* none; *Career* FCA; *Style*— The Rt Hon the Viscount Craigavon

CRAIGEN, Jeremy John; s of Desmond Craigen, of Parsons Green, London, and Elena Craigen (d 1995); *b* 7 May 1963; *Educ* Radley; *m* 15 May 1993, Philippa, da of Simon Cowley; 1 da (Lily Elena b 28 Feb 1997); *Career* jr copywriter Ted Bates (merged with Dorlands Advtg 1987) 1984; BMP DDB Needham (now BMP DDB): joined 1990, dir of creativity 1996, dep creative dir 2001, jt creative dir 2002; *Awards* 9 Cannes Lions, 10 Br TV Awards, 8 Campaign Press Awards, 5 D&AD nominations; *Recreations* golf, fine wine, travel, music; *Clubs* Hampton Court Palace Golf; *Style*— Jeremy Craigen, Esq; ✉ 42 Richmond Park Road, Kingston upon Thames, Surrey KT2 6AH (tel 020 8546 6276); BMP DDB, 12 Bishop's Bridge Road, London W2 6AA (tel 020 7258 3979, mobile 07767 407749, e-mail jeremy.craigen@bmpddb.com)

CRAIGIE, Cathie; MSP; *b* 14 April 1954; *Educ* Kilsyth Acad; *m* Arthur; 1 s (Andrew), 1 da (Karen); *Career* cncllr Cumbernaud and Kilsyth DC 1984–96, Cncl ldr 1994–96, parly asst to MP 1992–97, cncllr North Lanarkshire Cncl 1995–99, MSP (Lab) Cumbernaud & Kilsyth 1999–; Lab pty: memb 1974–, constituency pty sec 1992–99, Nat Policy Forum 1998–; chair housing, policy & resources and equal opportunities, vice-chair housing, environmental services, Kilsyth Local Area Ctee, Cumbernauld Housing Partnership; Lab spokesman: social exclusion, housing & voluntary sector; memb Audit Ctee, memb Scottish Parly ctees; rep of Cncl on Convention of Scottish Local Authorities; external audit team for chartered accountants; *Recreations* cycling, reading, family holidays; *Style*— Ms Cathie Craigie, MSP

CRAIGMYLE, 4 Baron (UK 1929); Thomas Columba Shaw; s of 3 Baron Craigmyle (d 1998); *b* 19 October 1960; *m* 25 April 1987, (Katharine) Alice, 2 da of David Floyd, OBE, of Combe Down, Bath; 4 s (Hon Alexander Francis b 1 July 1988, Hon Finnian Donald b 28 May 1990, Hon Callum Edward b 4 Jan 1993, Hon Joseph Thomas b 9 March 1996); *Heir* s Hon Alexander Shaw; *Style*— The Rt Hon Lord Craigmyle

CRAKE, Paul Alexander; *b* 16 November 1962; *Educ* King Edward VII GS King's Lynn Norfolk, Univ of Southampton (BA), Dorset Business Sch Bournemouth Poly, Columbia Univ Grad Sch of Business NY (Sr Exec Prog); *Career* admin World Archaeological Congress 1985–86, Southampton City Cncl 1986–91 (latterly mktg mangr), head of mktg and communications Stirling District Cncl 1991–95, communication dir Design Cncl 1995–98; RSA: fellowship and communication dir 1998–2003, prog dir 2003–07, acting sec faculty of Royal Designers for Industry 2004–07; memb: Ct Univ of Southampton 2000–, Univ of Southampton Devpt Tst 2005–; FRSA 1996; *Recreations* archaeology, architecture, art; *Style*— Paul Crake

CRAM, Prof (William) John; s of Rev Frederick Charles Cram, of Harby, Leics, and Laura Mary, *née* Redhead (d 1991); *b* 6 September 1940; *Educ* Kingswood Sch Bath, St John's Coll Cambridge (MA, PhD); *m* 25 July 1965, Patricia Jean, da of Reginald Middleditch (d 1987); 2 s (Nicholas b 1973, Roderick b 1976); *Career* sr res asst UEA 1967–68; Univ of Sydney: lectr in biology 1969, sr lectr 1975, reader 1979–84; Univ of Newcastle upon Tyne: prof of plant biology 1984–, head Dept of Plant Biology 1984–88, head Dept of Biology 1988–91; author of numerous scientific papers; memb Plant Biology Ctee Soc for Experimental Biology 1984–87; hon sec Aust Soc of Plant Physiologists 1976–79, exec sec XIII Int Botanical Congress 1981, sec Nat Conf of Univ Profs 1992–; *Recreations* violin, running, gardening; *Style*— Prof John Cram; ✉ Department of Biological and Nutritional Sciences, Agriculture Building, University of Newcastle upon Tyne NE1 7RU (tel 0191 222 7886, fax 0191 222 6720, e-mail w.j.cram@ncl.ac.uk)

CRAM, Stephen (Steve); MBE (1986); s of William Frank Cram, and Maria Helene, *née* Korte; *b* 14 October 1960; *Educ* Jarrow GS, Newcastle Poly (BA); *Family* 1 da (Josephine), 1 s (Marcus); *Career* middle distance runner; Cwlth Games: Gold medal 1500m 1982 and 1986, Gold medal 800m 1986; European Championships: Gold medal 1500m 1982 and 1986, Bronze medal 800m 1986; Gold medal 1500m World Championships 1983, Silver medal 1500m Olympic Games LA 1984, memb Br Olympic Squad 1980, 1984 and 1988; world mile record holder, former world record holder 1500m and 2000m; athletics presenter/commentator BBC TV; regular contributor to BBC Radio Live 5; motivational speaker and sports conslt; chm English Inst of Sport; chm and dir Comrades of Children Overseas (COCO); chm and tstee Northumberland Sport; pres London and Southern England Branch Sunderland AFC Supporters' Assoc; BBC Sports Personality of the Year 1983; hon fell Univ of Sunderland; Hon DUniv: Staffordshire, Sheffield Hallam; *Recreations* golf, football, snooker; *Clubs* Jarrow and Hebburn AC, Sunderland AFC; *Style*— Steve Cram, Esq, MBE; ✉ Third Floor, 14 Blandford Square, Newcastle upon Tyne NE1 4HZ (tel 0191 230 1124, e-mail stevecram1@msn.com)

CRAMER, Christopher Ranville (Chris); s of James Cramer, of Portsmouth, and Patricia Cramer (d 1993); *b* 3 January 1948; *Educ* Portsmouth Northern GS; *m* Helen Margaret; 1 da (Hannah Ruth b 24 Oct 1982); *Career* journalist Portsmouth News 1965–70; BBC: field prodr 1970–81 (various assignments incl Rhodesia ceasefire, held hostage at Iranian Embassy Siege London 1980), on secondment to estab new TV service for Sultan of Brunei 1975–77, dep foreign ed 1981–82, foreign ed then home ed 1982–86, news ed, intake ed then managing ed 1986–91, head of newsgathering BBC TV and Radio News 1991–96, vice-pres and managing ed CNN International 1996–; FRTS 1993 (memb Cncl 1992–94); *Books* Hostage (1981); *Recreations* rowing, jogging; *Style*— Chris Cramer, Esq

CRAMP, Prof Rosemary Jean; CBE (1987); da of Robert Raymond Kingston Cramp (d 1999), of Hallaton, Leics, and Vera Grace, *née* Ractliffe (d 1965); *b* 6 May 1929; *Educ* Market Harborough GS, St Anne's Coll Oxford (MA, BLitt); *Career* lectr St Anne's Coll Oxford 1950–55; Univ of Durham: lectr 1955–66, sr lectr 1966–71, prof 1971–90, prof emeritus 1990–; visiting fell All Souls Coll Oxford 1992; conslt archaeologist Durham Cathedral until 1997, memb Validation Panel Museum Trg Inst 1993–97, memb Review Ctee for Export of Works of Art 1994–2003; chm Archaeological Data Service 1997–2001; pres: Soc for Church Archaeology 1996–2000, Durham and Northumberland Architectural and Archaeological Soc 2000–02 (hon vice-pres 2005–), Soc of Antiquaries of London 2001–04; former pres: Cncl Br Archaeology (currently vice-pres), Cumberland and Westmorland Antiquarian and Archaeological Soc (hon vice-pres); vice-pres Royal Archaeological Inst 1992–97; cmmr Royal Cmmn of Ancient and Historical Monuments for Scotland 1974–99; tstee Br Museum 1978–98; Hon DSc: Univ of Durham 1995, Univ of Bradford 2002; Hon DLitt: UC Cork 2003, Univ of Leicester 2004; FSA; *Books* Corpus of Anglo Saxon Stone Sculpture (vol 1 1984, vol 2 with R N Bailey 1988, vol 7 2006), Studies in Anglo Saxon Sculpture (1992), Wearmouth and Jarrow Monastic Sites (2 vols, 2006); *Recreations* cooking, gardening, reading; *Clubs* Oxford and Cambridge; *Style—* Prof Rosemary Cramp, CBE, FSA; ✉ 5 Leazes Place, Durham DH1 1RE (tel and fax 0191 386 1843)

CRAMPIN, Peter; QC (1993); s of John Hames Crampin, of Oundle, and Gwendoline Edith, *née* Richardson; *b* 7 July 1946; *Educ* St Albans Sch, UC Oxford (open exhibitioner, MA); *m* 2 Oct 1975, Frida Yvonne, eld da of late Henri Helmut Schoemann; 1 s (Joseph Charles b 11 July 1990); *Career* admitted slr 1973, called to the Bar Middle Temple 1976, 2nd jr counsel to the Attorney-Gen in charity cases 1988–93, recorder 1995–; *Style—* Peter Crampin, Esq, QC; ✉ Radcliffe Chambers, 11 New Square, Lincoln's Inn, London WC2A 3QB (tel 020 7831 0081, fax 020 7405 2560)

CRAMPIN, Prof Stuart; s of Sydney Crampin (d 1968), of Tiptree, Essex, and Kate, *née* Ireson (d 1984); *b* 22 October 1935; *Educ* Maldon GS, KCL (BSc, Jelf medal), Pembroke Coll Cambridge (PhD, ScD); *m* 15 June 1963, Roma Eluned, da of Lloyd Williams; 2 da (Liss-Carin b 7 Sept 1964, Amelia Catharine b 26 Aug 1966); *Career* Nat Serv RAF 1954–56; res fell Seismological Inst Univ of Uppsala 1963–65, Gassiot fell in seismology NERC 1965–67, dep chief scientific offr Br Geological Survey 1986–92 (princ scientific offr 1967–76, sr princ scientific offr 1976–86), prof of seismic anisotropy Dept of Geology and Geophysics Univ of Edinburgh 1992–97, hon prof of seismic anisotropy 1997–; fndr dir Edinburgh Anisotropy Project 1988–92; organiser various int workshops on seismic anisotropy 1982–; Mombusho visiting prof Hokkaido Univ 1985; chm Cmmn on Wave Propagation in Real Media Int Assoc of Seismology and Physics of the Earth's Interior 1984–90; first successful stress-forecast of earthquake time and magnitude; author of over 250 papers in int res jls; memb: Royal Astronomical Soc 1961, Seismological Soc of America 1963, American Geophysical Union 1981, Soc of Exploration Geophysicists 1982 (Virgil Kauffman Gold medal 1988), Euro Assoc of Geoscientists and Engineers 1982 (Conrad Schlumberger award 1986), Euro Geophysical Soc 1985; FRSE 1986; *Recreations* hill walking, travelling, gardening; *Style—* Prof Stuart Crampin, FRSE; ✉ Department of Geology and Geophysics, Grant Institute, West Mains Road, Edinburgh EH9 3JW (tel 0131 650 4908, fax 0131 668 3184, e-mail scrampin@ed.ac.uk)

CRAMPTON, Prof Richard John; s of John Donald Crampton (d 1988), of Kidderminster, Worcs, and Norah, *née* Haden (d 2005); *b* 23 November 1940; *Educ* Queen Elizabeth's GS Hartlebury, Solihull Sch, Trinity Coll Dublin (MA), SSEES Univ of London (PhD); *m* 10 July 1965, Celia Primrose Mary, da of Dermot Marshall Harriss (d 1943), of Nyasaland; 2 s (Will b 1969, Ben b 1972); *Career* prof of E Euro history Univ of Kent at Canterbury 1988–90 (lectr in history 1967–78, sr lectr 1978–88), prof of E Euro history Unv of Oxford 1996–2006 (univ lectr 1990–96, fell St Edmund Hall 1990–); visiting fell Woodrow Wilson Int Center for Scholars Washington DC 1998–99; Dr (hc) Kliment Ohridski Univ Sofia; FRHistS; *Books* The Hollow Detente (1981), Bulgaria 1878–1918: A History (1983), A Short History of Modern Bulgaria 1987, Bulgaria (1989), Eastern Europe in the Twentieth Century (1994), Concise History of Bulgaria (1997), Eastern Europe in the Twentieth Century - and After (1997), Atlas of Eastern Europe in the Twentieth Century (jtly, 1997), The Balkans since the Second World War (2002), Bulgaria (in Oxford History of Modern Europe series, 2007); *Recreations* reading, cooking, listening to music, bird watching; *Style—* Prof RJ Crampton; ✉ St Edmund Hall, Oxford OX1 4AR (e-mail richard.crampton@politics.ox.ac.uk)

CRAMPTON SMITH, Gillian; da of Alexander Crampton Smith, of Oxford, and Rachel, *née* Lupton (d 1999); *b* 21 February 1946; *Educ* St Paul's Girls' Sch, Newnham Coll Cambridge (MA); *m* Philip, s of Owen Tabor; *Career* graphic designer: Sunday Times 1971–75, Times Literary Supplement 1975–78; freelance graphic designer 1978–84; lectr: Canterbury Coll of Art 1977–82, Central Sch of Art 1981–83, St Martin's Sch of Art 1982–88; prof of computer-related design RCA 1993–2000; dir Interaction Design Inst Ivrea 2000–; conslt: Apple Computer Cupertino 1992–94, Interval Research Palo Alto 1994–99; chm CONVIO EU Network of Excellence 2004; memb: Advsy Bd Wellcome Wing Science Museum 1999–2000, Art and Design Panel English AHRB 1999–2000, Advsy Panel EU Future and Emerging Technols 2000, Bd Grad Pioneer Scheme Nat Endowment for Science, Technol and the Arts (NESTA) 2003–; assessor Swedish Govt Research Fndn 1997–2000, distinguished advsr Special Interest Gp for Computer-Human Interaction American Computing Machinery 2000–03; assoc fell and memb Governing Body Newnham Coll Cambridge 1993–96, sr fell RCA; FRSA 1991; *Recreations* cooking, Venice; *Style—* Ms Gillian Crampton Smith

CRAMSIE, Marcus James Lendrum; s of Arthur Vacquerie Cramsie, of Co Tyrone, NI, and Susan Doreen, *née* Lendrum; *b* 24 April 1950; *Educ* Charterhouse, Trinity Hall Cambridge (MA); *m* 19 March 1983, Carol Lesley; 2 da (Camilla b 1984, Louise b 1986), 1 s (Rory b 1990); *Career* Price Waterhouse 1972–76, Kleinwort Benson Ltd 1976–91 (dir 1986–91), dir Singer & Friedlander Holdings Ltd 1991–98, ptnr KPMG Corporate Finance 1999–2002, dir Nabarro Wells & Co Ltd 2003–; FCA; *Recreations* golf, tennis; *Style—* Marcus Cramsie, Esq; ✉ 20 Lyford Road, London SW18 3LG; Nabarro Wells & Co Ltd, Saddlers House, Gutter Lane, London EC2V 6HS

CRAN, Mark Dyson Gordon; QC (1988); s of Gordon Cran (d 1972), and Diana, *née* Mallinson; *b* 18 May 1948; *Educ* Gordonstoun, Millfield, Univ of Bristol (LLB); *m* 29 July 1983 (m dis 1986), Prudence Elizabeth, *née* Hayles; *Career* called to the Bar Gray's Inn 1973; recorder 2000; in practice London; *Recreations* country sports, long walks, convivial disputation, wine and food, performing arts; *Clubs* Brooks's, MCC; *Style—* Mark Cran, Esq, QC; ✉ Brick Court Chambers, 7/8 Essex Street, London WC2R 3LD (tel 020 7379 3550, e-mail mark.cran@brickcourt.co.uk)

CRANBROOK, 5 Earl of (UK 1892); Gathorne Gathorne-Hardy; DL (Suffolk 1984); also Viscount Cranbrook (UK 1878), Baron Medway (UK 1892); s of 4 Earl, CBE (d 1978) by his 2 w, Dowager Countess Cranbrook, OBE, JP; *b* 20 June 1933; *Educ* Eton, CCC Cambridge (MA), Univ of Birmingham (PhD); *m* 9 May 1967, Caroline, o da of Col Ralph George Edward Jarvis, of Doddington Hall, Lincoln, by his w Antonia Meade (*see* Peerage, Earl of Clanwilliam); 2 s (John Jason, Lord Medway b 1968, Hon Argus Edward b 1973), 1 da (Lady Flora b 1971); *Heir* s, Lord Medway; *Career* Sarawak Museum 1956–58, Zoology Dept Univ of Malaya 1961–70, ed Ibis 1973–80; sat in House of Lords as hereditary peer 1978–99; memb: House of Lords Select Ctee on Science and Technol, Select Ctee on EU Affairs, EU Select Sub-Ctee on Environment (chm 1980–94, 1987–90 and 1998–99), Royal Cmmn on Environmental Pollution 1981–92, NERC 1982–88, Broads Authy 1988–99, UK Round Table on Sustainable Devpt 1995–99; chm: Long Shop Museum Project 1978–, Ind Environmental Advsy Bd Shanks plc 1988–2002, Stichting voor Eur Milieubeleid 1990–97, English Nature (Nature Conservancy Cncl for England) 1990–98, Inst for Euro Environmental Policy 1990–2005, ENTRUST (Regulator of Environmental Bodies under the Landfill Tax Regulations) 1996–2002, CEH Advsy Ctee 1998–2005, Int Tst for Zoological Nomenclature 2001–; dep chm Harwich Haven Authy 1995–97 (memb Bd 1989–97); memb Suffolk Coastal DC 1974–83; non-exec dir Anglian Water 1989–98; pres Suffolk Wildlife Tst; tstee Nat History Museum 1982–86; patron Suffolk Nat Soc; RGS Gold Medallist 1995; Skinner and Freeman of City of London; Hon DSc: Univ of Aberdeen, Cranfield Univ; Hon JBS and Hon PNBS Sarawak carrying title Dato Sri; Hon FIWM, Hon FCIWEM; FIBiol, Hon FLS, FZS, FRGS; OStJ; *Books* Mammals of Borneo (1965, 2 edn 1977), Mammals of Malaya (1969, 2 edn 1978), Birds of the Malay Peninsula (with D R Wells, 1976), Mammals of South-East Asia (1987, 2 edn 1990), Key Environments: Malaysia (ed, 1988), Belalong: a tropical rainforest (with D S Edwards, 1994), Wonders of Nature in South-East Asia (1997), The Ballad of Jerjezang (trans, 2001), Swiftlets of Borneo: builders of edible nests (with C K Lim, 2002); *Style—* The Rt Hon the Earl of Cranbrook, DL; ✉ Glemham House, Great Glemham, Saxmundham, Suffolk IP17 1LP (tel 07775 755825, fax 01728 663339)

CRANE, Sir Peter Francis Crane; s of Francis Roger Crane (d 2001), and Jean Berenice, *née* Hadfield (d 1987); *b* 14 January 1940; *Educ* Nottingham HS, Highgate Sch, Gonville & Caius Coll Cambridge (MA, LLM), Tulane Univ USA (LLM); *m* 1967, Elizabeth Mary, da of Noel Bawtry Pittman; 4 da (Anna b 1968, Kate b 1969, Rebecca b 1972, Lucy b 1974); *Career* barrister Midland & Oxford Circuit 1964–87, recorder 1982–87, circuit judge (Midland & Oxford Circuit) 1987–2000, resident judge Peterborough Combined Court 1992–2000, judge of the High Court of Justice 2000–07; memb: Senate of the Inns of Court and the Bar 1983–86, Sentencing Guidelines Ctee Cncl 2004–06; Judicial Studies Bd: memb Maid Bd 1993–96 and 2001–06, chm Criminal Ctee 2001–06; *Publications* Phipson on Evidence (co-ed 15 edn, 1999); *Recreations* reading, walking, gardening, wine; *Style—* Sir Peter Crane

C

CRANE, Prof Sir Peter Robert; kt (2004); s of Walter Robert Crane (d 1988), and Dorothy Mary, *née* Mills (d 2001); *b* 18 July 1954; *Educ* Univ of Reading (BSc, PhD); *m* 21 June 1986, Elinor Margaret Hamer-Crane, da of Paul Hamer Sr, of Chicago, IL; 1 da (Emily Elisabeth Mary b 9 August 1990), 1 s (Samuel Claire Robert b 26 July 1995); *Career* lectr Dept of Botany Univ of Reading 1978–81, postdoctoral scholar Dept of Biology Indiana Univ 1981–82, curator Field Museum of Natural History Chicago 1982–99 (vice-pres academic affrs 1994–99), dir Royal Botanic Gardens Kew 1999–2006, John and Marion Sullivan prof Univ of Chicago 2006–; pres: Palaeontological Soc, Palaeontological Assoc; author of more than 100 pubns in plant palaeontology and evolutionary biology; memb: Bd Nat Museum of Natural History Smithsonian Inst USA, Overseers Visiting Ctee Organic and Evolutionary Biology Harvard Univ, Bd Botanic Gardens Conservation Int, Bd WWF UK, Advsy Bd Royal Parks; Bicentenary Medal Linnean Soc 1984, Schuchert Award Paleontological Soc 1993, Henry Allan Gleason Award NY Botanical Garden 1998; patron Thomas Phillips Price Tst, memb Bd Lovaine Tst; Hon DDes Kingston Univ, Hon DSc Univ of Portsmouth, hon fell Royal Holloway Coll London; foreign assoc Nat Acad of Scis USA 2001, foreign memb Royal Swedish Acad of Scis 2002, memb Deutsche Akademie der Naturforscher Leopoldina; FRS 1998; *Recreations* travel, biographies; *Style—* Prof Sir Peter Crane, FRS; ✉ Department of Geophysical Science, University of Chicago, 5734 S Ellis Avenue, Chicago, IL 60637, USA

CRANFIELD, Richard William Lionel; s of Lionel Sydney William Cranfield (d 1965), and Audrey Cecil Martin, *née* Pank; *b* 19 January 1956; *Educ* Winchester, Fitzwilliam Coll Cambridge (MA); *m* 26 Sept 1981, Gillian Isabel, da of Archibald Spence Fleming (d 1979), of Kelso, Roxburghshire; 2 s (Edward, George), 2 da (Sophie, Henrietta); *Career* admitted slr 1980; head corporate dept Allen & Overy 2000– (ptnr 1985); Freeman City of London 1985, memb Worshipful Co of Merchant Taylors; memb Law Soc; *Recreations* golf, field sports; *Style—* Richard Cranfield, Esq; ✉ Allen & Overy, One New Change, London EC4M 9QQ (tel 020 7330 3000, fax 020 7330 9999)

CRANHAM, Kenneth; s of Ronald Cranham, of Hastings, East Sussex, and Margaret, *née* McKay Ferguson (d 2001); *b* 12 December 1944, Dunfermline; *Educ* Tulse Hill Sch, Nat Youth Theatre, RADA (Christine Silver Meml prize, Bancroft gold medal, Herbert Tree prize); *m* 25 July 1987, Fiona Victory; 2 da (Nancy Grace b 24 Oct 1982, Kathleen Mary Margaret b 24 Sept 1993); *Career* actor; *Television* Mayhew's London (BBC) 1966, Votzek (BBC) 1967, City '68 (Granada) 1968, Coronation Street (Granada) 1968, Sling Your Hook (BBC) 1969, Gangster Thirty Minute Theatre (BBC) 1969, The Changeling (BBC) 1974, Peer Gynt (BBC) 1976, Butterflies Don't Count (BBC) 1978, The Sound of the Guns (Granada) 1979, Danger UXB 1979, The Merchant of Venice (BBC) 1980, 'Tis Pity She's a Whore (BBC) 1980, Thérèse Raquin (BBC) 1980, Cribb (Granada) 1980, The Sin Bin (BBC) 1981, Brideshead Revisited (Granada) 1981, Harvey Moon in Shine on Harvey Moon (ATV) 1982–85, Iris Murdoch's The Bell (BBC) 1982, Heart of the High Country (ITV) 1985, Lady Windermere's Fan (BBC) 1985, The Birthday Party (BBC) 1985, The Dumb Waiter (BBC) 1985, The Caretaker (BBC) 1985, The Chauffeur and the Lady (BBC) 1985, A Sort of Innocence (BBC) 1986, Normal Service (BBC), The Black and Blue Lamp (BBC), Master of the Marionettes (BBC), The Vision Thing (BBC), Rules of Engagement (ITV), Dunrulin' (BBC), Oranges Are Not The Only Fruit (BBC), The Contractor (BBC), Chimera (ITV), A Little Bit of Lippy (BBC), El C.I.D. (Granada), The Party (BBC), Between the Lines (BBC), La Ronde (BBC), Royal Celebration (BBC), Requiem Apache (BBC), The Tenant of Wildfell Hall (BBC), Just Another Secret (ITV), Get Well Soon (BBC), Our Mutual Friend (BBC), The Murder of Stephen Lawrence (BBC), Without Motive (ITV), Justice in Wonderland (BBC), Lady Audley's Secret (ITV), The Sins (BBC), Night Flight (BBC), Dickens (BBC), The Sinking of the Lusitania (BBC), Pollyanna (ITV), Sparkling Cyanide (ITV), Leopold Mozart in The Genius of Mozart (BBC), Pompey in Rome (HBO), The Line of Beauty (BBC) 2005, Harold Wilson in The Lavender List (BBC) 2006, After Life (ITV) 2006, Lillies (ITV) 2006, W H Auden in The Addiction of Sin (BBC) 2007; *Films* incl: Prospero's Books, Stealing Heaven, A Good Year, Man Dancin', Trauma, Vampira, Layer Cake, The Rising: Ballad of Mangal Pandey, Joseph Andrews, Hellraiser II, Fratello Sole, Sorella Luna, The Clot, Chocolat, Under Suspicion, The Last Yellow, Women Talking Dirty, Gangster No 1, Shiner, Born Romantic, Two Men Went to War, A Man Sat Next to Me..., Hot Fuzz, Oliver, Tale of a Vampire, The Boxer; *Theatre* RSC: Ivanov, The Iceman Cometh, School for Scandal; RNT: The UN Inspector, Flight, An Inspector Calls (also Br tour, Aldwych, Broadway American tour, nomination Best Actor Olivier Awards 1994), Kick for Touch, Cardiff East, From Kipling to Vietnam, The Caretaker, Strawberry Fields, Love Letters on Blue Paper, The Passion, The Country Wife, Old Movies, Larkrise, Madras House; Royal Court Theatre: Narrow Road to the Deep North, Early Morning, Saved, Ruffian on the Stair, Samuel Beckett's Play, Cascando, The London Cuckolds, Tibetan Inroads, Magnificence, Cheek, Owners, Geography of a Horse Dreamer, Tooth of Crime, No One Was Saved, Their Very Own and Golden City, Ubu Roi; West End: Loot, Comedians, Entertaining Mr Sloane; other prodns incl: Doctor's Dilemma (Mermaid Theatre), Le Main Sal (Almeida), Paul Bunyan (ROH), The Entertainer (Greenwich), Gaslight (The Old Vic) 2007, Loot, End Game (Beckett Centenary Dublin) 2006, Scrawdyke in Little Malcolm and his Struggle Against the Eunuchs (European tour, Watford Palace and Traverse Theatre Edinburgh), A Midsummer Night's Dream (Manchester Royal Exchange); *Radio* The Barchester Chronicles, New Grub St, Sons and Lovers, Hard Times, Answered Prayers, Earthly Powers, Barrack Room Ballards; *Recreations* home, family, music, art, dining, friends, walking in London, drinking and thinking on rail journeys; *Style—* Kenneth Cranham, Esq; ✉ c/o Markham & Froggatt, 4 Windmill Street, London W1T 2HZ (tel 020 7636 4412)

CRANSTON, Ross Frederick; QC (1998); s of Frederick Hugh Cranston (d 1999), of Brisbane, Aust, and Edna Elizabeth, *née* Davies; *b* 23 July 1948; *Educ* Nundah State Sch, Wavell HS Brisbane, Univ of Queensland (BA, LLB), Harvard Univ (LLM), Univ of Oxford (DPhil, DCL); *m* 1, 5 March 1976 (m dis 1985), Prof (Barbara) Jane Stapleton, da of Colin Arthur Stapleton, of Sydney, Aust; m 2, 25 Aug 1988 (m dis 1998), Elizabeth Anna, da of Leslie Victor Whyatt, of Kent; 1 da (Imogen Molly); *Career* called to the Bar Gray's Inn 1976 (bencher 1998); recorder 1997– (asst recorder 1991–97); lectr in law Univ of Warwick 1975–77, ANU 1978–86, Lubbock prof of banking law Univ of London 1986–92, dir Centre for Commercial Law Studies Queen Mary & Westfield Coll London 1989–92 (dean Faculty of Laws 1988–91), Cassel prof of commercial law Univ of London 1993–97, visiting prof Law Dept LSE 1997–2005, Centennial prof of law LSE 2005–; MP (Lab) Dudley N 1997–2005 (Parly candidate (Lab) Richmond (Yorks) 1992); Slr-Gen for England

and Wales 1998–2001; chair: All-Pty Parly Gp on Alcohol Misuse 2002–05, All-Pty Parly Gp for the Bar 2002–05; conslt Ctee of Inquiry Concerning Public Duty and Private Interest 1979, memb Legal Advsy Panel Nat Consumer Cncl 1976–77 and 1987–97; conslt: World Bank, IMF, UNCTAD, Cwlth Secretariat, Lord Woolf's Inquiry into Access to Justice 1994–96; pres SPTL 1992–93 (vice-pres 1991–92), chm Bd of Tstees Public Concern at Work 1996–97 (dep chm 1993–96), chair Soc of Lab Lawyers 2003–; memb American Law Inst; *Books* Cranston's Consumers and the Law (1978, 3 edn (jtly) 2000), Regulating Business (1979), Law and Economics (jt ed, 1981), Delays and Efficiency in Civil Litigation (jtly, 1984, 3 ed 2000), Legal Foundations of the Welfare State (1985), Law, Government and Public Policy (1987), European Banking Law (1993, 2 ed 1999), The Single Market and the Law of Banking (ed, 1991, 3 edn 1995), Reform of Civil Procedure (jt ed, 1995), Legal Ethics and Professional Responsibility (ed, 1995), Making Commercial Law (ed, 1997), Principles of Banking Law (1997, 2 edn 2002), Banks, Liability and Risk (ed, 1990, 3 edn 2000), How Law Works (2006); *Clubs* Reform; *Style*— Ross Cranston, QC; ✉ 3 Verulam Buildings, Gray's Inn, London WC1R 5EA (tel 020 7831 8441, fax 020 7831 8479)

CRANWORTH, 3 Baron (UK 1899); Philip Bertram Gurdon; s of Hon Robin Gurdon (ka 1942, s of late 2 Baron, KG, MC, who d 1964) and late Hon Yoskyl Pearson, da of 2 Viscount Cowdray (who m 2, Lt-Col Alistair Gibb, and m 3, 1 Baron McCorquodale of Newton, KCVO, PC); *b* 24 May 1940; *Educ* Eton, Magdalene Coll Cambridge; *m* 18 Jan 1968, Frances Henrietta (d 2000), da of late Lord William Walter Montagu Douglas Scott, MC (s of 7 Duke of Buccleuch), and Lady Rachel Douglas-Home (da of 13 Earl of Home); 2 s (Hon (Sacha William) Robin b 1970, Hon (Brampton) Charles b 1975), 1 da (Hon Louisa-Jane, (Mrs Simon Hanbury) b 1969); *Career* late Lt Royal Wilts Yeo; *Style*— The Rt Hon the Lord Cranworth; ✉ Grundisburgh Hall, Woodbridge, Suffolk IP13 6TW

CRATHORNE, 2 Baron (UK 1959); Sir (Charles) James Dugdale; 2 Bt (UK 1945), JP (N Yorks 1999); s of 1 Baron, TD, PC (d 1977), and Nancy, OBE (d 1969), da of Sir Charles Tennant, 1 Bt; *b* 12 September 1939; *Educ* Eton, Trinity Coll Cambridge; *m* 1970, Sylvia Mary, da of Brig Arthur Montgomery, OBE, TD; 2 da (Hon Charlotte b 1972, Hon Katharine b 1980), 1 s (Hon Thomas Arthur John b 1977); *Heir* s, Hon Thomas Dugdale; *Career* with Sotheby and Co 1963–66, asst to pres Parke-Bernet NY 1966–69, James Dugdale and Associates London (ind fine art consultancy serv) 1969–77, James Crathorne and Assocs 1977–; fine art lectr, annual lectr tours to USA 1970–, lecture series Met Museum NY 1981, Aust Bicentennial Lectr Tour 1988; dir: Cliveden Hotel 1985–97, Woodhouse Securities 1989–99, Cliveden plc 1997–98, Hand Picked Hotels Ltd 2001–02; chm: Captain Cook Tst 1993– (tstee 1978–), Jt Ctee of the Nat Amenity Socs 1996–99; contribs to Apollo and The Connoisseur; memb: Cncl RSA 1982–88, Editorial Bd House Magazine 1983–, Exec Ctee Georgian Gp 1985– (chm 1990–99), Cons Advsy Gp on the Arts and Heritage 1988–98, Yorks Regnl Ctee Nat Tst 1974–84 and 1988–94; elected memb House of Lords 1999–; hon sec: All-Pty Parly Arts and Heritage Gp 1981–, All-Pty Photography Gp 1997–; memb Works of Art Sub-Ctee 1983–2002, chm Works of Art Ctee 2004–; pres: Cleveland Assoc of Nat Tst 1982–94, Yarm Civic Soc 1987–, Cleveland Family History Soc 1988–, Cleveland Sea Cadets 1988–, Hambledon Dist CPRE 1988–, Cleveland and N Yorks Magistrates Assoc 1997–2003, Cleveland and S Durham Magistrates Assoc 2003–, Yorks and Humberside RFCA 2006– (vice-pres 1999–2006); vice-pres: Cleveland Wildlife Tst 1990–, Public Monuments and Sculpture Assoc 1997–, N Yorks Co Scouts 1998–, North of England RFCA 2001–; govr Queen Margaret's Sch York 1986–99; memb Ct: Univ of Leeds 1985–97, Univ of York 1999–, Univ of Hull 1999–; tstee National Heritage Memorial Fund 1992–95; patron: Attingham Tst for the Study of the Br Country House 1991–, Cleveland Community Fndn 1990–; hon patron Friends of York Sculpture Park 1992–; church warden All Saints Crathorne 1977–; HM Lord-Lt N Yorks 1999– (DL: Cleveland 1983–96, N Yorks 1996–99); Queen's Golden Jubilee Medal 2002; FRSA 1972 (memb Cncl RSA 1982–88); KStJ 1999; *Exhibitions* Photographs (Middlesbrough Art Gallery) 1980, All-Pty Photography Gp annual exhbn (Westminster and touring) 1992–, Georgian Theatre Royal Richmond N Yorks 2005; *Books* Edouard Vuillard (1967), Tennants Stalk (jtly 1973), A Present from Crathorne (jtly, 1989), Cliveden: The Place and the People (1995), The Royal Crescent Book of Bath (1998), Parliament in Pictures (co-photographer, 1999); *Recreations* photography, travel, family life in the country, jazz; *Clubs* Brooks's, Pratt's; *Style*— The Lord Crathorne; ✉ Crathorne House, Yarm, North Yorkshire TS15 0AT (tel 01642 700431, fax 01642 700632, e-mail james@jcrathorne.fsnet.co.uk); House of Lords, London SW1A 0PW (tel 020 7219 5224, fax 020 7219 2772, e-mail crathornej@parliament.uk)

CRAUFURD, Sir Robert James; 9 Bt (GB 1781), of Kilbirney, N Britain; s of Sir James Gregan Craufurd, 8 Bt (d 1970), and Ruth Marjorie, *née* Corder (d 1998); *b* 18 March 1937; *Educ* Harrow, UC Oxford (MA); *m* 1, 1964 (m dis 1987), Catherine Penelope, yr da of late Capt Horatio Westmacott, RN, of Torquay, Devon; 3 da (Caroline Anne b 1965, Penelope Jane b 1967, Veronica Mary b 1969); m 2, 1987, Georgina Anne, da of late John Dennis Russell, of Lymington, Hants; *Heir* none; *Career* memb London Stock Exchange 1969; *Style*— Sir Robert Craufurd, Bt; ✉ East Grove, Grove Road, Lymington, Hampshire SO41 3RF (tel 01590 672406)

CRAUSBY, David Anthony; MP; s of Thomas Crausby (d 1993), and Kathleen, *née* Lavin (d 2002); *b* 17 June 1946; *Educ* Derby GS Bury, Bury Coll of FE; *m* 4 Sept 1965, Enid, da of William Noon; 2 s (David, Jason); *Career* skilled turner (former apprentice), former full time works convenor; MP (Lab) Bolton NE 1997–; *Recreations* watching football, cinema, walking; *Style*— David Crausby, Esq, MP; ✉ c/o Bolton North East Labour Party, 580 Blackburn Road, Bolton, Lancashire BL1 7AL (tel 01204 303340); House of Commons, London SW1A 0AA (tel 020 7219 3000)

CRAVEN, 9 Earl of (GB 1801); Benjamin Robert Joseph Craven; also Baron Craven (E 1665), Viscount Uffington (GB 1801); o s of 8 Earl of Craven (d following a motor accident 1990), and Teresa Maria Bernadette, da of Arthur John Downes, of Blackhall, Clane, Co Kildare; *b* 13 June 1989; *Style*— The Rt Hon the Earl of Craven

CRAVEN, Sir John Anthony; kt (1996); s of William Herbert Craven, and Hilda Lucy Craven; *b* 23 October 1940; *Educ* Michaelhouse SA, Jesus Coll Cambridge (BA), Queen's Univ Kingston Ontario; *m* 1, 1961, Gillian Margaret, *née* Murray; 1 s, 1 da; m 2, 1970, Jane Frances, *née* Stiles-Allen; 3 s; m 3, Ning Ning, *née* Chang; *Career* Clarkson Gordon & Co 1961–64, Wood Gundy 1964–67, S G Warburg & Co 1967–73 (dir 1969–73), chief exec White Weld & Co Ltd 1973–78, vice-chm S G Warburg & Co 1979, fndr and chm Phoenix Securities Ltd 1981–89, chief exec Morgan Grenfell Gp plc 1987–89, chm Deutsche Morgan Grenfell Gp plc (formerly Morgan Grenfell Gp plc) 1989–97, memb Bd of MDs Deutsche Bank AG 1990–96; non-exec chm: Tootal Gp plc 1985–90, Lonmin plc (formerly Lonrho plc) 1997–, GEMS Funds 1998–, Fleming Family & Ptnrs 2003–07 (non-exec dir 2001–), Patagonia Gold plc 2004–; non-exec dir: Société Generale de Surveillence SA 1986–95, Rothmans International BV 1991–99, Ducati SpA 1992–2001, Reuters Holdings plc 1997–2004; memb: Ontario Inst of CAs, Canadian Inst of CAs; *Style*— Sir John Craven; ✉ Lonmin plc, 4 Grosvenor Place, London SW1X 7YL

CRAVEN, Prof John Anthony George; s of George Marriot Craven (d 1989), and Dorothy Maude, *née* Walford (d 2003); *b* 17 June 1949; *Educ* Pinner GS, King's Coll Cambridge (Kennedy Meml Scholar, Adam Smith Essay Prize, Stephenson Essay Prize, MA), MIT; *m* 1974, Laura Elizabeth, da of Prof John Loftis; 1 s (Matthew Thomas b 1978), 1 da (Rebecca Mary b 1981); *Career* Univ of Kent: lectr in economics 1971–76, sr lectr 1976–80, reader 1980–86, prof of economics 1986–96, dean Faculty of Social Scis 1987–91, pro-vice-chllr 1991–93, dep vice-chllr 1993–96; vice-chllr Univ of Portsmouth 1997–; visiting assoc prof Univ of Guelph Canada 1982–83; memb Archbishops' Cncl 2006–; Hon DSc Univerisiti Teknologi Malaysia 2000; memb Royal Economic Soc 1971; *Books* Distribution of the Product (1979), Introduction to Economics (1984, 2 edn 1989), Social Choice (1992); *Recreations* choral singing, charity trustee; *Style*— Prof John Craven

CRAVEN, John Raymond; OBE (2000); s of Bill Craven (d 1990), and Marie, *née* Noble (d 1989); *Educ* Leeds Modern GS; *m* 27 March 1971, Jean Marilyn, da of Alfred (Blackie) Howe, CBE (d 1974); 2 da; *Career* journalist and television presenter; jr reporter The Harrogate Advertiser (later reporter The Yorkshire Post and freelance reporter for nat press); BBC: news writer 1965, TV reporter Points West (BBC Bristol) 1970, presenter Search (current affairs magazine for children) 1971, presenter and later ed John Craven's Newsround 1972–89, currently presenter Countryfile (BBC1) and Castle in the Country (BBC2); other TV credits incl: Swap Shop, Saturday Superstore, Animal Sanctuary, Craven's Collectables; winner: BAFTA Award (for best children's TV documentary) 1975, Pye TV Award (for distinguished services to TV) 1983, TV Times Award (for top children's personality) 1983, elected memb RTS Hall of Fame 1996, awarded The Baird Medal RTS 2002; patron: Whale and Dolphin Conservation Soc, The Soc for the Protection of Animals Abroad; pres YHA England and Wales; vice-pres Waterways Tst; *Recreations* walking in the countryside, aviation; *Style*— John Craven, Esq, OBE; ✉ c/o Unique Management Ltd, 114 Power Road, Chiswick, London W4 5PY (tel 020 8987 6400, e-mail london@uniquegroup.co.uk)

CRAVEN, Michael Anthony (Mike); s of Henry Craven (d 1996), and Hilary, *née* Willcox; *b* 1 February 1959; *Educ* Marist Coll Hull, Univ of Hull (BA); *Career* advsr to Rt Hon John Prescott, MP , *qv*, 1983–87; md Market Access 1995–97 (dir 1988–95), dir of communications Lab Pty 1998, founding ptnr Lexington Communications 1998–; Parly candidate (Lab) 1983; *Recreations* walking, reading; *Clubs* Soho House; *Style*— Mike Craven, Esq; ✉ 198 High Holborn, London WC1V 7BD (tel 020 7395 8949, e-mail michael.craven@lexcomm.co.uk)

CRAWFORD, Alexander Hamilton; JP (NE Hants) 2002; s of James Allison Crawford (d 1978), and Betsy Carroll, *née* Hughes (d 1950); *b* 15 January 1944; *Educ* Queen Mary's Sch Basingstoke, Imperial Coll London (BSc), Open Univ Business Sch (Dip Mgmnt), Farnborough Coll of Technol (Dip French); *m* 1, 6 Jan 1968 (m dis 1982), Lesley Sandra Jane; 2 da (Alison Mary b 6 Jan 1971, Sarah Louise b 30 May 1973), 1 s (Stephen Nicholas b 8 July 1981); m 2, 1 June 1982, Jennifer Mary Evans, *née* Stuart; *Career* managing ed IPC Sci & Technol Press 1967–72, sci ed Euro Physical Soc 1972–73, mathematics teacher Aldershot Manor Sch 1974–77, engr ed Electrical Review 1977–80, Euro ed Energy Developments 1981; publisher Milehouse 1999; ed: Health & Safety at Work 1982–87, Laboratory News 1987–92 and 1993–98, CORDIS News Euro Cmmn 1998–99, Chemistry & Industry 1999–2001, Pharmaceutical Business News 2001, Trends in Analytical Chemistry 2002–; managing ed: Laboratory Practice 1992, Laboratory News 1992; chm: Nat Fedn of Consumer Gps 1979–80, Occupational and Environmental Diseases Assoc 1991–93, Nat Science Centre Project 1994–96 (dir 1993–96); memb: Nat Consumer Cncl 1977–82, Bd Pavilion Housing Assoc 2004–05; generalist advsr Aldershot CAB 2002–, sec Blackwater Valley Housing Forum 2004–, sec Cargate Area Residents Assoc 2005–, govr Frimley Park Hosp NHS Fndn Tst 2005–; memb: Rushmoor BC 1976–85, Hants CC 1981–82; MInstP 1970, MIMgt 1990, FRMS 1990, AIL 1992; *Recreations* swimming, walking; *Style*— Alexander Crawford, Esq; ✉ 17 Cargate Avenue, Aldershot, Hampshire GU11 3EP (tel 01252 314708, e-mail alex@cargate.fsnet.co.uk)

CRAWFORD, Prof Alistair; s of John Gardiner Crawford (d 1991), of Fraserburgh, Aberdeenshire, and Mary Ann, *née* Holiday (d 1993), of Hull; *b* 25 January 1945; *Educ* Fraserburgh Acad, Glasgow Sch of Art (DA), Aberdeen Coll of Educn (Art Teacher's Cert); *m* 5 Nov 1971, Joan, da of Clifford Martin; *Career* art teacher Woodfarm HS Glasgow 1966–67, lectr in textile design Dept of Textile Industries Univ of Leeds 1968–71, sr lectr in graphic design Coventry Poly 1971–73; UCW Aberystwyth: lectr in graphic art 1974–83, sr lectr 1983–87, actg head Dept of Visual Art and curator of coll collections 1986–90, reader 1987–90, prof of graphic art and keeper of coll collections 1990–98, head Dept of Visual Art 1990–93, head School of Art 1993–95, research prof of art 1995–; painter, printmaker, photographer, art historian, performer, writer and ind curator; columnist Inscape jl of photography 1999–; memb Int Advsy Bd European Soc for the History of Photography 2004– (also co-ed photoresearcher (Vienna) of soc jl 2004–); Br School at Rome: Balsdon sr fell 1995–96, tstee 1996–2000, archive res fell 1997–2001; fell Printmakers' Cncl of GB 1978–93, MSTD 1977–97, FRSA 1983–86, MSIAD 1977–86 (ASIAD 1973), FRPS 1991–98, RCA 1993–; Hon RE 2000–; *Solo Exhibitions* incl: Curwen Gallery London 1981, Segno Grafico Venice 1981, Centro Iniziative Per l'Arte e la Cultura Palazzo Kechler Udine 1981, Cartesius Gallery Trieste 1982, Italian Journal (Curwen Gallery London) 1983, Printworks Gallery Chicago 1983, The Spirit of Place (Wales and Scot touring) 1986–88, Travel Journal (Tolquhon Gallery Aberdeenshire) 1992, Barcelona Tango (Printworks Gallery Chicago and Aberystwyth, Abulafia Gall Llandeilo) 1994–97, Vedute d'Italia (Casa Cinus Sardinia) 1994, It is in the Nature of My Gaze (Univ of Wales Aberystwyth) 1995, A Return to Wales, retrospective (Nat Library of Wales) 2000, Pictures for an even smaller room (Univ of Wales Aberystwyth) 2004–05, Landscape Capriccios: the landscape of the mind (Univ of Wales Aberystwyth, Martin's Gall Cheltenham and Denbighshire Arts Touring to Mold, Llanwrst, Denbigh) 2004–06, North by North West (Jersey Arts Centre) 2006, Pictures for a small room (Toko Gall Aberystwyth, Rowley Gall London) 2006–07; *Group Exhibitions* incl: 4 times 20 (Oriel Theatre Clwyd Mold and touring, with Norman Ackroyd, David Hockney and Terry Willson) 1981–82, Vedute d'Italia/Alistair Crawford & Robert Greethem (Catherine Lewis Gallery Univ of Wales Aberystwyth and Wales touring 1987–88 and Printworks Gallery Chicago 1988), Pivot - 16 artists using photography (Oriel Mostyn Llandudno and Wales touring) 1991–92, Small Works (Printworks Gallery Chicago) 1997, Gardens of Wales (RCA, Conwy, Nat Library of Wales) 1999, National Print Exhibition (Mall Galleries London) 2000, 2001 and 2002, Off Cuts (Bankside Gallery London) 2001, Ogwyn Davies & Alistair Crawford (RCA, Conwy) 2001, Stark Gallery London at Glasgow Art Fair 2005, Prima Luce Fotografia da Edward Weston a Mario Giacomelli (Universita' Politecnica delle Marche, Ancona and Palazzo del Monte di Pietà Padova) 2005–06; *Work in Collections* incl: Glasgow Sch of Art, Nat Museum of Wales, Hunterian Museum and Art Gallery Glasgow, Welsh Arts Cncl, SW Thames HA, Continental Bank Collection Chicago, Mazda Cars (UK), Br Sch at Rome, P&O London, Fleetwood, Newport, Leicester, Norwich, Hove, Arbroath, Buckie, Carmarthen, Grimsby, Haverfordwest and Peterhead Museums, Br Cncl, Nat Library of Wales, Imperial Coll London, Contemporary Art Soc of Wales, Frito-Lay Corporation Dallas, Eton Coll, The Getty Group Chicago, Town Docks Museum Hull, The Beckman Inst Univ of Illinois at Champaign, The Scottish Fisheries Museum Anstruther, MOMA Wales, United Airlines, The Royal National Mission to Deep Sea Fishermen London, Maritime Museum Great Yarmouth, American Dairy Assoc Chicago, Seidman Jackson & Fisher Chicago, Greenberger & Kaufmann Chicago, Morse-Diesel Engineering Co Chicago, F I Torchia & Associates Chicago, International Minerals Corp Northbrook Illinois, Ashmolean Museum Oxford, Aberdeen Maritime Museum, Penlee House Museum Penzance, Univs of Aberystwyth, Bangor, Leeds, Liverpool, Northampton and Swansea, Leighton Park Sch Reading, London Oratory Sch, West Bromwich Coll, Walsall Educn Authy, Coates Inks UK, Moore Stephens Accountants Jersey, Nat Screen and Sound Archive of Wales, Denbighshire CC; *Touring Exhibitions* as designer and curator incl: Elio Ciol photographer (Welsh Arts Cncl and N Wales Arts Assoc) 1977–81, John

Thomas 1838–1905 photographer (Welsh Arts Cncl) 1977–81, Mario Giacomelli - a retrospective 1955–83 (Visiting Arts Unit of GB and Fotogallery Cardiff) 1983–86, Carlo Bevilacqua Il Maestro (Visiting Arts Unit of GB and UW Aberystwyth) 1987–90, Mario Giacomelli (Printworks Gallery Chicago) 1994, The Welsh Lens (MOMA Wales, Zirpoli Gallery Switzerland, Museo Genna Maria Sardinia) 1997–99, Immagini del passato, the photography of Father Peter Paul Mackey 1851–1935 (Museo Nazionale Sassari, Exma Cagliari, Galleria Comunale Nuoro Sardinia) 2000, Eric Lessing. Vom Festhalten der Zeit. Reportage-Fotografie 1948–1973 (Kunsthistorisches Museum Vienna); performance: An Evening with Eugénie Strong (Tabernacle Arts Centre Machynlleth, Br Sch at Rome, Lambeth Palace, Aberystwyth Arts Centre, Drovers Festival Lampeter, Girton Coll Cambridge) 1996–, Brief Exposure (Tabernacle Arts Centre Machynlleth, Aberystwyth Arts Centre, Drovers Festival Lampeter, Jersey Arts Centre, Steiner Theatre London, Shrewsbury Visual Art Festival) 2001–; *Awards* incl: Welsh Arts Cncl Design Award 1976, Welsh Arts Cncl/Editions Alecto Major Printmaking Award 1977, W Wales Arts Assoc Cmmn Award 1977, Welsh Arts Cncl Travel Award 1978, Br Cncl 1981, Sir Winston Churchill travelling fellowship in Photography 1982, Royal Nat Eisteddfod Gold Medal in Fine Art 1985, Royal Nat Eisteddfod Photography Prize 1989, Krazna-Krausz Photograhy Award 1992, winners Tabernacle Art Competition (Machynlleth) 2004 and 2005; *Publications* incl: John Thomas 1838–1905 Photographer (with Hilary Woollen, 1977), The Print Collection of the University College of Wales Aberystwyth (1984), Mario Giacomelli (1985), Elio Ciol - Italia Black & White (1986), Carlo Bevilacqua (1986), Elio Ciol - Assisi (1991 and 1992), Will Roberts (1994), Kyffin Williams (1995), It is in the Nature of My Gaze, Alistair Crawford Collected Photographs 1989–94 (1995), The Welsh Lens (1997), Robert Macpherson 1814–1872, the foremost photographer of Rome (1999), Made of Wales (2000), Immagini del passato, the photography of Father Peter Paul Mackey 1851–1935 (2000), Mario Giacomelli (2001, 2002, 2005 and 2006), Erich Lessing, Reportage-Fotography 1948–1973 (2002, 2003 and 2005); *Recreations* gardening; *Style*— Prof Alistair Crawford; ✉ Brynawel, Aberystwyth, Ceredigion SY23 3BD (website www.alistaircrawford.co.uk)

CRAWFORD, (Robert Hardie) Bruce; JP, MSP; *Career* civil servant with Scottish Office 1974–99; Perth and Kinross: cncllr 1988–99, leader 1996–99; MSP (SNP): Mid & Fife 1999–2007, Stirling 2007–; chief whip 1999–2000, shadow min for tport and environment 2000–01, shadow min for environment and energy 2001–03, shadow min for Parl 2003–05, chm SNP 2005–07, min for Parly business 2007–; chm Perth and Kinross Recreational Facilities Ltd 1996–99; *Recreations* politics, golf, football; *Style*— Bruce Crawford, Esq, MSP; ✉ The Scottish Parliament, Edinburgh EH99 1SP (tel 0131 348 5686, fax 0131 348 5708, mobile 0771 3651298, e-mail bruce.crawford.msp@scottish.parliament.uk)

CRAWFORD, HE Charles Graham; CMG (1998); s of Graham Wellington James Crawford, of Hemel Hempstead, Herts, and Edith Ellen, *née* Orrah; *b* 22 May 1954; *Educ* St Albans Sch, St John's Coll Oxford (BA), Lincoln's Inn (Part II Bar Exams), Fletcher Sch of Law and Diplomacy USA (MA); *m* 1990, Helen Margaret, *née* Walsh; 2 s (James b 1991, Robert b 1993), 1 da (Ellen b 1999); *Career* HM Dip Serv: Indonesia Desk FCO 1979–81, second then first sec (press/info) Belgrade 1981–84, Civil Aviation Desk then speechwriter FCO 1984–87, first sec (political) Pretoria/Cape Town 1987–91, Soviet then Eastern Dept FCO 1991–93, political cnsllr Moscow 1993–96, ambass to Bosnia and Herzegovina 1996–98, Weatherhead Center for Int Affrs Harvard Univ 1998–99, dep political dir FCO 1999–2000, ambass to Fed Repub of Yugoslavia 2001–03, ambass to Poland 2003–07; *Recreations* chess, music; *Style*— HE Mr Charles Crawford, CMG; ✉ e-mail charles.crawford@fco.gov.uk

CRAWFORD, Prof Dorothy Hanson; OBE (2005); da of Sir Theo Crawford (d 1993, pres RCPath 1969–72), and Margaret, *née* Green (d 1973); *b* 13 April 1945, Glasgow; *Educ* Univ of London (MB BS, MD, DSc), Univ of Bristol (PhD); *m* 1968, Dr William Alexander; 2 s (Daniel b 1970, Theodore b 1973); *Career* sr lectr and reader Royal Postgrad Medical Sch 1985–90, prof of medical microbiology LSHTM 1990–97, prof of medical microbiology Univ of Edinburgh 1997–; FRCPath 1993 (MRCPath 1981), FRSE 2001, FMedSci 2001; *Publications* The Invisible Enemy (2000); author of more than 200 scientific papers; *Style*— Prof Dorothy Crawford, OBE; ✉ The Royal (Dick) School of Veterinary Studies, The University of Edinburgh, Summerhall, Edinburgh EH9 1QH

CRAWFORD, Sir Frederick William; kt (1986), DL (W Midlands 1995); s of William Crawford (d 1955), and Victoria Maud, *née* Careless (d 1988); *b* 28 July 1931; *Educ* George Dixon GS Birmingham, Univ of London (BSc(Eng), MSc, DSc), Univ of Liverpool (PhD, DipEd, DEng), OU (DipStat); *m* 21 Oct 1963, Béatrice Madeleine Jacqueline, da of Roger Hutter, of Paris; 1 da (Isabelle (Mrs Peter Sutton) b 1965), 1 s (Eric b 1968 d 1992); *Career* scientist NCB Mining Research Estab Middx 1956–57, sr lectr in electrical engrg Coll of Advanced Technol Birmingham 1958–59; Stanford Univ Calif 1959–82: prof of electrical engrg 1969–82, chm Inst for Plasma Research 1973–80; vice-chllr Aston Univ 1980–96; chm Criminal Cases Review Cmmn 1996–2003, chm Haruspex Consulting Ltd 2004–; non-exec dir: Legal & General Group plc 1988–97, Rexam plc (formerly Bowater plc) 1989–97, PowerGen plc 1990–2002; vice-pres Parly and Scientific Ctee 1992–95; vice-chm Ctee of Vice-Chllrs and Princs 1993–95; High Sheriff W Midlands 1995–96; Freeman City of London 1986, Master Worshipful Co of Engineers 1996–97, Master Worshipful Co of Info Technologists 2000–01; hon bencher Inner Temple 1996; Hon DSc Univ of Buckingham 1996; FREng 1985, FInstP 1964, FAPS 1965, FIEE 1965, FIEEE 1972, FIMA 1978, CIMgt 1986, Hon FIL 1987; *Clubs* Athenaeum; *Style*— Sir Frederick Crawford, DL; ✉ 47 Charlbury Road, Oxford OX2 6UX (tel 01865 554707)

CRAWFORD, Maj-Gen Ian Campbell; CBE (1982); *b* 17 June 1932; *Educ* Dumfries Acad, Univ of Edinburgh (MB ChB); *m* 4 April 1959, Phyllis Mary; 1 da (Fiona b 1960), 1 s (Niall b 1967); *Career* conslt physician (Cardiology) Queen Elizabeth Mil Hosp Woolwich 1977–83 and 1985–90; dir Army Med and consltg physician to the Army 1990–92, hon physician to HM The Queen 1990–92; private consultant practice (cardiology and gen internal med) 1992–; FRCPE 1972, FRCP 1986; *Style*— Maj-Gen Ian C Crawford, CBE; ✉ The Arbour, Bobbing, Kent (tel 01795 842292, fax 01795 843753)

CRAWFORD, Prof James Richard; s of James Allen Crawford, of Hahndorf, S Australia, and Josephine Margaret, *née* Bond; *b* 14 November 1948; *Educ* Univ of Adelaide (BA, LLB, Stow scholar), Univ of Oxford (DPhil); *m* 1, Marisa Luigina, *née* Ballini; 2 da (Rebecca Jane b 5 Aug 1972, Emily Jessica Teresa b 17 Aug 1975); m 2 (m dis), Patricia Hyndman; 2 da (Alexandra Vijayalalitha b 26 Sept 1992, Natasha Mihiri b 3 Jan 1994); m 3, Joanna Gomula; 1 s (James Tadeusz b 26 April 1999); *Career* Univ of Adelaide: lectr 1974–77, sr lectr 1977–82, reader 1982–83, prof of law (personal chair) 1983–86; cmmr Australian Law Reform Cmmn 1982–84 (pt/t cmmr 1984–90), Challis prof of int law Univ of Sydney 1986–92 (dean Faculty of Law 1990–92), Whewell prof of int law Univ of Cambridge 1992–, professorial fell Jesus Coll Cambridge 1992–, dir Lauterpacht Research Centre for Int Law 1997–2003 and 2006–; barr of High Court of Australia and of the Supreme Court of NSW (SC NSW 1997), memb of Matrix Chambers London; dir of studies Int Law Assoc London 1991–98; memb: Advsy Ctee on the Australian Judicial System The Constitutional Cmmn 1985–87, Institut de Droit Int 1991 (assoc 1985), UN Int Law Cmmn 1992–2001; judge Admin Tbnl OECD 1993–; hon bencher Gray's Inn 1991; FBA 2000; *Publications* The Creation of States in International Law (1981, Creative Scholarship award American Soc of Int Law, 2 edn 2006), The Rights of Peoples (ed, 1988), Australian Courts of Law (3 edn 1993, 4 edn 2004), The ILC's Articles on State Responsibility (2002); *Recreations* cricket, reading, walking; *Style*— Prof James Crawford, SC, LLD, FBA; ✉ Lauterpacht Research Centre for International Law, Cambridge CB5 8BL (tel 01223 335358, fax 01223 311668, e-mail jrc1000@hermes.cam.ac.uk)

CRAWFORD, Lincoln; OBE (1998); s of Norman Crawford (d 1983), and Ena Crawford (d 1972); *b* 1 November 1946; *Educ* Univ Tutorial Coll London, Brunel Univ (LLB); *m* 1, 26 July 1976 (m dis), Janet, da of John Clegg (d 1987); 3 s (Douglas Luke b 4 Dec 1978, Paul David b 26 Aug 1981, Jack Justin b 7 Sept 1988); m 2, 5 June 1999, Bronwen, da of Clive Jenkins (d 1999); 1 da (Ella Charlotte 7 Jan 1999), 1 s (Mostyn Clive b 5 March 2001); *Career* called to the Bar 1977, recorder 1997–; advsr to Lord Scarman following Brixton disorders 1981, exec memb Prison Reform Tst; pt/t chm Employment Tbnls Judicial Studies Bd; chm: Inquiry into the care and treatment of Martin Mursell, Inquiry into the employment practices of the London Borough of Hackney, Standards Panel London Borough of Camden (Sleezebuster), Bar Race Relations Ctee, Champion of the Community Legal Services; memb: Cmmn for Racial Equality 1984, Parole Bd 1985–88, Br Boxing Bd of Control, Black-Jewish Forum; chm: Prince's Tst Sports Ctee 1989, Ind Adoption Serv; S of England chm Special Needs Appeals Panel FEFC; vice-chm Charta Mede Tst; participant Duke of Edinburgh Study Conf 1989, govr Hampstead Comprehensive Sch; Hon LLD Brunel Univ; *Recreations* squash, swimming; *Clubs* Commonwealth; *Style*— Lincoln Crawford, Esq, OBE; ✉ 12 Kings Bench Walk, Temple, London EC4 (tel 020 7583 0811, fax 020 7583 7228)

C

CRAWFORD, Michael; OBE (1987); *b* 19 January 1942; *Educ* St Michael's Coll Bexley, Oakfield Sch Dulwich; *Career* actor 1955–; in original prodn of Britten's Noyes Fludde and of Let's Make an Opera; *Theatre* incl: Come Blow Your Horn (Prince of Wales) 1961, Travelling Light 1965, The Anniversary 1966, No Sex Please We're British (Strand) 1971, Billy (Drury Lane) 1974, Same Time Next Year (Prince of Wales) 1976, Flowers for Algernon (Queen's) 1979, Barnum (Palladium) 1981–83 and (Victoria Palace) 1985–86, The Phantom of the Opera (Her Majesty's) 1986 (also NY 1988, LA 1989, and tour of USA, Canada, Aust and UK), The Music of Andrew Lloyd Webber 1991–92, EFX (MGM Grand Las Vegas) 1995, Dance of the Vampires 2002–03, The Woman in White 2004–; *Television* incl: Some Mothers Do 'Ave 'Em, Chalk and Cheese; *Film* incl: Soap Box Derby, Blow Your Own Trumpet, Two Left Feet, The War Lover, Two Living One Dead, The Knack 1964, A Funny Thing Happened on the Way to the Forum 1965, The Jokers, How I Won the War 1966, Hello Dolly 1968, The Games 1969, Hello and Goodbye 1970, Alice in Wonderland 1972, The Condorman 1980; *Albums* Michael Crawford performs Andrew Lloyd Webber (1991), A Touch of Music in the Night (1993), With Love (1994), In Concert (1998), On Eagle's Wings (1998), Christmas (1999), The Disney Album (2001); cast albums incl: Alice in Wonderland, Billy, Flowers For Algernon, Barnum, The Phantom of the Opera, Songs from the Stage and Screen (1987) EFX (1995); *Awards* Variety Club Award for Most Promising Newcomer (for The Knack), TV Times Awards for Funniest Man on TV (for Some Mothers Do 'Ave 'Em), Sun Award for TV Actor of the Year (for Some Mothers Do 'Ave 'Em), Variety Club Show Business Personality of the Year and Silver Heart Award (for Billy), Variety Club Show Business Personality of the Year (for Barnum), Oliver Award for Best Actor in a Musical (for Barnum), Broadways' Tony Award (for Phantom of the Opera), Olivier Award for Best Actor in a Musical (for Phantom of the Opera), Drama Desk and Outer Critics Circle Award, Los Angeles' Dramalogue Award and Drama Critics Award; *Books* Parcel Arrived Safely, Tied with String (autobiography, 2000); *Style*— Michael Crawford, Esq, OBE; ✉ c/o Knight Ayton Management, 114 St Martins Lane, London WC2N 4BE (tel 020 7836 5333, fax 020 7836 8333)

CRAWFORD, Prof Michael Angus; s of Thomas Crawford (d 1954), and Lilian Crawford (d 1990); *b* 9 July 1930, Edinburgh; *Educ* Fort Augustus Sch, Univ of Edinburgh (BSc), Royal Postgraduate Medical Sch (PhD); *m* 8 Dec 1998, Amanda, *née* Walton; 1 s (Adam), 1 da (Lyndsay), 2 adopted da (Cleo, Olivia); *Career* Royal Canadian Air Force 1952–54 (rising to Flying offr); research asst to Prof M D Milne Francis Frazer Labs Royal Postgrad Med Sch London 1956–60, lectr and head Dept of Biochemistry Makerere Univ Medical Sch Uganda 1960–65, head Dept of Biochemistry Nuffield Inst of Comparative Medicine 1965–89; dir Inst of Brain Chemistry and Human Nutrition: Queen Elizabeth Hosp for Children 1989–96, London Met Univ 1996–; Wellcome visiting research fell to Prof Ernst Baranay Univ of Uppsalla Sweden 1963, special chair in biochemistry Univ of Nottingham 1980–90, Danone chair Univ of Ghent 2000, hon prof Albert Schweitzer Int Univ Geneva 2000; pres Congress of the Int Soc for the Study of Fats and Lipids 2001; tstee and fndr dir Mother and Child Fndn, fndn dir Little Fndn; Centenary Award Hoffman la Roche 1966, Gold Medal 1st Int Congress on Essential Fatty Acids and Prostaglandins 1981, Int Award for Modern Nutrition 1995, Gold Medal for Science and Peace Albert Schweitzer Int Univ 2003; chair McCarrison Soc; memb: American Soc for Biochemistry and Molecular Biology, BAAS, American Soc for the Advancement of Science, Nutrition Soc, RSM; CBiol 1988, FIBiol 1988, FRCPath 1996; *Publications* What We Eat Today (with S M Crawford, 1972), Conservation (1976), Nutrition and Evolution (1995); author of over 290 papers, several chapters, symposium proceedings; *Recreations* music, beekeeping, skiing, scuba diving, gardening; *Style*— Prof Michael Crawford; ✉ 36 Regent's Park Road, London NW1 7SX (tel 020 7133 2926, e-mail michael@macrawf.demon.co.uk)

CRAWFORD, Prof Michael Hewson; s of Brian Hewson Crawford, and Margarethe Bettina, *née* Nagel; *b* 7 December 1939; *Educ* St Paul's, Oriel Coll Oxford (MA), Br Sch at Rome (scholar); *Career* Jane Eliza Procter visiting fell Princeton Univ 1964–65; Christ's Coll Cambridge: res fell 1964–69, fell 1969–86, lectr 1969–86; prof of ancient history UCL 1986–; visiting prof: Univ of Pavia 1983, École Normale Supérieure Paris 1984, Univ of Padua 1986, Sorbonne Paris 1989, Univ of San Marino 1989, Univ Statale Milan 1990, Univ of L'Aquila 1990, Univ of Pavia 1992, École des Hautes Etudes Paris 1997, École des Hautes Etudes en Sciences Sociales Paris 1999; jt dir: Excavations of Fregellae 1980–86, Valpolcevera Project 1987–94, Veleia Project 1994–95, S Martino Project 1996–2003; chm Jt Assoc of Classical Teachers 1992–95 (chm Ancient History Ctee 1978–84), vice-pres Roman Soc 1981–; tstee Entente Cordiale Scholapships 2000; ed: Papers of the Br Sch at Rome 1975–79, Jl of Roman Studies 1980–84; Joseph Crabtree orator 2000; foreign memb Istituto Lombardo 1990, memb Academia Europaea 1995, Reial Acadèmia de Bones Lletres 1998, corresponding memb Académie des Inscriptions et Belles-Lettres Paris 2006; Officier de l'Ordre des Palmes Académiques de la République Française 2001; FBA 1980; *Books* Roman Republican Coin Hoards (1969), Roman Republican Coinage (1974), Archaic and Classical Greece (with D Whitehead, 1982), Coinage and Money under the Roman Republic (1985), La Moneta in Grecia e a Roma (1986), L'impero romana e la struttura economica e sociale delle province (1986), The Coinage of the Roman World in the Late Republic (ed with A Burnett, 1987), Medals and Coins from Budé to Mommsen (ed with C Ligota and J B Trapp, 1991), Antonio Agustin between Renaissance and Counter-reform (ed, 1993), Roman Statutes (ed, 1996); contribs to Annales, Economic History Review, Jl of Roman Studies, Oxford DNB; *Style*— Prof Michael Crawford; ✉ Department of History, University College, Gower Street, London WC1E 6BT (tel 020 7679 7396)

CRAWFORD, Prof Robert; s of Robert Alexander Nelson Crawford (d 1997), and Elizabeth Menzies Crawford; *b* 23 February 1959; *Educ* Hutchesons' GS Glasgow, Univ of Glasgow (MA), Univ of Oxford (DPhil); *m* 2 Sept 1988, Alice, *née* Wales; 1 s (Lewis Robert b 17 June 1994), 1 da (Blyth Iona b 14 Aug 1996); *Career* poet and critic; Elizabeth Wordsworth jr research fell St Hugh's Coll Oxford 1984–87, Br Acad post doctoral fell Univ of Glasgow 1987–89; Univ of St Andrews: lectr in modern Scottish literature

1989–95, prof 1995–, head Sch of English 2002–05; poetry ed Polygon 1992–99; FRSE 1998, fell English Assoc 1998; *Awards* Scot Arts Cncl Book Award 1992 and 1999, selected as one of the best 20 UK New Generation Poets Arts Cncl of Eng 1994, recommendation Poetry Book Soc 1990, 1992, 1996 and 2003; *Poetry* major works: A Scottish Assembly (1990), Sharawaggi (with WN Herbert, 1990), Talkies (1992), Masculinity (1996), The Penguin Book of Poetry from Britain and Ireland since 1945 (ed with Simon Armitage, 1998), Spirit Machines (1999), The New Penguin Book of Scottish Verse (ed with Mick Imlah, 2000), The Tip of My Tongue (2003), Selected Poems (2005), Apollos of the North (2006); *Prose* works incl: The Savage and the City in the Work of TS Eliot (1987), Devolving English Literature (1992, 2 edn 2000), Identifying Poets (1993), The Modern Poet (2001), Scotland's Books: The Penguin History of Scottish Literature (2007); *Recreations* walking, painting; *Style*— Prof Robert Crawford; ✉ School of English, University of St Andrews, St Andrews, Fife KY16 9AL (tel 01334 462666, fax 01334 462655, e-mail rc4@st-and.ac.uk)

CRAWFORD, Robert Gammie; CBE (1990); s of William Crawford (d 1980), of Aberdeen, and Janet Beveridge, *née* Gammie (d 1974); *b* 20 March 1924; *Educ* Robert Gordon's Coll Aberdeen; *m* 4 Sept 1947, Rita (d 2004), da of August Daniel Veiss (d 1975), of Latvia; 1 da (Fiona b 1959); *Career* Flt Lt navigator RAF 1942–47; admitted slr 1950; ptnr Ince and Co (int shipping lawyers) 1950–73; dir: AVDEL plc 1983–94, Sturge Aviation Syndicate Management Ltd 1994–96, L R Integrity Management Ltd (formerly Marine Offshore Management Ltd) 1994–96, Ockham Aviation Agencies Ltd 1996–97; chm: Highlands and Islands Airports Ltd 1986–93, Independent Claims Services Ltd 1993–99; memb Lloyd's 1975–95; memb Bd: Lloyd's Register of Shipping 1982–94, Gen Ctee Lloyd's Register of Shipping 1982–2006, Civil Aviation Authy 1984–93; vice-chm Port of London Authy 1985–92; chm Silver Line Ltd 1974–91, chm UK War Risk Club 1982–; dir: UK Protection and Indemnity Club 1983–94 (chm 1984–91), UK Freight Demurrage Defence Club 1976– (chm 1987–90); farmer 1966–99; tstee Lloyd's Register Superannuation Fund 1982–2006; Freeman City of London, Freeman Worshipful Co of Watermen and Lightermen 1985; FInstD; *Recreations* shooting, reading, conversation; *Clubs* Royal Northern and University (Aberdeen); *Style*— Robert G Crawford, Esq, CBE; ✉ 9 London House, Avenue Road, London NW8 7PX (tel and fax 020 7483 2754, e-mail r.g.crawford@btinternet.com)

CRAWFORD, Prof Robert James; *b* 6 April 1949; *Educ* Lisburn Tech Coll, Queen's Univ Belfast (BSc, PhD, DSc); *m* 1974, Isobel Catherine (Renee) Allen; 2 s, 1 da; *Career* tech serv engr Plastics Div ICI; Queen's Univ Belfast: lectr 1974–82, sr lectr 1982–84, reader 1984–88, actg head of dept 1988–89, prof 1989–2005, head Sch of Mech and Process Engrg 1989–2005, pro-vice-chllr 2001–05; prof of mech engrg Univ of Auckland 1999–2001, vice-chllr Univ of Waikato 2005–; dir: Rotosystems Ltd 1991–, Hughes and McLeod Ltd 1991–, University Bookshop Ltd 1993–99; memb Bd of Invest NI 2002–; external examiner to univs throughout Ireland and UK; conslt to various bodies Ireland and abroad; former chm Plastics and Rubber Inst (PRI) NI, former memb Ctee NI Branch IMechE; winner: various awards of PRI 1979–92, Engrg Employers' Fedn Trophy 1992; memb: Soc of Plastics Engrs, Polymer Processing Soc; CEng, FIM, FIMechE, FREng 1997; *Books* Mechanics of Engineering Materials (jtly, 1987, latest edn 1996), Plastics and Rubber - Engineering Design and Applications (1985), The Packing of Particles (jtly, 1987), Mechanics of Engineering Materials (jtly, 1987), Mechanics of Engineering Materials - Solutions Manual (jtly, 1987), Rotational Moulding of Plastics (ed, 1992, 2 edn 1996), Plastics Engineering (3 edn, 1997), Rotational Moulding Technology (jtly, 2002); also contrib various other books and author of numerous articles in professional and learned jls; *Style*— Prof Robert Crawford, FREng; ✉ The University of Waikato, Gate 1, Knighton Road, Private Bag 3105, Hamilton, New Zealand

CRAWFORD, Prof Robert MacGregor Martyn; s of Dr Robert MacGregor Cleland Crawford (d 1981), and Bethia Rankin, *née* Martyn (d 1976); *b* 30 May 1934; *Educ* Glasgow Acad, Univ of Glasgow (BSc), Liège (Docteur en Sciences Naturelles); *m* 20 June 1964, Barbara Elizabeth, da of Percy Hall (d 1979); 1 s (Magnus b 29 Oct 1971); *Career* Univ of St Andrews: lectr in botany 1962–72, reader 1972–77, prof of plant ecology 1977–99 (currently emeritus prof); assoc memb Belgian Royal Acad 2000; FRSE 1974; *Books* Studies in Plant Survival (1989); *Recreations* photography, music; *Style*— Prof Robert Crawford, FRSE; ✉ Kincaple Cottage, St Andrews, Fife KY16 9SH (tel 01334 850214); Sir Harold Mitchell Building, The University, St Andrews, Fife KY16 9AL (tel 01334 463370, fax 01334 463366, e-mail rmmc@st-and.ac.uk)

CRAWFORD, Sir Robert William Kenneth; kt (2007), CBE (2002); s of Hugh Merrall Crawford (d 1982), of West Bergholt, Colchester, Essex, and Mary, *née* Percival (d 2001); *b* 3 July 1945; *Educ* Culford Sch, Pembroke Coll Oxford (BA); *m* 9 Dec 1975, Vivienne Sylvia, da of Boghdan Andre Polakowski; 1 da (Helen b 1984), 1 s (Alistair b 1987); *Career* Imperial War Museum: head res and info office 1971–89, keeper Dept of Photographs 1975–83, asst dir 1979–82, dep DG 1982–95, DG 1995–; chm: UK Nat Inventory of War Memls 1995–, Nat Museums Dirs Conf 2001–06; tstee: IWM Devpt Tst 1982–, Sir Winston Churchill Archives Tst 1995–2006, Florence Nightingale Museum 1999–, Royal Logistic Corps Museum 2000, Fleet Air Arm Museum 2000, Horniman Museum & Public Park Tst 2001–; memb Bd: mda (Europe) 1998–, Nat Historic Ships Ctee 2000–06; Freeman City of London 1998, Liveryman Worshipful Co of Glovers 1998; *Style*— Sir Robert Crawford, CBE; ✉ Imperial War Museum, Lambeth Road, London SE1 6HZ (tel 020 7416 5206)

CRAWFORD, Susan Louise (Mrs Jeremy Phipps); da of late Lt Cdr Wilfrid Hornby Crawford, RN, and late Patricia Mary, *née* McCosh; *b* 11 May 1941; *Educ* St Denis Sch Edinburgh, Prior's Field Godalming, Studio Simi Florence Italy; *m* 12 Oct 1974, Jeremy Joseph Julian Phipps, s of Lt Alan Phipps (ka 1943); 1 s (Jake Shimi Alan b 29 Aug 1975), 1 da (Jemma Louise Rose b 21 July 1977); *Career* artist and equestrian portrait painter; portrait cmmns incl: HM The Queen (mounted), HRH The Prince of Wales, HM Queen Elizabeth the Queen Mother (for the Black Watch Regt), HRH The Princess Margaret, Countess of Snowdon (for The Royal Highland Fusiliers), HRH The Princess Royal (mounted), HH The Sultan of Brunei and HM Sultan Qaboos of Oman, 21 Epsom Derby winners and steeplechasers incl Red Rum, Arkle and Desert Orchid; collections worldwide; work exhibited at: The Royal Scot Acad, The Nat Portrait Gallery, The Royal Acad of Arts, The Royal Soc of Portrait Painters, The Queen's Gallery, V&A, The National Gallery of Pahang Pinang Malaysia, Arthur Akermann & Son, The David Ker Gallery, The Tryon Gallery, Nat Horseracing Museum Newmarket; *Style*— Susan Crawford; ✉ website www.slcrawford.com

CRAWFORD, His Hon William Hamilton Raymund; QC (1980); s of Col Mervyn Crawford, DSO, JP, DL (d 1977), of Dunscore, Dumfriesshire, and Martha Hamilton, *née* Walker (d 1991); *b* 10 November 1936; *Educ* Winchester, Emmanuel Coll Cambridge; *m* 1965, Marilyn Jean, da of John Millar Colville; 1 s, 2 da; *Career* Lt Royal Scots Greys 1956–57; called to the Bar 1964, dep chm Agric Land Tbnl 1978, recorder of the Crown Court 1979–86, circuit judge (NE Circuit) 1986–2001, ret; *Recreations* fishing, shooting; *Clubs* Northern Counties; *Style*— His Hon William Crawford, QC; ✉ c/o The Crown Court, Newcastle upon Tyne

CRAWFORD AND BALCARRES, 29 (and 12) Earl of (S 1398, 1651 respectively); Robert Alexander Lindsay; KT (1996), GCVO (2002), PC (1972); also Lord Lindsay (of Crawford; *ante* 1143), Lord Lindsay of Balcarres (S 1633), Lord Lindsay and Balniel (S 1651), Baron Wigan of Haigh Hall (UK 1826), Baron Balniel (Life Peer UK 1974); Premier Earl of Scotland in precedence; maintains private officer-of-arms (Endure Pursuivant); s of 28 Earl of Crawford and Balcarres, KT, GBE, FSA (d 1975), and Mary Katherine (d 1994), da of late Col the Rt Hon Lord Richard Cavendish, CB, CMG, PC (gs of 7 Duke of Devonshire); *b* 5 March 1927; *Educ* Eton, Trinity Coll Cambridge; *m* 27 Dec 1949, Ruth Beatrice, da of Leo Meyer-Bechtler, of Zürich; 2 s, 2 da; *Heir* s, Lord Balniel; *Career* Grenadier Gds 1945–49; MP (Cons): Hertford 1955–74, Welwyn and Hatfield Feb-Sept 1974; PPS to Fin Sec of Treasy 1955–57, min Housing and Local Govt 1957–60; memb Shadow Cabinet (Health and Social Security) 1967–70, min of state Def 1970–72, min of state Foreign and Cwlth Affrs 1972–74; chm Lombard North Central Bank 1976–80; vice-chm Sun Alliance Insurance Group 1975–91; dir: National Westminster Bank 1975–88, Scottish American Investment Trust 1978–88; first Crown Estate cmmr and chm 1980–85; pres RDCs Assoc 1959–65; chm: Nat Assoc for Mental Health 1963–70, Historic Buildings Cncl for Scotland 1976–83, Royal Cmmn on the Ancient and Historical Monuments for Scotland 1985–95; chm: Bd of Nat Library of Scotland 1990–99; Lord Chamberlain to HM Queen Elizabeth The Queen Mother 1992–2002; DL (Fife) until 2003; *Style*— The Rt Hon the Earl of Crawford and Balcarres; ✉ House of Lords, London SW1A 0PW

CRAWLEY, Baroness (Life Peer UK 1998), of Edgbaston in the Co of West Midlands; Christine Crawley; *b* 9 January 1950; *Educ* Notre Dame Catholic Secdy Girls' Sch Plymouth, Digby Stuart Trg Coll Roehampton; *Career* former drama teacher and youth theatre leader, town and dist cncllr in Oxon, Parly candidate (Lab) SE Staffs 1983; MEP (Lab) Birmingham East 1984–99; Euro Parl: chair Women's Rights Ctee 1989–94, dep leader European PLP 1994–99, memb Civil Liberties Ctee and Women's Rights Ctee; Baroness in Waiting (Govt whip) House of Lords 2002–; chm Women's Nat Cmmn 1999–, chm W Midlands Regnl Cultural Consortium 1999–; memb: Fabian Soc, Co-operative Party, CND, Mfrg Sci and Fin Union; *Recreations* Latin American literature, amateur dramatics, attending local football matches in Birmingham; *Style*— The Rt Hon Baroness Crawley; ✉ c/o Euro Office, 5 Barnsley Road, Edgbaston, Birmingham B17 8EB (tel 0121 429 7117, fax 0121 420 3836, e-mail ccrawley@enterprise.net)

CRAWLEY, Peter Stanbridge; s of William John Crawley (d 1965), and Grace Loelia, *née* Pegg; *b* 5 December 1923; *Educ* UCS London; *m* 20 May 1950, Joan Elizabeth Spicer Crawley, FRCPE, da of Dr Percy Peter James Stewart, OBE (d 1924); 2 s (Richard b 1951, Patrick b 1952 d 1999), 1 da (Jane b 1957); *Career* WWII RAC RASC Capt 1942–47; princ dir Faber & Faber Ltd 1964–73 (dir 1961–64), dir Faber Music Ltd 1965–73; ind publisher in assoc with: Victor Gollancz Ltd 1973–2000, Cassell, Weidenfeld & Nicolson 2000–, Yale University Press 2005–; publisher: Master Bridge Series, architectural history books, some general; illustrated (photographs) many architectural history books; *Recreations* golf, reading, photography, music, bird watching, ceramics; *Clubs* Savile; *Style*— Peter Crawley, Esq; ✉ Garth House, Hertingfordbury, Hertfordshire SG14 2LG (tel 01992 582963, fax 01992 505014)

CRAWLEY, Thomas Henry Raymond; s of Charles William Crawley (d 1992), of Cambridge, and Kathleen Elizabeth, *née* Leahy (d 1982); *b* 17 May 1936; *Educ* Rugby, Trinity Coll Cambridge (MA); *m* 22 April 1961, Felicity Merville, da of Gerald Ashworth Bateman (ret Cdr RN, d 1995); 1 s (Charles b 1965), 2 da (Alice b 1967, Tessa b 1969); *Career* Martin's Bank Ltd 1959–61; admitted slr 1965, slr Hong Kong 1986; ptnr: Turner Kenneth Brown 1967–94, Radcliffes 1994–2002; conslt 2002–; City of London Solicitors prize and Charles Steele prize 1964; Freeman City of London 1985, Liveryman Worshipful Co of Solicitors 1987; memb Law Soc; *Clubs* Travellers, Hong Kong; *Style*— Thomas Crawley, Esq; ✉ 12 Cavendish Road, London W4 3UH (tel 020 8994 8643, fax 08701 615800, e-mail tomcr@wley.co.uk)

CRAWLEY-BOEVEY, Sir Thomas Michael Blake; 8 Bt (GB 1784), of Highgrove, Glos; s of Sir Launcelot Valentine Hyde Crawley-Boevey, 7 Bt (d 1968), and Elizabeth Goodeth, da of Herbert d'Auvergne Innes; *b* 29 September 1928; *Educ* Wellington, St John's Coll Cambridge (MA); *m* 16 Feb 1957, Laura (d 1979), da of late Jan Pouwels Coelingh, of Wassenaar, Netherlands; 2 s (Thomas Hyde b 1958, William Walstan b 1960); *Heir* s, Thomas Crawley-Boevey; *Career* former shipping agent; ed: Money Which? 1968–76, Which? 1976–80 (ed-in-chief 1980–82); Master Worshipful Co of Girdlers 1992–93; *Style*— Sir Thomas Crawley-Boevey, Bt; ✉ 47 Belvoir Road, Cambridge CB4 1JH (tel 01223 365698)

CRAWSHAW, 5 Baron (UK 1892); Sir David Gerald Brooks; 5 Bt (UK 1891); s of 3 Baron Crawshaw (d 1946), and Sheila, da of late Lt-Col P R Clifton, CMG, DSO; suc bro, 4 Baron (d 1997); *b* 14 September 1934; *Educ* Eton, RAC Cirencester; *m* 1970, Belinda Mary, da of G P H Burgess, of Sandringham, Melbourne, Australia; 4 da (Hon Susanna b 1974, Hon Amanda b 1975, Hon Elisabeth b 1976, Hon Katharine b 1978); *Heir* bro, Hon John Brooks; *Career* High Sheriff Leics 1985–86; pres NW Leics Cons Assoc 2001–; *Style*— The Rt Hon the Lord Crawshaw; ✉ Whatton House, Loughborough, Leicestershire LE12 5BG (tel 01509 842225)

CRAWSHAW, Gillian Anne (Jill); da of William Sumner Crawshaw (d 1983), and Trudy, *née* Riding; *Educ* West Kirby GS for Girls, St Anne's Coll Oxford (MA); *m* 1973, Stephen Rudolf Danos, s of Sir Laszlo Danos (d 1935); 2 s (Toby William Laszlo b 1974, Dominic Stephen Robert b 1977); *Career* freelance travel writer for numerous publications 1966–71; travel ed: Daily Mail 1971–82, Evening Standard 1982–87, Sunday Express and Sunday Express Magazine 1987–92, The European 1992–93; currently weekly travel columnist The Times; regular contrib to various magazines, radio and TV progs incl: The Observer, Landmark Travel TV; sole travel contrib The Doomsday Book project; three times Travel Writer of the Year, commended Br Press Awards, twice awarded French Govt Writers' Awards, Scottish Special Writer of the Year 1997, Travel Journalist of the Year 1997, Top Foreigners Prize Franciacorte 2000; memb Br Guild of Travel Writers; *Books* Holidays with Children at Home & Abroad (1982); *Recreations* Oriental carpets, Georgian architecture, skiing, obsessional travel, food, deserts; *Style*— Mrs Jill Crawshaw; ✉ Pond House, 54 Highgate West Hill, London N6 6DA (tel 020 8340 0307, fax 020 8348 3782)

CRAWSHAW, Steven John; s of John Crawshaw, of Eastbourne, E Sussex, and Serena, *née* Chennel; *b* 15 April 1961; *Educ* Eastbourne Coll, Univ of Leicester (LLB), Coll of Law Guildford, CIM (DipM), IPM, Cranfield Sch of Mgmnt (MBA); *m* 29 June 1991, Brigid, *née* Rushmore; 2 s (James, Antony); *Career* Cheltenham & Gloucester plc: mangr Legal Dept 1990–95, strategic planner 1995–96, head of strategy 1996–97; PA to gp dir of customer finance Lloyds TSB Gp plc 1997–98, flotation prog dir Bradford & Bingley Building Soc 1999–2000; Bradford & Bingley plc: gp strategy dir 2000–01, gp strategy, HR and IT dir 2001–02, md lendings and savings 2003–04, gp chief exec 2004–; *Recreations* family, hill walking, cooking; *Style*— Steven Crawshaw, Esq; ✉ Bradford & Bingley plc, Croft Road, Crossflatts, Bingley, West Yorkshire BD16 2UA (tel 01274 555555, e-mail steven.crawshaw@bbg.co.uk)

CRAWSHAY, Martin Richard Charles; s of Capt Walter Stanley Cubitt Crawshay (d 1955), of Norwich, Norfolk, and Elaine Grace (Betty), *née* Osborne (d 1972); *b* 16 January 1928; *Educ* Eton, RMA Sandhurst; *m* 24 Oct 1967, Joanna Deborah Grania, da of Maj Thomas Henry Bevan, MC (d 1964), of Castlebellingham, Co Louth; 1 s (Charles Martin b 1969); *Career* Adj: 16/5 The Queen's Royal Lancers 1956–57 (cmmnd 1948), Univ of Oxford OTC 1959–61; racing liaison exec Horserace Betting Levy Bd 1963–91, pres Nat Pony Soc 1992, pres Br Percheron Horse Soc 1993; hon memb Br Equine Veterinary Assoc; gardens co-ordinator Suffolk Red Cross 1991–2000; Freeman City of London, Liveryman Worshipful Co of Farriers; *Publications* Rien Ne Va Plus (2002); *Recreations* protecting the countryside; *Clubs* Cavalry and Guards; *Style—* Martin Crawshay, Esq; ✉ The Old Vicarage, Leavenheath, Colchester, Essex CO6 4PT (tel 01787 210384)

CRAXTON, John Leith; RA; s of late Harold Craxton, OBE, LRAM, and Essie; *b* 3 October 1922; *Educ* various private schs, Westminster and Central Sch of Art, Goldsmiths Coll London, Acad Julian Paris; *Career* artist; first solo exhibition Leicester Gallery 1944, worked in Pembrokeshire with Graham Sutherland and in Scilly Isles and Greece with Lucian Freud 1944–47; designed sets for Daphnis & Chlöe, Royal Ballet 1951 and Apollo 1966; Cotterel Meml Tapestry for Univ of Stirling *Solo Exhibitions* St Georges Gallery 1943, Galerie Gasser Zurich 1946, Br Cncl Athens 1946–49, Leicester Gallery 1951, 1956, 1961 and 1966, Christopher Hall Gallery 1982, 1985, 1987 and 1993, Pallant Gallery Chichester 1998–99; *Recreations* music, archaeology; *Style—* John Craxton, Esq, RA; ✉ c/o Royal Academy of Arts, Burlington House, Piccadilly, London W1V 0DS

CRAY, Rt Rev Graham Alan; *see:* Maidstone, Bishop of

CREAGH, Mary; MP; *b* 2 December 1967, Coventry; *Educ* Bishop Ullathorne Comp Coventry, Pembroke Coll Oxford, LSE; *m*; 1 c; *Career* cncllr Islington BC 1998–2005, leader Lab Gp Islington BC 2000–04; MP (Lab) Wakefield 2005–; lectr Cranfield Sch of Mgmnt 1997–2005, tstee Rathbone Training 1998–2005; memb: GMB, Co-op Soc, Fabian Soc, Amnesty Int, RNID; *Style—* Ms Mary Creagh, MP; ✉ House of Commons, London SW1A 0AA

CREAMER, Brig Dr Ian Stephen; MC (1973); s of Joseph and Ruth Creamer; *Educ* St Joseph's Coll Blackpool, Univ of Liverpool Med Sch, LSHTM (MSc); *Career* MO Southport Gen Infirmary 1966–67, locum neurosurgical houseman Mil Hosp Colchester 1967; army MO: NI 1968, Catterick Camp Yorks 1968–69, BAOR Minden 1969–71, Weeton Camp Lancs 1971–72; regtl MO 1 Bn The King's Regt 1972–74, second in cmd 19 Field Ambulance Colchester 1974–76, psc 1976, med staff offr HQ 1 Armoured Div BAOR 1978–80, CO 1 Armoured Field Ambulance 1980–83, sr lectr in preventive med Royal Army Med Coll 1984–85, Br liaison offr (med) to USA and Canada 1985–87, dep cdr med Br Army of the Rhine 1987–90, CO 33 Gen Surgical Hosp Al Jubayl Saudi Arabia 1990–91, CO Cambridge Mil Hosp Aldershot 1991–92, DACOS Med HQ UK Land Forces 1992–94, cdr med 3 UK Div 1994–97, cdr med 5 Div 1997–2000, dir Army Primary Health Care Project 2000–02; vice-pres Three Ships Appeal Trinity Sailing Tst 2004–; MRCS, LRCP, memb Inst of Health Mgmnt 1993; FCIM 1992, FFPHM 1999; OStJ 2000; *Publications* numerous papers in med jls; *Recreations* offshore sailing, skiing, gliding, scuba diving, painting; *Clubs* RSM; *Style—* Brig Dr Ian Creamer, MC; ✉ Owl Corner, 4 Parkhill Road, Torquay, Devon TQ1 2AL (e-mail owlman@doctors.org.uk)

CREASE, David Plaistow; s of Gilbert Crease (d 1971), and Margaret Frances Plaistow (d 1981); *b* 22 July 1928; *Educ* Christ's Hosp, Gonville & Caius Coll Cambridge (MA), Edinburgh Coll of Art (Dip); *m* 15 Aug 1969, Jane Rosemary, da of Harold Leonard Goodey, of Reading, Berks; 1 da (Hermione b 1970); *Career* architect Public Works Dept Hong Kong 1955–59, office of Oscar Niemeyer and in own practice Brasilia 1960–63, chief architect Design Unit Univ of York 1966–81 (awards incl 3 Medals and Civic Tst Award for housing schemes in Yorkshire), in own practice York 1981–; princ works of practice incl: univ housing at Heslington York 1967–74, housing at Beverley Minster (commended by RIBA 1990), Bishop's Wharf York (Housing Design Award 1993), Minerva Mews Yarm Teesside 1995, housing at Owlthorpe Sheffield 1995; chm Ryedale Constituency Liberal Democrats 1998–2001; RIBA; *Recreations* hunting the clean boot (human scent) with bloodhounds; *Clubs* Pickering Liberal; *Style—* David P Crease, Esq; ✉ Deer Park, Scampston, Malton, North Yorkshire YO17 8HW; Crease Strickland Parkins, Architects, Bishopgate House, Skeldergate Bridge, York YO23 1WH (tel 01904 641289, fax 01904 611229, e-mail dpcrease@fsmail.net)

CREASEY, Richard John; s of John Creasey, MBE (d 1973), and (Evelyn) Jean, *née* Fudge; *b* 28 August 1944; *Educ* Malvern; *m* 1, 5 Jan 1968, Wendy; 2 s (Simon b 19 July 1972, Guy b 1 May 1974), 1 da (Sarah b 19 Jan 1980); m 2, 4 June 1999, Vera; *Career* Granada TV: researcher 1965–72, prodr 1972–74; ATV Network: prodr 1974–77, exec prodr 1977–78, head of documentaries 1978–81; Central TV: controller of features 1981–90, dir of special projects 1990–94; fndr Siguy Films 1987–; dir of factual progs Meridian Broadcasting 1992–94, ed-in-chief The Digital Village 1995–2001, exec prodr BBC New Media 2001–04, dir BFC Media 2004–; expdn ldr Ford London-New York Overland Challenge 1993–94; chm Soviet Br Creative Assoc 1989–99, chm and co fndr Television Tst for the Environment (TVE); memb BAFTA; *Style—* Richard Creasey, Esq; ✉ 11 Regent's Park Road, London NW1 7TL (tel 020 7482 6549, e-mail richard.creasey@bfcmedia.co.uk)

CREBER, Frank Paul; s of Dr Geoffrey Tremain Creber and Hilda, *née* Lewey (d 1994); *b* 12 January 1959; *Educ* Dr Challoner's GS Amersham, Univ of Newcastle upon Tyne (BA), Chelsea Sch of Art (MA); *m* 1982, Marguerite Honor Blake, da of Rev Canon Peter Douglas Stuart Blake; 2 s (Theodore Sebastion Peter b 1983, Nicholas Tremaine b 1986); *Career* artist; most important works: White Light/Yellow Light 1987, Within One Flame go Two As One 1987, Open State 1988, Man with Bird 1989, Cliff Dance 1990, The Bather 1991, White Rock 1991, The Family 1993, The Planets 1995, Community Picnic 2004; exhibitions incl: Barclays Bank Young Painters Competition (Henry Moore Gallery, RCA London) 1987, Picker Fellowship Show (Kingston Poly) 1988, two man show (Diorama Gallery London) 1988, solo show (Sue Williams Gallery Portobello Rd London) 1988, 1989, 1991 and 1992, Picker Fellows at Kingston (Watermans Art Centre Brentford) 1989, Artist of The Day (Flowers East London) 1989, two persons show (Paton Gallery) 1990, gp show (ROI at Lloyd's London) 1990, Painting Today (auction at Bonham's Knightsbridge) 1991, Where Art Meets Community (Tobacco Dock London) 1992, Bow's Arts (Sedgewick's Aldgate East London) 1992, Inner City Blues (gp show, Barbican Concourse Gallery) 1993, gp show (Great Banquet Exhibition Banqueting House Whitehall) 1995, gp show (Homerton Hosp London) 1996, solo show (Mosaic Highgate London) 1996, Travelling Light (Big Issue Clerkenwell Road London) 1997, Picker Fellows (Stanley Picker Gallery Kingston) 1997, Community Action Network London 1998, Arthur Anderson Group Show 1998, solo show (Stanton Guildhouse) 1999, gp show (Community Action Network Haymarket London) 2000, gp show (Middlesex Hosp London) 2000, solo show (Art Space Gallery London) 2004; exhibitions organised and curated: Art Meets Community (Tobacco Dock London) 1992, gp show (Bow's Arts Gallery London) 1992, Inner City Blues (Barbican) 1993; works in collections: Unilever plc, Arthur Andersen & Co, Art for Hosps, Stanhope Construction Ltd, Leicestershire Collection, Int Business Machines; artist in residence The Bromley-by-Bow Centre London 1992–; awards: prizewinner Avon Open (Artsite Gallery Bath) 1984, prizewinner Brewhouse Open (Taunton) 1985, Herbert Read fellowship Chelsea Sch of Art 1986, jt winner Barclays Bank Young Painters award 1987, Picker fellowship Kingston Poly (now Kingston Univ) 1987–88; *Recreations* sailing; *Style—* Frank Creber, Esq; ✉ 49 Darnley Road, Hackney, London E9 6QH (tel 020 8533 5104); The Bromley-by-Bow Centre, 1 Bruce Road, London E3 3HN (tel 020 8980 4618, fax 020 8880 6608)

CREDITON, Bishop of 2004–; Rt Rev Robert John Scott Evens; s of Reginald Evens (d 1997), and Sheila, *née* Scott (d 1995); *b* 29 May 1947; *Educ* Maidstone GS, Trinity Coll Bristol (DipTh); *m* 1972, Susan, *née* Hayes; 1 s (Tom b 1979), 1 da (Claire b 1982); *Career* in banking 1965–74; archdeacon of Bath 1995–2004; ACIB; *Recreations* gardening, caravanning; *Style—* The Rt Rev the Bishop of Crediton

CREED, Martin; *b* 1968, Wakefield, W Yorks; *Educ* Slade Sch of Fine Art; *Career* artist; winner Turner Prize 2001; *Solo Exhibitions* incl: Work No 78 (Starkmann Ltd London) 1993, Camden Arts Centre London 1995, Work No 203 (The Portico London) 1999, Work No 160 (Space 1999 London) 1999, MARTINCREEDWORKS (Southampton City Art Gallery, Leeds City Art Gallery, Bluecoat Gallery Liverpool, Camden Arts Centre London) 2000, Art Now: Martin Creed (Tate Britain London) 2000, The Lights Going On and Off (Gavin Brown's Enterprise NY) 2000, Work No 225 (cmmnd by Public Art Fund Times Square/42nd Street NY) 2000, Work No 252 (St Peter's Church Cologne) 2000–, A large piece of furniture partially obstructing a door (Alberto Peola Arte Contemporanea Turin) 2002, SMALL THINGS (Galerie Analix Forever Genève) 2003, Work No 289 (The Br Sch at Rome) 2003, Work No 300 (GBE Modern NY) 2003–, Centre for Contemporary Art Ujazdowski Castle Warsaw 2004, Hauser & Wirth London 2004. Gavin Brown's Enterprise 2005, I LIKE THINGS Fondazione Nicola Trussardi 2006, Hauser & Wirth Coppermill 2007; *Group Exhibitions* incl: Ace! Arts Cncl Collection (Hayward Gallery London) 1996, nerve (ICA London) 1999, Intelligence: New British Art 2000 (Tate Britain London) 2000, Art/Music: Rock, Pop, Techno (Museum of Contemporary Art Sydney) 2001, Space-Jack! (Yokohama Museum) 2001, Turner Prize 2001 (Tate Britain London) 2001, State of Play (Serpentine Gallery London) 2004; *Recordings* incl: I Can't Move (7 song CD, 1999), Work Nos 207, 208 and 209 'EVERYTHING IS GOING TO BE ALRIGHT' (3 song CD, 1999), Work No 320 'I don't know what I want' (1 song CD, 2004); *Style—* Martin Creed, Esq; ✉ c/o Hauser & Wirth London, 196A Piccadilly, London W1J 9DY (tel 020 7287 2300, fax 020 7287 6600, website www.hauserwirth.com)

CREEGOR, Vivien; da of Leonard Creegor (d 1996), and Stella, *née* Myers (d 2001); *b* 10 April 1955; *Educ* Orange Hill Girls' GS, City of London Poly; *m* 27 May 1990; *Career* presenter, newsreader, journalist; travel writer Mail on Sunday; chm 3 UN confs on women's health for WHO (Geneva Switzerland, Beijing China (incl speeches by Hillary Clinton, Julius Nyrere and Jane Fonda)); BBC Amateur Actress of the Year Award 1979; memb: Greenpeace, BAFTA; *Television and Radio* BBC: prodn assistant Radio Drama Department 1977–80, announcer and newreader Radio 4 1980–81, presenter/reporter Points West Bristol TV News 1982–88, newsreader News After Noon BBC1 1984, sub-editor/scriptwriter TV News 1985–86, presenter/reporter Transit (Sports & Events) 1987, newsreader Newsview BBC2 1988; also for BBC: The Small Business Programme, Breakthrough, Radio 2 newsreader, abridger for A Book at Bedtime Radio 4, reader of Morning Story, numerous in-house videos; presenter Sky News 1989–; *Recreations* reading, writing, cinema; *Clubs* Groucho; *Style—* Ms Vivien Creegor; ✉ c/o Cunningham Management, London House, 271 King Street, London W6 9L2 (tel 020 8233 2824, fax 020 8233 2825)

CREER, Kenneth Ernest; MBE (1993); s of Ernest Lyons Creer (d 1989), of Isle of Man, and Robina, *née* Kelly (d 1975); *b* 29 August 1937; *Educ* Douglas HS Isle of Man, Salisbury Sch of Art, Central London Poly, BIPP; *m* 5 Dec 1964 (m dis 1996), Pauline Winifred, da of Leslie James Artis; 3 s (Colin Leslie b 12 Dec 1965, Peter b 21 May 1968, Paul Robin b 18 March 1976); m 2, 31 May 1996, Jean Maureen, da of Charles Lucas; *Career* forensic imaging conslt; apprentice photographer S R Keig Ltd Isle of Man 1954–57, photographer 16 Ind Parachute Bde 1957–60, photographic printer Speedy Photographic London 1960–61, sr photographer Metropolitan Police New Scotland Yard 1963–68 (photographer 1961–63); Metropolitan Police Forensic Sci Lab (now Forensic Sci Service): head Photographic Section 1968–97, princ photographer 1969–83, chief photographer 1983–97; Forensic Imaging Consultant 1997–, responsible for the introduction of specialist criminological photographic techniques; lectr and author of numerous papers on criminological photographic matters; Richard Farrant Meml trophy for distinction in applied photography 1983; FBIPP 1983 (MBIPP 1964), FRPS 1986; *Recreations* sailing, golf; *Style—* Kenneth Creer, Esq, MBE; ✉ 5 College Road, Enfield, Middlesex EN2 0QE (tel 020 8367 0665)

CREER, (Dahlis) Virginia; da of Cdre Bruce Loxton, RAN (ret), of Sydney, Aust, and Dahlis Ailsa, *née* Robertson; *b* 4 February 1948; *Educ* Ascham Sch Sydney Aust, Univ of Sydney (BA); *m* 1971, David Victor Charles Creer, s of Victor Charles Hamish Creer; 1 s (Benjamin Fulke Matthew b 7 Sept 1976), 1 da (Camilla Dahlis Elizabeth b 12 July 1979); *Career* Mktg Div Unilever Ltd 1969–72, asst brand mangr then brand mangr Schweppes Ltd 1972–77 (mktg mangr 1976), account dir Grey Advertising Ltd 1978–80; Davidson Pearce Ltd: sr planner 1980, Bd dir 1982, agency devpt dir 1985–87, exec planning and devpt dir 1987–88; asst md BMP Davidson Pearce Ltd 1988–89, managing ptnr BMP DDB Needham Ltd 1989, jt md BMP 4 1990–2000, ptnr The Yardley Creer Partnership 2000–; memb: Mktg Soc 1976, MRS 1980, IPA 1982, Forum 1992; *Recreations* running, riding, sailing; *Clubs* Women's Advertising Club of London, Royal Sydney Golf; *Style—* Mrs Virginia Creer; ✉ (tel 020 8741 3484, e-mail virginiacreer@ycpartnership.co.uk)

CREGEEN, Peter Geoffrey; s of Geoffrey Hugh Stowell Cregeen (d 1980), and Viola Gertrude Dorothea, *née* Butler; *b* 28 January 1940; *Educ* St Christopher's Sch Hove, Hove Coll, Guildhall Sch of Music and Drama; *m* Carole, da of Frederick Walker; 3 da (Lucy b 5 May 1969, Maria b 23 Aug 1971, Emma b 6 April 1974), 1 s (Tom (twin) b 6 April 1974); *Career* actor Palace Theatre Watford 1959–60, dir and actor Salisbury Playhouse 1960–63 (returned as assoc artistic dir 1969), television dir 1964–87 for BBC (also prodr), ATV, Yorkshire TV, LWT (also prodr) and Thames TV (also prodr), exec prodr The Bill (Thames) 1988, head of drama series BBC Television 1989–93, prodr BBC 1994–95, prodn dir Stoll Moss Theatres 1995–97 (conslt 1998–), TV dir Pearson Television and Cloudnine NZ 1998 (TV dir Pearson Television 1999 and 2000), TV prodr and dir Bentley Productions 1999, exec prodr LWT United Productions 2001–02, TV dir BBC Television 2003–, devpt exec prodr IA Prodns 2003–04; conslt D L Tafner 1998; dir Ludlow Festival 1982–84; lectr: Guildhall Sch of Music and Drama 2004–, East 15 Acting Sch 2004–, Guildford Conservatoire 2004, Acad of Live and Recorded Arts 2005–; memb Cncl: Dirs' Guild of GB 1988, RTS 1989–92, BAFTA 1992–97; memb Bd: Actors Centre 1989– (chm 1995–), TAPS 1994– (chm 1997–), Jerusalem Productions 1998–2002 (chm 1999–), Tara Arts 2003–; FGSM; *Recreations* music, gardening; *Style—* Peter Cregeen, Esq; ✉ 2 Ormond Road, Richmond upon Thames, Surrey TW10 6TH (tel 020 8332 3081)

CRERAR, Lorne Donald; s of Ronald Crerar, of Wester Ross, and Isobel Scott, *née* Pollok; *b* 29 July 1954; *Educ* Kelvinside Acad, Univ of Glasgow (LLB, Shaws Stewart Meml Prize and Bennet Miller Prize for Best Private Law Student); *m* 29 Oct 1994, Susan Mary, da Gerard Reilly; *Career* qualified slr 1978; Harper Macleod: ptnr 1985–, co-founding ptnr Business Law Div, head Commercial Property Dept and Banking Law Unit, also currently managing ptnr Harper Macleod; non-exec chm InsureDirect.co.uk; chm Appeals Ctee European Rugby Cup Ltd, chm Scottish Rugby Union Discipline Ctee, former pres Scottish Sports Law Forum; convenor of Standards Cmmn to Scot Exec; princ legal advsr several fin instns, non-exec dir Justice Dept Scottish Exec; pt/t prof Univ of Glasgow; NP; memb Law Soc of Scotland; *Recreations* hill climbing, golf; *Clubs* Arlington Baths; *Style—* Prof Lorne Crerar; ✉ Harper Macleod, 45 Gordon Street, Glasgow G1 3PE (tel 0141 221 8888, fax 0141 226 4198)

CRESSWELL, HE Jeremy Michael; CVO (1996); s of John Cresswell (d 1982), and Jean, *née* Lewis; *b* 1 October 1949, Windsor; *Educ* Sir William Borlase's Sch Marlow, Exeter Coll Oxford (BA), Johannes-Gutenberg Univ Mainz; *m* 1974 (m dis 2006), Ursula Petra, *née* Forwick; 1 da (Julia b 1978), 1 s (David b 1985); partner, Dr Barbara Munske; *Career* diplomat; entered HM Dip Serv 1972, desk offr West African Dept FCO 1972–73, third then second sec (Chancery) Brussels 1973–77, second then first sec (Chancery) Kuala Lumpur 1977–78; FCO: desk offr Trade Relations and Export Dept 1978–81, private sec Parly Under Sec's Office 1981, private sec Min of State's Office 1982; dep political advsr British Mil Govt Berlin 1982–86, dep head of dept Press Office FCO 1986–88, asst head of dept South America Dept FCO 1988–90, cnsllr and head of Chancery UK Delgn to

NATO Brussels 1990–94, dep head of mission Prague 1995–98, sr dir RCDS 1998, head Western European Dept FCO 1998–99, head EU (Bilateral) Dept FCO 1999–2001, min and dep head of mission Berlin 2001–05, high cmmr to Jamaica and the Cwlth of the Bahamas 2005–; *Recreations* choral music, sport (especially tennis); *Style—* Mr Jeremy Cresswell; ✉ c/o Foreign & Commonwealth Office (Kingston), King Charles Street, London SW1A 2AH (tel 00 1 876 510 0700, e-mail jeremy.cresswell@fco.gov.uk)

CRESSWELL, Dr Lyell Richard; s of Jack Cecil Cresswell (d 1986), and Muriel Minnie, *née* Sharp (d 1982); *b* 13 October 1944; *Educ* Victoria Univ of Wellington NZ (BMus), Univ of Toronto (MusM), Univ of Aberdeen (PhD); *m* 4 Jan 1972, Catherine Isabel, da of Keith James Mawson, of Otaki, NZ; *Career* composer; works incl: Concerto for Violin and Orchestra 1970, Salm 1977, Prayer for the Cure of a Sprained Back 1979, The Silver Pipes of Ur 1981, Le Sucre du Printemps 1982, O! 1982, Concerto for Cello and Orchestra 1984, The Fallen Dog 1984, Our Day Begins at Midnight 1985, To Aspro Pano Sto Aspro 1985, Speak For Us Great Sea 1985, A Modern Ecstasy 1986, The Pumpkin Massacre 1987, Sextet 1988, Passacagli 1988, Ixion 1988, Voices of Ocean Winds 1989, Ylur 1990, Il Suono di Enormi Distanze 1993, Dragspil 1995, Concerto for Orchestra and String Quartet 1997, KAEA (trombone concerto) 1997, Of Whirlwind Underground 1999, The Voice Inside (concerto for violin and soprano) 2001, Shadows without Sun 2004; memb: British Acad of Composers and Songwriters, Composers Assoc of NZ; various works recorded on Continuum label and Linn, NMC and Metier Records; Hon DMus Victoria Univ of Wellington 2002, Inaugural Elgar Bursary 2002; *Recreations* illustrating the book of Ezekiel; *Style—* Dr Lyell Cresswell; ✉ 4 Leslie Place, Edinburgh EH4 1NQ (tel and fax 0131 332 9181)

CRESSWELL, Hon Mr Justice; Sir Peter John Cresswell; kt (1991); s of Rev Canon JJ Cresswell, and Madeleine, *née* Foley; *b* 24 April 1944; *Educ* St John's Sch Leatherhead, Queens' Coll Cambridge (MA, LLM); *m* 29 April 1972, Caroline (d 2003), da of Maj Gen Sir Philip Ward, KCVO, CBE, LL, of Sussex; 2 s (Oliver b 11 Nov 1973 d 1988, Mark b 25 Sept 1975); *Career* called to the Bar Gray's Inn 1966 (bencher 1989), QC 1983, recorder of the Crown Court 1986–91, judge of the High Court of Justice (Queen's Bench Div) 1991–, judge in charge of the Commercial List 1993–94; chm London Common Law and Commercial Bar Assoc 1985–87, memb Senate of Inns of Ct and Bar 1981–86, memb Civil Justice Cncl 1999–2003; chm Gen Cncl of the Bar 1990 (memb 1987–90, vice-chm 1989); tstee Cystic Fibrosis Research Tst; hon memb Canadian Bar Assoc 1990; pres Flyfishers' Club 2003–05; *Books* Encyclopaedia of Banking Law (1982–); *Recreations* fly fishing, river management, the Outer Hebrides; *Clubs* Flyfishers'; *Style—* The Hon Mr Justice Cresswell; ✉ Royal Courts of Justice, Strand, London WC2A 2LL

CRESWELL, Alexander Charles Justin; s of Sir Michael Justin Creswell, KCMG (d 1986), and Baroness Charlotte Mea thoe Schwartzenberg en Hohenlandsberg (d 2002); *b* 14 February 1957; *Educ* Winchester, W Surrey Coll of Art & Design, Byam Shaw Sch of Drawing & Painting; *m* 4 July 1992, Mary Curtis, da of John Green, of Calamansac, Cornwall; 1 s (Theodore b 1999), 2 da (Cicely b 2000, Constance b 2003); *Career* artist; tutor The Prince of Wales's Inst of Architecture London 1992–99; memb: Inst of Classical Architecture, Int Network for Traditional Building Architecture and Urbanism; pres Ewhurst Village Soc; Knight of the Order of Francis the First (KFO) *Exhibitions* contrib numerous gp exhbns 1982–; solo: White Horse Gallery London 1982, 1983 and 1984, Anima Gallery London 1983, Jonathan Poole Gallery London 1983, 1985 and 1987, Sally Le Gallais Gallery Jersey 1984, Addison Ross Gallery London 1984, 1985 and 1986, Crake Gallery Johannesburg 1984, Bulstrode Gallery London 1985, Brussels Europa Hotel 1985, Ritz Hotel London 1987, Fine Art Trade Guild Gallery London 1989, Arthur Andersen & Co London 1989, Spink & Son London 1991, 1994 and 1997, Atlantic Hotel Jersey 1991, Cadogan Gallery London 1992, China Club Hong Kong 1995, New Academy Gallery 1999, Windsor Castle 2000, Hirschl & Adler NYC 2001, 2004 and 2006, John Martin of London 2002, Portland Gallery 2008; *Commissions* incl: The Royal Collection, English Heritage, Parliamentary Art Coll, Duchy of Cornwall, Royal Bank of Scotland, HSBC, The BBC, London Capital Club, The Frick Collection NYC; *Books* The Silent Houses of Britain (1991), Out of the Ashes - Watercolours of Windsor Castle (2000); *Recreations* gardening, sailing, classic cars; *Clubs* Art Workers Guild, Port Navas Yacht; *Style—* Alexander Creswell, Esq; ✉ Copse Hill, Ewhurst, Surrey (tel 01483 277493, website www.alexandercreswell.com)

CRESWELL, Brig David Hector Craig; s of Lt-Col John Hector Creswell, OBE (d 2004), of Colchester, Essex, and Laurette Maxwell, *née* Craig; *b* 12 May 1942; *Educ* Wellington, RMA Sandhurst; *m* 30 Sept 1967, Pamela Mary Scott (d 2002), da of Dr Denis Dearman Matthews (d 1986), of Winchester, Hants; 2 s (Edward b 1969, Nicholas b 1972); *Career* reg cmmn RA 1962, asst def attaché Copenhagen 1979–81, CO 40 Field Regt RA 1981–84, directing staff Royal Mil Coll of Sci 1984–85, superintendent Proof and Experimental Estab Shoeburyness 1985–87, dir Rapier 1988–91; dir of mktg Matra BAe Dynamics plc (formerly British Aerospace Defence plc) 1991–2002, md Eastern Aerospace Alliance 2002–05, chm RA Museum Ltd; FIMgt 1986; *Recreations* sailing, golf, skiing, walking, reading; *Clubs* Army and Navy; *Style—* Brig David Creswell; ✉ 26 Whitelands House, Cheltenham Terrace, London SW3 4QX (tel 020 7730 0603, e-mail david.creswell@btinternet.com)

CRETNEY, Dr Stephen Michael; Hon QC (1992); s of Fred Cretney (d 1980), and Winifred Mary Valentine, *née* Rowlands (d 1982); *Educ* Cheadle Hulme Sch, Magdalen Coll Oxford (DCL, MA); *m* 7 July 1973, Rev Antonia Lois, da of Cdr Anthony George Glanusk Vanrenen, RN, of Fordingbridge, Hants; 2 s (Matthew b 1975, Edward b 1979); *Career* Nat Serv 1954–56; admitted slr 1962; ptnr Macfarlanes 1964–65, Kenya Sch of Law Nairobi 1966–67, Univ of Southampton 1968–69, fell Exeter Coll Oxford 1969–78, law cmmr 1978–83, prof of law Univ of Bristol 1984–93 (dean of faculty 1984–88), fell All Souls Coll Oxford 1993–2001 (emeritus fell 2001–); hon bencher Inner Temple 2006; Hon LLD Univ of Bristol 2007; FBA 1985; *Books* Principles of Family Law (1974, 7 edn with Prof J M Masson and Prof R Bailey-Harris, 2002), Elements of Family Law (1987, 4 edn, 2000), Law, Law Reform and the Family (1998), Family Law in 20th Century Britain: A History (2003), Same Sex Relationships (2006); author of other legal texts and articles in learned jls; *Clubs* Oxford and Cambridge; *Style—* Dr Stephen Cretney; ✉ 8 Elm Farm Close, Wantage, Oxfordshire OX12 9FD (e-mail smcretney@aol.com)

CREWE, Candida Annabel; da of Quentin Hugh Crewe (d 1998), and Angela Maureen Huth, *qv*; *b* 6 June 1964; *Educ* The Manor Sch Great Durnford, St Mary's Sch Calne, Headington Sch Oxford; *m* Jan 1997; 2 s; *Career* bookshop asst 1983–86, jr ed Quartet Books Ltd London 1985–86, journalist weekly column London Evening Standard 1985–86; freelance journalist 1986–: The Spectator, The Guardian, The Independent, The Times, The Daily Telegraph, The Sunday Telegraph, The Observer, The Sunday Times, Tatler, Harpers & Queen, Marie-Claire, You Magazine, The Evening Standard; *Awards* runner-up for Catherine Pakenham meml award for Journalism 1987, winner Catherine Pakenham award for Journalism 1990, shortlisted for the John Llewellyn Ryhs meml award for Falling Away 1997; memb PEN Int; *Books* Focus (1985), Romantic Hero (1986), Accommodating Molly (1989), Mad About Bees (1991), Falling Away (1996), The Last to Know (1998); *Recreations* photography; *Clubs* Groucho; *Style—* Miss Candida Crewe

CREWE, Prof Sir Ivor Martin; kt (2006), DL (Essex 2002); s of late Francis Crewe, of West Didsbury, Gtr Manchester, and Lilly Edith, *née* Neustadtl; *b* 15 December 1945; *Educ* Manchester Grammar, Exeter Coll Oxford (MA), LSE (MSc); *m* 3 July 1968, Jill Barbara, da of late Dr Theo Gadian, of Salford, Gtr Manchester; 1 da (Deborah b 1972), 2 s (Ben b 1974, Daniel b 1977); *Career* asst lectr Dept of Politics Lancaster Univ 1967–69, jr research fell Nuffield Coll Oxford 1969–71; Univ of Essex: lectr 1971, sr lectr 1974, dir ESRC data archive 1974–82, prof Dept of Govt 1982–, pro-vice-chllr (academic) 1992–95, vice-chllr 1995–; chair: 1994 Gp of Univs 1998–2001, Fndn Degree Gp DfES 2000–03; Eng and NI Cncl Universities UK 2001–03; pres Universities UK 2003–05; co-dir British Election Study 1973–82, ed British Jl of Political Sci 1977–82 and 1984–92; commentator on elections and public opinion for Channel 4, The Guardian and The Observer; memb: Political Studies Assoc, American Political Studies Assoc; hon fell Exeter Coll Oxford 1998; Hon DLitt Univ of Salford; High Steward Colchester 2003–; *Books* A Social Survey of Higher Civil Service (1969), Decade of Dealignment (1983), The British Electorate 1963–1987 (1991), SDP: The Birth, Life and Death of the Social Democratic Party (1995), The New British Politcs (1998, 3 edn 2004); *Recreations* opera, walking, skiing; *Style—* Prof Sir Ivor Crewe, DL; ✉ University of Essex, Colchester, Essex CO4 3SQ (tel 01206 872000, fax 01206 869493, e-mail vc@essex.ac.uk)

CREWE, Susan Anne; da of late Richard Cavendish, and late Pamela Cavendish; *b* 31 August 1949; *Educ* St Mary's Sch Wantage, Cheshire Coll of Agric; *m* 1, 1970 (m dis), Quentin Crewe; 1 s (Nathaniel Richard b 1971), 1 da (Charity b 1972); *m* 2, 1984 (m dis), Nigel Ryan; *Career* journalist, freelance writer and broadcaster; contrib: The Times, Daily Telegraph, Evening Standard, Literary Review; social ed Harpers & Queen 1991–92, ed House & Garden 1994–; fndr Friends of the Rehabilitation of Addictive Prisoners Tst (Rapt); vice-patron Royal Soc of Sculptors; *Recreations* gardening, riding, travelling, theatre, music; *Clubs* The Academy; *Style—* Mrs Susan Crewe; ✉ House & Garden, Vogue House, Hanover Square, London W1S 1JU (tel 020 7499 9080, fax 020 7629 2907)

CRIBBENS, Dr Alan Hugh; MBE (1993); s of Eddie Victor Cribbens (d 2001), and Stella, *née* Penwill; *b* 1 November 1942; *Educ* Aylesbury GS, UCL (BSc Eng, PhD); *m* 1, 1968 (m dis 2003), Christine Lesley, da of Leslie James Schofield; 2 da (Sarah Catherine b 1971, Emma Jane b 1974); m 2, 2003, Linda, da of Norman Domkowicz; *Career* engr; trained Marconi Wireless Telegraph Co 1961–62; BR: various appointments R&D Div 1970–76, team ldr Electronic Interlocking 1976–81, head Microelectronics Unit R&D Div (responsible for devpt of Solid State Interlocking, the standard railway signalling system in the UK) 1981–88, head Safety Critical Systems Unit BR Res 1988–94, technical strategist BR Res 1994–97; conslt to railway signalling industry 1997–; visiting prof in railway engrg ICSTM 2002; FIEE 1986 (MIEE 1972), FIRSE 1991, FREng 2001; *Publications* Microwave polarisation measurements of four solar radio bursts (1969), High time resolution swept-frequency microwave polarimeter (1970), Microprocessors in Railway Signalling: The Solid State Interlocking (1987), Solid State Interlocking (SSI): an integrated electronic signalling system for main line railways (1987), Long distance transmission of safety information for the Solid State Interlocking (1989), The application of advanced computing techniques to the generation and checking of SSI data (1992), SSI - Ten Years of Electronic Interlocking (1995); *Recreations* walking, gardening, music, DIY; *Style—* Dr Alan Cribbens, MBE, FREng; ✉ Birchwood House, Birchwood Farm, Portway, Coxbench, Derby DE21 5BE (e-mail alan.cribbens@btconnect.com)

CRICHTON, District Judge Nicholas; s of late Charles Ainslie Crichton, and Vera Pearl McCallum, *née* Harman-Mills; *b* 23 October 1943; *Educ* Haileybury, Queens Univ Belfast (LLB); *m* 29 March 1973, Ann Valerie, da of late Col John Eliot Jackson, of Lopcombe Corner, Wilts; 2 s (Simon b 25 Feb 1975, Ian b 12 Jan 1977); *Career* admitted slr 1970; asst slr Currey & Co 1970–71 (articled 1968–70), ptnr Nicholls Christie & Crocker 1974–86 (asst slr 1972–74); District Judge (Magistrates' Court) 1987–, recorder of the Crown Court 1995– (asst recorder 1991–95); memb Family Justice Cncl; *Recreations* cricket, golf, watching rugby, gardening, birdwatching, walking; *Style—* District Judge Crichton; ✉ c/o Inner London and City Family Proceedings Court, 59–65 Wells Street, London W1A 3AE

CRICK, Prof Sir Bernard Rowland; kt (2002); s of Harry Edgar Crick (d 1968), and Florence Clara, *née* Cook (d 1987); *b* 16 December 1929; *Educ* Whitgift Sch, UCL (BSc), LSE (PhD), Harvard Univ; *m* 18 Sept 1953 (m dis 1980), Joyce Pumpfrey Morgan; 2 s (Oliver, Tom); *Career* lectr LSE 1957–65; prof of politics: Univ of Sheffield 1965–71, Birkbeck Coll London 1971–84; hon fell Politics Dept Univ of Edinburgh 1986–, visiting fell Woodrow Wilson Centre 1995–96; literary ed The Political Quarterly 1993–2000 (jt ed 1966–80), winner Yorks Post Book of the Year Award 1980; memb Cncl Hansard Soc 1962–92, hon pres Politics Assoc 1970–76, hon pres Assoc for Teaching of Citizenship, hon vice-pres Political Studies Assoc 1994–; chm: The Political Quarterly Publishing Co 1980–93, Orwell Memorial Tst 1981–, British Ctee of British and South African Conf 1991–94; chief judge Orwell Prize for Political Writing 1981–2006; advsr on citizenship: DfEE 1998–2001 (chm Advsy Gp The Teaching of Citizenship in Schools DfEE 1997–98), Home Office 2005–05; advsr Immigrant Educn; Hon DSSc Queen's Univ Belfast 1988, Hon Dr of Arts Univ of Sheffield 1990; Hon DLitt: E London Univ 1990, Kingston Univ 1996, Univ of Glasgow 2006; hon fell: Birkbeck Coll London 1998, UCL 2001; *Books* The American Science of Politics (1958), In Defence of Politics (1962, latest edn 1992), The Reform of Parliament (1964), Crime, Rape and Gin (1975), George Orwell, A Life (1980, latest edn 2000), Socialism (1987), Essays on Politics and Literature (1989), Political Thoughts and Polemics (1990), Essays on Citizenship (2000), Crossing Borders (2001), Democracy (2002); *Recreations* polemicising, book and theatre reviewing, hill walking; *Clubs* Savile; *Style—* Prof Sir Bernard Crick; ✉ 8A Bellevue Terrace, Edinburgh EH7 4DT (tel and fax 0131 557 2517, e-mail bernard.crick@ed.ac.uk)

CRICK, Charles Anthony; s of Maurice Arthur Crick, TD (d 1979), of Peterborough, and Margaret Matilda, *née* Edney (d 2001); *b* 7 May 1949; *Educ* Oundle, UCL (LLB); *m* 1997, Jennifer Claire, *née* Luckham; 2 c; *Career* admitted slr 1974, articled clerk and asst slr Allen and Overy 1972–80, asst slr Middleton Potts and Co 1980–81, ptnr D J Freeman and Co 1981–96, dir Numis Corp plc 1996–2004, head of corp fin Numis Securities Ltd 1996–2004, ptnr Longbow Capital LLP 2005–; Freeman City of London Slrs' Co 1986; memb Law Soc; *Recreations* golf, music, painting; *Clubs* Hunstanton Golf, The Addington Golf, Royal Aberdeen; *Style—* Charles Crick, Esq

CRICK, Richard William; s of Cyril Albert Edden Crick (d 1988), of Easton-in-Gordano, Avon, and Blanche Helen, *née* Prewett; *b* 7 June 1946; *Educ* Clifton, BNC Oxford (MA); *Children* 1 s (James b 1974), 1 da (Sally b 1977); *Career* accountant Deloitte Haskins and Sells 1967–71; banker: Hill Samuel & Co Ltd 1972–87 (dir 1981–87), md Hill Samuel Merchant Bank (SA) Ltd 1981–85, dir Barclays de Zoete Wedd Ltd 1988–96, md Corp Finance Div Barclays Tokyo 1992–95, vice-chm Corp Finance Div Barclays de Zoete Wedd Ltd 1995–96; ret 1996; FCA; *Recreations* golf, skiing, sailing, travel, wine; *Clubs* St Enodoc Golf, Cannes Mandelieu Golf; *Style—* Richard W Crick, Esq; ✉ 2 Craven Hill Mews, London W2 3DY (tel and fax 020 7402 8096)

CRICKHOWELL, Baron (Life Peer UK 1987), of Pont Esgob in the Black Mountains and County of Powys; (Roger) Nicholas Edwards; PC (1979); s of (Herbert Cecil) Ralph Edwards, CBE, FSA (d 1977), and Marjorie Ingham Brooke; *b* 25 February 1934; *Educ* Westminster, Trinity Coll Cambridge (MA); *m* 1963, Ankaret, da of William James Healing, of Kinsham House, Glos; 1 s (Hon Rupert Timothy Guy b 1964), 2 da (Hon Sophie Elizabeth Ankaret b 1966, Hon Olivia Caroline b 1970); *Career* 2 Lt Royal Welch Fusiliers 1952–54; employed at Lloyd's by Wm Brandt's 1957–76 (memb Lloyd's 1968–2002), chief exec Insurance Gp; dir: Wm Brandt's Ltd 1974–76, R W Sturge (Holdings) Ltd 1970–76, PA International and Sturge Underwriting Agency Ltd 1977–79, Globtik Tankers Ltd 1976–79, Ryan International plc and subsids 1987–89, Associated British Ports Holdings plc 1987–99; dep chm Anglesey Mining plc 1988–2000; chm: ITNET plc 1996–2004, HTV Group Ltd 1997–2002 (dir 1987–97); MP (Cons) for

Pembroke 1970–87 (ret), memb Shadow Cabinet and Cons Front Bench spokesman on Welsh Affairs 1974–79, sec of state of Wales 1979–87; chm: Advsy Ctee Nat Rivers Authy 1988–89, Nat Rivers Authy 1989–96; memb Ctee Automobile Assoc 1988–98; pres: Univ of Wales Cardiff 1988–98, Contemporary Art Soc for Wales 1988–93, SE Wales Arts Assoc 1987–94; Hon LLD Univ of Glamorgan; hon fell Cardiff Univ; *Books* Opera House Lottery: Zaha Hadid and the Cardiff Bay Opera House (1997), Westminster, Wales and Water (1999); *Recreations* fishing, gardening, collecting drawings and watercolours; *Clubs* Brooks's; *Style*— The Rt Hon Lord Crickhowell, PC; ✉ Pont Esgob Mill, Fforest Coal Pit, Abergavenny NP7 7LS; 4 Henning Street, London SW11 3DR

CRIGHTON, Dr Gordon Stewart; s of Allan Crighton (d 1971), of Balbeggie, Perthshire, and Margaret, *née* Stewart; *b* 29 April 1937; *Educ* Perth Acad, Univ of St Andrews (BSc); *m* 25 Aug 1962, Margaret, da of late James Stephen; 4 da (Suzanne Elizabeth b 18 Sept 1963, Isla Margaret b 16 March 1966, Heather Frances b 17 March 1967, Jennifer Rhona b 13 March 1968), 1 s (Andrew Gordon b 5 Feb 1965); *Career* Mott Hay & Anderson Consulting Engrs 1959–63 and 1965–66, Sir William Halcrow & Partners Consulting Engrs 1963–65 and 1967–78, L N Henderson & Associates Consulting Engrs 1966–67 and 1969–71, project mangr Kinhill Project Mangrs and Engrs 1971–72, Brian Colquhoun & Partners Consulting Engrs 1975–78, dir Valentine Laurie & Davies Consulting Engrs 1972–75 and 1978–82; Balfour Beatty 1982–93: head Civil Engrg Dept Project Engrg Div 1982–86, engrg dir Channel Tunnel 1986–92, engrg dir Kuala Lumpur Int Airport Malaysia 1992–93; sr exec mangr (project mangr Lantau and Airport Railway) Mass Transit Railway Corporation 1993–99; vice-pres Taiwan High Speed Rail Corp 1999–; author of numerous papers on civil engrg worldwide; Hon DSc Univ of Kent 1992; fell American Soc of Civil Engrs 1982, FICE 1982, fell Instn of Engrs Hong Kong 1994, FREng 1995; *Recreations* golf; *Style*— Dr Gordon S Crighton, FREng; ✉ 11 The Haystacks, High Wycombe, Buckinghamshire HP13 6PY (tel 01494 440638); Taiwan High Speed Rail Corp, 100 Hsin Yi Road, Sec. 5, Taipei, Taiwan 110, R.O.C. (tel 00 886 2 8725 1452, fax, 00 886 2 8725 1586)

CRIGMAN, David Ian; QC (1989); s of Jack Crigman (d 1987), and Sylvia, *née* Rich; *b* 16 August 1945; *Educ* King Edward's Sch Birmingham, Univ of Leeds (LLB); *m* 20 Aug 1980, Judith Ann, da of Mark Penny; 1 s (Sam Mark b 7 April 1982); *Career* called to the Bar Gray's Inn 1969, recorder of the Crown Court 1985–; *Recreations* writing, tennis, skiing; *Style*— David Crigman, Esq, QC; ✉ St Philips Chambers, 55 Temple Row, Birmingham B2 5LS (tel 0121 246 7000, fax 0121 246 7001, e-mail dcrigman@st-philips.co.uk)

CRIPPS, Michael Frederick; s of late Maj Charles Philip Cripps, TD, and Betty Christine, *née* Flinn; *b* 22 October 1947; *Educ* Felsted, Medway Coll (HNC); *m* 23 April 1982, Carolyn Louise, da of Elie Gabriel Farah; 3 s (Alexander Timothy James (step s) b 1974, Nicholas Frederick b 1985, Christopher Philip b 1988); *Career* exec search; dist mangr Johnson Group 1969–72, branch mangr Drake Consltss 1972–73; Cripps Sears & Partners Ltd: ptnr 1973–78, chm and md 1978–; memb Bd Transearch International 1997–99, memb World Search Gp 2003–; memb Ctee Japan Assoc 1990–2001; MIPM, MEI; FInstD 1985; *Recreations* sport generally, rowing, rugby football, cycling, sailing, people, travel, contemporary and classical live music; *Clubs* City of London, MCC, Bembridge Sailing; *Style*— Michael Cripps, Esq; ✉ Cripps Sears & Partners, Sardinia House, 52 Lincoln's Inn Fields, London WC2A 3LZ (tel 020 7440 8999, fax 020 7242 0515, e-mail london@crippssears.com)

CRISP, Dr Adrian James; s of Bertram William Crisp (d 1999), of Harrow Weald, Middx, and Mary Louise, *née* Butland (d 1999); *b* 21 November 1948; *Educ* UCS London, Magdalene Coll Cambridge (MA, MB BChir, MD), UCH London; *m* 6 July 1974 (m dis 2005), Lesley Roberta, da of Archibald Shaw (d 1981), of Harrow, Middx; 1 s (Alasdair James Gavin b 1977 d 1990), 1 da (Alison Victoria b 1979); *Career* house offr and SHO UCH and Northwick Park Hosp Harrow 1974–78, med registrar UCH 1978–80, sr registrar Guy's Hosp 1980–85, res fell Massachusetts Gen Hosp and Harvard Univ 1982–83; Addenbrooke's Hosp Cambridge: conslt rheumatologist 1985–, dir Bone Density Unit 1989–91, postgrad clinical tutor 1990–97; conslt rheumatologist: Newmarket Hosp 1985–, Princess of Wales Hosp Ely 1993–, Saffron Walden Hosp 2003–; assoc lectr Univ of Cambridge 1985–, dir of studies in clinical med and fell Churchill Coll Cambridge 1992–, assoc dean Clinical Sch Univ of Cambridge 1998–2003, assoc postgrad dean (pre-registration house offrs) Eastern Deanery 2003–05; memb: Br Soc for Rheumatology, Bone Research Soc; DRCOG 1977, FRCP 1991 (MRCP 1977); *Publications* Oxford Textbook of Rheumatology (contrib), Blackwell's Textbook of Diabetes (contrib), Management of Common Metabolic Bone Disorders (jtly); *Recreations* military history, golf, pre-1960 British films; *Clubs* RSM, Gog Magog Golf; *Style*— Dr Adrian Crisp; ✉ The Old Forge, 83 High Street, Great Abington, Cambridge CB21 6AE (tel 01223 892860); Addenbrooke's Hospital, Cambridge CB2 2QQ (tel 01223 216254, e-mail ajcrisp@addenbrookes.nhs.uk)

CRISP, Baron (Life Peer UK 2006), of Eaglescliffe in the County of Durham; Sir (Edmund) Nigel Ramsay; KCB (2003); *b* 14 January 1952; *Educ* Uppingham, St John's Coll Cambridge (MA); *m* 1 May 1976; 1 s, 1 da; *Career* Halewood Community Cncl 1973–76, Trebor Ltd 1977–81, Cambridgeshire Community Cncl 1981–86, unit gen mangr East Berks HA 1986–92; chief exec: Heatherwood and Wexham Park Hosps NHS Tst 1992–93, Oxford John Radcliffe Hosp NHS Tst 1993–97; regnl dir NHS Exec: South Thames Region 1997–99, London Region 1999–2000; chief exec NHS 2000–06, perm sec Dept of Health 2000–06; licentiate Inst of Health Serv Mgmnt; *Style*— The Rt Hon the Lord Crisp, KCB

CRISPE, Simon Leslie Hare; *b* 31 July 1955, New Zealand; *Educ* BArch (NZ); *m* 28 April 1979, Marianne Denise; 2 c; *Career* assoc dir Lister Drew and Associates (before acquisition by W S Atkins) 1989–91, tech dir W S Atkins 1993–; projects incl: project mangr Chicago Beach Resort Dubai 1993–95 (project design dir 1997–99), project design dir BA World Cargo Centre UK 1995–97, commercial dir W S Atkins and Ptnrs Overseas Dubai 2000–; ARCUK, RIBA; *Recreations* motor sport, classic car restoration, wood carving and cabinet making; *Clubs* Daimler and Lanchester Owners', Porsche Club of GB, Ferrari Owners; *Style*— Simon Crispe, Esq; ✉ W S Atkins, Woodcote Grove, Ashley Road, Epsom, Surrey KT18 5BW (tel 01372 726140, fax 01372 740055, e-mail scrispe@wsatkins-dxb.co.ae)

CRITCHLEY, Tom; s of Leonard Critchley (d 1986), and Jessie, *née* Turner (d 1988); *b* 17 August 1928; *Educ* Sheffield Coll of Technol; *m* 15 Dec 1951, Margaret, da of Frederick Bland (d 1934); 1 s (Andrew b 1959); *Career* Davy-Ashmore Group 1951–66, Cammell Laird and Upper Clyde Groups 1966–69, JCB Group 1969–70, EMI Group 1970–80, head Investment Casting Mission to Canada; sr ptnr Int Consultancy Practice 1980–85, under sec Dept of Health 1986–90, int business advsr 1990–; business devpt advsr: SE Regional Arts Centre 2000–01, Royal Berkshire Fire and Rescue Service 2002–03; md: UK High Technology Co 1991–95, UK/Polish Jt Venture Polish Acad of Sciences 1991–95; head industry missions to Japan, SE Asia, Soviet Union and Poland 1988–91; UN advsr: Tanzanian Govt, High Cmmn for Refugees; chm Anglo Soviet Healthcare Gp 1988–91, memb Bd Nat Inst of Govt Purchasing USA 1977–78, UK delg Int Fedn of Purchasing and Materials Mgmnt 1978–82, faculty memb Mgmnt Centre Europe 1980–86, dir Int Mgmnt Inst 1984–88; Chartered Inst of Purchasing and Supply: fell 1967, chm of Cncl 1974–75, pres 1977–78, chm External Affrs 1978–82, memb Int Cncl 1979–82; memb NHS Mgmnt Bd for Procurement and Distribution 1986–90, chm UK Leisure Trade Assoc 1990–93, dir of govt and regulatory affairs Pan-European Trade Fedn 1992–93, dir Ctee for Int Students Imperial Coll London 1996–97, chm Huntleigh Fndn 1997–2003; Millennium advsr: The Children's Soc 1996–98, Friends of the Elderly 1998–2000; co-ordinator Harlington Hospice Capital Appeal 2003–05; vice-patron Br Assoc for Servs to the Elderly 2006–; *Recreations* competitive sports, live theatre, performing arts, North American history; *Style*— Tom Critchley, Esq; ✉ 3 Lincoln Close, Stoke Mandeville, Aylesbury, Buckinghamshire HP22 5YS (tel 01296 612511, fax 01296 614203)

CRITCHLOW, His Hon Judge Christopher Allan; s of Charles Brandon Critchlow (d 1996), and Eileen Marjorie, *née* Bowers; *b* 8 July 1951; *Educ* Royal GS Lancaster, Univ of Exeter (LLB), Inns of Court Cncl of Legal Educn; *m* 7 Sept 1974, Wendy Anne, da of Anthony Lucey; 1 s (Samuel Brandon b 19 Nov 1979), 2 da (Abigail Lucey b 16 Sept 1981, Clementine Rose b 17 Aug 1984); *Career* called to the Bar Inner Temple 1973 (memb 1970, bencher 2003); appointed: asst recorder 1987, recorder 1991, circuit judge (SE Circuit) 2000–; govr Royal GS Guildford; *Recreations* golf, bridge, tennis, reading history; *Clubs* Reform; *Style*— His Hon Judge Critchlow; ✉ c/o Reading Crown Court, Reading, Berkshire (tel 0118 468500)

CRITCHLOW, Howard Arthur (Harry); s of Arthur Critchlow (d 1997), of Nottingham, and Edith Ellen, *née* Evans (d 1972); *b* 22 April 1943; *Educ* Nottingham HS, Univ of Sheffield (BDS); *m* 5 Dec 1970, Avril, da of George Pyne, of Sheffield; 1 s (Edward b 1972), 1 da (Bridget b 1974); *Career* conslt oral surgn 1976–: Glasgow Dental Hosp, Stobhill Gen Hosp, Royal Hosp for Sick Children Southern General Hosp Glasgow; dir Dental Examinations RCPS Glasgow; res work in: cryosurgery, laser surgery, dental implants; memb BDA 1965, FBAOMS 1976, FDSRCS (England), FDSRCP (Glasgow); *Recreations* hill walking, running, gardening, DIY, keep fit; *Clubs* 41, LMG; *Style*— Harry Critchlow, Esq; ✉ Glasgow Dental Hospital, 378 Sauchiehall Sreet, Glasgow G2 3JZ (tel 0141 211 9600)

CRITCHLOW, Prof Keith Barry; s of Michael Bernard Critchlow (d 1972), and Rozalind Ruby, *née* Weston-Mann (d 1983); *b* 16 March 1933; *Educ* Summerhill Sch, St Martin's Sch of Art London (Inter NDD), RCA (ARCA); *m* Gail Susan, da of Geoffrey W Henebery; 1 s (Matthew Alexander), 3 da (Louise Penelope, Amanda Jane, Amelia Poppy); *Career* Nat Serv RAF 1951–53; lectr at most art and architecture schools in the UK; teaching appts at: Harrow, Sir John Cass, Hornsey, Watford, Wimbledon, The Slade, The Royal Coll; appts abroad incl: Ghana, Kuwait, Sweden, Aust, India, USA, Canada, Jordan, Iran, Saudi Arabia; formerly: tutor and res dir The Architectural Assoc, tutor in painting Sch of the Royal Coll of Art, tutor Slade Sch, dir Visual Islamic Arts Unit Royal Coll of Art; The Prince of Wales's Inst of Architecture: formerly actg dir Research, formerly actg dir of Visual Islamic and Traditional Arts (VITA); currently pt/t tutor (also emeritus prof); fndr of own architectural design office Keith Critchlow and Assocs; buildings designed in: USA, Kuwait, Saudi Arabia, Iran, UK (incl Krishnamurti Study Centre), India (incl SS Baba Inst of Higher Med Sciences Hosp Puttaparthi - second largest hosp in Asia); research dir KAIROS educnl charity; FRCA 1986 (Higher Dr 1989), FDIH (USA) 1987; *Books* Order in Space (1969, 2 edn 2000), Chartres Maze - A Model of the Universe?, Into the Hidden Environment (1972), Islamic Patterns - A Cosmological Approach (1976, 2 edn 1999), Time Stands Still (1979), The Sphere, Soul & Androgyne (1980), The Whole Question of Health (with Jon Allen, 1995); *Recreations* painting, writing, geometry, walking, photography, meditation; *Style*— Prof Keith Critchlow; ✉ VITA, Prince's Foundation, 19–22 Charlotte Road, London EC2A 3SG (tel 020 7613 8500); KAIROS tel 01803 732135

CRITCHLOW, Stafford; s of Rex Critchlow, of Lincs, and Jenifer, *née* Pye; *b* 17 November 1965, Lincs; *Educ* Uppingham, Univ of Newcastle (BA, William Bell meml scholar, BArch), Instituto Universitario di Architettura Venezia; *m* 20 March 1999, Harriet Lane, da of David Lane, CMG, of London, former ambass to the Holy See; 1 da (Poppy b 23 Nov 2001), 1 s (Barnaby b 25 Jan 2005); *Career* architect; Boilerhouse Project V&A Museum 1984–85, Gaul Assocs Chicago 1986, Skidmore Owings and Merrill Inc 1988–89, Chris Wilkinson Architects 1992–99, Wilkinson Eyre Architects: joined 1999, assoc 2000, dir 2005; exhbn 40 Under 40 (V&A) 2006; memb Design Review Panel CABE 2007–; RIBA 1994, FRSA 1996; *Style*— Stafford Critchlow, Esq; ✉ Wilkinson Eyre Architects, 24 Britton Street, London EC1M 5UA (tel 020 7608 7900, fax 020 7608 7901)

CRITTENDEN, Eur Ing Prof Barry David; s of Henry John Crittenden (d 1990), and Rosina Katie, *née* Hedley (d 1969); *b* 23 May 1947; *Educ* Chislehurst and Sidcup GS (Hugh Oddy meml prize), Univ of Birmingham (BSc, PhD); *m* 30 Oct 1971, Janet Mary, da of Raymond Charles Pinches; 1 da (Lucy Rosina b 2 April 1979), 1 s (Daniel Charles b 4 Aug 1981); *Career* chemical engr UKAEA Aldermaston 1971–73; Univ of Bath: lectr 1973–88, sr lectr 1988–91, reader 1991, prof of chemical engrg 1991–, head of dept 2004–; CEng, Eur Ing, FIChemE, FREng; *Books* Management of Hazardous and Toxic Wastes in the Process Industries (with S T Kolaczkowski, 1987), Waste Minimization: A Practical Guide (with S T Kolaczkowski, 1995), Adsorption Technology and Design (with WJ Thomas, 1998); *Recreations* photography, cycling; *Style*— Eur Ing Prof Barry Crittenden; ✉ Department of Chemical Engineering, University of Bath, Claverton Down, Bath BA2 7AY (tel 01225 386501, fax 01225 385713)

CROAN, Sheriff Thomas Malcolm; s of John Croan (d 1951), of Edinburgh, and Amelia, *née* Sydney (d 1989); *b* 7 August 1932; *Educ* St Joseph's Coll Dumfries, Univ of Edinburgh (MA, LLB); *m* 2 April 1959, Joan Kilpatrick, da of George Law; 1 s (Nicholas Miles Law b 14 April 1960), 3 da (Gillian Carol Mary b 4 April 1963, Karen Margaret Sylvia 3 Aug 1965, Larissa Anne Sydney b 7 April 1973); *Career* admitted to Faculty of Advocates 1956, standing jr counsel to Queen and Lord Treasurer's Remembrancer 1963–64, standing jr counsel to Scottish Devpt Dept 1964–65 (for highways work 1967–69), advocate depute 1965–66, memb Legal Aid Supreme Court Ctee 1968–69, sheriff of Grampian, Highland and Islands (formerly Aberdeen, Kincardine and Banff) 1969–83, sheriff of N Strathclyde 1983–; *Recreations* sailing; *Style*— Sheriff Thomas Croan; ✉ Sheriff Court House, St Marnock Street, Kilmarnock KA1 1ED

CROCKARD, Prof (Hugh) Alan; s of Hugh Crockard (d 1988), and Mary, *née* McKimm (d 1988); *b* 24 January 1943; *Educ* Royal Belfast Acad Instn, Queen's Univ Belfast (MB BCh, BOA, DSc, Sinclair Medal in Surgery); *m* 1978, Dr Caroline Orr; 2 s (Michael Charles b 30 Jan 1984, Thomas Hugh b 18 Jan 1987); *Career* Wellcome sr surgical fell 1973–74, Hunterian prof (treatment of head injury) RCS 1973–74, Fogarty int postdoctoral fell Chicago 1974–75, sr lectr in neurosurgery Queen's Univ Belfast 1974–78, conslt neurosurgn The Nat Hosp for Neurology and Neurosurgery 1978–2006, prof of surgical neurology Univ of WA and Inst of Neurology London; dir Raven Dept of Educn RCS 1998–2003, nat dir Modernising Medical Careers 2004–07; numerous visiting professorships; pres: Br Cervical Spine Soc 1998 (co-fndr 1986, sec), European Cervical Spine Research Soc 1999; Calvert medal 1972, Morrow lectr Belfast 1984, Jameson medal (Neurosurgical Soc of Australasia) 1989, Lund neurosurgical medal 1987, Olivacrona lectr 1995, Harrington medal 1995, Wylie McKissock medal 1996; memb: Soc of Br Neurological Surgns, American Acad of Neurological Surgery, American Assoc of Neurological Surgns, Soc of Neurological Surgns, Hungarian Spine Soc; FRCSEd 1970, FRCS 1971, FDSRCS 2001, FRCP 2003; *Books* Trauma Care (with W M Odling-Smee, 1981), Neurosurgery: The Scientific Basis of Clinical Practice (with R Hayward and J T Hoff, 3 edn 2000); also author of over 330 original articles; *Recreations* music, travel, sailing, photography; *Clubs* Athenaeum, Royal Ocean Racing; *Style*— Prof Alan Crockard; ✉ c/o Victor Horsely Department of Neurosurgery, National Hospital for Nervous Diseases, Queen Square, London WC1N 3BG (e-mail alan.crockard@uclh.nhs.uk)

CROCKETT, Rt Rev (Phillip) Anthony; *see:* Bangor, Bishop of

CROFT, 3 Baron (UK 1940); Sir Bernard William Henry Page Croft; 3 Bt (UK 1924); s of 2 Baron Croft (d 1997), by his w, Lady Antoinette Fredericka Hersey Cecilia Conyngham (d 1959), da of 6 Marquess Conyngham; *b* 28 August 1949; *Educ* Stowe, Univ of Wales (BSc Econ); *m* 1993, Mary Elizabeth, da of late James Richardson, of Co Tyrone; *Heir* none; *Career* publishing; *Recreations* shooting, fishing, skiing; *Clubs* Hurlingham, Naval and Military; *Style*— The Rt Hon the Lord Croft; ✉ Croft Castle, Leominster, Herefordshire HR6 9PW

CROFT, Charles Beresford; s of Arthur James Croft (d 1979), and Margaret Bays Conyers, *née* Wright; *b* 14 January 1943; *Educ* Worksop Coll, Leeds Univ Medical Sch (MB ChB Hon); *m* 23 March 1968, Hilary Louise Whitaker, da of Ronald Whitaker (d 1968); 1 da (Emma Louise b 1972); *Career* conslt surgn and assoc prof Albert Einstein Sch of Med NY 1974–79; conslt surgn: The Royal Free Hosp London, The Nat Heart and Chest Hosp London 1979–; civil conslt in laryngology RAF 1983–; FRCS 1970, FRCSEd 1972; *Recreations* golf, tennis, sailing; *Clubs* MCC, Moor Park Golf, RSM; *Style*— Charles B Croft, Esq; ✉ Rye Lodge, 91 Copsewood Way, Northwood, Middlesex (tel 01923 823793); 48 Crawford Street, London W1 (tel 020 7262 7837); 55 Harley Street, London W1N 1DD (tel 020 7580 2426, fax 020 7436 1645, e-mail cbq@uk-consultants.co.uk)

CROFT, David Michael Bruce; s of Eric David Croft (d 2000), and Catherine Margaret, *née* Kelly; *b* 2 April 1955; *Educ* Epsom Coll, Magdalen Coll Oxford (MA, pres JCR); *m* 1 Sept 2001, Angela Jane, *née* Murray; *Career* began career with Ocean Transport & Trading 1976–82; various positions: Nat Freight Consortium 1982–87, Thames Television 1987–91, Channel Four Television 1992–96; currently dir: Anglia Television, Border Television, Granada Television, Meridian Broadcasting, Tyne Tees Television, Yorkshire Television; *Recreations* horse racing, travel, golf; *Clubs* Royal Liverpool Golf; *Style*— David Croft, Esq; ✉ Flat 51, 5 Concordia Street, Leeds LS1 4ES; Yorkshire Television Ltd, The Televsion Centre, Leeds LS3 1JS (tel 0113 222 7184, fax 0113 242 3867, mobile 07770 578468, e-mail david.croft@itv.com)

CROFT, Giles Laurance; s of John Rothschild Croft, of Perrymead, Somerset, and Nikki, *née* Geal; *b* 20 June 1957; *Educ* Monckton Combe Sch, City of Bath Tech Coll; *Career* artistic director; dir Bath Young People's Theatre Co 1978–80, regnl ed Bananas magazine 1979–80, admin Le Metro Theatre Co Bath 1980–82, artistic dir Gate Theatre 1985–89, series ed Absolute Classics 1988–90, literary mangr Royal Nat Theatre 1989–95; artistic dir: Palace Theatre Watford 1995–99, Nottingham Playhouse 1999–; vice-pres European Theatre Convention, memb Bd Paines Plough 1997–; prodns incl: Conversations with a Cupboard Man (Lyric Hammersmith) 1983, Written in Sickness (Upstream) 1984, Orphee (Upstream) 1984, Elmer Gantry (Gate) 1986, The Boxer (Edinburgh Festival) 1986, Naomi (Gate) 1987, The Infant (Gate) 1989, The Secret Life (BBC Radio 4) 1993; Watford credits incl: Anna Karenina 1995, Foreign Lands 1996, Kind Hearts and Coronets 1997 (also adapted), The Talented Mr Ripley 1998; Nottingham Playhouse credits incl: Wonderful Tennessee 2000, Because It's There 2000, Polygraph 2001, Ratpack Confidential 2002–03, Chicken Soup with Barley 2005; adapted for nat tour: The Ladykillers 1999, Passport to Pimlico 2000, Whisky Galore 2007; author of many short stories and articles (published and broadcast); FRSA; *Clubs* Blacks; *Style*— Giles Croft, Esq; ✉ Nottingham Playhouse, Wellington Circus, Nottingham NG1 5AF (tel 0115 947 4361)

CROFT, Judith Mary; da of Thomas Edwin Hirst, of Wakefield, and Kathleen Mary, *née* Scholefield; *b* 16 August 1956; *Educ* Wakefield Girls HS, De Montfort Univ (BA), Bristol Old Vic Theatre Sch; *m* 28 Oct 1978, Robert Frank Croft; 1 da (Rosie Frances b 1 Aug 1986), 1 s (Lewis George b 13 Nov 1988); *Career* stage designer; assoc designer Gateway Theatre Chester 1981–83, head of design Oldham Coliseum Theatre 1983–86, freelance designer 1987–90, head of design Library Theatre Co Manchester 1991–; memb: Br Soc of Theatre Designers, Equity Designers Ctee; *Theatre* Gateway Theatre Chester: The Elephant Man, A Streetcar Named Desire, Tragical History Tour, Cider With Rosie, A Midsummer Night's Dream; Oldham Coliseum Theatre: Tartuffe, The Railway Children, Girlfriends; Library Theatre Co Manchester prodns incl: The Lion, the Witch and the Wardrobe, Assassins, Laughter on the 23rd Floor (also Guildford, Queen's Theatre West End and nat tour, nominated Olivier Award 1997), My Night with Reg, Neville's Island, Pygmalion, Perfect Days, The Borrowers (also nat tour with Watershed Prodns, nominated Best Design and Best Special Prodn Manchester Evening News Awards 2000), The Memory of Water, Beauty Queen of Lenanne (nominated Best Design Manchester Evening News Awards 2001), Falstaff (winner Best Prodn of an Opera Manchester Evening News); other credits incl: Top Girls (Lancaster Dukes), Falstaff (Royal Northern Coll of Music, winner Best Prodn of an Opera Manchester Evening News Awards 2001), Cinderella and Jack and the Beanstalk, Rock and Roll Pantos (Clwyd Theatr Cymru); *Style*— Mrs Judith Croft; ✉ 18 Lache Lane, Chester CH4 7LR (tel 01244 676046); Head of Design, Library Theatre, St Peter's Square, Manchester M2 5PD

CROFT, Sir Owen Glendower; 14 Bt (E 1671), of Croft Castle, Herefordshire; s of Sir Bernard Hugh Denman Croft, 13 Bt (d 1984), and Helen Margaret, *née* Weaver (d 1995); *b* 26 April 1932; *m* 1959, Sally Patricia, da of Dr Thomas Montagu Mansfield, of Brisbane, Australia; 2 da (Patricia Alice b 1960, Georgiana b 1964), 1 s (Thomas Jasper b 1962); *Heir* s, Thomas Croft; *Style*— Sir Owen Croft, Bt; ✉ Salisbury Court, Uralla, NSW 2358, Australia

CROFT, Rodney John; s of late Ronald Croft, of Bolton, Lancs, and late Joan Constance, *née* Bolton; *b* 26 February 1944; *Educ* Bolton Sch, Selwyn Coll Cambridge and Middx Hosp Med Sch (Berkley fell, MA, MB BChir, MChir); *m* 28 July 1973, Hazel Ann, da of late Bernard Dudley Cattermole, and late Eva Cattermole; 2 s (Alexander James b 25 Nov 1974, Alistair Charles b 7 April 1977), 1 da (Antonia Jane b 9 April 1980); *Career* surgical registrar Ipswich Hosps 1971–73, surgical registrar in neurosurgery Maida Vale Hosp 1973; The Middx Hosps and Central Middx: surgical registrar 1973–75, sr surgical registrar 1975–80, research sr registrar 1976; North Middx Univ Hosp: conslt gen and vascular surgn 1980–2004, RCS surgical tutor 1983–89, undergrad tutor 1986–2001, co-clinical dir of surgery 2004–05, clinical governance lead Dept of Surgery and Anaesthetics 2005–06; Royal Free Hosp Med Sch: clinical sub dean 1988–2001, memb Sch Cncl 1991–98, School Medal 1993, hon conslt vascular surgn 2001–04; St George's Univ Sch of Med Grenada: assoc prof of surgery 1989–2000, prof of surgery 2000–, chm UK surgical faculty 2000–04, dean clinical studies UK 2004–; hon conslt vascular surgn Whittington Hosp 2001–04; hon sr lectr in surgery Univ of London 1994–; examiner in surgery (final MB BS) Univ of London 1989–2004; memb BSI Ctees for Vascular Implants 1986–, princ UK expert ISO Ctees for vascular implants, princ UK expert CEN Ctee for vascular implants 1993–; pres Cambridge Univ Med Soc 1964–65; Capt RAMC TAVR 1972–74, Surgn Lt rising to Surgn Lt Cdr RNR 1974–83; Freeman City of London, Liveryman Worshipful Soc of Apothecaries; memb: BMA 1968–2007, Int Soc of Chirugie 1976–2007, Vascular Surgical Soc of GB and Ireland 1981–, Military Surgical Soc 1988–; FRSM 1975–2007, fell Assoc of Surgns of GB and Ireland 1980–, FRCS, FACS 1984; *Recreations* music (classical, choral and jazz), rowing; *Clubs* Garrick, MCC, Lord's Taverners; *Style*— Rodney J Croft, Esq; ✉ 127 Queen's Road, Buckhurst Hill, Essex IG9 5BH (tel 020 8505 7813); North London Nuffield Hospital, Cavell Drive, Uplands Park Road, Enfield, Middlesex EN2 7PR (tel 020 8366 2122)

CROFT, Sir Thomas Stephen Hutton; 6 Bt (UK 1818), of Cowling Hall, Yorks; s of Maj Sir John Archibald Radcliffe Croft, 5 Bt (d 1990), and Lucy Elizabeth, *née* Jupp; *b* 12 June 1959; *Educ* King's Sch Canterbury, UCL (BSc), RCA (MA); *m* 28 April 2001, Maxino Julia Benato; 1 da (Katharine Amelia Rosalind b 23 Nov 2003); *Heir* unc, Cyril Croft; *Career* architect; buildings incl: Royal Yacht Squadron Pavilion Cowes 2000; RIBA; *Style*— Sir Thomas Croft, Bt; ✉ 9 Ivebury Court, 325 Latimer Road, London W10 6RA (tel 020 8962 0066, e-mail tc@thomascroft.com, website www.thomascroft.com)

CROFT, Trevor Anthony; *b* 9 June 1948; *Educ* Belle Vue Boys' GS Bradford, Univ of Hull (BSc), Univ of Sheffield (Dip Town and Regnl Planning); *m* 1980, Janet Frances Halley; 2 da (Hazel, Jennifer); *Career* with: Ministry of Development NI 1971–72, Countryside Cmmn for Scotland 1972–75, Govt of Malawi (Town and Country Planning Dept, Nat Parks and Wildlife Dept) 1976–81; National Trust for Scotland: planning offr 1982–84, head of policy research 1984–88, regnl dir for Central and Tayside 1988–95, dep dir and dir of countryside 1995–96, dir designate 1996–97, dir 1997–2001, conslt 2001–03; reporter Scot Exec Directorate for Plannine and Environmental Appeals 2002–; memb S Scotland Advsy Ctee Forestry Cmmn 1988–90; memb Cncl Europa Nostra 1999–2001; property convenor and memb Congregational Bd St Fillan's Church Aberdour 1986–88; hon treas and memb Exec Ctee Euro Network of Nat Heritage Orgns 2000–01; chm Br Equestrian Vaulting Ltd 2002–03, memb Bd Br Equestrian Fedn 2002–03; assoc RSGS (memb Cncl 1998–2001 and 2002–05, memb Fin Ctee 2002–); chm Kinross Civic Tst Awards Ctee 2005–; memb RTPI, FRSA; *Recreations* restoring my Series One Land Rover, travel, motorcycling, sailing; *Clubs* Royal Scots (Edinburgh); *Style*— Trevor A Croft, Esq; ✉ Glenside, Tillyrie, Kinross KY13 0RW (tel 01577 864105)

CROFTON, 7 Baron (I 1797); Guy Patrick Gilbert Crofton; 10 Bt (I 1758); s of 5 Baron Crofton (d 1974); suc bro, 6 Baron 1989; *b* 17 June 1951; *Educ* Theresianistische Akademie Vienna, Midhurst GS; *m* 1985, Gillian Susan Burroughs, o da of late Harry Godfrey Mitchell Bass, CMG, of Reepham, Norfolk; 2 s (Hon (Edward) Harry Piers, Hon (Charles) Marcus George (twins) b 23 Jan 1988); *Heir* s, Hon Harry Crofton; *Career* Lt-Col 9/12 Royal Lancers (Prince of Wales's); defence attaché, Berne, Switzerland 1995–97, HQ LANDJUT Rendsburg Germany 1998, HQ SFOR Sarajevo Bosnia 1999, Defence Evaluation and Research Agency Farnborough 2000–02, defence attaché Luanda Angola 2003–06, ret; *Clubs* Cavalry and Guards', St Moritz Tobogganing; *Style*— The Rt Hon the Lord Crofton; ✉ Hamilton House, High Street, Bruton, Somerset BA10 0AH

CROFTON, Sir John Wenman; kt (1977); s of Dr William Mervyn Crofton; *b* 1912; *Educ* Tonbridge, Sidney Sussex Coll Cambridge (MA, MD), St Thomas' Hosp London (MB BCh); *m* 1945, Eileen Chris Mercer, MBE; *Career* sr lectr in med Postgrad Med Sch of London 1947–51; Univ of Edinburgh: prof of respiratory diseases and tuberculosis 1952–77, dean Faculty of Med 1963–66, vice-princ 1970–71; pres RCPEd 1973–76; conslt WHO; Edinburgh Medal for Sci and Society 1995, Galen Medal for Therapeutics Soc of Apothecaries 2001, Union Medal Int Union Against Tuberculosis and Lung Diseases 2005; Liveryman Worshipful Soc of Apothecaries; Dr (hc) Univ of Bordeaux 1994, DSc (hc) Univ of London 2001; hon memb: Acad of Med Argentina, Acad of Med Catalonia, Acad of Med Singapore; FRCP, FRCPEd, FACP, FRACP, FRCPI, FFCM, Hon FRSE 1997; *Recreations* mountains, music, reading, science, history; *Style*— Sir John Crofton; ✉ 13 Spylaw Bank Road, Edinburgh EH13 0JW (tel 0131 441 3730, fax 0131 441 5105)

CROFTON, Dr Richard Wenman; s of Sir John Wenman Crofton, *qv*, and Eileen Chris Crofton, MBE; *b* 2 October 1947; *Educ* The Edinburgh Acad, Sidney Sussex Coll Cambridge, Univ of Edinburgh (MA, MB ChB); *m* 26 April 1975, Susan Anne, da of William Henry James (d 1979), of Beverley, E Yorks; 1 s (David b 8 Aug 1978), 1 da (Eilidh b 17 Nov 1984); *Career* MRC res fell Dept of Therapeutics Univ of Edinburgh 1973–77, res fell Dept of Infectious Diseases Leiden Univ The Netherlands 1974–76, registrar Aberdeen Teaching Hosps 1977–79, lectr Dept of Med Univ of Aberdeen 1979–83, conslt physician Law Hosp Carluke 1983–; memb Br Soc of Gastroenterology; FRCPEd 1986, FRCPGlas 1998; *Recreations* family life, the outdoors, bird watching; *Style*— Dr Richard Crofton; ✉ 22 Silverdale Crescent, Lanark, Lanarkshire ML11 9HW (tel 01555 661394); Wishaw Hospital, Wishaw, Lanarkshire ML2 0DP (tel 01698 361100)

CROFTS, Prof Roger Stanley; CBE (1999); s of Stanley Crofts (d 1995), and Violet, *née* Dawson; *b* 17 January 1944; *Educ* Hinckley GS, Univ of Liverpool (BA), Univ of Leicester (PGCE), Univ of Aberdeen (MLitt); *m* Lindsay Manson; 1 s (Tim), 1 da (Catharine); *Career* research asst Univ of Aberdeen 1966–72, research fell UCL 1972–74; Scottish Office: North Sea Oil Support Gp 1974–81, Central Research Unit 1981–84, Highlands and Tourism 1984–88, Rural Affrs 1988–91; chief exec Scottish Natural Heritage 1991–2002; hon prof of geography Univ of Aberdeen 1997–, visiting prof of environmental mgmnt Royal Holloway Coll London (later Royal Holloway Univ of London) 1997–2004, visiting prof of geoscience Univ of Edinburgh 2004–; The World Conservation Union (IUCN): chair UK Ctee 1999–2002, chair WCPA Europe 2001–; chair The Sibthorp Tst; memb: Cncl and Bd National Tst for Scotland (also chm Conservation Ctee), Ctee Scottish Assoc of Marine Science, Bd Plantlife, Bd Scot Agric Coll; Hon DSc Univ of St Andrews; FRSA 1996, FRSE 2001, FRSGS 2001; *Publications* Scotland: The creation of its natural landscape (co-author, 1999), Scotland's Environment: The Future (co-author, 2000), Conserving Nature: Scotland and the Wider World (co-ed, 2005), Land of Mountain and Flood (co-author, 2007); author of several articles and ed of books on environmental mgmnt, rural devpt, earth history and coastal processes; *Recreations* cooking without a book, garden design, singing in private, wildflower photography, hill walking; *Style*— Prof Roger Crofts, CBE; ✉ 6 Old Church Lane, Duddington Village, Edinburgh EH15 3PX (tel 0131 661 7858)

CROHAM, Baron (Life Peer UK 1978), of the London Borough of Croydon; Sir Douglas Albert Vivian Allen; GCB (1973, KCB 1967, CB 1963); s of Albert John Allen (ka 1918), of Croydon, Surrey; *b* 15 December 1917; *Educ* Wallington GS, LSE (BSc); *m* 1941, Sybil Eileen (d 1994), da of John Marco Allegro (d 1964), of Carshalton, Surrey; 1 da (Hon Rosamund Sybil (Hon Mrs Sulyak) b 1942), 2 s (Hon John Douglas b 1945, Hon Richard Anthony b 1950); *Career* perm sec: Treasy 1968–74, Civil Serv Dept 1974–77; dir: Pilkington plc 1978–92, Guinness Mahon & Co Ltd 1989–92; chm: British National Oil Corporation 1982–86 (dep chm 1978–82), Guinness Peat Group 1983–87, Trinity Insurance Ltd 1988–92; industrial advsr to Govr Bank of England 1978–83; chm: Anglo-German Fndn 1981–98, Review of Univ Grants Ctee 1985–87; *Recreations* woodwork, bridge; *Clubs* Reform, Civil Service; *Style*— The Rt Hon the Lord Croham, GCB; ✉ 9 Manor Way, South Croydon, Surrey CR2 7BT (tel 020 8688 0496)

CROISDALE-APPLEBY, Prof David; JP (Thames Valley 2003); s of Mark Appleby (d 1980), of Belford, Northumberland, and Florence Isabel, *née* White; *b* 6 February 1946; *Educ* Royal GS Newcastle upon Tyne, Univ of London (MA), Univ of Newcastle (BSc), Brunel Univ (MSc), Open Univ (MA) Univ of Lancaster (PhD); *m* 3 Aug 1968, Rev Carolynn Elizabeth, da of Maj Alan Cuthbert Croisdale, MBE (d 1974); 3 s (Mycroft b 1971, Lindsay b 1973, Merton b 1976), 1 da (Catriona b 1984); *Career* chief exec: De Villiers & Schonfeldt Ltd 1976–79, Allen Brady & Marsh Ltd 1979–82; worldwide ops dir SSC&B:Lintas Ltd 1982–84, chm and chief exec Creative Synergy Ltd 1984–99, dir of strategy, mktg and communications Univ for Industry (learndirect) 1999–2001; chm: The DCA Co Ltd 1985–99, Utilities Research Ltd 1986–99, Yarrow Housing Ltd 2001–, Radian Gp 2006–; dir: Centrex 2002–, Food from Britain 2002–, Turning Point 2003–, Postwatch 2006–; chm: NHS Ind Review Panels 1996–2002, Careplus 2002–04, Bucks Hosps NHS Tst 2002–06, Prog Devpt Gp for Longterm Sickness and Incapacity NICE 2007–; dep chm: Bucks Mental Health NHS Tst 2001–02, Cncl for the Registration of Forensic Practitioners 2002–; dir NHS Confedn 2005–, inspr of medical educn GMC and PMETB 2004–; visiting prof of strategic mktg and communications Univ of Strathclyde 1996–, visiting prof Durham Business Sch 2002–; memb Cncl Univ of Durham 2000–, chm Ustinov Coll Univ of Durham 2005–; tstee Colin Javens Spinal Injury Tst 2005–; memb Strategic Advsy Gp Durham Cathedral 2006–; FRSA 1988; *Recreations* 18th Century

English literature, art history; *Style*— Prof David Croisdale-Appleby; ✉ Abbotsholme, Hervines Road, Amersham, Buckinghamshire HP6 5HS (tel 01494 725194, e-mail croisdaleappleby@aol.com); Waren Lea Hall, Bamburgh, Northumberland

CROLL, Prof James George Arthur; s of Keith Waghorn Croll (d 1976), and Jean, *née* Campbell (d 1994); *b* 16 October 1943, Palmerston North, NZ; *Educ* Palmerston North Boy's HS, Univ of Canterbury Christchurch (BE, PhD); *m* 16 Dec 1966 (m dis 1996), Elisabeth Joan, da of Robert Colston Sprackett (d 1993), of Auckland, NZ; 1 s (Nicolas James b 1974), 1 da (Katherine Elisabeth b 1978); partner, Patricia Jean Hindmarsh; *Career* asst engr NZ Miny of Works 1961–67; UCL: res fell 1967–70, lectr 1970–82, reader in structural engrg 1982–85, prof of structural engrg 1985–92, Chadwick prof of civil engrg and head Dept of Civil Engrg 1992–2004, prof of civil engrg 2004–; currently: chm Jt Bd of Moderators ICE, IStructE and CIBSE; former: memb Cncl IStructE, sec and chm Br Soc for Social Responsibility in Sci; CEng, CMath, FICE, FIStructE, FIMA, FREng 1990; *Books* Elements of Structural Stability (1973), Force Systems & Equilibrium (1975); *Recreations* music, sailing, skiing, cycling, painting; *Clubs* Natural Science; *Style*— Prof James Croll, FREng; ✉ 8 Chester Place, Regent's Park, London NW1 4NB (tel 020 7486 4310); Department of Civil and Environmental Engineering, University College London, London WC1E 6BT (tel 020 7679 2723, fax 020 7380 0986, e-mail j.croll@ucl.ac.uk)

CROLY, Colin Vernon; s of Dr Vernon Robert Arthur Croly (d 2006), and Martha Maria, *née* Albertyn (d 2003); *b* 9 October 1949; *Educ* St Andrew's Coll Grahamstown S Africa, Univ of Cape Town (BCom, LLB), UCL (LLM); *m* 24 Feb 1973, Clare Margaret, *née* Stroebel; *Career* admitted slr 1976; ptnr Barlow Lyde & Gilbert 1980–; sec gen Int Assoc of Insurance Lawyers 1994–, memb Bd Fedn of Defence and Corp Counsel 2004–06, govt appointee IBRC 1997–98; Who's Who Legal Int Insurance and Reinsurance Lawyer of the Year 2005, 2006 and 2007; memb: Law Soc 1976, Int Bar Assoc; *Publications* Reinsurance Practice and the Law (jt ed, 1993); *Recreations* gardening, reading, opera, theatre; *Clubs* RAC; *Style*— Colin Croly, Esq; ✉ 36 Blomfield Road, Little Venice, London W9 2PF; Barlow Lyde & Gilbert, Beaufort House, 15 St Botolph Street, London EC3A 7NJ (tel 020 7643 8460, fax 020 7071 9318, e-mail ccroly@blg.co.uk)

CROMARTIE, 5 Earl of (UK 1861); John Ruaridh Grant Mackenzie; also Viscount Tarbat (UK 1861), Baron Castlehaven (1861), Baron MacLeod of Castle Leod (UK 1861); Chief of the Clan Mackenzie; s of 4 Earl of Cromartie, MC, TD (d 1989), and his 2 w, Olga, *née* Laurance (d 1996); *b* 12 June 1948; *Educ* Rannoch Sch Perthshire, Univ of Strathclyde; *m* 1, 1973 (m dis 1983), Helen, da of John Murray; 1 s (decd); m 2, 1985, Janet Clare, da of Christopher James Harley, of Strathpeffer; 2 s (Colin Ruaridh, Viscount Tarbat b 7 Sept 1987, Hon Alasdair Kenelm Stuart b 6 Dec 1989); *Heir* s, Viscount Tarbat; *Career* sat as cross-bencher in House of Lords until 1999; explosives conslt, past editor Explosives Engineering; tstee John Muir Tst; memb Inst of Explosive Engrs 1982, pres Mountaineering Cncl of Scotland 2003– (exec memb 1994); *Books* Rock and Ice Climbs in Skye (SMT); part author: Cold Climbs, Classic Rock, Wild Walks and many magazine articles both in the climbing and explosives press; *Recreations* mountaineering, geology, art; *Clubs* Scottish Mountaineering, Army and Navy, Pratt's; *Style*— The Rt Hon the Earl of Cromartie; ✉ Castle Leod, Strathpeffer, Ross-shire IV14 9AA

CROMBIE, Prof Alexander Leaster; s of Richard Crombie (d 1987), and Annie Drummond (d 1983); *b* 7 August 1935; *Educ* Cork GS, Galashiels Acad, Univ of Edinburgh (MB ChB); *m* 1, 26 Aug 1961, Margaret Ann (d 2000), da of David Alexander Adamson (d 1981); 2 s (Richard David, David Alexander), 2 da (Pauline Ann, Louise Margaret); m 2, 12 June 2003, Ann, da of Abraham Feldstein (d 1959); *Career* clinical tutor in ophthalmology Univ of Edinburgh 1964–67, MRC fell Johns Hopkins Univ Baltimore 1965–66, conslt ophthalmologist Royal Victoria Infirmary Newcastle upon Tyne 1967–95; Univ of Newcastle upon Tyne: prof of ophthalmology 1976–95, assoc dean Med Sch 1981–89, dean of med 1989–95 (now emeritus); author of chapters in books on ophthalmology, medical ethics and medical education; former vice-pres Coll of Ophthalmologists, former pres Age Concern Newcastle, tstee Northumbria Calvert Tst; FRCSEd 1964, Hon FRCOphth 1994 (FRCOphth 1989); *Recreations* golf, reading, music, art, walking; *Clubs* East India, Northern Counties (Newcastle upon Tyne); *Style*— Prof Alexander Crombie; ✉ 19 Graham Park Road, Gosforth, Newcastle upon Tyne (tel 0191 285 2378)

CROMER, 4 Earl of (UK 1901); Evelyn Rowland Esmond Baring; also Baron Cromer (UK 1892), Viscount Cromer (UK 1899), and Viscount Errington (UK 1901); s of 3 Earl of Cromer, KG, GCMG, MBE, PC (d 1991), and Hon Esme Mary Gabrielle Harmsworth, CVO, da of 2 Viscount Rothermere; *b* 3 June 1946; *Educ* Eton; *m* 1, 1971 (m dis 1992), Plern Isarankura na Ayudhya; m 2, 1993, Shelley Hu, da of Hu Guo-qin; 1 s (Alexander Rowland Hamsworth, Viscount Errington b 5 Jan 1994), 1 da (Lady Venetia Esme Mei b 22 Feb 1998); *Heir* s, Viscount Errington; *Career* md: Inchcape China Ltd 1979–94, Inchcape Vietnam Ltd 1987–94, Inchcape Special Markets Ltd 1990–94; chm: LGSC China Fund Ltd (Hong Kong), Phillipine Discovery Investments Co Ltd, Jardine Fleming China Region Fund Inc (USA), Korea Asia Fund Ltd 1995–2001; dep chm: Land-Ocean Inchcape Int Container Transport Co Ltd (China) 1985–94, Motor Transport Co of Guangdong & Hong Kong Ltd (China) 1979–94; dir: Inchcape Pacific Ltd 1985–94, Schroder AsiaPacific Fund plc 1995–, Somerset TEC 1996–2001, Western Provident Assoc 2004–, Pacific Basin Shipping 2004–, Cluff Oil China Ltd (Hong Kong); chm Business Link Somerset 1997–; memb St John's Cncl (Hong Kong) 1980–85; *Recreations* mountain climbing, deep sea diving; *Clubs* White's, Oriental, Hong Kong (Hong Kong); *Style*— The Rt Hon the Earl of Cromer; ✉ 6 Sloane Terrace Mansions, London SW1X 9DG

CROMIE, Stephen John Henry; s of Dr Brian William Cromie, of Kings Cliffe, Northants, and Heather Anne Howie, *née* Wood; *b* 13 January 1957; *Educ* Abingdon Sch, Downing Coll Cambridge (MA); *m* 28 Aug 1982, Marianne Frances, da of John Edward Burton, East Ewell, Surrey; 1 s (Jonathan b 1989), 1 da (Charlotte b 1996); *Career* admitted slr 1981; ptnr Linklaters 1987–2001 (joined 1979), judicial asst to Royal Courts of Justice 2001–06, Treasy Slrs Dept 2006–; FCIArb; *Books* International Commercial Litigation (jtly, 1990, 2 edn 1997), Merger Control in Europe (1991); *Recreations* wine, cooking, cycling; *Style*— S J H Cromie, Esq; ✉ 21 Regents Park Terrace, London NW1 7ED (tel 020 7485 5328)

CROMPTON, Prof David William Thomasson; OBE (1999); s of Arthur Thomasson Crompton (d 1995), of Bolton, Lancs, and Gladys, *née* Mather (d 2003); *b* 5 December 1937; *Educ* Bolton Sch, Univ of Cambridge (MA, PhD, ScD); *m* 14 April 1962, Effie Mary, da of Robert Marshall (d 1989), Lancs; 1 s (John b 1963), 2 da (Tessa b 1964, Virginia b 1967); *Career* Nat Serv 2 Lt King's Own Royal Regt 1956–58; lectr Univ of Cambridge 1968–85 (asst in res 1963–68), vice-master Sidney Sussex Coll 1981–83 (res fell 1964–65, fell 1965–85), adjunct prof Div of Nutritional Sciences Cornell Univ NY 1981–; Univ of Glasgow: John Graham Kerr prof of zoology 1985–2000, vice-dean of science 1993–95; Scientific medal The Zoological Soc of London 1977; fndr memb Br Soc for Parasitology 1962, co ed Parasitology 1972–82; memb: Aquatic Life Sciences Ctee NERC 1981–84, WHO Expert Ctee for Parasitic Diseases 1985–; chm Co of Biologists Ltd 1994–2000, head of WHO Collaborating Centre for Soil-transmitted Helminthiases at Univ of Glasgow 1989–2004, md St Andrew's Clinics for Children 1992–; hon memb: The Slovak Parasitology Soc 1999, American Soc of Parasitologists 2001, The Helminthological Soc of Washington 2002; hon fell Univ of Glasgow 2005; fell Royal Soc of Tropical Med and Hygiene 1986–2000, FIBiol 1979, FZS 1980–2001, FRSE 1989; *Books* An Ecological Approach to Acanthocephalan Physiology (1970), Parasitic Worms (jtly, 1980), Parasites and People (1984), Biology of the Acanthocephala (jt ed), Ascariasis and its Public Health Significance (jt ed, 1985), Ascariasis and its Prevention and Control (jt ed, 1989), A Guide to Human Helminths (jtly, 1991), Helminth Control in School-Age Children (jtly, 2002), Controlling Disease due to Helminth Infections (jt ed, 2003), Handbook of Helminthiasis for Public Health (jtly); *Recreations* walking, books, dogs; *Style*— Prof D W T Crompton, OBE, FRSE; ✉ Melrose Cottage, Tyndrum, Perthshire FK20 8SA; Institute of Biomedical and Life Sciences, University of Glasgow, Glasgow G12 8QQ (e-mail dwtc@tyndrum.demon.co.uk)

CROMPTON, Sarah Melanie; da of Donald Walker Crompton (d 1982), and Mary, *née* Barnes; *b* 30 August 1957; *Educ* Headington Sch Oxford, Hertford Coll Oxford (BA), UC Cardiff (Dip Journalism); *m* 1995, Icaro Kosak; 1 s (Augusto b 1997); *Career* features writer Coventry Evening Telegraph 1983–85 (reporter 1980–83), dep features ed Woman Oct 1986– April 1987 (researcher and features writer 1985–86), asst ed Woman's Own 1989–90 (features ed April 1987–89), asst ed Telegraph Magazine 1990–94, arts ed The Daily Telegraph 1994–; *Recreations* watching Manchester United and other forms of armchair sport; *Style*— Ms Sarah M Crompton; ✉ The Daily Telegraph, 1 Canada Square, Canary Wharf, London E14 5DT (tel 020 7538 5000)

CROMWELL, 7 Baron (E 1375); Godfrey John Bewicke-Copley; s of 6 Baron Cromwell (d 1982; Barony abeyant 1497 to 1923, when abeyance terminated in favour of present Baron's gf, 5 Baron); *b* 4 March 1960; *m* 23 June 1990, Elizabeth A, da of John Hawksley; 1 da (Hon Helen Tatiana b 18 March 1995), 3 s (Hon David Godfrey b 21 Sept 1997, John William, Ralph Thomas (twins) b 14 Nov 2000); *Heir* s, Hon David Bewicke-Copley; *Career* dir: Britain-Russia Centre 2000–, British East-West Centre 2000–, Russo-British C of C 2004–, British-Georgian C of C 2007–; *Style*— The Rt Hon the Lord Cromwell

CRONIN, Tacey Marguerite (Mrs David Bain); da of Flt Lt Anthony Arthur Cronin (d 1972), and Margaret Elizabeth, *née* Roberts (d 2003); *b* 28 June 1959; *Educ* Stamford HS, Bristol Univ (LLB); *m* 3 Jan 1987, David Ian Bain, s of Capt David Walter Bain (d 1972); 3 da (Athene Margaret b 1990, Esmé Rose b 1993, Cecily Mary b 1996); *Career* called to the Bar Middle Temple 1982; dep dist judge 2005; mediator; memb: Bar Cncl 1985–86, Gen Cncl of the Bar 1987; dir BMIF 1988–2002; govr Westbury Park Primary Sch 1996–2004 (chm 2001–03); *Recreations* theatre, motor sport, travel, Scottish country dancing; *Style*— Miss Tacey Cronin; ✉ Albion Chambers, Broad Street, Bristol BS1 1DR (tel 0117 927 2144, fax 0117 926 2569)

CROOK, Anthony Derek Howell (Tony); s of Ernest Henry William Crook (d 1982), and Hilda Muriel, *née* Howell (d 1996); *b* 22 December 1944; *Educ* St Paul's, Univ of Bristol (BA), Univ of London (MPhil), Univ of Sheffield (PhD); *m* 1967, Jennifer Rose, *née* Miller; 2 da (Emily Jane b 1972, Hannah Louise b 1976); *Career* offr res branch GLC 1967–68; Dept of Town and Regional Planning Univ of Sheffield: lectr 1968–86, sr lectr 1986–95, reader 1990–94, personal chair 1994, head, prof 1994–; Univ of Sheffield: acting head Dept of Landscape, dep dean Faculty of Architectural Studies, pro-vice-chllr 1999–; chm Conf of Heads of Planning Schs 1969–99; adsvr to Institute of Planning; also lectr, res and advsr overseas incl Canada, China, Hong Kong and Malaysia; chair: ConneXions S Yorks 2001–, Sheffield Homes; memb Bd: S Yorks Housing Asoc 1973–, Nat Housing Fedn 1980–86; tstee Shelter; RTPI: memb Housing and Renewal Panel, memb Research Ctee; FRSA 1999, FRTPI 2001 (MRTPI 1977), AcSS 2004; *Publications* author of various books, res reports, refereed journal articles and published conference papers on housing policy; *Style*— Professor Tony Crook; ✉ University of Sheffield, Western Bank, Sheffield S10 2TN (tel 0114 222 6303, fax 0114 272 2199, e-mail a.crook@sheffield.ac.uk)

CROOK, Anthony Donald (Tony); s of Thomas Roland (d 1926), of Hoghton, Lancs, and Emily, *née* Allsup; *b* 16 February 1923; *Educ* Clifton, Sidney Sussex Coll Cambridge; *m* 28 June 1943, Dianne Ada, *née* Smith; 1 da (Carole Anne); *Career* RAF 1939–46 (twice mentioned in Dispatches), Flt Lt; formed racing car partnership with Raymond Mays of Lincoln 1945, won first motor race to be held in post war Britain 1946, formed own racing team 1946 and developed, raced and distributed Bristol cars made by Bristol Aeroplane Co (over 400 races incl Formula One Grand Prix, Formula 2 and sports cars with Bristol engines 1946–55), with late Sir George White bought Bristol Cars Ltd from Bristol Aeroplane Co 1960, sole owner, chm and md Bristol Cars Ltd 1973–; *Clubs* British Racing Drivers'; *Style*— Tony Crook, Esq; ✉ Bristol Cars Ltd, Head Office, 368–370 Kensington High Street, London W14 8NL

CROOK, Colin; s of Richard Crook (d 1970), and Ruth Crook (d 1971); *b* 1 June 1942; *Educ* Harris Coll Preston, Liverpool Poly; *m* 1965, Dorothy Jean, da of Alfred Edward Taylor, of Wallasey; 2 da; *Career* Motorola (USA) 1969–79, dir advanced systems gp ops MGR Microcomputers 1975–78; md: Zynar Holdings BV, BT Telecom Enterprises, Rank Precision Industries 1978–80; chm: HBS Ltd (UK) 1980–83, Nestar Systems (USA) 1980–83; memb Main Bd BT 1983–1984, sr vice-pres Data General Corpn 1984–89, chm Corp Technol Ctee Citicorp NY USA 1990–97; sr fell Wharton Sch; currently ind conslt and researcher; FREng 1981, MIEE, MIERE, MIEEE, MACM (USA); *Publications* Power of Impossible Thinking; *Recreations* digital photography, books, science, wine, walking, travel, gardening; *Style*— Colin Crook, Esq, FREng; ✉ Penberen House, Seifton, Shropshire SY7 9BY (e-mail colin_crook@msn.com)

CROOK, Frances Rachel; da of Maurice Crook (d 1977), of London, and Sheila Sibson-Turnbull (d 1999); *b* 18 December 1952; *Educ* Camden Sch London, Univ of Liverpool (BA), Lancaster Univ (PGCE); 1 da (Sarah Rose Eleanor b 27 May 1988); *Career* campaign organiser Amnesty Int 1980–85, dir Howard League for Penal Reform 1986–; memb Bd Sch Food Tst 2005–; cncllr Barnet Borough 1982–90, govr Greenwich Univ (chair Staff and General Ctee) 1996–2002; Freedom City of London 1997; *Style*— Ms Frances Crook; ✉ The Howard League, 1 Ardleigh Road, London N1 4HS (tel 020 7249 7373)

CROOK, Prof Joseph Mordaunt; CBE (2003); s of Austin Mordaunt Crook (d 1967), and Florence Irene, *née* Woolfenden (d 1986); *b* 27 February 1937; *Educ* Wimbledon Coll, BNC Oxford (MA, DPhil); *m* 1, 4 July 1964, Margaret Constance, da of James Mulholland (d 1974); m 2, 9 July 1975, Susan Mayor, *qv*, da of Frederick Hoyland Mayor (d 1972); *Career* lectr Bedford Coll London 1965–75, res fell Warburg Inst 1970–71, reader in architectural history Univ of London 1975–81, Slade prof of fine art Univ of Oxford 1979–80, visiting fell BNC Oxford 1979–80, prof of architectural history Univ of London 1981–99 (now prof emeritus), visiting fell and Waynflete lectr Magdalen Coll Oxford 1985, visiting fell Gonville & Caius Coll Cambridge 1986, public orator Univ of London 1988–91; supernumerary fell BNC Oxford 2002–; memb Historic Bldgs Cncl for Eng 1974–84, pres Soc of Architectural Historians (GB) 1980–84, memb Advsy Bd for Redundant Churches 1991–99, vice-chm Fabric Cmmn Westmister Abbey 2002– (memb 1998–); Freeman Worshipful Co of Goldsmiths 1978 (Liveryman 1984); Hon DLit Univ of London; FBA, FSA; *Books* The British Museum (1972), The Greek Revival (1972 and 1995), The History of The King's Works (1973–76), William Burges and the High Victorian Dream (1981), The Dilemma of Style: Architectural Ideas from the Picturesque to the Post-Modern (1987), John Carter and the Mind of the Gothic Revival (1995), The Rise of the Nouveaux Riches: Style and Status in Victorian and Edwardian Architecture (1999), The Architect's Secret: Victorian Critics and the Image of Gravity (2003); *Recreations* strolling; *Clubs* Athenaeum, Brooks's; *Style*— Prof J Mordaunt Crook, CBE, FBA, FSA; ✉ 55 Gloucester Avenue, London NW1 7BA; West Wing, Maristow, Devon PL6 7BZ

CROOK, Paul; s of William Giles Crook, of Poole, Dorset, and Helen Margaret, *née* Swales; *b* 6 March 1952; *Educ* Ruzawi Sch Zimbabwe, Peterhouse Sch Zimbabwe, Jesus Coll Cambridge (MA, LLM); *m* 11 Sept 1976, Dr Susan Jill, da of Dr Andrew Ernest Dossetor, of Newmarket, Suffolk; 1 da (Anne b 1986), 2 s (John b 1988, Peter b 1990); *Career* admitted slr 1978, admitted Paris Bar 1994; Allen & Overy: ptnr 1984–2003, Global Head of Corp Know-How and Training 2003–; Freeman City of London Slrs Co 1984; memb Law Soc; *Recreations* golf, hockey, skiing, squash, tennis; *Style*— Paul Crook, Esq; ✉ Allen & Overy, One Bishops Square, London E1 6AO (tel 020 3088 0000, fax 020 3088 0088)

CROOK, 3 Baron (UK 1947), of Carshalton, Co Surrey; Robert Douglas Edwin Crook; s of 2 Baron Crook (d 2001), and Ellenor, *née* Rouse (d 1998); *b* 29 May 1955; *m* 29 May 1981, Suzanne Jane, da of Harold Robinson, of Farnsfield, Notts; 2 s (Hon Matthew Robert b 28 May 1990, Hon James Nicholas b 16 June 1992); *Heir* s, Hon Matthew Crook; *Style*— The Rt Hon the Lord Crook

CROOKALL, Prof John Roland; s of Dr Robert Crookall, DSc, PhD (d 1981), and Gladys Kate, *née* Stoneham (d 1969); *b* 5 May 1935; *Educ* Dorking County GS, Willesden Coll of Technol (HNC), Imperial Coll (DIC), Univ of Nottingham (PhD); *m* 19 June 1965, Gretta Mary, da of Basil Blaxley Inger; 2 s (Barry Nicholas b 5 Oct 1966, Andrew Spencer b 1 Oct 1967), 1 da (Sheila Elizabeth Anne b 8 May 1972); *Career* performance and design engr aero-engines de Havilland Engine Co Ltd 1957–61 (engrg apprentice 1952–57), visiting lectr Willesden Coll of Technol 1958–62, PhD res Univ of Nottingham 1962–65, lectr and course mangr MSc course in prodn technol Imperial Coll London 1965–74; Cranfield Univ: prof of mfrg systems 1974–90 (emeritus prof of mfrg 1990), head Dept for Design of Machine Systems 1982–84, fndr and chm Computer Integrated Manufacturing Inst 1985–90; fndr and head Coll of Manufacturing Cranfield 1985–90; chm Bd CIM Technology Ltd 1985–90, chm CIRP (UK) Ltd 1988–91; int conslt in intellectual property and patents and int speaker on global mfrg 1990–; memb numerous ctees and professional bodies incl: Advsy Ctee on Sci and Technol 1988–92, Parly and Scientific Ctee 1985–91, Br Library Advsy Cncl 2000–; chm UK Bd Int Inst for Prodn Engrg Res (CIRP) 1988–91, pres Gp on Electrical and Physical Processes CIRP 1979–83 and 1989–92, pres Int Symposium on Electromachining 1980–86, memb and UK rep Int Fedn of Info Processing (IFIP); external examiner to 11 prodn and mechanical engrg courses within UK, external assessor Univ Grants Ctee Hong Kong 1991–; tstee Panasonic Tst 1995–; memb Royal Coll of Organists, dir of music Elstow Abbey Bedford and chm Friends of Elstow Abbey; sr memb American Soc of Mfrg Engrs, assoc Chartered Inst of Patent Agents; FREng 1990, FCGI, CEng, FIMechE, AMIoD, MAE; *Awards* Instn of Mechanical Engrs: James Clayton fellowship 1962, James Clayton prize 1965, E Midlands Branch prize 1965; meritorious commendation Indust Year Awards DTI 1986, LEAD award SME (USA) 1991; *Books* Numerically Controlled Machine Tools (1970); author of over 100 papers on mfrg; *Recreations* music; *Style*— Prof John R Crookall, FREng; ✉ 12 Hall Close, Harrold, Bedford MK43 7DU (tel 01234 720475, fax 01234 720675)

CROOKENDEN, Simon Robert; QC (1996); s of late Maj Spencer Crookenden, CBE, MC, of Kendal, Cumbria, and late Jean, *née* Dewing; *b* 27 September 1946; *Educ* Winchester, Corpus Christi Coll Cambridge (MA); *m* 20 Aug 1983, Sarah Anne Georgina Margaret, da of late George Leonard Pragnell; 2 da (Rebecca Jean b 9 Nov 1985, Alice Lily b 5 Aug 1991), 1 s (Thomas Henry b 19 Sept 1987); *Career* called to the Bar Gray's Inn 1974; *Recreations* rowing; *Clubs* London Rowing; *Style*— Simon Crookenden, Esq, QC; ✉ Essex Court Chambers, 24 Lincoln's Inn Fields, London WC2A 3EG (tel 020 7813 8000, fax 020 7813 8080)

CROOKS, Stanley George; s of Wallace George Crooks (d 1978), and Alice Mary, *née* Clancy (d 1989); *b* 3 March 1925; *Educ* St Marylebone GS London, Univ of London (BSc, BSc Econ); *m* 22 July 1950, Gwendoline May, da of Arthur George Hatch; 1 s (Andrew b 1959), 1 da (Julia b 1961); *Career* Royal Artillery 1943–47 (service Burma 1944–45, Indochina 1945, Malaya 1946, Hong Kong 1947); Pirelli Group of Companies 1950–97; md Pirelli General Ltd Southampton 1967–71 (joined 1950), gen mangr Société Internationale Pirelli Basle 1974–82 (dep gen mangr 1971–74), dir and gen mangr Pirelli Société Générale Basle 1982–87; chm: Pirelli Construction Co Ltd 1982–91, Pirelli Ltd 1987–91, Pirelli Focom Ltd 1987–91, Pirelli Tyres UK 1991–92; vice-chm: Pirelli UK plc 1989–97, Pirelli General plc 1994–97 (chm 1987–94); chm: Southampton Innovations Ltd 1996–99, Photonic Innovations Ltd 1998–99; pres Southern Sci and Technol Forum 1977–93, chm CBI Educn Policy Panel 1995–97; vice-chm Cncl Univ of Southampton 1987–96, chm of govrs Southampton Inst of Higher Educn 1988–90, chm Univ of Southampton Mgmnt Sch 1990–92; chm Advsy Bd Thorneycroft Meml Fund 1999–; dir Winchester Housing Tst Ltd 1995–; Hon DSc Univ of Southampton 1977; FIEE 1965, CCMI (CIMgt 1970); *Books* Twyford - Ringing the Changes (1999), Twyford - 20th Century Chronicles (2000), Alfred Waterhouse in Twyford (2003), Peter Thorneycroft (2007); *Recreations* gardening, music, reading; *Style*— Stanley Crooks, Esq; ✉ Bournewood House, Bourne Lane, Twyford, Winchester, Hampshire SO21 1NX

CROOKSTON, Peter Christian; s of Robert Crookston (d 1969), and Nancy Hedley (d 2004); *b* 30 December 1936; *Educ* Clegwell Secdy Modern Sch Hebburn-on-Tyne, Newcastle upon Tyne Coll of Commerce; *m* 1 (m dis 1974), Julia Hampton; 1 s (James b 21 Feb 1970); m 2, 31 March 1988, Zoe Zenghelis, da of John Tsakiris (d 1985), and Anastasia Gabriel (d 1994), of Athens, Greece; *Career* trainee journalist Newcastle Journal and Evening Chronicle, sub ed Daily Express 1959–61, picture ed The Observer 1961–64, asst ed/dep ed Sunday Times Magazine 1964–69, ed Nova magazine 1969–71; features ed: Sunday Times 1971–73, The Observer 1973–77; ed: The Observer Magazine 1977–82, Geo International 1988–90; dep ed Departures 1990–91, ed WORLD Magazine 1991–93, contributing ed Telegraph Magazine 1993–94, ed English Heritage Magazine 1994–99, travel ed Sainsbury's The Magazine 1999–2001, conslt ed The Queen's Golden Jubilee Official Souvenir Programme 2002; freelance contrib The Observer, The Guardian, Condé Nast Traveller, Saga Magazine and The Independent 2001–; *Books* Villain (1967), Village London (ed, 1978), Village England (ed, 1979), Island Britain (ed, 1981), The Ages of Britain (ed, 1982); *Recreations* sailing, cycling, singing; *Clubs* Chelsea Arts, Itchenor Sailing; *Style*— Peter Crookston, Esq; ✉ 84 Portland Road, London W11 4LQ (fax 020 7243 4280)

CROPPER, James Anthony; s of Anthony Charles Cropper (d 1967), of Tolson Hall, Kendal, and Philippa Mary Gloria, *née* Clutterbuck; *b* 22 December 1938; *Educ* Eton, Magdalene Coll Cambridge (BA); *m* 30 June 1967, Susan Rosemary, da of Col F J N Davis (d 1988), of Northwood, Middx; 2 s (Charles Michael Anthony b 1969, d 1974, Mark b 1974), 1 da (Sarah b 1972); *Career* dir: James Cropper plc papermakers 1966– (chm 1971–), East Lancs Paper Group plc 1982–84, NW Water Group plc 1989–90; pres Br Paper and Bd Industry Fedn 1987–89; dir Cumbria Rural Enterprise Agency 1987–, chm govrs of Abbot Hall Art Gallery and Museum 1983–88; memb: S Westmorland RDC 1967–74, Lancs River Authy 1968–74, NW Water Authy 1973–80 and 1987–89, S Lakeland Dist Cncl 1974–77; High Sheriff Westmorland 1971, HM Lord-Lt Cumbria 1994– (Vice Lord-Lt 1991, DL 1986); Liveryman Worshipful Co of Stationers & Newspaper Makers; FCA; KStJ 1997; *Recreations* shooting, skiing, golf; *Clubs* Brooks's; *Style*— James Cropper, Esq; ✉ Tolson Hall, Kendal, Cumbria (tel 01539 722011); James Cropper plc, Burneside Mills, Kendal, Cumbria (tel 01539 722002)

CROPPER, Peter John; s of Samuel Duncan Cropper (d 1961), and Anna Southwell, *née* Parkinson (d 1990); *b* 7 February 1940; *Educ* Salford GS, Univ of Manchester, RAC Cirencester (Postgrad Dip Advanced Farm Mgmnt); *m* 16 Sept 1963, Hilary Mary (d 2004), da of Arnold Trueman, of Bollington, Cheshire; 2 da (Elizabeth b Dec 1969, Charlotte b Feb 1973), 1 s (Carl b Oct 1971); *Career* various tech and mgmnt appts AEI and English Electric 1960–68, software devpt mangr ICL 1968–75, gen mangr Computer Gp CWS Ltd 1975–80; md: STC IDEC Ltd 1980–85, STC Technology Ltd 1985–87; dir corporate info systems STC plc 1987–91, vice-pres info systems Northern Telecom Ltd (following merger with STC plc) 1991–97, chm Consarc Consulting Architects Ltd 1997–, dir Zephen Ltd 1997–, dir Zephen Properties Ltd 2003–; Freeman City of London 1988, Liveryman Worshipful Co of Scientific Instrument Makers, Past Master Worshipful Co of Information Technologists; CEng, FBCS, CITP; *Recreations* bridge, theatre; *Clubs* Naval and Military; *Style*— Peter Cropper, Esq; ✉ Zephen Ltd, Somerton Randle Farm, Somerton, Somerset TA11 7HW (tel 01458 274900, fax 01458 274901, e-mail peter@zephen.com)

CROSBIE, Annette; OBE (1998); *b* 12 February 1934; *Career* actress; *Theatre* Citizens Theatre Glasgow: View from a Bridge, The Crucible, Anne Frank, The Cherry Orchard, Guy Landscape (also Royal Court); Bristol Old Vic: Romeo and Juliet, The Tempest, A Taste of Honey, Caesar and Cleopatra; Comedy Theatre: Tinker, My Place, A Singular Man; other: Mr Bolfry (Aldwych), The Changeling (Royal Court), Twelfth Night (City of London Festival and tour), The Winslow Boy (New Theatre), The Family Dance (Criterion), Curse of the Starving Class (Royal Court), Corn is Green (Yvonne Arnaud Theatre Guildford), The Undertaking (Greenwich and Fortune), Tiger at the Gate (NT), Forty Years On (Chichester), Tramway Road (Lyric), Talk of the Devil (Palace Theatre Watford), Collier's Friday Night (Greenwich), Curtains (Whitehall), The Way South (Bush), I Thought I Heard A Rustling (Stratford Theatre Royal), Karate Billy Comes Home (Theatre Upstairs Royal Court); *Television* BBC: Catherine of Aragon in The Six Wives of Henry VIII (BAFTA Best Actress 1970), The Seagull, East Lynne, Auntie's Niece, Waste, Twelfth Night, Langrish Go Down, Find Me First, Henrick Ibsen, Of Mycenae and Men, Tolstoy, The Misanthrope, Jessie, Richard III, Pericles, Nobody's Property, Paying Guests, Watch With Mother, Take Me Home, Beyond the Pale, Summers Lease, Colin's Sandwich, One Foot in the Grave (2 series), Jute City; other: Queen Victoria and Edward VII (ATV, BAFTA and TV Times Best Actress 1975), The Portrait (LWT), Lilly Langtry (LWT), The House on the Hill (STV), Lowry - A Private View (Granada), Sunday Night Thriller (LWT), Charles Dilk Trilogy (Granada), Northern Lights (STV), The Pyramid Game (LWT), Off Peak (STV), Que Sera (TVS), Paradise Postponed (Euston Films), Taggart (STV), Game Set and Match (Granada), Bon Esperance (French TV), Heartbeat (Yorkshire), The Speaker of Mandarin (TVS), An Unsuitable Job for a Woman, Oliver Twist, Anchor Me; *Films* The Slipper and the Rose (Best Actress Evening News Drama Awards 1976), Hawk the Slayer, The Disappearance of Harry, Ordeal By Innocence, Final Warning, The Pope Must Die, The Debt Collector, Calendar Girls; *Style*— Ms Annette Crosbie, OBE

CROSBIE, Neil; s of James Steele Crosbie (d 1973), and Doreen, *née* Bell; *b* 28 January 1953; *Educ* Royal GS Newcastle upon Tyne, Aston Univ (BSc); *m* 2 Aug 1975, Christine Mary, da of John Fletcher Tully; 1 da (Ciaran b 9 March 1979), 2 s (Andrew b 1 Dec 1980, Iain b 9 May 1983); *Career* Forward Trust (Finance) Ltd 1973–74, Universities and Colleges Christian Fellowship 1975–79; British & Foreign Bible Soc 1979–2001, gen sec United Bible Socs 2002–04, chief exec SGM Lifewords 2004–; memb ACEVO 1993; MIMgt 1985; *Recreations* reading, walking, sleeping; *Style*— Neil Crosbie, Esq

CROSBY, Sir James Robert; kt (2006); s of John Philip Crosby (d 1991), and Ruth, *née* Harrison; *b* 14 March 1956, Leeds; *Educ* Lancaster Royal GS, BNC Oxford (scholar); *m* 17 June 1988, Una, *née* McLaughlin; 4 da (Kate b 7 Dec 1990, Harriet b 17 Nov 1992, Louise b 27 May 1994, Imogen b 28 May 1998); *Career* Scottish Amicable 1977–94 (fund mangr until 1987, then sr positions in IT, mktg and finance), joined Halifax for launch of bancassurance business 1994, memb Bd Halifax plc 1996, chief exec Halifax plc 1999–2001, chief exec HBOS plc (following merger) 2001–06; non-exec dir: St James's Place Capital 2000–06 (fndr dir predecessor co J Rothschild Assurance 1991), ITV plc (formerly Granada) 2002–, FSA 2004–, Compass Gp plc 2007–; memb: European Advsy Bd Bridgepoint Capital 2006–, Delegacy Finance Ctee Oxford Univ Press 2006–; chm Govt's Public-Private Forum on Identity Mgmnt 2006–; FFA 1980; *Recreations* sport, fitness training; *Style*— Sir James Crosby

CROSBY, John Rutherford; s of John Charles Crosby (d 1938), of Colchester, and Florence Nightingale, *née* Rutherford (d 1982); *b* 1 May 1933; *Educ* Univ of Durham (BA), Univ of London (MA), UC Cardiff (Dip Personnel Mgmnt); *m* 10 March 1962, Rosalind Elizabeth, da of Gilbert Baynon Williams (d 1968); 1 da (Sarah (Mrs Perrin) b 1963), 2 s (Neil b 1966, David b 1968); *Career* personnel mgmnt appts with EMI and Costain Group 1958–68, sr consit Hay MSL 1968–76, personnel dir British American Tobacco Co 1983–88 (head of personnel servs 1976–83), dir of gp personnel BAT Industries 1988–92; IPM (now CIPD): vice-pres 1979–81, pres 1985–87, chm IPM servs 1985–87, chm IPM Advsy Ctee on Nominations 1987–89; memb: Cncl VSO 1983–92, Business Liaison Ctee London Business Sch 1984–90, Civil Serv Final Selection Bd 1984–2000, NEDO Steering Gp on Human Resource Devpt 1986–87, Employment Appeal Tbnl 1991–2004, Jt Steering Gp Social Servs Inspectorate 1993–98, Armed Forces Pay Review Body 1993–99, Civil Serv Arbitration Panel 1993–; memb Bd: Ind Assessment and Research Centre 1988–, Legal Aid Bd 1994–97; ind assessor NHS 1996–; memb Cncl Farnham Castle 2002–06 (govr tstee 1983–2002), govr Croydon Coll 1987– (vice-chm 1989–93, chm 1993–97, immediate past chm 1997–2001), tstee Overseas Students Tst 1988–93; govr Univ of Westminster 1994–2003 (chm Personnel Ctee 1995–2003); memb Ct Univ of Sussex 2000– (memb Cncl 1995–2000), memb Ct City Univ 2007–; memb Ctee BAT Pensioners Assoc 2005– (chm 1998–2005); Freeman City of London, Freeman of Colchester, Liveryman Guild of Tobacco Pipe Makers and Tobacco Blenders; DLitt (hc) Univ of Westminster 2003; CCIPM 1980, CIMgt 1983, FCInstD 1984, FRSA 2001; *Books* Handbook of Management Development (contrib, 1986 and 1991); *Recreations* music (particularly opera), theatre, avoiding all gardening; *Clubs* Oriental, IOD; *Style*— John Crosby, Esq; ✉ 70 Woodcote Valley Road, Purley, Surrey CR8 3BD (tel 020 8660 2717, fax 020 8763 9324)

CROSET, Paul John Francis; OBE (1967); s of Louis Paul Croset (d 1982), and May Eveline, *née* Garrett (d 1989); *b* 15 March 1919; *Educ* Rishworth Sch, Stamford Sch; *m* 1, 26 Aug 1944 (m dis 1985), (Margaret) Vivien, da of William Suckling, of Radlett, Herts; 3 da (Jacqueline b 1946, Jane b 1948, Louise b 1956); m 2, 27 May 2005, Pamela Joanne Sykes, da of Jack Baxter (d 1967); 2 step da (Mandy (Mrs Whone), Kieran); *Career* served WWII Maj RE with BEF, BNAF, CMF; engr; chm and fndr Holset Engineering Co Ltd 1952–98, md BHD Engineers 1959–73, chm Readicut Int plc 1977–84 (dir 1969–89, dep chm 1984–89), local dir Barclay Bank plc Leeds 1977–84; dir: Cummins Engine Co Ltd 1981–84, Hepworth plc 1985–89; consit to Dept of Engrg Univ of Warwick 1989–92; underwriting memb Lloyd's 1968–97; Freeman City of London 1972, Liveryman Worshipful Co of Founders 1973; MSAE 1964, FRSA 1973, CIMgt 1980; *Recreations* fishing, shooting, horology; *Clubs* Army and Navy; *Style*— Paul Croset, Esq, OBE; ✉ 16 Thomas a Becket Walk, Hampsthwaite, North Yorkshire HG3 2FS

CROSFIELD, Lesley; da of William Chapman Sharp (d 1965), and Joan Mary, *née* Wiltshire; *b* 27 July 1950; *Educ* Tal Handaq Malta, Bell Baxter HS, Duncan of Jordanstone Coll of Art Dundee; *Partner* Colin Craig; *Career* ceramics and pottery art study: pottery sch Aarhus Denmark, Sir John Cass, Middx Poly 1970–77; ind travel 1977–80: 2–handed Atlantic crossing, one year spent in NY; hotelier Altskeith Hotel Trossachs 1980–87, organiser Altskeith Alefest 1983–86, co-chef and hotelier The Albannach 1990– (Michelin BIB Gourmand 1997, McAllan Award Overall Excellence 1998, McAllan Award Best Restaurant with Rooms 1998, Good Food Guide W Coast Newcomer of the Year 2000, Scotland the Best Award for Excellence 2000, Which? Hotel Guide Hotels of the Year category 2002, 2 AA Rosettes 2002, Scottish Hotel Bedroom of the Year Hotel Review Scotland 2007); *Books* Scotland on a Plate (2001); *Recreations* sailing, hill walking, the arts, food, wine, conversation; *Clubs* RYA; *Style—* Ms Lesley Crosfield; ✉ The Albannach, Lochinver, Sutherland IV27 4LP (tel 01571 844407, fax 01571 844285, e-mail the.albannach@virgin.net, website www.thealbannach.co.uk)

CROSLAND, Neisha; da of C R H Crosland, and Felicity, *née* d'Abreu; *b* 11 December 1960; *Educ* Convent of the Sacred Heart Woldingham, Hatfield Girls Grammar Herts, Camberwell Schs of Arts and Crafts (BA), RCA (MA); *m* Stephane Perche; 2 s (Oscar Maurice b 1996, Samuel Alphonso b 1999); *Career* freelance textile designer; pt/t external teaching appts at Glasgow Sch of Art, Winchester Sch of Art and Northbroke College 1988–94; designed Romagna collection for Osborne & Little 1988, designed Carnaval Collection (wallpapers and furnishing fabrics) Harlequin Wallcoverings Ltd 1990–94, contrib First Eleven portfolio 1991, fndr Neisha Crosland Scarves 1994, launched Neisha at Debenhams 1998, fndr Ginka ready-to-wear 1999, first wallpaper collection 1999, opened first retail outlet London 2000–01, stationery collection 2002, licensed collection for Hankyu Dept Stores Japan 2002, first home furnishings collection 2003, opened Neisha Crosland flagship store London 2003; exhibitions: Egg London, Jeffrye Museum London, work curated by V&A; collaborations: Charlotte Crosland 2004, Mario Testino's Diana Princess of Wales (Kensington Palace), Bill Amberg, V&A, The Rug Company, Veedon Fleece 2005; judge RSA Bursary Awards 2006 and 2007; MA external examiner RCA 2007; Design and Decoration award 2004, Elle Decoration award 2005; nominated: Peugeot design award 2000, Homes & Gardens award 2000; RDI 2007; *Clubs* Chelsea Arts; *Style—* Miss Neisha Crosland; ✉ Unit 40, Battersea Business Centre, 99 Lavender Hill, London SW11 5QL (tel 020 7978 4389, fax 020 7924 2873, e-mail info@neishacrosland.com, website www.neishacrosland.com)

CROSS, Andrew John; s of Colin Cross, and Mary, *née* McMurray; *Educ* St George's Sch Mayfair, Riverside Sch; *Career* RN 1979–84; prison offr: HMP Feltham 1985–87, HMP The Verne 1987–91; princ offr and govr HMP (level 5) Long Lartin 1991–93, govr (level 4) HMP The Mount 1994–97, dep govr HMP and YOI Bullwood Hall 1997–2000, govr HMP Bedford 2000–05, govr Feltham YOI 2005–; *Style—* Andrew Cross, Esq

CROSS, Prof Anthony Glenn; s of Walter Sidney Cross (d 1941), and Ada, *née* Lawson (d 2004); *b* 21 October 1936; *Educ* High Pavement Sch Nottingham, Trinity Hall Cambridge (Wootton Isaacson scholar, MA, PhD) Harvard Univ (AM), UEA (DLitt), Fitzwilliam Coll Cambridge (LittD); *m* 11 Aug 1960, Margaret, da of Eric Arthur Elson (d 1986); 2 da (Jane b 1964, Serena b 1967); *Career* Nat Serv 1955–57; Frank Knox meml fell Harvard Univ 1960–61, reader UEA 1972–81 (lectr 1964–69, sr lectr 1969–72); visiting fell: Centre for Advanced Study Univ of Illinois 1968–69, All Souls Coll Oxford 1977–78; dir Norwich Summer Russian Course 1969–81; Roberts prof of Russian Univ of Leeds 1981–85; Univ of Cambridge: prof of Slavonic studies 1985–2004, fell Fitzwilliam Coll 1986–2004; chm Br Academic Ctee for Liaison with Russian Archives 1981–95, memb Br Univs Assoc of Slavists (pres 1982–84), chm Academia Rossica 2001–05; gen ed: Russia through European Eyes 1968–75, Anglo-Russian Affinities 1989–95; reviews ed Jl of European Studies 1971–, ed Study Gp on Eighteenth-Century Russian Newsletter 1973–; Alec Nove Prize in Russia Studies 1997, Antsiferov Prize St Petersburg 1997, Dashkova Medal Moscow 2003; fell Russian Acad for the Humanities 1996; FBA 1989; *Books* N M Karamzin (1971), Russia Under Western Eyes (ed, 1971), Russian Literature in the Age of Catherine the Great (ed, 1976), Anglo-Russian Relations in the Eighteenth Century (1977), By the Banks of The Thames - Russians in Eighteenth Century Britain (1980), The 1780s: Russia under Western Eyes (1981), The Tale of the Russian Daughter and Her Suffocated Lover (1982), Eighteenth Century Russian Literature, Culture and Thought: A Bibliography of English-Language Scholarship and Translations (jtly, 1984), The Russian Theme in English Literature (1985), Russia and the World of the Eighteenth Century (ed jtly, 1986), An English Lady at the Court of Catherine the Great (ed, 1989), Anglophilia on the Throne - The British and Russians in the Age of Catherine the Great (1992), Anglo-Russica - Selected Essays on Anglo-Russian Cultural Relations (1993), Engraved in the Memory - James Walker and his Russian Anecdotes (ed, 1993), Literature, Lives and Legality in Catherine's Russia (jt ed, 1994), By the Banks of the Neva: Chapters from the Lives and Careers of the British in Eighteenth-Century Russia (1996), Russia in the Reign of Peter the Great: Old and New Perspectives (ed, 1998), Britain and Russia in the Age of Peter the Great: Historical Documents (jt ed, 1998), Peter the Great through British Eyes: Perceptions and Representations of the Tsar since 1698 (2000), Catherine the Great and the British: A Pot-Pourri of Essays (2001), St Petersburg, 1703–1825 (ed, 2003); *Recreations* food, travel, collecting books, watching cricket; *Style—* Prof Anthony Cross, FBA; ✉ Fitzwilliam College, Storey's Way, Cambridge CB3 0DG (tel 01223 332046, fax 01223 477976, e-mail agc28@cam.ac.uk)

CROSS, Prof (Margaret) Claire; da of Frederick Leonard Cross (d 1964), of Boston, Lincs, and Rebecca *née* Newton (d 1984), of Boston, Lincs; *b* 25 October 1932; *Educ* Wyggeston GS Leicester, Girton Coll Cambridge (BA, PhD); *Career* co archivist for Cambridgeshire 1958–61, int fell American Assoc of Univ Women 1961–62, subsequently res fell Univ of Reading, prof of history Univ of York (formerly lectr, sr lectr then reader, ret 2000); numerous pubns in jls; memb: Royal Historical Soc, Ecclesiastical History Soc, Historical Assoc; FRHistS; *Books* The Free Grammar School of Leicester (1953), The Puritan Earl - The Life of Henry Hastings (1966), The Royal Supremacy in the Elizabethan Church (1969), Church and People 1450–1660 - The Triumph of the Laity in the English Church (1976), York Clergy Wills 1520–1600 - 1: The Minister Clergy (1984), Urban Magistrates and Ministers - Religion in Hull and Leeds from the Reformation to the Civil War (1985), Law and Government under the Tudors - Essays Presented to Sir Geoffrey Elton on his Retirement (1988), York Clergy Wills 1520–1600 - 2: The City Clergy (1989), The End of Medieval Monasticism in the East Riding of Yorkshire (1993), Monks, Friars and Nuns in Sixteenth Century Yorkshire (ed with N Vickers, 1995), Patronage and Recruitment in the Tudor and Early Stuart Church (1996), Mass and Parish in Late Medieval England: The Use of York (ed with P S Barnwell and A Rycraft, 2005); *Recreations* gardening; *Style—* Prof Claire Cross; ✉ 17 Pear Tree Court, York YO1 7DF (tel 01904 654221); Centre of Medieval Studies, The King's Manor, University of York, York YO1 7EP (tel 01904 433961, e-mail mcc1@york.ac.uk)

CROSS, Emma-Jane; da of Bryan Cross (d 1981), and Susan, *née* Surridge; *b* 7 October 1967, Harlow, Essex; *Educ* BA, MPhil; *partner* Sarah Dyer; *Career* academic and researcher 1997–99, fndr and ceo beatbullying 1999– (Children's Charity of the Year 2005, UK Charity of the Year 2005 and 2006); dir: Socialpreneurial Ltd, Primary Contact Solution; *Style—* Ms Emma-Jane Cross; ✉ beatbullying, Rochester House, 67–69 Belvedere Road, London SE19 2HP (tel 020 8771 3888, e-mail emma-jane@beatbullying.org)

CROSS, Gillian Clare; da of James Eric Arnold (d 1988), and Joan Emma, *née* Manton; *b* 24 December 1945; *Educ* N London Collegiate Sch for Girls, Somerville Coll Oxford (MA), Univ of Sussex (DPhil); *m* 1967, Martin Cross; 2 s (Jonathan b 1967, Anthony b 1984), 2 da (Elizabeth b 1970, Katherine b 1985); *Career* children's author; memb Soc of Authors; *Books* The Runaway (1979), The Iron Way (1979), Revolt at Ratcliffe's Rags (1980), Save Our School (1981), A Whisper of Lace (1981), The Demon Headmaster (1982), The Dark Behind the Curtain (1982), The Mintyglo Kid (1983), Born of the Sun (1983), On the Edge (1984), The Prime Minister's Brain (1985), Swimathon (1986), Chartbreak (1986), Roscoe's Leap (1987), A Map of Nowhere (1988), Rescuing Gloria (1989), Wolf (1990, Carnegie medal Library Assoc), The Monster from Underground (1990), Twin and Super-Twin (1990), Gobbo the Great (1991), Rent-a-Genius (1991), The Great Elephant Chase (1992, winner first prize Smarties Awards, Whitbread children's book award), The Furry Maccaloo (1992), Beware Olga! (1993), The Tree House (1993), Hunky Parker is Watching You (1994), What Will Emily Do? (1994), New World (1994), The Crazy Shoe Shuffle (1995), Posh Watson (1995), The Roman Beanfeast (1996), The Demon Headmaster Strikes Again (1996), Pictures in the Dark (1996), The Demon Headmaster Takes Over (1997), The Goose Girl (1998), Tightrope (1999), Down With the Dirty Danes (2000), The Treasure in the Mud (2001), Calling a Dead Man (2001), Beware of the Demon Headmaster (2002), Facing the Demon Headmaster (2002), The Dark Ground (2004), The Black Room (2005), Sam Sorts it Out (2005), The Nightmare Game (2006), Brother Aelred's Feet (2007); *Recreations* orienteering, playing the piano; *Style—* Mrs Gillian Cross; ✉ c/o Oxford Children's Books, Oxford University Press, Great Clarendon Street, Oxford OX2 6DP

CROSS, Dr Neil Earl; s of Sidney Cross (d 1993), and Winifred, *née* Earl (d 1980); *b* 17 March 1945; *Educ* Drayton Manor Co GS, Univ of Exeter (BSc), Univ of Edinburgh (PhD); *m* 7 Oct 1972, Carol Christian Buchan, *née* Gillan; 1 s (Alastair b 1976), 1 da (Georgina b 1980); *Career* various positions with 3i Group plc 1969–96 (incl main int bd dir 1988–96); chm: BMT Gp Ltd, Close Technol & Gen VCT plc, European Venture Capital Assoc 1986–87; dir: Business in the Environment 1994–96, Babraham Inst 1995–2003, Taylor Nelson Sofres plc 1996–2005, Perkins Foods plc 1997–2001, Alliance Unichem plc 1997–2006, Dawson Holdings plc 1997–2007; non-exec dir: Bernard Matthews Holdings Ltd (dep chm), Bayard Fund, Caliburn Absolute Strategies spc; advsr: Unilever UK Pension Fund 1997–2006, Baring European Private Equity Fund, Fifth Causeway Development Capital Fund; vice-pres RSA 2003– (chm 2001–03); visiting prof Cranfield Business Sch 1992–93; memb Lottery Advsy Panel of the Arts Cncl of England 1996–99; tstee The Mary Kinross Charitable Tst; FCIS 1981 (ACIS 1972), FRSA 1992; *Recreations* walking, theatre, reading; *Clubs* Savile; *Style—* Dr Neil Cross; ✉ Sycamore House, Bluntisham, Cambridgeshire PE28 3LA

CROSS, Nicholas John; s of John Cross, CBE, of Ixworth, Suffolk, and Janet, *née* Devitt; *b* 13 August 1962; *Educ* Uppingham, Univ of Cambridge (BA); *m* Non, da of Rt Hon John Morris, QC, MP, *qv*; 2 s (Henry John Caradog, Llewelyn John Edmund (twins) b 14 June 1996); *Career* dir SRU Ltd mgmnt consultancy 1992–93 (joined 1984), int planning dir Bartle Bogle Hegarty Ltd advtg agency 1993–96, mktg dir (i/c advtg, direct mail catalogues and storecard ops) Selfridges Ltd dept store 1996–; memb Mgmnt Ctee Nat Youth Agency (formerly Nat Youth Bureau) 1988–93; *Recreations* shooting, sailing; *Clubs* Farmers'; *Style—* Nicholas Cross, Esq; ✉ 14 St Paul Street, London N1 7AB; Selfridges Ltd, 400 Oxford Street, London W1A 1AB (main tel 020 7629 1234, sec's tel 020 7318 3035)

CROSS, Philippa Jane (Pippa); da of Robert Lionel Cross (d 1977), and Jill Patricia Abbott, MBE, of Ipswich, Suffolk; *b* 13 May 1956; *Educ* Ipswich HS GPDST, St Anne's Coll Oxford; *m* 1982, Graham Ronald Lee; 1 da (Maisie Victoria Kelda b 2 May 1983), 1 s (Pierrot Robert Alexander b 6 Aug 1991); *Career* entertainments mangr Wembley Conf Centre 1977–80; Granada Television Manchester mangr 1980–85; mangr factual progs TVS Television Maidstone 1985–88; Granada Television London 1988– (prodn exec My Left Foot, prodn exec The Field), head of devpt feature films and films for TV 1990–, head of film 1993–2002 (prodr: Jack & Sarah, August, Seeing Red, The Hole, The Gathering, Gifted; exec prodr: Heart, The Misadventures of Margaret, Girl's Night, Rogue Trader, Essex Boys, Longitude, Ghostworld, Bloody Sunday), dir CrossDay Productions Ltd 2002– (prodr: Gifted, Shooting Dogs, Knife Edge); *Recreations* horse riding, cinema, theatre; *Style—* Ms Pippa Cross; ✉ e-mail pippacro@aol.com

CROSS, Stefan Tylney; s of Brian Cross, of Bournemouth, and Jackie, *née* Kirby; *b* 5 October 1960; *Educ* Univ of Southampton (LLB), Univ of Leicester (LLM); *m* 18 Jan 1986, Dr Alison Steele; 2 da (Anna b 22 Jan 1991, Rachael b 3 Feb 1993), 2 s (Michael b 31 July 1996, Daniel b 5 Sept 2004); *Career* slr; trainee slr G A Mooning Aldridge & Brownlee 1983–85, Thompsons Slrs 1986–2002 (equity ptnr 1990–2002), fndr Stefan Cross Solicitors 2002–; Wig and Pen Award Bournemouth and Dist Law Soc 1983, TSB Articled Clerks Award 1984 and 1985; cncllr (Lab) Newcastle CC 1990–98; memb Law Soc 1985; *Recreations* politics, football, trashy crime thrillers, indie rock music, travel; *Clubs* Newcastle United FC; *Style—* Stefan Cross, Esq; ✉ 23 Montagu Avenue, Newcastle upon Tyne NE3 4HY (tel 0191 285 6110); Stefan Cross Solicitors, Buddle House, Buddle Road, Newcastle NE4 8AW (tel 0191 226 6686, e-mail stc@stefancross.co.uk)

CROSS, Tom; *b* London; *Educ* Univ of Exeter (BSc); *m*; 3 c; *Career* early career as petroleum engr and economist with Conoco, Thomson and LL&E, research dir Petroleum Sci & Tech Inst, fndr and chief exec Dana Petroleum plc; currently non-exec chm AUPEC Ltd; currently chm Assoc of Br Ind Oil Cos (BRINDEX), former chm Soc of Petroleum Engrs, memb Governing Cncl UK Offshore Operators Assoc; advsr BBC Radio (on oil and gas affrs), editorial advsr Jl of Petroleum Technology, advsr Bd Trawlpac Seafoods (export and financing), currently co-dir Parkmead Gp plc; MEI, FInstD (chartered dir); *Recreations* outdoor sporting activities; *Style—* Tom Cross, Esq; ✉ Dana Petroleum plc, 17 Carden Place, Aberdeen AB10 1UR

CROSS, Dr Trevor Arthur; *b* 14 May 1960, Chelmsford, Essex; *Educ* BSc, PhD, Anglia Poly (Dip); 1 s; *Career* various roles rising to business unit mangr Space Solar Cell until 1999, business dir Communications Business Gp then business systems dir MTech (Marconi Applied Technologies) 1999–2001; e2v Gp: co-fndr and tech dir e2v technologies 2002 (following MBO of Marconi Applied Technologies), co listed on London Stock Exchange 2004, chief technol offr 2006–; memb Cncl PPARC 2005–; author of 30 tech papers and 4 patents; *Recreations* hill walking, travel, skiing, squash, theatre, cinema; *Style—* Dr Trevor Cross; ✉ e2v technologies Ltd, 106 Waterhouse Lane, Chelmsford, Essex CM1 2QU (tel 01245 453417)

CROSS BROWN, Tom; s of Christopher James Cross Brown (d 1998), and Georgina, *née* Forrester (d 1999); *b* 22 December 1947; *Educ* Uppingham, BNC Oxford (MA), INSEAD (MBA); *m* 1972, Susan Rosemary, da of Col Mansel Halkett Jackson (d 1967); 1 s (Nicol b 1975 d 1998), 3 da (Gemma b 1977, Amelia, Claire (twins) b 1982); *Career* md Lazard Brothers & Co Ltd 1994–97 (dir 1985), chief exec Lazard Brothers Asset Management Ltd 1994–97; ABN AMRO Asset Management Ltd: chm 1997–2003, global chief exec 2000–03; non-exec chm: ABN AMRO Trustees Ltd 2001–04, ABN AMRO GSTS Ltd 2004–06, Pearl Assurance plc 2005–, National Provident Life Ltd 2005–, NPI Ltd 2005–, London Life Ltd 2005–, Just Retirement (Holdings) plc 2006–; non-exec dir: Whitegate Leisure plc 1987–92, Artemis Investment Management Ltd 2002–06, Pearl Gp Ltd 2005–, Quintain Estates and Development plc 2005–06, PAT (Pensions) Ltd 2005–, Artemis Alpha Tst plc 2006–, Blue Bay Asset Management plc 2006–; tstee: Cancer Care and Haemotology Fund Stoke Mandeville Hosp 2004–, Lazard Brothers Directors Pension Scheme 2007–; hon sec The Benedict Soc 2005– (memb 2001–); chm Heathfield Sch 2005– (govr 2000–); *Style—* Tom Cross Brown, Esq; ✉ Shipton Old Farm, Winslow, Buckinghamshire MK18 3JL

CROSSAN, Denis Gerard; s of Denis Crossan (d 1995), and Mary, *née* McGinley; *Educ* St Mungo's Acad, Glasgow Sch of Art (BA), Nat Film Sch; *m* 1987, Gillian Louise, *née* Barclay; 1 s (Maxwell James b 1987), 2 da (Rachel Louise b 1990, Juliet Renée b 1997); *Career* cinematographer; dir of photography working on various music videos and commercials 1983–; memb BSC 1993; *Films* credits incl: The Real McCoy, I Know What You Did Last Summer, Clandestine Marriage (Newport Beach Film Festival Best Cinematography 2000), The Hole, Me Without You, Agent Cody Banks; *Awards* Best

Cinematography D&AD 1991, Creative Circle 1991, Clio Gold Award 1994; *Recreations* surfing; *Style*— Denis Crossan, Esq; ✉ c/o McKinney McCartney Management Ltd, 10 Barley Mow Passage, London W4 4PH (tel 020 8995 4747, fax 020 8995 2414); c/o Grant, Savic, Kopaloff & Associates, 6399 Wilshire Boulevard, Suite 414, Los Angeles, CA 90048 USA (tel 00 1 323 782 1854, fax 00 1 323 782 1877)

CROSSETT, Robert Nelson (Tom); s of Robert Crossett (d 1961), and Mary, *née* Nelson (d 1988); *b* 27 May 1938; *Educ* Campbell Coll Belfast, Queen's Univ Belfast (BSc, BAgric), Lincoln Coll Oxford (DPhil), UEA; *m*; 2 c; *Career* cmmnd pilot Gen Duties Branch RAFVR 1959; gp ldr Environmental Studies Aust Atomic Energy Cmmn Res Establishment Sydney 1966–69, sr sci offr ARC Letcombe Laboratory 1969–72, crop devpt offr Scot Agric Devpt Cncl 1972–75 (sec Crops Ctee), agric res advsr Sci Advsrs' Unit Dept of Agric and Fisheries Scot 1975–78; MAFF: sci liaison offr Horticulture and Soils 1978–84, head Food Sci Div 1984–85, chief scientist Fisheries and Food 1985–89; environment dir National Power 1989–91, gen sec Nat Soc for Clean Air and Environmental Protection 1992–96 (vice-pres 1997–); DG Int Union of Air Pollution Prevention and Environmental Protection Assoc (IUAPPA)1997–98; chm: Steering Gp on Food Surveillance 1985–89, Southern Regnl Environmental Protection Advsy Ctee of Environment Agency 1996–2002; dir: Environmental Research Gp SE Inst of Public Health 1998–2000; former chair Nat Flood Forum, currently chair Thames Flood Forum; memb: AFRC 1985–89, CMO's Ctee on Med Aspects of Food Policy 1985–89, NERC 1985–89, Supervisory Bd of the Laboratory of the Govt Chemist 1985–89, UK Govt Roundtable on Sustainable Devpt 1995–97, Advsy Gp to Sec of State for Environment (on environmental mgmnt and audit) 1994–96; visiting fell Science Policy Research Unit Univ of Sussex 1997–2002, sr visiting fell Sch of Health and Life Sciences KCL 1999–; *Publications* papers on plant physiology, marine biology and food science; *Recreations* walking, gardening, orienteering, boats; *Style*— Tom Crossett, Esq

CROSSICK, Prof Geoffrey Joel; s of Louis Crossick (d 1989), of London, and Rebecca Naomi, *née* Backen (d 2001); *b* 13 June 1946, London; *Educ* Haberdashers' Aske's, Gonville & Caius Coll Cambridge (open scholar, MA), Birkbeck Coll Univ of London, Univ of London (PhD); *m* 1973, Rita Vaudrey; 2 s (Matthew Samuel b 10 Feb 1978, Joshua b 7 Nov 1980); *Career* research fell Emmanuel Coll Cambridge 1970–73, lectr in economic and social history Univ of Hull 1973–78; Univ of Essex: lectr in history 1979–83, sr lectr then reader in history 1983–91, prof of history 1991–2002, pro-vice-chllr (academic devpt) 1997–2002; chief exec AHRB 2002–05, warden Goldsmiths Univ of London 2005–; memb: Advsy Cncl Br Library, Bd of Dirs London Higher, Business and Community Ctee HEFCE, Bd Universities UK, Bd UCEA, London Cultural Consortium; hon fell Emmanuel Coll Cambridge 2004; FRHistS 1986; *Books* The Lower Middle Class in Britain 1870–1914 (ed, 1976), An Artisan Elite in Victorian Society (1978), Shopkeepers and Master Artisans in Nineteenth-Century Europe (ed with H G Haupt, 1984), The Petite Bourgeoisie in Europe 1780–1914 (with H G Haupt, 1995), The Artisan and the European Town (ed, 1997), Cathedrals of Consumption: The Department Store in European Society 1850–1940 (ed, 1999); *Recreations* music, Tottenham Hotspur FC; *Style*— Prof Geoffrey Crossick; ✉ Goldsmiths, University of London, New Cross, London SE14 6NW (tel 020 7919 7901)

CROSSLAND, Prof Sir Bernard; kt (1990), CBE (1980); s of Reginald Francis Crossland (d 1976), and Kathleen Mary, *née* Rudduck (d 1950); *b* 20 October 1923; *Educ* Simon Langton GS Canterbury, Derby Regnl Tech Coll, UC Nottingham (BSc, MSc, PhD, DSc); *m* 25 July 1946, Audrey, da of Frank Elliott Birks (d 1961); 2 da (Jennifer b 1948, Mary Anne b 1952); *Career* tech asst Rolls Royce Ltd 1943–45 (apprentice 1940–44), lectr Luton Tech Coll 1945–46, sr lectr in mechanical engrg (formerly asst lectr and lectr) Univ of Bristol 1946–59; Queen's Univ of Belfast: prof and head Dept of Mechanical and Industrial Engrg 1959–84, dean Engrg Faculty 1964–67, pro-vice-chllr 1978–82, emeritus prof of mechanical engrg 1984–; assessor King's Cross Underground Fire Investigation 1988, expert witness for prosecution Port Ramsgate Walkway Disaster Case 1997; chm: NI Youth Careers Guidance Cmmn 1975–81, NI Manpower Cncl 1981–86, Bd of Engrs Registration 1983–86, NI Postgrad Awards Advsy Bd 1982–95, Public Hearing into the Bilsthorpe Colliery accident 1994; memb: NI Trg Cncl 1964–81, NI Econ Cncl 1981–85, AFRC 1981–87, NI Ind Devpt Bd 1982–87, Engrg Cncl 1983–88; Freeman City of London 1987, memb Worshipful Co of Engrs 1988; lectrs for IMechE: Leonardo da Vinci 1970, George Stephenson 1989 and Thomas Lowe Gray 1999; IMechE: George Stephenson Research Prize 1956, Thomas Hawksley Gold Medal 1968, James Watt Int Gold Medal 1999; ICE Kelvin Medal 1992, RIA Cunningham Medal 2001, Lifetime Achievement Award Engrs Ireland 2007; Hon DSc: Nat Univ of Ireland 1984, Univ of Dublin 1985, Univ of Edinburgh 1987, Queen's Univ Belfast 1988, Aston Univ 1988, Cranfield Inst of Technol 1989; Hon DEng: Univ of Bristol 1992, Univ of Limerick 1993, Univ of Liverpool 1993; hon fell Univ of Luton 1994; Hon FIMechE (pres 1986–87), Hon FWeldI (pres 1995–98), Hon MASME, Hon FIEI, MRIA 1976, FREng 1979, FRS 1979 (vice-pres 1984–86), FIAcadE 1998, Hon FIStructE 2001; *Publications* An Introduction to the Mechanics of Machines (1964), Explosive Welding of Metals and its Application (1982), The Lives of Great Engineers of Ulster - Vol 1 (2003), The Anatomy of an Engineer (2006); author of numerous papers on high pressure engrg, explosive welding and forming of metals, fatigue of metals, history of technology, safety engrg and the educn and trg of engrs in jls of learned societies and conf proceedings; *Recreations* walking, music, travel; *Clubs* Athenaeum; *Style*— Prof Sir Bernard Crossland, CBE, FREng, FRS; ✉ 16 Malone Court, Belfast BT9 6PA (tel 028 9066 7495); The Queen's University, Belfast BT7 1NN (tel 028 9095 4238, e-mail b.crossland@qub.ac.uk)

CROSSLEY, Prof Michael; s of Kenneth Crossley, and Kathleen, *née* Lumb (d 1975); *b* Halifax, Yorks; *Educ* Keele Univ (BEd), Univ of London (MA), La Trobe Univ Melbourne (PhD); *m* 1978, Anne, da of Dennis Morgan and Beryl Morgan; 2 s (Martin b 1987, Sam b 1990); *Career* Grad Sch of Educn Univ of Bristol: prof of comparative and int educn, co-ordinator Research Centre for Int and Comparative Studies, dir Educn in Small States Research Gp; former assoc dean Faculty of Educn Univ of PNG, assoc memb and memb Editorial Advsy Bd Comparative Educn Research Centre Univ of Hong Kong; former chair British Assoc for Int and Comparative Educn (BAICE); memb: Br Educn Research Assoc (BERA), Comparative and Int Educn Soc (CIES) USA, Cncl for Educn for the Cwlth, Royal Cwlth Soc; founding series ed Bristol Papers in Educn, ed Comparative Educn; memb Editorial Bd: Research in Post-compulsory Educn, Int Jl of Educnl Devpt, Compare, Int Review of Educn; FRSA 2001, AcSS 2005; *Books* Research Training and Educational Management: International Perspectives (jt ed, 1994), Qualitative Educational Research in Developing Countries: Current Perspectives (jt ed, 1997), Learning and Teaching in an International Context: Research, Theory and Practice (jt ed, 1998), Educational Development in the Small States of the Commonwealth: Retrospect and Prospect (jtly, 1999), Globalisation, Educational Transformation and Societies in Transition (jt ed, 2000), Comparative and International Research in Education: Globalisation, Context and Difference (jtly, 2003), Research and Evaluation for Educational Development (jtly, 2005), Changing Educational Contexts, Issues and Identities: 40 Years of Comparative Education (jt ed, 2007); *Recreations* badminton, tennis, squash, surfing, windsurfing; *Style*— Prof Michael Crossley; ✉ The Graduate School of Education, University of Bristol, 35 Berkeley Square, Bristol BS8 1JA (website www.smallstates.net)

CROSSLEY, Paul Christopher Richard; CBE (1993); s of Frank Crossley (d 1948), and Myra, *née* Barrowcliffe (d 1979); *b* 17 May 1944; *Educ* Silcoates Sch Wakefield, Mansfield Coll Oxford; *Career* pianist; int concert career with world's leading orchs, ensembles, and conductors; solo recitalist and regular broadcaster; works specially written for him by leading composers incl: Adams, Berio, Gorecki, Henze, Takemitsu, Tippett; artistic dir London Sinfonietta 1988–94; sixteen TV progs on prominent composers; recordings incl: Liszt: A Recital 1983, Ravel: Complete Piano Music 1983, Fauré: Complete Piano Music 1983–87, Tippett: Sonatas 1–4 1985, Messiaen: Turangalila-Symphonie 1986, Messiaen Des Canyons aux Etoiles Oiseaux Exotiques, Couleurs de la Cité Celeste 1988, Poulenc: Complete Piano Music 1989, Stravinsky: Complete Music for Piano and Orchestra 1990, Adams: Eros Piano 1991, Takemitsu: Riverrun 1991, Debussy: Complete Piano Music 1993, Franck: Symphonic Variations 1994 and Piano Music 1994, Lutoslawski: Piano Concerto 1995, Takemitsu: Quotation of Dream 1998, Takemitsu: Complete Piano Music 2000, Scriabin: Late Piano Works 2007, Grieg: Lyric Pieces 2007; hon fell Mansfield Coll Oxford 1991; *Recreations* mah-jongg, reading; *Style*— Paul Crossley, Esq, CBE; ✉ c/o Connaught Artists Management Ltd, 2 Molasses Row, Plantation Wharf, London SW11 3UX (tel 020 7738 0017, e-mail classicalmusic@connaughtartists.com)

CROSSLEY-HOLLAND, Kevin John William; s of Peter Charles Crossley-Holland (d 2001) of Dyfed, and Joan Mary Crossley-Holland, MBE, *née* Cowper (d 2005); *b* 7 February 1941; *Educ* Bryanston, St Edmund Hall Oxford (MA); *m* 19 March 1999; Linda Waslien; 2 s (Kieran b 1963, Dominic b 1967), 2 da (Oenone b 1982, Eleanor b 1986); *Career* ed Macmillan & Co 1962–69, Gregory fell in poetry Univ of Leeds 1969–71, talks prodr BBC 1972, editorial dir Victor Gollancz 1972–77, lectr in English Tufts in London program 1969–78, lektor Regensburg Univ 1979–80, Arts Cncl fellow in writing Winchester Sch of Art 1983 and 1984, visiting prof St Olaf Coll Minnesota 1987, 1988 and 1989, endowed chair in the humanities and fine arts Univ of St Thomas Minnesota 1991–95; editorial conslt Boydell and Brewer 1987–89; chm E Arts Assoc Literature Panel 1986–89; dir American Composers Forum 1991–96; chm Poetry next-the-Sea Festival 1999–2006; patron: Soc for Storytelling, Thomas Lovell Beddoes Soc; tstee Wingfield Coll 1986–99; hon fell St Edmund Hall Oxford 2001; FRSL; *Books* poetry: vols incl Waterslain (1986), The Language of Yes (1996), Poems from East Anglia (1997), Selected Poems (2001), Moored Man (2006); for children: The Green Children (1966, Arts Cncl Award), Storm (1985, Carnegie Medal), British Folk Tales (1987), Short! (1998), The King Who Was and Will Be (1998), Arthur: The Seeing Stone (2000, Guardian Children's Fiction Award, Tir na n-Og Award), At the Crossing-Places (2001), King of the Middle March (2003), How Many Miles to Bethlehem? (2004), Gatty's Tale (2006); translations from Old English: Beowulf (1968), The Exeter Book of Riddles (revised edn, 1993); mythology: The Norse Myths (1981); travel and history: Pieces of Land (1972), The Stones Remain (1989); edited: The Anglo-Saxon World (1982), Folk-Tales of The British Isles (1985), The Oxford Book of Travel Verse (1986), Young Oxford Book of Folk-Tales (1998), Light Unlocked (with Lawrence Sail, 2005); opera: The Green Children (with Nicola LeFanu, 1990), The Wildman (with Nicola LeFanu, 1995), The Sailor's Tale (with Rupert Bawden, 2002); musical settings: A Knot of Riddles (with Sir Arthur Bliss), Riddles (with William Mathias), Pilgrim Jesus (with Stephen Paulus), The Nine Gifts (with Steve Heitzeg); *Recreations* music, walking, wine, travel; *Clubs* Garrick; *Style*— Kevin Crossley-Holland, Esq, FRSL; ✉ Chalk Hill, Burnham Market, Norfolk PE31 8JR (tel 01328 730167, fax 01328 730169, e-mail kevin@crossley-holland.com)

CROSTHWAITE, Andrew Donald; s of Donald Rothery Crosthwaite, of Lytham, Lancs, and Jean Mary, *née* Cavill; *b* 16 March 1957; *Educ* Manchester Grammar, Worcester Coll Oxford (BA); *Children* 2 s (Matthew Andrew, Sam Neil (twins) b 14 May 1990), 1 da (Katie Louisa b 19 Aug 1991); *Career* advtg exec; Ogilvy & Mather 1978–81, McCormick Publicis 1981–82, Doyle Dane Bernbach 1982–85; FCO Ltd: joined 1985, dir 1986, planning ptnr until 1993; dir of planning Euro RSCG Wnek Gosper 1993–96, fndr Euro RSCG Upstream (Brand Consultancy) 1996–99, brand conslt and memb Global Innovation Network 1999–, dir Off the Back Burner 2004–, inventor Eureka Inventing 2005–; memb Marketing Soc; FIPA; *Recreations* sailing, drinking, walking; *Style*— Andrew Crosthwaite; ✉ Brendon House, 10 Orchehill Avenue, Gerrards Cross, Buckinghamshire SL9 8PX (e-mail andrewcrosthwaite@yahoo.com)

CROSTHWAITE, Peregrine Kenneth Oughton (Perry); s of Kenneth Alan Crosthwaite, and Nora Elsie, *née* Oughton; *b* 24 March 1949; *Educ* St Paul's, Trinity Coll Oxford (MA); *m* 29 Oct 1982, Valerie Janet, yr da of Sir Albert Jonas Cahn, Bt, *qv*; 2 s (Nicholas Anthony b 22 Jan 1985, Thomas William b 23 Oct 1986), 1 da (Sally-Anne Claire b 8 May 1989); *Career* joined Fenn & Crosthwaite 1972 (merged with George Henderson to become Henderson Crosthwaite 1975), ptnr Henderson Crosthwaite 1979–86, chm Investec Investment Bank & Securities (formerly Investec Henderson Crosthwaite) 1997–2004, chm Jupiter Green Investment Tst; non-exec dir: ToLuna plc, Melrose plc; memb: Nordoff-Robbins Music Therapy Fundraising Ctee, Trinity Coll Oxford Investment Ctee; tstee CIDA Fndn UK; memb: Worshipful Co of Merchant Taylors, Freeman City of London; memb London Stock Exchange 1975; *Recreations* cricket, tennis, skiing, music, books, theatre; *Style*— Perry Crosthwaite, Esq; ✉ 30 Larpent Avenue, London SW15 6UU (tel 020 8788 2073)

CROUCH, Prof Colin John; s of Charles John Crouch (d 1990), of Charlbury, Oxon, and Doris Beatrice, *née* Baker (d 1990); *b* 1 March 1944; *Educ* Latymer Upper Sch, LSE (BA), Univ of Oxford (DPhil); *m* 10 June 1970, Joan Ann, da of David Freedman (d 1972), of London; 2 s (Daniel b 1974, Benjamin b 1978); *Career* lectr in sociology: LSE 1969–70, Univ of Bath 1972–73; reader LSE 1980–85 (lectr 1973–79, sr lectr 1979–80); Univ of Oxford: fell and tutor in politics Trinity Coll 1985–98, faculty lectr in sociology 1985–96, chm Sub-Faculty of Sociology 1987–89, proctor 1990–91, chm Social Studies Faculty Bd 1994, prof of sociology 1996–98; Euro Univ Inst Florence: prof of sociology 1995–2004, chm Dept of Political and Social Studies 2001–04; prof of governance and public mgmnt Univ of Warwick Business Sch 2005–; research interests in the comparative sociology of Western Europe and economic sociology and in public servs mgmnt and policy; curator Bodleian Library 1990–95, delegate Oxford Univ Press 1992–98; memb Standing Ctee of Ct of Govrs LSE 1980–84, jt ed The Political Quarterly 1985–95; chm: Fabian Soc 1976 (memb Exec Ctee 1969–78), Political Quarterly 2000–; memb: Max Planck Soc Cologne 1997–, Regnl Policy Forum 2000–03; referee class 3 Oxfordshire Football Assoc; FBA 2005; *Editor* Stress and Contradiction in Modern Capitalism (with Lindberg et al, 1975), Br Political Sociology Yearbook Vol III Participation in Politics (1977), The Resurgence of Class Conflict in Western Europe since 1968 vol I Nat Studies vol II comparative Analyses (with A Pizzorno, 1978), State and Economics in Contemporary Capitalism (1979), Int Yearbook of Organizations Democracy vol I Organizational Democracy and Political Processes (with F Heller, 1983), The New Centralism (with D Marquand, 1989), Corporatism and Accountability Organised Interests in Br Public Life (with R P Dore, 1990), European Industrial Relations: the Challenge of Flexibility (with G Baglioni, 1990), The Politics of 1992 (with D Marquand, 1990), Towards Greater Europe? (with D Marquand, 1992), Social Research and Social Reform (with A Heath, 1992), Ethics and Markets (with D Marquand, 1993), Organized Industrial Relations in Europe (with F Traxler, 1995), Reinventing Collective Action (with D Marquand, 1995), Les capitalismes en Europe (with W Streeck, 1996), Political Economy of Modern Capitalism (with W Streeck, 1997), After the Euro (2000), Citizenship, Markets and the State (with C Eder and D Tambini, 2001); *Books* The Student Revolt (1970), Class Conflict and the Industrial Relations Crisis (1977), The Politics of Industrial Relations (2 edn 1982), Trade Unions: the Logic of Collective Action (1982), Industrial Relations and European State Traditions (1993), Are Skills the Answer (jtly, 1999), Social Change in Western Europe (1999), Local Production Systems in Europe: Rise or Demise? (jtly, 2001),

Postdemocrazia (2003), Changing Governance of Local Economics: Response of European Local Production Systems (jtly, 2004), Capitalist Diversity and Change: Recombinant Governance and Institutional Entrepreneurs (2005); *Recreations* playing violin, listening to music, gardening; *Style—* Prof Colin Crouch; ⊠ University of Warwick Business School, Coventry CV4 7AL (tel 024 7652 4505, fax 024 7652 4410, e-mail colin.crouch@wbs.ac.uk)

CROUCH, Julian David; s of David James Frederick Crouch, and Barbara Victoria, *née* Heywood; *Educ* Ayr Acad, Univ of Edinburgh; *Career* theatre designer; maskmaker and designer Trickster Theatre Co, co-fndr Improbable Theatre (with Phelim McDermott and Lee Simpson) 1996, co-dir and co-designer Shockheaded Peter (Best Dir TMA Awards 1998, Best Designer Critics Soc Awards 1998, Best Entertainment Olivier Awards 2002), designer and assoc dir Jerry Springer The Opera (NT) 2003 (Best Musical Evening Standard Awards, Olivier Awards and Critics Soc Awards 2004); other prodns incl: 70 Hill Lane (Improbable, OBIE Best Prodn 1997), A Midsummer Nights Dream (English Shakespeare Co, Best Touring Prodn TMA Awards 1997); *Style—* Julian Crouch, Esq; ⊠ Improbable, 4th Floor, 43 Aldwych, London WC24 4DN (tel 020 7240 4556, e-mail crouch@dircon.co.uk)

CROUCH, Sunny; OBE; da of Frederick Charles Moore, of London, and Edith Joyce, *née* Budd; *b* 11 February 1943; *Educ* Lancaster Univ (MA), Dip CIM, Dip MRS; *m*; *Career* mktg mgmnt Brocades (GB) Ltd 1966–72; course dir (honours degree in business studies) Univ of Portsmouth Business Sch 1972–83, visiting course dir (market research) Coll of Chartered Inst of Mktg 1977–83; mktg conslt 1972–83, chief mktg and tourism offr City of Portsmouth 1983–88 (Tourist Authy of the Year Award 1985, English Tourist Bd's first England for Excellence Award for Cities 1988), dir of mktg London Docklands Devpt Corp 1988–98 (nine years' winner Property Marketing Awards), md World Trade Centre London 1998–; non-exec bd dir: Melody Radio 1989–92, Scottish Radio Holdings 1997–2005, London First 2002–, Thurrock Urban Devpt Corp 2004–, Places for People plc 2005–; chm: DOBRIC Publications 1990–98, TourEast London 1993–98; vice-pres Docklands Business Club 1989–98; memb: Tourism Soc 1983– (Nat Cncl 1989–98, vice-chm 1994–97), First Forum 1988– (Nat Exec Ctee 1989–98), Industrial and Economic Affrs Ctee Gen Synod C of E 1991–98; govr: City of Portsmouth Girls' Sch 1977–88, Portsmouth Coll of Art, Design and FE 1984–88, Univ of East London 2000–; memb Cncl Friends of the National Maritime Museum 1999–2006; London Borough of Tower Hamlets Civic Award 2004, SHINE Woman of the Year Award 2005, Lifetime Achievement Award Tourism Soc 2006; Freeman: City of London 1993, Worshipful Co of World Traders 1998; FCIM 1970, full memb MRS 1975, FTS 1985, MInstD 1990; *Publications* Mass Media and Cultural Relationship (jtly, 1975), Marketing Research for Managers (1984 and 1985, 3 edn 2003); *Style—* Mrs Sunny Crouch, OBE; ⊠ 99 Caledonian Wharf, London E14 3EN (tel 07775 603193, e-mail sunny.crouch@btopenworld.com)

CROW, Bob; s of George Crow (d 1996), and Lillian Crow; *b* 13 June 1961; *Educ* Kingswood Secdy Modern Hainault; *m* Nicola, *née* Hoarau; 1 s (Anthony), 3 da (Kerrie, Natasha, Tanya); *Career* gen sec RMT 2002– (asst gen sec 1995–2002), memb Bd Transport for London 2002; *Recreations* football, boxing, darts; *Style—* Bob Crow, Esq; ⊠ RMT, Unity House, 39 Chalton Street, London NW1 1JD (tel 020 7387 4771, mobile 07799 893801)

CROW, Dr Julie Carol; da of Dr Eric George Hemphill Carter, and Phyllis Elsie, *née* Crump; *b* 26 February 1942; *Educ* Chislehurst and Sidcup Girls GS, London Hosp Med Coll Univ of London; *m* 22 Jan 1966, Dr Timothy John Crow, s of Percy Arthur Crow; 1 s (Oliver b 10 April 1971), 1 da (Louise b 21 Feb 1974); *Career* house physician and surgn Aberdeen 1966; Univ of Aberdeen: lectr in pathology 1968–71, pt/t lectr 1971–73; Northwick Park Hosp: pt/t registrar 1975–76, pt/t sr registrar 1976–82, locum conslt in histopathology 1983–85; sr lectr in histopathology Royal Free Hosp Sch of Med and hon conslt Royal Free Hosp 1985–; registrar Royal Coll of Pathologists 1996–2001; memb: BMA, MWF, IAP, Pathological Soc of GB and Ireland; FRCPath 1989; *Recreations* chinese brush painting, tennis, reading, watching TV; *Style—* Dr Julie Crow; ⊠ Department of Histopathology, Royal Free Hospital, Pond Street, London NW3 2QG (tel 020 7830 2227, fax 020 7435 3289, e-mail julie.crow@royalfree.nhs.uk)

CROWCROFT, Prof Jonathan Andrew (Jon); s of Prof Andrew Crowcroft, and Prof Kyla Greenbaum; *b* 23 November 1957; *Educ* Univ of Cambridge (BA), Univ of London (MSc, PhD); *m* 1988, Noreen, da of Leo McWeever; 1 da (Alice b 1989), 2 s (Daniel b 1996, Patrick b 1998); *Career* lectr rising to prof of networked systems Computer Science Dept UCL 1982–2001, Marconi prof of communications Univ of Cambridge 2001–; memb Internet Architecture Bd; SMIEEE, FIEE, FBCS, FREng, FACM; *Recreations* cycling; *Style—* Prof Jon Crowcroft; ☎ tel 01223 763 633

CROWDEN, James Gee Pascoe; CVO (2003), JP (Wisbech 1969); yr s of Lt-Col R J C Crowden, MC (d 1977), of Peterborough, and Nina Mary, *née* Gee (d 1981); *b* 14 November 1927; *Educ* Bedford Sch, Pembroke Coll Cambridge (MA); *m* 1, 1955, Kathleen Mary (d 1989), da of late Mr and Mrs J W Loughlin, of Upwell, and wid of Capt F A Grounds; 1 s (decd), 1 step s; *m* 2, 2001, Margaret, da of late Rev and Mrs Wilfred Cole, of Oundle, and wid of John Reginald Crowden; 4 step da; *Career* cmmnd Royal Lincs Regt 1947; chartered surveyor; sr ptnr Grounds & Co 1974–88; former pres Agric Valuers' Assocs of Cambs, Herts Beds and Bucks, Lincs, Norfolk and Wisbech; rowed in Oxford and Cambridge Boat Race 1951 and 1952 (pres 1952), Capt GB VIII Euro Championships Macon 1951 (Gold medallists), rowed 1950 Euro Championships Milan (Bronze medal) and Olympic Games Helsinki 1952, coached 20 Cambridge crews 1953–75, steward Henley Royal Regatta 1959– (memb Ctee of Mgmnt 1964–92); memb Cncl Amateur Rowing Assoc 1957–77; chm Cambs Olympic Appeals 1984, 1988, 1992, 1996 and 2000; vice-pres Br Olympic Assoc 1988–; dep pres East of England Agric Soc 2000; pres: Cambs Fedn of Young Farmers 1971–73, Cambs Scouts 1992–2002, Cambs TAVRA and Cadet Ctee 1992–2002, E Anglia TAVRA 1996–2000 (vice-pres 1992–96 and 2001–02), Old Bedfordians' Club 1996–98, Royal Naval Assoc Peterborough 2001–06; patron: Cambs Red Cross 1992–2002, Cambs Royal British Legion 1992–2006, Cambs Regt Old Comrades' Assoc 1998–; Hon Col Cambs ACF 1996–2002; govr: March GS 1960–70 (chm 1967–70), King's Sch Peterborough 1980–90, St Hugh's Sch Woodhall Spa 1981–92; chm Cncl Order of St Etheldreda 1992–2002; memb: Ely Diocesan Pastoral Ctee 1969–89, Ely Cathedral Fabric Ctee 1986–90; churchwarden All Saints' Walsoken 1964–76 and 1983–84; chm Appeal Exec Ctee Peterborough Cathedral 1979–80; High Sheriff Cambs and Isle of Ely 1970, HM Lord-Lt and Custos Rotulorum of Cambs 1992–2002 (DL 1971, Vice Lord-Lt 1985–92); Freeman Town of Wisbech 2001, Freeman Tri-Base United States Air Force (RAF Alconbury, Molesworth and Upwood) 2001; hon memb Ct Co of Watermen and Lightermen of the River Thames (Master 1991–92); hon fell Pembroke Coll Cambridge 1993; FCIArb 1977, FRSA 1990, KStJ 1992; *Recreations* rowing, shooting; *Clubs* East India, Devonshire, Sports and Public Schs, Hawks' (Cambridge), Univ Pitt, Cambridge County, Leander, Sette of Odd Volumes; *Style—* J G P Crowden, Esq, CVO; ⊠ 19 North Brink, Wisbech, Cambridgeshire PE13 1JR (tel 01945 583320); The Manor House, Elton, Peterborough, Cambridgeshire PE8 6RE (tel 01832 280206)

CROWE, David Edward Aubrey; s of Norman Ronald Aubrey Crowe (d 1983), and Barbara Lythgoe, *née* Jones; *b* 31 August 1939; *Educ* Cranleigh Sch Surrey, Christ Church Oxford (MA); *m* 8 June 1963, Helen Margaret, da of George Denis Dale (d 1983); 2 da (Sarah b 1967, Lucy b 1971); *Career* slr 1964; ptnr: HA Crowe and Co 1964–68, Gouldens 1968–89; Pty candidate (Lib): Bromley 1970, Ravensbourne 1974; ldr Lib Gp Bromley Cncl 1974–78, vice-chm London Lib Pty 1975, chm Bromley Consumer Gp 1978–79, cncllr

(Lib Dem) Bromley Cncl 1994–; Mayor London Borough of Bromley 2000–2001; chm Beckenham and Bromley Nat Tst 1975–79 (hon sec 1979–88); memb Law Soc; *Recreations* opera, gardening; *Clubs* Oxford and Cambridge, National Liberal; *Style—* David Crowe, Esq

CROWE, Victoria Elizabeth; OBE (2004); da of Philip Farrands Crowe (d 1980), and Aziel, *née* Rowe; *b* 8 May 1945; *Educ* Kingston Sch of Art, RCA (MA); *Career* artist; pt/t lectr Edinburgh Coll of Art, sr visiting scholar St Catharine's Coll Cambridge 2004–07; RSW 1982, ARSA 1987; *Solo Exhibitions* incl: The Scottish Gallery Edinburgh 1970, 1973, 1977, 1982, 1995, 1998, 2001, 2004 and 2006, Thackeray Gallery London 1983, 1985, 1987, 1989, 1991, 1994, 1999, 2001, 2003, 2005 and 2007, Fine Art Society Glasgow and Edinburgh 1988, Bruton Gallery 1989, 1993 and 1998, Scottish Nat Portrait Gallery 2000, A Shepherd's Life (touring Scotland, also at Hatton Gallery Newcastle upon Tyne and Mercer Art Gallery Harrogate) 2003, Alchemy (Drumcroon and Wigan Educn Authy) 2003; *Group Exhibitions* incl: Artist and Teacher (Fine Art Society Edinburgh and Glasgow), Contemporary Art from Scotland (touring exhbn), Light from the Window (Nat Gallery of Scotland), Portrait 84 (National Portrait Gallery London), Portraits on Paper (Scottish Arts Cncl touring exhbn) 1984–85, Sunday Times/Singer Friedlander Watercolour Exhbn 1988, 1990, 1991, 1992 and 1993, Scottish Art in the 20th Century (RWEA Bristol) 1991, Portrait of a Living Marsh (work from Artists for Nature Fndn Polish project, touring exhbn throughout Europe and USA with book) 1993, Artists for Nature in Extremadura (touring exhbn throughout Europe and USA with book, 1995), ANF Indian Project, Wild Tigers of Bhandhavgarh (Burrel Collection, Glasgow) 2000; regular exhibitor at Royal Acad of Arts London, RSA Edinburgh, Royal Scottish Watercolour Soc; *Public Collections* incl: RCA, Royal Acad of Arts, Scottish Nat Gallery of Modern Art, Univ of Edinburgh, Contemporary Art Soc, NT for Scotland, Scottish Nat Portrait Gallery, City Art Centre Edinburgh, Nat Portrait Gallery London; *Commissioned Portraits* incl: R D Laing (for SNPG), Tam Dalyell MP, Lord Wemyss (for Nat Tst Scotland), Kathleen Raine, Dame Janet Vaughn (Nat Portrait Gallery), Ole Lippmann (Danish Nat Portrait Collection), Thea Musgrave (Scottish Nat Portrait Gallery) 2005; *Awards* incl: Daler/Rowney Prize for Watercolour Royal Acad of Arts 1987, Hunting Gp major award 1988, Chris Beetles Prize RWS, Sir William Gillies Bequest RSA 1992 and 2004; *Publications* Painted Insights (monograph, 2001); *Style—* Ms Victoria Crowe, OBE; ⊠ c/o Scottish Gallery, 16 Dundas Street, Edinburgh EH3 6HZ; c/o Thackeray Gallery, Thackeray Street, Kensington Square, London W8 5ET

CROWLEY, Graham Neil; s of Victor Matthew Crowley, and Veronica Mary, *née* Lee; *b* 3 May 1950; *Educ* St Martin's Sch of Art (DipAD), RCA (MA); *m* 16 Dec 1978, Sally Ann, da of Warwick Arthur Townshend; 2 s (Robin Merrick 1 Aug 1982, Pearse Max Gary 20 July 1985); *Career* artist; artist in residence Univ of Oxford 1982–83, memb Fine Art Faculty British Sch at Rome 1982–88, sr fell in painting S Glamorgan Inst of HE Cardiff 1986–89, drawing residency Riverscape Int Cleveland 1991–92, head of fine art City & Guilds of London Art Sch 1997–98, prof of painting RCA 1998–2006; memb Advsy Bd ICA 1985–89, Fine Art Working Ctee Nat Advsy Bd DES 1987–88; *Solo Exhibitions* Air Gallery London 1982, Home Comforts (MOMA Oxford and touring) 1983, Reflections (Riverside Studios) 1984, Night Life (ICA) 1984, Table Manners (Edward Totah Gallery London) 1984, Forum Zurich Art Fair 1984, Domestic Crisis (Totah Gallery NYC) 1986, In Living Memory and Other Paintings (Edward Totah Gallery) 1987, Law and Order (Cleveland Gallery Middlesbrough) 1989, More Paintings About Speculating and Flower Arranging (Edward Totah Gallery) 1989, Ballads and Folk Songs - Paintings 1981–89 (Howard Gdns Gallery S Glamorgan Inst of HE) 1990, Somewhere Else (Edward Totah Gallery) 1991, Northern Seen (Northern Centre for Contemporary Art Sunderland) 1992, Lamont Gallery (London) 1995 and 1997, Lamont Gallery 1998, Familiar Ground (Beaux Arts London) 2001), Beaux Arts London 2003 and 2005; *Group Exhibitions* incl: John Moores Exhbn (Walker Art Gallery Liverpool) 1976, 1980, 1982, 1983, 1985, 1987, 1993, 2004 and 2006 (prize winner 1983 and 2006), Drawing (Barbara Toll Gallery NYC) 1984, Venice Biennale (Anthony Reynolds Gallery) 1984, The Proper Study (Br Cncl New Delhi) 1985, Still Life - A New Life (Harris Museum and Art Gallery Preston and touring) 1985, Figuring Out the '80's (Laing Art Gallery Newcastle) 1988, The New British Painting (USA) 1988, Real Life Stories (Spacex Exeter) 1989–90, The New British Painting (Queen's Museum NYC) 1990, The Brew House Open Taunton (first prize) 1990, Riverscape (Middlesborough and Cleveland Galleries) 1993, John Jones/London Open (first prize), finalist Jerwood Painting Prize 2002; *Murals* Brompton Hosp London 1982, Chandler's Ford Library 1983; *Work in Public Collections* Imperial War Museum, Museum of Auckland NZ, Arts Cncl Collection, Ipswich Museum, Leicester Educn Authy, Leeds Educn Authy, V&A, Br Cncl Collection, Contemporary Arts Soc, Kettles Yard Cambridge, Castle Museum Nottingham, Univ of Northumbria at Newcastle; *Books* Gogol's Overcoat (1984, ICA for Nighlife Exhbn); *Recreations* reading, motor cycling, gardening; *Style—* Graham Crowley; ⊠ Rineen, Skibbereen, Co Cork, Ireland (tel 00 353 28 36421)

CROWLEY, Jane Elizabeth Rosser; QC (1998); da of Robert Jenkyn Rosser (d 1967), and Marion, *née* Davies; *Educ* Howell's Sch Llandaff (head girl), King's Coll London (LLB), Inns of Court Sch of Law; *m* 1986, Mark Crowley; 1 s (Huw b 1988), 1 da (Sara b 1990); *Career* called to the Bar Gray's Inn 1976; recorder 1992, dep High Court judge 1999; memb: Gray's Inn, Wales & Chester Circuit; pt/t pres Mental Health Review Tbnls 1999; assocs: Family Law Bar Assoc, Liberty; *Recreations* family, food and wine, countryside, music, sport; *Style—* Mrs Jane Crowley, QC; ⊠ 30 Park Place, Cardiff CF10 3BS (tel 029 2039 8421, fax 029 2039 8725); 1 Garden Court, Temple, London EC4Y 9BJ (tel 020 7797 7900, fax 020 7797 7929, e-mail janecrowley@aol.com)

CROWLEY, John; QC (1982); s of John Joseph Crowley (d 1998), and Anne Marie, *née* Fallon (d 1987); *b* 25 June 1938; *Educ* St Edmund's Coll Ware, Christ's Coll Cambridge (MA, LLB); *m* 1977, Sarah Maria, da of Christopher Gage Jacobs; 2 da (Rachel Maria b 1979, Rose Abigail b 1982); *Career* called to the Bar Inner Temple 1962 (bencher 1989), called to Irish Bar 1997; recorder 1980–2004, dep judge of the High Court 1991–2004; memb Criminal Injuries Compensation Bd 1985–2000, memb Criminal Injuries Compensation Appeals Panel 2000–02; chm Appeals Ctee ICAEW 2000–2004 (vice-chm 1998–2000); govr St Edmund's Coll Ware 1990–98; *Recreations* music, the turf, wine; *Style—* John Crowley, Esq, QC; ⊠ 37 Viceroy Road, London SW8 2HA (tel 020 7622 4742, fax 020 7622 7008)

CROWLEY, Robert (Bob); *Career* designer for theatre, opera and film; assoc artist: Royal Shakespeare Co, Nat Theatre; directing debut The Cure at Troy (Field Day Theatre Co); RDI; *Theatre* credits with the RSC: The Irish Play, Thirteenth Night, The Forest, The Taming of the Shrew, King Lear, Measure for Measure, The Time of Your Life, A New Way to Pay Old Debts, Henry V, Love's Labour's Lost, As You Like It, Les Liaisons Dangereuses (also West End, NY, Los Angeles and Tokyo), The Two Noble Kinsmen, Flight, Principia Scriptoriae, Macbeth, The Jew of Malta, The Plantaganets, Henry IV Parts I and II, tours of Romeo and Juliet, A Midsummer Night's Dream, The Winter's Tale, The Crucible, Othello and Hamlet; credits with the NT: A Midsummer's Night Dream, Ghetto, Hedda Gabler, Ma Rainey's Black Bottom, Racing Demon, White Chameleon, Richard III, Murmuring Judges, The Sea, Night of the Iguana, Carousel (also West End and Broadway), Macbeth, Absence of War, The Prince's Play, The Designated Mourner, The Cripple of Inishmaan, King Lear, Amy's View (also Broadway), His Girl Friday, Mourning Becomes Electra (Critics Circle Award), The History Boys; other credits incl: Timon of Athens, A View from a Bridge and Destiny (all Bristol Old Vic), A

Midsummer Night's Dream (Bristol Old Vic and London), The Duchess of Malfi (Royal Exchange, Roundhouse and Paris), Dr Faustus (Royal Exchange), One of Us (Greenwich Theatre), After Aida (Welsh Nat Opera and The Old Vic), Two Way Mirror (The Young Vic), Saint Oscar (Field Day Theatre Co), Madame de Sade (Tokyo), The Three Sisters (Gate Theatre Dublin and The Royal Court London), When She Danced (with Vanessa Redgrave, The Globe Theatre), The Importance of Being Earnest (with Maggie Smith, The Aldwych), No Man's Land (with Harold Pinter, Almeida and Comedy Theatres), Moonlight (Almeida Theatre and West End), The Cryptogram (Ambassadors Theatre), Cunning Little Vixen (Chatelet Paris), Judas Kiss (transferred Broadway), The Iceman Cometh (The Old Vic and Broadway), Twelfth Night (with Helen Hunt, Lincoln Center Theater NY), Sweet Smell of Success (Broadway, 2002, Tony Award), Into the Woods (Donmar Warehouse), Elton John and Tim Rice's Aida for Disney (Chicago, Broadway and US tour, Tony Award), Cressida (Albery Theatre), Orpheus Descending (Donmar Warehouse), The Witches of Eastwick for Cameron Mackintoch (Drury Lane), Mary Poppins (Prince Edward Theatre and Broadway), Tarzan (dir and designer, Broadway and The Netherlands), The Year of Magical Thinking (set designer, Broadway), The Coast of Utopia (set designer, Lincoln Center Theater); *Ballet* credits as designer of set and costumes (for Royal Ballet): Anastasia, Pavane; *Opera* Don Giovanni (Kent Opera), Alcina (Spitalfields Festival and Los Angeles), The King Goes Forth to France, The Knot Garden and La Traviata (all Royal Opera House), The Magic Flute (ENO), Eugene Onegin (WNO, Opera North and the Lyric Opera Queensland), Don Giovanni (Bavarian State Opera); *Film* Othello, Tales of Hollywood (with Jeremy Irons and Alec Guinness), Suddenly Last Summer (for BBC, dir Richard Eyre, with Maggie Smith), The Crucible (with Daniel Day-Lewis and Winona Ryder); *Awards* eleven Olivier Award nominations (incl two for Les Liaisons Dangereuses and two for Henry V), two Drama Desk Award nominations and two Tony Award nominations (for Les Liaisons Dangereuses on Broadway), Olivier Award for Designer of the Year 1990, Tony Award and Outer Critics Circle Award (for Carousel on Broadway) 1994, Tony Award nomination for Iceman Cometh and Twelfth Night 1999, Drama Desk Award for Twelfth Night 1999, RSA Royal Designer for Industry, Tony Award for Mary Poppins and The Coast of Utopia 2007; *Style—* Mr Bob Crowley; ✉ c/o David Watson, Simpson Fox Associates Ltd, 52 Shaftesbury Avenue, London W1V 7DE (tel 020 7434 9167, fax 020 7494 2887, e-mail cary-parsons@simpson-fox.com)

CROWN, Giles Humphry; s of Sidney Crown, and June, *née* Downes; *b* 13 July 1969, London; *Educ* St Paul's, Jesus Coll Cambridge (MA), UCL (LLM), Inns of Court Sch of Law; *m* Nicola (Nicki), *née* Wilson; 1 da (Zoë), 1 s (Alexander); *Career* called to the Bar Middle Temple 1994 (Astbury scholar), admitted slr 2003; pupillage Blackstone Chambers and One Brick Court 1993–95, barr specialising in media law One Brick Court 1995–2000 (Inns of Court Pegasus scholar seconded to Potter Anderson & Corroon USA 1996), head of legal and business affrs TBWA UK Gp 2000–01, Lewis Silkin Slrs 2001– (ptnr 2003–, dep head Media Brands and Technol Dept 2005–); memb Secretariat: Royal Cmmn on Criminal Justice 1992, Court of Appeal (Civil Div) Review Ctee 1997; memb: Advtg Lawyers Gp, Advtg and Mktg Ctee Int C of C, Exec Ctee Branded Content Mktg Assoc; chair and dir Westminster CAB, Lib Dem candidate for Westminster's Hyde Park Ward 1998, membership sec Cities of London and Westminster Lib Dems 1998–2001; *Publications* Advertising Law and Regulation (1999); regular commentator and contrib in legal jls, trade press and nat media; *Recreations* travel, theatre, opera, cinema, keen triathlete; *Style—* Giles Crown, Esq; ✉ Lewis Silkin LLP, 5 Chancery Lane, Clifford's Inn, London EC4A 1BL (tel 020 7074 8090, e-mail giles.crown@lewissilkin.com)

CROWTHER, Prof (Margaret) Anne; da of William Broughton Worden (d 1970), and Margaret, *née* Fenwick; *b* 1 November 1943; *Educ* Walford Sch Adelaide, Univ of Adelaide (BA), Somerville Coll Oxford (DPhil); *m* 1969, John McCauley Crowther; 1 s (Geoffrey John b 1980); *Career* lectr in history: Univ of Kent 1968–73, Univ of Stirling 1973–75; fell New Hall Cambridge 1975–78; Univ of Glasgow: successively lectr, sr lectr then reader 1979–94, prof of social history 1994–2006, hon research fell 2006–; chm Scottish Records Advsy Cncl 1995–2001 (memb 1993–); FRHistS 1992, FRSE 1997; *Books* The Workhouse System 1834–1929 (1981), Social Policy in Britain 1914–1939 (1988), On Soul and Conscience: the Medical Expert and Crime (jtly, 1988), Medical Lives in the Age of the Surgical Revolution (jtly, 2007); *Recreations* gardening; *Style—* Prof Anne Crowther, FRSE; ✉ Centre for the History of Medicine, University of Glasgow, Lilybank House, Bute Gardens, Glasgow G12 8RT (tel 0141 330 6071, fax 0141 330 4889)

CROWTHER, His Hon Judge Thomas Rowland; QC (1981); s of Dr Kenneth Vincent Crowther (d 1996), and Winifred Anita, *née* Rowland (d 1992); *b* 11 September 1937; *Educ* Newport HS, Keble Coll Oxford (MA); *m* 1969, Gillian Jane, da of William Leslie Prince (d 1978); 1 s (Thomas b 1970), 1 da (Lucy b 1971); *Career* called to the Bar Inner Temple (bencher 2005); barr 1960, in practice Oxford Circuit 1960–69, in practice Wales & Chester Circuit 1970–84 (jr 1974), recorder of the Crown Court 1980–84, circuit judge (Wales & Chester Circuit) 1985–2001, sr circuit judge (Western Circuit) and hon recorder of Bristol 2001–; dir Gwent Area Broadcasting Ltd 1982–84; *Recreations* garden, trout fishing; *Style—* His Hon Judge Crowther, QC; ✉ Lansor, Caerleon NP18 1LS (tel 01633 450224)

CROXALL, Prof John Patrick; CBE (2004); s of Harold Eli Croxall (d 1990), and Marjorie, *née* Jones (d 1996); *b* 19 January 1946, Birmingham; *Educ* King Edward's Sch Birmingham, The Queen's Coll Oxford (open scholar, MA), Univ of Auckland (Cwlth scholar, PhD); *Partner* Alison Jane Statterfield, *née* Morris; *Career* dir Oiled Seabird Research Unit and sr research assoc in zoology Univ of Newcastle upon Tyne 1972–75; Br Antarctic Survey: PSO and head Birds and Mammals Section 1976–85, SPSO and head Higher Predators Section 1986–2000, DCSO and head Conservation Biology 2001–06; chair Global Seabird Prog Birdlife Int 2006–; pres Br Ornithologists' Union 1995–99 (memb Cncl 1974–78, vice-pres 1987–91), chm RSPB 1998–2003 (memb Cncl 1989–2003), memb Perm Exec Int Ornithological Ctee 1998–2006; author of 310 papers and books; Scientific Medal Zoological Soc of London 1984, Polar Medal 1992 and 2004, Pres's Medal Br Ecological Soc 1995, Murphy Prize and Medal Int Waterbird Soc 1997, Marsh Award of Conservation Zoological Soc of London 2002, Godman-Salvin Medal Br Ornithologists' Union 2004; hon prof: Univ of Birmingham 1998–, Univ of Durham 1998–; memb Br Ornithologists' Union 1965, memb Int Ornithological Ctee 1990, corresponding fell American Ornithologists' Union 2004; FRS 2005; *Recreations* birdwatching, walking, rebuilding houses; *Style—* Prof John Croxall, CBE, FRS; ✉ 3 Oakington Road, Girton, Cambridge CB3 0QH (tel 01223 234287); Birdlife International, Wellbrook Court, Girton Road, Cambridge CB3 0NA (tel 01223 277318, fax 01223 277200, john.croxall@birdlife.org)

CROXFORD, David; s of Frederick William Gordon Croxford (ka 1944), and late Lucy May, *née* Williams; *b* 3 October 1937; *Educ* Hinchley Wood Co Sch Esher; *m* 5 July 1975, Victoria Wendy, da of late Robert Francis Fort; *Career* chartered accountant; trained and qualified with Hagley Knight & Co 1955–62, Tansley Witt & Co (now part of MacIntyre Hudson) 1962–64, Ogden Parsons & Co (now part of PricewaterhouseCoopers) 1964–67, mangr Bird & Partners 1968–71; Moore Stephens: sr and managerial positions Bermuda 1972–77, relocated to Jersey 1977, accounts controller 1977, special servs mangr 1979, ptnr 1980–95; ind practitioner and conslt 1996–2005, dir Atlas Trust Co (Jersey) Ltd 2001–; memb: ICAEW 1962, Jersey Soc of Chartered and Certified Accountants 1977, Jersey Assoc of Practising Chartered and Certified Accountants 1981, Jersey Taxation Soc 1986, Licenced Insolvency Practitioner 1989–2005, Soc of Tst and Estate Practitioners 1996; MInstD 1988; *Recreations* singing (choral and sacred), golf, music, gardening; *Clubs* La Moye Golf (Jersey), Jersey Gilbert and Sullivan Soc, The Mayfair Health (Jersey); *Style—* David Croxford, Esq; ✉ La Chaumiere, College Hill, St Helier, Jersey JE2 4RE (tel 01534 872751, fax 01534 872752, e-mail dc@psilink.co.je, website www.croxford.co.je)

CROXFORD, Ian Lionel; QC (1993); s of Peter Patrick Croxford, BEM, and Mary, *née* Richardson; *b* 23 July 1953; *Educ* Westcliff HS for Boys, Univ of Leicester (LLB); *m* Sandra; 1 da, 1 s; *Career* called to the Bar Gray's Inn 1976 (Bacon scholar, bencher 2001), ad eundem Lincoln's Inn; *Recreations* watching sport; *Style—* Ian Croxford, Esq, QC; ✉ Wilberforce Chambers, 8 New Square, Lincoln's Inn, London WC2A 3QP (tel 020 7306 0102, fax 020 7306 0095)

CROXON, Raymond Patrick Austen; QC (1983); *b* 31 July 1928; *Educ* Strand Coll and St Thomas' Hosp (MSR), King's Coll London (LLB); *m* Hara, *née* Marinou; *Career* served RAMC 1946–49; radiographer 1950–59, called to the Bar Gray's Inn 1960; publishing co 1960–63, practising barr 1963–, head of chambers; *Recreations* travel, walking, swimming, reading, listening to music, attending concerts and theatre, learning modern Greek language; *Clubs* Savage; *Style—* Raymond Croxon, Esq, QC; ✉ Regency Chambers, Peterborough PE1 1NA

CROXSON, Andrew James; s of David Croxson, and Lucy, *née* Paterson; *b* 28 April 1973, Merton, Surrey; *Educ* King's Sch Chester, Mansfield Coll Oxford (exhibitioner, BA), Trinity Hall Cambridge (MPhil); *m* 25 Aug 2002, Siân, *née* Davies; 1 s (James Llewelyn Wilfred b 5 March 2005), 1 da (Marianne Bronwen b 12 March 2007); *Career* assoc rising to sr Tax Dept Finance and Real Estate Gp Arthur Andersen 1996–2000, assoc rising to ptnr Spectrum Strategy Conslts 2000– (roles incl head of strategy and innovation BBC account Siemens IT Solutions and Services 2004–); ACA 1999; *Recreations* snowboarding, motor racing; *Style—* Andrew Croxson, Esq; ✉ 6A Woodland Grove, Weybridge, Surrey KT13 9EF (tel 01932 848191, e-mail acroxson@msn.com); Spectrum Strategy Consultants, Greencoat House, Francis Street, London SW1P 1DH (tel 020 7630 1400)

CROYDON, Archdeacon of; *see:* Davies, Ven (Vincent) Anthony (Tony)

CROYDON, David John; s of John Farley Croydon, of Stourbridge, West Midlands, and Patricia Ethel, *née* Lloyd; *b* 26 February 1949; *Educ* King Edward VI GS Stourbridge, Univ of London (BA); *m* 29 July 1972, Catherine Mary (d 2005), da of James Goddard (d 2005), of Birmingham; 1 s (Luke James b 20 Jan 1981), 1 da (Madeleine Lucy b 26 June 1986); *Career* advertising exec 3M Corporation 1977–80, account mangr MSW Promotions 1980–81, account dir Counter Products Marketing 1981–86, fndr and md Marketing Principles Ltd (sales promotion consultancy) 1986–99, chief exec DraftWorldwide 1999–2000, fndr and md Hilltop Publishing Ltd and Force Majeure Records Ltd 2001–, fndr Impartial Business Advice Ltd 2006; memb Ind Publishers Gp; *Recreations* rugby football; *Clubs* Chinnor, Saracens, Middx; *Style—* David Croydon, Esq; ✉ Monks Hill, South Hills, Brill, Aylesbury, Buckinghamshire (tel 01844 237450, mobile 07836 334150, e-mail dave@hilltoppublishing.co.uk)

CROYDON, Bishop of 2003–; Rt Rev Nicholas Baines; s of Frank Baines, and Beryl Baines; *Educ* Holt Comp Sch Liverpool, Univ of Bradford (BA), Trinity Coll Bristol (BA); *Career* linguist specialist GCHQ Cheltenham 1980–84; asst curate St Thomas Kendal 1987–91, assoc min Holy Trinity Leicester 1991–92, vicar of Rothley 1992–2000, rural dean of Goscote 1995–2000, archdeacon of Lambeth 2000–03; non-exec dir The Ecclesiastical Insurance Gp 2002–; memb Gen Synod C of E 1995–2003; *Books* Hungry for Hope (1991), Speedbumps and Potholes (2003), Jesus and People Like Us (2004), Marking Time (2005); *Recreations* music, reading, sport; *Style—* The Rt Rev the Bishop of Croydon; ✉ 53 Stanhope Road, Croydon, Surrey CR0 5NS; St Matthew's House, 100 George Street, Croydon, Surrey CR0 1PE (tel 020 8256 9630, fax 020 8256 9631, e-mail bishop.nick@southwark.anglican.org)

CROZIER, Adam; *b* Falkirk; *m* Annette; 2 da (Molly, Grace); *Career* Saatchi & Saatchi: joined 1988, bd dir 1990–94, jt chief exec 1994–2000; chief exec: Football Association 2000–02, Royal Mail Group plc 2003–; non-exec dir Debenhams plc 2006–; *Style—* Adam Crozier, Esq; ✉ Royal Mail Group plc, 148 Old Street, London EC1V 9HQ

CROZIER, Brian Rossiter; s of Robert Henry Crozier (d 1939), and Elsa, *née* McGillivray (d 1957); *b* 4 August 1918; *Educ* Lycée Montpellier France, Peterborough Coll Harrow, Trinity Coll of Music London; *m* 1, 7 Sept 1940, Mary Lillian (Lila) (d 1993), da of Charles Augustus Samuel (d 1965); 3 da (Kathryn-Anne (Mrs Choguill) b 1941, Isobel (Mrs Colbourn) b 1944, Caroline (Mrs Wyeth) b 1953), 1 s (Michael b 1948); m 2, Jacqueline Marie, 18 Dec 1999; *Career* conslt and writer on int affairs; WWII aeronautical inspection 1941–43; music and art critic London 1935–39; reporter and sub ed: Stoke-on-Trent, Stockport, London 1940–41, News Chronicle 1944–48; sub ed and writer Sydney Morning Herald Aust 1948–51, correspondent Reuters 1951–52 (sub ed 1943–44), features ed Straits Times Singapore 1952–53, leader writer and corr, ed of Foreign Report The Economist 1954–64, commentator for the BBC Overseas Servs 1954–65, chm Forum World Features 1965–74, co-fndr Inst for the Study of Conflict 1970 (dir 1970–79); contrib ed: National Review NY 1978–93, Now! London 1980–81, The Times 1982–84; adjunct scholar Heritage Fndn Washington DC 1984–95, distinguished visiting fell Hoover Instn Stanford CA 1996–99; named in The Guinness Book of Records 1988 as the writer who has interviewed most heads of state and govt in the world (58) 1948–92 (now 67); *Books* The Rebels (1960), The Morning After (1963), Neo-Colonialism (1964), South-East Asia in Turmoil (1965), The Struggle for the Third World (1966), Franco (1967), The Masters of Power (1969), The Future of Communist Power (1970), De Gaulle (1973), A Theory of Conflict (1974), The Man Who Lost China (Chiang Kai-Shek) (1977), Strategy of Survival (1978), The Minimum State (1979), Franco: Crepúsculo de un hombre (1980), The Price of Peace (1980), Socialism Explained (jtly, 1984), This War Called Peace (jtly, 1984), The Andropov Deception (under pseudonym John Rossiter, 1984), The Grenada Documents (ed 1987), Socialism: Dream and Reality (1987), The Gorbachev Phenomenon (1990), Communism: Why Prolong its Death-Throes? (1990), Free Agent (autobiography, 1993), The KGB Lawsuits (1995), Le Phénix Rouge (jtly, 1995), The Rise and Fall of the Soviet Empire (1999), The Other Brian Croziers (2002); *Recreations* piano, taping stereo; *Clubs* RAC; *Style—* Brian Crozier, Esq; ✉ 18 Wickliffe Avenue, Finchley, London N3 3EJ (tel 020 8346 8124, fax 020 8346 4599)

CRUDDAS, Jonathan (Jon); MP; s of John and Pat Cruddas; *Educ* Oaklands RC Comp Portsmouth, Univ of Warwick (BSc, MA, PhD); *m* Anna, *née* Healy; 1 s; *Career* policy offr Lab Pty 1989–94, chief asst to gen sec of Lab Pty 1994–97, dep political sec to the PM 1997–2001; MP (Lab) Dagenham 2001–; memb TGWU; *Recreations* golf, angling; *Clubs* Dagenham Working Men's, White Heart Angling, Dagenham Royal Naval Assoc; *Style—* Jon Cruddas, Esq, MP; ✉ House of Commons, London SW1A 0AA (tel 020 7219 8161)

CRUDDAS, Peter Andrew; s of John Cruddas, and Lilian Frances, *née* Grover; *b* 30 September 1953; *Educ* Shoreditch Comp Sch; *m* 4 June 1987, Fiona Jane, *née* French; 1 s (Stephen), 3 da (Sarah, Annabel, Lucinda); *Career* money markets trader at various banks 1970–88, fndr chm and ceo CMC Gp plc (pioneer of internet trading) 1989–; memb Mensa; London Entrepreneur of the Year 2004; *Recreations* golf (handicap 5), reading, chess; *Clubs* Royal Mougin Golf, Monte Carlo Golf; *Style—* Peter Cruddas, Esq; ✉ CMC Group plc, 66 Prescot Street, London E1 8HG (tel 020 7170 8200, fax 020 7207 8499)

CRUICKSHANK, David John Ogilvie; s of Ogilvie Cruickshank (d 2004), of Scotland, and Rosemary Elizabeth, *née* Philip; *b* 20 February 1959; *Educ* Waid Acad Anstruther, Univ of Edinburgh (BCom); *m* 1984, Rona, da of Rowland Dalgliesh; 2 da (Lindsay Alexandra b 28 Aug 1990, Fiona Jacqueline b 4 June 1992); *Career* Deloitte: trainee chartered accountant Edinburgh 1979–82, tax mangr 1982–88, tax ptnr 1988–, ptnr i/c London

Tax Practice 1995–99, managing ptnr Tax (UK) 1999–2006, chm UK Bd 2007–; MICAS 1982; *Recreations* work, family, golf, tennis, travel, good company, current affairs; *Clubs* Caledonian, Pyrford Golf, Newtonmore Golf, Isle of Purbeck Golf; *Style*— David Cruickshank, Esq; ✉ Deloitte, 180 The Strand, London WC2R 1BL(direct tel 020 7007 1826, direct fax 020 7007 1064, e-mail dcruickshank@deloitte.co.uk)

CRUICKSHANK, Sir Donald Gordon (Don); kt (2006); s of Donald Campbell Cruickshank, of Moray, Scotland, and Margaret Buchan *née* Morrison; *b* 17 September 1942; *Educ* Fordyce Acad, Univ of Aberdeen (MA), Manchester Business Sch (MBA), Univ of Aberdeen (LLD); *m* 17 Oct 1964, Elizabeth Buchan, da of Alexander Watt Taylor, of Fraserburgh, Scotland; 1 s (Stewart b 1965), 1 da (Karen b 1969); *Career* McKinsey and Co Inc 1972–77, dir and gen mangr Sunday Times Times Newspapers Ltd 1977–80, dir Pearson Longman Ltd 1980–84, md Virgin Group plc 1984–89, chief exec NHS in Scotland 1989–93, DG of telecommunications Office of Telecommunications 1993–98, chm UK Banking Review 1998–2000, non-exec chm SMG plc 1999–2004, chm London Stock Exchange 2000–03, non-exec chm FormScape 2004–, non-exec chm Clinovia 2005–; non-exec dir Christian Salvesen plc 1993–95, T&F Informa plc 2004–05 (chm Taylor & Francis plc 2004), Qualcomm Inc 2005–; chm: Wandsworth DHA 1986–89, Action 2000 1997–2000; memb Financial Reporting Cncl 2002–; memb of Ct Univ of Aberdeen 2005–; *Recreations* opera, theatre, golf, sport; *Style*— Sir Don Cruickshank

CRUICKSHANK OF AUCHREOCH, Martin Melvin; s of Brig Martin Melvin Cruickshank, CIE (d 1964), and Florence Watson Cruickshank (d 1976); *b* 17 September 1933; *Educ* Rugby, Eaton Hall, CCC Cambridge; *m* 1 March 1958, Rona, da of Mary Fenella Paton of Grandhome (d 1949), of Grandhome House, Aberdeen; 1 da (Fenella b 1959), 3 s (Martin b 1960, Nicholas b 1961 d 1973, Paul b 1963); *Career* cmmnd Gordon Highlanders 1952, serv Malaya 1952–53 (despatches), Cyprus 1955–56, Germany 1960–61, Congo 1962 (Co cmd), Nigeria 1962–64 (chief instr Offr Cadet Sch, Bde Maj, Dep Cmdt Nigerian Military Coll), ret 1967; landowner; sec and past pres Strathfillan Golf Club; Order of St John in Scotland: memb Cncl 1970–75, memb Chapter 1970–96, Sword Bearer 1977–96; FRGS; KStJ 1982 (OStJ 1965, CStJ 1974); *Recreations* travel (particularly deserts), bird watching, golf, music, oenology, rally driving (British Army Team 1961, 1965 and 1966); *Clubs* Army and Navy, Optimists'; *Style*— M M Cruickshank of Auchreoch; ✉ Auchreoch, Crianlarich, Perthshire (tel 01838 400218, fax 01838 400217)

CRUISE, Prof (Adrian) Michael (Mike); s of Ambrose John Cruise (d 1972), and Ellen Florence Cruise (d 1997); *b* 12 May 1947, Rhwbina, Glamorgan; *Educ* Dorking Co GS, UCL (BSc, PhD); *m* 1971, Elizabeth Jennifer; 2 da (Becca b 30 Sept 1976, Rachel b 28 July 1978); *Career* UCL 1968–86 (lectr and dep dir Mullard Space Science Lab), Rutherford Appleton Lab 1986–95 (div head 1987, assoc dir and head Space Science Dept 1994–95), dep dir British Nat Space Centre 1994–95, prof of astrophysics and space research Univ of Birmingham 1995– (head Sch of Physics and Astronomy 1997–2002, currently pro-vice-chllr (research and knowledge transfer)); visiting prof: Univ of Leicester, Cranfield Univ, Univ of Kent; UK delg Science Prog Ctee European Space Agency 1996–2000; chair Astrophysics Div and memb Cncl European Physical Soc, chm Scientific Ctee H CoSPAR, memb Cncl for the Central Lab of the Research Cncls (CCLRC); NASA Gp Achievement Award 1984, BMFT Award FRG 1984, ESA Hipparcos Science Team Award 1997, Geoffrey Pardoe Award RAeS 1998; CPhys, CSci, FRAS 1973, FInstP 1998; *Publications* Principles of Space Instrument Design (jtly, 1998); author of more than 60 scientific papers; *Recreations* music, cryptography; *Clubs* Royal Astronomical Soc Dining, Univ of Birmingham Dining, Lunar Soc; *Style*— Prof Mike Cruise; ✉ University of Birmingham, Edgbaston, Birmingham B15 2TT (tel 0121 414 3974, fax 0121 414 4534, e-mail a.m.cruise@bham.ac.uk)

CRUM EWING, Humphry John Frederick; s of Humphry William Erskine Crum Ewing (d 1985), and Winifred Mary, *née* Kyle (d 1988); *b* 11 May 1934; *Educ* Marlborough, ChCh Oxford (MA); *m* 1, 30 April 1964, Carolyn Joan Maule (d 1975), da of Lt-Col Ian Burn-Murdoch, OBE, IA (d 1963), and formerly w of 3 Baron Wrenbury; 1 s (Alexander b 1966), 2 da (Arabella b 1967, Nicola b and d 1969); m 2, 14 Feb 1980, Mrs Janet Angela Tomlinson, da of L R Bates (d 1965), of Leicester; *Career* public and int affrs consltt; pres OUCA 1956, Parly candidate (Cons) Swansea East 1959; chm: Ingersoll Gp 1966–69, Rajawella Cos 1976–79; advsr to: Shadow Foreign Sec 1977–79, Min for Consumer Affrs 1981–83, Min for HE and Sci 1987–90, Min for Training 1990–92, Parly Sec Office of Public Servs & Sci 1992–93, Political Office of PM 1992; specialist advsr to House of Commons Defence Ctee 1999–2001; treas Secs and Assts' Cncl House of Commons 1990–94, an advsr to Oppn Spokesmen on Defence 1997–; chm Standish Gp 2004–; memb: EuroDéfense UK 2000–, Cncl RIIA 2000–03, IISS, Organising Ctee Oxford Intelligence Gp 2004–; ed Bailrigg Publications 1995–2003; assoc fell RUSI; fell Lancaster Univ Centre for Defence & Int Security Studies 1992–2003, academic assoc Strategic and Combat Studies Inst (SCSI) 1993–; pres Reading East Constituency Cons Assoc 2007–; Liveryman Worshipful Co of Clockmakers; *Publications* incl: Overseas Aid: A Policy of Enlightened Self-Interest (1979), A Question for Ministers (1992), British Opinion and Missile Defence (1995), Defence Diplomacy: What Is It? (1999), Around and About Westminster (2003), Military Tasks & Planning Assumptions in the Defence White Paper (2004); *Recreations* bridge, cooking, travelling, collecting; *Style*— Humphry Crum Ewing, Esq; ✉ 63 Baker Street, Reading, Berkshire RG1 7XY (tel and fax 0118 958 5096, e-mail crum.ewing@ntlworld.com)

CRUSH, His Hon Harvey Michael; s of George Stanley Crush (d 1970), of Chislehurst, Kent, and Alison Isabel, *née* Lang (d 1992); *b* 12 April 1939; *Educ* Chigwell Sch Essex; *m* 1, 21 Aug 1965 (m dis 1982), Diana, da of Frederick Joseph Bassett (d 1965), of Coulsdon, Surrey; 1 s (Nicholas b 1 Dec 1967), 1 da (Emily b 21 May 1971); m 2, 9 Dec 1982, Margaret (Maggie) Rose, da of Nicholas Dixson (d 1986); *Career* admitted slr 1963; ptnr Norton Rose 1968–91, dir TOSG Trust Fund Ltd 1970–95; memb Supreme Court Rule Ctee 1984–88, recorder of the Crown Court 1992–95 (asst recorder 1987–92); advocate Higher Courts 1994, circuit judge (SE Circuit) 1995–2001 (dep circuit judge 2001–04); called to the Bar 2001; vice-pres and chm City of London Law Soc 1989–91; memb: Law Soc, Swanley & Dist CAB Mgmnt Ctee 1991–2001 (chm 1991–93), Local then General Ctee London Legal Aid Area 1969–82 (memb Area Ctee 1982–95); dir Br Assoc of Aviation Conslts 1991–95 and 2001– (hon slr 1991–94, dep chm 2001–02 and 2004–05, chm 2002–04); hon life memb: Sevenoaks and Dist Motor Club (chm 1968–71), Slrs' Assoc of Higher Courts Advocates, London Slrs' Litigation Assoc; Liveryman Worshipful Co of Slrs 1982 (memb Ct of Assts 1987, Master 1994–95), Liveryman Worshipful Co of Farriers 1984 (memb Ct of Assts 1997–2003); Guild of Air Pilots and Air Navigators: Freeman 1991, Liveryman 2000; MRAeS 1980, FRAeS 2004; *Recreations* flying, travel; *Style*— His Hon Harvey Crush; ✉ Quadrant Chambers, 10 Fleet Street, London EC4Y 1AU

CRUTE, Prof Ian; *Educ* Univ of Newcastle upon Tyne (BSc, PhD); *Career* research scientist Nat Vegetable Research Station 1973–87 (promoted princ scientific offr 1981), Fulbright fell Dept of Plant Pathology Univ of Wisconsin Madison 1986–87, head Crop and Environment Protection Dept Horticulture Research Int (HRI) East Malling 1987, head Plant Pathology and Weed Science Dept HRI Wellesbourne 1993–99 (site dir 1995–99), dir Rothamsted Research (formerly Inst of Arable Crops Research) 1999–; visiting prof of plant pathology Univ of Oxford 1997; chm Cncl Sainsbury Lab; pres British Soc for Plant Pathology 1995; Research Medal RASE 1992, BCPC Medal 1995; *Style*— Prof Ian Crute; ✉ Rothamsted Research, Rothamsted, Harpenden, Hertfordshire AL5 2JQ

CRWYS-WILLIAMS, Air Vice Marshal David Owen; CB (1990); s of late Gareth Crwys-Williams, OBE, of Llangollen, Clwyd, and Frances Ellen, *née* Strange (d 1999); *b* 24 December 1940; *Educ* Oakham Sch, RAF Coll Cranwell; *m* 1, 1963 (m dis 1972), Jennifer Jean, *née* Pearce; 1 da (Jacqueline Lara b 23 Feb 1967), 1 s (Geraint Miles Vickery b 27 April 1971); m 2, 1973, Irene (Suzie), da of late D J T Whan, of Kendal, Cumbria; 1 s (Huw David b 20 Nov 1975), 2 da (Kirsty Jane b 20 Feb 1977, Claire Elizabeth b 4 Nov 1981); *Career* RAF Coll Cranwell 1958–61, cmmnd as pilot 1961, 30 Sqdn Kenya 1961–63, 47 Sqdn RAF Abingdon 1964–66, ADC to C-in-C RAF Trg Cmd 1966–68, Sqdn Ldr 1969, OC 46 Sqdn RAF Abingdon 1969–71, OC Ops RAF Masirah Oman 1972, Army Staff Coll 1973, Personal Staff Offr to C-in-C Near East Air Force 1974–75, Wing Cdr 1975, OC 230 Sqdn RAF Odiham 1975–77, Personnel Offr MOD 1977–79, Gp Capt 1979, Dep Dir Air Plans MOD 1979–81, Station Cdr RAF Shawbury 1982–84, RCDS 1985, Air Cdre 1985, Dir of Air Support (later Dir of Air Staff Duties) 1986–88, Air Vice Marshal 1988, Cdr Br Forces Falkland Islands 1988–89, DG RAF Personnel Services MOD 1989–92; md: Services Sound and Vision Corp 1993–, Visua Ltd 1996–98; chm: Columbia Communications Europe 1994–98, Teleport London International 1994–98, New Island Conservation Tst 1995–; tstee: Amersham and Wycombe Coll 1997– (vice-chm 1999–2000, chm 2001–03), Br Forces Fndn 1999–, RAF Museum 2002–; memb Cncl Cinema and Television Benevolent Fund 1994; Freeman City of London 2002, Liveryman Guild of Air Pilots and Navigators 2002; FCIPD 1991, FCMI (FIMgt 1993); *Recreations* building, fishing, walking; *Clubs* RAF; *Style*— Air Vice Marshal David Crwys-Williams, CB; ✉ c/o Barclays Bank, PO Box 354, Abingdon, Oxfordshire OX14 1FL

CRYAN, His Hon Judge Donald Michael; s of Thomas Cryan (d 1997), of Ireland, and Helen McBeath, *née* Munro (d 1974); *b* 18 January 1948; *Educ* Salvatorian Coll, UCL (LLB); *m* 1973, Pamela; 2 s; *Career* called to the Bar Inner Temple 1970 (bencher 1991); recorder 1993–96, circuit judge (SE Circuit) 1996–; designated family judge: Medway 2001–05, Kent 2005–; chm Lord Chllr's Working Pty on Delay in Family Proceedings Courts (FPC) 2002–03; memb: Lord Chllr's Advsy Ctee on Judicial Case Mgmnt in Public Law Children Act Cases 2002–, Unified Admin Judicial Ctee 2003–05, Family Ctee Judicial Studies Bd 2003–; chair Family and Magisterial Sub-Ctee 2005, judicial memb Courts Bd for Kent; memb Ctee: Centre for Child and Family Law Reform, Marshall Hall Tst 1992–2005; Freeman City of London 1978, Master Worshipful Co of Fruiterers 1999 (Liveryman 1978, Upper Warden 1998); *Recreations* opera and walking; *Clubs* RAC; *Style*— His Hon Judge Cryan; ✉ 4 Paper Buildings, Temple, London EC4Y 7EX (tel 020 7583 0816, e-mail hhjudge.cryan@judiciary.gsi.gov.uk)

CRYER, (Constance) Ann; JP, MP; da of Allen Place (d 1973), and Margaret Ann, *née* Ratcliffe (d 1996); *b* 14 December 1939; *Educ* Spring Bank Secdy Modern Darwen, Bolton Tech Coll, Keighley Tech Coll; *m* 1, 3 Aug 1963, George Robert (Bob) Cryer, MP, MEP (d 1994), s of John Arthur Cryer; 1 s (John Robert (MP for Hornchurch 1997–2005) b 11 April 1964), 1 da (Jane Ann b 17 Nov 1965); m 2, 6 Sept 2003, Rev John Hammerley (d 2004); *Career* cleric ICI 1955–61, telephonist GPO 1961–64, researcher Sociology Dept Univ of Essex 1969–70, PA to Bob Cryer, MP, MEP 1974–94, MP (Lab) Keighley 1997–; memb: Cncl Euro Parly Assembly 1997–2003, Lord Chllr's Dept Select Ctee 2003–05, Home Office Select Ctee 2005–; backbench rep on Parly Ctee 2005–; cncllr Darwen BC 1962–65; pres Keighley and Worth Valley Railway Preservation Soc; chair PLP/CND 1999–, memb Campaign Gp of Lab MPs 1997–; pres-elect Keighley Agric Show 2007; memb: Lab Pty, Co-op Pty, Friends of the Earth, CND, T&GWU; memb Cncl Bradford Cathedral 2000– (hon lat canon 2005–); *Publications* Boldness be my Friend - Remembering Bob Cryer (compiler, 1997); *Recreations* gardening, cinema, theatre, time spent with six grandchildren and two step grandchildren; *Style*— Mrs Ann Cryer, MP; ✉ 32 Kendall Avenue, Shipley, West Yorkshire; Bob Cryer House, 35 Devonshire Street, Keighley, West Yorkshire BD21 2BH; House of Commons, London SW1A 0AA (tel 020 7219 3000 or 01535 210083)

CRYSTAL, Prof David; OBE (1995); s of Samuel Cyril Crystal, of London, and Mary Agnes, *née* Morris; *b* 6 July 1941; *Educ* St Mary's Coll Liverpool, UCL (BA), Univ of London (PhD); *m* 1, 1 April 1964, Molly Irene (d 1976), da of Capt Robert Stack (d 1965); 2 s (Steven David b 1964, Timothy Joseph b 1969 d 1972), 2 da (Susan Mary b 1966, Lucy Alexandra b 1973); m 2, Hilary Frances, da of Capt Kenneth Norman (d 1990), of Cuffley, Herts; 1 s (Benjamin Peter b 1977); *Career* res asst Survey of English Usage UCL 1962–63, asst lectr linguistics Univ Coll of North Wales 1963–65; Univ of Reading: lectr 1965–69, reader 1969–75, prof of linguistics 1975–85; hon prof of linguistics Univ of Wales (Bangor) 1985–; writer and ed of ref books 1985–; ed: Journal of Child Language 1974–85, The Language Library 1978–, Applied Language Studies 1980–84, Child Language Teaching and Therapy 1985–96, Linguistics Abstracts 1985–96; assoc ed Journal of Linguistics 1970–73, co-ed Studies in Language Disability 1974–2006, consulting ed English Today 1984–94, usage ed Great Illustrated Dictionary (Readers Digest, 1984), conslt AND Reference 1997–2001, chm Crystal Reference Systems 2001–06 (dir of research 2006–); Sam Wanamaker fell Shakespeare's Globe 2003; author of numerous pubns connected with the English language and linguistics; dir The Ucheldre Centre Holyhead 1990–; memb Bd: Br Cncl 1996–2001, English Speaking Union 2001–06; vice-pres: Inst of Linguistics 1998–, Soc for Eds and Proofreaders 2004–; patron: Nat Assoc of Professionals Concerned with Language-Impaired Children 1986–2002, Int Assoc of Teachers of English as a Foreign Language 1993–, Assoc for Language Learning 2007–; fell Coll of Speech Therapists 1983, FRSA 1983, FBA 2000; *Books* incl: The Cambridge Encyclopedia of Language (1987, 2 edn 1997), The English Language (1988, 2 edn 2001), The Cambridge Encyclopedia (ed, 1990, 4 edn 2000), The Cambridge Encyclopedia of the English Language (1995, 2 edn 2003), Language Play (1998), Language Death (2000), Language and the Internet (2001, 2 edn 2006), The Penguin Encyclopedia (ed, 2002, 3 edn 2006), The Stories of English (2004), Shakespeare's Words (with Ben Crystal, 2002), The Language Revolution (2004), A Glossary of Netspeak and Textspeak (2004), Pronouncing Shakespeare (2005), The Shakespeare Miscellany (with Ben Crystal 2005), Dr Johnson's Dictionary (2005), How Language Works (2006), Words, Words, Words (2006), The Fight for English (2006), As They Say in Zanzibar (2006), By Hook or By Crook (2007), Think on my Words (2007); *Recreations* cinema, music, bibliophily, progressing the arts; *Style*— Prof David Crystal, OBE; ✉ Akaroa, Gors Avenue, Holyhead, Anglesey LL65 1PB (tel 01407 762764, fax 01407 769728, e-mail davidcrystal1@googlemail.com)

CRYSTAL, Jonathan; s of Dr Samuel Cyril Crystal, OBE, of London, and Rachel Ethel, *née* Trewish; *b* 20 December 1949; *Educ* Leeds GS, QMC London (LLB); *m* Giselle Satya, *née* Jeremie; 2 s (Petros, Jeremie), 1 da (Sophie); *Career* called to the Bar Middle Temple 1972; dir: Tottenham Hotspur FC 1991–93, Cardiff City FC 2000–07; *Recreations* sports, travel; *Style*— J Crystal, Esq; ✉ Cloisters, 1 Pump Court, Temple, London EC4Y 7AA (tel 020 7827 4007, fax 020 7827 4100, e-mail jc@cloisters.com)

CRYSTAL, Michael; QC (1984); s of late Dr Samuel Cyril Crystal, OBE, and Rachel Ettel Crystal; *b* 5 March 1948; *Educ* Leeds GS, QMC London (LLB), Magdalen Coll Oxford (BCL); *m* 1972, Susan Felicia Sniderman; 1 s, 1 da; *Career* called to the Bar: Middle Temple 1970 (bencher 1993), Gray's Inn (ad eundem) 1989; dep judge of the High Court 1995–; lectr in law Pembroke Coll Oxford 1971–76; visiting prof Dept of Laws UCL 2002–; DTI inspr into: County NatWest Ltd and County NatWest Securities Ltd 1988–89, National Westminster Bank plc 1992; memb: Insolvency Rules Advsy Ctee 1993–97, Advsy Cncl Centre for Commercial Law Studies Queen Mary & Westfield Coll London 1996–, Fin Law Panel 1996–2002, FA Premier League Panel for Insolvency Matters

2004–; sr visiting fell Queen Mary & Westfield Coll London 1996, hon fell Soc for Advanced Legal Studies 1997; govr RSC 1988–2006 (hon govr 2006–); memb Int Insolvency Inst 2005–, fell American Coll of Bankruptcy 2006–; fell Royal Instn of GB 2004–; *Publications* various legal textbooks; *Recreations* travel, music, theatre; *Clubs* RAC, MCC; *Style—* Michael Crystal, QC; ✉ 3–4 South Square, Gray's Inn, London WC1R 5HP (tel 020 7696 9900, fax 020 7696 9911)

CRYSTAL, Peter Maurice; s of Boris Leonard Crystal, of Leeds, and Pauline Mary, *née* Fox; *b* 7 January 1948; *Educ* Leeds GS, St Edmund Hall Oxford (MA), McGill Univ Montreal (LLM); *m*; 1 s (Philip), 3 da (Emma, Anna, Carla); *Career* sr ptnr Memery Crystal slrs; Parly candidate: Leeds NE (SDP) 1983 and 1987, Fulham (Lib Dem) 1992; memb Law Soc; *Recreations* sports, travel; *Clubs* Reform, Athenaeum, Vincent's (Oxford); *Style—* Peter Crystal, Esq; ✉ Memery Crystal, 44 Southampton Buildings, London WC2A 1AP (tel 020 7242 5905, fax 020 7242 2058, e-mail pmcrystal@memerycrystal.com)

CUCKNEY, Lady ; *see:* Newell, (Priscilla) Jane

CUCKNEY, Baron (Life Peer UK 1995), of Millbank in the City of Westminster; Sir John Graham Cuckney; kt (1978); s of Air Vice-Marshal Ernest John Cuckney, CB, CBE, DSC* (d 1965), and Lilian, *née* Williams (d 1976); *b* 12 July 1925; *Educ* Shrewsbury, Univ of St Andrews; *m* 1, 1960, Muriel (d 2004), da of late Walter Scott Boyd; m 2, 12 April 2007, (Priscilla) Jane Newell, *qv*; *Career* war serv with Royal Northumberland Fusiliers and King's African Rifles, attached to War Office (asst to Gen Staff); former chm The Orion Publishing Group Ltd 1994–97; former chm: Royal Insurance Holdings plc, 3i Group plc, Westland Group plc, The Crown Agents for Overseas Govts and Admins, The Thomas Cook Group, John Brown plc, Brooke Bond Group plc, International Military Services Ltd, Port of London Authority, Bd Mersey Docks and Harbour, Standard Industrial Trust; former dep chm TI Group plc, former vice-chm Glaxo Wellcome plc; former dir: Brixton Estate plc, Lazard Bros & Co Ltd; advsr to Sec of State for Social Security (on Maxwell pension affair) 1992–95, fndr chm Maxwell Pensioners Tst 1992–95; Freeman City of London 1977, Elder Brother Trinity House 1980; *Style—* The Rt Hon Lord Cuckney; ✉ House of Lords, London SW1A 0PW

CUDDEFORD, Norman Allan; s of Charles Leonard Allan Cuddeford (d 1986), of Leigh-on-Sea, and Gwendoline May, *née* Hockley (d 1985); *b* 8 January 1933; *Educ* Felsted; *m* 1, 1963 (m dis 1975), Penelope Alexandra Cuddeford; 1 s (Alastair b 1964); m 2, 12 April 1975, Maria, da of Dr Erasmo Hoyo Hernandez, of Mexico City; 1 da (Vanessa b 1980), 1 step da (Ana Gabriela b 1971); *Career* Nat Serv RAF 1952–54, cmmnd 1953, later CO RAF Sennen (at that time the youngest CO in RAF); associated with Lloyd's of London since 1955; freelance sports commentator (covering athletics, cricket, tennis) BBC Radio 1965–98; conslt: SBJ Stephenson Ltd, Steel Burrill Jones Ltd; memb Rottingdean Preservation Soc; Freeman City of London 1956, Liveryman Worshipful Co of Glass Sellers; *Recreations* travel, good company and convivial conversation, cricket; *Clubs* RAF, MCC; *Style—* Norman Cuddeford, Esq; ✉ Point Clear, Lustrells Road, Rottingdean, East Sussex BN2 7DS (tel 01273 304 943); Steel Burrill Jones Ltd, 100 Whitechapel Road, London E1 (tel 020 7816 2000)

CULE, Dr John Hedley; MBE (2005); s of Walter Edwards Cule (d 1942), of Glamorgan, and Annie, *née* Russ (d 1940); *b* 7 February 1920; *Educ* Porth Co Sch, Kingswood Sch Bath, Trinity Hall Cambridge (MA, MD), King's Coll Hosp London; *m* 23 March 1944, Joyce Leslie (d 1999), da of Henry Phillips Bonser (d 1962); 2 s (Simon b 1949, Peter b 1951), 1 da (Myfanwy b 1955); *Career* WWII Capt RAMC served Italy (despatches) 1943–46; surgical registrar Addenbrooke's Hosp Cambridge 1947, med registrar KCH London 1948, princ NHS partnership Camberley 1948–71, psychiatrist St David's Hosp Carmarthen and Psychiatric Unit W Wales Gen Hosp 1972–86; Soc of Apothecaries lectr in the history of med Univ of Wales Coll of Med 1972–2003; pres: Osler Club London 1972, History of Med Soc of Wales 1978–80, Br Soc for History of Med 1985–87 (vice-pres 1984, treas 1972–82), Int Soc for History of Med 1992–96 (vice-pres 1989–92); memb Cncl Harveian Soc 1964; chm: Welsh Branch Br Driving Soc 1986–94, Sanders Watney Tst (Driving for the Disabled) 1994–2000 (vice-chm 1986–94); keynote address 350th anniversary celebrations RCPI 2005; High Sheriff Co of Dyfed 1985–86; Freeman City of London 1964, Liveryman Worshipful Soc of Apothecaries 1962; emeritus fell American Osler Soc, hon fell Faculty of the History and Philosophy of Med Soc of Apothecaries 1997; MRCS, FRCP, FRCGP, FSA 1996, Hon FRSM 1996; *Books* Wreath on the Crown (1967), A Doctor for the People (1980), Child Care through the Centuries (jt ed, 1986), The Great Maritime Discoveries and World Health (jt ed, 1991), Russia and Wales. Essays on the History of State Involvement in Health Care (jt ed, 1994), Medicine: a History of Healing (contrib, 1997); ed Vesalius (jl Int Soc for the History of Med, 1995–2002), Osler Oration (jl of medical biography, vol 8, 2000), Clio in the Clinic: History in Medical Practice (contrib, 2005); *Recreations* horse carriage driving trials, fly fishing; *Clubs* Royal Perth Golfing Soc and County and City; *Style—* Dr John H Cule, MBE; ✉ Abereinon, Capel Dewi, Llandysul, Ceredigion SA44 4PP (tel 01559 362229, fax 01559 362238, e-mail john@cule.demon.co.uk)

CULHANE, Prof (John) Leonard; s of late John Thomas Culhane, and late Mary Agnes, *née* Durkin; *b* 14 October 1937; *Educ* Clongowes Wood Coll, UCD (BSc, MSc), UCL (PhD); *m* 7 Sept 1961, Mary Brigid, da of late James Smith; 2 s (Simon b 22 Sept 1963, Laurence b 18 Feb 1966); *Career* Dept of Physics UCL: res asst 1963, lectr 1967, reader 1976, prof 1981–94, dir Mullard Space Sci Laboratory 1983–; head and prof Dept of Space and Climate Physics UCL 1994–; sr scientist Lockheed Palo Alto Laboratory 1969–70; author of more than 290 scientific papers on solar and cosmic X-ray astronomy, X-ray instrumentation and spectroscopy; chm: Space Sci Prog Bd 1989–94, Brit Nat Ctee Space Res 1989–93, COSPAR Cmmn E 1994–2002; UK delegate and vice-chm ESA SPC 1990–95; chm ESF Euro Space Sci Ctee 1996–2002; memb: Cncl Univ of Surrey 1985–88, Astronomy Plan Sci Bd SERC 1989–93, Particle Physics and Astronomy Res Cncl 1996–2000, IAU, American Astronomical Soc, RAS; foreign memb Norwegian Acad of Sci and Letters 1996; FRS 1985; *Books* X-Ray Astronomy (with P Sanford, 1981); *Recreations* music, racing cars; *Style—* Prof J Leonard Culhane, FRS; ✉ 24 Warnham Road, Horsham, West Sussex RH12 2QU (tel 01403 263475); Mullard Space Science Laboratory, University College London, Holmbury St Mary, Dorking, Surrey RH5 6NT (tel 01483 274111, fax 01483 278312, e-mail jlc@mssl.ucl.ac.uk)

CULL-CANDY, Prof Stuart Graham; s of Stanley William Cull-Candy, and Margaret Cull-Candy; *b* 2 November 1946; *Educ* Univ of London (BSc), UCL (MSc), Univ of Glasgow (PhD); *m* Dr Barbara Paterson Fulton; 1 da (Sophie); *Career* postdoctoral fell Inst of Pharmacology Univ of Lund 1974–75; UCL: Beit meml research fell and assoc research staff Dept of Biophysics 1975–82, Wellcome Tst reader in pharmacology Dept of Pharmacology 1982–90, prof of neuroscience (personal chair) 1990–, Gaddum chair of pharmacology 2006–; int research scholar Howard Hughes Med Inst 1993–98; memb: Neuroscience Ctee MRC 1975–82, Int Interest Gp Grants Ctee Wellcome Tst 1991–97, Research Fellowship Ctee Royal Soc 2003–, Research Grants Ctee Royal Soc 2005–, Sr Research Fellowships Panel Leverhulme Tst 2006–; ed: Jl of Physiology 1987–95, European Jl of Neuroscience 1988–, Neuron 1994–98; external editorial advsr in neuroscience Nature 1993–97, reviewing ed Jl of Neuroscience 2000–, guest ed Current Opinions in Neurobiology 2007; memb: American Neuroscience Soc, Physiological Soc, Br Neuroscience Soc, Int Brain Research Orgn (IBRO); G L Brown Award Physiological Soc 1996, Wolfson Award Royal Soc 2003; FRS 2002, FMedSci 2004, fell British Pharmacological Soc 2005, Faculty of 1000 2006–; *Publications* author of various book chapters and numerous articles on synaptic transmission and glutamate receptors in the brain and peripheral nervous system in scientific jls; *Recreations* natural history, local history, antiquarian books relating to medicine and natural history, the Arts and Crafts movement; *Style—* Prof Stuart G Cull-Candy, FRS, FMedSci; ✉ Department of Pharmacology, University College London, Gower Street, London WC1E 6BT (tel 020 7679 3766, fax 020 7679 7298, e-mail s.cull-candy@ucl.ac.uk)

CULLEARN, David Beverley; s of Jack Cullearn (d 1944), of Bradford, and Gladys Irene, *née* Earnshaw; *b* 22 April 1941; *Educ* Grange GS Bradford, Leeds Sch of Architecture (DipArch); *Career* architect and painter in watercolours; ptnr Edmund Kirby Manchester, Liverpool and London; awards: Structural Steel Design Award 1987, Malcolm Dean Design Award 1987, Office of the Year award (Volvo HQ) 1987–88, various Civic Tst Awards; exhibitions: Phillips Gallery, Manchester Art Gallery, The Gallery London, Royal Acad; PP Soc of Architect Artists; RIBA; *Recreations* mountain walking, horse racing, architecture, painting; *Style—* David Cullearn, Esq; ✉ High Royd, Northgate, Honley, Huddersfield HD9 6QL (tel 01484 663633, fax 01484 660837, e-mail cullearn@msn.com); EK Architects Limited, 8 King Street, Manchester M2 6AQ (tel 0161 832 3667, fax 0161 832 3795)

CULLEN, Prof Christopher Noel (Chris); JP; s of Patricia, *née* Cody; *b* 25 December 1949; *Educ* N Manchester GS, UCNW Bangor (BA, PhD); *Career* dir of clinical psychology servs to people with mental handicaps Salford HA 1983–86, SSMH chair of learning difficulties Univ of St Andrews 1986–95, prof Keele Univ 1995–, clinical dir psychological therapies Staffs Combined Healthcare NHS Tst 1995–; former pres Br Psychological Soc; fell Br Psychological Soc 1983; *Books* Human Operant Conditioning and Behaviour Modification (ed with G Davey, 1988); *Recreations* climbing, fell running, ski mountaineering; *Clubs* Mynydd Climbing; *Style—* Prof Chris Cullen; ✉ Psychology Department, Keele University, Staffordshire ST5 5BG (e-mail c.cullen@keele.ac.uk)

CULLEN, Sir (Edward) John; kt (1991); s of William Henry Pearson Cullen, and Ellen Emma Cullen; *b* 19 October 1926; *Educ* Univ of Cambridge (MA, MEng, PhD), Univ of Texas (MS); *m* 1954, Betty Davall Hopkins; 2 s, 2 da; *Career* dep chm Rohm and Haas (UK) Ltd until 1983; chm Health and Safety Cmmn 1983–93; pres: Inst of Chemical Engrs 1988–89, Pipeline Industries Guild 1996–98, Br Safety Industries Fedn 1997–; vice-pres: Instn of Occupation Health and Safety, Nat Health and Safety Gps Cncl; chm: Br Nat Ctee for Int Engrg Affrs 1991–96, Robens Inst Advsy Ctee 1993–94, Fédération Européenne d'Associations Nationales d'Ingénieurs (FEANI) 1996–99, MacRobert Award Ctee 1999–2003 (memb 1995–99); memb: HRH the Duke of Edinburgh's Cwlth Study Conf Cncl 1990, Cncl (now Senate) Engrg Cncl 1990–95, Cncl Royal Acad of Engrg until 1994, Exec Ctee RoSPA 1993–2002; tstee Br Occupational Health Research Fund 1992–98; Hon DSc Univ of Exeter 1993; FREng 1987, FRSA 1988; *Recreations* gardening, swimming, reading, walking; *Clubs* Athenaeum; *Style—* Sir John Cullen, FREng; ✉ 34 Duchess of Bedford House, Kensington, London W8 7QW

CULLEN, Dr Michael Henry; s of Charles Gavin Cullen, and Olive, *née* Walker; *b* 29 March 1947; *Educ* Queen Elizabeth's Sch Barnet, Univ of Bristol (BSc, MB ChB, MD); *m* 1, 2 July 1972 (m dis 1988), Rosemary Elizabeth; 3 s (Matthew Jacob b 13 March 1974, Alexander James b 11 Dec 1976, Thomas Oliver b 7 May 1980); m 2, 20 Aug 1989, Alison Helen, da of David Machin; 1 da (Flora Ruth b 28 March 1991); *Career* conslt med oncologist Queen Elizabeth Hosp Birmingham 1982–, clinical dir Oncology and Haematology Servs Univ Hosp Birmingham NHS Tst 1990–98, hon reader in med oncology Univ of Birmingham 1997–; chm: Jt Collegiate Cncl for Oncology 1998–2002, RCP Ctee on Med Oncology 1998–; memb NCRI Working Pty on Testicular Tumours; author of pubns on: lung cancer, testicular cancer, lymphoma; memb: Int Assoc for the Study of Lung Cancer, Br Assoc for Cancer Res, Assoc of Cancer Physicians; UK nat rep Euro Soc of Med Oncology; memb Bd W Midlands Arts 1997–2002, memb W Midlands Regnl Arts Cncl 2002–04; FRCP 1988, FRCR 2001; *Recreations* tennis, skiing, wine tasting, music, fine art; *Style—* Dr Michael Cullen; ✉ Priory Hospital, Edgbaston, Birmingham B5 7UG (tel 0121 446 1670); Queen Elizabeth Hospital, Edgbaston, Birmingham B15 2TH (tel 0121 627 2444, fax 0121 697 8428, e-mail michael.cullen@uhb.nhs.uk)

CULLEN, (Charles) Nigel; OBE (1987), TD (1976, and 2 Bars 1982 and 1990), DL (Notts 1991); s of Peter Carver Cullen (d 1990), and Dorothy, *née* Woodward (d 1992); *b* 26 September 1944; *Educ* Trent Coll; *m* 15 April 1981 (m dis 2000), Brenda Suzanne, da of Flt Offr Franklin Paul Bowen, US Army, of Oklahoma, USA; 1 s (Stephen James b 1971), 1 da (Emily Josephine b 1979); *Career* TA: cmmnd 1964, platoon cdr 5/8 Bn Sherwood Foresters 1964–67, platoon cdr Mercian Vol 1967–72, co cdr 3 WFR 1972–78, GSO 2 V Notts 1978–81, 2 i/c 3 WFR 1981–83, SO 2 G3 V 54 Inf Bde 1984, CO 3 WFR 1984–87, SO 1 G3 V E Dist 1987–88, dep cdr 54 Inf Bde 1988–91, TA Col SPT DARC 1991–92, ADC (TA) 1991–93; admitted slr 1970, NP; memb Freeth Cartwright LLP; pres: Notts C of C and Indust 1991–92, Notts City Business Club 1989–90; chm: Assoc of E Midlands C of C and Industry 1994–96, Notts Business Venture Enterprise Agency 1996–2003; dir Business Link Greater Nottingham 1996–98; memb and sec E Midlands Branch STEP 1996–2000; Dep Under Sheriff of Derbyshire 1994–96; memb: Notts Law Soc, The Notaries' Soc, Law Soc; *Recreations* theatre, cinema; *Style—* Nigel Cullen, Esq, OBE, TD, DL; ✉ 2 William Close, Duffield, Belper, Derbyshire DE56 4HN (tel 01332 842730); Freeth Cartwright LLP, Cumberland Court, 80 Mount Street, Nottingham NG1 6HH (tel 01159 369385, fax 01158 599653, e-mail nigel.cullen@freethcartwright.co.uk)

CULLEN, Timothy William Brian (Tim); s of (James) Brian Cullen, CBE (d 1972), and (Sybil) Kathleen, *née* Jones (d 1991); *b* 23 March 1944; *Educ* King William's Coll IOM, Trinity Coll Dublin (MA); *m* 19 July 1980, Nora, da of Vytautas Meskauskas; 1 da (Jura b 1982), 1 s (Brian b 1986); *Career* English teacher St Edward's Sch FL 1967–69, press spokesman Ford Motor Co Ltd Warley England 1969–73, int press spokesman Ford Motor Co Dearborn MI 1973–75, int public affairs admin Continental Bank Chicago 1975–78, various external affairs posts World Bank Washington DC 1978–84, chief of external affairs Euro Office World Bank Paris 1984–90, chief Information and Public Affrs Div and chief spokesman World Bank Washington DC 1990–96, sr advsr external and UN affrs World Bank 1996–99, fndr and md Tim Cullen Assocs (TCA) Ltd (Int Policy Mgmnt) 1999–, chm The International Leadership Programme at Oxford (ILPO) Ltd 2001–, chm and publisher Plain Words Media Ltd 2003–, programme dir Oxford Programme on Negotiation and Oxford Programme on Investment Decision-Making Univ of Oxford 2004–; pres Bd of Dirs Int Sch of Paris 1988–89; memb: Jt UN Information Ctee 1990–96, UNESCO Experts Gp on Information and Communication 2000–01; cmmr IOM Fin Supervision Cmmn 2001–; tstee Bishop Barrow's Charity King William's Coll IOM 2004–; sr assoc memb St Antony's Coll Oxford 2000–; *Books* Yugoslavia and The World Bank (1979); *Recreations* writing, cooking, photography, fishing; *Clubs* East India; *Style—* Tim Cullen, Esq; ✉ Tim Cullen Associates, The Plain, Boars Hill, Oxford OX1 5DD (tel 01865 326323, fax 01865 326363, e-mail tcullen@timcullen.com or tim.cullen@sbs.ox.ac.uk, website www.timcullen.com)

CULLEN OF WHITEKIRK, Baron (Life Peer UK 2003), of Whitekirk in the County of East Lothian (William) Douglas Cullen; PC (1997); s of Sheriff Kenneth Douglas Cullen (d 1956), and Gladys Margaret, *née* Douglas-Wilson (d 1992); *b* 18 November 1935; *Educ* Dundee HS, Univ of St Andrews (MA), Univ of Edinburgh (LLB); *m* 1961, Rosamond Mary, da of William Henry Nassau Downer, OBE, of NI; 2 s, (Christopher, Adrian), 2 da (Sophia, Felicity); *Career* advocate 1960, standing jr counsel to HM Customs and Excise 1970–73, QC 1973, Advocate-Depute 1978–81, a senator Coll of Justice in Scotland (Lord of Session) 1986–2005, Lord Justice Clerk of Scotland 1997–2001, Lord Justice Gen of

Scotland and Lord Pres of the Ct of Session 2001–05; memb Civil and Commercial Courts Qatar Financial Centre 2007–; chm: Med Appeal Tbnl 1977–86, Ct of Inquiry into Piper Alpha Disaster 1988–90, Review of Business of the Outer House of the Ct of Session 1995, Tbnl of Inquiry into the shootings at Dunblane Primary Sch 1996, Ladbroke Grove Rail Inquiry 1999–2001; memb Royal Cmmn on Ancient and Historical Monuments of Scot 1987–97; memb Bd The Signet Accreditations Ltd 2007–; pres SACRO 2000–, Saltire Soc 2005–; memb Ct Napier Univ 1996–2005; chm: Cncl The Cockburn Assoc (Edinburgh Civic Tst) 1984–86, Govrs St Margaret's Sch Edinburgh 1994–2001; Hon LLD: Univ of Aberdeen 1992, Univ of St Andrews 1997, Univ of Dundee 2000, Univ of Edinburgh 2000, Glasgow Caledonian Univ 2000; Hon DUniv Heriot-Watt Univ 1995; FRSE 1993, Hon FREng 1995; *Recreations* gardening, natural history; *Clubs* Caledonian, New (Edinburgh); *Style—* The Rt Hon the Lord Cullen of Whitekirk; ✉ House of Lords, London SW1A 0PW

CULLEY, Kenneth (Ken); CBE (1998); s of James Culley (d 1970), of Cheshire, and Lily Valentine, *née* Dale (d 1970); *b* 3 June 1942; *Educ* Kings Sch Macclesfield; *m* 1, 1964 (m dis 1984), Barbara May, da of Frank Hooley; 2 da (Alison Jane b 1966, Johanne Helen b 1968), 1 s (Nicholas James b 1971); m 2, 1985, Eleanor Pamela Broomhead, da of Dr David Alexander Whyte Fairweather; *Career* accountant Bradford & Bingley Building Society 1965–69, gen mangr Cheshire Building Society 1969–83, chief exec and dir Portman Building Society 1983–99; dir The Building Societies Trust Ltd 1995–97; chm: JPMorgan Fleming Elect plc 2004–, 1st Credit (Funding) Ltd 2005–, Marks and Spencer Financial Servs plc 2005– (non-exec dir 2000–05); non-exec dir: Fleming Managed Income plc 1999–2003, Fleming Managed Growth plc 1999–2004, BRIT Insurance Ltd 2000– (chm 2003–07), Football Licencing Authy 2000–04, Financial Markets Compensation Scheme Ltd 2000–05, BRIT Insurance (UK) Ltd 2003–, BRIT Syndicates Ltd 2004–, BRIT Insurance Hldgs plc 2007–; memb Cncl: Building Socs Assoc 1986–99 (dep chm 1994–95, chm 1995–96), Int Union of Housing Fin Instns 1995–99 (dep pres 1997–99); memb Cncl of Mortgage Lenders 1994–97; FCIB; *Recreations* sport: fishing, horse riding, rugby football, soccer; *Style—* Ken Culley, Esq, CBE; ✉ Coombesbury Cottage, Boxford, Newbury, Berkshire RG16 8DE (tel 01488 608509, fax 01488 608806, e-mail kenculley@hotmail.com)

CULLINAN, Edward Horder; CBE; s of Dr Edward Revill Cullinan, CBE (d 1965), and Dorothea Joy, *née* Horder; *b* 17 July 1931; *Educ* Ampleforth, Univ of Cambridge (BA), AA Sch of Architecture (AADipl), Univ of Calif Berkeley; *m* Rosalind, *née* Yeates; 2 da (Emma Louise b 1962, Kate b 1963), 1 s (Thomas Edward b 1965); *Career* Nat Serv Lt RE 1949–51; architect in practice London 1959, fndr Edward Cullinan Architects 1968–; Bannister Fletcher prof Univ of London 1978–79; visiting critic 1973–85: Toronto, Cincinnati, MIT; Graham Willis prof Univ of Sheffield 1985–87, George Simpson prof Univ of Edinburgh 1987–89, visiting prof Univ of Nottingham 2004–; tstee: Academy Enterprises, Koestler Award Tst 1998–; Hon Dr Univ of Sheffield 2001–; Hon DUniv: Lincolnshire and Humberside, E London; FRSA 1981, RA 1991, Hon FRIAS 1995; *Books* Edward Cullinan Architects (1984 and 1995), Ends Middles Beginnings (2005); *Recreations* building, horticulture, silviculture, surfing; *Style—* Edward Cullinan, Esq, CBE, RA; ✉ Gib Tor, Quarnford, Buxton, Derbyshire SK17 0TA; Edward Cullinan Architects Ltd, 1 Baldwin Terrace, London N1 7RU (tel 020 7704 1975, fax 020 7354 2739)

CULLINANE, John Patrick; s of John Cullinane, of London, and Pauline Mary Elizabeth, *née* Rourke; *b* 4 March 1955; *Educ* St Benedict's Sch Ealing, Wadham Coll Oxford (MA); *m* 30 July 1983, Jane Margaret Dacre, *née* Spokes; 1 da (Laura Jane Elizabeth b 30 Aug 1985), 1 s (Ruairi John Spokes b 10 March 1987); *Career* Dept of Employment Gp 1977–86, Arthur Andersen 1986–2002 (ptnr 1995), Deloitte 2002–; pres Chartered Inst of Taxation 2006–07 (dep pres 2005–06); Freeman City of London; memb: Co of Tax Advsrs, Guild of Investment Bankers; *Recreations* squash, skiing; *Style—* John Cullinane, Esq; ✉ Deloitte, 180 Strand, London WC2R 1BL (tel 020 7303 2803, fax 020 7303 5909, e-mail jcullinane@deloitte.co.uk)

CULLIS, Prof Anthony George; s of George Thomas Cullis (d 1966), and Doris Mary, *née* Bowen (d 2003); *b* 16 January 1946, Worcester; *Educ* Univ of Oxford (MA, DPhil, DSc); *m* 6 Oct 1979, Ruth Edith; 1 s (Richard Anthony), 1 da (Elizabeth Ruth); *Career* memb tech staff Bell Labs Murray Hill NJ 1972–75; Defence Research Agency (Royal Signals and Radar Estab) Malvern: sr scientific offr 1975–78, princ scientific offr 1978–83), sr princ scientific offr 1983–95; Dept of Electronic and Electrical Engrg Univ of Sheffield: prof 1995–, head Semiconductor Materials and Devices Research Gp 1999–; dir Sheffield Field Emission Gun Transmission Electron Microscope Facility 1998–, dir Sheffield Focused Ion Beam Facility 2001–; pres Scientific Cncl TASC Italian Nat Lab Trieste 2001–03; chm: Microscopy of Semiconducting Materials Series of Int Confs 1977–, Electron Microscopy and Analysis Gp Inst of Physics 1980–82, Department of Industry Working Party on Transient Annealing 1981–84, SERC MSEC Instrumentation Panel 1988–93; memb Functional Materials Coll EPSRC 1997–; co-ordinating ed Materials Science and Engrg Reports 1994–; Holliday Award Inst of Materials Minerals and Mining 1984; FInstP, FRSC, FIMMM, FRS 2004; *Style—* Prof Anthony Cullis; ✉ 3 Dore Close, Dore, Sheffield S17 3PU (tel 0114 235 3343); Department of Electronic and Electrical Engineering, University of Sheffield, Mappin Street, Sheffield S1 3JD (tel 0114 222 5407, e-mail a.g.cullis@sheffield.ac.uk)

CULLUM, Peter Geoffrey; s of Geoffrey Cullum (d 1994), and Doreen, *née* Cozens (d 2001); *b* 10 September 1950, Norwich; *Educ* City Business Sch (MBA); *m* 7 May 2000, Ann, *née* Gray; 1 s (Simon b 22 Dec 1977), 2 da (Claire-Louise b 1 March 1981, Abigail b 8 Jan 1986); *Career* trainee Royal Insurance Group 1969–74, mktg exec Commercial Union 1975–82, mktg dir London & Edinburgh Insurance Co 1982–91, ceo Economic Insurance Co Ltd 1991–96, chm and fndr Towergate Partnership Ltd 1996–; memb Advsy Bd Cass Business Sch; Ernst & Young UK Entrepreneur of the Year 2005; memb RSA; FCII 1971, ACIM 1999; *Publications* plethora of articles in the tech insurance trade press; *Recreations* golf, tennis, spectator of rugby and soccer; *Style—* Peter Cullum, Esq; ✉ Towergate Partnership Ltd, Towergate House, 2 County Gate, Staceys Street, Maidstone, Kent ME14 1ST (tel 01622 754754, fax 01622 754999, e-mail peter.cullum@towergate.co.uk)

CULSHAW, Jonathan Peter (Jon); s of James Culshaw, of Lancs, and Theresa Culshaw; *b* 2 June 1968; *Educ* St Bede's HS Ormskirk, St John Rigby Sixth Form Coll; *Career* comedian; voice artist Spitting Image 1994–96 (telephoned 10 Downing St using voice of William Hague, was put through to Tony Blair and the incident was reported in Hansard 1998), impersonator Dead Ringers BBC Radio 4 1999– and BBC2 2002–, voice artist 2DTV 2001–; Royal Variety Performance 2001 and 2002, Alter Ego ITV Specials 2001 and 2002, Meet The Dead Ringers (Arena documentary) BBC2 2001 and 2002, Secret Policeman's Ball 2006, The Sky at Night 50th Anniversary Edition 2007; *Awards* for Dead Ringers: Br Comedy Awards 2001, Gold Sony Radio Award 2001, Programme of Year Broadcasting Press Guild 2001, Best Comedy Spoken Word Awards 2001, Voice of the Listener Award 2002, Best Political Satire Award Political Studies Assoc; Montreux Rose D'Or Press Award 2002 (for 2DTV); *Style—* Jon Culshaw, Esq; ✉ Billy Marsh Associates, 76A Grove End Road, St John's Wood, London NW8 9ND

CULSHAW, Robert Nicholas; MVO (1979); s of late Ivan Culshaw, and Edith Marjorie Jose, *née* Barnard; *b* 22 December 1952; *Educ* UCS Hampstead, King's Coll Cambridge (univ classics scholar, MA); *m* 19 March 1977, Elaine Ritchie, da of Alan Clegg; 1 s (Robin Alexander b 20 June 1992); *Career* HM Dip Serv: FCO 1974–75, MECAS 1975–76, Muscat 1977–79, Khartoum 1979–80, Rome 1980–84, FCO London 1984–88, dep head of mission and consul-gen Athens 1988–93, head News Dept and FCO spokesman 1993–95, min-cnsllr Washington 1995–99, consul-gen Chicago 1999–2003, dir (Americas and Overseas Territories) FCO 2003–05; dep dir British Antarctic Survey 2006–; MCIL, FRSA; *Recreations* singing, skiing, hiking, poetry; *Style—* Robert Culshaw, Esq, MVO; ✉ Piney Lodge, 66 Cow Lane, Fulbourn, Cambridge CB21 5HB

CULVERHOUSE, Lavinia Jane; da of Alan Frederick John Culverhouse, of Arizona, USA, and Mavis, *née* Budd; *b* 9 April 1965; *Educ* St Mary's Sch Gerrards Cross, Coll of Distributive Trades (Dip CAM); *m* 29 Sept 2000, Peter Thomas Dobie; 2 s (Lucas Christian b 2003, Fraser Alexander Fulton b 2006); *Career* media planner and buyer BBDO Ltd 1979–85, account dir Abbot Mead Vickers/BBDO 1989–92, gp account dir Doner Cardwell Hawkins 1992–94, md Design House Consultants Ltd 1994–; dir DBA 1999; FRSA 2000; *Recreations* literature, cinema, yoga, fashion; *Clubs* Groucho; *Style—* Ms Lavinia Culverhouse; ✉ Design House Consultants Ltd, 4 Duke Street, Richmond, Surrey TW9 1HP (tel 020 8439 9360, fax 020 8439 9373, e-mail laviniaculverhouse@designhouse.co.uk)

CULYER, Prof Anthony John (Tony); CBE (1999); s of Thomas Reginald Culyer (d 1979), and Betty Ely, *née* Headland; *b* 1 July 1942; *Educ* Sir William Borlase's Sch Marlow, King's Sch Worcester, Univ of Exeter (BA), UCLA; *m* 26 Aug 1966, Sieglinde Birgit, da of Kurt Kraut (d 1947); 1 s, 1 da; *Career* Fulbright scholar 1964–65, lectr Univ of Exeter 1965–69; Univ of York 1969–: lectr, sr lectr, reader, prof of economics; head Dept of Economics and Related Studies 1986–2001, pro-vice-chllr 1991–94, dep vice-chllr 1994–97, dir of health devpt 1997–2001; chief scientist Institute for Work and Health Toronto 2003–06; visiting prof: Queens Univ Canada 1976, Trent Univ Canada 1985–86, Medis Inst Munich 1990, Toronto Univ Canada 1991 (hon prof 1991–), Central Inst of Technol NZ 1997; adjunct prof Department of Health Policy Mgmnt and Evaluation Univ of Toronto 2003–; William Evans visiting prof Univ of Otago NZ 1979, Woodward lectr Univ of Br Columbia Canada 1986, Perey lectr McMaster Univ Canada 1991, Champlain lectr Trent Univ Canada 1991; chm: NHS Task Force on Funding of R&D 1993–94, Methodology Panel NHS Technology Assessment R&D Programme 1992–97, Central R&D Ctee Sub-Gp on Culyer Implementation 1997; vice-chm: N Yorks HA 1995–99, Nat Inst for Clinical Excellence 1999–2003; memb: Central R&D Ctee for the NHS 1991–2001, Yorkshire Region R&D Ctee, Review Advsy Ctee on the London Special Health Authorities 1993, Subject Area Panel (Economics) ESRC, Br Cncl Health Advsy Ctee 1995–97, Central R&D Ctee Nat Working Gp on R&D in Primary Care 1996–97, Research Advsy Ctee Institute for Work and Health 1997–2002, Scientific Advsy Ctee Institute for Work and Health 1997–2003, Research and Devpt Ctee NICE 1999–, External Review Team for Cancer Care Ontario Research 2003–04, Ontario Health Technol Assessment Ctee 2005–; memb WHO two person mission to Kazakhstan on the privitisation and reform of health care services 1997; special advsr to: R&D Ctee High Security Psychiatric Services Commissioning Bd 1995–99, NHS Exec Comprehensive Spending Review Gp 1997–98, dir of R&D NHS 1997–99, Canada Health Cncl 2005–; professional conslt to: UK Dept of Health, OECD, EEC, WHO, Govt of Canada, Govt of NZ; Office of Health Economics: chair Policy Ctee 1997–, chair Editorial Ctee 1997–, chair Mgmnt Ctee 1997–, chair 2001– (dep chair 1997–2001); co-ed Jl of Health Economics 1982–; memb Editorial Bd: Br Med Jl 1995–99, Med Law International, Clinical Effectiveness in Nursing, Jl of Medical Ethics; memb Conf of Heads of Univ Depts of Economics 1987–2001; memb Kenneth J Arrow Award Prize Ctee 1996–98, memb Canadian Institutes for Health Research Michael Smith Prize in Health Research Ctee 2005–; memb and founding chm Health Economists Study Gp; memb: Royal EC Soc, Research Advsy Ctee Canadian Inst for Advanced Research, Acad Advsy Cncl Univ of Buckingham; tstee The Canadian Health Services Research Fndn Ottawa 2000–03; church organist and choirmaster, memb Liturgy and Music Advsy Gp Diocese of York 1995–2000, chm North East Yorkshire Area Royal Sch of Church Music 1995–2004, memb Advsy Cncl Royal Sch of Church Music 2002–, tstee and memb Cncl Royal Sch of Church Music 2003–; Hon DEcon Stockholm Sch of Econs Sweden 1999; FMedSci 1999, FRSA 1999, Hon FRPC 2005; *Publications* incl: Health Economics (1973), Economics of Social Policy (1973), Benham's Economics (1973), Economic Policies and Social Goals (1974), Need and the National Health Service (1976), Annotated Bibliography of Health Economics (1977), Human Resources and Public Finance (1977), Economic Aspects of Health Services (1978), Measuring Health (1978), Political Economy of Social Policy (1980 and 1991), Economic and Medical Evaluation of Health Care Technologies (1983), Health Indicators (1983), Economics (1985), Public Finance and Social Policy (1985), International Bibliography of Health Economics (1986), Public and Private Health Services (1986), Health Care Expenditures in Canada (1988), Perspectives on the Future of Health Care in Europe (1989), Standards for Socioeconomic Evaluation of Health Care Products and Services (1990), Competition in Health Care (1990), The Economics of Health (1991), International Review of the Swedish Health Care System (1991), Recent Developments in Health Economics (1992), Equity in Health Care Policy (1992), Supporting Research and Development in the NHS (1994), Reforming Health Care Systems: Experiments with the NHS (1996), Being Reasonable About the Economics of Health: Selected Essays by Alan Williams (1997), Handbook of Health Economics (2001), The Dictionary of Health Economics (2005); also over 200 articles and pamphlets; *Recreations* music and gardening; *Style—* Prof Tony Culyer, CBE; ✉ 80 Front Street East 804, Toronto, Ontario M5E 1T4, Canada (tel 00 1 416 359 9973); Institute for Work and Health, 481 University Avenue Suite 800, Toronto, Ontario M5G 2E9, Canada; Department of Economics and Related Studies, University of York, Heslington, York, YO10 5DD (tel 01904 433762/433789/433752, fax 01904 433759, e-mail ajc17@york.ac.uk, website www.users.york.ac.uk/ajc17)

CUMANI, Luca Matteo; s of Sergio Cumani (d 1980), and Elena, *née* Cardini; *b* 7 April 1949; *Educ* Milan; *m* 1979, Sara Doon, da of Simon Patrick Conyngham Plunket; 1 s (Matthew Sergio Simon b 1981), 1 da (Francesca Deepsea b 1983); *Career* racehorse trainer; rider of 85 winners in Italy, France and UK incl Moet and Chandon on Meissen and Prix Paul Noel de la Houtre on Harland 1972, champion amateur Italy 1972; formerly asst trainer to: S Cumani, H R A Cecil 1974–75; first held trainer's licence 1976; horses trained incl: Falbrav, Kahyasi, Freeze The Secret, Old Country, Tolomeo, Commanche Run, Free Guest, Bairn, Embla, Then Again, Celestial Storm, Half a Year, Infamy, Markofdistinction, Barathea, Only Royale, High-Rise, One So Wonderful, Gossamer; Gp One races won incl: The English Derby (twice), Irish Derby, St Léger, Italian Derby, Premio Roma (twice), Arlington Million, Rothmans International, E P Taylor Stakes (twice), Juddmonte International Stakes (three times), Phoenix Champion Stakes, St James's Palace Stakes (twice), Cheveley Park Stakes, Prix Royal Oak, Queen Elizabeth II Stakes (twice), Sussex Stakes, Ascot Fillies Mile (three times), Irish 2000 Guineas, Yorkshire Oaks (twice), Breeders Cup Mile, Irish 1000 Guineas (twice), Singapore International Cup, Coral Eclipse, Hong Kong Cup, Prix Ispahan; *Style—* Luca Cumani, Esq; ✉ tel 01638 665432, fax 01638 667160, e-mail luca.cumani@bedfordhousestables.co.uk

CUMBERLAND, Prof David Charles; s of Frank Charles Cumberland (d 2000), of Pleasington, nr Blackburn, Lancs, and Edna Constance, *née* Hodson (d 1997); *b* 17 August 1944; *Educ* Queen Elizabeth GS Blackburn, Univ of Edinburgh Med Sch (MB ChB); *m* 1, 26 Dec 1970 (m dis 2000), Marilyn Susan, da of Colin Rowley (d 1974); 2 da (Louise Helen b 21 Aug 1973, Melanie Claire b 9 April 1976); m 2, 25 May 2000, Norazlina Yusof; 1 s (Matthew Charles b 9 Dec 2000), 1 da (Sarah Charlotte b 16 Jul 2002); *Career* prof of interventional cardiology Univ of Sheffield and Northern General Hosp specializing in treatment of coronary artery disease by angioplasty and associated research until 2000; conslt in cardiovascular intervention Kuala Lumpur Malaysia 2000–03, conslt in cardiac intervention Northern Gen Hosp Sheffield 2003–; memb: London Cardiovascular Associates 2003, BMA, Br Cardiac Assoc, Br Cardiovascular Intervention Soc, Malaysian Heart Assoc; fndr chm Br Coronary Angioplasty Gp; author of numerous articles in jls; Rohan Williams Medal 1973, Trent Medal for Excellence in Healthcare 1990; FRCR 1973, FRCPEd 1986, FACC 1993, FRCS 1994, FESC 1994; *Books* Endovascular Surgery (jtly, 1989), Handbook of Coronary Stents (jtly, 2002), Textbook of Interventional Cardiology (jtly, 2003); *Recreations* jiu jitsu, country walking; *Style—* Prof David Cumberland; ✉ Cardiology Unit, Northern General Hospital, Sheffield S5 7AU (tel 0114 271 4953, fax 0114 236 6233, mobile 07770 471045, e-mail cumberlanddavid@aol.com)

CUMBERLEGE, Baroness (Life Peer UK 1990), of Newick in the County of East Sussex; Julia Frances Cumberlege; CBE (1985), DL (E Sussex 1986); da of Dr Lambert Ulrich Camm (d 1997), of Newick, E Sussex, and Mary Geraldine Gertrude, *née* Russell (d 1962); *b* 27 January 1943; *Educ* Convent of the Sacred Heart Kent; *m* 14 Jan 1961, Patrick Francis Howard Cumberlege, s of Geoffrey Fenwick Jocelyn Cumberlege, DSO, MC (d 1979); 3 s (Hon (Christopher) Mark b 1961, Hon Justin Francis b 1964, Hon Oliver Richard b 1968); *Career* memb: Lewes DC 1966–79 (ldr 1977–78), E Sussex CC 1974–85 (chm Social Servs Ctee 1979–82); JP 1973–85; memb E Sussex AHA 1977–81; chm: Brighton HA 1981–88, Nat Assoc of Health Authorities 1987–88, SW Thames RHA 1988–92; Parly under sec of state for health in House of Lords 1992–97, memb Jt Select Ctee on Draft Mental Health Bill 2004–05; exec dir MJM Healthcare Solutions 1997–2001; dir: Huntsworth plc 2001–03; sr assoc Kings Fund; memb: Cncl St George's Med Sch (chm 2000–06), Press Cncl 1977–83, Appts Cmmn 1984–90, NHS Policy Bd 1989–97, Cncl ICRF 1997–2001, Cncl Cancer Research UK 2001–; chm: Review of Community Nursing for England 1985, Review of Maternity Servs for England 1993, Tstees of Chailey Heritage 1998–, HR and Communications Cmmn Cancer Research UK, RCP Working Pty on Med Professionalism 2004–05; vice-pres RCN 1988, vice-pres RCM 2001; chm and govr several schs, memb Cncl Brighton Poly 1987–89 (memb Formation Ctee 1988–89), memb Cncl Univ of Sussex 2001–; tstee Leeds Castle Fndn 2005–; Vice Lord-Lt E Sussex 1991; hon degree: Univ of Surrey, Univ of Brighton, Univ of London; FRSA, Hon FRCP, Hon FRCGP; *Clubs* RSM; *Style—* The Rt Hon Baroness Cumberlege, CBE, DL; ✉ Snells Cottage, The Green, Newick, Lewes, East Sussex BN8 4LA (tel 01825 722154, fax 01825 723873); House of Lords, London SW1A 0PW (e-mail cumberlegej@parliament.uk)

CUMING, Frederick George Rees; s of Harold Albert Cuming (d 1976), of Welling, Kent; and Grace Madeleine, *née* Rees; *b* 16 February 1930; *Educ* Sidcup Sch of Art, RCA; *m* Oct 1962, Audrey, da of Eric Lee, of Ashton-under-Lyme; 1 s (Daniel Lee b 5 Nov 1964), 1 da (Rachel Joanna b 25 Aug 1971); *Career* Nat Serv Sgt RAEC 1949–51; painter; winner grand prix fine art Monaco Ingot Industrial Expo, Sir Brinsley Ford award New English Arts Club, House and Garden Prize RA 1994; adviser New Metropole Arts Centre Folkestone, tstee Rye Art Gallery and Eastern Rooms Gallery; memb: Nat Tst, New English Arts Club 1960; Hon DLitt Univ of Kent 2004; ARCA 1964, RA 1974; *Solo Exhibitions* New Metropole Arts Centre Folkestone 1972–75, Jonleigh Guildford 1975, Thackeray London 1976, Chichester 1976, Grafton London 1983, 1985, 1987, 1988, 1990, 1992, 1994, 1996, and 1998, Drew Canterbury 1983–86, Easton Rooms Rye 1983, Nat Tst Fndn for Arts (Agnews), Salute to Turner (Agnews), Edinburgh Festival 1995, Johannesburg SA 1996–97, Dallas USA 1999, Greenwick Connecticut USA 1999, featured artist RA Summer Show 2001 (afforded solo exhbn Small Weston Room), portrait of Prof Stephen Hawking (Nat Portrait Gall London) 2007; *Group Exhibitions* incl: Royal Soc of Portrait Painters, John Moores Liverpool, Leicester Gallery, Pictures for Schools, 12 Royal Academicians Chichester, Little Studio NY, Artists of Fame and Promise (Brandler Galleries Brentwood) 1993; *Public Collections* incl: Royal Acad, Miny of Works, Monte Carlo Museum, Brighton and Hove Museum, St John's and Worcester Colls Oxford, New Metropole Arts Centre, Farringdon Tst, W H Smith, LWT, Southend Museum and Art Gallery, Canterbury Museum and Art Gallery, Scunthorpe Museum and Art Gallery, Preston Museum and Art Gallery, Kendall Museum and Art Gallery, Greenwich Conn USA, Dallas, San Francisco, Florida; *Publications* Figure in a Landscape (book), The Art of Fred Cuming, RA (video); *Recreations* reading, music, travelling, walking; *Clubs* Chelsea Arts, Dover St Arts; *Style—* Frederick Cuming, Esq, RA; ✉ The Gables, Wittersham Road, Iden, Rye, East Sussex TN31 7UY (tel 01797 280322)

CUMMING, Maj-Gen Andrew Alexander John Rennie; CBE (1993); s of Donald Alexander Cumming (d 1995), and Evelyn Julia, *née* Rennie (d 1995); *b* 12 March 1948; *Educ* Bradfield Coll, Army Staff Coll, HCSC; *m* 1 Sept 1979, Gilly, *née* Thompson; 3 da (Camilla, Henrietta (twins) b 21 Sept 1982, Georgina b 7 Sept 1987); *Career* CO 17/21 Lancers 1988–91, Cdr 20 Armd Bde/11 Armd Bde 1992–93, ACOS (Ops) HQ Land 1993–95, Chief Jt Ops Intervention Force Sarajevo 1995–96, Cdr Initial Trg Gp 1996–99, Cdr Land Warfare Centre 1999–2002, co-ordinator Kosovo Protection Corps 2002–04, controller SSAFA Forces Help 2004–; Hon Col Queen's Royal Lancers 2006–; dir Wincanton Race Course 2004–; *Recreations* field sports, skiing, sailing, walking, reading; *Clubs* Cavalry and Guards'; *Style—* Maj-Gen Andrew Cumming, CBE; ✉ c/o SSAFA Forces Help, 19 Queen Elizabeth Street, London SE1 2LP

CUMMING, David John; s of Patrick Gordon Cumming (d 1979), and Mildred Joan Cumming; *b* 23 October 1948, Hull; *Educ* Charterhouse, Grenoble Univ; *m* 5 Jan 1974, Helen Madeleine Parker; 2 da (Oonagh b 6 Feb 1975, Harriet b 22 Jan 1978); *Career* BAA: joined as exec trainee 1968, various posts rising to airport duty mangr Heathrow Airport 1970–84, onward travel mangr Heathrow 1984–87, mangr South Terminal Gatwick Airport 1987–89, gen mangr Terminal 2 Heathrow 1989–92, gen mangr Terminal 1 Heathrow 1992–97, ops dir Gatwick 1997–2002, md Southampton Int Airport 2002–06; *Recreations* fly fishing, skiing, photography, mountain biking; *Style—* David Cumming, Esq; ✉ e-mail djc@davidcumming.com

CUMMING, Ian Roy; OBE (2003); s of Roy Langdon Cumming, and Jean Evelyn, *née* Maxwell; *b* 10 September 1964; *Educ* William Hulmes GS, Manchester Metropolitan Univ; *m* 1993, Gail Deborah, *née* Cox; *Career* gen mangr Manchester Royal Infirmary 1990–93 (joined 1983), asst chief exec NW RHA 1993–95; chief exec: Lancaster Acute Hosps NHS Tst 1995–98, Univ Hosps of Morecambe Bay NHS Tst 1998–; chm Ski Crazy Ltd 1991–95; FIBMS, MHCM, FCMI; *Recreations* skiing, sailing, travel, private pilot; *Style—* Ian Cumming, Esq, OBE; ✉ Long Barn, Tearnside, Kirkby, Lonsdale, Cumbria LA6 2PU; University Hospitals of Morecambe Bay NHS Trust, Westmorland General Hospital, Burton Road, Kendal, Cumbria LA9 7RG (tel 01539 795366, fax 01539 795313, e-mail ian.cumming@virgin.net)

CUMMING, Dr (William James) Kenneth; s of Wallace Cumming, of Manchester, and Kathleen Margurite, *née* Lavery; *b* 29 August 1946; *Educ* Royal Belfast Academical Instn, Queen's Univ Belfast (BSc, MB BCh); *Children* 2 da (Emma b 27 Dec 1973, Claire b 25 Aug 1975); *Career* registrar and sr registrar Newcastle upon Tyne 1972–79, conslt neurologist Withington Hosp Univ of Manchester 1979–96; pres NW Myasthenic Assoc, chm South Manchester Imaging plc; BAO 1971, Hon MD Queen's Univ Belfast 1979; accredited Cardiff University Expert Witness; MInstD; fell Acad of Experts, FRCP, FRCPI, fell Royal Acad of Med in Ireland; *Recreations* golf; *Clubs* East India; *Style—* Dr Kenneth Cumming; ✉ Manchester Business Park, 3000 Aviator Way, Manchester M22 5TG (tel 0161 932 6162, fax 0161 932 6362, e-mail cummingkc@regusnet.com)

CUMMING, Robert Alexander; s of Alexander Ian Cumming (d 1962), and Bery Mary Stevenson (d 2000); *b* 31 May 1945; *Educ* Trinity Hall Cambridge (MA); *m* 7 June 1975, Alison Carolyn, da of John George Jenkins, CBE; 2 da (Hester Chloe Mary b 2 June 1983, Phoebe Alice Elizabeth b 5 June 1988); *Career* author, art critic, broadcaster, curator; called to the Bar Middle Temple 1967 (Harmsworth scholar); practising barrister 1967–69, Hambros Bank 1970–71, lectr Tate Gallery 1974–78, dir Christie's Fine Arts Course 1978–88, chm Christie's Education 1988–2000, chm Christie's International Art Studies 1998–2000; pres: Christie's Education Inc (USA), Christie's Education (France); tstee: Christie's Educn Trust 1986–2000, Project Street Life 2004–06; memb: Exhbns Sub-Ctee Arts Cncl 1984–88, Cncl Friends of the Tate Gallery 1983–1995, Thames and Chiltern Regnl Ctee Nat Trust 1990–96; chm Contemporary Art Soc 1988–90; patron Royal Soc of Br Sculptors 1998–2006; ptnr Jenkins & Beckers Wine Merchants 1994–; external examiner: Univ of London 1976–80, Univ of Glasgow 1988–92; Buckingham Partnership 1998–2005, dean and dir of British progs Boston Univ London 2005–; writing awards: Silver Pencil Award Utrecht 1982, TES Sr Info Book Award 1983, Premio Europeo di Letteratura Giovainle Pier Paolo Vergerio Padua 1985; memb Gray's Inn 1969; FRSA 1990; *Books* Macmillan Encyclopedia of Art (1977), Just Look (1979), Just Imagine (1982), Christie's Guide to Collecting (1984), Looking into Paintings (1985, with TV programme), Working with Colour (exhbn catalogue, 1985), The Colour Eye (1990), Discovering Turner (1990), Paolozzi Mythologies (exhbn catalogue, 1990), Annotated Art (1995), Great Artists (1998), ART a no nonsense guide to art and artists (2001), Art: Eyewitness Guide (2006); *Recreations* all things European, family life, making and collecting, golf, shooting, wine; *Clubs* Arts, Anatema, Aula; *Style—* Robert Cumming, Esq; ✉ The Old Mill House, Maids Moreton, Buckingham MK18 7AR (tel 01280 816226, fax 01280 821574, e-mail robertcumming@onetel.com, website www.robertcumming.net); Boston University, 43 Harrington Gardens, London SW7 4JU (tel 020 7373 9430)

CUMMING-BRUCE, Edward Simon Hovell-Thurlow; s of late Rt Hon Sir Roualeyn Cumming-Bruce, and Lady Sarah Cumming-Bruce, *née* Savile (d 1991); *b* 7 June 1958; *Educ* Ampleforth, Magdalen Coll Oxford (MA); *m* 1984, Antonia, da of C S Gaisford-St Lawrence, of Howth Castle, Dublin, Eire; 2 s (Michael b 1985, William b 1987), 1 da (Isabelle b 1990); *Career* Laurence Prust & Co 1980–90, dir Schroder Securities Ltd 1990–91, head of equity capital markets Dresdner Kleinwort Benson Ltd 1999– (dir 1992–99); *Recreations* fishing, shooting; *Style—* Edward Cumming-Bruce, Esq; ✉ Dresdner Kleinwort Benson Ltd, 20 Fenchurch Street, London EC3 (tel 020 7623 8000, fax 020 7283 4667)

CUMMINGS, John Andrew; *b* 15 May 1949; *Educ* Eastbourne GS, Univ of Kent (BA), Univ of Nottingham (CertEd), Univ of London (MA); *m* Claire; 1 s, 1 da; *Career* teacher; Theatre in Education Dovecot Arts Centre 1973–75; asst master: Glasgow Acad 1975–80, Tonbridge Sch 1980–89, Melbourne GS 1985; head of English and head of Sixth Form Wycliffe Coll 1989–93, headmaster Keil Sch Dumbarton 1993–99, headmaster Duke of York's Royal Military Sch Dover 1999–; *Recreations* theatre, tennis, squash, hill walking; *Style—* John Cummings, Esq; ✉ School House, Dover, Kent CT15 5EQ (tel 01304 245024)

CUMMINGS, John Scott; MP; s of George Cummings, and Mary, *née* Cain; *b* 6 July 1943; *Educ* Murton Cncl Sr Sch, Easington and Durham Tech Coll; *Career* colliery electrician Murton Colliery 1958–87, sec Murton Colliery Mechanics 1967–87, MP (Lab, NUM sponsored) Easington 1987–; memb: Miners Gp of Lab MPs, Easington Rural DC 1970–73, Easington DC 1973–87 (chm 1975–76, leader 1979–87), Northumbrian Water Authy 1977–83, Peterlee and Aycliffe Devpt Corp 1980–87, Cncl of Europe 1992–97, WEU 1992–97; vice-chm Coalfield Community Campaign 1984–87, former hon pres Co Durham Branch Stonham Housing Assoc; *Recreations* Jack Russell terriers, walking, foreign travel; *Clubs* Murton Victoria, Murton Demmi, Murton Ex Servicemens', Thornley Catholic, Peterlee Lab; *Style—* John Cummings, Esq, MP; ✉ Constituency Office, Seaton Holme, Easington Village, Peterlee, County Durham SR8 3BS (tel 0191 527 3773, fax 0191 527 9640); House of Commons, London SW1A 0AA (tel 020 7219 5122)

CUMMINS, Andrew; *m*; 2 c; *Career* formerly with: BHP Ltd, McKinsey & Company, Elders IXL Ltd/Foster's Brewing Gp Ltd, Inchcape plc; chm: Cummins Assocs Ltd 1998–, Advsy Bd CVC Asia Pacific Ltd 2000–, Nixela Investments Pty Ltd, Rocla Concrete Tie Inc (USA); non-exec dir: Pacific Brands Ltd (Australia), DCA Gp Ltd (Australia), Edible Concepts Hldgs Pty Ltd (Australia); former directorships incl: Affinity Health Ltd, Techpac Hldgs Ltd, Amatek Gp (Australia), Li & Fung (Distribution) Ltd (Hong Kong), Inchcape plc, ITT London & Edinburgh Ltd, Toyota (GB) Ltd, Bain Hogg Gp plc, Hudson Conway Ltd (Australia), Courage Ltd, Impulse Airlines Ltd; memb Inst of Engrs Australia; *Clubs* Athenaeum (Melbourne), Union (Sydney), RAC (London); *Style—* Andrew Cummins, Esq

CUMMINS, Gus; s of Harold George Cummins (d 1986), of London, and Honor, *née* Bird (d 1978); *b* 28 January 1943; *Educ* Sutton Art Sch, Wimbledon Art Sch (NDD, sr drawing prize), RCA (MA); *m* 1968, Angela, da of Arthur C Braven; 2 s (Casper b 1968, Marcus b 1970), 1 da (Rosie b 1979); *Career* artist; taught pt/t 1969–: Hammersmith, Sutton, Croydon, Chelsea, Ravensbourne, Wimbledon, City & Guilds, RA Schs of Art; sculptural work for exhbn display during 1970s, exhibited paintings since 1970s; memb Rye Soc of Artists 1979–, memb London Gp 1982; memb Cncl Royal Acad of Arts 2002; RA 1992; *Solo Exhibitions* Gardner Art Centre Brighton 1991, Stormont Studios Rye 1991, Metropole Art Centre Folkestone 1992, Brian Sinfield Gallery Oxford 1993, Hastings Museum Gallery 1993, Lamont Gallery London 1995, St Mary-in-the-Castle Arts Centre Hastings 1999; two persons shows: Eastern Rooms Gallery Rye 1987, New Grafton Gallery London 1993, Star Gallery Lewes; *Group Exhibitions* incl: London Gp 1981–, RA 1982–, Hastings Museum 1979–, Eastern Rooms Gallery Rye 1984–, Spirit of London 1983 and 1984, Odette Gilbert Gallery 1984 and 1985, paintings and sculptural installations Dordrecht Festival 1986, Lloyds of London Travelling 1986 and 1987, Gardner Art Centre Brighton Univ 1988, Hunting Group Mall Gallery 1989 and 1990, President's Choice RA and Arts Club 1989, Academicians Choice Mall Gallery and Eye Gallery Bristol 1990, Looking Glass Appeal (Riverside One London) 1990, Discerning Eye (Mall Gallery and tour) 1991–92, Barbican Centre 1992, New Grafton Gallery 1992, Singer Friedlander/Sunday Times Water Colour Competition Mall Gallery 1992, Woodlands Gallery London (with Anthony Green and Anthony Wishaw) 2002; also exhibited United Arab Emirates and USA; *Awards* Henry Moore Prize (London Gp) 1982, Second Prize Spirit of London 1983, Daler-Rowney Prize RA 1987, First Prize Hunting Gp Mall Gallery 1990, House & Garden Prize RA 1992, Blackstone Award RA 1992, First Prize Hunting Gp RCA 1999, Royal Watercolour Soc Prize 2001, Jack Goldhill Award for Sculpture RA 2005; *Recreations* music, poetry, swimming, snooker; *Clubs* Chelsea Arts, Dover St Arts; *Style—* Gus Cummins, Esq, RA; ✉ Harpsichord House, Cobourg Place, Hastings, East Sussex TN34 3HY (tel 01424 426429); c/o Royal Academy of Arts, Piccadilly, London W1V 0DS

CUMMINS, Jack; s of Arthur Cummins (d 1987), and Jessie, *née* Milton (d 1981); *b* 17 June 1952, Irvine, Ayrshire; *Educ* Kilmarnock Acad, Univ of Glasgow (MA, LLB); *m* 17 March 1980, Josephine, *née* Donaldson; *Career* R & J M Hill Brown & Co: apprentice then asst 1976–80, ptnr 1980–, sr ptnr 2005–; memb: Nicholson Ctee on liquor licensing law in Scotland 2001, expert Reference Gp on Licensing (Scotland) Bill 2003, Nat Licensing Forum; ed Scottish Licensing Law and Practice 1995–, columnist Scottish Licensed Trade News; contrib to radio and TV progs; regular speaker at confs; memb Law Soc of Scotland 1978; *Publications* Licensing Law in Scotland (1993, 2 edn 2000), Scottish

Licensed Trade Handbook (contrib, 2003), Licensing Law Guide (contrib, 2003), Licensed Premises: Law and Practice (contrib, 2005), The Licensing (Scotland) Act 2005 (2006); *Style—* Jack Cummins, Esq; ✉ R & J M Hill Brown & Co, 3 Newton Place, Glasgow G3 7PU (tel 0141 333 0636, fax 0141 332 8558, e-mail jcc@hillbrown.co.uk)

CUMPSTY, Nicholas Alexander; s of Norman Cumpsty (d 1980), and Edith A; *b* 13 January 1943; *Educ* Haberdashers' Aske's Hampstead, Imperial Coll London (BSc), Trinity Coll Cambridge (PhD); *m* 1, 1966, Annette Tischler (d 1982); 1 s (Daniel), 1 da (Megan); m 2, Mary Cecily Hamer, *née* Turner; 2 step da (Emily D Hamer, Camilla R Hamer); *Career* res fell Peterhouse Cambridge 1966–69, sr noise engr Rolls Royce 1969–71; Univ of Cambridge: fell Peterhouse 1972–, prof of aerothermal technol 1989–99 (lectr then reader 1972–89); chief technologist Rolls Royce plc 2000–05; prof of engrg Imperial Coll London 2005–; memb: Royal Cmmn on Environmental Pollution 2005–, Defence Scientific Advsy Cncl 2005–; fell: American Soc of Mechanical Engrs 1975, American Inst of Aero and Astronautics 1996; emeritus fell Peterhouse Cambridge 2005–; FIMechE 1992, FREng 1995; *Books* Compressor Aerodynamics (1989), Jet Propulsion (1997); *Recreations* reading, music, photography, walking; *Style—* Mr Nicholas Cumpsty, FREng; ✉ Imperial College, London SW7 2AZ (e-mail n.cumpsty@imperial.ac.uk)

CUNARD, Peter John; s of Basil Charles Henry Cunard (d 1962), and Christine May, *née* Tremer (d 1995); *b* 21 August 1945; *Educ* Latymer Fndn; *m* 1970, Susan Margaret Ethel, da of James Coleridge; 2 s (Nicholas Peter b 30 Oct 1971, Sebastian James b 29 Dec 1972), 1 da (Catherine Jane b 27 Nov 1976); *Career* press offr Assoc Television 1964–69, press and PR offr English Stage Co Royal Court Theatre 1969, PR advsr Duke of Bedford 1969–73, head of PR Trust House Forte 1973–76, dir Durden-Smith Communications 1976–80, fndr and md Granard Communications 1980–90, chief exec The Rowland Co (after merger of Granard Communications with Kingsway PR) 1990–92, memb Exec Ctee Rowland Worldwide Ltd, ptnr Tolman Cunard Ltd (strategic conslts) 1992–99, chm Cunard Communications Ltd 1983–, non-exec dir Creston Gp plc 2002–07; chm Devpt Ctee Public Relations Consultants Assoc 1985; tstee Sick Children's Trust 1984–; MInstD 1980; *Books* Public Relations Case Book (1990); *Recreations* gardens, photography, wine, horse racing; *Clubs* Lord's Taverners, Solus; *Style—* Peter Cunard, Esq; ✉ The Mill House, Stanningfield, Suffolk IP29 4RX

CUNDALL, Dr Peter Alan; s of Lester Alan Cundall, of Cowes, IOW, and Emmie Pamela, *née* Johnson (d 2000); *b* 9 April 1944, Llandudno, Conwy; *Educ* Purley Co GS, Imperial Coll London (BSc, PhD); *m* 12 Nov 1966, Christine Ann, *née* Martin; 2 da (Alison Joyce b 6 Oct 1967, Anita Pamela b 26 Feb 1972); *Career* princ and sr engr Dames & Moore 1974–79, assoc prof Dept of Civil and Mineral Engrg Univ of Minnesota 1982–86 (asst prof 1972–74, adjunct prof 1990–), princ Itasca Consulting Gp Inc 2000– (sr conslt 1989–2000); author of 70 scientific papers; Award for Outstanding Contributions to Rock Mechanics American Rock Mechanics Assoc 2003, Rock Mechanics Award Soc for Mining, Metallurgy and Exploration 2003; FREng 2005; *Recreations* sailing, oil painting; *Style—* Dr Peter Cundall; ✉ Itasca Consulting Group, Inc, 111 Third Avenue South, Suite 540, Minneapolis, MN 55401, USA (tel 00 1 612 371 4711, fax 00 1 612 371 4717, e-mail icg@itascacg.com)

CUNDEY, Angus Howard; s of Samuel Howard Cundey (d 1982), and Eileen Florence, *née* Fitter; *b* 7 June 1937, London; *Educ* Downside, Framlingham Coll, Tailor and Cutter Acad London (Dip); *m* 1, 1968, Gudrun, *née* Munck; 1 s (Simon Howard b 29 Sept 1968), 1 da (Sarah Howard b 10 Dec 1971); m 2, 2002, Myranda, *née* Grainger Smith; *Career* apprentice Lanvin Paris 1955; Henry Poole & Co (Savile Row) Ltd: joined as cutter 1958, chm 1980–; dir Savile Row Bespoke Ltd; dir: Br Clothing Industries Assoc, UK Fashion Export; Liveryman Merchant Taylors Co 1990; *Publications* Henry Poole: Founders of Savile Row (2003); *Recreations* motoring, gardening; *Clubs* Vintage Sports Car; *Style—* Angus Cundey, Esq; ✉ Old Well Cottage, Milden, Ipswich, Suffolk IP7 7AL (tel 01787 247430); Henry Poole & Co (Savile Row) Limited, 15 Savile Row, London W1S 3PJ (tel 020 7734 5985, fax 020 7287 2161, e-mail office@henrypoole.com)

CUNDY, Rt Rev Ian Patrick Martyn; *see:* Peterborough, Bishop of

CUNINGHAME, *see:* Fairlie-Cuninghame, Montgomery Cuninghame

CUNLIFFE, Prof Sir Barrington Windsor (Barry); kt (2006), CBE (1994); s of George Percival Windsor (d 1942), and Beatrice Emma, *née* Mersh; *b* 10 December 1939; *Educ* Northern GS Portsmouth, St John's Coll Cambridge (BA, MA, PhD, LittD); *m* 1, 1962 (m dis 1979), Frances Ann, *née* Dunn; 1 s (Daniel b 1966), 1 da (Charlotte b 1969); m 2, 4 Jan 1979, Margaret, da of late Robert Herdman, of Brockworth, Glos; 1 s (Thomas b 1981), 1 da (Anna b 1984); *Career* asst lectr Univ of Bristol 1963–66, prof of archaeology Univ of Southampton 1966–72, prof of Euro archaeology Univ of Oxford 1972–; vice-pres: Soc of Antiquaries 1982–85 (pres 1991–95), Prehistoric Soc 1983–86; cmmr English Heritage 1986–92 and 2006–, a govr Museum of London 1995–98, tstee British Museum 2000–; memb: Roman Soc, Soc of Medieval Archaeology, Royal Archaeological Inst; Hon DLitt Univ of Sussex 1983, Hon DSc Univ of Bath 1984, Hon DUniv Open Univ 1995; FSA 1964, FBA 1979, correspondent memb Deutschen Archaologischen Instituts, hon memb Royal Irish Acad; *Books* incl: The Cradle of England (1972), Rome and the Barbarians (1975), Rome and her Empire (1978), The Celtic World (1979), Roman Bath Discovered (1984), The City of Bath (1986), Greeks, Romans and Barbarians (1988), Iron Age Communities in Britain (1991), Wessex to AD 1000 (1993), The Oxford Illustrated Prehistory of Europe (1994), The Ancient Celts (1997), Facing the Ocean (2001), The Extraordinary Voyage of Pytheas the Greek (2001), The Celts: A Very Short Introduction (2003), Iron Age Britain (2005); *Clubs* Athenaeum; *Style—* Prof Sir Barry Cunliffe, CBE, FBA, FSA; ✉ Institute of Archaeology, 36 Beaumont Street, Oxford (tel 01865 278240)

CUNLIFFE, Sir David Ellis; 9 Bt (GB 1759), of Liverpool, Lancashire; s of Sir Cyril Henley Cunliffe, 8 Bt (d 1969), and Eileen Mary, *née* Parkins; *b* 29 October 1957; *Educ* St Alban's GS for Boys; *m* 1983, Linda Carol, da of John Sidney Batchelor, of Harpenden; 3 da (Emma Mary b 1986, Katherine Alice b 1990, Bridget Carol b 1991); *Heir* bro, Andrew Cunliffe; *Career* business development manager; *Style—* Sir David Cunliffe, Bt; ✉ Sunnyside, Burnthouse Lane, Needham, Harleston, Norfolk IP20 9LN

CUNLIFFE, 3 Baron (UK 1914); Roger Cunliffe; s of 2 Baron Cunliffe (d 1963), and his 1 w, Joan Catherine, da of late Cecil Lubbock (n of 1 Baron Avebury); *b* 12 January 1932; *Educ* Eton, Trinity Coll Cambridge (MA), Architectural Assoc (AADipl), Open Univ; *m* 27 April 1957, Clemency Ann, da of late Maj Geoffrey Benyon Hoare, DL, of Aldeburgh, Suffolk; 2 s, 1 da; *Heir* s, Hon Harry Cunliffe; *Career* consulting architect (ret); memb Ct of Assts Worshipful Co of Goldsmiths (Prime Warden 1997–98); RIBA, MCMI; *Books* Office Buildings (with Leonard Manasseh, 1962), Tomorrow's Office (with Santa Raymond, 1997); *Recreations* pottery, planting trees, cycling; *Style—* The Rt Hon Lord Cunliffe; ✉ The Broadhurst, Brandeston, Woodbridge, Suffolk IP13 7AG

CUNNINGHAM, Allen; s of late Sir Graham Cunningham, KBE, and late Marjorie, *née* Harris; *Educ* Leighton Park Sch Reading, Univ of Liverpool (BArch); *m* 1958, Sandra Lynne, da of late Edmund Bainbridge; 2 s (Graham b 1959, Neve b 1961), 1 da (Aldona b 1965); *Career* project architect: Sir Leslie Martin Cambridge 1957–60, Marcel Breuer & Associates NY 1960–63, Marcel Breuer Paris 1963–66; gp ldr City Architect's Office Nottingham 1966–68, princ architect Llewelyn-Davies, Weeks, Forestier-Walker & Bor London 1968–72, head of architecture Poly of Central London 1974–97; visiting prof Univ of Westminster 1997–2001; fndr The Jl of Architecture (chm Editorial Bd 1996–, exec ed 1997–); memb Scientific Ctee DOCOMOMO Int 1999–; memb Bd of Architectural Educn ARCUK 1978–92; RIBA: memb Cncl RIBA Cities of London and Westminster Soc of Architects 1974–97, memb Educn and Professional Devpt Ctee 1980–84 and 1996–98, elected London regnl rep to RIBA Cncl 1996–99, fndr memb RIBA Reform Gp 1996–, juror RIBA Pres's Royal Gold Medal 1993, juror EAAE Prize 2005–07; co-fndr and vice-pres Terre Romane; registered ARCUK 1959, ARIBA 1959, FRSA 1993; *Publications* Modern Movement Heritage (ed, 1998); *Recreations* creating tableaux objets; *Style—* Mr Allen Cunningham; ✉ 38 Rue de l'Engin, 24500 Eymet, France (tel 00 33 5 53 74 29 73, e-mail cunning@wanadoo.fr)

CUNNINGHAM, Andrew; s of Robert Cunningham (d 1998), and Lily, *née* McGalloway; *b* 22 July 1956, Fife; *Educ* King Edward VI GS Nuneaton, Christ's Coll Cambridge; *m* 29 Sept 1989, Deborah, *née* Moran; 3 s (James b 14 Feb 1992, Harry b 11 March 1994, Patrick b 21 June 1996), 1 da (Elspeth b 2 Aug 1999); *Career* ptnr Deloitte Haskins & Sells (latterly Coopers & Lybrand Deloitte) 1989–96 (joined 1978); Grainger Tst plc: finance dir 1996–2002, dep ceo 2002–; non-exec dir The Local Shopping REIT plc 2007–; FCA 1981; *Style—* Andrew Cunningham, Esq; ✉ Grainger Trust plc, Citygate, St James Boulevard, Newcastle upon Tyne NE1 4JE (e-mail acunningham@graingertrust.co.uk)

C

CUNNINGHAM, Lt-Gen Sir Hugh Patrick; KBE (1975, OBE 1966); s of Sir Charles Banks Cunningham, CSI (d 1967), of Campbelltown, Argyll and Grace, *née* Macnish; *b* 4 November 1921; *Educ* Charterhouse; *m* 1, 1955, Jill (d 1992), da of J S Jeffrey (d 1978), of E Knoyle, Wilts; 2 s, 2 da; m 2, 1995, Zoë, da of T S Andrew; *Career* 2 Lt RE 1942, GOC SW Dist 1971–74, ACGS (OR) MOD 1974–75, Lt-Gen 1975, Dep Chief of Def Staff (OR) 1976–78, ret; Col Cmdt RE 1976–81, Col Queen's Gurkha Engrs 1976–81, Col Bristol Univ OTC 1977–87; HM Lt Tower of London 1983–86; dir: Fairey Holdings 1978–87, Fairey Engineering 1981–86, MEL 1982–89, Trend Communications Ltd 1983–86; chm: LL Consultants 1983–89, The Trend Group 1986–89; pres Old Carthusian Soc 1982–87, govr Suttons Hosp in Charterhouse 1983–96, chm Port Regis Sch 1980–94 (visitor 1994–); hon memb Ct of Assts Worshipful Co of Glass Sellers (Master 1980–81); *Clubs* Army and Navy, MCC; *Style—* Lt-Gen Sir Hugh Cunningham, KBE; ✉ Granary Mill House, Fontmell Magna, Shaftesbury, Dorset SP7 0NY (tel 01747 812025, fax 01747 811965)

CUNNINGHAM, James Dolan (Jim); MP; s of Adam Cunningham, and Elizabeth, *née* Farrel; *b* 4 February 1941; *Educ* St Columbia HS, Tillicoultry Coll (Dip Industrial Law, Dip Social Sciences); *m* 1 March 1985, Marion, da of late Frank Muir Podmore; 1 s (Andrew), 1 da (Jeanette), 1 step s (Paul A Douglas), 1 step da (Jacqueline (Mrs Stevenson)); *Career* engr Rolls Royce until 1988; Coventry City Cncl: sometime vice-chm Fin Ctee, chm Leisure Ctee, vice-chm Tport and Highways Ctee, chief whip, dep ldr of the Cncl, and ldr 1988–92 (memb 1972–93); chief steward and shop steward MSF; sec then chm Coventry SE CLP; MP (Lab) Coventry S 1992–; *Recreations* walking, reading, music, football, politics, history, archaeology, political philosophy; *Style—* Jim Cunningham, Esq, MP; ✉ House of Commons, London SW1A 0AA

CUNNINGHAM, Prof John; *b* 27 June 1949; *Educ* Magdalen Coll Sch Oxford, Trinity Hall Cambridge (BA), Oxford Univ Clinical Med Sch (Nuffield travel award, BM BCh, DM); *Career* house physician and house surgn Radcliffe Infirmary Oxford 1974, SHO (rotating) Whittington Hosp London 1974–75, SHO (thoracic med) Brompton Hosp 1975, med registrar Cardiothoracic Dept Central Middx Hosp 1976–77, lectr in med Med Unit London Hosp Med Coll 1977–80, fell Div of Endocrinology and Metabolism Washington Univ Sch of Med St Louis Missouri USA 1980–82, conslt physician and nephrologist Royal London Hosp 1982–; St Bartholomew's and the Royal London Sch of Med & Dentistry (formerly Royal London Hosp Sch of Med): hon sr lectr in med 1986–, sub-dean for student admissions 1990–97, prof of renal and metabolic med 2001–05, prof of nephrology UCL 2003–, conslt nephrologist UCL Hosp and The Royal Free Hospital 2003–; physician to: The Royal Household 1993–05, King Edward VII's Hosp for Officers 1993–, HM The Queen and Head of the Medical Household 2005–; special tstee Royal London Hosp 1985–, recognised teacher Univ of London 1985–, Jan Brod Meml lectr Prague 1993; over 100 presentations to nat/int learned gps and societies; memb Editorial Bd: Nephrology Dialysis Transplantion 1993–, Int Procceedings Jl (Nephrology Section) 1993–; memb: RSM, American Soc of Nephrology, Renal Assoc, American Soc for Bone and Mineral Res, Euro Calcified Tissue Soc, Bone and Tooth Soc, Euro Dialysis and Transplant Assoc - Euro Renal Assoc, Int Soc of Nephrology; FRCP 1988 (MRCP); *Publications* author of chapters in med and scientific textbooks, invited reviews and over 70 original articles in scientific jls; *Recreations* music, various sports - active and passive; *Style—* Prof John Cunningham; ✉ The Centre for Nephrology, The Royal Free Hospital, Rowland Hill Street, London NW3 2PF

CUNNINGHAM, John Roderick; s of John Cunningham (d 1952), of Kent, and Millicent, *née* Seal (d 1929); *b* 13 May 1926; *Educ* Beckenham Sch, Queen's Univ Belfast (BSc(Econ)); *m* 1964, Monica Rachel, da of Cedric George (d 1964), of Surrey; 2 da (Meryl b 1955 (from previous m), Clare b 1970), 1 s (Roderick b 1965); *Career* RAF Aircrew 1943–47; dir Coutts & Co 1980–87 (various exec posts 1950–80), chm Nikko Bank (UK) plc 1987–92; memb: Bd of Govrs Cordwainers' Coll 1981–92, Cncl City Branch IOD 1985–97, Cncl City Livery Club 1990–2001; vice-pres City Branch Royal Soc of St George (chm 1990); chm Tonbridge Cons Assoc (Vauxhall Ward) 1990–98; memb: Guild of Freemen of City of London, United Wards' Club of City of London, Aldersgate Ward, Bishopsgate Ward, Castle Baynard Ward, Portsoken Ward; memb Ct of Assts Worshipful Co of Loriners (Master 1984); FCIB; *Recreations* City of London activities; *Clubs* IOD, City Livery; *Style—* John R Cunningham, Esq; ✉ 25 Mote Avenue, Mote Park, Maidstone, Kent ME15 7SU (tel 01622 672697)

CUNNINGHAM, Mark James; QC (2001); s of James Arthur Cunningham, and late Carole Kathleen, *née* Wood; *b* 6 June 1956; *Educ* Stonyhurst, Magdalen Coll Oxford (BA), Poly of Central London (Dip Law); *m* 19 July 1980 (m dis 1995); 2 da (Clementine b 1981, Susannah b 1985), 2 s (Charles b 1984, Edward b 1989); *Career* called to the: Bar Inner Temple 1980, East Caribbean Bar 2005; jr counsel to the Crown Chancery 1992, inspr DTI 1998–99, jr counsel to the Crown A Panel 1999; *Recreations* tennis, cricket, horses, food; *Style—* Mark Cunningham, QC; ✉ Maitland Chambers, 7 Stone Buildings, Lincoln's Inn, London WC2A 3SZ (tel 020 7406 1200, fax 020 7406 1300, e-mail mcunningham@maitlandchambers.com)

CUNNINGHAM, (Harold) Michael Clunie; s of Harold Cunningham, and Margaret Isabel, *née* McPherson; *b* 18 November 1947; *Educ* Rossall Sch, RMA Sandhurst; *m* 22 Dec 1970, Virginia Pamela Liege, da of Col Sir Thomas Butler, Bt, CVO, DSO, OBE (d 1994); 2 da (Sophia Louisa Caroline b 31 July 1973, Henrietta Maria Charlotte b 17 Dec 1975), 2 s (Charles Alexander Clunie b 9 Dec 1978, Rupert Jasper Clunie b 25 May 1984); *Career* cmmnd 2 Lt Queen's Own Hussars 1968, ret as Capt 1976; ptnr Neilson Hornby Crichton stockbrokers 1981–86 (joined 1976), dir Neilson Milnes 1986–91, dir Rathbone Neilson Cobbold (formerly Neilson Cobbold) 1991–99, chm Pennine Fund Managers Ltd 1994–98; dir: Rathbone Investment Management 1996–, Rathbone Unit Trust Managers Ltd 1997–; chm Nu Nu plc 2002–; FSI (memb Stock Exchange 1981); *Recreations* field sports, fishing, sailing; *Style—* Michael Cunningham, Esq; ✉ Dolhyfryd, Lawnt, Denbigh, Denbighshire LL16 4SU (tel 01745 814805); Rathbone Investment Management, Port of Liverpool Building, Pier Head, Liverpool L3 1NN (tel 0151 236 6666, fax 0151 243 7036)

CUNNINGHAM, Phyllis Margaret; CBE (1997); da of Andrew Cunningham (d 1992), of Manchester; *b* 15 September 1937; *Educ* Chorlton Central Sch Manchester, Loreburn Coll Manchester (Dip Business Studies), Univ of York; *Career* trainee admin Withington Hosp Manchester 1956–59, personal/res asst to Med Dir Geigy Pharmaceutical Co Manchester 1959–62, unit admin Roosevelt Hosp NY 1962–64, planning offr Royal Free Hosp London 1964–74, dep house govr and sec to the Bd Royal Marsden Hosp London 1974–80; chief exec: Royal Marsden Hosp Special HA 1980–94, Royal Marsden NHS Tst 1994–98; tstee

St Christopher's Hospice Sydenham 1999–; memb Ministerial Advsy Bd Med Devices Agency 2001–03; chm Abbeyfield, Richmond, Thames & Dist Soc Ltd 2002–04, tstee Headley Ct Tst 2001–, tstee Lady Capel's Charity 2003–, tstee and memb Bd Abbeyfield UK 2004–07; govr: Christ's Sch Richmond 1995–99, Queen's Sch Richmond 2002–; Veuve Clicquot Business Woman of the Year 1991; FRSA 1993; *Recreations* travel, gardening, theatre, music; *Style*— Miss Phyllis Cunningham, CBE; ✉ 12 Augustus Close, Brentford Dock, Brentford, Middlesex TW8 8QE (tel 020 8847 1067)

CUNNINGHAM, Roseanna; MSP; da of Hugh Cunningham (d 1993), and Catherine, *née* Dunlay; *b* 27 July 1951; *Educ* Univ of West Australia (BA), Univ of Edinburgh (LLB), Univ of Aberdeen (DipLP); *Career* asst research offr SNP 1977–79, slr Dumbarton DC 1986 (trainee slr 1983–85); slr: Glasgow DC 1986–89, Ross Harper & Murphy Glasgow 1989–90; admitted Faculty of Advocates 1990; MP (SNP): Perth and Kinross 1995–97, Perth 1997–2001; MSP (SNP) Perth 1999–; shadow justice min 1999–, convener Scottish Parl Justice and Home Affrs Ctee 1999–2000, sr vice-convenor and dep leader SNP 2000–04, convener Scottish Parl Health and Community Care Ctee 2004–07, convener Rural Affrs and Environment Ctee 2007–; *Recreations* reading, arguing, music; *Style*— Ms Roseanna Cunningham, MSP; ✉ The Scottish Parliament, Edinburgh EH99 1SP; Algo Business Centre, Glenearn Road, Perth (tel 01738 450408 and 0131 348 5697, fax 01738 450409 and 0131 348 5952, e-mail rcmp.perth@snp.org or roseanna.cunningham.msp@scottish.parliament.uk)

CUNNINGHAM, Thomas Anthony (Tony); MP; s of Daniel Cunningham (d 1987), and Bessie, *née* Lister; *Educ* Workington GS, Univ of Liverpool (BA), Didsbury Coll (PGCE), St John's Coll Manchester (RSA TESL); *m* 1985, Anne, da of Albert and Margaret Gilmore; 1 da (Angela b 1992), 1 s (Daniel b 2004), 1 step s (David b 1978), 1 step da (Marie b 1981); *Career* history teacher Alsager Comp Sch 1976–80, English teacher (VSO) Mikunguni Trade Sch Zanzibar 1980–82, history teacher Netherhall Sch Maryport 1983–93; MEP (Lab) Cumbria and Lancs N 1994–99, MP (Lab) Workington 2001–; cncllr Allerdale BC 1987–94 (ldr 1992–94), Mayor of Workington 1990–91; govt whip 2005–; *Recreations* sports, reading; *Clubs* Station Road; *Style*— Tony Cunningham, Esq, MP; ✉ House of Commons, London SW1A 0AA; Moss Bay House, 40 Heart Road, Derwent Howe, Workington, Cumbria CA14 3YT

CUNNINGHAM, Prof Valentine David; s of Rev Valentine Cunningham, of Lutterworth, Leics, and Alma Lilian, *née* Alexander; *b* 28 October 1944; *Educ* Lawrence Sheriff Sch Rugby, Keble Coll Oxford (scholar, MA), St John's Coll Oxford (DPhil); *m* 6 August 1966, Carol Ann, da of Joseph Shaw; 2 s (Joseph Valentine Asa b 23 Dec 1970, Willoughby Buz Raphael Bunyan b 29 Jan 1975); *Career* jr res fell St John's Coll Oxford 1969–72; Univ of Oxford: lectr in English 1972–, chm English Faculty 1984–87, prof of English language and literature 1996–; CCC Oxford: fell and tutor in English 1972–, dean 1980–91, sr tutor 1991–94; permanent visiting prof Univ of Konstanz Germany 1994–2001; frequent broadcasts on BBC Radio; judge literary prizes incl: Booker Prize 1992 and 1998, Commonwealth Writers Prize 2000 and 2001; memb Labour Pty, memb St Margaret's Church N Oxford; *Publications* Everywhere Spoken Against: Dissent in the Victorian Novel (1975), The Penguin Book of Spanish Civil War Verse (ed, 1980), Spanish Front: Writers on the Civil War (ed, 1986), British Writers of the Thirties (1988), Cinco Escritores Britanicos/Five British Writers (ed, 1990), In the Reading Gaol: Postmodernity, Texts, and History (1994), George Eliot: Adam Bede (ed, 1996), The Victorians: An Anthology of Poetry and Poetics (ed, 2000), Reading After Theory (2002); numerous articles and introductions in books and learned jls; *Recreations* jazz trumpet and piano (ldr Dark Blues Jazz Band); *Clubs* Ronnie Scott's; *Style*— Prof Valentine Cunningham; ✉ Corpus Christi College, Oxford OX1 4JF (tel 01865 276700, fax 01865 276767, e-mail valentine.cunningham@ccc.ox.ac.uk)

CUNNINGHAM-JARDINE, Ronald Charles (Ronnie); CVO (2007); s of Charles Frederick Cunningham (d 1973), of Jardine Hall, Lockerbie and Woodend House, Banchory, and Dorothy Agnes Jessie, *née* Jardine (d 1964); *b* 19 September 1931; *Educ* Ludgrove, Eton, RMA Sandhurst; *m* 19 Sept 1958, (Constance Mary) Teresa, da of John Inglis (d 1959), of West Nisbet, Jedburgh; 1 s (John Charles b 11 Nov 1961), 1 da (Rachel Mary (Mrs Andrew Wardall) b 28 Dec 1963); *Career* served Royal Scots Greys 1950–58, ret Capt; Lord Lt Dumfries & Galloway Region (Dists of Nithsdale and Annandale & Eskdale) 1991–2006 (Vice Lord Lt 1988–91); farmer 1960–95; pres Lockerbie Branch Royal Br Legion 1974–2006, chm BFSS Dumfries & Galloway 1988–93; sec and chm Dumfriesshire Hunt 1960–88; *Recreations* all country sports; *Clubs* White's, Muthaiga (Kenya); *Style*— Ronald Cunningham-Jardine, Esq; ✉ Fourmerkland, Lockerbie, Dumfriesshire DG11 1EH (tel 01387 810226, fax 01387 811375, car 078 6091 4947)

CUNNINGHAM OF FELLING, Baron (Life Peer UK 2005), of Felling in the County of Tyne & Wear; Dr John Anderson (Jack) Cunningham; PC (1993), DL (Cumbria 1991); s of Andrew Cunningham; *b* 4 August 1939; *Educ* Jarrow GS, Bede Coll Univ of Durham (BSc, PhD); *m* 1964, Maureen; 1 s, 2 da; *Career* formerly research chemist Univ of Durham, then lectr and Trades Union official, cncllr Chester-Le-Street DC (chm Fin Ctee 1969–74); MP (Lab): Whitehaven 1970–83, Copeland 1983–2005; PPS to Rt Hon James Callaghan 1972–76, Parly under sec of state Dept of Energy 1976–79; front bench oppn spokesman on: Industry 1979–83, Environment 1983–92; memb Shadow Cabinet 1983–97, shadow ldr House of Commons and Lab campaign coordinator 1989–92; chief oppn spokesman on: foreign and Cwlth affrs (shadow foreign sec) 1992–94, trade and industry 1994–95, National Heritage 1995–97; min for: Agriculture, Fisheries and Food 1997–98, Cabinet Office 'enforcer' and chllr of the Duchy of Lancaster 1998–99; *Recreations* gardening, fell walking, fly fishing, music, books, ornithology, theatre; *Style*— The Rt Hon the Lord Cunningham of Felling, PC, DL

CUNYNGHAME, Sir Andrew David Francis; 12 Bt (NS 1702), of Milncraig, Ayrshire; s of Sir (Henry) David St Leger Brooke Selwyn Cunynghame, 11 Bt (d 1978), and Hon Pamela Margaret (d 1991), da of late 5 Baron Stanley of Alderley; *b* 25 December 1942; *Educ* Eton; *m* 1, 1972, Harriet Ann, da of Charles Thomas Dupont, of Montreal, Canada; 2 da (Ann Marie Albinia b 1978, Tania Albinia Pamela Jean b 1983); m 2, 19 Aug 1989, Isabella, da of late Edward Everett Watts, Jr; *Heir* bro, John Cunynghame; *Career* former chm City Vintagers Ltd; Liveryman Worshipful Co of Pattenmakers; FCA; *Clubs* Brooks's; *Style*— Sir Andrew Cunynghame, Bt; ✉ 12 Vicarage Gardens, London W8 4AH

CUPITT, Rev Don; s of late Robert Cupitt, of Wendover, Bucks, and late Norah Cupitt; *b* 22 May 1934; *Educ* Charterhouse, Trinity Hall Cambridge (BA), Westcott House Cambridge; *m* 28 Dec 1963, Susan Marianne, da of Frank Cooper Day (d 1941); 1 s (John b 1965), 2 da (Caroline b 1966, Sally b 1970); *Career* Nat Serv 2 Lt Royal Signals 1956–57; curate St Philip's Salford 1959–62, vice-princ Westcott House Cambridge 1962–65; Emmanuel Coll Cambridge: dean 1965–91, asst univ lectr 1968–73, univ lectr 1973–96; Hon DLitt Univ of Bristol 1985; hon fell The Jesus Seminar 2001; *Books* Christ and the Hiddenness of God (1971), Crisis of Moral Authority (1972), The Leap of Reason (1976), The Worlds of Science and Religion (1976), Who Was Jesus? (with Peter Armstrong, 1977, BBC TV documentary, 1977), The Nature of Man (1979), Explorations in Theology (1979), The Debate about Christ (1979), Jesus and the Gospel of God (1979), Taking Leave of God (1980), The World to Come (1982), The Sea of Faith (1984, BBC TV series 1984), Only Human (1985), Life Lines (1986), The Long-Legged Fly (1987), The New Christian Ethics (1988), Radicals and the Future of the Church (1989), Creation out of Nothing (1990), What is a Story? (1991), The Time Being (1992), After All (1994), The Last Philosophy (1995), Solar Ethics (1995), After God (1997), Mysticism After Modernity (1998), The Religion of Being (1998), The Revelation of Being (1998), The New Religion of Life in Everyday Speech (1999), The Meaning of it All in Everyday Speech (1999), Kingdom Come in Everyday Speech (2000), Philosophy's Own Religion (2000), Reforming Christianity (2001), Emptiness and Brightness (2002), Is Nothing Sacred? (2002), Life, Life (2003), The Way to Happiness (2005), The Great Questions of Life (2006), The Old Faith and the New (2006), Radical Theology (2006), Impossible Loves (2007); *Recreations* family life; *Style*— The Rev Don Cupitt; ✉ Emmanuel College, Cambridge CB2 3AP (tel 01223 334267, fax 01223 334426)

CURBISHLEY, Alan Charles; s of William George Curbishley, of Barkingside, Essex, and Cordielia Maud, *née* Foley (d 1982); *b* 8 November 1957; *Educ* South West Ham Tech Sch for Boys; *m* 15 July 1983, Carol, da of Robert Henry John Watson; 1 da (Claire b 14 March 1985), 1 s (Michael Alan b 27 July 1988); *Career* professional football player and manager; West Ham United 1974–79 (finalist European Cup Winners' Cup 1976), Birmingham City 1979–83 (promotion to Division 1 1980), Aston Villa 1983–84, Charlton Athletic 1984–87 (promotion to Division 1 1986), Brighton & Hove Albion 1987–90 (promotion to Division 2 1988); Charlton Athletic: rejoined as player 1990, jt player mangr (with Steve Gritt) 1991–95, sole mangr June 1995– (promotion to Premier League 1998); represented England at schoolboy, Under 18 (World Youth Cup winners 1975) and Under 21 level; FA full coaching licence 1991; *Style*— Alan Curbishley, Esq; ✉ c/o Charlton Athletic FC, The Valley, Floyd Road, London SE7 3BL

CURIEL, Raul Morris; s of Isaac Curiel Segura, of Montevideo, Uruguay, and Clara, *née* Margounato; *b* 31 March 1946; *Educ* Colegio Nacional Jose P Varela Scdy Sch Montevideo Uruguay, Univ de la Republica Montevideo Uruguay, Iowa State Univ USA (BArch), Univ of Minnesota USA (MArch); *m* 26 May 1976, Linda, da of Ronald Webb; 2 da (Alessandra Stephanie b 5 May 1985, Melanie Jane b 30 May 1989); *Career* formerly architect São Paulo, dir Fitzroy Robinson Ltd UK 1983– (architectural asst 1978–83); major architectural projects incl: The Standard Chartered Bank, Sedgwick House, HQ for the Moscow Narodny Bank, interiors for London HQ of Drexel Burnham Lambert, a mixed conservation/new office building at 75 King William St, numerous business parks; awarded: AIA merit award, selected design Sch of Architecture ISU 1971, selected design UNESCO's Int Design Competition 1972, Mason's award 1990 and Tiler's and Bricklayer's award 1990 for building at 75 King William St; memb: IAB 1977, RIBA 1979; *Recreations* theatre, reading, swimming, viewing buildings, sketching; *Style*— Raul Curiel, Esq

CURL, Prof Emeritus James Stevens; s of George Stevens Curl (d 1974), and Sarah, *née* McKinney (d 1995); *b* 26 March 1937; *Educ* Cabin Hill, Campbell Coll, Queen's Univ Belfast, Belfast Coll of Art, Oxford Sch of Architecture, UCL (DiplArch, DipTP, PhD); *m* 1, 1960 (m dis 1986), Eileen Elizabeth, da of John Blackstock (d 1984), of Belfast; 2 da (Dr Astrid James b 1962, Ingrid Teesdale b 1964); m 2, 1993, Prof Dorota Iwaniec, *qv*; *Career* architect, town planner, antiquarian, architectural historian; architectural ed Survey of London 1970–73, conslt architect to Scottish Ctee for European Architectural Heritage Year 1973–75, sr architect Herts CC 1975–7; De Montfort Univ Leicester: sr lectr 1978–88, prof of architectural history Dept of Architecture 1988–95, prof of architectural history and research Centre for Conservation Studies 1995–98, emeritus prof of architectural history 1998–, research fell Sch of Architecture 1998–2000; Queen's Univ Belfast: sr res fell Sch of Architecture 2000–02 (hon sr res fell 2002), prof of architectural history 2000–02; practising assoc Acad of Experts; visiting fell Peterhouse Cambridge 1991–92 and 2002; memb Advsy Cncl Friends of Kensal Green Cemetery 1998–2003 (memb Fabric Ctee 2003–); memb: Fabric Advsy Ctee Leicester Cathedral 1992–2000, Educn Ctee Royal Soc of Ulster Architects 1997–99, Conservation Ctee Royal Soc of Ulster Architects 2000–01; author of numerous articles and reviews; Liveryman Worshipful Co of Chartered Architects; RIBA, AABC, MRTPI, MRIAI, ARIAS, FSA Scot, FSA; *Books* The Erosion of Oxford (1977), The Life and Work of Henry Roberts 1803–76, Architect (1983), The Londonderry Plantation 1609–1914 (1986), English Architecture (1987), Victorian Architecture (1990), The Art and Architecture of Freemasonry (1991, new edn 2002, Sir Banister Fletcher Award 1992), Encyclopaedia of Architectural Terms (1993), Egyptomania (1994), Victorian Churches (1995), Dictionary of Architecture (1999 and 2000), The Honourable The Irish Society and the Plantation of Ulster, 1608–2000: The City of London and the Colonisation of County Londonderry in the Province of Ulster in Ireland (2000), The Victorian Celebration of Death (2000 and 2004), Kensal Green Cemetery 1824–2001 (2001), Classical Architecture (2001), Piety Proclaimed (2002), Death and Architecture (2002), Georgian Architecture (2002), The Egyptian Revival (2005), Oxford Dictionary of Architecture and Landscape Architecture (2006), Victorian Architecture: Diversity and Invention (2007); *Recreations* music, opera, travel, literature, ecclesiology food, wine, poetry, painting; *Clubs* Art Workers' Guild, Oxford and Cambridge; *Style*— Prof Emeritus James Stevens Curl, FSA; ✉ 15 Torgrange, Holywood, Co Down BT18 0NG (tel and fax 028 90 425 141, e-mail jscurl@btinternet.com)

CURL, His Hon Judge Philip; s of Dr Oliver Curl, and Joan, *née* Crooks; *b* 31 October 1947; *Educ* Radley, Univ of Southampton (LLB); *m* 22 Oct 1983, Nicola Ruth, da of late Richard Quentin Gurney; 2 da (Olivia Elisabeth b 17 Jan 1986, Eleanor Rose b 16 May 1989); *Career* called to the Bar Gray's Inn 1970, recorder 1995–96 (asst recorder 1991), circuit judge (SE Circuit) 1996–, designated family judge Norwich Combined Court 1998–; *Recreations* playing and watching sport, art, travel; *Clubs* Boodle's, MCC, Norfolk (Norwich); *Style*— His Hon Judge Curl; ✉ Norwich Combined Courts Centre, Bishopgate, Norwich NR3 1UR

CURNOCK, Dr David Anthony; s of George Henry Reginald Curnock, of Bramcote Hills, Notts, and Vera Marjorie, *née* Bucknell; *b* 17 August 1946; *Educ* Chigwell Sch, St John's Coll Cambridge (MA, MB BChir), Charing Cross Hosp Med Sch; *m* 13 Nov 1971, Anne Elizabeth, da of John Ruff, of Holmbury-St-Mary, Surrey; 3 da (Ruth b 1972, Elizabeth b 1974, Esther b 1980), 1 s (Michael b 1982); *Career* lectr in child health Univ of Benin Nigeria 1977–79, sr registrar of paediatrics Derbys Children's Hosp and Nottingham City Hosp 1979–82, conslt paediatrician Nottingham City Hosp 1982–2006; FRCP 1989, FRCPCH 1997; *Recreations* printing, railway history; *Style*— Dr David Curnock; ✉ 39 Sevenoaks Crescent, Bramcote Hills, Nottinghamshire NG9 3FP

CURNOCK COOK, Jeremy Laurence; s of Colin Curnock Cook (d 2003), and Doris, *née* Wolsey (d 2002); *b* 3 September 1949, Bromley, Kent; *Educ* Westminster, TCD (MA); *m* 1, Elizabeth Joanna Badgett; m 2, Mary Elisabeth Thomasson; m 3, Sara Jane, *née* O'Donahue; 2 da (Jessica b 22 Aug 1989, Hannah b 12 Nov 1992), 1 s (Rory b 8 Feb 1991); *Career* md and fndr Int Biochemicals Gp plc 1975–87, dir responsible for Bioscience Unit Rothschild Asset Mgmnt Ltd 1988–2000, chm and fndr Bioscience Mangrs Ltd 2001–; chm: Targeted Genetics Inc USA 1995–, Inflazyme Pharmaceuticals Inc Canada 1996–; dir: Biocompatibles Int plc 1992– (former chm), Sirna Therapeutics USA 1995–2007, Angiotech Pharmaceuticals Inc Canada 1995–2001, Silence Therapeutics plc 2005–, Osteologix Inc USA 2006–; memb Soc of Gen Microbiology 1971; FInstD 1983, FRSA 1995; *Recreations* theatre, music, skiing, keeping fit; *Clubs* Univ and Kildare St (Dublin), RAC of Victoria (Melbourne); *Style*— Jeremy Curnock Cook, Esq; ✉ 2 Balfern Grove, London W4 2JX (tel 020 8742 8354, fax 020 8995 6304, e-mail biojlcc@aol.com); Bioscience Managers Limited, 243 Knightsbridge, London SW7 1DN (tel 020 7225 4400, fax 020 7052 9121, e-mail jlcc@biosciencemanagers.com)

CURNOW, (Elizabeth) Ann Marguerite; QC (1985); da of Cecil Curnow (d 1944, as Japanese POW), and Doris, *née* Behr (d 1964); *b* 5 June 1935; *Educ* St Hilda's Sch Whitby, KCL

(LLB, AKC), Sorbonne (Cours de Civilisation Française); *m* 28 Sept 1981, His Hon (William) Neil Denison, QC; 3 step s; *Career* called to the Bar Gray's Inn 1957 (bencher 1985), prosecuting counsel to the Crown Middx Crown Court 1972–77, sr prosecuting counsel to the Crown Central Criminal Court 1981–85 (jr prosecuting counsel 1977–81), recorder of the Crown Court 1980–2001; memb: Parole Bd 1992–94, Criminal Injuries Compensation Bd 1996–2002, Mental Health Review Tbnl 2000–04; chm Victim Support Lambeth 1987–2003; *Recreations* music (especially opera), tapestry, Burmese cats, gardens; *Style—* Miss Ann Curnow, QC; ✉ 6 King's Bench Walk, Temple, London EC4Y 7DR (tel 020 7583 0410, fax 020 7353 8791, e-mail ann.curnow@6kbw.com)

CURNOW, Barry John; s of Stuart John Curnow (d 1986), and Margaret Agnes (Daisy), *née* Parkhouse (d 2001); *b* 19 May 1948; *Educ* Sutton HS Plymouth, Univ of Exeter (BA), Univ of London (MA); *m* 1, 23 Oct 1971, Patricia Margaret, da of late Dr D R L Newton; m 2, 24 Dec 1987, Penelope Ann, da of Henry S J de Haas; *Career* certified mgmnt conslt and group analyst; personnel mangr GLC 1969–73, joined Hay-MSL 1974, gp md Hay-MSL Management Consultants 1984–86, chief exec Hay Management Consultants Asia Hong Kong 1986–87, worldwide dir Hay Group 1987–90, chm and chief exec MSL Group International 1987–91, fndr dir Future Perfect 1987 (exec chm 1991–), non-exec dir and advsr to several cos, chm Independent Counselling and Advsy Servs (ICAS) Ltd 1991–97, princ Maresfield Curnow Sch of Mgmnt Consulting 1991–; pres: UK Inst of Personnel Mgmnt 1989–91 (vice-pres pay and employment conditions 1984–86), Inst of Mgmnt Conslts 1996–97 (chm Int Ctee 2000–); chm Int Cncl Mgmnt Consulting Institutes 2003–05; tstee dir Tavistock Inst of Human Relations 1997–; hon psychotherapist Barts 1998–2000; res assoc Henley Mgmnt Coll 1974–83; visiting prof: Mgmnt Consltg CASS Business Sch City Univ 2001–, Univ of Durham 2003; former chair Educ Ctee and asst Worshipful Co of Mgmnt Conslts; memb Inst of Gp Analysis 2001–; Freeman City of London, Freeman Worshipful Co of Chartered Secs and Admins; CCIPD, FCMC, FIOD; *Publications* Managing Third Age Careers - The Corporate Challenge (with John McLean Fox, 1994), The Chance to Live More Than Once (companion vol to Third Age Careers - The Corporate Challenge, with John McLean Fox, 1996); International Guide to Management Consultancy (jt consltg ed 2001 and 2003); *Recreations* amateur radio licence G3UKI 1965; *Style—* Barry Curnow, Esq; ✉ tel 020 7788 4017, fax 020 7691 0206, mobile 07810 285403, e-mail barry_curnow@compuserve.com and maresfieldcurnow@aol.com

CURR, Surgn Rear Adm Ralph Donaldson; s of George Curr (d 1999), of Bromley, Kent, and Florence, *née* Poole (d 2002); *b* 25 September 1943; *Educ* Dulwich Coll, KCH London (MB BS, AKC); *m* 2 Aug 1972, Susan, *née* Brereton; 2 s (Iain b 25 July 1973, Alan b 9 March 1981), 3 da (Rachael b 17 Jan 1975, Sarah b 27 Oct 1976, Helen b 7 Aug 1978); *Career* base MO HMS Tamar Hong Kong 1984–86, princ MO HMS Intrepid and staff MO COMAW 1986–88, princ MO HMS Drake and advsr in gen practice 1990–95, dir of med personnel 1995–97, dep med DG (Naval) 1997–2000, dir of med ops CINCFLEET 2000–02, med DG (Naval) 2002–03; sec Tamar Faculty RCGP; memb Royal Naval Med Club 1976– (pres 2002); tstee: UK National Defence Assoc, Pentewan Viallge Tst, Lord Caradon Lecture Tst; chm St Austell Sea Cadets, memb Cncl of St John Cornwall; involved with: Nat Tst, St Austell Parish Church; Alan Hirst Meml Prize for Naval Gen Practice 1996; Queen's Golden Jubilee Medal 2002, Defence Med Services Gen Practice Medal 2003; memb BMA 1989; LRCP, MRCS, DRCOG 1975, FRCGP 1992 (MRCGP 1974), Hon FRCGP (Hong Kong) 1993; OStJ 2001; *Recreations* tennis, walking, church; *Clubs* Naval, Scottish Malt Whisky Soc; *Style—* Surgn Rear Adm Ralph Curr; ✉ Seagarth, Pentewan Hill, Pentewan, St Austell, Cornwall PL26 6DD (tel 01726 843106, mobile 07919 374192, e-mail rdcurr@hotmail.com)

CURRAN, Edmund Russell; OBE (2006); s of William John Curran (d 1973), of Dungannon, NI, and Elizabeth, *née* Russell (d 1945); *b* 29 September 1944; *Educ* Royal Sch Dungannon, Queen's Univ Belfast (BSc, DipEd); *m* 1, 1969 (m dis 1992), Romaine, da of William Carmichael; 2 s (Jonathan William b 18 Sept 1973, Andrew Edmund Simon b 13 Oct 1976), 2 da (Cathryn Ruth b 1 Sept 1975, Claire Susannah b 10 March 1978); m 2, 1994, Pauline Beckett, da of Jack Beckett; *Career* Belfast Telegraph: grad trainee journalist 1966–67, reporter, feature writer then ldr writer 1967–72, asst ed 1973–74, dep ed 1974–88; ed Sunday Life (Belfast) 1988–92 (seconded as ed Wales on Sunday 1991), ed Belfast Telegraph 1993–2005, ed-in-chief NI newspapers Independent News and Media 2005–; pres UK Soc of Editors 2001; UK Regnl Newspaper Ed of the Year 1992; memb PCC 2002–; *Recreations* tennis, golf; *Clubs* Belvoir Park Golf, Royal Co Down Golf; *Style—* Edmund Curran, Esq, OBE

CURRAN, Margaret Patricia; MSP; da of James Curran (d 1991), of Glasgow, and Rose, *née* McConnellogue (d 2004); *b* 24 November 1958; *Educ* Our Lady & St Francis Sch (MA); *m* 1986, Rab Murray, s of George Murray; 2 s (Christopher b 16 March 1987, David b 3 May 1989); *Career* community worker 1982–87, sr community worker 1987–89, lectr Community Educn Univ of Strathclyde 1989–99, MSP (Labour) Glasgow Baillieston 1999–; Scot Parl: convenor Social Inclusion Ctee 1999–2000, convenor Housing Ctee 1999–2000, min for social justice 2002–03 (dep min 2000–02), min for communities 2003–04, min for Parl 2004–; donor: Oxfam, Amnesty Int; memb TGWU; *Recreations* reading, arts, cinema, family (especially children); *Style—* Ms Margaret Curran, MSP; ✉ 75 Langside Drive, Glasgow G43 2ST (tel 0141 637 3254, e-mail mag.curran@virgin.net); Constituency Office, Westwood Business Centre, Easterhouse, Glasgow (tel 0141 771 4844, fax 0141 771 4877)

CURRAN, Patrick David; QC (1995); *Educ* Ratcliffe Coll, The Queen's Coll Oxford (MA); *m*; 2 da, 2 s; *Career* called to the Bar Gray's Inn 1972 (bencher 2005), recorder 1992–, memb King's Inns and the Bar of Ireland 1994–; asst cmmr Parly Boundary Cmmn 1993–, legal memb Mental Health Review Tbnls 1995–; memb: Ctee Personal Injury Bar Assoc 1995–2000, Academic Editorial Bd London Law Review 2005; govr Westminster Cathedral Choir Sch 1999–; fell Soc for Advanced Legal Studies 1998–, memb Soc of Legal Scholars 2003–; *Publications* Personal Injuries and Quantum Reports (ed, 1992–); Criminal Law Review (contrib, 1992), Personal Injury Handbook (contrib and ed, 1997), Personal Injury Pleadings (1994, 3 edn 2004), Criminal Law and Forensic Psychiatry (contrib, 1995); *Style—* Patrick Curran, Esq, QC; ✉ 9–12 Bell Yard, Temple Bar, London WC2 (tel 020 7400 1800, fax 020 7404 1405)

CURRAN, Stephen William; s of Dr Richard Desmond Curran, CBE (d 1985, Capt RNVR), and Marguerite Claire, *née* Gothard; *b* 9 March 1943; *Educ* Marlborough House Sch, Wellington, RMA Sandhurst; *m* 21 June 1969, Anne Beatrice, da of late Harry Grumbar, of Rats Castle, Roughway, nr Tonbridge, Kent; 1 s (Charles b 1972), 1 da (Louise b 1979); *Career* Lt 1 The Queen's Dragoon Gds 1963–66; Permutit Co Ltd 1966–67, Bowater Co Ltd 1967–71, analyst Grumbar and Sée 1971–75, managing conslt Coopers and Lybrand Assocs 1975–79, project fin mangr NCB Pension Funds 1979–81; Candover Investments plc: dep chief exec 1981–90, chief exec 1991–99, chm 1999–2006, non-exec dir 2006–; non-exec dir: Jarvis Hotels plc, Greggs plc; FCCA 1973; *Recreations* skiing, swimming, tennis, riding; *Clubs* Cavalry and Guards', Hurlingham; *Style—* Stephen Curran, Esq; ✉ c/o Candover Investments plc, 5th Floor, 20 Old Bailey, London EC4M 7LN (tel 020 7489 9848, fax 020 7248 5483)

CURRAN, Susan; da of Norman Griffin, of Lincoln, and Maureen, *née* McGinnity; *b* 14 May 1952; *Educ* Abbeydale GS for Girls Sheffield, Univ of Sussex (BA), Univ of East Anglia (MBA); *m* 1, 1976 (m dis 1980), Timothy Curran; m 2, 1980 (m dis 1987), Raymond Curnow; 2 s (Rufus b 7 Nov 1980, Evan b 14 Dec 1982); m 3, 1997, Paul Simmonds; *Career* underwriter FM Insurance Co 1973–78, dir and sec Probit Consultancies Ltd 1979–87, freelance writer 1985–, md Rampant Horse Ltd 1993–95, md Curran Publishing Serices Ltd 1999–; memb Norwich City Cncl (Lab) 1990–95; *Books* fiction: The Mouse God (1987), The Heron's Catch (1989), Mrs Forster (1991), Mine (1994), Communion With Death (1995); non-fiction incl: How to Write a Book and Get it Published (1990), The Penguin Computing Book (with Ray Curnow, 1983), The Driver's Handbook (1997), The Environment Handbook (1999); *Recreations* politics, cooking, collecting contemporary art, other people; *Style—* Ms Susan Curran; ✉ 2 St Giles Terrace, Norwich NR2 1NS (tel 01603 665843, fax 01603 624627, e-mail susan@curranpublishing.com)

CURRIE, Andrew Buchanan; s of Buchanan Currie, of Loughborough, Leics, and Wilma, *née* Livingston; *b* 16 April 1954; *Educ* Loughborough GS, Univ of Birmingham (BA); *Career* employment research exec Inst of Dirs 1983–86, sr account exec Profile Public Relations 1986–88, dep dir and head of research Shopping Hours Reform Cncl 1988–94, ed Making Sense of Shopping 1988–94; BAA: asst dir of public affrs 1994–2000, dir of community relations 2000–03, dir of employee communications 2003–07, head CEO's Office 2007–; FRSA; *Recreations* opera, reading, writing; *Style—* Andrew Currie, Esq; ✉ Flat 3, 52 Cumberland Street, London SW1V 4LZ; BAA Limited, World Business Centre 1, 1206 Newall Road, Middlesex UB3 5AP (tel 020 8745 9964, fax 020 8745 2435)

CURRIE, Brian Murdoch; s of William Murdoch Currie (d 1984), and Dorothy, *née* Holloway (d 1995); *b* 20 December 1934; *Educ* Blundell's (open scholar), Oriel Coll Oxford (open scholar, MA); *m* 21 Oct 1961, Patricia Maria, da of Capt Frederick Eaton-Farr (d 1945); 3 s (Murdoch b 1964, Lachlan b 1967, Gregor b 1975), 1 da (Lucinda b 1966); *Career* Subaltern RTR 1957–59; Arthur Andersen: articled clerk 1959–62, qualified CA 1962, ptnr 1970–90, managing ptnr London 1977–82; fin memb HMSO Bd 1972–74, inspr Dept of Trade 1978–81; memb: Restrictive Practices Court 1979–2004, Take-over Panel 1989–97; dep chm Fin Reporting Cncl 1996–98; ICAEW: memb Cncl and Mgmnt Ctee 1988–99, vice-chm Fin Reporting and Auditing Group 1990–92, chm Practice Regulation Directorate 1992–93, chm Chartered Accountants Jt Ethics Ctee 1994–95, vice-pres 1994–95, dep pres 1995–96, pres 1996–97; chm Public Sector Liaison Gp of Accounting Standards Ctee 1984–86; memb IFAC Compliance Ctee 2000–2002, memb Euro Ctee of Br Invisibles 1991–95; lay memb GDC 1994–99; tstee Oriel Coll Devpt Tst 1979–94; govr Blundell's Sch 2000–02, chm Peter Blundell Soc 1997–2002; hon treas The Glass Assoc 1999–2003 (jt ed The Glass Cone); Exmoor Soc Fndr's Award 2002 (treas 1993–2002); memb Worshipful Co of Chartered Accountants (memb Court of Assts 1994–97); fell Inst of Ops Mgmnt (memb Nat Cncl 1970–73); FIMC; *Recreations* study of glass; *Clubs* Athenaeum, Pluralists; *Style—* Brian Currie, Esq; ✉ Westbrook House, Bampton, Devon EX16 9HU (tel 01398 331418, e-mail brian@currie.co.uk)

CURRIE, Sir Donald Scott; 7 Bt (UK 1847); s of George Donald Currie (d 1980), and Janet, *née* Scott; suc unc, Sir Alick Bradley Currie, 6 Bt (d 1987); *b* 16 January 1930; *m* 1, 1948 (m dis 1951), Charlotte, da of Charles Johnstone, of Arizona; 1 s (Donald Mark b 1949 d 1994), 2 da (Julia Ann (Mrs Eugene R Gangaware), Janet Sue (Mrs Robert E Buck) (twins) b 1950); m 2, 1952, Barbara Lee (d 1993), da of A P Garnier, of California; 1 s (Gary Dwayne b 1953), 2 da (Tina Marie (Mrs Linneman) b 1955, Kathren Evelyn (Mrs Earl Avara) b 1959); m 3, 1994, Barbara Lou Lebsack, da of Joshua I Fenn, of Kansas; *Career* US Dept of the Interior, US Nat Park Serv (ret); ranch hand Aristocrat Angus Ranch; *Style—* Sir Donald Currie, Bt

CURRIE, Ian Hamilton; s of John Currie (d 1984), and Vera Matilda Currie, *née* Lea; *b* 9 March 1948; *Educ* Portsmouth Northern GS; *m* 22 Feb 1972, Catherine Helen, da of Ernest William Pink (d 1983); 2 da (Victoria Catherine b 1979, Jacqueline Neoma b 1983); *Career* fin dir: Gieves Group plc 1981–97, Chivers Communications plc 2000–01, Sirrus Gp plc, Binns & Co PR Ltd; chm: Syrinx Securities Ltd, Pullingers (Furnishers) Ltd; FCA (England and Wales) 1970; *Recreations* cruiser sailing; *Clubs* Portchester Sailing (tstee); *Style—* Ian Currie, FCA; ✉ Clear Cottage, Manor Road, Hayling Island, Hampshire PO11 0QT (tel 023 9246 2966, fax 023 9246 1240, car 07836 270166, e-mail ianhcurrie@aol.com)

CURRIE, James McGill; s of late David Currie, of Kilmarnock, Scotland, and Mary, *née* Smith; *b* 17 November 1941; *Educ* St Joseph's Sch Kilmarnock, Blairs Coll Aberdeen, Royal Scots Coll, Valladolid Spain, Univ of Glasgow (MA); *m* 27 June 1968, Evelyn Barbara, da of Alexander Malcolm Macintyre, of Glasgow; 1 s (Alister John b 1971), 1 da (Jennifer b 1973); *Career* civil servant; asst princ Scot Home and Health Dept 1968–72, Scot Educn Dept 1972–75; asst sec: Tport Policy 1977–80, Industrial Devpt 1981–82; cnsllr for Social Affrs and Tport at UK Perm Representation to EEC in Brussels 1982–86, dir Euro Regnl Devpt Fund of Euro Cmmn (Brussels) 1987–89, chef de cabinet to Sir Leon Brittan 1989–92, dep ambass at EC Delgn to US in Washington 1993–96, DG Customs and Indirect Taxation 1996–97, DG Environment 1997–2001; non-exec dir: Royal Bank of Scotland 2001–, Total UK 2004–; int advsr Eversheds LLP, sr advsr Burson-Marsteller; *Recreations* guitar, tennis, golf, good food; *Clubs* New (Edinburgh); *Style—* James M Currie, Esq

CURRIE, Kenneth Alexander (Ken); s of Alexander Currie, of Barrhead, and Georgina, *née* Ruddie; *b* 9 March 1960; *Educ* Barrhead HS, John Nielson Sch Paisley, Paisley Coll of Technol, Glasgow Sch of Art (Elizabeth Greenshields Fndn scholar, Cargill scholar, BA, Dip Postgrad Studies, Newberry medal); *m* July 1992, Marie Barbour; 2 da (Eilidh Barbour b 27 Dec 1993, Kirsty Fraser b 26 Nov 1996), 1 s (Andrew Galloway (twin) b 26 Nov 1996); *Career* artist; visiting prof Glasgow Sch of Art 2002; *Selected Solo Exhibitions* New Work from Glasgow (Arnolfini Bristol) 1986, Third Eye Centre Glasgow 1988, Raab Galerie Berlin 1988, Story from Glasgow (Kelvingrove Museum Glasgow) 1990, Raab Gallery London 1991, Raab Gallery Berlin 1993, Galerie Christian Dam Copenhagen 1994, Raab Boukamel Gallery London 1995 and 1996, Galerie Christian Dam Oslo 1997, Boukamel Contemporary Art London 1999, BCA Gallery London 2001, Tullie House Museum and Art Gallery Carlisle 2002, Mackintosh Museum Glasgow Sch of Art 2002, Flowers East London 2003, Flowers NY 2004; *Group Exhibitions* incl: New Image Glasgow (Third Eye Centre and tour) 1985–86, The Vigorous Imagination (Scottish Nat Gallery of Modern Art) 1987, Art History (Hayward Gallery) 1987, The Lion Rampant: New Scottish Paintings & Photography (Artspace, San Francisco) 1988–89, Scottish Art since 1900 (Scottish Nat Gallery of Modern Art and Barbican Art Gallery) 1989–90, Mischaire le Carte Immague Speculare (Gian Ferrari Arte Contemporánea) 1990–91, Shocks to the System (Hayward Gallery) 1991, VI Biennale d'Arte (Sacra Teramo Italy) 1994, Bad Blood (Glasgow Print Studio) 1996, XXXVIII Premio Suzzara Italy 1998, Narcissus 20th Century Self-Portraits (Scottish Nat Portrait Gall) 2001, Goya, Köllowitz and Currie (Glasgow Print Studio/Sanctuary Gall of Modern Art Glasgow) 2003; *Works in Public Collections* Scottish Nat Gallery of Modern Art, Macmaster Univ Art Gallery Toronto, Br Cncl, Aberdeen Art Gallery, Nottingham Castle Museum, City of Manchester Art Gallery, Glasgow museums and art galleries, MOMA Copenhagen, Yale Center for British Art Connecticut, Gulbenkian Fndn Lisbon, Br Museum, Boston Museum of Fine Arts, Scot Nat Portrait Gallery, British Museum; *Style—* Ken Currie, Esq; ✉ 34 Riverside Road, Glasgow G43 2EF

CURRIE, Maj-Gen (Archibald) Peter Neil; CB (2001); s of Dr Donald Currie, and Ysobel Marion, *née* Garland; *b* 30 June 1948, Dar es Salaam, Tanzania; *Educ* Monkton Combe, Univ of Nottingham (BA), RMA Sandhurst, Army Cmd and Staff Course, Higher Cmd and Staff Course; *m* 3 Aug 1974, Angela Margaret, *née* Howell; 2 s (Donald Jeremy James b 3 Sept 1977, Angus Peter Robert b 28 March 1979); *Career* CO 12 Regt RA 1987–90, instr Army Staff Coll 1990–91, Col Mil Ops 1 1991–93, Cdr Artillery Allied Rapid Reaction Corps 1994, Dep Cdr Multination Div Centre (Airmobile) 1995, Dir Personal Services (Army) 1996–98, mil advsr to high rep Bosnia-Herzegovina 1998–99, Dep

C

Adj-Gen and DG Service Conditions (Army) 1999–2002; chm: Army Central Fund 1999–2002, Army Dependants' Tst 1999–2002, Army Sports Control Bd 1999–2002; conslt 2003–04; dir Blue Forces Group Ltd 2002–, non-exec dir Close Brothers Military Services 2003–06; tstee Combat Stress 2006–; memb: Bd Services Sound and Vision Co, Cncl Forces Pension Soc, Bd Race for Opportunity 1999–2002; Col Cmdt RA 2002–; Lt Govr Royal Hosp Chelsea 2005–; memb HAC; Queen's Commendation for Valuable Service 1999; *Recreations* skiing, tennis, squash, history, opera and jazz, oriental rugs, walking in wild places; *Style*— Maj-Gen Peter Currie, CB

CURRIE, Raymond Frank (Ray); s of William Murdoch Currie (d 1984), and Dorothy, *née* Holloway (d 1995), of South Molton, Devon; *b* 11 May 1945; *Educ* Blundell's, The Loomis Sch Windsor CT, CCC Cambridge (exhibitioner, BA); *m* 1, 1 July 1972 (m dis 2001), Edwina Currie, da of Simon Cohen; 2 da (Deborah Josephine b 30 Oct 1974, Susannah Elizabeth b 19 May 1977); m 2, 27 May 2003, Sharon Frances Attwal, da of Anthony Munro; *Career* Arthur Andersen: articled clerk 1967–70, qualified 1970, London 1970–73, fndr memb Birmingham practice 1973–79, dir of training 1979–96; dir Tower House Training Ltd 1996–; memb Bd of Accreditation of Educn Courses CCAB 1985–95 (chm 1992–95); ICAEW: chm Dist Training Bd 1986–90, memb Educn and Training Directorate 1989–2001 (chm 1999–2000), chm Educn and Assessment Ctee 1995–99, memb Cncl 1994–2001; memb: Business and Mgmnt Studies Ctee CNAA 1986–91, Audit Ctee Qualifications and Curriculum Authy (QCA) 1998–; pres Derby Soc of Chartered Accountants 1999–2000; FCA 1974 (ACA 1970), MITD 1983, MIPM 1987, MAAT 1998; *Recreations* all sports - playing some slowly, following all enthusiastically, reading, cinema; *Clubs* Le Beaujolais, MCC, Yorkshire CCC, N Devon CC; *Style*— Ray Currie, Esq; ✉ Tower House Training Limited, 160 Western Road, Micklever, Derby DE3 9GT (tel 01332 549280, e-mail ray@currie.co.uk)

CURRIE OF MARYLEBONE, Baron (Life Peer UK 1996), of Marylebone in the City of Westminster; David Anthony Currie; s of Kennedy Moir Currie (d 1972), of London, and Marjorie, *née* Thompson; *b* 9 December 1946; *Educ* Battersea GS, Univ of Manchester (BSc), Univ of Birmingham (M Soc Sci), Univ of London (PhD); *m* 9 July 1975 (m dis), Shaziye, da of Hussein Gazioglu, of Nicosia, Cyprus; 2 s (Hon James Mehmet b 9 April 1978, Hon Timothy Timur b 8 May 1982); m 2, 24 March 1995, Angela Mary Piers Dumas; *Career* Hoare and Govett Co 1971–72, Economic Models 1972; QMC London: lectr 1972–79, reader 1979–81, prof of economics 1981–88; London Business Sch: prof of economics 1988–2000, dir of Centre for Economic Forecasting 1988–95, dep princ 1992–95, dep dean external relations 1999–2000; dean Cass Business Sch City Univ 2001–; chm Ofcom 2002–; non-exec dir Abbey National plc 2001–02; memb: HM Treasy Panel of Independent Forecasters 1992–95, Advsy Bd for the Research Cncls 1992–93, Advsy Cmmn RPI 1992–93, Mgmnt Bd Ofgem 1999–2002; tstee Joseph Rowntree Reform Tst 1991–2002; Hon DLitt Univ of Glasgow 1998, hon fell Queen Mary Coll London; memb Royal Econ Soc; *Books* Advances in Monetary Economics (ed, 1985), The Operation and Regulation of Financial Markets (ed, 1986), Macroeconomic Interactions between North and South (ed, 1988), Macroeconomic Policies in an Interdependent World (ed, 1989), Rules, Reputation and Macroeconomic Policy Coordination (1993), EMU: Problems in the Transition to a Single European Currency (ed, 1995), North-South Linkages and International Macroeconomic Policy (ed, 1995), The Pros and Cons of EMU (1997), Will the Euro Work? (1998); *Recreations* music, literature, swimming; *Style*— The Rt Hon Lord Currie of Marylebone

CURRY, Rt Hon David Maurice; PC (1996), MP; s of Thomas Harold Curry and late Florence Joan, *née* Tyerman; *b* 13 June 1944; *Educ* Ripon GS, CCC Oxford, Kennedy Sch of Govt Harvard Univ (Kennedy scholar); *m* 1971, Anne Helene Maud Roullet; 1 s, 2 da; *Career* reporter: Newcastle Journal 1967–70, Financial Times 1970–79 (trade ed, international companies ed, Brussels correspondent, Paris correspondent, European news ed); sec Anglo-American Press Assoc of Paris 1978–79, fndr Paris Cons Assoc 1977; European Parliament: MEP (EDG) NE Essex 1979–89, chm Agric Ctee 1982–84 (yst ctee chm in Euro Parliament's history), Cons spokesman Budget Ctee 1984–, rapporteur gen EEC Budget 1987; MP (Cons) Skipton and Ripon 1987–; min of state MAFF 1992–93 (Parly sec 1989–92); min of state DOE: for planning and local govt 1993–94, for local govt, housing and urban regeneration 1994–97; shadow min of agriculture, fisheries and food 1997 (resigned Nov 1997), shadow sec of state for Local and Devolved Govt Affrs 2003–04; chm Agriculture Select Ctee 1999–2001, chm Select Ctee on Environment, Food and Rural Affrs 2001–03, memb Public Accounts Ctee 2005–, memb Ctee on Standards and Privileges 2006–; chm Dairy UK 2005–; columnist: Yorkshire Post, Local Govt Chronicle; *Books* The Food War: the EEC-US Conflict in Food Trade (1982), The Conservative Tradition in Europe (ed, 1998), Lobbying Government: Chartered Institute of Housing (1999), The Sorcerer's Apprentice: Local Government and the Sate (2000); *Recreations* digging, windsurfing; *Style*— The Rt Hon David Curry, MP; ✉ Newland End, Arkesden, Essex CB11 4HF; Constituency office: 19 Otley Street, Skipton, North Yorkshire BD19 1DY (tel 01756 792092)

CURRY, John Arthur Hugh; CBE (1997); s of Col Alfred Curry (d 1975), and Mercia, *née* Friedlander (d 2001); *b* 7 June 1938; *Educ* KCS Wimbledon, St Edmund Hall Oxford (MA, Rugby and Tennis blues), Harvard Graduate Sch of Business Admin (MBA); *m* 1962, Anne Rosemary, *née* Lewis; 3 s, 1 da; *Career* CA; Arthur Andersen 1962–64, dir Unitech plc 1971–86 (non-exec dir 1986–96); chm: ACAL plc 1986–2005, All England Lawn Tennis and Croquet Club Ground Co plc 1989– (dir 1986–), Foreign & Commonwealth Smaller Companies plc 2001–04 (dir 1996–2004); non-exec dir: Dixons Group plc 1993–2001, Terence Chapman Gp plc 1999–2003; Liveryman Worshipful Co of Chartered Accountants; FCA; *Recreations* tennis, rugby, travel; *Clubs* All England Lawn Tennis and Croquet (chm 1989–99), Int Lawn Tennis Club of GB, Queen's, Farmers', IOD; *Style*— John Curry, Esq, CBE; ✉ Stokewood Park House, Droxford, Hampshire SO32 3QY

CURRY, (Thomas) Peter Ellison; QC (1973); s of Maj F R P Curry, RA (d 1955), and Sybil, *née* Woods (d 1996); *b* 22 July 1921; *Educ* Tonbridge, Oriel Coll Oxford (MA); *m* 30 March 1950, Pamela Joyce, da of Gp Capt A J Holmes, AFC (d 1950); 2 s (Guy b 1952, Iain b 1953), 2 da (Fleur b 1956, Jilly b 1959); *Career* enlisted 1939, offr cadet 1940, OCTU Bangalore and Deolali India 1941, 1 Indian Field Regt Indian Artillery (India, North West Frontier, Burma, Assam) 1941–44, air trg course Peshawar 1944, Capt Air Force Devpt Centre Amesbury 1944, air directorate War Office GSO 3 1945–46; called to the Bar Middle Temple 1953, QC 1966 (resigned 1967), slr Freshfields 1967, returned to Bar 1970, bencher Middle Temple 1979, head of chambers; pres Aircraft and Shipbuilding Industries Arbitration Tbnl 1978–80; GB athletics rep Olympic Games 1948, Br 3000m steeplechase champion 1948, winner Oxford and Cambridge Cross Country 1947 and 1948; squash: represented Army, Oxford Univ, Sussex; asst scoutmaster Stepney Sea Scouts 1946; chm: Walston House Boys and Girls' Club 1951, Cobham Cons Assoc 1958; vice-chm Barristers Benevolent Assoc 1990–91 (treas 1964–71 and 1984–90), chm Chancery Bar Assoc 1980–85, tstee Stable Lads Welfare Tst 1986–92; *Recreations* lawn tennis, gardening, farming, the turf; *Style*— Peter Curry, Esq, QC; ✉ Hurlands, Dunsfold, Surrey GU8 4NT (tel 01483 200356); 4 Stone Buildings, Lincoln's Inn, London WC2A 3AA (tel 020 7242 5524, fax 020 7831 9152

CURRY, Stephen Robert; s of Stanley Curry (d 1964), of Clitheroe, Lancashire, and Norah, *née* Rowlinson; *b* 17 October 1942; *Educ* Clitheroe Royal GS, Manchester Coll of Commerce (journalism course); *m* Angela, *née* Blackshaw; 1 s (Michael b 27 Jan 1970); *Career* journalist; The Blackburn Times 1959–62, Lancashire Evening Post 1963, sports reporter Head Office United Newspapers London 1964–66, chief football writer Daily Express 1980–96 (football reporter 1966–80), former football columnist Sunday Telegraph, currently football columnist Daily Mail; *Style*— Stephen Curry, Esq

CURTEIS, Ian Bayley; s of late John Richard Jones, of Lydd, Kent, and late Edith Marion Pomfret Cook, *née* Bayley; *b* 1 May 1935; *Educ* Slough GS, Univ of London; *m* 1, 8 July 1964, Mrs Joan MacDonald; 2 s (Tobit b 1966, Mikol b 1968); m 2, 12 April 1985, Joanna Trollope, OBE, DL, *qv*, da of A G C Trollope, of Overton, Hants; 2 step da (Louise b 1969, Antonia b 1971); m 3, 20 Oct 2001, Lady Deirdre Freda Mary Hare, er da of 5 Earl of Listowel, GCMG, PC (d 1997) and wid of 7 Baron Grantley, MC (d 1995); 2 step s (Richard, 8 Baron Grantley , *qv*, b 1956, Francis Norton b 1960); *Career* TV playwright and dir; BBC TV script reader 1956–63, staff dir (drama) BBC and ATV 1963–67 (dir of plays by John Betjeman, John Hopkins, William Trevor and others); pres Writers' Guild of GB 1998–, chm Ctee on Censorship Writers' Guild of GB 1981–85, tstee Joanna Trollope Charitable Tst 1995–, pres Writers' Guild of Great Britain 1998–2001; author of numerous newspaper articles, speeches and lectures on the ethics and politics of British broadcasting; FRSA 1984; *Television Plays* incl: Beethoven, Sir Alexander Fleming (BBC entry at Prague Festival 1973), Mr Rolls and Mr Royce, Long Voyage out of War (trilogy), The Folly, The Haunting, Second Time Round, A Distinct Chill, The Portland Millions, Philby, Burgess and Maclean (Br entry Monte Carlo Festival 1978, BAFTA nomination Best Play of the Year, performed RNT and BBC 4 2002), Hess, The Atom Spies, Churchill and the Generals (Grand Prize for Best Programme of 1981 New York Int Film and TV Festival and BAFTA nomination Best Play of the Year), Suez 1956 (BAFTA Nomination Best Play of the Year), Miss Morison's Ghosts (British entry Monte Carlo Festival), BB and Lord D, The Mitford Girls, The Falklands Play; *Radio Plays* Eroica, Love. The Falklands Play, After the Break, More Love, Yet More Love; *Screenplays* Miss Morison's Ghosts, Andre Malraux's La condition humaine, Lost Empires (adapted from J B Priestley), Graham Greene's The Man Within (TV), The Nightmare Years (TV), The Zimmerman Telegram, Gorbachov, The Choir (BBC serial), Yalta (BBC); *Published Plays* A Personal Affair, Long Voyage out of War (1971), Churchill and the Generals (1979), Suez 1956 (1980), The Falklands Play (1987); *Recreations* dissidence; *Clubs* Garrick, Beefsteak; *Style*— Ian Curteis, Esq; ✉ 2 Warwick Square, London SW1V 2AA; Markenfield Hall, Ripon, North Yorkshire HG4 3AD; c/o Alexander Cann Representation, 2 St Thomas Square, Newport, Isle of Wight PO30 1SN (tel 01983 556866, mobile 07796 954969)

CURTICE, Prof John Kevin; s of Thomas John Curtice (d 1978), and Mildred Winifred, *née* Menear (d 2006); *b* 10 December 1953, Redruth, Cornwall; *Educ* Magdalen Coll Oxford (MA), Nuffield Coll Oxford; *m* 1978, Lisa Joan; 1 da (Ruth Anne b 9 Aug 1984); *Career* research fell Nuffield Coll Oxford 1981–83, lectr in politics Univ of Liverpool 1983–88, successively lectr, sr lectr, reader and prof of politics Univ of Strathclyde 1988–; co-dir British General Election Study 1983–98, dep dir Centre for Research into Elections and Social Trends (CREST) 1994–, research conslt Scottish Centre for Social Research 2001–; conslt British Social Attitudes series 1985–; conslt to BBC election progs 1979–, regular contrib to newspapers and broadcast media; Political Communication Prize Political Studies Assoc 2004; FRSA 1992, FRSE 2004; *Books* How Britain Votes (jtly, 1985), Understanding Political Change (jtly, 1991), Labour's Last Chance (co-ed, 1994), Labour's Last Chance (co-ed, 1994), British Social Attitudes Report (co-ed, annually 1994–), On Message (jtly, 1999), The Rise of New Labour (jtly, 2001), New Scotland, New Politics (jtly, 2001), New Scotland, New Society (co-ed, 2001), Devolution - Scottish Answers to Scottish Questions? (co-ed, 2003), Has Devolution Delivered? (jtly, 2006); *Recreations* music, gardening; *Clubs* Nat Liberal; *Style*— Prof John Curtice; ✉ Department of Government, University of Strathclyde, 16 Richmond Street, Glasgow G1 1XQ (tel 0141 548 4223, fax 0141 552 5677, e-mail j.curtice@strath.ac.uk)

CURTIS, Prof Adam Sebastian Genevieve; s of Herbert Lewis Curtis, DSM (d 1974), of London, and Nora, *née* Stevens (d 1954); *b* 3 January 1934; *Educ* Aldenham, King's Coll Cambridge (MA), Univ of Edinburgh (PhD); *m* 3 May 1958, Ann, da of William Park (d 1993), of Berwick-upon-Tweed; 2 da (Penelope Jane b 1961, Susanna Clare b 1964); *Career* lectr in zoology UCL 1962–67 (hon res asst Dept of Anatomy 1957–62); Univ of Glasgow: prof of cell biology 1967–2004, head Molecular and Cellular Biology Div 1994–95, co-dir Centre for Cell Engrg 1997–; pres Scot Sub-Aqua Club 1972–75, memb Cncl RSE 1983–86, pres Soc for Experimental Biology 1991–93, pres Tissue of Cell Engrg Soc 2001–03; fell in Biomaterials Science and Engrg (FBSE) European Soc for Biomaterials 2004; FIBiol 1968, FRSE 1969; *Books* The Cell Surface (1967), Cell-Cell Recognition (ed, 1978); *Recreations* gardening, sports diving, making mosaics; *Style*— Prof Adam Curtis, FRSE; ✉ 2 Kirklee Circus, Glasgow G12 0TW (tel 0141 339 2152, e-mail a.curtis@bio.gla.ac.uk); Centre for Cell Engineering, University of Glasgow, Glasgow G12 8QQ (tel 0141 330 5147, fax 0141 330 3730)

CURTIS, Anthony Samuel; s of Emanuel Curtis (d 1979), of London, and Eileen, *née* Freedman; *b* 12 March 1926; *Educ* Midhurst GS, Merton Coll Oxford (MA); *m* 3 Oct 1960, Sarah Curtis, *qv*; 3 s (Job b 1961, Charles b 1963, Quentin b 1965); *Career* served RAF 1945–48; lectr Br Inst of Sorbonne 1950–51, freelance journalist and critic (The Times, New Statesman, BBC) 1952–55, on staff Times Literary Supplement 1955–58 (dep ed 1959–60), Harkness fell in journalism Yale Univ and elsewhere USA 1958–59, literary ed Sunday Telegraph 1960–70; Financial Times: arts and literary ed 1970–72, literary ed 1972–89, chief book critic 1989–94; theatre articles London Magazine; numerous broadcasts on Radio 3 and 4, author of features and radio plays, regular appearances on Critics Forum; Br Cncl lectr France & India; treas Royal Lit Fund 1982–98, memb Soc of Authors (tstee pension fund); tstee London Library 2004–06; FRSA 1990; *Publications* The Pattern of Maugham (1974), Somerset Maugham (biography, 1977), The Rise and Fall of the Matinée Idol (ed, 1977), The Critical Heritage - Somerset Maugham (ed with John Whitehead, 1987), The Nonesuch Storytellers - Somerset Maughan (ed and intro, 1990), Lit Ed: on reviewers and reviewing (1998), Before Bloomsbury (2002), Virginia Woolf (2006), Golden Opportunities (adaptation, performed Warehouse Theatre Croydon, 2006); *Recreations* internet chess, backgammon; *Clubs* Garrick, Travellers, Beefsteak, Literary Soc; *Style*— Anthony Curtis, Esq; ✉ 9 Essex Villas, London W8 7BP (tel and fax 020 7937 7798, e-mail anticurtis@aol.com)

CURTIS, Prof Charles David; OBE (2001); s of Flt Lt Charles Frederick Curtis, and Kate Margaret, *née* Jackson (d 1988); *b* 11 November 1939; *Educ* High Storrs GS Sheffield, Imperial Coll London, Univ of Sheffield (BSc, PhD); *m* 24 Nov 1963, Diana Joy, da of Lionel Sidney Saxty (d 1990), of Sheffield; 2 da (Sarah b 1965, Kate b 1968); *Career* Univ of Sheffield 1965–88 (successively lectr, reader, prof); Univ of Manchester: head of Dept 1989–92, prof 1989–, research dean Faculty of Science and Engrg 1994–2000, dir Environment Centre 1996–2002, emeritus prof 2004–; head R&D strategy Radioactive Waste Mgmnt Div Nucelar Decommissioning Authy; visiting prof UCLA 1970–71, industrial fell Marathon Oil Co Denver 1973, CSPG visiting prof Univ of Calgary 1981, visiting prof Tongji Univ Shanghai 1984, res assoc Br Petroleum Res Centre 1987–88, conslt BP Research International 1988–94, conslt ENRICERCHE Milan 1994–97; various pubns in jls; memb Cncl Natural Environment Research Cncl 1990–93; pres Geological Soc of London 1992–94; memb: Scientific and Educn Ctees Royal Soc 1977–89, CNAA 1980–89, Radioactive Waste Management Advsy Ctee 1994– (chm 2000–); Murchison Medal 1987; FGS 1977 (pres 1992–94); *Recreations* mountaineering, reading, writing; *Style*— Prof Charles Curtis, OBE; ✉ Townhead Cottage, Edale Road, Hope S33 6SF (e-mail ccurtis355@aol.com); Nuclear Decommissiong Authority Radioactive Waste Management Division, Curie Avenue, Harwell, Didcot OX11 0RH (tel 01235 825415)

CURTIS, James William Ockford; QC (1993); s of Eric William Curtis, MC (d 2005), of Bedford, and Margaret Joan, *née* Blunt (d 1998), of Bedford; *b* 2 September 1946; *Educ* Bedford Sch, Worcester Coll Oxford (MA); *m* 1985, Genevra Fiona Penelope Victoria Caws, QC (d 1997), da of Richard Byron Caws, CBE (d 1997); 1 da (Polly Joanna Sarah Clare b 26 Nov 1987); *Career* called to the Bar Inner Temple 1970, pupillages with William Gage (now Hon Lord Justice Gage), and Neil Denison (formerly The Common Serjeant of London), recorder of the Crown Court 1991–; *Recreations* farming, field sports, skiing, classics; *Clubs* Reform, Flyfishers'; *Style—* James Curtis, Esq, QC; ✉ 6 King's Bench Walk, Temple, London EC4Y 7DR (tel 020 7583 0410, fax 020 7353 8791)

CURTIS, Monica Anne; da of Maj H L Seale (d 1986), and M Seale, *née* Ferrigno (d 1998); *b* 26 May 1946; *Educ* Bournemouth Sch for Girls, Univ of Manchester (BA); *m* 1968, Dr Timothy Curtis (d 1986); 2 s (Patrick b 1974, James b 1976); *Career* dep head Kesteven and Grantham Girls' Sch 1991–98, head Chelmsford Co HS for Girls 1998–; govr Felsted Sch; *Recreations* skiing, walking, reading, theatre, film, arts; *Style—* Mrs Monica Curtis; ✉ Chelmsford County High School for Girls, Broomfield Road, Chelmsford, Essex CM6 3DR (tel 01245 352592, fax 01245 345746, e-mail cchs@btconnect.com)

CURTIS, Oliver; s of Lionel Curtis, and Brenda Curtis; *Educ* London Coll of Printing (BA); *m* 15 Feb 2002, Andi Marie, *née* d'Sa; *Career* cinematographer; D&AD Gold Pencil for Poems on the Box; memb BSC 1998; *Film* dir of photography: Madagascar Skin 1993, Love and Death on Long Island 1995, Wisdom of Crocodiles 1997, Vanity Fair 1998 (BAFTA nomination), Saltwater 1999, Final Curtain 2000, Owning Mahowny 2001, Something Borrowed 2003, Uncle Adolf 2004, The Wedding Date 2005, Death at a Funeral 2006; dir of documentaries incl: Trotsky's Home Movies 1990, Pontecorvo 1991, Affairs of the Heart 1992; *Recreations* tennis, squash; *Style—* Oliver Curtis, Esq; ✉ c/o ICM, Oxford House, 76 Oxford Street, London W1D 1BS (tel 020 7636 6565, fax 01844 261740)

CURTIS, Paul Francis; s of Thomas Joseph Curtis (d 1943), of Oxford, and Kathleen Mary, *née* Philips; *b* 15 November 1940; *Educ* S Bonaventures GS, LSE (BSc (Econ), dep pres Union); *m* 24 Aug 1968, Maria Victoria, da of Adam Manduke; 1 s (Rupert Paul b 1 Sept 1977); *Career* Euro merchandising mangr Electric Storage Battery Co 1963–66, advtg exec Philips Electrical Ltd 1966–67, brands mangr Ranks Hovis McDougall Ltd 1967–69, sr brands mangr Van den Berghs 1969–70, mktg dir Mars Confectionery Slough 1970–85, exec dir and pres int mktg International Distillers & Vintners 1985–96, gp mktg dir Grand Metropolitan plc 1996–97; non-exec dir Royal Doulton plc 1996–2005; advsr Tomorrow's People Tst; memb: Mgmnt Bd Getting London Working 1999–2001, Mktg Gp City and E London Bond (BOOST); *Recreations* shooting, theatre, opera; *Style—* Paul Curtis, Esq; ✉ Walnut Tree House, Swinbrook, Burford, Oxfordshire OX18 4ED (tel 01993 824363, fax 01993 824175, e-mail paul@curtispf.fsnet.co.uk)

CURTIS, Dr Penelope; da of Adam S G Curtis, of Glasgow, and Ann, *née* Park; *b* 24 August 1961; *Educ* Westbourne Sch, CCC Oxford (BA), Courtauld Inst Univ of London (MA, PhD); *Career* Tate Gall Liverpool 1988–94, curator Henry Moore Inst 1994–; memb Advsy Ctee: UK Govt Art Collection, Imperial War Museum Art Cmmns; *Exhibitions* incl: Modern British Sculpture from the Collection (Tate Gall Liverpool) 1988, Barbara Hepworth - A Retrospective (Tate Gall Liverpool) 1994, Taking Positions: Figurative Sculpture and The Third Reich (Henry Moore Inst) 2001, Scultura Lingua Morta: Sculpture from Fascist Italy 2003, Figuring Space: Sculpture/Furniture from Mies to Moore 2007; *Publications* Sculpture 1900–1945 (1999); *Style—* Dr Penelope Curtis; ✉ Henry Moore Institute, 74 The Headrow, Leeds LS1 3AH (tel 0113 246 7467, fax 0113 246 1481)

CURTIS, Penelope Jane Hamilton (Mrs Christopher Crouch); da of Thomas Curtis, of Buckland, Surrey, and Nancy Frances Mary, *née* Pearson; *b* 20 February 1957; *Educ* St Michael's Sch Oxted, Univ of Exeter (LLB, Lloyd Parry prize, Maxwell law prize); *m* 22 Aug 1987, Christopher Charles Crouch; 2 da (Alexandra b 1991, Serena b 1994); *Career* Freshfields: articled clerk 1979–81, slr 1981–87; N M Rothschild: head Compliance Dept 1987–97, dir 1989–97; dir UBS 1997–; memb City of London Slrs Co; Freeman City of London, hon ward clerk Coleman St Ward; memb Law Soc; *Recreations* theatre, opera, walking; *Style—* Ms Penelope Curtis; ✉ Church Woods, The Street, Wonersh, Surrey GU5 0PG; UBS Investment Bank, 3 Finsbury Avenue, London EC2M 2PA (tel 020 7567 8000)

CURTIS, Sir Richard Herbert Curtis; kt (1992); *b* 24 May 1933; *Educ* Univ of Oxford (MA); *Career* called to the Bar Inner Temple 1958 (bencher 1985); recorder of the Crown Court 1974–89, QC 1977; hon recorder City of Hereford 1981–92, recorder City of Birmingham and sr circuit judge Oxford & Midland Circuit 1989–92; judge of the High Court of Justice (Queen's Bench Div) 1992–2005; presiding judge Wales & Chester Circuit 1994–97; dep chief steward of City of Hereford 1996–; a pres Mental Health Review Tbnls 1983–92; *Style—* Sir Richard Curtis

CURTIS, Sarah; da of Dr Carl Myers (d 1963), of Preston, Lancs, and Ruth, *née* Stross (d 1973); *b* 21 May 1936; *Educ* Roedean (scholar), Sorbonne, St Hugh's Coll Oxford (exhibitioner, MA, pres OU Lib Club, fndr Jt Action Ctee Against Racial Intolerance); *m* 3 Oct 1960, Anthony Curtis, *qv*; 3 s (Job b 1961, Charles b 1963, Quentin b 1965); *Career* Times Educnl Supplement 1958–59, The Times 1959–61, freelance journalist and reviewer (The Times, New Society, TES, TLS, Financial Times, Sunday Times, New Statesman & Society, BBC Radio 4 and World Service) 1961–, educn and info offr Family Planning Assoc SW London 1971–73, res project dir Wandsworth Cncl for Community Relations 1975–76, ed Adoption & Fostering (jl of British Agencies for Adoption & Fostering) 1976–87, ed RSA Jl and head of communications RSA 1989–95; Parly candidate (Lib) Enfield N Feb and Nov 1974; memb: Exec Bd UK Ctee for UNICEF 1971–84, Lord Chllr's Advsy Ctee on JPs for Inner London 1982–89; tstee Ind Adoption Serv 1988–2004; JP (Youth and Family Courts) Inner London 1978–2001; FRSA 1995; *Books* New Orbits (jt author, 1959), High Time for Radicals (jt author, 1960), Thinkstrip series (1976–79), Looking at Handicap (ed, 1982), It's Your Life series (jt author, 1983), From Asthma to Thalassaemia (ed, 1986), St Hugh's - 100 Years of Women's Education in Oxford (contrib, 1986), Juvenile Offending (1989); The Journals of Woodrow Wyatt: Vol I (ed, 1998), Vol II (ed, 1999), Vol III (ed, 2000); Children Who Break the Law or 'Everybody Does It' (1999), The Russell House Companion to Youth Justice (contrib, 2005); *Recreations* reading novels, gardening and cooking; *Style—* Mrs Sarah Curtis; ✉ 9 Essex Villas, London W8 7BP (tel and fax 020 7937 7798, e-mail santicurtis@aol.com)

CURTIS, Stephen Russell; s of Barry Russell, and Joyce Muriel, *née* Smith; *b* 27 February 1948; *Educ* Forest Sch, Univ of Exeter (BA); *m* 1972, Gillian Mary, *née* Pitkin; 3 s, 1 da; *Career* asst statistician Business Statistics Office 1970–72; DTI: joined 1972, statistician Export Statistics 1975–78, statistician 1978–83, chief statistician 1983–85; Business Statistics Office: registrar of cos 1985–90, chief exec 1988–90; chief exec DVLA 1990–95, chief exec designate Employment Tbnl Serv 1996, md Professional Servs Div Jordans Ltd 1997–; *Recreations* walking, travel, photography; *Clubs* Civil Service; *Style—* Stephen Curtis, Esq; ✉ Jordans Ltd, 21 St Thomas Street, Bristol BS1 6JS

CURTIS, Prof Tony; s of Leslie Thomas Curtis (d 1978), and Doris Eileen, *née* Williams; *b* 26 December 1946, Carmarthen; *Educ* UC Swansea, Goddard Coll VT, Univ of Glamorgan (DLitt); *m* 1970, Margaret, *née* Blundell; 1 s (Gareth Wyn b 1973), 1 da (Bronwen Beatrice 1976); *Career* poet and writer; incl in The Oxford Companion to English Literature and The New Companion to the Literatures of Wales; chair Welsh Acad of Writers 1984–89; Univ of Glamorgan: dir MPhil in writing 1993–, prof of poetry 1994–; Eric Gregory Award 1972, National Poetry Prize 1984, Dylan Thomas Award 1994, Cholmondeley Award 1997; FRSL 2000; *Books* 26 books of poetry, literary criticism and art criticism incl: The Art of Seamus Heaney (1982), How to Study Modern Poetry (1990), Welsh Painters Talking to Tony Curtis (1997), Welsh Artists Talking to Tony Curtis (2001), Heaven's Gate (poems, 2001), Dal Confine: Selected Poems of Tony Curtis (2001), Related Twilights: Notes from an Artist's Diary (by Josef Herman, ed, 2002), Scelti Poesie: Dannie Abse (ed, 2003), Considering Cassandra (poems and a story, 2003); *Recreations* golf, tennis; *Style—* Prof Tony Curtis

CURTIS-THOMAS, Claire; MP; *b* 30 April 1958; *Educ* Mynyddback Comprehensive Sch Swansea, Fareham Tech Coll (TEC), Cosham Tech Coll (HNC), UC Cardiff (BSc), Aston Univ (MBA); *Children* 3 c (Georgina b 28 Dec 1987, Carla b 14 July 1990, Lewis b 29 Nov 1997); *Career* site mechanical engr rising to mangr environmental strategy Shell Chemicals UK Ltd 1986–92, head R&D Laboratory then head Strategy and Business Planning Birmingham City Cncl 1992–95, Aston Univ (MBA) 1995–96, dean Faculty of Business and Engrg Univ of Wales Coll Newport 1996–97; MP (Lab) Crosby 1997–; memb DTI Select Ctee, chair App Party Gp for False Allegations; fndr Waterloo Partnership; involved with: SET (educn charity), Amnesty Int, Discovery North West (educnl tst), Ramblers' Assoc, Women's Engrg Soc, Soroptimist Int; CEng, FIMechE (MIMechE 1994), FInstCES 1998, FCGI 2000, FIEE 2001; *Recreations* walking, travel, music; *Style—* Ms Claire Curtis-Thomas, MP; ✉ House of Commons, London SW1A 0AA (e-mail curtisthomasc@parliament.uk); Constituency Office, The Minster, 16 Beach Lawn, Waterloo, Liverpool L22 8QA (tel 0151 928 7250, fax 0151 928 9325)

CURWEN, Andrew; *b* 15 August 1958; *Educ* Bishops Stortford Coll, Univ of Bradford (BSc); *m* Anne; 2 s (Edward, George); *Career* ptnr and head of M&A Deloitte; treas St Stephens Etton PC; FCA 1985, MSI 1995; *Recreations* fishing (salmon), wine (drinking and collecting), France, sport (rugby, skiing, cricket, tennis); *Clubs* East India, Devonshire Sportsmen and Public Schs; *Style—* Andrew Curwen, Esq; ✉ Deloitte & Touche LLP, Athene Place, 66 Shoe Lane, London EC4A 3BQ

CURWEN, Michael Jonathan; s of Dr Montague Curwen, and Thelma, *née* Freiberger; *b* 13 November 1943; *Educ* Clifton, The Queen's Coll Oxford (BA); *m* 28 June 1970, (Helena) Sandra, da of Dr Charles Norman Faith; 1 da (Nicola b 1971), 1 s (Robert b 1974); *Career* called to the Bar Inner Temple 1966, recorder of the Crown Court 1989–; *Recreations* theatre, golf, gardening; *Style—* Michael Curwen, Esq; ✉ 100 Wildwood Road, London NW11 6UD (tel 020 8209 1743)

CURZON, Prof Martin Edward John; s of Stanley Arthur Curzon, of Selsdon, Surrey, and Antoinette Carmela, *née* Davies; *b* 11 May 1940; *Educ* Univ of London (BDS, PhD), Univ of Rochester (MS); *m* 1, 1964 (m dis 1992), Jennifer Anne; 3 s (Richard Martin b 1967, Thomas Paul b 1972, Neil Simon b 1974); *m* 2, 1994, Anne; *Career* extern Govt of BC 1965–66, lectr Univ of Bristol 1968–70, sr dental offr Govt of Canada 1970–73, chm Oral Biology Eastman Dental Center 1973–83 (fell 1966–68), prof Univ of Leeds 1983–2000 (emeritus 2000–); pres: Br Paedodontic Soc 1987–88, Euro Acad of Paediatric Dentistry 1990–94; memb: ORCA, EAPD, CAPD, AAPD, IADR; life hon memb: Belgian Acad of Paediatric Dentistry, Canadian Acad of Paediatric Dentistry; DSc (hc) Univ of Athens 2003; FDS 1993; *Books* Trace Elements and Dental Disease (1983), Paediatric Operative Dentistry (4 edn, 1996), Handbook of Dental Trauma (2001); *Recreations* gardening; *Style—* Prof Martin Curzon

CUSACK, Mark Paul John; s of Capt Robert Joseph Cusack, of Dublin, and Olive Mary, *née* Byrne; *b* 28 February 1958; *Educ* St Paul's Sch Dublin, Trinity Coll Dublin (BBS); *m* 1990, Susan Jane Williams; 2 da; *Career* Arthur Andersen & Co 1979–83; dir: Hoare Govett 1983–91 (head UK Research), BZW 1992–95, UBS 1995–98, Deutsche Bank 1998–; FCA; *Recreations* squash, tennis, golf; *Clubs* Riverside, Fitzwilliam (Dublin); *Style—* Mark P Cusack, Esq

CUSACK, Niamh; da of Cyril Cusack (d 1993), and Maureen (d 1977); *b* 20 October 1959; *Educ* Scoil Lorcan Dublin, Colaiste Iosagain, Royal Acad of Music, Guildhall Sch of Music and Drama; *Career* actress; *Theatre* Gate Theatre Dublin: Hester Worsley in A Woman of No Importance, Irina in Three Sisters, Nora in A Doll's House; RSC: Desdemona in Othello, Juliet in Romeo and Juliet, Jane Hogarth in The Art of Success, Rosalind in As You Like It; West Yorkshire Playhouse: Pegeen Mike in The Playboy of the Western World, Gemma in Captain Swing; Lady Mary in The Admirable Crichton (Theatre Royal Haymarket), Gustchen in The Tutor (Old Vic), Nora Clitheroe in The Plough and the Stars (Young Vic), Irina in Three Sisters (Royal Exchange Manchester), Helena in The Faerie Queen (Aix-en-Provence), The Maids (Donmar), Nabokov's Gloves, Molière's Learned Ladies, Portia in The Merchant of Venice (Chichester Festival Theatre), Serafina Pekkala in His Dark Materials, Ghosts (Gate London); *Television* Lucky Sunil, Poirot, Till We Meet Again, Jeeves and Wooster, Heartbeat, Angel Train, Shadow of the Sun, Colour Blind, Rhinoceros, Little Bird, A&E, Loving You, Too Good to be True, State of Mind; *Films* Paris By Night, Fools of Fortune, The Playboys, The Closer You Get; *Awards* Irish Life Award, Irish Post Award; *Recreations* walking, cooking, reading, dreaming; *Style—* Ms Niamh Cusack; ✉ PFD, Drury House, 34–43 Russell Street, London WC2B 5HA (tel 020 7344 1000)

CUSACK, Sinead Mary; da of the actor Cyril James Cusack (d 1993), and his 1 w, Maureen, *née* Kiely (d 1977); *m* 23 March 1977, Jeremy Irons, *qv*; 2 s (Samuel b 16 Sept 1978, Maximilian b 17 Oct 1985); *Career* actress; *Theatre* for RSC incl: Lady Amaranth in Wild Oats, Lisa in Children of the Sun, Isabella in Measure For Measure, Celia in As You Like It, Evadne in The Maid's Tragedy, Lady Anne in Richard III, Portia in The Merchant of Venice, Daisy in The Custom of the Country, Ingrid in Peer Gynt, Kate in Taming of the Shrew, Beatrice in Much Ado About Nothing, Roxanne in Cyrano de Bergerac, Lady Macbeth in Macbeth, Cleopatra in Antony and Cleopatra; other credits incl: Desdemona in Othello (Ludlow Festival), Raina in Arms And The Man (Oxford Festival), Alice in Aristocrats (Hampstead), Masha in The Three Sisters (Gate Dublin and Royal Court), Ruth in Map of the Heart (Globe), Grace in Faith Healer (Royal Court), Mai in Our Lady of Sligo (Nat Theatre), Abby in The Mercey Seat (Almeida); *Television* for BBC incl: Playboy of the Western World, Menace - The Solarium, Shadow of a Gunman, George Sand - Notorious Woman, Affairs of the Heart, Quiller, Love's Labour Lost, Trilby, Supernatural - Ghost in Venice, The Kitchen, The Henhouse, Twelfth Night, Tales From Hollywood, Oliver's Travels (also film), Have Your Cake and Eat It (winner of Best Actress RTS Awards 1998); other credits incl: The Eyes Have It (ATV), Romance: The Black Knight (Thames), Scoop (LWT), God on the Rocks (Channel 4); *Films* Alfred the Great, Tamlyn, David Copperfield, Hoffman, Revenge, Horowitz in Dublin Castle, The Last Remake of Beau Geste, Rocket Gibraltar, Venus Peter, Waterland, Bad Behaviour, Cement Garden, The Sparrow, Flemish Board, Stealing Beauty, Dream, I Capture the Castle, Matilde; *Style—* Ms Sinead Cusack

CUSCHIERI, Prof Sir Alfred; kt (1998); s of Saviour Cuschieri (d 1990), and Angela Galeá; *b* 30 September 1938; *Educ* Malta (MD), Univ of Liverpool (ChM); *m* Marguerite, *née* Holley; *Career* Univ of Liverpool: lectr in surgery 1968–70, sr lectr 1970–74, reader 1974–76; prof of surgery and head Dept of Surgery Univ of Dundee 1976–; dir Minimal Access Therapy Trg Unit for Scotland 1993–; ed: Surgical Endoscopy, Seminars in Laparoscopic Surgery; pres: Br Soc of Surgical Oncology 1986–87, European Assoc of Endoscopic Surgery 1996–97; memb: Surgical Research Soc 1970, Br Soc of Gastroenterology 1970, BASO 1974, SAGES 1987, EAES 1991; FRSE, FRCS, FRCSEd, FRCSGlas, FMedSci, FIBiol; *Publications* author of 19 textbooks on surgery, and over 300 articles on research related to surgery and oncology; *Clubs* Athenaeum; *Style—* Prof Sir Alfred Cuschieri; ✉ Department of Surgery, Ninewells Hospital and Medical School,

University of Dundee, Dundee DD1 9SY (tel 01382 660111, fax 01382 641795, e-mail a.cuschieri@dundee.ac.uk)

CUSHING, Philip Edward; *Educ* Highgate Sch, Christ's Coll Cambridge; *Career* formerly with Norcros plc then LEGO Group, chief exec international ops Norton Opax until 1990; Inchcape plc: joined as chief exec Inchcape Berhad 1990, main bd dir 1992–, dir i/c testing servs, shipping servs and buying servs 1992–95, also i/c mktg and distribution 1994–95, md 1995–99, gp chief exec 1996–99; gp chief exec Vitec Gp plc 2000–01; chm: Pelican Restaurants Ltd 2001–02, Paragon Print and Packaging Ltd 2002–, DCI Biologicals Inc 2002–, Tecmail Ltd 2003, Fosbel International Holdings Ltd 2003–; non-exec dir Ikon Office Solutions Inc; MCIM; *Style*— Philip Cushing, Esq; ✉ Warren End, Warren Cutting, Coombe Hill, Kingston upon Thames KT2 7HS

CUSINE, Sheriff Douglas James; s of James Fechney Cusine (d 1987), and Catherine, *née* McLean (d 1975); *b* 2 September 1946; *Educ* Hutchesons' Boys' GS Glasgow, Univ of Glasgow (LLB); *m* 21 July 1973, Marilyn Calvert, da of George Ramsay (d 1988), of Johnstone, Renfrewshire; 1 da (Jane b 19 Sept 1981), 1 s (Graeme b 2 Jan 1984); *Career* admitted slr 1971; lectr in private law Univ of Glasgow 1974–76; Dept of Conveyancing Univ of Aberdeen: lectr 1976–82, sr lectr 1982–90, head of dept 1987–98, prof 1990–2000; memb and examiner for Law Soc of Scotland 1988–96; memb: Cncl Law Soc 1988–2000, Lord President's Advsy Cncl for Messengers at Arms and Sheriff Offrs 1989–2000; chm Bd of Examiners Soc of Messengers at Arms and Sheriff Offrs 1990–92; Sheriff of Grampian, Highland and Islands at Aberdeen; *Books* The Impact of Marine Pollution (jt ed, 1980), Scottish Cases and Materials in Commercial Law (jt ed, 1987), A Scots Conveyancing Miscellany (ed, 1988), New Reproductive Techniques: A Legal Perspective (1988), Law and Practice of Diligence (jtly, 1990), Standard Securities (1991, 2 edn (jtly) 2002), Missives (jtly, 1993, 2 edn 1999), Requirements of Writing (jtly, 1995), McDonald's Conveyancing Manual (jt ed, 6 edn 1997), Servitudes and Rights of Way (jtly 1998); *Recreations* swimming, walking, bird watching; *Style*— Sheriff Douglas Cusine; ✉ Sheriff's Chambers, Sheriff Court House, Castle Street, Aberdeen AB10 1WP (tel 01224 657200)

CUSITER, Christopher Peter (Chris); s of Stan Cusiter, of Aberdeen, and Ruth, *née* Gibson; *b* 13 June 1982, Aberdeen; *Educ* Robert Gordon's Coll Aberdeen, Univ of Edinburgh (LLB); *Career* rugby union player (scrum half); clubs: Boroughmuir, Watsonians, Border Reivers (provincial team, Player of the Year 2003–04); Scotland: 31 caps, debut v Wales 2004; memb British and Irish Lions touring squad NZ 2005; memb Scottish Inst of Sport; nominated Spirit of Scotland Awards 2004; *Recreations* guitar; *Style*— Mr Chris Cusiter; ✉ c/o Border Reivers, Netherdale, Nether Road, Galashiels TD1 3HE

CUSK, Rachel Emma; da of Peter Cusk, of Bury St Edmunds, and Carolyn, *née* Woods; *b* 8 February 1967; *Educ* St Mary's Convent Cambridge, New Coll Oxford (BA); *Career* novelist; patron UN Year for Tolerance 1995, memb Bd London Arts Bd 1997–; *Books* Saving Agnes (1993, Whitbread First Novel Award 1993), The Temporary (1995), The Country Life (1997, Somerset Maugham Award 1998), A Life's Work: On Becoming a Mother (2001), The Lucky Ones (2003, shortlisted Whitbread Novel Award), In the Fold (2005); various short stories; *Recreations* piano, walking; *Style*— Ms Rachel Cusk

CUSSINS, Peter Ian; s of Philip Cussins (d 1976), of Newcastle upon Tyne, and Doreen Cussins; *b* 18 March 1949; *Educ* Bootham Sch York, Univ of London (BSc); *m* 18 Sept 1973, Vandra Jean (d 1998), da of Maynard Stubley, of Alnmouth, Northumberland; 3 da (Abigail b 1976, Alexandra b 1978, Lydia b 1983), 1 s (Jabin b 1980); m 2, 24 Oct 2000, Susan Deirdre, da of Kenneth Saxby (d 2001), and Gill Saxby, of Corbridge, Northumberland; 2 step da (Amy b 1979, Sophie b 1981); *Career* chm: Cussins Homes Ltd 1973–99, Cussins Investment Properties Ltd 1981–99, Cussins Commercial Developments Ltd 1981–99, Cussins Property Gp plc 1981–99, NBP Whitelam Homes Ltd 2000–, Cussins Ltd; dir: Hotspur Investments Ltd 2000–, Regent Homes Ltd 2001–; chm: Tyneside Foyer Appeal, Royal Victoria Infirmary Breast Cancer Appeal; *Recreations* golf, shooting, fishing; *Style*— Peter I Cussins, Esq; ✉ West Bitchfield Tower, Belsay, Newcastle upon Tyne NE20 0JP

CUSTIS, Patrick James; CBE (1981); er s of Alfred William Custis (d 1945), of Dublin, and Amy Custis; *b* 19 March 1921; *Educ* The HS Dublin; *m* 1954, Rita, yr da of Percy William Rayner (d 1968), of Bognor Regis; 1 s; *Career* Josolyne Miles Co CAs 1946–51, RTZ 1951–55, Glynwed International 1956–67, fin dir Guest Keen and Nettlefolds (GKN) 1974–81 (joined 1967), ret; dir: New Court Property Fund Managers Ltd 1978–91, Lloyds Bank Midlands and N Wales Regnl Bd 1979–91, Prisons Bd (Home Office) 1980–85, Associated Heat Services plc 1981–90, Wolseley plc 1982–90, Leigh Interests plc 1982–96 (chm 1994–96), Birmingham Technology Ltd 1983–93, MCD Group plc (chm) 1983–86, Wyko Group plc 1985–94, Benford Concrete Machinery plc 1985–86; chm Midlands Indust Gp of Fin Dirs 1977–80, co-opted memb Cncl ICAEW 1979–85, memb Monopolies and Mergers Cmmn 1981–82; pres Wolverhampton Soc of CAs 1985–86; Liveryman Worshipful Co of CAs in England and Wales; FCA, FCMA, FCIS, JDipMA, FRSA; *Recreations* gardening, walking, reading; *Style*— Patrick Custis, Esq, CBE; ✉ 18 Richmond Village, Stroud Road, Painswick, Gloucestershire GL6 6UH

CUSWORTH, (George Robert) Neville; s of George Ernest Cusworth (d 1966), of Bad Homburg, Germany, and Violet Helene, *née* Cross (d 1969); *b* 14 October 1938; *Educ* St Paul's, Keble Coll Oxford (MA), Courtauld Inst (Cert in Euro Art), Stanford Univ; *m* 6 Sept 1963, (Vivien) Susan, da of Philip Glynn Grylls, of Worthing, W Sussex; 1 s (Nicholas b 20 March 1964), 1 da (Juliet b 30 Jan 1966); *Career* Butterworth Group: chief exec 1987–99, chm 1990–99; chm Bowker-Saur Ltd 1989–92, dir Reed Publishing Ltd 1989–93, chm Butterworth-Heinemann Ltd 1990–93, chief exec Professional Div Reed International Books Ltd 1990–95, dir and chm Legal Div Reed Elsevier plc 1995–99, dir Elsevier NV 1995–99, chm Jordan Publishing Ltd 2003– (non-exec dir 2000–), non-exec dir The West of England Tst Ltd 2003–; dir Int Electronic Publishing Research Centre 1985–88, memb Cncl Publishers' Assoc 1988–91, chm Bd Book House Trg Centre 1989–93; chm Caradon Dist CPRE 2000–02, govr Univ of Plymouth 2000–06; Freeman City of London 1982, Master Worshipful Co of Stationers and Newspaper Makers 2006–07; *Publications* author of articles on Cornish local history in Journal of the Royal Inst of Cornwall 2003 and 2005; *Recreations* local history, art history, walking; *Clubs* Garrick; *Style*— Neville Cusworth, Esq; ✉ Garrick Club, Garrick Street, London WC2E 9AY

CUTHBERT, Prof Alan William; s of Thomas William Cuthbert (d 1989), and Florence Mary, *née* Griffin (d 1970); *b* 7 May 1932; *Educ* Deacon's GS Peterborough, Leicester Coll of Technol (BPharm), Univ of St Andrews (BSc), Univ of London (PhD), Univ of Cambridge (MA, ScD); *m* 22 April 1957, Harriet Jane (Hetty), da of Charles McLagan Webster (d 1969); 2 s (Adrian b 1960, Bruce b 1962); *Career* Instr Lt RN 1956–59; Univ of Cambridge: reader in pharmacology 1973–79, prof of pharmacology and head Pharmacology Dept 1979–99, master Fitzwilliam Coll 1991–99, dep vice-chllr 1995–99; author of over 300 scientific papers; Hon DSc: De Montfort Univ 1993, Aston Univ 1995; Hon LLD Univ of Dundee 1995; elected Acadèmia Europaea 1996, memb Academie Royal de Medicine de Belgique 1996; FRS 1982, FMedSci 1990; *Recreations* growing orchids, travelling, tennis, working; *Clubs* Royal Society Club, Hawks' (Cambridge); *Style*— Prof Alan Cuthbert, FRS; ✉ 7 Longstanton Road, Oakington, Cambridge CB4 5BB (tel 01223 233676); Department of Medicine, University of Cambridge, Addenbrooke's Hospital, Hill's Road, Cambridge CB2 2QQ (tel 01223 336853, e-mail awc1000@cam.ac.uk)

CUTHBERT, Michael William; s of Thomas Cuthbert (d 1977), of Coventry, Warks, and Thelma Josephine, *née* O'Hehir; *b* 6 July 1956; *Educ* Archbishop Ullathorne RC Comp Sch, UCL (LLB); *m* 29 July 1989 (m dis 2001), Stephanie Edith, da of David Henry Tate (d 1994), of Leigh, Surrey; 1 da (Caroline Isabella Louise b 13 Aug 1991); *Career* slr; Slaughter and May: articled clerk 1978–80, asst slr 1980–82; Clifford-Turner: asst slr 1982–86, ptnr 1986–87; ptnr Clifford Chance London 1987–89 and 1993–99 (ptnr New York 1989–93), ptnr Clifford Chance LLP 2000–2003, sr ptnr Clifford Chance Moscow 2002–, regnl managing ptnr Central and Eastern Europe and Russian Fedn Clifford Chance 2003–; memb: Law Soc 1980, City of London Slrs' Co; Slr of the Supreme Court of: the Judicature of England and Wales 1980, Hong Kong 1986; *Recreations* opera, food and wine, the cinema; *Clubs* Raffles, Home House; *Style*— Michael Cuthbert, Esq; ✉ Clifford Chance CIS Ltd, 24/27 Ul Sadovaya-Samotechnaya, 127051 Moscow, Russian Federation (tel 00 7 501 258 5050, fax 00 7 501 258 5051, e-mail michael.cuthbert@cliffordchance.com)

CUTHBERT, Stephen Colin (Steve); CBE (2005); s of Colin Samuel Cuthbert (d 1975), formerly of Sanderstead, Surrey, and Helen Mary Cuthbert, *née* Scott (d 1986); *b* 27 October 1942; *Educ* Trinity Sch of John Whitgift, Univ of Bristol (BSc); *m* 1, 22 Feb 1969 (m dis 1986), Jane Elizabeth, da of late David Bluett, of Sydney, Aust; 1 da (Nicola b 1971), 2 s (Simon b 1974, Ian b 1974); m 2, 27 Oct 1987, Susan Melanie, da of late Kenneth Gray, of Brighton; 2 step da (Joanna b 1971, Nicola b 1974), 1 step s (Christopher b 1982); *Career* md Brent International plc 1980–93 (dir 1976–93), DG The Chartered Inst of Mktg 1994–99, chief exec Port of London Authy 1999–2004; chm CBI Southern Region 1992–93 (vice-chm 1990), chm UK Major Ports Gp 2002–; dir London C of C and Industry 2000–02; *Recreations* cruising sailing, family interests; *Style*— Steve Cuthbert, Esq, CBE

CUTHBERTSON, Ian; s of James Cuthbertson, of Glasgow, and Catherine, *née* Jardine; *b* 8 May 1951, Glasgow; *Educ* Jordanhill Coll Sch, Univ of Glasgow (LLB); *m* 1974, Sally, *née* Whittick; 1 s (Gavin b 1978), 2 da (Erin b 1980, Eilidh b 1982); *Career* admitted slr 1974; ptnr Boyds 1978, jt fndr Dorman Jeffrey 1979, ptnr (specialising in corporate recovery) Dundas & Wilson (merger with Dorman Jeffrey) 1997–; memb Law Soc of Scotland, founding memb Int Insolvency Inst; fell: Insolvency Practitioners Assoc, Assoc of Business Recovery Professionals, Inst of Contemporary Scotland; FInstD; *Recreations* watching soccer, rugby and sport generally, reading, music; *Style*— Ian Cuthbertson, Esq; ✉ 121 Mugdock Road, Milngavie, East Dunbartonshire G62 8NW (tel 0141 563 8772, e-mail ijcuthbertson@aol.com); Dundas & Wilson, 191 West George Street, Glasgow G2 6LD (tel 0141 222 2200, fax 0141 222 2201, e-mail ian.cuthbertson@dundas-wilson.com)

CUTHBERTSON, James Gordon (Jim); *b* 1942; *Educ* BArch; *m*; 2 da (Helen b 1970, Jacqueline b 1973); *Career* architect, arbiter and adjudicator; Keppie Henderson and Partners Glasgow 1966–78, liaison architect Bldg Div CSA, Cuthbertson Architects 1978–; mangr Ian Darby Partnerships Glasgow 2000–; memb Assoc of Planning Supervisors; memb Cncl: Glasgow Inst of Architects 1981–84 and 1985–88 (sr vice-pres 1985 and 1987), RIAS 1985–88 and 1995– (memb Practice Ctee and chm Insurance Ctee 1985–99), RIBA 1995– (memb Practice Bd 1995–97, chm Disciplinary Ctee 1995–2001); MCIArb 1984; *Recreations* sailing, photography, birdwatching, computers; *Style*— Jim Cuthbertson, Esq; ✉ 206 Nithsdale Road, Glasgow G41 5EU (tel and fax 0141 423 6856, e-mail cuthj@aol.com)

CUTHBERTSON, Michael James; s of J R Cuthbertson, MC (d 1997), and A V Cuthbertson (d 1997); *b* 1 May 1948; *Educ* Merchant Taylors' (scholar), Queens' Coll Cambridge (scholar, MA, Cert Ed); *m* 16 July 1994, Elizabeth Dawn, da of Canon G M Guinness; *Career* head of history Bradfield Coll 1974–78 (asst master 1971–74), head of history Radley Coll 1978–88 (dir sixth form studies 1984–90), headmaster Monkton Combe Sch 1990–2005; inspr Ind Schools Inspectorate 2001–05; memb: HMC 1990–2005, SHA 1990, Admiralty Interview Bd 1991–2004; reviser for History A-Level Oxford and Cambridge Bd 1992–93; govr Castle Court Sch 1992– (chm of govrs 2006–); tstee The Ind Schs Christian Alliance (TISCA) 2007–; *Recreations* walking, watching sport, reading, travel, numismatics, photography, model railways; *Clubs* Thames Hare and Hounds; *Style*— Michael Cuthbertson, Esq

CUTHBERTSON, District Judge; Peter; s of late Peter Brentley Cuthbertson, and Edna, *née* Stockdale; *b* 3 March 1949; *Educ* Robert Richardson's GS Ryhope, Pembroke Coll Oxford (MA, chm Blackstone Soc); *m* 26 May 1971, Carole Margaret, da of Sydney White and Margaret Alice Humphrey White; 1 da (Caroline Helen b 7 Feb 1976), 1 s (Timothy Peter b 18 Aug 1979); *Career* admitted slr 1973; Latimer, Hinks, Marsham & Little (now Latimer Hinks): articled to late Eric Nelson Marsham 1971–73, ptnr 1975–92; district judge 1992–; memb Law Soc; *Recreations* golf, sailing, theatre, tennis, walking; *Clubs* Oxford Union Society; *Style*— District Judge Cuthbertson; ✉ Teesside Combined Court Centre, Russell Street, Middlesbrough TS1 2AE

CUTLER, His Hon Judge Keith Charles; s of Henry Walter Cutler, of Woburn Sands, Bucks, and Evelyn Constance, *née* Butcher; *b* 14 August 1950; *Educ* Rickmansworth GS, Cedars Sch, Univ of Bristol (LLB); *m* 30 Aug 1975, Judith Mary, da of Ronald Philip Haddy (d 1974); 1 s (James b 1982), 1 da (Anna b 1985); *Career* called to the Bar Lincoln's Inn 1972 (bencher 2005); recorder 1993–96 (asst recorder 1989–93), circuit judge (Western Circuit) 1996–, resident judge Salisbury 2003–, liaison judge to Wilts magistrates 2006–, hon recorder of Salisbury 2007–; memb: Cncl of HM Circuit Judges 2001– (asst sec 2003, hon sec 2005–), Parole Bd 2001–04, Judges' Cncl 2005–; vice-pres Wiltshire Magistrates Assoc 2001–; chm Mediation (Salisbury & District) 2001–, dep chllr Dio of Portsmouth 2003–; *Style*— His Hon Judge Cutler

CUTT, Mike; s of Ronald Cutt (d 1998), and Margaret, *née* Langley; *b* 2 July 1958, Redhill; *Educ* Univ of Exeter (BA), Chartered Inst of Bankers, Thames Valley Univ (Dip); *m* 3 March 1995, Julie, *née* Adams; 2 s (Toby b 19 Aug 1995, Frasier b 16 March 1998); *Career* Nationwide Building Soc: head of gp mgmnt devpt 1979–91, head of gp profitability 1991–92, head of retail planning 1992–94, head of retail HR 1994–97; dir of resourcing and reward Kingfisher plc 1997–2000, HR dir B&Q plc 2000–05, gp HR dir Boots Gp plc 2005–; non-exec dir Land Registry 2005–; govr New Coll Swindon 1996–99; FCIB 1981, FCIPD 1989; *Recreations* following the England and British Lions rugby teams; *Style*— Mike Cutt, Esq; ✉ Boots the Chemist Ltd, 1 Thane Road, Nottingham NG90 1BS (tel 0115 959 5902, fax 0115 847 2802, e-mail mike.cutt@boots.co.uk)

CUTTS, John William; s of William George Cutts (d 1951), and Ingeborg Ernestine, *née* Walter (d 2003); *b* 27 September 1950; *Educ* Dean Close Sch Cheltenham, Univ of Sussex (BSc), INSEAD Fontainebleau (MBA); *m* 1, 18 Sept 1976 (m dis); 4 da (Samantha Mady Nicola b 23 Feb 1985, Dominique Lara Elisabeth b 24 July 1986, Tatiana Rebecca Sara b 5 Feb 1988, Natasha Tara Josephine b 21 Jan 1991); m 2, 15 Sept 2001, Monika Christine Lipken; *Career* apprentice Rolls Royce Ltd 1968–72, technical export mangr Ansafone Ltd 1972–75, gen mangr H & B Real Gewerbebau GmbH 1976–79, gen mangr Eupic Services BV (property investment) 1979–81, md mergers and acquisitions Amsterdam Rotterdam Bank NV 1981–88, dir Euro mergers and acquisitions Corporate Fin Dept Samuel Montagu & Co Ltd 1988–92, md corporate fin WestLB Panmure Ltd (formerly West Merchant Bank Ltd 1992–2000), chief exec Pall Mall Capital Ltd 2000–; non-exec chm: BPL Holdings Ltd, DCM Holdings (Jersey) Ltd; *Recreations* opera, sailing; *Clubs* Royal Thames Yacht, Hurlingham; *Style*— John W Cutts, Esq; ✉ Pall Mall Capital Ltd, 18A St James's Place, London SW1A 1NH (tel 020 7518 7301, e-mail john.cutts@pallmallcapital.com)

CYMERMAN, Dr Anthony; s of Alfred Cymerman, of Highgate, London, and Annette, *née* Loufer; *b* 4 December 1944; *Educ* La Sainte Union Convent, Hargrave Park Sch, Dame Alice Owen's Sch, Univ of Leeds (BChD); *m* 28 March 1976, Cherry, da of Maj R Keal,

MBE; 1 s (James Alexander b 9 June 1977), 1 da (Kate Elizabeth b 28 Dec 1981); *Career* qualified from Leeds Dental Sch 1970, assoc London 1970–72, started own private practice in Harley St 1971 (second practice in NW London 1974); conslt BUPA and Private Patients Plan 1982; former memb: Camden and Islington FPC (now Area Health Authy), Camden and Islington Local Dental Ctee, Camden and Islington Dental Serv Ctee, Dental Advsy Ctee UCH, Fedn London Area LDC's; hon tutor London Hosp Dental Sch 1986; memb: BDA 1970, RSM 1987; *Recreations* cricket, clay pigeon shooting; *Clubs* MCC; *Style*— Dr Anthony Cymerman; ✉ 2 Bisham Gardens, Highgate, London N6 6DD (tel 020 8341 9922, e-mail anthony@cymerman.co.uk)

CYPRUS AND THE GULF, Bishop of 2007–; Rt Rev Michael Augustine Owen Lewis; s of John Desmond Lewis, of Swaythling, Hants, and Jean Beryl, *née* Pope; *b* 8 June 1953; *Educ* King Edward VI Sch Southampton, Merton Coll Oxford (BA Oriental Studies, BA Theology, MA); *m* 1979, Julia Donneky, *née* Lennox; 2 s (Paul b 18 June 1969, George Isaac Andrew b 17 May 1983), 1 da (Eleanor Hannah Mary b 8 March 1982); *Career* ordained: deacon 1978, priest 1979; curate Christ the King (Salfords, Southwark) 1978–80, chaplain Thames Poly 1980–84, vicar St Mary the Virgin (Welling, Southwark) 1984–91, team rector Worcester SE 1991–99, rural dean Worcester East 1993–99, bishop of Middleton 1999–2007; chm House of Clergy (Worcester Diocesan Synod) 1997–99, chm Diocesan Advsy Ctee Worcester 1998–99, hon canon Worcester Cathedral 1998–99, chm Manchester Diocesan Bd of Educn 2000–; governing tstee St Michael's Coll Llandaff 2006–; warden of Readers and Lay Assts Diocese of Manchester 2001–; *Recreations* enjoying architecture, food and drink, Middle Eastern and Caucasian travel; *Style*— The Rt Rev the Bishop of Cyprus and the Gulf; ✉ Bishop of Cyprus and the Gulf, PO Box 22075, 1517 Nicosia, CYPRUS (tel +357 22 671220, fax +357 22 674553, e-mail bishop@spidernet.com.cy)

C

D

D'ALBIAC, James Charles Robert; s of Air Marshal Sir John D'Albiac, KCVO, KBE, CB, DSO (d 1963), and Lady Sibyl Mary, *née* Owen; *b* 14 October 1935; *Educ* Winchester, Magdalen Coll Oxford (BA); *m* 2 May 1964, Carole Ann, da of Robert Percy Garner (d 1988); 1 da (Jane Sibyl b 22 Sept 1966); *Career* Nat Serv 2 Lt Lincolnshires serv Malaya 1954–56; stockbroker, ptnr Rowe & Pitman stockbrokers London 1968–86; dir: Mercury Asset Management 1986–91, Jupiter Asset Management Ltd 1991–; MSI, AIIMR; *Recreations* golf, chess; *Clubs* Berkshire Golf, Huntercombe Golf, Oxford and Cambridge; *Style—* James D'Albiac, Esq; ✉ 65 Pont Street, London SW1X 0BD

d'ANCONA, John Edward William; CB (1994); s of Adolph d'Ancona (d 1970), of Malta, and Margaret Simpson Gilbert, *née* Arnott (d 1977); *b* 28 May 1935; *Educ* St Edward's Coll Malta, St Cuthbert's GS Newcastle, King's Coll Durham (BA, DipEd); *m* 27 Dec 1958, (Mary) Helen, da of Sqdn Ldr Ralph Taylor Hunter (d 1957), of Newcastle upon Tyne; 3 s (Matthew R, *qv*, b 1968, Patrick D b 1972, Michael P b 1974); *Career* teacher 1959–61; Civil Serv: asst princ Miny of Educn 1961–64, PPS to Min of State for Educn 1964–65; princ: Miny of Educn 1965–67, Miny of Technol 1967–70, DTI 1970–74; asst sec Dept of Energy 1974–81, under sec and dir gen Offshore Suppliers Office Dept of Energy 1981–94 (conslt 1994–); dir Spearhead Exhibitions Ltd 1996–99, chm and ceo Maris Int 2000–04; pres Soc for Underwater Technol 1997–99; chm UK Maritime Forum 2000–; *Recreations* cricket, philately, winebibbing; *Style—* John d'Ancona, Esq, CB

d'ANCONA, Matthew Robert Ralph; s of John d'Ancona, CB, *qv*, and Helen, *née* Hunter; *b* 27 January 1968, London; *Educ* St Dunstan's Coll, Magdalen Coll Oxford (BA, Demy, HWC Davis History Prize); *m* 13 March 2002, Sarah Schaefer; 2 s (Zac b 2 April 2001, Teddy b 7 June 2003); *Career* asst ed The Times 1994–95 (joined 1991), dep ed The Sunday Telegraph 1998–2006 (dep ed Comment 1996–98), contributing ed GQ 2006–, ed The Spectator 2006–; memb: Bd of Dirs Centre for Policy Studies 1998–2006, Advsy Cncl Demos 1998–2006, Br Exec Int Press Inst 1998–2006, Policy Advsy Bd Social Market Fndn 2002–06, Millennium Cmmn 2001–06, Hansard Soc Cmmn on Parliament in the Public Eye 2004–05; Charles Douglas-Home Meml Tst Prize 1995, Political Journalist of the Year Br Press Awards 2004, Political Journalist of the Year Political Studies Assoc 2006; prize fell All Souls Coll Oxford 1989–96; FRSA 2004; *Books* The Jesus Papyrus (co-author, 1996), The Quest for the True Cross (co-author, 2000), Going East (novel, 2003), Tabatha's Code (2006); *Recreations* cinema; *Clubs* Garrick; *Style—* Matthew d'Ancona, Esq; ✉ The Spectator, 22 Old Queen Street, London SW1H 9HP (e-mail editor@spectator.co.uk)

D'ARCY, Gordon; s of John D'Arcy, of Wexford, and Peggy, *née* Versey; *b* 10 February 1980, Wexford; *Educ* Clongowes Wood Coll, Dublin Inst of Technol; *Career* rugby union player (back); clubs: Lansdowne, Leinster (provincial team) 1998– (over 80 appearances); Ireland: 31 caps, debut v Romania 1999, memb squad World Cup 1999, winners Triple Crown 2006; memb British and Irish Lions touring squad NZ 2005; *Style—* Mr Gordon D'Arcy

D'ARCY, Robert John Bruce; s of Cecil Vivian Robert D'Arcy (d 1995), of Holbrook, Suffolk, and Margery Mary, *née* Bailey (d 1987); *b* 12 August 1942; *Educ* Marlborough, Univ of Munich, Coll of Estate Management; *m* 22 Nov 1969, Janet Maxwell, da of Maxwell Heron Matheson (d 1978), of Woodbridge, Suffolk; 2 s (Justin b 6 Sept 1971, Toby b 26 Jan 1977), 2 da (Annabel (twin) b 6 Sept 1971, Charlotte b 12 Jan 1973); *Career* chartered surveyor; Chestertons 1966–68, Donaldsons 1968–69, ptnr James Crichton and Co 1969–; FRICS; *Recreations* sailing, shooting, golf; *Clubs* Royal Thames Yacht; *Style—* Robert D'Arcy, Esq; ✉ The Old Rectory, Bredfield, Woodbridge, Suffolk IP13 6AX (tel 01394 385223)

d'ASCOLI, Bernard; s of Georges d'Ascoli, of Aubagne, France, and Marcelle, *née* Thermes; *b* 18 November 1958; *Educ* Marseille Conservatoire; *Partner*, Eleanor Harris; 1 s (Stéphane b 1996); *Career* pianist; debuts: Queen Elizabeth Hall, Barbican and Royal Festival Hall 1982, Concertgebouw Amsterdam 1984, Houston TX 1985, The Proms Royal Albert Hall 1986, Tokyo 1988, Paris 1989; performed as soloist with: RPO, LPO, Philharmonia, BBC Symphony Orch, CBSO, Chamber Orch of Euro, English Chamber Orch, Montreal Symphony, Boston Symphony, Dresden Philharmonic; played under conductors incl: Paavo Berglund, Andrew Davis, Sergiu Comissiona, Kurt Sanderling, Sir Yehudi Menuhin, Andrew Litton, Yevgeny Svetlanov, Michel Plasson, Sir John Pritchard, Gunter Herbig, Ivan Fischer, Andrew Parrott; various int tours; *Awards* Best Young Talent in France 1976, First Prize Int Maria Canals Competition Barcelona 1978, Chopin Prize Santander 1980, Third Prize Leeds Int Piano Competition 1981; prize winner: Marguerite Long Competition Paris, Bach Competition Leipzig, Chopin Competition Warsaw; *Recordings* Liszt Sonata, La Legierezza; Franck: Prelude Chorale and Fugue (1982); Schumann: Carnaval, Papillons, Fantasie Stücke op 111 (1989), Piano Quintet with Schidlof Quartet (2001); Chopin: 4 Ballades, Nocturne in C Sharp Minor, Berceuse, Tarantelle, Andante Spianato and Grande Polonaise (1990), Chopin: Impromptus, Scherzi (2005), Complete Nocturnes (2005); *Recreations* philosophy, psychology, sport; *Style—* Bernard d'Ascoli, Esq; ✉ c/o CLB Management, 28 Earlsmead Road, London NW10 5QB (tel 020 8964 4513, fax 020 8964 4514, e-mail clebris@clbmanagement.co.uk)

D'CRUZ, Dr David Pascal; s of Joseph C D'Cruz, of London, and Albertina, *née* De Sousa; *b* 22 June 1959; *Educ* Mount St Mary's Coll, St Mary's Hosp Med Sch London (MB BS, MD); *m* 9 March 1986, Dr Maria B Y Saldanha; 2 da (Rebecca b 1 May 1987, Olivia b 8 March 1990); *Career* pre-registration house offr St Mary's Hosp London 1983–84, SHO UCHL 1984–85, registrar in med Royal London Hosp 1986–88, registrar in rheumatology St Thomas' Hosp London 1988–93, sr registrar then conslt rheumatologist Bart's and Royal London Hosp 1993–2000, conslt rheumatologist Lupus Unit St Thomas' Hosp 2000–; managing ed Lupus; ed-in-chief Jl of Autoimmune Diseases; tstee Hughes Syndrome Fndn; FRCP 1998 (MRCP 1986); *Publications* author of 100 peer reviewed pubns on systemic lupus erythematosus and systemic vasculitis, and 12 book chapters on autoimmune connective tissue diseases; *Recreations* trout fishing; *Style—* Dr David D'Cruz; ✉ The Louise Coote Lupus Unit, St Thomas' Hospital, London SE1 7EH (tel 020 7188 7188, fax 020 7960 5698)

D'EYNCOURT, *see:* Tennyson-d'Eyncourt

d'INVERNO, Isobel Jane; da of Raymond Shaw, of Wembury, Devon, and Margaret, *née* Newall; *b* 1 September 1957, Withington, Manchester; *Educ* Cheadle Hulme Sch, Univ of St Andrews (MA); *m* 1983, Joseph d'Inverno; 3 s (Monty b 18 April 1988, Cospatric b 17 Sept 1990, Louis b 11 Sept 1995), 1 da (Lucia b 17 April 1994); *Career* CA 1983; Ernst & Whinney 1980–84, corporate tax supervisor and mangr Ernst & Young (formerly Arthur Young) 1984–90, head of corporate tax Brodies 1990–97, dir corporate tax MacRoberts 1997– (head of charities gp 2005–); memb: Law Soc of Scotland (convenor Tax Law Ctee), Stamp Duty Land Tax Practitioners Gp, Stamp Duty Land Tax Working Together Steering Gp (with HMRC), ICAEW; CIOT 1984; *Recreations* reading novels, theatre; *Style—* Mrs Isobel d'Inverno; ✉ MacRoberts, Excel House, 30 Semple Street, Edinburgh EH3 8BL (tel 0131 229 5046, fax 0131 229 0846, e-mail isobel.dinverno@macroberts.com)

D'JANOEFF, Alexander Constantine Basil; s of Constantine V D'Janoeff (d 1986), of Windsor, and Margarita, *née* Rotinoff; *b* 27 March 1952; *Educ* Eton, Strasbourg Univ France; *m* 22 June 1991, Hon Anne, da of 9 Baron Rodney (d 1992); *Career* qualified CA 1977; Coopers & Lybrand: joined 1972, Paris Office 1977–80, London Office 1980–85, seconded Schroder Ventures (Mgmnt Buy Out Fund) 1985, ptnr corp fin 1986–96, dir i/c Euro Corp Fin 1989–96; md Credit Suisse First Boston Private Equity 1996–; FCA, FRSA; *Recreations* golf, mountain walking in Switzerland; *Clubs* Brooks's, Annabel's, Guards Polo; *Style—* Alexander D'Janoeff, Esq; ✉ Credit Suisse First Boston, One Cabot Square, London E14 4QJ (tel 020 7888 3232, fax 020 7888 3477)

D'SOUZA, Baroness (Life Peer UK 2004), of Wychwood in the County of Oxfordshire; Dr Frances Gertrude Claire D'Souza; CMG (1998); da of Robert Anthony Gilbert Russell (d 1979), of Ardingly Farm, W Sussex, and Pauline, *née* Parmet (d 1988); *b* 18 April 1944; *Educ* St Mary's Princethorpe, UCL (BSc), Univ of Oxford (DPhil); *m* 1, 1959 (m dis 1973, remarried 2003), Stanislaus Joseph D'Souza; 2 da (Hon Christa Claire b 1960, Hon Heloise b 1962); m 2, 1985 (m dis 1994), Martin John Griffiths; *Career* Ford Fndn research fell Wellcome Inst of Comparative Physiology 1973–77, pt/t lectr Dept of Anthropology LSE 1974–80, sr lectr in physical anthropology Dept of Humanities Oxford Poly (now Brookes Univ) 1977–79, res dir Relief and Development Inst 1983–86 (fndr dir 1979–83), dir Article 19 Int Centre against Censorship 1989–98; dir The Redress Tst 2003–05; fndr memb: AfghanAid 1981–89, Int Broadcasting Tst, Cncl for Arms Control 1982–85, Int Alert 1982–92, Int Freedom of Expression Exchange (IFEX) 1992 (convenor 1994); govr Westminster Fndn for Democracy 1999–; memb Ind Monitoring Bd HMP Wormwood Scrubs 2006–; *Publications* author of numerous scientific papers, journalism and human rights pubns; regular broadcaster; *Recreations* music, especially opera, string quartets, serious walking; *Style—* The Lady D'Souza, CMG; ✉ e-mail dsouzaf@parliament.uk

DABYDEEN, Prof David; *b* 9 December 1955, Guyana; *Educ* Univ of Cambridge (BA), Univ of London (PhD); *Career* author; research fell: Yale Univ 1982, Wolfson Coll Oxford 1983; prof of literary studies Univ of Warwick 1997; ambass-at-large Govt of Guyana 1993–, memb Exec Bd UNESCO 1993–97, Guyanan ambass and perm delg to UNESCO 1997–; Quiller Couch Prize Univ of Cambridge 1978, Cwlth Poetry Prize 1989, Guyana Literature Prize 1992, Medal of Honour for Literary Achievement Schoelcher Martinique; FRSL; *Publications* Slave Song (1984), Coolie Odyssey (1988), The Intended (1991), Disappearance (1993), Turner (1995), The Counting House (1997), A Harlot's Progress (1999), Our Lady of Demerara (2004); *Style—* Prof David Dabydeen; ✉ University of Warwick, Coventry CV4 7AL (tel 024 7652 3467, fax 024 7652 3473, e-mail d.dabydeen@warwick.ac.uk)

DACKER, Philip Andrew; s of Frederick Andrew Dacker (d 1992), and Margaret Chisholm, *née* Greig; *b* 20 June 1949; *Educ* Edinburgh Acad, Univ of Edinburgh (LLB); *m* 30 Dec 1972, Ellinor Lindsay (Lyn), da of Dr Hugh McLeod Tunstall MacDonald; 1 da (Vicki b 16 Dec 1989); *Career* apprentice J & F Anderson WS Edinburgh 1970–72, asst slr Alexander Hendry & Son Denny 1972–73; Dundas & Wilson: asst slr 1973–76, ptnr Commercial Property Dept 1976, managing ptnr 1991–96, ptnr Banking Gp 1996–99; managing ptnr Henderson Boyd Jackson WS 1999–; memb: Law Soc of Scotland 1973, Int Bar Assoc; NP 1978, WS 1978; *Recreations* golf, travel; *Style—* Philip Dacker; ✉ Henderson Boyd Jackson WS, Exchange Tower, 19 Canning Street, Edinburgh EH3 8EH (tel 0131 228 2400)

DACRE, Myles Randell; s of Peter Dacre (d 2003), and Joan, *née* Hill; *b* 8 February 1958; *Educ* Univ Coll Sch, Camberwell Sch of Art, Univ of Reading (BA); *Career* sr art dir Corporate Annual Reports 1982–86, assoc dir Addison Design 1986–88; md: Citigate Design 1988–93, Lloyd Northover Citigate 1993–; *Style—* Myles Dacre, Esq

DACRE, Nigel; s of Peter Dacre (d 2003), and Joan, *née* Hill; *b* 3 September 1956; *Educ* UCS Hampstead, St John's Coll Oxford (MA); *m* Prof Jane Elizabeth Dacre, da of Peter Verrill; 2 da (Claire b 1986, Anna b 1995), 1 s (Robert b 1989); *Career* graduate trainee BBC 1978, BBC Bristol 1980, TV journalist News at Ten ITN 1982, prog ed World News ITN 1987, exec prodr News At One and News at 5:40 1990–92, head of prog output and exec prodr News at Ten 1992–93, ed ITV News 1995–2002, dean Media Sch London Coll of Printing 2002–03, media conslt 2002–03, chief exec Teachers' TV 2003–06, dir Ten Alps Digital 2006–; FRTS 2002; *Style—* Nigel Dacre, Esq

DACRE, Paul Michael; s of Peter Dacre (d 2003), and Joan, *née* Hill; *b* 14 November 1948; *Educ* UCS London, Univ of Leeds (BA); *m* Kathleen, da of Charles James Thomson; 2 s (James Charles b 21 May 1984, Alexander Peter b 6 Aug 1987); *Career* Daily Express: reporter Manchester 1970–71, reporter, feature writer and assoc features ed London 1971–76, NY corr 1976–79; Daily Mail: bureau chief NY 1980, dep news ed London 1981, news ed 1983, asst ed news and foreign 1986, asst ed features 1987, exec ed 1988, assoc ed 1989–91; ed: Evening Standard 1991–92, Daily Mail 1992–; ed-in-chief Associated Newspapers 1998–; dir: Associated Newspaper Holdings 1991–, DMGT 1998–, Teletext Holdings Ltd 2000–; memb: Press Complaints Cmmn 1998–, Press Bd of Fin 2004–; *Clubs* Garrick; *Style—* Paul Dacre, Esq; ✉ The Daily Mail, Northcliffe House, 2 Derry Street, London W8 5TT (tel 020 7938 6000)

DACRE, Baroness (E 1321) Rachel Leila; *née* Brand; da of 4 Viscount Hampden, who was also 26 Baron Dacre, following whose death (1965) the Viscountcy passed to his bro while the Barony fell into abeyance between the two surviving daughters, until terminated in favour of Rachel, the elder, 1970; *b* 24 October 1929; *m* 26 July 1951, Hon William Douglas-Home (d 1992); 1 s, 3 da; *Heir* s, Hon James Douglas-Home; *Style—* The Rt Hon Lady Dacre

DADA, Feroze Ahmad; s of Ahmad Valimohamed Dada, of Pakistan, and Halima; *b* 21 April 1952; *Educ* St Patrick's Sch Karachi, Univ of Karachi (BCom); *m* 4 Feb 1984, Farida, da of H L A Maung, of Burma; 1 da (Sumaya b 1986), 1 s (Nadir b 1990); *Career* sr ptnr Freeman & Partners Chartered Accountants 1981–; dir: FSI Group plc 1986–2004, Brook

Hotels plc 1994–2004, Reyker Investments Ltd 1995–, European Middleware Consulting Co Ltd 1997–, Tpoll Market Intelligence Ltd 2001–07, Boxbrands Ltd 2005–; CTA 1978, FCA 1983, MCIArb 1999; *Books* Interest Relief for Companies (1981); *Recreations* cricket; *Clubs* Brondesbury Cricket; *Style*— F A Dada, Esq; ✉ Northfield, 158 Totteridge Lane, Totteridge, London N20 8JJ (tel 020 8446 7846); Freeman & Partners Chartered Accountants, 30 St James's Street, London SW1A 1HB (tel 020 7925 0770, fax 020 7925 0726, e-mail ferozed@freemanpartners.com)

DAFIS, Cynog Glyndwr; s of late Rev George Davies, and Annie Davies; *b* 1 April 1938; *Educ* Aberaeron County Secdy Sch, Neath Boys' GS, UCW Aberystwyth; *m* 1 Jan 1962, Llinos Iorwerth, da of Iorwerth and Eluned Jones; 2 s, 1 da; *Career* teacher of English and Welsh Pontardawe Coll of FE 1960–62, head of English Newcastle Emlyn Secdy Modern Sch 1962–80, teacher of English Aberaeron Comp Sch 1980–84, head of English Dyffryn Teifi Comp Sch Llandysul 1984–91, res offr Dept of Adult Continuing Educn UC Swansea 1991–92; MP (Plaid Cymru): Ceredigion and Pembroke N 1992–97, Ceredigion 1997–2000; AM (Plaid Cymru) Mid and West Wales 1999–2003; *Publications* Mab y Pregethwr (authobiography, 2005); *Recreations* literature, music, walking, jogging; *Style*— Cynog Dafis, Esq; ✉ Cedrwydd, Llandre, Bow Street, Ceredigion SY24 5AB

DAGLESS, Prof Erik Leslie; s of Alec W Dagless (d 2001), and Johanne, *née* Petersen (d 1975); *b* 4 November 1946; *Educ* Orton Longueville GS, Univ of Surrey (BSc, PhD); *m* 23 Aug 1969, Christine Annette, da of Leslie Lansbury; 1 da (Helen b 1972), 2 s (Niels b 1973, Stephen b 1975); *Career* lectr Univ Coll Swansea 1971–78, sr lectr UMIST 1981 (lectr 1978–81); Univ of Bristol: prof of microelectronics 1982–, head of dept 1985–88, dean Faculty of Engrg 1988–91, Leverhulme Tst Royal Soc Sr Res Fell 1991–92; hon ed Part E IEE Proceedings, conslt ed ESES Addison Wesley; memb Exec Ctee UCNS 1989–92; FIEE, FRSA; *Books* Introduction to Microprocessors (1979); *Style*— Prof Erik Dagless; ✉ Department of Electrical and Electronic Engineering, Merchant Venturer's Building, Woodland Road, Bristol BS8 1UB (tel 0117 954 5205, e-mail erik.dagless@bristol.ac.uk)

DAGWORTHY, Wendy; *b* 4 March 1950; *Educ* Medway Coll of Art, Hornsey Coll of Art (DipAD); *Career* fashion designer with Radley (Quorum) 1971, designer/dir own label Wendy Dagworthy Ltd 1972–88 (outfit exhibited at V&A), freelance designer and conslt for Laura Ashley, Liberty and Betty Jackson; has exhibited internationally (London, Milan, NY, Paris), participating designer The Courtelle Awards, Fashion Aid and many other charity shows; dir London Designer Collections 1982–90, conslt to CNAA Fashion/Textiles Bd 1982, judge RSA Bd 1982; lectr at numerous colls since 1972 incl: Bristol, Kingston, Liverpool, Manchester, Newcastle and Lancashire Polys, Gloucester and Medway Colls of Art & Design, Salisbury Coll of Art, RCA; external assessor (fashion courses) for numerous colls incl: St Martin's Sch of Art 1986–88, Swire Coll of Design Hong Kong Poly 1989; judge of art and design projects, awards and competitions for various cos incl: Br Wool Textile Corp, Br Fashion Awards, Tissavel Fur, BP, Courtelle Awards, Lennard's Bursary Award, Fil d'Or Int Linen Award Monte Carlo 1985, Irish Designer Awards 1988, Smirnoff Awards 1989, Lloyd's Bank Fashion Challenge (chm) 1990–91, Nat Nescafe Design Competition 1991, ICI Fibres Tactel Awards Paris 1992, The Clothes Show Competition 1993; course dir (BA Hons Fashion) Central St Martin's Coll of Art and Design 1989–98, prof of Fashion RCA 1998–; course and document advsr Birmingham Poly 1991; has appeared regularly on TV and radio shows nationwide; hon memb Fashion Acts; *Style*— Prof Wendy Dagworthy; ✉ Royal College of Art, School of Fashion and Textiles, Kensington Gore, London SW7 2EU (tel 020 7590 4444)

DAHRENDORF, Baron (Life Peer UK 1993), of Clare Market in the City of Westminster; Sir Ralf Dahrendorf; KBE (1982); s of Gustav Dahrendorf (d 1954), and Lina, *née* Witt (d 1980); *b* 1 May 1929; *Educ* Hamburg Univ (DPhil), LSE (PhD); *Career* lectr Saarbrücken 1957; prof of sociology: Hamburg 1958–60, Tübingen 1960–64, Konstanz 1966–69 (vice-chm Funding Ctee Konstanz Univ 1964–66); Parly sec of state FO 1969–70, memb EEC Cmmn Brussels 1970–74, dir LSE 1974–84; non-exec dir: Glaxo Holdings plc 1984–97, Bankgesellschaft Berlin (UK) plc 1996–2001; warden St Antony's Coll Oxford 1987–97, dir and chm Newspaper Publishing plc 1992–93; memb: Hansard Soc Cmmn on Electoral Reform 1975–76, Royal Cmmn on Legal Servs 1976–79; tstee Ford Fndn 1976–88; Hon DLitt: Univ of Reading, Univ of Dublin, Univ of Malta; Hon LLD: Univ of Manchester, Wagner Coll NY, York Univ Ontario, Columbia Univ NY; Hon DHL: Kalamazoo Coll, Johns Hopkins Univ; Hon DSc: Univ of Ulster, Univ of Bath, Univ of Bologna; Hon DUniv: Open Univ, Maryland, Surrey; Hon Dr: Université Catholique de Louvain; Hon DSSc: Queen's Univ Belfast, Univ of Birmingham; Hon Dr in International Relations The American Univ Washington, Hon Dr in Sociology Univ of Urbino; Hon Degree Univ of Buenos Aires, Hon DPhil Univ of Haifa in Israel, Hon Dr Université René Descartes Paris; hon fell: Imperial Coll, LSE; Hon MRIA, FBA, FRSA; Grand Cross de l'Ordre du Mérite (Sénégal) 1971, Grosses Bundesverdienstkreuz mit Stern und Schulterband (W Germany) 1974, Grand Croix de l'Ordre du Mérite (Luxembourg) 1974, Grosses Goldenes Ehrenzeichen am Bande für Verdienste (Austria) 1975, Grand Croix de l'Ordre de Léopold II (Belgium) 1975, Cdr's Grand Cross Order of Civil Merit (Spain) 1990, Knight Grand Cross Order of Merit (Italy) 2002, Orden pour le Mérite (Germany) 2003; *Clubs* Reform, Garrick; *Style*— The Rt Hon Lord Dahrendorf, KBE, FBA; ✉ House of Lords, London SW1A 0PW

DAINTITH, Prof Terence Charles; s of Edward Daintith (d 1942), and Irene, *née* Parsons; *b* 8 May 1942; *Educ* Wimbledon Coll, St Edmund Hall Oxford (MA), Univ of Nancy (Leverhulme Euro scholar); *m* 1965, Christine Anne, da of Sqdn Ldr Charles Edward Bulport; 1 s (Edward Charles b 1967), 1 da (Alexandra b 1968); *Career* called to the Bar 1966; assoc in law Univ of Calif 1963–64, lectr in constitutional law Univ of Edinburgh 1964–72, prof of public law and head Dept of Public Law Univ of Dundee 1972–83 (fndr and dir Centre for Petroleum and Mineral Law Studies 1977–83), prof of law Euro Univ Inst Florence 1981–87; Univ of London: prof of law 1988–2002, dir Inst of Advanced Legal Studies 1988–95, dean Insts of Advanced Study 1991–94, dean Sch of Advanced Study 1994–2002; prof of law Univ of WA Aust 2002–; additional bencher Lincoln's Inn 2000; Parsons scholar Univ of Sydney 1988; ed Jl of Energy and Nat Resources Law 1983–92; memb Academia Europaea 1989 (convenor legal ctee 1993–96, chm Soc Sciences Section 1996–98); Hon LLD De Montfort Univ 2001; *Publications* The Economic Law of the United Kingdom (1974), United Kingdom Oil and Gas Law (with G D M Willoughby, 1977, 3 edn 2000), The Legal Character of Petroleum Licences (ed and contrib, 1981), European Energy Strategy - The Legal Framework (with L Hancher, 1986), Contract and Organisation - Social Science Contributions to Legal Analysis (with G Teubner 1986), The Legal Integration of Energy Markets (with S Williams, 1987), Law as an Instrument of Economic Policy - Comparative and Critical Approaches (1988), Harmonization and Hazard - Regulating Workplace Health and Safety in the European Community (with G R Baldwin, 1992), Implementing EC Law in the United Kingdom: Structures for Indirect Rule (1995), The Executive in the Constitution (with A C Page, 1999), Discretion in the Administration of Offshore Oil and Gas (2006); *Recreations* cycling and carpentry; *Clubs* Athenaeum; *Style*— Prof Terence Daintith; ✉ Institute of Advanced Legal Studies University of London, 17 Russell Square, London WC1B 5DR (tel 020 7862 5839/5840)

DAINTON, (Hon) Prof John Bourke; s of Baron Dainton, FRS (Life Peer, d 1997), and Barbara Hazlitt, *née* Wright; *b* 10 September 1947, Cambridge; *Educ* Bradford GS, Merton Coll Oxford (MA, DPhil); *m* Josephine Zilberkweit; *Career* SRC research student Dept of Nuclear Physics Univ of Oxford 1969–72, lectr in physics Merton Coll Oxford 1972–73, research assoc SRC Daresbury Lab 1973–77, research assoc Dept of Physics Univ of Sheffield 1977–78, lectr in physics Dept of Natural Philosophy Univ of Glasgow 1978–81 and 1982–85; Univ of Liverpool: lectr in physics 1986–88, sr lectr in physics 1988–91, reader in physics 1991–94, prof of physics 1994–2002, Sir James Chadwick chair of physics 2002–; founding dir Cockcroft Inst of Accelerator Science and technol 2005–07; Deutsches Elektronen-Synchrotron (DESY) Hamburg: visiting scientist 1981–82 and 1997–99, spokesman UK Insts in H1 experiment 1992–98, memb Exec Ctee H1 experiment 1993–95, physics co-ordinator H1 experiment 1995–97, spokesman H1 experiment 1997–99; author of over 250 papers in peer reviewed scientific jls incl Physics Letters, Nuclear Physics, Zeitschrift fuer Physik and European Jl of Physics; memb Editorial Bd Jl of High Energy Physics 1999–; referee: The Physical Review 1988–, Jl of Modern Physics 1991–, Physics Letters 1995–, European Jl of Physics 1999–, INTAS projects EU 2000–, DTI/Research Cncl Faraday Partnerships 2000; SERC: sr fell 1992–97, memb Particle Physics Experiments Selection Panel 1981–83, memb Particle Physics Ctee 1989–92; chair SPS Ctee CERN 2003; memb: High Energy and Particle Physics Sub-Ctee Inst of Physics 1985–88, High Energy and Particle Physics Bd European Physical Soc 1986–93, Gen Cncl and Gen Ctee BAAS 1989–91 (recorder Section A Physics 1988–91, sec 1987), LHC Detector Research Bd CERN 1995–96, LEP Ctee CERN 1996–98, Large Hadron Collider Ctee CERN 1999–2003, Science Ctee PPARC 2001–03 chair and memb Scientific Advsy Ctee Nat Inst for Nuclear Physics and High Energy Physics Amsterdam 2001–08, chair INFN review of SuperB proposal 2007–08; UK delg European Ctee for Future Accelerators 1989–92, external memb Helsinki Inst of Physics 2001; Max Born Medal Inst of Physics and German Physical Soc 1999; Freeman City of London 1983, Liveryman Worshipful Co of Goldsmiths 1983; distinguished fell Alexander von Humboldt Stiftung Germany 2003; CPhys 1986, FInstP 1986, FRS 2002, FRSA 2003; *Recreations* travel, having time to think; *Style*— Prof John Dainton; ✉ Department of Physics, Oliver Lodge Laboratory, University of Liverpool, Oxford Street, Liverpool L69 7ZE (tel 0151 794 7769); Cockcroft Institute of Accelerator Science, Daresbury Science and Innovation Campus, Warrington WA4 4AD (tel 01925 864229)

DALDRY, Stephen David; CBE (2004); s of Patrick Daldry (d 1976), and Cherry, *née* Thompson; *b* 2 May 1961; *Educ* Huish GS Taunton, Univ of Sheffield (BA); *m* 2001, Lucy Sexton, the dancer and performance artist; 1 da (Annabel Clare b 2003); *Career* film and theatre director; appt incl: Metro Theatre 1984–86, artistic assoc Crucible Theatre Sheffield 1986–88 (trainee dir (Arts Cncl) 1985–86); artistic dir: Gate Theatre London 1989–92, Royal Court Theatre London 1992–97; prodns incl: Damned for Despair (Gate Theatre (winner best dir London Fringe Awards and Critics' Circle)), An Inspector Calls (NT (winner best dir, Olivier Awards, Evening Standard Awards, Critics' Circle Awards, Drama Desk Awards, Tony Awards)), Machinal (RNT (winner best dir Olivier Awards)), Judgement Day (Old Red Lion Theatre (winner best dir London Fringe Awards)), Ingolstadt (Gate Theatre (winner best dir London Fringe Awards and Time Out Awards)), Figaro gets Divorced (Gate Theatre (winner best dir Time Out Awards)), The Kitchen (Royal Court) 1995, Billy Elliot the Musical (Victoria Palace Theatre London) 2005; film prodn work incl: Eight (nominated for BAFTA Best Short Film Award) 1998, Billy Elliot (nominated for best dir Academy Award, winner Alexander Korda Award BAFTA) 2000, The Hours 2001; memb: Equity, Soc of Dirs (USA); *Style*— Stephen Daldry, Esq, CBE; ✉ Working Title Films, 76 Oxford Street, London W1V 8HQ (tel 020 7307 3000, fax 020 7307 3002)

DALE, Iain Leonard; CBE (2002, OBE 1989); s of Leonard H Dale, CBE, DL (d 1986), fndr of Dale Electric International plc 1935, and Doris Anne Smithson (d 1984); *b* 9 June 1940; *Educ* Scarborough Coll; *m* Maria, da of Josef Lanmuller (d 1973), of Pottendorf-Landegg, Austria; 3 s (Jonathan Iain b 1963, Paul Josef b 1967, David Leonard b 1969); *Career* creative dir Streets Advertising 1969–71, md Hicks Oubridge Public Affairs 1971–74; chm: Dale Electric International plc 1992–94 (dir 1972–94), Dale Power Systems plc 1992–94; dir: Ottomotores Dale Sa De Cv (Mexico) 1981–94, Dale Electric Power Systems Ltd (Thailand) 1985–94, Witt & Busch Ltd (Nigeria) 1986–94; chm Henderson TR Pacific Investment Trust plc 1994– (dir 1990–), Bioflame Ltd 2002–; non-exec dir: Chevalier International Holdings Ltd Hong Kong 1992–2002, Vislink plc 1995–2001, Bowman Power Systems Ltd 1995–2002; chm: Assoc of Br Generating Set Manufacturers 1984–85, South East Asia Trade Advsy Gp (SEATAG) 1988–92, Southern Asia Advsy Group (SAAG) 1994–2000, Br Cncl's BOND (Br Overseas Industrial Placement) Scheme 1994–; memb: NEDO Generating Set Sub Gp 1982–87, Nat Cncl CBI 1984–94 (memb Fin and Gen Purpose Ctee 1992–93), Latin American Trade Advsy Gp 1985–92, Br Overseas Trade Bd 1992–96, Bd of Govrs SOAS Univ of London 1992–94, FCO Business Panel 1994–2000; ambass for British Business (FCO appointment) 1997–; pres Scarborough Economic Action Ltd 1994–, pres Flowerfund Homes 1986–; memb Co of Merchant Adventurers of City of York; *Recreations* walking, photography; *Style*— Iain L Dale, Esq, CBE; ✉ Grove House, Low Marishes, Malton, North Yorkshire YO17 6RQ (tel 01653 668119, fax 01653 668356, e-mail Iaindale@aol.com)

DALE, John; s of Kenneth Dale, of Cleethorpes, and Eileen, *née* Minchin; *b* 1 May 1946; *Educ* Wintringham GS Grimsby; *Career* Daily Mail 1968–78, The Observer 1978–79, Now! magazine 1979–81; ed Take a Break magazine 1991–; memb BSME 1991; *Books* The Prince and The Paranormal (1985); *Style*— John Dale, Esq

DALE, Laurence Vincent; s of George Robert Dale, of Keymer, W Sussex, and Thelma Jean, *née* Singleton; *b* 10 September 1957; *Educ* Brighton Hove & Sussex GS, Guildhall Sch of Music and Drama, Salzburg Mozarteum; *Career* tenor; memb Royal Opera Co Covent Garden 1980–81, professional debut as Camille in The Merry Widow (ENO) 1981; awarded Medaille de la Ville de Paris for contrib to French culture; stage dir 2000–; artistic dir: Opéra Théâtre de Metz 2002–04, Evian Festival 2001–; *Roles* incl: Don José in Peter Brook's La Tragedie de Carmen (cr role) 1981, title role in Orfeo (ENO 1983, Salzburg Festival 1993), Ulysses (ENO) 1989, Don Ottavio in Don Giovanni (Nice, Munich, Salzburg Festival, WNO, Berlin, Marseille, Genova), Ferrando in Cosi fan Tutte (WNO, Holland Festival, Frankfurt, Berlin), Alfredo in La Traviata (WNO), Fenton in Falstaff (Brussels, Aix-en-Provence, NY, Milano, Covent Garden, Buenos Aires), Eisenstein in Die Fledermaus (WNO), Tamino in The Magic Flute (Vienna Staatsoper, Salzburg, Zurich, Brussels, Toronto, Stuttgart, Berlin, Opera Bastille Paris), Romeo in Gounod's Romeo and Juliet (Basel, Zurich), Idamante in Idomeneo (Holland Festival), Ramino in La Cenerentola (Glyndebourne, Marseille), Pelléas et Mélisande (Bruxelles), Belfiore in La Finta Giardiniera (Salzburg Festival debut) 1992, title role in Werther (Lille and Paris) 1993, Debussy's Rodrigue et Chimene (world premiere Lyon Opera) 1993; *Recordings* incl: Recital of French Opera and Opera-Comique Arias (under Kenneth Montgomery, 1988), Gounod's St Cecilia Mass, Mozart's Mass in C Minor, Honegger's Le Roi David, Debussy's Rodrigue et Chimene, Purcell's The Fairy Queen, Cavalli's La Didone, Monteverdi's Orfeo, Chausson's La Tempete; *Productions* La Tragedie de Carmen (Opéra de Bordeaux) 2000, Der Zarewitsch (Bad Ischl Operetta Festival) 2000, L'Incontro Improvviso (HaydenTage Festival Eisenstadt and EXPO 2000 Hannover) 2000, Dido and Aeneas (NY) 2001, Les Malheurs d'Orphee (NY) 2001, Powder Her Face (French premiere, Nantes and Metz) 2002, Land des Lächelins (Salzburg, Bad Ischel, Metz) 2002, Graf von Luxemburg (Innsbruck, Bad Ischl) 2002, Turn of the Screw 2003, Gustave III (Metz) 2003, Gustavo III (French premiere, Metz) 2003, Les Huguenots 2004, Opera Seria (Dutch premiere, Reis Opera) 2005; *Style*— Laurence Dale, Esq

DALE, Peter David; s of David Howard Dale (d 2006), and Betty Marguerite, *née* Rosser, of Cambs; *b* 25 July 1955; *Educ* King Henry VIII Sch Coventry, Univ of Liverpool (BA);

D

m 1988, Victoria, *née* Pennington, 1 s (Christopher Leo b 1988), 2 da (Georgia Hope b 1997, Madeleine Grace b 1997); *Career* journalist; BBC Television: film ed 1979–80, research and traineeship 1980, dir/prodr BBC documentaries 1982–98; Channel 4: commissioning ed documentaries 1998–2000, head of documentaries 2000–05, head More4 2005–; *Awards* journalism prize Anglo-German Fndn 1992, best documentary award RTS 1994, best documentary series award RTS 1996, Prodr of the Year Award Broadcast Magazine 1997, BFI Grierson Award for best documentary 1997; *Recreations* family, sailing; *Style*— Peter Dale, Esq; ✉ Head of More4, Channel Four Television Corporation, 124 Horseferry Road, London SW1P 2TX (tel 020 7306 8314, fax 020 7306 8358, e-mail pdale@channel4.co.uk)

DALE, Prof Peter Grenville Hurst; s of Thomas Calvert Dale (d 1964), of Gosforth, Newcastle upon Tyne, and Phyllis, *née* Addison; *b* 14 February 1935; *Educ* Dame Allan's Boys' Sch, Rutherford Coll, King's Coll Durham (DipArch), Leeds Met Univ (MA); *m* 1 (m dis 1985); 3 s (Ruarigh b 1966, Patrick b 1968, Robert b 1971); m 2, 14 Sept 1988; *Career* chartered architect; former posts in: Kingston upon Thames, Surrey Co, Gateshead Borough, Newcastle City; asst dir Lothian Region 1974–77, Co architect Humberside 1977–87, self-employed 1987–; sr lectr Leeds Met Univ 1987–96, prof Univ of Leeds 1994–2000 (emeritus prof 2000–); author of 5 RIBA open learning packages in practice mgmnt, briefing processes, price control, selecting contractors and tendering procedures; former memb Cncl ARCUK (vice-chm 1994), chm ARB RIBA Jt Validation Panel 1996–2001, former memb Cncl SCALA and RIAS; RIBA: thrice vice-pres, memb Cncl, memb Educn Ctee, former chm Yorks Region, thrice former pres Humberside Branch, chm York and N Yorks Branch; former dep chm Lothian Region Children's Panels; project mangr CISC NCVQ Future of the Built Environment; chm: BSI Tech Ctee for Contractor Standards in EC (also Euro delegateand BSI-Euro Chm and Secretariat), Govt Advsy Panel for DETR Research 1994–99; memb Yorks and Humberside Arts Advsy Gp; Yorkshire advsr to Civic Tst, tstee York Civic Tst 2005–; recipient 33 local and nat awards in architecture; memb tbnls for: child support, social security, disability; Hon Letters London Coll of Mgmnt and IT 2003; Freeman City of London 1990, Millennium Master Worshipful Co of Chartered Architects 2000; Jubilee Master Guild of Building City of York 2003, vice-pres Freemen of England and Wales 2004, Master Guild of Cordwainers City of York 2006; RIBA 1961, FRIAS 1971; *Recreations* painting, golf, fishing, shooting; *Style*— Prof Peter G H Dale; ✉ 19 Mile End Park, Pocklington, York YO42 2TH (tel and fax 01759 302996)

DALE, Stephen Hugh; s of Frederick Francis George Dale, of Lewes, E Sussex, and Margaret Brenda Nancy, *née* Beales; *b* 12 July 1955; *Educ* Bolton Sch, Univ of Manchester (BA); *m* Corinne Jenny, *née* David; 1 da (Claire Jenny Margaret b Nov 1994); *Career* chartered accountant Deloitte Haskins & Sells Manchester 1976–80 (articled clerk 1976–79); PricewaterhouseCoopers (formerly Price Waterhouse before merger): joined Tax Dept Manchester 1980, specialised in VAT and transferred to London office 1983, ptnr 1989– (Paris office 1991–); ICAEW: memb Tax Ctee, chm VAT Ctee 1988–96; pres Indirect Tax Ctee FEE 1993–, dep pres Int VAT Assoc 1996– (pres 1994–96); memb: VAT Practitioners Gp 1983–91 (memb Exec Ctee), Jt VAT Ctee 1990–93, VAT Ctee Centre Français du Commerce Extérieur 1994–, Conseil de L'Association des Practiciens de la TVA Européenne; ACA 1980; *Books* Advanced VAT Planning, Property and Financial Services (1989), Guide Pratique de la TVA (1999); *Recreations* music, walking, golf; *Style*— Stephen Dale, Esq; ✉ Landwell & Associés, 61, rue de Villiers, 92208 Neuilly-sur-Seine, France (tel 00 33 1 56 57 41 61, fax 00 33 1 56 57 49 81, e-mail stephen.dale@fr.landwellglobal.com)

DALE-THOMAS, Philippa Mary; da of Peter Alan Dale-Thomas, of Taunton, Somerset, and Thirle Wynette Alpha, *née* Tribe; *b* 5 March 1960; *Educ* Cheltenham Ladies' Coll, Cambridge Coll of Arts and Technol (HND); *Career* bd dir Edelman Public Relations 1989–93 (joined 1982); dep chm Fishburn Hedges 2004– (bd dir 1993–, md 2000–03); IPR Awards for: public affairs 1987 and 1991, commerce and industry 1989 and 1990, internal communications 1989, long-term PR programmes 1991; MIPR 1988, FIPR 1999; *Recreations* horse riding, scuba diving, gardening, playing the piano; *Style*— Miss Philippa Dale-Thomas; ✉ Fishburn Hedges, 77 Kingsway, London WC2B 5BW (tel 020 7839 4321, fax 020 7839 2858, e-mail philippa.dt@fishburn-hedges.co.uk)

DALEY, Michael John William; s of late Desmond William Daley and late Alma Joan, *née* Ellen; *b* 23 September 1953; *Educ* Hatfield Sch; *m* 1993, Elizabeth Jane, *née* Hobson; 1 s (Nicholas William b 28 May 1995), 1 da (Jessica Isabel b 8 Dec 1997); *Career* S G Warburg & Co Ltd 1973–77, Credit Suisse First Boston Ltd 1977–86, vice-pres and head Fixed Income Group Morgan Stanley International 1986–91, exec dir Morgan Stanley Asset Management Ltd 1988–91; md Strategic Value Management Ltd 1992–, memb Gp Exec Ctee and dir various subsids Guinness Flight Hambro Asset Management Ltd 1994–99; pres Avebury Asset Management Ltd 2000–; FInstD 1984, MCMI (MIMgt 1986), FSI 2005; *Recreations* golf, skiing, mountaineering, motoring, shooting; *Clubs* Carlton, RAC; *Style*— Michael Daley, Esq; ✉ Avebury Asset Management Ltd, 500 Chiswick High Road, London W4 5RG (tel 020 8956 2400, e-mail michael.daley@globalfixedincome.com)

DALEY, Paul; *b* 23 December 1962; *Career* musician; former memb Leftfield; remixer for artists incl: Fatboy Slim, David Bowie, Stereo MC's, Renegade Soundwave, Tricky, David Arnold (co-prodr); contrib to film soundtracks incl: Shallow Grave 1995, Trainspotting 1996, Go 1999, The Beach 2000; *Albums* Leftism 1995 (UK no 3), Rhythm and Stealth 1999 (UK no 1), Stealth Remixes 2000; *Singles* Not Forgotten 1990, More Than I Know 1991, Release the Pressure 1992, Song of Life 1992, Open Up 1993, Original 1995, The Afro-Left EP 1995, Africa Shox 1999, Dusted 1999, Swords 2000; *Style*— Paul Daley, Esq; ✉ c/o Lisa Horan Management, Studio 123, Westbourne Studios, 242 Acklam Road, London W10 5JJ (tel 020 8968 0637, fax 020 8968 0665, e-mail info@lhmanagement.com)

DALGETY, Hon Ramsay Robertson; QC (Scot 1986); s of late James Robertson Dalgety, of Dundee, and Georgia Alexandra, *née* Whyte; *b* 2 July 1945; *Educ* Dundee HS, Univ of St Andrews (LLB); *m* 13 Nov 1971, Mary Margaret, da of late Rev Neil Cameron Bernard, of Edinburgh; 1 s (Neil b 1975), 1 da (Caroline b 1974); *Career* advocate at the Scottish Bar 1972, temp sheriff 1987–91, judge of the Supreme Court Tonga 1991–95 (sometimes actg chief justice of Tonga 1991–94); dir and chm: Archer Transport Ltd and Archer Transport (London) Ltd 1982–85, Venture Shipping Ltd 1983–85; dir: Scottish Opera Ltd 1980–90, Scottish Opera Theatre Trust Ltd 1987–90; memb: Faculty of Advocates 1972, IOD 1982–89; cncllr City of Edinburgh DC 1974–80, chm Opera Singers' Pension Fund London 1991–92 (tstee 1983–92, dep chm 1987–91); dep traffic cmmr for Scotland 1988–92, dep chm Edinburgh Hibernian Shareholders' Assoc 1990–92; vice-pres Tonga Int Game Fishing Assoc 1996– (treas 1994–96), tournament dir Tonga Int Billfish Tournament 1996; *Recreations* gamefishing, boating, golf, cricket, football, opera, travel; *Clubs* Surrey County Cricket, Nuku'alofa (Tonga); *Style*— Hon Ramsay R Dalgety, QC; ✉ PO Box 869, Nuku'alofa, Kingdom of Tonga, South Pacific (tel chambers 00 676 23400, home 00 676 23348, fax 00 676 24538, e-mail dalgety@candw.to)

DALGLEISH, Prof Angus George; s of Ronald Dalgleish, and Eileen Anna Dalgleish; *b* 14 May 1950; *Educ* Harrow Co GS for Boys, UCL (MRC scholar, BSc, MD), UCH (MB BS); *m* 28 Sept 1984, Judy Ann, da of Geoffrey Riley; 1 s (Tristan Amadeus b 7 Dec 1988); *Career* house surgn in gen surgery and orthopaedics and locum casualty offr St Stephen's Hosp 1975, house physician in gen med and oncology Poole District Hosp 1975, flying doctor serv Queensland 1976–77, gen med registrar Princess Alexandra Hosp Brisbane 1978–80 (resident MO 1977–78), gen med registrar Princess Alexandra Hosp and cardio-thoracic registrar Prince Charles Hosp 1980–81, registrar in radiotherapy Queensland Radium Inst Royal Brisbane Hosp 1981–82, sr registrar in oncology Royal Prince Alfred Hosp Sydney 1982–83, sr registrar in clinical immunology and haematology Clinical Immunological Research Centre Univ of Sydney and Kanematsu Inst Royal Prince Alfred Hosp 1983–84, clinical res fell Inst of Cancer Research and hon sr registrar Royal Marsden Hosp 1984–86, clinical scientist MRC/CRC and hon conslt physician, immunologist and oncologist Northwick Park Hosp 1986–88, head Retrovirus Research Gp CRC 1988–91, head of clinical virology, sr lectr and hon conslt physician Royal London Hosp Med Coll 1991–, prof and fndn chair of oncology St George's Hosp Med Sch (now St George's Univ of London) 1991–; fndr and research dir Onyvax Ltd 1997, research dir Cancer Vaccine Inst, involved with major research progs; FRCPath 1995, FRACP 1984, FRCP 1993, FMedSci 2001; *Publications* AIDS and the New Viruses, Tumour Immunology (co-ed), Inflamation and Cancer; author of numerous medical pubns and chapters in books; *Recreations* hiking, sailing, tennis, skiing, piano, opera; *Style*— Prof Angus Dalgleish; ✉ Cellular Molecular Medicine, St George's University of London, Cranmer Terrace, Tooting, London SW17 0RE (tel 020 8725 5815, e-mail a.dalgleish@sgul.ac.uk)

DALHOUSIE, 17 Earl of (S 1633); James Hubert Ramsay; DL (Angus 1993); s of 16 Earl of Dalhousie, KT, GCVO, GBE, MC, JP, DL (d 1999), by his w Margaret, da of late Brig-Gen Archibald Stirling of Keir (2 s of Sir John Stirling-Maxwell, 10 Bt, KT, DL, which Btcy has been dormant since 1956) and Hon Margaret Fraser, OBE, da of 13 Lord Lovat; suc f 1999; *b* 17 January 1948; *Educ* Ampleforth; *m* 1973, Marilyn, 2 da of Maj Sir David Henry Butter, KCVO, MC, and Myra Alice, da of Sir Harold Wernher, 3 and last Bt, GCVO, TD, by his w Lady Zia, *née* Countess Anastasia Mikhailovna; 2 da (Lady Lorna b 1975, Lady Alice b 1977), 1 s (Simon David, Lord Ramsay b 1981); *Heir* s, Lord Ramsay; *Career* cmmnd 2 Bn Coldstream Gds 1968–71; dir Hambros Bank 1981–82; exec dir Enskilda Securities 1982–87; dir: Central Capital Ltd 1987–91, Capel-Cure Myers 1987–91, Jamestown Investments Ltd 1987–, Edinburgh Japan Trust plc (formerly Dunedin Japan Investment Trust plc until 1996) 1993–99; chm: William Evans 1990–2000, Scottish Woodlands Ltd 1998–2005 (dir 1993–98), Dunedin Smaller Companies Investment plc 1998–; pres British Deer Soc 1987, cmmr Deer Cmmn Scotland 2005–; chm of govrs Unicorn Preservation Soc 2002–; Vice Lord-Lt Angus 2003; OStJ; *Clubs* White's, Pratt's, Turf, Caledonian (pres 1990–); *Style*— The Rt Hon the Earl of Dalhousie; ✉ Brechin Castle, Brechin, Angus DD9 6SH; Flat 15, 41 Courtfield Road, London SW7 4DB (tel 020 7373 3724)

DALKEITH, Countess of; Lady Elizabeth Marian Frances; *née* Kerr; 4 da of 12 Marquess of Lothian, KCVO (d 2004); *b* 8 June 1954; *Educ* London Sch of Economics (BSc); *m* 31 Oct 1981, Earl of Dalkeith; 2 s, 2 da; *Career* radio journalist BBC; chm The Scottish Ballet 1990–95, chm Heritage Educn Tst 1999–; memb Dumfries and Galloway Health Bd 1987–90, patron CRUSAID Scotland, tstee Nat Museums of Scotland 1991–99; memb Bd Br Museum 1999–; *Recreations* music, reading, theatre, television; *Style*— Countess of Dalkeith; ✉ Dabton, Thornhill, Dumfriesshire DG3 5AR; 24 Lansdowne Road, London W11 3LL

DALLAGLIO, Lawrence; MBE (2004); *b* 10 August 1972; *Educ* Ampleforth, Kingston Univ; *Career* professional rugby union player; Wasps RFC: joined 1990, capt 1st XV 1995–, League Champions 1997, 2003, 2004 and 2005, winners Tetleys Bitter Cup 1999 and 2000, winners Heineken Cup 2004 and 2007; England: 81 caps, also former memb England colts, Under 21, students and A teams, memb winning 7's team World Cup Murrayfield 1993, debut v South Africa 1995, capt 1997–99 and 2003–04, winners Six Nations Championship 2000, 2001 and 2003, winners World Cup Aust 2003, memb squad World Cup France 2007; memb Br and Irish Lions touring squad South Africa 1997, Aust 2001 and NZ 2005; Player of the Year RFU 1995–96; *Style*— Lawrence Dallaglio, Esq, MBE; ✉ c/o Sportscast, 11A Laud Street, Croydon, Surrey CR0 1SU (tel 020 8405 0401)

DALLAS, George Sherman; s of Dr Sherman F Dallas (d 1997), and Betty Lou Sears Dallas (d 2002); *b* 24 July 1956, Terre Haute, IN; *Educ* Stanford Univ (BA), Haas Sch of Business Univ of Calif Berkeley (MBA); *m* 20 April 1991, Katherine Mary Johnston; 2 s (Zachary Sherman, William Peter (twins) b 9 June 1998); *Career* assoc Int Affrs Dept Govr's Office Atlanta 1979, corp banking offr Wells Fargo Bank San Francisco and NY 1981–83; Standard & Poor's: corp credit rating analyst NY 1983–88, regnl practice ldr Corp Ratings Europe 1988–92, head of London office 1992–93, md and regnl head Western Europe 1993–97, md and regnl head Eastern Europe, ME and Africa 1997–2000, md Global Emerging Markets 2000–01, md and global practice ldr Governance Servs London 2001–; McGraw-Hill Excellence in Leadership Award 2003; memb European Corp Governance Inst 2002–; memb Highgate Choral Soc; *Publications* Governance and Risk (2004); *Recreations* choral music, bluegrass banjo, sailing, tennis; *Clubs* Coolhurst Lawn Tennis; *Style*— George Dallas, Esq; ✉ Standard & Poor's, 20 Canada Square, Canary Wharf, London E14 5LH (tel 020 7176 3505, fax 020 7176 3790, e-mail george_dallas@standardandpoors.com)

DALLAS, James Anthony; s of John Anthony Dallas (d 2003), and Joy, *née* Marriott (d 2002); *b* 21 April 1955; *Educ* Eton, St Edmund Hall Oxford (MA); *m* 7 Sept 1979, Annabel, *née* Hope; 1 s (Edward b 29 Nov 1984), 2 da (Katherine b 15 May 1986, Matilda b 15 Oct 1988); *Career* with City legal firm 1976–81, sr legal advsr Int Energy Devpt Corp 1981–84; Denton Hall (now Denton Wilde Sapte): joined 1984, appointed to Mgmnt Bd 1990, chm 1996–; non-exec dir AMEC plc 1999–2007; memb Int Bar Assoc; memb Bd MS Corporate Devpt Bd, memb Ctee Action for the River Kennet, tstee Thames Rivers Restorations Tst; *Recreations* fishing, tennis, ornithology; *Style*— James Dallas, Esq; ✉ Denton Wilde Sapte, One Fleet Place, London EC4M 7WS (tel 020 7246 7579, fax 020 7246 7794, e-mail james.dallas@dentonwildesapte.com)

DALLAS, Michael John Linwood; s of Linwood Forbes Dallas (d 1982), and Helen, *née* Ralston (d 1990); *b* 2 February 1944; *Educ* Diocesan Coll Cape Town, Univ of Cape Town (BCom); *m* 28 April 1973, Elizabeth, da of John McGill Dick; 2 s (James Robert Linwood b 9 March 1976, Edward John McGill b 1 Aug 1979); *Career* PricewaterhouseCoopers (formerly Coopers & Lybrand before merger): trainee Cape Town, joined London office 1969, ptnr 1985–2001, ptnr i/c Public Services Assurance and Business Advsy Serv 1993–2001; memb: South African Inst of Chartered Accountants 1968, Public Sector Ctee Accounting Standards Bd 1991–2002, Dept of Health Audit Ctee 1999–2006 (chair 2002–06); chair Audit Cmmn Technical Advsy Gp 2002, Audit Ctee Gt Ormond St Hosp 2007–; CIPFA 1992, FRSA 1996; *Recreations* walking, gardening, antiques, the Cotswolds, skiing; *Style*— Michael Dallas, Esq; ✉ Ashley Manor Barn, Ashley, Tetbury, Gloucestershire GL8 8SX (tel 01666 577336)

DALLEY, Janet Elizabeth (Jan); da of Christopher Mervyn Dalley (d 1999), and Elizabeth Alice, *née* Gammell (d 2001); *b* 2 January 1952; *Educ* Univ of Bristol (BA), Univ of Oxford (MSc); *m* 1985, Andrew Motion, FRSL, *qv*; 2 s (Andrew Jesse b 1986, Lucas Edward b 1988), 1 da (Sidonie Gillian Elizabeth (twin) b 1988); *Career* journalist; literary ed Independent on Sunday 1993–97, literary ed Financial Times 1999–; *Books* Diana Mosley: A Life (1999), The Black Hole: Money, Myth and Empire (2006); *Style*— Ms Jan Dalley; ✉ Financial Times, One Southwark Bridge, London SE1 9HL (tel 020 7873 4782, fax 020 7873 3929, e-mail jan.dalley@ft.com)

DALRYMPLE, *see also:* Hamilton-Dalrymple

DALRYMPLE, James Stewart; s of Andrew Dalrymple (d 1973), of Motherwell, Scotland, and Margaret, *née* Craig; *b* 19 August 1941; *Educ* Dalziel HS Motherwell; *m* 13 Dec 1971, Margaret Elizabeth, *née* Stevenson; 1 s (William b 24 Aug 1971), 1 da (Jean Eileen b 13

Feb 1973); *Career* jr reporter Hamilton Advertiser 1960–61; news reporter: Scottish Daily Record Glasgow 1961–63, Scottish Daily Express Glasgow 1963–65; crime reporter Daily Express London 1965–70, mangr Mirror Group Newspapers Trg Scheme 1970–81, London ed Scottish Daily Record 1981–86; writer: The Independent 1986–89 and 1999–, Independent on Sunday 1989–90, Sunday Times 1990–96, Daily Mail 1996–99; Granada 'What The Papers Say' Reporter of the Year 1988, UK Press Awards Feature Writer of the Year 1991 (nominated 1998 and 2000); *Recreations* golf; *Style—* James Dalrymple, Esq

DALRYMPLE, William Benedict (HAMILTON-); s of Major Sir Hew Hamilton-Dalrymple, Bt, KCVO, *qv*, and Lady Anne-Louise, *née* Keppel; *Educ* Ampleforth, Trinity Coll Cambridge (exhibitioner, sr history scholar, MA), St Andrews Univ (DLit); *Career* writer, broadcaster and historian; contrib to jls and newspapers incl: TLS, Granta, New Yorker, New York Review of Books, The Guardian; patron: Sabeel, Palestinian Solidarity Gp; Mungo Park Medal RSGS 2002, Sir Percy Sykes Memorial Medal RSAA 2005; FRSL 1993, FRGS 1993, FRAS 1998; *Television* Stones of the Raj 1997, Indian Journeys 2000 (Grierson Award for Best Documentary Series 2000–01), Sufi Soul (2005); *Radio* The Long Search 2002 (winner Sandford St Martin Prize for Religious Broadcasting 2003), Three Miles an Hour 2002; *Books* In Xanadu (1989, Best First Work Award Yorkshire Post, Spring Book Award Scottish Arts Cncl 1990), City of Djinns (1993, Thomas Cook Travel Book Award, Young British Writer of the Year Award Sunday Times 1994), From the Holy Mountain (1997, Autumn Book Award Scottish Arts Cncl), The Age of Kali (collected journalism, 1998), The White Mughals: Love and Betrayal in 18th-Century India (2002; winner Wolfson History Prize 2003, Scottish Book of the Year 2003; shortlisted: Pen Hessel-Tiltman Prize 2003, Kiryama Prize 2004, James Tait Black Meml Prize 2004), The Last Mughal: The Fall of a Dynasty, Delhi 1857 (2006, Duff Cooper Memorial Prize 2006); *Recreations* walking, travelling, listening to music, reading, my children; *Style—* William Dalrymple, Esq; ✉ 1 Pages' Yard, Church Street, Chiswick, London W4 2PA (tel 020 8742 3233, e-mail wdalrymple1@aol.com, website www.williamdalrymple.com); c/o David Godwin, DGA, 55 Monmouth Street, London WC2H 9DG (tel 020 7240 9992)

DALTON, Andrew Searle; s of Frederick James Searle Dalton (d 1953), and Mary, *née* Whittaker (d 1973); *b* 18 May 1949; *Educ* Oundle, Magdalen Coll Oxford; *m* 16 Oct 1982, Jennie Kelsey, da of Edward Webb Keane, of New York; 2 da (Abigail Mary b 1985, Elizabeth Ann b 1992), 2 s (Frederick Victor Burdell, Benjamin Edward Alexander (twins) b 1986); *Career* S G Warburg Gp plc 1972–95, dir Mercury Asset Management Gp plc 1986–98, md Merrill Lynch Investment Managers 1998–2002, managing ptnr Dalton Strategic Partnership LLP 2002–; chm: Dalton Capital (Guernsey) Ltd, Dalton Strategic Servs Ltd, Dalton Capital (Hong Kong) Ltd; dir: Dalton Capital Advsrs (India) Pvt, Melchior Japan Investment Tst; cncllr Royal Borough of Kensington and Chelsea (mayor 2007–08); chm Oundle Sch Fndn, govr Oundle Sch; tstee and treas: Ridley Hall Cambridge, Wycliffe Hall Oxford; tstee Titus Tst; memb: Advsy Cncl Sulgrave Manor, City and Guilds of London Art Sch; farmer; dir: Corsock Farms Ltd, Corsock Forestry Ltd; Third Warden Ct of Assts Worshipful Co of Grocers; *Clubs* Carlton, Pilgrims, Ends of the Earth; *Style—* Andrew Dalton, Esq; ✉ Dalton Strategic Partnership LLP, Princes Court, 7 Princes Street, London EC2R 8AQ (tel 020 7367 5413, e-mail andrew.dalton@daltonsp.com); 20 South End, London W8 5BU (tel 020 7937 5116); Crofts, Castle Douglas, Kirkcudbrightshire DG7 3HX (tel and fax 01556 650235); The Manor House, Fritwell, Bicester, Oxfordshire OX27 7QR (tel 01869 346587, fax 01869 345652)

DALTON, Annie; da of late Cecil Henry James Dalton, and Audrey Beryl, *née* Harris; *b* 18 January 1948; *Educ* Felixstowe Secdy Modern, Ipswich Civic Coll, Univ of Warwick (BA); *m* (m dis); 1 da (Anna Rachel b 1 Jan 1971), 1 adopted s (Reuben Alexander 24 Nov 1973), 1 adopted da (Maria Jane b 5 Nov 1976); *Career* children's writer; formerly writer in residence HM Prison Wellingborough, writer's exchange in Jamaica; *Books* Nightmaze (shortlisted Carnegie Award 1990), The Alpha Box, Swan Sister, Naming the Dark, The Real Tilly Beany (commended for Carnegie Award 1992), The Afterdark Princess (winner Nottingham Oak Children's Book Award 1991), Angels Unlimited; *Style—* Ms Annie Dalton

DALTON, Ian Mark Marshall; s of Douglas Vivien Marshall Dalton, of Bournemouth, and Helgard, *née* Herzog; *b* 14 January 1964, Welwyn Garden City; *Educ* Verulam Sch St Albans, Univ of York (BA, MA), Univ of Durham (MBA); *m* 1 Aug 1992, Juliet, *née* Kearsley; 1 s (Max Joshua b 23 Sept 1998), 1 da (Alexandra Rachel Beth b 23 Sept 1998); *Career* residential care offr N Yorks CC Social Servs 1985–86, project offr then district offr Royal Soc for Mentally Handicapped Children and Adults 1986–90, devpt mangr community mental health Durham CC Social Servs 1990–91, various posts incl actg dir commissioning Northern RHA/Northern and Yorks RHA 1991–95; Northern and Yorks regnl office NHS Exec: head of primary and community care 1995–96, head of purchaser performance devpt 1996–97; dir of devpt and planning Hartlepool and E Durham NHS Tst 1997–99, dir of acute servs planning and devpt N Tees and Hartlepool NHS Tst 1999–2000; Dept of Health: regnl dir of performance mgmnt Northern and Yorks 2000–02, dir of performance North 2002–03; head of health Coalition Provisional Authy Southern Iraq (seconded to FCO) 2003; chief exec: N Cheshire Hosps NHS Tst 2003–05, N Tees and Hartlepool NHS Tst 2005–07, NE SHA 2007–; Hon Col B (250) Sqdn (V) 5 Gen Support Regt RAMC; *Style—* Ian Dalton, Esq; ✉ North East Strategic Health Authority, Riverside House, Goldcrest Way, Newcastle-upon-Tyne NE15 8NY

DALTON, Robert Anthony (Tony); *Educ* Dame Allan's Boys' Sch Newcastle upon Tyne; *m* Joanne; 1 s (Simon), 1 da (Julia); *Career* mktg mangr Van Den Berghs Ltd (Unilever) 1958–71, sales and mktg mangr Littlewoods 1971–73, dep chm Saatchi & Saatchi Advertising and chm and chief exec Ted Bates (Saatchi & Saatchi) 1973–88, chm and chief exec FCB Advertising until 1992, subsequently self employed in creative and mktg servs consultancy, dep chm Saatchi & Saatchi Advertising (London) 1995–96 (non-exec dir Laing Henry until bought by Saatchi & Saatchi 1995), sr exec Saatchi & Saatchi (New York) 1997–; FIPA; *Recreations* opera, theatre, literature, sport, horse racing; *Clubs* RAC, Mosimann's, Harry's Bar; *Style—* Tony Dalton, Esq; ✉ Saatchi & Saatchi, 375 Hudson Street, New York, NY 10014–3660, USA (tel 00 1 212 463 2000)

DALTON, Timothy; *b* 21 March 1946; *Educ* RADA; *Career* actor; *Theatre* began career in regnl theatre: lead roles in The Merchant of Venice, Richard II, The Doctor's Dilemma, St Joan; London debut as Malcolm in Little Malcolm and His Struggle Against the Eunuchs (Royal Court); other credits incl: Arthur in A Game Called Arthur, Edgar in King Lear, Berowne in Love's Labour's Lost (Aldwych), Prince Hal in Henry IV (parts I and II), King Henry in Henry V (Roundhouse), Romeo in Romeo and Juliet, The Samaritan (Shaw), Black Comedy and White Liars, The Vortex (Greenwich), Lord Byron in Lunatic Lover and Poet (Old Vic), Mark Antony in The Romans (New Mermaid), Hotspur in Henry IV (part I (Barbican)), Antony & Cleopatra, The Taming of the Shrew (Haymarket), A Touch of the Poet (with Vanessa Redgrave, Young Vic), Lord Asriel in His Dark Materials (RNT); *Television* incl: Candida (BBC), Five Finger Exercise, Centennial (mini-series), Charlie's Angels, Mr Rochester in Jane Eyre (BBC), The Master of Ballantrae (HTV), Mistral's Daughter (US mini-series, with Lee Remick, Stephanie Powers & Stacey Keach), Florence Nightingale (US mini-series, with Jaclyn Smith, Timothy West), Sins (mini-series, with Joan Collins), Philip von Joel in Framed (mini-series, Anglia), In the Company of Wolves (Anglia), Rhett Butler in Scarlett (mini-series, Sky TV), Salt Water Moose (movie, USA/Canada), Chief Inspector Rennie in The Informant, Darrow in The Reef (CBS), Sheriff Dex in Made Men, Julius Caesar in Cleopatra, Father William Bowdern in Possessed (Showtime), Matt in Time Share (Fox Family Channel); *Film* incl: King of France in The Lion Winter (with Peter O'Toole and Katharine Hepburn), Prince Rupert in Cromwell (with Alec Guinness and Richard Harris), Heathcliffe in Wuthering Heights, Darnley in Mary, Queen of Scots (with Vanessa Redgrave and Glenda Jackson (Brit Film Award nomination)), Charles Lord in Permission to Kill (with Dirk Bogarde and Ava Gardner), Juan de Dios in The Man Who Knew Love, lead in Sextette (with Mae West, Tony Curtis and Ringo Starr), Col Christie in Agatha (with Dustin Hoffman and Vanessa Redgrave), Prince Barin in Flash Gordon, Chanel Solitaire (with Marie-France Pisier), Dr Rock in The Doctor and the Devils, Basil St John in Brenda Starr (with Brooke Shields), Bancroft in Hawks, James Bond in The Living Daylights and Licence to Kill, The King's Whore, Neville Sinclair in The Rocketeer, Boris in The Beautician and the Beast, Allan Pinkerton in American Outlaws, Looney Tunes - Back in Action, Amphitryon in Hercules 2004; *Style—* Timothy Dalton; ✉ c/o ICM, Oxford House, 76 Oxford Street, London W1D 1BS

DALTREY, Roger Harry; CBE (2005); s of Harry Daltrey, and Irene Daltrey; *b* 1 March 1944, Hammersmith, London; *Educ* Acton Co GS; *Children* 5 c; *Career* fndr and lead singer The Who (formerly The Detours) 1963–; albums: My Generation 1965, A Quick One 1966, The Who Sell Out 1967, Tommy 1969, Who's Next 1971, Quadrophenia 1973, The Who By Numbers 1975, Who Are You 1978, Face Dances 1981, It's Hard 1982; solo albums: Daltrey 1973, Ride a Rock Horse 1975, One of the Boys 1977, McVicar 1980, Parting Should be Painless 1984, Under a Raging Moon 1985, Can't Wait to See the Movie 1987, Rocks in the Head 1992; actor on stage and TV and in more than thirty films incl Tommy 1975 (nominated Golden Globe Best Acting Debut in a Motion Picture) and McVicar 1980; *Recreations* history; *Style—* Roger Daltrey, Esq, CBE; ✉ c/o Jools Broom, Trinifold, 12 Oval Road, London NW1 7DH (tel 020 7419 4300)

DALWOOD, Dexter; *b* 1960, Bristol; *Educ* St Martin's Sch of Art (BA), RCA (MA); *Career* artist; *Solo Exhibitions* Clove Building London 1992, Galerie Unwahr Berlin 1995, Dexter Dalwood: New Paintings (Gagosian Gallery London) 2000, Dexter Dalwood: New Paintings (Gagosian Gallery LA) 2002, Dexter Dalwood: New Paintings (Gagosian Gallery NY) 2004, Recent History (Gagosian Gallery London) 2006; *Group Exhibitions* incl: Whitechapel Open London 1992, 1994 and 1996, Wild (Ikon Gallery Birmingham and Harris Museum Preston) 1993, Base (Salama-Caro Gallery London) 1994, John Moores 19 (Walker Art Gallery Liverpool) 1995, Remaking Reality (Kettles Yard Cambridge) 1996, Thoughts (City Racing London) 1997, Humdrum (The Trade Apartment London) 1998, Die Young Stay Pretty (ICA London) 1998, Facts and Fictions (In Arco Turin) 1998, Dirty Realism (Robert Pearre Fine Art Tucson) 1999, Rebecca (Sali Gia London) 1999, Heart and Soul (60 Long Lane London and Sandroni Rey Venice LA) 1999, Young and Serious-Recycled Image (Ernst Museum Budapest) 1999, Caught (303 Gallery NY) 1999, Neurotic Realism: Part Two (Saatchi Gallery London) 1999, Sausages and Frankfurters: Recent British and German Paintings from the Ophiuchus Collection (The Hydra Workshop Hydra) 2000, Twisted: Urban and Visionary Landscapes in Contemporary Painting (van Abbe Museum Eindhoven) 2000, Arthur C Rose presents... (Vilma Gold London) 2001, Generator 3 (Baluardo di San Regalo Lucca) 2001, View Five: Westworld (Mary Boone Gallery NY) 2001, Remix (Tate Liverpool) 2002, Sydney Biennale 2002, Tate Triennial Exhibition of Contemporary British Art (Tate Britain) 2003, My Way Home (Galerie Thaddaeus Ropac Salzburg) 2003; *Film* 1800; *Style—* Dexter Dalwood, Esq; ✉ c/o Gagosian Gallery, 6–24 Britannia Street, London WC1X 9JD (tel 020 7841 9960, website www.gagosian.com)

DALY, Alexander (Alec); CBE; *b* 1 March 1936; *Educ* Univ of Edinburgh; *Career* formerly with ICL, various positions rising to head of truck mfrg ops Ford Motor Co 1962–78; GKN plc: joined as exec chm GKN Sankey 1978, main bd dir 1986–94, latterly md Engineered and Agritechnical Products; CBI: dep dir-gen 1994–2000, chm National Mfrg Cncl 1995–2000; chm: Capital Safety Group Limited, Brent International plc, Anite plc 1995–2005; non-exec dir Robert Bosch (UK) Ltd; Freeman: Worshipful Co of Glaziers, City of London; CIMgt, FIMI, FRSA; *Recreations* reading, rugby football, theatre; *Clubs* RAC; *Style—* Alec Daly, CBE

DALY, His Eminence Cardinal Cahal Brendan; s of Charles Daly (d 1939), of Loughguile, Co Antrim, and Susan Daly (d 1974); *b* 1 October 1917; *Educ* St Malachy's Coll Belfast, Queen's Univ Belfast (MA), St Patrick's Coll Maynooth (DD), Institut Catholique Paris (LPh); *Career* ordained (RC) 1941, classics master St Malachy's Coll Belfast 1945–46, reader in scholastic philosophy Queen's Univ Belfast 1963–67 (lectr 1946–63); consecrated bishop 1967; bishop of: Ardagh and Clonmacnois 1967–82, Down and Connor 1982–90; Archbishop of Armagh (RC) and Primate of All Ireland 1990–96 (Archbishop Emeritus 1996–), created Cardinal 1991; Hon D Univ: Trinity Coll Dublin, Queen's Belfast, Nat Univ of Ireland Dublin, Notre Dame Indianapolis Ind, St John's NY, Sacred Heart Fairfield CT; *Books* Morals, Law and Life (1962), Natural Law Morality Today (1965), Violence in Ireland and Christian Conscience (1973), Peace, the Work of Justice (1979), The Price of Peace (1991), Morals and Law (1993), Tertullian The Puritan (1993), Northern Ireland - Peace - Now is the Time (1993), Moral Philosophy in Britain from Bradley to Wittgenstein (1996), Steps on my Pilgrim Journey (1998), The Minding of Planet Earth (2004); *Recreations* reading, writing; *Style—* His Eminence Cardinal Cahal B Daly, DD; ✉ Ard Mhacha, 23 Rosetta Avenue, Belfast BT7 3HG (tel 028 9064 2431, fax 028 9049 2684)

DALY, Francis D; s of Edward M Daly (d 1983), of Montenotte, Cork, and Clare, *née* Egan (d 1987); *b* 16 September 1943; *Educ* Glenstal Abbey, UC Cork (BCL); *m* 21 Feb 1970, Patricia Mary, da of late H P O'Connor, of Cork; 2 s (Teddy b 14 Nov 1970, Ken b 22 April 1972), 2 da (Aiveen b 14 Nov 1973, Alex b 6 Oct 1976); *Career* admitted slr 1966; ptnr Ronan Daly Jermyn 1970– (joined 1966); pres Law Soc of Ireland 1996–97, chm Slrs' Disciplinary Tbnl 2004–; *Recreations* golf, sailing; *Clubs* Cork Golf, Cork Constution RFC; *Style—* Francis D Daly, Esq; ✉ Cleveland, Blackrock Road, Cork; Corthna, Schull, Co Cork (tel 00 353 214 294 279); Ronan Daly Jermyn, 12 South Mall, Cork (tel 00 353 214 802700, fax 00 353 214 802790)

DALY, James; CVO (1994); s of late Maurice Daly, and Christine Daly; *b* 8 September 1940; *Educ* St Thomas More Chelsea, UCL (BScEcon); *m* 1970, Dorothy Lillian, *née* Powell; 2 s; *Career* served RM 1958–67; HM Dip Serv: joined FO 1968, third sec Accra 1971–73, third sec Moscow 1973–76, second sec Karachi 1976–78, first sec FCO 1978–79, first sec Sofia 1979–86, consul-gen Paris 1986–92, cnsllr and consul-gen Moscow 1992–95, high cmmr to Vanuatu 1995–97, high cmmr to Mauritius 1997–2000, with FCO 2001–; memb Special Immigration Appeals Cmmn 2003–; *Recreations* reading, music, walking; *Clubs* In & Out; *Style—* James Daly, Esq, CVO; ✉ 10 Cardinal Mansions, Carlisle Place, London SW1P 1EY

DALY, (Gerald) James; *b* 1953, Glasgow; *Educ* Heriot-Watt Univ (BA); *m* (m dis); 3 s; *Career* early career in mktg with Heinz and Dunlop; admitted slr 1986, in-house lawyer 1987–2001, equity ptnr in private practice 2001–04, sole practitioner specialising in consumer finance law 2004–; regular contrib on legal issues to Leasing Life, Motor Finance and Credit Today; former memb Legal Ctee Finance & Leasing Assoc; memb: Consumer Credit Trade Assoc, Law Soc 1986; *Recreations* theatre, writing, racehorses (sometime jt owner); *Style—* James Daly, Esq; ✉ Suite 543, Andover House, George Yard, Andover SP10 1PB

DALY, John; s of John Daly, and Emilie Daly; *Educ* St Clement Danes GS; *Career* asst cameraman Film Dept BBC 1976–1987, dir of photography BBC 1987–98, freelance dir of photography 1998–; memb: BAFTA, BSC 1995; *Television* credits incl: Persuasion

(Photography and Lighting BAFTA 1995), Our Friends in the North (nomination Photography and Lighting BAFTA Awards 1996), Far From the Madding Crowd (Photography and Lighting BAFTA 1998), 20,000 Streets under the Sky 2005 (nomination Photography and Lighting BAFTA Awards 2005); *Film* credits incl: Titanic Town 1998, Fanny & Elvis 1999, Essex Boys 2000, Dog Eat Dog 2000, The Parole Officer 2001, Greenfingers 2001, Johnny English 2003 (second unit), Lila Dit Câ 2003, Life and Lyrics 2006; *Style*— John Daly, Esq, BSC; ✉ c/o ICM, Oxford House, 76 Oxford Street, London W1D 1BS (tel 020 7636 6565)

DALY, Margaret Elizabeth; da of Robert Bell (d 1978), of Belfast, and Evelyn Elizabeth, *née* McKenna; *b* 26 January 1938; *Educ* Methodist Coll Belfast; *m* 1964, Kenneth Anthony Edward Daly, s of Edward Joseph Daly (d 1983), of Ireland; 1 da (Denise b 1971); *Career* trade union official ASTMS 1959–70, conslt Cons Central Office 1976–79, dir Cons Trade Union Orgn 1979–84, MEP (EPP) Somerset and Dorset West 1984–94 (Hon MEP 1994); dir Margaret Daly Associates 1996–; memb Mgmnt Bd Euro Movement 2000–; Parly candidate (Cons) Weston-super-Mare 1997; fell Industry and Parliament Tst 1993; *Style*— Mrs Margaret Daly; ✉ Margaret Daly Associates, The Old School House, Aisholt, Bridgwater, Somerset TA5 1AR (tel 01278 671688, fax 01278 671684, e-mail dalyeuropa@aol.com)

DALYELL, Hon Mrs (Kathleen Mary Agnes); OBE (2005), DL (W Lothian); da of Baron Wheatley (Life Peer, d 1988); *b* 17 November 1937; *Educ* Convent of Sacred Heart, Queens Cross Aberdeen, Univ of Edinburgh (MA); *m* 26 Dec 1963, Tam Dalyell, *qv*; 1 s, 1 da; *Career* teacher of history; NT Scot property mangr (vol) House of the Binns 1972–, memb Historic Buildings Cncl of Scotland 1975–87; dir: Heritage Education Tst 1987–2005, Weslo Housing Mgmnt 1994–2003, SCAN (Scottish Archive Network Ltd) 1998–2004; chm Bo'ness Heritage Tst 1988–95, memb Ancient Monuments Bd of Scotland 1989–2000, chm Royal Commission on Ancient and Historical Monuments of Scotland 2000–05; cmmr Royal Fine Art Cmmn for Scotland 1992–2000; tstee: Paxton Tst 1988–92, Carmont Tst 1997–, Hopeloun Preservation Tst 2005–, Museum of Scotland Charitable Tst 2005–; memb Ct Univ of Stirling; Dr (hc) Univ of Edinburgh 2006; FSA Scot; *Recreations* reading, travel, hill walking, chess; *Style*— The Hon Mrs Dalyell, OBE, DL, FSA Scot; ✉ The Binns, Linlithgow EH49 7NA

DALYELL, (Sir) Tam; 11 Bt (NS 1685), of the Binns (but does not use title); s of Lt-Col Gordon Loch Dalyell, CIE, and (Dame) Eleanor Isabel Dalyell of The Binns, *de jure* Baronetess (d 1972); *b* 9 August 1932; *Educ* Eton, King's Coll Cambridge, Univ of Edinburgh; *m* 26 Dec 1963, Hon Kathleen Mary Agnes Dalyell, *qv*, da of Baron Wheatley (Life Peer, d 1988); 1 s (Gordon Wheatley b 26 Sept 1965), 1 da (Moira Eleanor b 25 May 1968); *Heir* s, Gordon Dalyell; *Career* Nat Serv Royal Scots Greys 1950–52; King's Coll Cambridge 1952–56, teacher Bo'ness Acad 1956–60, seconded to British India Steam Navigation Co as dir of studies on Ship Sch Dunera 1960–62, MP (Lab): West Lothian 1962–83, Linlithgow 1983–2005; Father of the House of Commons 2001–05; memb: Public Accounts Ctee, Select Ctee on Sci and Technol 1965–68, Nat Exec Ctee of Lab Pty 1986–87, Educn Inst of Scot; ldr Parly Union Delgn to: Brazil 1976, Zaïre 1990, Peru 1999, Bolivia 2000, Libya 2001; weekly columnist New Scientist 1967–2005; rector Univ of Edinburgh 2002–06; Hon DSc: Univ of Edinburgh 1994, City Univ 1998; Hon Dr: Univ of St Andrews 2001, Univ of Northumbria 2005, Univ of Stirling 2005, Napier Univ Edinburgh 2005, Open Univ 2006; FRSE 2003; *Books* Case for Ship Schools (1960), Ship School Dunera (1962), Devolution: the End of Britain? (1978), One Man's Falklands (1983), A Science Policy for Britain (1983), Misrule - How Mrs Thatcher Misled Parliament (1987), Dick Crossman: A Portrait (1989); *Style*— Tam Dalyell, Esq; ✉ Binns, Linlithgow EH49 7NA

DALZIEL, Ian Martin; s of John Calvin Dalziel, FRCO (d 1983), and Elizabeth Roy, *née* Bain; *b* 21 June 1947; *Educ* Daniel Stewart's Coll Edinburgh, St John's Coll Cambridge, Université Libre de Bruxelles, London Business Sch; *m* 1972, Nadia Maria Iacovazzi; 4 s; *Career* Mullens & Co 1970–72, Manufacturers Hanover Ltd (London and NY) 1972–83, co fndr and dep md Adam & Co Group plc 1983–92; chm: Continental Assets Tst plc 1989–98, Invesco Continental Smaller Companies Tst plc 1998–; dir Lepercq-Amcur Fund NV 1988–; cncllr London Borough of Richmond upon Thames 1978–79; MEP (EDG) Lothians 1979–84; memb Queen's Body Guard for Scotland (Royal Co of Archers); *Recreations* golf, skiing, shooting, tennis; *Clubs* Brooks's, Racquet and Tennis (NY), New (Edinburgh), Royal and Ancient Golf (St Andrews), Honourable Co of Edinburgh Golfers (Muirfield), Country Club of Charleston, Yeamans Hall, Sunningdale Golf; *Style*— Ian Dalziel, Esq; ✉ 210 route de Jussy, 1243 Presinge, Geneva, Switzerland (tel 00 41 22 759 90 50); 96 King Street, Charleston, SC 29401, USA

DALZIEL, Malcolm Stuart; CBE (1984); s of Robert Henderson Dalziel (d 1979), and Susan Aileen, *née* Robertson (d 1981); *b* 18 September 1936; *Educ* Banbury GS, St Catherine's Coll Oxford (MA); *m* 1961, Elizabeth Anne, da of Major Philip Collins Harvey (d 1977); 1 s (Rory), 2 da (Caroline, Annabel); *Career* Nat Serv 1955–57, Lt The Northamptonshire Regt; Br Cncl: SOAS 1960, educn offr Lahore Pakistan 1961–63, regnl dir Penang Malaysia 1963–67, regnl rep Lahore 1967–70, rep Sudan 1970–74, dir Mgmnt Serv Dept and dep controller Estab Div 1974–79, controller HE Div 1983–87; cnsllr cultural affrs Br Embassy Cairo 1979–83, sec Int Univ and Poly Cncl 1983–87; dep chm Cncl for Educn in the Cwlth 1990–2003 (memb Exec Ctee 1983–2003), affiliate Queen Elizabeth House Int Devpt Centre Univ of Oxford, chm Restoration and Devpt Tst St Mary Magdalene Oxford 2002–; dir CERES (Conslts in Economic Regeneration in Europe Servs) 1988–97, int funding conslt 1991–2004; memb Ct Univ of Essex 1983–88; memb Exec Ctee Methodology Soc 2003–; *Recreations* theatre, ballet, rugby football, walking; *Clubs* Oxford and Cambridge, Northampton CCC; *Style*— Malcolm Dalziel, Esq, CBE; ✉ 368 Woodstock Road, Oxford OX2 8AE (tel 01865 558969)

DALZIEL, Dr Maureen; *b* 7 April 1952; *Educ* Notre Dame HS Glasgow, Univ of Glasgow (MB ChB), Univ of London (MD); *m*; *Career* jr hosp doctor Glasgow and Lanarkshire Hosps 1976–79, GP E Kilbride Glasgow 1979–81, registrar then sr registrar in public health med Brent and SW Herts HAs 1981–85, assoc dir NW Thames RHA 1989 (conslt in public health med 1985–89); chief exec: SW Herts DHA 1990–93 (dir of public health 1989–90), Hillingdon Health Agency 1993–95; dir of public health N Thames Regional Office NHS Exec 1995–98, med dir NHS Litigation Authy 1999, dir Nat Co-Ordinating Centre for Serv Delivery and Orgn Research and Devpt 1999–2001, chief exec Human Fertilisation and Embryology Authy (HFEA) 2001–2002, md Health Consultancy 2004–; hon sr lectr in public health med London Sch of Hygiene and Tropical Med 2000– (lectr 1981–85, sr lectr 1989–90); dir CSK 2002–05; memb: ICN ARC, RHA 2005–07, Br Pregnancy Advsy Serv 2007–; chair European Steering Gp "Megapoles" Social Disadvantage in Capital Cities 1997–2001; numerous articles in learned jls and papers presented at nat confs; MFCM 1985, FFPHM 1990, FRSA 1999; *Recreations* skiing, reading novels and biographies, golf (Par 3), watching old films; *Style*— Dr Maureen Dalziel; ✉ e-mail dalziel@btinternet.com

DAMANT, David Cyril; s of William Alexander Arthur Damant (d 1983), and Mary Edith Damant (d 2001); *b* 15 March 1937; *Educ* Queens' Coll Cambridge; *Career* former ptnr Investment Research Cambridge, ptnr Quilter Goodison 1982–86; md Paribas Asset Management (UK) Ltd 1987–91; chm MAP Fund Managers Ltd 1991–93, conslt Credit Suisse Investment Management Group 1993–96, Cowell and Partners 1996–2002; pres European Fedn of Fin Analysts Socs 1995–2000, chm UK Soc of Investment Professionals1980–82 (fell 1986), co chm Int Cncl of Investment Assocs 1995–2000, chm Accounting Advocacy Ctee UK Soc of Investment Professionals 2000–04, chm Consultative Advsy Gp Int Auditing and Assurance Standards Bd 2004– (memb 2001–); sr advsr Int Center for Accounting Reform Moscow 1998–2003, treas Inst for Quantitative Investment Research 1988–2004; memb: Bd Int Accounting Standards Ctee 1986–2000 (del to Russian Int Advsy Bd on Accounting and Auditing 1992–96, memb Standards Advsy Ctee 2001–05), UK Accounting Standards Ctee 1987–90, CFA Inst; *Recreations* opera, food and wine; *Clubs* Beefsteak, Garrick, RAF; *Style*— David Damant, Esq; ✉ Agar House, 12 Agar Street, London WC2N 4HN (tel 020 7379 6926, mobile 07770 938374, e-mail david.damant@totalise.co.uk)

DAMAZER, Mark David; s of Stanislau Damazer (d 1997), and Suzanne, *née* Buchs; *b* 15 April 1955; *Educ* Haberdashers' Aske's, Gonville & Caius Coll Cambridge (BA), Harvard Univ (Harkness fell); *m* Rosemary, *née* Morgan; *Career* trainee ITN 1979–81, BBC World Service 1981–82, TV-AM 1982–84; BBC: 6 O'Clock News 1984–86, output ed Newsnight 1986–88, ed 9 O'Clock News 1990–94 (dep ed 1988–90), ed TV News Progs 1994–96, head of Current Affrs 1996–98, head of Political Progs 1998–2000, dep dir BBC News 2000–04, controller Radio 4 and BBC 7 2004–; vice-chm and Br exec Int Press Inst, memb Bd Inst for Contemporary History; Home News and News Programme of the Year RTS 1993, New York TV Festival (Gold) 1994; *Recreations* opera, poor tennis, gardening, Tottenham Hotspur; *Style*— Mark Damazer, Esq; ✉ 29 Killieser Avenue, London SW2 4NX (tel 020 8674 9611, fax 020 8678 0636); BBC - White City, Room 1103, Wood Lane, London W12 7TS (tel 020 8752 7005, fax 020 8752 7009, mobile 07850 762171)

DANAHER, Timothy (Tim); s of Anthony Danaher, and Madeleine, *née* Hewett; *b* 17 November 1975, London; *Educ* Alleyns Sch, Univ of York (BA); *Career* various roles Property Week Magazine 1999–2005, ed Retail Week 2005–; regular media commentator on retail issues, freelance writer for various nat newspapers; *Style*— Tim Danaher, Esq; ✉ Retail Week, 33–39 Bowling Green Lane, London EC1R 0DA (tel 020 7520 3505, fax 020 7520 3519, e-mail tim.danaher@emap.com)

DANCE, Charles Walter; OBE (2006); s of Walter Dance (d 1950), of Birmingham, and Eleanor, *née* Perks (d 1985); *b* 10 October 1946; *Educ* Widey Tech Sch Plymouth, Plymouth Sch of Art, Leicester Coll of Art and Design; *m* 18 July 1970, Joanna Elizabeth Nicola Daryl, da of Francis Harold Haythorn, of Plymstock, Devon; 1 s (Oliver b 1974), 1 da (Rebecca b 1980); *Career* actor 1970–; *Theatre* seasons at repertory theatres: Leeds, Oxford, Windsor, Swindon, Chichester, Greenwich; joined Royal Shakespeare Company 1975; leading roles in RSC prodns incl: Richard III, As You Like It, Henry IV Parts 1 and 2, Henry V, Henry VI Part 2, The Changeling, Perkin Warbeck, The Jail Diary of Albie Sachs, title roles in Henry V and Coriolanus, The Three Sisters, Good, Long Day's Journey into Night; *Television* incl: The Fatal Spring, Rainy Day Women, The Secret Servant, The Jewel in the Crown (BAFTA Best Actor nomination), First Born, Out on a Limb, The Macguffin, Saigon - The Last Day, Rebecca, In the Presence of Mine Enemies, Randall & Hopkirk Deceased, Murder Rooms, Nicholas Nickleby, Foyle's War, Trial and Retribution, To the Ends of the Earth, Fingersmith, Last Rights, Bleak House, Fallen Angel, Wolfenden; *Radio* Frederick Delius in The Paradise Garden Attained, Sydney Carton in A Tale of Two Cities; *Film* For Your Eyes Only, Plenty, The Golden Child, Good Morning Babylon, Hidden City, White Mischief, Pascali's Island, China Moon, Alien 3, La Valle de Pietra, Century, Last Action Hero, Kabloonak (Best Actor Paris Film festival 1996), Exquisite Tenderness, Shortcut to Paradise, Undertow, Michael Collins, Space Truckers, GoldenEye, The Blood Oranges, Us Begins With You, What Rats Won't Do, Hilary and Jackie, Dark Blue World, Jurij, Gosford Park, Black and White, Ali G Inda House, Swimming Pool, Ladies in Lavender (writer and dir), Starter for Ten, Remake; *Style*— C W Dance, Esq, OBE; ✉ c/o ICM, Oxford House, 76 Oxford Street, London W1N 0AX (tel 020 7636 6565); c/o Susan Smith, 121 North San Vicente Boulevard, CA 90211 USA

DANCER, Eric; CBE (1991), JP; s of Joseph and Mabel Dancer; *b* 17 April 1940; *Educ* King Edward VII Sch Sheffield, Sheffield Poly, Inst of Mgmnt, Chartered Inst of Purchasing and Supply; *m* Aug 1980, Carole Anne Moxon; *Career* surveying asst Fowler Standford & McNab Sheffield 1956–59, asst buyer Moorwood Vulcan Ltd 1959–63, buyer Balfour-Darwins Ltd 1963–67, asst purchasing offr Brightside Foundry & Engineering Co Ltd 1965–1967, chief buyer Metro Cammell Ltd Birmingham 1967–68, supplies mangr Jensen Motors Ltd 1969–72, dir Anglo Nordic Holdings plc London 1972–1980, tstee Dartington Hall Tst 1984–87, chm English Country Crystal 1983–87, md Dartington Hall Corp 1980–87, md Dartington Crystal Ltd 1987–2001; fndr chm: Devon and Cornwall TEC 1989–93, G10; chm Rural Devpt Cmmn Devon 1981–86; chm Magistracy Ctee; memb Bd: Prince's Youth Business Tst 1989–92, SW Regnl Devpt Bd 1984–91; TEC Nat Cncl memb SW Regnl Cncl CBI; memb Wedgwood plc Gp Mgmnt Ctee; memb Nat Cncl (CBI); pres: Duke of Edinburgh Awards (Devon), Devon Historic Churches Tst, Income Tax Cmmrs, Devon RFCA, Devon Playing Fields Assoc, Community Cncl of Devon, Devon Community Fndn, St John Cncl for Devon, Devon Conservation Forum; county pres Scouts; vice-pres: St Loyes Exeter, The West of England Sch; patron: Malay and Borneo Veterans Assoc, Army Devpt Fund (Devon), Devon Historic Buildings Tst, Cancer Research UK, Royal Albert Memorial Museum Appeal, Torquay Natural History Soc, NSPCC Devon Full Stop Appeal; county patron SSAFA; tstee: Exeter Cathedral Music Fndn Tst, Exeter Cathedral Preservation Tst; govr Univ of Plymouth 1992–96; contrib Open Univ course material on effective mgmnt; HM Lord-Lt Devon 1998–; Hon Capt Royal Naval Reserve 2001; Freeman City of London 1992, Liveryman Worshipful Co of Glass Sellers 1992; Hon DUniv Sheffield Hallam 1999; FRSA; KStJ 1998; *Recreations* motor boats, reading, music; *Clubs* Royal Dart Yacht, Army and Navy; *Style*— Eric Dancer, CBE, JP; ✉ Lieutenancy Office, County Hall, Exeter EX2 4QD

DANCEY, Roger Michael; s of Michael Dancey (d 1997), of Farnham Common, Bucks, and Rosalind, *née* Clarke; *b* 24 November 1945; *Educ* Lancing, Univ of Exeter (BA, MA), Loughborough Univ; *m* Nov 1988, Elizabeth Jane Shadbolt, da of Frank Porter; 1 step da (Carolyn Jane b 17 July 1969), 1 step s (Robert William b 20 Dec 1970); *Career* teacher; head of careers Whitgift Sch 1972–76, head of sixth form Greenshaw HS 1976–82, sr master Royal GS Worcester 1982–86, headmaster King Edward VI Camp Hill Sch for Boys 1986–95, headmaster City of London Sch 1995–98, chief master King Edward's Sch Birmingham 1998–2005; govr: Warwick Schs Fndn, King's Sch Worcester; dep pro-chllr Univ of Birmingham; *Recreations* cinema, theatre, cricket, golf; *Clubs* Edgbaston Golf; *Style*— Roger Dancey, Esq; ✉ 110 Gough Road, Edgbaston, Birmingham B15 2JQ

DANCY, Hugh; *Career* actor; *Theatre* Billy and the Crab Lady (Soho Theatre), To the Green Fields Beyond (Donmar Warehouse); *Television* Kavanagh QC, Dangerfield, Trial & Retribution, Cold Feet, Madame Bovary, Relic Hunter, Daniel Deronda, Elizabeth Regina; *Film* David Copperfield, Young Blades, The Sleeping Dictionary, Black Hawk Down, Tempo, Ella Enchanted, King Arthur, Shooting Dogs, Basic Instinct 2; *Style*— Hugh Dancy, Esq; ✉ c/o PFD, Drury House, 34–43 Russell Street, London WC2B 5HA (tel 020 7344 1010, fax 020 7836 9544)

DAND, Dr Ian William; s of William Slight Dand (d 1988), and Mary Audrey Beryl, *née* Hepworth (d 1996); *b* 14 February 1941; *Educ* Bishop Vesey's GS Sutton Coldfield, Univ of Glasgow (BSc, PhD); *m* 7 April 1971 (m dis 2004), Rosemary Patterson, da of late Lt Cdr Arthur Winter; 2 s (James Alexander b 1973, John Ross Patterson b 1977); *Career* tech apprentice John I Thornycroft & Co 1959–64; Ship Div National Physical Laboratory: sr scientific offr 1970–76, princ scientific offr 1976–81, sr princ scientific offr (IM) 1981; sr scientist NMI Ltd 1982–85, mangr Vessel Hydrodynamics Gp British Maritime Technology Ltd 1985–94, dir BMT SeaTech Ltd 1994–2007; Silver Medal RINA 1976 and 1982, Bronze Medal RINA 1999; companion Nautical Inst 1976, FRINA 1993,

FREng 1994, FRSA 1996; *Recreations* woodwork, model-making, sketching, DIY, playing the guitar; *Style*— Dr Ian Dand, FREng; ✉ BMT SeaTech Ltd, Southampton, Hampshire SO14 3TJ (tel 02380 635122, fax 02380 635144)

DANDO, Stephen; *b* 13 February 1962, Scotland; *Educ* Univ of Strathclyde, Univ of Edinburgh (MBA); *Career* grad trainee Austin Rover 1984–85; various positions: Ferranti Int 1985–89, United Distillers 1989–97, Diageo 1997–99, UDV Europe 1999–2000; global HR dir Guinness Ltd 2000–01; BBC: dir HR and internal cmmns 2001–04, dir BBC People 2004–06, memb Exec Bd, dir BBC Pension Tst; gp HR dir Reuters plc 2006–; memb Editorial Advsy Bd Human Resources Magazine; CFCIPD, FRSA; *Style*— Stephen Dando, Esq

DANDY, David James; s of James Dandy (d 2000), and Margaret, *née* Coe (d 1984); *b* 30 May 1940; *Educ* Forest Sch, Emmanuel Coll Cambridge, London Hosp Med Coll (MD, MA, MChir); *m* 17 Sept 1966, (Stephanie) Jane, da of Harold Vaughan Essex (d 1985), of Wellington, Somerset; 1 s (James b 1971), 1 da (Emma b 1973); *Career* sr fell Toronto Gen Hosp Canada 1972–73, conslt orthopaedic surgn Addenbrooke's Hosp Cambridge and Newmarket Gen Hosp 1975–2002, hon conslt Addenbrooke's Hosp Cambridge 2002–; civilian advsr in knee surgery RN and RAF 1980–2006; Br Orthopaedic Assoc: fell 1975, Robert Jones prize 1991, Naughton Dunn meml lecture 1991, memb Cncl 1992–94, pres 1998–99; RCS: James Berry prize 1985, Hunterian prof 1994, memb Cncl 1994–2006, chm External Affairs Bd 1998–2002, hon treas 2002–06, vice-pres 2005–06; pres: Int Arthroscopy Assoc 1989–91, Br Orthopaedic Sports Trauma Assoc 1993–95, Br Assoc of Surgery of the Knee 1996–98, Combined Servs Orthopaedic Soc 2001–04; chm Granta Decorative and Fine Arts Soc 2007–; Freeman: City of London, Worshipful Soc of Apothecaries 1987; FRCS; *Books* Arthroscopy of the Knee (1973), Arthroscopic Surgery of the Knee (1981), Arthroscopy of the Knee - A Diagnostic Atlas (1984), Essentials of Orthopaedics and Trauma (1989); *Recreations* gardening, writing; *Clubs* East India, RSM; *Style*— Mr David Dandy; ✉ The Old Vicarage, Great Wilbraham, Cambridgeshire CB21 5JF (tel 01223 880276, fax 01223 880006)

DANDY, Gillian Margaret (Gill); da of George Thomas Dandy (d 2002), and Marjorie Walker Dandy, of Heddington, Wilts; *b* 17 August 1957; *Educ* Ancaster House Sch Bexhill-on-Sea, Birmingham Coll of Food and Domestic Arts; *Career* Harrison Cowley Public Relations Ltd Birmingham 1980–83, assoc dir Leslie Bishop Company Ltd London 1983–90, bd dir Shandwick Communications Ltd London 1990–96, dir of devpt and PR London Bible Coll 1996–2002, communications dir Evangelical Alliance 2002–04, dir Vision Communications 2004–; non-exec dir Shared Interest Society Ltd 2004–, tstee Shared Interest Fndn 2004–; MInstF, FCIPR, FRSA; *Recreations* travel, skiing, theatre, active memb of St Barnabas Church Kensington and London Bible Coll; *Style*— Miss Gill Dandy; ✉ 56 Southerton Road, Hammersmith, London W6 0PH (tel 020 8748 0809, e-mail gill.dandy@btinternet.com)

DANDY, Katherine; *b* 9 August 1960, Wigan, Gtr Manchester; *Educ* Wigan Girls HS, Univ of Sheffield; *Career* slr specialising in pensions litigation; slr Nabarro Nathanson 1993–96, head of dispute resolution Sackers LLP 1999–; lectures on pension law; memb: Assoc of Pension Lawyers, Law Soc; *Recreations* skiing, trekking, cooking, Wigan Athletic; *Style*— Ms Katherine Dandy; ✉ Sacker & Partners LLP, 29 Ludgate Hill, London EC4M 7NX (tel 020 7615 9507, e-mail katherine.dandy@sackers.com)

DANG, Mohinder Singh; s of Mohan Singh, of Amritsar, India, and Shakuntal, *née* Kaur; *b* 2 April 1946; *Educ* Med Coll Amritsar (MB BS), Punjab Univ (MS Ophth), Univ of Dublin (DO); *m* 5 Dec 1975, Sona Singh, da of Aya Ram (d 1989); 2 da (Neetika b 24 Jan 1977, Tarana b 11 May 1982); *Career* SHO: Charing Cross Hosp London 1973, Canterbury Hosp 1973–74; registrar in ophthalmology: Birkenhead Hosp 1974–78, Bournemouth Hosp 1978–80; sr registrar in ophthalmology Manchester Royal Eye Hosp 1980–83; conslt in ophthalmology: Darlington Meml NHS Tst 1983– (former memb Tst Mgmnt Bd, former chm Med Exec Ctee, chm Med Staff Ctee), Friarage NHS Tst Northallerton, SW Durham NHS Tst 1983–; memb various working gps and ctees Darlington HA, memb UK, Euro and Int Intraocular Implant Socs; author of numerous articles in jls; Int Excellence Award NRI Inst UK 1992; memb Exec: Sikh Community Gp Darlington, Overseas Doctors Assoc UK, Indian Doctors of Cleveland; hon res fell Indian Cncl of Medical Res 1970–72; Bharat Gaurav Award 2005, Glory of India Award 2005; Masters in Surgery (Ophth) 1973; FRCSEd 1979, FCOphth 1988, FRCOphth 1993; *Recreations* walking, reading, travel, golf; *Style*— Mohinder Singh Dang, Esq; ✉ Mussoorie House, 8 Compton Grove, Darlington, Durham DL3 9AZ (tel 01325 486371); Memorial Hospital, Darlington, Durham (tel 01325 743417, fax 01325 743413, e-mail m.dang@ntlworld.com)

DANGAN, Viscount; Garret Graham Wellesley; s (by 1 m) and h of 7 Earl Cowley, *qv*; *b* 30 March 1965; *m* 30 June 1990, Claire L, da of Peter Brighton, of King's Lynn, Norfolk; 2 s (Hon Henry Arthur Peter b 3 Dec 1991, Hon Bertram Garret Graham b 12 April 1999), 1 da (Hon Natasha Rose b 28 June 1994); *Career* banker; traded options: Hoare Govett Ltd, money markets Banque Indosuez, ING (derivatives) Ltd, subsequently with Geldermann Ltd; chief exec IFX Ltd 1995–, gp chief exec IFX Group plc (formerly Zetters plc) 2000–03, chm ODL Gp Ltd 2004–; *Clubs* Brooks's; *Style*— Viscount Dangan; ✉ Ashbourne Manor, High Street, Widford, Hertfordshire SG12 8SZ

DANIEL, Barbara Mary; da of Arthur Boote (d 1989), of Colehill, Dorset, and Joan, *née* West (d 1980); *b* 8 June 1954; *Educ* Bromley GS; *m* 19 Dec 2003, Tim Daniel; *Career* sec and editorial asst: Coronet Books 1973–77, Magnum Books 1977–80; Macdonald Sphere: editorial mangr 1981–86, editorial dir 1986–89, publishing dir 1989–92; editorial dir Little Brown and Co (UK)/Time Warner Books 1992–2005, gp administration dir Little, Brown Book Gp 2006–; *Style*— Barbara Daniel; ✉ Little, Brown Book Group, Brettenham House, Lancaster Place, London WC2 7EN (tel 020 7911 8100, e-mail barbara.daniel@littlebrown.co.uk)

DANIEL, His Hon Judge Gruffydd Huw Morgan; DL (Gwynedd 1993); s of Prof John Edward Daniel (d 1962), and Catherine Megan Parry-Hughes (d 1972); *b* 16 April 1939, Bangor; *Educ* Ampleforth, UC Wales (LLB), Inns of Court Sch of Law; *m* 10 Aug 1968, Phyllis Margaret Bermingham, da of Walter Ambrose Bermingham, of Clifden, Connemara, Eire (d 1988); 1 da (Antonia Siwan Bermingham); *Career* Nat Serv 1958–60, served 24 Foot the South Wales Borderers, cmmnd 2 Lt 23 Foot the Royal Welch Fusiliers, Capt 6/7 RWF 1965, served MELF (Cyprus) and UK; called to the Bar Gray's Inn 1967; recorder 1980–86, asst parly boundary cmmr for Wales 1981–82 (Gwynedd Enquiry) and 1985, circuit judge (Wales & Chester Circuit) 1986–, liaison judge for Gwynedd 1988–96 (dep liaison judge for N Wales 1984–88), liaison judge N Wales 1996–2004, sr judge (non-resident) Sovereign Base Areas Cyprus 2002– (dep sr judge 1995–2002), chm N Wales Area Judicial Forum 2004–; chm Mental Health Review Tbnl 2002–; pres Student Law Soc 1962–63; tstee Royal Welch Fusiliers Museum 1995–2003, Hon Col 6 (Cadet) Bn RWF 1996–2003; HM Lord-Lt Gwynedd 2005–; *Recreations* shooting, sailing, gardening; *Clubs* Reform, Royal Anglesey Yacht, Bristol Channel Yacht; *Style*— His Honour Judge Daniel, DL

DANIEL, Sir John Sagar; kt (1994); *b* 31 May 1942; *Educ* Christ's Hosp, St Edmund Hall Oxford (open scholar, MA), Univ of Paris (NATO scholar, Joliot-Curie scholar, DSc), Thorneloe Coll (ATh), Concordia Univ (MA); *m* 1966, Kristin Anne Swanson; 1 s, 2 da; *Career* assoc prof Dept of Metallurgical Engrg Univ of Montreal 1971–73 (asst prof 1969–71), dir of studies Télé-Université Univ of Quebec 1974–77 (co-ordinator 1973–74), vice-pres Learning Servs Athabasca Univ Alberta 1978–80, vice-rector academic affrs Concordia Univ Montreal 1980–84, pres Laurentian Univ Ontario 1984–90, vice-chllr The Open Univ 1990–2001, pres The US Open Univ 1998–2001; assoc cmmr Nat Cmmn on Educn 1992–93, asst dir-gen for educn UNESCO 2001–04, pres Commonwealth of Learning Vancouver 2004–; pres: Canadian Soc for the Study of HE 1982–83 (vice-pres and prog chm 1981–82), Int Cncl for Distance Educn 1982–85 (prog chm 12th World Conf Vancouver 1978–82), Canadian Assoc for Distance Educn 1988–89; memb Editorial Bd: Distance Education 1980–90, Canadian Jl of Higher Education 1980–90, Jl of Distance Education 1988–90, British Jl of Educational Technology 1988–90; numerous opening and keynote addresses at int conferences; vice-pres Organizing Ctee World Jr Athletics Championships Sudbury 1986–88, dir Milton Keynes and N Bucks Trg and Enterprise Cncl 1990–95; tstee Carnegie Fndn for the Advancement of Teaching 1993–2001; memb Cncl: Fndn International Baccalaureate 1992–99, Univ of Buckingham 1994–2001, Coll of St Mark and St John 1994–96, Central Sch of Speech and Drama 1994–96, Univ for Indust 1998–2001; memb: Nat Defence Coll Canada 1989–90, HE Quality Cncl 1992–94, Advsy Cncl Royal Naval Engrg Coll 1993–96, Defence Trg Review 2000–01, Conseil d'Administration Centre National d'Education à Distance 1994–97, Br North American Ctee 1995–2001 and 2006–, Canadian Cncl on Learning 2005–; reader C of E: Dio of St Albans 1991–2001, Dio in Europe 2003–05; hon chm Royal Overseas League Vancouver Branch; hon life memb: Canadian Assoc for Distance Educn 1990, Int Cncl for Distance Educn 1988; Distinguished Young Memb Award American Soc for Metals 1973, Frank Oppenheimer Award American Soc for Engrg Educn Annual Conf NY 1974, Cwlth of Learning Award of Excellence 1995, Morris D Keeton Award, Cncl for Adult and Experiential Learning USA 1999; hon fell St Edmund Hall Oxford 1990, hon conslt prof TV Univ Shanghai 1998, hon fell Open Univ 2002; Hon DSc: Royal Mil Coll St Jean Canada 1988, Open Univ of Sri Lanka 1994, Univ of Paris VI 2001, Univ of Educn Winneba Ghana 2006; Hon DEd CNAA 1992, Hon LLD Univ of Waterloo Canada 1993, Univ of Wales 2002; Hon DUniv: Universidade Aberta Portugal 1996, Anadolu Univ Turkey 1998, Sukhothai Thammathirat Open Univ Thailand 1999, Open Univ of Hong Kong 2001, Stirling 2003, Thompson Rivers Univ BC 2005; Hon DLitt: Deakin Univ Aust 1985, Univ of Lincolnshire and Humberside 1996, Athabasca Univ Alberta 1998, Indira Gandhi Nat Open Univ India 2003, Laurentian Univ Canada 2006, Kota Open Univ India 2007; Hon DHumLett: Thomas Edison State Coll New Jersey 1997, Richmond American International Univ London 1997, Univ du Québec Télé-université 1999, Univ of Derby 2000, New Bulgarian Univ 2000; W Bengal Netaji Subhas Open Univ 2005; Hon FCP 1997; Officier de l'Ordre des Palmes Académique (France) 1992 (Chevalier 1986), Queen's Jubilee Medal Canada 2003; *Books* Mega-universities and Knowledge Media: Technology Strategies for Higher Education; author of numerous articles in professional jls; *Style*— Sir John Daniel; ✉ 205–3133 Cambie Street, Vancouver, V52 4N2, Canada; Commonwealth of Learning, 1055 West Hastings Street, Suite 1200, Vancouver, BC, V6E 2E9, Canada (tel 00 1 604 775 8200, e-mail jdaniel@col.org)

DANIEL, Prof Nicholas; s of Jeremy Daniel (d 2006), and Margaret Louise (Billie) *née* Tomkins (d 1993); *b* 9 January 1962; *Educ* Salisbury Cathedral Sch, Purcell Sch, Royal Acad of Music; *m* 1986, Joy, *née* Farrall; 2 s (Alastair William b 23 May 1994, Patrick Nicholas b 1 March 1996); *Career* oboist; prof Univ of Indiana USA 1997–99, Prince Consort prof of music Royal Coll of Music 1999–2002, artistic dir Osnabruck Festival Germany 2002–04, artistic dir Leicester Int Music Festival 2004–, artistic dir Barbirolli Isle of Man Int Oboe Festival 2005–, co-fndr, dir and princ oboe Britten Sinfonia, fndr memb Haffner Wind Ensemble; prof of Oboe Staatliche Hochschule für Musick Trossingen 2004–, winner BBC Young Musician of the Year 1980 and competitons in Italy, Germany and Austria; duo with Julius Drake 1980–; regularly appears with: Lindsay Quartet, Brindisi Quartet, Vanburgh String Quartet; debut BBC Proms 1992; recent performances incl: BBC Symphony, CBSO, New Symphony Orch, Britten Sinfonia, Scottish Chamber Orch, Bulgaria, Korea, Canada, Finland, Australia; premieres incl: works by John Taverner, John Woolrich, Michael Berkeley, Sir Harrison Birtwistle, Sir Peter Maxwell Davies, Oliver Knussen, Colin Matthews, David Matthews, Thea Musgrave, Sir Michael Tippett, Sir Richard Rodney Bennett; 30 CDs on Chandos, Collins, Hyperion, Virgin, Leman Classics; Artist of the Week BBC Radio 3; memb: Liedloff Continuum Network, Natural Nurturing Network, Assoc of Radical Midwives, The Informed Parent; ARAM 1986, FGSM 1995, FRAM 1997; *Recreations* Star Trek, cooking, walking, theatre, ballet, cinema, music, home birth studies; *Style*— Prof Nicholas Daniel

DANIEL, Paul Wilson; CBE (2000); s of Alfred Daniel, of Sutton Coldfield, Warks, and Margaret, *née* Poole; *b* 5 July 1958; *Educ* King Henry VIII Sch Coventry, King's Coll Cambridge, Guildhall Sch of Music and Drama; *m* 1988, Joan Rodgers, CBE, *qv*; 2 da (Eleanor Elizabeth b 4 Sept 1990, Rose Imogen b 14 May 1993); *Career* conductor; music dir Opera Factory London 1987–90, music dir Opera North 1990–97, princ conductor English Northern Philharmonia (Opera North Orchestra) 1990–97, music dir ENO 1997–2005; studied with Sir Adrian Boult and Sir Edward Downes; conducted numerous major international orchs incl: London Symphony Orchestra, Philharmonia, London Philharmonic, Royal Philharmonic, BBC Symphony, London Sinfonietta, City of Birmingham Symphony Orchestra, Royal Liverpool Philharmonic, Scottish Chamber Orchestra, Hallé Orchestra, Royal Scottish Nat Orchestra, Bournemouth Symphony Orchestra, BBC Nat Orchestra of Wales, Orchestra of the Age of Enlightenment, Czech Philharmonic, National Orchestra of Belgium, Royal Flanders Philharmonic, Ensemble Intercontemporain, Ensemble Modern (Germany), Suisse Romande Orchestra, Orchestre de Paris, the Cleveland Orchestra, NY Philharmonic Orch, Gothenburg Symphony Orchestra, MDR Leipzig, Swedish Radio Symphony Orchestra; operas conducted with Opera North incl: Verdi's Jerusalem (Br stage première) and Attila, Dukas' Ariane et Barbe-Bleue, Tippett's King Priam, Boris Godunov (BBC Proms 1992), Don Carlos, Wozzeck, Schrecker's Der Ferne Klang, Britten's Gloriana, Janáček's Jenufa; operas conducted at ENO incl: The Flying Dutchman, Falstaff, From the House of the Dead, Manon, Otello, Boris Godunov, La Traviata, The Carmelites, Pelléas and Mélisande, Mark Anthony, Turnage's The Silver Tassie (world première), Nixon in China, War and Peace, Lulu, Peter Grimes, The Rape of Lucretia, A Midsummer Night's Dream, The Ring Cycle; other operas conducted incl: King Priam (for Nancy Opera, awarded French Critics' Prize), Mitridate (at Royal Opera House), Beatrice and Benedict and Khovanshchina (at La Monnaie Brussels), Erwartung and Duke Bluebeard's Castle (for Geneva Opera), La Clemenza di Tito (Aix Int Festival); has also conducted The Marriage of Figaro, Katya Kabanova and Hans-Jurgen von Bose's new opera Slaughterhouse 5 (with the Bayerische Staatsoper); recordings with various artists and orchestras incl: LSO and John Williams (Sony Classics), Scottish Chamber Orchestra and Evelyn Glennie (BMG), English Northern Philharmonia and Opera North companion to Harry Enfield's Guide to Opera (EMI), Boris Godunov (Chandos), Mendelssohn Elijah (Decca), Walton Series (Naxos), Bryn Terfel (Deutsche Grammophon), Elgar with LPO (BMG), Elgar 3rd Symphony (Naxos), Falstaff (Chandos), Belshazzar's Feast (Naxos); winner of Olivier Award for Outstanding Achievement in Opera; *Style*— Paul Daniel, CBE; ✉ c/o Ingpen & Williams Ltd, 7 St George's Court, 131 Putney Bridge Road, London SW15 2PA

DANIEL, Dr Reginald; s of Reginald Daniel (d 1988), and Alice, *née* Youell (d 1993); *b* 7 December 1939; *Educ* Palmers Sch Grays, Univ of London, Westminster Hosp Med Sch (MB BS, LRCP, DO, AKC, ECFMG); *m* Carol; 1 s (Lorne Piers b 23 July 1968), 1 da (Claire Suzanne b 2 Dec 1969); *Career* conslt ophthalmic surgn Guy's and St Thomas' Hosps, ophthalmic private practice Harley Street and London Bridge Hosp; lectr Univ of London; author of medical books and many ophthalmic papers in professional jls; memb: BMA, Euro Intraocular Implant Soc, American Academy of Ophthalmology, Contemporary Soc of Ophthalmologists in USA, Moorfield Hosp Surgns' Assoc; Freeman City of London,

Liveryman Worshipful Co of Spectacle Makers; FRCS, FRCOpth; *Recreations* golf, tennis, skiing; *Clubs* City of London Livery; *Style—* Dr Reginald Daniel; ✉ 152 Harley Street, London W1G 7LH (tel 020 7935 3834, fax 020 7224 2574)

DANIEL, William Wentworth; CBE (1997); s of George Taylor Daniel, and Margaret Elizabeth, *née* Hopper; *b* 19 November 1938; *Educ* Univ of Manchester (BA, MSc); *m* 1, 22 Sept 1961 (m dis 1974), Lynda Mary, *née* Garrett; m 2, 6 July 1990, Eileen Mary, *née* Loudfoot (d 1996); *Career* asst lectr Univ of Manchester 1962–63, directing staff Ashorne Hill Mgmnt Coll Warwickshire 1963–65, research offr Research Services Ltd London 1965–67, res fell Univ of Bath 1967–68, dir The Policy Studies Inst (formerly Political and Economic Planning London) 1986–93 (res fell 1968–83, dep dir 1983–86), chief exec NTBN 1998–2000; memb: ESRC 1992–96, Ctee of Experts European Fndn for the Improvement of Living and Working Conditions (EFILWC) 1992–96; *Books* incl: Racial Discrimination in England (1968), The Right to Manage? (1972), Sandwich Courses in Higher Education (1975), Where Are They Now? - A Follow up Survey of the Unemployed (1977), Maternity Rights - The Experience of Women (1980), Workplace Industrial Relations in Britain (1983), Workplace Industrial Relations and Technical Change (1987), The Unemployed Flow (1990); *Recreations* golf, tennis; *Clubs* National Liberal, Bude & North Cornwall Golf; *Style—* William Daniel, Esq, CBE; ✉ Bryn-Mor, 7 Maer Down Road, Bude, North Cornwall EX23 8NG (tel 01288 359239, e-mail bill@wwdaniel.fsnet.co.uk)

DANIELL, Gillian Mary; da of John Averell Daniell, of Lutterworth, Leicestershire, and Nancy Helen Law; *b* 23 February 1947; *Educ* The Sch of Sts Mary and Anne Abbots Bromley, Loughborough Coll of Art, Slade Sch of Fine Art (Dip Theatre Design), Goldsmiths Coll of Art (BA), RCA (MA); *m* 1972 (m dis 1987), Vaughan, s of Herman Grylls; 1 da (Sarah Hope b 22 June 1979); *Career* theatre designer, university lecturer and artist; memb: CNAA (examiner for fine art BA Hons) 1984–87, Soc of Br Theatre Designers 1989–; pt/t lectr variously at: Portsmouth Poly, Croydon Coll of Art, Homerton Coll Cambridge, International Agrarische Hoge Sch Larenstein Netherlands, The Chinese Univ of Hong Kong; currently at: Univ of Greenwich, Sch of Architecture and Construction (subject leader for Art and Design); co sec Invisible Films 2003–; contrib to a number of publications; FRSA 2002; *Exhibitions* incl: Young Contemporaries 1969, mixed show RCA 1970 and 1971, mixed show Trinity Coll Cambridge 1971, Art Spectrum Alexandra Palace London 1971, Past students of the Environmental Media Dept RCA 1972, mixed staff show Croydon Coll of Art 1973, Art Into Landscape exhbn Serpentine Gall 1974 (awarded second prize); Scaling Up Guild Hall Manchester 1986, From Wilson to Callaghan 1997; *Theatre* fndr Calliope Theatre Co Williamstown Mass; co-designer and dir: The Zoo Story (Royal Court) 1970, Fallen Woman 1985; designer credits incl: As Cuecas (The Bloomers 1975, German Inst Lisbon Portugal 1985), The Winter Dancers (Royal Court) 1977; freelance designer for Durham Theatre Co Darlington 1982–85; Liverpool Playhouse: Rat In The Skull 1987, Macbeth 1988, Second Lady 1988, Of Mice And Men (also UK tour) 1989; other prodns incl: Diary of A Somebody - The Orton Diaries (NT) 1987, Monopoly (The Old Red Lion) 1987, Two Acts Of Love (Prince of Wales Theatre) 1987, The Orton Diaries (The King's Head) 1987, Every Good Boy Deserves Favour (Queen Elizabeth Hall) 1987, A Slice of Saturday Night (The King's Head and The Arts Theatre) 1989; *Television* documentary prodr, formed own TV prodn co 1982; *Awards* nomination for Best Design in Charrington London Fringe Award (for Slice of Saturday Night) 1990; *Style—* Ms Gillian Daniell; ✉ 79 Mortimer Road, London N1 5AR (tel 020 7254 4579, e-mail g.m.daniell@gre.ac.uk or gilliangrylls@hotmail.com)

DANIELS, Ann; *b* 24 July 1964; *Children* 4 c (Joseph, Rachel, Lucy (triplets) b 23 March 1994, Sarah b 16 April 2003); *Career* key team memb in first all-women expedition to North Pole McVites Penguin North Pole Relay 1997, memb first all-Br women's team to ski to South Pole 2000, memb M&G Investments North Pole Expedition 2002 (becoming first all-women's team to ski to both poles); now motivational speaker and presenter and polar guide for the Arctic and Antarctic regions; memb James Caird Soc; involved with: Special Olympics, Expeditions Charity; judge and hon speaker for Avon in praise of women's awards; entry in: Guiness Book of Records, National Book of Statistics; Pride of Britain Award 2000; Freedom of Yeovil Town; Hon LLD; *Recreations* climbing, mountaineering, canoeing, outdoor activities; *Style—* Mrs Ann Daniels; ✉ SFX Entertainment, 35–36 Grosvenor Street, London W1X 9FG (tel 020 7529 4300, fax 020 7529 4301, mobile 0797 1821122, e-mail rhesus@ukonline.co.uk)

DANIELS, Brian Russell; s of Samuel Peter Daniels, and Anita Faye, *née* Gittleson, of Leeds; *b* 11 March 1953; *Educ* Allerton Grange Sch Leeds, Leeds Poly (RSA Teaching Cert); *m* 1982, Eileen Ruth Christopher, da of Pluto Christophides, and Madeleine Cohen-Chaco; 1 da (Alexa Kate Sara Christopher-Daniels b 7 Feb 1986); *Career* fndr Daniels Bates Partnership Ltd 1983–94, chief exec Stars + Angels Ltd, chief exec and artistic dir Pluto Productions Ltd (on behalf of New End Theatre Hampstead), chief exec Off West End Theatres Ltd and Shaw Theatre Ltd, chm Daniels Smalley Partnership Ltd; prodns incl: She Knows You Know (nominated Olivier award 1997), The Disputation 2001, Lady Day at Emerson's Bar and Grill 2002–03, Sit and Shiver 2006, From the Hart 2007, Dionne Warwick - My Music & Me, Eartha Kitt - Live at the Shaw Theatre; *Recreations* theatre, cinema, dining, travel; *Style—* Brian Daniels, Esq; ✉ Stars + Angels Ltd, c/o New End Theatre, 27 New End, Hampstead, London NW3 1JD (tel 020 7794 7088, e-mail briandaniels@newendtheatre.co.uk)

DANIELS, Jack; s of David John Daniels (d 2002), of Swanage, Dorset, and Margaret Ann, *née* Owen; *b* 8 June 1963; *Educ* Lode Heath Comp Sch Solihull, Warblington Comp Sch Havant, Portsmouth Coll of Art (OND), Bournemouth Coll of Art (HND); *m* 1, (m dis 1999), Teresa Ann, da of Bernard Appleby; 2 s (Jake b 11 Jan 1989, Jaxon b 29 July 1991); m 2, 6 March 2000, Karla-Joy, da of Dr Neil Cherry, OMNZ (d 2003); 1 da (Poppy-Joy Tokohana b 5 May 2005); *Career* former apprentice electrical engr; photographer (specialising in animal portraits) 1988–; editorial cmmns for: Sunday Times, Daily Telegraph, The Observer, Daily Mail, The Field, GQ, The New Scientist, Country Life, Elle, The Express Magazine, The Sunday Correspondent, Evening Standard, Esquire, BBC Wildlife, Loaded, The Guardian, Time Magazine etc; advtg cmmns for clients incl: Renault Kangoo, BSkyB, Ford Focus, Arthurs, MAFF Pet Passports, Cadbury's, Farleys, Citroën Austria, Birmingham Mint, Spillers Pet Foods, Winalot packaging and POS, Kitekat packaging, Bonio packaging, British Coal, Twickenham Rugby Club, Nationwide Building Society, National Westminster Bank, TSB/Our Price, Virgin Net, Jacobs Bakeries, Budget Car Hire, Nickelodeon TV, Pentax, NCDL, RSPCA, Prudential, IBM, Orange, London Zoo, British Telecom, Coca-Cola, Barclays Bank, The Prince's Youth Business Tst, British Gas, Nissan, Vicks, Logitech, British Airways/Airmiles, Chesterfield-Bieffe Helmets Milan, Conservative Pty Lion Campaign, Whiskas 1998 and 1999 Calendar, Yellow Pages, Bonjela; Anya Hindmarch handbag vending at Harrods/Liberty etc; other cmmns for book covers and record sleeves; work published throughout Europe, USA and Far East; contrib to Getty Images; lectr AoP @ Holborn Studios; tutor: Salisbury Coll, Bournemouth Arts Inst 2000–; exhibited at: AoP Gallery 'Urban Animals' 2000, Special Photographers Gallery, Hamilton's, Barbican, Royal Photographic and Smith's Galleries; memb Assoc of Photographers 1988; *Awards* Zig-Zag/Pentax Photographer of the Year 1988, Gold Medal Royal Photographic Soc 133rd Print Awards 1989, Merit Assoc of Photographers 11th Awards 1993; *Recreations* sea fishing, target shooting, computing, frequenting The Square & Compass; *Clubs* Tennessee Squire, Victoria, Swanage Gun, Glastonbury '95 Vets, Square & Compass Hat (Worth Matravers, Dorset); *Style—* Jack Daniels, Esq; ✉ tel 01929 427429, mobile 07831 356719, website www.jackdaniels.me.uk

DANIELS, Patrick Deane; s of Gerald Ernest Deane Daniels (d 1942), and Marcelle Barbara Mary Daniels (d 2003); *b* 20 April 1940; *Educ* St George's Coll Weybridge, Univ of Durham (LLB), Coll of Law; *m* Heide Marie, da of Friedrich Mumm (d 1944); 1 s (Mark Frederick), 1 da (Nina Marie); *Career* asst slr Bulcraig and Davis 1965–66 (articled clerk 1962–65), attended course in German law and worked in Germany 1966–67, asst slr Freshfields 1968–72, ptnr Simmons and Simmons 1973–97 (asst slr 1972–73); memb Ctee: City of London Law Soc 1992–99, Br-German Jurists' Assoc 1992–2000; memb: Br Inst of Int and Comparative Law, Soc for Advanced Legal Studies; memb Clare Parish Cncl, churchwarden St Peter and St Paul parish church Clare; Freeman and Liveryman City of London Slrs' Co 1990 (memb Ct of Assts 1995–97); *Recreations* travel, arts, wine; *Clubs* Carlton; *Style—* Patrick Daniels, Esq; ✉ The White House, Nethergate Street, Clare, Sudbury, Suffolk CO10 8NP (tel 01787 277255, fax 01787 278979, e-mail pddaniels@btconnect.com)

DANIELS, (Newton Edward) Paul; s of Handel Newton Daniels, and Nancy, *née* Lloyd; *b* 6 April 1938; *Educ* Sir William Turner's GS Coatham Redcar; *m* 1, 26 March 1960 (m dis 1975); 3 s (Paul Newton b 9 Sept 1960, Martin b 19 Aug 1963, Gary b 15 March 1969); m 2, 2 April 1988, Debbie, *née* McGee; *Career* magician and entertainer; Nat Serv Green Howards (served Hong Kong)1957–59, clerk (later internal auditor) local govt, mobile grocery business (later shop owner), turned professional 1969; memb: Inner Magic Circle, The Grand Order of Water Rats; *Theatre* It's Magic (Prince of Wales) 1980–82, An Evening With Paul Daniels (Prince of Wales) 1983; Christmas season Savoy 1989; summer seasons: Great Yarmouth 1979, Bournemouth 1980, Blackpool 1983; appeared in 5 Royal Variety Shows; role of Alain in School For Wives (Comedy Theatre) 1997; *Television* debut Opportunity Knocks 1970; subsequent series incl: The Paul Daniels Magic Show, Odd One Out, Every Second Counts, Wizbit (childrens series), Wipeout, Secrets; *Awards* winner: Magician of the Year Award, Hollywood's Acad of Magical Arts Golden Rose of Montreux Trophy 1985 (for Paul Daniels Easter Magic Show BBC); *Books* Paul Daniels Magic Book (1980), More Magic (1981), Paul Daniels Magic Annual (1983), 77 Popular Card Games and Tricks (1985), The Paul Daniels Magic Showcase (1992), 50 Easy Card Tricks (1993); *Recreations* golf; *Clubs* The Magic Circle; *Style—* Paul Daniels, Esq; ✉ 140 Beckett Road, Doncaster DB2 4BA (tel 01302 321233, fax 0118 9403904, e-mail newton_edward@msn.com)

DANIELS, Prof Peter George; s of Frederick James Daniels, of Ilford, Essex, and Eileen Bertha, *née* Galley; *b* 30 September 1950; *Educ* Ilford Co HS, Univ of Bristol (BSc), UCL (PhD, DSc); *m* 12 July 1975, Anne Elizabeth, da of Robert Latham, of London; 1 da (Katherine b 1986), 1 s (Geoffrey b 1989); *Career* Dept of Mathematics City Univ: lectr 1977, reader 1981, prof of applied mathematics 1985–, head of Dept 1987–97; *Recreations* cycling, gardening; *Style—* Prof Peter Daniels; ✉ Centre for Mathematical Science, City University, Northampton Square, London EC1V OHB (tel 020 7040 8450, fax 020 7040 8597, e-mail p.g.daniels@city.ac.uk)

DANIELS, Susan Tracy; OBE (2006); da of Sidney Daniels (d 2006), and Zena, *née* Deyong (d 1987); *b* 18 February 1959, London; *Educ* Keele Univ (BA), City Lit Adult Training Unit, Garnett Coll (Cert HE), Hatfield Poly (Cert for Teachers of Hearing Impaired Children); *Partner* Christopher; 2 da (Zoe, Nysa); *Career* lectr ILEA City Lit Centre for the Deaf 1984–88; RNID: HE devpt offr 1988–89, head of educn, employment and training 1989–91, head of policy, research and devpt 1991–92; chief exec National Deaf Children's Soc 1992–; cmmr Disability Rights; chair: UK Cncl of Deafness, Groundbreakers; memb ACEVO; Young Jewish Care Award 1992, Coverdale Training Bursary 1993; *Publications* Deaf with Honours: A Guide (1990), Cochlear Implants - Deaf People's Views (1993); *Style—* Ms Susan Daniels, OBE; ✉ The National Deaf Children's Society, 15 Dufferin Street, London EC1Y 8UR (tel 020 7490 8656, fax 020 7251 5020, e-mail ndcs@ndcs.org.uk)

DANKWORTH, Sir John Philip William; kt (2006), CBE (1974); *b* 20 September 1927; *Educ* Monoux GS, RAM; *m* 18 March 1958, Clementine Dinah (Dame Cleo Laine, DBE, *qv*); 1 s (Alex b 1960), 1 da (Jacqui b 1963); *Career* musician, closely involved with post-war devpt of Br jazz 1947–60; pops music dir LSO 1985–90, princ guest pops conductor San Francisco Orch 1987–89; cmmnd compositions incl: Improvisations (with Matyas Seiber) 1959, Escapade (Northern Sinfonia Orchestra) 1967, Tom Sawyer's Saturday (Farnham) 1967, String Quartet 1971, Piano Concerto (Westminster Festival) 1972, Grace Abounding 1980, The Diamond and The Goose 1981, Reconciliation (for silver jubilee of Coventry Cathedral) 1987, Woolwich Concerto (clarinet concerto for Emma Johnson) 1995, Lady in Waiting (Houston Ballet), Man of Mode (RSC), Edward II (Nat Theatre), Double Vision (for BBC Big Band, world premiere BBC Proms) 1997, Dreams '42 (string quartet for Kidderminster Festival) 1997, Objective 2000 (for combined orchestras of Harpur Trust Schools), Mariposas: A Tribute to Stuff Smith, Joe Venuti, Stephane Grappelli and Ray Nance for Violin and Piano (for Peter Fisher) 1996 (rescored for violin and string orchestra 2001; film scores incl: We Are the Lambeth Boys, The Criminal, Saturday Night and Sunday Morning 1964, Darling, The Servant 1965, Modesty Blaise, Sands of Kalahari, Morgan, Return From the Ashes (Academy Award nomination) 1966, Accident 1969, Salt and Pepper 1969, Fathom 1969, 10 Rillington Place 1971, The Last Grenade 1971, Gangster No 1 2000; musical theatre incl: Boots with Strawberry Jam (with Benny Green) 1968, Colette (starring Cleo Laine) 1979; TV theme for the Avengers series; numerous records incl: Echoes of Harlem, Misty, Symphonic Fusions, Moon Valley; formed Wavendon Stables Performing Arts Centre (with Cleo Laine) 1970; Variety Club of GB Show Business Personality Award (with Cleo Laine) 1977, ISPA Distinguished Artists Award 1999, Back Stage Bob Harrington Lifetime Achievement Award (with Cleo Laine) 2001, BBC British Jazz Awards Lifetime Achievement Award (with Cleo Laine) 2002, fell British Acad of Composers and Songwriters 2005; Liveryman Worshipful Co of Musicians; hon fell Leeds Coll of Music 1999; Hon MA Open Univ 1975; Hon DMus: Berklee Sch 1982, Univ of York 1993, Univ of Cambridge 2004; Hon DA Univ of Luton 2006; FRAM 1973; *Books* Sax From The Start (1996), Jazz in Revolution (1998); *Recreations* driving, household maintenance; *Style—* Sir John Dankworth, CBE; ✉ The Old Rectory, Wavendon, Milton Keynes, Buckinghamshire MK17 8LU (tel 01908 583151, fax 01908 584414)

DANN, Trevor John; *b* 6 November 1951; *Educ* Nottingham HS, Univ of Cambridge (MA); *m* 5 Feb 1991, Maureen Patricia, *née* Gunn; 1 da (Celia b 22 Nov 1992), 1 s (Henry b 25 June 1994); *Career* writer, broadcaster and prodr; reporter and prodr Radio Nottingham 1974–79, prodr BBC Radio 1 1979–83, BBC TV progs incl Live Aid and Whistle Test 1983–88; freelance TV prodr 1988–91, managing ed BBC Greater London Radio 1991–93 (prog organiser 1988–91), md Confederate Broadcasting 1993–96, head of prodn BBC Radio 1 1995–96, head BBC Music Entertainment 1996–2000, md pop music Emap 2000–02 (developed Smash Hits Chart), exec prodr Smash Hits Pollwinners Party, Q Awards and Kerrang Awards (Channel 4) 2001, fndr ind prodn co 2002–, presenter breakfast show BBC Radio Cambridgeshire 2002–04; dir and fell Radio Acad; currently: presenter Classic Gold network, prodr BBC Radio 2, prodr podcasts FT and New Media Age magazine, contrib Word magazine; sometime contrib: The Times, Sunday Telegraph, The Guardian, The Independent, Evening Standard, Q, Music Week, Mojo; FRSA; *Publications* Darker Than The Deepest Sea (2006); *Clubs* Notts County Supporters; *Style—* Trevor Dann, Esq; ✉ website www.trevordann.com

DANNATT, Gen Sir (Francis) Richard; KCB (2004), CBE (1996), MC (1973); s of Anthony Richard Dannatt, and Mary Juliet, *née* Chilvers; *b* 23 December 1950; *Educ* Jr Sch Felsted, St Lawrence Coll, RMA Sandhurst, Univ of Durham (BA, pres Durham Union Soc); *m* 19 March 1977, Philippa Margaret, da of Archibald James Gurney; 3 s (Thomas Richard James b 25 Oct 1978, Edward Robert Samuel b 12 Jan 1981, Oliver William Jack 10 May 1984) 1 da (Richenda Juliet Rose b 5 Oct 1988); *Career* CO 1 Bn Green Howards 1989–91, Col Higher Cmd and Staff Course 1992–94, Col Green Howards 1994–2003, Cdr 4 Armd Bde 1994–96, dir Def Prog Staff (MOD) 1996–99, Cdr 3 UK Div 1999–2000, Dep Col Adj Gen's Corps (Provost) 1999–2005, Dep Cdr (ops) Stabilisation Force Bosnia 2000–01, Col Cmdt The King's Div 2001–05, ACGS 2001–02, Cdr Allied Rapid Reaction Corps 2003–05, Col Cmdt AAC 2004–, C-in-C Land Cmd 2005–06, Chief of the Gen Staff 2006–; vice-pres Offrs' Christian Union 1998–, pres Soldiers' and Airmen's Scripture Readers Assoc 1999–, pres Army Rifle Assoc 1999–; Queen's Commendation for Valuable Service 2000; *Recreations* tennis, cricket, skiing, fishing, shooting, reading; *Clubs* Army and Navy; *Style*— Gen Sir Richard Dannatt, KCB, CBE, MC; ✉ RHQ The Green Howards, Trinity Church Square, Richmond, North Yorkshire (tel 01748 822133)

DANON, Pierre; *b* 14 May 1956; *Educ* Ecole Nationale des Ponts et Chausses Paris, Univ of Paris II, HEC Paris (MBA); *Career* Xerox Corp: memb Straegy Ctee Worldwide 1981–2000, sr vice-pres USA 1997–2000, pres Europe 1998–2001; exec dir BT Gp plc and ceo BT Retail 2000–05, chief operating offr Capgemini 2005, sr advsr JP Morgan 2005–; non-exec dir: Hays plc 2001–, Emap plc 2004–; memb European Fndn for Quality Mgmnt (EFQM) 1998–2001; *Recreations* golf, swimming, opera; *Style*— Mr Pierre Danon

DANTZIC, Roy Matthew; s of David A Dantzic (d 2002), of Whitecraigs, Glasgow, and Renee, *née* Cohen; *b* 4 July 1944; *Educ* Brighton Coll Sussex; *m* 3 June 1969, Diane, da of Abraham Clapham (d 1984), of Whitecraigs, Glasgow; 1 da (Emma Lucy b 23 Sept 1973), 1 s (Toby Alexander b 15 Feb 1975); *Career* Coopers & Lybrand 1962–69, Kleinwort Benson Ltd 1970–72, Drayton Corporation Ltd 1972–73, Samuel Montagu & Co Ltd 1974–80 (dir 1975), fin dir Britoil plc (formerly Br National Oil Corporation) 1980–84; dir: Pallas SA 1984–85, Wood Mackenzie & Co 1985–89, Stanhope Properties plc 1989–95, Merrill Lynch International Ltd 1995–96; md: Port Greenwich Ltd 1996–97, British Gas Properties 1997–2003 (non-exec dir 2003–04); non-exec chm: Premier Portfolio Gp plc 1985–92, ABC Cinemas 1998–2000, Development Securities plc 2003–, Interior Services Gp plc 2004–; non-exec dir: Moor Park (1958) Ltd 1980–90, Saxon Oil plc 1984–85, British Nuclear Fuels plc 1987–91, Total Oil Holdings Ltd 1995–96, Airplanes Ltd 1996–, AeroUSA Inc 1996–, Architectural Heritage Fund 2003–, Blenheim Bishop Ltd 2004–; tstee Portman Estate 2005–; govr Brighton Coll 1990–98, pt/t memb CEGB 1984–87; FICAS 1968; *Recreations* golf, theatre, sitting in the shade; *Clubs* MCC, Moor Park Golf; *Style*— Roy Dantzic, Esq

DANZIGER, Daniel Guggenheim (Danny); s of Edward Danziger (decd), of Palm Beach, Los Angeles, and Gigi, *née* Guggenheim; *b* 1 February 1953; *Educ* Harrow, Rollins Coll Florida (BA); *m* (m dis 1991), Victoria Constance Baillieu; *Career* author and journalist; formerly with family businesses, writer Sunday Times; columnist: The Independent 1990–95, Daily Mail 1996–97, Sunday Times Magazine 1999–; co-fndr Cover magazine 1997; nominated Columnist of the Year 1991, nominated Ed of the Year BSME 1999; *Books* The Happiness Book (1980), All in a Day's Work (1987), Eton Voices (1988), The Cathedral (1989), The Noble Tradition (1990), Lost Hearts (1992), The Orchestra (1995), Year 1000 (1999), 1215: The Year of Magna Carta (2003), Hadrian: When Rome Ruled the World (2005), Museum: Behind the Scenes at the Metropolitan Museum of Art (2007); *Recreations* swimming, golf, running; *Clubs* Wentworth, RAC, Epicurean Soc, Hillcrest CC; *Style*— Danny Danziger, Esq; ✉ c/o Georgina Capel (tel 020 7734 2414, e-mail georgina@capelland.co.uk)

DANZIGER, Nick; s of Harry Lee Danziger, and Angela, *née* King; *b* 22 April 1958; *Educ* Switzerland, Chelsea Art Sch (BA, MA); *Career* painter, photographer, author and documentary filmmaker; visiting lectr various arts schs and univs 1980–; numerous solo exhbns USA, Japan, Europe, features in nat and int newspapers and magazines; works in public collections incl: The Royal Photographic Soc, Nat Museum of Photography Film and Television, Julia Margaret Cameron Tst, The Gallery of Modern Art Glasgow, Hillsborough Castle NI; fndr orphanage Kabul Afghanistan; memb Cncl Winston Churchill Memorial Tst 1998–, memb Mission Enfance 2001–, vice-pres Action Innocence Monaco 2002–; FRGS 1982; *Television* incl: War Lives & Videotape (BBC) 1991, Adventures in the Land of SPLAJ (Channel 4) 1993, Down & Out in Paris and London (Channel 4) 1993, French Letters (Channel 4) 1994, Postcards from the Edge (Channel 4) 1996, The Fight for Hearts and Minds (Channel 4) 1994, Orphans of War (Channel 4) 1998, The Establishment (Channel 4) 1999, Out of Kosovo (Channel 4) 1999, Mongolia (Discovery Channel), Afghanistan (Discovery Channel) 2000, Niger/Mali (Discovery Channel), Nomads of the Sahara (Discovery Channel) 2000, Aids The Global Killer (Channel 4) 2000, The Unquiet Peace (BBC) 2001, To the Roof of the World (NMO), Women Facing War (ICRC/Channel 4/BBC) 2002, Jacques Henri Lanfigue: The Boy Who Never Grew Up (BBC) 2004, Digital Picture of Britain (BBC) 2005; *Awards* Winston Churchill Memorial Tst Fellowship 1982, winner Prix Italia (best tv documentary for War Lives & Videotape) 1992, fell in photography Nat Museum of Photography Film & Television 1994, Prix Italia 1992, Special Award The World Television Festival Japan 1993, Broadcast Award Best Single Documentary UK 1999, Journalist of the Year AMADE 1999, Ness Award RGS 2000, Photography of the Year Face Value geographical magazine 2001, Special Award Festival Nord-Sud Geneva 2002, Journalist of the Year Premio Russo Italy 2002, runner-up Best Short Documentary IFCT NY 2003, first prize Single Portrait Award World Press Photo 2004, Nikon Photo Essay of the Year Special Award 2004, Silver Award China Int Press Photo Contest on Peace and Development 2005; *Books* Danziger's Travels (1987), Danziger's Adventures (1992), Danziger's Britain (1996), The British (2001); *Style*— Nick Danziger; ✉ c/o Mark Lucas, Lucas Alexander Whiteley, 14 Vernon Street, London W14 0RJ (tel 020 7471 7900)

DARBON, Mark; *Educ* Thames Poly (now Univ of Greenwich, BA, Dipl Arch); *Career* architect; David A Croydon 1982–85, Spence & Webster 1985–86, Pawson Williams 1988–90, Richard Rogers Partnership 1990– (assoc dir 1999–, dir 2001–); *Projects* incl: Montevetro Battersea, Ashford Designer Retail Outlet, St Katherine's Docks, Kew Bridge Residential Project, SmithKline Beecham Masterplan, Channel 4 TV HQ, Greenwich Millennium Project Competition, Greenwich Pennisula Masterplan, Potsdamer Platz Masterplan Competition Germany, DTB Tower Frankfurt Competition Germany; *Style*— Mark Darbon, Esq; ✉ Richard Rogers Partnership, Thames Wharf, Rainville Road, London W6 9HA

DARBY, Adrian Marten George; OBE (1996); s of Col C G Darby, MC (d 1971), of Kemerton Court, Tewkesbury, Glos, and Monica, *née* Dunne (d 1958); *b* 25 September 1937, London; *Educ* Eton (Oppidan scholar), ChCh Oxford (MA); *m* 30 March 1964, Lady Meriel Kathleen, *née* Douglas-Home; 1 da (Catherine Monica b 1964), 1 s (Matthew George b 1967); *Career* lectr ChCh Oxford 1962–63, fell and tutor in economics Keble Coll Oxford 1963–85 (bursar 1968–82), self-employed farmer 1964–; chm: RSPB 1986–93 (vice-pres 1996–), Kemerton Conservation Tst 1989–, Plantlife Int 1994–2002 (pres 2005–), Planta Europa 1998–2004, Jt Nature Conservation Ctee (JNCC) 2004–; Plantlife Award for Outstanding Contrib to Plant Conservation 2002; chm Kemerton PC, memb Wychavon DC 1998–; fell Eton Coll 1979–94, hon fell Keble Coll Oxford 1998; *Style*— Adrian Darby, Esq, OBE; ✉ Kemerton Court, Kemerton, Tewkesbury, Gloucestershire GL20 7HY (tel 01386 725254)

DARBY, Catherine; da of Harry Peters, of Caernarvon, North Wales, and Vera, *née* Knight; *b* 3 March 1935; *Educ* Caernavon GS, UCNW (scholarship, DipEd, Ida Esling Award); *m* 1 (m dis), Malcolm Black, s of Vernor Black; m 2 (m dis), George Ratcliffe; 3 c (Martin Peters b 1958, Rachel Peters b 1963, Emily Peters b 1965); *Career* teacher of retarded children 1956–58; author 1958–; Brontë Poetry Prize 2001, winner Cardiff Int Playwriting Competition 2001; *Publications* incl: Moon Chalice Series (6 vols, 1975–), Falcon Series (12 vols, 1976–), A Dream of Fair Serpents (1979), Sabre Series (6 vols, 1980–), Rowan Series (6 vols, 1982–), a further 100 novels under other pseudonyms (Maureen Peters, Veronica Black, Levanah Lloyd, Belinda Grey, Sharon Whitby and Elizabeth Law), 15 magazine serials, 25 short stories, 12 articles; *Recreations* travel, tapestry work, study of occult, reading; *Style*— Ms Catherine Darby; ✉ c/o Robert Hale Ltd, Clerkenwell House, 45–47 Clerkenwell Green, London EC1R 0HT (tel 020 7251 2661)

DARBY, Gavin J; *b* 15 February 1956; *Educ* Cranleigh Sch, Univ of Manchester (BSc Mgmnt Science); *m*; 2 da, 1 s; *Career* early positions in brands and mktg mgmnt with Spillers and S C Johnson; Coca-Cola 1984–2001: joined as mktg mangr (later mktg dir) 1984, devpt assignment Coca-Cola Enterprises (USA) 1988–89, ops dir UK 1989–91, based Brussels (responsible for Denmark, Holland, Belgium and Luxembourg) 1991–93, pres Northwest Europe Div 1993–98 (responsible for above and France), based UK (adding Br and Irish businesses to territories) 1995–98, also sr vice-pres Coca-Cola International and memb Euro Operating Bd, pres Central Europe Div 1998; Vodafone: chief operating offr then chief exec Vodafone UK 2001–04, chief executive Americas region 2004–; *Recreations* golf, running, current affairs and economics; *Style*— Gavin Darby, Esq

DARBY, George; s of late Norman Darby, and Joanna Eleanor, *née* Willock; *b* 20 July 1942; *Educ* Bolton Sch, Univ of Nottingham (BA); *m* 1, Constance Smith; 2 da (Susanne b 28 Sept 1966, Amanda b 21 Nov 1975), 2 s (Antony b 9 Feb 1969, Christopher b 31 May 1978); m 2, Helene Feger; 1 da (Stephanie b 22 April 1996), 1 s (Benjamin b 29 Aug 1999); *Career* Westminster Press grad trainee Keighley News 1964–65; sub-ed: Northern Echo 1965–67, Daily Mirror 1967–68; The Sunday Times 1968–85: personal asst to Harold Evans (ed), editorial mangr, asst ed, assoc managing ed features, assoc magazine ed, chief asst to Frank Giles (ed), exec features ed, ed The Times Royal Wedding Magazine 1981 and The Times Bicentenary Magazine 1984; managing ed then ed Sunday Today 1985–86, dep ed Today 1987, exec ed The Observer Magazine 1987–88, conslt ed The Independent Magazine 1988, dep ed The Telegraph Magazine 1988–96, editorial projects dir The Telegraph Group Ltd 1996–; adjunct prof Univ of Missouri Sch of Journalism 1985–86, proprietor Jigsaw Productions design consultancy 1970–; *Books* various ghosted autobiographies; ed: The Sunday Times Bedside Book (1983 and 1984), Thalidomide Children and the Law (1977); contrib Pictures on a Page (by Harold Evans, 1978); *Clubs* Garrick; *Style*— George Darby, Esq; ✉ The Telegraph Group Ltd, 1 Canada Square, London E14 5DT (tel 020 7538 5000)

DARBYSHIRE, (John) Anthony Charles; s of (Leslie) Noel Darbyshire (d 1981), of Normanton, Derbys, and Marjorie Darbyshire (d 1947); *b* 7 May 1939; *Educ* Uppingham, Keble Coll Oxford (MA), McGill Univ Montreal; *m* 1, 3 June 1967 (m dis 1982), (Faith) Lorraine, da of Noel William Hempsall, of Walesby, Notts; 1 s (Markham Noel Charles b 10 June 1968); m 2, 28 Aug 1982, Sheena Nanette Mabel, da of Capt Thomas Wilson Taylor, of Barnby Moor, Retford, Notts; 1 s ((John) Hamish McGregor b 26 Sept 1984), 1 da (Keturah Mona Ellen b 8 Dec 1986); *Career* prodn mangr John Darbyshire & Co Ltd 1964–66, conslt Urwick Orr & Ptnrs 1966–67, chm AH Turner Gp Ltd 1967–90, princ ADA Communications 1990–2001, md ADA Assessment Solutions Ltd 2001–; memb: Mgmnt Ctee Br Vehicle Rental and Leasing Assoc 1980–90, Cncl CBI 1982–90 (Smaller Firms Cncl 1979–89, E Midlands Regnl Cncl 1980–90); chm Bassetlaw Industry Assoc 1986–89 (memb Mgmnt Ctee 1986–98), memb Nat Exec Bd Young Enterprise 1989–90 (chm Notts area Bd 1986–90), chm N Notts Trg and Enterprise Cncl 1989–90, dir N Notts Bus Link 1995–96; tstee Comino Fndn 1993–; chm Pilgrim Fathers Origins Assoc 2006–; FInstD 1976, FRSA 1988, CCMI (CIMgt 1989, MIMgt 1971, FIMgt 1983); *Recreations* skiing, golf, gardening and improving the quality of life; *Style*— Anthony Darbyshire, Esq; ✉ Firs Farm House, Bilby, Retford, Nottinghamshire DN22 8JB (tel 01777 711141, e-mail ad@improver.co.uk, website www.improver.co.uk)

DARBYSHIRE, David Glen; s of Thomas Leslie Darbyshire (d 1979), and Alice, *née* Moss; *b* 20 May 1944; *Educ* Wigan GS, Liverpool Coll of Art, Univ of Newcastle upon Tyne (BA, BArch); *m* 7 July 1973 (m dis 1990), Jane Helen; 1 da (Kate); *Career* architect Ryder and Yates Ptnrs 1972–75, princ architect Washington Devpt Corp 1975–79, ptnr Jane and David Darbyshire 1979–87; Civic Tst Award for Dukes Cottages Backworth; Civic Tst Commendation for: Church St Cramlington, St John's Green Percy Main; winner of: St Oswald's Hospice Special Category Regnl Ltd Competition and Civic Tst Award, RIBA Nat Award Building of the Year 1988, The Times/RIBA Community Enterprise Scheme Commendation, Housing Design Award for Collingwood Ct Morpeth 1989; princ Darbyshire Architects 1987–; RIBA; *Recreations* music, mechanical engineering, fine art; *Clubs* Bristol Owners'; *Style*— David Darbyshire, Esq; ✉ 10 Lily Crescent, Jesmond, Newcastle upon Tyne (tel 0191 281 0501); Darbyshire Architects, Hawthorn Cottage, Hawthorn Road, Gosforth, Newcastle upon Tyne NE3 4DE (tel 0191 284 2813)

DARBYSHIRE, David Stewart; s of Wing Cdr Rupert Stanley Darbyshire (ka 1941), and Ann, *née* Todd; *b* 14 November 1940; *Educ* Radley, Oriel Coll Oxford (MA); *m* 24 Jan 1970, Elizabeth, da of Eric Watts; 1 s (Rupert b 1975), 2 da (Sophie b 1973, Alice b 1978); *Career* Capt SAS AVR 1964–70; called to the Bar 1965, in practice 1965–66; Arthur Andersen: London 1966–72, Paris 1972–79, ptnr 1976–, Leeds 1979–85, London 1985–94, Moscow 1994–; treas Hakluyt Soc 1989; vice-pres Federation des Experts Comptables Européens 1990, memb Ordre des Experts Comptables and Compagnie des Commissaires aux Comptes 1977; FCA 1970, ATII 1971; *Recreations* sailing, hill walking; *Clubs* Royal Thames Yacht, Sea View Yacht; *Style*— David Darbyshire, Esq; ✉ Arthur Anderson, Staraya, Basmannaya 14, 103064 Moscow, Russia (tel 00 7 502 222 4600, fax 00 7 502 222 4603)

DARBYSHIRE, Jane Helen; OBE (1994); da of Gordon Desmond Wroe (d 1994), of Brixham, Devon, and Patricia, *née* Keough; *b* 5 June 1948; *Educ* Dorking GS, Univ of Newcastle upon Tyne (BA, BArch); *m* 1, 7 July 1973 (m dis), David Glen Darbyshire, s of Thomas Darbyshire (d 1980), of Wigan, Lancs; 1 da (Kate b 1979); m 2, 25 July 1993, Michael Murray Walker; *Career* chartered architect in private practice; ptnr Jane and David Darbyshire 1979–87, princ Jane Darbyshire Associates 1987–94, dir Jane Darbyshire and David Kendall Ltd 1995–2000 (conslt 2000–); memb Cncl RIBA 1998–2001; exhibitor Women in Architecture (RIBA) 1983, winner St Oswalds Hospice Design Competition 1981, exhibitor DLI Museum Durham 1981; Civic Tst: award for restoration 1982, commendation for Cramlington Housing 1983, commendation for flat refurbishment Percy Main 1986, award for St Oswalds Hospice Gosforth Newcastle upon Tyne 1987; award for housing design Morpeth 1988, Nat RIBA award 1988, Building of the Year Award 1988, Nat Housing Design award 1989, 2 housing design awards 1991, RIBA award for St Cuthbert's Church Durham 1991, Civic Tst Award 1992 and 1993; features: Channel 4 Design Matters, BBC Townscape; Civic Tst assessor, RIBA Awards assessor 1984–90, memb Bd Tyne & Wear Urban Devpt Corp 1993–98, external examiner Univ of Newcastle upon Tyne 1992–, memb Bd Culture North East 2000–01; *Recreations* music, art, history of architecture, horses; *Style*— Ms Jane Darbyshire-Walker, OBE; ✉ White Gables, Stock Lane, Grasmere, Cumbria LA22 9SJ; Jane Darbyshire and David Kendall Ltd, Millmount, Ponteland Road, Newcastle upon Tyne NE5 3AL

DARCY DE KNAYTH, Baroness (18 in line, E 1332); Dame Davina Marcia Ingrams; DBE (1996); da of 17 Baron Darcy de Knayth (Viscount Clive), *né* Hon Mervyn Herbert, 2 s of 4 Earl of Powis by his w (Violet) Countess of Powis, in whose favour the abeyance existing in the Barony of Darcy de Knayth was terminated in 1903, and Vida (d 2003), da of late Capt James Harold Cuthbert, DSO; *b* 10 July 1938; *m* 1 March 1960, Rupert George Ingrams (k in a motor accident 28 Feb 1964), s of late Leonard St Clair Ingrams, OBE, and bro of Richard Ingrams, *qv*; 1 s, 2 da; *Heir* s, Hon Caspar Ingrams; *Career* sits as Independent in House of Lords; *Style*— The Lady Darcy de Knayth, DBE; ✉ Camley Corner, Stubbings, Maidenhead, Berkshire SL6 6QW (tel 01628 822935)

DARELL, Brig Sir Jeffrey Lionel; 8 Bt (GB 1795), of Richmond Hill, Surrey, MC (1945); o s of Col Guy Marsland Darell, MC (d 1947), 3 s of 5 Bt; suc cous, Sir William Oswald Darell, 7 Bt (d 1959); *b* 2 October 1919; *Educ* Eton, RMC Sandhurst; *m* 30 June 1953, Bridget Mary, da of Maj-Gen Sir Allan Henry Shafto Adair, 6 Bt, GCVO, CB, DSO, MC; 2 da (Katherine Mary (Mrs Richard J Astor) b 1954, Camilla Viola (Mrs Henry R T Adeane) b 1956), 1 s (Guy Jeffrey Adair b 1961); *Heir* s, Guy Darell; *Career* Brig (ret) Coldstream Guards, served WWII 1939–45 (The Coats Mission 1940–41), Lt-Col 1957, cmd 1 Bn Coldstream Guards 1957–59, AAG War Office 1959–61, Coll Cdr RMA Sandhurst 1961–64, Regimental Lt-Col cmdg Coldstream Guards 1964, cmd 56 (London) Inf Bde TA 1965–67, vice-pres Regular Commissions Bd 1968–70, Cmdt Mons Officer Cadet Sch 1970–72, ADC to HM The Queen 1973–74; tstee and memb London Law Tst 1981–98; High Sheriff Norfolk 1985–86; *Clubs* Army and Navy, MCC; *Style*— Brig Sir Jeffrey Darell, Bt, MC; ✉ Denton Lodge, Harleston, Norfolk IP20 0AD (tel 01986 788206)

DARESBURY, 4 Baron (UK 1927), of Walton, Co Chester; Sir Peter Gilbert Greenall; 5 Bt (UK 1876), DL (Cheshire 1994); eldest s of 3 Baron Daresbury (d 1996), and his 1 w, Margaret Ada, *née* Crawford; *b* 18 July 1953; *Educ* Eton, Magdalene Coll Cambridge (MA), London Business Sch (Sloan fellowship); *m* 11 Sept 1982, Clare Alison, da of Christopher Nicholas Weatherby, MC, of Whaddon House, Whaddon, Bucks; 4 s (Hon Thomas Edward b 1984, Hon Oliver Christopher b 1986, Hon Toby Peter b 1988, Hon Jonathan James (Jake) b 1992); *Heir* s, Hon Thomas Greenall; *Career* De Vere Group plc (formerly Greenalls Brewery then Greenalls Gp): joined 1977, dir 1984, md 1989, chief exec 1997–99, non-exec chm 1999–2006; chm: Aintree Racecourse Co Ltd 1988–, Highland Gold Mining Ltd 2002–04, Naastar plc; non-exec dir: KazakhGold Gp Ltd 2005–07, Mallett plc 2007–, Jockey Club Racecourses; High Sheriff Cheshire 1992; *Clubs* Jockey, MCC, Royal & Ancient; *Style*— The Lord Daresbury, DL; ✉ Hall Lane Farm, Daresbury, Warrington, Cheshire WA4 4AF (tel 01925 740212); Office tel 01925 740427, fax 01925 740884, e-mail peter.daresbury@daresburyltd.co.uk

DARKE, Christopher; s of late Derek Herbert Darke, and Helen Navina, *née* Davies; *b* 5 August 1949; *m* 1, Marian; 1 s (Cerith James), 1 da (Joanna Siân); m 2, Lorraine Julie; 2 da (Ellen Cordelia, Anna Madeleine); *Career* engrg draughtsman 1970–77, TU offr AUEW-TASS 1977–82, nat offr AUEW-TASS/MSF 1982–92, gen sec Br Air Line Pilots' Assoc (BALPA) 1992–2002, currently gen mangr of regnl servs BMA; memb Competition Cmmn 1998–; *Recreations* flying, travel, reading, gardening; *Style*— Christopher Darke, Esq

DARKE, Geoffrey James; s of Harry James Darke (d 1983), and Edith Annie Darke (d 1973); *b* 1 September 1929; *Educ* Prince Henry's GS, Birmingham Sch of Architecture (DipArch); *m* 1959, Jean Yvonne, da of Edwin Rose (d 1971); 1 s (Christopher), 2 da (Elizabeth, Sarah); *Career* cmmnd RE 1954–56, Malaya; sr architect Stevenage New Town Devpt Corp 1952–58, private practice 1958–61, ptnr Darbourne & Darke Architects and Landscape Planners 1961–87 (work incl several large cmmns, particularly public housing also commercial and civic bldgs), fndr Geoffrey Darke Associates 1987–; successes in nat and int competitions incl: Stuttgart 1977, Hanover 1979, Bolzano 1980, Hanover (Misburg) 1982; memb Union of Int Architects Co-ordinating Gp 1982–93; RIBA: memb Cncl 1977–83, chm Competitions Working Gp 1979–84, memb EC Affrs Ctee 1990–96, RIBA rep Access Ctee for Eng 1992–97; memb Aldeburgh Festival Snape Maltings Fndn 1979–98; ARIBA, FRSA; numerous medals and awards for architectural work; co-recipient (with John Darbourne) Fritz Schumacher award for servs to architecture and town planning (Hamburg) 1978; *Recreations* music; *Style*— Geoffrey Darke, Esq; ✉ Geoffrey Darke Associates, 2 Murray Court, 80 Banbury Road, Oxford OX2 6LQ (tel 01865 514575)

DARKE, Simon Geoffrey; s of Dr Geoffrey Darke (d 1995), of Leicester, and Margaret Winifred, *née* Wadsworth (d 1987); *b* 14 December 1941; *Educ* Downside, London Hosp Med Coll (MB BS, MS, LRCS); *m* 31 Jan 1970, Patricia Elizabeth, da of Philip Wreaks Mason, CBE (d 1975); 1 da (Tiffanie Jane b 18 Aug 1972), 2 s (Nicholas Gregory Simon b 18 June 1974, Christopher Michael Mason b 4 June 1979); *Career* London Hosp: house surgn 1965, rotating surgical resistrar 1969–71, sr registrar 1973–76, lectr professorial surgical unit 1976–77; Addenbrooke's Hosp Cambridge: accident offr 1967–68, sr house offr 1968; surgical registrar Bethnal Green Hosp 1968–69; sr registrar: Whipps Cross Hosp 1972–73, London Hosp 1973–75; conslt vascular and gen surgn: E Dorset Health Authy, Royal Bournemouth Hosp and Poole Gen Hosp 1977–; numerous presentations and lectures to learned socs, numerous pubns in med jls; memb, past pres and former sec Vascular Surgical Soc GB and Ireland, fndr exec memb and former treas Euro Soc Vascular Surgery, memb Assoc of Surgns; MRCP, FRCS; *Publications* contrib book chapters on vascular surgery; *Recreations* golf, fishing, shooting, skiing; *Style*— Simon Darke, Esq; ✉ Royal Bournemouth Hospital, Castle Road East, Bournemouth, Dorset BH7 7DW (tel 01202 303626)

DARLEY, Kevin Paul; s of Clifford Darley, of Wolverhampton, W Midlands, and Dorothy Thelma, *née* Newby; *b* 5 August 1960; *Educ* Colton Hills Comp Sch; *m* 22 Nov 1982, Debby, da of Donald Ford; 2 da (Lianne Kerry b 1983, Gemma Louise b 1988); *Career* flat race jockey; apprenticed to Reg Hollinshead 1976, rode out claim 1978, Champion apprentice 1978 (70 winners); first winner Dust-Up Haydock 1977, first group winner Borushka Gp 2 Park Hill Stakes 1983, Cock of the North (champion northern jockey) 1990, 1992, 1993, 1995, 1997, 1999, 2000, 2001, 2002 and 2003, champion jockey 2000; 158 winners Best Season 2001 (155 winners in 2000), first Gp 1 winner River North Aral Pokal Gp 1 1994, winner first Classic French Derby Chantilly (riding Celtic Swing) 1995, winner first British Classic St Leger (riding Bollin Eric) 2002, 2000 domestic winners as at Oct 2002 (2000th winner Heir to Be), winner 55 Gp races in Britain, winner 17 Gp 1 races; jt pres Jockeys' Assoc 2001–; *Recreations* gardening, listening to music, DIY, shooting, fishing, skiing; *Style*— Kevin Darley, Esq; ✉ Ascot House, Lower Dunsforth, York YO26 9RZ (tel 01423 323611, fax 01423 323891, e-mail kevindarley@btopenworld.com)

DARLEY, Sylvia Juliet; OBE (1987); da of Thomas Bladworth Darley (d 1983), of Cantley Hall, Doncaster, and Gladys Gordon Norrie Darley (d 1987); *b* 15 March 1923; *Educ* Southover Manor Sch Lewes, Doncaster Tech Coll; *Career* served WRNS 1943–46; sec (later mangr) to Sir Malcolm Sargent 1947–67, fndr and chief exec Malcolm Sargent Cancer Fund for Children 1967–95 (pres 1995–), fndr Malcolm Sargent Cancer Fund for Children in Aust (NSW 1984, Victoria 1988, WA1990); dir Charity Christmas Card Cncl (chm 1981–86, dep chm 1986–91); chm Malcolm Sargent Festival Choir; *Recreations* music, cooking, bird watching, organising concerts; *Style*— Miss Sylvia Darley, OBE; ✉ 26 Lamont Road, London SW10 0JE (tel 020 7352 6805)

DARLING, Rt Hon Alistair Maclean; PC (1997), MP; s of Thomas Young Darling (d 1995), and Anna Darling; *b* 28 November 1953; *Educ* Loretto, Univ of Aberdeen (LLB); *m* 12 Nov 1986, Margaret McQueen Vaughan; 1 s (Calum), 1 da (Anna); *Career* slr 1978–82, admitted advocate 1984; memb Lothian Regnl Cncl 1982–87; MP (Lab): Edinburgh Central 1987–2005, Edinburgh SW 2005–; oppn front bench spokesman on: home affairs 1988–92, Treasy and economic affrs 1992–96; chief sec to the Treasy 1997–98 (shadow chief sec 1996–97), sec of state for Social Security 1998–2001, sec of state for Work and Pensions 2001–02, sec of state for Tport 2002–06, sec of state for Scotland 2003–06, sec of state for trade and industry 2006–07, chllr of the Exchequer 2007–; memb Lab Pty's Economic Cmmn 1994–97; govr Napier Coll Edinburgh 1985–87; *Style*— The Rt Hon Alistair Darling, MP; ✉ House of Commons, London SW1A 0AA (tel 020 7219 4584)

DARLING, Sir Clifford; kt (1977), GCVO (1994); s of Charles and Aremelia Darling; *b* 6 February 1922; *Educ* Acklins Public Sch, several public schs in Nassau; *Career* senator 1964–67, dep speaker House of Assembly 1967–69, Min of State 1969, Min of Labour and Welfare 1971, Min of Labour and National Insurance 1974–77, speaker House of Assembly 1977, MP Bahamas 1977–92, Governor-General The Bahamas 1992–94; past chm Tourist Advsy Bd; memb: Masonic Lodge, Elks Lodge; *Style*— Sir Clifford Darling, GCVO; ✉ PO Box N-1050, Nassau, Bahamas

DARLING, 3 Baron (UK 1924); (Robert) Julian Henry Darling; s of 2 Baron Darling (d 2003), and Rosemary, *née* Dickson (d 1997); *b* 29 April 1944, Lyndhurst, Hants; *Educ* Wellington, RAC Cirencester; *m* 1 Oct 1970, Janet Rachel, *née* Mallinson; 2 s (Hon (Robert) James Cyprian b 6 March 1972, Hon (Henry) Thomas Unthank b 27 Aug 1978), 1 da (Hon (Rachel) Pollyanna Margaret b 4 March 1974); *Heir* s, Hon James Darling; *Career* chartered surveyor; ptnr Smith-Woolley 1971–89, sole princ Julian Darling 1990–; md Intwood Farms Ltd 1972–; chm Land Use Panel Nat Trust; chm Great Yarmouth and Waveney MIND, memb Nat Exec Nat Assoc of Official Prison Visitors; G R Judd Prize for Estate Economy 1965, Nuffield scholar 1984; FRICS 1975; *Recreations* fishing, gardening; *Clubs* Norfolk; *Style*— The Rt Hon the Lord Darling; ✉ Intwood Hall, Norwich NR4 6TG (tel 01603 250450, fax 01603 250520, e-mail jdarling@paston.co.uk)

DARLING, Paul Antony; QC (1999); *b* 15 March 1960; *Educ* Tonstall Sch Sunderland, Winchester, St Edmund Hall Oxford (BA, BCL); *Career* called to the Bar 1983, in private practice Keating Chambers 1985–, bencher Middle Temple 2004; ed Construction Law Letter 1991–95, memb editorial team Keating on Building Contracts (edn 5, 6, 7 and 8); lectr on construction and engineering law; chm TECBAR; tstee Free Representation Unit; non-exec dir Horseracing Totalisator Bd 2006–; *Recreations* supporting Newcastle United FC, horse racing; *Style*— Paul Darling, Esq, QC; ✉ Keating Chambers, 15 Essex Street, Outer Temple, London WC2R 3AA (tel 020 7544 2600, fax 020 7544 2700, e-mail pdarling@keatingchambers.com)

DARLINGTON, Gavin Leslie Brook; s of Arthur Brook Darlington, and Pamela Leslie, *née* Roberts; *b* 27 June 1949; *Educ* Rugby, Downing Coll Cambridge (LLB); *m* 11 April 1977, Pavla Ann, da of Karel Kucek; 1 s (Nicholas James b 7 Jan 1986), 1 da (Georgina Ruth b 19 Nov 1989); *Career* Freshfields: articled clerk 1972–74, asst slr 1974–80, ptnr 1980–2005, head of corp law London 1996–99 and Paris 1999–2002, global head of corp law 2003–05; memb Law Soc; *Recreations* gardening, golf, swimming, theatre, cinema; *Style*— Gavin Darlington, Esq

DARLINGTON, Jonathan Philip; s of John Oliver Darlington, of Kidderminster, and Bernice Constance Elizabeth, *née* Murphy; *b* 1 February 1956; *Educ* King's Sch Worcester, Univ of Durham, Royal Acad of Music; *m* 1, 8 Dec 1979 (m dis 1999), Katherine Theresa, da of Lt Col Anthony Wynter Lister; 2 s (William John Anthony b 8 Aug 1988, Edmund Harry b 2 April 1992); m 2, 1 June 2003, Clotilde Vayer; 1 s (Max Virgil Louis David b 19 April 2003); *Career* conductor and pianist; has conducted various major orchs and opera cos, particularly in France, given numerous concerts as pianist and chamber musician; dep music dir Paris Opera 1992–94, music dir Vancouver Opera and Duisburg Philharmonic 2002–; first res conductor Düsseldorf Opera 1997–, princ guest conductor Deutsche Oper am Rhein 1998–; conductor: The Marriage of Figaro (Paris Opera debut) 1991, A Midsummer Night's Dream (Paris Opera, also tour to Bolshoi) 1991, The Barber of Seville (Paris Opera), Swan Lake (Paris Opera, also video recording) 1992, The Nutcracker (Paris Opera) 1993, The Magic Flute (Paris Opera) 1994, Das Lied von der Erde (Paris Opera) 1994, Marriage of Figaro (Lausanne) 1995, Metropolitan Opera NY (with Paris Opera Ballet) 1996, Barber of Seville (Lausanne) 1997, Katya Kabanova (Deutsche Oper am Rhein) 1997, La Cerentola (Deutsche Oper) 1997, Tosca (Deutsche Oper), Der Freischutz (Deutsche Oper), Madame Butterfly (Deutsche Oper) 1997, Tamerlano (Deutsche Oper) 1997, L'Elisir d'Amore (Lausanne Opera) 1998, Matrimonio Segreto (Lausanne Opera) 1998, Le Finta Giardiniera (Deutsche Oper am Rhein) 1998, Jenufa (Deutsche Oper) 1998, Cosi fan Tutte (Lausanne Opera) 1998, The Rake's Progress (Lausanne Opera) 1999, Cosi fan Tutte (Naples Opera) 1999, Haydn's Orfeo (Lausanne Opera) 1999, Alcina (Deutsche Oper am Rhein) 1999, Romeo et Juliette (Bordeaux Opera) 2000, Freischutz (Lausanne Opera) 2000, Cenerentola (Lausanne Opera) 2001, The Marriage of Figaro (Vancouver Opera) 2001, Macbeth (Bordeaux Opera) 2002, Cunning Little Vixen (TCE Paris) 2002, La Boheme (Vancouver Opera) 2003, Eugene Onegin (ENO) 2005, Traviata (ENO) 2006, La Clemenzia di Tito (Opera Australia) 2006; Chevalier de l'Ordre des Arts et des Lettres (France) 1992; *Recreations* mountaineering, skiing, wind-surfing, reading, chamber music; *Style*— Jonathan Darlington, Esq

DARLINGTON, Stephen Mark; s of John Oliver Darlington, MBE, and Bernice Constance Elizabeth, *née* Murphy; *b* 21 September 1952; *Educ* King's Sch Worcester, ChCh Oxford (MA); *m* 12 July 1975, Moira Ellen, da of Noel Edward Lionel Hill; 3 da (Rebecca b 1979, Hannah b 1981, Olivia b 1985); *Career* asst organist Canterbury Cathedral 1974–78, master of music St Albans Abbey 1978–85, artistic dir Int Organ Festival 1979–85, organist and student in music ChCh Oxford and lectr Univ of Oxford 1985–; pres RCO 1998–2000; DMus (Lambeth, Oxford) 2001; FRCO; *Recreations* travel, wine, canoeing; *Style*— Dr Stephen Darlington; ✉ Christ Church, Oxford OX1 1DP (tel 01865 276195)

DARNELL, Jennie; da of John Darnell, and Jean, *née* Martin; *Educ* Richmond-upon-Thames Coll, Royal Holloway and Bedford New Coll London (BA), Univ of Sheffield (MA); *Career* freelance theatre and television dir; previously assoc dir: West Yorkshire Playhouse 1995–96, Plymouth Theatre Royal 1996–2007, Hampstead Theatre 2001–04; winner Regnl Theatre Young Dirs Scheme Central TV 1993; patron Scene and Heard; *Recreations* travel, cinema; *Style*— Ms Jennie Darnell; ✉ c/o Clare Vidal-Hall Agency, 57 Carthew Road, London W6 0DU

DARNLEY, 11 Earl of (I 1725); Adam Ivo Stuart Bligh; sits as Baron Clifton of Leighton (E 1608); also Baron Clifton of Rathmore (I 1721), Viscount Darnley (I 1723); s of 9 Earl of Darnley (d 1955), and his 3 w, Rosemary, da of late Basil Potter; suc half-bro, 10 Earl, 1980; *b* 8 November 1941; *Educ* Harrow, ChCh Oxford; *m* 14 Oct 1965, Susan Elaine, JP, da of Sir Donald Forsyth Anderson (d 1973), by his w Margaret, sis of Sir Harry Llewellyn, 3 Bt, CBE, DL (d 1999); 1 s (Ivo Donald Stuart, Lord Clifton of Rathmore b 1968), 1 da (Lady Katherine Amanda b 1971); *Heir* s, Lord Clifton of Rathmore; *Style*— The Rt Hon Earl of Darnley; ✉ Netherwood Manor, Tenbury Wells, Worcestershire WR15 8RT

DARROCH, His Hon Judge Alasdair; s of Ronald George Darroch (d 1957), and Diana Graburn Smith (d 1992); *b* 18 February 1947; *Educ* Harrow, Trinity Coll Cambridge; *m* 15 July 1972, Elizabeth Lesley, *née* Humphrey; 1 s (Gordon b 30 July 1974); *Career* admitted slr 1971; ptnr Mills & Reeve 1974 (articles 1969–71), recorder 1998, circuit judge (SE Circuit) 2000–; past pres Norwich and Norfolk Law Soc; tstee St Raphael Club Norwich; *Recreations* gardening, antique collecting, real ale; *Style*— His Hon Judge Darroch; ✉ Norwich Combined Court, Bishopgate, Norwich, Norfolk NR3 1UR

DARROCH, (Nigel) Kim; CMG (1997); s of Alastair Macphee Darroch, and Enid Thompson; step s of Monica, *née* Davis; *b* 30 April 1954, S Stanley, Co Durham; *Educ* Abingdon Sch, Univ of Durham (BSc); *m* 25 March 1978, Vanessa Claire, *née* Jackson; 1 s (Simon Alastair b 25 June 1983), 1 da (Georgina b 17 April 1986); *Career* joined FCO 1976, news dept and planning staff FCO 1976–80, third, second then first sec Tokyo 1980–84, FCO 1985, private sec to Min of State FCO 1986–88, first sec Rome 1989–92, dep head European Integration Dept FCO 1993–95, head E Adriatic Dept FCO 1995–97, cnsllr UK rep to EU 1997–98, head News Dept FCO 1998–2000, dir EU Cmd FCO 2000–02, DG Europe FCO 2003–04, EU advsr to PM and head European Secretariat Cabinet Office 2004–; *Recreations* sailing, cinema, skiing, squash; *Style—* Kim Darroch, Esq, CMG

DART, Geoffrey Stanley; s of Wilfrid Stanley Dart, of Torquay, and Irene Jean, *née* Crews; *b* 2 October 1952; *Educ* Devonport HS, Torquay Boys' GS, St Peter's Coll Oxford (scholar, MA); *m* 17 Aug 1974, Rosemary Penelope, da of late Gordon Frederick Hinton; 1 s (Thomas James b 15 Nov 1978), 1 da (Rebecca Clare b 17 Oct 1980); *Career* civil servant; researcher Electricity Cncl 1974–77, various positions Dept of Energy 1977–84, cabinet sec Cabinet Office 1984–85, princ private sec to Sec of State for Energy 1985–87; Dept of Energy: asst sec Electricity Div 1987–89, asst sec Offshore Safety Div 1989–91, head Finance Branch 1991–92; DTI: asst sec Competitiveness Div 1992–94, dir De-Regulation Unit 1994, head Regnl Devpt Div 1995–96, dir Simplification Project 1996–97, dir Insurance Directorate 1997–98, dir Oil and Gas 1998–2002, head Strategy Unit 2003–05, dir Corporate Law and Governance 2005–; non-exec dir Laing Engineering Ltd 1991–95, dir European Investment Bank 1994–96; FRSA; *Recreations* reading, listening to music, films, football, cricket; *Style—* Geoffrey Dart, Esq; ✉ Department of Trade and Industry, 1 Victoria Street, London SW1H 0ET (tel 020 7215 0206, fax 020 7215 0235, e-mail geoff.dart@dti.gsi.uk)

DARTMOUTH, 10 Earl of (GB 1711); William Legge; also Baron Dartmouth (E 1682) and Viscount Lewisham (GB 1711); s of 9 Earl of Dartmouth (d 1997), and his 1 w (now Raine, Countess Spencer); *b* 23 September 1949; *Educ* Eton, ChCh Oxford, Harvard Business Sch (MBA); *Heir* bro, Hon Rupert Legge; *Career* chm and fndr Kirklees Cable; contested (Cons): Leigh Lancs 1974, Stockport South 1974, European Parl Yorkshire Region 1999; FCA; *Style—* The Rt Hon the Earl of Dartmouth

DARTON, Prof Richard Charles; s of Allan John Darton, and Beryl Clare, *née* Davies; *b* 1 July 1948; *Educ* King's Sch Rochester (King's scholar), Univ of Birmingham (BSc), Downing Coll Cambridge (PhD); *m* 27 April 1974, Diana Mildred, da of Alan Theophilus Warrell; 2 s (Nicholas John b 3 Aug 1976, Thomas Charles b 15 Jan 1978), 1 da (Frances Clare b 27 Feb 1982); *Career* ICI postdoctoral res fell Univ of Cambridge 1973–75; various appointments Shell Int Petroleum The Netherlands 1975–91, on secondment Shell UK 1991; prof Dept of Engrg Science Univ of Oxford 2000– (head of dept 2004–), reader in chemical engrg, sr research fell and tutor Keble Coll Oxford 2001–; Stephen Anderman visiting lectr: Mendelev Univ 1999, Kurnakov Inst Moscow 1999, Univ of St Petersburg 2000; Cncl Medal IChemE 2005 (dep pres 2007–08); hon memb Czech Soc of Chemical Engrg 2000; memb American Chemical Soc 1997; FIChemE 1987, FREng 2000; *Recreations* Scottish country dancing, reading history; *Style—* Prof Richard Darton; ✉ 3 Cameron Avenue, Abingdon, Oxfordshire OX14 3SR (tel 01235 526069); University of Oxford, Department of Engineering Science, Parks Road, Oxford OX1 3PJ (tel 01865 273002, fax 01865 283310, e-mail richard.darton@eng.ox.ac.uk)

DARVILL, Keith; s of Ernest Darvill (d 1989), and Ellen, *née* Clark; *b* 28 May 1948; *Educ* Norlington Secdy Modern Leytonstone, East Ham Tech Coll, Thurrock Coll of FE, Poly of Central London, Coll of Law Chester; *m* 1971, Julia; 1 da (Nicole b 1974), 2 s (Andrew b 1977, Simon b 1988); *Career* Port of London Authy: various clerical positions 1963–73, asst slr 1973–84; ptnr Duthie Hart and Duthie Solicitors 1984–93, sole practitioner 1993–99, ptnr Kenneth Elliott & Rowe Solicitors 1999–; MP (Lab) Upminster 1997–2001, memb Select Ctee on Procedure 1997–2001; memb: Law Soc 1981–, Soc of Lab Lawyers, Havering Fedn of Community Assocs, T&GWU, Fabian Soc; *Recreations* tennis, badminton, gardening; *Clubs* Cranston Park Lawn Tennis (Upminster); *Style—* Keith Darvill, Esq

DARWALL-SMITH, Lucy Ellen; da of Herbert Francis Eade, and Anne Barbara, *née* Forbes; *b* 1 June 1955; *Educ* Micklefield Sch for Girls; *m* (m dis); 1 da (Daisy b 26 Nov 1985); *Career* assoc dir Lopex 1979–81, chm Darwall Smith Associates Ltd 1981–; MInstD, MRCA; *Recreations* theatre, ballet, food, friends; *Clubs* Commonwealth, Sloane; *Style—* Ms Lucy Darwall-Smith; ✉ Middleham House, Ringmer, Lewes, East Sussex BN8 5EY (tel 01273 813503, fax 01273 814019); Darwall Smith Associates Ltd, 60 Ironmonger Row, London EC1V 3QR (tel 020 7553 3700, fax 020 7553 3701)

DARWALL SMITH, Her Hon Judge Susan Patricia; DL (Bristol 2004); da of George Kenneth Moss, JP (d 1991), and Jean Margaret, *née* Johnston; *b* 27 October 1946; *Educ* Howell's Sch Denbigh; *m* 15 Sept 1968, Simon Crompton Darwall Smith, s of Randle Frederick Hicks Darwall Smith (d 1999); 2 da (Belinda Claire b 1 Aug 1972, Emma Louise b 7 Nov 1974); *Career* called to the Bar Gray's Inn 1968; in practice Western Circuit 1968–92, recorder 1986–92, circuit judge (Western Circuit) 1992–; govr The Redmaids' Sch Bristol 1990–; *Recreations* travel, opera, ballet, theatre, gardening; *Clubs* Army and Navy; *Style—* Her Hon Judge Darwall Smith, DL; ✉ Bristol Crown Court, The Law Courts, Small Street, Bristol BS1 2HL

DARWEN, 3 Baron (UK 1946), of Heys-in-Bowland, W Riding of Yorkshire; Roger Michael Davies; eldest s of 2 Baron Darwen (d 1988), and Kathleen Dora, *née* Walker; *b* 28 June 1938; *Educ* Bootham Sch York; *m* 1961, Gillian Irene, da of Eric G Hardy, of Valley View, Leigh Woods, Bristol; 2 s (Hon Paul b 1962, Hon Benjamin b 1966), 3 da (Hon Sarah b 1963, Hon Naomi b 1965, Hon Mary b 1969); *Heir* s, Hon Paul Davies; *Style—* The Rt Hon the Lord Darwen; ✉ Labourer's Rest, Green Street, Pleshey, Chelmsford, Essex

DARZI OF DENHAM, Baron (Life Peer UK 2007), of Gerrards Cross in the County of Buckinghamshire; Prof Sir Ara Warkes Darzi; KBE (2002); *b* 7 May 1960; *Educ* RCSI (MB, BCh, BAO, LRCPI, LRCSI), TCD (MD); *m* Wendy; 2 c (Freddie, Nina); *Career* conslt surgn Central Middlesex Hosp London 1994–95; currently hon conslt surgn St Mary's Hosp NHS Tst, conslt Royal Marsden Hosp NHS Tst, Paul Hamlyn chair of surgery, head Dept of Surgical Technology and Biosurgery and Divn of Surgery, Oncology, Reproductive Biology and Anaesthesia Faculty of Med Imperial Coll London, hon prof Inst of Cancer Research; min of state Dept of Health 2007–; tutor in gastrointestinal and minimal access surgery RCS 1995–2001; memb Cncl: RSM (Surgical Section) 1995–99, Assoc of Coloproctology GB representing AESGBI 1997–99; sec and memb Cncl Soc of Minimal Invasive Therapy 1998–99; chm London Modernisation Bd 2000–03; memb: Policy and Evaluation Advsy Gp The Nuffield Tst 1997–2001, Steering Ctee (Cncl) Surgical Research Soc (SRS) 1998, Educn Bd Raven Dept of Educn RCS 1998–, Steering Ctee of New and Emerging Application of Technologies NHS Exec Health, Tech R&D 1999–, Educn Ctee Euro Assoc of Endoscopic Surgeons (EAES) 1999–, Modernisation Action Gp NHS Exec Dept of Health (Profession and NHS Force) 2000–03; EPSRC memb Integrated Healthcare Technologies Sector Programme Ctee, parly advsr to Health Select Ctee, memb MRC Research Panel; research in all aspects of minimal access surgery and allied technologies incl robotic surgery; Hunterian prof RCS 1997–98, James IV travelling fell 1999–2000, Robert Smith Lecture, Zachary Cope Lecture, Sylvester O'Halron Lecture, Sir Peter Freyer Lecture, Hunterian e-Master Class, Farady Lecture; FACS, FRCS, FRCSI, FCGI, FRCSEd, Hon FRCPGlas, FMedSci, Hon FREng; *Publications* author of over 300 papers and 5 books; reviewer for: Br Jl of Surgery, Annals of Surgery, Surgery; *Clubs* Athenaeum, Mossimans; *Style—* Prof the Lord Darzi of Denham, KBE; ✉ Imperial College London, St Mary's Hospital, South Wharf Road, London W2 1NY (tel 020 7886 1310, fax 020 7413 0470, e-mail a.darzi@imperial.ac.uk)

DAS, Dr Sankar Kumar; s of D Das (d 1974), of Calcutta, India, and late Nilima, *née* Roy Chondbury; *b* 1 December 1933; *Educ* Univ of Calcutta (MB BS); *m* 26 Nov 1977, Enakshi, da of P K Roy (d 1976); 1 s (Shumit b 1 June 1979), 1 da (Priya b 27 Feb 1984); *Career* med registrar Victoria Hosp Blackpool 1964–66, fell of internal, chest and nuclear med and asst instr in med VA Hosp Milwaukee 1966–69, sr med registrar King's Coll Hosp and St Francis Hosp London 1970–74; conslt physician in geriatric med: Manor Hosp Derby and Derby City Hosp 1974–77, St Helier Gp Hosp and London Borough of Sutton 1977–; hon sr lectr Univ of London 1977–, recognised teacher St George's Hosp Tooting 1977–; conslt Specialists' Assoc; inventor of: hind paddle walker Mark I, II and III, exercising machine, DAK mobile Mark I and II walking frames, disc computer for analytical prog on geriatric med, clinical audi urinary incontinence gadgets (male and female); memb Panel on Residential Accommodation Sutton Borough; Mother India Int Award for servs to the elderly and disabled people in the UK 1989, Man of the Year (American Biographical Assoc) for servs to the elderly 1990; memb: Br Geriatric Soc 1966, NY Acad of Sciences 1992, Royal Inst of GB, Br Geriatric Soc, American Coll of Chest Physicians; fell: Int Biographical Assoc 1980, Int Youth in Achievement 1980; FRSH 1966, FRCP 1974 (MRCP), FCCP (USA) 1974; *Publications* Lecture Notes on Medical Infirmities, Europe (1981), Fits, Faints and Falls (1985), contrib to med jls and author of papers on computers in medicine; *Recreations* flying, polo, horse riding, cricket; *Style—* Dr Sankar Das; ✉ 62 Rose Hill, Sutton, Surrey SM1 3EX (tel 020 8644 1639); St Helier Hospital, Wrythe Lane, Carshalton, Surrey SM5 1AA (tel 020 8644 4343)

DASGUPTA, Prof Sir Partha Sarathi; kt (2002); s of Prof Amiya Dasgupta (d 1992), of Santiniketan, India, and Shanti, *née* Dasgupta (d 2001); *b* 17 November 1942; *Educ* Univ of Delhi (BSc), Univ of Cambridge (BA, Stevenson prize, PhD); *m* 29 June 1968, Carol Margaret, da of Prof James Edward Meade (d 1995); 2 da (Zubeida b 11 Jan 1974, Aisha b 3 July 1983), 1 s (Shamik b 13 Aug 1977); *Career* supernumery fell Trinity Hall Cambridge 1971–74 (research fell 1968–71); LSE: lectr 1971–75, reader 1975–78, prof of economics 1978–84; Univ of Cambridge: prof of economics 1985–, fell St John's Coll Cambridge 1985–, Frank Ramsay prof of economics 1994–; prof of economics, prof of philosophy and dir Programme in Ethics in Society Stanford Univ 1989–92; visiting asst prof Carnegie-Mellon Univ 1968–69, visiting fell Delhi Sch of Economics 1970–71, Ford visiting prof Inst of Economic Growth Univ of Delhi 1981; visiting prof: Jawaharlal Nehru Univ 1978, Stanford Univ 1983–84 (visiting assoc prof 1974–75), Harvard Univ 1987, Princeton Univ 1988; Royal Economic Soc: memb Cncl 1988–93, pres 1998–2001; European Economic Assoc: memb Cncl 1989–93, pres 1999; memb Cncl: Econometric Soc 1984–90, European Soc for Populaton Economics 1987–91; assoc ed: Jl of Development Economics 1972–76, Social Choice and Welfare 1984–96, Jl of Environmental Economics and Management 1985–89; memb Advsy Bd Environment and Development Economics 1996–; memb Panel of Experts of Environmental Health WHO 1975–85, prog dir for applied economic theory and econometrics Centre for Public Policy Research London 1984–86 (research fell 1983–93), research advsr UNU/World Inst for Devpt Economics 1991–94, memb Scientific Bd Santa Fe Inst 1991–96, chm Beijer Int Inst of Ecological Economics Royal Swedish Acad of Sciences 1991–97, sr research fell Inst for Policy Reform Washington DC 1992–94; foreign hon memb American Acad of Arts and Sciences 1991, foreign memb Royal Swedish Acad of Sciences 1991, hon fell LSE 1994, hon memb American Economic Assoc 1997, memb Pontifical Acad of Soc Scis 1998, foreign assoc US Nat Acad of Scis 2001, fell Third World Acad of Sci 2002, foreign memb American Philosophical Soc 2005; fell Econometric Soc 1975; Volvo Environment Prize (jtly with K G Mäler) 2002, John Kenneth Galbraith Award American Agricultural Economics Assoc 2007; Dr (hc): Wageningen Univ 2000, Catholic Univ of Louvain 2007; FBA 1989, FRS 2004; *Books* Guidelines for Project Evaluation (with S A Marglin and A K Sen, 1972), Economic Theory and Exhaustible Resources (with G M Heal, 1979), The Control of Resources (1982), Environmental Decision-Making (jt ed, 1984), Economic Organizations as Games (jt ed, 1986), The Economics of Bargainning (jt ed, 1987), An Inquiry into Well-Being and Destitution (1993), The Environment and Emerging Development Issues (jt ed with K-G Maler, 1997), Human Well-Being and the Natural Environment (2001); author of numerous articles in jls, lectrs and reviews; *Clubs* MCC; *Style—* Prof Sir Partha Dasgupta, FBA, FRS; ✉ 1 Dean Drive, Holbrook Road, Cambridge CB1 7SW (tel 01223 212179); University of Cambridge, Sidgwick Avenue, Faculty of Economics, Cambridge CB3 9DD (tel 01223 335207)

DASHWOOD, Sir Edward John Francis; 12 Bt (Premier Bt of GB, cr 1707), of West Wycombe, Buckinghamshire; s (by 1 m) of Sir Francis John Vernon Hereward Dashwood, 11 Bt (d 2000); *b* 25 September 1964; *Educ* Eton, Univ of Reading (BSc); *m* 10 April 1989, Lucinda Nell, o da of Gerrard Herman Francis Miesegaes and Mrs D Parker; 1 da (Victoria Lucinda b 21 March 1991), 2 s (George Francis b 17 June 1992, Robert Edward b 15 Nov 1993); *Heir* s, George Dashwood; *Career* land agent, landowner; ARICS; *Recreations* shooting, fishing, tennis; *Style—* Sir E J F Dashwood, Bt; ✉ West Wycombe Park, Buckinghamshire (tel 01494 524412, fax 01494 471617)

DASHWOOD, Sir Richard James; 9 Bt (E 1684), of Kirtlington Park, Oxfordshire, TD (1987); s of Sir Henry George Massy Dashwood, 8 Bt (d 1972), and Susan Mary (d 1985), da of late Maj Victor Robert Montgomerie-Charrington; *b* 14 February 1950; *Educ* Eton; *m* 1984 (m dis 1993), Kathryn Ann er da of Frank Mahon, of Eastbury, Berks; 1 s (Frederick George Mahon b 1988); *Heir* s, Frederick Dashwood; *Career* Lt 14/20 King's Hussars 1969, TA & VR 1973–94 (Major 1992); ptnr Harris Allday Stockbrokers; *Clubs* Boodle's; *Style—* Sir Richard Dashwood, Bt; ✉ Ledwell Cottage, Sandford St Martin, Oxfordshire OX7 7AN (tel 01608 683267)

DATTA, Dr Shreelata; da of T Datta, and M Datta; *b* 1979, London; *Educ* St Albans HS for Girls (scholar), Imperial Coll Sch of Medicine London (BSc, MB BS, Arthur Macey scholar, travelling scholar); *Career* house offr Hemel Hempstead Gen Hosp and Queen Mary's Hosp 2003–04, SHO Queen Charlotte's and Chelsea Hosp and Hillingdon Hosp 2004–; memb: Exec Ctee Medical Women's Fedn 2003–, Cncl BMA 2004– (jr drs rep Obstetrics and Gynaecology Central Conslts and Specialists Ctee and Medico-Legal Ctee); advsr: Elsevier Sciences 1999–, Oxford Univ Press 1999–, Blackwell Sciences 1999–, Unimed Sciences Publishing 2003–; *Publications* Oxford Handbook of the Foundation Programme (co-author, 2005); *Recreations* travel, mystery shopping, tennis; *Style—* Dr Shreelata Datta; ✉ British Medical Association, BMA House Tavistock Square, London WC1H 9JP

DAUBENEY, Philip Edward Giles; s of Cyril Walter Philip Daubeney (d 1969), and Emily Margaret, *née* Gleed; *b* 27 March 1938; *Educ* Hardye's Sch Dorchester, Balliol Coll Oxford (MA); *m* 12 Aug 1961, Heather Margaret; 1 s (Piers Edward Francis b 25 March 1964), 1 da (Clare Elizabeth b 19 April 1966); *Career* served: Parachute Regt 1956–58 (Nat Serv 2 Lt), TA (Maj); ICI 1961–93 (ceo ICI India 1983–90, regnl chief exec ICI African and Eastern Region 1990–93), chief exec Electricity Assoc 1993–2002, chm JP Morgan Fleming Indian Investment Tst 2002–, chm EAQA Ltd 2002–; chm: South Africa Business Assoc 1993–95, South Africa Area Advsy Gp BOTB 1993–95, Int Air Compressor Mfrs Assoc 2002–; *Recreations* gardening, shooting, watercolours; *Clubs* Oxford and Cambridge; *Style—* Philip Daubeney, Esq; ✉ Durmast House, Burley, Hampshire BH24 4AT

DAUBNEY, Christopher Paul (Chris); s of Rev Kenneth Crocker Daubney (d 1992), of Alton, Hants, and Evelyn Blanche, *née* Knight (d 1987); *b* 14 September 1942; *Educ* Clifton, St

D

John's Coll Cambridge (MA); *m* 23 Sept 1995, Vanessa; *Career* various posts BBC 1964–73; IBA: princ engr quality control 1973–81, head of quality control 1981–83, head of engrg info servs 1984–87, head Engrg Secretariat 1987, asst dir of engrg (policy and projects) 1987–88; chief engr Channel 4 1988–96, dir of strategic planning Samsung Electronics Research Inst 1996–97, md Panasonic Broadcast Europe 1998–99 (sr dir 1997–98), owner The Daubney Consultancy 1999–; CEng 1973, FIEE 1990 (MIEE 1973), MIOA 1978; *Recreations* walking, music, cooking, do-it-yourself, family life; *Style*— Chris Daubney, Esq; ✉ tel 01494 671482, fax 01494 671482, e-mail chris@daubney.plus.com

DAUNCEY, Brig Michael Donald Keen; DSO (1945), DL (Gloucester 1983); s of Thomas Gough Dauncey (d 1965), of Crowthorne, Berks, and Alice, *née* Keen (d 1988); the name Dauncey was first recorded in Uley, Glos, c1200s; *b* 11 May 1920; *Educ* King Edward's Sch Birmingham; *m* 1945, Marjorie Kathleen, da of Hubert William Neep (d 1967); 1 s (John), 2 da (Gillian, (Margaret) Joy); *Career* cmmnd 22nd (Cheshire) Regt 1941, seconded to Glider Pilot Regt 1943, Arnhem 1944 (wounded, taken prisoner, later escaped), MA to GOC-in-C Greece 1946–47, seconded to Para Regt 1947–49, Staff Coll 1950, instr RMA Sandhurst 1957–58, CO 1st Bn 22 (Cheshire) Regt 1963–66 (BAOR and UN Peace-keeping Force Cyprus), DS Plans JSSC 1966–68, Cmdt Jungle Warfare Sch 1968–69, Cmdt Support Weapons Wing Sch of Inf Netheravon 1969–72, Brig 1973, def and mil attaché Br Embassy Madrid 1973–75, ret from Army 1976; Col 22nd (Cheshire) Regt 1978–85, Hon Col 1 Cadet Bn Glos Regt (ACF) 1981–90; pres The Glider Pilot Regtl Assoc 1994–98; ldr The Airborne Pilgrimage to Arnhem 2000, pres Double Hills Arnhem Commemoration 1978 1999–; *Recreations* travelling, tennis, under-gardener; *Clubs* Army and Navy; *Style*— Brig Michael Dauncey, DSO, DL; ✉ Uley Lodge Coach House, Uley, Dursley, Gloucestershire GL11 5SN (tel 01453 860216)

DAUNTON, Prof Martin James; s of Ronald James Daunton, and Dorothy May, *née* Bellett; *b* 7 February 1949; *Educ* Barry GS for Boys, Univ of Nottingham (BA), Univ of Kent (PhD), Univ of Cambridge (LittD); *m* 1984, Claire Hilda Gabriel, da of Philip Gobbi; *Career* lectr in economic history Univ of Durham 1973–79, successively lectr, reader and then Astor prof of Br history UCL 1979–97; Univ of Cambridge: prof of economic history 1997–, fell Churchill Coll 1997–2004, chm Faculty of History 2001–2003, chm Sch of Humanities and Social Sciences 2003–05, master Trinity Hall 2004–; visiting fell ANU 1985 and 1994, visiting prof Nihon Univ 2000; chm Inst of Historical Research 1994–98, tstee Nat Maritime Museum 2002–; vice-pres Royal Historical Soc 1996–2000 (hon treas 1986–91); convenor Editorial Bd Studies in History 1994–2000, conslt ed Oxford DNB 1993–98; FRHistS 1980 (pres 2004–), FBA 1997; *Books* Coal Metropolis: Cardiff 1870–1914 (1977), House and Home in the Victorian City (1983), Royal Mail: The Post Office Since 1840 (1985), A Property Owning Democracy? (1987), Progress and Poverty: An Economic & Social History of Britain 1700–1850 (1995), Trusting Leviathan: The Politics of Taxation in Britain, 1799–1914 (2001), Just Taxes: The Politics of Taxation in Britain 1914–79 (2002), Wealth and Welfare: An Economic and Social History of Britain 1851–1951 (2007); *Recreations* architectural tourism, collecting modern ceramics, walking; *Clubs* Reform, Oxford and Cambridge; *Style*— Prof Martin Daunton, FBA; ✉ Trinity Hall, Trinity Lane, Cambridge CB2 1TJ (tel 01223 332540, fax 01223 332537, e-mail mjd42@cam.ac.uk)

DAVAN WETTON, Hilary John; s of Eric Davan Wetton, CBE (d 1986), of Nairn, and Valerie, *née* Edwards (d 1970); *b* 23 December 1943; *Educ* Westminster, Royal Coll of Music, BNC Oxford; *m* 1, 19 Sept 1964, Elizabeth Jane Tayler; 3 da (Charlotte, b 1966, Venetia b 1969, Fenella b 1972); m 2, 5 Jan 1989, Alison Mary Moncrieff, da of Prof Alexander Kelly; 1 s (Alexander b 1991), 1 da (Camilla b 1995); *Career* dir of music: St Albans Sch 1965–67, Cranleigh Sch 1967–74, Stantonbury Educn Campus and Music Centre 1974–79, St Paul's Girls Sch 1979–94, Tonbridge Sch 1994–; conductor: St Albans Choral Soc 1965–67, Guildford Choral Soc 1968–, Woking Symphony Orch 1971–74, Milton Keynes Chorale 1974–79, Milton Keynes City Orch (formerly Chamber Orch) 1975–, The Holst Singers of London 1978–91, Birmingham Schs' Symphony Orch 1983–85, Scottish Schs' Orch 1984–95, Buckinghamshire Youth Orch 1985–89, Wren Orch 1989–, Canticum 1992–94, Edinburgh Youth Orch 1994–97; guest conductor with orchs in Australia, Bulgaria, Denmark, Iceland, Norway, Singapore and USA; performances on Radio 3 (with Ulster Orch and BBC Concert Orch), BBC 2 and Thames Television; conslt for Classic FM Masterclass 1994–97; author of articles in Music and Musicians, Musical Times, Choir and Organ and Classic FM Magazine; Hon MA Open Univ 1983, Hon DMus De Montfort Univ 1994; memb RSA; *Recordings* with LPO 1988: Mozart Jupiter Symphony, Holst Planets, Elgar Enigma Variations; other recordings incl: Vaughan Williams 5 Tudor Portraits and Holst Golden Goose (with Philharmonia and Guildford Choral Soc), Holst Choral Symphony (with RPO and Guildford Choral Soc, winner of Diapason D'Or 1994), works by Britten, Bliss and Holst (with Holst Singers), 5 CDs of 19th century British symphonists (with Milton Keynes City Orch); *Recreations* tennis; *Clubs* Garrick; *Style*— Hilary Davan Wetton, Esq; ✉ c/o Richard Haigh, Performing Arts Management, 6 Windmill Street, London W1P 1HF (tel 020 7255 1362, fax 020 7631 4631)

DAVENPORT, *see also:* Bromley-Davenport

DAVENPORT, Hugo Benedick; s of (Arthur) Nigel Davenport, and Helena Margaret, *née* White (d 1979); *b* 6 June 1953; *Educ* Westminster, Univ of Sussex (BA); *m* 10 Aug 1988, Sarah, da of Hugh Mollison; 1 s, 1 da; *Career* Visnews Ltd 1976–77, Liverpool Daily Post and Echo 1977–80, freelance journalist 1980–81, NI corr The Observer 1984–85 (reporter and feature writer 1981–84), feature writer Mail on Sunday 1985–87, film critic Daily Telegraph 1989–96 (news feature writer 1987–89), freelance writer-broadcaster 1996–97, ed FT New Media Markets 1998–2000, launch ed Broadband Media 2002–; memb Hon Advsy Devpt Bd Booktrust 2003; prize for population and environmental reporting Population Inst Washington 1988; FRSA 2003; *Books* Days that Shook the World (2003); *Recreations* reading, walking, drawing, music; *Style*— Hugo Davenport, Esq; ✉ 6 Ann's Close, Kinnerton Street, London SW1X 8EG (tel and fax 020 7235 0559); Office: (tel 020 7017 4247, e-mail hugo1@btconnect.com)

DAVENPORT, Ian Richard; s of Ellis Davenport, of Cheshire, and Shirley, *née* Silk; *b* 8 July 1966; *Educ* King's GS Macclesfield, Goldsmiths Coll London (BA), Northwich Coll of Art and Design; *m* 6 July 2004, Sue Arrowsmith; *Career* artist; exhibited Freeze (Surrey Docks London) 1988, retrospective (Ikon Birmingham) 2004; Contemporary Art Soc cmmn for wall painting at Univ of Warwick 2004, Western Bridge Southwark St cmmn; *Awards* prizewinner John Moores 21 Liverpool Exhibition 1999, prizewinner Primo del Golfo La Spezia Italy 2000, winner Prospects Essor Project Space London 2002; nominated Turner Prize 1991; *Recreations* arts, music, walking, cooking; *Style*— Ian Davenport, Esq; ✉ Waddington Galleries, 11 Cork Street, London W1S 3LT

DAVENPORT, Ian Richard; s of Martin Robert Davenport, of Cannes, France, and Ann Maxwell, *née* Fyfe (d 2000); *b* 27 May 1960, Chicoutimi, Canada; *Educ* Bloxham Sch, Univ of Durham (BA); *m* 1987, Katherine, *née* Bates; 1 s (Samuel b 1995), 1 da (Ella b 1999); *Career* Arthur Andersen & Co 1983–85, Morgan Stanley Int Ltd 1985–87, Kleinwort Benson 1987–88, St George's Coll Weybridge 1988–92, Radley Coll 1992–2004, headmaster Blundell's Sch 2004–; memb HMC 2004; author of articles in Politics Assoc jls; *Recreations* American political biographies, fell running, skiing, opera, contemporary music; *Clubs* East India, Lansdowne, Jesters; *Style*— Ian Davenport, Esq; ✉ Blundell's School, Tiverton, Devon EX16 4DN (tel 01884 232301, fax 01884 243232, e-mail headmaster@blundells.org)

DAVENPORT, Jack; s of Nigel Davenport, and Maria Aitken; *b* 1 March 1973, Wimbledon; *Educ* Cheltenham Coll, UEA; *m* 2000, Michelle Gomez; *Career* actor; *Theatre* incl: The Tempest, Hamlet, The Servant, Lady Windermere's Fan, How to Lose Friends and Alienate People, Enemies; *Radio* A Clockwork Orange 1998; *Television* incl: This Life 1996, The Moth 1997, Macbeth 1998, Ultraviolet 1998, The Wyvern Mystery 2000, Coupling 2000–02, Swingtown 2007; *Film* incl: Fierce Creatures 1997, Talos the Mummy 1998, The Wisdom of Crocodiles 1998, The Talented Mr Ripley 1999, The Cookie Thief 1999, Not Afraid Not Afraid 2001, The Bunker 2001, The Pirates of the Caribbean: The Curse of the Black Pearl 2003, The Pirates of the Caribbean: Dead Man's Chest 2006, Pirates of the Caribbean: At World's End 2007, The Key Man 2007; *Style*— Jack Davenport, Esq; ✉ c/o Hamilton Hodell, Fifth Floor, 66–68 Margaret Street, London W1W 8SR

DAVENPORT, Prof John; s of William Kenneth Davenport, of Coventry, and Eda Bessie, *née* Taylor; *b* 12 February 1946; *Educ* Bablake Sch Coventry, St Mary's Hosp Med Sch, Univ of London (BSc, DSc), Univ of Southampton (MSc), UC Wales (PhD); *m* 1970, Julia Lesley, *née* Ladner; 2 da (Emma b 9 Nov 1973, Kate b 19 April 1976); *Career* demonstrator Dept of Marine Biology UC Wales 1970–72; Unit of Marine Invertebrate Biology NERC: higher scientific offr 1972–74, sr scientific offr 1974–80, princ scientific offr 1980–83; UCNW: sr lectr Sch of Animal Biology 1987–88 (lectr 1983–87), reader Sch of Ocean Sciences 1989–91 (sr lectr 1988–89); dir Univ Marine Biological Station and chair Marine Biology Univ of London 1991–99; prof and head: Dept of Zoology and Animal Ecology UC Cork 1999–, Dept Zoology, Ecology and Plant Science 2002–; dir Environmental Res Inst UC Cork 2000–02; MRIA 2001; FIBiol 1987, FRSE 1995; *Books* Animal Osmoregulation (with J C Rankin, 1981), Environmental Stress and Behavioural Adaptation (1985), Animal Life at Low Temperature (1992), Aquaculture: The Ecological Issues (jtly, 2003); author of numerous articles in scientific jls; *Recreations* skiing, sailboarding, walking, birding; *Style*— Prof John Davenport, FRSE; ✉ e-mail jdavenport@zoology.ucc.ie

DAVENPORT-HINES, Dr Richard Peter Treadwell; s of John Hines (d 2003), and June Pearson, *née* Treadwell; *b* 21 June 1953, London; *Educ* St Paul's, Selwyn Coll Cambridge (exhibitioner, MA, PhD); *m* 20 May 1978, Frances Jane, *née* Davenport; 2 s (Hugo Denzil Rufus b 11 Oct 1983, Cosmo Rory Hector Albertyn b 14 June 1986); *Career* historian; res fell LSE 1982–86, freelance historian and reviewer 1986–; res assoc Oxford DNB 1995–2004, tstee London Library 1996–2005; Wolfson Prize for History and Biography 1985, Wadsworth Prize for History 1986; FRHistS 1984, FRSL 2005; *Publications* Dudley Docker (1984), Speculators and Patriots (ed, 1986), Business in the Age of Reason (ed, 1987), British Business in Asia since 1860 (ed, 1989), Sex, Death and Punishment (1990), The Macmillans (1992), Glaxo (1992), Vice (1993), Auden (1995), Gothic (1998), The Pursuit of Oblivion (2001), A Night at the Majestic (2006), Hugh Trevor-Roper's Letters from Oxford (ed, 2006), Ettie: The Life and Friendships of Lady Desborough (2008); *Clubs* Athenaeum; *Style*— Richard Davenport-Hines, Esq; ✉ 51 Elsham Road, London W14 8HD

DAVENTRY, 4 Viscount (UK 1943) James Edward FitzRoy Newdegate; s of 3 Viscount Daventry, JP, DL (d 2000); gf assumed the additional surname of Newdegate by Royal Licence 1936; *b* 27 July 1960; *Educ* Milton Abbey, RAC Cirencester; *m* 10 Sept 1994, Georgia, yr da of John Stuart Lodge, of Daglingworth Place, Cirencester, Glos; 1 s (Humphrey John b 23 Nov 1995), 2 da (Hester Anne b 31 Dec 1997, Sophia Hebe b 8 March 2001); *Career* dir R K Harrison Insurance Brokers Ltd; *Recreations* shooting, fishing, racing, golf, farming, occasional gardening; *Clubs* White's, Turf, MCC; *Style*— The Rt Hon the Viscount Daventry; ✉ Arbury, Nuneaton, Warwickshire CV10 7PT

DAVEY, Andrew Paul (Andy); s of Peter Anthony Cecil Davey, of Bristol, and Joan Venville, of Alverstoke, Hants; *b* 12 July 1962; *Educ* W Sussex Coll of Design, RCA (MDes); *Children* 1 s (Joseph Stephen b 4 Feb 2002), 1 da (Eleanor Grace b 18 Jan 2005); *Career* product designer fndr princ TKO Product Design Consultants London 1990–; clients incl: Seiko, Yamaha, Tomy, Olympus, Honda; lectr on design issues at various venues incl Japan; featured in various articles and pubns incl: AXIS (int design magazine Japan), The I.D. 40 (int design magazine NY) 1996 and Terence Conran on Design 1996, The Design Museum Directory of 20th Century Design 1997, The International Design Yearbook 1998, 2000 and 2001, The Product Book (D&AD) 1999, Design Report (int design magazine South Korea) 2000, Power of Ten 2001, Design Directory - Great Britain 2001, Designing the 21st Century 2002, Designers on Design 2005, British Design 2007/8 2007; work in the perm collection of Design Museum London; various appearances on TV incl: Rough Guide to Design (BBC2) 1992, BBC Design Awards (BBC2) 1996, Style Tribes 'Design' (FCO) 2000; memb D&AD; *Exhibitions* incl: 'thinkteck!' (Tokyo Design Network Design Museum London) 1995, Baygen Clockwork Radio 1996 (selected by Design Museum as one of 25 top designs in museum's 25th Year 2007), Design of the Times - One Hundred Years of the Royal College of Art (RCA) 1996, Shiny and New: Contemporary British Design in Metal (San Francisco) 1997, Design for Creative Britain (FCO London) 1998, Powerhous::uk (DTI London) 1998, Millennium Products (Design Cncl Millennium Dome) 1999, creativebritain (stilverk Berlin) 2000, Great Expectations (Design Cncl Exhbn NY) 2001, Designed for Use (Design Cncl-Br Cncl Europe) 2002–03; *Awards* Red Dot Award for High Design Quality (Germany) 1999, G-Mark Good Design Award (Japan) 2001, IF Design Award (Germany) 2002; *Publications* Detail, Exceptional Japanese Design (2003); *Recreations* sailing, multimedia; *Style*— Andy Davey, Esq; ✉ TKO Design (e-mail mail@tkodesign.co.uk, website www.tkodesign.co.uk)

DAVEY, Christopher Stephen (Chris); s of John James Murrell Davey, and Nan W Pattison; *Educ* Guildhall Sch of Music and Drama; *Career* lighting designer; memb Assoc of Lighting Designers; *Theatre* My One and Only (Piccadilly Theatre and Chichester Festival Theatre), Dangerous Corner (Garrick Theatre), Jekyll and Hyde (Northern Ballet Theatre), The Car Man (Old Vic and int tour, winner Best Musical Event Evening Standard Awards), Honk! (nat tour), Closer (Abbey Theatre Dublin), Baby Doll (Albery Theatre, RNT, Birmingham Rep), The Colour of Justice (RNT, Victoria Palace, Tricycle Theatre), Shining Souls (Old Vic), In a Little World of Our Own (Donmar Warehouse), Endgame (Donmar Warehouse), Blood Wedding (Young Vic), Grimm Tales (Young Vic), 21 (Rambert Dance Co), Romeo and Juliet (Chichester Festival Theatre), The Vagina Monologues (national tour), Iphigenia at Auslis (RNT), Rattle of a Simple Man (Comedy Theatre), Yellowman (LiverpoolEveryman/Hampstead), Beasts and Beauties (Bristol Old Vic), The Quare Fellow (OSC), The Sugar Syndrome (Royal Court), Crazyblackmuthaf***inself (Royal Court), The Force of Change (Royal Court), The Taming of the Shrew (nat tour), The Deep Blur Sea (nat tour), Sunday Father (Hampstead), Out in the Open (Hampstead); for RSC: Night of the Soul, Alice in Wonderland, Romeo and Juliet, A Midsummer Night's Dream (also NY), Everyman (also NY), A Month in the Country, Troilus and Cressida, The Comedy of Errors (world tour), Mysteria, Easter; for Shared Experience Theatre: Madame Bovary, After Mrs Rochester, A Passage to India, Mill on the Floss, Jane Eyre, Anna Karenina, The Tempest, War and Peace, Desire Under the Elms, The Danube; extensive designs for: Shared Experience Theatre, West Yorkhire Playhouse, Royal Exchange Manchester, Royal Lyceum Edinburgh, Traverse Theatre Edinburgh, Birmingham Rep; *Opera* incl: The Fool (Gogmagogs), The Picture of Dorian Gray (Opera de Monte Carol), La Traviata (Castleward Opera Belfast), Gli Equivoci Nel Sebiante (Batignano Opera Tuscany), Jeptha (WNO); three seasons at Grange Park Opers; *Recreations* swimming; *Style*— Chris Davey, Esq; ✉ 326B Bethnal Green Road, London E2 0AG (tel and fax 020 7739 4378, e-mail chris@davey1x.fsnet.co.uk); c/o Jeffrey Cambell Management, 11a Greystone Court, South Street, Eastbourne, East Sussex BN21 4LP (tel 01323 411444, fax 01323 411373, e-mail jeffreycambell@btinternet.com)

DAVEY, Edward Jonathon; MP; s of John George Davey (d 1970), and Nina Joan, *née* Stanbrook (d 1981); *b* 25 December 1965; *Educ* Nottingham HS, Jesus Coll Oxford (BA, pres JCR), Birkbeck Coll London (MSc); *m* July 2005, Emily Gasson; *Career* sr econs advsr to Lib Dem MPs (primarily Paddy Ashdown and Alan Beith) 1989–93, conslt Omega Partners 1993–97, MP (Lib Dem) Kingston and Surbiton 1997–; Lib Dem econ affrs and London economy spokesman 1997–2001, Lib Dem shadow chief secretary to the Treasy 2001–02, Lib Dem shadow to the Office of the Dep PM 2002–05, Lib Dem shadow educn and skills spokesman 2005–06, Lib Dem shadow trade and industry spokesman 2006–; memb: Fin Bill Standing Ctee 1997, 1998, 1999, 2000 and 2001, Bank of England Standing Ctee 1997, Procedure Select Ctee 1997–99, Greater London Authy Standing Ctee 1999, Treasy Select Ctee 2000–01; awarded Hon Testimonial of the Royal Humane Soc and Certificate of Commendation by the Chief Constable of the Br Tport Police 1994; FRSA 2001; *Publications* Making MPs Work for Our Money (2000); *Recreations* walking, hiking, tennis; *Clubs* National Liberal; *Style—* Edward Davey, Esq, MP; ✉ House of Commons, London SW1A 0AA (tel 020 7219 3512, fax 020 7219 0250, e-mail daveye@parliament.uk, website www.edwarddavey.co.uk)

DAVEY, Jon Colin; s of Frederick John Davey (d 1991), and Dorothy Mary, *née* Key (d 1969); *b* 16 June 1938; *Educ* Raynes Park GS; *m* 1962, Ann Patricia, da of Maj Stanley Arthur Streames (d 1977); 2 s (Simon b 1964, Jonathan b 1967), 1 da (Jennifer b 1972); *Career* asst sec Broadcasting Dept Home Office 1981–85 (asst sec of Franks Ctee on Official Secrets 1971–72, sec of Williams Ctee on Obscenity and Film Censorship 1977–79, sec of Hunt Inquiry into Cable Expansion and Broadcasting Policy 1982); DG Cable Authy 1985–90, dir Cable and Satellite Independent Television Commission 1991–96, chm Media Matrix Partnership1996–2003, dir Communications Equity Associates International Ltd 1996–98; ed Insight 1997–; ind advsr on public appts DCMS 1999–2007; memb British Screen Advsy Cncl 1990–96, hon fell Soc of Cable Telecommunication Engrs 1994; RTS Silver Medal 1999; *Recreations* music, lawn-making, English countryside; *Style—* Jon Davey, Esq; ✉ 71 Hare Lane, Claygate, Esher, Surrey KT10 0QX (tel 01372 810106, e-mail jondavey@fish.co.uk)

DAVEY, Prof Kenneth Jackson; OBE (1997); s of Reginald Alfred Davey (d 1962), and Vera Elizabeth, *née* Jackson (d 1973); *b* 7 December 1932; *Educ* Silcoates Sch, Merton Coll Oxford (MA), Univ of Birmingham (MSocSc); *m* 18 Aug 1962, Beryl Joyce, da of John Iliff Herbert (d 1975); 2 s (Guy b 1964, Julian b 1966), 1 da (Stephanie b 1971); *Career* RA 1954–56: 2 Lt 1955, Lt 1956; HM Overseas Admin Serv in Uganda 1957–69, dir of studies E African Staff Coll 1970–72; Inst of Local Govt Studies Univ of Birmingham 1972–: assoc dir 1974–83, prof of devpt admin 1981– 2000, dir 1983–89, emeritus prof 2000–; conslt to govts of: Kenya 1975–76, Indonesia 1978–98, Pakistan 1981–82, Georgia 2000–01, Ukraine 2000–02; conslt to World Bank on urban fin 1982– (in Bangladesh, Brazil, China, Jordan, Kenya, Mexico, Poland, Russia, South Africa, Tanzania, Turkey and Uganda); co-ordinator British assistance to local govt reform in Czech Republic, Slovakia and Hungary 1991–2003, chm Steering Ctee Local Govt Initiative Open Soc Inst 2005–; vice-chm Cncl Malvern Coll 1994–2007; FRSA 1988; Offr's Cross Order of Merit of the Repub of Hungary 2004; *Books* Taxing a Peasant Society (1974), Financing Regional Government (1983), Strengthening Municipal Government (1989), Urban Management (1996), Balancing National and Local Responsibilities: Education Finance and Management in four Central European Countries (ed, 2002); *Recreations* choral singing, walking; *Style—* Prof Kenneth Davey, OBE; ✉ Haymesbrook, Haymes Drive, Cleeve Hill, Cheltenham, Gloucestershire GL52 3QQ (tel 01242 526232, e-mail k.j.davey@bham.ac.uk)

DAVEY, Nigel Thomas; s of Leslie Douglas, and Elsie Alice, *née* Hummerston; *b* 8 May 1947; *Educ* Ilford Co HS, Trinity Coll Cambridge (MA); *m* 19 Aug 1972, Ruth Mary; 3 s (James b 1975, Andrew b 1977, Richard b 1979); *Career* chartered accountant; ptnr: Spicer & Oppenheim 1980–90, Touche Ross (now Deloitte & Touche) 1990–2006; FCA 1972, FTII 1994; *Books* The Business of Partnerships (with P J Oliver, 1991), Ray: Partnership Taxation (with J C Clarke 2003, revised edn 2006); *Recreations* tennis, badminton, music; *Style—* Nigel Davey, Esq; ✉ 31 Middleton Road, Shenfield, Brentwood, Essex CM15 8DJ (tel 01277 211954)

DAVEY, Peter John; OBE (1998); s of John Davey (d 1981), and Mary, *née* Roberts; *b* 28 February 1940; *Educ* Oundle, Univ of Edinburgh (BArch); *m* 1968, Carolyn Frances, da of Maj Francis Harvey Pulford (d 1978); 2 s (Pelham Francis John b 1977, Meredith William Thorold b 1979); *Career* architect, journalist, writer and critic; dir: EMAP Architecture 1994–95, EMAP Construct 1995–2005; publishing dir Architectural Research Quarterly 1995–97; managing ed Architects' Journal 1978–82, ed The Architectural Review 1982–2005; memb Cncl RIBA 1990–93 (vice-pres and hon librarian 1991–93); Int Union of Architects Jean Tschumi Prize for Architectural Criticism 2005, Médaille d'Argent de l'Analyse Architecturale Académie d'Artictecture Paris 2005, Pierre Yogo Award Int Ctee of Architectural Critics 2005; RIBA 1972, FRSA 1998; Knight (first class) Order of White Rose of Finland 1991; *Books* Arts and Crafts Architecture (1982, new edn 1995), Peter Zumthor (1998); contrib to many books and professional jls; *Clubs* Athenaeum; *Style—* Peter Davey, Esq; ✉ 44 Hungerford Road, London N7 9LP

DAVEY, Richard H; s of Hubert H Davey, and May, *née* Harding; *b* 22 July 1948; *Educ* Lancing, Lincoln Coll Oxford (BA); *m*; 5 c (Anna b 17 Jan 1974, Edward b 30 July 1981, Nicholas b 10 Feb 1984, Benedict b 31 Aug 1989, Thomas b 14 Sept 1991); *Career* Slater Walker 1970–76, NM Rothschild & Sons 1976–83, dir Exco International plc 1983–87; md Merrill Lynch International 1987–89, exec vice-chm N M Rothschild & Sons 1989–99; non-exec chm London Capital Group Holdings plc 2007–; non-exec dir: Scottish Widows Life Insurance 1996–2000, Freeserve plc 1999–2001, Yorkshire Building Soc 2005–, Amlin plc 2005–, Severn Trent plc 2006–; *Style—* Richard Davey, Esq

DAVEY SMITH, Prof George; *b* 9 May 1959; *Educ* Univ of Oxford (MA, DSc), Univ of Cambridge (MB BChir), London Sch of Hygiene and Tropical Med (MSc), Univ of Cambridge (MD); *Career* clinical research fell and hon clinical med offr Welsh Heart Prog 1985–86, Wellcome research fell in clinical epidemiology Univ Coll and Middx Sch of Med Dept of Community Med 1986–89, lectr in epidemiology London Sch of Hygiene and Tropical Med 1989–92, sr lectr in public health and epidemiology and hon sr registrar then conslt in public health med Dept of Public Health Univ of Glasgow 1992–94, prof of clinical epidemiology Univ of Bristol and hon conslt in public health med Avon Health 1994–; hon prof Dept of Public Health Univ of Glasgow, visiting prof LSHTM; conslt ODA/Govt of India Nat AIDS Control Prog; memb Steering Ctee Nat Fitness Survey 1987–91; memb Editorial Bd: Jl of Health Psychology, Critical Public Health; ed Int Jl Epidemiology; author of numerous pubns in academic jls and book chapters; memb: Int Epidemiological Assoc, Soc for Social Med; FFPHM 1996 (MFPHM 1992), FRCP 2005, FMedSci 2006; *Style—* Prof George Davey Smith; ✉ Department of Social Medicine, University of Bristol, Canynge Hall, Whiteladies Road, Bristol BS8 2PR (e-mail zetkin@bristol.ac.uk)

DAVID, Craig Ashley; *b* 5 May 1981, Southampton; *Career* singer; *Albums* Born To Do It 2000 (UK no 1, US release 2001, US no 11, over 7 million copies sold), Slicker Than Your Average 2002 (UK no 4), The Story Goes 2005; *Singles* Fill Me In 2000 (UK no 1, youngest Br male solo artist to have a no 1 single), 7 Days 2000 (UK no 1), Walking Away 2000 (UK no 3), Rendezvous 2001, What's Your Flava? 2002, Hidden Agenda 2003, Rise & Fall 2003 (UK no 2), Spanish 2003, World Filled With Love 2003, You Don't Miss Your Water ('Til The Well Runs Dry) 2003, All the Way 2005; *Videos* Off The Hook...Live At Wembley 2001; *Style—* Craig David, Esq; ✉ c/o Helter Skelter, The Plaza, 535 Kings Road, London SW10 0SZ (tel 020 7376 8501); website www.craigdavid.co.uk

DAVID, Joanna; da of Maj John Almond Hacking, and Davida Elizabeth, *née* Nesbitt; *b* 17 January 1947; *Educ* Altrincham GS, Elmhurst Ballet Sch, Royal Acad of Dancing, Webber Douglas Acad of Dramatic Art; *Partner* (since 1972), Edward Charles Morice Fox, *qv*; 1 da (Emilia Rose Elizabeth Fox , *qv* b 31 July 1974), 1 s (Frederick Samson Robert Morice b 5 April 1989); *Career* actress; memb Ctee: Theatrical Guild, Unicorn Theatre for Children; tstee and dir Ralph and Meriel Richardson Fndn, memb Cncl King George V Fund; *Theatre* incl: Chichester Festival Theatre 1971, The Family Reunion 1973 and Uncle Vanya (Royal Exchange Manchester) 1977, The Cherry Orchard 1983 and Breaking the Code (Theatre Royal Haymarket) 1986, Stages (RNT) 1992, The Deep Blue Sea (Royal Theatre Northampton) 1997, Ghost Train Tattoo (Royal Exchange) 2000, Copenhagen (Salisbury Playhouse) 2003, The Importance of Being Earnest (Royal Exchange) 2004, A Voyage Round My Father (Donmar Warehouse and Wyndhams Theatre) 2006; *Television* incl: War and Peace, Sense and Sensibility, Last of the Mohicans, Duchess of Duke Street, Rebecca, Carrington and Strachey, Fame is the Spur, First Among Equals, Paying Guests, Unexplained Laughter, Hannay, Children of the North, Secret Friends, Inspector Morse, Maigret, Rumpole of the Bailey, Darling Buds of May, The Good Guys, Sherlock Holmes - The Cardboard Box, Pride and Prejudice, A Touch of Frost, Bramwell, A Dance to the Music of Time, Midsummer Murders - Written in Blood, Dalziel and Pascoe, Blind Date, Heartbeat, The Mill on the Floss, The Dark Room, The Glass, The Way We Live Now, The Forsyte Saga, He Knew He Was Right, Brides in the Bath, Monarch of the Glen 2004, Falling 2004, Heartbeat 2004, Bleak House 2005; *Films* In the Name of the Pharoah 1998, Cotton Mary 1999, Soulkeeper 2002, The Tulse Hill Suitcase 2003, These Foolish Things 2004; *Style—* Miss Joanna David; ✉ c/o Angharad Wood, Tavistock Wood Management Limited, 32 Tavistock Street, London WC2E 7PB (tel 020 7257 8725, fax 020 7240 9029, e-mail wood@tavistockwood.com)

DAVID, Baroness (Life Peer UK 1978), of Romsey in the City of Cambridge; Nora Ratcliff David; JP (Cambridge City 1965); da of George Blockley Blakesley, JP (d 1934); *b* 23 September 1913; *Educ* Ashby-de-la-Zouch Girls' GS, St Felix Southwold, Newnham Coll Cambridge (MA); *m* 1935, Richard William David, CBE (d 1993), s of Rev Frederick Paul David (d 1955); 2 s (Hon Nicholas Christopher b 1937, Hon (Richard) Sebastian b 1940), 2 da (Hon Teresa Katherine (Hon Mrs Davies) b 1944, Hon Elizabeth Sarah (Hon Mrs Forder) b 1947); *Career* sits as Lab Peer in House of Lords, Baroness-in-Waiting to HM The Queen (Govt whip) 1978–79, oppn whip 1979–83, dep chief oppn whip 1983–87 and oppn spokesman for environment and local govt in Lords 1986–88, oppn spokesman for educn 1979–83 and 1986–97; former Cambridge city cncllr, Cambs co cncllr 1974–78; memb: Bd Peterborough Devpt Corp 1976–78, EC Select Ctee 1991–94, EC Agric Ctee 1993–97; hon fell: Newnham Coll Cambridge 1986, Anglia HE Coll (now Anglia Ruskin Univ) 1989; Hon DLitt Staffs Univ 1994; *Recreations* theatre, reading, travel, walking; *Style—* The Rt Hon Baroness David; ✉ 50 Highsett, Cambridge CB2 1NZ (tel 01223 350376); House of Lords, London SW1A 0PW (tel 020 7219 3159, e-mail davidn@parliament.uk)

DAVID, Peter Howard; s of George Maurice David (d 1969), and Ruth, *née* Bloch; *b* 7 September 1951; *Educ* Liverpool Coll, Univ of London (BA); *m* 1 July 1978, Celia, da of Norman Binns; 1 s (Ian George b 8 Jan 1980), 1 da (Tessa b 12 Feb 1982); *Career* formerly on staff The Teacher Newspaper; The Times Higher Education Supplement: chief reporter until 1981, Washington ed 1981–83; Washington ed Nature 1983–84; The Economist: tech corr 1984, on foreign staff 1985, int ed 1986–93, business affrs ed 1993–98, political ed 1998–2002, foreign ed 2002–; *Books* Star Wars and Arms Control (1984), Triumph in the Desert (1990); *Clubs* RAC; *Style—* Peter David, Esq; ✉ The Economist, 25 St James's Street, London SW1A 1HG (tel 020 7830 7000)

DAVID, Prof Timothy J; *Educ* Clifton Coll, Univ of Bristol (MB ChB, PhD, MD), DCH; *Family* 2 s; *Career* prof of child health and paediatrics Univ of Manchester and hon conslt paediatrician Booth Hall Children's Hosp Manchester 1991–; proceedings ed Jl of Royal Soc of Medicine 1995–; memb Manchester Family Justice Cncl 2005–; FRCP 1986 (MRCP 1976), FRCPCH 1997; *Publications* Recent Advances in Paediatrics (vols 9–23, 1991–2006), Food and Food Additive Intolerance in Childhood (1993), Symptoms of Disease in Childhood (1995), Problem-Based Learning in Medicine (jtly, 1999); author or ed of more than 350 pubns; *Recreations* classical music, opera, watching cricket, cricket photography; *Style—* Prof Timothy J David; ✉ University of Manchester, Booth Hall Children's Hospital, Manchester M9 7AA (tel 0161 918 5536, fax 0161 904 9320)

DAVID, Timothy James; s of Herman Francis David (d 1974), of Wimbledon, London, and Mavis Jeanne, *née* Evans; *b* 3 June 1947; *Educ* Stonyhurst, New Coll Oxford (MA), Univ of Rhodesia (Grad CertEd), Univ of London; *m* 24 Feb 1996, Rosemary, da of Josef Kunzel, and Prudence Kunzel; 1 s, 1 da; *Career* vol teacher Southern Rhodesia 1965–66, New Coll Oxford 1966–69, headmaster St Peter's Community Secdy Sch Salisbury and memb Conf of The Heads of African Secdy Schs 1970–71, Univ of Rhodesia 1972, Br Cncl 1973, educn dir Help the Aged 1974 (concurrently pt/t Univ of London); HM Dip Serv: entered FCO by open competition 1974, second later first sec Dar es Salaam 1977–80 (concurrently first sec (non-resident) Antananarivo 1978–80), Cwlth Coordination Dept FCO 1980–82 (sec to UK Delgn to Cwlth Heads of Govt Meeting 1981), UK Mission to UN NY 1982, on loan to Central and Southern Africa Dept ODA 1983–84, UK Mission to UN Geneva 1985–88, head Int and Planning Section and dep head Aid Policy Dept ODA 1988–89, cnsllr and head Narcotics Control and Aids Dept FCO 1989–91, ambass to Fiji and high cmmr to Nauru and Tuvalu 1992–95 (concurrently high cmmr to Kiribati 1994–95), cnsllr Middle East Dept 1995, dep high cmmr to Zimbabwe 1996–98, high cmmr to Belize 1998–2001 (dean Dip Corps of Belize 2001), high cmmr to Zambia 2002–05, ret; UK dir Tuvalu Tst Fund 1992–95, memb Cncl Univ of the S Pacific 1993–95, patron Save the Children (Fiji) 1993–95, memb Rhodes Scholarship Selection Ctee Zambia 2002–05, tstee Oaksey Playing Fields Assoc 2006–, govr Oaksey Village Sch 2006–, tstee and dir Emmaus (Glos) 2006–; *Recreations* friends, reading, music, travel, tennis, squash, walking; *Clubs* Commonwealth Trust, All England Lawn Tennis and Croquet; *Style—* Tim David, Esq; ✉ c/o The Old House, Oaksey, Malmesbury, Wiltshire SN16 9TD

DAVID, Wayne; MP; s of David Haydn David, of Bridgend, Mid Glamorgan, and Edna Amelia, *née* Jones; *b* 1 July 1957; *Educ* Cynffig Comp Sch, UC Cardiff (BA, PGCE FE, Charles Morgan prize in Welsh history), UC Swansea; *m* 8 June 1991 (m dis 2007), Catherine Thomas; *Career* teacher of history Brynteg Comp Sch 1983–85, tutor organiser Workers' Educn Assoc Mid Glamorgan 1985–89, MEP (Lab) South Wales 1989–94 and South Wales Central 1994–99, Lab candidate Nat Assembly for Wales election 1999, advsr Youth Serv 1999–2001, MP (Lab) Caerphilly 2001–; European Parl: treas European PLP 1989–91, first vice-pres Regnl Policy Ctee 1992–94, vice-pres Socialist Gp 1994–98, ldr European PLP 1994–98; House of Commons: memb EU Scrutiny Select Ctee 2001–, chair All-Pty Poland Gp 2003– (sec 2001–03), PPS to Min of State MOD 2005–06, chair All-Pty EU Gp 2006–; sec: Dept for Work and Pensions Ctee PLP 2002–, Welsh Gp PLP 2003–; pres: Cncl for Wales of Vol Youth Services, Aber Valley Male Voice Choir, Caerphilly Local History Soc; memb: Bd European Movement 2002–06 (pres Wales Cncl), Fabian Soc; fell Univ of Cardiff 1995; *Recreations* music, reading; *Style—* Wayne David, Esq, MP; ✉ Constituency Office, The Community Council Offices, Bedwas, Caerphilly

D

CF83 8YB (tel 029 2088 1061, e-mail davidw@parliament.uk); House of Commons, London SW1A 0AA (tel 020 7219 8152)

DAVID-WEILL, Michel Alexandre; s of Pierre David-Weill, and Berthe, *née* Haardt; *b* 23 November 1932; *Educ* Institut de Sciences Politiques Paris, Lycée Français New York; *m* 1956, Helene Lehideux; 4 da; *Career* Brown Brothers Harriman 1954–55, Lehman Brothers New York 1955–56; Lazard Frères & Co New York: joined 1956, ptnr 1961–, sr ptnr 1977–; Lazard Brothers & Co London: dir 1965–, chm 1990–91, dep chm 1992–; ptnr Lazard Frères et Cie Paris 1965–, vice-chm Lazard Frères & Co LLC 1995–; non-exec dir Pearson plc 1970–; Chevalier Legion d'Honneur; *Clubs* Knickerbocker (NY), Brook (NY), Creek (Locust Valley); *Style*— Michel David-Weill, Esq; ✉ Lazard Freres & Co, 30 Rockefeller Plaza, New York, NY 10020, USA (tel 00 1 212 632 6000, fax 00 1 212 632 6060); Lazard Brothers & Co Ltd, 21 Moorfields, London EC2P 2HT (tel 020 7588 2721, fax 020 7628 2485)

DAVIDOVITZ, (Robert Hyman) Colin; BEM (1954); s of Lambert Samuel Davidson, and Rose-Marie Davidson; *b* 18 August 1930; *Educ* Tynecastle Secdy Sch Edinburgh; *m* 20 Sept 1958, Catherine, da of Archibald Callaghan; 2 da (Judith b 1959, Theresa b 1963), 2 s (Philip b 1961, Robert b 1964); *Career* RN: boy telegraphist 1946, telegraphist 1948, leading telegraphist (special) 1951, PO telegraphist (PROV) 1954; Assoc-Rediffusion telerecordist 1955, sr engr Scottish TV 1957; Southern TV: sr engr 1958, prodn mangr 1964, prodn controller 1975; West Midland studio controller ATV/Central 1981, dir ops TV-am 1987–92, dir Kingsway Production Services Ltd 1992–; cncllr: Eastleigh BC 1996– (dep ldr Cons Gp), Hants CC 2001– (memb Cabinet); pres Catenians Southampton 1976; memb Rotary Club of Itchen Valley 2001–; *Recreations* photography, painting, yachting; *Style*— Colin Davidovitz, Esq, BEM; ✉ 55 Kingsway, Chandlers Ford, Hampshire SO5 1FH (tel 023 8025 1342)

DAVIDSON, Anthony Beverley (Tony); s of Dr Ronald Beverley Davidson (d 1972), and Edna Robina Elizabeth, *née* Cowan; *b* 25 December 1947; *Educ* Morgan Acad Dundee, Univ of St Andrews (MA); *m* 21 Dec 1971, Avril Rose, da of John Pearson Duncan, of Dundee; 2 s (Ronald John b 1975, Duncan Anthony b 1982), 2 da (Amanda Beverley b 1977, Laura Rose b 1979); *Career* CA 1974; mangr Deloitte Haskins & Sells (Edinburgh) 1970–75, sr mangr Whitelaw Wells & Co 1975–76, chief accountant Highways Dept Lothian Regnl Cncl 1976–77, chief inspr TSB (Tayside and Central Scotland) 1977–79, head Inspection Div TSB Gp 1979–82, gen mangr TSB (Tayside and Central Scotland) 1982–83, sr exec dir TSB Scotland plc 1987–90 (gen mangr 1983–87); md UAP Provincial Insurance plc 1990–98; exec dir Sun Life and Provincial Holdings plc 1996–98; dir Gleneagles Forestry Ltd 1998, chm Fleming Worldwide Income Investment Tst plc 1999; non-exec dir: Sun Life Assurance Company of Canada (UK) Ltd 2000, RLG with Profits Ltd 2004, JP Morgan Fleming Fledgeling Investment Tst plc 2005; FCMA 1975, FCIBS 1984; *Recreations* golf, photography; *Clubs* Gullane Golf, Wentworth, Gleneagles Country, Valderrama Golf (Spain); *Style*— Tony Davidson, Esq; ✉ Pinnerwood Estate, Tullibardine, Auchterarder, Perthshire PH3 1JS (tel 01764 660382, e-mail tonydavidson@gleneaglesforestry.co.uk)

DAVIDSON, Arthur; QC (1978); *b* 7 November 1928; *Educ* Liverpool Coll, King George V Sch Southport, Trinity Coll Cambridge; *Career* served Merchant Navy; called to the Bar Middle Temple 1953; Parly candidate (Lab) Blackpool South 1955, Preston North 1959, Hyndburn 1983; MP (Lab) Accrington 1966–83, PPS to Slr-Gen 1968–70, Parly sec Law Offrs Dept 1974–79, memb Home Affairs Select Ctee 1980–83; oppn spokesman on: defence 1980–81, legal affairs 1981–83 (shadow AG 1982–83); memb: Cncl Consumers' Assoc 1970–74, Exec Ctee Soc of Labour Lawyers 1981–; formerly chm PLP Home Affairs Gp; legal dir: Associated Newspaper Holdings 1987–90, Mirror Group Newspapers 1991–93; memb: Nat Fabian Soc, Cncl Nat Youth Jazz Orch; chm House of Commons Jazz Club 1973–83; *Style*— Arthur Davidson Esq, QC; ✉ 1 Pump Court, Temple, London EC4Y 7AA (tel 020 7827 4000, fax 020 7827 4100)

DAVIDSON, Christopher William Sherwood (Bill); s of Thomas Leigh Davidson (d 1998), and Donaldine, *née* Brown (d 1982); *b* 29 July 1940; *Educ* Uppingham, Univ of Nottingham (BA); *Career* articles with R K Denby (later Sir Richard Denby) 1962–65, admitted slr 1966; asst slr: Winkworth & Pemberton Westminster 1966–67, Coward Chance 1968–70; ptnr Ashton Hill & Co Nottingham 1971–75, gp slr and co sec NUS Holdings Ltd 1975–77; fndr (later sr ptnr) Christopher Davidson & Co 1977–2004; co sec: Endsleigh Insurance Services Ltd 1968–2004, NUS Holdings Ltd 1971–2006; conslt slr Christopher Davidson Co 2004–06, ret 2006; memb Ctee N Gloucester Circle Newman Assoc; *Recreations* cooking and crime fiction (with special interest in humorous and ecclesiastical who-done-its); *Style*— Bill Davidson, Esq; ✉ The Old Rectory, Kemerton, Tewkesbury, Gloucestershire GL20 7HY (tel 01386 725244); Christopher Davidson & Co, 2/3 Oriel Terrace, Oriel Road, Cheltenham, Gloucestershire GL20 7HY (tel 01242 581481, fax 01242 221 210)

DAVIDSON, David; s of John Davidson, and Marjory, *née* Cormack; *b* 25 January 1943; *Educ* Trinity Acad Edinburgh, Heriot-Watt Univ (MRPharmS), Manchester Business Sch (DpBA); *m* 9 Nov 1968, Christine, da of George Hunter; 3 s (Alasdair Michael b 14 Feb 1970, Giles Thomas b 26 Sept 1972, Quintin Edward b 15 Oct 1976), 2 da (Jennifer Lucy b 5 May 1974, Suzanne Victoria b 25 May 1979); *Career* manager community pharmacy 1966–69, community pharmacy proprietor 1969–74, developed own chain of pharmacies in NW England, Yorkshire and Glasgow 1974–93, UniChem Ltd: advsr 1975–79, dir 1979–90; regnl chm UniChem plc 1990–93; memb advsy Ctee Glaxo 1988–93, memb Scottish Pharmaceutical Advsy Ctee 1997–98, memb Postgraduate Educn Bd for NHS Pharmacists 1997–98, memb Royal Pharmaceutical Soc of Great Britain; dir Stirling Enterprise and Stirling Business Links 1995–99, memb Rural Stirling Economic Partnership 1995–99; MSP (Cons) Scotland North East 1999–2007 (Scots parly candidate Banff & Buchan 1998); chm Strathard Community Cncl 1990–94, Scottish Cons dep spokesman on local govt 1998, finance spokesman 1999, dep industry spokesman 1999, finance and tourism spokesman 2001, Cons health spokesman 2003–05; chair Cross Pty Diabetes Gp, co-chair Cross Pty Cancer Gp, convenor Justice 2 Ctee; vice-chm: Cross Pty Oil and Gas Gp, Cross Pty Asthma Gp, Cross Pty Tourism Gp; memb: Rifkind Policy Commission Ind Gp 1998–99, fndr chm: Assoc of Scottish Community Councils 1993–95, Stirling Community Council Forum 1994–95; exec memb Conservatives in Local Govt 1998–99, Stirling Cncl Trossachs Ward 1995–99; hon memb Aberdeen and Grampian C of C; tstee Stirling Landfill Tax 1998–99; school govr Bexley 1974–75, chm St Ambrose Coll 1986–88, parish cncllr 1975–79; *Recreations* country pursuits, pedigree cattle, rugby football, sailing, travel; *Clubs* Country, Unionist; *Style*— David Davidson, Esq; ✉ North Hilton, Netherley, By Stonehaven, Aberdeenshire, AB39 3QL (tel 01569 730449, fax 01569 731316)

DAVIDSON, Prof Donald Allen; s of John Forsyth Davidson (d 1976), and Jean, *née* Cole (d 1984); *b* 27 April 1945; *Educ* Robert Gordon's Coll Aberdeen, Univ of Aberdeen (MacFarlane Prize in geography, BSc), Univ of Sheffield (PhD); *m* 3 April 1969, Caroline Elizabeth, *née* Brown; 2 da (Caroline Louise b 29 May 1971, Lorna Elizabeth b 5 Dec 1973), 1 s (Alan John MacDonald b 9 Feb 1986); *Career* jr research fell and temp lectr Dept of Geography Univ of Sheffield 1967–71, lectr Dept of Geography St David's UC Univ of Wales at Lampeter 1971–76; Dept of Geography Univ of Strathclyde: lectr, sr lectr then reader 1976–86; prof Dept of Environmental Science Univ of Stirling 1991– (reader 1986–91, head of dept 1993–99), managing ed Progress in Environmental Science jl; chm: Geography Panel Scottish Exam Bd 1986–90, Geography Panel Higher Skill Prog 1995–97, Advsy Ctee on Sites of Special Scientific Interest (SSSI) 2004–; memb: science-based archaeology ctee SERC 1992–95, Terrestrial Sciences Ctee NERC 1995–98; memb Editorial Bd: Geoarchaeology 1988–95, Soil Use and Management 1995– (currently ed-in-chief), NERC Coll 2003–; hon pres Scottish Assoc of Geography Teachers 1990–92; FRSE 1997; *Books* Geoarchaeology: Earth Science and the Past (ed jtly with M L Shackley, 1976), Science for Physical Geographers (1978), Timescales in Geomorphology (ed jtly with R Cullingford and J Lewin, 1980), Principles and Applications of Soil Geography (ed jtly with E M Bridges, 1982), Landscape Ecology and Land Use (ed jtly with A Vink, 1983), Land Evaluation (ed, 1986), Soil Erosion (ed jtly with R P C Morgan, 1986), Conceptual Issues in Environmental Archaeology (ed jtly with J Bintliff and E G Grant, 1988), The Evaluation of Land Resources (1992); also author of numerous articles and papers in academic jls incl Journal of Archaeological Science, Geoarchaeology, Int Journal of Geographical Information Systems, Applied Soil Ecology, Environment Int; *Recreations* maintaining an old house and large garden; *Style*— Prof Donald Davidson, FRSE; ✉ Beechwood, Glen Road, Dunblane, Perthshire FK15 0DS (tel 01786 823599, fax 01786 823599, e-mail d.a.davidson@stir.ac.uk)

DAVIDSON, Duncan Henry; s of Col Colin Keppel Davidson, CIE, OBE (ka 1943), and Lady (Mary) Rachel Davidson (later Lady (Mary) Rachel Pepys DCVO); *b* 29 March 1941; *Educ* Ampleforth; *m* 22 Sept 1965, Sarah Katherine, *née* Wilson; 4 da (Camilla b 7 Feb 1968, Natasha b 10 Oct 1969, Flora b 11 Aug 1975, Rose b 12 April 1979); *Career* Lt Royal Scots Greys 1959–63; mangr George Wimpey plc 1963–65, fndr and chm Ryedale Homes Ltd 1965–72, fndr and chm Persimmon plc 1972–; non-exec dir Wm Morrison Supermarkets plc 2004–05; memb Ct Univ of Newcastle upon Tyne; *Recreations* country pursuits; *Clubs* White's, Turf; *Style*— Duncan Davidson, Esq; ✉ Lilburn Tower, Alnwick, Northumberland NE66 4PQ (tel 01668 217291, fax 01668 217371); Persimmon plc, Persimmon House, Fulford, York YO19 4FE (tel 01904 642199, fax 01904 630924)

DAVIDSON, Dr Duncan Lewis Watt; s of Lewis Davidson, CBE, DD (d 1981), and Jean Davidson; *b* 16 May 1940; *Educ* Knox Coll Jamaica, Univ of Edinburgh (BSc, MB ChB); *m* 22 July 1964, Anne Veronica McDougall, da of Dr Arthur Maiden, OBE, of St Andrews, Fife; 4 s (Simon Lewis Tweedie, Mark Oliver Tweedie (twins) b 9 July 1965, (Julian) Anthony b 6 Feb 1967, Peter Duncan b 2 June 1970), 1 da (Kathleen Anne b 2 Jan 1978); *Career* various appts in med and neurology in Edinburgh and Montreal 1966–76, conslt neurologist Tayside Univ Hospitals Tst and hon sr lectr in med Univ of Dundee 1976–2002, conslt in med educn 2002–; FRCPEd 1979; *Books* Neurological Therapeutics (with Jar Lenman, 1981); *Recreations* gardening, photography; *Style*— Dr Duncan Davidson; ✉ Oliver, Tweedsmuir, By Biggar, Lanarkshire ML12 9QW (tel 01899 880278)

DAVIDSON, Edward Alan; QC (1994); s of Alan Thomas Davidson (d 1977), of Sheffield, and Helen Muriel, *née* Johnston (d 1952); *b* 12 July 1943; *Educ* King's Sch Canterbury, Gonville & Caius Coll Cambridge (scholar, Tapp Postgrad scholar, MA, LLB); *m* 19 May 1973, Hilary Jill, da of Norman S Fairman; 2 s (Mark b 14 June 1976, Philip b 27 Aug 1978); *Career* called to the Bar Gray's Inn 1966 (Atkin & Birkenhead scholar, bencher 2002); in practice Chancery Bar 1968–; sec The Institute 2001–06; memb: Chancery Bar Assoc, Professional Negligence Bar Assoc, Soc of Tst and Estate Practitioners, Assoc of Contentious Tst and Probate Specialists; *Recreations* tennis, bridge, gardening; *Style*— Edward Davidson, Esq, QC; ✉ Radcliffe Chambers, 11 New Square, London WC2A 3QB (tel 020 7831 0081, fax 020 7405 2560, e-mail clerks@radcliffechambers.com)

DAVIDSON, Erick Stanley; s of Stanley Davidson, of Berwick-upon-Tweed, Northumberland, and Agnes Sanderson Turnbull, *née* Mackay; *b* 10 February 1949; *Educ* Berwick-upon-Tweed GS, Hull Sch of Architecture, Newcastle Coll of Art (Dip Business Studies and Design); *m* 1977, Yvonne Jean Grace, da of Archibald Dickson (d 1981); 2 da (Carolyne b 1 May 1978, Linsey b 2 April 1982); *Career* mangr Marks & Spencer 1971–72, asst to MD of Pubns RIBA 1972–74, business mangr The Jenkins Group 1974–76, mktg dir Ads Graphics 1976–78, fndr and chm The Tayburn Group 1978–; govr Edinburgh Coll of Art 2003–; *Recreations* golf, football; *Clubs* Dunbar, Gullane; *Style*— Erick Davidson, Esq; ✉ Beech House, 25A Dalrymple Crescent, Edinburgh EH9 2NX (tel 0131 667 7421); Tayburn Ltd, 15 Kittle Yards, Causewayside, Edinburgh EH9 1PJ (tel 0131 662 0662, fax 0131 662 0606)

DAVIDSON, Ian; MP; *Educ* Jedburgh GS, Galashiels Acad, Univ of Edinburgh (MA), Jordanhill Coll Glasgow; *m*; 1 s, 1 da; *Career* MP (Lab/Co-op): Glasgow Govan 1992–97, Glasgow Pollok 1997–2005, Glasgow SW 2005–; memb Backbench: Overseas Aid Ctee, Trade & Industry Ctee, Defence Ctee; former chm: MSF Gp, Co-op Gp; chair Br Bermuda Gp, vice-chair Construction Gp; sec: Tribune Gp, Parly Rugby Team, Br-Japan Gp, German Gp, Trade Union Gp, Shipbuilding and Ship Repair Gp, New Europe All-Pty Gp, Aerospace Gp; memb All-Pty Royal Marines Gp, memb All-Pty Br Russia Gp; memb All-Pty Country Gps: America, Canada, ANZAC, Zimbabwe, South Africa, Japan, China, Germany (vice-chair), Gibraltar, Cayman Islands, Falkland Islands, Nigeria (chair 2001), India, UK and Arab Repub of Egypt; memb Pub Accounts Select Ctee; chair: Lab Against the Euro 2002, Lab Against European Superstate, Centre for a Social Europe; treas British Cncl; capt Parl rugby team; *Recreations* running, swimming, rugby union; *Style*— Ian Davidson, Esq, MP; ✉ House of Commons, London SW1A 0AA (tel 020 7219 3000)

DAVIDSON, Jane Elizabeth; AM; da of Dr Lindsay Alexander Gordon Davidson, and Dr Joyce Mary; *b* 19 March 1957; *Educ* Malvern Girls' Coll, Univ of Birmingham (BA), Univ of Wales Aberystwyth (PGCE); *m* 1994, Guy Roger Stoate; 1 da (Hannah), 2 step s (Joe, Lewis); *Career* teacher 1981–83, devpt offr YHA 1983–86, youth and community worker 1986–89; researcher to Rhodri Morgan MP 1989–94, Welsh co-ordinator Nat Local Govt Forum Against Poverty 1994–96, head of Social Affairs Welsh Local Govt Assoc 1996–99, memb Nat Assembly for Wales (Lab) Pontypridd 1999–, dep presiding offr 1999–, min for educn and lifelong learning 2000–; *Publications* The Anti Poverty Implications of Local Government Reorganisation (LGIU, 1990), Freeing the Dragon (1999); various articles in social policy jls; *Recreations* theatre, walking, swimming; *Style*— Ms Jane Davidson, AM; ✉ National Assembly for Wales, Cardiff Bay, Cardiff CF99 1NA; c/o Unit 10, Maritime Offices, Woodland Terrace, Maes y Coed, Pontypridd CF37 1DZ (tel 01443 406400)

DAVIDSON, Jim; OBE (2001); *b* 13 December 1954; *Educ* St Andrew's Sch Charlton; *Career* entertainer, comedian, TV presenter, theatre prodr and dir; *Theatre* stage seasons incl: Great Yarmouth 1986, 1989, 1991, 1994, 1995 and 1996, Torquay 1987, 1988, 1990 and 1992, Cardiff 1987, Blackpool 1993, Cinderella (Apollo Oxford, Hippodrome Bristol, Alhambra Theatre Bradford) 1985, 1986 and 1989, Dick Whittington (London Palladium) 1980, Cinderella (Dominion Theatre London) 1988, Buttons in Sinderella (Cambridge Theatre, Shaftesbury Theatre and Blackpool Opera House) 1993, 1994 and 1996, Dick Whittington (Bristol Hippodrome) 1996 and 2002 (also at Manchester Palace 1997, London Apollo 2000 and Mayflower Southampton 2001), Aladdin (Mayflower Southampton) 2003, Sinderella II (UK tour) 2004; many cabaret and club engagements and UK theatre tours; *Television* shows incl: New Faces (debut ITV) 1976, What's On Next, The Jim Davidson Show (five series, TV Times Award Funniest Man on TV 1980), Up The Elephant And Round The Castle (four series), Home James (four series), Stand Up Jim Davidson, Jim Davidson Special 1984, Jim Davidson's Falkland Specials 1985, Jim Davidson In Germany 1986, Jim Davidson's Comedy Package 1987, Wednesday At Eight 1988, Telethon 1988, Big Break 1991–, The Generation Game 1995–2002, Jim Davidson So Far 1998, Jim Davidson Presents 2000, Homeward Bound for Christmas 2000, Jim Davidson Falklands Bound 2002, Jim Davidson Basra Bound 2003, Jim Davidson's Commercial Breakdown 2004; *Videos* incl: The Unedited Jim Davidson Live,

Something Old, Something New, Something Borrowed, Something..., Unseen Big Break, Jim Davidson Xposed, The Truth, The Whole Truth..., Sinderella, Jim Davidson and The Boys Live (filmed with the Br Troops in Poland), Jim Davidson's Silver Jubilee Video, Vote for Jim; *Film* Colour Me Kubrick 2007; *Recordings* LPs incl: The Jim Davidson Album, A Dirty Weekend with Jim Davidson, Another Dirty Weekend, The Full Monty; *Awards* Variety Club of GB Showbusiness Personality of the Year 1997, Comic Heritage Showbusiness Personality of the Year 1997, Grand Order of Water Rats Showbusiness Personality of the Year 1998; *Books* incl: Too Risky, Too Frisky, Jim Davidson Gets Hooked, Jim Davidson's True Brit, The Full Monty, Close to the Edge (autobiography); *Clubs* Carlton; *Style*— Jim Davidson, Esq, OBE; ✉ c/o Lake-Smith Griffin Associates, Walter House, 418 Strand, London WC2R 0PT (tel 020 7836 1020, fax 020 7836 1040)

DAVIDSON, 2 Viscount (UK 1937); John Andrew Davidson; s of 1 Viscount Davidson, GCVO, CH, CB, PC (d 1970), and Hon Dame Frances Davidson, DBE (Baroness Northchurch, d 1985); *b* 22 December 1928; *Educ* Westminster, Pembroke Coll Cambridge; *m* 1, 30 June 1956 (m dis 1974), Margaret Birgitta (who m 2, 1974, as his 2 w, 4 Viscount Colville of Culross), da of Maj-Gen Cyril Henry Norton, CB, CBE, DSO; 4 da (1 decd); m 2, 1975, Pamela Joy Dobb (d 2006), da of John Vergette; *Heir* bro, Hon Malcolm Davidson; *Career* served with Black Watch and 5 Bn KAR 1947–49; dir Strutt & Parker (Farms) Ltd 1960–75; lord-in-waiting 1985–86; Capt Queen's Body Guard of the Yeomen of the Guard (dep chief whip in House of Lords) 1986–91; memb: Cncl CLA 1965–75, RASE 1973–75; *Style*— The Viscount Davidson; ✉ 19 Lochmore House, Cundy Street, London SW1W 9JX

DAVIDSON, Prof John Frank; s of John Davidson, and Katie Davidson; *b* 7 February 1926; *Educ* Heaton GS Newcastle, Trinity Coll Cambridge (BA, PhD, ScD); *m* 1948, Susanne Hedwig Ostberg; 1 s, 1 da; *Career* Mechanical Devpt Dept Rolls Royce Derby 1947–50 (apprentice 1947); Univ of Cambridge: res fell Trinity Coll 1949–53, res in Engrg Laboratory 1950–52, univ demonstrator in chemical engrg 1952–54, univ lectr 1954–75, fell and steward Trinity Coll 1957, prof of chemical engrg and head Dept of Chemical Engrg 1975–78, Shell prof of chemical engrg 1978–93, vice-master Trinity Coll 1992–96; visiting prof: Univ of Delaware 1960, Univ of Sydney 1967, MIT 1981, Univs of Delaware, Oregon and Houston 1981, Univ of Notre Dame IN 1988; visiting lectr Univs of Cape Town and Johannesburg 1964, Wilhelm lectr Princeton 1988; memb: Ct of Enquiry for Flixborough Disaster 1974–75, Advsy Ctee on Safety of Nuclear Installations HSE 1977–87, Advsy Cncl for Applied Res and Devpt 1980 (memb Jt Working Pty on Biotechnology), Governing Body AFRC Inst of Engrg Res 1982, Advsy Bd AFRC Inst of Food Res 1986; Int Fluidization Award of Achievement (Engrg Fndn Conf Banff) 1989, Royal Medal of Royal Soc 1999; Docteur (hc) Institut National Polytechnique de Toulouse 1979, Hon DSc Aston Univ 1989; foreign assoc US Nat Acad of Engrg 1976, fell Indian Nat Sci Acad 1990, foreign assoc Russian Acad of Engrg 1998; FIChemE (pres 1970–71), MIMechE, fndr FREng 1976 (memb Acid Emissions Ctee 1985), FRS 1974 (vice-pres 1989); *Books* Fluidised Particles (with D Harrison, 1963), Fluidization (1971, 2 edn with R Clift and D Harrison, 1985); *Recreations* hill walking, gardening, mending bicycles and other domestic artefacts; *Style*— Prof John Davidson, FRS, FREng; ✉ 5 Luard Close, Cambridge CB2 8PL (tel and fax 01223 246104); University of Cambridge, Department of Chemical Engineering, Pembroke Street, Cambridge CB2 3RA (tel 01223 334775)

DAVIDSON, John Roderick; OBE (2004); yr s of (Alexander) Ross Davidson (d 1977), of Portsmouth, and Jessie Maud, *née* Oakley (d 1984); *b* 29 January 1937; *Educ* Portsmouth Northern GS, Univ of Manchester (BA, Wadsworth Memorial award); *Career* advsr to students Chelsea Sch of Art 1966–68, asst sch sec Royal Post Grad Med Sch 1968–74; Imperial Coll London: asst sec 1974–77, personnel sec 1977–85, admin sec 1985–89; Univ of London: clerk of the Senate 1989–94, clerk of the Cncl 1994–2004, dir of admin 1991–2004; memb Univ of London Examinations and Assessment Cncl 1991–2000, memb Bd Br Inst Paris 1993–2004; chm Lansdowne (Putney) Ltd 1999–; dir: London East Anglian Group Ltd 1991–96, SAUL Trustee Co Ltd 1993–98, London Area South Eastern Library Region 1995–2001, Senate House Services Ltd 1996–2004; tstee: Univ of London Convocation Tst 1997–2004, St Stephen's AIDS Tst 2003–; govr: Charterhouse 1994–2004, More House School 2000– (chm 2005–), Wimbledon HS 2001–; memb Soc of Genealogists 1988–; *Recreations* opera, theatre, genealogy; *Clubs* Athenaeum; *Style*— John Davidson, Esq, OBE; ✉ 10 Lansdowne, Carlton Drive, London SW15 2BY (tel 020 8789 0021)

DAVIDSON, Dr (William) Keith Davidson; CBE (1982), JP (Glasgow 1962); s of James Fisher Keith Davidson (d 1978), of Bearsden, Glasgow, and Martha Anderson, *née* Milloy (d 1956); *b* 20 November 1926; *Educ* Coatbridge Secdy Sch, Univ of Glasgow; *m* 6 Feb 1952, Dr Mary Waddell Aitken, da of Dr George Jamieson (d 1967), of Chryston, Strathclyde; 1 s (Keith b 1954), 1 da (Mhairi b 1956); *Career* Med Offr 1 Bn RSF 1950, Maj 2 i/c 14 Field Ambulance 1950–51, Med Offr i/c Holland and Belgium 1952; gen med practitioner 1953–90; DPA Univ of Glasgow 1965, chm Glasgow Local Med Ctee 1971–75, chm Scottish Gen Med Servs Ctee 1972–75, memb Scottish Cncl on Crime 1972–75, dep chm Gen Med Servs Ctee (UK) 1975–79, memb Scottish Med Practices Ctee 1968–80; chm Scottish Cncl BMA 1978–81, vice-pres BMA 1983–, memb GMC 1984–94; hon pres Glasgow Eastern Med Soc 1984–85, chm Scottish Health Servs Planning Cncl 1984–89, memb Scottish Health Servs Policy Bd 1985–89, memb Gtr Glasgow Health Bd 1989–91; chm: Strathclyde AIDS Forum 1990–92, Gtr Glasgow Health Bd AIDS Forum 1990–93, Gtr Glasgow Health Bd Drugs and Alcohol Forum 1990–93; chm Chryston HS Bd 1995–98 (vice-chm 1990–95); Elder Church of Scotland 1956–; session clerk: Ruchazie Parish Church 1961–71, Stepps Parish Church 1983–97; memb Bonnet Makers and Dyers Craft; fell BMA 1975, FRCGP 1980; SBStJ 1976; *Recreations* gardening; *Style*— Dr Keith Davidson, CBE; ✉ Dunvegan, 2 Hornshill Farm Road, Stepps, Glasgow G33 6DE (tel 0141 779 2103)

DAVIDSON, Kenneth Muir (Ken); *b* 11 November 1948; *m* 1973, Judy, *née* Dick; *Career* dir Bain Dawes (Scotland) Ltd 1977–80, chief devpt exec Bowring (UK) Ltd 1980–83, chm and md Frizzell Insurance Brokers Ltd 1983–92, chief exec FirstCity Insurance Gp Ltd 1992–94 (non-exec dir 1994–99); chm: Harel (UK) Ltd 1987–, Davidson Partnership Ltd 1994–, Netquote Ltd 1995–97, Kingsmead Underwriting Agency Ltd 1995–2003, Crispin Speers and Partners Ltd 1999–, Associated Insurance Experts 2001–, CSP Holding Ltd 2005–, Ascent Insurance Brokers Ltd 2006–; dir: CII Enterprises Ltd 1992–97, Simplemethod Ltd 1992–99, Educn and Trg Tst Chartered Inst Ltd 1993–, Insurance Solutions Ltd 1995–97, Soc of Fin Advsrs Ltd 1997–98, B F Caudle Agencies Ltd 2001–03; dep pres Insurance Charities Ltd 2006–; conslt Barlow Lyde & Gilbert 1995–2003; pres CII 1997–98, vice-pres Insurance Inst of London 1999–; Liveryman: Worshipful Co of Insurers, Worshipful Co of Wheelwrights; chm Br Insurance Law Assoc 2002–04; ACIArb, ACII; *Books* Insuring Environmental Risks (1987); *Style*— Ken Davidson, Esq

DAVIDSON, Prof Marilyn Joy; da of Wallace Eyre, and Joyce Mary, *née* Robinson, of Queniborough, Leics; *b* 22 November 1951; *Educ* Melton Mowbray Upper Sch, Bolton Inst of Technol (external BA Univ of London), Barnet Coll London (CertEd), Univ of Queensland (MA), UMIST (PhD); *m* (m dis); 1 da (Fern Eyre-Morgan b 8 Oct 1986), 1 s (Lloyd Eyre-Morgan b 16 Aug 1988); *Career* lectr Dept of Community Studies Barnet Coll of Further Educn 1974–75, tutor in psychology Univ of Queensland 1975–79, guest psychology lectr and supervisor Dept of Mgmnt Sciences UMIST 1980–83, guest lectr Univ of Manchester and Manchester Business Sch 1980–84, prof in work psychology Manchester Business Sch Univ of Manchester (formerly Manchester Sch of Mgmnt UMIST) 1998– (lectr 1984–89, sr lectr 1989–98); ed Women in Management Review 1991–96, former assoc ed Occupational and Organizational Psychology; assoc editorial memb: Gender, Work and Organisations, The International Review of Women and Leadership, The International Journal of Police Science and Management; CPsychol, FBPsS (memb Div of Occupational Psychology, memb Div of Psychology Women Section), FRSA; *Books* with C L Cooper: High Pressure: The Working Lives of Women Managers (1982), Stress and the Woman Manager (1983), Working Women - An International Survey (1984), Women in Management (1984), Women and Information Technology (ed, 1987), The Stress Survivors (1991), Shattering the Glass Ceiling - The Woman Manager (1992), European Women in Business and Management Europe 1992 (ed, 1993); others: Reach for the Top: A Woman's Guide to Success in Business and Management (1985), Vulnerable Workers - Psychological and Legal Issues (jt ed, 1991), Women in Management - Current Research Issues (jt ed, 1994), The Black and Ethnic Minority Woman Manager - Cracking the Concrete Ceiling (1997), Women in Management - Current Research Issues Vol II (jt ed, 2000), Individual Diversity and Psychology in Organizations (jt ed, 2003), International Handbook of Women and Small Business Entrepreneurship (jt ed, 2005), Managing Diversity and Equality in Construction (ed with A Gale, 2006), Gender and Communication at Work (jt ed, 2006); author of numerous articles and chapters in jls and pubns; *Recreations* playing cello, horse riding, theatre, cinema; *Style*— Prof Marilyn Davidson; ✉ Manchester Business School, The University of Manchester, Booth Street West, Manchester M15 6PB (tel 0161 306 3449, fax 0161 306 3450, e-mail marilyn.davidson@mbs.ac.uk)

D

DAVIDSON, Dr Neil McDonald; s of John Mackinnon Davidson (d 1980), and Alice Mary Stewart, *née* McDonald (d 1993); *b* 15 May 1940; *Educ* Merton Coll Oxford (MA, DM), St Thomas' Hosp London; *m* 31 Dec 1963, Jill Ann, da of Ernest Ripley; 3 s (Angus b 1966, Alastair b 1970, Calum b 1981), 1 da (Fiona b 1967); *Career* lectr then sr lectr in med Ahmadu Bello Univ Zaria Nigeria 1969–74, conslt physician Eastern Gen Hosp Edinburgh 1979–92, hon sr lectr Univ of Edinburgh 1979–92 (lectr then sr lectr in med 1975–79), asst dir of studies (med) Edinburgh Postgrad Bd for Med 1985–92; chief of internal med NWAF Hosp Tabuk Saudi Arabia 1992–95, head Dept of Med Zayed Military Hosp Abu Dhabi UAE 1995–96, sr conslt physician Armed Forces Hosp Kuwait 1996–98, conslt physician Al-Zahra Hosp Sharjah UAE 1998–99, int mgmnt team med dir European Gaza Hosp Palestine 1999–2001, chief Internal Med Beijing United Family Hosp China 2001–02, med dir Nat Hosp Abuja Nigeria 2002–04, med dir Reddington Multi-Specialist Hosp Lagos Nigeria 2005–; visiting prof of med Royal Coll of Surgns in Ireland 1992–95; author of papers on peri-partum cardiac failure, endocrinology and metabolism, tropical diseases; memb GMC 1989–94; FRCPE 1982, FRCP 1984; *Recreations* collecting antique maps, squash; *Style*— Dr Neil Davidson; ✉ 43 Blackford Road, Grange, Edinburgh EH9 2DT (tel 0131 667 3960, fax 0131 667 0973, e-mail nd99@hotmail.com)

DAVIDSON, Nicholas Ranking; QC (1993); s of Brian Davidson, CBE (d 1995), and Priscilla Margaret, *née* Chilver (d 1981); *b* 2 March 1951; *Educ* Winchester (scholar), Trinity Coll Cambridge (exhibitioner, MA, vice-pres Cambridge Union); *m* 7 Sept 1978, Gillian Frances, da of Michael Leslie Watts; 2 da (Alexandra Frances Priscilla b 20 July 1983, Elizabeth Frances Hermione b 9 April 1989); *Career* called to the Bar Inner Temple 1974 (Inner Temple scholar, Cert of Honour, Treasurer's prize, Hughes Parry prize, bencher 1998); dep judge of the High Court 2000–; chm Professional Negligence Bar Assoc 1998–99 (treas 1990–95, dep chm 1996–97); govr St Mary's Sch Ascot 1996–2006; MCIArb; *Publications* contrib Professional Negligence and Liability (ed Simpson, 2000); *Recreations* bridge, music, skiing; *Style*— Nicholas Davidson, Esq, QC; ✉ 4 New Square, Lincoln's Inn, London WC2A 3RJ (tel 020 7822 2000, fax 020 7822 2001, e-mail n.davidson@4newsquare.com)

DAVIDSON, Peter John; s of John Frank Davidson, and Susanne, *née* Ostberg; *b* 25 July 1954; *Educ* Perse Sch, Trinity Coll Cambridge (sr scholar, MA), IMD, INSEAD; *Career* process engr; ICI Agricultural Division Billingham: process engr Projects & Engrg Dept 1977–81, NITRAM plants mangr 1981–83, ammonia section mangr res 1983–86, res mangr 1986–89; process engrg mangr ICI Engineering 1989–94, gp research and technol mangr Tioxide plc 1994–98, vice-pres R & T Quest Foods 1998; currently non-exec dir D1 Oils plc; corporate memb Inst of Chemical Engrs and Chartered Engrs 1983, FIChemE, MEng, FREng 1992, FRSA 1995; *Recreations* hill walking, planning gardens, skiing, sailing, watercolours, cooking; *Style*— Peter Davidson, Esq, FREng

DAVIDSON, Philomena Mary; da of Thomas Oliver Grant Davidson, violinist (d 1985), and Mary Bridget Bourke; *b* 24 March 1949; *Educ* City & Guilds of London Art Sch (Edward Stott travel scholarship, Dip Sculpture), Royal Acad Schs London (RAS Dip Sculpture, Gold Medal for sculpture, Bronze Medal for work from the figure); *m* 7 Dec 1974, Michael Frank Davis; 2 da (Lucy Victoria b 3 June 1977, Ruth Alexandra b 18 Jan 1982); *Career* sculptor; studied Japanese language arts and architecture Japan 1973–76, opened Bronze Foundry Milton Keynes 1980; exhibitions: Royal Acad Summer Exhibition, Royal West of England Acad Annual Show, Westminster City Gallery, Bircham Gallery, Margam Sculpture Park, Woodlands Gallery, Well Hung Gallery, Artspace 2000, Study Gallery 2002; dir Chelsea Harbour Sculpture 1993 and 1996, md The Sculpture Co Ltd 1994–98, md Davidson Arts Partnership 1999–; first one woman show Coopers & Lybrand Atrium Gallery 1997; first woman pres Royal Soc of Br Sculptors 1990–96; FRSBS 1990 (assoc fell 1984), FRSA 1990, RWA 1996; *Recreations* swimming, reading biographies; *Style*— Ms Philomena Davidson; ✉ 34 Quainton Street, Neasden Village, London NW10 0BE (tel 020 8438 0299, e-mail phil@davidsonarts.com)

DAVIDSON, Roderick Macdonald; JP (1976); s of late Dr Stephen Moriarty Davidson, of Plymouth, and late Kathleen Flora, *née* Macdonald; *b* 2 January 1938; *Educ* Clifton, St John's Coll Cambridge; *m* 17 June 1961, Jane Margaret, da of late Dr Basil Stanley Kent, of Kingsclere; 2 da (Emma b 1963, Juliet b 1969), 1 s (Michael b 1965); *Career* Nat Serv RM 1956–58, cmmnd 1957; former dir Albert E Sharp stockbrokers; chm Close Brothers Devpt VCT 1999–, non-exec dir Close Bros VCT 1996–; cncllr Bristol City Cncl 1969–74, chm Cncl Bristol Cathedral 2005–; chm SSAFA Forces Help Avon & Severnside 1999–2005; memb: Ancient Soc of St Stephens Ringers, Dolphin, Canynges Colston, Colston Research; High Sheriff Avon 1981–82; memb: Worshipful Co of Curriers, Soc of Merchant Venturers of Bristol; *Recreations* golf, fishing, music; *Clubs* MCC, Clifton, Thurlestone Golf, Bristol and Clifton Golf, Burnham and Berrow Golf, Royal Dornoch Golf; *Style*— Roderick Davidson, Esq; ✉ tel and fax 0117 946 6844

DAVIDSON, Stephen Robert; DL (W Yorks 2002); s of Cecil Robert Davidson, of Tynemouth, and Joan, *née* Robinson (d 2003); *b* 20 October 1950; *Educ* Tynemouth GS, UMIST (BSc), Univ of Newcastle upon Tyne (PGCE); *m* 1983, Carol Anne, da of Ralston Smith; 1 s (Jamie b 1993); *Career* grad trainee Tube Investments Gp 1972–73; former sch appts: Lord Wandsworth Coll 1974–83, middle sch master Manchester GS 1983–96; currently headmaster Bradford GS 1996–; *Recreations* sport, travel, civil aviation; *Clubs* East India, MCC, Bradford, Ilkley Golf; *Style*— Stephen Davidson, Esq, DL; ✉ Bradford Grammar School, Keighley Road, Bradford BD9 4JP (tel 01274 553702, fax 01274 548129, e-mail hmsec@bradfordgrammar.com)

DAVIDSON KELLY, (Charles) Norman; s of (Frederick) Nevill Davidson Kelly (d 1976), of Edinburgh, and Mary Lyon Campbell (Molly), *née* MacLeod (d 1993); *b* 2 June 1945; *Educ* Edinburgh Acad, Exeter Coll Oxford (BA), Univ of Edinburgh (LLB); *m* 2 Sept 1972, Annabella Daphne Pitt, da of Herbert Alasdair Pitt Graham, of the Bahamas; 1 s (John b 1977), 1 da (Suzanna b 1979); *Career* law apprentice/asst slr W & J Burness, WS

Edinburgh; slr with Ivory & Sime Edinburgh, co sec Oil Exploration (Holdings) Ltd 1974–79, corp devpt dir LASMO plc 1986–94, gp gen mangr Business Devpt BHP Petroleum Ltd 1995–2001, chief exec Mena Energy Ltd 2001–02, pres Tigris Petroleum Pty Ltd 2002–; memb Bd Sidro SA 1990–2003; *Clubs* Puffins; *Style*— Norman Davidson Kelly, Esq; ✉ Little Boarhunt, Liphook, Hampshire GU30 7EE

DAVIDSON OF GLEN CLOVA, Baron (Life Peer 2006), of Glen Clova in Angus; Neil Forbes Davidson; QC (Scot 1993); *b* 13 September 1950; *Educ* Univ of Stirling (BA), Univ of Bradford Mgmnt Centre (MSc), Univ of Edinburgh (LLB, LLM); *m* 1980, Regina Anne, *née* Sprissler; *Career* analyst J & A Scrimgeour 1972; admitted to Faculty of Advocates 1979; slr-gen for Scotland 2000–01, advocate-gen for Scotland 2006–; dir: Scot Cncl for Int Arbitration 1990–2006, City Disputes Panel 1994–2000; ICJ chef de mission Egypt 1997 and 1998; pres Clan Davidson Assoc 2002–; *Books* Judicial Review in Scotland (1986); *Style*— Lord Davidson of Glen Clova, QC; ✉ c/o Advocates' Library, Parliament House, Parliament Square, Edinburgh EH1 1RF (tel 0131 226 5071, fax 0131 225 3642)

DAVIE, Alan; CBE (1972); *b* 28 September 1920; *Educ* Edinburgh Coll of Art (DA); *m* 1947, Janet Gaul, 1 da; *Career* painter, poet, musician, silversmith and jeweller; numerous solo and group exhbns worldwide since 1946 incl: London, Edinburgh, New York, Florida, Arizona, Perth, Delphi, Geneva, Hong Kong, Sweden; solo shows: Paris 1982, 1987 and 1988, ACA Gallery Munich 1994, Gimpel Gallery London 1997, 1999 and 2003, ACA Gallery NY 1997, Inverness Museum and Gallery 1997, The Pier Arts Centre Stromness Orkney 1998, Faggionata Fine Art London 1998, Nothelfer Gallery Berlin 2003, James Hyman Gallery London 2003, Open Eye Gallery Edinburgh 2004; retrospective exhbns: Edinburgh Festival and RSA Galleries 1972, Braunschweig and Karlsruhe 1972, SW Arts touring Scotland 1988–89, 54 Years of Paintings (McLellen Galleries Glasgow and Talbot Rice Gallery Univ of Edinburgh) 1992, Bristol RWA Galleries 1992, touring exhbn to Scotland, Brussels, Brazil, Argentina, Columbia, Venezuela, Chile, Mexico, Peru and Costa Rica 1992–94, Barbican London 1993, Ireland Kilkenny Castle (ACA Gallery NY, Bineth Gallery Tel Aviv, Univ of Brighton), Drawings Retrospectives (Scottish Nat Gallery of Modern Art) 1997, Scottish Nat Gallery of Modern Art Edinburgh 2000, Tate St Ives 2003–04; Small Painting: Univ of Brighton 2000, Univ of Edinburgh 2001; work included in: Br Painting 1700–1960 (Moscow), Br Painting and Sculpture 1960–70 (Washington), Br Paintings (Hayward Gallery) 1974, 25 years of Br Art (RA London) 1977, Retro Gouaches (Br Cncl Brussels) 1992, Il Mago (Art Gallery & Museum Glasgow) 1993; many works in public collections worldwide; external assessor Art Degrees 1967–; visiting prof Univ of Brighton 1997; music concerts and broadcasts with Tony Oxley Sextet 1974–75; monographs: Alan Davie (1967 and 1991), Alan Davie: The Quest for the Miraculous (1993), Alan Davie Drawings (1997); Gregory fell Univ of Leeds, sr fell RCA London; Guthrie Award (Royal Scot Acad Edinburgh) 1942; graphic prizes: Kraków 1966, Ibiza Museum 1976; Best Foreign Painter (VII Bienal de São Paulo) 1963, Saltire Award 1977; Hon DLitt: Heriot-Watt Univ 1994, Univ of Hertfordshire 1995; Hon DUniv Edinburgh 2003; HRSA, RWA; *Recreations* sailing, gliding, underwater swimming, music; *Style*— Alan Davie, Esq, CBE; ✉ Gamels Studio, Rush Green, Hertford SG13 7SB (tel 01920 463684, fax 01920 484406)

DAVIE, Jonathan Richard; s of Richard Davie, of Wimbledon, and Anne Christine Margaret, *née* Wilmot; *b* 21 September 1946; *Educ* Tonbridge, Univ of Neuchâtel; *m* 13 Sept 1986, Belinda Mary, da of Wing Cdr M V Blake; 2 da (Samantha Jane b 4 Jan 1991, Francesca Louise b 23 Aug 1995); *Career* articled to J Dix Lewis Caesar Duncan & Co (now Robson Rhodes) CAs 1965–69; Wedd Durlacher Mordaunt & Co: joined 1969, memb Stock Exchange 1974, ptnr 1976–86, sr dealing ptnr 1986; main bd dir Barclays de Zoete Wedd Holdings 1986–97 (md Fixed Income 1986–91), chief exec BZW Global Equities 1991–96, dep chm BZW 1996–97, vice-chm Credit Suisse First Boston 1997–2007, chm First Avenue Ptnrs LLP 2007–; non-exec chm IG Index plc 2004–, non-exec dir Credit Suisse (UK) Ltd 2003–; FCA (ACA 1970); *Recreations* golf, tennis, skiing; *Clubs* City of London, Queen's, Royal and Ancient, Royal St George's Golf, Prestwick Golf, Berkshire Golf, Sunningdale Golf, Rye Golf; *Style*— Jonathan Davie, Esq; ✉ First Avenue Partners LLP, Fitzroy House, 20 Grafton Street, London W1S 4DZ

DAVIE, Dr Ronald; s of Thomas Edgar Davie (d 1956), and Gladys May, *née* Powell; *b* 25 November 1929; *Educ* King Edward VI GS Aston, Univ of Reading (BA), Univ of Manchester (CertEd, Dip Teaching the Deaf), Univ of Birmingham (Dip Educnl Psychology), Univ of London (PhD); *m* 3 Aug 1957, Kathleen, da of William Wilkinson (d 1976); 1 da (Alison Catherine (Mrs Gray) b 1960), 1 s (Neil Adrian John b 1961); *Career* educnl and child psychologist; county educnl psychologist Isle of Wight 1961–64, co-dir Nat Child Devpt Study 1968–71, dep dir and dir of res Nat Children's Bureau 1972–73 (princ res offr 1965–68), prof of educnl psychology UC Cardiff 1974–81, dir Nat Children's Bureau 1982–90, consulting psychologist 1990–99, visiting prof Univ of Glos (formerly Cheltenham and Gloucester Coll of HE) 1997–; memb SEN Tbnl 1994–2003; hon res fell UCL 1991–, visiting fell Univ of Newcastle upon Tyne 1995–; vice-pres Young Minds charity 1990–, tstee Eden Valley Hospice 1997–2007 (chm 1999–2000); Hon DEd, Hon DLitt; FBPsS, Hon FRCPCH; *Books* 11,000 Seven-Year-olds (1966), Living with Handicap (1970), From Birth To Seven (1972), Children Appearing Before Juvenile Courts (1977), Change in Secondary Schools (1985), Child Sexual Abuse: The Way Forward After Cleveland (1989), Listening to Children in Education (1996), The Voice of the Child (1996); *Recreations* photography, antiques, calligraphy; *Style*— Dr Ronald Davie; ✉ Bridge House, Upton, Caldbeck, Cumbria CA7 8EU (tel and fax 016974 78364, e-mail rdavie29@aol.com)

DAVIE, Tim Douglas; s of Douglas Davie, of Herstmonceux, Sussex, and Alicia, *née* Higson; *b* 25 April 1967, Croydon; *Educ* Whitgift Sch Croydon, Univ of Cambridge (MA); *m* 1997, Anne, *née* Shotbolt; 3 s (James b 18 Feb 2000, William b 16 Sept 2002, Edward b 14 Jan 2006); *Career* brand mangr Proctor and Gamble 1989–93; PepsiCo: UK mktg dir 1993–2000, vice-pres int mktg 2000–05; dir Mktg, Cmmns and Audiences BBC 2005–; dir: Freeview, Digitaluk; memb Mktg Gp of GB 2000; *Recreations* running, skiing, reading; *Clubs* Soho House; *Style*— Tim Davie, Esq; ✉ BBC, 201 Wood Lane, London W12 7TQ (tel 020 8752 5252, e-mail tim.davie@bbc.co.uk)

DAVIES, Alan; *Career* comedian and actor; *Television* for BBC incl: The Stand Up Show, Top of the Pops, Have I Got News For You, Room 101, Jonathan Creek (winner of Best Drama BAFTA Awards 1998, winner of Most Popular Drama Series National Television Awards 1998), QI, Urban Trauma (also video 1998); other credits incl: The Clive James Show (ITV), A Many Splintered Thing (ITV), Bob and Rose (ITV), The Brief (ITV); *Radio* shows for BBC incl: Sick as a Parrot (Radio 5), Alan's Big One FM (Radio 1); *Tours* UK Tour, Melbourne Comedy Festival, Auckland Comedy Festival, Montreal Comedy Festival; *Video* Live From the Lyric Theatre (1995); *Awards* Best Young Comic Time Out Awards 1991, Festival Critics Award Edinburgh Festival 1994; *Recreations* supporter of Arsenal FC; *Style*— Alan Davies, Esq; ✉ c/o ARG, 4 Great Portland Street, London W1W 8PA (tel 020 7436 6400)

DAVIES, Alun Huw; *b* 16 January 1960; *Educ* Bishop Gore GS Swansea, Emmanuel Coll Cambridge (Windsor scholar, BA), Magdalen Coll Oxford and Univ of Oxford Med Sch (BM BCh), Univ of Oxford (MA, DM); *m*; 2 c; *Career* house surgn Nuffield Dept of Surgery Univ of Oxford and John Radcliffe Hosp 1984–85, house physician Northampton Gen Hosp 1985, demonstrator in anatomy Univ of Cambridge and supervisor in anatomy Downing, Girton and Wolfson Colls 1985–86, hon research worker Dept of Anatomy RCS 1986; SHO: John Radcliffe Hosp 1986–87, Bristol Royal Infirmary 1987–88; surgical registrar Churchill and John Radcliffe Hosps Oxford and Milton Keynes Hosp 1988–90, research fell, hon registrar and tutor in surgery Bristol Royal Infirmary and Univ of Bristol 1990–92, research fell and hon registrar Royal United Hosp Bath 1992, lectr Univ of Bristol 1992–95, sr registrar Derriford Hosp Plymouth 1992–93, sr registrar Bristol Royal Infirmary 1993–95, sr lectr and hon conslt in surgery Charing Cross and Westminster Med Sch 1995–97; Imperial Coll of Med and Charing Cross Hosp: sr lectr and hon conslt in surgery 1997–99, dir of undergraduate trg and dep head Div of Surgery, Anaethesia and Intensive Care 1998–2002, reader in surgery 1999–; currently hon conslt surgn: Hammersmith Hosps NHS Tst, Chelsea and Westminster NHS Tst, St Mary's Hosp Tst, Kingston and Roehampton NHS Tst; regnl advsr in vascular surgery 2003–07; ed Phlebology 2003–; reviewer: Br Jl of Surgery, Annals of RCS, BMJ, Br Jl of Radiology, European Jl of Vascular & Endovascular Surgery, Br Jl of Neurology & Psychiatry, Lancet, Cochrane Database, European Jl of Cardiology, Jl of Vascular Surgery; sometime examiner: Univ of Bristol, Univ of London, Univ of Leicester; memb NHS Panel of Experts Dept of Health; Sir Jules Thorn research fell 1991, Hunterian prof RCS 1993, Abdol Islami int guest scholar American Coll of Surgns 2000–01; RSM: memb Cncl Quality and Mgmnt Section 1998–, memb Cncl Venous Forum 1999–, memb Cncl Section of Surgery 2000–; memb: BMA, European Soc of Vascular Surgery, European Venous Forum (memb Bd 2000–, pres 2006–07), Surgical Research Soc, Soc of Academic Surgns, American Inst of Ultrasound in Med, Int Soc of Cardiovascular Surgery (UK rep European Chapter), Vascular Surgery Soc of GB and I (memb Cncl 1994–96), Br Assoc of Atherosclerosis, Vascular Soc of GB and I (memb Cncl 2002–07); fell: Assoc of Surgns of GB and I, Soc of Vascular Med and Biology, American Venous Forum; FRCS 1988, FRSM, FHEA 2007; *Publications* incl: Fast Facts: Vascular Surgery Highlights (published annually 1999–), Essential Vascular Surgery (co-author, 1999), Essential Postgraduate Surgery (co-ed, 2000), An Atlas of Endovascular and Vascular Surgery (co-author, 2001), Renal Access (co-ed, 2003) Leg Ulcers (co-author, 2003); numerous chapters in books, papers and articles in learned jls; *Style*— Alun Davies, Esq; ✉ Department of Surgery, Charing Cross Hospital, London W6 8RF (tel 020 8846 7320, fax 020 8846 7362, e-mail a.h.davies@imperial.ac.uk)

DAVIES, Prof Alwyn George; s of Rev John Lewis Davies (d 1986), of Hunstanton, Norfolk, and Victoria May, *née* Rowe (d 1996); *b* 1926; *Educ* Hamonds GS Swaffham Norfolk, UCL (BSc, PhD, DSc); *m* 11 Aug 1956, Margaret, da of Geoffrey Drake (d 1980), of Menai Bridge, Anglesey; 1 da (Sarah b 1958), 1 s (Stephen b 1960); *Career* lectr Battersea Poly 1949, prof of chemistry UCL 1969– (lectr 1953, reader 1964); fell UCL 1991; FRSC; FRS 1989; *Books* Organic Peroxides (1961), Organotin Chemistry (1997, 2 edn 2004); *Style*— Prof Alwyn Davies, FRS; ✉ 26 South Approach, Moor Park, Northwood, Middlesex HA6 2ET (tel 01923 823528); Chemistry Department, UCL, 20 Gordon Street, London WC1H 0AJ (tel 020 7679 4701, fax 020 7679 7463, e-mail a.g.davies@ucl.ac.uk)

DAVIES, (David) Andrew; AM; s of Wallace Morton Davies (d 1987), of Hereford, and Elizabeth Muriel Jane Davies, *née* Baldwin (d 1987); *Educ* Univ of Swansea (BSc); *m* 1978 (m dis 1990), Deborah, *née* Frost; *Career* memb Nat Assembly for Wales (Lab) Swansea W 1999–, min for Assembly Business 1999–; memb Yes for Wales Campaign and co-ordinator Lab assembly referendum campaign 1997, former memb Exec Ctee and regnl official Wales Labour Pty; former head of employee devpt Ford Motor Co; assoc dir public affairs co, memb SW Wales Regnl Ctee; pres Caer Las Housing Assoc, vice-pres Longfields Spastic Assoc, govr Swansea Coll and Dynevor Comp Sch; memb: Fabian Soc, Socialist Health Assoc, Liberty, Amnesty International; *Recreations* reading, the arts (especially contemporary music and dance), cooking, gardening; *Clubs* Swansea RFC (patron), Dunfant RFC, Swansea Business; *Style*— Andrew Davies, Esq, AM; ✉ National Assembly for Wales, Cardiff Bay, Cardiff CF99 1NA (tel 029 2089 8249, fax 029 2089 8419, e-mail andrew.davies@wales.gsi.gov.uk)

DAVIES, Andrew Wynford; *b* 20 September 1936; *Educ* Whitchurch GS Cardiff, UCL; *m* 1960; *Career* author, screenwriter and playwright; Hon DLitt: Coventry Univ 1994, Univ of Warwick 2004, Open Univ 2004, UCL 2006; Hon Dr Arts De Montfort Univ 2003; hon fell Univ of Wales 1997; fell BAFTA 2003, FRSL 1996; *Awards* Guardian Children's Fiction Award 1979, Boston Globe Horn Award 1979, Broadcasting Press Guild Award 1980, 1990, 1998, 1999 and 2002, Pye Colour TV Award Best Children's Writer 1981, RTS Writer's Award 1986,1987 and 2006, BAFTA Writer's Award 1989, BAFTA Award 1989, 1993, 1999, 2002 and 2006, Primetime Emmy Award 1991, Writers' Guild Award 1991, 1993, 1994, 1996, 1998 and 2006, Samuelson Award (Lifetime Achievement) 2004; *Television* scripts/adaptations: To Serve Them All My Days 1979 (from R F Delderfield novel, BBC1), A Very Peculiar Practice 1986–87, Mother Love 1989, House of Cards (from Michael Dobbs novel) 1990, Filipina Dreamers 1991, The Old Devils (from Kingsley Amis novel) 1992, Anglo-Saxon Attitudes 1992, A Very Polish Practice 1992, To Play the King (Michael Dobbs, BBC1) 1993, Middlemarch (from George Eliot novel, BBC1) 1994, Pride and Prejudice (Jane Austen, BBC1) 1995, Game On (with Bernadette Davis) 1995, The Final Cut (Michael Dobbs, BBC1) 1995, Emma (Jane Austen, ITV) 1996, Wilderness (with Bernadette Davis) 1996, Moll Flanders (Defoe, ITV) 1996, Bill's New Frock (Channel 4) 1997, Getting Hurt (BBC) 1998, Vanity Fair (BBC) 1998, A Rather English Marriage (BBC) 1998, Wives and Daughters (BBC) 1999, Take a Girl Like You 2000, The Way We Live Now (Anthony Trollope, BBC) 2001, Othello (ITV) 2001, Daniel Deronda (from George Eliot novel, BBC) 2002, Tipping the Velevet (BBC) 2002, Dr Zhivago (ITV) 2002, Boudica (ITV) 2002, He Knew He Was Right 2004, Falling (ITV) 2005, Bleak House (BBC) 2005, The Chatterley Affair (BBC) 2006, The Line of Beauty (BBC) 2006; *Stage Plays* Rose 1981, Prin 1990; *Films* Circle of Friends 1995, Bridget Jones's Diary 2001, The Tailor of Panama 2001, Bridget Jones: The Edge of Reason 2004; *Fiction* A Very Peculiar Practice (1986), The New Frontier (1987), Getting Hurt (1989), Dirty Faxes (1990); *Children's books* The Fantastic Feats of Dr Boox (1972), Conrad's War (1978), Marmalade and Rufus (1981), Marmalade Atkins in Space (1981), Educating Marmalade (1982), Danger Marmalade at Work (1983), Marmalade Hits the Big Time (1984), Alfonso Bonzo (1987), Poonam's Pets (with Diana Davies, 1990), Marmalade on the Ball (1995); *Recreations* tennis, food, alcohol; *Style*— Andrew Davies, Esq, FRSL; ✉ c/o The Agency, 24 Pottery Lane, London W11 4LZ (tel 020 7727 1346, fax 020 7727 9037)

DAVIES, Anna Elbina; *see:* Morpurgo Davies, Prof Anna

DAVIES, Barry; MBE (2005); *b* 24 October 1939; *Educ* Cranbrook Sch, Univ of London; *m* Penny; 1 da (Giselle), 1 s (Mark); *Career* sports broadcaster; cmmnd RASC (broadcaster Br Forces Network Cologne) 1962; with BBC Radio and corr The Times 1963–66; joined ITV (first TV football commentary Chelsea v AC Milan 1966), covered World Cup 1966 and Olympic Games 1968; joined BBC 1969; has covered Olympic Games, World Cup, Cwlth Games and Wimbledon; sports commentated and presented: football, tennis, rowing (boat race), hockey, ice hockey, ice skating, badminton, gymnastics, water skiing, cycling, volleyball; presenter Maestro (series, BBC); commentator: Lord Mayor's Show (BBC) 1996–, last Royal Tournament 1999, All The Queen's Horses 2002; *Recreations* family, sport, theatre; *Clubs* Hawks' (Cambridge), Wentworth; *Style*— Barry Davies, Esq, MBE; ✉ c/o Essentially Sport, Sir Walter Raleigh, 4th Floor, 48–50 Esplanade, St Helier, Jersey JE2 3QB (tel 01534 840888, fax 01534 840999)

DAVIES, Betty Alicia; JP (Nottingham 1971); da of Charles William Pearl, of Nottingham, and Alice, *née* Stevenson; *Educ* Haywood Sch Nottingham, Guildhall Sch of Music and Drama (LGSM); *Career* fashion/textile designer and corp branding specialist; chm and chief exec Betty Davies SFI (design and mgmnt conslts, corp and ceremonial dress) 1990–, princ Perform PR Scotland 2003; designer: Royal Bank of Scotland, Royal

Collections 1993–, Bank of Scotland 1997–2003, Levee dress for first woman Herald Ct of the Lord Lyon, Royal Scot Acad robes 2002–03, new ceremonial robes Moderator of the General Assembly of the Church of Scotland 2004, academic robes Edinburgh Coll of Art; public memb Press Cncl 1983–90; memb Ct Univ of Nottingham, memb Bd of Govrs Nottingham Girls' HS 1987–94, govr Edinburgh Coll of Art 1989–2002 (hon fell 2003); conslt dir and vice-chm Edinburgh Coll of Art Alumni Assoc 2003–, ed Decades 2003; chm Nottingham Cncl for Voluntary Serv 1981–84; fndr chm Edinburgh Theatre Workshop; organiser Lunch-time Proms Nottingham Playhouse 1966–89 and Royal Scottish Acad 1989–94; MIMgt 1982; *Recreations* visual and performing arts; *Style—* Mrs Betty Davies; ✉ 5 Blackie House, Lady Stair's Close, Edinburgh EH1 2NY (tel 0131 225 6065, fax 0131 220 2755, mobile 07720 441363, e-mail betty.davies@bettydavies.co.uk)

DAVIES, Bob; *b* 12 October 1948; *Educ* Univ of Edinburgh (LLB); *m* 1971, Eileen; 1 s (Christopher b 1978); *Career* Ford Motor Co: joined 1970, mangr treasy analysis Ford Motor Credit 1982–83, dir of fin Ford Spain 1983–85; dir Coopers & Lybrand Assoc 1985–87, chief fin offr Waterford Wedgewood plc 1987–91, fin dir Ferranti International plc 1991–93, chief exec East Midlands Electricity plc 1997–98 (fin dir 1994–97), chief exec Arriva plc 1998–2006, chm Biffa plc 2006–; non-exec dir: Geest plc 1998–2004, Barratt Devpts 2004–, British Energy Group plc 2006–; chm NE Regnl Cncl CBI 2007–, dir Sunderland Urban Regeneration Co 2002–07, chm Bd of Govrs Univ of Sunderland; CIMgt, fell CIMA; *Recreations* golf, vintage cars; *Style—* Bob Davies, Esq; ✉ Biffa plc, Coronation Road, Cressex, High Wycombe, Buckinghamshire HP12 3TZ

DAVIES, Prof (John) Brian; s of John Kendrick Davies (d 1966), and Agnes Ada Davies (d 1971); *b* 2 May 1932; *Educ* Univ of Cambridge (MA), Univ of London (MSc, PhD, DSc); *m* 11 Aug 1956, Shirley June, da of Frederick Ralph Abrahart; 1 s (Jeremy b 1960), 2 da (Fiona b 1961, Nicola b 1970); *Career* res scientist Mullard Research Laboratories 1955–63, lectr Univ of Sheffield 1963–67; UCL: sr lectr 1967–70, reader 1970–85, prof 1985–97 (emeritus prof 1997–), dean of engrg 1989–91; FIEE 1982, FREng 1988, FIEEE 1995; *Books* Electromagnetic Theory (vol 2, 1972); *Recreations* music, mountaineering; *Style—* Prof Brian Davies, FREng; ✉ 14 Gaveston Drive, Berkhamsted, Hertfordshire HP4 1JE (e-mail bdavies@gaveston.u-net.com); Department of Electrical Engineering, University College, Torrington Place, London WC1E 7JE

DAVIES, Charles Simon Hartley; s of Graham Hartley Davies, and Carolyn, *née* Murrell; *b* 2 April 1970; *Educ* Shrewsbury, Univ of Durham (BA); *Career* Cargill 1992–93, Sunrise Asset Co Ltd 1993–98, fndr and ceo The Link Asset & Securities Co Ltd 1998–, fndr Linkbrokers Inc (NY) 2003, fndr Link Securities (HK) 2005; Deloitte 5th Fastest Gp Company in UK 2004; *Recreations* swimming, fly fishing; *Style—* Charles Davies, Esq; ✉ The Link Asset and Securities Co Ltd, The Courtyard, 12 Sutton Row, London W1D 4AD (tel 020 7663 4300, fax 020 7851 6630, e-mail charlie@linkbrokers.co.uk)

DAVIES, Chris; MEP (Lib Dem) NW England; *b* 7 July 1954; *Educ* Cheadle Hulme Sch Stockport, Gonville & Caius Coll Cambridge (MA), Univ of Kent at Canterbury; *m* 27 Oct 1979, Carol; 1 da; *Career* chm Housing Liverpool City Cncl 1982–83, marketing and communications conslt 1983–95 and 1997–99; MP (Lib Dem) Littleborough and Saddleworth 1995–97, MEP (Lib Dem) NW England 1999–, environment spokesman European Parl; *Recreations* fell running; *Style—* Chris Davies, Esq, MEP; ✉ 87A Castle Street, Stockport SK3 9AR (tel 0161 477 7070, fax 0161 477 7007, e-mail chrisdaviesmep@cix.co.uk); European Parliament, Room 10G 218, Rue Wiertz, B-1047, Brussels (tel 0032 2284 5353/7353, e-mail chris.davies@europarl.europa.eu)

DAVIES, Colin Godfrey; *b* 1934; *Educ* Kings Sch Bruton, Loughborough Univ of Technol (BSc); m; 2 s; *Career* cmnd offr RAF 1952–54; bank official National Provincial Bank 1951–55; Cable and Wireless plc: technician rising to sr mangr commercial and technical fields 1955–77, chief engr Long Distance Servs Abu Dhabi 1978–79, mangr Int Servs Qatar 1980–82, general mangr Qatar 1983–87, dir of Corp Technol 1988–90; DG Projects and Engrg CAA 1990–97, ret; CEng, FIEE, FRAeS; *Recreations* sport; *Style—* Colin Davies, Esq; ✉ Ibex House, Church Lane, Worplesdon, Guildford, Surrey GU3 3RU (tel and fax 01483 233214, e-mail cgdavies@btopenworld.com)

DAVIES, David; s of Paul Davies, and Susan, *née* Stark; *b* 3 March 1985, Cardiff; *Educ* St Cyres Comp Sch Penarth; *Career* swimmer; achievements incl: Silver medal 200m freestyle and Silver medal mixed 4 x 200m freestyle relay European Youth Olympics 2001, Silver medal 400m freestyle and Bronze medal 4 x 200m freestyle relay European Jr Long-Course Championships 2002, Silver medal 1500m freestyle European Short-Course Championships 2002, Gold medal 1500m freestyle, Silver medal 200m freestyle and Bronze medal 400m freestyle European Jr Long-Course Championships 2003, Bronze medal 1500m freestyle Olympic Games Athens 2004, Bronze medal 1500m freestyle World Championships Montreal 2005, Gold medal 1500m freestyle and Bronze medal 400m freestyle Cwlth Games Melbourne 2005; *Style—* David Davies, Esq

DAVIES, 3 Baron (UK 1932), of Llandinam, Co Montgomery; David Davies; DL (Powys); s of 2 Baron Davies (ka 1944), by his w, Ruth Eldrydd (d 1966), da of Maj W M Dugdale, CB, DSO, of Glanyrafon Hall, Llanyblodwell, Salop; *b* 2 October 1940; *Educ* Eton, King's Coll Cambridge; *m* 1972, Beryl, da of W J Oliver; 2 da (Hon Eldrydd Jane b 1973, Hon Lucy b 1978), 2 s (Hon David Daniel b 1975, Hon Benjamin Michael Graham b 1985); *Heir* s, Hon David Davies; *Career* chm Welsh National Opera Co 1975–2000; CEng, MICE; *Style—* The Rt Hon the Lord Davies, DL; ✉ Plas Dinam, Llandinam, Powys

DAVIES, Dr David Denison; s of Samuel Davies (d 1958), and Ethel Mary, *née* Dennison (d 1980); *Educ* Salt GS, Univ of Leeds (MRCS, LRCP), Univ of London (PhD); *m* 26 Feb 1977, Kay; 1 s (Edward b 1978), 1 da (Philippa b 1980); *Career* res fell Anaesthetics Res Dept RCS London 1967–70, conslt anaesthetist and pain specialist Central Middx Hosp London 1970–; memb: Anaesthetic Res Soc, Pain Soc; author of numerous publications on gas chromatography, pharmacokinetics of anaesthetic agents, morbidity and mortality in anaesthesia and pain therapy; FRCA, FRSM; *Books* Gas Chromatography in Anaesthesia: Thesis (1975); *Recreations* history, painting, traditional jazz; *Style—* Dr David Denison Davies; ✉ 10 Beaufort Place, Bray, Maidenhead, Berkshire SL6 2BS (tel and fax 01628 671003); Department of Anaesthesia, Central Middlesex Hospital, Acton Lane, London NW10 7NS (tel 020 8453 2160, fax 020 8453 2194)

DAVIES, Prof Sir David Evan Naunton; kt (1994), CBE (1986); s of David Evan Davies (d 1935), and Sarah, *née* Samuel (d 1982); *b* 28 October 1935; *Educ* West Monmouth Sch, Univ of Birmingham (MSc, PhD, DSc); *m* 1, 21 July 1962, Enid (d 1990), da of James Edwin Patilla; 2 s (Christopher James b 1965, Michael Evan b 1967); m 2, 19 Nov 1992, Jennifer Eason Rayner; *Career* lectr and sr lectr Univ of Birmingham 1961–67, hon sr princ sci offr Royal Radar Estab Malvern 1966–67, asst dir Res Dept BR Derby 1967–71, prof of electrical engrg UCL 1971–86 (vice-provost 1986–88), vice-chllr Loughborough Univ of Technol 1988–1993, chief scientific advsr MOD 1993–99; pres Royal Acad of Engrg 1996–2001; pro-chllr Univ of Sussex 1998–2001; chm: Railway Safety 2001–03, Hazard Forum 2003–; memb Bd: ERA Technology Ltd 1994–2003, Lattice plc 2001–02, ERA Fndn 2001–07; memb and chm of numerous ctees of: MOD, DES, Cabinet Office; Rank Prize for Optoelectronics 1984, Callendar Medal (Inst of Measurement and Control) 1984, Centennial Medal (Inst of Electrical and Electronic Engrs USA) 1984, Faraday Medal (IEE) 1987, President's Medal Royal Acad of Engrg; Hon DSc: Loughborough Univ 1994, Univ of Bradford 1995, Univ of Warwick 1997, Univ of Wales 2002; Hon DEng: Univ of Birmingham 1994, South Bank Univ 1994, Herriot Watt Univ 1999, UMIST 2000; Hon DUniv Surrey 1996; hon fell UCL 2006; FIEE 1967, FREng 1979, FRS 1984; *Publications* author of publications on radar and fibre optics; *Style—* Prof Sir David Davies, CBE, FRS, FREng; ✉ Church Hill House, Church Lane, Danehill, East Sussex RH17 7EY; 29 Victoria House, 25 Tudor Street, London EC4Y 0DD (tel 01825 790321, e-mail den@easonestates.freeserve.co.uk)

DAVIES, David Johnston; OBE (2007); s of John Edwardes Davies, MBE (d 1948), and Margaret Frances, *née* Morrison (d 1999); *b* 28 May 1948; *Educ* Royal Masonic Sch for Boys, Univ of Sheffield (BA(Econ)), Univ of Oxford (CertEd); *m* July 1977, Susan Anne, *née* Cuff; 2 da (Amanda Jane b March 1980, Caroline Frances b April 1983); *Career* Thomson Regional Newspapers (Belfast Telegraph) 1970–71, BBC corr and presenter 1971–94 (variously BBC TV News political corr, BBC TV News educn corr, presenter/corr Grandstand and Match of the Day, assignments incl General Elections and World Cups); The FA: dir public affrs 1994–98, exec dir 1998–2000, dir int strategy 2000–06, exec dir 2004–06; sports/media conslt 2006–; memb: RTS 1985–, Football Writers Assoc 1990–, Media Ctees/Panel UEFA 1996–2006, Govt Football Task Force 1997–99, BOA 2000–06, Assistance Progs Ctee UEFA 2002–03; Duke of Edinburgh's Gold Award 1965, Clear Speaking Award Birmingham Inst for the Deaf 1993; fell Univ of Sheffield 2000–; *Recreations* family, watching cricket, tennis, theatre; *Clubs* Lancashire CCC; *Style—* David Davies, Esq, OBE; ✉ Tregaron Associates, Apartment 9, The Iceworks, 34–36 Jamestown Road, London NW1 7BY (tel 01242 631345, e-mail david.davies@wiggin.co.uk)

DAVIES, David Thomas Charles; MP, AM; s of Peter Hugh Charles Davies, and Kathleen Diane, *née* Elton, of Newport; *b* 27 July 1970; *Educ* Bassaleg Comp Sch Newport; *m* 2003, Aliz, *née* Harnisföger; *Career* Br Steel Corp 1988–89, seasonal jobs in Australia 1989–91, gen mangr tea importing and shipping co 1991–99, memb Nat Assembly for Wales (Cons) Monmouth 1999–; Parly candidate (Cons) Bridgend 1997, MP (Cons) Monmouth 2005–; led NO campaign Newport 1997; memb: Inst of Traffic Admin, Inst of Freight Forwarding; MILog; *Recreations* surfing, long distance running, keeping fit; *Clubs* Oriental, Cardiff and County, Abergavenny Constitutional, Chepstow Cons, Monmouth Cons, Usk Cons; *Style—* David Davies, Esq, MP, AM; ✉ The Grange, 16 Maryport Street, Usk, Monmouthshire (tel 01291 672780); National Assembly for Wales, Cardiff Bay, Cardiff CF99 1NA (tel 029 2089 8325, fax 029 2089 8326, e-mail david.davies@wales.gov.uk)

DAVIES, David Yorwerth; s of Hywel Morris Davies (d 1985), and Marjory Winnifred Davies (d 1970); *b* 24 February 1939; *Educ* Grove Park GS Wrexham, Univ of Durham (DipArch); *m* 31 May 1969, Angela, da of Jack Theed (d 1966); 2 s (Andrew b 1970, Gareth b 1972); *Career* fndr D Y Davies Associates Chartered Architects 1969, exec chm D Y Davies plc 1986–96, conslt GHM Group 1996–2002; cmmnd bldgs incl: Heathrow Terminal 3, Blue Circle Industries HQ Aldermaston; dir Docklands Development Corp 1988–90; RIBA (vice-pres 1987), Hon FAIA; *Recreations* golf, food, wine; *Clubs* Sunningdale Golf, Royal and Ancient; *Style—* David Davies, Esq; ✉ Heatherside, Ridgemount Road, Sunningdale, Berkshire SL5 9RL (tel 01344 620027)

DAVIES, Derek; s of John Davies (d 1965), and Alice, *née* Heap (d 1996); *b* 27 October 1933; *Educ* Bolton Sch, Trinity Hall Cambridge (MA, MB BChir); *m* 2 May 1959, Barbara Jean, da of William Helsby (d 1969); 2 s (Christopher b 1960, Timothy b 1969), 2 da (Alison b 1964, Amanda b 1967 d 1980); *Career* sr med house offr Manchester Royal Infirmary 1960–62 (resident clinical pathologist 1959–60); med registrar: Derbyshire Royal Infirmary 1962–63, UCH 1963–65; lectr then sr lectr in clinical endocrinology Victoria Univ of Manchester 1968–88 (hon conslt 1972–88), conslt physician Manchester Royal Infirmary 1988–95 (med clinical dir 1991–94), chm Clinical Bd Manchester Central Hosps and Community Care NHS Tst 1991–92; pt/t med memb Pensions Appeal Tribunals (England & Wales); ret; fell Manchester Med Soc; FRSM, FRCP; *Recreations* choral music, fell walking; *Style—* Derek Davies, Esq; ✉ tel 01204 811220, e-mail daviesbltndc@btinternet.com

DAVIES, Edward Rodney; *b* 25 May 1958; *Educ* Leeds GS, Univ of Manchester (LLB), Coll of Law, King's Coll London (MSc); *m* Juliet; *Career* admitted slr 1982; ptnr specialising in construction and engrg law Masons slrs Manchester 1989–; trained as mediator American Arbitration Assoc (San Francisco); course lectr in construction and engrg law, visiting research fell UMIST; memb: Law Soc 1982, American Arbitration Assoc 1994; *Recreations* walking; *Style—* Edward Davies, Esq; ✉ Masons, 100 Barbirolli Square, Manchester M2 3SS (tel 0161 234 8234, fax 0161 234 8235)

DAVIES, Edwin; OBE (2000); s of Edwin Davies (d 1983), and Hannah, *née* Kelly (d 1979); *b* 18 June 1946, Salford, Gtr Manchester; *Educ* Farnworth GS, Univ of Durham (BA); *m* 1, 22 Aug 1969 (m dis 1987), Jean, *née* Ellison; 1 da (Sarah Jane b 22 March 1971), 1 s (Roger John b 14 Feb 1974); m 2, 30 June 1989, Susan Chinn, *née* Crellin; *Career* various positions rising to asst gp md Scapa Group plc 1968–84, chm STRIX Group Ltd 1984–2006; dir Bolton Wanderers FC 1999–; tstee V&A 2007–; CMI 1996; FCMA 1985; *Recreations* soccer, shooting, travel; *Style—* Edwin Davies, Esq, OBE; ✉ Morrecroft, Crossag Road, Isle of Man IM9 3EF (tel 01624 828730, fax 01624 824578, e-mail gilly@fildraw.com)

DAVIES, Elsa Myfanwy; LVO (2004); da of Mary, *née* Williams, and John Rees; *Educ* Univ of Wales (Teacher's Cert), Open Univ (BA), Univ of London (DipEd, MA); *Career* teacher Glamorgan CC 1965–70, dep head London Borough of Hillingdon 1970–74; head teacher: Surrey CC 1974–83, London Borough of Hillingdon 1983–87; mangr Chartered Mgmnt Inst 1988–91, dir National Playing Fields Assoc (NPFA) 1991–2004, chief exec NPFA Services Ltd 1991–2004, chief exec Millenium Centres Devpt Co Ltd 1997–2004, chief exec Mackworth Ltd 2004–; conslt to various bodies incl: Univ of London, Moorhead State Univ MN, Univ of Ulster, Univ of Leicester, Manchester Poly, Brighton Poly, BBC Enterprises, Welsh Consumer Cncl, The Spastics Soc (now Scope), National Foundation for Educn and Research, Commission of the European Communities; lectr to various orgns, local authorities and colleges incl: Capita Training, The Engineering Cncl, The Industrial Soc, Surrey, Hants, Essex and Sheffield Local Authorities, Univ of Antwerp, Univ of Birmingham, Kingston Poly, Poly of Wales, Mid Kent Coll of HE; govr Royal Welsh Coll of Music and Drama 2001–06; memb: Central Cncl of Physical Recreation (CCPR), Cncl for Nat Academic Awards Educnl Orgn, Mgmnt Bd and Initial Teacher Educn Bd 1985–91, Nat Curriculum Working Gp on Design and Technol 1989–91, Cncl Advsy Centre for Educn 1977–90 (former chm), Cncl British Educnl Mgmnt and Admin Soc 1980–92, ESU 1980–2000 (Page scholar 1981), UK/US Teacher Exchange Ctee Central Bureau for Educnl Visits and Exchanges 1981–92 (former vice-chm), Euro Forum for Educn Mgmnt 1981–92, Commonwealth Cncl for Educnl Admin 1981–92, Educn 2000 1983, Court Univ of Wales Coll of Cardiff 1989–92, Ct Nat Library of Wales 2002–06, Organising Ctee Educn Mgmnt Int Intervisitation Prog 1990, Cncl Action for Govrs Info and Trg Sponsorship Ctee 1990–91, Working Gp Human Resource Devpt Partnership 1990–91, Belgravia Breakfast Club 1991–2000, Lady Taverners 1992–97, London Businesswomen's Network 1992–97, City of London Sport and Recreation Cncl 1992–94, Shadow Sec of State's Nat Lottery Gp 1996, Cncl Univ of Wales 2006–, Glas Cymru; hon advsr World Educn Fellowship (GB) 1977– (former chm); external examiner Wales Poly 1985–91; author of several chapters and articles in educnl pubns; FCMI 1987, FRSA 1989 (memb Examinations Bd Educnl Policy Ctee and chm Advsy Ctee on Initial Educn 1990), MILAM 1997–2001; *Style—* Mrs Elsa Davies, LVO

DAVIES, Emrys Thomas; CMG (1987); s of Evan William Davies (d 1954), and Dinah, *née* Jones (d 1995); *b* 8 October 1934; *Educ* Parmiters Fndn Sch London, Sch of Slavonic Studies Univ of Cambridge, SOAS Univ of London, Inst of Fine Arts Hanoi Univ; *m* 1960, Angela Audrey, da of Paul Robert Buchan May (d 1952), and Esme May; 1 s (Robert),

2 da (Victoria, Elizabeth); *Career* RAF 1953–55; HM Dip Serv: served Peking and Shanghai 1956–59, FO 1959–60, Political Residence Bahrain 1960–62, UN Gen Assembly NY 1962, FO 1962–63, asst political advsr to Hong Kong Govt 1963–68, Br High Cmmn Ottawa 1968–71, FCO 1972–76, commercial cnsllr Peking 1976–78 (in charge 1976 and 1978), Univ of Oxford Business Summer Sch 1977, NATO Defense Coll Rome 1979, dep high cmmr Ottawa 1979–82, Dip Serv overseas inspr 1982–83, dep perm rep to OECD Paris 1984–87, ambass to Vietnam 1987–90, high cmmr to Barbados, Antigua and Barbuda, St Kitts and Nevis, Dominica, St Lucia, St Vincent and the Grenadines and Grenada 1991–94, ret; head UK Delgn to the EC Monitoring Mission Zagreb 1995, sec gen Tripartite Cmmn for the Restitution of Monetary Gold Brussels 1995–98, memb Ind Panel of Advsrs to Welsh Office 1997, head of UK Delgn EC Monitoring Mission Sarajevo 1998 and 1999, political advsr EU Police Mission Sarajevo 2003; *Books* Albigensians and Cathars (trans); *Recreations* golf, theatre, painting, walking; *Clubs* RAF; *Style*— Emrys Davies, Esq, CMG; ✉ Edinburgh House, 8 Alison Way, Winchester, Hampshire SO22 5BT

DAVIES, Sir Frank John; kt (1999), CBE (1993); s of Lt-Col F H Davies (d 1991), of Lincoln, and Veronica Josephine Davies (d 1943); *b* 24 September 1931; *Educ* Monmouth, UMIST; *m* 1956, Sheila Margaret, da of Geoffrey Bailey (d 1938), and Frances Bailey (d 1971); 3 s (James, Stephen, Jonathan); *Career* gp chief exec and md Rockware Gp plc 1983–93; dir: Ardagh plc 1985–2002, BTR Nylex Ltd 1991–94, Aggregate Industries plc (formerly Bardon Group plc) 1994–2002, Investor Champions plc 2000–05, Ardagh Glass Group plc 2002–; chm: Nuffield Orthopaedic Centre NHS Tst 1990–98, Health and Safety Cmmn 1993–99, Backcare (Nat Back Pain Assoc) 1998–2005, Mediwatch 2003–05; pres: Glass Mfrs Fedn 1986 and 1987, Fedn Européene de Verre d'Emballage 1988–89; govr Inst of Occupational Med 2000–, govr and chm Br Safety Cncl 2000–06, dep chm Railway Safety 2001–03, non-exec dir Railway Safety and Standards Bd 2003–; vice-pres St John Ambulance Oxon 1973–2000; memb: Oxon HA 1983–91, Cncl CBI 1986–93, Packaging Standards Cncl 1992–93; chm St Mary's Church Appeal Banbury 2000–06; Freeman: City of London, Worshipful Co of Basketmakers, Worshipful Co of Glass Sellers; CIMgt, FRSA; OStJ 1987; *Recreations* gardening, music, history, theatre; *Clubs* Carlton, RAC; *Style*— Sir Frank Davies, CBE; ✉ Stonewalls, Castle Street, Deddington, Oxfordshire OX15 0TE (tel 01869 338131)

DAVIES, (David) Gareth; s of John Davies (d 1978), and Annie Ceridwen, *née* Evans (d 1949); *b* 7 February 1939; *Educ* Aberdare GS for Boys, Univ of Wales Coll of Cardiff (BA); *m* 1963, Sonia Eileen, da of Harry Ludlow; 1 s (Ioan Geraint b 14 March 1968); *Career* museum asst in charge Chelmsford and Essex Museum 1964–65, asst curator Colchester and Essex Museum 1965–70, dir Verulamium and City Museum St Albans 1970–86, dir Cncl of Museums in Wales 1986–96; heritage conslt/lectr/advsr; chair Contemporary Art Soc for Wales, tstee/advsr Welsh Regnl Museum Royal Regiment of Wales, art/museum conslt Univ of Glamorgan, memb Arts Cncl of Wales Capital Grants Ctee; author of numerous articles and papers; FMA 1979 (AMA 1970), FSA 1978; *Recreations* rugby and cricket (spectator), theatre, reading and music, food and wine, walking, collecting contemporary art; *Style*— Gareth Davies, Esq, FSA; ✉ 1 Court Cottages, Michaelston Road, St Fagans, Cardiff CF5 6EN (tel 029 2059 5206)

DAVIES, His Hon Gareth Lewis; s of David Edward Davies (d 1960), and Glynwen Lewis (d 1992); *b* 8 September 1936; *Educ* Brecon Co GS, Univ of Wales (LLB); *m* 1, 1962; 2 da (Sally b 1963, Lucy 1965), 2 s (Simon b 1967, Jonathan b 1967); m 2, 2001, Emma Jayne; *Career* qualified slr 1962, ptnr Ottaways St Albans 1965–90, recorder 1987–90, circuit judge 1990–2002 (dep circuit judge 2002–); *Recreations* sailing instructor, ski guide, cycling, classic cars; *Style*— His Hon Gareth Davies

DAVIES, Gareth Robert; s of Tegfryn Davies, and Ethel, *née* Roberts; *Educ* Chetham's Sch Manchester, RMA Sandhurst; *Career* cmmnd Royal Regt of Artillery (5RA and 3RHA) 1966, Maj Sultan of Oman's Artillery 1977–80; joined Prison Service 1980, govr HMP Canterbury 1995–98, ldr Kosovo Prisons Project DFID 1999, govr HMP Pentonville 2000–, dir of law and order Iraq 2004–; memb Prison Govrs Assoc; Churchill fell 1995; *Recreations* opera (performance, direction and appreciation), growing fruit, reading, poetry, music, watching rugby (played for Army and Hong Kong Colony); *Clubs* In and Out; *Style*— Gareth Davies, Esq

DAVIES, Gavyn; OBE (1979); s of W J F Davies, of Southampton, and M G Watkins; *b* 27 November 1950; *Educ* Taunton's Sch Southampton, St John's Coll Cambridge (BA), Balliol Coll Oxford; *m* 1989, Susan Jane Nye; 1 da (Rosie b 31 Jan 1990), 2 s (Ben b 14 March 1995, Matthew b 2 July 1998); *Career* econ advsr Policy Unit 10 Downing St 1974–79, UK economist Phillips and Drew 1979–81, chief UK economist Simon and Coates 1981–86, chief int economist Goldman Sachs 1986–2001 (ptnr 1988–2001, advsy dir 2001–), chm BBC 2001–04 (vice-chm 2001), currently co-fndr Prisma Capital Ptnrs; memb HM Treasy independent panel of economic forecasting advisers 1992–97; chm UK govt inquiry into The Future Funding of the BBC 1999; visiting prof LSE 1988–98; fell Univ of Wales Aberyswyth 2002–; Hon DSc Univ of Southampton 1998, Hon LLD Univ of Nottingham 2002; *Recreations* sport; *Style*— Gavyn Davies, Esq, OBE

DAVIES, (John) Geoffrey; s of Leonard Churchman Davies (d 1990), of Cardiff, and Olive Winnifred Davies; *b* 12 May 1942; *Educ* Oundle, Univ of London (BSc(Econ)); *m* 15 July 1978, Penelope Antoinette Jeanne, *née* Cracroft-Rice; 1 s (Benjamin John b 5 Oct 1979); *Career* apprentice then prodn mangr British Ropes 1961–67, mgmnt conslt Inbucon AIC 1968–71, mangr Messrs Man Judd 1975–76 (articled clerk 1971–74); Touche Ross (now Deloitte & Touche): jt ptnr in charge Jersey 1977, regnl ptnr in charge Touche Ross UK Offshore Region 1991; currently memb Administrative Appeals Panel Jersey; FCA (ACA 1974); *Recreations* swimming, walking, boating, cycling, reading and wine; *Clubs* Cardiff & County, Victoria, United; *Style*— Geoffrey Davies, Esq

DAVIES, George William; s of George Davies (d 1987), of Southport, Lancs, and Mary, *née* Wright; *b* 29 October 1941; *Educ* Bootle GS, Univ of Birmingham, Northumbria Univ (DCL); *m* 1, 25 Sept 1965 (m dis 1985), Anne Margaret, da of Maj Donald Dyson Allan; 3 da (Melanie b 8 Aug 1966, Emma b 23 Sept 1968, Alexandra b 7 Sept 1973); m 2, 7 Dec 1985 (m dis 1992), Mrs Elzbieta Krystyna (Liz) Devereux-Batchelor, da of Stanislaw Ryszard Szadbey; 2 da (Lucia b 22 May 1988, Jessica b 2 June 1989), m 3, 16 Oct 1992, Fiona Teresa, da of Donovan Karl Shead; 2 s (George Jeremy b 19 Feb 1992, Barnaby Charles b 9 Dec 1993); *Career* stock merchandise controller Littlewoods Stores 1967–72, School Care (own business) 1972–75, Party Plan and Pippadee Lingerie 1975–81; J Hepworth & Son: joined 1981, responsible for launch of Next Feb 1982, jt gp md 1984, chief exec 1985, chm and chief exec 1987–88; chm and md The George Davies Partnership plc 1989, md George Clothing (part of Asda Group plc) 1995–2000, fndr S'porter (themed designer clothing for football clubs) 1995; launched Per Una into Marks and Spencer stores 2001, launched George Davies postgrad course in Retail in Mktg Heriot-Watt Univ 2005; Guardian Young Businessman of the Year 1985, Wood MacKenzie Retailer of the Year 1987, Marketing Personality of the Year 1988, Drapers Lifetime Achievement Award 2003, Prima Designer of the Decade 2004 (also High Street Designer of the Decade), TextilWirtschaft Magazine Forum Award 2004; Hon DBA Liverpool Poly 1989, Hon DDes Nottingham Trent Univ 1996, Hon DDes Middlesex Univ 2002, Hon DLitt Heriot-Watt Univ 2003, Hon DCL Northumbria Univ 2005, Hon DDes De Montfort Univ 2006; FRSA 1987, sr fell RCA 1988, hon fell Soc of Dyers and Colourists 2004; *Books* incl: What Next? (1989); *Recreations* golf, tennis, cycling; *Clubs* Formby Golf, Blackwell Golf; *Style*— George Davies, Esq; ✉ PO Box 19, Gloucestershire GL56 9TL (tel 01386 852862, fax 01386 852180)

DAVIES, Geraint Talfan; s of Aneirin Talfan Davies, OBE (d 1980), of Cardiff, and Mary Anne, *née* Evans (d 1971); *b* 30 December 1943; *Educ* Cardiff HS for Boys, Jesus Coll Oxford (MA); *m* 9 Sept 1967, Elizabeth Shan, da of Thomas Vaughan Yorath, of Cardiff; 3 s (Matthew b 1969, Rhodri b 1971, Edward b 1974); *Career* asst ed Western Mail 1974–78, head of news and current affairs HTV Wales 1978–82, asst controller of programmes HTV Wales 1982–87, dir of programmes Tyne Tees TV 1987–90, controller BBC Wales 1990–2000; chm: Inst of Welsh Affrs 1992–, CBAT The Arts and Regeneration Agency 1996–2003, Int Film Festival of Wales 1998–2001, WNO 2000–03 and 2006–, Arts Cncl of Wales 2003–06, Town and Country Broadcasting Ltd 2006–; dir Screen Wales 1994–2000; non-exec dir: Wales Millennium Centre 2000–03 and 2006–, Glas Cymru Cyf 2000–; memb: Mgmnt Ctee Northern Sinfonia 1989–90, Mgmnt Ctee Northern Stage 1989–90, Prince of Wales Ctee on the Environment 1993–96, NCVQ 1996–97, Radio Authy 2001–03, BT Wales Advsy Forum 2001–; govr: Welsh Coll of Music and Drama 1993–97, Univ of Wales Inst Cardiff (UWIC) 2001–; chm Newydd Housing Assoc 1975–78; tstee: Tenovus Cancer Appeal 1984–87, Br Bone Marrow Donor Appeal 1987–95, Media Standards Tst 2006–; Hon FRIBA; *Style*— Geraint Talfan Davies, Esq; ✉ 15 The Parade, Whitchurch, Cardiff CF14 2EF (tel 029 2062 6571, e-mail geraint.talfan@btopenworld.com)

DAVIES, Sir Graeme John; kt (1996); s of Harry John Davies, and Gladys Edna, *née* Pratt; *b* 7 April 1937; *Educ* Sch of Engrg Univ of Auckland NZ (BE, PhD), Univ of Cambridge (MA, ScD); *m* Florence Isabelle; 1 s (Michael b 1960), 1 da (Helena b 1961); *Career* lectr Dept of Metallurgy and Materials Science Univ of Cambridge 1962–77, fell St Catharine's Coll Cambridge 1967–77, prof Dept of Metallurgy Univ of Sheffield 1978–86, vice-chllr Univ of Liverpool 1986–91; chief exec: UFC 1991–93, PCFC 1992–93, HEFCE 1992–95; princ and vice-chllr Univ of Glasgow 1995–2003, vice-chllr Univ of London 2003–; author and co-author of more than 120 scientific papers on forming processes, welding, solidification and casting, mechanical properties of materials; Rosenhain medal Inst of Metals 1982; Freeman City of London 1987, Freeman and Burgess holder City of Glasgow 1996; Liveryman Worshipful Co of Ironmongers 1989 (Master 2005–06); CEng, FIM, FIMechE, FRSA, FREng 1988, FRSE 1996; *Books* Solidification and Casting (1973), Texture and the Properties of Materials (co-ed, 1976), Solidificacao e Fundicao das Metals e Suas Ligas (jtly, 1978), Hot Working and Forming Processes (co-ed, 1980), Superplasticity (jtly, 1981), Essential Metallurgy for Engineers (jtly, 1985); *Recreations* birdwatching, Times crossword; *Clubs* Athenaeum; *Style*— Sir Graeme Davies, FRSE, FREng; ✉ Senate House, University of London, London WC1E 7HU (tel 020 7862 8004, e-mail graeme.davies@lon.ac.uk)

DAVIES, Ven Graham; s of James Stanley Davies (d 1968), of Llanelli, and Dorothy May, *née* James (d 1965); *b* 5 November 1935; *Educ* Llanelli Boys' GS, St David's UC Lampeter (BA, BD, Rugby colours), St Michael's Coll Llandaff, Episcopal Theol Sch Cambridge MA; *m* Janet Flora, da of Rev W R Nicholas; 3 s (Robert b 1963, Hugh b 1965, Alexander b 1970); *Career* ordained: deacon 1959, priest 1960; curate Steynton and Johnston 1959–62, curate Llangathen 1962–64, minor canon St David's Cathedral 1964–66, rector Burton 1966–71, rector Hubberston 1971–74, youth tutor Swadelands Sch Lenham and chaplain Lenham 1974–80, vicar Cwmdeuddwr St Harmon and Llanwrthwl 1980–86, bishop's advsr for schs 1983–86, vicar Cydweli and Llandyfaelog 1986–97, examining chaplain to Bishop of St David's (with responsibility for post-ordination trg) 1986–96, clerical sec Diocesan Conf 1992–97, canon of St David's Cathedral 1992–96, archdeacon of St David's 1996–, vicar of Steynton 1997–; *Recreations* rugby football, cricket; *Style*— The Ven the Archdeacon of St David's; ✉ The Vicarage, Steynton, Milford Haven, Pembrokeshire SA73 1AW (tel 01646 692867)

DAVIES, Prof Graham Arthur; s of Evan Henry Davies (d 1978), and Esther Alice, *née* Powell (d 1979); *b* 2 July 1938; *Educ* Wolverhampton Municipal GS, Univ of Birmingham (BSc, PhD), Victoria Univ of Manchester (DSc, Sir John Cadman Medal, Moulton Medal IChemE); *m* July 1963, Christine Pamela, da of Frederick Charles Harris; 1 s (Andrew Simon Craig), 1 da (Joanna Elizabeth); *Career* Procter & Gamble Ltd Newcastle upon Tyne 1963–65; UMIST (now Univ of Manchester): lectr in chemical engrg 1965–70, sr lectr 1970–76, reader 1976–88, prof 1988–, head Dept of Chemical Engrg 1993–; FIChemE, CEng, FREng 1995; *Books* Recent Advances in Liquid-Liquid Extraction (co-author, 1970), Science & Practice of Liquid-Liquid Extraction (1993); *Recreations* golf; *Style*— Prof Graham Davies, FREng; ✉ Chemical Engineering Department, University of Manchester, PO Box 88, Manchester M60 1QD (tel 0161 200 4342)

DAVIES, Prof Graham James; s of William Thomas Davies (d 1992), and Amy, *née* Lewis (d 1995); *b* 2 July 1946, Swansea; *Educ* Univ of Wales Aberystwyth (BSc, PhD), Univ of Wales (DSc); *m* 1975, Frances Vivienne, *née* Martin; 2 s (Steffan James b 22 Nov 1976, Timothy Martin b 28 Nov 1982); *Career* research offr King's Coll London 1971–72; BT Research Labs: jr research fell and exec engr 1972–79, head Surface Science and Epitaxy Gp 1979–84, head Advanced Materials Section 1984–90, mangr Technol Analysis Unit 1991–93, mangr Corporate Research Prog 1993–98, gen mangr (vice-pres) Technol Acquisition and Int Devpt 1998–2001; Sir James Timmins Chance prof of engrg and exec head (dean) Sch of Engrg Univ of Birmingham 2001–; dir: Birmingham Research and Development Ltd, Diamond Light Source; cncl memb Cncl for the Central Lab of the Research Cncls (CCLRC); author of over 150 pubns and four patents, contrib to seven books; Duddell Premium IEE 1974; Liveryman Worshipful Co of Engrs; MRSC, FIEE, FInstP, FIMMM, FREng; *Recreations* golf, walking, reading; *Style*— Prof Graham Davies

DAVIES, (Andrew) Gregory Simon (Gregg); s of Jack Coppenhall (d 1979), and Joan Davies (d 2006); *b* 1 December 1960, Wales; *Educ* Shrewsbury, Kent Sch CT USA, Univ of St Andrews (BSc); *m* 20 April 1987, Alison Margaret Elizabeth, *née* McVeigh; 1 da (Anna Alice Elizabeth b 12 Feb 1998); *Career* Haberdashers' Aske's Sch 1984–89; Fettes Coll: appointed 1989, housemaster 1993–99, dep headmaster 1999–2004, actg headmaster Fettes Coll Prep Sch 2000–03; headmaster Shiplake Coll 2004–; memb: Boarding Schs Assoc, HMC, SHMIS; *Recreations* rugby refereeing, loud singing, log chopping, cabinet making; *Clubs* Leander, Stewards; *Style*— Gregg Davies, Esq; ✉ Shiplake College, Henley-on-Thames, Oxfordshire RG9 4BW (tel 0118 940 2455, fax 0118 940 5204)

DAVIES, (Stephen) Howard; s of Thomas Emrys Davies, and (Eileen) Hilda, *née* Bevan (d 1991); *b* 26 April 1945; *Educ* Christ's Hosp, Univ of Durham (BA), Univ of Bristol; *m* Susan, da of Rt Rev Eric St Q Wall (former Bishop of Huntingdon); 2 da (Hannah Clare b 1973, Katherine Sian (Kate) b 1978); *Career* theatre dir; assoc dir Bristol Old Vic 1971–73 (prodns incl: Troilus and Cressida, Candida, Spring Awakening), fndr memb Avon Touring Co, asst dir RSC 1974; freelance dir 1974–76: The Caucasian Chalk Circle (Birmingham Rep), The Threepenny Opera (York Rep), The Iceman Cometh (RSC Aldwych), Man is Man (RSC); assoc dir RSC 1976–86, fndr and dir The Warehouse RSC 1977–82 (prodns incl: Piaf, Good, Les Liaisons Dangereuses), visiting dir RNT 1987–88 (prodns incl: The Shaughraun, Cat on a Hot Tin Roof, The Secret Rapture), assoc dir RNT 1989– (prodns incl: Hedda Gabler, The Crucible, Piano, A Long Day's Journey into Night, Mary Stuart, Chips with Everything), former assoc dir Almeida, currently assoc dir RNT (prodns incl Mourning Becomes Electra); dir: The Iceman Cometh (Almeida, Old Vic and Broadway) 1999 (Evening Standard and Olivier Awards for Best Dir 1999), All My Sons (Cottesloe, Olivier Award for Best Dir 2001), Private Lives (Albery Theatre) 2001 (nomination Olivier Award for Best Dir 2002); opera dir: Idomeneo, Eugene Onegin; TV dir: Tales from Hollywood, Armadillo, Copenhagen, Blue Orange; dir film The Secret Rapture; *Recreations* travel, hill walking, watching rugby, drawing and painting; *Style*—

Howard Davies, Esq, FRSA; ✉ c/o Royal National Theatre, South Bank, London SE1 9PX (tel 020 7928 2033, fax 020 7620 1197)

DAVIES, (Sir) Howard John; kt (2000); s of Leslie Powell Davies (d 1989), of Rochdale, Lancs, and Marjorie, *née* Magowan; *b* 12 February 1951; *Educ* Manchester Grammar, Memorial Univ of Newfoundland, Merton Coll Oxford (MA), Stanford Univ (MS); *m* 30 June 1984, Prudence Mary, da of Eric Phillipps Keely, CBE (d 1988), of Findon; 2 s (George b 1984, Archibald b 1987); *Career* FO 1973–74, private sec to HM Ambass Paris 1974–76, HM Treasy 1976–82, McKinsey and Co 1982–85, special advsr to Chllr of the Exchequer 1985–86, re-joined McKinsey and Co 1986–87, controller Audit Cmmn for Local Authorities and the NHS (formerly for Local Authorities) 1987–92, DG CBI 1992–95, dep govr Bank of England 1995–97 (non-exec dir Bank of England 1998–2003), chm FSA (formerly SIB) 1997–2003, dir LSE 2003–; non-exec dir: GKN plc until 1995, Morgan Stanley 2004–; tstee Tate Gallery 2002–; *Recreations* cricket, writing; *Clubs* Barnes Common Cricket; *Style—* Mr Howard Davies

DAVIES, Hugh Llewelyn; CMG (1994); s of Vincent Ellis Davies, OBE (d 2002), and Rose Trench, *née* Temple (d 1993); *b* 8 November 1941; *Educ* Rugby, Churchill Coll Cambridge (BA); *m* 21 Sept 1968, Virginia Ann, da of Hugh Lucius; 1 da (Charlotte b 1970), 1 s (Jonathan b 1973); *Career* HM Dip Serv: FO 1965, Chinese language studies Hong Kong 1966–68, second sec and HM consul Peking 1969–71, China Desk FCO 1971–74, first sec (econ) Br Embassy Bonn 1974–77, head of Chancery Br High Cmmm Singapore 1977–79, asst head Far Eastern Dept FCO 1979–82, secondment Barclays Bank Int 1982–83, commercial cnsllr Br Embassy Peking 1984–87, dep perm UK rep OECD Paris 1987–90, head Far East Dept FCO 1990–93, sr Br trade cmmr Hong Kong 1993, Br sr rep (ambass) on the Sino-British Jt Liaison Gp Hong Kong 1993–97, special co-ordinator for China, Hong Kong FCO 1998–99; exec dir Prudential Corporation Asia 1999–2005, conslt on Asia 2002–, sr China business advsr Old Mutual plc 2005–06, sr ptnr Orient Ptnrs 2005–; *Recreations* travel, sports, art, gardens; *Clubs* Hong Kong; *Style—* Hugh Davies, Esq, CMG

DAVIES, (Edward) Hunter; s of John Davies (d 1958), of Cambuslang, and Marion, *née* Brechin (d 1987); *b* 7 January 1936; *Educ* Creighton Sch Carlisle, Carlisle GS, Univ of Durham; *m* 1960, Margaret Forster, *qv*; 1 s, 2 da; *Career* author, broadcaster, publisher; journalist Sunday Times 1960–84 (ed Sunday Times Magazine 1975–77); columnist: Punch 1979–89, Stamp News 1981–86, Evening Standard 1987, The Independent 1989–95, New Statesman 1996–; presenter BBC Radio Four's Bookshelf 1983–86; memb: Br Library Consultative Gp on Newspapers 1987–89, Bd Edinburgh Book Festival 1990–95; pres Cumbria Wildlife Tst 1994–; *Books* fiction incl: Here We Go Round the Mulberry Bush (1965, filmed 1968), A Very Loving Couple (1971), Flossie Teacake's Fur Coat (1982), Come on Ossie! (1985), Saturday Night (1989), Striker (1992); non-fiction incl: The Other Half (1966), The Beatles (1968, 3 edn 2002), The Glory Game (1972, 2 edn 1985), A Walk Around the Lakes (1979), William Wordsworth (1980), Father's Day (1981, TV series 1983), The Joy of Stamps (1983), The Good Guide to the Lakes (also publisher, 1984, 4 edn 1993), In Search of Columbus (1991), Hunting People (1994), Teller of Tales (1994), Wainwright (1995), Living on the Lottery (1996), Born 1900 (1998), A Walk Around the West Indies (2000), The Quarrymen (2001), The Eddie Stobart Story (2001), Boots, Balls and Haircuts (2003), Relative Strangers (2003), The Fan (2003), My Story So Far (with Wayne Rooney, 2006), The Beatles, Football and Me (2006), The Bumper Book of Football (2007); *Recreations* collecting footbal memorabilia, Lakeland books; *Style—* Hunter Davies, Esq; ✉ 11 Boscastle Road, London NW5; Grasmoor House, Loweswater, Cockermouth, Cumbria

DAVIES, Prof Huw Cathan; *b* 5 February 1944, Wales; *Educ* Univ of Wales (BSc), Imperial Coll London (DIC), Univ of London (PhD); *m* 20 Aug 1966, Marian, *née* Williams; 1 s (Rhys b 13 May 1968), 1 da (Rebecca b 20 Oct 1970); *Career* lectr Univ of Reading 1968–82, prof ETH Zürich 1982– (head Dept of Environmental Science 2002–04); pres Int Assoc for Meteorology and Atmospheric Science 1999–2003, memb Cncl NERC 2005–; memb Academia Europaea 1990; FRMetS; *Style—* Prof Huw Davies; ✉ Institute for Atmospheric and Climate Science, ETH, Universitdtsstrasse 16, CH-8092 Zrich, Switzerland (tel 00 41 44 633 3506, fax 00 41 44 633 1058, e-mail huw.davies@env.ethz.ch)

DAVIES, Huw Humphreys; s of William Davies (d 1984), of Llangynog, and Harriet Jane, *née* Humphreys (d 1991); *b* 4 August 1940; *Educ* Llandovery Coll, Pembroke Coll Oxford (MA); *m* 1966, Elizabeth Shân, da of William Harries; 2 da (Elin Mari b 25 April 1969, Catrin Humphreys b 23 Sept 1971); *Career* prog dir and prodr TWW 1964–68; HTV Wales: programme dir and prodr 1968–78, asst controller of programmes 1978–79, controller of programmes 1979–81, dir of programmes 1981–89, chief exec 1987; gp dir of TV HTV Group 1989–94, pres HTV International 1994–96; fndr independent TV prodn co Square Circle 1996–2002, dir Winchester Entertainment plc 1996–; chief exec Channel Television Ltd 2000–; chm Winchester Entertainment plc 2003–04, dir Content Film plc 2004–; memb Gorsedd of Bards; FRSA 1989; *Recreations* walking, reading; *Style—* Huw Davies, Esq; ✉ 27 Victoria Road, Penarth, Cardiff CF64 3HY

DAVIES, Prof Hywel Aled; s of David Charles Davies (d 1966), and Hilda Williams (d 2000); *b* 2 January 1941, Denbigh, N Wales; *Educ* Abergele GS, Imperial Coll London (BSc, PhD); *m* 26 Feb 1966, Mair, *née* Evans; 3 da (Bronwen Mair b 12 July 1967, Gwyneth Aledwen b 3 May 1969, Rhian Eleri b 6 Nov 1972); *Career* postdoctorate research assoc Brookhaven Nat Lab USA 1966–67, postdoctorate research fell Yale Univ 1967–68, SRC and univ research fell Univ of Nottingham 1968–69; Univ of Sheffield: lectr in metallurgy 1969–79, sr lectr 1979–86, reader 1986–89, prof of physical metallurgy 1989–2003, research prof in physical metallurgy and magnetic materials 2003–06, emeritus prof 2006–; visiting research fell G E Corporate R&D Centre Schenectady USA 1981, visiting scientist CSIRO West Lindfield Aust 1986, visiting prof Tohoku Univ Japan 2000; industrial conslt for numerous cos incl: Wilkinson Sword Ltd, Lucas Electrical Ltd, PSI plc; former chm Mgmnt Panel EPSRC Advanced Magnetics Prog; pres Sheffield and District Cambrian Soc 1994–96 and 2005–06; FREng 2003, FIMMM, CEng, MInstP, CPhys; *Publications* The Properties of Liquid Metals (jt ed, 1967), Solidification and Casting of Metals (jt ed, 1979); author or co-author of over 400 pubns in scientific jls on rapidly solidified alloys and ferromagnetic materials; *Recreations* history, walking, motor sport; *Style—* Prof Hywel Davies; ✉ Department of Engineering Materials, University of Sheffield, Sheffield S1 3JD (tel 0114 222 5518, fax 0114 222 5943, e-mail h.a.davies@sheffield.ac.uk)

DAVIES, Dr Ivor John; s of David Howell Davies, of Penarth, S Glamorgan, and Gwenllian, *née* Phillips (d 1990); *b* 9 November 1935; *Educ* Penarth Co Sch, Cardiff Coll of Art (NDD), Swansea Coll of Art (ATD), Univ of Lausanne, Univ of Edinburgh (PhD); *Career* artist; teacher of art and craft Little Ealing Secdy Modern Boys Sch London 1957–59, asst teacher of English Univ of Lausanne and Gymnases 1959–61, pt/t lectr in history of art Extra Mural Dept Cardiff 1961–63, lectr i/c History of Art 19th and 20th Century Dept of Fine Art Univ of Edinburgh 1963–78, first curator Talbot Rice Art Centre Univ of Edinburgh 1971–78, lectr in history of art and head School of Cultural Studies Faculty of Art and Design Gwent Coll of HE Newport 1978–88; lectr and external examiner for numerous bodies; author of numerous articles and reviews in art magazines; involved in destruction-in-art, multi-media and experimental theatre in the 1960s; memb: AICA (Int Assoc of Art Critics), GWELED (Welsh arts movement), AAH (Assoc of Art Historians); vice-pres Royal Cambrian Acad 1995– (memb 1992–); *Exhibitions* solo exhbns incl: Oriel (Welsh Art Cncl Gallery Cardiff) 1974, City Art Gallery Leeds 1975, Talbot Rice Art Centre Univ of Edinburgh 1972, 1973, 1974 and 1977, Holsworthy Gallery New King's Road London 1980 and 1981, Newport Museum and Art Gallery 1987, Max Rutherson/Roberts Gallery Bond St London 1989, Jeddah Saudi Arabia 1990, Mandarin Hong Kong 1992, Wrexham Library touring exhbn 1991–93, Victoria Art Gallery Bath 1993, Legends of the White Book touring exhbn 1999, retrospective exhbn Brno 2006; numerous gp exhbns nationally and internationally 1953–2004 incl: Blast to Freeze: 20th Century British Art (Wolfsburg and Toulouse) 2002–03, The Art and the Sixties (Tate Modern and tour Aust and NZ) 2004; *Work in Public Collections* incl: Welsh Arts Cncl, Scottish Arts Cncl, City Art Gallery Leeds, Nat Museum of Wales, Arts Cncl of GB, Newport Museum and Art Gallery, Deal Collection Dallas; *Books* The Age of the Vanguards, Discovering Welsh Art (co-ed and contrib), Certain Welsh Artists (1999); *Recreations* languages; *Style—* Dr Ivor Davies; ✉ 99 Windsor Road, Penarth, South Glamorgan CF64 1JF (tel 029 2070 3492)

D

DAVIES, James Baumann; s of Anthony Baumann Davies, of Farndon, Cheshire, and Anne, *née* Richardson; *b* 26 February 1962, Corbridge, Northumberland; *Educ* Ysgol Gyfun David Hughes Menai Bridge, Univ of Leicester (LLB, LLM), Univ of Strasbourg (Dip); *m* 30 Dec 1989, Priska Carel, *née* Johnston; *Career* slr; Denton Hall 1986–90, Lewis Silkin 1992– (currently ptnr and jt head Employment and Incentives Dept); memb Bd ius laboris, tstee and memb Advsy Bd Advice on Individual Rights in Europe; contrib to various employment law pubns; memb: Employment Lawyers Assoc (sometime treas), European Employment Lawyers Assoc; *Recreations* sports, travel, France; *Clubs* Glamorgan CCC; *Style—* James Davies; ✉ Lewis Silkin LLP, 5 Chancery Lane, Clifford's Inn, London EC4A 1BL (tel 020 7074 8035, fax 020 7864 1737, e-mail james.davies@lewissilkin.com)

DAVIES, James Selwyn (Joe); s of John Selwyn Davies (d 2000), of Cardiff, and Joan, *née* Williams (d 2002); *b* 29 June 1956; *Educ* Christ Coll Brecon, St John's Coll Cambridge (MA, Sir Joseph Lamour prize, Rugby blue), UC Cardiff (PGCE); *m* 28 March 1981, Virginia Felicity, da of Jeffrey Graham; 3 s (Edward Selwyn b 22 Sept 1982, Charles Alan b 13 June 1984, James Peter b 24 Nov 1986), 1 da (Rebecca Helen b 11 Dec 1989); *Career* housemaster Tonbridge Sch 1980–94, exchange teacher Anglican Church GS Brisbane Aust 1988, dep head St John's Sch Leatherhead 1994–2000, headmaster Sutton Valence Sch 2000–; govr: Rose Hill Sch, Yardley Court Sch, Fetcham Village Infants' Sch 1996–2000 (also chair Personnel Ctee); memb: HMC 2001, SHA 2001, Nat Tst; *Recreations* rugby (played for Cardiff, Penarth, Bedford and London Welsh), cricket, squash, reading, cycling, camping, marathon running; *Clubs* Hawks' (Cambridge), East India; *Style—* Joe Davies, Esq; ✉ Sutton Valence School, Sutton Valence, Maidstone, Kent ME17 3HL (tel 01622 842381, e-mail hm@svs.org.uk)

DAVIES, Janet; AM; da of David Rees (d 1963), and Jean Wardlaw, *née* Arbuckle (d 1963); *b* 29 May 1938; *Educ* Howell's Sch Llandaff, Trinity Coll Carmarthen (BA), Open Univ (BA); *m* 1965, Basil Peter Ridley Davies (d 2000), s of John Davies; 1 s (Richard Thomas b 1966), 1 da (Sara Sian b 1968); *Career* memb Nat Assembly for Wales (Plaid Cymru) South Wales West 1999–; memb: Plaid Cymru, Party of Wales, CND Cymru; *Recreations* gardening, sailing; *Style—* Ms Janet Davies, AM; ✉ National Assembly for Wales, Cardiff Bay, Cardiff CF99 1NA (tel 029 2089 8289, e-mail janet.davies@wales.gov.uk)

DAVIES, Jocelyn Ann; AM; da of Thomas Davies, and Majorie, *née* Smith, of Newbridge, Gwent; *b* 18 June 1959; *Children* 1 s (Lewis b 5 May 1980), 2 da (Anna b 4 Nov 1989, Katie b 29 Dec 1990); *Career* borough cncllr 1987–91, Pty by-election candidate Islwyn 1995, memb Nat Assembly for Wales (Plaid Cymru) South Wales East 1999–; memb: Railway Devpt Soc, Amnesty Int, Friends of the Earth; *Recreations* drawing, walking, people watching; *Style—* Ms Jocelyn Davies, AM; ✉ National Assembly for Wales, Cardiff Bay, Cardiff CF99 1NA (tel 029 2089 5289); Constituency Office, 10 High Street, Newport, Gwent NP20 1FQ (tel 01633 220022, fax 01633 220603)

DAVIES, John; s of John Charles Davies (d 1987), of Birmingham, and Kathleen Anne, *née* Snipe (d 2004); *b* 12 July 1946; *Educ* Bournville Boys' Tech Sch Birmingham; *m* 6 Nov 1971, Jacqueline, da of William Springall Wheeler; 1 s (Charles William b 26 Nov 1974), 3 da (Alison Jane b 29 April 1976, Nicola Kate b 23 March 1978, Lucy Anne b 25 June 1980); *Career* trainee investment analyst Midland Assurance Ltd Birmingham 1964–67; investment analyst: J M Finn & Co (Stockbrokers) 1968–71, Nat Coal Bd Pension Fund 1971–73; Confederation Life Insurance Co: asst mangr equity investment 1973–74, mangr pension investment 1974–76, mangr segregated funds investment 1976–79, dep investment mangr 1979–82; investment mangr 3i Group plc 1982–84, md 3i Asset Management 1984–2002; dir: Merrill Lynch British Smaller Companies Trust plc 1999–, Baronsmead AIM VCT plc 2006–; trustee St Michael Sch Sunninghill; ASIP, FSI; *Recreations* music, reading, hill walking; *Clubs* Girt Clog Climbing; *Style—* John Davies, Esq; ✉ c/o Caroline Driscoll, Merrill Lynch Investment Managers, 33 King William Street, London EC4R 9AS (tel 020 7743 2427, e-mail john.davies1@btinternet.com)

DAVIES, John Booth; s of Harry Davies, and Nora, *née* Booth; *Educ* Haslingden GS, Univ of Leeds (BA); *Career* managing ed Phoebus Publishing (later Macdonald Phoebus) 1976–81, estab Grub Street Book Packagers 1982, estab Grub Street Publishing Ltd 1992 (International Cookbook Publisher of the Year World Cookbook Awards 2000); father of chapel NUJ 1980–81, memb Guild of Aviation Artists; *Books* Octopus Book of Aircraft and Aviation (1977); *Recreations* cricket, chess, watching Blackburn Rovers, travel, reading; *Style—* John Booth, Esq; ✉ Grub Street, 4 Rainham Close, London SW11 6SS (tel 020 7924 3966, fax 020 7738 1009, e-mail john@grubstreet.co.uk)

DAVIES, Prof John Christopher Hughes (Christie); s of Christopher George Davies (d 1984), and Marian Eileen, *née* Johns (d 1975); *b* 25 December 1941; *Educ* Dynevor Sch, Emmanuel Coll Cambridge (MA, PhD); *Career* tutor in economics Univ of Adelaide 1964, radio prodr BBC Third prog 1967–69, lectr in sociology Univ of Leeds 1969–72, visiting lectr in sociology Indian univs incl Univ of Bombay and Univ of Delhi 1973–74, prof of sociology Univ of Reading 1984–2002 (lectr then sr lectr then reader 1972–84), distinguished scholars interdisciplinary lectr Inst of Humane Studies George Mason Univ VA 1986; *Books* Wrongful Imprisonment (with R Brandon, 1973), Permissive Britain (1975), Censorship and Obscenity (with R Dhavan, 1978), Ethnic Humor Around the World (1990), The Corporation under Siege (with M Neal, 1998), Jokes and Their Relation to Society (1998), The Mirth of Nations (2002), Esunikku Joku (with Goh Abe, 2003), The Right to Joke (2004), The Strange Death of Moral Britain (2004); *Recreations* travel, art exhibitions, jokes; *Clubs* Cambridge Union (pres 1964); *Style—* Prof Christie Davies; ✉ Department of Sociology, University of Reading, Whiteknights, Reading, Berkshire RG6 6AA (tel 0118 986 3775, e-mail j.c.h.davies@reading.ac.uk)

DAVIES, Very Rev John David Edward; s of William Howell Davies, of Newport, Gwent, and Doiran Rallison, *née* Watkins; *b* 6 February 1953; *Educ* Bassaleg GS, Univ of Southampton (LLB), Coll of Law Chester, St Michael's Coll Llandaff, Univ of Wales Cardiff (DipTh), Univ of Wales (LLM); *m* 1986, Joanna Lucy, da of Allen Aulton, and Sylvia, *née* Hamer; 1 da (Kate Frances Lucy b 1 Aug 1988), 1 s (Christopher James Gerald b 11 July 1990); *Career* articled clerk 1975, slr 1977–82; asst curate Chepstow 1984–86, curate i/c Michaelston-y-Fedw with Rudry 1986–88, rector of Bedwas with Rudry 1988–95, vicar of Newport (Maindee) 1995–2000, dean of Brecon 2000–; chm of tstees St David's Fndn Hospice Care 2000–03; *Recreations* music especially opera, organ and 60s and 70s pop, walking, cricket, golf, reading, entertaining; *Style—* The Very Rev the Dean of Brecon; ✉ The Deanery, The Cathedral Close, Brecon, Powys LD3 9DP (tel 01874 623344, office 01874 623857, fax 01874 623716, e-mail admin@breconcathedral.org.uk)

DAVIES, Prof John Kenyon; s of Harold Edward Davies (d 1990), and Clarice Theresa, *née* Woodburn (d 1989); *b* 19 September 1937; *Educ* Manchester Grammar, Wadham Coll Oxford (BA), Merton Coll Oxford (MA), Balliol Coll Oxford (DPhil); *m* 1, 8 Sept 1962 (m dis 1978), Anna Elbina Laura Margherita, da of A Morpurgo (d 1939), of Rome; m 2, 5 Aug 1978, Nicola Jane, da of Dr R M S Perrin; 1 s (Martin b 1979), 1 da (Penelope b 1981); *Career* Harmsworth scholar Merton Coll Oxford 1960–63, jr fell Center for Hellenic Studies Washington DC 1961–62, Dyson jr fell Balliol Coll Oxford 1963–65, lectr Univ of St Andrews 1965–68, fell in ancient history Oriel Coll Oxford 1968–77; Univ of Liverpool: Rathbone prof of ancient history and classical archaeology 1977–2003, pro-vice-chllr 1986–90, head Sch of Archeology, Classics and Oriental Studies 1990–95 and 2000–02; Leverhulme research prof 1995–2000; ed: Jl of Hellenic Studies 1973–77, Archaeological Reports 1972–74; chm: St Patrick's Isle (IOM) Archaeological Tst 1982–85, NW Archaeological Tst 1982–91; auditor CVCP Academic Audit Unit 1990–93; corresponding memb Deutsche Archäologische Institut 2000, visiting sr fell Istituto de Studi Avanzati Unv of Bologna 2006; FBA 1985, FSA 1986, FRSA 1988; *Books* Athenian Propertied Families 600–300 BC (1971), Democracy and Classical Greece (1978, 2 edn 1993), Wealth and the Power of Wealth in Classical Athens (1981), The Trojan War: Its Historicity and Context (ed with L Foxhall, 1984), Hellenistic Economies (ed jtly, 2000), Making, Moving and Managing: The New World of Ancient Economies 323–31 BC (ed jtly, 2005); *Recreations* choral singing; *Clubs* Royal Over-Seas League; *Style*— Prof John K Davies; ✉ 20 North Road, Grassendale Park, Liverpool L19 0LR (tel 0151 427 2126, e-mail jkdavies@liv.ac.uk)

DAVIES, Rt Rev John Stewart; *see:* St Asaph, Bishop of

DAVIES, Prof Kay Elizabeth; CBE (1995); da of Harry Partridge and Florence, *née* Farmer; *b* 1 April 1951; *Educ* Stourbridge Girls' HS, Somerville Coll Oxford (Kirkaldy Prize, MA, DPhil); *m* 1973 (m dis 2000), Stephen Graham Davies; 1 s; *Career* Guy Newton jr research fell Wolfson Coll Oxford 1976–78, Royal Soc Euro post-doctoral fell Service de Biochimie Centre d'Études Nucleaires de Saclay Gif-sur-Yvette France 1978–80; St Mary's Hosp Med Sch Dept of Biochemistry: Cystic Fibrosis research fell 1980–82, MRC sr research fell 1982–84; Nuffield Dept of Clinical Med John Radcliffe Hosp Oxford: MRC sr research fell 1984–86, MRC external staff 1986–89, univ research lectr 1990; MRC research dir MRC Clinical Scis Centre Royal Post Graduate Med Sch Hammersmith and prof of molecular genetics Univ of London 1992–94, MRC external staff head Molecular Genetics Gp Inst of Molecular Med Oxford 1994–95 (MRC external staff 1989–92); Univ of Oxford: prof of genetics 1995–98, assoc head for external rels Dept of Biochemistry 1996–, Dr Lee's prof of anatomy 1998–, co-dir Oxford Centre for Gene Function 2001–; hon dir MRC Functional Genetics Unit 1999–; fell: Green Coll Oxford 1989–92 and 1994–95, Keble Coll Oxford 1995–98, Hertford Coll Oxford 1998–; memb MRC 2002–; Bristol-Myers visiting prof USA 1986, James and Jean Davis Prestige visitorship Univ of Otago NZ 1996; memb: Advsy Ctee Euro Cell and Tissue Bank 1989–, Med Ethics Advsy Gp Lambeth Palace 1994–, Scientific Advsy Panel CIBA Fndn 1994–, Genetics Interest Gp Wellcome Tst 1996–; founding ed Human Molecular Genetics 1992–; memb numerous Editorial Bds incl: Jl of Biotherapeutics and Gene Therapy 1994–, Gene Therapy 1994–, Molecular Medicine Society 1994–, Molecular Medicine Today 1994–; memb: Academia Europaea, EMBO, Biochemical Soc, Genetics Soc, Euro Human Genetics Soc; 7th Annual Colleen Giblin distinguished lectr Columbia Univ USA 1992, distinguished lectr Mayo Clinic 1994; Annual Medal Int Inst of Biotechnology 1993, Wellcome Tst Award 1996, SCI Medal 1999; hon fell Somerville Coll Oxford 1995; Hon DSc Univ of Victoria BC 1990, Hon DUniv Open 1999; Hon FRCP 1994, FRCPath 1997 (MRCPath 1990), FMedSci 1998, FRS 2003; *Books* Molecular Analysis of Inherited Diseases (with A P Read, 1988, revised edn 1992), Human Genetics Diseases. A Practical Approach (ed, 1988), Genome Analysis. A Practical Approach (ed, 1988), The Fragile X Syndrome (ed, 1989), Application of Molecular Genetics to the Diagnosis of Inherited Disease (ed, 1989), Genome Analysis Review (ed with S Tilghman, 1990–); also author of numerous articles for learned jls; *Style*— Prof Kay Davies, CBE; ✉ Department of Physiology, Anatomy and Genetics, University of Oxford, South Parks Road, Oxford OX1 3QX (tel 01865 285880, fax 01865 285878, e-mail kay.davies@dpag.ox.ac.uk)

DAVIES, Kenneth Seymour; s of George Seymour Davies (d 1997), of Eastcote, Middx, and (Isobel) Dorothy, *née* Corfield (d 1995); *b* 11 February 1948; *Educ* St Nicholas GS Northwood; *m* 15 May 1971, Brenda Margaret, da of William George Cannon (d 1987), of Ruislip, Middx; 4 s (Mark b 1972, Peter b 1974, Robert b 1976, Trevor b 1982), 1 da (Kirsty b 1980); *Career* CA 1970; ptnr Pannell Kerr Forster 1974–; hon treas Willing Wheels Club (cancer charity); FCA; *Recreations* gardening, walking; *Style*— Ken Davies, Esq; ✉ PKF, Farringdon Place, 20 Farringdon Road, London EC1M 3AP (tel 020 7831 7393, fax 020 7405 6736, e-mail ken.davies@uk.pkf.com)

DAVIES, Laura Jane; CBE (2000, MBE 1988); da of David Thomas Davies, and Rita Ann, *née* Foskett; *b* 5 October 1963; *Educ* Fullbrook Co Secdy Sch; *Career* golfer; memb Curtis Cup Team 1984, turned professional 1985, Br Open Ladies Golf champion 1986, US Open champion 1987, memb winning European Solheim Cup team 1992, 2000 and 2003; ranked world No 1 in 1995 and 1996; 66 tournament wins in professional career incl 4 Majors; *Recreations* all sport, cars, music; *Style*— Miss Laura Davies, CBE; ✉ c/o Rob Alter, IMG Golf Client Division, McCormack House, Burlington Lane, London W4 2TH (tel 020 233 5300)

DAVIES, (Robert) Leighton; QC (1994); s of Robert Brinley Davies (d 1978), of Cwm-parc, Mid Glamorgan, and Elizabeth Nesta, *née* Jones; *b* 7 September 1949; *Educ* Rhondda County GS Porth, CCC Oxford (BA, BCL, Boxing blue); *m* 25 Aug 1979, Linda Davies, da of David Fox, of Cwm-parc, Mid Glamorgan; 2 s (Rhoss b 30 May 1980, Greg b 9 Jan 1991), 1 da (Rhia b 12 Nov 1985); *Career* called to the Bar Gray's Inn 1975 (bencher 2002); practising barr: Cardiff 1975–97, Farrar's Building Temple 1997–; recorder of the Crown Court 1994– (asst recorder 1990); memb Criminal Bar Assoc 1988; memb Greenpeace; *Recreations* fly fishing, gardening, watching rugby football; *Style*— Leighton Davies, Esq, QC; ✉ Bryn Corun, Glyncoli Road, Treorchy, Rhondda, Mid-Glamorgan CF42 6SB (tel 01443 774559, fax 01443 774573, e-mail leightondaviesqc@msn.com); Farrar's Building, Temple, London EC4Y 7BD (tel 020 75839241, fax 020 7583 0090)

DAVIES, (Edward) Leslie; s of Robert Davies (d 1956), of North Ferriby, and Mabel Joyce, *née* Roberts (d 1965); *b* 23 December 1931; *Educ* Ruthin Sch, Jesus Coll Oxford (MA); *m* 4 Feb 1995, Pauline Ann Molyneux; *Career* admitted slr 1956, ptnr Ivesons 1960–97, conslt 1997; pres Hull Inc Law Soc 1965, memb Cncl Law Soc of England and Wales 1976–98 (chm Educn and Trg Ctee 1983–86); govr Coll of Law 1983–; Under Sheriff Kingston upon Hull 1965; memb Law Soc 1960; *Recreations* golf; *Clubs* Royal Over-Seas League, Brough Golf (former pres, former capt); *Style*— Leslie Davies, Esq; ✉ 30 Parkfield Avenue, North Ferriby, East Yorkshire HU14 3AL (tel 01482 631312)

DAVIES, Prof Lindsey Margaret; CBE (2004); da of Dr Frank Newby, of Horsham, W Sussex, and Margaret, *née* Thomsett; *b* 21 May 1953; *Educ* Univ of Nottingham (BMedSci, BM BS); *m* 21 Sept 1974 (m dis 1994), Dr Peter Davies; 2 s (James b 11 July 1979, Adam b 30 Sept 1980); *Career* house surgn Mansfield Gen Hosp 1975, house physician Nottingham City Hosp 1976, clinical med offr (child health and occupational med) Nottingham HA 1977–80, sr clinical med offr (community child health) Nottingham DHA 1981–83, registrar then sr registrar in community med Trent RHA 1983–85, dir of public health Southern Derbyshire HA 1985–90 (seconded as visiting scholar Georgetown Univ 1988), dir of public health Nottingham HA 1990–93; NHS Exec: head Public Health Div 1993–94, regnl dir of public health (E Midlands) 1994–2006, nat dir of pandemic influenza preparedness 2006–; special prof Univ of Nottingham Med Sch 2000– (special lectr 1991–2000); memb various Dept of Health working parties; memb Cncl and Cncl Exec BMA 1991–93 (chm Ctee for Public Health Med and Community Health 1992–93); author of various articles in learned jls; govr Henry Mellish Sch Bulwell 2001–06; MHSM, FFPH, FRCP; *Style*— Prof Lindsey Davies, CBE; ✉ Department of Health, Richmond House, 79 Whitehall, London SW1A 2NS

DAVIES, Ven Lorys Martin; s of Evan Tudor Davies (d 1952), and Eigen Morfydd, *née* Davies (d 2003); *b* 14 June 1936; *Educ* St Mary's C of E Sch, Whitland GS, St David's Coll Univ of Wales (organ exhibitioner, Philips history scholar, BA), Wells Theol Coll; *m* 8 Oct 1960, Barbara Ethel, da of Charles David Walkley; 2 s (Christopher Martin b 6 Oct 1961, Stephen Mark b 22 Sept 1964); *Career* asst curate St Mary's Tenby 1959–61, chaplain Brentwood Sch 1962–66, chaplain and head of dept Solihull Sch 1966–68, vicar of Moseley (St Mary's) Birmingham 1968–81; chaplain: Uffculme Clinic 1968–71, Sorrento Maternity Hosp 1968–81, Moseley Hall Hosp 1968–81; hon canon 1981; residentiary canon Birmingham Cathedral 1981–92, diocesan dir of ordinands 1982–90, chm House of Clergy 1990–92, archdeacon of Bolton 1992–2001 (now emeritus); General Synod: memb 1998–2001, memb Hospital Chaplaincies Cncl (vice-chm 2003–05) and National Stewardship Ctee; chm: Elisabeth Dowell Housing Assoc 1969–91, Robert Stevens Tst 1973–, Freda and Howard Ballance Tst 1982–; memb: CFAS Medical Ctee Univ of Cambridge 2001–05, Healthcare Cmmn (formerly Community Health Improvement) 2001–05; memb Birmingham Rotary Club 1982–90; JP Birmingham 1978–92; ALCM 1952; *Recreations* sport, music, theatre, reading, travel; *Style*— The Ven Lorys M Davies; ✉ Heolcerrig, 28 Penshurst Road, The Oakalls, Bromsgrove B60 2SN (tel and fax 01527 577337)

DAVIES, Mark Edward Trehearne; s of Denis Norman Davies, of Slinfold, W Sussex, and Patricia Helen, *née* Trehearne; *b* 20 May 1948; *Educ* Stowe; *m* 1, 8 June 1974 (m dis 1984), Serena Barbara, *née* Palmer; m 2, 20 Nov 1987, Antonia Catharine, da of Jeremy Barrow Chittenden, of Lytes Cary Manor, Somerset; 2 da (Sophia b 13 May 1988, Mollie b 18 March 1993), 2 s (Hugo b 5 Oct 1989, Harry b 24 Sept 1996); *Career* commodity broker Ralli International 1969, fndr Inter Commodities 1972 (awarded Queen's Award for Export Achievement 1981); chm and chief exec Inter Commodities 1972–84, chm and chief exec GNI Ltd 1984–94 (chm 1994–2001), dir Gerrard Group plc 1986–2001 (chief exec 1995–2001); chm: Greig Middleton Holdings 1999–2001, Thornhill Holdings Ltd 2001–, FF&P Asset Mgmnt Ltd 2003; dir: The Rank Fndn Ltd 1991–, Thornhill Investment Management Ltd 2001–, Racing Welfare 2001–, Thornhill Nominees Ltd 2001–, Thornhill Unit Tst Managers Ltd 2001–, Ascot Authority (Holdings) Ltd 2002–, Caledonia Investments plc 2002–, OMFS Central Services Ltd 2003–, Fleming Family & Partners Ltd 2003–, FCM SEED LLP 2006–, Racing Welfare (Enterprises) Ltd 2006–; chm: Admington Hall Farms Ltd 1995–, FF&P Capital Management Ltd 2004–; *Books* Trading in Commodities (co-author, 1974); *Recreations* hunting, racing; *Clubs* White's; *Style*— Mark Davies, Esq; ✉ 26 Chester Street, London SW1X 7BL; Fleming Family & Partners Ltd, Ely House, 37 Dover Street, London W1S 4NJ (tel 020 7409 5678, fax 020 7409 5791)

DAVIES, Mefin; *b* 2 September 1972, Nantgaredig, Carmarthen; *Career* rugby union player (hooker); clubs: Carmarthen Quins, Dunvant, Neath, Pontypridd (winners Principality Cup 2002, finalists Parken Pen Trophy 2002), Celtic Warriors 2003–04, Neath-Swansea Ospreys 2004–05, Gloucester 2005–; Wales: 29 caps (1 as capt), debut v South Africa 2002, memb squad World Cup 2003, winners Six Nations Championship and Grand Slam 2005; control systems engr and ptnr Process and General Technology Bridgend; *Style*— Mr Mefin Davies; ✉ c/o Gloucester Rugby Football Club, Kingsholm, Kingsholm Road, Gloucester GL1 3AX

DAVIES, (Evan) Mervyn; CBE (2002), JP (Hong Kong 2000); s of Richard Aled Davies, and Margaret Davies; *b* 21 November 1952; *Educ* Rydal Sch, Harvard Business Sch; *m* 3 March 1979, Jeanne Marie, *née* Gammie; 1 da (Laura Jane), 1 s (Thomas Gwyn); *Career* md (UK banking) and sr credit offr Citibank 1983–93; Standard Chartered plc: joined 1993 then worked in Hong Kong and Singapore, gp exec dir (with responsibility for Hong Kong, China and NE Asia and technol and ops) 1997–2001, gp chief exec 2001–06, chm 2006–; non-exec dir: Tesco plc 2003–, Tottenham Hotspur FC 2004–, Fleming Family & Partners 2006–; memb: Dep PM's Special Taskforce on China, Corp Bd Royal Acad, Advsy Bd Corsair, Bd Business Sch Univ of Bangor; chm Interim Exec Ctee Int Centre for Financial Regulation (ICFR); past chm: Hong Kong Assoc of Banks, Hong Kong Youth Arts, Asian Youth Orch, Br Chamber of Commerce Hong Kong; chm Appeal Fundraising Bd Breakthrough Breast Cancer 2004–, tstee Sir Kyffin Williams Tst 2007–; FCIB; *Recreations* soccer, cricket, golf, rugby, Welsh art, antiques; *Clubs* Oriental, Hong Kong, Mark's, Shek O (Hong Kong), Annabels; *Style*— Mervyn Davies, Esq, CBE; ✉ Standard Chartered plc, 1 Aldermanbury Square, London EC2V 7SB (tel 020 7280 7088, fax 020 7600 2546, e-mail emd@uk.standardchartered.com)

DAVIES, (Angie) Michael; *b* 23 June 1934; *Educ* Shrewsbury, Queens' Coll Cambridge (MA); *m* 1960, Jane Priscilla; 2 c; *Career* chm and chief exec Imperial Foods and dir Imperial Gp until May 1982; chm: Tozer Kemsley and Millburn Holdings plc 1985–86 (non-exec dir 1982–86), Bredero Properties plc 1986–94, Worth Investment Tst plc 1986–95 (non-exec dir 1984–95), Perkins Foods plc 1987–2001, Berk Ltd 1988–95, Wiltshier plc 1988–95, Calor Gp plc 1988–97 (non-exec dir 1987–88), National Express Gp Ltd 1992–2004, Simon Gp plc (formerly Simon Engineering plc) 1993–2003, Corporate Services Gp plc 1999–2002; dep chm: Manpower plc 1989–92 (non-exec dir 1987–92), TI Gp plc 1990–93 (non-exec dir 1984–93), AerFi Gp plc 1993–2000; non-exec dir: The Littlewoods Organisation plc 1982–88, TV-am plc 1983–89, Avdel plc 1983–94, British Airways plc 1983–2002, Worcester Gp 1991–92; FCA; *Style*— A Michael Davies, Esq; ✉ Little Woolpit, Ewhurst, Cranleigh, Surrey GU6 7NP (tel 01483 277344)

DAVIES, Prof (John) Michael; s of Alfred Ernest Davies (d 1975), of Walsall, and Mavis Muriel, *née* Wildgoose (d 1979); *Educ* Queen Mary's GS Walsall, Victoria Univ of Manchester (BSc, PhD, DSc); *m* 24 June 1967, Anthea Dorothy, da of Rex Henry Percy, MBE, DL, of Guildford; 1 s (Peter b 18 Nov 1972), 1 da (Claire b 16 Oct 1974); *Career* lectr Victoria Univ of Manchester 1962–65, engr Ove Arup & Partners Edinburgh 1965–70, visiting prof Univ of Karlsruhe 1980–81; Univ of Salford: reader 1971–80, prof of civil engrg 1981–95, chm Civil Engrg Dept 1988–91; prof of structural engrg Victoria Univ of Manchester 1995–2002, prof of structural engrg UMIST (now Univ of Manchester) 2002–; memb: Br Standards Ctees, Ctee Euro Convention for Constructional Steelwork (chm 1991–99); ctee coordinator Int Bldg Cncl 1985–89; FIStructE 1976, FICE 1977, FREng 1997; *Books* Manual of Stressed Skin Diaphragm Design (with E R Bryan, 1982), Plastic Design to BS 5950 (with B A Brown, 1996), Lightweight Sandwich Construction (2001); *Recreations* tennis, golf, skiing; *Style*— Prof Michael Davies, FREng; ✉ 83 Park Road, Hale, Altrincham, Cheshire WA15 9LQ (tel 0161 980 2838); Manchester Centre for Civil and Construction Engineering, University of Manchester, PO Box 88, Manchester M60 1QD

DAVIES, Michael; CBE (2000); s of Leonard Gwerfyl Davies (d 1996), of London, and Nancy Hannah, *née* Jones; *b* 23 January 1942; *Educ* Architectural Assoc (Dipl, M Arch), UD (UCLA), RIBA; *m* 1, 3 March 1966, Isabel Christina, *née* Hogg; 1 s (Oliver Joanne Pascal Schafer b 5 July 1972), 1 da (Dio Andromeda Mistral b 4 June 1977); m 2, 8 Dec 1977, Elizabeth Renee Yvonne, da of Marius Escalmel; *Career* architect; Airstructures Design 1967–69, Chrysalis USA 1969–72, Piano + Rogers 1972–77, Chrysalis Architects (London) 1979–83; Richard Rogers Partnership: fndr ptnr 1977, River CADS Ltd; projects incl:

Pompidou Centre, IRCAM, Lloyd's Bldg, Inmos, terminal 1 and Europier at London Heathrow Airport, London Royal Docks masterplan, City of Dunkirk masterplan, Greenwich Peninsula masterplan, Millennium Dome; currently dir T5 Project London Heathrow; lectr: Architectural Assoc, Univ of Calif, Univ of Texas, Calif Poly; memb: Cncl Architectural Assoc Sch of Architecture, advsy panel Sunday Times 'A Future for London' 1990, Docklands Urban Design Panel, Millennium Experience Litmus gp; tstee Camden Arts Centre; FICPD, FRGS, FRSA; *Style—* Michael Davies, Esq, CBE, FRSA; ✉ Richard Rogers Partnership, Thames Wharf, Rainville Road, London W6 9HA

DAVIES, Michael Thomas (Mike); *b* 16 August 1947; *Educ* Aston Univ (BSc); *Career* early career with British Alcan Aluminium (latterly divnl md), dir Williams plc 1988–96 (joined 1986), chief exec Newmond plc 1997–2000; Baxi Group Ltd: gp chief exec 2000–02, chm 2003–04, non-exec dir 2004–05; chm: Vi-Spring 2003–06, Marshalls plc 2004–, Royal Mint 2007–; non-exec dir: Taylor Woodrow plc 2003–, Pendragon plc 2003–; *Clubs* RAC, MCC; *Style—* Mike Davies, Esq; ✉ Marshalls plc, Birkby Grange, Birkby Hall Road, Birkby, Huddersfield HD2 2YA (tel 01484 438900); Royal Mint, Llantrisant, Pontyclun CF72 8YT

DAVIES, Neil Llewellyn; s of Thomas Davies (d 1988), and Beatrice, *née* Croker; *b* 19 March 1961, Aberdare; *Educ* Aberdare Boys GS, Univ of Kent (BA); *Partner* Benjamin Marc Powis; *Career* slr and mediator specialising in family law; Morgan Bruce Slrs Cardiff 1986–94, ptnr and head Private Client Div Paris Smith & Randall Southampton 1994–; memb: Hampshire Resolution (also press spokesman), Skills and Support Ctee Resolution; memb UK Coll of Family Mediators; *Recreations* art and philosophy (when not playing tennis); *Style—* Neil Davies, Esq; ✉ Paris Smith & Randall LLP, 1 London Road, Southampton SO15 2AE (tel 023 8048 2482, fax 023 8048 2230)

DAVIES, Neil Valentine; s of late Isadore Edward Davies, of Brighton, E Sussex, and Carmel, *née* Greenberg; *b* 14 February 1957; *Educ* Harrow Co Boys' GS, King's Coll Cambridge (MA), QMC London (MSc); *Partner* Suzanne Farrell; *Career* econ asst rising to econ advsr Dept of Employment Gp 1978–86; HSE: econ advsr 1986–89, head Econ Advsrs Unit 1989–94, head Mgmnt, Small Firms and Trg Unit 1994–96; sr econ advsr MOD 1996–; memb Soc of Business Economists 1996; contrib various articles to learned jls; chair of govrs Geoffrey Chaucer Sch Southwark 1982–83; *Style—* Neil Davies, Esq; ✉ Ministry of Defence, Level 3, Main Building, Whitehall, London SW1A 2HB (tel 020 7218 2573, fax 020 7218 1656, e-mail neil.davies765@mod.uk)

DAVIES, Nick; *b* 28 March 1953; *Educ* Royal Latin GS Buckingham, Stowe, UC Oxford (BA); *Career* BR guard Cambridge 1974–75; messenger boy The Guardian 1975–76, trainee Mirror Gp 1976–78, with Evening Standard Diary 1978–79, news reporter The Guardian 1979–84, home affrs corr The Observer 1984–86, chief feature writer London Daily News 1986–87, Washington columnist The Scotsman 1987–88; freelance writer 1988–: The Guardian, World in Action; writer My Kingdom (film) 2002; *Awards* Crime Reporter of the Year 1980, Br Press Awards Commendations 1981, 1982, 1983, 1991, 1993, Feature Writer of the Year 1997, Journalist of the Year 1998, Reporter of the Year 1999, Martha Gellhorn Award 1999, European Journalism Prize 2003; *Books* White Lies (1991), Murder on Ward Four (1993), Dark Heart, The Shocking Truth About Hidden Britain (1997), The School Report (2000); *Style—* Nick Davies, Esq; ✉ The Guardian, c/o News Desk, 119 Farringdon Road, London EC1R 3ER (tel 002 7278 2332, e-mail mail@nickdavies.net)

DAVIES, Nicola Velfor; QC (1992); *b* 13 March 1953; *Educ* Bridgend Girls' GS, Univ of Birmingham (LLB); *Career* called to the Bar Gray's Inn 1976 (bencher 2001), recorder 1998–, dep judge of the High Court 2003–; *Style—* Nicola Davies, QC; ✉ 3 Serjeants Inn, London EC4Y 1BQ (tel 020 7353 5537, fax 020 7353 0425)

DAVIES, Rev Dr Noel Anthony; OBE (2003); s of Rev Ronald Anthony Davies (d 1967), of Pontycymer, Glamorgan, and Anne, *née* Morgans; *b* 26 December 1942; *Educ* Garw GS Pontycymer Glamorgan, UCNW Bangor (BSc), Mansfield Coll Oxford (BA Theol), Univ of Wales (PhD); *m* 10 Aug 1968, Patricia, da of John Cyril Barter (d 1986), of Lyme Regis; *Career* min Welsh Congregational Church Glanaman Dyfed 1968–77; gen sec: Cncl of Churches for Wales and Cmmn of The Covenanted Churches in Wales 1977–90, Cytun: Churches Together in Wales 1990–98; min Ebeneser Newydd Congregational Church Swansea 1996–, min of congregations in Clydach 1999–, chm Cncl of Welsh Congregational Union 1990–93, moderator Churches' Cmmn on Mission 1991–95, pres Welsh Congregational Union 1998–99, memb Bd of Christian Aid 1999–; pt/t lectr in theology Trinity Coll Carmarthen, hon res fell Univ of Wales Cardiff 1999; *Publications* Wales: Language, Nation, Faith and Witness (1996), Wales: A Moral Society? (jt ed with Bishop Rowan Williams, 1996), Un Er Mwyn y Byd (1998), God in the Centre (1999); also author of collections of prayers and meditations in Welsh; *Recreations* gardening, music, West Highland terriers, Oriental cooking; *Style—* The Rev Dr Noel Davies, OBE; ✉ 16 Maple Crescent, Uplands, Swansea SA2 0QD (e-mail noeldavies@aol.com)

DAVIES, Noel Anthony Thomas; s of Thomas Herbert Davies (d 1998), and Vera May, *née* Smith (d 1995); *b* 1 January 1945; *Educ* Hereford Cathedral Sch (George Robertson Sinclair music scholar), Royal Coll of Music (ARCM organ performance, ARCM piano accompaniment, Michael Mudie Award for opera conducting); *Career* conductor; studied under Melville Cook, Hubert Dawkes and Sir Adrian Boult; specialises in operas by Mozart, Verdi, Puccini and operas of Eastern Europe; ENO (formerly Sadler's Wells Opera): repetiteur 1967, conducting debut 1969, resident conductor 1974–2003; conductor ENO tour to Metropolitan Opera NY, regular guest conductor at RNCM; guest appearances incl: Houston Grand Opera, Iceland Opera, Bergen Festival, Bayerische Staatsoper Munich, Royal Opera Covent Garden, Canadian Opera Co Toronto (nominated by Bd of Canadian Theatre for Most Outstanding Musical Direction), Opera Ireland Dublin; ed several works by Handel which have had been performed internationally; charity work incl: Catholic Stage Guild, Cardinal Hume Centre (for young people at risk in London), Terrence Higgins Tst, various other charities for AIDS sufferers; *Books* Handel's Xerxes (co-ed with Sir Charles Mackerras, Chester Music Ltd); *Recreations* cuisine, British countryside, supporter of West Ham United FC; *Style—* Noel Davies, Esq; ✉ 9 Avenue Road, Abergavenny, Monmouthshire NP7 7DA (tel 01873 853257)

DAVIES, Owen Handel; QC (1999); s of David Trevor Davies, and Mary Davies; *b* 22 September 1949; *Educ* Hazelwick Comp, Magdalene Coll Cambridge; *m* Caroline Jane Davies; 1 s (Jack Andrew Bowen 30 May 1982), 1 da (Mary Laura Caroline b 22 Feb 1988); *Career* called to the Bar Inner Temple 1973 (bencher 2001); recorder of the Crown Court 2000–, head Garden Court Chambers; ed LND Journal; memb: Amnesty Int Lawyers' Gp, Environmental Law Assoc, Administrative Law Assoc, Criminal Bar Assoc, Liberty, Immigration Law Practitioners' Assoc, Haldane Soc; *Publications* articles and pamphlets on law and disarmament and human rights; *Clubs* India; *Style—* Owen Davies, QC; ✉ Garden Court Chambers, 57–60 Lincoln's Inns Fields, London WC2A 3LS (tel 020 7933 7600, fax 020 7993 7700, e-mail owend@gclaw.co.uk)

DAVIES, Owen Mansel; s of D Mansel Davies, of Penarth, S Glamorgan, and Margaret Phyllis, *née* Hunt; *b* 3 June 1934; *Educ* Swansea GS, Clifton, Peterhouse Cambridge (MA); *m* 1960, Elisabeth Jean Leedham; 2 da (Catherine Elisabeth b 30 July 1961, Susan Margaret b 12 July 1966), 1 s (Timothy Mansel b 8 May 1963); *Career* Nat Serv Lt RA 1953–55; BP International technologist Aden Petroleum Refinery 1960–64, process engr London 1965–68, project engr BP Italia Rome 1969, mangr Catalytic Branch BP Trading Ltd 1970–72, mangr Projects Div Refineries Dept BP Trading Ltd 1972–75, md BP SE Asia Singapore 1975–78, pres Sohio Construction Co San Francisco 1978–80, gen mangr Projects London 1981–88, gen mangr Business Services BP Engineering London 1988–92, ind conslt 1992–; memb Northamptonshire Police Authy 1995–2003; FEI (FInstPet 1978), FIChemE 1985, FREng 1989, CEng, Eur Ing; *Recreations* sailing, gardening, photography; *Style—* Mr Owen Davies, FREng; ✉ 63 High Street, Braunston, Daventry, Northamptonshire NN11 7HS (tel and fax 01788 890076)

DAVIES, Prof Paul Charles William; s of Hugh Augustus Robert Davies, of London, and Pearl Vera, *née* Birrell; *b* 22 April 1946; *Educ* Woodhouse GS Finchley, UCL (BSc, PhD); *m* 1, 13 July 1968 (m dis 1972), Janet Elaine, *née* Hammill; m 2, 28 July 1972, Susan Vivien Corti, da of Corti Woodcock (d 1958); 1 s (Charles Hugh Aidan b 1981), 1 da (Annabel Rebecca Eleanor b 1977); *Career* formerly: lectr in applied mathematics King's Coll London, prof Dept of Physics Univ of Newcastle upon Tyne; currently prof of natural philosophy Univ of Adelaide (formerly prof of mathematical physics); former govr Dame Allan's Schs Newcastle upon Tyne, vice-pres Teilhard de Chardin Centre; ABC Eureka Prize for the Promotion of Science 1991; Advance Australia Award 1993, Templeton Prize for Progress in Religion 1995; FInstP 1984, FAIP 1990, FRSL 1999; *Books* non-fiction: The Physics of Time Asymmetry (1974 and 1977), Space and Time in the Modern Universe (1977), The Forces of Nature (1979, 2 edn 1986), The Search for Gravity Waves (1980), The Runaway Universe (1978), The Edge of Infinity (1981), The Accidental Universe (1982), Quantum Fields in Curved Space (with N D Birrell, 1982), God and the New Physics (1983), Quantum Mechanics (1984), Superforce (1984), The Ghost in the Atom (with J R Brown, 1986), The Cosmic Blueprint (1987), Superstrings (with J R Brown, 1988), The New Physics (ed, 1989), The Matter Myth (1991), The Mind of God (1992), The Last Three Minutes (1994), Are We Alone? (1995), About Time (1995), More Big Questions (1998), The Fifth Miracle (1998), How to Build a Time Machine (2001), The Goldilocks Enigma (2006); fiction: Fireball (1987); numerous tech papers incl: Scalar Particle Production in Schwarzschild and Rindler Metrics (1975), The Thermodynamic Theory of Black Holes (1977), Perturbation Technique for Quantum Stress Tensors in a General Robertson-Walker Spacetime (with W G Unruh, 1979), Journey through a Black Hole (with I G Moss, 1989); *Recreations* travel, making radio and television programmes; *Style—* Prof Paul Davies

DAVIES, Pauline Elizabeth; da of Gordon White, of Guildford, Surrey, and Petroula, *née* Theohari; *b* 8 April 1950, London; *Educ* Guildford Co GS for Girls, Univ of Manchester (BSc, PGCE, MEd); *m* 4 July 1970, Alan Henry Davies, s of Denis Mercer Davies; 2 s (Luke Mercer b 13 July 1978, Nathan Henry b 21 April 1982); *Career* teacher Urmston GS for Girls 1972–76, various positions incl head of dept, sr teacher and dep head King Edward VI GS for Boys Chelmsford 1978–90, headmistress Croydon HS GDST 1990–98, headmistress Wycombe Abbey Sch 1998–; memb: SHA 1988, GSA 1990; involved with Build Africa; *Recreations* theatre, ballet, music, literature, travel; *Clubs* Lansdowne; *Style—* Mrs Pauline Davies; ✉ Wycombe Abbey School, High Wycombe, Buckinghamshire HP11 1PE (tel 01494 520381, fax 01494 447404, e-mail daviesp@wycombeabbey.com)

DAVIES, Prof Peter David Owen; s of Herbert Lewis Owen Davies (d 2000), of Caldy, Wirral, and Mary Ann Lockerbie, *née* Curry (d 1983); *b* 30 April 1949; *Educ* Marlborough, UC Oxford, St Thomas' Hosp London (MA, BM BCh, DM); *m* 1975, Eleanor Mary Baskerville, da of David Mynors (d 1999); 3 s (Richard b 1976, Edward b 1978, Michael b 1985), 1 da (Mary b 1982); *Career* various jr posts London Hosps until 1978, clinical offr MRC Tuberculosis and Chest Diseases Unit Brompton Hosp 1978–80, subsequently various posts Cardiff 1980–88, conslt respiratory physician Aintree Hosps and Cardiothoracic Centre Liverpool 1988–; licenced reader (Anglican Church) Dio of Chester; memb: BMA 1973, Br Thoracic Soc 1979, American Thoracic Soc 1987; sec TB Alert 1999; FRCP, RSM 1996; *Books* Clinical Tuberculosis (ed), Cases in Clinical Tuberculosis (co-author); also author of papers on many aspects of tuberculosis particularly epidemiological; *Style—* Prof Peter Davies; ✉ Tuberculosis Research Unit, Cardiothoracic Centre, Thomas Drive, Liverpool L14 3PE (tel 0151 228 1616, fax 0151 293 2254, e-mail p.d.o.davies@liverpool.ac.uk)

DAVIES, Peter Donald; s of Stanley Davies (d 1991), of Aberystwyth, Dyfed, and Dorothy Margaret, *née* Addicott (d 1987); *b* 14 May 1940; *Educ* Ardwyn Sch Aberystwyth, Guy's Hosp Univ of London (MB BS); *m* 23 May 1965 (m dis 1989), Penelope Anne, da of Wilfred Reginald Dawes; 2 da (Lucy Bronwen b 1969, Emma Sian b 1971); m 2, 24 Dec 1993, Margaret Ruth, da of Horace Gallant; *Career* lectr in experimental ophthalmology Inst of Ophthalmology London 1967–70, resident Moorfields Eye Hosp 1970–74, sr registrar Middx Hosp and Moorfields Eye Hosp 1974–78, conslt ophthalmic surgn Norwich Health Dist 1978–2001, initiated the devpt of out-patient cataract surgery in the UK 1983–, dir East Anglian Eye Bank 1993–2001; author of pubns on ophthalmology and corneal surgery; FRCS 1973, FRCOphth 1989, hon reader Biological Sciences UEA 1998; *Recreations* horse riding, shooting; *Style—* Peter Davies, Esq; ✉ Consulting Rooms, Hill House, BUPA Hospital, Old Watton Road, Colney, Norwich NR4 7SZ (tel 01603 255508 ext 408)

DAVIES, Peter Douglas Royston; CMG (1994); s of late Douglas Davies, of Christchurch, Dorset, and late Edna, *née* Dingle; *b* 29 November 1936; *Educ* Brockenhurst Co HS, LSE (BSc (Econ)); *m* 28 Jan 1967, Elizabeth Williams; 1 s (Simon Leslie Peter b 1968), 2 da (Eleanor Catherine b 1971, Jane Olivia b 1974); *Career* FO (now FCO): second sec Nicosia 1966–67, FO 1967–68, first sec Budapest 1968–71, FCO 1971–74, consul Rio de Janeiro 1974–78, cnsllr The Hague 1978–82, dep high cmmr Kuala Lumpur 1982–85, RCDS 1986, head Arms Control and Disarmament Dept FCO 1987–91, consul-gen and DG Trade and Investment Canada Toronto 1991–96; fndr Peter Davies and Assocs 1996–; *Recreations* cosmology, golf, skiing; *Style—* Mr Peter Davies, CMG; ✉ Peter Davies, South Wing, The Manor, Moreton Pinkney, Northamptonshire NN11 3SJ

DAVIES, Rear Adm Peter Roland; CB (2005), CBE (1996, MBE 1984); s of Roland Davies (d 1982), and Winifred, *née* Stephen; *b* 2 April 1950; *Educ* Thornleigh GS Bolton, KCL (BSc), RMCS Shrivenham (MSc); *m* 13 July 1974, Dianne Helen, *née* Whittaker; 1 s (Malcolm b 1977), 1 da (Louise b 1979); *Career* univ cadet entry RN 1969; submarine weapon engr offr HMS Opportune, HMS Narwhal and HMS Courageous, staff posts Faslane, Devonport and Northwood, staff course NATO Defence Coll Rome; MOD and Procurement posts incl: RN SUB Harpoon project, Directorate of Operational Requirements, project mangr TOMAHAWK prog, Directorate of Naval Communication and Info Systems; Cdre HMS Collingwood 1998–2001, Flag Offr Trg and Recruiting and chief exec Naval Recruiting and Trg Agency 2001–04; princ and chief exec City Lit 2004–; FIEE 1995; *Recreations* swimming, sailing (RYA offshore skipper); *Style—* Rear Adm Peter Davies; ✉ 7 Merchant Court, 61 Wapping Wall, London E1W 3SJ; City Lit, Keeley Street, Covent Garden, London WC2B 4BA (e-mal p.davies@citylit.ac.uk)

DAVIES, Maj-Gen Peter Ronald; CB (1991); s of Lt-Col Charles Henry Davies (d 2004), of Crookham Village, Hants, and Joy, *née* Moore; *b* 10 May 1938; *Educ* Llandovery Coll, Welbeck Coll, RMA Sandhurst; *m* 12 Sept 1960, (Rosemary) Julia, da of David Felice (d 1961), of Douglas, IOM; 1 s (Tristan David Henry b 1961), 1 da (Cecily Harriet b 1963); *Career* cmmnd Royal Signals 1958, served BAOR Berlin, Cyprus, Borneo and UK 1958–72, Bde Maj 20 Armd Bde 1973–74, Instr Staff Coll Camberley 1975–76, CO 1 Armd Div Signal Regt 1976–79, Col GS SD HQ UKLF 1979–82, Bde Cdr 12 Armd Bde 1982–84, RCDS 1985, Dep Cmdt and Dir of Studies Army Staff Coll 1985–86, Cdr Communications BAOR 1987–90, GOC Wales 1990–91; Col King's Regt (8th, 63rd, 96th) 1986–94, Chm Regtl Cncl and King's Liverpool and Manchester Regts' Assoc 1986–94, Col Cmdt Royal Signals 1991–96, life pres Jullunder Bde Assoc 1996–; DG RSPCA 1991–2002, DG World SPA 2003– (vice-pres 1998–99, pres 2000–02), exec dir Euro Gp for Animal Welfare 1992–2002, dir Flora and Fauna 2001–, chm Freedom Food Ltd

D

1994–2002; conslt Int Strategic Planning Advsy Bd Andrew Corporation USA 1991–92; memb Exec Ctee: Forces Help Soc and Lord Robert's Workshops 1994–96, Addaction 1997–99, Wildlife Information Network 2002–04; chm Animals in War Meml Fund 1997–; govr Welbeck Coll 1980–81, tstee Llandovery Coll 1992–2004; Queen Victoria Silver Medal RSPCA 2003, Massachusetts SPA George T Angell Meritorious Award 2003; CIMgt 1994 (FIMgt 1991), FIPD 1991, FRSA 2002; *Recreations* perpetual motion, Welsh nostalgia; *Clubs* Buck's, Army and Navy, Fadeaways, Kennel; *Style*— Maj-Gen Peter Davies, CB; ✉ World Society for the Protection of Animals, 89 Albert Embankment, London SE1 7TP (e-mail peterdavies@wspa.org.uk)

DAVIES, Dr Peter Thomas; CBE (2003); s of Thomas Henry Davies (d 1980), and Molly Rose, *née* Gardner; *b* 24 February 1948; *Educ* Sweyne Sch Rayleigh, Univ of Reading (BSc), Univ of London (PhD); *m* 1972, Phyllis, *née* Campbell; 2 s (Alan b 1975, Bryan b 1976); *Career* postdoctoral res fell Physics Dept QMC London 1972–73; SERC: memb Engrg Div 1973–78, private sec to chm Prof Sir Geoffrey Allen 1978–80, memb Astronomy Div 1980–82; memb Central Policy Review Staff and princ advsr to Chief Scientist at Cabinet Office 1982–84, ops dir and sec Royal Greenwich Observatory 1984–85, fndr dir Rover Advanced Technol Centre Univ of Warwick 1985–96, chief exec Pera International 1999– (md 1996–99); industrial prof Univ of Nottingham; memb Design Cncl 1999–2005; *Style*— Dr Peter Davies, CBE; ✉ Pera, Innovation Park, Melton Mowbray, Leicestershire LE13 0PB (tel 01664 501501)

DAVIES, Philip; MP; *b* 5 January 1972, Doncaster; *Educ* Old Swinford Hosp Sch, Univ of Huddersfield; *Career* Asda: cashier 1993–95, trainee customer servs mangr 1995–97, customer rels supervisor 1997–99, customer servs project mangr 1999–2004, sr mktg mangr 2004–05; MP (Cons) Shipley 2005– (Parly candidate (Cons) Colne Valley 2001), memb Culture Media and Sport Select Ctee 2006–; memb Cons Pty 1988–; *Style*— Philip Davies, Esq, MP; ✉ House of Commons, London SW1A 0AA (e-mail daviesp@parliament.uk); Constituency Office tel 01274 592248, website www.philip-davies.org.uk

DAVIES, Philip John; CB (2001); s of Glynn Davies (d 1997), and Catherine Mary, *née* Adams; *b* 19 September 1954; *Educ* St Julian's HS Newport, Hertford Coll Oxford (BA, BCL); *m* 5 Sept 1981, Jacqueline Sara, da of George Boutcher; 1 da (Helen Louise Amanda b 5 June 1989); *Career* barr; lectr Univ of Manchester 1977–1982; Parly Counsel Office: successively asst, sr asst then dep counsel 1982–1994, Parly counsel 1994–; author of articles and notes in various legal periodicals; tstee Mickleham Village Hall; *Recreations* family, Welsh terriers, the garden; *Style*— Philip Davies, Esq, CB; ✉ Pinecroft, The Downs, Givons Grove, Leatherhead, Surrey KT22 8JY (tel 01372 373915); Office of the Parliamentary Counsel, 36 Whitehall, London SW1A 2AY (tel 020 7210 6630, fax 020 7210 6632, e-mail philip.j.davies@cabinet-office.x.gsi.gov.uk)

DAVIES, Quentin; MP; s of late Dr Michael Ivor Davies, and late Thelma Davies; *b* 29 May 1944; *Educ* Leighton Park Sch Reading, Gonville & Caius Coll Cambridge (MA), Harvard Univ (Frank Knox fell); *m* 1983, Chantal, da of late Lt-Col R L C Tamplin, Military Knight of Windsor, and late Claudine Tamplin; 2 s (Alexander, Nicholas); *Career* HM Dip Serv: third sec FCO 1967–69, second sec Moscow 1969–72, first sec FCO 1973–74; Morgan Grenfell & Co Ltd: asst dir 1974–78, DG and pres Morgan Grenfell France SA 1978–81, dir and head of Euro Corp Fin 1981–87, conslt 1987–93; MP (Cons until 2007, then Lab): Stamford and Spalding 1987–97, Grantham and Stamford 1997–; oppn spokesman on pensions 1998–99, shadow Paymaster General 1999–2000, oppn spokesman on defence 2000–01, shadow sec of state for NI 2001–03; memb: Euro Standing Ctee 1990–97, Treasy Select Ctee 1992–98, Standards and Privileges Ctee 1996–98, Euro Legislation Ctee 1997–98, Int Devpt Select Ctee 2003–; dir: Dewe Rogerson International 1987–96, SGE 1999–2000, Vinci SA and Vinci plc 2003–; advsr: Chartered Inst of Taxation 1993–, NatWest Markets 1993–2000, Royal Bank of Scotland Global Markets 2000–03; memb Cncl Lloyd's of London 2004; Freeman City of London, Liveryman Worshipful Co of Goldsmiths; MCIT 1993; *Recreations* reading, walking, riding, skiing, travel; *Clubs* Beefsteak, Brooks's, Travellers, Grantham Cons; *Style*— Quentin Davies, Esq, MP; ✉ House of Commons, London SW1A 0AA

DAVIES, Dr Rachel Bryan; da of John Edwards (d 1960), and Gweno, *née* Davies Bryan (d 1981); *b* 6 October 1935; *Educ* Friends' Sch Sibford, Friends' Sch Sidcot, UCW Aberystwyth (LLB, BA), QMC London (LLM), KCL (PhD); *m* 1958, Geraint Tim Davies, s of David Evan Davies; 4 da (Angharad b 1960, Crisiant b 1963, Manon b 1965, Rhianon b 1968), 1 s (Siôn b 1967); *Career* called to the Bar Gray's Inn 1965; res asst Law Faculty Univ of Melbourne 1958–62, lectr in law Kingston Poly 1965–67, law reporter The Times 1975–81, commercial law reporter Financial Times 1981–92; chm Rent Tbnls 1981–86, exec and consultative ed Kluwer Law Publishing 1985–89, chm Employment Tbnls 1992– (pt/t chm 1986–92), vice-pres Univ of Wales Swansea 1994–2005, memb Cncl and Ct of Govrs Univ of Wales 1995–2005; tstee Tenovus 1999–2001; De Lancey and De La Hantey prize for medico-legal journalism 1981; hon fell Univ of Wales Aberystwyth 2001; FRSA 1990; *Recreations* walking, music, reading; *Style*— Dr Rachel Davies; ✉ Gelli Heblyg, Llangynwyd, Maesteg, Pen-y-Bont ar Ogwr CF34 0DT (tel 01656 739115)

DAVIES, (William) Rhodri; QC (1999); s of His Hon Judge (Lewis) John Davies, QC, and Janet Mary, *née* Morris; *b* 29 January 1957; *Educ* Winchester, Downing Coll Cambridge (BA); *m* 28 July 1984, Hon Victoria Catherine (Vicky), da of Stewart Platt, of Writtle, Essex; 3 da (Rachael b 1985, Joanna b 1987, Jessica b 1990); *Career* called to the Bar Middle Temple 1979, practising in London 1980–; *Recreations* running, sailing, swimming, family; *Clubs* Thames Hare & Hounds; *Style*— Rhodri Davies, Esq, QC; ✉ 1 Essex Court, Temple, London EC4Y 9AR (tel 020 7583 2000)

DAVIES, His Hon Sir Rhys Everson; kt (2000), QC (1981); s of Evan Davies (d 1986), of Neath, W Glamorgan, and Nancy Caroline, *née* Everson (d 1947); *b* 13 January 1941; *Educ* Cowbridge and Neath GS, Univ of Manchester (LLB); *m* 9 Feb 1963, Katharine Anne, da of Walter William Yeates; 1 s (Mark Everson b 24 July 1965), 1 da (Carolyn Alison b 16 Feb 1969); *Career* called to the Bar Gray's Inn 1964 (bencher 1993); in practice Northern Circuit 1964–90, recorder 1980–90, sr circuit judge until 2003, resident judge for Manchester and hon recorder of Manchester 1990–2003; chm Gtr Manchester Area Criminal Justice Strategy Ctee 1992–2003, pres Manchester and Dist Medico-Legal Soc 2002–04 (patron 2004–), memb Sentencing Advsy Panel 2000–05, ind monitor Criminal Records Bureau 2003–; memb Ct and Cncl Univ of Manchester 1993–2004 (dep chm 2000–04, visitor 2004–); *Recreations* music, walking; *Style*— His Hon Sir Rhys Davies, QC; ✉ Manchester Crown Court, Crown Square, Manchester M3 3FL

DAVIES, Richard James Guy; s of George Glyn Davies, MBE, of Frinton-on-Sea, Essex, and Cynthia Joan, *née* Franklin; *b* 7 December 1953; *Educ* Felsted, St Catharine's Coll Cambridge (MA); *m* 19 July 1980 (m dis 1992); 2 s (Michael b 1985, Christopher b 1987); *Career* with Lazard Bros & Co Ltd 1976–93, chief exec LET Ventures Ltd 1993–95; British Linen Bank Ltd: joined as dir 1995, head of corp fin 1995–99, dir British Linen Advisers 1999–; *Recreations* sailing, music, literature; *Clubs* Royal Thames Yacht, Royal Corinthian Yacht; *Style*— Richard Davies, Esq; ✉ Highfield Farm, Fordham Road, West Bergholt, Colchester C06 3DP; British Linen Advisers Ltd, 8 Frederick's Place, London EC2R 8HY (tel 020 7710 8800, fax 020 7710 8813, e-mail richard.davies@britishlinen.co.uk)

DAVIES, Richard John; s of Sydney John Davies, and Valerie Reynolds Davies; *b* 12 August 1949; *Educ* King's Coll Taunton, Univ of Liverpool (BA, MA); *m* Margaret Mary, *née* Goddard; 1 s (John), 1 da (Emelye); *Career* teaching asst Dept of Political Theory and Institutions Univ of Liverpool 1972–73; entered Civil Serv 1973, served MOD, FCO, MPO etc 1973–84, asst sec Welsh Office 1985; head of div Welsh Office: Health Mgmnt, Systems and Personnel 1985–87, Health and Social Servs Policy 1987–89, Housing 1989–94, School Performance 1994–99; dir Welsh Office Dept of Educn; Welsh Assembly Govt: dir Dept for Trg and Educn 1997–2006, dir Mgmnt Bd 2000–, head Dept for Public Servs and Performance 2006–; visiting prof Univ of Glamorgan; Nuffield-Leverhulme fell 1990–; MCMI, FRSA; *Recreations* family, walking, swimming, music; *Style*— Richard Davies, Esq; ✉ Department for Public Services and Performance, Welsh Assembly Government, Cathays Park, Cardiff CF10 3NQ (tel 029 2082 3207, fax 029 2082 5524, e-mail richard.john.davies@wales.gsi.gov.uk)

DAVIES, Dr Robert James; s of Canon Dilwyn Morgan Davies (d 2000), of Ilmington, Warks, and Kate, *née* Maltby (d 1987); *b* 24 February 1943; *Educ* St John's Sch Leatherhead, St Catharine's Coll Cambridge (MA, MB BS, MD), Univ of Greenwich (MSc, PGCE, Cert CMT); *m* 1, 1969 (m dis 1979); 2 s (Mark b 10 Oct 1972, James b 27 May 1975); m 2, 1981, Karen, da of Dennis Stanley Seymour Henley, of Bexley, London; *Career* res fell Brompton Hosp London 1971–73, lectr in med St Thomas' Hosp London 1973–76, med res Univ of Tulane New Orleans 1976–77; Bart's: conslt physician 1977–99, dir Asthma and Allergy Res Dept 1981–99, conslt in charge Dept of Respiratory Med 1987–99, prof of respiratory med 1991–99 (reader 1983–90); dir Gen and Emergency Med Royal Hosps Tst 1994–96, dir of R&D Royal Hosps NHS Tst 1996–97; pres: Br Soc for Allergy and Clinical Immunology 1987–90, Br Allergy Fndn 1996–2000; second vice-pres Int Assoc for Allergy and Immunology 1997–99 (treas 1985–94); md masters-in-science.com 2004–; lectr in computing NW Kent Coll 2004–; Medal of Faculty of Med Univ of Montpellier France 1981; FRCP 1982, fell American Acad of Allergy and Immunology 1984, hon memb Argentinian Soc for Allergy and Immunology 1997; *Publications* Respiratory Medicine (ed, 1988–94), Allergy - The Facts (ed, 1989), Understanding Hay Fever and Other Allergies (1995); *Recreations* hill walking, horse breeding; *Style*— Dr Robert J Davies; ✉ 96 Vanbrugh Park, Blackheath, London SE3 7AL (tel 020 8858 9215, e-mail drrobertdavies@gmail.com)

DAVIES, Roger Guy; s of Cyril Graham Davies, OBE (d 1974), and Hettie Susannah, *née* Lewis; *b* 5 November 1946; *Educ* Kingswood Sch Bath, Fitzwilliam Coll Cambridge (MA); *m* 30 May 1970, Diana June, da of Harold Charles Perks (d 1967); 3 s (Tom b 23 Sept 1973, William b 8 Nov 1974, Edward b 17 Dec 1977), 1 da (Georgina b 18 Oct 1982); *Career* ptnr Allen & Overy: articled clerk 1970–72, asst slr 1972–76, ptnr 1976–, Freeman Worshipful Co of Slrs; memb Law Soc; *Recreations* golf, tennis, shooting, horse racing, eventing, music; *Clubs* Royal St George's Golf, Ashridge Golf, Oxford and Cambridge Golfing Soc, Hawks' (Cambridge); *Style*— Roger Davies, Esq

DAVIES, (Robert) Russell; s of John Gwilym Davies, of Llanbedr, Merioneth, and Gladys, *née* Davies; *b* 5 April 1946; *Educ* Manchester Grammar, St John's Coll Cambridge (scholar, BA, Tiarks German award); *m* 23 March 1972 (m dis), Judith Anne, da of Noel Stephen Slater; 1 s (Steffan John b 5 Feb 1979); m 2, Emma Jane, da of Gerald Kingsley; 3 s (Joseph Philip b 14 July 2000, Matthew Gwilym, Oliver Nathaniel (twins) b 14 Nov 2003); *Career* freelance journalist and broadcaster; TV actor and presenter 1970–71, cartoonist Liberal News 1971, caricaturist Times Literary Supplement 1972–74; The Observer: football reporter 1973–76, film critic 1973–78, contracted writer 1983–88; sports columnist New Statesman 1978–79, TV critic Sunday Times 1979–83 (columnist 1978–), dep ed Punch 1988 (contrib 1976–92); sports columnist: Sunday Telegraph 1989–94, Daily Express 1996–; radio critic Sunday Telegraph 1996–97; radio incl: documentaries on American culture for Radio 3, biographies of jazz and blues singers, plays for radio, sports documentaries, Midweek 1979–81, Jazz Century, Beethoven or Bust, Russell Davies Song Show, Friday Night Is Music Night, Just Before Goonrise, Spike Milligan: 21 Goon Salute, Oh What A Beautiful Evening, Living In Harmony, The Guv'nor: The Rober Farnon Story, Radio Roots, Pick of the Week, Opening Nights, The Bix Beiderbecke Story, Brain of Britain 2004, The Archive Hour: Charles Chilton, George on George (Radio 4), biographical series (Cole Porter, Irving Berlin, George Gershwin, Harry Warren, Johnny Mercer, Richard Rogers, Louis Armstrong, Nat King Cole, Fats Waller, Bing Crosby, Ella Fitzgerald), radio series (When Housewives had the Choice, Radio Fun, Seven Deadly Singsongs, What An Institution, Quad Wrangles, Turns of the Century, Word of Mouth (Ondas Prize Barcelona 1996)); script editor Frank Sinatra: Voice of the Century (Radio 2), author of radio scripts for Denis Norden, David Jacobs, Harry Connick Jr, Al Jarreau, Pat Boone, Stewart Copeland, Henry Goodman, Ruthie Henshall; television incl: What The Papers Say, What The Papers Say Annual Awards 1989–97, presenter Saturday Review, presenter Jazz Week and Jazz On a Summer's Day weekend BBC2, music documentaries BBC2 (Laughing Louie, Duke Ellington and his Famous Orchestra, Le Jazz Hot, The Lowest of the Low, Buddy Bolden's Children, A Musical Nation?, The Honky Tonk Professor), Statements (arts series BBC Wales), Knowing My Place (HTV), Dudley Moore: After the Laughter (BBC 4), Artie Shaw: Quest for Perfection (BBC 4), University Challenge (BBC 2), script editor Private Life of a Masterpiece (BBC 2); formerly: librettist Love And The Ice Cream Vendor (Roundhouse and South Bank Show LWT), actor Charles Charming's Challenges (Apollo Theatre); recorded The World of Buddy Bolden (with Humphrey Lyttelton) 1986; *Books* Peregrine Prykke's Pilgrimage (illustrator, 1976), Vicky (with Liz Ottaway, 1987), Ronald Searle (1990), The Diaries of Kenneth Williams (ed), The Kenneth Williams Letters (ed), Foreign Body: The Secret Life of Robert Maxwell (1996); *Recreations* jazz and jazz history, trombone, tuba, bass saxophone and piano playing, comic art, cartooning, tidying up; *Style*— Russell Davies, Esq; ✉ c/o PFD, Drury House, 34–43 Russell Street, London WC2B 5HA (tel 020 7344 1000)

DAVIES, Ryland; s of late Gethin Davies, and Joan Davies; *b* 9 February 1943; *Educ* Royal Manchester Coll of Music (studied with Frederic R Cox, OBE); *m* 1, 1966 (m dis 1981), Anne Elizabeth Howells; m 2, 1983, Deborah Rees; 1 da (Emily); *Career* tenor, operatic prodr and voice teacher; debut as Almaviva in The Barber of Seville WNO 1964, debut as prodr L'Elisir d'Amore 1991; pt/t prof of singing RNCM 1987–94; performed at venues incl Covent Garden, Glyndebourne, NY Met, Milan, Paris, Vienna, Salzburg, Berlin, Hamburg, Stuttgart, Buenos Aires, Bonn, Geneva, Nice, Madrid, Barcelona, Palermo, Rome, Edinburgh Festival; worked with orchs incl: London Symphony, London Philharmonic, English Chamber Orch, Chicago Symphony, Philadelphia Orch, Vienna Symphony, Boston Symphony, Cleveland Symphony, Bavarian Radio Orch; worked under conductors incl: Sir John Pritchard, Sir Colin Davis, Sir Charles Mackerras, Daniel Barenboim, Sir Georg Solti, Richard Bonynge, Simon Rattle, Andrew Davis, Erich Leinsdorf, Karl Böhm, Zubin Mehta, Claudio Abbado, Herbert von Karajan, Bernard Haitink, James Levine, John Eliot Gardiner; made numerous recordings, given performances on radio, TV and film; Boyce and Mendelssohn Fndn scholarship 1964, John Christie award 1965; fell Royal Manchester Coll of Music 1971, fell Welsh Coll of Music and Drama 1996; *Roles* incl: Belmonte in Die Entführung aus dem Serail (Glyndebourne, Paris, Amsterdam and Lyons), Fenton in Falstaff (Scottish Opera and Covent Garden), Ferrando in Cosi Fan Tutte (Covent Garden, Met Opera NY), Flamand in Capriccio (Glyndebourne), Tamino in The Magic Flute (Glyndebourne, WNO, Scottish Opera), Essex in Britten's Gloriana (Sadler's Wells), Hylas in The Trojans, Don Ottavio in Don Giovanni (Covent Garden), Cassio in Otello, Ernesto in Don Pasquale (Covent Garden), Lysander in A Midsummer Night's Dream (Covent Garden, Glyndebourne), The Prince in The Love for Three Oranges (Glyndebourne), Eisenstein in Die Fledermaus (ENO), Nemorino in L'Elisir d'Amore (Covent Garden), Le Duc, Chérubin and Basilio in Le Nozze di Figaro (Covent Garden), Arbace in Idomeneo (Met Opera NY), Don Basilio in Le Nozze di Figaro (New Israeli Opera), Don Basilio in Figaro's Wedding (ENO 1999), Rev Horace Adams in Peter Grimes (ENO 1999, Saito Kinen Festival Japan 2002, Florence 2002), Don Basilio in Le Nozze Di Figaro (Glyndebourne) 2001; other productions incl: Dialogue of the Carmelites (Netherlands Opera) 1997 and 2002, Le Nozze di Figaro (Chicago Lyric Opera 1998), Die Zauberflöte (Santa Fe Opera 1998), Carmen (Netherlands Opera 1999), Dialogue of the Carmelites (ENO, Santa Fe Opera 1999), Turk in Italy LA Boheme (ENO) 2000, Monostatos-Zauberelöte (Met Opera NY) 2001, The Makropulos Case (Houston Grand Opera) 2002, Arbace in Idomeno (Opera North) 2003, Monostatos (Amsterdam and Covent Garden) 2003, Francis Flute in A Midsummer Night's Dream (La Fenice Venice) 2004, Rev Horace Adams in Peter Grimes (Salzburg Easter Festival and Berlin Philharmonie) 2005, The Makropulos Case (Lyon) 2005, Dialogue of the Carmelites (ENO) 2005, Monsieur Triquet in Eugene Onegin (ROH) 2006; *Style*— Ryland Davies, Esq; ✉ Elm Cottage, Loseberry Road, Claygate, Surrey KT10 9DQ

DAVIES, Prof Sally Claire; da of Prof J G Davies (d 1990), and E M Davies, *née* Tordoff; *b* 24 November 1949, Birmingham; *Educ* Edgbaston High Sch for Girls, Manchester Univ MB ChB; *m* 7 Oct 1989, Dr Willem H Ouwehand; 2 da (Olivia b 26 Nov 1991, Isa b 3 Feb 1995); *Career* conslt haematologist Central Middx Hosp 1995–, prof of haemoglobinopathies Faculty of Med Imperial Coll London 1997–, dir of R&D NHS London Region 1999–2004, dir of R&D Dept of Health 2004–; ed Int Cochrane Collaboration 1999–; chair UK Clinical Research Collaboration 2004–, memb Advsy Ctee on Health Research WHO 2006–; govr Ashridge Mgmnt Sch 2006–; FRCP 1992, FRCPath 1997, FRCPCH 1997, FFPHM 1999, FMedSci 2002; *Publications* author of more than 50 peer-reviewed pubns, 19 chapters in books and more than 80 other articles in the fields of sickle cell disease and R&D strategies for health; *Recreations* opera, cooking, skiing; *Clubs* RSM; *Style*— Prof Sally C Davies; ✉ Department of Health, Richmond House, 79 Whitehall, London SW1A 2NL (tel 020 7210 5982, e-mail sally.davies@dh.gsi.gov.uk)

DAVIES, (Hilary) Sarah Ellis; da of Michael E Davies, of Bungay, Suffolk, and Maureen Davies; *b* 11 January 1962; *Educ* Cheltenham Ladies' Coll, Wimbledon Sch of Art (fndn course), Kingston Poly; *m* 26 July 1997, Jeremy F Bourke, s of Ben Bourke; 1 da (Natasha Ellis b 15 July 2000), 1 s (Samuel Ellis b 25 Feb 2004); *Career* Lambie-Nairn & Co Ltd: runner 1982–84, TV commercials prodr 1984–85, head of TV (responsible for commercials prodn, brand identity for TV Cos and TV graphics) 1985–93, md Lambie-Nairn & Co Ltd 1993–97; commercial dir The Brand Union Ltd (incorporating Lambie-Nairn and Tutssels) 1997–99; corp branding conslt 1999– (clients incl: Royal Acad of Arts, Music Choice, 3i, Pearson Television, Thames Television, Red Bee Media Ltd (formerly BBC Broadcast)); produced Marketing for Television Companies Promax Europe 1999; memb: Commissioning Design Panel Promax UK 1997, Promax Europe 1998 (seminar ctee Promax UK 1998, 1999, 2000 and 2001), Marketing Soc 1997, Women in Marketing and Design 1997, RTS 1997 (Multichannel Ctee 1999, 2000 and 2001); tstee Media Tst, tstee ONE20 (TimeBank); Lambie-Nairn & Co recipient of Queen's Award for Export Achievement 1995; *Publications* Building the Brand (Spectrum magazine, 1995); *Recreations* skiing, scuba diving, fly fishing, travel; *Clubs* Chelsea Arts; *Style*— Ms Sarah Davies; ✉ 98 Bennerley Road, London SW11 6DU (tel and fax 020 7350 2239, e-mail sarah@sarahdavies.demon.co.uk)

DAVIES, Sharron Elizabeth; MBE (1993); da of Terry Davies, and Sheila, *née* Conybeare; *b* 1 November 1962; *Educ* Kelly Coll Devon; *Children* 1 s (Elliott Anthony Mark b 4 Nov 1993), 1 da (Grace Elizabeth b 14 June 1998); *Career* swimmer; memb Br Olympic Team 1976 (youngest memb), 1980 (Silver medal 400m individual medley) and 1992, Bronze medal 400m European Championships 1977, Gold medals 200m and 400m individual medley Cwlth Games 1978, Bronze medal 4 x 100m freestyle relay Cwlth Games 1990, Silver medal 4 x 200m freestyle relay Cwlth Games 1990; has broken over 200 Br records; Sportswoman of the Year 1978 and 1980; regular swimming presenter BBC Sport; interior design and fashion conslt; Amazon in Gladiators (ITV) 1995–96, presenter The Big Breakfast (Planet 24 for Channel 4) 1996–97; *Style*— Ms Sharron Davies, MBE; ✉ c/o BBC Sport, BBC Television Centre, Wood Lane, London W12 7RJ; website www.sharrondavies.tv

DAVIES, Dr Sheilagh; da of Arthur Brython Davies (d 1967), and Rachel Edith, *née* Penn (d 1965); *b* 4 March 1946; *Educ* Moreton Hall Oswestry, Royal Free Hosp Sch of Med Univ of London (LRCP MRCS, MB BS, DObstRCOG, DPsycholM, Laughlin prize); *m* (m dis); 1 da (Gwenllian Catherine Mary b 25 Dec 1985); *Career* SHO/registrar in psychiatry Nat Hosp for Nervous Diseases UCH and the Maudsley and Bethlem Hosps 1972–76, sr registrar in gen adult psychiatry then in psychotherapy Maudsley and Bethlem Hosps 1976–80, conslt psychiatrist in psychotherapy, head Psychotherapy Unit and hon sr lectr Royal Free Hosp 1981– (divnl med dir and chm Psychiatric Specialty Gp 1994–97), clinical tutor Inst of Psychiatry 1981–87, hon conslt psychiatrist in psychotherapy Tavistock Clinic 1994–; Br Psychoanalytical Soc: memb Cncl 1987–89, hon sec 1989–92, memb Scientific Ctee 1995– (chm 1999–), memb Ct of Electors 1999–; chm Psychotherapy Faculty Royal Coll of Psychiatrists 1994–99; fndr memb: Assoc for Psychoanalytical Psychotherapy in the NHS (memb Cncl 1982–86 and 1994–), Int Assoc for Forensic Psychotherapy (memb Steering and Advsy Ctee 1992–), NI Inst of Human Rels; FRCPsych 1990 (MRCPsych 1975); *Recreations* walking, dogs, Wales, opera, classical music, theatre; *Clubs* Groucho, RSM; *Style*— Dr Sheilagh Davies; ✉ Royal Free Hospital, Psychotherapy Unit, Second Floor, Pond Street, London NW3 2QG (tel 020 7830 2046, fax 020 7830 2139)

DAVIES, Simon; s of Arthur Rees Davies (d 1982), of Newcastle Emlyn, Cardiganshire, and Catherine Elizabeth, *née* Jones (d 1991); *b* 12 March 1937; *Educ* Cardigan GS, Coll of Estate Mgmnt (pres SU); *m* 1, Oct 1959 (m dis 1989), Anja Ilse, *née* Körner; 1 s (Michael Stephen b 1 April 1960 d 1978), 1 da (Kathleen Anja b 1 June 1964); m 2, March 1990, Sheila Jane, *née* Henderson; *Career* md J Simon Davies Ltd Chartered Valuation Surveyors; vice-pres Central London Valuation Tbnl; hon memb Gorsedd of Bards; Freeman City of London; FRICS, FCIArb; *Recreations* rugby, opera; *Clubs* East India; *Style*— Simon Davies, Esq; ✉ 9 Hyde Park Crescent, London W2 2PY (tel 020 7706 4321, fax 020 7262 7789, e-mail simon@simondavies.biz)

DAVIES, Siobhan; CBE (2002, MBE 1995); *b* 18 September 1950; *Educ* London Contemporary Dance Studio; *Career* choreographer; lead dancer and choreographer London Contemporary Dance Theatre (cr 17 works) 1972–87, assoc choreographer Rambert Dance Co 1988–93; fndr (with Richard Alston and Ian Spink) Second Stride, fndr Siobhan Davies Dance Co 1988; composers worked with incl: Steve Reich, Kevin Volans, Gerald Barry, Max Eastley, Matteo Fargion; others worked with incl: David Buckland (set designer), Peter Mumford (lighting designer), Sasha Keir (costume designer), Antony McDonald (costume designer), Caryl Churchill (text), David Ward (artist); Hon DUniv Surrey 1999, Hon Dr Univ of Leicester 2003; *Works created* for Rambert Dance Co: Embarque 1988, Sounding 1989, Signature 1990, Winnsboro Cotton Mill Blues 1992; for Siobhan Davies Dance Co: White Man Sleeps 1988, Wyoming 1988, Cover Him With Grass 1989, Drawn Breath 1989, Different Trains 1990, Arctic Heart 1991, White Bird Featherless 1992, Make Make 1992, Wanting to Tell Stories 1993, The Glass Blew In 1994, Wild Translations 1995, The Art of Touch 1995, Trespass 1996, Affections 1996, Bank 1997, Eighty Eight 1998, Wild Air 1999, Of Oil and Water 2000, Plants and Ghosts 2002, Bird Song 2004, In Plain Clothes 2006; for Royal Ballet: A Stranger's Taste 1999, Thirteen Different Keys 1999 (cmmnd by Artangel, dancers from Royal Ballet and Siobhan Davies Dance Co); other credits: Dancing Ledge (for Eng Nat Ballet) 1990; *Awards* Fulbright Arts Fellowship 1986–87, Digital Dance Award 1988, 1989, 1990 and 1992, Prudential Award for the Arts (commendation) 1991, 1992, 1993 and 1995, Laurence Olivier Award for Outstanding Achievement in Dance 1993, Prudential Award for the Arts 1996, Time Out Award 1998 and 1999, South Bank Award for Dance 2000, Creative Briton Award 2000; *Style*— Ms Siobhan Davies, CBE; ✉ Siobhan Davies Dance, Siobhan Davies Studios, 85 St Georges Road, London SE1 6ER (tel 020 7091 9650, fax 020 7091 9669, e-mail info@siobhandavies.com, website www.siobhandavies.com)

DAVIES, Dr Stevie; da of Henry James Davies (d 1974), of Swansea, and Mona Joan Davies; *b* 2 December 1946; *Educ* Priory Girls' GS Shrewsbury, Univ of Manchester (BA, MA, PhD); *m* 1; 2 da (Emily Jane b 1977, Grace Hannah b 1980), 1 s (Robin Harry (twin) b 1980); m 2, 1990, Frank Regan; *Career* lectr in English lit Univ of Manchester 1971–84, author and pt/t tutor 1984–2001, sr res fell Roehampton Inst 1994–2001, Royal Literary Fund writing fell Univ of Wales Swansea 2001–03; dir of writing Univ of Wales Swansea 2004–; memb Greenpeace, involved in the peace movement and feminism; Arts Cncl Writer's Award 1996; FRSL 1998, fell Academi Cymreig 2000 (memb 1999); *Books* literary criticism: Emily Brontë: The Artist as a Free Woman (1983), Images of Kingship in 'Paradise Lost' (1983), The Idea of Woman in Renaissance Literature (1986), Emily Brontë (1988), Virginia Woolf's 'To the Lighthouse' (1989), John Milton (1991), Shakespeare's 'Twelfth Night' (1993), John Donne (1994), Emily Brontë: Heretic (1994), Shakespeare's Taming of the Shrew (1995), Henry Vaughan (1995); novels: Boy Blue (1987, Fawcett Soc Book Prize 1989), Primavera (1990), Arms and the Girl (1992), Closing the Book (1994, shortlisted Fawcett Soc Prize 1994), Four Dreamers and Emily (1996), The Web of Belonging (1997, shortlisted Arts Cncl of Wales Book of the Year 1998), Unbridled Spirits: Women of the English Revolution (1998), Impassioned Clay (1999, shortlisted Arts Cncl of Wales Book of the Year 2000), The Element of Water (2001, winner Arts Cncl of Wales Book of the Year 2002), Kith & Kin (2004); *Recreations* playing piano, listening to music, reading; *Style*— Dr Stevie Davies, FRSL

DAVIES, Susan Elizabeth (Sue); OBE; da of Stanworth Wills Adey (d 1980), and Joan Mary Margaret Charlesworth (d 1967); *b* 14 April 1933; *Educ* Nightingale-Bamford NY USA, Eothen Caterham, Triangle Secretarial Coll; *m* 11 Sept 1954, John Ross Twiston Davies (d 2004), s of John Harold Twiston Davies (d 1990); 2 da (Joanna Lyn Twiston b 27 Dec 1955, Stephanie Jane Twiston b 27 March 1958 d 1988); *Career* photography; Municipal Jl 1953–54, various voluntary jobs, Artists Placement Gp 1966–67, ICA 1967–70, fndr and dir Photographers' Gallery 1971–91 (first photography gallery in Europe), photography conslt and curator 1991–; district and parish cncllr 1995–2003; Progress medal Royal Photographic Soc 1982, Kulturpreis German Photographic Soc 1990; memb: CNAA Photography Ctee 1982–86, CNAA Design Panel 1986–88; Hon FRPS 1980; *Recreations* jazz, gardens, grandchildren; *Clubs* Chelsea Arts; *Style*— Mrs Sue Davies, OBE; ✉ 57 Sandlilands Road, Fulham, London SW6 2BD (tel 020 7731 7262, e-mail sue.ristic@btinternet.com)

DAVIES, Terence; s of Thomas Davies (d 1952), of Liverpool, and Helen, *née* O'Brien (d 1997); *b* 10 November 1945; *Educ* Sacred Heart RC Boys' Sch, Coventry Drama Sch, Nat Film and TV Sch; *Career* actor, writer and director (film) 1973–; shipping office clerk 1960–61, unqualified book-keeper and accountant 1961–73; dir: The Terence Davies Trilogy (7 int prizes), Distant Voices Still Lives (17 int prizes), The Long Day Closes (2 int prizes), The Neon Bible, The House of Mirth (1 prize); *Books* Hallelujah Now (novel, 1983), A Modest Pageant (1992); subject of Terence Davies: A Critical Study (by Wendy Everett); *Recreations* reading, listening to music, dining, humour; *Style*— Terence Davies, Esq; ✉ 7 The Green, Mistley, Manningtree, Essex CO11 1EU (e-mail terencedavies@aol.com)

DAVIES, Thomas; s of David Charles Davies (d 1967), and Henrietta Florence, *née* Sutton (d 1984); *b* 25 June 1932; *Educ* Pinner Co GS; *m* 1959, Ursula Jane, da of Leonard Theodore Freeman; 3 da (Virginia Jane b 1962, Gillian Karina b 1964, Kristina Louise b 1968); *Career* Sydenham & Co (now Baker Tilly) Chartered Accountants Hereford office 1948–97 (ptnr 1967–97); vice-pres Hereford Cathedral Perpetual Trust Ltd; FCA; *Recreations* game fishing, ornithology, crosswords; *Style*— Thomas Davies, Esq; ✉ Hunters Moon, Breinton, Hereford HR4 7PB (tel 01432 266746, fax 01432 291367)

DAVIES, Prof Trevor; *b* 1946; *Educ* Univ of Sheffield (BSc, PhD); *Career* UEA: lectr, reader in atmospheric sciences 1988, dir Climatic Research Unit 1993–98, prof of environmental sciences 1998–, dean Sch of Environmental Sciences 1998–2004, currently pro-vice-chllr (research); memb NERC; fndr CRed (carbon reduction prog) 2003; *Style*— Prof Trevor Davies; ✉ Vice-Chancellor's Office, University of East Anglia, Norwich NR4 7TJ

DAVIES, Tristan David Henry; s of Maj-Gen Peter Ronald Davies, and Julia Rosemary, *née* Felice; *b* 26 October 1961; *Educ* Douai Sch, Univ of Bristol; *Children* 2 s (Thomas Charles Brook, Guy Robert Brook), 1 da (Harriet Rosemary Brook); *Career* journalist; ed Covent Garden Courier 1983–86, Piazza magazine 1986–87; The Independent: joined 1987, listings ed 1988–90, arts and weekend ed 1990–95, dep features ed 1993–96; asst ed Night and Day magazine Mail on Sunday 1996–98, exec ed The Independent 1998–2001, ed Independent on Sunday 2001–; *Recreations* singing, football; *Clubs* Groucho; *Style*— Tristan Davies, Esq; ✉ Independent on Sunday, 191 Marsh Wall, London E14 9RS (tel 020 7005 2000, fax 020 7005 2628)

DAVIES, Ven Vincent Anthony (Tony); s of late Vincent Davies, of Knighton, Leicester, and Maud Mary Cecilia, *née* Hackett; *b* 15 September 1946; *Educ* Green Lane Boys' Secdy Modern, Charles Keene Coll Leicester, Brasted Place Theol Coll, St Michael's Theol Coll Llandaff; *Career* Walkers (Organ Builders) Ltd 1961, Messrs Pearce & Son jewellers Leicester 1962–63, Furse (Wholesale) Electrical Ltd Leicester 1963–67, works study offr Leicester Mercury 1967–69, Theol Coll 1969–73, curate St James Owton Manor (Dio of Durham) 1973–76, curate St Faith Wandsworth (Dio of Southwark) 1976–78 (vicar 1978–81), vicar St John Walworth 1981–94, rural dean of Southwark and Newington 1988–93, archdeacon of Croydon and canon of Southwark Cathedral 1994–; FRSA; *Recreations* swimming, walking, architecture, history, Italy; *Clubs* National Liberal; *Style*— The Ven the Archdeacon of Croydon; ✉ Croydon Area Episcopal Office, St Matthew's House, 100 George Street, Croydon, Surrey CR0 1PE (tel 020 8256 9630, fax 020 8256 9631, e-mail tony.davies@southwark.anglican.org)

DAVIES, (William) Vivian; s of late Walter Percival Davies, of Llanelli, Carmarthenshire, and Gwenllian, *née* Evans; *b* 14 October 1947; *Educ* Llanelli GS, Jesus Coll Oxford (MA), The Queen's Coll Oxford (Randall-MacIver student in archaeology); *m* 1, 30 Oct 1970 (m dis 1994), Janet Olwen May, da of late Laurie Frederick Foat, DFM, of Llanelli, Carmarthenshire; 1 da (Elen Mai b 24 May 1971), 1 s (Thomas Dafydd Robert b 30 June 1974); m 2, 11 Aug 1996, Renée Frances, da of Lester Friedman, of LA, USA; *Career* Egyptologist; dep keeper Dept of Egyptian Antiquities Br Museum 1981–88 (asst keeper 1974–81), keeper of Egyptian Antiquities Br Museum 1988–; visiting prof of Egyptology Univ of Heidelberg 1984–85; hon librarian Egypt Exploration Soc 1975–85, reviews ed Jl of Egyptian Archaeology 1975–85, gen ed EES Publications 1989–99; chm Sudan Archaeological Research Soc 1991–; memb: Governing Cncl Br Inst in Eastern Africa 1989–2005, German Archaeological Inst 1992–; FSA 1980; *Books* Egyptian Sculpture (with T G H James, 1983), Saqqara Tombs (with A B Lloyd and A J Spencer, 1984), Problems and Priorities in Egyptian Archaeology (ed with J Assmann and G Burkard, 1987), Egyptian Hieroglyphs (1987), Catalogue of Egyptian Antiquities in the British Museum VII Axes (1987), Egypt and Africa Nubia from Prehistory to Islam (ed, 1991), Biological Anthropology and the Study of Ancient Egypt (ed with Roxie Walker, 1993), Time Machine, Ancient Egypt and Contemporary Art (ed with James Putnam, 1994),

D

Egypt, the Aegean and the Levant (ed with Louise Schofield, 1995), Egypt (with Renée Friedman, 1998), Studies in Egyptian Antiquities: A Tribute to T G H James (ed, 1999), Colour and Painting in Ancient Egypt (ed, 2001), Uncovering Ancient Sudan: A Decade of Discovery by the Sudan Archaeological Research Soc (ed with Derek Welsby, 2002); *Style*— Vivian Davies, Esq, FSA; ✉ Department of Ancient Egypt and Sudan, British Museum, London WC1B 3DG (tel 020 7323 8306, fax 020 7323 8303, e-mail wdavies@thebritishmuseum.ac.uk)

DAVIES, Prof Wendy Elizabeth; da of late Douglas Charles Davies, and late Lucy, *née* Evans; *b* 28 August 1942; *Educ* Maynard Sch, Univ of London (BA, PhD); *Career* lectr Univ of Birmingham 1970–76; UCL: lectr 1977–81, reader 1981–85, prof 1985–, head of dept 1987–92, dean 1991–95, pro-provost 1995–; visiting fell All Souls Coll Oxford 1986; vice-pres Br Acad 2003–05; memb: Cncl Soc for Medieval Archaeology 1983–86, Ancient Monuments Bd for Wales 1993–2003, Humanities Research Bd 1996–98; a govr Museum of London 1995–2001; FRHistS 1979, FSA 1988, FBA 1992; *Books* An Early Welsh Microcosm (1978), The Llandaff Charters (1979), Wales in the Early Middle Ages (1982), Small Worlds, The Village Community in Early Medieval Brittany (1988), Patterns of Power (1990), The East Brittany Survey, Field Work and Field Data (1994), A Breton Landscape (1997), The Inscriptions of Early Medieval Brittany (2000), Acts of Giving (2007); *Recreations* gardening, early music; *Style*— Prof Wendy Davies; ✉ History Department, University College London, Gower Street, London WC1E 6BT (tel 020 7679 1348)

DAVIES, Windsor; *b* 28 August 1930; *Career* actor; former school teacher; *Theatre* credits incl: Sir John Brute in The Provok'd Wife, Fluellon in The Battle of Agincourt, Under Milk Wood, Sir Toby Belch in Twelfth Night, Tartuffe and the Bacchae, Sink or Swim, Roll on 4 O'Clock, Run for Your Wife, My Wife Whatshername, It Runs in the Family, Capt Hook in Peter Pan, The Rocky Horror Show, Doctor in the House, Cardiff East; numerous pantomime incl: Cinderella, Babes in the Wood, Dick Whittington, Humpty Dumpty, Jack and the Beanstalk, Sleeping Beauty; *Television* credits incl: Shadow of the Tower, The View from Daniel Pyke, The Perils of Pendragon, The Donati Conspiracy, Pathfinders, Grand Slam, The New Statesman, Love Story, New Scotland Yard, Callan, The Main Chance, Crown Court, Thriller, Billy Liar, Sam, Paris, Battery Sgt Maj Williams in It Ain't Half Hot Mum, Never the Twain, Mosley, Mortimers, Vanity Fair, Sunburn, Gormenghast, Cor Blimey!; *Film* credits incl: The Family Way, Department K, Crimine, Hammerhead, Frankenstein Must Be Destroyed, Endless Battles, Adolf Hitler - My Part in His Downfall, Soft Beds Hard Battles, Carry On Behind; *Style*— Windsor Davies, Esq

DAVIES OF COITY, Baron (Life Peer UK 1997), of Penybont in the County of Mid Glamorgan (David) Garfield Davies; CBE (1996); s of David John Davies (d 1976), of Bridgend, Glamorgan, and Lizzie Ann, *née* Evans (d 1993); *b* 24 June 1935; *Educ* Heolgam Secdy Modern Bridgend, Bridgend Tech Coll, Port Talbot Sch of Further Educn; *m* 12 March 1960, Marian, da of Raymond Jones, of Trelewis, nr Treharris, Glamorgan; 4 da (Hon Helen Claire b 16 Jan 1961, Hon Susan Karen b 22 May 1962, Hon Karen Jayne b 16 June 1965, Hon Rachel Louise b 24 Jan 1969); *Career* Nat Service Sr Aircraftsman RAF 1956–58; British Steel Corp: jr operative Corp 1950–51, apprentice electrician 1951–56, electrician 1958–69; Union of Shop Distributive and Allied Workers (USDAW): area organiser 1969–73, dep divnl offr 1973–78, nat offr 1978–86, gen sec 1986–97; TUC: memb Gen Cncl 1986–97, memb Employment Appeal Tbnl 1991–2006, chm Int Ctee TUC 1992–97; cncllr Penybont RDC 1966–69; JP Ipswich 1972–78; *Style*— The Lord Davies of Coity, CBE; ✉ 64 Dairyground Road, Bramhall, Stockport, Cheshire SK7 2QW (tel 0161 439 9548)

DAVIES OF OLDHAM, Baron (Life Peer UK 1997), of Broxbourne in the County of Hertfordshire; Bryan Davies; s of George William Davies (d 1989), and Beryl Davies (d 1989); *b* 9 November 1939; *Educ* Redditch Co HS, UCL (BA), Inst of Educn Univ of London, LSE (BSc); *m* 1963, Monica Rosemary Mildred, da of Jack Shearing (d 1980), and Doris Shearing; 2 s (Hon Roderick Gareth b 1964, Hon Gordon Huw b 1966), 1 da (Hon Amanda Jane b 1969); *Career* teacher Latymer Sch 1962–65, lectr Middx Poly 1965–74; Parly candidate (Lab) Norfolk Central 1966, MP (Lab) Enfield North Feb 1974–1979, Parly candidate (Lab) Newport West 1983, MP (Lab) Oldham Central and Royton 1992–97; sec Parly Lab Pty 1979–92; PPS: to dep PM 1975–76, Dept of Educn 1976, Treasy 1977; Govt whip 1979, Lord in Waiting (Govt whip) 2000–03, Capt HM's Body Guard of Yeomen of the Guard (dep govt chief whip in Lords) 2003–; memb Select Ctee on: Overseas Devpt 1975–78, Public Expenditure 1975–78, Nat Heritage 1992–93; shadow higher educn min 1993–97; memb MRC 1977–79; chair FE Funding Cncl 1998–2000, pres RoSPA 1999–2001; *Recreations* literature, sport; *Style*— The Lord Davies of Oldham

DAVIS, *see also:* Hart-Davis

DAVIS, Albert Edward; s of Albert Ellerd Davis (d 1954), of Luton, Beds, and Kate Elizabeth, *née* Sell (d 1962); *b* 15 July 1928; *Educ* Luton GS; *m* 1 March 1952, Rhona, da of Walter Maurice Temple-Smith (d 1980), of Harpenden, Herts; 1 s (Andrew Albert b 1956); *Career* sr ptnr Davis & Co (chartered certified accountants) 1964– (joined 1945, jr ptnr 1950–64); dir Beacon Private Tst 1960–; memb: City of London Branch Royal Soc of St George, United Wards Club City of London, Farringdon Ward Club; past pres Ward of Cheap Club; Freeman City of London 1984, Liveryman Worshipful Co of Arbitrators 1984; FTII 1951, FCCA 1952, FCIArb 1968; *Recreations* music, walking, travel, horticulture; *Clubs* City Livery (past chm Music Section, chm Motoring Section); *Style*— Albert Davis, Esq; ✉ e-mail davis@debrett.net

DAVIS, Andrew; s of Brendon G F Davis, and Catharine Agnes, *née* Smyth; *b* 22 February 1964; *Children* 1 s (Joscelyn Andrew b 24 June 1992); *Career* formerly farmer, property devpt and investment, art consulting; fndr and exec chm von Essen gp of companies 1997–, exec chm PremiAir Aviation Services Ltd 2007–; *Style*— Andrew Davis, Esq; ✉ von Essen hotels Ltd, Ston Easton Park, Ston Easton, Bath BA3 4DF (e-mail chairman@vonessenhotels.co.uk)

DAVIS, Sir Andrew Frank; kt (1999), CBE (1992); *b* 2 February 1944; *Educ* Watford GS, Royal Acad of Music, King's Coll Cambridge (organ scholar); *Career* conductor; continuo player for Eng Chamber Orch and Acad of St Martin-in-the-Fields, studied conducting with Franco Ferrara in Rome; Festival Hall debut 1970 conducting BBC Symphony Orch; asst conductor BBC Scottish Symphony Orch 1970–72, assoc conductor The Philharmonia Orch 1973–77, princ guest conductor Royal Liverpool Philharmonic Orch 1974–77, music dir Toronto Symphony Orch 1975–88 (conductor laureate 1988–), music dir Glyndebourne Festival Opera 1988–2000, chief conductor BBC Symphony Orch 1989–2000 (incl tours to Hong Kong, Europe and Japan, conductor laureate 2000–), princ guest conductor Royal Stockholm Philharmonic Orch 1995–98, music dir and princ conductor Lyric Opera of Chicago 2000–; has worked with other orchs incl: Berlin Philharmonic, Frankfurt Radio Symphony, Tonhalle, Stockholm Philharmonic, Israel Philharmonic, NY Philharmonic, Boston, Chicago and Philadelphia Orchs, LA Philharmonic; appeared at venues incl: Bayreuth Festival, Paris Opera, Royal Opera House Covent Garden, Met Opera NY, Chicago Lyric Opera, La Scala Milan, BBC Proms (conductor Last Night 1993–), All Saints' Day Concert Musikverein Vienna, various Br and Euro festivals, numerous other venues in N America, Europe and Far East; work for Glyndebourne Festival Opera incl: Eugene Onegin, Falstaff, Ariadne auf Naxos, Don Giovanni, Katya Kabanova 1988, Jenufa 1989, Tippett's New Year 1990, The Marriage of Figaro 1991, La Clemenza di Tito 1991, The Magic Flute 1991, Peter Grimes 1992, Pique Dame 1992, Onegin 1994, Makropulos Case, Ermione 1995, Lulu 1996 (Gramophone Award for Best Video 1997), Conte Ory 1997; other operatic work incl: The Marriage of Figaro (Chicago Lyric Opera), La Clemenza di Tito (Chicago Lyric Opera), Peter Grimes (Bavarian Staatsoper) 1991; awarded Royal Philharmonic Soc/Charles Heidsieck Conductor's Award 1990; *Recordings* incl: all Dvořák Symphonies (with The Philharmonia), Mendelssohn Symphonies (with Bavarian Radio Symphony Orch), Tippett The Mask of Time (with BBC Symphony Orch, following Euro premiere BBC Proms 1984, winner Gramophone Record of the Year 1987, Grand Prix du Disque 1988), Birtwistle Mask of Orpheus (with BBC Symphony Orch, Gramophone Award for Best Contemporary Recording 1998), Shostakovich Violin Concertos, Brahms Piano Concertos, Nielsen Symphonies 4 and 5, various by Elgar, Vaughan Williams, Britten, Delius and Tippett; over 25 recordings with Toronto Symphony Orch incl: Strauss Four Last Songs and Salome final scene, Holsts Planets Suite, Handel Messiah; *Style*— Sir Andrew Davis, CBE; ✉ c/o Askonas Holt, Lonsdale Chambers, 27 Chancery Lane, London WC2A 1PF (tel 020 7400 1700, fax 020 7400 1799, e-mail info@askonasholt.co.uk)

DAVIS, (John) Barry; s of Wilfred John Davis (d 1973), of Birmingham, and Edna Olive, *née* Chester (d 1988); *b* 6 January 1936; *Educ* George Dixon GS Birmingham; *m* 10 Sept 1960, Brenda Margaret, da of William Henry Barnes; 1 da (Elizabeth Jayne b 20 Jan 1972); *Career* articled clerk Jacob Cavenagh & Skeet Chartered Accountants Birmingham 1952–57, qualified 1958; ptnr Mazars Birmingham 1965–96 (joined when Dixon Hopkinson 1958), sole practitioner in private practice 1996–2003; dir Inc Assoc of Organists 1999–, dir IAO Trading Ltd 1999–; methodist local preacher; hon consul Finland; FCA (ACA 1958), MIPA, LLCM, ALCM; Knight First Class of the Order of the Lion of Finland; *Recreations* classical music, opera, ballet, gardening; *Clubs* Birmingham Consular Association, Birmingham Organists Association; *Style*— Barry Davis, Esq; ✉ 31 Mirfield Road, Solihull, West Midlands B91 1JH (tel and fax 0121 705 4937)

DAVIS, Prof Bryn Derby; s of William Derby Davis (d 1995), and Joan, *née* Stansfield (d 1994); *b* 22 March 1938; *Educ* Archbishop Holgate's GS York, Univ of London (Sister Tutor's Dip/RNT, BSc, PhD); *m* 1, 1962 (m dis 1979), Valerie; 2 s (Timothy, Jonathan); m 2, 1979, Catherine; 1 s (Robert), 1 da (Sarah); *Career* princ tutor (mental health) Holloway Sanatorium NW Surrey Gp of Hosps 1970–73, DHSS nursing research fell 1973–76, dep dir Nursing Research Unit Univ of Edinburgh 1976–84 (univ fell 1983–84), princ lectr and dir of nursing research Brighton Poly 1984–89, prof of nursing educn, head dept and dean Sch of Nursing Univ of Wales Coll of Med Cardiff 1989–99, emeritus prof Univ of Wales Coll of Med 1999–; visiting prof of psychology Univ of Wales Bangor, visiting prof of nursing NE Wales Inst Wrexham; ed Jl of Psychiatric and Mental Health Nursing 1997–2004; non-exec dir Pontypridd and Rhondda NHS Tst 2000–04; memb: UKCC 1998–2002, Royal Coll of Nursing Pain Forum (chm 1991–97), UK Pain Soc; *Books* Research into Nurse Education (ed, 1983), Transcultural Psychiatry (contrib, 1986), Psychiatric Nursing Research (contrib, 1986), Nursing Education: research and developments (ed, 1987), Empathy in the Helping Relationship (contrib, 1990), Perspectives on Pain: mapping the territory (contrib, 1998), Caring for People in Pain (1999); *Recreations* sailing, amateur astronomy, reading, writing, painting, music, theatre, walking; *Style*— Prof Bryn Davis

DAVIS, Calum; s of Roy Albert George Davis (d 2002), of Rockford, Hants, and Catherine Jessie Davis, of Oban, Scotland; *b* 18 June 1951; *Educ* Taunton Sch, Canterbury Sch of Architecture (DipArch); *m* 1, 20 Aug 1977 (m dis 1996); 1 s (Jamie b 1981), 1 da (Josie b 1984); m 2, 9 April 2004, Hayley Ann Tasmin Bebb; 1 da (Rosy Bebb-Davis b 1998); *Career* architect; sr ptnr Architon LLP architects, interior designers, video animations, 3D modelling and planning supervisors; dir: Architon Developments Ltd 1986–, Architon Services Ltd 1986–, Trefoil Properties Ltd 1988–, Architon Media Graphics Ltd 1995–; ARCUK 1979, RIBA 1979; Eng trialist under 19 rugby 1969; rep: SW Eng Schs rugby 1969, S Eng under 19 rugby 1969; *Recreations* golf, skiing, conservation of historic buildings; *Clubs* RAC; *Style*— Calum Davis, Esq; ✉ Architon LLP, Regency House, 17 West Street, Epsom, Surrey KT18 7RL (tel 01372 745600, fax 01372 745016, mobile 07831 837908, e-mail calum@architon.com)

DAVIS, Carl; Hon CBE (2005); *b* 28 October 1936; *m* Jean Boht, *qv*; 2 da (Hannah b 1 Jan 1972, Jessie b 3 May 1974); *Career* composer and conductor; studied with: Paul Nordoff and Hugo Kauder NY, Per Norgaad Copenhagen; asst conductor New York City Opera 1958, artistic dir and princ conductor Royal Liverpool Philharmonic Orch Summer Pops 1992–2000; BAFTA Lifetime Achievement Award 2003; hon fell Liverpool John Moores Univ 1992, Hon DMus Univ of Liverpool 2002; Chevalier de l'Ordre des Arts et des Lettres (France) 1983; *Musical Theatre* Diversions (Obie Prize Best Review) 1958, Twists (Arts Theatre London) 1962, The Projector and Cranford (Theatre Royal Stanford East), Pilgrim (Edinburgh Festival), The Wind in the Willows (Haymarket) 1985, Alice in Wonderland (Hammersmith) 1987, The Vackees (Haymarket) 1987; *Incidental Music for Theatre* incl: The Prospect Theatre Co, The National Theatre, The Royal Shakespeare Co; *Ballet* A Simple Man 1987, Lipizzaner 1988, Liaison Amoureuses (Northern Ballet Theatre) 1988, Madly, Badly, Sadly, Gladly, David and Goliath, Dances of Love and Death (London Contemporary Dance Theatre), The Picture of Dorian Gray (Sadler's Wells Royal Ballet), A Christmas Carol (Northern Theatre Ballet) 1992, The Savoy Suite (English Nat Ballet) 1993, Alice in Wonderland (English Nat Ballet) 1995, Aladdin (Scottish Ballet) 2000, Pride and Prejudice (Ballet Central) 2002, Cyrano (Birmingham Hippdrome) 2007; *Music for Television* incl: The Snow Goose (BBC TV) 1971, The World at War (Thames TV, Emmy Award) 1972, The Naked Civil Servant (Thames TV) 1975, Our Mutual Friend (BBC TV) 1978, Hollywood (Thames TV) 1980, Churchill - The Wilderness Years (Southern TV) 1981, Silas Marner (BBC TV) 1985, Hotel du Lac (BBC TV) 1986, The Accountant 1989 (BAFTA Award), The Secret Life of Ian Fleming 1989, Separate but Equal 1991, The Royal Collection 1991, A Year in Provence 1992, Fame in the 20th Century - Clive James 1992, Ghengis Cohn 1993, Thatcher - The Downing Street Years 1993, Message for Posterity (Dennis Potter) 1994, Pride and Prejudice 1995, Oliver's Travels 1995, British Film Music (BBC TV) 1995, European Cinema 1995, Anne Frank Remembered (BBC TV) 1995, Celtic Symphony 1996, Real Women (BBC TV) 1997, A Dance to the Music of Time (Channel 4) 1997, The Cold War (Turner), Seasaw (ITV), Coming Home (ITV), Good Night Mr Tom (Carlton), The Queen's Nose (five series, BBC), The Great Gatsby 2000, Back Home (film) 2001, The Cranford Chronicles (BBC) 2007; *Music for Radio* Carl Davis Classics (Radio 2) 1997–; *Operas for Television* The Arrangement, Who Takes You to The Party, Orpheus in the Underground, Peace; *Film Music* The Bofors Gun 1969, The French Lieutenant's Woman 1981 (BAFTA award), Champions 1984, The Girl in a Swing 1988, Rainbow 1988, Scandal 1988, Frankenstein Unbound 1989, The Raft of the Medusa 1991, The Trial 1992, The Voyage 1993, Widow's Peak 1994, Topsy Turvy 2000; series of Thames Silents incl Napoleon (revised and enlarged score 2000), The Wind, The Big Parade, Greed, The General, Ben Hur, Intolerance, Safety Last, The Four Horsemen of Apocalypse 1992, Wings 1993, Waterloo 1995, Phantom of the Opera (Channel 4) 1996, Wedding March, Topsy Turvey, Book of Eve 2002, An Angel for May 2001 (Best Score Ale Kino Film Festival Poland 2003), Promoted to Glory 2003, Mothers & Daughters 2004; *Silent Film Music* The Wedding March 1998, Old Heidelberg 1999, Iron Mask 1999, The Adventurer 2000; several Chaplin Mutuals incl: Behind the Screen, The Rink, The Cure, The Immigrant, The Adventurer, The Crowd, Easy Street 2002, Charlie Chaplin The Mutual Films Vol 1 DVD 2003, The Mutual Films Vol 2 2005, The Godless Girl 2007; *Concert Works* Music for the Royal Wedding, Variations on a Bus Route, Overture on Australian Themes, Clarinet Concerto 1984, Lines on London Symphony 1984, Fantasy for Flute and Harpsichord 1985, The

Searle Suite for Wind Ensemble, Fanfare for Jerusalem 1987, The Glenlivet Fireworks Music 1988, Norwegian Brass Music 1988, Variations for a Polish Beggar's Theme 1988, Pigeons Progress 1988, Jazz Age Fanfare 1989, Everest 1989, Landscapes 1990, Paul McCartney's Liverpool Oratorio (with Paul McCartney) 1991, the BBC Proms 1999; *Recordings* incl: Christmas with Kiri (with Kiri Te Kanawa) 1986, Beautiful Dreamer (with Marilyn Horne) 1986, The Silents 1987, Ben Hur 1989, A Simple Man 1989, The Town Fox and Other Musical Tales (text by Carla Lane) 1990, Paul McCartney's Liverpool Oratorio 1991, Liverpool Pops At Home 1995, Pride and Prejudice 1995, The World at War, Pride and Prejudice and other Great Themes 1996, Phantom of the Opera 1997, Carl Davis 1997, Classics for a Summer Evening from Leeds Castle 1997, A Classical Celebration from Leeds Castle 1999, The Silents 2000, The World at War 2003, Christmas Album with Halle 2003, CD with Willard White and BBC Concert Orch 2005; *DVDs* A Simple Man, A Christmas Carol, Unknown Chaplin, Mutuals - Chaplin Vols 1, 4 and 11; *Composition* On the Beach At Night Alone (premièred at Leeds Castle) 1999; *CDs* Aladdin 2006, Show Music 2007; *Style*— Carl Davis, Esq, CBE; ✉ c/o Threefold Music, 2 The Court Yard, London SW3 4EE (tel 020 7730 9477, fax 020 7730 9199, e-mail admin@threefoldmusic.co.uk)

DAVIS, Christine Agnes Murison; CBE (1997); da of William Russell Aitken (d 1998), and Betsy Mary, *née* Murison (d 2000); *b* 5 March 1944; *Educ* Ayr Acad, Univ of St Andrews (MA), Univ of Aberdeen (DipEd); *m* 27 July 1968, Robin John Davis; 2 da (Marion Elizabeth, Alison Joan (twins) b 11 Oct 1969); *Career* history teacher: Cumbernauld HS 1967–68, Stirling HS 1968–69, supply work 1971–75; HM Inst Cornton Vale 1979–87; memb: Dunblane Town Cncl (Dean of Guild 1974–75) 1972–75, Perth and Kinross Joint CC 1972–75, Scottish Examination Bd 1982–86, North of Scotland Hydro Electric Bd 1980–90, Scottish Economic Cncl 1987–95, Scottish Ctee of the Cncl on Tribunals 1989–95, Hansard Soc Cmmn on Election Campaigns 1990–91; memb Ctee: Central Region Valuation Appeal 1975–89, Legal Aid Central 1980–87, Information Technol Awareness 1983–84; chm: Electricity Consultative Cncl for the North of Scotland District 1980–90 (memb 1974–77, dep chm 1978–79), Scottish Legal Aid Bd 1991–98 (memb 1986–89 and 1990–91), Scottish Agricultural Wages Bd 1995–2004 (memb 1990–95); vice-chair Information Technol Year Scottish Ctee 1981–82; memb Rail Passenger Ctee for Scotland 1997–2005; ind advsr on public appointments in Scotland 1998–2002; convenor Energy Action Scotland 2004 (special dir 1992–2002 and 2003–), dir and tstee Nat Energy Fndn 1990–2003; tstee: Joseph Rowntree Charitable Tst 1996–, Falkland Heritage Tst 2001–; memb Ct Univ of St Andrews 2000; *Recreations* embroidery, walking, gardening; *Clubs* Penn; *Style*— Christine Davis, CBE; ✉ 24 Newton Crescent, Dunblane, Perthshire FK15 0DZ (tel 01786 823226, fax 01786 825633, e-mail camdavis@gn.apc.org)

DAVIS, Christopher John Dusser; s of John Frank Davis (d 1988), and Pamela Mary Wilson, *née* Boyle (d 2001); *b* 28 June 1941; *Educ* Bradfield Coll, ChCh Oxford (MA); *m* 15 Aug 1969, Linda Lee, da of late Lee Oberholtz; 1 s (Benjamin James b 28 May 1977); *Career* ed Hamlyn Gp 1968–72, managing ed Mitchell Beazley 1972–74; Dorling Kindersley: ed dir 1974–82, publishing dir 1982–, dep chm 1987–2000, gp publisher 2000–05; publisher-at-large Weldon Owen 2006–; hon dep marshal Ford County Historical Assoc Dodge City Kansas 1975; *Books* North American Indian (1969), World Soccer (1972, 2 edn 1974), Olympic Games (1972); *Recreations* arts, sport, travel, dogs, wine; *Clubs* Groucho, 2 Brydges; *Style*— Christopher Davis, Esq; ✉ 34 Half Moon Lane, London SE24 9HU (tel and fax 020 7733 1898, e-mail christo.davis@virgin.net)

DAVIS, Clive Timothy; s of Sherman Alexander Davis, of Bath, and Betty Mavis, *née* Savery; *b* 8 October 1959; *Educ* Culverhay Comp Sch, St Catherine's Coll Oxford (BA); *m* 2 May 1986, Mohini, da of Mohanbhai Patel; 3 s (Shivan Clive b 7 Sept 1990, Krishan Alexander b 11 March 1993, Anand Anthony b 20 June 1997); *Career* journalist; books ed West Indian World newspaper 1981–85 (gen reporter and arts ed 1981–82), BBC News trainee 1982–84, sub ed BBC Radio News 1984–86, freelance feature writer and gen reporter The Guardian 1985–86, feature writer London Daily News 1986–87, writer The Times 1987–, feature writer Sunday Times 1994–; based New York 1994; contrib: Wilson Quarterly (Woodrow Wilson Center for Int Scholars Washington DC) 1997–, Washington Times 1997–; politics/culture blogger The Spectator 2007–; writer and presenter: Richard Wright - A Native Son (Radio 4 documentary), Eyewitness - William L Shirer (Radio 4 documentary); media fell Hoover Instn Stanford Univ; *Recreations* piano; *Style*— Clive Davis, Esq; ✉ The Times, 1 Pennington Street, London E98 1TA (e-mail clivedav@aol.com)

DAVIS, Sir Colin Rex; kt (1980), CH (2001), CBE (1965); s of Reginald George Davis (d 1944), of Weybridge, Surrey, and Lillian; *b* 25 September 1927; *Educ* Christ's Hosp, Royal Coll of Music; *m* 1, 1949 (m dis 1964), April Cantelo; 1 s, 1 da; m 2, 1964, Ashraf Naini, da of Abeolvahab Naini Assar (d 1978); 3 s, 2 da; *Career* formerly conductor: BBC Scottish Orchestra, Sadler's Wells (musical dir 1961–65); chief conductor BBC Symphony Orchestra 1967–71, conducted Bayreuth 1977, musical dir ROH 1971–86, music dir Bayerischer Rundfunk Orchestra Munich 1983–92, princ conductor LSO 1995–2007 (pres 2007–); princ guest conductor: Boston Symphony Orchestra 1972–84, LSO 1975–95, NY Philharmonic 1998–2003; hon conductor Dresden Staatskapelle 1990; Hon DMus: Keele Univ 2002, Royal Acad of Music 2002; winner Pipesmoker of the Year (32nd recipient) 1995; Freeman City of London 1992, Hon Freeman Worshipful Co of Musicians 2005; Commendatore of Republic of Italy 1976, Chev de la Legion d'Honneur 1982, Cdr's Cross of the Order of Merit of Fed Republic of Germany 1987, Cdr L'Ordre des Lettres (France) 1990, Bayerischen Verdienstorden 1992, Cdr First Class Order of the Lion of Finland 1992, Bavarian Order of Merit 1993, Royal Philharmonic Gold Medal 1995, Sibelius Birthplace Medal 1998, Officer de L'Ordre National de la Legion d'Honneur 1999, Maximiliansorden of the Federal Land of Bavaria 2000; *Recreations* reading, gardening, knitting; *Clubs* Athenaeum; *Style*— Sir Colin Davis, CH, CBE; ✉ 39 Huntingdon Street, London N1 1BP (tel 020 7609 5864, fax 020 7609 5866); c/o Columbia Artists Management Inc, 1790 Broadway, New York, NY 10019–1412, USA

DAVIS, Rt Hon David Michael; PC (1997), MP; s of Ronald Alexander Davis, and Elizabeth, *née* Brown; *b* 23 December 1948; *Educ* Bec GS, Univ of Warwick (BSc), London Business Sch (MSc), Harvard Univ (AMP); *m* 28 July 1973, Doreen, da of Alfred John Cook; 2 da (Rebecca b 1974, Sarah b 1977), 1 s (Alexander b 1987); *Career* strategic planning dir Tate & Lyle plc 1984–87 (non-exec dir 1987–90); MP (Cons): Boothferry 1987–97, Haltemprice and Howden 1997–; Govt whip 1989–93, Parly sec Office of Public Service and Science 1993–94, min of state for Europe FCO 1994–97; chm Cons Pty 2001–02, shadow sec of state for the Office of the Dep PM 2002–03, shadow sec of state for home, constitutional and legal affrs and shadow home sec 2003–, candidate Cons Pty leadership election 2005; chm Public Accounts Ctee 1997–2001; memb Cons Pty Policy Bd 2001–; dir Globe Investment Trust plc 1989–90; *Recreations* flying, mountaineering, writing; *Style*— The Rt Hon David Davis, MP; ✉ House of Commons, London SW1A 0AA (tel 020 7219 3000)

DAVIS, David William; s of George Henry Davis (d 1999), of Beaconsfield, and Lucy Ada, *née* Tylee (d 1959); *b* 29 October 1942; *Educ* Emanuel Sch; *m* 25 Nov 1967, Jennifer, da of Wilfred Snell; 1 da (Jacqueline b 25 Feb 1970), 1 s (Kenneth b 28 May 1971); *Career* CA 1966; ptnr: Fryer Sutton Morris & Co 1967–, Fryer Whitehill & Co 1971–, Clark Whitehill 1982– (now Horwath Clark Whitehill); FCA 1975; *Recreations* bridge; *Clubs* Phyllis Court; *Style*— David Davis, Esq; ✉ Blue Hills, Ibstone, Buckinghamshire HP14 3XT (tel 01491 638245)

DAVIS, Derek Richard; s of late Stanley Lewis Davis, OBE, of Malta, and late Rita Beatrice Rachel Davis, MBE, *née* Rosenheim; *b* 3 May 1945; *Educ* Clifton, Balliol Coll Oxford (BA); *m* 25 Jan 1987, Diana, da of late Ellis Levinson, of Chelsea; 1 da (Rebecca b 1988), 1 s (Joshua b 1990); *Career* asst princ Bd of Trade 1967, princ DTI 1972; Dept of Energy: asst sec 1977, under sec 1985; head Oil and Gas Div DTI 1987–93, DG British National Space Centre 1993–99; dir Chemicals and Biotechnology, Consumer Goods and Postal Services DTI 1999–2002, dir Nuclear and Coal Liabilities DTI 2002–04, chm Br Geological Survey 2005–; memb BBSRC 2000–02; *Style*— Derek Davis, Esq; ✉ 6 Roman Road, Bedford Park, London W4 1NA (tel and fax 020 8747 3931, e-mail derekrdavis@msn.com)

DAVIS, Prof Edward Arthur; s of Edward Davis (d 1988), and Elizabeth, *née* Smith (d 2000); *b* 26 November 1936; *Educ* Univ of Birmingham (BSc), Univ of Reading (PhD), Univ of Cambridge (MA); *m* 30 Oct 1960, Christine Elizabeth, da of Philip Edwyn Riley (d 1987); 2 s (Philip b 1962, Andrew b 1964); *Career* res asst prof Physics Dept Univ of Illinois 1963–64, scientist Xerox Corp Rochester NY 1964–67, lectr Physics Dept Univ of Cambridge 1973–80 (Royal Soc Mr and Mrs John Jaffé Donation res fell Cavendish Laboratory 1968–73), prof of experimental physics Univ of Leicester 1980–2002 (dean Faculty of Science 1987–90), distinguished research fell Dept of Materials Science and Metallurgy Univ of Cambridge 2002–; ed/conslt ed Philosophical Magazine; CPhys, FInstP, fell American Physical Soc; *Books* Electronic Properties of Non-Crystalline Materials (with N F Mott, 1971, 2 edn 1979), Science in the Making (Vol I 1995, Vol II 1997, Vol III 1998, Vol IV 1999), JJ Thomson and the Discovery of the Electron (with I Falconer, 1997), Nevill Mott: Reminiscences and Appreciations (1998); *Recreations* tennis, rock climbing, golf; *Style*— Prof Edward Davis; ✉ Department of Materials Science and Metallurgy, University of Cambridge, Pembroke Street, Cambridge CB2 3QZ

DAVIS, Emma; da of P K B Davis, and Jennifer Davis; *Educ* Univ of York (MA), Université Catholique Lyon, Central Sch London (Advanced Dip Fine Art), Slade Sch of Fine Art (MA, bursary); *Career* designer and artist; freelance ed Routledge 1996–; memb: BECTU, Mensa; *Theatre* set/costume designer White Horse Theatre Co Germany (prodns: The Comedy of Errors, Brain-Catch-Fire, The Empty Chair) 1999, costume designer Macbeth: False Memory (Lyric Hammersmith and UK tour) 2000, set/costume designer Cavalcade (Mount View Theatre London) 2000, set/costume designer The Apple Tree (Mount View Theatre London) 2000, asst dir Whose Life is it Anyway? (Comedy Theatre London) 2005, asst designer Peter Hall Season (prodns Much Ado About Nothing, Waiting for Godot and You Never Can Tell; Theatre Royal Bath and nat tour) 2005; *Film, Television and Video* designer The Templar (film) 2000, art dept Dirty Pretty Things (film) 2001–02, prodn buyer The Miller's Tale (TV, The Canterbury Tales series) 2003, asst art dir Nokia N-Gage (commercial) 2003, asst art dir Mrs Henderson Presents (film) 2004, prodn buyer Alien Autopsy (film) 2005, prodn buyer United 93 (film) 2005–06, prodn buyer Celebration (TV) 2006, prodn buyer The Bank Job (film) 2006–07; *Art Exhibitions* Keeley St Studios London 2000, Bolt Court Centre London 2001, Soc of Women Artists (Mall Galleries London) 2005; *Recreations* painting, photography, sculpture, reading, writing; *Style*— Ms Emma Davis

DAVIS, Evan Harold; s of Quintin Visser Davis, of Leatherhead, Surrey, and Hazel Noreen, *née* Groves; *b* 8 April 1962; *Educ* The Ashcombe Sch Dorking, St John's Coll Oxford (MA, ed Cherwell), Kennedy Sch of Govt Harvard Univ (MPA); *Career* research offr Inst for Fiscal Studies 1984–86, Harvard Univ 1986–88, research fell Centre for Business Strategy London Business Sch 1988–92, co-ordinator corporate policy research Inst for Fiscal Studies 1992–93, economics ed BBC 2001– (corr 1993–2001); *Books* The Penguin Dictionary of Economics (with G Bannock and R Baxter, 1987), Public Spending (1998), The New Penguin Dictionary of Business (with G Bannock, P Trott and M Uncles, 2003); *Style*— Evan Davis; ✉ Room 4220, BBC Television Centre, Wood Lane, London W12 7RJ

DAVIS, Gareth; *b* 13 May 1950; *Educ* Univ of Sheffield; *Career* Imperial Tobacco plc: joined W D & H O Wills as mgmnt trainee1972, manufacturing dir 1987, md Imperial Tobacco Int 1987, chief exec 1996–; non-exec dir Wolseley plc 2003–; *Style*— Gareth Davis, Esq; ✉ Imperial Tobacco Group plc, Upton Road, Southville, Bristol BS99 7UJ

DAVIS, Grahame Watson; s of William Henry Davis (d 1944), of Chatham, Kent, and Georgina, *née* Watson (d 1985); *b* 9 September 1934; *Educ* King's Sch Rochester; *m* 29 Aug 1963, Wendy Lovelace Davis, JP, da of Antony Lovelace Wagon (d 1978), of Rochester, Kent; 1 da (Helena b 1966), 1 s (Piers b 1971); *Career* slr; formerly sr ptnr Hextall Erskine & Co London, chm Employment Tbnls 1993–; memb Law Soc; *Recreations* golf, cricket; *Clubs* Wig & Pen, Castle; *Style*— Grahame W Davis, Esq

DAVIS, Ian Edward Lamert; s of (Walter) Patrick Carless Davis (d 1996), of Roehampton, and Jane, *née* Lamert (d 1987); bro of James Patrick Lamert Davis, *qv*, Sir Crispin Henry Lamert Davis, and Sir Nigel Anthony Lamert Davis (Hon Mr Justice Davis), *qv*; *b* 10 March 1951; *Educ* Charterhouse, Balliol Coll Oxford (MA); *m* 1, 1977, Sally Fuller; 1 s, 1 da; m 2, 1994, Penny Thring; *Career* with Bowater 1972–79; McKinsey & Co: assoc 1979–85, princ 1985–90, dir 1990–, UK md 1996–2003, worldwide md 2003–; memb: Int Business Cncl World Economic Forum, Advsy Bd Judge Inst of Mgmnt; *Recreations* sport, opera; *Style*— Mr Ian Davis; ✉ McKinsey & Company, 30 Kensington Church Street, London W8 4HA

DAVIS, Ian Paul; *b* 26 December 1954; *Educ* Univ of Liverpool (BEng), Open Univ (MBA); *Career* site engr Head Wrightson Process Engrg 1976–78, design engr Simpson Coulson and Partners 1978–80, design and project engr Davy International 1980–83; National House Building Cncl (NHBC): regnl engr 1983–90, dir of Technical Services 1990–94, dep chief exec (ops) 1994–97, dir 1994–97; DG Fedn of Master Builders 1997–2006; chm NHBC Services Ltd 1995–97; dir: PRC Homes Ltd 1990–97, NHBC Building Control Services Ltd 1994–99, Soha Housing 1996–2004 (chm 1999–2003), Builders Information Services Ltd 1997–98, Trade Debt Recovery Services Ltd 1997–99, National Register of Warranted Builders Ltd 1997–, Building Industry Certification Scheme Ltd 1997–, Constructing Better Health Ltd 2004–, Trustmark (2005) Ltd 2005–; advsr Joseph Rowntree Fndn Housing Standards Inquiry 1993–94; memb Cncl: Confedn of Registered Gas Installers 1990–94, National Inspection Cncl for the Electrical Contracting Industry 1990–94, CIC 1990–94; memb: BSI Tech Ctees 1987–97, Examination Bd National Energy Fndn 1992–96; tech sec European Union of Promoters and Contractors; govr John Hampden Sch 1996–2000; CEng 1981, MICE; *Style*— Ian Davis, Esq

DAVIS, Prof Ian Robert; s of David Davis (d 1988), of Paignton, S Devon, and Theodora, *née* Rawson; *b* 2 March 1937; *Educ* Northern Poly (DipArch), Georgia Inst of Technol, UCL (PhD); *m* 8 July 1961, Judith Margaret, da of Roy Cardwell (d 1975), of Bognor Regis, W Sussex; 2 da (Amanda b 1962, Caroline b 1964), 1 s (Simon b 1969); *Career* architect in practice 1961–70, princ lectr Sch of Architecture Oxford Poly 1970–89; advsr UN Post-Disaster Shelter Provision, Reconstruction and Disaster Risk Reduction 1975–2003, memb Nat Acad of Sci Int Ctee on the Implications of Disaster Assistance Washington DC 1976–79, leader Housing and Hazards Section Int Karakoram Expedition 1980, chm Int Panel on Disaster Risk Reduction 1981–86, dir Disaster Mgmnt Centre 1982–89, dir Int Training and Research Centre (INTRAC) 1991–96; memb Nat Co-ordination Ctee on the Int Decade for Nat Disaster Reduction (IDNDR) 1990–99; dir International Development and Emergency Relief Consits Ltd (IDRC) Oxford Centre for Disaster Studies (OCDS) 1993–98, prof of development and disaster management Cranfield Univ 1998–, visiting prof Cranfield Univ 2002; dir Safe Trust 1995–; Sasakawa-DHA (UN) Disaster Prevention Award 1996; visiting fell Univ of York 1995;

hon fell Oxford Brookes Univ 1991; FRSA; *Books* Shelter and Disaster (1978), Disasters and Small Dwelling (ed, 1982), Dunroamin - The Suburban Semi and Its Enemies (with P Oliver and I Bentley, 1982, reprinted 1994), Disasters and the Small Dwelling - Perspectives for the UN IDNDR (ed with Y Aysan, 1992), Christian Perspectives on Disaster Management (ed with M Wall, 1993), At Risk: Natural Hazards and People's Vulnerability and Disasters (with P Blaikie, T Cannon and B Wisner, 1994, 2 edn 2003), Building for Safety Compendium (with A Clayton, 1994), Developing Building for Safety Programmes (with Y Aysan, A Clayton, A Cory and D Sanderson, 1995), Disaster Mitigation, Preparedness and Response. An Audit of UK Assets (with D Sanderson, J Twigg and B Cowden, 1995), Forecasts and Warnings, IDNDR Flagship Programme - Project 5 The Dissemination of Warnings (with D Sanderson, D Parker and J Stack, 1998); *Recreations* grandfather, photography, painting, music, travel; *Style*— Prof Ian Davis; ✉ 97 Kingston Road, Oxford OX2 6RL (tel 01865 556473, fax 01865 516865, e-mail i.davis@n.oxford.demon.co.uk); Disaster Management Centre, Cranfield University, RMCS, Shrivenham, Swindon SN6 8LA (tel 01793 785287, fax 01793 785883)

DAVIS, James Gresham; CBE (1988); s of Col Robert Davis, OBE, JP (d 1963), and Josephine, *née* Edwards (d 1976); *b* 20 July 1928; *Educ* Bradfield Coll, Clare Coll Cambridge (MA); *m* 24 Nov 1973, Adriana Johanna (Hanny), da of Evert Verhoef (d 1978), and Petronella Verhoef-Stuy, of Rhoon, Holland; 3 da (Mariske b 1974, Katrina b 1978, Charlotte b 1980); *Career* RN 1946–49; P&O Steam Navigation Co: joined 1952, Calcutta 1953–54, Kobe (Japan) 1954–56, Hong Kong 1956–57, dir P&O Lines 1967–72; chm: British Rail Anglian Bd 1988–92, Bromley Shipping plc 1989–94, TIP Europe plc 1990–93, P Wigham Richardson 2003–; dep chm Hanjin Eurobulk 2003–07; dir: Kleinwort Benson Ltd 1973–88, DFDS Ltd 1975–96 (chm 1984–95), DFDS Travel Ltd 1975–96, Pearl Cruises of Scandinavia Inc 1982–86, Rodskog Shipbrokers (Hong Kong) Ltd 1983–88, Associated British Ports Holdings plc 1983–97, Transport Development Group plc 1984–91, Sedgwick Marine Energy & Cargo Ltd 1988–2000, Global Ocean Carriers Ltd 1988– (chm 1996–), British International Freight Assoc 1989–, Hempel Paints Ltd 1992–2000, Trinitas Services Ltd 1993–99, Tsavliris Salvage (International) Ltd 1994–99, 2M Invest Copenhagen 1996–99; dir Catenas Ltd 2000–02; memb Advsy Bd: J Lauritzen A/S Copenhagen 1981–85, DFDS A/S Copenhagen 1981–85; advsr Tjaereborg (UK) Ltd 1985–87; pres: Chartered Inst of Tport 1981–82, World Ship Soc 1969, 1971, 1984, 1985,1986 and 2003–, Harwich Lifeboat (RNLI) 1984–, Inst of Freight Forwarders Ltd 1984–86, National Waterways Tport Assoc 1986–92, Inst of Supervisory Mgmnt 1989–93, Inst of Chartered Shipbrokers 1990–92 (vice-pres 1988–90), Inst of Export 1995–2002 (vice-pres 1991–95), Danish-UK C of C 2000– (chm 1992–2000); vice-pres: Br Maritime League 1984–89, The Marine Soc 1986– (chm Cncl 1987–93); chm: Int Maritime Industries Forum 1981–, Simpler Trade Procedures Bd (SITPRO) 1987–98, Marine Risk Mgmnt Services Ltd 1995–99, Liberia Maritime Advsy Bd 1998–2000, Br Ctee Nippon Kanji Kyokai 2003–; memb: Cncl Mission to Seafarers 1981–, Int and Br Ctee Bureau Veritas 1989–, Gen Ctee Lloyd's Register; pt/t memb Br Transport Docks Bd 1981–83; tstee National Maritime Museum 1993–98, govr World Maritime Univ 1985– (chm Friends of the World Maritime Univ 1985–); memb: Baltic Exchange 1973–, Greenwich Forum 1982–; delivered: Thomas More Meml Lecture 1983, Reginald Grout Lecture 1989, Wakefield Meml Lecture 1989; Seatrade Personality of the Year 2002–03; Freeman City of London 1973, Liveryman and Asst to the Ct Worshipful Co of Shipwrights, Master Worshipful Co of World Traders 1996–97, Younger Br Trinity House; FCIT 1969, Hon FNI 1985, Hon FInstFF 1986, FRSA 1986, FISM 1989, FICS 1990; Knight Cdr Order of Dannebrog (Denmark) 1995; *Recreations* golf, family, ships; *Clubs* Brooks's, Hurlingham, Golfers, Harwich and Dovercourt Golf, Royal Calcutta Golf, Fanlingerers, Holland Park Lawn Tennis; *Style*— James Davis, Esq, CBE; ✉ 115 Woodsford Square, London W14 8DT (tel 020 7602 0675); Summer Lawn, Dovercourt, Essex CO12 4EF (tel 01255 502981); c/o Baltic Exchange, 38 St Mary Axe, London EC3A 8BH (tel 020 7929 6429, fax 020 7929 6430, e-mail imif@btconnect.com)

DAVIS, James Patrick Lamert; s of (Walter) Patrick Carless Davis (d 1996), of Roehampton, and Jane, *née* Lamert (d 1987); er bro of Sir Nigel Anthony Lamert Davis (Hon Mr Justice Davis), and Ian Edward Lamert Davis, *qqv*; *b* 23 September 1946; *Educ* Charterhouse, Balliol Coll Oxford; *m* 18 May 1974, Sally Anne, da of Noel Kemball, and Margaret Kemball; 1 s (Andrew b 23 March 1978), 3 da (Nicola b 23 March 1980, Sarah b 9 June 1982, Clare b 30 June 1986); *Career* Freshfields (now Freshfields Bruckhaus Deringer): articled clerk 1969, ptnr 1976–, ptnr i/c Singapore Office 1980–84; *Recreations* fishing, golf; *Clubs* MCC, Singapore Cricket, Berkshire Golf; *Style*— James Davis, Esq; ✉ Freshfields Bruckhaus Deringer, 65 Fleet Street, London EC4Y 1HS (tel 020 7936 4000, fax 020 7832 7001)

DAVIS, John Patrick; s of Ralph Patrick Davis, formerly of Chaldon, Surrey, and Vivian Hilda, *née* Braund; *b* 12 June 1944; *Educ* Tonbridge, Univ of Nottingham (BSc); *m* 5 Aug 1972, Fenella Irene, da of Guy Charles Madoc, CBE, KPM, of Ramsey, Isle of Man; 1 s (Michael b 23 June 1975), 1 da (Rosemary b 11 June 1976); *Career* gen mangr mech engrg Redpath Dorman Long Ltd 1979–83; chm: Intelek plc 1990–99 (chief exec and gp md 1985–90), 3s Group Ltd 2000, Drew Scientific Group plc 2003–; CEng 1971, MIWeldE 1983, FIEE 1986, FIMechE 1992, FInstD 1997; *Recreations* mountain rescue, bee keeping, sailing; *Style*— John Davis, Esq; ✉ Sandwath, Newbiggin-on-Lune, Cumbria CA17 4LY (tel 01539 623298, e-mail john@davisj.com)

DAVIS, Leonard Andrew (Leon); s of Leonard Harold Davis (d 1966), and Gladys, *née* Lacey (d 1968); *b* 3 April 1939; *Educ* South Aust Inst of Tech; *m* 1963, Annette, *née* Brakenridge; 2 da (Megan, Amanda); *Career* md Pacific Coal 1984–89, gp exec CRA Ltd 1989–91, mining dir RTZ Corp 1991–94, md and chief exec CRA Ltd 1994–95, chief operating offr RTZ-CRA 1996, chief exec Rio Tinto plc and Rio Tinto Ltd 1997–2000 (jt dep chm 2000–), chm Westpac Banking Corp 2000–; Hon DSc Curtin Univ WA; FRACI, fell Australasian Inst of Mining and Metallurgy; *Clubs* Melbourne, Brisbane; *Style*— Leon Davis, Esq; ✉ c/o Rio Tinto plc, 6 St James's Square, London SW1Y 4LD (tel 020 7930 2399, fax 020 7753 2480)

DAVIS, Lindsey Margaret; da of late William Alfred Davis, and late Joan Margaret, *née* Barker; *b* 21 August 1949; *Educ* King Edward VI HS for Girls Birmingham, Lady Margaret Hall Oxford (MA); *Career* civil servant Property Services Agency 1972–85, full time writer 1986–; memb: Soc of Authors, The Detection Club; chair Crimewriters' Assoc 2002–03, hon pres The Classical Assoc 1997–98; shortlisted Georgette Heyer Historical Novel prize 1985, 1986 and 1988; winner Crimewriters' Assoc (CWA) Dagger in the Library award 1995, winner CWA Ellis Peters Historical Dagger 1999; author of various romantic serials for Woman's Realm; *Books* The Course of Honour (1997); incl The Falco series: The Silver Pigs (1989, Authors' Club Best First Novel award 1990), Shadows in Bronze (1990), Venus in Copper (1991), The Iron Hand of Mars (1992), Poseidon's Gold (1993), Last Act in Palmyra (1994), Time to Depart (1995), A Dying Light in Corduba (1996), Three Hands in the Fountain (1997), Two for the Lions (1998), One Virgin Too Many (1999), Ode to a Banker (2000), A Body in the Bath House (2001), The Jupiter Myth (2002), The Accusers (2003), Scandal Takes a Holiday (2004), See Delphi and Die (2005); contrib author: No Alibi (1995), Perfectly Criminal (1997), Past Poisons (1998), Great Stories of Crime and Detection (2002), Mysterious Pleasures (2003), Saturnalia (2007); *Recreations* gardening, travel, theatre; *Style*— Ms Lindsey Davis; ✉ c/o Heather Jeeves Literary Agency, 9 Kingsfield Crescent, Witney, Oxfordshire OX28 6JB (tel 01993 700253); e-mail pt@lindseydavis.co.uk, website www.lindseydavis.co.uk

DAVIS, Lionel Edward; s of Sidney Edward Davis, MBE (d 1983), and Lendorana Florence Minnie, *née* Brignell (d 1984); *b* 26 April 1935; *Educ* Univ of Nottingham (BScEng), UCL (PhD, DScEng); *m* 22 Feb 1964, Hilary Frances, *née* Farmer; 3 s (Andrew Lionel, b 26 Nov 1965, Brandon Neil b 21 May 1971, Marcus Christopher b 27 Oct 1973), 1 da (Claire Frances b 17 Oct 1967); *Career* section ldr Mullard Research Laboratories 1959–64, assoc prof Rice Univ Houston TX 1964–72, prof and head of electrical engrg Paisley Coll Scotland 1972–87; UMIST (now Univ of Manchester): prof of communication engrg and head of microwave engrg gp 1987–2002, professorial fell 2002–03, prof emeritus 2003–; memb various Ctees IEE and IEEE; IEEE Microwave Theory and Techniques Soc (MTT-S) distinguished microwave lectr 2003–05; FIEE 1977, FInstP 1993, FIEEE 1995; *Publications* numerous academic papers published in learned jls: IEEE Trans on Microwave Theory and Techniques, Proc IEE Microwave Antennas Propag, Microwave and Optical Technology Letters; *Recreations* reading, travelling, gardening; *Style*— Prof Lionel Davis

DAVIS, Margaret Ann McLeod Leo (Meg); da of John Alexander Bede McLeod Davis (d 1976), of Montréal, Canada, and Barbara Ann Lusby; *b* 26 September 1957; *Educ* École Classique Sécondaire Villa Maria, McGill Univ Montreal (BA); *m* 19 March 2006, J Pimblett; *Career* dir MBA Literary Agents 1988– (joined 1984); sec Assoc of Authors' Agents 1998–2001; co-chair Dramatists' section Personal Mangrs Assoc 2004–; *Style*— Ms Meg Davis; ✉ MBA Literary Agents Ltd, 62 Grafton Way, London W1T 5DW (tel 020 7387 2076, fax 020 7387 2042, e-mail meg@mbalit.co.uk)

DAVIS, Prof Mark Herbert Ainsworth; s of Christopher Ainsworth Davis (d 1951), and Frances Emily Davis, JP, *née* Marsden, of Moulsford, Oxon; *b* 1 May 1945; *Educ* Oundle, Clare Coll Cambridge (MA, ScD), Univ of Calif Berkeley (MS, PhD); *m* 15 Oct 1988, Jessica Isabella Caroline, da of Robert Sinclair Smith, of Broadstairs, Kent; *Career* research asst Electronics Research Laboratory Univ of Calif Berkeley 1969–71; Imperial Coll London: lectr 1971–79, reader 1979–84, prof of system theory 1984–95; dir and head of research and product devpt Tokyo-Mitsubishi International plc 1995–99, prof of mathematics Imperial Coll London 2000–; sometime visiting prof: Harvard Univ, MIT, Univ of Oslo, TU Vienna; FSS 1985, FIMS 1994, Hon FIA 2001; *Books* Linear Estimation and Stochastic Control (1977), Stochastic Modelling and Control (1985), Markov Models and Optimization (1993), Louis Bachelier's Theory of Speculation (jtly, 2006); *Recreations* classical music (violin and viola); *Style*— Prof Mark Davis; ✉ Department of Mathematics, Imperial College, London SW7 2AZ (tel 020 7594 8486, e-mail mark@chartfield.org)

DAVIS, Dr Michael; s of Harry Tyrrell Davis (d 1970), of London, and Joan, *née* Latcham (d 2003); *b* 8 July 1943; *Educ* Charterhouse, St Thomas' Hosp Med Sch Univ of London (MB BS, MD); *m* 1, 5 Dec 1970 (m dis 1994), Elizabeth Maureen, da of Hedley Victor Billing (d 1984); 1 da (Joelle b 18 May 1972), 2 s (Justin b 10 May 1974, Julian b 29 Jan 1978); m 2, 2 Sept 1994, Catherine Susan Jones; 1 da (Annabelle b 7 Jan 1996), 1 s (William b 9 July 1997); *Career* jr hosp posts 1967–74, sr lectr and conslt physician Liver Unit KCH London 1974–82; consIt physician: Dudley Rd Hosp Birmingham 1982–86, Royal United Hosp Bath 1986–; clinical examiner RCP 1989–; author scientific papers and chapters med textbooks relating to gastroenterology; MBSG 1972, FRCP 1984 (MRCP); *Books* Drug Reactions and the Liver (1981), Therapy of Liver Disease (1989); *Recreations* woodwork, music, walking; *Style*— Dr Michael Davis; ✉ Royal United Hospital, Combe Park, Bath BA1 3NG (tel 01225 824131, fax 01225 825516)

DAVIS, Michael Edward; s of Capt Raymond Norris Davis, of Sevenoaks, Kent, and Margaret, *née* Pierce; *b* 14 August 1951; *Educ* Sevenoaks Sch, Univ of London (BA); *m* 17 Aug 1974, Helen Frances, da of William Podmore, OBE, JP, of Wetley Rocks, Staffs; 1 s (Paul Michael William b 4 July 1983), 1 da (Laura Helen Margaret b 2 Feb 1986); *Career* admitted slr 1977, ptnr Herbert Smith 1986– (joined 1975), higher rights (civil); non-exec dir CEDR, non-exec dir London Ct of Int Arb; Freeman Worshipful Co of Slrs; memb: Law Soc, Int Bar Assoc, Acad of Experts, Soc of Construction Law; *Recreations* horse riding, water skiing, travel, landscaping, rugby football; *Style*— Michael Davis, Esq; ✉ Herbert Smith, Exchange House, Primrose Street, London EC2A 2HS (tel 020 7374 8000)

DAVIS, Hon Mr Justice; Sir Nigel Anthony Lamert Davis; kt (2001); s of (Walter) Patrick Carless Davis (d 1996), of Roehampton, and Jane, *née* Lamert (d 1987); bro of James Patrick Lamert Davis, and Ian Edward Lamert Davis, *qqv*; *b* 10 March 1951; *Educ* Charterhouse, UC Oxford (MA); *m* 1, (m dis 1992), Sheila Ann Gillies Nickel; 3 da (Louisa Mary, Katherine Elizabeth (twins) b 6 Dec 1980, Marianna Jane b 10 July 1984); m 2, 2001, Emma Douglas; *Career* called to the Bar Lincoln's Inn (Hardwicke scholar, Kennedy scholar) 1975 (bencher 2000), jr Treasy counsel 1985–92, QC 1992, recorder of the Crown Court 1995–2001, judge of the High Court of Justice (Queen's Bench Div) 2001–; *Clubs* MCC, Vincent's (Oxford), Riverside; *Style*— The Hon Mr Justice Davis; ✉ Royal Courts of Justice, Strand, London WC2A 2LL

DAVIS, Nigel Ruscoe; s of John Haydn Davis, of Lichfield, Staffs, and Marion, *née* Ruscoe; *b* 30 November 1949, Solihull, Warks; *Educ* Tudor Grange GS Solihull, Fitzwilliam Coll Cambridge (MA); *m* 24 Feb 1973, Susan Mary, *née* Porter; 3 s (Edwin Thomas Ruscoe b 18 Aug 1975, Ancel Philip Ruscoe b 28 March 1978 d 1979, Benjamin William Ruscoe b 21 Feb 1981), 2 da (Sophie Agnetha Klara b 7 Feb 1982, Stephanie Ruth Emily b 2 Sept 1985); *Career* slr specialising in agric law; articled clerk then asst slr Wedlake Bell 1972–76, ptnr Holland Rigby & Williams 1977–85 (asst slr 1976–77); ptnr and head Agric Law Unit: Flint Bishop & Barnett 1985–94, Shakespeares 1994–96, Roythorne & Co 1996–2000; princ Nigel Davis slrs 2000–; chm Agric Law Assoc; memb Ctee Br Estonian, Latvian and Lithuanian Law Assoc, Derbyshire Co Ctee CLA, various agric and livestock breed socs; memb: Law Soc, UK Environmental Law Assoc, Environmental Law Fndn, Br Hungarian Law Assoc, NFU; fndr memb AgriLaw Gp of Legal Practices; contrib to Legal Network TV on agric matters, legal advsr to livestock and agric show socs, conslt ed on agric law Amicus Curiae (Soc for Advanced Legal Studies jl); livestock panel judge (sheep); govr Derbyshire Agric & Hort Soc; accredited mediator 1997, fell Soc of Advanced Legal Studies 1998; *Publications* Agricultural Precedents Handbook (co-author, 2001), CLA handbook on farm business tenancy agreements (co-author), Agric Law Assoc compilation of European Regulations on the Sheepmeat and Goatmeat regime and Beef and Suckler Cow regimes (ed); various articles in jls and farming press; *Recreations* agric history, farming (sheep and beef), exhibiting and judging sheep, emergence and devpt of Central and Eastern Europe and the Baltic states, watching most sports especially rugby and cricket; *Style*— Nigel Davis, Esq; ✉ The Sheepfold, Carr Hall Farm, Turnditch, Belper, Derbyshire DE56 2LW (tel 01335 372889, fax 01335 372891, e-mail nigeldavis@agriculturalsolicitors.co.uk)

DAVIS, Peter Anthony; *b* 10 October 1941; *Educ* Winchester, Lincoln Coll Oxford (MA); *m*; 2 s (b 1975 and 1977); *Career* gen audit ptnr Price Waterhouse 1974–80 (joined 1963), exec dep chm Harris Queensway 1980–87; Sturge Holdings plc: gp fin dir 1988–93, dep chm 1991–93; DG National Lottery (OFLOT) 1993–98; non-exec dir: Symphony Group plc 1984–87, Horne Brothers plc 1984–89, Avis Europe plc 1987–89, Abbey National Building Society then Abbey National plc 1982–94 (dep chm 1988–94), Provident Financial plc 1994–2000, Equitable Life Assurance Society 1995–2001, Boosey & Hawkes plc 1998–2003 (chm 2002–03), Ascent Gp (chm 2001–); memb Cncl ICAEW 1989–95 (chm Bd for Chartered Accountants in Business 1990–93); Liveryman Worshipful Co of Chartered Accountants; FCA (ACA 1967); *Recreations* tennis, fishing, football, theatre; *Style*— Peter Davis, Esq

DAVIS, Sir Peter John; kt (1997); s of John Stephen Davis, and Adriantje, *née* de Baat; *b* 23 December 1941; *Educ* Shrewsbury; *Career* mgmnt trainee and salesman Ditchburn Organisation 1959–65, mktg and sales General Foods Ltd 1965–72, Fitch Lovell Ltd 1973–76, mktg dir and md Key Markets 1973–76, dir and asst md J Sainsbury plc 1976–86, chief exec Reed International plc 1986–92, chm Reed International plc 1990–94, chief exec and co-chm Reed Elsevier plc (following merger) 1993–94 (memb Supervisory Bd Elsevier NV 1993–94 and Aegon NV 1993–94), gp chief exec Prudential Corporation plc 1995–2000 (non-exec dir 1994–95), chief exec J Sainsbury plc 2000–04, chm J Sainsbury plc 2004; non-exec dir: The Boots Company plc 1991–2000, Cadbury Schweppes plc 1999–2000; memb Bd UBS AG 2001–07, memb Advsy Bd Permira Advisers Ltd; chm: Basic Skills Agency 1991–97, Nat Advsy Cncl for Educn and Trg Targets 1993–97, Business in the Community (BITC) 1997–2002 (memb 1992–2006), New Deal Taskforce 1997–2000; vice-pres CIM; chm Marie Curie Cancer Care 2006–; tstee: ROH 1994–2005 (dep chm 1999–2001, memb Bd 1999–2005), V&A 1994–97; chm Royal Opera House Fndn 2001–03; *Recreations* sailing, opera, wine; *Clubs* Trearddur Bay Sailing (Cdre 1982–84); *Style*— Sir Peter Davis

DAVIS, Peter Kerrich Byng; s of Frank C Davis, MC (d 1979), and Barbara, *née* Hartshorne; *b* 4 May 1933; *Educ* Felsted, Univ of London, St Thomas' Hosp Med Sch (MB BS); *m* 24 April 1965, Jennifer Anne, da of Brig-Gen (Creemer) Paul Clarke (d 1971); 1 s (Paul b 14 Aug 1966), 1 da (Emma b 9 Aug 1968); *Career* sr registrar in plastic surgery Churchill Hosp Oxford 1968–71; conslt plastic surgn 1971–: St Thomas' Hosp London (now emeritus), Queen Mary's Hosp Roehampton, Kingston Hosp; Br Assoc of Aesthetic Plastic Surgns: memb 1977–, vice-pres 1981, pres 1982–84, hon sec 1988–91; memb: BMA 1959, BAPS 1971, RSM 1971, ICPRS 1971, ISAPS 1979; *Books* Operative Surgery (contrib, 1982), Maxillo-Facial Injuries (contrib, 1985 and 1996); *Recreations* fishing; *Style*— Peter Davis, Esq

DAVIS, Peter Robert Christian; OBE (1993); s of Robert Henry Davis (d 1990), and Ruth Anna Louise, *née* Larsen; *b* 25 February 1949; *Educ* Archbishop Tenison's GS, SW London Coll (HNC, Dip Mktg); *m* Nov 1984, Anne Klitgaard, da of Finn Bertelsen; 1 da (Sarah Maria Klitgaard b 26 April 1985), 1 s (Thomas Casper b 11 June 1988); *Career* Inco Europe Ltd: sales asst German Div 1967–69, asst to Customer Servs Mangr 1969–73; asst to Product Mangr Metal Box Ltd 1973–75, mktg co-ordinator Medical Products 3M UK plc 1976–77, product mangr then gp project mangr Dylon International Ltd 1977–84, special advsr to Rt Hon Kenneth Baker DOE 1984–86, head Home Affairs Cons Res Dept 1986–87, head General Election Media Monitoring Unit Cons Central Office 1992, dir of Mktg Membership and Overseas Affairs RIBA 1988–93, chief exec The Industry Cncl for Packaging and the Environment (Incpen) 1993–97, DG The British Plastics Fedn (BPF) 1997–; dir and tstee Tidy Br Gp 1996–2005; cncllr (Cons) Lambeth 1978–84, dep ldr Lambeth Cncl 1982; chm: Cons Greater London Area Local Govt Ctee 1988–91, Croydon S Cons Assoc 1995–98; dep chm The Enterprise Forum 2001; appointed goodwill ambass for the City of Copenhagen 1997, memb Anglo-Danish Soc, memb Danish Church Regents Park; Liveryman Worshipful Co of Horners 2000; FCIM (MCIM 1973), FIP, FRSA 2006; *Recreations* walking, reading, gardening, European history; *Clubs* Athenaeum, 107 Pall Mall; *Style*— Peter Davis, Esq, OBE, FRSA; ✉ 64 Woodcote Valley Road, Purley, Surrey CR8 3BD (tel 020 8668 3915); The British Plastics Federation, 6 Bath Place, Rivington Street, London EC2A 3JE (tel 020 7457 5000, e-mail pdavis@bpf.co.uk)

DAVIS, Richard Charles; s of Joseph Arthur Davis, of Fairford, Glos, and Dorothy Ellen, *née* Head; *b* 15 May 1949; *Educ* Queen's Coll Taunton, Univ of Leeds (LLB); *m* 21 Sept 1974, Margaret Jane, da of William Dixon, OBE; 1 da (Sarah Margaret b 8 Sept 1981), 1 s (James William Richard b 14 March 1984); *Career* admitted slr 1974; ptnr Barber Titleys; memb Law Soc; *Recreations* art, music, travel, sailing; *Clubs* Morgan Sports Car, The Harrogate; *Style*— Richard C Davis, Esq; ✉ The Gables, Bishop Thornton, Harrogate, North Yorkshire HG3 3JR (tel 01423 770172); Barber Titleys, 6 North Park Road, Harrogate, North Yorkshire HG1 5PA (tel 01423 502211, fax 01243 503835, e-mail richard.davis@barbertitleys.co.uk)

DAVIS, Roger O'Byrne; s of Paul Patterson Davis (d 1984), of Burnham Market, Norfolk, and Mabel Beryl Davis; *b* 1 August 1943; *Educ* Wrekin Coll; *m* 11 March 2006, Dr Jutta Maria Huesmann, da of Dr Josef Huesmann, of Meppen, Germany; *Career* articled clerk Chantrey Button & Co 1960–66; Cooper Brothers & Co (now PricewaterhouseCoopers): joined 1966, ptnr 1975–2003, seconded to HM Treasy 1975–77, head of audit Coopers & Lybrand 1992–98, head of professional affrs 1999–2003; dep chm Turnbull Ctee on Corporate Governance 1999; memb Company Law Consultative Ctee DTI 2000–01, rapporteur (global movement of people) European Services Forum 2001–03, memb Professional Oversight Bd for Accountancy and Actuaries 2004–, memb Competition Cmmn 2005–; memb RSA; FCA; *Recreations* English countryside, sailing, music; *Clubs* Carlton; *Style*— Roger Davis, Esq; ✉ 15 Blackheath Park, London SE3 9RW (tel 020 8852 7339, e-mail rogerobdavis@aol.com)

DAVIS, Sandra Sharon; da of Josef Martin Davis, and Milly Edith Davis; *b* 3 July 1956; *Educ* South Hampstead HS, Univ of Sussex (BA), Univ of Aix-en-Provence, Coll of Law; *m* 6 Sept 1987, Avron Woolf Smith, of South Africa; 2 s (Zakari Louis Smith b 5 Sept 1989, Elliott Nathan Smith b 8 Dec 1991); *Career* Mishcon de Reya (formerly Victor Mishcon & Co): articled clerk 1979–81, ptnr 1984–, head of Family Dept; memb: Slrs' Family Law Assoc, Lord Chllr's Child Abduction Panel, Int Bar Assoc; fell Int Acad of Matrimonial Lawyers; *Books* International Child Abduction (1993); *Recreations* photography, travel, theatre, art, family; *Style*— Ms Sandra Davis; ✉ Mishcon de Reya, Summit House, 12 Red Lion Square, London WC1R 4QD (tel 020 7440 7000, e-mail sandra.davis@mischon.co.uk)

DAVIS, His Hon Judge (Richard) Simon; s of Peter Richard Davis, of Great Missenden, Bucks, and Evelyn, *née* Richmond; *b* 29 July 1956, Frome, Somerset; *Educ* Wellington, Univ of Leicester (LLB); *m* 26 July 1980, Caroline Jane, *née* Neal; 2 s (Toby William Neal b 15 Feb 1987, Guy Hugo Hobson b 1 April 1989), 1 da (Imogen Caroline b 24 Dec 1990); *Career* called to the Bar Inner Temple 1978 (bencher 2007), recorder 2000–04 (asst recorder 1998–2000), circuit judge (South Eastern Circuit) 2004–; *Recreations* tennis, swimming, skiing, cycling; *Clubs* Lansdowne; *Style*— His Hon Judge Simon Davis; ✉ Inner London Crown Court, Sessions House, Newington Causeway, London SE1 6AZ (tel 020 7234 3100, e-mail hhjudgesimon.davis@judiciary.gsi.gov.uk)

DAVIS, Simon Ward; s of Anthony Davis, of Glos, and Susan, *née* Hames; *b* 26 June 1959, Mauritius; *Educ* Wellington, Magdalen Coll Oxford (Kitchener scholar, Underhill exhibitioner); *m* 13 Dec 1997, Jane, *née* Ray; 1 s (Gabriel b 23 Feb 1999), 1 da (Lara b 13 April 2001); *Career* slr; ptnr Clifford Chance (formerly Clifford Turner) 1994– (joined 1982); pres London Slrs Litigation Assoc, memb Law Soc 1982 (memb Cncl); *Recreations* family and friends; *Style*— Simon Davis, Esq

DAVIS, Prof Stanley Stewart; s of William Stanley Davis, of Warwick, and Joan, *née* Lawson; *b* 17 December 1942; *Educ* Warwick Sch, Univ of London (BPharm, PhD, DSc); *m* 24 Nov 1984, Lisbeth, da of Erik Illum (d 1986), of Denmark; 3 s (Benjamin b 1970, Nathaniel b 1974, Daniel b 1984); *Career* lectr Univ of London 1967–70, sr lectr Aston Univ 1970–75, Lord Trent prof of pharmacy Univ of Nottingham 1975–2003; fndr chm: Pharmaceutical Profiles Ltd, Danbiosyst (UK) Ltd; FRSC, FRPharmS; *Books* Imaging in Drug Research (1982), Microspheres in Drug Therapy (1984), Site Specific Drug Delivery (1986), Delivery Systems for Peptides (1987), Polymers for Controlled Drug Delivery (1987), Pharmaceutical Applications of Cell and Tissue Culture in Drug Transport (1991); *Recreations* skiing, tennis, painting; *Style*— Prof Stanley Davis; ✉ 19 Cavendish Crescent North, The Park, Nottingham NG7 1BA; School of Pharmaceutical Sciences, University of Nottingham, University Park, Nottingham (tel 0115 951 5121, fax 0115 951 5122, e-mail stanley.davis@nottingham.ac.uk)

DAVIS, Steven Ilsley; s of Lt-Col George Ilsley Davis, of Tinmouth, Vermont, and Marion Brown Davis; *b* 6 November 1934; *Educ* Phillips Acad Mass, Amherst Coll Mass (BA), Harvard Business Sch (MBA); *m* 27 Feb 1960, Joyce Ann, da of Theodore S Hirtz (d 1962), of NY; 2 s (Andrew Tinmouth b 1962, Christopher Stamer b 1963), 1 da (Stephanie b 1975); *Career* private US Army Reserve 1958; asst vice-pres JP Morgan & Co 1959–66, US Agency for Int Devpt 1966–68, first vice-pres Bankers Trust Co 1968–72; md: First International Bancshares Ltd 1972–79, Davis International Banking Consultants 1979–; asst dir US Govt Agency for Int Devpt 1966–68; Hon Phi Beta Kappa Amherst Coll; *Books* The Eurobank (1975), The Management of International Banks (1979), Excellence in Banking (1985), Managing Change in the Excellent Banks (1989), Leadership in Conflict - The Lessons of History (1996), Leadership in Financial Institutions (1998), Bank Mergers: Lessons for the Future (2000); *Recreations* skiing, tennis, hiking; *Clubs* Vanderbilt; *Style*— Steven Davis, Esq; ✉ 66 South Edwardes Square, London W8 (tel 020 7602 6348); Davis International Banking Consultants, 42 Brook Street, London W1K 5DB (tel 020 7958 9008, fax 020 7958 9275)

D

DAVIS, Rt Hon Terence Anthony Gordon (Terry); PC (1999); s of Gordon Davis; *b* 5 January 1938; *Educ* King Edward VI GS Stourbridge, UCL, Univ of Michigan; *m* 1963, Anne, *née* Cooper; 1 s, 1 da; *Career* Parly candidate (Lab): Bromsgrove 1970, 1971 (by-election), 1974 (twice), Birmingham Stechford March 1977 (by-election); MP (Lab): Bromsgrove 1971–74, Birmingham Stechford 1979–83, Birmingham Hodge Hill 1983–2004; oppn front bench spokesman: Health Serv 1981–83, Treasy and Econ Affrs 1983–86, Industry 1986–87; memb: Public Accounts Ctee 1987–94, Advsy Cncl on Public Records 1989–94, Cncl of Europe Assembly 1992–2004 (ldr UK Delegation 1997–2002, ldr Socialist Gp 2002–04), WEU Assembly 1992–2004 (ldr Socialist Gp 1996–2000, ldr UK Delegation 1997–2002), OSCE Assembly 1997–2004 (ldr UK Delgn 2002–04); sec gen Cncl of Europe 2004–; memb MSF, former memb Yeovil RDC, business exec (MBA) and motor industry mangr; *Style*— The Rt Hon Terry Davis

DAVIS-GOFF, Sir Robert William; 4 Bt (UK 1905), of Glenville, Parish of St Patrick's, Co Waterford; s of Sir Ernest William Davis-Goff, 3 Bt (d 1980); *b* 12 September 1955; *Educ* Cheltenham Coll; *m* 1978, Nathalie Sheelagh, da of Terence Chadwick, of Lissen Hall, Swords, Co Dublin; 3 s (William Nathaniel b 1980, Henry Terence Chadwick b 1986, James Sammy Chadwick b 1989), 1 da (Sarah Chadwick b 1982); *Heir* s, William Davis-Goff; *Career* picture dealer, property investment; *Recreations* shooting; *Style*— Sir Robert Goff, Bt; ✉ Lissen Hall, Swords, Co Dublin; Eairy Moar Farm, Glen Helen, Isle of Man; Ballinacor, Rathdrum, Co Wicklow

DAVIS-WHITE, Malcolm; QC (2003); s of Bret Davis-White, and Valerie, *née* Bates; *b* 18 September 1960, Ongar, Essex; *Educ* St Edmund's Coll Ware, Hertford Coll Oxford (MA, BCL); *m* Sarah Louise, *née* O'Hara; 1 da (Harriet b 27 May 1994), 2 s (Alexander b 14 Sept 1995, Edmund b 7 May 1998); *Career* called to the Bar; jr counsel to the Crown (Chancery) 1994–2003; *Publications* Atkins Court Forms (Vol 9, Companies General 2004, Companies Insolvency 2006), Directors Disqualification and Bankruptcy Restrictions (jtly, 2 edn 2005); ✉ Malcolm Davis-White, Esq, QC

DAVISON, Clive Phillip; s of Maj Laurence Napier Davison (d 1966), and Rosa Rachel Louisa, *née* Parker (d 1994); *b* 14 March 1944; *Educ* Grange Sch Christchurch, South Bank Poly, Thames Poly; *m* 1, 1968 (m dis 1982), Sandra, da of Thomas Keith Lord, of Billericay, Essex; *m* 2, 1993, Jane Elise, da of Roger Howorth, of West Moors, Dorset; 1 s (Alexander Napier b 2 Oct 1988), 1 da (Hannah Louise b 26 Jan 1990); *Career* chartered architect; assoc Trehearne & Norman Preston & Partners 1974–77, ptnr Trehearnes 1977–79, design and site supervisor of Min of P T T Riyadh 1977–83, co sec and dir I M Coleridge Ltd 1987, princ Davison Associates, md Davison Partnering Ltd; designer of various hosp and healthcare projects for NHS trusts; RIBA; *Recreations* squash, guitar, reading, skiing; *Style*— Clive Davison, Esq; ✉ 157 Bure Lane, Christchurch, Dorset BH23 4HB (tel 01425 280 749); Davison Associates, 87 Southbourne Road, Bournemouth, Dorset BH6 3QL (tel and fax 01202 434453, e-mail clive.davison@btconnect.com)

DAVISON, Ian Frederic Hay; CBE (2003); *b* 30 June 1931; *Educ* LSE (BSc(Econ)), Univ of Michigan; *Career* managing ptnr Arthur Andersen & Co 1966–82, dep chm and chief exec Lloyd's of London 1983–86; chm: Hong Kong Securities Review Ctee 1987–88, Credit Lyonnais Capital Markets 1988–91, Storehouse plc 1990–96, The NMB plc 1992–2000, Newspaper Publishing plc 1993–94, MDIS plc (now Northgate) 1993–99, Dubai Financial Services Authy 2002–04, Ruffer LLP 2003–; non-exec dir: Cadbury Schweppes plc 1990–2000; pres Nat Cncl for One Parent Families 1991–2004; chm: V&A Enterprises 1994–2002, Sadler's Wells 1995–2003, RCA 1996–2007, SANE 2000–02; FCA; *Books* A View of the Room, Lloyd's, Change and Disclosure (1987); *Recreations* music, opera, gardening, bellringing; *Clubs* Athenaeum, Beefsteak; *Style*— Ian Hay Davison, Esq, CBE; ✉ 13 Catharine Place, Bath BA1 2PR (e-mail ihdavison@aol.com)

DAVOUD, Nicole Matilde; OBE (1994, MBE 1982); *b* 6 October 1939; *Educ* Lyceo Nacional No 1 Buenos Aires, Univ of Buenos Aires; *m* 31 March 1960, Raymond Davoud (decd); 1 s (Alexander Joseph b 5 April 1966); *Career* fndr and dir Nicole Davoud Associates (qualitative research consltts) 1963–74, ind researcher and advsr disability policy issues 1974–; fndr Crack MS (young arm of Multiple Sclerosis Soc) 1974–76; memb: MRS 1970–95, Cncl Multiple Sclerosis Soc 1976–80, Ctee Int Year of Disabled 1979–82, N London Ctee for Employment of People with Disabilities 1991–97, Presidential Working Party Disability Appeal Tbnl 1991–92, Disability Living Allowance Advsy Bd 1995–2000, Disability Benefits Forum 1998–, Innovative Schemes Tender Bd 1998–99; *Publications* Turning Objectives into Realities - the Challenge of 1981 (1979), Multiple Sclerosis and Its Effect on Employment (1980), Part Time Employment - Time For Recognition, Organisation and Legal Reform (1980), Where Do I Go From Here? (autobiography, 1985), Disability Employment Credit - The Way Ahead (1990), Employing People With Disabilities - Employers' Perspective (1992), Welfare to Work: Disability Perspective (1996), Disability Living Allowance - An Alternative Approach (1998), Disability in the Millennium (1999); *Recreations* meditation, friends and the arts; *Style*— Mrs Nicole Davoud, OBE

DAWBER, George Arthur; s of Arthur Dawber (d 1986), of Calgary, Canada, and Gladys, *née* Garrett (d 1989); *b* 15 September 1939; *Educ* Alma Park, UMIST; *m* 19 March 1966, Glenys, da of Eric Ernest Whalley; 2 da (Zoë Cordelia b 29 July 1968, Aimie Camilla b 9 March 1980), 1 s (Howard Jason b 20 May 1972); *Career* professional photographer: nat serv station photographer RAF, trained in photographic transmissions 1956–59, professional cricketer Lancashire CCC 1959–60, industrial photographer 1960–70, general photographer 1970–75, freelance with own studio 1975– (specialising in wedding, portrait and PR photography), former princ lectr Fuji Professional Sch of Photography UK (has lectured widely UK and Overseas), course dir Photo Trg Overseas; memb Admissions and Qualifications Bd: BIPP (nat pres BIPP 1983–84), Master Photographers Assoc (pres 2002); winner Kodak Bride of the Year Competition, winner Kodak Portraits in Uniforms Competition, awarded Craftsmen Degree of Professional Photographers of America (CrPhotog) and Presidential award for services to his profession 1984; FBIPP, FMPA; *Style*— George Dawber, Esq; ✉ The Cottage, 159 Dialstone Lane, Offerton, Stockport, Cheshire SK2 6AU (tel 0161 483 3114, studio fax 0161 483 6063, e-mail george@dawberphoto.co.uk)

DAWES, Prof Edwin Alfred; s of Harold Dawes (d 1939), of Goole, E Yorks, and Maude, *née* Barker (d 1967); *b* 6 July 1925; *Educ* Goole GS, Univ of Leeds (BSc, PhD, DSc); *m* 19 Dec 1950, Amy, da of Robert Dunn Rogerson (d 1980), of Gateshead, Tyne & Wear; 2 s (Michael b 1955, Adrian b 1963); *Career* lectr in biochemistry Univ of Leeds 1950 (asst lectr 1947–50), sr lectr in biochemistry Univ of Glasgow 1961–63 (lectr 1951–61); Univ of Hull: Reckitt prof of biochemistry 1963–92 (emeritus 1993), dean of sci 1968–70, pro-vice-chllr 1977–80, dir Biomedical Res Unit 1981–92; ed Biochemical Jl 1958–65, ed-in-chief Jl Gen Microbiology 1976–81; Fedn of Euro Microbiological Socs: ed-in-chief FEMS Microbiology Letters, pubns mangr 1982–90, archivist 1990–; chm Sci Advsy Ctee Yorks Cancer Res 1978–2006 (campaign vice-chm 1987–); visiting lectr Biochemical Soc Aust and NZ 1975, American Med Alumni lectr Univ of St Andrews 1980–81; hon vice-pres: The Magic Circle London (memb 1959–, historian 1987–, Maskelyne Award 1998, David Devant Int Award 2002); hon life pres: Scot Conjurers' Assoc 1973–, Scot Assoc Magical Soc 1996–; pres: Br Ring Int Brotherhood of Magicians 1972–73, Hull Lit and Philosophical Soc 1976–77 (memb Cncl 1973–); chm Centre for the Magic Arts Ltd 2005–; historical conslt The Mysteries of Magic (The Learning Channel) 1997–98, Extreme Magic - Extreme Danger (LWT) 1999; memb Hall of Fame Soc of American Magicians 1984; chm Philip Larkin Soc 1995–; Milbourne Christopher Fndn (USA) Literary Award 1999; Hon DSc Univ of Hull 1992; FRSC 1956, FIBiol 1964; *Books* The Great Illusionists (1979), Isaac Fawkes: Fame and Fable (1979), Quantitative Problems in Biochemistry (6 edn, 1980, trans into 6 languages), Biochemistry of Bacterial Growth (jtly, 3 edn 1982), The Biochemist in a Microbial Wonderland (1982), Vonetta (1982), The Barrister in The Circle (1983), The Book of Magic (1986, re-issued as Making Magic, 1992), Microbial Energetics (1986), The Wizard Exposed (1987), Philip Larkin: the Man and His Work (contrib, 1989), Henri Robin: Expositor of Science and Magic (1990), Novel Biodegradable Microbial Polymers (ed, 1990), Molecular Biology of Membrane-Bound Complexes in Phototrophic Bacteria (ed, 1990), The Magic of Britain (1994), Charles Bertram: The Court Conjurer (1997), Stodare: The Enigma Variations (1998), Stanley Collins: Conjurer, Collector and Iconoclast (2002), The Annals of Conjuring (jt ed, 2001), Harry Leat (2003), Out of the Rich Cabinet (2004), The Great Lyle (2005), Circle Without End (jtly, 2005); *Recreations* conjuring, book collecting; *Style*— Prof Edwin Dawes; ✉ Dane Hill, 393 Beverley Road, Anlaby, East Yorkshire HU10 7BQ (tel 01482 657998, fax 01482 655941, e-mail eadawes@hotmail.com); Department of Biological Sciences, University of Hull, Hull, East Yorkshire HU6 7RX (tel 01482 465316, fax 01482 466443)

DAWES, Howard Anthony Leigh; s of George Roland Dawes (d 1965), and (Phyllis) Kathleen, *née* Reeves; *b* 4 August 1936; *Educ* Uppingham; *m* 1 (m dis); 1 s, 3 da; m 2, Aug 1991, Judith Ann, *née* Bolton; *Career* chm and chief exec: Neville Industrial Securities 1965–88, Dawes Trust Ltd 1965–; dir Velcourt Group plc 1968–99, chm Wine & Dine plc 1997–2000; chm Nuffield Hosp 1984–89; past chm Ctee of Friends of Birmingham Museums and Galleries, hon treas Birmingham Cons Assoc 1968–76, memb Midland Industrial Cncl 1977–97, vice-pres Scientific Instrument Soc 1997– (chm 1994–97); chm Pershore Abbey Appeal 1991–; Freeman City of London, Liveryman Worshipful Co of Glaziers; FCA, FRAS 1960, FRSA 1975; *Recreations* history of science; *Clubs* Buckland; *Style*— Howard Dawes, Esq; ✉ Craycombe House, Fladbury, Worcestershire WR10 2QS; PO Box 15, Pershore, Worcestershire WR10 2RD (tel 01386 861075, fax 01386 861074, e-mail daweshal@aol.com)

DAWES, Dr Peter Terence; s of John Geoffrey Dawes, of Stone, Staffs, and Lorna Graham, *née* Wholey; *b* 1 May 1953; *Educ* Herbert Strutt GS Belper (Rugby capt), Univ of Liverpool (MB ChB, Rugby capt); *m* 1, 1974 (m dis 1992), Barbara, da of Frank Charnley; 2 da (Georgina Martell b 21 Feb 1981, Hannah Elisabeth b 27 July 1982), 2 s (John Mansfield b 13 Jan 1984, Samuel Edward b 25 May 1987); m 2, 1998, Carol Anne Stanton, da of late Norman Loweth; 2 step da (Claire Louise Stanton b 4 Sept 1980, Gemma Victoria Stanton b 27 Nov 1982); *Career* house offr Whiston Hosp Merseyside 1976–77, SHO then registrar (med) St Helens Hosp and Whiston Hosp Merseyside 1977–80, registrar (rheumatology) Middlesbrough Gen Hosp 1981–82, conslt rheumatologist Staffs Rheumatology Centre Haywood Hosp Stoke-on-Trent 1987– (sr registrar (rheumatology) 1982–87), clinical sr lectr in postgrad med Keele Univ 1987–, head of div Locomotor Directorate N Staffs Hosp Tst 1987–; memb: MSSC Audit Advsy Gp 1989–90, N Staffs Audit Res Gp 1989–91, N Staffs MRCP Course Working Pty 1989–, Awards Ctee N Staffs Med Inst 1990–92, Drugs and Therapeutics Ctee 1994–97, N Staffs Rehabilitation Strategy Gp 1997–99, Discretionary Points Ctee 1997–, N Staffs Estates Strategy Gp 1997–, N Staffs Musculoskeletal Bd 1997–, Devpt of Integrated Care Packages Serv Devpt Bd 1998–, Waiting List Task Force 1999–, Benchmarking Gp 1999–; BSR: memb Educn Ctee 1988–90, Advsy Gp for Read coding in Rheumatology 1990–96, rep on BSR/Br Orthopaedic Assoc/Arthritis and Rheumatism Cncl (ARC)/Primary Care Rheumatology Soc/RCGP/Br League Against Rheumatism Working Pty devising a Musculoskeletal Undergrad Curriculum, sec 2002–; conslt advsr Primary Care Rheumatology Soc 1990–92, chm Fastrak Users Gp 1995–98, clinical assessor Jt Conslts Ctee Ind Review, exec memb Midlands Rheumatology Soc 1996–99; memb: BSR/Res Unit RCP Jt Working Gp 1990–, Int League of Assocs for Rheumatology/Outcome Measures in Rheumatoid Arthritis Clinical Trials Gp developing outcome measures in Rheumatoid Arthritis 1993–, People to People Prog 1993–, Cochrane Musculoskeletal Advsy Gp 1994–97, ARC Educn Working Gp 1995–, Br Rheumatology Outcome Study Gp (BROSG), Rheumatology Regnl Specialists Gp; chair, convenor and rapporteur at numerous confs and symposia; memb: Assoc of Liverpool Med Sch, Nat Ankylosing Spondylitis Soc, N Staffs Med Inst, NW Rheumatology Club, Nat Osteoporosis Soc (local chm 1995–97), W Midlands Physicians; assoc ed Rheumatology in Practice 1988–90, memb Editorial Bd Br Jl of Rheumatology (now Rheumatology) 1989– (guest ed 1988), editorial advsr Medicom Excel Newsletter, book assessor OUP; external reviewer for jls incl: The Lancet, Jl of Rheumatology, Annals of Rheumatic Diseases, Arthritis and Rheumatism, Drugs & Therapeutics Bulletin, Prescribers Jl; grant reviewer: ARC, Med Inst, Haywood Fndn; memb: American Coll of Rheumatology, Br Health Professionals in Rheumatology, BMA, Br Soc of Immunology, BSR, Br Soc of Inflammation; supporter Haywood Rheumatism R&D Fndn; Sr Registrar Prize in Rheumatology Annual Sr Registrar Meeting 1983 and 1985 (runner-up 1984), Syntex Award Midland Rheumatology Soc 1984, BSR UK Travelling Fellowship 1986; FRCP 1994 (MRCP 1980); *Publications* author of over 350 pubns in books and med jls; *Recreations* hill walking, fishing, music, campanology; *Style*— Dr Peter Dawes; ✉ Staffordshire Rheumatology Centre, The Haywood, High Lane, Burslem, Stoke-on-Trent ST6 7AG (tel 01782 556302, fax 01782 813419, e-mail pt.dawes@whns.nhs.uk)

DAWID, Prof (Alexander) Philip; s of Israel Dawid, and Rita, *née* Abel; *b* 1 February 1946; *Educ* City of London Sch, Trinity Hall and Darwin Coll Cambridge (MA, Dip Math Statistics, ScD); *m* 18 March 1974, (Fatemeh) Elahe, da of Mohamed Ali Madjd; 1 s (Jonathan b 10 May 1975), 1 da (Julie b 29 July 1979); *Career* prof of statistics City Univ 1978–81, prof UCL 1982–2007 (lectr 1969–78, reader 1981–82), prof Univ of Cambridge 2007–; medicines cmmr 1988–91; ed Biometrika 1992–96; pres Int Soc for Bayesian Analysis 2000; memb ISI 1978, FIMS 1979, Chartered Statistician 1993; *Recreations* music; *Style*— Prof Philip Dawid; ✉ Department of Pure Mathematics and Mathematical Statistics, Wilberforce Road, Cambridge CB3 0WL

DAWKINS, Prof Marian Ellina Stamp; da of Hon A Maxwell Stamp (d 1984), and Alice Mary, *née* Richards (d 2000); *b* 13 February 1945; *Educ* Queen's Coll Sch London (E E Florence scholar), Somerville Coll Oxford (BA, Nuffield exhibitioner), Univ of Oxford (DPhil); *m* 1967 (m dis 1984); *Career* res offr Animal Behaviour Res Gp Dept of Zoology Univ of Oxford 1969–74, jr res fell Wolfson Coll Oxford 1974–78, departmental demonstrator in animal behaviour Dept of Zoology Univ of Oxford 1974–80; Somerville Coll Oxford: lectr in zoology 1977–80, fell and tutor in biological sciences 1980–, vice-princ 2005–; Univ of Oxford: res lectr 1991–96, reader 1996–97, prof of animal behaviour 1998–, head Animal Behaviour Res Gp Dept of Zoology; dir John Krebs Field Lab; memb: Standing Advsy Ctee on Standards for Psychological Res and Teaching Involving Animals Br Psychological Soc 1981–84, Farm Animal Welfare Cncl 1983–89, Farm Livestock Advsy Cncl RSPCA 1980–89, Animal Experiments Ctee Royal Soc 1982–97; sec Ethical Ctee Assoc for the Study of Animal Behaviour 1986–90; ed: Animal Behaviour 1994–96, Animal Welfare 1996–; sec gen Int Ethological Congress 1995–99; RSPCA/Br Soc for Animal Protection prize 1991; memb: Int Soc for Applied Ethology, Assoc for the Study of Animal Behaviour; Hon DSc Univ of Guelph Canada 2000; *Publications* Animal Suffering: The Science of Animal Welfare (1980), Unravelling Animal Behaviour (1986, 2 edn 1995), The Tinbergen Legacy (ed with T R Halliday and R Dawkins, 1991), Through Our Eyes Only? The Search for Animal Consciousness (1993), An Introduction to Animal Behaviour (with A Manning, 5 edn 1998), Observing Animal Behaviour: Design and Analysis of Quantitative Data (2007), The Future of Animal Farming: Renewing an Ancient Contract (2008); *Recreations* windsurfing, photography, music, natural history; *Style*— Prof Marian Dawkins; ✉ Dept of Zoology, University of Oxford, South Parks Road, Oxford OX1 3PS (tel 01865 271215, fax 01865 310447, e-mail marian.dawkins@zoo.ox.ac.uk)

DAWKINS, Prof (Clinton) Richard; s of Clinton John Dawkins, and Jean Mary Vyvyan, *née* Ladner; *b* 26 March 1941; *Educ* Oundle, Balliol Coll Oxford (MA, DPhil, DSc); *m* 1; m 2; 1 da (Juliet Emma); m 3, 1992, Hon Sarah Ward (the actress Lalla Ward), only da of 7 Viscount Bangor (d 1993); *Career* asst prof of zoology Univ of Calif Berkeley 1967–69; Univ of Oxford: univ lectr in zoology and fell New Coll 1970–90, univ reader in zoology 1990–95, Charles Simonyi prof in public understanding of sci 1995–; RSL Award 1987, Los Angeles Times Literary Prize 1987, Silver Medal Zoological Soc of London 1989, Michael Faraday Award Royal Soc of London 1990, Royal Instn Christmas Lectures 1991, Nakayama Prize 1994, Int Cosmos Prize 1997, Kistler Prize 2001, Shakespeare Prize 2005, Lewis Thomas Prize 2007; Hon DLitt: Univ of St Andrews 1995, ANU 1996; Hon DSc: Westminster Coll 1997, Univ of Hull 2001, Univ of Sussex 2005, Univ of Durham 2005, Free Univ of Brussels 2005; Hon DUniv Open Univ 2003; hon fell Regent's Coll London 1988; FRSL 1997, FRS 2001; *Books* The Selfish Gene (1976, 2 edn 1989), The Extended Phenotype (1982), The Blind Watchmaker (1986), River Out of Eden (1995), Climbing Mount Improbable (1996), Unweaving the Rainbow (1998), A Devil's Chaplain (2003), The Ancestor's Tale (2004), The God Delusion (2006); *Style*— Prof Richard Dawkins, FRS; ✉ New College, Oxford OX1 3BN (tel 01865 514103, website www.richarddawkins.net)

DAWKINS, Simon John Robert; s of Col William John Dawkins, and Mary, *née* King; *b* 9 July 1945; *Educ* Solihull Sch, Univ of Nottingham (BA), Queens' Coll Cambridge (PGCE), Birkbeck Coll London (MA); *m* 20 July 1968, Janet Mary, da of Gordon Harold Stevens; 1 da (Sarah Mary Louise b 2 Oct 1972), 1 s (Thomas Peter James b 16 Nov 1974); *Career* formerly head of econs and housemaster Dulwich Coll, headmaster Merchant Taylors' Sch Crosby 1986–2005; HMC: chm NW Div 1995–96, memb Membership Ctee 1996–99, memb Academic Policy Ctee 1999–2003; govr Arnold Sch Blackpool; Freeman Worshipful Co of Merchant Taylors; *Recreations* sport, gardening; *Clubs* Formby Golf; *Style*— Simon Dawkins, Esq; ✉ Brackenwood, St George's Road, Hightown, Liverpool (tel 0151 929 3546); Merchant Taylors' School, Crosby, Liverpool L23 (tel 0151 928 3308)

DAWKINS, William; *b* 28 October 1956; *Educ* Westminster, Trinity Coll Cambridge (MA, Rowing blue 1978, Goldie 1976–77); *m*; 4 c; *Career* journalist; trainee journalist Buckinghamshire Advertiser; Financial Times: foreign desk sub-ed and page ed 1981–83, UK company news reporter 1983–84, small business ed 1984–86, EC corr Brussels 1986–89, Paris corr 1989–93, Tokyo Bureau chief 1993–97, dep managing ed 1997–98, foreign ed 1998–2001, publishing ed 2001–04; ptnr Odgers Ray & Berndtson 2004–; memb Foreign Correspondents' Club of Japan (pres 1996–97); *Clubs* Hawks' (Cambridge), Leander, Army and Navy; *Style*— William Dawkins, Esq; ✉ 11 Hanover Square, London W1S 1JJ (tel 020 7529 1111)

DAWN, Elizabeth; MBE (2000); da of Albert Butterfield (d 1984), of Leeds, W Yorks, and Annie, *née* Shaw (d 1975); *b* 8 November 1939; *Educ* St Patrick's, Corpus Christi Leeds; *m* 1, 1957; 1 s (Graham b 1958); m 2, Donald Ibbetson, s of Arthur Ibbetson; 3 da (Dawn b 1963, Ann b 1967, Julie b 1968); *Career* actress; Vera Duckworth in Coronation Street (Granada) 1974–; other credits incl: Kisses at Fifty (BBC) 1972, Speech Day (BBC) 1972, Leeds United (BBC) 1973, Sunset Across The Bay (BBC) 1974, How's Yer Father (Granada) 1974, Sam (BBC) 1974, Z Cars (BBC) 1974, Village Hall 1974, Crown Court 1975, Green Hill Pals 1975, Larry Grayson Special 1975, Lie Detector (commercial) 1975; Royal Variety Show (Palladium) 1989, Royal Show (Prince's Trust, Opera House Manchester); recorded single Passing Strangers (with Joe Longthorne) 1994; patron: Booth Hall Hosp, Manchester Taxi Drivers' Assoc, Liz Dawn Breast Cancer Appeal (for St James Hospital Leeds); Lady Mayoress of Leeds 2000–01; Yorkshire Women of the Year Award 1996/97; Hon Degree Univ of Leeds 1998; *Recreations* charity work with mentally handicapped children; *Style*— Ms Elizabeth Dawn, MBE; ✉ c/o Arena Entertainments, Regent's Court, 39 Harrogate Road, Leeds LS7 3PD (tel 0113 239 2222, fax 0113 239 2016)

DAWNAY, Caroline Margaret; da of Capt Oliver Payan Dawnay, CVO (d 1988), of Longparish and Wexcombe, and Lady Margaret Boyle, da of 8 Earl of Glasgow; *b* 22 January 1950; *Children* 1 s (Hugo Ronald Alexander MacPherson b 28 Jan 1980); *Career* dir A D Peters & Co Ltd Writers' Agents 1981–94 (joined 1977, merger to form Peters Fraser & Dunlop 1988), dir June Hall Agency 1989–93, dir Peters Fraser & Dunlop 1993–; pres Assoc of Authors' Agents 1994–97 (treas 1991–94); *Books* An Alphabet of Aunts (jtly, 2007); *Clubs* 2 Brydges Place; *Style*— Ms Caroline Dawnay; ✉ 14 Sterndale Road, London W14 0HS; PFD, Drury House 34–43 Russell Street, London WC2B 5HA (tel 020 7344 1000)

DAWNAY, (Charles) James Payan; s of Capt Oliver Payan Dawnay, CVO (d 1988), and Lady Margaret Stirling-Aird, *née* Boyle; *b* 7 November 1946; *Educ* Eton, Trinity Hall Cambridge (MA); *m* 10 June 1978, Sarah, da of Edgar David Stogdon, MBE, of Balaroulin, Pitlochry; 3 da (Alice b 1979, Olivia b 1981, Fenella b 1988), 1 s (David b 1985); *Career* dir S G Warburg 1984–85, dir Mercury Asset Management Group plc 1985–91, chm Mercury Fund Managers Ltd 1987–91, dir Martin Currie Ltd 1992–2000, dep chm Martin Currie Ltd 1999–2000; chm: China Heartland Fund Ltd 1997–2004, Northern AIM VCT plc 2000–, Invesec High Income Tst plc 2001–, Gurr Johns Ltd 2001–04, Penicuik House Preservation Tst 2003–, CCLA Investment Mgmnt Ltd 2004–, Resources Investment Tst 2005–, Biggar Museum Tst 2005–; dir Taiwan Opportunities Tst plc; tstee Nat Galleries of Scotland 2004–; *Recreations* fishing, collecting; *Clubs* Brooks's, Pratt's, New (Edinburgh), Biggar; *Style*— James Dawnay, Esq; ✉ Symington House, by Biggar, Lanarkshire ML12 6LW (tel 01899 308211, fax 01899 308727, e-mail jdawnay@yahoo.co.uk)

DAWS, Andrew Michael Bennett; s of Victor Sidney Daws (d 1978), and Doris Jane Daws (d 1997); *b* 11 March 1943; *Educ* King's Sch Grantham, Univ of Exeter (LLB), Coll of Law; *m* 1, 1969 (m dis 1979), Edit, *née* Puskas; m 2, 27 Aug 1981, Phoebe, da of Clifford Hughes (d 2003); 1 da (Constance Clemency Jane Bennett b 1984), 2 s (Harry Arthur

Victor Bennett b 1986, Guy Cromwell George Bennett b 1990); *Career* admitted slr 1967, ptnr Denton Hall 1975–97; conslt: Ernst & Young 1997–2000, Shook, Hardy and Bacon 2001–03; non-exec dir West Middlesex University NHS Trust 2002–; memb Ethics Standards Bd 2001–03, memb Ethics and Conduct Ctee RICS 2004–; *Recreations* golf; *Clubs* Royal Mid-Surrey Golf; *Style*— Andrew M B Daws, Esq

DAWSON, (Ian) Grant; s of Stanley Dawson, and Marian, *née* Haswell; *b* 17 March 1959; *Educ* Holmemead Secdy Modern Sch, Bedford Coll of FE, Univ of Leicester (BA), Inns of Court Sch of Law; *Children* 2 da (Faye b 12 April 1991, Eve b 21 Jan 1997), 1 s (Elliot b 30 Oct 1994); *Career* general counsel and co sec Centrica plc 1996–; previously with: Racal Gp 1984–86, STC plc 1986–91, Northern Telecom Europe Ltd 1991–96; called to the Bar Lincoln's Inn; *Recreations* golf, scuba diving, sailing, opera; *Style*— Grant Dawson, Esq; ✉ Centrica plc, Millstream, Maidenhead Road, Windsor, Berkshire SL4 5GD (tel 01753 494000, fax 01753 494001)

DAWSON, Sir Hugh Michael Trevor; 4 Bt (UK 1920), of Edgwarebury, Co Middlesex; s of Maj Sir (Hugh Halliday) Trevor Dawson, 3 Bt (d 1983), and Caroline Jane, *née* Acton; *b* 28 March 1956; *Educ* at home; *Heir* bro, Nicholas Dawson; *Style*— Sir Hugh Dawson, Bt; ✉ 11 Burton Court, Franklin's Row, London SW3

DAWSON, Prof John; *Educ* UCL (BSc, MPhil), Univ of Nottingham (PhD); *Career* various posts Univ of Wales, chair in distributive studies Univ of Stirling until 1990, prof of mktg and head Mktg Gp Univ of Edinburgh 1990–2005 (head Dept of Business Studies 1993–98), prof of retail studies Univ of Stirling 2005–; distinguished prof Univ of Mktg Kobe 2002–; founding ed: Cambria, Int Jl of Retailing 1984, Int Review of Retail, Distribution and Consumer Research (currently co-ed); author of several books on the retail industry in Europe and Asia; FRSE 2004; *Style*— Prof John Dawson

DAWSON, John A L; s of James Lawrence Dawson (d 1984), and Olive Joan, *née* Turner; *b* 6 February 1950; *Educ* Mill Hill Sch, Univ of Southampton (British Rail engrg scholar); *m* 21 June 1980, Frances Anne Elizabeth, *née* Whelan; 2 da (Alice Anne Louise b 27 June 1983, Grace Emily Rose b 3 July 1987); *Career* DOE 1972–76, Dept of Tport 1976–81, overseas tport conslt 1981–85, dir of tport London Regnl Office Dept of Tport 1985–88, chief road engr Scottish Devpt Dept 1988, dir of roads Industry Dept Scottish Office 1989–95; AA: gp public affrs dir 1995–2002, policy and int dir 2003–04, dir The AA Motoring Tst 2003–04; currently chm and md EuroRAP AISBL, chm and md Int Road Assessment Prog (iRAP) 2005–; dir Nat Assoc of Air Ambulance Services 1999–2002; sec FIA Fndn for the Automobile and Soc 2001–; FIHT 1987, FICE 1996 (MICE 1976); *Recreations* touring; *Style*— John Dawson, Esq; ✉ EuroRAP AISBL, Worting House, Basingstoke, Hampshire RG23 8PX (tel 01256 345598)

DAWSON, Lynne; da of Francis Lewis Dawson, of Newton-on-Ouse, N Yorks, and Rita, *née* Slater; *Educ* Easingwold Sch, Guildhall Sch of Music and Drama London, Britten-Pears Sch Snape; *Career* soprano; initially worked as French translator; has performed with orchs incl: Berlin Philharmonic, Vienna Philharmonic, Boston Symphony, San Francisco Symphony, all major Br orchs; concert venues incl: Lincoln Center NY, La Scala Milan, Colon Buenos Aires, Aix-en-Provence Festival, Salzburg Festival, Edinburgh Festival, Royal Albert Hall, Wigmore Hall, South Bank; *Operatic performances* incl: Constanze in Mozart's Die Entführung aus dem Serail (La Monnaie Brussels) 1990, Teresa in Berlioz' Benvenuto Cellini (Amsterdam Opera) 1991, Countess in the Marriage of Figaro (Strasbourg Festival) 1991, Fiordiligi Cosi Fan Tutte (Naples) 1992, Amenaide in Rossini's Tancredi (Berlin State Opera) 1994, Cleopatra in Handel's Julius Caesar (Berlin Staatsopera) 1996, Pamina in The Magic Flute (Berlin Staatsopera) 1997, Dido in Dido Aeneas (De Vlaamse Opera) 1998; *Recordings* over 65 recordings incl: Bach's B Minor Mass, Beethoven Choral Symphony, Gluck's Iphigenie en Aulide, Handel's Messiah, Haydn's Creation, Mozart's C Minor Mass, Requiem, Don Giovanni and Die Entführung aus dem Serail, Orff's Carmina Burana; sang Verdi Requiem Libera Me At Funeral of Diana, Princess of Wales 1997; *Style*— Miss Lynne Dawson; ✉ c/o IMG Artists Europe Ltd, Lovell House, 616 Chiswick High Road, London W4 5RX (tel 020 8233 5800, fax 020 8742 8758, website www.lynnedawson.com)

DAWSON, Mark Patrick; s of Douglas George Damer Dawson; *b* 19 October 1941; *Educ* Wellington; *m* 1, 1970 (m dis 1983), Carol Anne, da of John Dudley Groves; 2 s; m 2, 1987 (Constance) Clare Power, *née* Mumford; *Career* Lt Essex Yeo; chm and md Pickford Dawson & Holland Ltd 1970–78; md: Jardine Matheson Insurance Brokers UK Ltd 1978–79, Jardine Matheson Underwriting Agencies Ltd 1979; dep chm: Jardine Lloyd's Underwriting Agencies Ltd (formerly Jardine Glanvill Underwriting Agencies Ltd) 1991–95 (md until 1990), Jardine Lloyd's Advisers Ltd 1994–95 (conslt 1995–97); qualified Cert in Teaching English as a Foreign Language to Adults (CTEFLA) 1996; fndr The Friends of Holy Innocents Church Lamarsh 2001 (treas and tstee 2001–), memb Ctee Colne-Stow Countryside Assoc 2006–; *Style*— Mark Dawson, Esq; ✉ Cooks Green, Lamarsh, Bures, Suffolk CO8 5DY (tel 01787 227088 and 01787 228593, e-mail markdawson@ace-webs.com)

DAWSON, Matthew James Sutherland (Matt); MBE (2004); s of Ronald Sutherland Dawson, and Lois, *née* Thompson; *b* 31 October 1972; *Educ* Royal GS High Wycombe; *Career* rugby union player; clubs: Northampton Saints RFC 1991–2003 (over 240 appearances, winners European Cup 2000), London Wasps RFC 2003–06 (winners Zurich Premiership 2005); England: 77 caps (9 as capt), winners 6 Nations Championship 2000, 2001 and 2003 (winners Grand Slam 2003), winners World Cup Aust 2003; memb squad Br & I Lions tour South Africa 1997, Aust 2001 and NZ 2005 (5 test caps); RFU Player of the Year 2000; ret from rugby 2006; resident capt A Question of Sport (BBC TV); supporter NSPCC; *Recreations* golf, football, cricket, theatre, exhibitions; *Style*— Matt Dawson, Esq, MBE; ✉ c/o Merlin Elite, 37 Lower Belgrave Street, London SW1W 0LS (tel 020 7823 5990, e-mail richard.thompson@merlinelite.co.uk)

DAWSON, Michael John; OBE (1986), DL; *b* 20 January 1943; *Educ* King James's GS Knaresborough; *m*; 2 da; *Career* chm: Tunstall Group plc 1980–99 (joined 1970), Mion Electronics plc 1993–2002; The Prince's Youth Business Tst: chm N Yorks Bd 1986–99, tstee 1996–99; memb: Bd YORTEK 1985– (founding chm 1985–90), Ct Univ of York 1998–; chm York Minster Fundraising Steering Ctee 2003–; tstee: York Minster Fund 1992–2002, Martin House Children's Hospice 2000–04; FCCA 1970, FRSA 1997; *Recreations* game fishing, racing, showjumping, travel; *Style*— Michael Dawson, Esq, OBE, DL; ✉ Mill House, Sutton upon Derwent, York YO41 4BN

DAWSON, Prof Peter; s of Frederick Dawson, of Sheffield, S Yorks, and May, *née* Pierrepoint; *b* 17 May 1945; *Educ* Firth Park Sch Sheffield, KCL (BSc, PhD), Westminster Med Sch (MB BS); *m* 20 July 1968, Hilary Avril, da of Kenneth Reginald Sturley, of Amersham, Bucks; 1 da (Kate b 1976), 1 s (James b 1978); *Career* SHO in: gen and renal med Hammersmith Hosp 1979–80, med oncology Royal Marsden Hosp 1980; registrar in radiology Guy's Hosp 1980–82, sr registrar in radiology Middx Hosp 1982–85, prof of diagnostic radiology Royal Postgrad Med Sch and Hammersmith Hosp 1996– (reader and hon conslt 1985–96); conslt UCL Hosps London 1999–, chm and clinical dir UCL Hosps 2002–; prof of radiology Univ of London 1999–; author of various scientific med res papers; pres British Inst of Radiology, Roentgen prof RCR; Barclay Medal Br Inst of Radiology 2000; MInstP 1966, FRCR 1984 (memb Cncl), FRCP 1994 (MRCP 1980); *Recreations* grand opera, wine, snooker; *Style*— Prof Peter Dawson; ✉ Beechers, Green Lane, Chesham Bois, Amersham, Buckinghamshire HP6 5LQ (tel 01494 728222); UCL Hospitals, Department of Radiology, Mortimer Street, London W1N 8AA (tel 020 7636 8333, fax 020 7380 9068, e-mail phd728222@aol.com)

DAWSON, Prof Dame Sandra June Noble; DBE (2004); da of Wilfred Denyer (d 1996), of Corton Denham, Dorset, and Joy Victoria Jeanne, *née* Noble; *b* 4 June 1946; *Educ* Dr Challoner's Sch Amersham, Keele Univ (BA); *m* 23 Aug 1969, Henry Richards Currey Dawson, s of Horace Dawson (d 1952), of Sotik, Kenya; 2 da (Hannah Louise Joy b 1976, Rebecca Annie Brenda b 1978), 1 s (Tom Stephen John b 1983); *Career* Imperial Coll London: res offr 1969–70, lectr then sr lectr 1971–90, prof of organisational behaviour 1990–95; KPMG prof of mgmnt studies 1995–, dir Judge Business Sch Univ of Cambridge 1995–2006, fell Jesus Coll Cambridge 1995–99, master Sidney Sussex Coll Cambridge 1999–; chm Riverside Mental Health Tst 1992–95; non-exec dir: Public Health Lab Serv 1996–99 (memb Strategic Review Gp 1994–96), Fleming Claverhouse Investment Tst 1996–2003, Cambridge Econometrics 1996–2007, Barclays plc 2003–; memb: Res Strategy Bd Offshore Safety Div HSE 1990–95, N Thames NHS Regnl R&D Ctee 1994–95, HEFCE Business and Mgmnt Research Assessment Panel 1995–97 and 2000–01, Sr Salaries Review Bd 1997–2003, DTI Futures and Innovation Bd 1998–2001, ESRC Research Priorities Bd 2000–03, DTI Taskforce Accounting for People 2003, UK India Roundtable 2006–; tstee RAND Europe (UK) 2001–04; *Books* Analysing Organisations (1986, 3 edn 1996), Safety at Work: The Limits of Self Regulation (1988), Managing in the NHS: a Study of Senior Executives (1995), Future Health Organisations and Systems (ed, 2005); *Recreations* music, walking; *Style*— Prof Dame Sandra Dawson, DBE; ✉ Judge Business School, University of Cambridge, Trumpington Street, Cambridge CB2 1AG (tel 01223 339700)

DAWSON, William Strachan; s of John Oliver Hanbury Dawson, of South Cadbury, Somerset, and Elizabeth Sutherland, *née* Strachan; *b* 10 September 1955; *Educ* Winchester, Selwyn Coll Cambridge (MA); *m* 1, 8 Sept 1984 (m dis), Alison Jill, da of John Eric Aldridge, of Halland, E Sussex; 1 da (Lucinda b 1986), 2 s (Henry b 1988, Archie William b 1994); m 2, 25 August 2007, Anna Ward; 1 step da (Isabella), 1 step s (Ruairi); *Career* admitted slr 1980, ptnr Simmons & Simmons 1986–2007 (head of int employment law 2001–07), ptnr Farrer & Co 2007–; *Books* Tolley's Company Acquisitions Handbook (contrib, 1989, 7 edn 2004); *Recreations* piano, skiing, cooking, classical music; *Clubs* Broadgate; *Style*— William Dawson, Esq; ✉ Farrer & Co, 66 Lincoln's Inn Fields, London WC2A 3LH

DAY, Prof Bill; *Educ* Univ of Cambridge (PhD); *m* 25 May 1973, Virginia Lesley Elisabeth; 2 s (Benjamin b 9 Aug 1979, Nicholas b 14 March 1984), 1 da (Elisabeth b 12 March 1982); *Career* research and research mgmnt Inst for Arable Crops Resarch until 1988, head Process Engrg Div Silsoe Research Inst 1988–99, dir Silsoe Research Inst 1999–2006; visiting prof of agric engrg Nat Soil Resources Inst (NSRI) Cranfield Univ at Silsoe; ed-in-chief Biosystems Engrg; *Style*— Prof Bill Day

DAY, Dr Christopher Duncan; s of Roger William Elmsall Day (d 1984), and Kathleen Margaret, *née* Bell (d 1996); *b* 19 July 1941; *Educ* Hymers Coll Hull, Kings Coll Durham (MB BS); *m* 1, 5 Nov 1966, Pamela (d 1979), da of William Corbet Barnsley (d 1981), of Newcastle upon Tyne; 1 da (Elizabeth b 1972), 1 s (William b 1977); m 2, 21 Aug 1982, Rosemary Ann, da of Charles Darby, of Datchet, Berks; *Career* house offr in surgery and med Newcastle upon Tyne Gen Hosp 1964–65, sr house offr in anaesthetics Dudley Rd Hosp Birmingham 1965–66, registrar and sr registrar in anaesthetics Sheffield Hosps 1966–70, conslt in anaesthetics 1970–2001; med dir Chesterfield and N Derbyshire Royal Hosp NHS Tst 1993–2000; memb: CSA, AAGBI; *Style*— Dr Christopher Day; ✉ Alghero, 44 Matlock Road, Walton, Chesterfield, Derbyshire S42 7LE (tel 01246 270942)

DAY, Colin Norman; *Career* sr advsr Henderson Investors; pt/t chm Grandfield Ltd (formerly Grandfield Rork Collins PR), ind dir Rolfe & Nolan plc; vice-chm Govrs Anglia Poly Univ; memb CIPFA; magistrate; *Style*— Colin Day, Esq; ✉ Henderson Investors, 3 Finsbury Avenue, London EC2M 2PA (tel 020 7410 4100)

DAY, Corinne; da of Antony Day, and Hazel Day; *Career* photographer; former fashion model; self-taught photographer, began taking photographs of friends 1989, with The Face magazine 1990–93 (photography launch career of Kate Moss , *qv*); fashion photography for magazines incl: i-D, British Vogue, American Vogue, Vogue Homme, L'Uomo Vogue, Vogue Italia, French Vogue; advertising campaigns for fashion cos incl: Barney's NY 1992, Joseph 1994, Miu Miu 1994 and 1995, Paul & Joe 2002; worked with bands and musicians incl: Blur, Beck, Ian Brown, Beta Band, Clinic, Pearl Jam, Pusherman, Spiritualized, Moby (photography for Play album sleeve); video work: second unit camera work Oasis 'Cigarettes and Alcohol' video 1993, art dir for Everything But The Girl and Oasis 1993–95 co-dir MTV short films, Agent Provocateur promotions and Pusherman videos 1993–97; photography for Saatchi & Saatchi Anti-Child Abuse Campaign 1997; work exhibited: The Photographers' Gallery London, Gimpel Fils Gallery London, Whitney Museum NYC, Warhol Museum Philadelphia, Br Arts Cncl, Canon Photography Gallery V&A, ICA Boston; patron: Chicken Shed Theatre, Dystrophic Epidermolysis Bullosa Res Assoc; *Books* Diary (2000), Imperfect Beauty (2000); *Recreations* travel, gym, taking photographs; *Style*— Miss Corinne Day; ✉ c/o Susan Babchick, 6 Brewer Street, Unit 4, London W1F 0SD (020 7827 1497)

DAY, Elinor Jane; da of Barry Day, and Jean, *née* Walker; *b* 9 November 1962, London; *Educ* St Stephen's Coll Broadstairs, Malvern Boys Coll, Emmanuel Coll Cambridge (MA); *Career* ind theatre dir (Sadlers Wells, fringe, tours) 1985–88, BBC: script ed 1988–90, drama prodr 1990–98; dep head prodn FilmFour 1998–2002, launched The Light Club (ind prodn co) 2002; memb BAFTA; *Film* produced BBC: Loved Up (BAFTA Best Schools Drama 1995), Killing Me Softly, In Your Dreams, The Perfect Blue, Face; exec prodr FilmFour: Some Voices, Jump Tomorrow (Sundance Film Festival 2000), Late Night Shopping, Lucky Break, Miranda, Gangster No 1, Crush, The Warrior (winner Sutherland Trophy London Film Festival 2001), East is East, Charlotte Gray; *Recreations* theatre, cinema, travel; *Style*— Ms Elinor Day; ✉ 57 Elms Cresent, London SW4 8QE (tel 020 7622 5933, e-mail elinor@thelightclub.fsnet.co.uk)

DAY, Prof John; s of Horace John Ernest Day (d 1996), and Violet Augusta, *née* Liggitt (d 1993); *b* 13 September 1948, London; *Educ* Bexley GS, Christ's Coll Cambridge (scholar MA, PhD, Sr Hebrew Prize), Univ of Oxford (DD); *m* 20 June 1981, Jane Mary, *née* Osborn; 1 adopted da (Lisa Marie b 11 Dec 1982), 1 adopted s (Sebastian John b 26 June 1984); *Career* John Goodenday fell Hebrew Univ of Jerusalem 1972–73, res fell in arts Univ of Durham 1977–80, fell and tutor in theology Lady Margaret Hall Oxford 1980–; Univ of Oxford: lectr in Old Testament 1980–96, reader in biblical studies 1996–2004, prof of Old Testament studies 2004–; sr res fell Br Acad/Leverhulme Tst 1995–96; book list ed Soc for Old Testament Study 2006–; memb Soc of Biblical Lit (USA); Dahood Meml Prize Soc of Biblical Lit 1984; *Publications* Oxford Bible Atlas (ed, 3 edn 1984), God's Conflict with the Dragon and the Sea: Echoes of a Canaanite Myth in the Old Testament (1985), Molech: A God of Human Sacrifice in the Old Testament (1989), Psalms (1990), Wisdom in Ancient Israel: Essays in Honour of J A Emerton (ed with R P Gordon and H G M Williamson, 1995), William Robertson Smith's Lectures on the Religion of the Semites (ed 2 and 3 series, 1995), King and Messiah in Israel and the Ancient Near East: Proceedings of the Oxford Old Testament Seminar (ed, 1998), Yahweh and the Gods and Goddesses of Canaan (2000), In Search of Pre-Exilic Israel: Proceedings of the Oxford Old Testament Seminar (ed, 2004), Temple and Worship in Biblical Israel: Proceedings of the Oxford Old Testament Seminar (ed, 2005), Society for Old testament Study Book List (ed, 2007); author of over 50 articles and over 120 reviews; *Recreations* travel in the Near East, attending congresses, collecting books; *Style*— Prof John Day; ✉ Lady Margaret Hall, Oxford OX2 6QA (e-mail john.day@theology.ox.ac.uk)

DAY, Air Chief Marshal Sir John Romney; KCB (1999), OBE (1985); s of John George Day (d 1987), and Daphne Myrtle, *née* Kelly (d 1979); *b* 15 July 1947; *Educ* King's Sch Canterbury, Imperial Coll London (BSc(Eng)); *m* April 1969, Jane Richards; 2 s (Mark John b 19 Sept 1970, Jonathan Philip b 18 Aug 1974); *Career* flying trg RAF 1968–70, pilot Wessex helicopters 72 Sqdn 1970–73, flying instr Jet Provosts RAF Linton-on-Ouse 1973–76, OC Oxford Univ Air Sqdn 1976–79, Flt Cdr 18 Sqdn 1979–80, RAF Staff Coll Bracknell 1981, PSO to Air Member for Personnel 1982–83, OC 72 Sqdn 1983–85, Gp Capt Support Helicopters HQ No 1 Gp 1986–87, OC RAF Odiham 1987–89, RCDS 1990, Dir Air Force Plans and Progs MOD 1991–94, AOC No 1 Gp 1994–97, DCDS (Commitments) MOD 1997–2000, Air Memb for Personnel and C-in-C Personnel and Trg Command 2000–01, C-in-C Strike Command 2001–03, sr military advsr BAE Systems 2003–; FCGI 2002 (ACGI 1968), FRAeS 2003; *Clubs* RAF; *Style—* Air Chief Marshal Sir John Day, KCB, OBE; ✉ BAE Systems, Stirling Square, 6 Carlton Gardens, London SW1Y 5AD

DAY, Dr Kenneth Arthur; s of Arthur Day (d 1989), and Irene Laura, *née* Pope (d 1993); *b* 18 July 1935; *Educ* Greenford Co GS, Bristol Univ Med Sch (MB ChB, DPM); *m* 1, 27 June 1959 (m dis 1993), Sheila Mary Day, da of Albert Torrance (d 1971); 1 da (Caroline b 1960), 2 s (Paul Vincent b 1961, Matthew Charles b 1964); m 2, 6 Nov 1993, Diana Ruth Day, JP, da of John Snowden Lee (d 1993); *Career* house offr Bristol Royal Infirmary 1961–62, registrar Barrow Hosp Bristol 1962–66, registrar and sr registrar Dept of Psychiatry Univ of Newcastle 1966–69, conslt psychiatrist Northern RHA and Newcastle HA 1969–92, sr lectr Dept of Psychiatry Univ of Newcastle 1986–96 (hon sec 1996–), conslt psychiatrist and med dir Northgate and Prudhoe NHS Tst Morpeth 1992–96 (hon conslt 1996–2007); Mental Health Act cmmr 1987–94; vice-pres Int Assoc for the Scientific Study of Mental Deficiency 1992–96 (sec 1985–92), vice-chm Mental Retardation Section World Psychiatric Assoc 1989–96 (sec 1983–89), vice-pres Euro Assoc for Mental Health in Mental Retardation 1993–98; Dept of Health (formerly DHSS): memb Hosp Advsy Serv 1972, sci advsr 1981–87, memb Standing Med Advsy Ctee 1984–88, memb Nat Devpt Team 1977–86, med memb Mental Health Review Tbnl 1988–, memb Hosp Advsy Gp Reed Ctee on Mentally Disordered Offenders; RCPsych: memb Cncl, Ct of Electors, Fin and Exec Ctee and numerous other ctees, chm Section for Psychiatry of Mental Handicap 1983–87; pres Northern Region Mencap 1978–90, WHO advsr on mental handicap to the People's Republic of China 1991; Winston Churchill Meml Fellowship 1972, Burden Gold medal and Res prize 1985–86, Blake Marsh lectr RCPsych 1989, WHO Fellowship 1990, Penrose Lecture 1998; writer and presenter: The Special Child (YTV) 1977, The Special Child Teenage Years (YTV) 1979; conslt and writer BBC TV series incl: Homes from Home 1976, Accident of Birth 1978, Aspects of Mental Handicap 1979, The Handicapped Family 1979, Let's Go 1979, 1980 and 1982; winner Animal Portraits category Wildlife Photographer of the Year 1989; Freeman City of London 1989, Liveryman Worshipful Soc of Apothecaries 1993 (Yeoman 1988); hon offr and fell Int Assoc for the Scientific Study of Intellectual Disability 1996; FRCPsych 1978 (fndn memb 1972), FRSM 1983, FRSA 1997, FRGS 1999, ARPS 2005; *Publications* The Special Child (1977), The Special Child - The Teenage Years (1979), Behaviour Problems in The Mental Handicapped: An Annotated Bibliography (1988), Prudhoe & Northgate Hospitals: A History 1914–99 (2000), Treating Mental Illness and Behaviour Disorders in Children and Adults with Mental Illness (2001); numerous scientific papers, articles and chapters on mental handicap; photographs published in natural history books and magazines; *Recreations* squash, badminton, tennis, golf and other sports, natural history, painting, carving, photography; *Clubs* City Livery; *Style—* Dr Kenneth Day; ✉ 28 Percy Gardens, Tynemouth, Tyne & Wear NE30 4HQ

DAY, Lucienne; OBE (2004); da of Felix Conradi (d 1957), and Dulcie Lilian, *née* Duncan-Smith; *Educ* Convent Notre Dame De Sion Worthing, Croydon Sch of Art, RCA; *m* 5 Sept 1942, Robin Day, OBE, RDI, *qv*, s of Arthur Day (d 1956), of High Wycombe, Bucks; 1 da (Paula b 1954); *Career* teacher Beckenham Sch of Art 1942–47, freelance designer 1948– (dress fabrics, furnishing fabrics, carpets, wallpapers, table-linen); cmmnd by: Heal's Fabrics, Edinburgh Weavers, Cavendish Textiles, Tomkinsons, Wilton Royal, Thos Somerset, firms in USA, Scandinavia and Germany; designed china decoration for Rosenthal China Bavaria 1956–68, currently designing silk mosaic tapestries; conslt (with Robin Day) John Lewis Partnership 1962–87; major retrospective exhbn (with Robin Day) Barbican Gallery London 2001; work in permanent collections incl: V&A, Trondheim Museum Norway, Cranbrook Museum Michigan, Röhsska Museum Gothenburg Sweden, Musée des Arts Décoratifs Montreal, Art Inst of Chicago, Whitworth Art Gallery Univ of Manchester; awards incl: Design Cncl Awards 1957, 1960 and 1968, American Inst of Dirs First Award 1950; Triennale Di Milano: Gold Medal 1951, Gran Premio 1954; memb: Rosenthal Studio-Line Jury 1960–68, Ctee Duke of Edinburgh Prize for Elegant Design 1960–63, Cncl RCA 1962–67, Design Bursary Juries RSA; Hon DDes: Univ of Southampton 1995, Univ of Buckingham 2003; RDI 1962 (Master 1987–89), ARCA 1940, FSIAD 1955, Hon FRIBA 1998, sr FRCA 1999; *Recreations* plant collecting in Mediterranean regions, gardening; *Style—* Mrs Lucienne Day, OBE; ✉ 21 West Street, Chichester, West Sussex PO19 1QW (tel 01243 781429, fax 01243 531207)

DAY, Martin James; s of Clifford Day (d 1961), and Molly, *née* Dale (d 2002); *b* 12 April 1944; *Educ* City of London Sch, Univ of Durham (BA), Christ's Coll Cambridge (LLM), City of London Poly (MSc); *m* 1 (m dis 1976), Elizabeth Mary, da of Thomas H Sykes (d 1999); m 2 (m dis 1995), Loraine Frances, da of Frank Leslie Hodkinson (d 1984); 1 s (James b 1978), 1 da (Philippa b 1983), m 3, Reiko Ishibashi, da of Yoichi Inaba (d 1975); *Career* articled clerk Austin Wright & Co 1966–68, admitted slr 1969, ptnr Linklaters & Paines 1976–94 (asst slr 1969–76); memb Disciplinary and Appeal Tbnls IMRO 1994–99, gp legal and compliance advsr Guinness Flight Hambro Asset Management Ltd 1995–98, conslt Arnheim & Co Slrs 1997–98, dir Pricewaterhouse Coopers CAs 1997–98, ind legal conslt 1999–2003, slr Herbert Smith 2003–05, conslt Farrer & Co 2005–; chm: Hampton Music Festival 1969–71, Tstees of the Hampton Arts Tst 1969–72, Thameside Arts Tst 1973–74, Westminster Children's Charitable Fndn 1976–90, Kibogora Hosp Tst 1989–91; memb: Ct of Common Cncl (Ward of Aldersgate) 1977–79 and 1986–87, Governing Body SOAS Univ of London 1978–79, Ward of Cripplegate 2005–; dir Slrs' Benevolent Assoc 1988–96, vice-chm Br Korean Law Assoc 2005–; govr: Christ's Hosp 2006–, Lady Eleanor Holles Sch 2006–07; memb: Law Soc, Int Cmmn of Jurists (Br Section), Tst Law Ctee, Ctee City of London Law Soc 2005–07; Liveryman City of London Slrs' Co 1976; FRGS 1965; *Books* Unit Trusts: The Law and Practice (with P I Harris, 1974), Tolley's Trust Law International (memb Editorial Bd 1989–99); *Recreations* music, country pursuits; *Style—* Martin J Day, Esq; ✉ c/o Messrs C Hoare & Co, 37 Fleet Street, London EC4P 4DQ

DAY, Martyn; s of Brian Day (d 1983), and Hazel Mules Berry, *née* Abraham; *b* Ossett, Yorks; *partner* Carol Hatton; 2 s (Harry b 19 Oct 1990, Jack b 28 March 1992), 3 da (Martha b 10 Oct 1993, Sally b 29 April 1996, Evie b 20 Dec 2004); *Career* admitted slr 1981; Colombotti & Ptnrs until 1981, Clifford & Co 1981, Bindman & Ptnrs 1981–87, sr ptnr Leigh Day & Co 1987–; memb Exec Ctee Soc of Labour Lawyers; dir Greenpeace Environmental Tst; memb Assoc of Professional Injury Lawyers; *Books* Toxic Torts, Personal Injury Handbook, Multi-Party Actions, Environmental Action: A Citizen's Guide; *Style—* Martyn Day, Esq; ✉ Leigh Day & Co, Priory House, 25 St John's Lane, London EC1M 4LB (tel 020 7650 1234, fax 020 7253 4433, e-mail mday@leighday.co.uk)

DAY, Prof Nicholas Edward; CBE (2001); s of John King Day (d 1997), and Mary Elizabeth, *née* Stinton (d 1993); *b* 24 September 1939; *Educ* Gresham's, Univ of Oxford (BA, Jr Univ prize), Univ of Aberdeen (PhD); *m* 19 Sept 1961, Jocelyn Deanne, da of Henry George Broughton (d 1988); 1 da (Sheenagh Louise b 4 April 1963), 1 s (Owen John b 5 May 1965); *Career* res fell Univ of Aberdeen 1962–66, fell Australian Nat Univ 1966–69, statistician then head Unit of Biostatistics and Field Studies Int Agency for Res on Cancer Lyon 1969–86, cancer expert Nat Cancer Inst USA 1978–79, dir MRC Biostatistics Unit Cambridge 1986–89 (hon dir 1989–99), prof of public health Univ of Cambridge 1989–99, MRC research prof of epidemiology Univ of Cambridge 1999–2004; chm MRC Ctee on the Epidemiology and Surveillance of Aids 1988–92; fell: Churchill Coll Cambridge 1986–91, Hughes Hall Cambridge 1991–; fell Royal Statistical Soc, RCPath, Academy of Medical Science, FRS 2004; *Books* Statistical Methods in Cancer Research Vol 1 (1980) and Vol 2 (1988), Screening For Cancer of the Uterine Cervix (1986), Screening For Breast Cancer (1988); *Recreations* sea fishing, tree growing; *Style—* Prof Nicholas Day, CBE, FRS; ✉ La Cordonnerie, La Bellieuse, St Martin's, Guernsey GY4 6RP (tel 01481 238740); Strangeways Research Laboratory, 1 Wort's Causeway, Cambridge CB1 8RN (tel 01223 740151, fax 01223 740177, e-mail nick.day@srl.cam.ac.uk)

DAY, Prof Peter; *b* 20 August 1938; *Educ* Maidstone GS, Wadham Coll Oxford (Gibbs prize in chemistry, MA, DPhil); *m* 1964, Frances Mary Elizabeth, *née* Anderson; 1 da (Alison b 1968), 1 s (Christopher b 1971); *Career* jr res fell St John's Coll Oxford 1963–65, departmental demonstrator Inorganic Chemistry Laboratory Oxford 1965–68, fell and tutor in inorganic chemistry St John's Coll Oxford (jr dean 1967–70, vice-pres 1974), lectr in inorganic chemistry Univ of Oxford 1965–88, dir Institut Laue-Langevin Grenoble 1989–91, (Br assoc dir 1988–89), dir and resident prof of chemistry Royal Instn of GB 1991–94, Fullerian prof Royal Instn of GB 1994–; ad hominem prof of solid state chemistry Univ of Oxford 1988–91, visiting prof UCL 1991–; professeur associé Faculté des Sciences Université de Paris-Sud Orsay 1975, guest prof H C Ørsted Inst Univ of Copenhagen 1978, visiting fell Res Sch of Chemistry ANU Canberra 1980, visiting prof Univ of Valencia 2002–06; visiting appts at res laboratories: Cyanamid Euro Res Inst Geneva 1962, Bell Laboratories Murray Hill NJ 1966, IBM Res Laboratories San José CA 1974, Xerox Corp Webster Res Center Rochester NY 1978; memb Cncl: Parly and Scientific Ctee 1991–98, COPUS 1991–98; memb Medicines Cmmn 1999–2005; chm Royal Soc Res Grant Bd for Chemistry 1992–95 (memb 1983–85 and 1991–95); Br Cncl: memb Science Advsy Ctee 1991–98, chm Anglo-French Advsy Ctee 1992–97; Royal Soc of Chemistry: memb Dalton Div Cncl 1983–88, memb Books and Review Ctee 1984–85, vice-pres 1986–88, memb Pubn and Information Bd 1997–2003; memb numerous ctees SERC 1976–92; memb: Nat Ctee on Superconductivity 1987–89, Univ of Oxford Superconductivity Gp 1988–91 (chm Steering Ctee 1987), ISIS Science Advsy Cncl 1988–91 (chm Experimental Selection Panel (Structures) 1988); memb Physics and Engrg Sci Ctee Europe Euro Sci Fndn 1994–2000; memb Editorial Advsy Bds: Nouveau Journal de Chimie, Synthetic Metals, Review of Solid State Sciences, Dictionary of Inorganic Compounds, Journal of Materials Chemistry (scientific advsy ed 1999–2003), Chemistry of Materials; rep govr Sevenoaks Sch 1977–88, govr Birkbeck Coll London 1994–2001; hon fell: Wadham Coll Oxford 1991, Indian Acad Sci 1994, St John's Coll Oxford 1996, UCL 2003; Hon DSc: Univ of Newcastle 1994, Univ of Kent 1999; memb Academia Europaea 1992– (treas Cncl 2000–, tstee 2002–); FRS 1986; *Publications* The Philosopher's Tree (1999), Nature Not Mocked (2005), Molecules in Materials (2007); ed seven chemistry books; *Style—* Prof Peter Day, FRS; ✉ The Royal Institution, 21 Albemarle Street, London W1X 4BS (tel 020 7670 2901, fax 020 7670 2958, e-mail pday@ri.ac.uk)

DAY, Robin; OBE (1983); s of Arthur Day (d 1956), and Mary, *née* Shersby (d 1956); *b* 25 May 1915; *Educ* High Wycombe Sch of Art, RCA; *m* 5 Sept 1942, Lucienne Day, OBE, *qv*, da of Felix Conradi (d 1957), of Croydon, Surrey; 1 da (Paula b 1954); *Career* princ of own design practice 1940–; worldwide success with design of seating for sports stadia, concert halls, airports, etc; interior design of Super VC10 aircraft; Robin and Lucienne Day exhibition (Barbican and book) 2001; jt first prize MOMA NY competition for design of furniture, Gold medal Milan Triennale exhbn 1951, Design Centre award 1957, 1961, 1965 and 1966, Design medal CSID 1957; Hon FRIBA, ARCA, RDI 1959; *Recreations* walking, mountaineering, ski touring; *Clubs* Alpine, Eagle Ski; *Style—* Robin Day, Esq, OBE, RDI; ✉ 21 West Street, Chichester, West Sussex PO19 1QW (tel 01243 781429)

DAY, Rosemary; da of Albert Rich (d 1985), and Alice, *née* Wren (d 2000); *b* 20 September 1942; *Educ* Christ's Hosp, Bedford Coll London (BA); *m* (m dis); *Career* asst dir gen GLC 1979–82 (joined 1964), dir of admin London Tport 1983–87, chief exec Data Networks plc 1986–88, ops dir Allied Dunbar Assurance plc 1988–94; non-exec dir: Nationwide Anglia Building Society 1983–88, London Buses Ltd 1988–93, London Transport 1993–98, Milk Marketing Bd 1993–94, Legal Aid Advsy Ctee 1993–94, Senior Salaries Review Body 1994–2000, UKAEA 1999–, NI Regnl Devpt Dept Bd 2007–; dir Picker Inst Europe 2002–05; chm: London Ambulance Serv Trust 1996–99, Govt Offices Mgmnt Bd 1996–98, National Air Traffic Servs 1997–2001; chm Joyful Co of Singers 1987–2001 (Gran Premio Citta D'Arezzo 1994), tstee Railway Children 1999–, tstee Chiswick House and Gardens 2005–; ATII 1980, FRSA 1983, CIMgt 1988; *Recreations* singing, conversation, the arts; *Style—* Mrs Rosemary Day; ✉ 63A Barrowgate Road, London W4 4QT (tel 020 8995 4390, fax 020 8995 6720, e-mail rday@joyfulco.demon.co.uk)

DAY, Stephen Peter; CMG (1989); s of Frank William Day (d 1956), and Mary Elizabeth Day (d 1968); *b* 19 January 1938; *Educ* Bancroft's Sch, CCC Cambridge (MA); *m* 24 Feb 1965, Angela Doreen, da of William Attwood Waudby, of Kenya; 2 da (Belinda b 1966, Philippa b 1968), 1 s (Richard b 1972); *Career* HMOCS; political advsr S Arabian Fedn 1961–67, first sec Political Adviser's Office Singapore 1970, first sec (press) UK mission to UN NY 1972–75, cnsllr Beirut 1977–78, consul-gen Canadian Prairie Provinces 1979–81, ambass Doha 1981–84, head of ME Dept FCO 1984–86, attached to household of HRH The Prince of Wales 1986, ambass Tunisia 1987–92, sr Br trade cmmr Hong Kong 1992–93, dir Cncl for the Advancement of Arab-Br Understanding 1993–94; chm: Br-Tunisian Soc 1994–, Palestine Exploration Fund 1995–2000, Br-Yemeni Soc 1998–2000, MBI Tst SOAS Univ of London 2000–03, MBI Fndn 2002–; dir: Claremont Associates 1994–, SATUCO (Tunisia) 2000–05, Sindbad Productions 2000–; *Recreations* walking, reading; *Clubs* Hong Kong, Athenaeum; *Style—* Stephen Day, Esq, CMG; ✉ e-mail s.day@claremontassociates.net

DAY, William Michael; s of Sir Derek Day, KCMG, of Goudhurst, Kent, and Sheila, *née* Nott; *b* 26 June 1956; *Educ* Tonbridge, Univ of Exeter (BA); *m* 1986, Kate Susanna, da of Bill Gardener; 1 s (Rupert b 7 Sept 1987), 2 da (Eleanor b 21 April 1989, Susanna b 6 Dec 1991); *Career* Save the Children Fund: Uganda 1983, Ethiopia 1983–84, Sudan 1984; prodr/presenter BBC World Serv for Africa 1985–87, relief co-ordinator Oxfam Ethiopia 1987–88, grants dir Africa Charity Projects/Comic Relief 1988–94, dir Opportunity Tst 1994–96, chief exec CARE International UK 1996–2004; sr assoc Univ of Cambridge Prog for Industry 2003–, special advsr UN Devpt Prog 2004–; non-exec dir South Kent Hosps NHS Tst 1994–96; chm: Central Appeals Ctee BBC 1997–2003 (memb 1992–2003), Water and Sanitation for the Urban Poor (WSUP) 2006–; memb Grants Cncl Charities Aid Fndn 1990–94; tstee: Disasters Emergency Ctee 1997–2004, BBC Children in Need 1998–; memb Cncl ODI 2000–; ind assessor Public Appointments DCMS 1999–; *Style—* William Day, Esq

DAY-LEWIS, Daniel; s of Cecil Day-Lewis, CBE (Poet Laureate, d 1972), by his 2 w, Jill Balcon, actress, da of late Sir Michael Balcon, film prodr; *Educ* Bristol Old Vic Theatre Sch; *Family* 1 s (Gabriel b 1995); m, 1996, Rebecca Miller, da of Arthur Miller, of USA; *Career* actor; *Theatre* Bristol Old Vic Co: The Recruiting Officer, Troilus and Cressida, Funny Peculiar, Old King Cole, A Midsummer Night's Dream (transferred to Old Vic),

Class Enemy, Edward II, Oh! What A Lovely War; Little Theatre Co: Look Back in Anger, Dracula; other roles incl: Guy Bennet in Another Country (Queen's) 1982, Romeo in Romeo and Juliet (RSC tour) 1983–84, Mayakovsky in The Futurists (NT) 1986, title role in Hamlet (NT) 1989; *Television* Shoestring, Artemis II, The Lost Traveller, The Sugar House, Beyond the Glass, How Many Miles to Babylon, Thank You PG Woodhouse, Dangerous Corner, My Brother Jonathan, Insurance Man; *Films* Gandhi 1981, The Saga of HMS Bounty 1983, My Beautiful Launderette 1985, A Room With A View 1985, Nanou 1985, The Unbearable Lightness of Being 1986, Stars and Bars 1987, My Left Foot 1988, Ever Smile New Jersey 1988, Last of the Mohicans 1991, Age of Innocence 1992, In the Name of the Father 1993, The Crucible 1995, The Boxer 1998, The Gangs of New York 2001; *Awards* Best Supporting Actor NY Critics' Awards for My Beautiful Launderette and A Room With A View 1986; Best Actor Awards for My Left Foot incl: Evening Standard Film Awards 1989, Rehab Entertainment Awards 1989, Boston Soc of Film Critics 1989, Oscar 1990, BAFTA 1990, NY Critics' 1990, LA Critics'1990, Nat Soc of Film Critics' 1990, London Critics' Film Circle 1990, Montreal Critics' 1990, Dublin Independent 1990; Variety Club Best Film Actor Award for Last of the Mohicans 1992; *Style*— Daniel Day-Lewis, Esq; ✉ c/o Julian Belfrage Associates, 46 Albemarle Street, London W1X 4PP (tel 020 7491 4400, fax 020 7493 5460); Simpson Fox Associates Ltd, 52 Shaftesbury Avenue, London W1V 7DE (tel: 020 7434 9167, fax: 020 7494 2887)

DAYKIN, Dr Andrew Philip; s of Philip William Daykin (d 2002), of St Albans, Herts, and Eileen Elizabeth, *née* Sales (d 1985); *b* 27 December 1950; *Educ* St Albans Sch, Univ of Oxford (MA), St Mary's Hosp Med Sch (MB BS); *m* 1, 10 Sept 1977 (m dis 2003), Chrystal Margaret, da of Anthony George Mitsides, of London; 2 da (Eleni b 1981, Ariana b 1983); m 2, 10 June 2006, Lorraine Margaret, da of Mrs Margaret Walker, of Knaresborough, Yorks; *Career* SHO Whittington Hosp London 1977, SHO and registrar in anaesthetics St Mary's Hosp London 1978–81, sr registrar Winchester and Southampton Hosps 1981–86, clinical fell in anaesthesia Ottawa Children's Hosp 1984; Taunton and Somerset Hosp: conslt anaesthetist and dir of intensive care 1986–, dir of anaesthetics 1994–99; regnl advsr Intensive Care Med 1999–; FFARCS 1980, FRCP 2006 (MRCP 1978); *Recreations* canoeing, sailing; *Style*— Dr Andrew Daykin; ✉ Fourways Cottage, Wheelbarrow Lane, Hemyock, Devon EX15 3PF (tel 01823 680916); Musgrove Park Hospital, Taunton, Somerset TA1 5DA (tel 01823 333444)

DAYKIN, Christopher David; CB (1993); s of John Francis (d 1983), and Mona, *née* Carey; *b* 18 July 1948; *Educ* Merchant Taylors', Pembroke Coll Cambridge (MA); *m* 1977, Kathryn Ruth, da of Harold William Tingey; 1 da (Rachel b 1981), 2 s (Jonathan b 1982, Jeremy b 1984); *Career* Govt Actuary's Dept: 1970, 1972–78 and 1980–, princ actuary 1982–84, directing actuary 1985–89, govt actuary 1989–; princ (Health and Social Servs) HM Treasy 1978–80; VSO Brunei 1971; FIA 1973 (pres 1994–96); *Recreations* travel, photography, language; *Style*— Christopher Daykin, Esq, CB; ✉ Government Actuary's Department, 15/17 Furnival Street, London EC4A 1AB (tel 020 7211 2620, fax 020 7211 2650, e-mail chris.daykin@gad.gov.uk)

DAYMOND, Prof Terence John; s of late Deric Alfred Daymond, and Ethel Anne, *née* Bird; *b* 24 February 1942; *Educ* Rutlish Sch, Univ of Edinburgh (MB ChB), DipObstRCOG, Dip Phys Med; *m* 18 Jan 1969, Jacqueline Mary, da of late Bernard Joffre Martin, of Wisbech, Cambs; 3 da (Carolyn b 1969, Joanna b 1971, Charlotte b 1986), 1 s (Benjamin b 1983); *Career* acting CMO Dhariwal nr Amritsar Punjab India 1969–70, med registrar King's Lynn Norfolk 1971–73, rheumatology registrar Aylsham Norfolk 1973–76, sr registrar in rheumatology Royal Victoria Infirmary Newcastle upon Tyne 1976–79, conslt in rheumatology and rehabilitation City Hosps Sunderland 1979–2007, conslt Breakspear Hosp 2007–; patron ME Assoc (Sunderland and S Tyneside); memb: BMA, BSR; FRCP 1987 (MRCP), FRSM, FRCPEd 1998; *Books* Treatment in Clinical Medicine Rheumatic Disease (with Hilary H Capell, T J Daymond, W Carson, 1983); *Recreations* swimming; *Style*— Prof Terence Daymond; ✉ 34 Eslington Terrace, Jesmond, Newcastle upon Tyne NE2 4RN

DAZELEY, Peter William; s of late William Henry George Dazeley, of London, and Freda Kathleen, *née* Ward, MBE (d 2006); *b* 29 June 1948; *Educ* Holland Park Comp; *m* 1, (m dis); 1 da (Tiger Itasca Shin-Yee b 19 Oct 2000); m 2, 31 March 2007, Jannith Chit Ying Wong; *Career* photographer specialising in prodn of fine art and creative images for leading advtg agencies; memb Creators' Cncl Design and Artists Copyright Soc; life memb Assoc of Photographers (formerly AFAEP); *Recreations* golf; *Clubs* Queen's, Coombe Hill Golf; *Style*— Peter Dazeley, Esq; ✉ Peter Dazeley, The Studios, 5 Heathmans Road, Parsons Green, Fulham, London SW6 4TJ (tel 020 7736 3171, fax 020 7731 8876, website www.peterdazeley.com)

de ARANDA, Corinne Andree Reppin; da of Jameson Reppin Bates, of S Benfleet, Essex, and Andree Josephine Amand Eugenie, *née* Eyskens; *b* 18 March 1961; *Educ* Queenswood Sch; *m* 1, 1989 (d 1991); m 2, 19 Sept 1997, Pedro de Aranda; 1 s (Juan b 15 Dec 1998); *Career* dir Co-ordinated Properties Ltd, trainee asst buyer Harrods 1979–84, conslt Ligne Roset (UK) Ltd 1984–86, sales mangr Van Cleef and Arpels 1987, sales dir Elizabeth Gage 1987–89, md Chaumet (UK) 1989–90, vice-pres DeAranda & Associates 1991–94, Jawharat al Imrat 1995–97, co sec Prologue (UK) Ltd 1998–, Prologue SARL 2003; FRSA 2001; *Style*— Corinne de Aranda; ✉ e-mail corinne@prologueworld.com

de BERNIÈRES, Louis Henry Piers; s of Maj Reginald Piers Alexander de Bernière-Smart; *b* 8 December 1954, London; *Educ* Bradfield Coll, Victoria Univ of Manchester (BA), Leicester Poly (PGCE), Inst of Educn Univ of London (MA); *Career* novelist; former jobs incl teacher, landscape gardener, car mechanic and bookshop asst; named Granta Best of Young British Novelists list 1993, Author of the Year British Book Awards 1997; *Publications* as Louis de Bernières: The War of Don Emmanuel's Nether Parts (1990, Best First Book Eurasia Region Cwlth Writers' Prize 1991), Señor Vivo and the Coca Lord (1991, Best Book Eurasia Region Cwlth Writers' Prize 1992), The Troublesome Offspring of Cardinal Guzman (1992), Captain Corelli's Mandolin (1994, shortlisted Book of the Year Sunday Express 1994, Best Book Cwlth Writers' Prize 1995, stage adaptation 1999, film adaptation 2001), Labels (1997), The Book of Job (introduction, 1998), Red Dog (2001), Sunday Morning at the Centre of the World (radio play, 2001, broadcast BBC Radio 4 1999), Birds Without Wings (2004, shortlisted Whitbread Novel Award 2004), A Partisan's Daughter (2008); regular contrib of short stories to newspapers and magazines; *Style*— Louis de Bernières, Esq; ✉ c/o Publicity, Random House, 20 Vauxhall Bridge Road, London SW1V 2SA (tel 020 7840 8617, fax 020 7932 0761)

de BLOCQ van KUFFELER, John Philip; s of Capt F de Blocq van Kuffeler (d 2005), of Royal Netherlands Navy, and Stella, *née* Hall; *b* 9 January 1949; *Educ* Atlantic Coll, Clare Coll Cambridge (MA); *m* 3 April 1971, Lesley, da of Dr E M Callander; 2 s (Hugo b 1974, Alexander b 1979), 1 da (Venetia b 1977); *Career* Peat Marwick Mitchell & Co 1970–77, head of corp fin Grindlay Brandts Ltd 1980–82 (mangr 1977–80); Brown Shipley & Co Ltd: dir 1983–91, head of corp fin 1983–88, memb Exec Ctee 1985–91, head of investment banking UK and USA 1986–88; gp chief exec Brown Shipley Holdings plc 1988–91; chm: Provident Financial plc 1997– (chief exec 1991–97), Huveaux plc 2001–, Eidos plc 2002–05; dir: Medical Defence Union Ltd 2001–04, TV Eye Ltd 2003–05; memb Ctee Issuing Houses Assoc 1984–88; FCA 1979 (ACA 1973); *Recreations* fishing, shooting, tennis; *Clubs* City; *Style*— John de Blocq van Kuffeler, Esq; ✉ Huveaux plc, 4 Grosvenor Place, London SW1X 7DL (tel 020 7245 0270, fax 020 7245 0271)

de BOER-KRUYT, Dien; da of Henk Kruyt (d 1991), and Fiet Ferman (d 1998); *b* 18 August 1944, Netherlands; *Educ* Groningen Univ, Harvard Univ (MA); *m* 15 June 1985, Hans de Boer; 6 s (Ivan b 22 April 1973, Andreas b 21 Sept 1975 d 1998, Dimitri b 4 Oct 1976, Hugo b 24 May 1978, Alexander b 29 May 1978, Michael b 4 Dec 1987), 2 da (Naomi b 1 Sept 1977, Sarah b 18 Jan 1989); *Career* teacher Harvard Univ 1974, researcher MIT 1974–75, strategy and policy conslt Bosboon and Hegener (KPMG) 1975–80, dir Inst for Strategy and Policy 1980–87, coach (in Asia and Europe) 1987–; non-exec dir: Sara Lee Int 1994–, HBG Construction 1994–2001, Imtech Installation 1999–, Reed Elsevier 2000–, Allianz NL 2002–; involved with Dutch Peace Corps and Inst for Home Care; *Recreations* coaching, sailing, reading, travelling, Chinese Chi Kung, dancing, singing; *Style*— Mrs Dien de Boer-Kruyt; ✉ Hoofdgracht 65, 1411 LB Naarden, The Netherlands (tel 00 31 35 69 44455, e-mail dien@diendeboer.com, website www.diendeboer.com); c/o Reed Elsevier Group plc, 1–3 Strand, London WC2N 5JR

D

de BOINVILLE, Simon Murdoch Chastel; s of Charles Alfred Chastel de Boinville (d 1985), of Farnham, Surrey, and Frances Anne, *née* Morrison (d 1984); *b* 16 March 1955; *Educ* Radley, RAC Cirencester; *m* 4 Oct 1980, Shaunagh Elisabeth, da of Dermott Bibby Magill, of Baughurst, Hants; 3 s (Reuben b 1986 d 1988, Nicolai b 1989, Lucian b 1991), 1 da (Cornelia b 1988); *Career* ptnr Cluttons Chartered Surveyors 1989–91 (joined 1979), dir John D Wood & Co (Residential and Agricultural) Ltd 1991–96, dir INIGO Business Centres Ltd 1997–2002, dir Lonsdale Insurance Brokers (Lloyd's brokers); FRICS; *Clubs* Farmers'; *Style*— Simon de Boinville, Esq; ✉ Grantham Farm, Baughurst, Tadley, Hampshire RG26 5JT (tel 0118 981 1364, fax 0118 982 0989, e-mail simon@granthamfarm.org)

de BONO, Edward Francis Charles Publius; s of late Prof Joseph Edward de Bono, CBE, of St Julian's Bay, Malta, and Josephine, *née* Burns; *b* 19 May 1933; *Educ* St Edward's Coll Malta, Royal Univ of Malta (BSc, MD), ChCh Oxford (Rhodes scholar, DPhil), Univ of Cambridge (PhD); *m* 1971 (m dis 2006), Josephine, da of Major Francis Hall-White; 2 s; *Career* Univ of Cambridge: asst dir of res Dept of Investigative Med 1963–76, lectr in med 1976–83; fndr and dir Cognitive Research Trust Cambridge 1971–83, sec gen Supranational Independent Thinking Orgn (SITO) 1983–, fndr Int Creative Forum 1990–, prof of thinking Univ of Pretoria 2002–, fndr The World Centre for New Thinking 2004, Da Vinci prof of thinking Univ of Advancing Technol Arizona 2006; chm Cncl Young Enterprise Europe 1998–; invited to be king: Geraldton WA 2000, Margaret River WA 2000, Launceston Tasmania 2002; the planet formerly known as DE 73 named Edebono by the Naming Ctee of the Int Astronomic Union; TV series: de Bono's Course in Thinking (BBC), The Greatest Thinkers (WDR Germany); lectured extensively worldwide; Carl Sloane Award Int Assoc of Mgmnt Consulting Firms 2006; Hon LLD Univ of Dundee 2005; *Books* incl: The Use of Lateral Thinking (1967), Lateral Thinking; A Textbook of Creativity (1970), Wordpower (1977), de Bono's Thinking Course (1982), Six Thinking Hats (1985), Letters to Thinkers (1987), I am Right, You are Wrong (1990), Handbook for the Positive Revolution (1991), Six Action Shoes (1991), Teach Your Child to Think (1992), Serpetition (1992), Serious Creativity (1992), Textbook of Wisdom (1993), Teach Yourself to Think (1994), Water Logic (1995), Parallel Thinking (1996), How to be More Interesting (1997), Mind Pack (1997), Simplicity (1998), Super Mind Pack (1998), Why I Want to be King of Australia (1999), New Thinking for the New Millennium (1999), Textbook of Wisdom (2000), The de Bono Code (2000), Why So Stupid: How the Human Race has Never Learned to Think (2003), How to Have a Beautiful Mind (2004), Six Value Medals (2005), H+ a new religion? (2006), How to Have Creative Ideas: 62 exercises to develop the mind (2007), Are Americans Really Free? (2007); *Recreations* travel, toys, thinking; *Clubs* Athenaeum; *Style*— Dr Edward de Bono; ✉ L2 Albany, Piccadilly, London W1V 9RR (website www.edwdebono.com and www.edwarddebono.com)

de BORMAN, (Chevalier) Jean-Marc (John); s of Alexandre de Borman (d 1999), and Genevieve, *née* Froisset (d 1966); *b* 14 December 1954; *Educ* Stowe, Chelsea Sch of Art (BA); *m* 6 May 1982, Julia, *née* Murray; 2 c (Arthur Alexandre David, Rosie Genevieve Ann (twins) b 19 Feb 1983); *Career* cinematographer; memb: BSC 1996–, BAFTA 1997–; *Film* Small Faces 1995, Trojan Eddie 1995, The Full Monty 1996, Photgraphing Fairies 1996, The Mighty 1997, Hideous Kinky 1997 (Evening Standard Award for Technical Achievement 1999), Gregory's 2 Girls 1998, Hamlet 1998 (nominee Best Cinematography Independent Spirit Awards 2001), New Year's Day 1999, Saving Grace 1999, There's Only One Jimmy Grimble 1999, Serendipity 2000, The Guru 2001, Pure 2002, Ella Enchanted 2002, Shall We Dance 2003, A Lot Like Love 2004, Tara Road 2005, Fade to Black 2005; *Recreations* watching rugby, tennis; *Clubs* Soho House, Chelsea Arts, Electric Cinema; *Style*— John de Borman, Esq; ✉ c/o McKinney Macartney Management, 10 Barley Mow Passage, London W4 4PH (tel 020 8995 4747, fax 020 8995 2414); c/o Skouras Agency, Los Angeles (tel 00 1 310 901 0701)

de BOTTON, Hon Janet Frances; CBE (2006); da of Baron Wolfson (Life Peer), *qv*, and Ruth, *née* Sterling; *b* 31 March 1952, London; *Educ* St Paul's Girls Sch; *m* 1, 1972 (m dis 1989), Michael Philip Green; 2 da (Rebecca Sarah b 27 April 1974, Catherine Victoria b 1 Sept 1976); m 2, 1990, Gilbert de Botton (d 2000); *Career* dir Christie's Int 1994–98, chair Tate Modern 1999–2002; tstee: Wolfson Fndn 1987–, Tate Gallery 1992–2002, Tate Fndn 2006–; *Style*— The Hon Mrs de Botton, CBE; ✉ c/o Tate Gallery, Millbank, London SW1P 4RG (tel 020 7887 8000)

de BRAUX, John Andrew; s of Cecil Hubert de Braux, of Watford, Herts, and Vera Nellie, *née* Ford (d 2001); *b* 5 July 1950; *Educ* Watford Boys' GS, St Albans Coll (HNC), Univ of Westminster (MBA); *m* 21 Aug 1971, Judith Gwendoline, *née* Stanton; 2 da (Anna Katherine b 1 Jan 1975, Alexandra Claire b 24 Feb 1978); *Career* British Railways: tech offr/IT project asst 1968–82, permanent way engr 1982–88; infrastructure mangr British Rail Network SouthEast 1988–90; chief exec: Hillingdon Community Health NHS Tst 1990–93, W Middx Univ Hosp NHS Tst 1994–2001, Epsom and St Helier NHS Tst 2001–03, Beds and Herts SHA 2003–06; md debraux consulting limited 2006–; sometime chair W London Orthopaedic Network and Cancer Collaborative, memb Action on Orthopaedics Steering Bd, estab Learning Partnership for Acute Tsts (in partnership with NW London Hosp's Tst); MInstD 1998; *Recreations* choral singing, walking, canal boating; *Clubs* Old Fullerians Assoc; *Style*— John de Braux, Esq; ✉ debraux consulting limited, 71 Kenilworth Drive, Croxley Green, Rickmansworth, Hertfordshire WD3 3NN (tel 01923 231173, fax 01923 237067, mobile 07831 559269, e-mail john@debraux.com)

DE BURGH, Christopher John (né Davison); s of Charles John Davison, of Wexford, Ireland, and Maeve Emily, *née* de Burgh; *b* 15 October 1948; *Educ* Marlborough, Trinity Coll Dublin (MA); *m* Diane Patricia, da of Arthur Morley; 1 da (Rosanna Diane b 17 April 1984), 2 s (Hubie Christopher b 29 March 1988, Michael Charles Arthur b 30 Oct 1990); *Career* singer and songwriter; has released 18 albums to date, debut album Far Beyond These Castle Walls 1974, other albums incl Notes From Planet Earth - The Ultimate Collection 2001 and Timing Is Everything 2002; single The Lady in Red, album Into the Light (both 1986) and album Flying Colours reached number one in UK, USA and elsewhere; toured extensively in Europe, Aust, Japan, UK and Ireland; winner of over 80 Gold, Silver and Platinum discs since 1976 in USA, Canada, England, Ireland, Germany, Belgium, Holland, Switzerland, Austria, Norway, Sweden, Spain, South Africa, Aust, Hong Kong, Brazil, Denmark, France and Israel; other awards incl: Beroliner award (Germany), Bambi award (Germany), Midem Int Trophy (France), ASCAP award (UK and America, 1987, 1988, 1990, 1991 and 1997), IRMA awards (Ireland 1985–1990); *Recreations* swimming, scuba diving, golf, fine wine collecting, antiques, Persian rugs; *Style*— Chris De Burgh, Esq; ✉ c/o Kenny Thomson Management, 754 Fulham Road, London SW6 5SH (tel 020 7731 7074, fax 020 7736 8605, e-mail ktmuk@dircon.co.uk)

DE BURGH, Lydia Anne; da of Capt Charles De Burgh, DSO, RN (d 1973), of Seaforde, and Isabel Caroline Berkeley, *née* Campbell (d 1969); *b* 3 July 1923; *Educ* privately, Byam Shaw Sch of Art; *Career* WRNS 1942 (ULTRA/Enigma), Br Red Cross 1943–45; professional portrait, wildlife and landscape painter; apprenticed to late Sonia Mervyn RP; exhbns at: Royal Soc of Portrait Painters, Royal Soc of Br Artists, Royal Birmingham Soc, Royal Ulster Acad of Art, Glasgow Inst of Fine Arts, Chelsea Art Soc (memb 1957–69), Soc of Wildlife Artists London, Soc of Equestrian Artists, Ulster Watercolour Soc; solo exhbns incl: NI Office, Vose Gallery Boston MA 1957, HQ NI 1975 and 1978, Gordon Gallery London, Wildlife Gallery Eastbourne; retrospective exhbns: Down County Museum then The Malone Gallery Belfast 1993, St Patrick's Museum Co Down 2003, Hillsborough Castle (Govt House) Co Down 2006–07; cmmns incl: Princess Alice HRH The Duchess of Gloucester 1954, HM The Queen 1955, 1956 and 1959, HRH the late Princess Royal 1956 and 1957, the late Marquess and Marchioness of Headfort, African wildlife in Kenya for Rowland Ward Ltd, Crossroads of Sport (Sportsmans Gallery NY) 1960–70, Maze Prison 1972; lectr worldwide, numerous interviews on BBC; HRUA 1985 (ARUA 1956), hon memb Ulster Water Colour Soc, memb Chelsea Art Soc 1956–72; *Books* Lydia's Story (1991, recorded for Blind and Disabled Listening Libraries RNIB 1993), Another Way of Life (1999); *Recreations* travelling, reading, gardening, fine arts; *Style*— Lydia De Burgh, HRUA; ✉ 4 Church Court, Castlewellan Road, Clough, Downpatrick, County Down BT30 8QX

de CANDOLE, (Mark) Andrew Vully; s of Eric Armar Vully de Candole, CMG, CBE (d 1989), and Elizabeth Marion, *née* Constable-Roberts (d 1997); *b* 15 April 1953; *Educ* Marlborough; *Career* md City Gate Estates plc 1985–90, md Pathfinder Group 1991–2000, co-fndr Private Equity Investor plc 2000–05; fndr Einstein Fund 2004; non-exec dir Queen Victoria Hospital NHS Trust 1994–96; *Recreations* garden design, skiing, sailing; *Style*— Andrew de Candole, Esq; ✉ Courtyard Offices, Al Quoz, PO Box 211317, Dubai, UAE

de CHASSIRON, Charles Richard Lucien; s of Brig H E C de Chassiron (d 1974), and Deane, *née* Richardson (d 1996); *b* 27 April 1948; *Educ* Rugby, Jesus Coll Cambridge (MA), Kennedy Sch of Govt Harvard Univ (MPA); *m* 28 Sept 1974, Britt-Marie Sonja, da of Nils G Medhammar; 1 da (Anna b 1975), 1 s (Hugo b 1976); *Career* HM Dip Serv: joined FCO 1971, Stockholm 1972–75, Maputo 1975–78, memb UK Delgn at Lancaster House Rhodesia Conf 1979, Salisbury 1980, Brasilia 1982–85, head of S American Dept 1988–89, cnsllr (econ and commercial) Rome 1989–94, ambass Estonia 1994–97, DG for trade and investment in Italy and consul-general Milan 1997–2001, head Protocol Div FCO 2002–06, Vice Marshal of the Diplomatic Corps 2002–06; currently diplomatic conslt Royal Garden Hotel; chm Spencer House; chm Br-Italian Soc; *Recreations* walking, history of art; *Clubs* Beefsteak, RAC; *Style*— Charles de Chassiron, Esq

de CLIFFORD, 27 Baron (E 1299); John Edward Southwell Russell; er s of 26 Baron de Clifford, OBE, TD (d 1982), by his 1 w, Dorothy Evelyn (d 1987), da of Ferdinand Meyrick, MD, of Kensington Court, London, and Kate Meyrick the nightclub owner; *b* 8 June 1928; *Educ* Eton, RAC Cirencester; *m* 27 June 1959, Bridget Jennifer, yst da of Duncan Robertson, of Llantysilio Hall, Llangollen, by his w Joyce (aunt of Sir Watkin Williams-Wynn, 11 Bt,, *qv*); *Heir* bro, Hon William Russell; *Career* farmer, ret; *Clubs* Naval and Military; *Style*— The Rt Hon Lord de Clifford; ✉ Riggledown, Pennymoor, Tiverton, Devon EX16 8LR (tel 01363 866301)

de COURCY, Anne Grey; da of Maj John Lionel Mackenzie Barrett (d 1940), of Tendring, Essex, and Evelyn Kathleen Frances, *née* Ellison-Macartney; *Educ* Wroxall Abbey Leamington Spa; *m* 1, 1951, Michael Charles Cameron Claremont Constantine de Courcy (d 1953), elder son of Lt Cdr Hon Michael John Rancé de Courcy, RN (d 1940); m 2, 24 Jan 1959, Robert Armitage, 2 s of Gen Sir (Charles) Clement Armitage, KCB, CMG, DSO, DL, of Downington House, Glos; 1 s (John b Dec 1959), 2 da (Sophy b June 1961, Rose b March 1964); *Career* Evening News: writer, columnist, woman's ed 1972–80; Evening Standard: writer, columnist, section ed 1982–92; Daily Mail 1993–; *Books* Kitchens (1973), Starting From Scratch (1975), Making Room at the Top (1976), A Guide to Modern Manners (1985), The English in Love (1986), 1939 - The Last Season (1989, new edn 2003), Circe - The Life of Edith, Marchioness of Londonderry (1992, new edn (as Society's Queen) 2004), The Viceroy's Daughters (2000), Diana Mosley (2003), Debs at War (2005); *Recreations* reading, writing, swimming, gardening; *Style*— Ms Anne de Courcy

DE FEO, Joseph; s of Ralph and Jean De Feo; *b* 31 May 1947; *Educ* Adelphi Univ New York (BA, MBA, MS); *m* Anna Julie; 1 s (Christian Joseph), 1 da (Danielle Julie); *Career* asst mangr Computer Ops Interstate Stores Inc 1969–71, systems programmer Chemical Bank New York 1971–72, mangr Systems Software Blyth & Co Inc 1972, sr systems programmer Federal Reserve Bank of New York 1972–74, vice-pres Info Servs Smith Barney, Harris Upham 1974–77, vice-pres Int Bank Servs Chase Manhattan Bank 1982–84 (vice-pres Bank Support Servs 1977–82), vice-pres Systems Devpt and User Support Gp Goldman Sachs & Co 1984–87, dir Gp Systems and Ops Morgan Grenfell & Co Ltd 1988–89, dir Gp Ops and Technol Barclays Bank plc 1989–96, chief exec Open Gp 1996–98 (former non-exec dir), chief exec CLS Gp Hldgs 2000–, pres and ceo CLS Bank International; author of numerous articles in indust and mgmnt pubns and nat newspapers, frequent lectr and speaker; memb Cncl APACS, fndr memb Group of 20, chm CHAPS Clearing Co (formerly Cheque and Credit Clearing Co); non-exec dir Dept of Social Security, sr rep for Barclays Gp in SWIFT, memb Advsy Bd Cross Border Exchange Inc; Freeman Worshipful Co of Information Technologists; *Style*— Joseph De Feo, Esq; ✉ CLS Group Holdings, Exchange Tower, 1 Harbour Exchange Square, London E14 9GE; CLS Bank International, 39 Broadway, New York, NY 1006, USA (e-mail jdefeo@cis-bank.com)

de FONBLANQUE, John Robert; CMG (1993); s of Maj-Gen Edward Barrington de Fonblanque (d 1981), of Lyndhurst, Hants, and Elizabeth Flora Lutley, *née* Sclater (d 2005); *b* 20 December 1943; *Educ* Ampleforth, King's Coll Cambridge (MA), LSE (MSc); *m* 24 March 1984, Margaret, da of Harry Prest; 1 s (Thomas b 1985); *Career* HM Dip Serv 1968–2003: second sec Jakarta 1969–71, first sec UK rep to EC 1971–77, princ HM Treasy 1977–79, FCO 1979–83, asst sec Cabinet Office 1983–85, cnsllr Delhi 1986–87, cnsllr and head of Chancery UK Rep to EC 1988–93, visiting fell Royal Inst for International Relations 1993, dir for global issues 1994–97, dir Europe 1998–99; ambass to Orgn for Security and Cooperation in Europe (OSCE) 1999–2003; dir Office of OSCE High Cmmn on Nat Minorities 2004–07; *Recreations* mountain walking; *Style*— John R de Fonblanque, Esq, CMG

DE FREYNE, 7 Baron (UK 1851); Francis Arthur John French; s of 6 Baron, JP, DL (d 1935), by Victoria, da of Sir John Arnott, 2 Bt; *b* 3 September 1927; *m* 1, 30 Jan 1954 (m dis 1979); 2 s (Hon Fulke b 1957, Hon Patrick b 1969), 1 da (Hon Vanessa b 1958); m 2, 1978, Sheelin Deirdre, da of Col Henry O'Kelly, DSO, of Co Wicklow, and wid of William Walker Stevenson; *Heir* s, Hon Fulke French; *Career* KM; *Style*— The Rt Hon Lord De Freyne; ✉ The Old School, Sutton Courtenay, Oxfordshire OX14 4AW

DE GELSEY, William Henry Marie; s of Baron Henry de Gelsey (d 1963), formerly of Hungary, and Marguerite, *née* Lieser (d 1965); *b* 17 December 1921; *Educ* Roman Catholic Univ Public Sch Budapest, Trinity Coll Cambridge (MA); *Career* investment banker (exec dir) Hill Samuel and Co Ltd 1959–71, md Orion Bank Ltd 1971–80, dep chm Orion Royal Bank Ltd 1980–88; sr advsr to the Managing Bds: Creditanstalt-Bankverein (Vienna and London) 1988–97, Bank Austria Creditanstalt Gp and CA IB Investmentbank (Vienna and London) 1997–, CA IB Corp Fin Gp (Vienna, Budapest and London) 2001–07, CA IB Corporate Finance Ltd; chm Gedeon Richter Rt Budapest 1995–; memb: Economic Advsy Cncl of PM of Hungary 1998–2002, UniCredit Markets and Investment Banking Div 2007–; KCSG 2005; *Recreations* travelling; *Clubs* Annabel's, Mark's, Harry's Bar, The Walbrook, George; *Style*— William de Gelsey, Esq, KCSG; ✉ CA IB Corporate Finance, c/o Schottengasse 6, 1010 Vienna, Austria (tel 00 43 50505 43311, fax 00 43 50505 43397, e-mail degelseyw@ca-ib.com); c/o 80 Cheapside, London EC2V 6EE (tel 020 7309 7866, fax 020 7823 9452); Palais Saint-Pierre, 32 Boulevard d'Italie, Monte-Carlo, MC 98000 Monaco

de GREY, Lady; *see:* Irwin, Flavia

de GREY, Michael John; *b* 6 September 1942; *m* 1, 1966 (m dis 1988), Carolyn Blackie; 2 da (Rachel Emma b 1969, Helen Sarah b 1971); m 2, 1989, Charlotte Ashe; 1 da (Annabel Louise b 1994); *Career* schoolmaster Elstree Sch 1961, district mangr Courages Brewery 1962–70, concerts mangr Victor Hochhauser Ltd 1970–72, gen mangr London Mozart Players 1972–81, gen mangr Royal Choral Soc 1976–79, admin dir London Sinfonietta 1981–88 (admin dir Opera Factory 1985–88), conslt SE Arts and London Handel Orch 1988–89, gen mangr LAMDA 1989, head of mktg Soundalive Tours 1990–91, chief exec Nat Youth Orch of GB 1991–2002, gen mangr West of England Philharmonic Orchestra 2003–; dir: Assoc of Br Orchs 1984–89, LPO 1987–89; memb Music Advsy Panel SE Arts 1986–90; *Style*— Michael de Grey, Esq; ✉ West of England Philharmonic Orchestra, PO Box 886, Trinity Quay, Avon Street, Bristol BS99 5LJ

de GREY, Spencer Thomas; CBE (1997); s of Sir Roger de Grey, KCVO, PPRA (d 1995), and Flavia Irwin, RA, *qv*; *b* 7 June 1944; *Educ* Eton, Churchill Coll Cambridge (MA, DipArch); *m* 3 Sept 1977, Hon (Amanda) Lucy, da of Baron Annan, OBE (Life Peer, d 2000); 1 da (Georgia Catherine b 22 Aug 1988), 1 s (Felix Nicholas b 29 Aug 1992); *Career* architect London Borough of Merton 1969–73; Foster & Partners (formerly Foster Associates): joined 1973, estab Hong Kong office 1979, dir 1981 (responsible for Third London Airport at Stansted and Sackler Galleries Royal Acad), design ptnr 1991–, sr exec/head of design 2007–; projects as design ptnr incl: Commerzbank HQ Frankfurt, Lycée Albert Camus Fréjus, EDF regional operational centre Bordeaux, Law Faculty Univ of Cambridge, Great Court British Museum, Alexander Fleming Bldg and Tanaka Business Sch Imperial Coll London, Nat Botanical Gardens for Wales, World Squares for All, The Sage music centre Gateshead, Boston Museum of Fine Arts, Opera House Dallas, Avery Fisher Hall Lincoln Center NY, Dresden Railway Station, HM Treasy Whitehall London, Smithsonian Inst Washington DC; architectural advsr Royal Botanic Gardens Kew 1995–, chm Building Centre Tst, chm Sch of Architecture Advsy Bd Univ of Cambridge; ARCUK 1969, RIBA 1993, FRSA 2006; *Recreations* music, theatre, travel; *Style*— Spencer de Grey, Esq, CBE; ✉ Foster & Partners, Riverside 3, 22 Hester Road, London SW11 4AN (tel 020 7738 0455, fax 020 7738 1107, e-mail sdegrey@fosterandpartners.com)

DE GROOSE, Tracy; da of Colin Darwen, of Cadiz, Spain, and Pauline Darwen; *b* 11 March 1968, Darwen, Lancs; *Educ* West Kirby GS, Brunel Univ (LLB); *m* Andrew De Groose; *Career* various positions rising to mktg controller Stella Artois Interbrew UK 1992–98, business dir Starcom Motive 1998–2002, md Naked Communications 2002–; Mktg Soc Award for work on Stella Artois brand 1997; memb Mktg Soc; *Style*— Mrs Tracey De Groose; ✉ Naked Communications, 159–173 St John Street, London EC1V 4QJ (tel 020 7663 1774, e-mail tracy@nakedcomms.com)

de GRUBEN, HE Baron Thierry; s of Baron Guy de Gruben (d 1977), and Monique, *née* Dierckx de Casterlé; *b* 17 November 1941, Antwerp, Belgium; *m* 15 Nov 1980, Françoise, *née* Francq; 1 s (Christopher b 1982); *Career* Belgian diplomat; diplomatic trainee NATO Brussels 1969–70, Press Serv Miny of Foreign Affrs 1970–71, attaché then sec Moscow 1971–76, sec then first sec London 1976–80, consul-gen Bombay 1980–82, Private Office of the Min of External Relations Brussels 1982–85, ambass Warsaw 1985–90, ambass Moscow 1990–95, dep political dir Brussels and special envoy for Eastern Slavonia 1995–97, ambass and perm rep to NATO Brussels 1997–2002, ambass to the Ct of St James's 2002–; *Clubs* Travellers, Athenaeum, Caledonian, RAC; *Style*— HE Baron Thierry de Gruben; ✉ Embassy of Belgium, 17 Grosvenor Crescent, London SW1X 7EE (e-mail london@diplobel.be)

de GUINGAND, Anthony Paul; s of Paul Emile de Guingand (d 1976), and Olwen Doreen, *née* Witts (d 1999); *b* 7 August 1947; *Educ* Ampleforth; *m* 24 Nov 1973, Diana Mary, da of John Harrington Parr (d 1998); 2 s (Marcus b 1977, Peter b 1982), 1 da (Emily b 1979); *Career* exec dir International Commodities Clearing House Ltd 1973–86; md London Traded Options Market 1986–92, dir fin LIFFE 1992–2002, md Paul E de Guingand Ltd 2002–; FCA, MSI; *Recreations* rugby, golf; *Style*— Anthony de Guingand; ✉ Playfoots, Bramble Reed Lane, Matfield, Kent TN12 7ET

de HAAN, Kevin Charles; QC (2000); s of Michael James de Haan (d 1988), and Barbara Ada, *née* Wood; *b* 30 October 1952; *Educ* Davenant Fndn GS, QMC London (LLB), Univ of Brussels; *m* 1983, Katy Monica, da of Kenneth Martin Foster; *Career* barrister; called to the Bar Inner Temple 1976 (bencher 1997); recorder; *Books* Food Safety Law (contrib, 1995), Pollution in the UK (contrib, 1995), The Law of Betting, Gaming and Lotteries (ed, 2001); *Recreations* skiing, flying light aircraft, aerobatics, cycling, walking, music; *Clubs* Ski Club of GB; *Style*— Kevin de Haan, Esq, QC; ✉ Francis Taylor Building, Temple, London EC4Y 7BY (tel 020 7353 8415, fax 020 7353 7622, e-mail mgoba@mgoba.demon.co.uk)

de HAAS, Her Hon Judge Margaret Ruth; QC (1998); da of Joseph de Haas, of London, and Lisalotte Herte, *née* Meyer; *b* 21 May 1954; *Educ* Townsend Girls' Sch Bulawayo, Univ of Bristol (LLB); *m* 18 May 1980, Iain Saville Goldrein, s of Neville Clive Goldrein; 1 s (Alastair Philip b 1 Oct 1982), 1 da (Alexandra Ann b 22 Feb 1985); *Career* called to the Bar Middle Temple 1977; practised Northern Circuit, recorder 1999–2004 (asst recorder 1995–99), dep judge of the High Court 2000, circuit judge (Northern Circuit) 2004–; memb: Personal Injury Bar Assoc, Professional Negligence Bar Assoc, Family Law Bar Assoc; FRSA; *Books* Property Distribution on Divorce (2 edn with Iain S Goldrein, 1985), Personal Injury Litigation (with Iain S Goldrein, 1985), Domestic Injunctions (1987 and co-author 1998), Butterworths Personal Injury Litigation Service (with Iain S Goldrein), Family Court Practice (contrib, 1993), Structured Settlements (jt ed-in-chief with Iain S Goldrein, 1993), Medical Negligence: Cost Effective Case Management (with Iain S Goldrein, 1996), Civil Court Practice (co-ed, 2000); *Recreations* family, swimming, theatre; *Style*— Her Hon Judge de Haas, QC

de HAMEL, Dr Christopher Francis Rivers; s of Dr Francis Alexander de Hamel, and Joan Littledale, *née* Pollock; *b* 20 November 1950; *Educ* Univ of Otago (BA), Univ of Oxford (DPhil); *m* 1, 1978 (m dis 1989); 2 s; m 2, 1993, Mette Tang Simpson, *née* Svendsen; *Career* Sotheby's: cataloguer of medieval manuscripts 1975–77, asst dir 1977–82, dir western manuscripts 1982–2000, Donnelley fell librarian CCC Cambridge 2000–; visiting fell All Souls Coll Oxford 1999–2000, Sandars reader in bibliography Univ of Cambridge 2003–04; memb Comité international de paléographie latine 2004; Hon LittD St John's Univ Minnesota 1994, Hon DLitt Univ of Otago 2002, PhD Univ of Cambridge 2005; FSA 1981, FRHistS 1986; *Books* Glossed Books of the Bible and the Origins of the Paris Booktrade (1984), A History of Illuminated Manuscripts (1986, 2 edn 1994), Medieval & Renaissance Manuscripts in New Zealand (with M Manion and V Vines, 1989), Syon Abbey, the Library of the Bridgettine Nuns and their Peregrinations after the Reformation (1991), Scribes and Illuminators (1992), British Library Guide to Manuscript Illumination (2001), The Book: A History of the Bible (2001), The Rothschilds and their Collections of Illuminated Manuscripts (2005); various reviews, articles and catalogues; *Clubs* Roxburghe, Grolier (NY), Association Internationale de Bibliophilie (Paris); *Style*—

Dr Christopher de Hamel, FSA; ✉ Corpus Christi College, Trumpington Street, Cambridge CB2 1RH

de HAVILLAND, John Anthony; s of Maj-Gen Peter Hugh de Havilland, CBE, DL (d 1989), and Helen Elizabeth Wrey (d 1976), da of William Whitmore Otter-Barry, of Horkesley Hall, Colchester; *b* 14 April 1938; *Educ* Eton, Trinity Coll Cambridge; *m* 1964, Hilary Anne, da of Robert Ewen MacKenzie (d 1993), of Ulceby, Lincs; 2 da (Lucinda b 1965, Victoria b 1968), 1 s (Piers b 1970); *Career* joined J Henry Schroder Wagg & Co Ltd 1959 (md 1971–90), ret 1990; non-exec dir Cadogan Estate; chm Nat Rifle Assoc 1990–2001, capt English VIII 1979–93, shot for England 1961–92, 1996, 1998, winner Match Rifle Championship at Bisley nine times since 1963; *Recreations* shooting; *Style*— John de Havilland, Esq; ✉ Blommenberg Farm, PO Box 1212, Stanford, Western Cape, South Africa

de HOGHTON, Sir (Richard) Bernard Cuthbert; 14 Bt (E 1611), of Hoghton Tower, Lancashire, DL (Lancs); s of Sir Cuthbert de Hoghton, 12 Bt (d 1958), and half-brother of Sir (Henry Philip) Anthony Mary de Hoghton, 13 Bt (d 1978); *b* 26 January 1945; *Educ* Ampleforth, McGill Univ Montreal (BA), Univ of Birmingham (MA); *m* 1974, Rosanna Stella Virginia, da of Terzo Buratti, of Florence; 1 da (Elena Susannah Isabella b 1976), 1 s (Thomas James Daniel Adam b 1980); *Heir* s, Thomas de Hoghton; *Career* landowner; Turner and Newall & Co Ltd 1967–71; sr exec: Vickers da Costa & Co 1971–77, de Zoete & Bevan & Co 1977–86 (ptnr 1984–86); dir BZW Securities Ltd 1986–89, dir Brown Shipley & Co 1990–94, assoc Teather & Greenwood & Co 1994–98, dir Tutton & Saunders Ltd (Savoy Asset Mgmnt Gp plc) 1998–99; memb: CLA, Historic Houses Assoc; patron: Int Spinal Research Tst, Auto-Cycle Union, Br Red Cross (Lancs branch); vice-pres Int Tree Fndn; assoc European Soc of Investment Analysts; UN special ambass 1995; lay rector Preston Minster; FSI; Knight SMOM, Knight Constantinian Order of St George; *Recreations* skiing, shooting, tennis; *Style*— Sir Bernard de Hoghton, Bt, DL; ✉ Hoghton Tower, Hoghton, Preston, Lancashire PR5 0SH (tel 01254 852986, fax 01254 852109, e-mail mail@hoghtontower.co.uk)

de JONQUIERES, Guy; s of Maurice de Fauque de Jonquières (d 2001), of London, and late Pauline de Jonquières; *b* 14 May 1945; *Educ* Lancing, Exeter Coll Oxford; *m* 1977, Diana Elizabeth, da of T V N Fortescue; 2 s (Alexander b 1981, Julian b 1983); *Career* graduate trainee Reuters 1966–68; Financial Times: staff corr 1968–80 (Paris, Washington, Saigon, NY, Brussels), electronics industry corr 1980–86, int business ed 1986–90, consumer industries ed 1990–94, world trade ed 1994–2004, Asia columnist and commentator 2005–; *Recreations* reading, travel; *Style*— Guy de Jonquières, Esq; ✉ The Financial Times, Suite 2903–2909, Two International Finance Centre, 8 Finance Street, Central, Hong Kong (tel 00 852 2230 5823)

de la BÉDOYÈRE, Guy Martyn Thorold Huchet; s of Count de la Bédoyère , *qv*, and Countess Irene T P de la Bédoyère; *b* 28 November 1957; *Educ* KCS Wimbledon, Wimbledon Coll, Univ of Durham (BA), Univ of London (BA), UCL (MA); *m* 4 July 1981, Rosemary Anne, da of Canon R C A Carey; 4 s (Hugh b 27 Jan 1985, Thomas b 19 Nov 1986, Robert b 16 Oct 1988, William b 16 Aug 1990); *Career* freelance historian, archaeologist, writer and broadcaster; presenter: The Romans in Britain (BBC Radio 4) 1997, The Romans in Britain (BBC 2/Open Univ); co-presenter My Famous Family (UKTV History) 2006; regular guest Time Team (Channel 4) 1998–, Chm of the War Cabinet in The 1940s House (Channel 4); history teacher Kesteven and Sleaford HS 2007–; memb Soc for Promotion of Roman Studies 1997–; FRNS 2002, FSA 2007; *Publications* Samian Ware (1988), Finds of Roman Britain (1989), Buildings of Roman Britain (1991, reprinted 2001), Towns of Roman Britain (1992, revised edn 2003), Roman Villas and the Countryside (1993), The Writings of John Evelyn (1995), The Diary of John Evelyn (1995), Particular Friends. The Correspondence of Samuel Pepys and John Evelyn (1997, 2 edn 2005), Hadrian's Wall. A History and Guide (1998), The Golden Age of Roman Britain (1999, shortlisted Br Archaeological Book of the Year 2000), Companion to Roman Britain (1999), Battles over Britain. The Archaeology of the Air War (2000), Voices of Imperial Rome (2000), Pottery in Roman Britain (2000), Aviation Archaeology in Britain (2001), Eagles over Britannia. The Roman Army in Britain (2001), The Home Front (2002), Architecture in Roman Britain (2002), Gods with Thunderbolts. Religion in Roman Britain (2002), Defying Rome. The Rebels of Roman Britain (2003), A New History of Roman Britain (2006), The Letters of Samuel Pepys (2006), The Romans for Dummies (2006); *Recreations* coin collector, piano, travelling in the USA, photography, aviation (private pilot's licence 2000), genealogy; *Style*— Guy de la Bédoyère, Esq; ✉ The Old Post House, Welby, Grantham, Lincolnshire NG32 3LN (tel 01400 231190, e-mail guydelabed@yahoo.co.uk)

de la BÉDOYÈRE, Count Quentin Michael Algar; s of Count Michael de la Bédoyère (d 1973), and Catherine, *née* Thorold (d 1959); *b* 23 November 1934; *Educ* Beaumont Coll, LAMDA; *m* 28 July 1956, Irene Therese Philippa, da of late Martyn Gough; 2 s (Guy Martyn Thorold Huchet de la Bédoyère , *qv*, b 28 Nov 1957, Raoul Maurice Greville Huchet de la Bédoyère, *qv* b 20 Aug 1959), 3 da (Catherine Christina Mansel b 20 April 1961, Camilla Louise Nugent b 27 Sept 1963, Christina Sibyl Montagu b 15 April 1966); *Career* Nat Serv 2 Lt RASC 1953–55; Jacqmar Ltd 1956–57; Sun Life of Canada: sales rep 1957, field mgmnt 1960, London Head Office 1972, field trg offr 1972–76, mktg offr 1976–79, dir mktg devpt and PR 1980, vice-pres individual product mktg 1984, vice-pres planning and devpt 1987–90, vice-pres product mgmnt 1990–94, md Sun Life of Canada Unit Managers Ltd 1994–96 (dir 1990–96), ptnr IQ Productions 1997–; *Books* The Doctrinal Teaching of the Church (1963), The Family (1975), Barriers and Communication (1976), The Remaking of Marriages (1978), Managing People and Problems (1988), How to Get Your Own Way in Business (1990), Getting What You Want (1994), Autonomy and Obedience in the Catholic Church (2003); *Recreations* freelance writing (columnist and reviewer Catholic Herald 2001–), public speaking, painting, motorcycling; *Style*— Count de la Bédoyère; ✉ 10 Edge Hill, Wimbledon, London SW19 4LP (e-mail quentin@blueyonder.co.uk)

de la BÉDOYÈRE, (Count) Raoul Maurice Greville Huchet; s of Count Quentin de la Bedoyere, *qv*, of London, and Irene, *née* Gough; *b* 20 August 1959; *Educ* KCS Wimbledon, Wimbledon Coll, Univ of Birmingham (BA); *m* 24 Nov 1989, Sally Jean, da of Frank Carswell; 1 da (Eléonore Frances Kallisto b 2 April 1993), 1 s (Zacharie Adam Kronos b 28 Jan 1996); *Career* media sales VNU Publications 1982–84, media buyer Foote Cone and Belding advtg 1984–86, media planner Davidson Pearce 1986–87, bd account planner Gold Greenlees Trott 1991–92 (media planner 1987–91); planning dir: Woollams Moira Gaskin O'Malley 1994–95 (account planner 1992–94), Burkitt Edwards Martin 1995; account planner rising to bd planning dir Bates Dorland 1995; *Style*— Raoul de la Bédoyère, Esq

DE LA BERE, Sir Cameron; 2 Bt (UK 1953), of Crowborough, Co Sussex; s of Sir Rupert De la Bère, 1 Bt, KCVO (d 1978), Lord Mayor of London 1952–53, and Marguerite (d 1969), eldest da of Lt-Col Sir John Humphery; *b* 12 February 1933; *Educ* Tonbridge and abroad; *m* 20 June 1964, Clairemonde, only da of Casimir Kaufmann, of Geneva; 1 da (Réjane (Mrs Michel Lacoste) b 1965); *Heir* bro, Adrian De la Bère; *Career* jeweller; Liveryman Worshipful Co of Skinners; *Clubs* Société Litéraire (Geneva), Hurlingham; *Style*— Sir Cameron De la Bère, Bt; ✉ 1 Avenue Theodore Flournoy, 1207 Geneva, Switzerland (tel 00 41 22 786 00 15)

de la CRUZ, Angela; *b* 1965, La Coruna, Spain; *Educ* Santiago de Compostela (BA), Chelsea Coll of Art, Goldsmiths Coll London (BA), Slade Sch of Fine Art (MA); *Career* artist; commissions incl At Any Time - New Work (stage set) for Ballet Rambert 2001; *Solo Exhibitions* Untitled (Premises London) 1993, Galerie In Situ (Aalst Belgium) 1997, Everyday Painting (John Weber Gallery NY) 1998, 4xSolo (De Markten Brussels) 1998, Larger Than Life (commission, Royal Festival Hall London) 1998, Everyday Painting (Anthony Wilkinson Gallery London 1998) and (Galerie Krinzinger Vienna) 1999, One Painting (Lift Gallery London) 1999, John Weber Gallery NY 2000, Anthony Wilkinson Gallery London 2001, Perth Int Arts Festival 2002, Galleri Bouhlou Norway, Weterling Gallery Stockholm, Anna Schwarz Gallery Melbourne; *Group Exhibitions* Rubber Works Installation (Spitalfields Market Project London) 1993, Surface Tension (Curwen Gallery London) 1994, Making Mischief (St James's St London) 1994, Memory (Riverside Studios London) 1995, Abstract Eroticism (MOCA London) 1996, Art and Design (Academy Editions London) 1996, Wasted (Hyena Co website) 1996, Stepping Out (33 Gt Sutton St London) 1996, Lineart (Galerie in Situ Aalst) 1997, Shuttle (Anthony Wilkinson Fine Art London) 1997, Fasten Seatbelt (Galerie Krinzinger Vienna) 1997, Dissolution (Laurent Delaye Gallery London) 1997, Take Off (Benger Fabrik Bregenz Hamburg) 1997, Destroyer/Creator (John Weber Gallery NY) 1998, Speed (New Langton Arts Centre San Francisco) 1998, Contemporary Women Painters (Hillwood Art Museum NY) 1998, UK Maximum Diversity (Benger Fabrik Bregenz Hamburg and Atelierhaus der Akademie der bildenden Kunste Wien) 1998, 54x54 (MOCA London) 1999, Peinture sur PEINTURE (Salle de Bal Vienna) 1999, Fundacion Lazaro Guadiano Madrid 1999, French Inst Vienna 1999, I'm a Virgin (The Waiting Room Wolverhampton) 1999, Links - Schilderkunst in extremis? (Provincehuis Maastricht) 1999, Europe on a Shoestring (John Weber Gallery NY) 1999, Transgressions and Transformations (Yale Univ) 1999, Getting the Corners (Or Gallery Vancouver) 1999, John Moores 21 (prizewinner, Walker Museum & Art Gallery Liverpool) 1999, White Out (Gallery Fine London) 1999, Aktuelle Kunst (The Water Tower Vlissingen) 1999, My Old Man Said Follow the Van (Rosemary Branch London) 1999, Art for the 21st Century (John Weber Gallery NY) 2000, Point of View I/II (Richard Salmon Gallery London) 2000, The Wreck of Hope (The Nunnery London) 2000, 3 Rooms (Anthony Wilkinson Gallery London) 2000, Landscape (Barbara Gillman Gallery Miami) 2000, Makeshift (Univ of Brighton Gallery) 2001, Nothing: Exploring Invisibilities (Northern Gallery Contemporary Art) 2001, Record Collection (VTO Gallery London) 2001, Ingenting (Rooseum Malmo) 2001, Melancholy (Sunderland) 2001, Sitting Tenants (Lotta Hammer Projects London) 2002, Beauty (Laing Art Gallery Newcastle) 2002; *Work in Public Collections* Br Cncl Collection, Contemporary Art Soc; *Style*— Ms Angela de la Cruz; ✉ c/o Lisson Gallery, 52–54 Bell Street, London NW1 5DA (tel 020 7724 2739)

de la MARE, (Walter) Giles Ingpen; s of Richard Herbert Ingpen de la Mare (d 1986), of Much Hadham, Herts, and Amy Catherine, *née* Donaldson (d 1968); *b* 21 October 1934; *Educ* Eton, Trinity Coll Oxford (MA); *m* 10 Aug 1968, Ursula Alice, da of Nigel Oliver Willoughby Steward, OBE (d 1991), of Cullompton, Devon; 1 s (Joshua b 1969), 1 da (Catherine b 1971); *Career* Nat Serv RN 1953–55, Midshipman RNVR 1954 (Sub Lt 1955); dir: Faber and Faber Ltd 1969–98, Faber Music Ltd 1977–87, Geoffrey Faber Holdings Ltd 1990–, Giles de la Mare Publishers 1995–; Publishers Assoc: chm Univ Coll and Professional Publishers Cncl 1982–84, memb Cncl 1982–85, chm Copyright Ctee 1988, chm Freedom to Publish Ctee 1992–95 and 1998–2000; memb: Stefan Zweig Ctee Br Library 1986–95, Freedom to Publish Ctee Int Publishers Assoc 1993–96, Translation Advsy Gp Arts Cncl of England 1995–98, Exec Ctee Patrons of Br Art Tate Gallery 1998–2001; literary tstee Walter de la Mare 1982–, fndr Walter de la Mare Soc 1997; *Books* The Complete Poems of Walter de la Mare (ed, 1969), Publishing Now (contrib gen chapter, 1993), Short Stories 1895–1926 by Walter de la Mare (ed, 1996), Short Stories 1927–1956 by Walter de la Mare (ed, 2001), Short Stories for Children by Walter de la Mare (ed, 2006); *Recreations* music (performance and listening), art and architecture, photography, exploring remote places; *Clubs* Garrick; *Style*— Giles de la Mare, Esq; ✉ PO Box 25351, London NW5 1ZT (e-mail gilesdelamare@dial.pipex.com, website www.gilesdelamare.co.uk)

de la RUE, Sir Andrew George Ilay; 4 Bt (UK 1898), of Cadogan Square, Chelsea, London; s of Sir Eric Vincent de la Rue, 3 Bt (d 1989), and his 1 w, Cecilia (d 1963), da of Maj Walter Waring, DL, MP (d 1930), and Lady Clementine Hay; *b* 3 February 1946; *Educ* Millfield; *m* 1984, Tessa Ann, er da of David Dobson, of Stragglethorpe Grange, Lincoln; 2 s (Edward Walter Henry b 25 Nov 1986, Harry William John b 27 July 1989); *Heir* s, Edward de la Rue; *Style*— Sir Andrew de la Rue, Bt; ✉ Stragglethorpe Grange, Brant Broughton, Lincolnshire (tel 01636 626505); London (tel 07967 629221)

de la TOUR, Frances; da of Charles de la Tour (d 1983), and Moyra de la Tour, *née* Fessas (now Mrs Silberman); family of the painter Georges de la Tour (d 1652); *b* 30 July 1945; *Educ* Lycée Français de Londres, Drama Centre London; *Children* 1 da (Tamasin Kempinski b 12 Nov 1973), 1 s (Josh Kempinski b 7 Feb 1977); *Career* actress; hon fell Goldsmiths Coll London 1999 *Theatre* RSC 1965–71: various roles incl Hoyden in Trevor Nunn's prodn of The Relapse, Helena in Peter Brook's prodn of A Midsummer Night's Dream; other credits incl: Violet in Small Craft Warnings (Hampstead and Comedy) 1973 (Best Supporting Actress Plays and Players Awards), Ruth Jones in The Banana Box (Apollo) 1973, Rosalind in As You Like It (Oxford Playhouse) 1974, Isabella in The White Devil (Old Vic) 1976, Eleanor Marx in Landscape of Exiles (Half Moon) 1978, title role in Hamlet (Half Moon) 1979, Stephanie in Duet for One (Bush and Duke of York's) 1980 (Standard Best Actress, Critics' Best Actress, SWET Best Actress in a New Play Awards), Jean in Skirmishes (Hampstead) 1982, Sonya in Chekhov's Uncle Vanya (Haymarket) 1982, Josie in A Moon for the Misbegotten (Riverside and Mermaid) 1983 (SWET Best Actress in a Revival Award), title role in St Joan (NT) 1984, Dance of Death (Riverside) 1985, Sonya and Masha in Chekhov's Women (Lyric) 1985, Brighton Beach Memoirs (NT) 1986, Lillian (Lyric and Fortune) 1986, Façades (Lyric Hammersmith) 1988, Regan in King Lear (Old Vic) 1989, Olga Knipper in Chekhov's Women (Moscow Lytcée Theatre and a special performance at Moscow Arts Theatre) 1990, When She Danced (Globe) 1991 (Best Supporting Actress Olivier Awards 1992), The Pope and the Witch (Comedy) 1992, Greasepaint (Lyric Hammersmith) 1993, Les Parents Terribles (RNT) 1994 (nominated Olivier Award for Best Actress), Three Tall Women (Wyndham's) 1995, The Fire Raisers (Riverside Studios) 1995, Blinded by the Sun (RNT) 1996, The Play About the Baby (Almeida) 1998, The Forest (RNT) 1998–99, Antony and Cleopatra (RSC) 1999–2000, Fallen Angels (Apollo) 2001 (Variety Club Best Actress Award), The Good Hope (RNT) 2001–02, Dance of Death by Strindberg (Lyric) 2003, The History Boys (RNT) 2004 and (Broadway NY) 2006 (Best Featured Actress Tony Awards); *Television* incl: Play for Today 1973 and 1975, Rising Damp (series) 1974–76, Flickers (series) 1980, Duet for One 1985 (BAFTA Best Actress nomination), Clem by Andy de la Tour, Ghengis Cohn (TV film) 1994, Dennis Potter's Cold Lazarus (TV Film) 1996, Tom Jones (series) 1997, The Egg by Partrick Arber 2002, Death on the Nile 2003; *Film* incl: Rising Damp 1979 (Standard Best Film Actress Award 1980), The Cherry Orchard 1998, Harry Potter and the Goblet of Fire 2004, The History Boys 2006; *Style*— Ms Frances de la Tour; ✉ c/o Claire Maroussas, ICM, Oxford House, 76 Oxford Street, London W1N 0AX (tel 020 7636 6565, fax 020 7323 0101)

DE LA WARR, 11 Earl (GB 1761); William Herbrand Sackville; also Baron De La Warr (E 1299 and 1570), Viscount Cantelupe (GB 1761), and Baron Buckhurst (UK 1864); er s of 10 Earl De La Warr, DL (d 1988); *b* 10 April 1948; *Educ* Eton; *m* 1978, Anne, *née* Leveson, former w of Earl of Hopetoun (s of 3 Marq of Linlithgow); 2 s (William Herbrand Thomas, Lord Buckhurst b 1979, Hon Edward b 1980); *Heir* s, Lord Buckhurst; *Career* farmer and stockbroker; Mullens & Co 1976–81, Credit Lyonnais Securities 1981–2004,

D

dir Shore Capital Stockbrokers 2004–; jt pres Youth Clubs Sussex, pres Bowles Rock Outwards Bound Centre; patron De La Warr Pavilion Tst; tstee: Retraining of Racehorses, Moorcroft Racehorse Welfare Centre; *Recreations* country pursuits; *Clubs* White's, Turf; *Style*— The Rt Hon the Earl De La Warr; ✉ Buckhurst Park, Withyham, East Sussex TN7 4BL; 14 Bourne Street, London SW1W 8JU

de LACY, Richard Michael; QC (2000); *b* 4 December 1954; *Educ* Hymers Coll Hull, Clare Coll Cambridge (open scholar, MA); *m* 1980 (m dis 2003), Sybil, *née* del Strother; 1s, 2 da; *Career* called to the Bar Middle Temple 1976 (Harmsworth scholar), bencher 2001; in practice Chancery Bar 1978–; practising arbitrator 1991–; memb: Panel Practice Regulation Review Ctee ICAEW 1997–2003, Tbnl Panel Accountancy and Actuarial Disciplinary Bd 2005–; hon treas Barristers' Benevolent Assoc 1989–99 (memb Ctee 1984–89); chm Endeavour Trg 2004– (hon treas 2001–04), memb Cncl Royal Br Legion Poppy Factory 2005–; accredited mediator CEDR 1997; FCIArb 1991; *Publications* Precedents of Pleadings (specialist ed, 16 edn 2007); articles on property law and arbitration; *Recreations* music, equestrianism, modern history; *Clubs* Travellers; *Style*— Richard de Lacy, Esq, QC; ✉ 9 Devereux Court, London WC2R 3JJ; 3 Stone Buildings Lincoln's Inn WC2A 3XL (tel 020 7242 4937, fax 020 7405 3896, e-mail rdelacy@3sb.law.co.uk)

de LANDTSHEER, Jan; s of Karel de Landtsheer (d 1971), of Antwerp, and Virginia, *née* Petre; *b* 27 December 1950; *Educ* KA Antwerp, RUC Antwerp (BA), Vrije Universiteit Brussel (MSc); *m* Christine, *née* Schaeken; *Career* Vrije Universiteit Brussel: res asst 1973, teaching asst 1979; publisher De Sikkel 1979, publishing ed Wiley Europe 1992, sr publishing ed Wiley 1997–; memb: Int Assoc of Computational Mechanics 1992, Euromech 1997; *Recreations* long distance swimming and running, sea sailing, saxophone-playing in concert bands; *Clubs* Trinity Triathlon (Littlehampton), Bognor Regis Concert Band, Harmonie Sainte Jeanne-d'Arc (France); *Style*— Jan de Landtsheer, Esq; ✉ John Wiley & Sons, Baffins Lane, Chichester, West Sussex PO19 1UD (tel 01243 70 147, e-mail jdelandt@wiley.co.uk)

de LANGE, (Rabbi) Prof Nicholas Robert Michael; s of George Douglas de Lange, of London, and Elaine, *née* Jacobus; *b* 7 August 1944; *Educ* ChCh Oxford (MA, DPhil, James Mew Rabbinic Hebrew prize), Leo Baeck Coll London (Rabbinic Dip); *Career* Parkes Library fell Univ of Southampton 1969–71; Univ of Cambridge: lectr in Rabbinics 1971–95, fell Wolfson Coll 1984–, reader in Hebrew and Jewish studies 1995–2001, prof of Hebrew and Jewish Studies 2001–; memb: Br Assoc for Jewish Studies 1974– (past pres), Cncl Jewish Historical Soc of England 1975–, Ctee The Translators Assoc 1990–93 and 1998–2001 (chm 2001), Soc of Authors; founding ed (with Judith Humphrey) Bulletin of Judeo-Greek Studies 1987–; *Books* Origen and the Jews (1976), Apocrypha - Jewish Literature of the Hellenistic Age (1978), Origène - Philocalie 1–20 (with Marguerite Harl, 1983), Atlas of the Jewish World (1984), Judaism (1986, 2 edn 2003), Greek Jewish Texts from the Cairo Genizah (1996), Illustrated History of the Jewish People (ed, 1997), An Introduction to Judaism (2000), Hebrew Scholarship and the Medieval World (ed, 2001); many literary translations; author of numerous articles in jls and pubns; *Style*— Prof Nicholas de Lange; ✉ Faculty of Divinity, West Road, Cambridge CB3 9BS (tel 01223 763002, fax 01223 763003)

de LASZLO, Damon Patrick; only s of Patrick David de Laszlo (d 1980), and Deborah, *née* Greenwood (d 1980), da of 1 Viscount Greenwood PC, KC, and gs of Philip de Laszlo (d 1937), the portrait painter; *b* 8 October 1942; *Educ* Gordonstoun; *m* 1972, Hon Sandra Daphne, da of 2 Baron Hacking (d 1971); 1 da (Lucy b 1975), 2 s (Robert b 1977, William b 1979); *Career* co dir Trust Co of the West Inc (USA) 1980–; chm Economic Res Cncl 1980–, chm Harwin plc; dir INTELLECT (industry body for IT, telecoms and electronics in the UK) 2002–06; *Recreations* shooting, scuba diving, economics; *Clubs* Boodle's, City of London, East India, RGS; *Style*— Damon de Laszlo, Esq; ✉ A2 Albany, Piccadilly, London W1J 0AL (tel 020 7437 1982); Pelham Place, Newton Valence, Alton, Hampshire GU34 3NQ (tel 01420 588212)

de LISI, Benedetto (Ben); s of Vincent Michael de Lisi, of Long Island, NY, and Palma Aida, *née* Afflitto; *b* 31 May 1955; *Educ* Hauppauge HS Long Island NY, Suffolk Community Coll Long Island NY, Pratt Inst of Fine Arts Brooklyn NY; *Career* fashion designer; fndr: Benedetto Inc menswear 1980–82, Ci Boure restaurant Belgravia (with ptnr J L Journade) 1982, Benedetto Ltd producing Ben de Lisi label 1982–91; fndr dir BDL (Design) Ltd 1991–; first London shop opened 1998; IWS Freestyle Awards 1987, nominated Most Innovative Designer of the Year 1990, winner Glamour category British Fashion Awards 1994 and 1995 (nominated 1992), nominated Glamour Awards in 1996, 1997 and 1998; *Style*— Ben de Lisi, Esq; ✉ 40 Elizabeth Street, London SW1W 9NZ (tel 020 7730 2994, e-mail feedback@bendelisi.com)

DE L'ISLE, 2 Viscount (UK 1956), of Penshurst, Co Kent; Maj Philip John Algernon Sidney; 10 Bt (UK 1806), of Castle Goring, Co Sussex, and 8 Bt (UK 1818), of Penshurst Place, Co Kent; MBE (1977), DL (Kent 1996); also Baron De L'Isle and Dudley (UK 1835); o s of 1 Viscount De L'Isle, VC, KG, GCMG, GCVO, PC (d 1991), and his 1 w, Hon Jacqueline Corinne Yvonne, *née* Vereker (d 1962), da of FM 6 Viscount Gort, VC, GCB, CBE, DSO, MVO, MC; *b* 21 April 1945; *Educ* Tabley House Cheshire; *m* 15 Nov 1980, Isobel Tresyllian, da of Sir Edmund Gerald Compton, GCB, KBE; 1 da (Hon Sophia Jacqueline Mary b 25 March 1983), 1 s (Hon Philip William Edmund b 2 April 1985); *Heir* s, Hon Philip Sidney; *Career* cmmnd Grenadier Gds 1966, served BAOR, NI and Belize, GSO3 Ops/SD HQ 3 Inf Bde NI 1974–76, ret 1979; Hon Col 5 Bn Princess of Wales Royal Regt (Queen's and Royal Hampshires) 1992–99; farmer and landowner; Vice Lord-Lt Kent 2002–; memb Lord Chllr's Advsy Cncl on Nat Records and Archives 2004–; Hon Col Kent Army Cadet Force (KACF) 2006–; Freeman City of London, Liveryman Worshipful Co of Goldsmiths; *Clubs* White's, Pratt's; *Style*— The Viscount De L'Isle, MBE, DL; ✉ Penshurst Place, Penshurst, Tonbridge, Kent TN11 8DG (tel 01892 870307, fax 01892 870866, e-mail delisle@penshurstplace.com, website www.penshurstplace.com)

de LISLE, Timothy John March Phillipps (Tim); s of Everard de Lisle, DL (d 2003), of Stockerston, Leics, and Hon Mary Rose, *née* Peake, da of 1 Viscount Ingleby (d 1966); *b* 25 June 1962; *Educ* Eton, Worcester Coll Oxford (exhibitioner, BA); *m* 1991, Amanda, da of Clive Barford, of Aldworth, Berks; 1 s (Daniel b 24 Jan 1994), 1 da (Laura b 20 April 1998); *Career* freelance journalist 1979–86, fndr Undergraduate Tutors 1983–87; The Daily Telegraph: diary reporter 1986–87, chief rock critic 1986–89, gen reporter 1987, news feature writer 1987–89, ed Weekend Section 1989–90; arts ed The Times 1989; The Independent on Sunday: cricket corr 1990–91, arts ed 1991–95; freelance arts and sports writer 1995– (cricket columnist The Independent 1995–96 and 1999–2000, and Evening Standard 1997–98, arts feature writer The Daily Telegraph, rock critic The Mail on Sunday 1999–); ed Wisden Cricket Monthly 1996–2000, ed Wisden.com website 1999–, ed Wisden Cricketers' Almanack 2003; Editor of The Year (Special Interest Magazines) Br Society of Magazine Editors 1999; memb NUJ 1983–; *Publications* Lives of the Great Songs (ed, 1994, revised and expanded edn 1995); *Recreations* swimming, television, books, photography; *Clubs* Cricket Writers', Eton Ramblers; *Style*— Tim de Lisle, Esq; ✉ c/o Wisden, 136 Bramley Road, London W10 6SR (tel 020 7565 3114, fax 020 7565 3051)

DE LYON, Hilary Barbara; da of Leonard John De Lyon (d 1984), and Margaret Vera De Lyon; *b* 8 April 1956, Epsom, Surrey; *Educ* Rosebery GS Epsom, Univ of Liverpool (BA, MPhil); *m* 1, 5 Aug 1978 (m dis), Stephen Williams; m 2, 3 May 1997, Martin Webster; *Career* lectr in English and drama Milton Keynes Coll 1980–83, educn/equal opportunities policy offr NUT 1983–86, princ policy offr (educn) Assoc of Metropolitan Authorities 1986–94, asst educn offr London Borough of Sutton (secondment) 1992–93, sec (conduct and admin) Lord Chllr's Advsy Ctee on Legal Educn and Conduct 1994–99; chief exec: Soc of Chiropodists and Podiatrists 1999–2002, RCGP 2002–; co-fndr: Labour Women's Network, Emily's List UK; memb ACEVO 1999; former memb: First Division Assoc Equal Opportunities Cttee, Soc of Educn Offrs Equal Opportunities Cttee, Fawcett Soc Educn Cttee; chair Friends of Castle Acre Church; former sch govr; *Publications* Women Teachers: Issues and Experiences (co-ed, 1989), The Good Employers' Guide: An essential guide for school governors (1998), Production Values: Futures for Professionalism (contrib, 2006); columnist Podiatry Now 1999–2002; contrib: The New Generalist, British Journal of General Practice 2002–; various pubns on educn and equal opportunities 1984–1994; *Recreations* theatre, opera, chamber music, gardens and gardening; *Clubs* RSM; *Style*— Ms Hilary De Lyon; ✉ Royal College of General Practitioners, 14 Princes Gate, Hyde Park, London SW7 1PU (tel 020 7581 3232, fax 020 7225 2389, e-mail hdelyon@rcgp.org.uk)

de MAULEY, 7 Baron (UK 1838); Rupert Charles Ponsonby; TD (1988); s of Hon Thomas Maurice Ponsonby, TD (d 2001), and Maxine Henrietta, *née* Thellusson; suc unc, 6 Baron de Mauley, 2002; *b* 30 June 1957, Oxford; *Educ* Eton; *m* 2002, Hon Lucinda Katherine Fanshawe Royle, da of Baron Fanshawe of Richmond, KCMG (Life Peer, d 2001); *Heir* bro, Hon George Ponsonby; *Career* dir: Samuel Montagu & Co Ltd 1990–93, Standard Chartered Merchant Bank Asia Ltd Singapore 1994–99 (md 1996–99), FixIT Worldwide Ltd 1999–2006; CO Royal Wessex Yeo (TA) 2003–04 (cmmnd 1976); oppn whip and DTI spokesman House of Lords and shadow min Cabinet Office; FCA 1990 (ACA 1980); *Style*— The Rt Hon the Lord de Mauley, TD

de MILLE, His Hon Judge Peter Noël; s of Noël James de Mille (d 1995), and Ailsa Christine de Mille, *née* Ogilvie (d 2002); *b* 19 November 1944; *Educ* Fettes, Trinity Coll Dublin (BA, LLB); *m* 17 Dec 1977, Angela Mary, da of Peter Cooper; 1 da (Charlotte Elizabeth b 17 June 1981); *Career* called to the Bar Inner Temple 1968; recorder of Crown Court (Midland & Oxford Circuit) 1987–92, circuit judge (Midland & Oxford Circuit) 1992–2002, circuit judge (SE Circuit) 2002–; *Recreations* music, theatre, sailing; *Clubs* Aldeburgh Yacht; *Style*— His Hon Judge de Mille; ✉ Peterborough Crown and County Court, Crown Building, Rivergate, Peterborough PE1 1EJ (tel 01733 349161)

de MOLLER, June Frances; *b* 25 June 1947; *Educ* Roedean, Hastings Coll, Sorbonne; *m* 1967 (m dis 1980); m 2, 1996, J R Giles Crisp; *Career* md Carlton Communications plc 1993–99 (dir 1983–99); non-exec dir: Anglian Water plc 1992–99, Riverside Mental Health NHS Trust 1992–96, Lynx Gp plc1999–2002, Cookson Gp plc 1999–2004, British Telecommunications plc 1999–2002, J Sainsbury plc 1999–2005, Archant Ltd 2002– (non-exec dir Eastern Counties Newspapers Gp 1999–2002), London Merchant Securities plc 2002–07, Temple Bar Investment Tst plc 2005–, Derwent London plc 2007–; memb: Advsy Bd Judge Inst Mgmnt Studies 1996–2003, Home of Rest for Horses 1999–2005, Cncl Aldeburgh Productions 2000–, Cncl UEA 2002–; *Recreations* reading, tennis, the arts, breeding Red Poll Cattle; *Style*— Mrs June de Moller

DE NARDIS DI PRATA, Mainardo; s of Balduccio de Nardis di Prata, of London, and Simonetta Vallarino Gancia; *b* 24 November 1960; *Educ* Aiglon Coll Switzerland, Bedales, Univ Bocconi Milan (Economics); *m* 2 July 1988, Cristiana Clerici di Cavenago; 2 s (Alberico b 14 Feb 1992, Gherardo b 14 March 1994); *Career* McCann Erickson Rome 1980–81, Young and Rubicam Milan 1981–85, fndr ptnr of advtg agency Alberto Cremona 1985–87, vice-chm Medianetwork Group Italy 1987–93 (merged with CIA Group plc 1993), chm MNI (Assoc of Euro Media Independents) 1988–93, ceo CIA Medianetwork Europe Holdings and chm various gp cos in Europe 1993–; exec dir F.lli Gancia & C SpA Canelli Italy; *Books* La Mappa dei Media in Europa (The Map of European Media) (1994); *Recreations* ski, sailing, classic cars; *Clubs* Il Clubino Milan Italy (affiliated to Boodle's London); *Style*— Mainardo de Nardis di Prata, Esq; ✉ 111 Old Church Street, London SW3 6DX (tel 020 7352 6340, fax 020 7352 1287); Mediaedge:cia, 1 Paris Garden, London SE1 8NU (tel 020 7803 2254, fax 020 7803 2094, mobile 077 1017 1623, e-mail mdenardi@cia-group.com)

de NAVARRO, Michael Antony; QC (1990); s of Alma José Maria de Navarro (d 1979), of Broadway, Worcs, and Agnes Dorothy McKenzie, *née* Hoare (d 1987); *b* 1 May 1944; *Educ* Downside, Trinity Coll Cambridge (BA); *m* 20 Dec 1975, Jill Margaret, da of Charles Walker, of Southwell, Notts; 1 s (Antony Charles b 1980), 2 da (Katharine Mary b 1978, Frances Anne b 1982); *Career* called to the Bar Inner Temple 1968 (bencher 2000), recorder Western Circuit 1990–; chm Personal Injury Bar Assoc 1997–99; *Recreations* opera, cricket; *Clubs* MCC; *Style*— Michael de Navarro, QC; ✉ 2 Temple Gardens, Temple, London EC4Y 9AY (tel 020 7822 1200, fax 020 7822 1300, e-mail mdenavarro@2templegardens.co.uk)

de PASS, David Vincent Guy; s of Lt Cdr John Gerald Irvine de Pass, RN (d 1981), and Marie Elizabeth, *née* Eberhardt (d 1988); *b* 27 August 1949; *Educ* Harrow, Coll of Law, George Washington Univ (MCL), LSE (LLM); *Career* admitted slr 1973; admitted to the Bar of Dist of Columbia 1978, ptnr and head of private client dept Holman Fenwick & Willan 1986–2002, with Specialist Advice Dept Coutts & Co 2002–; pubns in law jls and magazines, contrib to legal precedents book; memb: Law Soc, Phi Delta Phi Legal Fraternity; *Recreations* cricket, philately, music; *Clubs* Harrovian Rifle Assoc, Harrow Wanderers, Hurlingham; *Style*— David de Pass, Esq

de PURY, Christopher Mark; s of Andrew de Pury, and Lois, *née* Costen; *b* 11 February 1968, London; *Educ* Aylesbury GS, ChCh Oxford (MA); *m* 5 Feb 2000, Carolyn, *née* Rice-Oxley; 2 s (Sebastian, Theo), 1 da (Olivia); *Career* ptnr Herbert Smith; tstee Stock Exchange Drama Soc; *Recreations* family, theatre, drama; *Style*— Christopher de Pury, Esq; ✉ c/o Herbert Smith, Exchange House, Primrose Street, London EC2A 2HS (tel 020 7466 2095, e-mail christopher.de-pury@herbertsmith.com)

de QUINCEY, Paul Morrison; s of Ronald Anthony de Quincey, and Margaret Winifred Claire, *née* Dingley (d 1990); *b* 23 June 1954; *Educ* Sutton HS Plymouth, Univ of Leeds (MA, PGCE); *m* 1 May 1976, Teresa Elizabeth Patricia, *née* Casabayo; 1 da (Lara Claire b 8 April 1983), 1 s (Thomas Anthony b 16 Oct 1985); *Career* English teacher Esan Teacher Trg Coll Nigeria 1976–78, English master Wakefield Girls' HS 1979–81; British Council: asst rep Korea 1981–84, conslt 1984–87, asst rep Algeria 1987–91, dep dir Czechoslovakia 1991–93, dir Venezuela 1993–98, dir Americas 1998–2000, dir UK 2000–02, dir GFS and memb Sr Mgmnt Team 2002–04, dir France 2004–; *Recreations* fishing, shooting, theatre; *Style*— Paul de Quincey, Esq; ✉ The British Council, 9 Rue de Constantine, 75340 Paris cedex 07, France

DE RAMSEY, 4 Baron (UK 1887); John Ailwyn Fellowes; DL (Cambs 1993); s of 3 Baron De Ramsey, KBE, TD, DL (d 1993), and Lilah Helen Suzanne, *née* Labouchere (d 1987); *b* 27 February 1942; *Educ* Winchester, Writtle Inst of Agric; *m* 1, 1973 (m dis 1983), Phyllida Mary, da of Philip Athelstan Forsyth; 1 s (Hon Freddie John b 1978); m 2, 1984, Alison Mary, er da of Sir Archibald Birkmyre, 3 Bt (d 2001); 1 s (Hon Charles Henry b 1986), 2 da (Hon Daisy Lilah b 1988, Hon Flora Mary b 1991); *Heir* s, Hon Freddie Fellowes; *Career* farmer; dir Cambridge Water Co 1974–94 (chm 1983–89), pres CLA 1991–93, Crown Estate cmmr 1994–2002, chm Environment Agency 1995–2000; pres RASE 2002–03; Hon DSc; FRAgS 1993; *Recreations* fishing; *Clubs* Boodle's; *Style*— The Rt Hon Lord De Ramsey, DL, FRAgS; ✉ Abbots Ripton Hall, Abbots Ripton, Huntingdon, Cambridgeshire PE28 2PQ

de RIVAZ, Vincent; s of François de Rivaz, and Isabelle de Buttet; *b* 4 October 1953; *Educ* Ecole Nationale Superieure d'Hydraulique de Grenoble; *m* 10 May 1980, Anne, *née* de Valence de Minardière; 3 c (Ailred b 5 June 1981, Albéric b 29 Oct 1982, Amaury b 22

April 1987); *Career* hydroelectric engr; EDF: joined External Engrg Centre 1977–, mangr Far East Div 1985–91, md Hydro Power Dept 1991–94, dep head Int Div and mangr New Projects Dept 1995–98, dep chief fin offr 1999–2000, head of strategy and fin 2000–03, chief exec London Electricity Gp (now EDF Energy) 2003– (memb Exec Ctee 2004–); Melchett Medal 2006; *Style*— Vincent de Rivaz, Esq; ✉ EDF Energy, 40 Grosvenor Place, London SW1X 7EN (tel 020 7752 2101, fax 020 7752 2104, e-mail vincent.de-rivaz@edfenergy.com)

de ROS, 28 Baron (E 1264); Peter Trevor Maxwell; Premier Baron of England; s of 27 Baroness de Ros (d 1983), and Cdr David Maxwell, RN; gs of Hon Mrs (Angela) Horn; *b* 23 December 1958; *Educ* Headfort Sch Kells, Stowe, Down HS Downpatrick; *m* 5 Sept 1987, Angela Siân, da of late Peter Campbell Ross; 1 s (Hon Finbar James b 14 Nov 1988), 2 da (Hon Katharine Georgiana b 26 Oct 1990, Hon Jessye Maeve b 8 July 1992); *Heir* s, Hon Finbar James Maxwell b 14 Nov 1988; *Style*— The Rt Hon the Lord de Ros

de ROTHSCHILD, Baron (Eric Alain Robert) David; s of Baron (James Gustave Jules) Alain de Rothschild (d 1982), and Mary Germaine, *née* Chauvin du Treuil; *b* 3 October 1940; *Educ* Lycée Janson de Sailly Paris, Polytechnicum of Zürich; *m* 21 Dec 1983, (Donna) Maria Beatrice, da of Don Alfonso Caracciolo di Forino (d 1990); 2 s (James Alain Robert Alexandro b 7 Dec 1985, Pietro Noè Genaro b 21 March 1991), 1 da (Anna Saskia Esther b 29 April 1987); *Career* managing ptnr Chateau Lafite Rothschild 1974–; chm: Paris Orleans SA 1975–, Rothschild Continuation Ltd London 1977–, N M Rothschild Asset Management Ltd London 1997– (dir 1989–), Rothschild Bank AG 2000–, N M Rothschild & Sons Ltd London 2004– (dir 1978–); ptnr Rothschild et Compagnie Banque 1987–; dir Chalone Inc San Francisco 1989–; *Style*— Baron David de Rothschild; ✉ Rothschild & Co Banque, 17 Avenue Matignon, 75008 Paris, France (tel 00 33 1 40 74 40 06, fax 00 33 1 40 74 98 16)

de ROTHSCHILD, Edmund Leopold; CBE (1997), VMH (2005), TD (and 2 Bars); s of Maj Lionel Nathan de Rothschild, OBE, JP (d 1942), of Exbury House, Exbury, nr Southampton, and Marie-Louise, *née* Beer; bro of Leopold de Rothschild, CBE, *qv*; *b* 2 January 1916; *Educ* Harrow, Trinity Coll Cambridge (MA); *m* 1, 22 June 1948, Elizabeth (d 1980), da of Marcel Lentner, of Vienna; 2 da (Katherine Juliette b 11 July 1949, Charlotte Henrietta b 28 Nov 1955), 2 s (Nicholas David b 10 Oct 1951, David Lionel (twin) b 28 Nov 1955); m 2, 26 April 1982, Anne Evelyn, JP, widow of J Malcolm Harrison, OBE; *Career* Maj RA (TA), served WWII, BEF, BNAF, CMF, France, N Africa, Italy (wounded); merchant banker; dir Rothschild Continuation Ltd 1975–95 (ptnr 1946, sr ptnr 1960–70, chm 1970–75); chm AUR Hydropower Ltd 1980–91; dep chm British Newfoundland Corp Canada 1963–69 (dir 1953–63); dep chm Churchill Falls (Labrador) Corp (Canada) 1966–69; pres Assoc of Jewish Ex-Servicemen and Women, fndr Res into Ageing; HM Govt tstee Freedom from Hunger Campaign 1965–97, vice-pres Queens Nursing Inst; memb: Asia Ctee BNEC 1970–71 (chm 1971), Cncl Royal Nat Pension Fund for Nurses until 1996; Victoria Medal of Honour (VMH) RHS 2005; Freeman City of London, Liveryman Worshipful Co of Fishmongers 1949; Hon LLD Memorial Univ of Newfoundland 1961, Hon DSc Univ of Salford 1983; Order of the Sacred Treasure (first class) Japan 1973; *Books* Window on the World (1949), A Gilt Edged Life (memoir, 1998); *Recreations* fishing, gardening; *Clubs* White's, Portland; *Style*— Edmund de Rothschild, Esq, CBE, TD; ✉ New Court, St Swithin's Lane, London EC4P 4DU (tel 020 7280 5000); Exbury House, Exbury, Southampton, Hampshire SO45 1AF (tel 023 8089 1203)

de ROTHSCHILD, Leopold David; CBE (1985), RD; 2 s of Maj Lionel de Rothschild, OBE, MP (d 1942); bro of Edmund de Rothschild, CBE, TD, *qv*; *b* 12 May 1927; *Educ* Harrow, Trinity Coll Cambridge; *Career* dir: Sun Alliance & London Insurance 1982–95, Bank of England 1970–83, N M Rothschild & Sons 1970–; pres: English Chamber Orchestra and Music Soc Ltd 2001–, Bach Choir 2002–; tstee: Glyndebourne Arts Tst 1975–97, Nat Museum of Sci and Industry 1987–97; chm Cncl Royal Coll of Music 1988–99; memb Cncl Winston Churchill Meml Tst 1990–2000; Hon DUniv York 1991; Liveryman Worshipful Co of Musicians; FRCM; Order of Francisco de Miranda 1 class (Venezuela) 1978, Gran Oficial Order de Merito (Chile) 1993, Ordem Nacional Do Cruzeiro Do Sul (Brazil) 1993, Order of the Aztec Eagle Encomienda (Mexico) 1994; *Style*— Leopold de Rothschild Esq, CBE, RD; ✉ N M Rothschild & Sons, New Court, St Swithin's Lane, London EC4P 4DU (tel 020 7280 5000, fax 020 7220 7543)

de SALIS, 9 Count (Holy Roman Empire 1748, cr by Francis I); John Bernard Philip Humbert de Salis; TD; also Hereditary Knight of the Golden Spur (1571); s of 8 Count de Salis (Lt-Col Irish Gds, d 1949), of Lough Gur, Co Limerick, and (Mary) Camilla, *née* Presti di Camarda (d 1953); descended from Peter, 1 Count de Salis-Soglio (1675–1749), Envoy of the Grisons Republic to Queen Anne; Jerome, 2 Count de Salis, was naturalised Br by Act of Parliament 1731 following his marriage to Mary, da and co-heiress of the last Viscount Fane; an earlier member of the family, Feldzeugmeister Rudolph von Salis, was cr a Baron of the HRE by the Emperor Rudolf II in 1582 for gallantry against the Turks; through Sophia, da of Adm Francis William Drake, w of Jerome, 4 Count de Salis, the family is heir-gen of Sir Francis Drake; the 8 Count's mother was Princess Hélène de Riquet, da of Prince Eugène de Caraman-Chimay (Prince of Chimay 1527 HRE by Maximilian I, Belgium 1889 by Leopold II), who was a descendant of Jean de Croy killed at Agincourt 1415 and gs of Thérèse de Cabarrus (Madame Tallien); *b* 16 November 1947; *Educ* Downside, CCC Cambridge (LLM); *m* 1, 1973 (m dis and annulled); m 2, Marie-Claude, 3 da of Col René-Henri Wüst, Swiss Army, of Zürich and Geneva; 1 s (Count John-Maximilian Henry b 3 Nov 1986), 2 da (Countess Lara, Countess Camilla (twins) b 20 Dec 1995); *Heir* s, Count John-Maximilian de Salis; *Career* late Brevet Maj 9/12 Royal Lancers (Prince of Wales's), special offr Panzergrenadiers Swiss Army; called to the Bar Gray's Inn; delegate Int Ctee Red Cross Missions in Middle East, Africa, head of delgn Iraq 1980–81, Thailand 1981–84, special envoy in Lebanon 1982; ptnr Gautier Salis et Cie Geneva 1989–96, vice-chm Bank Lips Zurich 1996–98, md European Capital Partners (Switzerland) SA 1999–, dir Amadeus SA Geneva 2000–; ambass of the Order of Malta: to Thailand 1986–98, to Cambodia 1993–98; pres Swiss Assoc of the Order of Malta 1995–2000, pres Comité International de l'Ordre de Malte (CIOMAL) 2000–; Gold Medal with Swords (Beirut) 1982, Knight of Justice Constantinian Order of St George, Knight Grand Cross Order of the White Elephant (Thailand), Knight Grand Cross of the Order of Merit of the Order of Malta with Swords, Knight Grand Cross of Honour and Devotion Sov Mil Order of Malta 2000 (Knight 1974); *Recreations* melancholia; *Clubs* Cavalry and Guards', Beefsteak, Cercle de la Terasse (Geneva), Royal Bangkok Sports; *Style*— The Count de Salis, TD; ✉ Maison du Bailli, CH-1422 Grandson, Switzerland (tel 00 41 24 445 1466, fax 00 41 24 445 3403, e-mail john.de.salis@worldcom.ch)

de SAUMAREZ, 7 Baron (UK 1831); Sir Eric Douglas Saumarez; er twin s of 6 Baron de Saumarez (d 1991), and Joan Beryl (Julia), *née* Charlton (d 2004); *b* 13 August 1956; *Educ* Milton Abbey, Univ of Nottingham, RAC Cirencester; *m* 1, 14 July 1982 (m dis 1990), Christine Elizabeth, yr da of Bernard Neil Halliday, OBE, of Woodford Green, Essex; 2 da (Claire b 1984, Emily b 1985); m 2, 4 Sept 1991, Susan, *née* Hearn; *Heir* bro, Hon Victor Saumarez; *Career* farmer; *Recreations* shooting, fishing, flying; *Style*— The Rt Hon the Lord de Saumarez; ✉ Les Beaucamps de Bas, Cbtel, Guernsey GY5 7PE

de SAVARY, Peter John; *Educ* Charterhouse; *m* 1 (m dis), Marcia (now Hon Lady (John) Astor); 2 da (Lisa, Nicola); m 2 (m dis), Alice, *née* Simms; m 3, (Lucille Lana), *née* Paton; 3 da (Tara, Amber, Savannah); *Career* entrepreneur (petroleum, property and maritime interests); America's Cup challenger 1983 and 1987; chm The Carnegie Club; Tourism Personality of the Year (English Tourist Bd) 1988; *Recreations* sailing, riding, carriage driving; *Clubs* Royal Thames Yacht, Royal Burnham Yacht, Royal Torbay Yacht, Royal Corinthian Yacht, New York Yacht, Carnegie (fndr and chm); *Style*— Peter de Savary Esq; ✉ Carnegie Club, 69 Cadogan Gardens, London SW3 2RB

de SEGUNDO, Karen Maria Alida; da of Gerard Jacobus Platerink (d 1995), and Hendrika Alida, *née* Bolk; *b* 12 December 1946, The Hague; *Educ* Leiden Univ (LLM), Michigan State Univ (MBA); *m* 29 Nov 1975, William Nigel de Segundo; 3 s (Charles Sempill b 15 Dec 1977, Robert Daniell b 23 April 1980, Julian William Alexander b 8 May 1986); *Career* Royal Dutch Shell 1971–2005; dir Merril Lynch New Energy Technology plc 2000–, memb Supervisory Bd Koninklijke Ahold 2004–, dir Poÿry Oyj 2005–, non-exec dir Lonmin plc 2005–, non-exec dir Ensus Ltd 2006–, memb Eco Advsy Bd General Electric Co; memb Advsy Cncl Anglo Netherlands Soc; *Style*— Mrs Karen de Segundo; ✉ Lonmin plc, 4 Grosvenor Place, London SW1X 7YL

D

de SILVA, (George) Desmond Lorenz; QC (1984); s of Edmund Frederick Lorenz de Silva, MBE (d 1994), and Esme Norah Gregg de Silva (d 1982); *b* 13 December 1939; *Educ* privately; *m* 5 Dec 1987, HRH Princess Katarina of Yugoslavia, o da of HRH Prince Tomislav of Yugoslavia, and HGDH Princess Margarita of Baden, and ggggda of Queen Victoria; 1 da (Victoria Marie Esme Margarita b 6 Sept 1991); *Career* called to the Bar: Middle Temple 1964, Sierra Leone 1968, Gambia 1981, Gibraltar 1992, Botswana 2001; dep circuit judge 1976–80, head of chambers 1987–; dep chief prosecutor UN War Crimes Tbnl Sierra Leone 2002 (at level of asst sec-gen of UN), prosecutor (at level of under sec-gen of UN) 2005, UNDP envoy to Belgrade 2005; memb: Home Affrs Standing Ctee Bow Gp 1982, Editorial Advsy Bd Crossbow 1984; vice-pres St John Ambulance London (Prince of Wales Dist) 1984–; councilman City of London (Ward of Farringdon Without) 1980–95; landowner (Taprobane Island in the Indian Ocean); memb Racehorse Owners Assoc; patron Memorial Gates Tst; Freeman City of London, Liveryman Worshipful Co of Gunmakers; KStJ 1994 (CStJ 1985, OStJ 1980); *Recreations* politics, shooting, travel; *Clubs* Brooks's, Carlton, Naval and Military, Orient (Colombo); *Style*— Desmond de Silva Esq, QC; ✉ Marlands House, Itchingfield, Horsham, West Sussex RH13 0NN; Taprobane Island, Weligama Bay, Weligama, Sri Lanka; 2 Paper Buildings, Temple, London EC4Y 7ET (tel 020 7556 5500)

de SILVA, Harendra Aneurin Domingo; QC (1995); s of Annesley de Silva (d 1978), of Colombo, Sri Lanka, and Maharani of Porbandar (d 1989); *b* 29 September 1945; *Educ* Millfield, Queens' Coll Cambridge (MA, LLM); *m* 10 June 1972, Indira; 1 da (Ayesha Annette b 30 July 1975), 1 s (Nihal Ceri b 17 Jan 1979); *Career* called to the Bar Middle Temple 1970 (bencher); recorder of the Crown Court; *Recreations* golf, bridge, tennis; *Clubs* Roehampton, Oxford and Cambridge; *Style*— Harendra de Silva, Esq, QC; ✉ 2 Paper Buildings, Temple, London EC4Y 7ET (tel 020 7556 5500)

DE SILVA, Dr Stephanie Gwendoline; da of Muthumadinage Piyasena (d 1990), of Sri Lanka, and Esther, *née* Dabare (d 1989); *b* 11 December 1938; *Educ* Methodist Coll Colombo Sri Lanka, Med Sch Univ of Colombo Sri Lanka; *m* 19 Oct 1967, Ariyapala De Silva, s of K A De Silva (d 1971), of Sri Lanka; 1 da (Gitanjali Tania b Aug 1968); *Career* conslt psychiatrist Hounslow and Spelthorne Community Tst (based West Middlesex Hosp Isleworth) 1981–2000, ret (sr registrar 1978–80); clinical tutor and regnl tutor for NW Thames RHA 1985, lead clinician Learning Disability Serv Hounslow and Spelthorne Community Mental Health Tst 1999–2000, locum conslt psychiatrist Hounslow and Spelthorne Community and Mental Health Tst 2000–; chairperson Med Exec Ctee Leavesden Hosp 1988; NHS Meritorious Service Award 1991; MRCPsych, FRCPsych 1992; *Style*— Dr Stephanie De Silva; ✉ Flat 7, Greville Lodge, Woodside Park Road, London N12 8RJ

de SOUZA, Christopher Edward; s of Denis Walter de Souza (d 2002), and Dorothy Edna, *née* Woodman (d 1984); *b* 6 June 1943; *Educ* Prior Park Coll Bath, Univ of Bristol, Old Vic Theatre Sch Bristol; *m* 1971 (m dis 1981), Robyn Ann Williams; partner, Elinor Ann Kelly; 2 s (Tristan Edward b 17 June 1987, Sebastian Denis b 19 April 1993); *Career* broadcaster, also composer, opera producer and director; head of music St Bernadette's Sch Bristol 1966–70, staff prodr Sadler's Wells/ENO 1971–75, arts prodr BBC Radio London 1975–79, music prodr BBC Radio 3 1980–86, prodr BBC Promenade Concerts 1987–88, presenter BBC Radio 3 1988–, own prog Tuning Up focusing on young musicians 1990–92, awarded NY Radio Show Silver Medal 1992), artistic dir Southern Sinfonia 1998–; fndr dir Liszt Festival of London 1977; prodr of over 100 operas for BBC Radio, Abbey Opera, Northern Ireland Opera, Handel Opera, Opera East, Royal Coll of Music, Aldeburgh Festival, Bologna Festival, Kraków Festival and Miami Festival; dir Br stage premières of: Liszt's Don Sanche 1977, Virgil Thompson's The Mother of Us All 1979, Pfitzner's Palestrina 1983, Gretry's William Tell 1984; regular competition adjudicator, contributed articles to The Listener, Music and Musicians, Musical Times, The Strad, BBC Proms Guides; chm: SE Branch Composers' Guild of GB 1974–76, AVANTI (agency for young musicians) 1985–91; memb: Park Lane Group 1984–92, Redcliffe Concerts 1985–90, British Youth Opera 1986–99; memb: Equity, Br Acad of Composers and Songwriters, Performing Rights Soc, Royal Soc of Musicians, Royal Phiharmonic Soc, Liszt Soc; *Compositions* incl: 8 Epithalamia for Organ (1966–71), Sonata for Flute and Piano (1974), Maharajahs (music for BBC2 series), Four Brecht Songs (1991), Six-foot Cinderella (music for BBC2), Symphonic Suite from Britten's music for The Rescue, The Ides of March (a capella, 1993), Children of the Light (with Adrian Morris, 2001), Missa Douensis (2003); *Recordings* incl first modern prodn of Liszt's opera Don Sanche (BBC Studio Recording with BBC Scottish Symphony Orch); *Books* A Child's Guide to Looking at Music (1980); *Recreations* entertaining, travel, languages, painting, drawing; *Clubs* Royal Over-Seas League; *Style*— Christopher de Souza, Esq; ✉ Westbrook Farm Cottage, Boxford, Newbury, Berkshire RG20 8DL (tel and fax 01488 608010, e-mail chris@chrisdesouza.co.uk)

de SOUZA, Howard Gareth; s of Joseph Anthony de Souza, and Rose de Souza; *b* 1 October 1956; *Educ* Watford Boys' GS, Lancaster Univ (BSc); *m* 1995, Nicole, *née* Stalker; 1 s (Joseph), 1 da (Kitty); *Career* State of the Art London 1982–85, Burson Marsteller London 1985–89, Bell Pottinger Communications 1989–2000, Ogilvy Public Relations Worldwide 2000–02, currently with The Seven Partnership; *Recreations* enjoying myself; *Style*— Howard de Souza, Esq

DE STEMPEL, Sophie Christina; da of Baron Michael De Stempel, of Crosfield Road, Hampstead, and Cristina MacDonald; *b* 31 December 1960; *Educ* Lady Eden's Sch London, Convent of the Sacred Heart Woldingham, City and Guilds Sch of Art Kennington; *m* 2003, Sir Ian Holm, *qv*; *Career* artist; exhibitions incl: Gallery 24 Powis Terrace 1985, Conway Hall 1986, Albemarle Gallery 1987, The Mall Galleries 1988, and many mixed shows; most important works: The Unmade Bed 1986 (Saatchi collection), Profile of Gillian Melling 1988 (Catherine Parma collection), interior 1989 (Berry collection), Interior Bathroom 1989 (Saatchi collection), India Jane Birley 1990 (Pigoztsi collection), India Jane in an Interior 1990–91 (Saatchi collection); currently prof The Prince's Drawing Sch; *Style*— Sophie De Stempel

de SWIET, Prof Michael; s of John de Swiet (d 2001), of Trewen Pentrych, Cardiff, and Mary Marguerite, *née* Smith (d 2002); *b* 15 August 1941; *Educ* Cheltenham Coll, Univ of Cambridge (MD); *m* 12 Sept 1964, (Eleanor) Jane de Swiet, da of Richard Miles Hawkins, of Broadwas-on-Teme, Worcs; 1 da (Harriet Kate b Aug 1968), 2 s (Thomas Michael b 12 May 1970, Charles Richard John b 12 Dec 1972); *Career* SHO Nat Hosp for Nervous Diseases 1968; UCH: house physician 1966–67, SHO 1967–68, res fell 1968–70; res fell Univ of Calif San Francisco 1970–71, registrar Radcliffe Infirmary Oxford 1971–73; conslt physician Queen Charlotte's Hosp, UCH and Whittington Hosp 1973–; prof of obstetric medicine Imperial Coll Sch of Med London; *Books* Basic Science in Obstetrics

Gynaecology (co-ed, 3 edn 2002), Medical Disorders in Obstetric Practice (4 edn, 2002); *Recreations* the arts, gardening, woodwork, walking; *Style*— Prof Michael de Swiet; ✉ 60 Hornsey Lane, London N6 5LU; Institute of Reproductive and Developmental Biology, Queen Charlotte's Hospital, Hammersmith Campus, Du Cane Road, London W12 0NN (tel 020 7594 2151, fax 020 7594 2154, e-mail m.deswiet@imperial.ac.uk)

de THAME, Rachel; da of Michael Cohen, and Ghita Cohen, of Hadley Wood, Herts; *Educ* Royal Ballet Sch, City Lit Inst, English Gardening Sch; *m* 1, 1986, Stephen Colover; 1 da (Lauren Lucy b 1989), 1 s (Joseph David Simon b 1991); m 2, 1999, Gerard de Thame; 1 da (Emma Grace b 2004); *Career* TV presenter and writer; previously fashion model and actress, film credits incl Merlin and Bodywork; contrib: Daily Telegraph, The Guardian, Gardeners' World Magazine, Garden News, New Eden; *Television* for BBC: Gardeners' World 1999–, Small Town Gardens 2001, Going for a Song 2001, Call My Bluff 2002, Gardening with the Experts 2003; Heart of the Country (ITV) 1999; *Books* Small Town Gardens (2001), Rachel de Thame's Top 100 Star Plants (2002), Gardening with the Experts (jtly, 2003); *Recreations* reading, theatre, antiques, country walks; *Style*— Mrs Rachel de Thame; ✉ c/o Hilary Murray-Watts, Arlington Enterprises Ltd, 1–3 Charlotte Street, London W1T 1RD (tel 020 7580 0702, fax 020 7580 4994, website www.arlingtonenterprises.co.uk); c/o Luigi Bonomi, Sheil Land Associates Ltd, 43 Doughty Street, London WC1N 2LH (tel 020 7405 9351, fax 020 7831 2127, e-mail info@sheilland.co.uk)

de TRAFFORD, Sir Dermot Humphrey; 6 Bt (UK 1841), of Trafford Park, Lancs; VRD; s of Sir Rudolph Edgar Francis de Trafford, 5 Bt, OBE (d 1983), and his 1 w, June Isabel, MBE (d 1977), only da of Lt-Col Reginald Chaplin; *b* 19 January 1925; *Educ* Harrow, ChCh Oxford (MA); *m* 1, 26 June 1948 (m dis 1973), Patricia Mary, o da of late Francis Mycroft Beeley, of Long Crumples, Hants; 6 da (Mary Annette b 1949, Elizabeth Eugenie (Mrs John A Langdon) b 1951, Patricia Clare (Mrs P W U Corbett) b 1955, Victoria Mary (Mrs Andrew Roberts) b 1958, (Cynthia) June Bernadette (Mrs Nicholas C Kirkman) b 1958, (Antonia) Lucy Octavia (Mrs David Carotti) b 1966), 3 s (John Humphrey b 1950, Edmund Francis b 1952, Gerard Thomas Joseph b 1968); m 2, 1974, Xandra Carandini (d 2002), da of Lt-Col Geoffrey Trollope Lee, and former w of Roderick Walter (d 1996); *Heir* s, John de Trafford; *Career* md GHP Group Ltd 1961 (chm 1966–77), dep chm Imperial Continental Gas Assoc 1972–87 (dir 1963–87), chm Low & Bonar plc 1982–90 (dep chm 1980); vice-pres IOD 1993–95 (formerly chm); CIMgt, FRSA; *Recreations* grandchildren; *Clubs* White's, Royal Ocean Racing; *Style*— Sir Dermot de Trafford, Bt, VRD; ✉ 1 Ropers Orchard, Danvers Street, London SW3 5AX (tel 020 7351 9123)

de TRAFFORD, John Humphrey; eldest s and h of Sir Dermot Humphrey de Trafford, 6 Bt, VRD, *qv*, and his 1 w, Patricia Mary, *née* Beeley; *b* 12 September 1950; *Educ* Ampleforth, Univ of Bristol (BSc); *m* 1975, Anne, da of Jacques Faure de Pebeyre; 1 s (Alexander Humphrey b 28 June 1978), 1 da (Isabel June b 1980); *Career* vice-pres American Express Europe Ltd 1987–92, vice-pres and gen mangr American Express International (Taiwan) Inc 1992–94, vice-pres American Express Travel Related Services Inc 1994–96, sr vice-pres, country mangr for the UK and Ireland American Express 1996–2000, regnl pres Northern Europe American Express 2000–; *Clubs* Royal Ocean Racing; *Style*— John de Trafford, Esq

de VESCI, 7 Viscount (I 1776); Thomas Eustace Vesey; 9 Bt (I 1698); also Baron Knapton (I 1750); s of 6 Viscount de Vesci (d 1983), by his w Susan Anne (d 1986), da of late Ronald Owen Lloyd Armstrong-Jones, MBE (and sis of Earl of Snowdon, *qv*); *b* 8 October 1955; *Educ* Eton, St Benet's Hall Oxford; *m* 5 Sept 1987, Sita-Maria Arabella, o da of Brian de Breffny (d 1989), of Castletown Cox, Co Kilkenny, and Maharaj Kumari Jyotsna Devi, da of late Maharajadhiraja Bahadur Uday Chand Mahtab, KCIE, of Burdwan; 2 s (Hon Damian John b 1985, Hon Oliver Ivo b 16 July 1991), 1 da (Hon Cosima Frances b 1988); *Heir* s, Hon Oliver Vesey; *Career* md Horticultural Coir Ltd; *Clubs* White's; *Style*— The Rt Hon the Viscount de Vesci; ✉ 14 Rumbold Road, London SW6 2JA

de VILLIERS, 4 Baron (UK 1910); Alexander Charles de Villiers; s of 3 Baron de Villiers (d 2001); *b* 29 December 1940; *m* 1966; *Style*— The Rt Hon the Lord de Villiers

de VINK, Peter Henry John; s of Dr Ludovicus Petrus Hendricus Josephus de Vink (d 1987), and Catharina Louisa Maria, *née* Van Iersel; *b* 9 October 1940; *Educ* Univ of Edinburgh (BCom); *m* 1, 27 May 1967 (m dis 1993), Jenipher Jean, da of Ranald Malcolm Murray-Lyon, MD (d 1969); 1 da (Natalie b 1970), 1 s (Patrick b 1971); m 2, 23 Sept 1994, Julia Christine Quarles van Ufford (d 2007); *Career* Nat Serv 1961–63, cmmnd Dutch Army; dir Ivory & Sime 1975 (joined 1966, ptnr 1969), fndr dir Edinburgh Financial & General Holdings Ltd 1978–; dir: Viking Resources Oil & Gas Ltd 1972–88, Viking Resources Tst plc 1972–88, Wereldhave NY 1973–90, Benline Offshore Contractors Ltd 1974–96, Albany Oil & Gas Ltd 1987–91, Capital Copiers (Edinburgh) Ltd 1989–90, Screen Consultants NV 1994–2002, Oxford Philanthropic 1994–96; former memb: Exec Scot Cncl (Devpt and Ind), Bd of Govrs Napier Univ, Scottish Industrial Development Advsy Bd, Scottish Ctee Game Conservancy Cncl, Scottish Cons Bd of Fin; *Recreations* shooting, golf, fishing; *Clubs* New (Edinburgh); *Style*— Peter H J de Vink, Esq; ✉ Edinburgh Financial & General Holdings Ltd, 3A Charlotte Square, Edinburgh EH2 4DR (tel 0131 225 6661, fax 0131 556 6651, mobile 07836 702335, e-mail pdev@efgh.co.uk)

de VOGÜÉ, Count Ghislain Alain Marie Melchior; s of Comte Robert Jean de Vogüé, and Anne, *née* d'Eudeville; *b* 11 August 1933; *Educ* Univ of Le Havre; *m* 1 July 1960, Catherine Marie Monique, *née* Fragonard; 1 da (Laurence b 1 Feb 1976), 1 s (Marc b 14 Dec 1979); *Career* mgmnt attaché Banque de l'Union Européenne 1959–64, md Moët et Chandon Epernay 1969–75 (joined 1965), dir Jas Hennessy (France) 1976–2004, vice-chm of bd Moët-Hennessy Paris 1988–94, chm Domaine Chandon (USA) 1989–2002; memb Bd: Moët et Chandon (France), Chandon SA (Spain) 1989–2001, Domaine Chandon Pty (Aust) 1990–2000, Louis Vuitton Moët Hennessy 1990–2001, Iomedio 2000–02, Actium Developpement 2002–, Access2Net 2002–; *Recreations* music, skiing, golf, sailing; *Style*— Count Ghislain de Vogüé; ✉ 21 Quai de la Tournelle, 75005 Paris

de WECK, Paul Louis; s of Eugene P de Weck (d 1984), of Wimbledon, and Mary Eileen, *née* French; *b* 6 May 1937; *Educ* Beaumont Coll; *m* 27 April 1963, Ann Eileen, da of Wilfrid Frederick John Ward (d 1973), of Worcester Park; *Career* Nat Serv 1955–57, Sr Aircraftman RAF, Photographic Reconaissance Course; ret; memb Baltic Exchange 1970–; Freeman City of London 1978, Liveryman Worshipful Co of Gardeners 1978; FIFP 1974, FICS 1987; *Recreations* gardening, horse racing, swimming, riding, photography; *Clubs* Beaufort Hunt, Racehourse Owners' Assoc, Castle Baynard Ward; *Style*— Paul de Weck, Esq; ✉ Nettleton Lodge, Nettleton, Chippenham, Wiltshire SN14 7NS (tel 01249 782556)

de WILDE, (Alan) Robin; QC (1993); s of Capt Ronald Cedric de Wilde (d 1985), and Dorothea Elizabeth Mary, *née* Fenningworth (d 2005); *b* 12 July 1945; *Educ* Dean Close Sch Cheltenham, RAF Coll Cranwell; *m* 16 April 1977, Patricia Teresa, da of Gerald Ivan Bearcroft (d 1980), and Kathleen Mary, *née* O'Toole (d 1975); 3 s; *Career* called to the Bar Inner Temple 1971 (bencher 1996); chm Professional Negligence Bar Assoc 1995–97; Liveryman Worshipful Co of Bowyers; *Style*— Robin de Wilde, Esq, QC; ✉ London Chambers, 218 Strand, London WC2R 1AT (tel 020 7353 3936)

DE WITT, Sir Ronald Wayne (Ron); kt (2002); s of James Goldwyn De Witt, of Saskatoon, Canada, and Una Doreen, *née* Lane; *b* 31 March 1948; *Educ* Sch of Advanced Nursing Wellington NZ (Dip Nursing), Univ of Humberside (BA, MA); *Career* student nurse Misericordia Hosp 1967–70, staff nurse Winnipeg Children's Hosp 1970, charge nurse Stoke Mandeville Hosp 1971–73 (staff nurse 1971), nursing offr Queen Mary Hosp Roehampton 1973–75, asst princ nurse Auckland Hosp 1980–83 (supervisor 1975, sr supervisor 1976–80), dir of nursing Green Lane Hosp Auckland 1983–86, chief nurse Auckland Health 1988–90 (dep chief nurse 1986–88), dist mangr Auckland City 1989–90, gen mangr Auckland Hosp 1990–91; chief exec: Royal Hull Hosp NHS Tst 1991–96, Leeds HA 1996–99, King's Healthcare NHS Tst 1999–2002, NW London SHA 2002–04, Her Majesty's Courts Service (HMCS) 2004–; visiting prof of health and educn commissioning Sheffield Hallam Univ 1997–2005; chm Eng Nat Bd for Nursing, Midwifery and Health Visiting 1997–2002 (now emeritus prof); Dow Corning Int Award for Plastic Surgery 1973; hon fell Univ of Humberside and Lincolnshire; DCL (hc) UEA 2004; *Style*— Sir Ron De Witt

de ZULUETA, Dr Felicity Ines Soledad (Mrs Kahya); da of Dr Julian de Zulueta, and Gillian Owtram de Zulueta; *b* 26 March 1948; *Educ* UEA (BSc), Univ of Cambridge (MA), Univ of Sheffield (MB ChB); *m* 30 Sept 1977, Sedat Kahya, s of late Samuel Kahya, of Istanbul, Turkey; 1 s (Damian Samuel Hakan b 10 Nov 1979); *Career* private psychotherapist, qualified gp analyst, systemic therapist and EMDR therapist; SHO, registrar and sr registrar Maudsley Hosp where trained in psychotherapy, trained at Tavistock Clinic in family therapy, hon sr lectr Inst of Psychiatry, conslt psychiatrist in psychotherapy and lead clinicain Traumatic Stress Serv Maudsley Hosp; memb: Med Section Amnesty Int, Inst of Group Analysis, European Soc for Traumatic Stress Studies; fndr memb Int Attachment Network; FRCPsych (MRCPsych); *Books* From Pain to Violence: The Traumatic Roots of Destructiveness (1993, 2 edn 2006); also contrib chapters to various books; *Recreations* travelling, photography, walking, scuba diving; *Style*— Dr Felicity de Zulueta; ✉ Traumatic Stress Service, Maudsley Hospital, Denmark Hill, London SE5 8AZ (tel 020 3228 2969, fax 020 3228 3573, e-mail f.dezulueta@iop.kcl.ac.uk)

DE ZULUETA, Paul Gerald; *see:* Torre Diaz, Count of

DEACON, John Richard; s of Arthur Henry Deacon, and Lilian Deacon; *b* 19 August 1951; *Educ* Gartree HS, Beauchamp GS Leicester, Chelsea Coll; *m* Veronica; 5 s (Michael, Robert, Joshua, Cameron, Luke), 1 da (Laura); *Career* guitarist and songwriter; first band Opposition, joined Queen 1971 (with Freddie Mercury (d 1991), Brian May, *qv*, Roger Taylor, *qv*); albums: Queen (1973, Gold), Queen II (1974, Gold), Sheer Heart Attack (1974, Gold), A Night at the Opera (1975, Platinum), A Day at the Races (1976, Gold), News of the World (1977, Gold), Jazz (1978, Gold), Live Killers (1979, Gold), The Game (1980, Gold), Flash Gordon Original Soundtrack (1980, Gold), Greatest Hits (1981, 9 times Platinum), Hot Space (1982, Gold), The Works (1984, Platinum), A Kind of Magic (1986, double Platinum), Live Magic (1986, Platinum), The Miracle (1989, Platinum), Queen at the Beeb (1989), Innuendo (1991, Platinum), Greatest Hits Two (1991), Made in Heaven (1995), Greatest Hits Three (1999), Queen on Fire: Live at the Bowl (2004); number 1 singles: Bohemian Rhapsody (1975 and 1991), Under Pressure (1981), Innuendo (1991); numerous tours worldwide, performed at Live Aid Concert Wembley Stadium 1985; voted Best Band of the Eighties ITV/TV Times 1990, Br Phonographic Indust award for Outstanding Contribution to Br Music 1990; *Style*— John Deacon, Esq; ✉ Queen Productions Ltd, 46 Pembridge Road, London W11 3HN (tel 020 7727 5641)

DEACON, Richard; CBE, RA (1999); s of Gp Capt Edward William Deacon (d 2004), of Somerset, and Dr Joan Bullivant Winstanley (d 1973); *b* 15 August 1949; *Educ* Plymouth Coll, Somerset Coll of Art, St Martin's Sch of Art (DipAD), RCA (MA), Chelsea Sch of Art; *m* 1977 (m dis 2000), Jacqueline Poncelet; 1 s (Alexis b 1978), 1 da (Alice b 1982); *Career* artist; prof Ecole Nationale Supérieure des Beaux Arts 1998–; tstee Tate Gallery 1992–97, vice-chm Baltic Centre for Contemporary Art Tst 1999–2005; Turner Prize 1987, Chevalier de l'Ordre des Arts et des Lettres (France) 1998; *Exhibitions* incl: Tate Gallery 1985, Bonnefanten Museum 1987, Whitechapel Art Gallery 1989, Hannover Kunstverein 1993, British Cncl touring exhibition S America 1996–97, Tate Gallery Liverpool 1999, DCA Dundee 2001, Ludwig Museum Cologne 2003, Atelier Brancusi Paris 2004, Tate Gallery St Ives 2005, Museo Artium Vitonia-Gasteiz 2005, Sara Hilden Art Museum Tampere 2005–06, Arp Museum Germany 2006, Ikon Gallery Birmingham 2007, Wales at the Venice Biennale of Art 2007; *Commissions* Toronto, Plymouth, Gateshead, Krefeld, Villeneuve d'Ascq, Auckland, Tokyo, Beijing, Haarlem, San Francisco, Niigata, Assen; *Publications* Richard Deacon - Monograph (1995 and 2000); *Style*— Prof Richard Deacon, CBE, RA; ✉ c/o Lisson Gallery, 67 Lisson Street, London NW1 5DA (tel 020 7724 2739, fax 020 7724 7124, website www.richarddeacon.net)

DEACON, Susan Catherine; MSP; da of James Deacon (d 1980), and Barbara, *née* Timmins; *b* 2 February 1964, Musselburgh, E Lothian; *Educ* Musselburgh GS, Univ of Edinburgh (MA, MBA); *partner* John Boothman; 1 da (Clare b 10 Aug 1997), 1 s (James b 9 June 2002); *Career* admin offr and research asst W Lothian DC 1987–89, sr admin offr then ctee and office servs mangr East Lothian DC 1990–94, sr conslt Eglinton Mgmnt Centre Edinburgh 1994, MBA dir of progs Edinburgh Business Sch Heriot-Watt Univ 1994–98, business and mktg conslt 1998–99, MSP (Scottish Lab Party) Edinburgh East and Musselburgh 1999–; min for health and community care Scottish Exec 1999–2000; memb: Strategic Advisory Gp Scottish Rugby Union 2004, RSA Cmmn on Illegal Drugs, Communities and Public Policy 2005–; various advsy roles to business, public sector and voluntary orgns; contrib to various books, jls and newspapers; Frontbencher of the Year Scottish Politician of the Year Awards 2000; MCIPD 1993; *Recreations* family activities, walking, cycling, reading, playing piano; *Style*— Ms Susan Deacon, MSP; ✉ Scottish Parliament, Edinburgh EH99 1SP (tel 0131 348 5753, fax 0131 348 5904, e-mail susan.deacon.msp@scottish.parliament.uk)

DEAKIN, Michael; s of Sir William Deakin, DSO (d 2005), and Margaret, *née* Beatson Bell; bro of Prof Nicholas Deakin, CBE, *qv*; *b* 21 February 1939; *Educ* Bryanston, Universite d'Aix Marseilles, Emmanuel Coll Cambridge (MA); *Career* writer, documentary and film maker; fndr ptnr Editions Alecto (fine art publishers) 1960–64, prodr BBC Radio Current Affairs Dept 1964–68, prodr then editor Documentary Unit Yorkshire TV 1968–81; prodns incl: Out of Shadow into the Sun - The Eiger, Struggle for China, Whicker's World - Way Out West, Johnny Go Home (Br Acad award, 1976), David Frost's Global Village, The Frost Interview - The Shah, Act of Betrayal 1987, Not a Penny More, Not a Penny Less 1989, Secret Weapon 1990, Doomsday Gun 1993, The Good King 1994; fndr memb TV-am Breakfast Time Consortium 1980; TV-am: dir of progs 1982–84, memb Bd 1984–85, conslt 1984–87; dir Griffin Productions Ltd 1985–, sr vice-pres Paramount/Revcom 1987–93; *Books* Restif de la Bretonne - Les Nuits de Paris (translated with Nicholas Deakin, 1968), Gaetano Donizetti (1968), Tom Grattan's War (1970), The Children on the Hill (1972, 9 edn 1982), Johnny Go Home (with John Willis, 1976), The Arab Experience (with Antony Thomas, 1975, 2 edn 1976), Flame in the Desert (1976), I Could Have Kicked Myself (with David Frost, 1982), Who Wants to be Millionaire (with David Frost, 1983), If You'll Believe That You'll Believe Anything... (1986); *Recreations* motorcycling, eating, music, dalmatians; *Clubs* BAFTA; *Style*— Michael Deakin, Esq

DEAKIN, Prof Nicholas Dampier; CBE (1997); s of Sir William Deakin, DSO (d 2005), and Margaret, *née* Beatson Bell; bro of Michael Deakin, *qv*; *b* 5 June 1936; *Educ* Westminster, Milton Acad USA, ChCh Oxford (MA), Univ of Sussex (DPhil); *m*; 3 c, 3 step c; *Career* civil servant (admin class) 1959–63: asst princ Home Office, private sec to Minister of State 1962–63; asst dir Nuffield Survey of Race Rels 1963–68, res fell Centre for Multi-Racial Studies Univ of Sussex 1969–71, lectr Sch of African and Asian Studies Univ of Sussex 1971–72, head Social Studies then Central Policy Unit GLC 1972–80; Univ of Birmingham: prof of social policy and admin 1980–98, head Dept Social Admin 1980–91, dean Faculty of Commerce and Social Science 1986–89 (dep dean 1984–86), hon prof 1998–2001, emeritus prof 2001–, fndn fell 2006; public orator 1992–95; visiting fell Adlai Stevenson Inst of Int Affrs Univ of Chicago 1972, visitor Centre for Environmental

Studies 1971–72 (then memb Res Advsy Ctee), visiting prof Local Government Centre Univ of Warwick 1997–2000, visiting prof Dept of Social Policy and Administration, Centre for Civil Soc LSE 1999–2005; held European Union Chair of Social Policy Eötvös Lorant Univ Budapest 1998; memb Social Affrs Ctee Econ and Social Res Cncl 1982–86 (vice-chm 1984–86), scientific advsr Personal Servs DHSS 1986–91; chm: Birmingham Standing Conf for the Single Homeless 1983–86, Cncl for Voluntary Service Nat Assoc 1982–85, Nat Cncl for Vol Orgns Cmmn on Future of Vol Sector in England 1995–96 (report published as Meeting the Challenge of Change 1996), Birmingham City Pride 1999–2001; memb Exec Ctee Nat Cncl for Voluntary Orgns 1982–85 and 1988–91; govr: Royal Inst of Public Admin 1981–88, Family Policy Studies Centre 1984–2001; memb Ctee W Midlands Low Pay Unit 1983–84; regular lectr for Civil Serv; external examiner: UCL, Univ of Glasgow, Brunel Univ, Southampton Univ, Univ of Edinburgh, Univ of Exeter, Univ of Bath, LSE, Univ of Nottingham, Loughborough Univ; author of numerous articles in various learned publications; *Publications* incl: Colour and Citizenship (co-author, 1969), Colour and the British Electorate (ed, 1965), Policy Change in Government (ed, 1986), The Politics of Welfare (1987, 2 edn 1994), The Enterprise Culture and the Inner Cities (co-author, 1993), Contracting for Change (co-author, 1997), The Treasury and Social Policy (with Richard Parry, 2000), In Search of Civil Society (2001); contrib: The Yearbook of Social Policy in Britain (eds Catherine Jones and June Stevenson, 1984), Party Ideology in Britain (eds L J Tivey and A W Wright, 1989), Consuming Public Services (with A W Wright, 1990), The Costs of Welfare (jt ed and contrib, 1993), Transforming British Governments (ed with R A W Rhodes, 2000), The Student's Companion to Social Policy (eds A Erskine, P Alcock, M May, 2001, 2 edn 2004), Welfare and the State (jt ed, 2003), A Companion to Contemporary Britain (eds P Addison and H Jones, 2005), Angleterre ou Albion, entre Fascination et Répulsion (ed G Millat, 2006); *Style*— Prof Nicholas Deakin, CBE; ✉ Chedington, Lynmouth Road, London N2 9LR (tel 020 8883 8659)

DEAKIN, Pippa Caroline; da of (Iver) Tim Deakin, of Botesdale, Suffolk, and (Elizabeth) Joyce, *née* Knuckey; *b* 30 October 1965; *Educ* The Manor House Great Durnford, Princess Helena Coll Temple Dinsley; *Career* hotelier; teacher Hill House prep sch 1982, nursery sch teacher 1983–86, governess and nursery sch teacher abroad 1986–91, fndr proprietor Pippa Pop-Ins (first children's nursery hotel) 1992–, childcare and educnl conslt 1997–, 2nd Pippa Pop-Ins opened Oct 1999, public speaker and lectr on childcare and education; nat and Euro schs interior design and mktg conslt Le Rosey Swizerland 2001–; England Tourist Bd England for Excellence award 1992, Which? Hotel Guide London Hotel of the Year 1994, Entrepreneur of the Year BAWE 1996, Most Original New Business for GB and Europe 1996, represented GB as the most original new business in the FCEM World Awards 1996; Focus on Food RSA advsr Children's Act 1989, govr Princess Helena Coll Herts 1993–96, tstee St Nicholas Montessori Centre London/Int 1996–2001; memb RSA Millennium Educnl Ctee for under 8s 1997–98, memb Br Assoc of Women Entrepreneurs; FRGS, Hon FRSA 1995; *Recreations* riding, skiing, sailing, the Arts, charity fund-raising and illustration for children; *Style*— Miss Pippa Deakin; ✉ Pippa Pop-Ins, 430 Fulham Road, London SW6 1DU (tel 020 7385 2458 or 020 7731 1445, fax 020 7385 5706, e-mail pippadeakin@hotmail.com)

DEALTRY, Prof (Thomas) Richard; s of George Raymond Dealtry (d 1966), and Edith, *née* Gardiner (d 1990); *b* 24 November 1936; *Educ* Cranfield Univ (MBA); *m* 17 Sept 1963 (m dis 1982), Pauline Sedgwick; 1 s (Roger Paul b 7 June 1968), 1 da (Claire Elizabeth b 1 Nov 1972); *Career* Nat Serv 1959–61, Capt RAEC 1960; under sec Scottish Office and Industrial Advsr for Scotland 1977–78, regnl dir and conslt industrial advsr Gulf Orgn for Industrial Consulting Arabian Gulf Territories Orgn 1978–82, business and mgmnt devpt conslt 1982–, md Intellectual Partnerships Consultancy Ltd 1996–; dir: BAA plc, Corp Mgmnt Progs Univ of Surrey 1999–; company broker and prof in strategic mgmnt IMCB 1982–; CEng, MIMechE, MCIM; *Publications* The Corporate University Blueprint (2000), A Chronology of Corporate University Thinking (2000); *Recreations* golf, rugby union; *Style*— Prof Richard Dealtry; ✉ 43 Hunstanton Avenue, Harborne, Birmingham B17 8SX (tel 0121 427 6949, fax 0121 427 8491, e-mail prof.dealtry@dial.pipex.com, website www.corporateuniversity.org.uk)

DEAN, Janet Elizabeth Ann; MP; da of Harry Gibson (d 1982), of Biddulph, Staffs, and Mary, *née* Walley (d 1981); *b* 28 January 1949; *Educ* Winsford Verdin County GS; *m* 3 Aug 1968, Alan Dean (d 1994), s of George Dean (d 1998); 2 da (Carol b 3 April 1970, Sandra b 3 July 1972); *Career* Staffs CC: memb 1981–97, vice-chair Highway Ctee 1985–93, vice-chair Social Servs Ctee 1993–95; memb: E Staffs BC 1991–97 (mayor 1996–97), Uttoxeter Town Cncl 1995–97; MP (Lab) Burton 1997–; memb: Lupus UK, Lab Pty 1971–, Home Affairs Select Ctee, Chm's Panel; *Recreations* grandsons, reading; *Style*— Mrs Janet Dean, MP; ✉ House of Commons, London SW1A 0AA (tel 020 7219 6320, fax 020 7219 3010)

DEAN, (Catherine) Margaret; da of Thomas Day Scrimgeour (d 1969), and Catherine Forbes, *née* Sunderland; *b* 16 November 1939; *Educ* George Watson's Ladies Coll, Univ of Edinburgh (MA); *m* Brian Dean, MBFRCS MCh (Orth), s of Thomas Brown Dean; 3 da (Rosalyn b 26 Dec 1962, Alison b 29 Jan 1966, Joanna b 14 Dec 1970); *Career* HM Lord-Lt Fife 1999–; *Style*— Mrs Margaret Dean; ✉ c/o Assistant Clerk to the Lieutenancy, Fife House, Fife Council, Glenrothes, Fife KY7 5LT (tel 01592 416303, fax 01592 414200)

DEAN, Mark; s of Robert M Dean, and Barbara L Dean; *b* 1958; *Educ* Brighton Poly (BA), Goldsmiths Coll London (MA); *Career* artist; BT New Contemporaries Award 1993, awarded Imaginaria Cmmn ICA 1999; *Solo Exhibitions* City Racing London 1996, Laurent Delaye Gallery London 1999 and 2000, IMAGO Univ of Salamanca 2000, Summer Video Screenings by Mark Dean (IKON Gallery Birmingham) 2001, The Return of Jackie & Judy (+ Joey) (Laurent Delaye Gallery London) 2002, Disco Maquette (Sketch London) 2004, project for Lightsilver Beaconsfield 2005; *Group Exhibitions* A Simple Twist of Fate (Riverside Studios London) 1992, Dean/Furneaux/Wright (City Racing London) 1992, BT New Contemporaries 93 (UK tour) 1993, Lost Property 1 (W139 Amsterdam) 1995, Lost Property 2 (Great Western Studios London) 1995, I Beg to Differ (Milch London) 1996, Flag (Clink Wharf London) 1996, Silent/Still (Hit & Run London) 1996, BONGO (Bricks & Kicks Vienna) 1997, Big Blue (Coins London and Café Adler/Café Fix Berlin) 1997, Afternoon in the Park (Laurent Delaye Gallery London, incl Jam in the Park) 1997, Chez l'un, l'autre (Galerie Anton Weller Paris) 1997, Ne me quitte pas (GlassBox Paris) 1997, Instantaneous (Beaconsfield London) 1998, Back in Love (Coins London) 1998, Heavier than Air (Imperial War Museum London) 1998, Driving Towards Distraction (Laurent Delaye Gallery London) 1998, Host (Tramway Glasgow) 1998, Synchronicity (Laurent Delaye Gallery London) 1999, Klega's Flat (Sali Gia Gallery London) 1999, Mondo (Flag London) 1999, Imaginaria (ICA London) 1999, A Quoi tu joues? (Attitudes Geneva) 2000, Realm of the Senses (Turku Art Museum) 2000, Mommy Dearest (Gimpel Fils London) 2000, Video Vibe (Gallery of the Br Sch in Rome) 2000, Black Box Recorder (Br Cncl Int Touring Show Museum Ludwig Cologne) 2000, The Wreck of Hope (Nunnery Gallery London) 2000, Exit: Art and Cinema at the end of the century (Chisenhale Gallery London) 2000, VideoVideoVideoVideo (Galerie Anton Weller Paris) 2001, Why Me Not You? (Polish Cultural Inst London) 2001, Mute Loops (Lux Gallery London) 2001, Video Vibe (Contemporary Arts Centre of Vilnus) 2001, VideoROM (Valencia Biennial) 2001, Black Box Recorder (Br Cncl Int Touring Show MOMA Buenos Aires) 2001, WR001 (WRO Centre Wroclaw) 2001, Invitation à...Laurent Delaye Gallery invitée par la galerie Anton Weller (Galerie Anton Weller Paris) 2001, Self Portrayal (Laurent Delaye Gallery London) 2001, Video in the City (HEDAH film festival Centrum voor Hedendaagse Kunst Maastricht) 2001, New Acquisitions: Video Works by Mark Dean & Mark Wallinger (Leeds City Art Gallery) 2001, Century City: Art and Culture in the Modern Metropolis (Tate Modern London) 2001, City Racing 1988–98: A Partial Account (ICA London) 2001, Geometers (Nylon London) 2002, Game On (Barbican Gallery London) 2002, Thug Life (Smart Project Space Amsterdam) 2002, About Belief (South London Gallery) 2002, So Jackie! (Galerie P Brussells) 2002, Mark Dean & Janice McNab (Galerie Volker Diehl Berlin) 2002, Corpa Nova (27 Spital Sq London) 2003, Independence (South London Gallery) 2003, Game On (City Art Gallery Helsinki) 2003 (also at Lille Capital of Culture 2004), The Last Show (Galerie P Brussels) 2003, Platform for Art (London Underground) 2003, Atomic Art Bomb (Modern Art Oxford) 2004, Love Story (Danielle Arnaud Gallery London) 2004, Planet B (Palais Thurn und Taxis and Magazin 4 Bregenz) 2004, Vinyl 2 (Redux London) 2004, Lightsilver (Beaconsfield London) 2005, Art Futures (Bloomberg Space London) 2005, Off Loop (Barcelona) 2005; *Work in Public Collections* Leeds City Art Gallery, Fondation Musée d'Art Moderne Grand-Duc Jean Luxembourg; *Style*— Mark Dean, Esq; ✉ c/o Tailbiter, 76 Essendine Road, London W9 2LY (e-mail mail@tailbiter.com)

D

DEAN, Peter Henry; CBE (1993); s of Alan Walduck Dean, and Gertrude, *née* Bürger; *b* 24 July 1939; *Educ* Rugby, Univ of London (LLB); *m* 31 July 1965, Linda Louise, da of Rev William Edward Keating; 1 da (Amanda b 1967); *Career* admitted slr 1962; RTZ Corporation plc: joined 1966, sec 1972–74, dir 1974–85; freelance business conslt 1985–96; dep chm Monopolies and Mergers Cmmn 1990–97 (memb 1982–97), Investment Ombudsman 1996–2001, chm Gaming Bd for GB 1998–2005, chm Gambling Cmmn 2005–; dir G H Dean & Co Ltd 1999– (chm 2002–); non-exec dir: Associated British Ports Holdings plc 1980–2001, Liberty Life Assurance Co Ltd 1986–95, Seeboard plc 1993–96; chm: English Baroque Choir 1985–89 and 1999–2000, City Chamber Choir 2003–; chm Cncl of Mgmnt Highgate Counselling Centre 1991–2002 (memb 1985–2002); memb Law Soc; *Recreations* music (especially choral singing), skiing; *Clubs* Ski Club of GB; *Style*— Peter Dean, Esq, CBE; ✉ 52 Lanchester Road, Highgate, London N6 4TA (tel 020 8883 5417, fax 020 8365 2398, e-mail peter@deann64ta.freeserve.co.uk)

DEAN, Raymond Frank (Ray); s of Mario Frank Dean (d 1957), and late Leah Marsh Shannon; *b* 29 July 1936; *Educ* Britannia HS Vancouver, Guildford Coll of Art; *m* 26 Oct 1971, Anne Elisabeth, *née* Young; *Career* engine room apprentice RCN 1953–56; draughtsman Alcan Canada 1956–59 (chief shop steward United Steelworkers of America); photographer 1961–; assignments incl: still photography for Oscar winning documentary Dylan Thomas by Jack Howells, first exhbn Wig & Pen Club, work published by Br Jl of Photography and Photography Magazine; theatre and ballet photography incl: The Royal Opera House, Nureyev, Fonteyn, Marcel Marceau, Le Coq Mime, Comedie Française; design work for Derek Jarman incl: The Devils, Jazz Calendar; jt fndr Job Magazine 1973–84; int industrial photographer; clients incl: Shell International, Elf Oil, Buitoni, Honeywell, Design Magazine, British Steel, Coutts Bank, Hill Samuel, Lloyd's, Alcan, Michelin, ICI; *Recreations* France and NY, eating, drinking, taking pictures; *Style*— Ray Dean, Esq; ✉ e-mail macdean.zinphotog@btinternet.com, website raydean-photography.com

DEAN, Stafford Roderick; s of Eric Edwin Dean, and Vera Standish, *née* Bathurst; *b* 20 June 1937; *Educ* Epsom Coll, Royal Coll of Music (opera scholar); *m* 1, 1963, Carolyn Joan, *née* Lambourne; 4 s (Russell Edwin b 9 Feb 1966, Mark Roderick b 24 Aug 1967, Warwick Ashcroft b 19 March 1969, Ashley Jameson b 15 Aug 1974); m 2, 1981, Anne Elizabeth, *née* Howells; 1 s (Matthew Stafford Howells b 12 May 1981), 1 da (Laura Elizabeth Howells b 27 April 1983); *Career* bass; with: Glyndebourne Chorus and Opera For All 1962–64, Sadler's Wells Opera 1964–69, Covent Garden Opera 1969– (now guest singer); Sadler's Wells Opera debut as Zuniga in Carmen 1964, Royal Opera House debut as Masetto in Don Giovanni 1969, int debut as Leporello in Don Giovanni Stuttgart 1971, performed with all major Euro and American opera cos (especially in prodns of Mozart repertoire); *Performances* operatic roles incl: Figaro in Le Nozze di Figaro (Scottish Opera, Munich, Hamburg, Cologne, Bonn, Covent Garden, Chicago, Met NY), Leporello in Don Giovanni (ENO, Scottish Opera, Stuttgart, Munich, Hamburg, Cologne, Bonn, San Francisco, Chicago, Covent Garden), Alfonso d'Este in Lucrezia Borgia (Covent Garden), Osmin in Die Entführung aus dem Serail (Scot Opera, Hamburg, Geneva), Bottom in A Midsummer Night's Dream (Covent Garden), Rangoni in Boris Godunov (Covent Garden, Orange, Florence), Rocco in Fidelio (Scottish Opera and WNO), The Count in Jacobin (Scottish Opera), The King of Portugal in Ines de Castro (Scottish Opera), Waldner in Arabella, Dr Bartolo in Le Nozze di Figaro (Covent Garden), Don Alfonso in Cosi fan Tutte (Madrid, Barcelona, Covent Garden), Swallow in Peter Grimes (Covent Garden, San Francisco, Paris, Genoa, Nancy, Tours, Toulouse, Glyndebourne, Florence, Saito Kinen Fest Japan, recording with Haitink), Prof Bieganski in Sophie's Choice (Covent Garden); recital repertoire incl: Beethoven 9th Symphony and Missa Solemnis, Mozart, Verdi and Penderecki Requiems, Shostakovich 14th Symphony; *Style*— Stafford Dean, Esq; ✉ Kingswood House, Mark Way, Godalming, Surrey GU7 2BW

DEAN, Tacita Charlotte; *b* 1965, Canterbury; *Educ* Kent Coll Canterbury, Canterbury Coll of Art, Falmouth Sch of Art (BA), Slade Sch of Fine Art (Dip); *Career* artist; Greek govt scholar Supreme Sch of Fine Art Athens 1989–90, artist in residence Ecole Nationale des Beaux-Arts Bourges 1995, Screenwriters' Lab Sundance Inst 1997, artist in residence Wexner Center for the Arts Columbus 1999, scholarship Deutscher Akademischer Austauschdienst Berlin 2000–01; creator Berlin Project: Between the Ears (Radio 3) 2002; Barclays Young Artist Award 1999, shortlisted Turner Prize 1998; *Solo Exhibitions* The Martyrdom of St Agatha and Other Stories (Galerija Skuc Ljubljana and Umetnosta Galerija Maribor) 1994, Clear Sky, Upper Air (Frith Street Gallery London) 1995, Galerie 'La-Box' Ecole Nationale des Beax-Arts Bourges 1995, Foley Artist (Art Now Tate Gallery) 1996, Witte de With Center for Contemporary Art Rotterdam 1997, The Drawing Room The Drawing Center NY 1997, Frith Street Gallery London 1997, Galerie Gebauer Berlin 1998, Statements (Frith Street Gallery and Art Basel '98) 1998, De Pont Fndn Tilburg 1998, ICA Univ of Pennsylvania 1998, Madison Art Center 1999, Sadler's Wells Theatre 1999, Marian Goodman Gallery Paris 1999, Cranbrook Gallery Bloomfield Hills 1999, The Sea, with a Ship: afterwards an Island (Dundee Contemporary Arts) 1999, Banewl (Newlyn Art Gallery) 1999, Millennium Sculpture Project London 1999, Marian Goodman Gallery NY 2000, Museum für Gegenwartskunst Basel 2000, Art Gallery of York Univ Toronto 2000, Banewl (Berkeley Art Museum Univ of Calif Berkeley) 2000, Museu d'Art Contemporani de Barcelona 2001, Tate Britain 2001, Hirshhorn Museum Washington 2001; *Group Exhibitions* BT New Contemporaries (Newlyn Orion Penzance, Cornerhouse Manchester, Orpheus Gallery Belfast, Angel Row & Bonnington Gallery Nottingham and ICA London) 1992, Barclays Young Artists Award (Serpentine Gallery London) 1993, Peripheral States (Benjamin Rhodes Gallery London) 1993, Watt (Witte de With Center for Contemporary Arts and Kunsthal Rotterdam) 1994, Coming Up for Air (144 Charing Cross Road and the agency London) 1994, Mise en Scène (ICA London) 1994, Mysterum Alltage, Hammoniale der Frauen (Kampnagel Hamburg) 1995, Kine[kunst]'95 (Casino Knokke Knokke-Heist) 1995, Video Forum (Art Basel '95) 1995, Speaking of Sofas (nat touring exhbn) 1995, Whistling Women (Royal Festival Hall London) 1995, Videos and Films by Artists (Ateliers d'Artistes de la ville de Marseille) 1995, The British Art Show 4 (nat touring exhbn) 1995, Lisbeth Bik, Tacita Dean, Jos van der Pol, Peter Fillingham (Cubitt Street Gallery London) 1995, CCATV (Centre for Contemporary Art London) 1996, Art Node Fndn Stockholm 1996, State of Mind

(Centrum Beelende Kunst Rotterdam) 1996, Swinging the Lead (Int Festival of the Sea Bristol) 1996, Berwick Ramparts Project (Berwick-upon-Tweed) 1996, Container '96: Art Across the Oceans (Parkhus Quay Copenhagen) 1996. Tacita Dean & Stephen Wilks (Galerie Paul Andriesse Amsterdam) 1996, Found Footage (Klemens Gasser & Tanja Grunert Cologne) 1996, Exploding Cinema (26th Int Film Festival Rotterdam) 1997, Challenge of Materials (Science Museum London) 1997, A Case for a Collection (Towner Art Gallery Eastbourne) 1997, Contemporary British Drawings - Marks & Traces (Sandra Gering Gallery NY) 1997, Celluloid Cave (Thread Waxing Space NY) 1997, Flexible (Museum für Gegenwartskunst Zurich) 1997, The Frame of Time - Openmuseum (Museum van Hedenaagse Kunst Limburg) 1997, Screenwriters' Lab (Sundance Inst) 1997, At One Remove (Henry Moore Inst Leeds) 1997, 20:20 (Marian Goodman Gallery NY) 1997, Social Space (Marian Goodman Gallery Paris) 1997, New Found Landscape (Kerlin Gallery Dublin) 1997, Voiceover: Sound and Vision in Current Art (nat touring exhbn) 1998, Wounds: Between Democracy and Redemption in Contemporary Art (Moderna Museet Stockholm) 1998, A-Z (The Approach London) 1998, Video/Projection/Film (Frith Street Gallery London) 1998, La Terre est Ronde - Nouvelle Narration (Musée de Rochechouart) 1998, La Mer n'est pas la Terre (FRAC Bretagne La Criée Rennes) 1998, Disrupting the Scene (Cambridge Darkroom) 1998, Breaking Ground (Marian Goodman Gallery NY) 1998, Sharawedgi (Felsenvilla Baden) 1998, The NatWest Art Prize 1998 (Lothbury Gallery London) 1998, The Turner Prize 1998 (Tate Gallery) 1998, New Media Projects (Orchard Gallery Derry) 1999, Exploding Cinema (28th Int Film Festival Rotterdam) 1999, 1264–1999 Une Légende a Suivre (Le Credac Ivry) 1999, Appliance of Science (Frith Street Gallery London) 1999, Hot Air (GranShip Shizuoka Convention and Arts Center and Marian Goodman Gallery Paris) 1999, Geschichten des Augenblicks (Städitsche Galerie im Lenbachhaus Munich) 1999, Go Away: Artists and Travel (RCA) 1999, New Visions of the Sea (Nat Maritime Museum London) 1999, Fourth Wall (Public Art Devpt Tst at RNT London) 1999, 0 to 60 in 10 Years (Frith Street Gallery London) 1999, Laboratorium (Antwerp Open) 1999, Un Monde réel (Fondation Cartier Paris) 1999, Tacita Dean, Lee Ranaldo, Robert Smithson (Dia Center for the Arts NY) 1999, Landscape (ACC Gallerie Weimar and int tour organised by Br Cncl) 2000, The Sea and the Sky (Beaver Coll Art Gallery Philadelphia and Royal Hibernian Gallery Dublin) 2000, L'ombra della ragione (La Galleria d'Arte Moderna Bologna) 2000, Intelligence: New British Art 2000 (Tate Britain) 2000, On the Edge of the Western World (Yerba Buena Center for the Arts San Francisco) 2000, Amateur/Liebhaber (Kunstmuseum, Kunsthallen & Hasselblad Gothenburg) 2000, Mixing Memory and Desire (Neues Kunstmuseum Luzerne) 2000, Artifice (Deste Fndn Museum and Br Cncl int tour) 2000, Somewhere Near Vada (Project Art Center Dublin) 2000, Another Place (Tramway Glasgow) 2000, media_city Seoul 2000 (Seoul Metropolitan Museum) 2000, Tout le Temps (La Biennale de Montréal) 2000, Vision and Reality (Louisiana Museum of Art) 2000, Arcadia (Nat Gallery of Canada Ottawa) 2001, Humid (Spike Island Bristol) 2001, Nothing: Exploring Invisibilities (Northern Gallery of Contemporary Art Sunderland) 2001, Double Vision (Galerie für Zeitgenoessische Kunst Leipzig) 2001; *Publications* Teignmouth Electron (1999), Floh (2001); *Style—* Ms Tacita Dean; ✉ Frith Street Gallery, 60 Frith Street, London W1D 3JJ (tel 020 7494 1550, fax 020 7287 3733, e-mail info@frithstreetgallery.com)

DEAN, Timothy Nicholas; s of Geoffrey Dean, of Penzance, Cornwall, and Hilda, *née* Floyd; *b* 23 April 1956; *Educ* Dr Challoner's GS, Guildhall Sch of Music and Drama (ATCL), Univ of Reading (BA), Royal Coll of Music (ARCM); *m* 1981, Ruth Mary, da of Dr Peter Reid Duncan; 3 s (Jonathan Andrew b 26 Sept 1983, Thomas Carey b 28 Dec 1986, Duncan Matthew b 26 Dec 1992); *Career* head of music/chorus master Kent Opera 1983–90, asst music dir D'Oyly Carte Opera Co 1990–91, music dir The Opera Co Tunbridge Wells 1991–94, head of opera RSAMD 1994–, artistic dir British Youth Opera 2002–07 (music dir 1987–2001), chorus dir Royal Scottish Nat Orchestra 2006–; conductor London Bach Soc 1988–90; conducting debuts: ENO 1991, Scottish Opera 1991; festival appearances incl: City of London, Bath, Spitalfields, Aldeburgh, Covent Garden, Stour, Cheltenham, Brighton, Canterbury; conductor: Queen Elizabeth Hall, Purcell Room, Sadler's Wells, Theatre Royal Drury Lane, Royal Opera House, St John's Smith Square, Wigmore Hall, St Martin-in-the-Fields, St James's Palace, Chequers, 10 Downing St; FRSA; *Recreations* walking, reading, theatre, racquet sports; *Style—* Timothy Dean, Esq; ✉ Braeval, 4 Ellergreen Road, Bearsden, Glasgow G61 2RJ (tel 0141 942 8121); Royal Scottish Academy of Music and Drama, 100 Renfrew Street, Glasgow G2 3BD (tel 0141 270 8318, fax 0141 270 8352, e-mail t.dean@rsamd.ac.uk); British Youth Opera, c/o South Bank University, 103 Borough Road, London SE1 0AA (tel 020 7815 6090/1/2/3, fax 020 7815 6094)

DEAN OF HARPTREE, Baron (Life Peer UK 1993), of Wedmore in the County of Somerset; Sir (Arthur) Paul Dean; kt (1985), PC (1991); s of Arthur Dean (d 1961), of Weaverham, Cheshire; *b* 14 September 1924; *Educ* Ellesmere Coll, Exeter Coll Oxford (MA, BLitt, pres OUCA); *m* 1, 1957, Doris Ellen (d 1979), da of Frank Webb (d 1960), of Sussex; m 2, 1980, Mrs Margaret Frances (Peggy) Parker, *née* Dierden (d 2002); *Career* WWII Capt Welsh Gds, ADC to Cdr 1 Corps BAOR; former farmer; CRD 1957, resident tutor Swinton Cons Coll 1956–57, asst dir CRD 1962–64, Parly candidate (Cons) Pontefract 1962; MP (Cons): N Somerset 1964–83, Woodspring 1983–92; oppn front bench spokesman on health and social security 1969–70, Parly under sec DHSS 1970–74, chm Cons Health and Social Security Ctee 1979–82; memb: Commons Servs Select Ctee 1979–82, Exec Ctee Cwlth Parly Assoc UK Branch 1975–92, Commons Chm's Panel 1979–82; second dep chm House of Commons and dep chm Ways and Means 1982–87, first dep chm Ways and Means and dep speaker 1987–92; dep speaker House of Lords 1995–; memb Exec Ctee Assoc of Conservative Peers 1995–; former: memb Church in Wales Governing Body, govr BUPA, chm Cons Watch-Dog Gp for Self-Employed; dir: Charterhouse Pensions, Watney Mann and Truman Hldgs; govr Cwlth Inst 1981–89; *Clubs* Oxford Carlton (pres), Oxford and Cambridge; *Style—* The Rt Hon Lord Dean of Harptree, PC; ✉ House of Lords, London SW1A 0PW

DEAN OF THORNTON-LE-FYLDE, Baroness (Life Peer UK 1993), of Eccles in the County of Greater Manchester; Brenda Dean; PC (1998); da of Hugh Dean, of Thornton, Lancs; *b* 29 April 1943; *Educ* St Andrews Sch Eccles, Stretford GS; *m* 30 April 1988, Keith Desmond McDowall, CBE; *Career* admin sec Manchester Branch SOGAT 1959–71 (asst branch sec 1971, sec 1976), gen sec SOGAT 1985–91 (pres 1983–85), dep gen sec GPMU 1991–92; chm Ind Ctee for the Supervision of Standards of Telephone Information Servs 1993–99; non-exec Bd memb Univ Coll Hosps London 1993–98; memb: Women's Nat Cmmn (co-chm 1975–78), NEDC 1985–92, BBC Gen Advsy Cncl 1985–89, TUC Gen Cncl 1985–92, TUC Econ Ctee 1987–92, Cncl Assoc of Business Sponsorship of the Arts 1989–95, Cncl City Univ 1991–95, Advsy Ctee Carnegie 3rd Age Enquiry, Press Complaints Cmmn 1993–98, Broadcasting Complaints Cmmn 1993–94, Armed Forces Pay Review Body 1993–94 (chm 1999–), LSE Governing Body 1994–98, Cncl Open Univ 1995–97, Dearing Ctee 1996–97; govr Ditchley Fndn 1992–; non-exec dir: Inveresk plc 1993–97, Chamberlain Phipps plc 1994–96, Care First plc (formerly Takare plc) 1995–98, Assured British Meat 1997–2001, Sr Salaries Review Body 1999–, Gen Insurance Standards Cncl 1999–, Dawson Holdings 2004–; pres Coll of Occupational Therapists 1995–; chm Housing Corporation 1997–2003, chm Covent Garden Market Authy 2005–; House of Lords: jr spokesman on employment 1994–96, jr spokesman to Lord Donoughe 1996–97, Lab whip 1995–97; memb Ctee on reform of House of Lords 1999, memb House of Lords Appointments Cmmn 2000–; tstee: Pension Scheme of Inveresk plc 1994–97, Prince's Youth Business Tst 1994–2000, Industry & Parliament Tst 1997–; Hon MA Univ of Salford 1986, Hon BA City Univ 1993, Hon MA South Bank Univ 1995, Hon LLD Univ of North London 1996, Hon LLD De Montfort Univ 1998, Hon MA Univ of Nottingham 2002; hon fell Univ of Central Lancashire 1991; FRSA; *Recreations* family, cooking, sailing, and theatre; *Clubs* Reform, Royal Cornwall Yacht; *Style—* The Rt Hon Baroness Dean of Thornton-le-Fylde, PC; ✉ House of Lords, London SW1A 0PW

DEANE, Derek; OBE (2000); s of Gordon Shepherd, and Margaret, *née* Seager; *Career* sr princ Royal Ballet 1980–89 (joined 1972, later choreographer), dep artistic dir/res choreographer Teatro dell'Opera Rome 1990–92, artistic dir English National Ballet and English National Ballet Sch 1993–2001; prodns for English Nat Ballet incl: restaging of Marius Petipa's Grand Pas from Paquita, Giselle 1994, Alice in Wonderland (2 Olivier Award nominations) 1995, Swan Lake 1997, The Nutcracker 1997, Romeo & Juliet 1998; choreographer for Royal Ballet and Birmingham Royal Ballet; various prodns in USA, France, Japan, Australia, South Africa; subject of BBC television documentary 1995; *Style—* Derek Deane, Esq, OBE; ✉ English National Ballet, Markova House, 39 Jay Mews, London SW7 2ES (tel 020 7581 1245, fax 020 7225 0827)

DEANE, Michael; s of Ted Deane, and Ellen Deane (d 1998); *b* 19 March 1961; *m* Kate, *née* Smith; 1 s (Marco Chokdee b March 2000); *Career* chef prop: Restaurant Michael Deane, Deane's Brasserie, Deane's Deli; *Awards* Northern Ireland Chef of the Year 1993, 1 Michelin Star 1997–, 3 AA Rosettes 1997–2004, Restaurant of the Year Jameson Guide 2000, Chef of the Year Jameson Guide 2001, AA Restaurant of the Year 2001, Craft Guild of Chefs UK Restaurant Chef of the Year 2002, 2 Stars Jameson Guide to Ireland; *Style—* Michael Deane, Esq; ✉ Restaurant Michael Deane, 38–40 Howard Street, Belfast BT1 6PD (tel 028 9033 1134, fax 028 9056 0001)

DEANE, Seamus; *b* 9 February 1940; *Educ* Queens' Univ Belfast (BA, MA), Univ of Cambridge (PhD); *Career* visiting Fulbright and Woodrow Wilson scholar Reed Coll OR 1966–67, visiting lectr Univ of Calif Berkeley 1967–68; visiting prof: Univ of Notre Dame IN 1977, Univ of Calif Berkeley 1978; prof of modern English and American literature UC Dublin 1980–93; Walker Ames prof Univ of Washington Seattle 1987, Julius Benedict distinguished visiting prof Carleton Coll MN 1988, Keough prof of Irish studies Univ of Notre Dame IN 1993–; dir Field Day Theatre and Publishing Co; memb: Royal Irish Acad, Aosdana (Irish Artists' Cncl); *Awards* AE Meml Award for Literature 1973, American-Irish Fund for Literature 1989, Guardian Fiction Prize 1996, South Bank Award for Literature 1996, Irish Times Literature Prize for Fiction 1997, Irish Times Int Prize for Fiction 1997, Ruffino Antico Fattore International Literature Award 1998; *Poetry* Gradual Wars (1972), Rumours (1977), History Lessons (1983), Selected Poems (1988), Quatorze elegies pour l'Irlande suivies de Guerre Civile (1982); *Fiction* Reading in the Dark (1996); *Critical* Celtic Revivals: Essays in Modern Irish Literature 1880–1980 (1985), A Short History of Irish Literature (1986), The French Revolution and Enlightenment in England 1789–1832 (1988), Strange Country: Ireland, Modernity and the Nation (1997), Foreign Affections: Essays on Edmund Burke (2005); *Edited* The Adventures of Hugh Trevor (by Thomas Holcroft, 1973), Sale Catalogues of the Libraries of Eminent Persons (1973), Atlantis (1969–74), Field Day Pamphlet Series (6 series), The Field Day Anthology of Irish Writing (3 vols, 1991), Penguin Twentieth Century Classics: James Joyce (5 vols, 1992), Field Day Essays: Critical Conditions (12 vols, 1996–2002), Future Crossings (ed with K Ziarek, 2002), Field Day Review I (2005); *Style—* Seamus Deane, Esq; ✉ c/o Institute of Irish Studies, 1145 Flanner Hall, University of Notre Dame, Notre Dame, IN 46556, USA (tel 00 1 219 631 7120, fax 00 1 219 631 3620)

DEAR, Alan Ferguson; s of Frank McKenzie Rae Dear, and Kathleen Ferguson Dear, *née* Ferguson; *b* 16 January 1965; *Educ* Forfar Acad, Royal Scottish Acad of Music and Drama (BA), UC Cardiff (Dip Theatre); *Career* dir Sherman Youth Project Sherman Theatre Cardiff 1985–87, dir Dundee City Festival 1987–89, arts offr City of Westminster 1989–91, dir Roadmender Arts Centre Roadmender Trust Northampton 1991–92, head of Educn and Community WNO Cardiff 1992–97, chief exec Royal Coll of Organists 1997–2005, dir Sexual Health UK 2005–; tstee Hackney Music Devpt Tst 1998–2002, advsr Bird Coll 2005–; *Recreations* theatre, travel, the visual arts, singing; *Style—* Alan Dear, Esq; ✉ e-mail alan.dear@atmosprojects.co.uk

DEAR, Baron (Life Peer 2006), of Willersey in the County of Gloucestershire; Sir Geoffrey James Dear; kt (1997), QPM (1982), DL (1985); s of Cecil William Dear, and Violet Mildred, *née* Mackney; *b* 20 September 1937; *Educ* Fletton GS, UCL (LLB); *m* 1, 1958, Judith Ann (d 1996), da of J W Stocker (d 1972), of Peterborough; 2 da (Catherine b 1961, Fiona b 1966), 1 s (Simon b 1963); m 2, 1998, Alison Jones; *Career* joined Peterborough Combined Police after cadet serv 1956, various posts rising to supt Mid Anglia Constabulary 1970–72, asst chief constable Nottinghamshire Constabulary 1972, dep asst cmmnr Met Police 1980–81, asst cmmr Met Police 1981–85, chief constable West Midlands Police 1985–90, HM inspr of constabulary 1990–97; non-exec chm: Skyguard Technologies Ltd 2001–, Image Metrics plc 2001–03, Action Against Business Crime 2004–, Key Forensic Services Ltd 2005–, Omniperception Ltd 2005–; non-exec dir: Reliance Security 1997–2005, Reliance Secure Task Management 2001–05; Vice Lord-Lt Worcs 1998–2002; Queen's Commendation for Bravery 1979; fell UCL 1990; FRSA 1989; *Recreations* field sports, rugby football, fell walking, music, reading, gardening; *Clubs* East India, Special Forces; *Style—* The Lord Dear, QPM, DL

DEAR, Jeremy; s of John Dear, of Bruges, Belgium, and Jan Dear; *b* 6 December 1966; *Educ* Br Sch Brussels, Coventry Poly (BA), Univ of Wales Cardiff (Dip Journalism); *m* 16 Oct 1999, Paula, *née* Jolly; *Career* former Midlands ed Big Issue; NUJ: former nat organiser Newspapers and Agencies, pres 1997–98, gen sec 2001–; memb: Gen Cncl TUC 2002–, NCTJ, Int Fedn of Journalists (IFJ) European Labour Rights Expert Gp; *Style—* Jeremy Dear, Esq; ✉ National Union of Journalists, Headland House, 308 Gray's Inn Road, London WC1X 8DP (tel 020 7843 3728, fax 020 7278 6617, e-mail jeremyd@nuj.org.uk)

DEARDEN, Dr Andrew Richard; s of Philip Dearden (d 2000), and Wendy Saville, *née* Protheroe; *b* 7 November 1962, Wales; *Educ* Laverton HS Aust, Church Coll of NZ, Tonyrefail Comp Sch Porth, Welsh Nat Coll of Med (MB, BCh); *m* 24 Aug 1985, Ann, *née* Evans; 3 da (Eleanor b 25 March 1988, Melissa b 8 Nov 1990, Lois b 26 March 1995); *Career* princ GP Cardiff practice 1994–; chm Welsh Assoc of GP Trainees 1991–93, chm GP Ctee Wales 2002– (memb 1996–, dep chm 1999–2002), memb Bro Taf Local Med Ctee 1994–, memb UK GP Ctee 1997–, exec memb Cardiff Local Health Gp 1999–2003, chm BMA Ctee on Community Care 2000–04, chm Pensions Ctee BMA 2004–; asst registrar of marriages 1987–2000; DCCH (Dip in Community Child Health) 1992, DGM (Dip in Geriatric Med) 1992, DFFP 1994; MRCGP 1993, FRSA 2004, fell BMA 2006; *Publications* Successful Negotiation in the New Contract (2004), The Insider's Guide to the New GMS Contract (2004), The A-Z Reference Book of the New GMS Contract (2005), The Enhanced Service Handbook (2006); author author of articles in med jls; *Recreations* science fiction, eating out, collecting ancient Egyptian amulets and antiquities, owned classic motor car 1999–2004; *Style—* Dr Andrew Dearden; ✉ 116 Newport Road, Cardiff CF24 1YT (tel 02920 494537, fax 02920 498086)

DEARDEN, Dr (Norman) Mark; s of Norman Gerald Dearden, of Leeds, and Mary Isobel Emily, *née* Mosby; *b* 30 June 1953; *Educ* Lord William's GS, Univ of Leeds (BSc, MB ChB); *m* 6 Sept 1986, Margaret Ruth, da of Eric Burkinshaw; 2 s (Paul b 1988, Richard b 1989); *Career* jr doctor Leeds 1977–81, lectr in anaesthetics Univ of Leeds 1981–84, conslt neuro anaesthetist and pt/t sr lectr in anaesthetics Edinburgh 1985–92, conslt anaesthetist and clinical sr lectr in anaesthesia Leeds 1992–; contrib to: Lancet, BMJ, Br Jl of Anaesthesia, Br Jl of Hospital Medicine, Jl of Neurosurgery, Jl of Neurosurgical

Anaesthesiology, Anaesthesia, Current Opinion in Anaesthesiology, Current Anaesthesia and Critical Care, Jl of Physiology, Br Jl of Intensive Care, Jl of Neurotrauma, Behavioural Brain Res, Clinical and Laboratory Haematology, Care of the Critically Ill, Jl of Anatomy, Jl of Neurology Neurosurgery and Psychiatry; Br rep Intensive Care Gp of The World Fedn of Neurology; memb: Yorks Soc of Anaesthetists 1980, Intensive Care Soc 1983, Scottish Soc of Anaesthetists 1985, E of Scotland Soc of Anaesthetists 1985, World Fedn of Neurologists 1988, Euro Intensive Care Soc 1989, Exec Euro Brain Injury Consortium (EBIC, also sec), Neuroanaesthesia Soc of GB and Ireland 2000; *Books* Brain Protection (1983), The Clinical Use of Hypnotic Drugs in Head Injury (contrib), Advances in Brain Resuscitation (1991), Management of Brain Edema in Head Injury (contrib), Réanimation et Neurologie (contrib, 1995), Neurochemical Monitoring in the Intensive Care Unit (contrib, 1995), Management of Cerebral Oedema and Raised Intracranial Pressure - Principles and Practice of Critical Care (contrib,1997), Diagnosis of Raised Intracranial Pressure, Medical Management of Head Injury, Oxford Textbook of Critical Care (contrib, 1999); *Recreations* horticulture, DIY, swimming; *Style—* Dr Mark Dearden; ✉ Nan Tan House, Dixon Lane, Wortley, Leeds LS12 4AD; Department of Anaesthesia, Leeds General Infirmary, Great George Street, Leeds LS1 3EX (tel 0113 243 2799, fax 0113 231 6821, mobile 07885 211717, e-mail richard.dearden@aol.com)

DEARDEN, Michael Bailey (Mike); s of John Skelton Dearden (d 1962), and Doris Dearden (d 1969); *b* 15 September 1942; *Educ* Manchester Grammar, Merton Coll Oxford (MA); *m* 16 July 1964, Monica Tatiana (d 2002), da of Gordon Hewlett Johnson; 1 s (Jonathan Michael b 31 Jan 1965), 1 da (Kathryn Tatiana b 2 Feb 1969); *Career* Castrol Ltd: mktg mangr 1980–84, chief exec Castrol Malaysia 1984–86, gen mangr New Ventures Castrol Ltd 1986–88, regnl dir Castrol Ltd 1988–91; chief exec Foseco International 1991–95; Burmah Castrol plc: chemicals dir (main bd) 1995–98, lubricants dir 1998–2000; chm: The Brick Business 2003–04, Minova International Ltd 2003–06; non-exec dir: Johnson Mathey plc 1999–, Travis Perkins plc 2000–, The Weir Gp 2003–; Liveryman Worshipful Co of Coachmakers and Coach Harness Makers; ACIM 1965, MIMC 1975; *Recreations* gardening, bridge, rugby, opera, scuba diving, shooting, wine; *Clubs* Oxford and Cambridge; *Style—* Mike Dearden, Esq

DEARDEN, Neville; s of Maj Issac Samuel Dearden (d 1979), and Lilian Anne, *née* Claxton (d 1983); *b* 1 March 1940; *Educ* Rowlinson Tech Sch Sheffield, King Alfred Coll Winchester, Univ of Southampton; *m* 1, 4 April 1963, Jean Rosemary, da of Walter Francis Garratt, of Sheffield; 1 da (Karen b 1966), 2 s (Adrian b 1968, David b 1970); m 2, 3 May 1980, Eileen Bernadette, da of Dr William John Sheehan; 4 s (Michael b 1981, Patrick b 1984, Ciaran b 1987, Liam b 1990); *Career* head of Science Dept Lafford Sch Lincs 1961–67; md: W Garratt & Son Ltd 1972–78, M & H Fabrications Ltd 1972–77; chief exec S W Fabrications Ltd 1980–84, md Sheffield Brick Group plc 1982–87, chief exec Pan Computer Systems Ltd 1982–85; chm: Parker Winder and Achurch Ltd 1983–85, C H Wood Security Ltd 1983, Mylnhurst Limited 1996–; Smith Widdowson Eadem Ltd: chm 1983, md 1986; md F G Machin Ltd 1983; chief exec: JCL Engineering Services Ltd, Crompton Engineering (Lancs) Ltd 1989, Doncaster C of C and Enterprise 1997–, Doncaster Business Link Ltd 1997–; Comyn Ching Ltd: gp manufacturing dir 1990, gp sales and mktg dir 1995; independent dir Marshall Bros (Bury) Ltd 1993; dir: SRC Advanced Systems Ltd 1996–, Yorks and Humber C of C 1997–, South Yorks Small Business Serv, DBIC Ltd, Donbac Ltd, Newcastle Sports Injury Clinic Ltd; sr conslt Quantum Enterprise Development 1996; FIMgt, FIIM, FICM, FinstD, DMS; *Recreations* game and sea fishing, boating, practical craft work; *Style—* Neville Dearden, Esq; ✉ Doncaster Chamber of Commerce and Enterprise, Icon, First Point, Balby Carr Bank, Doncaster DN4 5JQ (home tel 0114 236 4386, fax 0114 235 4382, e-mail chamber@dcce.co.uk and neville.dearden@dcce.co.uk)

DEARING, Baron (Life Peer UK 1998), of Kingston upon Hull in the County of the East Riding of Yorkshire; Sir Ronald Ernest (Ron) Dearing; kt (1984), CB (1979); s of Ernest Henry Ashford Dearing (d 1941), and M T Dearing; *b* 27 July 1930; *Educ* Doncaster GS, Univ of Hull (BSc), London Business Sch (Sloane fell); *m* 1954, Margaret Patricia, *née* Riley; 2 da; *Career* regnl dir N Region DTI 1972–74, under sec DTI and Dept of Industry 1972–76, dep sec Dept of Industry 1976–80; chm: Post Office 1981–87 (dep chm 1980–81), Camelot Group plc 1994–95; gp chm Nationalised Industries Chairmen's Gp 1983–84; non-exec dir: Prudential Corp 1987–91, Whitbread Co plc 1988–90, Br Coal Corp 1988–91, Ericsson Ltd 1988–93, IMI plc 1988–94, SDX plc 1996–98; chm: Co Durham Devpt Corp 1987–90, CNAA 1987–88, Polys and Colls Funding Cncl 1988–92, Northern Devpt Corp 1990–94, Fin Reporting Cncl 1989–93, Review Ctee on Accounting Standards, Universities Funding Cncl 1991–92, Higher Educn Funding Cncl for England 1992–93, Nat Curriculum Cncl, Sch Examinations and Assessment Cncl 1993, Sch Curriculum and Assessment Authy 1993–96, Nat Ctee of Inquiry into Higher Educn 1996–97; chair: Write Away 1996–2000, University for Industry (ufi) 1999–2000, Higher Educn Policy Inst 2002–; chm Churches Schools Review Gp (C of E) 1999–2001, chllr Univ of Nottingham 1994–2000; memb Governing Body Univ of Melbourne 1997–2000; first pres Inst of Direct Mktg 1994–97, pres Assoc of Church Colleges 2000–02, vice-pres: Local Govt Assoc 2000–, Nat Centre for Young People with Epilepsy; chair of tstees HE Policy Inst 2002–04; tstee: TRAC until 1997, The Sascha Lasserson Meml Tst, Home of Compassion 2003–; patron: Music in Allendale, ufi, Trident, Christ's Coll Guildford 2003–; author or chair of reports on: accounting standards 1988, schs curriculum and assessment 1993–94, review of qualifications for 16–19 year olds 1995–96, HE 1996–97, C of E schs 200–01, foreign languages in schs 2006–07; Gold Medal Inst of Mgmnt 1994, McKechnie Lecture Univ of Liverpool 1995, Menzies Lecture Univ of Melbourne 1998; Hon Dr: Univ of Brighton, Univ of Durham, Univ of Exeter, Univ of Nottingham, Univ of Hull, Univ of Humberside, Univ of Melbourne, Univ of Glos; fell: London Business Sch, Univ of Sunderland, Open Univ; Hon FREng 1992, Hon FCGI; *Recreations* music, gardening, car boot sales; *Style—* The Lord Dearing, CB; ✉ House of Lords, London SW1A 0PW

DEARLOVE, Sir Richard Billing; KCMG (2001), OBE (1984); *b* 23 January 1945; *Educ* Monkton Combe Sch, Kent Sch CT, Queens' Coll Cambridge (MA); *m* 1968, Rosalind, *née* McKenzie; 2 s, 1 da; *Career* joined FCO 1966; served: Nairobi 1968–71, FCO 1971–73, 1976–80 and 1984–87, Prague 1973–76, Paris 1980–84, UKMIS Geneva 1987–91, Washington 1991–93; Secret Intelligence Service: dir personnel and admin 1993–94, dir ops 1994–98, asst chief 1998–99, chief 1999–2004; master Pembroke Coll Cambridge 2004–; memb Advsy Bd American Int Gp 2005–, advsr to Monitor Gp 2005–; tstee Kent Sch CT 2001–; hon fell Queens' Coll Cambridge 2004; *Style—* Sir Richard Dearlove, KCMG, OBE; ✉ The Master's Lodge, Pembroke College, Cambridge CB2 1RF

DEARY, Prof Ian J; s of Hugh McCulloch Deary, of Carluke, Lanarkshire, and Isobelle Ferguson, *née* Higgins; *b* 17 May 1954, Carluke, Lanarkshire; *Educ* Hamilton Acad, David Dale Coll Glasgow (ONC), Glasgow Coll of Technol (HNC), Univ of Edinburgh (BSc, MB ChB, PhD); *m* 26 June 1978, Ann Marie, *née* Barclay; 2 da (Elayne b 1 April 1979, Joanna Frances Halla b 5 Aug 1982), 1 s (Matthew John Hugh b 5 May 1988); *Career* house physician, house surgn, locum sr house surgn and SHO in psychiatry Edinburgh and London 1983–85, registrar in psychiatry Royal Edinburgh Hosp 1989–90; Univ of Edinburgh: lectr A 1985–90, sr lectr 1990–92, reader 1992–95, prof of differential psychology (personal chair) 1995–; fndr memb Int Soc for Intelligence Research (memb Advsy Ctee), memb Standing Ctee Psychology Div Br Acad; Int Soc for the Study of Individual Differences: memb, chair Ctee to Select Distinguished Young Scientist Award, memb Publication Ctee, memb Bd of Dirs 1993–2003, pres 1999–2001, past pres 2001–03; Chllr's Award Univ of Edinburgh 2003, Royal Soc-Wolfson Research Merit Award 2003–; CPsychol, MRCPsych 1991, FRCPE 1996, FRSE 2003, FBA 2003, FMedSci 2007; *Publications* Foundations of Personality (jt ed, 1993), Personality Psychology in Europe, volume 4 (jt ed, 1993), Personality Traits (jtly, 1998, 2 edn 2003), Personality Psychology in Europe, volume 7 (jt ed, 1999), Looking Down on Human Intelligence: From Psychometrics to the Brain (2000, Br Psychology Soc Book Award 2002), Intelligence: A Very Short Introduction (2001); also author of numerous book chapters and refereed jl articles; *Recreations* cycling, saxophone, lyric writing, English romantic composers, late Victorian novelists, Motherwell FC; *Style—* Prof Ian J Deary; ✉ Department of Psychology, University of Edinburgh, 7 George Square, Edinburgh EH8 9JZ (tel 0131 650 3452, fax 0131 651 1771, e-mail i.deary@ed.ac.uk)

DEAS, Roger Stewart; s of George Stewart (d 1983), of Motherwell, and Winifred Mary, *née* Ogden (d 1996); *b* 1 August 1943; *Educ* The HS of Glasgow, Univ of Glasgow (BSc); *m* 27 June 1970, Carole, da of Percy Woodward, of Nottingham; 2 da (Angela Elizabeth b 1972, Wendy Jane b 1974); *Career* fin dir: Brown Bros Ltd 1974–81, Currys Group plc 1981–85, Heron Corporation plc 1985–86; nat fin ptnr Coopers & Lybrand 1986–95; md Bridewell Group plc 1995–; FCMA 1986 (ACMA 1974); *Recreations* sailing; *Clubs* Royal Motor Yacht; *Style—* Roger Deas, Esq; ✉ Sunset House, 10 Chaddesley Glen, Canford Cliffs, Poole, Dorset BH13 7PF (tel 01202 709394); The Bridewell Group plc, Bridewell House, Reading, Berkshire RG1 1JG (tel 0118 960 7550)

D

DEASLEY, Prof Peter John; s of Reginald George Deasley (d 1979), of Newmarket, Suffolk, and Eileen Violet, *née* Bray (d 1964); *b* 26 January 1943; *Educ* Soham GS, The King's Sch Ely, Univ of Nottingham (BSc, PhD), Univ of Cambridge (MA); *m* 1, 1969 (m dis 1980); m 2, 1985, Irène Margossian (d 2006); *Career* research asst Univ of Cambridge 1965–67, engr and gp ldr English Electric Valve Co 1968–72; PA Technology: conslt then sr conslt UK 1972–78, mangr Germany 1978–80, mangr Switzerland 1980–83, mangr Benelux 1983–85; dir Ingersoll Engineers 1985–88, md Cambridge Control Ltd 1988–90; Cranfield Univ: dir Business Servs CIM Inst 1990–99, prof of mechatronics 1993–2005, emeritus prof 2006–; dir Cranfield Innovative Manufacturing Research Centre 2002–05; Royal Acad of Engrg visiting prof Univ of Hull 1989–94; winner Tony Goldsmith Cup IProdE 1988; author of 100 papers in scientific jls and two book chapters; FIET (FIEE 1986), FRSA 1987, FREng 1997; *Recreations* golf, watching cricket, music; *Clubs* Royal Over-Seas League, Rugby Golf, Newmarket Links Golf; *Style—* Prof Peter Deasley, FREng; ✉ Cranfield University, Cranfield, Bedfordshire MK43 0AL (tel 01234 750111)

DEAYTON, (Gordon) Angus; s of Roger Davall Deayton, of Caterham, Surrey, and Susan Agnes, *née* Weir; *b* 6 January 1956; *Educ* Caterham Sch Surrey, New Coll Oxford (BA); *Career* writer and broadcaster; with Oxford Revue at Edinburgh Festival 1978 and 1979, memb Hee Bee Gee Bees pop parody gp 1979–85, writer and performer Radio Active (BBC Radio 4) 1980–87 (various awards incl from BPG and Sony); writer/performer: Brunch (Capital Radio) 1985–88, Uncyclopaedia of Rock (Capital Radio) 1986–87 (Monaco Radio award 1986), Rowan Atkinson Stage Show (UK, Aust and NY) 1986–90, Alexei Sayle's Stuff (BBC2) 1988–91, One Foot in the Grave (BBC1) 1989–2000; writer/presenter: KYTV (BBC2) 1989–93 (Grand Prix and Silver Rose of Montreux 1992), TV Hell (BBC2) 1992, Have I Got News For You 1990–2002, In Search of Happiness 1995, End of the Year Show 1995, 1996, 1997, 1998 and 2000, The Lying Game 1997, Before They Were Famous 1997–2005, The Temptation Game 1998, History of Alternative Comedy 1999, Not Another Awards Show 1999, Millenium Sketch Show 1999, Not Another Gameshow, News Bulletin, Eurovision Song Contest 2002, Posh'n'Becks: The Reign in Spain 2003–05, Nighty Night 2003–05; presenter: BAFTA Awards 1996 and 2001, Hell's Kitchen 2004–05, Bognor or Bust 2004, New Year's Dishonours List 2005, Heartless 2005, Comic Relief Does University Challenge 2003 and 2005, Absolute Power 2005, Stick to What You Know 2005, Help Your Self 2006, Only Fools on Horses 2006, Would I Lie to You? 2007; other awards incl: Newcomer of the Year TV Comedy Awards 1991, Best TV Performance in a non-acting role BPG Awards 1992, New Talent of the Year TV and Radio Industry Club Awards 1992, BBC TV Personality of the Year TV and Radio Industry Club Awards 1995; *Books* Radio Active Times (1986), The Uncyclopaedia of Rock (1987), In Search of Happiness (1995); *Recreations* soccer (former Crystal Palace FC triallist), tennis, skiing; *Clubs* Groucho, Soho House, Home House, Garrick; *Style—* Angus Deayton; ✉ c/o ICM, Oxford House, 76 Oxford Street, London W1D 1BS (tel 020 7636 6565, e-mail nickforgacs@icmlondon.co.uk)

DEBLONDE, Eric; *b* 24 April 1951; *m* Evelyne Blondel; 1 s (Olivier b 24 Jan 1978); *Career* chef; Henri IV Restaurant Dunkirk 1967–69, second de cuisine Hotel de Dieppe Rouen 1972 (joined 1969, CAP de cuisine 1970–72), mil serv 1972–73, second de cuisine Auberge de l'Ecu de France Rouen Aug-Sept 1973, chef saucier Inn on the Park London 1973–74, chef garde mangr Hôtel du Golf Crans Sur Sierre Switzerland 1974–75, chef rôtisseur Belles Rives Juan les Pins May-Sept 1975, sous chef Inn on the Park London 1975–76, chef de cuisine La Marine Caudebec en Caux 1976, exec chef Hotel Tunis Hilton Tunisia 1977–79 (1 sous chef 1976–77), chef de cuisine Le Kilal Château Baie de St Tropez March-Nov 1979, chef de cuisine Frantei Bordeaux 1980–86, exec chef Four Seasons Inn on the Park 1986–2002, exec chef Four Seasons Amman 2002–; chef Challenge Anneka (BBC Television) 1994; awards incl: Grand Prix de l'Académie Nationale de Cuisine, Craft Guild of Chefs Banqueting Award 1995; pres Association Culinaire Française 1992–, memb Académie Culinaire de France; Chevalier de l'Ordre du Mérite Agricole 1995, Maître Cuisiniër de France 1996, vice-consul Ordre des Canardiers GB; *Style—* Eric Deblonde, Esq; ✉ The Four Seasons, Amman (tel 00 962 6 550 5555, fax 00 962 6 550 5556)

DECIES, 7 Baron (I 1812); Marcus Hugh Tristam de la Poer Beresford; only s of 6 Baron Decies (d 1992), and his 2 w, Diana, *née* Turner Cain; *b* 5 August 1948; *Educ* St Columba's Coll, Univ of Dublin (MLitt); *m* 1, 1970 (m dis 1974), Sarah Jane, only da of Col Basil Gunnell; m 2, 1981, Edel Jeanette, da of late Vincent Ambrose Hendron, of Dublin; 2 da (Hon Louisa Katherine de la Poer b 23 Oct 1984, Hon Jessica Laragh Marion de la Poer b 16 Nov 1996), 2 s (Hon Robert Marcus Duncan de la Poer b 14 July 1988, Hon David George Morley Hugh de la Poer b 4 May 1991); *Heir* s, Hon Robert Beresford; *Career* lawyer and historian; FCIArb; *Clubs* MCC, Kildare St and Univ (Dublin); *Style—* The Rt Hon Lord Decies; ✉ Straffan Lodge, Straffan, Co Kildare, Ireland

DEDMAN, His Hon Judge Peter George; s of George Stephen Henry Dedman (d 1971), and Jessie Maud, *née* Hanson; *b* 22 May 1940; *Educ* Tottenham GS; *m* 4 April 1965, Patricia Mary Gordon, JP, RGN, da of Gawn Orr and Irene Gordon; 1 da (Clare Victoria b 23 June 1972); *Career* Magistrates' Courts Service Brentford, Tottenham and Newham until 1969; called to the Bar Gray's Inn 1968, recorder of the Crown Court 1992; memb Age Link, memb Musicians' Union; *Recreations* music - playing piano and trombone, film/concert/theatre-going; *Style—* His Hon Judge Peter Dedman; ✉ Chelmsford Crown Court, New Street, Chelmsford, Essex CM1 1EL (tel 01245 603000, fax 01245 603011)

DEE, Michael James Damian; s of Kenneth William Dee (d 1977), of Bath, and Dorothy Josephine, *née* Whittern-Carter (d 1999); *b* 12 June 1946; *Educ* Douai Coll, Univ of Edinburgh (BSc); *m* 28 April 1973 (m dis 1997), Pamela Sarah, da of Cecil George Moore, of Jersey; 5 da (Samantha b 1974, Joanna b 1976, Nicola b 1977, Belinda b 1980, Emily b 1991); partner, Jane Elizabeth Dee, *née* Baker (surname changed by deed poll); *Career* dir Damian Investment Tst 1972–73, md Europlan Financial Services 1976–, chm Europlan Continuation Ltd 1984–; FInstD; *Recreations* sailing, golf, motor racing, shooting; *Clubs* Royal Channel Islands Yacht, La Moye Golf; *Style—* Michael Dee, Esq; ✉ Le Fromentel, La Grande Route de la Cote, St Clement, Jersey JE2 6SD; Europlan

Continuation Ltd, International House, The Parade, St Helier, Jersey JE2 3QQ (tel 01534 505800, fax 01534 505805, e-mail admin@europlantrust.com)

DEECH, Baroness (Life Peer UK 2005), of Cumnor in the County of Oxfordshire; Dame Ruth Lynn Deech; DBE (2002); da of Josef Asher Fraenkel (d 1987), of London, and Dora, *née* Rosenfeld (d 1989); *b* 29 April 1943; *Educ* Christ's Hosp, St Anne's Coll Oxford (BA), Brandeis Univ USA (Fulbright award, MA); *m* 23 July 1967, Dr John Stewart Deech, s of Max Deech; 1 da (Hon Sarah Rosalind Phyllis b 13 Nov 1974); *Career* legal asst Law Cmmn 1966–67, called to the Bar 1967, research asst to Leslie Scarman (later Rt Hon Lord Scarman) 1967–68, asst prof of law Univ of Windsor Canada 1968–70, fell and tutor in law St Anne's Coll Oxford 1970–91, pupillage 1981, princ St Anne's Coll Oxford 1991–2004; visiting prof Osgoode Hall Law Sch York Univ Canada 1978; Univ of Oxford: sr proctor 1985–86, memb Hebdomadal Cncl 1986–2000, chm Admissions Ctee 1993–97 and 2000–03, pro-vice-chllr 2001–04; visiting lectr Faculty of Law Univ of Cape Town 1994; memb Ctee of Inquiry into Equal Opportunities on the Bar Vocational Course 1993–94, memb Exec Cncl of Int Soc of Family Law, chm Human Fertilisation and Embryology Authy 1994–2002; ind adjudicator for HE 2004–; govr: Carmel Coll Wallingford 1980–90, Oxford Centre for Hebrew and Jewish Studies 1994–2000, UCS 1997–2002; chm Stuart Young Awards 1988–, Rhodes tstee 1996–2006; Hon Freeman Worshipful Co of Drapers 2003; hon bencher Inner Temple 1996; Hon LLD: Univ of Strathclyde 2003, Richmond the American Int Univ 2006; hon fell Soc for Advanced Legal Studies 1997–; FRSM 2001; *Recreations* after dinner speaking, music, entertaining; *Style*— The Lady Deech, DBE; ✉ Office of the Independent Adjudicator, Thames Tower, 5th Floor, Station Road, Reading RG1 1LX (tel 0118 959 9813)

DEEDES, Hon Jeremy Wyndham; s of Baron Deedes, MC, PC, DL (Life Peer, d 2007), and Evelyn Hilary, *née* Branfoot (d 2004); *b* 24 November 1943; *Educ* Eton; *m* 1973, Anna Rosemary, da of late Maj Elwin Gray; 2 s (George William b 28 Feb 1976, Henry Julius b 8 June 1978); *Career* reporter: Kent & Sussex Courier 1963–66, Daily Sketch 1966–69; dep ed Daily Express 1976–79, managing ed Evening Standard 1979–85 (ed Londoner's Diary 1970–76), managing ed Today 1985–86; Daily and Sunday Telegraph: exec ed 1986–92, editorial dir 1992–96; Telegraph Group: md 1996–2003, chief exec 2004, vice-chm 2004; exec chm The Sportsman 2006, non-exec chm Pelham PR 2007–; chm Newspaper Publishers Assoc 1998; dir Warwick Racecourse, memb Horserace Totalisator Bd 1992–98; *Recreations* cricket, racing, golf, cabinet making; *Clubs* Boodle's, Royal Cape Golf, Sunningdale Golf, Huntercombe Golf; *Style*— The Hon Jeremy Deedes; ✉ Hamilton House, Compton, Newbury, Berkshire RG16 0QJ (tel 01635 578 695)

DEEGAN, Terence Leslie (Terry); s of Gilbert Leslie Deegan (d 1970), and Doris Elsie, *née* Barnet (d 2002); *b* 26 September 1942; *Educ* Dartford GS; *m* Susan Philippa; 1 s (Paul b 24 Sept 1969), 2 da (Tara Joanna b 18 Nov 1982, Naomi Rachel b 12 Aug 1985); *Career* with Customs & Excise 1959–67, full time union official Customs & Excise Gp (Trade Union) 1967–71, asst sec Soc of Civil and Public Servants 1971–80; Communication Mangrs' Assoc (CMA): dep gen sec 1980–89, elected gen sec 1989–98 (re-elected 1994), CMA chief exec and Mfrg Sci and Fin (MSF) nat offr 1998–2002; ed CMA News 1989–2002; memb: HM Prisons Ind Monitoring Bd 2001–05, Easterton PC 2003–; *Recreations* theatre, poultry keeping, walking, cycling and family; *Clubs* Lansdowne, Theatre Royal Bath; *Style*— Terry Deegan, Esq; ✉ TD Consultancy Services, Highlands House, Easterton, Devizes, Wiltshire SN10 4PG (tel and fax 01380 813488)

DEELEY, Michael; s of John Hamilton-Deeley (d 1979), and Josephine Frances Anne, *née* Deacon; *b* 6 August 1932; *Educ* Stowe; *m* 1, 1955 (m dis 1967), Teresa Harrison; 2 da (Catherine Anne b 26 Aug 1956, Isobel b 16 July 1957), 1 s (Manuel b 4 Jan 1964); m 2, 1970, Ruth Vivienne Emilie, da of Vivian George Stone-Spencer (d 1995); *Career* Nat Serv 1950–52, 2 Lt IRWK serv Malaya 1951–52; film prodr; md: Br Lion Films 1972–76, EMI Films Ltd 1976–79; pres EMI Films Inc (USA) 1977–79, chm and ceo Consolidated Entertainment Inc 1984–90; prodr of more than thirty motion pictures incl: The Deer Hunter (Best Film Oscar 1978), The Italian Job, Convoy, Murphy's War, The Man Who Fell to Earth, Blade Runner, Robbery, A Gathering of Old Men (NAACP Image Award); dep chm Br Screen Advsy Cncl; fndr memb: PM's Working Party on the Film Industry 1975, Interim Action Ctee on the Film Industry; memb Motion Picture Acad Arts & Sciences (US), BECTU (formerly ACTT); *Recreations* sailing; *Clubs* Garrick, New York Yacht; *Style*— Michael Deeley, Esq; ✉ 1010 Fairway Road, Santa Barbara, CA 93108, USA; 36 Elizabeth Court, London SW10 0JU

DEELEY, Peter Anthony William; s of George William Deeley (d 1985), of Warks, and Bridie Deeley, of Balsall Common, nr Coventry; *b* 30 August 1942; *Educ* Ratcliffe Coll, Coventry Poly; *m* 9 July 1966, Patricia Ann, da of Walter Edgar Jones (d 1983), of Coventry; 3 da (Eleanor Elizabeth Jude b 28 Sept 1976, Anna Shahida Jude b 10 Aug 1982, Rosemary Lucy Jude b 27 Nov 1984); *Career* dep md GW Deeley Ltd 1968 (joined 1958); chm Deeley Group Ltd 1985; pres Builder Employers' Confedn (Coventry) 1970–; vice-chm: Coventry Hosps Tst (chm 1992–), Coventry Tech Coll (chm 1991–95); Freeman City of Coventry 1963; memb Inst of Bldg; *Recreations* golf, walking; *Style*— Peter Deeley, Esq; ✉ Eathorpe Hall, Eathorpe, Leamington Spa, Warwickshire CV33 9DF (tel 01926 632755); Deeley Group Ltd, William House, Torrington Avenue, Coventry, Warwickshire CV4 9GY (tel 024 7646 2521, fax 024 7646 9533)

DEEM, Prof Rosemary; da of Lesley George Deem (d 1986), of Liff, Dundee, and Peggy, *née* Stoyle, of Liff, Dundee; *b* 18 January 1949, Plymouth, Devon; *Educ* Queen Eleanor's GS Dunstable, Univ of Leicester (BA, MPhil), Open Univ (PhD); *m* 12 March 1985, Prof Kevin Joseph Brehony, s of Eddie Joseph Brehony (d 1984), of Birmingham; *Career* tutorial asst in sociology Univ of Leicester 1972–73; temp lectr in sociology: Loughborough Univ 1973–74, Univ of York 1974–75; lectr in sociology N Staffs Poly 1975–79; Open Univ: lectr in sociology of educn 1980–87, sr lectr in sociology of educn 1987–91, sub dean (research) Faculty of Educn 1986–91; Lancaster Univ: prof of educnl research 1991–2000, dean of social sciences 1994–97, founding dir Grad Sch 1998–2000; prof of educn Univ of Bristol 2001–; dir ESCalate (UK Learning and Teaching Support Network Educn Subject Centre) 2001–04; chair: Research Ctee Univs Cncl on the Educn of Teachers 1991–93, Pubns Ctee Soc for Research in HE 2003–; memb: HE Funding Bodies Research Assessment Panel for Educn 1996, 2001 and 2008, Grants Bd ESRC 1999–2003; elected memb Cncl BERA 1993–97; jt managing ed The Sociological Review 2001–05; chair Br Sociological Assoc 1986–87 and 1994–96 (treas 1985–86), chair R&D Ctee 2007–, vice-chair Soc for Res into HE 2007–; *Publications* Women and Schooling (1978), Schooling for Women's Work (ed, 1980), Co-education Reconsidered (ed, 1984), All Work and No Play (1986), Work, Unemployment and Leisure (1988), Active Citizenship and the Governing of Schools (with K J Brehony and S J Heath, 1995), Knowledge, Higher Education and the New Managerialism (with M Reed and S Hillyard, 2007); also author of over 70 academic articles and chapters in social science jls and books; *Recreations* hill walking, cycling, photography, caravanning, reading, theatre, visiting art galleries, travel; *Style*— Prof Rosemary Deem; ✉ Graduate School of Education, University of Bristol, Helen Wodehouse Building, 35 Berkeley Square, Bristol BS8 1JA (tel 0117 928 7013, fax 0117 925 1537, e-mail r.deem@bristol.ac.uk)

DEENY, Hon Mr Justice; Sir Donnell Justin Patrick Deeny; kt (2005); *b* 25 April 1950; *Educ* Clongowes Wood Coll, TCD, Queen's Univ Belfast; *m* 1998, Alison Jane, *née* Scott; 2 da (Grace b 1999, Eless b 2006), 1 s (Alexander b 2001), 2 da from previous m (Maeve, Rebecca); *Career* called to the Bar NI 1974, bencher Middle Temple and NI, QC (NI) 1989, SC Repub of Ireland 1996, judge of the High Court of Justice in NI 2004–; chm: Opera NI 1988–92, Arts Cncl of NI 1993–98 (memb 1991–98); pres Ulster Architectural Heritage Soc 2006; tstee Ulster Museum 1983–85; memb (Alliance) Belfast City Cncl 1981–85, High Sheriff Belfast 1983; *Recreations* books, the arts, skiing; *Style*— The Hon Mr Justice Deeny; ✉ c/o Royal Courts of Justice, Chichester Street, Belfast BT1 3JF

DEERING, Christopher (Chris); s of Claude V Deering, and Helen Bruno; *b* 15 January 1945, Boston, MA; *Educ* Boston Coll (BS), Harvard Business Sch (MBA); *m* 1 Sept 1968, Jane van Dyke; 1 s (J Claude b 12 Dec 1981), 1 da (Abigail van Dyke 18 March 1985); *Career* product mangr int mktg Gillette Corp 1968–70, assoc mktg McKinsey & Co 1970–73, mktg dir Europe Gillette Corp 1979–83, vice-pres int mktg Atari Warner Communications 1983–85, sr vice-pres int sales Columbia Pictures Home Video 1985–90, exec vice-pres and chief operating offr int Columbia TriStar Home Video 1990–95, pres Sony Computer Entertainment Europe 1995–2004, pres Sony Europe 2004–05; Lifetime Achievement Award (Interactive Arts) BAFTA 2003; *Recreations* sailing, skiing, piano, history; *Clubs* Union, Soho House; *Style*— Chris Deering, Esq

DEERY, Dr Alastair Robin Stewart; s of late Sgt-Major Michael John Stewart Deery, MM, and Isabella Stout, *née* Murray; *b* 5 October 1953; *Educ* Alleynes Sch, Univ of London (BSc, MB BS); *m* 1, 24 Dec 1981 (m dis 1993), Dr Clare Constantine Davey, da of Dr Charles James Constantine Davey; m 2, April 1994, Dr Valerie Thomas, da of David Thomas; 2 s (Andrew, Michael), 1 da (Charlotte); *Career* house offr UCH London 1979, SHO Manchester 1980, registrar in histopathology Western Infirmary Glasgow 1981–83, sr registrar in histopathology and cytopathology Charing Cross Hosp London 1984–86, conslt, hon sr lectr in histopathology and cytopathology and dir cytopathology unit Royal Free Hosp London 1986– (chm of pathology 1994–96, unit trg dir 1996–); med lab head London Regnl QAT; memb: Br Soc of Clinical Cytology, Pathological Soc of UK, London Regnl Cncl, NHSCSP, RCPath 2001–; chm LNC 2000–; FRCPath 1996; *Recreations* collecting writing instruments, skiing; *Style*— Dr Alastair Deery

DEFRIES, Jeffrey; *b* 14 February 1948; *Educ* Univ of Birmingham (BCom); *m* Dr Elizabeth Defries; 2 s; *Career* asst to fin sec Imperial Coll of Science and Technol London 1972–73, asst sec Inst of Devpt Studies Univ of Sussex 1974–76, sec Inst of Cancer Research 1982–88 (dep sec 1977–82), asst dir The Science Museum 1988–98, dep dean and sec London Business Sch 1998–2001, sec and head of corp affrs NHSU 2002–05, chief exec Careers Research and Advisory Centre (CRAC) and dir Nat Inst for Careers Educn and Counselling (NICEC) 2006–; fundraising advsr Int Cncl of Nurses 2002–, sr advr European Fndn for Mgmnt Devpt; lectr Civil Service Coll; numerous conference presentations on mgmnt of change, corp governance and fin mgmnt; local voluntary positions incl chm Northwood and Pinner Lib Synagogue; CPFA; *Style*— Jeffrey Defries, Esq

DEFRIEZ, Alistair Norman Campbell; s of Norman William Defriez, and Helen Catherine, *née* Maclean (d 1991); *b* 2 November 1951; *Educ* Dulwich Coll, UC Oxford (open Gladstone scholar, MA); *m* 1978, Linda Phillips; 1 da (Rachel Philippa b 1982), 2 s (Richard Alistair James b 1984, Henry Alistair William b 1985); *Career* Coopers & Lybrand 1973–78, md UBS Investment Bank (formerly S G Warburg & Co Ltd then UBS Warburg) 1987– (joined 1978), on secondment as DG Panel on Takeovers and Mergers 1996–99; FCA 1978 (ACA 1976); *Recreations* golf, rugby, music, reading; *Clubs* St George's Hill Golf, Royal Wimbledon Golf, London Scottish RFC, Bankers'; *Style*— Alistair Defriez, Esq

DEGEN, Dr Richard Mark; s of William Degen (d 1986), of Vienna, and Bertha, *née* Weinlös; *b* 18 February 1938; *Educ* Christ's Coll GS, KCL, Royal Dental Hosp London (Prosthetics prize, Baldwin scholar, Dolamore prize), Charing Cross Hosp London, St George's Hosp London, Univ of London (BDS); *m* 1973, Bernice Janet, da of Cyril Roles; 3 s (Jonathan Howard b 24 Feb 1965, Antony Craig b 6 Dec 1966, Robbie Benjamin b 21 July 1976), 1 da (Danielle Lisbeth b 30 March 1978); *Career* dental surgeon and prosthodontist; NHS 1961, oral surgery, dental reconstruction and conscious sedation specialist in private practice 1966–; demonstrator in conservative dentistry Royal Dental Hosp Sch of Dental Surgery London, accredited implant surgeon for Bicon implant system Faulkener Hosp Tufts Univ; memb: Br Soc of Med and Dental Hypnosis 1983, Soc for Advancement of Anaesthesia in Dentistry 1986; The Royal Humane Soc Award 1971; peer review convenor and teacher RCS; memb: Faculty of Dental Surgery RCS England (memb Advsy Bd), Assoc of Dental Implantology UK; LDSRCS 1961; *Recreations* private aviation, electronics, swimming; *Style*— Dr Richard M Degen; ✉ 135 Harley Street, London W1G 6BE (tel 020 7486 2207 and 020 8455 3122, fax 0870 169 1670, mobile 07973 612613, e-mail degen@dsl.pipex.com, website www.bicon.co.uk)

DEGHY, Julian; s of Guy Deghy (d 1992), of London, and Mari, *née* Hooper; *b* 16 October 1960; *Educ* St Clement Danes GS for Boys; *Career* freelance photographic asst 1980–82, photographic asst to James Cotier, *qv* 1983–86, freelance photographer 1987–; various exhbns incl Assoc of Photographers Awards exhbns 1993 and 1999; solo exhbn of the art bronze foundry Museum of London 1999, photographic exhbn of Elizabeth Frink's work River and Rowing Museum Henley 2000–01; memb Assoc of Photographers 1987; *Recreations* racing, theatre, music, travel, food and wine; *Clubs* Chelsea Arts, Groucho; *Style*— Julian Deghy; ✉ 43 Carol Street, London NW1 0HT (tel 020 7267 7635, fax 020 7267 8706, website www.deghy.com)

DEHN, Conrad Francis; QC (1968); s of Curt Gustav Dehn (d 1948), of London, and Cynthia, *née* Fuller (d 1987); *b* 24 November 1926; *Educ* Charterhouse, ChCh Oxford (MA); *m* 1, 1954, Sheila, da of William Kilmurray Magan (d 1967), of London; 2 s (Hugh b 1956, Guy b 1957), 1 da (Katharine b 1959); m 2, 1978, Marilyn, da of Peter Collyer (d 1979), of Oxon; *Career* RA 1945–48, best cadet Mons Basic OCTU 1946, 2 Lt 1947; called to the Bar Gray's Inn 1952 (bencher 1977, treas 1996); recorder of the Crown Court 1974–98, head of Fountain Court Chambers 1984–89, dep judge of the High Court 1988–96; dir Bar Mutual Insurance Fund 1988–; chm: London Univ Disciplinary Appeals Ctee 1986–90, Advsy Ctee Gen Cmmrs of Income Tax Gray's Inn 1994–2003; hon legal advsr Southwark Action for Voluntary Orgns 2003–; memb Advsy Bd Inns of Court Sch of Law 2002– (govr 1996–2002); pres Camberwell Soc 1996–2007, vice-pres Age Concern London 2001–02; Hon Liberty of the Old Metropolitan Borough of Camberwell 2006; *Recreations* theatre, living in France; *Clubs* Reform; *Style*— Conrad Dehn, QC; ✉ Fountain Court, Temple, London EC4Y 9DH (tel 020 7583 3335, fax 020 7353 0329, e-mail cdehn@fountaincourt.co.uk)

DEHN, Thomas Clark Bruce; s of Harold Bruce Dehn, and Jean Margaret Henderson, *née* Ewing; *b* 6 March 1949; *Educ* Harrow, RAF Coll Cranwell, Bart's Med Coll London (MB BS, MS, LRCP); *m* 15 Sept 1984, (Dorothea) Lorraine, da of Gilbert Maurice Baird, of Dunbartonshire; 2 da (Henrietta b 1986, Emily b 1988); *Career* gen surgn; conslt gen surgn Royal Berks Hosp Reading, clinical lectr in surgery Nuffield Dept of Surgery John Radcliffe Hosp Oxford 1984–88, lectr in surgery Bart's Med Coll London 1980–84; conslt surgn Royal Berks Hosp Reading 1990–; examiner in surgery Faculty of Dental Surgeons RCS 1990–95, examiner Intercollegiate Bd in Gen Surgery 2001–; chm Oxford Deanery Gen Surgery Higher Surgical Trg Ctee 1995–2001, chm Oesophageal Section Br Soc of Gastroenterology 2006– (sec 2000–05); memb: Hosp Jr Staff Ctee 1987–88, Cncl Section of Surgery RSM 1993–96, RCS Comparative Audit Serv Ctee 1992–98, MRC Working Pty on Oesophageal Cancer 1994–96, Grey Turner Surgical Club 1994–, Br Oesophageal Gp 1994–, Cncl Assoc of Surgeons of GB and I 2005–, Br Soc of Gastroenterologists, Cncl Assoc of Laparoscopic Surgns of GB and I; Freeman City of London, Liveryman and Steward Worshipful Co of Distillers; FRCS; *Publications* author of research publications on oesophageal cancer, surgery and physiology of hiatus hernia, and laparoscopic (key-hole) surgery; *Recreations* flying, rowing, shooting, sailing; *Style*— Thomas Dehn, Esq; ✉ Department of Surgery, Royal Berkshire Hospital, Reading,

Berkshire RG1 5AN (tel 0118 322 8623); Capio Hospital, Reading, Berkshire RG1 6UZ (tel 0118 902 8012, website www.lapsurg.info)

DEIGHTON, Gary; s of Eric Deighton, and Joan Margaret, *née* Brittle; *b* 2 August 1961, Nottingham; *Educ* Glaisdale Sch Nottingham, Bilborough Coll Nottingham, Univ of Dundee (MA), Humberside Coll (PGCE), Univ of Nottingham (MA), Henley Coll (Dip), Br Assoc for Counselling and Psychotherapy (Dip); *m* 1 July 1989, Alison, *née* Davies; 1 s (Alexander Huw b 8 March 1998), 1 da (Anastasia Helen b 8 Aug 2000); *Career* teacher 1984–86, asst govr HM Prison Serv 1986–96, auditor HM Prison Serv 1995–97, govr HMP Swansea 1997–99, govr HMP Exeter 1999–2002, HM inspr of prisons 2002–05, govr HMP Pentonville 2005–07, head Professional Standards Unit Prison Serv 2007–een's Golden Jubilee Medal 2002; *Recreations* the sea; *Style*— Gary Deighton, Esq; ✉ Corporate Security Group, HM Prison Service Headquarters, Cleland House, Page Street, London SW1P 4LN (tel 020 7217 3000, e-mail gary.deighton01@hmps.gsi.gov.uk)

DEIGHTON, Jane Elizabeth; da of Herbert Stanley Deighton (d 1976), and Mary Elizabeth Anne, *née* Duncan; *b* 18 March 1952; *Educ* Univ of Sussex (BA), Coll of Law; *Career* admitted slr 1985; slr Seifert Sedley Williams 1983–90, ptnr Deighton Guedalla 1990–; memb Law Soc; *Publications* Human Rights in Malawi (1992), Emergency Powers in Northern Ireland (1998); *Style*— Ms Jane Deighton; ✉ Deighton Guedalla, 382 City Road, London EC1V 2QA (tel 020 7713 9434, fax 020 7837 7473, e-mail jd@deightonguedalla.com)

DELACOURT-SMITH OF ALTERYN, Baroness (Life Peer UK 1974), of Alteryn in the County of Gwent; Margaret Rosalind; da of F J Hando; *b* 5 April 1916; *Educ* Newport High Sch, St Anne's Coll Oxford; *m* 1939, Baron Delacourt-Smith, PC (Life Peer; d 1972); 1 s, 2 da; m 2, 1978, Prof Charles Blackton; *Career* cncllr of Royal Borough of New Windsor 1962–65, JP 1962–67; *Style*— The Rt Hon the Lady Delacourt-Smith

DELAMERE, 5 Baron (UK 1821); Hugh George Cholmondeley; s of 4 Baron Delamere (d 1978, whose gf 2 Baron was fifth cous of 1 Marquess of Cholmondeley) and his 1 w, Phyllis, da of Lord George Montagu Douglas Scott (3 s of 6 Duke of Buccleuch); *b* 18 January 1934; *Educ* Eton, Magdalene Coll Cambridge (MA); *m* 1964, Ann Willoughby, da of Sir Patrick Renison, GCMG, and formerly w of Michael Tinné; 1 s; *Heir* s, Hon Thomas Cholmondeley; *Career* farmer; sr settlement officer Kinangop 1962–63; landowner (57,000 acres); *Recreations* racing, shooting, flying; *Clubs* Pitt, Muthaiga Country, Jockey (Kenya); *Style*— The Rt Hon the Lord Delamere

DELANEY, Francis James Joseph (Frank); 5 s of Edward Joseph Delaney (d 1968), of Tipperary, Ireland, and Elizabeth Josephine, *née* O'Sullivan (d 1990); *b* 24 October 1942; *Educ* Abbey Schs Tipperary, Rosse Coll Dublin; *m* 1, 1966 (m dis 1980), Eilish, *née* Kelliher; 3 s (Edward b 1968, Bryan b 1971, Owen b 1976); m 2, 1988 (m dis 1997), Susan, *née* Collier; m 3, 1998, Salley, *née* Vickers; m 4, Diane Meier; *Career* writer, broadcaster, journalist; work incl: RTE News Dublin, current affrs with BBC N Ireland, BBC TV and BBC Radio 4; *Non-Fiction* James Joyce's Odyssey (1981), Betjeman Country (1983), The Celts (1986), A Walk in the Dark Ages (1988), Legends of the Celts (1989), A Walk to the Western Isles (1993), Simple Courage (2006); *Novels* My Dark Rosaleen (novella, 1989), The Sins of the Mothers (1992), Telling the Pictures (1993), A Stranger in their Midst (1995), The Amethysts (1997), Desire and Pursuit (1998), Pearl (novel, 1999), At Ruby's (2001), Jim Hawkins and the Curse of Treasure Island (2002), Ireland, A Novel (2005); *Clubs* Athenaeum, Chelsea Arts; *Style*— Frank Delaney, Esq; ✉ e-mail frankdelaney@frankdelaney.com

DELANEY, Ven Peter Anthony; MBE (2001); s of Anthony Mario Delaney (d 1949), of Venice, Italy, and Ena, *née* Bradbury; *b* 20 June 1939; *Educ* KCL, St Boniface Coll Warminster; *Career* ordained: deacon 1966, priest 1967; curate St Marylebone Parish Church 1966–70, chaplain London Unity Church of Christ the King 1970–74, canon residentiary and precentor Southwark Cathedral 1974–77, vicar All Hallows by the Tower 1977–2004, canon St Paul's Cathedral Nicosia and sr commissary Dio of Cyprus and the Gulf 1984, prebendery St Paul's Cathedral 1995–99, guild vicar St Katherine Cree City of London 1997–2000, archdeacon of London 1999–, rector St Stephen Walbrook 2002–; govr St Dunstan's Coll Catford 1977–2004; dir City Arts Tst 1980–93, chm City Churches Devpt Gp 1995–2002; Master Worshipful Co of World Traders 1994–95, Master Worshipful Co of Gardeners 1999–2000; Freeman Co of Watermen & Lightermen; Kt Cdr SMO of Knights Templars; fell Sion Coll City of London, AKC; *Books* The Canon Law of the Church of England (1975), The Artist and his Explorations into God (1981); *Recreations* gardening, painting, theatre, the arts in general; *Style*— The Ven the Archdeacon of London, MBE; ✉ Archdeacon of London's Office, The Old Deanery, Dean's Court, London EC4V 5AA (tel 020 7236 7891)

DELANEY, Theo John Samuel; s of Barry John Samuel Delaney, of Hamilton Terrace, London, and Brenda Jean, *née* Darby; *b* 31 December 1965; *Educ* Shene Sch, Richmond Coll; *Career* prodn runner John Clive & Co 1984–86, prodn asst Berkofsky Barrett Productions 1986–87, news ed Direction Magazine (Haymarket Publishing) 1988–89; film dir: Tony Kaye Films 1990–91 (film prodr 1989–90), Spots Film Services 1991–96, Tomboy Films 1996–2002, Hotspur and Argyle 2002–; *Awards* Bronze (NY Advtg Festival) 1990, Gold (Creative Circle Awards) 1990, Silver Lion (Int Advtg Festival Cannes) 1990 and 1991, work accepted for D&AD Annual 1992 and 1997, Best New Director (Saatchi and Saatchi New Directors Showcase/Int Advtg Festival Cannes) 1993; memb D&AD 1992; *Clubs* Groucho; *Style*— Theo Delaney, Esq

DELBRIDGE, Richard; s of Tom Delbridge, and Vera, *née* Lancashire; *b* 21 May 1942; *Educ* LSE (BSc), Univ of Calif Berkeley (MBA); *m* 19 March 1966, Diana Genevra Rose, da of H W Bowers-Broadbent; 2 da (Roseanna b 1970, Cressida b 1982), 1 s (Mark b 1973); *Career* CA 1966; Arthur Andersen: articled clerk 1963–66, mgmnt conslt 1968–, ptnr 1974–76; md and gen mangr London office J P Morgan & Co Inc 1987–89 (int operations 1976–79, comptroller 1979–85, asst gen mangr 1985–87), gp fin dir Midland Bank plc 1989–92, gp fin dir HSBC Holdings plc (following takeover of Midland Bank) 1993–95, dir and chief fin offr Nat Westminster Bank plc 1996–2000; non-exec dir: Innogy plc 2000–2002, Egg plc 2000–2003, Tate & Lyle plc 2000– (sr non-exec dr 2003–), Gallaher Gp plc 2001–, Balfour Beatty plc 2002–05, Cazenove Group plc 2002–05, Fortis Gp 2004–, JP Morgan Cazenove 2005–; dir City Arts Tst 1997–2001, tstee Wordsworth Tst 2000–, memb Cncl and treas Open Univ 2001–; memb: Bd Securities Assoc 1988–89, Financial Reporting Review Panel 1999–; FCA 1972; *Recreations* hill walking, swimming, books; *Style*— Richard Delbridge, Esq

DELEVINGNE, Charles Hamar; s of (Edward) Dudley Delevingne (d 1974), and Hon Angela Margo Hamar, *née* Greenwood; *b* 25 June 1949; *Educ* Embley Park; *m* 18 June 1983, Pandora Anne, da of Sir Jocelyn Stevens, CVO, *qv*, of Testbourne, Hants; 3 da (Chloe b 1984, Poppy b 1986, Cara Jocelyn b 1992); *Career* chm Property Investment Co; *Recreations* shooting, fishing; *Clubs* Buck's; *Style*— Charles Delevingne, Esq; ✉ 95 Albert Bridge Road, London SW11 (tel 071 585 0301); Testbourne Lodge, Hampshire (tel 026 472 569); Kimbolton Lodge, Fulham Road, SW3 (tel 071 589 1126)

DELLA SALA, Prof Sergio; *b* 23 September 1955; *Educ* Univ of Calif Berkeley (pre-med), Univ of Milan Medical Sch (MD, PhD); *Career* Univ of Milan: registrar in neurology 1980–84, conslt in neurology 1987–93, head of Neuropsychology Unit 1989–93; Univ of Aberdeen: prof of psychology 1994–2004, hon conslt in neurology; Univ of Edinburgh: prof of human cognitive neuroscience 2004–, hon conslt in neurology; *Style*— Prof Sergio Della Sala; ✉ Department of Psychology, University of Edinburgh, 7 George Square, Edinburgh EH8 9JZ (tel 0131 651 3242, fax 0131 651 3230, e-mail sergio@ed.ac.uk)

DELLIÈRE, John Peter; s of Robert Fernand George Dellière, of Haslemere, Surrey, and Elaine Gorton, *née* Hobbs; *b* 6 August 1944; *Educ* Whitgift Sch; *m* 28 June 1969, Elizabeth Joan, da of late Gordon Keith Harman, of Lower Kingswood, Surrey; 3 s (Christian John b 10 Jan 1972, James Peter b 26 Aug 1976, Michael Robert Gordon b 2 Oct 1979); *Career* Mellors Basden & Co (City Accountants) 1963–68, Arthur Andersen & Co 1968–70, dir The White House (Linen Specialists) Ltd 1970, md The White House Ltd and subsidiary cos 1982– (dir 1980–, jt md 1982–85); memb Cncl Bond St Assoc 1977–96 (chm 1981–83); FCA 1979 (ACA 1967), ATII 1967; *Recreations* golf, tennis; *Clubs* RAC, Monte's; *Style*— John Dellière, Esq; ✉ Mill Wey House, Mill Lane, Ripley, Surrey GU23 6QT (tel 01483 224975); The White House Ltd, 102 Waterford Road London SW6 2HA (tel 020 7629 3521, fax 020 7629 8269, mobile 078 3620 6362, e-mail john@the-white-house.co.uk)

DELLOW, Jeffrey (Jeff); s of Ernest Dellow (d 1966), of Heworth, Co Durham, and Edith, *née* Greenwell; *b* 19 January 1949; *Educ* Bill Quay Sch, St Martin's Sch of Art, Maidstone Coll of Art, Slade Sch of Fine Art (Cheltenham Fellowship); *m* June 1976, Paula Jean Alison, da of Lt Col Roy Cleasby, MBE; 1 da (Bryony Grace b 27 Jan 1987); *Career* artist; lectr: Hull Coll of Art 1977–86, Roehampton Inst London 1978–80, NE London Poly 1978–86, Slade Sch of Fine Art (postgrad painters) 1980–82, Winchester Sch of Art 1982–86, Central Sch of Art 1982–84; head of painting and print lectr Hull of Coll of Art 1986–88, princ lectr in fine art Kingston Univ 1988–; visiting artist: RAF Brüggen 1974–75, Hull Coll of Art 1977, NE London Poly 1978, Roehampton Inst London 1978, Maidstone Coll of Art 1979, Slade Sch of Fine Art 1979, Manchester Poly Fine Art 1980, Norwich Sch of Art 1981, Winchester Sch of Art 1981; work in collections incl: Arts Cncl of GB, Unilever, James Capel, Coopers & Lybrand, Arthur Andersen & Co, BASF UK, Grand Valley State Univ Michigan; Boise travelling scholarship, Arts Cncl of GB minor bursary, prizewinner Athena Art Awards Barbican 1988; *Solo Exhibitions* solo show New Paintings Castlefield Gallery 1987, Recent Paintings (Cafe Gallery London) 1995, paintings and works on paper Grand State Univ Michigan 1996, Jeff Dellow Recent Paintings (Standort Ausstellungshalle) 2000, Recent Small Paintings (Deli Art) 2001, Beyond Surface (APT Gallery) 2004; *Group Exhibitions* incl: John Moores 10 Liverpool 1976, Drawing in Action (Arts Cncl Touring Show) 1978–79, Open Attitudes (MOMA Oxford) 1979, Small Works by Younger Br Artists 1980, Small Works (Roehampton Inst) 1980, Sculpture and Painting from the Greenwich Studios (Woodlands Gallery Blackheath) 1981, Opening Show (Hull Artists Assoc) 1982, Small Works (Newcastle upon Tyne Poly Gallery) 1982, Marseille Art Present (Artis Gallery Marseille and Maison du Peuple Gardance) 1983, Whitechapel Open 1983–91, 100 Artists (The Showroom Gallery London) 1984, Drawings and Watercolours (Hull Coll of Art) 1984, Greenwich Festival Studio Open 1985–93, Summer in the City (Ikon Gallery Birmingham) 1985, Three Painters (Arteast Gallery collective) 1986, Three Abstract Painters (Todd Gallery) 1987, Art for Sale (Minories Gallery) 1988, Idylls (Todd Gallery Summer Show) 1989, Bath Art Fair 1989, John Moores 16 Liverpool 1989, Art 90 Islington Art Fair 1990, Todd Soho Gallery 1990, Olympia Art Fair 1990, Creative Assets (Harris Museum Preston) 1990, Works on Paper (Todd Gallery) 1990, Pachipamwe III (Nat Gallery of Zimbabwe Harare) 1990, Broadgate Art Week 1990, John Moores 17 (prizewinner) 1991, Whitechapel Studio Open 1992, Greenwich Studios Painting and Sculpture (Woodlands Gallery Blackheath) 1992, Leeds Poly Artists Symposium/Workshop 1992, Watercolour Curwen Gallery (Windmill St London), Sunday Times Singer & Friedlander Watercolour Competition (Mall Galleries London), Sans Frontiers (Waterman Art Centre) 1993, Delight (Manchester Metropolitan Univ) 1996, Delight (Stanley Picker Gallery Kingston Univ) 1997, Art in Perpetuity (Trust Studio Open Deptford) 1997, Cheltenham Fellows Tricentennial Exhbn Cheltenham 1997, Critical Faculty (Stanley Picker Gallery) 1998, Critical Faculty (Grand Valley State Univ Michigan) 1998, Forks and Hope (Sun and Doves Gallery London), Deptford X open studios at Art in Perpetuity Tst, Open Studios APT 2001, Open Studios Brockley Artists London 2002, Ten Days in Deptford Brockley Artists Woodlands Gallery London 2002, Open Studios APT On Show Art in Perpetuity Tst 2003, Nues aus den Ateliers de Kunstler 2003; *Style*— Jeff Dellow, Esq; ✉ Kingston University, School of Fine Art, Knights Park, Kingston upon Thames KT1 2QJ (tel 020 8547 2000, e-mail j.dellow@kingston.ac.uk, website www.anderssonhall.com or www.jeffdellow.com)

DELMAR-MORGAN, Michael Walter; s of Curtis Delmar Morgan (d 1987), and Susan Henrietta, *née* Hargreaves Brown (d 2007); *b* 1 March 1936; *Educ* Eton; *m* 17 Feb 1962, Marjorie, da of John Kennedy Logan (d 1984); 1 s (Benjamin b 1966), 2 da (Katharine b 1968, Alexandra (Mrs Ben Crofts) b 1971); *Career* banker; dir: Brown Shipley & Co Ltd 1966–88, Columbus Financial Services Ltd 1989–2005; tstee St Dunstan's (The Blinded Servicemen's Charity); ret 2006; *Recreations* sailing; *Clubs* Royal Yacht Sqdn; *Style*— Michael W Delmar-Morgan, Esq

DELPY, Prof David Thomas; *Educ* Brunel Univ (BSc), Univ of London (DSc); *Career* Dept of Med Physics and Bioengineering UCL: sr physicist 1976–82, princ physicist1982–86, sr lectr 1986–91, Hamamatsu prof of med photonics 1991–, head of dept 1992–99; vice-provost UCL; memb Cncl BBSRC; *Recreations* music, SF stories; *Style*— Prof David Delpy; ✉ Department of Medical Physics and Bioengineering, University College London, London WC1E 6BT

DEMARCO, Prof Richard; CBE (2007, OBE 1984); s of Carmine Demarco (d 1975), of Edinburgh, and Elizabeth Valentine Fusco (d 1982); *b* 9 July 1930; *Educ* Holy Cross Acad Edinburgh Coll of Art, Moray House Teachers Coll; *m* 1956, Anne Carol, da of Robert Muckle; *Career* artist, arts organiser, broadcaster, lectr; art master Duns Scotus Acad Edinburgh 1956–67, illustrator of BBC pubns 1958–61, fndr memb and vice-chm Traverse Theatre Club 1963–67, dir Traverse Art Gallery 1963–67; artistic dir: Richard Demarco Gallery 1966–, Euro Youth Parl 1993– (artistic advsr 1994–); tstee Kingston-Demarco Euro Cultural Fndn 1993–95, dir Demarco Euro Art Fndn 1993– (tstee 1992), artistic advsr Demarco Euro Culture Initiative 1995–; introduced avant-garde visual art to Edinburgh Festival Prog 1967 and presented avant-garde art from abroad 1968–92; responsible for promotion of nat and int art and theatre; visiting lectr at over 150 schs of art and univs, Stanley Picker fell and lectr Kingston Poly 1991, prof of European cultural studies Kingston Univ 1993–2000 (emeritus prof 2001–); dir Sean Connery's Scot Int Educn Tst 1972, memb Bd of Govrs Carlisle Sch of Art 1973–77, contrib ed Studio International 1982–84; external examiner: Stourbridge Sch of Art 1987–89, Wolverhampton Sch of Art 1990; vice-pres Kingston Tst 2000–; memb: Association International des Critiques d'Art 1994, Int Assoc of Independent Exhbn Curators (IKT) 2001–, SSA, RSW; chm Caroline Park Assoc 2002–; Scot Arts Cncl Award for services to the Arts in Scotland 1975, Br International Theatre Inst Award 1992, Polish International Theatre Inst Award (Stanislaw Witkiewicz Award) 1992, Arts Medal Royal Philosophical Soc of Glasgow 1996, The Herald Edinburgh Festival Archangel Award 2000; Hon DFA Atlanta Coll of Art 1993, LLD (hc) Univ of Dundee 1996; hon FRIAS 1991, hon fell Inst of Contemporary Scotland 2002; FRSA 1997, Hon RSA 2001; Gold Order of Merit of the Polish People's Republic 1976, Cavaliere della Repubblica d'Italia 1988, Chevalier de l'Ordre des Arts et des Lettres (France) 1991; *Books* artist represented in over 1600 collections; illustrator of books incl: The Edinburgh Diary 1980, The Royal Mile 1990, Literary Edinburgh 1992; regular broadcaster TV and radio in Britain, N America and Poland; progs incl: One Man's Week (1971), Images (5 progs Grampian TV, 1974), The Demarco Dimension (1988), The Green Man (BBC Omnibus, 1990), Portrait of Richard Demarco (BBC2, 1991); *Publications* incl: The Artist as Explorer (1978), The Road to Meikle Seggie (1978), The Celtic Consciousness (1978), A Life in

D

Pictures (1994), Kunst = Kapital (Fife Coll Adam Smith Lecture, 1995); weekly columnist: Edinburgh and Lothian Post 1987–89, Sunday Times (Scotland) 1988; *Recreations* exploring The Road to Meikle Seggie towards the Hebrides in the footsteps of the Roman Legions, St Servanus and the Celtic Saints, and the medieval scholars, onwards into the Mediterranean and Eastern Europe; *Clubs* Scottish Arts (Edinburgh); *Style—* Prof Richard Demarco, CBE; ✉ 23A Lennox Street, Edinburgh EH4 1PY (tel 0131 343 2124); Demarco European Art Foundation, Building Two, New Parliament House, 5–7 Regent Road, Edinburgh EH7 5LB (tel 0131 557 0707, fax 0131 557 5972)

DEMERY, Edward Peter; CVO (2005); s of Peter Demery, and Cecilia Gwyneth Nepean, *née* Clifford-Smith; *b* 12 December 1946; *Educ* Bradfield Coll; *m* 16 Jan 1971, Alexandra, da of Harold Paillet Rodier, of Leatherhead, Surrey; 1 s (Rupert b 1972), 1 da (Miranda b 1973); *Career* dir Clifford-Smith (Underwriting Agencies) Ltd 1976–85; Justerini & Brooks Ltd wine merchants: joined 1967, dir 1977–, sales dir 1986–93, md 1993–2003, chm 2004–; Clerk of the Royal Cellars 1992–; Master Worshipful Co of Vintners 2006–07; *Recreations* golf, cricket, tennis; *Clubs* I Zingari, Band of Brothers, R&A, Royal St George's Golf, Boodle's, Saintsbury, Hon Co of Edinburgh Golfers (Muirfield), All England Lawn Tennis and Croquet, Royal Wimbledon Golf; *Style—* Edward Demery, Esq, CVO; ✉ 72 Vineyard Hill Road, Wimbledon, London SW19 7JJ (tel 020 8946 7056); Justerini & Brooks Ltd, 61 St James's Street, London SW1A 1LZ (tel 020 7484 6402, fax 020 7484 6499, e-mail edward.demery@justerinis.com)

DEMIDENKO, Nikolai; s of Anatoli Antonovich Demidenko; *b* 1 July 1955; *Educ* Moscow Conservatoire; *m* Julya Borisovna Dovgiallo; *Career* pianist; visiting prof: Univ of Surrey, Yehudi Menuhin Sch; medallist: Concours International de Montreal 1976, Tchaikovsky Int Competition 1978; performances incl: Br debut with Moscow Radio Symphony Orch 1990, Piano Masterworks series Wigmore Hall 1993; 1994–95 appearances incl: Hollywood Bowl, Berlin with Berliner Symphoniker, Royal Festival Hall with RPO and Yuri Temirkanov, various Scottish venues with Scottish Chamber Orch, Toronto, Haskil-Kempff Festival Luxembourg, St John's Smith Square for BBC, Belfast, Chester and Ribble Valley Festivals, complete Mussorgsky song cycles with Anatoli Safiulin St John's Smith Square, Rouen and Verbier Festival, Int Piano Series Royal Festival Hall, Gramophone Award Winners Festival Wigmore Hall; 1995–96 season incl: Celebrity Recital Series Barbican, Scriabin Concerto with Netherlands Radio Philharmonic, Prokofiev Second Concerto with LPO, Gershwin Rhapsody in Blue with BBC Philharmonic Orch, series with Israel Philharmonic, tour of Australia for ABC, Int Piano Festival Singapore, Gramophone Award Winners Festival Wigmore Hall; 1996–97 season incl: recitals in Amsterdam, Istanbul, Munich, Prague, Toronto, Warsaw, Bristol, Windsor Festival, Barbican Great Orchs of the World Series (with Moscow Philharmonic), Polish Radio Symphony Orch, Orchestre Philharmonique de Luxembourg; 1997–98 season incl: A Romantic Voyage (3 part recital series) Wigmore Hall, recitals in Brisbane, Melbourne, Perth and Sydney; 1998–99 season incl: Barbican Celebrity Recital Series, Beethoven's Diabelli Variations with Twyla Tharp Dance Co in Paris and London; 1999–2000 season incl: Int Piano Series recital at Royal Festival Hall; *Recordings* for Hyperion Records incl: works by Bach-Busoni, Chopin, Liszt, Medtner Second and Third Piano Concertos with BBC Scottish Symphony Orch (winner Gramophone Award 1992), Rachmaninov Music for Two Pianos with Dmitri Alexeev (nominated Classic CD Instrumental Award 1995), Live at Wigmore double album, Tchaikovsky First Piano Concerto, Scriabin Piano Concerto (winner Classic CD Award 1994), Weber Concertos, Clementi Sonatas, Mussorgsky Song Cycles, Schubert Impromptus, Prokofiev Piano Concerto cycle (with London Philharmonic and Alexander Lazarev); *Style—* Nikolai Demidenko, Esq; ✉ c/o Georgina Ivor Associates, 28 Old Devonshire Road, London SW12 9RB (tel 020 8673 7179, fax 020 8675 8058)

DEMPSEY, Michael Bernard; s of John Patrick Dempsey (d 1993), latterly of Ramsgate, Kent, and Britannia May, *née* Thompson (d 1993); *b* 25 July 1944; *Educ* Bishop Ward RC Secdy Modern Dagenham; *m* 1, 21 Oct 1967 (m dis 1988), Sonja, da of George Mathew Green; 1 da (Polly b 15 Oct 1969), 2 s (Joe, Ben (twins) b 2 Jan 1972); m 2, 15 Aug 1989, Charlotte Antonia, da of David Elliot Richardson; 3 da (Daisy b 2 May 1990, Fleur May b 15 July 1994, Jemima b 20 May 1998); *Career* asst designer Chevron Studio 1963–64, in-house designer Bryan Colmer Artist Agents 1964–65, freelance designer 1965–66, designer Cato Peters O'Brien 1966–68; art dir: William Heinemann Publishers 1968–74, William Collins/Fontana Publishers 1974–79, RSA Journal 1997–2002; fndr ptnr Carroll & Dempsey 1979–85, chm and creative dir CDT Design (formerly Carroll Dempsey & Thirkell) 1985–; conslt designer Dept for Culture, Media and Sport 1997–98, conslt art dir Royal Mail 1999 Millennium Stamp Programme 1998–99, designer Royal Mail Definitive Stamps 2006, designer Raoyal Mail special issue stamps Sounds of Britain 2006; feature writer: Design Week 2001–, Blueprint magazine; memb: D&AD 1968 (memb Exec 1996–98, pres 1997–98), Design Cncl Millennium Products Selection Panel 1998–99, BAFTA 2003–; FCSD 1980, RDI 1994 (master 2005–), AGI 1998, FRSA 2005 (memb Cncl 2005–); *Awards* D&AD Silver 1981 (most outstanding technical lit) and 1984 (most outstanding book jacket), D&AD Gold and Silver 1985 (most outstanding book design), 2 D&AD Silvers 1989 (most outstanding annual report and album covers), 2 D&AD Silvers 1992 (most outstanding corp ID and logo), CSD Minerva Award 1993 (most outstanding corp ID), D&AD Silver 2000 (most outstanding use of illustration), D&AD Silver 2001 (most outstanding use of photography); *Books* Bubbles - Early Advertising Art of A & F Pears (1978), The Magical Paintings of Justin Todd (1978), Pipe Dreams - Early Advertising Art of The Imperial Tobacco Company (1982); *Recreations* living; *Clubs* Groucho; *Style—* Michael Dempsey, Esq; ✉ The Hayloft, Church Lane, Osmington, Dorset DT3 6EW (tel 01305 832520); CDT Design Ltd, 21 Brownlow Mews, London WC1N 2LA (tel 020 7242 0992, fax 020 7242 1174, e-mail mike.d@cdt-design.co.uk)

DEMPSEY, Noel; TD; s of Michael Dempsey, of Longwood, Co Meath, Ireland, and Maureen, *née* Byrne; *b* 6 January 1953, Trim, Co Meath; *Educ* St Michael's Christian Bros Sch Trim, UCD (BA, Dip), St Patricks Coll Maynooth (Dip, HDipEd); *m* 18 Sept 1979, Bernadette, *née* Rattigan; 4 c (Shane, Aileen, Aisling, Cathal); *Career* memb: Meath CC 1977–92 (chm 1986–87), Trim Urban DC 1981–92 (chm 1981–82, 1985–86 and 1991–92); TD (Fianna Fáil) Meath 1987–; Govt chief whip 1991–92, min of state Dept of Def 1991–92, min of state Dept of Finance 1992, oppn spokesman on environment 1995–97, min for the environment and local govt 1997–2002, min for educn and sci 2002–04, min for communications, marine and natural resources 2004–07, min for tport and maritime affrs 2007–; dir Dublin and East Regnl Tourism Orgn 1985–90, nat sec Local Authy Memb's Assoc 1997–2002; memb: Gaelic Athletic Assoc, Macra na Feirme, Muintir na Tire, Tidy Towns; *Recreations* golf, reading; *Style—* Noel Dempsey, TD; ✉ Newtown, Trim, Co Meath, Ireland (tel 00 353 46 94 31146, fax 00 353 46 94 36643, e-mail info@noeldempsey.ie); Department of Transport and Maritime Affairs, Kildare Street, Dublin 2, Ireland

DEMPSTER, Alastair Cox; CBE (2005); *b* 22 June 1940, Glasgow; *Educ* Paisley GS; *m* Kathryn; 2 s (Stuart b 4 Oct 1968, Ross b 6 Nov 1971); *Career* Royal Bank of Scotland plc: various branch banking appts W of Scotland 1955–62, Branch Dept (Inspection and Advances) Head Office 1962–68, exec asst Head Office 1968–70, asst personnel mangr 1970–72, rep New York Office 1972–73, rep SE Asia Office Hong Kong and md Royal Scot Finance Co Ltd 1973–77, controller, supt then asst gen mangr International Div 1977–86; TSB Group plc: dir of commercial banking and international/exec dir 1986–91, chief exec TSB Bank Channel Islands Ltd 1991–92 (dep chm 1992–), chief exec TSB Bank Scotland plc 1992–98; chm: Aberforth Geared Capital and Income Tst plc, Deanway Developments Ltd; dir: Office of the Banking Ombudsman 1990–98, Scottish Homes 1994–98, Scottish Fin Enterprise 1994–98, Aberforth Split Level Investment Tst plc; pres Chartered Inst of Bankers in Scotland 1994–97, chm Ctee of Scottish Clearing Bankers 1993–95; chm: The Scottish Community Fndn, Scottish Sports Cncl; memb: Scottish Hosps Endowments Research Tst 1998–2002, UK Sport Cncl, Glasgow Housing Assoc (chm Audit Cmmn); tstee: St Andrews Links Tst (chm), Scottish Football Partnership, Commonwealth Games Cncl Fund; memb Ct Heriot-Watt Univ (convener Audit Ctee 1991–97), vice-chm Bd of Govrs Edinburgh Art Coll 1993–2002; a High Constable City of Edinburgh; Hon Dr Univ of Paisley; FCIBS; *Recreations* golf, tennis, bridge, world affairs, reading, gardening; *Clubs* Luffness New Golf, New (Edinburgh); *Style—* Alastair Dempster, Esq, CBE

DEMPSTER, John William Scott; s of Dr David Dempster (d 1981), of Plymouth, and Mary Constance, *née* Simpson (d 1985); *b* 10 May 1938; *Educ* Plymouth Coll, Oriel Coll Oxford (MA); *Career* civil servant; princ private sec to the Sec of State for the Environment 1976–77, fin offr Dept of Tport 1977–81, princ establishment and fin offr Lord Chancellor's Dept 1981–84; Dept of Tport: head of marine directorate 1984–89, princ establishment and fin offr 1989–91, DG highways 1991–94, dep sec aviation and shipping 1994–95; dir Bahamas Maritime Authy 1995–99, currently dir UK Major Ports Gp; *Recreations* mountaineering, sailing; *Clubs* Swiss Alpine (pres Assoc of Br Membs); *Style—* John Dempster, Esq, CB

DEMPSTER, Maj Malcolm Maclagan; s of Henry Maclagan Dempster (d 1983), and Ruth Appleby, *née* Rowan (d 2001); *b* 17 March 1940; *m* (m dis 1984); 1 da (Sarah Georgina b 1982), 1 s (Roy W); *Career* qualified aeronautical engr HM Forces, served Malayan, Borneo conflicts (incl secondment to Gurkha Forces) and NI, cmmnd 1974, PSO Staff of Flag Offr Naval Air Cmd 1977–79, SO MOD Procurement 1979–81, SO HQ 1 Br Corps Germany 1981–83, cmd appt UK 1983–85, SO MOD responsible for NATO Air (Army) matters 1985–88; UK del: NATO Air Forces Ctee for Int Interoperability 1985–88 (chm 1988), NATO Advsy Gp on Aeronautical Res and Devpt 1986–88, NATO Ctee for Future Aircraft and Equipment Requirements 1986–88, Int Aeronautical Ctee for Standardisation 1986–88; md: Goldenlogic Ltd 1988–91, Express Thurston Helicopters Ltd 1989–91; dir Express Aviation Mktg 1989–91, vice-pres (UK) Octrin Corp 1989–99, md Spearhead Envotech Ltd 1999– (commercial dir 1991–99, md Anglo Turkish Trading Ltd 1992–; conslt on aeronautical matters to Crown Agents 1989; chief exec Biggin Hill Airport Business Assoc, co-opted memb Biggin Hill Int Air Fair Ctee 1988–91; md EG Operations Ltd 1999–2001, md Warning Systems (GB) Ltd 2000–, memb HM Govt Industry Advsy Gp Aeronatical Research and Devpt 2002–06; SERC visiting tutor to univ PhD courses; FInstD, MRAeS, MIIE; *Publications* author of various scientific and tech articles; *Recreations* golf, music, country pursuits, a constant battle with a 200 year old country property; *Clubs* IOD, The Arts, Royal Aeronautical Soc; *Style—* Maj Malcolm Dempster; ✉ Well Cottage, Monxton, Andover, Hampshire SP11 8AS (tel 01264 710535); Clarendon Court, Stockbridge, Hampshire SO20 8HU (tel 01264 781993)

DEMPSTER, Prof Michael Alan Howarth; s of late Cedric William Dempster, and late Honor Fitz Simmons, *née* Gowan; *b* 10 April 1938; *Educ* Univ of Toronto (BA), Carnegie Inst of Technology (MS, PhD), Univ of Oxford (MA), Univ of Cambridge (MA); *m* 1 (m dis), Ann Laura, *née* Lazier; 1 da (Trinity Catherine Laura Fitz Simmons); m 2, Elena Anatolievna, *née* Medova; 1 da (Anna Medova); *Career* jr research fell Nuffield Coll Oxford 1966; Balliol Coll Oxford: fell and tutor in mathematics 1967–79, sr research fell 1979–81, lectr in mathematics 1981–87; univ lectr in industrial mathematics Univ of Oxford 1967–81, fell Center for Advanced Study in Behavioural Sciences Stanford Calif 1974–75, sr research scholar System and Decision Sciences International Inst for Applied Systems Analysis Laxenburg Austria 1979–81, prof of mathematics, statistics and computing science/R A Jodrey research prof of mgmnt and information sciences Dalhousie Univ 1981–93, prof of mathematics Univ of Essex 1990–95 (dir Inst for Studies in Fin 1993–95); Judge Business Sch Univ of Cambridge: dir Centre for Financial Research 1996, dir of research 1997–2001, dir PhD prog 1997–2002, currently emeritus prof of finance and mgmnt sciences; fell Hughes Hall Cambridge 2003–; resident participant progs on financial mathematics and devpt in quantitative finance Isaac Newton Inst for Mathematical Sciences Cambridge 1995; Oxford Systems Associates Ltd: md 1974–79, chm 1974–80; chm and md Cambridge Systems Assocs Ltd 1996–; conslt to various cos incl: BT, Citigroup, CSFB, HSBC, Fujitsu, Frank Russell Co, Morgan Stanley; founding co-ed-in-chief Quantitative Finance 2000–; visiting prof: Univ of Rome, Univ of Toronto, Univ of Melbourne, Univ of Calif Berkeley; visiting sr fell Manchester Business Sch, visiting fell Princeton Univ; memb: London Mathematical Soc, American Mathematical Soc, Canadian Mathematical Soc, Mathematical Programming Soc, Operational Research Soc, Inst for Operations Research and Mgmnt Sciences, Assoc for Computing Machinery, Inst of Mathematical Statistics, American Statistical Assoc, Econometric Soc, Oxford Political Economy Club, American Inst of Decision Science, Public Choice Soc, Sigma Xi Hon Scientific Fraternity; FIMA, Hon FIA; *Publications* Introduction to Optimization Methods (with P R Adby, 1974), Stochastic Programming (contrib and ed, 1980), Analysis and Optimization of Stochastic Systems (co-ed with M H A Davis, C J Harris, O L R Jacobs, P C Parks, 1980), Large-Scale Linear Programming (co-ed with G B Dantzig and M Kallio, 1981), Deterministic and Stochastic Scheduling (contrib and co-ed with J K Lenstra and A H G Rinnooy Kan, 1982), Proceedings of the IIASA Task Force Meeting on Stochastic Optimization (guest ed, 1983), Mathematical Models in Economics (contrib and co-ed with M O L Bacharach and J L Enos, 1997), Mathematics of Derivative Securities (contrib and co-ed with S R Pliska, 1997), Risk Management: Value at Risk and Beyond (contrib and ed, 2002); also ed translations and author of numerous articles in various learned jls; *Recreations* reading, gardening, tennis, sailing, skiing; *Style—* Prof M A H Dempster; ✉ Judge Business School, University of Cambridge, Trumpington Street, Cambridge CB2 1AG (tel 01223 339641, fax 01223 339652, e-mail mahd2@cam.ac.uk, website www-cfr.jims.cam.ac.uk)

DENARO, Maj-Gen Arthur George; CBE (1996, OBE 1991); s of late Brig George Tancred Denaro, CBE, DSO, and Francesca Violet Denaro; *Educ* Downside, RMA Sandhurst; *m* 1980, Margaret Roney, *née* Acworth, wid of Maj M J Kealy, DSO (d 1979); 1 da (b 1982), 1 s (b 1985), 2 step da, 1 step s; *Career* cmmnd QRIH 1968; Staff Coll 1979–80; CO QRIH 1989–91, Cdr 33 (later 20) Armd Brigade 1992–94, RCDS 1994, COS HQ UNIPROFOR Former Yugoslavia 1994–95, COS HQ Br Forces Cyprus 1995–96, Chief Combat Support HQ ARRC 1996–97, Cmdt RMA Sandhurst 1997–2000, GOC 5th Div 2001–03; Middle East advsr to the Sec of State for Defence 1997–2002, Extra Equerry to HRH The Prince of Wales 2000–, sr advsr Olive Gp 2003–07, advsr The Court of HH The Crown Prince of Bahrain 2003–07, Middle East and military advsr JCB 2004–; memb Cncl Prince's Tst 2000–, Hon Col The Royal Wessex Yeomanry 2003–, Col The Queen's Royal Hussars (Queen's Own and Royal Irish) 2004–; chm Army Benevolent Fund (Hereford) 2003–, steward Hurlingham Polo Assoc (HPA) 2005–; *Recreations* field sports, polo, skiing; *Clubs* Cavalry and Guards'; *Style—* Maj-Gen Arthur Denaro, CBE

DENBIGH AND DESMOND, 12 and 11 Earl of (E1622 and I 1622); Alexander Stephen Rudolph Feilding; also Baron Feilding, Viscount Feilding (both E 1620), Baron Feilding, Viscount Callan (both I 1622), and Baron St Liz (E 1663); o s of 11 Earl of Denbigh and 10 Earl of Desmond (d 1995), and Caroline Judith Vivienne, *née* Cooke; *b* 4 November 1970; *Educ* Stowe; *m* 27 Jan 1996, Suzanne Jane, yr da of Gregory R Allen, of Brixham, Devon; 1 s (Peregrine Rudolph Henry, Viscount Feilding b 19 Feb 2005), 1 da (Hester

Imelda Florence b 5 July 2006); *Heir* s, Viscount Feilding; *Style*— The Rt Hon the Earl of Denbigh and Desmond; ✉ Newnham Paddox House, Monks Kirby, Warwickshire CV23 0RX (tel 01788 833291, e-mail info@newnhampaddox.com, website www.newnhampaddox.com)

DENBY, Georgia; da of Raymond Ridgwell, and Joyce Ridgwell; *Educ* N Devon Art Coll; *Career* photographer; travelling exhibitions: worldwide BIPP 2000, 2001, 2002, 2003 and 2004, worldwide Master Photographers Assoc (MPA) 2001, GB and I Photographic Alliance of GB (PAGB) 2001 and 2002, Euro Qualification of the Euro Photographer (QEP) 2001–02; cmmns incl: Amber Books, Advision Advtg, Turton Advtg, Visual Language Prodns, Safetylite Ltd, Napthans Photography, Seven Security Servs, A&C Black; work sold at Bonhams London 2005; patron Stiff Upper Lip (NY drama co); supporter: Norfolk Deaf Assoc (NDA), VLM (sign language channel); BIPP Photographer of the Year Central Region 2000, 2001, and 2003, 4 MPA Awards of Excellence 2001, QEP 2001, credit Photographic Alliance of GB 2001, Br Professional Photography Awards Oskar 2004; also numerous Gold, Silver and Bronze BIPP awards; ARPS 2000, FBIPP (ABIPP 2000), assoc MPA (AMPA) 2000; *Publications* Psychic Detectives (2001), Image 26 (2002), Tudor Flashbacks (series, 2002); *Recreations* art in all forms, computer software, jazz and classical music; *Style*— Mrs Georgia Denby; ✉ Orchard Farmhouse, Saxlingham Green, Norwich, Norfolk NR15 1TG (tel 01508 498431, e-mail georgia@safetylite.com, website www.georgiadenby.co.uk)

DENCH, Dame Judith Olivia (Judi); CH (2005), DBE (1988, OBE 1970); da of Dr Reginald Arthur Dench (d 1964), of York, and Eleanora Olave Dench; *b* 9 December 1934; *Educ* The Mount Sch York, Central Sch of Speech and Drama; *m* 5 Feb 1971, Michael Williams (d 2001); 1 da (Finty b 24 Sept 1972); *Career* actress and director; fndr memb Surrey Soc CPRE; Hon DLitt: Univ of York 1978, Univ of Warwick 1980, Univ of Birmingham 1989, Loughborough Univ 1991, Open Univ 1992, Univ of London 1994; hon degree Royal Scottish Acad of Music and Drama; assoc memb RSC 1969–; The Patricia Rothermere Award for Outstanding Service to Theatre 1997, Lifetime Achievement Award Women in Film and Television Awards 1997, Special Award for Services to British Theatre Olivier Awards 2004; *Theatre* stage roles for RSC incl: The Gift of the Gorgon, The Cherry Orchard, Measure for Measure, A Midsummer Night's Dream, Penny for a Song, Twelfth Night, The Winter's Tale, The Comedy of Errors, Macbeth (SWET Best Actress Award), Pillars of the Community, Juno and the Paycock (SWET, Standard, Plays and Players and Variety Club Awards), Waste, All's Well That Ends Well, Merry Wives the Musical 2006–07; roles in the West End incl: The Promise, Cabaret, The Wolf, The Good Companions, The Gay Lord Quex, Pack of Lies (SWET and Plays & Players Best Actress Award), Mr and Mrs Nobody, The Plough and the Stars, Filumena, The Royal Family, The Breath of Life, The Breath Of Life (Haymarket Theatre Royal); roles at RNT incl: The Importance of Being Earnest (Evening Standard Best Actress Award), Other Places (Standard, Plays & Players and Drama Awards), Antony and Cleopatra (Olivier, Drama Magazine, and Evening Standard Best Actress Awards), Entertaining Strangers, Hamlet, The Sea, The Seagull, Absolute Hell (Olivier Award for Best Actress 1996), A Little Night Music (Olivier Award for Best Actress in a Musical 1996), Esme Allen in Amy's View (also Broadway, Tony Award 1999); as dir: Much Ado About Nothing, Look Back in Anger (Renaissance Theatre Co), Macbeth (Central School), The Boys from Syracuse (Regent's Park, Best Revival of a Musical Olivier Awards 1992), Romeo and Juliet (Regent's Park) 1993; *Television* incl: Marching Song, Hilda Lessways, Pink String and Sealing Wax, An Age of Kings, Major Barbara, Talking to a Stranger (BAFTA Best TV Actress Award), A Fine Romance (BAFTA Best TV Actress Award), Going Gently (BAFTA Best TV Actress Award), Saigon Year of the Cat, The Browning Version, Mrs & Mrs Edgehill (ACE Award for Best Actress), Absolute Hell, As Time Goes By, Last of the Blonde Bombshells; *Film* incl: Four in the Morning (BAFTA Award for Most Promising Newcomer), Wetherby, A Room With a View (BAFTA Award for Best Supporting Actress), 84 Charing Cross Road, A Handful of Dust (BAFTA Award for Best Supporting Actress), Henry V, Jack & Sarah, Hamlet, Mrs Brown (winner of Best Actress Golden Globe Awards 1997, Oscar nomination for Best Actress 1997, BAFTA Award for Best Leading Actress 1997), M in GoldenEye, Tomorrow Never Dies and The World is Not Enough, Shakespeare in Love (Oscar winner for Best Supporting Actress 1999, BAFTA Award for Best Supporting Actress 1999), Tea with Mussolini, Chocolat (Oscar nomination for Best Supporting Actress 2001, winner Best Supporting Actress Screen Actors Guild Awards 2001), Iris (Oscar nomination for Best Actress 2002, BAFTA Award for Best Actress, Variety Club Award), The Shipping News 2002, The Importance of Being Ernest 2002, Die Another Day 2002, The Chronicles of Riddick 2003, Ladies in Lavender 2003, Mrs Henderson Presents 2005, Casino Royale 2006, Notes on a Scandal 2006 (Best Actress Evening Standard British Film Awards 2007, nomination Best Actress Oscars 2007); *Style*— Dame Judi Dench, CH, DBE; ✉ c/o Julian Belfrage Associates, 46 Albemarle Street, London W1S 4DF (tel 020 7491 4400, fax 020 7493 5460)

DENCH, Robert Graham (Bob); BEM (1972); s of Eric Leslie Dench (d 2007), and Gladys May, *née* Knowles (d 1980); *b* 14 February 1950, Surrey; *Educ* John Ruskin GS Shirley; *m* 9 Sept 1972, Christina Mary, *née* Norman; 2 da (Anna Elizabeth b 1974, Melanie Louise b 1976); *Career* Metropolitan Police 1969–76, Barclays Bank 1976–2004 (chm Barclays Stockbrokers, md Barclays Life, md Barclays Mortgages); chm Paragon Gp plc 2007– (non-exec dir 2004–); non-exec dir: Clipper Ventures plc 2003–, AXA plc 2004–; *Recreations* sailing, golf, reading; *Clubs* Carlton, Addington Palace Golf, Wentworth; *Style*— Robert Dench, Esq, BEM; ✉ e-mail bob.dench@paragon-group.co.uk

DENHAM, 2 Baron (UK 1937); Sir Bertram Stanley Mitford Bowyer; 10 Bt (E 1660), of Denham, and 2 Bt (UK 1933), of Weston Underwood; PC (1981), KBE (1991); s of 1 Baron Denham (d 1948), and Hon Daphne Freeman-Mitford (d 1996, aged 100), da of 1 Baron Redesdale; suc to Btcy of Denham on death of kinsman 1950; *b* 3 October 1927; *Educ* Eton, King's Coll Cambridge; *m* 14 Feb 1956, Jean, da of Kenneth McCorquodale, MC, TD; 3 s, 1 da; *Heir* s, Hon Richard Bowyer; *Career* late Lt Oxf and Bucks LI; a Lord-in-Waiting to HM The Queen 1961–64 and 1970–71, Capt of Yeomen of the Gd (dep chief whip in House of Lords) 1971–74, Capt Hon Corps Gentlemen-at-Arms 1979–91 (govt chief whip House of Lords), oppn dep chief whip 1974–78, oppn chief whip 1978–79, an Extra Lord-in-Waiting to HM The Queen 1998–; memb Countryside Cmmn 1993–99; *Books* The Man Who Lost His Shadow (1979), Two Thyrdes (1983), Foxhunt (1988), Black Rod (1997); A Thing of Shreds and Patches (audio book, reading own choice of verse, 2000); *Clubs* White's, Pratt's, Garrick; *Style*— The Rt Hon the Lord Denham, PC, KBE; ✉ The Laundry Cottage, Weston Underwood, Olney, Buckinghamshire MK46 5JZ (tel 01234 711535)

DENHAM, Gary George; s of Maurice Denham, and Patricia Denham; *b* 4 July 1951; *Educ* Bennets End Secdy Sch; *m* 6 May 1972, Vivienne, da of Roy Howlett; 4 s (Nathan b 10 Dec 1975, Jacob b 3 Oct 1979, Joshua b 31 Aug 1983, Elijah b 13 June 1986), 1 da (Krsna b 14 June 1977); *Career* art dir The Kirkwood Company advtg agency 1971–73, head of art Maisey Mukerjee Russell 1973–74; art dir: French Gold Abbott 1974–76, Greys Sydney 1976–77; freelance art dir/photographer 1977–83; art dir: Bartle Bogle Hegarty 1983–84, Boase Massimi Pollitt 1984–86; head of art Holmes Knight Ritchie 1986–87, jt creative dir Aspect Hill Holliday 1987–89, art dir/gp head Bartle Bogle Hegarty 1989–92, head of art CME KHBB 1992–95, sr creative Leagas Delaney 1995, freelance art dir/photographer/painter 1995–; awards incl: Bronze Irish Int Advtg Awards, Silver Campaign Press Awards, Gold Pegasus (Readers Digest) Awards, Gold NY Art Dirs Show; photography exhibited: New Australian Photography 1977, Venezia 1979, Pompidou Centre 1980; work in The Polaroid Collection Boston USA; memb D&AD 1975; *Recreations* gardening, painting; *Style*— Gary Denham, Esq

DENHAM, Grey; *b* 11 February 1949; *Educ* Handsworth GS, Brooklyn Tech Coll, Bristol Coll of Commerce, Univ of London (LLB), Inns of Court Sch of Law, Columbia Univ Grad Sch of Business (CSEP); *m* 3 July 1976, Janet Miranda, *née* Lea; 1 s (Matthew Giles b 8 Aug 1982); *Career* called to the Bar Inner Temple 1972; lectr in law Leicester Poly 1972–74, sr lectr in law Nottingham Law Sch 1974–76 and 1977–78; co legal offr Alfred Herbert Ltd 1978–80; GKN plc: co lawyer 1980–83, dep head of legal 1983–86, head of legal 1986–95, chm GKN Gp Services Ltd 1995–97 (exec dir 1997–), pres GKN North America Inc 1996–2001, exec dir GKN (UK) plc 1996–, gp sec 1996–, chm GKN Charitable Appeals Ctee 1998–, pres GKN America Corp 2001–, exec dir GKN Hldgs plc 2001–, exec dir Westland Group plc 2001–; non-exec dir Charter plc 2005–; regnl chm W Midlands CBI 2005– (regnl vice-chm 2004–05); non-exec dir Young Enterprise 2006–; memb: Legal Ctee SMMT 1985–95, Regnl Advsy Gp London Stock Exchange 1996–2000, Cncl Birmingham C of C and Industry 1996–, W Midlands Cncl CBI 1998–, Exchange Markets Gp London Stock Exchange 2000–04, Primary Markets Gp London Stock Exchange 2000–05 (chm 2000–04), Young Enterprise Business Leadership Cncl 2003–05, Chairman's Ctee CBI 2005–, Hon Soc of the Inner Temple, Inst of European Law, Alumni Soc of Univ of London, Alumni Soc of Columbia Univ; govr memb RNLI; FRSA 1992; *Recreations* watching and playing cricket, watching Aston Villa, watching ballet; *Clubs* Warwickshire CCC, Knowle and Dorridge LTC; *Style*— Grey Denham, Esq; ✉ GKN plc, PO Box 55, Redditch, Worcestershire B98 0TL (tel 01527 517715, fax 01527 533463, e-mail grey.denham@gkn.com)

DENHAM, Rt Hon John; PC (2000), MP; *b* 15 July 1953; *Educ* Woodroffe Comp Lyme Regis, Univ of Southampton (BSc); *m* (m dis), Ruth Dixon; 1 s, 1 da; partner, Sue Littlemore; 1 s; *Career* voluntary sector work; MP (Lab) Southampton Itchen 1992– (contested Southampton Itchen 1983 and 1987); Parly under-sec of state DSS 1997–98 (min of state 1998), min of state Dept of Health 1998–2001, min of state for Crime Reduction, Policing and Community Safety Home Office 2001–03, sec of state for Innovation, Univs and Skills 2007–, chm Home Affrs Select Ctee; elected memb: Hampshire CC 1981–89 (dep ldr and spokesperson on educn), Southampton City Cncl 1989–93 (chair Housing Ctee); memb MSF; *Style*— The Rt Hon John Denham, MP; ✉ House of Commons, London SW1A 0AA (tel 020 7219 3000)

DENHAM, Pamela Anne; CB (1997), DL (Tyne & Wear 2000); da of Matthew Gray Dobson (d 1970), and Jane, *née* Carter (d 1962); *b* 1 May 1943; *Educ* Central Newcastle HS, KCL (BSc, PhD); *m* 1965 (m dis 1980), Paul Denham (d 1988); partner, Brian Murray (d 1993); *Career* Miny of Technol then DTI 1967–98, under sec and regnl dir Government Office for the North East until 1998; chair Project North East 1998–, memb Bd Community Fndn Serving Tyne & Wear and Northumberland 2002–07, non-exec memb Newcastle Primary Care Tst 2001–; tstee Age Concern Newcastle 2000–, tstee Age Concern England 2002–05; memb Governing Body Univ of Sunderland 1998–2007, chair of govrs Central Newcastle HS GDST 2001–06; Hon LLD Univ of Sunderland 1994; FRSA; *Recreations* walking, cooking, reading; *Style*— Pamela Denham, CB, DL

DENHAM, Hon Mrs Justice Susan Gageby; da of R J D Gageby (d 2004), and Dorothy Mary, *née* Lester (d 2002); *b* 22 August 1945, Dublin; *Educ* Alexandra Coll Dublin, TCD, Columbia Univ NY; *m* 18 July 1970, Dr Brian Denham; 1 da (Niamh b 1979), 3 s (Niall b 1980, Colm, Cian b 1984 (twins)); *Career* called to the Bar King's Inns Dublin; jr counsel 1971–87, sr counsel 1987–, judge of the High Court of Ireland 1991–92, judge of the Supreme Court of Ireland 1992–; chair: Working Gp on a Courts Cmmn 1995–98, Working Gp on a Court of Appeal 2007–; pro-chllr TCD 1996–; hon bencher Middle Temple 2005; Hon LLD Queen's Univ Belfast 2002; *Recreations* horses, gardening, reading; *Style*— The Hon Mrs Justice Susan Denham; ✉ The Supreme Court, The Four Courts, Dublin 7, Ireland (tel 00 353 1 888 6533)

DENHOLM, (James) Allan; CBE (1992); s of James Denholm (d 1959), and Florence Lily Keith, *née* Kennedy (d 1972); *b* 27 September 1936; *Educ* Hutchesons' Boys' GS Glasgow; *m* 10 Sept 1964, Elizabeth Avril, da of John Stewart McLachlan (d 1994), of Larbert, Stirlingshire; 1 s (Keith b 7 Sept 1966), 1 da (Alison b 24 May 1969); *Career* dir: William Grant & Sons Ltd 1975–96, Scottish Mutual Assurance plc 1987–2003 (dep chm 1992), Abbey National plc 1992–97, Abbey National Life plc 1993–2003, Scottish Provident plc 2001–03; memb Supervisory Ctee Scottish Provident 2001–06, tstee Scottish Provident and Scottish Mutual Staff Pension Funds 2001–06; dir Scottish Cremation and Burial Reform Soc 1980–; pres Inst of Chartered Accountants of Scotland 1992–93; tstee Inst of Chartered Accountants Staff Pension Fund 1994–2007; chm: Glasgow Jr C of C 1972–73, E Kilbride Devpt Corp 1983–95 (memb 1979–95); visitor Incorporation of Maltmen in Glasgow 1980–81, pres 49 Wine and Spirit Club of Scotland 1983–84, tstee Scottish Cot Death Tst 1985–94, dir Weavers' Soc of Anderson 1987 (pres 1994–95), pres Assoc of Deacons of the Fourteen Incorporated Trades of Glasgow 1994–95, collector The Trades House of Glasgow 1996–97 (deacon convener 1998–99), dir The Merchants House of Glasgow 1996–97, memb Advsy Bd The Salvation Army 1996–, dir The Soc of Deacons and Free Preseses of Glasgow 1996– (deacon 1999–2000), patron Royal Incorp of Hutcheson's Hosp 1998–, dir Assoc for the Relief of Incurables in Glasgow 1998–; elder New Kilpatrick Parish Church Bearsden 1971–; CA 1960, FSA Scot 1987, FRSA 1992; *Recreations* shooting, golf; *Clubs* Western (Glasgow, chm 2004–05); *Style*— J Allan Denholm, Esq, CBE; ✉ Greencroft, 19 Colquhoun Drive, Bearsden, Glasgow G61 4NQ (tel and fax 0141 942 1773)

DENHOLM, John Clark; s of Robert Denholm (d 1986), of Lower Largo, Fife, and Ann King, *née* Clark; *b* 10 September 1950; *Educ* Buckhaven HS, Univ of St Andrews (MA); *m* 16 Dec 1978, Julia Margaret, da of Ben Gregory; 1 da (Katy b 16 April 1986), 1 s (Michael b 19 Sept 1988); *Career* product mangr The Boots Co Nottingham 1972–76, brand mangr Scottish & Newcastle Breweries 1976–80, account dir Hall Advertising 1980–84, chm The Leith Agency Edinburgh 1995– (md 1984–95), gp md Silvermills (holding co) 1995–; MIPA 1986; *Recreations* golf; *Style*— John Denholm, Esq; ✉ The Leith Agency, 37 The Shore, Leith, Edinburgh EH6 6QU (tel 0131 561 8600)

DENIS, Germain; s of Joseph Denis, and Elizabeth, *née* Veilleux; *Educ* Laval Univ Canada; *Career* public serv int trade and domestic econ devpt issues Canadian Govt 1965–95, served GATT, WTO and NAFTA panels, memb team for free trade with USA; exec dir Int Grains Cncl and Food Aid Ctee 1995–; memb: Int Food and Agribusiness Mgmnt Assoc (IAMA), RIIA, World Trade Law Assoc, Canning House, Hong Kong Assoc; MInstD; Medal Alimentos Argentinos Secretario de Agricultura 1997, Medal Ordre du Mérite Agricole de France 1998, Medal Mérite Professionnel Bourse de Commerce de Paris 1998; *Publications* author of a broad range of articles related to global food markets, globalisation and int trade, int devpt issues, and domestic trade matters; *Recreations* gardening, golfing, reading; *Style*— Germain Denis, Esq; ✉ International Grains Council, 1 Canada Square, Canary Wharf, London E14 5AE (tel 020 7513 1122, fax 020 7513 0630)

DENMAN, 5 Baron (UK 1834); Sir Charles Spencer Denman; 2 Bt (UK 1945), of Staffield, Co Cumberland; CBE (1976), MC (1942), TD; s of Hon Sir Richard Denman, 1 Bt (d 1957); suc cous, 4 Baron, 1971; *b* 7 July 1916; *Educ* Shrewsbury; *m* 11 Sept 1943, Sheila Anne (d 1987), da of Lt-Col Algernon Bingham Anstruther Stewart, DSO; 3 s, 1 da; *Heir* s, Hon Richard Denman; *Career* served WWII Duke of Cornwall's LI (TA), Maj 1943, served India, Middle East and Mediterranean; contested Leeds Central (Cons) 1945; former chm Marine & General Mutual Life Assurance Soc; former dir: Consolidated Gold Fields,

D

Close Bros Gp, British Water, Wastewater Ltd, C Tennant Sons & Co; sr advsr: Close Bros, Merchant Bridge; memb Ctee of Middle East Trade, former memb Ctee on Invisible Exports; pres: Royal Soc for Asia Affairs, NZ-UK C of C; vice-pres: Middle East Soc, Saudi-British Soc; tstee: Kitchener Meml Fund, Arab British Charitable Fndn; formerly govr Windlesham House School; Knight Grand Cross of the Order of St Francis; *Clubs* Brooks's; *Style*— The Rt Hon Lord Denman, CBE, MC, TD

DENNING, (Michael) John; s of Frederick Edward Denning (d 1985), of Bath, and Linda Agnes Albertine, *née* Young (d 1953); *b* 29 November 1934; *Educ* Benedicts; *m* 12 March 1966, Elizabeth Anne, da of Ralph William Beresford, of Ben Rhydding, W Yorks; 2 da (Jacqueline (Mrs Clive Roberts) b 1968, Nicola (Mrs Quentin Johnson) b 1972), 1 s (Simon b 1969); *Career* owner of Burghope Manor (13th century); fndr The Heritage Circle of Country Houses and Castles, lectr and after-dinner speaker on the stately homes of GB, organiser of tours for overseas gps to visit and stay in stately homes; *Recreations* shooting, travel; *Style*— John Denning, Esq; ✉ Burghope Manor, Winsley, Bradford-on-Avon, Wiltshire BA15 2LA (tel 01225 723557/722695, e-mail info@burghope.co.uk)

DENNING, Prof the Hon Robert Gordon; only child of Baron Denning, PC; *b* 3 August 1938; *Educ* Winchester, Magdalen Coll Oxford (MA, PhD); *m* 30 Dec 1967, Elizabeth Carlyle Margaret, da of E R Chilton, of Oxford; 2 c; *Career* 2 Lt KRRC 1957–58; fell and tutor in inorganic chemistry Magdalen Coll Oxford 1968–, prof of chemistry Univ of Oxford 1996–; *Publications* author of approximately 90 articles on the optical properties of materials; *Style*— Prof the Hon Robert Denning; ✉ Magdalen College, Oxford OX1 4AU

DENNIS, Caspian Michael; s of John Peter Leslie Dennis, of the Isle of Bute, and Veronica Helen, *née* Demoore; *b* 11 September 1977, Margate, Kent; *Educ* Stantonbury Campus Milton Keynes, Univ of Manchester (BA), Birkbeck Coll London (MA); *Partner* Tara Louise Hiatt; 1 da (Manon, b 12 Aug 2005); *Career* rights asst rising to rights exec Faber and Faber Ltd 1999–2002, literary agent Abner Stein 2002–; *Style*— Caspian Dennis, Esq; ✉ Abner Stein, 10 Roland Gardens, London SW7 3PH (tel 020 7373 0456, fax 020 7370 6316, e-mail caspian@abnerstein.co.uk)

DENNIS, Cathy Roseanne; *b* 25 March 1969; *Career* singer and songwriter; songwriter and prodr for artists incl: Britney Spears (incl Toxic (UK no 1 2004, Ivor Novello Most Performed Work 2004, ASCAP Award 2004)), Celine Dion, Delta Goodrem, Enrique Iglesias, Janet Jackson, Kelly Clarkson (incl Before Your Love (USA no 1 2002)), Kylie Minogue (incl Can't Get You Out of My Head (UK no 1 2001, Ivor Novello Dance, Most Performed Work and Int Hit of the Year Awards 2002, ASCAP Award 2003), Come into My World (UK no 8 2002, Best Dance Song Grammy Awards 2004)), Pink, S Club 7 / S Club (incl Never Had a Dream Come True (UK no 1, nominated Ivor Novello Award for Best Song Musically and Lyrically 2001) and Have You Ever (UK no 1 2001)), S Club 8, Spice Girls, Will Young (incl Anything is Possible (UK no 1 2002, Best Selling UK single, Ivor Novello Award 2003)), Rachel Stevens (incl Sweet Dreams My LA Ex (UK no 2 2003, nominated Record of the Year 2003, nominated Best British Single Brit Awards 2004)); songwriter American Idol theme music (ASCAP Award 2003, 2004 and 2005); Billboard Award for Top New Female Artist 2001; *Singles* with DMob: C'Mon and Get My Love 1989, That's the Way of the World 1990, Why 1994; as solo artist: Touch Me (All Night Long) 1991, Just Another Dream 1991 (ASCAP Award 1991), Too Many Walls 1991 (ASCAP Award 1991, ASCAP (LA) Award 1992), Everybody Move 1991, You Lied to Me 1992, Irresistible 1992, Falling 1993, West End Pad 1996, Waterloo Sunset 1997, When Dreams Turn to Dust 1997; *Albums* Move to This 1991, Into the Skyline 1993, Am I the Kind of Girl 1996; *Style*— Cathy Dennis; ✉ c/o 19 Entertainment, 33 Ransomes Dock, 35–37 Parkgate Road, London SW11 4NP

DENNIS, Geoffrey; *Career* early career as dir Economics and Fin Div Ewbank Preece Consltg and md Travers Morgan Environmental Consultancy; formerly: int dir Br Red Cross, head S Asia Int Fedn of the Red Cross (IFRC); chief exec: Friends of the Elderly 2000–04, CARE Int 2004–; *Style*— Geoffrey Dennis, Esq; ✉ CARE International,10–13 Rushworth Street, London SE1 0RB (tel 020 7934 9334, fax 020 7934 9335)

DENNIS, Prof Ian Howard; s of Flt Lt Bernard Cecil Dennis (d 1982), of Altrincham, Cheshire, and Jean Harrison, *née* Dennis; *b* 17 September 1948; *Educ* Manchester Grammar, Queens' Coll Cambridge (MA, PhD); *m* 17 July 1982, Dr Susan Mary Bower, da of Ivan William Bower (d 1989), of Southsea, Hants; 1 s (Robert William b 1984), 1 da (Katherine Mary b 1986); *Career* called to the Bar Gray's Inn 1971; lectr in law Cncl of Legal Educn 1971–73; UCL: lectr 1974–82, reader 1982–87, prof 1987–, head of dept 2002–; Allen, Allen and Hemsley visiting professorial fell Univ of Sydney 1995; special conslt Law Cmmn 1986–87 (memb criminal codification team 1981–89); ed Criminal Law Review; *Books* Codification of the Criminal Law, a Report to the Law Commission (with J C Smith and E J Griew, 1985), The Law of Evidence (3 edn 2007); *Recreations* chess, cycling, wine, mountain walking; *Style*— Prof Ian Dennis; ✉ Faculty of Laws, University College London, Bentham House, Endsleigh Gardens, London WC1H 0EG (tel 020 7679 1431)

DENNIS, Dr John Stephen; s of Patrick John Dennis (d 1990), and Audrey, *née* Martin (d 1971); *b* 26 September 1955; *Educ* Churchfields Sch Swindon, Selwyn Coll Cambridge (nat engrg scholar, BA, N Carolina State Univ prize, Coll Book prize, res scholar, PhD); *m* 5 Sept 1981, Ruth Dennis, MRCVS, da of Rev Dr John Wall; *Career* lectr Dept of Chemical Engrg Univ of Cambridge 1984–88, self employed conslt chem engr 1989–, mangr LINK Biochemical Engrg Prog 1989–, biochemical engrg co-ordinator SERC 1991–; visiting prof UCL 1996–; Steetley Award Inst of Energy 1989; memb Ctee Biotechnology Gp SCI; corporate memb IChemE 1986, CEng 1986; *Publications* author of numerous articles and symposia on combustion, heat transfer, fluidisation and biochemical engrg; *Recreations* rowing (formerly memb Cambridge Univ 2nd VIII), sculling, running, reading; *Style*— Dr John Dennis; ✉ 20 High Street, Stetchworth, Newmarket, Suffolk CB8 9TJ (tel 01638 508171, fax 01638 508344)

DENNIS, Mark Jonathan; QC (2006); s of Edward John Dennis, and Patricia Edna, *née* Roberts; *b* 15 March 1955; *Educ* Battersea GS, Peterhouse Cambridge (BA, MA); *m* 26 July 1985, Christabel Harriet, *née* Birbeck; 1 s, 1 da; *Career* called to the Bar Middle Temple 1977; jr Treasy counsel 1993–98, sr Treasy counsel 1998–2006, recorder of the Crown Court 2000–; memb Criminal Bar Assoc; *Style*— Mark Dennis, Esq, QC; ✉ 6 King's Bench Walk, Temple, London EC4Y 7DR (tel 020 7583 0410, fax 020 7353 8791, e-mail clerks@6kbw.com)

DENNIS, Dr Richard Benson; s of Alfred Benson Dennis, of Weymouth, Dorset, and Valentine Betty, *née* Smith; *b* 15 July 1945; *Educ* Weymouth GS, Univ of Reading (BSc, PhD); *m* 17 Dec 1971, Beate, da of Wilhelm Stamm (d 1974), of W Germany; 2 da (Andrea b 1974, Angela b 1976); *Career* Alexander von Humboldt fell Munich Univ 1976–78, sr lectr Heriot-Watt Univ 1978–91 (lectr 1971), fndr Mütek GmbH W Germany 1980, md Edinburgh Instruments Ltd 1983–, dir Edinburgh Sensors Ltd 1987–; dir and co sec UK Consortium for Photonics and Optics; memb Scottish Consultative Cncl on the Curriculum 1990–94; chm Sch Bd Balerno HS 1989–93; *Recreations* bridge, golf; *Clubs* Carlton Bridge, Dalmahoy Country; *Style*— Dr Richard Dennis; ✉ St Leonards, 480 Lanark Road, Juniper Green, Edinburgh EH14 5BL (tel 0131 453 5682); Edinburgh Instruments Ltd, 2 Bain Square, Livingston EH54 7DQ (tel 01506 425300, 01506 425320, e-mail richard.dennis@edinst.com)

DENNIS, Rodney John; s of William Gordon Dennis, and Shiela Dennis; *b* 7 November 1952; *Educ* Univ of Cape Town (BBusSci); *m* 27 Aug 1979, Pamela Mary, *née* Hartnady; *Career* chief investment offr Prudential Portfolio Managers Ltd March 1996–; *Recreations* flying, sailing, skiing, reading, music; *Style*— Rodney Dennis, Esq

DENNIS, Ronald (Ron); CBE; s of Norman Stanley Dennis (d 1986), of Woking, Surrey, and Evelyn, *née* Reader; *b* 1 June 1947; *Educ* Guildford Tech Coll (Vehicle Technol Course); *m* 31 Dec 1985, Lisa Ann, da of Gary K Shelton; 2 da (Charlotte Victoria b 25 Aug 1987, Francesca Olivia b 11 Nov 1993), 1 s (Christian Shelton b 27 Oct 1990); *Career* apprentice Thomson & Taylor, owner/mangr Project Four team (winning ProCar Championship 1979 and Formula 3 Championship 1979–80), merged with McLaren team 1980; McLaren Formula One racing team: winners Constructors' Cup 1984–85 and 1988, 1989, 1990, 1991 and 1998, nine driving championships; McLaren F1 winner Le Mans 24 hour race 1995 (first attempt); chm and ceo McLaren Gp (incl: McLaren Racing Ltd, McLaren Marketing Ltd, McLaren Cars Ltd, McLaren Electronic Systems Ltd, McLaren Composites Ltd, McLaren Applied Technologies Ltd); memb Formula One Cmmn; tstee Tommy's Campaign; Hon DTech De Montfort Univ 1996, Hon DSci City Univ 1997, Hon DUniv Surrey 2000; *Recreations* golf, shooting, snow and water skiing; *Clubs* Morton's, Tramp, British Racing Drivers'; *Style*— Ron Dennis, Esq, CBE; ✉ McLaren Technology Centre, Chertsey Road, Woking, Surrey GU21 4YH (tel 01483 261002, fax 01483 261261)

DENNY, Sir Anthony Coningham de Waltham; 8 Bt (I 1782), of Castle Moyle, Kerry; s of Rev Sir Henry Lyttelton Lyster Denny, 7 Bt (d 1953); *b* 22 April 1925; *Educ* Clayesmore, Anglo-French Art Centre, Regent St Poly Sch of Architecture; *m* 1 Sept 1949, Anne Catherine, er da of late Samuel Beverley; 2 s (Piers Anthony de Waltham b 1954, Thomas Francis Coningham b 1956), 1 adopted da (Sophy Elinor Sisophanh b 1974); *Heir* s, Piers Denny; *Career* serv RAF (air crew) 1943–47; designer; ret ptnr and conslt to Verity and Beverley (Architects and Designers), offices in: NY, Tetbury and Lisbon, Portugal; hereditary Freeman of Cork; MCSD, FRSA; *Clubs* Chelsea Arts; *Style*— Sir Anthony Denny, Bt; ✉ Almonry Cottage, Muchelney, Langport, Somerset TA10 0DG (tel 01458 252621)

DENNY, Sir Charles Alistair Maurice; 4 Bt (UK 1913), of Dumbarton, Co Dunbarton; s of Sir Alistair Maurice Archibald Denny, 3 Bt (d 1995), and Elizabeth Hunt, da of Maj Sir (Ernest) Guy Richard Lloyd, 1 Bt, DSO; *b* 7 October 1950; *Educ* Wellington, Univ of Edinburgh; *m* 1981 (m dis 2002), Belinda (Linda) Mary, yr da of James Patrick McDonald, of Dublin; 1 s (Patrick Charles Alistair b 1985), 1 da (Georgina Mary b 1989); *Heir* s, Patrick Denny; *Career* assoc dir HSBC; *Recreations* golf, racing, gardening; *Clubs* R&A; *Style*— Sir Charles Denny, Bt; ✉ The Ridge, 2 Oakfield, Hawkhurst, Kent TN18 4JR; HSBC, 8 Canada Square, London E14 5HQ (tel 020 7991 5741, e-mail charles.a.m.denny@hsbcgroup.com)

DENNY, John Ingram; CMG (1997); s of Thomas Ingram Denny, of Macclesfield, Cheshire, and Claire Dorothy, *née* Lewis; *b* 28 May 1941; *Educ* Normain Coll Chester, Poly of N London (DipArch), Univ of Reading (MSc); *m* 2 June 1967, Carol Ann Frances, da of Walter James Hughes, of St Leonards, Bournemouth, Hants; 1 s (Paul b 7 Oct 1969), 2 da (Louise (Mrs Adrian Myers) b 23 July 1971, Sarah b 31 Jan 1974); *Career* md Cecil Denny Highton Partnership, jt md HOK International Ltd 1995–2001 (joined 1970, ptnr 1971, sr ptnr 1990, incorporated 1995), md Property Consulting Ltd 2002–04; conslt architect to: FCO, Home Office, Parly Works Office, Royal Household, HM Treasy, Cabinet Office, PACE, Crown Estate and Natural History Museum; memb RIBA; *Recreations* golf, photography; *Style*— John Denny, Esq, CMG

DENNY, (Edward) Michael Patrick; s of Edward Maynard Donald Denny, of Cowfold, W Sussex, and Patricia, *née* Musprett-Williams; *b* 8 April 1943, Sussex; *Educ* Eton; *m* March 1968, Gay Amanda Louise, *née* Hobrow; 1 s (Charles Henry b 1973), 1 da (Joanna Elizabeth Louise b 1975); *Career* fndr Northern Investors Co 1984, chm NVM Private Equity 1988–; chm Br Venture Capital Assoc 1990; govr Univ of Durham 1989–96; MSI; *Recreations* golf, shooting, skiing; *Clubs* New (Edinburgh); *Style*— Michael Denny, Esq; ✉ Westsidewood House, Carnwath, South Lanarkshire ML11 8LJ (tel 01501 785236, fax 01501 785444); Northern Venture Managers Limited, Northumberland House, Princess Square, Newcastle upon Tyne NE1 8ER (e-mail michael.denny@nvm.co.uk)

DENNY, Neill Quentin William; s of Alfred Christopher Denny, of Alresford, Hants, and Alison Mary, *née* McLellan; *b* 31 July 1966, Cheam, Surrey; *Educ* Dulwich Coll (scholar), Hounslow Borough Coll (HND, pres Student Union); *m* 2 June 2001, Anne, *née* Whitaker; 1 da (Alexandra Kathleen Elizabeth b 11 March 2003), 1 s (Jack Alfred Charles b 18 Sept 2005); *Career* reporter Direct Response 1989, reporter then news ed Precision Marketing 1990–94, dep ed Promotions & Incentives 1994–95, reporter Marketing magazine 1995, launch ed Marketing Direct 1995–98, dep ed Marketing magazine 1998–99, ed Retail Week 1999–2004, ed-in-chief The Bookseller 2004–; Freeman City of London 2001; highly commended PPA Ed of the Year 2002; *Recreations* reading, wine, football, cycling; *Style*— Neill Denny, Esq; ✉ The Bookseller, 5th Floor, Endeavour House, 189 Shaftesbury Avenue, London WC2H 8TJ (tel 020 7420 6109, fax 020 7420 6103, e-mail neill.denny@bookseller.co.uk)

DENNY, Ronald Maurice; s of Maurice Ellis Louis Denny (d 1981), and Ada Beatrice, *née* Bradley (d 1999); *b* 11 January 1927; *Educ* Gosport County Sch; *m* 1, 7 Nov 1952, Dorothy (d 2003), da of William Hamilton (d 1933); 1 s (Andrew b 1964), 2 da (Jane b 1957, Elizabeth b 1958); m 2, 5 Oct 2005, Kathleen (Audrey) Halls; *Career* Rediffusion plc: chief exec 1979–89, chm 1985–89 (ret); dir: BET plc 1982–89 (ret), Thames Television 1980–89, Electrocomponents plc 1984–95, TCC Ltd Malta 1991–2004; memb Philharmonia Orchestra Tst 1984–92; CEng, FIEE 1948, FRSA 1985, Hon RCM 1984; *Recreations* music, reading; *Clubs* Arts; *Style*— Ronald Denny, Esq; ✉ 7 The Holt, Bishop's Cleeve, Cheltenham GL52 8NQ (tel 01242 677151)

DENNYS, Nicholas Charles Jonathan; QC (1991); s of John Edward Dennys, MC (d 1973), and Hon Lavinia Mary Yolande Lyttelton; *b* 14 July 1951; *Educ* Eton, BNC Oxford (BA); *m* 19 Feb 1977, Frances Winifred, da of Rev Canon Gervase William Markham, of Morland, Cumbria; 4 da (Harriet b 5 Feb 1979, Sophie b 2 Feb 1981, Romilly Mary b 31 March 1984, Katharine b 14 July 1986); *Career* called to the Bar Middle Temple 1975; recorder 1999– (asst recorder 1997–99); *Recreations* golf, windsurfing, reading; *Style*— Nicholas Dennys, Esq, QC; ✉ 1 Atkin Buildings, Gray's Inn, London WC1R 5AT (tel 020 7404 0102)

DENOON DUNCAN, Russell Euan; s of Douglas Denoon Duncan (d 1955), of Johannesburg, South Africa, and Ray, *née* Reynolds (d 1981); gs of James Denoon Duncan, a senator in the Senate of the Union of South Africa; *b* 11 March 1926; *Educ* Michaelhouse Natal; *m* 28 Jan 1956, Caroline Jane Lloyd, da of Noel Wynne Spencer Lewin (d 1980), of London; 2 s (James b 1957, Angus b 1960); *Career* SA Artillery 1943–45, served Egypt and Italy, rising to Lance Bombardier; admitted attorney SA 1949, admitted slr 1961; ptnr Webber Wentzel Johannesburg 1952–61; Cameron McKenna (former Markbys then Cameron Markby Hewitt): ptnr 1963–90, sr ptnr 1987–90, conslt 1990–97; chm National Australia Group (UK) Limited (UK holding co of National Australia Bank) 1987–92; vice-pres Br Hungarian Law Assoc 1991–94, pres Br Polish Legal Assoc 1995–2000 (vice-chm 1989–91, chm 1991–95), patron Euro Law Students' Assoc 2004–05; Adwokatura Zasluzonym, Polish Bar Assoc 2003; former chm Thames Ditton Residents' Assoc; Freeman Worshipful Co of Slrs 1987; FInstD, Offr Order of Merit of Poland 1995; *Recreations* mountain walking, tennis, painting; *Clubs* City of London, City Law, Royal Tennis Ct, Rand, Johannesburg Country; *Style*— Russell Denoon Duncan, Esq; ✉ Rose Cottage, Watts Road, Thames Ditton, Surrey KT7 0BX (tel 020 8398 5193, mobile 07711 418982, e-mail redd@clara.co.uk)

DENSHAM, (Peter) Ryan Cridland; s of Humphrey Ashley (d 1979), and Mary Constance, *née* Cridland; *b* 8 February 1949; *Educ* Clifton; *m* Melinda Jane, da of Peter Lowell Baldwin; 1 da (Emily b 1980), 2 s (Henry b 1981, George b 1987); *Career* CA; with Chalmers Impey & Co London 1967–73 (articled clerk 1967–71), with Thornton Baker (now Grant Thornton) 1973–83 (ptnr 1979), ptnr PricewaterhouseCoopers (formerly Price Waterhouse before merger) 1983–2004; tstee and dir Bristol Old Vic Theatre Sch, dir Conservatoire of Dance and Drama; vestryman St Mary Redcliffe Bristol, secretaire Commanderie de Bordeaux à Bristol; former Master Antient Soc of St Stephens Ringers, former pres Grateful Soc; ACA 1971; *Recreations* fishing, sailing, golf, skiing; *Style*— Ryan Densham, Esq; ✉ mobile 07710 703327, e-mail thedenshams@btinternet.com

DENT, Helen Anne; da of Frederick Dent, of Grays, Essex, and Muriel, *née* Antcliffe; *b* 29 June 1951; *Educ* Grays Convent Thurrock, Lancaster Univ (BEd), South Bank Univ (MSc), Salford Univ; *Career* various social work posts London 1974–78, lectr in social work and social policy 1978–81, with London Borough of Enfield 1981–86, asst dir Cambs CC 1986–90, dir of external affrs Nat Children's Homes 1990–96, currently chief exec Family Welfare Assoc; non-exec dir Gt Ormond St Hosp for Children NHS Tst; memb Cncl ESRC; tstee: Child Poverty Action Gp (CPAG), End Child Poverty (ECP); *Recreations* opera, singing, choral music (London Welsh Choral), gardening, reading; *Clubs* Cwlth Soc; *Style*— Ms Helen Dent; ✉ 14 Cloudsley Place, London N1 0JA (tel 020 7837 6065); The Family Welfare Association, 501–505 Kingsland Road, London E8 4AU (tel 020 7254 6251, e-mail helen.dent@fwa.org.uk)

DENT, Jeremy Francis; s of Cdr Adrian James Dent, of Sway, Hants, and Diana Elizabeth, *née* Buxton; *b* 24 January 1952; *Educ* Bradfield Coll, Univ of Southampton (BSc); *Career* trainee accountant KPMG 1974–77; lectr in accounting: Univ of Southampton 1977–82, London Business Sch 1982–88; prof of accounting Manchester Business Sch 1988–90; fell in accounting: London Business Sch 1999–, LSE 1999– (reader 1991–99); visiting prof: Stockholm, Copenhagen, Turku, Paris, Sydney; FCA 1977; *Style*— Jeremy Dent, Esq; ✉ 560 Hamilton House, 6 St George Wharf, London SW8 2JE (tel 020 7582 4598, e-mail jdent@jeremydent.com)

DENT, Julie Elizabeth; CBE (2006); da of Thomas Michael Patrick Delaney (d 1985), and Kathleen Rose, *née* Stratford; *b* 3 April 1956; *Educ* Rosebury GS Epsom, Lanchester Poly (BA), Brunel Univ (MA), Cornell Univ (Exec Devpt Prog); *m* 25 March 1978, Anthony Middleton Dent, s of Montague Middleton Dent (d 2000); 1 s (Thomas Isambard Middleton b 22 Oct 1979), 1 da (Emily Elizabeth Middleton b 8 April 1982); *Career* ceo Ealing, Hammersmith and Hounslow Family Health Services Authy 1991–95, dir Ealing, Hammersmith and Hounslow HA 1995–2000, dir performance mgmnt Dept of Health 2000–02, ceo SW London SHA 2002–; mgmnt conslt 2007–; chm: Secure Health 2007–, London Probation Bd 2007–; govr Orley Farm Prep Sch Harrow; *Recreations* travelling, reading, music, gardening; *Style*— Mrs Julie Dent, CBE; ✉ London Probation Board, 71–73 Great Peter Street, London SW1P 2ZY (tel 020 7222 5656)

DENT-BROCKLEHURST, Henry; s of Mark Dent-Brocklehurst, and Mary Elizabeth Chipps; *b* 6 May 1966; *Educ* Stowe, Univ of Southern Calif; *m* 9 May 1998, Lili Maltese; 2 s (Mark b 27 April 2001, Lucas b 10 Feb 2002); *Career* landowner; owner Sudeley Castle; film and documentary maker; *Recreations* surfing, tennis, golf; *Clubs* Annabel's; *Style*— Henry Dent-Brocklehurst, Esq

DENTON, Charles Henry; s of Alan Denton; *b* 20 December 1937; *Educ* Reading Sch, Univ of Bristol (BA); *m* 1961, Eleanor Mary, *née* Player; 1 s, 2 da; *Career* deckhand 1960, advtg trainee 1961–63, BBC TV 1963–68, freelance TV prodr with Granada, ATV and Yorkshire TV 1969–70, dir Tempest Films Ltd 1969–71, md Black Lion Films 1979–81, controller of progs ATV 1977–81 (head of documentaries 1974–77), dir of progs Central Independent TV 1981–84, dir Central Independent Television plc 1981–87, chief exec Zenith Productions 1984–93, head of drama BBC TV 1993–96; chm: Zenith North Ltd 1988–93, Action Time Ltd 1988–93, Cornwall Film 2001–; chm PACT until 1993, govr Br Film Inst 1993–2000, dir Film Cncl 2000–, memb Arts Cncl of England 1996–98; FRSA 1988, FRTS 1988; *Style*— Charles Denton, Esq

DENTON, Nicholas John (Nick); s of John Richard Denton, and Jennifer Jane, *née* Forbes; *b* 18 October 1955; *Educ* Winchester, Magdalene Coll Cambridge (MA); *m* 23 March 1991, Katie, da of Michael Benzecry; 1 s (Toby John b 19 May 1993), 2 da (Rebecca Louisa b 2 June 1995, Eliza Lucy b 30 Oct 1998); *Career* Dewe Rogerson Ltd: account dir London 1981–86, dir Australia 1986–87; corp affrs mangr Eurotunnel plc 1987–88, dir Shandwick Consultants Ltd 1988–97, fndr ptnr The Hogarth Partnership 1997; *Recreations* tennis, history, reading, opera, walking; *Style*— Nick Denton, Esq; ✉ The Hogarth Partnership, No 1 London Bridge, London SE1 9BG (e-mail ndenton@hogarthpr.co.uk)

DENTON, Prof Richard Michael (Dick); s of Arthur Benjamin Denton (d 1968), of Chippenham, Wilts, and Eileen Mary, *née* Evans (d 2002); *b* 16 October 1941; *Educ* Wycliffe Coll, Christ's Coll Cambridge (MA, PhD), Univ of Bristol (DSc); *m* 1965, Janet Mary, *née* Jones; 2 da (Sally Catherine b 1967, Hannah Rachel b 1972), 1 s (Stephen Richard b 1969); *Career* Dept of Biochemistry Univ of Bristol: MRC Metabolism Control Gp 1966–72, lectr 1973–78, reader 1978–87, prof of biochemistry (personal chair) 1987–, head of dept 1995–2000, chm of med sciences 2000–04, dean of med and veterinary science 2003–04; MRC sr research leave fellowship 1984–88; memb: MRC Grants Ctee and Physiological Systems Bd 1977–85, MRC Cncl 1999–04, Research Ctee Br Diabetic Assoc 1986–92 (chm 1990–92), Molecular and Cell Biology Panel Wellcome Tst Research Ctee 1993–96; R D Lawrence lecture Br Diabetic Assoc 1981; memb Biochemical Soc 1965; FMedSci 1998, FRS 1998; *Publications* over 220 research papers in Nature, Biochemical Jl and other int research jls on topics incl molecular basis of the control of metabolism by insulin and other hormones; *Recreations* family, fell walking, keeping fit, cooking, reading; *Style*— Prof Dick Denton, FRS; ✉ Dept of Biochemistry, School of Medical Sciences, University of Bristol, Bristol BS8 1TD (tel 0117 331 2184, fax 0117 331 2168, e-mail r.denton@bristol.ac.uk)

DENYER, Roderick Lawrence; QC (1990); s of Oliver James Denyer (d 1982), and Olive Mabel, *née* Jones; *b* 1 March 1948; *Educ* Grove Park GS for Boys Wrexham, LSE (LLM); *m* 21 April 1973, Pauline; 2 da (Hannah b 4 March 1978, Alexandra b 10 Feb 1981); *Career* called to the Bar Inner Temple 1970 (bencher 1996); lectr in law Univ of Bristol 1971–73, practising barr 1973–2002, former head of chambers, recorder of the Crown Court 1990–2002, circuit judge (Wales & Chester Circuit) 2002–; *Publications* Personal Injury Litigation and Children (1993, 2 edn 2002), various pubns in legal jls; *Recreations* cricket, 1960s pop music; *Style*— His Hon Judge Denyer, QC

DENYER, Stephen Robert Noble; s of Wilfred Denyer, of Sherborne, Dorset, and Joy Victoria Jeanne, *née* Noble; *b* 27 December 1955; *Educ* Fosters GS Sherborne, Univ of Durham (BA); *m* 3 Sept 1988, Monika Maria, da of Heinrich Christoph Wolf, of Lübeck, Germany; 3 s (Martin, Timothy, Frank), 1 da (Helen); *Career* admitted slr 1980; ptnr Allen & Overy 1987–, regnl managing ptnr for Europe 1998–; Freeman Worshipful Co of Slrs 1986; memb Law Soc 1980; memb Int Bar Assoc 1987; *Recreations* walking, travel, gardening; *Style*— Stephen Denyer, Esq; ✉ Allen & Overy, Taunustor 2, 60311 Frankfurt am Main, Germany

DENZ, Silvio Werner; s of Werner Josef Denz, and Doris, *née* Steiger; *b* 14 September 1956, Basle, Switzerland; *Educ* Basler Kantonalbank Basel, Swiss Business Sch Basel; *Family* 1 s (Claudio Werner b 31 Jan 1988); *Career* Swiss Army 1976, finance dept André & Cie Lausanne 1977–79, mktg dept Miller Brewing Milwaukee WI 1979–80, creator chain of perfumeries (120 stores) Switzerland 1980–2000, fndr Art and Fragrance Ltd Zurich 2000, fndr Jaguar Fragrance Ltd London 2001; prop vineyards: Clos d'Agon Spain 1999, Chateau Faugeres Saint-Emilion 2005, Chateau de Chambrun Lalande-de-Pomerol 2007; property buying and renovating London 2002–; *Recreations* skiing, diving, flying, biking, tennis, collecting art; *Style*— Silvio Denz, Esq; ✉ 130 Wigmore Street, London W1U 3SB (tel 020 3230 2005, fax 020 3230 2004)

DENZA, Eileen; CMG (1984); da of Alexander Young (d 1995), and Ellen Duffy (d 1981); *b* 23 July 1937; *Educ* Univ of Aberdeen (MA), Univ of Oxford (MA), Harvard Univ (LLM); *m* 1966, John Denza; 1 da (Antonia b 1967), 2 s (Mark b 1969, Paul b 1971); *Career* asst lectr in law Univ of Bristol 1961–63, called to the Bar Lincoln's Inn 1963, asst legal advsr FCO 1963–74, legal cnsllr FCO 1974–86, legal advsr to UK Representation to Euro Community 1980–83, pupillage and practice at Bar 1986–87, second counsel to the Chm of Ctees, counsel to Euro Communities Ctee House of Lords 1987–95, visiting prof of law UCL 1997– (sr res fell 1996); memb: European Community Law Section Advsy Bd Br Inst of Int and Comparative Law, Expert Panel on Human Rights in the EU, Justice; FRSA; *Books* Diplomatic Law (1976, 2 edn 1998), The Intergovernmental Pillars of the European Union (2002); contrib: Satow, Diplomatic Practice, Essays in Air Law, Airline Mergers and Co-operation in the European Community, Consular Law and Practice, Institutional Dynamics of European Integration, The European Union and World Trade Law, Evans' International Law (2 edn 2006), EU Law for the 21st Century; *Style*— Prof Eileen Denza, CMG

DERBY, Bishop of 2005–; Rt Rev Dr Alastair Llewellyn John Redfern; s of Victor Redfern (d 1995), and Audrey, *née* Musty; *b* 1 September 1948; *Educ* ChCh Oxford, Trinity Coll Cambridge, Univ of Bristol; *m* 1, 21 Dec 1974, Jane Valerie (d 2004), da of Kenneth Straw; 2 da (Elizabeth Jane b 3 April 1978, Zoë Louise 30 June 1980); m 2, 6 May 2006, Caroline Elizabeth Boddington; *Career* curate Tettenhall Wolverhampton 1976–79, lectr and vice-princ Ripon Coll Cuddesdon 1979–87, curate All Saints Cuddesdon 1983–87, canon theologian Bristol Cathedral 1987–97, bishop of Grantham and dean of Stamford 1997–2005; *Books* Ministry and Priesthood (1999), Being Anglican (2000); *Recreations* reading, walking; *Style*— The Rt Rev the Bishop of Derby; ✉ The Bishop's House, 6 King Street, Duffield, Belper, Derbyshire DE56 4EU (tel 01332 840132, fax 01332 842743, e-mail bishop@bishopofderby.org)

DERBY, 19 Earl of (E 1485); Edward Richard William Stanley; 12 Bt (E 1627), DL (Merseyside 1999); also Baron Stanley of Bickerstaffe (UK 1832) and Baron Stanley of Preston (UK 1886); s of Hon Hugh Henry Montagu Stanley (d 1971, gs of 17 Earl of Derby), and Mary Rose (who m 2, William Spiegelberg) da of late Charles Francis Birch, of Rhodesia; suc uncle, 18 Earl of Derby, MC, DL (d 1994); *b* 10 October 1962; *Educ* Eton, RAC Cirencester; *m* 21 Oct 1995, Hon Caroline Emma Neville, da of 10 Baron Braybrooke, *qv*; 1 da (Lady Henrietta Mary Rose b 6 February 1997), 2 s (Edward John Robin, Baron Stanley of Bickerstaffe b 21 April 1998, Hon Oliver Hugh Henry b 26 April 2002); *Heir* s, Baron Stanley of Bickerstaffe; *Career* cmmnd Grenadier Gds 1982–85; dir incl: Fleming Private Asset Management Ltd 1992–2000, Robert Fleming & Co Ltd 1996–98, Robert Fleming Int Ltd 1998–2001, Haydock Park Racecourse Co Ltd 1994–, Fleming Family and Ptnrs 2001–; pres: Liverpool C of C 1995–, Royal Liverpool Philharmonic Soc 1995–, Royal Lytham & St Annes Golf Club 1995–, Formby Golf Club 1995–, Royal Botanical and Horticultural Soc of Manchester and the Northern Counties 1995–, Henshaw's Soc for the Blind 1996–2007, Sefton C of C 1998–, Knowsley C of C 1995–; vice-pres PGA 2001–; chm: Knowsley Ltd 1998–, FF&P Tstee Co Ltd 2004–; hon pres: Liverpool Cncl of Social Services, Boys Brigade Liverpool Battalion 1995–; tstee: Nat Museums and Galleries on Merseyside 1995–2005, Aintree Racecourse Charitable Appeal Tst 1995–; memb Cncl Univ of Liverpool 1998–2004; patron: Friends of Liverpool Cathedral 1995–, Liverpool Branch RNLI 1995–, Liverpool Area Prince's Tst, numerous other charities; life pres Rugby Football League 1996–; *Clubs* White's, Jockey Club Rooms; *Style*— The Rt Hon the Earl of Derby, DL; ✉ Knowsley, Prescot, Merseyside L34 4AF (tel 0151 489 6147, office fax 0151 482 1988, e-mail private.office@knowsley.com, website www.knowsley.com)

DERBY, Peter Jared; s of Samuel Jonathan James Derby (d 1974), of Belfast, and Frances Emma, *née* Leckie (d 1997); *b* 21 February 1940; *Educ* Inchmarlo Sch, Royal Belfast Academical Inst, Queen's Univ Belfast (BSc); *m* 3 Aug 1968, Rosemary Jane, da of Charles Euan Chalmers Guthrie (d 1985), of Edinburgh; 2 da (Lucy b 1969, Polly b 1973), 1 s (Andrew b 1971); *Career* jt asst actuary Scottish Widows Fund 1965–67 (joined 1961), ptnr Wood Mackenzie and Co 1970–86 (joined 1967); dir: Hill Samuel and Co Ltd 1986–88, Ashton Tod McLaren 1988–89, Citigroup Quilter (formely Quilter & Co Ltd) 1989–2004; sidesman Christ Church Shamley Green; memb Guildry of Brechin Angus 1973; Freeman: City of London, Worshipful Co of Actuaries 1979 (Master 2001–02); FFA 1965, memb Stock Exchange 1970; *Recreations* golf, tennis, music; *Clubs* New (Edinburgh), Woking Golf, Royal Co Down Golf; *Style*— Peter J Derby, Esq; ✉ Haldish Farm, Shamley Green, Guildford, Surrey GU5 0RD (tel 01483 898461, fax 01483 898606, e-mail peter@thederbys.co.uk)

DERBYSHIRE, Benjamin Charles Edward; s of Sir Andrew George Derbyshire, and Lily, *née* Binns; *b* 15 May 1953; *Educ* Bryanston, Hatfield GS, Sch of Architecture Birmingham Poly, Sch of Architecture Univ of Cambridge (DipArch); *m* 14 April 1979 (m dis 2003), Annie Anoja Sapumali, da of I D S Weerawardina; 1 s (Albert Guy Devakumara b 24 April 1987), 1 da (Millicent Grace Ranjani b 15 Jan 1990); *Career* architect; Hunt Thompson Assocs (now HTA Architects Ltd): joined 1976, assoc 1979–, ptnr 1986–98, dir 1998–2004, md 2004–; chm USER Research 1991–95 (fndr dir 1989); memb: RIBA Community Architecture Gp 1983–87, Campaign Gp Business in the Community Professional Firms Gp 1990–93, Ctee Nat Tenants' Resource Centre 1991–95, Bd Prince's Trust 1992–95 (memb Ctee Faith in Estates 1986–87); winner of numerous architectural and building construction awards; contrib to architectural pubns; chair of Govrs Columbia Primary Sch 1995–98; RIBA 1977, FRSA 1993; *Recreations* walking, cycling, music; *Style*— Benjamin Derbyshire, Esq; ✉ HTA Architects Ltd, 79 Parkway, London NW1 7PP (tel 020 7485 8555, fax 020 7485 1232, e-mail bd@hta-arch.co.uk)

DERBYSHIRE, Prof Edward; s of late Edward Derbyshire, of Timonium, Maryland, and late Kathleen, *née* Wall; *b* 18 August 1932; *Educ* Alleyne's GS Stone, Keele Univ (BA, DipEd), McGill Univ Montreal (MSc), Monash Univ (PhD); *m* 2 June 1956, Maryon Joyce, da of late Arthur John Lloyd, of Keele, Staffs; 3 s (Edmund Lloyd b 20 Jan 1959, Edward Arthur b 13 April 1965, Dominic Giles b 17 Nov 1968); *Career* RAEC 1954–56; lectr in geography Univ of NSW 1960–62, sr lectr in geography Monash Univ 1965–66 (lectr 1963–65); Keele Univ: lectr in physical geography 1967–70, sr lectr 1970–74, reader 1974–84, prof of geomorphology 1984; Univ of Leicester: prof of physical geography 1985–90, res prof 1990–92, prof emeritus 1991–; res prof of physical geography Royal Holloway Coll London (now Royal Holloway Univ of London) 1991–, hon res prof Gansu Acad of Sciences PRC 1991–, Belle Van Zuylen prof Univ of Utrecht 1992; pres Br Geomorphological Res Gp 1982–83 (hon sec 1971–75), pres Section E BAAS 1989–90, sec-gen Int Union for Quaternary Res (INQUA) 1991–95, chm Int Geological Correlation Prog (UNESCO/IUGS) 1996–2001, chm Ctee for Research Directions Int Union of Geological Sciences (IUGS) 2002–06, chm Science Prog Ctee Int Year of Planet Earth (UNESCO/IUGS) 2002–; Geological Soc London: sec foreign and external affrs 2007–, chm External Rels Ctee 2007– (memb 1999–2006); hon life memb: INQUA 1999, Quaternary Res Assoc; FGS 1974, FRGS 1980; Antarctic Serv Medal USA 1974; *Books* The Topographical Map (1966), Climatic Geomorphology (ed, 1973), Geomorphology and Climate (ed, 1976), Geomorphological Processes (with J R Hails and K J Gregory, 1980), Genesis and Properties of Collapsible Soils (ed with I J Smalley and T A Dijkstra, 1995),

Landslides in the Thick Loess Terrain of Northwest China (ed with X M Meng and T A Dijkstra, 2000), Palaeoenvironmental Reconstruction in Quaternary Arid Lands (ed with A K Singhi, 1999); *Recreations* photography, music, poetry, painting; *Style*— Prof Edward Derbyshire; ✉ Department of Geography, Royal Holloway, University of London, Egham, Surrey TW20 0EX (tel 01273 748919, e-mail e.derbyshire@rhul.ac.uk)

DERBYSHIRE, Eileen; da of Frank Derbyshire (d 1976), of Manchester, and Mary Edna, *née* Taylor (d 1993); *b* 6 October 1931; *Educ* Manchester HS for Girls, Northern Sch of Music; *m* 1 April 1965, Thomas Wilfrid Holt, s of George Wrangham Holt; 1 s (Oliver Charles Thomas b 22 May 1966); *Career* actress; first broadcast in 1948, has taken part in numerous radio prodns; first appeared in rep 1952 (toured with Century Theatre and others); plays role of Emily Bishop in Coronation Street (joined in first year 1961); LRAM; *Style*— Miss Eileen Derbyshire; ✉ c/o Granada Television Ltd, Granada TV Centre, Quay Street, Manchester M60 9EA

DERBYSHIRE, Nicholas Crawford (Nick); s of Arnold Clifford Derbyshire (d 1974), and Eileen, *née* Crawford (d 1999); *b* 20 July 1943; *Educ* St Edward's Sch Oxford, Sch of Architecture Gloucester Coll of Art and Design (DipArch), Manchester Business Sch (Dip Business Studies), Hochschule Für Gestaltung Ulm Germany; *m* 18 July 1970, Winifred, da of Donald Blenkinsop; 2 s (William George b 1971, Thomas Henry b 1974); *Career* architect; British Rail: joined Regnl Architects' Office York 1970, southern regnl architect 1986–89, architect for Network SE 1989–91, dir Architecture and Design Gp 1991–95; dir: Nick Derbyshire Design Associates Ltd 1995–97, Nick Derbyshire Architects 1997–; visiting prof Dept of Design Nottingham Trent Univ 1996–; RIBA, FRSA; *Awards* Civic Tst Award 1976 and FT Architectural Award 1978 (for Bradford Transport Interchange), FT Architectural Award (for travel centre at Newcastle station) 1986, Civic Tst Award (for scheme at Poole station) 1990, RICS Building Conservation Award and Lord Montagu Trophy (for Liverpool St Station) 1992, RIBA Award 1996 and Civic Tst Award 1997 (for Ashford International Terminal); *Books* Liverpool Street: A Station for the Twenty-First Century (1991); *Recreations* sailing, hill walking; *Clubs* Tinker Class Owners Assoc; *Style*— Nick Derbyshire, Esq; ✉ Nick Derbyshire Architects, PO Box 37865, London SE23 3RQ (tel 020 7833 1515, fax 020 8291 9305, e-mail nick@ndarch.co.uk)

DERBYSHIRE, Victoria A; da of Pauline Derbyshire, *née* Mulrooney; *b* 2 October 1968, Bury, Gtr Manchester; *Educ* Univ of Liverpool, Lancashire Poly (Dip); *Career* journalist and broadcaster; BRMB Birmingham 1991–92, BBC Coventry and Warks Radio 1992–95, co-host breakfast show BBC GMR Manchester 1995–98, co-host Breakfast Show then Victoria Derbyshire Show BBC Radio Five Live 1998– (Radio Show of the Year TRIC Award 1999, Best Breakfast Show Sony Gold Radio Award 1999 and 2002); Radio Personality of the Year Variety Club of GB 2006; *Style*— Miss Victoria Derbyshire; ✉ c/o Knight Ayton Management, 114 St Martin's Lane, London WC2N 4AZ (tel 020 7836 5333)

DEREGOWSKI, Prof Jan Bronisław; s of Jan Deregowski (d 1964), and Szczestawa Helena, *née* Enskajt (d 1987); *b* 1 March 1933; *Educ* schooling abroad and N Copernicus Polish Coll, Univ of London (BSc, BA, PhD), Univ of Aberdeen (DSc); *m* 14 August 1958, Eva Loft, da of Eiler Gudmund Nielsen; 2 s (Sven Marek b 2 Dec 1966, Niels Tadeusz b 12 Feb 1969), 1 da (Anna Halina b 16 Nov 1976); *Career* various engrg appts 1960–65, Miny of Overseas Devpt research fell Univ of Zambia 1965–69; Univ of Aberdeen: lectr 1969–77, sr lectr 1977–81, reader 1981–88, prof 1988–; memb Soc Polonaise des Sciences et des Lettres a l'Etranger 1990; fell Netherlands Inst for Advanced Studies; FBPsS, FRSE 1994; *Books* Illusions, Patterns and Pictures (1980), Distortion in Art: The Eye and the Mind (1984), Perception and Artistic Style (co-author, 1990); *Recreations* reading, history of the Grand Duchy of Lithuania, Polish language; *Style*— Prof Jan Deregowski, FRSE; ✉ Department of Psychology, University of Aberdeen, King's College, Old Aberdeen, Aberdeen AB9 2UB (tel 01224 272246 and 01224 272228, fax 01224 273426, e-mail psy022@abdn.ac.uk)

DERHAM, Katie; *Educ* Magdalene Coll Cambridge; *m* 1999; 2 da (Natasha, Eleanor); *Career* broadcaster; *Radio* researcher Moneybox BBC Radio 4 1993–94, presenter Moneycheck BBC Radio 5 Live 1995–96 (Bradford and Bingley Personal Fin Broadcaster Award), ed Financial World Tonight BBC Radio 4, presenter Classic FM 2002–, presenter LBC 2003; *Television* BBC: reporter Film 96 and Film 97, consumer affairs corr 1996–97, reporter Here and Now 1997; ITV: media and arts corr 1998–2001, media and arts ed 2001–03, newscaster ITV News, currently presents ITV Lunchtime News and London Tonight; presenter Wide Angle ITV2 1998–99; The People's Review 2006, Tour de France 2007; presenter Classical Brit Awards 2001, 2002, 2003 and 2004; New TV Talent of the Year TRIC Awards 1999; *Style*— Ms Katie Derham; ✉ ITN, 200 Gray's Inn Road, London WC1X 8XZ (tel 020 7833 3000)

DERHAM, Dr Kenneth Walter; s of Kenneth Reginald Derham, of Southampton, Hants, and Edith Sybil, *née* Harden; *b* 16 May 1949; *Educ* Univ of Bath (BSc), Univ of Essex (PhD); *m* 16 April 1977, Janet Mary, da of Edgar Victor Garton (d 1984), of Enfield, Middx; 1 da (Anna Rose b 1980); *Career* commissioning ed Elsevier Applied Science Publishers 1974–77, sr ed Plenum Publishing Co 1977–99, md Plenum UK & Euro 1978–91, md Plenum Publishing Co Ltd 1991–98, publishing dir Kluwer Academic/Plenum Publishers 1998–2003, editorial dir Springer 2004–; MRSC, CChem; *Style*— Dr Kenneth Derham; ✉ Springer Science and Business Media, Ashbourne House, The Guildway, Old Portsmouth Road, Guildford, Surrey GU3 1LP (tel 01483 734427, fax 01483 734411)

DERING, Christopher John; s of Dr John Charles Dering, of Southampton, and late Annette Joan, *née* Green; *b* 21 September 1964; *Educ* Weymouth GS, Exeter Coll Oxford (scholar, Maxwell Law Prize, Slaughter & May Contract Prize, proxime accessit Martin Wronker Prize, BA, MA); *m* 18 July 1987, Julie Ann, da of late Harry Alfred Killick; 1 da (Lucy Ann b 18 May 1993), 1 s (James Christopher b 11 Nov 1999); *Career* lectr in law Exeter Coll Oxford 1986–88, called to the Bar Middle Temple 1989, admitted slr 1992, admitted slr (Hong Kong) 1999, ptnr Pinsent Masons 1992–2005 (joined 1989, memb Partnership Bd 1998–2001, head Int and Energy Div 2002–03), princ vice-pres Civil GBU Bechtel and dir Bechtel Ltd 2006– (princ counsel 2005); visiting lectr KCL Centre of Construction Law 2005–; memb Cncl Soc of Construction Law 2004–06; govr Canadian Int Sch of Hong Kong 2000–02; FRSA; *Books* Jersey Law Reports (ed, 1987–88), Service Level Agreements (contrib, 1993), Eco-Management and Eco-Auditing (contrib and co-ed, 1993), Health and Safety Law for the Construction Industry (consulting ed, 1997, 2 edn 2004), Environmental Law for the Construction Industry (consulting ed, 1998, 2 edn 2002), Facilities Management Legal Update (memb ed bd, 1997–98), Employment Law for the Construction Industry (consulting ed, 2000); *Recreations* caravanning; *Style*— Christopher Dering, Esq; ✉ 11 Pilgrim Street, London EC4V 6RN (tel 020 7861 7878, fax 020 7651 7955, e-mail cdering@bechtel.com)

DERRICK, Robin James; s of Ivor Charles Derrick (d 1998), and Jean Mary Derrick (d 2001); *b* 29 May 1962, Bristol; *Educ* Clerk GS Bristol, Filton Tech Coll, St Martin's Sch of Art London (BA); *Children* 1 s (Luke William b 1995); *Career* creative dir and photographer; art dir: The Face 1986–87 (designer 1984–86), Elle (Italy) 1987–89, Glamour (France) 1989–91, Arena 1991–93 (contrib ed 1986); Vogue: art dir 1993–2001, creative dir 2001–, conslt on numerous int edns; former guest art dir: Per Lui (Milan), Actuel (Paris); co-fndr Studio Box 1988; photographer for various magazines incl: British, German, Spanish, Russian and Japanese Vogue, Nylon (USA), Dolce Vita, i-D; co-curator Unseen Vogue Design Museum 2003, Big Head (solo exhbn, Galerie Gordon Pym & Fils Paris) 2004; *Books* The Impossible Image (co-ed, 2000), Unseen Vogue (co-ed, 2002), People in Vogue (co-ed, 2003); *Style*— Robin Derrick, Esq; ✉ Vogue, Vogue House, Hanover Square, London W1S 1JU (rderrick@condenast.co.uk)

DERRINGTON, John Anthony; CBE; s of late John Derrington; *b* 24 December 1921; *Educ* Battersea Poly (BSc), Imperial Coll London (DIC); *m* 1971, Beryl June, *née* Kimber; 1 s, 3 da; *Career* chartered civil engrg conslt, formerly with Sir Robert McAlpine & Sons; former pres ICE; FREng 1979; *Recreations* gardening, travel, reading; *Style*— John Derrington, Esq, CBE, FREng; ✉ 3 Gorham Avenue, Rottingdean, Brighton BN2 7DP

DERRY-EVANS, Robert Stephen; *b* 2 March 1952; *Educ* Univ of Oxford (MA); *Career* McKenna & Co: asst slr 1977–84, ptnr Hong Kong 1984–89, ptnr London 1989–94, managing ptnr 1994–97; managing ptnr Cameron McKenna 1997, exec ptnr CMS 2003–; author of numerous articles and speaker at confs worldwide; memb: Law Soc, Law Soc of Hong Kong, Int Bar Assoc; *Style*— Robert Derry-Evans, Esq

DERVAIRD, Hon Lord; John Murray Dervaird; s of John Hyslop Murray (d 1984), of Beoch, Stranraer, and Mary, *née* Scott (d 1993); *b* 8 July 1935; *Educ* Cairnryan Sch, Edinburgh Acad, CCC Oxford (MA), Univ of Edinburgh (LLB); *m* 30 July 1960, Bridget Jane, 2 da of Sir William Maurice Godfrey, 7 Bt (d 1974); 3 s (Alexander Godfrey b 12 Feb 1964, William John b 21 Oct 1965, David Gordon b 4 June 1968); *Career* Lt Royal Signals 1954–56; advocate 1962, QC (Scot) 1974, Lord of Session (Senator of the Coll of Justice) 1988–89; memb Scottish Law Cmmn 1979–88; chm: Agric Law Assoc 1981–85 (vice-pres 1985–91), Scottish Cncl of Law Reporting 1978–88, Scottish Lawyers Euro Gp 1975–78, Med Appeal Tbnls 1978–79 and 1985–88, Scottish Ctee on Arbitration 1986–96, Scot Cncl for Int Arbitration 1989–2003; Univ of Edinburgh: Dickson Minto prof of company law 1990–99, dean Faculty of Law 1994–96, emeritus prof 1999–; designated by UK to Panel of Arbitrators for Int Centre for Settlement of Investment Disputes 1998–2004; hon pres Advocates Business Law Gp 1988–, vice-pres Comité Européen de Droit Rural 1989–93, chm Panel of Professional Adjudicators in Scotland 2004–; memb: City Disputes Judicial Panel 1994–, Advsy Bd Int Arbitration Inst Paris 1999–; chm: BT Scottish Ensemble (formerly Scottish Baroque Ensemble) 1990–99, Luss Estates Tst 1991–; tstee David Hume Inst 1992–; grand chaplain Von Poser Soc of Edinburgh 1994– (knight 1996); FCIArb 1991; *Books* Stair Encyclopedia of Scots Law - Title 'Agriculture' (1987, 2 edn 2001), Corporate Law - The European Dimension (contrib, 1991), Butterworths European Law Vol 1 - Companies (contrib, 1992), Handbook International Commercial Arbitration (Scotland) (1995); *Recreations* music, farming, gardening, birdwatching, curling; *Clubs* New (Edinburgh), Puffins, Aberlady Curling, Int Arbitrators; *Style*— The Hon Lord Dervaird; ✉ 4 Moray Place, Edinburgh EH3 6DS (tel 0131 225 1881, fax 0131 220 0644, e-mail murraydervaird@talk21.com); Auchenmalg House, Auchenmalg, Wigtownshire DG8 0JR (tel 01581 500205, fax 01581 500324); Wood of Dervaird Farm, Glenluce, Wigtownshire (tel 01581 300222)

DERWENT, Henry Clifford Sydney; CB (2006); s of Clifford Sydney Derwent (d 1995), of Daventry, Northants, and Joan Kathleen, *née* Craft; *b* 19 November 1951; *Educ* Berkhamsted Sch, Worcester Coll Oxford; *m* 26 Nov 1988, Rosemary Patricia Jesse, da of Reginald Meaker; 2 da (Olivia Christiana Maud b 28 June 1989, Romola Henrietta Rose b 8 Nov 1993), 1 step da (Rachel Patricia Alice Milnes-Smith b 5 March 1978); *Career* DOE and PSA 1974–85 (seconded to Midland Bank 1984), Dept of Tport 1986–96 (various posts 1986–92, dir Nat Roads Policy 1992–96, seconded to SBC Warburg Dillon Read 1996), dir Environment Risks and Atmosphere DETR 1999–2002, dir Climate, Energy and Environmental Risks DEFRA 2002–, PM's special rep on climate change 2005; *Recreations* music, riding, watercolours; *Style*— Henry Derwent, Esq, CB

DERWENT, 5 Baron (UK 1881); Sir Robin Evelyn Leo Vanden-Bempde-Johnstone; 7 Bt (GB 1796), LVO (1957), DL (N Yorkshire 1991); s of 4 Baron Derwent, CBE (d 1986), and Marie Louise, *née* Picard (d 1985); *b* 30 October 1930; *Educ* Winchester, Clare Coll Cambridge (MA); *m* 12 Jan 1957, Sybille Marie Louise Marcelle, da of Vicomte de Simard de Pitray (d 1979); 3 da (Hon Emmeline Veronica Louise (Hon Mrs Winterbotham) b 1958, Hon Joanna Louise Claudia (Hon Mrs Matthews) b 1962, Hon Isabelle Catherine Sophie (Hon Mrs Tabain) b 1968), 1 s (Hon Francis Patrick Harcourt b 1965); *Heir* s, Hon Francis Johnstone; *Career* 2 Lt Kings Royal Rifle Corps 1949–50, Lt Queen Victoria's Rifles (TA Res) 1950–53; second sec FO 1954–55 and 1958–61, private sec to Br Ambass Paris 1955–58, second sec Mexico City 1961–65; first sec: Washington 1965–68; FO 1968–69; N M Rothschild & Sons Ltd 1969–85, dep chm Hutchison Whampoa (Europe) Ltd 1998– (md 1985–98), chm Scarborough Museums Tst 2003–; dir: F and C (Pacific) Investment Trust 1989–2001, Scarborough Building Society 1991–2001; memb N York Moors Nat Park Authy 1996–99; Chev Legion of Hon 1957, Officier de l'Ordre Nationale du Mérite (France) 1978; *Recreations* shooting, fishing; *Clubs* Boodle's; *Style*— The Rt Hon the Lord Derwent, LVO, DL; ✉ Hackness Hall, Scarborough, North Yorkshire YO13 0BL; Flat 6, Sovereign Court, Wrights Lane, London W8 5SH

DESAI, Anita; da of Toni Nimé, of Berlin, and D N Mazumdar, of Dhaka, Bangladesh; *b* 24 June 1937; *Educ* Queen Mary's Sch for Girls Delhi, Univ of Delhi (BA); *Career* writer; Helen Cam fell Girton Coll Cambridge 1986–87, Purington prof of English Mount Holyoke Coll US 1988–93, John E Burchard prof of writing MIT 1993–; visiting prof: Elizabeth Drew prof Smith Coll USA 1987–88, Gildersleeves prof Barnard Coll NY 1989, American Univ of Cairo Egypt 1992; visiting fell Clare Hall Cambridge 1989, visiting scholar Rockefeller Foundation Bellagio Itlay 1992; author of several reports for UN and UNICEF; book reviewer for numerous litereray jls and newspapers; hon fell: Girton Coll Cambridge, Clare Hall Cambridge; hon memb American Acad of Arts and Letters; FRSL; *Books* Cry, The Peacock (1963), Voices in the City (1965), Bye-Bye, Blackbird (1971), Where Shall We Go This Summer? (1975), Fire on the Mountain (Winnifred Holtby Prize, National Acad of Letters Award India, 1978), Games At Twilight And Other Stories (short stories, 1979), Clear Light of Day (1980), In Custody (1984, filmed by Merchant Ivory Productions 1994), Journey To Ithaca (1995), The Peacock Garden (for children), Cat On A Houseboat (for children), The Village By The Sea (for children, Guardian Award for children's fiction 1984, filmed by BBC 1992), Fasting Feasting (1999, Shortlisted for Booker Prize), Diamond Dust and Others Stories (2000), The Zig Zag Way (2004); *Style*— Ms Anita Desai, FRSL; ✉ c/o Deborah Rogers, Rogers, Coleridge & White Ltd, 20 Powis Mews, London W11 1JN

DESAI, Baron (Life Peer UK 1991), of St Clement Danes in the City of Westminster; Meghnad Jagdishchandra Desai; s of Jagdishchandra Chandulal Desai (d 1984), of Baroda, India, and Mandakini, *née* Majmundar (d 1989); *b* 10 July 1940; *Educ* Univ of Bombay (BA, MA), Univ of Pennsylvania (PhD); *m* 1 (m dis 2004), Gail Graham, da of George Ambler Wilson, CBE (d 1978), of London; 2 da (Hon Tanvi b 1972, Hon Nuala b 1974), 1 s (Hon Sven b 1975); m 2, Kishwar Ahluwalia, *née* Rosha; 1 step s (Gaurav b 1981), 1 step da (Mallika b 1982); *Career* assoc specialist Dept of Agric Econ Univ of Calif 1963–65; LSE: lectr 1965–77, sr lectr 1977–80, reader 1980–83, prof 1983–2003 (emeritus prof 2003–), head Devpt Studies Inst 1990–95, dir Centre for the Study of Global Governance 1992–2003; memb: Exec Ctee Fabian Soc 1991–92, Cncl Royal Econ Soc 1991–94; chm Islington South and Finsbury Constituency Lab Pty 1986–92; pres Assoc of Univ Teachers in Economics 1987–90; Hon DSc Kingston Univ 1992, Hon DPhil London Guildhall Univ 1996, Hon LLD Monash Univ 2005; Hon DUniv: Middx 1993, E London 1994; FRSA 1991; *Books* Marxian Economic Theory (1974), Applied Econometrics (1976), Marxian Economics (1979), Testing Monetarism (1981), Cambridge Economic History of India vol 2 (co-ed, 1983), Agrarian Power and Agricultural Productivity in South Asia (co-ed, 1984), Lectures on Advanced Econometric Theory (ed, 1988), Lenin's Economic Writings (ed, 1989), Marx's Revenge: The Resurgence of

Capitalism and the Death of Statist Socialism (2002), Nehru's Hero: Dilip Kumar in the Life of India 1944–1964 (2004), Development and Nationhood: Essays in the Political Economy of South Asia (2004), Why is India a Democracy (2005), The Route of All Evil: The Political Economy of Ezra Pound (2006); *Recreations* reading, politics; *Style*— The Rt Hon Lord Desai; ✉ 3 Deepdene Road, London SE5 8EG (e-mail m.desai@lse.ac.uk); House of Lords, London SW1A 0AA (tel 020 7219 5066)

DESMOND, Daniel Frank (Danny); s of Frank Albert Desmond (d 1973), and Beatrice Eva, *née* Mitchison (d 1998); *b* 10 January 1940, Feltham Middlesex; *Educ* St Mary's Sch Northampton; *m* 8 Nov 1980, Diana Chalkley, *née* Mayne; 3 s (Nicholas b 24 Aug 1963, Nigel 14 Aug 1967, Charles b 22 Sept 1983), 2 da (Louise b 26 Nov 1970, Lara 19 Nov 1981); *Career* gp md Hunting Gate Gp 1969–83; fndr Bride Hall Gp 1983 (currently chm and chief exec); dir: GL Portland Estates 1983–92, Nick Faldo Design (Overseas) Ltd, Faldo J Series; *Recreations* family, golf; *Clubs* Mark's, Harry's Bar, Annabel's, George; *Style*— Danny Desmond, Esq

DESMOND, Denis Fitzgerald; CBE (1989); s of Maj James Fitzgerald Desmond, JP, DL, of Killaloo, Londonderry, and Harriet Ivy, *née* Evans (d 1972); *b* 11 May 1943; *Educ* Castle Park Dublin, Trinity Coll Glenalmond; *m* 25 July 1965, Annick Marie Marguerite Francoise, da of M Jean Faussemagne, of Nancy, France; 1 da (Stephanie b 1970); *Career* 2 Lt and Lt RCT (TA) 1964–69; Hon Col 1 Bt (NI) ACF 2005–; chm and md Desmond & Sons Ltd Londonderry 1970–2004 (dir 1966–70), chm Adria Ltd Strabane 1976–81, dir Ulster Development Capital Ltd Belfast 1985–90, regnl dir Nationwide Anglia Building Society 1986–90, dir Ulster Bank Ltd 1990–97; chm Altnagelvin Hosps Health Tst 1996–2004; High Sheriff Co Londonderry 1974; HM Lord-Lt County Londonderry 2000 (DL 1992–2000); ADC to Govr NI 1967–69; Hon DSc: Queen's Univ Belfast 1987, Univ of Ulster 1991; *Recreations* fishing, tennis; *Style*— Denis Desmond, Esq, CBE; ✉ Bellarena, Limavady, Co Londonderry BT49 0HZ

DESMOND, Dermot; *b* 1950, Cork, Republic of Ireland; *Educ* Scoil Mhuire Marino, Good Counsel Coll New Ross; *Career* stockbroker; early career with Citibank, Investment Bank of Ireland and Price Waterhouse Coopers (banking conslt Afghanistan); fndr and chm: NCB 1981–94, International Investment and Underwriting Ltd (IIU) 1995– (cos incl Daon, Betdaq, London City Airport, Intuition Publishing and Espatial); owner London City Airport; non-exec dir of several cos incl Celtic plc 1995–, also investor in numerous cos incl Manchester United plc, Mountain Province Diamond, Unidare and Datalex; tstee Chester Beatty Library; *Recreations* golf; *Style*— Mr Dermot Desmond; ✉ International Investment and Underwriting, IFSC House, Custom House Quay, Dublin 1, Ireland

DESMOND, Richard Clive; s of Cyril Desmond (d 1987), and Millie, *née* Harris; *b* 8 December 1951, London; *Educ* Christ's Coll Finchley; *m* 4 Aug 1983, Janet, *née* Robertson; 1 s (Robert b 10 June 1989); *Career* publisher; early career: advtg exec Thomson Newspapers, advtg mangr Beat Pubns Ltd, publisher Int Musician & Recording World magazine, De Monde Advtg Ltd; prop: Northern and Shell plc 1982– (pubns incl OK! magazine (launched 1993)), Express Newspapers 2000– (pubns incl Daily Express, Sunday Express and Daily Star), Portland TV; charitable involvement incl: Richard Desmond Charitable Tst, Disability Fndn, Richard Desmond Children's Eye Centre, pres Norwood, RD Crusaders Supergroup (with Roger Daltrey) for Teenage Cancer Tst; supporter: Jewish Care, Niger Appeal, Elton John's AIDS Fndn, Darfur- Not on Our Watch; *Style*— Mr Richard Desmond; ✉ Northern & Shell plc, The Northern & Shell Building, 10 Lower Thames Street, London EC3R 6EN

DESPONTIN, Dr Brenda; da of Telford Griffiths, and Nancy Betty Griffiths; *Educ* Lewis Girls' GS, Penarth GS, Univ of Cardiff (BA, MA, PhD), Univ of Bath (PGCE), Univ of Hull (MBA); *Career* princ girls' div King's Sch Macclesfield 1992–97, headmistress Haberdashers' Monmouth Sch for Girls 1997–; memb: GSA 1997 (pres 2006), Boarding Schools Assoc 1997; Promethean Award for Sch Leadership in a Secdy Sch in Wales Teaching Awards 2003; MIMgt 1992, MIIP 1999; *Recreations* the arts, reading, writing, theatre; *Clubs* Univ Women's; *Style*— Dr Brenda Despontin; ✉ Haberdashers' Monmouth School for Girls, Hereford Road, Monmouth NP25 5XT (tel 01600 711100, fax 01600 711233)

DETMER, Prof Don Eugene; s of Lawrence O Detmer (d 1962), of Great Bend, KS, and Esther B, *née* McCormick (d 1997); *b* 2 February 1939; *Educ* Univ of Durham, Univ of Kansas, Univ of Cambridge; *m* 26 Aug 1961, Mary Helen McFerson; 2 da (Mary Catherine b 28 June 1963, Emily Anne b 28 Oct 1966); *Career* surgical educn: Johns Hopkins Univ 1965–67, NIH 1967–69, Duke Med Center 1969–72; health policy trg: Inst of Med Nat Acads 1972, Harvard Business Sch 1973; asst and assoc prof of surgery and preventive med Univ of Wisconsin Madison 1973–74, vice-pres for health sciences and prof of surgery and med informatics Univ of Utah 1984–88, vice-pres and provost for health sciences, sr vice-pres and prof of surgery, business admin and health evaluation sciences Univ of Virginia 1988–99 (prof emeritus and prof of med educn 1999–), Dennis Gillings prof of health mgmnt and dir Cambridge Univ Health Univ of Cambridge 1999–2003 (sr associate 2004–); fell Clare Hall Cambridge; chm Nat Ctee on Vital and Health Statistics Dept of Health and Human Servs Washington DC (also chair Bd of Regents), chair Bd on Health Care Servs Inst of Med, co-chair Blue Ridge Academic Health Gp; memb Bd: Assoc of Academic Health Centers, China Med Bd of NY Inc, Nuffield Tst; memb Editorial Bd Quality and Safety in Healthcare; Chancellor's Award for Distinguished Teaching Univ of Wisconsin Madison, President's Award American Med Informatics Assoc 1996 and 1998, Medal Mongolian State Univ 2001; Distinguished Med Alumnus Duke Univ Med Center Alumni Assoc 1993; nat assoc Nat Academies Washington DC; fell: AAAS 1998, American Coll of Med Informatics, Acad of Health, American Coll of Sports Med; memb: Inst of Med, RSM, Soc of Med Administrators; FACS; *Publications* author of numerous papers in learned jls; *Recreations* fly fishing, crafts, wilderness canoeing, horse riding; *Clubs* Cosmos (Washington DC); *Style*— Prof Don Detmer; ✉ Judge Institute of Management, University of Cambridge, Trumpington Street, Cambridge CB2 1AG (tel 01223 339700, fax 01223 339701, e-mail d.detmer@jims.cam.ac.uk)

DETSINY, (Anthony) Michael; s of Rudolph Detsiny, JP (d 1987), and Edith, *née* Scheff (d 1993); *b* 25 July 1941; *Educ* Highgate Sch; *m* 2 Dec 1967, Angela Hazel, da of Francis Charles Cornell (d 1977); 2 s (Warren Rodney b 1969, Stephen Charles b 1978), 1 da (Hazel Karen b 1972); *Career* dir: Cadbury Ltd 1977–83, Allied Breweries 1983–86; md The Creative Business Ltd 1986–91, chm and chief exec Foote Cone and Belding (London) 1991–96, dir The Marketing and Communications Business 1996–97, DG The Marketing Soc 1997–; MInstD; *Recreations* gardening, reading; *Style*— Michael Detsiny, Esq; ✉ The Willows, Moor End Common, Frieth, Henley-on-Thames, Oxfordshire RG9 6PU (tel 01494 881176); The Marketing Society, St George's House, 3–5 Pepys Road, London SW20 8NJ (tel 020 8879 3464, fax 020 8879 0362)

DETTORI, Lanfranco (Frankie); MBE (2001); s of Gianfranco Dettori, and Maria, *née* Nieman; *b* 15 December 1970; *Career* flat race jockey; apprenticed to Luca Cumani, champion apprentice 1990 (100 winners), retained by John Gosden; major races won: Queen Elizabeth II Stakes 1990, World Young Jockey Championship Japan 1992/93, Ascot Gold Cup (twice), French Derby (on Polytain) 1992, Nunthorpe Stakes 1993, Prix de L' Abbeye de Longchamp, Sussex Stakes, Fillies Mile, Heinz 57, Irish Derby (on Balanchine) 1994, The Oaks (on Balanchine) 1994 and (on Moonshell) 1995, St Léger (on Classic Cliché) 1995 and (on Shantou) 1996, King George VI and Queen Elizabeth Diamond Stakes (on Lammtarra) 1995 and (on Daylami) 1999, Prix de l'Arc de Triomphe (on Lammtarra) 1995, 2,000 Guineas (on Mark of Esteem) 1996 and (on Island Sands) 1999, Breeders Cup Turf (on Daylami) 1999, Dubai World Cup (on Dubai Millennium) 2000, Prix du Jockey Club (on Lawman) 2007, Epsom Derby (on Authorized) 2007; winner Golden Spurs Award 1989, Derby Award 1990; winner all seven races on one card at Ascot 28 Sept 1996; Cartier Award of Merit 1996; champion jockey 1994, 1995 and 2004; *Recreations* football, swimming, snooker, golf, sport in general; *Style*— Frankie Dettori, Esq, MBE; ✉ c/o Classic Management Ltd, 5th Floor, 140 Brompton Road, London SW3 1HY (tel 020 7808 0233, fax 020 7584 7933, e-mail info@classicmanagement.biz)

DEUCHAR, Patrick Lindsay; s of David Deuchar (d 1998), and Marian, *née* Davies; *b* 27 March 1949; *Educ* Christ's Hosp, Wilts Coll of Agric; *m* 1 (m dis), Gwyneth; 1 s (David Lindsay b 3 March 1976), 1 da (Patricia Margaret b 5 April 1978); m 2, Liz Robertson, *qv*; 1 da (Briony Elizabeth Veronica b 4 July 1991); *Career* unit mangr farm in Berks 1968–70, journalist and info offr Agric Div IPC Business Press 1970–71; PR offr The Royal Show 1971–74, PR mangr Earl's Court & Olympia exhibition halls 1974–78, own PR consultancy 1978–81, dir London Office World Championship Tennis 1983–89 (joined as Euro PR dir 1981), chief exec Royal Albert Hall 1989–97, md Royal Albert Hall Developments Ltd 1989–97; winner Int Facility Mangr of 1993 (Performance Magazine); bd dir: London First 1994 (memb Visitors Cncl 1995), Trafalgar Square 2000; tstee: Cardiff Bay Opera House 1993–96, Albert Meml Tst 1994–2000; memb Cncl Royal Coll of Music 1995–2001; chm SPARKS (sporting charity) 1992–96, memb Nat Fundraising Ctee The Muscular Dystrophy Gp 1991–95, barker Variety Club of GB 1992, memb Ctee Royal Marsden Hosp Appeal 1990–92; Freeman Worshipful Co of Armourers & Braziers 1966; MInstD 1986, FRSA 1992; *Style*— Patrick Deuchar, Esq

DEUCHAR, Dr Stephen John; s of late Rev John Deuchar, and Nancy Dorothea, *née* Jenkyns; *b* 11 March 1957; *Educ* Dulwich Coll (scholar), Univ of Southampton (BA), Westfield Coll London (PhD); *m* 1982, Dr Katie Scott; 1 s, 3 da; *Career* Andrew W Mellon fell in Br art Yale Univ 1981–82; Nat Maritime Museum: curator of paintings 1985–87, curator Armada exhbn 1987–88, corp planning mangr 1988–89, organiser of exhbns and display projects 1990–95, dir Neptune Court Project 1995–97; dir Tate Britain 1998–; memb Cncl Govt Art Collection; tstee Metropole Arts Tst 2005–; memb Cncl Univ of Southampton 2004–; *Books* Noble Exericse: the sporting ideal in 18th century British art (1982), Paintings, Politics and Porter: Samuel Whitbread and British Art (1984), Concise Catalogue of Oil Paintings in the National Maritime Museum (jtly, 1988), Sporting Art in 18th Century England: a social and political history (1988), Nelson: an illustrated history (jtly, 1995); *Style*— Dr Stephen Deuchar; ✉ Tate Britain, Millbank, London SW1P 4RG (tel 020 7887 8048)

DEUTSCH, Antonia Sara; da of Ronald Leopold Deutsch, of Ilmington, Warks, and Jill Patricia, *née* Davis; *b* 24 June 1957; *Educ* The Abbey Sch, Sorbonne; *m* 31 May 1980, Colin David Guy Robinson, s of Guy Martyn Robinson; 1 s (Oscar Charles Thomas b 4 Nov 1989), 1 da (Eliza Alice Louise b 10 Aug 1991); *Career* photographic asst 1981–84, freelance photographer specialising in people, landscapes and black and white images 1984–; awards incl: Assoc of Photographers Silver Award 1989, Gold and Merit Awards 1991 and Judges' Choice 1996, Ilford Print of the Year 1989; memb Assoc of Photographers (formerly AFAEP) 1988; *Recreations* photography, independent rough travel, family; *Style*— Ms Antonia Deutsch; ✉ tel mobile 07836 344972, e-mail ad@antoniadeutsch.co.uk

DEUTSCH, Renée; da of Maurice Deutsch, and Matilda Deutsch; *b* 2 August 1944; *Educ* Hendon Co GS, Northern Poly Sch of Architecture; *m* (m dis); m 2, 10 June 1995, Robert Cooper; *Career* architecture and design for 10 years, mgmnt consultancy for 6 years; appeals co-ordinator (3 years): Almeida Theatre, Half Moon Theatre, London Contemporary Dance; head of consumer PR Dennis Davidson Assocs, vice-pres and md Consumer Products Div The Walt Disney Co Ltd until 1991, ind mktg conslt 1991–93, md The Licensing Syndicate Ltd 1993–2006, prop Renée Deutsch 2007–; *Recreations* performing arts, visual arts, reading, tennis; *Clubs* Groucho, IOD; *Style*— Ms Renée Deutsch; ✉ 93A Camden Mews, London NW1 9BU (tel 020 7482 4347); 125 Parkway, London NW1 7PS (tel 020 7387 7871, fax 020 7388 1211, e-mail licensing.syndicate@btinternet.com)

DEVA, Niranjan Joseph (Nirj); DL (Greater London) 1985, MEP (Cons) SE England; s of late Thakur Dr Kingley de Silva Deva Aditya, and Zita de Silva Deva, da of Sen Dr M G Perera, MVO; *b* 11 May 1948; *Educ* St Joseph's Coll Colombo, Loughborough Univ; *m* Indra, da of late Romy Govindia; 1 step s; *Career* company dir and scientific advsr, memb Cncl RCS 1977–79, chm Bow Gp 1981 (sec Foreign Affrs Ctee 1985–87), former advsr to Viscount Whitelaw and Rt Hon David Howell, MP, memb Nat Consumer Cncl 1985–88, chm DTI/NCC Ctee on deregulation of Euro air tport 1985–87; MP (Cons) Brentford and Isleworth 1992–97 (first Asian Cons MP elected this century, Parly candidate (Cons) Hammersmith 1987); memb: Euro Standing Ctee B 1992–97, All-Pty Mfrg Gp 1993–97; memb Standing Ctee on: Immigration Bill 1992–97, Parly Admin (Ombudsman) 1993–97; jt sec Cons Pty Aviation Ctee 1992–97; PPS Scottish Office 1996–97, Select Ctee on Educn 1994–96; MEP (Cons) South East England 1999–; Euro Parl: front bench spokesman Devpt and Co-operation Ctee 1999–, memb Environment Ctee 1999–, memb UK Cons Delgn, delg EU-ACP Jt Parly Assembly 1999–, rapporteur Trade, WTO and Devpt 2000–, delg to Asean countries 2002–, memb Regnl Economy Tport and Tourism Ctee 2002–, delg to UN Gen Assembly 2003, delg to SAARC countries 2004–, coordinator EPP-ED Gp Devpt Cmmn 2004–, rapporteur on Financial Perspectives 2005–, memb Foreign Affrs Ctee 2005, chm delgn to World Summit UN Gen Assembly 2005, chm Working Gp A Devpt Ctee 2007–; Cons Pty special advsr on ethnic affrs 2001–03; currently DG Policy Research Centre for Business; hon ambass at large Govt of Sri Lanka 2003–, hon advsr to PM of Sri Lanka 2003–; candidate for UN Sec Gen 2006; chm Symphony Plastics Ltd; dir: Erabodagama Estates Ltd 1990–, Waulngalle Distilleries Ltd 1990–, Distilleries Co of Sri Lanka Ltd 2004–, Aitken Spence Ltd Sri Lanka 2005; patron CHASE (Childrens Hospice Service); author of various articles and pamphlets on Chile, Zimbabwe, Rhodesia, enterprise zones, air tport, deregulation; FRSA; Vishwa Kirthi Sri Lanka Abhimani 2006; *Recreations* tennis, riding, reading; *Clubs* Carlton, Hownslow Conservative; *Style*— Nirj Joseph Deva, Esq, DL, FRSA, MEP; ✉ Policy Research Centre for Business, 169B Kennington Road, London SE11 6SF (tel 01784 432070, fax +32 22 849245, e-mail office@nirjdeva.com, website www.nirjdeva.com)

DEVANEY, John F; *b* 1946; *Educ* BEng, Harvard Univ (Advanced Mgmnt Prog); *Career* Perkins Engines: grad trainee 1968–76, project mangr Canton Ohio 1976–78, dir quality control then dir mfrg UK 1978–82, dir sales and business devpt Engines Div 1982–83, pres Engines Div 1983–88, gp vice-pres European Components Gp (now Perkins Gp) Peterborough 1988; gp vice-pres Kelsey-Hayes Corporation Romulus Michigan 1989–92; Eastern Group plc (formerly Eastern Electricity plc): md 1992–95, chief exec 1993–95, exec chm 1995–98, dir subsids EA Technology Ltd; chm: Exel plc 2000–02, Liberata until 2002, Marconi Corp plc 2002–; fndr and chm BizzEnergy; non-exec dir: Midland Bank plc 1994–, NFC plc 1996–, Norwich Capital Investments Ltd 1996–, MEL Ltd 1997–, British Steel plc 1998–; pres Electricity Assoc 1994–95; CEng, FIEE, FIMechE; *Clubs* Reform; *Style*— John Devaney, Esq; ✉ Marconi Corporation plc, New Century Park, Coventry CV3 1HJ

DEVAS, Michael Campbell; MC (1945); only s of Geoffrey Charles Devas, MC (d 1971; whose mother was Edith, da of Lt-Col Hon Walter Campbell, 3 s of 1 Earl Cawdor), by his w Joan (d 1975), great niece of Rt Hon Sir Henry Campbell-Bannerman, the Liberal PM (1906–08); *b* 6 June 1924; *Educ* Eton; *m* 1, 28 June 1952 (m dis 1966), Patience

D

Merryday, da of late Sir Albert Gerald Stern, KBE, CMG (d 1966); 1 s, 1 da; m 2, 12 Oct 1967, Gillian Barbara, da of late Col H M P Hewett, and formerly w of Charles Arthur Smith-Bingham; 1 s; *Career* served Welsh Gds NW Europe 1942–47, Capt 1946; banker; joined M Samuel & Co 1947, dir 1960; dir Kleinwort Benson Ltd 1965–86; chm: Colonial Mutual Life Assurance (UK Bd) 1982–94, Kleinwort Charter Investment Trust plc 1970–1992; dir Dover Corporation (USA) 1967–94; Liveryman Worshipful Co of Drapers; *Recreations* sailing, skiing; *Clubs* White's, Royal Yacht Sqdn; *Style—* Michael Devas, Esq, MC; ✉ Hunton Court, Maidstone, Kent ME15 0RR (tel 01622 820307)

DEVAUX, His Hon Judge John Edward; s of Henry Edward Devaux (d 1988), and Anne Elizabeth Devaux (d 1984); *b* 1947; *Educ* Beaumont Coll, Univ of Bristol (LLB); *m* 1979, Fiona Mary, *née* O'Conor; 2 da; *Career* called to the Bar Lincoln's Inn 1970; recorder of the Crown Court 1989–93, circuit judge (SE Circuit) 1993–, resident judge Ipswich 1998–2006, hon recorder of Ipswich 2000–; *Style—* His Hon Judge Devaux; ✉ Ipswich Crown Court, The Courthouse, 1 Russell Road, Ipswich, Suffolk IP1 2AG (tel 01473 228585)

DEVERELL, Brig John Duncan; CBE (2007, OBE 1998); s of John Christopher Byron Deverell (d 1998), and Elizabeth Letitia, *née* Duncan; *b* 1 May 1955; *Educ* Eton, RMA Sandhurst, Christ's Coll Cambridge (MPhil); *m* 1993, Susanne Christiane, *née* Kampert; 1 s (John Conrad Christopher b 1993), 2 da (Georgina Elisabeth Mary b 1994, Flora Sophia b 1996); *Career* cmmnd Royal Scots Dragoon Guards 1975; served: UK, Germany, Belize, former Yugoslavia, Kuwait, Saudi Arabia, Yemen, Iraq; Royal Irish Regt 1995–2006; dir defence diplomacy MOD 2006–; *Recreations* horses, hunting, music, art; *Clubs* Cavalry; *Style—* Brigadier John Deverell, CBE

DEVERELL, Gen Sir John Freegard (Jack); KCB (1999), OBE (1987, MBE 1979); s of Harold James Frank Deverell (d 1986), of Bath, and Joan Beatrice, *née* Carter; *b* 27 April 1945; *Educ* King Edward's Sch Bath, RMA Sandhurst, RNC Greenwich; *m* 15 Dec 1973, Jane Ellen, da of Gerald Tankerville Norris Solomon, of Hindon, Wilts; 1 da (Emma b 23 Nov 1976), 1 s (Simon b 21 Oct 1978); *Career* RMA Sandhurst 1964–65, cmmnd Somerset and Cornwall Light Infantry 1965, Cmd 3 Bn Light Infantry 1984–86, Dir of Studies Royal Mil Coll of Sci 1986–88, Cdr UK Mobile Force 1988–90, DG Army Manning and Recruiting 1993–95, Cmdt Royal Mil Acad Sandhurst 1995–97, Dep C-in-C Land 1997–, Dep Commander Mil Ops SFOR 1998–99, Dep C-in-C Land 1999–2001, C-in-C Allied Forces N Europe 2001–2004; FRSA, FICPD; *Recreations* cricket, golf, horses; *Clubs* Cavalry and Guards', I Zingari, Free Foresters, Mounted Infantry; *Style—* Gen Sir Jack Deverell, KCB, OBE

DEVEREUX, Alan Robert; CBE (1980), DL; s of Donald Charles Devereux, and Doris Louie Devereux; *b* 18 April 1933; *Educ* Colchester Sch, Clacton Co HS, Mid-Essex Tech Coll; *m* 1, 1959, Gloria Alma, *née* Hair (d 1985); 1 s (Iain b 1964); m 2, 1987, Elizabeth, *née* Docherty; *Career* ceo Scotros plc 1970–80; dir: Scottish Mutual Assurance Society 1972–2003, Walter Alexander plc 1980–90, Gleneagles plc 1990–2003; chm: Hambros Scotland Ltd 1984–90, Scottish Ambulance Serv NHS Tst 1994–97; fndr dir Quality Scotland Fndn 1991–; chm: CBI Scotland 1977–79, Scottish Tourist Bd 1980–90; memb Br Tourist Authy 1980–90; chm Mission Aviation Fellowship 2003–; CEng, MIEE; *Recreations* reading, antique clock restoration, charities; *Clubs* East India, Devonshire, Sports and Public Schools; *Style—* Alan Devereux, Esq, CBE, DL; ✉ South Fell, 24 Kirkhouse Road, Blanefield, Stirlingshire G63 9BX (tel 01360 770464, fax 01360 771133, e-mail aland@post.almac.co.uk)

DEVEREUX, Richard; s of Austin Augustus Devereux (d 1970), of Lincoln, and Vera Evelyn, *née* Whylde (d 2005); *b* 3 April 1956; *Educ* Bishop King Sch Lincoln, Portsmouth Coll of Art (scholar, DipAD); *m* 20 Aug 1977, Christine Anne, da of Stanley Holmes; 1 da (Hannah Galadriel b 22 March 1988); *Career* artist; *Solo Exhibitions* Recent Works (Axis Gallery Brighton) 1979, Recent Works (Hiscock Gallery Portsmouth) 1980, Circles (Usher Art Gallery Lincoln) 1984, Assembled Rites (Artsite Bath) 1987, On Sacred Ground (Cairn Gallery Glos) 1988, Beyond the Hall of Dreams (New Art Centre London) 1989, In Stillness and In Silence (Usher Art Gallery Lincoln then The Gallery Cork Street London) 1994, Primordium (Cairn Gallery Glos) 1994–95, Casting Visions (Angel Row Gallery Nottingham) 1997, Source (Hart Gallery London) 1998, Thresholds (Hart Gallery London) 2000, Silent Portals (Yorkshire Sculpture Park) 2002, Seeing Silence (Atrium Gallery Bournemouth Univ) 2003, Works: 1999–2005 (Bend in the River, Gainsborough) 2005; *Selected Group Exhibitions* Rufford Arts Centre 1982, Ogle Gallery Cheltenham 1984, Sculpture to Touch (Usher Gallery Lincoln, Ferens Gallery Hull and Normanby Hall Scunthorpe) 1986, 20th Century Br Sculpture (Roche Court Wilts) 1988–2006, New Art Centre London 1989 and 1990, The Journey (Lincoln) 1990, Southampton City Art Gallery 1990, Shared Earth (Peterborough Art Gallery and 6 venue tour) 1991–92, 20th Century Br Sculpture (Millfield Sch) 1992, The Solstice (Cairn Gallery Glos) 1992, Painting the Earth (The Gallery at John Jones London) 1993, ARCO (Madrid) 1994, Art 25! (Basel) 1994, Art 26! (Basel) 1995, Alchemy (Bury St Edmunds Art Gallery and Ickworth House) 1995, Art 27 (Basel) 1996, Peter Bartlow Gallery (Chicago) 1999, Art 99 (Miami) 1999, Gathering Light (Maltby Contemporary Art Winchester) 2001, Lacerta (Dorset) 2006 and 2007; *Collections* incl: Bodleian Library Oxford, Nat Library of Scotland, Tate Gallery Library London, Trinity Coll Dublin, The Nat Tst, Vancouver Art Gallery and various private collections UK and abroad; *Published Limited Edition Books* Quiet Flame (1986), Assembled Rites (1987), The Bowl of Grain (1989–90), In Stillness and In Silence (1991), From the Angel's Palm (1992), Marked by Ritual (1992), Travaux Publics (1996), Silent Umbra (2003), Within Voids (2003), Iren/Iron (2003), Ferrum Portal (2003), Intervention 1 (2003), Guide to Thresholds (2005), Viodwhispers (2005); subject of several articles in various pubns; *Style—* Richard Devereux, Esq; ✉ tel and fax 01522 887621, e-mail info@devereuxart.co.uk, website www.devereuxart.co.uk

DEVINE, Prof Fiona; da of Patrick Noel Devine (d 1990), and Martha, *née* Daly; *b* 6 June 1962, London; *Educ* Univ of Essex (BA, MA, PhD); *Partner* James B Husband; *Career* research offr Social Science Branch Dept of Employment 1988, research offr Policy Studies Inst 1988–89, lectr in sociology Univ of Liverpool 1989–94; Univ of Manchester (formerly Victoria Univ of Manchester): lectr in sociology 1994–97, sr lectr in sociology 1997–99, reader in sociology 1999–2001, prof of sociology 2001–, head of sociology Sch of Social Sciences 2004–07; memb Cncl and chair Int Advsy Ctee ESRC 2003–07; visiting scholar Kennedy Sch of Govt Harvard Univ (Leverhulme Tst grant) 1999; memb: British Sociological Assoc 1985, American Sociological Soc 1995; *Books* Affluent Workers Revisited: Privatism and the Working Class (1992), Social Class in America and Britain (1997), Sociological Research Methods in Context (with Sue Heath, 1999), Class Practices: How Parents Help their Children get Good Jobs (2004); *Recreations* swimming, walking, classical and world music; *Style—* Prof Fiona Devine; ✉ Sociology, School of Social Sciences, University of Manchester, Arthur Lewis Building, Oxford Road, Manchester M13 9PL (tel 0161 275 2508, fax 0161 275 2514, e-mail fiona.devine@manchester.ac.uk)

DEVINE, Rt Rev Joseph; *see:* Motherwell, Bishop of (RC)

DEVINE, Prof Thomas Martin; OBE (2005); *b* 30 July 1945; *Educ* Univ of Strathclyde (BA, PhD, DLitt); *m*; 2 s (twins), 3 da; *Career* Univ of Strathclyde: asst lectr in econ history 1969–70, lectr in history 1970–78, sr lectr 1978–83, reader in Scottish history 1983–88, prof of Scottish history 1988–98, chm Dept of History 1989–92, dean Faculty of Arts and Social Sciences 1993–94, dir Research Centre in Scottish History 1993–98, dep princ 1994–97; Univ of Aberdeen: dir Research Inst of Irish and Scottish Studies 1998–2003, research prof of Scottish history 1998–2004, Louis and Loretta B Glucksmann research prof in Irish and Scottish studies 2004–06; dir AHRB (now AHRC) Centre for Irish and Scottish Studies 2001–06, Sir William Fraser prof of Scottish history and palaeography Univ of Edinburgh 2006–; Univ of Guelph Canada: visiting prof of Scottish history 1983 and 1988, adjunct prof of Scottish history Faculty of Graduate Studies 1989–; adjunct prof of history Univ of N Carolina 1997–; British Acad/Leverhulme Tst sr research fell 1992–93; chm Cncl of Economic and Social History Soc of Scotland 1984–88 (memb Cncl 1989–90); ed Scottish Economic and Social History 1981–86; convener Section Ctee Archaeology and Historical Studies RSE 1994–98 (memb 1993–98); memb: Cncl Scottish History Soc 1976–79, Cncl Scottish Catholic Historical Soc 1977–82 (convenor of Cncl 1991–95), Company of Scottish History 1981–, Bd of Govrs St Andrew's Coll of Educn 1990–95, Cncl British Acad 1998–2001, Research Advsy Ctee Leverhulme Tst, Advsy Ctee ESRC Devolution Research Prog; tstee: Nat Museums of Scotland 1995–2002, Edinburgh UNESCO World City of Literature; chair Euro Ethnological Research Centre 1998–2002; Sr Hume Brown Prize in Scottish History Univ of Edinburgh 1976, Royal Gold Medal RSE 2001; Hon DLitt Queen's Univ Belfast, Hon DLitt Abertay Univ Dundee, Hon DUniv Univ of Strathclyde 2006; FRHistS 1980, FRSE 1992 (Henry Duncan Prize and lectr 1993), FBA 1994, Hon MRIA 2001; *Books* The Tobacco Lords: A Study of the Tobacco Merchants of Glasgow and their Trading Activities 1740–1790 (1975), Lairds and Improvement in the Scotland of the Enlightenment (ed, 1979), Ireland and Scotland 1600–1850: Parallels and Contrasts in Economic and Social Development (ed with D Dickson, 1983), Farm Servants and Labour in Lowland Scotland 1770–1914 (1984), A Scottish Firm in Virginia: William Cunninghame and Co 1767–1777 (1984), People and Society in Scotland 1760–1830 (ed with R Mitchison, 1988), The Great Highland Famine: Hunger, Emigration and the Scottish Highlands in the Nineteenth Century (1988, Agnes Muir MacKenzie Prize Saltire Soc 1991), Improvement and Enlightenment (ed, 1989), Conflict and Stability in Scottish Society 1700–1850 (ed, 1990), Irish Immigrants and Scottish Society in the Eighteenth and Nineteenth Centuries (ed, 1991), Scottish Emigration & Scottish Society (ed, 1992), The Transformation of Rural Scotland: Social Change and Agrarian Development 1660–1815 (1994), Clanship to Crofters' War: The Social Transformation of the Scottish Highlands (1994), Scottish Elites (ed, 1994), Industry, Business and Society in Scotland since 1700 (ed with A J G Cummings, 1994), Glasgow, Vol I, Beginnings to 1830 (ed with G Jackson, 1995), Exploring the Scottish Past: Themes in History of Scottish Society (1995), Scotland in the Twentieth Century (ed with R J Finlay, 1996), Eighteenth Century Scotland: New Perspectives (ed with J R Young, 1998), Celebrating Columba: Irish-Scottish Connections 597–1997 (ed with J F McMillan, 1998), The Scottish Nation 1700–2000 (1999), Scotland's Shame? Bigotry and Sectarianism in Modern Scotland (ed, 2000), Being Scottish: Personal Reflections on Scottish Identity Today (ed, 2002), Scotland's Empire, 1600–1815 (2003), Scotland's Empire and the Shaping of the Americas (2004), The Transformation of Scotland (jt ed, 2005), Clearance and Improvement: Land, Power and People in Scotland 1700–1900 (2006); also author of nearly 100 book chapters and contribs to learned jls; *Recreations* grandchildren, watching skilful football, exploring the Hebrides, visiting Italy; *Style—* Prof Thomas M Devine, OBE, FRSE, Hon MRIA, FBA; ✉ School of History, Classics and Archaeology (Scottish History), University of Edinburgh, 17 Buccleuch Place, Edinburgh EH8 9LN (tel 0131 650 1000, e-mail t.m.devine@ed.ac.uk)

DEVITT, Sir James Hugh Thomas; 3 Bt (UK 1916), of Chelsea, Co London; s of Lt-Col Sir Thomas Gordon Devitt, 2 Bt (d 1995), and his 3 w, Janet Lilian, da of late Col Hugh Sidney Ellis, CBE, MC; *b* 18 September 1956; *Educ* Sherborne, Corpus Christi Coll Cambridge (MA); *m* 20 April 1985, Susan Carol, er da of Dr (Adrian) Michael Campbell Duffus, of Woodhouse Farm, Thelbridge, Crediton, Devon; 1 da (Gemma Florence b 1987), 2 s (Jack Thomas Michael b 1988, William James Alexander b 1990); *Heir* s, Jack Devitt; *Career* chartered surveyor CB Richard Ellis Hotels; MRICS; *Clubs* Ipswich Town FC; *Style—* Sir James Devitt, Bt

DEVLIN, Es; da of Timothy Devlin, and Angela, *née* Laramy; *b* 24 September 1971; *Educ* Cranbrook Sch, Univ of Bristol, Central St Martins, Motley Design Sch; *Career* set and costume designer; teacher: Wimbledon Sch of Art 2000, Br Cncl Bangladesh 2001, Anglo American Educn 2002; *Theatre* Edward II (Bolton Octagon) 1996, Piano (TPT Tokyo) 1997, Love and Understanding (Bush Theatre) 1997, Snake in the Grass (Peter Hall Co at the Old Vic) 1997, Yard Gal (Royal Court Theatre) 1997, Love You Too (Bush Theatre) 1998, Betrayal (RNT) 1998, Howie the Rookie (Bush Theatre) 1999, The Death of Cool (Hampstead Theatre) 1999, Drink, Dance, Laugh, Lie (Bush Theatre) 1999, Hamlet (Young Vic) 1999, Perapalas (Gate Theatre) 2000, Rita, Sue and Bob Too/A State Affair (Soho Theatre and Out of Joint) 2000, Henry IV (RSC) 2000, Meat (Plymouth Theatre Royal) 2000, Credible Witness (Royal Court Theatre) 2000, Closer to Heaven - the Pet Shop Boys Musical (Arts Theatre) 2001, The Prisoner's Dilemma (RSC) 2001, A Day in the Death of Joe Egg (Comedy Theatre) 2001 (Broadway 2003), Hinterland (RNT and Out of Joint) 2001, That was Then (Abbey Theatre Dublin) 2002, Arabian Night (Soho Theatre and ATC) 2002, Antony and Cleopatra (RSC) 2002, Five Gold Rings (Almeida) 2003, Wire/Dinos and Jake Chapman/Es Devlin (Only Connect Festival Barbican) 2003; *Opera* The Cunning Peasant (Guildhall Sch of Music and Drama) 1997, Live Culture (ENO Works) 1998, Don Giovanni (Br Youth Opera) 1999, Fidelio (English Touring Opera) 1998, Powder Her Face (Ystad Festival) 1999, National Opera Studio Showcase (Queen Elizabeth Hall) 1999, Hansel and Gretel (Scottish Opera Go Round) 2001, Macbeth (Klangbogen Festival Vienna) 2003; *Dance* Four Scenes (Rambert Dance Co) 1998, Gods Plenty (Rambert Dance Co) 2000, A Streetcar Named Desire (Northern Ballet Theatre) 2002, I Remember Red (Cullberg Ballet Sweden) 2002; *Film* A Tale of Two Heads 1998, Beggar's Belief 1999, Brilliant 2000, Snow on Saturday 2001, Victoria Station 2002; *Exhibitions* work included in: Prague Quadrennial 1999, Make Space (SBTD) 1998, 2D > 3D (SBTD) 2002; *Awards* Linbury Prize for Stage Design 1995–96, TMA Award for Best Design 1999 (nominated 2000); *Recreations* travel; *Style—* Miss Es Devlin; ✉ c/o Sally Hope Associates, 108 Leonard Street, London EC2A 4RH (tel 020 7613 5353, fax 020 7613 4848, e-mail sally@sallyhope.biz); website www.esdevlin.com

DEVLIN, His Hon Keith Michael; s of Francis Michael Devlin (d 1996), of Goring-by-Sea, W Sussex, and Norah Devlin (d 1996); *b* 21 October 1933; *Educ* Price's Sch, KCL (LLB, MPhil), Brunel Univ (PhD); *m* 12 July 1958, Pamela Gwendoline, da of Francis James Phillips (d 1984), of Inverkeithing, Fife; 2 s (Stephen b 1964, Philip b 1966), 1 da (Susan b 1968); *Career* cmmnd Nat Serv 1953–55; called to the Bar Gray's Inn 1964; dep chief clerk Met Magistrates' Courts Serv 1964–66, various appts as a dep met stipendiary magistrate 1975–79; asst recorder 1980–83, recorder 1983–84, circuit judge (SE Circuit) 1984–95, dep circuit judge 1995–99; liaison judge Beds 1990–93, resident judge Luton Crown Court 1991–93; a chm Mental Health Review Tbnl 1991–93 and 1995–98; Brunel Univ: univ lectr in law 1966–71, reader in law 1971–84, assoc prof of law 1984–96 professorial research fell 1996–, memb Court 1984–88; memb Court Univ of Luton 1994–99; fell Netherlands Inst for Advanced Study in the Humanities and Social Sciences Wassenaar 1975–76, memb Consumer Protection Advsy Ctee 1976–81; Magistrates' Assoc: memb 1974–, memb Legal Ctee 1974–88, vice-chm 1984–88, co-opted memb Cncl 1980–88, a vice-pres Buckinghamshire branch 1994–; JP Inner London (Juvenile Court Panel) 1968–84 (chm 1973–84); jt fndr and ed Anglo-American Law Review 1972–84; memb Inst of Cancer Research: 1999– (memb Cncl 1999–2001, chm Ethics Ctee 2000–03); Liveryman Worshipful Co of Feltmakers (memb Court of Assts 1991–, Master 1998–99); memb Royal Instn (memb Fin Ctee 1987–97, memb Cncl 1994–97); FRSA; *Publications* Sentencing Offenders in Magistrates' Courts (1970), Sentencing (Criminal Law Library No 5, with Eric Stockdale, 1987), articles in legal journals; *Recreations* Roman Britain, watching cricket, fly fishing; *Clubs* Athenaeum, MCC, Hampshire Cricket; *Style*— His Hon Keith Devlin, PhD; ✉ Aylesbury Crown Court, Market Square, Aylesbury, Buckinghamshire HP20 1XD (tel 01296 434401)

DEVLIN, Roger William; s of William Devlin, of Lancs, and Edna, *née* Cross; *b* 22 August 1957; *Educ* Manchester Grammar, Wadham Coll Oxford (MA); *m* 1983, Louise Alice Temlett, da of John Frost Tucker, of Somerset; 2 da (Sophie Victoria Temlett b 29 Nov 1989, Grace Katherine b 4 March 1993); *Career* dir: Hill Samuel & Co Ltd 1978–91, Corning Europe 1991–94, Henry Ansbacher & Co Ltd (head of corp fin) 1994–96; corp devpt dir: Hilton Group 1996–, Ladbroke Worldwide Betting 1996–; non-exec chm: First Residential Properties 1991–03, The Monitor Group Ltd 1994–2000, Baydrive Group 2003–; non-exec dir: PGA European Tour 2000–03, RPS Group 2002–; advsr Phoenix Private Equity 2002–; *Recreations* golf, horse racing, Blackburn Rovers; *Clubs* Racehorse Owners Assoc, Worplesdon, Royal St George's Golf, Royal & Ancient; *Style*— Roger Devlin, Esq; ✉ Hilton Group, Maple Court, Central Park, Reeds Crescent, Watford, Hertfordshire WD1 1HZ (tel 020 7856 8788, fax 020 7856 8409)

DEVLIN, Stuart Leslie; AO (1988), CMG (1980); *b* 9 October 1931; *Educ* Gordon Inst of Technol Geelong, Royal Melbourne Inst of Technol, RCA; *m* 1986, Carole; *Career* goldsmith, silversmith and designer; Royal Warrant as Goldsmith Jeweller to HM The Queen 1982; Freeman City of London 1966, Prime Warden Worshipful Co of Goldsmiths 1996–97; Dr (hc) RMIT Univ Melbourne; DesRCA (Silversmith), DesRCA (Industrial Design-Engrg); *Style*— Dr Stuart Devlin, AO, CMG; ✉ 52 Angmering Lane, East Preston, West Sussex BN16 2TA (tel 01903 858939)

DEVLIN, Timothy Robert (Tim); s of (Hugh) Brendan Devlin, CBE (d 1998), and Ann Elizabeth, *née* Heatley; gs of Maj John Joseph Devlin, OBE; *b* 13 June 1959; *m* 1, 1987 (m dis 1989); m 2, 1991 (m dis 2002); *Career* with Cons Res Dept 1981, accountant 1981–84, called to the Bar Lincoln's Inn 1985; MP (Cons) Stockton S 1987–97; PPS: to Sir Nicholas Lyell, QC, MP as Attorney Gen 1992–94, to Anthony Nelson, MP as Min of Trade 1995–97; in practice as barr 1997–, Attorney Gen's list of approved prosecutors 1998–; conslt Stanbrook & Hooper Brussels, sr expert TACIS Legislative Early Warning System Kiev Ukraine 1997–99, dep chm NHS Tbnl 2002–; former chm Northern Gp of Cons MPs, pres Northern Cons Trade Unions; memb: GB-East Europe Centre, Stockton-on-Tees Cons Assoc, Soc of Cons Lawyers, Bow Gp; former chm LSE Cons, chm Islington N Cons Assoc 1986 (sec 1985); memb Bd of Tstees NSPCC 1994–96; *Style*— Tim Devlin, Esq; ✉ 32 Furnival Street, London EC4A 1JQ

DEVON, 18 Earl of (E 1553); Sir Hugh Rupert Courtenay; 14 Bt (I 1644), DL (Devon 1991); patron of four livings; s of 17 Earl of Devon (d 1998); *b* 5 May 1942; *Educ* Winchester, Magdalene Coll Cambridge; *m* 9 Sept 1967, Diana Frances, elder da of late Jack Watherston, of Menslaws, Jedburgh, Roxburghshire; 3 da (Lady Rebecca Eildon Wharton b 1969, Lady Eleonora Venetia Clarkson b 1971, Lady Camilla Mary Duff b 1974), 1 s (Charles Peregrine, Lord Courtenay b 14 Aug 1975); *Heir* s, Lord Courtenay; *Career* chartered surveyor, farmer and landowner; former pres Devon Branch CLA, pres Devon Co Show 2003; Vice Lord-Lt Devon 2002–; *Style*— The Rt Hon the Earl of Devon, DL; ✉ Powderham Castle, Devon EX6 8JQ (tel 01626 890252)

DEVONISH, Marlon; MBE (2005); *b* 1 June 1976; *Career* athlete; memb Coventry Godiva Harriers; achievements incl: Gold medal 4x100m relay World Jr Championships 1994, Gold medal 100m and Gold medal 4x100m relay European Jr Championships 1995, Gold medal 4x100m relay and Bronze medal 100m European Under 23 Championships 1997, Silver medal 4x100m World Championships 1999 and 2003, Gold medal 4x100m relay and Bronze medal 100m European Championships 2002, Gold medal 4x100m relay and Silver medal 100m Cwlth Games 2002 (memb England team), Gold medal 200m World Indoor Championships 2003, Gold medal 4x100m Olympic Games Athens 2004; *Style*— Marlon Devonish, Esq, MBE

DEVONPORT, 3 Viscount (UK 1917); Sir Terence Kearley; 3 Bt (UK 1908); also Baron Devonport (UK 1910); s of 2 Viscount Devonport (d 1973); *b* 29 August 1944; *Educ* Aiglon Coll Switzerland, Selwyn Coll Cambridge (BA, DipArch, MA), Univ of Newcastle upon Tyne (BPhil); *m* 1, 7 Dec 1968 (m dis 1979), Elizabeth Rosemary, 2 da of late John G Hopton, of Chute Manor, Andover; 2 da (Hon Velvet b 1975, Hon Idonia b 1977); m 2, 7 May 2000, Dr Meiyi Pu, da of Prof Wan Jan Pu, of Beijing; 1 da (Hon Minya Dandie, b 24 Nov 2000); *Heir* kinsman, Chester Kearley; *Career* architect: David Brody NY 1967–68, London Borough of Lambeth 1971–72, Barnett Winskill Newcastle upon Tyne 1972–75; landscape architect Ralph Erskine Newcastle upon Tyne 1977–78, in private practice 1979–84; forestry mangr 1973–, farmer 1978–; md Tweedswood Enterprises 1979; dir various other cos 1984–; chm Millhouse Developments Ltd 1989–; memb: Lloyd's 1976–90, Int Dendrology Soc 1978–, TGEW Northern Advsy Ctee 1978–92, TGUK Nat Land Use and Environment Ctee 1984–87, CLA Northern Advsy Ctee 1980–85; pres: Arboricultural Assoc 1995–, Forestry Cmmn Ref Panel 1987–93; House of Lords: vice-chm All-Pty Parly Forestry Ctee, memb Parly Select Ctee on Public Bldgs and Architecture; RIBA, ALI, FRSA 1996; *Recreations* nature, travel, the arts, good food, trees, music, country sports; *Clubs* Beefsteak, Farmers', RAC, MCC, Royal Over-Seas League, Northern Counties (Newcastle upon Tyne); *Style*— The Rt Hon the Viscount Devonport; ✉ Ray Demesne, Kirkwhelpington, Newcastle upon Tyne NE19 2RG

DEVONSHIRE, Dowager Duchess of; Hon Deborah Vivien; *née* Mitford; DCVO (1999); 6 da of 2 Baron Redesdale (d 1958), and sis of Nancy, Pamela, Unity and Jessica Mitford, also of Hon Lady Mosley; *b* 31 March 1920; *Educ* private; *m* 19 April 1941, 11 Duke of Devonshire (d 2004); 1 s, 2 da; *Career* dir: Chatsworth House Tst, Peacock Hotel Baslow, Devonshire Arms Hotel Bolton Abbey; pres of many local charitable orgns; *Books* The House: A Portrait of Chatsworth (1982), The Estate: A View From Chatsworth (1990), Farm Animals (1990), Treasures of Chatsworth (1990), The Garden at Chatsworth (1999), Counting My Chickens...And Other Home Thoughts (2001), Chatsworth: The House (2002), The Duchess of Devonshire's Chatsworth Cookery Book (2003), Round About Chatsworth (2005); *Style*— Her Grace the Dowager Duchess of Devonshire, DCVO; ✉ Chatsworth, Bakewell, Derbyshire DE45 1PP (tel 01246 582204, fax 01246 582937)

DEVONSHIRE, 12 Duke of (E 1694); Peregrine Andrew Morny Cavendish; CBE (1997); also Baron Cavendish of Hardwicke (E 1605), Earl of Devonshire (E 1618), Marquess of Hartington (E 1694), Earl of Burlington and Baron Cavendish of Keighley (both UK 1831); s of 11 Duke of Devonshire, KG, MC, PC (d 2004), and Hon Deborah Mitford (Dowager Duchess of Devonshire, DCVO, *qv*), da of 2 Baron Redesdale; *b* 27 April 1944; *Educ* Eton, Exeter Coll Oxford; *m* 28 June 1967, Amanda Carmen, da of late Cdr Edward Gavin Heywood-Lonsdale, RN; 1 s (William, Earl of Burlington b 1969), 2 da (Lady Celina Imogen (Lady Celina Carter) b 1971, Lady Jasmine Nancy (Lady Jasmine Dunne) b 1973); *Heir* s, Earl of Burlington; *Career* sr steward The Jockey Club 1989–94, chm British Horseracing Board 1994–97, HM's Representative and Chm at Ascot Racecourse 1997–; dep chm Sotheby's Holdings Inc; *Style*— The Duke of Devonshire, CBE; ✉ Chatsworth, Bakewell, Derbyshire DE45 1PP (tel 01246 565300, fax 01246 565436, e-mail beamsley2@aol.com)

DEWAR, *see:* Beauclerk-Dewar

DEWAR, Hamish Richard John; s of Richard John Gresley Dewar (d 1991), of Hay Hedge, Bisley, nr Stroud, Glos, and Andrena Victoria Dewar; *b* 15 January 1956; *Educ* Sherborne, Downing Coll Cambridge (MA); *m* 21 May 1983, Anna Maria, da of Patrick Cloonan, of Sawbridgeworth, Herts; 2 s (Lachlan b 18 July 1987, Woody b 25 Feb 1991), 1 da (India b 3 Jan 1989); *Career* specialist in conservation and restoration of paintings; studied under Richard Maelzer at Edward Speelman Ltd 1977–81, own practice 1982–; main restoration works incl: David with Head of Goliath by Guido Reni, Seed of David (altar piece from Llandaff Cathedral) by D G Rossetti, Angel di Soto by Picasso, The Light of the World by Holman Hunt (for St Paul's Cathedral); *Recreations* golf, football; *Clubs* Sunningdale Golf; *Style*— Hamish Dewar, Esq; ✉ 14 Mason's Yard, Duke Street, St James's, London SW1Y 6BU (tel 020 7930 4004, fax 020 7930 4100, e-mail hamish@hamishdewar.co.uk)

DEWAR, Robert James; CMG (1969), CBE (1964); s of Dr Robert Scott Dewar (d 1939); *b* 1923; *Educ* Glasgow HS, Univ of Edinburgh, Wadham Coll Oxford; *m* 1947, Christina Marianne, da of late Olaf August Ljungberger, of Stockholm, Sweden; 2 s, 1 da; *Career* Colonial Forest Serv Nigeria and Nyasaland 1944–60, chief conservator of forests Nyasaland 1961–64, perm sec Natural Resources Malawi 1964–69, memb staff World Bank 1969–84, chief Agric Div Regnl Mission for E Africa 1974–84, conslt to the World Bank 1984–86; chm: Zimbiala Tst, Friends of Malawi Assoc; *Recreations* golf, angling, gardening; *Clubs* Cwlth Trust, New Cavendish; *Style*— Robert Dewar Esq, CMG, CBE; ✉ Dundurn, 5 Knock Road, Crieff, Perthshire PH7 4AH (tel 01764 654830)

DEWAR OF THAT ILK AND VOGRIE, Col Michael Kenneth O'Malley; Chief of the Name and Arms of Dewar; *b* 15 November 1941; *Educ* Downside, Pembroke Coll Oxford (MA), RMA Sandhurst; *m* 6 July 1968, Lavinia Mary, o da of late Dr Jack Souttar Minett, of Stony Stratford, Bucks; 3 s (Alexander Malcolm Bretherton b 1970, James Michael Bretherton b 1973, Edward Jack Bretherton b 1978), 1 da (Katharine Victoria Lavinia b 1981); *Career* cmmnd 2 Lt The Royal Green Jackets 1962, psc, Lt-Col 1982, CO Light Division Depot 1985–87, Col 1987, Col Defence Studies Staff Coll Camberley 1987–90 (ret); dep dir Int Inst for Strategic Studies 1990–94, dir The Albemarle Connection 1994–96; md: MDA Communications 1996–, Airtime Communications 1996–, MDA Publishing Ltd 1998–; defence conslt 1990– (BBC TV, ITV News, BSkyB News, BBC Radio 4 and Radio 5); Knight of Honour and Devotion SMO Malta 1988; *Books* Internal Security Weapons and Equipment of the World (1978), Brush Fire Wars, Campaigns of the British Army since 1945 (1984, revised 1987), The British Army in Northern Ireland (1985, revised 1996), Weapons and Equipment of Counter-Terrorism (1987), The Art of Deception in Warfare (1989), The Defence of the Nation (1989), An Anthology of Military Quotations (1990), Northern Ireland Scrapbook (jtly, 1986), Campaign Medals (jtly, 1987), War in the Streets (1992), The Gulf War: A Photographic History (1992); *Style*— Col Michael Dewar of that Ilk and Vogrie

DEWE, Roderick Gorrie (Roddy); s of Douglas Percy Dewe (d 1978), and Rosanna Clements Gorrie, *née* Heggie (d 1971); *b* 17 October 1935; *Educ* abroad, UC Oxford (BA); *m* 1964, Carol Anne, da of Michael Beach Thomas (d 1941), of Herts; 1 da (Sarah b 1965), 1 s (Jonathan 1967); *Career* chm Dewe Rogerson Gp Ltd 1969–98; Hon FCIPR; *Recreations* golf, fly fishing, travel; *Clubs* Beefsteak, Savile, City of London; *Style*— Roddy Dewe, Esq; ✉ 55 Duncan Terrace, London N1 8AG (tel 020 7359 7318); Booking Hall, Southill Station, Biggleswade, Bedfordshire SG18 9LP (tel 01462 811 274, e-mail dewedrop@aol.com)

DEWE MATHEWS, Bernard Piers; CBE (1996), TD (1967); s of Denys Cosmo Dewe Mathews (d 1985), of London, and Elizabeth Jane, *née* Davies (d 1937); *b* 28 March 1937; *Educ* Ampleforth, Harvard Business Sch; *m* 10 Feb 1977, Catherine Ellen, da of Senator John Ignatius Armstrong (d 1977), of NSW, Aust; 3 da (Jacqueline b 1978, Laura b 1979, Chloe b 1982), 1 s (Charles-Frederick (Freddie) b 1985); *Career* Nat Serv 2 Lt Malaya 1956–57, TA Maj 21 SAS Regt 1957–67; Edward Moore & Sons CAs 1957–62, BP Co Ltd 1962–65, Coopers & Lybrand & Assocs 1965–69, dir and head Int Projects Div J Henry Schroder & Co Ltd 1978–97 (joined 1969); dir: CEPR 1998–2003, Nat Musicians Symphony Orch (NMSO) 2000–02, Chief of Jt Ops (MOD) Mgmnt Bd 2000–2004; memb: SEATAG 1985–89, OPB 1989–95, EGAC 1993–97; memb Cncl London C of C 1986–87; dep chm and tstee Outward Bound Tst 1997–2000, treas and tstee Farm Africa 2000–06, tstee VLF (Sisters of Nazareth) 2006–; govr St Paul's Girls' Prep Sch 1988–93; FCA 1972 (ACA 1962); *Books* Blowing my own Trumpet (2000), The Mallinckrodt-Bischoff Partnership (2004); *Recreations* music, sport, landscape gardening, painting watercolours; *Clubs* Garrick, Tadmarton Heath Golf; *Style*— Bernard Dewe Mathews, Esq, CBE, TD; ✉ 112 Castelnau, Barnes, London SW13 9EU (tel 020 8741 2592, fax 020 8748 7669)

DEWEY, Sir Anthony Hugh; 3 Bt (UK 1917), of South Hill Wood, Bromley, Kent; JP (1961); s of Maj Hugh Grahame Dewey, MC (d 1936), and gs of Rev Sir Stanley Daws Dewey, 2 Bt (d 1948); *b* 31 July 1921; *Educ* Wellington, RAC Cirencester; *m* 22 April 1949, Sylvia Jacqueline Rosamund, da of late Dr John Ross MacMahon, of Branksome Manor, Bournemouth; 3 da (Delia Mary (Mrs Nicholas J Wingfield-Digby) b 1951, Carola Jane (Mrs Robert H Sutton) b 1955, Angela Rosamund (Mrs Ivan Hicks) b 1957), 2 s (Rupert Grahame b 1953, Charles Ross b 1960); *Heir* s, Rupert Dewey; *Career* Capt RA NW Europe 1940–46; farmer Somerset; *Clubs* Army and Navy; *Style*— Sir Anthony Dewey, Bt; ✉ The Rag, Galhampton, Yeovil, Somerset BA22 7AJ (tel 01963 440213)

DEWEY, Prof John Frederick; s of John Edward Dewey (d 1982), of London, and Florence Nellie Mary, *née* Davies (d 2000); *b* 22 May 1937; *Educ* Bancroft's Sch Woodford Green, Univ of London (BSc, DIC, PhD), Univ of Cambridge (MA, ScD), Univ of Oxford (MA, DSc); *m* 4 July 1961, Frances Mary, da of William Blackhurst (d 1971), of Wistow, Cambs; 1 da (Ann Penelope b 1963), 1 s (Jonathan Peter 1965); *Career* lectr: Univ of Manchester 1960–64, Univ of Cambridge 1964–70; prof: Albany Univ NY 1970–82, Univ of Durham 1982–86, Dept of Earth Sciences Univ of Oxford 1986–2000, Dept of Geology Univ of Calif Davis; fell UC Oxford 1986–; memb Academy of Europe 1989, foreign memb US Nat Acad of Sciences 1997; FGS 1960, FRS 1985; *Recreations* British and Irish music, watercolour painting, model railways, skiing, cricket; *Style*— Prof John Dewey, FRS; ✉ Sherwood Lodge, 93 Bagley Wood Road, Kennington, Oxford OX1 5NA (tel 01865 735525, e-mail dewey@geology.ucdavis.edu)

DEWHIRST, Timothy Charles; DL (E Yorks); s of Alistair Jowitt Dewhirst, CBE, of Driffield, E Yorks, and Hazel Eleanor, *née* Reed; *b* 19 August 1953; *Educ* Worksop Coll; *m* 1, 15 July 1978 (m dis 1997), Prudence Rosalind, née Horsell; 1 s (Charles Alistair Geoffrey b 4 June 1980), 1 da (Samantha Prudence b 26 June 1983); m 2, 28 April 1999, Charlotte Edwina Mary, née Birkett; 1 da (Matilda Charlotte b 2 May 2001); *Career* chm Dewhirst Group plc (clothing and toiletry mfrs) 1993– (chief exec 1986–93); vice-chm BCIA 1990–; memb Cncl BATC 1993–; *Recreations* shooting, golf, fishing, sailing; *Style*— Timothy C Dewhirst, Esq, DL; ✉ Nafferton Heights, Nafferton, Driffield, East Yorkshire YO25 0LD; Dewhirst Group Ltd, Dewhirst House, Westgate, Driffield, East Yorkshire YO25 6TH (tel 01377 252561, fax 01377 252030)

DEWHURST, Philip Anthony; s of Alfred John Dewhurst, and Rosalind Georgina Dewhurst; *b* 25 September 1949; *Educ* Mark Hall Sch; *m* Joan Catherine; 1 da (Grace b 14 June 1983), 1 s (Tom b 27 March 1987); *Career* mgmnt trainee then copywriter Longman Group Ltd 1968–71, int publicity controller Evans Publishing Ltd 1971–73; PRO: Havering London BC 1973–76, Hackney London BC 1976–77; head of PR and publicity City of Canterbury 1977–80, PRO Surrey CC 1980–84; dir of public affrs: Chemical Industries Assoc 1984–88, Sterling Public Relations 1988–92; md public affrs GCI Group 1992–94, gen mangr GCI Europe 1993–94; chief exec The Rowland Company (Saatchi & Saatchi PR) 1994–95, dir of corp affrs Railtrack plc 1995–99, UK chief exec Shandwick Int 1999–2001, gp dir Corp Affrs BNFL Gp 2001–07, head of PR Gazprom Mktg and Trading 2007–; pres IPR (now CIPR) 1999– (chm CIPR Excellence Awards 2004–05), chm Nuclear Industry Assoc 2004–, hon sec NATPRO 2003–; visiting fell Bournemouth Univ 2004–; FCIPR (FIPR 1989), FRSA 1989; *Recreations* art, travel; *Style*— Philip Dewhurst, Esq

D

DEWS, Vivienne Margaret; da of Albert Dews, and Eva Margaret, *née* Hayman; *b* 29 December 1952; *Educ* Northampton HS for Girls, Univ of Cambridge (BA), Univ of Warwick (Dip); *m* 1, 1972 (m dis), Stephen Ladner; m 2, 1979, Alan Cogbill; 1 s, 1 da (and 2 da decd); *Career* civil servant; joined Home Office 1974, private sec to Min for Police and Prisons 1979, dep dir Top Mgmnt Prog 1987, head immigration policy 1989, head after entry casework and appeals 1991, head consulting efficiency and market testing Home Office 1994, dir fin and services Immigration and Nationality Directorate 1995, chief exec Police IT Org (PITO) 1999, dir (modernising corp support) Inland Revenue 2002, dir Resources and Planning Health and Safety Exec 2002–; memb CIPFA; *Recreations* family, home, garden; *Style*— Miss Vivienne Dews; ✉ Health and Safety Executive, Rose Court, Southwark Bridge Road, London SE1 9HS

DEXTER, Colin; OBE (2000); *b* 29 September 1930; *Educ* Stamford Sch, Christ's Coll Cambridge (MA); *m* 30 March 1956, Dorothy; 1 da (Sally b 1960), 1 s (Jeremy b 1962); *Career* author; Nat Serv; sr asst sec Univ of Oxford Delegacy of Local Examinations 1966–87; six times nat crossword champion of Ximenes and Azed Competitions; memb: CWA, Detection Club; recipient of the Cartier Diamond Dagger Award for services to crime fiction 1997, Sherlock Holmes Award 1999; Freedom City of Oxford 2001; Hon MA (by incorporation) Univ of Oxford 1966, hon fell St Cross Coll Oxford 2005; *Books* Inspector Morse crime novels: Last Bus to Woodstock (1975), Last Seen Wearing (1976), The Silent World of Nicholas Quinn (1977), Service of All The Dead (1979, Silver Dagger Award CWA), The Dead of Jericho (1981, Silver Dagger Award CWA), The Riddle of the Third Mile (1983), The Secret of Annexe 3 (1986), The Wench is Dead (1989, Gold Dagger Award CWA), The Jewel That Was Ours (1991), The Way Through the Woods (1992, Gold Dagger Award CWA), Morse's Greatest Mystery (1993), The Daughters of Cain (1994), Death is Now My Neighbour (1996), The Remorseful Day (1999); *Recreations* Wagner, crosswords, reading; *Style*— Colin Dexter, OBE; ✉ 456 Banbury Road, Oxford OX2 7RG

DEXTER, Emma; da of Colin Hall Dexter, of London, and Carteret, France, and Mercia, *née* Ife; *b* 25 June 1959, London; *Educ* Croydon HS for Girls, Somerville Coll Oxford (MA), Courtauld Inst (MPhil); *m* 19 March 2003, Adrian Jackson; 2 s (Silas b 7 May 1992, Zachary b 12 Feb 1997); *Career* asst curator Stoke-on-Trent City Museum and Art Gallery 1985–87, dir Chisenhale Gallery London 1987–90; Inst of Contemporary Arts (ICA) London: dep dir of exhbns 1990–92, dir of exhbns 1992–99; sr curator Tate Modern 2000–; visiting lectr: Goldsmiths Coll, Christies Contemporary Art, De Montfort Univ, Essex Univ; memb Critical Curating (London Univ); mentor RCA Curating Course 2005–06, Nesta mentor for artist Joy Gregory 2004–06, mentor for Inspire Fell at Tate Modern 2005–; jury memb and chair Becks Futures Awards ICA 2000; memb jury: Present Future section Artissima Fair Turin 2002–05, Deutsche Börse Photography Prize London 2006, Spectrum Int Prize for Photography Germany 2008; *Exhibitions* prog at ICA introducing: Marlene Dumas, Charles Ray, Luc Tuymans, John Currin, Thomas Schiebitz, Steve McQueen, Jake and Dinos Chapman, Mark Leckey; at Tate: Cruel and Tender 2003 (Tate's first photography show), Luc Tuymans and Bruce Nauman 2004, Frida Kahlo 2005; *Publications* Cruel and Tender (ed and contrib, 2003), Luc Tuymans (ed and contrib, 2004), Raw Materials (ed and contrib, 2004), Frida Kahlo (ed and contrib, 2005), Vitamin D: New Perspectives in Drawing (contrib, 2005); *Recreations* cooking, foreign languages; *Style*— Ms Emma Dexter; ✉ Tate Modern, Exhibitions and Displays, Bankside, London SE1 9TG (tel 020 7401 5207, e-mail emma.dexter@tate.org.uk)

DEXTER, Dr (Thomas) Michael; s of Thomas Richard Dexter (d 1976), and (Gertrude) Agnes, *née* Depledge (d 1991); *b* 15 May 1945; *Educ* Manchester Central GS, Univ of Salford (BSc, DSc), Univ of Manchester (PhD); *m* 10 Aug 1966 (m dis 1978), (Frances) Ann, da of John Sutton, of Hurdsfield, Cheshire; 2 s (Alexander Michael b 1972, Thomas b 1987), 2 da (Katrina Ann (twin) b 1972, Rachel b 1985); *Career* visiting fell Sloan Kettering Inst NY 1976–77, sr scientist Paterson Laboratories Manchester 1977–87 (scientist 1973), life fell Cancer Research Campaign 1978–98, head of Dept of Experimental Haematology Paterson Inst for Cancer Research Manchester 1982–98, prof of haematology (personal chair) Univ of Manchester 1985–98, dir Paterson Inst 1997–98 (dep dir 1994–97), dir Wellcome Trust 1998–2003, chm Stem Cell Sciences Holdings 2003–, scientific advsr Rothschild Asset Management 2003–; Gibb research fell 1992–98; author of 300 papers in jls; pres Int Soc for Experimental Haematology 1988–89; memb: Scientific Ctee Leukaemia Research Fund 1985–88, Grants Ctee Cancer Research Campaign 1986–93, Scientific Advsy Bd Biomedical Research Center Univ of Br Columbia 1988–91, Ctee on Effects of Ionising Radiation 1988–93, Steering Ctee Electro-Magnetic Fields National Grid 1989–98, Scientifc Ctee Gunnar Nilsson Research Tst Fund 1991–97; memb Editorial Bd of 10 scientific jls; memb: Ctee SERC 1991–94, Ctee AFRC (now BBSRC) 1991–94, Cncl MRC 1993–96 (chm MCMB 1994–96, chm Human Genome Co-ordinating Ctee 1996–98), Ctee on Med Affects of Radiations in the Environment (COMARE) 1993–98, World Ctee IACRLD 1994–99, Cncl Royal Soc 1995–96 and 2002–04, Ctee SEBCC 1998–2000, NE Science Cncl 2003–; chm Int Centre for Life Newcastle, chair Cockroft Inst 2004–; Hon DSc: UMIST 1999, Univ of Salford 2000, Mahidol Univ Thailand 2001, Imperial Coll London 2002, Univ of Newcastle 2006; FRS 1991, FRCPath 1997 (MRCPath 1987), FIBiol 1997 (CIBiol), FMedSci 1997 (founding fell), Hon FRCP 1998 (Hon MRCP 1994); *Recreations* folk singing, poetry, gardening; *Style*— Dr Michael Dexter, FRS; ✉ e-mail tmdexter@btinternet.com

DEYERMOND, Prof Alan David; s of Maj Henry Deyermond (d 1966), and Margaret, *née* Lawson (d 1958); *b* 24 February 1932; *Educ* Quarry Bank HS Liverpool, Victoria Coll Jersey, Pembroke Coll Oxford (MA, BLitt, DLitt); *m* 30 March 1957, Ann Marie, da of William Bracken (d 1943), and Mary, *née* Burke (d 1985); 1 da (Ruth Margaret b 1971); *Career* Westfield Coll London (later Queen Mary & Westfield Coll London, now Queen Mary Univ of London): asst lectr 1955–58, lectr 1958–66, reader 1966–69, sr tutor 1967–72, prof of Spanish 1969–97 (research prof 1997–), dir Medieval Hispanic Research Seminar 1967–97, dean Faculty of Arts 1972–74 and 1981–84, vice-princ 1986–89; assoc dir Inst of Romance Studies Univ of London 1991–93; gen ed Papers of the MHRS 1995–; visiting prof: Univ of Wisconsin 1972, UCLA 1977, Princeton Univ 1978–81, Univ of Victoria Canada 1983, Northern Arizona Univ 1986, Johns Hopkins Univ 1987, Univ Nacional Autónoma de México 1992, Univ da Coruña Spain 1996; consejo superior de investigaciones científicas Madrid 2002–; distinguished visiting prof Univ of Calif Irvine 1997–99; Taylorian lectr Univ of Oxford 1999; pres Asoc Internacional de Hispanistas 1992–95 (hon life pres 1995–); chm Hendon S Liberal Assoc 1959–64; pres London Medieval Soc 1970–74; sidesman St Peter's Church St Albans 1990–98, chm Kentish's Educnl Fndn 1992–98; corresponding fell: Medieval Acad of America 1979, Real Academia de Buenas Letras de Barcelona 1982; memb Hispanic Soc of America 1985; Premio Internacional Elio Antonio de Nebrija 1994; Hon LHD Georgetown Univ 1995, hon fell Queen Mary & Westfield Coll London 1999, Dr (Hc) Univ de Vale ncia 2005; FSA 1987, FBA 1988; *Books* incl: The Petrarchan Sources of 'La Celestina' (1961, 2 edn 1975), Epic Poetry and the Clergy - Studies on the 'Mocedades de Rodrigo' (1969), A Literary History of Spain - The Middle Ages (1971), 'Lazarillo de Tormes' - A Critical Guide (1975, 2 edn 1993), Historia y crítica de la literatura española: Edad Media (1980, first supplement 1991), El 'Cantar de Mio Cid' y la épica medieval española (1987), Tradiciones y puntos de vista en la ficción sentimental (1993), La literatura perdida de la Edad Media castellana Vol I (1995), Point of View in the Ballad (1996), The Libro de Buen Amor in England (2004), Poesía de cancionero del siglo XV (2007), A Century of British Medievalists (ed, 2007); *Recreations* psephology, vegetarian cookery; *Style*— Prof Alan Deyermond, FBA; ✉ 20 Lancaster Road, St Albans, Hertfordshire AL1 4ET (tel 01727 855383, e-mail alandeyermond@waitrose.com); Department of Hispanic Studies, Queen Mary, University of London, Mile End Road, London E1 4NS

DEYES, Anthony Francis (Tony); s of William Francis Deyes (d 1948), and Marjorie, *née* Ridgway; *b* 9 July 1944; *Educ* Kingswood Sch Bath, KCL (BA), Inst of Educn Univ of London (PGCE), Aston Univ (MPhil), Middlesex Univ (MBA); *m* 1968, Maya, da of Emil Koch; 3 s (Philip Francis b 27 Feb 1969 d 1971, Marcus Eugene b 11 March 1972, Robert Anthony b 21 Feb 1973); *Career* teacher King's Sch of English Bournemouth 1968–69, dir Language Inst Univ of Deusto Bilbao 1973–76 (lectr in English and linguistics 1969–73); British Council: dir Coimbra 1976–77, dir of studies Lisbon 1977–80, visiting prof of linguistics Catholic Univ of São Paulo 1980–85, sr advsr English Language Div 1987–90 (conslt 1985–87), dir Rio de Janeiro 1990–93, dir and cultural attaché Ecuador 1993–99, dir Wales 1999–; author of over 60 articles in professional and academic jls; *Recreations* reading, swimming, golf, amateur dramatics, music (opera and Mozart), walking, speech-making; *Style*— Tony Deyes, Esq; ✉ 28 Park Place, Cardiff CF10 3QE (tel 029 2039 7346, fax 029 2023 7494, deyes@heimat77.fsnet.co.uk)

DHAMIJA, Dinesh; *b* 28 March 1950; *Educ* King's Sch Canterbury, Univ of Cambridge (MA); *m* Tani, *née* Malhotra; 2 s (Biren b 11 Sept 1978, Darun b 6 April 1980); *Career* with IBM and other cos until 1979, estab (with Tani Dhamija) Dabin Travel Ltd 1980, estab (with Tani Dhamija) Flightbookers 1983, gen sales agent UK & I for various airlines 1987–95, fndr and chm ebookers plc (originally Flightbookers' internet div) 1999–; *Recreations* golf; *Clubs* Roehampton, Wentworth, RAC, Oxford and Cambridge; *Style*— Dinesh Dhamija, Esq

DHANDA, Parmjit Singh; MP; s of Balbir Singh Dhanda, and Satvinder Kaur, *née* Johal; *b* 17 September 1971, London; *Educ* Mellow Lane Comp Sch Hayes, Univ of Nottingham (BEng, MSc); *Career* organiser Lab Pty W London, Hants and Wilts 1996–98, asst nat organiser Connect 1998–2001, MP (Lab) Gloucester 2001–; asst Govt whip 2005–06, Parly under sec of state (children, young people and families) DfES 2006–; memb: Sci and Technol Select Ctee 2001–03, Educn and Skill Policy Cmmn 2001–05; cncllr Hillingdon BC 1998–2002, European Parly candidate (Lab) SE 1999; vice-chair: Lab Friends of India, Progress; memb: Lab Pty 1988– (memb NEC Working Pty on Equal Opportunities 1998–2001), USDAW, TGWU, Fabian Soc; *Recreations* watching football and rugby, playing most sports, reading; *Clubs* Gloucester RFC, Gloucester City FC; *Style*— Parmjit Dhanda, Esq, MP; ✉ House of Commons, London SW1A 0AA (website www.parmjitdhanda.com)

DHANDSA, Dr Narinder S; s of Shiv Dhandsa (d 1971), and Samitar Dhandsa; *b* 29 February 1956; *Educ* Gillingham GS, St Thomas' Hosp Med Sch (MB, BS); *Career* jr hosp doctor NHS 1979–82, chief exec Associated Nursing Services plc 1984–2005; currently dir: Rickshaw Restaurants Ltd, Vigour Ltd; *Recreations* skiing, golf, art; *Style*— Dr Narinder Dhandsa

DHARGALKAR, Suresh Dinkar; LVO (1994); s of Dinkar Laxman Dhargalkar (d 1979), of Bombay, India, and Sushila, *née* Belwalkar (d 1993); *b* 16 December 1934; *Educ* Hind Vidhylaya HS Bombay, Sch of Architecture Sir J J Sch of Art Bombay, Sch of Architecture Regent Street Poly London, Poly Coll of Architecture and Advance Building Technol London; *m* 3 Aug 1962, Hildegard (d 1991), da of Oswald Bente (d 1964); 2 s (Hans b 1963, Martin b 1967 d 1985); *Career* architectural asst in private architectural practice: Bombay 1952–55, London 1955–70; architect in private practice London 1970–74, princ architect with PSA/DOE for Royal Palaces 1979–90 (architect 1975–79), actg consIt architect project mangr with Royal Household 1995– (superintending architect 1990–95); dep keeper of the Royal Philatelic Collection 2003–06; special interest in environmental control for preservation of historic artefacts, lighting and precaution against fire and theft in historic bldgs, palaces and museums; works undertaken in restoration and new works at: Windsor Castle, St James's Palace, Hampton Court Palace, British Museum, National Maritime Museum; active participant in organising seminars for conservation of cultural historic properties for ICCROM until 1989 (Cert 1984), conservation architect Egypt Exploration Soc 1997–; Freeman City of London 1965; corp memb RIBA 1970, memb ARCUK 1970; FRPSL 2002; *Recreations* travel, cooking, watercolour painting, philately; *Style*— Suresh Dhargalkar, Esq, LVO, RIBA, FRPSL; ✉ 3 Elmer Gardens, Edgware, Middlesex HA8 9AR (tel 020 8952 3075)

DHINSA, Jojar Singh; s of Joginder Singh Dhinsa (d 2002), and Gurmej Kaur Dhillon; *b* 12 February 1975, Coventry; *Educ* Sidney Stringer Sch and Community Coll Coventry, UCE (BSc); *Career* fndr and prop JK Trading 1989–96, chm and ceo Athlone Gp 2000–; pres Alchamist Assoc; Newcomer of the Year Asian Business Awards 2004 (nomination Businessman of the Year); ambass Coventry City; *Style*— Jojar S Dhinsa, Esq; ✉ Athlone Group, 200 Brook Drive, Green Park, Reading RG2 6UB (e-mail jdhinsa@athloneinternational.com)

DHOLAKIA, Baron (Life Peer UK 1997), of Waltham Brooks in the County of West Sussex; Navnit; OBE (1994), DL (W Sussex 1999); s of Permananddas Mulji Dholakia, of Bhavnagar, India; *b* 4 March 1937; *Educ* Home Sch and Inst of Science Bhavnagar Gujarat, Brighton Tech Coll; *m* 1967, Ann, da of Harold McLuskie, of London; 2 da (Hon Anjali, Hon Alene); *Career* med lab technician 1960–66, devpt offr Nat Ctee for Commonwealth Immigrants 1966–68 (sr devpt offr 1968–74, princ offr and sec 1974–76), with Cmmn for Racial Equality 1976–94; previous appts with: Police Complaints Cmmn, Ethnic Minority Advsy Ctee of the Judicial Studies Bd, Lord Carlisle's Ctee of the Parole Ststems Review; chm Brighton Young Liberals 1959–62, chm Brighton Liberal Assoc 1962–64, memb (Lib) Brighton CBC 1961–64; sits as Lib Dem peer House of Lords, spokesman in home affrs, memb House of Lords Appointments Cmmn, pres Lib Dems 2000–04; pres: NACRO 2003– (chm 1998–2003, chm Race Issues Advsy Ctee), Friends Circle Int; vice-pres The Family Welfare Assoc; vice-chm and memb Mgmnt Bd Policy Research Inst on Ageing and Ethnicity, memb Cncl: Save the Children Fund 1992–98, Howard League for Penal Reform 1992–2002, Indian Jewish Assoc UK, Cmmn on the Future of Multi-Ethnic Britain, The Caine Prize for African Writing; memb: Editorial Bd Howard Jl, Mannheim Centre for Criminology and Criminal Justice LSE, Home Sec's Race Forum; memb Advsy Bd: Centre for Reform, Human Rights Act Research Unit, Centre for Ethnic Minority Studies Royal Holloway Univ of London, Int Trade & Law Inst; tstee: The Ghandi Tst, Dr L M Singhvi Fndn, Police Fndn, The Apex Tst, British Empire and Cwlth Museum Bristol, Parly Appeal for Romanian Children, Shrimati Pushpa Wati Loomba Meml Tst, Br Indian Golden Jubilee Fund, Pallant House Gallery Chichester; patron and vice-patron of numerous charities; govr Commonwealth Inst 1998–2005; assoc RPS Rainer; former magistrate and memb Bd of Visitors HM Prison Lewes; Asian Who's Who Int Asian of the Year Award 2000, Pravasi Bharatiya Sanman Award 2003; *Style*— The Rt Hon the Lord Dholakia, OBE, DL; ✉ House of Lords, London SW1A 0PW (tel 020 7219 5203, fax 020 7219 2082, e-mail dholakian@parliament.uk)

DHOLAKIA, Uday Kumar; s of Dhiru Bhagwandas Dholakia, of Oadby, Leicester, and Chandrika Dhiru, *née* Bhatti; *b* 2 January 1958; *Educ* Westlain GS Brighton; *m* 9 July 1989, Hardika, da of late Rangitlal Modi; 2 da (Saffron Banita b 25 Aug 1997, Serene Devashree b 19 Nov 1999); *Career* small business advsr Dept of Planning and Transportation Leics CC 1984–86, princ business conslt Chief Exec's Dept Leicester City Cncl 1986–88, dep dir Leics Business Venture (DTI) 1990–91, ptnr planning and corp affrs Global Consulting IJK Ltd 1991–; non-exec dir: Leicester Boiler Engineers Ltd 1990–93, Watford Electronics Ltd 1993–95; vice-pres Small Business Bureau 1998–, fndr dir Westminster African Caribbean Business Initiative 1997–2000, cmmr Broadcasting

Standards Cmmn 1999–2003, tstee Nat Employment Policy Inst 1995–2000, fndr memb Euro Ethnic Minority Business Network 1999; memb: Ctee Leicester Family Services Unit 1985–87, Leiceser and Co C of C and Industry 1987–88 (fndr chm Leics Business Awards), Advsy Bd Central Television plc (later Carlton Television plc) 1993–95, Bd Leics and Rutland Probation Bd 1994– (chm Complaints and Appeals Ctee), E Midlands Electricity Consumer Ctee 1997–2000, Oftel Small Business Taskforce 2001–, Minority Media and Telecommunications Cncl of USA 2003–, Leics Police Authy 2006–, Bd Local Better Regulation Office Cabinet Office 2007–; tstee: Leics Orgn for the Relief of Suffering (LOROS) 2001–, Leics and Rutland Community Fndn 2005–; assoc Inst of Export, MIMC, MBCS, MCIM, MIMgt, FRSA, FIBC; hon citizen Haskovo City Bulgaria 2005; *Awards* Young Stockbroker of the Year 1978, Young Entrepreneur of the Year 1979, NE Enterprise Tst Award 1983, Cmmn for Racial Equality Bursary to US 1986, Asian Times/Caribbean Times Community Award 1989, Leicester Common Purpose grad 1991–92, E Midlands Ethnic Minority Business Award 1998; *Recreations* wine, marine antiques, travelling, cricket, television; *Clubs* Royal British Club of Portugal; *Style—* Uday Dholakia, Esq; ✉ Global House, 2 Spinney Hill Road, Leicester LE5 3GG (tel 0116 251 5225, fax 0116 290 2045, mobile 07973 757601, e-mail uday@global-consulting.com)

di VITA, Charlotte; MBE (1998); *b* 5 September 1966; *Educ* Univ of Edinburgh (MA); *Career* early career as voluntary research, mktg and fundraising conslt for environmental, human rights and medical orgns, co-ordinator Anglo-Brazilian Conference on the Environment 1990, founder Trade plus Aid 1997–; launched: Charlotte di Vita Collections 1998–2007, Trade plus Aid Design Studio South Africa; memb Business Gp Co-ordinating Ctee Amnesty Int 1990–92, environmental conslt 1990–92; goodwill ambass Nelson Mandela Children Fund 2003–, launched 21st Century Leaders project 2004–; Pilkington Window to the World Award Woman of the Year Awards 2003, Honorary Acheivement Award UK Gift Industry Awards 2004; Hon DBA Huddersfield Univ; *Style—* Ms Charlotte di Vita; ✉ Trade plus Aid, 1–3 Shelgate Road, London SW11 1BD

DIAMOND, Prof Derek Robin; s of Baron Diamond (Life Peer, d 2004), of Little Chalfont, Bucks, and Sadie, *née* Lyttleton; *b* 18 May 1933; *Educ* Harrow Co GS, Univ of Oxford (MA), Northwestern Univ (MSc); *m* 12 Jan 1957, Esme Grace, da of Richard Bryant Passmore (d 1982); 1 s (Andrew Richard b 1961), 1 da (Stella Ruth b 1963); *Career* lectr in geography Univ of Glasgow 1957–68; LSE: reader in regnl planning 1968–82, prof of geography (specialising in urban and regnl planning) 1982–95, emeritus prof 1995–, hon fell 2006–; hon prof of human geography Inst of Geography Beijing 1990; vice-pres Town and Country Planning Assoc, past pres Inst of Br Geographers, hon pres Regional Studies Assoc, hon memb RTPI 1989; FRGS; *Books* Regional Policy Evaluation (1983), Infrastructure & Industrial Costs in British Industry (1989), Metropolitan Governance: its contemporary transformation (1998); *Recreations* philately; *Clubs* Geographical; *Style—* Prof Derek Diamond; ✉ 9 Ashley Drive, Walton-on-Thames, Surrey KT12 1JL (tel 01932 223280, e-mail derek@diamondwot.fsnet.co.uk); London School of Economics and Political Science, Houghton Street, London WC2A 2AE (tel 020 7955 7496, fax 020 7955 7412)

DIAMOND, Prof Ian; s of Harold Frederick Diamond (d 1985), of Torquay, Devon, and Sylvia Betty Diamond; *b* 14 March 1954, Kingskerswell, Devon; *Educ* LSE (BSc, MSc), Univ of St Andrews (PhD); *m* 1997, Jane; 1 s (Tom b 8 Sept 1999), 1 step da (Alexandra b 20 March 1991), 1 step s (Mark b 3 Sept 1992); *Career* lectr Heriot-Watt Univ 1979–80; Univ of Southampton: lectr 1980–88, sr lectr 1988–92, prof 1992–2003; chief exec ESRC 2003–; chair Exec Gp Research Cncls UK 2004–07; author of 120 articles in learned jls; Clifford C Clogg Prize Population Assoc of America 2000; AcSS 2000, FBA 2005; *Recreations* swimming, running, Southampton FC, Torquay United FC; *Clubs* Bradford on Avon Swimming; *Style—* Prof Ian Diamond; ✉ 25 Green Lane, Hinton Charterhouse, Bath BA2 7TL; Economic and Social Research Council, Polaris House, North Star Avenue, Swindon SN2 1UJ (tel 01793 413004, fax 01793 413002, e-mail ian.diamond@esrc.ac.uk)

DIBBLE, Robert Kenneth; s of Herbert William Dibble (d 1973), and Irene Caroline Dibble (d 1995); *b* 28 December 1938; *Educ* Westcliff HS for Boys; *m* 26 Aug 1972, Teresa Frances, da of James Vincent MacDonnell; 4 s (William b 5 July 1973, Thomas b 12 April 1975, Edward b 7 Feb 1979, Matthew b 31 Dec 1980); *Career* RNC Dartmouth 1955–58, HMS Belton 1958–59, Lt HM Yacht Britannia 1959–60, HMS Caesar 1961–62, Russian interpreter's course 1962–64, mixed manned ship USS Claude V Ricketts 1964–65, long communications course 1965–66, Sqdn Communications Offr HMS Ajax 1966–67, Lt Cdr HMS Hampshire 1967–68, head of electronic warfare HMS Mercury 1968–70, def fell KCL 1970–71, Staff Ops Offr to Sr Naval Offr W Indies 1971–72, Cdr naval staff and head of electronic warfare policy MOD 1972–75, i/c HMS Eskimo 1975–76, DS Maritime Tactical Sch 1976–77; admitted slr 1980; slr Linklaters and Paines 1980–81 (articled clerk 1978–80); ptnr: Wilde Sapte 1982–98, LeBoeuf Lamb Greene & MacRae 1998–2002; chm Dover Harbour Bd 2000– (dir 1998); Freeman: City of London, City of London Solicitors' Co, Worshipful Co of Shipwrights; *Recreations* family, walking, music, reading, languages; *Style—* Robert Dibble, Esq; ✉ Dover Harbour Board, Harbour House, Dover, Kent CT17 9BU (e-mail robert.dibble@doverport.co.uk)

DICK, (John) Antony; s of Cdre John Mathew Dick, CB, CBE (d 1981), and Anne Moir, *née* Stewart; *b* 23 March 1934; *Educ* Trinity Coll Glenalmond, Worcester Coll Oxford (BA); *m* 1, 15 May 1967, Marigold Sylvia, da of Rev Cecil B Verity; 1 s (Crispin b 1971), 2 da (Amy-Clare b 1972, Jasmine b 1974); m 2, 19 Oct 2002, Sarah Jane Goodman; *Career* RN 1952–54; qualified CA 1956; investment mangr: Iraq Petroleum Co Ltd 1961–67, J Henry Schroder Wagg and Co Ltd 1967–68; md Kingsdrive Investment Management Ltd 1969–70, dir GT Management plc 1970–91; non-exec dir: USDC Investment Trust 1987–93, S R Pan European Investment Trust 1987–99, Makepeace Ltd 1988–97, Foreign & Colonial Eurotrust 1989–2004, The Technology Broker Ltd 1990–2000, Hotspur Investments 1993–95, Saracen Value Trust 1993–97, Aquarian Explosion Wall Co 1994–98, Chescor Indian Investment Trust 1994–2000, Invesco Tokyo Trust 1995–2002, St Andrew Trust plc 1998–2000; *Recreations* sailing, psychological astrology; *Style—* Antony Dick, Esq; ✉ 26 Chalcot Square, London NW1 8YA (tel and fax 020 7722 5126); Mill House, Postlip Lodge, Winchcombe, Gloucestershire GL54 5AQ (tel and fax 01242 602098, e-mail antonydick@aol.com)

DICK, Frank William; OBE (1989); s of Frank Dick, of Edinburgh, and Diana May, *née* Sinclair; *b* 1 May 1941; *Educ* Royal HS Edinburgh, Loughborough Coll (DLC), Univ of Oregon (BSc); *m* 1, 1970 (m dis 1977), Margaret Fish; 1 s (Frank Sinclair Shacklock b 3 Oct 1972); m 2, 1980, Linda Elizabeth, da of Frank Brady; 2 da (Erin Emma Louise b 18 July 1981, Cara Charlotte Elizabeth b 18 May 1985); *Career* dep dir of physical educn Worksop Coll 1965–69, nat athletics coach for Scotland 1970–79, dir of coaching Br Athletics Fedn 1979–94 (resigned), coaching conslt 1995–; athletics coach: European Cup 1979–93, Olympic Games 1980–92, European Championships 1982–90, World Championships 1983–93; coach to: Daley Thompson (athletics) 1983–92, Boris Becker (conditioning tennis) 1986–89, Jeff Thompson (conditioning karate) 1986–, Mark MacLean (conditioning squash) 1987–, Gerhard Berger (conditioning Formula One) 1990–, Katarina Witt (conditioning skating) 1991–, Ronnie Irani (cricket) 1998–, Denise Lewis (athletics) 2002–, Justin Rose (golf) 2003–; leadership devpt dir Optical Express 2007–; chm Br Assoc of Nat Coaches 1985–86; pres: Euro Athletics Coaches Assoc 1985–, Br Inst of Sports Coaching 1990–91; memb Bd of Dirs Scottish Inst of Sport 1998–; winner Geoffrey Dyson Award and memb UK Coaches' Hall of Fame 1998, Golden Pin European Athletics Assoc 2003; Hon DTech Loughborough Univ 2003; FBISC 1989; *Books* Sports Training Principles (1980, 1989, 1995, 2002 and 2007), Winning (1992), Winning Lines (2004); *Recreations* music, public speaking, jogging; *Style—* Frank Dick, Esq, OBE; ✉ The Highland, East Hill, Sanderstead, Surrey CR2 0AL (tel 020 8651 4858, fax 020 8657 3247); Rosedale House, Rosedale Road, Richmond, Surrey TW9 2SZ (tel 020 8939 9019, fax 020 8939 9080, e-mail fwd.coaching@btinternet.com)

DICK, Dr Jeremy Peter Rose; s of Peter Dick (d 2001), and Diana, *née* George (d 1983); *b* 29 September 1953; *Educ* Marlborough (exhibitioner), King's Coll Cambridge (exhibitioner, MA), KCH (MB BChir, PhD); *m* 21 Sept 1985, Bridget Mary, da of Roger Gates; 1 s (Andrew b 1988), 2 da (Madeleine b 1989, Catherine b 1994); *Career* SHO Douera Hosp Algeria and house physician St Luke's Hosp Guildford 1977–78, house surgn KCH and SHO St Nicholas Hosp Plumstead 1978–79, SHO Maudsley Hosp, KCH and Brompton Hosp 1979–80, registrar in cardiology Papworth Hosp and in nephrology Addenbrooke's 1980–82, SHO in neurology Nat Hosp 1982–83, res registrar in neurology Maudsley Hosp and KCH 1983–86, registrar in neurology N Manchester Gen Hosp and Manchester Royal Infirmary 1987–89, sr registrar in neurology Charing Cross Hosp 1989–91; conslt in neurology: Royal London, Newham Gen and St Andrew's Hosps 1991–97, Bart's 1994–97, Manchester Royal Infirmary 1997–2001, Withington and Wythenshaw Hosps 1997–, Hope Hosp 2001–; Pfizer prize for res in clinical med Manchester Med Soc 1989; chm NW Regional Training Ctee in neurology 1999–2006, memb RCP: Part II Question Gp 1992– (examiner 1999–, memb Bd 2003); memb: Assoc of Br Neurologists, American Acad of Neurology, RSM (memb Cncl Neurology Section 1994–96); FRCP 1996; *Recreations* squash, golf, skiing; *Clubs* Jesters, Royal Cinque Ports Golf; *Style—* Dr Jeremy Dick; ✉ Department of Neurology, Withington Hospital, Nell Lane, Manchester M20 2LR (tel 0161 291 4320, fax 0161 291 4172, e-mail jeremy@jprd.demon.co.uk)

DICK, Stewart John Cunningham; s of John David Cunningham Dick (d 1990), of Edinburgh, and Jessie Anderson Calder (d 1985); *b* 14 January 1946; *Educ* George Watson's Coll Edinburgh, Univ of Edinburgh (MA, LLB); *m* 12 April 1974, Alison Aileen Mackintosh, *née* Dickson; *Career* Wallace and Sommerville (became Whinney Murray) 1968–72, dir of corp banking Brown, Shipley and Co Ltd 1980–92 (joined 1972), dir and head of banking Ansbacher & Co Ltd 1993–2001, head of int private banking Singer & Friedlander Ltd 2001–06, dir private client finance Arbuthnot Latham & Co Ltd 2006–; non-exec dir Hampshire Trust plc 1993–2001; MICAS 1972; *Recreations* gardening, golf; *Clubs* Caledonian, RAC, MCC; *Style—* Stewart Dick, Esq; ✉ Dunvegan, 2 Oak Park, Old Avenue, West Byfleet, Surrey KT14 6AG (tel 01932 342755); Arbuthnot Latham & Co Limited, Arbuthnot House, 20 Ropemaker Street, London EC2Y 9AR (tel 020 7012 2699)

DICKENS, Barnaby John; s of Archie Bernard Dickens, and June Mary McNeile; *b* 9 June 1954; *Educ* Dulwich Coll, Trinity Coll Cambridge (scholar, MA); *m* 13 Oct 1983, Lucy Anne, da of Sir Oliver Nicholas Millar, GCVO, FBA; 3 s (Roland Oliver Porter b 9 April 1979, Max John Porter b 27 Aug 1981, Archie Dickens b 2 March 1994), 1 da (Marnie Dickens b 13 Nov 1985); *Career* account exec: The Creative Business 1977–78, WS Crawford 1978–79; Public Advertising Cncl LA 1980, account dir Marsteller 1984 (account mangr 1981), Bd account dir GGK London 1986–92, md Crammond Dickens Lerner 1993–; *Style—* Barnaby Dickens, Esq; ✉ Crammond Dickens Lerner & Partners Ltd, 1 Earlham Street, London WC2H 9LL (tel 020 7240 8100)

DICKETTS, Simon Charles Hedley; s of Brian John Dicketts, of Glastonbury, Somerset, and Daphne Francis, *née* Little; *b* 13 September 1954; *Educ* Corchester Sch Corbridge Northumberland, St Edward's Sch Oxford; *Career* porter Christie's auctioneers 1975, employed at J Walter Thompson 1976–80; Saatchi & Saatchi: joined as copywriter 1985, creative gp head 1985–92, jt creative dir 1992–95 (resigned); M&C Saatchi: founding memb and creative dir 1995–2002, exec creative dir 2002–; awards incl: 3 Gold Lions Cannes Film Advtg Awards, 13 Campaign Press Silver Awards; memb D&AD; *Recreations* food, wine, bridge, tennis, snooker; *Clubs* Soho House; *Style—* Simon Dicketts, Esq; ✉ M&C Saatchi Ltd, 34–36 Golden Square, London W1R 4EE (tel 020 7543 4500, fax 020 7543 4501)

DICKIE, John; s of John Dickie (d 1977), and Gladys, *née* O'Neil (d 2000); *b* 31 August 1965, Glasgow; *Educ* Morecambe HS, Worcester Coll Oxford (BA), London Business Sch (MBA); *m* July 1991, Sue, *née* Grunstein; 1 s (Jack b 1998), 1 da (Eve b 2000); *Career* Swiss Bank Corp 1987–88, public policy conslt Prima Europe 1988–98 (md 1997–98), md GPC Market Access London 1997–98, head Int Regulatory Practice GPC Int 1998–2000, regulatory affrs dir European Competitive Telecommunications Assoc (ECTA) 2000–03, head Political and Parly Affrs BBC 2003–, head corporate affrs BBC 2006–; cncllr Camden BC 1994–2003 (dep leader 2000–03); chair Go Neighbourhood Mgmnt Pathfinder; *Recreations* reading, keeping fit, cinema, opera; *Clubs* Reform; *Style—* John Dickie, Esq; ✉ BBC Media Centre, White City, 201 Wood Lane, London W12 7TQ (tel 020 8008 2896, fax 020 8008 2130, e-mail john.dickie@bbc.co.uk)

DICKIE, Dr Nigel Hugh; s of John Dickie, OBE, of Oxshott, Surrey, and Inez Campbell, *née* White; *b* 4 October 1956; *Educ* KCS Wimbledon, Queen Elizabeth Coll London (BSc, The Copping Prize in Nutrition, PhD); *m* 24 Aug 1986, Alison Susan May, da of John Michael Duffin; 2 s (Andrew James John b 27 Feb 1988, Alexander Stuart b 8 Oct 1990); *Career* nutritionist Van den Berghs and Jurgens Ltd 1982–83, conslt nutritionist Slimming Magazine, Slimming Magazine Clubs and various leading food companies 1983–85, md Counsel PR co (formerly Holmes & Marchant Counsel Gp) 1992–2005 (dir 1985), exec dir Huntsworth Gp Ltd 2001–05, dir corp and govt affrs H J Heinz Co Ltd 2005–; Freeman City of London 1989; memb Nutrition Soc 1978; registered nutritionist (RNutr) 2000; FRSH 1991, FIFST 1991, MCIPR (MIPR 1991), CSci 2004; *Recreations* good food and wine, family and home; *Style—* Dr Nigel Dickie; ✉ H J Heinz Company Limited, South Building, Hayes Park, Hayes, Middlesex UB4 8AL (tel 020 8573 7757)

DICKIE, Robert Stewart; s of Robert Dickie, of Hamilton, Strathclyde, and Helen, *née* Hutton; *b* 31 October 1959, Glasgow; *Educ* Hamilton GS, Strathclyde Grad Business Sch Glasgow (MBA); *m* 20 Aug 1982, Karen; 4 s (Cameron b 23 Feb 1986, Jonathan b 3 Dec 1987, Matthew b 23 May 1990, Gregor b 1 June 1995); *Career* various retail banking roles Clydesdale Bank plc 1976–97, on secondment Nat Australia Bank Gp Melbourne 1993–97, head of ops and customer services and head of direct and channel mgmnt Nat Australia Gp (Europe) 1997–2000, md (UK enterprise) Zurich Financial Services (UKISA) Ltd 2000–02, gp ops dir Braford & Bingley plc 2003–; Scottish Young Banker of the Year 1991; FCIBS 1994 (ACIBS 1984, memb Cncl), FRSA 2004; *Recreations* hill walking, rugby union, reading; *Style—* Robert Dickie, Esq; ✉ Bradford & Bingley plc, PO Box 88, Croft Road, Crossflatts, West Yorkshire BD16 2UA (tel 01274 806911, fax 01274 551022, e-mail robert.dickie@bbg.co.uk)

DICKINS, Julian Grahame; s of Grahame John Dickins, of Newbury, Berks, and Claire Daisy, *née* Myers; *b* 31 December 1957; *Educ* St Bartholomew's Sch Newbury, Univ of Southampton (LLB), Coll of Law Guildford; *m* 1997, Ellie, da of Ian and Lesley Hickling; *Career* admitted slr 1983; ptnr: Penningtons 1986–96 (joined 1983), Dickins Hopgood Chidley LLP 1996–; sec: PCC St Michael's and All Angels Church Enborne Berks, Law Soc 1983; *Recreations* amateur dramatics, travelling, skiing, piano; *Clubs* Rotary; *Style—* Julian Dickins, Esq; ✉ Dickins Hopgood Chidley, The Old School House, 42 High Street, Hungerford RG17 0NF (tel 01488 683555, fax 01488 681919, e-mail jdickins@dhc-solicitors.co.uk)

DICKINSON, (Paul) Bruce; s of Bruce Dickinson, of Aachen, Germany, and Sonja, *née* Hartley; *b* 7 August 1958; *Educ* Oundle, King Edward VII GS Sheffield, QMC London (BA); *m* 1, 1984 (m dis 1987), Jane Barnett; m 2, Paddy Bowden, da of late Col Walter

Bowden, of USA; 2 s (Austin Matthew, Griffin Michael), 1 da (Kia Michelle); *Career* singer, songwriter, broadcaster and author; first professional group Samson: joined 1979, left 1981; Iron Maiden: joined 1981, left 1993, rejoined 1999; 5 solo albums; currently radio presenter BBC 6 Music; winner Silver Sony Radio Award 1994; charity involvements incl: Prince's Tst ambass, NSPCC, Make A Wish Fndn USA, Rock Aid Armenia; qualified nat fencing referee and amateur coach, ranked no 7 in UK 1989; *Books* The Adventures of Lord Iffy Boatrace (1990), The Missionary Position (1992); *Recreations* flying, fencing, railways; *Style*— Bruce Dickinson, Esq; ✉ c/o The Sanctuary Group plc, Sanctuary House, 43–45 Sinclair Road, London W14 0NS (tel 020 7602 6351)

DICKINSON, Prof Harry Thomas; s of Joseph Dickinson (d 1979), and Elizabeth Stearman, *née* Warriner (d 1979); *b* 9 March 1939; *Educ* Gateshead GS, Univ of Durham (BA, DipEd, MA), Univ of Newcastle upon Tyne (PhD), Univ of Edinburgh (DLitt); *m* 26 Aug 1961, Jennifer Elizabeth, da of Albert Galtry, of Kilham, E Yorks; 1 s (Mark James b 1967), 1 da (Anna Elizabeth b 1972); *Career* Earl Grey fell Univ of Newcastle upon Tyne 1964–66; Univ of Edinburgh: asst lectr 1966–68, lectr 1968–73, reader 1973–80, prof of Br history 1980–; concurrent prof of history Nanjing Univ China 1987–, Douglas Southall Freeman prof Richmond Univ USA 1997; author of many historical essays and articles, ed History 1993–2000; FRHistS, FRSE 1998; *Books* The Correspondence of Sir James Clavering (1967), Bolingbroke (1970), Walpole and the Whig Supremacy (1973), Politics and Literature in the Eighteenth Century (1974), Liberty and Property (1977), Political Works of Thomas Spence (1982), British Radicalism and the French Revolution (1985), Caricatures and the Constitution (1986), Britain and the French Revolution (1989), The Politics of the People in Eighteenth-Century Britain (1995), Britain and the American Revolution (1998), The Challenge to Westminster (with M Lynch, 2000), The Blackwell Companion to Eighteenth-Century Britain (2002), Constitutional Documents of the United Kingdom 1782–1835 (2005), Reactions to Revolutions (jtly, 2007), British Pamphlets on the American Revolution (4 vols, 2007); *Style*— Prof Harry Dickinson, FRSE; ✉ 44 Viewforth Terrace, Edinburgh EH10 4LJ (tel 0131 229 1379); History Department, University of Edinburgh, Edinburgh EH8 9JY (tel 0131 650 3785, fax 0131 650 3784, e-mail harry.dickinson@ed.ac.uk)

DICKINSON, Prof John Philip; s of George Snowden Dickinson (d 1974), of Morecambe, and Evelyn, *née* Stobbart; *b* 29 April 1945; *Educ* Univ of Cambridge (MA), Univ of Leeds (MSc, PhD); *m* 17 Feb 1968, Christine, da of Maurice Houghton (d 1980), of Morecambe; 1 s (Anthony), 2 da (Rachel, Vanessa); *Career* lectr: Univ of Leeds 1968–71, Lancaster Univ 1971–75; sr lectr: Univ of Western Aust 1975–80, Univ of Dundee 1980–81; prof of accounting Univ of Stirling 1981–85; Univ of Glasgow: prof of accounting and fin 1985, head Dept of Accounting and Fin 1987–91, dir Glasgow Business Sch 1987–89, dean Faculty of Law and Fin Studies 1989–92; princ King Alfred's Coll Winchester 1992–2001, hon prof Univ of Southampton 2000–; chm Br Accounting Assoc 1994–95; dir and tstee National Autistic Soc 2002– (nat cncllr 2000–), gen sec Autism Europe 2004–, tstee Research Autism 2005–; dist organiser Christian Aid 1989–92; FASA CPA 1976, FIMgt 1980, FRSA 1980, FCIS 1992 (ACIS 1976); *Books* Portfolio Analysis (1974), Risk and Uncertainty in Accounting and Finance (1974), Statistics for Business Finance and Accounting (1976), Portfolio Analysis and Capital Markets (1976), Management Accounting: An Introduction (1988), Statistical Analysis in Accounting and Finance (1990); *Recreations* photography, travel, languages, poetry; *Style*— Prof John Dickinson; ✉ Swans Mead, Haverbreaks Road, Lancaster LA1 5BJ (tel 01524 68792, e-mail swansmead@hotmail.com)

DICKINSON, Lorna; MVO (2002); da of Michael Eugene Dickinson, and Barbara, *née* Benfield; *b* 20 December 1958; *Educ* Univ of Warwick (BA); *m* 4 June 1983, Michael Ingham, BBC football corr; 1 s (Marshall Quincy Ingham b 7 Aug 1993); *Career* TV prodr; credits incl: A Royal Celebration in Honour of HRH the Prince of Wales 50th Birthday, An Audience with Elton John, An Audience with Rod Stewart, An Audience with Ken Dodd, An Audience with Billy Connolly, Robin Williams in the Wild with Dolphins, Goldie Hawn in the Wild with Elephants, The Trouble with Michael Caine, 30 Years of James Bond, The Full Wax, Page Three, Aspel and Company, Schofield in Hawaii, Two Rooms - A Celebration of the Songs of Elton John and Bernie Taupin, The World According to Smith and Jones, Clive James meets Katharine Hepburn, The Dame Edna Experience; *Awards* BAFTA Awards 1994 and 1996, Gold Award NY Int Film Festival & TV Festival; *Style*— Ms Lorna Dickinson, MVO; ✉ Original Productions (tel 079 6636 2792)

DICKINSON, Mark; s of Stanley Park Dickinson, and Beatrice Joan Dickinson; *b* 20 January 1951; *Educ* Dame Alice Owen Sch, Univ of Manchester (BA); *m* Pauline; 2 da (Emily b 1982, Megan b 1985), 2 s (Samuel (twin) b 1985, Josiah b 1990); *Career* trainee Macmillan Journals 1974–76, ed New Manchester Review 1976–81, sub ed and TV writer Daily Telegraph 1976–86, author 1986–88, asst chief sub ed Evening Leader (Wrexham) 1988–89, chief sub ed Tonight (Chester) 1989–90, chief sub ed Evening Express (Aberdeen) 1991–92, asst ed The Journal (Newcastle) 1992–93, dep ed-in-chief Chronicle Newspapers 1993–96, ed The Journal (Newcastle) 1996–2000, ed Liverpool Echo 2000–05, ed-in-chief Trinity Mirror NW and N Wales, editorial dir Trinity Mirror Midlands 2005–; memb Guild of Eds; *Publications* The Manchester Book, Goodbye Piccadilly; *Recreations* football, rugby, golf, tennis, wine and food, countryside; *Style*— Mark Dickinson, Esq; ✉ Birmingham Post & Mail, Weaman Street, Birmingham B4 6AT (e-mail rina_chaukar@mrn.co.uk)

DICKINSON, Patric Laurence; LVO (2006); s of John Laurence Dickinson (d 2003), and April Katherine, *née* Forgan (d 1998); *b* 24 November 1950; *Educ* Marling Sch, Exeter Coll Oxford (MA, pres Oxford Union); *Career* res asst Coll of Arms 1968–78, Rouge Dragon Pursuivant of Arms 1978–89, Richmond Herald 1989–, treas Coll of Arms 1995–, Earl Marshal's sec 1996–, sec Order of the Garter 2004–; called to the Bar Middle Temple 1979; hon treas: English Genealogical Congress 1975–91, Bar Theatrical Soc 1978–; hon sec and registrar Br Record Soc 1979–; pres: Bristol and Glos Archaeological Soc 1998–99, Soc of Genealogists 2005– (vice-pres 1997–2005); vice-pres Assoc of Genealogists and Researchers in Archives (AGRA) 1988–; chm Anthony Powell Soc 2003–07; FSG 2000; *Recreations* music, cycling, swimming, walking, talking, attending memorial services; *Clubs* Brooks's; *Style*— P L Dickinson, Esq, LVO; ✉ College of Arms, Queen Victoria Street, London EC4V 4BT (tel 020 7236 9612); 13 Old Square, Lincoln's Inn, London WC2A 3UA

DICKINSON, Prof Peter; s of Frank Dickinson (d 1978), and Muriel, *née* Porter (d 2003); *b* 15 November 1934; *Educ* The Leys Sch Cambridge, Queens' Coll Cambridge (MA), Juilliard Sch of Music NY, Univ of London (DMus); *m* 29 July 1964, Bridget Jane, da of Lt Cdr Edward Philip Tomkinson, DSO (ka 1942); 2 s (Jasper b 1968, Francis b 1971); *Career* composer, pianist and writer; recorded works incl: piano concerto and organ concerto, Outcry, Mass of the Apocalypse, The Unicorns, Rags, Blues and Parodies, Songcycles, Surrealist Landscape, American Trio, Sonatas; pianist; recorded works largely with sister Meriel Dickinson (mezzo); academic posts incl: prof Keele Univ 1974–84 (now emeritus), prof of music Goldsmiths Coll London 1991–97 (now emeritus), head of music Inst of US Studies Univ of London 1997–2004; numerous contribs to books periodicals and BBC radio; memb Bd Trinity Coll of Music 1984–98; tstee: Bernarr Rainbow Tst, Berners Tst; memb: Soc for American Music, RSM, RMA; Hon DMus Keele Univ 1999; LRAM, ARCM, FRCO, FRSA, Hon FTCL; *Books* Twenty British Composers (ed, 1975), The Music of Lennox Berkeley (1989, 2 edn 2003), Marigold: the

Music of Billy Mayerl (1999), Copland Connotations: Studies and Interviews (ed, 2002), CageTalk: Dialogues with and about John Cage (2006), Lord Berners: Portrait of a Polymath (2008); *Recreations* rare books; *Clubs* Garrick; *Style*— Prof Peter Dickinson; ✉ c/o Novello and Co Ltd, 14–15 Berners Street, London W1T 3LJ

DICKINSON, Hon Peter Malcolm de Brissac; s of Hon Richard Sebastian Willoughby Dickinson, DSO (s of 1 Baron Dickinson); raised to the rank of a Baron's s 1944; *b* 16 December 1927; *Educ* Eton, King's Coll Cambridge; *m* 1, 25 April 1953, Mary Rose (d 1988), elder da of Vice Adm Sir Geoffrey Barnard, KCB, CBE, DSO, of Bramdean, Hants; 2 da (Philippa Lucy Ann b 1955, Polly b 1956), 2 s (John Geoffrey Hyett b 1962, James Christopher Meade b 1963); *m* 2, 3 Jan 1992, J C Robin McKinley, of Blue Hill, ME; *Career* author; asst editor Punch 1952–69; chm Mgmnt Ctee Soc of Authors 1978–80; has published numerous children's books and detective novels; FRSL 1999; *Style*— The Hon Peter Dickinson; ✉ 1 Arlebury Park Mews, The Avenue, Alresford, Hampshire SO24 9ER

DICKINSON, 2 Baron (UK 1930); Richard Clavering Hyett Dickinson; s of Hon Richard Sebastian Willoughby Dickinson, DSO (d 1935) and gs of 1 Baron (d 1943); *b* 2 March 1926; *Educ* Eton, Trinity Coll Oxford; *m* 1, 1957 (m dis), (Margaret) Ann, da of Brig Gilbert R McMeekan, CB, DSO, OBE, JP (d 1982); 2 s; *m* 2, 1980, Rita Doreen Moir; *Heir* s, Hon Martin Dickinson; *Style*— The Rt Hon Lord Dickinson; ✉ The Stables, Gloucester Road, Painswick GL6 6TH

DICKINSON, Robert Henry; CBE (1998), DL (Northumberland 1999); s of Robert Joicey Dickinson (d 1981), and Alice Penelope, *née* Barnett (d 1985); *b* 12 May 1934; *Educ* Harrow, ChCh Oxford (MA); *m* 3 Aug 1963, Kyra Irina, da of Laurence Boissevain; 1 s (Robert Alexander b 23 June 1964), 2 da (Emma b 19 March 1967, Laura b 23 May 1970); *Career* admitted as slr 1960; sr ptnr Dickinson Dees Slrs until 1997; chm: Northern Rock plc (formerly Northern Rock Building Society) until 1999, Grainger Trust plc until 2007, Northern Investors plc until 2006, Aon-Minet Group Pension & Life Assurance Scheme; *Clubs* Boodle's, Pratt's, Beefsteak, Northern Counties; *Style*— Robert Dickinson, Esq, CBE, DL; ✉ Styford Hall, Stocksfield-on-Tyne, Northumberland NE43 7TX; Grainger plc, St James' Boulevard, Newcastle upon Tyne NE1 4JE (tel 0191 261 1819, fax 0191 269 5901)

DICKINSON, Simon Clervaux; s of Peter Dickinson, of Northumberland, and Anne, *née* Chayter; *b* 26 October 1948; *Educ* Aysgarth Sch, Harrow (art scholar, first cricket and football XIs); *m* Hon Jessica, da of 2 Baron Mancroft (d 1987); 2 da (Phoebe Victoria b 27 Sept 1984, Octavia Jessica b 18 Feb 1986), 1 s (Milo Clervaux Mancroft b 28 June 1989); *Career* art dealer; Christies: joined 1968, dir 1974–93, sr picture dir 1990–93; chm Simon C Dickinson Ltd and Simon Dickinson Inc 1993–; paintings discovered/re-discovered incl: Titian's Portrait of Giacomo Delfino 1977 (last previously recorded in 16th century), Watteau's Allegory of Spring 1983, Van Dyck's Portrait of Ann Carr 1983, Constable sketch for The Young Waltonians 1984, Guido Reni's Portrait of St James the Greater 1988, Claude Landscape 1989, Titian's Venus and Adonis 1991 (subsequently sold to Getty Museum for £7.5m), Hendrick Goltzius' The Crucifixion 1991 (missing since 1604), Guido Reni self-portrait 1992, Botticelli's Virgin Adoring The Christ Child 1999 (subsequently sold to the National Galleries of Scotland); *Recreations* gardening, shooting, fishing, tennis, golf; *Clubs* White's, Boodle's; *Style*— Simon Dickinson, Esq; ✉ Simon C Dickinson Ltd, 58 Jermyn Street, London SW1Y 6LX (tel 020 7493 0340, fax 020 7493 0796, e-mail simon@simondickinson.com)

DICKINSON, Stephen; s of Rev Arthur Edward Dickinson (d 1989), and Ada Violet, *née* Hickey (d 1972); *b* 12 October 1934; *Educ* Aysgarth, St Edward's Sch Oxford, King's Coll Newcastle, Univ of Durham (BA); *m* 23 March 1968, Mary Elisabeth, da of Maj Richard Quintin Gurney (d 1980), of Bawdeswell Hall, East Dereham, Norfolk; 2 s (Michael Edward b July 1969, James Stephen b May 1971); *Career* Nat Serv Flying Offr RAF 1957–59; CA 1962; CA Br Virgin Islands 1963–74; Grainger Trust plc: md 1974–2002, dep chm 2002–; chm Deutsche Land plc 2006–; former Br Virgin Islands rep UK Overseas Territories Assoc 1993–2004; *Recreations* field sports, cricket, golf; *Clubs* White's, Northern Counties, RAF; *Style*— Stephen Dickinson, Esq; ✉ Crow Hall, Bardon Mill, Hexham, Northumberland NE47 7BJ (tel 01434 344495, fax 01434 344115); Grainger Trust plc, Citygate, St James' Boulevard, Newcastle upon Tyne NE1 4JE (tel 0191 261 1819, fax 0191 269 5901)

DICKSON, Prof James Holms; s of Peter Dickson (d 1973), and Jean, *née* Holms (d 1951); *b* 29 April 1937; *Educ* Bellahouston Acad Glasgow, Univ of Glasgow (BSc), Univ of Cambridge (MA, PhD); *m* 6 June 1964, Camilla Ada (d 1998), da of George Bruce Lambert (d 1970); 1 s (Peter b 1965), 1 da (Kate b 1968); *Career* fell (former res fell) Clare Coll Cambridge 1963–70, sr res asst Univ of Cambridge 1961–70; Univ of Glasgow: joined as lectr in botany 1970, later sr lectr, reader in botany, prof of archaeobotany and plant systematics until 2002 (ret), currently hon sr res fell; botanist Royal Soc expedition to Tristan da Cunha 1961, ldr Trades House of Glasgow expedition to Papua New Guinea 1987; investigator of bryophytes found with Tyrolean Iceman 1994–, investigator of plants found with Br Columbian Iceman 2000–; pres: Nat History Soc Glasgow, Botanical Soc Scotland; conslt to Britoil Exhibition Glasgow Garden Festival 1988; Leverhulme Tst emeritus fell (archaeobiology of ancient icemen) 2006–07; FLS 1964, FRSE 1993 (Neill Medal 1995); *Books* Bryophytes of the Pleistocene (1973), Wild Plants of Glasgow (1991), A Naturalist in the Highlands - James Robertson and his Life and Travels in Scotland (with Prof Douglas Henderson, 1994), The Changing Flora of Glasgow (with P Macpherson and K J Watson, 2000), Plants and People in Ancient Scotland (with Camilla Dickson, 2000); *Recreations* gardening; *Style*— Prof James Dickson, FRSE; ✉ 113 Clober Road, Milngavie, Glasgow (tel 0141 577 9533); Department of Environmental and Evolutionary Biology, University of Glasgow (tel 0141 330 4297, fax 0141 330 5971, e-mail j.dickson@bio.gla.ac.uk)

DICKSON, Dr Jennifer; da of John Liston Dickson (d 1975), of Cape Town, South Africa, and Margaret Joan, *née* Turner (d 1980); *b* 17 September 1936; *Educ* Eunice HS for Girls Bloemfontein, Goldsmiths Coll Sch of Art London, Atelier 17 Paris; *m* 13 April 1961, Ronald Andrew Sweetman; 1 s (William David (Bill) b 17 Aug 1965); *Career* artist, photographer, garden historian; teacher Eastbourne Sch of Art 1959–62, directed and developed Printmaking Dept Brighton Coll of Art 1962–68, graphics atelier Saidye Bronfman Centre Montreal 1970–72; sessional instr: Concordia Univ Montreal 1972–79, Université d'Ottawa 1980–85; head Dept of Art History Saidye Bronfman Centre Montreal 1985–88; visiting artist: Ball State Univ 1967, Univ of WI 1968, Univ of Wisconsin 1972, Ohio State Univ 1973, W Illinois Univ 1973, Haystack Mountain Sch of Crafts Maine 1973, Queen's Univ 1977–78; subject of CBC Special TV progs 1980, 1982, 1990 and 1995; fndr memb: Br Printmakers' Cncl, Print and Drawing Cncl Canada; Hon LLD Univ of Alberta 1988; fell Royal Soc of Painter-Etchers & Engravers, RA 1976 (ARA 1971), CM 1995; *Exhibitions* incl: The Secret Garden 1975, The Earthly Paradise 1980 and 1981, The Last Silence (Canadian Museum of Contemporary Photography) 1993 and on tour 1995; *Public Collections* incl: Nat Gallery of Canada Ottawa, Nat Film Bd of Canada, Metropolitan Museum NY, V&A London, The Hermitage Museum St Petersburg, Bibliothèque Nationale Paris; *Awards* incl: Prix de Jeunes Artistes pour Gravure Biennale de Paris 1963, Special Purchase Award World Print Competition (San Francisco Museum of Art) 1974, Biennale Prize 5th Norwegian Int Print Biennale 1980, Victor Tolgesy Award for the Arts Cncl for the Arts Ottawa 2002; *Books* The Hospital for Wounded Angels (1988), The Royal Academy Gardener's Journal (1991); *Recreations* opera, film, visiting gardens; *Style*— Dr Jennifer Dickson, CM, RA; ✉ 20 Osborne Street,

Ottawa, Ontario K1S 4Z9, Canada (tel 00 1 613 730 2083, fax 00 1 613 730 1818, studio tel 00 1 613 233 2315); Wallack Galleries, 203 Bank Street, Ottawa, Ontario K2P 1W7, Canada (tel 00 1 613 235 4339, fax 00 1 613 235 0102)

DICKSON, Jeremy David Fane; s of Lt-Col J D L Dickson, MC (d 1959), and Elizabeth Daphne, *née* Fane (d 2002); *b* 23 June 1941; *Educ* Marlborough, Emmanuel Coll Cambridge (MA); *m* 9 Oct 1965 (m dis 2002), Patricia, da of Laurence Cleveland Martin (d 1980); 1 s (James David Laurence b 30 Jan 1970), 1 da (Lucy Camilla b 25 June 1971); *Career* ptnr PricewaterhouseCoopers (formerly Coopers & Lybrand and Deloitte Haskins & Sells before mergers) 1977–2000 (ret); FCA; *Recreations* cricket, shooting, philately; *Clubs* MCC; *Style*— Jeremy Dickson, Esq

DICKSON, Michael Douglas (Mike); s of Dr (William) Powell Greenlie Dickson (d 1986), of Lancaster, and Muriel Constance, *née* MacKinnon; *b* 25 January 1948; *Educ* Sedbergh, Coll for Distributive Trades London (HNC Business Studies); *m* 30 Aug 1986, Elizabeth Anne, da of Graham George Giles; 2 s (Edward Alexander Dickson b 4 Sept 1987, William George Dickson b 20 June 1989); *Career* KMP Partnership advtg agency London 1967–71, broadcaster Radio Hong Kong 1971, Lintas London 1972–76, TBWA 1976–80, dep md Astral Advertising 1980–82, dir Aspect Advertising 1982–85, ptnr Edwards Martin Thornton 1985–88, mgmnt bd dir D'Arcy 1988–; memb Mktg Soc 1980; *Publications* Marketing: Communicating with the Consumer (contrib, 1992); *Recreations* sailing (former vice-chm Sigma Class Assoc); *Clubs* Royal Ocean Racing; *Style*— Mike Dickson, Esq; ✉ D'Arcy, Warwick Building, Kensington Village, Avonmore Road, London W14 8HQ (tel 020 7071 2052, fax 020 7071 1024, mobile 07768 448443, e-mail mike.dickson@darcyww.co.uk)

DICKSON, Niall Forbes Ross; s of Sheriff Ian Anderson Dickson (d 1982), and Margaret Forbes, *née* Ross (d 1981); *b* 5 November 1953; *Educ* Glasgow Acad, Edinburgh Acad, Univ of Edinburgh (MA, DipEd), Moray House Coll (CertEd); *m* 1979, Elizabeth Selina, da of James Mercer Taggart, of Lisburn, Co Antrim; 2 da (Jennifer Margaret b 1982, Julia Amy Victoria b 1987), 1 s (Andrew James Ross b 1984); *Career* teacher Broughton HS Edinburgh 1976–78, publicity offr National Corporation for the Care of Old People 1978–79, head of publishing Age Concern England 1980–82 (press offr 1979–80); ed: Therapy Weekly 1982–83, Nursing Times 1983–88; BBC: health corr 1988–90, chief social affairs corr 1990–95, social affrs ed 1995–2004; chief exec The King's Fund 2004–; chm: Dept of Health Direct Payments Steering Gp 2004–06, Dept of Health Individual Budgets Reference Gp; memb: NHS Modernisation Bd 2004–05, NHS Leadership Network 2004–, Sec of State for Health's Sounding Bd 2006–; visiting fell Office for Public Mgmnt 1994–2004; winner Business and Professional Periodical of the Year Award 1985 and 1988, Charles Fletcher Medical Broadcaster of the Year Award 1997; hon fell: Univ of Cardiff 2006, Inst of Educn Univ of London 2007; Hon FRCP 2007; *Books* Ageing in the 80's - What Prospects for the Elderly? (1981); *Recreations* tennis, golf; *Clubs* Reform,Golf House (Elie) Hever Castle; *Style*— Niall Dickson, Esq; ✉ The King's Fund, 11–13 Cavendish Square, London W1G 0AN (tel 020 7307 2487, fax 020 7307 2803, e-mail n.dickson@kingsfund.org.uk)

DICKSON, Prof Peter George Muir; s of William Muir Dickson (d 1956), of London, and Regina, *née* Dowdall-Nicolls (d 1968); *b* 26 April 1929; *Educ* St Paul's, Worcester Coll Oxford (MA, DPhil, DLitt); *m* 27 Oct 1964, Ariane Flore, da of Ennemond Raoul Marie Faye, of Clifton Down, Bristol; 1 da (Olimpia b 1975); *Career* res fell Nuffield Coll Oxford 1954–56, tutor St Catherine's Soc Oxford 1956–60, fell St Catherine's Coll Oxford 1960–; Univ of Oxford: reader in modern history 1978–89, prof of early modern history 1989–96, emeritus prof 1996; FBA 1988, FRHistS 1970; *Books* The Sun Insurance Office 1710–1960 (1960), The Financial Revolution in England 1688–1756 (1967, 2 edn 1993), Finance and Government under Maria Theresia 1740–1780 (1987); *Recreations* tennis, swimming, cinema, art; *Style*— Prof P G M Dickson, FBA; ✉ Field House, Iffley, Oxford OX4 4EG (tel 01865 779599); St Catherine's College, Oxford OX1 3UJ (tel 01865 271700)

DICKSON, Sheriff Robert Hamish; WS (1969); s of Sheriff Ian Anderson Dickson, WS (d 1982), of Glasgow, and Margaret Forbes, *née* Ross (d 1981); *b* 19 October 1945; *Educ* Glasgow Acad, Drumtochty Castle, Glenalmond Coll, Univ of Glasgow (LLB); *m* 12 Aug 1976, Janet Laird (d 2004), da of Alexander Campbell (d 1987), of Port of Menteith; 1 s (Graeme Ross Campbell b 13 Nov 1977); *Career* legal asst Edinburgh 1969–71, ptnr Brown Mair Gemmill & Hislop Solicitors 1973–86 (joined 1971), Sheriff of S Strathclyde, Dumfries and Galloway at Airdrie 1988– (floating Sheriff 1986–88); pres Sheriffs Assoc 2006; *Books* Medical and Dental Negligence (1997); also author of various articles on med legal matters; *Recreations* golf, music, reading; *Clubs* Royal & Ancient, Elie Golf (capt 1997–99); *Style*— Sheriff Robert Dickson, WS; ✉ Airdrie Sheriff Court, Graham Street, Airdrie ML6 6EE (tel 01236 751121, fax 01236 747497)

DIDSBURY, (Michael) Peter Townley; s of William Didsbury (d 1975), and Edith Pomfrett, *née* Brown (d 1995); *b* 10 April 1946; *Educ* Hymers Coll Hull, Balliol Coll Oxford (Elton exhibitioner), Univ of Durham (MPhil); *m* Patricia Ann, da of Leonard Cooley; 1 da (Sarah Louise b 10 June 1983); *Career* schoolmaster Humberside Educn Authy 1974–80, archaeologist Humberside CC Archaeology Unit 1987–96, freelance archaeological conslt 1996–; *Books* The Butchers of Hull (1982), The Classical Farm (1987), That Old-Time Religion (1994), Scenes from a Long Sleep: New and Collected Poems (2003); *Awards* Poetry Book Soc Recommendation for The Classical Farm 1987 and for That Old-Time Religion 1994, The Cholmondeley Award for Poetry 1989; *Style*— Peter Didsbury, Esq; ✉ 4 Victoria Avenue, Princes Avenue, Hull HU5 3DR; c/o Bloodaxe Books, PO Box 1SN, Newcastle upon Tyne NE99 1SN

DIEHL, His Hon Judge John Bertram Stuart; QC (1987); s of late Ernest Henry Stuart Diehl, and Caroline Pentreath *née* Lumsdaine; *b* 18 April 1944; *Educ* Bishop Gore Sch Swansea, UCW Aberystwyth (LLB); *m* 29 July 1967, Patricia; 2 s (Robert b 1973, Stephen b 1975); *Career* asst lectr and lectr Univ of Sheffield 1965–69; called to the Bar Lincoln's Inn 1968; recorder 1984, circuit judge (Wales & Chester Circuit) 1990–, hon recorder Swansea 2001–; *Recreations* golf, gardening, walking; *Clubs* Bristol Channel Yacht; *Style*— His Hon Judge J B S Diehl, QC; ✉ The Law Courts, St Helens Road, Swansea, SA1 4PF (tel 01792 637000)

DIEPPE, Prof Paul; *b* 20 May 1946; *Educ* Caterham Sch, St Bartholomew's Hosp London; *m* 14 Aug 1971, Elizabeth Anne; 2 da (Clare Rachel b 29 April 1974, Victoria Louise b 30 April 1977); *Career* registrar Guy's Hosp 1973–74, sr registrar Bart's 1976–78 (res fell 1974–76); Univ of Bristol: sr lectr in med 1978–86, ARC prof of rheumatology 1987–, dean Faculty of Med 1995–97; dir MRC Health Services Res Collaboration (HSRC) 1997–; FRCP 1983; *Books* Crystals and Joint Disease (1983), Rheumatological Medicine (1985), Slide Atlas of Rheumatology (1985), Arthritis (1988), Rheumatology (1993, 2 edn 1998); *Recreations* sailing, cycling, reading novels; *Style*— Prof Paul Dieppe; ✉ MRC HSRC, Department of Social Medicine, University of Bristol, Canynge Hall, Whiteladies Road, Bristol BS8 2PR (tel 0117 928 7343, fax 0117 928 7236)

DIERDEN, Kenneth Norman (Ken); s of Norman William Dierden (d 1984), of Havant, and Marjorie Harvey, *née* Nicholas; *b* 26 February 1952; *Educ* Bancroft's Sch Woodford Green, Univ of Southampton (BA); *Children* 1 da (Isabella b 1988); *Career* Freshfields Slrs 1980– (ptnr 1987–); chm Assoc of Pension Lawyers 1995–97; memb Worshipful Co of Slrs; memb Law Soc; CTA; *Books* Tolley's Company Law (contrib, 1988), Tolley's Director's Handbook (contrib, 1990), The Guide to the Pensions Act 1995 (ed, 1995); *Recreations* cycling; *Style*— Kenneth Dierden, Esq; ✉ Freshfields Bruckhaus Deringer, 65 Fleet Street, London EC4Y 1HS (tel 020 7936 4000, fax 020 7832 7001)

DIGBY, 12 Baron (I 1620 and GB 1765); Sir Edward Henry Kenelm Digby; KCVO (1999), JP (1959); s of 11 Baron Digby, KG, DSO, MC (d 1964), and Hon Pamela, *née* Bruce (d 1978), da of 2 Baron Aberdare; bro-in-law of late Averell Harriman; *b* 24 July 1924; *Educ* Eton, Trinity Coll Oxford, RMC; *m* 18 Dec 1952, Dione Marian, yr da of Rear Adm Robert St Vincent Sherbrooke, VC, CB, DSO; 2 s (Hon Henry Noel Kenelm b 1954, Hon Rupert Simon b 1956), 1 da (Hon Zara Jane (Hon Mrs Percy) b 1958); *Heir* s, Hon Henry Digby; *Career* Capt Coldstream Gds 1947, ADC to C-in-C Far E Land Forces 1950–51; Hon Col 4 Bn Devonshire and Dorset Regt 1992–96; dir: Beazer plc 1983–91, Gifford Hill (Dallas) Inc 1986–91, Paccar (UK) Ltd 1990–96; memb Dorchester RDC 1962, cncllr Dorset CC 1966–81 (vice-chm 1974–81); pres: Royal Bath and W Soc 1976, Wessex Branch IOD 1982–98, Dorset SSAFA - Forces Help 1984–99, Cncl St John for Dorset 1984–99, Relate (Dorset) 1989–99, Eastern Wessex TAVRA 1993–96; chm RAS of the Cwlth 1967–79, dep chm SW Econ Planning Cncl 1972–79, chm Dorset Magistrates' Courts Ctee 1984–96; HM Lord-Lt Dorset 1984–99 (DL 1957, Vice Lord-Lt 1965–84); patron Dorset BRCS; KStJ 1984; *Recreations* skiing, tennis; *Clubs* Pratt's; *Style*— The Rt Hon the Lord Digby, KCVO; ✉ West Wing, Minterne House, Minterne Magna, Dorchester, Dorset DT2 7AX (tel 01300 341425)

D

DIGBY-BELL, Christopher Harvey; s of Lt-Col Horatio Arthur Digby-Bell (d 1997), and Elizabeth Margaret Ann, *née* Cochrane; *b* 21 June 1948; *Educ* Marlborough; *m* 7 Sept 1974, Claire, da of Stephen Sutherland Pilch, of Finchampstead, Berks; 1 da (Melissa b 1980), 2 s (Timothy b 1981, William b 1984); *Career* admitted slr 1972; Taylor & Humbert 1966–82, managing ptnr Taylor Garrett 1987–89 (joined 1982); Frere Cholmeley Bischoff: joined as ptnr 1989, sometime mktg and business devpt ptnr, int managing ptnr until 1998; chief exec and gen counsel Palmer Capital Partners 1998–; hon legal advsr Down's Syndrome Assoc 1990; memb Law Soc 1972 (memb Ruling Cncl for City of London 2001–03, memb Ruling Cncl for Beds and Cambs 2005–); *Recreations* cricket, golf, collecting cricket prints, photography, cooking, cinema, pop music, American football; *Clubs* MCC, Leander, Stewards (Henley), Berkshire Golf; *Style*— Christopher Digby-Bell, Esq; ✉ Palmer Capital Partners, Time & Life Building, 1 Bruton Street, Mayfair, London W1J 6TL (tel 020 7409 5500, fax 020 7409 5501, e-mail chdb@palmercapital.co.uk)

DIGGLE, Prof James; s of James Diggle, and Elizabeth Alice, *née* Buckley; *b* 29 March 1944; *Educ* Rochdale GS, St John's Coll Cambridge (Henry Arthur Thomas scholar, Pitt scholar, Browne scholar, Allen scholar, BA, MA, PhD, LittD, Hallam prize, Montagu Butler prize, 2 Browne medals, Porson prize, Members' Latin essay prize, Chllr's classical medal); *m* 8 June 1974, Sedwell Mary, da of Preb Frederick Alexander Routley Chapman (d 1988); 3 s (Charles James b 1975, Julian Alexander b 1977, Nicholas Marcel b 1978); *Career* Univ of Cambridge: fell Queens' Coll 1966–, librarian Queens' Coll 1969–77, asst lectr in classics 1970–75, praelector Queens' Coll 1971–73 and 1978–, lectr in classics 1975–89, univ orator 1982–93, chm Faculty of Classics 1989–90 (librarian 1975–81), reader in Greek and Latin 1989–95, prof of Greek and Latin 1995–; pres Cambridge Philological Soc 1996–98 (hon sec 1970–74, jt ed Proceedings 1970–82), jt ed Cambridge Classical Texts and Commentaries 1977–, chm Classical Jls Bd 1990–97 (treas 1979–90); Corresponding memb Acad of Athens 2001–; FBA 1985; *Books* The Phaethon of Euripides (1970), Flavii Cresconii Corippi Iohannidos... Libri VIII (jt ed, 1970), The Classical Papers of A E Housman (jt ed, 1972), Studies on the text of Euripides (1981), The Textual Tradition of Euripides' Orestes (1991), Euripidis Fabulae (vol 2 1981, vol 1 1984, vol 3 1994), Cambridge Orations 1982–93: A Selection (1994), Euripidea: Collected Essays (1994), Tragicorum Graecorum Fragmenta Selecta (1998), The Characters of Theophrastus (2004), Odysseus Unbound: The Search for Homer's Ithaca (jtly, 2005); *Style*— Prof James Diggle; ✉ Queens' College, Cambridge CB3 9ET (tel 01223 335527, fax 01223 335522, e-mail jd10000@cam.ac.uk)

DIGGORY, Dr Colin; s of John Harold Diggory (d 2002), of Redcar, Cleveland, and Olga, *née* Midcalf (d 1985); *b* 22 July 1954; *Educ* Sir William Turner's Sch Redcar, Grey Coll Durham (BSc, PGCE), Open Univ (MA, EdD); *m* 10 Aug 1976, Susan Janet, da of R A Robinson; 2 da (Sarah b 24 Sept 1979, Ruth b 13 Sept 1981), 1 s (Mark b 11 Nov 1982); *Career* asst master Manchester Grammar 1976–83, asst master St Paul's Sch 1983–87, head of maths Merchant Taylors' Sch 1987–90, headmaster Latymer Upper Sch 1991–2002 (second master 1990–91), headmaster Alleyn's Sch 2002–; chief examiner A Level maths Univ of London 1989–91; chm: London Div HMC 1999, Jr Schs Sub-Ctee HMC 1999–2001; govr Highgate Sch 2003–, tstee Soc of Schoolmasters and Schoolmistresses 2004–; tstee Dulwich Picture Gallery 2005–; Open Univ vice chancellor Sir John Daniel Award 2005; CMath 1994, FIMA 1994, FRSA 1994; *Recreations* theatre, walking, reading; *Clubs* East India, Devonshire, Sports and Public Schs, Dulwich; *Style*— Dr Colin Diggory; ✉ Alleyn's School, Dulwich SE22 8SU (tel 020 8693 1500, e-mail headmaster@alleyns.org.uk)

DIK, Prof Wim; *Educ* Delft Univ of Technol; *Career* with Unilever 1964–88 (held various positions in food and chemical divs rising to chm Nederlandse Unilever Bedrijven BV); min for foreign trade Holland 1981–82; joined Post Telegraph Telephone (PTT) 1988, chm and chief exec Koninklijke PTT Nederland (KPN) 1989–98, chm and ceo Koninklijke KPN (Royal Dutch Telecom) 1998–2000; prof of mgmnt of ICT-oriented orgns Delft Univ of Technology 2000–; memb Supervisory Bd: ABN AMRO Holding NV 1993–2005, Van Gansewinkel Gp BV 1999–2004, Casema NV (chm), Tele Atlas NV (chm); non-exec dir: Aviva (formerly CGNU) 1999– (previously chm Nuts Ohra), Unilever 2001–, LogicaCMG (formerly CMG) 2001–; Grand Offr Royal Order of Oranje Nassau (Holland), Cdr Royal Order of the North Star (Sweden); *Style*— Prof Wim Dik; ✉ Faculty of Technology, Policy and Management, Delft University of Technology, PO Box 5015, 2600 GA Delft, Netherlands; Aviva plc, St Helen's, 1 Undershaft, London EC3P 3DQ

DILBERT, Jennifer Pearl; MBE (2005); da of Vernon L Jackson, OBE, and Francine Jackson; *Educ* Brock Univ Ontario, Univ of Western Ontario; *m* Leonard Dilbert; 2 da (Rita, Juliette); *Career* Dept of Fin and Devpt Cayman Islands Govt: higher exec offr 1980, higher exec offr and admin offr 1981–84, mangr Cayman Islands Currency Bd 1984–86, inspr of banks and trust companies 1991–93 (dep inspr 1987–91), inspr of fin servs Fin Servs Supervision Div 1993–96; exec dir Deutsche Bank (Cayman) Ltd 1996–99, Cayman Islands Govt rep UK 2000–; analyst Banking Supervision Div Bank of England 1986–87; Cayman Islands Monetary Authy: memb Bd 2000–02, md (on secondment) 2002; vice-pres Cayman Islands Bankers' Assoc 1999–2000, memb Cncl Cayman Islands Stock Exchange 1997–99; treas Nat Ctee Duke of Edinburgh's Award 1996–99 (Gold Award 1983), head Fin Ctee and memb Bd of Elders John Gray Meml Church 1996–99; Miss Cayman Islands 1979; *Style*— Mrs Jennifer Dilbert, MBE; ✉ Cayman Islands Government Office, 6 Arlington Street, London SW1A 1RE (tel 020 7491 7772, fax 020 7491 7944, e-mail info@cigo.co.uk)

DILHORNE, 2 Viscount (UK 1964); Sir John Mervyn Manningham-Buller; 5 Bt (UK 1866); also Baron Dilhorne (UK 1962); s of 1 Viscount Dilhorne, sometime Lord High Chllr and Lord of Appeal in Ordinary (d 1980, ggs of Sir Edward M-B, 1 Bt, who was bro of 1 Baron Churston) by his w Lady Mary Lindsay (4 da of 27 Earl of Crawford and Balcarres); *b* 28 February 1932; *Educ* Eton, RMA Sandhurst; *m* 1, 8 Oct 1955 (m dis 1973), Gillian Evelyn, er da of Col George Cochrane Stockwell, JP; 3 s, 1 da; m 2, 17 Dec 1981, Prof Susannah Jane Eykyn, da of late Cdr W C Eykyn, RN, and former w of Colin Gilchrist; *Heir* s, Hon James Manningham-Buller; *Career* Lt Coldstream Gds 1952–57, served Egypt, Germany, Canal Zone; cncllr Wilts CC 1964–66; called to the Bar 1979; md Clarkson de Falbe (LP&M) Ltd 1969–70, md Stewart Smith (LP&M) Ltd 1970–74;

memb: Jt Parly Ctee on Statutory Instruments 1981–88, EEC Select Ctee (Law & Institutions) 1986–89, Consolidated Bills Ctee 1988–; chm VAT Tbnl 1989–97; fell Chartered Inst of Taxation (memb Cncl 1969–82); *Recreations* skiing, opera singer (bass), shooting, walking, fishing; *Clubs* Buck's, Pratt's, Royal St George's, Swinley Forest Golf, Beefsteak; *Style*— The Rt Hon Viscount Dilhorne

DILLON, Andrew Patrick; CBE (2003); *b* 9 May 1954; *Educ* St Ambrose Coll Hale Barns, N Cheshire Coll of FE Altrincham, Univ of Manchester (BSc); *Career* unit gen mangr The Royal Free Hosp London 1986–91, chief exec St George's Healthcare NHS Tst London 1991–99, chief exec Nat Inst for Health and Clinical Excellence (NICE) 1999–, dir Health Technol Assessment Int 2003–05; memb Nat Cncl NHS Tst Fedn 1995–97; MHSM 1975; *Recreations* family; *Style*— Andrew Dillon, Esq, CBE; ✉ National Institute for Health and Clinical Excellence, MidCity Place, 71 High Holborn, London WC1V 6NA (tel 020 7067 5800, fax 020 7067 5801, e-mail andrew.dillon@nice.org.uk)

DILLON, 22 Viscount (I 1622); Harry Benedict Charles Dillon; also Count Dillon (Fr cr of Louis XIV 1711 for Hon Arthur Dillon, 3 s of 7 Viscount and father of 10 and 11 Viscounts, who was Col proprietor of the Dillon Regt, promoted to Lt-Gen in the Fr service, govr of Toulon, and cr titular Earl Dillon 1721/22 by the Chevalier de St Georges, otherwise known as the Old Pretender or, to his supporters, James III); s of 21 Viscount Dillon (d 1982); *b* 6 January 1973; *Heir* unc, Hon Richard Dillon; *Style*— The Rt Hon the Viscount Dillon; ✉ e-mail studiodillon@btinternet.com

DILLWYN-VENABLES-LLEWELYN, *see also:* Venables-Llewelyn

DILLY, Prof (Peter) Noel; GM, RD; s of George Frederick Dilly (d 1979), of Walsall, and Annie Winifred, *née* Fox (d 1982); *b* 25 December 1935; *Educ* Howardian HS Cardiff, UCH (MB BS), RCS (Dip Ophthalmology); *m* 1, 22 Nov 1957 (m dis), Muriel Daphne, *née* Holmshaw; 1 s (Stephen George b 22 May 1958); m 2, 5 July 1979 (m dis 2002), Susan Ann, *née* Butcher; 1 da (Sarah Ann b 26 Sept 1981), 1 s (Simon George b 8 July 1983); *Career* res asst to Prof J Z Young FRS, 1960–62, house surgn UCH 1966 (house physician 1965–66), lectr in anatomy UCL 1966–67, res asst MIT USA 1969–70, sr lectr in anatomy UCL 1970–74, prof and chm Dept of Structural Biology St George's Hosp Med Sch 1974–2001; hon res assoc Dept of Chemistry UCL 1975–2001, hon assoc specialist in ophthalmology St George's Hosp 1989–2001 (hon occulist 1984–89); yachtmaster ocean examiner RYA 1983, tstee Royal Inst of Navigation; MRIN; fell Royal Coll of Ophthalmologists (FRCOphth); *Recreations* anything dangerous, polar exploration and deep ocean cruising, Himalayan mountaineering (4 expeditions), potholing and caving, astronomical telescope building; *Clubs* Alpine, Medway Yacht, Walton and Frinton Yacht, Wimbledon Park Golf; *Style*— Prof Noel Dilly, GM, RD; ✉ 11 Westwood Park, Forest Hill, London SE23 3QB (tel 020 8699 7876); Department of Anatomy, St George's Hospital Medical School, Cranmer Terrace, London SW17 0RE (tel 020 8725 5207, fax 020 8725 3326, e-mail noel@pndilly.fsnet.co.uk)

DILNOT, Andrew William; CBE (2000); s of A W J Dilnot, and P J Dilnot, *née* Ozmond; *b* 19 June 1960; *m* Catherine, *née* Morrish; 2 da (Rosemary b 29 Sept 1990, Julia b 30 March 1993); *Career* Inst for Fiscal Studies: research asst rising to sr research offr 1981–86, dir of personal sector research 1987–90, dep dir 1990–91, dir 1991–2002; coll lectr in economics LMH Oxford 1987–88, dir of studies and coll lectr in economics Exeter Coll Oxford 1988–89; princ St Hugh's Coll Oxford 2002–; hon research fell UCL 1985–91, visiting fell ANU Canberra 1986, visiting prof of social economics (Downing meml fell) Univ of Melbourne 1989; pt/t presenter Analysis (BBC Radio 4), presenter More or Less (BBC Radio 4); regular contrib to TV and radio news and current affrs progs, also articles in national broadsheets; special advsr to House of Lords Select Ctee enquiries into harmonisation of European social security systems and withholding tax on investment income; memb: Social Security Advsy Ctee 1992–2002, Cncl Royal Economic Soc 1993–98, Fiscal Studies Task Force of the Effect of the Tax System on Innovative Activity Office of Science and Technol 1993–94, Retirement Income Enquiry (Anson Ctee) 1994, Costs of Continuing Care Enquiry (Barclay Ctee) 1995; *Books* The Reform of Social Security (1984), The Economics of Social Security (1989), Pensions Policy in the UK: An Economic Analysis (1994); also author of numerous book chapters, articles, reports and other papers; *Style*— Andrew Dilnot, Esq, CBE

DILWORTH, Stephen Patrick Dominic; s of Patrick Dilworth, of London, and Ida Dilworth; *b* 20 October 1951; *Educ* St Joseph's Acad Blackheath, Open Univ (BA), UMIST (BSc); *m* Siobhan, da of Brendan and Marie Anglin; 2 da (Louise b 1972, Laura b 1982), 1 s (Nicholas b 1981); *Career* regnl mangr Leeds Permanent Building Soc: Thames Valley 1982–86, London 1986–88; asst gen mangr of mktg Town and Country Building Soc 1988–92, Stephen Dilworth Marketing Consultancy 1992–94, head of corp affrs Bank of Ireland (GB) 1994–99; Foresters UK: head of gp mktg and communications 1999–2002, UK membership dir 2002–; dir: Soho Ltd, Yamada International plc; chm Soho Housing Assoc; pres Chartered Inst of Bankers (London Centre); FCBSI 1977, MCIM 1992, AIPR 1992, FCIB 1993, FCIM 2007; *Books* More Than A Building Society (1987); *Recreations* theatre, golf, films, football, history, economics, scuba diving; *Clubs* RAC; *Style*— Stephen Dilworth, Esq; ✉ 3 Hayes Road, Bromley, Kent BR2 9AF (tel 020 8290 1823); Foresters UK (tel 020 8628 3435, e-mail steve.dilworth@foresters.co.uk)

DIMBLEBY, David; s of Richard Dimbleby, CBE (d 1965), and Dilys, *née* Thomas; *b* 28 October 1938; *Educ* Charterhouse, ChCh Oxford, Paris Univ, Perugia Univ; *m* 1, 1967 (m dis 2000), Josceline Rose, *qv*, da of late Thomas Gaskell; 1 s, 2 da; m 2, 2000, Belinda Giles; 1 s; *Career* broadcaster; news reporter BBC Bristol 1960–61; presenter and interviewer on network programmes incl: Quest (religion), What's New (science for children), In My Opinion (politics), Top of the Form 1961–63; documentary films incl: Ku-Klux-Klan, The Forgotten Million, Cyprus - The Thin Blue Line 1964–65, South Africa - The White Tribe 1979 (RTS supreme documentary award), The Struggle for South Africa 1990 (US Emmy award, Monte Carlo Golden Nymph award), US-UK Relations - An Ocean Apart (7 films) 1988, David Dimbleby's India 1997, Rebellion 1999; special corr CBS News New York, film reports (and documentary film Texas-England) for 60 minutes 1966–68, commentator Current Events 1969, presenter 24 Hours (BBC1) 1969–72, chm The Dimbleby Talk-In 1971–74, films for Reporter at Large 1973, Election Campaign Report 1974; presenter: Panorama (BBC1) 1974–77 and 1980–82 (reporter 1967–69), People and Power 1982–83, BBC General Election Results programmes 1979, 1983, 1987, 1992, 1997 and 2001, This Week Next Week 1984–86, Question Time 1994–, A Picture of Britain (BBC) 2005; live commentary on public occasions incl: State Opening of Parliament, Trooping the Colour, wedding of Prince Andrew and Sarah Ferguson, Queen Mother's 90th birthday parade (RTS outstanding documentary award), meml services incl Sir Laurence Olivier (RTS outstanding documentary award); chm Dimbleby and Sons Ltd 1986–2001 (md 1966–86); winner of Richard Dimbleby Award for Personal Contribution in Factual TV BAFTA 1998; *Books* An Ocean Apart (with David Reynolds, 1988); *Style*— David Dimbleby, Esq; ✉ 14 King Street, Richmond, Surrey TW9 1NF

DIMBLEBY, Jonathan; s of Richard Dimbleby, CBE (d 1965), and Dilys, *née* Thomas; *b* 31 July 1944; *Educ* UCL (BA); *m* 1968 (m dis 2006), Bel Mooney, *qv*; 1 s (Daniel Richard b 1974), 1 da (Katherine Rose b 1980); *Career* freelance journalist, broadcaster and author; TV and radio reporter BBC Bristol 1969–70, World at One (BBC Radio) 1970–71, This Week (Thames TV) 1972–78 and 1986–88, prodr and presenter Jonathan Dimbleby in South America (Thames) 1979, Jonathan Dimbleby in Evidence - The Police 1980 (Thames), The Bomb (Thames) 1980, The Eagle and the Bear (Thames) 1981, The Cold War Game (Thames) 1982, The American Dream (Thames) 1984, Four Years On - The Bomb (Thames) 1984, assoc ed and presenter First Tuesday series (Thames) 1982–85, ed documentary series Witness (Thames) 1986–88, presenter and ed Jonathan Dimbleby on Sunday (TV-am) 1985–86, presenter On the Record (BBC TV) 1988–93, writer and presenter Review of the Year 1989 and 1990 and Russia at the Rubicon (BBC) 1990, interview with President Gorbachov (BBC) 1990, Election Call (BBC) 1992, chm Any Questions? (BBC Radio) 1987–, presenter Any Answers? (BBC Radio) 1988–, co-deviser and host The Brain Game (Channel 4) 1992: writer and presenter Charles - The Private Man, The Public Role (Central) 1994, presenter Jonathan Dimbleby (LWT) 1995–, writer and presenter The Last Governor (BBC TV) 1997, presenter The General Election '97 and 2001 (ITV); writer and presenter: An Ethiopian Journey (LWT) 1998, A Kosovo Journey (LWT) 2000, Michael Heseltine - A Life in the Political Jungle (LWT) 2000; awards incl Soc of Film and TV Arts Richard Dimbleby Award (for most outstanding contrib to factual TV) 1974; pres: Soil Assoc 1998–, VSO 1999–, RSPB 2001–, Bath Festivals Tst 2003–; vice-pres Cncl for Protection of Rural England 1997– (pres 1992–97); tstee Richard Dimbleby Cancer Fund; *Books* Richard Dimbleby (1975), The Palestinians (1979), The Prince of Wales: A Biography (1994), The Last Governor: Chris Patten and the Handover of Hong Kong (1997); *Recreations* farming, music, sailing, tennis, riding; *Style*— Jonathan Dimbleby, Esq; ✉ c/o David Higham Associates Ltd, 5–8 Lower John Street, London W1R 4HA (tel 020 7437 7888)

DIMBLEBY, Josceline Rose; da of late Thomas Josceline Gaskell; *b* 1 February 1943; *Educ* Cranborne Chase Sch, Guildhall Sch of Music; *m* 1967 (m dis 2000), David Dimbleby, *qv*; 1 s, 2 da; *Career* cookery writer for Sainsbury's 1978–, cookery ed Sunday Telegraph 1982–97; regular contrib: BBC Good Food Magazine 1993–94, Ideal Home Magazine 1999–2000; regular demonstrator annual BBC Cooking & Kitchen shows, House & Garden Show, Country Living Show and others, after dinner speaker and occasional TV incl Masterchef and Good Food Prog (both BBC), Carlton Food Network; André Simon Award 1979, Glenfiddich Cookery Writer of the Year Award 1993; contrib travel articles: Condé Nast Traveller, Mail on Sunday; *Books* A Taste of Dreams (1976), Party Pieces (1977), Josceline Dimbleby's Book of Puddings, Desserts and Savouries (1979), Favourite Food (1983), The Essential Josceline Dimbleby (1989), The Practically Vegetarian Book (USA edn, 1995), The Cooking Enthusiast (USA edn, 2000), A Profound Secret (2004), May and Amy (USA edn, 2005); for Sainsbury's: Cooking for Christmas (1978), Family Meat and Fish Cookery (1979), Cooking with Herbs and Spices (1979), Curries and Oriental Cookery (1980), Salads for all Seasons (1981), Marvellous Meals with Mince (1982), Festive Food (1982), Sweet Dreams (1983), First Impressions (1984), The Josceline Dimbleby Collection (1984), Main Attractions (1985), A Traveller's Tastes (1986), The Josceline Dimbleby Christmas Book (1987), The Josceline Dimbleby Book of Entertaining (1988), The Cook's Companion (1991), The Almost Vegetarian Cookbook (1994), The Christmas Book (1994), Josceline Dimbleby's Complete Cookbook (1997), Josceline Dimbleby's Cooking Course (1999), Josceline Dimbleby's Almost Vegetarian Cookbook (2000); *Recreations* singing, travel; *Style*— Josceline Dimbleby; ✉ 18 Ashchurch Park Villas, London W12 9SP (tel 020 8743 1216, fax 020 8332 1356, e-mail jossy@dircon.co.uk)

DIMMOCK, Charlie; da of Terry Dimmock, and Sue Dimmock; *b* 1966, Romsey, Hampshire; *Career* gardener; TV presenter; *Style*— Ms Charlie Dimmock; ✉ c/o Arlington Enterprises Ltd, 1–3 Charlotte Street, London

DIMMOCK, Prof Nigel John; s of Herbert Douglas Dimmock (d 1987), of Brookwood, Surrey, and Doreen Agnes, *née* Robinson (d 1984); *b* 14 April 1940; *Educ* Woking GS, Univ of Liverpool (BSc), Univ of London (PhD); *m* 1, 27 April 1963 (m dis), Jennifer Ann, da of John Glazier, of Bulawayo, Zimbabwe; 2 s (Nicholas b 1 Feb 1964, Simon b 26 Dec 1965), 1 da (Samantha b 1 Nov 1967); m 2, 30 Oct 1987, Jane Elizabeth Mary, da of Dr Samuel Ballantine, of Leicester (d 1985); *Career* virologist and teacher; MRC Salisbury 1961–66, Aust Nat Univ Canberra 1966–71; Univ of Warwick: lectr 1971, sr lectr 1975, reader 1982, prof 1986; visiting res fell: Melbourne 1977, Munich 1979, Vancouver 1981, Perth Aust 1987; memb: American Soc for Microbiology, Soc for Gen Microbiology; ed Jl of Gen Virology 1980–88; *Books* Introduction to Modern Virology (jtly, 1987, 6 edn 2007), Neutralization of Animal Viruses (1993), Mims' Pathogenesis of Infectious Disease (jtly, 1995); *Recreations* theatre, books, working with wood, road running, triathlon; *Style*— Prof Nigel Dimmock; ✉ Department of Biological Sciences, University of Warwick, Coventry CV4 7AL (tel 024 7652 3593, fax 024 7652 3568, e-mail n.j.dimmock@warwick.ac.uk)

DIMMOCK, Rear Adm Roger Charles; CB (1988); s of Frank Charles Dimmock (d 1992), and Ivy Annie May, *née* Archer (d 1989); *b* 27 May 1935; *Educ* Price's Sch; *m* 1958, Lesley Patricia Reid; 3 da (Sandra b 1959, Jacqueline b 1960 d 1987, Nicola b 1963); *Career* entered RN 1953; pilot's wings FAA 1954, USN 1955, qualified flying instr 1959; Master Mariner Foreign Going Cert of Serv 1979; served RN Air Sqdns and HM Ships Bulwark, Albion, Ark Royal, Eagle, Hermes, Anzio, Messina, Murray, Berwick (i/c), Naiad (i/c); CSO to FO Carriers and Amphibious Ships 1978–80, cmd RNAS Culdrose 1980–82, cmd HMS Hermes 1982–83, dir Naval Air Warfare MOD 1983–84, Naval Sec 1985–87, Flag Offr Naval Air Cmd 1987–88; chm tstees Fleet Air Arm Museum 1987–88; dir Charnauds Ltd 1992–98, md Archer Mullins Ltd 1997– (dir 1990–); pres: RN Hockey Assoc 1985–90, Combined Services Hockey Assoc 1987–93, Denmead-Hambledon Branch RNLI 1981–; memb Ctee of Mgmnt RNLI 1987–; MInstD 1994; *Recreations* hockey, cricket, golf, family and friends; *Style*— Rear Adm Roger Dimmock, CB; ✉ Beverley House, 19 Beverley Grove, Farlington, Portsmouth, Hampshire PO6 1BP (e-mail 101530.1655@compuserve.com)

DIMOND, Paul Stephen; CMG (2005); s of Cyril James Dimond (d 1979), and Dorothy, *née* Knight; *b* 30 December 1944, Bournemouth; *Educ* St Olave's & St Saviour's GS for Boys Bermondsey; *m* 18 Sept 1965, Carolyn Susan, *née* Davis-Mees; 2 s (Mark James b 17 March 1968, Matthew David b 12 Sept 1970); *Career* diplomat; Japanese language offr 1966–68; served: Tokyo, Osaka, Stockholm, The Hague (dep head of mission), LA (consul-gen); ambass to The Philippines 2002–04, ret; dir: Intralink Ltd, Baillie Gifford Japan Tst plc 2006–, Japan 21; chm Westminster Gardens Ltd; memb for fund devpt Br Neurological Research Tst; outplacement advsr FCO; conslt; FRSA 1980, FCIL 1988, FCIM 1989; *Recreations* vintage Batsfords; *Clubs* Travellers, Royal Over-Seas League; *Style*— Paul Dimond, Esq, CMG; ✉ c/o Travellers Club, 106 Pall Mall, London SW1Y 5EP

DIMSON, Prof Elroy; s of David Dimson, of London, and Phyllis, *née* Heilpern; *b* 17 January 1947; *Educ* Univ of Newcastle upon Tyne (BA), Univ of Birmingham (MCom), Univ of London (PhD); *m* 1 July 1969, Dr Helen Patricia Dimson, da of Max Sonn, of Whitley Bay, Tyne & Wear; 3 s (Jonathan Ashley b 1971, Benjamin Simon b 1979, Daniel Marc b 1986), 1 da (Susanna Rachel b 1973); *Career* Tube Investments 1969–70, Unilever Ltd 1970–72; London Business Sch: joined 1972, dean MBA Progs 1986–90, chair Fin Faculty 1992–94, chair Accounting Faculty 1999–2002, govr 2000–03 and 2007–, currently BGI prof of investment mgmnt; chm The German Investment Trust plc 1995–97; dir: Mobil Trustee Co Ltd 1984–2003, Hoare Govett Indices Ltd; memb Bd: Jl of Banking and Finance, European Financial Management, Jl of Investing, Jl of Investment Mgmnt; memb Advsy Bd Edward Jones Ltd; former visiting prof: Univ of Chicago, Univ of Calif Berkeley, Univ of Hawaii, Euro Inst Brussels, Bank of England; author of numerous published papers; *Books* Risk Measurement Service (jtly, 1979, and subsequent edns to 2007), Cases in Corporate Finance (jtly, 1988), Stock Market Anomalies (1988), The Millennium Book: A Century of Investment Returns (jtly, 2000), Triumph of the Optimists: 101 Years of Global Investment Returns (jtly, 2002), Endowment Asset

Management (jtly, 2007); *Style—* Prof Elroy Dimson; ✉ London Business School, Regents Park, London NW1 4SA (tel 020 7000 7000, e-mail edimson@london.edu)

DIN, Russhied Ali; s of Matab Ali Din, of Rawalpindi, Pakistan, and Hilda Rose, *née* Dring (d 1985); *b* 8 April 1956; *Educ* Ordsall Secdy Modern, Salford Coll of Technol, Birmingham Poly (BA); *Career* designer: City Industrial Shopfitters 1978, Fitch & Co 1979, Italy Studios Giardi Rome 1980, Thomas Saunders Architects 1981, Peter Glynn Smith Assoc 1982–84 (BAA Gatwick refurbishment 1983), Allied Int Designers 1984–86; formed DIN Associates 1986– (became Ltd Co 1988); design conslt to: Next Retail plc 1987, French Connection, Nicole Farhi, Escada, Joop!; other projects incl: Polo Ralph Lauren Paris 1991, Tommy Hilfiger, Selfridges, Habitat, Diana, Princess of Wales Museum & Visitors Centre Althorp 1998; external assessor Kingston Poly and École Superiure D'Arts Graphiques & D'Architecture Interiure (ESAG), judge Student Design Awards 1998; Young Business Person of the Year (Observer and Harvey Nichols) 1991; MCSD 1991, FRSA; *Recreations* equestrian pursuits, tennis; *Style—* Russhied Din, Esq; ✉ DIN Associates Ltd, 32 St Oswalds Place, London SE11 5JE (tel 020 7582 0777)

DINARDO, Carlo; s of Nicandro Dinardo (1987), and Rosaria, *née* Iannacone; *b* 5 July 1939; *Educ* St Patrick's HS Coatbridge Scotland, Paddington Tech Coll, Tech Coll Coatbridge Scotland, Univ of Strathclyde; *m* 30 Aug 1962, Irene Rutherford, da of William James Niven (d 1977), of Helensburgh; 2 da (Karen b 24 Oct 1965, Lorraine b 7 Aug 1973), 1 s (Mark b 27 April 1967); *Career* fndr ptnr own practice of consulting engrs 1969; princ: Dinardo & Ptnrs 1978–, Dinardo Partnership 1990–; dir Scottish Conslts Int 1987–90; memb Ctee: Educn Task Gp Inst of Structural Engrs 1987–89, Industrial Trg Advsy Bd Paisley Coll of Technol, Inst of Engs and Shipbuilders Scotland 1994– (pres 1999–2001); memb Bd of Govrs of Westbourne Sch for Girls Glasgow 1984–91, memb Bd Renfrewshire Learning Bus Partnership; CEng 1965, MIStructE 1965, MICE 1967, FIStructE 1976, FICE 1976, MIHT 1979, FInstPet 1979, MCIA 1980, FGS 1982, FIHT 1982, MConsE 1984, MASCE 1991, FEANI, FHKIE 1992, FIES 1994; *Publications* author of papers published in learned jls; *Recreations* golf, skiing, fishing, rugby, curling, historical travels; *Clubs* Royal Northern & Univ (Aberdeen), Buchanan Castle Golf (Drymen), Glasgow Golf, Royal Aberdeen Golf; *Style—* Carlo Dinardo, Esq; ✉ Cleveden, Main Street, Killearn, Glasgow G63 9NE (tel 01360 550459); Dinardo Partnership Ltd, Mirren Court, 119 Renfrew Road, Paisley, Renfrewshire PA3 4EA (tel 0141 889 1212, fax 0141 889 5446, car 0860 836757)

DINGEMANS, James Michael; QC (2002); s of Rear Adm P G V Dingemans, CB, DSO, of Sussex, and Faith, *née* Bristow; *b* 25 June 1964; *Educ* Mansfield Coll Oxford (BA, Rugby Union blue), Inns of Court Sch of Law; *m* 20 April 1991, Janet Elizabeth, *née* Griffiths; 2 da (Phoebe b 10 Aug 1992, Freya b 29 Jan 1997), 1 s (Alexander b 16 April 1994); *Career* called to the Bar Inner Temple 1987; recorder 2002–; leading counsel Hutton Inquiry 2003; vice-chm Int Rels Ctee Bar of Eng and Wales 2006; memb: Exec Ctee and Cncl Cwlth Lawyers' Assoc, Organising Ctee Cwlth Law Conf London 2005, Advsy Panel Rugby Football League; *Books* Employers Liability Cases (2003); *Recreations* rugby, sailing, cricket; *Clubs* Broadhalfpenny Brigands Cricket, Bar Yacht; *Style—* James Dingemans, Esq, QC; ✉ 3 Hare Court, Temple, London EC4Y 7BJ (tel 020 7415 7800, fax 020 7415 7811, e-mail jamesdingemans@3harecourt.com)

DINGLE, Dr John Thomas; s of T H Dingle (d 1990), and Violet, *née* Tolman; *b* 27 October 1927; *Educ* King Edward Sch Bath, Univ of London (BSc, DSc), Univ of Cambridge (PhD); *m* 11 July 1953, Dorothy Vernon; 2 s (Jonathan b 1957, Timothy b 1959); *Career* Mil Serv RN 1946–49; res asst Royal Nat Hosp for Rheumatic Diseases Bath 1951–59; Strangeways Research Lab: sr res asst 1959, head Physiology Dept 1969, dep dir (MRC external staff) 1971–79, chm Pathophysiology Lab 1976–, dir 1979–93; CCC Cambridge: fell 1968–, warden of Leckhampton 1981–86, steward of Estates 1987–93, Life fell 1998–; pres Hughes Hall Cambridge 1993–98 (hon fell 1998–); chm Editorial Bd The Biochemical Jl 1976–82, author of numerous papers in scientific learned jls; pres Br Connective Tissue Soc 1980–86; Heberden Medal 1978, Steindler Award 1980; pres Cambridge Univ RUFC 1990–2002 (treas 1983–90); *Recreations* rugby, sailing; *Clubs* Hawks' (Cambridge); *Style—* Dr John Dingle; ✉ Middle Watch, Mount Boone Hill, Dartmouth, Devon TQ6 9NZ; Corpus Christi College, Cambridge CB2 1RH

DINKEL, Philip Charles Christian; s of Prof Ernest Michael Dinkel (d 1983), and Emmy Gerarda Mary Dinkel, *née* Keet (d 2003); *b* 3 October 1946; *Educ* Ampleforth, AA Sch of Architecture; *m* 3 Oct 1981, Lucia, *née* Stevens; 1 da (Charlotte b 7 Feb 1986), 2 s (Henry b 5 Oct 1988, Theodore b 15 June 1990); *Career* architect; Sir Hugh Casson project architect Hobhouse Ct Trafalgar Square 1973–77 (Civic Tst Award 1981), in private practice specialising in conservation work, commercial and residential projects in UK, Albania and Far East 1977–; AA Prize 1970; fndr chm Lloyd's of London WRG 1994; RIBA; *Recreations* the arts, cello, conservation matters; *Style—* Philip Dinkel, Esq; ✉ Aycote House, Rendcomb, Gloucestershire GL7 7EP (tel 01285 831866, fax 01285 831855); 3 Montpelier Mews, London SW7 1HB

DINKIN, Anthony David; QC (1991); s of Hyman Dinkin (d 2004), of London, and Mary, *née* Hine (d 1992); *b* 2 August 1944; *Educ* Henry Thornton GS Clapham, Coll of Estate Mgmnt London (BSc); *m* 20 Oct 1968, Derina Tanya, MBE, da of Benjamin Green (d 1994); *Career* called to the Bar Lincoln's Inn 1968 (bencher 2003); recorder of the Crown Court 1989–; memb: Lands Tbnl 1997–98, Mental Health Review Tbnl 1999–; examiner in law Univ of Reading 1985–92, external examiner in law City Univ 2003–; former memb Anglo-American Real Property Inst; pres Estate Mgmnt Club 1998; *Recreations* gardening, theatre, music, travel; *Style—* Anthony Dinkin, Esq, QC; ✉ 2–3 Gray's Inn Square, London WC1R 5JH (tel 020 7242 4986, fax 020 7405 1166, e-mail adqc@ukonline.co.uk)

DINSDALE, Owen Malcolm; s of Malcolm George Frank Dinsdale, and Suzanne, *née* van Rooyen; *b* 15 January 1947; *Educ* King Edward VII Sch Johannesburg, Univ of Witwatersrand; *m* 9 July 1972, Bernice, da of William Greenblatt; 3 s (Tarquin Ian b 24 April 1974, Ryan Stuart b 22 Nov 1976, Ewan Anthony b 5 May 1980); *Career* md Telerama Redifussion 1979–81; md: Barlow Manufacturing Co 1984–86 (gen mangr 1981–84), Imperial Cold Storage 1986–87, Gerber Foods Holdings 1987–88; chief exec Acsis Group plc until 1994, dir Premier Health Group plc, currently chm Didata Ltd; *Recreations* fly fishing, hockey, tennis, golf; *Clubs* Country (Johannesburg), Wanderers, Woburn Golf and Country; *Style—* Owen Dinsdale, Esq; ✉ Ridge End, 82 West Hill, Aspley, Guise, Bedfordshire MK17 8DX (tel 01908 583318)

DINWIDDIE, Ian Maitland; s of Lauderdale Maitland Dinwiddie (d 1978), and Frances Lilian Pedrick; *b* 8 February 1952; *Educ* Sherborne, Univ Exeter (BA); *m* 1978, Sally Jane, da of Leslie Ronald Croydon; 2 da (Laura b 1981, Lucy b 1991), 1 s (Andrew b 1984); *Career* audit mangr Ernst & Young 1972–82, fin controller Arbuthnot Savory Milln Holdings Ltd 1982–86, gen mangr Savory Milln Ltd 1986; fin dir: Arbuthnot Latham Bank Ltd 1987, gp fin dir Guinness Mahon Holdings plc until 1990; currently fin dir Allen & Overy LLP; *Recreations* sailing, golf; *Style—* Ian Dinwiddie; ✉ Allen & Overy LLP, One Bishops Square, London E1 6AO (tel 020 3088 0000, fax 020 3088 0088)

DINWIDDIE, Dr Robert; s of Noel Alexander Williamson Dinwiddie (d 1994), of Dumfries, and May Stirling, *née* Kennedy (d 1996); *b* 23 February 1945; *Educ* Dumfries Acad, Univ of Aberdeen (MB ChB); *m* 23 Oct 1971, Mary McCalley, da of James Saunderson (d 1984), of Dumfries; 1 s (Robert b 1973), 1 da (Jane b 1974); *Career* conslt paediatrician: Queen Charlotte's Maternity Hosp London 1977–86, Great Ormond St Hosp for Children London 1977–2005; hon sr lectr Inst of Child Health Univ of London 1977–2005; author of numerous scientific pubns on paediatrics especially cystic fibrosis and the chest; memb RSM; FRCP 1984, FRCPCH 1997; *Books* The Diagnosis and Management of Paediatric Respiratory Disease (1997); *Recreations* gardening, walking, sailing; *Clubs* RSM; *Style—* Dr Robert Dinwiddie; ✉ 1 Circle Gardens, Merton Park, London SW19 3JX; Great Ormond Street Hospital for Children, Great Ormond Street, London WC1N 3JH (tel 020 7405 9200, fax 020 7813 8514, e-mail rdinwiddie@doctors.org.uk)

DINWIDDY, Bruce Harry; CMG (2003); s of Thomas Lutwyche Dinwiddy (d 1992), and Ruth, *née* Abbott (d 1996); *b* 1 February 1946; *Educ* Winchester, New Coll Oxford (MA); *m* 29 June 1974, Emma Victoria, da of Sir David Llewellyn (d 1992); 1 da (Celia Rose (Mrs James Stone) b 22 Sept 1976), 1 s (Thomas Rhidian b 13 May 1979); *Career* economist Govt of Swaziland (ODI Nuffield fell) 1967–70, reseach offr ODI 1970–73; HM Dip Serv: entered 1973, first sec UK delgn to MBFR talks Vienna 1975–77, FCO 1977–81, head of Chancery Cairo 1981–83, FCO 1983–86, asst sec Cabinet Office 1986–88, cnsllr Bonn 1989–91, dep high cmmr Ottawa 1992–95, head African Dept (Southern) FCO 1995–98, cmmr (non-resident) Br Indian Ocean Territory 1996–98, high cmmr to Tanzania 1998–2001, govr Cayman Is 2002–05, ret; *Publications* Promoting African Enterprise (1974); *Recreations* golf, swimming, lawn tennis, music (piano), travel; *Clubs* Vincent's (Oxford), Aldeburgh Golf, Royal Wimbledon Golf; *Style—* Bruce Dinwiddy, Esq, CMG; ✉ 8 Connaught Avenue, London SW14 7RH

D

DIPPLE, Christine; da of James Henry Brown, and Isabel Brown; *m* Teesdale Sch Barnard Castle, Univ of Leeds (BA), Univ of Oxford (PGCE), L'Université de Lille (Maitre ès Lettres); *Career* teacher of French Teesdale Sch 1979–81, teacher of French (i/c Italian) Millfield Sch 1981–84, head of modern languages Sherborne Sch for Girls 1984–88, head of modern languages and day housemistress St Swithun's Sch Winchester 1988–91, head Talbot Heath Sch 1991–; memb: GSA 1991, SHA 1991; govr: Sunninghill Prep Sch, Horlde Walhampton Sch; chm Grange Choral Soc Christchurch; *Recreations* choral singing, reading, walking, concert and theatre-going, foreign travel; *Clubs* Univ Women's; *Style—* Mrs Christine Dipple; ✉ Talbot Heath School, Rothesay Road, Bournemouth, Dorset BH8 9LJ (tel 01202 761881)

DISKI, Jenny; da of James Simmonds (d 1966), of London and Banbury, Oxford, and René, *née* Rayner; *b* 8 July 1947; *Educ* St Christopher Sch Letchworth, King Alfred Sch Golders Green, UCL; *m* Dec 1976, Roger Diski, s of Ralph Marks; 1 da (Chloe b 1 July 1977); *Career* author; formerly shop asst, Eng and history teacher Haggerston Sch Hackney 1973–77 (free sch teacher 1972–73), home tutor ILEA 1977–83, teacher Islington Sixth Form Centre 1985–89; FRSL; *Books* Nothing Natural (Methuen), Rainforest (Methuen and Penguin), Like Mother (Bloomsbury and Vintage), Then Again (Bloomsbury and Vintage), Happily Ever After (Hamish Hamilton), Monkey's Uncle (Weidenfeld and Nicolson, 1994), The Vanishing Princess (Phoenix, 1996), The Dream Mistress (Weidenfeld & Nicholson, 1996), Skating to Antarctica (Granta, 1997), Don't (1998); *Television plays* A Fair and Easy Passage (Channel 4), Seduction (Channel 4), Murder in Mind (BBC1); *Style—* Ms Jenny Diski; ✉ c/o A P Watt, 20 John Street, London WC1N 2DR (tel 020 7405 6774)

DISLEY, John Ivor; CBE (1979); s of Harold Disley, and Marie Hughes; *b* 20 November 1928, Corris, Gwynedd; *Educ* Oswestry HS, Loughborough Coll; *m* 1958, Sylvia Cheeseman; 2 da; *Career* former Br steeplechase record holder and former Welsh mile record holder; Bronze medal Olympic Games Helsinki 1952, Sportsman of the Year 1955; vice-chm Sports Cncl 1974–82; dir Reebok UK Ltd 1984–95, fndr dir London Marathon Ltd, chm London Marathon Tst 2006; chm British Olympians 1996–2002; memb Royal Cmmn on Gambling 1976–78; pres Snowdonia Soc 2003–; *Books* Tackle Climbing, Orienteering, Expedition Guide, Your Way with Map and Compass; *Recreations* mountaineering, orienteering; *Clubs* Climbers, Southern Navigators, Alpine; *Style—* John Disley, Esq, CBE; ✉ Hampton House, Upper Sunbury Road, Hampton, Middlesex TW12 2DW (tel 020 8979 1707, e-mail johnapdisley@aol.com)

DISMORE, Andrew; MP; s of Ian Dismore (d 1965), and Brenda Hartley; *b* 2 September 1954; *Educ* Bridlington GS, Univ of Warwick (LLB), LSE (LLM), Coll of Law Guildford; *Career* slr: Robin Thompson and Partners 1978–95, Russell Jones and Walker 1995–; MP (Lab) Hendon 1997–; cncllr Westminster City Cncl 1982–97 (ldr Lab Gp 1990–97); *Recreations* gardening, opera, Greece, Greek culture; *Style—* Andrew Dismore, Esq, MP; ✉ House of Commons, London SW1A 0AA (tel 020 7219 4026)

DISPENZA, Adriano; s of late Mario Dispenza, of France, and Lina, *née* Inzirillo; *b* 24 September 1948; *Educ* QMC (BSc), Paris (Dip Faculté de Droit et Sciences Economiques); *m* 12 March 1979, Rallia Jean, da of John Adam Hadjipateras, of Greece; 1 da (Carolina b 5 March 1981); *Career* Morgan Grenfell & Co Ltd 1973–77, Amex Bank Ltd 1977–79, md First Chicago Ltd 1979–88, md Merrill Lynch Int Ltd 1988–95, md Folio Corp Fin Ltd; *Recreations* reading, travel, crosswords; *Style—* Adriano Dispenza, Esq

DISS, Eileen (Mrs Raymond Everett); da of Thomas Alexander Diss, and Winifred, *née* Irvine; *b* 13 May 1931; *Educ* Ilford Co HS, Central Sch of Art and Design; *m* 18 Sept 1953, Raymond Terence Everett, s of Elmo Terence Everett; 1 da (Danielle Claire b 1956), 2 s (Timothy Patrick b 1959, Matthew Simon Thomas b 1964); *Career* BBC TV designer 1952–59, freelance designer 1959–; RDI 1978, FRSA; *Theatre* designs for Nat Theatre and West End Theatres; *Television* designs for BBC incl: Maigret, Cider with Rosie; designs for ITV incl: The Prime of Miss Jean Brodie, Porterhouse Blue, Jeeves and Wooster, A Dance to the Music of Time, Longitude; *Film* Joseph Losey's A Doll's House 1972, Sweet William 1978, Harold Pinter's Betrayal 1982, Secret Places 1984, 84 Charing Cross Road 1986, A Handful of Dust 1988, August 1994 (dir Anthony Hopkins, *qv*); *Awards* BAFTA Awards 1961, 1965, 1974, 1992, 2001 and 2006; *Style—* Miss Eileen Diss; ✉ 4 Gloucester Walk, London W8 4HZ (tel 020 7937 8794)

DISS, Paul John; *b* 30 November 1951; *Educ* St Catharine's Coll Cambridge; *m* Janice Fletcher; 1 da (Nicola), 2 s (Jonathan, Matthew); *Career* slr Linklaters & Paines 1976–77 (articled clerk 1974–76); ptnr: Stephenson Harwood & Lo Hong Kong 1981–84, Stephenson Harwood 1982–99 (slr 1977–81), SJ Berwin 1999–; Freeman City of London Slrs' Co 1986; memb: Law Soc, Int Bar Assoc; *Recreations* collecting books, cricket coaching; *Style—* Paul Diss, Esq; ✉ SJ Berwin, 222 Gray's Inn Road, London EC4R 1BE (tel 020 7111 2222, fax 020 7111 2000)

DITCHBURN, (John) Blackett Dennison; s of Thomas Dennison Ditchburn, and Elaine, *née* Walton; *b* 7 January 1957; *Educ* Strode's Sch Egham, Walthamstow Tech Coll, NE London Poly; *m* 1985, Judy, da of Jack Regis, of Northwood, Middx; 1 da (Hayley Juliette b 31 March 1987), 1 s (Loic Jack Dennison b 2 Nov 1988); *Career* land surveyor 1973–80, PR and advertising exec 1980–86, Prudential Corporation 1986–94, Carat Advertising 1994–98, dir Transacsys plc 1999–, chief exec Girovend Ltd 1999–; memb Mktg Soc 1992, assoc memb D&AD 1993; *Books* Superbiking (1983); *Recreations* cooking, reading, anything on wheels; *Style—* Blackett Ditchburn, Esq

DITTMAR, Hank; *m*; *Career* former head Reconnecting America; chief exec Prince's Fndn for the Built Environment 2005–; chm Congress for the New Urbanism Bd America; *Style—* Hank Dittmar, Esq; ✉ Prince's Foundation for the Built Environment, 19–22 Charlotte Road, London EC2A 3SG

DIX, Wing Cdr Kenneth John Weeks; OBE (1975), AFC (1958), QC (1967); adopted s of Eric John Dix (d 1982), of Dorset, and Kate, *née* Weeks (d 1986); *b* 12 September 1930; *Educ* HMC Canford, RAF Colls Cranwell, Bracknell, Manby (PSC, AWC); *m* 1, 1953 (m dis); 1 da (Linda b 1954), 1 s (Michael b 1956); m 2, 1969 (m dis); *Career* RAF 1948–83 (Europe, ME, Far E, USA), ret with rank of Wing Cdr; conslt for electronic defence systems and mil advsr (Eldecon), specialist in avionics, navigation, weapons and reconnaissance systems; dir Electronic Defence Assoc; represented various counties,

RAF, Combined Servs and Oxbridge combined XV at rugby 1953; Queen's Commendation 1967; MRAeS, MIMgt, MIEE, memb BHS; *Recreations* fly fishing, horse riding, shooting, studying antiques; *Clubs* RAF, Royal Over-Seas League, SFC; *Style*— Wing Cdr Kenneth J W Dix, OBE, AFC, QC, RAF; ✉ c/o Lloyds Bank, Bournemouth BH1 1ED

DIXEY, Judy; da of John Dixey, and Jane, *née* Dobson; *Educ* St Hilda's Coll Oxford (MA); *Career* charity dir; qualified as CA with Peat Marwick Mitchell 1975–78; asst dir Eastern Arts Assoc 1985–89, dir Bankside Gallery 1993–2004; exec dir Vocaleyes 2004–; tstee Gemini; CA 1979; *Recreations* singing; *Style*— Ms Judy Dixey; ✉ e-mail jmdixey@hotmail.com

DIXON, Prof Adrian Kendal; s of Kendal Dixon, and Annette, *née* Darley; *b* 5 February 1948; *Educ* Uppingham, King's Coll Cambridge (MA, MB BChir, MD), Bart's Med Coll London (Golf purple); *m* 1979, Anne Hazel, *née* Lucas; 2 s (Charles Kendal b 21 Jan 1981, Thomas Christopher b 12 March 1987), 1 da (Emily Louise b 3 Feb 1983); *Career* jr hosp posts Bart's, Nottingham Gen Hosp and Hosp for Sick Children Great Ormond St 1972–79, lectr in radiology and hon conslt radiologist Addenbrooke's Hosp Cambridge 1979–94, prof of radiology Univ of Cambridge 1994–; ed-in-chief European Radiology 2008–; fell Peterhouse Cambridge 1986–; FRCR 1978, FRCP 1991, FMedSci 1998, Hon FFRRCSI 1999, Hon FRANZCR 2001, FRCS 2003; *Books* Body CT (1983), Human Cross Sectional Anatomy (1991), Diagnostic Radiology (2007); *Recreations* family, golf; *Style*— Prof Adrian Dixon

DIXON, Andrew Gareth; s of Geoff Dixon, and Maureen, *née* Young; *b* 5 December 1958; *Educ* Univ of Bradford Mgmnt Centre (BSc); *m* 16 July 1988, Charlotte, da of Richard Kendall; 1 s (Elliott b 8 July 1996), 1 da (Lilly b 6 January 1998); *Career* sec social and cultural affrs Univ of Bradford 1979–80, administrator and youth projects dir Major Road Theatre Company 1981–84, county arts offr Humberside CC 1984–89; Northern Arts: asst dir 1989–92, dep chief exec and head regnl devpt 1992–97, chief exec 1997–2002; exec dir Arts Cncl 2002–05, chief exec Newcastle Gateshead Initiative 2005–, exec dir Tourism Tyne & Wear 2006–; *Recreations* arts, skiing, photography, vegetarian cookery; *Style*— Andrew Dixon, Esq; ✉ Newcastle Gateshead Initiative, 4th Floor, Central Square South, Orchard Street, Newcastle upon Tyne NE1 3AZ

DIXON, Prof Anthony Frederick George (Tony); s of George Edward Dixon (d 1988), and Rose Emma, *née* Middlemiss (d 1986); *b* 4 May 1932; *Educ* E Ham GS, UCL (BSc), Jesus Coll Oxford (DPhil); *m* 20 Aug 1957, (Theodora) June, da of Michael Phil Theodore White (d 1995); 1 da (Fiona b 1963), 1 s (Keith b 1965); *Career* Univ of Glasgow: asst lectr 1957–59, lectr 1959–69, sr lectr 1969–74; prof of biology UEA 1974–97 (emeritus prof 1997–), prof Nat Univ of La Plata Argentina 1994; Gregor Mendel Gold Medal 1992, Medal of Honour Akademia Podlaska 2000, Laureateship Univ of S Bohemia 2001; Dr (hc) Univ of S Bohemia 2006; *Books* Biology of Aphids (1973), Simulation of Lime Aphid Population Dynamics (with N D Barlow, 1980), Cereal Aphid Populations: Biology Simulation and Prediction (with N Carter and R Rabbinge, 1982), Aphid Ecology (1985, 2 edn 1998), Insect Predator - prey dynamics: ladybird beetles and biological control (2000), Insect Herbivore-Host Dynamics: Tree Dwelling Aphids (2005); *Recreations* reading; *Style*— Prof Tony Dixon; ✉ 20 Newfound Drive, Cringleford, Norwich, Norfolk NR4 7RY; School of Biological Sciences, University of East Anglia, Norwich NR4 7TJ (tel 01603 592260, e-mail a.f.dixon@uea.ac.uk)

DIXON, Baron (Life Peer UK 1997), of Jarrow in the County of Tyne & Wear; Donald (Don) Dixon; PC (1996), DL (Tyne & Wear 1997); s of late Christopher Albert Dixon, and Jane Dixon; *b* 6 March 1929; *Educ* Ellison Street Elementary Sch Jarrow; *m* Doreen Morad; 1 s, 1 da; *Career* shipyard worker 1947–74, branch sec GMWU 1974–79, cncllr S Tyneside MDC 1963–; MP (Lab) Jarrow 1979–97, formerly Lab dep chief whip until 1996; Freeman: Borough of Jarrow 1972, Metropolitan Borough of South Tyneside 1997; *Recreations* football, boxing, reading; *Clubs* Jarrow Labour, Ex Servicemen's (Jarrow), Hastings (Hebburn); *Style*— The Rt Hon Lord Dixon, PC; ✉ 1 Hillcrest, Jarrow, Tyne & Wear NE32 4DP (tel 0191 897635); House of Lords, London SW1A 0PW

DIXON, Isobel; *b* Umtata, South Africa; *Educ* Univ of Stellenbosch, Univ of Edinburgh; *Career* poet and literary agent; agent Blake Friedmann Literary Agency Ltd; contrib to numerous poetry jls and anthologies, trans South African novels into English; Sanlam Literary Award 2000, Olive Schreiner Award 2004; *Books* Weather Eye (2000), A Fold in the Map (2007); *Style*— Ms Isobel Dixon; ✉ Blake Friedmann Literary Agency Ltd, 122 Arlington Road, London NW1 7HP

DIXON, Sir (David) Jeremy; kt (2000); s of Joseph Lawrence Dixon, and Beryl Margaret, *née* Braund; *b* 31 May 1939; *Educ* Merchant Taylors', AA Sch of Architecture (AADipl); *m* 1 (sep); 1 s, 2 da; partner, Julia Somerville; *Career* architect: in private practice since 1973: princ Jeremy Dixon 1975–90 (with Fenella Dixon), Jeremy Dixon BDP 1983–90, Jeremy Dixon Edward Jones and Jeremy Dixon Edward Jones BDP 1991–2003, Dixon Jones 2003–; winner int competitions: Northampton Co offices 1973, Royal Opera House 1983, Piazzale Roma Venice 1990; other competition wins: Tate Gallery coffee shop and restaurant 1984, study centre Darwin Coll Cambridge 1988, Robert Gordon Univ residence Aberdeen 1991, Univ of Portsmouth science building 1993, Nat Portrait Gallery extension 1994, Saïd Business Sch Univ of Oxford 1996, Magna Carta Bldg Salisbury Cathedral 2001, Panopticon UCL 2001, Kings Place devpt 2002, Exhibition Rd project 2004; other works incl: reconstruction of the Tatlin Tower 1971, housing in St Mark's Road London 1975, Henry Moore Sculpture Inst Leeds 1988, Compass Point Docklands 1989, Plymouth Superstore for J Sainsbury 1991, Regent Palace devpt 2005; chm RIBA Regnl Awards Gp 1991–; tutor: AA Sch 1972–82, RCA 1980–83; RIBA; *Exhibitions* Venice Biennale 1980 and 1991, Paris 1981, Bordeaux Chateau Exhibition Paris 1998; *Publications* Jeremy Dixon and Edward Jones: Buildings & Projects 1959–2002 (2002); *Recreations* walking in English landscape, contemporary sculpture and painting, music; *Style*— Sir Jeremy Dixon; ✉ Dixon Jones Ltd, Unit 6C, 44 Gloucester Avenue, London NW1 8JD (tel 020 7483 8888, fax 020 7483 8899, e-mail jeremydixon@dixonjones.co.uk)

DIXON, (Henry) Joly; CMG (2004); s of Gervais Joly Dixon (d 1996), and Kay, *née* Russell (d 1996); *b* 13 January 1945, Warrington; *Educ* Shrewsbury (head of sch), Univ of York (BA); *m* 1976, Mary Minch; 2 da (Joanna b 1969, Rachel b 1974), 3 s (Noel b 1971, David b 1984, Michael b 1986); *Career* lectr in economic statistics: Univ of York 1970–72, Univ of Exeter 1972–75; sr administrator European Cmmn Brussels 1975–82, financial cncllr Delgn of the European Cmmn Washington DC 1982–85, economic advsr to Jacques Delors 1985–1992, dir for int economic affrs European Commn Brussels 1992–2003, dep special rep to UN Sec Gen Kosovo 1999–2000, chm Bd of Govrs Indirect Tax Authy Bosnia 2004–; statistics cmmr 2006–; *Recreations* photography, garden design, cabinet making; *Style*— Joly Dixon, Esq, CMG; ✉ Statistics Commission, Artillery House, 11–19 Artillery Row, London SW1P 1RT

DIXON, Sir Jonathan Mark; 4 Bt (UK 1919), of Astle, Chelford, Co Palatine of Chester; s of Capt Nigel Dixon, OBE, RN (d 1978), and Margaret Josephine, da of late Maurice John Collett (d 2004); suc unc, Sir John George Dixon, 3 Bt (d 1990); *b* 1 September 1949; *Educ* Winchester, UC Oxford (MA); *m* 1978, Patricia Margaret, da of James Baird Smith; 1 da (Katherine Anne b 1980), 2 s (Mark Edward b 1982, Timothy Nigel b 1987); *Heir* s, Mark Dixon; *Recreations* fishing; *Style*— Sir Jonathan Dixon, Bt

DIXON, Josie; da of Brian Hugh Dixon, and Ailsa Mary Pauline, *née* Harrison; *Educ* Lord Williams's Sch Thame, UC Oxford (open scholarship, Violet Vaughan Morgan Prize, BA), Wolfson Coll Oxford (MPhil); *m* 2002, Dr Bryan Wells; 2 s (Marcus Julian b 2003, Orlando Lucian b 2005); *Career* A-level examiner Oxford and Cambridge Examinations Bd 1986–89; CUP: ed 1989–91, commissioning ed 1992–94, sr commissioning ed for literature 1995–98, assoc editorial manager for humanities 1998–99; publishing dir Academic Div Palgrave Macmillan 1999–2003, publishing conslt 2003–; vol work with tuberculosis patients Hosp del Niño Lima 1983, lifelong Oxfam supporter; Sir Stanley Unwin Travelling Scholar 1993; *Publications* essays published in Revolution and English Romanticism: Politics and Rhetoric (ed Hanley and Selden, 1990) and The Cambridge Companion to Coleridge (ed Newlyn, 2002); reviews in The Times Higher Education Supplement; *Recreations* music (recordings of Renaissance polyphony made with the Cambridge Taverner Choir), Italy; *Style*— Ms Josie Dixon; ✉ e-mail josiedixon@jasmine-winchester.fsnet.co.uk

DIXON, Kenneth Herbert Morley; CBE (1996); s of Arnold Morley Dixon (d 1975); *b* 19 August 1929; *Educ* Cranbrook Sch Sydney Aust, Univ of Manchester (BA), Harvard Business Sch (AMP); *m* 1955, Patricia Oldbury, *née* Whalley; 2 s (Michael, Giles b 1969); *Career* Lt Royal Signals BAOR Cyprus 1947–49; Calico Printers Association Ltd 1952–56; Rowntree & Co: joined 1956, mktg UK Confectionery Div 1966, dir Rowntree Mackintosh Ltd and dep chm UK Confectionery Div 1970, chm UK Confectionery Div 1973, dep chm Rowntree Mackintosh Ltd 1978, chm Rowntree Mackintosh plc (Rowntree plc from 1987) 1981–89; vice-chm Legal and General Group plc 1986–94 (dir 1984–94), dir Yorkshire Tyne-Tees Television Holdings plc (formerly Yorkshire Television Holdings plc) 1989–97, dep chm Bass plc 1990–94 (dir 1988–96, chm Remuneration and Audit Ctees); memb: Cncl for Indust and Higher Educn 1986–, Cncl Nat Forum for Mgmnt Educn and Devpt 1987–; pt/t memb British Railways Bd 1990–; Univ of York: memb Hon Degrees Ctee 1983–, memb Fin Ctee 1986, chm Jt Ctee on Jarratt Report 1986, memb Policy and Resources Ctee 1987–, memb Ctee on Appts to Court and Cncl 1988–, pro-chllr 1987–, chm Cncl 1990 (memb Cncl 1983); chm Open Univ Visiting Ctee 1990; FRSA, CIMgt; *Recreations* reading, music, fell walking; *Style*— Kenneth Dixon, Esq, CBE

DIXON, Dr Michael; s of Walter Dixon, of Weybridge, Surrey, and Sonia Ivy, *née* Doidge (d 1997); *b* 16 March 1956, Plymouth; *Educ* Tiffin Boys' Sch Kingston upon Thames, Imperial Coll London (BSc, ARCS), Univ of York (DPhil); *m* 1, 1988; 1 da (Isabel Richenda b 4 June 1990), 1 s (Samuel John b 20 Jan 1992); m 2, 29 Dec 2001, Deborah Mary, *née* McMahon; 1 s (Noah b 10 Sept 1999); *Career* sponsoring ed Pitman Publishing Ltd 1980–83, publisher then publishing dir John Wiley & Sons Ltd 1983–96, md Thomson Science Europe 1996–98, gp md Sweet & Maxwell Ltd 1998–99, DG Zoological Soc of London 2000–04, dir Natural History Museum 2004–; chief scientific advsr Dept for Culture Media and Sport 2006–, memb Cncl Royal Albert Hall 2004–, memb Bd Ecsite 2005–; tstee Int Tst for Zoological Nomenclature 2004–; memb Ct of Imperial Coll 2006–; *Recreations* natural history, photography, music; *Clubs* RSM; *Style*— Dr Michael Dixon; ✉ The Natural History Museum, Cromwell Road, London SW7 5BD (tel 020 7942 5471, e-mail m.dixon@nhm.ac.uk)

DIXON, Peter John; s of George Edward Dixon, and Violet Jose, *née* Bell; *b* 4 February 1949; *Educ* King Edward VI GS, Wellingborough GS, LSE (BSc), London Inst of Educn (postgrad CertEd), Brunel Univ (MEd); *m* 28 July 1973, (Elizabeth) Susan, da of Joseph Arthur Butterworth; 2 s (Simon Peter b 29 Sept 1979, Nicholas Jonathan b 8 Nov 1981); *Career* head of history and integrated studies Hayes Co GS 1972–80, chef and proprietor White Moss House Cumbria 1980–; winner of food and wine awards in all leading guide books; Master Chef of GB (memb Exec Ctee); *Recreations* walking, tennis, wine tasting, bridge, chess; *Style*— Peter Dixon, Esq; ✉ White Moss House, Rydal Water, Grasmere, Cumbria LA22 9SE (tel 01539 435295, fax 01539 435516, e-mail dixon@whitemoss.com)

DIXON, Peter John Bellett; *Educ* CCC Cambridge (MA, open exhibitioner), London Business Sch (MSc); *Career* arbitrage trader Vickers da Costa stockbrokers 1967–73, asst dir Edward Bates and Sons Ltd merchant bankers 1973–77, dir then md Turner Curzon Ltd 1977–86, dir and head of capital markets Den norske Bank plc 1986–90, non-exec dir and business conslt 1990–; chm: Union Discount Ltd (also non-exec dir Union plc), Optoplast plc, Megamode Ltd, Manifest Voting Agency Ltd; former chm: Ketlon (UK) Ltd, Welpac plc; chm Enfield and Haringey HA 1998–2001, currently chm UCL Hosps NHS Fndn Tst, memb Cncl and tstee NHS Confedn; chm The Housing Corporation, chm Office for Public Mgmnt, former chm N Thames region London & Quadrant Housing Tst and New Islington and Hackney Housing Assoc, former cncllr London Borough of Islington (chm Planning Application Ctee 1973–74); lay memb Info Tbnl Lord Chllr's Dept; *Style*— Peter Dixon, Esq; ✉ University College London Hospitals NHS Foundation Trust, 250 Euston Road, London NW1 2PG (tel 020 7380 9634)

DIXON, Air Cdre Ray L; *b* 7 May 1948; *Educ* Univ of Liverpool (BSc); *m*; 1 s, 1 da; *Career* cmmnd RAF 1970, fighter pilot 1970–, RAAF Staff College 1984, sr personnel offr 1990–94, Station Cdr RAF Mt Pleasant 1994–95, Chief Plans Branch Allied Forces Central Europe HQ 1995–97, sr air advsr NATO Forces Bosnia Herzegovina 1997, Cdr Br Forces Falkland Is 1998–99, sr mangr Air Def systems and sites UK and abroad 1999–2000, Inspr of Flight Safety RAF 2000–02, Dir Def Aviation Safety Centre 2002–; Upper Freeman Guild of Air Pilots and Air Navigators; FRAeS; *Recreations* game fishing, nature conservation, DIY, music; *Style*— Air Commodore R L Dixon, FRAeS, RAF (ret); ✉ Woodland House, Broadwoodkelly, Devon EX19 8EA

DIXON, Prof Richard Newland; s of Robert Thomas Dixon (d 1985), of Borough Green, Kent, and Lilian, *née* Newland (d 1973); *b* 25 December 1930; *Educ* Judd Sch Tonbridge, KCL (BSc), St Catharine's Coll Cambridge (PhD, ScD); *m* 18 Sept 1954, Alison Mary, da of Gilbert Arnold Birks (d 1966), of Horsforth, Leeds; 1 s (Paul b 1959), 2 da (Joan b 1961, Sheila b 1962); *Career* post doctoral fell Nat Res Cncl of Canada 1957–59, ICI fell lectr in chem Univ of Sheffield 1959–69, Sorby research fell Royal Soc 1964–69; Univ of Bristol: prof of chemistry 1969–96, dean of sci 1979–82, pro-vice-chllr 1989–92, Alfred Capper Pass prof of chemistry 1990–96, prof emeritus 1996, sr research fell 1996–; Leverhulme emeritus fell 1996–98; visiting scholar Stanford Univ USA 1982–83; non-exec dir United Bristol Healthcare NHS Tst 1994–2003 (chm 2006–); memb: Faraday Cncl RSC (vice-pres 1989–98), SERC Ctees; tstee Charitable Trustees for United Bristol Hospitals 2003– (vice-chm 2005–); CChem 1976, FRSC 1976, FRS 1986; *Books* Spectroscopy and Structure (1965), Theoretical Chemistry (Vol 1 1971, Vol 2 1973, Vol 3 1975); author of 200 papers in research jls; *Recreations* mountain walking, travel, theatre, concerts, photography; *Style*— Prof Richard Dixon, FRS; ✉ 22 Westbury Lane, Bristol BS9 2PE (tel 0117 968 1691); School of Chemistry, University of Bristol, Cantock's Close, Bristol BS8 1TS (tel 0117 928 7661 fax 0117 925 1295, e-mail r.n.dixon@bris.ac.uk)

DIXON, Dr Stella; da of Harold Dixon, of Langport, Somerset, and Edna, *née* Norman; *b* 20 December 1947; *Educ* Elmhurst GS, Univ of London (BSc), Univ of Bath (PhD); *m* 17 Dec 1977, Howard Burton; 2 s (David Alexander William b 15 Jan 1979, Matthew Oliver James b 18 Oct 1982); *Career* social work lectr and mangr 1969–90, with FE Unit/FE Devpt Agency 1991–2000; Magistrates' Court Serv Inspectorate: HM sr inspr 2000–02, HM dep chief inspr 2002–03, HM chief inspr 2003–05; *Recreations* walking, swimming, music; *Style*— Dr Stella Dixon; ✉ 5 Larkhall Place, Bath BA1 6SF (tel 01225 424726)

DIXON, Tom; OBE (2000); *b* 21 May 1959; *Educ* Holland Park Comp; *Career* designer; professional musician Funkopolitans 1980–82, nightclub promotion and event organisation 1981–84; inauguration of Creative Salvage 1984; launched: Space and Space Studio (manufacturing and retail venture) 1991, Eurolounge 1994; creative dir: Habitat 2001– (head of design 1998–2001), Art & Technology 2004–; launched Tom Dixon design shop 2001; Hon Dr UCE Birmingham 2004; *Publications* International Design Yearbook, One Hundred Chairs (1987), The Modern Chair (1988), Tom Dixon (1989), New British Designers (1990), The Modern Chair (1993), 100 Designs/100 Years (1999), Rethink (2000),

Design Directory Great Britain (2001), The Eco-design Handbook (2002), 30–30 Vision (2003), The International Design Year Book (2003), 100 Future Products 2004 (2003), The Official Point of View Milan 03 (2003), Who's Who in Design Vol 2 (2004), The International Design Year Book (ed, 2004), Designers on Design (2004), Love Your Home (2004), The Lighthouse Book; featured in various catalogues and exhbn papers; *Style*— Tom Dixon, Esq, OBE; ✉ Tom Dixon, 28 All Saints Road, London W11 1HG (tel 020 7792 5335, fax 020 7792 2156, e-mail info@tomdixon.net, website www.tomdixon.net)

DIXON-SMITH, Baron (Life Peer UK 1993), of Bocking in the County of Essex; Robert William (Bill) Dixon-Smith; DL (Essex 1986); 2 s of Dixon Smith (d 1995) of Braintree, Essex, and his 1 w, (Alice) Winifred, *née* Stratton (d 1976); *b* 30 September 1934; *Educ* Oundle, Writtle Agric Coll; *m* 13 Feb 1960, Georgina Janet, da of George Cook, of Halstead, Essex; 1 da (Hon Sarah Jane (*see* Christopher Henry St John Hoare) b 16 Dec 1960), 1 s (Hon Adam William George b 11 Jan 1963); *Career* Nat Serv 2 Lt King's Dragoon Gds 1955–57; farmer; memb Essex CC 1965–93 (chm 1986–89), memb Assoc of CCs 1983–93 (chm 1992–93), memb Local Govt Mgmnt Bd 1991–93, chm Anglia Poly Univ 1992–93 (Hon Dr 1994), memb Cncl Essex Univ 1991–94, govr Writtle Coll 1967–94 (chm of govrs 1973–85, fell 1993); memb: Select Ctee for European Communities, Sub-ctee 4 1994–96, Select Ctee for Science and Technology House of Lords 1994–98; oppn House of Lords spokesman on: environment, tport and the regions 1998–2001, home affrs 2001–02, environment 2003–; Freeman City of London 1988, Liveryman Worshipful Co of Farmers 1991; *Recreations* shooting, fishing, golf; *Style*— The Rt Hon Lord Dixon-Smith, DL; ✉ Lyons Hall, Braintree, Essex CM7 6SH (tel 01376 326834)

DIXSON, Maurice Christopher Scott; s of H G (George) Dixson (d 1992), and E E (Lilla) Dixson, *née* McCartney (d 1999); *b* 5 November 1941; *Educ* Palmers GS, UC Swansea (BA), Carleton Univ Ottawa (MA), Pembroke Coll Oxford (DPhil); *m* Anne Beverley, da of late Wilfred Morris; *Career* mgmnt trainee and commercial exec Hawker Siddeley Aviation 1969–74; BAC (British Aerospace): dir Al Yamamah Defence Project and commercial dir Military Aircraft Div 1983–86, chief exec Royal Ordnance 1986–88, md Commercial Aircraft Co 1988–90; exec dir and md Smaller Companies Gp GEC 1990–93, chief exec Simon Gp plc 1993–2002, non-exec dir Swan Hill plc 1994–2003, exec chm Cranfield Aerospace Ltd 2003–, chm Southside Thermal Sciences (STS) Ltd 2004–; memb Econ Policy Ctee Engrg Employers Assoc 1994–2002; memb Cons Pty; FRAeS 1986, FInstPS 1989; *Recreations* shooting, fishing, soccer (played for Br Universities), watching rugby, fine arts; *Clubs* RAC; *Style*— Dr Maurice Dixson; ✉ Pound House, Middle Common, Kington Langley, Wiltshire SN15 5NW (tel 01249 758171, fax 01249 758880)

DJALILI, Omid; s of Ahmad Djalili, and Parvaneh Samii Djalili; *b* 1965, London; *Educ* Holland Park Sch London, Univ of Ulster Coleraine; *Career* comedian and actor; Edinburgh Festival shows: Short Fat Kebab Shop Owner's Son 1995, Arab and the Jew 1996, Omid Djalili is Ethnic 1997, The Iranian Ceilidh 1999, Warm to My Winning Smile 2000, Behind Enemy Lines 2002 (Perrier Award nominee); Freedom City of Montreal 1986; *Television* Bloody Foreigners (Best Documentary One World Media Awards 2001), Small Potatoes, Whoopi (US), Casanova, HBO half hour stand-up special, Jack Dee Live at the Apollo half hour stand-up special; *Film* The Calcium Kid, Anita and Me, The Mummy, The World is Not Enough, Gladiator, Spy Game, Modigliani, Sky Captain and the World of Tomorrow, Deadlines; *Awards* Time Out Comedy Award 2001, Best Stand-Up EMMA Awards 2002, nominee Best Comedy South Bank Awards 2002, nominee Canadian Gemini Award; *Recreations* tennis, football; *Style*— Omid Djalili, Esq; ✉ c/o Scott Marshall, 54 Poland Street, London W1V 7NR; c/o Bound & Gagged Comedy, 25 Melrose Avenue, Willesden Green, London NW2 4LH

DJANOGLY, Jonathan; MP; *Educ* Oxford Brookes Univ (BA), Guildford Law Sch, ICAEW; *Career* slr 1990–98, ptnr SJ Berwin LLP 1998–; cncllr Regent's Park Westminster London BC 1994–2001; Parly candidate (Cons) Oxford E 1997, MP (Cons) Huntingdon 2001–, shadow min for home, constitutional and legal affrs 2004–05, shadow slr-gen 2005–, shadow min for trade and industry 2005–; memb Trade and Industry Select Ctee 2001–05; memb Law Soc 1991; *Style*— Jonathan Djanogly, Esq, MP; ✉ House of Commons, London SW1A 0AA (tel 020 7219 2367)

DOBASH, Prof Rebecca Emerson; da of I M Emerson, and Helen, *née* Cooper; *b* 3 February 1943; *Educ* Arizona State Univ (BA, MS), Washington State Univ (PhD); *m* 5 June 1965, Russell P Dobash, s of Paul Dobash; *Career* social research Faculty of Law Univ of Manchester; memb: American Criminology Soc, Br Criminology Assoc, European Criminology Soc; awards for outstanding research and pubns Int Soc of Victimology and American Soc of Criminology, August Vollmer Award; fell: Rockefeller Centre Bellagio 1981 and 1992, Univ of Melbourne 1996; *Books* Violence Against Wives (1979), The Imprisonment of Women (1986), Women, Violence and Social Change (1992), Women Viewing Violence (1992), Gender and Crime (1995), The Simulated Client (1996), Research Evaluation and Programmes for Violent Men (1996), Rethinking Violence Against Women (1998), Changing Violent Men (2000); *Recreations* travel, food, gardening; *Style*— Prof Rebecca Emerson Dobash; ✉ School of Law (Criminology), University of Manchester, Oxford Road, Manchester M13 9PL (tel 0161 275 4490, fax 0161 275 4922)

DOBBIE, Dr Robert Charles (Bob); CB (1996); *b* 16 January 1942; *Educ* Dollar Acad, Univ of Edinburgh (BSc), Univ of Cambridge (PhD); *m* 18 Sept 1964, Elizabeth Charlotte, *née* Barbour; 3 s; *Career* ICI fell Univ of Bristol 1967–68, lectr in chemistry Univ of Newcastle upon Tyne 1968–76, tutor Open Univ 1975–85; DTI: princ 1976–83, asst sec 1983–90, under sec 1990–95 (on secondment to DOE 1990–92); under sec Cabinet Office 1995–97, dir Competitiveness Unit DTI 1997–, regnl dir Govt Office for the North East 1998–2001; author 40 research pubns in chemistry 1964–78; *Recreations* theatre, malt whisky, mountains; *Style*— Dr Bob Dobbie, CB; ✉ 38 Albert Street, London NW1 7NU

DOBBIE, Scott Jamieson; CBE (1998); s of Scott Dobbie (d 1943), and Isobel, *née* Jamieson (d 1969); *b* 24 July 1939; *Educ* Dollar Acad, Univ of Edinburgh (BSc); *m* 1962, Brenda, *née* Condie; 2 da; *Career* with Unilever 1961–66, with ICI 1966–72; Wood Mackenzie & Co Stockbrokers: ptnr 1975–82, managing ptnr 1982–88; NatWest Securities: md 1988–93, chm 1993–98; chm: CRESTCo Ltd 1996–2001, Securities Inst 2000–, Standard Life European Private Equity Tst 2001–, The Edinburgh Investment Tst plc 2003– (dir 1998); vice-chm Bankers Tst Int 1998–99; dir: SFA 1993–2001, Murray VCT4 plc 2000–03, Premier Oil plc 2000–, Scottish Fin Enterprise 2001–06; sr advsr Deutsche Bank AG 1999–; cmmr Jersey Fin Servs Cmmn 2000–; memb: Regulatory Decisions Ctee FSA 2001–06; ind memb Standards Ctee Corp of London; Hon FSI 1996; *Recreations* mechanical objects, buildings, books; *Style*— Scott Dobbie, Esq, CBE; ✉ Securities Institute, Centurion House, 24 Monument Street, London EC3R 8AQ (tel 020 7645 0603. fax 020 7626 3068, e-mail scott.dobbie@sii.org.uk)

DOBBIN, Jim; MP; s of William Dobbin, and Catherine Dobbin; *b* 26 May 1941; *Educ* St Columba's RC HS Cowdenbeath, St Andrew's RC HS Kirkcaldy, Napier Coll Edinburgh; *m* 1964, Pat; 2 s (Barry, Patrick), 2 da (Mary, Kerry); *Career* microbiologist Royal Oldham Hosp 1973–94 (with NHS for 30 years), MP (Lab/Co-op) Heywood and Middleton 1997–; chair All-Pty Pro-Life Gp; memb Backbench Ctees on: Environment, Tport and the Regions 1997–, Health 1997–, NI 1997–; memb Standing Ctee C for Euro Legislation 1997–; memb European Scrutiny Ctee 1998–; Rochdale MBC: cncllr 1983–97, chm Housing 1986, chm Neighbourhood Servs 1989, dep ldr 1990–92, ldr 1996–97; contested Bury N 1992; memb AMICUS; *Recreations* walking, gardening, theatre, cinema, football (Glasgow Celtic FC); *Style*— Jim Dobbin, MP; ✉ House of Commons, London SW1A 0AA (tel 020 7219 3000)

DOBBIN, Rev Dr Victor; CB (2000), MBE (1980), QHC (1993); s of Vincent Dobbin (d 1995), of Bushmills, and Annie, *née* Doherty (d 1957); *b* 12 March 1943; *Educ* Bushmills GS, Magee UC, Trinity Coll Dublin (MA), Queen's Univ Belfast (MTh, PhD); *m* Aug 1967, Rosemary, *née* Gault; 1 da (Anona b 1973), 1 s (Nigel b 1975); *Career* Royal Army Chaplains Dept: joined 1972, D warden RAChD Centre 1982–86, sr chaplain 3 Armd Div 1986–89, staff chaplain BAOR 1989–91, ACG Southern Dist 1991–95, Chaplain Gen 1995–2000; dir Leadership and Ethics Centre 2002–, memb Learning Advsy Cncl PSNI 2004–; Churchill fell 2000; Hon DD Presbyterian Theol Faculty in Ireland 1995; *Style*— Rev Dr V Dobbin, CB, MBE, DD; ✉ Glenview, 20 Cushendall Road, Bonamargy, Ballycastle, Antrim BT54 6QR (tel 028 2076 3841, e-mail victordobbin@aol.com)

DOBBS, Hon Mrs Justice; Dame Linda Penelope; DBE (2004); *b* 3 January 1951; *Educ* Moreton Hall, Univ of Surrey (BSc), LSE (LLM, PhD); *Career* called to the Bar Gray's Inn 1981 (bencher 2002); QC 1998, dep judge of the High Court 2003–04, judge of the High Court of Justice (Queen's Bench Div) 2004–; vice-pres NACRO, govr Expert Witness Inst, patron S African Legal Educn Fndn; tstee Oxford Sch of Drama; hon doctorate Univ of Sheffield 2006; *Publications* Road Traffic Law and Practice (1995), Archbold (contrib ed), Road Traffic Bulletin, Fraud: Law, Practice and Procedure; *Recreations* reading, music, travel, food and wine; *Style*— The Hon Mrs Justice Dobbs, DBE

D

DOBBS, Michael John; s of Eric William Dobbs (d 1990), and Eileen, *née* Saunders (d 1974); *b* 14 November 1948; *Educ* Hertford GS, ChCh Oxford (MA), Fletcher Sch of Law and Diplomacy USA (PhD, MALD); *Career* novelist; advsr to Margaret Thatcher, MP as ldr of the Oppn 1977–79, govt special advsr 1981–87, chief of staff Cons Pty 1986–87, jt dep chm Cons Pty 1994–95; dep chm Saatchi & Saatchi 1983–91, presenter Despatch Box (BBC2) 1999–2001; judge Whitbread Book Awards 2003; *Books* Salt on the Dragon's Tail (PhD thesis, 1975), House of Cards (1989, televised 1991), To Play the King (1992, televised 1993), The Final Cut (1995), Goodfellowe MP (1997), The Buddha of Brewer Street (1998), Whispers of Betrayal (2000), Winston's War (2002), Never Surrender (2003), Churchill's Hour (2004), Churchill's Triumph (2005), First Lady (2006), The Lords' Day (2007); *Recreations* losing weight, genealogy; *Style*— Michael Dobbs, Esq; ✉ Newton House, Wylye, Wiltshire BA12 0QS (mobile 07836 201967)

DOBBY, John Michael; s of Herbert Charles Dobby (d 1982), of Dover, and Gwendoline Dobby; *b* 21 November 1941; *Educ* Nautical Sch Mercury, City of London Coll; *m* 23 July 1966, Janet Constance, da of Albert Victor Williams; 3 s (Timothy James b 2 Jan 1968, Simon John b 30 March 1970, Martin Jason b 5 June 1972); *Career* apprentice timber importer 1959; Meyer International plc: md subsid Gabriel Wade (Southern) Ltd 1976–80 (dir 1972–80), gen mangr Meyer Merchants 1980–82, jt md Jewson Ltd 1983 (sometime chm), dir MI Nederland 1984–97, dir Van Hoorebeke et Fils 1985–99, chm Pont Meyer NV 1993–97 (dir 1986–97), also former chm Meyer Forest Products Ltd, chief exec Meyer International plc 1993–97 (dir 1983–97); supervisory dir: Jongeneel Holding BV 2000–06, NV Deli Universal 2006–; FIWSc; *Recreations* swimming, gardening, sailing; *Clubs* RYA, Royal Southern Yacht; *Style*— John Dobby, Esq; ✉ Hill Rise, High Street, Meonstoke, Hampshire SO32 3NH (tel 01489 878657, e-mail j.dobby@virgin.net)

DOBKIN, His Hon Judge Ian James; s of Morris Dobkin (d 1979), and Rhoda, *née* Saipe; *b* 8 June 1948; *Educ* Leeds GS, The Queen's Coll Oxford (Hastings exhibitioner, MA); *m* Oct 1980, Andrea Ruth, da of Jack Dante, and Rose Dante; 2 s (Matthew Jacob b 6 July 1983, Jonathan Edward b 4 Aug 1985); *Career* called to the Bar Gray's Inn 1971; in practice NE Circuit 1971–95, recorder of the Crown Court 1990–95 (asst recorder 1986–90), circuit judge (NE Circuit) 1995–; judicial memb W Yorks Probation Bd 2001–; liaison judge Leeds Area Magistrates Courts 2002–05; Parly candidate (Cons) Penistone 1978 and 1979; United Hebrew Congregation Leeds: vice-pres 1981–84 and 1992–96, pres 1984–88, 1996–99 and 2005–06, hon life vice-pres 2003; vice-chm Leeds Hillel Fndn, memb Advsy Ctee Leeds Centre for Criminal Justice Studies Univ of Leeds 1987–; *Recreations* crosswords, music, theatre, reading; *Clubs* Moor Allerton Golf (Leeds), Yorks CCC; *Style*— His Hon Judge Dobkin; ✉ Leeds Crown Court, Oxford Row, Leeds LS1 3BG

DOBLE, Michael John; s of Brian Sinclair Doble (d 1979), and Margaret Ingham, *née* Eastwood; *b* 31 October 1951; *Educ* St George's Sch Harpenden, Coll of Law; *m* 8 Sept 1984, Nandika Shankari, da of Dr Victor Thevathasan; 2 s (George Michael b 28 Aug 1985, Edward Oliver b 8 Nov 1987), 2 da (Harriett Victoria Rose b 27 April 1993, Anna Elizabeth b 26 Nov 1994); *Career* slr; articled clerk Denton Hall & Burgin, ptnr Denton Hall 1981, ptnr Denton Wilde Sapte 2000–04 (head Energy and Infrastructure Dept 2000–04), dir (energy) Denton Wilde Sapte 2004–; *Recreations* golf, cricket, country sports; *Clubs* MCC, Tanglin, Dulwich and Sydenham Golf, Sherborne Golf; *Style*— Michael Doble, Esq; ✉ Denton Wilde Sapte, One Fleet Place, London EC4M 7WS (tel 020 7246 7000, fax 020 7246 7777)

DOBRES, Charlie; *m* Karen; 1 da (Millicent-Muriel), 1 s (Alfie); *Career* account mangr Lowe Howard-Spink 1995, fndr Lowe Digital 1996, co-fndr (with Andrew Walmsley, *qv*) i-level 1998 (ceo 1998–2007, non-exec advsr 2007–); fndr gen sec Interactive Advtg Bureau 1998, fndr memb Digital Mktg Gp; *Style*— Charlie Dobres, Esq; ✉ i-level, 26–30 Strutton Ground, London SW1P 2HR (tel 020 7340 2700, fax 020 7340 2701)

DOBSON, Andrew Charles; s of Raymond Dobson, FRICS, of Rowlands Gill, Tyne & Wear, and Dr Mary Dobson, *née* Meikle; *b* 20 February 1956; *Educ* Oundle, St Catharine's Coll Cambridge (MA), Coll of Law Guildford; *m* 10 Aug 1985, Janet Margaret, da of Eric Shiells (decd); 1 s (Patrick Archie Shiells b 18 Jan 1988), 2 da (Alexandra Emma b 30 Dec 1989, Laura Poppy b 19 Nov 1991); *Career* litigation slr Macfarlanes 1980–86 (joined 1978), litigation ptnr Knapp Fishers 1986–87, head Commercial Litigation Lawrence Graham 1987–92 and 1995– (ptnr 1987–); memb: Law Soc 1980, Int Bar Assoc 1990; *Style*— Andrew Dobson, Esq; ✉ Lawrence Graham, 190 Strand, London WC2R 1JN (tel 020 7379 0000, fax 020 7379 6854)

DOBSON, Carolan; da of Thomas Michael Geekie, of Glasgow, and June, *née* Lusk; *b* 4 December 1954, Glasgow; *Educ* Univ of St Andrews (BSc); *m* 19 Dec 1981, James Kenneth Dobson; 2 da (Charlotte Isobel b 5 June 1986, Anna Elizabeth 5 Dec 1989); *Career* dir: Murray Johnstone Ltd 1987–93, Abbey Asset Mangrs Ltd 1997–2003, Shires Smaller Companies plc 2004–; non-exec dir: British Waterways plc 1998–2001, Securities and Investment Inst 1997–2003, Sport Scotland and Scottish Sports Cncl Tst Cos; ind investment advsr to pension funds of: Environment Agency 2004–, London Borough of Enfield, Rhondda Cynon Taf BC; memb Competition Cmmn 2005–; chm Lomond Sch 2002–; MSI 1993; *Recreations* skiing, tennis; *Style*— Mrs Carolan Dobson; ✉ Competition Commission, Victoria House, Southampton Row, London WC1B 4AD

DOBSON, Prof Christopher Martin; s of Arthur Dobson (d 1973), and Mabel, *née* Pollard; *b* 8 October 1949; *Educ* Abingdon Sch, Keble Coll Oxford (scholar, BSc, MA, Gibbs award), Merton Coll Oxford (sr scholar, DPhil); *m* 1977, Dr Mary Janet Dobson, da of Dr Derek Justin Schove; 2 s (Richard James b 16 Aug 1982, William Thomas b 11 March 1986); *Career* research fell Univ of Oxford 1975–77, asst prof of chemistry Harvard Univ and visiting scientist MIT 1977–80; Univ of Oxford: lectr BNC 1980–2001, fell LMH 1980–2001, univ lectr in chemistry 1980–95, reader 1995–96, prof (Aldrichian praelector) of chemistry 1996–2001, dir Oxford Centre for Molecular Sciences 1998–2001 (dep dir 1989–98); John Humphrey Plummer prof of chemical and structural biology Univ of Cambridge 2001–; St John's Coll Cambridge: fell 2001–, master 2007–; pres Protein Soc 1999–2001 (memb 1995–); author of over 500 papers in learned jls; nat lectr Biophysical Soc 1998; named lectureships incl: Sackler Distinguished Lecture Univ of Cambridge 2002, Bakerian Lecture Royal Soc 2003, Wills Lecture Univ of London 2003, Bayer

Distinguished Lecture Univ of Washington 2003, Anfinsen Meml Lecture Johns Hopkins Univ 2003, Joseph Black Lecture Univ of Glasgow 2003, Centenary Lecture Andersonian Chemical Soc Univ of Strathclyde 2004, EMBO Lecture Biochemical Soc 2004, Presidential Lecture Scripps Research Inst La Jolla 2005, Burroughs Wellcome Lectures Univ of E Carolina 2005, Fiftieth Anniversary Lecture Int Union of Biochemistry and Molecular Biology 2005, Sir John Kendrew Lecture Weizmann Inst 2005, William H Stein Meml Lecture Rockefeller Univ 2006, John D Ferry Lectures Univ of Wisconsin 2006, Linus Pauling Lecture and Medal Stanford Univ 2006; Sammet guest prof Johann Wolfgang Goethe Univ Frankfurt 2007; Corday Morgan Medal and Prize Royal Soc of Chemistry 1983, Brunauer Award American Ceramic Soc 1996, Dewey and Kelly Award Univ of Nebraska 1997, Interdisciplinary Award Royal Soc of Chemistry 1999, Bijovet Medal Univ of Utrecht 2002, Silver Medal Italian Soc of Biochemistry 2002, Stein and Moore Award Protein Soc 2003, Davy MEdal Royal Soc 2005, Hans Neurath Award Protein Soc 2006; Presidential visiting prof Univ of Calif San Francisco 2001–02; int research scholar Howard Hughes Med Inst USA 1992, Leverhulme Tst sr research fell Royal Soc 1993; fell Eton Coll 2001–; Dr (hc) Univ of Leuven 2001, Hon MD Umea Univ 2005, Hon MD Univ of Florence 2006, Dr (hc) Univ of Lège 2007; memb: Biochemical Soc 1988, Biophysical Soc 1998, EMBO 1999; hon memb National Magnetic Resonance Soc India 2004, hon foreign memb American Acad of Arts and Sciences 2007; CChem, FRSC 1996 (MRSC 1973), FRS 1996, FMedSci 2005; *Recreations* family, friends, travel; *Style—* Prof Christopher Dobson, FRS; ✉ Department of Chemistry, University of Cambridge, Lensfield Road, Cambridge CB2 1EW (tel 01223 763070, fax 01223 763418, e-mail cmd44@cam.ac.uk); The Master's Lodge, St John's College, Cambridge CB2 1TP

DOBSON, Rt Hon Frank Gordon; PC (1997), MP; s of James William Dobson, and Irene Shortland, *née* Laley; *b* 15 March 1940; *Educ* Archbishop Holgate's GS York, LSE; *m* 1967, Janet Mary, da of Henry Alker, and Edith Alker; 3 c; *Career* former administrator CEGB and Electricity Cncl; asst sec Cmmn for Local Admin 1975–79; MP (Lab, RMT sponsored): Holborn and St Pancras South 1979–83, Holborn and St Pancras 1983–; oppn front bench spokesman on: educn 1981–83, health 1983–87, energy 1989–92; shadow leader of the House and Lab Pty campaign co-ordinator 1987–89; chief oppn spokesman on: employment 1992–93, transport and London 1993–94, environment and London 1994–97; sec of state for health 1997–99; mayoral candidate (Lab) London 2000; *Style—* The Rt Hon Frank Dobson, MP; ✉ 22 Great Russell Mansions, Great Russell Street, London WC1B 3BE; House of Commons, London SW1A 0AA

DOBSON, Michael William Romsey; s of Sir Denis Dobson, KCB, OBE, QC (d 1995), of London, and Lady Mary Elizabeth, *née* Allen; *b* 13 May 1952; *Educ* Eton, Trinity Coll Cambridge (MA); *m* 1998, Frances Mary Josephine, *née* de Salis; 1 da (Olivia Carolyn Romsey); *Career* Morgan Grenfell Group plc: joined 1973, chief exec Morgan Grenfell Asset Mgmnt 1987–88, gp chief exec Morgan Grenfell Gp plc 1989–93, chief exec Deutsche Morgan Grenfell 1993–96; memb Bd of MDs Deutsche Bank AG 1996–2000 (responsible for: investment banking 1996–98, asset mgmnt 1998–2000), chief exec Schroders plc 2001–; non-exec dir Gen Enterprise Mgmnt Servs Ltd; *Style—* Michael Dobson, Esq

DOBSON, Dr Nicholas; s of Martin Dobson (d 2004), of Ellesmere Park, Manchester, and Mary Frances, *née* Ormonde; *b* Southport; *Educ* De La Salle Coll Pendleton, Univ of Leeds (BA, CertEd), Univ of Manchester (Dip), Coll of Law (Dip), Univ of Sheffield (PhD); *m* 16 April 1977, Jennifer Ruth Elizabeth, *née* Mercer; 1 da (Victoria Jane b 15 April 1986), 2 s (Matthew James b 20 Aug 1988, Benjamin Joseph b 10 Oct 1992); *Career* admitted slr 1984; early career as teacher (incl at St Bede's Coll Manchester) and social worker, articled clerk Leak, Almond and Parkinson, lawyer Bolton MBC, Tameside MBC, Bradford MBC then Calderdale MBC, asst head of legal servs Leicester City Cncl, chief slr Doncaster Cncl, ptnr and head of local govt law Pinsent Masons (formerly Pinsent Curtis) 1999–; past serv memb Assoc of Cncl Secs and Slrs; memb Law Soc; *Publications* TUPE, Contracting Out and Best Value (1998), Best Value, Law and Management (2000); contrib to professional jls; *Recreations* walking, swimming, reading, writing, music (eclectic tastes), opera, art, digital photography, playing blues guitar; *Style—* Dr Nicholas Dobson; ✉ Pinsent Masons, 1 Park Row, Leeds LS1 5AB (tel 0113 244 5000, fax 0113 244 8000, e-mail nicholas.dobson@pinsentmasons.com)

DOBSON, Nigel Hewitt; s of George Hewitt Dobson (d 1984), of Beckenham, Kent, and Ethel Grace, *née* Boxshall (d 2004); *b* 13 August 1949; *Educ* St Dunstan's Coll; *Career* Whinney Murray & Co (now Ernst & Young) 1968–2001: Ernst & Ernst St Louis Missouri 1974–75, Corporate Advsy Servs Div Whinney Murray 1976–93, seconded Corporate Fin Dept Midland Bank 1978–80, ptnr 1981–2001, i/c Restructuring and Reorganisation Servs 1994–99, Corp Fin 1999–2001; FCA (ACA 1972), MSI 1993; *Recreations* sailing, gardening, reading; *Style—* Nigel Dobson, Esq; ✉ Red Lodge, The Parade, Minnis Bay, Birchington, Kent CT7 9LX; Port St Charles, St Peter, Barbados, West Indies

DOBSON, Prof Peter James; s of Cyril James Dobson (d 1991), and Mary, *née* Bright; *b* 24 October 1942; *Educ* Newquay GS, Univ of Southampton (BSc, PhD); *m* 6 Nov 1965, Catherine, *née* Roberts; 2 da (Laura b 22 Sept 1969, Emma b 25 Jan 1973); *Career* sr lectr in physics Imperial Coll London 1980–84 (lectr 1968–80), sr princ scientist Philips Research Labs 1984–88; Univ of Oxford: lectr Dept of Engrg Science 1988–96, prof of engrg science 1996–2002, academic dir Begbroke Science Park 2002–; fell The Queen's Coll Oxford 1988; holder of over 30 patents, author of over 130 papers in refereed jls; MA (by incorporation) Univ of Oxford 1988; memb American Chemical Soc 2001; FInstP 2003 (MInstP 1966); *Recreations* gardening, jazz, cooking, surfing; *Style—* Prof Peter Dobson; ✉ University of Oxford Begbroke Science Park, Sandy Lane, Kidlington, Oxfordshire OX5 1PF (tel 01865 283780, fax 01865 374992, e-mail peter.dobson@begbroke.ox.ac.uk)

DOBSON, Roger Swinburne; OBE (1987); s of Sir Denis William Dobson, KCB, OBE, QC (d 1995), and Thelma Swinburne (d 1964); *b* 24 June 1936; *Educ* Bryanston, Trinity Coll Cambridge (MA), Stanford Univ (DEng), Golden Gate Univ; *m* Deborah Elizabeth Sancroft, da of Richard James Burrough (d 1998); 1 s (William b 27 April 1977), 1 da (Serena b 5 July 1979); *Career* Binnie & Partners 1959–69; Bechtel Ltd: joined 1969, gen mangr PMB Systems Engineering 1984–86, md Laing Bechtel Petroleum Development Ltd 1986–90; dep chm Thomas Telford Ltd 1990–99; DG and sec ICE 1990–99; md Hill Farm Orchards Ltd 2000–; chm: Computer Aided Design Working Gp Process Plant Econ Devpt Cncl 1982–87, Energy Industry Cncl 1987–90; hon treas and dir Quinco Campaign to Promote Engrg 1997–2002; memb: Construction Industry Sector Gp (NEDO) 1988–92, DTI Action for Engrg Initiative 1994–96; dir Year of Engrg Success (YEARCO) 1997–99; MBCS 1969, FICE 1990 (MICE 1963), FREng 1993; *Publications* Some Applications of a Digital Computer to Hydraulic Engineering (1967), Effective CADCAM Data Exchange (1985), Offshore Structural Design Advances & Trends (1986), Keynote Address (CADCAM Data Exchange Tech Centre, 1986), Cost Effective R&D for Topsides Development (1987), Private Participation in Infrastructure Projects (1989); *Recreations* sailing, tennis, fishing, gardening; *Clubs* Royal Ocean Racing; *Style—* R S Dobson, Esq, OBE, FREng; ✉ Etchilhampton House, Etchilhampton, Devizes, Wiltshire SN10 3JH (tel 01380 722927, fax 01380 729020, e-mail roger.dobson2@btinternet.com)

DOBSON, Susan Angela (Sue); da of Arthur George Henshaw (d 1994), and Nellie, *née* Flower (d 1978); *b* 31 January 1946; *Educ* Holy Family Convent, Assumption Convent Ramsgate, Ursuline Convent Westgate-on-Sea, NE London Poly (BA, Dip HE); *m* 1966 (m dis 1974), Michael Dobson; *Career* fashion, cookery and beauty ed Femina 1965–69, contributing ed Fair Lady 1969–71; ed: SA Inst of Race Rels 1972, Wedding Day and First Home 1978–81, Successful Slimming 1981, Woman & Home 1982–94; ed-in-chief Choice 1994–2002, travel ed Choice 2002–; memb: British Guild of Travel Writers, Bd Plan International UK 1993–2004; *Books* The Wedding Day Book (1981, 2 edn 1989); *Recreations* travel, books, photography, theatre, music, exploring Britain; *Style—* Ms Sue Dobson; ✉ Choice Magazine, 2 King Street, Peterborough, Cambridgeshire PE1 1LT (e-mail sue@choicemag.co.uk)

DOCHERTY, Dr David; s of David Docherty (d 1972); *b* 10 December 1956; *Educ* St Mungo's Acad Glasgow, Univ of Strathclyde (BA), LSE (PhD, MSc); *m* 1992, Kate, da of Rt Hon Sir Murray Stuart-Smith, *qv*; 2 da (Flora b 17 Oct 1993, Polly b 9 July 1997); *Career* fell Broadcasting Research Unit 1984–89, research dir Broadcasting Standards Cncl 1989–91; BBC Television: head of broadcasting analysis 1991–93, head of planning and strategy 1993–95, controller of planning and strategy 1995–96, dir of strategy and channel devpt 1996–97, dep dir of TV 1997, dir of new services BBC Bd of Mgmnt 1999; md broadband content Telewest Communications 2000–03, chief exec Yoo Media 2003–05, ceo CSC Media Gp 2007–; chm Bd of Govrs: Univ of Luton 2001–06, Univ of Bedfordshire 2006–; *Books* The Last Picture Show (1989), Keeping Faith? Channel 4 and its Audience (1989), Running the Show: 21 Years of London Weekend Television (1990), Violence in Television Fiction (1991), The Spirit Death (2000), The Killing Jar (2002), The Fifth Season (2002); *Style—* Dr David Docherty; ✉ Serge Hill, Abbots Langley, Hertfordshire WD5 0RY; CSC Group, 37 Harwood Road, London SW6 4QY (tel 020 7371 5999)

DOCHERTY, Paul; s of Joseph Docherty (d 1997), and Elizabeth Eileen, *née* Waters; *b* 17 September 1951, Fayid, Egypt; *Educ* Queen Victoria Sch Dunblane, Univ of Strathclyde (BA, MLitt); *Children* 3 s (Thomas b 13 April 1989, Edward b 6 Dec 1992, Harry b 23 Sept 1994); *Career* lectr in English Univ of Moscow 1983–84; British Cncl: posted London and Helsinki 1985–93, dep dir Moscow 1993–96 (concurrently cultural attaché British Embassy Moscow), sec 1996–2000, dir Czech Repub 2000–03 (concurrently cultural cnsllr British Embassy), dir Italy 2003– (concurrently cultural cnsllr British Embassy); govr: British Inst Florence, Keats Shelley House Museum Rome; *Recreations* playing the guitar (blues), music (especially opera), film; *Style—* Paul Docherty, Esq; ✉ c/o British Council, 10 Spring Gardens, London SW1A 2BN; British Council, Via delle Quattro Fontane 20, 00184 Rome, Italy (tel 00 39 06 478141, e-mail paul.docherty@britishcouncil.it)

DOD, Bernard Geoffrey; s of Arthur Edwin Ashton Dod, and Hilda Edith, *née* Crammond; *Educ* Collyers Sch Horsham, Downing Coll Cambridge, Lincoln Coll Oxford (BLitt); *Career* copy-ed OUP 1969–76, ed Elsevier Int Projects 1976–79, sr ed Phaidon Press 1979–; cncllr Charlbury Town Cncl; *Books* Aristoteles Latinus: Analytica Posteriora (ed with L Minio-Paluello, 1968), Aristoteles Latinus: De Sophisticis Elenchis (1975), The Cambridge History of Later Medieval Philosophy (contrib chapter, 1982); *Recreations* walking, gardening, reading, music; *Style—* Bernard Dod, Esq; ✉ Phaidon Press Ltd, Regent's Wharf, All Saints Street, London N1 9PA (tel 020 7843 1023, fax 020 7843 1213, e-mail bdod@phaidon.com)

DODD, Kenneth Arthur (Ken); OBE (1982); s of late Arthur Dodd, and Sarah Dodd; *b* 8 November 1932; *Educ* Holt HS Liverpool; *Career* singer, comedian, actor, entertainer; professional debut Empire Theatre Nottingham 1954, London Palladium debut 1965 (created record by starring in own 42 week season), appeared in over 20 pantomimes, Shakespearean debut as Malvolio in Twelfth Night (Liverpool) 1971; records incl: Tears (number 1 for 6 weeks), Love Is Like a Violin, Happiness; *Recreations* racing, soccer, reading, people; *Style—* Ken Dodd, Esq, OBE; ✉ 76 Thomas Lane, Knotty Ash, Liverpool L14 5NX

DODDS, Brig Geoffrey Charles William; OBE (2000, MBE 1993); s of Denis Dodds, of Bromley, Kent, and Jean, *née* Church; *b* 27 August 1958; *Educ* St Olave's Sch, RMCS Shrivenham (BSc); *m* 1 June 1985, Cate, *née* Macauley; 3 da (Camilla b 9 Jan 1989, Imogen b 29 Feb 1992, Sophie b 10 Jan 1995); *Career* Dep COS 33 Armd Bde 1991–92, mil planning offr UN NY 1994–96, CO 35 Engr Regt 1997–2000, Cdr Royal Engrs Theatre Troops 2002–03, Dir Ops JFC (Naples) 2004–; RCDS 2007–; Queen's Commendation for Valuable Service 1994; *Style—* Brig Geoffrey Dodds, OBE

DODDS, Prof John Allan; s of John Dodds (d 1966), and Violet, *née* Allen (d 1989); *b* 24 October 1942, Redcar, N Yorks; *Educ* St Mary's Coll Middlesbrough, Loughborough Univ (BTech, PhD); *m* 16 Sept 1965, Kate, *née* Moscrop; 2 da (Ellen b 1966, Jennifer b 1973), 1 s (John Michael b 1967 d 1989); *Career* contract researcher Nancy France 1968–72, Centre Nationale de la Recherche Scientifique (CNRS) researcher Laboratoire des Sciences du Genie Chimique (LSGC) Nancy 1972–96, prof Ecole des Mines Albi France 1996–; dir: Centre Poudres et Procedes 1996–2004, UMR CNRS Albi 2005–; chm Working Party on Particle Systems Characterisation European Fedn of Chem Engrg; author of 150 pubns in scientific jls and 200 presentations at symposia; Sr Moulton Medal IChemE 2003; CEng 1978, FIChemE 2002, FREng 2005; *Recreations* history, music; *Style—* Prof John Dodds; ✉ Ecole des Mines d'Albi, Campus Jarland, 81013 Albi, France (tel 00 33 563 49 30 07, fax 00 33 563 49 30 25)

DODDS, Nigel Alexander; OBE (1997), MP, MLA; s of Joseph Alexander Dodds, of Enniskillen, Co Fermanagh, and Doreen Elizabeth, *née* McMahon; *b* 20 August 1958; *Educ* Portora Royal Sch, St John's Coll Cambridge (univ scholarship, McMahan studentship, BA, Winfield prize for law), Inst of Professional Legal Studies Belfast; *m* 17 Aug 1985, Diana Jean, da of James Harris, of Loughbrickland, Banbridge, Co Down; 2 s ((Nigel Andrew) Mark b 5 Aug 1986, Andrew James Joseph b 5 Jan 1990), 1 da (Robyn Elizabeth Helen b 17 Aug 1996); *Career* called to the Bar NI 1981; pty sec Ulster Democratic Unionist Party; elected memb Belfast City Cncl 1985–, Lord Mayor of Belfast 1988–89 and 1991–92; MLA (DUP) Belfast N 1998–, MP (DUP) Belfast N 2001–; NI Assembly: min for social devpt 1999–2000 and 2001–02, min for enterprise, trade and investment 2007–; deleg NI Forum 1996–98; vice-pres Assoc of Local Authorities of NI 1988–89; memb Senate Queen's Univ Belfast 1988–93; *Style—* Nigel Dodds, Esq, OBE, MP, MLA; ✉ House of Commons, London SW1A 0AA; Constituency Office, 210 Shore Road, Belfast BT15 3PB (tel 028 9077 4774)

DODDS, (John) Nigel William; *b* 18 June 1949; *Educ* Barnard Castle Sch, Univ of Nottingham (LLB), Coll of Law; *Career* admitted slr 1973; ptnr Alderson Dodds; memb Cncl Law Soc 1994–, chm Law Soc Tstees Ltd (Law Soc charity) 2000–; memb Law Soc 1973; *Style—* Nigel Dodds, Esq; ✉ Alderson Dodds, 4/8 Stanley Street, Blyth, Northumberland NE24 2BU (tel 01670 352293, fax 01670 354166)

DODDS-SMITH, Ian Charles; *b* 1951; *Educ* Solihull Sch, Downing Coll Cambridge (MA); *Career* admitted slr 1976; specialises in product liability and the law relating to pharmaceuticals and healthcare; Cameron McKenna (formerly McKenna & Co): asst slr 1976–83, seconded to Schering Health Care Ltd 1978–83, ptnr 1984–2002; ptnr Arnold & Porter LLP 2002– (currently co-head of food, drug and medical devices gp and head of European product liability gp); memb: Legal Ctee Assoc of the Br Pharmaceutical Industry, various Royal Coll and MRC working parties on research and liability issues, Defence Research Inst, Fedn of Insur and Corp Counsel Fndn; FRSM; *Publications* contrib to pubns incl: Medical Negligence, Early Phase Human Drug Evaluation in Man, Pharmaceutical Medicine; *Style—* Ian Dodds-Smith, Esq; ✉ Arnold & Porter (UK) LLP, Tower 42, 25 Old Broad Street, London EC2N 1HQ (tel 020 7786 6216, fax 020 7786 6299, e-mail ian.dodds-smith@aporter.com)

DODGSHON, Prof Robert Andrew; s of Robert Dodgshon (d 1964), and Dorothy, *née* Owens; *b* 8 December 1941; *Educ* Univ of Liverpool (BA, PhD); *m* 1969, Katherine, *née* Simmonds; 2 da (Clare b 1971, Lucy b 1973); *Career* Univ of Wales Aberystwyth: lectr

1970, sr lectr 1980, reader 1984, prof 1988, dir Inst of Geography and Earth Sciences 1998–2003, Gregynog prof 2000–07; pres Soc for Landscape Studies; memb: Cncl Countryside Cncl for Wales, Cncl Nat Tst, Jt Nature Conservation Ctee; Murchison Award RGS 1996; FBA 2002; *Books* Land and Society in Early Scotland (1981), The European Past (1987), From Chiefs to Landlords (1998), Society in Time and Space (1998); *Recreations* music, walking, landscape, travel; *Style*— Prof Robert Dodgshon; ✉ Institute of Geography and Earth Sciences, University of Wales, Aberystwyth SY23 3DB (tel 01970 622631, fax 01970 622659, e-mail rad@aber.ac.uk)

DODGSON, Clare; da of William Baxter, and Ann, *née* Mattimoe; *b* 10 September 1962; *m* 1988, Gerard Dodgson; *Career* administrative posts NHS Newcastle upon Tyne 1980–90, dir of planning and service devpt 1990–92, chief exec Sunderland HA 1993–99, chief operating offr Employment Serv 2001–2002 (dir jobcentre servs 1999–2001), chief operating offr Jobcentre Plus 2002–03 (actg chief exec 2003), chief exec Legal Services Cmmn 2003–07; non-exec dir: Prescription Pricing Authority 1993–1997, Contributions Agency 1997–99, Child Support Agency 1999–2001, NW London HA 2002; *Style*— Ms Clare Dodgson

DODGSON, Elyse Anne; da of Samuel Kramer (d 1991), and Mildred, *née* Seltzer; *b* 26 August 1945; *Educ* Abraham Lincoln HS NY, Northwestern Univ (BSc), Guildhall Sch of Music and Drama, Univ of Essex; *Family* 1 da (Tamsin Rebecca Dodgson b 8 July 1970), 1 s (Matthew Jesse William Dodgson b 18 April 1972); m, 2 July 1988, Prof Gerd R Hoff; *Career* actor and theatre dir and prodr; actor with Brighton Combination 1968–69, head of drama Vauxhall Manor Sch 1979–82 (dir Motherland 1981–82), ILEA advsy teacher for equal opportunities 1984–85; Royal Court Theatre: dir Young People's Theatre 1985–91, prodr Young Writers' Festival 1986–91, fndr and dir int residency 1989–, assoc dir (educn) 1992–95, assoc dir (int) 1996–, prodr Int Seasons 1997–; prodn credits for Royal Court Int Dept incl: Via Dolorosa 1998, Mr Kolpert 2000, Alive from Palestine (Al Kasaba Theatre) 2001 and 2002, Plasticine 2002, Black Milk 2003, Terrorism 2003, Ladybird 2004, At the Table/Almost Nothing 2004, New Cuban Playwrights 2004, Way to Heaven 2005, On Insomnia and Midnight 2006; memb Bd Out of Joint 1999–; tstee Nat Life Story Collection 1990–2000; Int Theatre Inst Award for Excellence in Int Theatre 1999, Young Vic Award 2004; *Books* Motherland: West Indian Women to Britain (1984, The Other Award 1984), First Lines (ed, 1988), New German Plays (ed, vol 1 1997, vol 2 1998), New Spanish Plays (co-ed, 1999); *Style*— Ms Elyse Dodgson; ✉ Royal Court Theatre, Sloane Square, London SW1W 8AS (tel 020 7565 5050, fax 020 7565 5001, e-mail international@royalcourttheatre.com)

DODGSON, His Hon Judge Paul; s of late Reginald Dodgson, and Kathleen Slyvia, *née* Jay; *b* 14 August 1951; *Educ* Tiffin Sch Kingston upon Thames, Univ of Birmingham; *m* 20 Feb 1982, Jan, da of Geoffrey Hemingway (d 1966); 2 da (Eleanor b 17 Sept 1984, Laura b 22 July 1986), 1 s (William Geoffrey b 1 Feb 1991); *Career* called to the Bar Inner Temple 1975, in practice criminal law, recorder of the Crown Ct 1996–2001 (asst recorder 1992–96), circuit judge 2001–; judicial memb Parole Bd 2003–; *Recreations* sailing; *Style*— His Hon Judge Dodgson; ✉ c/o Southwark Crown Court, 1 English Grounds, Southwark, London SE1 2HU

DODSON, Joanna; QC (1993); da of Jack Herbert Dodson, and Joan Muriel, *née* Webb; *b* 5 September 1945; *Educ* James Allen's Girls' Sch, Newnham Coll Cambridge (entrance exhibitioner, MA); *m* 1974 (m dis 1981); *Career* called to the Bar Middle Temple 1971 (bencher 2000); memb: SE Circuit, Family Law Bar Assoc; govr James Allen's Girls' Sch 1999–; *Style*— Miss Joanna Dodson, QC; ✉ Renaissance Chambers, 5th Floor, Gray's Inn Chambers, Gray's Inn, London WC1R 5JA (tel 020 7404 1111, fax 020 7430 1522/1050, e-mail clerks@renaissancechambers.co.uk)

DODSON, (Peter) Mark Loveys; s of Peter Sidney Dodson, OBE, of Colchester, Essex, and Elizabeth Katherine Loveys, *née* Davis; *b* 6 October 1957; *Educ* St Helena Sch Colchester, Colchester Inst of HE (Dip); *m* 28 Dec 1991, Sarah Margaret McGregor, da of Derek Charles Ralph Burn (d 2003); 3 da (Alexandra Grace b 12 April 1997, Charlotte Rosemary b 21 May 1999, Louisa Mae b 31 Jan 2003); *Career* chef; Portman Hotel London 1978–79 and 1980–81, Old Court House Hotel Jersey 1979–80, sous chef Le Talbooth Dedham 1981–83, head chef The Waterside Inn Bray 1988–2001 (joined 1983, sous chef 1986–88), exec head chef Cliveden 2001–05, chef and prop The Masons Arms Knowstone 2005– (Michelin Star 2006–, Egon Ronay Star 2006); memb Académie Culinaire de France (now Acad of Culinary Arts) 1988–; second prize Mouton Rothschild Menu Competition 1986, Domaines Drouhin Prix des Deux Cartes 1993; *Books* Advanced Practical Cookery (contrib, 1995); *Recreations* record collecting, sport; *Style*— Mark Dodson, Esq; ✉ The Masons Arms, Knowstone, Devon EX36 4RY

DODSON, Richard Charles; s of John Summerville Dodson, of Woodford Green, Essex, and Muriel Edith, *née* Bunce; *b* 2 January 1951; *Educ* Buckhurst Hill County HS, UCL (BSc); *m* 14 April 1979, Barbara, da of Allan Carrington, of Kenilworth, Warks; 1 s (Lee b 1968); *Career* media res dir Foote Cone and Belding Ltd 1984–87 (media res mangr 1972), md Telmar Communications Ltd 1988–, pres Telmar Group Inc NY 1989–; treas Woodford Green CC; FIPA 1987; *Recreations* racing horses, cricket, bridge; *Style*— Richard Dodson, Esq; ✉ 15 Fairlight Avenue, Woodford Green, Essex IG8 9JP (tel 020 8491 6626); Curlew Cottage, Talland Street, Polperro, Cornwall; Telmar Communications Ltd, 46 Chagford Street, London NW1 6EB (tel 020 7569 7500, fax 020 7569 7501, mobile 077 1035 5777)

DODSWORTH, *see also:* Smith-Dodsworth

DODWELL, Christina; da of Christopher Bradford Dodwell, of Sussex, and Evelyn, *née* Beddow; *b* 1 February 1951; *Educ* Southover Manor Lewes, Beechlawn Coll Oxford; *m* 1991, Stephen Hobbs; *Career* explorer and author; 3 year journey through Africa by horse 1975–78; 2 year journey through Papua New Guinea by horse and canoe 1980–81, presenter BBC film River Journey-Waghi 1984 (winner BAFTA award); sr attaché Madagascar Consulate, chm Dodwell Tst; Freedom Sepik River region of Papua New Guinea 1984, winner Mungo Park medal Royal Scottish Geographical Soc 1989; FRGS 1982, FRSA 1985; *Books* Travels with Fortune (1979), In Papua New Guinea (1982), An Explorers Handbook (1984), A Traveller in China (1986), A Traveller on Horseback (1987), Travels with Pegasus (1989), Beyond Siberia (1993), Madagascar Travels (1995); *Recreations* fossil hunting, walking; *Style*— Ms Christina Dodwell; ✉ The Dodwell Trust, 16 Lanark Mansions, Pennard Road, London W12 8DT (e-mail dodwell@madagascar.freeserve.co.uk)

DODWORTH, Air Vice Marshal Peter; CB (1994), OBE (1982), AFC (1971), DL (Lincs 2004); s of Eric Albert Dodworth (d 1988), of Southport, and Edna, *née* Barker (d 1988); *b* 12 September 1940; *Educ* Southport GS, Univ of Leeds (BSc); *m* 1963, Kay, da of Hugh Parry; 4 s (Antony b 18 March 1965, Christopher b and d 1965, Bruce b 6 Aug 1967, Jonathan b 6 Feb 1976); *Career* cmmnd RAF 1961, flying trg (Jet Provosts and Vampires) 1961–63, No 54 Sqdn (Hunters) 1963–65, No 4 Flying Trg Sch (Gnats) 1965–67, advanced instr Central Flying Sch (Gnats) 1967–69, Harrier Conversion Team 1969–72, Air Staff HQ RAF Germany 1972–76, OC Ops Wing RAF Wittering (Harriers) 1976–79, Nat Defence Coll 1980, Air Cdr Belize 1980–82, Directing Staff RAF Staff Coll 1982–83, Station Cdr RAF Wittering 1983–85, Cmd Gp Exec HQ Allied Air Forces Central Europe Ramstein Germany 1985–87, RCDS 1987, Dir of Personnel MOD 1988–91, Defence Attaché and head of Br Defence Staff Br Embassy Washington DC 1991–94, head Operations Branch Implementation Team 1994, Sr Directing Staff (Air) RCDS 1994–96, ret; mil advsr Bombardier Services Defence 1997–2000, def advsr Vosper Thorneycroft Aerospace 2000–02; chm of govrs Stamford Endowed Schs 2005; Liveryman GAPAN 2004; FRAeS 1996; *Recreations* golf, DIY, reading, gardening; *Clubs* RAF (chm 1994–96); *Style*— Air Vice Marshal Peter Dodworth, CB, OBE, AFC, DL; ✉ tel 01780 740340, fax 01780 740598, e-mail peterdodworth@onetel.com

DOE, Prof William Fairbank; s of Asa Garfield Doe (d 1985), and Hazel Thelma, *née* Young (d 2002); *b* 6 May 1941; *Educ* Newington Coll, Univ of Sydney (MB BS), Univ of London (MSc); *m* 20 March 1982, Ms Dallas Elizabeth Ariotti, da of James D McIntosh; 2 s (Jamie b 28 April 1985, Thomas b 6 July 1986); *Career* MRC fell 1970–71, lectr in med RPMS 1973–74, conslt Hammersmith Hosp 1973–74, Lilly int fell 1974–75, Nat Inst for Health Research fell Scripps Clinic and Research Fndn 1975–77, assoc prof Univ of Sydney and hon physician Royal N Shore Hosp 1978–81; John Curtin Sch of Med Research ANU: prof 1982–98, head Dept of Med and Clinical Science 1982–88, head Div of Molecular Med 1988–98; dir of gastroenterolgy Canberra Hosp 1991–97, prof of med Univ of Sydney 1995–98, prof of med and dean Sch of Med Univ of Birmingham 1998– (memb Univ Senate 1998–, memb Cncl 2002–), hon conslt physician Univ Hosp Birmingham NHS Tst and City Hosp NHS Tst 1998–; distinguished visiting fell Christ's Coll Cambridge 1988–89; non-exec dir Birmingham and Black Country Strategic HA 1998–; sr ed Jl of Gastroenterology and Hepatology 1993–2002 (memb Editorial Bd 1987–, tstee 2002–06), assoc ed Inflammatory Bowel Disease 1994–98; memb Editorial Bd: Cell Biochemistry and Function 1985–87, Australian Prescriber 1987–90; author of numerous scientific papers on molecular cell biology of mucosal inflammation and colon cancer; WHO conslt Beijing 1987; memb: Advsy Ctee Social Psychiatry Research Unit Nat Health and Med Research Ctee Aust 1982–95, Cncl Nat Centre for Epidemiology Population Health 1987–98, Aust Drug Evaluation Ctee 1988–95, Cncl RACP 1993–98, Research Strategy Ctee Nat Health and Med Research Ctee Aust 1997–98, Cncl of Heads of Med Schs 1998– (memb Exec 2000–); memb: Gastroenterological Soc of Aust (pres 1989–91), Br Soc of Gastroenterology, American Gastroenterology Assoc, BMA, Aust Coeliac Soc; tstee Canberra Arts Patrons Orgn 1983–86, involved with Canberra Cancerians 1990–98, govr Univ of Worcester 2005–; Distinguished Research Prize and Medal Gastroenterolgy Soc of Australia 1997; FRACP 1978, FRCP 1993 (MRCP 1969), FMedSci 1999; *Recreations* opera, reading, oriental rugs, wine, tennis; *Clubs* Cwlth; *Style*— Prof William Doe; ✉ The Medical School, University of Birmingham, Edgbaston, Birmingham B15 2TT (tel 0121 414 4046, fax 0121 414 7149, e-mail w.f.doe@bham.ac.uk)

DOEH, Doran; *b* 14 May 1948; *Educ* Dartmouth Coll USA (Reynolds scholar, BA), Univ of Oxford (MA), Univ of London (LLB); *Career* barrister 1973; legal advsr: Burmah Oil North Sea Limited 1975–76, The British National Oil Corporation 1977–82, Britoil plc 1982–86; admitted slr 1987; Allen & Overy: joined 1986, ptnr Moscow 1995–98, ptnr London 1998–99; ptnr Denton Wilde Sapte 1999–; hon assoc Centre for Petroleum, Mineral Law Policy Univ of Dundee; memb: Law Soc, Int Bar Assoc, RIIA; FSALS; *Recreations* cooking, wine, opera; *Style*— Doran Doeh, Esq; ✉ Denton Wilde Sapte, 1 Fleet Place, London EC4M 7WS (tel 020 7242 1212, fax 020 7246 7777); Bolshaya Dmitrovka 7/5, Boulevard 2, 103009 Moscow, Russia (tel 00 7 095 255 7900, fax 00 7 095 255 7901)

DOEL, District Judge John Michael; s of Harry and Edith Doel; *Educ* Brockley CGS London, UC Cardiff (BSc, Welsh vest in rowing), Washington State Univ; *m*; 2 s (Owen, Lewis); *Career* articled A C Hepburn Slr, admitted slr 1974; district judge (Wales & Chester Circuit) 2000– (dep district judge 1991–2000); govr Barry Comp Sch; *Recreations* opera, gardening, walking, yoga; *Style*— District Judge Doel; ✉ c/o Wales & Chester Circuit Secretariat, 2nd Floor, Churchill House, Churchill Way, Cardiff CF1 4HH (e-mail jdoel@lix.compulink.co.uk)

DOEL, Air Cdre Martin Terry; OBE (1998); s of Terry Doel, of Hythe, Hants, and Brenda Doel; *b* 21 November 1956, Romsey, Hants; *Educ* Totton GS, King Alfred's Coll Winchester (BEd), KCL (MA), RAF Coll Cranwell, RAF Staff Coll, Jt Servs Cmd and Staff Coll; *m* 9 Aug 1980, Angela, *née* Ransom; 2 s (Matthew b 14 Nov 1985, Andrew b 12 Sep 1989); *Career* various appts as jr offr RAF 1980–89, OC Personnel Mgmnt Sqdn RAF Marham 1988–90, personal staff offr to C-in-C Strike Cmd 1990–93, RAF Staff Coll 1994, OC Admin Wing RAF Laarbruch 1995–97, directing staff JSCSC 1998–2000, station cdr RAF Brampton Wyton Henlow 2000–03, dir RAF Div JSCSC 2003–04, dir Personnel & Trg Strategy RAF 2004–; chm RAF FA, pres RAF Volleyball Assoc; Alistair Black Meml Trophy for War Studies 1981; FRAeS; *Publications* Humanitarian Intervention (RUSI jl, 1995, Trench Gasgoigne Essay Prize); *Recreations* football (UEFA grade B coach), cricket; *Clubs* RAF; *Style*— Air Commodore M T Doel, OBE; ✉ Headquarters Personnel and Training Command, RAF Innsworth, Gloucester GL3 1EZ (tel 01452 712612, e-mail dpt.cos@ptc.raf.mod.uk)

DOGGART, Anthony Hamilton (Tony); s of James Hamilton Doggart (d 1989), of Albury, Surrey, and his 2 w Leonora Margaret, *née* Sharpley (d 1994); *b* 4 May 1940; *Educ* Eton, King's Coll Cambridge (MA); *m* 1 May 1964, Caroline Elizabeth, da of Nicholas Gerard Voute, of The Hague, Netherlands; 1 s (Sebastian Hamilton b 6 April 1970), 1 da (Nike Henrietta b 16 March 1972); *Career* called to the Bar Middle Temple 1962 (memb Lincoln's Inn); head of Special Business Dept Save & Prosper Gp 1970–74, pres First Investment Annuity Co of America 1974–78, int exec vice-pres Insurance Co of N America 1978–80, fin dir Save & Prosper Gp 1986–94 (sales dir 1980–86); chief exec: Jardine Fleming Unit Trusts 1994, Fleming European Fund Management Div 1994–97; fin dir: Robert Fleming Asset Management 1997–99, Robert Fleming & Co Ltd 1999–2000; non-exec dir Hamilton Life Insurance Co Ltd 1999–; chm Contemporary Applied Arts 1999–2006, vice-chm The Crafts Cncl 1988–94; hon treas Marie Curie Cancer Care 2003–; *Books* Tax Havens and Offshore Funds (1972); *Recreations* skiing, wild mushrooms, oak furniture; *Clubs* Garrick, Brooks's, City of London, Hurlingham; *Style*— Tony Doggart, Esq; ✉ 23 Ovington Gardens, London SW3 1LE (tel 020 7584 7620, fax 020 7589 1794, e-mail tony@doggart.net)

DOGGART, John Victor; s of John Doggart, of Macclesfield, Cheshire, and Sara Doggart; *b* 9 May 1941; *Educ* Uppingham, Clare Coll Cambridge (MA), UCL (MA); *Partner* Zoë Coward; 1 da (Tamzin b 1973); *Career* architect: Robert Matthew Johnson Marshall 1962, Urban Resources Administration (NY) 1966, Richard and Su Rogers (now Richard Rogers Assocs) 1967–69; energy conslt Milton Keynes Development Corp 1970–80, ptnr ECD Partnership (architects and energy conslts) 1980–95, md ECD Energy and Environment Ltd 1995–2001, dir Faber Maunsell 2001–05; memb: Nat Energy Rating Ctee, BREEAM Steering Ctee; memb Panel Sustainable Devpt Cmmn; chm: Energy Conservation and Solar Centre, Sustainable Energy Acad; CEng, MInstE; *Recreations* canoeing, sailing, skiing, jigsaws, reading; *Style*— John Doggart, Esq; ✉ The Coach House, Belsize Park Gardens, London NW3 4LA (tel 07785 360218, e-mail johndoggart@talktalk.net)

DOHERTY, Dr Ciaran Conor; s of John Doherty, and Kathleen, *née* Hunter; *b* 29 March 1948; *Educ* St Mary's CBS GS Belfast, Queen's Univ Belfast (MB, MD); *m* Kathleen Mary, da of John Michael Collins, of Belfast; 2 da (Karen b 1978, Catherine b 1981), 1 s (Conor b 1981); *Career* NI kidney res fell 1976–78, clinical fell in nephrology Univ of S Calif 1979–81, conslt renal physician Belfast City Hosp and Royal Victoria Hosp 1981–, special lectr Dept of Med Queen's Univ Belfast 1983– (jr tutor 1973–75, clinical teacher in nephrology 1981–), postgrad clinical tutor Belfast Postgrad Med Centre 1985–90, clinical dir of nephrology Belfast City Hosp 1996–2001; author and co-author of 65 papers on kidney disease, contrib to 10 nephrology textbooks; pres Irish Nephrology Soc 1986–88, NI rep and memb Cncl Nat Assoc of Clinical Tutors 1986; memb Assoc of Physicians of GB and NI 1988, fell Royal Acad of Med in Ireland 1990, censor RCPI 1999–2002, hon sr lectr Dept of Med Queen's Univ Belfast 1999–; FRCP 1992 (MRCP), FRCPI 1992;

Recreations boating, golf, gardening; *Clubs* Corrigan; *Style*— Dr Ciaran Doherty; ✉ Regional Nephrology Unit, Belfast City Hospital Tower, Lisburn Road, Belfast BT9 5JY (tel 028 9032 9241, e-mail ciaran.doherty@bch.n-i.nhs.uk)

DOHERTY, Kenneth (Ken); s of Anthony Doherty (d 1983), and Rose, *née* Lawler; *b* 17 September 1969; *Educ* Westland Row CBS; *Career* snooker player; turned professional 1990; amateur career: memb Rep of Ireland Sr Int team 1984–88 (Jr Int team 1984–87), Irish Jr champion 1983–86, World Jr champion 1987, Irish Amateur Sr champion 1987 and 1989, World Amateur Sr champion 1989; winner: B & H Masters 1990, Regal Welsh Masters 1993 and 2001, Regal Scottish Masters 1993, Irish Professional Championships 1993, Pontins Professional International 1993 and 1994, Embassy World Championship 1997 (runner-up 2003), Rothmans Malta Grand Prix 2000, Thailand Masters 2001; runner-up UK Championship 2002; highest world ranking no 3; Ireland Sports Personality of the Year 1997; *Recreations* golf, movies, swimming, soccer; *Style*— Ken Doherty, Esq

DOHERTY, Prof Michael; s of Donald Doherty (d 2006), of Upton, Devon, and Eileen May, *née* Fairchild (d 1980); *b* 7 March 1951; *Educ* City of London Freemen's Sch, St John's Coll Cambridge (MA, MB BChir, MD); *m* 27 Sept 1980, Sally Anne; 2 da (Emma b 1982, Jill b 1983); *Career* prof of rheumatology Univ of Nottingham; ed Annals of Rheumatic Diseases 1992–99; Freeman City of London 1984; fell Higher Educn Acad (FHEA), FRCP; *Books* Rheumatological Medicine (1985), Pyrophosphate Arthropathy - A Clinical Study (1988), Clinical Examination in Rheumatology (1992), Rheumatology Examination and Injection Techniques (1992); *Recreations* cinema, opera, osteology, art; *Style*— Prof Michael Doherty; ✉ Academic Rheumatology, City Hospital, Nottingham NG5 1PB (tel 0115 823 1756)

DOHERTY, Pat; MP, MLA; *Educ* St Joseph's Coll Belfast; *Career* vice-pres Sinn Féin 1988–, memb NI Assembly (Sinn Féin) Tyrone W 1998–, MP (Sinn Féin) Tyrone W 2001– (Parly candidate (Sinn Féin) Tyrone W 1997); *Style*— Pat Doherty, Esq, MP, MLA; ✉ House of Commons, London SW1A 0AA; Northern Ireland Assembly, Parliament Buildings, Stormont Estate, Belfast BT4 3XX

DOHERTY, (Joseph) Raymond; QC (1997); s of James Doherty, of Stirling, and Mary, *née* Woods; *b* 30 January 1958; *Educ* St Joseph's Coll Dumfries, Univ of Edinburgh (LLB), Hertford Coll Oxford (BCL), Harvard Law Sch (LLM); *m* 23 July 1994, Arlene Elizabeth, da of Tony Donaghy; 2 da (Lucy Catherine b 1996, Clara Elizabeth b 2000), 1 s (Rory James b 1997); *Career* admitted as advocate 1984 (Lord Reid scholarship 1983–85); standing jr counsel to: MOD in Scotland 1990–91, Scottish Office Industry Dept 1992–97; clerk of Faculty of Advocates 1990–95, advocate depute 1998–2001; *Publications* Armour on Valuation for Rating (jt ed, 1990–), Stair Memorial Encyclopaedia of the Laws of Scotland (contrib); *Style*— J R Doherty, QC; ✉ Advocates Library, Parliament House, Edinburgh EH1 1RF (tel 0131 226 5071, fax 0131 225 3642)

DOHMANN, Barbara; QC (1987); *Educ* Univ of Erlangen, Univ of Mainz, Univ of Paris; *Career* called to the Bar 1971; recorder 1990–2002, dep judge of the High Court (Commercial Court Queen's Bench and Chancery Div) 1994–2002; sometime arbitrator and mediator; memb Ctee: Commercial Bar Assoc (chm 1999–2001), European Circuit, London Common Law & Commercial Bar Assoc (LCLCBA); memb: Gen Cncl of the Bar (memb Legal Services Ctee 1999–2001), Learned Soc for Int Procedure Law; founding memb Chllr's Forum of the Univ of the Arts London; former memb Court of Govrs London Inst HE Corp; *Clubs* Athenaeum; *Style*— Miss Barbara Dohmann, QC; ✉ Blackstone Chambers, Blackstone House, Temple, London EC4Y 9BW

DOIG, Alan David; CBE (2006), QFSM (2004); s of Alexander Doig (d 1997), and Myra Bisset, *née* Reid; *b* 11 May 1957, Kirkcaldy, Fife; *Educ* Kirkcaldy HS, Kirkcaldy Tech Coll (HNC), Inst of Industrial Mangrs (Cert), Open Univ (BSc); *m* 7 June 1975, Senga, *née* Somerville; 2 da (Maxine b 9 March 1976, Rachael b 27 Sept 1988), 1 s (Christopher b 24 June 1992); *Career* Fife Fire Brigade 1976–88 (seconded: Scottish Fire Serv Trg Sch 1979–81, Fire Servs Coll 1985–87); Staffs Fire and Rescue Serv: joined 1988, asst chief fire offr 1993–95, dep chief fire offr 1995–99, chief fire offr and chief exec 1999–; non-exec dir Govt Decontamination Serv Defra; author of numerous articles in fire specialist media; FIFireE 1997; *Recreations* golf, reading; *Style*— Alan Doig, Esq, CBE, QFSM; ✉ 29 Fountain Road, Draycott-in-the-Clay, Derbyshire DE6 5HP (e-mail thedoigs@btopenworld.com); Staffordshire Fire & Rescue Service, Pirehill, Stone, Staffordshire ST15 0BS (tel 01785 898667, fax 01785 897510, e-mail a.doig@staffordshirefire.gov.uk)

DOIG, Caroline May; o da of Lt George William Lowson Doig (d 1942), and May Desson Doig, *née* Keir (d 1997); *b* 30 April 1938; *Career* house offr and registrar Dundee, gen surgery trg Darlington and Durham, SHO in paediatric surgery Glasgow, further paediatric surgery trg Hosp for Sick Children Gt Ormond St London and Hosp for Sick Children Edinburgh; sr lectr in paediatric surgery Univ of Manchester then conslt Booth Hall Children's Hosp and St Mary's Hosp Manchester 1975–2000; memb: Paediatric Speciality Trg Gp NHS 1976–78, Surgical Div Manchester DHA, N Manchester AHA 1990, Admissions Ctee Univ of Manchester, Univ of Manchester Working Pty on Clinical Academic Provision 1991, Cncl Manchester Med Soc 1980–83 and 1990–93, Cncl Paediatric Section RSM 1984–87, Med Advsy Bd Br Cncl 1990–; RCSEd: examiner primary 1980–, examiner part II 1982–2003, memb Cncl 1984–94 and 1996–2001, dir of heritage 2001–03, memb Sci and Educn Sub-Ctee 1985–89 and 1990–94, memb Educn and Training Bd 1998, memb Nominations Ctee 1994–97, memb Devpt Ctee 1995–98, memb Fin Ctee 1996–98, chm Paediatric Surgical Advsy Bd until 1993, examiner in Singapore 1987 and 1994, Kuwait 1989, Kuala Lumpur 1990, Hong Kong 1990, 1993, 1997 and 2000; GMC: memb 1989–2003, memb Overseas Review Appeal Bd 1990–91, chm Overseas Ctee 1994–98 (memb 1990–98), memb Registration Ctee 1998–2000, memb Assessment Referral Ctee 1997–2004 (chm 1999–2003), memb Interim Orders Ctee 2000–04; Med Women's Fedn: memb 1962–, memb Cncl 1980–87, memb Exec 1981–87, nat pres 1985–86, pres Manchester Branch 2000–01, pres SE Assoc 2002–04 and 2006, memb Sub-Ctee on Postgrad Trg, memb Med Educn and Ethical Ctee, former liaison offr, former sec/treas Manchester and Dist Branch; Mason Brown Lecture RCSEd 1989; memb: Br Assoc of Paediatric Surgns, Assoc of Surgns of GB and I, Scot Paediatric Surgical Soc; FRSA; *Publications* Colour Atlas of Inguinal Hernias and Hydroceles in Infants and Children (1983), Recent Advances in Surgery (contrib, 1988), Gastroenterology, Clinical Science and Practice (contrib various chapters in vols I and II, 1993), Constipation (contrib, 1994 and 1995), Upper Digestive Surgery (contrib, 1994), Hirschsprung's Disease (contrib, 1994), Surgery of the Anus, Rectum and Colon (contrib, 1997), Pediatric Surgery (contrib, 1998), Paediatric Surgery (contrib, 1998), Upper Gastrointestinal Surgery (contrib, 1999); *Recreations* golf, swimming, gardening, theatre, cooking, stamp collecting, dolls houses, painting; *Clubs* Lansdowne, New (Edinburgh); *Style*— Miss Caroline Doig; ✉ Lea Cottage, Borthwick Hall Estate, Heriot, Midlothian EH38 5YE (tel 01875 835 719)

DOIG, John; s of David Doig (d 1994), and Mary (Mamie), *née* Maguire (d 1991); *b* 2 August 1958; *Educ* Holyrod Sch Glasgow, St Mary's Music Sch Edinburgh (first pupil enrolled at request of Lord Menuhin); *Career* violinist; BBC Symphony Orch 1975–78, princ first violin BBC Philharmonic Orch 1979–81; Scottish Chamber Orch: co ldr 1986–88, guest ldr and dir 1988–90; ldr Scottish Opera Orch 1990–97; fndr and dir Scottish Bach Consort 1994–99 (memb Bd of Dirs), fndr and artistic dir Killearn Series 1994; performances with Scottish Chamber Orch incl: Flanders Festival, Edinburgh Int Festival, BBC Proms, Carnegie Hall NY; *Recordings* with Scottish Chamber Orch: Bach Brandenburg Concerto No 2, Stravinsky Apollon Masagète, Tchaikovsky/Stravinsky Entr'Acte From The Sleeping Beauty (world premiere), Tchaikovsky Mozartiana, Britten Young Apollo and Les Illuminations; *Recreations* horse riding, dogs, water sports, country walks; *Style*— John Doig, Esq; ✉ Endrick Mews, Killearn, Stirlingshire G63 9ND

DOIG, (Robertson) Lindsay; s of Isaac Doig (d 1977), of Dundee, and Jean Ann Durno, *née* Robertson (d 1986); *b* 30 August 1938; *Educ* Univ of St Andrews (MB ChB), Univ of Dundee (ChM); *m* 24 Sept 1966, Roslyn, da of James Mayo Buchanan (d 1989), of Toorak, Melbourne; 3 s (Geoffrey b 1971, Roger b 1974, Colin b 1978); *Career* lectr in surgery and sr surgical registrar St Thomas' Hosp 1968–76, surgn to the Gen Infirmary Leeds and hon sr lectr in surgery Univ of Leeds 1976–; former tutor RCS; fell: Assoc of Surgns, Vascular Surgical Soc, RSM; memb: Br Assoc of Endocrine Surgns, Leeds Medico-legal Soc (memb Ctee, pres 1990–93), Leeds Medico-Chirurgical Soc; Freeman City of London 1978, Liveryman Worshipful Soc of Apothecaries; FRCSEd 1967, FRCS 1969; *Recreations* shooting, history, fine arts, music; *Clubs* Cheselden; *Style*— R Lindsay Doig, Esq; ✉ Strathleven, 439 Harrogate Road, Leeds LS17 7AB (tel 0113 268 0053); General Infirmary at Leeds LS1 3EX (tel 0113 243 2799); Leeds Nuffield Hospital, Leighton Street, Leeds LS1 3EB (tel 0113 388 2000, fax 0113 388 2100); BUPA Hospital, Leeds LS8 1NT (tel 0113 269 3939)

DOIG, Maxwell Kirkcaldy; s of David Thomas Doig, and June Doig; *b* 21 February 1966; *Educ* Manchester Sch of Art (BA), Slade Sch of Art (scholar); *Career* artist in residence Hochshule Der Künst Berlin 1991–92; travelled extensively through USA, Mexico and Aust 1997; *Solo Exhibitions* Univ of Manchester 1986, Hart Gallery Nottingham 1990 and 1994, Hart Gallery London 1992, 1995 and 1997, Hart Gallery Edinburgh Festival 1992, Paintings & Drawings 1987–97 (touring), L Albemarle Gallery London 2002, 2004 and 2006, Ettinger Gallery NY 2005; *Group Exhibitions* Young Contemporaries (Whitworth Gallery Manchester) 1986, One Hundred and Fifty Years of Art in Manchester (Cavendish Building Manchester Poly) 1988, Bankside Open Exhibition (London) 1989 and 1990, Intaglio Gallery (London) 1990, East West Gallery (London) 1990, Strang Print Room (Univ of London) 1990, Images of the Yorkshire Landscape (Civic Hall Leeds) 1991, Gulascy Gallery (Budapest) 1991, 6 Int Art Fair Olympia 1991, The Green Book Exhibition (Dean Clough Halifax) 1991, Art 92, Art 93, Art 94 and Art 96 (London Art Fairs), Hart Gallery (London) 1994, Mercer Gallery (two-man exhbn, Harrogate) 1994, Geneva Art Fair 1995, Young Masters (Mercer Gallery Harrogate) 1995, Ghent Art Fair 1996, Twentieth Century Br Art Fair (London) 1996, Int Summer Show (L Abermarle Gallery London) 2003 and 2004, Summer Exhibition (Eleanor Ettinger Gallery NY) 2003, Art London (Burtons Court Chelsea) 2003, London Art Fair (Business Centre Islington) 2004, Int Realism Exhibition (L Abermarle Gallery London) 2005; *Public Collections* Univ of Manchester, Univ of London, Mercer Gallery Harrogate, Provident Financial Group, Huddersfield Art Gallery, Prudential plc, Holman Fenwick and Willan; *Awards* Landscape Drawing Award Manchester Acad Open Exhibition 1986, Joseph Webb Prize for Draughtsman under 35 1990, Villiers David Prize 1997 (shortlisted 1995); *Style*— Maxwell Doig, Esq; ✉ c/o Albemarle Gallery, 49 Albemarle Street, London W1S 4JR (tel 020 7499 1616)

DOIG, Peter; *b* 1959; *Educ* Wimbledon Sch of Art, St Martin's Sch of Art (BA), Chelsea Sch of Art (MA); *Career* artist; tstee Tate Gallery 1996–; *Solo Exhibitions* Metropolitan Gallery 1984, The Naked City (Air Gallery) 1986, Articule (Montreal) 1990, Whitechapel Artist Award (Whitechapel Gallery) 1991, Victoria Miro Gallery 1994, Enterprise (NY) 1994; *Group Exhibitions* New Contemporaries (ICA) 1982 and 1983, Things as They Are (Riverside Studios) 1985, Into the Nineties (Mall Galleries) 1990, Barclays Young Artist Award (Serpentine Gallery) 1991, Inside a Microcosm (Laure Genillard Gallery) 1992, New Voices (Centre Albert Borschette) 1992, Moving into View (Royal Festival Hall) 1993, Twelve Stars (Barbican Centre) 1993, Projet Unite Firminy (Firminy Vert) 1993, John Moores Liverpool Exhbn 18 (1st prize) 1993, Prix Eliette von Karajan (tour, 1st prize) 1994, Unbound: Possibilities in Painting (Hayward Gallery) 1994, New Voices (Br Cncl tour to Spain) 1994, Enterprise 1994, Imprint '93 (Cabinet Gallery) 1994, Here and Now (Serpentine Gallery) 1994, Turner Prize (Tate Gallery) 1994; *Work in Collections* Contemporary Arts Soc, John Moores, Br Cncl, Arts Cncl, Euro Parliament; *Style*— Peter Doig, Esq

DOLBY, Dr Richard Edwin; OBE (2000); s of James Edwin Dolby (d 1991), of Northampton, and Kathleen Florence, *née* Clarke (d 1978); *b* 7 July 1938; *Educ* Northampton GS, Selwyn Coll Cambridge (BA, MA, PhD); *m* Jean Elizabeth; 2 da (Catherine Julia b 30 Aug 1965, Elizabeth Jane b 1 July 1968), 2 step da (Jane Nicola b 11 May 1973, Gillian Emily b 15 Dec 1976); *Career* Nat Serv REME 1956–58, graduate trainee Alcan Industries 1962–63, GEC Hirst Research Laboratories 1963–65; The Welding Institute (formerly Br Welding Research Assoc): joined as research metallurgist 1965, head Materials Dept 1978–80, research mangr 1980–86, dir of research & technol 1986–2003; current pres Inst of Materials, Minerals and Mining; current memb: Nuclear Safety Advsy Ctee Health and Safety Cmmn, UK Tech Advsy Ctee for Structural Integrity of Nuclear Plant, Materials Bd UK Defence Scientific Advsy Cncl; cnslt MOD Defence Scientific Advsy Cncl; former vice-pres Int Inst of Welding (chm Tech Mgmnt Bd and Research Strategy Gp); Pfeil prize Inst of Metals 1972, Sir William Larke Medal The Welding Inst 1982, Brooker Medal The Welding Inst 1990, Arata Prize Int Inst of Welding 2003, Int Award American Welding Soc 2004; Hon Dr Univ of Sheffield; hon memb Japan Welding Soc; FIM 1977, FREng 1987, Hon FWeldI 2005 (FWeldI 1977); *Recreations* golf, philately, gardening, music; *Style*— Dr Richard Dolby, OBE, FREng

DOLBY, Trevor John; s of Kenneth Douglas Dolby (d 1999), of Ellastone, Derbys, and Elsie Dolby; *b* 24 April 1957; *Educ* King Edward VI Sch Lichfield, Lanchester Poly (BSc); *m*; 2 c; *Career* writer and ed New Leaf Books 1979–82, science ed John Murray Publisher 1982–84, publishing manager Reed Illustrated Div 1990–92, ed Natural History div rising to publishing manager Illustrated div Hamlyn/Reed 1984–92, publishing dir Pavilion Books 1992–96, publishing dir Orion Non-Fiction and Orion Audio 1996–2003, md and publisher HarperEntertainment 2003–06, publisher Preface 2007–; non-exec dir Maverick Television 2000–04; memb Fundraising Ctee English PEN; Ed of the Year Br Book Awards 2003 (shortlisted 2002); *Recreations* 1964 Mercedes-Benz 220SEBC, collecting modern first editions; *Clubs* Mornington Crescent (offr and memb), Academy, Hospital; *Style*— Trevor Dolby, Esq; ✉ Random House Publishers, 20 Vauxhall Bridge Road, London SW1V 2SA

DOLLERY, Prof Sir Colin Terence; kt (1987); *b* 14 March 1931; *Educ* Lincoln Sch, Univ of Birmingham (Queen's scholar, BSc, MB ChB, Leith Newman prize in pathology); *m*; 1 s, 1 da; *Career* house physician: Queen Elizabeth Hosp Birmingham 1957 (house surgn 1956), Hammersmith Hosp London 1957, Brompton Hosp London 1958; Hammersmith Hosp: med registrar 1958–60, sr registrar 1960–63, conslt physician 1963–96; Royal Postgrad Med Sch (Imperial College Sch of Medicine at Hammersmith Hosp following merger 1997): asst lectr in med 1960–61, tutor in med 1961–63, lectr in clinical therapeutics 1963–66, hon dir Med Research Cncl Clinical Pharmacology Research Gp 1966–67, sr lectr in clinical therapeutics Dept of Med 1967–69, prof of clinical pharmacology 1969–87, prof and chm Dept of Med 1987–91, dean 1991–96; dir of R&D Hammersmith, Queen Charlotte's and Chelsea Hosps London 1991–94, pro-vice-chllr for med and dentistry Univ of London 1992–96; Dept of Health: memb Ctee on Safety of Meds 1966–75, conslt advsr on clinical pharmacology to Chief MO 1979–81; Univ Grants Ctee: memb Med Sub-Ctee 1971–80, chm Panel on Pharmacy 1973–77, memb Ctee and chm Med and Dental Sub-Ctees 1984–89; memb: Univs Funding Cncl (concurrently chm

Med Ctee) 1989–91, Med Ctee CVCP 1992–; first chm Cncl of Deans of UK Med Schs and Faculties 1992–93; memb: MRC (concurrently chm Physiological Systems Bd) 1982–84, Panel of Independent Assessors Nat Health and Med Research Cncl of Australia 1984–; chm: Clinical Pharmacology Section Br Pharmacological Soc 1970–75, Clinical Pharmacology Section Int Union of Pharmacology, Organising Ctee First World Conf on Clinical Pharmacology 1980; pres Int Union of Pharmacology 1987–90 (memb Cncl 1978–81, vice-pres 1981–84); memb: Expert Advsy Panel on Drug Evaluation WHO 1982–, Int Cncl of Scientific Unions 1990–93, Univ Grants Ctee Hong Kong 1989–2000 (chm Med Sub-Ctee 1990–2000, memb Institutional Devpt Sub-Ctee 1993); visiting professorships: McMaster Univ Ontario 1972, UCLA 1973, Univ of Queensland 1974, Med Univ of S Carolina 1976, Mayo Med Sch Minnesota 1977, Flinders Univ Adelaide, Beijing Med Univ 1987, Harvard Univ 1989, Univ of Chicago 1991, Mount Sinai Hosp NY 1992; numerous named lectures; non-exec dir: Life Sciences plc 1988–98, Larson-Davis Inc 1998–99, Discovery Partners Inc 2001–, Predict Inc 2001–; conslt Zeneca plc 1992–99, sr conslt SmithKline Beecham plc 1996–2000, sr conslt GlaxoSmithKline 2001–; memb: MRS, Research Defence Soc, Physiological Soc, Br Cardiac Soc, Br Pharmacological Soc, Assoc of Physicians of GB and I, Euro Soc for Clinical Investigation (past pres); Int Soc of Hypertension Astra Award 1986; Hon MD Liège Univ 1986, Hon DSc Univ of Birmingham 1988; hon memb Assoc of American Physicians 1981; FRCP, FRSM, FFPM, FAMS; Chevalier dans l'Ordre National du Mérite (France) 1976; *Publications* numerous papers in scientific jls concerned with high blood pressure, clinical pharmacology and therapeutics; *Style*— Prof Sir Colin Dollery; ✉ 101 Corringham Road, London NW11 7DL

DOLLOND, Steven; s of Charles Dollond; *b* 28 November 1943; *Educ* Quintin Sch, Lincoln Coll Oxford (MA), Harvard Business Sch (MBA); *Career* called to the Bar Middle Temple; private office of Ldr of the Oppn 1968–70, contested (Cons) Eton and Slough Feb and Oct 1974; mgmnt conslt Arthur D Little 1972–77, mktg dir Br Technol Gp 1977–86, dir Heritage Projects 1989–2002, chief exec Decatur Mgmnt 1994–, conslt Thales 1998–; Liveryman Upholders Co; *Recreations* exotic travel; *Clubs* Carlton; *Style*— Steven Dollond, Esq; ✉ Flat 16 Berkeley Court, Glentworth Street, London NW1 5NA (tel 020 7935 1432)

DOLMAN, Edward James (Ed); s of James William Dolman, and Jean, *née* Angles (d 2006); *b* 24 February 1960, Wimbledon; *Educ* Dulwich Coll, Univ of Southampton (BA); *m* 1987, Clare Maureen, *née* Callaghan; 1 da (Esther Maria b 15 Nov 1988), 1 s (Alexander William b 17 Aug 1990); *Career* joined Christie's 1984, dir and head of furniture Christie's South Kensington 1990–96, md Christie's Amsterdam 1996–97, dir Christie Manson & Woods 1997, md Christie's Europe 1998–99 (commercial dir 1997–98), md Christie's America 1999–2000, ceo Christie's International plc 1999–; memb: Cncl Specialist Schs and Acads Tst, Int Advsy Bd Br American Business Inc; Chevalier de la Légion d'Honneur 2007; *Recreations* art history, rugby, sailing, Chelsea FC; *Clubs* RAC, Old Alleynians; *Style*— Ed Dolman, Esq; ✉ Christie's, 8 King Street, St James's, London SW1Y 6QT

DOLMAN, Julian Henry; s of Arthur Frederick Dolman (d 1976), and Margaret Mary, *née* McKinnon; *b* 16 September 1939; *Educ* Sherborne, St Catharine's Coll Cambridge (MA); *m* 1, 29 Nov 1962 (m dis 1974), Juliet, da of James White, of Charmouth, Dorset; 2 da (Catherine b 1964, Sarah b 1966); m 2, 21 Sept 1974, Susan Jennifer, da of Roy Frederick Palmer, of Little Aston, Staffs; 2 s (Charles b 1975, Edward b 1976); *Career* admitted slr 1966, ptnr Wall James and Davies; memb Law Soc Panel of Specialist Planning Lawyers 1991–; legal assoc Royal Town Planning Inst 1992–; author of numerous articles on town planning law and occasional lectr at univs; Freeman City of London 1979; memb Law Soc 1966; *Recreations* Africana 1840–52, history, gardening; *Style*— Julian Dolman, Esq; ✉ Forge Mill Farm, Shelsley Beauchamp, Worcestershire WR6 6RR (fax 01226 812 814, e-mail forgemill@btinternet.com); Wall James and Davies, 19 Hagley Road, Stourbridge, West Midlands DY8 1QW (tel 01384 371 622, fax 01384 374 057, e-mail j.dolman@wjandd.co.uk)

DOMINICZAK, Prof Marek Henryk; s of Dr Tadeusz Dominiczak, of Gdansk, Poland, and Dr Aleksandra Dominiczak; *b* 12 March 1951; *Educ* Copernicus HS Gdansk, Med Acad of Gdansk (MB, PhD), Univ of Cambridge (Cert English Language Teaching to Adults (CELTA)); *m* 26 Dec 1976, Prof Anna Felicja Dominiczak, da of Prof Jakub Penson (d 1971); 1 s (Peter b 1985); *Career* conslt pathologist St Luke's Hosp Malta 1979–82, registrar and sr registrar Glasgow Royal Infirmary 1982–85, conslt biochemist West Glasgow Hosps Univ NHS Tst 1985– (head Biochemistry Dept 1996–2000); Univ of Glasgow: hon lectr 1986–90, hon sr lectr 1990–2006, hon prof 2007–; dir Med Humanities Unit Gartnavel Gen Hosp Glasgow 2002–; fndr ArtScience Lab Inst for Art History Univ of Glasgow 2001; special prof: Univ of Oslo 1974, Rockefeller Univ NY 1989; co-ordinator EC TEMPUS: Jt Euro Project Poland 1991–93, Jt Euro Network 1994–, Structural Jt Euro Project Estonia 1994–97; ed Clinical Chemistry and Laboratory Med 1998–2003; memb: Assoc of Clinical Biochemists, Nat Acad of Clinical Biochemistry USA, Scottish Cardiac Soc; FRCPath, FRCPGlas; *Books* Joint European Project Management Handbook (1994), Handbook of Lipoprotein Testing (ed, 1997 and 2000), International Collaboration in Laboratory Medicine: a model programme (ed, 1998), Medical Biochemistry (ed, 1999), Flesh and Bones of Metab and Nutrition (2007); *Recreations* photography, art history (memb Tate Friends and Friends of the Royal Acad of Arts); *Style*— Prof Marek Dominiczak; ✉ Department of Biochemistry, Gartnavel General Hospital, Glasgow G12 0YN (tel 0141 211 2788, fax 0141 211 3452, e-mail mhd1b@clinmed.gla.ac.uk)

DON, Robert Seymour; s of Air Vice-Marshal Francis Percival Don, OBE, DL (d 1964), of North Elmham, Norfolk, and Angela Jane, *née* Birkbeck (d 1995); *b* 5 April 1932; *Educ* Eton, Trinity Coll Cambridge (MA); *m* 2 July 1955, Judith Henrietta, da of Geoffrey Nicholas Holmes, of Shotesham All Saints, Norfolk; 4 da Charlotte (Mrs Timothy Laing) b 1956, Joanna Mary (Mrs Thomas Fitzalan Howard) b 1958, Fiona (Mrs James Gibson Fleming) b 1962, Henrietta (Mrs Mark Burdon) b 1965); *Career* Nat Serv 1 The Royal Dragoons 1950–52, TA Fife and Forfar Yeomanry 1953–54; John Harvey & Sons Ltd 1957–65, dir Hicks & Don Ltd Wine Merchants (formerly RS Don Ltd) 1965–2002, dir Elmham Wines Ltd 1967–; former chm: E Counties Wine and Spirit Assoc, English Vineyards Assoc, Norfolk Fruit Growers Assoc; gen cmmr of Income Tax 1975–2007; MW 1965; memb Inst of Masters of Wine; *Books* Off the Shelf (1967), Teach Yourself Wine (1968); *Recreations* shooting, fishing, deer stalking, skiing, photography; *Clubs* Cavalry and Guards'; *Style*— Robert Don, Esq; ✉ Garden Cottage, Elmham House, North Elmham, Dereham, Norfolk NR20 5JY (tel 01362 668363, fax 01362 668571, e-mail rsdon@btconnect.com)

DON, Robin Cameron; s of John Buttercase Don (d 1970), of Newport-on-Tay, Fife, Scotland, and Elizabeth Seath, *née* Fairbairn (d 1986); *b* 9 June 1941; *Educ* Bell Baxter HS Cupar; *Career* theatre designer; trained at Dundee Art Coll and studied engrg in Edinburgh; apprentice to theatre designer Ralph Koltai 1967–71; designs for Open Space Theatre 1971–77: Four Little Girls, Othello, Tooth of Crime, How Beautiful with Badges, The Taming of the Shrew, And They Put Handcuffs on the Flowers, Sherlock's Last Case, Measure for Measure, Hamlet, The Merchant of Venice; designs for other prodns: Mary Queen of Scots (Scot Opera) 1977, Bartholomew Fair (Round House) 1978, Les Mamelles de Tiresias (RAM/Opera North 1978, ENO 1979), Eugene Onegin (Aldeburgh 1979, Ottawa 1982, San Francisco Opera 1986), The Marriage of Figaro (Opera North) 1979, A Midsummer Night's Dream (Aldeburgh 1980, Royal Opera House Covent Garden 1986), The Flying Dutchman (Opera North) 1980, The Ticket of Leave Man (NT) 1981, Shakespeare's Rome (Mermaid) 1981, Hotel Paradiso (NT of Iceland) 1981, The Trumpet Major (RNCM and WNO) 1981, The Last Elephant (Bush) 1981, Cosi Fan Tutti (NIOT Belfast) 1981, The Birthday Party (Pitlochry) 1981–82, Song and Dance (Palace London) 1982, Madame Butterfly (Opera North) 1982, L'Elisir d' Amore (NIOT Belfast) 1982, The Midsummer Marriage (San Francisco Opera) 1983, Peter Grimes (WNO 1983, Aust Opera Sydney 1986), Twelfth Night (RSC Stratford 1983 and RSC Barbican 1984), The Boyfriend (Old Vic) 1984, Tamerlano (Opera de Lyon) 1984, When I Was a Girl I Used to Scream and Shout (Bush 1984, Edinburgh Festival 1985, Sydney and Whitehall 1986), Giasone (Buxton Festival) 1984, Kiss of the Spiderwoman (Bush) 1985, On The Edge (Hampstead) 1985, Chicago (NT of Iceland) 1985, Man of Two Worlds (Westminster) 1985, Don Quixote (NY City Opera) 1986, More Light (Bush) 1987, Norma (Covent Garden) 1987, Carmen (Sydney) 1987, La Forza del Destino (Toronto) 1987, Fat Pig (Haymarket Leicester) 1987, Spookhouse (Hampstead) 1987, The Brave (Bush) 1988, Ziegfeld (London Palladium) 1988, A Walk in the Woods (Comedy) 1988, Cavalleria Rusticana (Sydney) 1989, Hidden Laughter (Vaudeville) 1990, The Rocky Horror Show (Piccadilly) 1990, Macbeth (Santiago Ballet) 1991, The Magic Flute (Iceland) 1991, (Sweden) 1992, Someone Who'll Watch Over Me (Hampstead Theatre 1992, Broadway 1992, Dublin 1993), Beautiful Thing (Bush) 1993, Eugene Onegin (Iceland) 1993, Black Comedy (Zurich) 1993, The Rocky Horror Show (Minneapolis) 1993, Il Pagliacci (Sydney) 1994, Darwin's Flood (Bush) 1994, The Knocky (Royal Court) 1995, The Winter Guest 1995 (Almeida, West Yorkshire Playhouse (TMA Regional Theatre Awards for Best Design)), The Maiden Stone (Hampstead) 1995, Boom Bang A Bang (Bush) 1995, Hamlet (Royal Lyceum Theatre Co Edinburgh) 1995, Les Enfants du Paradis (RSC) 1996, A Perfect Ganesh (West Yorkshire Playhouse) 1996, Fool for Love (Donmar) 1996, Steaming (Picadilly) 1997, Cracked (Hampstead) 1997, Of Mice and Men (West Yorkshire Playhouse) 1997, The Rocky Horror Show (Wolfsburg and Euro tour) 1997, The Winter Guest (Venice Film Festival) 1997, The Weeping of Angels (Dublin Festival) 1997, Romeo and Juliet (Royal Ballet of Flanders) 1998, Hey Persephone! (Aldeburgh Festival and Almeida Festival) 1998, A Long Day's Journey into Night (Gate Theatre Dublin) 1999, The Gin Game (Savoy and nat tour) 1999, The Storm (Almeida Theatre, Br entry at Prague Quadriennale 1999) 1999, Carmen (Chicago) 2000, Arms and the Man (Gate Theatre Dublin) 2000, Il Corsaro (Athens Megaron) 2001, Turandot (ballet, China) 2001, The Girl with Red Hair (Royal Lyceum Theatre Co Edinburgh, Hampstead Theatre London) 2005, The Flint Street nativity (Liverpool Playhouse) 2006, Bent (Trafalgar Studios) 2006, Salome (Nuffield Theatre) 2006, The Emperor Jones (RNT) 2007, The Winter's Tale (Royal Lyceum Edinburgh) 2007; dir Int Scenography Course Central St Martin's Sch of Art and Design London 1990–95, dir 1st term project at Motley Theatre Design Course 1999; memb: Exec Ctee Soc of Br Theatre Designers 1975–91, British Theatre Design 1979–1983, British Theatre Design 1983–87; winner Golden Troika (for Eugene Onegin) at Prague Quadriennale 1979, Best Designer Award (Critics' Circle) 1996, first prize Garden of Islington competition 1999–2000; *Recreations* exploration of natural phenomena; *Style*— Robin Don, Esq; ✉ e-mail robin@robindon.com, website www.robindon.com

DON-WAUCHOPE, Sir Roger Hamilton; 11 Bt (NS 1667), of Edmonstone and Newton Don; elder s of Sir Patrick George Don-Wauchope, 10 Bt (d 1989), and Ismay Lilian Ursula, *née* Hodges; *b* 16 October 1938; *Educ* Hilton Coll Natal, Durban and Pietermaritzburg Univ; *m* 14 Dec 1963, Sallee, yr da of Lt-Col Harold Mill-Colman, OBE, ED, of Durban, South Africa; 2 s, 1 da; *Heir* s, Andrew Don-Wauchope; *Career* ptnr Deloitte & Touche Chartered Accountants South Africa 1972–98 (joined 1959), ret; CA(SA), HDipTax; *Clubs* Victoria (past chm), Durban Country, Prince's Grant, Old Hiltonian (past nat chm, vice-pres), Sr Golfers' Soc of KwaZulu-Natal (memb Ctee); *Style*— Sir Roger Don-Wauchope, Bt; ✉ Newton, 53 Montrose Drive, Pietermaritzburg 3201, Natal, South Africa (tel 00 27 33 347 1107, e-mail don-wuachope@intekom.co.za)

DONACHIE, Prof William David; s of Charles Donachie (d 1966), and Jessie, *née* Leiper (d 1997); *b* 27 April 1935; *Educ* Dunfermline HS, Univ of Edinburgh (BSc, Sir David Baxter scholar, PhD); *m* 1965, Dr Millicent Masters; 1 s (David b 1974); *Career* asst lectr in genetics Univ of Edinburgh 1958–61; research assoc in biochemical scis Princeton Univ 1962–63; lectr in genetics Univ of Edinburgh 1963–65; on staff: MRC Microbial Genetics Research Unit Hammersmith Hosp 1965–68, Molecular Genetics Unit Edinburgh 1968–74; Univ of Edinburgh: sr lectr in molecular biology 1974–80, reader 1980–93, prof of bacterial genetics 1993–2000, prof emeritus 2000–; visiting prof: Univ of Copenhagen 1978, Univ of Paris (VII) 1988; memb Academia Europaea 1989; fell American Acad for Microbiology 1999; FRSE 1998; *Recreations* natural history, drawing, t'ai chi, gardening and other good things; *Style*— Prof William D Donachie, FRSE; ✉ Institute of Cell and Molecular Biology, University of Edinburgh, Darwin Building, King's Buildings, Mayfield Road, Edinburgh EH9 3JR (tel 0131 650 5354, fax 0131 668 3870, e-mail william.donachie@ed.ac.uk)

DONAGHY, Rita Margaret; CBE (2005, OBE 1998); da of William Scott Willis (d 1963), of Leamington Spa, and Margaret Brenda, *née* Howard (later Mrs Bryan, d 2006); *b* 9 October 1944, Bristol; *Educ* Univ of Durham (BA); *m* Feb 2000, Edward Easen-Thomas; *Career* perm sec to Students' Union Inst of Educn Univ of London 1984–2000 (joined registry 1968), chair ACAS 2000–; memb: NALGO/UNISON Nat Exec Cncl 1973–2000 (pres NALGO 1989–90), Gen Cncl TUC 1987–2000 (pres 1999–2000), Advsy Ctee on Employment of People with Disabilities 1995–97, Low Pay Cmmn 1997–2000, Ctee on Standards in Public Life 2001– (interim chair 2007); Hon DUniv: Open Univ 2003, Keele 2004; Hon DBA Univ of Greenwich 2005; FCIPD 2003, FRSA 2004; *Recreations* theatre, gardening, watching cricket; *Clubs* Surrey CCC; *Style*— Mrs Rita Donaghy, CBE; ✉ ACAS, Brandon House, 180 Borough High Street, London SE1 1LW (tel 020 7210 3670, e-mail rdonaghy@acas.org.uk)

DONAGHY, Roger; s of George Gerald Donaghy (d 1989), of Co Armagh, NI, and Florence, *née* Thompson; *b* 10 February 1940; *Educ* Portadown Tech Coll, Univ of Adelaide; *m* 17 Nov 1962, Rachael, da of Joseph Watson, of Co Armagh, NI; 1 da (Nina Diane b 1968); *Career* reporter and feature writer Portadown Times 1955–61, feature writer Advocate Newspapers Tasmania 1961–63, TV reporter and industrial corr Aust Broadcasting Corp Adelaide 1963–65; BBC World Serv News 1966–: journalist, duty ed, newsroom ed; FDR memb Rotary Club of Danson; *Recreations* golf, travel, reading, photography; *Style*— Roger Donaghy, Esq; ✉ 41 Bean Road, Bexleyheath, Kent DA6 8HW (tel 020 8303 5109); BBC, Bush House, Strand, London WC2 (tel 020 7240 3456)

DONALD, Prof Athene Margaret; da of Walter Griffith, of London, and Annette Marian, *née* Tylor; *b* 15 May 1953; *Educ* Camden Sch for Girls, Univ of Cambridge (BA, PhD); *m* 3 July 1976, Dr Matthew J Donald; 1 s (James George b 19 May 1986), 1 da (Margaret Frances b 27 July 1988); *Career* postdoctoral assoc Dept of Materials Sci and Engrg Cornell Univ 1977–81, SERC fell Dept of Metallurgy and Materials Sci Univ of Cambridge 1981–83, res fell Cavendish Lab Cambridge 1983–85, prof of experimental physics Dept of Physics Univ of Cambridge 1998– (lectr 1985–95, reader in experimental physics 1995–98); memb: OST Foresight Technol Panel on Food/Drink 1994–97, Biology Neutron Advsy Panel 1995–99, EPSRC Coll 1995–, Large Scale Structures Instr Beam Scheduling Panel 1996–99, Prog Mgmnt Ctee for LINK Prog on Competitive Industrial Materials from Non-Food Crops 1997, Editorial Bd Polymer Int 1998–, BBSRC Agrifood Ctee 1999–2002, Governing Cncl and Science Sub-Ctee IFR 1999–2003, Advsy Bd Jl Macromolecular Sci 1999–, Editorial Advsy Bd Int Jl of Biological Macromolecules 1999–, Steering Advsy Ctee ISIS 2nd Target Station 2002–, EPSRC Physics SAT 2002–04, BBSRC Strategy Bd 2003–04, 2008 RAE Physics Sub Panel; chm BBSRC JREI Ctee

1999–2000, ed-in-chief European Physics Jl E 1999–2004, symposium organiser on Materials Sci of Food MRS Boston 1998–99; Charles Vernon Boys Prize Inst of Physics 1989, Samuel Locker Award in Physics 1989, Rosenhain Medal and Prize Inst of Materials 1995, William Hopkins Prize Cambridge Philosophical Soc 2003, Mott Medal and Prize Inst of Physics 2005, Bakerian Prize lectr Royal Soc 2006; fell Robinson Coll Cambridge; fell APS, FInstP, FRS 1999; *Publications* Liquid Crystalline Polymers (with A H Windle, 1992, 2 edn 2006), Starch: Structure and Function (1997 and 2001); also author of over 220 papers in learned jls and numerous book chapters and reviews; *Style—* Prof Athene Donald, FRS; ✉ Cavendish Laboratory, J J Thomson Avenue, Cambridge CB3 0HE (tel 01223 337382, fax 01223 337000, e-mail amd3@cam.ac.uk)

DONALD, Chris Mark; s of Hugh Ernest James Donald, of Newcastle upon Tyne, and late Kathleen Evelyn, *née* Rickard; *b* 25 April 1960; *Educ* Heaton Comp Newcastle, Newcastle Coll of Arts; *m* 15 May 1988, Dolores Clare, da of Charles Doherty; 1 s (Dale Thomas b 30 Sept 1989), 1 da (Jamie Clare b 15 Sept 1991); *Career* clerical offr DHSS Central Office Newcastle 1978–80, founded Viz Magazine 1979, ed Viz 1979–, student Newcastle Coll of Arts 1981–82, set up House of Viz to publish Viz full time 1984 (signed publishing agreement Virgin Books 1985 then John Brown Publishing Ltd 1987); Br Magazine Publishing Awards Youth Magazine Ed of the Year 1989; *Books* Viz: The Big Hard One (1986), Viz: The Big Hard Number Two (1987), Viz: The Big Pink Stiff One (1988), Viz: Holiday Special (1988), Viz: The Dog's Bollocks (1989), The Viz Book of Crap Jokes (1989), The Billy the Fish Football Yearbook (1989), Viz: The Spunky Parts (1990), Viz: The Sausage Sandwich (1991), Viz: The Fish Supper (1992), Viz: The Pork Chopper (1993), The Viz Book of Absolute Shite for Boys and Girls (1993), Viz: The Pan Handle (1994), The Viz Book of Top Tips (1994), Viz: The Bell End (1995), Top Tips Two (1995), Viz: The Turtle's Head (1996), Viz Letterbocks (1996), Viz: The Joy of Sexism (1996), The Full Toss (1997); *Recreations* railway station restoration, Newcastle United supporter, signwriting; *Style—* Chris Donald, Esq; ✉ House of Viz, PO Box 1PT, Newcastle upon Tyne NE99 1PT

DONALD, George Malcolm; s of George Donald (d 2000), of Bieldside, Aberdeen, and Margaret, *née* Tait (d 1947); *b* 12 September 1943; *Educ* Robert Gordon's Coll Aberdeen, Aberdeen Acad, Edinburgh Coll of Art (Andrew Grant scholar, postgrad scholar, DA), Benares Hindu Univ (travelling scholar), Hornsey Coll of Art (ATC), Univ of Edinburgh (MEd); *m* 1969 (m dis 1986); 1 da (Saskia b 1971), 1 s (Ninian Fraser b 1973); *Career* artist and printmaker; dir Centre for Continuing Studies Edinburgh Coll of Art until 2001, dir Edinburgh Coll of Art Summer Sch until 2004; currently keeper RSA; visiting prof: Univ of Central Florida 1981, 1996, 2002, 2003, 2004 and 2005, Chinese Acad of Fine Art 1993 and 1994, Kyoto Saga Univ of Arts 2002, Univ of Sharjah 2003, American Coll of Dubai 2004; memb Printmaker's Workshop; RSA 1992; *Solo Exhibitions* 57 Gall 1971, Pool Theatre Gall 1972, Shed 50 Gall 1974, Edinburgh Scottish Gall 1981, Bohun Gall 1984, Chine Collé 1984 and 1987, Peacock Printmakers' Gall 1985, Glasgow Print Workshops Gall 1985, Helsinki Festival 1985, Finnish Assoc of Printmakers' Gall 1985, New Paintings (Open Eye Gall) 1985, 1995, 1998, 2002 and 2003, Galerija Fakulteta Likovnih Umetnosti 1987, From the Edge (tour) 1990, New Paintings from China (Open Eye Gall) 1991, Christopher Hull Gall 1992, Far East · New Paintings from China and Japan (Open Eye Gall) 1993, 9 Translations from the Chinese 1994, Open Eye Gall 2000, 2003, 2005 and 2007; *Group Exhibitions* Marjorie Parr Gall 1968 and 1971, Edinburgh Int Festival 1968, Pernod Exhbn 1968, Scottish Graphics (57 Gall) 1971, Int Graphics (Carnegie Festival) 1971, Richard Demarco Gall 1972, Goosewell Gall 1972, McLellan Galls 1974, Mall Gall 1974, Among the Quiet Weavers (Weavers' Workshop) 1974, 20 x 57 Exhbn (57 Gall) 1975, Compass Gall 1975 and 1981, Young Scottish Artists (Scottish Gall) 1976, Scottish Print Open (Scottish Arts Cncl) 1976, New Prints (Printmakers' Workshop) 1976, Alamo Gall 1978, Scottish Gall 1978, Photo-Graphic (Printmakers' Workshop) 1979, Contemporary Papermakers (City Art Centre Edinburgh) 1980, UCF Gall 1981, Print Annual 2 (PMW) 1981, NY Festival City Gall 1983, Open Eye Gall 1983 and 1986, Mercury Gall 1983, 1984 and 1986, Sue Rankin Gall 1984 and 1987, Fine Art Soc 1984 and 1985, Nicholson Gall 1986, Charter House Gall 1986, Christopher Hull Gall 1987 and 1990, Smiths Galls 1987, Sarajevo Winter Festival 1988, Graphica Creativa 90 (Alvar Aalto Museum) 1990, One Hundred Years of Scottish Printmakers (Hunterian Museum) 1990, Bohun Gall 1990, Images of the Orient (Kingfisher Gall) 1990, Cormund Gall 1990, Gall 41 1992, RSW (annually) 1992–, RSA (annually) 1992–, Open Eye Gall 1992, 1994, 1995, 1998, 2000, 2001, 2002, 2003, 2004 and 2005, Loomshop Gall 1993, Thompsons Gall 2003; *Works in Collections* V&A, Nat Library of Scotland, Hunterian Museum, Scottish Arts Cncl, BBC, Nuffield Fndn, Miro Fndn Mallorca, Sharjah Gall of Fine Art UAE, Univ of Central Florida, Dubai Racing Club, Univ of Edinburgh; *Awards* Latimer Award RSA 1970, Guthrie Award RSA 1973, Gillies prize RSA 1982, May Marshall Brown Award RSW 1983, Gillies Award RSA 2003; *Recreations* fiddling, pottering, travelling; *Style—* George Donald, Esq, RSA; ✉ e-mail g.donald@care4free.net

DONALD, Hugh Robertson; OBE (1999); s of Robert Donald, of Edinburgh, and Anne Mary, *née* Watt (d 1994); *b* 5 November 1951; *Educ* Melville Coll Edinburgh, Univ of Edinburgh (LLB); *m* 16 Aug 1975, Margaret Grace; 1 s (Euan Christopher b 6 July 1979), 1 da (Morag Elizabeth b 21 July 1981); *Career* slr and mediator; Shepherd & Wedderburn: apprentice 1973–75, slr 1975–77, ptnr 1977–, managing ptnr 1994, chief exec 1995–99, chm 2005–; chm Family Mediation Scotland; WS 1979; *Recreations* walking, gardening, family, church; *Style—* Hugh Donald, Esq; ✉ Shepherd & Wedderburn WS, Saltire Court, 20 Castle Terrace, Edinburgh EH1 2ET (tel 0131 228 9900, fax 0131 228 1222, e-mail desk@shepwedd.co.uk)

DONALD, John Alistair; *b* 6 December 1928; *Educ* Farnham GS, Farnham Sch of Art, RCA (travel scholarship); *m* (m dis); 4 s, 1 da; *Career* Nat Serv 1947–49; self-employed designer, goldsmith and silversmith; design conslt: Hadley Co 1956–75, Antler Luggage 1958–68, Halex hairbrushes 1960–65; exhibitor with Goldsmiths Co NY 1960, fndr own workshop Bayswater 1960; proprietor: retail shop and workshop Cheapside 1968–2004, retail shop (with Tecla Pearls) Bond St London 1969–72, additional workshop Sussex 1970; external assessor to various maj arts and crafts schs, chief assessor Chamber of Mines jewellery competition SA 1972 and 1973; work incl: civic and presidential regalia, silver for Birmingham Cathedral, Oxford and Cambridge Colls and City Livery Cos; work in the private collections of: HRH The Queen Mother, HRH Princess Margaret, HRH Prince Charles, Duchess of Gloucester, Queen Margrethe of Denmark, Rt Hon Mrs Thatcher; badges of office incl: Sheriff of Nottingham, Mayor of Lincoln, Sheriff City of London; Liveryman Worshipful Co of Goldsmiths 1972 (Freeman 1959); *Recreations* golf; *Style—* John Donald, Esq; ✉ Brightling Place, Brightling, Robertsbridge, East Sussex TN32 5HD (tel 01424 838287, fax 01424 838196)

DONALDSON, Antony Christopher; s of Sqdn Ldr John William Donaldson, DSO, AFC (ka 1940), and Sheila Richardson, *née* Atchley; *b* 2 September 1939; *Educ* Charterhouse, Regent Street Poly, Slade Sch, UCL; *m* 1960, Patricia Anne, da of Charles William Marks; 2 s (Matthew John b 1961, Lee b 1963); *Career* artist; teacher Chelsea Sch of Art 1962–66, Harkness fell USA; solo exhbns incl: Rowan Gallery London 1963, 1965, 1966, 1968, 1970, 1979 and 1981, Nicholas Wilder Gallery Los Angeles 1968, Galleria Milano Milan 1971, Galerie du Luxembourg Paris 1973, 1976 and 1977, Bonython Gallery Adelaide Australia 1983, Juda Rowan Gallery London 1984, Daniel Gervis Paris 1985, Corcoran Gallery Los Angeles 1985, Mayor Rowan Gallery London 1989, Daniel Gervis Cannes 1992, First works (Mayor Gallery London) 1999, Hollywood Remade (Mayor Gallery London) 2004; work in public collections incl: Arts Cncl of GB, Arts Cncl of NI, Art Gallery of NSW Sydney, Berado Collection Sintra Museum of Modern Art Portugal, Bradford City Art Gallery, British Cncl, British Museum, Contemporary Art Soc London, Ferrens Art Gallery Hull, Folkwang Museum Essen, Govt Art Collection London, Graves Art Gallery Sheffield, Gulbenkian Fndn Lisbon, Hedendaagse Kunst Utrecht, Leicester Educn Authy, National Museum of Wales Cardiff, Olinda Museum Brazil, Porto Allegre Museum Brazil, Stuyvesant Fndn, Tate Gallery London, Wilde Theatre Bracknell, Williams College and Museum of Art Williamstown MA, Ulster Museum Belfast, UCL, Walker Art Gallery Liverpool; films: Soft Orange 1969, Pix 1972; *Style—* Antony Donaldson, Esq

DONALDSON, (William) Blair MacGregor; s of Dr William Donaldson (d 2003), and Janet Thompson, *née* Orr (d 1970); *b* 24 December 1940; *Educ* Edinburgh Acad, Univ of Edinburgh (MB ChB), FRCS, FRCOphth, DO; *m* 27 July 1966, Marjorie Stuart, da of Hugh Gordon Mackay (d 1958); 1 da (Lesley Elizabeth b 1972); *Career* jr hosp appts in Tasmania and Scotland 1966–79, conslt ophthalmic surgn, sr univ lectr 1979–, md BID Instruments Ltd; memb: BMA, American Acad of Ophthalmology, RSM; *Recreations* silversmithing, oil painting, antique restoration, skiing, golf; *Style—* Blair Donaldson, Esq; ✉ Kindrochit Lodge, Braemar, Deeside, Aberdeenshire; 45 Carlton Place, Aberdeen (tel 01224 641166)

DONALDSON, Brian; s of William Donaldson (d 1992), and Elsie Josephine, *née* Longstaff; *b* 6 April 1946; *m* 30 Aug 1969, Elizabeth Claire, *née* Sumner; 3 s (Charles Stewart b 11 Nov 1971, Christopher Paul b 25 Oct 1973, Benjamin James b 10 July 1979); *Career* Miny of Civil Aviation 1963–65; HM Dip Serv: joined 1965, mgmnt offr Algiers 1968–71, archivist La Paz 1971–73, Communications Ops Dept FCO 1974–75, entry clearance offr Lagos 1975–79, vice-consul Luxembourg 1979–81, Trade Rels and Exports Dept FCO 1981–83, asst private sec to Malcolm Rifkind as Min of State FCO 1983–85, second then first sec Port Louis 1985–89, dep head of mission Yaoundé 1989–92, first sec Dhaka 1992–96, Personnel Mgmnt Dept FCO 1996–97, dep head Info Dept FCO 1997–98, high cmmr to Namibia 1999–2002, ambass to Madagascar 2002–05 (concurrently non-resident ambass to Comoros); dir gen Pres of Madagascar's Small Grants Scheme 2005–; chm: Grant's Ctee, Kitchen Task Charities Tst 2006–; memb Cncl Assoc of Business Executive 2006–, tstee Equitrade Fndn 2007–; *Recreations* family, people watching; *Style—* Brian Donaldson, Esq; ✉ Rose Cottage, High Street, Milverton, Somerset TA4 1LL

DONALDSON, Prof Gordon Bryce; s of Alexander Walls Donaldson, of Glasgow, and Margaret Merry, *née* Johnston; *b* 10 August 1941; *Educ* Glasgow Acad, Univ of Cambridge (major open scholar, English Electric scholar, MA, PhD); *m* 15 Aug 1964, Christina, da of John Alexander Martin; 1 s (Ian Martin b 21 July 1966), 1 da (Anne Dunlop b 14 Oct 1968); *Career* lectr in physics Lancaster Univ 1966–75, visiting scientist Univ of Calif Berkeley (Fulbright scholar) 1975; Univ of Strathclyde: lectr 1976–78, sr lectr 1978–85, head Dept of Applied Physics 1984–86, personal prof 1985–88, prof of applied physics 1988–2006 (emeritus prof 2006–), head Dept of Physics and Applied Physics 1993–98; visiting prof Univ of Virginia Charlottesville 1981; hon ed Superconductor Science and Technology 1998–; nat co-ordinator for superconductivity SERC/DTI 1990–93, EPSRC Peer Coll for Functional Materials 1994–; hon fell CSIRO Australia 1999–2000; FInstP, CPhys, FRSE 1991; *Publications* author of over 100 scientific papers concerned chiefly with the science and applications of superconductivity, including chapters (some co-authored) in: Active and Passive Thin Film Devices (1978), Superconducting Electronics (1990), Concise Encyclopaedia of Magnetic and Superconducting Materials (1992), The New Superconducting Electronics (1993), SQUID Sensors: Fundamentals, Fabrication and Applications (1996); *Style—* Prof Gordon B Donaldson, FRSE; ✉ 108 Springkell Avenue, Pollokshields, Glasgow G41 4EW (tel 0141 427 3668); Department of Physics, John Anderson Building, University of Strathclyde, Glasgow G4 0NG (tel 0141 553 4134, fax 0141 552 7143, e-mail g.b.donaldson@strath.ac.uk)

DONALDSON, Hugh Montgomery; s of Dr Ian Montgomery Kerr Donaldson (d 1968), of Glasgow, and Annie Meek May, *née* Ferrier; *b* 21 December 1941; *Educ* Kelvinside Acad Glasgow, Univ of Glasgow (BSc), Univ of Strathclyde (MSc); *m* 8 Oct 1965, (Shirley) Rosemary, da of Shirley Edwin McEwan (Sem) Wright; 2 s (Richard Ian Montgomery b 14 Oct 1966, Nicholas Phillip Kerr b 19 Sept 1968), 1 da (Susannah Jane b 29 Nov 1971); *Career* sandwich apprentice Fairfield Shipbuilding and Engineering Co Ltd 1959–63; ICI: various maintenance research jobs Nobel Div until 1971 (joined as engr 1964), Organics Div 1971–73, area engr Huddersfield works 1973–76, project gp mangr Engrg Dept 1976–78, works engr Huddersfield Works 1978–81, chief engr ICI plc Engrg Dept NW and Fine Chemicals 1981–85, ops dir ICI Organics Div and Fine Chemicals Manufacturing Organisation 1985–90, gen mangr (personnel) ICI plc 1991–93, gen mangr (corp res) Zeneca Plc (following demerger from ICI) 1993–95; chief exec: Holliday Chemical Holdings Plc 1995–96, Spillers Petfoods 1997–98, Jarvis Porter Group plc 1998; dir: Atic Industries Bombay 1988–91, Fletcher Joseph Ltd 1994–97; memb Review Body on Doctors' and Dentists' Remuneration 2002–; MIChemE 1985, FREng 1989, FIMechE 1989; *Recreations* sailing, golf, jogging, gardening; *Style—* Hugh M Donaldson, Esq, FREng

DONALDSON, Prof Iain Malcolm Lane; s of Archibald Thomson Donaldson (d 1981), of Edinburgh, and Milly, *née* Bailey (d 1986); *b* 22 October 1937; *Educ* Fettes, Univ of Edinburgh (MB ChB, BSc), Univ of Oxford (MA, by special resolution); *m* 18 July 1961, Jean Patricia, da of John Patrick Maule, OBE (d 2002), of Edinburgh; 1 s (David b 1971); *Career* jr med and res posts Univ of Edinburgh 1962–69, Anglo-French res scholar Université de Paris 1969–70, res offr Laboratory of Physiology Univ of Oxford 1973–79 (MRC clinical res fell 1970–73), fell and tutor in med St Edmund Hall Oxford 1973–79 (emeritus fell 1979–), prof of zoology Univ of Hull 1979–87, prof of neurophysiology Univ of Edinburgh 1987–2003 (prof emeritus 2003–); hon librarian RCP Edinburgh 2000–; author of papers on physiology of the central nervous system and on the history of medicine; MRCP 1965, FRCPEd 1981 (MRCPEd 1965); *Recreations* studying the past; *Style—* Prof I M L Donaldson; ✉ Division of Neuroscience, University of Edinburgh, Appleton Tower, Crichton Street, Edinburgh EH8 9LE (tel 0131 650 3526, e-mail i.m.l.d@ed.ac.uk)

DONALDSON, Prof (Charles) Ian Edward; s of Dr William Edward Donaldson, and Elizabeth, *née* Weigall; *b* 6 May 1935; *Educ* Melbourne GS, Univ of Melbourne (BA), Magdalen Coll Oxford (MA); *m* 1, 1962 (m dis 1990), Tamsin Jane Procter; 1 s, 1 da; m 2, 1991, Grazia Maria Therese Gunn; *Career* sr tutor in English Univ of Melbourne 1958; Univ of Oxford: Harmsworth sr scholar Merton Coll 1960–62, fell and lectr in English Wadham Coll 1962–69; CUF lectr in English 1963–69, prof of English ANU Canberra 1969–91, fndn dir Humanities Res Centre ANU 1974–90, regius prof of rhetoric and English literature Univ of Edinburgh 1991–95; Univ of Cambridge: Grace I prof of English 1995–2002, fell King's Coll 1995–, chm English Faculty 1999–2001, dir Centre for Research in the Arts, Social Sciences and Humanities 2001–03; dir Humanities Research Centre ANU Canberra 2003–07; visiting appts: Univ of Calif Santa Barbara, Gonville & Caius Coll Cambridge, Cornell Univ, Univ of Melbourne; Syndicate, CUP 1997–2001; professional fell Sch of Culture and Communication Univ of Melbourne 2007–; fell Aust Acad of the Humanities (FAHA) 1975, FBA 1987, FRSE 1993; *Books* The World Upside-Down: Comedy from Jonson to Fielding (1970), Ben Jonson: Poems (ed, 1975), The Rapes of Lucretia (1982), Jonson and Shakespeare (ed, 1983), Transformations in Modern European Drama (ed, 1983), Seeing the First Australians (ed with Tamsin Donaldson, 1985), Ben Jonson (ed, 1985), Shaping Lives: Reflections on Biography (jt ed,

1992), Ben Jonson: Selected Poems (ed, 1995), Jonson's Magic Houses (1997); *Style*— Prof Ian Donaldson, FAHA, FBA, FRSE; ✉ School of Culture and Communication, University of Melbourne, VIC 3010, Australia

DONALDSON, Jeffrey Mark; PC (2007), MP, MLA; s of James Alexander Donaldson, and Sarah Anne, *née* Charleton; *b* 7 December 1962; *Educ* Kilkeel HS, Castlereagh Coll Belfast (Dip Electrical Engrg); *m* 26 June 1987, Eleanor Mary Elizabeth, da of late Gilbert Cousins; 2 da (Claire Victoria b 21 Nov 1990, Laura Alexandra b 13 April 1992); *Career* agent to Rt Hon J Enoch Powell, MBE, MP 1983–84, personal asst to Rt Hon James Molyneaux, MP 1984–85, memb NI Assembly 1985–86, ptnr in fin servs/estate agency practice 1986–; MP (UUP until 2003, now DUP) Lagan Valley 1997–, MLA (DUP (elected as UUP)) Lagan Valley 2003–; Parly spokesman (UUP) trade and industry and defence 1997–2003, currently Parly spokesman (DUP) tport and int devt; memb Select Ctees on: NI 1997–2000, Tport 2000–01 and 2005–, Statutory Instruments and Regulatory Reform 2001–05; hon sec Ulster Unionist Cncl 1988–2000 (vice-pres 2000–03), memb Northern Ireland Forum 1996–98; asst grand master Loyal Orange Order 1994–97; alderman Lisburn City Cncl 2005–; *Recreations* reading, local history, church activities, hill walking, music, travelling; *Style*— The Rt Hon Jeffrey Donaldson, Esq, MP, MLA; ✉ House of Commons, London SW1A 0AA (tel 020 7219 3407, fax 020 7219 0696)

DONALDSON, Prof John Dallas; s of John Donaldson (d 1988), of Elgin, Moray, and Alexandrina Murray Ross, *née* Dallas (d 1985); *b* 11 November 1935; *Educ* Elgin Acad, Univ of Aberdeen (BSc, PhD), Univ of London (DSc); *m* 22 March 1961, Elisabeth Ann, da of George Edmond Forrest, of Eastbourne, E Sussex; 2 da (Claire b 1962, Sarah b 1965), 1 s (Richard b 1969); *Career* asst lectr Univ of Aberdeen 1958–61, chemistry lectr Chelsea Coll London 1961–72, reader in inorganic chemistry Univ of London 1972–80; City Univ: prof of industrial chemistry 1980–90, dir Industrial & Biological Chemistry Res Centre 1988–91; Brunel Univ: head Dept of Chemistry 1990–97, dir Centre for Environmental Research 1991–2005; visiting prof Imperial Coll London 2006– chm: J D Donaldson Research Ltd 1984–, Hopeman Associates Ltd 1991–; dir Oxford Forecasting Services Ltd 1994–2002; jt dep chm WAMITAB; memb Nat Ctee for Chemistry 1985–89; tstee Zimbabwe Tech Mgmnt Trg Tst 1983–94; Freeman (by redemption) City of London 1982, memb Ct of Assts Worshipful Co of Pewterers 2005 (Liveryman 1983); fell Soc of Industrial Chemistry, FRSC 1959, CChem, FRSA 1986, hon fell Chartered Inst of Wastes Mgmnt 2002; *Books* Symmetry & Sterochemistry (with S D Ross, 1972), Cobalt in Batteries (with S J Clark and S M Grimes, 1986), Cobalt in Electronic Technology (with S J Clark and S M Grimes, 1988), Cobalt in Medicine Agriculture and the Environment (with S J Clark and S M Grimes, 2000); *Clubs* Roehampton; *Style*— Prof John Donaldson; ✉ 21 Orchard Rise, Richmond, Surrey TW10 5BX (tel 020 8876 6534, e-mail jd.donaldson@btinternet.com); Hopeman Associates Limited, Brunel Science Park, Kingston Lane, Uxbridge, Middlesex UB8 3PQ (tel 01895 266869, fax 01895 269753)

DONALDSON, Hon Michael John Francis; o s of Baron Donaldson of Lymington, PC (Life Peer, d 2005), and Dame (Dorothy) Mary Donaldson, GBE (d 2003); bro of Jenny Williams, *qv*; *b* 16 November 1950; *Educ* Stanbridge Earls Sch; *m* 11 Nov 1972, Judith Margaret, da of late Edgar William Somerville, of Garsington, Oxon; 2 s (William Michael Somerville, James John Francis (twins) b 29 Aug 1977); *Career* negotiator Knight Frank & Rutley London 1969–71; dir: Edwood Property Co Ltd 1972–75, Nab Properties Ltd 1972–80, Marquis & Co Chartered Surveyors 1975–; Incorporated Soc of Valuers and Auctioneers: chm SW London branch 1982–85, memb Nat Cncl 1985–96; Freeman City of London 1972, memb Ct of Assts Worshipful Co of Cutlers 2001– (Liveryman 1975–2001, Master 2005–06); ASVA, ARVA, FSVA, IRRV 1981–99, MAE 1995, MCIArb 1999 (ACIArb 1973), FRICS 2000; *Recreations* sailing, skiing; *Clubs* Royal Lymington Yacht, City Livery Yacht, Guildford Coastal Cruising; *Style*— The Hon Michael Donaldson; ✉ Windlesham, Surrey GU20 6LT (tel 01344 626909, fax 01344 622006, e-mail donaldson.westwood@btinternet.com); Marquis & Co, Marquis House, 54 Richmond Road, Twickenham, Middlesex TW1 3BE (tel 020 8891 0222, fax 020 8892 6215, e-mail mjfd@marquisandco.com)

DONALDSON, Prof Simon Kirwan; s of Peter Eden Kirwan Donaldson, and Edith Jane, *née* Stirland; *b* 20 August 1957; *Educ* St Faith's Sch Cambridge, Sevenoaks Sch, Pembroke Coll Cambridge (Sailing blue), Worcester Coll Oxford; *m* (Ana) Nora, *née* Hurtado; 2 s (Andres b 1984, Nicholas b 1993), 1 da (Jane b 1987); *Career* Univ of Oxford: jr res fell All Souls Coll 1983–85, Wallis prof of mathematics 1985–97, prof Stanford Univ 1997–98, prof Imperial Coll London 1998–; Royal Soc research prof 2001–; Jr Whitehead Prize London Mathematical Soc 1985, Fields Medal Int Congress of Mathematicians 1986, Sir William Hopkins Prize Cambridge Philosophical Soc 1991, Royal Medal Royal Soc 1992, Crafoord Prize Royal Swedish Academy of Sciences 1994; FRS 1986; *Books* The Geometry of 4–Manifolds (with P B Kronheimer, 1990); *Recreations* sailing; *Style*— Prof Simon Donaldson, FRS; ✉ Department of Mathematics, Imperial College, 180 Queen's Gate, London SW7 2BZ (tel 020 7594 8559, fax 020 7594 8517, e-mail s.donaldson@ic.ac.uk)

DONALDSON, Hon Thomas Hay; o s of late Baron Donaldson of Kingsbridge, OBE (Life Peer), and Frances Annesley, *née* Lonsdale (d 1994); *b* 1 June 1936; *Educ* Eton, Cincinnati Univ, Trinity Coll Cambridge (BA); *m* 1962, Natalie, da of late Basil Wadkovsky, of Miami Beach; 2 s, 4 da; *Career* with Empire Trust Co NY 1958–62, W E Hutton and Co NY 1962–63; Morgan Guaranty Trust Co of NY London Office 1963–96: vice-pres 1972–90, Euro credit offr 1982–91, md 1990–96, chm Euro Credit Policy Ctee 1991–94, sr credit advsr Europe 1994–96; dir: Abbey National Treasury Services plc 1994–97, JP Morgan Life Assurance Ltd 1997–2003, JP Morgan Int Bank 1999–; memb: Bucks Ctee Game Conservancy Tst 1999–2006 (chm 2002–04); FCIB; *Books* Lending in International Commercial Banking, The Medium Term Loan Market (with J A Donaldson), Understanding Corporate Credit, How to Handle Problem Loans, Thinking About Credit, Credit Risk and Exposure in Securitisation and Transactions, Project Lending, The Treatment of Intangibles, Credit Control in Boom and Recession, More Thinking About Credit; *Recreations* bridge, reading, writing, shooting; *Clubs* Brooks's; *Style*— The Hon Thomas Donaldson; ✉ The Old Lodge, Mayertorne, London Road, Wendover Dean, Wendover, Buckinghamshire HP22 6QA (tel and fax 01296 622309, e-mail t.donaldson576@btinternet.com)

DONCASTER, Archdeacon of; *see:* Fitzharris, Ven Robert Aidan

DONCASTER, Bishop of 2000–; Rt Rev Cyril Guy Ashton; s of William Joseph Ashton (d 1958), and Margaret Anne, *née* Todd (d 1994); *b* 6 April 1942; *Educ* Grangefield GS, Oakhill Theol Coll London, Lancaster Univ (MA); *m* 3 July 1965, Muriel; 3 s (Jonathan, Simon, Timothy), 1 da (Elizabeth); *Career* curate St Thomas Blackpool 1967–70, vocation sec Church Pastoral Soc 1970–74, vicar of St Thomas' Lancaster 1974–91, dir of training Dio of Blackburn 1991–2000; course dir Post-Grad Dip Cliff Coll Derbys 1995–; *Books* Church on the Threshold (1991), Threshold God (1992), A Faith Worth Sharing? (jtly, 1995); *Recreations* motorcycling, vintage cars, swimming, cycling, music, wine, walking; *Style*— The Rt Rev the Bishop of Doncaster; ✉ Bishop's House, 3 Farrington Court, Wickersley, Rotherham S66 1JQ (tel 01709 730130, fax 01709 730230)

DONEGALL, 7 Marquess of (I 1791); Dermot Richard Claud Chichester; LVO; sits as Baron Fisherwick (GB 1790); also Viscount Chichester of Carrickfergus and Baron Chichester of Belfast (I 1625), Earl of Donegall (I 1647), Earl of Belfast (I 1791), Baron Templemore (UK 1831); Hereditary Lord High Admiral of Lough Neagh and Govr of Carrickfergus Castle; s of 4 Baron Templemore, KCVO, DSO, OBE, PC, JP, DL (d 1953), and Hon Clare Meriel Wingfield (d 1969), da of 7 Viscount Powerscourt; suc kinsman, 6 Marquess of Donegall 1975, having suc as 5 Baron Templemore 1953; *b* 18 April 1916; *Educ* Harrow, RMC; *m* 16 Sept 1946, Lady Josceline Gabrielle Legge (d 1995), da of 7 Earl of Dartmouth, GCVO, TD (d 1958); 1 s, 2 da; *Heir* s, Earl of Belfast; *Career* 2 Lt 7 Hussars 1936 (POW 1941–44), Maj 1944, served in Egypt, Libya, Italy; one of HM's Body Guard, Hon Corps of Gentlemen at Arms 1966; grand master Masonic Order Ireland, sr grand warden England, grand warden United Grand Lodge (Masonic) 1982–, Standard Bearer HM Body Guard of Hon Corps of Gentleman at Arms 1984–86; *Recreations* shooting, fishing; *Clubs* Cavalry and Guards', Kildare St (Dublin); *Style*— The Most Hon the Marquess of Donegall, LVO; ✉ Dunbrody Park, Arthurstown, Co Wexford, Republic of Ireland (tel 00 353 51 389104)

DONEGAN, Kathleen (Kate); *b* 1953, Fife; *Educ* Univ of Stirling (BA); *m* Dr Chris Donegan; 2 s; *Career* former memb Scottish Office Home Dept; joined Prison Serv 1977, asst govr HMP Cornton Vale 1977–84, asst govr HMP Barlinnie 1984–87, dep govr HMP Reading 1987–89, govr (resources and services) HMP Glenochil 1989, dep govr HMP Perth 1989–91, head Operational Manpower Planning Unit Scottish Prison Serv HQ 1991–93, dep project mangr Staffing Structure Review (SSR) 1993–94, dep govr HMP Barlinnie 1994–95, HM inspr then dep chief inspr of prisons for Scot 1995–96, govr HMP & YOI Cornton Vale 1996–2001, govr HMP Glenochil 2001–06, govr HMP Perth 2006–; *Recreations* computing, reading; *Style*— Mrs Kate Donegan; ✉ HM Prison Perth, 3 Edinburgh Road, Perth PH2 8AT (tel 01738 622293, fax 01738 630545)

DONERAILE, 10 Viscount (I 1785); Richard Allen St Leger; also Baron Doneraile; s of 9 Viscount Doneraile (d 1983), and Melva, Viscountess Doneraile; *b* 17 August 1946; *Educ* Orange Coast Coll Calif; *m* 1969, Kathleen Mary, da of Nathaniel Simcox; 1 s (Hon Nathaniel b 1971), 1 da (Hon Maeve b 1974); *Heir* s, Hon Nathaniel St Leger; *Career* air traffic control specialist Missippi Univ; *Style*— The Rt Hon Viscount Doneraile; ✉ 405 Eve Circle, Placentia, California 92670, USA

DONLEAVY, James Patrick Michael; s of Patrick John Donleavy (d 1957), of NY, and Margaret, *née* Walsh (d 1987); *b* 23 April 1926; *Educ* Fordham Prep Sch NYC, Roosevelt HS Yonkers, Manhattan Prep Sch NYC, US Naval Acad Prep Sch Port Deposit Maryland, TCD; *m* 1, 1949 (m dis 1969), Valerie, da of John McMichael Heron (d 1950), of Ilkley, W Yorks and Port-e-Vullen, IOM; 1 s (Philip b 22 Oct 1951), 1 da (Karen b 31 March 1955); m 2, 1969 (m dis 1988), Mary Wilson Price; 1 s (Rory b 27 July 1980), 1 da (Rebecca b 28 Dec 1979); *Career* WWII US Navy 1944–46; author and playwright; *Novels* The Ginger Man (1955), A Fairy Tale of New York (1961), A Singular Man (1963), The Saddest Summer of Samuel S (1966), The Beastly Beatitudes of Balthazar B (1968), The Onion Eaters (1971), The Destinies of Darcy Dancer Gentleman (1977), Schultz (1980), Leila (1983), JP Donleavy's Ireland In All Her Sins and In Some of Her Graces (1986), A Singular Country 1989, Are You Listening Rabbi Löw (1987), That Darcy, That Dancer, That Gentleman (1990), The Lady Who Liked Clean Rest Rooms (1996), Wrong Information is Being Given Out at Princeton (1997), The Dog on the Seventeenth Floor (2007); *Plays* Fairy Tales of New York (1960), What They Did in Dublin with The Ginger Man (with introduction) (1961), A Singular Man (1964), The Saddest Summer of Samuel S (1967), The Beastly Beatitudes of Balthazar B (1981); *Short Stories* Meet My Maker The Mad Molecule (1964); *Manuals* The Unexpurgated Code: A Complete Manual of Survival and Manners, De Alfonce Tennis: The Superlative Game of Eccentric Champions, Its History, Accoutrements, Rules, Conduct and Regimen (1984); *Autobiography* The History of the Ginger Man: An Autobiography (1994), An Author and his Image and Other Pieces (1997); *Art Exhibitions* Printers Gallery Dublin 1950 and 1951, Bronxville NY 1959, Langton Gallery London 1975, Caldwell Gallery Belfast 1987, Anna-Mei Chadwick Gallery 1989, Alba Fine Gallery London 1991, Front Lounge Dublin 1995, Walton Gallery London 2002, Molesworth Gallery Dublin 2006, National Arts NY 2007; *Recreations* farming, De Alfonce tennis; *Clubs* Kildare St and Univ (Dublin), NY Athletic; *Style*— J P Donleavy, Esq; ✉ Levington Park, Mullingar, Co Westmeath, Ireland

DONNACHIE, Prof Alexander; s of Cdr John Donnachie, RNVR (d 1979), of Kilmarnock, and Mary Ramsey, *née* Adams (d 2001); *b* 25 May 1936; *Educ* Kilmarnock Acad, Univ of Glasgow (BSc, PhD); *m* 9 April 1960, Dorothy, da of Thomas Paterson (d 1979), of Kilmarnock; 2 da (Susan b 1963, Lynn b 1965); *Career* lectr UCL 1963–65 (DSIR res fell 1961–63), res assoc CERN Geneva 1965–67, sr lectr Univ of Glasgow 1967–69; Univ of Manchester: prof of physics 1969–2002, head of theoretical physics 1975–85, dean Faculty of Sci 1985–87, dir Physical Laboratories 1989–94, dean Faculty of Sci and Engrg 1994–97; CERN: chm SPS Ctee 1988–93, memb Scientific Policy Ctee 1988–93, memb Res Bd 1988–95, memb Cncl 1989–94; sec C11 Cmmn IUPAP 1987–90, memb SERC 1989–94 (chm Nuclear Physics Bd 1989–93); FInstP; *Books* Electromagnetic Interactions of Hadrons Vols 1 and 2 (1978), Pomeron Physics and QCD (2002), Electromagnetic Interactions of Hadronic Structure (2007); *Recreations* sailing, walking; *Style*— Prof Alexander Donnachie; ✉ Physics Department, University of Manchester, Manchester M13 9PL (tel 0161 275 4200, fax 0161 275 4218)

DONNACHIE, Ian Louis; s of late Louis Donnachie, and Dorothy Donnachie; *b* 4 June 1947; *Educ* DLit, DBA, MMS, MHSM, DipHSM, Graduate Prog Hosp Mgmnt Chicago; *m* (m dis); 2 da (Samantha, Elspeth); *Career* chief exec St James's Univ Hosp NHS Tst Leeds 1981–90, chief exec Chelsea and Westminster, Charing Cross and Hammersmith Hosps 1990–94, chief exec Bradford HA 1994–2002, sr vice-pres Nations Healthcare Inc 2003–; memb HRH The Duke of Edinburgh's Sixth Cwlth Study Conf Australia; dir and memb Bd Martin House Children's Hospice; Hon DLit Univ of Bradford; *Recreations* sculpture, theatre, walking, reading; *Clubs* East India; *Style*— Ian Donnachie, Esq; ✉ 2 Rossett Green Lodge, Rossett Green Lane, Harrogate, North Yorkshire HG2 9LL (tel 01423 879707, e-mail ianldonnachie@aol.com); Nations Healthcare (UK Office), Greencoat House, Francis Street, London SW1P 1DH (tel 020 7592 0860, e-mail idonnachie@nationshealthcare.com)

DONNE, David Lucas; s of late Dr Cecil Lucas Donne, of Wellington, NZ, by his w Marjorie Nicholls Donne; *b* 17 August 1925; *Educ* Stowe, ChCh Oxford (MA), Syracuse Univ NY; *m* 1, 1957, Jennifer Margaret Duncan (d 1975); 2 s, 1 da; m 2, 1978, Clare, da of Maj F J Yates; *Career* called to the Bar Middle Temple 1949; with Charterhouse Gp 1953–64, William Baird 1964–67; chm: Dalgety 1977–86 (dep chm 1975–77), Crest Nicholson plc 1973–92, Steetley plc 1983–92 (dep chm 1979–83), Asda Gp plc 1986–88, Argos plc 1990–95; dir: Royal Trust Bank 1972–93 (dep chm 1989–93), Sphere Investment Tst 1982–95 (chm 1989–95), Marathon Asset Management 1989–, Guinness Flight Extra Income Tst 1995–2003; memb: Nat Water Cncl 1980–83, Bd British Coal (formerly NCB) 1984–87, Stock Exchange Listed Cos Advsy Ctee 1987–91; tstee: Royal Opera House Devpt Land Tst 1985–90, The Game Conservancy 1987–91; *Recreations* shooting, opera, sailing; *Clubs* Royal Thames Yacht; *Style*— David Donne, Esq; ✉ 8 Montagu Mews North, London W1H 2JU

DONNELLAN, Declan Michael Dominic Martin; s of Thomas Patrick John Donnellan, of Ballinlough, Co Roscommon, and Margaret Josephine Donnellan; *b* 4 August 1953; *Educ* St Benedict's Sch Ealing, Queens' Coll Cambridge (MA); *Career* called to the Bar Middle Temple 1978; artistic dir Cheek By Jowl Theatre Co 1981–, assoc dir RNT 1989–97, first dir RSC Acad Stratford-upon-Avon, assoc dir Russian Theatre Confedn; awards in Paris, London, Moscow and NY incl Observer Award for outstanding achievement; Chevalier de l'Ordre des Arts et des Lettres; *Productions* for Cheek By Jowl Theatre Co incl: Twelfth Night 1987, Lady Betty 1989, As You Like It 1992 and 1995, Measure for Measure 1994, The Duchess of Malfi 1996, Much Ado About Nothing 1998, Othello 2004,

Cymbeline 2007; for RNT: Fuente Ovejuna 1989, Peer Gynt 1990, Angels in America Part 1 Millennium 1991 and Part 2 Perestroika 1993, Sweeney Todd 1992, The Mandate 2004; for RSC: The School for Scandal 1998, King Lear 2002, Great Expectations 2005; for Russian Theatre Confedn: Boris Godunov 2000, Twelfth Night 2003, Three Sisters 2005; other prodns incl: The Winter's Tale (Maly Theatre St Petersburg) 1997, Le Cid (Avignon Festival) 1998, Falstaff (Saltzburg Festival) 2001, Homebody/Kabul (NY Theatre Workshop) 2001, Romeo and Juliet (Bolshoi Ballet Moscow) 2003; *Publications* incl The Actor and the Target (2000); *Style—* Declan Donnellan, Esq; ✉ c/o Michelle Braidman Associates, 10–11 Lower John Street, London W1R 3PE (fax 020 7439 3600); website www.cheekbyjowl.com

DONNELLY, Sir (Joseph) Brian; KBE (2003), CMG (1998); s of Joseph Donnelly (d 1986), and Ada Agnes, *née* Bowness (d 1971); *b* 24 April 1945, Workington, Cumbria; *Educ* Workington GS, The Queen's Coll Oxford (Wyndham scholar, MA, ed Cherwell), Univ of Wisconsin (MA); *m* 1, 20 Aug 1966 (m dis 1994), Susanne Gibb; 1 da (Kathryn Charlotte b 27 Oct 1970); m 2, 6 Nov 1997, Julia Mary Newsome; 1 step da (Alexandra Petch b 5 Sept 1977), 1 step s (Andrew Petch b 23 July 1980); *Career* joined HM Dip Serv 1973, second sec FCO 1973–75, first sec (Economic and Social Cncl (ECOSOC)) UKMIS NY 1975–79, first sec and head of Chancery Singapore 1979–82, asst head Personnel Policy Dept FCO 1982–84, dep to chief scientific advsr Cabinet Office 1984–87, cnsllr and consul-gen Athens 1988–90, RCDS 1991, head Non-Proliferation Dept FCO 1992–95, min and dep perm rep UK Delgn to NATO and WEU Brussels 1995–97, ambass to Serbia and Montenegro 1997–99, dir FCO 1999–2000, on secondment to Standard Chartered Bank and BP (Southern Africa) 2000–01, high cmmr to Zimbabwe 2001–03, ambass to Zimbabwe 2003–04, ret; special advsr to Sec of State for Foreign and Cwlth Affrs 2005–06; tstee Senhouse Roman Museum 2007–; memb Cwlth Scholarships Cmmn 2006–; *Recreations* golf, reading, kite flying; *Clubs* Royal Cwlth Soc, Maryport Golf; *Style—* Sir Brian Donnelly, KBE, CMG

DONNELLY, Declan; *b* 25 September 1975, Newcastle upon Tyne; *Career* actor and presenter; performed with Ant McPartlin, *qv*, as 'Ant & Dec' since 1993; jt winner (with Ant McPartlin): Best Double Act Carling Loaded Awards 2000, People's Choice Comedy Awards 2000, Entertainment Personality of the Year Nat TV Awards 2001, TV Personality of the Year Variety Club Awards 2002, TV Personality of the Year TRIC Awards 2002, Special Recognition Award Nat TV Awards 2002, Most Popular Entertainment Presenter TV Quick Awards 2003, TV Personality Award GQ 2003 and 2004, Best Comedy Duo Loaded Awards 2003; *Television* as actor incl: Byker Grove (as Duncan) 1989–93, A Tribute to the Likely Lads 2002; as presenter incl: The Ant & Dec Show 1995 (BAFTA, RTS Award), Ant and Dec Unzipped 1997 (BAFTA), SM:TV Live 1998–2001 (Best Entertainment Prog Children's BAFTAs 2000, Best Children's Show TV Quick Awards 2000 and 2001, Best Children's Entertainment Prog RTS Awards 2000, Best Children's Prog Broadcast Awards 2001, Best Children's Prog Indie Awards 2001, Best Presenters RTS Awards 2001, Kids Award Disney Channel 2001, TV Presenters of the Year RTS Awards 2002), CD:UK 1998–2001 (Best Teen Show TV Hits Awards 2000), Ant and Dec's Secret Camera Show 2000, Friends Like These 2000 (Bronze Rose Montreux Awards 2000), Slap Bang with Ant and Dec 2001, Pop Idol 2001 (Entertainment Prog of the Year TRIC Awards 2002, Best Entertainment Prog BAFTA Awards 2002, Golden Rose Montreaux Awards 2002, Best Entertainment Prog Nat TV Awards 2002), Brit Awards 2001, Party in the Park 2001, Comic Relief: Say Pants to Poverty 2001, Record of the Year 2001 and 2002, Ant & Dec's Saturday Night Takeaway 2002 (Best Entertainment Presenter Nat TV Awards 2002, 2003 and 2004, Best Entertainment Prog TV Quick Awards 2003 and 2004, Best Entertainment Prog Nat TV Awards 2003 and 2004, People's Choice and Best Comedy Entertainment Performance Comedy Awards 2003, Best Comedy Entertainment Performance and Best Comedy Entertainment Prog Comedy Awards 2004, Best Entertainment Presenter RTS Awards 2005, Best Entertainment Prog Broadcast Awards 2006), I'm a Celebrity, Get Me Out of Here! 2002– (Best Reality Prog TV Quick Awards 2003 and 2004, Lew Grade Award for Entertainment Prog or Series BAFTAs 2005), Pride of Britain Awards 2003, Comic Relief: The Big Hair Do 2003, World Idol 2003, British Comedy Awards 2003 and 2004, Comic Relief: Red Nose Night Live 2005; *Films* incl Love Actually 2003; *Albums* with Ant McPartlin: Psyche 1994, Top Katz 1995, The Cult of Ant & Dec 1997; *Style—* Declan Donnelly; ✉ c/o James Grant Management, Syon Lodge, 201 London Road, Isleworth TW7 5BH (tel 020 8232 4100, fax 020 8232 4101)

DONNELLY, Dougie; s of Robert Donnelly, of Glasgow, and Jane, *née* Wright; *b* 7 June 1953; *Educ* Hamilton Acad, Univ of Strathclyde (LLB); *m* 22 Aug 1980, Linda, da of David A Sommerville; 3 da (Kim b 20 Aug 1982, Laura b 9 Dec 1985, Lisa b 3 Oct 1991); *Career* booker MAC Entertainments Glasgow 1974–76, Radio Clyde 1976–92 (presenter Mid Morning Show, Rock Show, Music Week and Sunday File), presenter, commentator and reporter BBC TV Sport 1978–; coverage incl: Olympic Games, World Cup, European Football Championships, Cwlth Games; presenter: Grandstand, Sportscene, Friday Night with Dougie Donnelly, Embassy World Snooker Championship, International Survival of the Fittest, Benson & Hedges Snooker Masters, Open Golf Championship, US Masters, Ryder Cup; presenter/commentator The Golf Channel (US); sports videos presenter and writer; columnist Glasgow Evening Times 1983–2005; chm: Bd of Tstees Cwlth Games (Scotland) Endowment Fund, Scottish Inst of Sport; *Awards* incl: Scottish TV Personality of the Year 1982, Scottish Radio Personality of the Year 1979, 1982 and 1985, Best Dressed TV Presenter 1985, nomination RTS Award 2003, Sunday Mail Great Scot 2005; *Recreations* golf, reading, music, socialising, after-dinner speaking; *Clubs* Variety, Glenearn Golf (Gleneagles); *Style—* Dougie Donnelly, Esq; ✉ c/o David Meehan, David John Associates, 16a Winton Drive, Glasgow G12 0QA (tel 0141 357 0532)

DONNELLY, Martin Eugene; CMG (2002); *b* 4 June 1958; *Educ* St Ignatius Coll, Campion Hall Oxford (BA), Coll of Europe Bruges (Dip Euro Studies), Ecole Nationale d'Administration Paris; *Children* 3 da; *Career* HM Treasury: admin trainee Public Enterprises Div 1980–81, External Fin Div 1981–82, private sec to Fin Sec to the Treasury 1982–83, seconded to Ecole Nationale d'Administration Paris 1983–84, princ European Community Gp 1984–87, private sec to Sec of State on secondment to NI Office (London) 1988–89, at Cabinet of Cmmn EC Brussels 1989–92, head of Defence Team 1993–95, seconded to French Trésor Monetary Affrs and Govt Debt Bureau 1995–96, head of Treasury Econ and Monetary Union Div 1997–98; dep head Cabinet Office European Secretariat 1998–2003, dep DG (policy) Immigration and Nationality Dept Home Office 2003–04, DG (europe and globalisation) FCO 2004–; *Recreations* family, reading, hill walking, music; *Style—* Martin Donnelly, Esq, CMG; ✉ Foreign & Commonwealth Office, King Charles Street, London SW1A 2AA (tel 020 7008 2207, fax 020 7008 2326, e-mail martin.donnelly@fco.gov.uk)

DONNELLY, Prof Peter Duncan; *b* 27 January 1963; *Educ* Univ of Edinburgh (MB ChB, MD), DA (RCS Eng), Univ of Stirling (MBA), Univ of Wales Coll of Med (MPH), Harvard Univ (PMD); *m* Joan; 3 s; *Career* jr hosp dr positions 1985–88, NHS MDG scholar Stirling MBA Prog 1988–89; South Glamorgan HA: registrar 1989–90, sr registrar 1990–92, conslt in public health med 1992–93, actg dir of planning and procurement 1993–94, dep chief admin MO/dep dir of public health med 1994–96; dir of public health and exec memb Bd Morgannwg HA 1996–2000; dir Public Health and Health Policy Lothian Health Bd 2000–04, dep chief medical offr Scottish Executive 2004–; sr lectr in public health med Univ of Wales Coll of Med 1992–96 (lectr 1989–92); pres Assoc of Dirs of Public Health 1999–2001, vice-pres Faculty of Public Health Med RCP 2001–04 (treas 1999–2001); hon sr lectr in public health med Univ of Wales Coll of Med and Univ of Wales Swansea 1996–2000, hon prof of public health Univ of Edinburgh 2002–; Hon DSc Napier Univ; FFPH, FRCP, FRCPE; *Publications* author of articles in the scientific and professional press on public health and resuscitation; *Style—* Prof Peter D Donnelly, MD; ✉ Scottish Executive Health Department, St Andrew's House, Regent Road, Edinburgh EH1 3DG (tel 0131 244 2270, e-mail peter.donnelly@scotland.gsi.gov.uk)

DONNELLY, Prof Peter James; s of Augustine Stanislaus Donnelly, of Brisbane, Aust, and Sheila Bernadette, *née* O'Hagan; *b* 15 May 1959; *Educ* St Joseph's Coll Brisbane, Univ of Queensland (BSc, DPhil), Balliol Coll Oxford (Rhodes scholar, DPhil); *m* 28 June 1986 (m dis 2006), Sarah Helen, da of Robert John Harper; 2 da (Imogen Clare b 1990, Caroline Emma b 1996), 1 s (Giles James b 1993); *Career* research fell UC Swansea 1984–85, lectr UCL 1985–88, prof of mathematical statistics and operational research Queen Mary & Westfield Coll London 1988–94, prof of statistics and ecology and evolution Univ of Chicago 1994–96; Univ of Oxford: head Dept of Statistics 1996–2001, prof of statistical science, fell St Anne's Coll; visiting asst prof Univ of Michigan 1983–84; Mitchell Prize 2002, Guy Medal in Silver RSS 2004; memb: Int Statistical Inst, RSS; FIMS, Hon FIA, FRS 2006; *Publications* author of many articles in academic jls; *Recreations* sport, music, children; *Style—* Prof Peter Donnelly, FRS; ✉ Department of Statistics, University of Oxford, 1 South Parks Road, Oxford OX1 3TG (tel 01865 272860, fax 01865 272595, e-mail donnelly@stats.ox.ac.uk)

DONNELLY, Peter Lane; Baron of Duleek; s of Col Paul J Donnelly Jr, of Oyster Bay, Long Island, USA, and Marian, *née* Kinsley; *b* 18 March 1947; *Educ* Georgetown Univ Washington DC (BSc), Fordham Univ Law NY (Juris Dr), NYU Grad Sch of Business, Templeton Coll Oxford; *m* 1 (m dis 1982), Joyce Arbon; m 2, 23 May 1983, Georgina Mary, da of late Dennis Dallamore, of Johannesburg, South Africa; 2 s (Sebastian b 1986, Octavian b 1989); *Career* vice-pres The European-American Bank & Tst Co NY 1969–77, ptnr Kuhn Loeb Lehman Brothers Int NY 1977–82, md (Int) The First Boston Corp NY 1982–86, md (Europe) Prudential-Bache Capital Funding London 1986–91, sr advsr FirstCorp (Johannesburg) 1991–93, dir FNB of Southern Africa (UK) Ltd 1992–93; sr advsr European Privatisation and Investment Corp (Vienna) 1991–2003, gen mangr UK and Western Europe ABSA Bank Limited Johannesburg 1994–99, md Banco Finantia Gp Lisbon 1999–; dir: ABSA Manx Holdings Isle of Man 1995–99, ABSA Syndicate Investments (Holdings) Ltd 1995–99, Aureus Capital Partners Ltd Jersey 2000–; *Recreations* lawn tennis, golf, painting; *Clubs* Piping Rock (NY), Union (NY), Brooks's, Queen's, City of London, Bembridge Sailing, Inanda Polo (Johannesburg); *Style—* Peter Donnelly, Esq

DONNELLY, Roisin Jane Catherine; da of Thomas John Donnelly, of Glasgow, and Catherine Joyce, *née* Doherty; *b* 17 June 1961, Paisley; *Educ* Notre Dame HS Glasgow, Univ of Glasgow (MA); *m* 29 April 1995, Robert George Hughes; 3 da (Lorna Catherine b 22 Oct 1996, Cordelia Georgia b 18 May 1999, Juliet Aurora b 13 Feb 2001), 1 s (Angus John b 24 March 1998 d 1998); *Career* Procter & Gamble: mktg dir cosmetics and fragrances UK 1992–94, mktg dir cosmetics and male toiletries Western Europe, Eastern Europe, ME and Africa 1994–96, mktg dir fine fragrance Western Hemisphere (USA and S America) 1996–98, corp mktg dir and head of mktg UK and Ireland 1998–; memb Bd Cosmetic Exec Women, memb Marketing Gp of GB, memb WACL; fell Marketing Soc; *Style—* Ms Roisin Donnelly; ✉ Procter & Gamble, The Heights, Brooklands, Surrey KT13 0XP (tel 01932 896500, fax 01932 896554, mobile 07787 105607, e-mail donnelly.rj@pg.com)

DONOGHUE, Barbara Joan; *b* 16 July 1951, Canada; *Educ* McGill Univ Canada (Ontario scholar, Univ scholar, Govt of Canada fell, BCom, MBA); *m* 1976, Stefanos Vavalidis; 2 s (Alexander Charles b 27 Nov 1984, Philip Zacharias b 8 May 1989); *Career* Canadian Pacific Ltd 1973–77, Bank of Nova Scotia 1977–79, vice-pres int and corporate banking Bankers Tst Co 1979–93, md Hawkpoint Ptnrs and Natwest Markets 1994–98, dir Noventus Ptnrs 2004–06; non-exec dir and chm Audit Ctee Eniro AB 2003–; chair Co regulatory Design Gp Office of Communications 2005; memb: ITC 1999–2003, Bd Centre for Creative Business London Business Sch 1999– (teaching fell Strategic and Int Mgmnt Faculty 1999–2004), Broadcasting Policy Gp 2004–, Competition Cmmn 2005–; *Clubs* Hurlingham; *Style—* Barbara Donoghue; ✉ e-mail barbara.donoghue@btinternet.com

DONOGHUE, Dr Emma; da of Denis Donoghue, and Frances, *née* Rutledge; *b* 24 October 1969; *Educ* Muckross Park Convent Sch Dublin, UCD (BA), Univ of Cambridge (PhD); *Partner* Dr Christine Roulston; 1 s (Finn Roulston b 15 Nov 2003); *Career* writer; *Publications* Passions Between Women: British Lesbian Culture 1668–1801 (1993), What Sappho Would Have Said: Four Centuries of Love Poems between Women (ed, 1997), We Are Michael Field (1998), The Mammoth Book of Lesbian Short Stories (ed, 1999); fiction: Stir-Fry (1994), Hood (1995, winner American Library Assoc Gay, Lesbian and Bisexual Book Award 1997), Kissing the Witch (linked fairytales, 1997), Slammerkin (2000, Ferro-Grumley Award for Lesbian Fiction 2002), The Woman Who Gave Birth to Rabbits (stories, 2002), Life Mask (2004), Touchy Subjects (2006), Landing (2007); stage plays: I Know My Own Heart (Dublin, Glasshouse, 1993), Ladies and Gentlemen (Dublin, Glasshouse, 1996), Kissing the Witch (San Francisco Magic Theatre, 2000); radio plays: Trespasses (RTE Radio, 1996), Don't Die Wondering (BBC Radio 4, 2000), Exes (BBC Radio 4, 2001), Humans and Other Animals (BBC Radio 4, 2003), Mix (BBC Radio 3, 2003); *Style—* Emma Donoghue; ✉ c/o Caroline Davidson Literary Agency, 5 Queen Anne's Gardens, London W4 1TU (tel 020 8995 5768, 020 8994 2770, e-mail emma@emmadonoghue.com, website www.emmadonoghue.com)

DONOHOE, Brian; MP; s of George Donohoe, and Catherine Donohoe; *b* 10 September 1948; *Educ* Irvine Royal Acad, Kilmarnock Tech Coll; *m* 16 July 1973, Christine, da of Raymond Pawson; 2 s; *Career* draughtsman Ailsa Shipyard 1970–77 (engrg apprentice 1965–70), Hunterston Nuclear Power Station 1977, draughtsman ICI Organics Div 1977–81; convener Political and Educn Ctee TASS 1969–81, sec Irvine Trades Cncl 1973–82, chm Cunninghame Industrial Devpt Ctee 1975–85, dist offr NALGO 1981–92, treas Cunninghame S Constituency Lab Pty 1983–91; MP (Lab) Cunninghame S 1992–; sec All-Pty Parly Gardening & Horticultural Gp 1994–, sec All-Pty Parly Scotch Whisky Gp 1996–, hon treas Br-American Parly Gp 2002–, chm PLP Transport Ctee 2004–, jt chm All-Pty Parly Gp against Fluoridation 2005– (vice-chm 1996–2005); memb: Tport Select Ctee 1993–97 and 2002–05, Environment, Tport and the Regions Select Ctee 1997–2002; tstee Thrive 2003–; *Recreations* gardening; *Style—* Brian H Donohoe, Esq, MP; ✉ House of Commons, London SW1A 0AA (tel 020 7219 6230, constituency 01294 276844, mobile 07774 646 600, pager 07644 066 100)

DONOUGHMORE, 8 Earl of (I 1800); Richard Michael John Hely-Hutchinson; also Viscount Hutchinson of Knocklofty (UK 1821), Baron Donoughmore of Knocklofty (I 1783) and Viscount Donoughmore of Knocklofty (I 1797); s of Col 7 Earl of Donoughmore (d 1981), and Jean, Countess of Donoughmore, MBE, *née* Hotham (d 1995); *b* 8 August 1927; *Educ* Winchester, Groton USA, New Coll Oxford (BM BCh, MA); *m* 1, 1 Nov 1951, Sheila (d 1999), da of late Frank Frederick Parsons and Mrs Roy Smith-Woodward; 4 s; m 2, Margaret, former w of Cdr John Morgan; *Heir* s, Viscount Suirdale; *Career* Capt RAMC 1954–56; fin conslt, company dir; chm Hodder Headline plc (formerly Headline Book Publishing plc) until 1997; sat as Viscount Hutchinson of Knocklofty in House of Lords until 1999; *Recreations* fishing, shooting, racing; *Style—* The Rt Hon the Earl of Donoughmore; ✉ The Manor House, Bampton, Oxfordshire OX18 2LQ

DONOUGHUE, Baron (Life Peer UK 1985), of Ashton in the County of Northamptonshire; Bernard Donoughue; s of Thomas Joseph Donoughue and Maud Violet, *née* Andrews; *b* 8 September 1934; *Educ* Northampton GS, Lincoln Coll Oxford (BA), Harvard Univ, Nuffield Coll Oxford (MA, DPhil); *m* 1959 (m dis 1990), Carol Ruth, da of late Abraham Goodman; 2 da (Hon Rachel Anne b 1965, Hon Kate Miriam b 1967), 2 s (Hon Paul Michael David b 1969, Hon Stephen Joel b 1969); *Career* lectr, sr lectr, reader LSE 1963–74, sr policy advsr to PM 1974–79, devpt dir Economist Intelligence Unit 1979–81, asst ed The Times 1981–82, head of res and investment policy Grieveson Grant & Co 1984–86 (ptnr 1983), dir Kleinwort Benson Securities 1986–88, exec vice-chm LBI 1988–91; oppn House of Lords spokesman on Treasy matters and energy 1991–92, on National Heritage 1993–97; Parly sec MAFF (min for Farming and Food) 1997–99; visiting prof in govt LSE 2003–; sec All Pty Parly Gp on Racing and Bloodstock, chm Starting Price Regulatory Cmmn 2004–, chm Future Funding of Horseracing Gp 2005–06, chm Review of Regulation of Greyhound Racing 2007; memb: Advsy Bd Wissenschaftszentrum Berlin 1978–90, London Arts Bd 1991–97, Cncl LSE, Cncl LSO, Int League for the Protection of Horses (ILPH); hon fell: Lincoln Coll Oxford, LSE, Northampton Univ; Hon LLD Univ of Leicester; FRHistS; *Books* Trade Unions in a Changing Society (1963), British Politics and the American Revolution (1964), The People into Parliament (with W T Rogers, 1966), Herbert Morrison: Portrait of a Politician (with G W Jones, 1973), Prime Minister (1987), The Heat of the Kitchen (2003), Downing Street Diaries (2005); *Clubs* Pratt's; *Style*— The Rt Hon the Lord Donoughue; ✉ House of Lords, London SW1A 0PW

DONOVAN, Ian Alexander; s of Ivar Kirkwood Donovan (d 1983), and Marion Sutherland, *née* Esslemont (d 1995); *b* 19 December 1945; *Educ* Malvern Coll, Univ of Birmingham (MB ChB, MD); *m* 3 May 1975, Rosamund Mary, da of Reginald Vickors, of Worcs; 2 da (Amy b 1980, Lorna b 1982), 1 s (Robert b 1985); *Career* sr lectr in surgery Univ of Birmingham 1979–87, conslt surgn W Midlands RHA 1987–; memb: Cncl Assoc of Surgns GB and Ireland, Advsy Ctee Admin of Radioactive Substances DHSS, Ct of Examiners Royal Coll of Surgns of Eng, Intercollegiate Bd of Examiners in Gen Surgery; hon sec and pres W Midland Surgns Soc, RCS regnl advsr W Midlands Region; FRCS; *Recreations* woodwork, photography, family; *Clubs* East India; *Style*— Ian Donovan, Esq; ✉ 57 Birmingham Road, Hagley, Worcestershire DY9 9JY (tel 01562 884625)

DONOVAN, Ian Edward; s of John Walter Donovan (d 1986), and Ethel Molyneux Studdy Hooper (d 1990); *b* 2 March 1940; *Educ* Leighton Park Sch Reading; *m* 26 July 1969, Susan Betty da of William Harris (d 1993), of Abbotsbury, Dorset; 2 s (Christopher George b 1971, James William b 1974); *Career* fin dir: Lucas Girling Koblenz 1978–81, Lucas Electrical 1982–84; CAA: gp dir fin and central servs 1985–88, memb for fin 1986–88; dir Smiths Industries Aerospace & Defence Systems Ltd 1988–2000; chm ChartCo Ltd 1999–2000; pres Lambda Advanced Analog Inc 2000–01, dir Cranfield Aerospace Ltd 2002–06; memb Cncl Soc of Br Aerospace Companies 1995–97, dir Aeronautical Tsts Ltd 2002–; dir English Symphony Orch 2000–02; tstee Air League Educnl Tst 1994–2000 and 2002–05; hon treas: The Air League 1994–2000 and 2002–05, Homeless Network 2000–02; chm of tstees: RAeS, Pension and Life Assurance Scheme 2007–; FRAeS, FCMA; *Recreations* sailing, golf, fly fishing, music; *Clubs* RAF; *Style*— Ian E Donovan, Esq; ✉ Lawn Farm, Church Lane, Tibberton, Droitwich, Worcestershire WR9 7NW

DONOVAN, Judith; CBE (1997); da of Ernest Nicholson, of Bradford, W Yorks, and Joyce, *née* Finding; *b* 5 July 1951; *Educ* St Joseph's Coll Bradford, Woking Girls' GS, Univ of Hull (BA); *m* 12 Nov 1977, John Patrick Donovan, s of William Donovan, of Darlington; *Career* mktg trainee Ford Motor Co 1973–75, account mangr J Walter Thomson 1976, advertising mangr Grattan 1977–82, chm JDA (formerly Judith Donovan Associates) 1982–2000, chm DIY Direct Marketing 2001–; pres Bradford Jr C of C 1980, pres Bradford C of C 1999–2001 (memb Cncl 1998–2003); chm: Bradford Business Club 1985, Bradford TEC 1990–98, Millennium Cmmn 2000–06, Direct Mktg Assoc 1999–2001 (dir 1991–), Health and Safety Cmmn 2000–08, Northern Postwatch 2001–08, Yorks Tourist Bd 2005–; memb UK Bd Big Lottery Fund 2007–; ed-in-chief Direct Marketing Strategies 1999–2001; dir: Northern Ballet Theatre 1990–, Business Link W Yorks 2000–03; pres Bradford Samaritans 1999–2002, govr Friends of Bradford Art Galleries & Museums 1984–89, govr Legacy Tst, tstee Yorkshire Dales Millennium Tst 2003–05, fndr patron Women Mean Business, patron Small Business Bureau, memb Forum; Freeman City of London, Liveryman Worshipful Co of Marketors 1999; Hon DUniv Leeds Met Univ 2003; MInstM 1977, MCIM 1978, MCAM 1979, memb Mktg Soc 1987, CIMgt, FRSA 1995, FCAM, FCIM, FInstD (MInstD 1983), FIDM 2001; *Recreations* reading, the Western Front, pets; *Style*— Mrs Judith Donovan, CBE; ✉ Biggin Grange, Kirkby Malzeard, Ripon, North Yorkshire HG4 3QG; DIY Direct Marketing, Biggin Barns, Ringbeck, Kirkby Malzeard, Ripon, North Yorkshire HG4 3TT (tel 01765 650000, fax 01765 650153, e-mail judith@diydirectmarketing.co.uk)

DONOVAN, Michael John (Mike); *b* 11 May 1953; *m* Helen; 2 s (Adam, Ross); *Career* product validation engr rising to project ops manager Land Rover Ltd 1976–87, project dir Land Rover Discovery 1988–89, dir mfrg planning Rover Gp 1989–90, regnl dir Rover Cars 1990–91, dir of strategic planning and new progs then md (commercial) Rolls-Royce Motor Cars 1991, with Vickers plc 1991–94; British Aerospace plc: chief exec Avro Int Aerospace 1994–96, chief exec BAe Regnl Aircraft 1996–97, pres Aero Int Asia 1997, gp md defence systems 1997–98; chief exec Marconi Systems and Marconi Capital 1998–2001, chief operating offr Marconi Gp plc 2001–04 (dir 2000); non-exec dir Balfour Beatty plc 2006–; *Style*— Mike Donovan, Esq

DONOVAN, Paul James Kingsley; s of Brian Donovan (d 1992), of Croydon, Surrey, and Enid Constance, *née* Shaylor (d 1992); *b* 8 April 1949; *Educ* Queen Elizabeth's GS Barnet, Oriel Coll Oxford (MA); *m* 27 Oct 1979, Hazel Margaret, da of William Hubert Case (d 1987), of Kenya; 1 s (Toby b 1981), 2 da (Emily b 1987, Mary b 1989); *Career* journalist and writer; trainee Mirror Group Newspapers 1970–73, night news ed and reporter Sunday Mirror 1973–78, reporter, showbusiness writer and critic Daily Mail 1978–85, showbusiness ed, TV critic and media corr Today 1986–88; self-employed 1988–; TV previewer Hello! 1988–2001; radio columnist Sunday Times 1988–, contrib Oxford Dictionary of National Biography; memb: Devonshire Assoc, Dartmoor Museum Assoc, Oxford Univ Soc; *Books* Roger Moore (1983), Dudley (1988), The Radio Companion (1991), All Our Todays (1997); *Recreations* birds, Devon, walking; *Style*— Paul Donovan, Esq; ✉ 11 Stile Hall Gardens, London W4 3BS (tel 020 8994 5316); office (tel 020 8747 8387, fax 020 8747 4850, e-mail pauldon@scribbler.freeserve.co.uk)

DONOVAN, Prof Robert John; OBE (2007); s of Francis Alexander Donovan (d 1991), of Sandbach, Cheshire, and Ida, *née* Brooks; *b* 13 July 1941; *Educ* Sandbach Sch, UCW (BSc), Univ of Cambridge (PhD); *Children* 1 da (Jane Frances); *Career* res fell Gonville & Caius Coll Cambridge 1966–70; Univ of Edinburgh: lectr in physical chemistry 1970, reader 1974, appointed to personal chair of physical chemistry 1979, head Dept of Chemistry 1984–87 and 1995–97, chair of chemistry 1986–2006, sr hon professorial fell 2006–; visiting scientist Max-Planck Inst für Strömungsforshung Göttingen 1975, JSPS sr visiting fell Inst of Molecular Sci Okazaki Japan 1982 (visiting fell 1983 and 1989), visiting fell Aust Nat Univ Canberra 1993, Erskine fell Univ of Christchurch NZ 2001, visiting prof Tokyo Inst of Technol Japan 2005; SERC: chm Laser Facility Ctee 1988–92, chm Facilities Cmmn 1993–95; memb Cncl for the Central Lab of the Research Cncls (CCLRC) 2004–; FRSE 1976 (vice-pres 1998–2001), FRSC 1980; *Publications* incl Laser Chemistry (2007); *Recreations* riding, skiing and hill walking; *Style*— Prof Robert Donovan,OBE, FRSE; ✉ School of Chemistry, The University of Edinburgh, West Mains Road, Edinburgh EH9 3JJ (tel 0131 650 4722, fax 0131 650 6453)

DORAN, Andrew Michael (Andy); s of Kevin Reginald Doran, of Portsmouth, Hants, and Penelope Jean, *née* Hotton; *b* 24 February 1967, Portslade, E Sussex; *Educ* Kingston Poly (BSc), Univ of Bath (MSc); *m* 4 Dec 1992, Lucy Anne, da of Richard Cartwright; 1 da (Rebecca Jean b 1 Aug 1997), 1 s (Harvey Richard b 17 April 1999); *Career* team ldr Alcan Aluminium Can Recycling 1991–93, recycling offr London Borough of Hillingdon 1993–94; Surrey CC: dep head of sustainable devpt 1994–2001, exec asst to Ldr of the Cncl 2001–03, seconded as project offr County Cncls Network 2003–04, corporate policy offr 2004–05, head Local Authy Waste Performance DEFRA 2005–06, nat mangr Novelis Recycling 2006–; chm Local Authy Recycling Advsy Ctee (LARAC) 2003– (policy offr 2000–03); memb Chartered Inst of Wastes Mgmnt (CIWM), assoc memb Inst of Environmental Mgmnt and Assessment (IEMA); *Recreations* wine, football, cycling, sailing, running; *Style*— Andy Doran, Esq; ✉ Novelis UK Limited, Latchford Locks Works, Warrington, Cheshire WA4 1NP (e-mail andy.doran@novelis.com)

D

DORAN, Frank; MP; s of Francis Doran, and Betty, *née* Hedges; *b* 13 April 1949; *Educ* Leith Acad, Univ of Dundee (LLB); *m* 1967 (m dis), Patricia Ann (Pat), *née* Govan; 2 s (Frank, Adrian); *Career* admitted slr 1977; MP (Lab): Aberdeen S 1987–92, Aberdeen Central 1997–2005, Aberdeen N 2005–; shadow spokesman on oil and gas 1988–92, chm House of Commons Admin Ctee 2005–, sec Trade Union Gp of Lab MPs; fndr memb Scottish Legal Action Gp, fndr memb and former chm Dundee Assoc for Mental Health; *Recreations* cinema, football, art, sport; *Style*— Frank Doran, Esq, MP; ✉ House of Commons, London SW1A 0AA (tel 020 7219 3000)

DORAN, Gregory; s of John Doran, and Margaret, *née* Freeman; *b* 24 November 1958; *Educ* Univ of Bristol (BA), Bristol Old Vic Theatre Sch; *partner* Sir Antony Sher, KBE, *qv*; *Career* theatre dir; assoc dir RSC 1997–; *Theatre* RSC prodns incl: The Odyssey 1992, Henry VIII 1996, Cyrano de Bergerac 1997, The Merchant of Venice 1997, The Winter's Tale 1998, Oroonoko 1999 (Best Prodn Emma Awards 2000), Timon of Athens 1999, Macbeth 1999, As You Like It 2000, Jubilee 2001, King John 2001, Much Ado About Nothing 2002, The Island Princess 2002, The Jacobean Season 2003 (Olivier Award for Outstanding Achievement of the Year 2003), The Taming of the Shrew 2003, The Tamer Tamed 2003, All's Well That Ends Well 2003, Othello 2004, Venus and Adonis 2004, A Midsummer Night's Dream 2005, Sejanus 2005, The Canterbury Tales 2005, Antony and Cleopatra 2006, Merry Wives: the Musical 2006, Coriolanus 2007; other credits incl: Titus Andronicus (Market Theatre Johannesburg and RNT) 1995, The Real Inspector Hound/Black Comedy (Donmar Warehouse Prodns Comedy Theatre) 1998, The York Mystery Plays (York Minster) 2000 (Best Prodn TMA Awards); *Film* Macbeth, A Midsummer Night's Dreaming (BBC4 documentary); *Books* Woza Shakespeare! (with Antony Sher, 1996); *Style*— Gregory Doran, Esq; ✉ Royal Shakespeare Company, Waterside, Stratford-upon-Avon, Warwickshire CV37 6BB (tel 01789 412624)

DORCHESTER, Bishop of 2000–; Rt Rev Colin William Fletcher; OBE (2000); s of Alan Philip Fletcher, and Annette Grace Fletcher; *Educ* Marlborough, Trinity Coll Oxford, Wycliffe Hall Oxford; *m* 1980, Sarah; 1 s (b 1982), 2 da (b 1984, 1986); *Career* asst curate St Peter Shipley 1975–79, asst curate St Andrew Oxford and tutor Wycliffe Hall Oxford 1979–84, vicar Holy Trinity Margate 1984–93, rural dean Thanet 1988–93, domestic chaplain to the Archbishop of Canterbury 1993–2000; *Recreations* ornithology, walking, sport; *Style*— The Rt Rev the Bishop of Dorchester; ✉ Arran House, Sandy Lane, Yarnton, Oxfordshire OX5 1PB (tel 01865 375541, fax 01865 379890, e-mail bishopdorchester@oxford.anglican.org)

DORÉ, Katharine Emma; da of Robert Edward Frederick Doré, of Herefordshire, and Estelle Margaret, *née* Smith; *b* 13 February 1960; *Educ* St Brandon's Sch for Girls, Central Sch of Speech & Drama; *Children* 1 s (Toby b 27 Aug 1993); *Career* freelance stage mangr and admin; cos worked for 1981–88 incl Leicester Haymarket, Whirligig Children's Theatre, Scottish Ballet, English Touring Opera (now City of Birmingham Opera) and Watermans Arts Centre, co dir and prodr (with Matthew Bourne) Adventures in Motion Pictures (modern dance co) 1988–2004 (prodn incl: Swan Lake (London, UK tour, Los Angeles and Broadway), Cinderella (London and Los Angeles), The Car Man (London and UK, Europe, American and Japanese tours)), prodr KD Management and Productions Ltd (prodns incl: A Midsummer Night's Dream, Arsenic & Old Lace), prodr Magic Times Prodns; tstee and co-fndr Treehouse Tst 1996– *Awards* Barclays New Stages Award 1990, Manchester Evening News Award and Olivier Award 1995, Time Out Dance Award, South Bank Show Award and Evening Standard Ballet Award 1996, US Dramalogue Award 1997, US Drama Critics Circle Award 1999, 3 Tony Awards 1999, Manchester Evening News Theatre Award 2000, Evening Standard Award 2000; *Recreations* contemporary arts, gardening, travel, Italy; *Style*— Ms Katharine Doré; ✉ Magic Times, Horseshoe Wharf, 6A Clink Street, London SE1 9FE (tel 020 7407 7772, e-mail katherine@magictimesproductions.com)

DORE, Prof Ronald Philip; CBE (1989); s of Philip Brine Dore, and Elsie Constance Dore; *b* 1 February 1925; *Educ* Poole GS, SOAS Univ of London (BA); *m* 1957, Nancy Macdonald; 1 s, 1 da; 1 s (with Maria Paisley); *Career* lectr in Japanese Instns SOAS Univ of London 1951, prof of Asian Studies Univ of British Columbia 1956, reader then prof of sociology LSE 1961 (hon fell 1980), fell IDS 1969–82, asst dir Tech Change Centre 1982–86; Imperial Coll London: visiting prof 1982–86, dir Japan-Europe Industry Research Centre 1986–91; adjunct prof MIT 1989–94, assoc Centre for Economic Performance LSE 1992–; memb Accademia Europaea, hon foreign memb American Acad of Arts and Scis 1978, hon foreign fell Japan Acad 1986; Order of the Rising Sun (3rd Class) Japan 1988; FBA 1975; *Books* City Life in Japan (1958, 2 edn 1999), Land Reform in Japan (1959, 2 edn 1984), Education in Tokugawa Japan (1963, 2 edn 1983), Aspects of Social Change in Modern Japan (ed, 1967), British Factory, Japanese Factory (1973, 2 edn 1990), The Diploma Disease (1976, 2 edn 1997), Shinohata: Portrait of a Japanese Village (1978, 2 edn 1993), Community Development: Comparative Case Studies in India, the Republic of Korea, Mexico and Tanzania (ed with Zoe Mars, 1981), Energy Conservation in Japanese Industry (1982), Flexible Rigidities: Structural Adjustment in Japan (1986), Taking Japan Seriously: A Confucian Perspective on Leading Economic Issues (1987), Japan and World Depression, Then and Now: Essays in Memory of E F Penrose (ed jtly, 1987), How the Japanese Learn to Work (with Mari Sako, 1988, revised edn 1998), Corporatism and Accountability: Organized Interest in British Public Life (ed jtly, 1990), Will the 21st Century be the Age of Individualism? (1991), The Japanese Firm: The Sources of Competitive Strength (ed jtly, 1994), The Return of Incomes Policy (ed jtly, 1995), Japan Internationalism and the UN (1997), Stockmarket Capitalism, Welfare Capitalism, Japan and Germany versus Anglo-Saxons (2000), Social Evolution, Technology and Culture (2001), Collected Writings of Ronald Dore (2002), New Forms and Meanings of Work (2004); *Style*— Prof Ronald Dore, CBE, FBA; ✉ 157 Surrenden Road, Brighton BN1 6ZA (01273 501370)

DORE, Simon Peter George Taylor; s of Peter George Dore, of Hants, and Gillian Helena Read, *née* Martin; *b* 10 October 1961; *m* 4 May 1996, Kate, da of John Ayers; 4 s (William b 14 June 1990, George b 10 Jan 1992, Peter b 14 July 1994, Thomas b 12 Aug 1997); *Career* studio mangr BBC Radio 1987–88, prodr/presenter BBC World Service Radio for Europe 1988–90, sr presentation dir British Satellite Broadcasting Ltd (BSB) 1990–91 (presentation dir 1990), freelance promotions prodr 1991; BBC: asst ed World Service TV 1991–92, ed Worldwide TV 1992–93, managing ed Worldwide TV 1993–95; managing dir BTAS Advsy Ltd 1995–96, dir of broadcasting Granada Sky Broadcasting 1996–98, dir of channel devpt Granada Media 1998–99, chief technol offr ITV Digital 1999–2003, chief technol offr ITV 2001–03, sr vice-pres Technol and Ops Showtime 2003–, chief technol offr Top UpTV 2006–; FRSA; *Style—* Simon Dore, Esq; ✉ Top Up TV, Riverview House, Hampton Wick, Kingston, Surrey KT1 4BU (tel 020 8614 0380, e-mail simon.dore@topuptv.com)

DOREY, Sir Graham Martyn; kt (1993); s of late Martyn Dorey, and late Muriel, *née* Pickard; *b* 15 December 1932; *Educ* Kingswood Sch Bath, Ecole des Roches Verneuil, Univ of Bristol (BA), Univ of Caen (Cert d'Études Juridiques); *m* 1, 5 Sept 1962, Penelope Cecile (d 1996), da of late Maj E A Wheadon, ED; 2 s (Robert b 1970, Martyn b 1972), 2 da (Suzanne b 1963, Jane b 1964); m 2, 15 Aug 1998, Cicely Ruth Lummis; *Career* advocate of the Royal Court 1960, people's dep States of Guernsey 1970–73, slr-gen Guernsey 1973, attorney-gen Guernsey 1977, dep bailiff Guernsey 1982–92, bailiff of Guernsey 1992–99, pres Ct of Appeal Guernsey 1992–99, judge Court of Appeal Jersey 1992–99; KStJ 1996 (CStJ 1992); *Recreations* sailing, maritime history; *Style—* Sir Graham Dorey

DORKEN, (Anthony) John; s of late Oscar Roy Dorken, of Birmingham, and Margaret, *née* Barker; *b* 24 April 1944; *Educ* Mill Hill Sch, King's Coll Cambridge (MA); *m* 1972, Satanay, da of Fawzi Mufti; 1 da (Marina Charlotte b 1976), 1 s (Adam Alexander b 1981); *Career* VSO Libya 1965–66, asst princ Bd of Trade 1967–71, private sec to Parly under sec of state for Industry 1971–72, princ Dept of Trade and latterly Dept of Energy 1972–77, seconded to Cabinet Office 1977–79, asst sec Dept of Energy 1980–86, seconded to Shell UK Exploration and Production 1986–89, dir of resource mgmnt Dept of Energy 1989–92, dep DG Office of Gas Supply 1992–93, head Consumer Affairs Div DTI 1993–96; dir Br Rubber Manufacturers' Assoc 1997–2005 (dep dir 1996–97), ceo Br Tyre Manufacturers' Assoc 2006–; sec and treas Medical Aid and Relief for the Children of Chechnya; *Recreations* reading, walking, music, squash, tennis; *Clubs* Stormont Lawn Tennis and Squash Rackets; *Style—* John Dorken, Esq; ✉ 10 Connaught Gardens, London N10 3LB (tel 020 8372 6213, e-mail dorken24@aol.com)

DORKING, Bishop of 1996–; Rt Rev Ian James Brackley; s of Frederick Arthur James Brackley (d 1987), of Westcliff-on-Sea, Essex, and Ivy Sarah Catherine, *née* Bush (d 1980); *b* 13 December 1947; *Educ* Keble Coll Oxford, Cuddesdon Theol Coll; *m* 12 June 1971, Penelope (Penny) Ann, da of Arthur William Saunders; 2 s (Christopher James b 7 April 1973, Alexander Jonathan b 1 Aug 1975); *Career* ordained deacon 1971, priest 1972; asst curate St Mary Magdalene with St Francis Lockleaze Bristol 1971–74; Bryanston Sch: asst chaplain 1974–76, chaplain 1976–80, master i/c cricket 1975–80; vicar St Mary's E Preston with Kingston 1980–88, rural dean Arundel and Bognor 1982–87; team rector St Wilfrid's Haywards Heath 1988–96, rural dean Cuckfield 1989–95; proctor in convocation and memb Gen Synod 1990–95, memb House of Bishops 2001; *Recreations* cricket, golf, pipe organs, theatre, reading; *Style—* The Rt Rev the Bishop of Dorking; ✉ 13 Pilgrims Way, Guildford, Surrey GU4 8AD (tel 01483 570829, fax 01483 567268, e-mail bishop.ian@cofeguildford.org.uk)

DORMAN, Sir Philip Henry Keppel; 4 Bt (UK 1923), of Nunthorpe, Co York; s of Richard Dorman (d 1976), and Diana Keppel, *née* Barrett; suc kinsman, Sir Charles Geoffrey Dorman, 3 Bt, MC (d 1996); *b* 19 May 1954; *Educ* Marlborough, Univ of St Andrews; *m* 1, 12 April 1982 (m dis 1992); 1 da (Megan Bay Keppel b 1984); m 2, 15 June 1996 (m dis 2004), Sheena Alexandra Faro; *Heir* none; *Career* tax accountant; life protector Dorman Museum Middlesbrough; *Recreations* golf; *Clubs* MCC, Lewes Golf; *Style—* Sir Philip Dorman, Bt

DORMANDY, Prof John Adam; s of Paul Szeben, and Klara, *née* Engel; *b* 5 May 1937; *Educ* St Paul's, Univ of London (MB BS); *m* 29 Jan 1983, Klara Dormandy, da of Prof I Zarday; 1 s (Alexis b 1969), 1 da (Xenia b 1972); *Career* conslt vascular surgn St George's Hosp, prof of vascular sciences Univ of London; awarded: Fahreus Medal, Hamilton Bailey Prize, Hunterian Professorship RCS; chm: section on clinical measurement RSM, Venous Forum RSM; ed jls on various aspects of circulatory disease; chm Intercontinental Consensus on Critical Limb Ischaemia; DSc 1990; FRCSEd 1974, FRCS 1975; *Books* Clinical Haemorheology (1987), Critical Limb Ischaemia (1990); *Recreations* skiing, tennis, golf, Savoie; *Style—* Prof John Dormandy; ✉ Department of Vascular Surgery, Ingleby House, St George's Hospital, Blackshaw Road, London SW17 0QT (tel 020 8767 8346, fax 020 8682 2550, e-mail dormandyjohn@aol.com)

DORMENT, Richard; *b* 15 November 1946; *Educ* Georgetown Prep Sch MD, Princeton Univ (BA), Columbia Univ NYC (MA, MPhil, PhD); *m* 1, 1970 (m dis 1981), Kate Ganz; 1 s (Anthony Ganz b 1975), 1 da (Lily Sophia b 1977); m 2, 1985, Harriet Waugh; *Career* faculty fell Columbia Univ NYC 1968–72, asst curator of paintings Philadelphia Museum of Art 1973–76; guest curator for the exhbn Alfred Gilbert - Sculptor and Goldsmith (Royal Acad of Arts London) 1985–86; art critic: Country Life 1986, Daily Telegraph 1986–; frequent contrib: Times Literary Supplement, NY Review of Books; guest curator James McNeill Whistler Exhbn (Tate Gallery, Musée d'Orsay, Nat Gallery of Art Washington DC) 1994–95; memb: Reviewing Ctee on the Export of Works of Art 1995–2002, Advsy Ctee Govt Art Collection 1995–2005; tstee: Watts Gallery 1996–, Wallace Collection 2003–; winner Hawthornden Prize for art criticism 1992, Critic of the Year Br Press Awards 2000; *Books* Alfred Gilbert (1985), British Painting in the Philadelphia Museum of Art (1986), James McNeill Whistler (with Margaret MacDonald, 1994); *Style—* Richard Dorment, Esq; ✉ 10 Clifton Villas, London W9 2PH (tel 020 7266 2057, e-mail rdorment@btclick.com)

DORMER, Robin James; s of Dudley James Dormer (d 1983), and Jean Mary, *née* Brimacombe; *b* 30 May 1951; *Educ* Int Sch of Geneva, UCW Aberystwyth (LLB); *Career* Coward Chance 1976–80; admitted slr 1980, memb legal staff Law Cmmn 1980–87, asst Parly Counsel Office 1987–90, asst slr Solicitor's Office Dept of Health 1992–99 (joined 1990), dep counsel Parly Counsel Office 2000–05 (rejoined 1999), parly counsel 2005– (at law Cmmn 2006–); memb (vol) Legal Servs Gp Terrence Higgins Tst 1987–99, co sec (vol) The Food Chain 2003–06; *Style—* Robin Dormer, Esq; ✉ Law Commission, Conquest House, 37/38 John Street, Theobald's Road, London WC1N 2BQ (tel 020 7453 1206, fax 020 7453 1297)

DORRELL, Rt Hon Stephen James; PC (1994), MP; s of Philip George Dorrell (d 1994) and Christine Dorrell; *b* 25 March 1952; *Educ* Uppingham, BNC Oxford; *m* 1980, Penelope Anne (Annette) Wears Taylor, da of Maurice James Taylor, of Windsor, Berks; 1 da (Alexandra Elizabeth Nancy b 11 July 1988), 3 s (Philip James Andrew b 13 Nov 1992, William Edward Charles b 27 March 1997, Christopher George Robert b 11 March 1999); *Career* PA to Rt Hon Peter Walker MP 1974; Parly candidate (Cons) Kingston upon Hull E Oct 1974; MP (Cons): Loughborough 1979–97, Charnwood 1997–; PPS to Rt Hon Peter Walker MP (sec of state for Energy) 1983–87, asst Govt whip 1987–88, a Lord Cmmr of HM Treasy (govt whip) 1988–90, Parly under sec of state Dept of Health 1990–92, financial sec to Treasy 1992–94, sec of state for Nat Heritage 1994–95, sec of state for Health 1995–97, shadow sec for Educn and Employment 1997–98; *Recreations* walking, reading; *Style—* The Rt Hon Stephen Dorrell, MP; ✉ House of Commons, London SW1A 0AA (tel 020 7219 4472, fax 020 7219 5838, e-mail dorrells@parliament.uk)

DORRIAN, Hon Lady; Leeona June Dorrian; da of Thomas Michael Dorrian (d 1975), of Edinburgh, and June Sylvia, *née* Neill; *b* 16 June 1957; *Educ* Cranley Sch Edinburgh, Univ of Aberdeen (LLB); *Career* admitted to Faculty of Advocates 1981, standing jr counsel to Health & Safety Exec in Scotland 1987–94, advocate depute 1988–91, standing jr counsel to Dept of Energy 1991–94, QC (Scot) 1994, temporary judge 2002–05, senator Coll of Justice in Scot and Lord of Session 2005–; memb Criminal Injuries Compensation Bd 1997–2002; *Clubs* RAC, Scottish Arts (Edinburgh), Royal Forth Yacht (Edinburgh); *Style—* The Hon Lady Dorrian; ✉ 23 Dundas Street, Edinburgh EH3 6QQ (tel 0131 556 2256, fax 0131 556 8398, e-mail ljdorrian@lineone.net); Court of Session, Parliament Square, Edinburgh EH1 1RF (tel 0131 225 2595)

DORRIES, Nadine; MP; *b* Liverpool; *Career* early career as nurse; advsr to Dr Oliver Letwin, MP, *qv*, memb shadow Treasy team steering ctee; memb Kirkhope Cmmn for Asylum; MP (Cons) Bedfordshire Mid 2005–; *Style—* Mrs Nadine Dorries, MP; ✉ House of Commons, London SW1A 0AA

DOTRICE, Roy; s of Louis Dotrice and Neva, *née* Wilton; *b* 26 May 1925; *Educ* Dayton Acad, Intermediate Sch Guernsey, Elizabeth Coll; *m* 1946, Kay Newman; 3 da (Michéle (m 1987 Edward Woodward, *qv*, the actor), Karen (m 1994 Ned Nalle, pres Universal TV), Yvette (m 1985 John E R Lumley)); *Career* actor; *Theatre* with Royal Shakespeare Co 1957–65, over 30 West End performances; 12 Broadway appearances incl 3 one-man shows: Winston Churchill, Abraham Lincoln, Brief Lives (in Guinness Book of World Records as longest running solo performance (1770 shows)), Moon for the Misbegotten (Broadway Critics Circle, Drama Desk and Tony Awards); *Television* British TV: For the Greater Good, Life Begins, Casualty; American TV incl: Beauty and the Beast, Going to Extremes, Wings, The Equaliser, LA Law, Picket Fences, Mr & Mrs Smith, Arliss, Sliders, The Colour of Funny, Madigan Men; *Film* incl: The Cutting Edge, Lounge People, Amadeus, Eliminators, Corsican Brothers, The Scarlett Letter, Swimming with Sharks, These Foolish Things; *Awards* Best Actor Awards for: Brief Lives (TV) UK 1969, The Caretaker USA 1966; Tony nomination for A Life 1981; *Recreations* fishing, riding, golf; *Clubs* Garrick; *Style—* Roy Dotrice Esq; ✉ c/o Eric Glass Ltd, 25 Ladbroke Crescent, Notting Hill, London W11 1PS (tel 020 7629 7162); c/o Nancy Schmidt, Boutique Agency, 10 Universal City Plaza, Suite 2000, CA 91608, USA (tel 00 818 753 2385, fax 00 818 753 2386)

DOUBLEDAY, John Vincent; s of Gordon Vincent Doubleday (d 1993), of Great Totham, Essex, and Margaret Elsa Verder, *née* Harris (d 1992); *b* 9 October 1947; *Educ* Stowe, Goldsmiths' Coll Sch of Art; *m* 1969, Isobel Jean Campbell, da of Maj Frederick Robert Edwin Durie (d 1995), of Argyll; 3 s (Robert b 1974, Edwin b 1976 d 2000, James b 1978); *Career* artist; *Exhibitions* incl: Waterhouse Gallery 1968–69 and 1970–71, Richard Demarco Gallery Edinburgh 1973, Laing Art Gallery Newcastle, Bowes Barnard Castle 1974, Pandion Gallery NY, Aldeborough Festival 1983; *Portraits/Portrait Sculpture* incl: Prince Philip Duke of Edinburgh, Earl Mountbatten, Golda Meir 1976, Maurice Bowra 1979, Lord Olivier, Mary and Child Christ (Rochester Cathedral), Caduceus (Harvard Mass), Isambard Kingdom Brunel (two works in Paddington and Bristol), Charlie Chaplin (Vevey and London) 1982, Beatles (Liverpool), Dylan Thomas (Swansea) 1984, Commando Memorial 1986, Arthur Mourant (St Helier Museum Jersey) 1990, Sherlock Holmes (Town Square Meiringen) 1991, Graham Gooch (Chelmsford) 1992, Johann Pflug (Biberach) 1994, Nelson Mandela (United World Colls) 1996, Gerald Durrell (Jersey) 1999, Sherlock Holmes (Baker St Station London) 1999, The Dorset Shepherd (Dorchester) 2000, Child in the Park (Billericay) 2001, Col Jabara (USAF Acad Colorado Springs) 2004, Nelson (Gibraltar) 2005; *Work in Public Collections* Ashmolean, Br Museum, Herbert F Johnson NY, Tate Gallery, V&A, Nat Museum of Wales; *Recreations* impractical projects; *Style—* John Doubleday, Esq; ✉ Goat Lodge, Goat Lodge Road, Great Totham, Maldon, Essex (tel 01621 892085)

DOUEK, Ellis Elliot; s of Cesar Douek, of London, and Nelly, *née* Sassoon; *b* 25 April 1934; *Educ* English Sch Cairo Egypt, Westminster Med Sch (MRCS, LRCP); *m* 1, 1964; 2 s (Daniel b 1965, Joel b 1967); m 2, 1994, Gill Green; *Career* Capt RAMC 1960–62; registrar ENT Royal Free Hosp 1965, sr registrar King's Coll Hosp 1968, conslt otologist Guy's Hosp 1970; FRCS 1967, RSM, BAO; *Books* Sense of Smell and Its Abnormalities (1974); contrib chapters in: Textbook of Otology and Laryngology 1988, Robbs Surgery 1976, A Middle East Affair (2004); *Recreations* painting; *Clubs* Athenaeum; *Style—* Ellis Douek, Esq; ✉ 14 Heathcroft, Hampstead Way, London NW11 7HH (tel 020 8455 6427)

DOUETIL, Dane Jonathan; CBE (2007); *b* 28 July 1960; *Educ* Univ of Birmingham; *m* Antonia Clare; 3 da (Grace Caroline b 18 Nov 1991, Abigail Nicola b 12 Dec 1993, Kate Isobel b 8 Jun 1997); *Career* Willis Faber Group: joined 1982, exec dir Political and Risk Div 1988; founding shareholder and dir Special Risk Servs 1989–94, conslt for various financial instns 1994–98, conslt Benfield Gp 1997; Brit Insurance Holdings plc: chief exec Brit Insurance Ltd 1998, memb Bd 1999, chief exec Brit Syndicates Ltd 2002, dep chief exec 2004, gp chief exec 2005–; former chm Lloyd's Market Assoc, chm Market Reform Gp 2006, memb Contract Certainty Steering Ctee Lloyd's; *Recreations* shooting, fishing; *Clubs* Boodles; *Style—* Dane Douetil, Esq, CBE; ✉ Brit Insurance, 55 Bishopsgate, London EC2N 3AS (tel 020 7984 8803, fax 020 7984 8801, e-mail dane.douetil@britinsurance.com)

DOUGAL, Andrew James Harrower; s of Andrew J H Dougal (d 1987), and Muriel, *née* Macdonald; *b* 2 September 1951, Glasgow; *Educ* Greenock Academy, Paisley GS, Univ of Glasgow (BAcc); *m* 21 July 1978, Margaret, *née* Carmichael; 1 da (Alison b 28 Dec 1979), 2 s (Gavin b 21 July 1982, Calum b 2 June 1992); *Career* CA 1975; successively articled clerk and asst mangr Ernst & Young 1972–77, chief accountant Scottish & Universal Investments Ltd 1977–86; Hanson plc: finance comptroller 1986–89, finance dir ARC Ltd (subsid) 1989–92, md ARC Southern (subsid) 1992–93, dep finance dir 1993–95, finance dir 1995–97, chief exec 1997–2002; dir: Taylor Woodrow plc 2002–07, BPB plc 2003–05, Celtel Int BV 2004–05, Premier Farnell plc 2006–, Taylor Wimpey plc 2007–, Creston plc 2007–; MICAS 1975 (memb Qualification Bd 2000–06), CCMI 1999, FRSA 2005; *Recreations* family, sports, travel, history; *Style—* Andrew Dougal, Esq; ✉ Taylor Wimpey plc, 2 Princes Way, Solihull, West Midlands B91 3ES (tel 0121 600 8000, fax 0121 600 8001)

DOUGAL, Malcolm Gordon; s of Eric Gordon Dougal (d 1970), and Marie, *née* Wildermuth (d 1998); *b* 20 January 1938; *Educ* Ampleforth, The Queen's Coll Oxford (MA); *m* 1, 1964 (m dis 1995), Elke Urban; 1 s (Gordon b 17 June 1982); m 2, 30 Sept 1995, Mrs Brigid J C Pritchard, *née* Turner (d 2000); 2 step s (William, Anthony); m 3, 5 Sept 2003, Diana Blade, *née* Price; 2 step s (Christopher, Simon); *Career* 2 Lt Royal Sussex Regt served Korea and Gibraltar 1956–58; De Havilland Aircraft 1961–64, Ticket Equipment Ltd (Plessey) 1964–66, Harris Lebus 1967–69, FCO London 1969–72; first sec: Paris 1972–76, Cairo 1976–79; FCO London 1979–81, consul-gen Lille 1981–85, dep high cmmr Canberra 1986–89, RCDS London 1990, dir FCO/DTI Jt Directorate (Overseas Trade Services) 1991–94, consul-gen San Francisco 1994–98; warden John Spedan Lewis Tst for the Advancement of the Natural Sciences 1998–2005; memb: RSPB, Nat Tst, Butterfly Conservation; *Recreations* natural history, books, wine, history; *Style—* Malcolm Dougal, Esq

DOUGLAS, Alasdair Ferguson; s of George Douglas, of Perth, Scotland, and Christina, *née* Ferguson; *b* 16 March 1953; *Educ* Perth Acad, Univ of Edinburgh (LLB), Univ of London (LLM); *m* Kathryn Veronica Cecile, da of Cecil Kennard, OBE (d 1971); 1 s (Robert Ferguson), 1 da (Alice Jane); *Career* admitted slr 1981; sr ptnr Travers Smith (ptnr 1985–, managing ptnr 1995–2001); memb City of London Slrs' Co; memb: Law Soc, Law Soc of Scotland; fell Soc for Advanced Legal Studies; *Books* contrib: Tolley's Tax Planning, Tolley's Company Law; *Recreations* family, bagpiping; *Clubs* City of London, Royal Scottish Pipers' Soc, Scottish Piping Soc of London; *Style—* Alasdair Douglas, Esq; ✉ Travers Smith, 10 Snow Hill, London EC1A 2AL (tel 020 7295 3000, fax 020 7295 3500, e-mail alasdair.douglas@traverssmith.co.uk)

DOUGLAS, Anthony Jude (Tony); s of Arthur Sydney Douglas (d 1976), and Margaret Mary, *née* Farey; *b* 14 December 1944; *Educ* Cardinal Vaughan GS, Univ of Southampton

(BA); *m* 24 Aug 1968, Jacqueline, *née* English; 2 da (Amy Jane b 2 Oct 1978, Laura Claire b 28 May 1984); *Career* Lintas Advertising: graduate trainee 1967, various account mgmnt posts, client serv dir 1980; D'Arcy McManus & Masius (D'Arcy Masius Benton & Bowles following merger 1985): gp account dir 1982, jt md 1985, jt chm and chief exec 1987–95; chief exec COI 1996–98; chm FCB Europe 1998–99; currently non-exec chm Real Affinity Gp; FIPA, memb Mktg Soc; *Recreations* cooking, walking, reading, travel, anthropology; *Clubs* RAC; *Style—* Tony Douglas, Esq

DOUGLAS, Barry; OBE (2002); s of Barry Douglas (d 1988), and Sarah Jane, *née* Henry; *b* 23 April 1960; *Educ* RCM (with John Barstow, further study with Maria Curcio); *Career* concert pianist and conductor; debut London 1981, Gold medal Tchaikovsky Int Piano Competition Moscow 1986; worldwide concert career; tours: USA, Japan, Far East, USSR, Europe; worked with conductors incl: Ashkenazy, Davis, Masur, Jansons, Maazel, Temirkanov, Tilson Thomas, Janowski, Mackerras, McFerrin; subject of TV documentary After The Gold, appeared in Dudley Moore's TV series Concerto; former visiting fell Oriel Coll Oxford, Prince Consort prof Royal Coll of Music; music dir Camerata Ireland; Hon DMus Queen's Univ Belfast; FRCM 1988; *Recordings* Tchaikovsky Piano Concerto Nos 1, 2 and 3, Mussorgsky Pictures at an Exhibition, Brahms Piano Quintet in F Minor, Beethoven Hammerklavier, Brahms Piano Concerto No 1, Tchaikovsky Sonata in G, Liszt Piano Concertos, Prokofiev Sonatas 2 and 7, Berg Sonata, Liszt Sonata in B Minor, Beethoven Sonata Op 53, 57, 90, Rachmaninov Piano Concerto No 2, Corigliano Piano Concerto, Britten Piano Concerto, Reger Piano Concerto Op 114, Strauss Burleske, Britten Piano Concerto Op 13, Debussy Fantasie for piano and orchestra, Debussy Pour le piano; *Recreations* driving, reading, food and wine; *Style—* Barry Douglas, Esq, OBE; ✉ c/o IMG Artists, Lovell House, 616 Chiswick High Road, London W4 5RX (tel 020 8233 5800, fax 020 8233 5801)

DOUGLAS, Elizabeth Ann; da of late Alfred Graham Douglas, DFC, and Ann Welch, OBE (d 2002); *b* 17 February 1945; *Educ* Farnham Sch of Art, Univ of Southampton (BSc); *Career* photographer; exhibitions incl: Nationwide HQ, Sir Harold Hillier Gardens and Arboretum, several one day shows; photographic library Insect Field Photography; glider pilot 1962–69; sailing instr RYA 1969–73, winner Lark Class Cowes Dinghy Week 1971; FBIPP 1999; *Recreations* sailing, gardening, music; *Style—* Miss Elizabeth Ann Douglas

DOUGLAS, Dr (John) Graham; s of Dr Keith Douglas, of Menston, nr Ilkley, and Mavis Douglas; *b* 20 October 1949; *Educ* Bradford GS, Univ of Edinburgh (BSc, MB ChB); *m* 1 Oct 1977, Alison, da of John Menzies, of Dalkeith, Edinburgh; 1 s (Jamie b 5 Oct 1980), 1 da (Catriona Douglas b 7 June 1983); *Career* jr med and surgical house offr Edinburgh Royal Infirmary 1974–75, SHO and registrar in gen medicine, gastroenterology and renal medicine Eastern Gen Hosp and Edinburgh Royal Infirmary 1975–81, sr registrar in chest med and infection Edinburgh Royal Infirmary and Northern Gen Hosp 1981–86, conslt physician with an interest in thoracic med and infection Aberdeen 1986–, sr lectr in med 1986–; author of 100 scientific publications on gen and thoracic med and infection; FRCP, FSA Scot; *Recreations* hill walking, cycling, golf, DIY, history; *Style—* Dr Graham Douglas; ✉ Respiratory Unit, Aberdeen Royal Infirmary, Aberdeen AB25 2ZN (tel 01224 681818 ext 51212, e-mail j.g.douglas@arh.grampian.scot.nhs.uk)

DOUGLAS, Hilary; CB (2002); da of James Robert Keith Black (d 1992), and Joan Margaret, *née* Boxall; *b* 27 July 1950; *Educ* Wimbledon HS, New Hall Cambridge (BA); *m* 1972, Robert Harold Douglas, s of Robert Francis Douglas; 2 s (Robert b 5 Oct 1979, Andrew b 11 July 1982); *Career* press librarian RIIA 1971–73; DES: joined 1973, worked on educn policy 1973–89, freelance work Netherlands 1989–91, fndr FEFC 1991–92, fndr Sch Curriculum and Assessment Authy 1992–93, head Personnel Dept 1993–94, dir Admin and Finance Office For Standards of Educn 1994–96; dir Civil Service Employer Gp and Top Mgmnt Prog Cabinet Office 1996–97, dir Personnel and Support Services DfES 1997–2000; md Corp Services and Devpt HM Treasy 2000–; *Recreations* travel, European languages, singing, family; *Style—* Mrs Hilary Douglas, CB; ✉ HM Treasury, 1 Horse Guards Road, London SW1A 2HQ (tel 020 7270 4400, fax 020 7451 7639, e-mail hilary.douglas@hm-treasury.gsi.gov.uk)

DOUGLAS, Prof Ian; s of Prof Ronald Walter Douglas (d 2000), and Edna Maud, *née* Cadle (d 1995); *b* 2 December 1936; *Educ* Merchant Taylors', Balliol Coll Oxford (MA, BLitt), Aust Nat Univ (PhD); *m* 16 Nov 1963, Maureen Ann, da of Frank Bowler (d 1988); 2 s (David b 1965 d 1981, Aidan b 1967), 1 da (Fiona b 1972); *Career* Nat Serv Bombardier RA 1956–58; lectr Univ of Hull 1966–71, prof of geography Univ of New England Armidale NSW 1971–78, prof of physical geography Univ of Manchester 1979–97 (emeritus and research prof 1997–); sci co-ordinator NERC Lowland Permeable Catchment Directed Research Programme (LOCAR) 2000–06; dir Salford and Trafford Groundwork Tst 1993–2002; pres Inst of Aust Geographers 1978; chm: Br Geomorphological Res Gp 1980–81, UK/MAB Urban Forum 1993–97; organiser first Int Conf On Geomorphology Manchester 1985, treas Scientific Ctee on Problems of the Environment (SCOPE) 2001–; Australia Int Medal Inst of Australian Geographers 2006; MCIWEM 1975; *Books* Humid Landforms (1977), The Urban Environment (1983), Environmental Change and Tropical Geomorphology (co-ed, 1985), Encyclopaedia of Global Environmental Change Vol 3 (ed, 2002), Companion Encyclopaedia of Geography (co-ed, 2 edn 2007); *Recreations* walking in rainforests, swimming, gardening; *Style—* Prof Ian Douglas; ✉ 21 Taunton Road, Sale, Cheshire M33 5DD; School of Geography, University of Manchester M13 9PL (tel 0161 275 3642, fax 0161 275 7878, e-mail i.douglas@manchester.ac.uk)

DOUGLAS, Prof James; s of James Douglas (d 1936), of Edinburgh, and Mary Helen Douglas (d 1933); *b* 4 July 1932; *Educ* Heriot-Watt Coll, Paris Conservatoire, Mozarteum Salzburg, Hochschule Munich; *m* 1, 1959, Mary Henderson Irving (d 1967); 2 s (Stephen James b 1961, Gavin John b 1962); m 2, 16 April 1968, Helen Torrance Fairweather; 1 da (Katharine Helen b 1971); *Career* composer, accompanist, organist; prof l'Académie des Sciences Universelles Paris 1992–; md: Eschenbach Editions 1986–, Caritas Records 1989–; compositions incl: 15 symphonies, 15 string quartets, 20 orchestral works, chamber music (incl The Christ Church Sequence, 75 chamber works, 2001–06), The Glorious Sequence (33 instrumental works), The Highlands and Islands (66 works, 1968–2007), piano music, organ music, choral music and over 200 songs; operas: Mask, The King, Molière, Cuthbert; recordings: Visions of Glory (1990), Cry of the Deer (1991), A Vision (2000), Cloud of Unknowing (2001), 11 CDs in the Caritas Live series (2007); memb: Music Publishers' Assoc, Performing Right Soc, Mechanical-Copyright Protection Soc, Br Acad of Composers and Songwriters, Br Phonographic Inst Ltd; LRAM, ARCM; *Books* The Music of Hermann Reutter (1966); *Recreations* reading, café society; *Style—* Prof James Douglas; ✉ c/o Eschenbach Editions, Achmore, Moss Rd, Ullapool, Ross-shire IV26 2TF (tel and fax 01854 612 938, e-mail j.douglas@caritas-music.co.uk, website www.caritas-music.co.uk)

DOUGLAS, Dr James Frederick; s of Capt Rev James Douglas, CF (ka 1944), and Annie Hildegarde, *née* Harte; *b* 22 September 1938; *Educ* Portora Royal Sch Enniskillen, Wadham Coll Oxford (MA, BM BCh, BCL), Queen's Univ Belfast (MB BCh); *m* 27 April 1973, Giselle Sook An Lim; 3 s (Jeremy b 1975, Timothy b 1978, Andrew b 1981); *Career* lectr Coll of Law 1963–64, called to the Bar Middle Temple 1964; houseman Royal Victoria Hosp Belfast 1969–70, tutor in pharmacology Queen's Univ Belfast 1970–71, casualty posts Oxford and Belfast 1971–72, nephrologist 1972, conslt Belfast City and Royal Victoria Hosps 1975, sr nephrologist Belfast City Hosp 1988–2003 (dir 1990–96), lectr Dept of Clinical Pharmacology Queen's Univ Belfast 2003–; med advsr NI Kidney Research Fund 1988–2003 (patron 2003–), chm NI Transplant Games Ctee 1996–; memb: UK Transplant Support Assoc 1996–2002, ULTRA (Unrelated Living Transplant Regulatory Authy) 1996–2006; author of various pubns on: renal transplantation, renal failure, renal toxicology, the law and renal failure; memb: Renal Assoc, Euro Dialysis and Transplantation Assoc, Br Transplant Soc (memb Cncl 2002–), Transplantation Soc, Int Soc of Nephrology, American Soc of Nephrology; FRCP 1987 (MRCP 1973); *Recreations* astronomy, chess, cricket, country pursuits; *Style—* Dr James Douglas; ✉ e-mail jamesfdouglas38@hotmail.com

DOUGLAS, Prof Kenneth Thomas (Ken); s of Thomas William Douglas, and Irene, *née* Cluney; *b* 10 January 1948, Folkestone, Kent; *Educ* Belfast Royal Acad (Sir Hans Sloane Medal, Royal Inst of Chem Prize), Balliol Coll Oxford (MA), Univ of Kent at Canterbury (PhD); *m* 29 July 1972, (Sylvia) Claire, *née* Shrigley; 1 da (Rosalind Kate b 10 July 1979), 1 s (Jeremy Shrigley b 29 May 1982); *Career* postdoctoral res fell Univ of Chicago 1973–75, asst prof of chemistry and biochemistry Duquesne Univ Pittsburgh 1975–78 (assoc prof 1978), lectr in biological chemistry Univ of Essex 1978–87; Univ of Manchester: prof of medicinal chemistry and ldr Drug Design and Action Gp 1987–, head Dept of Pharmacy 1991–94, fndr Discovery To Medicines Ltd 2007; dir and fndr Wolfson Centre for Structure-Based Rational Design of Molecular Diagnostics 2003; exchange prof Univ de Paris-Sud 1978, hon prof Univ of Nagasaki 1983, visiting prof Univ Paul-Sabatier Toulouse 1991–92; ed Biochimica et Biophysica Acta 1985–95 and 2002–, editorial advsr Biochemistry Jl; Matsumae Medal and int fell Japan 1983, RSC Silver Medal and Prize 2002; ed and editorial advisor on numerous professional jls, author of over 200 articles and 4 patents; memb panel Res Assessment Exercise 2008 2004; memb: Biochemical Soc, Soc for Drug Res, Br Assoc for Cancer Res, European Assoc for Cancer Res, UK Assoc of Pharmaceutical Scientists; served on numerous nat and int grants ctees and panels; refereed grants and funding proposals to various instns; FRSC, CChem, CSci; *Recreations* painting as badly as possible, reading as much as possible, listening to others sing but never singing myself; *Style—* Prof Ken Douglas; ✉ School of Pharmacy & Pharmaceutical Sciences, University of Manchester, Oxford Road, Manchester M13 9PL (tel 0161 275 2371, fax 0161 275 2481, e-mail ken.douglas@manchester.ac.uk)

D

DOUGLAS, Margaret Elizabeth (Mrs Terence Lancaster); OBE (1994); *b* 22 August 1934; *Educ* Parliament Hill GS London; *Career* BBC: joined as sec 1951, later worked in Current Affairs Dept, chief asst to DG 1983–87, chief political advsr 1987–93; supervisor of Parly Broadcasting House of Commons 1993–99; *Recreations* watching politics and football; *Style—* Miss Margaret Douglas, OBE; ✉ Flat 49, The Anchor Brewhouse, 50 Shad Thames, London SE1 2LY (tel 020 7403 3568)

DOUGLAS, Michael John; QC (1997); s of James Murray Douglas, and Julie Friederike Douglas; *b* 7 August 1952; *Educ* Westminster, Balliol Coll Oxford (MA); *Career* called to the Bar Gray's Inn 1974, recorder 2000; *Recreations* theatre, cinema, eating out, football, travel; *Style—* Michael Douglas, Esq, QC; ✉ 4 Pump Court, Temple, London EC4Y 7AN (tel 020 7842 5555, fax 020 7583 2036)

DOUGLAS, Prof Neil James; s of Prof Sir Donald Douglas (d 1993), and Margaret Diana, *née* Whitley; *b* 28 May 1949; *Educ* Glenalmond Coll, Univ of St Andrews (scholar), Univ of Edinburgh (MB ChB, MD, DSc); *m* 16 July 1977, Dr Susan McLaren Galloway, da of Dr Thomas McLaren Galloway; 1 s (Sandy Donald b 6 Jan 1983), 1 da (Kirsty McLaren b 21 Feb 1985); *Career* lectr in med Univ of Edinburgh 1974–83, MRC fell Univ of Colorado 1980–81; Univ of Edinburgh: sr lectr in med 1983–91, reader in med/respiratory med 1991–95, prof of respiratory and sleep med 1995–; physician Royal Infirmary Edinburgh 1983–, dir Scottish Nat Sleep Labs 1983–; pres Royal Coll of Physicians Edinburgh 2004– (vice-pres 2000–04); formerly: chm Editorial Bd Clinical Sci, hon sec Br Thoracic Soc, chm Br Sleep Soc; *Style—* Prof Neil Douglas; ✉ Respiratory Medicine, Royal Infirmary, Edinburgh EH16 4SA (tel 0131 242 1836, fax 0131 242 1766, e-mail n.j.douglas@ed.ac.uk)

DOUGLAS, Sue; *see:* Douglas Ferguson, Susan Margaret

DOUGLAS, Torin Stuart; s of Stuart Douglas (d 1994), of Reigate, and Hazel Joyce, *née* Smith (d 1989); *b* 24 September 1950; *Educ* Eastbourne Coll, Univ of Warwick (BA); *m* 6 Oct 1973, Carol Sheila, da of Kenneth Douglas Winstanley; 2 s (Richard Torin Winstanley b 18 Oct 1981, Michael Stuart b 6 March 1985), 1 da (Eleanor Frances b 20 April 1991); *Career* trainee journalist D C Thomson 1972–73, media writer then features ed Campaign 1973–76, information offr IBA 1976–78, assoc ed Marketing Week 1978–82, ed Creative Review 1980–82, advtg and mktg writer The Times 1982–84, advtg and media writer The Economist 1982–84, presenter Advertising World LBC Radio 1984–89, media page columnist The Independent 1988–89, media corr BBC News 1989–; columnist Marketing Week 1979–2006, also contrib to Sunday Times, The Observer, The Guardian, Radio Times, Punch and The Listener; Mktg Soc Journalism Award 1983, Magazine Publishing Awards Best Business Columnist 1987; chm Broadcasting Press Guild 1996–98; memb NUJ; fell CAM Fndn; *Books* The Complete Guide to Advertising (1985); *Style—* Torin Douglas, Esq; ✉ BBC Room G690, BBC News Centre, Wood Lane, London W12 7RJ (tel 020 8624 9052, fax 020 8624 9096, e-mail torin.douglas@bbc.co.uk)

DOUGLAS FERGUSON, Susan Margaret; da of Kenneth Frank Douglas, of London, and Vivienne Mary, *née* Harris; *b* 29 January 1957; *Educ* Tiffin Girls' Sch Kingston upon Thames, Univ of Southampton (BSc); *m* 26 July 1994; 2 s (Felix b 1994, Lachlan b 1999), 1 da (Freya b 1995); *Career* Arthur Andersen & Co Mgmnt Consultancy 1978–79, Mims Magazine Haymarket Publishing 1979–80; reporter: Sunday Express Johannesburg 1980–81; Mail on Sunday 1982–87: med corr, features ed, asst ed, assoc ed; asst ed Daily Mail 1987–91, dep ed Sunday Times 1992–95, ed Sunday Express 1996, conslt ed The European, The Scotsman, Scotland on Sunday and Gear Magazine NY 1997–2001, pres of new business Condè Nast 2001–; *Recreations* riding; *Style—* Ms Susan Douglas Ferguson

DOUGLAS-HAMILTON, The Rt Hon Lord James Alexander; *see:* Selkirk of Douglas, The Rt Hon Lord

DOUGLAS-HOME, (Alexander) Sholto; s of Robin Douglas-Home (d 1968), and Sandra Howard, *née* Paul; step s of Rt Hon Michael Howard, QC, MP, *qv*; *b* 1 September 1962; *Educ* Bradfield Coll, Univ of Warwick (BSc); *m* 1992, Alexandra Jane, da of Ben Miller; 1 s (Louis Robin b 1999), 1 da (Tallula Elizabeth b 2001); *Career* account handler in various advtg agencies 1983–93, head of advtg and PR BT plc 1993–98, on secondment from BT as dir of mktg and sales New Millennium Experience Co 1998–2001, mktg dir (Kalends) Reuters plc 2001–02, publisher Reuters Magazine 2001–04, global head Mktg Communications Reuters plc 2001–; chm NABS Charity Ctee 2001–02; chm MGGB 2006–07 (memb Cncl 1999–), memb Cncl ISBA 2006– (memb Exec Ctee 1997–2006); Grand Prix and Gold Award IPA Advtg Effectiveness Awards (for BT's 'It's Good to Talk' campaign) 1996; ed Zagat Survey 1997–; FCIM 2002; *Recreations* horse racing, restaurants, photography; *Clubs* Morton's, George, Mark's, Harry's Bar; *Style—* Sholto Douglas-Home, Esq; ✉ Reuters Ltd, The Reuters Building, South Colonnade, Canary Wharf, London E14 5EP (tel 020 7250 1122, e-mail sholtodh@yahoo.com)

DOUGLAS MILLER, Robert Alexander Gavin; s of Maj Francis Gavin Douglas Miller (d 1950), and Mary Morison, *née* Kennedy (d 2002); *b* 11 February 1937; *Educ* Harrow, Univ of Oxford (MA); *m* 9 March 1963, Judith Madeleine Smith, da of Richard Michael Desmond Dunstan, OBE, of Firbeck, nr Worksop, Notts; 3 s (Andrew Gavin b 30 Sept 1963, Robert Peter b 15 Jan 1965, Edward James b 20 May 1966), 1 da (Emma Lucy Jane b 8 Jan 1969); *Career* served in 9 Lancers 1955–57; joined Jenners Edinburgh 1962: md 1972–96, chm 1982–; chm and md Kennington Leasing; dir: First Scottish American

Investment Tst, Northern American Tst; memb Kyle of Sutherland Fishery Bd; landowner (5850 acres); *Recreations* fishing, shooting, gardening; *Clubs* New (Edinburgh); *Style*— Robert Douglas Miller, Esq; ✉ Bavelaw Castle, Balerno, Midlothian (tel 0131 449 3972); Jenners, 48 Princes Street, Edinburgh EH2 2YJ (tel 0131 260 2324)

DOUKAS, Sarah; da of Dr John Chambers, and Noelle, *née* Strange; *b* 21 December 1952; *m* 1; 1 da (Noelle b 10 Nov 1979); m 2, 14 Feb 1994, Tim Garner; 2 da (Genevieve b 30 Sept 1991, Poppy b 2 Oct 1997); *Career* formerly model, punk band mangr and antiques business prop Clignancourt Market Paris, jr booker Laraine Ashton Model Agency (now IMG) 1980–87, fndr and md Storm Model Mgmnt 1987–; *Style*— Ms Sarah Doukas; ✉ Storm Model Management, 1st Floor, 5 Jubilee Place, London SW3 3TD (tel 020 7376 7764, fax 020 7376 5145, e-mail sarah@stormmodels.co.uk)

DOURO, Marquess of; (Arthur) Charles Valerian Wellesley; OBE (1999), DL (Hampshire 1999); s and h of 8 Duke of Wellington, KG, LVO, OBE, MC; *b* 19 August 1945; *Educ* Eton, ChCh Oxford; *m* 3 Feb 1977, Antonia (chm Guinness Trust), da of HRH Prince Frederick von Preussen (d 1966, s of HIH Crown Prince Wilhelm, s and h of Kaiser Wilhelm II), and Lady Brigid Ness; 2 s (Arthur Gerald, Earl of Mornington b 31 Jan 1978, Lord Frederick Charles b 30 Sept 1992), 3 da (Lady Honor Victoria b 25 Oct 1979, Lady Mary Luise b 16 Dec 1986, Lady Charlotte b 8 Oct 1990); *Heir* s, Earl of Mornington; *Career* chm: Dunhill Holdings plc 1991–93 (dep chm 1990–91), Framlington Group plc 1994–, Vendôme Luxury Group plc 1993–99, Sun Life & Provincial plc 1995–2000; dep chm: Thames Valley Broadcasting 1975–84, Deltec Panamerica SA 1985–89, Guinness Mahon Holdings plc 1988–91; dir: Transatlantic Holdings plc 1983–95, Sun Life Corporation plc 1988–96, GAM Worldwide Inc, Eucalyptus Pulp Mills 1979–88, Sanofi-Aventis 2002–, Pernod Ricard 2003–; MEP (Cons) Surrey West 1979–89, Parly candidate Islington N (Cons) 1974; cmmr English Heritage 2003–; chm Cncl KCL 2007–; *Style*— Marquess of Douro, OBE, DL; ✉ Richemont Holdings plc, 15 Hill Street, London W1J 5QT (tel 020 7499 2539); Stratfield Saye House, Hampshire RG7 2BZ; Apsley House, Piccadilly, London W1J 7NT

DOVE, Ian William; QC (2003); s of Jack Richard Dove, of Northampton, and Janet Yvonne, *née* Clarke; *b* 31 December 1963, Northampton; *Educ* Northampton Sch for Boys, St Catherine's Coll Oxford (MA), Inns of Court Sch of Law; *m* 4 June 1988, Juliet Caroline, *née* Gladston; 2 s (Tobias John b 3 Sept 1993, Wilfred Henry b 30 Jan 1996); *Career* called to Bar Inner Temple 1986, pt/t immigration judge 2000, recorder 2003; *Style*— Ian Dove, Esq, QC; ✉ No 5 Chambers, Fountain Court, Steelhouse Lane, Birmingham B4 6DR (tel 0121 606 0500, fax 0121 606 1501, e-mail id@no5.com)

DOVE, John; s of Anthony Dove, and Betty Margaret, *née* Curran; *b* 24 July 1944; *Educ* Ampleforth, Univ of Durham (BA), Univ of Manchester (Dip Drama); *Career* theatre director; Arts Cncl trainee dir under Philip Hedley Birmingham 1971–72, assoc dir to Jane Howell Northcott Theatre Exeter 1973–74 (co dir Bingo), freelance dir 1974–84 (worked with Richard Eyre at Nottingham, Richard Cotterell at Bristol Old Vic, Toby Robertson at Old Vic), assoc dir Hampstead Theatre 1984–; *Productions* for Hampstead Theatre incl: A Little Like Drowning (Plays and Players Award), Ask for the Moon, The Daughter in Law, The Awakening, Hedda Gabler, Bold Girls (Evening Standard Award), A Colliers Friday Night, Flight into Egypt, My Boy Jack 1997; other prodns incl: Rafts and Dreams (Royal Court), Goodnight Siobhan (Royal Court), A Muse of Fire (Edinburgh Festival), adaptation of Angelic Avengers for Denmark, Backstroke in a Crowded Pool (Bush Theatre, Susan Smith Blackburn Award), Democracy (Bush Theatre), Someone Who'll Watch Over Me (West Yorkshire Playhouse), Morning and Evening (Hampstead), Crossing the Equator (Bush), The Soldiers Song (Theatre Royal Stratford East), Prayers of Sherkin (Peter Hall Co, Old Vic) 1997, The Airman Who Would Not Die (Radio 4) 1997, Man and Boy (Radio 3) 1998, Saigon - Year of the Cat (Radio 4) 1998, wrote Mother Teresa in Kilburn (Radio 4) 1998, Falling (Hampstead) 1999, The Good Samaritan (Hampstead) 2000, La Grande Terese (Radio 4), Be Not Afraid - A Life of Handel (Radio 4) 2001, Vita Virginia (Stuttgart State Theater Germany), Darwin in Malibu (Birmingham Theatre), Death of a Salesman (Royal Lyceum Edinburgh), Measure for Measure (Globe Theatre London and USA tour), The Winter's Tale (Globe Theatre), In Extremis (Globe Theatre) 2006, All My Sons (Royal Lyceum) 2006 (Scottish Critics Award), Living Quarters (Royal Lyceum) 2007, I am Shakespeare (Chichester Theatre) 2007; *Recreations* painting, music, athletics, writing; *Style*— John Dove, Esq; ✉ c/o Simpson Fox Associates, 52 Shaftesbury Avenue, London W1

DOVER, Den; MEP (Cons) NW England; s of Albert Dover (d 1971), and Emmie, *née* Kirk (d 1971); *b* 4 April 1938; *Educ* Manchester Grammar, Univ of Manchester (BSc); *m* 1989, Kathleen, da of John Thomas Fisher (d 1986); 1 s and 1 da (by previous m); *Career* civil engr; chief exec Nat Building Agency 1971–72, projects dir Capital and Counties Property plc 1972–75, contracts mangr Wimpey Laing Iran 1975–77, dir of Housing Construction GLC 1977–79; MP (Cons) Chorley 1979–97; MEP (Cons) NW England 1999–; MICE, CEng; *Recreations* cricket, hockey, golf; *Style*— Den Dover, Esq, MEP; ✉ 30 Countess Way, Euxton, Chorley, Lancashire; 166 Furzehill Road, Borehamwood, Hertfordshire (e-mail ddover@europarl.eu.int)

DOVER, Sir Kenneth James; kt (1977); s of Percy Henry James Dover (d 1978), and Dorothy Valerie Anne Healey (d 1973); *b* 11 March 1920; *Educ* St Paul's, Balliol Coll Oxford (MA, DLitt), Merton Coll Oxford; *m* 1947, Audrey Ruth, da of Walter Latimer (d 1931); 1 s, 1 da; *Career* served WWII RA; tutorial fell Balliol Coll Oxford 1948–55; Univ of St Andrews: prof of Greek 1955–76, dean Faculty of Arts 1960–63 and 1973–75, chllr 1981–2005; visiting lectr Harvard Univ 1960, Sather visiting prof Univ of Calif 1967, prof-at-large Cornell Univ 1983–89, prof of classics Stanford Univ (Winter Quarter) 1987–92; pres: Soc for Promotion of Hellenic Studies 1971–74, Classical Assoc 1975, Corpus Christi Coll Oxford 1976–86 (hon fell 1986), Br Acad 1978–81; hon foreign memb American Acad of Arts and Sciences 1979–, foreign memb Royal Netherlands Acad of Arts and Sciences 1979–; hon fell Balliol Coll Oxford 1977, hon fell Merton Coll Oxford 1980; Hon LLD: Univ of Birmingham 1979, Univ of St Andrews 1981; Hon DLitt: Univ of Bristol, Univ of London 1980, Univ of St Andrews 1981, Univ of Liverpool 1983, Univ of Durham 1984; Hon DHL Oglethorpe Univ 1984; FBA 1966, FRSE 1975; *Publications* Greek Word Order (1960), Lysias and the Corpus Lysiacum (1968), Aristophanic Comedy (1972), Greek Popular Morality in the time of Plato & Aristotle (1974), Commentaries on various classical Greek texts, Greek Homosexuality (1978), Greek and the Greeks (1987), The Greeks and their Legacy (1988), Marginal Comment (memoirs, 1994), The Evolution of Greek Prose Style (1997); papers in learned journals; *Recreations* gardening, historical linguistics; *Style*— Sir Kenneth Dover, FRSE, FBA; ✉ 49 Hepburn Gardens, St Andrews, Fife KY16 9LS (tel 01334 473589)

DOVER, Michael Grehan; s of Maj E J Dover (d 1983), and Ida, *née* Grehan (d 2001); *b* 22 October 1948; *Educ* The King's Sch Canterbury, Trinity Coll Dublin (BA); *m* 1972, Ruth, da of Capt T A Pearson (d 1972); 2 s (Alexander b 1975, Linden b 1983), 1 da (Katherine b 1979); *Career* Penguin Books 1972–83, publisher Weidenfeld Publishers Ltd 1987 (editorial dir 1983), dir Orion Publishing Group Ltd 1992–99, publisher and dir Cassell & Co 1999–2001, ed-in-chief and dir Weidenfeld & Nicolson 2002–; *Clubs* Chelsea Arts, London Rowing, Kildare St and University (Dublin); *Style*— Michael Dover, Esq; ✉ Jasmine House, 190 New King's Road, London SW6 4NF; Weidenfeld & Nicolson Ltd, Wellington House, 125 Strand, London WC2R 0BB (tel 020 7420 5525, e-mail mgd@orionbooks.co.uk)

DOVER, Bishop of (Bishop in Canterbury) 1999–; Rt Rev Stephen Squires Venner; s of Thomas Edward Venner (d 1979), and Hilda Lester, *née* Boon, of Weymouth, Dorset; *b* 19 June 1944; *Educ* Hardye's Sch Dorchester, Univ of Birmingham (BA), Linacre Coll Oxford (MA), Inst of Educn Univ of London (PGCE); *m* 29 July 1972, Judith, da of Arthur Sivewright Johnstone; 2 s (Edward Stephen Squires b 24 April 1974, Thomas William Johnstone b 9 Jan 1980), 1 da (Alice Victoria b 15 Dec 1976); *Career* curate St Peter's Streatham 1968–71; hon curate: St Margaret Streatham Hill 1971–72, Ascension Balham 1972–74; head of RE St Paul's Girls' Sch Hammersmith 1972–74, vicar St Peter's Clapham 1974–76, Bishop of Southwark's chaplain to overseas students 1974–76; vicar: St John's Trowbridge 1976–82, Holy Trinity Weymouth 1982–94; rural dean of Weymouth 1988–93, canon and preb of Salisbury Cathedral 1989–94, bishop of Middleton 1994–99; bishop for the Falklands 2006–; chm: Salisbury Diocesan Bd of Educn 1989–94, Salisbury Diocesan House of Clergy 1992–94; memb: Gen Synod C of E 1985–95, Gen Synod Bd of Educn 1985–(vice-chm 2000–); chaplain to Lord Warden of Cinque Ports 2004–; pres Woodard Corp 1999–2002 (vice-pres 1995–98); pro-chllr Canterbury Christ Church Univ 2005–; *Books* All God's Children? (chm of Working Pty, 1991); *Recreations* reading, walking, the family; *Style*— The Rt Rev the Bishop of Dover; ✉ Upway, 52 St Martin's Hill, Canterbury, Kent CT1 1PR (tel 01227 464537); Bishop's Office, Old Palace, Canterbury, Kent CT1 2EE (tel 01227 459382, fax 01227 784987, e-mail bishop@bishcant.org)

DOVER, Prof William Duncan; s of Joseph Dover (d 1940), and Sarah Jane Graham, *née* Wilson (d 1989); *Educ* Bishopshalt Sch, Univ of Surrey (DipTech), UCL (PhD); *m* 27 July 1968, Dilys, da of John Richard Edwards (d 1989); 1 s (James William b 1973), 1 da (Elizabeth Mary b 1976); *Career* asst Faculté Polytechnique De Mons Belgium 1966–67, lectr City Univ London 1967–69, Shell prof of mechanical engrg UCL 1987– (lectr 1969–78, reader 1978–83, prof of mechanical engrg 1983–87); chm Dover & Partners Ltd 1979–86; dir: UCL NDE Centre 1985–, TSC Ltd 1985–, NDE Technology Ltd 1994–; visiting prof City Univ 1985–; CEng, FIMechE, fell Br Inst of Nondestructive Testing (FInstNDT); *Books* Fatigue and Crack Growth in Offshore Structures (ed, 1986), Fatigue of Offshore Structures (ed, 1989), Fatigue of Large Scale Threaded Connections (ed, 1989), Non Destructive Testing of Materials (ed 1995); 200 tech and sci papers; *Recreations* golf, swimming, skiing; *Style*— Prof William Dover; ✉ Coniston House, Orchehill Avenue, Gerrards Cross, Buckinghamshire SL9 8QH (tel 01753 886097); NDE Centre, Department of Mechanical Engineering, University College London, Torrington Place, London WC1E 7JE (tel 020 7380 7184, fax 020 7383 0831, e-mail wddover@btinternet.com)

DOW, Rt Rev (Geoffrey) Graham; *see:* Carlisle, Bishop of

DOW, Prof Julian Alexander Thomas; s of William Alexander Nicholas Dow, of Glos, and Eirona Elizabeth Dow; *b* 1957; *Educ* King's Sch Gloucester, St Catharine's Coll Cambridge (scholar, MA, PhD, ScD, Athletics blue); *m* 2001, Shireen-Anne Davies; 1 s (Nicholas), 1 step s (Benjamin), 2 step da (Sofya, Clara); *Career* Harkness fell 1981–83, research fell St Catharine's Coll Cambridge 1983–84; Univ of Glasgow: lectr in cell biology 1984–94, sr lectr in cell biology 1994–97, reader in genetics 1997–99, prof of molecular and integrative physiology 1999–, head Div of Molecular Genetics 2001–05; BBSRC: memb Investigating Gene Function Panel 1998, memb Genomics in Animal Function Panel 1999, memb Animal Sciences Panel 1999–2002, memb Research Equipment Initative Panel 1999–2001; chair UK Drosophila Genomics Steering Ctee 2000–02; memb: Soc for Experimental Biology 1981–, Royal Entomological Soc of London 1985–, Physiological Soc 1998–; President's Medal Soc for Experimental Biology 1992, Bidder lectr Soc for Experimental Biology; *Books* Dictionary of Cell and Molecular Biology (3 edn, 1999); *Recreations* skiing, diving; *Clubs* Achilles, Hawks' (Cambridge); *Style*— Prof Julian Dow; ✉ Molecular Genetics, Institute of Biomedical and Life Sciences, University of Glasgow, Glasgow G11 6NU (tel 0141 330 5101, e-mail j.a.t.dow@bio.gla.ac.uk)

DOWD, George Simon Edmund; s of George Francis Edmund Dowd, of Scarborough, N Yorks, and Lily, *née* Clay; *b* 9 November 1946; *Educ* Scarborough HS for Boys, Univ of Liverpool Med Sch (MB ChB, FRCS, MCh (Orth), MD); *m* Angela Christine, da of John Anthony Sedman; 3 da (Olivia Jayne b 13 Oct 1975, Caroline Suzanne b 19 Oct 1977, Charlotte Louise b 12 Nov 1980); *Career* house surgn and physician David Lewis Northern Hosp Liverpool 1971–72, lectr in orthopaedics Univ of Liverpool 1978–81; sr lectr and conslt orthopaedic surgn: Royal Liverpool Hosp and Royal Liverpool Children's Hosp 1981–82, Univ of London and Royal Nat Orthopaedic Hosp 1982–87; conslt orthopaedic surgn St Bartholomew's Hosp and sr lectr Univ of London 1987–96; currently: conslt orthopaedic surgn Royal Free Hosp, hon sr lectr Royal Free Med Sch, dir Knee Surgery Unit Wellington Hosp London; Hunterian prof RCS 1985; ABC travelling fell, Heritage visiting prof Calgary Canada 1986; Norman Roberts medal 1978, President's medal BR Orthopaedic Res Soc 1986; memb: BMA, Br Orthopaedic Assoc, Br Orthopaedic Res Soc, Br Assoc for Surgery of the Knee; *Publications* Multiple Choice Questions In Orthopaedics and Trauma (1987), Self-assessment on Trauma and Orthopaedics (co-author); also papers on trauma, arthritis and knee disorders in leading med jls; *Recreations* sailing, tennis and travel; *Style*— George Dowd, Esq; ✉ Royal Free Hospital, Pond Street, London NW3 2QG (tel 020 7794 0500); Wellington Knee Surgery Unit, Wellington Hospital, Wellington Place, London NW8 9LR (tel 020 7586 5959)

DOWD, James (Jim); MP; s of late James Dowd, and Elfriede Dowd; *b* 5 March 1951; *Educ* Sedgehill Comp Sch London, London Nautical Sch; *Career* apprentice Post Office telephone engr 1967–72, station mangr Heron Petrol Stations 1972–73, telecommunications engr Plessey 1973–92; London Borough of Lewisham: cncllr 1974–94, sometime chm Fin Ctee, dep mayor 1987 and 1991, mayor 1992; former memb Lewisham and N Southwark DHA; Parly candidate (Lab) Beckenham 1983, MP (Lab) Lewisham W 1992– (also contested 1987), London whip 1993–95, memb Shadow NI Team 1995–97, a Lord Cmmr of HM Treasy (Govt whip) 1997–2001, memb Health Select Ctee 2001–, chair All Pty Parly Small Shops Gp 2002–; memb: Lab Pty 1970–, Co-op Pty, Int Fund for Animal Welfare, Amicus, GMB; *Style*— Jim Dowd, Esq, MP; ✉ House of Commons, London SW1A 0AA (tel 020 7219 4617, fax 020 8699 2001, e-mail jimdowd.newlabour@care4free.net)

DOWD, Prof Peter Alan; s of Andrew James Dowd, of NSW, Aust, and Lorna May, *née* Harris; *b* 21 July 1946; *Educ* Marist Brothers' Coll Broken Hill Aust, Univ of New England (BSc), Ecole Polytechnique de l'Université de Montréal Canada (MSc), Univ of Leeds (PhD); *m* 1978, Ingrid Elizabeth, da of Stanley Crystal Gittings; 1 s (Dylan Benjamin b 15 June 1979); *Career* operational research offr Zinc Corp/New Broken Hill Consolidated Ltd NSW 1967–71, res fell Ecole Poly Montréal 1971–75; Dept of Mining and Mineral Engrg Univ of Leeds: BP research fell 1975–78, lectr 1978–86, sr lectr 1986–90, reader in mining geostatistics and operational research 1990–92, prof of mine design and geostatistics 1992, prof of mining engrg 1993–2004, head of dept 1995–2001, acting head Dept of Chem Engrg 1997–2000, head Sch of Process Environmental and Materials Engrg 1997–2003; exec dean of Faculty of Engrg, Computer and Mathematical Sciences Univ of Adelaide Aust; visiting prof: Ecole Nationale Supérieure des Mines de Paris 1981–83, Dept of Mine Planning and Mineral Processing Tech Univ of Lisbon 1977–91, Dept of Chem, Materials, Mining and Metallurgical Engrg Univ of Rome 1985–86; visiting lectr: Dept of Mining Engrg Univ of Queensland 1982, Otago Sch of Mines Univ of Dunedin 1983, China Univ of Mining and Technol 1986–87; Inst of Mining and Metallurgy: sec North of England Section 1983–98, Exec Ctee 1993, vice-pres 1996–98, pres 1998–99; chm: Int Assoc for Mathematical Geology Geostatics Ctee 1990–95, Nat Mining Industry Conference Organising Ctee 1992–95, Serial Pubs Ctee 1992–2000, Univ of Leeds Mining Assoc; UK ed De Geostatisticus 1987–2002; memb: Soc of Mining

Professors 1993–, Leeds GS Bd of Governors 1997–2004, Canadian Inst of Mining and Metallurgy (fell 1973–), Int Assoc for Mathematical Geology, Int Geostatistics Assoc; fell Australasian Inst of Mining and Metallurgy 1983; FREng 1998, FTSE 2006, FRSA, FIMM, FIChemE, FIQ; *Publications* author of numerous papers and parts of books and articles in learned jls; *Recreations* cross country running, cinema, theatre, opera, cricket; *Style—* Prof Peter Dowd, FREng; ✉ Executive Dean, Faculty of Engineering, Computer and Mathematical Sciences, University of Adelaide, Adelaide, SA 5005, Australia (tel +61 8 8303 4700, fax +61 8 8303 4361, e-mail peter.dowd@adelaide.edu.au)

DOWDEN, Richard George; s of Peter John Dowden (d 2003), of Fairford, Glos, and Eleanor Isabella, *née* Hepple (d 2005); *b* 20 March 1949; *Educ* St George's Coll, Bedford Coll London (BA); *m* 3 July 1976, (Mary Catherine) Penny, da of Stanley William Mansfield (d 1977); 2 da (Isabella Catherine b 1981, Sophie Elizabeth b 1983); *Career* sec Cmmn for Int Justice and Peace RC Bishops Conf 1972–75, ed Catholic Herald 1976–79, journalist The Times 1980–86, Africa ed The Independent 1986–94, dip ed The Independent 1994, foreign affairs writer The Economist 1995–2001, exec dir Royal African Soc 2002–; *Style—* Richard Dowden, Esq; ✉ The Royal African Society, School of Oriental and African Studies, Russell Square, London WC1H 0XG

DOWDESWELL, Prof Julian Andrew; s of Robert Dowdeswell, of Oxford, and Joan Marion, *née* Longshaw; *b* 18 November 1957; *Educ* Magdalen Coll Sch Oxford, Jesus Coll Cambridge (scholar, BA, PhD), Univ of Colorado (MA); *m* 20 Aug 1983, Evelyn Kae, *née* Lind; 1 da (Victoria Marie b 16 June 1988), 1 s (Adam Robert b 26 Feb 1992); *Career* research assoc Scott Polar Research Inst Univ of Cambridge 1985, lectr Univ of Wales Aberystwyth 1986–89, sr asst in research then asst dir of research Scott Polar Research Inst Univ of Cambridge 1989–94, prof of glaciology and dir Centre for Glaciology Univ of Wales Aberystwyth 1994–98, prof of physical geography and dir Bristol Glaciology Centre Univ of Bristol 1998–2001, prof of physical geography and dir Scott Polar Research Inst Univ of Cambridge 2001–, fell Jesus Coll Cambridge 2002–; NERC: memb Polar Science and Technol Bd 1995–97, Earth Sciences Research Grants and Trg Awards Ctee 1996–2000, Polar Sciences Expert Gp 1997–99, Earth Sciences Bd 1997–2000, Peer Review Coll 2002–; head Glaciers and Ice Sheets Div Int Cmmn for Snow and Ice 1999–; memb Cncl Int Glaciology Soc 1993–96, UK memb Cncl of Int Arctic Science Ctee 2001–, chair UK Nat Antarctic Research Ctee 2002–, UK alternate delg Cncl of Scientific Ctee on Antarctic Research 2002–; govr Plascrug Sch Aberystwyth 1996–98; Polar Medal 1995, Gill Meml Award RGS 1998; FRGS 1985; *Publications* Glacimarine Environments: Processes and Sediments (jt ed, 1990), The Arctic and Environmental Change (jt ed, 1996), Glacial and Oceanic History of the Polar North Atlantic Margins (jt ed, 1998), Glacially Influenced Sedimentation on High Latitude Continental Margins (jt ed, 2002), Islands of the Arctic (2002); author of articles on glaciology, glacier-marine interactions, cryosphere and climate change, and satellite sensing of ice; *Recreations* hill walking, skiing, watching Oxford United FC; *Style—* Prof Julian Dowdeswell; ✉ Scott Polar Research Institute, University of Cambridge, Cambridge CB2 1ER (tel 01223 336541, fax 01223 336549, e-mail jd16@cam.ac.uk); Jesus College, Jesus Lane, Cambridge CB5 8BL

DOWDING, Prof Keith Martin; s of Jeffrey William Dowding, and Sheila Leanora, *née* Patton; *b* 6 May 1960, Swindon, Wilts; *Educ* Noel-Baker Comp Sch, Keele Univ (BA), Nuffield Coll Oxford (DPhil); *m* Anne Vivienne Gelling; 2 s (Jonathon, Christopher); *Career* lectr in politics: St Catherine's Coll Oxford 1984–88, Univ Coll Oxford 1986–87, Brunel Univ 1988–93; lectr in political theory Poly of N London 1987, Hallsworth fell Univ of Manchester 1993–94; LSE: lectr in public choice and public policy 1993–96, reader in public choice and public admin 1996–2000, prof of political science 2000–07; visiting fell: ANU 2000–02, Netherlands Inst for Advanced Study 2006; Br Acad research readership 2005–07, assoc memb Nuffield Coll Oxford 2005–, prof of political sci ANU 2007–; *Publications* Rational Choice and Political Power (1991), Preferences, Institutions and Rational Choice (ed with Desmond King, 1995), The Civil Service (1995), Power (1996), Challenges to Democracy (ed with James Hughes and Helen Margetts, 2001), The Ethics of Stakeholding (ed with Jurgen De Wispelaere and Stuart White, 2003), Justice and Democracy (ed with Robert E Goodin and Carole Pateman, 2004); numerous chapters, articles and reviews in jls and books; *Style—* Prof Keith Dowding; ✉ Department of Government, London School of Economics and Political Science, Houghton Street, London WC2A 2AE (tel 020 7955 7176, fax 020 7831 1707, e-mail k.m.dowding@lse.ac.uk)

DOWDING, Nicholas Alan Tatham; QC (1997); s of Alan Lorimer Dowding, of Witney, Oxon, and Jennifer Mary, *née* Hughes; *b* 24 February 1956; *m* 23 March 2007, Alison Denise Oakes; 3 da (Eleanor Clare b 24 Aug 1985, Rebecca Judith b 9 Sept 1987, Katherine Sarah b 14 May 1989); *Career* called to the Bar Inner Temple 1979; chm Property Bar Assoc; memb: Chancery Bar Assoc, London and Common Law Bar Assoc; Hon MRICS; *Publications* ed Handbook of Rent Review (jtly, 1980–85), ed Woodfall on Landlord and Tenant (jtly, 1994), Dilapidations: The Modern Law and Practice (jtly, 1994, 3 edn 2005), ed Landlord and Tenant Reports; *Recreations* sailing, chamber music, juggling, limericks; *Style—* Nicholas Dowding, Esq, QC; ✉ Falcon Chambers, Falcon Court, Temple, London EC4Y 1AA (tel 020 7353 2484, fax 020 7353 1261, e-mail dowding@falcon-chambers.com)

DOWDING, 3 Baron (UK 1943); Piers Hugh Tremenheere Dowding; s of 2 Baron Dowding (d 1992), and his 2 w, Alison Margaret, *née* Bannerman; *b* 18 February 1948; *Educ* Fettes, Amherst Coll Mass (BA); *m* 1973, Noriko Shiho; 2 da (Hon Rosemary June b 25 Sept 1975, Hon Elizabeth Yuki b 16 Feb 1989); *Heir* bro, Hon Mark Dowding; *Career* prof of English Okayama Shoka Univ 1999– (assoc prof 1977–); life pres Dumfries and Galloway Branch Aircrew Assoc; *Style—* The Rt Hon Lord Dowding

DOWDS, Donal Joseph; s of William James Dowds (d 1992), and Mary, *née* Noone (d 2002); *b* 3 May 1953, Burnfoot, Co Donegal; *Educ* Paisley Coll of Tech (BSc), Univ of Glasgow (MBA); *m* 29 July 1978, Jane Marie; 3 c (Mark b 2 May 1981, Ruari b 27 Nov 1982, Grainne b 8 Jan 1985); *Career* BAA plc: joined 1979, ops dir Glasgow Airport 1988–92, md Glasgow Airport Ltd 1992–96, dep md BAA Scottish Airports 1995, md Edinburgh Airport Ltd 1996–99, md BAA Scotland 1999–2003, divnl md BAA Scotland & USA 2003–, chm and pres BAA USA Hldgs Inc 2003–07, chm and pres BAA USA Inc 2003–07; former chm: Scottish Airports Ltd, Aberdeen Airport Ltd, Edinburgh Airport Ltd, Glasgow Airport Ltd; former dir: BAA Int Ltd, BAA (Int Hldgs) Ltd; non-exec dir BAA Naples Airport; memb Bd Airport Operators' Assoc (chm until 2004); former vice-chm Scottish Tourism Forum, dir Glasgow C of C until 2000, vice-chm Edinburgh Lothians and Borders Tourist Bd until 2000, memb Bd VisitScotland 2000–06, memb Bd Scottish Cncl for Devpt and Industry 2001–; CEng, MICE; *Recreations* reading, music, shooting, golf, fishing; *Style—* Donal Dowds, Esq; ✉ BAA Limited, Worl Business Centre 1, 1206 Newall Road, Hounslow, Middlesex UB3 5AP (tel 020 8745 9969, fax 020 8745 2435, e-mail donal_dowds@baa.com)

DOWELL, Sir Anthony James; kt (1995), CBE (1973); s of Arthur Henry Dowell (d 1976), and Catherine Ethel, *née* Raynes (d 1974); *b* 16 February 1943; *Educ* Hampshire Sch, Royal Ballet Sch; *Career* Royal Ballet: sr princ 1967–, asst to dir 1984–85, assoc dir 1985–86, dir 1986–2001; *Clubs* Marks; *Style—* Sir Anthony Dowell, CBE; ✉ The Royal Opera House, Covent Garden, London WC2E 9DD (tel 020 7240 1200)

DOWELL, Prof John Derek; s of William Ernest Dowell, of Ellistown, Leics, and Elsie Dorothy, *née* Jarvis; *b* 6 January 1935; *Educ* Coalville GS, Univ of Birmingham (BSc, PhD); *m* 19 Aug 1959, Patricia, da of Lesley Clarkson, of Maltby, S Yorks; 1 da (Laura b 1962), 1 s (Simon Jeremy b 1964); *Career* research fell Univ of Birmingham 1958–60, research assoc CERN Geneva 1960–62, lectr in physics Univ of Birmingham 1962–68, visiting scientist Argonne Nat Laboratory 1968–69, sr lectr Univ of Birmingham 1970–73 (lectr 1969–70), scientific assoc CERN Geneva 1973–74; Univ of Birmingham: sr lectr 1974–75, reader 1975–80, prof of elementary particle physics 1980–, Poynting prof of physics 1997–2002, emeritus prof 2002–; scientific assoc CERN Geneva 1985–87; chm SERC Particle Physics Ctee 1981–85 (memb Nuclear Physics Bd 1974–77 and 1981–85), chm CERN LEP Ctee 1993–96, chm Rutherford Appleton Laboratory Users Advsy Ctee 1993–98, chm ATLAS Collaboration Bd (CERN) 1996–98, memb CERN Scientific Policy Ctee 1982–90 and 1993–96, UK memb Euro Ctee for Future Accelerators 1989–93; memb: BBC Sci Consultative Gp 1992–94, DESY Extended Scientific Cncl 1992–98, Ct Univ of Warwick 1992–2001, Particle Physics and Astronomy Research Cncl 1994–97, Cncl Royal Soc 1997–98 (vice-pres 1998), HEFCE RAE Panel (Physics) 1999–2001; lay chair Birmingham Children's Hosp NHS Tst 2004–; author of over 200 papers in scientific jls; fell American Physical Soc 2004; FRS 1986, FInstP 1987 (Rutherford medal and prize 1988), CPhys 1987; *Recreations* piano, amateur theatre, skiing; *Style—* Prof John Dowell, FRS; ✉ 57 Oxford Road, Moseley, Birmingham B13 9ES (tel 0121 449 3332); School of Physics and Astronomy, The University of Birmingham, Birmingham B15 2TT (tel 0121 414 4658, fax 0121 414 6709, e-mail j.d.dowell@bham.ac.uk)

D

DOWER, Prof Michael Shillito Trevelyan; CBE (1996); s of John Gordon Dower (d 1947), and Pauline, *née* Trevelyan (d 1988); *b* 15 November 1933; *Educ* The Leys Sch Cambridge, St John's Coll Cambridge (MA), UCL (DipTP); *m* 1 Sept 1960, Nan, da of late Allan Done; 3 s (John b 1961, Daniel b 1964, Alexander b 1968); *Career* town planning asst LCC 1957–60, town planner Civic Trust 1960–65, amenity and tourism planner UN Special Fund Ireland 1965–67, dir Dartington Amenity Res Trust 1967–81, dir Dartington Inst 1981–85, nat park offr Peak Park Joint Planning Bd 1985–92, DG Countryside Cmmn 1992–96, prof of European rural devpt Univ of Glos (formerly Cheltenham and Gloucester Coll of HE) 1996–2002; memb: UK Sports Cncl 1965–72, English Tourist Bd 1969–76; fndr chm Rural Voice 1980–82; vice-pres: Euro Cncl for the Village and Small Town 1990–94 and 2000–04 (pres 1986–90, sec-gen 1996–2000), Br Tst for Conservation Volunteers 1996–, Youth Hostels Assoc 1996–; patron Landscape Design Tst 1996–, tstee Afghanaid 2002–03; chm Northumberland Foot and Mouth Inquiry 2002; Freeman City of Dallas TX; Hon DSc Univ of Plymouth; MRICS, MRTPI, FRSA, Hon FLI; Conseilleur d'Honneur de la Connêtablie de Guyenne; *Books* Fourth Wave: The Challenge of Leisure (1965), Hadrian's Wall: A Strategy for Conservation and Visitor Services (1976), Leisure Provision and People's Needs (co-author, 1981); *Recreations* walking, landscape painting, sculpture, travel; *Style—* Prof Michael Dower, CBE; ✉ 56 Painswick Road, Cheltenham, Gloucestershire GL50 2ER (tel 01242 226511)

DOWER, Robert Charles Philips (Robin); DL (Northumberland 2002); s of John Gordon Dower (d 1947), and Pauline Dower, CBE, JP, *née* Trevelyan; *b* 27 October 1938; *Educ* The Leys Sch Cambridge, St John's Coll Cambridge (MA), Univ of Edinburgh (BArch), Univ of Newcastle upon Tyne (DipLD); *m* 4 Nov 1967, Frances Helen, da of Henry Edmeades Baker, of Owletts, Kent; 1 s (Thomas b 1971), 2 da (Beatrice b 1974, Caroline b 1976); *Career* architect, historic buildings conslt; Yorke Rosenberg Mardall London 1964–71, in private practice as princ Spence & Dower (chartered architects) Newcastle upon Tyne 1974–; memb: Northumberland and Newcastle Soc 1971– (chm 1997–), Northern Cncl for Sport and Recreation 1976–86, Countryside Cmmn for England and Wales 1982–91, Diocesan Advsy Ctee (Newcastle Dio) 1995–; minister's nominee to Northumberland Nat Park 1978–81, Cathedrals Fabric Cmmn for England nominee to Fabric Ctee Durham Cathedral 1991– (chm 1997–); ARIBA 1965; *Recreations* wood engraving, lettering inscriptions, walking, gardening; *Style—* Robin Dower, Esq, DL; ✉ Cambo House, Cambo, Morpeth, Northumberland NE61 4AY (tel 01670 774297); c/o Spence & Dower, Column Yard, Cambo, Morpeth NE61 4AY (tel 01670 774448)

DOWLEY, (Laurence) Justin; s of Laurence Edward Dowley, of Great Bowden, Leics, and Virginia, *née* Jorgensen; *b* 9 June 1955; *Educ* Ampleforth, Balliol Coll Oxford (MA); *m* 2, 11 Oct 1986, Emma, da of Martin Lampard, of Theberton, Suffolk; 2 da (Laura b 1987, Florrie b 1994), 2 s (Myles b 1989, Finn b 1992); *Career* Price Waterhouse 1977–80, Morgan Grenfell & Co Ltd 1981–96 (dir 1988–96); Merrill Lynch: md 1996–, co-head M&A Europe 1997–99, co-head investment banking Europe 1999–2001; currently ptnr Tricorn Partners LLP; non-exec dir: Bridgewell Gp Ltd 2001–, Intermediate Capital Gp plc 2006–; ACA 1980; *Clubs* MCC (memb Fin Ctee 1997–, treas 2006–), Boodle's; *Style—* Justin Dowley, Esq; ✉ Tricorn Partners LLP, 27 Knightsbridge, London SW1X 7LY

DOWLING, Prof Dame Ann Patricia; DBE (2007, CBE 2002); da of Mortimer Joseph Patrick Dowling, of Birchington, Kent, and Joyce, *née* Barnes; *b* 15 July 1952; *Educ* Ursuline Convent Sch Westgate, Girton Coll Cambridge (MA, PhD); *m* 31 Aug 1974, Dr Thomas Paul Hynes, s of Thomas Hynes; *Career* Sidney Sussex Coll Cambridge: research fell 1977–78, dir of studies in engrg 1979–90, fell 1979–; Univ of Cambridge: asst lectr in engrg 1979–82, lectr 1982–86, reader in acoustics 1986–93, dep head Engrg Dept 1990–93 and 1996–99, prof of mechanical engrg 1993–, dir Univ Gas Turbine Partnership 2001–; Jerome C Hunsaker visiting prof MIT 1999–2000, Moore distinguished scholar Caltech 2001; non-exec dir DRA 1995–97; chm: EPSRC Technical Opportunities Panel 2002–06 (memb 1998–2002), Rolls-Royce Propulsion and Power Advsy Bd; vice-pres Royal Acad of Engrg 1999–2002 (memb Cncl 1998–2002), memb Cncl EPSRC 2001–06; ind memb Defence Science Advsy Cncl 1998–2001; tstee Ford of Britain Tst 1993–2002, tstee Nat Museum of Science and Industry 1999–; govr Felsted Sch 1994–99; winner A B Wood Medal Inst of Acoustics 1990; memb AIAA 1990; fell: Inst of Acoustics 1989, Cambridge Philosophical Soc 1993; foreign assoc French Acad of Science 2002; CEng 1990, FIMechE 1990, FREng 1996, FRS 2003, FRAeS; *Books* Sound and Sources of Sound (with J E Ffowcs Williams, 1983), Modern Methods in Analytical Acoustics (with D G Crighton et al, 1992), contribs to various scientific jls; *Recreations* opera, walking; *Style—* Prof Dame Ann Dowling, DBE, FRS, FREng; ✉ Engineering Department, University of Cambridge, Trumpington Street, Cambridge CB2 1PZ (tel 01223 332739, fax 01223 330282, e-mail apd1@cam.ac.uk)

DOWLING, Prof Patrick Joseph; CBE (2001), DL (Surrey 1999); s of John Dowling (d 1951), of Dublin, and Margaret, *née* McKittrick; *b* 23 March 1939; *Educ* Christian Brothers Sch Dublin, UCD(BE), Imperial Coll London (DIC, PhD); *m* 14 May 1966, Dr Grace Carmine Victoria Dowling, da of Palladius Mariano Agapitus Lobo, of Zanzibar; 1 da (Rachel b 8 March 1967), 1 s (Tiernan b 7 Feb 1968); *Career* bridge engr Br Constructional Steelwork Assoc 1965–68, Imperial Coll London 1968–94 (latterly prof, head Civil Engrg Dept 1985–94), vice-chllr and chief exec Univ of Surrey 1994–2005, chm BAAS 2005–; fndr ptnr Chapman & Dowling 1981–94, chair Surrey Satellite Technol Ltd 1994–2005; Steel Construction Inst: memb Exec Ctee and Cncl 1985–, chm 1998–2002; pres Inst of Structural Engrs 1994–95; memb Senate Engrg Cncl 1996–2002 (chm 2001–02), memb Engrg & Technol Bd 2001–; pres City & Guilds Coll Assoc (CGCA) 1999–2000; memb Cncl Royal Holloway Univ of London 1991–95; chm: Daphne Jackson Tst 1994–2005, Surrey Community Fndn, Education Ctee Royal Soc; elected corresponding memb: Argentine Nat Acad of Engrg 2002, Argentine Nat Acad of Exact, Physical and Natural Sciences 2002; Gustave Trasenster Medal, Assoc des Ingénieurs Sortis de L'Université de Liège; Hon LLD: NUI 1995, Roehampton Univ 2005; Hon DSc: Vilnius Tech Univ Lithuania 1996, Univ of Ulster 1998, Univ of Kuopio 2005; Hon DUniv Surrey 2006; FIStructE 1978, FICE 1979, FREng 1981, FRINA 1985, FCGI 1989, FRS 1996, FIC 1997, FIAE 2000, Hon MRIA 2007; *Publications* ed: Journal of Constructional Steel Research, Steel Plated Structures (1977), Buckling of Shells in Offshore Stuctures (1982), Design of

Steel Structures (1988), Constructional Steel Design (1992); *Recreations* reading, travelling, performing arts; *Clubs* Athenaeum, Chelsea Arts, County (Guildford), National Yacht Club of Ireland; *Style—* Prof Patrick Dowling, CBE, DL, DSc, FREng, FRS; ✉ Apartment A4, Trinity Gate, Epsom Road, Guildford GU1 3PJ (e-mail p.dowling@surrey.ac.uk)

DOWN, Lesley-Anne; da of P J Down, of London, and Isabella, *née* Gordon-Young; *b* 17 March 1955; *Educ* Professional Children's Sch; *m* 1, 1982 (m dis 1985), William Friedkin; 1 s (Jack b 1982); m 2, 1986, Don E FauntLeRoy, s of Donald FauntLeRoy; *Career* actress 1967–; *Theatre* incl: The Marquise, Hamlet, Great Expectations, Pygmalion; *Television* incl: The Snow Queen, Upstairs Downstairs, The One and Only Phyliss Dixie, Heartbreak House, Unity Mitford, The Hunchback of Notre Dame, The Last Days of Pompeii, Arch of Triumph, North And South (books 1, 2 and 3), Indiscreet, Ladykillers, Nightwalk, Frog Girl, The Brewery, Sunset Beach, The Bold and the Beautiful; *Film* incl: The Smashing Bird I Used to Know, All the Right Noises, Countess Dracula, Assault, Scalawag, Tales from Beyond The Grave, Brannigan, The Pink Panther Strikes Again, A Little Night Music, The Betsy, Hanover Street, The Great Train Robbery, Rough Cut, Sphinx, Scenes from A Goldmine, Nomads, Munchie Strikes Back, The Unfaithful, Meet Wally Sparks; *Awards* nominee Golden Globe Best Actress for North And South; winner: Evening Standard Award Best New Actress for The Pink Panther Strikes Again, Bravo Award Best Actress for North And South; *Style—* Ms Lesley-Anne Down

DOWN, Michael Kennedy; s of John Down (d 1952), and Irene Beryl, *née* Kennedy (d 1982); *b* 4 February 1930; *Educ* Sevenoaks Sch; *m* Barbara Joan, *née* West; 2 da (Clare b 1958, Laura b 1960), 1 s (Ian b 1962); *Career* Nat Serv RAF 1948–50; CA 1955; Moores Rowland (formerly Edward Moore & Sons): articled clerk 1950–55, ptnr 1960, jt managing ptnr 1974–85, exec dir Moores Rowland Int 1980–93; tstee The Ulverscroft Fndn 1996–; pres Br Glove Assoc 1997–2001; Freeman City of London, Master Worshipful Co of Glovers 1997–98; FCA; *Recreations* travel, country life; *Style—* Michael Down, Esq; ✉ 8 Eylesden Court, Bearsted Green, Maidstone, Kent ME14 4BF (tel 01622 631729)

DOWN, Rt Rev William John Denbigh; s of late William Leonard Frederick Down (Flying Offr, RAFVR), and late Beryl Mary, *née* Collett; *b* 15 July 1934; *Educ* Farnham GS, St John's Coll Cambridge (MA), Ridley Hall Theol Coll Cambridge; *m* 29 July 1960, Sylvia Mary, da of Martin John Aves (d 1985); 2 s (Andrew b 1962, Timothy b 1975), 2 da (Helen (The Rev Mrs H Burn) b 1964, Julia b 1968); *Career* chaplain: RANR 1972–74, HMAS Leeuwin Fremantle WA 1972–74; ordained: deacon 1959, priest 1960; asst curate St Paul's Church Fisherton Anger Salisbury 1959–63, sr chaplain The Missions to Seamen South Shields 1964–65 (asst chaplain 1963–64), port chaplain The Missions to Seamen Hull 1965–71, sr chaplain The Missions to Seamen Fremantle WA 1971–74, gen sec The Missions to Seamen London 1976–90 (dep gen sec 1975), chaplain St Michael Paternoster Royal City of London 1976–90, bishop of Bermuda 1990–95, asst bishop of Leicester and priest i/c St Mary Humberstone 1995–2001, ret; hon asst bishop Dio of Oxford 2001–; hon canon: Holy Trinity Cathedral Gibraltar 1985, St Michael's Cathedral Kobe Japan 1987; hon chaplain: Worshipful Co of Carmen 1978 (Hon Liveryman 1981), Worshipful Co of Farriers 1983 (Hon Liveryman 1986), Worshipful Co of Innholders 1983–90; Freeman City of London 1981; Hon Memb Hon Co of Master Mariners 1989; FNI 1991; *Books* On Course Together (1989), Chaplaincy (contrib, 1999), Down To The Sea (2004), The Bishop's Bill of Fare (2005); *Recreations* golf, watching cricket, ships and seafaring; *Clubs* MCC, Royal Cwlth Soc, Chipping Norton Golf; *Style—* The Rt Rev William Down; ✉ 54 Dark Lane, Witney, Oxfordshire OX28 6LX (tel 01993 706615, e-mail bishbill@aol.com)

DOWN AND CONNOR, Bishop of (RC) 1991–; Most Rev Patrick Joseph Walsh; s of Michael Walsh (d 1966), and Nora, *née* Hartnett (d 1988); *b* 9 April 1931; *Educ* St Mary's Christian Brothers GS, Queen's Univ Belfast (MA), Christ's Coll Cambridge (MA), Pontifical Lateran Univ Rome (STL); *Career* teacher St MacNissi's Coll Garron Tower 1958–64, chaplain Queen's Univ Belfast 1964–70, pres St Malachy's Coll Belfast 1970–83, aux bishop of Down and Connor 1983–91; *Recreations* walking, music, theatre; *Style—* The Most Rev the Bishop of Down and Connor; ✉ Lisbreen, 73 Somerton Road, Belfast BT15 4DE (tel 028 9077 6185, fax 028 9077 9377)

DOWN AND DROMORE, Bishop of 1997–; Rt Rev Harold Creeth Miller; s of Harold Miller (d 1984), of Belfast, and Violet, *née* McGinley (d 1991); *b* 23 February 1950; *Educ* Belfast HS, Trinity Coll Dublin (BA, MA), Univ of Nottingham (BA), St John's Coll Nottingham (DPS); *m* 2 Jan 1978, Elizabeth Adelaide, *née* Harper; 2 s (Kevin Samuel b 18 July 1981, Niall Matthew Harold b 21 Sept 1988), 2 da (Ciara Elizabeth Maeve b 17 Feb 1983, Laura Ruth b 27 Sept 1985); *Career* ordained: deacon 1976, priest 1977; curate St Nicholas' Carrickfergus 1976–79, chaplain and dir of extension studies St John's Coll Nottingham 1979–84, chaplain Queen's Univ Belfast 1984–89, rector Carrigrohane Union of Parishes 1989–97; canon: St Fin Barre's Cathedral, Cork and Cloyne Cathedral, St Patrick's Cathedral Dublin; memb Advsy Ctee TEAR Fund; *Recreations* caravanning, music, phillumeny; *Style—* The Rt Rev the Bishop of Down and Dromore; ✉ The See House, 32 Knockdene Park South, Belfast BT5 7AB (tel 028 9047 1973, fax 028 9065 0584, e-mail bishop@down.anglican.org)

DOWNER, Prof Martin Craig; s of Dr Reginald Lionel Ernest Downer (d 1937), of Shrewsbury, and Eileen Maud Downer, *née* Craig (d 1962); *b* 9 March 1931; *Educ* Shrewsbury, Univ of Liverpool (LDS, RCS), Univ of London (DDPH, RCS), Univ of Manchester (PhD, DDS); *m* 1961, Anne Catherine, da of R W Evans; 4 da (Stephanie b 1962, Caroline b 1965, Diana b 1968, Gabrielle b 1972); *Career* area dental offr Salford 1974–79; chief dental offr: Scottish Home and Health Dept 1979–83, DHSS 1983–90; prof of dental health policy Eastman Dental Inst 1990–96 (now emeritus); hon prof Univ of Manchester 1996–; hon sr lectr Univs of Edinburgh and Dundee 1979–83; former memb: WHO, Expert Panel on Oral Health; ed Community Dental Health; *Books* contributor: Cariology Today (1984), Strategy for Dental Caries Prevention in European Countries (1987), Evolution in Dental Care (1990), Risk Markers for Oral Diseases 1 - Dental Caries (1991), Cariology for the Nineties (1993), Oral Health Promotion (1993), Introduction to Dental Public Health (co-author, 1994), Oral Health Diet and Other Factors (1999), Community Oral Health (2003); *Style—* Prof Martin Downer; ✉ Oral Health Consultancy Services, 16A Westbury Park, Bristol BS6 7JA (tel 0117 974 3703, e-mail m.downer@mailbox.ulcc.ac.uk)

DOWNER, Philip John; s of John Downer, and Judith, *née* Brentnall; *b* 29 September 1960; *Educ* Uppingham; *m* 21 Sept 1991, Julia, *née* Watson; 1 da; *Career* personnel and trg dir Our Price Records 1990–94 (retail ops 1980–90), vice-pres Waterstone's Inc 1994–96, ops dir Thomas Pink 1996–97; Borders (UK) Ltd: ops dir Superstores 1997–2000, md Superstores 2000–03, md 2003–06, retail dir 2006–; chm World Book Day 2007; memb Cncl Booksellers' Assoc 2003; *Recreations* books, music, travel; *Style—* Philip Downer, Esq; ✉ Borders (UK) Ltd, Stillerman House, 120 Charing Cross Road, London WC2H 0JR (tel 020 7395 3403, fax 020 7836 0914, e-mail pdowner@bordersgroupinc.com)

DOWNES, Justin Alasdair; s of Patrick Downes (d 1978), and Eileen Marie, *née* Mackie; *b* 25 September 1950; *Educ* The Oratory; *Career* dir: Financial Strategy 1980–85, Streets Financial Strategy 1985–86; fndr Financial Dynamics Ltd 1986–87; dir: London Financial News 1996–97, Rizwan Nash Ltd 1996–, Corporate Dynamics Ltd 1999–; non-exec dir Hansard Group plc 1999–; various private cos; memb Cncl Family Holidays Assoc 1990; memb Somerset CC 1976–; *Style—* Justin Downes, Esq; ✉ e-mail jd@downes.com

DOWNES, His Hon Judge Paul Henry; s of Eric Downes, of Clwyd, and Lavinia, *née* Starling; *b* 23 November 1941; *Educ* Ducie HS Manchester, Coll of Commerce UMIST, Coll of Law London, Inns of Court Sch of Law, Univ of Cardiff (LLM); *m* 1, Joyce; 2 s (Andrew Paul b 21 May 1965, Nicholas John b 22 Oct 1969), 1 da (Alison Jayne b 25 May 1968); m 2, Beverly Jill, da of Jack Cowdell; 1 s (Christopher Francis (Kit) b 26 May 1986); *Career* dep magistrates clerk: Manchester 1956–62, Sheffield 1962–63, Nottingham 1967–69; county prosecuting advocate Suffolk 1969–72, in practice at Bar Norwich 1972–95, recorder of the Crown Court 1993–95 (asst recorder 1991), circuit judge (SE Circuit) 1995–; dep diocesan chllr Dio of Ipswich and St Edmundsbury 1999–, diocesan chllr Dio of Wakefield 2007–, diocesan chllr Dio of Norwich 2007– (Bishop's selector of ordinands 2004–); *Recreations* music, chamber choir singing, playing instruments, reading, sailing; *Clubs* Norfolk (Norwich), Sloane; *Style—* His Hon Judge Downes; ✉ Norwich Combined Court Centre, Bishopgate, Norwich NR3 1UR (tel 01603 728200)

DOWNHILL, Ronald Edward; s of John Edward Downhill (d 1986), of Burghfield Common, Berks and Lily, *née* Darraugh; *b* 11 August 1943; *Educ* Hyde Co GS; *m* 1969, Olwen Elizabeth, da of Ronald Siddle; 3 da (Helen Louise b 1972, Rebecca Clare Elizabeth b 1975, Victoria Ruth b 1984); *Career* called to the Bar 1968, admitted slr 1974; Inland Revenue: Chief Inspector's Branch 1960–64, Estate Duty Office 1964–69, Slr's Office 1969–74; self employed tax conslt in partnership 1977–82, tax specialist Berwin Leighton Paisner (joined 1974, ptnr 1976–77 and 1982–); advsr to Inland Revenue Tax Rewrite Project 1996; chm Revenue Law Ctee of Law Soc 1997–2000 (memb 1989–); memb: Law Soc 1974, STEP 1993; ATII 1978; *Recreations* watching soccer, theatre; *Style—* Ronald Downhill, Esq; ✉ Berwin Leighton Paisner Solicitors, Adelaide House, London Bridge, London EC4R 9HA (tel 020 7760 1000, fax 020 7760 1111, e-mail ron.downhill@blplaw.com)

DOWNIE, Robert MacKenzie (Robin); s of Robert Thom Downie (d 1978), and Margaret Jean, *née* Livingston; *b* 7 December 1950; *Educ* Glasgow HS; *m* 16 Sept 1985, Frances Catherine, da of Harold Bremner Reid; 2 s (Adam Robert b 3 Aug 1989, Marcus MacKenzie b 12 Jan 1991), 1 da (Rhoda Frances Margaret b 22 May 1993); *Career* CA 1973, Mann Judd Gordon Glasgow 1968–79; ptnr: Neville Russell 1979–98, Mazars Neville Russell 1998–2002, Mazars 2002–; chm Glasgow Student Villages Ltd 2002–; dir RSFS Forest Tst Co 2002–; ICAS (convenor Area Trg Ctee 1987–91), memb Cncl Scottish Chartered Accountants Benevolent Assoc 1997–2004, chm Scottish Crusaders 1990–94, govr RSAMD 1989–2000; FRSAMD 1998, FRSA 1998; *Style—* Robin Downie, Esq; ✉ Mazars, 90 Vincent Street, Glasgow G2 5UB (tel 0141 226 4924, fax 0141 204 1338, e-mail robin.downie@mazars.co.uk)

DOWNIE, Prof Robert Silcock; s of Capt Robert Mackie Downie (d 1980), of Glasgow, and Margaret Barlas, *née* Brown (d 1974); *b* 19 April 1933; *Educ* HS of Glasgow, Univ of Glasgow (MA), The Queen's Coll Oxford (BPhil); *m* 15 Sept 1958, Eileen Dorothea, da of Capt Wilson Ashley Flynn (d 1942), of Glasgow; 3 da (Alison, Catherine, Barbara); *Career* Russian linguist Intelligence Corps 1955–57; Univ of Glasgow: lectr in philosophy 1959–69, prof of moral philosophy 1969–2002, professorial research fell 2002–; visiting prof of philosophy Syracuse Univ NY 1963–64; Stevenson lectr in medical ethics 1986–88; FRSE 1986, FRSA 1999; *Books* Government Action and Morality (1964), Respect for Persons (1969), Roles and Values (1971), Education and Personal Relationships (1974), Caring and Curing (1980), Healthy Respect (1987), Health Promotion (1990), The Making of a Doctor (1992), Francis Hutcheson (1994), The Healing Arts: An Illustrated Oxford Anthology (1994), Palliative Care Ethics (1995), Medical Ethics (1996), Clinical Judgement Evidence in Practice (2000), Palliative Care Philosophy: Critique and Reconstruction (2006), Bioethics and the Humanities (2007); *Recreations* music; *Style—* Prof Robert Downie, FRSE, FRSA; ✉ 17 Hamilton Drive, Glasgow G12 8DN; Kilnaish, by Tarbert, Argyll PA29 6XZ (tel 0141 339 1345); Department of Philosophy, University of Glasgow, Glasgow G12 8QQ (tel 0141 330 4273, fax 0141 330 4112, e-mail r.downie@philosophy.arts.gla.ac.uk)

DOWNING, John; MBE (1992); *b* 17 April 1940; *Career* photographer; apprentice photographic printer Daily Mail 1956–61; The Express: perm freelance photographer 1962–64, staff photographer 1964–2001, chief photographer 1985–2001; freelance photographer 2001–; maj news events covered incl: Vietnam, Beirut, The Falklands, Nicaragua, Afghanistan, The Gulf, Bosnia, Somalia and Rwanda; fndr Press Photographers' Assoc (now Br Press Photographers' Assoc) 1984 (pres until 1986); memb judging panel: Ian Parry Scholarship 2002, Picture Editor Awards (student section) 2002; memb NUJ; memb London Welsh Male Voice Choir 1998; *Awards* Rothman's Br Press Pictures of the Year (human interest) 1971, runner up (news feature) World Press Photo Competition 1972 and 1978, Ilford Br Press Photgrapher of the Year 1977, 1979, 1980, 1981, 1984, 1988 and 1989, IPC Br Press Photographer of the Year 1977 and 1980 (runner-up 1991), UN Photography Gold Medal 1978, Photokina Gold Medal 1978, Martini Royal Newspaper Photographer of the Year 1990, Kodak Feature Photographer of the Year 1992/93, runner up Photographer of the Year Br Picture Editors' Awards 1994, 1995 and 1999, La Nacion (Argentina) Int Photographer of the Year 1994–95, overall winner Br Airways London Eye Photography Competition 2001, Br Picture Editors' Guild Lifetime Achievement Award 2001; *Style—* John Downing, Esq, MBE; ✉ 3B China Wharf, Mill Street, London SE1 2BQ (tel 020 7232 2498, fax 020 7064 9150)

DOWNING, Richard; s of John Clifford Downing, of Stourbridge, W Midlands, and Greta Irene, *née* Kelley; *b* 8 February 1951; *Educ* King Edward VI Sch Stourbridge, Univ of Birmingham (BSc, MB ChB, MD); *m* 24 July 1976, Stella Elizabeth, da of Stefan Kolada, of Chaddesley Corbett, Worcs; 2 s (Benjamin Louis b 1978, Thomas Kolada b 1982), 2 da (Alice Elizabeth Gwendoline b 1984, Lily Anastazia b 1991); *Career* lectr in anatomy Univ of Birmingham 1976–77, res assoc Washington Univ St Louis MO 1977–78; surgical registrar: Birmingham AHA 1979–80, Worcester Royal Infirmary 1980–83; sr lectr and hon conslt in surgery Univ of Birmingham 1986–90 (lectr 1983–86), conslt vascular surgn and dir Islet Res Lab Worcester Royal Infirmary 1990–; author of pubns on vascular surgery and pancreatic islet transplantation, memb Editorial Bd Br Jl of Diabetes and Vascular Disease; examiner Faculty of Dental Surgery RCS, advsr in surgery Int Hosps Gp 1987–90; memb: BMA, Diabetes UK, Br Transplantation Soc, European Soc Vascular Surgery, Pancreatic Soc GB and Ireland, Surgical Vascular Soc GB and Ireland; FRCS 1980; *Recreations* antiquarian books, the countryside; *Style—* Richard Downing, Esq; ✉ Department of Vascular Surgery, Worcestershire Royal Hospital, Worcester WR5 1DD (tel 01905 760725, fax 01905 760681, e-mail r_downing@btinternet.com)

DOWNING, Stewart; *b* 22 July 1984, Middlesbrough; *Career* professional footballer; Middlesbrough FC: joined as apprentice, first team debut 2002, winners League Cup 2004, runners-up UEFA Cup 2006; England: 2 caps, debut v Holland 2005, memb squad World Cup 2006; *Style—* Stewart Downing, Esq; ✉ c/o Middlesbrough Football Club, Riverside Stadium, Middlesbrough TS3 6RS

DOWNS, Prof Anthony John (Tony); s of Henry James Downs (d 1986), of Sutton Courtenay, Oxon, and Florence Elizabeth, *née* Dooley (d 1980); *b* 28 January 1936; *Educ* Lincoln Sch, St John's Coll Cambridge (BA, PhD); *m* 7 Oct 1961, Mary Bronwen, da of Leslie George Diamond; *Career* Salter's fell Dept of Inorganic Chemistry Univ of Cambridge 1961–1962; sr demonstrator then lectr Univ of Newcastle upon Tyne 1962–66; Univ of Oxford: sr res offr 1966–71, lectr 1971–96, prof of chemistry 1996–, dep/actg head Inorganic Chemistry Lab 1996–2003; Jesus Coll Oxford: fell and tutor 1966–2003, tutor for admissions 1973–76 and 1980, vice-princ 1986–89 and 1994, emeritus fell 2003–; memb numerous ctees of RSC and Engineering and Physical Sciences Res Cncl (and its earlier incarnations), memb various editorial bds of scientific jls; memb Bd of Govrs Colfe's Sch 1983–98; *Publications* Spectroscopy of Matrix Isolated Species (jtly, 1989), Chemistry of

Aluminium, Gallium, Indium and Thallium (ed and author, 1993); author of numerous papers and review articles in Jl of the ACS and other learned jls 1960–; *Recreations* travel, walking, opera, cricket, (steam) railways; *Style*— Prof Tony Downs; ✉ 11 St Swithun's Road, Kennington, Oxford OX1 5PT (tel 01865 739698); Inorganic Chemistry Laboratory, University of Oxford, South Parks Road, Oxford OX1 3QR (tel 01865 272673, fax 01865 272690, e-mail tony.downs@chemistry.oxford.ac.uk)

DOWNSHIRE, 9 Marquess of (I 1789); (Arthur Francis) Nicholas Wills Hill; also Earl of Hillsborough (I 1751 and GB 1772), Viscount Hillsborough (I 1717), Viscount Fairford (GB 1772), Viscount Kilwarlin (I 1771), Baron Harwich (GB 1756), and Baron Hill (I 1717); Hereditary Constable of Hillsborough Fort; s of 8 Marquess of Downshire (d 2003), and Hon Juliet Mary, *née* Weld Forester (d 1986); *b* 4 February 1959; *Educ* Eton, RAC Cirencester, Poly of Central London; *m* 28 April 1990, Diana Jane (Janey), o da of Gerald Leeson Bunting, DL, of Northallerton, N Yorks; 3 da (Lady Isabella Diana Juliet b 3 April 1991, Lady Beatrice Hannah Georgina b 10 Feb 1994, Lady Claudia Lucy Helena b 15 March 1998), 1 s (Edmund Robin Arthur, Earl of Hillsborough b 21 May 1996); *Heir* s, Earl of Hillsborough; *Career* with Touche Ross & Co 1981–87, gp fin dir and co sec Scheduling Technology Gp (STG) Ltd 1988–2000, actg fin dir STG as subsid of Manugistics Inc 2001–02, co dir 2002–; co-dir: Ritchey plc, Fearing International, Identify UK Ltd, base2stay Ltd; chm of govrs Aysgarth Sch; memb: Woodard Fndn, Historic Houses Assoc, CLA; MICA; *Recreations* shooting and country pursuits, skiing, keen player of many sports including soccer, tennis, golf and cricket; *Style*— The Most Hon the Marquess of Downshire

DOWNTON, Dr Christine Veronica; da of Henry Devereux Downton (d 1962), and Christina Vera, *né e* Threadgold; *b* 21 October 1941; *Educ* Caerphilly GS, LSE (BSc, PhD); *Career* vice-chm Pareto Ptnrs; former dir Investment Mgmnt Regulatory Orgn; ceo: Archimedes Assocs, County NatWest Investment Management; sr conslt to the pres Federal Reserve Bank of NY, asst dir N M Rothschild, asst advsr Bank of England; govr LSE; *Recreations* reading, walking; *Style*— Dr Christine V Downton

DOWSON, Antony Peter; s of John Robert Dowson, and Sheila Margret, *née* Horstead; *b* 27 January 1958; *Educ* Royal Ballet Sch White Lodge, ARAD, PDTC; *m* 1, 17 March 1990 (m dis), Fiona Jane Chadwick; 1 da (Emily b 23 April 1991); m 2, 28 Aug 1997, Ruth Spivak; 1 da (Sophie b 24 Nov 1998), 1 s (Jacob b 1 March 2002); *Career* currently princ teacher English National Ballet Sch, former princ dancer Royal Ballet Co; leading roles with Royal Ballet incl: Mayerling, Manon, Sleeping Beauty, La Fille Mal Gardée, Prince of the Pagodas; *Recreations* watching football, Chelsea FC, listening to music, cooking; *Style*— Antony Dowson, Esq; ✉ c/o English National Ballet School, Carlyle Building, Hortensia Road, London SW10 0QS

DOWSON, Prof Duncan; CBE (1989); s of Wilfrid Dowson (d 1970), of Kirkbymoorside, N Yorks, and Hannah, *née* Crosier (d 1987); *b* 31 August 1928; *Educ* Lady Lumley's GS Pickering, Univ of Leeds (BSc, PhD, DSc); *m* 15 Dec 1951, Mabel, da of Herbert Strickland (d 1961), of Kirkbymoorside, N Yorks; 2 s (David Guy b 1953, Stephen Paul b 1956 d 1968); *Career* Sir W G Armstrong Whitworth Aircraft Co 1952–54; Univ of Leeds 1954–: lectr 1954–63, sr lectr 1963–65, reader 1965–66, prof of fluid mechanics and tribology 1966–93, dir Inst of Tribology 1967–86, head Dept of Mechanical Engrg 1967–92, pro-vice-chllr 1983–85, dean for int relations 1988–93, prof emeritus 1993, research prof 1995–98, 1998–2001 and 2001–, memb Ct 2002–; visiting prof Univ of NSW Sydney 1975, hon prof Univ of Bradford 1996–, external prof Loughborough Univ 2001–03; memb: Educn and Sci Working Pty on Lubrication Educn and Res 1972–76, Orthopaedic Implant Ctee DHSS 1974–77, Regnl Sci Ctee YRHA 1977–80, Res Ctee Arthritis and Rheumatism Cncl 1977–85, various SERC ctees 1987–90; memb Cncl IMechE 1988–97 (vice-pres 1988–90, dep pres 1990–92, pres 1992–93); Liveryman Worshipful Co of Blacksmiths; Hon DTech Chalmers Univ of Technol Göteborg Sweden 1979; Docteur (hc) Institut National Des Sciences Appliquées de Lyon France 1991, Hon DSc Univ of Liège Belgium 1996, DEng (hc) Univ of Waterloo Canada 2001, Hon DEng Univ of Bradford 2003; fell: ASME, ASLE; foreign memb Royal Swedish Acad of Engrg Sci 1986; FIMechE 1973, FREng 1982, FRS 1987, FRSA (chm Yorks Region 1992–97), FCGI 1996; *Books* Elastohydrodynamic Lubrication (2 edn, 1977), History of Tribology (1979, abridged Japanese edn 1997, 2 edn 1998), Biomechanics of Joints and Joint Replacements (1981), Ball Bearing Lubrication (1981); *Recreations* walking; *Style*— Prof Duncan Dowson, CBE, FRS, FREng; ✉ Ryedale, 23 Church Lane, Adel, Leeds LS16 8DQ (tel 0113 267 8933, fax 0113 281 7039); School of Mechanical Engineering, The University of Leeds, Leeds LS2 9JT (tel 0113 233 2153, fax 0113 233 4611, e-mail d.dowson@leeds.ac.uk)

DOWSON, Dr Jonathan Hudson; s of John Heaton Dowson (d 1994), and Margot Blanche, *née* Hudson (d 1992); *b* 19 March 1942; *Educ* The Leys Sch Cambridge, Queens' Coll Cambridge (MA, MB BChir, MD), St Thomas' Hosp, Univ of Edinburgh (DPM, PhD); *m* 29 Dec 1965, Lynn Susan, *née* Dothie; 1 da (Emma b 1967), 2 s (James b 1968, Jonathan b 1972); *Career* lectr in psychiatry Univ of Edinburgh 1973–75 (lectr in anatomy 1969–72), conslt psychiatrist Addenbrooke's Hosp Cambridge 1977–, lectr in psychiatry Univ of Cambridge 1977–, dir Studies in Clinical Med Queens' Coll Cambridge 1999–; visiting prof Univ of Florida 1983; examiner: RCPsych 1981– (regnl advsr 1990–95), Univ of Cambridge 1988–; papers on ageing, brain lipopigment, personality disorders and adult attention-deficit disorder; fell commoner Queens' Coll Cambridge 1985; FRCPsych; *Books* Personality Disorders: Recognition and Clinical Management (with A T Grounds, CUP, 1995); *Recreations* theatre; *Clubs* Oxford and Cambridge; *Style*— Dr Jonathan Dowson; ✉ Old Vicarage, Church Lane, Sawston, Cambridge CB2 4JR; Department of Psychiatry, Level 4, Addenbrooke's Hospital, Hills Road, Cambridge CB2 2QQ (tel 01223 336965)

DOWSON, Sir Philip Manning; kt (1980), CBE (1969), PPRA; s of Robert Manning Dowson, of Geldeston, Norfolk; *b* 16 August 1924; *Educ* Gresham's, UC Oxford, Clare Coll Cambridge (MA), AA Sch of Architecture (AADipl); *m* 1950, Sarah Albinia (Lady Dowson, MBE), da of Brig Wilson Theodore Oliver Crewdson, CBE (d 1961), by his w Albinia Joane, 2 da of Sir Nicholas Henry Bacon, 12 Bt, of London; 1 s, 2 da; *Career* Lt RNVR 1943–47; architect; Ove Arup and Partners: joined 1953, sr ptnr 1969–89, conslt 1989–; fndr ptnr Arup Associates architects and engrs 1963; pres Royal Academy of Arts 1993–99 (ARA 1979, RA 1986); memb Royal Fine Art Cmmn 1971–97; tstee: The Thomas Cubitt Tst 1978–98, The Royal Armouries 1984–89, National Portrait Gallery 1993–99, Coram Fndn 1993–99; memb Bd of Tstees Royal Botanic Gardens Kew 1983–95; Royal Gold Medal for Architecture RIBA 1981; hon fell: Clare Coll Cambridge, Royal Coll of Art, Duncan Jordanstone Coll of Arts, American Inst of Architects, RIAS; Hon Dr Art De Montfort Univ 1999; RIBA, FSIAD; *Style*— Sir Philip Dowson, CBE, PPRA; ✉ Royal Academy of Arts, Piccadilly, London W1V 0DS (tel 020 7300 5690)

DOYLE, Prof Anthony (Tony); s of John Francis Doyle, of Leeds, and Eileen, *née* Simpson; *b* 28 January 1963, Leeds; *Educ* Cardinal Heenan HS Leeds, Univ of Manchester (BSc, PhD); *m* 15 July 1989, Jacqueline Ann, *née* Halliday; 3 s (Liam Matthew b 9 Jan 1990, Craig Robert b 11 Aug 1991, Adam Russell b 4 Oct 1994); *Career* SERC res assoc Univ of Manchester 1987–90; Univ of Glasgow: lectr 1990–99, reader 1999–2002, GridPP project ldr 2001–, prof 2002–; DESY visiting research scientist 1994–97, Alexander von Humboldt fell Univ of Hamburg 1998, PPARC sr res fell 2000; author of more than 200 pubns on particle physics and grid computing; FInstP 2001, FRSE 2005; *Style*— Prof Tony Doyle; ✉ Dept of Physics and Astronomy, Kelvin Building, Univ of Glasgow G12 8QQ

DOYLE, Avril; MEP; da of Dr Richard Belton (d 1974), and Dr Freda Belton, *née* Ryan (d 2004); *b* 18 April 1949, Dublin; *Educ* Holy Child Convent Killiney, UCD (BSc); *m* Dec 1971, Frederick Doyle; 3 da (Christina b 1972, Elizabeth b 1973, Kate b 1979); *Career* memb (Fine Gael) Wexford Corp and CC 1974–95 (mayor of Wexford 1976), TD (Fine Gael) Wexford 1982–89 and 1992–97, memb (senator) Seanad Éireann (Fine Gael) Agric Panel 1989–92 and 1997–2002, MEP (Fine Gael) Leinster 1999–; min of state Depts of Finance and Environment Ireland 1986–87, memb shadow cabinet 1992, min of state Taoiseach's Dept, Dept of Finance and Dept of Tport Energy and Communications Ireland 1995–97, ldr Irish Delgn European People's Party and European Dems 1999–, currently vice-chm Delgn for rels with the Gulf States, vice-chm Ctee on Fisheries, memb Ctee on the Environment, Public Health and Food Safety and Ctee on Industry, Research and Energy European Parl; pres Equestrian Fedn of Ireland 2001–05; memb: Royal Dublin Soc, Show Jumping Assoc of Ireland, Eventing Ireland, Fédération Equestre Internationale EU Working Gp; hon memb Br Veterinary Assoc; *Style*— Mrs Avril Doyle, MEP; ✉ Kitestown House, Wexford, Ireland (tel 00 353 53 914 2873, fax 00 353 53 914 7810, e-mail office@avrildoyle.ie); European Parliament, Rue Wiertz, BE-1047, Brussels, Belgium (tel 0032 2 28 47 784, fax 0032 2 28 49 784, e-mail avril.doyle@europarl.europa.eu)

D

DOYLE, (Frederick) Bernard; s of James Hopkinson Doyle, and Hilda Mary, *née* Spotsworth; *b* 17 July 1940; *Educ* Univ of Manchester, Harvard Business Sch (MBA); *m* Ann, *née* Weston; 2 s (Stephen Francis, Andrew John), 1 da (Elizabeth Ann); *Career* chartered engr; mgmnt conslt London, Brussels and USA 1967–72, Booker McConnell 1973–81 (dir 1979, chm Engrg Div to 1981); chief exec: SDP 1981–83, Welsh Water Authy 1983–87; dir ops MSL Search and Selection International (UK) Ltd (formerly MSL International (UK) Ltd) 1988–90, md Hamptons 1990–94, md MSL Search and Selection International (UK) Ltd 1994–99, head Public Sector Practice Hoggett Bowers 1999–2000, dir KPMG Exec Search and Selection 2001–05, ptnr Gatenby Sanderson 2005–; chair Sustainability West Midlands 2003–; vice-chair NE Worcs Coll 1999–; crew memb Times Clipper 2000 Round the World Yacht Race 2000–01; CIMgt, FICE, FIWES, FRSA; *Recreations* reading, theatre, bird watching, walking, sailing; *Style*— Bernard Doyle, Esq; ✉ 38A West Road, Bromsgrove, Worcestershire B60 2NQ

DOYLE, Craig; s of Sean Doyle, of Dublin, and Eithne, *née* Hannigan; *b* 17 December 1970; *Educ* Blackrock Coll Dublin, Nat Univ of Ireland Maynooth (BA), London Coll of Printing (Dip Broadcast Journalism); *m* 2001, Doon, *née* Hutson; 1 s (Quin b 14 Dec 2002); *Career* formerly staff reporter then staff prodr News and Current Affairs BBC Radio; presenter/host: Tomorrow's World and Tomorrow's World Live (BBC1), Midweek (BBC Radio 4), Holiday on a Shoestring (BBC1), 50 Places to See Before You Die (BBC1), Holiday Prog (BBC1), Innovation Nation (BBC1); reporter: Grandstand (BBC TV), Wimbledon (BBC TV); New TV Talent of the Year TRIC Awards 2001; *Recreations* a range of badly played sports incl running (ran NY marathon 2001 and Dublin marathon 2002), golf, football and canoeing; nappy changing; *Style*— Craig Doyle, Esq; ✉ c/o Diane Evans, Noel Gay Management, Shepperton Studios, Studios Road, Shepperton, Middlesex TW17 0QD (tel 01932 572569, fax 01932 572712)

DOYLE, Dr David; RD (1973, and bar 1983); s of Edward Doyle, of Edinburgh, and Mary Stevenson, *née* Shand; *b* 28 September 1937; *Educ* George Heriot's Sch Edinburgh, Univ of Edinburgh (MD); *m* 1, 24 Oct 1964, Janet Caryl (d 1984), da of Phyllis and late Stanley Maurice Gresham Potter, of Nottingham; 5 s (Michael b 1966, Stanley b 1968, Edward b 1970, Arthur b 1972, Quintin b 1977); m 2, 28 Sept 1996, Catherine Ford Whitley, wife of late John Whitley, da of late Dr A G and Anna Cruikshank, of Edinburgh; *Career* RAFVR 1958–61, Univ of Edinburgh Air Sqdn, RAuxAF 1962–67, RNR 1967–; house offr in med and surgery Edinburgh Royal Infirmary 1961–62, anatomy demonstrator Univ of Edinburgh 1962–63, SHO in surgical neurology Edinburgh 1963; appts in academic pathology and neuropathology 1963–71: Edinburgh, KCH London; conslt neuropathologist Glasgow 1971–; Dip in Forensic Med, Cert in Aviation Med; CBiol, FIBiol, FRAeS, FFPathRCPI, FRCPEd 1996; *Recreations* Highland bagpiping, flying, climbing with Kate; *Clubs* RSM, Royal Scottish Piping Soc, Glasgow Highland; *Style*— Dr David Doyle, RD; ✉ Neuropathology, 35 Thorn Road, Bearsden, Glasgow G61 4BS

DOYLE, Ian Thomas; s of James Doyle (d 1994), and Catherine Forgie Workman (d 1989); *b* 13 March 1940; *Educ* Whitehill Sr Secdy Sch Glasgow; *m* 2 Sept 1961 (m dis 1980), Maureen Marshall, da of Samuel Sunderland; 1 da (Gillian Stuart b 10 April 1967), 1 s (Lee Grant Marshall b 30 March 1968); m 2, 15 Oct 1982, Irene Dick Scott (d 2004), da of Peter Dick; *Career* fndr and dir Doyle Cruden Group 1967– (sold 2001), fndr and chm Cuemasters Ltd 1988– (sold 2001), chm 110sport Management Ltd 2003–; snooker clients incl: Stephen Hendry, Mark Williams, Ken Doherty, Stephen Maguire, Joe Perry, Allister Carter, David Gray, Marco Fu, Anthony Hamilton; golf clients incl: Dean Robertson, Stephen Gallacher, Alastair Forsyth, Stephen O'Hara, Marc Warren, Catriona Matthews; other sports clients incl rugby and football; *Recreations* golf and sport generally; *Style*— Ian Doyle, Esq; ✉ 110sport Management Ltd, Pavilion 1, Castlecraig Business Park, Players Road, Stirling FK7 7SH (tel 01786 462 634, fax 01786 450 068, e-mail i.doyle@110sport.com)

DOYLE, Dr Peter; CBE (1992); s of Peter Doyle (d 1969), and Joan, *née* Murdoch (d 1987); *b* 6 September 1938; *Educ* Eastwood Secdy Sch Clarkson Glasgow, Univ of Glasgow (BSc, PhD); *m* 7 Aug 1962, Anita, *née* McCulloch; 1 da (Elaine b 13 Sept 1965), 1 s (Alan b 28 Feb 1967); *Career* ICI plc: joined ICI Pharmaceuticals Div 1963, head Chemicals Dept ICI Pharmaceuticals Div 1975–77, research dir then R&D dir ICI Plant Protection Div (now ICI Agrochemicals) 1977–86, dep chm and technical dir ICI Pharmaceuticals 1986–89, gp research and technol dir and main bd dir 1989–93, chm BBSRC 1998–2003; exec dir Zeneca Group plc (following its demerger from ICI) 1993–99 (i/c R&D, safety, health and environment, mfrg and E & W Europe); non-exec dir: Oxford Molecular Gp plc 1997–2000, Oxagen 1999–2002, Syngenta 2000, Avidex 2001; Royal Soc Zeneca lectr 1993; chm Steering Ctee Cambridge Interdisciplinary Research Centre for Protein Engrg 1990–95, vice-pres Cncl Royal Instn 1991; memb: Cncl UCL 1985–98, Cncl Centre for the Exploitation of Sci and Technol 1989–, PM's Advsy Cncl on Sci and Technol 1989–94, MRC 1990–94, SERC Nat Ctee on Superconductivity 1990–94, Steering Ctee Oxford Interdisciplinary Research Centre for Molecular Sciences 1990–93, Bd of Dirs Rothstamsted Experimental Station 1991–98, Bd Salters' Inst of Industrial Chemistry 1993–, Standing Gp on Health Technol Central R&D Ctee NHS 1994–98, Royal Cmmn on Environmental Pollution 1994–98, UK Round Table on Sustainable Development 1998–2000; tstee The Nuffield Fndn 1998–, patron Astra Zeneca Science Teaching Tst 2002–; Hon DSc: Univ of Glasgow 1992, Univ of Nottingham 1993, Univ of Sussex 1995; Hon LLD Univ of Dundee 1994; memb Ct of Assts Worshipful Co of Salters 1996 (Freeman 1982, Liveryman 1983, Master 2003–04); FRSE 1993; *Style*— Dr Peter Doyle, CBE, FRSE; ✉ Salters' Hall, 4 Fore Street, London EC2Y 5DE

DOYLE, Philip John; s of Albert Edward Doyle (d 1980), and Veronica Mary, *née* Jackson; *b* 30 September 1951; *Educ* West Park GS St Helens, Queens' Coll Cambridge (foundation scholar); *m* 1 July 1972, Anne Elizabeth, da of Francis William Frankland Dobby; 1 da (Lorna Mary b 19 June 1978), 2 s (Edward Francis b 22 Nov 1980, Howard William b 7 April 1984); *Career* Arthur Andersen: joined 1972, ptnr 1983–, head of Tax Div (London) 1993–; FCA 1977; *Recreations* walking, cricket, football, completed London Marathon 1993; *Clubs* RAC; *Style*— Philip Doyle, Esq; ✉ Arthur Andersen, 1 Surrey Street, London WC2R 2PS (tel 020 7438 3450, fax 020 7831 1133)

DOYLE, Prof William; s of Stanley Joseph Doyle (d 1973), of Scarborough, N Yorks, and Mary Alice, *née* Bielby (d 2003); *b* 4 March 1942; *Educ* Bridlington Sch, Oriel Coll Oxford (MA, DPhil); *m* 2 Aug 1968, Christine, da of William Joseph Thomas (d 1969), of Aberdare, Glamorgan; *Career* sr lectr in history Univ of York 1978–81 (asst lectr 1967–69, lectr 1969–78), prof of modern history Univ of Nottingham 1981–85, prof of history Univ of Bristol 1986–2008; visiting prof: Columbia SC 1969–70, Bordeaux 1976, Paris 1988; visiting fell All Souls Coll Oxford 1991–92, Hans Kohn memb Inst for Advanced Study Princeton 2004; pres Soc for the Study of French History 1992–95; Hon DUniv Bordeaux III France; FRHistS, FBA 1998; *Books* The Parlement of Bordeaux and the End of the Old Regime 1771–90 (1974), The Old European Order 1660–1800 (1978), Origins of the French Revolution (1980), The Ancien Regime (1986), The Oxford History of the French Revolution (1989), Officers, Nobles and Revolutionaries (1995), Venality. The Sale of Offices in Eighteenth Century France (1996), Jansenism (1999), Robespierre (jt ed with Colin Haydon, 1999), La Vénalité (2000), Old Regime France (ed, 2001), The French Revolution: A Very Short Introduction (2001); *Recreations* books, decorating, travelling about; *Clubs* Athenaeum, Oxford and Cambridge; *Style—* Prof W Doyle, FBA; ✉ Linden House, College Road, Lansdown, Bath, Somerset BA1 5RR (tel 01225 314341, e-mail william.doyle1@btinternet.com)

DRABBLE, Jane; OBE (2000); da of late Walter Drabble, of Hilton, Dorset, and Molly, *née* Boreham; *b* 15 January 1947; *Educ* Clayton Hall GS Newcastle-under-Lyme, Plympton GS Plymouth, Univ of Bristol (BA); *Career* BBC: studio mangr BBC Radio 1968–73, prodr Radio Current Affrs 1973–75, asst prodr, prodr, then sr prodr TV Current Affrs 1975–86, ed London Plus 1986–87, ed Everyman 1987–91, asst md Network TV 1991–94, concurrently head of factual progs Network TV 1993–94, dir of educn and memb Bd of Mgmnt 1994–99; cmmr for judicial appointments 2001–06; chair Mental Health Media 2002–06, vice-chair Basic Skills Agency 2001–04, memb Nat LSC 2000–06; dir Birmingham Royal Ballet 2002–, govr and memb Bd RSC 2002–; *Recreations* music, theatre, walking; *Style—* Ms Jane Drabble, OBE; ✉ 2 Greenend Road, London W4 1AJ

DRABBLE, Margaret; CBE (1980); da of His Hon John Frederick Drabble, QC (d 1982), by his w Kathleen, *née* Bloor; *b* 5 June 1939; *Educ* The Mount Sch York, Newnham Coll Cambridge; *m* 1, 1960 (m dis 1975), Clive Walter Swift, *qv*; 2 s, 1 da; m 2, 1982, Michael Holroyd, CBE, FRSL, *qv*; *Career* author; Hon DLitt: Univ of Sheffield, UEA 1994; FRSL 1973; *Books* A Summer Birdcage (1962), The Garrick Year (1964), The Millstone (1966), Wordsworth (1966), Jerusalem the Golden (1967), The Waterfall (1969), The Needle's Eye (1972), London Consequences (ed with B S Johnson, 1972), Arnold Bennett - A Biography (1974), The Realms of Gold (1975), The Genius of Thomas Hardy (ed, 1976), New Stories 1 (co-ed, 1976), The Ice Age (1977), For Queen and Country (1978), A Writer's Britain (1979), The Middle Ground (1980), The Oxford Companion to English Literature (ed 5 edn, 1985), The Radiant Way (1987), The Concise Oxford Companion to English Literature (with Jenny Stringer, 1987), A Natural Curiosity (1989), Safe As Houses (1989), The Gates of Ivory (1991), Angus Wilson: A Biography (1995), The Witch of Exmoor (1996), The Oxford Companion to English Literature (ed 6 edn, 2000), The Peppered Moth (2001), The Seven Sisters (2002); *Style—* Ms Margaret Drabble, CBE; ✉ c/o PFD, Drury House, 34–43 Russell Street, London WC2B 5HA (tel 020 7344 1000)

DRABBLE, Richard John Bloor; QC (1995); s of His Hon Frederick John Drabble, QC (d 1982), and Kathleen Marie, *née* Bloor (d 1984); *b* 23 May 1950; *Educ* Leighton Park Sch Reading, Downing Coll Cambridge (BA); *m* 31 May 1980, Sarah Madeleine Hope, da of Lt Cdr John David Walter Thomas Lewis (d 1966); 3 s (William b and d 1981, Frederick b 1982, Samuel b 1985); *Career* called to the Bar Inner Temple 1975 (bencher 2002); jr counsel to the Crown Common Law 1992–95; chm Administrative Law Bar Assoc 1998–2000; fell Inst of Advanced Legal Studies 1998; *Publications* Halsburys Laws Social Security (contrib), Goudie & Supperstone Judicial Review (contrib), Local Authorities and Human Rights (jt edn); numerous articles; *Recreations* reading, walking, dogs; *Style—* Richard Drabble, Esq, QC; ✉ Landwark Chambers, 180 Fleet Street, London EC4A 2HG (tel 020 7430 1221, fax 020 7421 6060)

DRABBLE, William Alexander; s of William Alan Drabble, and Gladys Edith, *née* Johnson; *b* 10 August 1971; *Educ* Reepham HS, Norwich City Coll (Dip Catering, Outstanding Student of the Year 1990); *m* Claudine Erica, *née* Barbour; *Career* chef; Mirabelle restaurant Grand Hotel Eastbourne 1990–93, Capital Hotel Knightsbridge 1993–94, Nico Central London 1994, jr sous chef Nico Park Lane London 1994–96, sous chef Pied à Terre London 1996–97, head chef Michaels Nook Grasmere 1997–98 (1 Michelin Star, 4 AA Rosettes), head chef Aubergine Restaurant London 1998– (1 Michelin Star, 4 AA Rosettes, French Restaurant of the Year 2000); winner Nat Final Assoc Culinaire Française Coupe Emile Fêtu 1991, memb GB jr nat team Culinary Olympics Frankfurt 1992 (winners Silver and Bronze medals); *Publications* London on a Plate: Recipes from London's Finest Chefs (contrib, 2002); *Recreations* walking, skiing, reading, relaxing with friends and family; *Style—* William Drabble, Esq; ✉ Aubergine Resturant, 11 Park Walk, London SW10 0AJ (tel 020 7352 3449, fax 020 7351 1770)

DRABU, Dr Yasmin Jeelani (Mrs Naqushbandi); da of Dr Ghulam Jeelani Drabu, of Hale, Cheshire, and Ayesha Jeelani, *née* Ashai; *b* 21 June 1950; *Educ* N Manchester GS, Univ of Manchester Med Sch (MB ChB); *m* 17 Aug 1975, Dr Khalid Naqushbandi, s of Ghulam Nabi Naqushbandi, of Srinagar Kashmir; 3 da (Lara Hennah b 3 Feb 1981, Shama, Sabah (twins) b 10 Oct 1983); *Career* sr registrar UCH 1980–82, conslt microbiologist N Middx Hosp 1982–; Royal Free Hosp: hon sr lectr 1989–, clinical dir of pathology 1993–95, clinical dir of diagnostic and therapy servs 1995–97, chm Supplies Evaluation Ctee 1997–2000, med dir 2000–; memb GMC working gp for medical microbiology performance procedures 1999–; dep ed Jl of Clinical Pathology 2000– (med exec dir 2001–); memb Kashmiri Assoc of GB; DCH, FRCPath; *Style—* Dr Yasmin Drabu; ✉ Department of Microbiology, North Middlesex Hospital, Sterling Way, London N18 1QX (tel 020 8887 2892, fax 020 8887 4227)

DRAGUN, Richard Eugenjusz; s of Jan Dragun (d 1996), of Anlaby, nr Hull, and Genowefa, *née* Hulnicka (d 1990); *b* 13 May 1951; *Educ* Marist Coll Hull, London Coll of Printing (DipAD); *Career* designer Nat Car Park Ltd 1973–74, dir Design Research Unit Ltd 1980–89 (designer 1974–80); conslt designer British Mass Transit Consultants, Taipei Metro project Taiwan 1986–87, sr designer Baghdad Metro project 1981–84; head of graphic design BDP Design 1993– (ptnr 1989–93); exhibition and museum design incl: Nat Sound Archive London (permanent exhibition), Spaceworks (Nat Maritime Museum London), Charing Cross Station (London Transport), History and Culture of Oman (Smithsonian Inst Washington DC), Gulf Cooperation Cncl (Summit Conf Exhibition Oman), Nat History Museum and Travelling Exhibitions for Miny of Heritage and Culture (Sultanate of Oman); conslt JV Gp (Dar Es Salaam, Int Trade Fair 1989–); work selected for pubn and exhibition in UK Graphic Design 1984–85, Best in Exhibition Design, Best in Retail Identity Design 1996, Graphis Diagrams (Switzerland), Design (Republic of China), World Graphic Design (Japan), Typographic Writings 2001; author of various articles; dir Sign Design Soc 1997 (memb Steering Gp 1996–, co sec 2000–); memb Governing Body of Southwark Coll, chm Art and Design Consultative Ctee 1988–92; FCSD 1998 (MCSD 1978); *Recreations* fine art, modern prints, books; *Style—* Richard Dragun, Esq; ✉ 31 Sidney Road, St Margarets, Twickenham TW1 1JP; Building Design Partnership (tel 020 7812 8000, fax 020 7812 8399, e-mail re-dragun@bdp.co.uk)

DRAKES, David Hedley Foster; s of Donald Frank Drakes (d 1986), and Kathleen, *née* Caldecott; *b* 20 September 1943; *Educ* Wyggeston GS for Boys Leicester, St Catharine's Coll Cambridge (exhibitioner, MA); *m* Patricia Margaret Mary, da of Edward Henshall; *Career* advtg account mangr: Doyle Dane Bernbach London 1966–70; Aalders Marchant Weinreich London 1970–72; fndr and dir Intellect Games 1973–76; md Marketing Solutions Limited 1977–82; fndr managing ptnr and majority shareholder The Marketing Partnership Limited 1983–; past chm: Inst of Sales Promotion, The Sales Promotion Conslts Assoc; memb Mktg Soc 1978; FCIM 2001; *Recreations* opera, ballet, theatre, playing squash; *Clubs* RAC; *Style—* David Drakes, Esq; ✉ The Marketing Partnership Ltd, 69 Hatton Garden, London EC1N 8JT (tel 020 7400 7200, fax 020 7400 7201)

DRAKES, Paul William Foster; s of Donald Frank Drakes (d 1986), and Kathleen, *née* Caldicott; *b* 6 November 1950; *Educ* Wyggeston GS; *m* 1, 1973 (m dis 1980), Janet Bell; 2 s (Oliver b 30 Dec 1975, William b 3 Jan 1979); m 2, 1981, Stephanie Anne, da of Melvyn Moffatt; 2 s (Jonathan b 18 Dec 1986, Harry b 4 July 1989); *Career* trainee Sun Life Co Leicester 1967, mgmnt trainee Dunlop Leicester 1967, trainee media planner and buyer Gee Advertising Leicester 1968, media planner and buyer C R Cassons London 1969, media gp head Allardyce Hampshire 1970, appointed media gp head The Media Department Ltd 1973; Primary Contact Ltd: media mangr 1973, media dir and Bd dir 1976, account gp head 1986, dir of client servs 1988; client servs dir ACGB Nottingham 1991; ptnr CHCchoir 1992–2006 (following merger 2002, formerly Drakes Jardine Ltd (fndr ptnr), then choir), ptnr 23red Central 2006–; MIPA; *Recreations* four sons, a love for Leicester City FC and a successful company; *Style—* Paul Drakes, Esq; ✉ 2 Huntingdon Drive, The Park, Nottingham NG7 1BW (tel 0115 941 8776); 23red Central, 32A Stoney Street, Nottingham NG1 1AA (tel 0115 9247157)

DRANSFIELD, Graham; s of Gordon Dransfield, of Linthwaite, W Yorks, and Barbara, *née* Booth; *b* 5 March 1951; *Educ* Colne Valley HS Huddersfield, St Catherine's Coll Oxford (coll scholar, BA, Soccer blue); *m* 21 June 1980, Helen Frances, da of Lawrence Demchy; 1 da (Louise Jane b 14 Feb 1981), 1 s (Mark Lucas b 21 Dec 1984); *Career* articled clerk then asst slr Slaughter & May 1974–82; Hanson plc: slr 1982–86, co sec 1986, assoc dir 1989, dir 1992–; memb Law Soc 1976; *Recreations* squash, tennis, running, cycling, golf; *Clubs* Beckenham CC, The Addington Golf; *Style—* Graham Dransfield, Esq; ✉ Hanson plc, 1 Grosvenor Place, London SW1X 7JH (tel 020 7259 4114, fax 020 7245 9939, e-mail graham.dransfield@hansonplc.com)

DRAPER, Christopher (Chris); s of Lawrie Draper, of Landford, Wilts, and Susan, *née* Davey; *b* 20 March 1978, Sheffield; *Career* yachtsman; achievements in 49er class incl: Gold medal World Championships 2003 (Silver medal 2002 and 2004), Gold medal European Championships 2004 (Silver medal 2002 and 2003), Bronze medal Olympic Games Athens 2004; *Recreations* surfing, mountain biking; *Style—* Chris Draper, Esq; ✉ Woodlands, Pear Tree Drive, Landford, Salisbury SP5 2AY (e-mail c.draper2@ukonline.co.uk)

DRAPER, Nigel Francis; s of Geoffrey Walter Draper, and Rosa Elizabeth Snell, *née* Pitcher; *b* 22 August 1953; *Educ* Mitcham GS, Frome GS, LSE (BSc); *m* 1975, Cheryl Ann, *née* Fry; 1 da (Sara b 1980); *Career* Kensington, Chelsea and Westminster AHA: purchasing asst 1974–76, admin St Mary Abbot's Hosp 1976–77; asst sector admin Brent Health Dist 1977–79, capital planning offr NE Thames RHA 1979–80, planning offr W Lambeth HA 1980–83, area admin offr Royal N Shore Hosp Sydney Aust 1983–84, admin W Lambeth HA 1984–85; Llewelyn-Davies (architects, urban designers and planners, health planners, interior and graphic designers) 1985–99, with Secta (health servs conslts) 1999– (currently dir); MHSM (DipHSM); *Recreations* supporting Leeds United; *Style—* Nigel Draper, Esq

DRAPER, Prof Paul Richard; s of James Krishen Draper, of York, and Dorothy Jean Draper; *b* 28 December 1946; *Educ* Univ of Exeter (BA), Univ of Reading (MA), Univ of Stirling (PhD); *m* Janet Margaret, *née* Grant; 1 s (Timothy James Jonathan b 29 Sept 1977), 1 da (Lucy Jane Jessica b 30 April 1980); *Career* research fell Univ of Stirling 1972–73, lectr Univ of St Andrews 1973–75, lectr Univ of Edinburgh 1976–78; Univ of Strathclyde: Esmée Fairbairn sr lectr 1978–86, prof 1986–97, head Dept of Accounting & Finance 1990–95, vice-dean Strathclyde Business Sch 1993–97; Walter Scott and Partners prof of fin Univ of Edinburgh 1997–2001, head Sch of Business and Economics and prof of fin Univ of Exeter 2002–; Research Prize Inst for Quantitative Investment (with G Brown and E McKenzie) 1992; *Books* The Scottish Financial Sector (with I Smith, W Stewart and N Hood, 1988), The Investment Trust Industry in the UK (1989); *Recreations* commuting; *Style—* Prof Paul Draper; ✉ Streatham Lodge, Streatham Rise, Exeter EX4 4PE (tel 01392 274973); School of Business and Economics, The University of Exeter, Streathan Court, Rennes Drive, Exeter EX4 4PU (tel 01392 263218, e-mail p.r.draper@exeter.ac.uk)

DRAYSON, Baron (Life Peer UK 2004), of Kensington in the Royal Borough of Kensington and Chelsea; Paul Rudd Drayson; s of Michael Rudd Drayson, of Lymington, Hants; *b* 5 March 1960; *Educ* Aston Univ (PhD); *m* 1994, Elspeth Jane, da of Prof Brian John Bellhouse, of Islip, Oxon; 2 da (Hon Olivia Grace Georgina b 1996, Hon Francesca Alice Celina b 2003), 3 s (Hon James Alexander b 1997, Hon George Edward b 1999, Hon Charles Frederick b 2001); *Career* fndr and md Lambourn Food Co 1986–91, fndr and dir Genisys Development Ltd 1991–95, fndr and chief exec Powderject Pharmaceuticals plc 1993–2003, entrepreneur in residence Saïd Business Sch Univ of Oxford 2003–05; chm UK Bioindustry Assoc 2001–02; memb Investment Advsy Ctee Isis Coll Venture Fund 1999–2004; sits as Lab peer in House of Lords, min for defence procurement 2005–07, min of state for defence equipment and support 2007–; memb Advsy Bd Oxford Univ Challenge Seed Fund 1999–2004, chm fundraising campaign Oxford Children's Hosp 2002–05; FRSA 1998; *Style—* The Rt Hon the Lord Drayson

DRECHSLER, Paul Joseph; *b* 16 April 1956; *Educ* TCD (BA BAI), INSEAD (IEP); *m* Jan 1979, Wendy Isobel, *née* Hackett; 2 s (Mark, Jonathan), 1 da (Sophie); *Career* Imperial Chemical Industries plc: various positions 1978–92, chm and pres ICI Brasil SA 1992–93, chief exec ICI Acrylics Inc (USA) 1993–96, chief exec ICI Polyester 1996–98, chm and chief exec Quest Int 1998–, exec dir ICI plc 1999–2003, exec chm Wates Gp Ltd 2006– (ceo 2004); sr ind dir Filtrona plc 2005–; *Recreations* family, music, skiing, political science; *Style—* Paul Drechsler, Esq; ✉ 17 Ardbeg Road, Dulwich, London SE24 9JL (e-mail wdrechsler@aol.com)

DRESCHER, Derek Peter; s of Clifford Drescher (d 1966), and Joan Ringrose, *née* Jackson (d 2001); *b* 13 March 1940; *Educ* Pocklington Sch, Univ of Birmingham; *m* 11 April 1966, Gillian Mary, da of Ronald Harry Eden, of Oxford; 2 da (Lucy, Alison); *Career* lighting designer Lincoln and Oldham Repertory Theatre Cos 1961–63; BBC Radio: studio mangr 1963–71, music prodr 1971–89, sr prodr (jazz) 1989–99; freelance prodr and photographer 1999–, dir New Vortex Jazz Club 2003–; memb Ctee Cheltenham Jazz Festival 1996–2006; documentaries incl: Constant Lambert, Jelly Roll Morton, Charlie Parker, Little Titch, Shostakovich, Miles Davis (The Phoenix, nominated Sony award 1991), George Russell (The Invisible Guru), Billy Mayerl (A Formula for Success); series incl: Man-Woman of Action, Desert Island Discs 1976–89, Jazz Today, Concerto, Highway to Heaven, Before the Blues (Sony award for best specialist music prog 1988), This Week's Composer (Duke Ellington), Play as I Please (Humphrey Lyttelton), Touch of Genius (George Shearing), Impressions, A Man for All Music (André Previn), Misterioso (Thelonious Monk), Kiri (Dame Kiri Te Kanawa), Saxophone Colossus (Sonny Rollins), Bright Size Life (Pat Metheny); exhbn of photographs of jazz musicians at Vortex Jazz Club and Bloomsbury Theatre 1999, enlarged exhbn at Cheltenham International Jazz Festival 2000, exhbn of photgraphs at Laine Dankworth Centre Wavendon 2002–03; jt first prize winners exhbn Lauderdale House Highgate 2001; *Books* Desert Islands Lists (with Roy Plomley, 1984); *Recreations* theatre, music, travel, books; *Style—* Derek Drescher, Esq; ✉ 10 Fortismere Avenue, Muswell Hill, London N10 3BL (tel 020 8883 8081)

DREW, Dan Hamilton; s of Daniel Edward Drew (d 1974), of Petworth, W Sussex, and Rena Frayer, *née* Hamilton (d 1990); *b* 31 January 1938; *Educ* Stubbington House, Tonbridge; *m* 1, 1963 (m dis), Carol Ann, da of Dr Robert Gibson Miller, of Helston, Cornwall; 1 da (Xanthe b 1966) 1 s (Angus b 1967); m 2, 1976, Beverley, da of Alan Lestocq Roberts (d 1981), of Graffham, W Sussex; 1 da (Frances b 1979); *Career* chartered accountant; gp fin dir Interlink Express plc 1982–92; chm Bath and Wessex Opera Ltd 1992–97; *Recreations* OU student, fishing, shooting, golf; *Style—* D H Drew, Esq; ✉ Lower Poswick, Whitbourne, Worcester WR6 5SS (tel 01886 821275, fax 01886 822027, e-mail danhdrew@msn.com)

DREW, David Elliott; MP; s of Ronald Montague Drew, and late Maisie Joan Drew; *b* 13 April 1952; *Educ* Kingsfield Sch, Univ of Nottingham (BA), Univ of Birmingham (PGCE), Bristol Poly (MA), UWE (MEd); *m* Anne; 4 c; *Career* teacher 1976–86, lectr UWE 1986–97; MP (Lab/Co-op) Stroud 1997–, chm PLP Backbench Ctee on Agric 1997–2001, vice-chair PLP Backbench Rural Affairs Gp; memb Select Ctee DEFRA; town, and former dist and county cncllr; *Style—* David Drew, Esq, MP; ✉ House of Commons, London SW1A 0AA (tel 020 7219 6479, fax 020 7219 0910)

DREW, Dorothy Joan; da of Francis Marshall Gant (d 1956), of Reading, Berks, and Wilhelmina Frederica, *née* Dunster (d 1982); *b* 31 March 1938; *Educ* The Sch of St Helen and St Katharine, Univ of London (LLB); *m* 12 Dec 1959, Patrick Drew, s of Alec Charles Drew (d 1967), of Reading, Berks; 2 s, 1 da; *Career* called to the Bar Gray's Inn 1981, pt/t chm Social Security Appeal Tbnls 1986–92; adjudicator Immigration Appeals Tbnl 1989–93 (special adjudicator 1993–2000, regnl adjudicator 1998–2000); chm Child Support Appeals Tbnl 1993–94; vice-pres Immigration Appeal Tbnl 2000–01; JP Reading 1975–95; *Recreations* music, theatre, family; *Style—* Mrs Dorothy Drew; ✉ Handpost, Swallowfield, Berkshire RG7 1PU; Cosawes Barton, Ponsanooth, Truro, Cornwall TR3 7EJ

DREW, Prof John Sydney Neville; s of John William Henry Drew (d 1989), and Kathleen Marjorie, *née* Wright (d 1991); *b* 7 October 1936; *Educ* King Edward's Sch Birmingham, St John's Coll Oxford (MA), Fletcher Sch of Law and Diplomacy, Tufts Univ (AM), Middle East Centre for Arabic Studies; *m* 22 Dec 1962, Rebecca Margaret Amanda, *née* Usher; 2 s (Jason b 1965, David b 1972), 1 da (Emma b 1967); *Career* Lt Somerset LI 1955–57; HM Dip Serv 1960–73: third sec Paris 1962–64, second sec Kuwait 1965–67, first sec Bucharest 1968–70; dir of mktg and exec programmes London Business Sch 1973–79, dir of corp affairs Rank Xerox 1979–84, dir of European affrs Touche Ross Int 1984–86, head of UK Offices European Cmmn 1987–93; visiting prof of European mgmnt: Imperial Coll of Sci and Technol London 1987–90, Open Univ 1992–99; visiting prof of European business mgmnt Univ of Durham 1995–2003; sr advsr European Business Sch 2006–; dir: Europa Times 1993–94, The Change Group International plc 1996–2003; pres Inst of Linguists 1993–99, pres Eurotas 1998–2003, chm Durham Inst 1995–2003, dep chm Enterprise Support Group 1993–95, tstee Thomson Fndn 1994–2006; Sloan fell London Business Sch 1970, assoc fell Templeton Coll Oxford 1982–87; Hon MBA Univ of Northumbria 1991; *Books* Doing Business in the European Community (1979, 3 edn 1991), Networking in Organisations (1986), Europe 1992 - Developing an Active Company Approach to the European Market (1988), Readings in International Enterprise (1994, 2 edn 1999), Ways through the Wall (2005); *Recreations* travel, golf, personal development; *Clubs* Oxford and Cambridge; *Style—* Prof John Drew; ✉ 49 The Ridgeway, London NW11 8PQ (tel 020 8455 5054, e-mail profdrew@eurotas.org)

DREWRY, Prof David John; s of Norman Tidman Drewry (d 1984), of Grimsby, Lincs, and Mary Edwina, *née* Wray (d 1993); *b* 22 September 1947; *Educ* Havelock Sch Grimsby, QMC London (BSc), Emmanuel Coll Cambridge (PhD); *m* 10 July 1971, Gillian Elizabeth, da of Clifford Francis Holbrook (d 1979); *Career* Univ of Cambridge: Sir Henry Strakosh fell 1972, sr asst in res 1978–83, asst dir of res 1983, sr visiting scholar 1999; dir Scott Polar Res Inst 1984–87, dir Br Antarctic Survey 1987–94, dir of science and technology and dep chief exec NERC 1994–98, DG British Cncl 1998; visiting fell Green Coll Oxford 1995–96, visiting prof Univ of London 1996–, vice-chllr Univ of Hull 1999–, guest prof Xiamen Univ China 2006–; pres Int Arctic Sci Ctee 1997–2002; non-exec dir Hull Urban Regeneration Co 2002–, Humber Economic Partnership 2002–; chm Yorkshire Univs 2002–04; memb: Int Glaciological Soc 1969– (vice-pres 1991–96), Royal Geographical Soc (vice-pres 1990–93, Cuthbert Peek Award 1979, Patron's Medal 1998), Cncl of Mangrs of Nat Antarctic Programmes (chm 1989–91), European Science Fndn 1989–98, FCO Panel 2000; tstee Antarctic Heritage Tst; patron: Robert Gordon Fndn; memb: Univs UK 1999–, Bd Yorkshire Science 2005–; US Antarctic Serv Medal 1979, Polar Medal 1986, Gold Medal (Prix de la Belgica) Royal Acad of Belgium 1995; Hon DSc: Robert Gordon Univ 1993, Univ of Humberside 1994, Anglia Poly Univ 1998; hon fell Queen Mary Coll London 1991; FRGS 1972, FRSA 1998, CGeog, CCMI 2002; *Books* Antarctica: Glaciological and Geophysical Folio (1983), Glacial Geologic Processes (1986), Antarctica and Environmental Change (1993); *Recreations* hill walking, skiing, classical music, theatre, gastronomy; *Style—* Prof David J Drewry; ✉ University of Hull, Hull HU6 7RX (fax 01482 466557, e-mail david.drewry@hull.ac.uk)

DREYFUS, James; *Career* actor; patron of Kairos, Lesbian and Gay Bereavement Centre; *Theatre* Russell Paxton in Lady in the Dark (RNT), Medvedenko in The Seagull (Thelma Holt Productions), Grimald in King Arthur (Centro Cultural de Belém); with Birmingham Repetory: Cassius in Julius Caesar, Gentlemen Prefer Blondes, Al in The Grapes of Wrath, Sean in Playing by the Rules; Gary in Eurovision (Vaudeville), Christopher/Patrick in Elegies for Angels, Punks and Raging Queens (Criterion), Ned Lowenscroft in Elizabeth Rex 2002, Billy, Rupert, Michael and Pierre Hickory-Wood in One for the Pot 2002–03, Carmen Ghia in The Prodcuers (Theatre Royal) 2004–05; *Television* Paris 1994, Thin Blue Line 1995, Absolutely Fabulous 1996, Gimme, Gimme, Gimme 1999, Gormenghast 2000, Oscar in Bette 2000, Waking the Dead 2004, Willo the Wisp (voice for animation) 2004, The Lenny Henry Show 2005, The Man and the Mouse 2005, My Hero 2005, The All New Alexei Sayle Show, The Complete and Utter History of Everything, Frontiers, Dame Edna Nurses it Better; *Radio* Robbie Ross in Friends of Oscar, The Short Straw; *Film* Thin Ice 1995, Richard III 1995, Boyfriends 1996, Notting Hill 1999, Being Considered 2000, Cody Banks II: Destination London 2003, Churchill: The Hollywood Years 2004, Fat Slags 2004, Colour Me Kubrick 2004; *Awards* Television Comedy Newcomer Award 1996, second prize Ian Charleson Award 1997 (for Julius Caesar), Olivier Award 1998 (for Lady in the Dark); *Recreations* lounging, loafing, napping and writing; *Style—* James Dreyfus, Esq; ✉ c/o Cassie Mayer Ltd, 5 Old Garden House, The Lanterns, Bridge Lane, London SW11 3AD

DRIFE, Prof James Owen; s of Thomas John Drife (d 1993), of Ancrum, Jedburgh, and Rachel Coldwell, *née* Jones (d 1986); *b* 8 September 1947; *Educ* Muirkirk JS Sch, Cumnock Acad, Univ of Edinburgh (BSc, MB ChB, MD); *m* 16 June 1973, Diana Elizabeth, da of Prof Ronald Haxton Girdwood, of 2 Hermitage Drive, Edinburgh; 1 s (Thomas b 20 Dec 1975), 1 da (Jennifer b 23 Nov 1977); *Career* house offr Edinburgh Royal Infirmary 1971–72, MRC res fell Edinburgh 1974–76, registrar Eastern Gen Hosp Edinburgh 1976–79, lectr Univ of Bristol 1979–82, sr lectr Univ of Leicester 1982–90, prof of obstetrics and gynaecology Univ of Leeds 1990– (dean of students 1996–99), hon conslt obstetrician and gynaecologist Leeds Gen Infirmary 1990–; UK ed European Jl of Obstetrics and Gynaecology 1985–95 (co-ed 2003–); co-ed: Contemporary Reviews in Obstetrics and Gynaecology 1988–97, British Jl of Obstetrics and Gynaecology 1994–2002; hon sec Blair-Bell Res Soc 1988–91; jr vice-pres RCOG 1998–2001, chm Assoc of Profs of Obstetrics and Gynaecology 2002–07, pres N of England Obstetrical and Gynaecological Soc 2007–; memb: Cases Ctee Med Protection Soc 1985–94 (dir Med Claims Mgmnt Servs 1994–98), Cncl RCOG 1993–2008, Midwifery Ctee UKCC 1993–98, GMC 1994–2005; Hon FCOG (SA) 2002; FRCSEd 1981, FRCOG 1990 (MRCOG 1978), FRSA 1997, FRCPEd 1998; *Books* Dysfunctional Uterine Bleeding and Menorrhagia (ed, 1989), Micturition (co-ed, 1990), HRT and Osteoporosis (co-ed, 1990), Antenatal Diagnosis (co-ed, 1991), Prostaglandins and the Uterus (co-ed, 1992), Infertility (co-ed, 1992), Contraception (co-ed, 1993), Caesarean Section (co-ed, 2000), Clinical Obstetrics and Gynaecology (co-ed, 2004), Obstetrics and Gynaecology for the MRCOG (co-ed, 2004); *Recreations* songwriting; *Clubs* Athenaeum, RSM, National Liberal; *Style—* Prof James Drife; ✉ Department of Obstetrics and Gynaecology, D Floor, Clarendon Wing, Belmont Grove, Leeds LS2 9NS (tel 0113 392 3888, fax 0113 392 3902, e-mail j.o.drife@leeds.ac.uk)

DRISCOLL, Fiona Elizabeth Lawrence; da of James Patrick Driscoll, and Jeanne L Williams; *b* 27 April 1958; *Educ* Sorbonne (Dip), Somerville Coll Oxford (MA); *m* 1992, Suresh Hiremath; *Career* mktg advsr Republican Campaign NY 1976, fin servs broker FPC 1976–80, mgmnt conslt Deloitte Haskins and Sells 1980–84, account dir Collett Dickenson Pearce 1984–87, sr conslt Bell Pottinger Communications (formerly Lowe Bell Communications) 1987–94, jt md The Rowland Company 1994–95, chief exec Ogilvy Adams Rinehart 1995–97, chief exec Driscoll Communications 1997–, mktg dir DERA 1999–2001, strategy dir Hedra plc 2003–06; memb Waste Implementation Prog (WIP) Steering Ctee DEFRA 2003–05; dir Inst of Leadership 1998–; non-exec chair: NHS Lotteries Ltd 2006–, Health Lottery Ltd 2007–; non-exec dir: Horserace Totalisator Bd 1999–2006, Fleming Managed Growth plc 1999–2004, Thomson Intermedia plc 2000–; chm: 300 Group 1994–6, City Women's Network 1996–98, Non Executive Directors Forum Alumni Cncl 2000–; memb: Nat Youth Cncl 1975, Public Services Productivity Panel 2000–06; librarian (vice-pres) Oxford Union 1979; A Millennium Woman of the Year 2000; *Style—* Ms Fiona Driscoll; ✉ e-mail fiona@driscoll.org.uk

D

DRISCOLL, Helen Deborah; da of John Cupitt, and Doris, *née* Jones; *b* 22 November 1956, Bromley, Kent; *Educ* Univ of Leicester (LLB); *Children* 2 s (James b 14 April 1977, Rory b 5 May 1979), 1 da (Sophie b 3 Nov 1982); *Career* slr; Eversheds 1991–97, Freeth Cartwright 1997–2001, Martineau Johnson 2001–; memb Law Soc 1993, MENSA; *Style—* Ms Helen Driscoll; ✉ Martineau Johnson, 1 Colmore Square, Birmingham B4 6AA (tel 0870 763 1635, fax 0870 763 2035, e-mail helen.driscoll@martjohn.com)

DRISCOLL, Dr James Philip (Jim); s of Reginald Driscoll, and Janetta Bridget Driscoll; *b* 29 March 1943; *Educ* St Illtyd's Coll Cardiff, Univ of Birmingham (BSc, PhD), Manchester Business Sch; *m* 1969, Josephine Klapper; 2 s, 2 da; *Career* teacher St Illtyd's Coll Cardiff 1964, res Joseph Lucas Ltd 1968–69; British Steel Corporation: sr res offr 1969–72, Supplies Dept 1972–75, mangr Divnl Supplies 1975–78, project proposals mangr 1978–80, regnl mangr BSC (Industry) S Wales 1980–82; econ and industrial advsr to Sec of State for Wales, seconded at under-sec level Welsh Office Indust Dept 1982–85; Mgmnt Consultancy Div PriceWaterhouseCoopers (formerly Coopers & Lybrand): assoc dir 1985–87, dir 1987–90, ptnr 1990–2000, ret; memb Inst of Welsh Affairs, memb Welsh Industrial Devpt Advsy Bd; CEng, MIChemE 1975, MInstGasE 1975, MInstE 1975; *Publications* author of various tech papers; *Recreations* family, sport; *Clubs* Cardiff Athletic, Peterston FC (Cardiff); *Style—* Dr Jim Driscoll; ✉ 6 Cory Crescent, Wyndham Park, Peterston-super-Ely, Cardiff CF5 6LS (tel 01446 760372)

DRISCOLL, Lindsay Jane; da of Clement Milligan Woodburn (d 2005), and Evelyn Miriam Woodburn (d 1978); *b* 17 April 1947, Lowestoft, Suffolk; *Educ* The Queen's Sch Chester, St Hugh's Coll Oxford (MA); *m* 29 Dec 1978, Rev Canon David Driscoll; 2 s (Richard Woodburn b 7 July 1980, Jonathan Peter b 13 May 1983); *Career* slr Biddle & Co 1971–73 (articled clerk 1969–71), asst registrar gen Kenya 1973–78, lectr Kenya Sch of Law 1973–78, charity law conslt 1980–87, legal advsr NCVO 1987–95, ptnr Sinclair Taylor and Martin 1995–2003, legal cmmr Charity Cmmn for England and Wales 2003–; memb Bd Int Centre for Not for Profit Law 1995–2003, memb Exec Ctee Charity Law Assoc 1996–2003; tstee: Womankind Worldwide 1998–2006, Widows Rights Int 2002–05, Balkans Community Initiatives Fund 2002–06, Historia Theatre Co, Dance United, St Katherine's and Shadwell Tst; memb Law Soc 1971; *Recreations* walking, travel, theatre; *Style—* Mrs Lindsay Driscoll; ✉ Charity Commission for England and Wales, Harmsworth House, 13–15 Bouverie Street, London EC4Y 8DP (tel 020 7674 2550, fax 020 7674 2308, e-mail lindsay.driscoll@charitycommission.gsi.gov.uk)

DRISCOLL, Prof Michael John; s of Michael Driscoll (d 1987), and Catherine, *née* Nash; *b* 27 October 1950; *Educ* Boteler GS Warrington, Trent Poly (Lord Kings Norton Prize, BA); *Children* 1 da (Alice b 2 June 1981), 1 s (Jack b 10 Aug 1984); *Career* research asst Univ of Sheffield 1973–77, lectr Univ of Birmingham 1977–89; head Sch of Economics Middlesex Poly 1989–91; Middlesex Univ: dean and pro-vice-chllr 1991–95, dep vice-chllr 1995–96, vice-chllr 1996–; economist OECD Paris 1985–88; chair: Standing Conf of Princs (SCOP)/Univs UK (UUK) Sector Gp on Sustainability 2000, Coalition of Modern Univs (CMU) 2003–; memb: Bd Coll of NE London 1997, Steering Gp London Higher Bd UUK 2001–; patron N London Hospice 2001; FRSA, CCIM; *Publications* author of numerous articles and books on monetary policy and macroeconomics; *Recreations* walking, cinema, theatre, watching Aston Villa FC; *Clubs* IOD; *Style—* Prof Michael Driscoll; ✉ Middlesex University, Trent Park, Bramley Road, London N14 4YZ (tel 020 8411 5606, fax 020 8411 5465, e-mail m.driscoll@mdx.ac.uk)

DRISSELL, Air Cde Peter James; s of Anthony Drissell (d 1978), of Bristol, and Alicia, *née* Miller; *b* 24 November 1955, Bristol; *Educ* Hartcliffe Sch Bristol, City Univ (BSc), RAF Coll Cranwell, KCL (MA), JSDC Greenwich (Advanced Staff Course), RCDS; *m* 27 Feb 1982, Pauline, *née* Anderson; *Career* cmmnd RAF Regt 1974, Sqdn Ldr 1988 OC 48 Sqdn RAF Regt 1989–91, Wing Cdr 1994, OC Ops Wing RAF Honington 1996–97, personal staff offr CAS 1997–98, RCDS 2003, Provost Marshal RAF 2004–05, Cmdt Gen RAF Regt and AO RAF Police 2005–07; dir Plan UK 2004–, tstee Chilterns Multiple Sclerosis Centre 2005–; FInstD 2006 (MInstD 1997), FCGI 2007; *Recreations* horse riding, fly fishing, walking, music; *Clubs* RAC, RAF; *Style—* Air Cdre Peter Drissell; ✉ 1 Farm Grove, Knotty Green, Buckinghamshire HP9 2UA (tel 07789 542982, e-mail peterdrissell@aol.com)

DRIVER, David John; s of Denis Alan Driver (d 1968), of Cambridge, and Mona Eileen, *née* Scott; *b* 4 August 1942; *Educ* Perse Sch Cambridge, Cambridge Sch of Art; *m* 27 Nov 1976, Sara Penelope, da of Ashley Rock; 1 s (Paul Robert Thomas b 28 Dec 1979), 1 da (Helen Rachel b 5 April 1984); *Career* freelance illustrator and designer for various publications since 1963 incl: Town, Queen, Vogue, Penguin Books, Observer Magazine, Sunday Times, Harpers Bazaar (re-design 1969), The Listener (re-design 1980); art ed Farm and Country (Thomson Organisation) 1963–67, asst art ed Woman's Mirror (IPC) 1967–68, art dir Cornmarket Press 1968–69, art ed and dep ed Radio Times 1969–81, freelance art dir Francis Kyle Gallery 1979–, head of design and asst ed The Times (News International) 1981–; designer: Royal Mail Christmas stamps 1991, Queen's Golden Wedding stamps 1997; winner various awards incl: Gold & Silver awards for Radio Times D&AD 1976, Editorial Award of Excellence Soc of Newspaper Design Awards (USA) 1987, 1989 and 1997, Newspaper Design Awards 1989 and 1994, Colour Newspaper of the Year and Features Design Awards 1992, Hon Dr of Letters Anglia Poly Univ 2001; *Books* The Art of Radio Times (ed, compiler and designer, 1981); designer: Graham Greene Country (by Paul Hogarth and Graham Greene), The Windsor Style (by Suzy Menkes), The Mediterranean Shore (by Paul Hogarth and Lawrence Durrell); *Recreations* cricket; *Style—* David Driver, Esq; ✉ The Times, Times

Newspapers Ltd, 1 Pennington Street, London E1 9XN (tel 020 7782 5000, fax 020 7782 5639, e-mail david.driver@thetimes.co.uk)

DRIVER, Olga Lindholm; *see:* Aikin, Olga Lindholm

DROGHEDA, 12 Earl of (I 1661); Henry Dermot Ponsonby Moore; also Baron Moore (I 1616 and UK 1954, by which latter title he sat in House of Lords) and Viscount Moore (I 1621); s of 11 Earl of Drogheda, KG, KBE (d 1989), and Joan Eleanor, *née* Carr (d 1989); *b* 14 January 1937; *Educ* Eton, Trinity Coll Cambridge (BA); *m* 1, 15 May 1968 (m dis 1972), Eliza, da of Stacy Barcroft Lloyd, Jr, of Philadelphia; m 2, 1978, Alexandra, da of Sir Nicholas Henderson, GCMG; 2 s (Benjamin Garrett Henderson, Viscount Moore b 1983, Hon Garrett Alexander b 1986), 1 da (Lady Marina Alice b 1988); *Heir* s, Viscount Moore; *Career* Lt Life Gds 1957; photographer (professional name Derry Moore); *Books* The Dream Come True, Great Houses of Los Angeles (with Brendan Gill, 1980), Royal Gardens (with George Plumptre, 1982), Stately Homes of Britain (with Sybilla Jane Flower, 1982), Washington, Houses of the Capital (with Henry Mitchell, 1982), The English Room (with Michael Pick, 1984), The Englishwoman's House (with Alvilde Lees-Milne, 1984), The Englishman's Room (with Alvilde Lees-Milne, 1986), The Gardens of Queen Elizabeth The Queen Mother (with the Marchioness of Salisbury, 1988), Evening Ragas, a photographer in India (1997), Inside the House of Lords (with Clive Aslet, 1998); *Clubs* Brooks's; *Style*— The Earl of Drogheda; ✉ 40 Ledbury Road, London W11 2AB (tel 020 7229 5950, fax 020 7221 8135, e-mail moorederry@aol.com)

DROMGOOLE, Dominic; *b* 1963; *Educ* Univ of Cambridge; *Career* prodr and dir; artistic dir Bush Theatre London 1990–96 (nat tour 1994), new plays dir Old Vic (working alongside Sir Peter Hall) 1997, artistic dir Oxford Stage Co 1998–2005 (prodr and dir of numerous prodns, plays directed incl Troilus and Cressida and Hay Fever), artistic dir Shakespeare's Globe Theatre 2005–; regular contributor to The Guardian and The Sunday Times; *Books* The Full Room (2001), Will and Me: How Shakespeare Took Over My Life (2006); *Style*— Dominic Dromgoole, Esq; ✉ Shakespeare's Globe, 21 New Globe Walk, Bankside, London SE1 9DT (tel 020 7902 1400, fax 020 7902 1401)

DROMGOOLE, June Kell; da of Robert Bonar Valentine (d 1982), of Dundee, and Alexandrina, *née* Kell (d 1958); *b* 1 August 1947; *Educ* Harris Acad Dundee, WRAC Coll Camberley; *m* 1, 1977 (m dis 1991), Peter Morrow; 1 s (Jamie Richard b 25 Aug 1980); m 2, 3 Aug 1991, Patrick Dromgoole; *Career* 2 Lt WRAC 1966–68; with Global Television Services Ltd 1968–70, asst ITV Network buyer Granada Television Ltd 1970–73, dir of sales (and 50 per cent shareholder) AML International Ltd 1973–84, md Southbrook International Television Co 1985–87, chief operating offr Palladium International Television Ltd 1987–90, head of purchased progs BBC Television 1990–97, head of prog acquisition BBC Broadcast 1997–98, controller Prog Acquisitions Channel Four TV Corporation 1998–2005; memb BAFTA; *Recreations* French food and wine, theatre, cinema; *Style*— Mrs June Dromgoole

DROMORE, Bishop of 1999–; Most Rev John (Thomas) McAreavey; s of John McAreavey (d 1980) and Mary Elisabeth (May); *b* 2 February 1949; *Educ* St Colman's Coll Newry, Nat Univ of Ireland Maynooth (BA), Pontifical Univ Maynooth (BD, STL), Pontifical Gregorian Univ Rome (JCD); *Career* ordained priest Maynooth 1973; prof of canon law Pontifical Univ Maynooth 1988–99, memb Armagh Regnl Marriage Tbnl 1979–92; sec Exec Ctee Int Cmmn on English in the Liturgy (ICEL) 2002; *Recreations* hill walking, swimming, reading; *Style*— The Most Rev the Bishop of Dromore; ✉ Bishop's House, 44 Armagh Road, Newry, Co Down BT35 6PN (tel 028 302 62444, fax 028 302 60496, e-mail bishopofdromore@btinternet.com)

DRONKE, Prof (Ernst) Peter Michael; s of A H R Dronke, and M M Dronke, *née* Kronfeld; *b* 30 May 1934; *Educ* Victoria Univ NZ (MA), Magdalen Coll Oxford (MA), Univ of Cambridge (MA); *m* 1960, Ursula Miriam, *née* Brown; 1 da; *Career* res fell Merton Coll Oxford 1958–61; Univ of Cambridge: lectr in medieval Latin 1961–79, fell Clare Hall 1964–, reader 1979–89, prof of medieval Latin lit 1989–; guest lectr Univ of Munich 1960, guest prof Centre d'Études Médiévales Poitiers 1969, Leverhulme fell 1973, W P Ker lectr Univ of Glasgow 1976, guest prof Univ Autónoma Barcelona 1977, visiting fell Humanities Res Centre Canberra 1978, visiting prof of medieval studies Westfield Coll London 1981–86, Matthews lectr Birkbeck Coll London 1983, Carl Newell Jackson lectr Harvard Univ 1992, O'Donnell lectr Univ of Toronto 1993, Barlow lectr UCL 1995; co ed: Mittellateinisches Jahrbuch 1977–, Premio Internazionale Ascoli Piceno 1988; author of essays in learned jls and symposia; hon pres Int Courtly Literature Soc 1974, corresponding fell Real Academia de Buenas Letras 1976; FBA 1984; *Books* Medieval Latin and the Rise of the European Love-Lyric (2 volumes, 1965–66), The Medieval Lyric (1968), Poetic Individuality in the Middle Ages (1970), Fabula (1974), Abelard and Heloise in Medieval Testimonies (1976), Barbara et Antiquissima Carmina (with Ursula Dronke, 1977), Bernardus Silvestris Cosmographia (ed, 1978), Introduction to Francesco Colonna Hypnerotomachia (1981), Women Writers of the Middle Ages (1984), The Medieval Poet and his World (1984), Dante and Medieval Latin Traditions (1986), Introduction to Rosvita, Dialoghi Drammatici (1986), A History of Twelfth Century Western Philosophy (1988), Hermes and the Sibyls (1990), Latin and Vernacular Poets of the Middle Ages (1991), Intellectuals and Poets in Medieval Europe (1992), Verse with Prose from Petronius to Dante (1994), Nine Medieval Latin Plays (1994); *Recreations* music, film, Brittany; *Style*— Prof Peter Dronke, FBA; ✉ 6 Parker Street, Cambridge CB1 1JL (tel 01223 359942); Clare Hall, Cambridge CB3 9AL (tel 01223 332360)

DROWNE, Steve John; s of Michael Drowne (d 2002), and Tina, *née* Viggers; *b* 10 December 1971, Launceston, Cornwall; *Educ* Shebbear Coll Devon; *m* 21 Nov 1999, Clare, *née* Hartfall; *Career* jockey 1997–; winner: Chively Park CPI, Molyglare Stakes, Prix D'Abbaye 2003 and 2005; Flat Race Ride of the Year 2002; *Recreations* shooting, skiing; *Style*— Stephen Drowne, Esq; ✉ 23 Hamblin Meadow, Hungerford, Berkshire RG17 0HJ (tel 01488 681145, e-mail dronste@aol.com)

DRUCKMAN, Paul Bryan; s of Leonard Druckman, of Sutton, Surrey, and Phoebe, *née* Hodes; *b* 23 December 1954, Bulawayo, Zimbabwe; *Educ* KCS Wimbledon, Univ of Warwick (PGCE); *m* 1983, Angela, *née* Samuel; 1 s (Alan b 9 Feb 1985), 1 da (Emma 21 Feb 1988); *Career* chartered accountant; dir Orchard Business Systems 1985–90, fndr and md Dit 1991–2001, md Orange Consulting 2001–04, pres ICAEW 2004–05, chm Clear Gp 2005–; non-exec dir: Access Accounts Ltd 2004–, Business Links for London 2004–07, Allen & Allen Gp 2006–, Rugged Logic 2007–; chm Consultative Ctees of Accounting Bodies (CCAB) 2004–05, dir Fin Reporting Cncl 2004–, memb Takeover Panel 2004–05, chm M Inst 2006–; FCA 1979, assoc memb Inst of Environmental Mgmnt 2002; *Recreations* sport particularly golf, tennis and scuba diving; *Style*— Paul Druckman, Esq; ✉ Clear Group, Charlton House, 179 Kingston Road, Surrey KT3 3SS (tel 020 8329 4900, e-mail paul.druckman@thecleargroup.com)

DRUMMOND, Colin Irwin John Hamilton; s of Rev William Balfour Drummond (d 1981), and Annie Rebecca, *née* Roy; *b* 22 February 1951, Belfast; *Educ* Trinity Coll of Music (LCTL, Colman Prize), Wadham Coll Oxford (MA), Harvard Grad Sch of Business Admin (Harkness fell, MBA); *m* 28 June 1975, Georgina, *née* Lloyd; 2 s (Colin Hugh Lloyd b 27 Nov 1981, Alexander George Balfour b 10 July 1984); *Career* official Economic Intelligence Dept Bank of England 1973–78, conslt Boston Consulting Gp 1978–84, exec dir Renold plc 1984–86, chief exec Yarns Div Coats Viyella plc 1986–92, chief exec Viridor Waste and exec dir Pennon Gp plc 1992–; memb Advsy Ctee on Business and the Environment 2003–05, chm Govt's Environmental Sector Advsy Gp 2005–, chm Integrated Pollution Mgmnt Knowledge Transfer Network 2007–; sr visiting fell Dept of Earth Sciences Univ of Oxford; organist and choirmaster St John the Baptist Church Wellington 1993–2006; Master Worshipful Co of Water Conservators 2007–08; CCMI 2002; *Recreations* sport, music, gardening; *Clubs* Oxford and Cambridge; *Style*— Colin Drummond, Esq; ✉ Pennon Group plc, Great Western House, Station Approach, Taunton TA1 1QW (tel 01823 721485, e-mail cdrummond@viridor-waste.co.uk)

DRUMMOND, David James; s of James Drummond, of Edinburgh, and Audrey Joan, *née* Morrison; *b* 4 August 1956; *Educ* George Watson's Coll Edinburgh, Univ of Edinburgh (BMus), RNCM Manchester; *m* 1, 25 June 1983 (m dis 1988), Jane Caroline, da of Derek Tregilges, of Perranporth, Cornwall; m 2, 9 April 1994, Elizabeth Kate, da of Tom Hutchinson; 2 da (Imogen Mary b 9 July 1997, Katherine Phyllis b 5 March 2004), 1 s (William Tavis b 26 Nov 2000); *Career* staff conductor and chorus master Stora Teatern Gothenburg 1982–84 (conducted Katerina Ismailova, The Turn of the Screw, Don Giovanni, Spöket på Canterville, Lo Sposo Senza Moglie), asst chorus master ENO 1984–88 (conducted Die Fledermaus, The Mikado, The Magic Flute), chorus master Scottish Opera 1988–90 (conducted Street Scene), musical dir London Oriana Choir 1996– (recordings incl: Everyman (by Walford Davies) 2004, If Love could say God's Name (DVD with Beth Nielsen Chapman) 2006); dir Music and Opera UCL 1990–2001: conducted Le Roi d'Ys 1992, Ruslan & Ludmilla 1993, César Franck's opera Hulda 1994 (world première), La Wally 1995, Ballad of Baby Doe 1996 and Heise's Drot og Marsk 1997 (both Br premières), Mignon 1998 Mazeppa 1999, Jewels of the Madonna 2000, Aulis Sallinen's Kullervo 2001 (Br première); conducted Boris Godunov (Kharkov Opera House, 1998); orchestras conducted include: Kharhov Philharmonic, London Mozart Players, BBC Concert Orch (recorded music for BBC Olympics 2000), Royal Philharmonic; currently: freelance conductor and vocal coach, opera coach Royal Coll of Music and Royal Acad of Music; *Recreations* squash, golf, hill walking, tai-kwon-do, football, languages, travel; *Style*— David Drummond, Esq; ✉ 50 Pinner View, Harrow, Middlesex HA1 4QD (tel 020 8861 1511, fax 020 8861 6092, e-mail upbeat@freeuk.com)

DRUMMOND, Gillian Vera (Gilly); DL (Hants 1994); da of Gavin Clark (d 1997), of Fawley, Hants, and Vera, *née* Royden (d 1998); *b* 15 September 1939, Clatterbridge, Cheshire; *Educ* Roedean, Poggio Imperiale Florence; *m* 1, 1958 (m dis 1978), Graham Turner Laing; 3 da (Sophie (Mrs Comninos) b 1960, Ariane (Mrs Koopman) b 1963, Laura b 1969); m 2, 1978, Maldwin Andrew Cyril Drummond; 1 s (Aldred b 1978); *Career* cmmr English Heritage 2002– (memb Historic Parks and Gardens Advsy Ctee 1988–2001, chm Historic Parks and Gardens Panel 2001–07); pres: Waterside Charities 1981–95, Blackfield Gardening Soc 1993–, Assoc of Gardens Tsts 1995– (chm 1992–95); vice-pres: Royal Southampton Horticultural Soc 1986–, Hampshire Gardens Tst 1996– (fndr chm 1984–); chm SW Region Historic Houses Assoc 2000–05; memb: Gardens and Parks Ctee RZS 1986–88, Gardens Ctee Historic Houses Assoc 1986–2000, Jt Mgmnt Ctee Sir George Staunton Country Park Havant 1988–96, Cncl of Mgmnt Sir Harold Hillier Gardens and Arboretum 1989–, Croome Park Forum 1996–, Advsy Gp Educn and Historic Built Environment Survey Attingham Tst 2001–03, Urban Green Spaces Taskforce ODPM 2001–; tstee: Solent Rescue 1988–98, Learning through Landscapes Tst 1991–, Gilbert White's House and the Oates Meml Museum 1992–, Chawton House Library 1993–, Countryside Educn Tst 1999–, Nat Maritime Museum 2005–, Chiswick House and Gardens Tst 2006–; advsr St Martin-in-the-Fields Appeal 2005–; sr judge Southern Region in Bloom 1986–2001; county pres St John Ambulance Hants 1990–2003; govr Millbrook Community Sch Southampton 1988–2005; Gold Veitch Meml Medal RHS 1996; *Recreations* gardening, sailing, art, architecture; *Clubs* Royal Yacht Squadron (lay assoc memb), Royal Cruising; *Style*— Mrs Gilly Drummond, DL, VMH; ✉ Stanswood Farm House, Fawley, Southampton SO45 1AB (tel 023 8089 1543); Wester Kames Castle, Port Bannatyne, Isle of Bute PA20 0QW

DRUMMOND, Maldwin Andrew Cyril; OBE (1990), JP (1963), DL (Hants 1976); s of Maj Cyril Augustus Drummond, JP, DL (d 1945), of Cadland House, and Mildred Joan, *née* Humphreys (d 1976); *b* 30 April 1932; *Educ* Eton, RAC Cirencester, Univ of Southampton; *m* 1, 1955 (m dis 1977), Susan, da of Sir Kenelm Cayley; 2 da (Frederica (Mrs Templer) b 1957, Annabella (Mrs Villers) b 1959); m 2, 18 Jan 1978, Gillian Vera (Gilly), da of Gavin Clark, of Fawley, Hampshire; 1 s (Aldred b 1978); *Career* Nat Serv The Rifle Bde 1950–52, Capt Queen Victoria's Rifles TA 1952–65; farmer and owner Manor of Cadland; dir: Southampton Harbour Bd and Br Tports Docks Bd 1965–75, Rothesay Seafoods 1968–92, Southern Water Authy 1983–86, Ocean Sound Ltd 1985–91; chm: Bldg Ctee STS Sir Winston Churchill 1964–66, Sail Trg Assoc 1967–72, Warrior (formerly Ships) Preservation Tst 1979–91, Maritime Tst 1980–89, Boat Ctee RNLI 1984–92, New Forest 9th Centenary Tst 1987–94, Heritage Coast Forum 1988–96, New Forest Ctee 1990–96; past pres Hampshire Field Club and Archaeological Soc, pres Shellfish Assoc of GB and NI 1987–; tstee: Mary Rose Tst 1976–91, Royal Naval Museum 1986–96; memb Ctee of Mgmnt RNLI 1971–2005; memb: New Forest DC 1957–65, Hampshire CC 1965–75; High Sheriff Hants 1980–81, countryside cmmr 1980–86; verderer of the New Forest 1961–90, official verderer 1999–2002; Freeman City of London 1986, Prime Warden Worshipful Co of Fishmongers 1996–97 (memb Ct 1986); younger bro Trinity House 1991–; Hon DSc: Bournemouth Univ 1994, Nottingham Trent Univ 1996; FRGS, FRSA, FSA 2003; *Books* Conflicts in an Estuary (1973), Secrets of George Smith Fisherman (ed and illustrator, 1973), Tall Ships (1976), Salt-Water Palaces (1979), The Yachtsman's Naturalist (with Paul Rodhouse, 1980), The New Forest (with Philip Allison, 1980), The Riddle (1985), West Highland Shores (1990), John Bute, An Informal Portrait (ed, 1996), The Book of the Solent (ed with Robin McInnis, 2001), After You Mr Lear 92007); *Recreations* sailing; *Clubs* Royal Yacht Squadron (cdre 1991–96), Royal Cruising, White's, Pratt's, Leander; *Style*— Maldwin Drummond, Esq, OBE, DL, DSc, FSA; ✉ Stanswood Farm House, Fawley, Southampton SO45 1AB (tel 023 8089 1543, e-mail office@cadland.org.uk); Manor of Cadland, Cadland House, Fawley, Southampton SO45 1AA (tel 023 8089 2039, fax 023 8024 3308); Wester Kames Castle, Isle of Bute PA20 0QW (tel 01700 503983)

DRUMMOND, Prof Michael Frank; s of Kenneth John Drummond (d 1973), and Ethel Irene, *née* Spencer; *b* 30 April 1948; *Educ* Atherstone GS, Univ of Birmingham (BSc, MCom), Univ of York (DPhil); *m* 8 June 1973, Margaret, da of James Brennan, of Tamworth, Staffs, 1 s (Thomas b 1980), 1 da (Kate b 1987); *Career* Univ of Birmingham: lectr 1978–84, sr lectr 1984–86, prof of health services management 1986–90; Univ of York: prof of economics 1990–, dir Centre for Health Economics 1995–; memb: North Warwickshire Health Authy 1982–90, Med Comm 1988–91; *Books* Principles of Economic Appraisal in Health Care (1980), Studies in Economic Appraisal in Health Care (1981), Economic Appraisal of Health Technology in the European Community (1987), Methods for the Economic Evaluation of Health Care Programmes (1987, 2nd ed 1997); *Recreations* walking, running, travel; *Style*— Prof Michael Drummond; ✉ Centre for Health Economics, University of York, Heslington, York YO10 5DD (tel 01904 213409, fax 01904 213402)

DRUMMOND, Rev Norman Walker; s of Edwin Payne Drummond (d 1971), of Greenock, and Jean Drummond, *née* Walker (d 1992); *b* 1 April 1952; *Educ* Merchiston Castle Sch Edinburgh, Fitzwilliam Coll Cambridge (MA), New Coll Edinburgh (BD); *m* 1976, Lady Elizabeth Kennedy, da of 7 Marquess of Ailsa (d 1994); 3 s (Andrew b 1977, Christian b 1986, Ruaraidh b 1993), 2 da (Margaret b 1980, Marie Clare b 1981); *Career* ordained as minister Church of Scot, cmmnd to serv as Chaplain to HM Servs Army 1976; chaplain: Depot Parachute Regt and Airborne Forces 1977–78, 1 Bn The Black Watch (Royal Highland Regt) 1978–82, Fettes Coll 1982–84, to Moderator of Gen Assembly of Church of Scot 1980, to Govr Edinburgh Castle 1990–92; headmaster Loretto Sch

1984–95, min of Kilmuir and Stenscholl Isle of Skye 1996–98; BBC nat govr and chm Broadcasting Cncl for Scot 1994–99, chm BBC Children in Need 1997–99; chaplain to HM The Queen in Scotland, memb Queen's Body Guard for Scotland (Royal Co of Archers); fndr and chm Columba 1400, Community and Int Leadership Centre Isle of Skye 1997–; chm: Drummond International 1999–, Community Action Network Scotland 2001–03, Lloyds TSB Fndn for Scotland 2003–; non-exec chm dir The Change Partnership Scotland 1999–2003, non-exec dir J & J Denholm Ltd 2002–; pres: Edinburgh Battalion The Boys' Brigade 1993–98, Victoria League for Overseas Students in Scot 1995–98; govr Gordonstoun Sch 1995–2000, govr The New Sch Butterstone 1999–2002, chm Aiglon Coll Switzerland 1999–2005; memb Scottish Ctee ICRF 1995–98, former tstee Fndn for Skin Research; former memb: Scottish Ctee Duke of Edinburgh's Award Scheme, Ct Heriot-Watt Univ; former chm Musselburgh and District Social Services; *Books* The First 25 Years - the Official History of the Kirk Session of The Black Watch (Royal Highland Regiment), Mother's Hands, The Spirit of Success - How to Connect Your Heart to Your Head in Work and Life; *Recreations* rugby football, cricket, golf, curling, traditional jazz; *Clubs* MCC, Free Foresters, New (Edinburgh), Hawks' (Cambridge); *Style*— Norman Drummond; ✉ 35 Drummond Place, Edinburgh EH3 6PW

DRUMMOND-MORAY OF ABERCAIRNY, William George Stirling Home; Laird of Abercairny; 2 (but eldest surviving) s of Maj James Drummond-Moray, twenty-first of Abercairny, and of Ardoch, Perthshire, JP, DL, by his w Jeanetta (twin da of Lt-Col Lord George Scott, OBE, JP, DL, 3 s of 6 Duke of Buccleuch and (8 of) Queensberry); *b* 22 August 1940; *Educ* Eton, RAC Cirencester; *m* 1, 7 Jan 1969 (m dis 1991), (Angela) Jane, da of Lt Cdr Michael Baring, RN (d 1954); 3 da (Anna b 1971, Frances b 1974, Georgina b 1979); m 2, 1991, Emma Moyra Rattray, er da of Capt James Rattray of Rattray; 1 da (Caroline b 1992); *Career* estate mangr; *Recreations* shooting, polo; *Style*— William Drummond-Moray of Abercairny; ✉ Abercairny, Crieff, Perthshire (tel 01764 653114, fax 01764 65206)

DRUMMOND-MURRAY OF MASTRICK, (William Edward) Peter Louis; s of Edward John Drummond-Murray of Mastrick (d 1976), and Eulalia Ildefonsa Wilhelmina Heaven (d 1988); *b* 24 November 1929; *Educ* Beaumont Coll; *m* 12 June 1954, Hon Barbara Mary Hope, 4 and yst da of 2 Baron Rankeillour, GCIE, MC (d 1958); 4 s, 1 da; *Career* dir of banks and financial cos until 1998; stockbroker; chief exec Hosp of St John and St Elizabeth London 1978–82; Slains Pursuivant of Arms to the Lord High Constable of Scotland the Earl of Erroll 1981–; Kt of Honour and Devotion SMOM 1971, Grand Cross of Honour and Devotion in Obedience 1984, genealogist SMOM 2000–05 (Chllr Br Assoc 1977–89), Delegate of Scotland and the Northern Marches 1989–98; former pres Murray Clan Soc, former chm Heraldry Soc of Scotland; Freeman City of London; KStJ 1988 (CStJ 1977); *Recreations* archaeology, genealogy, heraldry, baking, brewing, bookbinding, bookplate collecting; *Clubs* New (Edinburgh), Puffin's (Edinburgh); *Style*— Peter Drummond-Murray of Mastrick, Slains Pursuivant of Arms; ✉ 6/2 Huntingdon Place, Edinburgh EH7 4AT (tel and fax 0131 556 2913, e-mail p.drummond-murray@lineone.net)

DRUMMOND OF MEGGINCH, Capt Humphrey; MC (1945); formerly Humphrey ap Evans, changed name by decree of Court of Lord Lyon 1966; s of Maj James John Pugh Evans, MBE, MC (d 1974), of Lovesgrove, Aberystwyth; *b* 18 September 1922; *Educ* Eton, Trinity Coll Cambridge; *m* 2 June 1952, Cherry Drummond, Lady Strange (sixteenth holder of the peerage; d 2005); 3 s (one of whom, 17 Baron Strange, *qv*), 3 da; *Career* served 1942–45 with 1 Mountain Regt; Indian Political Serv 1947; gen sec Cncl for Preservation of Rural Wales 1947–51, Welsh rep of Nat Tst 1949–54; Gold Staff Offr coronation of HM Queen Elizabeth II; author and magazine contributor; fndr Kilspindie Basset Hounds; chm Soc of Authors (Scot) 1975–81; proprietor: Freeman City of London; *Books* Our Man in Scotland, The Queen's Man, The King's Enemy, Falconry, Falconry For You, Falconry in the East, Nazi Gold, Balkan Assault (ed); *Clubs* Garrick, New (Edinburgh); *Style*— Capt Humphrey Drummond of Megginch, MC; ✉ Tresco, 160 Kennington Road, London SE11 (tel 020 7735 3681); Megginch Castle, Errol, Perthshire PH2 7SW (tel 01821 642222, fax 01821 642708, e-mail 113400–250@compuserv.com)

DRUMMOND YOUNG, Hon Lord; James Edward Drummond Young; s of the late Duncan Drummond Young, MBE, DL, of Edinburgh, and Annette, *née* Mackay; *b* 17 February 1950; *Educ* John Watson's Sch Edinburgh, Sidney Sussex Coll Cambridge (BA), Harvard Law Sch (Joseph Hodges Choate Meml fell, LLM), Univ of Edinburgh (LLB); *m* 1991, Elizabeth Mary, da of John Campbell-Kease; 1 da; *Career* admitted to Faculty of Advocates 1976, standing jr counsel Bd of Inland Revenue 1986–88, QC 1988, advocate depute 1999–2001, senator Coll of Justice 2001–, chm Scottish Law Cmmn 2007–; *Books* The Law of Corporate Insolvency in Scotland (with J B St Clair, 3 edn 2004), Stair Memorial Encyclopaedia of the Laws of Scotland (contrib, 1989); *Recreations* music, travel; *Style*— The Hon Lord Drummond Young; ✉ Parliament House, Edinburgh EH1 1RQ (tel 0131 225 2595, fax 0131 240 6711)

DRURY, David Robert; s of Albert Drury (d 1970), of Leeds, and Anne, *née* Crewe (d 1970); *Educ* Temple Moor GS Leeds, Leeds Coll of Art (BA); *m* 1, 1970 (m dis), Pamela Mary, da of George Ratcliffe; 1 s (Benjamin b 4 Sept 1975), 1 da (Rebecca b 8 Jan 1977); m 2, 1984 (m dis), Janet Elizabeth, da of Reginald Carter; 1 s (Samuel b 23 Sept 1984); 2 da by Judith Anne Hayes (Bethan b 29 July 1991, Rhiannon b 8 Dec 1993); *Career* film and television director and producer; dir: Forever Young 1984, Intrigue 1988, Children of the North 1990 (winner RTS Award for best series), The Secret Agent 1992, Bad Company 1993 (winner Samuelson Int Film and TV Award for best series), Prime Suspect III 1993 (winner BAFTA Award for best drama series, American Critics Award and Banff TV Festival Award for best series, Emmy for best mini-series), Runway One 1995, Rhodes (series) 1995, Hostile Waters 1997, The Unknown Soldier 1998, Trust 1999, Tough Love 2000, Bomber 2000, The Swap 2002, The Cry 2002, Family (series) 2003, The Crooked Man 2003, Messiah: The Promise 2004, Marian, Again 2005, The Brief 2005, Love Lies Bleeding 2006, Fallen Angel 2006; film dir: Defence of the Realm 1986 (selected for dirs' fortnight Cannes Film Festival, winner Rimini Film Festival Award for best dir, Madrid Film Festival Award best film); *Clubs* Groucho, Century; *Style*— David Drury, Esq; ✉ c/o PFD, Drury House, 34–43 Russell Street, London WC2B 5HA

DRURY, Ian Charles; s of Arthur Drury, of Winchester, and Mary Drury; *b* 13 February 1961, Hemel Hempstead, Herts; *Educ* Peter Symonds' GS Winchester, New Coll Oxford (MA); *m* 20 May 2005, Joanna, *née* Abercrombie-Gould-Fletcher; 1 s (James Edward Browning b 20 Dec 1991), 1 da (Sophie Anne Marie b 20 May 1994); *Career* ed Aerospace Publishing 1984–94, editorial dir HarperCollins Publishers 1994–2001, publishing dir Cassell & Co 2001–03, publishing dir Weidenfeld & Nicholson 2003–; memb: Br Cmmn for Military Hist 1996–, RUSI 2001–; *Publications* The Russo-Turkish War (1990), Verdun (1992), Jutland (1994), Hitler's War on Russia (2007); *Recreations* freemasonry, long distance running, film and theatre; *Style*— Ian Drury, Esq; ✉ Weidenfeld & Nicolson, The Orion Publishing Group, 5 Upper St Martin's Lane, London WC2H 9EA (tel 020 7420 5620, e-mail ian.drury@orionbooks.co.uk)

DRURY, John Kenneth; s of John Kenneth Drury, of Paisley and Elizabeth Laird McNeil, *née* Pattison; *b* 23 January 1947; *Educ* Paisley GS, Univ of Glasgow (MB ChB, PhD); *m* 16 July 1974, Gillian Ruth Alexandra, da of Dr Thomas Gilmore, of Paisley; 1 da (Sarah b 1978), 1 s (Colin b 1981); *Career* res fell Inst of Physiology Univ of Glasgow, conslt gen surgn with interest in peripheral vascular surgery and clinical dir of gen surgery Victoria Infirmary NHS Tst Glasgow 1987–, hon clinical sr lectr Univ of Glasgow 1987– (memb Faculty of Med 1992–95, memb Univ Senate 1993–2000); RCPS Glasgow: hon registrar for surgical examinations 2001–04, dir of surgical examinations 2004–; RCS Glasgow: examiner in fellowship, memb Intercollegiate Ctee for Basic Surgical Examinations 2003–; Scottish Audit Surgical Mortality: memb Mgmnt Ctee 2003–, vascular coordinator 2004–; author of papers on gen and vascular surgery; memb: Ctee Paisley RNLI, Cncl Southern Med Soc, Vascular Soc GB 1987, European Soc of Vascular Surgery; FRCS 1978; *Recreations* yachting, squash, golf, skiing, local art; *Style*— John Drury, Esq; ✉ 10 Main Road, Castlehead, Paisley, Renfrewshire PA2 6AJ (tel 0141 8894512); Department of Surgery, Victoria Infirmary, Langside, Glasgow G42 9TY (tel 0141 201 5464)

DRURY, Jolyon Victor Paul; s of Alfred Paul Dalou Drury (d 1987), and Enid Marie, *née* Solomon (d 1996); *b* 19 November 1946; *Educ* Tonbridge, Pembroke Coll Cambridge (exhibitioner, DipArch, MA); *m* 25 April 1975, Christine Evelyn Cary, da of Dr John Gilson, CBE; 2 s (Adrian John Jolyon b 24 Nov 1977, Charles Worthington Paul b 26 May 1981); *Career* Arup Assocs 1971–75, fndr Jolyon Drury Consultancy 1975–2000, Arup JDC 2000–03, dir Surge Logistics Conslts 2005–; Lt-Col Engineer and Logistics Staff Corps 2004–; Freeman City of London 2005, Liveryman Worshipful Co of Carmen 2005; RIBA 1972, FIMH 1984, FILog 1993, FILT 2000, FCIT 2000, FCILT 2004; *Publications* Building and Planning for Industrial Storage and Distribution (with Peter Falconer, 1975, updated 2003), Factories, Planning, Design and Modernisation (1981), Automated Warehouses (1988), Revelation to Revolution: The Legacy of Samuel Palmer (2005); *Recreations* small holding, France, etchings; *Style*— Jolyon Drury, Esq; ✉ Woodside, Potters Corner, Ashford, Kent TN26 1AE

DRURY, Martin Dru; CBE (2001); s of Walter Neville Dru Drury, TD (d 1999), of Edenbridge, Kent, and Rae, *née* Sandiland (d 2002); *b* 22 April 1938; *Educ* Rugby; *m* 5 Jan 1971, Elizabeth Caroline, da of Hon Sir Maurice Bridgeman, KBE (d 1980), of Selham, W Sussex; 2 s (Matthew b 8 Aug 1972, Joseph b 18 June 1977), 1 da (Daisy b 6 Sept 1974); *Career* 2 Lt 3 Hussars 1957; broker at Lloyd's 1959–65, Mallett & Son (Antiques) Ltd 1965–73; National Tst: historic bldgs rep and advsr on furniture 1973–81, historic bldgs sec 1981–95, dep DG 1992–96, DG 1996–2001, memb Arts Panel 2004–; chm Landmark Tst 1992–95 and 2001–, chm Stowe Advsy Panel 2005, dir Arundel Castle Tst Ltd 1987–95, vice-chm Attingham Tst; memb: Fabric Advsy Ctee St Paul's Cathedral 1991–, Cncl Georgian Gp 1994–, Cncl UK Overseas Territories Conservation Forum 2000–06, Exec Ctee Soc for the Protection of Historic Buildings 2006–; tstee: Heritage of London Tst 1996–, The Wallace Collection 2001–; cmmr Royal Hosp Chelsea 2002–; Esher Award for services to the protection of historic buildings 2002; memb Ct of Assts Worshipful Co of Goldsmiths (Prime Warden 2005–06); Hon Dr Arts Univ of Greenwich 2000; FSA 1992; *Clubs* Brooks's, Pratt's, Seaview Yacht; *Style*— Martin Drury, Esq, CBE, FSA; ✉ 3 Victoria Rise, London SW4 0PB (tel and fax 020 7622 9688, e-mail drury@vicrise.fsworld.co.uk)

DRURY, Stephen Patrick; s of Patrick Keith Drury (d 1992), and Anne Rosemary, *née* Major-Lucas; *b* 20 May 1954; *Educ* Charterhouse, Oriel Coll Oxford (MA); *m* 25 June 1983, Deborah Ann, da of late Wilfred McBrien Swain, OBE; 2 s (Patrick b 1984, Benjamin b 1993), 1 da (Frances b 1987); *Career* called to the Bar 1977, admitted slr 1980, admitted slr Hong Kong 1984, ptnr Holman Fenwick & Willan 1985– (joined 1978); visiting lectr in ship fin law Business Sch City Univ 1990–; memb Cncl: Amateur Rowing Assoc 1980–84, Hong Kong Amateur Rowing Assoc 1984–87; licensed umpire Amateur Rowing Assoc 1999; Freeman City of London, Liveryman Worshipful Co of Merchant Taylors 1988; *Books* Arrest of Ships (vol 6, 1987); *Recreations* rowing, golf; *Clubs* Kingston Rowing, Royal Hong Kong Yacht, Effingham Golf, Lansdowne; *Style*— Stephen Drury, Esq; ✉ Holman Fenwick & Willan, Marlow House, Lloyds Avenue, London EC3N 3AL (tel 020 7488 2300, fax 020 7481 0584, e-mail stephen.drury@hfw.co.uk)

DRYDEN, Sir John Stephen Gyles; 11 Bt (GB 1733), of Ambrosden, Oxon; and 8 Bt (GB 1795), of Canons-Ashby, Northants; s of Sir Noel Percy Hugh Dryden, 10 Bt (d 1970; 6 in descent from Sir Erasmus Dryden, 6 Bt, bro of the poet John Dryden), and Rosamund Mary, *née* Scrope (d 1994); *b* 26 September 1943; *Educ* The Oratory; *m* 1970, Diana Constance, da of Cyril Tomlinson (d 2000), of Wellington, NZ; 1 s (John Frederick Simon b 1976), 1 da (Caroline Diana Rosamund b 1980); *Heir* s, John Dryden; *Style*— Sir John Dryden, Bt; ✉ Spinners, Fairwarp, East Sussex TN22 3BE

DRYSDALE, Prof David Douglas (Dougal); s of David Drysdale (d 1979), of Dunfermline, Fife, and Christina Campbell, *née* Rae (d 1988); *b* 30 September 1939; *Educ* Edinburgh Acad, Univ of Edinburgh (BSc), Univ of Cambridge (PhD); *m* 8 Aug 1964, Judyth, *née* McIntyre; 3 s (David John b 22 July 1965, Andrew James b 8 July 1967, Peter Robert b 4 May 1971); *Career* post doctoral research fell Dept of Chemistry Univ of Toronto 1966–67, research lectureship Dept of Physical Chemistry Univ of Leeds 1971–74 (post doctoral research fell 1967–71); Univ of Edinburgh: lectr Dept of Fire Engrg 1974–90, reader in fire safety engrg Dept of Civil and Environmental Engrg 1990–98, prof of fire safety engrg 1998–2004 (prof emeritus 2004–); visiting prof Centre for Firesafety Studies Worcester Poly Inst MA 1982, visiting prof Tianjin Inst of Technol 2001; co-ordinator ODA China Fire Science Trg Project 1993–98; chm Int Assoc for Fire Safety Science 2002–05; memb: Soc of Fire Protection Engrs (USA), Combustion Inst, Forensic Science Soc, Int Assoc of Fire Safety Science; ed Fire Safety Jl, memb Editorial Bd Soc of Fire Protection Engrs Handbook of Fire Protection Engrg (fourth edn); author of numerous papers in learned jls; Fire Research lectr Fire Research Station Building Research Estab 1995, Howard W Emmons lectr Worcester Poly Inst MA 1995; Man of the Year Soc of Fire Protection Engrs (USA) 1983, Arthur B Guise Medal Soc of Fire Protection Engrs (USA) 1995, Kawagoe Medal Int Assoc for Fire Safety Science 2002, Rasbash Medal Inst of Fire Engrs 2005; CEng 1999, FRSE 2002, FSFPE 2004, MRSC, FIFireE; *Books* Introduction to Fire Dynamics (1985, 2 edn 1998); *Recreations* music, hill walking, golf; *Style*— Prof Dougal Drysdale

du BOULAY, Prof Clair Evelyn; da of Malcolm Munday, of Speen, Berks, and Maureen, *née* Marshall; *b* 27 December 1952, Adelaide, Aust; *Educ* St Albans HS for Girls, Univ of Southampton (BM, DM), Univ of Wales Coll of Med (MSc); *m* 1, 22 Jan 1977, Mark du Boulay; 1 da (Alexandra b 16 Nov 1983), 1 s (Edward b 6 May 1986); m 2, 24 Feb 1996, Frank Smith; *Career* house surgn Surgical Unit Royal S Hants Hosp Southampton 1976–77, house physician Royal Hants Co Hosp Winchester 1977, med offr Wessex Regnl Blood Transfusion Serv 1977, SHO and registrar Dept of Pathology Southampton Gen Hosp 1978–80, lectr in pathology Univ of Southampton 1980–84, clinical scientist MRC Radiobiology Unit Harwell 1984–86; Southampton Univ Hosps Tst: sr lectr in pathology 1984–2005, conslt in histopathology 1987–2005, postgrad clinical tutor 1997–2000, dir of med educn 2000–2005; dean Wessex Inst of Postgrad Educn 2005–; memb MRC Soft Tissue Tumour Panel 1984–89; RCPath: dir of continuing professional devpt 1998–2001, dir Professional Standards Unit 2001–03, vice-pres 2002–05, rep Faculty of Pathology Coll of Physicians Ireland 2002–; memb: Pathological Soc of GB and I 1984–99, Br Soc of Gastro-Enterology, Assoc of Clinical Pathologists, Int Acad of Pathology (memb Cncl 1989–92), Assoc for the Study of Med Educn (memb Cncl 1996–2000, treas 1997–2000); FRCPath 1994 (MRCPath 1982), Hon FRCPI 2006; *Publications* Pathology: a core text of basic pathological processes with self-assessment (co-author, 1997), The Good CPD Guide (co-author, 1999), Master Medicine: Pathology (co-author, 2 edn 2003); author of 35 peer reviewed pubns on pathology and med educn; *Style*— Prof Clair du Boulay; ✉ Wessex Institute, Highcroft, Romsey Road, Winchester SO22 5DH (tel 01962 892737, e-mail clair.duboulay@nesc.nhs.uk)

du CROS, Sir Claude Philip Arthur Mallet; 3 Bt (UK 1916), of Canons, Middlesex; s of Capt Sir Philip Harvey du Cros, 2 Bt (d 1975), and Matilde Dita, *née* Mallet (d 1993); *b* 22 December 1922; *m* 1, 1953 (m dis 1974), Christine Nancy (d 1988), da of F E Bennett, of Spilsby, Lincs, and former w of George Tordoff; 1 s (Julian Claude Arthur Mallet b 1955); m 2, 1974 (m dis 1982), Margaret Roy, da of late Roland James Frater, of Gosforth, Northumberland; *Heir* s, Julian du Cros; *Career* farmer; *Style*— Sir Claude du Cros, Bt; ✉ Longmeadow, Ballaugh Glen, Ramsey, Isle of Man

DU-FEU, Vivian John; *Educ* Univ of Cardiff; *Career* admitted slr 1979, early career in Employment Law, joined Eversheds Phillips & Buck (now Eversheds) 1983, currently chm Eversheds Human Resources Gp; pt/t lectr in labour law Univ of Cardiff 1983–87 (pt/t tutor 1981–83); dir Principle Training Ltd; memb Croner Editorial Advsy Bd; FIPD; *Books* The Conduct of Proceedings Before Industrial Tribunals, Protecting Your Business and Confidential Information (co-author 1992), Collective Labour Law (co-author 1992), Procedure in Industrial Tribunal Cases (co-author 1992), Flexible Working Practices (contrib 1996), Employment Law in the NHS (co-author 1996), EU Comparative Labour Law (co-ed, 2001); *Style*— Vivian Du-Feu, Esq; ✉ Eversheds, 1 Callaghan Square, Cardiff CF10 5BT (tel 029 2047 1147, fax 029 2046 4347, DX 33016 Cardiff, e-mail vivdufeu@eversheds.com)

DU NOYER, Paul Anthony; s of Anthony George Du Noyer, of Liverpool, and Jean, *née* Moran; *b* 21 May 1954; *Educ* Bootle Salesian Coll, Wigan Tech Coll, LSE (BScEcon); *m* 25 June 1977, Una Mary O'Farrell, da of Edward Farrell; 2 s (Edward Paul b 22 Feb 1984, Daniel Paul b 25 June 1992); *Career* freelance journalist 1978–80, asst ed New Musical Express 1983–85 (staff writer 1980–83), ed Q magazine 1990–92 (asst ed 1986–90), ed Mojo magazine 1993–95, ed dir Emap Digital Music 1999–2001, assoc ed Word magazine 2002–; *Books* The Story of Rock'n'Roll (1995), We All Shine On: John Lennon's Solo Songs (1997), Liverpool: Wondrous Place (2002); *Style*— Paul Du Noyer, Esq; ✉ c/o Word magazine, 90 Pentonville Road, London N1 9HS (tel 020 7520 8625)

du PLESSIS, Jan Petrus; *b* 22 January 1954; *Educ* Univ of Stellenbosch SA; *Career* with International Div Rembrandt Group Ltd 1981–88, fin dir Compagnie Financière Richemont AG Switzerland (ultimate parent co of Rothmans International) 1988–2004, dir Richemont International Ltd 1990–2004; non-exec chm: British American Tobacco plc 2004– (non-exec dir 1999–), RHM plc 2005–07; non-exec dir Lloyds TSB 2005–; *Style*— Jan du Plessis, Esq

DU SAUTOY, Prof Marcus Peter Francis; *Career* prof of mathematics Univ of Oxford, fell Wadham Coll Oxford; EPSRC sr media fell; memb: Science and Society Ctee Royal Soc 1999–2005, Dialogue in Med Science and Society Assoc of Med Research Charities 2003–; judge: Crighton Medal London Mathematical Soc 2003 and 2006, Aventis Science Book Prize 2003, BBC 4 Samuel Johnson Non-Fiction Book Prize 2005; Royal Instn Christmas lectr 2006; presenter Mindgames (BBC 4), presenter The Music of the Primes (BBC4) 2005; Berwick Prize London Mathematical Soc 2001; *Books* The Music of the Primes: Why an Unsolved Problem in Mathematics Matters (2003), Finding Moonshine: A Mathematician's Journey Through Symmetry (2008); *Style*— Prof Marcus du Sautoy; ✉ Mathematical Institute, University of Oxford, 24–29 St Giles', Oxford OX1 3LB

du VIVIER, Dr Anthony Wilfred Paul; s of Maj Paul Edward du Vivier (d 1967), and Joan Beryl, *née* Swann; *b* 16 June 1944; *Educ* Ampleforth, Bart's Med Sch (MD); *m* 13 Aug 1977, Judith Vivienne, da of late Cdr Reginald Sidney Brett, RN; *Career* conslt dermatologist KCH London 1978–; FRCP; *Clubs* RSM; *Style*— Dr Anthony du Vivier; ✉ Department of Dermatology, King's College Hospital, London SE5 9RS (tel 020 7346 3258/3579); 62 Wimpole Street, London W1G 8AJ (tel 020 7935 6465, fax 020 7935 5014, e-mail anthonyduvivier@aol.com)

DUBERLY, (Archibald) Hugh; CBE (1996); s of Cdr Archibald Gray, RN, DSO, DL (d 1991), and Grey Cunliffe, *née* Duberly; name changed by deed poll 1963; *b* 4 April 1942, Huntingdon; *Educ* Winchester; *m* 4 Nov 1967, Sarah Elizabeth Duberly, DL, da of Maj-Gen I A Robertson, CB, MBE, DL; 2 s (James Gray b 24 Sept 1968, Harry Grey b 9 Oct 1975), 1 da (Kate Saffron b 2 April 1971); *Career* cncllr Hunts DC 1979–2004; High Sheriff Cambs 1991–92, HM Lord-Lt Cambs 2003– (DL 1989); cmmr Crown Estate 2002–; dir Agricultural Mortgage Corp plc 1995–2002; pres CLA 1993–95; chm: Kimbolton Sch 1992–2000, Ely Diocesan Bd of Fin 1992–, Papworth Tst 1995–, Shuttleworth Tst 2001–; *Clubs* Boodle's, Nairn Golf; *Style*— Hugh Duberly, Esq, CBE

DUBOWITZ, Prof Victor; s of Charley Dubowitz, and Olga, *née* Schattel; *b* 6 August 1931; *Educ* Beaufort West Central HS, Univ of Cape Town (BSc, MB ChB, MD), Univ of Sheffield (PhD); *m* 10 July 1960, Lilly Magdalena Suzanne, *née* Sebok; 4 s (David b 1963, Michael b 1964, Gerald b 1965, Daniel b 1969); *Career* res assoc (histochemistry) Royal Postgrad Med Sch 1958–60, clinical asst Queen Mary's Hosp for Children Carshalton 1958–60, lectr in clinical pathology Nat Hosp for Nervous Diseases 1960–61, lectr in child health Univ of Sheffield 1961–65 (sr lectr 1965–67), reader in child health and developmental neurology Univ of Sheffield 1967–72, prof of paediatrics Univ of London 1972–96 (prof emeritus 1996–), hon conslt paediatrician Hammersmith Hosp 1972–; dir Muscle Res Centre 1972–96, dir Therapeutic Studies European Neuromuscular Centre (ENMC) Holland 1999–2003; pres: Br Paediatric Neurology Assoc 1992–1994, European Paediatric Neurology Soc 1993–97, World Muscle Soc 1995–, Med Art Soc 1997–2000; Jean Hunter Prize RCP 1987; FRCP 1972, Hon FRCPCH 2000; Cdr Order Constantine the Great 1980, Arvo Ylppo Gold Medal Finland 1982, Gaetano Conte Gold Medal Italy 1991, Cornelia de Lange Medal The Netherlands 1997, James Spence Gold Medal RCPCH 2007; *Books* Developing and Diseased Muscle A Histochemical Study (1968), The Floppy Infant (2 edn, 1980), Muscle Biopsy - A Modern Approach (2 edn, 1985, 3 edn 2006), Gestational Age of the Newborn - A Clinical Manual (1977), Muscle Disorders in Childhood (2 edn, 1995), Neurological Assessment of the Preterm and Full-term Infant (1981, 2 edn 1999), A Colour Atlas of Muscle Disorders in Childhood (1989), A Colour Atlas of Brain Disorders in the Newborn (1990), Ramblings of a Peripatetic Paediatrician (2005); *Recreations* sculpting, hiking, photography; *Style*— Prof Victor Dubowitz; ✉ Dubowitz Neuromuscular Centre, Department of Paediatrics, Imperial College London, Hammersmith Campus, Du Cane Road, London W12 0NN (tel 020 8383 3148, fax 020 8905 5922)

DUBS, Baron (Life Peer UK 1994), of Battersea in the London Borough of Wandsworth; Alfred (Alf) Dubs; *Educ* LSE (BSc); *Career* MP (Lab) Battersea S (later Battersea) 1979–87, Parly under sec NI Office 1997–99; dir Refugee Cncl 1988–95, dep chm ITC 2000–01, chm Broadcasting Standards Cmmn 2001–04; sits as Lab peer in House of Lords, chair Lab Pty in House of Lords 2000–05, memb House of Lords Select Ctee on the EU; *Recreations* walking in the Lake District; *Style*— The Rt Hon the Lord Dubs; ✉ House of Lords, London SW1P 0PW (tel 020 7219 3590)

DUCIE, 7 Earl of (UK 1837); David Leslie Moreton; also Baron Ducie (GB 1763) and Baron Moreton (UK 1837); s of 6 Earl of Ducie (d 1991), and Alison May, *née* Bates; *b* 20 September 1951; *Educ* Cheltenham Coll, Wye Coll London (BSc); *m* 1975, Helen, da of M L Duchesne, of Brussels; 1 s (James Berkeley, Lord Moreton b 1981), 1 da (Lady Claire Alison b 1984); *Heir* s, Lord Moreton; *Style*— The Rt Hon the Earl of Ducie; ✉ e-mail office@tortworthestate.com

DUCKWORTH, His Hon Brian Roy; DL (Lancs); s of Eric Roy Duckworth (d 1972); *b* 26 July 1934; *Educ* Sedbergh, Univ of Oxford (MA); *m* 1964, Nancy Carolyn, da of Christopher Holden (d 1972); 3 s, 1 da; *Career* called to the Bar 1958; recorder of the Crown Court 1972–83, circuit judge (Northern Circuit) 1983–2004 (dep circuit judge 2004–), liaison judge to Chorley and S Ribble Magistracy 1992–2004; hon pres S Cumbria Magistracy 1987–92; memb: Lancs Probation Ctee 1990–2001, Lord-Lts' Magistracy Ctee 1992–2004, Ctee Cncl of Circuit Judges 1996–2004, dep sr judge Sovereign Base Area Ct Cyprus 1998–; chm Samlesbury Hall Tst 1992–; memb Ct Lancaster Univ 2002–; vice-pres Blackburn Branch Prayer Book Soc; *Recreations* golf, sailing, gardening; *Clubs* Pleasington Golf; *Style*— His Hon Brian Duckworth, DL

DUCKWORTH, Simon D'Olier; s of John Alexander D'Olier Duckworth (d 1988), of Wimbledon, and Anne Judith, o c of Brig P M Medill, DSO; *b* 16 November 1964, London; *Educ* KCS, Girton Coll Cambridge (organ exhibitioner, MA); *Career* Coll of Arms 1993–2001, clerk Gunmakers' Co 2001–03; dir: Fidelity European Values plc 2003–, Barings Common Investment Fund 2004–; memb: Ct of Common Cncl City of London 2000– (memb Finance and Investment Ctees 2002–), City of London Police Authy 2002– (dep chm 2006–), Strategic Policing Policy Gp Assoc of Police Authorities (APA) 2007–, Advsy Bd City Univ 2006– (memb Cncl 2001–06); clerk Queen's Chapel of the Savoy 1999–; tstee: Lord Mayor's 800th Anniversary Awards Tst 2003–, Cobra Fndn 2006–; memb RFCA 2002–; Liveryman Skinners' Co 1998–, memb Parish Clerks' Co 2000–; OStJ 2005 (SBStJ 2001); *Recreations* cooking, collecting claret, church music; *Clubs* Brooks's, University Pitt (hon sec 1989), Guildhall, Newmarket and Suffolk Real Tennis; *Style*— Simon Duckworth, Esq; ✉ 4 City Wall House, Wormwood Street, London EC2M 1RQ (tel 020 7588 6670, e-mail simon.duckworth@cityoflondon.gov.uk)

DUCKWORTH-CHAD, Anthony Nicholas George; OBE (1999), DL (Norfolk 1994); s of A J S Duckworth (d 1993), of Southacre House, King's Lynn, Norfolk; *b* 20 November 1942; *Educ* Eton, RAC Cirencester; *m* 6 May 1970, Elizabeth Sarah, da of Capt C B H Wake-Walker (d 1998), of East Bergholt Lodge, Suffolk; 2 s (James b 1972, William b 1975), 1 da (Davina b 1978); *Career* farmer and landowner; memb: Walsingham RDC 1963–74, North Norfolk DC 1974–95 (chm 1987–89); pres: Norfolk branch CLA 1997–2002 (chm 1977–78), Royal Norfolk Agricultural Assoc 2006; govr Greshams Sch 1974– (chm 2005–); High Sheriff Norfolk 1992; Prime Warden Worshipful Co of Fishmongers 2004; *Recreations* country sports; *Clubs* White's, Pratt's; *Style*— Anthony Duckworth-Chad, Esq, OBE, DL; ✉ 5 Cumberland Street, London SW1V 4LS; Pynkney Hall, East Rudham, King's Lynn, Norfolk PE31 6TF

DUDBRIDGE, Prof Glen; s of George Victor Dudbridge, and Edna Kathleen, *née* Cockle; *b* 2 July 1938; *Educ* Bristol GS, Magdalene Coll Cambridge (MA, PhD), New Asia Inst of Advanced Chinese Studies Hong Kong; *m* 16 Sept 1965, Sylvia Lo Fung-Young, da of Lo Tak-Tsuen (d 1981); 1 s (Frank b 1967), 1 da (Laura b 1968); *Career* Nat Serv RAF 1957–59; jr res fell Magdalene Coll Cambridge 1965, fell Wolfson Coll Oxford 1966–85 (emeritus fell 1985); visiting prof Univ of Calif Berkeley 1998 (visiting assoc prof 1980); visiting assoc prof Yale Univ 1972–73, fell Magdalene Coll and prof of Chinese Univ of Cambridge 1985–89; Univ of Oxford: lectr in modern Chinese 1965–85, fell UC 1989–2005 (emeritus fell 2005), prof of Chinese 1989–94, Shaw prof of Chinese 1994–2005; hon memb Chinese Acad of Social Scis 1996; FBA 1984; *Books* The Hsi-yu chi: a study of antecedents to the 16th century Chinese novel (1970), The legend of Miao-shan (1978 (revised 2004), Chinese edn 1990), The Tale of Li Wa: study and critical edn of a Chinese story from the 9th century (1983), Religious Experience and Lay Society in T'ang China (1995), Lost Books of Medieval China (2000), Books, Tales and Vernacular Culture: papers on China (2005); *Style*— Prof Glen Dudbridge, FBA; ✉ University College, Oxford OX1 4BH

DUDDING, Richard Scarbrough; s of Sir John Scarbrough Dudding (d 1986), and Enid Grace, *née* Gardner; *b* 29 November 1950; *Educ* Cheltenham Coll, Jesus Coll Cambridge (MA); *m* 11 July 1987, Priscilla Diana, *née* Russell; 2 s (Edwin Charles Scarbrough b 19 Sept 1987, John Russell b 4 April 1989); *Career* DOE (latterly DETR, then DTLR): joined 1972, private sec to John Smith, MP 1976–78, princ 1977, seconded to Overseas Containers Ltd 1983–85, asst sec 1984, sec to Ctee of Enquiry into Conduct of Local Govt 1985–86, head Fin, Gen and Housing Div 1986–88, Water Privatisation Team 1989–90, under sec 1990, dir Central Fin 1990–93, dir Pollution Control and Waste 1993–96, princ establishments offr 1996–97, DG Strategy and Corp Servs 1997–2002; dir for environment and economy Oxon CC 2003–; *Recreations* family, gardening, walking; *Style*— Richard Dudding

DUDDING, Rodger Ian; s of Arthur Leopold Frederick Dudding (d 1970), and Lorna Iris, *née* Sayer (d 1999); *b* 21 December 1937, Gillingham, Kent; *Educ* various schs, Royal Naval Tech Sch Chatham Naval Dockyard; *m* 7 Jan 1961, Gloria Elaine, *née* Davies; 1 s (Guy Oliver b 28 March 1966), 1 da (Harriet Louise b 25 Jan 1968); *Career* qualified naval engr 1959 (discharged due to injury), sales and mktg positions Rembrandt/Rothmans Cigarette Gp 1959–67, sales rising to vice-pres American Machine and Foundry 1967–70; fndr: Lonsto (Int) Ltd 1970– (introduced queue mgmnt systems to UK), Dudrich (Hldgs) Ltd 1970– (largest portfolio of lock-up garages in UK); FIP 1962, FBIM 1965, FInstD 1970; *Recreations* business, classic cars and motorcycles; *Clubs* Bentley Drivers; *Style*— Rodger Dudding, Esq; ✉ Lonsto (International) Limited, Lonsto House, 276 Chase Rd, London N14 6HA (tel 020 8882 8575, fax 020 8886 6676, website www.lonsto.co.uk)

DUDDRIDGE, James; MP; *Educ* Crestwood Sch, Huddersfield New Coll, Wells Blue Sch, Univ of Essex; *m* Katy; *Career* retail and merchant banker Barclays Bank 1993–95 (joined as grad trainee), Barclays Bank of Swaziland 1995–96, sales dir Banque Belgolaise Ivory Coast 1997–98, nat sales mangr Barclays Bank 1998, former service delivery dir Barclays Bank Botswana; conslt YouGov 2000–05; dir Okavango Ltd 2002–05; MP (Cons) Rochford and Southend E 2005– (Parly candidate (Cons) Rother Valley 2001); *Style*— James Duddridge, Esq, MP; ✉ House of Commons, London SW1A 0AA (tel 020 7219 4830, e-mail james@jamesduddridge.com, website www.jamesduddridge.com)

DUDLESTON, Barry; s of Percy Dudleston (d 1979), and Dorothy Vera, *née* Jones; *b* 16 July 1945; *Educ* Stockport Sch; *m* 1 (m dis); 1 da (Sharon Louise b 29 Oct 1968); m 2 (m dis); 1 s (Matthew Barry b 12 Sept 1988); m 3, 19 Oct 1994, Louise Wendy; 1 s (Jack Nicholas b 29 April 1998); *Career* cricket umpire; professional cricketer: Leics CCC 1965–80, Glos CCC 1981–83; represented Rhodesia 1976–79; first class record: 295 matches, 32 centuries, highest score 202 v Derbys 1979; shared Leics record partnership 1st wicket 390 with J Steele v Derbys 1979, 206 with J Steele v Staffs (Gilette Cup) 1975; first class umpire 1984–, appointed to Test Match Panel 1991– (debut 4th Test England v W Indies Edgbaston 1991); *Clubs* MCC; *Style*— Barry Dudleston, Esq; ✉ Sunsport Ltd, Hamilton House, 66 Palmerston Road, Northampton NN1 5EX (tel 01604 631626, fax 01604 631628, e-mail barry@sunsport.co.uk, website www.sunsport.co.uk)

DUDLEY, Anne Jennifer; da of late William James Beckingham, of Brighton, and Dorothy Thelma Beckingham; *Educ* Eltham Hill GS, Royal Coll of Music (Performer's Dip, BMus), KCL (MMus); *m* 1978, Roger Dudley, s of Leonard William Dudley; 1 da (Angela b 7 April 1992); *Career* musician, composer, arranger, prodr; composer in assoc with the BBC Concert Orch 2002–05; keyboard player and arranger with: ABC (Lexicon of Love album), Wham! (Young Guns, Bad Boys and Everything She Wants), Malcolm McLaren (co-wrote Buffalo Gals and other tracks on Duck Rock), Frankie Goes to Hollywood (Two Tribes and The Power of Love); fndr memb Art of Noise (performed, wrote and co-produced all six albums); freelance arranger and musician with: Phil Collins, Paul McCartney, Wham, Lisa Minelli, Lloyd Cole, Rod Stewart, Marc Almond, Seal, Tina Turner, Cher, Elton John, Pulp, Boyzone, Will Young, Pet Shop Boys, Jaz Coleman of Killing Joke (songs From the Victorious City 1990); solo albums: Ancient and Modern 1995, A Different Light 2002, Seriously Chilled 2004; composer of soundtracks for cinematic feature films incl: Hiding Out, Buster, Wilt, Silence Like Glass, Say Anything,

Mighty Quinn, The Pope Must Die, Disorderlies, The Miracle, The Crying Game, Knight Moves, When Saturday Comes, The Grotesque, Hollow Reed, The Full Monty, Pushing Tin, American History, The Miracle Maker, Monkeybone, Lucky Break, The Gathering, Bright Young Things, Perfect creature, Tristan and Isolde, Black Book, The Walker; composer of soundtrack music for TV: Jeeves and Wooster 1990–93, Krypton Factor, Down to Earth, Anna Lee, Kavanagh QC, Crime Traveller, The Perfect Blue, The Tenth Kingdom, The Key; composer of music for TV and cinema commercials incl: Spanish Sherries, Volvo, World Wildlife Fund, Commercial Union, Reebok, Guinness, Stella Artois; concert music: Music and Silence, Winter Solstice, Northern Lights; Grammy Award for Peter Gunn 1988, Midsummer Award for Volvo (Twister) 1996, Academy Award (Oscar) for The Full Monty 1997; memb: BAFTA, Academy of Motion Picture Arts and Sciences; FRCM; *Style—* Anne Dudley; ✉ c/o Karen Elliot, Hothouse Music Ltd, Greenland Place, 115–123 Bayham Street, London NW1 0AG (tel 020 7446 7446, fax 020 7446 7448, e-mail annedud@aol.com)

DUDLEY, Bishop of 2000–; Rt Rev David Stuart Walker; s of Fred Walker, and Joyce, *née* Garside; *b* 30 May 1957; *Educ* Manchester Grammar, King's Coll Cambridge (MA, Table Tennis capt), Queens' Coll Birmingham (DipTh); *m* Susan Ann, *née* Pearce; 1 s, 1 da; *Career* curate St Mary Handsworth 1983–86, team vicar Maltby 1986–91, vicar of Bramley and Ravenfield 1981–95, team rector Bramley and Ravenfield with Hooton Roberts and Braithwell 1995–2000; memb Gen Synod C of E 2005–, memb C of E Pensions Bd 2006–; chair S Yorks Housing Assoc 1995–2001, memb Cncl Nat Housing Fedn 1996–2002, memb Govt Policy Action Team on Housing Mgmnt 1998–2001, chair Housing Assocs Charitable Tst 2005–; FRSA 2007; *Recreations* cricket, hill walking, various needlecrafts, reading; *Style—* The Rt Rev the Bishop of Dudley; ✉ Bishop's House, Bishop's Walk, Cradley Heath, West Midlands B64 7RH (tel 0121 550 3407, 0121 550 7340, e-mail bishop.david@cofe-worcester.org.uk)

DUDLEY, His Hon Judge Michael John; s of John Kenneth Dudley (d 1982), and Ruby Marguerite, *née* Curtis (d 1991); *b* 24 January 1947, Bristol; *Educ* Magdalen Coll Sch Brackley, Univ of Birmingham (LLB), Univ of Leeds (GCertEd); *m* 27 April 1968, Barbara, *née* Taranienko; 1 s (Robert Michael b 28 Dec 1968), 1 da (Kate b 16 Sept 1972); *Career* called to the Bar Lincoln's Inn 1972; practising barr Birmingham 1972–2003, recorder until 2003, circuit judge 2003–; tstee Sutton Coldfield Recreational Tst; *Recreations* music, golf, rugby, walking; *Clubs* Sutton Coldfield Rugby, Sutton Coldfield Golf; *Style—* His Hon Judge Dudley; ✉ Wolverhampton Combined Court, Pipers Row, Wolverhampton WV1 3LQ (tel 01902 481002)

DUDLEY, Rev Dr Martin Raymond; s of Ronald Frank Dudley, and Joyce Mary, *née* Gardiner, of Birmingham; *b* 31 May 1953; *Educ* King Edward's Sch Birmingham, RMA Sandhurst, KCL (BD, MTh, PhD, AKC), St Michael's Coll Llandaff and UC Cardiff, Cass Business Sch City Univ (MSc); *m* Paula, *née* Jones; 2 s (Thomas Edward b 1989, Joseph Nicholas b 1994); *Career* ordained: deacon 1979, priest 1980; asst curate Whitchurch Cardiff 1979–83; vicar Weston 1983–88; priest-in-charge Ardeley 1986–88; vicar Owlsmoor Sandhurst 1988–95; lectr Simon of Cyrene Theological Inst 1992–94; rector St Bartholomew the Great Smithfield 1995–; vice-chm St Bartholomew the Great Heritage Tst 1999–; vice-pres American Friends of St Bartholomew the Great 2000–; non-exec dir Whitehall Consultants 2001–03; memb: Bar Cncl Professional Conduct and Complaints Ctee 2000–06, London Diocesan Synod 2003–06, Bishop's Cncl 2003–06; tstee: Butchers and Drovers Charitable Inst 1997–2004, Field Lane Fndn 2000–01, The London Library 2003–07, City Parochial Fndn 2005–; govr: The City Literary Inst 2001–03, City of London Sch for Girls 2002–, City of London Acad (Southwark) 2003–; memb: Corp of London Libraries Archives and Guildhall Art Gallery Ctee 2002–, Hampstead Heath Mgmnt Ctee 2003–04, Ct Bridewell Royal Fndn 2003–, Corp of London Licensing Ctee 2004–, Corp of London Planning and Transportation Ctee 2005–, City of London City Bridge Tst 2007–, Standards Ctee 2007–; chm Resource Centre (London) Ltd 2007–; Common Councilman Corp of London (Aldersgate Ward) 2002–05; chaplain to: Master Butcher 1995–, Imperial Soc of Knights Bachelor 1995–, Chartered Secretaries and Administrators 1995–2000, Hackney Carriage Drivers 1998–, Master Farmer 1999–2000 and 2002–03, Information Technologists 2001–, Master Fletcher 2001–02 and 2004–, PR Practitioners 2001–, Tax Advsrs 2002–, Royal Soc of St George (City of London branch) 2003–, Alderman & Sheriff Anstee 2003–04; jr vice-pres Farringdon Ward Club 2006–07 (sr vice-pres 2007–08); memb: ctee City of London Archeological Tst 2006–, Corporation of London Community & Children's Servs Ctee 2006–, Professional Conduct & Complaints Ctee CIArb 2005–; Limborough Lecturer Worshipful Co of Weavers 2005; Freeman City of London 1996, Liveryman Worshipful Co of Farriers 2000, Hon Freeman Worshipful Co of Farmers 2000, Hon Freeman City of London Guild of Public Relations Practioners 2005; FRHistS 1995, FSA 1997, FRSA 2006; SBStJ 1998; *Publications* Confession and Absolution (jt ed, 1990), The Oil of Gladness (jt ed, 1993), The Collect in Anglican Liturgy (ed, 1994), Like a Two-Edged Sword (ed, 1995), A Manual of Ministry to the Sick (1997), Humanity and Healing (1998), Ashes to Glory (1999), A Herald Voice (2000), Risen, Ascended, Glorified (2002), Crowning the Year (2003), Churchwardens: A Survival Guide (jtly, 2003), The Parish Survival Guide (jtly, 2004), Serving the Parish (jtly, 2006); contrib: Studies in Church History, Anglican Theological Review, Heythrop Jl, Contemporary Review, Church Times and numerous dictionaries and encyclopaedias; *Clubs* Athenaeum, Guildhall; *Style—* The Rev Dr Martin Dudley, FSA, FRHistS; ✉ SBG Parish Office, 6 Kinghorn Street, London EC1A 7HW (tel 020 7606 5171 (office), 020 7628 3644 (home), fax 020 7600 6909, e-mail martin.dudley@btinternet.com)

DUDLEY, 4 Earl of (UK 1860); William Humble David Ward; also Baron Ward of Birmingham (E 1664) and Viscount Ednam (UK 1860); s of 3 Earl of Dudley, MC (d 1969), by his 1 w, Lady Rosemary, *née* Sutherland-Leveson-Gower, RRC (d 1930), da of 4 Duke of Sutherland; *b* 5 January 1920; *Educ* Eton, ChCh Oxford; *m* 1, 1946 (m dis 1961), Stella, da of Miguel Carcano, KCMG, KBE, sometime Argentinian ambass to UK; 1 s, 2 da (twins); m 2, 1961, Maureen, da of James Swanson; 1 s, 5 da; *Heir* s, Viscount Ednam; *Career* sat as Cons in House of Lords 1969–99; 2 Lt 10 Hussars 1941, Capt 1945; ADC to The Viceroy of India 1942–43; memb House of Lords Ctee on Euro Secdy Legislation 1972–74 (chm Sub-Ctee on EEC Economics, Finance and Regnl Policy 1973–74); pres Baggeridge Brick Co Ltd; *Clubs* White's, Pratt's; *Style—* The Rt Hon the Earl of Dudley; ✉ c/o White's Club, 37 St James's Street, London SW1A 1JG (tel 020 7493 6671)

DUDLEY, William Stuart; s of William Stuart Dudley, and Dorothy Irene, *née* Stacey; *b* 4 March 1947; *Educ* Highbury GS, St Martin's Sch Art (BA), Slade Sch of Art UCL (Post Grad Dip Fine Art); *Career* theatre designer; assoc designer RNT 1981– (res stage designer 1970–81); hon pres Tower Theatre 1988, hon dir Irish Theatre Co London; fndr memb folk band Morris Minor and the Austin Seven 1980; memb Soc of Br Theatre Designers, RDI 1989; *Theatre* RNT incl: Lavender Blue, Larkrise to Candleford, Lost Worlds, The World Turned Upside Down, Undiscovered Country (SWET Award), Dispatches, Don Quixote, Schweyk in the Second World War, Cinderella, The Mysteries, The Real Inspector Hound, The Critic (Olivier Award for Best Costume Design 1993), Entertaining Strangers, Waiting for Godot, Cat on a Hot Tin Roof, The Shaughraun, The Changeling, Bartholomew Fair, The Voysey Inheritance, The Crucible, The Coup, Pygmalion, The Rise and Fall of Little Voice, On The Ledge, Johnny on a Spot, Under Milk Wood 1995, Wild Oats 1995, Mary Stuart 1996, The Homecoming 1997, All My Sons 2000 (Olivier Award for Best Set Design 2001); RSC incl: Ivanov, That Good Between Us, Richard III, A Midsummer Night's Dream, The General from America; Royal Court incl: Small Change, The Fool, Hamlet, Edmund, Kafka's Dick, Etta Jenks; other prodns incl: Hamlet (Neue Schauspielhaus Hamburg), The Ship, I Claudius, Mutiny!, Kiss me Kate, Girlfriends, Matador, Heartbreak House, My Night with Reg, A Street Car Named Desire; *Opera* WNO incl: Anna Christie, The Barber of Seville, Indomeneo; Royal Opera House incl: Don Giovanni, Tales of Hoffman, Der Rosenkavalier, The Cunning Little Vixen; other opera incl: Billy Budd (Metropolitan Opera), The Ring (Bayreuth) 1983, Un Ballo in Maschera (Salzburg Festival) 1989, Lucia di Lammermoor (Lyric Opera of Chicago), The Big Picnic (Harland and Wolff, Glasgow), Lucia di Lammermoor (Opera National de Paris); *Television* Persuasion (BBC (BAFTA Award for Production Design 1996)); *Recreations* playing the concertina and the cajun accordion; *Style—* William Dudley, Esq

DUDLEY-WILLIAMS, Sir Alastair Edgcumbe James; 2 Bt (UK 1964), of City and Co of the City of Exeter; s of Sir Rolf Dudley Dudley-Williams, 1 Bt (d 1987); *b* 26 November 1943; *Educ* Pangbourne Coll; *m* 1972, Diana Elizabeth Jane, twin da of late Robert Henry Clare Duncan, of Haslemere, Surrey; 3 da (Marina Elizabeth Catherine (Mrs Kieran Clifton) b 1974, Lorna Caroline Rachel b 1977, Eleanor Patricia Rosemary b 1979); *Heir* bro, Malcolm Dudley-Williams; *Career* field salesman Hughes Tool Co Texas 1962–64, oil well driller Bay Drilling Corporation (Louisiana) 1964–65; driller: Bristol Siddeley Whittle Tools Ltd 1965–67, Santa Fe Drilling Co (N Sea and Libya) 1967–72, Inchcape plc 1972–86, Wildcat Consultants 1986–; chm Pirrie Hall Ctee Brook 1990–92; memb: Stewards Enclosure Henley Royal Regatta, Standing Cncl Baronetage; *Recreations* gardening, fishing, shooting; *Style—* Sir Alastair Dudley-Williams, Bt

DUDMAN, Graham Michael; s of Andrew Alistair Dudman, and Elaine Mary, *née* Brown; *b* 2 October 1963; *Educ* Whitehaven GS, Preston Poly; *Career* reporter: Stockport Express 1983–85, Middlesbrough Evening Gazette 1985–87, Daily Mail 1987–89 (freelance), Daily Express 1989–90; The Sun 1990–: reporter, News Editor, Head of News, Associate Editor, Asst Ed (Features); *Recreations* tennis, watching cricket; *Style—* Graham Dudman, Esq; ✉ Head of News, The Sun, 1 Virginia Street, London E1 9XP (tel 020 7782 4000, fax 020 7782 4108)

DUERDEN, Prof Brian Ion; s of late Cyril Duerden, of Burnley, Lancs, and Mildred, *née* Ion; *b* 21 June 1948; *Educ* Nelson GS, Univ of Edinburgh (BSc, MB ChB, MD); *m* 5 Aug 1972, Marjorie, da of late Thomas Blakey Hudson, and Letitia Margaret, *née* Kenyon; *Career* house offr thoracic surgery and infectious diseases City Hosp Edinburgh 1972–73, lectr and hon registrar in bacteriology Univ of Edinburgh Med Sch 1973–76; Univ of Sheffield Med Sch: lectr and hon sr registrar in med microbiology 1976–79, sr lectr and hon conslt in med microbiology 1979–83; prof and hon conslt microbiologist and infection control dr Children's Hosp Sheffield 1983–90; Univ of Wales Coll of Med: prof of med microbiology 1991–, dir Cardiff Public Health Laboratory 1991–95, dir of med microbiology S Glamorgan 1991–95; dep dir Public Health Laboratory Service Bd 1995–2002 (med dir 2000–03, actg dir 2002–03), dir of clinical quality Health Protection Agency 2003, inspr of microbiology and infection control Dept of Health 2004–; chm Editorial Bd Jl of Med Microbiology 1987–2002 (ed-in-chief 1982–2002); memb Editorial Ctee: Reviews Med Microbiology 1989–2002, Anaerobe 1989–; chm Assoc of Profs of Med Microbiology 1994–2000 (hon sec 1989–94), chm Jt Working Pty on Infection in Renal Units 1995–2002; memb: Nat Quality Assurance Advsy Panel 1986–91, Microbiology Advsy Ctee 1988–94 and 2004–, Advsy Ctee on Dangerous Pathogens 1991–94 and 2004–, Jt Dental Ctee MRC 1989–93, SMAC Sub-Gp on Antimicrobial Resistance 1997–98, Int Gp on Antimicrobial Resistance Clinical Prescribing and Research Sub-Gps 1999–2002, CMO UK Zoonoses Gp 1999–, CVO Gp on Surveillance of Diseases and Infections in Animals 1999–, Healthcare Assoc Infections Surveillance Steering Gp 2000–02, Specialist Advsy Ctee on Antimicrobial Resistance 2002–07, Nat Expert Panel on New and Emerging Infections 2004–, Advsy Ctee on Antimicrobial Resistance and Healthcare Associated Infections 2007–; RCPath: memb Cncl 1986–89 and 1990–93, examiner 1981–, memb Specialist Advsy Ctee on Medical Microbiology 1982–99 and 2004–, memb Exec Ctee 1990–93, memb Examiners Sub-Ctee 1994–2004, chm microbiology examiners 1994–99, membership by published works 1999–2004; memb: Soc for Anaerobic Microbiology 1976– (chm 1989–93), Assoc of Med Microbiologists 1983– (hon sec 1984–87, memb Exec Ctee 1984–94), Pathological Soc of GB and I 1974–2002 (memb Ctee 1981–2002), Anaerobe Soc of the Americas; fell Infectious Diseases Soc of America, FRCPath 1990 (MRCPath 1978), FRCPEd 2005; *Books* Short Textbook of Medical Microbiology (5 edn, 1983), A New Short Textbook of Microbial and Parasitic Infection (1987), Topley and Wilson's Principles of Bacteriology, Virology and Immunity (contrib 7 edn, 1983–84, ed and contrib 8 edn, 1990 and 9 edn, 1998), Anaerobes in Human Disease (1991), Medical and Environmental Aspects of Anaerobes (1992), Microbial and Parasitic Infection (1993), Medical and Dental Aspects of Anaerobes (1995); *Recreations* cricket, photography, travel, music; *Style—* Prof Brian Duerden; ✉ Pendle, Welsh Street, Chepstow, Monmouthshire NP16 5LU; Department of Medical Microbiology, Cardiff University College of Medicine, Heath Park, Cardiff CF14 4XN (tel 029 2074 2168, fax 029 2074 2169, e-mail brian.duerden@dh.gsi.gov.uk)

DUFF, Andrew Nicholas; OBE (1997), MEP (Lib Dem) Eastern England; s of Norman Bruce Duff (d 1997), and Diana, *née* Wilcoxon; *b* 25 December 1950; *Educ* Sherborne, St John's Coll Cambridge (MA, MLitt); *Career* res offr Hansard Soc 1974–76, res fell Joseph Rowntree Reform Tst 1989–92, dir Federal Tst for Educn and Res 1993–99; cnclr Cambridge City 1982–90, vice-pres Liberal Democrat Pty 1994–97; MEP (Lib Dem) Eastern England 1999–, ldr Lib Dems in European Parl 2007–, spokesman on constitutional affrs; memb European Convention 2002–03; *Publications* Treaty of Amsterdam (1997), Reforming the European Union (1997), Understanding the Euro (1999), The Struggle for Europe's Constitution (2005); *Recreations* music; *Clubs* Nat Liberal; *Style—* Andrew Duff, Esq, OBE, MEP; ✉ Orwell House, Cowley Road, Cambridge CB4 0PP (tel 01223 566700, fax 01223 566698, e-mail mep@andrewduffmep.org, website www.andrewduff.eu)

DUFF, Prof (Robin) Antony; s of The Rt Hon Sir Antony Duff, GCMG, CVO, DSO, DSC (d 2000), of Dorset, and Lady Duff, *née* Pauline Bevan; *b* 9 March 1945; *Educ* Sedbergh, ChCh Oxford (BA); *Career* visiting lectr Univ of Washington Seattle 1968–69, currently prof Dept of Philosophy Univ of Stirling (joined 1970); research readership British Acad 1989–91, Leverhulme major research fellowship 2002–05; FRSE 1996, FBA 2004; *Books* Trials and Punishments (1986), Intention, Agency and Criminal Liability (1990), Criminal Attempts (1996), Punishment, Communication and Community (2001); *Style—* Prof R A Duff, FRSE, FBA; ✉ Department of Philosophy, University of Stirling, Stirling FK9 4LA (tel 01786 467555, fax 01786 466233)

DUFF, Dr Keith Leslie; s of Leslie Alexander George Duff (d 2001), of London, and Elsie Muriel Janet, *née* Evans (d 1990); *b* 16 July 1949; *Educ* Haberdashers' Aske's, UC Cardiff (BSc), Univ of Leicester (PhD); *m* 21 June 1975, Janet, da of Dr William Smith Russell, of Leicester; 2 da (Katy b 1977, Elizabeth b 1979); *Career* Geology and Physiography Section Nature Conservancy Cncl: joined 1975, dep head 1978–85, head Earth Sci Conservation 1985–87; asst chief scientist Nature Conservancy Cncl 1987–91, chief scientist English Nature 1991–2006, environmental conslt 2006–; Geologists' Association: memb Cncl 1976–85, sec Field Meetings 1978–82, vice-pres 1982–85, hon memb 1996; Inst of Geologists: memb Cncl 1987–90, sec External Rels Ctee 1987–90; memb: Geological Soc (memb Conservation Ctee 1977–89, memb Cncl 1994–97), Palaeontographical Soc (memb Cncl 1979–82), Environmental Advsy Bd Shanks plc 1989–2004, Euro Working Gp on Earth Science Conservation 1988– (fndr memb), Science and Innovation Strategy Bd NERC 2003–07, Univ Collaboration Ctee Br Geological

D

Survey 2005–, Cncl Scottish Assoc for Marine Sciences 2006–, Research Policy Ctee RICS 2006–; pres Earth Sci Teachers' Assoc 1997–99; hon res fell Dept Geology Univ of Leicester; ldr several geological study tours to Western USA for Centre for Extra-Mural Studies Univ of London and GA 1981–92, assessor Marine Sciences Ctee NERC 1988–91, external examiner for MSc in Earth Sci and the Environment Kingston Univ 1998–2002; dir Nat Stone Centre 1985–88; memb Editorial Bd Geology Today 1985–2000; judge BIGGA (Br and Int Golf Greenkeepers' Assoc) Golf Environment Competition 1997–2002, advsy memb R&A Golf Course Ctee 2004–; recipient Foulerton Award; CGeol 1990; *Books* Bivalvia of the Lower Oxford Clay of Southern England (1978), New Sites for Old (ed, 1985), Fossils of the Oxford Clay (contrib, 1991); author of numerous papers and articles in jnls; *Recreations* golf, skiing, travel; *Clubs* Burghley Park Golf; *Style*— Dr Keith Duff

DUFF, Prof Michael John Benjamin; s of George Benjamin Duff (d 1976), and Joan Emily, *née* Reynolds (d 1999); *b* 17 January 1933; *Educ* Emanuel Sch, UCL (BSc, PhD); *m* 20 April 1963, Susan Mary, da of Alfred Jones (d 1986); 1 da (Charlotte Fiona b 1964), 1 s (Robert Michael b 1967); *Career* devpt engr EMI Electronics Ltd 1956–58; Dept of Physics and Astronomy UCL: res asst 1958–62, lectr 1962–77, reader 1977–84, prof 1985–96, emeritus prof of physics 1997–, res collaborator St George's Hospital 2000–; visiting lectr Univ of Ife Nigeria 1965, visiting prof Univ of Arizona 1987; hon sec Br Pattern Recognition Soc 1976–84, chm BPRA 1984–86, pres Int Assoc for Pattern Recognition 1990–92 (sec 1984–90), distinguished fell Br Machine Vision Assoc 2000–; CEng 1966, FIEE 1981, FRSA 1986, FIAPR (fell Int Assoc for Pattern Recognition) 1994; *Books* numerous pubns incl: Conference on Recent Developments in Cloud Chamber and Associated Techniques (ed with N Morris, 1956), Computing Structures for Image Processing (ed, 1983), Modern Cellular Automata (with K Preston, 1984), Intermediate-Level Image Processing (ed, 1986); *Recreations* travelling, music, gardening, photography; *Style*— Prof Michael Duff; ✉ e-mail michaeljbduff@aol.com

DUFF, Rev Timothy Cameron; s of Timothy Duff (d 1974) of Tynemouth, and Marjory Magdalene, *née* Cameron (d 2004); *b* 2 February 1940; *Educ* Royal GS Newcastle upon Tyne, Gonville & Caius Coll Cambridge (MA, LLM); *m* 23 June 1966, Patricia, da of Capt John Munby Walker DLI (d 1955), of North Shields; 2 s (John b 1968, James b 1970), 1 da (Emma b 1973); *Career* admitted slr 1965, sr ptnr Hadaway & Hadaway 1988–2000; sec and clerk to tstees Tyne Mariners Benevolent Inst 1984–2006; dir: Tynemouth Building Society 1985–94, Universal Building Society 1994–2005; ordained 1993; hon curate N Shields parish; grand offr United Grand Lodge of England 1998–; *Recreations* sailing, beagling, freemasonry, gardening; *Clubs* Northern Counties; *Style*— The Rev Timothy Duff; ✉ 24A Percy Gardens, Tynemouth, North Shields NE30 4HQ (tel 0191 2571463, e-mail timothy@timothyduff.co.uk)

DUFF GORDON, Sir Andrew Cosmo Lewis; 8 Bt (UK 1813), of Halkin, Ayrshire; s of Sir Douglas Frederick Duff Gordon, 7 Bt (d 1964, whose ggf, Sir William Duff Gordon, 2 Bt, was paternal gs of 2 Earl of Aberdeen); *b* 17 October 1933; *m* 1, 1967 (m dis 1975), Grania Mary, da of Fitzgerald Villiers-Stuart, of Villerstown, Co Waterford; 1 s (Cosmo Henry Villiers b 1968); m 2, 1975, Eveline (Evie) Virginia Soames, *qv*, yst da of Samuel Soames, of Newbury, Berks; 3 s (William Andrew Lewis b 1977, Thomas Francis Cornewall b 1979, Frederick Samuel Douglas b 1981); *Heir* s, Cosmo Duff Gordon; *Clubs* Sunningdale Golf, Kington Golf, Herefordshire Bow Meeting Society; *Style*— Sir Andrew Duff Gordon, Bt; ✉ Downton House, Walton, Presteigne, Powys (tel 01544 21223)

DUFFELL, Lt Gen Sir Peter Royson; KCB (1992), CBE (1988, OBE 1981), MC (1966); s of Roy John Duffell (d 1979), of Lenham, Kent, and Ruth Doris, *née* Gustaffson; *b* 19 June 1939; *Educ* Dulwich Coll; *m* 9 Oct 1982, Ann Murray, da of Col Basil Bethune Neville Woodd (d 1975), of Rolvenden, Kent; 1 da (Rachel Leonie Sylvia b 9 April 1985), 1 s (Charles Basil Royson b 20 Oct 1986); *Career* cmmnd 2 KEO Gurkha Rifles 1960, Staff Coll Camberley 1971, Brigade Maj 5 Brigade 1972–74, MA to C in C UKLF 1976–78, Cmdt 1 Bn 2 KEO Gurkha Rifles 1978–81, Col GS MOD 1981–83, Cdr Gurkha Field Force 1984–85; COS 1 (BR) Corps 1986–87, RCDS 1988, Cabinet Office 1989, Cdr Br Forces Hong Kong 1989–92, Inspr Gen of Doctrine and Trg 1992–95; Col Royal Gurkha Rifles 1994–99; chief exec Dechert LLP 1995–2006 (conslt 2006–); tstee Foyle Fndn 2006–; govr Sandroyd Sch 1995–, memb Advsy Bd SOAS 2006–; pres: Alleyn Club 2006–07, Sirmoor Rifles Assoc 2006–; Freeman City of London; FRGS 1975, FRAS 1992; *Recreations* family, collecting pictures, skiing, elephant polo, wine, armchair and country pursuits; *Clubs* Travellers, Pratt's, MCC; *Style*— Sir Peter Duffell

DUFFERIN AND CLANDEBOYE, 11 Baron (I 1800); Sir John Francis Blackwood; also 12 Bt (I) of Ballyleidy, and 8 Bt (UK 1814) (claim to the Irish titles is yet to be proved); s of 10 Baron Dufferin and Clandeboye (d 1991), and Margaret, *née* Kirkpatrick (d 1999); *b* 18 October 1944; *Educ* Barker Coll Hornsby, Univ of NSW (BArch); *m* 1971, (Annette) Kay, da of Harold Greenhill, of Seaforth, Sydney, NSW; 1 da (Hon Freya Jodie b 1975), 1 s (Hon Francis Senden b 6 Jan 1979); *Heir* s, Hon Francis Blackwood; *Career* architect in private practice; ARAIA; *Style*— The Rt Hon Lord Dufferin and Clandeboye; ✉ PO Box 1815, Orange NSW 2800, Australia

DUFFETT, Christopher Charles Biddulph; s of Capt Charles Henry Duffett, CBE, DSO, RN (d 1981), and Leonora Biddulph; *b* 23 August 1943; *Educ* Bryanston, Peterhouse Cambridge (MA), Wharton Sch Univ of Pennsylvania (MBA); *m* 1973, Jennifer Edwards; 2 s (Samuel Owen Salisbury b 1975, Daniel Charles William Biddulph b 1977); *Career* Nat Devpt Office 1965–67, S G Warburg and Co Ltd 1969–71, Inco Ltd NY 1971–74, treas Inco Europe Ltd 1974–77, gp treas Rank Organization Ltd 1977–79, gp fin dir The Economist Newspaper Ltd 1979–88, ceo The Law Debenture Corp plc 1988–, chm Assoc of Investment Tst Cos 1999–; dir City Disputes Panel Panel Ltd 2000–; FCT; *Recreations* gardening, sailing, walking; *Clubs* Royal Ocean Racing, City of London; *Style*— Christopher Duffett, Esq

DUFFETT, Michael Terence; s of Francis Duffett (d 1993), of Beckenham, Kent, and Marjorie, *née* McCarthy (d 1988); *b* 1 August 1939; *Educ* Hill Sch Stillness, Central Poly, London Coll of Printing and Graphic Art; *m* Janet, da of Stanley Spencer; 4 da (Rachel b 1 Dec 1966, Emma b 24 Feb 1968, Rebecca b 9 May 1969, Sarah b 19 April 1970); *Career* photographer of fine art/museum and gallery photographic mgmnt; med photographer Royal Nat Orthopaedic Hosp 1959, photographer for Tate Gallery 1962, freelance commercial photographer and design conslt 1967–70, conslt to Slater Walker 1970, advsr on creation of new Photographic Dept Tate Gallery 1974, princ photographer Photographic Dept Tate Gallery 1977–, began collection of photographic equipment (1860–1960) 1977, lectr 1979–, head of photography Tate Gallery 1984–94, chief Govt photographer 1985–, organiser and mangr photographic recording prog of 30,000 Turner watercolours and drawings for the Clore Gallery 1985–, undertook complete photographic survey of entire collection Dulwich Picture Gallery 1988 and Bedford Coll; judge: Kodak Ltd Exposure Project 1989, 1990 and 1991, BIPP Nat Print Competition 1990, Inst of Med and Biological Illustrators 1990; chm and fndr Assoc for Historical and Fine Art Photography 1986; exhibitions incl: Guildhall 1961, Gallery Las 1963, Kings Gallery 1964, Kings Road Gallery 1972; ARPS 1965, FRSA 1987, FBIPP 1988; *Style*— Michael Duffett, Esq; ✉ 1 Queens Road, Beckenham, Kent BR3 4JN (tel 020 8650 2944)

DUFFIELD, HE Linda Joy; CMG (2002); da of late Bryan Charles Duffield, of Northwood, Middx, and Joyce Eileen, *née* Barr; *b* 18 April 1953; *Educ* St Mary's GS Northwood Hills, Univ of Exeter (BA), Ecole Nationale d'Administration Paris; *Career* grad trainee DHSS 1976; entered HM Dip Serv 1987, EU Dept FCO 1987–88, language trg 1988, first sec (commercial) Moscow 1989–92, dep head Eastern Dept FCO 1993–94, head Transcaucasus and Central Asia Dept FCO 1994–95, dep high cmmr Ottawa 1995–99, high cmmr to Sri Lanka 1999–2002 (concurrently non-resident high cmmr to the Maldives), dir wider Europe FCO 2002–04, ambass to Czech Repub 2004–; *Recreations* skiing, skating, classical music, reading; *Style*— HE Miss Linda Duffield, CMG; ✉ c/o Foreign & Commonwealth Office (Prague), King Charles Street, London SW1A 2AH

DUFFIELD, Dame Vivien Louise; DBE (2000, CBE 1989); da of Sir Charles Clore (d 1978), and Francine, *née* Halphen (d 1993); *b* 26 March 1946; *Educ* French Lycée London, Cours Victor Hugo Paris, Heathfield Sch Ascot, LMH Oxford (MA); *m* 1969 (m dis 1976), John Duffield; 1 da (Arabella Elizabeth b 1971), 1 s (George Lincoln b 1973); *Career* chm Clore Fndn UK and Israel 1978–; NSPCC: memb Centenary Appeal Ctee 1983, memb Fin Devpt Ctee 1985, vice-chm National Appeal Bd 1998–2002; Royal Opera House Trust: dir 1985–, dep chm 1988–95, chm 1995–2002, chm Devpt Appeal 1996; dir Royal Opera House 1990–2002 (dep chm 1998–); vice-chm: Wishing Well Appeal Great Ormond St Hosp 1987–90, Cancer Appeal Royal Marsden Hosp 1990–95; chm Eureka children's museum Halifax 1986–, dir Royal Ballet 1990–97 (govr 2002–), govr South Bank Bd 2002–; tstee Dulwich Picture Gallery 2002; benefactor of the year NACF; Hon DPhil Weizmann Inst 1985, Hon DLitt Univ of Buckingham 1990; FKC, Hon RCM 1987, Hon FRAM 2003; *Recreations* skiing, shooting, opera, ballet; *Style*— Dame Vivien Duffield, DBE; ✉ c/o The Clore Foundation, Unit 3, Chelsea Manor Studios, Flood Street, London SW3 5SR

DUFFIN, Stuart; s of Ian Duffin (d 1984), of Glasgow, and Isobel Wands; *b* 13 June 1959; *Educ* Gray's Sch of Art Aberdeen; *Career* artist; Scottish Arts Cncl Award (to study and travel in Italy) 1987, exchange artist to Moscow 1992, exchange artist to Jerusalem Printmakers Workshop 1996; RE 1995, RSA 2005 (ARSA 1996); *Solo Exhibitions* Laughter and Forgetting (Edinburgh) 1989, Nostalgia (Glasgow Print Studio) 1989, Colour of Ashes (Glasgow Print Studio) 1995, Dreaming of Jerusalem (Gallery of Jerusalem Printmakers Workshop) 1998, Sacred Science (Glasgow Print Studio) 2001; *Group Exhibitions* incl: etching and intaglio techniques (Scottish Arts Cncl tour) 1983, Int Contemporary Art Fair LA 1988, Ka De We (exhbn of Scottish printmaking, Berlin) 1988, Royal Festival Hall London 1990, Int Miniature Prints (NY and tour of USA) 1991, Scottish Contemporary Printmaking (Moscow) 1991, Int Exhbn of Graphic Art (Kharkov Museum Ukraine) 1993, Nat Print Open (Mall Galleries London) 1995, Out of Darkness (Glasgow Print Studio) 2004; *Recreations* reading, music; *Style*— Stuart Duffin, Esq; ✉ 40 Cromarty Avenue, Glasgow G43 2HG (tel 0141 632 7432, e-mail info@stuartduffin.com, website www.stuartduffin.com)

DUFFY, Carol Ann; CBE (2002, OBE 1995); da of Francis Duffy, and Mary, *née* Black; *b* 23 December 1955; *Educ* St Joseph's Convent Stafford, Stafford Girls' HS, Univ of Liverpool (BA); *Career* freelance writer and poet; FRSL; *Awards* Eric Gregory Award 1984, C Day Lewis fellowship 1982–84, Somerset Maugham Award 1988, Dylan Thomas Award 1990, Scottish Arts Cncl Book Award of Merit 1985 and 1990, Whitbread Award for Poetry 1993; *Books* Standing Female Nude (1985), Selling Manhattan (1987, 4 edn 1994), The Other Country (1990), Mean Time (1993), Selected Poems (1994), Anvil New Poets (ed, 1994), The World's Wife (2000), Feminine Gospels (2002), Rapture (2005, T S Eliot Prize); *Style*— Ms Carol Ann Duffy, CBE; ✉ c/o Picador Books, Pan Macmillan Publishers, 20 New Wharf Road, London N1 9RR

DUFFY, Dr Francis Cuthbert (Frank); CBE (1997); s of John Austin Duffy (d 1944), and Annie Margaret, *née* Reed (d 2000); *b* 3 September 1940; *Educ* St Cuthbert's GS Newcastle upon Tyne, Architectural Assoc Sch London (AADipl), Univ of Calif (MArch), Princeton Univ (MA, PhD); *m* 4 Sept 1965, Jessica Mary, da of Philip Bear, of Chiddingstone, Kent; 3 da (Sibylla b 1966, Eleanor b 1969, Katya b 1970); *Career* asst architect Nat Bldg Agency 1964–67, Cwlth Fund Harkness fell (in USA)1967–70, estab and head of London Office JFN Associates 1971–73, fndr ptnr DEGW plc architects 1973–; fndr and chm Bldg Use Studies 1980–88, fndr and chief ed Facilities (newsletter) 1984–90, consIt on the working environment to many cos and instns; chair: Design Selection Panel Stratford City 2006–, Architecture Design and Workplace Advsy Cncl BBC 2006–; visiting prof: MIT 2001–04, Univ of Reading 2007–; pres: Architects' Cncl of Europe 1994, RIBA 1993–95 (memb Cncl 1989–99); tstee Architecture Fndn 2000–; memb Architects Registration Bd (ARB) 1997–2003; British Cncl of Offices (BCO) Pres's Award 2004; *Books* Planning Office Space (jtly, 1976), The Orbit Study (princ author, 1984), Orbit 2 (jtly, 1985), The Changing City (jtly, 1989), The Changing Workplace (1992), The Responsible Workplace (jtly, 1993), The New Office (1997), New Environments for Working (jtly, 1998), Architectural Knowledge (jtly, 1998); *Clubs* Architectural Association, Athenaeum, Reform, Princeton (NY); *Style*— Dr Francis Duffy, CBE; ✉ DEGW plc, 8 Crinan Street, London N1 9SQ (tel 020 7239 7777, fax 020 7278 5613, e-mail fduffy@degw.com); Threeways, The Street, Walberswick, Suffolk IP18 6UE (tel 01502 723814)

DUFFY, James Bernard; s of Bernard Duffy, and Teresa Duffy; *b* 10 September 1955; *Educ* St Mary's Coll Middlesbrough, Univ of Newcastle Sch of Architecture (BA, BArch); *m* 1, 27 May 1985, Fiona (d 1996); 1 da (Sarah Catherine b 26 Oct 1986); m 2, 29 June 2002, Susie; *Career* architect; assoc dir Fitch & Co London 1984–86, assoc dir McColl London 1986–88, princ James Duffy Associates 1988–95 (sold practice to BDG McColl London 1995), dir of architecture BDG McColl London 1995–2000, architect dir Building Design Partnership (BDP) 2000–; sr competitions assessor RIBA 1994, memb Br Cncl of Shopping Centres (BCSC) 1995–; author of conference papers and occasional magazine articles; regular conference speaker incl 66 airport conferences worldwide; Bunz Travelling Studentship 1980, Urban Infill Award Irish Planning Inst 1992, Civic Tst Award 1995; memb Parish Cncl St Theodore's RC Church; ARB 1982, RIBA 1982; *Recreations* gym, singing and guitar, running, walking, skiing; *Clubs* Cannons (Surbiton), Stragglers, Ramblers, Ski Club of GB, Nat Tst; *Style*— James Duffy, Esq; ✉ Building Design Partnership, 16 Brewhouse Yard, Clerkenwell, London EC1V 4LJ (tel 020 7812 8000, fax 020 7812 8399, mobile 07876 397536)

DUFFY, Prof John Alastair; s of John Duffy (d 1952), of Birmingham, and Edna Frances, *née* Walker (d 1996); *b* 24 September 1932; *Educ* Solihull Sch, Univ of Sheffield (BSc, PhD), Univ of Aberdeen (DSc); *m* 19 Dec 1959, Muriel Florence Lyon, da of Edward Ramsay (d 1977), of Hamilton; 1 s (Alastair b 1965), 1 da (Penelope b 1968); *Career* res chemist Albright & Wilson 1958–59, lectr Wolverhampton Poly 1959–61, sr lectr NE Wales Inst 1961–65, lectr, sr lectr, reader, prof of chem then emeritus prof Univ of Aberdeen 1966–; quality assessor for Scottish HE Funding Cncl 1993–94; conslt: Schott Glaswerke W Germany 1984–86, Br Steel Corp 1986–89; author of 150 scientific pubns; chm NE Scotland Section Royal Soc of Chemistry 1978–81; Blackwell Prize Univ of Aberdeen 1992; fell Soc of Glass Technol, FRSC, CChem; *Books* General Inorganic Chemistry (1966), Bonding, Energy Levels and Bands in Inorganic Solids (1990); *Recreations* music, romantic opera; *Style*— Prof John Duffy; ✉ 35 Beechgrove Terrace, Aberdeen AB15 5DR (tel 01224 641752); Department of Chemistry, The University, Aberdeen (tel 01224 273409, fax 01224 272921, e-mail j.a.duffy@abdn.ac.uk)

DUFFY, Most Rev Joseph Augustine; *see:* Clogher, Bishop of (RC)

DUFFY, Maureen; da of late Hugh Andrew Duffy, and Mary, *née* McAtamney; *b* 4 May 1959; *Educ* Kingston Univ (BA, MBA), Univ of London (Dip Mgmnt); *Career* J Walter Thompson Co Ltd: grad to sr media exec 1982–87, assoc media dir 1987–89, gp media dir 1989–95, world ptnr 1996–98, strategic communication dir 1996–98; controller of mktg BBC TV 1998–2000, controller of daytime ITV 2000–02, ceo Newspaper Marketing Agency 2003–; *Recreations* keeping fit, squash, film, theatre, reading, antiques, travel; *Style*— Ms Maureen Duffy

DUFFY, Maureen Patricia; da of Grace Wright; *b* 1933; *Educ* Trowbridge HS, Sarah Bonnell HS for Girls, KCL (BA); *Career* author, playwright and poet; co fndr Writers' Action Gp; chm: Authors Licensing and Collecting Soc 1980–95, Copyright Licensing Agency 1996–99; pres Writers' Guild of GB 1986–89 (jt chm 1977–88), hon pres Br Copyright Cncl 2003– (chm 1989–98, vice-pres 1998–2003); hon pres Authors Licensing and Collecting Soc 2002–, pres European Writers Congress 2003–05 (vice-pres 1991–2003); Int Confedn of Socs of Authors and Composers (CISAC) Gold Medal for Literature 2002, Benson Medal for Literature RSL 2004; FKC 2002, FRSL; *Books* incl: Illuminations (1991), Occam's Razor (1993), Henry Purcell (1994), Restitution (1998), England: the making of the myth (2001), Alchemy (2004), Family Values (2008); *Style*— Ms Maureen Duffy; ✉ 18 Fabian Road, London SW6 7TZ (fax 020 7385 2468)

DUFFY, Patrick G; s of Dr J B Duffy, and Mrs E C Duffy; *b* 8 January 1949; *Educ* MB, BCh, BAO; *m* 13 July 1987, Dr Zara Anne, *née* McClenahan; 2 s (Frederick b 16 July 1989, Peter b 12 July 1991), 2 da (Emmylene b 28 Oct 1993, Sarah-Jane b 24 Aug 1995); *Career* conslt paediatric urologist London, hon sr lectr in paediatric urology Inst of Child Health Gt Ormond St Hosp for Children London; memb: European Soc of Paediatric Urology (ESPU), Br Assoc of Urological Surgeons (BAUS), BMA, RSM; FRCSI; *Recreations* sailing, squash, music; *Style*— Patrick Duffy, Esq; ✉ Portland Consulting Suite, 234 Great Portland Street, London W1W 5QT (tel 020 7390 8322, fax 020 7390 8324)

DUFFY, Philip Edmund; s of Walter Duffy (d 1991), and Ellen Dalton (d 1995); *b* 21 January 1943; *Educ* St Edward's Coll W Derby, Royal Manchester Coll of Music (GRSM, ARMCM), Univ of London; *Career* master of the music Liverpool Metropolitan Cathedral 1966–96; Liverpool Hope Univ: princ lectr 2000–06, dir of performance 2006–; hon fell Guild of Church Musicians 1994; ISM 1966; KSG 1981; *Recreations* reading, theatre, walking; *Style*— Philip Duffy, Esq; ✉ 2 South Court, Wexford Road, Oxton CH43 9TD (e-mail pipduf@aol.com)

DUFFY, Simon; *b* 27 November 1949; *Educ* Univ of Oxford (BA), Harvard Business Sch (Harkness fell, MBA); *Career* analyst N M Rothschild and Sons 1973–76, analyst Shell UK 1978–80, conslt Bain and Company 1980–82, gen mangr planning and treasy Consolidated Gold Fields plc 1982–86, dir of corp fin Guinness plc 1986–89, ops dir Guinness subsid United Distillers Ltd 1989–92, dep chm and gp fin dir EMI Group plc (formerly Thorn EMI) 1992–99, chief exec and dep chm World Online 1999–2000, ceo End2End 2001–02, chief financial offr and exec vice-pres Orange 2002–03, pres and ceo NTL 2003–05, exec vice-chm NTL 2006–07, exec chm QXL ricardo plc 2007–; FRSA; *Clubs* Brooks's; *Style*— Simon Duffy

DUFFY, Terence John; s of John Edward Duffy (d 1989), of Birkenhead, Cheshire, and Theresa, *née* Williamson (d 1961); *b* 24 August 1947; *Educ* St Anselm's Coll Cheshire, Jesus Coll Cambridge (BA, MA), New Coll Oxford (BM BCh); *m* 6 Aug 1971, Rowena Siriol, da of Henry Vaughan-Roberts, BM, of Conwy, N Wales; 1 s (Elliot Edward Vaughan b 1977), 1 da (Alexandra Margaret Theresa (Sasha) b 1983); *Career* house appts Bedford and Oxford 1972–73, demonstrator in anatomy Univ of Cambridge 1973–74 (supervisor Jesus Coll 1973–74), SHO and registrar Bedford and Cambridge Hosp 1974–78, registrar Swansea 1978–79, Wellcome res fell Cambridge 1979–80, lectr in surgery Univ of Cambridge and fell Jesus Coll 1980–84, sr lectr in surgery Keele Univ 1984–89, conslt in gen and breast surgery N Staffs Hosp 1984–; author of numerous pubns on gen and transplant surgery 1978–; memb: W Midlands Surgical Soc, BMA 1969, BTS 1980, BASO 1990; FRCS 1977, FRSM 1989; *Recreations* music, sport; *Style*— Terence Duffy, Esq; ✉ University Hospital North Staffordshire, City General Hospital, Newcastle Road, Stoke-on-Trent, Staffordshire ST4 6QG (tel 01782 552741, fax 01782 680199, e-mail tjduffy@merrytree.net)

DUFTON, Robert; s of Maj Felix Dufton, RE, and Rosemary, *née* Orpin; *b* 20 March 1962; *Educ* Sevenoaks Sch, Univ of Bristol (LLB), Coll of Law, Ashridge Mgmnt Coll (Dip Gen Mgmnt); *Career* slr Lovells 1984–90, conslt AEA 1991, prog dir and co sec Arts and Business 1992–94, dep dir of ops Heritage Lottery Fund 1995–2002, dir Rayne Fndn 2002–04, dir Paul Hamlyn Fndn 2004–; memb: Cncl Univ of Bristol, Bd of Govrs Museum of London; memb Law Soc 1986; *Style*— Robert Dufton; ✉ Paul Hamlyn Foundation, 18 Queen Anne's Gate, London SW1H 9AA (tel 020 7227 3500, fax 020 7222 0601)

DUGDALE, Hon David John; DL (N Yorks 1998); s of 1 Baron Crathorne, PC, TD (d 1977), and Nancy, OBE (d 1969), da of Sir Charles Tennant, 1 Bt; *b* 4 May 1942; *Educ* Eton, Trinity Coll Cambridge; *m* 1972, Susan Louise, da of Maj L A Powell (d 1972); 1 da (Clare Nancy Louise b 1978), 1 s (Jonathan William Sean b 1980); *Career* farmer and engr; dir: United Oilseeds Marketing Ltd 1996–, Dairy Crest Gp plc 2002–; High Sheriff for Co of Cleveland 1995; CEng, MIMechE; *Recreations* building, photography, shooting; *Style*— The Hon David Dugdale, DL; ✉ Park House, Crathorne, Yarm, North Yorkshire TS15 0BD (tel 01642 700225, work 01642 700295)

DUGDALE, Keith Stuart; JP (1967); s of George Dugdale (d 1954), of Norwich, and Dorothy Elizabeth, *née* Parkerson (d 1970); *b* 27 September 1930; *Educ* Gresham's, Magdalen Coll Oxford (MA); *m* 1957, Rev Angela Marion, *née* Willey, MBE, DL Norfolk 1992; 1 da (Hilary Ruth b 1964), 2 s (Christopher John b 1966, Jeremy Keith b 1969); *Career* CA; Martin & Acock: articled clerk 1951, ptnr 1956–94; pt/t memb VAT and Duties Tbnls 1992–; chm Norfolk and Norwich Triennial Festival 1977–82, pres E Anglian Soc of CAs 1978–79, vice-chm Norfolk Family Health Servs Authy 1990–96, memb E Norfolk HA 1996–99, memb Norfolk HA 1999–2002 (vice-chm 2001–02), chm Norwich Bench 1996–98; FCA 1955; *Recreations* books, music, gardening; *Clubs* Norfolk; *Style*— Keith Dugdale, Esq; ✉ Beck House, Kelling, Holt, Norfolk NR25 7EL (tel 01263 588389, e-mail dugdale@freeuk.com)

DUGDALE, Sir William Stratford; 2 Bt (UK 1936), of Merevale and Blyth, Co Warwick; CBE (1982), MC (1943), DL (1955); s of Sir William Francis Stratford Dugdale, 1 Bt (d 1965); *b* 29 March 1922; *Educ* Eton, Balliol Coll Oxford; *m* 1, 13 Dec 1952, Lady Belinda Pleydell-Bouverie (d 1961), da of 7 Earl of Radnor, KG, KCVO; 3 da (Laura (Hon Mrs Arthur Hazlerigg) b 1953, Matilda (Mrs Marcus May), Charlotte (Hon Mrs Gerard Noel) (twins) b 1955), 1 s ((William) Matthew Stratford b 1959); m 2, 17 Oct 1967, Cecilia Mary, da of Lt-Col Sir William Malcolm Mount, 2 Bt, ED, DL (d 1993); 1 da (Adelaide Margaret Victoria Jane b 1970), 1 s (Thomas Joshua Stratford b 1974); *Heir* s, Matthew Dugdale; *Career* Capt Grenadier Gds 1944, served in Africa and Italy (despatches); slr 1949; chm: Trent River Authy 1965–73, Severn Trent Water Authy 1974–84, Nat Water Cncl 1982–84, General Utilities plc 1988–99; dir Phoenix Assurance 1985 (and other cos); chm Aston Villa FC 1973–81; JP Warks 1951–97, High Sheriff Warks 1971–72; High Steward Stratford-upon-Avon 1976–; *Clubs* Brooks's, White's, MCC, Jockey; *Style*— Sir William Dugdale, Bt, CBE, MC, DL; ✉ Blyth Hall, Coleshill, Birmingham B46 2AD (tel 01675 462203, fax 01675 465071); Merevale Hall, Atherstone, Warwickshire (tel 01827 712181, fax 01827 714903); 24 Bryanston Mews West, London W1 (tel and fax 020 7262 2510, e-mail billydug@aol.com)

DUGGIN, Sir Thomas Joseph; kt (2004); s of Joseph Duggin (d 1986), of Bury, Lancs, and Alice Lilian, *née* Mansfield; *b* 15 September 1947; *Educ* Thornleigh Salesian Coll; *m* 1, 1968 (m dis); 2 s (Nicholas James b 1973, Alistair Richard b 1975); m 2, 1983 (m dis); m 3, 1999, Janette Mortimer, *née* David; *Career* HM Dip Serv: joined 1967, desk offr Cwlth Policy and Planning Dept FCO 1967–68, desk offr Protocol Dept FCO 1969, third sec (commercial) Oslo 1969–73, third later second sec (commercial) Bucharest 1973–76, asst private sec Private Office FCO 1976–79, second sec (Chancery/info) Bangkok 1979–82, first sec S America Dept FCO 1982–85, head of Chancery and consul La Paz 1985–88, head of Chancery Mexico City 1989–91, high cmmr to Vanuatu 1992–95, cnsllr FCO 1995–2001, ambass to Colombia 2001–05; dir Global Strategies Gp UK 2006–, vice-pres Global Stategies Gp (Colombia) 2006–; memb Bd Br Colombian C of C 2005–; *Recreations* reading, music, tennis; *Style*— Sir Thomas Duggin; ✉ e-mail tjduggin@yahoo.co.uk

DUKE, Prof Christopher (Chris); s of Frederick Alexander Duke, of London, and Edith, *née* Page; *b* 4 October 1938; *Educ* Eltham Coll, Jesus Coll Cambridge (BA, CertEd, MA), KCL (PhD); *m* 1 (m dis 1981), Audrey Ann, *née* Solomon; 1 s (Stephen b 1968), 2 da (Annie b 1970, Cathy b 1972); m 2, Jan 1982, Elizabeth Ann, da of E Lloyd Sommerlad, of Sydney, Aust; 2 s (Alex b 1978, Paul b 1981 (d 2007)); *Career* lectr: Woolwich Poly 1961–66, Univ of Leeds 1966–69; fndn dir of continuing educn ANU 1969–85, fndn prof, chm of continuing educn and dir of open studies Univ of Warwick 1985–96 (pro-vice-chllr 1991–95), formerly dep vice-chllr Univ of NSW and pres Univ of Western Sydney Nepean, currently prof of regnl partnerships and learning RMIT Univ Melbourne 2002–07 (dir of community and regnl partnerships 2002–03); dir of HE NIACE 2002–05, asssoc dir of adult learning Action on Access 2003–05, ceo Pascal Internat Observatory 2004–; ed Int Jl of Univ Adult Educn 1971–96; vice-chm Universities Assoc for Continuing Educn 1994–96 (sec 1989–94), various other int and local continuing educn positions; hon prof of lifelong learning: Inst of Educn Univ of Scotland, Univ of Leicester; Hon DLitt Keimyung Univ Korea; FACE, FRSA; *Books* incl: The Learning University (1992), The Adult University (1999), Managing the Learing University (2002); *Recreations* gardening, bird-watching, reading, conversation, learning French; *Style*— Prof Chris Duke

DUKE, Timothy Hugh Stewart; s of William Falcon Duke (d 1954), of Sway, Hants, and Mary Cecile, *née* Jackson (d 2003); *b* 12 June 1953; *Educ* Uppingham, Fitzwilliam Coll Cambridge (MA); *Career* Peat Marwick Mitchell & Co 1974–81; College of Arms: research asst 1981–89, Rouge Dragon Pursuivant of Arms 1989–95, Chester Herald of Arms 1995–; Registrar Coll of Arms 2001–07; Liveryman Worshipful Co of Broderers 1987; hon sec Harleian Soc 1994–; *Clubs* Travellers; *Style*— Timothy Duke, Esq, Chester Herald of Arms; ✉ College of Arms, Queen Victoria Street, London EC4V 4BT (tel 020 7236 7728, fax 020 7248 6448)

DULVERTON, 3 Baron (UK 1929); Sir (Gilbert) Michael Hamilton Wills; 4 Bt (UK) 1897; s of 2 Baron Dulverton, CBE, TD, DL (d 1992), and his 1 w Judith Betty, *née* Leslie Melville (d 1983); *b* 2 May 1944; *Educ* Gordonstoun; *m* 1, 1980 (m dis 1999), Rosalind van der Velde; 1 da (Hon Charlotte Alexandra Hamilton b 1981), 1 s (Hon Robert Anthony Hamilton b 20 Oct 1983); m 2, 2000, Mrs Mary Vicary; *Heir* s, Hon Robert Wills; *Career* farmer, forester and industrialist; chm Thwaites Ltd 1995–; dir: West Highland Woodlands Ltd, Batsford Estate Co (1983) Ltd; tstee Dulverton Tst; *Clubs* Turf; *Style*— The Rt Hon the Lord Dulverton

DUMA, Alexander Agim; s of Dervish Duma (d 1998), and Naftali, *née* Andoni (d 1966); *b* 30 March 1946; *Educ* UCL (LLB); *m* 1980 (m dis 1983), Mary Gertrude, da of Surgn-Col E W Hayward; *Career* called to the Bar Gray's Inn 1969; Parly candidate (Cons) 1979, GLC candidate (Cons) Bermondsey 1977; Barton Mayhew & Co 1968–72, Philips Industries 1973–75, Barclays Merchant Bank 1975–87; dir: Blackfriars Settlement 1977–84 and 1986–89, Barclays de Zoete Wedd Ltd 1983–87, Chase Investment Bank Ltd 1987–89, Equity & General plc 1987–90, Torday & Carlisle plc 1988–92, The London & Northumberland Estates Co Ltd 1988–, Smith New Court Corporate Finance Ltd 1989–92 (conslt 1992–94), The New Plastics Co Ltd 1990–94, Lady Clare Ltd 1994–99, Headgear Investments Ltd 1997–, Richmond Theatre Prodns Ltd 2006–; chm: Pickett Ltd 1988–, Poundfloat Ltd 1992–95, EC-1 Ltd 1999–2001, The Plain English Gp Ltd 2000–03, Opera Players Ltd 2000–03 (dir 1995), Room Service Gp plc 2001–03, Sky Capital Holdings plc 2002–03 and 2005–07, Sky Capital Enterprises plc 2005–07; conslt Granville & Co Ltd 1992–94, UK rep Deloitte & Touche Albania 1993–95; memb Cncl Newcomen Collett Fndn 1977–94, tstee Devas Club 1996–2000, tstee Denys Holland Scholarship 1996–, memb Finance Ctee Terrence Higgins Tst 1997–2003, chm of tstees Terrence Higgins Pension Fund 2002–, pres Crabtree Fndn 2004; pres Bermondsey Cons Assoc 1979–83; hon consul Republic of Albania 1992–94; chm: The Centre for Albanian Studies 1998–, Br-Albanian Cncl 1998–, Anglo-Albanian Assoc 2005– (memb Cncl 1966–2005); pres Friends of UCL 2001–07, fell UCL 2005; FCA; *Clubs* Brooks's; *Style*— Alexander Duma, Esq; ✉ 39 Donne Place, London SW3 2NH (tel 020 7823 7422, fax 020 7581 0982); Le Grès, 82110 Lauzerte, France (tel 00 33 563 95 70 23, fax 00 33 563 95 70 44)

DUMFRIES, Johnny; *see:* Bute, 7 Marquess of

DUMMETT, Prof Sir Michael Anthony Eardley; kt (1999); s of George Herbert Dummett (d 1970), and Mabel Iris, *née* Eardley-Wilmot (d 1980); *b* 27 June 1925; *Educ* Sandroyd Sch, Winchester, ChCh Oxford, Univ of Oxford (DLitt); *m* 1951, Ann, *née* Chesney (Lady Dummett); 3 s, 2 da (1 s and 1 da decd); *Career* Univ of Oxford: fell All Souls Coll 1950–79 (sr res fell 1974–79, emeritus fell), reader philosophy of mathematics 1962–74, Wykeham prof of logic 1979–92 (emeritus prof), fell New Coll Oxford 1979–92 (hon fell); Hon DPhil Univ of Nijmegen 1983; Hon DLitt: Univ of Caen 1993, Univ of Aberdeen 1993, Univ of Stirling 2002, Univ of Athens 2004; FBA 1968–81 and 1995–; *Books* Frege: Philosophy of Language (1973), Elements of Intuitionism (1977), Truth and Other Enigmas (1978), The Game of Tarot (1980), Voting Procedures (1984), Frege: Philosophy of Mathematics (1991), The Logical Basis of Metaphysics (1991), Origins of Analytical Philosophy (1993), The Seas of Language (1993), Principles of Electoral Reform (1997), On Immigration and Refugees (2001), Truth and the Past (2005), Thought and Reality (2006); *Recreations* playing exotic card games; *Style*— Prof Sir Michael Dummett, FBA; ✉ 54 Park Town, Oxford OX2 6SJ (tel and fax 01865 558698); New College, Oxford (tel 01865 279555)

DUMVILLE, Prof David Norman; s of Norman Dumville (d 1958), and Eileen Florence Lillie, *née* Gibbs (d 1996); *b* 5 May 1949; *Educ* St Nicholas GS Northwood, Emmanuel Coll Cambridge (open entrance exhibitioner, sr scholar, MA), Univ of Edinburgh (PhD, Jeremiah Dalziel Prize); *m* 23 Nov 1974, Sally Lois, *née* Hannay (d 1989); 1 s (Elliott Thomas b 19 July 1978); *Career* Univ of Wales fell Dept of Welsh UC Swansea 1976–77, asst prof Dept of English Univ of Pennsylvania 1977–78; Univ of Cambridge: univ lectr Dept of Anglo-Saxon, Norse and Celtic 1978–91, reader in early mediaeval history and culture of the British Isles 1991–95, prof of palaeography and cultural history 1995–2004; Girton Coll Cambridge: fell 1978–2004 (life fell 2005–), dir of studies in Anglo-Saxon, Norse and Celtic 1978–2004, coll lectr 1978–99, (moral) tutor 1980–82, memb Cncl 1981–82, memb various Coll ctees; external dir of studies in Anglo-Saxon, Norse and Celtic: Emmanuel Coll and St Catharine's Coll Cambridge 1978–85, Fitzwilliam Coll Cambridge 1991–2003; prof of history, palaeography and Celtic Univ of Aberdeen 2005–; visiting prof and Pepys lectr Center for Medieval and Renaissance Studies UCLA 1995, visiting prof Sch of Celtic Studies Dublin Inst for Advanced Studies 1996–97, distinguished visiting prof of mediaeval studies Univ of Calif Berkeley 1997, visiting fell Huntington Library San Marino CA 1984; vice-pres Centre Int de Recherche et de Documentation sur le Monachisme Celtique (Daoulas) 1986–; Br Acad research reader in the humanities 1985–87, research assoc Sch of Celtic Studies Dublin Inst for Advanced Studies 1989–; managing ed Mediaeval Scandinavia and Jl of Celtic Studies 2002–; memb Editorial Advsy Bd: Anglo-Saxon Studies in Archaeology and History 1978–85, Toronto Medieval Texts and Translations 1978–, Cambridge Medieval Celtic Studies 1980–93, Cambrian Medieval Celtic Studies 1993–2002; author of numerous reviews and articles in learned jls; memb jt Br Acad and Royal Historical Soc Ctee on Anglo-Saxon Charters 1986–90 and 1993–2003; O'Donnell lectr in Celtic Studies: Univ of Oxford 1977/78, Univ of Edinburgh 1980/81, Univ of Wales 1982/83; FRHistS 1976, FSA 1983, FRSAIre 1989, FSA Scot 1999; *Books* Chronicles and Annals of Mediaeval Ireland and Wales: The Clonmacnoise-group Texts (with K Grabowski, 1984), The Historia Brittonum: The 'Vatican' Recension (1985), Britain's Literary Heritage: The Early and Central Middle Ages c650–c1200 AD (1986), Histories and Pseudo-histories of the Insular Middle Ages (1990), Wessex and England from Alfred to Edgar: Six Essays on Political, Cultural, and Ecclesiastical Revival (1992), Liturgy and the Ecclesiastical History of Late Anglo-Saxon England: Four Studies (1992), English Caroline Script and Monastic History: Studies in Benedictinism AD 950–1030 (1993), Saint Patrick AD 493–1993 (jtly, 1993), Britons and Anglo-Saxons in the Early Middle Ages (1993), The Churches of North Britain in the First Viking-Age (1997), Three Men in a Boat: Scribe, Language, and Culture in the Church of Viking-Age Europe (1997), Councils and Synods of the Gaelic Early and Central Middle Ages (1997), A Palaeographer's Review: The Insular System of Scripts in the Early Middle Ages (2 vols, 1999–2005), Saint David of Wales (2001), Annales Cambriae (2002–), The Annals of Ulster (2005–), Cáin Adomnáin and Canones Adomnani (with P P Ó Néill, 2003), Abbreviations used in Insular Script (2004), The Early Mediaeval Insular Churches and the Preservation of Roman Literature (2004), Brenhinoedd y Saeson, 'The Kings of the English' (2005–); *Recreations* travel in North America, politics and other arguments; *Style—* Prof David Dumville; ✉ Department of History, University of Aberdeen, Crombie Annexe, Meston Walk, Old Aberdeen AB24 3FX (tel 01224 272195, fax 01224 272003)

DUNALLEY, 7 Baron (I 1800, but does not use his title); (Henry) Francis Cornelius Prittie; s of 6 Baron Dunalley (d 1992), and (Mary) Philippa, *née* Cary; *b* 30 May 1948; *Educ* Gordonstoun, Trinity Coll Dublin (BA), Bedford Coll London (CQSW); *m* 1978, Sally Louise, er da of late Ronald Vere, of Heaton Chapel, Cheshire; 3 da (Hon Rebecca Louise b 1979, Hon Hannah Beatrice b 1983, Hon Rachel Sarah b 1987), 1 s (Hon Joel Henry b 1981); *Heir* s, Hon Joel Prittie; *Career* probation offr: Inner London Probation Serv 1977–80, Oxfordshire and Buckinghamshire Probation Serv 1980–2001, Thames Valley Probation Serv 2001–03, Shetland Islands Cncl Criminal Justice Unit 2003–; *Style—* Francis Prittie, Esq; ✉ e-mail prittiefamily@ntlworld.com

DUNANT, Sarah; da of David Dunant, and Estelle, *née* Joseph; *Educ* Godolphin & Latymer Sch, Newnham Coll Cambridge (BA); *m*; 2 da (Zoe b 12 March 1987, Georgia b 30 Dec 1990); *Career* prodr BBC Radio 3 and 4 1974–76; freelance journalist, writer and broadcaster 1976–; presenter The Late Show (BBC2), co-writer Thin Air (BBC1), presenter Nightwaves (BBC Radio 3); also appeared on other Radio 4 and Radio 3 progs, BBC World Service and Capital Radio; critic and writer: The Guardian, The Times and The Observer; *Books* Exterminating Angels (jtly, 1983), Intensive Care (jtly, 1986), Snow Storms In A Hot Climate (1988), Birth Marks (1991), Fatlands (1993), War of the Words (ed, 1994), Under My Skin (1995), The Age of Anxiety (ed, 1996), Transgressions (1997), Mapping The Edge (1999), Birth of Venus (2003), In the Company of the Courtesan (2006); *Recreations* travel; *Style—* Ms Sarah Dunant; ✉ c/o Aitken & Stone Ltd, 18–21 Cavaye Place, London SW10 9PT (tel 020 7373 6002, e-mail reception@gillonaitken.co.uk)

DUNBAR, *see also:* Hope-Dunbar

DUNBAR, Sir Archibald Ranulph; 11 Bt (NS 1700), of Northfield, Moray; s of Maj Sir (Archibald) Edward Dunbar, 10 Bt, MC (d 1969); *b* 8 August 1927; *Educ* Wellington, Pembroke Coll Cambridge, Imperial Coll of Tropical Agric Trinidad; *m* 1974, Amelia Millar Sommerville, da of late Horace Campbell Davidson, of Currie, Midlothian; 2 da (Harriet Sophie b 1974, Stephanie Clare b 1975), 1 s (Edward Horace b 1977); *Heir* s, Edward Dunbar; *Career* Colonial Serv: entered 1953, agric offr Uganda, ret 1970; Hon Sheriff Sheriff Ct Dist of Moray; Knight of Honour and Devotion SMOM 1989; *Books* A History of Bunyoro-Kitara (1965), Omukama Chwa II Kabarega (1965), The Annual Crops of Uganda (1969); *Style—* Sir Archibald Dunbar, Bt; ✉ The Old Manse, Duffus, Elgin IV30 5QD (tel 01343 830270)

DUNBAR, Sir James Michael; 14 Bt (NS 1694), of Mochrum, Wigtownshire; er s of Sir Jean Ivor Dunbar, 13 Bt (d 1993), and his 1 w, Rose Jeanne, *née* Hertsch; *b* 17 January 1950; *m* 1, 1978 (m dis 1989), Margaret Marie, da of Albert Jacobs; 2 s (Michael Joseph b 5 July 1980, David Scott b 22 May 1983), 1 da (Stacy Beth b 29 July 1985); m 2, 1989, Margaret Elizabeth, da of Gordon Talbot; 1 da (Cassandra Talbot b 23 July 1991); *Heir* s, Michael Dunbar; *Career* Col USAF, ret; *Style—* Sir James Dunbar, Bt; fax 00 1 704 321 5966, e-mail jmdunbar2@earthlink.net

DUNBAR, Lennox Robert; *b* 17 May 1952; *Career* Peacock Printmakers Aberdeen: etching technician 1978–81, educn offr 1981–86; Grays Sch of Art Aberdeen: lectr in painting and printmaking 1986–87, head of printmaking 1987–97, acting head of fine art 1997–; visiting artist/tutor Louisiana State Univ and Univ of Kansas 1986; visiting lectr: Duncan of Jordanstone Coll of Art Dundee 1987, Coll of Santa Fe New Mexico 1999–, Acad of Fine Art Prague; RSA 2006 (ARSA 1990); *Exhibitions* Scottish Print Open 2 (tour Scotland and Australia) 1980, Peacock Printmakers (Finland) 1980, RSA Award Winners 1945–79 (Artspace Gallery Aberdeen) 1980, Five Artists from Aberdeen (Third Eye Centre Glasgow) 1982, Printmakers Drawings (Printmakers Workshop Edinburgh) 1982, New Scottish Prints (City Gallery NY then tour of USA and Canada 1983–84) 1983, Printmaking in Scotland (Festival Exhibition) 1983, RSA Galleries (Edinburgh) 1983, Etching (Scottish Arts Cncl touring exhbn) 1983, Scottish Print Open 3 (tour of Scotland) 1983, Four North East Artists (Fruitmarket Gallery Edinburgh & Aberdeen Art Gallery) 1983, Eight Br Print Biennale (Bradford) 1984, Lennox Dunbar and Ian Howard (Glasgow Arts Centre) 1984, Contemporary Scottish Drawings (Fine Art Soc) 1984, Double Elephant - Br Prints (Barbican Arts Centre) 1985, Peacock Printmakers (Talbot Rice Gallery Edinburgh and Aberdeen Art Gallery) 1986, Scottish Print Open 4 (tour of Scotland) 1987, Humberside Print Open 1987, Art of the Print - A Century of Scottish Printmaking (Fine Art Soc) 1987, Premio Biella Per L'Inlusione (Italy) 1987, Printmakers Drawings (Mercury Gallery Edinburgh) 1987, Six North East Artists (369 Gallery Edinburgh, Pier Arts Centre Orkney and Artspace Gallery Aberdeen) 1988, Scottish Art (Collegium Artisticum Sarajevo) 1988, Cleveland Drawing Biennale (Middlesbrough) 1989, Humberside Print Open (tour of USSR) 1989, Intergrafik 90 (Berlin) 1990, Fruitmarket Open (Fruitmarket Gallery Edinburgh) 1990, Guthrie Award Winners (RSA, Fine Art Soc) 1990, RGI (Mall Galleries London) 1990, Inverclyde Biennial 1990, Paperworks IV (Seagate Gallery Dundee) 1993, Five Printmakers (RSA) 1995, New Work on Paper (Hatton Gallery Newcastle upon Tyne and Peacock Printmakers Aberdeen) 1995, Cheltenham Drawing Open 1996, Peacock 21 (Aberdeen Art Gallery) 1996, Int Print Triennal (Cracow) 1997, The Large Edition (Quicksilver Gallery London and Malvern Gallery) 1997, Contemporary Scottish Painters & Printmakers (Beatrice Royal Contemporary Art Gallery Hants) 1997, 36 Units (Compass Gallery Glasgow) 1999, Peacock Printmakers Aberdeen 1999, Bonhoga Gallery Shetland 1999, Trondheim Biennale (Norway and Touring USA) 1999; *Awards* RSA Meyer Oppenheim Award for Painting 1976, RSA Latimer Award for Painting 1978, Scottish Arts Cncl Bursary 1981, Scottish Arts Cncl Travel Award (to NY) 1983, RSA Guthrie Award for Painting 1984, winner Paisley Art Inst Drawing Competition 1987 (2nd prize 1985), maj prizewinner Cleveland Drawing Biennale 1989, Shell Expro Premier Award 1991, 1993 and 2006, RSA Highland Soc of London Award 1992, SSA Whyte and Mackay Award 1995, RSA Gillies Award 1999, prizewinner Int Print Biennale Varna 2001; *Style—* Lennox Dunbar, Esq

DUNBAR, Sir Robert Drummond Cospatrick; 10 Bt (NS 1698), of Durn, Banffshire; s of Sir Drummond Dunbar, 9 Bt (d 2000); *b* 17 June 1958; *Educ* Harrow, ChCh Oxford; *m* 1994, Sarah Margaret, da of Robert Brooks, of Hattingley, Hants; 1 s (Alexander b 1 March 1995), 1 da (Rosanna b 12 July 1999); *Heir* s, Alexander Dunbar, Younger of Durn; *Career* admitted slr 1982, with Private Client Dept Allen & Overy 1980–86, investment mangr Mercury Warburg Investment Management (subsequently Merrill Lynch Investment Managers) 1986–2003; ASIP 1986; *Style—* Sir Robert Dunbar, Bt

DUNBAR, Prof Robin Ian MacDonald; s of George MacDonald Dunbar (d 1998), and Betty Lilian, *née* Toon (d 1998); *b* 28 June 1947; *Educ* Magdalen Coll Sch Brackley, Magdalen Coll Oxford (BA), Univ of Bristol (PhD); *m* 1971, Eva Patricia, *née* Melvin; 2 s (Jared Ian MacDonald b 1975, Arran Joseph William b 1982), 1 da (Zaila Yvette b 1979); *Career* SERC research fell King's Coll and Dept of Zoology Univ of Cambridge 1977–82, lectr Zoological Inst Univ of Stockholm 1983, research fell Zoology Dept Univ of Liverpool 1985–87, successively lectr, reader and prof Anthropology Dept UCL 1987–94, prof of psychology Psychology Dept Univ of Liverpool, prof of evolutionary psychology Sch of Biological Sciences Univ of Liverpool 1997–2007, prof of evolutionary anthropology Univ of Oxford 2007–; memb Home Office Animal Procedures Ctee 1997–2004, memb Scientific Advsy Ctee Fondacion J-M Delwast 2000–04; memb: Assoc for Study of Animal Behaviour, Primate Soc of GB, International Behavioural Ecology Soc, American Psychological Assoc, Br Ecological Soc, Br Assoc for Advancement of Sci, American Assoc for the Advancement of Science, Save British Science, Galton Inst, Human Behaviour and Evolution Soc; FRAI 1989, FBA 1998; *Books* Social Dynamics of Gelada Baboons (jtly, 1975), Current Problems in Sociobiology (jt ed, 1982), Reproductive Decisions: An Economic Analysis of Gelada Baboon Social Strategies (1984), The World of Nature (1986), Primate Social Systems (1988), The Trouble with Science (1995), Human Reproductive Decisions: Biological and Social Perspectives (ed, 1995), Grooming, Gossip and the Evolution of Language (1996), Evolution of Culture and Language in Primates and Humans (jt ed, 1996), The Evolution of Culture (jt ed, 1999), Primate Conservation Biology (jtly, 2000), Cousins (jtly, 2000), Human Evolutionary Psychology (jtly, 2001), The Human Story (2004), Evolutionary Psychology (jtly, 2005), Oxford Handbook of Evolutionary Psychology (jt ed, 2007); *Recreations* hill walking, medieval, Renaissance and Baroque music, ecclesiastical architecture, archaeology; *Clubs* Ramblers' Assoc; *Style—* Prof Robin Dunbar; ✉ Institute of Cognitive and Evolutionary Anthropology, University of Oxford, 51 Banbury Road, Oxford OX2 3PE

DUNBAR OF HEMPRIGGS, Sir Richard Francis; 9 Bt (NS 1706), of Hempriggs, Caithness-shire; s of Leonard James Blake (d 1989), and Dame Maureen Daisy Helen Dunbar of Hempriggs (baronetess in her own right, d 1997); suc mother 1997, having assumed the name of Dunbar of Hempriggs in lieu of Blake 1965; *Educ* Charterhouse; *m* 1969, (Elizabeth Margaret) Jane, o da of George Lister, of Gloucester; 2 da (Emma Katherine b 9 Nov 1977, Fiona Blake b 2 Sept 1981); *Heir* da, Emma Dunbar of Hempriggs, yr; *Style—* Sir Richard Dunbar of Hempriggs, Bt; ✉ PO Box 1423, Burlinghame, California 94011, USA; Reiss, Wick, Caithness

DUNBOYNE, 29 Baron (19 by Patent) (I 1324 and 1541); John Fitzwalter Butler; s of 28 Baron Dunboyne, VRD (d 2004), and Anne Marie, *née* Mallet; *b* 31 July 1951; *Educ* Winchester, Trinity Coll Cambridge (MA), London Business Sch (Sloan fell); *m* 1975, Diana Caroline, yr da of Sir Michael Williams, KCMG; 3 da (Hon Genevieve b 1977 d 2006, Hon Imogen b 1979, Hon Cleone b 1986), 1 s (Hon Richard b 1983); *Heir* s, Hon Richard Butler; *Career* Hill Samuel Group 1974–75, Stolt Neilsen Inc 1977–78, Lazard Brothers & Co Ltd 1979–80, mgmnt conslt 1980–, dir Fitzwalter & Co Ltd 1985–; projects incl: EU Consortium for Privatisation in Kazakhstan 1994, project co-ordinating team ldr for Western Siberia EU Tacis Enterprise Support Centres for large and medium sized enterprises 1998–99, ISCRA Investment Support Centres in Russia London Business Sch/DFID 2000–02, EU Tacis Assistance to Miny of Economics and Finance Kabardino-Balkarian Repub Russia 2004; transatlantic voyage in small sailing boat 1975–76; *Recreations* international relations, sailing, country pursuits, quixotic causes; *Clubs* Butler Soc (vice-pres), Irish Peers Assoc, Cruising Assoc; *Style—* The Rt Hon the Lord Dunboyne

DUNCAN, Alan J C; MP; *b* 31 March 1957; *Educ* Merchant Taylors', St John's Coll Oxford (pres Oxford Union, cox coll 1st VIII), Harvard Univ (Kennedy scholar); *Career* with Shell International Petroleum 1979–81, oil trader and conslt on oil supply and refining industries 1982–92 (in Singapore 1984–86), MP (Cons) Rutland and Melton 1992– (Parly candidate (Cons) Barnsley W and Penistone 1987); PPS to: min of state for Health 1993–94 (resigned), Dr Brian Mawhinney as chm Cons Pty 1995–97; Parly political sec to Rt Hon William Hague MP, Leader of the Oppn 1997–98, vice-chm Cons Pty until 1998, oppn front bench spokesman on health 1998–99, oppn front bench spokesman on trade and industry 1999–2001, shadow min for foreign and Cwlth affrs 2001–03, shadow sec of state for constitutional affrs 2003–04, shadow int devpt sec 2004–05, shadow sec of state for tport 2005, shadow sec of state for trade and industry 2005–07, shadow sec of state for business, enterprise and regulatory reform 2007–; Freeman City of London, Liveryman Worshipful Co of Merchant Taylors; *Books* Saturn's Children, How the State Devours Liberty, Prosperity and Virtue (with Dominic Hobson, 1995); *Publications* An End to Illusions (1993); *Recreations* fishing, shooting; *Style—* Alan Duncan, Esq, MP; ✉ House of Commons, London SW1A 0AA (e-mail duncana@parliament.uk)

DUNCAN, Rev Canon Bruce; MBE (1993); s of Andrew Allan Duncan (d 1984), and Dora, *née* Young; *b* 28 January 1938; *Educ* St Albans Sch, Univ of Leeds (BA), Cuddesdon Theol Coll; *m* 17 Dec 1966, Margaret Holmes, da of late Ralph Lister Smith; 3 da (Sarah (Mrs Simon Lagden) b 17 Sept 1967, Kate b 27 June 1969, Helen b 24 Jan 1971); *Career* fndr dir: Children's Relief Int 1960–65, Northorpe Hall Tst 1960–65; asst curate St Bartholomew's and i/c St Mary of Bethany Armley Leeds (concurrently asst chaplain Armley Prison) 1967–79, hon curate St Mary the Less Cambridge 1969–70, chaplain Order of the Holy Paraclete and St Hilda's Sch Whitby 1970–71, chaplain to HM Ambassadors in Austria, Hungary and Czechoslovakia (based Vienna) 1971–75, vicar Collegiate Church of the Holy Cross and the Mother of Him Who Hung Thereon Crediton 1975–86, rural dean Cadbury 1976–81, rector Crediton and Shobrooke 1982–86, residentiary canon Manchester Cathedral and fell Coll of Christ Manchester 1986–95, princ Sarum Coll (formerly Salisbury and Wells Theol Coll) 1995–2002, canon Salisbury Cathedral and prebendary Chesenbury with Chute 1995–2002, canon emeritus Salisbury Cathedral 2002–, Lazenby chaplain Univ of Exeter 2003–04; archbishops' advsr for foreign rels 1971–75, chm Diocesan Bd for Mission and Unity 1975–86, chm Bd of Int Conslts Trinity Inst for Christianity and Culture 2002–; chm Cathedral Fabric Ctee Manchester 1988–91; memb: Exeter Diocesan Synod 1975–86, Bishop's Cncl 1975–86, Diocesan Advsy Ctee Manchester 1987–93, Cathedral Fabric Advsy Ctee Bradford 1997–2002, Salisbury Diocesan Synod 1997–2002; The Northorpe Hall Tst: tstee 1965–97, chm 1977–97, pres 1997–; memb Int Ctee of Vol Agencies Working for Refugees Geneva 1960–65, govr Hayward's Sch 1975–86, lectr S Manchester Coll Dip in Counselling 1986–95, dir Manchester Cathedral Devpt Tst 1986–95; memb Int Conslts Bd Trinity Inst for Christianity and Culture 2004–; memb Br Assoc of Psychological Type 1989 (memb Bd 1990–93); chm of tstees: St Luke's Coll Fndn 2006 (tstee 2005–), Families for Children Adoption Agency 2006–; Commissary in the UK for the Bishop of the North Eastern Caribbean & Aruba 2006; awarded Archbishop of Canterbury's Cross of St Augustine 2004; Hon DD Grad Theol Fndn Indiana 2002, hon fell Sarum Coll 2006–; FRSA 1989; *Books* Children at Risk (ed A H Denny, 1968), Sich Selbst Verstehen (1993), Pray Your Way: Your Personality and God (1993); *Recreations* travel, walking, five grandchildren, music, cookery, bookbinding, depth psychology, growing clematis; *Clubs*

Athenaeum; *Style*— The Rev Canon Bruce Duncan, MBE; ✉ Church Path Cottage, St David's Hill, Exeter, Devon EX4 4DU (tel 01392 422485, e-mail churchpath@fsmail.net)

DUNCAN, Clive; John Charles Duncan (d 1973), of Dublin, and Irene Florence, *née* Boys (d 1973); *b* 5 September 1944; *Educ* John Colet Sch Wendover, High Wycombe Coll of Art, Camberwell Sch of Art (NDD), City & Guilds Sch of Art; *m* Jan 1970, Janet, *née* McQueen; 1 da (Catharine), 1 s (Alexander); *Career* sculptor and teacher; head of sch Heatherley Wilson Sch of Art 1969–71, head of sculpture and princ lectr Sir John Cass Faculty of Art and Design London Guildhall Univ 1973–93, pres Thomas Heatherley Educational Tst 1973–93; visiting lectr City & Guilds Sculpture Sch, UCL, Slade Summer Sch; exhibitions design conslt Sothebys London; gall lectr on bronze casting V&A; FRBS 1984, RBA 1984, memb Soc of Portrait Sculptors 2005; *Selected Exhibitions* Royal Acad Summer Show 1968, 1969, 1971, 1975, 1979, 1981, 1982, 1987, 1988, 1993 and 1996, Glasgow Inst of Fine Art 1968, The Guildhall London 1974 and 1978, Nicholas Treadwell Gall London 1978, Portland Sculpture Park Dorset 1981, RBA 1983, Playhouse Gall Harlow 1983, Henley Mgmnt Coll 1993, Oxfordshire Artists Culham 1994 and 1995, Henley Arts Festival 1996, Soc of Portrait Sculptors; Trafalgar Crown and fifty pence piece both commissioned by Royal Mint, other commissions incl portraits, head studies, sculptures and inscriptions; work featured in Museum of Reading and in sculpture collections in US, Spain, England and Scotland; *Awards* Bucks Art Scholarship 1963, Leon Underwood Drawing Prize 1965, Surdival Meml Award for Sculpture 1998; *Publications* From Lost Wax to Found Bronze (booklet and video); *Style*— Clive Duncan, Esq; ✉ Holme Cottage, Station Road, Shiplake, Henley-on-Thames, Oxfordshire RG9 3JS

DUNCAN, Grant Stuart; s of Stuart Duncan, of London, and Pat, *née* Wollen; *b* 15 April 1958, Singapore; *Educ* Dulwich Coll, Univ of St Andrews (MA), INSEAD; *m* 1989 (m dis), Penny, *née* Marson; 1 s (Louis b 2 June 1995), 1 da (Nina b 3 July 1998); *Career* grad trainee rising to client services dir Collett Dickenson Pearce 1982–93, md Gold Greenlees Trott/TBWA 1993–99, md rising to chief exec Publicis 1999–2007, ptnr Grace Blue Worldwide 2007–; bd dir Mktg Soc, non-exec dir World Archipelago; tstee Prostate Cancer Charity; FIPA 2004; *Recreations* watching Chelsea, collecting art, loving my children; *Clubs* Soho House, The Hospital; *Style*— Grant Duncan, Esq; ✉ mobile 07770 271068

DUNCAN, Very Rev Dr Gregor Duthie; s of Edwin John Duncan, of Largs, and Janet Brown, *née* Simpson; *b* 11 October 1950; *Educ* Allan Glen's Sch Glasgow, Univ of Glasgow (MA), Clare Coll Cambridge (PhD), Oriel Coll Oxford (BA), Ripon Coll Cuddesdon; *Career* research asst Univ of Oxford 1976–80; ordained: deacon 1983, priest 1984; curate Oakham with Hambleton and Egleton and Braunston with Brooke 1983–86, chaplain Edinburgh Theol Coll 1987–89, rector St Columba's Largs 1989–99, rector St Ninian's Glasgow 1999–, dean Dio of Glasgow and Galloway 1996–; memb Gen Synod Scottish Episcopal Church 1990–98, 2000–03 and 2006– (former tutor Theol Inst); *Style*— The Very Rev Dr Gregor Duncan; ✉ St Ninian's Rectory, 32 Glencairn Drive, Glasgow G41 4PW (tel 0141 423 1247, fax 0141 424 3332, e-mail dean@glasgow.anglican.org)

DUNCAN, Ian Alexander; s of Kenneth George Duncan (d 1979), and Peggy Pauline, *née* Stuchbury (d 2004); *b* 21 April 1946; *Educ* Central GS Birmingham, Coll of Commerce Birmingham; *m* Carol Hammond, da of William Wilford Smith (d 1991), of Watnall, Notts; 2 s (Adam Harvey b 1966, Alexander James b 1975), 1 da (Tavira Caroline b 1975); *Career* CA; European controller Otis Elevator 1970–72, dir treasy ops Europe Rockwell Int 1972–75, treas int ops Avis Rent a Car 1975–79, vice-pres Leasco 1979–80, vice-pres Reliance World Trade Co 1979–80, fin dir Pentos plc 1980–84; Tomkins plc: fin dir 1984–92, md fin 1992–99, dep chm 1995–99; ptnr: Compass Partners Int 2000–02, Dimitra Capital Partners LLP 2002–07; chm: Volution Holdings 2003–06, Darchem Holdings 2002–04; chm various private equity interests; Freeman City of London, Liveryman Worshipful Co of Glaziers; CCMI, Fndn FCT, FCCA, FRSA; *Recreations* field sports, the Arts, travel, flying helicopters, scuba diving; *Style*— Ian A Duncan, Esq; ✉ Durham House, Durham Place, London SW3 4ET (fax 020 7823 3642, e-mail ianaduncan@email1000.fsnet.co.uk); Kildermorie Estate, Ardross, Easter Ross IV17 0YH (fax 01349 880655)

DUNCAN, Jacqueline Ann; da of late Sonia Whitaker, *née* Bromley; *b* 16 December 1931; *Educ* Convent of the Sacred Heart Brighton, House of Citizenship London; *m* 1, 1955 (m dis 1963), Michael Inchbald; 1 s (Courtenay Charles b 1958), 1 da (Charlotte Amanda b 1960); m 2, 5 June 1974, Brig Peter Trevenen Thwaites (d 1991); m 3, 10 Feb 1994, Col Andrew Duncan, LVO, OBE; *Career* fndr and princ: Inchbald Sch of Design 1960–, Inchbald Sch of Fine Arts 1970–, Inchbald Sch of Garden Design 1972–; memb: Monopolies Cmmn 1972–75, Whitfield Ctee on Copyright and Design 1974–76, London Electricity Conservation Cncl 1973–76, Visiting Ctee RCA 1986–90; tstee St Peter's Res Tst 1987–90; cncllr Westminster City Cncl (Warwick Ward) 1974–78; acting pres Int Soc of Interior Designers (London Chapter) 1987–90; govr Oaklands Primary Sch Welwyn Herts 2003; JP South Westminster 1976–94; fell Int Soc of Interior Designers 1994 (chm 1990–92), fell Interior Designers and Decorators Assoc 1996; *Books* Directory of Interior Designers (1966), Bedrooms (1968), Design & Decoration (1971); *Recreations* arboriculture, fishing, historical research; *Clubs* Cavalry and Guards', Guards Polo; *Style*— Mrs Andrew Duncan; ✉ Inchbald School of Design, 32 Eccleston Square, London SW1V 1PB (tel 020 7630 9011, fax 020 7976 5979, e-mail principal@inchbald.co.uk)

DUNCAN, John; s of John Duncan (d 1976), of Henfield, W Sussex, and Doris Annie, *née* Withers (d 1980); *b* 20 April 1936; *Educ* Steyning GS; *m* 1 (m dis); 2 s (Alistair John b 12 Feb 1959, Graham Michael b 23 July 1961); m 2, 22 Jan 1997, Helen Ruth; *Career* National Westminster Bank (formerly Westminster Bank): various positions rising to dep mangr City of London 1952–74, chief info offr and dep head of public affrs 1974–79; dir of PR Dewe Rogerson Ltd 1979–83, divnl vice-pres (public affrs) American Express Travel Related Servs EMEA 1983–86, gp corp affrs dir Inchcape plc 1986–95; writer and commentator 1995–; chm Banner Duncan Assocs 1997–; FCIB, FIPR; *Books* How to Manage Your Bank Manager (1982); *Recreations* sport, particularly golf and cricket, theatre, music, travel; *Clubs* Lord's Taverners, Highgate Golf, MCC; *Style*— John Duncan, Esq; ✉ 34 Prebend Street, London N1 8PS (tel and fax 020 7359 8259, mobile 07808 293988, e-mail jdjd@blueyonder.co.uk)

DUNCAN, Kathleen Nora; OBE (2007); da of George James Denis Dale (d 1983), and Nellie Logan, *née* Jamieson (d 2001); *b* 26 September 1946; *Educ* Christ's Hosp, St Aidan's Coll Durham (BA), Poly of Central London (Dip Arts Admin); *m* 11 Jan 1975 (m dis 1983), Neil Stuart Duncan (d 1997); *Career* head of arts servs London Borough of Havering 1971–73, dep dir SE Arts 1974–76, chief exec Composers and Authors Soc of Hong Kong 1977–79, gen mangr Archer Travel Hong Kong 1979–82, int mktg dir Boosey & Hawkes Music Publishers Ltd 1983–86, mktg dir Order of St John 1986–89, mktg conslt The Performing Rights Soc Ltd 1989–90, DG Lloyds TSB Foundation for England and Wales 1990–2005; memb Bd Crime Concern 1993–2000 (dep chm 1994–2000), memb Exec Ctee Assoc of Charitable Fndns 1994–2000 (dep chair 1999–2000), chm DfES Parenting Fund 2005–06; tstee: Nat Family and Parenting Inst 1999–2006, Cmmn for the Future of Volunteering 2005–07, New Philanthropy Capital 2006–, Changing Faces 2006–07, Youth Music 2006–, Br Inst of Human Rights 2006–, Hosking Houses Tst 2006–; govr Christ's Hosp 1974– (almoner 1984–1998); *Recreations* music, travel, walking; *Clubs* Reform; *Style*— Mrs Kathleen Duncan, OBE; ✉ 148 Cranmer Court, London SW3 3HF (tel 020 7589 6777)

DUNCAN, Lindsay Vere; *b* 7 November 1950; *m* Hilton McRae; 1 s (Cal); *Career* actress; *Theatre* incl: Progress (Bush Theatre), Hedda Gabler (Hampstead Theatre), Top Girls (Royal Court London and Jo Papps Public Theatre NY, awarded NY Obie), The Merry Wives of Windsor, Les Liaisons Dangereuses (West End and Broadway, Olivier Award, Theatre World Award and Tony nomination for Best Actress) and Troilus & Cressida (all RSC), Berenice, Cat on a Hot Tin Roof (Evening Standard Best Actress Award), Plenty, The Provok'd Wife and The Prince of Homburg (all NT), Three Hotels (Tricycle Theatre), The Cryptogram (Ambassadors Theatre), A Midsummer Night's Dream (RSC), Ashes to Ashes (Royal Court and Gramercy Theatre NYC), The Homecoming (NT), Celebration and The Room (both Almeida and Pinter Festival NYC), Mouth to Mouth (Royal Court and Albery Theatre, won Critics Circle Best Actress Award), Private Lives (Albery Theatre, winner of Critics Circle, Olivier, Variety Club, Tony and Drama Desk (NY) Awards for Best Actress), A Midsummer Night's Dream (US Tour and Broadway), That Face (Royal Court) 2007; also performed in the opening season at Royal Exchange Theatre; *Television* incl: Rainy Day Women (BBC), Grown Ups (BBC), GBH (Channel 4, Bafta nomination for Best Actress), Traffik (Channel 4, FIPA D'Or (Cannes)), Redemption (BBC), A Year in Provence (BBC), The Rector's Wife (Channel 4, Best Actress Monte Carlo TV Festival), Jake's Progress (Channel 4), Tom Jones (BBC), Shooting the Past (BBC), Oliver Twist (ITV), Dirty Tricks (ITV), Perfect Strangers (BBC, Bafta nomination for Best Actress), Rome (HBO), Poirot: The Mystery of the Blue Train, Spooks, Longford, Rome (series 2); *Film* incl: Loose Connections, Prick Up Your Ears, The Reflecting Skin, City Hall, A Midsummer Night's Dream, An Ideal Husband, Mansfield Park, Under the Tuscan Sun, Afterlife (Best Actress Bratislava Film Festival and Bowmore Scottish Screen Award), Starter for Ten; *Style*— Lindsay Duncan; ✉ c/o Paul Lyon-Maris, ICM, Oxford House, 76 Oxford Street, London W1D 1BS (tel 020 7636 6565, fax 020 7323 0101)

DUNCAN, Mary (Mrs Adrian White); da of Kenneth Playfair Duncan (d 1999), and Gillian Duncan; *b* 19 November 1958, Warrington; *Educ* Bicester Comp, Univ of Exeter (LLB), Coll of Law; *m* Sept 1985, Adrian White; 2 s (Alexander b 31 Oct 1991, Thomas b 4 Feb 1994); *Career* admitted slr 1983; articled clerk then asst slr Henmans 1981–85, asst slr Greenwoods 1985–86, asst slr then ptnr Henmans LLP 1986–; memb Personal Injury Panel Law Soc; *Books* Fatal Accident Claims (1993), Trauma Care: A Team Approach (contrib, 2000), Health and Safety at Work Essentials (co-author, 2003); *Recreations* family, music, tennis, gardening; *Style*— Mrs Mary Duncan; ✉ Henmans LLP, 500 Oxford Business Park South, Oxford OX4 2BH (tel 01865 781000, fax 01865 778687, e-mail mary.duncan@henmansllp.co.uk)

DUNCAN, Michael Greig; s of Alec Greig Duncan (d 1979), and Betty, *née* Shaw; *b* 9 September 1957; *Educ* King Williams Coll IOM, Downing Coll Cambridge (MA); *m* 2 July 1983, Fiona Helen, da of Michael John Carlisle Glaze, CMG; 2 s (Rory b 8 March 1985, Adam b 12 June 1989), 1 da (Chloe b 14 Oct 1986); *Career* admitted slr 1981, ptnr Allen & Overy 1987– (asst slr 1981–86, currently chm Global Banking Practice); memb City of London Law Soc; *Style*— Michael Duncan, Esq; ✉ Allen & Overy LLP, One Bishops Square, London E1 6AO

DUNCAN, Dr Peter Watson; s of Arthur Alexander Watson Duncan, of Edinburgh, and Catherine Bowes, *née* Williamson; *b* 14 April 1954; *Educ* George Heriot's Sch, Univ of Edinburgh (MB ChB); *m* 16 April 1983, Fiona Margaret, da of Arthur Murray Grierson, of Tetbury, Glos; 2 da (Meg b 3 April 1985, Jane b 18 Aug 1989), 1 s (Ian b 27 Feb 1987); *Career* registrar in anaesthetics Royal Infirmary of Edinburgh 1979–82; sr registrar in anaesthetics: Newcastle upon Tyne 1982–85, Univ of Natal Durban 1983–84; Royal Preston Hosp: conslt in anaesthetics and intensive care 1985–, clinical dir (anaesthetics) 1991–97; chm Assoc of NW Intensive Care Units 1996–2000, memb Guidelines Advsy Gp Nat Inst for Clinical Excellence (NICE) 2003–; memb Intensive Care Soc; FRCA 1981; *Recreations* photography, music; *Style*— Dr Peter Duncan; ✉ Royal Preston Hospital, Sharoe Green Lane, Preston, Lancashire (tel 01772 522555, e-mail peter.duncan@lthtr.nhs.uk)

DUNCAN, Richard; *see:* Rudin, Richard Duncan

DUNCAN, His Hon Judge Sean Bruce; s of Joseph Alexander Duncan (d 1994), and Patricia Pauline Duncan (D 2006); *b* 21 December 1942; *Educ* Shrewsbury, St Edmund Hall Oxford (MA); *m* 20 April 1974, Diana Bowyer Courtney; 3 s (Thomas Alexander Courtney b 26 Dec 1976, Hugo Patrick Miles b 13 Nov 1978, Joel Renvyle Charles b 1 March 1981), 1 da (Hannah Rose b 26 Feb 1983); *Career* called to the Bar Inner Temple 1966 (scholar); in practice Northern Circuit 1966–88, circuit judge (Northern Circuit) 1988–; pres Cncl of HM's Circuit Judges 2002 (hon sec 1996–99), hon sec Ctee Northern Circuit 1985–88; memb Cheshire Yeo (TA) 1963–69; chm Old Swan Boys Club 1974–77, vice-chm Liverpool Cncl of Social Serv 1981–88, memb ctee Shrewsbury House Youth Club 1990–; *Recreations* boating, golf, opera, jazz, cinema; *Clubs* Liverpool Ramblers AFC (pres 2000–02), Royal Liverpool Golf (capt 2003); *Style*— His Hon Judge Duncan; ✉ Queen Elizabeth II Law Courts, Derby Square, Liverpool L2 1XA (tel and fax 0151 255 0485)

DUNCAN-JONES, Prof Katherine Dorothea; da of Prof Austin Duncan-Jones (d 1964), and Elsie Elizabeth, *née* Phare (d 2003); *b* 13 May 1941; *Educ* King Edward VI HS for Girls Birmingham, St Hilda's Coll Oxford (Violet Vaughan Morgan scholarship, Charles Oldham Shakespeare Prize, Matthew Arnold Prize); *m* 1971 (m dis 1989), A N Wilson, *qv*; 2 da (Emily b 20 Nov 1971, Beatrice b 7 April 1974); *Career* fell: New Hall Cambridge 1964–65, Somerville Coll Oxford 1965–2001 (sr res fell 2001–); author numerous articles on Renaissance literature and theatre reviews; memb Cncl: Malone Soc, Mgmnt of the Friends of the Bodleian Library; first recipient Ben Jonson Discoveries Prize 1997, awarded prof as title of distinction Univ of Oxford 1998; fell Folger Shakespeare Library 1998, memb Shakespeare Birthplace Tst 2000, hon res fell UCL; FRSL 1991; *Books* Sir Philip Sidney: Courtier Poet (1991), Shakespeare's Sonnets (1997), Ungentle Shakespeare: Scenes from His Life (2001), Shakespeare's Life and World (2004), Shakespeare's Narrative and Other Poems (jtly, 2007); *Recreations* swimming, theatre-going; *Clubs* Summerfields Sch Pool (Oxford); *Style*— Prof Katherine Duncan-Jones, FRSL; ✉ Somerville College, Oxford OX2 6HD (tel 01865 511024, e-mail katherine.duncan-jones@some.ox.ac.uk)

DUNCAN-JONES, Dr Richard Phare; s of Austin Ernest Duncan-Jones, and Elsie Elizabeth Duncan-Jones (d 2003); *b* 14 September 1937; *Educ* King Edward's Sch Birmingham, King's Coll Cambridge (MA, PhD); *m* 1986, Julia Elizabeth, *née* Poole; *Career* Gonville & Caius Coll Cambridge: W M Tapp research fell 1963–67, domestic bursar 1967–84, official fell 1967–, coll lectr and dir of studies in classics 1984–; memb Inst for Advanced Study Princeton 1971–72; FBA 1992, FSA 2000; *Books* The Economy of the Roman Empire (1974, 2 edn 1982), Structure and Scale in the Roman Economy (1990), Money and Government in the Roman Empire (1994); also author of articles in learned jls; *Recreations* walking, wine tasting, continental cinema; *Style*— Dr Richard Duncan-Jones, FBA, FSA; ✉ Gonville & Caius College, Cambridge CB2 1TA (tel 01223 332394)

DUNCAN SMITH, Rt Hon (George) Iain; PC (2001), MP; s of late Gp Capt Wilfred George Gerald Duncan Smith, DSO (and bar), DFC (and 2 bars), and Pamela Duncan Smith; *b* 9 April 1954; *Educ* Conway, Univ per Stranieri di Perugia, RMA Sandhurst, Dunchurch Coll; *m* 1982, Hon Elizabeth Wynn, da of 5 Baron Cottesloe, *qv*; 2 s, 2 da; *Career* cmmnd Scots Gds 1975, ADC to Gen Sir John Acland and Cdr of Cwlth Monitoring Force in Zimbabwe 1979; with GEC Marconi 1981–88; dir: Bellwinch Property Ltd 1988–89, Jane's Information Group 1989–92; Parly candidate (Cons) Bradford W 1987; MP (Cons): Chingford 1992–97, Chingford and Woodford Green 1997–; shadow sec of state for Social

D

Security 1997–99, shadow sec of state for Defence 1999–2001, ldr Cons Pty and ldr HM Opposition 2001–03; chm Centre for Social Justice 2004–; jt sec: Cons Back Bench Foreign and Cwlth Affrs Ctee 1992–97, Cons Back Bench Def Ctee 1995–96; chm Cons Back Bench Social Security Ctee 1997–99, chm Cons Back Bench Defence Ctee 1999–; memb Select Ctee: Health 1993–95, Administration 1993–97, Standards in Public Life (Standards and Privileges Ctee) 1995–97; chm: Cons Pty Policy Bd 2001–03, Cons Pty Social Justice Policy Gp 2005–; vice-chm Fulham Cons Assoc 1991; Freeman City of London 1993; *Publications* The Devil's Tune (novel), Who Benefits (Social Security), Game, Set and Match? (Maastricht), Facing the Future (Defence and Foreign and Commonwealth Affairs), 1994 and Beyond, A European Germany or A German Europe?, Five Years and Counting ... Britain and Europe's Growing Vulnerability to Missile Attack, A Race Against Time, Britian's conservative Majority: Good for Me Good for My Neighbour; *Style*— The Rt Hon Iain Duncan Smith, MP; ✉ House of Commons, London SW1A 0AA

DUNCANSON, Neil; s of Jack Duncanson (d 1994), and Olive, *née* Smith, of Saxmundham, Suffolk; *b* 14 February 1960; *Educ* Coopers' Co and Coborn Sch Upminster Essex, Harlow Tech Coll Essex, NCTJ (full cert), Nat Film and TV Sch (directors' course); *m* 1980, Julie, da of Reginald Green; 1 s (Sam b 7 Dec 1988), 1 da (Jessica b 12 Aug 1993); *Career* chief reporter Newham Recorder 1978–84, news journalist (on and off screen) Thames TV 1984–86, deviser/prodr Men on Earth series and others for Thames TV Sport 1986–88 (news ed ITV Olympic Games Seoul 1988), prodr/dir 2 Eyewitness series and 7–Sport for LWT 1988–90, freelance prodr 1990–91, with Chrysalis Television 1991–92, md Chrysalis Television 1992–; credits incl: Italian Football (Channel 4), Rugby Special/Bowls (BBC), NBA (Channel 4), Graham Taylor: Cutting Edge (Channel 4), Formula One (ITV), Spanish Soccer, Baseball, Angling (BSkyB), Gazza's Coming Home (Channel 4 and ITV), Nick Hancock videos, Arsenal videos, Inside Rugby (Channel 4), It's Only A Game (Channel 4), No Balls Allowed (Channel 4), Reg and Harry's Classic Fight Night (ITV 2), Top Ten Series (Channel 4); awards incl: Silver Shot (for The Fastest Men on Earth) Euro Film and TV Festival 1989, Gold Medal (for 7–Sport) NY Film and TV Festival 1990, Indie Award for Best Sports Programming (for Italian Football 1993 and Formula One 1999, Sports Video of the Year Award 1994 and 1995, RTS Sports Journalism Award (for Graham Taylor: Cutting Edge) 1995, RTS Best Live Sports Coverage (for Formula One) 1998; dir: Queen's Park Rangers FC, Wasps RUFC; memb RTS 1994; *Books* The Fastest Men on Earth (1988), Sports Technology (1991), The Olympic Games (1992), Tales of Gold (with Patrick Collins, 1992), Crown of Thorns (with Norman Giller, 1992); *Recreations* soccer, tennis, movies, writing, Egyptology, sports history, collecting sports memorabilia; *Style*— Neil Duncanson, Esq; ✉ Chrysalis TV Building, 46–52 Pentonville Road, London N1 9HF (tel 020 7502 6000, fax 020 7502 5600)

DUNCOMBE, *see*: Pauncefort-Duncombe

DUNDAS, James Frederick Trevor (Jamie); s of Sir Hugh Dundas, CBE, DSO, DFC (d 1995), and Hon Lady Dundas; *b* 4 November 1950; *Educ* Eton, New Coll Oxford, Inns of Court Sch of Law; *m* 27 June 1979, Jennifer Ann, da of John Daukes; 1 s, 2 da; *Career* called to the Bar Inner Temple 1972; dir Morgan Grenfell & Co Ltd 1981–91, fin dir Hong Kong Airport Authy 1992–96; MEPC Ltd: fin dir 1997–99, chief exec 1999–2003; non-exec dir: J Sainsbury plc 2000–07, Standard Chartered plc 2004–, Drax Gp plc 2005–; chm Macmillan Cancer Relief 2001–; *Style*— Jamie Dundas, Esq

DUNDAS, Kevin John; s of A M Dundas, of Mid Glamorgan, and D V Dundas; *b* 6 October 1961; *Educ* King Edward VI Sch Bury St Edmunds, Trinity & All Saints' Coll Leeds (BSc); *m* 29 Oct 1994, Elizabeth, *née* Ede; 2 s (Hamish James b 24 Jan 1997, Oliver William b 5 Oct 1998), 1 da (Isabella Daisy b 3 Nov 2002); *Career* account planner Publicis 1986–89, bd dir Young & Rubicam London 1989–93, sr vice-pres and dir of planning Saatchi & Saatchi San Francisco 1993–95, exec vice-pres and dir of planning FCB Advtg San Francisco 1995–99; Saatchi & Saatchi London: exec planning dir 1999–2002, md 2002–03, ceo 2003–05; worldwide strategy dir Saatchi & Saatchi 2005–; memb Cncl IPA 2003–; *Recreations* flying (PPL); *Clubs* White Waltham Aero, Century, Soho House, Wentworth Golf; *Style*— Kevin Dundas, Esq; ✉ Saatchi & Saatchi, 80 Charlotte Street, London W1A 1AQ (tel 020 7462 7005, e-mail kevin.dundas@saatchi.co.uk)

DUNDEE, 12 Earl of (S 1660); Alexander Henry Scrymgeour of Dundee; also Viscount Dudhope (S 1641), Lord Scrymgeour (S 1641), Lord Inverkeithing (S 1660), Baron Glassary (UK 1954); Baron of Barony of Wedderburn; Hereditary Royal Standard Bearer for Scotland; s of 11 Earl of Dundee (d 1983), and Patricia, Countess of Dundee; *b* 5 June 1949; *Educ* Eton, Univ of St Andrews; *m* 1979, Siobhan Mary, da of David Llewellyn, of Sayers, Great Somerford, Wilts; 3 da (Lady Marina Patricia Siobhan b 21 Aug 1980, Lady Flora Hermione Vera b 30 Sept 1985, Lady Lavinia Rebecca Elizabeth b 5 Nov 1986), 1 s (Henry David, Lord Scrymgeour b 1982); *Heir* s, Lord Scrymgeour; *Career* contested (Cons) Hamilton by-election 1978; *Style*— The Rt Hon the Earl of Dundee; ✉ Farm Office, Birkhill, Cupar, Fife FY15 4QP

DUNDERDALE, Sue; da of John Mason Dunderdale (d 1988), and Dorothy, *née* Alderson (d 1997); *Educ* Morecambe GS, Univ of Manchester; *Career* dir; fndr and first artistic dir Pentbus Theatre Co; artistic dir: Soho Poly Theatre 1984–88, Greenwich Theatre 1988–89; BBC drama dirs course 1989; TV drama dir 1991–; writer and dir Last Laugh (short film, selected Brisbane, LA and Chicago Film Festivals) 2004; co-chair Dirs' Guild of GB 1986–87, chair Dir's Guild 2001–03; *Style*— Ms Sue Dunderdale; ✉ c/o Peter MacFarlane, MacFarlane Chard Associates, 3 Percy Street, London W1T 1DF (tel 020 7636 7750)

DUNDONALD, 15 Earl of (S 1669); (Iain Alexander) Douglas Blair; also Lord Cochrane of Dundonald (S 1647), Lord Cochrane of Dundonald, Paisley and Ochiltree (S 1669), and Marquis of Maranhão (Empire of Brazil 1823 by Dom Pedro I for 10 Earl); s (by 1 m) of 14 Earl of Dundonald (d 1986); *b* 17 February 1961; *Educ* Wellington, RAC Cirencester (DipAg); *m* 4 July 1987, (M) Beatrice (L), da of Adolphus Russo, of Gibraltar; 2 s (Archie Iain Thomas, Lord Cochrane b 14 March 1991, Hon James Douglas Richard b 10 May 1995), 1 da (Lady Marina Aphra Mariola b 26 Nov 1992); *Heir* s, Lord Cochrane; *Career* dir property investment and technology start ups; hon Chilean consul to Scotland; *Recreations* skiing, sailing, country pursuits; *Style*— The Rt Hon the Earl of Dundonald; ✉ Lochnell Castle, Ledaig, Argyll PA37 1QT

DUNFORD, David John; s of Alfred George Dunford (d 1962), and Kate, *née* Spearman (d 2002); *b* 30 January 1948; *Educ* Univ of Essex (BA); *m* 7 Sept 1978, Anne Wilson, da of James Fleming (d 1981); *Career* asst ed then dep chief sub ed Essex Co Newspapers 1973–78; BBC: joined 1978, successively sub ed, chief sub ed and duty ed BBC Radio News, fin journalist for BBC radio TV and World Service, former ed BBC General News Serv providing comprehensive news and current affairs coverage to BBC local and regnl radio and TV stations, ret; memb EBU Working Pty on the Devpt of Local Radio, co-organiser and contrib European Conf on Local Radio 2002 and 2004; visiting lectr London Coll of Communication Univ of the Arts London 2006–07; Gillard Award for outstanding contrib to BBC local radio 2002; *Recreations* horse riding, trivial pursuit; *Style*— David Dunford, Esq; ✉ Long Gardens, 68 Brook Lane, Galleywood, Chelmsford, Essex CM2 8NN (tel 01245 474220, e-mail ddunford@beeb.net)

DUNFORD, Martin; s of Stan Dunford, of Hants, and Margaret, *née* Lines; *b* 7 June 1959, London; *Educ* Roan Sch Blackheath, Univ of Kent at Canterbury (BA); *m* 31 May 2003, Caroline Osborne; 2 da (Daisy b 14 Oct 2003, Lucy b 10 April 2007); *Career* co-fndr and publishing dir Rough Guides; *Publications* Rough Guides to: Amsterdam, The Netherlands, Brussels, Belgium and Luxembourg, New York, Italy, Rome; *Style*— Martin Dunford; ✉ Rough Guides, 80 Strand, London WC2R 0RL (tel 020 7010 3710, e-mail martin.dunford@roughguides.com)

DUNHILL, Richard; s of Vernon Dunhill (d 1938), and Helen, *née* Field Moser (d 1984); Co Alfred Dunhill formed by gf 1907; *b* 27 October 1926; *Educ* Beaumont Coll; *m* 5 April 1952, Patricia Susannah, da of Henry B Rump (d 1965); 1 da (Susan Mary b 1953), 3 s (Christopher John b 1954, (Alfred) Mark b 1961, Jonathan Henry b 1962); *Career* army conscript 1944–48; Alfred Dunhill Ltd: joined 1948, dir 1961, dep chm 1967, chm 1977, pres 2000, life pres 2007; chm Dunhill Holdings plc 1981–89 (pres 1989–93); former Barker Variety Club of GB; Master Worshipful Co of Pipemakers and Tobacco Blenders 1987–88; *Recreations* gardening, backgammon; *Style*— Richard Dunhill, Esq

DUNKELD, Bishop (RC) of 1981–; Rt Rev Vincent Paul Logan; s of Joseph Logan (d 1975), and Elizabeth, *née* Flannigan (d 1998); *b* 30 June 1941; *Educ* Blairs Coll Aberdeen, St Andrew's Coll Drygrange Melrose, CCC London (DipRE); *Career* ordained priest Edinburgh 1964; asst priest: St Margaret's Davidsons Mains Edinburgh 1964–66, CCC London 1966–67; chaplain St Joseph's Hosp Rosewell Midlothian 1967–77, advsr in religious educn Archdiocese of St Andrews and Edinburgh 1967–77, parish priest St Mary's Ratho Midlothian 1977–81, episcopal vicar for educn Archdiocese of St Andrews and Edinburgh 1978–81; *Style*— The Rt Rev the Bishop of Dunkeld; ✉ Bishop's House, 29 Roseangle, Dundee DD1 4LS (tel 01382 224327, fax 01382 205212)

DUNKELS, Paul Renton; QC (1993); s of George Antony Dunkels (d 1985), and Mollie, *née* Renton (d 1991); *b* 26 November 1947; *Educ* Harrow; *m* 2 Sept 1972, Melanie Gail, da of Lawrence Taverner; 2 da (Cynthia Leigh b 7 March 1975, Eleanor Claire b 6 Sept 1982), 1 s (Antony Lawrence Renton b 31 May 1977); *Career* called to the Bar Inner Temple 1972, in practice Western Circuit 1974–, recorder of the Crown Court 1988–, currently head of chambers Walnut House Chambers; *Style*— Paul Dunkels, Esq, QC; ✉ Walnut House, 63 St David's Hill, Exeter, Devon EX4 4DW (tel 01392 279751, fax 01392 412080)

DUNKERLEY, Christopher; s of George William Dunkerley (d 1994), of Smallfield, Surrey, and Diana Margaret, *née* Lang; *b* 12 December 1951; *Educ* Charterhouse, Pembroke Coll Oxford (MA); *m* 16 Sept 1983, Kathleen Jane, *née* Hansen; 1 s (Jonathan b 18 Oct 1986), 1 da (Laura b 8 Sept 1988); *Career* graduate trainee William Brandts 1973–75, mangr Orion Bank 1975–76, asst gen mangr Saudi International Bank 1977–87, asst dir James Capel & Co 1987–89, chief exec Dartington & Co Gp plc 1989–92, md Glen House Associates 1992–96, chief exec Swire Fraser Financial Management 1993–95, ptnr Coutts & Co 1996–2000, dir Dunkerley Financial Planning Ltd 2000–; non-exec dir Henderson High Income Tst plc 1989–; govr Clifton Coll 2002–; *Recreations* ocean racing, golf; *Clubs* Royal Ocean Racing, Lansdowne; *Style*— Christopher Dunkerley, Esq; ✉ Glen House, Sandy Lane, Abbots Leigh, Bristol BS8 3SE (tel 01275 375200, fax 01275 375047)

DUNKLEY, Christopher; s of Robert Dunkley (d 1989), and Joyce Mary, *née* Turner (d 1993); *b* 22 January 1944; *Educ* Haberdashers' Aske's; *m* 1967 (m dis 2005), Carolyn Elizabeth, da of Lt-Col Arthur Philip Casey Lyons (d 1976), of Hampstead, London; 1 s (Damian b 1969), 1 da (Holly b 1971); *Career* journalist and broadcaster; feature writer and news ed UK Press Gazette 1965–68, reporter then specialist correspondent and critic The Times 1968–73, TV critic Financial Times 1973–2002, feature writer Daily Mail 2002–; presenter Feedback BBC Radio 4 1986–98; occasional TV presenter: Man Alive, Panorama, This Week, Viewpoint; *Awards* Br Press Awards Critic of the Year 1976 and 1986, TV-am Broadcast Journalist of the Year 1989, Judges' Award 1990, Voice of the Listener and Viewer Best Individual Contribution to Radio 1998; *Books* Television Today and Tomorrow - Wall to Wall Dallas?; *Recreations* motorcycling, collecting, books, eating Italian food; *Style*— Christopher Dunkley, Esq

DUNLEATH, 6 Baron (UK 1892); Brian Henry Mulholland; 3 Bt (UK) 1945); o s of 5 Baron Dunleath (d 1997), and his 2 w, Elizabeth M, *née* Hyde (d 1989); *b* 25 September 1950; *Educ* Eton, Royal Agricultural Coll Cirencester; *m* 1, 1976 (m dis 2004), Mary Joan, yst da of Maj Robert John Fuller Whistler, of Camberley, Surrey; 1 da (Hon Tara Miranda b 15 April 1980), 2 s (Hon Andrew Henry b 15 Dec 1981, Hon William Alexander b 15 Feb 1986); m 2, 2006, Vibeke Lunn, yr da of late Col Jens Christian Lunn, of Knabstrup Hovedgaard Denmark; *Heir* s, Hon Andrew Mulholland; *Career* landowner and co dir; production mangr Finsbury Distillery Co Ltd 1972–82, brands mangr Matthew Clark Gp plc with responsibility for Irish Distillers 1982–85, dir Lanyon Developments Ltd 1985–91, admin Belle Isle Estate 1991–94, chm Dunleath Estates Ltd 1997– (dir 1994–97), dir Downpatrick Race Club Ltd 1999–; *Recreations* shooting, fishing, gardening; *Clubs* MCC, Kildare Street and Univ (Dublin); *Style*— The Rt Hon the Lord Dunleath; ✉ Ballywalter Park, Ballywalter, Newtownards BT22 2PP; Dunleath Estates Ltd, Ballywalter Park Estate Office, Newtownards BT22 2PA (tel 028 4275 8264, fax 028 4275 8818, e-mail bd@dunleath-estates.co.uk)

DUNLOP, Andrew Alexander; s of Andrew Roberts Jeffrey Dunlop, of Renfrewshire, and Merope Jane, *née* Haggart; *b* 22 June 1964, Perthshire; *Educ* HS of Glasgow, Univ of Aberdeen; *m* 16 Feb 1991, Jusna; 2 da (Octavia Taqiyah b 4 Nov 1999, Alyssa Kamilah b 25 May 2003); *Career* slr; Arthur Andersen 1991, Freshfields 1993, ptnr Shaw Pittman Potts and Trowbridge 1998, ptnr Burges Salmon 2001–; dir: Nat Outsourcing Assoc 1998–, European Outsourcing Assoc 2005–; memb Law Soc 1991; *Recreations* flyfishing, golf, skiing; *Style*— Andrew Dunlop, Esq; ✉ Burges Salmon, Narrow Quay House, Bristol BS1 4AH (tel 0117 939 2000)

DUNLOP, Rear Adm Colin Charles Harrison; CB (1972), CBE (1963), DL (Kent 1976); s of Rear Adm Samuel Harrison Dunlop, CB (d 1950), of Surrey, and Hilda Dunlop (d 1965); *b* 4 March 1918; *Educ* Marlborough; *m* 1, 1941, (Moyra) Patricia O'Brien (d 1991), da of John Albert Gorges (d 1968); 3 s (Angus, Robin (d 1946), Graham); m 2, 1995, Cmdt Elizabeth (Liz) Craig-McFeely, CB, DL, WRNS; *Career* RN 1935–74: served WWII HM Ships Kent, Valiant, Diadem and Orion in Far East, Med and Atlantic, cmd HMS Pembroke 1964–66, dir Def Policy 1968–69, Rear Adm 1969, cmd Br Naval Staff Washington 1969–71, Flag Offr Medway 1971–74, ret; DG Cable TV Assoc and Nat TV Rental Assoc 1974–83; *Recreations* cricket, country pursuits; *Clubs* Army and Navy, MCC, I Zingari, Free Foresters, Band of Bros; *Style*— Rear Adm C C H Dunlop, CB, CBE, DL; ✉ 1 The Gatehouse, Elliscombe Park, Holton, Wincanton, Somerset BA9 8EA (tel 01963 31534)

DUNLOP, Eileen Rhona; da of James Dunlop (d 1982), and Grace, *née* Love (d 1977); *b* 13 October 1938; *Educ* Alloa Acad, Moray House Coll of Educn Edinburgh (Dip, Steele Prize); *m* 1979, Antony Kamm, s of George Kamm, and Josephine Kamm; *Career* author; teacher Eastfield Sch Penicuik 1959–61, teacher Abercromby Sch Alloa 1961–63, dep head Sunnyside Sch Alloa 1963–79, headmistress Prep Sch of Dollar Acad 1980–90; memb Pen Scottish Centre; *Books* Robinsheugh (1975), A Flute in Mayferry Street (1976), Fox Farm (1978), The Maze Stone (1982), A Book of Old Edinburgh (jt ed with Antony Kamm, 1983), Scottish Verse to 1800 (jt ed with Antony Kamm, 1985), Scottish Traditional Rhymes (jt ed with Antony Kamm, 1985), Clementina (1985), The House on the Hill (1987), The Valley of Deer (1989), Finn's Island (1991), Green Willow's Secret (1993), Finn's Roman Fort (1994), Stones of Destiny (1994), Castle Gryffe (1995), The Ghost by the Sea (1996), Waters of Life (1996), Warrior's Bride (1998), A Royal Ring of Gold (1999), Ghoul's Den (1999), The Haunting of Alice Fairlie (2001), Nicholas Moonlight (2002), Weerdwood (2003), Queen Margaret of Scotland (2005); *Recreations* reading, theatre, gardening; *Style*— Miss Eileen Dunlop; ✉ 46 Tarmangie Drive, Dollar, Clackmannanshire FK14 7BP (tel 01259 742007, fax 01259 742077)

DUNLOP, Graeme Dermott Stuart; OBE (2006); *b* 1942; *Educ* Charterhouse, Magdalene Coll Cambridge; *Career* P&O SNCO: joined as mgmnt trainee 1964, (attached to Mackinnon

Mackenzie Bombay until 1967), asst mangr Personnel Container Fleets Ltd 1967–70, asst to the sec Australia 1970, devpt asst General Cargo Div (GCD) 1971–72, asst devpt mangr GCD 1972–74, devpt mangr 1974–75, dir P&O Strath Services Ltd 1975–77, general mangr Arabian Peninsular Container Line 1977–79, md North Sea Ferries Rotterdam 1979–87, md P&O European Ferries Ltd 1987–2003, memb Bd 1991–2003, chm P&O European Ferries Ltd 1993–2003, chm P&O Trans European (Holdings) Ltd (formerly P&O European Transport Services) 1996–2003; pres: Chamber of Shipping 1999–2000, EC Shipowners Assoc 2003–; chm: Standard Steamship Owners' P&I Assoc (Bermuda) Ltd 1997–, AWSR Shipping Ltd 2003–; *Style—* Graeme Dunlop, Esq, OBE

DUNLOP, Ian Charles Grant; s of James Andrew Merson Dunlop (d 1990), and Jean Margaret Dunlop; *b* 2 January 1950; *Educ* Tonbridge, Univ of Leeds (BA); *m* 12 April 1990, Setsuko, da of Masahide Uematsu; 1 da (Emily Aya b 7 June 1990); *Career* gp product mangr Bass Charrington 1971–74, account mangr (Colgate-Palmolive account) D'Arcy McManus & Masius 1974–77, account mangr and account dir (accounts incl Cadbury Schweppes and Smiths Food Gp) Dorlands 1977–79, account dir (Sony and Zanussi accounts) BBDO 1979, bd dir Norman Craig & Kummel 1979–82, bd dir and client serv dir (accounts incl NatWest, Whitbread and Post Office) Owen Wade Delmonte (became Roose OWD 1987) 1982–90, dep md (accounts incl Twinings and British Coal) Alliance Advertising (formerly Alliance International) 1990–93, sr vice-pres/gp div dir McCann-Erickson Inc Tokyo 1993–, sr vice-pres/md DDB Japan Inc 1995–; memb Marketing Soc 1989; *Recreations* Rhododendrons and Azaleas, Art Nouveau, Far Eastern cuisine, travel; *Style—* Ian Dunlop, Esq; ✉ DDB Needham Japan Inc, Hiroo Plaza 9F, 5–6–6 Hiroo, Shiuya-Ku, Tokyo 150–0012, Japan

DUNLOP, John Leeper; OBE (1996); s of Dr John Leeper Dunlop, MC (d 1959), and Margaret Frances Mary, *née* Fiffett (d 1972); *b* 10 July 1939; *Educ* Marlborough; *m* 22 June 1965, Susan Jennifer, da of Gerard Thorpe Page (d 1985), of Harpole, Northants; 3 s (Timothy b 1966 d 1987, Edward b 1968, Harry b 1976); *Career* Nat Serv 2 Lt Royal Ulster Rifles 1959–61; racehorse trainer 1964–, trained over 3,000 winners incl the Derby 1978 (Shirley Heights) and 1994 (Erhaab); memb Ctee: Racing Welfare, Br Racing Sch; dir Goodwood, memb Cncl Sports Horse Breeding GB, pres Royal Int Horse Show; *Recreations* breeding racehorses, owning show horses; *Clubs* Turf; *Style—* John Dunlop, Esq, OBE; ✉ House on the Hill, Arundel, West Sussex (tel 01903 882106); Castle Stables, Arundel, West Sussex (tel 01903 882194, fax 01903 884173, car tel 07860 339805)

DUNLOP, Robert Fergus; AE (1956); s of A Fergus Dunlop, OBE, TD (d 1980), and Gwendolen Elizabeth, *née* Coit; *b* 22 June 1929; *Educ* Marlborough, St John's Cambridge (MA), MIT (MSc); *m* 1966, Jane Clare, da of Lt-Col George Hervey McManus (d 1959), of Canada; 1 s, 2 da; *Career* cmmnd 2 Lt RA, later Flt Lt 501 (Co of Glos) Fighter Sqdn RAuxAF; Sloan fell 1960; Bristol Aeroplane Co Ltd and Br Aircraft Corp 1952–66, Westland Aircraft Ltd 1966–70, dep chm Lonrho plc 1992–94 (joined 1970, dir 1972–94), actg chm Observer Ltd 1992–93; CEng, MRAeS; *Style—* Robert Dunlop, Esq, AE; ✉ 42 Woodsford Square, London W14 8DP (tel 020 7602 2579); PO Box 62142, 8061 Paphos, Cyprus (tel 00 357 26 939787)

DUNLOP, Sir Thomas; 4 Bt (UK 1916), of Woodbourne, Co Renfrew; s of Sir Thomas Dunlop, 3 Bt (d 1999); *b* 22 April 1951; *Educ* Rugby, Univ of Aberdeen (BSc); *m* 1984, Eileen, er da of Alexander Henry Stevenson (d 1990); 1 da (Nicola Mary b 1987), 1 s (Thomas b 11 March 1990); *Heir* s, Thomas Dunlop; *Career* ptnr Abbey Forestry Pershore; memb Inst of Chartered Foresters; *Style—* Sir Thomas Dunlop, Bt; ✉ Bredon Croft, Bredon's Norton, Tewkesbury, Gloucestershire GL20 7HB

DUNLOP, Prof William; CBE (2005); s of Alexander Morton Dunlop, and Annie Denham Rennie, *née* Ingram; *b* 18 August 1944; *Educ* Kilmarnock Acad, Univ of Glasgow (MB ChB), Univ of Newcastle upon Tyne (PhD); *m* 25 March 1968, Sylvia Louise, da of Dr Irwin Krauthamer; 1 s (Keith b 1972), 1 da (Emma b 1973); *Career* various jr posts in Obstetrics and Gynaecology Dept, regius prof Univ of Glasgow 1969–74, seconded as lectr Univ of Nairobi 1972–73, MRC scientific staff Newcastle 1974–75, visiting assoc prof Med Univ of S Carolina 1980, prof and head of Dept Obstetrics and Gynaecology Univ of Newcastle upon Tyne 1982–99 (sr lectr 1975–82), head Sch of Surgical and Reproductive Sciences 1999–2001; pres RCOG 2001– (hon sec 1992–98); chm: Blair-Bell Res Soc 1989–92, Assoc of Profs of Obstetrics and Gynaecology 1999–, Jt Conslts Ctee 2003–; vice-chm: Specialist Trg Authy 2002–, Acad of Med Royal Colls 2002–; treas: European Bd and Coll of Obstetrics and Gynaecology 2000–, Section of Obstetrics and Gynaecology Union Européenne de Médecins Spécialistes 2001–; ed-in-chief Fetal and Maternal Med Review 1989–99; ed Recent Advances in Obstetrics and Gynaecology 2003–; memb South African Soc of Obstetricians and Gynaecologists 2003–; fell Acad of Med Singapore 2002, hon fell American Coll of Obstetricians and Gynaecologists 2003; FRCSEd 1971, FRCOG 1984 (MRCOG 1971), FRCPSGlas 2003; *Recreations* music, drama, literature; *Style—* Prof William Dunlop, CBE; ✉ Department of Obstetrics and Gynaecology, University of Newcastle upon Tyne, 4th Floor, Leazes Wing, Royal Victoria Infirmary, Newcastle upon Tyne NE1 4LP (tel 0191 232 5131, fax 0191 222 5066, e-mail william.dunlop@ncl.ac.uk)

DUNLUCE, Viscount Randal Alexander St John McDonnell; s and h of 9 Earl of Antrim, *qv*; *b* 2 July 1967; *Educ* Gresham's, Worcester Coll Oxford (BA); *m* Oct 2004, Aurora Gunn; *Career* investment mangr: NCL Investments Ltd 1993–97, Sarasin Investment Management Ltd 1998– (also currently dir); dir: Antrim Estates Co, Northern Salmon Co; tstee: Irish Landmark Tst, Glenarm Buildings Preservation Tst, Irish Grouse Conservation Tst; *Recreations* country pursuits, conservation, vintage cars; *Clubs* Beefsteak, White's; *Style—* Viscount Dunluce; ✉ Glenarm Castle, Glenarm, Ballymena, Co Antrim BT44 0BD (tel 02828 841229, e-mail randal@glenarmcastle.com); Juxon House, 100 St Paul's Churchyard, London EC4M 8BU (tel 0207 038 7000)

DUNMORE, Helen; da of Maurice Ronald Dunmore, and Betty, *née* Smith; *b* 12 December 1952; *Educ* Nottingham HS for Girls, Univ of York (BA); *m* 24 Oct 1980, Francis Benedict Charnley; 1 s (Patrick Maurice b 28 July 1981), 1 da (Teresa Mary Benedicta b 11 Feb 1994), 1 step s (Oliver Benjamin b 13 Feb 1977); *Career* poet and novelist; FRSL; *Poetry* incl: The Apple Fall (1983), The Sea Skater (1986, winner Poetry Soc's Alice Hunt Bartlett Award 1987), The Raw Garden (1988, Poetry Book Soc Choice winter 1988–89), Short Days, Long Nights, New and Selected Poems (1991), Recovering a Body (1994), Secrets (1994, The Signal Poetry Award 1995), Bestiary (1997), Out of the Blue (2001); *Children's Novels* Going to Egypt (1992), In the Money (1993), Amina's Blanket (1996), Go Fox (1996), Fatal Error (1996), Brother Brother Sister Sister (1999), Zillah and Me (2000), The Zillah Rebellion (2001); *Fiction* Zennor in Darkness (1993, The McKitterick Prize 1994), Burning Bright (1994), A Spell of Winter (1995, winner inaugural Orange Prize for women fiction writers 1996), Talking to the Dead (1996), Love of Fat Men (1997), Your Blue-Eyed Boy (1998), With Your Crooked Heart (1999), Ice Cream (2000), The Siege (2001), Mourning Ruby (2003), House of Orphans (2006); *Recreations* family life and friendships; *Style—* Ms Helen Dunmore, FRSL; ✉ c/o Caradoc King, A P Watt Ltd, 20 John Street, London WC1N 2DR (tel 020 7405 6774, fax 020 7831 2154)

DUNMORE, 12 Earl of (S 1686); Malcolm Kenneth Murray; also Viscount of Fincastle, Lord Murray of Blair, Moulin and Tillimet (Tullimet; both S 1686); er s of 11 Earl of Dunmore (d 1995), and Margaret Joy, *née* Cousins (d 1976); *b* 17 September 1946; *Educ* Queechy HS, Launceston, Schs' Bd 'A' certificate and various other technical qualifications; *m* 1970, Joy Anne, da of Arthur Partridge (d 1987), of Launceston, Tasmania; 1 s (Leigh Kenneth b 1977), 1 da (Elisa Anne b 1980) (both adopted); *Heir* bro, Hon Geoffrey Murray; *Career* electrical tech offr Air Services Australia 1968–99, licensed aircraft maintenance engr, ret; pte pilot; patron: Armorial & Heraldry Soc of Australasia, Co of Armigers Inc (Australian chapter), Scottish Australian Heritage Cncl, Murray Clan Socs of Edinburgh, New Zealand Soc, Victoria and Queensland, St Andrew Soc Tasmania, Tasmanian Caledonian Cncl, Launceston Caledonian Soc; patron Sunny Bank RSL Sub-Branch Inc; past master Concord Masonic Lodge; sat in House of Lords 1998; *Recreations* flying, astronomy; *Clubs* Soaring Club of Tasmania; *Style—* The Rt Hon the Earl of Dunmore; ✉ PO Box 100E, East Devonport, Tasmania 7310, Australia (e-mail malc5@bigpond.com)

DUNN, Angus Henry; s of Col Henry George Mountfort Dunn (d 1969), and Catherine Mary (d 1986); *b* 30 December 1944; *Educ* Marlborough, King's Coll Cambridge (MA), Pennsylvania Univ; *m* 1973, Carolyn Jane, da of Alan Bartlett, of Cranbook, Kent; 2 s (Thomas b 1974, James b 1977), 1 da (Eliza b 1983); *Career* HM Diplomatic Service 1968–73 (FCO, Kuala Lumpur, Bonn); joined Morgan Grenfell & Co Ltd 1972 (dir 1978–88), exec deputy chm Morgan Grenfell (Asia) Ltd Singapore 1983–85; dir: Julianas Holdings plc 1983–85, Manufacturers Hanover Ltd 1988–91, OPERIS 1999– (chm 2005); independent PFI conslt 1992–94 and 1997–99; head: Group Private Fin Unit Tarmac plc 1994–96, Private Fin Unit DOE 1996; *Books* Export Finance (co-author, 1983), Personal Accountant Tax Reckoner (software pubn, 1990–93); *Recreations* riding, sailing; *Clubs* Royal Thames Yacht; *Style—* Angus Dunn, Esq; ✉ Dower House, Oxon Hoath, Tonbridge, Kent (tel 01732 810330)

D

DUNN, Prof Douglas Eaglesham; OBE (2003); s of William Douglas Dunn (d 1980), and Margaret, *née* McGowan; *b* 23 October 1942; *Educ* Renfrew HS, Camphill Sch Paisley, Scottish Sch of Librarianship, Univ of Hull (BA); *m* 1, Lesley Balfour, *née* Wallace (d 1981); m 2, 10 Aug 1985, Lesley Jane, da of Robert Bathgate (d 1979); 1 s (William Robert Bathgate b 5 Jan 1987), 1 da (Lillias Ella Bathgate b 18 June 1990); *Career* writer; head Sch of English Univ of St Andrews 1995–99 (prof 1991–), St Andrews Scottish Studies Inst 1993– (fell in creative writing 1989–91); Somerset Maugham Award 1972, Geoffrey Faber Meml Prize 1975, Hawthornden Prize 1982, Whitbread Book of the Year Award for 1985 (1986), Cholmondeley Award 1989; Hon LLD Univ of Dundee 1987, Hon DLitt Univ of Hull 1995; hon prof Univ of Dundee 1987, hon fell Humberside Coll; FRSL 1981; *Books* books of poetry incl: Terry Street (1969), The Happier Life (1972), Love or Nothing (1974), Barbarians (1979), St Kilda's Parliament (1982), Elegies (1985), Selected Poems (1986), Northlight (1988), Dante's Drum-kit (1993), The Donkey's Ears (2000), The Year's Afternoon (2000), Selected Poems 1964–2000 (2003); other books: Secret Villages (short stories, 1985), Andromache (translation, 1990), Poll Tax: The Fiscal Fake (1990), The Essential Browning (ed, 1990), Scotland: An Anthology (ed, 1991), Faber Book of Twentieth Century Scottish Poetry (ed, 1992), Boyfriends and Girlfriends (short stories, 1995), Oxford Book of Scottish Short Stories (ed, 1995), 20th Century Scottish Poems (ed, 2000); *Recreations* music, philately; *Style—* Prof Douglas Dunn, OBE, FRSL; ✉ School of English, Castle House, University of St Andrews, St Andrews, Fife KY16 9AL (tel 01334 462666, fax 01334 462655, e-mail ded@st-andrews.ac.uk)

DUNN, Geoffrey Richard; s of late Kenneth Grayson Dunn, of Crawley, W Sussex, and Nila Jane, *née* Griffiths; *b* 10 July 1949; *Educ* Ifield GS, Univ of Manchester (BSc, MSc), Manchester Business Sch (Dip); *m* 12 Sept 2003; *Career* investment controller ICFC Ltd 1975–78, corp fin exec SG Warburg & Co Ltd 1978–80, asst gp treas GKN plc 1980–83, head of fin and planning Midland Bank plc 1984–87, gp fin dir Exco International plc 1987–92, conslt 1993–94; chief fin offr: SWIFT SC Brussels 1994–97, GlobalOne Telecommunications SA Brussels 1997–98; fin dir Xansa plc 1999–2002, ind interim dir and conslt 2003–; non-exec dir Datamonitor plc 2001–02; FCT 1997; *Recreations* mountaineering, skiing, opera and music; *Clubs* Alpine, London Mountaineering; *Style—* Geoffrey Dunn, Esq; ✉ 10 Carlisle Road, London NW6 6TJ (tel 020 8968 5547, e-mail grdunn@grdunn.co.uk)

DUNN, His Hon (William) Hubert; QC (1982); s of William Patrick Millar Dunn (d 1964), of Tudor Hall, Co Down, and Isobel, *née* Thompson (d 1954); *b* 8 July 1933; *Educ* Winchester, New Coll Oxford (BA); *m* 23 Sept 1971, Maria Henriquetta Theresa D'Arouje Perestrello, da of George Hoffacker de Moser, 3 s of Count de Moser in the nobility of Portugal; 1 da (Eugenia b 27 May 1972), 1 s (Sebastian b 29 Aug 1973); *Career* 2 Lt The Life Gds 1956–57, Household Cavalry Reserve of Offrs 1957–64; called to the Bar Lincoln's Inn 1958; local govt cmmr 1963; recorder of the Crown Court 1980–93, circuit judge (SE Circuit) 1993–2005; pres Women Caring Tst 2004– (chm of tstees 1995–2004); *Recreations* travel, literature; *Clubs* Boodle's; *Style—* His Hon Hubert Dunn, QC

DUNN, Jane Ellinor; da of David Rolf Thesen (d 2002), and Ellinor Hodder Thesen, *née* Wilson; *b* Durban, South Africa; *Educ* Bentley GS, Clifton HS Bristol, UCL; *m* 1, (m dis 1985), Philip Martin Dunn; 1 s (Benjamin David Harald b 19 Oct 1971), 1 da (Lily Caroline b 19 Oct 1973); m 2, 22 Feb 1996, Nicholas David Maclachlan Ostler; *Career* author; formerly with Copy Dept Vogue magazine, co-fndr and editorial dir Pierrot Publishing; freelance journalist: Vogue, Brides, Sunday Times, Guardian, Observer, Literary Review, Sunday Telegraph; FRSL 1999; *Publications* Moon In Eclipse: A Life of Mary Shelley (1978), A Very Close Conspiracy: Vanessa Bell and Virginia Woolf (1990), Virginia Woolf: An Illustrated Anthology (1994), Antonia White: A Life (1998), Elizabeth and Mary: Cousins, Rivals, Queens (2003), Shall We Ever Be So Happy?: Dorothy Osborne and Sir William Temple (2008); *Style—* Ms Jane Dunn; ✉ c/o AP Watt Ltd, 20 John Street, London WC1N 2DR (tel 020 7405 6774, fax 020 7831 2154, e-mail apw@apw.co.uk)

DUNN, Prof John Montfort; s of Col Henry George Montfort Dunn (d 1970), and Catherine Mary, *née* Kinloch (d 1986); *b* 9 September 1940; *Educ* Winchester, Millfield, King's Coll Cambridge (BA); *m* 1, 1965 (m dis 1971), Susan Deborah, *née* Fyvel; m 2, 1973 (m dis 1987), Judith Frances Bernal; 2 s (Thomas William b 8 Dec 1989 d 1990, Charles Montfort b 11 Jan 1991); m 3, 1997, Ruth Ginette Scurr; 2 da (Polly Anna Montfort b 15 May 1998, Rosalind Jean Monfort b 23 April 2003); *Career* Univ of Cambridge: fell Jesus Coll 1965–66, fell King's Coll 1966–, lectr in political science 1972–77, reader in politics 1977–87, prof of political theory 1987–; visiting prof: Univ of Ghana, Univ of Br Columbia, Univ of Bombay, Tokyo Met Univ, Tulane Univ, Univ of Minnesota; Olmsted visiting prof Yale Univ 1991; Br Acad: chm Political Studies Section 1994–97, memb Cncl 2004–07; foreign hon memb: American Acad of Arts and Sciences 1991, Bd of Conslts Kim Dae-Jung Fndn for the Asia-Pacific Region 1994; FBA 1989, FSA 1993; *Books* The Political Thought of John Locke (1969), Modern Revolutions (1972), Dependence and Opportunity (with A F Robertson, 1973), Western Political Theory in the Face of the Future (1979), Political Obligation in its Historical Context (1980), The Politics of Socialism (1984), Rethinking Modern Political Theory (1985), Interpreting Political Responsibility (1990), Democracy: the unfinished journey 508 BC - 1993 AD (ed, 1992), Contemporary Crisis of the Nation State? (ed, 1995), The History of Political Theory and Other Essays (1996), Great Political Thinkers (ed with Ian Harris, 1997), The Cunning of Unreason (2000), Pensare la Politica (2002), Locke: A Very Short Introduction (2003), Setting the People Free: The Story of Democracy (2005); *Style—* Prof John Dunn, FBA, FSA; ✉ The Merchant's House, 31 Station Road, Swavesey, Cambridge CB24 4QJ (tel 01954 231451); King's College, Cambridge CB2 1ST (tel 01223 331258, fax 01223 331315, e-mail jmd24@cam.ac.uk)

DUNN, Prof Judith Frances (Judy); da of Dr James Pace Dunn, and Jean, *née* Stewart; *b* 6 June 1939; *Educ* St George's Sch Harpenden, New Hall Cambridge (MA, PhD, Frank Smart Prize); *m* 1987, Prof Robert Plomin; 1 da (Sophia b 1963), 2 s (William b 1964, Paul b 1964); *Career* fell King's Coll Cambridge 1978, sr scientific offr MRC Unit on Devpt of Behaviour Univ of Cambridge, distinguished prof Pennsylvania State Univ

1990, MRC research prof King's Coll London 1996; Outstanding Achievement Award Pennsylvania State Univ 1988, Guggenheim Fellowship 1992, Distinguished Scientific Contrib Soc for Research in Child Development (SRCD) 2000; FBA 1996, FMedSci 2000, FKC 2001; *Books* incl: Siblings (1982), Beginnings of Social Understanding (1988), Separate Lives (1990), Young Children's Close Relations (1993), From One Child to Two (1995); *Recreations* music; *Style*— Prof Judy Dunn; ✉ Institute of Psychiatry, King's College, Denmark Hill, London SE5 8AF (tel 020 7848 0893, e-mail judy.dunn@iop.kcl.ac.uk)

DUNN, Baroness (Life Peer UK 1990), of Hong Kong Island in Hong Kong and of Knightsbridge in the Royal Borough of Kensington and Chelsea; Lydia Selina Dunn; DBE (1989, CBE 1983, OBE 1978), JP (1976); da of Yen Chuen Yeh Dunn (d 1965), and Chen Yin-chu (d 1990); *b* 29 February 1940; *Educ* St Paul's Convent Sch Hong Kong, Univ of Calif Berkeley; *m* 1988, Michael David Thomas, CMG, QC, *qv*; *Career* dir: John Swire & Sons (Hong Kong) Ltd 1978–, Swire Pacific Ltd 1981–, Cathay Pacific Airways Ltd 1985–97 (Bd advsr 1997–2002), Christie's International plc 1996–98, John Swire & Sons Ltd 1996–, Marconi plc (formerly GEC plc) 1997–2002, Christie's Fine Art Ltd 1998–2000; dep chm: Hongkong and Shanghai Banking Corp 1992–96 (dir 1981–96), HSBC Holdings plc 1992– (dir 1990–); memb Hong Kong Exec Cncl 1982–88 (sr memb 1988–95), memb Hong Kong Legislative Cncl 1976–85 (sr memb 1985–88); chm: Hong Kong Trade Devpt Cncl 1983–91, Hong Kong/Japan Business Co-operation Ctee 1988–95 (memb 1983–88), Lord Wilson Heritage Tst 1993–95; dir Volvo AB 1991–93 (memb Int Advsy Bd 1985–91), memb Hong Kong/US Econ Co-operation Ctee 1984–93; Prime Minister of Japan's Trade Award 1987, US Sec of Commerce's Peace and Commerce Award 1988; Hon LLD: Chinese Univ of Hong Kong 1984, Univ of Hong Kong 1991, Univ of Br Columbia 1991, Univ of Leeds 1994; Hon DSc Univ of Buckingham 1995, hon fell London Business Sch; *Books* In the Kingdom of the Blind (1983); *Recreations* study of antiquities; *Style*— The Baroness Dunn, DBE; ✉ John Swire & Sons Ltd, Swire House, 59 Buckingham Gate, London SW1E 6AJ

DUNN, Martin; *b* 26 January 1955; *Educ* Dudley GS; *Career* journalist; Dudley Herald 1973–76; reporter: Birmingham Evening Mail 1975–76, Birmingham Post 1976–77, Daily Mail 1977–79; freelance journalist USA 1979–84, Bizarre ed The Sun 1984–90 (NY corr 1983–84), dep ed The Sun 1990–91, ed Today 1991–92; ed-in-chief: Boston Herald 1992–93, New York Daily News 1993–97; md: Associated New Media 1996–2000, DMG Front of Mind Ltd 2000–03; dep publisher and ed-in-chief New York Daily News 2003–; *Recreations* squash, running, golf; *Style*— Martin Dunn, Esq

DUNN, Richard Carl Edward Christy (Rick); s of David Christy Dunn (d 1998), and Anne, *née* Collet; *b* 8 March 1976; *Educ* Oundle, Imperial Coll London (BSc), St Edmund's Coll Cambridge (BA, Rowing blue); *Career* amateur rower; memb Leander Club; honours incl: Bronze medal eights World Jr Championships 1994, Gold medal coxless fours World Under 23 Championships 1996, winner Grand Challenge Cup Henley Royal Regatta 1996, fourth place eights World Championships 1997, eighth place coxed fours World Championships 1998, Silver medal coxed fours World Championships 1999, Gold medal coxed fours World Championships 2000, winner Prince Philip Challenge Cup Henley Royal Regatta 2000, winner coxless fours World Cup 2001, Gold medal coxless fours World Championships 2001, winner Stewards Challenge Cup Henley Royal Regatta 2001, Silver medal coxless fours World Championships 2002, second place coxless fours World Cup 2002, second place coxless fours World Cup 2003, Silver medal coxless fours World Championship 2003; spare for Olympic team 2000, memb Cambridge crew Boat Race 2001–02; patron: Project Oarsome, Sports Aid Fndn; nominated one of Top 50 Most Eligible Bachelors Company magazine; *Recreations* spear fishing, snowboarding, food; *Clubs* Hawks' (Cambridge), The Bears, Leander; *Style*— Rick Dunn, Esq; ✉ c/o Benchmark Sport, 83 Charlotte Street, London W1T 4PR (tel 020 7462 0002, fax 020 7462 0003, e-mail matt@benchmarksport.com)

DUNN, Sam; s of Nicholas Dunn, and Jennifer, *née* Hazelwood-Randall; *b* 28 December 1972, Bristol; *Educ* Univ of Birmingham (BA), Univ of Wales Cardiff (Dip); *Career* journalist; reporter Evening Herald Plymouth 1998–99, sr business corr Western Daily Press 1999–2002, sr reporter Financial Adviser/Investment Adviser 2002–03; Independent on Sunday: dep personal fin ed 2003–04, personal fin ed 2004–; Personal Fin Journalist of the Year Harold Wincott Award 2005, Journalist of the Year Headlinemoney Awards 2006; *Recreations* long-distance running, guitar, disco; *Style*— Sam Dunn, Esq; ✉ The Independent, Independent House, 191 Marsh Wall, London E14 9RS (tel 020 7005 2357, e-mail s.dunn@independent.co.uk)

DUNN OSTLER, Jane; *see:* Dunn, Jane

DUNNE, Philip; MP; *Educ* Univ of Oxford; *Career* formerly: SG Warburg, ptnr Phoenix Securities; chm Ottakar's plc 1998–2006 (co-fndr 1987); chm Baronsmead 4 VCT plc 2001–, non-exec dir Ruffer LLP 2002–; MP (Cons) Ludlow 2005–; cncllr (Cons) South Shropshire DC 2001–07; memb Public Accounts Ctee 2006–; dir Juvenile Diabetes Research Fndn 1999–2005; *Style*— Philip Dunne, MP; ✉ House of Commons, London SW1A 0AA

DUNNE, Sir Thomas Raymond; KCVO (1995), JP (Hereford and Worcester 1977); s of Philip Dunne, MC (d 1965), of East Clandon, Surrey, and his 1 wife Margaret Ann Willis, CBE, *née* Walker; *b* 24 October 1933; *Educ* Eton; *m* 17 July 1957, Henrietta Rose, da of Cosmo Stafford Crawley (d 1989); 2 s (Philip b 1958, Nicholas b 1970), 2 da (Camilla (Hon Mrs Rupert Soames) b 1960, Letitia b 1965); *Career* RMA Sandhurst 1951–53, cmmnd RHG 1953–58, farmer; Hon Col: 2 (volunteer) Bn Mercian Volunteers 1985–87, 4 (volunteer) Bn The Worcestershire and Sherwood Foresters Regt 1987–93 (formerly 2 Bn Mercian Volunteers), 5 (Shropshire and Herefordshire) Bn The Light Infantry (Volunteers) 1993–98; memb Hereford CC 1962–68; High Sheriff Herefordshire 1970, DL Hereford and Worcester 1974 (Herefordshire 1973), HM Lord-Lt and Custos Rotulorum Hereford and Worcester 1977–98, HM Lord-Lt for the separate counties of Herefordshire and Worcestershire on the formation of those counties April 1998–2001, HM Lord-Lt of Herefordshire 2001–, chm Lord-Lts Assoc 2001–; pres Three Counties Agricultural show 1977 and 1997; memb W Mercia Police Authy 1979–99, dir W Midland Regnl Bd Central TV, chm of tstees Worcester Museum of Porcelain 1985–2000, chm Hereford Cathedral Cncl 2001–; pres W Midlands TAVRA 1989–98, dir Hereford Race Club Ltd 1989–98; KStJ 1977; *Style*— Sir Thomas Dunne, KCVO; ✉ Clerk to the Lieutenancy, Herefordshire Council, PO Box 239, Hereford HR1 1ZU

DUNNETT, Anthony Gordon; CBE (2004); s of Peter Sydney Dunnett (d 1988), and Margaret Eileen, *née* Johnson, of Wadhurst, East Sussex; *b* 17 June 1953; *Educ* St Dunstan's Coll London, McGill Univ Montreal (Dip CS, BCom), Univ of Exeter (MA); *m* 1975, Ruth Elizabeth, da of Dennis Henry Barker; 1 s (Timothy b 1978), 2 da (Penelope b 1980, Emily b 1982); *Career* Nat Westminster Bank plc 1975–77; Royal Bank of Canada: Montreal 1977–80, Curacao 1980–82, Montreal 1982–86; corp banking dir Midland Bank 1986–88, corp dir Samuel Montagu 1988–89, corp dir Midland Bank 1990–91, fin dir Corp & Institutional Banking Midland Bank plc London 1991–94, on secondment as dir Industrial Devpt Unit DTI 1994–96; chief exec: English Partnerships 1996–98, South East England Devpt Agency 1998–2003; pres International Health Partners UK 2004–, chm Two-Five-Four-O LLP 2004–07; dir: Kingsmead Homes 1997–99, Countryside Maritime 1997–2003, City Life 2002–03; memb Urban Task Force 1998–; memb Advsy Bd: Insolvency Agency 1994–96, Relationships Fndn 2000–; memb local church; FCIB 1981, FRSA 1997, MInstD 1999; *Recreations* gardening, theatre, opera, music; *Style*— Anthony Dunnett, Esq, CBE; ✉ Shepherds Fold, Beech Hill, Wadhurst, East Sussex TN5 6JR (e-mail a.dunnett@ihpuk.org)

DUNNIGAN, David; s of Walter Dunnigan, and Jean, *née* Johnston; *b* 10 December 1961; *Educ* Univ of Nottingham (LLB), Chester Coll of Law; *m* 23 Jan 1993, Lavinia, *née* Buswell; 2 da (Anna b 31 March 1993, Clara b 10 July 1998), 1 s (William b 16 Nov 1994); *Career* admitted slr; articled clerk Turner Kenneth Brown 1984–86; Clifford Chance: joined 1987, ptnr 1992–, memb World Firm Mgmnt Ctee, global practice ldr capital markets; *Recreations* opera, fine wine, family; *Style*— David Dunnigan, Esq; ✉ Clifford Chance LLP, 10 Upper Bank Street, London E14 5JJ

DUNNILL, Prof Peter; OBE (1999); s of Eric Dunnill (d 1980), of Rustington, W Sussex, and Majorie (d 1985); *b* 20 May 1938; *Educ* Willesden Tech Sch, UCL (BSc 1961, DSc 1978), Royal Inst (PhD); *m* 11 Aug 1962, Patricia Mary, da of Sidney Lievesley (d 1992), of Winchmore Hill, London; 1 s (Paul b 2 April 1971); *Career* staff MRC Royal Inst 1963–64; UCL: lectr 1964–79, reader 1976–84, prof of biochemical engrg 1984–, fell 1991, dir BBSRC (formerly SERC) Interdisciplinary Research Centre for Biochemical Engineering 1991–95, dir BBSRC sponsored Advanced Centre for Biochemical Engrg 1996–2001, chm Advanced Centre for Biochemical Engrg 2001–; memb: SERC Biotechnology Directorate Management Ctee 1982–88 and 1993–94, Biotechnology Advsy Gp to the Heads of Res Councils 1987–90, Biotechnology Joint Advsy Bd 1989–92, Cncl BBSRC 1993–95, Bioscience Innovation and Growth Team Steering Gp DTI and Dept of Health 2002–03; Donald Biochemical Engrg Medal IChemE 1995, Heatley Medal Biochemical Soc 1997; FRSC 1979, FIChemE 1981, FREng 1985; *Books* Fermentation and Enzyme Technology (1979), Enzymic and Non-enzymic Catalysis (1980); *Recreations* music; *Style*— Prof Peter Dunnill, OBE, FREng; ✉ The Advanced Centre for Biochemical Engineering, Department of Biochemical Engineering, UCL, Torrington Place, London WC1E 7JE (tel 020 7679 7031, fax 020 7209 0703, e-mail p.dunnill@ucl.ac.uk)

DUNNING, Prof Eric Geoffrey; s of Sydney Ernest Dunning (d 1981), and Florence Daisy, *née* Morton (d 1987); *b* 27 December 1936; *Educ* Acton Co GS for Boys, Univ of Leicester (BSc, MA, PhD); *m* 1, 12 July 1962 (m dis 1965), Ellen Adrienne, da of Col Nathaniel Sweets (d 1988), of St Louis, Missouri; m 2, 17 July 1969 (m dis 1986), (Ursula) Judith Clare Hibbert; 1 s (Michael James b 1976), 1 da (Rachel Clare b 1978); *Career* Univ of Leicester: asst lectr 1962, lectr 1963, sr lectr 1972, prof of sociology 1988–98 (emeritus prof of sociology 1998–), res dir Centre for Research into Sport and Society 1992–98; visiting prof of sociology UC Dublin 1998–, visiting prof Univ of Ulster Jordanstown; visiting lectureships: Univ of Warwick 1966–69, Univ of Nottingham 1974; visiting professorships: Brooklyn Coll NY 1964, Univ of Minnesota 1968, SUNY 1970, Instituto Nacional de Educacion Fisica de Catalunya 1990, 1991 and 1992; assoc ed International Review for the Sociology of Sport; memb Br Sociological Assoc; *Books* The Sociology of Sport (1971), Barbarians Gentlemen and Players (1979), Hooligans Abroad (1984), Quest For Excitement (1986), The Roots of Football Hooliganism (1988), Football on Trial (1990), Sport and Leisure in the Civilizing Process (1992), The Sports Process (1993), Sport Matters (1999), Handbook of Sport Studies (2000), Fighting Fans (2002), Norbert Elias (2003); *Recreations* music, theatre; *Style*— Prof Eric Dunning; ✉ Sociology Department, University of Leicester, University Road, Leicester LE1 7RH (direct tel 0116 252 5940, e-mail ed15@le.ac.uk)

DUNNING, Graham; QC (2001); s of Maj James Edwin Dunning, of Romsey, Hants, and Jane Priscilla, *née* Hunt; *b* 13 March 1958, Aldershot, Hants; *Educ* King Edward VI Sch Southampton, RMA Sandhurst, Emmanuel Coll Cambridge (entrance scholar, Squire law scholar, MA), Harvard Law Sch (Kennedy scholar, LLM); *m* 26 July 1986, Claire Abigael, da of Dr W S C Williams, of Oxford; 3 s (William, Thomas, Samuel), 1 da (Sophie); *Career* short serv ltd cmmn 3 RTR 1977; called to the Bar Lincoln's Inn 1982; practising barr specialising in commercial law and arbitration, memb Essex Court Chambers (formerly 4 Essex Court) 1983–; memb: Br Insur Law Assoc, Br Maritime Law Assoc, Commercial Bar Assoc (COMBAR), London Law and Commercial Bar Assoc, London Court of Int Arbitration, London Maritime Arbitrators Assoc; *Recreations* golf, skiing, family; *Clubs* Woking Golf, Rye Golf; *Style*— Graham Dunning, Esq, QC; ✉ Essex Court Chambers, 24 Lincoln's Inn Fields, London WC2A 3EG (tel 020 7813 8000, fax 020 7813 8080, e-mail gdunning@essexcourt.net)

DUNNING, Prof John Harry; s of John Murray Dunning (d 1966), and Anne Florence, *née* Baker (d 1965); *b* 26 June 1927; *Educ* John Lyons Harrow, UCL (BSc Econ), Univ of Southampton (PhD); *m* 1, (m dis 1975); 1 s (Philip John b 1957); m 2, 4 Aug 1975, Christine Mary, da of Ernest Stewart Brown (d 1992); *Career* Sub Lt RNVR 1945–48; lectr and sr lectr in economics Univ of Southampton 1952–64; Univ of Reading: fndn prof of economics 1964–75, Esmée Fairbairn prof of int investment and business studies 1975–88; ICI res prof in int business 1988–92 (emeritus prof of int business 1992–); prof of int business Rutgers Univ 1989–2000; chm Economists Advisory Group Ltd; conslt to UK Govt depts, OECD, UNCTAD and UNIDO; memb: Royal Econ Soc, Acad of Int Business, Int Trade and Fin Assoc (pres 1994); AIB: pres 1987–88, dean of fellows 1994–96; Dr (hc) Universidad Autónoma Madrid 1990; Hon PhD: Uppsala Univ Sweden 1975, Antwerpen Univ 1997, Chinese Culture Univ Taiwan 2007, Lund Univ Sweden 2007; hon prof of int business Univ of Int Economics and Business Beijing 1995; *Books* incl: American Investment in British Manufacturing Industry (1958, rev and updated 1998), British Industry - Change and Development in the Twentieth Century (with C J Thomas, 2 edn 1963), The Economics of Advertising (with D Lees and others, 1967), An Economic Study of the City of London (with E V Morgan, 1971), Readings in International Investment (1972), Economic Analysis and the Multinational Enterprise (1974), The World's Largest Industrial Enterprises 1962–77 (1981), International Capital Movements (with John Black, 1982), Multinational Enterprises, Economic Structure and International Competitiveness (1985), Japanese Participation in British Industry (1986), Explaining International Production (1988), Multinationals, Technology and Competitiveness (1988), Structural Change in the World Economy (with Allan Webster, 1990), Multinational Enterprises and the Global Economy (1993, revised edn (jtly) 2007), The Globalization of Business (1993), Foreign Direct Investment and Governments (with Rajneesh Narula, 1996), Globalization and Developing Countries (with Khalil Hamdani, 1997), Alliance Capitalism and Global Business (1997), Governments, Globalization and International Business (1997), Globalization, Trade and Foreign Direct Investment (1998), Regions, Globalization and the Knowledge Based Economy (2000), Global Capitalism at Bay? (2001), Theories and Paradigms of International Business Activity (2002), Global Capitalism, FDI and Competitiveness (2002), Making Globalization Good (2003), Multinationals and Industrial Competitiveness (with Rajneesh Narula, 2004), Multinational Enterprises and Emerging Challenges of the 21st Century (with Tsai-Mei Lin, 2007); *Recreations* gardening, walking; *Clubs* Athenaeum; *Style*— Prof John H Dunning; ✉ c/o University Business School, Reading Whiteknights, Reading, Berkshire RG6 2AA

DUNNING, Sir Simon William Patrick; 3 Bt (UK 1930), of Beedinglee, Lower Beeding, Sussex; s of Sir William Leonard Dunning, 2 Bt (d 1961), and Kathleen Lawrie, *née* Cuthbert (d 1992); *b* 14 December 1939; *Educ* Eton; *m* 1975, Frances Deirdre Morton, da of Maj Patrick William Morton Lancaster, of Wapsbourne Manor, Sheffield Park, E Sussex, and formerly w of Capt Nigel Edward Corbally Stourton; 1 da (Mariota Kathleen Masika b 1976); *Heir* none; *Clubs* Turf; *Style*— Sir Simon Dunning, Bt; ✉ Low Auchengillan, Blanefield, Glasgow G63 9AU (tel 01360 770323, fax 01360 771375)

DUNNINGTON-JEFFERSON, Sir Mervyn Stewart; 2 Bt (UK 1958), of Thorganby Hall, East Riding of Yorkshire; s of Lt-Col Sir John Alexander Dunnington-Jefferson, 1 Bt, DSO (d 1979), and (Frances) Isobel, *née* Cape; *b* 5 August 1943; *Educ* Eton; *m* 1971, Caroline Anna, da of John Bayley, of Hillam Hall, Monk Fryston, N Yorks; 2 da (Annabelle Mary b 1973, Emma Elizabeth b 1978), 1 s (John Alexander b 1980); *Heir* s, John Dunnington-Jefferson; *Career* ptnr Marldon; *Recreations* sport; *Clubs* MCC, Queen's; *Style—* Sir Mervyn Dunnington-Jefferson, Bt; ✉ 7 Bolingbroke Grove, London SW11 6ES (tel 020 8675 3395)

DUNRAVEN AND MOUNT-EARL, 7 Earl of (I 1822); Sir Thady Windham Thomas Wyndham-Quin; 7 Bt (GB 1781); also Baron Adare (I 1800), Viscount Mount-Earl (I 1816), Viscount Adare (I 1822); s of 6 Earl of Dunraven and Mount-Earl, CB, CBE, MC (d 1965), and Nancy, *née* Yuille (d 1994); *b* 27 October 1939; *Educ* Le Rosey Switzerland; *m* 1969, Geraldine, da of Air Cdre Gerard W McAleer, CBE; 1 da (Lady Ana b 1972); *Heir* none; *Career* farming and property devpt; *Clubs* Kildare Street (Dublin); *Style—* The Rt Hon The Earl of Dunraven and Mount-Earl

DUNSANY, 20 Baron (I 1439); Edward John Carlos Plunkett; s of 19 Baron Dunsany (d 1999), and Vera de Sà Sottomaior (d 1986); *b* 10 September 1939; *Educ* Eton, Slade Sch of Fine Art, Ecole des Beaux Arts Paris; *m* 1982, Maria Alice Villela de Carvalho; 2 s (Randal b 1983, Oliver b 1985); *Heir* s, Hon Randal Plunkett; *Career* artist and architectural designer, princ de Marsillac Plunkett Architecture Associates Inc (architects); *Recreations* chess; *Style—* The Rt Hon the Lord Dunsany

DUNSTAN, (Andrew Harold) Bernard; s of Dr Albert Ernest Dunstan (d 1963), and Louisa, *née* Cleaverley (d 1960); *b* 19 January 1920; *Educ* St Paul's, Byam Shaw Sch of Art, Slade Sch of Art (Slade scholar); *m* 1949, Diana Maxwell Armfield, RA, *qv*; 3 s (Andrew Joseph b 1950, David James b 1952, Robert Maxwell b 1955); *Career* painter; teacher at art schs 1947–73 incl: W of England Coll of Art, Camberwell, Byam Shaw, City and Guilds London; has exhibited regularly at London galleries, biennially at Roland Browse and Delbanco 1952–70 and regularly at Agnews 1973–; work in public collections incl: London Museum, Arts Cncl, Royal W of England Acad, Royal Collection; work in numerous private collections; tstee Royal Acad 1980–85; memb New English Art Club 1946 (hon memb 1992); RA 1968 (ARA 1956), RWA (pres 1976–82); *Books* incl: Pictures in Progress, Painting Methods of the Impressionists (1976, revised 1983), Ruskin's Elements of Drawing (ed, 1991), The Paintings of Bernard Dunstan (1993); *Recreations* music; *Clubs* Arts; *Style—* Bernard Dunstan, RA; ✉ 10 High Park Road, Kew, Richmond, Surrey TW9 4BH

DUNSTONE, Charles; *b* 21 November 1964; *Educ* Uppingham; *Career* former computer salesman NEC; estab Carphone Warehouse 1989 (currently chief exec); non-exec dir: HBOS plc, Daily Mail General Tst; chm Prince's Tst Trading Bd; *Recreations* sailing; *Style—* Charles Dunstone, Esq; ✉ Carphone Warehouse, 1 Portal Way, London W3 6RS (tel 020 8896 5000, fax 020 8896 5160)

DUNT, Vice Adm Peter; CB (2002); s of Hugh Dunt, of Prestatyn, N Wales, and Margaret, *née* Morgan; *b* 23 June 1947; *Educ* Duke of York Sch Nairobi, Merchant Taylors'; *m* 3 Aug 1974, Lesley Rae, *née* Gilchrist; 2 da (Rebecca b 21 Nov 1979, Sarah b 6 Aug 1981); *Career* Supply and Secretariat Offr RNC 1965, various RN sea and shore appointments incl Sec to Adm Woodward and Gp Logistics Offr (Falklands conflict) HMS Hermes 1982; subsequent MOD appointments incl: Dep Dir New Mgmnt Strategy (Directorate of Naval Staff Duties) and Sec to Second Sea Lord, Cmd HMS Raleigh (Navy's Ratings' New Entry Trg Estab) 1992, Dir Naval Personnel Corp Programming until 1997; RCDS 1997, appointed Rear Adm 1998, COS and DG Naval Personnel Strategy and Plans to the Second Sea Lord and C-in-C Naval Home Cmd 1998–2000, Chief Naval Supply Offr 2000–02, sr directing staff RCDS 2001–02, promoted Vice Adm 2002, chief exec Defence Estates 2002–07, Chief Naval Logistics Offr 2005; FCIPD 2001; *Recreations* all sport, gardening, DIY; *Clubs* I Zingari, Free Foresters, Incogniti, The Mount; *Style—* Vice Adm Peter Dunt, CB

DUNTHORNE, John William Bayne; s of Philip Bayne Dunthorne (d 2003), of Alton, Hants, and Ruth Mabelle, *née* Sturch; *b* 26 August 1946; *Educ* Abingdon Sch, Oxford Sch of Architecture (DipArch); *m* 16 Aug 1974, Maggie Alice, da of John Edgar Taylor (d 1988), of Blofield, Norfolk; 1 da (Joanna b 1981), 1 s (Oliver b 1983); *Career* assoc ptnr Chapman Lisle Assocs 1972–74, jt sr ptnr Dunthorne Parker Architects 1978–, dir DPSL 1985–; RIBA 1973; *Projects* incl: offices for BUPA, Brooke Bond and Swiss Life, industrial parks, historic shopping schemes in Oxford, Colchester, High Wycombe and Bury St Edmunds, restoration of Grade I listed buildings Golden Cross in Oxford, Red Lion in Colchester, Grade II offices in Clifton, residential schemes in Whitehall and Featherstone St London; *Awards* incl: Robertson Award, Ideas in Architecture Award, Oxford Preservation Tst Award, Royal Tunbridge Wells Civic Soc Conservation Award, Civic Tst Award; *Books* An Airport Interface (with M P Parker, 1971); *Recreations* cricket, golf, skiing; *Clubs* MCC, Chelsea Arts, Forty, Lord Gnome's CC; *Style—* J W B Dunthorne, Esq; ✉ 5 Aspley Road, London SW18 2DB; Dunthorne Parker, Architects, 16 Hampton Gurney Street, London W1H 5AL (tel 020 7258 0411)

DUNWOODY, Hon Mrs (Gwyneth Patricia); MP; o da of Baroness Phillips (Life Peer, d 1992), and Morgan Phillips (sometime Gen Sec of the Lab Pty, d 1963); *b* 12 December 1930; *Educ* Fulham County Secdy Sch, Convent of Notre Dame; *m* 1954 (m dis 1975), Dr John Elliot Orr Dunwoody; 2 s, 1 da (Tamsin Dunwoody-Kneafsey, AM, *qv*); *Career* former journalist for Fulham local newspaper and writer for radio, also former memb Totnes Cncl; MP (Lab): Exeter 1966–70, Crewe 1974–83, Crewe and Nantwich 1983–; parly sec Bd of Trade 1967–70, UK memb of Euro Parl 1975–79, memb Lab NEC 1981–90, chm NEC Local Govt Sub-Committee Nov 1981–90, oppn front bench spokesman Health Service 1981, memb Lab Home Policy Ctee 1982–89, chair Select Ctee on Transport; dir Film Prodn Assoc of GB 1970–74; responsibility for co-ordinating Lab Party campaigns 1983–89, life pres Lab Friends of Israel 1993–; *Style—* The Hon Mrs Dunwoody, MP; ✉ House of Commons, London SW1A 0AA (tel 020 7219 3000)

DUNWOODY, (Thomas) Richard; MBE (1993); s of George Rutherford Dunwoody, of Clanfield, Oxon, and Gillian Margaret, *née* Thrale; *b* 18 January 1964; *Educ* Rendcomb Coll; *m* 16 July 1988, Carol Ann, da of Robert Ronald George Abraham, of Wantage, Oxon; *Career* nat hunt jockey; all time record holder most National Hunt winners (1699), first winner 1983 (on Game Trust at Cheltenham), 3rd in Amateur Championship 1983–84; runner-up Jockeys Championship: 1989–90 (102 winners), 1990–91 (127 winners), 1991–92 (137 winners), 1992–93 Champion Jockey (173 winners), 1993–94 Champion Jockey (197 winners), 1994–95 Champion Jockey (163 winners); major wins: Grand National 1986 (West Tip), Cheltenham Gold Cup 1988 (Charter Party), King George VI Chase 1989 and 1990 (Desert Orchid) and 1996 and 1997 (One Man), Champion Hurdle 1990 (Kribensis), Breeders Cup Chase 1989 and 1992 (Highland Bud), Grand National 1994 (Miinnehoma); former jt pres Jockeys' Assoc of Great Britain; *Recreations* motorsport, rugby football, fitness; *Style—* Richard Dunwoody, Esq, MBE

DUNWOODY, (Moyra) Tamsin; da of late Dr John Dunwoody, and Hon Gwyneth Dunwoody, MP, *qv*; *b* 3 September 1958, Totnes, Devon; *Educ* Grey Coat Hosp Westminster, Univ of Kent (BA), South Bank Univ (AHSM); *m* 23 July 1994, Mark Kneafsey; 2 s (Daniel, Michael), 3 da (Demelza, Morgana, Clarissa); *Career* formerly hosp mangr: St Mary's Hosp London, Whittington Hosp London, Royal Free Hosp London; co sec St Davids Care in the Community, small business advsr, tutor ICT accountancy; memb Nat Assembly for Wales (Lab) Preseli Pembrokeshire 2003–07, dep min for enterprise, innovation and networks 2005–, dep min for environment, planning and countryside 2005–; *Style—* Mrs Tamsin Dunwoody

DUPLEIX, Jillian Edith (Jill); da of Edward Anzac Dupleix, of Victoria, Aust, and Rosemary Ann, *née* Campbell; *Educ* Hermitage C of E Girls' GS Geelong; *m* 26 June 1981, Terry Peter Durack; *Career* food writer, cookery editor, author and photographer; food columnist Melbourne Age 1981–87 and 1990–95, restaurant critic Melbourne Herald 1987–90; food ed: New Woman 1991–94, Elle Australia 1994–98, Sunday Age 1994–98, Sydney Morning Herald 1994–2000; The Times Cook and cookery ed The Times 2000–; ed (with Terry Durack) Sydney Morning Herald Good Food Guide 1994–2001; Cookery Journalist of the Year Br Guild of Food Writers 2002; *Books* incl: Hot Food Cool Jazz (1993), New Food (1994), Allegro Al Dente (1995), Old Food (1998), Simple Food (2002), Very Simple Food (2003), Good Cooking (2005); *Recreations* eating and drinking; *Style—* Ms Jill Dupleix; ✉ e-mail info@jilldupleix.com, website www.jilldupleix.com

DUPPLIN, Viscount; Charles William Harley Hay; s and h of 15 Earl of Kinnoull, Arthur William George Patrick Hay, and Countess of Kinnoull, Gay Ann Hay, *née* Lowson; *b* 20 December 1962; *Educ* Eton, ChCh Oxford (MA), City Univ, Inns of Court Sch of Law; *m* 15 June 2002, Catherine Clare Crawford, da of His Hon William Crawford, of Dalgonar, Dumfriesshire; 3 da (Hon Alice, Hon Catriona (twins) b 25 Sept 2003, Hon Auriol b 15 March 2007); *Career* called to the Bar Middle Temple 1990; investment banker with Credit Suisse First Boston Ltd 1985–88, underwriter with Hiscox Group at Lloyd's 1990; dir: Hiscox Underwriting Ltd 1995–97, Construction and General Guarantee Insurance Company Ltd 2001–, Heritage Group Ltd 2001–05; md Europe Hiscox Insurance Co Ltd 1995–2001, dir Amorphous Sugar Ltd 2001–; tstee Royal Caledonian Ball Tst 1992– (chm 1996–); dir M&A Hiscox plc 2000– (memb Exec Mgmnt Ctee 2004–); memb Devpt Ctee ChCh Oxford 2003–; Lt Atholl Highlanders 1992–, memb Queen's Body Guard for Scotland (Royal Co of Archers) 2000–; pres (London membs) Nat Tst for Scotland 2007–; FRPSL 2006 (MRPSL 1999); *Recreations* skiing, real tennis, philately, motor cars, racing; *Clubs* White's, Turf, Royal Perth, MCC, Jockey (Vienna); *Style—* Viscount Dupplin; ✉ 17 Cumberland Street, London SW1V 4LS (tel 020 7976 6973); Pitkindie House, Abernyte, Perthshire (tel 01828 686342, e-mail charles.dupplin@hiscox.com)

DUPREE, Sir Peter; 5 Bt (UK 1921), of Craneswater, Portsmouth, Co Southampton; s of Capt Sir Victor Dupree, 4 Bt (d 1976); *b* 20 February 1924; *m* 1947, Joan, da of late Capt James Desborough Hunt; *Heir* kinsman, David Dupree; *Career* Liveryman Worshipful Co of Farriers; *Style—* Sir Peter Dupree, Bt; ✉ 15 Hayes Close, Chelmsford, Essex CM2 0RN

DURAND, Sir Edward Alan Christopher David Percy; 5 Bt (UK 1892), of Ruckley Grange, Salop; elder s of Rev Sir (Henry Mortimer) Dickon Marion St George Durand, 4 Bt (d 1992), and Stella Evelyn, *née* L'Estrange; *b* 21 February 1974; *Educ* St Columba's Coll Dublin, Milltown Inst Dublin, Univ of Ulster at Coleraine (BA); *m* 5 June 2004, Rachel Ramona, *née* King; 1 da (Mary Magdalena Sophia Durand b 7 April 2005); *Heir* bro, David Durand; *Recreations* mysticism; *Style—* Sir Edward Durand, Bt; ✉ Lisnalurg House, Sligo, Republic of Ireland

DURANTE, Viviana; da of Giulio Durante, and Anna Maria Durante; *b* 8 May 1967, Rome; *Educ* White Lodge, Royal Ballet Sch; *Career* ballet dancer; Royal Ballet Co: joined 1984, first artist 1986–87, soloist 1987–89, princ dancer 1989–96; regularly dances with Irek Mukhamedov (and has toured with his company), has also danced with Errol Pickford, Bruce Sansom and Tetsuya Kumakawa; subject (with Darcey Bussell) of South Bank Show profile and documentary (LWT) 1992; appeared in Italian short film Ogri 27 Agosto; *Roles* debuts in 1988–89 season incl: Odette/Odile in Swan Lake (Australian tour 1988, London 1989), Princess Aurora in The Sleeping Beauty, title roles in Sir Frederick Ashton's Ondine and Cinderella, Juliet in Sir Kenneth MacMillan's Romeo and Juliet, leading roles in Natalia Makarova's La Bayadère, Ashton's Rhapsody and George Balanchine's Rubies; debuts in 1989–90 season incl: Lise in Ashton's La Fille mal Gardée, leading roles in MacMillan's The Prince of the Pagodas, Requiem and My Brother My Sisters; debuts in 1990–91 season incl: title role in MacMillan's Manon, the Golden Hours Girl in MacMillan's Elite Syncopations, Irina in MacMillan's Winter Dreams (created role), Sugar Plum Fairy in The Nutcracker, Roxane in David Bintley's Cyrano, Saturn Pas de Deux in The Planets, leading roles in MacMillan's Danses Concertantes, Balanchine's Stravinsky Violin Concerto (first Royal Ballet prodn of the work), Ashley Page's Bloodlines (created role), Ashton's Scenes de Ballet (USA tour), The Girl in Blue in Nijinska's Les Biches; debuts in 1991–92 season incl: title role in Giselle, Masha in Winter Dreams, Titania in Ashton's The Dream (Japan tour), The Woman in The Judas Tree (world première 1992, Sir Kenneth MacMillan's last one-act work), Ashton's Thais Pas de Deux, leading roles in Balanchine's Symphony in C, William Tuckett's Present Histories; 1996 season incl: Ashton's Rhapsody, Ashton's Symphonic Variations, title role in Sir Peter Wright's Giselle, Aurora in Anthony Dowell's Sleeping Beauty 1996; roles with Irek Mukhamedov and Company incl Diana and Actaeon Pas de Deux and Summer Pas de Deux from MacMillan's The Four Seasons; performed in Anna Karenina Tokyo 1998; *Awards* incl: Time Out/01 For London Dance Award 1989, Dance & Dancers magazine Dancer of the Year 1989, Evening Standard Ballet Award 1989, Positano Prize (Italy) 1991; *Recreations* reading, swimming, writing, relaxing; *Style—* Miss Viviana Durante

DURBIN, Dr Richard Michael; *Educ* Univ of Cambridge; *m* Julie; 1 da (Zoe b 26 Dec 1997), 1 s (Benjamin b 19 Feb 2000); *Career* research posts: Lab of Molecular Biology Univ of Cambridge, Harvard Univ, Stanford Univ; dep dir and head of informatics Wellcome Tst Sanger Inst; FRS 2004; *Books* The Computing Neuron (jt ed, 1989), Biological Sequence Analysis: Probabilistic Models of Proteins and Nucleic Acids (jtly, 1998); *Style—* Dr Richard Durbin; ✉ Wellcome Trust Sanger Institute, Wellcome Trust Genome Campus, Hinxton, Cambridge CB10 1SA

DURCAN, Paul; s of John James Durcan (d 1988), and Sheila MacBride (d 2004); *b* 16 October 1944; *Educ* Gonzaga Coll Dublin, UC Cork (BA); *m* 1 Aug 1967 (sep), Nessa, *née* O'Neill; 2 da (Sarah O'Neill b 22 June 1969, Siabhra O'Neill b 20 July 1970); *Career* poet; Patrick Kavanagh Award 1974, Irish American Cultural Institute Poetry Award 1989, Whitbread Poetry Award 1990, Heinemann Bequest Royal Soc of Literature 1995, Cholmondley Award for Poetry 2001; Ireland prof of poetry 2004–; memb Aosdána 1981; *Poetry* O Westport In The Light of Asia Minor (1975), Teresa's Bar (1976), Sam's Cross (1978), Selected Poems (1982), The Berlin Wall Café (1985, Poetry Book Soc Choice 1985), Going Home To Russia (1987), Jesus and Angela (1988), Daddy, Daddy (1990), Crazy About Women (1991), A Snail In My Prime (1993), Give Me Your Hand (1994), Christmas Day (1996, Poetry Book Soc Recommendation 1996), Greetings to Our Friends in Brazil (1999, Poetry Book Soc Recommendation 1999), Cries of an Irish Caveman (2001), Paul Durcan's Diary (2003), The Art of Life (2004), The Laughter of Mothers (2007); *Recreations* walking; *Style—* Paul Durcan, Esq; ✉ 14 Cambridge Avenue, Ringsend, Dublin 4 (tel and fax 00 353 01 668 2276)

DURDEN-SMITH, Neil; OBE (1997); s of Anthony James Durden-Smith MB, BS, FRCS (d 1963), of Middx, and Grace Elizabeth, *née* Neill (d 1938); *b* 18 August 1933; *Educ* Aldenham, BRNC Dartmouth; *m* 3 Jan 1964, Judith Chalmers, OBE, *qv*, da of David Norman Chalmers, FRICS (d 1952), of Cheshire; 1 da (Emma (Mrs Gordon Dawson) b 1967), 1 s (Mark b 1968); *Career* RN 1952–63; ADC to Govr-Gen of NZ 1957–59; played cricket and hockey for RN, Combined Services and Herts; prodr BBC Outside Broadcasts Dept (special responsibility 1966 World Cup) 1963–66; radio and TV broadcasting incl: Test Match and Co Cricket, Olympic Games 1968 and 1972, Trooping the Colour, Royal Tournament, Money Matters, Sports Special; chm and md Durden-Smith

D

Communications 1974–81, dir Ruben Sedgwick 1987–95, dir Tangible Securities; chm: Sports Sponsorship Int 1982–87, The Altro Group 1982–94, Woodside Communications 1992–; conslt AON 1995–; dir: BCM Grandstand 1993–, Children in Crisis 1993–95, The Anglo-American Sporting Clubs 1969–74; chm Lord's Taverners 1980–82 (pres Middx Region 1993–), pres Lord's Taverners Buccaneers; vice-pres: Eng Schools Cricket Assoc, Northwood Cricket Club, Eng Indoor Hockey Assoc, The Peter May Meml Appeal; chm The Brian Johnston Meml Tst 1994–99; patron: Motor Neurone Disease Assoc, Aspire, Westminster Soc for People with Hearing Difficulties; tstee: ISIS Assoc, Charlie Waller Meml Tst; pres Vale do Lobo Club Members' Assoc; Freeman City of London; *Books* Forward for England (1967), World Cup '66 (1967); *Recreations* theatre, current affairs, cricket, rugby, golf, reading the newspapers; *Clubs* MCC, Lord's Taverners, Saints & Sinners, I Zingari, Wig & Pen, Free Foresters, Lords & Commons Cricket, RN Cricket, County Cricketers Golf, Cricket Writers, Home House, Castaways, Highgate Golf, Vale do Lobo Golf, Ladykillers, Surbiton Hockey, Forty; *Style*— Neil Durden-Smith, Esq, OBE; ✉ 28 Hillway, Highgate, London N6 6HH (tel 020 8348 2340, fax 020 8348 8224)

DURGAN, Graham Richard; *b* 7 January 1957; *Educ* BSc; *m* Jane; 2 s, 1 da; *Career* Coopers & Lybrand 1977–82, fin trg 1982–85, md BPP Accountancy Courses Ltd 1985–88, dir Esprit Ltd 1988–90; chief exec: Business Training Network 1990–92, Accountancy Tuition Centres 1992–, BNB Resources plc 1997–2000, Durgan Monstein 2001–; chm: Emile Woolf International 2002–, Foulks Lynch plc 2002–; memb Cncl ICAEW 1995–; ACA; *Recreations* sailing, skiing, tennis; *Style*— Graham Durgan, Esq; ✉ Durgan Monstein plc, 10 Station Road, Henley on Thames, Oxfordshire RG9 1AY; Emile Woolf International, 4 Tannery House, Tannery Lane, Send, Surrey GU23 7EF

DURHAM, Archdeacon of; *see:* Jagger, Ven Ian

DURHAM, Dean of; *see:* Sadgrove, Very Rev Michael

DURHAM, Kenneth John; s of John Clifford Durham, of Thames Ditton, Surrey, and Geraldine Mary, *née* Trinder; *b* 23 October 1953; *Educ* St John's Sch Leatherhead, Brasenose Coll Oxford (BA), Inst of Education London (PGCE); *m* 1984, Vivienne Mary, da of Donald Edward Johnson; *Career* head of economics St Albans Sch 1975–87; KCS Wimbledon: head of economics 1987–91 dir of studies 1991–96; headmaster UCS Hampstead 1996–; memb HMC 1996; ESU Scholarship 1989; *Books* The New City (1992); *Recreations* music, theatre, opera, film, books, walking; *Style*— Kenneth Durham, Esq; ✉ University College School, Frognal, Hampstead, London NW3 6XH (tel 020 7435 2215)

DURHAM, 94 Bishop of 2003–; Rt Rev Dr (Nicholas) Thomas (Tom) Wright; s of Nicholas Irwin Wright, of Morpeth, Northumberland, and Rosemary, *née* Forman; *b* 1 December 1948; *Educ* Sedbergh, Exeter Coll Oxford (MA, DPhil, DD, Rugby Fives half blue), Wycliffe Hall Oxford; *m* 14 Aug 1971, Margaret Elizabeth Anne, da of Frank Albert Fiske; 2 s (Nicholas Julian Gregory b 9 June 1974, Oliver Thomas Irwin b 1 March 1981), 2 da (Rosamund Sarah Margaret b 17 March 1976, Harriet Elizabeth Ruth b 9 Feb 1979); *Career* ordained: deacon 1975, priest 1976; Merton Coll Oxford: jr res fell 1975–78, jr chaplain 1976–78; fell and chaplain Downing Coll Cambridge 1978–81, asst prof of New Testament lit McGill Univ Montreal 1981–86, hon prof Diocesan Coll Montreal 1981–86, fell, tutor and chaplain Worcester Coll Oxford 1986–93, univ lectr in theol Univ of Oxford 1986–93, canon theologian Coventry Cathedral 1992–99, dean of Lichfield 1993–99, canon theologian of Westminster 2000–03; memb: Doctrine Cmmn C of E 1979–81 and 1989–95, Int Anglican Doctrinal Cmmn 2001–, Lambeth Cmmn 2004; fell Inst for Christian Studies Toronto 1992–; memb: Soc of Biblical Lit 1982, Soc of New Testament Studies 1988; conslt and participant in numerous documentaries on Jesus and early Christianity incl: The Lives of Jesus 1996, Jesus Then and Now 1996, Heart of the Matter 1997, The Jesus Files 1998, Son of God 2001, The Apostles 2001, John Meets Paul 2002, Spring Journey 2004, Resurrection 2004; poetry: Easter Oratorio (music by Paul Spicer, 2000); participant in The Brains Tst 1999 and 2001; devised and presented numerous broadcast services 1995–2001; Hon DD: Univ of Aberdeen 2001, Nashotah House 2006, Wycliffe Coll Toronto 2006, Univ of Durham 2007; Hon fell Downing Coll Cambridge 2003, Hon fell Merton Coll Oxford 2004; *Books* Small Faith, Great God (1978), The Work of John Frith (1983), The Epistles of Paul to the Colossians and to Philemon (1987), The Glory of Christ in the New Testament (1987), The Interpretation of the New Testament 1861–1986 (1988), The Climax of the Covenant (1991), New Tasks for a Renewed Church (1992), The Crown and the Fire (1992), The New Testament and the People of God (1992), Who Was Jesus? (1992), Following Jesus (1994), The Lord and His Prayer (1996), Jesus and the Victory of God (1996), The Original Jesus (1996), For All God's Worth (1997), What St Paul Really Said (1997), Reflecting the Glory (1997), The Meaning of Jesus: Two Visions (with Marcus J Borg, 1999), The Way of the Lord (1999), The Myth of the Millennium (1999), Romans and the People of God (with S K Soderlund, 1999), Holy Communion for Amateurs (1999), The Challenge of Jesus (2000), Twelve Months of Sundays (3 vols, 2000, 2001 and 2002), Mark for Everyone (2001), Luke for Everyone (2001), Matthew for Everyone (2 vols, 2002), Paul for Everyone: Galatians and Thessalonains (2002), Paul for Everyone: The Prison Letters (2002), John for Everyone (2002), Romans (in New Interpreter's Bible, vol 10, 2002), The Meal Jesus Gave Us (2002), Paul for Everyone: 1 Corinthians (2003), Paul for Everyone: 2 Corinthians (2003), The Resurrection of the Son of God (2003), Quiet Moments (2003), Hebrews for Everyone (2003), Paul for Everyone: The Pastoral Letters (2003), For All the Saints? Remembering the Christian Departed (2003), Paul for Everyone: Romans (2004), The Scriptures, the Cross, and the Power of God (2005), Paul: Fresh Perspectives (2005), Scripture and the Authority of God (2005), Dictionary for Theological Interpretation of Scripture (jt ed, 2005), Judas and the Gospel of Jesus (2006), Evil and the Justice of God (2006), Simply Christian (2006), The Resurrection of Jesus: John Dominic Crossan and N T Wright in Dialogue (2006), The Cross and the Colliery (2007), Acts for Everyone (2007), Surprised by Hope (2008); *Recreations* music, poetry, golf; *Style*— The Rt Rev the Lord Bishop of Durham; ✉ Auckland Castle, Co Durham DL14 7NR (tel 01388 602 576, fax 01388 605264, e-mail bishop@bishopdunelm.co.uk)

DURHAM, Vivienne Mary; da of Donald Johnson, of Chichester, W Sussex, and Patricia, *née* Wiltshire; *b* Rustington, W Sussex; *Educ* St Hilda's Coll Oxford (MA), PGCE; *m* 1984, Kenneth Durham; *Career* teacher; Haberdashers' Aske's Sch for Girls 1983–87, Godolphin & Latymer Sch 1987–91, head of Eng Guildford HS 1991–93, head of Eng Haberdashers' Aske's 1993–97, dep head South Hampstead HS 1997–2004, headmistress Francis Holland Sch 2004–; accredited inspr Ind Schs Inspectorate 2000; govr: Sarum Hall Sch London, Woldingham Sch; memb: GSA 2004, SHA; *Recreations* reading, theatre, opera, riding, tennis, skiing; *Clubs* Univ Women's, Lansdowne; *Style*— Mrs Vivienne Durham; ✉ Francis Holland School, Clarence Gate, Ivor Place, London NW1 6XR (tel 020 7723 0176, fax 020 7706 1522, e-mail headmistress@fhs-nw1.org.uk)

DURHAM HALL, His Hon Judge Jonathan David; QC (1995); *b* 2 June 1952; *Educ* King Edward VII Sch Sheffield, Univ of Nottingham (LLB); *m* 1, Patricia Helen Bychowska; 1 da (Antonia b 14 July 1977), 1 s (Christian b 29 Oct 1980); m 2, Hilary Hart; *Career* called to the Bar Gray's Inn 1975; in practice NE Circuit, recorder 1995–2003 (asst recorder 1991–95), head of chambers 1995–2003, circuit judge (Wales & Chester Circuit) 2003–; memb Gen Cncl of the Bar 1994–95, chm Mental Health Review Tbnl, legal assessor GMC; memb Gray's Inn Barristers' Ctee; former memb Parochial Deanery and Diocesan Synod; served TA The Hallamshire Regt 1969–72; *Recreations* walking, all things countryside especially creation of rural woodland, plays of Shakespeare; *Style*— His Hon Judge Durham Hall, QC; ✉ Bradford Law Courts, Exchange Square, Bradford BD 1 1JA

DURIE, (William Howard) Robert; s of Kenneth Robert Durie (d 1989), and Enid, *née* Butler (d 1993); *b* 14 October 1941, Bristol; *Educ* Clifton; *m* 19 June 1965, Joanna Mary, *née* Silvey; 1 da (Emma (Mrs Brewer) b 28 March 1967), 2 s (James b 26 April 1969, Daniel b 15 April 1973); *Career* joined as trainee surveyor Stanley Alder & Price 1959, J P Sturge & Sons Chartered Surveyors 1962–95, rejoined Alder King 1995; non-exec dir Coutts & Co 1988–93; surveyor to Soc of Merchant Venturers and local Bristol charities and tsts; pres Bristol C of C 1986; dir: Business West, Destination Bristol; chm Lady Haberfield's Almshouse Charity, vice-patron Nat Assoc of Almshouses; pres Anchor Soc 1994; High Sheriff City of Bristol 2007–08; FRICS, FRSA 2005; *Recreations* sailing, walking, riding, rugby, golf, bridge, cricket; *Clubs* Royal Thames Yacht, MCC, Clifton RFC; *Style*— Robert Durie, Esq; ✉ Deerhurst, Church Road, Abbots Leigh, Bristol BS8 3QU (tel 01275 374833, fax 01275 375132, e-mail bob@whrd.co.uk)

DURIE OF DURIE, Andrew Maule Dewar; CBE (2000), DL (Dunbartonshire 1996); s of Lt-Col Raymond Varley Dewar Durie of Durie (d 1999), and Wendy, *née* Frances St John Maule; *b* 13 November 1939; *Educ* Wellington; *m* 25 Aug 1972, Marguerite Jamila, da of Graf Kunata Kottulinsky, of Vienna, Austria; 1 da (Nicola Louise b 19 Sept 1974), 2 s (James Alexander b 26 April 1978, Philip Anthony b 29 Aug 1986); *Career* cmmnd Argyll & Sutherland Highlanders 1958–68; served: UK, BAOR, SE Asia, Aden; ret Capt 1968; White Horse Distillers 1968–83: dir 1973–82, sr export dir 1982–83; int sales dir Long John International (Whitbread & Co plc) 1983–88; James Burrough Distillers: Euro sales dir 1988, dep md 1988–89, md 1989–90, ceo 1990–91; chm Allied Distillers Ltd (subsid of Allied Domecq plc) 1997–99 (md 1991–97); chm CBI Scotland Cncl 1997–99 (vice-chm 1996), chm Seafish Industry Authy 2002– (vice-chm 2000–02); dir Edinburgh Military Tattoo 2001–; memb Incorporation of Maltmen 1995, Liveryman Worshipful Co of Distillers 1986; *Recreations* sailing, tennis, rough shooting, skiing; *Clubs* Western; *Style*— Andrew Durie of Durie, Esq, CBE, DL; ✉ Finnich Malise, Croftamie, West Stirlingshire G63 0HA (tel 01360 660257, fax 01360 660101)

DURKAN, (John) Mark; MP, MLA; s of Brendan Durkan, and Isobel, *née* Tinney; *b* 26 June 1960; *Educ* St Columb's Coll Derry, Queen's Univ Belfast; *Career* asst to John Hume MP 1984–98; memb Derry City Cncl 1993–2000; chairperson SDLP 1990–95, Multi-Party Talks Negotiator SDLP 1996–98, MLA (SDLP) Foyle 1998–; min of finance and personnel 1999–2001, dep first min 2001–02; ldr SDLP 2001–; MP (SDLP) Foyle 2005–; *Style*— Mark Durkan, Esq, MP, MLA; ✉ 23 Bishop Street, Derry BT48 6PR (tel 02871 360700, fax 02871 360808, e-mail m.durkan@sdlp.ie); Northern Ireland Assembly, Parliament Buildings, Stormont Estate, Belfast BT4 3XX (tel 028 9052 1649, fax 028 9052 1329); House of Commons, London SW1A 0AA (tel 020 7219 5096, e-mail durkanm@parliament.uk)

DURKIN, Dr Michael Anthony Patrick; s of John Durkin (d 1986), of Cheltenham and Wimbledon, and Philomena, *née* O'Shea (d 1999); *b* 26 July 1950; *Educ* Whitefriars Sch Cheltenham, Middx Hosp Med Sch London (MB BS); *m* 19 July 1978, Susan Claire, da of Lawrence Paul Cotterell, of Cheltenham; 3 s (Luke b 1979, Jack b 1981, James b 1983), 1 da (Ellen b 1990); *Career* registrar in anaesthesia St Thomas' Hosp London 1976–79, res registrar Middx Hosp London 1980–81, sr registrar S Western RHA 1981–85; Gloucestershire Royal Hosp: conslt in anaesthesia and intensive care 1985–, clinical dir and chm Med Staff Ctee; med dir Gloucestershire Royal NHS Tst 1993–2002, med dir and dir of clinical quality Avon, Gloucestershire and Wiltshire Strategic HA 2003– (exec dir of clinical performance 2002–03), visiting prof Yale Univ Sch of Med (asst prof 1982–84, visiting assoc faculty 1989); lectr Keele Univ 1996–, med dir tutor NHS Leadership Prog 2001–; chapters in books and articles in jls on anaesthesia, intensive care and monitoring, ed Anaesthesia Points West; referee: BMJ, Intensive Care Med, Critical Care Med, Br Jl of Hosp Med; chair: Quality Taskforce NHS Exec SW, Clinical Governance Taskforce for South West, Genetics Steering Bd for South; memb Ctee: Soc of Anaesthetists of S Western Region, Gloucestershire Clinical Advsy Gp, Medical Workforce Advsy Gp, Cancer Strategy Gp, Research and Devpt Gp Gloucestershire HA; memb Cncl: Inst of Medical Sciences Cranfield Univ, Gloucestershire Royal Hosp, Univ for Gloucester Steering Gp; memb: Regnl Modernisation Bd NHS Exec SW, Emergency Planning Steering Gp DH; co-leader Clinical Governance and Leadership Review Team Ethiopia; tstee Intensive Care Charity; memb: Euro Intensive Care Soc, Int Anaesthesia Res Soc, Intensive Care Soc, Assoc of Anaesthetists GB, Assoc of Trust Medical Dirs, Br Assoc of Medical Mangrs, BMA; FRCA 1981, FCAnaes; *Books* Post Anaesthetic Recovery (3 edn, 1996); *Recreations* skiing, tennis, watching rugby; *Clubs* Lilleybrook; *Style*— Dr Michael Durkin

DURLACHER, Nicholas John; CBE (1995); s of John Sydney Durlacher, MC; *b* 20 March 1946; *Educ* Stowe, Magdalene Coll Cambridge; *m* 1971, Mary Caroline, da of Maj Guy Lewis Ian McLaren (d 1978); 1 s (David Michael b 1976); *Career* memb London Stock Exchange 1971–86; chm: LIFFE 1992–95, Securities and Futures Authy 1995–2001, Ennismore Smaller Cos 1999–, EMX Co 2000–07, Elexon Ltd 2000–, Electricity Balancing and Settlement Code Panel 2000–, Quilter Global Enhanced Income Tst plc 2000–05, FFastFill plc 2000–02; *Recreations* skiing, tennis, golf, shooting; *Clubs* White's; *Style*— Nicholas Durlacher, Esq, CBE; ✉ Elexon Ltd, 350 Euston Road, London NW1 3AW (tel 020 7380 4252, e-mail nick.durlacher@elexon.co.uk)

DURLACHER, Peter Laurence; s of Adm Sir Laurence Durlacher, KCB, OBE, DSC (d 1986), of Mougins, France, and Rimma Durlacher, MBE, *née* Sass-Tissovsky (d 1997); *b* 27 April 1935; *Educ* Winchester, Inst of Political Science Paris, Magdalene Coll Cambridge; *m* 1 (m dis), Jennifer Ann, da of Hugh Blauvelt (d 1967), of Drumnadrochit, Inverness; 2 da (Fenella b 1961, Sophie b 1968), 2 s (Christopher b 1963, Julian b 1966); m 2, Mary Cresswell-Turner (d 2000), da of Richard Girouard (d 1989), of London; *Career* Henry Ansbacher: joined 1957, dir 1966–72, an md 1970–72; i/c Overseas Dept Wedd Durlacher Mordaunt 1972–76, conslt to Stock Exchange and IMF 1976–80, ptnr Laurie Milbank Stockbrokers 1981–86, dir Parrish Stockbrokers 1986–90, chm Durlacher & Co (formerly Durlacher West Ltd) 1990–95, dir Nabarro Wells & Co Ltd 1995–98, IO Group plc 1998–99; chm Sunnybank Anglo-American Assoc 2001–; tstee Schoolmistresses and Governesses Benevolent Inst 1968–99, hon treas Nat Youth Bureau 1977–89; Liveryman Worshipful Co of Cutlers; *Recreations* walking, opera; *Clubs* City of London, Beefsteak; *Style*— Peter Durlacher, Esq; ✉ Mas Tournamy, 405 Chemin des Peyroues, 06250 Mougins, France (tel 00 33 49 39 00 216)

DURLESTEANU, HE Mariana; da of Ion Durlesteanu, and Serafima Durlesteanu; *b* 5 September 1971, Moldova (then part of USSR); *Educ* Babes-Bolyai Univ Romania, IEDC Brdo pri Kranju Slovenia (MBA); *m* 10 Nov 2004, Iurii Solopa; 1 s (Alexandru b 19 Aug 2003), 1 da (Iuliana b 19 Aug 2003); *Career* Moldovan diplomat; Miny of Finance Republic of Moldova: economist 1995–96, chief External Debt Serv Div 1996–97, head of foreign financing and external debt direction Treasy Dept 1997–2001, dir Project Implementation Unit World Bank's Projects Private Sector Devpt I & II 1998–2001, dep min of finance 2001–02, first dep min 2002–04, chm Savings Bank 2004–; ambass to the Ct of St James's 2005–; Gloria Muncii (Republic of Moldova) 2002; *Style*— HE Mrs Mariana Durlesteanu; ✉ Embassy of the Republic of Moldova, 5 Dolphin Square, Edensor Road, London W4 2ST

DURLING, David; *b* 15 October 1946; *Educ* Sir Philip Magnus Secdy Tech Sch London, Barnet Coll of FE (fndn course), Buckinghamshire Inst High Wycombe (BA), RCA (MA), Open Univ (PhD 1996); *m*; 1 c (b 1987); *Career* industrial and furniture designer; design asst then sr designer and assoc i/c industrial design team Graphics + Industrial Design Ltd Richmond Surrey 1971–75 (clients incl Royal Navy, Vickers Ship Engineering, ICI), freelance designer London 1975–76, sr designer Architect's Dept Notts CC 1976–83 (i/c interiors, furniture design and building graphics), sr lectr in industrial design Sheffield City Poly 1983–84, fndr dir EDGE Ltd design and R&D consltts 1984–96 (pt/t dir 1984–89), course ldr and sr lectr in 3D design (furniture) Sch of Industrial Design Leicester Poly 1986–89, md Lab Systems Ltd mfrs of laboratory furniture and equipment in UK 1991–93, dir Advanced Research Inst Sch of Art and Design Staffs Univ 1996, prof of design Sch of Arts and Educn Middlesex Univ; various visiting lectureships, visiting prof in design Univ of Central Lancashire, external examiner for industrial deisgn Nat Univ of Singapore; registered inspr FE Funding Cncl 1993–96; Chartered Soc of Designers: memb Nat Cncl 1987–91, local organiser Sheffield Area 1987–91, chm NE Regnl Cncl 1987–91; memb Nat Cncl Design Res Soc 1993–2006 (ed DR News 1996–, chm 1998–2006, fell), exec memb Int Assoc of Socs of Design Research, memb various tech ctees BSI; memb Ergonomics Soc 1981–, appointed memb panel for Art and Design Res Assessment Exercise 2001 HEFCE 1999–2001, FRSA; *Recreations* yacht cruising, sea fishing, cycling, reading and cyberspace; *Style—* Dr David Durling

DURRANI, Prof Tariq Salim; OBE (2003); s of Mohammed Salim Khan Durrani (d 1980), of London, and Bilquis Jamal; *b* 27 October 1943; *Educ* EPUET Dacca Bangladesh (BEng), Univ of Southampton (MSc, PhD); *m* 6 Aug 1972, Clare Elizabeth, da of late Howard Kellas; 2 da (Monise Nadia b 1977, Sophia Jasmine b 1981), 1 s (Jamiel Tariq b 1986); *Career* res fell Univ of Southampton 1970–76; Univ of Strathclyde: lectr 1976–79, sr lectr 1979–82, prof of signal processing 1982–, chm Dept of Electronic and Electrical Engrg 1986–90, dep princ (IT) 1990–91, dep princ 2000–06, sr advsr 2006–; IEEE: pres Signal Processing Soc 1994–96, chm Periodicals Cncl 1996–97, former chm Professional Gps on Signal Processing and Image Processing, vice-chair Technical Activities Region 8, pres Engrg Mgmnt Soc 2006–07; chm: Centre for Parallel Signal Processing, Scottish Electronics Technol Gp; dir Inst of System Level Integration 2000–; memb: Scottish Science Advsy Ctee 2002–04, Scottish Funding Cncl 2006–; IEEE Millennium Medal 2000, IEEE Signal Processing Soc Meritorious Service Award 2000, GG2 Leadership and Diversity Award as Asian Man of the Year 1999; dir: Scottish Inst for Enterprise 2001–04, Glasgow C of C 2002–, Leadership Foundation for Higher Educn 2004–; FIEE 1983, FIEEE 1989, FRSE 1994 (memb Cncl 2003–06, vice-convenor Int Ctee 2006–), FREng 1996; *Books* Laser Systems in Flow Measurements (with C Greated, 1977), Geophysical Signal Processing (with E A Robinson, 1986), Signal Processing (co-ed with J L Lacoume and R Stora, 1987), Mathematics and Signal Processing (ed, 1987), Transputer Applications 3 (ed, 1991); *Recreations* swimming; *Clubs* Ross Priory; *Style—* Prof Tariq Durrani, OBE, FRSE, FREng; ✉ 14 Duchess Park, Helensburgh, Dunbartonshire G84 9PY (tel 01436 676590); University of Strathclyde, Department of Electronic and Electrical Engineering, 204 George Street, Glasgow G1 1XW (tel 0141 548 2540, fax 0141 552 2487, e-mail durrani@strath.ac.uk)

DURRANT, Hugh Russell; s of Derek Walter Durrant (d 1990), and Elsie Violet, *née* Russell (d 1980); *b* 12 July 1947; *Educ* Latymer Upper Sch, Magdalene Coll Cambridge (MA); *Career* costume, set and fashion designer; head of design: Birmingham Repertory 1973–76, Theatre Royal York 1976–78, Northcott Theatre Exeter 1979–81; assoc dir Nottingham Playhouse 1982–85; fashion posts held incl: Emanuel couture 1985, head of design Cojana Ltd London 1985–90, couture designer Rafa Abu Dhabi 1991–92; estab own couture label 1988; design conslt (scenery) Holland America Westours Ltd 1993–2003; visiting prof: Nat Theater Inst Eugene O'Neill Center USA 1996–98, London Acad of Theatre 1999–2001; memb Acad of Television Arts and Scis USA; *Theatre* designed over 14 prodns Regent's Park Open Air Theatre, 12 pantomimes for Paul Elliott; costume design credits incl: Mystery of Irma Vep (Ambassadors) 1990, Seven Brides for Seven Brothers (Old Vic and Prince of Wales, London and Canada), The Mikado (Cambridge and Prince of Wales), Barry Manilow's Copacabana (Prince of Wales) 1994–95 (also UK tour 1995–96, Holland and America 1998, Australia 1999), Cher Farewell Tour and NBC special (USA) 2002 (Emmy Award Best Costume Design 2003); set and costume credits incl: Sister Mary Ignatius (Ambassadors) 1984, The Hot Shoe Show (Palladium) 1984, Cinderella (Palladium) 1985, Babes in the Wood (Palladium) 1986–87, Lock Up Your Daughters (Chichester and Savoy Theatre London) 1996, Lady Windermere's Fan (Chichester) 1997, Sandy Wilson's Divorce Me Darling (Chichester) 1997 (TMA Award for Best Musical), Jerry Herman's The Best of Times (Vaudeville) 1998, Nymph Errant (Chichester) 1999, Midnight Fantasy (Luxor Las Vegas) 2000, Dreamcatcher (UK) 2001, Ann-Margret...Here, Now! (USA tour) 2003, The Boyfriend (UK tour, 50th anniversary prodn) 2003, Jack and the Beanstalk (Nelson Mandela Theatre Johannesburg) 2003, Full Circle with Joan Collins (Triumph Prodns) 2004, The Merry Widow (Carl Rosa Opera) 2004, Wonderland (Harrah's Casino Reno) 2004, New Fantasies (Luxor Las Vegas) 2005, Manilow: Music and Passion (Las Vegas and USA tour), Babes in Arms (Chichester and West End) 2007; UK tours incl: Amadeus, A Little Night Music, Company, Naked Justice, Hot Flush; Br premieres incl: Mack and Mabel, Lady in the Dark; *Dance* credits incl: Symphony in Waves (Dutch Nat Ballet), Frankenstein (Royal Ballet, La Scala Milan, Dutch Nat Ballet (sets only)), Footnotes (Nederland Dans), Window & Sleeping Birds (Rambert), Dash and Hot Shoe Show (for Wayne Sleep, *qv*); *Other Credits* incl: Thomas Hardy's The Dynasts (Exeter Cathedral 900th anniversary (adapted and designed)), Voices from the Great War (Nottingham Playhouse (adapted, designed and directed)); concert costumes for: Sarah Brightman 1985–97, Cher, Ruthie Henshall, Gloria Hunniford, Barry Manilow; photographic styling for Cher 2002; *Television* and film incl: Ivanhoe (costumes), Boadicea (prodn designer), Young Alexander (costume designer), Telephone Detectives (prodn and costume designer); videos: Sarah Brightman, Andrea Bocelli, The Hey-Makers; *Clubs* Home House; *Style—* Hugh Durrant, Esq; ✉ 22 Alwyne Road, London N1 2HN (tel 020 7354 2851); c/o Jean Diamond, Diamond Management, 31 Percy Street, London W1T 2DD (tel 020 7631 0400, e-mail setsquare1@hotmail.com)

DURRANT, John; s of Edward Henry Samual Stokes Durrant (d 1972), and Phyllis, *née* Howard-Spink (d 1988); *b* 6 July 1949; *Educ* N Paddington Sch, Oxford Poly (now Oxford Brooks Univ) (DMS); *m* June 1974, Susan, da of Thomas Clark, of Cliftonville, Kent; 3 s (Oliver Jon b 20 Nov 1975, Thomas Edward b 22 Sept 1978, William Jack b 3 Dec 1981); *Career* promotion mangr W B Saunders medical publishers London 1969–73, mktg dir European Bibliographical Centre Oxford 1973–78; Clio Press Ltd Oxford: jt md 1978–81, chm and md 1981–94, currently dir; chm and md: Isis Publishing Ltd Oxford and Orlando USA 1994–, Soundings Ltd Newcastle upon Tyne; *Books* Microcomputer Software Guide (1982), Microcomputer Software Guide Vol II (1982); *Style—* John Durrant, Esq; ✉ Isis Publishing Ltd, 7 Centremead, Osney Mead, Oxford OX2 0ES (tel 01865 250333, fax 01865 790358)

DURRANT, Sir William Alexander Estridge; 8 Bt (GB 1784), of Scottow, Norfolk; s of Sir William Henry Estridge Durrant, 7 Bt, JP (d 1994), and Georgina Beryl Gwendoline, *née* Purse (d 1968); *b* 26 November 1929; *m* 1953, Dorothy, da of Ronal Croker, of Quirindi, NSW; 1 s (David Alexander b 1960), 1 da (Susan Elizabeth b 1962); *Heir* s, David Durrant; *Career* farmer and grazier; Capt 12/16 Hunter River Lancers; *Style—* Sir William Durrant, Bt; ✉ Red Hill, Nundle Road, Nemingha, NSW 2340, Australia

DURRELL, Prof Martin; s of Leslie Hay Durrell (d 1972), of Coltishall, Norfolk, and Audrey Lillian, *née* Easton; *b* 6 November 1943; *Educ* Manchester Grammar, Jesus Coll Cambridge (MA), Univ of Manchester (DipLing), Univ of Marburg (DPhil); *m* 30 Aug 1969, Ruth, da of Geoffrey Loy Barlow (d 1977), of Bury, Lancs; 1 s (John b 1975), 1 da (Ann b 1978); *Career* sr lectr (formerly lectr) Univ of Manchester 1967–86, guest prof Univ of Alberta 1983–84; prof of German: Univ of London 1986–90, Univ of Manchester 1990–; vice-pres Int Assoc of Germanists 2004–05, corresponding memb Int Academic Cncl Institut für Deutsche Sprache 1984–; Philological Soc: memb Cncl 1989–, hon treas 1994–; Cross Order of Merit of the Federal Repub of Germany 2002; *Recreations* music, theatre, ornithology; *Style—* Prof Martin Durrell; ✉ The German Department, University of Manchester, Manchester M13 9PL (tel 0161 275 3182, e-mail martin.durrell@man.ac.uk)

DURRINGTON, Prof Paul Nelson; s of late Alec Edward Durrington, of Wilmslow, Cheshire, and May Ena, *née* Nelson; *b* 24 July 1947; *Educ* Chislehurst and Sidcup GS, Univ of Bristol (BSc, MB, ChB, MD); *m* 13 Dec 1969, Patricia Joyce, da of late Capt Alfred Newton Gibbs, MBE, MC, of Barming, Kent; 2 da (Hannah Jane b 1975, Charlotte Lucy b 1987), 1 s (Mark Christopher Newton b 1977); *Career* house offr and sr house offr appts 1972–76 (Bristol Royal Infirmary, Bristol Royal Hosp for Sick Children, Frenchay Hosp Bristol); travelling fell: Br Heart Fndn, American Heart Assoc Univ of Calif San Diego 1979–80; Univ of Manchester: lectr in med 1976–82, sr lectr in med 1982–92, reader in med 1992–95, prof of med 1995–; hon conslt physician Manchester Royal Infirmary 1982–; med dir Family Heart Assoc 1995–2005, dir of R&D Central Manchester Healthcare Tst 1997–2001; chm Br Hyperlipidaemia Assoc 1992–95; memb Editorial Bd Atherosclerosis; FRCP 1987, FRCPath 1994, FMedSci 2001, fell American Heart Assoc (FAHA) 2001; *Books* Hyperlipidaemia Diagnosis and Management (1989, 3 edn 2007), Hyperlipidaemia (with Allan Sniderman 2000, 3rd edn 2005); *Recreations* angling; *Clubs* Prince Albert Angling Soc, Kirby Lonsdale Angling Assoc; *Style—* Prof Paul Durrington; ✉ Division of Cardiovascular and Endocrine Sciences, Core Technology Facility (3rd Floor), 46 Grafton Street, Manchester M13 9NT (tel 0161 275 1201, fax 0161 275 1183, e-mail pdurrington@manchester.ac.uk)

DURSTON, Trevor David; s of David Stanley Durston, and Margery Winnifred, *née* Dalton; *b* 15 February 1948; *Educ* Univ of Leeds (BSc), Aston Univ; *m* 25 July 1970, Janet Teresa, *née* Field; 2 da (Hannah Frances b 23 June 1979, Ruth Aimee b 22 June 1981); *Career* graduate trainee Tube Investments Ltd 1969–71, devpt engr Churchill Gear Machines Ltd 1971–72, project ldr Leslie Hartridge Ltd 1978–81 (devpt engr 1972–78), plant engr Himal Hydro and General Construction Co Nepal 1982–84, office mangr Butwal Power Co Nepal 1982–84, prodn mangr Butwal Engineering Works Ltd Nepal 1984–85, dir of devpt and consulting servs Nepal 1985–88; United Mission to Nepal: asst dir Engrg and Industrial Devpt Dept 1990–93, dir of personnel 1992–93; gen dir The Leprosy Mission Int 1993–; CEng 1978, MIMechE 1978, FCMI 1995; *Style—* Trevor Durston, Esq; ✉ The Leprosy Mission International, 80 Windmill Road, Brentford, Middlesex TW8 0QH (tel 020 8326 6767, fax 020 8569 7808)

DUTHIE, Sir Robert Grieve (Robin); kt (1987), CBE (1978); s of George Duthie, and Mary, *née* Lyle; *b* 2 October 1928; *Educ* Greenock Acad; *m* 5 April 1955, (Violetta) Noel, da of Harry Maclean; 2 s (David b 1956, Peter b 1959), 1 da (Susan b 1962); *Career* Nat Serv 1946–49; apprentice CA Thomson Jackson Gourlay & Taylor 1946–51, qualified CA 1952; chm: Black & Edgington plc 1972–83 (md 1962–80), R G Duthie and Company Ltd 1983–, Bruntons (Musselburgh) plc 1984–86, Britoil plc 1988–90, Capital House plc 1988–92, Tay Residential Investments plc 1989–96, Neill Clerk Group plc 1994–98; dir: British Asset Trust plc 1977–98, Royal Bank of Scotland plc 1978–99, Insight Gp plc 1983–90 (formerly Black and Edgington), Investors Capital Tst plc 1985–95, Carclo Engineering Gp plc 1986–98, Royal Bank of Scotland Gp plc 1986–99, Sea Catch plc 1987–93, British Polythene Industries plc 1988–99, Charterhouse plc 1991–93, Devol Engineering Ltd 1994–2003; chm: Made Up Textiles Assoc of Great Britain 1972, Clyde Port Authy 1978–81, Scottish Development Agency 1979–88; vice-chm BP Advsy Bd Scotland 1990–2002; treas Greenock West United Reform Church Greenock 1970–; memb: Scottish Telecommunications Bd 1972–78, Scottish Econ Cncl 1980–95, Ct Univ of Strathclyde 1988–94; Hon LLD Univ of Strathclyde 1984, Hon DTech Napier Univ 1989; CIMgt 1975, FRSA 1983, FScotvec 1988, FRIAS 1989; *Recreations* curling, golf; *Style—* Sir Robin Duthie, CBE; ✉ Fairhaven, 181 Finnart Street, Greenock, Strathclyde (tel 01475 722642)

DUTT, Trevor Peter; RD (1997); s of Dr Bishnu Pada Dutt (d 1970), of Mitcham, Surrey, and Phyllis Ida, *née* Roche (d 2000); *b* 14 September 1943; *Educ* Dulwich Coll, Bart's Med Coll (MB BS, MRCS, LRCP); *m* 27 May 1986, Pauline Deirdre (d 1997), da of Walter Edward Chapman, of Chigwell, Essex; 1 s (Alexander Philip b 24 Feb 1991); 1 step s (Damien Nicholas Edward Caracatsanis b 2 May 1974 d 2003); *Career* Surgn Cdr RNR (PMO London Div 1990–), SMO Royal Marines Res City of London 1987–90; jr med staff posts 1965–80 (Bart's, Whipps Cross, Royal Northern, City of London Maternity and Charing Cross Hosps), conslt in obstetrics and gynaecology Royal Northern and Whittington Hosps 1980–; hon conslt Hosp of St John and St Elizabeth; Freeman City of London 1967, Liveryman Worshipful Soc of Apothecaries 1967; FRCOG 1988 (MRCOG 1975), MAE 1994; *Publications* Gynaecology in Medico-Legal Practitioner Series (1999); *Recreations* flying, sailing, sub-aqua diving, horse riding; *Clubs* Athenaeum, Savage; *Style—* Trevor P Dutt, Esq, RD; ✉ 129 Mount View Road, London N4 4JH (tel 020 8348 7054, fax 020 8340 1352); 10 Harley Street, London W1G 9PF (tel 020 7580 1723, fax 020 7436 6053, mobiles 07768 056524 and 07860 746868, answering service 07659 122969, e-mail trevor.dutt@blueyonder.co.uk, website www.trevor-dutt.org)

DUTTON, Maj-Gen Bryan Hawkins; CB (1997), CBE (1990, OBE 1984, MBE 1978); s of George Ralph Neale Dutton (d 1983), and Honor Badcoe, *née* Morris (d 2007); *b* 1 March 1943; *Educ* Lord Weymouth Sch, RMA Sandhurst, RMCS Shrivenham, Staff Coll Camberley; *m* 15 July 1972, Angela Margaret, da of Harold Keith Wilson (d 1970); 1 s (Charles b 1974), 1 da (Sophie b 1977); *Career* cmmnd Devonshire and Dorset Regt 1963, Regtl serv 1963–73 (NI, Germany, Libya, Br Guiana, UK, Belize); C-in-C's Mission to Soviet forces in E Germany 1976–78, Regtl duty NI and BAOR 1978–79 (despatches 1979), staff security co-ordinator NI 1979–81, instr Staff Coll Camberley 1981–82, mil asst to Adj-Gen 1982–84, CO 1 Bn Devonshire and Dorset Regt NI and Berlin 1984–87, UKLF overseas ops 1987, cmd 39 Infantry Brigade Ulster 1987–89, Dir Public Relations (Army) 1990–92, Dir of Infantry 1992–94, Cdr Br Forces Hong Kong 1994–97 (Handover to PLA/PRC); Col Cmdt The Prince of Wales's Div 1996–99, Col The Devonshire and Dorset Regt 1998–2003; DG Leonard Cheshire 1998–; govr Holidaycare 1999–2003, govr E Hayes Dashwood Housing Assoc 1999–, tstee Hong Kong LEP Tst 1994–; chair Voluntary Organisations Disability Gp 2004–; CCIM 2003, FRSA 2003; *Recreations* offshore sailing, country pursuits, wildlife, music, history; *Clubs* Army and Navy; *Style—* Maj-Gen Bryan Dutton, CB, CBE; ✉ Leonard Cheshire, 30 Millbank, London SW1P 4QD (tel 020 7802 8202, e-mail bryan.dutton@lc-uk.org)

DUTTON, His Hon Judge Roger Thomas Dutton; s of Donald Roger Dutton, JP, of Wrexham, Clwyd, and Doreen May, *née* Ankers; *b* 24 March 1952; *Educ* Grove Park GS Wrexham, Univ of Kent at Canterbury (BA), Inns of Court Sch of Law; *m* 9 July 1977, Elaine Alison, *née* Dixon; 2 da (Katie Joanna b 23 Dec 1980, Sarah Louise b 5 Aug 1983), 1 s (James Roger George b 3 April 1991); *Career* called to the Bar Middle Temple 1974; in practice King St Chambers Chester 1974–96, asst recorder 1988–92, recorder 1992–96; circuit judge: (Wales & Chester Circuit) 1996–, (Northern Circuit) 2007–; liaison judge N Wales Magistrates 1999–2003, currently liaison judge Crewe, Nantwich and Macclesfield Justices; memb Cncl of Circuit Judges 1996–, memb Judicial Appt Cmmn's panel for interviewing for circuit judge and recorder applicants 1999, hon treas Cncl of HM's Circuit Judges 2005– (circuit rep Ctee 2004–05); occasional contrib New Law Jl; govr NE Wales Inst of HE 2001–; *Recreations* walking, golf, gardening, soccer, rugby and cricket

D

spectating; *Clubs* Chester City, Lansdowne, Wrexham Golf; *Style—* His Hon Judge Dutton; ✉ The Crown Court, The Castle, Chester CH1 2AN (tel 01244 317606)

DUTTON, Timothy James; QC (1998); s of James Derek Dutton, JP, of Richmond, N Yorks, and Joan Rosemary, *née* Parsons; *b* 25 February 1957; *Educ* Repton, Keble Coll Oxford (BA); *m* 1 April 1987, Sappho, da of B Raschid, of Washington DC, USA; 1 da (Pia Leila b 4 June 1988); *Career* called to the Bar Middle Temple 1979; recorder South Eastern Circuit 2000–, ldr South Eastern Circuit 2004–06; appeared in many leading commercial, public law and regulatory cases; vice-chm Bar Cncl 2007 (chm Carter Response Gp 2007, chair Working Pty into Advocacy Trg, chm Inns of Ct Advocacy Trg Ctee 2000–03; memb: Commercial Bar Assoc, Admin Law Bar Assoc, Employment Law Bar Assoc, Common Law and Commercial Bar Assoc, Advocacy Studies Bd 1999–; author of various articles and lectures on the law; *Recreations* French horn, sailing; *Clubs* Harbour; *Style—* Timothy J Dutton, Esq, QC; ✉ Fountain Court Chambers, Temple, London EC4Y 9DH (tel 020 7583 3335, fax 020 7353 0329, e-mail tdutton@fountaincourt.co.uk)

DUVAL, Robin Arthur Philip; CBE (2005); s of Arthur Edward Bickersteth Duval (d 1976), of Exeter, and Jane Elizabeth, *née* Evans (d 2001); *b* 28 April 1941; *Educ* King Edward's Sch Birmingham, UCL (BA), Univ of Michigan; *m* 20 Dec 1968, Lorna Eileen, da of Robert Watson, of Cardiff; 4 da (Polly b 1969, Sophie b 1971, Daisy b 1982, Martha b 1983), 1 s (Sam b 1976 d 1978); *Career* radio studio mangr BBC 1964–65, TV prodr J Walter Thompson 1965–68, princ Home Office 1981–83, head of UK prodn COI 1983–85 (TV prodr 1968–81), chief asst TV IBA 1985–90, dep dir of progs ITC 1991–98, dir BBFC 1999–2004; FRSA; *Recreations* music, Aston Villa, food; *Style—* Robin Duval, Esq, CBE

DUVALL, Len; OBE (1998), AM; *b* 26 September 1961; *Educ* Hawthorn Sch London; *Career* memb Greenwich Cncl 1990–2001 (ldr 1992–2000); GLA: memb London Assembly (Lab) Greenwich and Lewisham 2000–, vice-chair London Devpt Agency 2000–03, dep chair Budget Ctee 2001–04, memb Standards Ctee 2004–, memb Business Mgmnt and Appointments Ctee; chair: London Health Cmmn 2002–04, Met Police Authy 2004–; former memb London Fire Authy; vice-chair Local Govt Info Unit 1994–96, chair London Thames Gateway Partnership 1997–2000, former dep chair Assoc of London Govt, fndr memb New Local Govt Network, chair Cwlth Local Govt Forum 1998–2005; currently non-exec dir Tilfenland, former non-exec dir New Millennium Experience Ltd; chair Gtr London Lab Pty 2002–; a dir Royal Artillery Museums Tst 1997–; *Style—* Len Duvall, Esq, OBE, AM; ✉ Greater London Authority, City Hall, The Queen's Walk, Southwark, London SE1 2AA (tel 020 7983 4517/4408, fax 020 7983 4418, e-mail len.duvall@london.gov.uk)

DUXBURY, Prof Geoffrey; s of John Heap Duxbury (d 1972), and Nora, *née* Lightbown (d 1989); *b* 6 November 1942; *Educ* Cheadle Hulme Sch Cheshire, Univ of Sheffield (BSc, PhD, Turner Prize); *m* 8 Nov 1969, Mary Rose, da of Thomas John Tarrant; 1 s (Neil b 11 May 1973), 1 da (Elspeth b 9 Dec 1975); *Career* jr research fell Div of Electrical Sci Nat Physical Lab 1967–69, lectr in chemical physics Univ of Bristol 1970–80; Univ of Strathclyde: sr lectr in physics 1981–85, reader 1985–87, prof 1987–2006, emeritus prof 2006–, chm of Dept 1988–90; various visiting appts incl: Nat Research Cncl of Canada 1972, 1974 and 1980, Kitt Peak Nat Observatory USA 1980 and 1981, Univ of Nottingham (Kipping fell) 1983, Univ of Lille 1984, Univ of Colorado 1996, Univ de Paris Süd 1998 and 2005; memb: RSC, Optical Soc of America, IOP; awarded Marlow Medal Faraday Div RSC 1975; FInstP 1991, FRSE 1997; *Books* Infrared Vibration-Rotation Spectroscopy, From Free Radicals to the Infrared Sky (2000); author of numerous scientific papers in learned jls; *Style—* Prof Geoffrey Duxbury, FRSE; ✉ Department of Physics, University of Strathclyde, John Anderson Building, Glasgow G4 0NG (tel 0141 548 3271, fax 0141 552 2891, e-mail g.duxbury@strath.ac.uk)

DWEK, Joseph Claude (Joe); CBE; *b* 1 May 1940; *Educ* Carmel Coll, Univ of Manchester (BSc, BA); *m*; 2 c; *Career* chm: Bodycote International plc 1972–98, Penmarric plc; exec chm Worthington Group 1999–; dir: Jerome Group plc, Mercury Recycling Ltd, Opal Property Group; dir NWIDB DTI 1980–90, chm CBI NW 1994–96 (vice-chm 1994 and 1997), memb Bd NW Devpt Agency 2004– (chm Environmental Sub-Gp, vice-chm Business and Innovations Sub-Gp); past chm: Enworks, Mersey Basin Campaign DETR 1999–2004, Healthy Waterways Tst; chm Envirolink, past memb Cncl of Environmental Campaigns (ENCAMS), current memb Environmental Innovations Advsy Gp DTI/DEFRA; former dir: Royal Exchange Theatre, NORWIDA/INWARD, North West Broadcasting Ltd; currently memb Gen Assembly Univ of Manchester; past memb: Ct Victoria Univ of Manchester, Cncl UMIST, Manchester Business Sch; pres UMIST Assoc 1992–94; Hon DSc UMIST; FTI, AMCT; *Recreations* golf; *Style—* Joe Dwek, Esq, CBE; ✉ Penmarric plc, Suite One, Courthill House, 66 Water Lane, Wilmslow SK9 5AP (tel 01625 549081/2, fax 01625 530791, e-mail penjcdwek@aol.com)

DWEK, Prof Raymond Allen; s of Victor Joseph Dwek (d 1988), of Manchester, and Alice, *née* Liniado; *b* 10 November 1941; *Educ* Carmel Coll, Univ of Manchester (BSc, MSc), Lincoln Coll Oxford (DPhil), Exeter Coll Oxford (DSc); *m* 21 June 1964, Sandra, da of Dr David I Livingstone, of Manchester; 2 da (Juliet b 19 Dec 1965, Deborah b 3 Oct 1974), 2 s (Robert b 14 July 1967, Joshua b 23 March 1978); *Career* Univ of Oxford: res lectr in physical chemistry ChCh 1966–68, lectr in inorganic chemistry ChCh 1968–75, departmental demonstrator Dept of Biochemistry 1969–74, res lectr in biochemistry ChCh 1975–76, lectr in biochemistry Trinity Coll 1976–84, fell Exeter Coll 1976–, prof of glycobiology and dir Glycobiology Inst Dept of Biochemistry 1988–, assoc head Dept of Biochemistry (with special responsibilities for postgrad and post doctoral trg) 1996–2000, head Dept of Biochemistry 2000–06; visiting Royal Soc Res fell at Weizmann Inst Rehovot Israel 1969, Royal Soc Locke res fell 1974–76; visiting prof: Duke Univ NC 1968 (seconded to Inst of Exploratory Res Fort Monmouth NJ), Univ of Trieste 1974, Univ of Lund 1977, Inst of Enzymology Budapest 1980; author various articles in books and jls on physical chemistry, biochemistry and med; memb of various scientific ctees incl: Oxford Enzyme Gp 1971–88, Oxford Oligosaccharide Gp 1983–88, MRC AIDS Antiviral Steering Ctee 1987–92; dir and founding memb scientist Oxford GlycoScience Ltd (formerly Oxford GlycoSystems) 1988–, dir and memb Scientific Advsy Bd United Therapeutics Corp (USA) 2002–, dir Isis Innovation Univ of Oxford 2003–; special advsr to pres of Ben Gurion Univ of the Negev Israel 2000–; memb EMBO 1998–; holder 70 patents; Wellcome Tst Award 1994, award for research in biochemistry related to med 1996, Boyce Thompson Distinguished Lectr Series Cornell Univ 1997, Centennial Award Delaware Valley Coll Pennsylvania USA 1997, First Scientific Leadership Award Hepatitis B Fndn Philadelphia 1997, Fndn of Med Sciences Lectureship McGill Univ Montreal 2001, Lemieux Lecture Alberta 2003, Kluge Chair of Science and Society Library of Congress USA 2007; foreign memb American Philosophical Soc 2006–; Dr (hc): Katholieke Universitat Leuven 1996, Ben Gurion Univ 2001, Scripps Research Inst La Jolla CA 2004; CChem, CBiol, FRSC 1993, FRS 1998, FRSA 1998, FIBiol 1999; Cdr Order of Merit (Romania) 2000; *Books* Nuclear Magnetic Resonance in Biochemistry (1973), Principles and Problems in Physical Chemistry for Biochemists (jtly, 1975), Nuclear Magnetic Resonance in Biology (jtly 1977), Biological Spectroscopy (jtly, 1984); author over 450 scientific papers; *Style—* Prof Raymond Dwek, FRS; ✉ Glycobiology Institute, Department of Biochemistry, University of Oxford, South Parks Road, Oxford OX1 3QU (tel 01865 275344, fax 01865 275771)

DWORKIN, (Prof) Ronald Myles; s of David Dworkin, and Madeline Talamo; *b* 11 December 1931; *Educ* Harvard Coll, Univ of Oxford, Harvard Law Sch; *m* 1958, Betsy Celia Ross; 1 s, 1 da; *Career* prof of jurisprudence Univ of Oxford 1969–98 (now emeritus prof), fell UC Oxford 1969–98 (now emeritus fell), prof of law NY Univ Law Sch 1974– (Sommer prof of law and philosophy 1984–), Quain prof of jurisprudence UCL 1998–; hon QC 1998, hon bencher Middle Temple 1999; FBA 1979; *Style—* Ronald Dworkin

DWYER, Sir Joseph Anthony; kt (2001); *b* 20 June 1939; *m* Stella; 3 c; *Career* George Wimpey plc: joined 1955, qualified as civil engr, main bd dir 1988–2000, gp chief exec 1991–99, chm 1996–2000; co-chm Transmanche Link 1992–94; chm: Liverpool Vision, Construction for Merseyside; hon fell Liverpool John Moores Univ, Hon LLD Univ of Liverpool, Hon DSc Univ of Nottingham; FICE (pres), FCIOB (pres 1998–99), FREng 1997; *Style—* Sir Joseph Dwyer

DYER, Dr James A T; OBE (2003); s of Rev T J Dyer (d 1994), and Mary Watt, *née* Thomson; *b* 31 December 1946; *Educ* Robert Gordon's Coll, Univ of Aberdeen (MB, ChB, Ogston prize in surgery, Keith gold medal, Anderson gold medal and prize); *m* 1, 1969 (m dis 1994), Lorna, *née* Townson; 2 s (Paul b 1 Sept 1971, Euan b 22 Sept 1976), 1 da (Rowan b 11 Aug 1978); m 2, Suzanne, *née* Whitaker; 1 step s (Christopher b 4 April 1984), 2 step da (Sophie b 1 Sept 1989, Emily b 7 Nov 1990); *Career* various house jobs in Aberdeen Hosps 1970–71, trainee GP 1971–72; Royal Edinburgh Hosp: SHO and registrar posts in psychiatry 1972–75, sr registrar in psychiatry 1975–77; scientific offr MRC Unit for Epidemiological Studies in Psychiatry Edinburgh 1977–80, conslt in general and rehabilitation psychiatry Royal Edinburgh Hosp 1981–91, dir Mental Welfare Cmmn for Scotland 1993–2003 (HM med cmmr 1991–2003); hon sr lectr in psychiatry Univ of Edinburgh 1981–91; chm Section for social community and rehabilitation RCPsych 1994–97; author of papers on parasuicide, schizophrenia, care of long term mentally ill, mental health legislation and psychological aspects of nuclear war; Scottish Parly Standards Cmmr 2003–, medical memb Mental Health Tbnl Scotland 2005–; FRCPsych, FRSA, FFCS; *Recreations* family, photography, reading, theatre, walking; *Style—* Dr James Dyer, OBE; ✉ Scottish Parliament, Edinburgh EH99 1SP (tel 0131 348 6666, e-mail standards.commissioner@scottish.parliament.uk)

DYER, (Alexander) Patrick (Pat); s of John Alexander Dyer (d 1990), and Amie Moore Dyer (d 1956); *b* 30 August 1932; *Educ* US Military Acad (BS), Harvard Business Sch (MBA); *m* 1954; 1 s; *Career* various appts rising to exec vice-pres and bd dir Air Products and Chemicals Inc USA 1963–89; The BOC Group plc: md Gases and main bd dir 1989–96, dep chm and ceo 1993–96; non-exec dir Bunzl plc 1993– (non-exec chm 1993–96, non-exec dep chm 1996–); former chm: Int Oxygen Mfrs' Assoc, Compressed Gas Assoc; *Recreations* golf, skeet shooting; *Style—* Pat Dyer, Esq

DYER, Prof Sir (Henry) Peter Francis Swinnerton; 16 Bt (E 1678), of Tottenham, Middx; KBE (1987); s of Sir Leonard Schroeder Swinnerton Dyer, 15 Bt (d 1975), and Barbara, *née* Brackenbury (d 1990); *b* 2 August 1927; *Educ* Eton, Trinity Coll Cambridge; *m* 25 May 1983, Dr Harriet Crawford, er da of Rt Hon Sir Patrick Reginald Evelyn Browne, OBE, TD (d 1996); *Heir* kinsman, David Dyer-Bennet; *Career* Cwlth Fund fell Univ of Chicago 1954–55, res fell Trinity Coll Cambridge 1950–54 (fell 1955–73, dean 1963–73); master St Catharine's Coll Cambridge 1973–83; prof of mathematics Univ of Cambridge 1971–88 (lectr 1960–71, univ lectr Cambridge Maths Lab 1960–67); vice-chllr Univ of Cambridge 1979–81; visiting prof Harvard Univ 1971; chm: Ctee on Academic Orgn (London Univ) 1980–82, Steering Gp responsible for planning inst to replace New Univ of Ulster and Ulster Poly 1982–84; fellow Eton 1981–96, dir Prutec 1981–86, chm Univ Grants Ctee 1983–89, chief exec Univs Funding Cncl 1989–91, chm CODEST 1987–91 (memb 1984–91), memb Euro Science and Technol Assembly 1994–98; Hon DSc Univs of: Bath 1981, Ulster 1991, Wales 1991, Birmingham 1992, Nottingham 1992, Warwick 1993; Hon LLD Univ of Aberdeen 1991, Hon DMath Univ of Oslo 1992; hon fell: Worcester Coll Oxford, Trinity Coll Cambridge, St Catharine's Coll Cambridge; fell Academia Europaea, FRS; *Recreations* destructive gardening; *Style—* Prof Sir Peter Dyer, Bt, KBE, FRS; ✉ The Dower House, Thriplow, Cambridgeshire (tel 01763 208220)

DYER, Dr Richard George; OBE (2007); s of Cdr Charles William Dyer (d 1992), and Dorothy Patricia Victoria, *née* Vaughan-Hogan (d 1993); *b* 18 July 1943; *Educ* Churcher's Coll Petersfield, Univ of London (BSc), Univ of Birmingham (MSc), Univ of Bristol (PhD); *m* 1, 14 Sept 1967 (m dis 1995), Shirley James Foulsham; 2 s (James William b 3 June 1970, Matthew Charles b 30 Dec 1971), 1 da (Emilie Kate b 13 Jan 1976); m 2, 9 Dec 2000, Caroline Jane Edmonds, *née* Porter; 1 da (Françoise Callista b 25 Sept 2001); *Career* research Dept of Anatomy Med Sch Univ of Bristol 1968–74; ARC Inst of Animal Physiology (subsequently AFRC Inst of Animal Physiology and Genetics Res, and now The Babraham Inst): head Dept of Neuroendocrinology 1985–90, head Cambridge Research Station 1989–90, assoc dir of Inst 1991–93, exec dir 1993–94, dir The Babraham Inst 1994–2005; chief exec Biosciences Fedn 2006–; teacher of physiology Jesus Coll Cambridge 1977–90; research fellowships Germany and France; conslt WHO Shanghai 1983–86; memb Editorial Bd: Experimental Brain Research 1978–90, Jl of Endocrinology 1983–89; memb: Animals Research Bd AFRC 1992–93, Strategy Bd AFRC 1993, Animal Sci and Psychology Research Ctee BBSRC 1994–96, Exec Bd Univ of Cambridge Challenge Fund 1999–2004; European Sci Fndn (ESF): memb Exec Bd 1999–, vice-pres 2003–, memb Life and Environmental Sci Ctee 1995–2000, memb European Medical Research Cncls 1996–2000, chair Finance and Audit Ctee 2004–; Soc for Endocrinology Medal 1986, 50th Anniversary Medal of the Polish Physiological Soc 1987; *Publications* Brain opioid systems in reproduction (ed with R J Bicknell, 1989); also author of numerous papers on neuroendocrine topics in learned jls; *Recreations* finding bargains, escaping to mountains and the sea, lively conversation; *Style—* Dr Richard Dyer, OBE; ✉ Biosciences Federation, PO Box 502, Cambridge CB1 0AL (tel 01223 400181, fax 01223 246858, e-mail rdyer.bsf@physoc.org)

DYKE, *see also:* Hart Dyke

DYKE, Gregory (Greg); *b* 20 May 1947; *Educ* Hayes GS, Univ of York; *Career* journalist LWT 1977, ed-in-chief TV-am 1983–84, dir of progs TVS 1984–87; London Weekend Television: dir of progs 1987–90, md 1990, gp chief exec LWT (Holdings) plc 1991–94; chm Independent Television Association 1992–94, exec chm GMTV 1993–94, chief exec Pearson Television 1995–99, main bd dir Pearson plc 1996–99, chm Channel 5 Broadcasting Ltd 1997–99 (non-exec dir 1996–99), DG BBC 2000–04, chm HIT Entertainment 2005–; memb Media Advsy Bd Apax Partners 2004–; non-exec dir: Channel Four Television 1988–90, ITN Ltd until 1992; chllr Univ of York 2004–; chm Brentford FC 2006–; FRTS 1998; *Recreations* football, riding, skiing; *Style—* Greg Dyke

DYKE-COOMES, Martin; s of Ernest Thomas Dyke-Coomes (d 2005), and Gladys Dorothy, *née* Bignell (d 1995); *b* 14 August 1948; *Educ* Sarah Robinson Secdy Modern, Ifield GS, Architectural Assoc; *m* 24 June 1978, Maggie Pinhorn, *qv*, da of George Herbert Pinhorn (d 1996); 1 s (Ned Alexander b 1981), 1 da (Amy Elizabeth b 1983); 2 adopted s (Anthony b 1967, Claude b 1973); *Career* architect ARCUK 1973; fndr CGHP Architects in 1979; fndr Dyke Coomes Architects 1989; princ works: Hoxton St London N1 Regeneration (Times/RIBA award 1985), Jubilee Hall Redevelopment Covent Garden 1984–87 (Times/RIBA award 1988), Holland and Thurstan Dwellings 1982–86; participant in 1986 RIBA 40 under 40's exhibition; other works incl Stoke Newington Theatre and projects for Housing Assocs in Islington and Hackney; RIBA; *Recreations* thinking, fishing, wishing, eating, sleeping, dreaming, loving; *Clubs* Manchester United; *Style—* Martin Dyke-Coomes, Esq; ✉ Dyke Coomes Architects Ltd, Hothouse, 274 Richmond Road, London E8 3QW (tel 020 7923 2540, mobile 07914 010252, e-mail martin@dykecoomes.co.uk)

DYKER, Dr George Simpson; MBE (2002); s of Alexander Dyker (d 1981), and Sarah Helen, *née* Simpson, of Aberdeen; *b* 6 July 1941; *Educ* Hutchesons' GS, Univ of Glasgow (MB ChB); *m* 1; 1 s (Alexander George b 1966), m 2, 1969, Dr Elspeth Jean Chalmers Smith, da of John Kilpatrick Smith; 2 da (Karen Elizabeth Simpson b 1971, Morven Jean Kilpatrick b 1978); *Career* house physician Stobhill Hosp Glasgow 1964–65, house surgn Royal Infirmary Glasgow 1965, Faulds res fell Stobhill Hosp Glasgow 1965–66, princ in gen practice 1967–2002; dep regional advsr in gen practice 1989–96; memb BMA 1964; RCGP: dir of Hospital Visiting (Scotland) 1999–2003, hon sec Scottish Cncl 1997–2000; MRCP 1972, FRCGP 1987 (MRCGP 1972), FRCPGlas 1988; *Recreations* golf; *Style—* Dr George Dyker, MBE; ✉ 4 Old Coach Road, East Kilbride, Glasgow G74 4DP (tel 01355 220045, fax 01355 266795, e-mail ge.dyker@virgin.net)

DYKES, Dr David Wilmer; s of Capt David Dykes, OBE (d 1978), and Jenny, *née* Thomas (d 1971); *b* 18 December 1933; *Educ* Swansea GS, CCC Oxford (MA), Univ of Wales (PhD); *m* 22 Sept 1967, Margaret Anne, da of Harvey Clifford George (d 1969); 2 da (Elizabeth Anne b 28 July 1972, Rosemary Louise b 29 July 1978); *Career* cmmnd RN and RNR 1955–62; civil servant Bd of Inland Revenue 1958–59, admin appts Univ of Bristol and UC Swansea 1959–63, dep registrar UC Swansea 1963–69, registrar Univ of Warwick 1969–72; Nat Museum of Wales: sec 1972–86, actg dir 1985–86, dir 1986–89; hon lectr in history UC Cardiff (later Univ of Wales Coll of Cardiff) 1975–95; pres Br Numismatic Soc 1999–2003 (memb Cncl 1966–70 and 1997–); chllr Order of St John Priory for Wales 1991–98, bailiff of St Davids 1999–2002; awarded Parkes-Weber prize and medal RNS 1954; fndn memb Welsh Livery Guild 1993; Freeman City of London 1985, Liveryman Worshipful Co of Tin Plate Workers 1985; FRNS 1958, FRHistS 1965, FRSAI 1963, FSA 1973, FSA Scot 1996; KStJ 1993; *Books* Anglo-Saxon Coins in the National Museum of Wales (1977), Alan Sorrell: Early Wales Recreated (1980), Wales in Vanity Fair (1989), The University Coll of Swansea (1992), The Eighteenth Century Token (2007); author of articles and reviews in numismatic, historical and other jls; *Recreations* numismatics, writing, gardening; *Clubs* Athenaeum, Cardiff & County (Cardiff); *Style—* Dr David Dykes, FSA; ✉ 3 Peverell Avenue East, Poundbury, Dorchester, Dorset DT1 3RH

DYKES, Baron (Life Peer UK 2004), of Harrow Weald in the London Borough of Harrow; Hugh John Maxwell Dykes; s of Richard Dykes, of Weston-super-Mare, Somerset; *b* 17 May 1939; *Educ* Weston-super-Mare GS, Pembroke Coll Cambridge; *m* 1965, Susan Margaret, da of Elwand Smith of Wakefield, W Yorks; 3 s; *Career* investment analyst and stockbroker; ptnr Simon & Coates 1968–78, assoc memb Quilter Goodison & Co (formerly Quilter, Hilton, Goodison), dir Dixons plc Far Eastern Div 1985–; research sec Bow Group 1965–66, MP (Cons) Harrow E 1970–97 (Parly candidate (Cons) Tottenham 1966); PPS to: Parly under secs for Defence 1970–73, Parly under sec Civil Service Dept 1973; UK memb Euro Parl 1974, chm: Cons Parly European Ctee 1979–80 (former sec, vice-chm), Cons Gp for Europe 1979–80 (vice-pres 1982), UK European Movement 1990–95; joined Lib Dem Pty 1997, Lib Dem front bench EU spokesman House of Lords, chm Mid-Atlantic Club 2003–; *Clubs* Beefsteak, Garrick, English Speaking Union; *Style—* The Rt Hon the Lord Dykes

DYKES, Richard Thornton Booth; s of Alan Thornton Dykes (d 1979), and Myra McFie Booth (d 1991); *b* 7 April 1945; *Educ* Rossall Sch; *m* 1970 (m dis), Janet Rosemary, da of Cdr R J R Cundall; 1 s (Nicholas Thornton b 27 Oct 1972); *Career* articled clerk Dehn and Lauderdale slrs 1965–67, exec offr then higher exec offr Miny of Labour 1967–73, private sec to Sec of State for Employment 1973–76, princ Econ Policy Div Dept of Employment 1976–77, dir of industrial relations British Shipbuilders 1977–80, non-exec dir Austin & Pickersgill Ltd Sunderland 1979–80; Dept of Employment: princ private sec to Sec of State for Employment 1980–82, head Unemployment Benefit Serv 1982–85, sec Sr Mgmnt Gp 1985–86, head Inner Cities Central Unit 1986; Post Office Counters Ltd: gen mangr Gtr London 1986–87, dir of ops 1987–92, md 1992–96; md Royal Mail 1996–2001, currently chm Carrenza Ltd; chm DETR/HSC Work-related Road Safety Task Gp 2000–01; memb: Design Cncl 1976–2001, Forensic Sci Serv Advsy Bd 1993–98, Economic Devpt Ctee Business in the Community 1992–2003; non-exec dir Employment Serv 1998–2002; *Style—* Richard Dykes, Esq; ✉ The Old Rectory, Upper Slaughter, Gloucestershire GL54 2JB (tel 01451 810571)

DYMOND, Dr Duncan Simon; s of Dr Sydney Cyril Dymond (d 1978), and Adele, *née* Spector (d 1977); *b* 25 February 1950; *Educ* St Paul's, Bart's Med Sch Univ of London (MB BS, MD); *Family* 1 da (Francesca b 1979), 1 s (Daniel b 1982); *Career* asst prof of med and cardiology Mount Sinai Med Sch Univ of Wisconsin 1980–81, sr registrar in cardiology 1981–86, conslt cardiologist Bart's 1987–; fndr Br Nuclear Cardiology Gp, memb Cncl Br Cardiovascular Intervention Soc Scientific Ctee, hon sec Br Cardiac Soc 1990–94; memb: Br Nuclear Med Soc 1979, Br Cardiology Soc 1980, MRS 1981; fell American Coll of Cardiology 1983, fndr fell Euro Soc of Cardiology 1989; *Books* An Atlas of Myocardial Infarction (1994), The Jargon-Busters Guide to Heart Disease (1996), How to Cope with High Blood Pressure (2003); *Recreations* cricket, tennis, skiing, pianoforte, Italian opera, watercolours; *Clubs* MCC; *Style—* Dr Duncan Dymond; ✉ Cardiac Department, St Bartholomew's Hospital, London EC1A 7BE (tel 020 7601 8054); 84 Harley Street, London W1G 7HW (tel 020 7079 4260, e-mail dymondheart@hotmail.co.uk)

DYNEVOR, 9 Baron (GB 1780); Richard Charles Uryan Rhys; s of 8 Baron Dynevor, CBE, MC (d 1962, fifth in descent from Baroness Dynevor, herself da of 1 and last Earl Talbot, of the same family as the Earls of Shrewsbury); *b* 19 June 1935; *Educ* Eton, Magdalene Coll Cambridge; *m* 1959 (m dis 1978), Lucy, da of Sir John Rothenstein, CBE; 1 s, 3 da; *Heir* s, Hon Hugo Rhys; *Style—* The Rt Hon the Lord Dynevor; ✉ House of Lords, London SW1A 0PW

DYSART, Countess of (twelfth holder of title, S 1643); Katherine Grant of Rothiemurchus; *née* Greaves; also Lady Huntingtower (S 1643); 2 da of Countess of Dysart (10 holder of the title; d 1975) and Maj Owain Greaves, DL, RHG (d 1941); suc sis, Countess of Dysart (11 holder of the title; d 2003); *b* 1 June 1918; *m* 1941, Lt-Col John Peter Grant of Rothiemurchus, MBE (d 1987), s of late Col John P Grant of Rothiemurchus, CB, TD, JP, DL; 1 s (John Peter, Lord Huntingtower, DL, *qv*), 1 da (Jane (Lady Jane Buxton)); *Heir* s, Lord Huntingtower; *Style—* The Rt Hon the Countess of Dysart; ✉ Rothiemurchus, Aviemore, Inverness-shire PH22 1QH

DYSON, Sir James; kt (2007), CBE (1998); s of Alec Dyson (d 1956), of Holt, Norfolk, and Mary, *née* Bolton (d 1978); *b* 2 May 1947; *Educ* Gresham's, RCA (MDesRCA); *m* 1967, Deirdre, *née* Hindmarsh; 1 da (Emily b 26 Feb 1971), 2 s (Jacob b 21 Oct 1972, Sam b 26 Jan 1978); *Career* dir Rotork Marine 1970–74 (design and manufacture of Sea Truck high speed landing craft), md Kirk-Dyson 1974–79 (design and manufacture of Ballbarrow wheelbarrow), founded Dyson Research Ltd 1979 (developed and designed Dyson dual cyclone vacuum cleaner 1979–93), chm Dyson Ltd 1992–; memb Design Cncl 1997–, chm Design Museum 1999–2004, fndr Dyson Sch of Design Innovation 2007 (to open 2009), memb Cncl RCA (external examiner 1993–96), memb Advsy Bd MAK Vienna, cmmr for Royal Cmmn for the Exhbn of 1851; exhbn Doing a Dyson (Design Museum) 1996–97, other Dyson exhbns at Glasgow and Arnhem Holland; Dyson vacuum cleaners on perm display at: Sci Museum, Design Museum London, V&A, Boyman's Museum Rotterdam, San Francisco MOMA, Design Museum Zurich, Design Museum Lisbon, Museum fur Angewandte Kunst Cologne, Danish Design Centre Copenhagen, Centre Georges Pompidou Paris, Museum für Angewandte Kunst (MAK) Vienna; patron Nat Assoc of Inspectors and Advsrs in Design and Technol; chm Bath Coll of HE 1990–92, memb Ct Univ of Bath, dir Imperial Coll London; tstee The Roundhouse Theatre London 1998; hon fell Liverpool John Moores Univ 1997; Hon DLitt Staffs Univ 1990, Hon MIED Inst of Design 1997, Hon DSc Oxford Brookes Univ; Hon Dr: Univ of Bradford 1998, UWE, Univ of Middx, Brunel Univ, Bath Spa Univ, RCA, Univ of Bath; FCSD 1996, FREng 2005; *Awards* for Dyson designs incl Bldg Design and Innovation Award (for Ballbarrow) 1976; for Dyson Dual Cyclone vacuum cleaner: Int Design Fair Prize Japan 1991, Minerva Award CSD 1995, Award of Excellence Daily Mail 1995, Gerald Frewer Trophy Inst of Engrg Designers 1996, Industrial Design Prize of America 1996, Meilleure Acceptation and Meilleure Conception Galerie Lafayette Prix Innovation-Design 1996, Eversheds Grand Prix Award Design Cncl 1996, DBA Design Effectiveness Consumer Product Award 1996, DBA Design Effectiveness Eversheds Grand Prix Trophy 1996, Euro Design Prize 1997, Design Centrum Award for Design Prestige Czech Republic 1997, Prince Philip's Designers Prize 1997, Japan Industrial Design Promotion Organization Gold Award 1997, Design Cncl Award for Euro Design prize 1997, West of England Business of the Year Award 1997, Marketing Soc Award for Brand of the Year 1998, Marketing Soc Award for Marketer of the Year 1998, Designer of the Decade Award Design Week 1999, Good Design Award Japan 1999, Price Waterhouse West of England Business of the Year Award 1999, Franco-Br C of C and Industry Award for technol and innovation 1999, Prix Innovation Notre Temps du plus solide et du plus sûr France 1999, DC02 and DC03 awarded status of Millennium Products Design Cncl 1999, DC05 awarded oscar of innovation as best domestic appliance LSA magazine France 1999, Japan Super Good of the Year Silver Prize 1999, Int Design Prize Baden-Wurttenburg Germany, Etoile de l'Observeur du Design France 1999, 2000, 2001 and 2002, Mingay Award for best floor care product Australia 2000 and 2002, Kitchens Bedrooms and Bathrooms review for Appliance Innovation UK 2001, Homes and Gardens magazine Classic Design Reader's Award 2001, First Prize Domo household appliance fair Czech Republic 2001, Best Appliance Innovation Your Home magazine 2002, iF Design Award Germany 2002, Red Dot Product Design Award 2002, DC11 awarded Homes and Gardens Classic Design Award 2004, 2–drums awarded Br Allergy Fndn Seal of Approval 2004, DC11 awarded Best Appliance Home Beautiful Awards 2004, Br Consul-General Award 2004, Japan Best Design Award 2004, DC08 Telescope and DC11 awarded PLUS X Award for Innovation, Design and Ease of Use 2004, DC15 The Ball awarded PLUS X Award for Innovation, Design and Ease of Use 2005; awards for Dyson R&D Centre incl: Civic Tst Award Commendation 1999, Royal Fine Art Cmmn Tst/BSB Building of the Year Award Commendation 1999; other awards incl: Top Entrepreneur Enterprise Magazine 1997, Philanthropist of the Year Inst of Charity Fundraising Mangrs 1997, Designer of the Decade 2000, The Queen's Award for Enterprise (innovation category) 2003, Award for Business Excellence Wilts Business of the Year Awards 2003, Giant of Design (GOD) House Beautiful Awards USA 2004, Queens Award for Int Trade 2006, Plux X Lifetime Acheivement Award 2007; *Publications* Doing a Dyson (1996), Against the Odds (1997), History of Great Inventions (2001); *Recreations* running, garden design, bassoon and opera, tennis; *Clubs* Chelsea Arts, Bluebird; *Style—* Sir James Dyson, CBE; ✉ Dyson Ltd, Tetbury Hill, Malmesbury, Wiltshire SN16 0RP

DYSON, Jeremy Robert; s of Melvyn Dyson, and Elaine, *née* Saville; *b* 14 June 1966; *Educ* Leeds GS, Jacob Kramer Coll of Art and Design, Univ of Leeds (BA), Northern Sch of Film and TV (MA); *m* 20 April 2002, Nicola, *née* Clarke; 1 da (Eve b 2005); *Career* writer, memb The League of Gentlemen comedy gp (with Mark Gatiss, *qv*); performed oratorio The Same Dog (with Joby Talbot) Barbican 2000; Hon DLitt Univ of Huddersfield 2003; *Television* The League of Gentlemen (BBC 2) 1999, 2000 and 2002, The League of Gentlemen Christmas Special (BBC 2) 2000, 'Two Can Play at That Game' Randall and Hopkirk (Deceased) 2001, Funland (with Simon Ashdown, BBC 3 and BBC 2) 2005, Billy Goat (BBC 1) 2007; *Radio* On the Town with the League of Gentlemen (Radio 4) 1997, Ringing the Changes (Radio 4) 2000, Never Trust a Rabbit (Radio 4) 2001; *Awards* Perrier Award 1997, Sony Silver Award for Radio Comedy 1998, Golden Rose of Montreux 1999, BAFTA Award for Best Comedy 2000, RTS Award for Best Entertainment 2000, NME Award for Best TV Prog 2001, South Bank Show Award for Best Comedy 2003; *Books* The Essex Files (with Mark Gatiss, 1997), Bright Darkness: The Lost Art of the Supernatural Horror Film (1997), Never Trust a Rabbit (2000), A Local Book for Local People (2000), What Happens Now (2006); *Recreations* conjuring, music; *Style—* Jeremy Dyson, Esq; ✉ c/o PBJ Management, 7 Soho Street, London W1D 3DQ (tel 020 7287 1112)

DYSON, Rt Hon Lord Justice; Rt Hon Sir John Anthony; kt (1993), PC (2001); s of Richard Dyson (d 1988), of Leeds, and Gisella Elizabeth, *née* Kremsier; *b* 31 July 1943; *Educ* Leeds GS (fndn scholar), Wadham Coll Oxford (open classical scholar, MA); *m* 5 July 1970, Jacqueline Carmel, *née* Levy; 1 da (Michelle b 25 June 1971), 1 s (Steven b 21 May 1973); *Career* called to the Bar Middle Temple 1968 (Harmsworth scholar); QC 1982, recorder of the Crown Court 1986–93, judge of the High Court of Justice (Queen's Bench Div) 1993–2000, a Lord Jusice of Appeal 2001–, dep head of civil justice 2003–; judge in charge of Technology and Construction Court 1998–2000; memb: Cncl of Legal Educn 1992–96, Judicial Studies Bd 1994–98 (chm Ethnic Minorities Advsy Ctee 1994–98); hon fell Wadham Coll Oxford; *Recreations* music, walking, skiing, tennis; *Style—* The Rt Hon Lord Justice Dyson; ✉ Royal Courts of Justice, Strand, London WC2A 2LL

DYSON, Prof Robert Graham; s of Jack Dyson (d 1970), and Sylvia, *née* Schofield (d 1992); *b* 6 September 1942; *Educ* Hulme GS Oldham, Univ of Liverpool (BSc), Lancaster Univ (PhD); *m* 31 July 1965, Dorothy, da of Daniel Prestwich (d 1987), of Oldham, Lancs; 1 s (Michael), 1 da (Joanne); *Career* sr systems technologist Pilkington Bros plc 1968–70 (res mathematician 1964–68); Univ of Warwick: lectr 1970–77, sr lectr 1977–84, prof of operational res and systems 1984–, pro-vice-chllr 1989–95 and 1999–2005; chm Warwick Business Sch 1978–81 (dean 1998–2000); memb OR Panel SERC 1985–89, memb Maths Coll EPSRC 1997–; pres Operational Res Soc 1998–99; chm Ctee of Professors of Operational Research 1995–97; ed European Jl of Operational Research; President's Medal Operational Res Soc, Pergamon Prize for articles in Jl of Operational Res Soc; chm of govrs Kenilworth Sch 1993–97; *Books* Strategic Planning: Models and Analytical Techniques (1989), Strategic Development: Methods and Models (1998), Supporting Strategy (2007); *Recreations* cricket (played for Uppermill, Southport & Birkdale and Leamington CCs), theatre; *Clubs* Warwickshire CCC, Coventry RFC; *Style—* Prof Robert Dyson; ✉ Warwick Business School, University of Warwick, Coventry CV4 7AL (tel 024 7652 3775, e-mail r.g.dyson@warwick.ac.uk)

DYSON, Prof Tim; s of Geoffrey Harry George Dyson (d 1981), and Maureen Angela Jane, *née* Gardner (d 1974); *b* 1 August 1949; *Educ* Queens Univ Canada, LSE (BSc, MSc); *m* 17 May 1978, Susan Ann, da of Frank Borman (d 2002); 2 s (Tristram Simon b 25 Dec 1978, Nicholas Adam b 19 Oct 1983); *Career* res offr in demography Inst of Devpt Studies Univ of Sussex 1973–75, res fell Centre for Population Studies LSHTM 1975–80; LSE: lectr 1980–88, reader 1988–92, prof of population studies 1992–, chair Population Studies Gp 1995–99, convenor Dept of Social Policy 1997–99; memb numerous ctees at LSE incl: Social Res Div, Collegiate Ctee for the BSc (Econ), Res Ctee, Mgmnt Ctee Asia Res Centre, Mgmnt Ctee Centre for Global Governance, Standing Sub-Ctee Appointments Ctee; visiting fell Dept of Demography ANU 1986, visiting prof Inst for Developing Economies Tokyo 1996, visiting prof Faculty of Health Sciences American Univ of Beirut 1996–98; external examiner: LSHTM 1983–86, Univ of Surrey 1997–99, Univ of Southampton 1997–99, Univ of Liverpool 1998–2000; UN conslt: Int Inst for Population Studies Bombay 1981, Int Trg Prog on Population and Devpt Centre for Devpt Studies Trivandrum 1990; conslt Int African Inst and UNHCR Somalia 1985, demographic conslt USAID New Delhi 1986; advsr: FAO (on food prodn and population growth) 1996, UN Population Div (on population, devpt and the environment) 2000; various assignments: Health Statistics Div WHO, ODA, Office of Registrar Gen New Delhi; pres Br Soc for Population Studies

D

1994–96 (memb Cncl 1981–85, vice-pres 1991–93), vice-pres Population Investigation Ctee 1996– (memb 1991–); memb: US Nat Acad of Sciences Panel on India's Demography 1978–84, Ctee on Anthropological Demography Int Union for the Scientific Study of Population 1986–91, Population Studies Science Panel Wellcome Tst 1996–2001, Monitoring Panel on Food World Fedn of Scientists 2000; tstee Simon Population Tst 1992–2002; organiser of confs and seminars worldwide; co-ed Population Studies 1990–95; memb Editorial/Advsy Bd: Int Jl of Population Geography 1998–, Jl of Health and Population in Developing Countries 1998–; dir Options Consultancy Services (formerly Marie Stopes Consultancy) 1993–99; memb: Int Union for the Scientific Study of Population, Br Assoc of S Asian Studies, Soc for S Asian Studies, Indian Assoc for the Study of Population; FBA 2001; *Publications* incl: India's Historical Demography (ed, 1989), Population and Food: Global Trends and Future Prospects (1996), Famine Demography (jt ed, 2002), Twenty-first Century India (jt ed, 2004); author of numerous articles and papers in learned jls; *Style*— Prof Tim Dyson; ✉ 56 Beechwood Road, Sanderstead, London CR2 0AA (tel 020 8657 6834); Development Studies Institute, London School of Economics and Political Science, Houghton Street, London WC2A 2AE (tel 020 7955 7662, e-mail t.dyson@lse.ac.uk)

DYSON, Timothy John Bruce; s of Michael Bruce Dyson (d 1965), and Joyce Mary, *née* Simpson; *b* 3 December 1960; *Educ* Mirfield HS, Greenhead Coll, Loughborough Univ (BSc); *Career* Text 100: joined as graduate trainee 1984, account mangr 1986–87, assoc dir 1987–89, co dir 1989–90, gp md Text 100 International 1991– (dir 1990–); MIPR, MInstD; *Recreations* skiing, windsurfing, sailing; *Style*— Timothy Dyson, Esq

DYTOR, Clive Idris; MC (1982); s of Cecil Frederick Dytor (d 1976), of Milford Haven, Pembs, and Maureen Margaret, *née* Owen; *b* 29 October 1956; *Educ* Christ Coll Brecon, Trinity Coll Cambridge (MA), Wycliffe Hall Oxford (MA); *m* 17 Aug 1985, Sarah Louise, da of David Kingsley Payler; 1 s (Benjamin b 14 June 1989), 1 da (Francesca b 5 May 1995); *Career* Royal Marines: offr 1980–86, Commando Trg Centre 1980–81, troop cdre 45 Commando RM, staff instr Officers' Trg Unit 1982–83, trg instr Persian Gulf 1983–84, chief recruiting offr 1984–86; Commando medal 1981, Commandant's prize 1981; curate St Michael's Walsall 1989–92, chaplain Tonbridge Sch 1992–94, housemaster St Edward's Sch Oxford 1994–2000, head master The Oratory Sch 2000–; memb: HMC, SHA; patron: Police Rehabilitation Tst, Newman Soc; *Recreations* Hispanic studies, sport, music; *Clubs* Pitt (Cambridge), Leander, East India, Stewards' Enclosure (Henley); *Style*— Clive Dytor, Esq, MC; ✉ The Oratory School, Woodcote, Reading, Berkshire RG8 0PJ (website www.oratory.co.uk)

E

EADE, Robert Francis; s of Stanley Robert Eade (d 1994), and Kathleen Eade (d 1998); *Educ* Bromsgrove Sch, Univ of London (external BSc); *m* 1965, Mary Lindsay, da of Sidney John Coulson (d 1993), of Stratton-on-the-Fosse, Somerset; 2 s (Simon, James), 1 da (Jane); *Career* AEI (became GEC Group): sr design engr Industrial Electronics Div 1963–65 (engr 1960–63), asst chief engr Devpt 1965–68; Thorn EMI plc: gen mangr then md Avo Ltd 1972–76 (tech dir 1970–72), md Measurement and Components Div 1976–79, md Thorn EMI Technology 1979–83, dir Commercial Technology 1983–85, md Int 1985–87; non-exec dir: Lloyd's Register Quality Assurance Ltd 1985–98 (currently chm Tech Ctee), Northern Engineering Centre 1992–95, Engineering Centre for Wales 1993–95, Sussex Careers Ltd 1995– (chm 1998–), Lloyds Register Gen Ctee 1998–; dir Hurst Associates Ltd 1996–99; Crystalate Holdings plc: divnl dir 1987–88, gp chief exec 1988–90; conslt 1990–; dir Industry and Regions The Engrg Cncl 1992–95; memb Cncl: British Electrical and Allied Mfrs' Assoc (BEAMA) 1980–87, Standing Conf on Schs Science and Technol (SCSST) 1993–95; pres: Scientific Instrument Mfrs' Assoc (SIMA) 1981–82, Assoc for the Instrumentation, Control and Automation Industry (GAMBICA) 1982–84; formerly memb: Cncl ERA Technol, Sec of State for Industry Advsy Cncl on Calibration and Measurement, Sino Br Trade Cncl (and chm Electronics Ctee); chm Sussex Advice and Skills 2004–; CEng, FIEE, CCMI, FRSA; *Style—* Robert Eade, Esq; ✉ Furnace Lodge, Furnace Farm Road, Felbridge, East Grinstead, West Sussex RH19 2PU (tel 01342 713278, e-mail bob@eade.uk.com)

EADES, His Hon Judge Robert Mark; s of John Robert Eades (d 1982), of Staffs, and Margaret Ursula, *née* Megginson; *b* 6 May 1951; *Educ* Moffats Sch Bewdley, Leighton Park Sch Reading, Univ of Bristol; *m* 1982, Afsaneh (Sunny), da of Mohammed Atri; 2 da (Alexandra b 1984, Jessica b 1988); *Career* called to the Bar 1974; in practice 1975–2001, circuit judge (Midland Circuit) 2001–; *Recreations* gardening, historic buildings, local history; *Style—* His Hon Judge Eades

EADIE, Alastair Gordon; s of Col James Alister Eadie, DSO, TD, DL (d 1961), of Sudbury, Derbys; *b* 25 June 1940; *Educ* Eton; *m* 1, 14 April 1966, Hon Jacqueline (d 2002), da of 5 Baron Ashtown (d 1979); 3 s (James b 1967, Christopher b 1969, Edward b 1972); m 2, 31 Oct 2003, Caroline, da of Col John Conyers O'Dwyer (d 1986), of Ballinamallard, Co Fermanagh; *Career* trainee Crowleys Brewery 1958, trainee Labatts Brewery Canada 1959, clerk Shuttleworth & Howerth CAs 1960–61, trainee Watney Mann Breweries 1962–64, PA to md Watney Mann Breweries 1964–65, distribution dir Phipps Brewery 1965–66, dir Phipps Brewery Lankaster Wells Off-Licenses and Brown & Pank Wine and Spirit Merchants 1966–69, md Westminster Wine 1969–72, md IDV Retail Ltd, md W & A Gilbey/Mogan Furze Wine and Spirit Wholesalers 1977–87, dir External Affairs IDV UK Ltd 1987–98, dir External Affairs UDV UK Ltd 1998–2001; Ext Wine & Spirit Assoc of GB and NI (chm 1989–91, pres 1998–2000), Wine & Spirit Benevolent Soc (chm 1987–88), The Benevolent Soc of the Licensed Trade of Scotland (pres 1998–99); pres Licensed Victuallers Schools 1991–92, pres FIVS (int wine and spirit fedn) 1997–99; tstee: Wine and Spirit Educn Tst 2001–05, Licensed Trade Charities Tst 1997–, Hospitality Action 2000–07; memb Alcohol Educn & Research Cncl 1995–2001; Liveryman Worshipful Co of Distillers; *Recreations* gardening, shooting and stalking; *Style—* Alastair Eadie, Esq; ✉ West Hall, Blackford, Yeovil, Somerset BA22 7EB

EADIE, Craig Farquhar; *b* 22 April 1955; *Educ* Canford, Worcester Coll Oxford, Aix-Marseilles Univ France; *m* 3 Oct 1987, Deborah Ann, da of Leslie Burnett, of W Wycombe, Bucks; *Career* admitted slr 1980; ptnr Frere Cholmeley Bischoff 1986–98, fndr and ptnr Forsters 1998–; *Style—* Craig Eadie, Esq; ✉ Forsters, 67 Grosvenor Street, London W1K 3JN (tel 020 7863 8333, fax 020 7863 8444)

EADIE, Helen Stirling; MSP; da of James Miller, and Elizabeth Miller, *née* Stirling; *b* 7 March 1947; *m* Robert Eadie, s of Alex Eadie, BEM, JP (former MP for Midlothian); 2 da (Fiona b 28 July 1970, Jemma b 19 June 1983); *Career* MSP (Lab) Dunfermline E 1999–; vice-chm Fife Cncl Strategic Devpt Ctee, vice-pres North Sea Cmmn; former: full-time union official GMB, asst to Harry Ewing MP and Alex Eadie MP, project co-ordinator West Fife Enterprise, former hon pres Fife Cncl for Racial Equality, chm Equal Opportunities Ctee Fife Regnl Cncl, former sec Homeworkers Campaign London, former chm Child Care Now, former substitute memb Tport and Environment Ctee, convenor Cross-Party Working Gp on Strategic Rail Servs in Scottish Parl, former dep convener Scot Parl Public Petitions Ctee, vice-convenor Cross Pty Working Gp on Disability; previous Lab Pty positions: branch sec Larbert Lab Pty Young Socialists, branch sec and ward election agent Blackheath and Dulwich CLP, vice-chm Dulwich CLP, memb Exec Ctee Gtr London Lab Pty, memb Women's Nat Jt Trade Union and Lab Pty Advsy Ctee, memb former PM James Callaghan's Election Campaign Team 1979, sec Fife Regnl Cncl and Fife Cncl Lab Gps, chm Women's Section Dunfermline E CLP, memb Fife Cncl Lab Gp, vice-chair Exec Ctee Lab Movement in Europe in Scotland, former memb Scot Parl European Ctee, dep ldr Fife Regnl Cncl, memb Health Ctee, memb Exec Ctee Firtst Past the Post Campaign; memb: GMB, Co-op Pty, Fabian Soc, Lab Movement in Europe, Euro Movement, CPWG on Cancer; *Style—* Mrs Helen Eadie, MSP; ✉ 25 Church Street, Inverkeithing, Fife, KY11 1LG (tel 01383 412856, fax 01383 412855)

EADY, Anthony James; s of John James Eady (d 1995), and Doris Amy, *née* Langley (d 1988); *b* 9 July 1939; *Educ* Harrow, Hertford Coll Oxford (MA); *m* 23 June 1973, Carole June, da of Cyril Albert James Langley (d 1957); 2 s (Jeremy b 1974 d 1975, Nigel b 1976), 1 da (Joanna (Mrs Matthew Winn-Smith) b 1978); *Career* Theodore Goddard and Co 1962–66, admitted slr 1966, J Henry Schroder Wagg and Co Ltd 1966–79, sec Lazard Bros and Co Ltd 1979–98, asset tracing conslt 1998–; govr Sir William Perkins's Sch Chertsey 2000–, memb Exec Ctee Assoc of Governing Bodies of Ind Schs 2006–; Liveryman Worshipful Co of Slrs 1979; *Recreations* Hertford Soc (vice-pres and memb Ctee, chm 1995–2004), road running; *Clubs* Thames Hare and Hounds, Oxford and Cambridge (memb Gen, Mgmnt and other ctees), Road Runners (vice-pres and memb Cncl); *Style—* Anthony Eady, Esq; ✉ 10 Evelyn Close, Woking, Surrey GU22 0DG (tel 01483 762252)

EADY, Hon Mr Justice; Sir David Eady; kt (1997); s of Thomas William Eady (d 1978), and Kate, *née* Day (d 2001); *b* 24 March 1943; *Educ* Brentwood Sch, Trinity Coll Cambridge (MA, LLB); *m* 1974, Catherine, yr da of Joseph Thomas Wiltshire; 1 da (Caroline b 1975), 1 s (James b 1977); *Career* called to the Bar Middle Temple 1966 (bencher 1991); QC 1983, recorder of the Crown Court 1986–97, judge of the High Court of Justice (Queen's Bench Div) 1997–; memb Ctee on Privacy and Related Matters (The Calcutt Ctee) 1989–90; *Books* The Law of Contempt (2 edn with Prof A T H Smith, 1998); *Style—* The Hon Mr Justice Eady; ✉ Royal Courts of Justice, Strand, London WC2A 2LL

EAGLE, Angela; MP; da of André Eagle, and late Shirley Eagle; sis of Maria Eagle, MP, *qv*; *b* 17 February 1961; *Educ* Formby HS, St John's Coll Oxford (BA); *Career* various posts Crosby CLP 1978–80; COHSE: joined as researcher 1984, later nat press offr, Parly liaison offr until 1992; MP (Lab, UNISON sponsored) Wallasey 1992–; former memb: Backbench Health Ctee and Treasy Ctee, Select Ctee on Members Interests, Select Ctee on Employment 1992–96; memb PAC 1995–96, former oppn whip; Parly under sec of state: Tport 1997–98, DSS 1998–2001, Home Office 2001–02; chm Nat Conf of Lab Women 1991, chair Lab Backbench Employment Ctee; chm Oxford Univ Fabian Club 1980–83, sec Peckham CLP 1989–91; memb Lab Pty NEC Women's Ctee 1989–92; memb Exec Ctee: Socialist Health Assoc, Co-op Pty; memb NUJ, memb Br Film Inst; *Recreations* chess, cricket, cinema; *Style—* Ms Angela Eagle, MP; ✉ Home Office, 50 Queen Anne's Gate, London SW1H 9AT

EAGLE, Maria; MP; da of André Eagle, and late Shirley Eagle; sis of Angela Eagle, MP, *qv*; *Career* MP (Lab) Liverpool Garston 1997–; Parly under-sec of state Dept of Work and Pensions 2001–06, Parly under-sec of state NI Office 2006–; *Style—* Ms Maria Eagle, MP; ✉ House of Commons, London SW1A 0AA (tel 020 7219 3000)

EAGLEN, Jane; da of Ronald Eaglen (d 1970), and Kathleen, *née* Kent; *Educ* South Park GS Lincoln, RNCM; *Career* soprano; princ memb ENO 1983–90; Peter Moores Fndn scholarship, Carl Rosa Tst award, Countess of Munster scholarship; *Performances* incl: Leonora in Il Trovatore (ENO), Elizabeth I in Mary Stuart (ENO), Eva in Die Meistersinger (ENO), Tosca (ENO, Perth Opera Aust, Buenos Aires, Cleveland Symphony Orch), Donna Anna in Don Giovanni (ENO, Scottish Opera, Vienna State Opera, Bologna Opera, Metropolitan Opera NY), Turandot (at the Met and Bologna), Mimi in La Bohème (Scottish Opera), Fiordiligi in Cosi fan Tutte (Scottish Opera), Brünnhilde in Die Walküre (Scottish Opera, Costa Mesa USA, La Scala Milan and Vienna), Brünnhilde in Siegried (Chicago), complete Ring Cycle (Chicago, Met, Seattle, La Scala), Madam Butterfly (Brisbane Opera Aust), Amelia in Un Ballo in Maschera (Bologna Opera, Opera Bastille Paris 1995), Mathilde in William Tell (Geneva Opera, Royal Opera House), Norma (Scottish Opera, Seattle Opera, Ravenna Festival), La Gioconda (Chicago), Tristan und Isolde (Seattle), recitals for Wagner Socs in London, NY and Argentina, Verdi's Requiem (gave performance for Lockerbie Disaster Appeal), Mahler's Eighth Symphony (broadcast live by Channel 4), Turandot (Royal Opera House); exclusive recording contract with Sony Classical; *Recordings* incl: Norma, Third Norn in Götterdämmerung, Die Flammen, Medea in Corinto, Tosca, soundtrack for Sense and Sensibility, Bellini & Wagner, Mozart & Strauss; *Style—* Miss Jane Eaglen; ✉ c/o AOR Management Ltd (Personal Management), Westwood, Lorraine Park, Harrow Weald, Middlesex HA3 6BX (tel 020 8954 7646, fax 020 8420 7499)

EAGLES, Brian; s of David Eagles (d 1982), of London, and Anne, *née* Estrin (d 1994); *b* 4 February 1937; *Educ* Kilburn GS, Univ of London (LLB); *m* 30 May 1961, Marjorie, da of Leopold Weiss (d 1983), of London; 1 da (Karen b 1963), 2 s (Simon b 1965, Paul b 1967); *Career* slr; ptnr: J Sanson & Co 1960–67, Herbert Oppenheimer Nathan & Vandyk 1967–88, SJ Berwin & Co 1988–94, Hammond Suddards 1994–99, Howard Kennedy 1999–; arbitrator and mediator; panel memb: World Intellectual Property Orgn (WIPO), American Arbitration Assoc, Law Soc, Ind Film and Television Alliance, Sports Dispute Resolution; accredited CEDR mediator; Consensus Mediation, Intermediation; hon slr Celebrities Guild of GB 1983–; memb: Int Bar Assoc, Br Assoc of Lawyer Mediators (BALM), Int Assoc of Entertainment Lawyers, Law Soc 1960; regular contributor of articles to legal and entertainment industry publications; ACIArb; *Recreations* music, film, theatre, skiing, walking; *Style—* Brian Eagles, Esq; ✉ Montague House, 107 Frognal, Hampstead, London NW3 6XR; Howard Kennedy, 19 Cavendish Square, London W1A 2AW (tel 020 7546 8889, fax 020 7664 4489, e-mail brian.eagles@howardkennedy.com, website www.mediamediation.co.uk)

EAGLING, Wayne John; s of Eddie Eagling, and Thelma, *née* Dunsmore; *b* 27 November 1950, Montreal, Canada; *Educ* Robert Louis Stevenson Sch Pebble Beach CA, Royal Ballet Sch London; *Career* ballet dancer; Royal Ballet Co: joined 1969, soloist 1972–75, princ 1975–91; artistic dir: Dutch Nat Ballet 1991–2005, English Nat Ballet 2005–; created/choreographed new works incl: R B Sque (for Amnesty Int Gala 1983, Sadler's Wells Theatre 1984), Frankenstein - The Modern Prometheus (one act, for Royal Ballet 1985, La Scala Milan 1987, Dutch Nat Ballet 1993), Beauty and the Beast (one act, for Royal Ballet 1986), Manfred (two acts), Senso (three acts), Nijinsky (two acts), Pas de Deuxs (Naples, Mantova, on RAI TV), The Queen of Spades (opera at La Scala Milan), The Wall Concert (with Roger Waters, Berlin), I Want to Break Free (video for pop group Queen), Alma (two act ballet on life of Alma Mahler, La Scala Milan) 1994; for Dutch National Ballet: Ruins of Times 1993, Symphony in Waves 1994, Duet 1995; co-choregraphed: Nutcracker and Mouseking 1996 (with Toer van Schayk), Lost Touch (for Dancing for Duchenne, a Charity Gala Amsterdam) 1995, Holding a Balance (for opening of Vermeer exhbn, Mauritshuis The Hague) 1996, The Last Emperor (for The Hong Kong Ballet) 1997, Toverfluit (with Toer van Schayle) 1999, La Sacre du Printemps 2000, Frozen (for opening of Mintus von Weleer exbn Vermeer-Mauritshuis The Hague; *Roles* incl: Prince Siegfried in Swan Lake, Prince Florimund in The Sleeping Beauty, The Prince in The Nutcracker, The Poet in Les Sylphides, Solor in La Bayadère, Albrecht in Giselle; by Sir Frederick Ashton incl: Colas in La Fille Mal Gardée, Tirrenio in Ondine, The Prince in Cinderella, The Young Man in The Two Pigeons, Tuesday and Friday's Child in Jazz Calendar; by Sir Kenneth MacMillan incl: The Brother in Triad (first created role), des Grieux in Manon Lescaut, Prince Rudolf in Mayerling, Edward Gordon Craig and Oskar Beregi in Isadora, Romeo and Mercutio in Romeo and Mercutio, The Messenger of Death in Song of the Earth, The Chosen One in The Rite of Spring, title role in Orpheus; by Jerome Robbins incl: Requiem Canticles, In the Night, Dances at a Gathering; by Balanchine incl: The Four Temperaments, Violin Concerto, Agon, Apollo, The Prodigal Son, Bugaku, Serenade; others incl: The Boy with Matted Hair in Tudor's Shadowplay, title role in Robert Helpmann's Hamlet, Jean de Brienne in Rudolf Nureyev's Raymonda Act III, created role of Ariel in Rudolph Nureyev's The Tempest; *Recreations* scuba diving, golf; *Style—* Wayne Eagling, Esq

EALES, Darryl Charles; s of Barrie George Eales, of Birmingham, and Janet May, *née* Lewis; *b* 4 October 1960, Birmingham; *Educ* King Edward VI Camp Hill Sch for Boys, Univ of

Exeter (BA); *m* 4 July 1987, Joanne, *née* Stevenson; 2 da (Harriet Caroline Victoria b 28 March 1990, Caroline Georgina Grace b 4 Oct 1992); *Career* Price Waterhouse 1983–87 (latterly corporate finance mangr); Lloyds TSB Development Capital: joined 1987, dir 1994, regnl md 1997, chief exec 2003–; involved with: Acorns Children's Hospice, The Great Generation; CA 1986 (Tattersal Walker Prize ICAEW 1985); *Recreations* ball sports (increasingly as a spectator!), Birmingham City supporter, reading (especially military and political history), wine collecting; *Clubs* Copt Heath Golf; *Style*— Darryl Eales, Esq; ✉ Pinfield House, 27 Cherry Hill Road, Barnt Green, Birmingham B45 8LN (tel 0121 445 5754); Lloyds TSB Development Capital Limited, 2–5 Old Bond Street, London W1S 4PD (tel 020 7518 6810, fax 020 7518 6820, e-mail deales@ldc.co.uk)

EAMES, Brian A A; *b* 12 June 1942; *Educ* Stamford Sch; *Children* 1 da (Jessica b 19 Sept 1985), 1 s (Sandy b 7 Aug 1987); *Career* trainee East Midland Allied Press 1958–64, sub ed then chief sub ed Berrows Newspapers 1964–68, press offr then sr press offr Imperial Group 1968–74, PR mangr Unigate Group (Foods) 1974–78, PR conslt 1978–85 (PPR Int, Y&R London, Sam Weller Associates London, Tibbenham PR of Norwich and Nottingham), PR mangr Sea Fish Industry Authy Edinburgh and London 1985–89, head of press and PR Scottish Enterprise/Scottish Devpt Agency 1989–91, sole proprietor Brian Eames Associates Edinburgh 1991–2002, communications offr Perth and Kinross Cncl 2002–07, ret; former regnl chm: Br Assoc of Industrial Eds (now Br Assoc of Communicators in Business), Inst of PR; lectr in int corp communication, communication in orgn, PR and corp communication; Industrial Writer of the Year (Midlands) 1970, Best Newspaper (UK) 1988 and (Scotland) 1989, winner Inside Write UK Plain English Campaign award 2000; former MCIoM, former FCIPR, fell Br Assoc of Communicators in Business; *Style*— Brian Eames, Esq; ✉ Ruskin, Bowerswell Lane, Kinnoull, Perth PH2 7DL

EAMES, Philip Anthony William (Phil); s of Barry William Eames, and Gillian Eames; *Educ* Aylesbury GS, South Bank Univ; *m* 1991, Lucy Ann McNab; 3 s (Joshua b 1993, Henry b 1997, Oliver b 2004); *Career* dir ICL Media Business 1999–, md Incepta Online 2000–; *Recreations* golf, rugby; *Clubs* RAC; *Style*— Phil Eames, Esq; ✉ Incepta Online, 3 London Wall Buildings, London EC2M 5SY (tel 020 7638 9571, fax 020 7638 7091)

EAMES, Baron (Life Peer UK 1995), of Armagh in the County of Armagh; Most Rev Robert Henry Alexander Eames; OM (2007); s of William Edward Eames, of Belfast, and Mary Eleanor Thompson, *née* Alexander; *b* 27 April 1937; *Educ* Belfast Royal Acad, Methodist Coll Belfast, Queen's Univ Belfast (LLB, PhD), Trinity Coll Dublin (LLD); *m* 1966, (Ann) Christine, da of Capt William Adrian Reynolds Daly (d 1943), of London; 2 s (Hon Niall b 1967, Hon Michael b 1969); *Career* curate of Bangor Co Down 1963–66; incumbent of: Gilnahirk Down 1966–74, Dundela Down 1974–75; bishop of: Derry and Raphoe 1975–80, Down and Dromore 1980–86; archbishop of Armagh and Primate of All Ireland 1986–2006; chm: Archbishop of Canterbury's Int Cmmn on Communion and Women in the Episcopate 1988, Archbishop of Canterbury's Lambeth Int Cmmn on Anglican Structures 2004; govr Church Army 1985–; Archbishop of Canterbury's Award for Outstanding Serv to the Anglican Communion 2006, Tipperary Peace Int Prize 2007; hon bencher Lincoln's Inn 1998; Hon LLD Queen's Univ Belfast 1989, Hon DLitt Univ of Greenwich Univ; Hon DD: Univ of Cambridge 1994, Univ of Aberdeen 1997, Virginia Theological Seminary USA 2005, Yale Univ USA 2005; *Books* A Form of Worship for Teenagers (1965), The Quiet Revolution: Irish Disestablishment (1970), Through Suffering (1973), Thinking Through Lent (1978), Through Lent (1984), Chains to be Broken (1992); *Recreations* sailing, reading; *Clubs* Strangford Yacht, Ringhaddy Yacht, Kildare St and Univ (Dublin), Athenaeum; *Style*— The Most Rev the Rt Hon Lord Eames, OM; ✉ 3 Downshire Crescent, Hillsborough BT26 6DD; House of Lords, London SW1A 0PW

EARDLEY-WILMOT, Sir Michael John Assheton; 6 Bt (UK 1821), of Berkswell Hall, Warwickshire; s of Sir John Assheton Eardley-Wilmot, 5 Bt, LVO, DSC (d 1995), and Diana Elizabeth, *née* Moore; *b* 13 January 1941; *Educ* Clifton; *m* 1, 1971 (m dis 1985), Wendy, yr da of Anthony John Wolstenholme; 2 s (Benjamin John b 1974, Guy Assheton b 1979), 1 da (Holly Joanna b 1976); m 2, 1987, Diana Margaret, da of Robert Graham Wallis; 1 da (Poppy Clementine b 1987); *Heir* s, Benjamin Eardley-Wilmot; *Career* md Famous Names Holdings 1974–86, md Beaufort Hotel; *Style*— Sir Michael Eardley-Wilmot, Bt

EARL, Kimble David; s of late Leonard Arthur Earl, of Surrey, and late Margaret Lucy, *née* Pulker; *b* 29 November 1951; *Educ* Caterham Sch; *Career* former dep chief exec Argus Press Group, chief exec Newspaper Div and Consumer Publishing Div Argus Press Ltd 1988–1993, chm and chief exec The Bull Nelson Ltd 2000–, dir Wherecanwego.com 2004–, editorial dir Int Educn Today 2007–; mktg dir Oak Craft Traditional Buildings/Holmsley Mill Ltd, mktg conslt Field Seymour Parkes Slrs 1994–2003, mktg conslt Personal Injury Med Services 1996–; former chm: Reading Newspaper Co Ltd, Windsor Newspaper Co Ltd, London and North Surrey Newspapers Ltd, West London and Surrey Newspapers Ltd, Surrey and South London Newspapers Ltd, South London Press Ltd, Argus Specialist Publications, Trident Press, Reading Newspaper Printing Co Ltd, Thames Valley Publishing, Argus Consumer Magazines Ltd, Argus Books, Argus Specialist Exhibitions, West London and Surrey Newspapers; former dir: SM Distribution Ltd, Argus Press Holdings Inc, Team Argus Inc, Argus Business Publications Ltd, Argus Retail Services Ltd; *Recreations* walking, motor coach driving, travel; *Style*— Kimble Earl, Esq; ✉ The Bull Nelson Ltd, 2/12 Whitchurch Road, Pangbourne, Reading, Berkshire RG8 7BP (tel 0118 984 1394, fax 0118 984 5396, e-mail mail@bullnelson.co.uk)

EARL, Prof Michael John; s of Vincent Earl (d 1975), and Marjorie Earl (d 1990); *b* 11 January 1944, Cheadle, Cheshire; *Educ* Univ of Newcastle upon Tyne (BA), Univ of Warwick (MSc); *m* 1969, Alison Jennifer, *née* Eades; 1 s (Jonathan Christopher b 24 May 1983), 1 da (Justine Elizabeth b 17 June 1985); *Career* gp systems mangr GEC Telecommunications 1972–74, lectr in mgmnt control Manchester Business Sch 1974–76, fell in info mgmnt Templeton Coll Oxford 1976–90, prof of info mgmnt London Business Sch 1990–2002 (dep princ and actg princ 1998–2000), prof of info mgmnt Univ of Oxford 2002–, dean Templeton Coll Oxford 2002–; memb Advsy Cncl Oxford Philomusica Orch; FBCS 1992; *Books* Information Management: The Strategic Dimension (1988), Management Strategies for Information Technology (1989), Information Management: The Organisation Dimension (1996); *Recreations* golf, tennis, travel, music; *Clubs* Oxford and Cambridge, Frilford Heath Golf; *Style*— Prof Michael Earl; ✉ Templeton College, Oxford OX1 5NY (tel 01865 422722, fax 01865 422726, e-mail michael.earl@templeton.ox.ac.uk)

EARL, Peter Richard Stephen; s of late Peter Richard Walter Earl, and Patricia, *née* Lee; *b* 20 January 1955; *Educ* City of London Sch, Worcester Coll Oxford (open exhibitioner, MA, rowed for univ), Harvard Univ (Kennedy scholar, rowed for univ); *m* Emma Elizabeth, *née* Saunders; 1 s (Peter Richard William John b 10 March 1987), 1 da (Amelia Rose Elizabeth b 8 July 1985); *Career* conslt Boston Consulting Group 1978–79, assoc Blyth Eastman Dillon Inc 1979–80, mangr Orion Bank 1980–82, dir ABC International Ltd 1982–85, vice-pres Arab Banking Corporation 1982–85, chm Tranwood Earl & Co Ltd (formerly Ifincorp Earl & Co Ltd) 1985–91, chief exec Tranwood plc 1988–91, chm and chief exec Carter Organization Inc NYC 1990–, head of European corp fin Fieldstone Private Capital Group 1994–96, chief exec The Independent Power Corporation plc 1995–, md Rurelec plc 2004–, chief exec IPSA Gp plc 2005–; fndr: Demerger Corporation plc 1985–, Analysis Corporation plc 1986–, Integrated Energy Ltd 2001–; tstee: Everest Meml Tst, City of London Sch Bursary Tst; *Books* International Mergers & Acquisitions (1986); *Recreations* mountaineering (joint leader British 40th Anniversary Everest Expedition 1993), marathons, skiing; *Clubs* Vincent's (Oxford), Brooks's; *Style*— Peter Earl, Esq; ✉ Prince Consort House, 27–29 Albert Embankment, London SE1 7TJ (tel 020 7793 7676, fax 020 7793 7654, e-mail pearl@indpow.com)

EARL, Roger Lawrence; s of Lawrence William Earl (d 1994), of Hove, E Sussex, and Doris Florence, *née* Copelin (d 1997); *b* 4 October 1940; *Educ* St Christopher's Sch Kingswood, Hollingbury Ct Brighton, St Paul's; *m* 22 June 1968, Lynda Marion, da of late Harold Frederick Waldock, of Enfield, Middx; 2 da (Meredith Louise b 12 July 1970, Alexandra Kirsten b 20 June 1972); *Career* Arbon Langrish & Co (Lloyd's brokers) 1957–65; Bland Welch & Co/Bland Payne & Co (Lloyd's brokers): asst dir 1966–70, exec dir 1970–73, bd dir and md N American Div 1973–79; md and chief exec Fenchurch plc (Lloyd's brokers) 1979–96 (dep chm 1996–98), dir GPG plc 1987–89 (md 1989), dir Lambert Fenchurch Insurance Brokers Ltd 1998–2000, dir Heath Lambert Insurance Brokers Ltd 2000–, chm and ceo Carabela Conslts Ltd 2005–; dir and tstee Charles Letts Meml Tst 2002–; memb Kew Soc; memb Lloyd's 1970–96; Freeman Hon Co of Coachmakers and Coach Harness Makers; *Recreations* motor sport, skiing, scuba diving, tennis; *Clubs* Hurlingham, City of London, HSCC, Ferrari Owners', Maserati Owners, RAC, HGPCA, Automobile Club de Monaco (ACM), Automobile Club de l'Ouest (ACO), Lloyd's Motor (chm), LTA; *Style*— Roger Earl, Esq; ✉ 4 Cumberland Road, Kew, Surrey TW9 3HQ (tel 020 8948 1714, fax 020 8948 5737); Flouquet, Lacour de Visa, Tarn et Garonne, France; La Carabela, 28 Via Del Bosque, Canyamel, Mallorca, Spain (tel 00 34 971 841436)

EARL, Col Timothy James; OBE (1999); s of Rowland Earl (decd), and Elizabeth Walden, *née* Walton; *b* 2 July 1943; *Educ* Brentwood Sch, RMA Sandhurst; *m* 13 Jan 1968, Elizabeth, da of Count Guy de Pelet; 2 s (Philip b 18 June 1969, Alistair b 16 March 1973), 1 da (Charlotte b 18 Dec 1975); *Career* cmmnd 1 King's Own Border Regt 1964, served Guyana, Oman, Bahrain, Aden, Cyprus, NI and Jungle Warfare Sch Malaya, transferred Life Gds 1974, served Germany, NI, Belize and Norway, CO 1983–85, RCDS 1986, MOD 1987–90, sec Govt Hospitality Fund 1993–99, private sec to HRH The Princess Royal 1999–2002; *Recreations* country sports, planting trees; *Clubs* Flyfishers'; *Style*— Col Timothy Earl, OBE; ✉ Haddon, Stourton Caundle, Dorset DT10 2LB (tel 01963 362241, fax 01963 364501, mobile 07802 711344, e-mail timothy@earl2005.fsnet.co.uk)

EARLAM, Richard John; s of Francis Earlam, MD (d 1959), of Mossley Hill, Liverpool, and Elspeth Noeline (Elsie), *née* Skippers (d 1993); *b* 26 March 1934; *Educ* Liverpool Coll, Uppingham, Trinity Hall Cambridge (MA, MChir), Univ of Liverpool; *m* 6 Sept 1969, Roswitha, da of Alfons Teuber, playwright (d 1971), of Munich, Germany; 2 da (Melissa b 1976, Caroline b 1979); *Career* Capt RAMC 1960–62, surgical specialist Br Mil Hosp Hong Kong, TA MO 359 Field Regt RA; Fulbright scholar 1966, res asst Mayo Clinic USA 1966–67, clinical asst to Prof Zenker Munich 1968, Alexander von Humboldt fellowship W Germany 1968, conslt gen surgn The London Hosp 1972–98; chm: NE Thames Regnl Advsy Ctee in Gen Surgery, MRC Sub-Ctee on Oesophageal Cancer; memb MRC: Cancer Therapy Ctee, Manpower Ctee; examiner RCS 1982–86; memb RSM, FRCS; *Publications* Clinical Tests of Oesophageal Function (1976), ABC of Major Trauma (co-ed, 1991, 3 edn 2000), Trauma Care (ed, 1997); author of chapters and papers on abdominal surgery, oesophagus, stomach and gallbladder disease, epidemiology, surgical audit and coding; *Recreations* tennis, mountains summer and winter, beekeeping; *Clubs* Association of Surgeons, Collegium Internationale Chirurgiae Digestivae, Furniture History Soc, Bayerischer Yacht, British Dragon Assoc, Athenaeum; *Style*— Richard John Earlam, Esq; ✉ 4 Pembroke Gardens, London W8 6HS (tel and fax 020 7602 5255)

EARLE, Sir (Hardman) George Algernon; 6 Bt (UK 1869), of Allerton Tower, Woolton, Lancs; s of Sir Hardman Alexander Mort Earle, 5 Bt (d 1979), and Maie, Lady Earle (d 1986); *b* 4 February 1932; *Educ* Eton; *m* 24 Jan 1967, Diana Gillian Bligh, da of Col Frederick Ferris Bligh St George, CVO (d 1970), ggs of Sir Richard Bligh St George, 2 Bt; 1 da (Katharine Susan b 1968), 1 s (Robert George Bligh b 1970); *Heir* s, Robert Earle; *Career* Nat Serv Ensign in Grenadier Gds; memb of London Metal Exchange 1962–73; *Recreations* fox hunting, sailing; *Clubs* Royal Yacht Sqdn; *Style*— Sir George Earle, Bt

EARLE, Joel Vincent (Joe); s of James Basil Foster Earle (d 1989), of Kyle of Lochalsh, Ross-shire, and Mary Isabel Jessie, *née* Weeks (d 1992); *b* 1 September 1952; *Educ* Westminster, New Coll Oxford (BA); *m* 10 May 1980, Sophia Charlotte, da of Oliver Arbuthnot Knox, of London; 2 s (Leo b 1981, Martin b 1984); *Career* V&A: keeper Far Eastern Dept 1983–87 (res asst 1974–77, asst keeper 1977–83), head of public servs 1987–89; exhibitions co-ordinator and head of public affairs Japan Festival 1991, chair Dept of Art of Asia, Oceania, and Africa Museum of Fine Arts Boston 2003–07, vice-pres Japan Soc and dir Japan Soc Gallery 2007–; ind arts conslt 1991–2003; major exhbns: Japan Style 1980, Great Japan Exhibition 1981, Toshiba Gallery of Japanese Art 1986, Visions of Japan 1991, Songs of My People 1992, Shibata Zeshin 1997, Splendors of Meiji 1999, Netsuke: Fantasy and Reality in Japanese Miniature Sculpture 2001, Serizawa: Master of Japanese Textile Design 2001, Contemporary Clay: Japanese Ceramics for the New Century 2005, Contemporary Clay: Japanese Ceramics for the New Century 2005, Beyond Basketry: Japanese Bamboo Art 2006; tstee The Design Museum 1988–2002; *Books* The Great Japan Exhibition (contrib, 1981), The Japanese Sword (translator, 1983), Japanese Art and Design (ed, 1987), Masterpieces by Shibata Zeshin (1995), The Index of Inro Artists (ed, 1995), The Khalili Collection of Japanese Art: Lacquer (ed, 1995), Flower Bronzes of Japan (1995), Splendors of Meiji (1999), Infinite Spaces: The Art and Wisdom of the Japanese Garden (2000), Japanese Lacquer: The Chiddingstone Castle Collection (2000), The Robert S Huthart Collection of Iwami Netsuke (2000), Netsuke: Fantasy and Reality in Japanese Miniature Sculpture (2001), Splendors of Imperial Japan (2001), Lethal Elegance: Samurai Sword Fittings (2004), Contemporary Clay: Japanese Ceramics for the New Century (2005); catalogues for Christie's, Spink, Eskenazi and Barry Davies Oriental Art Ltd; *Style*— Joe Earle, Esq; ✉ 333 East 47th Street, New York NY 10017, USA (tel 00 1 212 715 1283, fax 00 1 212 715 1262, mobile 00 1 857 234 6992, e-mail jearle@japansociety.org)

EARLE, Laurence Foster; s of Robert Foster Earle, of London, and Joy, *née* Cartwright; *b* 11 July 1965; *Educ* Westminster, Univ of Sussex (BA); *m* 20 Sept 1997, Maria Christina, da of Robert Johnston Arnold; 1 s (Gabriel Harry Foster b 13 Oct 2001), 1 da (Eliza Constance b 13 Aug 2003); *Career* film ed iD Magazine 1989–91; Time Out Pubns: dep ed 1990–92; Independent on Sunday: arts ed 1995–96, ed Independent on Sunday Review 1996–98; The Independent: features ed 1999–2002, exec ed (features) 2002–03, ed The Independent Magazine 2003–; *Recreations* football, skiing, hill walking; *Style*— Laurence Earle, Esq; ✉ The Independent, 191 Marsh Wall, London E14 9RS (tel 020 7005 2000, fax 020 7005 2182, e-mail learle@independent.co.uk)

EARLS, Mark Benedict; s of Gerard Warmington Earls, of Harrow, Middx, and Kathleen Mary, *née* Orchard; *b* 12 July 1961; *Educ* John Lyon Sch Harrow, St Edmund Hall Oxford (BA); *Career* trainee Grey London (advtg agency) 1984–86, planner/sr planner Boase Massimi Pollit 1986–89, actg head of planning CDP Financial 1989–90; Ammirati and Puris/Lintas (formerly S P Lintas): sr planner/bd dir 1990–95, dir of planning Europe 1994–95; former bd planning dir Bates Dorland and St Luke's; exec planning offr Ogilvy & Mather 2001–; memb Ctee Account Planning Gp 1994–; memb Market Research Soc 1986; *Recreations* cricket (chm Wandsworth Gods CC), travel, walking, Italian cuisine, oysters; *Clubs* Vincent's (Oxford); *Style*— Mark Earls, Esq

EARNSHAW, Christopher Martin (Chris); s of Frank Earnshaw, of Hampton in Arden, W Midlands, and Bessie, *née* Smith; *b* 4 May 1954; *Educ* Wellington GS, Adams GS Newport, Univ of Sheffield (BSc); *m* 25 Aug 1979, Moira May, da of Donald Turner; 2 s (Nicholas b 4 Nov 1984, Matthew b 27 Sept 1992), 1 da (Rachel b 1 May 1987); *Career* British Telecommunications plc: dir Network BTUK 1989–91, md Worldwide Networks 1991–93, pres and ceo Concert Communications Inc 1993–95, md Networks and Systems/Info Servs 1995–99, gp engrg dir and chief technol offr 1999–2002; dep pres IEE 2006–, dir Engrg and Technol Bd (ETB) 2002–05, chm Police IT Orgn (PITO) 2004–07; fell Int Engrg Consortium; CEng, FIET, FREng 1999 FRSA 2000; *Style*— Chris Earnshaw, Esq, FREng; ✉ tel 01582 712753, e-mail chris@oakleighassoicates.com

EARWICKER, Martin John; s of George Allen Earwicker (d 1983), and Joan Mary, *née* West; *b* 11 May 1948; *Educ* Farnborough GS, Univ of Surrey (BSc); *m* 1970, Pauline Ann Josey; 2 s (Simon Paul b 1970, Alexander b 1977); *Career* various research posts ARE Portland 1970–86, dir Science (SEA) MOD 1986–89, head Attack Weapons Dept RAE 1989–90, head Flight Systems Dept DRA 1990–92, dir Op Studies DRA 1992–93, dir Air Systems Def Evaluation Res Agency (DERA) 1993–96, dep chief scientist Scrutiny and Analysis MOD 1996–98, DG Scrutiny and Analysis MOD 1998–99, md Analysis DERA 1998–99, head Science and Technology Base Office of Science and Technology DTI 1999–2001, chief exec Defence Science and Technol Lab 2001–06, dir Nat Museum of Science and Industry 2006–; pres: Assoc of European Research Establishments in Aeronautics (AEREA) 1995–96, Assoc for Science Educn 2008; visiting prof Imperial Coll London; chair Corporation Farnborough Coll of Technol 2004–; awarded AB Wood Silver Medal Inst of Acoustics 1984; CEng, FInstP 1998, FREng 2000; *Recreations* cycling, walking, woodwork, music; *Style*— Martin Earwicker, Esq; ✉ National Museum of Science and Industry, 165 Queen's Gate, London SW7 5HD

EAST ANGLIA, Bishop of (RC) 2003–; Rt Rev Michael Evans; s of late Ralph Evans, and Jeanette, *née* Barbyer, of Whitstable, Kent; *b* 10 August 1951, London; *Educ* Simon Langton GS for Boys Canterbury, St John's Seminary Wonersh, Heythrop Coll Univ of London (MA); *Career* asst priest Richmond Surrey 1975–77, lectr and vice-rector St John's Seminary Wonersh 1979–87 and 1993–95, univ chaplain South London Univs Chaplaincy 1987–93, parish priest Tunbridge Wells Kent 1995–2003; memb: British Catholic/Methodist Ctee 1991– (co-chm 2006–), International Catholic/Methodist Cmmn 1996–; chm Ctee for Christian Unity 2004–, jt pres Christian-Muslim Forum 2006–; memb Catholic Theological Assoc; *Publications* Let My People Go (1979), A Catholic Priest Today and Tomorrow (1993); author of numerous pamphlets and articles; *Recreations* supporting Leeds United FC, listening to music, everything Cambodian; *Style*— The Rt Rev the Bishop of East Anglia; ✉ The White House, 21 Upgate, Poringland, Norwich NR14 7SH (tel 01508 492202, fax 01508 495358, e-mail office@east-angliadiocese.org.uk)

EASSIE, Rt Hon Lord; Ronald David Mackay; PC (2006); *Educ* Univ of St Andrews (MA), Univ of Edinburgh (LLB); *Career* admitted Faculty of Advocates 1972; official at Court of Justice of the European Communities Luxembourg 1979–82, QC (Scot) 1986, advocate depute 1986–90, senator Coll of Justice 1997–; chm Scottish Law Cmmn 2002–04; *Style*— The Rt Hon Lord Eassie; ✉ Parliament House, Edinburgh EH1 1RQ

EASSON, Prof Angus; s of William Coleridge Easson (d 1987), and Olive Mary, *née* Hornfeck (d 1962); *b* 18 July 1940; *Educ* William Ellis GS, Univ of Nottingham (BA), Univ of Oxford (DPhil); *Career* lectr in English: Univ of Newcastle upon Tyne 1965–71, Royal Holloway Coll London 1971–77; Univ of Salford: prof of English 1977–2000, dean Faculty of Social Sciences and Arts 1986–89 and 1992–95, chm Modern Languages Dept 1989–92, chm English Dept 1992–99, research prof of English 2000–05, hon visiting fell 2005–; *Books* Elizabeth Gaskell (1979), Elizabeth Gaskell - Critical Heritage (1991); *Recreations* opera; *Style*— Prof Angus Easson; ✉ University of Salford, European Studies Research Institute, Salford, Greater Manchester M5 4WT (tel 0161 295 5614)

EASSON, Malcolm Cameron Greig; s of Prof Eric Craig Easson, CBE (d 1983), of Cheshire, and Moira McKechnie, *née* Greig (d 2005); *b* 7 April 1949; *Educ* Marple Hall GS, Univ of Manchester; *m* 6 July 1972, Gillian, da of Stanley Oakley (d 2003), of Cheshire; 1 s (James b 1979), 1 da (Helen b 1982); *Career* former princ of firm of chartered accountants specialising in taxation and finance for doctors of med, ret; FCA; *Recreations* golf, music; *Style*— Malcolm C G Easson, Esq; ✉ Cherry Garth, Scott Road, Prestbury, Cheshire SK10 4DN (tel 01625 827277)

EAST, John Hilary Mortlock; s of Grahame Richard East, CMG (d 1993), and Cynthia Mildred, *née* Beck; *b* 6 March 1947; *Educ* St Paul's, BNC Oxford; *m* 22 Aug 1970, (Dorothy) Diane, da of Roy Cuthbert Tregidgo; 2 da (Tamsyn b 1974, Emily b 1978), 2 s (Richard b 1976, Jonathan b 1985); *Career* admitted slr 1972; Clifford Chance: ptnr 1976–2004, managing ptnr Singapore 1983–85, managing ptnr Hong Kong 1991–95, sr ptnr Hong Kong 1998–99, regnl managing ptnr Asia 2000–01, chm Partner Selection Gp 2002–04; pres Rugby Fives Assoc 2005–; Freeman Worshipful Co of Slrs; memb Law Soc; *Recreations* rugby fives, real tennis, cricket, cinema, reading, theatre; *Clubs* Singapore Cricket, Hong Kong Cricket, Hong Kong, Jesters, The Royal Tennis Court (Hampton Court Palace), RAC; *Style*— John East, Esq; ✉ Clifford Chance, 10 Upper Bank Street, London E14 5JJ (tel 020 7006 1000, fax 020 7006 5555)

EAST, John Richard Alan; s of Bertram David (Barry) East (d 1996), of Eaton Square, London, and Gladys, *née* Stone (d 1957); *b* 14 May 1949; *Educ* Westminster; *m* 1, 14 May 1971 (m dis 1986), Judith Adrienne, da of Clive Hill, of Horshall, Surrey; 2 s (Robin b 1974, Christopher b 1978); m 2, 12 July 1986 (m dis 2001), Charlotte Sylvia, da of Lt Cdr Peter Gordon Merriman, DSC, RN (d 1965), and Alison Grace Merriman, *née* Williams (d 1997); m 3, 17 Jan 2007, Frances Ruth, da of Christopher John Ollard (d 1974) and Rachel Ollard MBE, *née* Swain, of Wold Newton, Lincs; *Career* Speechly Bircham (Slrs) 1967–70, Mitton Butler Priest & Co Ltd 1971–73, Panmure Gordon & Co 1973–77; Margetts & Addenbrooke (formerly Margetts & Addenbrooke East Newton, Kent East Newton & Co) 1977–86: sr ptnr 1977–80, managing ptnr 1980–86, sr ptnr 1983–86; dir: National Investment Group plc 1986–87, Guidehouse Group plc and subsids 1987–91; chm and chief exec John East & Partners Ltd (formerly Guidehouse Securities Ltd) 1987–; memb Stock Exchange 1974; co-fndr CISCO (now Quoted Cos Alliance); tstee and memb Ctee The Square Mile Charitable Tst, memb La Commanderie de Bordeaux à Londres; jt pres Dagenham and Redbridge FC; FSI 2000 (MSI (dip) 1992); *Recreations* music predominantly jazz (listening, playing and recording), non-league football, fine wine, travel; *Clubs* Carlton (dep chm 2003–), United & Cecil; *Style*— John East, Esq; ✉ John East & Partners Ltd, 10 Sinsbury Square, London EC2A 1AD (tel 020 7628 2200, fax 020 7628 4473, e-mail john.east@johneastpartners.com)

EAST, Prof Robin Alexander; s of Percy Alexander East (d 1981), of Romsey, Hants, and Winifred May, *née* Southwell (d 1993); *b* 11 December 1935; *Educ* Barton Peveril GS, Univ of Southampton (BSc, PhD); *m* 6 Oct 1962, June, da of George Henry Slingsby (d 1977), of Sheffield; 1 da (Jennifer Lynn b 1963); *Career* apprentice Vickers Supermarine 1953–57, visiting res fell Aust Nat Univ at Canberra 1973; Univ of Southampton: Sir Alan Cobham res fell 1960–63, lectr, sr lectr and reader in aeronautics 1963–85, head of Aeronautics Dept 1985–90, prof of aeronautics 1985–96 (emeritus prof 1996); memb various ctees and former chm Southampton Branch RAeS, chm Accreditation Ctee RAeS 1991–2004, chm Aerodynamics Gp Ctee 1997–2001; memb Aviation Ctee DTI 1995–99; assoc fell American Inst of Aeronautics and Astronautics 1991; CEng 1983, FRAeS 1985; *Books* Forty Years of the Spitfire (jt ed with I C Cheeseman, 1976), Spacecraft Systems Engineering (contrib, 1991); around 100 pubns on hypersonic aerodynamics and experimental facilities in int jls and conf proceedings; *Recreations* gardening, photography, ornithology, walking; *Style*— Prof Robin East; ✉ East Croft, North Common, Sherfield English, Romsey, Hampshire SO51 6JT (tel 01794 340444); School of Engineering Sciences, Aeronautics and Astronautics, University of Southampton, Southampton, Hampshire SO17 1BJ (tel 023 8059 2324, fax 023 8059 3058, e-mail rae@soton.ac.uk)

EASTAWAY, Nigel Antony; s of Kenneth George Eastaway, and Muriel, *née* Angus; *b* 17 November 1943; *Educ* Chigwell Sch; *m* 17 Aug 1968, Ann, da of Cecil Douglas Geddes; 1 da (Suzanne Emma Louise b 4 July 1980), 1 s (James Nigel Andrew b 18 May 1983); *Career* chartered accountant; former ptnr Moores Rowland; currently tech dir Chiltern plc; tstee Russian Aviation Res Tst; former chm Tax Policy Sub-Ctee, memb Corporate Tax Sub-Ctee, former chm Tech Ctee and Personal and Capital Sub-Ctees; memb: Cncl Chartered Inst of Taxation, Tech Ctee Tax Faculty ICAEW, Int Tax Planning Assoc; former memb Taxation Ctee London C of C and Industry; TEP, AIIT, MEWI, SBV, MBAE; fell Offshore Inst, hon fell Hong Kong Inst of Taxation, fell Hong Kong Inst of Certified Public Accountants; FCA, FCCA, FCMA, FCIS, FRSA, FBIS, CTA (fell); *Books* Chiltern's Yellow Tax Guide (formerly: BDO Stoy Hayward's, Moores Rowland's), Chiltern's Orange Tax Guide (formerly BDO Stoy Hayward's, Moores Rowland's), Moores Rowland's Taxation of Farmers and Farming, Moores Rowland's A to Z of Tax Planning, Moores Rowland's Tax Planning for Recording Stars, Tottel's Tax Advisers Guide to Trusts (formely Tolley's), WJB Chiltern's Visiting Entertainers and Sportsmen, Handbook on the Capital Gains Tax 1979, Tax and Financial Planning for Medical Practitioners, Tax and Financial Planning for Professional Partnerships, Practical Share Valuation, Share Valuation Cases, Utilising Personal Tax Losses and Reliefs, Tax Aspects of Company Reorganisations, Utilising Company Tax Losses and Reliefs, Intellectual Property Law and Taxation, Zurich Expatriate Tax and Investment Handbook, Taxation of Lloyd's Underwriters, Principles of Capital Transfer Tax, Hong Kong Stamp Duty, Tottel's Self-Assessment (formerly Tolley's), Tottel's Corporation Tax Self-Assessment (formerly Tolley's), Simons Taxes (contrib), ICAEW Taxation Service (contrib); Soviet Aircraft Since 1918 (ed), Aircraft of the Soviet Union (contrib), Encyclopaedia of Russian Aircraft (contrib), Mikoyan MiG-21 (contrib), The Soviet Air Force (contrib), Janes All the World's Aircraft (contrib); *Recreations* Russian aircraft history, playing with old cars, Bentleys, Jaguars and Morgans; *Clubs* Bentley Drivers', Vintage Sports Car, Morgan Sports Car, Air Britain; *Style*— Nigel Eastaway, Esq; ✉ Chiltern plc, 3 Sheldon Square, Paddington, London W2 6PS (tel 020 7339 9000, fax 020 7339 9022, e-mail neastaway@aol.com)

EASTEAL, Martin; s of Charles Owen Easteal (d 1994), of Seaton, Devon, and Iris Joan, *née* King; *b* 4 November 1947; *Educ* Buckhurst Hill Co HS, UC Oxford (MA), Harvard Univ (Knox fell); *m* 1972, Barbara Mary, *née* Clark; 2 da (Susanna b 1975, Sophie b 1980); *Career* asst princ then princ HM Treasy 1970–74, asst chief exec London Borough of Ealing 1974–79, general mangr Harlow Cncl 1979–83; dir: Public Policy PA Consulting Group 1983–88, Nat Audit Office 1988–92; chief exec: Local Govt Cmmn for England 1992–96, Chelmsford BC 1996–; chm Essex Millennium Festival Ctee; memb: NE Thames Regnl Health Authy, Eastern Arts Assoc, Electricity Consumers Ctee, Harlow Theatre Trust, Essex Police Authy, Princess Alexandra NHS Tst; fndr annual Redcliffe-Maud Meml Lecture; Freeman City of Norwalk California; FIMgt 1977, FIPD 1978, FRSA 1993, FRGS 1993; *Books* Nixon's Style of Government (1972), The Development of the General Manager (1985), Management Information Systems in Whitehall (1989); *Recreations* music, vintage cars; *Clubs* Reform; *Style*— Martin Easteal, Esq; ✉ Chelmsford Borough Council, Civic Centre, Duke Street, Chelmsford, Essex CM1 1JE (tel 01245 606901)

EASTELL, Prof Richard; *b* 12 February 1953, Shipley, W Yorks; *Educ* Univ of Edinburgh (BSc, MB ChB, MD); *m*; 3 c; *Career* Western Gen Hosp Edinburgh: house offr 1977–78 (also at Royal Infirmary Edinburgh), MRC research fell 1978–80, registrar 1980–82; registrar Northwick Park Hosp Harrow 1982–84, research assoc and sr clinical fell Mayo Clinic Rochester MN 1984–89; Dept Human Metabolism Clinical Biochemistry Univ of Sheffield: sr research fell and hon conslt 1989–92, sr lectr 1992–95, hon conslt physician 1992–, prof 1995–; Univ of Sheffield: research dean Sch of Med and Biomedical Sciences 2002–, dep dir Div of Clinical Sciences (N) 2003–, head Bone Metabolism Gp; dir of R&D Sheffield Teaching Hosps Tst; FRCP 1996 (MRCP 1981), Hon FRCPI 1998, FRCPath 2000, FMedSci 2000, FRCPEd 2000; *Publications* author and co-author of numerous research papers in learned jls; *Style*— Prof Richard Eastell; ✉ Division of Clinical Sciences (North), University of Sheffield, Clinical Sciences Centre, Northern General Hospital, Sheffield S5 7AU

EASTEN, Julian Maitland; s of George Maitland Easten (d 1961), of Newcastle upon Tyne, and Winifred, *née* Elliott (d 1987); *b* 14 February 1935; *Educ* Bedford Sch; *m* 1, 1957 (m dis 1989), Audrey, *née* Maris; 1 da (Linzi b 13 Jan 1957); m 2, Frances Penelope, da of Maurice Edward Cooke; 1 da (Alice Amelia b 13 Aug 1992); *Career* mgmnt trainee Rootes Group automobile mfrs Coventry 1952–53, asst mangr Competitions Dept Mintex Ltd responsibile for servs and PR for Grand Prix and Int Rally teams 1955–57, sales dir Rootes and Lotus Dealers (concurrently rally driver in nat and int events) 1958–61, zone then regnl rising to nat sales mangr Volkswagen UK 1962–72, ind consltt to motor industry 1972–75, photography student Poly of Central London 1975–77, freelance advtg and editorial photographer 1977–; currently reiki master/teacher; reg contrib various magazines incl Country Life; music industry credits incl Kiri te Kanawa (Arabella), Jorge Bolet, Sophie Rolland, Christopher Hogwood, The Lindsay String and The Purcell Quartets; *Books* Alexander Technique in Pregnancy (photographic contrib, 1993); *Recreations* motor sport; *Style*— Julian Easten, Esq

EASTERLING, Prof Patricia Elizabeth; da of Edward Wilson Fairfax (d 1978), and Annie, *née* Smith (d 1989); *b* 11 March 1934; *Educ* Blackburn HS for Girls, Newnham Coll Cambridge (BA, MA); *m* 22 Dec 1956, (Henry) John Easterling, s of Rev Claude Easterling (d 1962); 1 s (Henry Thomas Fairfax b 1963); *Career* asst lectr Univ of Manchester 1957–58; Newnham Coll Cambridge: asst lectr 1958–60, fell and lectr 1960–87, vice-princ 1981–86, hon fell 1987–94 and 2001–, professorial fell 1994–2001; univ lectr Univ of Cambridge 1969–87, prof of Greek UCL 1987–94, regius prof of Greek Univ of Cambridge 1994–2001; pres Classical Assoc 1988–89, pres Hellenic Soc 1996–99; chm: Ctees of Jt Assoc of Classical Teachers, Cncl of Univ Classical Depts 1991–93; memb Academia Europaea 1995–; hon doctorate Univ of Athens 1996, hon fell UCL 1997, Hon DLitt Univ of Bristol 1999, Hon DLit Univ of London (Royal Holloway) 1999, Hon DPhil Univ of Uppsala 2000, hon doctorate Univ of Ioannina 2002; correspondant de l'institut Académie des Inscriptions et Belles-Lettres Institut de France 2004; FBA 1998; *Books* Ovidiana Graeca (with E J Kenney, 1965), Sophocles Trachiniae (ed, 1982), Cambridge History of Classical Literature I (jt ed with B M W Knox, 1985), Greek Religion and Society (jt ed with J V Muir, 1985), The Cambridge Companion to Greek Tragedy (ed, 1997), Greek Scripts: an illustrated introduction (jt ed with C M Handley, 2001), Greek and Roman Actors (jt ed with E M Hall, 2002); *Recreations* walking; *Style*— Prof P E Easterling, FBA; ✉ Newnham College, Cambridge CB3 9DF (tel 01223 335700, fax 01223 357898)

EASTERMAN, Nicholas Barrie; s of Cyril Saul Herman Easterman (d 2003), of Lausanne, Switzerland, and Sheila, *née* Cope (d 1983); *b* 11 April 1950; *Educ* Millfield, UCL (LLB), Cncl of Legal Educn; *Career* called to the Bar Lincoln's Inn 1975 (bencher 1998); acting stipendiary magistrate 1995–2001, dep district judge 2001–; immigration judge 2003–; *Recreations* photography, driving, good wine and cognac; *Clubs* RAC, Wig & Pen, Bentham; *Style*— Nicholas Easterman, Esq; ✉ c/o Lincoln's Inn (e-mail nick.easterman@londonweb.net)

E

EASTHAM, Kenneth; s of late James Eastham; b 11 August 1927; Educ Openshaw Tech Coll; m 1951, Doris, da of Albert Howarth; Career former planning engr GEC Trafford Park; cncllr Manchester City Cncl 1962–80 (sometime dep ldr, chm Educn Ctee), memb NW Econ Planning Cncl 1975–79; MP (Lab, AUEW sponsored) Manchester Blackley 1979–97, former memb Employment Select Ctee; Style— Kenneth Eastham, Esq

EASTMAN, Brian Ralph; s of Leonard Eastman (d 1969), of Ashtead, Surrey, and Edith, née Beakhust (d 1993); b 31 May 1940; Educ Glyn Sch Epsom, Kingston Coll of Art (DipArch); m 16 May 1964, (Dorothy) Mary, da of Arthur Randall (d 1973), of Ashtead, Surrey; 2 s (Andrew b 5 May 1965, Mark b 18 June 1966), 1 da (Ruth b 10 Aug 1972); Career Philip Goodhew Partnership chartered architects: assoc 1960–74, ptnr 1974–79, princ 1979–2004; princ Brian Eastman 2005–; conslt architect: Wandsworth BC 1963–91, City of Westminster 1987–94; dir 54 Warwick Square Ltd; co sec: 52–53 Warwick Square Ltd, Tokenspin Ltd, Warwick Square Co Ltd 1994–2005; chm Crawley Planning Gp 1975–78; churchwarden Ifield Team 1984–89, ldr Scout Assoc; RIBA 1965; Clubs Crawley, S of England Agric Society; Style— Brian Eastman, Esq; ✉ 182 Buckswood Drive, Crawley RH11 8PS (home tel 01293 529414, office tel 01293 541666)

EASTMOND, Dr Clifford John; s of Charles John Henry Eastmond (d 1980), and Hilda, née Horrocks; b 19 January 1945; Educ Audenshaw GS, Univ of Edinburgh Med Sch (BSc, MB ChB, MD); m 25 March 1967, Margaret, da of Stanley Wadsworth (d 1976); 2 s (Nigel b 1970, Timothy b 1972), 1 da (Heather b 1975); Career house physician Northern Gen Hosp Edinburgh 1969, house surgn Royal Infirmary Edinburgh 1970, sr house offr Sefton Gen Hosp Liverpool 1970, registrar Liverpool Hosps 1971–74, res fell Univ of Liverpool Med Sch 1974–76, sr registrar Rheumatism Res Unit Leeds Univ and Gen Infirmary 1976–79, conslt rheumatologist Grampian Health Bd 1979–95; Grampian Univ Hosps Tst (formerly Aberdeen Royal Hosps NHS Tst): conslt rheumatologist 1995–, clinical dir of med 1995–99, assoc med dir 1999–2007; clinical sr lectr Univ of Aberdeen 1979–2007, rheumatologist in private practice Albyn Hosp Aberdeen 1997–; memb Scottish Soc of Rheumatology; elder Skene Parish Church, memb and past pres Westhill and Dist Rotary Club 1989–90, memb Cairngorm Mountaineering Club, memb Br Soc of Rheumatology (memb Cncl 1987–90); FRCPEd 1984, FRCP 1990; Recreations Scottish mountaineering, skiing, game shooting, music; Clubs Royal Northern and Univ; Style— Dr Clifford Eastmond; ✉ The Rowans, Skene, Aberdeenshire AB32 6YP (tel 01224 790370); Albyn Hospital, Albyn Place, Aberdeen, AB10 1RW (tel 01224 595993)

EASTOE, Roger; Career working on women's magazines with D C Thomson 1968–70, IPC Women's Magazines 1970–74 (latterly advertisement mangr Young Magazine Section), mgmnt positions at Punch Publications working on Punch and High Life (British Airways in-flight magazine) 1974–76; Mirror Group Newspapers: joined as sales devpt exec 1976, advertisement dir 1982, bd dir 1984–2000, dep md 1990–2000; chm Nat Readership Survey Ctee 1998–, memb numerous indust ctees incl Audit Bureau of Circulations (former chm); Style— Roger Eastoe, Esq

EASTON, Antony Miles; s of Peter Easton, of Dorset, and Bobbie Easton (d 1987); b 3 October 1963; Educ St Paul's, Chelsea Sch of Art, St Martin's Sch of Art; m Anna Claire, da of Richard Curtis; Career freelance graphic designer and TV prog maker 1983–87, bd dir Saatchi & Saatchi Advertising 1989–92 (art dir 1987–89), head of art Chiat/Day 1992–93, commercials dir Pagan Films 2004; Recreations art, politics, media, sport; Style— Antony Easton, Esq

EASTON, Dr Carole; Educ PhD; Career child and family psychotherapist 1980–92, counselling mangr ChildLine 1992–96, head of clinical servs Place to Be 1996–98, exec dir Cruse Bereavement Care 1998–2001, chief exec ChildLine 2001–; Style— Dr Carole Easton

EASTON, Ewan Reid; s of Norman Kidston Easton (d 1987), of Dumgoyne, Stirlingshire, and Alison Gray Easton; b 10 May 1958; Educ Kelvinside Acad Glasgow, Sedbergh, Univ of Glasgow; Career Maclay Murray & Spens LLP: apprentice 1980–82, slr 1982–84, seconded to Herbert Smith Slrs London 1984–85, ptnr 1985–, head Commercial Litigation Dept 1992–2000, head of mediation 2001–, memb Partnership Bd; CORE accredited mediator 2001, CEDR mediator 2002; legal advsr to Edinburgh Int Festival 1990–, memb Bd Edinburgh Book Festival 2001–; memb Law Soc of Scotland Arbitration Ctee 1999–; Recreations architecture, building restoration, Scottish paintings; Style— Ewan Easton, Esq; ✉ Maclay Murray & Spens LLP, 3 Glenfinlas Street, Edinburgh EH3 6AQ (tel 0131 226 5196, fax 0131 226 3174, e-mail ewan.easton@mms.co.uk)

EASTON, Sir Robert William Simpson; kt (1990), CBE (1980); s of James Easton and Helen Agnes, née Simpson; Educ Royal Technical Coll Glasgow; m 1948, Jean, da of H K Fraser; 1 s, 1 da; Career md Yarrow Shipbuilders Ltd 1979–91; chm: Yarrow Shipbuilders Ltd 1979–94, Clyde Port Authority 1983–93, GEC Scotland Ltd 1989–99, GEC-Marconi Naval Systems Ltd 1991–94, Clydeport Pension Trust 1993–2002; conslt GEC-Marconi Ltd 1994–96; dir: Glasgow Development Agency 1990–94, Merchants House of Glasgow 1993–2003, West of Scotland Water Authority 1995–97, Caledonian MacBrayne 1997–2000; chllr Univ of Paisley 1993–2003; Liveryman Worshipful Co of Shipwrights; Recreations walking, golf, gardening; Clubs Caledonian; Style— Sir Robert Easton, CBE

EASTON, Timothy Nigel Dendy; s of late Dendy Bryan Easton, of Tadworth, Surrey, and Iris Joan Easton; b 26 August 1943; Educ Mowden Sch, Christ Coll Brecon, Kingston Coll of Art, Scholarship Heatherley Sch of Art London; m 5 April 1967, Christine Margaret, da of late Flt Lt James William Darling (d 1984); 2 da (Lucy Kathryn Rebecca b 1969, Isabella b 1971); Career artist/sculptor and lectr and writer on art and architecture; works incl: mural Church of the Good Shepherd Tadworth 1969–71, mural Theological Coll Salisbury 1967–73 (drawings for Salisbury mural exhibited Chicago and Kansas USA 1968); first London exhibition Young Artists Upper Grosvenor Gallery 1970, began exhibiting sculptures in bronze 1971; various exhibitions of paintings and sculptures since 1970 in: England, Germany, Luxembourg, America; Chris Beetles Gallery London 1990, Cadogan Gallery 1991, Museum of Garden History 1999; portraits incl: Dr Glyn Simon as Archbishop of Wales, Gen Sir Geoffrey Musson; cmmn for Surgeons of Queen Victoria Hosp East Grinstead 1989; tstee Early English Organ Project; Elizabeth Greenshields Meml Fndn Award Montreal Canada 1973; Winston Churchill Travelling fell 1996; Books Timothy Easton, Oil Painting Techniques (1997), Encyclopaedia of Vernacular Architecture of the World (contrib, 1997); Recreations vernacular architecture in Suffolk, Irish and Scottish country dancing; Style— Timothy Easton, Esq; ✉ Bedfield Hall, Bedfield, Woodbridge, Suffolk IP13 7JJ (tel and fax 01728 628380)

EASTWELL, Nicholas Wakefield (Nick); s of Thomas William Eastwell, and Zena Diane, née Wakefield; Educ Westcliff HS, Trinity Hall Cambridge (Cooper scholar, MA); Career slr; Linklaters: articled clerk 1980–82, Hong Kong office 1983–89, ptnr (capital markets) 1989–, managing ptnr Central and Eastern Europe 1999–2005, global head Capital Markets 2003–; memb Listing Advsy Ctee UK Law Assoc (UKLA) 2000–02; hon lawyer and founding memb Hong Kong Capital Markets Assoc 1986–89; regular conf speaker; author of articles in various legal jls; memb Trinity Hall Assoc (Year Rep 1975); memb Law Soc 1982; Recreations family, history and archaeology, watching rugby and soccer, skiing, walking, travel; Clubs Aula (Trinity Hall), Hawks' (Cambridge); Style— Nick Eastwell, Esq; ✉ 5 Dartmouth Grove, London SE10 8AR; Linklaters, One Silk Street, London EC2Y 8HQ (tel 020 7456 4660, fax 020 7456 2222, mobile 07768 345683, e-mail nick.eastwell@linklaters.com)

EASTWOOD, Prof David Stephen; s of Colin Eastwood, of Sandbach, Cheshire, and Elaine Clara, née Hunt; b 5 January 1959, Oldham, Lancs; Educ Sandbach Sch, St Peter's Coll Oxford (open scholar, coll prize, MA, coll grad award), Univ of Oxford (DPhil); m 26 July 1980, Jan, née Page; 2 da (Miriam b 20 April 1984, Lydia b 21 Oct 1987), 1 s (Jonathan b 1 March 1989); Career stipendiary lectr in modern history St Peter's Coll Oxford 1984–85, research fell Keble Coll Oxford 1986–87 (jr research fell 1983–86), Br Acad postdoctoral fell 1986–87, fell and tutor in modern history Pembroke Coll Oxford 1988–95 (dean of grads 1989–92, sr tutor 1992–95); Univ of Wales Swansea: prof of history 1995–2000, head Dept of History 1996–2000, dean Faculty of Arts and Social Studies 1997–99, pro-vice-chllr 1999–2000; chief exec AHRB 2000–02 (memb Postgrad History Panel 1999–2000), vice-chllr UEA 2002–06, chief exec HE Funding Cncl 2006–; visiting lectr: Cornell Univ, Univ of Virginia; delg Univ of Oxford Delegacy of Local Examinations 1991–95; chair and co-fndr Nat Centre for Public Policy 1998–2000; chair: Benchmarking Gp Quality Assurance Agency (QAA) 2003–06, Assoc of Univs of E of England 2003–06, 1994 Gp of Univs 2005–06; memb: Jt Funding Cncls Working Gp on Interdisciplinary Research 1998–99, History Benchmarking Gp 1998–99, Steering Gp for DfES Review of Research Funding in the Arts and Humanities 2001–02, Science and Engrg Base Co-ordinating Ctee Office of Science and Technol (OST) 2001–02, DCMS Creative Industries/HE Forum 2001–04, Research Libraries Support Gp 2002–03, Research Assessment Exercise Review Gp 2002–03, Cncl John Innes Centre Norwich 2002– (also dep chair Cncl), Governing Cncl Sainsbury Lab John Innes Centre Norwich 2002–06, DfES Working Gp on 14–19 Reform 2003–04, Bd HE Policy Inst 2003–, Bd QAA 2004–06, Bd HEFCE 2005– (memb Research Ctee 2003–), cmmr Marshall Aid Meml Cmmn 2003– (dep chair 2005–); literary dir Royal Historical Soc 1994–2000; chair Editorial Bd Studies in History 2000–04 (memb 1994–2000); regular broadcaster for radio and TV; govr Bishopston Comp Sch 1996–2000; hon fell: St Peter's Coll Oxford 2002, Keble Coll Oxford 2006; Hon DLitt: UWE 2002, UEA 2006; FRHistS 1991; Publications Governing Rural England: Tradition and Transformation in Local Government 1780–1840 (1994, shortlisted History Today Prize), Government and Community in the English Provinces 1700–1870 (1997), A Union of Multiple Identities: The British Isles c1750–c1850 (ed with L Brockliss, 1997), The Social and Political Writings of William Cobbett (ed with N Thompson, 16 vols 1998); also author of more than 30 scholarly articles and book chapters; Recreations music, collecting CDs and books, current affairs, watching sport, walking, wine; Clubs Athenaeum; Style— Prof David Eastwood; ✉ The Chief Executive's Office, Higher Education Funding Council for England, Northaven House, Coldharbour Lane, Bristol BS16 1QD (tel 0117 931 7317, fax 0117 931 7203)

EASTWOOD, (Anne) Mairi; da of John Waddington (d 1979), and Helen Cowan, née MacPherson; b 11 July 1951; Educ St Leonards Sch, Imperial Coll London (BSc); m 1, 10 Aug 1974 (m dis 1987), James William Eastwood, s of late Donald Smith Eastwood; 1 da (Joanna Elizabeth Irene b 1980), 1 s (Donald James b 1983); m 2, 7 July 2001, Richard Napier Findlater, s of late George Richard Park Findlater; Career Arthur Young: chartered accountant 1976, ptnr in charge computer servs consultancy 1985–87, recruitment ptnr 1985–87, nat staff ptnr 1988–89; chief exec Eastwood Consulting Ltd 1989–99, ptnr Whitehead Mann 2000–05, managing ptnr Praesta Partners LLP 2005–; non-exec dir Kaisen Ltd 1992–95; memb Central Tport Consultative Ctee 1992–95; dir Royal Exchange Theatre Manchester 2002–04, govr Dragon Sch Oxford; FCA 1981; Clubs Lansdowne; Style— Mrs Mairi Eastwood; ✉ Flexney's House, Stanton Harcourt, Oxfordshire OX29 5RP; Praesta Partners LLP, 83 Pall Mall, London SW1Y 5ES

EASTY, Prof David Leonello; s of Arthur Victor Easty, and Florence Margaret Easty; b 6 August 1933; Educ King's Sch Canterbury, Univ of Manchester (MD); m 14 Jan 1963, Božana, da of Milan Martinović (d 1968); 3 da (Valerie, Marina, Julia); Career Capt RAMC 1959–62; Moorfields Eye Hosp City Rd London 1966–72; currently emeritus prof of ophthalmology Univ of Bristol; pres Ophthalmic Section RSM 1998–2000; Doyne lectr 1999, Mooney lectr 1999, Richardson Cross lectr 1999, Bowman lectr 2000, Castroviejo lectr 2002; Lang Medal 1998, Nettleship Medal for Research; memb BMA, FRCS, FRCOphth; Books Virus Diseases of The Eye (1984), External Eye Disease (ed, 1985), Immediate Eye Care (1990), Current Ophthalmic Surgery (1990), Oxford Textbook of Ophthalmology (2000); Recreations squash, jogging, tennis, fishing; Clubs Army and Navy, Clifton; Style— Prof David Easty; ✉ Department of Ophthalmology, Bristol University, Bristol Eye Hospital, Lower Maudlin Street, Bristol BS1 2LX (tel 0117 928 4827)

EASUN, William John; s of Michael John Easun, of Surrey, and Mary Patricia, née McKinstry; b 19 April 1955; Educ Haileybury, Guildford Coll of Law, Aix en Provence Univ (scholar); m 28 Sept 1991, Irene Ann, da of Bryce Luke; Career articled clerk Dale & Newbery Middx 1974–78, admitted slr 1979, Aix en Provence Univ 1979–80, asst slr Frere Cholmeley Paris and Monaco 1980–83, ptnr Frere Cholmeley Monaco 1983–89, ptnr i/c Monaco office Frere Cholmeley Bischoff 1989–98, ptnr i/c Lawrence Graham (formerly Eversheds (Monaco)) 2003; memb: Law Soc, Int Tax Planners' Assoc, STEP, Inst Art and Law; Recreations wine and food, bringing up three young daughters, mowing; Clubs Automobile (Monaco), The Monte Carlo, IOD (Monaco (chm)); Style— William Easun, Esq; ✉ Lawrence Graham, Est-Ouest, 24 Boulevard Princesse Charlotte, MC 98000, Monaco (tel 00 377 93 10 55 10, fax 00 377 93 10 55 11, e-mail william.easun@lawgram.com)

EATOCK TAYLOR, Prof (William) Rodney; s of William Taylor (d 1994), of Hadley Wood, Herts, and Norah O'Brien, née Ridgeway (d 2000); b 10 January 1944; Educ Rugby, King's Coll Cambridge (BA, MA), Stanford Univ (MS, PhD); m 16 Jan 1971, Jacqueline Lorraine Cannon, da of Desmond Cannon Brookes (d 1981); 2 s (Thomas b 1973, Henry b 1976); Career engr; Ove Arup and Partners 1968–70; UCL 1970–89: assoc res asst 1970–72, lectr 1972–80, reader 1980–84, prof of ocean engrg 1984–89, dean of engrg 1988–89; Univ of Oxford: prof of mechanical engrg 1989–, fell St Hugh's Coll 1989–, head Dept of Engrg Science 1999–2004; Royal Acad of Engrg: memb Cncl 2003–, vice-pres 2004–; author of numerous articles in jls; govr Queenswood Sch 1990–2003; FRINA 1986 (MRINA 1979), FIMechE 1989, FREng 1990; Recreations music; Clubs Athenaeum; Style— Prof Rodney Eatock Taylor, FREng; ✉ University of Oxford, Department of Engineering Science, Parks Road, Oxford OX1 3PJ (tel 01865 273144, fax 01865 273010)

EATON, Adm Sir Kenneth John; GBE (1994), KCB (1990); b 12 August 1934; Educ Fitzwilliam House Cambridge (BA); m 1959, Sheena; 2 s (Andrew b 1963, Richard b 1964), 1 da (Caroline b 1969); Career RN: asst dir communications planning 1979–81, asst dir command systems 1981–83, dir torpedoes 1983–85, DG Underwater Weapons (Navy) 1985–87, Naval Base Cdr Portsmouth 1987–89, Controller of the Navy 1989–94; dir Kenneth Eaton Associates Ltd 1994–2002; chm: Guy's & St Thomas' Hosps 1995–99, National Remote Sensing Centre Ltd/Infoterra Ltd 1995–2001, UKAEA 1996–2002, Mary Rose Tst 2001–07; Hon DSc Aston Univ; FIEE 1981, FREng 1994; Recreations countryside, theatre, opera, classical music; Style— Adm Sir Kenneth Eaton, GBE, KCB, FREng; ✉ c/o The Mary Rose Trust, College Road, HM Naval Base, Portsmouth PO1 3LX (tel 023 9275 0521, e-mail keneaton@globalnet.co.uk)

EATS, Richard John Drake; s of Thomas John Drake Eats (d 1978), of Effingham, Surrey, and Alma, née Holdham; b 11 September 1945; Educ Dulwich Coll, Emmanuel Coll Cambridge (MA), Cranfield Sch of Mgmnt (MBA); m 1980, Hilary Martelli, da of Eric Vernon Dawson; 2 s (Thomas Martin Drake b 1981, Matthew James Drake b 1986); Career inspr of taxes Inland Revenue 1968–69, Save & Prosper Ltd 1969–71, Britannia Group 1971–74, mktg dir Chieftain Trust Managers 1976–84, md GT Unit Managers 1989–92 (mktg dir 1984–89), md Henderson Touche Remnant Unit Trust Managers 1993–96, mktg dir Threadneedle Investments 1996–2007, dir Mahina Consulting 2007–;

Recreations golf; *Clubs* Roehampton, Royal Wellington Golf; *Style—* Richard Eats, Esq; ✉ 2 Muncaster Road, London SW11 6NT (tel 020 7978 5575)

EATWELL, Baron (Life Peer UK 1992), of Stratton St Margaret in the County of Wiltshire; John Leonard Eatwell; s of Harold Jack Eatwell (d 1998), and Mary, *née* Tucker (d 1987); *b* 2 February 1945; *Educ* Headlands GS Swindon, Queens' Coll Cambridge (BA, MA), Harvard Univ (AM, PhD); *m* 1, 24 April 1970 (m dis), Hélène, da of Georges Seppain, of Marly-le-Roi, France; 2 s (Hon Nikolai b 1971, Hon Vladimir b 1973), 1 da (Hon Tatyana b 1978); m 2, 1 July 2006, Hon Mrs Susan Digby; *Career* teaching fell Harvard Univ 1968–69; Univ of Cambridge: research fell Queens' Coll 1969–70, fell and dir of studies in economics Trinity Coll 1970–96, univ lectr in economics 1977–2002 (asst lectr 1975–77), pres Queens' Coll 1997–, prof of fin policy 2002–; visiting prof of economics New School for Social Research NY 1980–96; econ advsr to Rt Hon Neil Kinnock MP 1985–92, princ oppn spokesman (treasy and econ affairs) House of Lords 1993–97; chm British Screen Finance Ltd 1997–2000, dir Anglia Television Group Ltd 1994–2001, advsr EM Warburg Pincus & Co International Ltd 1996–, non-exec dir Cambridge Econometrics Ltd 1996–2007, dir and ind Bd memb SFA 1997–2002; memb Regulatory Decisions Ctee FSA 1997–2001; dir: Royal Opera House 1998–2002, Cambridge Endowment for Research in Fin 2002–; chm: Commercial Radio Companies Assoc 2000–04, Br Library Bd 2001–06; non-exec dir Rontech Ltd 2003–; memb: Cambridge Constituency Lab Pty, Royal Econ Soc, American Econ Assoc; *Books* An Introduction to Modern Economics (with Joan Robinson, 1973), Keynes's Economics and the Theory of Value and Distribution (with Murray Milgate, 1982), Whatever Happened to Britain? (1982), The New Palgrave Dictionary of Economics (with Murray Milgate and Peter Newman, 1987), The New Palgrave Dictionary of Money and Finance (with Murray Milgate and Peter Newman, 1992), Transformation and Integration: Shaping the Future of Central and Eastern Europe (1995), Global Unemployment (1996), Not 'Just Another Accession': The Political Economy of EU Enlargement to the East (1997), Global Finance at Risk (with Lance Taylor, 2000), Hard Budgets, Soft States: Social Policy Choices in Central and Eastern Europe (2000), International Capital Markets (with L Taylor, 2002); *Recreations* watching ballet, modern dance and rugby union football; *Clubs* Harvard (NY); *Style—* The Rt Hon Lord Eatwell; ✉ Queens' College, Cambridge CB3 9ET (tel 01223 335556, e-mail president@queens.cam.ac.uk)

EAVES, Prof Laurence; CBE (2003); *b* 13 May 1948; *Educ* Rhondda County GS, CCC Oxford (fndn scholar, MA), St John's Coll Oxford (sr scholar, DPhil); *m* Dr Ffiona Gilmore Eaves; *Career* research lectr ChCh Oxford and research fell Clarendon Laboratory Oxford 1972–74, Miller fell Univ of Calif Berkeley 1974–75; Univ of Nottingham: lectr in physics 1976–84, reader 1984–86, prof of physics 1986–2000, Lancashire-Spencer prof of physics 2000–; visiting prof Univ of Tokyo 1995, visiting fell Univ of Wollongong 1982, Royal Soc Leverhulme sr research fell 1993–94, EPSRC sr fell 1994–99; memb Cncl Royal Soc 2002–04; memb HEFCE RAE Physics Sub-Panel 2004–; Guthrie medal and prize Inst of Physics 2001; FInstP 1996, FRS 1997; *Publications* author of research articles in scientific jls; *Style—* Prof Laurence Eaves, CBE, FRS; ✉ School of Physics and Astronomy, University of Nottingham, Nottingham NG7 2RD (e-mail laurence.eaves@nottingham.ac.uk)

EBBSFLEET, Bishop of 2000–; Rt Rev Andrew Burnham; s of David Burnham, and Edith Eileen Burnham; *Educ* The Minister Sch Southwell, New Coll Oxford (MA), Westminster Coll Oxford; *Career* schoolmaster and freelance musician 1972–84; asst curate: Clifton Team Ministry 1983–85, Beeston 1985–87; vicar of Carrington Nottingham 1987–94, vice-princ St Stephen's House Oxford 1995–2000, prov episcopal visitor Ebbsfleet 2000–; proctor in convocation 1990–2000, hon asst to Bishops of Bath and Wells, Exeter, Lichfield, and Oxford; memb: C of E Liturgical Cmmn 1996–2000, Anglican-Methodist Formal Conversations 1998–2000; Choir Trg Dip (CHM) 1973; chorus master: English Sinfonia 1973–84 (also dir English Sinfonia Chorale), Nottingham Harmonic Soc 1981– (princ conductor 1973–85); ARCO; *Publications* The Deacon at the Eucharist (1992), A Manual of Anglo-Catholic Devotion (2001), A Pocket Manual of Anglo-Catholic Devotion (2004); various articles and reviews; *Recreations* liturgy, plainsong and churchmusic, reading; *Style—* The Rt Rev the Bishop of Ebbsfleet; ✉ Bishop's House, Dry Sandford, Abingdon, Oxfordshire OX13 6JP (tel 01865 390746, fax 01865 390611, e-mail bishop.andrew@ebbsfleet.org.uk)

EBDON, Prof Leslie Colin (Les); s of Harold Arthur Reid Ebdon (d 1989), and Doris, *née* Hasler (d 1979); *Educ* Imperial Coll London (BSc, DIC, PhD); *m* 6 June 1970, Judith Margaret, da of Rev Dr Stanley Thomas; 3 s (Benjamin Thomas b 1973 d 1982, Daniel Mark b 1975, Matthew Samuel b 1978), 1 da (Hannah Joy b 1983); *Career* lectr in chemistry Makerere Univ Uganda 1971–73, lectr rising to sr lectr in analytical chemistry Sheffield City Poly 1973–80; Plymouth Poly (later Poly SW then Univ of Plymouth): reader rising to prof of analytical chemistry 1981–89, head Dept of Environmental Science 1989, VG prof of analytical chemistry 1989–2003, dep vice-chllr (academic) 1989–2003; vice-chllr and chief exec: Univ of Luton 2003–06, Univ of Bedfordshire 2006–; dir Univ of Luton Enterprises Ltd 2003–; chair: Masters Courses in Chemistry Review Panel EPSRC 1997, Mass Spectrometry Serv Review Gp EPSRC 1998; memb: Central Science Lab Review Gp 1995, Structure and Bonding Coll EPSRC 1995–2006, Certification Evaluation Panel European Cmmn 1997, Research Proposal Evaluation Panel European Cmmn 1998; RSC: chair Pubns Bd 1991–97, memb Cncl 1991–, chair Strategy and Resources Bd 2003–05; Universities UK: memb Strategy Gp on Leadership, Mgmnt and Governance 2003–06, chair Policy Ctee on Student Experience 2006–, memb Health Ctee 2003–; chair Assoc of Univs in the E of England 2006–; DTI: memb Prog Mgmnt Ctee DTI/SERC LINK Prog on Techniques of Analytical and Physical Measurement 1990–95, SQMAC (Measurement Advsy Ctee) Steering Gp and Working Pty 1990–2007, memb Measurement Advsy Ctee 1999–2007, chair Valid Analytical Measurement Working Gp 1999–2007; chair Editorial Bd Chemistry World, author of over 250 papers in refereed jls and over 260 conf presentations; Schools lectr Analytical Div RSC 1986, 13th SAC Silver Medal for Analytical Chemistry RSC, Benedetti-Pichler Meml Award American Microchemical Soc 1995; dir: Centre for Competitiveness Ltd 2003, Luton Dunstable Partnership 2004; tstee Nat Marine Aquarium 1998–; memb Beds and Luton LSC 2004–; *Recreations* vegetable gardening, Baptist lay preacher; *Style—* Prof Les Ebdon; ✉ University of Bedfordshire, Park Square, Luton, Bedfordshire LU1 3JU (tel 01582 734111, fax 01582 743400)

EBDON, Peter David; s of Michael George Ebdon, and Barbara, *née* Cheeseman; *b* 27 August 1970; *Educ* Highbury Grove Secdy Sch; *m* 18 July 1992, Deborah Karen, da of Garry Baldrey; *Career* professional snooker player 1991–; winner Skoda Grand Prix 1993, runner-up Dubai Duty Free 1994, winner Benson & Hedges Irish Masters 1995, winner Regal Masters 1996, runner-up UK Championship 1996, runner-up World Championship 1996, winner Thailand Open 1997, winner british Open 2001, winner Regal Scottish Masters 2001, winner World Championship 2002; England rep at jr and sr level, world under 21 jr champion 1990; world record holder for most century breaks (4) in a 9–frame match Euro Open 1992 (also jt world record holder with 3 successive century breaks in same match); WPBSA Young Playerof the Year 1991; *Recreations* swimming, golf, cricket, chess, reading; *Style—* Peter Ebdon, Esq

EBRAHIM, Sir (Mahomed) Currimbhoy; 4 Bt (UK 1910), of Bombay; s of Sir (Huseinali) Currimbhoy Ebrahim, 3 Bt (d 1952), and Alhaja Amina Khanum, *née* Jairazbhoy; *b* 24 June 1935; *m* 15 Nov 1958, Dur-e-Mariam, da of Minuchehir Ahmed Nurudin Ahmed Ghulam Ally Nana, of Karachi; 3 s (Zulfiqar Ali b 1960, Murtaza Ali b 1963, Raza Ali b 1964), 1 da (Durre Najaf (Mrs Ahmed Raza Khan) b 1969); *Heir* s, Zulfiqar Ebrahim; *Career* memb Standing Cncl of the Baronetage; *Style—* Sir Currimbhoy Ebrahim, Bt

EBRAHIM, Prof Shaheen Brian John (Shah); s of Donald William Ebrahim, and Marjorie Sybil, *née* Evans (d 1971); *b* 19 July 1952; *Educ* King Henry VIII GS Coventry, Univ of Nottingham Med Sch (BMedSci, BM BS, DM), LSHTM (MSc), Univ of London (DCH); *m* 1, 8 Dec 1984 (m dis 2002), Julia Lesley, *née* Shaw; m 2, 3 July 2004, Fiona Clair, *née* Taylor; *Career* Univ of Nottingham Med Sch: Wellcome Tst clinical epidemiology trg fellowship 1981–83, lectr in geriatric med Dept of Health Care of the Elderly 1983–85; Wellcome Tst lectr in epidemiology Dept of Social Med and Gen Practice St George's Hosp Med Sch London 1985–86, conslt physician and sr lectr Dept of Geriatric Med Royal Free Hosp Sch of Med London 1987–89, prof of geriatric med London Hosp Med Coll and Bart's Med Coll 1989–92, prof of clinical epidemiology Royal Free Hosp Sch of Med London 1992–98, prof of epidemiology of ageing Univ of Bristol 1998–2005, prof of public health London School of Hygiene and Tropical Medicine 2005–; MRCGP 1981, FRCP 1993, FFPHM 1993; *Books* Clinical Epidemiology of Stroke (1990), The Health of Older Women (ed with J George, 1992), Essentials of Health Care in Old Age (with G Bennett, 1992, 2 edn 1995), Epidemiology in Old Age (1996), Stroke: Epidemiology, Evidence and Practice (1999), Handbook of Health Research Methods (jt ed, 2005); also author of scientific papers on clinical epidemiology and geriatric med; *Recreations* Capt Beefhart, Velvet Underground, coarse fishing; *Clubs* RSM; *Style—* Prof Shah Ebrahim; ✉ Department of Epidemiology & Population Health, London School of Hygiene & Tropical Medicine, London WC1E 7HT (tel 020 7927 2215, e-mail shah.ebrahim@lshtm.ac.uk)

EBSWORTH, Prof Evelyn Algernon Valentine; CBE (1996); s of Brig Wilfred Algernon Ebsworth, CB, CBE, (d 1978) of Cambridge, and Cynthia, *née* Blech (d 1975); *b* 14 February 1933; *Educ* Marlborough, Univ of Cambridge (MA, PhD, ScD); *m* 1, 1955, Mary (d 1987), da of Frank Reyner Salter, OBE; 3 da (Nicolette b 1958, Rachel b 1960, Lucy b 1964), 1 s (Jonathan b 1962); m 2, 1990, Rose, *née* Stinson, wid of Prof J J Zuckerman; *Career* Univ of Cambridge: fell King's Coll 1957–59, fell Christ's Coll 1959–67, demonstrator 1959–64, lectr 1964–67, tutor Christ's Coll 1964–67; Crum Brown prof of chemistry Univ of Edinburgh 1967–90, vice-chllr and warden Univ of Durham 1990–98; chm Cncl for the Registration of Forensic Practitioners 1998–2005; chm of govrs The Leys and St Faith's Schs Cambridge 2002–; author of numerous papers published in learned jls; former memb Scot Examinations Bd, corresponding memb Acad of Sciences Göttingen; DCL (hc) Univ of Durham 2002; FRSC, FRSE 1969; *Books* Volatile Silicon Compounds (1963), Structural Methods in Inorganic Chemistry (jtly, 1987); *Recreations* opera, gardening; *Clubs* Athenaeum; *Style—* Prof E A V Ebsworth, CBE, FRSE; ✉ c/o Royal Society of Chemistry, Burlington House, Piccadilly House, London W1V 0BN (tel 020 7437 8656)

ECCLES, George William; s of George Dunluce Eccles (d 1951), and Eileen Margaret Smith, *née* O'Neale; *b* 26 December 1950; *Educ* Downside, LSE (LLB); *m* 1986, Eve, *née* Wooler; 1 s (Dunluce b 1988), 1 da (Tabitha b 1991); *Career* Coopers & Lybrand (formerly Deloitte Haskins & Sells): trainee accountant 1974–77, worked in tech dept 1978–80, audit mangr 1980–87, ptnr UK 1987–94, ptnr Russia 1995–97; md Deloitte & Touche CIS 1997–99, chief operating offr Central Asian-American Enterprise Fund 2002–04 (dep chief operating offr 2000–01); chm: Media Group 1982–94, Hambleton Mining plc 2004–; dir Amur Minerals Corp; memb: RTS, Ctee Media Soc 1993–94, Standards Ctee EC Club Moscow 1996, St George's Soc Moscow 1997–99, Br Isles Club Moscow 1997–99, St George's Soc Kazakhstan 2001; FCA (ICAEW); *Publications* Accounting for Research and Development (1978), EEC Fourth Directive: Company Accounts (1978), EEC Third Directive: Mergers (1979), EEC Sixth Directive: Prospectuses (1979), Unfair Dismissal (1979), The Seventh Directive: Group Accounts (1980), Employment Act 1980 (1980), Company's Act 1980 (1980), Company's Act 1981 (1982), Climate for Cable: Legislation, SMATV and Marketing (1983), Television in Focus: Broadcasting in Europe (1990), Investing in UK Television (1991); *Recreations* horse racing, opera, Russian icons, Central Asia, France; *Clubs* Groucho, Special Forces, IOD, Cwlth, Br Soc of Var; *Style—* George Eccles, Esq; ✉ 9 Les Bastides, Quatier La Beilesse, 83600 Les Adrets, France; 27 Old Gloucester Street, London WC1N 3XX (e-mail eccles@compuserve.com)

ECCLES, 2 Viscount (UK 1964); John Dawson Eccles; CBE (1985); s of 1 Viscount Eccles, CH, KCVO, PC (d 1999), and his 1 w Hon Sybil Frances Dawson (d 1977), da of 1 Viscount Dawson of Penn; *b* 20 April 1931; *Educ* Winchester, Magdalen Coll Oxford (BA); *m* 29 Jan 1955, Diana Catherine (Baroness Eccles of Moulton (Life Peer), *qv*), 2 da of late Raymond Wilson Sturge, of Ashmore, Wilts; 3 da (Hon Alice Belinda (Hon Mrs Ward) b 1958, Hon Catherine Sara (Hon Mrs Gannon) b 1963, Hon Emily Frances (Hon Mrs Irwin) b 1970), 1 s (Hon William David b 1960); *Heir* s, Hon William Eccles; *Career* Capt TA; Head Wrightson & Co Ltd 1955–77; dir: Glynwed International plc 1972–96, Investors in Industry plc 1974–88, Davy International plc 1977–81, Courtaulds Textiles plc 1992– (non-exec chm 1995–2000); chm Chamberlin & Hill plc 1982–; memb: Monopolies & Mergers Cmmn 1976–85 (dep chm 1981–85), Cwlth Devpt Corp 1982–85 (chief exec 1985–94); sits as Cons peer in House of Lords, elected hereditary peer 2005; chm: Bd of Tstees Royal Botanic Gdns Kew 1983–91, The Georgian Theatre Royal Richmond Yorks until 2000, The Bowes Mus Barnard Castle 2000–; Hon DSc Silsoe Coll Cranfield Inst of Technol 1989; *Recreations* gardening, theatre; *Clubs* Brooks's; *Style—* The Rt Hon Viscount Eccles, CBE; ✉ Moulton Hall, Richmond, North Yorkshire DL10 6QH (tel 01325 377227); No 5, 30 Smith Square, London SW1P 3HF (tel 020 7222 4040)

ECCLES, His Hon Judge (Hugh William) Patrick; QC (1990); s of Gp Capt Hugh Haslett Eccles, of Esher, and Mary, *née* Cunnane; *b* 25 April 1946; *Educ* Stonyhurst, Exeter Coll Oxford (scholar, MA), Middle Temple London (Winston Churchill Pupillage prize); *m* 15 April 1972, (Rhoda) Ann, da of Patrick Brendan Moroney; 3 da (Katherine b 15 July 1974, Clare b 18 Oct 1976, Fiona b 18 Oct 1980); *Career* called to the Bar Middle Temple 1968 (bencher 1998); head of chambers 2 Harcourt Bldgs Temple 1985–2000, recorder of the Crown Court 1987–2000, dep judge of the High Court 1997–, circuit judge (Midland & Oxford Circuit) 2000–; legal memb Restricted Patients Panel Mental Health Review Tbnl 2000–, memb County Court Rule Ctee 1987–91, asst Parly boundary cmmr 1993–2000; memb Hon Soc of the Middle Temple 1964; govr Sch of St Helen and St Katharine Abingdon 1991–; *Recreations* tennis, opera and P G Wodehouse; *Style—* His Hon Judge Eccles, QC; ✉ Coventry Combined Court Centre, 140 Much Park Street, Coventry CV1 2SN

ECCLES OF MOULTON, Baroness (Life Peer UK 1990), of Moulton in the County of North Yorkshire; Diana Catherine Eccles (Viscountess Eccles); DL (N Yorks); 2 da of late Raymond Wilson Sturge, of Ashmore, Wilts, and late Margaret Sturge; *b* 4 October 1933; *Educ* St James's Sch West Malvern, Open Univ (BA); *m* 29 Jan 1955, 2 Viscount Eccles, CBE, *qv*, er s of 1 Viscount Eccles, CH, KCVO, PC (d 1999); 3 da (Hon Alice Belinda (Hon Mrs Ward) b 1958, Hon Catherine Sara (Hon Mrs Gannon) b 1963, Hon Emily Frances (Hon Mrs Irwin) b 1970), 1 s (Hon William David b 1960); *Career* chm: Ealing Dist HA 1988–93, Ealing, Hammersmith & Hounslow HA 1993–2000; dir: Tyne Tees Television 1986–94, J Sainsbury plc 1986–95, Yorkshire Electricity Group plc 1990–97; ind dir Times Newspapers Holdings Ltd 1998–; memb: North Eastern Electricity Bd 1974–85, British Railways Eastern Bd 1986–92, Yorkshire Electricity Bd 1989–90, National & Provincial Building Society 1991–96, Advsy Cncl for Energy Conservation 1982–84, Widdicombe Enquiry into Local Govt 1985–86, Home Office Advsy Panel on Licences for Experimental Community Radio 1985–86, Cncl Br Heart Fndn 1989–98,

E

Unrelated Live Transplant Regulatory Authy 1990–99; vice-chm: NCVO 1981–87, Durham Univ Cncl 1985– (lay memb 1981–85); chm Tyne Tees Television Programme Consultative Cncl 1982–84; dir Opera North 1998–; tstee: Charities Aid Fndn 1982–89, The London Clinic 2003; Hon DCL 1995; *Style—* The Rt Hon Lady Eccles of Moulton, DL; ✉ Moulton Hall, Moulton, Richmond, North Yorkshire DL10 6QH; 5/30 Smith Square, London SW1P 3HF

ECCLESHARE, (Christopher) William; s of Colin Forster Eccleshare (d 1989), and Elizabeth, *née* Bennett; *b* 26 October 1955, London; *Educ* William Ellis Sch Highgate, Trinity Coll Cambridge (MA); *m* 1980, Carol Ann, da of Arnold W Seigel; 2 s (Thomas Christopher b 2 Jan 1984, Charles David (Charlie) b 10 Dec 1986), 1 da (Rose Judith b 9 May 1989); *Career* J Walter Thompson Company Ltd advtg agency: joined as graduate trainee 1978, assoc dir 1983, sr assoc dir 1985, main bd dir 1986, head of account mgmnt 1988, md London 1990–92, ceo PPGH/JWT Amsterdam 1992–95, dir of worldwide strategic planning 1995–96; chm and ceo Northern Europe Ammirati Puris Lintas Ltd 1997–99, ptnr and ldr mktg practice McKinsey & Co 1999–2002, EMEA chm and ceo Young & Rubicam 2002–05 (also chm and ceo Wunderman Europe 2003–05), EMEA chm and ceo BBDO 2006–; non-exec dir Hays plc 2004–; memb Cncl Univ Coll Sch 2002–; FIPA 1994; *Recreations* theatre, marathon running, photography; *Style—* William Eccleshare, Esq; ✉ BBDO EMEA, 151 Marylebone Road, London NW1 5QE

ECCLESTON, Prof William (Bill); s of Henry Eccleston (d 1996), and Bertha Eccleston (d 1997); *b* 3 March 1941; *Educ* Harris Coll Preston, Univ of London (BSc, MSc, PhD); *m* 12 April 1966, Catherine Yvonne, *née* Daley; 2 s (John b 25 Jan 1967, Daniel b 13 July 1969); *Career* sr princ sci Plessey Res Laboratories 1966–71; Univ of Liverpool: lectr 1971–81, sr lectr 1981–85, prof of electronics 1985–86, Robert Rankin prof of electronic engrg 1986–, head Dept of Electrical Engrg and Electronics 1986–91, dean of Faculty of Engrg 1992–95; by-fell Churchill Coll Cambridge 1996–; numerous pubns in learned jls; chm: SERC/DTI VLSI Technology Sub-Ctee 1992–95, SERC/DTI IT Advsy Bd 1992–95; chm: EPSRC Microelectronics Centre Steering Ctee 1996–2001, Int Electron Devices Meeting Washington 1999–01; co-ord EPSRC Carbon Based Electronics Consortium 2000–06, memb Bd EC Integrated Project Poly Apply 2004–; Freeman Borough of Preston; FIEE 1985, CEng 1985, FREng 1997; *Recreations* music, football, walking, cricket; *Clubs* Lancashire Cricket, Preston North End; *Style—* Prof Bill Eccleston, FREng; ✉ Department of Electrical Engineering & Electronics, University of Liverpool, Liverpool L69 3BX (tel 0151 794 4502, e-mail beccle@liverpool.ac.uk)

ECHENIQUE, Prof Marcial Hernan; s of Marcial Echenique (d 1995), of Santiago, Chile, and Rosa, *née* Talavera; *b* 23 February 1943; *Educ* Catholic Univ Santiago, Univ of Barcelona (DipArch, DArch), Univ of Cambridge (MA); *m* 23 Nov 1963, Maria Louisa, da of Ernesto Holzmann (d 1978), of Santiago, Chile; 2 s (Marcial Antonio b 16 July 1964, Martin Jose b 25 Nov 1965 d 1994), 1 da (Alejandra b 1 Aug 1969); *Career* asst lectr in urbanism Univ of Barcelona 1963–65; Univ of Cambridge: lectr in architecture 1970–80, fell Churchill Coll 1972–, reader in architecture and urban studies 1980–93, prof of land use and tport studies 1993–, head Dept of Architecture 2004–; chm Marcial Echenique & Partners Ltd (architectural and planning conslts) 1990–2001; memb Bd: Banco de Bilbao y Vizcaya Spain 1988–94, Autopista Vasco-Aragonesa Spain 1994–99, Tecnologica SA Spain 1994–95, Ferrovial-Agroman Constructora Spain 1995–2000, Dockways Ltd Jersey 1996–99; memb Civic Soc Huntingdon and Godmanchester 1979; MRTPI 1991, RIBA 1997; *Books* Urban Development Models (jtly, 1975), Modelos de la Estructura Espacial Urbana (1975), La Estructura Del Espacio Urbano (jtly, 1975), Cambridge Futures (jtly, 1999), Cities for the New Millennium (jtly, 2001); *Recreations* music; *Style—* Prof Marcial Echenique; ✉ Farm Hall, Godmanchester, Cambridgeshire; Department of Architecture, University of Cambridge, 1 Scroope Terrace, Cambridge CB2 1PX (tel 01223 332958, fax 01223 332960)

EDBROOKE, Dr David Louis; s of Edward John Edbrooke, of Skelton, York, and Doris Edbrooke (d 1984); *b* 29 November 1946; *Educ* St Peter's Sch York, Guy's Hosp Med Sch (MRCS, LRCP, FRCA 1976); *m* 22 March 1975, Judith Anne, da of Douglas Rex Whittaker (d 1956); 1 s (Nicholas Robert), 1 da (Claire Diane); *Career* conslt anaesthetist Rotherham Dist Gen Hosp 1979–82; Royal Hallamshire Hosp: dir Intensive Care Unit 1982–92, clinical dir of critical care 1990–, clinical dir Intensive Care Unit 1992–, sec Consultant Med Staff Ctee 1993–95, dep chm Theatre Users Sub-ctee of Med Staff Ctee 1983–85, chm Disposables Subctee of Med Staff Ctee 1983–85; chm: Intensive Care Nat Audit and Research Centre Working Pty on Critical Care Costing Methodology, Southern Sector Div of Anaesthesia; vice-chm Euro Intensive Care Working Pty on Costs, dir Mercs (Medical Economics and Research Centre Sheffield), clinical dir Directorate of Critical Care; memb: Trent Regnl Advsy Subctee of Anaesthesia, Trent Regnl Advsy Ctee on Performance Supplements for Assoc Specialists; approx 50 published papers; memb: BMA 1971, Intensive Care Soc 1982, Casualty Surgns Assoc 1984; *Books* Basic Concepts for Operating Room and Critical Care Personnel (with S J Mather and D L Edbrooke, 1982), Multiple Choice Questions for Operating Room and Critical Care Personnel (with S J Mather and D L Edbrooke, 1983), Prehospital Emergency Care (with S J Mather and D L Edbrooke, 1986); *Recreations* golf; *Clubs* Lindrick Golf Notts; *Style—* Dr David Edbrooke; ✉ Intensive Care Unit, Royal Hallamshire Hospital, Glossop Road, Sheffield S10 2JF (tel 0114 271 2405)

EDDINGTON, Sir Roderick Ian (Rod); kt (2005); s of Gilbert Eddington, and April Eddington; *b* 2 January 1950; *Educ* Christ Church GS Perth WA, Univ of WA (BEng, MEngSci), Lincoln Coll Oxford (DPhil); *m* 1994, Young Sook; 1 s (James), 1 da (Michelle); *Career* md Cathay Pacific Airways 1992–96 (dir 1988–96), dir Swire Pacific (HK) 1992–1996, exec chm Ansett Holdings 1997–2000, chief exec British Airways plc 2000–05, non-exec chm Aust and NZ JPMorgan 2006–; chm: EU/Hong Kong Business Corp Ctee 2002–06, Assoc of European Airlines 2003; memb Bd: John Swire & Sons Pty Ltd 1997–, News Corp 1999–, Qantas 2001–02, Rio Tinto 2005–, CLP Holdings 2006–; hon fell Lincoln Coll Oxford, hon fell Pembroke Coll Oxford (res lectr 1978–79); Hon LLD Univ of WA; FRAeS 1993, FILT 2000; *Recreations* cricket, Australian rules football, rugby, bridge; *Clubs* Vincent's (Oxford), Shek-O (Hong Kong), Hong Kong CC, Lord's Taverners, Melbourne (Australia); *Style—* Sir Rod Eddington

EDDLESTON, Prof Adrian Leonard William Francis; s of Rev William Eddleston (d 1995), of Devon, and Kathleen Brenda, *née* Jarman; *b* 2 February 1940; *Educ* Queen Elizabeth's GS Blackburn, St Peter's Coll Oxford (MA, BM BCh, DM), Guy's Hosp; *m* 10 Sept 1966, Hilary Kay, da of Kenneth Radford (ka 1942); 1 da (Carolyn b 1968), 3 s (Stephen b 1969, Andrew b 1972, Paul b 1974); *Career* conslt physician King's Coll Hosp 1976–2000; Faculty of Clinical Med King's Coll Sch of Med & Dentistry: prof of liver immunology 1982–2000, sub dean curriculum 1984–89, vice-dean 1987–92, dean 1992–97; dean King's Coll Sch of Med & Dentistry 1997–98, head Guy's King's Coll & St Thomas' Hosps Sch of Med (following merger with UMDS of Guy's & St Thomas' Hosps) 1998–2000; memb Camberwell HA 1986–93; non-exec dir King's Healthcare Tst Bd 1993–; sec Euro Assoc Study of Liver 1982–84, Euro rep Cncl Int Assoc for Study of Liver 1984–88; FRCP 1974, memb Assoc of Physicians of GB and Ireland 1974; Hon FKC 1997; *Books* Immunology of Liver Disease (1979), Interferons in the treatment of chronic virus infections of the liver (1990); *Recreations* electronics, computing, model aircraft, music; *Clubs* Athenaeum; *Style—* Prof Adrian Eddleston

EDE, Maurice Gordon; s of William Gordon Ede, of Ashburton, Devon, and Phyllis Maud; *b* 12 December 1946; *Educ* Weymouth GS; *m* 1969, Margaret Anne, da of Robert Lockhart; 1 s (Simon Maurice b 1973), 1 da (Catherine Jane b 1976); *Career* articled clerk Butterworth Jones & Co Weymouth Dorset, CA Coopers & Lybrand, ptnr Finn-Kelcey and Chapman 1976–92, sole practitioner and co sec Hearn Engineering 1992–, chief exec Assoc of Br Independent Accounting Firms (ABIAF), currently dir Network 4m Ltd; memb: Ctee S Eastern Soc of CAs 1980– (pres 1987–88), Cncl ICAEW 1988–; FICE 1969; *Recreations* amateur dramatics, dancing; *Style—* Maurice Ede, Esq; ✉ Suite One, Park Farm Barn, Brabourne, Kent TN25 6RG (tel 01303 812811, fax 01303 814707, e-mail maurice@network4m.com)

EDELL, Stephen Bristow; s of Ivan James Edell (d 1958), and Hilda Pamela Edell (d 1976); *b* 1 December 1932; *Educ* Uppingham, Univ of London (LLB); *m* 20 Sept 1958, Shirley, da of Leslie Ross Collins (d 1984); 1 da (Theresa b 1964), 2 s (Philip b 1969, Nicholas b 1973); *Career* Nat Serv RA 2 Lt 1951–53; admitted slr 1958; ptnr: Knapp-Fishers 1959–75, Crossman Block & Keith 1984–87; law cmmr 1975–83, Building Societies Ombudsman 1987–94, Personal Investment Authy Ombudsman 1994–97, Waterways Ombudsman 1997–2005; chm of govrs Hurstpierpoint Coll 1997–2002; *Books* Inside Information on The Family and The Law (1969), The Family's Guide To The Law (1974); *Recreations* family life, music, opera, theatre, golf, tennis; *Clubs* City Livery; *Style—* Stephen B Edell, Esq

EDELMAN, Colin Neil; QC (1995); s of Gerald Bertram Edelman (d 1955), and Lynn Queenie, *née* Tropp; *b* 2 March 1954; *Educ* Haberdashers' Aske's, Clare Coll Cambridge (MA); *m* 26 Oct 1978, Jacqueline Claire, da of Hardy Wolfgang Seidel, of London; 1 da (Rachel Laura b 17 Sept 1982), 1 s (James Simon b 14 Jan 1984); *Career* called to the Bar Middle Temple 1977 (bencher 2003); recorder 1996– (asst recorder 1993), head of chambers 2002–; *Recreations* supporting Luton Town FC, walking, badminton, skiing; *Style—* Colin Edelman, Esq, QC; ✉ Devereux Chambers, Devereux Court, London WC2R 3JH (tel 020 7353 7534)

EDELMAN, David Laurence; s of Gerald Edelman (d 1955), and Lynn, *née* Tropp, JP; *b* 7 April 1948; *Educ* Haberdashers' Aske's, Univ of Leeds (BCom); *m* 4 July 1971, Sandra Marice, da of Ephraim Freeman; 2 da (Emma b 1976 d 1979, Tanya b 1981), 1 s (Jonathan b 1984); *Career* tax ptnr Edelman & Co (CAs) 1976–81, dir City Trust Ltd (bankers) 1981–86, dir Moorfield Estates plc 1983–94 (jt md 1986–92), md Northcliffe Properties Ltd 1992–, dir Moorfields Developments Ltd 1994–; chm London Borough of Hillingdon Wishing Well Appeal for Great Ormond St Hosp 1987–89; FCA 1972, MCT 1991; *Recreations* skiing, art, music; *Style—* David Edelman, Esq; ✉ 34 Links Way, Northwood, Middlesex HA6 2XB; Moorfield Developments Ltd, 1 Bennetthorpe, Doncaster, South Yorkshire (tel 01302 320446, fax 01302 340125, mobile 07714 721014, e-mail enquiries@moordev.co.uk)

EDELMAN, Dr Jack; CBE (1987); *b* 8 May 1927; *Educ* Sir George Monoux GS, Imperial Coll London (BSc), Univ of Sheffield (PhD), Univ of London (DSc); *m* 15 Aug 1958, Joyce Dorothy; *Career* reader in enzymology Imperial Coll London 1956–64, prof of botany Univ of London 1964–73, visiting prof Univs of Nottingham and London 1975–83; dir Ranks Hovis McDougall plc 1982–88; chm: Marlow Foods 1987–90, Br Industrial Biological Res Assoc 1978–83, The Latymer Fndn 1990–2000 (govr 1983–2000), The Miller Woodland Tst 2001–; vice-pres Inst of Biology 1984–86, chm Nutrition Ctee and tstee Rank Prize Funds 1984–, chm MAFF/DTI Link programme 1988–, vice-pres Br Nutrition Fndn 1989–2000; memb Cncl: Queen Elizabeth Coll London 1979–85, Univ of Kent at Canterbury 1983–91 (memb Ct 1991–2002), King's Coll London 1985–95; memb of Governing Cncl Inst of Food Research 1997–2000; author of various text books and children's science books; fell Linnean Soc of London (1997); *Clubs* Athenaeum; *Style—* Dr Jack Edelman, CBE; ✉ 55 Black Lion Lane, London W6 9BG

EDELMAN, Keith Graeme; *b* 10 July 1950; *Educ* Haberdashers' Aske's, UMIST (BSc); *m* 29 June 1974, Susan Margaret; 2 s (Daniel b 3 April 1978, Nicholas b 1 July 1980); *Career* dir Ladbroke Group plc and chm Texas Homecare subsid 1986–91, md Carlton Communications plc 1991–93, group chief exec Storehouse plc (and subsid BhS Ltd) 1993–99, md Arsenal FC 2000–; chm Glenmorangie plc 2002–03 (formerly non-exec dir), non-exec chm Metrobet 2006–; non-exec dir: Eurotunnel until 2004, Qualceram Shires plc 2005–; *Recreations* skiing, tennis, collecting antiques, cooking; *Style—* Keith Edelman, Esq; ✉ Arsenal Football Club, Highbury Stadium, Highbury, London N5 1BU

EDELMANN, Anton; *b* 2 July 1952, Bubesheim, W Germany; *Educ* Volkschule; *m*; 3 da; *Career* apprentice chef Ulm Bundesbahn Hotel W Germany, commis saucier The Savoy London 1969–70, first commis saucier and gardemanger Hotel de la Paix Geneva 1970–71, chef de partie, chef gardemanger and chef de partie saucier Franziskauer Düsseldorf 1971–72; Mil Serv German Air Force 1972–74; chef saucier Bayrischer-Hof Munich 1974–75, successively chef de partie saucier, poissonier chaud, gardemanger then sr sous chef the Dorchester London 1975–79, premier sous chef and actg head chef Portman Intercontinental Hotel 1979–80, head chef Grosvenor House Hotel 1980–82 (oversaw opening of Ninety Park Lane), maître chef des cuisines and dir The Savoy London 1982–2003 (recipient AA Rosette and The Ackerman Guide's Black Clover Award), chef/patron Allium (Dolphin Square Hotel) 2003–; Caterer & Hotelkeeper Chef of the Year Award 1985 and 1991; Christmas Cook (LBC Radio) since 1985, subject of profile in series The Real McCoy (Thames TV) 1990, regular appearances on Masterchef (BBC TV) since 1991, participant in Hot Chefs (BBC TV) 1992, subject of BBC Radio 4's Desert Island Discs prog 1993; memb British Branch Académie Culinaire; *Books* The Savoy Food and Drink Book (1989), Canapes and Frivolities (1991), Creative Cuisine (1993), Fast Feasts (1995), Christmas Feast (1996), Perfect Pastries (1996), Music and Food for Romance (1999), Tea at the Savoy (2000); *Style—* Anton Edelmann, Esq; ✉ Allium, Dolphin Square Hotel, Chichester Street, London SW1V 3LX

EDELSHAIN, Martin Bernard; s of Norman Israel Edelshain (d 1996), and Monna Annette Carlish; *b* 18 December 1948; *Educ* Clifton, Jesus Coll Cambridge (BA); *m* 1984, Yasuko, da of Yukitane Okada (d 1988); 1 s (Benjamin b 1986), 1 da (Deborah b 1987); *Career* dir: S G Warburg & Co Ltd 1983–86, S G Warburg, Akroyd, Rowe & Pitman, Mullens Securities Ltd 1986–88, S G Warburg & Co Ltd 1988–95, Chugai Pharma Europe Ltd 1995–2003, Gen-Probe Inc 2003–; *Recreations* cricket, swimming; *Clubs* MCC, Oriental; *Style—* Martin B Edelshain, Esq; ✉ The Hollow, Slade Oak Lane, Denham, Buckinghamshire UB9 5DW (tel 01895 833599, e-mail mbedel@attglobal.net)

EDEN OF WINTON, Baron (Life Peer UK 1983), of Rushyford in the County of Durham; Rt Hon Sir John Benedict Eden; 9 Bt (E 1672), of West Auckland, Durham, and 7 Bt (GB 1776), of Maryland, America; PC (1972); s of Sir Timothy Calvert Eden, 8 and 6 Bt (d 1963), and Patricia Eden, *née* Prendergast (d 1990); *b* 15 September 1925; *Educ* Eton, St Paul's Sch USA; *m* 1, 1958 (m dis 1974), Belinda Jane, da of late Sir (Frederick) John Pascoe; 2 s, 2 da; m 2, 1977, Margaret Ann, da of late Robin Gordon, former w of 18 Earl of Perth, *qv*; *Heir* (to baronetcies only) s, Hon Robert Eden; *Career* served WWII, Lt RB, 2 Gurkha Rifles, Adj The Gilgit Scouts 1943–47; MP (Cons) Bournemouth W 1954–83; UK delg to Cncl of Europe and WEU 1960–62, memb NATO Parliamentarians' conf 1962–66, oppn front bench spokesman for Power 1968–70, min of state Miny of Technol 1970, min for industry 1970–72, min of post and telecommunications 1972–74; memb Trade and Industry Sub-Ctee Commons Expenditure Ctee 1974–76; chm: Select Ctee European Legislation 1976–79, Select Ctee Home Affrs 1979–83; pres: Ind Schs Assoc 1969–71, Wessex Area of Nat Union of Cons and Unionist Assocs 1974–77; hon life vice-pres Assoc of Cons Clubs; chm: Lady Eden's Schools Ltd until 2001, WonderWorld plc 1982–98, Gamlestaden plc 1987–92, The Bricom Group Ltd 1990–93, Bullers plc 1992–94; chm: Bd of Tstees Royal Armouries 1986–94, The British Lebanese Association Ltd 1989–98; vice-pres Int Tree Fndn until 1998; *Recreations* gardening, shooting; *Clubs* Boodle's, Pratt's; *Style*— The Rt Hon Lord Eden of Winton, PC; ✉ House of Lords, London SW1A 0PW

EDER, Prof Andrew Howard Eric; s of Hans Eder (d 1998), of London, and Helga, *née* Fall (d 2001); bro of Bernard Eder, QC, *qv*; *b* 21 April 1964; *Educ* St Paul's, King's Coll Sch of Med and Dentistry London, Eastman Dental Inst London (BDS, MSc, LDS RCS, MRD RCS RCPS, MFGDP, FDS RCS, FHEA); *m* 31 July 1988, Rosina Jayne, da of Seymour Saideman, and Shirley Saideman; 2 s (David Philip b 16 Dec 1990, Daniel Lewis b 12 Aug 1993), 1 da (Deborah Ann b 11 Dec 1996); *Career* specialist in restorative dentistry and prosthodontics Wimpole St 1991–, recognised teacher in conservative dentistry Univ of London 1993–, examiner in conservative dentistry Univ of London 1999–, dir of continuing professional devpt and visiting prof Eastman Dental Inst UCL 2002–, hon conslt in restorative dentistry Eastman Dental Hosp UCLH Tst 2002–; visiting prof Univ of Middlesex 2002–; clinical dir London Tooth Wear Centre; Alpha Omega: memb 1984–, memb Cncl 1988–, treas 1989–93, tstee 1989–, chm 1994–95, chm of tstees 2003–; Odontological Section RSM: memb 1991–, jr fell 1991, Pres's award 1992, memb Cncl 1992–, hon sec 1993–96, hon treas 1996–98, vice-pres 1998–2001, pres 2001–02; Br Soc for Restorative Dentistry: memb 1987–, memb Cncl 1994–, hon fell 1997, pres-elect 2004–05, pres 2005–; memb Cncl Br Prosthodontic Conf 1998–; memb Editorial Advsy Bd Euro Jl of Prosthodontics and Restorative Dentistry 1996–, memb Bd of Advsrs British Dental Jl 2005–; memb SAC in Restorative Dentistry 2000–05; clinical advsr to Private Dentistry 1997–; memb: BDA 1984–, Med Defence Union 1987–, Faculty of Gen Dental Practitioners 1992–; Hon MFGDP Faculty of Gen Dental Practitioners RCS, Hon FHEA, FDS (ad eundum) RCSEd; *Publications* Tooth Surface Loss Book Br Dental Jl (co-ed, 2000); published articles in academic jls; *Recreations* tennis, swimming, skiing; *Style*— Prof Andrew H Eder, MRD FDS; ✉ 57A Wimpole Street, London W1G 8YP (tel 020 7486 7180, fax 020 7486 7182, e-mail andreweder@restorative-dentistry.co.uk, website www.restorative-dentistry.co.uk); Eastman Continuing Professional Development, 123 Gray's Inn Road, London WC1X 8WD (tel 020 7905 1234, fax 020 7905 1267, e-mail aeder@eastman.ucl.ac.uk, website www.eastman.ucl.ac.uk/cpd)

EDER, (Henry) Bernard; QC (1990); s of Hans Eder (d 1998), and Helga Eder (d 2001); bro of Prof Andrew H Eder, MRD FDS, *qv*; *b* 16 October 1952; *Educ* Haberdashers' Aske's, Univ of Cambridge (BA); *Children* 4 s (Simon b 1979, Michael b 1981, James b 1983, Benjamin b 1991), 1 da (Hannah b 1988); *Career* called to the Bar Inner Temple 1975; visiting prof Faculty of Laws UCL 1999–2003; *Recreations* tennis, skiing; *Style*— Bernard Eder, Esq, QC; ✉ Essex Court Chambers, 24 Lincoln's Inn Fields, London WC2A 3EG (tel 020 7813 8000, fax 020 7813 8080, e-mail beder@essexcourt.net)

EDEY, Russell Philip; s of Lt-Col Anthony Russell Edey (d 1994), of Johannesburg, South Africa, and Barbara Stephanie Ann, *née* Rees-Jones; *b* 2 August 1942; *Educ* St Andrew's Coll Grahamstown; *m* 8 June 1968, Celia Ann Malcolm, da of James Bisdee Malcolm Green, FRCS, of Colchester, Essex; 2 s (Philip b 1971, Anthony b 1975), 1 da (Kate b 1973); *Career* chartered accountant; N M Rothschild & Sons Ltd: dir 1981–, an md and head of corp fin 1990–96, non-exec dep chm N M Rothschild Corporate Finance 1996–, chm Anglogold Ashanti Ltd 2002–; non-exec dir: English China Clays plc 1995–99, FKI plc 1996–2006, Wassall plc 1997–2000, Express Dairies plc 1998–2002, Old Mutual plc 2004–, Paris Orleans SA 2004–, Associated British Ports Holdings plc 2006; dir The New Shakespeare Company Ltd 1990–2004; *Recreations* tennis, theatre, current affairs, wine; *Clubs* City of London, Australian (Melbourne); *Style*— Russell Edey, Esq; ✉ Starling Leeze, Coggeshall, Essex CO6 1SL; N M Rothschild & Sons Ltd, New Court, St Swithins Lane, London EC4P 4DU

EDGAR, David Burman; *b* 26 February 1948; *Educ* Univ of Manchester (BA); *m* 1979, Eve Brook (d 1998); *Career* author and playwright; Univ of Birmingham: dir of playwriting studies 1989–99, hon sr res fell 1988–, hon prof 1992–, prof of playwriting studies 1995–99; hon assoc artist RSC 1989, hon fell Birmingham Poly 1991, Hon MA Univ of Bradford 1984, Hon DUniv of Surrey 1993, Hon DLitt Univ of Birmingham 2002; FRSL; *Plays* The National Interest 1971, Excuses Excuses (Coventry) 1972, Death, Story (Birmingham Rep) 1972, Baby Love 1973, The Dunkirk Spirit 1974, Dick Deterred (Bush) 1974, O Fair Jerusalem (Birmingham Rep) 1975, Saigon Rose (Edinburgh) 1976, Blood Sports (Bush) 1976, Destiny (Aldwych) 1976 (John Whiting Award 1976), Wreckers 1977, Our Own People 1977, The Jail Diary of Albie Sachs (adaptation, Warehouse Theatre) 1978, Mary Barnes (adaptation, Birmingham Rep then Royal Court) 1978–79, Teendreams (with Susan Todd) 1979, Nicholas Nickleby (adaptation, Aldwych then Plymouth Theatre NY) 1980–81 (Soc of West End Theatres Best Play Award 1980, Tony Best Play Award (NY) 1981), Maydays (Barbican) 1983, Entertaining Strangers (NT 1987) 1985, That Summer (Hampstead) 1987, Heartlanders (with Stephen Bill and Anne Devlin, Birmingham Rep) 1989, The Shape of the Table (NT) 1990, The Strange Case of Dr Jekyll and Mr Hyde (Barbican) 1991, Pentecost (RSC Other Place, then Young Vic) 1994 (Evening Standard Best Play Award 1995, Olivier nomination for Best Play 1996), Albert Speer (adaptation, NT) 2000, The Prisoner's Dilemma (RSC) 2001, Daughters of the Revolution and Mothers Against (Continental Divide, Oregon Shakespeare Festival and Berkeley Rep Co) 2003, Playing with Fire (NT) 2005; *TV and Radio* The Eagle Has Landed 1973, Sanctuary 1973, I Know What I Meant 1974, Ecclesiastes 1977, Vote For Them (with Neil Grant) 1989, A Movie Starring Me 1991, Buying A Landslide 1992, Citizen Locke 1994, Talking to Mars (play, BBC) 1996, The Secret Parts (BBC) 2000; *Film* Lady Jane 1986; *Books* Destiny (1976), Wreckers (1977), The Jail Diary of Albie Sachs (1978), Teendreams (1979), Mary Barnes (1979), Maydays (1983), Entertaining Strangers (1985), Plays One (1987), That Summer (1987), The Second Time as Farce (1988), Vote For Them (1989), Heartlanders (1989), Edgar Shorts (1990), Plays Two (1990), The Shape of the Table (1990), Plays Three (1991), The Strange Case of Dr Jekyll and Mr Hyde (1992), Pentecost (1995), State of Play (ed, 1999), Albert Speer (2000), The Prisoner's Dilemma (2001), Continental Divide (2004); *Style*— David Edgar, Esq

EDGAR, (Christopher) George; s of Drs William M and F E Edgar, of Baildon, W Yorks; *b* 21 April 1960; *Educ* Univ of Cambridge (MA), Open Univ (MA); *m* 1994, Elena Ryurikovna, *née* Nagornichnykh; 2 da (Anna Laura b 1994, Katerina Maria b 1998); *Career* HM Dip Serv; FCO 1981–92 (resigned 1992, reinstated 1995), ambass to Cambodia 1997–2000, ambass to Repub of Macedonia 2001–04, consul gen St Petersburg 2004–06, FCO envoy for climate security in Africa 2006–; *Recreations* music; *Style*— George Edgar, Esq; ✉ c/o Foreign & Commonwealth Office, King Charles Street, London SW1A 2AH

EDGAR, Michael Alan; s of Alan Edgar (d 1992), of Christchurch, Hants, and Mary, *née* Robey (d 2000); *b* 6 July 1937; *Educ* Kingston GS, Univ of Cambridge (MA), St Thomas's Hosp (MB BChir, MChir); *m* Hilary, da of Arthur (Plum) Warner (d 1995); 3 da (Alison Jane b 7 July 1964, Jocelyn Ann b 15 April 1967, Claire Penelope b 6 Dec 1971); *Career* ret sr conslt orthopaedic and spinal surgn The Middx and UCH, now emeritus reader in surgery UCL and fell UCH, dir Dept of Spinal Deformities Inst of Orthopaedics UCL 1980–88; hon conslt to Royal Nat Orthopaedic Hosp, Nat Hosp for Neurology and Neurosurgery and Nat Hosp for Sick Children Great Ormond St, civil conslt advsr in orthopaedics to RAF, conslt to King Edward VII Hosp for Offrs; dean Inst of Sports Med 1992–95; examiner (MCH Orth) Liverpool 1989–92, referee in spinal surgery to RCS 1993; memb Editorial Bd Jl of Bone & Joint Surgery 1982–86, memb Advsy Editorial Bd Spine; memb Cncl RCS 1995–; chm Int Affrs Ctee Scoliosis Research Soc of USA; memb: Clinical Servs Ctee Br Orthopaedic Assoc until 1993, Academic Cncl Inst of Sports Med, Awards Ctee NE Thames RHA, Intercollegiate Bd of Orthopaedic Surgery; Br Orthopaedic Assoc Euro travelling fell 1972, Gold Medal lectr Robert Jones & Agnes Hunt Orthopaedic Hosp Oswestry 1983; pres Br Scoliosis Soc 1994–95, sec Br Orthopaedic Assoc 1989–92; tstee and chm Br Scoliosis Research Fndn, tstee Scoliosis Assoc of the UK, tstee ARISE (Royal Nat Orthopaedic Hosp Scoliosis Research Tst), memb Scoliosis Research Soc, bd memb Scoliosis Research Soc of USA; fell Orthopaedic Section RSM, FRCS 1967, FBOA; *Publications* author of various papers and proceedings mainly concerning scoliosis and other spinal conditions; *Recreations* Africa Mission Link, sailing, walking, antique restoration; *Clubs* Leander, Royal Lymington Yacht; *Style*— Michael Edgar, Esq; ✉ Hornbeams, Thackhams Lane, Hartley Wintney, Hampshire RG27 8JB (tel 01252 845940, fax 01252 845941, e-mail mae.hornbeams@googlemail.com)

EDGAR, Pauline Claire; da of Peter George Brown, of Kempsey, Worcs, and Christine Daisy, *née* Denley; *b* 13 March 1956, Birmingham; *Educ* Dudley Girls' HS, Bedford Coll Univ of London (BA), Inst of Educn Univ of London (PGCE); *m* 14 Aug 1982, James Patrick Hamish Edgar; 2 s (James Peter Campbell b 4 March 1984, Hamish Andrew b 7 Oct 1986), 1 da (Jessie Ann b 7 June 1990); *Career* history teacher Copthall Sch 1981–87, head of history and politics, head of sixth form and teaching and learning co-ordinator Francis Holland Sch 1987–2006, princ Queenswood Sch 2006–; memb: GSA 2006, Assoc of Sch and Coll Ldrs 2006; *Recreations* singing, running, swimming, sailing, travel; *Style*— Mrs Pauline Edgar; ✉ Queenswood School, Shepherd's Way, Brookmans Park, Hatfield, Hertfordshire AL9 6NS (tel 01707 602500, fax 01707 602597, e-mail principal@queenswood.herts.sch.uk)

EDGAR-JONES, Philip; s of Edward Jones, of Prestbury, Cheshire, and Isabella Jones; *b* 13 July 1966, Leeds; *Educ* Royal HS Edinburgh, Queen Margaret Coll Edinburgh (BA); *m* 14 July 1990, Wendy, *née* Edgar; 1 da (Daisy b 24 May 1998); *Career* co-presenter Moviewatch, journalist Sky magazine; series prodr The Big Breakfast 1994–97, series ed The Jack Docherty Show 1997–99, exec prodr The Priory 1999–2001, head of factual entertainment Endemol UK 2001– (exec prodr Big Brother, The Salon and Shattered); Nat Television Award for Big Brother 3 2002, Indie Award for Big Brother 3 2002; *Style*— Philip Edgar-Jones, Esq; ✉ Endemol UK, Shepherds Building Central, Charecroft Way, Shepherds Bush, London W14 0EE (tel 020 8222 4196, mobile 07801 868264, e-mail philip.edgar-jones@endemoluk.com)

EDGE, The; David Evans; s of Garvin Evans, of Dublin, and Gwenda Evans; *b* 8 August 1961; *Educ* Mount Temple Sch; *Career* guitarist and fndr memb U2 1978– (with Bono, Adam Clayton, and Larry Mullen, Jr, *qqv*); first U2 release U23 (EP) 1979; *Albums* Boy 1980, October 1981, War 1983 (entered UK chart at no 1), Under A Blood Red Sky 1983 (live album), The Unforgettable Fire 1984 (entered UK charts at no 1), Wide Awake in America 1985, The Joshua Tree 1987 (entered UK charts at no 1, fastest selling album ever in UK, Album of the Year Grammy Awards 1987), The Joshua Tree Singles 1988, Rattle & Hum 1988 (entered UK charts at no 1), Achtung Baby 1991, Zooropa 1993 (no 1 in 18 countries, Best Alternative Album Grammy Awards 1993), Pop 1997 (no 1), The Best of 1980–1990 1998, All That You Can't Leave Behind 2000 (no 1, Best Rock Album Grammy Awards 2002), The Best of 1990–2000 2002, How To Dismantle An Atomic Bomb 2004 (Album of the Year and Best Rock Album Grammy Awards 2006); *Singles* incl: Fire 1981, New Year's Day (first UK Top Ten hit) 1983, Pride (In the Name of Love) 1984, Unforgettable Fire 1985, With or Without You 1987, I Still Haven't Found What I'm Looking For 1987, Where The Streets Have No Name 1987 (Best Video Grammy Awards 1989), Desire (first UK no 1 single) 1988 (Best Rock Performance Grammy Awards 1989), Angel of Harlem 1988, When Love Comes to Town 1989, All I Want Is You 1989, Night & Day (for AIDS benefit LP Red Hot & Blue) 1990, The Fly (UK no 1) 1991, Stay 1993, Discotheque (UK no 1) 1997, Staring at the Sun 1997, Sweetest Thing 1998, Beautiful Day (UK no 1) 2000 (Record of the Year, Song of the Year and Best Rock Performance by a Duo or Group with Vocal Grammy Awards 2001), Stuck in a Moment You Can't Get Out Of 2001 (Best Song by a Pop Duo or Group Grammy Awards 2002), Elevation 2001 (Best Rock Performance by a Duo or Group with Vocal Grammy Awards 2002), Walk On 2001 (Record of the Year Grammy Awards 2002), Electrical Storm 2002, Vertigo (UK no 1) 2004 (Best Rock Performance by a Duo or Group with Vocal, Best Rock Song and Best Short Form Music Video Grammy Awards 2005), Sometimes You Can't Make It On Your Own (UK no 1) 2005 (Song of the Year, Best Rock Duo or Group Vocal and Best Rock Song Grammy Awards 2006); *Film* Rattle & Hum 1988; *Tours* incl: UK, US, Belgium and Holland 1980, UK, US, Ireland and Europe 1981–83, Aust, NZ and Europe 1984, A Conspiracy of Hope (Amnesty International Tour) 1986, Joshua Tree tour 1987, Rattle & Hum tour 1988, Zoo TV tour (played to 5 million people) 1992–93, Popmart tour 1997–98, Elevation 2001 tour 2001, Vertigo tour 2005; also appeared at: Live Aid 1985 (Best Live Aid Performance Rolling Stone Readers' Poll 1986), Self Aid Dublin, Smile Jamaica (Dominion Theatre, in aid of hurricane disaster relief) 1988, New Year's Eve concert Dublin (broadcast live to Europe and USSR) 1989; performed at venues incl: Wembley Stadium, Madison Square Garden NY, Longest Day Festival Milton Keynes Bowl, Croke Park Dublin, Sun Devil Stadium AZ; *Awards* Best Band Rolling Stone Readers' Poll 1986 (also jt winner Critics' Poll), Band of the Year Rolling Stone Writers' Poll 1984, Best International Act BPI Awards 1989 and 1990, Best Live Act BPI Awards 1993, Best International Group Brit Awards 2001, Outstanding Contribution to the Music Industry Brit Awards 2001, Outstanding Song Collection Ivor Novello Awards 2003, Golden Globe Award (for Hands that Built America) 2003, Oscar nomination (for Hands that Built America) 2003; *Style*— The Edge; ✉ c/o Regine Moylett Publicity, 2C Woodstock Studios, Woodstock Grove, London W12 8LE (tel 020 8749 7999)

EDGE, Geoffrey; s of John Edge (d 1977), of Tividale, Warley, W Midlands, and Alice Edith, *née* Rimell (d 1986); *b* 26 May 1943; *Educ* Rowley Regis GS, LSE (BA), Univ of Birmingham; *Career* asst lectr in geography Univ of Leicester 1967–70, lectr in geography Open Univ 1970–74, res fell Birmingham Poly 1979–80, sr res fell Preston and NE London Polys 1980–84; chm W M Enterprise 1982–, New Initiatives co-ordinator Copec Housing Tst 1984–87, sr assoc PE International 1987–97, assoc dir W S Atkins 1997–1999; chm Planning Ctee Bletchley UDC 1972–74, vice-chm Planning Ctee Milton Keynes BC 1973–76, MP (Lab) Aldridge Brownhills 1974–79 (Parly private sec, Dept Educn Science and Privy Cncl Office), chm Econ Devpt Ctee W Midlands CC 1981–86, leader Walsall MBC 1988–90 (chm Policy and Resources Ctee) 1988–90; memb: Regnl Studies Assoc; FRGS; *Books* Regional Analysis & Development (jt ed, 1973); *Recreations* gardening, walking, travel, reading, listening to classical music; *Style*— Geoffrey Edge, Esq; ✉ W M Enterprise, Wellington House, 31/34 Waterloo Street, Birmingham B2 5JT (tel 0121 236 8855, fax 0121 233 3942, e-mail geoffe@wm-enterprise.co.uk)

EDGE, Prof Kevin Anthony; s of George Edge, of Bristol, and Marion, *née* Leonard (d 1993); *b* 1 July 1949, Bristol; *Educ* Kingswood GS Bristol, Univ of Bath (BSc, PhD, DSc); *Partner* Delyth Ann Davies, *née* Jones; *Career* sr control systems engr Rolls Royce Ltd 1972–76 (engrg apprentice 1967–71); Univ of Bath: research offr 1976, lectr 1976–87, sr lectr 1987–91, reader 1991, prof 1991–, dep dir Centre for Power Transmission and Motion Control 1993–, head Dept of Mechanical Engrg 1997–2003, pro-vice-chllr (Research) 2003–; Bramah Medal IMechE 1990 (and various awards for proceedings papers 1986, 1987, 1990 and 1998); FIMechE 1990, FREng 2003; *Publications* contrib to numerous pubns and jls; co-ed of 17 conf proceedings; *Recreations* classical music, photography; *Style*— Prof Kevin Edge; ✉ University of Bath, Claverton Down, Bath BA2 7AY (tel 01225 386963, fax 01225 386928, e-mail k.a.edge@bath.ac.uk)

E

EDGE, Stephen Martin; s of Harry Hurst Edge (d 2003), of Bolton, Lancs, and Mary, *née* Rigg; *b* 29 November 1950; *Educ* Canon Slade GS Bolton, Univ of Exeter (LLB); *m* 6 Sept 1975, Melanie, da of Eric Stanley Lawler (d 1995), of Hassocks, W Sussex; 2 da (Charlotte Louise b 1982, Katharine Imogen b 1987); *Career* admitted slr 1975; ptnr (specialising in corp tax) Slaughter and May 1973–; various contribs to pubns and articles on tax; *Clubs* MCC; *Style*— Stephen Edge, Esq; ✉ Slaughter and May, 1 Bunhill Row, London EC1Y 8YY (tel 020 7600 1200, fax 020 7090 5000)

EDINBURGH, Bishop of 2001–; Rt Rev Brian Arthur Smith; s of Arthur Smith (d 1992), of Edinburgh, and Doris Marion, *née* Henderson; *b* 15 August 1943; *Educ* George Heriot's Sch Edinburgh, Univ of Edinburgh (MA), Univ of Cambridge (MA, MLitt); *m* 1 Aug 1970, Elizabeth Berring, da of Lt-Col Charles Francis Hutchinson (d 1980), of Longframlington, Northumberland; 2 da (Tessa b 1974, Alice b 1978); *Career* ordained: deacon 1972, priest 1973; curate of Cuddesdon 1972–79, tutor in doctrine Cuddesdon Theol Coll Oxford 1972–75, dir of studies Ripon Coll Cuddesdon 1975–78 (sr tutor 1978–79), dir of ministerial trg Diocese of Wakefield 1979–87; priest i/c Cragg Vale 1978–86, warden of readers Diocese of Wakefield 1981–87, hon canon of Wakefield Cathedral 1981–87, archdeacon of Craven 1987–93, bishop suffragan of Tonbridge 1993–2001; vice-chm Northern Ordination Course 1986–93, chm Churches Together in Kent 1999–2001; *Recreations* reading, music, walking, browsing in junk shops, short-wave radio listening, snorkelling; *Style*— The Rt Rev the Bishop of Edinburgh; ✉ 3 Eglinton Crescent, Edinburgh EH12 5DH; Diocesan Centre, 21A Grosvenor Crescent, Edinburgh EH12 5EL (tel 0131 538 7044, fax 0131 538 7088, e-mail bishop@edinburgh.anglican.org)

EDINGTON, (George) Gordon; CBE (2007); s of George Adam Edington (d 1994), and Phyllis Mary, *née* Allen (d 1971); *b* 7 September 1945; *Educ* St Mary's Sch Kenya, St Lawrence Coll Kent; *m* 23 June 1973 (sep), Jane Mary, da of Jack Jesson Adie, CMG; 4 s (Daniel Jesson b 18 Jan 1975, Joel Adam b 7 Oct 1976, Sam Gordon b 31 July 1980, Jack Jesson b 1 June 1985); *Career* with Knight Frank & Rutley 1964–68, ptnr Anthony Lipton & Co 1968–72, dir Sterling Land Co Ltd 1972–73, dir Westwood Commercial Holdings Ltd 1973–75, conslt Amalgamated Investment and Property Co Ltd and Deloitte Haskins & Sells/Price Waterhouse 1975–76, jt md Summerbridge Investments Ltd 1976–81, md Lynton plc 1981–94; BAA plc: joined following takeover of Lynton plc 1988, gp property dir (main bd appt) 1991–99 (resigned), chm BAA International 1992–99, chm Airports UK Ltd 1991–92, Scottish Express International 1991–93, BAA Hotels Ltd 1991–92 and Skycare Cargo Ltd 1991–94, BAA Art Prog 1994–99, chm BAA Lynton plc 1994–99 (resigned); non-exec chm: Greycoat Estates Ltd 1999–, Earls Court and Olympia Gp Ltd 2000–01 (resigned); non-exec dir Lend Lease Corp 1999–; past pres Br Property Fedn; chm: Michael Stuckey Tst (supporting young musicians) 1988–98, Public Art Devpt Tst 1992–98, Land and City Families Tst 1994–98; dir Snowshill Securities Ltd; dir Garden Park Investments Ltd; memb: Bd of Govrs The Wilson Centre Fitzwilliam Coll Cambridge 1993–98, Lord Mayor of London's 1997/98 Charity Appeal Steering Ctee; chair of tstees NCH (Nat Childrens Home) 2001–, tstee Tennis First Charitable Tst; Liveryman Worshipful Co of Chartered Surveyors; FRICS 1970, FRSA 1992; *Books* The Clowes Family of Chester Sporting Artists (Grosvenor Museum Chester, 1985), Property Management: A Customer Focused Approach (1997); *Recreations* tennis, fly fishing, golf, family, photography, historic Thames rivercraft, hill walking; *Clubs* Riverside Racquet, Royal Wimbledon Golf, Flyfishers', Henley Royal Regatta; *Style*— Gordon Edington, Esq, CBE

EDINGTON, Paul Tellet; s of Dr Francis Cameron Edington, of Penrith, and Anella Jean, *née* Munro; *b* 24 April 1943; *Educ* Sedbergh, Selwyn Coll Cambridge (MA, MB BCh), St Mary's Hosp Med Sch London; *m* 3 March 1973, Jane Margaret, da of Dr Geoffrey Howard Bulow, of Wellington Heath; 2 s (James b 1976, David b 1978), 1 da (Katherine b 1982); *Career* registrar St Mary's Hosp London 1973–76, exchange registrar Univ of Cape Town 1975–76; sr registrar in rotation Newcastle upon Tyne: Newcastle Gen Hosp, Royal Victoria Hosp, Princess Mary Maternity Hosp, Queen Elizabeth Hosp Gateshead; conslt obstetrician and gynaecologist Univ Hosp Nottingham 1981–2007, ret; LRCP, MRCS, FRCOG 1990 (MRCOG 1974); *Recreations* golf, cricket, gardening, skiing, music; *Clubs* Hawks' (Cambridge), Gynaecological; *Style*— Paul Edington, Esq; ✉ Baildon House, Baildon Close, Wollaton Park, Nottingham NG8 1BS (tel 0115 978 6187, e-mail ptedington@yahoo.co.uk); University Hospital, Queen's Medical Centre, Nottingham NG7 2UH (tel 0115 924 9924 ext 44196); Consulting Rooms, Nottingham Nuffield Hospital (tel 0115 920 9209)

EDIS, Andrew Jeremy Coulter; QC (1997); s of late Dr Peter Edis, of Liverpool, and late Barbara, *née* Creer; *b* 9 June 1957; *Educ* Liverpool Coll, UC Oxford (MA); *m* 16 Dec 1984, Sandy, da of Albert Wilkinson; 3 c (Sam b 6 July 1987, Philippa b 19 Oct 1989, Eleanor b 3 July 1996); *Career* called to the Bar Middle Temple 1980; jr of Northern Circuit 1983–84, hon sec Northern Circuit 1994–97, recorder of the Crown Court 1999 (asst recorder 1994), dep High Ct judge 2001–, head of chambers 2000–; memb Bar Cncl 1989–91; *Recreations* cricket, food and wine, history; *Clubs* Oxford and Cambridge, Liverpool Bar Cricket; *Style*— Andrew Edis, Esq, QC; ✉ Atlantic Chambers, 4–6 Cook Street, Liverpool L2 9QU (tel 0151 236 4421, fax 0151 236 1559, e-mail andrewedis@atlanticchambers.co.uk)

EDKINS, George Joseph (John); s of George Henry John Edkins (d 1981), and Olympia, *née* Izzillo (d 1971); *b* 18 June 1930; *Educ* Mitcham GS, Oxted GS; *m* 17 July 1954, Audrey Joan, da of Arthur James Paul; 2 s (Paul Anthony b 1 Aug 1956 (decd), Peter David b 19 Sept 1962), 1 da (Sara-Jane b 15 June 1965 (decd)); *Career* Served RAF Naval Fighter Intelligence 1948–50; Shell Int Petroleum 1950–55; chartered accountant: Frazer Whiting 1955–60, Pike Russell & Co 1960–70; sr ptnr: Russell Limebeer 1978–88, Fraser & Russell 1988–90 (ret 1990); Cystic Fibrosis Tst: vice-chm 1989–91, chief exec 1991–96; treas Int Cystic Fibrosis Assoc 1992–98, memb Cncl Assoc of Med Res Charities 1992–96; chm Inst of Meat 1999–2004; Liveryman Worshipful Co of Butchers (Master 2005); FCA 1965, FInstM; *Recreations* charity, rugby, all sports; *Clubs* RAC, City of London, Marylebone Cricket; *Style*— John Edkins, Esq; ✉ Birchwood Cottage, Mizen Way, Cobham, Surrey KT11 2RG (tel 01932 863017, e-mail john.edkins1@btopenworld.com)

EDLMANN, Stephen Raphael Reynolds; s of Capt Raphael Francis Reynolds Edlmann (d 1975), and Waltraud Helga Mathilde Edlmann (d 1984); *b* 13 March 1954; *Educ* Tonbridge, Trinity Hall Cambridge (MA); *m* 14 July 1979, Deborah Catherine, da of Roger John Nimmo Booth, of Co Durham; 5 s (Richard b 1980, Oliver b 1981, Nicholas b and d 1981, Lawrence b 1983, Joss b 1991); *Career* Linklaters: joined 1977, ptnr 1985–, head Int Finance Dept 1995–2000, memb Exec Ctee and Int Bd Linklaters & Alliance 1998–2001; govr Sherborne Sch; memb Worshipful Co of Slrs 1985; memb: Law Soc 1979, Int Bar Assoc 1986; *Recreations* entertaining, travelling, golf; *Clubs* Hawks' (Cambridge), MCC, Sherborne Golf, Harlequins; *Style*— Stephen Edlmann, Esq; ✉ Linklaters, One Silk Street, London EC2Y 8HQ (tel 020 7456 2000, fax 020 7456 2222)

EDMANS, Laurence Michael (Laurie); CBE (2006); s of Edmund Lionel Edmans, of Maidstone, Kent, and May Florence, *née* Paul; *b* 20 February 1948, London; *Educ* Chistlehurst and Sidcup GS, William Penn Comp Sch London, East London Coll of Commerce (Cert); *m* 6 Nov 1971, Linda Rose, *née* Spencer; 5 c (Jacqueline b 1965, Kirstie b 1974, Alexandra b 1976, Timothy b 1981, Robin b 1984); *Career* gen mangr employee benefits Crusader Insurance/CIGNA Corp 1964–89, mktg dir then dep chief exec National Provident Inst 1989–2000, dir of corp devpt AEGON UK plc 2000–06; dep chm: CPA Hldgs Ltd, bDifferent Ltd; memb Bd The Pensions Regulator, former chm Pensions and Savings Ctee ABI, chm Safe Home Income Plans, treas Family and Parenting Inst, govr and cncl memb Pensions Policy Inst, tstee CII Staff Pension Scheme, tstee Quest Sch for Autistic Children; FCII 1982, FPMI 1990; *Recreations* opera, ballet, golf, soccer (West Ham United season ticket holder); *Clubs* RAC; *Style*— Laurie Edmans, Esq, CBE; ✉ Allens Oast, Old Road, East Peckham, Kent TN12 5ER (tel 01622 871603, e-mail laurie_edmans@hotmail.com)

EDMISTON, Robert Norman; s of Vivian Randolph Edmiston, and Norma Margaret Edmiston; *b* 6 October 1946; *Educ* Abbs Cross Tech Sch, Barking Regnl Coll of Technol; *m* 1; 1 s (Andrew b 1969), 2 da (Deborah b 1971, Angela b 1975); m 2, 1998, Tracie Jacqueline, da of Donald Spicer; *Career* fin analyst Ford Motor Co, capital planning mangr Chrysler (mangr fin analysis), fin dir Jensen Motor Co, chm IM Group Ltd; *Recreations* Christian activities, swimming, windsurfing, flying, shooting, skiing; *Style*— Robert Edmiston, Esq; ✉ IM Group Ltd, IM House, South Drive, Coleshill B46 1DF

EDMONDS, David Albert; CBE (2003); s of Albert Edmonds, of Kingsley, Cheshire, and Gladys Edmonds; *b* 6 March 1944; *Educ* Helsby GS, Keele Univ (BA); *m* 1966, Ruth, da of Eric Beech, of Christleton, Chester; 2 s (Jonathan, Benedict), 2 da (Jane, Elizabeth); *Career* asst princ Miny of Housing and Local Govt 1966–69 (private sec/Parly sec 1969–71), princ DOE 1971–73, observer Civil Serv Selection Bd 1973–74, visiting fell Johns Hopkins Univ Baltimore 1974–75; DOE: private sec/permanent sec 1975–77, asst sec 1977–79, private sec to sec of state 1979–83, under-sec Inner Cities Directorate 1983–84; chief exec The Housing Corp 1984–91, dep chm New Statesman and Society 1988–90; pres Int New Towns Assoc 1988–91, dir The Housing Fin Corp 1988–91, md Group Central Servs NatWest Group 1991–98, DG Oftel 1998–2003 (memb Bd Ofcom 2002–05); chm NHS Direct Special HA 2004–, chm NHS Shared Business Services Ltd 2005–, chm designate NHS Direct NHS Tst 2006–; memb Bd: Hammerson plc 2003–, Wincanton 2005–, William Hill plc 2005–; memb Bd and chm Property Planning and Project Ctee English Partnerships 2000–01; tstee CRISIS 1994– (chm of tstees 1996–), memb Cncl Keele Univ 1996–2004 (treas 1997–2004); *Recreations* opera, golf, walking, films; *Clubs* Wimbledon Park Golf (captain 1997–98), Wimbledon Wanderers CC, Savile; *Style*— David Edmonds, Esq, CBE

EDMONDS, John Walter; s of Walter Edgar Edmonds (d 1986), and Maude Rose, *née* Edwards; *b* 28 January 1944; *Educ* Christ's Hosp, Oriel Coll Oxford (MA); *m* 30 Sept 1967, (Janet) Linden, da of Franklin Arthur Callaby (d 1978); 2 da (Lucinda Jane b 1969, Nanette Sally b 1972); *Career* GMB (formerly GMWU): res asst 1965–67, dep res offr 1967–68, regnl organiser 1968–72, nat offr 1972–85, gen sec 1986–2003; pres TUC 1997–98; visiting fell Nuffield Coll Oxford 1986–94; sr research fell KCL 2003–; formerly: dir Nat Building Agency, memb Royal Cmmn on Environmental Pollution; govr: LSE, Nat Inst of Economic and Social Research 1999–; pres Unity Bank 2000–03, memb Nat Economic Devpt Cncl 1986–92; chair Inland Waterways Advsy Cncl (IWAC) 2006–; non-exec dir: Carbon Tst 2001–, Environment Agency 2002–, Salix Finance 2003–; tstee: Inst of Public Policy Res 1990–2000, NSPCC 1997–2001; memb: Cncl ACAS 1990–2001, Cncl Consumers' Assoc 1993–96, Gen Cncl TUC, Forestry Cmmn 1995–2001; Hon LLD Univ of Sussex 1993; FRSA 1989–91; *Recreations* cricket, carpentry; *Clubs* Wibbandune CC, Thorpe CC; *Style*— Mr John Edmonds; ✉ 50 Graham Road, Mitcham, Surrey CR4 2HA; GMB, 22–24 Worple Road, London SW19 4DD (tel 020 8648 9991, e-mail johnedmonds1@hotmail.com)

EDMONDS, (Douglas) Keith; s of (Maxwell) John Edmonds, of Duffield, Derbys, and Margaret Agnes, *née* Morrison (d 1977); *b* 23 July 1949; *Educ* Ecclesbourne Sch, Univ of Sheffield Med Sch (MB ChB, capt Rugby Club); *m* 13 Oct 1990, Gillian Linda, da of Cyril Rose; 3 s (Alastair b 1991, Nicholas b 1992, Timothy b 1995); *Career* lectr Dept of Anatomy Univ of Sheffield 1975, SHO (obstetrics and gynaecology) Jessop Hosp for Women Sheffield 1975–77, registrar in obstetrics and gynaecology Southampton Hosp 1977–78; sr registrar in obstetrics and gynaecology: Queen Elizabeth Hosp Aust 1979–80, Southampton and Winchester Hosps 1980–82; conslt obstetrician and gynaecologist to Queen Charlotte and Chelsea Hosp and dir Nat Centre for Surgery of Congenital Malformations of Genital Tract 1982–, dir Inst of Obstetrics and Gynaecology Imperial Coll Sch of Med 2005–; author of many scientific pubns; pres Nat Endometriosis Soc 2000–04; memb: Blair-Bell Research Soc, Ovarian Club, Br Fertility Soc (and American), World Cncl of Paediatric and Adolescent Gynaecology; FRSM, FRANZCOG (Aust) 1982 (MRACOG 1979), FRCOG 1990 (MRCOG 1979); *Books* Practical Paediatric and Adolescent Gynaecology (1989), Textbook of Post-graduate Obstetrics and Gynaecology (1999); *Recreations* tennis, golf, rugby; *Clubs* Gynaecological Club of GB, Roehampton; *Style*— Keith Edmonds, Esq; ✉ Queen Charlotte's and Chelsea Hospital, DuCane Road, London W12 0HS (tel 020 8383 3586)

EDMONDSON, Prof Hugh Dunstan Christopher; s of Dr Dunstan Hugh Edmondson (d 1990), and Audrey Mary, *née* Burdon (d 1989); *b* 13 April 1936; *Educ* Stonyhurst, Univ of Birmingham (DDS, BDS, DA, MB ChB); *m* 13 May 1961, Eileen Margaret, da of William Burley; 2 da (Rowena Mary b 1962, Caroline Audrey b 1963), 1 s (Christopher Hugh b 1964); *Career* prof of oral surgery and oral med and head of dept Univ of Birmingham 1983–97 (lectr 1971–75, sr lectr 1975–83, emeritus prof 1997); conslt maxillofacial surgeon 1975–2003, service lead maxillofacial surgery 1997–2003; chm Dental Formulary Sub-Ctee 1987–2006; former memb: Medicines Control Agency, Ctee on Safety of Medicines Advsy Panel, Advsy Cncl on the Misuse of Drugs, Ctee on Dental and Surgical Materials, Advsy Ctee on NHS Drugs, Formulary Ctee BDA; chm Worcs branch Game Conservancy Tst; fell BAOMS, MRCS, LRCP, LDS RCS, FDS RCS; *Books* A Radiological Atlas of Diseases of the Teeth and Jaws (with R M Browne and P G J Rout, 1983), Atlas of Dental and Maxillofacial Radiology and Imaging (with R M Browne and P G J Rout, 1995); *Recreations* country pursuits, woodland management, gardening; *Style*— Prof Hugh Edmondson; ✉ Huddington Court, Huddington, Droitwich, Worcestershire WR9 7LJ (tel 01905 391247, fax 01905 391447, e-mail hugh@edmondson8239.freeserve.co.uk)

EDMONDSON, Mark Andrew; s of Lambert Edmondson (d 1967), of Carlisle and Derby, and (Ethel) Lally, *née* Atkins (d 2002); *b* 2 February 1963, Derby; *Educ* Noel Baker GS Derby, Nottingham Trent Univ (LLB), Anglia Ruskin Univ (LLM); *m* 15 June 1991, Judy, *née* Cooke; 2 da (Olivia Alyss b 11 Nov 1991, Francesca Elizabeth Grace b 4 March 1996); *Career* Smith Partnership Slrs until 1994, ptnr and co-fndr Edmondson Hall Slrs 1994–; lectr in sports law and equine law; author of various articles in Int Sports Law Jl; memb: Law Soc, Assoc Personal Injury Lawyers; *Recreations* football, horse racing and breeding, skiing, walking, gardening; *Clubs* Newmarket Golf, Bedford Lodge Leisure; *Style*— Mark Edmondson, Esq; ✉ Edmondson Hall Solicitors, 25 Exeter Road, Newmarket, Suffolk CB8 8AR

EDMONDSON, Dr Philip Charles; s of Dr Reginald Edmondson (d 1964), of Dunchurch, Rugby, and Phyllis Mary, *née* Elam (d 1996); *b* 30 April 1938; *Educ* Uppingham, Christ's Coll Cambridge (MA, MD, MB BChir), St Bartholomew's Hosp London; *m* 7 Sept 1968, Margaret Lysbeth, da of Stanley Bayston, of Saxton, N Yorks; 3 da (Camilla b 25 April 1970, Claire b 12 May 1972, Cordelia b 5 Jan 1980); *Career* physician to: Westminster Abbey 1979, KLM (Royal Dutch Airlines) London, Australian High Cmmn London; conslt physician to many major industrial cos; visiting med offr King Edward VII Hosp for Offrs London; Freeman City of London, Liveryman Worshipful Soc of Apothecaries; fell Med Soc of London, MRCP; *Recreations* fishing, country pursuits; *Clubs* Boodle's; *Style*— Dr Philip Edmondson; ✉ The Corderries, Abnash, Chalford Hill, Stroud, Gloucestershire GL6 8QL (tel 01453 883176)

EDMONDSON, Dr Robert Somerville; s of William Edmondson (d 1974), and Eileen Edmondson (d 1971); *b* 11 August 1937; *Educ* Bradford GS, St Bartholomew's Hosp Univ of London (MB BS); *m* 20 July 1962, Brenda Sigrid, da of John Woodhead (d 1964); 2 da (Sarah Jane b 1964, Ann-Marie b 1967), 2 s (Christopher Somerville b 1965, William Somerville b 1969); *Career* conslt anaesthetist Leeds Gen Infirmary 1969– (chairman of faculty 1986–88), hon lectr Univ of Leeds 1969–; pres Yorkshire Soc of Anaesthetists 1991– (sec and treas 1975–85); FFARCS; *Books* Intensive Care (contrib, 1983), Contemporary Neurology (1984); *Recreations* rowing, sailing, squash, photography, travel; *Style*— Dr Robert Edmondson; ✉ Department of Anaesthesia, Leeds General Infirmary, Great George Street, Leeds LS1 3EX (tel 0113 243 7172)

EDMONDSON, Stephen John; s of George Edmondson, of Scunthorpe, and Jean Mary, *née* Stanton; *b* 21 August 1950; *Educ* Scunthorpe GS, Middx Hosp Med Sch, Univ of London (BSc, MB BS); *m* 17 July 1976 (dis 1992), Barbara Bridget Alison, da of Dr Malcolm Nugent Samuel Duncan, TD; 2 c (Adam George b 1984, John David b 1989); m 2, 5 Feb 1994, Yolande Monique Laret; 3 c (Augustus b 1995, Sienna b 1998, Luca b 2000); *Career* conslt cardiothoracic surgn: Bart's 1984–, Heart Hosp 1997–; registrar: Hammersmith Hosp 1980–, Royal Post Grad Medical Sch 1980–, North Middlesex Hosp 1982–; memb: Soc of Cardiothoracic Surgns of GB and Ireland 1982, Br Cardiac Soc 1984, Euro Assoc of Cardiothoracic Surgery 1989; FRCS 1979, FRCP 1991 (MRCP 1980); *Recreations* tennis, football, skiing; *Clubs* Vanderbilt Racquet, Ealing Golf, Ulysses FC; *Style*— Stephen Edmondson, Esq; ✉ 50 Wimpole Street, London W1M 7DG (tel 020 7935 6375, fax 020 7224 3823, e-mail sedmondson@uk-consultants.co.uk)

EDMONSTONE, Sir Archibald Bruce Charles; 7 Bt (GB 1774), of Duntreath, Stirlingshire; s of Sir Archibald Charles Edmonstone, 6 Bt (d 1954), and Gwendolyn Mary, *née* Field (d 1989); *b* 3 August 1934; *Educ* Stowe; *m* 1, 17 Jan 1957 (m dis 1967), Jane, er da of Maj-Gen Edward Charles Colville, CB, DSO (d 1982) (s of Adm Hon Sir Stanley Colville, GCB, GCMG, GCVO); 1 da (Philippa Carolyn b 1958), 2 s (Archibald Edward Charles b 4 Feb 1961, Nicholas William Mark b 1964); m 2, 12 June 1969, Juliet Elizabeth, o da of Maj-Gen Cecil Martin Fothergill Deakin, CB, CBE; 1 s (Dru Benjamin Marshall b 26 Oct 1971), 1 da (Elyssa Juliet b 11 Sept 1973); *Heir* s, Archibald Edmonstone; *Career* 2 Lt Royal Scots Greys 1954–56; *Recreations* shooting, fishing; *Clubs* New (Edinburgh); *Style*— Sir Archibald Edmonstone, Bt; ✉ Duntreath Castle, Blanefield, by Glasgow (tel 01360 70215)

EDMONTON, Bishop of 1999–; Rt Rev Peter William Wheatley; er s of late William Nobes Wheatley, and late Muriel, *née* Ounsted; *b* 7 September 1947; *Educ* Ipswich Sch, The Queen's Coll Oxford (MA), Pembroke Coll Cambridge (MA), Coll of the Resurrection Mirfield, Ripon Hall Oxford; *Career* ordained deacon 1973, priest 1974; asst curate All Saints Fulham 1973–78; vicar: Holy Cross with St Jude and St Peter St Pancras 1978–82, St James W Hampstead 1982–95; priest i/c: All Souls Hampstead and St Mary Kilburn 1982–90, St Mary with All Souls Kilburn 1990–95; dir of post ordination trg (Edmonton Episcopal Area) 1985–94, area dean of N Camden (Hampstead) 1988–93; archdeacon of Hampstead 1995–99; *Style*— The Rt Rev the Bishop of Edmonton; ✉ 27 Thurlow Road, Hampstead, London NW3 5PP (tel 020 7435 5890, fax 020 7435 6049, e-mail bishop.edmonton@london.anglican.org)

EDMUND, John Humphrey; s of Charles Henry Humphrey Edmund (d 1995), of Swansea, and Vera May, *née* Warmington (d 1993); *b* 6 March 1935; *Educ* Swansea GS, Jesus Coll Oxford (MA); *m* 4 Sept 1965, (Elizabeth Ann) Myfanwy, da of William Lewis Williams (d 1975), of Newport, Pembrokeshire; *Career* Nat Serv RN 1953–55; admitted slr 1961; ptnr Beor, Wilson & Lloyd Swansea 1963–95 (conslt 1995–); Under Sheriff W Glamorgan 1983–2005, Clerk to Gen Cmmrs of Taxes (Swansea Div) 1986–; memb Law Soc 1962; *Clubs* Vincent's (Oxford), Bristol Channel Yacht; *Style*— John Edmund, Esq; ✉ 84 Pennard Road, Pennard, Swansea SA3 2AA (tel 01792 232526); Calvert House, Calvert Terrace, Swansea SA1 6AP (tel 01792 655178, fax 01792 467002, e-mail jedmund@clara.net)

EDNEY, Dr Andrew Thomas Bailey; s of Sydney George Edney (d 1986), and Dorothy Mary, *née* Smith (d 1990); *b* 1 August 1932; *Educ* Borden Sch, Univ of London, RVC (BVetMed, DVetMed), Open Univ (BA, MA); *Career* Nat Serv 201 Sqdn RAF 1950–52; gen practice Odiham Hants 1958–65, MAFF 1966–67, vet advsr in industry Waltham Centre Leics 1968–85, vet conslt, author and ed 1985–, vet ed Butterworth Heinemann plc 1985–2000; chm Round Table; BSAVA: sec 1976–77, nat pres 1979–80; WSAVA: sec 1982–86, vice-pres 1986–90, pres 1990–92, sr vice-pres 1992–94, hon memb 2000; chm Blue Cross Animal Charity 1999–2001 (memb Bd of Govrs 1994–, vice-chm 1998–99), hon memb Feline Advsy Bureau (FAB), membre d'honneur French Veterinary Soc (AFVAC) 2000–, pres Section of Comparative Med RSM 2001–03, govr Soc for Companion Animal Studies (SCAS) 2002– (chm 1986–88), memb Cncl Harveian Soc of London 2005–, pres Central Veterinary Soc 2007– (jr vice-pres 2006–07); Int Award for Service to the Veterinary Profession 1996; DVetMed Univ of London 1997; MRCVS 1958, FRSM 1970; *Books* Dog and Cat Nutrition (1982, 1988), Pet Care (1984), Dog and Puppy Care (1985), Practical Animal Handling (with R S Anderson, 1990), Manual of Cat Care (1992 and 2006), Cat (1999), The Complete Cat Handbook (with C Bessant, 2001); *Recreations* fine art related to animals, vintage aircraft, gardening; *Clubs* RSM, Kennel, Harveian Soc of London; *Style*— Dr Andrew Edney; ✉ Olde Dangstones, 147 Lower Street, Pulborough, West Sussex RH20 2DP

EDRIC, Robert; s of E H Armitage, of Sheffield; *b* 14 April 1956; *Educ* Firth Park GS Sheffield, Univ of Hull (BA, PhD); *m* Helen Sara, *née* Jones; 1 s (Bruce Copley Jones); *Career* novelist; *Awards* James Tait Black Fiction Prize 1985, runner up Guardian Fiction Prize 1986, Arts Cncl Bursary 1995; *Books* Winter Garden (1985), A New Ice Age (1986), A Lunar Eclipse (1989), In The Days of The American Museum (1990), The Broken Lands (1992), The Earth Made of Glass (1994), Elysium (1995), In Desolate Heaven (1997), The Sword Cabinet (1999), The Book of the Heathen (2000), Peacetime (2002), Cradle Song (2003), Siren Song (2004), Swan Song (2005), Gathering the Water (2006), In the Kingdom of Ashes (2007); *Style*— Robert Edric, Esq

EDRIDGE, Olga; da of Col Bernard Alfred Edridge, OBE, and Erica, *née* Mavrommati; *b* 22 March 1951; *Educ* Makris HS for Girls Athens Greece, London Film Sch (Dip Film Making), Univ of Reading (BA); *Career* BBC: asst film ed and acting ed 1975–79, grad prodn trainee 1979–81, asst prodr and dir 1981–83, prodr of religious progs 1983–86, series ed Heart of the Matter 1986–91, exec prodr BBC Corporate Prodr Choice 1992–93, project mangr BBC Corporate Performance Review 1993–94, project dir BBC World Services Prodr Choice 1994–95, dir Special Projects BBC Worldwide TV 1995–97, launch dir BBC/Telewest (jt venture UK TV channels) 1997–98, dir Joint Ventures and New Channels Devpt BBC Worldwide (DCI/Discovery, Telewest UKTV, Alliance Antlantis Canada, Jupiter Japan) 1998–2005, global strategic conslt Discovery Int Channels 2006–07; visiting prof of media arts St Mary's UC Univ of Surrey 1997–; Sandford St Martin Tst Award 1985, One World Broadcast Tst Award 1987; *Recreations* the cottage in Dartmoor, cooking for friends; *Style*— Olga Edridge; ✉ 33 Aldensley Road, London W6 0DH (e-mail oedridge@aol.com)

EDUR, Thomas; s of Enn Edur, of Estonia, and Liuda, *née* Mishustina, of Estonia; *b* 20 January 1969; *Educ* Tallinn Ballet Sch; *m* 1990, Agnes Oaks, *qv*, da of Juhan Oaks; *Career* ballet dancer; Estonia Ballet Theatre: Coppelia 1987, Giselle 1988, Paquita 1988, Sleeping Beauty 1989, Nostalgia 1989, Romeo and Juliet 1990, Swan Lake 1990, Estonian Ballads; English National Ballet: Coppélia 1990, The Nutcracker, Les Sylphides, Sphinx, 3 Preludes 1991–, Lucensio in The Taming of the Shrew, Lenski in Eugene Onegin, Études, Four Last Songs, Apollo, Stranger I Came, Cinderella 1992, Swan Lake, La Bayadère 1992, Spectre de la Rose, Ashton Romeo and Juliet, Sphinx 1993–, Impromptu, Sleeping Beauty, Don Quixote (pas de deux), Seven Silences of Salome (winner Time Out Award), D Deane's Paquita 1994, D Deane's Giselle 1994, Romeo and Mercutio in Nureyev Romeo and Juliet 1995, Alice in Wonderland 1995, Christopher Dean's Encounters 1996, Corda's Cinderella 1996, Our Waltzes 1997, Sanguine Fan 1997; joined Birmingham Royal Ballet 1996: Swan Lake 1996, Nutcracker Sweeties 1996, Peter Wright's Nutcracker 1996, Peter Wright's Sleeping Beauty 1997; freelance 1997–: Sleeping Beauty (Estonian Opera), Nutcracker (Sao Paolo Brazil and Tokyo Japan), Swan Lake 1998, Giselle (Balet de Nancy) 1998, D Deane's Romeo and Juliet (Albert Hall) 1998, D Deane's Swan Lake (Albert Hall and Hong Kong and Australia tour) 1998, Nureyev's Don Quixote (La Scala Milan) 1999, P Bart's Giselle (La Scala Milan) 1999, Cinderella (Zurich Ballet) 2000, Romeo and Juliet (Zurich Ballet) 2000, D Deane's Sleeping Beauty (Albert Hall) 2000, P Bart's Giselle (Berlin Staatsoper) 2000, Rest of the Cavalery (Tokyo) 2000, P Bart's Swan Lake (Berlin Staatsoper) 2001, Grand Pas Classique 2001, Romeo and Juliet (Estonian Nat Opera) 2001, Wedding Journey (Estonian Nat Opera) 2001, Swan Lake (Cape Town City Ballet) 2001, Romeo and Juliet (Albert Hall and Australian Tour) 2001; *Awards*: Best Couple (with Agnes Oaks) Int Ballet Competition Jackson Mississippi 1990, London Evening Standard Outstanding Performance in Ballet Award 1994, nominated for Laurence Olivier Award for Outstanding Achievement in Dance 1995 and 1997; Third Class Order of the White Star Estonia 2001; *Recreations* nature lover, scuba diving; *Style*— Thomas Edur, Esq; ✉ Continental Classics, 49 Tierney Road, London SW2 4QL

EDWARD, Prof the Rt Hon Sir David Alexander Ogilvy; KCMG (2004, CMG 1981), PC (2005), QC (Scot 1974); s of John Ogilvy Christie Edward (d 1960), of Perth, and Margaret Isabel, *née* MacArthur (d 1989); *b* 14 November 1934; *Educ* Sedbergh, UC Oxford (MA), Univ of Edinburgh (LLB); *m* 22 Dec 1962, Elizabeth Young, da of Terence McSherry, of Edinburgh; 2 da (Anne b 1964, Katherine b 1971), 2 s (Giles b 1965, John b 1968); *Career* Nat Serv Sub Lt RNVR 1955–57; advocate 1962, clerk and treas Faculty of Advocates 1967–77, pres Consultative Ctee of the Bars and Law Socs of the Euro Community 1978–80, Salvesen prof of European instns Univ of Edinburgh 1985–89 (hon prof 1990–), judge of European Court of First Instance 1989–92, judge of European Court of Justice 1992–2004, temp judge Court of Session Scotland 2004–; tstee: Nat Library of Scotland 1966–95, Industry and Parliament Tst, Carnegie Tst for the Univs of Scotland (chm 2003–), Trier Acad of European Law; memb: Law Advsy Ctee Br Cncl 1976–88, Panel of Arbitrators Int Centre for Settlement of Investment Disputes 1979–89 and 2004–; dir: Adam & Co Group plc 1983–89, The Harris Tweed Assoc Ltd 1984–89; chm Continental Assets Tst plc 1985–89; pres: Johnson Soc Lichfield 1995, Franco-Scottish Soc 1996–; vice-pres: Br Inst of Int and Comparative Law, Int Assoc for Business and Parliament; tstee Hopetoun Fndn; hon bencher Gray's Inn 1992, hon fell UC Oxford 1995; Hon LLD: Univ of Edinburgh 1993, Univ of Aberdeen 1997, Napier Univ 1998, Univ of Glasgow 2003; Dr (hc): Univ of Saarland 2001, Univ of Münster 2001; Hon DUniv Surrey 2003; FRSE 1990; *Clubs* Athenaeum, New (Edinburgh); *Style*— Prof the Rt Hon Sir David Edward, KCMG, QC, FRSE; ✉ 32 Heriot Row, Edinburgh EH3 6ES

EDWARDES, Sir Michael Owen; kt (1979); s of Denys Owen Edwardes, and Audrey Noel, *née* Copeland; *b* 11 October 1930; *Educ* St Andrew's Coll Grahamstown, Rhodes Univ (BA); *m* 1, 1958 (m dis), Mary Margaret, *née* Finlay; 3 da; m 2, 1988, Sheila Ann, *née* Guy; *Career* formerly non-exec chm Chloride Group plc (dir 1969–77 and 1986); chm: BL Ltd 1977–82, Mercury Communications Ltd 1982–83, ICL plc 1984, Dunlop Holdings plc 1984–85, Tryhorn Investments Ltd 1987–, Charter plc (formerly Charter Consolidated plc) 1988–96; dir: Hill Samuel Group 1980–87, Minorco SA 1984–93, Standard Securities plc 1985–87, Delta Motor Corporation (Pty) Ltd 1986–99, Flying Pictures Ltd 1987–, Kaye Organisation 1987–88, Jet Press Holdings BV 1990–, Strand Partners 1994–, Syndicated Services Co Inc 1995–; dep chm R K Carvill (International Holdings) Ltd 1988–; dir Int Mgmnt Devpt Inst Washington 1978–94; memb: NEB 1975–77, President's Ctee CBI 1981; tstee Thrombosis Res Inst 1991–2001; pres Squash Rackets Assoc 1991–95; Hon LLD Rhodes Univ; Hon FIMechE 1981; CIMgt (vice-chm 1977–80); *Books* Back from the Brink (1983); *Clubs* Veterans Squash Club of GB, RAC, Jesters, Rand (Johannesburg); *Style*— Sir Michael Edwardes

EDWARDS, Prof Anthony William Fairbank; s of Harold Clifford Edwards (d 1989), of Cambridge, and Ida Margaret Atkinson, *née* Phillips (d 1981); *b* 4 October 1935; *Educ* Uppingham, Trinity Hall Cambridge (MA, PhD, ScD, LittD); *m* 9 Aug 1958, (Elsa Helny) Catharina, da of Nils-Jonas Edlund, ADC to HM Gustav VI Adolf of Sweden; 2 da (Ann Ruth b 1959, Alice Margaret Charlotte b 1964), 1 s (David Thomas b 1960); *Career* Eugenics Soc Leonard Darwin research fell Dept of Genetics Univ of Cambridge 1960, research assoc Int Lab of Genetics and Biophysics Inst of Genetics Univ of Pavia 1961, actg asst prof Depts of Genetics and Mathematics Stanford Univ 1964, sr lectr Dept of Statistics Univ of Aberdeen 1965; Univ of Cambridge: asst dir of research Dept of Human Ecology (later Dept of Community Med) 1970, reader in mathematical biology (later biometry) 1978, sr proctor 1978–79, prof of biometry 2000–03 (ret), sometime memb Cncl of Senate and Gen Bd; fell Gonville & Caius Coll Cambridge 1970– (Berkeley bye-fell in med 1968, sometime memb Cncl); visiting prof of mathematics Dept of Theoretical Statistics Univ of Aarhus 1973; pres Br Regn Int Biometric Soc 1992–94, chm Cambridge Univ Library Syndicate 1993–98, chm Christiaan Huygens Ctee for the History of Statistics Int Statistical Inst 1999–2003, former memb Cncl Int Biometric Soc; Buehler lectr Univ of Minnesota 1992, II Fisher Meml lectr Univ of Adelaide 1992, XVIII Fisher Meml lectr GB 1994, Snedecor lectr Iowa State Univ 1996, Galton lectr Galton Inst 1997, VII Adriano Buzzati-Traverso lectr Univ of Pavia 1999, Zyskind lectr Iowa State Univ 1999; pres Cambridge Univ Gliding Tst Ltd 1978–96, chm Cambridge Univ Gliding Club 1968–77; fell Linnean Soc 1994, tstee and treas Sir Ronald Fisher Meml Tst 1969–, sometime memb Cambridge Dist HA; hon prof Univ of Pavia 1999; hon memb Genetics Soc; FRSS 1962, memb Int Statistical Inst 1976, CMath 1991, FIMA 1991; *Books* Likelihood (1972, 2 edn 1992), Foundations of Mathematical Genetics (1977, 2 edn 2000), Pascal's Arithmetical Triangle (1987, 2 edn 2002), Annotated Readings in the History of Statistics (with H A David, 2001), Cogwheels of the Mind (2004); *Recreations* gliding, skiing; *Style*— Prof A W F Edwards; ✉ tel 01223 332488, e-mail awfe@cam.ac.uk

EDWARDS, Arthur John; MBE (2003); s of late Arthur James Edwards, and late Dorothy May, *née* Ward; *b* 12 August 1940; *Educ* St Bernard's RC GS Stepney London; *m* 16 Sept 1961, Ann Patricia, *née* Heaphy; 2 s (John Gerard b 7 April 1964, Paul Patrick b 26 Feb 1966), 1 da (Annmarie b 26 March 1971); *Career* press photographer; formerly freelance, with The Sun 1975–; *Recreations* walking, watching West Ham Utd; *Style*— Arthur Edwards, Esq, MBE; ✉ c/o The Picture Desk, The Sun, 1 Virginia Street, London E1 9XP (tel 020 7782 4110)

EDWARDS, Prof (Gwilym) Barrie; CBE (2004); *b* 20 May 1938; *Educ* Univ of Liverpool (BVSc); *m*; 2 c; *Career* Univ of Liverpool: house surgn in Dept of Veterinary Clinical Studies 1961–63, lectr in large animal surgery 1963–70; sr lectr in large animal surgery at Royal Veterinary Coll London 1970–86; visiting lectr at Univs of: Cambridge, Edinburgh, Glasgow, Bristol, London, Pahlavi, Shiraz, Iran, Murdoch and Harare; external univ examiner: Bristol, Cambridge, Liverpool, Glasgow, Al Fatah, Libya; external examiner for PhD in Univs of: London, Edinburgh, Dublin, Tanzania; RCVS examiner; ed: Equine Veterinary Journal (EVJ) supplement on Equine Orthopaedic Injury and Repair, EVJ supplement on Gastroenterology; guest ed EVJ supplement on Equine Gastroenterology; memb Editorial Bd: In Practice, EVJ; memb Bd of Referees Jl of

E

Veterinary and Comparative Orthopaedics and Traumatology; rep of Racehorse Owners Assoc on SAC of Animal Health Tst; papers presented to numerous domestic and int confs; hon life memb Assoc of Veterinary Teachers and Research Workers 1998; memb: BVA, British Equine Veterinary Assoc (former pres), British Cattle Veterinary Assoc, Assoc of Veterinary Teachers and Research Workers, Assoc of Veterinary Clinical Teachers, Herts & Beds div BVA (form treas and pres), Lancashire Veterinary Assoc, Scientific Sub-Ctee of Home of Rest for Horses, Veterinary Advsy Ctee of the Horserace Betting Levy Bd; DVetMed; FRCVS; *Awards* Richard Hartley Meml Literary Award EVJ 1978 and 1981, EVJ Open Award 1986, Victory Medal Central Veterinary Soc 1993, Animal Health Tst Outstanding Scientific Achievement Award 1996, British Cattle Veterinary Assoc Bridge Award 1997, BBC Veterinary Award 2002; *Publications* over 120 papers in scientific jls, eight published books, several contributions to other publications; *Recreations* classical music, watching sport, golf; *Clubs* Caldy Golf; *Style*— Prof Barrie Edwards, CBE, FRCVS; ✉ Department of Veterinary Clinical Science and Animal Husbandry, University of Liverpool, Leahurst, Neston, South Wirral L64 7TE (tel 0151 794 6139, fax 0151 794 6034, e-mail gbedward@2.liv.ac.uk)

EDWARDS, Prof Brian; CBE (1988); s of John Albert Edwards (d 1979), of Bebington, and (Ethel) Pat, *née* Davis (d 1980); *b* 19 February 1942; *Educ* Wirral GS; *m* 7 Nov 1964, Jean, da of William Cannon, of Neston; 2 da (Penny Adrienne b 27 May 1967, Paula Michelle b 14 Nov 1968), 2 s (Christopher, Jonathan (twins) b 28 April 1973); *Career* various hosp posts 1958–69, lectr in health serv studies Univ of Leeds 1969–71, dep gp sec Hull Hosp Mgmnt Ctee 1971–73, dist admin Leeds Dist Health Authy 1973–76, area admin Cheshire AHA 1976–81, regnl gen mangr Trent RHA 1984–93 (regnl admin 1981–83), chief exec W Midlands RHA 1993–96, regnl dir NHS Exec (West Midlands) 1994–96, prof of health care devpt Sch of Health and Related Research Univ of Sheffield 1996–2002 (fndn dean 1996–98, emeritus prof 2002); visiting prof Keele Univ 1989–2000, leader Patient's Charter Team 1992–93; pres: Inst of Health Servs Mgmnt 1983, Health Supplies Assoc 2001–02, European Hospitals Fedn (HOPE) 2005–08; chm: Manpower Advsy Gp NHS 1983–85, Regnl Gen Mangrs Gp England 1986 and 1990–93, CPA (Ltd) 1992–2000, Health on the Box Ltd 2000–02, Cncl for the Professions Supplementary to Med 1997–2002, ATM Ltd 2000–, Notts Health NHS Tst 2001–06; memb: Fallon Judicial Inquiry 1997–98, Standing Advsy Ctee on Audit RCP, Hayes Review of Acute Health Services in NI 2000–01; conslt WHO in: India, Russia, Guyana, Czechoslovakia; ed: Health Servs Manpower Review, NHS 50th Anniversary Lectures 1999; Queen Elizabeth the Queen Mother Nuffield fell 1992; Hon DUniv Univ of Central England 1998; FHSA, CIMgt; Hon FRCPath 1996, Hon ACP; *Books* Si Vis Pacem (1973), Planning the Child Health Services (1975), Manager and Industrial Relations (1979), Merit Awards for Doctors (1987), Controlling Doctors (1991), Managing the NHS (1992), A Manager's Tale (1993, 2 edn 1995); ed: HOPE European Year Book (1998, 1999, 2000 and 2001), The Executive Years (2005), An Independent NHS (2007); *Recreations* golf; *Clubs* Bakewell Golf (capt 1991), Athenaeum, La Manga; *Style*— Prof Brian Edwards, CBE; ✉ 3 Royal Croft Drive, Baslow, Derbyshire DE45 1SN (tel 01246 583459)

EDWARDS, (David) Cenwyn; s of Alwyn John Edwards (d 1986), of Pontarddulais, and Edwina Jane, *née* Thomas; *b* 27 October 1945; *Educ* Llanelli Boys GS, Univ of N Wales Bangor (BA); *m* 1, 17 April 1971 (m dis 1990), Margaret Eluned, da of Thomas Owen Davies (d 1977); 1 da (Lowri b 1977), 1 s (Gruffudd b 1979); m 2, 12 Oct 1993 (m dis 2005), Meri Huws, da of Val Hughes, and Gwynne Hughes; *Career* joined HTV 1969, asst head of news and current affrs 1978–82, head of current affrs 1982–85, asst prog controller and N Wales exec 1985–89, controller of factual and general progs 1989–91, commissioning ed of factual progs S4C 1991, head of co-prodns S4C until 2005, dir of TV Tinopolis 2005–07; memb Nat Eisteddfod Court; *Recreations* drama, rugby, cricket; *Clubs* Llanelli RFC, Groucho; *Style*— Cenwyn Edwards, Esq

EDWARDS, Sir Christopher John Churchill; 5 Bt (UK 1866), of Pye Nest, Yorkshire; s of Sir (Henry) Charles Serrell Priestley Edwards, 4 Bt (d 1963), and Daphne Marjory Hilda, *née* Birt; *b* 16 August 1941; *Educ* Frensham Heights Sch, Loughborough Univ, Regis Univ Denver USA; *m* 1972, Gladys Irene Vogelgesang; 2 s (David Charles Priestley b 22 Feb 1974, Ryan Matthew Churchill b 16 April 1979); *Heir* s, David Edwards; *Career* fndr and gen mangr Kelsar Inc (American Home Products, San Diego, Calif) 1979–84, vice-pres Valleylab Inc (Pfizer Inc, Boulder Colorado) 1984–89, dir Ohmeda (BOC Group, Louisville, Colorado) 1989–92, pres Intermed Consultants Westminster Colorado 1992–; vice-pres Teledyne Water Pik Fort Collins Colorado 1994–95; exec vice-pres and gen mangr RAM Electronics Corp Fort Collins Colorado 1995–97; affiliate prof in Master of Sci in Mgmnt at Regis Univ and adjunct prof in Master of Technology Mgmnt at the Univ of Denver Colorado 1999–; US Nat Certified Soccer Coach, fndr and vice-pres Westminster Wolves Youth Soccer Club; memb Acad of Mgmnt; *Style*— Sir Christopher Edwards, Bt; ✉ 11637 Country Club Drive, Westminster, Colorado 80234–2649, USA (tel 001 30346 93156, fax 001 30363 51424, e-mail sir.chris@attbi.com)

EDWARDS, Prof Christopher Richard Watkin; s of Wing Cdr Thomas Archibald Watkin Edwards (d 1986), and Beatrice Elizabeth Ruby, *née* Telfer (d 1993); *b* 12 February 1942; *Educ* Marlborough, Univ of Cambridge (MB BChir, MD); *m* 6 April 1968, Sally Amanda Le Blount, da of Sqdn Ldr Gerald Le Blount Kidd, OBE, of Westerham, Kent; 2 s (Adam b 1969, Crispin b 1974), 1 da (Kate b 1971); *Career* sr lectr in medicine and hon conslt physician Bart's 1975, prof of clinical med Univ of Edinburgh and hon conslt physician to the Lothian Health Bd 1980–95, chm Dept of Med Western Gen Hosp Edinburgh 1981–91, dean Faculty of Med 1991–95, provost Faculty Gp of Med and Vet Med 1992–95, princ Imperial Coll Sch of Med 1995–2001 (fell 2003), vice-chllr Univ of Newcastle upon Tyne 2001–07; memb MRC Cncl 1992–95, govr Wellcome Tst 1994–2005; Hon DSc Univ of Aberdeen 2000; FRCP 1979, FRCPE 1981, FRSE 1990, FMedSci 1998; *Books* Essential Hypertension as an Endocrine Disease (co ed, 1985), Recent Advances in Endocrinology and Metabolism (co ed, 1992), Davidson's Principles and Practice of Medicine (co ed, 1995); *Recreations* golf, painting; *Clubs* Athenaeum; *Style*— Prof Christopher Edwards, FRSE

EDWARDS, Prof David John; s of late Percy Oliver Edwards, of Cwmbran, Gwent, and Ceinwen Elizabeth, *née* Salter; *b* 20 February 1951; *Educ* Croesyceiliog GS Gwent, Univ of Bristol (BSc, MSc, PhD), Univ of Oxford (MA); *m* 1973, Georgina Elizabeth, da of late R V Janson; 2 da (Eleanor Georgina b 24 Feb 1978, Charlotte Elizabeth b 15 Dec 1981); *Career* various positions in computer systems and satellite communications British Telecom 1973–85, New Blood lectr Univ of Bristol 1985–89; Univ of Oxford: fell Wadham Coll 1989– (admissions tutor 1993–98), lectr 1989–96, reader 1996–98, prof of engrg sci 1998–, sr pro-proctor 2006–07; IEE Prize for Innovation 1986, NPL Metrology Award 1990, IEEE Mountbatten Premium 1990, IEEE Neal Shepherd Meml Award 1990; approx 300 publications in scientific and technical jls and patents; curator Sheldonian Theatre; CEng 1985, FIEE 1997 (MIEE 1985), FRAS 1985; *Recreations* music, astronomy, clocks, classic/vintage motor cars, architecture; *Style*— Prof David Edwards; ✉ Wadham College, Oxford OX1 3PN (tel 01865 277900); University of Oxford, Department of Engineering, Parks Road, Oxford OX1 3PJ (tel 01865 273915, fax 01865 273906, e-mail david.edwards@eng.ox.ac.uk)

EDWARDS, David Michael; CMG (1989); s of Ernest William Edwards (d 1991), and Thelma Irene, *née* Foxley (d 1998); *b* 28 February 1940; *Educ* King's Sch Canterbury, Univ of Bristol (LLB); *m* 1 (m dis), Veronica Margaret, da of Robert Postgate, of Cannes, France (d 1997); 1 da (Vanessa Louise b 1967), 1 s (Capt Adrian David b 1969); m 2, Rain Ren; 1 s (Charles Ren b 1997), 1 da (Chloe Ren b 1999); *Career* admitted slr 1964, asst legal advsr FO 1967; legal advsr: Br Mil Govt Berlin 1972, Br Embassy Bonn 1974; legal cnsllr 1977, gen counsel and dir legal div IAEA Vienna 1977–79, legal cnsllr FCO 1979, agent of the UK Govt in cases before Euro Cmmn and Court of Human Rights 1979–82, cnsllr and legal advsr UK Mission to UN NY and HM Embassy Washington 1985–88, dep legal advsr FCO 1989–90, law offr (International Law) Hong Kong Govt 1990–95, sr counsel Bechtel Ltd 1995–97, vice-pres and region counsel Bechtel Asia Pacific (Singapore) 1997–2002, chief legal counsel Shell Petrochemicals Co Ltd and CNOOC's Petrochemical Complex Guangdong Province China 2002–, memb Panel of Mediators Singapore Mediation Centre 2002–; *Recreations* reading, travel, antique clocks; *Style*— David Edwards, Esq, CMG; ✉ tel 00 86 752 556 4132, e-mail edwards.david@cspc.net.cn

EDWARDS, (Ronald) Derek Keep; JP (Hants 1978); s of Ronald Allan George Edwards (d 1981), of Hants, and Edith Vere, *née* Keep (d 1974); *b* 22 November 1934; *Educ* Winchester; *m* 1, 6 June 1958 (m dis 1984), Sally Anne, da of Patrick Boyle Lake Coghlan, of Fernhurst, W Sussex; 4 s (David Christopher Keep b 1959, Simon Derek Keep b 1960, James Andrew Keep b 1962, Charles Peter Keep b 1969); m 2, 3 March 1988, Julia Ann, *née* Knock; *Career* King's Dragoon Gds 1953–55, Inns of Ct Regt (TA) 1955–61; memb Stock Exchange 1959; ptnr: R Edwards Chandler & Co 1960–69 (sr ptnr 1965–69), Brewin Dolphin & Co 1969–80, A H Cobbold & Co 1980–85; dir Cobbold Roach Ltd 1985–87; conslt: Rathbones 1991–98, St James's Place Partnership 1999–; dir City Arts Trust Ltd 1994–; memb Advsy Bd Berliner Bank AG 1991–98; chm: Guildhall Sch of Music and Drama 1994–97, Selborne Assoc 2000–; vice-chm: Gtr London Fund for the Blind 1986–96, Sheriffs and Recorders' Fund 1991–; vice-pres Bassishaw Ward Club (chm 1971); govr: Amesbury Sch 1970–88, Christ's Hosp Sch; memb Ct of Common Cncl 1978–97, Sheriff of London 1989–90; Freeman City of London 1971, Liveryman Worshipful Co of Loriners; Lord of the Manor of Winshill; FInstD, MSI, FIMgt; OstJ; *Books* Pudding on Fridays (memoir); *Recreations* field sports, riding, skiing, the arts; *Clubs* Cavalry and Guards', Guildhall; *Style*— Derek Edwards, Esq; ✉ Priors Lodge, Froxfield, Petersfield, Hampshire GU32 1BZ

EDWARDS, (John) Duncan; s of Dr Vernon Edwards (d 1991), and Jean, *née* Macgregor; *b* 28 March 1964, Watford; *Educ* Merchant Taylors', Univ of Sheffield (BA); *m* 2 Oct 1993, Sarah; 2 s (Freddie b 8 Oct 1994, Findlay b 7 Aug 1996); *Career* ceo The National Magazine Co Ltd; chm Comag Ltd; bd dir: PPA Ltd, NRS Ltd; Freeman City of London, memb Worshipful Co of Merchant Taylors; *Recreations* running, rugby, literature, history, politics; *Clubs* OMT FC, Soho House, George, Solus; *Style*— Duncan Edwards, Esq; ✉ The National Magazine Company, 72 Broadwick Street, London W1F 9EP (tel 020 7439 5000, e-mail duncan.edwards@natmags.co.uk)

EDWARDS, His Hon Judge (David) Elgan Hugh; DL (Cheshire 2000); s of Howell Dan Edwards, JP (d 1986), of Rhyl, Clwyd, and Dilys, *née* Williams (d 1994); *b* 6 December 1943; *Educ* Rhyl GS, UCW Aberystwyth (LLB); *m* 1, 29 July 1967 (m dis 1981), Jane Elizabeth Hayward; 1 da (Kathryn Sian Elizabeth b 1971), 1 s (Daniel Richard Hugh b 1974); m 2, 31 July 1982, Carol Anne, da of Arthur Smalls, of Saughall, Chester; 1 s (Thomas Huw Elgan b 1984), 1 da (Nia Alexandra b 1991); *Career* called to the Bar Gray's Inn 1967 (bencher 2004); recorder 1982–89, circuit judge (Wales & Chester Circuit) 1989–, sr circuit judge 2002–, resident judge Chester Castle, hon recorder of Chester 1997, resident judge for Cheshire 2006–; pres Cncl of HM Circuit Judges 2005; memb Chester City Cncl 1974–84, Sheriff City of Chester 1977–78; hon fell Univ of Wales Aberystwyth 2005; *Recreations* swimming, Manchester United supporter, Chester races; *Clubs* Chester City; *Style*— His Hon Judge Elgan Edwards, DL; ✉ c/o Chester Crown Court, The Castle, Chester CH1 2AN (tel 01244 317606, fax 01244 350073)

EDWARDS, Gareth Owen; CBE (2007, MBE 1976); s of Thomas Granville Edwards (d 1999), and Annie-Mary Edwards; *b* 12 July 1947; *Educ* Pontardawe Tech Sch, Millfield, Cardiff Coll of Educn; *m* 6 July 1972, Maureen, da of Luther Edwards (d 1985); 2 s ((Geraint) Owen b 29 April 1974, (Dafydd) Rhys b 20 Oct 1975); *Career* co dir and former rugby union player; Welsh secdy schs rugby int 1965–66, English schs 200 yds hurdles champion 1966 (UK under 19 record holder); Wales: 53 caps 1967–78, capt 13 times, youngest capt aged 20 1968; Cardiff RFC 1966–78, Barbarians 1967–78, Br Lions 1968, 1971 and 1974; dir: Euro-Commercials (South Wales) Ltd 1982–, Players (UK) Ltd 1983–88; chm Hamdden Ltd 1991–2000; chm Regnl Fisheries Advsy Ctee Welsh Water Authy 1983–89; dir Cardiff Rugby Club 1997–; regnl chm Coutts Bank 1998–2005; *Books* Gareth - an autobiography (1978), Rugby Skills (1979), Rugby Skills for Forwards (1980), Gareth Edwards on Fishing (1984), Gareth Edwards on Rugby (1986), Gareth Edwards' 100 Great Rugby Players (1987), Gareth Edwards - The Autobiography (1999), Tackling Rugby (2002); *Recreations* fishing, golf; *Style*— Gareth Edwards, Esq, CBE

EDWARDS, His Hon Judge Gareth Owen; QC (1985); s of Arthur Wyn Edwards (d 1974), and Mair Eluned Jones; *b* 26 February 1940; *Educ* Herbert Strutt GS, Univ of Oxford (BA, BCL); *m* 1967, Katharine Pek Har, da of Goh Keng Swee, of Kuala Lumpur, Malaysia; 1 da (Kim b 1968), 2 s (David b 1970, John b 1974); *Career* called to the Bar Inner Temple 1963; Capt Army Legal Serv Germany 1963–65; asst legal advsr Cwlth Office 1965–67, in practice Wales & Chester Circuit 1967–91, recorder of the Crown Court 1978–91, circuit judge (Wales & Chester Circuit) 1991–; asst cmmr Boundaries Cmmn 1975–80; *Recreations* chess, cricket, tennis, hill walking; *Clubs* Army and Navy; *Style*— His Hon Judge Gareth Edwards, QC

EDWARDS, Guy Richard Goronwy; QGM (1977), Austrian AC Gold Medal 1977; s of Sqdn Ldr Goronwy Edwards, DFC, RAF, of Liverpool, and Mary Christine Edwards; *b* 30 December 1942; *Educ* Liverpool Coll, Univ of Durham (BSc); *m* 26 April 1986, Daphne Caroline, da of William George McKinley, MRCVS, of Co Meath, Ireland; 1 s (Sean), 2 da (Natasha, Jade); *Career* professional racing driver 1965–85, winner 40 int races, drove as team mate to Graham Hill; Grand Prix Formula One: Lola 1974, Lord Hesketh 1976, BRM 1977; drove Le Mans Twenty Four Hour 9 times for Porsche, BMW and Lola (fourth 1985); awarded QGM for helping rescue Niki Lauda from burning Ferrari at German Grand Prix 1976; chm Guy Edwards Racing Ltd (organising sponsorship for motor racing) 1985–, responsible for Jaguar Car Co's commercial sponsorship prog (resulted in their winning World Championship 1987, 1988 and 1991, and Le Mans 1988 and 1990), dir of mktg Lotus Formula One Team; Freeman: City of London, Worshipful Co of Coachmakers and Coach Harness Makers; *Books* Sponsorship and the World of Motor Racing; *Recreations* country pursuits, reading, water sports, fishing; *Clubs* British Racing Drivers, Club International des Anciens Pilotes de Grand Prix F1 BARC; *Style*— Guy Edwards, Esq, QGM

EDWARDS, Prof Gwynne; s of William Edwards (d 1964), of Clydach Vale, Mid Glamorgan, S Wales, and Rachel Mary Lamb (d 1986); *b* 14 April 1937; *Educ* Porth Co GS, UC Cardiff, KCL (BA, PhD); *m* 1 Aug 1964, Gillian Marilyn Davies; 1 da (Eleri b 1968), 1 s (Gareth b 1971); *Career* lectr in Spanish Univ of Liverpool 1962–67; Dept of Euro Languages Univ of Wales Aberystwyth: lectr 1967–73, sr lectr 1973–80, reader 1980–83, prof 1983–2001, head of dept 1984–87, emeritus prof 2005–; *Theatre Productions*: Lorca's Blood Wedding 1987, 1992, 2001 and 2004, Lorca's Women 1987–88, Mario Vargas Llosa's La Chunga 1988, Lorca's Dona Rosita 1989 and 2004, Lorca's When Five Years Pass 1989 (winner of Scotsman Fringe First 2006), Lorca's The Shoemaker's Wonderful Wife 1990 and 1991, Carlos Muñiz's The Ink-Well 1990, Lope de Vega's Punishment Without Revenge 1991, Calderón's Three Judgements in One 1991, Life is a Dream 1992, Egon Wolff's Paper Flowers 1993 and 2003, José Triana's Medea in the Mirror 1996, Calderón's The Surgeon of Honour 1998, Sophocles' Antigone 1998, Poet in New York 1998, Francisco Ors' Contradance 1999, Garcia Márquez's Diatribe of Love 2001, Puccini's

Edgar 2001, Lorca's Mariana Pineda 2002 and 2006, Lorca's The House of Bernarda Alba 2003, Dylan Thomas in America (adaptation) 2003–05, Dylan Thomas in London (adaptation) 2006–07; *Books* The Prison and the Labyrinth: Studies in Calderonian Tragedy (1978), Lorca: The Theatre Beneath the Sand (1980), The Discreet Art of Luis Bunuel (1982), Dramatists in Perspective: Spanish Theatre in the Twentieth Century (1985), Lorca: Three Plays (1987), Lorca Plays: Two (1990), Calderón Plays: One (1991), Indecent Exposures: Buñuel, Saura, Erice, Almodóvar (1994), Lorca Plays: Three (1994), Burning the Curtain: Four Revolutionary Spanish Plays (1995), Lorca's Blood Wedding, student edn (1997), The House of Bernarda Alba, student edn (1998), Lope de Vega, Three Major Plays (1999), Flamenco (2000), Almodóvar: Labyrinths of Passion (2001), Lorca: Living in the Theatre (2003), Contemporary American Plays (2004), Three Spanish Golden Age Plays (2005), A Companion to Luis Buñuel (2005), Lorca's Yerma (2007); *Recreations* theatre, opera, music, sport, cinema, travel; *Style*— Prof Gwynne Edwards; ✉ 66 Maeshendre, Waun Fawr, Aberystwyth

EDWARDS, Jeffery; s of Walter Frederick (d 1983), and Hilda, *née* Fenemore; *b* 31 August 1945; *Educ* Orange Hill GS, Bushey GS, Leeds Coll of Art and Design (DipAD), RCA (MA, Printmaking prize); *m* 1969, Theresa, da of Cliff Tyrell; 1 s (Roland b 1970), 1 da (Chloë b 1972); *Career* artist; public collections incl: V&A, Tate Gallery, Br Cncl, Brooklyn Museum NY, Bradford City Art Gallery, Whitworth Art Gallery Manchester, Arts Cncl of Great Britain; sr lectr Chelsea Sch of Art 1982–; *Recreations* rhythm and blues, thoroughbred cars; *Clubs* Chelsea Arts; *Style*— Jeffery Edwards, Esq; ✉ Chelsea School of Art, Manresa Road, London SW3 6LS (tel 020 7351 3844)

EDWARDS, Jennifer; da of William Terence Edwards (d 1982), and Cora Marion Milton (d 1987); *b* 26 December 1954; *Educ* Torquay Girls' GS, Girton Coll Cambridge (BA); *m* Jean Pierre Ferraroli; 1 s (Jovan b 25 March 1995); *Career* civil servant 1976–81, local govt offr 1983–93; dep ldr of the oppn Westminster City Cncl 1990–94, nat campaigns organiser CND 1991–93, dir Nat Campaign for the Arts 1993–98, dir of external rels and devpt Arts Council England (formerly London Arts) 1998–; *Recreations* opera, family history, song, gardening; *Style*— Ms Jennifer Edwards; ✉ Arts Council England, 2 Pear Tree Court, London EC1R 0DS (tel 020 7608 6161, fax 020 7340 1095, e-mail jennifer.edwards@artscouncil.org.uk)

EDWARDS, Jeremy John Cary; s of William Philip Neville Edwards, CBE (d 1995), and Hon Mrs Sheila Edwards, *née* Cary (d 1976); *b* 2 January 1937; *Educ* Ridley Coll Ontario, Vinehall Sch, Haileybury and ISC; *m* 1, 18 April 1963 (m dis), Jenifer (decd), da of late Capt Langton Mould; 1 da (Venetia Hester b 16 Aug 1964), 1 s (Julian Peter Cary b 21 Jan 1967); m 2, 18 July 1974 (m dis), April Philippa Learmond, da of late Reginald Ernest Harding; 1 s (Benjamin Charles Cary b 17 Dec 1980); m 3, 1994, Amanda Mary Barber, da of Frank Rabone; *Career* Unilever Ltd 1955–57, Hobson Bates & Co Ltd 1957–59, Overseas Marketing & Advertising Ltd 1959–61, Courtaulds Ltd 1961–63, Vine Products Ltd 1963–66, Loewe SA 1966–68, Jessel Securities Ltd 1968–70, md Vavasseur Unit Trust Management 1970–74; Henderson Administration Group plc: joined 1974, jt md 1983, gp md 1989, ret 1995; former vice-chm C of E Children's Soc, former hon treas World Wide Fund for Nature UK, tstee Breast Cancer Haven; *Clubs* Boodle's, The Brook (NY); *Style*— Jeremy Edwards, Esq; ✉ 59 Dorothy Road, London SW11 2JJ (tel 020 7228 6055)

EDWARDS, Jeremy Paul; s of Peter Edwards, of Deli, N Cornwall, and Philippa, *née* Fielding; *b* 12 September 1962, Stroud; *Educ* Allhallows Sch Lyme Regis, Keele Univ (LLB), Coll of Law Guildford; *m* 29 July 1989, Kay, *née* Rawson; 1 da (Sophie), 2 s (Thomas, Rory); *Career* admitted slr 1989; Norton Rose: articled clerk 1987–89, Paris office 1992–95, ptnr 1997–, head of aviation 2002–, memb Bd 2005–; memb: Law Soc 1987, City of London Slrs Co 1989; *Recreations* fishing, sailing (yachts), golf, tennis, shooting; *Style*— Jeremy Edwards, Esq; ✉ Norton Rose, 3 More London Riverside, London SE1 2AQ (tel 020 7283 6000, e-mail jeremy.edwards@nortonrose.com)

EDWARDS, Rev Joel Nigel Patrick; *Educ* London Bible Coll (BA); *Career* probation offr 1978–88; min New Testament Church of God 1985–2003; gen sec African Caribbean Evangelical Alliance 1988–92, dir UK Evangelical Alliance 1992–97, gen dir Evangelical Alliance 1997–; hon canon St Paul's Cathedral; Hon DD: Caribbean Grad Sch of Theology Jamaica 2006, St Andrews Univ 2007; *Publications* Lord Make Us One - But Not All The Same! (1999), The Cradle, The Cross and The Empty Tomb (2000), Hope, Respect and Trust: Valuing These Three 92004); *Recreations* swimming, reading, the occasional jog; *Style*— The Rev Joel Edwards; ✉ Evangelical Alliance, Whitefield House, 186 Kennington Park Road, London SE11 4BT (tel 020 7207 2100, fax 020 7207 2150, e-mail j.edwards@eauk.org)

EDWARDS, John Frederick; s of late Fred Edwards, of Sheffield, and Lilian Ada Edwards; *b* 15 October 1948; *Educ* Henry Fanshaw GS Dronfield, Univ of Birmingham (BSc); *m* 1970, Linda; 1 s (Lewis Alexander James b 29 Sept 1974), 1 da (Frances Elizabeth b 8 March 1978); *Career* Massey Ferguson 1970, Chrysler UK 1971–75; Massey Ferguson 1975–79; finance dir: Jaguar Cars Ltd 1980–95, Northern Electric plc 1995–97, Meyer International plc 1997–2000, BNFL 2000–; FCMA 1984 (ACMA 1974); *Recreations* playing tennis, keeping fit, watching rugby; *Clubs* Warwick Boat, Leicester FC; *Style*— John Edwards, Esq

EDWARDS, John Neill Thesen; s of Maj John Herbert Edwards (d 1984), of Pretoria, South Africa, and Aorea Georgina, *née* Thesen; *b* 2 May 1946; *Educ* St Andrew's Coll Grahamstown, Univ of Pretoria (MB ChB); *m* 1 May 1976, Katherine Martine, da of Stanley Douglas Abercrombie, of Poole, Dorset; 4 s (John Patrick Abercrombie b 1978, Charles Thomas Thesen b 1979, Andrew Neill Douglas b 1983, Harison Martin Ashdown b 1988); *Career* registrar in obstetrics and gynaecology John Radcliffe Hosp Oxford, sr registrar in obstetrics and gynaecology UCH, conslt in obstetrics and gynaecology Poole Gen Hosp 1986–; FRCOG (MRCOG 1981), FRCSEd 1986; *Recreations* sailing, fishing, shooting; *Clubs* Royal Motor Yacht (Poole), Bournemouth Constitutional; *Style*— John Edwards, Esq; ✉ Sarum House, 29 Forest Road, Branksome Park, Poole, Dorset BH13 6DQ (tel 01202 765287)

EDWARDS, John Owen; s of Frederic V Edwards (d 1995), and Margaret, *née* Fergusson, of Congleton, Cheshire; *b* 7 August 1951; *Educ* Newcastle-under-Lyme HS, Worcester Coll Oxford (Hadow scholar, MA); *Career* prof Guildhall Sch of Music and Drama 1978–85, guest prof Hong Kong Acad of Performing Arts; musical dir: Travelling Opera 1979–81, D'Oyly Carte Opera Company 1992–2003; musical dir 1976–89: A Chorus Line, Annie, Oklahoma!, Evita, Chess, A Little Night Music, The Phantom of the Opera, Anything Goes; conductor: Kurt Weill's Johnny Johnson (RSC Summer Festival, Almeida Theatre) 1986, Street Scene (Palace Theatre) 1987, Offenbach's The Tales of Hoffmann (Victoria State Opera) 1992, The King and I 2001, Showboat (Opéra Du Rhin Strasbourg) 2002, Die Fledermaus 2004, The Merry Widow (Holland Park Opera) 2006; patron London Lighthouse; FGSM 1992; *Recordings* incl: West Side Story, My Fair Lady, Guys and Dolls, Kismet, The Student Prince, Kiss Me Kate, Showboat, The Most Happy Fella; *Publications* Wassail! (arrangement of Christmas carols for choir and harp, 1995); *Recreations* reading, travel; *Style*— John Owen Edwards, Esq; ✉ The Old Chapel, Finstock, Oxfordshire OX7 3BY

EDWARDS, John Robert; s of John Ellis Edwards (d 1981), of London, and Lillian Hannah Hall (d 1983); *b* 3 March 1938; *Educ* Hornsey Sch of Art, Leeds Inst of Educn, L'Ecole Nationale Superieure d'Architecture et d'Art Visuel Bruxelles (Br Cncl scholar); *Career* artist; visiting artist: Syracuse Univ NY 1976, Sch of Visual Arts New York City 1980; head Dept of Painting and Sculpture St Martin's Sch of Art London 1986–88 (head of painting 1980–86) currently lectr; exhbns incl: Br Cncl Delhi 2004, Nehru Centre London 2005; works in the collections of: Arts Cncl of GB, Br Cncl, Contemporary Art Soc London, Cncl for Nat Academic Awards, Govt Art Collection, Gulbenkian Fndn, Miny of Works Brussels, ICA, Solomon R Guggenheim Museum NY, Towner Art Gallery, Newcastle upon Tyne Poly; commissions: John Hansard Gallery Univ of Southampton 1989, Groundwork Hackney 1996; Winston Churchill travel fell Netherlands and Germany 1989, Pollock-Krasner Fndn Grant 1996; ARBS 1998; *Recreations* swimming; *Style*— John Edwards, Esq; ✉ 52 Isledon Road, London N7 7LD (tel 020 7503 1495, website www.johnedwardsindia.com)

EDWARDS, John Thomas; s of Jack Edwards (d 1953), and Gwendoline, *née* Davies (d 1982); *b* 16 November 1935; *Educ* Haverfordwest GS; *m* Iris Mary; *Career* reporter: West Wales Guardian 1953–54, Liverpool Daily Post 1955–57; US corr Daily Mirror 1961–63 (staff corr London 1958–61); Daily Mail: feature writer 1969–71, SE Asia corr 1971–75, sr writer 1975–84, columnist 1984–; British Press Awards: Reporter of the Year 1975, commended feature writer 1977, commended foreign corr 1981; Reporter of the Year Granada TV Awards 1976; *Recreations* sailing, gardening; *Clubs* Cardiff and County, Hong Kong Press; *Style*— John Edwards, Esq; ✉ The Daily Mail, Northcliffe House, 2 Derry Street, Kensington, London W8 5TT (tel 020 7938 6210)

EDWARDS, (Alfred) Kenneth; CBE (1989, MBE 1963); s of Ernest Edwards (d 1959), of London, and Florence May Branch (d 1983); *b* 24 March 1926; *Educ* Latymer Upper Sch, Magdalene Coll Cambridge, UCL (BSc); *m* 1, 17 Sept 1949, Jeannette Lilian (decd), da of David Louis Speeks, MBE; 1 s (Vaughan b 1951), 2 da (Vivien b 1954, Deryn b 1960); m 2, 3 April 2004, Jenefer, da of John Nicholas; *Career* Flying Offr RAF 1944–47 (RAF Coll Cranwell 1945); HM Overseas Civil Serv Nigeria 1952–63; gp mktg mangr Thorn Electrical Industries Ltd 1964, int dir Brookhirst Igranic Ltd (Thorn Gp) 1967, gp mktg dir Cutler Hammer Europa 1972, chief exec Br Electrical and Allied Manufacturers Association Ltd (BEAMA) 1976–82; chm: FPM plc 1989–91, Business Services Europe 1989–95; memb Bd: Polar Electronics plc 1989–96, Reliance Bank Ltd 1992–, Salvation Army Tstee Co 1996–, SATCOL Ltd 2003–; CBI: dep dir gen 1982–88, memb Cncl 1974 and 1976–82, memb Fin and Gen Purposes Ctee 1977–82, vice-chm Eastern Regnl Cncl 1974, Pres's Ctee 1982– (memb 1979–82); memb: Exec Ctee Organisme de Liaison des Industries Metalliques Européenes (ORGALIME) 1976–82, Bd Br Standards Inst (BSI) 1978–82 and 1984–; chm: Br Electrotechnical Ctee and Electrotechnical Divnl Cncl 1981–82, BSI Quality Policy Ctee 1988–93; memb: BOTB 1982–88, Salvation Army Nat Advsy Bd 1982–, BBC Consultative Gp on Industrial and Business Affrs 1983–88; dir BTEC 1983–88; pres: European Ctee for Electrotechnical Standardisation (CENELEC) 1977–79, Union des Industries de la Communauté Européene (UNICE) (memb Exec Ctee 1982–86, chm Fin Ctee 1983–86); memb Ct Cranfield Inst of Technol 1970–75; memb Bd and Exec Ctee Business in the Community 1987–89; *Recreations* music, books; *Clubs* RAF; *Style*— Kenneth Edwards, Esq, CBE; ✉ 51 Bedford Road, Rushden, Northamptonshire NN10 0ND (tel 01933 319110)

EDWARDS, Prof Kevin John; s of John Cyril William Edwards, of Northfleet, Kent, and Elsie May, *née* Clark; *b* 18 September 1949; *Educ* Northfleet Boys' Sch, Gravesend GS, Univ of St Andrews (MA), Univ of Aberdeen (PhD); *m* 25 July 1987, Rachel Ann, *née* Regan; 2 s (Fraser John Alf Regan b 17 Aug 1989, Calum Tom Regan b 6 Aug 1993); *Career* tutorial fell Dept of Geography Univ of Aberdeen 1972–75, lectr in environmental reconstruction Queen's Univ Belfast 1975–80; Univ of Birmingham: lectr in biogeography 1980–90, sr lectr in geography 1990–92, reader in palaeoecology 1992–94; Univ of Sheffield: prof of palaeoecology 1994–2000, head Dept of Archaeology and Prehistory 1996–99; prof of physical geography Univ of Aberdeen 2000–; adjunct prof Grad Sch City Univ of NY 2002–, research assoc Macaulay Land Use Research Inst 2002–; chm Users' Ctee Univ of Oxford Radiocarbon Accelerator Unit 1995–2000, dep chm Scottish Coastal Archaeology and Palaeoenvironment Tst 2001–; memb: Radiocarbon Ctees Natural Environment Research Cncl 1995–2000, Research Ctee Soc of Antiquaries of Scotland 2000–, Earth and Environmental Sciences Ctee RSE 2003–; memb Editorial Bd: Jl of Archaeological Science 1983–, Transactions of the Institute of British Geographers 1994–98, Environmental Archaeology 1997–, Landscapes 2003–; Univs Medal RSGS 1972; FRGS 1972, FSA Scot 1972, FSA 1999, FRSE 2002, CGeog RGS 2003; *Publications* Quaternary History of Ireland (1985), Scotland: Environment and Archaeology 8000 BC-AD 1000 (1997), Holocene Environments of Prehistoric Britain (1999); author of approximately 200 articles in geography, archaeology, botany and quaternary science; *Recreations* reading, archaeology, family history; *Style*— Prof Kevin Edwards; ✉ Department of Geography and Environment, University of Aberdeen, Elphinstone Road, Aberdeen AB24 3UF (tel 01224 272346, e-mail kevin.edwards@abdn.ac.uk)

EDWARDS, Lionel Antony (Tony); *b* 4 November 1944; *Educ* Univ of Birmingham (BSc), Harvard Business Sch (MBA with Distinction); *Career* apprenticeship and later sr mgmnt positions with Rolls-Royce, General Electric (USA), Motorola and Canadair 1962–89, md Lucas Aerospace (subsequently gp md) Lucas Industries plc 1989–92, chm Dowty Group and Main Bd dir TI Group plc 1992–98, chm and chief exec Messier-Dowty International 1994–98; head of Defence Export Services Organisation MOD 1998–2001; chm The Air League 2003–; former pres Soc of Br Aerospace Cos; past chm Def & Aerospace Sector Panel UK Technol Foresight Prog; past pres Royal Aeronautical Soc; tstee: RAF Museum Hendon, The Swordfish Heritage Tst, Battle of Britain Meml Tst; former memb Nat Def Industries Cncl, former memb Aviation Ctee DTI; CEng, FRAeS; *Recreations* farming, classic car restoration, historic aircraft preservation; *Style*— Tony Edwards, Esq; ✉ Wincotts Hill Farm, Whichford, Warwickshire CV36 5PQ

EDWARDS, Lyn; s of William David Edwards (d 1972), and Gwenllian, *née* Cox; *b* 28 August 1947; *Educ* Ogmore GS, Birmingham Sch of Architecture (DipArch), Aston Univ (BSc), Univ of Reading (MSc); *m* 1971, Lynne, *née* Williams; 1 s (Nicholas Lloyd b 1978); 2 da (Philippa Louise b 1982, Rebecca Kathryn b 1985); *Career* asst: Malcolm H Peck & Partners 1969–70, Oxfordshire Co Architect's Dept 1971–72; GMW Architects: project architect 1972, resident ptnr GMW International 1978, sr ptnr 1991– (ptnr 1980); projects incl: Royal Opera House master plan and extension, King Saud Univ Riyadh, bomb damage refurbishment NatWest Tower and 99 Bishopsgate London 1988–; chm: European Architects' Alliance, Br Conslts and Contractors Bureau; memb Assoc of Project Managers; RIBA 1972, FRSA; *Recreations* rugby football (RFU Coaching Award), reading, music, family; *Clubs* East India; *Style*— Lyn Edwards, Esq; ✉ GMW Architects, PO Box 1613, 239 Kensington High Street, London W8 6SL (tel 020 7937 8020, fax 020 7937 5818)

EDWARDS, His Hon Judge (Charles) Marcus; s of (John) Basil Edwards, CBE, JP (d 1996), and Molly Patricia, *née* Philips (d 1979); *b* 10 August 1937; *Educ* Rugby, BNC Oxford (BA); *m* 1, 1963, Anne Louise (d 1970), da of Sir Edmund Stockdale, of Hoddington House, nr Basingstoke; m 2, 1975, Sandra, da of James Mouroutsos, of Mass, USA; 1 da (Alexandra b 1983); *Career* 2 Lt Intelligence Corps 1955–56; HM Dip Serv 1960–65; third sec: Spain, South Africa, Laos, Whitehall; called to the Bar 1962; practising 1965–86, circuit judge (SE Circuit) 1986–; chm Pavilion Opera 1986–; *Recreations* gardening, walking, travel; *Clubs* Beefsteak; *Style*— His Hon Judge Marcus Edwards; ✉ Mathon Lodge, Mathon, Herefordshire WR14 4DW

EDWARDS, Mark John; s of Eric Edwards, of Penarth, and Mary O'Flynn; *b* 10 July 1954, Nairobi, Kenya; *Educ* St Mary's Sch Nairobi, Clongowes Wood Coll Kildare, Univ of Bristol (BSc); *m* 8 Sept 1979, Micheline; 2 s (Richard b 26 Aug 1981, Michael b 26 Nov 1985), 1 da (Georgina b 3 March 1983); *Career* accountant PricewaterhouseCoopers 1975–79, auditor Warner Lambert 1979–81, accountant Grant Thornton 1981–82,

E

subsidiary finance dir Whitbread plc 1982–89, divnl finance dir Williams plc 1989–96; Baxi Gp: finance dir 1996–2003, gp ceo 2003–; FCA 1979; *Recreations* golf, skiing, theatre; *Clubs* RAC, Kedleston Park Golf; *Style—* Mark Edwards, Esq; ✉ Baxi Group, Pentagon House, Sir Frank Whittle Road, Derby DE21 4XA (tel 01332 524804, fax 01332 524825, e-mail mark.edwards@baxigroup.com)

EDWARDS, (Kenneth) Martin; s of late Kenneth Reginald Edwards, and Joan Isabel, *née* Bradley; *b* 7 July 1955; *Educ* Sir John Deane's GS Northwich, Balliol Coll Oxford (MA, Jenkyns Prize, Keasbey bursary, David Paton studentship, Winter Williams Award, Martin Wronker Award), Chester Coll of Law; *m* 30 April 1988, Helena Mary Caroline, da of late Michael James Shanks; 1 s (Jonathan Michael b 28 Dec 1990), 1 da (Catherine Juliet Ruth b 5 June 1993); *Career* writer and slr; articled clerk Booth and Co Solicitors Leeds 1978–80, admitted slr 1980, ptnr Mace and Jones Liverpool 1984– (slr 1980–84); memb editorial bd Business Law Review; memb: Standing Ctee on Employment Law Law Soc 1987–97, Working Pty on Alternative Dispute Resolution Law Soc 1997–, Crime Writers' Assoc, Soc of Authors; ACIArb; *Books* Understanding Computer Contracts (1983), Understanding Dismissal Law (1984, 2 edn 1991), Managing Redundancies (1986), Executive Survival (1987, 2 edn 1991), Northern Blood (ed, 1992), Careers in the Law (1995, 6 edns), Anglian Blood (co-ed, 1995), Northern Blood 2 (ed, 1995), Know-How for Employment Lawyers (jtly, 1995), Perfectly Criminal (ed, 1996), Whydunit? (ed, 1997), Past Crimes (ed, 1998), Northern Blood 3 (ed, 1998), Missing Persons (ed, 1999), Scenes of Crime (ed, 2000), Tolley's Equal Opportunities Handbook (2000, 4 edns), Murder Squad (ed, 2001), Crime in the City (ed, 2002), Urge To Kill (2002), Green for Danger (ed, 2003), Mysterious Pleasures (ed, 2003), Crime on the Move (ed, 2004), ID (ed, 2006); *Novels* All The Lonely People (1991), Suspicious Minds (1992), I Remember You (1993), Yesterday's Papers (1994), Eve of Destruction (1996), The Devil in Disguise (1998), First Cut is the Deepest (1999), The Lazarus Widow (jtly, 1999), Take My Breath Away (2002), The Coffin Trail (2004), The Cipher Garden (2005), The Arsenic Labyrinth (2006); *Recreations* writing, music, cricket, travel, films; *Clubs* Athenaeum (Liverpool); *Style—* Martin Edwards, Esq; ✉ Watson Little Ltd, Capo di Monte, Windmill Hill, London (e-mail martinedwards10@btconnect.com, website www.martinedwardsbooks.com)

EDWARDS, Prof Michael; OBE (2006); s of Frank Ernest Walter Edwards (d 1995), and Irene Louise Dalliston (d 1985); *b* 29 April 1938; *Educ* Kingston GS, Christ's Coll Cambridge (BA, MA, PhD); *m* 7 July 1964, Danielle, da of Jacques Bourdin, of Lamotte-Beuvron, France; 1 s (Paul), 1 da (Catherine); *Career* lectr in French Univ of Warwick 1965–73, sr lectr then reader in lit Univ of Essex 1973–87, prof of English Univ of Warwick 1987–2002, prof of English Collège de France 2002–; visiting prof: Univ of Paris 1989–90, Collège de France and Univ of Witwatersrand 1997, Ecole Normale Supérieure 1998, European chair Collège de France 2000–01; memb Cncl Institut Collégial Européen; *Books* La Tragédie Racinienne (1972), To Kindle The Starling (poems, 1972), Eliot/Language (1975), Where (poems, 1975), The Ballad of Mobb Conroy (poems, 1977), Towards a Christian Poetics (1984), The Magic, Unquiet Body (poems, 1985), Poetry and Possibility (1988), Of Making Many Books (1990), Raymond Mason (1994), Eloge de l'Attente (1996), De Poetica Christiana (1997), Beckett ou le don des Langues (1998), Leçons de Poésie (2001), Ombres de Lune (2001), Un Monde Même et Autre (2002), Shakespeare et la Comédie de l'émerveillement (2003), Terre de Poésie (2003), Rivage Mobile (poems, 2003), Etude de la Création Littéraire en Langue Anglaise (2004), Racine et Shakespeare (2004), Shakespeare et L'Oeuvre de la Tragédie (2005), Le Genie de la Poesie Anglaise (2006); *Recreations* walking; *Clubs* Cambridge Union; *Style—* Prof Michael Edwards, OBE

EDWARDS, Dr Michael Frederick; OBE (1992); s of Henry Sandford Edwards (d 1965), and Jessie, *née* Wallwork; *b* 27 April 1941; *Educ* Tupton Hall GS, UC Swansea (BP scholarship, BSc, Harold Hartley Prize, PhD); *m* 30 Dec 1964, Margaret Roberta; 1 s (Peter Stephen b 22 April 1967), 1 da (Catherine Louise b 20 Aug 1969); *Career* lectr in engrg sci Univ of Warwick 1966–69, prof Chemical Engrg Dept Univ of Bradford 1981–87 (lectr then sr lectr 1969–81), princ engr Unilever Research 1987–2001; visiting prof of chemical engrg: UMIST (now Univ of Manchester), Univ of Wales Swansea; FIChemE, FREng 1992; *Books* Mixing in the Process Industries (ed, 1985, 2 edn 1992); *Recreations* walking, music; *Style—* Dr Michael Edwards, OBE, FREng; ✉ 44 Long Meadow, Gayton, Wirral CH60 8QQ (tel 0151 342 5602, e-mail coparran@btinternet.com)

EDWARDS, Paul David Thomas; s of Robert Thomas Edwards, and Ailsa Edith, *née* Brown; *Educ* Toowoomba GS, Queensland Univ of Technol (Dip Educn Art and Drama), RADA (Dip Scene Design); *Career* designer; assoc memb RADA, memb Soc of Br Theatre Designers; *Theatre* designs incl: Trojan Women (La Boite), Did You Say Love (La Boite), One Flew Over the Cuckoo's Nest (Brisbane Arts Theatre), Time and Time Again (Sydney Ensemble Theatre), The Young Idea (Chester Gateway), The Last Yankee (Leicester Haymarket), The Pleasure Principle (The Young Vic), No Flies On Mr Hunter (Chelsea Arts Theatre), Birdbath (Etc Theatre), Post of the Cosmos (Etc Theatre), Vita and Virginia (Sphinx Theatre Co), The Servant of Two Masters (Wolsey Theatre Ipswich), Brighton Beach Memories (Stephen Joseph Theatre), Little Women (Sheffield Crucible Theatre), Fair Game (Theatre Royal Plymouth), Kiss Me Kate (Norwich Playhouse), The Importance of Being Earnest (Nat Theatre of Israel), Boutique (London Studio Centre), Jyroscape (Sadlers Wells), The Taming of the Shrew (New Shakespeare Co), Is That All There Is? (Almeida and NY), Viva Espana, Trelawney of the Wells; designs for Harrogate Theatre: The Odd Couple, The Importance of Being Earnest, Private Lives, Jack and the Beanstalk, Gasping, On the Piste, Cat on a Hot Tin Roof, The Barber of Seville, Romeo and Juliet; designs for Queens Theatre Hornchurch: Noises Off, Great Expectations, The Sound of Music, The Turn of the Screw, Dames at Sea; designs for Theatre Clwyd: Pygmalion, Hamlet, The Seagull, School for Scandal; *Opera* designs incl: The Bartered Bride (Tel Aviv), Orfeo et Euridice (Tel Aviv), Little Magic Flute (Tel Aviv), L'Egoiste (RAM), La Finta Semplice (Nice, Vichy and Paris), The Marriage of Figaro (Dublin), The Secret Marriage (Paris), L'Italiana in Algeri (Garsington), Il Mondo Della Luna (Garsington), The Mikado (Cardiff), Orfeo et Euridice (Strasbourg, Valladolid and La Coruna), Jakobin (Wexford), Die Walküre (Caracas), The Pearl Fishers (Russia and Holland); *Recreations* skiing, sailing; *Style—* Paul Edwards, Esq; ✉ c/o Cassie Mayer Ltd, 5 Old Garden House, The Lanterns, Bridge Lane, London SW11 3AD

EDWARDS, Prof Paul Kerr; s of Ernest Edwards (d 1979), and Ida Vivienne, *née* Kerr; *b* 18 March 1952; *Educ* King Edward VI Sch Stratford-on-Avon, Magdalene Coll Cambridge (BA), Nuffield Coll Oxford (BPhil, DPhil); *m* 1975, Susan Jane, da of John Geeson Martin; 1 s (William John b 1980), 1 da (Rebecca Jane b 1983); *Career* Univ of Warwick: various research positions Industrial Relations Research Unit (IRRU) 1977–88, prof of industrial relations 1992–, dir IRRU 1998–2002 (dep dir 1988–98); sr fell Advanced Inst of Mgmnt Research 2004–07; chm Social Science Gp Br Acad 2006–; memb Br Sociological Assoc (1980); FBA 1998; *Books* Strikes in the United States (1981), The Social Organization of Industrial Conflict (co-author, 1982), Conflict at Work (1986), Managing the Factory (1987), Attending to Work (co-author, 1993), Managers in the Making (co-author, 1997), Industrial Relations (ed, 2003), The Politics of Working Life (co-author, 2005), Social Theory at Work (co-ed, 2006); *Recreations* cycling; *Style—* Prof Paul Edwards, FBA; ✉ Industrial Relations Research Unit, University of Warwick, Coventry, Warwickshire CV4 7AL (tel 024 7652 4270, fax 024 7652 4184, e-mail irrupe@wbs.warwick.ac.uk)

EDWARDS, Prof Peter Philip; s of late Ronald Goodlass, and Ethel Mary, who later m Arthur Edwards; *b* 30 June 1949; *Educ* Univ of Salford (Chemistry Prize, BSc, PhD); *m* 4 Sept 1970, Patricia Anne, da of John and Mary Clancy; 1 da (Kerrie b 13 Dec 1971), 2 s (Peter John b 23 April 1973, Karl b 17 March 1980); *Career* Fulbright scholar and Nat Science fell Baker Lab of Chemistry Cornell Univ 1975–77, SERC/NATO fell and Ramsay Meml fell Inorganic Chemistry Lab Univ of Oxford 1977–79; Univ of Cambridge: lectr and dir of studies in chemistry 1979–90, dir of studies in natural scis and fell Jesus Coll 1979–90, Nuffield Science Research fell 1986–87, co-fndr and co-dir first Interdisciplinary Research Centre in Superconductivity 1988, British Petroleum Venture Research fell 1988–90; Univ of Birmingham: prof of inorganic chemistry 1991–99, head Sch of Chemistry 1997–99, prof of chemistry and of materials 1999–2003; head and prof of inorganic chemistry Univ of Oxford 2003–; co-ordinator EPSRC UK Sustainable Hydrogen Energy Consortium 2003–; visiting prof Cornell Univ 1983–86, F S Kipping visitor Univ of Nottingham 1987, Royal Soc Leverhulme Tst sr research fell 1996–97; memb HEFCE: Research Assessment Exercise Panels 1996 and 2001, Non-Formula Funding Panel 1997; Royal Soc of Chemistry: Corday-Morgan Medal 1987, Tilden Medal 1992, vice-pres Dalton Div 1995; memb Materials Research Soc of India; Liversidge Medal 1999, Hughes Medal Royal Soc 2003; FRS 1996; *Books* The Metallic and Nonmetallic States of Matter (ed with C N R Rao, 1985), Metal-Insulator Transitions Revisited (ed with C N R Rao, 1995); *Style—* Prof Peter P Edwards, FRS; ✉ Inorganic Chemistry Laboratory, University of Oxford, South Parks Road, Oxford OX1 3QR (tel 01865 272646, fax 01865 272690)

EDWARDS, Peter Robert; s of Robert Edwards, of Worthing, West Sussex, and Doris Edith, *née* Cooper; *b* 30 October 1937; *Educ* Christ's Hosp; *m* 1, 1967, Jennefer Ann, da of Frederick Boys; m 2, 1970, Elizabeth Janet, da of Maitland Barrett; 1 s (Simon b 1970), 1 da (Sarah b 1971); *Career* Arthur Young 1955–90 (managing ptnr 1986–90), md Secretan plc 1990–92, ind memb Cncl FIMBRA 1990–94, currently public interest dir Personal Investment Authy; non-exec dir Blackwall Green Ltd 1993–96; Freeman City of London 1956, memb Worshipful Co of Merchant Taylors; ICAS 1960; *Recreations* ornithology; *Style—* Peter Edwards, Esq; ✉ River House, Church Lane, Bury, Pulborough, West Sussex RH20 1PB (tel 01798 831900, fax 01798 831774); The Personal Investment Authority, 25 The North Colonnade, Canary Wharf, London E14 5HS (tel 020 7676 1000, fax 020 7676 1099)

EDWARDS, (John) Richard Martin; OBE (2006); s of Arthur Crai Edwards (d 1989), of Stow-on-the-Wold, Glos, and Barbara Leslee Mary, *née* Hart (d 1997); *b* 2 September 1941; *Educ* Dulwich Coll; *m* Rowena Gail, da of Cdr George McCracken Rutherford, MBE, DSC, VRD, RNR (ret); 1 da (Melanie Jane b 13 July 1963), 1 s (James Lindsay b 3 Oct 1964); *Career* various admin and mgmnt posts Trust House Forte Ltd 1959–76, md Chester Grosvenor Hotel (Prestige) 1982–86 (gen mangr 1976–82), dir Exclusive Div Trust House Forte 1986–87, md Forte Classic Hotels 1987–90, quality serv dir Trust House Forte UK 1990, md Management Services International 1990–94; dir Grayshott Hall Health Fitness Retreat 1994–95, sec Phyllis Court Club 1995–2004; chm: Prestige Hotels 1981 and 1982, Thames and Chilterns Div BHA 1989–90 (chm Clubs Ctee BHA 1995–97), Master Innholders 1990–92, Acad of Food and Wine Service 1997–2005; first Hotelier of the Year 1983, Master Innholder 1986; Freeman City of London 1986; Chevalier du Tastevin 1981, Conseiller Culinaire de Grande Bretagne, Confrèrie de la Chaîne des Rotisseurs 1989–95; FHCIMA 1986; *Recreations* golf, painting, the South of France; *Clubs* Phyllis Court (Henley), Henley Golf; *Style—* Richard Edwards, Esq, OBE; ✉ 3 Bell Street Mews, Henley on Thames RG9 2BF (tel 01491 572959, e-mail riga546@hotmail.com); 546 Domaine des Canebières, 83490 Le Muy, Var, France (tel 00 33 66 83 61 945)

EDWARDS, Robert Charlton (Rob); s of Lawrence Edwin Edwards (d 1977), and Muriel Eugénie, *née* Peel (d 1989); *b* 24 May 1949; *Educ* Worcester Royal GS, Pembroke Coll Oxford, Bristol Old Vic Theatre Sch; *m* 1 Nov 1997, Markéta; 2 s (Oskar b 28 May 2001, Lukas b 16 Feb 2004); *Career* actor; *Theatre* RSC Stratford and the Aldwych 1980–81: Amintor in The Maid's Tragedy, Young Gobbo in The Merchant of Venice, Khomich in Lovegirl and the Innocent by Solzhenitsin, Charles Lamb in The Fool by Edward Bond; Young Vic 1986, 1989 and 1990: Lucio and The Duke in Measure for Measure, Mercutio in Romeo and Juliet; RSC Stratford and Barbican 1990–91: title role in Pericles (Barbican only), Pritikin in Barbarians by Maxim Gorky (Barbican only), First Citizen in Coriolanus; Apoo in Topakano's Martyrs' Day (Bush), Hamlet in Hamlet with the London Shakespeare Group (Far Eastern Tours for Br Cncl) 1985 and 1986, Max and Singer in Definitely the Bahamas by Martin Crimp and Angus in No More a-Roving by John Whiting (Orange Tree) 1987, Polynices in The Thebans (RSC) 1991, Poins in Henry IV (RSC) 1991, Horatio in Hamlet (RSC) 1992, Cassius in Julius Caesar (RSC) 1993, Quarlous in Bartholomew Fair (RSC) 1997, Walt Disney in Talk of the City (RSC) 1998, Scar in The Lion King (West End) 1999, Hippolito in Women Beware Women (RSC) 2006, Page in Merry Wives, the Musical (RSC) 2006–07; *Television* incl: Stephen Lovell in The Fourth Arm (BBC) 1981–82, John Fletcher in By the Sword Divided (BBC) 1983–84, Dr Chris Clarke in The Practice (Granada) 1985, Gilbert Whippet in Campion (BBC) 1988, Prince John in Henry IV Parts I & II and Henry V (BBC), Arthur Goslett in In Suspicious Circumstances 1993, John Drewe in Trail of Guilt (BBC) 1999, Richard Florian in Midsomer Murders (ITV) 2006, Geoff Holhurst in The Thick of It (BBC) 2007; *Recreations* scrambling, mountain walking; *Style—* Rob Edwards, Esq; ✉ c/o Gordon & French, 12–13 Poland Street, London W1V 3DE (tel 020 7734 4818, fax 020 7734 4832)

EDWARDS, Robert Philip (Rob); s of Robert Aelwyn Edwards, of Abbots Langley, Herts, and Kathleen Isobel, *née* Brockbank; *b* 13 October 1953; *Educ* Watford Boys' GS, Jesus Coll Cambridge (MA); *m* 8 June 1977, Dr Fiona Grant Riddoch, da of Thomas Grant Riddoch; 2 da (Robyn Edwards Riddoch b 20 Feb 1990, Lindsay Edwards Riddoch b 1 Jan 1993); *Career* journalist, television prodr and writer; organiser Scottish Campaign to Resist the Atomic Menace 1977–78, campaigns organiser Shelter (Scotland) 1978–80; work as Scottish corr Social Work Today 1981–83, res asst to Robin Cook MP 1980–83, co-ordinator of CND's case at Sizewell Inquiry 1982–85; Scottish corr: New Statesman 1983–89, The Guardian 1989–93; columnist Edinburgh Evening News 1989–94, environment ed Scotland on Sunday 1989–94, German corr New Scientist, Scotland on Sunday and The Scotsman 1994–96, conslt with New Scientist 1996–, environment ed Sunday Herald 1999–; prodr: documentary Children Under Fire (Channel 4) 1993, CCTV (Channel 4) 1999; Media Natura Regnl Journalist of the Year Br Environment and Media Awards 1989 (specially commended 1992), commended Industrial Soc Environment Award 1993, commended UK Press Gazette Regnl Awards 1993, Sunday Herald Br Environment and Media Award Newspaper of the Year 2001, shortlisted Journalist of the Year Br Environment and Media Awards 2006; memb NUJ; *Books* Fuelling the Nuclear Arms Race: the Links Between Nuclear Power and Nuclear Weapons (with Sheila Durie, 1982), Britain's Nuclear Nightmare (with James Cutler, 1988), Still Fighting for Gemma (with Susan D'Arcy, 1995); *Recreations* walking, opera, theatre, films and rock music; *Style—* Rob Edwards, Esq; ✉ 53 Nile Grove, Edinburgh EH10 4RE (tel 0131 447 2796, fax 0131 447 0647, e-mail rob.edwards@blueyonder.co.uk, website www.robedwards.com)

EDWARDS, Roger John; s of late Flt Lt John Alfred Edwards, of Ewhurst, Surrey, and Melva Joyce, *née* Burrell; *b* 30 November 1941; *Educ* Isleworth GS, Univ of Hull; *m* 4 July 1964, Janet Amelia, da of Stanley Victor Holmes (d 1971); 2 s (Nicholas St John b 29 July 1966, Barnaby James b 20 Aug 1969); *Career* McCann Erickson 1964–67, Chesebrough Ponds 1967–70, Davidson Pearce Ltd 1970–77, ceo Leo Burnett 1979–81, Grey Communications Group 1982– (formerly chm and chief exec, now md); FIPA 1983, FInstD; *Recreations* theatre, travel, walking, books, golf; *Clubs* Wisley Golf (dep chm);

Style— Roger Edwards, Esq; ✉ Grey Communications Group Ltd, 215–227 Great Portland Street, London W1N 5HD (tel 020 7636 3399)

EDWARDS, Ruth Dudley; da of Robert Walter Dudley Edwards (d 1988), and Sheila, *née* O'Sullivan (d 1985); *b* 24 May 1944; *Educ* Sacred Heart Convent Dublin, Sandymount HS Dublin, UCD (BA, MA, DLitt), Girton Coll and Univ (now Wolfson) Coll Cambridge, City of London Poly (Dip Business Studies); *m* 1, 31 July 1965 (m dis 1975), Patrick John Cosgrave (d 2001), s of Patrick Joseph Cosgrave (d 1952); m 2, 10 Jan 1976 (m dis 1991), John Robert Mattock, s of John Leonard Mattock (d 1986); *Career* teacher 1965–67, mktg exec Post Office 1970–74, principal DOI 1975–79, freelance writer 1979–, company historian The Economist 1982–2000, freelance journalist and broadcaster 1994–; memb Exec Ctee: Br Irish Assoc 1981–93, Crime Writers' Assoc 1995–98, Soc of Authors 1996–99; chm Br Assoc for Irish Studies 1986–93; *Books* An Atlas of Irish History (1973), Patrick Pearse: the triumph of failure (1977, Nat Univ of Ireland Historical Research Prize), James Connolly (1981), Corridors of Death (1981), Harold Macmillan: a life in pictures (1983), The Saint Valentine's Day Murders (1984), Victor Gollancz: a biography (1987, James Tait Black Memorial Prize), The School of English Murder (1990), Clubbed to Death (1992), The Pursuit of Reason: The Economist 1843–1993 (1993), The Best of Bagehot (1993), True Brits (1994), Matricide at St Martha's (1994), Ten Lords A-Leaping (1995), Murder in a Cathedral (1996), Publish and be Murdered (1998), The Faithful Tribe: an intimate portrait of the loyal institutions (1999), The Anglo-Irish Murders (2000), Newspapermen: Hugh Cudlipp, Cecil Harmsworth King and the glory days of Fleet Street (2003), Carnage on the Committee (2004), Murdering Americans (2007); *Recreations* friends; *Clubs* Academy, Reform; *Style—* Miss Ruth Dudley Edwards; ✉ 40 Pope's Lane, Ealing, London W5 4NU (tel 020 8579 1041, e-mail ruthdudleyedwards@ntlworld.com, website www.ruthdudleyedwards.co.uk)

EDWARDS, Prof Sir Samuel Frederick (Sam); kt (1975); s of Richard Edwards, of Swansea, and Mary Jane Edwards; *b* 1 February 1928; *Educ* Swansea GS, Gonville & Caius Coll Cambridge (MA, PhD), Harvard Univ; *m* 1953, Merriell E M Bland; 1 s, 3 da; *Career* prof of theoretical physics Univ of Manchester 1963–72; Univ of Cambridge: fell Gonville & Caius Coll 1972 (pres 1993–97), John Humphrey Plummer prof of physics 1972–84, Cavendish prof of physics 1984–95 (now emeritus), pro-vice-chllr 1993–95; chm SRC 1973–77, UK delg to Sci Ctee NATO 1974–79, memb Cncl Euro R&D (EEC) 1976–80; IMA: memb Cncl 1976–, vice-pres 1979, pres 1980–81; chm Def Scientific Advsy Cncl 1977–80 (memb 1973); non-exec dir: Lucas Industries plc 1981–93, Steetley plc 1985–92; sr scientific advsr Unilever and BP, chief scientific advsr Dept of Energy 1983–88 (memb Advsy Cncl on R&D 1974–77, chm 1983–88), pres BAAS 1988–89 (chm Cncl 1977–82); author of reports: Future of British Physics (HMSO) 1989, Evaluation of Science Programme EC 1990; memb Cncl AFRC 1990–94; Maxwell Medal and Prize Inst of Physics 1974, High Polymer Physics (Ford) Prize American Physical Soc 1982, Davy Medal Royal Soc 1984, Gold Medal Inst of Mathematics 1986, Guthrie Medal and Prize Inst of Physics 1987, Gold Medal Rheological Soc 1990, LVMH Prize (Science pour l'Art) 1993, Boltzmann Medal Int Union of Pure and Applied Physics 1995, Royal Medal Royal Soc 2001; Hon DSc Univs of: Bath, Birmingham, Cambridge, Edinburgh, Salford, Strasbourg, Wales, Sheffield, Dublin, Leeds, E Anglia, Mainz; Hon DTech Loughborough Univ, Hon PhD Tel Aviv; foreign memb: Académie des Sciences Paris, Nat Acad of Sciences Washington, Russian Acad; hon fell: Univ of Swansea, Inst of Physics, French Physical Soc, Euro Physical Soc; FRS, FInstP, FRSC, FIMA; *Books* Technological Risk (1980), Theory of Polymer Dynamics (with M Doi, 1986), Networks of Rod Molecules (with S Aharoni, 1994); *Clubs* Athenaeum; *Style—* Sir Sam Edwards, FRS; ✉ 7 Penarth Place, Cambridge CB3 9LU (tel 01223 366610); Cavendish Laboratory, Cambridge (tel 01223 337259, fax 01223 337000, e-mail sfe11@phy.cam.ac.uk)

EDWARDS, Prof Steven; s of William Edward Edwards (d 1976), of Wolverhampton, W Midlands, and Daisy May, *née* Candelent; *b* 9 March 1948; *Educ* Wolverhampton GS, Trinity Hall Cambridge (Vet MB, MA), Univ of Edinburgh (MSc, DVMS); *m* 15 May 1976, Virginia Elizabeth Marian Lynch, da of Charles Frederick Holt Evans, FSA, FSG; 2 s (Joseph Alexander b 28 Dec 1977, Peter William b 3 Oct 1979); *Career* gen vet practice 1972–76, vet investigation offr UK Overseas Devpt Miny El Salvador and Bolivia 1978–80; Virology Dept Central Vet Lab MAFF: vet res offr 1980–86, sr res offr 1986–92, head of dept 1992–98; MAFF (now DEFRA) Vet Labs Agency: dir of lab servs 1998–99, dir of surveillance and lab servs 1999–2000, chief exec 2000–; visiting prof: Faculty of Vet Sci Univ of Liverpool 2001–, RVC London 2002–; pres Vet Res Club 1995–96 (memb Cncl 1992–97), vice-pres Standards Cmmn Office International des Epizooties (OIE) 2000–03 (sec-gen 1991–2000), pres Biological Standards Cmmn (OIE) 2003–, sec Euro Soc for Vet Virology 1988–94 (hon memb 1997–); fndr tstee Fndn for Medieval Genealogy, chm St Lawrence Chobham Handbell Ringers 2004–06; MRCVS 1972; *Publications* author of more than 60 papers in peer-reviewed jls, contrib to books, conf proceedings and editorial work; *Recreations* railway preservation, genealogy, handbell ringing; *Style—* Prof Steven Edwards; ✉ Veterinary Laboratories Agency, New Haw, Addlestone, Surrey KT15 3NB (tel 01932 341111, fax 01932 347046, e-mail s.edwards@vla.defra.gsi.gov.uk)

EDWARDS, Tracy Karen; MBE (1990); da of Antony Herbert Edwards (d 1973), of Purley-on-Thames, Berks, and Patricia Edwards; *b* 5 September 1962; *Educ* Highlands Tilehurst, Arts Educn Tring, Gowerton Comp Swansea; *m* (m dis); 1 da (MacKenna Lily Jean Foy b 17 Dec 1999); *Career* yachtswoman; Whitbread Round the World Race: crew memb Atlantic Privateer 1985–86, skipper, navigator and project leader Maiden 1989–90 (first all female challenge, best result for a British boat since 1977, unbeaten 1997), skipper Royal SunAlliance 1998 (first British all female multihull crew, fastest all female crossing of the Atlantic, fastest time Cowes to Fastnet Rock, Channel record (fastest ocean sailing record in world at 22.7 knots), Australia to NZ record, Jules Verne trophy Feb 1998, dismasted Southern Ocean after 43 days at sea, reached Chile without assistance), Maiden II challenge 2002 (mixed crew, 24 hour record, Channel record, Antigua to Newport record, Round Br and Ireland record), mangr Oryx Quest 2005 (Qatar, first round the world race to start and finish in Middle East), currently conslt to cos doing business in Middle East, involved in TV projects and motivational, conference and after-dinner speaker; co-presenter Whitbread (Meridian) 1993–94, presenter National Geographic Science of Sailing; patron, Ahoy Centre, ambass NSPCC, ambass One Parent Families; voted Yachtsman of the Year by Yachting Journalists' Assoc of GB (first woman winner in the award's 35 year history), Daily Express Sportswoman of the Year 1990, RADAR People of the Year Award for Courage 1998; *Books* Maiden (1990), Living Every Second (2000); *Videos* Maiden Voyage (1990), Girls and Buoys (1998); *Recreations* horse riding, shooting, skiing, rugby; *Clubs* Royal Yachting Association, Royal Ocean Racing, Cape Horners, Mosimann's, Quintessentially; *Style—* Miss Tracy Edwards, MBE; ✉ c.o Mark Lucas, L A W, 14 Vernon Street, London W14 0RJ (tel 020 7471 7900, website www.tracyedwards.com)

EDWARDS, Dr Victoria Mary; OBE (2004); da of George Wade Brown Edwards, of Sway, Hants, and Betty Kathlene, *née* Mack; *b* 14 August 1963, Wallasey, Merseyside; *Educ* Univ of Reading (Strutt and Parker Award, BSc, PhD), Univ of Canterbury NZ (Cwlth scholar, MSc); *m* 15 May 1999, Richard Taylor; 1 step da (Stephanie Rose), 1 step s (Michael James); *Career* chartered surveyor Rural Dept Dreweatt-Neate 1984–87, conslt strategic devpt and mgmnt QEII Nat Tst Wellington NZ 1987–89; Univ of Portsmouth: sr lectr and dir of research 1989–94, princ lectr and dir of research Sch of Environmental Design and Mgmnt 1994– (head of sch 2006–); non-exec dir: Countryside Agency 1998–2004, Forestry Cmmn 1999–2006 (chair Research Strategy Mgmnt Bd), Macaulay Land Use Research Inst 2001–04; memb: Academic Advsy Cncl Environment Unit Inst of Economic Affrs 1990–95, Survey Courses Bd RICS 1991–96, Educn and Membership Ctee RICS 1992–96, Academic Ctee Cambridge Int Land Inst Fitzwilliam Coll Cambridge 1995–98, Advsy Ctee Sch of Rural Economy and Land Mgmnt RAC Cirencester 1996–2001, Burns Ctee (Inquiry into Hunting) 1999–2000, Steering Gp Promotion and Guidance for Recreation on Ecologically Sensitive Sites (PROGRESS) ODPM 2003–; tstee: Countryside Educn Tst 1998–2001, Habitat Research Tst; Carthage fell USA 1991, Winston Churchill travelling fell 1991, RICS teaching fell 1993–95, Jones Lang Wootton scholar 1995–96; fell Central Assoc of Agricultural Valuers 1985, FRICS 1986; *Books* Dealing in Diversity: America's Market for Nature Conservation (1995), Corporate Property Management: Aligning Business with Real Estate Strategy (jtly, 2004); *Recreations* local community interests in New Forest, walking, golf, skiing, fundraising for hospice movement (250km sponsored dog sled Arctic Circle 2006), wildlife filmmaking, cooking for friends; *Style—* Dr Victoria Edwards, OBE; ✉ University of Portsmouth, School of Environmental Design and Management, Portland Building, Portland Street, Portsmouth PO1 3AH (tel 023 9284 2918, fax 023 9284 2913, e-mail victoria.edwards@port.ac.uk)

EDWARDS-STUART, Antony James Cobham; QC (1991); s of Lt-Col Ivor Arthur James Edwards-Stuart (decd), and Elizabeth Aileen Le Mesurier, *née* Deck (d 2003); *b* 2 November 1946; *Educ* Sherborne, RMA Sandhurst (RAC Young Officers Prize), St Catharine's Coll Cambridge (MA); *m* 11 May 1973, Fiona Ann, da of (Albert) Paul Weaver, OBE (d 1993), of London; 2 s (Luke b 29 Sept 1973, Thomas b 4 Sept 1980), 2 da (Anna b 26 March 1976, Rachel b 25 Feb 1982); *Career* cmmnd 1 Royal Tank Regt 1966, Adj 1973–75, Adj Kent & Sharpshooters Yeo 1975–77; called to the Bar Gray's Inn 1976, recorder 1997– (asst recorder 1991–97), dep judge of the High Court 2003–, head of chambers 2005–; chm Home Office Advsy Ctee on Service Candidates 1995–98; MCIArb 2001; *Recreations* theatre, restoring property in France; *Style—* Antony Edwards-Stuart, Esq, QC; ✉ Crown Office Chambers, 2 Crown Office Row, Temple, London EC4Y 7HJ (tel 020 7797 8100, fax 020 7797 8101, e-mail edwards-stuart@crownofficechambers.com)

EFFINGHAM, 7 Earl of (UK 1837); David Mowbray Algernon Howard; DL (Essex); also 17 Baron Howard of Effingham (E 1554); s of Hon John Anthony Frederick Charles Howard (d 1971, s of 5 Earl of Effingham); suc uncle 6 Earl of Effingham (d 1996); *b* 29 April 1939; *Educ* Fettes, BRNC Dartmouth; *m* 1, 1964 (m dis 1975), Anne Mary, da of Harrison Sayer (d 1980), of Cambridge; 1 s (Edward Mowbray Nicholas, Lord Howard of Effingham b 1971); m 2, 29 Dec 1992, Mrs Elizabeth Jane Turner, da of Dennis Eccleston (d 1990), of Great Saling, Essex, and formerly w of Peter Robert Easton Turner; 2 step s (James Turner b 6 Sept 1971, Charlie Turner b 15 July 1974); *Heir* s, Lord Howard of Effingham; *Career* Cdr RN; pres Royal British Legion 2004–; Freeman Worshipful Co of Pewterers; *Recreations* racing, shooting, fishing; *Clubs* Royal Navy, Essex, Army and Navy; *Style—* Cdr The Earl of Effingham, DL; ✉ Readings Farm House, Blackmore End, Essex CM7 4DH (tel 01787 461182)

EFFORD, Clive; MP; *Career* MP (Lab) Eltham 1997–; *Style—* Clive Efford, Esq, MP; ✉ House of Commons, London SW1A 0AA (tel 020 7219 3000)

EFSTATHIOU, Prof George Petros; s of Petros Efstathiou, of London, and Christina, *née* Parperis; *b* 2 September 1955; *Educ* The Somerset Sch London, Keble Coll Oxford (BA), Univ of Durham (PhD); *m* 27 July 1976 (m dis 1997), Helena Jane (Janet), da of James Lewis Smart, of Poyntzpass, Newry, NI; 1 da (Zoe b 1986), 1 s (Peter b 1988); m 2, 23 May 1998, Yvonne, da of Gianfranco Nobis of Bournemouth, Dorset; 2 s (Francesco b 2002, Alexander b 2005); *Career* res asst Univ of Calif Berkley 1979–80, sr res fell King's Coll Cambridge 1984–88 (jr res fell 1980–84, fell 1997–), asst dir of res Inst of Astronomy Cambridge 1984–88 (SERC res fell 1980–84), Savilian prof of astronomy Univ of Oxford 1988–97 (head of astrophysics 1988–94), fell New Coll Oxford 1988–97, prof of astrophysics Univ of Cambridge 1997–; sr research fell PPARC 1994–99, dir Inst of Astronomy 2004–; memb: various ctees SERC, IAU 1980, PPARC; Maxwell Medal and Prize Inst of Physics 1990, Vainu Bappu Award Astronomical Soc of India 1988, Sherman Fairchild Distinguished Scholar Caltech 1991, Bodassaki Prize for astrophysics 1994, Robinson Prize in cosmology Univ of Newcastle upon Tyne 1997, Dannie Heineman Prize American Inst of Physics 2005; FRAS 1977, FRS 1994, FInstP 1995; *Recreations* running, guitar music; *Style—* Prof George Efstathiou, FRS; ✉ Institute of Astronomy, Madingley Road, Cambridge CB3 0HA (e-mail gpe@ast.cam.ac.uk)

EGAN, Sir John Leopold; kt (1986), DL (Warwickshire 1989); s of James Edward Egan (d 1982); *b* 7 November 1939; *Educ* Bablake Sch Coventry, Imperial Coll London (BSc), London Business Sch (MSc); *m* 1963, Julia Emily, da of George Treble, of Leamington Spa; 2 da (Catherine, Lydia); *Career* parts and service dir Leyland Cars 1971–76, corporate parts dir Massey Ferguson 1976–80, chm and chief exec Jaguar Cars Ltd 1980–90, chief exec BAA plc 1990–99; chm: Inchcape plc 2000–06, Harrison Lovegrove & Co 2000–06, Severn Trent plc 2005–; pres: London Tourist Bd 1993–, CBI 2002–04 (dep pres 2001–02); former chm Construction Task Force (report published 1998); fell Imperial Coll London 1985; hon prof: Dept of Engrg Univ of Warwick 1990–, Aston Univ 1990–; Hon Dr Cranfield Inst 1986, Hon DTech Loughborough Univ 1987, Hon DBA Int Business Sch 1988, Hon LLD Univ of Bath 1988, Hon DLitt Univ of Westminster 1999; hon fell: London Business Sch 1987, Wolverhampton Poly 1989; Hon FCIM 1989 (currently a vice-pres), Hon FCGI; Int Distinguished Entrepreneur Award Univ of Manitoba, RSA Bicentenary Medal 1995; Liveryman Worshipful Co of Coachmakers & Coach Harness Makers; *Recreations* skiing, walking, music; *Clubs* Warwick Boat, RAC, MCC; *Style—* Sir John Egan, DL

EGAN, Penny; da of Derek Morris (d 1994), and June, *née* Vorst; *b* 18 July 1951; *Educ* St Paul's Girls' Sch (dep head girl), Univ of Leicester (BA); *m* 1975, David Egan, s of Henry Lawrence Egan; 2 s (Oliver b 1980, Henry b 1982); *Career* museum asst Circulation Dept rising to press offr V&A 1972–75, press offr 10 Downing St 1975–77, press and publicity offr Crafts Advsy Ctee Crafts Cncl 1977–82, conference organiser Glass in the Environment 1984–86; RSA: lecture sec 1986–95, prog devpt dir 1995–97, exec dir 1998–2006; memb Bd Design Cncl 1999–, cmmr Mayor's Cmmn on the Creative Industries 2003–05; exec dir US-UK Fulbright Cmmn, non-exe dir Wardour Publishing and Design 2007–; tstee Campaign for Learning 1998–2005, tstee Geffrye Museum 2007–; memb Cncl Univ of Warwick 2007–; Hon FRSA, Hon Fell RCA; *Recreations* tennis, cooking, the Arts; *Clubs* Roehampton; *Style—* Mrs Penny Egan; ✉ tel 07885 398050, e-mail penny@pennyegan.com

EGAN, Peter; *Educ* RADA; *m* Myra Frances, actress; 1 da (Rebecca); *Career* actor; *Theatre* roles with RSC incl: Valentine in Two Gentlemen of Verona, Osric in Hamlet, Richmond in Richard II, Sergei Nikolayich Tsyganov in Barbarians 1990; most recently Casanova in Camino Real 1996–97; Chichester Festival Theatre roles incl: Apollodorus in Caesar and Cleopatra (with Sir John Gielgud), Jack Absolute in The Rivals (with Sir John Clements), Alexander in Dear Antoine; other stage credits incl: Stanhope in Journey's End (Cambridge, won Best Actor London Theatre Critics award) 1972, John Shand in What Every Woman Knows (Albery) 1973, Cheviot Hills in Engaged (NT) 1975, Charles Rolls in Rolls Hyphen Royce (Shaftesbury) 1977, Valentine in You Never Can Tell (Royal Gala opening Lyric) 1979, Sergius in Arms and the Man (Lyric) 1981, Rene Gallimard in M Butterfly (Shaftesbury) 1989, Astrov in Uncle Vanya (also dir, with Renaissance Theatre Co, Manchester Evening News Best Actor Award) 1991, Jimmy Porter in Déjà

Vu (Comedy Theatre) 1992, Three Hotels (Tricycle and West End) 1993, Casanova in Camino Real (RSC) 1997, Serge in Art (Wyndhams) 1999, Lloyd Dallas in Noises Off (NT) 2000 and (Picadilly Theatre) 2001, Tom in Secret Rapture (Lyric) 2003, Claudius and Ghost in Hamlet (Barbican) 2004, Sherlock Holmes in The Hound of the Baskervilles (nat tour); has also directed numerous plays at the Lyric and Savoy Theatres and at Mills Coll Oakland San Francisco; *Television* incl: Seth in Cold Comfort Farm 1967, the Earl of Southampton in Elizabeth R 1971, Millais in The Love School 1974, Oscar Wilde in Lillie Langtry 1978, title role in The Prince Regent 1978, Fothergill in Reilly Ace of Spies 1982, The Dark Side of the Sun 1983, Ever Decreasing Circles 1984, 1986, 1987 and 1989, A Woman of Substance, Pym in The Perfect Spy 1986, Joint Account 1988 and 1990, A Day in Summer 1988, The Price of the Bride 1989, Ruth Rendell's A New Lease Of Death 1991, MacGyver 1992, Vanity Dies Hard 1992, The Chief 1993, Chiller 1994, The Peacock Spring 1995, Edward Ellisson in Cater St Hangman 1998, A Touch of Frost 1998, Michael Cochrane in The Ambassador 1998, Dr Hook in Cry Wolf, Inspector Lynley Mysteries 2002, The Family 2004, Jericho (Granada) 2005, Whatever Love Means 2005, Home Again (BBC1) 2005; *Film* incl: The Hireling (BAFTA Best Actor Award) 1972, Hennessy 1973, Callan 1974, Chariots of Fire 1980, Henry Simcox in Paradise Postponed (Euston Films, winner TV Times Award 1986) 1985, Gobble 1996, Bean 1996, 2001: A Space Travesty 1999, Eye Inside 2002, Something Borrowed 2003, Man to Man 2004, Death at a Funeral 2006; *Style*— Peter Egan, Esq; ⊠ c/o ICM Ltd, Oxford House, 76 Oxford Street, London W1D 1BS (tel 020 7636 6565, fax 020 7323 0101)

EGDELL, Dr (John) Duncan; s of John William Egdell (d 1990), of Bristol, and Nellie Egdell (d 1996); *b* 5 March 1938; *Educ* Clifton, Univ of Bristol (MB ChB), Univ of Edinburgh (DipSocMed); *m* 9 Aug 1963, Dr Linda Mary Flint, da of Edmund Harold Flint (d 1974), of Barnehurst, Kent; 2 s (Brian, Robin), 1 da (Ann); *Career* house physician and surgn United Bristol Hosps 1961–62, in gen practice 1962–65, asst sr med offr Newcastle Regnl Hosp Bd 1968–69 (admin med offr 1966–67), regnl specialist in community med SW RHA 1974–76 (asst sr med offr 1969–72, princ asst sr med offr 1972–74), regnl med offr Mersey RHA 1977–86, community physician and conslt in public health med Clwyd Health Authy 1986–93 (hon conslt 1993–96), hon conslt in public health med N Wales Health Authy 1996–; FFPHM (1990, FFCM 1979); *Recreations* nature conservation, delving into the past; *Style*— Dr Duncan Egdell; ⊠ Ravenswood, Glen Auldyn, Lezayre, Isle of Man IM7 2AQ (tel 01624 818012)

EGEE, Dale Richardson; da of Wallace Caldwell Richardson (d 1979), of Vermont, USA, and Corinne Mitchell Richardson (d 1987); *b* 7 February 1934; *Educ* Sacred Heart Sch Greenwich CT, Rosemont Coll PA, Instituto D'Arte Florence; *m* 1, Peter H Lewis (d 1966); 1 da (Corinna *b* 1958), 2 s (Anthony *b* 1960, Adam *b* 1963); *m* 2, 4 Sept 1966, David Wayne Egee, s of Dr J Benton Egee; 1 da (Eliza *b* 1968); *Career* tapestry designer Beirut Lebanon 1968–85; works purchased or cmmnd by: Lebanese Govt 1972, BCCI Bank 1973 and 1977, Hyatt Hotels 1977, Govt of Qatar 1979, US Govt 1985, 1986 and 1988; art conslt and gallery owner 1979– (specialising in Middle Eastern art); gallery shows incl: Contemporary Islamic Calligraphy, Middle East Artists - Works on Paper; conslt to US State Dept for Art Collections for New Embassies 1985–2003: Saudi Arabia, Bangladesh, Yemen, Egypt, Jordan, Tel Aviv, Kuwait, Kenya, Tanzania; guest curator for Contemporary Arab Artists exhibition Rotterdam Museum of Ethnology 1994–95; assisted Br Museum and Jordan Nat Museum in acquisitions of contemporary Arab artists; articles in: Arts and the Islamic World 1988, 1993 and 1997, Eastern Art Report 1989; memb: Middle Est Assoc, Saudi-Br Soc; FRGS 1987; *Recreations* reading, cookery; *Clubs* Chelsea Arts; *Style*— Ms Dale Egee; ⊠ 9 Chelsea Manor Studios, Flood Street, London SW3 5SR (tel 020 7351 6818, e-mail egee.art@btinternet.com)

EGERTON-WARBURTON, Peter; o s of Col Geoffrey Egerton-Warburton, DSO, TD, JP, DL (d 1961; ggs of Rowland Egerton, bro of Sir John Grey-Egerton, 8 Bt, and Rev Sir Philip Grey-Egerton, 9 Bt), and Hon Georgiana Mary Dormer, MBE (d 1955), eldest da of 14 Baron Dormer, CBE, DL; *b* 17 January 1933; *Educ* Eton, RMA Sandhurst; *m* 1, 29 Jan 1955 (m dis 1958), Belinda Vera, da of James R A Young; *m* 2, 10 Nov 1960 (m dis 1967), Sarah Jessica, er da of Maj Willoughby Rollo Norman; 2 s; *m* 3, 6 June 1969, Hon Marya Anne, 2 da of Baron Glenkinglas, PC; 1 s, 1 da (twins); *Career* cmmnd Coldstream Gds 1953, ret 1962 with rank of Capt; Maj Cheshire Yeo 1963; ptnr John D Wood Estate Agents 1966–86, fndr and chm Egerton Ltd Estate Agents 1986–; landowner; Lord of the Manor of Grafton, patron of the livings of Plemstall and Guilden Sutton; *Clubs* White's, Beefsteak, Turf; *Style*— Peter Egerton-Warburton, Esq; ⊠ 54 Prince's Gate Mews, London SW7 2PR (tel 020 7589 9254); Mulberry House, Bentworth, Alton, Hampshire GU34 5RB (tel 01420 562360)

EGGAR, Timothy John Crommelin (Tim); PC (1995); s of John Drennan Eggar (d 1983), and Pamela Rosemary Eggar; *b* 19 December 1951; *Educ* Winchester, Magdalene Coll Cambridge, London Coll of Law; *m* 1977, Charmian Diana, da of Peter William Vincent Minoprio, CBE; 1 s, 1 da; *Career* barr, banker; PA to Rt Hon William Whitelaw 1974, MP (Cons) Enfield N 1979–97, PPS to min for Overseas Devpt 1982–85, Parly under-sec of state FCO 1985–89; min of state: Dept of Employment 1989–90, DES 1990–92, DTI 1992–96; dir Charterhouse Petroleum 1983–85; chm: M W Kellogg Group Ltd 1996–98, chm AGIP (UK) Ltd 1997–98, chief exec Monument Oil and Gas plc 1998–99 (non-exec dir 1997–98), vice-chm ABN AMRO Corp Finance 2000–03, vice-chm ABN AMRO UK 2004–, chm Harrison Lovegrove & Co 2005–; non-exec dir: LASMO plc 1999–2000, Expro plc 2004–07; sr advsr Int Gas Union; chm Anglo-Azeri Soc 1997–2001, pres Russo-British C of C 2003–; *Style*— The Rt Hon Tim Eggar; ⊠ ABN AMRO Corporate Finance, 250 Bishopsgate, London EC2M 4AA (tel 020 7678 1881)

EGLIN, Philip; s of Jack Eglin, and Mary, *née* Whitaker; *b* 29 November 1959, Gibraltar; *Educ* Harlow Tech Coll, Staffs Poly, RCA; *Career* ceramicist; various teaching posts: Brighton Poly, Univ of Wolverhampton, Dundee Coll of Art, Crewe and Alsager Coll, Camberwell Sch of Art, Loughborough Coll of Art, Staffs Univ, Falmouth Coll of Art, W Glamorgan Inst, RCA, Harbourfront Centre Toronto; *Solo Exhibitions* Stafford Art Gallery 1990, Oxford Gallery 1991, Philip Eglin - A Staffordshire Tradition? (South Bank Centre London) 1991, Crafts Cncl Shop at the V&A 1993, Scottish Gallery Edinburgh 1994, 1997, 2000 and 2004, Garth Clark Gallery NY 1995, 1999, 2000 and 2003, Barrett Marsden Gallery London 2001, 2003 and 2006, V&A 2001, Franklin Parrasch Gallery NY 2005, Nottingham Museum and Art Gallery 2007; *Group Exhibitions* RCA Exhibition (Japan and Korea) 1987, Contemporary Applied Arts London 1988, Garden Pots (Gainsborough's House Suffolk) 1989, A Summer Picnic (City Gallery Leicester) 1989, Clay Bodies (Contemporary Applied Arts London) 1989, The Decade Ahead (Scottish Gallery Edinburgh) 1990, Great Br Design Exhibition (Tokyo) 1990, EC Exhibition (Avignon) 1990, The Abstract Vessel (Oriel Cardiff) 1991, Aspects of Sculpture (Galerie für Englishe Keramik Sandhausen) 1991, Favourite Things (Crafts Cncl Gallery London) 1991, Colours of the Earth - 20th century British Ceramics (Br Cncl touring exhibition India) 1991, 25th Anniversary Exhibition (Contemporary Applied Arts London) 1992, 25th Anniversary Exhibition (Oxford Gallery) 1993, The Raw and the Cooked (MOMA Oxford and tour), One From the Heart (Aberystwyth Arts Centre and tour) 1995, The Nude in Clay (Perimeter Gallery Chicago) 1995, Hot off the Press (Tullie House Carlisle and tour) 1996, Living at Belsay Hall (Belsay Hall Northumberland) 1996, 10 Years Crafts (Scottish Gallery Edinburgh) 1996, Jerwood Prize Exhibition (Crafts Cncl Gallery London and German tour) 1996, Philip Eglin and Claire Curneen (Contemporary Applied Arts London) 1996, Objects of Our Time (Crafts Cncl Gallery London and tour) 1996, Selection

from the Collection (Ipswich Museum and Art Gallery) 1997, European Ceramics Workcentre s'Hertogenbosch 1998, A View of Clay (Contemporary Applied Arts London) 1998, Freighted with Wonders (Wolsey Art Gallery Ipswich) 1998, 541 Vases, Pots, Sculptures and Services (Stedelijk Museum Amsterdam) 1999, Only Human (Crafts Cncl Gallery London) 1999, 25th Anniversary Exhibition (Crafts Cncl Shop at the V&A) 1999, An Inaugural Gift: The Founders' Circle Collecton (Mint Museum N Carolina) 2000, British Ceramics.2000.dk (Grimmerhus Ceramics Museum Middelfart) 2000, Br Cncl touring show of Br Ceramics (Brazil and other venues in S America) 2000, Poetics of Clay: An International Perspective (Philadelphia Art Alliance and tour to Museum of Art and Design Helsinki) 2001–02, BLUR (Stedelijk Museum) 2002, Fragile, Think with Care (Univ of Essex) 2004; *Work in Public Collections* V&A, Crafts Cncl London, Contemporary Art Soc London, Br Cncl, Stedelijk Museum Amsterdam, Mint Museum N Carolina, Auckland Museum, Fitzwilliam Museum Cambridge, Brighton and Hove Museum and Art Gallery, Portsmouth Museum and Art Gallery, Shipley Museum and Art Gallery Gateshead, Liverpool Museum and Art Gallery, Hants CC, Potteries Museum Stoke-on-Trent, Norwich City Museum and Art Gallery, Nat Museum of Scotland, Aberystwyth Arts Centre; *Awards* Crafts Cncl setting-up grant 1987, Crafts Cncl Selected Index 1991, Arts Fndn Fellowship 1993, Jerwood Prize for Applied Arts 1996; *Publications* Philip Eglin (1997), Borrowings (2007); *Recreations* mangr Shamblers FC (under 13s) in Potteries Jr Youth League; *Style*— Philip Eglin, Esq; ⊠ c/o Barrett Marsden Gallery, 17–18 Great Sutton Street, London EC1 0DN (tel 7336 6396, fax 020 7336 6391)

EGLIN, Roger David; s of George Eglin (d 1968), of West Kirby, and Evelyn, *née* Sharrocks; *b* 29 June 1940, Bolton, Lancs; *Educ* Preston GS, Calday Grange GS, LSE (BSc Econ); *m* 5 Sept 1964, Judith Ann, da of Frederick Albert Kay; 2 da (Cordelia Jane *b* 26 Feb 1968, Penelope Lydia *b* 28 Jan 1970); *Career* journalist; res asst Financial Times 1960–61, economics corr Business Magazine 1962–66, business corr The Observer 1966–72; The Sunday Times: successively industrial and business ed, then managing ed, assoc business ed, currently supplements ed; *Books* Fly Me I'm Freddie (1980); *Recreations* sailing, walking dog, reading; *Clubs* Island Sailing, Royal Corinthian Yacht; *Style*— Roger Eglin, Esq; ⊠ The Sunday Times, 1 Pennington Street, London E1 9XW (tel 020 7782 5752, fax 020 7782 5100)

EGLINTON AND WINTON, 18 Earl of (S 1507 and UK 1859); Archibald George Montgomerie; Lord Montgomerie (S 1449), Baron Seton and Tranent (UK 1859), Baron Ardrossan (UK 1806); Hereditary Sheriff of Renfrewshire; s of 17 Earl of Eglinton and Winton (d 1966), and Ursula (d 1987), da of Hon Ronald Bannatyne Watson, s of Baron Watson (Life Peer, d 1899); *b* 27 August 1939; *Educ* Eton; *m* 7 Feb 1964, Marion Carolina, da of John Henry Dunn-Yarker, of Le Château, La Tour de Peilz, Vaud, Switzerland; 4 s (Hugh, Lord Montgomerie *b* 1966, Hon William *b* 1968, Hon James *b* 1972, Hon Robert *b* 1975); *Heir* s, Lord Montgomerie; *Career* ptnr Grieveson Grant Stockbrokers 1957–72, md Gerrard & National Hldgs plc 1972–80 (dep chm 1980–92), chm Gerrard Vivian Gray Ltd 1992–95; chm Edinburgh Investment Tst plc 1992–2003; chm Charities Investment Managers Ltd; tstee: Charibond, Nat Assoc of Almshouses Common Investment Fund; past asst grand master United Grand Lodge of England; *Style*— The Rt Hon the Earl of Eglinton and Winton; ⊠ Balhomie, Cargill, Perth PH2 6DS (tel 01250 883222)

EGMONT, 12 Earl of (I 1733); Sir Thomas Frederick Gerald Perceval; 16 Bt (I 1661); also Baron Perceval (I 1715), Viscount Perceval (I 1722), Baron Lovel and Holland (GB 1762), Baron Arden (I 1770), Baron Arden (UK 1802); s of 11 Earl of Egmont (d 2002); *b* 17 August 1934; *Style*— The Rt Hon the Earl of Egmont

EGREMONT, 2 Baron (UK 1963) and 7 Baron Leconfield (UK 1859); (John) Max Henry Scawen Wyndham; DL (W Sussex); s of 6 Baron Leconfield and 1 Baron Egremont, MBE (d 1972; as John Wyndham was private sec to Rt Hon Harold Macmillan, when PM); *b* 21 April 1948; *Educ* Eton, ChCh Oxford; *m* 15 April 1978, Caroline, da of Alexander Ronan Nelson, and Hon Audrey Paget (da of 1 and last Baron Queenborough, s of Lord Alfred Paget, 5 s of 1 Marquess of Anglesey); 3 da (Hon Jessica Mary *b* 27 April 1979, Hon Constance Rose *b* 20 Dec 1980, Hon Mary Christian *b* 4 Oct 1985), 1 s (Hon George Ronan Valentine *b* 31 July 1983); *Heir* s, Hon George Wyndham; *Career* farmer and writer; chm The Friends of the Nat Libraries 1985–, memb Royal Cmmn on Historical Manuscripts 1989–2001, memb National Manuscripts Conservation Tst 1995– (chm 2000–); tstee: The Wallace Collection, Br Museum 1990–2000; Liveryman Worshipful Co of Drapers; FRSL 2001, FSA 2005; *Books* The Cousins (1977), Balfour (1980), The Ladies Man (1983), Dear Shadows (1986), Painted Lives (1989), Second Spring (1993), Under Two Flags: The Life of Major General Sir Edward Spears (1997), Siegfried Sassoon (2005); *Style*— The Rt Hon Lord Egremont, DL, FRSL; ⊠ Petworth House, Petworth, West Sussex GU28 0AE (tel 01798 342447, fax 01798 344331, e-mail egremont@dial.pipex.com)

EHRET, Thomas (Tom); s of F X Ehret (d 2001), and J Ehret, *née* Giethlen; *b* 10 March 1952, Mulhouse, France; *Educ* Ecole Nationale Supérieure des Arts et Métiers Paris; *m* 6 July 1974, G Ehret, *née* Boisson; 2 s (Xavier *b* 21 July 1976, Charles *b* 5 Aug 1983); *Career* md Comex Houlder Diving Ltd 1983–88, ceo Stena Offshore BV 1989–95, chief operating offr Coflexip Stena Offshore SA 1996–2001, vice-chm Technip SA and pres Technip Offshore 2001–03, ceo Acergy Gp 2003–; non-exec dir Venture Prodn plc 2006–; *Recreations* music, reading; *Style*— Tom Ehret, Esq; ⊠ 601 Sovereign Court, 29 Wrights Lane, London W8 5SH (tel 07876 681379, e-mail tomehret@yahoo.com); Acergy Group, Dolphin House, Windmill Road, Sunbury on Thames, Surrey TW16 7HT (tel 01932 773700, fax 01932 773701, e-mail tom.ehret@acergy-group.com)

EICHELBERGER, Alyce Faye; da of Albert Clinton McBride (d 1973), and Frances Fay, *née* Mitchell (d 1962); *b* 28 October 1944; *Educ* Oklahoma State Univ USA (BSc), Baylor Univ (MA, MSc), Univ of London Inst of Educn (DPMC); *m* 1, 22 Jan 1966, Martin Davis Eichelberger, Jr, s of Martin Davis Eichelberger; 2 s (Martin Davis III *b* 28 Sept 1969, Clinton Charles *b* 14 March 1973); *m* 2, 28 Dec 1992, John Marwood Cleese, qv; *Career* teacher secdy sch 1962–69, teaching asst to Dean of Special Educn Baylor Univ 1974–75, educnl psychologist Waco Ind Sch Dist Texas 1975–78, child psychotherapist Notre Dame Clinic 1981–87; teacher in secdy sch for emotionally disturbed children 1980–83, teacher of children with med and emotional problems ILEA 1983–84; child psychotherapist: Tavistock Clinic, Chalcot Sch; educnl psychologist Educn Records Bureau NY; psychotherapist and psychologist: American Sch of London, American Embassy, Tasis Sch Thorpe Park Surrey; in private practice: Holland Park, Kensington and Chelsea; memb: Republicans Abroad, Int Jr League Assoc of Child Psychotherapy 1986; co-fndr lunchtime lectures RGS (fndr memb and conslt); ABPS 1980, fell American Psychological Assoc 1980, fell American Med Psychotherapist Assoc 1987, memb RSM 1988, assoc fell Br Psychological Soc 1988; *Books* Comparative Education of Gifted Children in France (1979), Corporate Education of Gifted Children in the USSR (1979), A Case Study of Maladjusted Children in a London Day School (1983), How to Manage your Mother (1999); also Another Revolutionary - A Case Study of Psychotherapy With a Five Year Old Rastafarian Boy; *Recreations* yoga; *Style*— Mrs Alyce Faye Eichelberger or Mrs John Cleese

EILBECK, Prof (John) Christopher; *b* 8 April 1945; *Educ* The Queen's Coll Oxford (BSc), Lancaster Univ (PhD); *Career* Royal Soc European fell ICTP Trieste 1969–70, research fell UMIST 1970–73; Heriot-Watt Univ 1973–: head Dept of Mathematics 1984–89, prof of scientific computing 1986–, dean of sci 1998–2001; visiting fell: Los Alamos Nat Lab New Mexico 1983–84, CCC Cambridge 2001; FRSE 1987; *Books* Solitons and Nonlinear

Wave Equations (jtly, 1982); also author of over 130 papers in learned jls; *Style*— Prof Chris Eilbeck, FRSE; ✉ Department of Mathematics, Heriot-Watt University, Edinburgh EH14 4AS (tel 0131 451 3220, fax 0131 451 3249, e-mail j.c.eilbeck@hw.ac.uk)

EILLEDGE, Elwyn Owen Morris; CBE (2001); s of Owen Eilledge (d 1991), of Oswestry, Shropshire, and Mary Elizabeth Eilledge (d 1973); *b* 20 July 1935; *Educ* Oswestry Boys' HS, Merton Coll Oxford (MA); *m* 30 March 1962, Ann, *née* Ellis; 1 da (Amanda Gail Caroline b 20 Nov 1968), 1 s (Julian Alexander Stephen b 15 June 1970); *Career* chartered accountant; Ernst and Young (formerly Ernst and Whinney): joined 1965, ptnr 1972–83, managing ptnr 1983–86, sr ptnr 1986–95, chm Ernst and Young International 1988–95; secondments: Govt of Liberia 1966–68, Hamburg 1968–71; chm BTR plc 1996–98 (dir 1995–); non-exec dir BG plc 1997–2005; memb Financial Reporting Cncl 1991–95, chm Financial Reporting Advsy Bd to the Treasy 1996–; Liveryman Worshipful Co of Chartered Accountants; FCA (ACA 1963); *Recreations* opera, gardening, snooker; *Clubs* Brooks's; *Style*— Elwyn Eilledge, Esq, CBE; ✉ Whitethorn House, Long Grove, Seer Green, Beaconsfield, Buckinghamshire (tel 01494 676 600)

EINSIEDEL, Andreas Jean-Paul (GRAF von); s of Wittigo Graf von Einsiedel (d 1980), of Frankfurt am Main, Germany, and Walburga, *née* Graefin von Oberndorff; *b* 28 January 1953; *Educ* Marquartstein Bavaria, PCL (BA); *m* 2 June 1979 (m dis 1992), Harriet Angela Victoria, da of Henry George Austen de L'Etang Herbert Duckworth (d 1992); 3 s (Orlando Ernle Benedict b 19 Aug 1980, Evelyn b 26 Aug 1982 d 2004, Robin b 12 April 1988), 1 da (Gwendolen b 24 Jan 1985); *Career* internationally renowned interiors photographer; work published regularly in many leading national and international interior magazines; *Style*— Andreas Graf von Einsiedel; ✉ 72–80 Leather Lane, London EC1N 7TR (tel 020 7242 7674, fax 020 7831 3712, e-mail andreas@einsiedel.com)

EISENBERG, Neville; s of Dr Benjamin Eisenberg (d 2006), of Pretoria, South Africa, and Masha, *née* Weinberg; *b* 12 April 1962, Cape Town, South Africa; *Educ* Pretoria Boys' HS, Univ of the Witwatersrand (BCom, LLB), LSE (LLM); *Career* admitted slr 1991; Werksmans Attorneys 1985–87; Berwin Leighton Paisner Slrs: slr 1989–95, ptnr 1996–, managing ptnr 1999–; memb London Cncl CBI; chm Br Israel Law Assoc, assoc govr Hebrew Univ of Jerusalem; chm South African Union of Jewish Students 1982–84, comptroller World Union of Jewish Students 1986–89; *Recreations* theatre, music, travel; *Clubs* Home House; *Style*— Neville Eisenberg, Esq; ✉ Berwin Leighton Paisner, Adelaide House, London Bridge, London EC4R 9HA (tel 020 7760 1000, fax 020 7760 4020, e-mail neville.eisenberg@blplaw.com)

EISENHAMMER, John Stephen Walworth; s of Stephen Eisenhammer, FRCS (d 1995), and Hannah Clare, *née* Maxted (d 1998); *b* 10 July 1956; *Educ* Clifton, ChCh Oxford, Coll of Europe Bruges, Nuffield Coll Oxford (DPhil), Fondazione Lelio Basso Rome; *m* 1987, Michèle, da of Robert Krieps; 2 s (Stephen b 14 March 1987, Maximilian b 18 Feb 1990); *Career* with BBC World Service 1983–85, with Business Magazine 1986; The Independent: dip writer 1986–87, ed European affrs 1987–89, corr Germany 1989–94, fin ed 1995–96, sr conslt Bell Pottinger Consultants 1996–98, dir Quiller Consultants 1998–; Foreign Correspondent Award Germany 1990; *Recreations* theatre, gardening, snowboarding; *Clubs* RAC; *Style*— John Eisenhammer, Esq; ✉ Quiller Consultants, 11–12 Buckingham Gate, London SW1E 6LB (tel 020 7233 9444, fax 020 7233 6577, e-mail eisen@quillerconsultants.com)

EISERMANN, Richard; *Educ* Int Sch of The Hague (Dip), Rhode Island Sch of Design (BFA); *Career* designer Chicago and Milan 1983–88, sr designer Sottsass Associati Milan 1988–94, asst prof of industrial design Rhode Island Sch of Design 1994–95, design gp dir and team leader IDEO Product Devpt Lexington MA 1995–99, design dir Whirlpool Europe 1999–2003, dir design and innovation Design Cncl 2003–06, co-fndr and strategic dir Prospect 2006–; fndr and pres Rhode Island Sch of Design Shoe Soc 1981; work exhibited: Axis Gallery Tokyo 1991, Municipal Museum Rotterdam 1991, Design Museum London (perm collection) 1992–; *Awards* Design Selection Award Austrian Design Cncl 1994, Good Design Award Industrie Forum Design Hannover 1994, Design Distinction Award ID Magazine Annual Design Review 1994, Bronze and Gold Industrial Design Excellece Awards (IDEA) Industrial Designers Soc of America (IDSA)/Business Week 2001, Nat Design Award Smithsonian Inst 2002, Gold IDEA IDSA/Business Week 2003 and 2004; *Style*— Richard Eisermann, Esq; ✉ Prospect, 4 Bath Street, London EC1V 9DX

EKERT, Prof Artur Konrad; *Educ* Jagiellonian Univ Kraków (MSc), Univ of Oxford (Soros scholar, Pirie-Reid scholar, DPhil); *Career* Merton Coll Oxford: jr res fell 1991–94, memb Governing Body 1991–98, jr dean 1992–93, res fell 1994–98, memb JRF Ctee 1995–96, tutor for grad admissions 1997–98, dean of graduates 1997–98; Keble Coll Oxford: fell and tutor in physics 1998–2002, memb Governing Body 1998–2002, head IT Ctee 2000–2002; prof of physics Univ of Oxford 1998–2002; prof of quantum physics Univ of Cambridge 2002–; fell King's Coll Cambridge 2002–; head Quantum Computation & Cryptography Gp (renamed The Oxford Centre for Quantum Computation 1999, acting dir 1999–) 1993–, memb Publicity Ctee Dept of Physics Univ of Oxford 1996; visiting posts: prof Univ of Innsbruck Austria 1993 and 1998, prof Univ of Camerino Italy 1999, prof NTT Atsugi Japan 2000, distinguished prof Nat Univ of Singapore; delivered over 100 invited lectures on quantum information science and public understanding of science incl: Roger Penrose 65th birthday conf, Br Assoc for the Advancement of Science at Festivals of Science 1994, 1996, and 2000, Nobel Symposium on the Foundations of Quantum Mechanics 1997, Dept of Continuing Educn Univ of Oxford 1993, 1995, and 2000; author of several articles on quantum cryptography and science, organized scientific conferences and programme committees, conslt for companies and govt agencies incl US Army and DRA/DERA; memb editorial bd The Proceedings of the Royal Society A, memb editorial bd New Jl of Physics; memb: European Science Fndn Steering Ctee for the Quantum Info Theory Prog, EPSRC Physics Coll, EPSRC fellowship panels, Euro Cmmn Pathfinder Ctee; *Style*— Prof Artur Ekert

EL BANNA, Dr Hany Abdel Gawad; OBE (2004); s of Abdel Gawad El Banna, of Mansoura, Egypt, and Nafisa Ahmed Al Jrisis, of Cairo, Egypt; *b* 9 December 1950, Egypt; *Educ* Al Azhar Univ Cairo (MbBCh), Medical Sch Univ of Birmingham (MD); *Partner* Youseria Labib; 3 da (Asmaa b 14 Aug 1984, Fatima Al Zahra b 10 Oct 1985, Maryam b 21 July 1989), 2 s (Al Hassan b 21 Nov 1986, Omar b 15 March 1994); *Career* doctor NHS 1977–94: radiotherapy Royal Berks Hosp, radiotherapy Belvedere Hosp, ENT Hosp Glasgow, gen surgery Stophill Gen Hosp, gen pathology Dudley Road Hosp, foetal pathology Maternity Hosp Queen Elizabeth Medical Centre Birmingham; co-fndr and pres Islamic Relief Worldwide 1984–, tstee's fndr Muslim Aid 1985–99; memb: Advsy Bd Three Faiths Forum, World Economic Forum West-Islamic World Dialogue Cncl of 100 Leaders, Advsy to the Int Prog Charity Cmmn; MInstD; *Awards* Hamilton Bailey Prize Dudley Road (City) Hosp 1981, Award for Service to Medicine and Humanity Egyptian Medical Syndicate 2004, Muslim News Award for Excellence Ibn Khaldun Award (for execellence in promoting peace and understanding between global cultures and faiths) 2004, Kashmiri and Pakistani Professional Assoc Award 2005, Asian Jewel Awards (for lifetime achievements) 2006, Muslim Power 100 Award (for lifetime achievements) 2007; *Style*— Dr Hany El Banna, OBE; ✉ Islamic Relief, 19 Rea Street South, Birmingham B5 6LB (tel 0121 622 0628, fax 0121 622 5003, e-mail president@islamic-relief.org.uk)

EL NAHAS, Prof (Abdel) Meguid; s of Hassan Khalil El Nahas (d 1978), of Cairo, Egypt, and Fatma Galal Selim, *née* El Hegazy; *b* 1 December 1949; *Educ* Jesuits' Coll Cairo, Univ of Geneva Med Sch, Univ of London (PhD); *m* 30 April 1983, Penelope Anne, da of Henry

Denys Hanan, DSC, of Shrewsbury; 2 da (Gemma b 1983, Holly b 1985); *Career* res Mass Gen Hosp Boston USA 1977–78; res fell in nephrology: Paris 1978–79, Royal Postgrad Med Sch London 1979–82; renal registrar Royal Free Hospital London 1982–84, lectr in nephrology Univ of Wales Coll of Med Cardiff 1984–86, conslt renal physician Sheffield Kidney Inst Northern Gen Hosp Sheffield 1986–, prof of nephrology Sheffield Kidney Inst Univ of Sheffield 1996–; memb: Nat and Int Socs of Nephrology, Assoc of Physicians, Assoc of Clinical Professors of Medicine; FRCP; *Recreations* sports, history, travelling; *Style*— Prof A Meguid El Nahas; ✉ Sheffield Kidney Institute, Northern General Hospital, Herries Road, Sheffield S5 7AU (tel 0114 271 4018, fax 0114 256 2514, e-mail m.el-nahas@sheffield.ac.uk)

ELAND, Michael John; CB (2006); s of George Eland, and Betty Eland; *b* 26 September 1952; *Educ* Worksop Coll, Trinity Coll Oxford (MA); *m* Luned Rhiannon, *née* Wynn Jones; 1 da (Charlotte Sophie Fairbairn b 1986), 1 s (Thomas George Benjamin b 1988); *Career* called to the Bar Middle Temple 1975; HM Customs and Excise: admin trainee 1975, private sec to Chm 1979–81; Cabinet Office 1982–87, private sec to Lord Pres of the Cncl (Viscount Whitelaw) 1987–88; HM Customs and Excise: asst sec 1988–92, cmmr 1992–97, dep DG (policy) Immigration and Nationality Directorate Home Office 1997–2000; HM Revenue and Customs (formerly Customs and Excise): cmmr 2000–, DG Business Servs and Taxes 2000–03, actg cmm 2003–04, DG Law Enforcement and Compliance 2004–; *Style*— Michael Eland, Esq, CB

ELCOMB, Brig (Christopher) Mark George; OBE (1993); s of Lt-Col Michael George Elcomb, of Codford St Mary, Wilts, and Elizabeth Mary, *née* Armour; *b* 2 July 1951; *Educ* Marlborough, RMA Sandhurst, Univ of Exeter (BA); *m* 26 May 1984, Nicola Gillian Branford, da of Maj Euan Hutchings; *Career* CO 2 Bn Light Infantry 1991–92, Cmdt Jr Div Staff Coll 1994–96, Cmd 24 Airmobile Bde and Colchester Garrison 1997–98, Dep Mil Sec 1999–2002, Asst Div Cmd 3 (UK) Div 2002–03, Cmd 1 Recce Bde/Chief ISTAR 2004–05, Cmd Multinational Task Force NW Bosnia 2005–06; Dep Col (Yorks) Light Infantry 1994–2005; chapter clerk Salisbury Cathedral 2006–; *Style*— Brig Mark Elcomb, OBE; ✉ Chapter Office, 6 The Close, Salisbury SP1 2EF (tel 01722 555100)

ELDEN, Jeremy Mark; s of Reginald Elden, and Sheilagh, *née* Carter; *b* 21 June 1958; *Educ* Northgate GS Ipswich, Hertford Coll (BA), Univ of Strathclyde (MSc); *m* 19 Sept 1987, Victoria Mary, *née* Bone; *Career* field engr Schlumberger Overseas SA 1980–82, reservoir engr Britoil 1982–83, oil analyst UBS Phillips & Drew 1984–90, dir oil research BZW 1990–94; UBS Ltd: dir oil research 1994–98, global head of oil and gas research 1997–98; head of oil and gas research Commerzbank Global Equities 1998–2000; head of oil and gas research Lehman Brothers International 2000–05; active business angel; dir TJ Composting Gp Ltd; *Style*— Jeremy Elden, Esq; ✉ Roziers, Wissington, Colchester CO6 4JQ (tel 01206 262526, e-mail jeremy@elden.us)

ELDER, Prof James Brown; s of David Elder (d 1988), of Linwood, Renfrewshire, and Margaret Helen, *née* Cowan (d 1982); *b* 20 May 1938; *Educ* Shawlands Acad Glasgow, Univ of Glasgow (MB ChB, MD); *m* 12 Dec 1964, Sheena Jean Reid Fyfe, da of Colin McLay, of Paisley (d 1996); 3 da (Jacqueline b 1966, Karen b 1967, Alison b 1969); *Career* sr registrar in gen surgery Glasgow Western Infirmary 1968–71 (registrar 1965–68), reader in surgery Manchester Royal Infirmary Univ of Manchester 1976–83 (sr lectr and conslt surgn 1971–76), prof of surgery Keele Univ Sch of Postgraduate Med 1983–2004 (now emeritus prof), conslt surgn to N Staffs Hosp Centre 1983–2004, hon conslt surgn Univ Hosp of N Staffs 2004–; examiner in surgery Univs of: Manchester 1976–83, Glasgow 1981–83, Sheffield 1986–89, Nottingham 1985–89, Hong Kong 1994–; examiner: RCPS Glasgow, Univ of Manchester 1992–96, Univ of Birmingham 1994–96 and 1999–2002, UCH London 1997–99, Univ of Malta 2003, Univ of Warwick 2006–; chm W Midlands Regnl Research Awards Cte 1994–2000, chm Midlands Regnl Evaluation Panel; past pres: W Midlands Surgical Soc, Midlands Gastroenterology Soc; memb: Prout Club, W Midlands Cancer Intelligence Unit; FRCSEd 1966, FRCS 1966, FRCS Glasgow 1981; *Recreations* hill walking, classical music, reading, photography, French wine; *Clubs* British Pottery Manufacturers' Fedn (Stoke-on-Trent); *Style*— Prof James B Elder; ✉ Keele University, School of Medicine, Thornburrow Drive, Hartshill, Stoke-on-Trent ST4 7QB (tel 01782 554047, fax 01782 747319, e-mail j.elder1@ntlworld.com)

ELDER, Mark Philip; CBE (1989); *b* 2 June 1947; *Educ* Bryanston, CCC Cambridge (music scholar, choral scholar, BA, MA); *m* 30 May 1980, Amanda Jane, *née* Stein; 1 da (Katherine Olivia b 13 April 1986); *Career* music dir: English National Opera 1979–93, Rochester Philharmonic Orchestra NY 1989–94; princ guest conductor City of Birmingham Orchestra 1992–95, music dir Hallé Orch 2000–; reg work with orchs worldwide incl London Philharmonic and Orch of Age of Enlightenment; freq appearances at int opera houses incl: ROH, Met Opera NY, Opéra National de Paris, Lyric Opera Chicago, Glyndebourne Festival; annual appearances at Proms, first Br conductor to conduct new prodn at Bayreuth Festival, involved in several TV projects; *Recordings* with orchs incl: Hallé, LPO, CBSO, BBC Symphony Orch, Orch of Age of Enlightenment, ROH, ENO; *Style*— Mark Elder, Esq, CBE; ✉ c/o Ingpen & Williams Ltd, 7 St George's Court, 131 Putney Bridge Road, London SW15 2PA (tel 020 8874 3222, fax 020 8877 3113)

ELDER, Prof Murdoch George; s of Archibald James Elder (d 1992), and Lotta Annie Catherine, *née* Craig (d 1998); *b* 4 January 1938; *Educ* Edinburgh Acad, Univ of Edinburgh (MB ChB, MD), Univ of London (DSc); *m* 3 Oct 1964, Margaret Adelaide, da of Dr James McVicker (d 1985), of Portrush, Co Antrim; 2 s (James b 1968, Andrew b 1970); *Career* Nat Serv Captain RAMC (TA&VR) 1964; lectr Univ of Malta 1969–71, sr lectr and reader Univ of London (Charing Cross Hosp Med Sch) 1971–78, res fell WHO 1976, travelling fell RCOG 1977, prof and head Dept of Obstetrics & Gynaecology Royal Postgraduate Med Sch Univ of London 1978–97, prof of obstetrics & gynaecology and chm Academic Div of Paediatrics and Obstetrics & Gynaecology Imperial Coll Sch of Med London (following merger) 1996–98, fell Imperial Coll Sch of Med London 2001–; dir: Obstetrics and Gynaecology Service Hammersmith, Queen Charlotte's Special Health Authy, WHO Clinical Res Centre 1980–92; visiting prof Univs of: Calif (LA), Singapore, Natal; examiner Univs of: London, Oxford, Cambridge, Edinburgh, Glasgow, Leeds, Liverpool, Birmingham, Bristol, Dundee, Malta, Malaysia, Cape Town, Singapore, Rotterdam, Helsinki; memb Hammersmith and Queen Charlotte's Special HA 1982–90, chm Hosp Med Ctee 1980–85, sec Assoc of Profs (O and G) 1984–86; memb: WHO Steering Ctee on Contraception 1980–86, WHO Research and Ethics Group 1994–; author of over 200 scientific pubns; Silver Medal Hellenic Obstetrical Soc 1983, Bronze Medal Helsinki Univ 1995; FRCSEd 1968, FRCOG 1979; *Books* Current Fertility Control (1978), Pre Term Labour (1982), Reproduction, Obstetrics and Gynaecology (1988), Pre Term Labour (1997), Obstetrics and Gynaecology (2001); *Recreations* golf, travel; *Clubs* 1942; *Style*— Prof Murdoch Elder; ✉ Easter Calzeat, Broughton, By Biggar, Lanarkshire ML12 6HQ (tel 01899 830359, fax 01899 830359, e-mail melder@eastercalzeat.fsnet.co.uk)

ELDER, Ronald David (Ron); CBE (1991); *b* 27 May 1946; *Educ* RAF Coll Cranwell; *m* Sue; 1 s, 1 da; *Career* cmmnd pilot 1968, early experience as weapons instr in Ground Attack and Fighter Reconnaissance, staff appointment AAFCE NATO HQ, Jaguar pilot 1976–81, RAF Staff Coll 1981, Central Tactics and Trials Orgn 1981–86, converted to Tornado GR1 1986, subsequently cmd No 20 Sqdn RAF Laarbruch, station cdr Tri-National Tornado Trg Estab RAF Cottesmore 1988–91, detached as RAF cdr to Tabuk Saudi Arabia (for early months of Operation Granby) 1990, RCDS 1991, Air Cdre 1991, Policy Area Central Staff MOD 1991–93, dir of Airspace Policy (responsible for strategy, planning and design of arrangements for UK airspace) 1993–98; CAA: head of general aviation 1998–2000, head of personnel licensing 2001–03, head Licensing Standards Div 2003–; FRAeS 1997; *Recreations* real tennis, golf, skiing; *Clubs* RAF; *Style*— Ron Elder, Esq; ✉ SRG, CAA, Aviation House, Gatwick Airport, West Sussex RH6 0YR (tel 01293 573079)

ELDERFIELD, Prof Henry; *b* 25 April 1943; *Educ* Univ of Liverpool (BSc, PhD), Imperial Coll London (DIC), Univ of Cambridge (MA, ScD); *Career* res fell Dept of Geology Imperial Coll London 1968–69, lectr Dept of Earth Sciences Univ of Leeds 1969–82; Univ of Cambridge: asst dir in res Dept of Earth Sciences 1982–89, fell and dir of studies St Catharine's Coll 1984–, reader in geochemistry 1989–99, prof of ocean geochemistry and palaeochemistry 1999–, exec sec Ctee for Interdisciplinary Environmental Studies (CIES) 2001–; visiting prof Univ of RI 1977–78, visiting scholar Woods Hole Oceanographic Instn 1982, Fulbright scholar 1988, visiting prof MIT 1988–89, Lady Davis visiting prof Hebrew Univ Jerusalem 1992; examiner for various univs incl: Liverpool, Reading, Amsterdam, Caen, Edinburgh, London, Newcastle upon Tyne, Oxford, Paris, Sheffield, Southampton, Utrecht, Toulouse, Lyon, Bergen; chm: Steering Ctee Biogeochemical Ocean Flux Study (BOFS), Int Steering Ctee Jt Global Ocean Flux Study (JGOFS) 1987–90, Ocean Drilling Project Sedimentary and Geochemical Processes Panel (SGPP) 1989–93, Scientific Ctee Prog Flux Oceaniques (PFO) 1989–94, French component JGOFS, Steering Ctee Br Mid Ocean Ridge Initiative (BRIDGE) NERC Community Res Assoc 1992–95, Scientific Gp on Decommissioning of Offshore Structures (NERC/DTI) 1996, Swedish Res Cncl Gp on Exogenic Geochemistry 1998, Internal Lithosphere Prog Project: Hydrogeology of the Oceanic Lithosphere 1998–, CEREGE (CNRS/ Univ of Aix-Marsailles) review of environmental research 1999; advsr on chairs and other academic posts and research profiles for various academic instns incl Harvard Univ, Univs of Wales, Southampton, Stockholm and Edinburgh and Woods Hole Oceanographic Instn; ed Geochemistry, Geophysics, Geosystems (G3) 1999–; assoc ed: Earth and Planetary Science Letters, Geochimica et Cosmochimica Aca, Geology, Marine Geology; author of 200 articles and papers in learned jls; NOAA Outstanding Scientific Paper for 1996, Newth lectr Scottish Inst for Marine Sciences 1997, Plymouth Marine Medal Marine Biological Assoc of the UK, Plymouth Marine Lab and Univ of Plymouth 1998, Prestwich Medal Geological Soc of London 2000, Patterson Medal Geochemical Soc 2002, Lyell Medal Geological Soc of London 2003, Urey Medal European Assoc of Geochemistry 2007; vice-pres Euro Fedn for Marine Sciences 1998–99, memb Challenger Soc for Marine Science (pres 1998–2000); fell: Geochemical Soc 2000, Euro Assoc for Geochemistry 2000, American Geophysical Union; hon fell Euro Union of Geosciences 2001; FRS 2001; *Style*— Prof Henry Elderfield; ✉ Department of Earth Sciences, Cambridge University, Downing Street, Cambridge CB2 3EQ (tel 01233 333400, fax 01233 333450, e-mail he101@esc.cam.ac.uk); St Catharine's College, Trumpington Street, Cambridge CB2 1RL

ELDON, David Gordon; CBE (2005), JP; s of Leslie Gordon Eldon (d 1945), and Mary Forbes, *née* Smith; *b* 14 October 1945; *Educ* Duke of York's Royal Military Sch Dover; *m* 14 May 1975, Maria Margarita, *née* Gaus; 2 s (Andrew Gordon b 1977, Paul Román b 1979), 1 da (Cristina Margarita b 1982); *Career* HSBC Gp 1968–2005, retired chm Asia Pacific and exec dir HSBC Holdings plc; sr advsr PricewaterhouseCoopers 2005–; chm Dubai Int Financial Centery Noble Gp; dir Mass Transit Railway Corp, dir Eagle Asset Mgmnt China Central Properties Ltd; memb: Seoul Int Business Advsy Cncl, Bretton Woods Ctee Int Cncl; advsr: Hong Kong Acad of Performing Arts, Unisys; dep chm Hong Kong Jockey Club, vice-patron The Community Chest; Hong Kong Businessman of the Year 2003, Asian Banker Lifetime Acheivement Award 2005; Hon DBA Hong Kong City Univ 2003; FCIB 1986 (ACIB 1972), fell Inst of Bankers Hong Kong (FIBHK) 1999; Gold Bahunia Star (GBS, Hong Kong) 2004; *Recreations* music, sports, reading; *Clubs* Hong Kong, China, Hong Kong Jockey (steward); *Style*— David Eldon, GBS, CBE, JP; ✉ 22nd Floor, Prince's Building, Central Hong Kong (tel 00 852 2289 8888, e-mail davideldon@eldon-online.com)

ELDON, 5 Earl of (UK 1821); John Joseph Nicholas Scott; Baron Eldon (GB 1799), Viscount Encombe (UK 1821); s of 4 Earl of Eldon, GCVO (d 1976, fifth in descent from the 1 Earl), and Hon Margaret Fraser, OBE (d 1969), da of 14 Lord Lovat; *b* 24 April 1937; *Educ* Ampleforth, Trinity Coll Oxford; *m* 1 July 1961, Countess Claudine, da of Count Franz von Montjoye-Vaufrey and de la Roche (originally a cr of Louis XV of France 1736, confirmed 1743 (also by Louis) and later by Emperor Franz Josef of Austria-Hungary 1888), of Vienna; 1 s (John Francis Thomas Marie Joseph Columba Fidelis, Viscount Encombe b 9 July 1962), 2 da (Lady Tatiana b 1967, Lady Victoria b 1968); *Heir* s, Viscount Encombe; *Career* 2 Lt Scots Gds, Lt Army Emergency Reserve; *Style*— The Rt Hon The Earl of Eldon

ELDON, HE Stewart Graham; CMG (1998), OBE (1991); s of John Hodgson Eldon, of Bridlington, E Yorks, and Rose Helen, *née* Stinton (d 2002); *b* 18 September 1953, Accra, Ghana; *Educ* Pocklington Sch, Christ's Coll Cambridge (MA, MSc); *m* Jan 1978, Christine Mary, *née* Mason; 1 da (Laura Madeleine b 24 Jan 1982), 1 s (Thomas Henry b 16 Aug 1985); *Career* diplomat; first sec Repub of Ireland Dept FCO 1982–83, private sec to min of state FCO 1983–86, first sec UK Mission to the UN NY 1986–90, asst head Middle Eastern Dept FCO 1990–91 (dep crisis mangr during Gulf War), cnsllr European Secretariat Cabinet Office 1991–93, cnsllr (political) UK Delgn to NATO and WEU Brussels 1994–97, dir (confs) FCO 1997–98, UK dep perm rep to UN NY (with personal rank of ambass) 1998–2002, ambass to Ireland 2003–06, UK perm rep to NATO (with personal rank of ambass) 2006–; fell Center for Int Affrs Harvard Univ 1993–94, visiting fell Yale Univ 2002; MIEE 2002; *Books* From Quill Pen to Satellite: Foreign Ministries in the Information Age (1994); *Recreations* travel, good food, reading science fiction, breaking computers; *Clubs* Athenaeum; *Style*— HE Mr Stewart Eldon, CMG, OBE; ✉ UK Delegation to NATO, OTAN/NATO, Autoroute Bruxelles-Zaventum, Evere, 1110 Brussels, Belgium (tel 00 32 2 707 7211, fax 00 32 2 707 7596)

ELDRED, Dr Vernon Walter; MBE (1970); s of Vernon Frank Eldred (d 1929), of Sutton Coldfield, and Dorothy, *née* Lyon (d 1968); *b* 14 March 1925; *Educ* Bishop Vesey's GS Sutton Coldfield, St Catharine's Coll Cambridge (MA, PhD); *m* 4 Aug 1951, Pamela Mary, da of Arthur Wood (d 1943), of Sutton Coldfield; 2 s (Andrew b 1952, John b 1958), 1 da (Sally b 1956); *Career* Dept of Scientific and Industrial Res Fuel Res Station Greenwich 1945–47, AERE Harwell 1947–48, Dept of Metallurgy Univ of Cambridge 1948–53, Nelson Res Labs English Electric Co Stafford 1953–55; Windscale Lab UKAEA: princ scientific offr 1955–59, res mangr metallurgy 1959–76, head Fuel Examination Div 1976–84, head Fuel Performance Div and dep head of lab 1984–87, head of lab 1987–90; Royal Soc Esso award for Conservation of Energy 1979; chm Ctee Nat Certificates and Dips in Metallurgy 1967–73; memb: Cncl Inst of Metallurgists 1966–69, Bd Br Nuclear Energy Soc 1974–77; fndr memb and first chm W Cumbria Metallurgic Soc; pres: Gosforth Dist Agric Soc Cumbria 1990, Gosforth and Dist Probus Club 1992–93; FIM 1968, FREng 1984, Hon FINucE 1988; *Recreations* beekeeping, fell walking, genealogy, gardening, computers; *Clubs* Oxford and Cambridge; *Style*— Dr Vernon Eldred, MBE, FREng; ✉ Fell Gate, Santon Bridge, Holmrook, Cumbria CA19 1UY (tel 01946 726275, e-mail vernon.eldred@which.net)

ELDRIDGE, David Albert; s of John Anthony Eldridge, of Hackney, London, and Linda Irene, *née* Benton; *b* 20 September 1973; *Educ* Brentwood Sch, Univ of Exeter (BA); *Career* playwright; playwright in residence: RNT 1997, Soho Theatre at TBWA-GGT (advtg agency) 2002; extensive work as dramaturg play-reader in London and Essex; stage plays: Serving It Up 1996, A Week With Tony 1996, Summer Begins 1997, Falling 1999, Under The Blue Sky 2000 (Time Out Live Award for Best New Play in the West End 2001), MAD 2004, Incomplete and Random Acts of Kindness 2005, Market Boy 2006; other work: Killers (BBC) 2000, Michael and Me (BBC Radio 4) 2001, The Nugget Run (short film) 2002; Hon DLitt Univ of Exeter 2007; *Publications* Serving It Up & A Week With Tony (1997), Under the Blue Sky (2001); *Recreations* friends, family, books, football; *Style*— David Eldridge, Esq; ✉ c/o ICM, Oxford House, 76 Oxford Street, London W1N 0AX (tel 020 7636 6565, fax 020 7323 0101)

ELDRIDGE, David John; s of Lt-Col Frederick George Eldridge (ret), of Haslemere, Surrey, and Irene Mary, *née* Buston; *b* 12 January 1935; *Educ* KCS Wimbledon; *m* 1, 14 May 1960, Diana Mary (d 1981), da of Eric Copp, of Hartlepool, Cleveland; 1 s (Charles b 1962), 2 da (Catherine b 1964, Victoria b 1966); m 2, 15 Dec 1984, Anna Maria, da of Jerzy Kowalski, of Warsaw, Poland; *Career* admitted slr 1956; ptnr: Stanley Attenborough & Co 1958–74, Martin & Nicholson 1975–77, Amhurst Brown Colombotti 1977–2003, Howard Kennedy 2003–, Wardynski & Ptnrs Warsaw Poland; tstee (since inception 1974) Museum of Islamic Art Jerusalem; donation govr Christ's Hosp Horsham; Freeman City of London, Liveryman and memb Ct of Assts Worshipful Co of Fletchers (Master 1984–86), memb Ct of Assts Guild of Freemen (Master 1983–84); memb Law Soc 1957; *Recreations* fine arts, sport; *Clubs* City Livery; *Style*— David Eldridge, Esq; ✉ 50A Howards Lane, London SW15 5QF (tel 020 8780 9084); Howard Kennedy, 19 Cavendish Square, London W1A 2AW (tel 020 7830 8133, fax 020 7830 8254)

ELDRIDGE, Mark; s of Bernard Derrick Eldridge, of Toronto, Canada (foster f George Hoare, of Liphook, Hants), and Anne May, *née* Murphy (foster mother Eileen Violet, *née* Luff); *b* 9 August 1954; *Educ* Churcher's Coll Petersfield, Lancaster Univ (BA), City Univ (Dip Law), Inns of Court Sch of Law; *m* 3 July 1982, Alexandra Catherine, da of John Watling Illingworth, of Wellingborough, Northants; 3 da (Charlotte b 27 March 1983, Elizabeth b 27 Sept 1984, Catherine b 31 Jan 1986), 1 s (Joseph b 10 July 1987); *Career* practising barr; called to the Bar Gray's Inn 1982, memb Inner Temple 1985, elected memb Gen Cncl of the Bar 1986–91, chm Young Bar of England and Wales 1989; memb Western Circuit; memb Criminal Bar Assoc; memb Bar European Gp; govr Thornhill Primary Sch 1986–88, chm Bd of Govrs Clerkenwell Parochial Sch 1993–96; Islington South and Finsbury Cons Assoc: vice-chm 1986–89, chm 1989–92, vice-pres 1992–2006; vice-pres Islington Cons Assoc 2006–07; *Recreations* swimming, golf, tennis; *Clubs* Carlton, IOD; *Style*— Mark Eldridge, Esq; ✉ 114 Liverpool Road, Islington, London N1 0RE (tel 020 7226 9863, fax 020 7704 1111, e-mail mark.eldridge3@btinternet.com); 3 Temple Gardens, Temple, London EC4Y 9AU (tel 020 7583 0010, fax 020 7353 3361)

ELEGANT, Robert Sampson; s of Louis Elegant (d 1965), and Lillie Rebecca, *née* Sampson (d 1984); *b* 7 March 1928; *Educ* Univ of Pennsylvania (BA), Yale Univ (Dip Chinese Language), Columbia Univ (MA, MS); *m* 1, 16 April 1956, Moira Clarissa Brady (d 1999); 1 da (Victoria Ann b 1958), 1 s (Simon David Brady b 1960); m 2, 10 May 2003, Rosemary Righter, *née* Douglas; *Career* Far East corr Overseas News Agency 1951–52, Int News Serv war corr Korea 1952–53; corr in Singapore and SE Asia for: Columbia Broadcasting Serv, McGraw-Hill News Serv and North American Newspaper Alliance 1954–55; S Asian corr & chief New Delhi Bureau Newsweek 1956–57, SE Asian corr & chief Hong Kong Bureau Newsweek 1958–61, chief Central Euro Bureau (Bonn-Berlin) Newsweek 1962–64, public lectr 1964–, chief Hong Kong Bureau Los Angeles Times 1965–69; foreign affrs columnist Los Angeles Times/Washington Post News Serv: Munich 1970–72, Hong Kong 1973–75; visiting prof of journalism and int affrs: Univ of South Carolina 1976, Boston Univ 1994–95; independent author and journalist 1976–; shortlisted (twice) Pulitzer Int Journalism Prize, Sigma Delta Chi Prize, Sch of Journalism Alumni Prize Columbia Univ; Pulitzer travelling fell 1951–52, fell Ford Fndn 1954–55, fell American Enterprise Inst 1976–78, sr fell Inst for Advanced Studies Berlin 1993–94, Edgar Allen Poe award Mystery Writers of America 1967, four Overseas Press Club awards; author of numerous articles in magazines; memb Int Inst for Strategic Studies; *Books* non-fiction: China's Red Leaders (1951), The Dragon's Seed (1959), The Centre of the World (1964, reprinted 1968), Mao's Great Revolution (1971), Mao vs Chiang: The Battle for China (1972), Great Citites: Hong Kong (1977), Pacific Destiny: Inside Asia Today (1990); novels: A Kind of Treason (1966), The Seeking (1969), Dynasty (1977), Manchu (1980), Mandarin (1983), White Sun, Red Star (published as From a Far Land in USA, 1986), Bianca (1992), The Big Brown Bears (1993), The Everlasting Sorrow (1994), Last Year in Hong Kong (1997), Cry Peace (2005); *Recreations* sailing, raising Shih Tzu dogs, collecting Chinese and Japanese objets d'art; *Clubs* Hong Kong Foreign Correspondents, Royal Hong Kong Yacht; *Style*— Robert Elegant, Esq; ✉ 10 Quick Street, London N1 8HL (tel and fax 020 7837 1009, mobile 07722 885925, e-mail relegant@yahoo.com); c/o Casalichiari, Torre Gentile, 06059 Todi PG, Italy (tel and fax 39 075 885 3194)

ELEY, Prof Barry Michael; s of Horace Henry Eley (d 1971), and Ena Maud, *née* Cast (d 1975); *b* 6 March 1940; *Educ* St Olave's & St Saviour's GS, The London Hosp Dental Sch (BDS, LDS RCS); *m* 1 June 1963, Julie Christina (d 1997), da of Arthur William Rumbold; 1 s (Peter John b 10 Dec 1965), 1 da (Esther Jane b 12 March 1968); *Career* house surgn London Hosp Med Sch 1963; KCH Dental Sch: asst lectr and registrar 1963–65, lectr in conservation dentistry 1965–74, sr lectr in periodontology 1974–80; King's Coll Sch of Med and Dentistry (now GKT): sr lectr and conslt 1980–89, head of Periodontal Dept 1980–99, dir Sch of Dental Hygiene 1980–99, conslt in periodontology, appointed prof of periodontology 1998 (now emeritus), head of division of periodontology and preventive dentistry 1999–2002; pres Br Soc of Periodontology 1993–94; author of over 100 scientific papers; memb: BDA, BSP, BSDR, RMS, IADR; FDS RCS 1972; *Books* Amalgam Tattoos (1982), Outline of Periodontics (with J D Mason, 2 edn 1989, Japanese edn 1992, 5 edn 2004), Dental Amalgam: a review of Safety (1993), The Future of Dental Amalgam: A Review of the Literature (1998); *Recreations* travel, reading, theatre, piano, listening to music, walking, astronomy; *Style*— Prof Barry Eley; ✉ 6 Pondfield Road, Orpington, Kent BR6 8HT (e-mail barry@bmeley.plus.com)

ELGAR, Edward James; s of Frank Elgar, and Mary, *née* Dee; *Educ* Tonbridge, Univ of Bristol (BA); *Career* publisher; coll sales rep George Allen & Unwin 1972–74; Martin Robertson Ltd: field ed 1974–76, editorial dir 1977–79; fndr memb and md Wheatsheaf Books 1979–86, fndr memb and md Edward Elgar Publishing Ltd 1986–; *Recreations* reading, rugby, cricket, wine, renovating house in France; *Style*— Edward Elgar, Esq; ✉ Edward Elgar Publishing Ltd, Glensanda House, Montpellier Parade, Cheltenham, Gloucestershire GL50 1UA (tel 01242 226939, fax 01242 262111)

ELGIN AND KINCARDINE, 11 and 15 Earl of (S 1633 and 1647); Andrew Douglas Alexander Thomas Bruce; KT (1981), CD (1985) JP (Fife 1951); also Lord Bruce of Kinloss (S 1604), Lord Bruce of Torry (S 1647), Baron Elgin (UK 1849); 37 Chief of the Name of Bruce; s of 10 Earl of Elgin, KT, CMG, TD (ggs of the 7 Earl who removed to safety the statuary known as The Elgin Marbles from the Parthenon in Athens), and Hon Dame Katherine Elizabeth Cochrane, DBE, da of 1 Baron Cochrane of Cults; *b* 17 February 1924; *Educ* Eton, Balliol Coll Oxford (MA); *m* 27 April 1959, Victoria Mary, o da of Dudley George Usher, MBE, TD, of Gallowridge House, Dunfermline; 2 da (Lady Georgiana Mary b 1960, Lady Antonia Katherine b 1964), 3 s (Charles Edward, Lord Bruce b 1961, Hon Adam Robert b 1968, Hon Alexander Victor b 1971); *Heir* s, Lord Bruce; *Career* served 3 Bn Scots Gds WWII (wounded); chm Nat Savings Ctee Scotland 1972–78; dir: Scottish Amicable Life Assurance Soc until 1994 (also former pres), Scottish Post Office Bd 1980–96; pres: Roy Caledonian Curling Club 1968–69, Royal Scottish Automobile Club; dir Royal Highland and Agric Soc 1973–76; Lord High Cmmr to Gen

Assembly of Church of Scotland 1980–81; bde pres Boys Bde 1963–85; memb Ct of Regents Royal Coll of Surgns of Edinburgh; Grand Master Mason of Scotland 1961–65, Capt Queen's Body Guard for Scotland (Royal Co of Archers); HM Lord-Lt Fife 1988–99 (DL 1955); Hon Col Elgin Regt of Canada (1969); Hon DLitt St Mary's NS 1976, Hon LLD Univ of Dundee 1977, Hon LLD Univ of Glasgow 1983; Order of Merit Norway 1994; *Style*— The Rt Hon the Earl of Elgin and Kincardine, KT, CD; ✉ Broomhall, Dunfermline KY11 3DU (tel 01383 872222, fax 01383 872904, e-mail lord.elgin@virgin.net)

ELIAS, Brian David; s of Albert Murad Elias, and Julie Sophie, *née* Ephraim; *b* 30 August 1948; *Educ* St Christopher Sch, RCM, and with Elisabeth Lutyens; *Career* composer: La Chevelure 1969, Peroration 1973, Somnia 1979, L'Eylah (cmmnd for BBC Promenade Concerts) 1984, Geranos (cmmnd by Fires of London) 1985, Variations (for solo piano) 1987, Five Songs to Poems by Irina Ratushinskaya (cmmnd by the BBC) 1989, The Judas Tree (cmmnd by Royal Opera House) 1992, Laments (cmmnd by the BBC) 1998, The House that Jack Built (cmmnd by the BBC) 2002, A Talisman (cmmnd by Cheltenham Festival) 2004; *Recreations* reading, gardening, theatre, art; *Style*— Brian Elias, Esq; ✉ Chester Music, 14–15 Berners Street, London W1T 3LJ (tel 020 7612 7400, fax 020 7612 7545)

ELIAS, Gerard; QC (1984); bro of Patrick Elias (The Hon Mr Justice Elias), *qv*; *b* 19 November 1944; *Educ* Cardiff HS, Univ of Exeter (LLB, capt cricket XI); *m* 14 March 1970, Elisabeth, da of Sir George Henry Kenyon, JP, DL, of Hyde, Cheshire; 3 s (David b 7 May 1971, Robert b 24 Feb 1973, James b 1 May 1976); *Career* called to the Bar Inner Temple 1968 (bencher 1993); recorder of the Crown Court 1984–, dep judge of the High Court 1996–; asst boundary cmmr for Wales 1984–, ldr Wales & Chester Circuit 1993–95 (treas 1990–92); leading counsel to N Wales Tbnl of Inquiry into Child Abuse 1996–98; memb Bar Cncl 1986–89, dir Bar Mutual Insurance Fund 1987–97, govr and memb Cncl Malvern Coll 1988–96; Glamorgan CCC: memb Exec Ctee 1985–93, dep chm 1993–98, chm 1998–2003; ECB: memb Registration Ctee 1993–96, chm Disciplinary Standing-Ctee 1996–; chllr Diocese of Swansea & Brecon 1999–; *Recreations* sailing, cricket, music; *Clubs* Cardiff & County; *Style*— Gerard Elias, Esq, QC

ELIAS, Hon Mr Justice; Sir Patrick Elias; kt (1999); s of Leonard Elias, and Patricia Mary, *née* O'Neill; bro of Gerard Elias, QC, *qv*; *b* 28 March 1947, Cardiff; *Educ* Cardiff HS, Univ of Exeter (LLB), King's Coll Cambridge (MA, PhD); *m* 15 Aug 1970, Wendy, *née* Kinnersley-Haddock; 3 s (James, Edward, Thomas), 1 da (Emily); *Career* called to the Bar Inner Temple 1973 (bencher 1995); fell Pembroke Coll Cambridge 1973–84, lectr Univ of Cambridge 1975–84, QC 1990, judge of the High Court of Justice (Queen's Bench Div) 1999–; pres Employment Appeal Tbnl 2006–; Hon LLD: Univ of Exeter 2001, City Univ London 2003; *Recreations* reading, music, cricket, rugby; *Style*— The Hon Mr Justice Elias; ✉ c/o Royal Courts of Justice, Strand, London WC2A 2LL; Employment Appeal Tribunal, Audit House, 58 Victoria Embankment, London EC4Y 0DS

ELIAS, Robin Pieter; s of Carel George Elias (d 2001), of Dorking, and Nancy Elizabeth, *née* Harvey; *b* 11 December 1953; *Educ* Therfield Comp Leatherhead; *m* 24 June 1978, Sally Anne, da of Malcolm Alfred Henry Holder; 1 s (Samuel Jeremy b 19 March 1987), 1 da (Amy Grace b 10 Aug 1990); *Career* reporter Surrey Advertiser Guildford 1971–77, sub ed Press Association 1977–79, sub ed London Evening News 1979–80; ITN: joined as prodr 1980, prog ed Lunchtime News 1990–92, prog ed News at Ten 1992–99, prog ed Evening News 1999–2000, head of Output 1996–99, dep ed ITV News 1999–2002, managing ed ITV News 2002–; *Style*— Robin Elias, Esq; ✉ ITN Ltd, 200 Gray's Inn Road, London WC1X 8XZ (tel 020 7833 3000, e-mail robin.elias@itn.co.uk)

ELIASCH, Johan Carl; *b* 15 February 1962, Sweden; *Educ* Royal Inst of Technol Sweden (MSc), Stockholm Univ; *m*; 2 c; *Career* chm and ceo Head 1995–, chm Investment Gp Equity Ptnrs Gp, chm London Films; sr dep party treas Cons Party until 2007, adviser on deforestation and green energy to the PM 2007–; memb Pres of the Repub of Austria's Trade Delegation; chm Young Cons Party Sweden 1979–82; memb: Bd Special Olympics Ctee, Advsy Bd Int Peace Fndn, Sports Advsy Bd Shimon Peres Peace Fndn, Int Advisory Bd Brasilinvest, Bd Sports on Addiction, Resources for Autism (founding memb), Advsy Bd Centre for Social Justice, World Econ Forum (also govr Retail and Consumer Goods Industry); chm The Duke of York NSPCC Challenge; patron Univ of Stockholm; exec prodr: Best of Friends 1991, Lady Chatterley 1993, Resort to Murder 1995, The Scarlet Pimpernel 1998 and 2000; *Recreations* golf (scratch handicap, played in British Open), curling (Swedish Rocky Mountain champion), skiing (forerunner downhill, super giant slalom and giant slalom, skied at World Cup and World Championships); *Style*— Mr Johan Eliasch

ELIBANK, 14 Lord (S 1643); Sir Alan D'Ardis Erskine-Murray; 14 Bt (NS 1628); s of Maj Robert Alan Erskine-Murray, OBE (d 1939), unc of 13 Lord; suc cous 1973; *b* 31 December 1923, Wynberg, South Africa; *Educ* Bedford, Peterhouse Cambridge; *m* 1962, Valerie Sylvia (d 1997), o da of late Herbert William Dennis, of St Margaret's, Twickenham; 2 s; *Heir* s, Master of Elibank; *Career* barr 1949–55, gen mangr and rep Shell Int Petroleum Co in Qatar 1977–80 (personnel 1955–77), personnel mangr Deminex Oil and Gas Ltd 1981–86; *Clubs* MCC; *Style*— The Rt Hon the Lord Elibank; ✉ Flat 80, Pier House, Cheyne Walk, London SW3 5HX

ELIOT, Simon; s of Geoffrey P Eliot (d 1976), and Hope, *née* Sykes (d 2006); *b* 20 July 1952; *Educ* Radley, Queens' Coll Cambridge (MA); *m* 10 Dec 1983, Olivia, *née* Roberts; 1 s (Henry b 17 May 1985), 1 da (Georgina b 20 Oct 1990); *Career* marine insurance broker Sedgwick-Forbes 1974–75, asst master Radley Coll 1975–76, asst master Winchester Coll 1976–2000 (house master 1988–2000), headmaster Sherborne Sch 2000–; govr: Old Malt House Sch, Sherborne Prep Sch, The Downs Wraxall; Freeman: City of London, Worshipful Co of Skinners; *Recreations* theatre, horse racing, music; *Style*— Simon Eliot, Esq; ✉ Abbey Grange, Hospital Lane, Sherborne, Dorset DT9 3JF (tel 01935 810410); Sherborne School, Abbey Road, Sherborne, Dorset DT9 3AP (tel 01935 810401)

ELIOTT OF STOBS, Sir Charles Joseph Alexander; 12 Bt (NS 1666), of Stobs, Roxburghshire; s of late Charles Rawdon Heathfield Eliott (himself s of half-bro of Sir Arthur Eliott of Stobs, 9 Bt), and Emma Elizabeth, *née* Harris; suc half second cousin, Sir Arthur Francis Augustus Boswell Eliott of Stobs, 11 Bt (d 1989); *b* 9 January 1937; *Educ* St Joseph's Christian Bros Rockhampton nr Brisbane; *m* 1959, Wendy Judith, da of Henry John Bailey, of Toowoomba, Queensland; 4 da (Elizabeth (Mrs Armanasco) b 1960, Jenny (Mrs Land) b 1961, Josephine (Mrs Grofski) b 1963, Clare Melinda b 1973), 1 s (Rodney Gilbert Charles b 1966) and 1 s decd (Stephen John); *Heir* s, Rodney Eliott; *Career* builder (C J & W J Eliott); *Style*— Sir Charles Eliott of Stobs, Bt; ✉ 11 Smythe Street, Toowoomba, Queensland 4350, Australia (tel 00 61 46 364284)

ELIS-THOMAS, Baron (Life Peer UK 1992), of Nant Conwy in the County of Conwy; Dafydd Elis-Thomas; PC (2004), AM; *b* 18 October 1946; *Educ* Ysgol Dyffryn Conwy, UCNW (PhD); *m* 1 (m dis), 1970, Elen M Williams; 3 s; m 2, 29 Dec 1993, Mair Parry Jones; *Career* tutor in Welsh studies Coleg Harlech 1971, subsequently taught at UCNW Bangor, Aberystwyth, Cardiff and Open Univ, former visiting fell Univ of St Andrews; MP (Plaid Cymru): Merionnydd Feb 1974–83, Meirionnydd Nant Conwy 1983–92 (Parly candidate (Plaid Cymru) Conway 1970); Plaid Cymru spokesman on agric and rural devpt 1974 and on educn and social policy 1975, memb Parly Select Ctee on Educn, Science and Arts 1979–83, served as memb of various other select ctees and standing ctees of House of Commons; memb Nat Assembly for Wales (Plaid Cymru) Merionnydd Nant Conwy 1999–, presiding offr Nat Assembly for Wales 1999–; pres Plaid Cymru 1984–91 (vice-pres 1979–81); writer, journalist and columnist, former broadcaster and prog presenter BBC Wales, HTV, S4C and Radio Wales; first chm Welsh Language Bd 1993–99; former memb: Welsh Arts Cncl, Wales Film Cncl, Welsh Film Bd, Gen Consultative Cncl BBC, BFI; pres Univ of Wales Bangor 2000–; hon sec: All-Pty Mental Health Gp, Mind, Inst for Workers Control and Shelter; *Recreations* environmental issues, hill walking, theatre, film, arts, music, active member Church in Wales; *Style*— The Rt Hon Lord Elis-Thomas, AM

ELKELES, Prof Robert Samuel; s of Dr Arthur Elkeles (d 1978), of London, and Margaret, *née* Stein (d 1970); *b* 1 June 1942; *Educ* Highgate Sch, Middx Hosp Med Sch London (Ken Clifford scholar, Boldero scholar in med, MB BS, LRCP, MD); *m* Jan 1971, Arran, *née* Miller; 1 s (Daniel Alexander b 4 May 1973), 1 da (Jennifer Margaret b 17 March 1976); *Career* house surgn in gen surgery Chase Farm Hosp Enfield 1965; house physician: Middx then Brompton Hosp 1966, Hammersmith Hosp 1967; asst to Sir George Pickering Radcliffe Infirmary Oxford 1967–68, registrar in endocrinology Hammersmith Hosp 1968–70, lectr in med Univ Hosp of Wales 1973–74 (registrar 1970–72), conslt physician Northwick Park Hosp and Clinical Research Centre Harrow 1974–78, conslt physician and sr lectr in med St Mary's Hosp Med Sch London 1978–, prof of diabetic medicine Imperial Coll London 2006–; chm: Div of Med Paddington and N Kensington Health Dist 1982–85, NW Thames Regnl Physicians in Diabetes and Endocrinology 1990–96, N Thames Specialist Trg Ctee in Diabetes and Endocrinology 1996–2000, St Mary's Hospital Tst Med Advsy Ctee 2000–06; Br Diabetic Assoc: past memb Professional Advsy Ctee, chm Nutrition Sub-Ctee, memb Med and Scientific Assoc Ctee 1992–95; memb: Ctee Br Hyperlipidaemia Assoc 1993–96, Cncl RCP London 1998–2001 and 2003–06; FRCP; *Books* Biochemical Aspects of Human Disease (with A S Tavill, 1983); *Recreations* music, tennis, cycling, walking; *Style*— Prof Robert Elkeles; ✉ 11 Askew Road, Moor Park, Northwood, Middlesex HA6 2JE (tel 01923 827341); St Mary's Hospital, Praed Street, London W2 1NY (tel 020 7886 6037)

ELKINGTON, Robert John; s of late John David Rew Elkington, OBE; *b* 7 October 1949; *Educ* Eton, Univ of Exeter (BA); *m* 1, 1974 (m dis 1983), Penelope Josephine, da of late Lt-Col Richard Ian Griffith Taylor, DSO; 1 s; m 2, 1984, Mary Patricia, da of late Maj Hon Antony John Ashley Cooper; 2 da; *Career* fin dir Gerrard Group plc (formerly Gerrard and National Holdings plc) until 2000, dir Old Mutual Fin Servs (UK) Ltd 2000–01, dir Thornhill Investment Management Ltd; *Recreations* gardening, shooting, golf; *Clubs* Boodle's, City of London, Sunningdale; *Style*— Robert Elkington, Esq; ✉ Cranbourne Grange, Sutton Scotney, Winchester, Hampshire SO21 3NA (tel 01962 760494, fax 01962 760312); Thornhill Investment Management Ltd, 77 South Audley Street, London W1K 1DX (tel 020 7629 0662)

ELL, Prof Peter Josef; s of Josef Ell (d 1957), of Lisbon, Portugal, and Maria Karola Ell (d 1990); *b* 7 May 1944; *Educ* Univ of Lisbon (MD), Univ of London (MSc), Univ of Bern (PD); *m* 1980, Yvonne, da of Jan Brink; 2 s (Georg Mischa b 2 March 1981, Patrick Sascha b 8 Dec 1983); *Career* conslt physician Landes Unfallkrankenhaus Feldkirch 1974–76, conslt physician i/c nuclear med Middx Hosp 1976–, dir Inst of Nuclear Med UC Med Sch London 1986–, prof of nuclear med and established chair Univ of London 1987–; dep dir Inst of Nuclear Med 1984–, hon conslt physician Middx Hosp 1976–; visiting prof: Univ of Saskatchewan 1982, Kuwait 1983, Islamabad 1983, Cairo 1984, Univ of Lisbon 1986; UK del: Euro Nuclear Med Soc 1981–82, World Fedn of Nuclear Med and Biology 1984, 1988 and 1990; annual prize Soc of Med Sciences Portugal 1976, annual prize Soc of Medical Sciences Vorarlberg Austria 1979, first and third prize for best scientific oral presentation Br Nuclear Med Soc 1990, Gold Medal Univ of Ghent 2004; pres Euro Assoc of Nuclear Med 1994–; corresponding memb: Finnish Soc of Nuclear Med 1984, Swiss Soc of Nuclear Med 1993, German Soc Nuclear Med 2000; fndr memb Euro Assoc of Nuclear Med 1985 (sec 1987–91 and 1991–93); Freeman City of Montpellier 1991; Dr (hc) Univ of Barcelona 2004; memb: American Soc of Nuclear Med 1974, Br Nuclear Med Soc 1974 (memb Cncl 1991–93, sec 1992–94), Br Inst of Radiology 1974 (memb Cncl 1984–87), NY Acad of Sciences 1976, Hosp Physicists Assoc 1977, RSM 1978, Br Cardiac Soc 1983, Assoc of Physicians of Great Br and Ireland 1994; FRCR 1984, FRCP 1990 (MRCP 1984), FMedSci 2004; *Recreations* the study of languages, the arts in general, photography and cinema; *Style*— Prof Peter Ell; ✉ Institute of Nuclear Medicine, University College London Hospitals NHS Trust, 235 Euston Road, London NW1 2BU (tel 020 7631 1066, fax 020 7436 0603, e-mail peter.ell@uclh.nhs.uk)

ELLARD, John Francis; s of (John) Edward Ellard (d 1999), and Marie, *née* Topping; *b* 5 April 1953; *Educ* John Fisher Sch Purley Surrey, King's Sch Chester, Trinity Hall Cambridge (MA); *m* 4 April 1987, Nicola Marigo, da of John David Pugh (d 1973); 2 s ((John) David b 12 Sept 1988, Robert Edward b 8 May 1990), 2 da (Caroline Francesca b 13 June 1992, (Sarah) Jane b 26 Dec 1993); *Career* admitted slr 1977; Linklaters & Paines: articled clerk 1975–77, asst slr 1977–83, ptnr 1983–2004, resident ptnr NY office 1986–89; of counsel Shearman & Sterling LLP 2004–; tstee The King's Consort 1998; memb Trinity Hall Devpt Bd 1998–, memb Law Soc; *Recreations* music, reading, mountain walking, photography; *Clubs* Oxford and Cambridge; *Style*— John Ellard, Esq; ✉ 38 Shawfield Street, London SW3 4BD; Shearman & Sterling LLP, Broadgate West, 9 Appold Street, London EC2A 2AP (tel 020 7655 5646, fax 020 7655 6315, e-mail john.ellard@shearman.com)

ELLEN, Eric Frank; QPM (1980); s of Robert Frank Ellen (d 1969), and Jane Lydia Ellen (d 1982); *b* 30 August 1930; *Educ* Univ of London (LLB); *m* 1949, Gwendoline Dorothy, da of John Thomas Perkins (d 1937); 1 s (Stephen), 1 da (Susan); *Career* Nat Serv; joined Port of London Police 1950, Chief Constable 1975, ret 1980; first dir ICC: Int Maritime Bureau 1981–99, Counterfeiting Intelligence Bureau 1985–99, Commercial Crime Bureau 1992–99; chief exec ICC Commercial Crime Services (incorporating Int Maritime Bureau, Counterfeiting Intelligence Bureau and Commercial Crime Bureau) 1990–99; conslt Commercial Crime Unit, special advsr on port security matters and maritime crime Int Assoc of Ports and Harbours, pres Int Assoc of Airport and Seaport Police 1977–79, chm Euro Assoc of Airport and Seaport Police 1975–78 (now life memb, exec sec 1980–88); chm: PEBs 1985, Electronic Intelligence Ltd 1985–86, Task Force on Commercial Crime 1996, ICC Commercial Crime Services; memb Bd ICC Commercial Crime Service 1999–2000, conslt on fraud to ICC 1999–2000; chm First Approach Ltd 2003–; memb: Hon Soc of the Middle Temple, Br Acad of Forensic Sciences, Ctee of Cons Lawyers Examining Maritime Fraud, Inst of Shipbrokers Ctee on Maritime Fraud; presented or chaired seminars on int commercial fraud and product counterfeiting in over 50 countries, advised Barbados Govt on formation of a new police force for the Barbados Port Authy 1983, reviewed security at ports of Jeddah and Dammam in Saudi Arabia, chm Cambridge Symposia on Commercial Crime 1985–, memb Anti-Corruption Working Gp Soc for Advanced Legal Studies 2000; frequent TV and radio appearances on the subject of marine fraud, terrorism, piracy and product counterfeiting; Freeman City of London; Police Long Serv and Good Conduct medal 1 class 1973, Repub of China Police medal 1 class 1979; CIMgt; *Publications* International Maritime Fraud (co-author), Air and Seaport Security International Reference Book (conslt ed, 1987–89), Violence at Sea (ed, 1987), Piracy at Sea (ed, 1989), Ports at Risk (ed, 1994), Shipping at Risk (ed 1997), A Guide to the Prevention of Money Laundering (1998), A Banker's Guide for the Prevention of Fraud and Money Laundering in Documentary Credits (co-ed, 1999), published many articles on varied subjects including specialist policemen, marine sabotage, piracy and terrorism, product counterfeiting and fraud; *Recreations* golf; *Clubs* Wig & Pen; *Style*— Eric Ellen, Esq, QPM; ✉ First Approach Ltd, 38 Tyle Green, Hornchurch, Essex RM11 2TB (tel 01708 442538)

ELLEN, Prof Roy Frank; s of Gerald Frank Ellen, of Mill Hill, London, and Nancy Eileen, *née* Childs; *b* 30 January 1947, London; *Educ* LSE (BSc, PhD), Univ of Leiden; *m* 18 Feb 1978, Nicola Jane, da of F Stanley Goward; 2 da (Philippa Louise b 23 Aug 1986, Olivia Grace b 6 Dec 1990); *Career* temp lectr LSE 1972–73; Univ of Kent at Canterbury: lectr in social anthropology 1973–80, sr lectr in social anthropology 1980–86, reader in social anthropology 1986–88, prof of anthropology and human ecology 1988–, head Dept of Anthropology 1996–99; visiting fell: Research Sch of Pacific Studies ANU 1981, Netherlands Inst for Advanced Study Wassenaar 1984; visiting prof Indonesian Environmental History Prog Univ of Leiden 1994; referee: ESRC, Leverhulme Tst, Nuffield Fndn, Carnegie Tst, Wenner-Gren Fndn, Nat Inst for Mental Health USA, Nat Science Fndn USA; pres Anthropology and Archaeology Section BAAS 2005; memb: Exec Ctee Cwlth Human Ecology Cncl 1978–81, Ctee Radcliffe-Brown Fund RAI 1982–85, Ctee Horniman Tst RAI 1982–85, Section H Ctee Br Assoc 1984, Cncl RAI 2003–, Bd Int Soc of Ethnobiology; managing ed Assoc of Social Anthropologists Research Methods Series 1980–85, ed Studies in Environmental Anthropology 1994–; memb Editorial Bd: Reviews in Anthropology, Cakalele: Maluku Research Jl; organiser of numerous confs, speaker at confs and symposia worldwide; memb: Assoc of Social Anthropologists of the Cwlth (memb Ctee 1981–85, hon sec 1982–85), Assoc of SE Asianists in the UK, European Assoc of Social Anthropologists, Koninklijk Instituut voor Taal, Land- en Volkenkunde, Cwlth Human Ecology Cncl; Nuffield Social Science Research Fellowship 1985–86, Munro Lectureship Univ of Edinburgh 1984; Hayter Travel Award 1973, Firth Award 1973; govr Powell-Cotton Museum Birchington 1983–2003; FRAI 1966 (vice-pres 2003–06), FLS 2001, FBA 2003; *Publications* Nuaulu Settlement and Ecology: the environmental relations of an eastern Indonesian community (1978), Social and Ecological Systems (ed with P H Burnham, 1979), Classifications in their Social Context (ed with D Reason, 1979), Environment, Subsistence and System: the ecology of small-scale social formations (1982), Ethnographic Research: a guide to general conduct (ed, 1984), Malinowski between Two Worlds: the Polish roots of an anthropological tradition (with E Gellner, G Kubica and J Mucha, 1988), The Cultural Relations of Classification: an analysis of Nuaulu animal categories from central Seram (1993), Nuaulu Ethnozoology: a systematic inventory (1993), Understanding Witchcraft and Sorcery in Southeast Asia (ed with C W Watson, 1993), Redefining Nature: ecology, culture and domestication (ed with K Fukui, 1996), Indigenous Environmental Knowledge and its Transformations: critical anthropological perspectives (ed with P Parkes and A Bicker, 2000), On the Edge of the Banda Zone: past and present in the social organization of a Moluccan trading network (2003), The Categorical Impulse: Essays in the anthropology of classifying behaviour (2006), Ethnobiology and the Science of Humankind (ed, 2006); also author of articles in refereed professional jls; *Style*— Prof Roy Ellen; ✉ Department of Anthropology, Eliot College, University of Kent, Canterbury CT2 7NS (tel 01227 823421, e-mail r.f.ellen@kent.ac.uk)

ELLEN, Susan Caroline; da of Albert John Davies, and Winifred Ivy Caroline, *née* Emberton; *b* 15 December 1948; *Educ* Cardiff HS for Girls, Malvern Girls' Coll, Univ of Bristol (BSc); *m* 2 March 1974, Simon Tudor Ellen, s of Wing Cdr R A G Ellen, Rtd, OBE; 2 da (Katie Louise b 14 Feb 1980, Joanna Caroline b 14 April 1982); *Career* BUPA Hosps: exec dir 1977–80, devpt dir 1980–82, op dir 1982–87; BUPA Health Services: business devpt dir 1987–90, md 1990–95; govr BUPA 1990–95; chm West Middx Univ Hosp Tst 2002–; md United Racecourses (Holdings) Ltd 1996–2002; non-exec dir: Asda Group plc 1992–98, Birmingham Midshires Building Society 1996–2000, Portman Building Soc 2001–; dep chm Independent Health Care Assoc 1990–95; memb: Fin Review Panel 1992–98, Fin Reporting Cncl 1995–97; MHSM 1972; *Recreations* national hunt racing, theatre, opera; *Style*— Mrs Susan Ellen; ✉ 47 Ennerdale Road, Kew, Richmond, Surrey TW9 2DN (tel 020 8948 0858)

ELLENBOROUGH, 8 Baron (UK 1802); Richard Edward Cecil Law; s of 7 Baron (d 1945); *b* 14 January 1926; *Educ* Eton, Magdalene Coll Cambridge; *m* 1, 9 Oct 1953, Rachel Mary (d 1986), da of late Maj Ivor Mathews Hedley, 17 Lancers; 3 s; m 2, 12 March 1994, Mrs Frances Kimberley (d 2004); *Heir* s, Hon Rupert Law; *Career* sat as Conservative Peer in House of Lords until 1999; former stockbroker; ptnr McAnally Montgomery 1962–78, former dir Towry Law & Co; pres Nat Union of Rate Payers 1960–90; *Style*— The Rt Hon Lord Ellenborough; ✉ Withypool House, Observatory Close, Church Road, Crowborough, East Sussex TN6 1BN (tel 01892 663139)

ELLERAY, Anthony John; QC (1993); s of late Alexander John Elleray, of Waddington, Lancs, and Sheila Mary, *née* Perkins; *b* 19 August 1954; *Educ* Bishop's Stortford Coll, Trinity Coll Cambridge (MA); *m* 17 July 1982, Alison Elizabeth, da of William Goring Potter, DFC, of Bollington, Cheshire; 1 da (Harriet b 29 Aug 1985), 1 s (Adam b 22 Sept 1989); *Career* called to the Bar Inner Temple 1977, barr Chancery Div Northern Circuit, dep judge of the High Ct 1997–, recorder 1999; memb: Chancery Bar Assoc, Northern Chancery Bar Assoc (chm); *Recreations* bridge, theatre, pictures, wine; *Clubs* Oxford and Cambridge, Manchester Tennis and Racquets; *Style*— Anthony Elleray, Esq, QC; ✉ Exchange Chambers, 7 Ralli Courts, West Riverside, Manchester M3 5FT (tel 0161 833 2722, fax 0161 833 2789, e-mail info@exchangechambers.co.uk)

ELLERAY, David Roland; s of Roland David Elleray, and Barbara Elizabeth, *née* Williams; *b* 3 September 1954; *Educ* Dover GS for Boys, Hertford Coll Oxford (Baring open scholar, MA, PGCE); *Career* teacher; Harrow Sch 1977–: head of geography 1985–91, house master Druries 1991–, dir of boarding 1999–, house master The Head Master's 2006–07; govr Harrow HS 2003–04; ISI Inspr 1995–2004, chm Bd of Mgmnt Harrow Club W10 1999–2002; ICSTM: memb Ct 2001–06, chm Sport and Leisure Ctee 2002–06; football referee 1968–2003, FA Premier League (formerly Football League Div One) referee 1986–2003, FIFA int referee 1992–99 (officiated 78 int matches); memb Cncl FA 2002–, hon pres Referees' Assoc of England 2004–, vice-chm Referees' Ctee 2005–, memb UEFA Referees' Ctee 2006–; maj honours as referee: FA Charity Shield (Leeds v Liverpool) 1992, FA Cup Final (Manchester United v Chelsea) 1994, World Club Championship Final Tokyo (Ajax v Gremio) 1995, Nelson Mandela Inauguration Trophy (South Africa v Brazil) 1996, UEFA Euro 96 Finals (Germany v Czech Republic) 1996, UEFA Super Cup Final (Barcelona v Borussia Dortmund) 1998, COSAFA Southern African Final (Namibia v Angola) 1999, Worthington Cup Final (Liverpool v Birmingham) 2001; memb Ctee Ind Schs FA 1982– (vice-chm 1999–2003, chm 2003–); subject of Football Stories: Men in Black (Channel 4) 2000 (RTS sports documentary of the year); *Books* Referee! (1998), The Man in the Middle (2004); *Recreations* travel; *Style*— David Elleray, Esq; ✉ Harrow School, Harrow on the Hill, Middlesex HA1 3HW (tel 020 8872 8000, fax 020 8423 3112)

ELLES, Baroness (Life Peer UK 1972), of the City of Westminster; Diana Louie Elles; da of Col Stewart Francis Newcombe, DSO (d 1956), and Elizabeth Chaki (d 1973); *b* 19 July 1921; *Educ* Univ of London (BA); *m* 1945, Neil Patrick Moncrieff Elles, s of Edmund Hardie Elles, OBE; 1 da (Hon (Elizabeth) Rosamund (Hon Mrs Lockhart-Mummery) b 1947), 1 s ((Hon) James Edmund Moncrieff Elles, MEP, *qv* b 1949); *Career* Flight Offr WAAF 1942–45; called to the Bar 1956; memb Care Ctee Kennington 1956–72; UK del to UN 1972, UK delg to European Parl 1973–75, memb UN Sub-Cmmn on Discrimination and Minorities 1974–75, oppn front bench spokesman on foreign and Euro affairs 1975–79, chm Cons Party Int Office 1973–78, MEP (EDG) Thames Valley 1979–89, vice-pres European Parl 1982–87, chm Legal Affairs Ctee 1987–89; House of Lords: memb Euro Communities Select Ctee 1989–94, chm Sub-Ctee Law and Institutions 1992 (memb 1995–99); govr: European Univ Inst Florence 1976–79, Br Inst of Florence 1994–96 (life govr 1997–); hon bencher Lincoln's Inn 1993; *Style*— The Baroness Elles; ✉ 75 Ashley Gardens, London SW1P 1HG (tel 020 7828 0175)

ELLES, (Hon) James Edmund Moncrieff; MEP (EPP-ED) SE England; s of Neil Elles, of London, and Baroness Elles, *qv*; *b* 3 September 1949; *Educ* Eton, Univ of Edinburgh; *m* 1977 (m dis), Françoise, da of François Le Bail; 1 da (Victoria b 27 July 1980), 1 s (Nicholas b 22 Aug 1982); *Career* admin external rels EC 1977–80, asst to Dep DG of Agric EC 1980–84; MEP (EPP-ED): Oxford and Bucks 1984–94, Bucks and Oxon E 1994–99, SE England 1999–; Euro Parl: vice-pres EPP-ED Gp, memb Budget Ctee, sub-memb Budget Control Ctee, sub-memb Foreign Affairs and Security Ctee, memb Delgn for Rels with US; co-fndr Euro Internet Fndn (EIF), fndr Transatlantic Policy Network (TPN); *Recreations* music, skiing, golf; *Clubs* Royal and Ancient Golf (St Andrews), Carlton; *Style*— James Elles, Esq, MEP; ✉ European Parliament, Rm E14 153, Rue Wiertz, B-1047 Brussels, Belgium (e-mail jelles@europe.eu.int)

ELLINGTON, Marc Floyd; DL (Aberdeenshire 1984); Baron of Towie Barclay, Laird of Gardenstown and Crovie; s of Homer Frank Ellington (d 1984), of Memsie, Aberdeenshire, and Vancouver, and Harriette Hannah Kellas; *b* 16 December 1945; *m* 21 Dec 1967, Karen Leigh, da of Capt Warren Sydney Streater; 2 da (Iona Angeline Barclay of Gardenstown b 1979, Kirstie Naomi Barclay b 1983); *Career* memb Historic Houses Assoc; vice-pres Buchan Heritage Soc, chm Heritage Press (Scot); dir: Grampian Enterprise Ltd 1992–96, Aberdeen Univ Research Ltd 1999–2004, Gardenstown Estates Ltd, Soundcraft Audio Guides; ptnr Heritage Sound Recordings; Saltire Award 1973, Euro Architectural Heritage Award 1975, Civic Tst Award 1975 and 1993; contrib various architectural and historical jls and periodicals, composer and recording artiste, communications, marketing conslt, prodr of documentary films and TV progs; non-exec dir Historic Scotland, chm Grampian Region Tourism Task Force, tstee Nat Galleries of Scot; memb: Historic Building Cncl for Scotland 1980–98, Heritage Lottery Fund Ctee for Scotland 1998–2004, Br Heritage Ctee, Performing Rights Soc; Convention of Baronage of Scotland; patron Banffshire Wildlife Rehabilitation Tst; FSA; OStJ; *Recreations* sailing, historic architecture, art collecting, music; *Style*— Marc Ellington of Towie Barclay, DL; ✉ Towie Barclay Castle, Auchterless, Turriff, Aberdeenshire AB53 8EP (tel 01888 511347)

ELLIOT, Alan Christopher; s of Ian Frederick Lettsom Elliot (d 1981), of London, and Madeline Adelaide Mary, *née* Maclachlan (d 1977); *b* 9 March 1937; *Educ* Rugby, ChCh Oxford (MA); *m* 20 Jan 1967, Tara Louise Winifred, da of Sir Thomas Brian Weldon, 8 Bt (d 1979), and Countess Cathcart, of Moor Hatches, W Amesbury, Wilts; 3 da (Sacha b 1968, Larissa b 1970, Natalya b 1978), 1 s (Dominic b 1975); *Career* Nat Serv 1958–60: 2 Lt Welsh Guards cmmnd 1959, sr under offr Mons Offr Cadet Sch; PA to MD Metropole Industries 1960, md Dufay Ltd 1963 (dir 1962), chm Blick Time Recorders 1971– (organised mgmnt buyout from Dufay Ltd 1966), chm Blick plc 1986–2002; *Recreations* shooting, fishing, bridge; *Clubs* White's, Portland; *Style*— Alan Elliot, Esq; ✉ The Old Rectory, Chilton Foliat, Hungerford, Berkshire RG17 OTF (tel 01488 682243, fax 01488 681139); 142 Pavilion Road, London SW1X 0AY (tel 020 7235 3382, fax 020 7235 2750)

ELLIOT, Graeme Arthur; s of Ian Frederick Lettsom Elliot (d 1981), and Madeleine Adelaide Mary, *née* Maclachlan (d 1977); *b* 28 August 1942; *Educ* Rugby, Magdalene Coll Cambridge (MA); *m* 1, 1966, Hermione, da of Lt-Col John Delano-Osborne, of Hants; 2 da (Alexandra b 1968, Victoria b 1971); m 2, 1983, Nicola Nella Simpson, da of Keith Alexander Taylor, of Queensland; *Career* RTZ Corporation plc 1968–85, exec vice-chm Slough Estates plc 1986–92; dir: Candover Investments plc 1988–94, Thames Valley Enterprise Ltd 1990–92, Southern Regnl Advsy Bd National Westminster Bank plc 1991–92, The William Hill Group Ltd 1992–98, Automated Securities (Holdings) plc 1993–96, American Endeavour Fund Ltd 1993–98, Automotive Precision Holdings plc 1994–, Speciality Shops plc 1994–98, NSM plc 1994–96, Euro Sales Finance plc 1995–98, Primary Health Properties plc 1996–, Emerald Energy 1998–2003, Five Arrows Chile Investment Tst Ltd 1998–2000; advsy dir Samuel Montagu & Co Ltd 1994–96; FCA; *Recreations* bridge, golf, tennis, skiing; *Clubs* White's; *Style*— Graeme A Elliot, Esq; ✉ 47 Breer Street, London SW6 3HE (tel 020 7731 4870)

ELLIOTT, Prof Alexander Thomas; *b* 1 February 1949; *Educ* Trinity Acad Edinburgh, Univ of Stirling (BA), Univ of Glasgow (PhD, DSc); *m* Barbara, *née* Idle; 2 da (Fiona b 6 Jan 1979, Elspeth b 1 July 1980); *Career* temporary lectr Nuclear Med Unit Univ of Strathclyde 1974–75, lectr Dept of Nuclear Med Middlesex Hosp Med Sch and hon sr physicist Middlesex Hosp 1975–77, princ physicist Dept of Nuclear Med Bart's and hon lectr Bart's Med Coll 1977–81, top grade physicist Western Infirmary/Gartnavel General Unit, West of Scotland Health Bds, Dept of Clinical Physics and Bioengineering Univ of Glasgow 1981–90, dir West of Scotland Health Bds Dept of Clinical Physics and Bioengrg and prof of clinical physics Univ of Glasgow 1990–, clinical dir Laboratory Med and Clinical Physics West Glasgow Hosps Univ NHS Tst 1997–2000; chm: Nat Consultative Ctee of Scientists in Med 1989– (memb 1982–), Clinical Services Div North Glasgow Univ Hosps NHS Tst 2000–; memb: Hosp Physicists' Assoc 1975 (memb Cncl 1984–86), American Soc of Nuclear Med 1978, British Nuclear Med Soc 1983 (memb Cncl 1987–90), Admin of Radioactive Substances Advsy Ctee 1988–98, Editorial Bd Euro Jl of Nuclear Med 1989–, Acute Healthcare Res Ctee Scottish Office 1993–99, American Soc of Nuclear Cardiology 1993, Ctee on Med Aspects of Radiation in the Environment 2000–; ed Nuclear Med Communications 1999–, author of over 200 papers, book chapters and presentations; FInstP 1983 (MInstP 1978), ARCP 2002; *Style*— Prof Alexander Elliott; ✉ Department of Clinical Physics and Bioengineering, Western Infirmary, Glasgow G11 6NT (tel 0141 211 2948, fax 0141 211 1920, alex.elliott.wg@northglasgow.scot.nhs.uk)

ELLIOTT, Ann Margaret; da of John Frederick Hildred (d 1976), and Evelyn Rose Collier (d 2003); *b* 23 February 1945; *Educ* Shurnhold Sch Melksham (now George Ward Sch), Chippenham GS, Bath Acad of Art (Dip Art and Design Graphics), Dept of Educn Univ of Bath (DipEd); *m* 1972, Robert Anthony Elliott; 2 s (b 1978 and 1983), 1 da (b 1980); *Career* art asst Cammell Hudson & Brownjohn Ltd (Films) 1967–68, curatorial asst Sheffield City Art Galleries 1969–72, gallery organiser Gardner Centre Gallery Univ of Sussex 1972–73, exhibition offr Fine Arts Dept Br Cncl 1973–77 and 1985–94 (temp offr 1972), head of sculpture The Hat Hill Sculpture Fndn (Sculpture at Goodwood) 1994–97, ind curator and exhbn organiser/asscoc curator Sculpture at Goodwood 1997–; pt/t res asst Aust Crafts Cncl 1977–78, advsr for SE Arts Visual Arts Bd; memb: Bd Gardner Arts Centre Univ of Sussex, Fabric Ctee of Portsmouth Cathedral 2006–; tstee: Ironbridge Open Air Museum of Steel Sculpture 1998–, Gabo Tst for Sculpture Conservation 1999–, Artpoint 2004–; projects incl: Rodin in Lewes 1999, Bronze: contemporary Br Sculpture (Holland Park) 2000, A Sculptor's Development: Anthony Caro 2001, Henry Moore: Land and Sea (Lewes and Dieppe) 2004; *Books* Sculpture at Goodwood, 6 vols (1995–2001), Sculpture at Goodwood Drawings and Models (1994–98), The Art of Prior's Court School (2002), Bleep: The Eric and Jean Cass Collection (2004), The Sculpture and Drawings of Bridget McCrum; *Recreations* art, running, King Charles Cavaliers; *Style*— Mrs Ann Elliott; ✉ Park Cottage, Wisborough Green, West Sussex RH14 0DF (tel 01403 700211, e-mail aelliott@aelliot.demon.co.uk)

ELLIOTT, Anthony Michael Manton (Tony); s of Alan Elliott, and Katherine Elliott; *b* 7 January 1947; *Educ* Stowe, Keele Univ; *m* 1, Nov 1976 (m dis 1978), Janet Street-Porter, *qv*; m 2, June 1989, Jane Laetitia, *née* Coke; 3 s (Rufus George b 19 April 1988, Bruce Roland, Lawrence John (twins) b 17 Oct 1990); *Career* fndr and chm Time Out Group 1968–, dir various Time Out cos; govr BFI 1997–2003 (chm Prodn Bd 1998–2000); dir: The Roundhouse Tst 1998–, Somerset House Tst 1999–, The Photographers Gallery

1999–, Soho Theatre Co 2000–04 (resigned); chair London Ctee Human Rights Watch 2003–; *Recreations* travel, watching TV, cinema going, eating out with friends, newspapers and magazines, being with family in time left from working; *Style*— Tony Elliott, Esq; ✉ Time Out Group, Universal House, 251 Tottenham Court Road, London W1T 7AB (tel 020 7813 3000, fax 020 7813 6001)

ELLIOTT, Maj-Gen Christopher Haslett; CVO (2004), CBE (1994); s of Lt-Col Blethyn Elliott, and Zara, *née* Codrington; *b* 26 May 1947; *Educ* Kelly Coll Tavistock, Mons Offr Cadet Sch, Staff Coll Camberley; *m* 1970, Annabel Melanie Emerson; 4 da; *Career* cmmnd SWB 1966; regtl appts 1967–79; COS Berlin Inf Bde 1981–83, memb Directing Staff Staff Coll Camberley 1985–87, CO 1 Bn Royal Regt of Wales 1987–90, Cdr Br Forces Belize 1990–93, dir Army Recruiting MOD 1993–94, Cdr Br Mil Advsy and Trg Team SA 1994–97, GOC UK Support Cmd Germany 1997–2000, Col Cmdt POW Div 1999–, Col Royal Regt of Wales 1999–, Defence Services Sec to HM The Queen 2001–04, mentioned in despatches; tstee Royal Regt of Wales Museum, patron Coral Cayes Conservation; *Recreations* fly fishing, rough shooting, skiing, walking, watersports; *Clubs* Army and Navy; *Style*— Maj-Gen Christopher Elliott, CVO, CBE

ELLIOTT, Maj-Gen Christopher Leslie; CB (1999), MBE (1969); s of Peter Archibald Elliott, and Evelyn Sarah, *née* Wallace; *b* 18 March 1947; *Educ* Pocklington Sch York, RMAS, RMCS (BSc(Eng)), Cranfield Inst of Technol (MPhil); *m* 1970, Margaret Bennett; 2 da (Naomi Sarah (d 2005), Georgina Nancy); *Career* cmmnd RE, OC 48 Field Sqdn RE 1980, CO 21 Engr Regt 1986–88, ACOS 1 (Br) Corps 1988–90, Cdr 6th Armoured Bde 1990–91, Dir of Studies Staff Coll Camberley 1991–92, Dir Mil Ops 1993–95, UK Mil Advsr to Chm Int Conf on former Yugoslavia 1995–96, DG Army Trg and Recruiting Agency 1996–99, COS HQ Quartermaster General 1999–2000, DG Doctrine and Devpt 2000–02; Col Commandant Corps of Royal Engrs 2000–; dir Doctrine and Strategic Analysis General Dynamics UK Ltd, conslt Over Arup and Partners; visiting prof Cranfield Univ; memb Senate Cranfield Univ 1996–99, memb Advsy Cncl RMCS 2000–02; pres Jt Services Paragliding and Hang Gliding Assoc 1993–2002, Cdre Royal Engr Yacht Club 1995–96, Cdre Army Sailing Assoc 2000– (Vice-Cdre 1993–94); cmmr The Royal Hosp Chelsea 1996–2002, tstee The Army Central Fund 1998–2000, pres Instn of Royal Engrs 2002–, pres Victim Support Wiltshire 2003–, parish cncllr Easton Royal 2003–; fell Instn of Royal Engrs (FInstRE) 2007; *Publications* Blast Damage to Buildings (contrib, 1995); *Recreations* sailing, paragliding, reading; *Clubs* Royal Ocean Racing, Royal Cruising (main ctee memb 2000–), Royal Engineers Yacht, Royal Lymington Yacht; *Style*— Maj-Gen Christopher Elliott, CB, MBE; ✉ e-mail cle@clelliott24.freeserve.co.uk

ELLIOTT, Sir Clive Christopher Hugh; 4 Bt (UK 1917), of Limpsfield, Surrey; s of Sir Hugh Francis Ivo Elliott, 3 Bt, OBE (d 1989), and Elizabeth Margaret, *née* Phillipson (d 2007); *b* 12 August 1945; *Educ* Bryanston, UC Oxford (BA), Cape Town Univ (PhD); *m* 1975, Marie-Thérèse, da of Johann Rüttimann, of Hohenrain, Switzerland; 2 s (Ivo Antony Moritz b 1978, Nicolas Johann Clive b 1980); *Heir* s, Dr Ivo Elliott; *Career* ornithologist and international civil servant; research offr Cape Town Univ 1968–75; FAO/UN Regnl Quelea Project Chad/Tanzania 1975–81; FAO project mangr: Arusha Tanzania 1982–86, Nairobi Kenya 1986–89; country projects offr FAO Headquarters Rome 1989–95, sr offr migratory pests AGPP 1995–2004, sr offr Locusts and Other Migratory Pests Gp 2004–06; conslt migrating pests; *Books* Quelea Quelea - Africa's Bird Pest (ed with R L Bruggers, 1989); *Recreations* tennis; *Style*— Sir Clive Elliott, Bt, PhD; ✉ 173 Woodstock Road, Oxford OX2 7NB

ELLIOTT, Sir David Murray; KCMG (1995), CB (1987); s of Alfred Elliott, ISM (d 1984), and Mabel Emily, *née* Murray (d 1960); *b* 8 February 1930; *Educ* Bishopshalt GS, LSE (Kitchener scholar, BSc Econ); *m* 22 Sept 1956, Ruth Marjorie, da of Gilbert Ingram (d 1979); 1 s (b and d 1963), 1 da (Rosalind Frances (Mrs Simon Pugsley) b 1968); *Career* Nat Serv RAF 1951–54; asst postal controller II Home Counties Region GPO 1954–57, tr offr Fed Miny of Communications Enugu Nigeria 1958–62, asst postal controller I then princ HQ GPO 1962–69, asst sec Miny of Posts and Telecommunications (later part of DTI) 1969–75, cnsllr (external trade) UK Perm Representation to EC Brussels 1975–78, under sec European Secretariat Cabinet Office 1978–82, min and dep UK perm rep to EC Brussels 1982–91, DG (internal market) Gen Secretariat Cncl of the EU Brussels 1991–95; advsr: EU affrs under UK Know-How Fund, EU PHARE Programmes 1995–98; memb Bd CARE International UK 1995–2001; *Clubs* Travellers; *Style*— Sir David Elliott, KCMG, CB; ✉ 31 Ailsa Road, St Margarets, Twickenham, Middlesex TW1 1QJ

ELLIOTT, David Stuart; s of Arthur Elliott (d 1979), of East Leake, Notts, and May, *née* Wright (d 1989); *b* 29 April 1949; *Educ* Loughborough GS, Univ of Durham (BA), Courtauld Inst of Art London (MA); *m* 23 Feb 1974 (m dis 2005), Julia Alison, da of Lt-Col John Debenham, MC, of Shrivenham, Wilts; 2 da (Joanna b 10 July 1977, Kate b 3 May 1979); *Career* regnl art offr Arts Cncl 1973–76, dir MOMA Oxford 1976–96, dir Moderna Museet Stockholm 1996–2001, dir Mori Art Museum Tokyo 2001–06, dir Istanbul Modern 2007–; museum winner Sotheby's prize for excellence in the visual arts, Museum of the Year award 1983, winner Nat Art Collections Fund Collect award 1988; advsr VAAC Br Cncl 1979–96, Centre for Int Contemporary Arts NY 1986–92; memb: Cncl Great Britain-Russia Soc, London Cncl Central Sch of Speech and Drama 1994–96, Art Panel of Arts Cncl of GB 1992–95; visitor Ashmolean Museum 1994–2001; exec and pres CIMAM (ICOM) 1998–2004; pres Int Jury Dakar Biennale des Arts Africains et Contemporains Senegal 2000; Hon Dr Arts Oxford Brookes Univ 1998; Orden de Mayo Argentina 2000; *Books* Alexander Rodchenko (ed 1979), José Clemente Orozco (1981), Tradition and Renewal - Art in the GDR (1984), New Worlds - Art and Society in Russia (1986), Eisenstein at Ninety (ed 1988), 100 Years of Russian Art (1989), Alexander Rodchenko - Works on Paper 1914–1920 (1991), Photography in Russia 1840–1940 (1992), Art in Argentina 1920–1994 (ed 1994), After the Wall: art and culture in Post-Communist Europe (ed with B Pejić, 1999), Organising Freedom: Nordic Art in the Nineties (2000), Happiness: A Survival Guide for Art and Life (2003), Hiroshi Sugimoto (2005), Tokyo-Berlin/Berlin-Tokyo (2006), Bill Viola: Hatsu-yume (First Dream) (2006); also author of numerous reviews, catalogues and articles; *Recreations* collecting art books; *Style*— David Elliott; ✉ Istanbul Modern, Meclis-i Mebusan.cad, Liman isletmeleri Sahasi, Antrepo No 4, 34433 Karakoy, Istanbul, Turkey (tel 00 90 212 334 7300, e-mail info@istanbulmodern.org)

ELLIOTT, Geoffrey Charles; CBE (2004), JP (Central Devon 2005); s of Alfred Stanley Elliott (d 1985), of Coventry, and Elsie, *née* Wilday; *b* 10 May 1945; *Educ* Bablake Sch Coventry; *m* 5 April 1969, Lynda Barbara, da of John Arthur Williams (d 1980), of Shipston-on-Stour, Warks, and Bessie, *née* Parkinson; 1 da (Joanne Marie b 1971), 1 s (Nicholas John b 1974); *Career* Coventry Evening Telegraph: reporter, feature writer, chief feature writer 1962–72, dep ed 1973–79, ed 1981–90; ed Kent Messenger 1979–80, ed and dir The News Portsmouth 1990–99, head of journalism Univ of Central Lancashire Preston 2000–03; Guild of Eds: chm Parly and Legal Ctee 1983–86, chm West Midlands 1987–88, chm Wessex 1993–94, pres 1998–99; memb: Press Cncl 1987–90, Press Complaints Cmmn 1995–97, Broadcasting Standards Cmmn 2000–03; exec chm Common Purpose Coventry 1989–90, memb Portsmouth Common Purpose Cncl 1995–; memb Round Table: Rugby Webb Ellis (chm 1977–78), Bearsted, Kent, Coventry Mercia; fell Soc of Eds 2003 (pres 1999); *Recreations* sport, gardening, music; *Style*— Geoffrey Elliott, Esq, CBE, JP

ELLIOTT, Giles Roderick McGregor; s of James McGregor Elliott (d 1996), and Drusilla Lucy Christine, *née* Juniper; *b* 6 February 1953; *Educ* Gresham's, Magdalene Coll Cambridge; *m* 1978, Charlotte Mary; 5 da (Alexandra, Laura, Orlanda, Victoria, Matilda), 1 s (Dominic); *Career* dir: J Henry Schroder & Co Ltd 1989–96, Guinness Mahon & Co Ltd 1996–97, HM Publishers Holdings Ltd 1996–, Singer & Friedlander Ltd 1997–2000, Bridgewell Gp Ltd 2000–; FCA, FRSA; *Recreations* golf, fishing, farming, shooting; *Clubs* Rye, Neville, Hong Kong; *Style*— Giles Elliott, Esq; ✉ Barelands Farm, Bells Yew Green, Tunbridge Wells TN3 9BD (tel 01892 750495, fax 01892 750010); Bridgewell Gp Ltd, 21 New Street, Bishopsgate, London EC2M 4HR (tel 020 7003 3000, fax 020 7003 3001)

ELLIOTT, Guy Robert; s of Robert Elliott, and Susan, *née* de Wend Fenton; *b* 26 December 1955, London; *Educ* Harrow, Exeter Coll Oxford, INSEAD; *m* 1988, Hon Sophia Sackville West; da of 6 Baron Sackville (d 2004); 1 s (Lucius Adam Robert b 3 July 2002); *Career* Kleinwort Benson 1977–79, Rio Tinto plc: joined 1980, pres Rio Tinto Brasil 1996–99, chief fin offr Rio Tinto plc and Rio Tinto Ltd 2002–; *Style*— Guy Elliott, Esq; ✉ Rio Tinto plc, 6 St James's Square, London SW1Y 4LD (tel 020 7930 2399, e-mail guy.elliott@riotinto.com)

ELLIOTT, Prof John; s of Alfred George Lewis Elliott (d 1989), and Mary Dorothy, *née* Greason (d 1992); *b* 20 June 1938; *Educ* Ashford GS, Univ of London (MPhil, Dip Philosophy of Educn); *m* 20 June 1998, Dr Christine, *née* O'Hanlon; 3 da from previous m (Dominique, Katherine, Jessica); *Career* sch teacher 1962–67, res offr Schs Cncl Humanities Project 1967–72, tutor Cambridge Inst of Educn 1976–84; UEA: prof of educn 1987–, lectr 1972–76, reader in educn 1984–86, dean Sch of Educn 1992–95, dir Centre for Applied Res in Educn 1996–99, professorial fell 2002–04, emeritus prof 2004–; advsy prof Hong Kong Inst of Educn 2000–, visiting prof Manchester Met Univ 2003–, hon prof Univ of Sheffield 2004–, assoc Von Hugel Inst St Edmund's Coll Cambridge 2004–; conslt on res devpt Hong Kong Curriculum Devpt Inst; tstee Keswick Hall Tst 1987–93, pres Br Educnl Res Assoc 1989–90 (memb Cncl 1987–92, vice-pres 1988–89); memb: Philosophy Educn Soc of GB, Norfolk LSC 2001–; Hon Dr: (in Education) Hong Kong Inst of Educn 2002, Autonomous Univ of Barcelona 2003; Hon DLitt UEA 2003; FRSA; *Books* Issues in Teaching for Understanding (ed with D Ebbutt, 1985), Case Studies in Teaching for Understanding (ed with D Ebbutt, 1986), Rethinking Assessment and Appraisal (ed with H Simons, 1989), La Investigacion-Accion en Educacion (1989), Action-Research for Educational Change (1991), Reconstructing Teacher Education (ed, 1993), The Curriculum Experiment (1998), Images of Educational Change (ed with H Altrichter, 2000), Images of Educational Change (co-ed, 2000), Reflecting Where the Action Is: the selected writings of John Eliott on Pedagogy and Action Research (2005); *Recreations* walking, golf, reading, travel; *Style*— Prof John Elliott; ✉ Centre for Applied Research in Education, University of East Anglia, Norwich NR4 7TJ

ELLIOTT, John; s of Leonard John Elliott (d 2001), and Elsie, *née* Maule; *b* 13 January 1949, London; *Educ* London Business Sch (MBA); *m* 1, April 1972; 1 s (Richard b Feb 1978); m 2, March 2005, Gillian, *née* Blythe; 3 da (Carrie b Oct 1985, Samantha b Nov 1987, Rebecca b Oct 1989); *Career* md Millwood Homes 1981–; FNAEA 1970; *Recreations* boats; *Style*— John Elliott, Esq; ✉ Millwood Designer Homes, Bordyke End, East Street, Tonbridge, Kent TN9 1HA (tel 01732 770991, fax 01732 770997, e-mail johne@mdh.uk.com)

ELLIOTT, John Charles Kennedy; MBE (1999); s of Charles Morris William Elliott (d 1967), of Altrincham, Cheshire, and Lesley Margaret, *née* Bush (d 1999); *b* 13 March 1937; *Educ* Merton House Sch Penmaenmawr, Mill Hill Sch London, Univ of Manchester; *m* 28 July 1962, Angela Mary, da of Col Geoffrey William Noakes OBE, JP, DL; 3 s (Charles Geoffrey b 3 Nov 1963, William James b 10 April 1965, Thomas Richard b 11 May 1969), 1 da (Vanessa Jane b 9 Feb 1967); *Career* admitted slr 1961; articled to Mr John Gorna 1956–61, James Chapman & Co 1961–62, Fentons Stansfield & Elliott 1962–68, fndr and sr ptnr Elliott & Co 1968–94 (conslt 1994–); dir: Northern Rock Building Society (Northern Bd) 1988–95, Bain Hogg Ltd UK Division 1994–99; chm Young Slrs' Gp of Law Soc 1973–74, pres Manchester Law Soc 1980, pres Euro-American Lawyers' Gp 1995–2001 (chm 1992–95); NSPCC: memb Central Exec Ctee 1980–87, chm Manchester and Salford Branch 1989–96, chm Gtr Manchester Area Ctee 1990–94; Liveryman Worshipful Co of Horners; memb Law Soc; *Clubs* The St James's (Manchester), Manchester Tennis and Racquets, BPMF (Stoke-on-Trent); *Style*— John C K Elliott, Esq, MBE; ✉ Bradwall House, Bradwall, Cheshire CW11 1RB (tel 01270 765369); (business tel 01270 768074, fax 01270 768004, car tel 078 6061 9346)

ELLIOTT, Prof Sir John Huxtable; kt (1994); s of Thomas Charles Elliott (d 1969), and Janet Mary, *née* Payne (d 1991); *b* 23 June 1930; *Educ* Eton, Univ of Cambridge (MA, PhD); *m* 1958, Oonah Sophia, da of Sir Nevile Butler; *Career* lectr in history Univ of Cambridge 1962–67 (asst lectr 1957–62), prof of history KCL 1968–73 (hon fell 1998), prof of history Inst for Advanced Study Princeton 1973–90, regius prof of modern history Univ of Oxford 1990–97; fell: Trinity Coll Cambridge 1954–67 (hon fell 1991), Oriel Coll Oxford 1990–98 (hon fell 1998); King Juan Carlos visiting prof NYU 1988, visiting hon prof Univ of Warwick 2003–06; memb American Philosophical Soc 1982; corr memb: Hispanic Soc of America 1975, Real Academia Sevillana de Buenas Letras 1976; foreign memb Academia Nazionale dei Lincei 2003; Wolfson Prize for History 1986, Gold Medal for the Fine Arts Spain 1990, Eloy Antonio de Nebrija Prize Spain 1993, Prince of Asturias Prize for Social Sciences Spain 1996, Balzan Prize for History 1500–1800 1999, Francis Parkman Prize 2007; Visitante Illustre de Madrid 1983; Medal of Honour Universidad Internacional Menéndez y Pelayo 1987; Hon Dr: Universidad Autónoma de Madrid 1983, Univ of Genoa 1992, Univ of Portsmouth 1993, Univ of Barcelona 1994, Univ of Warwick 1995, Brown Univ RI 1996, Univ of Valencia 1998, Univ of Lleida 1999, Universidad Complutense Madrid 2003, Coll of William and Mary Williamsburg VA 2005, Univ of London 2007; FBA 1972, FAAAS 1977; Cdr Order of Isabel la Católica 1987 (Grand Cross 1996), Grand Cross Order of Alfonso X El Sabio 1988, Cross of St George (Catalonia) 1999; *Books* The Revolt of the Catalans (1963), Imperial Spain 1469–1716 (1963), Europe Divided 1559–1598 (1968), The Old World and the New 1492–1650 (1970), Memoriales y Cartas del Conde Duque de Olivares Vol I (1978), Memoriales y Cartas del Conde Duque de Olivares Vol II (1980), A Palace for King (with Jonathan Brown, 1980), Richelieu and Olivares (1984), The Count-Duke of Olivares (1986), Spain and Its World 1500–1700 (1989), The World of the Favourite (ed with L W B Brockliss, 1999), Sale of the Century (Prado exhibition catalogue, ed with Jonathan Brown, 2002), Empires of the Atlantic World (2006); *Recreations* looking at paintings; *Style*— Prof Sir John Elliott, FBA; ✉ 122 Church Way, Iffley, Oxford OX4 4EG (tel 01865 716703); Oriel College, Oxford OX1 4EW

ELLIOTT, Judith Margaret; da of Thomas Charles Elliott, and Janet Mary, *née* Payne; *Educ* St Hilda's Coll Oxford (BA); *m* Donald Neil Davis; *Career* publishing dir Heinemann Young Books 1970–85, dir William Heinemann Ltd 1977–85, fndr md and publisher Orchard Books (part of The Watts Gp) 1985–92, chm Orion Children's Books 2003– (md and publisher 1992–2003); *Recreations* reading fiction, history and poetry, museums and galleries, enjoying being abroad; *Style*— Ms Judith Elliott

ELLIOTT, Keith; s of Wallace Elliott, and Celia, *née* Bradley; *b* 20 June 1941, Liverpool; *Educ* Quarry Bank GS Liverpool, Univ of Liverpool (BA, CertEd); *m* 1965, Valerie, *née* Chitham (d 2003); 2 s (Steven b 28 April 1978, Martin b 8 Dec 1980); *Career* teacher and univ lectr until 1996, self-employed motivational speaker, author and sports betting analyst 1996–; ind memb Horserace Betting Levy Bd 1997–2006; racing corr BBC Radio Merseyside 1980–97, sports analyst Fill Yer Boots (Sky TV) 2003–04, golf writer The Sportsman 2006; *Publications* Elliott's Golf Form (annually, 1994–); *Style*— Keith Elliott, Esq; ✉ 22 Burrell Close, Prenton, Birkenhead, Wirral CH42 8QE (tel 0151 609 1134, fax 0151 608 4860, e-mail kepos@btconnect.com, website www.keithelliott.co.uk)

ELLIOTT, Prof Marianne; OBE (2000); da of Terence J Burns (d 1982), and Sheila, *née* O'Neill; *b* 25 May 1948; *Educ* Dominican Coll Fortwilliam Belfast, Queen's Univ Belfast (BA), Lady Margaret Hall Oxford (DPhil); *m* 19 July 1975, Trevor Elliott, s of Clifford Elliott; 1 s (Marc b 11 Jan 1989); *Career* lectr II W London Inst of HE 1975–77, univ research fell UC Swansea 1977–79, temp lectr UC Swansea 1981–82, visiting prof Iowa State Univ 1983, visiting prof Univ of S Carolina 1984; Univ of Liverpool: univ research fell Dept of History 1984–87, hon fell Dept of History 1987–93, Andrew Geddes and John Rankin prof of modern history 1993–, dir of research 1995–, dir Inst of Irish Studies 1997–, dir of grad studies Dept of History, dir Humanities Grad Sch, chair Arts Faculty Res Ctee; pt/t course tutor Open Univ 1979–85, pt/t tutor Univ of Warwick 1980–81, Simon sr research fell Univ of Manchester 1988–89, lectr in history Birkbeck Coll London 1991–93, visiting prof history/Irish studies Boston Coll MA 1998; Leverhume Research Fell 1988–89, Nuffield Fndn Research Readership 1996–97, Br Acad Res Readership 2001–03, Royal Historical Soc Colin Matthew meml lectr 2002, Univ of Oxford Ford Lectures 2004–05; HE offr Br Assoc for Irish Studies 1985–88; external assessor for history chairs: Nat Univ of Ireland (UCD), Univ of Limerick, Nat Univ Maynooth; memb: Opsahl Cmmn on NI 1992–93, History and Archaeology Res Panel Br Acad/HRB 1995–98 (chair 1997–98), Bd Anglo-Irish Encounter 1997–, Br Acad Res Ctee 2002–05; FRHistS 1985, FBA 2002; *Publications* Partners in Revolution. The United Irishmen and France (1982, Leo Gershov Award American Historical Assoc 1983), The People's Armies (trans, 1987), Wolfe Tone. Prophet of Irish Independence (1989, Irish Independent/Irish Life Award for Biography 1990, American Conf for Irish Studies James R Donnelly Sr Prize for History 1992), A Citizens' Inquiry. The Opsahl Report on Northern Ireland (jtly, 1992), The Catholics of Ulster, A History (2000, runner-up Ewart-Biggs Meml Prize 2001), The Long Road to Peace in Northern Ireland (ed, 2001), Robert Emmet. The Making of a Legend (2003); author of numerous articles and contributions to edited collections; *Recreations* running, reading, music; *Style*— Prof Marianne Elliott, OBE, FBA; ✉ Institute of Irish Studies, The University of Liverpool, 1 Abercromby Square, Liverpool L69 7WY (tel 0151 794 3831, fax 0151 794 3836, e-mail lindam@liv.ac.uk)

ELLIOTT, Marianne; da of Michael Elliott, and Rosalind, *née* Knight; *Educ* St Hilary's Sch Alderley Edge, Stockport GS, Univ of Hull; *Career* artistic dir Royal Exchange Theatre Manchester, associate dir Royal Court Theatre London; *Theatre* Royal Exchange Theatre Manchester: Coyote Ugly 1996, I Have Been Here Before 1996, Poor Superman 1997, Mad For It 1997, The Deep Blue Sea 1997, Martin Yesterday 1998–99, Fast Food 1999, Nude With Violin 1999, A Woman of no Importance 2000, As You Like It 2000, Les Blancs 2001; other prodns incl: Terracotta (Hampstead Theatre and Birmingham Rep) 2000, Local (Royal Court Upstairs) 2000, The Little Foxes (Donmar Warehouse) 2001, The Sugar Syndrome (Royal Court) 2004, Notes on Falling Leaves (Royal Court) 2004, Pillars of the Community (RNT) 2005, Much Ado About Nothing (RSC) 2006, Therese Raquin (RNT) 2006; *Style*— Ms Marianne Elliott; ✉ Royal Court Theatre, Sloane Square, London SW1W 8AS (tel 020 7565 5050)

ELLIOTT, Prof Martin John; s of John Elliott, MBE, of Sheffield, S Yorks, and Muriel, *née* Dyson; *b* 8 March 1951; *Educ* King Edward VII GS, Univ of Newcastle upon Tyne (MB BS, MD); *m* 15 Jan 1977, Lesley Rickard, da of Alan Rickard (d 1989), of Puddletown, Dorset; 2 s (Becan b 3 June 1981, Toby b 12 May 1983); *Career* sr registrar and first asst in cardiothoracic surgery Freeman Hosp Newcastle upon Tyne 1978–83; Gt Ormond St Hosp: sr registrar 1984–85, conslt and sr lectr in cardiothoracic surgery1985–, clinical dir Cardio-respiratory and Critical Care Directorate 1997–2000, dep clinical dir 2000–01, dir of thoracic transplantation 2001–, dir Tracheal Team 2000–; visiting paediatric cardiac surgn: Malta 1989–, Tehran Heart Inst Iran 1991–, Sofia Bulgaria 1994–; hon conslt cardiothoracic surgeon: Harefield Hosp London 1994–, UCH London 1998–; prof of cardiothoracic surgery UCL 2004–; chm Int Nomenclature Gp; sec Euro Congenital Heart Surgeons Fndn; author of pubns relating to the results of cardiac surgery, pathophysiology of cardiopulmonary bypass and tracheal surgery; FRCS 1978; *Recreations* tennis, reading, cinema, music; *Style*— Prof Martin Elliott; ✉ The Cardiac Wing, The Great Ormond Street Hospital for Children, Great Ormond Street, London WC1N 3JH (tel 020 7405 9200, fax 020 7813 8262, e-mail elliom1@gosh.nhs.uk)

ELLIOTT, Martin John Henry; s of Patrick James Lawrence Elliott, of Boars Hill, Oxford, and Beryl Olivia Catherine, *née* Carroll; *b* 26 August 1955; *Educ* St Benedict's Sch Ealing, ChCh Oxford (BA); *m* 4 Aug 1984, Rosanna Lina, da of late Capt William James Gorard, of Ealing, London; 3 s (Benedict Edward Henry b 29 Nov 1988, Oliver James Ambrose b 16 Jan 1990, Edmund Giles Augustus b 4 Aug 1991), 3 da (Alice Clare Ianthe b 1 Aug 1993, Josephine Eleanor Naomi b 1 Sept 1995, Genevieve Elizabeth Cecilia b 24 Feb 1997); *Career* admitted slr 1979; Linklaters: articled clerk 1977–79, slr 1979–85, ptnr 1985–; memb Law Soc; *Recreations* rugby, cricket, tennis, golf, cycling, gardening; *Clubs* MCC; *Style*— Martin Elliott, Esq; ✉ Linklaters, One Silk Street, London EC2Y 8HQ (tel 020 7456 2000, fax 020 7456 2222)

ELLIOTT, Dr Michael; CBE (1982); *b* 30 September 1924, London; *Educ* The Skinner's Co Sch Tunbridge Wells, UC Southampton, Univ of London (external BSc, DSc, external PhD); *m* 2 Aug 1950, Margaret Olwen, *née* James; 2 da (Karen Mair b 19 Feb 1954, Fiona Anne b 28 Jan 1955); *Career* Insecticides and Fungicides Dept Rothamsted Experimental Station: scientific offr 1948–53, sr scientific offr 1953–61, princ scientific offr 1961–70, sr princ scientific offr 1970–79, dep chief scientific offr and head of dept 1979–84; Rothamsted Experimental Station: dep dir 1979–84, Lawes Tst sr fell 1989–; Div of Entomology Univ of Calif Berkeley: visiting lectr 1969 and 1974, visiting research scientist Pesticide Chem and Toxicology Lab 1986–88; visiting prof Imperial Coll London 1978; conslt on chemistry of insecticides 1984–85 and 1989–; author of numerous articles in pubns 1948–, over 120 patents and applications in field of insecticides 1962–; Hon DSc Univ of Southampton 1985, FKC 1984; foreign assoc Nat Assembly of Scis USA 1996; CChem, FRS 1979 (Mullard medallist 1982), FRSC 1984; *Awards* Burdick and Jackson Int Award for Pesticide Research (American Chem Soc) 1975, ARC Awards to Inventors 1977 and 1980, Second Holroyd Meml lectr and medallist SCI 1978, John Jeyes medallist and lectr Chem Soc 1978–79, La Grande Medaille de la Société Française de Phytiatrie et de Phytopharmacie 1983, RSC Fine Chems and Medicinals Gp Award 1984, Br Crop Protection Cncl Medal 1986, Br Technol Gp Awards to Inventors 1988 and 1992, Wolf Fndn Prize in Agric 1989, Prix de la Fondation de la Chimie Paris 1989, Environment Medal SCI 1993; *Style*— Dr Michael Elliott, CBE, FRS; ✉ c/o Rothamsted Research, Harpenden, Hertfordshire AL5 2JQ (tel 01582 763133, fax 01582 760981); home tel 01483 277506

ELLIOTT, Michael John; *b* 22 August 1953; *Educ* Manor Park GS Nuneaton, Sheffield City Coll of Educn (Univ of Sheffield Cert in Educn), Sheffield City Poly (Univ of Sheffield BEd); *Career* pt/t lectr Dept of Gen Studies Rotherham Coll of Technol 1978, res asst Dept of Educn Mgmnt Sheffield City Poly 1978–79, political advsr and res asst R G Caborn MEP 1979–82; Sheffield City Poly: gen mangr Union of Students 1982–84, asst to the princ 1984–86, head Publicity and Information Servs 1986; asst dir (resources) Yorkshire Arts Assoc 1987–88, dir West Midlands Arts Assoc 1989–91; chief exec: West Midlands Regnl Arts Bd 1992–96, Heart of England Tourist Bd 1996–2000; chair: Regnl Arts Bd Chief Execs' Gp 1990–94, RAB Services Ltd 1992, Aston Arts Advsy Bd 1995–98; chm Regnl Tourist Bd Director's Gp 1999–2000; chm Tourism Working Gp for English Heritage's Review of the Historic Environment 2000; treas Euro Forum for Arts and Heritage 1995–96, advsr Dept Culture Media and Sport on implementation of English tourism 1999; memb: Cncl Univ of Birmingham 1990–96, Arts Liaison Ctee 1990–96, Governing Body Herefordshire Coll of Arts and Design 1990–97, Governing Body Handsworth Coll 1995–98, Governing Body Clarendon Coll Nottingham 1997–98, Chief Offrs' Gp 1991–96, Information Mgmnt Policy Gp Arts Funding System 1991–95, Mgmnt Ctee English Regnl Arts Bds 1993–95, Exec of the Chief Offrs' Gp Integrated Arts Funding System 1993–95, Convocation Tst for the Arts Univ of Sheffield 1994–96, Sec of State for Culture's Strategic Planning Working Gp on Tourism 1997–2000, Sheffield City Hall Capital Devpt Advsy Bd 2001; chm Belgrade Theatre (Coventry) Tst ltd 1998–2001; govr Univ of Wolverhampton 2000–, chief exec Royal Liverpool Philharmonic Soc 2001–, memb Cncl Liverpool Inst of Performing Arts 2002–; fell Tourism Soc 1998, FRSA; *Publications* The Development of Consortia for Post 16 Provision in the Face of Falling Enrolments (with J A Mundy, 1978); *Recreations* walking, cycling, swimming, watching theatre, dance and football, listening to music, reading contemporary literature and keeping up to date with current affairs and good management practice, travel and continued learning through experience and practice; *Style*— Michael Elliott, Esq

ELLIOTT, Nicholas Blethyn; QC (1995); s of late Col B W T Elliott, of Wilts, and Zara, *née* Codrington; *b* 11 December 1949; *Educ* Kelly Coll Tavistock, Univ of Bristol (LLB); *m* Penelope Margaret Longbourne (Nemmy), da of Brig Hugh Browne; 2 s (Max Blethyn b 14 Aug 1982, George Hugh b 10 Feb 1984); *Career* pupillage chambers of Andrew Leggatt QC (now Sir Andrew Leggatt), called to the Bar Gray's Inn 1972 (bencher), currently in practice Gray's Inn; asst boundary cmmr 2000; *Publications* Banking Litigation (co-ed), Byles on Bills of Exchange and Cheques, Butterworths Money Laundering; *Recreations* tennis, bridge, bicycling, swimming, rock and roll dancing; *Style*— Nicholas Elliott, Esq, QC; ✉ 3 Verulam Buildings, Gray's Inn, London WC1R 5NT (tel 020 7831 8441, fax 020 7831 8479)

ELLIOTT, Paul; *b* 27 October 1949; *Educ* Latymer Upper Sch, Clare Coll Cambridge (MA); *m* Sharon Amanda Jordan; 1 da (Joanna b 6 Dec 1993), 1 s (Matthew b 1 April 1995); *Career* private sec to Min of Agric 1975–76, first sec (agric) Br Embassy Bonn 1984–89, head Milk Div MAFF 1989–94, princ fin offr MAFF (later DEFRA) 1996–2001, dir rural economies and communities DEFRA 2001–03, London Borough of Camden 2003–04, clerk to Worshipful Co of Scriveners 2007–; *Recreations* cricket, music, photography, travel; *Style*— Paul Elliott, Esq; ✉ e-mail paul.elliott149@btinternet.com

ELLIOTT, Robert James; s of Robert Alfred Elliott (d 1994), and Dorothy, *née* Pullar; *b* 3 July 1952, Newcastle upon Tyne; *Educ* Leeds GS, Univ of London (LLB), Coll of Law Lancaster Gate; *m* 1 April 1978, Sara Elizabeth, *née* Scott; 2 s (Robert Arthur John b 27 Oct 1981, James Henry Percival b 1 May 1988), 1 da (Katharine Frances b 24 Jan 1984); *Career* Wilde Sapte: slr 1976–79, ptnr 1979–90; ptnr Linklaters 1991– (joined 1990, currently global head of banking); memb: Law Soc, City of London Solicitors' Co; govr Tonbridge Sch; dir and tstee Surrey County Cricket Club; Freeman Co of Watermen & Lightermen of the River Thames; *Recreations* golf, sailing, theatre; *Clubs* Hurlingham, Royal Ocean Racing, New York Yacht; *Style*— Robert Elliott, Esq; ✉ Linklaters, One Silk Street, London EC2Y 8HQ (tel 020 7456 4478, fax 020 7456 2222, e-mail robert.elliott@linklaters.com)

ELLIOTT, Prof Sir Roger James; kt (1987); s of James Elliott (d 1932), and Gladys, *née* Hill; *b* 8 December 1928; *Educ* Swanwick Hall Sch, New Coll Oxford (MA, DPhil); *m* 1952, Olga Lucy, da of Roy Atkinson (d 1940); 2 da (Jane Susan b 1955, Rosalind Kira b 1957), 1 s (Martin James b 1962); *Career* research fell Univ of Calif Berkeley 1952–53, AERE Horwell 1953–55, lectr Univ of Reading 1955–57, fell St John's Coll Oxford 1957–74, Wykeham prof of physics Univ of Oxford 1974–88 (sr proctor 1969–70), fell New Coll Oxford 1974–96 (emeritus fell 1996–), prof of physics Univ of Oxford 1993–96 (emeritus prof 1996–); sec to delegates and chief exec OUP 1988–93 (delegate 1971–88); chm: Computer Bd for Univs and Res Cncls 1983–87, ICSU Press 1997–2002, Blackwell Ltd 1999–2002; non-exec dir Blackwells 1996–99; physical sec and vice-pres Royal Soc 1984–88, pt/t memb Bd UKAEA 1988–93, treas Int Cncl of Scientific Unions (ICSU) 2001–; memb Bd Br Cncl 1991–2000; chm Disability Info Tst 1998–2001, pres Publishers' Assoc 1993–94; hon fell: St John's Coll Oxford 1988, New Coll Oxford 1998; Hon DSc: Univ of Paris 1983, Univ of Bath 1991, Univ of Essex 1993; FRS 1976, fell Mexican Acad of Sciences 2003, FInstP 2005; *Clubs* Athenaeum; *Style*— Prof Sir Roger Elliott, FRS; ✉ 11 Crick Road, Oxford OX2 6QL; Theoretical Physics, 1 Keble Road, Oxford OX1 3NP (tel 01865 273997, fax 01865 273947, e-mail r.elliott1@physics.ox.ac.uk)

ELLIOTT, Prof Stephen Richard; s of Cyril Albert Elliott, and Mavis Mary, *née* Lumb; *b* 30 September 1952; *Educ* Trinity Coll and Cavendish Lab Cambridge (MA, PhD); *m* 3 Sept 1983, Penelope Ann Hylton, *née* Johnson; *Career* Trinity Coll Cambridge: prize (res) fell 1977–81, teaching fell 1981–; Univ of Cambridge: lectr 1979–94, reader in solid-state chemical physics 1994–99, prof of chemical physics 1999–; prof of physics Ecole Polytechnique France 1998–2000; ed Philosophical Magazine Letters; memb Editorial Bd: Philosophical Magazine, Jl of Non-Crystalline Solids, Current Opinion in Solid State and Materials Science, Jl of Optoelectronics and Advanced Materials; Zachariasen Prize 1992; *Books* Physics of Amorphous Materials (1983), Physics and Chemistry of Solids (1998); *Recreations* wine, 18th and 19th century caricatures, Italian life and culture; *Style*— Prof Stephen Elliott; ✉ Trinity College, Cambridge CB2 1TQ (tel 01223 336525/338512, fax 01223 336362, e-mail srel1@cam.ac.uk)

ELLIOTT, Prof (Charles) Thomas; CBE (1994); s of Charles Thomas Elliott (d 1970), and Mary Jane, *née* Higgins (d 1991); *b* 16 January 1939; *Educ* Washington Alderman Smith GS, Univ of Manchester (BSc, PhD); *m* Brenda; 1 s (David b 1962), 2 da (Catherine Ann b 1963, Elizabeth Mary b 1966); *Career* asst lectr and lectr Electrical Engrg Dept Univ of Manchester 1963–67, visiting scientist MIT Lincoln Laboratory 1970–71; Defence Evaluation and Research Agency (DERA, now QinetiQ): sr scientific offr 1967–73, princ scientific offr 1973–79, sr princ scientific offr (individual merit) 1979–86, dep chief scientific offr (individual merit) 1986–91, chief scientific offr (individual merit) 1991–, chief scientist Electronics Sector 1995–99, conslt 1999–; distinguished visiting scientist Jet Propulsion Laboratory Calif 1987, visiting prof of physics Heriot-Watt Univ 1992–99 (pt/t prof of physics 1999–); Rank Prize for Optoelectronics 1982, The Churchill Medal for Engrg (Soc of Engrs) 1986, MacRobert Award for Engrg (Royal Acad of Engrs) 1991, Patterson Medal (Inst of Physics) 1997, J J Thompson Medal (Instn of Electrical Engrs) 1998, Progress Medal RPS 2001; Hon FRPS 2001, FRS 1988, FInstP 1990; *Recreations* reading, music, travel, golf; *Style*— Prof Thomas Elliott, CBE, FRS; ✉ tel 01684 562474, fax 01684 892360

ELLIOTT, Timothy Stanley; QC (1992); *b* 2 April 1950; *Educ* Marlborough, Trinity Coll Oxford (exhibitioner, MA); *m* 1973, Katharine Barbara, *née* Lawrance; 1 s (b 1980), 1 da (b 1983); *Career* called to the Bar Middle Temple 1975; *Style*— Timothy Elliott, Esq, QC; ✉ 15 Essex Street, London WC2R 3AA (tel 020 7544 2600, fax 020 7240 7722)

ELLIOTT, Hon Lord; Walter Archibald Elliott; MC (1943), QC (1960); s of Prof Thomas Renton Elliott, CBE, DSO, FRS (d 1961), of Broughton, Peeblesshire, and Martha, *née* M'Cosh; *b* 6 September 1922; *Educ* Eton, Univ of Edinburgh; *m* 1954, Susan Isobel, da of late Phillip Mackenzie Ross; 2 s; *Career* Capt Scots Gds Italy, NW Europe WWII; barr and advocate 1950, pres Lands Tbnl for Scotland 1971–92, chm of Scottish Land Court with title Lord Elliott 1978–92; Ensign Queen's Body Guard for Scotland (Royal Co of Archers) until 2001 (ret); *Books* Us and Them, A Study of Group Consciousness (1986), Esprit de Corps (1996); *Recreations* gardening, travel; *Clubs* New (Edinburgh); *Style*— The Hon Lord Elliott, MC; ✉ Morton House, Fairmilehead, Edinburgh EH10 7AW (tel 0131 445 2548)

ELLIOTT OF MORPETH, Baron (Life Peer UK 1985), of Morpeth in the County of Northumberland and of the City of Newcastle upon Tyne; (Robert) William Elliott; kt (1974), DL (Northumbreland 1983); s of Richard Elliott (d 1957), of Low Heighley, Northumberland, and Mary Elizabeth, da of William Fulthorpe, of Morpeth; *b* 11 December 1920; *Educ* King Edward GS Morpeth; *m* 1956, (Catherine) Jane, da of Robert John Burton Morpeth, of Newcastle upon Tyne; 4 da (Hon Alison Mary (Hon Mrs Campbell Adamson) b 1957, Hon Catherine Victoria (Hon Mrs Taylor), Hon Sarah Anne (Hon Mrs Atkinson-Clark) (twins) b 1962, Hon Louise Jane b 1967), 1 s (Hon Richard John b 1959); *Career* farmer 1939–; chm, vice-pres and pres Northern Area Young Conservatives 1948–55; contested (Cons) Morpeth 1954 and 1955; MP (Cons) Newcastle upon Tyne N 1957–83; PPS to: Jt Parly Secs Miny of Transport and Civil Aviation 1958–59, Parly Under Sec of State Home Office 1959–60, Min of State Home Office 1960–61, Min for Technical Co-operation 1961–63; asst govt whip 1963–64, opposition whip 1966–70; comptroller of HM Household June-Oct 1970; vice-chm Conservative Party Organisation 1970–74; chm Select Ctee on Agriculture, Fisheries and Food 1980–83; chm United Artists Communications (North East); *Clubs* Northern Counties; *Style—* The Rt Hon Lord Elliott of Morpeth, DL; ✉ Crown House, Hall Yard, King's Cliffe, Northamptonshire PE8 6XQ (tel 01780 67888); 19 Laxford House, Cundy Street, London SW1 (tel 020 7730 7619)

ELLIS, Dr Adrian Foss; CB (2004); s of Henry James Ellis (d 1976), of Swindon, Wilts, and Marjorie Foss, *née* Smith (d 1975); *b* 15 February 1944; *Educ* Dean Close Sch Cheltenham, Univ of London (BSc(Eng)), Loughborough Univ (PhD); *m* 1, Lesley Maxted, *née* Smith (d 1970); m 2, 1973, Hilary Jean, da of Alfred Miles; 2 da (Sarah Louise b 23 June 1974, Joanna Katherine b 22 Dec 1976), 1 s (Nicholas Edward James b 10 July 1983); *Career* student apprenticeship Richard Thomas and Baldwins 1962–67, sr res offr British Steel Corp 1969–71, district alkali inspr HM Alkali Inspectorate 1976–83 (alkali inspr 1971–76); HSE: head of Major Hazards Assessment Unit 1985–86 (dep head 1983–85), dep chief inspr (Chemicals) 1986–90, regnl dir Field Ops, dir Technol and Hazardous Installations Policy 1990–91, dir Technol and Health Sciences 1991–96, dir of field ops 1996–2003; ILO conslt on major hazards: India 1985, Pakistan 1988, Thailand 1989, Indonesia 1990, Soviet Union and Soviet States 1991, China 1994; pres Int Assoc of Labour Inspection 2002–05 (sec gen 1999–2002); visiting prof Cranfield Univ 1992–99; FInstE 1977, FIChemE 1977 (memb Cncl), FREng 1995; *Books* The International Labour Office Manual on Major Hazards Control (co-author); *Recreations* travel, Swindon Town FC, exploring car boot sales; *Clubs* Athenaeum; *Style—* Dr Adrian Ellis, CB, FREng; ✉ 1 Wootton Oast, Garlinge Green Road, Petham, Canterbury, Kent CT4 5RJ

ELLIS, Anthony John; s of Jack Ellis, of Scunthorpe, S Humberside, and Nancy Doreen, *née* Reed; *b* 15 June 1945; *Educ* Univ of London (BD, MA); *m* 1, 1966 (m dis), Maureen Jane Anne Twomey; 2 da (Kate b 14 Feb 1973, Seònaid b 19 May 1975); m 2, 4 Sept 1980, Alice Anne, da of late James Stanley Stewart Findlay, of Helmsdale, Sutherland; 1 da (Bridget b 7 May 1985); *Career* sr lectr Dept of Moral Philosophy Univ of St Andrews 1987–90 (lectr 1971–1987, chm 1985–89), prof of philosophy Virginia Cwlth Univ Richmond VA 1990– (visiting prof 1987–88); univ fell Univ of Wollongong 1989; ed and author of various pubns and books; *Recreations* music, hill walking; *Style—* Anthony Ellis, Esq; ✉ Department of Philosophy, Virginia Commonwealth University, 915 W Franklin Street, Richmond, Virginia 23284, USA (tel 00 1 804 827 2188)

ELLIS, Prof Brian William; s of Frank Albert Ernest Ellis (d 1988), and Beryl Christine, *née* Holdsworth (d 1955); *b* 28 November 1947; *Educ* Harrow, St Mary's Hosp Med Sch London (MB BS); *m* 10 July 1976, Loveday Ann, da of David Ernest Pusey (d 1952), of Coleshill, Bucks; 1 da (Rebecca b 1978), 1 s (David b 1981); *Career* conslt urological surgn Ashford & St Peter's NHS Tst 1983– (dir of surgery 1999–2003), hon sr clinical res fell Academic Surgical Unit St Mary's Hosp Med Sch London 1985–, hon clinical tutor Charing Cross Med Sch London, visiting prof Middx Univ, clinical advsr to Medical Systems Ltd, dir Medical Software Ltd, clinical lead for NHS modernisation agency project 'Ultrasound in Urology'; former memb Cncl Br Assoc of Urological Surgns, former clinical advsr in surgery to British Airways; memb Travelling Surgical Soc; ed Jl of Integrated Care, referee for submissions to Br Jl of Surgery and BMJ, author of various papers on clinical audit, computing, prostate surgery; Best Videotape Prize Br Assoc of Urological Surgns 1997 and 1999, Hosp Doctor Urology Team of the Year Award 1998; FRCS 1977; *Books* Hamilton Bailey's Emergency Surgery (ed, 13 edn); *Recreations* wine, music, roses; *Style—* Prof Brian W Ellis; ✉ Graylands, 124 Brox Road, Ottershaw, Surrey KT16 0LG (tel and fax 01932 873254, e-mail brian.ellis@dial.pipex.com); Ashford Hospital, London Road, Ashford, Middlesex TW15 3AA (tel 01784 884429, fax 01784 884393)

ELLIS, Christopher Matthew (Chris); s of Dr John Matthew Ellis, and Mary Evelyn, *née* Ford; *Educ* Dean Close Sch Cheltenham; *m* Georgina, *née* Tilley; 2 s (Timothy, Benjamin); *Career* lighting designer; theatre dir and ceo Leicester Haymarket Theatre 1990–92, lighting advsr Leics Dio, theatre conslt Singapore Rep Theatre; memb Bd Derby Playhouse, memb Drama Panel E Midlands Arts; Lighting Designer of the Year Live 2000 Silver Award 2000; memb: Soc of Br Theatre Lighting Designers (now Assoc of Lighting Designers) 1972, Assoc of Br Theatre Technicians 1974; *Theatre* Chichester Festival Theatre: Pravda, 5/11, Government Inspector, How to Succeed in Business, Merchant of Venice, Blunt Speaking; RNT: St Joan, Lorenzaccio, The Ancient Mariner, Uncle Vanya, Hiawatha, The Mayor of Zalamea, Sir Gawain and the Green Knight, The Wonder of Sex, The Hypochondriac, Romans in Britain; RSC: The Venetian Twins, Romeo and Juliet, Hamlet, Love's Labour's Lost, Maysdays, A Midsummer Night's Dream, The Winter's Tale, The Knight of the Burning Pestle, They Shoot Horses Don't They, The Taming of the Shrew, Breaking the Silence, Faust Parts I and II; Savoy Theatre: Ute Lemper, HMS Pinafore, Lloyd George Knew My Father, Lady Harry; Old Vic: Hair, Henry IV Parts I and II, Henry V, Masterclass, The Importance of Being Earnest; Victoria Palace Theatre: High Society, Brigadoon, Soul Train; Deutsches Schauspielhaus Hamburg: Maria Stuart, Hamlet, Regie von Zalamea, Guys and Dolls; other credits incl: Rent (Prince of Wales Theatre), Annie Get Your Gun (Prince of Wales Theatre), Taboo (The Venue), La Cava (Piccadilly Theatre), Mac and Mabel (Piccadilly Theatre), Boyband (Gielgud Theatre), All You Need is Love (Queen's Theatre), The Pirates of Penzance (Queen's Theatre), Brief Encounter (Lyric Theatre), Hotstuff (Cambridge Theatre), West Side Story (Her Majesty's Theatre), Me and My Girl (Adelphi Theatre, Broadway and LA), Irma Vep (Duke of York's Theatre), Upon the Throne (Comedy Theatre), Signs of the Times (Vaudeville Theatre), Pygmalion (Shaftesbury Theatre), On Your Toes (Royal Festival Hall), The Mikado (Royal Festival Hall), Dance of the Vampires (Budapest), They're Playing Our Song (Singapore Rep Theatre), Sing to the Dawn (Singapore Rep Theatre), The Big Picnic (Glasgow Promenade Prodns/BBC), Telstar (New Ambassador's), Singing in the Rain (Sadlers' Wells); *Opera* ENO: The Gambler, La Traviata, Christmas Eve, Hansel and Gretel (also Netherlands, La Fenice and BBC); Scottish Opera: La Traviata, The Magic Flute, The Jacobin, Peter Grimes, Ariadne Auf Naxos (also Den Nortske Opera), From the House of the Dead (also WNO and Vancouver), Julius Caesar (also Ludwigshaven and Montpellier); other credits incl: The Nightingale's To Blame (Opera North), Wozzeck (Netherlands), A Midsummer Night's Dream (Netherlands and Tel Aviv), Donnerstag Aus Licht (ROH), The Chinese Conjuror (Almeida Opera); *Ballet* The Dancing Room (Dance Umbrella/BBC), Petrushka (Hong Kong Acad), Maxwell's Demons (Hong Kong Acad); *Recreations* sailing, photography, church organist; *Style—* Chris Ellis, Esq; ✉ 47 Shanklin Drive, Stoneygate, Leicester LE2 3QE (tel 0116 270 6442, fax 0116 270 0084, mobile 07885 581311, e-mail chrisellislighting@mac.com); Performing Arts, 6 Windmill Street, London W1P 1HF (tel 020 7255 1362, fax 020 7631 4631, e-mail info@performing-arts.co.uk)

ELLIS, David; *b* 13 February 1934; *Career* Nat Serv Army Special Investigations Branch 1952–55; Crusader Insurance plc: mgmnt 1956–60, regnl mangr Nigeria 1960–63, city branch mangr 1963–66, PA to Investment and Admin Mangr 1966–69, secondment to US parent gp 1969–70, mangr admin 1971–76, dir and gen mangr 1976–85 (mktg and sales 1976–83, parent group 1983–84, life ops 1984–85); sr vice-pres Cigna International Life Group and md Crusader 1986–89, chief exec Lane Clark & Peacock 1989–93, md Mast Organisation Ltd (int trg consultancy) 1993–, various directorships 1993–; memb Worshipful Co of Insurers 1987, Freeman City of London 1987; FCIS 1968 (two prizes), FCII 1972, FInstD 1986; *Recreations* golf, writing, reading, music; *Clubs* ESU; *Style—* David Ellis, Esq

ELLIS, His Hon Judge David Raymond; s of Raymond Ellis (d 1986), of Charney Bassett, Oxon, and Ethel, *née* Gordon; *b* 4 September 1946; *Educ* St Edward's Sch Oxford, ChCh Oxford (MA); *m* 18 December 1974, Cathleen Margaret, da of late Dr Albert Joseph Hawe, CBE, of Accra, Ghana; 1 s (Thomas b 1978), 1 da (Caroline b 1979); *Career* called to the Bar Inner Temple 1970, recorder of the Crown Court 1991–95 (asst recorder 1986), circuit judge (SE Circuit) 1995–; *Clubs* Leander; *Style—* His Hon Judge Ellis; ✉ The Law Courts, Altyre Road, Croydon CR9 5AB

E

ELLIS, Diana; QC (2001); da of Evan Henry Ellis (d 1970), and Irene Sarah Jeanette Ellis (d 1998); *Educ* Highbury Hill HS, LSE (Dip Social Admin), Univ of London (LLB); *m* 14 Jan 2001, Geoffrey Keith Watts, s of late Geoffrey Watts; *Career* former teacher; barr practising in int law and criminal law, recorder SE Circuit 1998–; on UN List of Counsel; *Style—* Ms Diana Ellis, QC; ✉ 25 Bedford Row, London WC1R 4HD

ELLIS, Diana Margaret; CBE (2004); da of Robert Hall (d 1981), of Twickenham, Middx, and Mabel Helen, *née* Steadman (d 1990); *b* 11 April 1938; *Educ* Perivale Girls' Sch, Guildford Coll of Technol (MRSH); *m* 3 Sept 1966, John David Ellis, s of Frederick Henry Ellis (d 1994); 1 da (Claire Suzanne b 24 Aug 1969); *Career* dist mangr Surrey CC; competitive career: Middx 1954–57, coxed winning crew Women's Eights Head of River Race 1969, 1971, 1972 and 1973 (stroked 1966–68), stroked GB eight European Championships 1966, coxed England 1972, Gold medal Nat Championships 1972 (Silver medal 1973); memb: Nat Championship Ctee 1977 (chm 1987–89), Women's Rowing Ctee 1977–, World Rowing Championship 1996 (vice-pres), Ctee Women's Eights Head of River Race 1980–93; chm: Women's Rowing Cmmn 1984–87, Serpentine Regatta 1987–89, Amateur Rowing Assoc 2000– (Exec Ctee 1989–2000); GB team mangr 1988; qualified umpire 1978–, elected Henley steward 1997; exec BOA 1997–, exec CCPR 2000– (dep chm 2005–); FRSA; *Recreations* rowing; *Clubs* Leander, Twickenham Rowing, St George's Ladies Rowing; *Style—* Mrs Diana Ellis, CBE; ✉ Amateur Rowing Association, 6 Lower Mall, Hammersmith, London W6 9DJ (tel 020 8237 6701, fax 020 8237 6749)

ELLIS, Prof Harold; CBE; s of Samuel and Ada Ellis; *b* 13 January 1926; *Educ* Univ of Oxford (BM BCh, MCh, DM); *m* 20 April 1958, Wendy, da of Henry Levine; 1 s (Jonathan b 1959), 1 da (Suzanne b 1962); *Career* Capt RAMC 1950–51; res surgical appts 1948–60, sr lectr Univ of London 1960–62, prof of surgery Univ of London at Westminster Hosp 1962–88, univ clinical anatomist Univ of Cambridge 1989–93, clinical anatomist Guy's Hosp 1993–; former vice-pres: RCS, RSM; pres Br Assoc of Surgical Oncology; FRCS, FRCOG; *Recreations* medical history; *Style—* Prof Harold Ellis, CBE; ✉ 16 Bancroft Avenue, London N2 0AS (tel 020 8348 2720); Department of Anatomy, King's College London (Guy's Campus), London Bridge, London SE1 1UL

ELLIS, Herbert Douglas (Doug); OBE (2005); s of Herbert Ellis; *b* 3 January 1924; *Educ* Chester Secdy Sch; *m* 1963, Heidi Marie, da of Rudolph Kroeger; 3 s; *Career* RN 1942–46; chm: Ellis Group of Cos (Ellmanton Construction Co Ltd, Ellmanton Investments Ltd), Aston Villa FC 1968–79 and 1982–2006, Aston Manor Brewery Co Ltd 1985–; *Recreations* football, salmon fishing, foreign travel; *Style—* Doug Ellis, Esq, OBE

ELLIS, Ian David; s of John D V Ellis (d 1998), and Heather, *née* Gosnell (d 1987); *b* 4 December 1955; *Educ* Sir Charles Lucas Sch; *m* 27 Oct 1998, Clare, *née* Poyner; 3 s (Stuart David b 17 Aug 1985, Adam John b 8 Sept 2000, Harry Alexander b 17 Nov 2003), 2 da (Sophie Louise b 27 Feb 1989, Lauren Daniel b 2 Oct 1992); *Career* Dist Valuers Office Ipswich 1974–83, Richard Ellis (now CBRE) 1983–98 (equity ptnr 1991, ceo Investment Mgmnt), md Corp Real Estate Gp Trillium 1998–2000, ceo Land Securities Trillium 2002– (dep ceo 2000–02), dir Land Securities plc 2002–; non-exec dir: ROK Property Solutions 2006–, Portman Settled Estates 2006–; memb Investment Property Forum; FRICS 1991; *Recreations* garden, history, family, team sports; *Style—* Ian Ellis, Esq; ✉ Land Securities Trillium, 140 London Wall, London EC2Y 5DN (tel 020 7796 5553, fax 0845 090 2900, e-mail ian.ellis@lstrillium.com)

ELLIS, Prof Ian Ogilvie; s of Philip Senior Ellis, of Cranford, Manchester, and Anna *née* Ure; *b* 24 August 1955; *Educ* Stockport GS, Univ of Nottingham Med Sch (BMed Sci, BM BS); *m* 1, 20 Oct 1979 (m dis 1997), Jane Elisabeth, da of Dudley John Stevens, of Westbere, Kent; 1 s (James Ogilvie b 1987), 1 da (Sophie Hannah b 1989); m 2, Eileen Jane, da of John Barrett (decd); 1 s (Tristan Alistair Malcolm b 1997); *Career* lectr pathology Univ of Nottingham 1980–87, conslt histopathologist specialising in breast disease City Hosp Nottingham 1987–, prof of cancer pathology Univ of Nottingham 2004– (reader in pathology 1997–2004); author of numerous pubns on breast cancer pathology and prognostic factors; chm National Coordinating Ctee for Breast Screening Pathology; lectr UK Breast Screening Prog Nottingham Trg Centre; MRCPath 1985; *Recreations* game fishing, wine tasting; *Style—* Prof Ian Ellis; ✉ Yew Tree House, 2 Kenilworth Road, The Park, Nottingham NG7 1DD (tel 0115 947 2186); Department of Histopathology, City Hospital, Hucknall Road, Nottingham NG5 1PB (tel 0115 969 1169, ext 46875, e-mail ian.ellis@nottingham.ac.uk)

ELLIS, John Norman; OBE (1995); s of Albert Edward Ellis (d 1990), and Margaret, *née* Thompson (d 1986); *b* 22 February 1939; *Educ* Osmondthorpe Secdy Modern Leeds, Leeds Coll of Commerce; *m* 1 (m dis); m 2, 5 Oct 1985, Diane; 1 s (Martin John), 1 da (Karen Elizabeth (Mrs Landricumbe)), 2 step s (Graham Anderson, Robert James Anderson); *Career* messenger Post Office 1954–57, postman 1957–58, clerical offr Miny of Works 1958–67, exec offr MPBW 1967–68; Civil and Public Servs Assoc (CPSA): full time offr 1968–82, dep gen sec 1982–86, gen sec 1986–92; sec Council of Civil Service Unions 1992–95, industrial relations conslt 1995–, chm Talking People Ltd 2000–, vice-chm Bd Tandridge Leisure Ltd 2000–, chm Cliff Crescent Mgmnt Ltd 2001–; former: exec cmmn memb Civil Service Pensioners Alliance, chm Caterham Branch Lab Pty, vice-chm Nat Whitley Cncl; sec Major Policy Ctee Cncl of Civil Service Unions; memb: Employment Tbnls London (S Region), Inst of Employment Rights, Labour Party; former memb: TUC Gen Cncl (memb Econ, Social Insurance and Industrial Welfare, Educn and Training, Equal Rights), TUC Public Services Ctee and Pension Special Ctee, Exec Bd Civil Serv Housing Assoc, Exec Bd Inst of Employment Rights, Civil Serv Occupational Health Serv Advsy Bd, Steering Ctee Centre for Public Sector Mgmnt Research, Advsy Bd Univ of Durham Business Sch; *Recreations* politics, motoring, dog walking, reading, gardening; *Style—* John Norman Ellis, Esq, OBE; ✉ 26 Hareston Valley Road, Caterham, Surrey CR3 6HD (tel 01883 380270, fax 01883 380271, e-mail johnellis60@aol.com)

ELLIS, Dr Jonathan Richard (John); s of Richard Ellis, of Potters Bar, Herts, and Beryl Lilian, *née* Ranger (d 1985); *b* 1 July 1946; *Educ* Lochinver House Sch, Highgate Sch, King's Coll Cambridge (BA, PhD); *m* 11 July 1985, Maria Mercedes, da of Alfonso Martinez (d 1982), of Cali, Colombia and Miami Beach, Florida; 1 s (Sebastian b 19 July

1990), 1 da (Jennifer b 17 Jan 1988); *Career* research assoc Stanford Linear Accelerator Centre 1971–72, Richard Chase Tolman fell Caltech 1972–73, ldr Theoretical Studies Div Euro Orgn for Nuclear Research (CERN) Geneva 1988–94 (memb staff since 1973), diplomatic advsr DG; Miller prof Univ of Calif Berkeley 1988; memb Cncl PPARC; FRS 1984, FIOP 1991; *Recreations* reading, listening to music, hiking in mountains; *Style—* Dr John Ellis, FRS; ✉ 5 Chemin du Ruisseau, Tannay, 1295 Mies, Switzerland (tel 00 41 22 776 48 58); Theoretical Studies Division, CERN, 1211–Geneva 23, Switzerland (tel 00 41 22 767 4142, fax 00 41 22 767 3850)

ELLIS, Dr Julia Peregrine; da of Cecil Montague Jacomb Ellis (d 1942), of London, and Pamela Sage, *née* Unwin; *b* 25 March 1936; *Educ* North Foreland Lodge, Middx Hosp Med Sch London (MB BS, DCH); *Career* St George's Hosp London 1966–69, sr registrar dermatology Oxford 1969–74, res dermatology Dept of Dermatology Univ of Miami Med Sch 1974; conslt dermatologist Princess Margaret Hosp Swindon and Marlborough NHS Tst 1975–2001; pres Dermatology Section RSM 2000–01, former pres St John's Hosp Dermatological Soc London, former treas and pres Dowling Club; FRCP; *Recreations* fishing; *Style—* Dr Julia P Ellis; ✉ 47 Oxford Street, Ramsbury, Wiltshire SN8 2PG (tel 01672 520436)

ELLIS, Michael Henry (Mike); OBE (2007); s of John Ellis (d 1988), of Sheffield, S Yorks, and Joan, *née* Lawton (d 2003); *b* 4 August 1951; *Educ* High Storrs GS Sheffield, Open Univ (BA); *m* 9 June 1973, Jeanette, *née* Booth; 2 da (Elizabeth Anne b 13 Oct 1978, Catherine Jane b 9 March 1980); *Career* worked in local govt sector 1967–87; Halifax Building Soc: gp treas 1987–92, gen mangr treasy and European ops 1992–95, md treasy and overseas ops 1995–96, banking and savings dir 1996–97; Halifax plc: banking and savings dir 1997–99, retail fin servs dir 1999, chief operating offr 1999–2001; gp fin dir HBOS plc 2001–04; non-exec dir WH Smith plc 2005–; memb: CIPFA 1973, ACT 1990; *Recreations* travel, reading, music, football; *Clubs* RAC; *Style—* Mike Ellis, Esq, OBE

ELLIS, Nigel George; s of George Ellis, of Selsey, W Sussex, and Ivy, *née* Howell; *b* 19 April 1939; *Educ* Farnborough GS; *m* 31 July 1965, Yvonne Meline Elizabeth, da of Norman Tracy (d 1976), of Crowborough, W Sussex; 1 da (Victoria b 1968), 1 s (Timothy b 1971); *Career* co sec City of London Real Property Co 1967–74; dir: Holland America UK Ltd 1974–79, Hammerson Property Development and Investment Corps 1979–88; fin dir BAA plc 1988–95; chm: Quintain Estates & Development plc 1995–2007, Hardy Underwriting Group plc 1997–2002; FCA 1963; *Recreations* philately, chess; *Style—* Nigel Ellis, Esq; ✉ Willmead Farm, Bovey Tracey, Newton Abbot, Devon TQ13 9NP (tel 01647 277599, fax 01647 277598)

ELLIS, Osian Gwynn; CBE (1971); s of Rev Thomas Griffith Ellis (d 1985), of Prestatyn, and Jennie, *née* Lewis (d 1976); *b* 8 February 1928; *Educ* Denbigh GS, Royal Acad of Music (Hovey scholar, Dr Joseph Parry prize, Vivian Dunn prize, Harriet Cohen award); *m* 5 Jan 1951, Irene Ellis, da of Richard Hugh Jones (d 1987), of Pwllheli; 2 s (Richard Llywarch b 1956, Tomos Llywelyn b 1959); *Career* concert harpist; played and recorded with: Melos Ensemble London 1954–, Lincoln Center Chamber Music Soc NY 1974–; prof of harp Royal Acad of Music 1959–89, princ harpist LSO 1960–94; has given concerts of poetry and music with Dame Peggy Ashcroft, Paul Robeson, Richard Burton, Lord David Cecil, Dorothy Tutin, Princess Grace and others; numerous recital tours with Sir Peter Pears Europe and USA; works written for him by Benjamin Britten: Harp Suite in C Major 1969, Canticle V (for performance with Pears) 1974, Birthday Hänsel 1975; harp concertos written for him by: Alun Hoddinott, William Mathias, Jorgen Jersild, Robin Holloway; solos and chamber music by: Malcolm Arnold, Elizabeth Maconchy, Colin Matthews, Menotti and William Schuman; awards: Grand Prix du Disque, French Radio Critics award; Hon DMus Univ of Wales 1970; FRAM 1960; *Style—* Osian Ellis, Esq, CBE; ✉ Arfryn, Yr Ala, Pwllheli, Gwynedd LL53 5BN

ELLIS, Dr Paul Anthony; s of Kevin Royce Ellis (d 1995), and Kathleen Margaret, *née* Gallagher; *b* 29 April 1963; *Educ* Christchurch Boys' HS NZ, Univ of Otago (MB ChB, MD); *m* 27 April 1996, Dr Isis Dove-Edwin, da of George Dove-Edwin, KCVO; 3 s (Alexander b 3 Aug 1998, Zachary b 6 Jan 2000, Cameron b 22 Sept 2004), 1 da (Georgia b 6 Oct 2001); *Career* registrar in oncology Christchurch Hosp NZ 1990–92; Royal Marsden Hosp: sr registrar in med oncology 1992–94, clinical res fell Royal Marsden Hosp 1994–96; conslt med oncologist Guy's and St Thomas' Hosps NHS Tst 1997–, hon sr lectr in med oncology KCL 1997–; co-chair CRUK Nat Adjuvant Breast Cancer Trial (TACT) 1999–; med advsr: UK Breast Cancer Care 1997–; memb various pharmaceutical industry advsy gps; memb: Assoc of Cancer Physicians 1993–, Br Breast Gp 1996–, American Soc of Clinical Oncology (ASCO) 1997–; memb Editorial Bd Jl of Clinical Oncology 2001–; delivered numerous presentations and invited lectures to int confs and learned socs; NZ Soc for Oncology Young Investigator of the Year 1992, 6th Odlin Res Fellowship 1994, Inaugural ASCO Fellowship Award Best Young Ivestigator ASCO annual meeting 1996; FRACP 1992; *Publications* author of peer reviewed articles, invited reviews, published abstracts and book chapters; *Recreations* golf, skiing, football, cricket; *Style—* Dr Paul Ellis; ✉ Department of Medical Oncology, Guy's Hospital, London SE1 9RT (tel 020 7188 4253, mobile 07775 783852, e-mail paul.ellis@gstt.nhs.uk); London Oncology Clinic, 95 Harley Street London (tel 020 7317 2535)

ELLIS, Dr Richard Mackay; s of Valentine Herbert Ellis, FRCS (d 1953), of London, and Angela Peart, *née* Robinson (d 1991); *b* 9 July 1941; *Educ* Wellington, Clare Coll Cambridge, St Thomas' Hosp Med Sch; *m* 14 Aug 1976, Gillian Ann, da of Samuel Cole (d 1975), of Reading; 1 da (Melissa b 1977), 1 s (William b 1978); *Career* assoc prof of orthopaedics Univ of Rochester NY 1975–80, sr lectr in rheumatology Univ of Southampton 1980, conslt in rehabilitation Salisbury Hosps 1980–2006; ed Jl of Orthopaedic Med, past pres Inst of Orthopaedic Med, past pres Soc of Orthopaedic Med; FRCS 1971, FRCP 1989; *Publications* Textbook of Musculoskeletal Medicine (co-ed, 2005); *Style—* Dr Richard Ellis; ✉ 161 Bouverie Avenue South, Salisbury, Wiltshire SP2 8EB

ELLIS, Prof Richard Salisbury; s of late Capt Arthur Ellis, MBE, of Colwyn Bay, Wales, and Marion, *née* Davies; *b* 25 May 1950; *Educ* Ysgol Emrys ap Iwan, UCL (BSc), Wolfson Coll Oxford (DPhil); *m* 28 July 1972, Barbara; 1 da (Hilary Rhona b 1976), 1 s (Thomas Marc b 1978); *Career* princ res fell Royal Greenwich Observatory 1983–85, prof of astronomy Univ of Durham 1985–93 (lectr 1981–83), sr res fell SERC 1989–94 (chm Large Telescope Panel), Plumian prof of astronomy and experimental philosophy Univ of Cambridge 1993–99, dir Inst of Astronomy Cambridge 1994–99, professorial fell Magdalene Coll Cambridge 1994–99, prof of obs astrophysics Univ of Cambridge 2000–03, Steele prof of astronomy Caltech 2002– (prof of astronomy 1999–2002), dir Palomar Observatory 2000–2002, dir Caltech Optical Observatories 2002–05; memb American Astronomical Soc; Hon DSc Univ of Durham 2002; fell UCL 1999; FRAS, FRS 1995, FInstP 1998, fell AAAS 2003; *Books* The Epoch of Galaxy Formation (with C S Frenk, 1988), Observational Tests of Inflation (with T Shanks, 1991), The Development of Large Scale Structure (1999); *Recreations* travel; *Style—* Prof Richard Ellis, FRS; ✉ Astronomy MS 105–24, California Institute of Technology, Pasadena, CA 91125, USA (tel 00 1 626 395 2598, fax 00 1 626 568 9352, e-mail rse@astro.caltech.edu)

ELLIS, Simon Edgar Hargreaves; s of John Edgar Hargreaves Ellis, of Cheshire, and Yvonne Valerie, *née* Nicholls; *b* 23 December 1964, Tidworth, Hants; *Educ* Pauline Meml Sch Colorado Springs USA, Abbey Gate Coll Chester, Univ of Hull (BA), RMA Sandhurst, Coll of Law Chester; *m* 2 Jan 1992, Susan Carey, *née* Watt; 2 s (James Edgar Hargreaves b 6 Dec 1992, Michael Edgar Hargreaves b 22 Jan 1997); *Career* served Army Cheshire Regt 1986–93; slr specialising in ecclesiastical and charity law particularly relating to property, currently ptnr Aaron & Ptnrs LLP Slrs; Cheshire Regt TA 1993– (currently Lt-Col cmdg Univ of Liverpool OTC); memb: Ecclesiastical Law Assoc, Charity Law Assoc, Law Soc 1997; memb Fell Running Assoc; *Recreations* fell and mountain running especially over longer distances, skiing; *Clubs* Tattenhall Running; *Style—* Simon Ellis, Esq; ✉ Aaron & Partners LLP, 5–7 Grosvenor Court, Foregate Street, Chester CH1 1HG (tel 01244 405555, fax 01244 405566, e-mail enquiries@aaronandpartners.com)

ELLIS, Susan Jacqueline; da of Michael John Irving Ellis, of Bridgwater, Somerset, and Juliette Wendy Scott, *née* Smith; *b* 30 April 1963; *Educ* Leamington Coll for Girls, City Univ Business Sch (BSc); *m*; 1 s; *Career* Midland Bank International 1981–85, National Opinion Polls 1985–86, PR mangr Broad Street Associates 1987–88, md Square Mile Communications 1992–2000 (jt fndr 1988), gp chief exec Weber Shandwick Square Mile 2000– (formerly Square Mile Communications); *Recreations* sport, cinema, theatre, literature; *Style—* Miss Susan Ellis; ✉ Weber Shandwick Square Mile, Fox Court, 14 Gray's Inn Road, London WC1X 8WS

ELLIS-BEXTOR, Sophie; da of Robin Bextor, and Janet Ellis; *b* 10 April 1979, W London; *Children* 1 s (Sonny b 23 April 2004); *Career* singer; *Albums* theaudience (with theaudience) 1998; solo: Read My Lips 2002 (UK no 2), Shoot From The Hip 2003; *Singles* with theaudience: I Know Enough (I Don't Get Enough) 1998, A Pessimist is Never Disappointed 1998, If You Can't Do It When You're Young When Can You Do It? 1998, I Got the Wherewithal 1998; Groovejet (If This Ain't Love) (with Spiller) 2000 (UK no 1); solo: Take Me Home 2001 (UK no 2), Murder on the Dancefloor 2001 (UK no 2), Get Over You 2002 (UK no 3), Music Gets the Best of Me 2002, Mixed Up World 2003, I Won't Change You 2003; *Videos* Watch My Lips 2003; *Style—* Ms Sophie Ellis-Bextor; ✉ website www.sophieellisbextor.net

ELLISON, Mark Christopher; s of Anthony Ellison (d 1959), and Arlette Maguire, *née* Blundell; *b* 8 October 1957; *Educ* Pocklington Sch, Skinners Sch, Univ of Wales (LLB), Inns of Court Sch of Law; *m* 21 Nov 1981, Kate Augusta, da of Michael Humphrey Middleton, CBE; 2 s (Ned, Rollo), 2 da (Flora, Maudie); *Career* called to the Bar Gray's Inn 1979; first sr treasy counsel Central Criminal Court 2005–; recorder; *Style—* Mark Ellison, Esq; ✉ Queen Elizabeth Building, Temple, London EC4Y 9BS (tel 020 7583 5766, e-mail barristers@holliswhiteman.co.uk)

ELLMAN, Louise Joyce; MP; *b* 14 November 1945; *Educ* Manchester HS for Girls, Univ of Hull (BA), Univ of York (MPhil); *m* Geoffrey David Ellman; 1 s, 1 da; *Career* vice-chm Lancashire Enterprises 1982–97; chm: Lancashire's Environment Forum 1989–97, NW Regnl Assoc 1992–97; memb: Lancashire Co-op Devpt Agency and Co-op Enterprise NW 1981–97, NW Partnership 1992–97; MP (Lab/Co-op) Liverpool Riverside 1997–; memb Environment, Tport and Regnl Affrs Select Ctee 1997–, memb Tport Select Ctee, chair Regeneration Gp, vice-chair Capital of Culture All Pty Parly Gp, jt sec All Pty Gp on Trafficking Women and Children, vice-chair PLP Regnl Govt Gp 2001– (sec 1997–99, chair 1999–2001); chair Jewish Lab Movement; vice-chair Lab Friends of Israel; memb W Lancs DC 1974–87, ldr Lancs CC 1981–97, ldr Lab Gp Lancs CC 1977–97; chm NW Regnl Exec Lab Pty 1993–98 (memb 1985–), vice-pres Local Govt Assoc 1997–; *Style—* Mrs Louise Ellman, MP; ✉ House of Commons, London SW1A 0AA (tel 020 7219 3000)

ELLMANN, Dr Maud; da of Richard David Ellmann (d 1987), of Oxford, and Mary Joan Donahue Ellmann (d 1989); *b* 16 January 1954; *Educ* Oxford HS, Université de Paris Sorbonne, King's Coll Cambridge (MA, Rylands prize), St Anne's Coll Oxford (DPhil); *m* 2000, John Wilkinson; *Career* lectr Dept of English Univ of Southampton 1979–89, Andrew W Mellon faculty fell in humanities Harvard Univ 1989–90; Univ of Cambridge: reader in modern literature Faculty of English 1989–2005, fell and dir of studies King's Coll 1989–2005; Notre Dame prof of English Univ of Notre Dame 2005; visiting prof: of Irish literature Northwestern Univ 2002, Universidade de Santiago de Compostela Spain; visiting asst prof: Smith Coll 1984–85, Amherst Coll 1985–86; Rose Mary Crawshay Award Br Acad 2004; fell American Cncl of Learned Socs, Bernhard fell Williams Coll Williamstown 1997–98, Guggenheim fell 1998–99, Knopf fell Harry Ransom Center Univ of Texas 2002, Margaret Bundy Scott visiting prof of English Williams Coll 2003, Keough distinguished prof of Irish studies Univ of Notre Dame 2004, founding fell English Assoc (FEA), FRSA; *Books* The Poetics of Impersonality: T S Eliot and Ezra Pound (1987), The Hunger Artists: Starving, Writing and Imprisonment (1993), Psychoanalytic Literary Criticism (1994), Elizabeth Bowen: The Shadow Across the Page (2003); *Style—* Dr Maud Ellmann; ✉ Keough Institute for Irish Studies, University of Notre Dame, Notre Dame, IN 46556, USA

ELLORY, Prof (John) Clive; s of Frederick Ronald Ellory, of Iver, Bucks, and Muriel, *née* Vanson; *b* 16 April 1944; *Educ* Latymer Upper Sch, Univ of Bristol (BSc, PhD), Univ of Cambridge (MA, ScD), Univ of Oxford (MA, DSc); *m* 1 Jan 1969, Jane Elisabeth, da of Donald Field Metcalfe; 1 da (Isabel b 24 May 1976), 1 s (Martin b 11 Nov 1979); *Career* research scientist Inst of Animal Physiology 1967–75, lectr Dept of Physiology Univ of Cambridge 1975–84, fell Queens' Coll Cambridge 1975–84, reader in human physiology Univ of Oxford 1985–96; visiting assoc prof Yale Univ 1971, guest fell Silliman Coll 1971, visiting assoc prof Univ of Illinois 1975 (visiting prof 1982), investigator US Antarctic Res Prog McMurdo Antarctica 1980, visiting prof Univ of Nice 1985 and 1993; memb: European Red Cell Ctee 1985–, Heads of Physiology Depts 1990–, Scientific Advsy Bd Quadrant Holdings Ltd Cambridge 1993–2000, Scientific Advsy Bd Action Research 2000–, Cncl British Heart Fndn (chair of project grants 2003–); awarded: MRC French Exchange Fellowship 1985, Maxime Hanss Prize (CNRS) 1994, Royal Soc Israel Research Professorship (Technion, Haifa) 1994; FMedSci 1999; *Books* Red Cell Membranes: a methodological approach (1982), The Binding and Transport of Anions in Living Tissues (1982), The Sodium Pump (1985), Membrane Transport in Red Cells (jtly, 1997), Patronage and Plate at Corpus Christi College, Oxford (1999), Red Cell Membrane Transport in Health and Disease (jtly, 2003); *Recreations* food, antique silver, hill walking; *Style—* Prof Clive Ellory; ✉ Sherrington Building, Department of Physiology, Anatomy and Genetics, Parks Road, Oxford OX1 3PT (tel 01865 272436, fax 01865 272488, e-mail jce@dpag.ox.ac.uk)

ELLWOOD, Peter David Roger; s of John Hassall George Stanley Ellwood (d 1984), and Eileen Eleanor, *née* Kenny (d 1990); *b* 17 October 1948; *Educ* Watford GS, Calday Grange GS, Univ of Cambridge (MA); *m* 1976, Susan Dianne, *née* Chester; 2 da (Emily b 1977, Katie b 1979), 1 s (Christian b 1985); *Career* various positions with Shell Mex and BP Ltd 1970–75; British Council: asst rep Nepal 1975–79, London 1979–83, dep dir Indonesia 1983–86, dir Cameroon 1986–89, dep dir France 1989–94, dir Sri Lanka 1994–95, dir Pakistan 1998–2002, regnl dir ME 2002–04, regnl dir North and Central Europe 2004–; *Recreations* travel, theatre-going, music, birdwatching; *Style—* Peter Ellwood, Esq; ✉ British Council, c/o British Embassy, Skarpögatan 6–8, PO Box 27819, S-115 93 Stockholm

ELLWOOD, Tobias; MP; *b* 12 August 1966, NY; *Educ* Vienna Int Sch, Loughbrough Univ, City Univ (MBA); *Career* Offr Royal Green Jackets 1991–96, served NI, Cyprus, Kuwait, Germany, Gibraltar, Bosnia; researcher to Rt Hon Tom King, MP 1996–97, sr business devpt mangr London Stock Exchange 1999; cncllr (Cons) Dacorum BC 1999; Parly candidate (Cons) Worsley 2001, MP (Cons) Bournemouth E 2005–; govr Queen's Park Infant Sch; *Publications* An Introduction to the Conservative Party (5 edn); *Style—* Tobias Ellwood, Esq, MP; ✉ House of Commons, London SW1A 0AA

ELLY, His Hon Judge (Richard) Charles; s of Harold Elly (d 1997), of Sherborne, Dorset, and Dora Ellen, *née* Luing (d 1988); *b* 20 March 1942; *Educ* Sir William Borlase's Sch Marlow, Hertford Coll Oxford (MA); *m* 7 Oct 1967, Marion Rose, da of Bernard Walter Blackwell (d 1987); 1 s (Mark b 1972), 1 da (Frances b 1975); *Career* admitted slr 1966, ptnr Reynolds Parry-Jones & Crawford 1968–98, recorder of the Crown Court 1995–98, circuit judge (SE Circuit) 1998–; memb Lord Chancellor's Advsy Ctee on Legal Educn and Conduct 1997–98; Law Soc: memb 1966–, memb Cncl 1981–97, chm Legal Aid Ctee 1984–87, chm Standards and Guidance Ctee 1987–90, chm Criminal Law Ctee 1991–92, dep vice-pres 1992–93, vice-pres 1993–94, pres 1994–95; pres: Berks Bucks & Oxon Law Soc 1988–89 (sec 1975–82), Criminal Law Slrs Assoc 1993–98, Hertford Coll Lawyers Assoc 1995–98; sec Southern Area Assoc of Law Socs 1975–82; chm Maidenhead Deanery Synod 1972–79, pres Cookham Soc 1987–97; govr Coll of Law 1985–2000, chm of govrs of Sir William Borlase's Sch Marlow 1996–2001; memb Berks CC 1980–81; Hon LLD Kingston Univ 1994; FRSA 1995; *Recreations* bird watching, theatre, walking, gardening; *Clubs* Oxford and Cambridge; *Style*— His Hon Judge Elly; ✉ c/o Reading County Court, 160–163 Friar Street, Reading, Berkshire RG1 1HE (tel 0118 987 0500)

ELMS, Marsha Marilyn; JP (Brentford 1982); da of James Frederick Carey (d 1992), and Carolyn Mary, *née* Fordham (d 1989); *b* 11 June 1946; *Educ* Tottenham Co GS, Bedford Coll London (BA), Brunel Univ (PGCE), Univ of Reading (MA); *m* Oct 1968, Richard Arthur Elms; 1 da (Lily Elizabeth Laura b 17 Nov 1975), 1 s (Edward James b 20 Nov 1979); *Career* teacher rising to dep head Featherstone HS 1969–89, dep head Magna Carta Sch Surrey 1989–93, head Kendrick Sch Reading 1993–, conslt head Ashmead Sch Reading 1997, exec headteacher Kendrick Fedn (Reading Girls' Sch and Kendrick Sch) 2007–; pres Assoc of Maintained Girls' Schs (AMGS) 2003, memb SHA Exec 1995–99 (memb Cncl 2004–), memb Bd of Tstees NFER; author of various SHA/ASCL pubns on equal opportunities and leadership; FRSA; *Recreations* skiing, art, antiques, food, family; *Style*— Mrs Marsha Elms; ✉ Kendrick School, London Road, Reading, Berkshire RG1 5BN (tel 0118 901 5859, fax 0118 901 5858, e-mail head.kendrickschool@reading.gov.uk)

ELMS-ELEY, (Elizabeth) Susan (Sue); da of Ernest Frederick Butler, and Renée, *née* Dale; *b* 2 April 1962; *Educ* Brynteg Comp Sch, Bridgend Tech Coll, Kingston Poly (BA, Postgrad Mktg Dip); *m* (m dis); m 2, 1996; *Career* student Kingston Poly 1981–85, research exec Leo Burnett advtg 1985–87, research mangr Lintas advtg 1987–89, bd dir Initiative Media London 1989–90, md Initiative Technologies Paris 1990–94, chief exec SP Consultants Worldwide 1994–95, int head of research Initiative Media Worldwide 1995–98, md Futures Worldwide Research Gp 1998–2001, md Carat Insight Ltd 2001–; former chm Media Research Group; memb: European Society for Opinion Surveys and Mkt Research (ESOMAR), IOD, MRS, IDM; *Recreations* cinema, travel; *Style*— Mrs Sue Elms-Eley; ✉ Carat Insight Ltd, Parker Tower, Parker Street, London (tel 020 7430 7000)

ELPHICKE, Natalie; *b* 5 November 1970, Welwyn Garden City; *Educ* Univ of Kent (LLB); *m* 1 June 1996, Charles Elphicke; 1 da (Anna Charlotte b 30 July 2000), 1 s (Thomas George b 27 Nov 2006); *Career* called to the Bar Lincoln's Inn 1994, admitted slr 1999; ptnr Addleshaw Goddard; memb Norwood Advice Centre 1995–99, cmmr Westminster Housing Cmmn 2005–06; memb Law Soc, Cons Party; Freeman City of London; *Recreations* housing policy, regeneration and social welfare, song writing, writing children's books, sailing; *Style*— Mrs Natalie Elphicke; ✉ 63 Chester Row, Belgravia, London SW1W 8JL; Addleshaw Goddard, Alder Castle, 10 Noble Street, London EC2V 7JW (tel 020 7160 3162, fax 020 7606 4390, e-mail natalie.elphicke@addleshawgoddard.com)

ELPHINSTON OF GLACK, Sir John; 11 Bt (NS 1701), of Logie, Co Aberdeen; s of Thomas George Elphinston (d 1967; s of de jure 9 Bt), and Gladys Mary, *née* Congdon (d 1973); suc unc, Sir Alexander Logie Elphinstone of Glack, 10 Bt (d 1970); *b* 12 August 1924; *Educ* Repton, Emmanuel Coll Cambridge (BA); *m* 29 May 1953, Margaret Doreen, da of Edric Tasker (d 1968), of Cheltenham, Glos; 4 s (Alexander b 1955, Charles b 1958, Andrew James b 1961, William Robert b 1963); *Heir* s, Alexander Elphinston; *Career* Lt RM 1942–47; chm Lancs, Cheshire and IOM Branches of RICS (Agric Div) 1975; pres Cheshire Agric Valuers' Assoc 1967, memb Lancs River Authy 1969–74; estates mangr Mond Div ICI, ret; conslt land agent with Gandy & Son Northwich Cheshire 1983–88; former sch govr; FRICS; *Recreations* church, country pursuits, cricket; *Style*— Sir John Elphinston of Glack, Bt

ELPHINSTONE, 19 Lord (S 1509); Alexander Mountstuart Elphinstone; also Baron Elphinstone (UK 1885); s of 18 Lord Elphinstone (d 1994), and Willa Mary Gabriel, *née* Chetwode; *b* 15 April 1980; *Educ* Eton, Univ of Newcastle upon Tyne, SOAS; *Heir* bro, Hon Angus Elphinstone; *Style*— The Lord Elphinstone; ✉ Whitberry House, Tyninghame, Dunbar, East Lothian EH42 1XL

ELPHINSTONE, Sir John Howard Main; 6 Bt (UK 1816), of Sowerby, Cumberland; s of Sir (Maurice) Douglas Warburton Elphinstone, 5 Bt, TD (d 1995), and (Helen) Barbara, *née* Main; *b* 25 February 1949; *Educ* Loretto; *m* 20 Oct 1990, Diane Barbara Quilliam, da of Dr Brian Quilliam Callow (d 1973), of Johannesburg, South Africa; *Heir* kinsman, Henry Elphinstone; *Recreations* DIY, food, gardening, wood carving; *Style*— Sir John Elphinstone, Bt; ✉ Garden Cottage, 6 Amherst Road, Sevenoaks, Kent TN13 3LS (tel 01732 459077)

ELSE, Martin Thomas; s of Richard Else (d 1992), and Lilian Margaret, *née* Stickells; *b* 21 May 1953; *Educ* Farnborough GS, Univ of Salford (BScEcon), Southampton Coll of Technol (qualified accountant IPFA), London Business Sch (Sloan fell with distinction); *m* 1 July 1978, Jennifer Louise, da of Timithy George Bridges; 1 s (David Thomas b 20 May 1980), 1 da (Sharon Louise b 29 Jan 1982); *Career* fin trainee City and Hackney HA and City and E London AHA 1975–79; NE Thames RHA: princ fin planning mangr 1979–82, princ asst treas 1982–83; Hampstead HA: dep treas 1983–86, dir of fin, operational planning and supplies 1986–90, dep dist gen mangr 1986–90, memb Tavistock and Portman Special Mgmnt Ctee and hon treas to the Special Tstees 1986–90; Royal Free Hampstead NHS Tst: dir of fin, planning and supplies 1990–94, dep chief exec 1990–94, hon sec and treas to the Special Tstees 1990–, chief exec 1994–, hon sec and treas to the Special Tstees Royal Free Hosp, tstee Appeal Tst for the Royal Free Hosp and chm Mgmnt Ctee Cancerkin charity 1994–96; variously memb nat NHS ctees incl: Costing for Contracting Steering Gp (chm 1994–97), Nat Steering Gp on Costing (chm 1997–2001), Estate Info Review Ctee 1994–97, Review of Financial Regime for NHS Tsts 1995–96, Nat Programme Co-ordination Bd 1996–98, Fin Issues Gp 1997–98, Regnl Advsy Ctee on Distinction Awards 1998–2001, Chief Executive's Information Mgmnt and Technol Forum 1998–2001; variously memb NHS nat influence gps incl: NAHAT (now NHS Confedn) Contracting and Resource Gp 1991–97, Tst Fedn Fin and Capital Standing Ctee 1994–97 (chm of Fin Dirs), Main Universities Teaching Hosps Tsts 1991–94 (fndr memb and former chm of Fin Dirs); CIPFA/Healthcare Fin Mangrs Assoc: memb Provider Mgmnt Gp 1993–94, memb Risk Mgmnt Review 1994; lectr to various orgns incl London Business Sch, Royal Free Sch of Med, City Univ, King's Fund, Audit Cmmn, Dept of Health Mgmnt Exec and CIPFA Conf and to professional health gps incl Coll of Radiographers and RCN; chair London Agency Project 1999–, tstee Hampstead Wells and Camden Tst 1996–; memb CIPFA 1979, MHSM 1994; *Style*— Martin Else, Esq; ✉ Chief Executive's Office, Royal Free Hampstead NHS Trust, Royal Free Hospital, Pond Street, London NW3 2QG (tel 020 7830 2176)

ELSON, Andrew Charles (Andy); s of Donald Frederick Elson (d 1995), and Phyllis Elson; *b* 9 June 1953; *m* (m dis); 2 da (Victoria, Emily); *Career* aeronautical engr and balloonist; apprentice Rolls Royce Technical Coll, estab own engrg co, currently researcher, designer and pilot of hot air balloons; pilot world's first hot air balloon flight over Mt Everest 1991, designer and co-pilot Brietling Orbiter II balloon flight Switzerland to Burma 1998 (9 days 17 hours, 55 mins), co-pilot Cable and Wireless balloon flight Spain to Japan 1999 (17 days, 18 hours, 25 mins, a record for non-stop sub-orbital flight), designed and constructed Solo Spirit gondola for Steve Fossett's solo around the world balloon attempt 2001, pilot, designer and project dir QinetiQ 1 project 2002–; Royal Aero Club: Salomons Trophy 1991, Gold Medal 1999; *Recreations* extreme sports, mountain biking, cave-diving, heliskiing, mountain climbing; *Style*— Andy Elson, Esq

ELSTEIN, David Keith; s of Albert Elstein (d 1983), and Millie Cohen (d 1985); *b* 14 November 1944; *Educ* Haberdashers' Aske's, Gonville & Caius Coll Cambridge (MA); *m* 16 July 1978, Jenny, da of Alfred Conway; 1 s (Daniel b 1981); *Career* prodr: BBC 1964–68, Thames Television 1968–72, LWT 1972–73; ed This Week and exec prodr documentaries Thames Television 1973–82, exec prodr Goldcrest TV 1982–83, md and exec prodr Brook Productions 1982–86, md and exec prodr Primetime TV 1983–86, dir of progs Thames Television 1986–93, head of programming Sky TV 1993–96, chief exec Channel 5 1996–2000; chm: Br Screen Advsy Cncl 1997–, Really Useful Theatres Ltd 2001–, Screen Digest Ltd 2003–, Broadcasting Policy Gp 2003–, Sports Network plc 2004–, Commercial Radio Companies Assoc 2004–, Sparrowhawk Investments Ltd 2004–, Digital Classics 2005–, Luther Pendragon Hldgs 2006–; vice-chm Kingsbridge Capital Ltd 2003–; non-exec dir NTL Inc 2003–; visiting prof: Univ of Stirling 1995–, Univ of Oxford 1998–99, Univ of Westminster 2001–04; James McTaggart meml lectr Edinburgh Int Television Festival 1991, Forman lectr 1995, Raymond Williams lectr 1997, Goodman lectr 1998, Bernard Simons lectr 1999; Media Achiever of the Year Campaign Media Awards 1998; *Publications* Beyond the Charter: The Future of the BBC (2004); *Recreations* cinema, theatre, bridge, reading; *Style*— David Elstein, Esq

ELSTON, John David; s of Lt-Col John William Elston (d 1984), and Alwyn, *née* Fawbert; *b* 2 August 1946; *Educ* Norwich Sch, Richmond Sch, Univ of Newcastle upon Tyne (BA); *m* 27 Sept 1980, Victoria Ann Harding (Vicky), da of Victor William Brown, of Toronto, Canada; 2 s (James b 1982, Henry b 1988), 1 da (Georgina b 1986); *Career* sr exec James Capel & Co 1985–94 (joined 1973), dir WestLB Panmure 1997–2004 (joined 1995), dir Panmure Gordon (Lazard & Co Ltd) 2004; FCA 1979; *Recreations* golf, tennis, bridge; *Style*— John Elston, Esq; ✉ Tara, Woodland Rise, Sevenoaks, Kent TN15 0HZ (tel 01732 762162)

ELSTON, John Scorgie; s of Charles Henry Elston, of West Kirby, Merseyside, and Hilda Constance Mary Elston (d 1986); *b* 22 March 1949; *Educ* St Bees Sch Cumberland, St Thomas' Hosp Med Sch (BSc, MB BS); *Partner* Frederika Estelle Smith; 1 da (Charlotte Rose Scorgie b 10 June 1990), 1 s (Guy Scorgie b 11 March 1993); *Career* med practitioner; house appts in gen med and surgery before specialising in ophthalmology; trg in ophthalmology: St Thomas' Hosp 1975–78, Moorfields Eye Hosp 1979–87, Hosp for Sick Children 1983–87; conslt ophthalmologist: Nat Hosp for Neurology and Neurosurgery 1987–91, St Mary's Hosp London 1987–91, Western Ophthalmic Hosp London 1987–91, Radcliffe Infirmary Oxford 1991–; FRCS 1982, FRSM 1988, FRCOphth 1989, MD 1990; *Books* Dystonia II (jtly, 1987), Pediatric Ophthalmology (jtly, 1990, 2 edn 1997), Scientific Basis of Neurosurgery (jtly, 1991, 2 edn 1999), Community Paediatrics (jtly, 1991); *Recreations* golf, tennis, walking, English literature; *Clubs* RSM; *Style*— John Elston, Esq; ✉ Radcliffe Infirmary, Oxford OX2 6HE (tel 01865 224201, fax 01865 224515, e-mail jselston@hotmail.com)

ELSTOW, Clare Marie Michelle; da of Geoffrey Charles Elstow, and Marie Patricia, *née* Ferriday; *Educ* Notre Dame HS Northampton, UCL (BA); *m*; 2 c; *Career* studio mangr BBC Radio 1977–82, studio mangr and composer BBC Radiophonic Workshop 1979, asst prodr rising to exec prodr BBC Educn 1983–2000, head of pre-school/CBeebies prodn BBC Children's 2000–06 (creative conslt 2006–); Hosa Bunka Award for Pre-School Excellence (Japan Prize) for Words and Pictures series 1992, RTS Educn Award for Numbertime 1994, RTS Educn Razzledazzle Award 2006, Bafta Award for (Boogie Beebies) 2006; govr Dr Challoner's HS for Girls; memb: Nat Childbirth Tst, NSPCC, Fawcett Soc, Friends of UCL, Amnesty Int, Friends of the Earth, Intermediate Technol; supporter Medical Fndn; *Recreations* music, creative writing, gardening, reading; *Style*— Ms Clare Elstow

ELSWORTH, David Raymond Cecil; s of Violet Kathleen Elsworth; *b* 12 December 1939; *m* 20 Dec 1969, Jennifer Jane Kimber, da of J K R Macgregor; 2 s (Simon David b 30 May 1972, Iain Robert David b 6 June 1975), 1 da (Jessica Jane b 9 June 1984); *Career* nat hunt jockey 1957–72, racehorse trainer 1978–; nat hunt winners: Rhyme 'N' Reason (Grand National) 1988, Heighlin (Triumph Hurdle), Barnbrook Again (twice winner Queen Mother Champion Chase), Desert Orchid (King George VI Rank Chase 1986 and 1988–90, Whitbread Gold Cup 1988, Cheltenham Gold Cup 1989, Jameson Irish Grand National 1990); trained on the flat: Mighty Flutter (third place, Derby) 1984, In the Groove (winner Goffs Irish One Thousand Guineas, first Classic and three further Group 1 races) 1990, Seattle Rhyme (Racing Post Trophy, Gp One Doncaster) 1991, Persian Punch (twice winner Henry II Stakes, twice third place Melbourne Cup, winner Sagaro Stakes), Salford Express (Dante Stakes) 1998, Lear Spear (Diomed Stakes, Prince of Wales Stakes) 1999; champion Nat Hunt trainer 1987–88; *Recreations* shooting, golf; *Style*— David Elsworth, Esq; ✉ Egerton House Stables, Cambridge Road, Newmarket, Suffolk CB8 0TH (tel 01638 668684, e-mail david.elsworth@virgin.net)

ELTON, Sir Arnold; kt (1987), CBE (1982); s of Max Elton (d 1953), and Ada, *née* Levy (d 1990); *b* 14 February 1920; *Educ* UCL (MS); *m* 9 Nov 1952, Billie Pamela, da of John Nathan Briggs; 1 s (Michael Jonathan b 1953); *Career* jr and sr Gold medal in surgery UCH, Gosse res scholarship Charing Cross Hosp 1951; formerly sr surgical registrar Charing Cross Hosp, house surgn, house physician and casualty offr UCH; conslt surgn: Mt Vernon Hosp 1960–70, Harrow Hosp 1951–70, Northwick Park Hosp 1970–85; med advsr and conslt surgn Wellington Hosp, hon conslt surgn Northwick Park Hosp 1985–, conslt emeritus surgn Clementine Churchill Hosp, conslt surgn British Airways 1988–96, conslt advsr Keltbray Ltd, conslt and advsr to Sir Robert McAlpine Ltd; exec chm Medical Consulting Services Ltd (formerly Medical and Political Services (MPS)) 1993–, exec chm Healthy Living (Durham) Ltd, chm and chief exec Healthy Living UK Ltd, chm and chief exec Universal Lifestyle, health exec Bovis Lend Lease 2001–; UK chm and exec memb European Div Int Med Parliamentarians Orgn 1995–; memb: Govt Ctee on Screening for Breast Cancer, Tricare Europe Preferred Provider Network (US Armed Forces) - Breast and Thyroid Surgery 1997–; chm Cons Med Soc 1975–92 (pres 1992–98, European rep 1992–), fndr chm Med and Scientific Div World Fellowship Duke of Edinburgh's Award 1997–, fndr chm Int Med and Sci Fundraising Ctee Br Red Cross; ed CMS Euro Bulletin 1994–96; memb Ct of Patrons and memb and chm Ct of Examiners to RCS, surgical tutor RCS 1970–82, dir and co-ordinator RCS Exchange of Surgns with China 1994–, previously examiner to Gen Nursing Cncl; memb: Assoc of Surgns, Br Assoc of Surgical Oncology (fndr memb), European Soc of Surgical Oncology 1995, World Fedn of Surgical Oncological Societies 1995– (memb Cncl and int advsr); Freeman City of London; Liveryman: Worshipful Soc of Apothecaries, Worshipful Co of Carmen; Jubilee Medal for Community Servs 1977; FRCS, FICS, FRSM; *Recreations* tennis, cricket, music; *Clubs* Carlton, RAC, MCC; *Style*— Sir Arnold Elton, CBE; ✉ Carlton Club, 69 St James's Street, London SW1A 1PJ; The Consulting Rooms, Wellington Hospital, Wellington Place, London NW8 9LE (tel 020 7935 4101, fax 020 7722 6638, mobile 07785 935264)

ELTON, Sir Charles Abraham Grierson; 11 Bt (GB 1717), of Bristol; s of Sir Arthur Hallam Rice Elton, 10 Bt (d 1973), and Margaret Ann, *née* Bjornson (d 1995); *b* 23 May 1953; *Educ* Eton, Univ of Reading (BA); *m* 2 March 1990 (m dis), Lucy Lauris, da of late Lukas Heller and Mrs Caroline Garnham; 1 da (Lotte Caroline b 15 Aug 1993), 1 s (Abraham

E

William b 27 Sept 1995); *Heir* s, Abraham William; *Career* with BBC Publications; *Style*— Sir Charles Elton, Bt; ✉ Clevedon Court, Clevedon, Somerset BS21 6QU; 25 Dartmouth Park Hill, London NW5 1HP

ELTON, Michael John; s of John Thomas Humphrey Elton (d 1981), and Kathleen Margaret, *née* Bird (d 1999); *b* 20 December 1933; *Educ* SW Essex Tech Coll, Royal Naval Electrical Sch; *m* 26 March 1965, Carole Elizabeth, da of William Saunby, of Kettering, Northants; 2 s (James Robert b 1967, Charles Lindsey b 1969); *Career* Nat Serv Sub Lt RNVR 1955–57; serv: 108 Minesweeping Sqdn Malta, base electrical offr Cyprus; Lt RNR 1958–62; engrg and sales positions STC London 1957–63, staff of mktg dir ITT Europe Paris 1963–64, mktg mangr STC Data Systems London 1964–69; Control Data: mangr int data servs Minneapolis 1969–70 and Brussels 1970–71, md Stockholm 1971–74, chm and md Helsinki 1973–74, gen mangr Brussels 1974–79, gen mangr London 1979–81; Technitron: vice-pres and gen mangr Technitron Int Inc 1981–86, md and chief exec Technitron plc 1986–90; CEng, FIEE, FBCS; *Recreations* golf, sailing, swimming; *Clubs* Naval, RNVR Yacht (Cdre 1999–2001); *Style*— Michael Elton, Esq; ✉ 3 Oriel Hill, Camberley, Surrey GU15 2JW

ELTON, 2 Baron (UK 1934); Rodney Elton; TD (1970); s of 1 Baron Elton (d 1973), and Dedi (d 1977), da of Gustav Hartmann, of Oslo, Norway; *b* 2 March 1930; *Educ* Eton, New Coll Oxford; *m* 1, 18 Sept 1958 (sep 1973, m dis 1979), Anne Frances, da of late Brig Robert Adolphus George Tilney, CBE, DSO, TD, DL; 1 s, 3 da; m 2, 24 Aug 1979, (Susan) Richenda (Lady Elton, CVO), yst da of late Sir Hugh Gurney, KCMG, MVO; *Heir* s, Hon Edward Elton; *Career* formerly: farmer, teacher and lectr; contested (Cons) Loughborough 1966 and 1970; oppn spokesman Educn and Welsh Affrs 1974–79, dep sec Int Affrs Ctee of Gen Synod of C of E 1976–78, dep chm Andry Montgomery Ltd 1977–79 and 1987–2003; memb Boyd Cmmn (Southern Rhodesia elections 1979); Parly under sec of state: NI Office 1979–81, DHSS 1981–82, Home Office 1982–84; min of state Home Office 1984–85, DOE 1985–86; memb: Select Ctee on the Scrutiny of Delegated Powers 1992–96, Select Ctee on the Constitution 2003–; a dep chm of Ctees and dep speaker House of Lords 1997–99 and 1999–, elected hereditary peer House of Lords 1999–; dep chm Assoc of Cons Peers 1988–93; memb Panel on Takeovers and Mergers 1987–90; chm: FIMBRA 1987–90, Enquiry into Discipline in Schs 1988, Intermediate Treatment Fund 1990–93, Divert Tst 1993–99 (pres 1999–2002); pres Bldg Conservation Tst 1990–95, tstee City Parochial Fndn & Tst for London 1991–97; chm Quality and Standards Ctee C&G 1999–2005; hon vice-pres Inst of Trading Standards Admin; licensed lay min C of E 1998–; Hon FCGI; *Clubs* Cavalry and Guards', Beefsteak, Pratt's; *Style*— The Rt Hon the Lord Elton, TD; ✉ House of Lords, London SW1A 0PW

ELVIDGE, Sir John William; KCB (2006); s of late Herbert William Elvidge, and late Irene Teresa, *née* Reynolds; *b* 9 February 1951; *Educ* Sir George Monoux Sch Walthamstow, St Catherine's Coll Oxford (BA); *m* Maureen Margaret Ann, *née* McGinn; *Career* Scottish Office: joined as admin trainee 1973, various posts in educn, housing and tport, higher exec offr (A) 1976–78, princ 1978–84, asst sec and fin offr Scottish Economic Planning and Devpt Depts 1984, seconded as dir of implementation Scottish Homes 1988–89, asst sec 1989–93, under sec Industry and Devpt Depts 1993–98; dep head Economic and Domestic Secretariat Cabinet Office 1998–99; sec and head Scottish Exec Educn Dept 1999–2002, sec and head Scottish Exec Fin and Central Services Dept 2002–03; permanent sec Scottish Executive 2003–; *Recreations* painting, film, theatre, modern novels, music, swimming, walking, food and drink; *Style*— Sir John Elvidge, KCB; ✉ Scottish Executive, Fifth Floor, St Andrews House, Edinburgh EH1 3DG (e-mail john.elvidge@scotland.gsi.gov.uk)

ELVIN, Jo; da of Harry Elvin, of Sydney, Aust, and Leonie, *née* Burgess; *b* 21 February 1970; *Educ* Cambridge Park HS, Univ of Western Sydney; *m* 29 Jan 2000, Ross Jones; 1 da (Evie); *Career* dep ed TV Hits magazine 1993–94; ed: Sugar magazine 1994–96, B magazine 1996–98, New Woman magazine 1998–2000, Glamour magazine 2000–; contrib of articles to The Independent, Evening Standard, The Observer and Media Week; featured in TV series Model Behaviour (Channel 4), also numerous TV, radio and public speaking appearances; memb: BSME, Women in Journalism; Ed of the Year BSME 1995, 1996 and 2002, Launch Ed of the Year BSME 2001, Editors' Ed of the Year BSME 2002; *Clubs* Groucho, Adam Street; *Style*— Ms Jo Elvin; ✉ Glamour Magazine, 6–8 Old Bond Street, London W1S 4PH (tel 020 7499 9080, fax 020 7491 2597, e-mail editor@glamourmagazine.co.uk)

ELWES, Henry William George; JP; s of Maj John Hargreaves Elwes, MC, Scots Gds (ka N Africa 1943), and Isabel Pamela Ivy, *née* Beckwith (later Mrs John Talbot, d 1993), gda of 7 Duke of Richmond and Gordon; *b* 24 October 1935; *Educ* Eton, RAC Cirencester; *m* 8 Sept 1962, Carolyn Dawn, da of Joseph William Wykeham Cripps (d 1958), of Ampney Crucis, Glos (3 cous of the post war chllr Sir Stafford Cripps); 3 s (John b 1964, Frederick b 1966, George b 1971 d 1993); *Career* late Lt Scots Gds; farmer and forester; chm Western Woodland Owners Ltd 1971–86 (pres 1986–2003), regnl dir Lloyds Bank plc 1985–91, dir Colebourne Estate Co; patron, pres or memb of many Glos tsts and socs; memb: Cirencester Rural Dist Cncl 1959–74, Glos CC 1971–91 (vice-chm 1976–83 and 1991, chm 1983–85); hon lay canon Gloucester Cathedral 2001–; High Sheriff Glos 1979–80; Hon Alderman Glos 1992; HM Lord-Lt Glos 1992– (DL 1982); Liveryman Worshipful Co of Gardeners; Hon DPhil Univ of Glos 2002, Hon LLD UWE 2006; *Clubs* Confrerie des Chevaliers du Tastevin; *Style*— H W G Elwes, Esq; ✉ Colesbourne Park, Gloucestershire GL53 9NP (tel 01242 870262, e-mail hwg@globalnet.co.uk)

ELWES, Sir Jeremy Vernon; kt (1994), CBE (1984); s of Eric Vincent Elwes (d 1985), of Sevenoaks, Kent, and Dorothea, *née* Bilton (d 1998); *b* 29 May 1937; *Educ* Wirral GS, Bromley GS, City of London Coll; *m* 1963, Phyllis Marion, da of George Herbert Harding Relf (d 2001), of Halstead, Kent; 1 s (Jonathan b 1969); *Career* chartered sec; dir Sevenoaks Constitutional Club Co Ltd 1977–2002; chm Cons Political Centre Nat Advsy Ctee 1981–84, personnel dir Reed Business Publishing Ltd 1982–93, human resources dir Reed Publishing Europe 1993–94; chm SE Area Provincial Cncl 1986–90, dir Sutton Enterprise Agency Ltd 1987–94 (chm 1987–90); Cons Pty Nat Union: memb Exec Ctee 1974–95, dep chm Europe Ctee 1991–95; memb Exec Ctee Gen Cncl Cons Gp for Europe 1977–96, hon sec Cons Med Soc 1997–2000, co-ordinator Specialist Gps for Cons Pty 2000–, pres Sevenoaks Cons Assoc 2007–; judge Int Wine and Spirits Competition Ltd 1983–99; chm: St Helier NHS Tst 1991–99, Walthamstow Hall 1984–2003 (govr 1977–2004); tstee and dir European Sch of Osteopathy 1999–2007; govr Eltham Coll 1977–96; St John Ambulance: pres Sevenoaks Div 2000–, dep county pres Kent 2001–; memb Cncl: Imperial Soc of Knights Bachelor 2002–, Printers' Charitable Corp 2002– (pres 2004, dep chm 2005–06, chm 2006–), Hospice in the Weald 2003–, Fndn for Liver Research 2005–; Liveryman: Worshipful Co of Stationers and Newspapermakers (chm Livery Ctee 2000–02, Livery rep in Ct 2005–07, memb Ct of Assts 2007–), Worshipful Co of Chartered Secretaries and Administrators 2003 (sec Livery Liaison Gp 2005–06, chm 2006–); ACIS, FRSA; Chevalier Ordre des Chevaliers Bretvins (Bailliage de GB, Maitre des Ceremonies 1984–88, Chancelier 1986–92), SBStJ 2006; *Recreations* wine, food, golf, reading; *Clubs* Knole, Nizels Golf, Admiralty Golf, Royal Over-Seas League; *Style*— Sir Jeremy Elwes, CBE; ✉ Crispian Cottage, Weald Road, Sevenoaks, Kent TN13 1QQ (tel 01732 454208, fax 01732 464153, e-mail jeremy.elwes@btopenworld.com)

ELWES, Nigel Robert; s of late Maj Robert Philip Henry Elwes, MBE, MC, of Ballinafad, Ireland, and his 1 wife, Vivien Elizabeth Fripp, *née* Martin-Smith; *b* 8 August 1941; *Educ* Eton; *m* 22 June 1965, Carolyn Peta, da of late Sir Robin McAlpine, CBE; 2 da (Serena (Mrs Jeremy Bradbeer) b 1967, Melisa (Mrs Nicholas Aikenhead) b 1973), 1 s (Andrew b 1969); *Career* CA, stockbroker, farmer and bloodstock breeder; ptnr Rowe & Pitman 1970–86, fin dir S G Warburg Securities 1986–91, chm Reyker Securities Ltd 1991–94; Stock Exchange: joined 1970, memb Cncl 1983–86 and 1988–91, chm Domestic Equity Market Ctee 1988–91, chm Special Ctee on Market Devpt (Elwes Ctee); ptnr: Aylesfield Farms 1991–, Aylesfield Farms Stud 1993–; dir Kempton Park Racecourse Co Ltd 2003–; chm: Cncl Thoroughbred Breeders' Assoc 1997–2003 and 2006–, Racing Welfare 2000– (vice-chm 1992–2000), Stable Lads Welfare Tst 2000–01 (vice-chm 1993–2000), Br Racing Sch 2004 (tstee 1992–2003); dir Br Horseracing Bd 1999–2003 (memb Race Planning Ctee 1996–99); dir Dorchester Hotel 1974–76; govr Lord Mayor Treloar Sch 1992–2000; MSI; FCA; *Recreations* hunting, shooting, racing; *Clubs* White's (chm House Ctee 1997–2000), Jockey; *Style*— Nigel Elwes, Esq; ✉ Manor Farmhouse, Kington Magna, Gillingham SP8 5EG (tel 01747 838700); Aylesfield Farms Stud Ltd (tel 01747 838928, fax 01747 839772, e-mail nigel@elwes.net)

ELWES, Peter John Gervase; s of Lt-Col Simon Edmund Vincent Paul Elwes, RA (d 1975), of Amberley, W Sussex, and Hon Gloria Elinor, *née* Rodd (d 1975); *b* 17 October 1929; *Educ* Eton, Miles Aircraft Tech Coll, Kingston and Gateshead Colls of Advanced Technol; *m* 7 May 1960, Hon Rosalie Ann, da of Brig James Brian George Hennessy, 2 Baron Windlesham (d 1962), of Askefield, Bray, Ireland; 3 s (Luke b 26 July 1961, Benedict b 4 May 1963, Marcus b 27 Nov 1964), 1 da (Harriet b 3 Dec 1968); *Career* 2 Lt Royal Scots Greys BAOR Germany 1950–52, Lt Northumberland Hussars 1953–56; Vickers Armstrong Ltd Weybridge and Newcastle 1948–53, Ransomes & Rapier Ltd Ipswich 1953–56, Rio Tinto plc 1956–73, md Hamilton Bros Oil and Gas Ltd 1973–77, dir Kleinwort Benson Ltd 1977–89, chief exec Enterprise Oil plc 1983–84, md Renown Energy Ltd 1988–89; Hardy Oil & Gas plc: dep chm and chief exec 1989–94, dep chm 1995–96; chm Aminex plc 1996–2006; non-exec dir Energy Africa Limited 1996–2004; FEI; *Recreations* painting, gardening, music; *Clubs* Hurlingham; *Style*— Peter Elwes, Esq

ELWORTHY, Air Cdre the Hon Sir Timothy Charles; KCVO (2001, CVO 1995), CBE (1986); eldest s of Marshal of the RAF Baron Elworthy, KG, GCB, CBE, DSO, LVO, DFC, AFC (Life Peer, d 1993), and Audrey, *née* Hutchinson (d 1986); *b* 27 January 1938; *Educ* Radley, RAF Coll Cranwell; *m* 1, 1961 (m dis 1969), Victoria Ann, eldest da of late Lt-Col H C W Bowring; 2 da (Katharine Emma Victoria b 1963, Lucinda Rose b 1965); m 2, 1971, Anabel, da of late Reginald Ernest Harding, OBE; 1 s (Edward Charles b 1974); *Career* RAF; Capt of The Queen's Flight 1989–94, Extra Equerry to HM The Queen 1991–, HM's Sr Air Equerry 1995–2001, dir of Royal Travel 1997–2001; Liveryman Guild of Air Pilots and Air Navigators; *Recreations* country pursuits, wine, travel; *Clubs* Boodle's; *Style*— Air Cdre the Hon Sir Timothy Elworthy, KCVO, CBE; ✉ Coates House, Swyncombe, Henley-on-Thames, Oxfordshire RG9 6EG

ELY, Bishop of 2000–; Rt Rev Dr Anthony John Russell; *b* 25 January 1943; *Educ* Uppingham, Univ of Durham (BA), Trinity Coll Oxford (DPhil), Cuddesdon Theol Coll; *m* 1967, Sheila Alexandra; 2 da (Alexandra b 1969, Serena b 1975), 2 s (Jonathan b 1971, Timothy b 1981); *Career* ordained: deacon 1970, priest 1971; curate Hilborough Gp of Parishes 1970–73, rector Preston-on-Stour, Atherstone-on-Stour and Whitchurch 1973–88, canon theologian Coventry Cathedral 1977–88, chaplain to HM The Queen 1983–88, dir Arthur Rank Centre (Nat Agric Centre) 1983–88, area bishop of Dorchester Dio of Oxford 1988–2000; memb Gen Synod 1980–88 and 2000–, hon chaplain Royal Agric Benevolent Inst 1983–2002; memb: Archbishops' Cmmn on Rural Affairs 1988–90, Rural Devpt Cmmn 1991–99; tstee Rural Housing Tst 2006; vice-patron RASE 2002– (chaplain1982–91, vice-pres 1991–2002, pres 2004–05), assoc Royal Agric Socs, pres East of England Agric Soc 2007; pres Woodward Corp 2003–; govr Radley Coll 2003–; Hulsean preacher Univ of Cambridge 2004; visitor: Jesus Coll Cambridge, St John's Coll Cambridge, Peterhouse Cambridge; hon fell: Wolfson Coll Cambridge, St Edmund's Coll Cambridge, St Chad's Coll Durham; *Books* Groups and Teams in the Countryside (ed, 1975), The Clerical Profession (1980), The Country Parish (1986), The Country Parson (1993); *Clubs* Oxford and Cambridge, Farmers'; *Style*— The Rt Rev the Bishop of Ely; ✉ The Bishop's House, Ely, Cambridgeshire CB7 4DW (tel 01353 662749, fax 01353 669477, e-mail bishop@ely.anglican.org)

ELYAN, David Asher Gremson; s of Max Elyan (d 2002), and Freda, *née* Gremson (d 2006); *b* 4 October 1940; *Educ* Cork GS, TCD (BA, BCom, MA); *Career* co sec Gordon & Gotch Hldgs plc 1970–74, assoc dir AGB Research plc 1980–87 (co sec 1974–87); dir: Attwood Research of Ireland Ltd 1981–90, Irish TAM Ltd 1981–90, Corporate Lease Mgmnt Ltd 1984–93, Elyan Estates Ltd 1987–93, Communication Investments Ltd 1987–, Langton Software Ltd 1987–2002, Bankside Gallery Ltd 1992–2003 (sec 1992–), CLM Fleet Mgmnt plc 1993–96, Wigmore Investments Ltd 1994–, Royal Albert Hall Devpts Ltd 2000–, Manx Public Art 2001–, Mediterranean Inst Malta 2003–; hon treas: TCD Dining Club 1968–94 (vice-chm 1994–), Friends of Royal Watercolour Soc 1990–1994; memb: Senate Univ of Dublin 1966–, Corp of Lloyds 1983–, Post Office Advsy Ctee (POAC) 1991–98, Cncl Royal Albert Hall 1996–, Isle of Man Arts Cncl (visual arts panel) 2000–02, Cncl Music Club of London 2003–06; chm Friends of Royal Acad of Music 1993–2000, tstee Fenton Arts Tst 2004–; Freeman City of London, Liveryman Worshipful Co of Chartered Secs 1978; hon fell Univ of Malta 2000; ACCS 1967, FRSA 1972, FCIS 1976 (ACIS 1969), Hon ARAM 1999; *Recreations* collecting first editions, tennis, art, music, bridge; *Clubs* MCC, Casino Maltese, Union (Malta); *Style*— David Elyan, Esq; ✉ 49 Chester Court, Regent's Park, London NW1 4BU; 31 Woodbourne Road, Douglas, Isle of Man IM2 3AB

ELYSTAN-MORGAN, Baron (Life Peer UK 1981), of Aberteifi in the County of Dyfed; (Dafydd) Elystan Elystan-Morgan; s of Dewi Morgan (d 1971), of Llandre, Aberystwyth, and Olwen Morgan (d 1947); *b* 7 December 1932; *Educ* Ardwyn GS Aberystwyth, UCW Aberystwyth; *m* 1959, Alwen (d 2006), *née* Roberts; 1 da (Hon Eleri (Hon Mrs Hurt) b 1960), 1 s (Hon Owain b 1962); *Career* sat as Lab Peer in House of Lords 1981–87, MP (Lab) Cardiganshire 1966–74, Parly under sec of state Home Office 1968–70, pres Welsh Local Authorities Assoc 1967–73, chm Welsh Parly Party 1967–68; called to the Bar Gray's Inn 1971 (formerly slr); recorder (Wales & Chester Circuit) 1983–87, circuit judge (Wales & Chester Circuit) 1987–2003, dep circuit judge 2003–05; hon fell UCW Aberystwyth 1991 (vice-pres 1992–97, pres and chm Cncl 1997–), pres Sch of Welsh Legal Affrs 2001–; *Style*— His Hon Lord Elystan-Morgan; ✉ House of Lords, London SW1A 0PW

EMANUEL, David Leslie; s of John Lawrence Morris Emanuel, and Elizabeth Emanuel (decd); *b* 17 November 1952, Wales; *Educ* Cardiff Coll of Art (dip), Harrow Sch of Art (dip), RCA (MA); *m* 1975 (sep), Elizabeth Emanuel, *qv*; 1 s (Oliver), 1 da (Eloise); *Career* fashion designer; early career experience at Hardy Amies, Cojana and Marcel Fenez (with Roland Klein); fndr ptnr (with wife) Emanuel 1977–90 (designers of HRH The Princess of Wales' wedding dress), fndr David Emanuel Couture 1990–; TV work incl: co-presenter Swank (ITV) 1994, Frock Doctor (ABC, USA) 1995, Designed by Emanuel (own series for HTV), The David Emanuel Fashion Show (GSB), co-hosted Afternoon Live (ITV) 1997; finale spot: Night of 100 Stars Gala Fashion Show (Radio City Hall NY) 1984, Fashion Aid (with Bob Geldof, Royal Albert Hall) 1985, Fashion Aid Japan (Tokyo) 1986, 150th Anniversary Celebration of RCA Art Gala Fashion Show 1987; designs for ballet prodns incl Frankenstein, the Modern Prometheus (Royal Opera House Covent Garden 1985 and La Scala Milan 1987); FCSD; *Books* Style for All Seasons (1983); *Recreations* sport (horse-riding, tennis, jet/water skiing), the arts; *Clubs* Royal Ascot Tennis, White Elephant; *Style*— David Emanuel, Esq

EMANUEL, Elizabeth Florence; da of Samuel Charles Weiner (Croix de Guerre), of Warfield, Berks, and Brahna Betty, *née* Charkham; *b* 5 July 1953; *Educ* City of London Sch for

Girls, Harrow Coll of Art, Royal Coll of Art (MA); *m* 12 July 1975 (sep 1990), David Leslie Emanuel, *qv*, s of John Lawrence Morris Emanuel; 1 s (Oliver b 21 March 1978), 1 da (Eloise b 25 Dec 1979); *Career* fashion designer; opened London Salon 1978, designed wedding dress for HRH Princess of Wales 1981, launched new shop and design studio 1996, launched own brand label (with backer Richard Thompson) 1999; theatre designs incl: costumes for Andrew Lloyd Webber's Song and Dance 1982, sets and costumes for ballet Frankenstein - The Modern Prometheus (Royal Opera House Covent Garden, La Scala Milan) 1985, costumes for Stoll Moss prodn of Cinderella 1985; designed uniforms for: Virgin Atlantic Airlines 1990, Britannia Airways 1996; launched international fashion label under own name 1992, costumes for film The Changeling 1995, designed new range for Berkertex Brides 1994, launched new wedding lifestyle range in Japan 1994, designed Elizabeth Hurley's dress for Esteé Lauder Beautiful campaign 1996–98 and Pleasures campaign 1999, costume design for short film Ros Beef 2003; active involvement with charities: Born Free Fndn, WWF, WSPA, London Lighthouse, IFAW; FCSD 1984; *Books* Style For All Seasons (with David Emanuel, 1983); *Recreations* music, ballet, cinema; *Clubs* Chelsea Arts; *Style*— Mrs Elizabeth Emanuel

EMBER, Michael George; s of Dr George Leslie Ember (d 1972), and Margaret Ilona, *née* Ungar (d 1996); *b* 13 May 1935; *Educ* The Gymnasium of Budapest Univ, Hungarian Acad of Drama, Univ of London (BA); *m* 1 April 1967, Elizabeth Ann, da of Sir Charles Sigmund Davis; 3 s (Nicholas Charles b 1969, Thomas Michael b 1972, Philip George b 1973); *Career* independent radio and TV prodr; formerly a chief prodr BBC Radio and originator of: Start the Week, Mid-Week, Stop the Week, In the Psychiatrist's Chair, All in the Mind (Radio 4), The Anthony Clare Interview (ITV); *Style*— Michael Ember, Esq; ✉ 48 Pemberton Road, East Molesey, Surrey KT8 9LH (tel 020 8979 5262, fax 020 8941 2779)

EMBERY, Prof Graham; s of Joseph Henry Embery (d 1987), and Elizabeth Jane; *b* 20 August 1939; *Educ* King Edward VI GS Stourbridge; *m* 14 Jan 1967, Vivienne Lacey, da of William Horace Powell (d 1973); 1 da (Philippa Jane b 24 June 1970), 2 s (Russell Geraint b 25 Nov 1971, James Toby William b 30 Dec 1973); *Career* lectr Queen's Univ Belfast 1968–70, lectr Royal Dental Hosp 1970–73, reader Univ of Liverpool 1984–87 (lectr 1973–77, sr lectr 1977–84), prof of basic dental sci Univ of Wales Coll of Med Cardiff 1987–2001, prof of dental sci and dean Univ of Liverpool Dental Sch 2001–; sec-gen Cncl of Euro Study Gp for Res on Surface and Colloidal Phenomena in the Oral Cavity; memb: Int Assoc for Dental Res, Br Connective Tissue Soc, Biochemical Soc, Jt Dental Ctee MRC 1991–95, Sci and Engrg Res Cncl and Health Authorities 1991–, Res Assessment Panel in Clinical Dentistry 1999–; pres: Br Soc for Dental Res 1994–96, Int Assoc for Dental Res 1999–; treas European Orgn for Caries Res 1994–96, Welsh Devpt Scheme for Health and Social Res 1995–99, Welsh NHS R&D Forum 1995–98; Colgate Prize 1973, IADR Distinguished Scientist Prize in Oral Biology; Hon DSc Univ of Wales; memb (fell) RSM; *Books* Clinical and Biological Aspects Dentifrizes (trans Japanese 2003); author of over 250 publications and articles; *Recreations* golf, oil painting, classic cars; *Style*— Prof Graham Embery; ✉ 16 Townfield Road, West Kirby, Wirral, Merseyside L48 7EZ (tel 0151 625 5954); Department of Clinical Dental Sciences, University of Liverpool Dental School, Edwards Research Building, Liverpool L69 3GN (tel 0151 706 5252/5275, fax 0151 706 5809, e-mail g.embery@liverpool.ac.uk)

EMBIRICOS, Epaminondas George; s of George Epaminondas Embiricos (d 1980), of Athens, and Sophie, *née* Douma (d 1999); *b* 15 July 1943; *Educ* Philips Exeter Acad New Hampshire USA, MIT (BSc, MSc); *m* 19 March 1977, Angela, da of Nicholas Pittas, of London; 2 s (George Epaminondas b 8 May 1978, Nicholas Epaminondas b 8 June 1980); *Career* chm: Embiricos Shipping Agency Ltd 1969–91, Embiricos Shipbrokers Ltd 1991–, Chartering Brokers Mutual Insurance Assoc 1999–2002; dir: Liberian Shipowners Cncl 1979–84, Baltic Exchange Ltd 1985–90; chm Greek Ctee Det Norske Veritas 1997–2001 (memb 1986–, vice-chm 1987–97), vice-chm Greek Shipping Co-op Ctee 1986–99; chm UK Freight Demurrage and Def Assoc 1993–96 (dir 1984–99), chm Greek Shipping Co-op Ctee 1999–; memb: American Bureau of Shipping 1990–, Br Ctee American Bureau of Shipping 1994–, Cncl of the Union of Greek Shipowners 1996–, Det Norske Veritas Classification Ctee 1997–2000, Visiting Ctee of the Dept of Ocean Engrg of MIT 1998–2002; ex officio memb Lloyd's Register Gen Ctee 2000–; Freeman City of London 1984, memb Ct of Assts Worshipful Co of Shipwrights 1994 (Liveryman 1985); *Recreations* sailing, reading; *Clubs* Royal Thames Yacht, Royal Yacht Club of Greece; *Style*— Epaminondas Embiricos, Esq; ✉ Commonwealth House, 1–19 New Oxford Street, London WC1A 1NU (tel 020 7404 0420, fax 020 7400 0887)

EMBLIN, Roslyn Inglis; JP (City of London 1996); da of Norman Inglis Emblin (d 1973), of Halifax, W Yorks, and Christabel Gardner Emblin; *b* 13 August 1943; *Educ* Princess Mary HS Halifax, Univ of London, Kings Fund Coll London; *Career* student nurse St Thomas' Hosp 1963–67, pupil midwife Queen Charlotte's Maternity Hosp London 1967–68; St Thomas' Hosp: ward sister 1968–71, admin sister 1971–72, nursing offr 1972–76; int sec RCN 1976–83 (fndr Int Summer Sch 1977); Moorfields Eye Hosp: chief nursing offr 1983, dir of nursing and dep chief exec 1985–2002, memb Govrs 1990–94, exec dir 1994–2002; dir St John Eye Hosp Jerusalem 1996–; memb Residential Property Tbnl (Office of the dep PM) 1997–; expert witness RCN 1995–2002, memb Immigration Appeal Tbnl (Lord Chllr's Dept) 2003–; memb: Victoria HA 1982–84, Frink Award Ctee Greater London Fund for the Blind 1987–95, Health Servs Ctee RNIB 1990–95, Bd Nat Care Standards Cmmn 2001–04; chm Chief Nurses Gp of the Special Health Authorities 1992–94; Sainsbury scholarship to study in USA and Canada 1981, Florence Nightingale scholarship to study in USA 1986; memb: RCN, Epsom Racecourse; CStJ 2003 (OStJ 1997); *Books* Nursing Education and Practice in the European Community (1980), Nursing in the EEC (1982); *Recreations* gardening, horse racing, travel; *Style*— Miss Roslyn Emblin; ✉ 46 Cranley Mews, South Kensington, London SW7 3BY (tel 020 7370 2383)

EMBREY, Derek Morris; OBE (1986); s of Frederick Embrey (d 1972), and Ethel May, *née* Morris; *b* 11 March 1928; *Educ* Wolverhampton Poly; *m* 1, 1951 (m dis 1996), Frances Margaret, da of Arthur Ewart Stephens (d 1971); 1 s (Stephen Adrian), 1 da (Fiona Jacquiline); m 2, 1999, Jean McKay Stevens, da of Norman McKay Fairegrieve (d 1962); *Career* Flight Lt RAFVR; group tech dir: AB Electronics Group plc 1973–91, AB Systems Ltd, AB Components Ltd, Voice Micro Systems Ltd; chm WAB 1987–90; sr assoc DME Assocs 1991–2001; Loughborough Univ: visiting prof 1977–86, external examiner 1984–88, visiting lectr 1988–96; visiting lectr Univ of Birmingham 1989–2000; chm Turnock Ltd 1998–2000; memb: Welsh Industries Bd 1982–85, Engrg Cncl 1982–86, Cncl UWIST 1983–89, NEC 1983–99, Engrg Cncl EGC2 Ctee 1988–95, USITT Bd Univ of Southampton 1988–96; chm M&D Bd IEE 1993–94 (vice-chm 1990–92), dir and memb Cncl BTEC 1993–96 (chm Engrg Advsy Ctee 1991–94); regnl chm for Wales ATC 1988–95, memb Air Cadet Cncl 1988–95; hon fell: Univ of Wolverhampton 1987, Univ of Wales Inst Cardiff 1992; Freeman City of London 1986, Liveryman Worshipful Co of Scientific Instrument Makers 1986, fndr memb Welsh Livery Guild 1992; CEng, FIET, FIMechE; *Recreations* music, archaeology, the fond remembrance of piloting and navigating aircraft; *Clubs* RAF; *Style*— Derek Embrey, Esq, OBE; ✉ 21 Rockfield Glade, Penhow, Caldicot NP26 3JF (tel and fax 01633 400995)

EMERSON, Michael Ronald; s of late James Emerson, of Wilmslow, Cheshire, and Priscilla Emerson; *b* 12 May 1940; *Educ* Hurstpierpoint Coll and Balliol Coll Oxford (MA); *m* 1966, Barbara Christine, da of late Harold Brierley; 1 s, 2 da; *Career* Price Waterhouse & Co London 1962–65; Orgn for Economic Cooperation and Devpt Paris: posts Devpt and Econs Depts, laterally head of General Economics Div 1966–73; EEC Brussels: head of Div for Budgetary Policy Directorate-Gen II 1973–76, econ advsr to President of the Commission 1977, dir for Nat Econs and Econ Trends 1978–81, dir Macroeconomic Analyses and Policy 1981–87, dir Econ Evaluation of Community Policies Directorate-Gen II EC Cmmn Brussels 1987–90, ambass and head of delgn of the EC to the Cwlth of Independent States 1991–96; fell Centre for Int Affairs Harvard Univ 1985–86; *Publications* Europe's Stagflation (ed, 1984), What Model for Europe (1987), The Economics of 1992 (1988), One Money, One Market (1990), The ECU Report (1991); contrib to various economic jls and ed of volumes on int and Euro economics; *Style*— Michael Emerson, Esq

EMERSON, Ronald Victor; s of Albert Victor Emerson, and Doris, *née* Hird; *b* 22 February 1947; *Educ* W Hartlepool GS, Univ of Manchester (BSc), Univ of Durham (MSc), Univ of Oxford (MLitt); *m* 1, 21 June 1969, Joan Margaret (d 1988), da of James Hubery Willis; 2 s (Christopher Mark b 28 May 1971, Simon Nicholas b 5 March 1975); m 2, 13 July 1996, Angela Jane, da of Dr K Stephenson; 2 s (Thomas Harry b 29 Nov 1996, William Alexander b 11 June 1998); *Career* De La Rue Gp 1970–75, commercial devpt controller Formica International; Bank of America: joined 1975, head of London corp office and UK country mangr 1985–89, head of payment servs and fin insts Europe Middle East and Africa 1989; dir and gen mangr Nomura Bank International 1989–91, regnl gen mangr UK/Europe Standard Chartered Bank 1991–94, ceo Standard Chartered Malaysia Berhad 1994–95, gp head corp banking Standard Chartered Bank 1995–96, sr advsr Bank of England 1997–98, sr advsr Fin Services Authy 1998–2000; non-exec dir Premier Oil 2001–; assoc fell Templeton Coll Oxford 2001–; FRSA; *Recreations* flying, sport, reading; *Style*— Ronald Emerson, Esq

EMERSON, Timothy John Peter; s of Col (Thomas) John Emerson, OBE, TD, DL, JP (d 2003), of Yelverton, Devon, and Rosemary Steeds, *née* White (d 1992); *b* 14 February 1942; *Educ* Kelly Coll Tavistock; *m* 9 June 1984, Susanna Jane, da of Sir Harry Evelyn Battie Rashleigh, 5 Bt (d 1984), of Stowford, Devon; 1 da (Charlotte b 9 June 1985), 1 s (Tom b 2 Sept 1987); *Career* admitted slr 1965, Notary Public; Stafford Clark London 1965–67, Heppenstalls Lyndhurst 1967–73, ptnr Foot & Bowden Plymouth 1973–99, conslt Gill Akaster Plymouth 1999–; slr to govrs Kelly Coll and Kelly Coll Prep Sch Tavistock; tstee: Lady Modiford Tst, Fortescue Garden Tst; memb: Law Soc 1965, Soc of Tst and Estate Practitioners; *Recreations* sailing, shooting, skiing, tennis; *Clubs* Royal Western Yacht; *Style*— Timothy Emerson, Esq; ✉ Coleraine, Yelverton, Devon PL20 6BN (tel 01822 852070); Gill Akaster, Scott Lodge, Milehouse, Plymouth PL2 3DD (tel 01752 512000, fax 01752 513553); Gill Akaster, 25 Lockyer Street, Plymouth PL1 2QW (tel 01752 203500, fax 01752 203503)

EMERTON, Baroness (Life Peer UK 1997), of Tunbridge Wells, in the County of Kent and of Clerkenwell in the London Borough of Islington; Dame Audrey Caroline Emerton; DBE (1989), DL (Kent 1992); da of George William Emerton (d 1971), of Tunbridge Wells, Kent, and Lily Harriet, *née* Squirrell; *b* 10 September 1935; *Educ* Tunbridge Wells GS, Battersea Coll of Technol; *Career* SRN 1956; sr tutor St George's Hosp London 1968, princ nursing offr teaching Bromley HMC 1968–70, chief nursing offr Tunbridge Wells and Leybourne HMC 1970–73, regnl nursing offr SE Thames RHA 1973–91; chief nursing offr St John Ambulance 1988–96 (co nursing offr 1970–84, Kent co cmmr 1984–88), chief offr Care in the Community 1996–98 (chief cdr 1998–2002); chm: Eng Nat Bd for Nurses Midwives and Health Visitors 1983–85, UK Central Cncl Nursing Midwives and Health Visitors 1985–93, Nurses Welfare Service 1992–98, Brighton Health Care NHS Trust 1994–2000, Nat Assoc of Hosp and Community Friends 2003–06; tstee: Kent Community Housing Tst 1992–98, Defence Med Welfare Serv 2001–, Burdett Nursing Tst 2002–04; lay memb GMC 1996–2001; pres Florence Nightingale Fndn 2004–; Hon DCL Univ of Kent 1989, Hon DUniv Central England 1997, Hon DSc Univ of Brighton 1997, Hon DSc Kingston Univ; hon fell Christ Church UC Canterbury 2003; memb RCN; FRSA; DGCStJ 2004 (DStJ 1993); *Style*— The Rt Hon Baroness Emerton, DBE, DL; ✉ Carlton House, 3 Strettitt Gardens, East Peckham, Tonbridge, Kent TN12 5ES; House of Lords, London SW1A 0PW

EMERTON, Rev Prof John Adney; s of Adney Spencer Emerton (d 1969), of Southgate, and Helena Mary, *née* Quin (d 1964); *b* 5 June 1928; *Educ* Minchenden GS Southgate, Corpus Christi Coll Oxford, Wycliffe Hall Oxford (BA, MA), Univ of Cambridge (MA, BD, DD); *m* 14 Aug 1954, Norma Elizabeth, da of Norman Bennington (d 1986); 2 da (Caroline Mary b 1958, Lucy Anne b 1966), 1 s (Mark Simon, *qv*, b 1961); *Career* ordained: deacon 1952, priest 1953; curate Birmingham Cathedral 1952–53, asst lectr in theology Univ of Birmingham 1952–53, lectr in Hebrew and Aramaic Univ of Durham 1953–55, lectr in divinity Univ of Cambridge 1955–62, visiting prof of Old Testament and Near Eastern studies Trinity Coll Toronto 1960, reader in Semitic philology Univ of Oxford 1962–68, fell St Peter's Coll Oxford 1962–68, regius prof of Hebrew Univ of Cambridge 1968–95 (emeritus prof 1995–), fell St John's Coll Cambridge 1970–; visiting fell Inst for Advanced Studies Hebrew Univ of Jerusalem 1983, visiting prof of Old Testament United Theol Coll Bangalore 1986, corresponding memb Göttingen Akademie der Wissenschaften 1990; ed Vetus Testamentum 1976–97; pres: Soc for Old Testament Study 1979 (memb 1952–), Int Orgn for the Study of the Old Testament 1992–95 (sec 1971–89); hon canon St George's Cathedral Jerusalem 1984–; Hon DD Univ of Edinburgh 1977, Burkitt medal for Biblical Studies British Acad 1991; FBA 1979; *Books* The Peshitta of the Wisdom of Solomon (1959), The Old Testament in Syriac - the Song of Songs (1966); *Style*— The Rev Prof John Emerton; ✉ 34 Gough Way, Cambridge CB3 9LN; St John's College, Cambridge CB2 1TP

EMERTON, Mark Simon; s of Rev Prof John Emerton, *qv*, of Cambridge, and Dr Norma Emerton, *née* Bennington; *b* 26 February 1961; *Educ* Perse Sch Cambridge, BRNC Dartmouth, St Peter's Coll Oxford (MA), City Univ (Dip), Univ of Portsmouth (LLM); *m* 16 July 1994, Hannah Kate, da of Martin Buckley, of Rudgwick, W Sussex; 3 da (Rebecca b 23 Sept 1997, Susanna b 24 Aug 1999, Martha b 7 April 2001); *Career* RN: joined 1979, various appts as supply offr and naval barr incl Supply Offr HMS Brilliant 1992–93, judge advocate at Naval Courts-Martial 1997–2002, dep chief naval judge advocate 1997–98, judge advocate Summary Appeal Court 2000–02, ret as Cdr; called to the Bar Gray's Inn 1991; cmmr Criminal Cases Review Cmmn 2002–; pt/t appts: parking adjudicator 2000–, immigration judge 2000–, chm Employment Tbnl 2000–, legal assessor to GMC 2002–; memb: Barrs Ctee Gray's Inn 2001–, Remuneration Ctee Bar Cncl 2003, Employed Barrs Ctee Bar Cncl 2004–; ind bd memb Office of the Ind Adjudicator for HE 2004–, ind scrutiny panel memb UK Sport Nat Anti-Doping Organisation 2005–; govr RNLI 1994– (branch ctee memb 1996–2007); govr Solent Infant Sch 2003–07; FRGS 1984, FCMI 2004 (MIMgt 1995); *Publications* Manual of Naval Law (ed, 1997), Halsbury's Laws of England (contrib, 4 edn 2003); *Recreations* family, theatre and the arts, conservation of the natural and built environment, travel, boats; *Clubs* Naval and Military; *Style*— Mark Emerton, Esq; ✉ The Criminal Cases Review Commission, Alpha Tower, Suffolk Street Queensway, Birmingham B1 1TT (tel 0121 633 1800, fax 0121 633 1804, e-mail mark.emerton@ccrc.x.gsi.gov.uk)

EMERY, Prof Alan Eglin Heathcote; s of Harold Heathcote-Emery (d 1977), and Alice, *née* Eglin (d 1972); *b* 21 August 1928; *Educ* Chester Coll, Univ of Manchester (BSc, MSc, MB ChB, MD, DSc), Johns Hopkins Univ USA (PhD); *m* 13 Oct 1988, Marcia Lynn, da of John Miller (d 1986), of Cleveland, USA; *Career* Nat Serv 14/20 Kings Hussars 1945–47; conslt physician 1966–; emeritus prof and hon fell Univ of Edinburgh 1983– (prof of human genetics 1968–83), hon visiting fell Green Coll Oxford 1986–2006 (hon fell 2006–), res dir and chm Euro Neuromuscular Center 1990–99 (chief scientific advsr 1999–), hon prof Peninsula Med Sch Exeter 2006–; foreign assoc RSS Africa; vice-pres Muscular Dystrophy Gp of GB 1999–; memb: Exec Ctee World Fedn Neurology 1994–2002, RSL; advsr Asian Myology Centre Tokyo 2000–; pres Medical Genetics section RSM 2002–04; author of various articles in learned scientific and medical jls; various professorships, lectureships and awards incl Nat Fndn Int Award (USA), Pro Finlandiae Gold Medal, Conte Prize (Italy) 2000, Association Francaise Contre Les Myopathies Prize 2001, Lifetime Achievement Award World Fedn of Neurology 2002; Hon MD: Univ of Naples, Univ of Würzburg; hon memb Gaetano Conte Acad (Italy); emeritus fell American Coll of Med Genetics; hon fell: Assoc Br Neurology, Netherlands Genetic Soc, Brazilian Muscular Dystrophy Assoc; FRCPEd 1970, FRSE 1972, FLS 1985, FRCP, FRSA, Hon FRSM; *Books* 20 books incl: Duchenne Muscular Dystrophy (3 edn 2003), Muscular Dystrophy - The Facts (2 edn 2000), The History of a History of a Genetic Disease (1995), Diagnostic Criteria for Neuromuscular Disorders (2 edn 1997), Neuromuscular Disorders: Clinical and Molecular Genetics (1998), The Muscular Dystrophies (2001), Medicine and Art (2003), Surgical and Medical Treatment in Art (2006), Mother and Child Care in Art (2007); *Recreations* oil painting, marine biology, fly fishing; *Style—* Prof Alan Emery, FRSE; ✉ 2 Ingleside Court, Budleigh Salterton, Devon EX9 6NZ (tel 01395 445847, fax 01395 443855); Green College, Oxford OX2 6HG

EMERY, Prof Paul; s of Lt Cdr Dr Leonard Lesley Emery RNVR, of Cardiff, and Beryl Olive, *née* Davis; *b* 30 November 1952; *Educ* Cardiff HS, Churchill Coll Cambridge (MB BChir, MA, MD), Guy's Hosp; *m* 19 July 1980, Shirley Macdonald, da of Sub Lt David Morton Bayne RNVR; 2 da (Lorna Megan b 25 Oct 1987, Joanna Louise b 17 March 1989); *Career* SHO Guy's Hosp Brompton, subsequently med registrar Guy's Hosp Lewisham 1980–83, sr registrar Guy's Hosp 1983–85, head of rheumatology Walter Eliza Hall and asst physician Royal Melbourne Hosp 1985–88, conslt and sr lectr Dept of Rheumatology Univ of Birmingham 1988–95, ARC prof of rheumatology Univ of Leeds 1995– (head Academic Unit of Musculoskeletal Disease); memb: Br Soc of Rheumatology, Br Soc of Immunology, BMA; FRCP 1992 (MRCP 1979); *Books* incl: The Role of Cytokines in Rheumatological Inflammation Autoimmunregation and Autoimmune Disease (jtly, 1987), Local Injection Therapy in Rheumatic Diseases (jtly, 1992), Management of Early Inflammatory Arthritis (ed, 1992), Clinical Rheumatology International Practice and Research (ed and contrib, 1992), Visual Diagnosis Self-Tests in Rheumatology (jtly, 1996, 2 edn 2001), What is Early Rheumatoid Arthritis? Definition and Diagnosis (jtly, 1997), Treatment of Rheumatoid Arthritis: New Drugs, New Hopes (1999), Rheumatology Highlights 1998–99 (jtly, 1999), How to Manage Rheumatoid Arthritis - A Quick Reference Guide (1999, 3 edn 2001), Lupus and the Joints - A GP Guide to Diagnosis (jtly, 2000), The Future of Cox-2 Inhibitors (jtly, 2001), Clinician's Manual on Cox-2 Inhibition and Arthritis (jtly, 2001), Rheumatology and the Kidney (jtly, 2001); also contrib numerous chapters to medical textbooks, author of more than 500 peer-reviewed papers; *Recreations* golf, squash; *Clubs* Pannal Golf; *Style—* Prof Paul Emery; ✉ Academic Unit of Musculoskeletal Disease, Second Floor, Chapel Allerton Hospital, Chapel Town Road, Leeds LS7 4SA (tel 0113 392 4884)

EMERY, Prof Vincent Clive; s of Ronald Emery (d 1985), and Doreen, *née* Tarr; *b* 9 May 1960, Hemel Hempstead, Herts; *Educ* Surbiton GS, Univ of Southampton (BSc, PhD); *m* 14 Sept 1991, Sarah Ann, *née* Stephens; 1 s (Timothy Simon b 16 Feb 1995); *Career* post-doctoral fell NERC Inst of Virology Univ of Oxford 1985–88; Royal Free Hosp Sch of Med: lectr in virology 1988–92, sr lectr in virology 1992–96, reader in virology 1996–2000; UCL: prof of virology 2000–, vice-head Grad Sch 2004–, pro-provost (S Asia and the Middle East) 2005–; memb Biochemistry and Cell Biology Ctee BBSRC, memb Advsy Panel Assoc of Cwlth Univs; Nat Physical Lab Prize for Measurement 1992; over 150 peer-reviewed pubns in jls and text books on virology; *Recreations* playing the piano and organ, bell ringing; *Clubs* Medical Research Club (sec 1997–2001), City Glee Club (pres 2003–05); *Style—* Prof Vincent Emery; ✉ Department of Infection, University College London, Rowland Hill Street, London NW3 2QG (tel 020 7830 2997, fax 020 7830 2854, e-mail v.emery@ucl.ac.uk)

EMIN, Tracey; *Educ* Maidstone Coll of Art (BA), Royal Coll of Art; *Career* artist; set designer Les Parents Terribles (Jermyn Street Theatre) 2004; *Solo Exhibitions* incl: The Shop (103 Bethnal Green Road London, with Sarah Lucas) 1993, My Major Retrospective (Jay Jopling/White Cube London) 1993, Exploration of the Soul - Journey Across America (tour) 1994, Tracey Emin Museum (221 Waterloo Road London) 1995–1998, Exorcism of the Last Painting I Ever Made (Galleri Andreas Brändström Stockholm) 1996, Istanbul Biennial (performance at Pera Palace Hotel Turkey) 1997, I Need Art Like I Need God (South London Gallery London, Gestellschaft für Aktuelle Kunst Bremen) 1997–1998, Sobasex (My Cunt is Wet With Fear) (Sagacho Exhibition Space Tokyo) 1998, Tracey Emin Every Part of Me is Bleeding (Lehmann Maupin NY) 1999, What do you Know About Love (Galerie Gebauer Berlin) 2000, Tracey Emin You Forgot To Kiss My Soul (White Cube London) 2001, I Think it's in my head (Lehmann Maupin Gall NY) 2002, Ten Years Tracey Emin (Stedelijk Muesum Amsterdam) 2002, Tracey Emin (Art Gall of NSW Aust) 2003, Menphis (Counter Gallery London) 2003, I'll Meet You in Heaven (Lorcan O'Neill Rome) 2004, Can't See Past My Own Eyes (Sketch London) 2004, Fear, War And The Scream (Roslyn Oxley Sydney/ City Gallery Wellington) 2004, Tracey Emin (BP British Art Displays Tate Britain) 2004, Tracey Istanbulda (Platform Garanti Contemporary Art Center Istanbul) 2004, Tracey Emin Monoprints (Museo de Ballas Artes Santiago) 2004, Death Mask (Nat Portrait Gallery) 2005, When I Think About Sex... (White Cube) 2005; *Group Exhibitions* incl: Sensation (Royal Acad of Arts London) 1997, Art from the UK: Angela Bulloch, Willie Doherty, Tracey Emin, Sarah Lucas, Sam Taylor-Wood (Sammlung Goetz, Munich) 1998, Turner Prize (Tate Gallery London) 1999, Art in Sacred Spaces (St. Mary's Church Islington London) 2000, Out There (White Cube Hoxton Square London) 2000, Peter Blake: About Collage (Tate Gallery London) 2000, Summer Exhibition (Royal Acad of Arts London) 2001, and 2004, A Bigger Splash: British Art from the Tate 1960–2003 (Pavilhão Lucas Nogueira Garcez São Paulo) 2003, Einleuchten (Museum der Moderne Salzburg) 2004, Critic's Choice (FACT Liverpool) 2005, 25 Twenty Five Years of the Deutsche Bank Collection (Duetsche Guggenheim Berlin) 2005, Body: New Art from the UK (Vancouver Art Gallery) 2005; *Works in Collections* incl: Arts Cncl of Br, Br Museum London, Museum of Contemporary Art San Diego, Pompidou Centre Paris, Saatchi Collection London, Tate Gallery London, Scottish Nat Gallery Edinburgh, Art Gall of NSW Sydney, Deutsche Bank, National Portrait Gall London, San Francisco MOMA, Guggenheim Museum NY, an Francisco MOMA, Stedelijk Museum Amsterdam; *Awards* Int Award for Video Art Baden-Baden 1997, Video Art Prize Südwest Bank Stuttgart 1997, Turner Prize nominee 1997, The Jury Prize Cairo Biennale Award 2001; RA 2007; *Publications* Strangeland (2005); *Style—* Ms Tracey Emin; ✉ c/o White Cube, 44 Duke Street, St James's, London SW1Y 6DD (tel 020 7930 5373, fax 020 7930 9973)

EMLEY, Miles Lovelace Brereton; s of Col Derek Brereton Emley, OBE, of Sturminster Newton, Dorset, and Mary Georgina, *née* Lovelace (d 1996); *b* 23 July 1949; *Educ* St Edward's Sch Oxford, Balliol Coll Oxford (MA); *m* 26 June 1976, Tessa Marcia Radclyffe, da of Radclyffe Edward Crichton Powell, MBE (d 1985); 2 s (Oliver b 1978, Alexander b 1982), 1 da (Katherine b 1980); *Career* dir: N M Rothschild & Sons Ltd 1982–89 (joined 1972), Virago Press Ltd 1988–90; md UBS Phillips & Drew Securities Ltd 1989–92, chm St Ives plc 1993– (dep chm 1992–93), dir Marston's plc (formerly Wolverhampton & Dudley Breweries plc) 1998–; Liveryman Worshipful Co of Leathersellers 1979; *Style—* Miles Emley, Esq; ✉ Whitehall House, Ashford Hill, Thatcham, Berkshire RG19 8AZ (tel 01635 268306); St Ives plc, St Ives House, Lavington Street, London SE1 0NX (tel 020 7928 8844)

EMLY, John Richard Keith; s of Charles Richard Lewis Emly (d 1975), of London, and Lillian Villette, *née* Jenner (d 1971); *b* 15 September 1941; *Educ* St Dunstan's Coll Catford; *m* 26 July 1969, Maria Joan, da of Frederic Jozef Jan Gumosz (d 1964), of Catford; 2 da (Gillian b 1972, Sarah b 1974), 2 s (Timothy b 1978, Benjamin b 1980); *Career* jt investment mangr The Law Debenture Corp Ltd 1971–75 (joined 1960), dir Robert Fleming Investment Management Ltd 1978–88, main bd dir Robert Fleming Holdings Ltd 1985–98 (joined 1975); dir: Fleming Investment Management Ltd 1988–2000, Fleming Income and Capital Investment Trust plc 1993–98, JP Morgan Mid-Cap Investment Trust plc 1996–, Robert Fleming Asset Management Ltd 1998–2000, F&C Income Growth Investment Trust plc 2001–05, F&C Capital and Income Investment Trust plc 2005–; investment dir CAA Pension Scheme 2000–; non-exec dir: Hemingway Properties plc 1995–99, Shaftesbury plc 2000–; memb Investment Ctee: P&O Pension Scheme 2003–, Balfour Beatty Pension Scheme 2003–; hon treas Scout Assoc 1996–2003; FRICS 1972, AIIMR, MSI; *Recreations* family life; *Style—* John Emly, Esq; ✉ The Civil Aviation Authority Pension Scheme, CAA House, London WC2B 6TE (tel 020 7453 6742)

EMMERSON, Ian Robert; OBE (1994); s of late Robert Leslie Emmerson, of Lincoln, and late Ida Kathleen, *née* Marshall; *b* 18 February 1944; *Educ* City GS Lincoln; *m* 23 Nov 1968, Sheila Margaret, da of Ernest Raymond (Dick) Barber (d 1968); 2 s (Nathan Robert b 1972, Richard Ian b 1974); *Career* GPO 1960–83 (asst exec engr BT), dir Impsport 1983–2003; chm Cwlth Games Cncl for Eng 1999–2007 (currently vice-pres), dir Manchester Cwlth Games Ltd, vice-pres Europe Cwlth Games Fedn; pres Br Cycling Fedn 1985–95, vice-pres Union Cycliste Internationale 1993–97; pres UCI Masters Cmmn 1993–2005; chm Velo Club Lincoln 1964–95, chm Lincs County Sports Partnership; Sheriff of Lincoln 1990–91; *Recreations* cycling, photography, travel; *Style—* Ian Emmerson, Esq, OBE; ✉ 5 Larkin Avenue, Cherry Willingham, Lincoln LN3 4AZ (tel 01522 750000, e-mail ian.emmerson@ntlworld.com)

EMMERSON, Prof (Alfred) Michael; OBE (1999); s of William Emmerson, and Elsie, *née* Barratt; *b* 17 October 1937; *Educ* UCH Med Sch (BSc, MB BS); *m* 30 April 1966, Elizabeth Barbara Mary, da of Dr John Lawn (decd), of Binbrook, Lincs; 1 da (Catherine b 8 Jan 1971), 1 s (Mark b 29 Sept 1972); *Career* Nat Serv class 1 mechanical engr and decoder RN 1957–59; trainee microbiologist UCH London 1966–73 (house offr 1965–66), conslt microbiologist Whittington Hosp London 1973–84, prof of clinical microbiology Royal Victoria Hosp Queen's Univ Belfast 1984–89, prof and head of dept Univ of Leicester 1989–91, prof and head Dept of Microbiology Univ Hosp Nottingham 1991–2000; pres Hosp Infection Soc UK 2002–, past pres Assoc of Medical Microbiologists; former chm: Microbiology Advsy Ctee MDA London, Central Sterilising Club; former chm: Br Standards Instn HCC/67 and CEN/TC 204, Specialist Advsy Ctee (microbiology) CPA (Accreditation) UK; memb Assoc of Professors in Med Microbiology; former memb PHLS Bd; Liveryman Worshipful Soc of Apothecaries 1975; MRCS, FRCP (LRCP), FRCP(G), FRCPath (memb Cncl 1996–99), FMedSci, Hon DipHIC; *Books* The Microbiology and Treatment of Life Threatening Infections (1982), Surveillance of Nosocomial Infections (1996), Principles of Practice of Clinical Bacteriology (1997); *Recreations* rugby, long distance running, vintage cars, gardening; *Clubs* Rugby Football; *Style—* Prof Michael Emmerson, OBE; ✉ 92 Southwood Lane, Highgate, London N6 55Y (tel 020 8341 7443, fax 020 874 6113)

EMMERSON, Robert Frank; s of Harold Claude Emmerson (d 1993), and Gladys Amy, *née* Gautrey (d 1991); *b* 5 October 1938; *Educ* Perse Sch Cambridge, Trinity Coll Cambridge (MA); *m* 26 April 1962, Anne, *née* Crabtree; 1 da (Nancy Victoria b 11 June 1970), 1 s (John Philip b 23 Feb 1972); *Career* project engr W J Lemessurier Cambridge MA 1965–67; Ove Arup & Partners: project and gp engr 1960–65 and 1967–77, dir 1977; Arup Gp: gp bd dir 1984, tstee dir 1995–, dep chm 1995–2000, chm 2000–04; projects supervised as design gp ldr incl: Bracken House London, Royal Mint Devpt London, HQ for Trustees Savings Bank Edinburgh, Fitzwilliam Coll Cambridge, John Lewis Dept Store Kingston, Patscenter Princeton, Derngate Theatre Northampton, Dental Teaching Hosp Hong Kong, ROH London, Glyndebourne Theatre, Millennium Bridge London; projects supervised as project engr incl: Inst of Educn and Law Univ of London, SOAS Univ of London, Christ's Coll Cambridge, Colby Coll ME, Newport Jazz Festival RI, Adult Educn Centre NH; projects as structual engr incl: Queen Elizabeth Hall London (as project engr), Hayward Gall London (as project engr), Sydney Opera House; dir Ove Arup Fndn 1995–; memb Exec Ctee Assoc Parly Engrg Gp, industrial advsr Churchill Coll Cambridge; tstee Architectural Assoc Fndn; author of numerous articles in professional pubns and jls; MCIBSE, FREng, FICE, FRSA; *Recreations* skiing, golf, art; *Clubs* Coombe Hill Golf; *Style—* Robert Emmerson, Esq; ✉ Arup Group Ltd, 13 Fitzroy Street, London W1T 4BQ (tel 020 7755 3373, fax 020 7755 3666, e-mail bob.emmerson@arup.com)

EMMETT, Robert; *Educ* UK and Switzerland; *Career* fashion designer; clothes and material design Geneva, moulage and further design Paris, opened London shop 1992; *Style—* Robert Emmett, Esq

EMMOTT, William (Bill); *b* 1956; *Educ* Magdalen Coll Oxford; *Career* The Economist: Brussels corr 1980–82, dep economics writer 1982–83, Tokyo corr 1983–86, fin ed 1986–89, business affairs ed 1989–93, ed 1993–2006; memb Exec Ctee Trilateral Cmmn 1998–; Hon LLD Univ of Warwick 1999, Hon DLitt City Univ 2001; hon fell Magdalen Coll Oxford; *Books* The Pocket Economist (1983), The Sun Also Sets (1989), Japan's Global Reach (1993), 20:21 Vision (2003); *Style—* Bill Emmott, Esq; ✉ The Economist, 25 St James's Street, London SW1A 1HG

EMMS, Gail Elizabeth; da of Anthony Charles Emms, of Bedford, and Janice Dorothy Barnes, *née* Barton; *b* 23 July 1977, Hitchin, Herts; *Educ* Dame Alice Harpur Sch Bedford, Kingston Univ (BSc); *Career* badminton player; achievements incl: winner women's doubles USA Open 2000, winner mixed doubles Dutch Open 2001, winner BMW Open 2001, winner mixed doubles Malaysia Open 2002, team Gold medal and Bronze medal women's doubles Cwlth Games 2002, Gold medal mixed doubles European Championships 2004, winner mixed doubles Thailand Open 2004, Silver medal mixed doubles Olympic Games Athens 2004, winner mixed doubles All-England Championships 2005, winner mixed doubles China Open 2005, Gold medal ladies doubles European Championships 2006, Gold medal mixed doubles, Silver medal team event and Bronze medal ladies doubles Cwlth Games Melbourne 2006, winner mixed doubles World Championships Madrid 2006; *Style—* Miss Gail Emms; ✉ c/o Professional Sports Group, The Town House, 63 High Street, Chobham, Surrey GU24 8AF (tel 01276 858930, fax 01276 856974)

EMSLEY, Kenneth; s of Clifford Briggs Emsley, and Lily, *née* Goldsborough; *b* 7 December 1921; *Educ* Bingley GS, Loughborough Coll, St John's Coll Cambridge (MA), Univ of Newcastle upon Tyne (LLM); *m* 1, 14 May 1959, Nancy Audrey (d 1997), da of Alfred Ernest Slee; m 2, 11 Feb 2006, Destiny May, da of Joseph Briggs (d 1953); *Career* served WWII; chm Smith & Hardcastle Ltd 1955–65; painter of watercolour drawings and miniature paintings, author of books and articles, lectr in law, ret 1980; sr visiting scholar St Edmund's Coll Cambridge 1977–78, guest memb Law Faculty Univ of Newcastle upon Tyne 1978–79, hon research fell Univ of Bradford 1992–2003; pres: The Br Watercolour Soc, The Bradford Arts Club until 1985 (former chm), The Br Soc of Miniaturists 1985–; memb: Cncl Yorks Archaeological Soc Leeds, Brontë Soc; hon sec Wakefield Manorial Court Rolls Series; FRSA 1945, ACIS 1970, MSEng 1948, FRHistS 1989, FRGS 1989;

Books Tyneside (with C M Fraser, 1973), Northumbria (with C M Fraser, 1979, rewritten 1989), The Courts of the County Palatine of Durham (1984), Wakefield Manorial Court Rolls (with C M Fraser, vol 1 1979 and vol 5 1987), Historical Introduction of Durham Quarter Sessions Rolls 1471–1625 (Surtees Soc, vol 199), Historic Haworth Today (1995); also numerous articles on local and legal history; *Recreations* formerly cricket, rugby, tennis; now bowls, art and music; *Clubs* The Bradford, Bradford and Bingley Sports (fndr memb), Cambridge Union, Cambridge Univ Cricket; *Style*— Kenneth Emsley, Esq; ✉ 34 Nab Wood Drive, Shipley, West Yorkshire BD18 4EL; The Yorkshire Archaeological Society, Claremont, Clarendon Road, Leeds LS2 9NZ

EMSLIE, Donald; *m* 1; 2 da (Sarah, Jenny); m 2, Sarah; *Career* Scottish TV (now part of SMG plc): joined 1985, commercial dir 1994, md Broadcasting Div 1997, chief exec SMG Television 1999–2007, memb Bd SMG plc 1999–2007; chm: Cncl ITV, Bd GMTV 2002–04; memb Bd: Scottish Screen, Skillset UK (chm Scottish Industry Skills Panel Skillset Scotland), Film Acad Scotland (chm Advsy Bd); chm Royal Lyceum Theatre Co; FRTS (vice-pres); *Recreations* golf; *Style*— Donald Emslie, Esq

EMSLIE, Hon Lord; (George) Nigel Hannington Emslie; eldest s of Baron Emslie, MBE, PC (Life Peer, d 2002); bro of Rt Hon Lord Kingarth, and Dr the Hon Richard Emslie, *qqv*; *b* 1947; *Educ* Edinburgh Acad, Trinity Coll Glenalmond, Gonville & Caius Coll Cambridge (BA), Univ of Edinburgh (LLB); *m* 1973, Heather Ann, da of late Arthur Frank Davis, of Bristol; 1 s, 2 da; *Career* advocate; admitted Faculty of Advocates 1972, QC (Scot) 1986, Dean of the Faculty of Advocates 1997–2001, senator Coll of Justice (Lord of Session) 2001–; *Style*— The Hon Lord Emslie; ✉ Parliament House, Edinburgh EH1 1RQ

EMSLIE, Dr the Hon Richard Hannington; 3 and yst s of The Rt Hon Lord Emslie, MBE, PC, FRSE (d 2002); bro of Hon Nigel Hannington Emslie (Hon Lord Emslie) and Rt Hon Lord Kingarth, *qqv*; *b* 28 July 1957; *Educ* Edinburgh Acad, Trinity Coll Glenalmond, Gonville & Caius Coll Cambridge (MA), Univ of Stellenbosch (PhD); *Partner* Keryn Adcock; *Career* wildlife biologist, res into applied white rhino grazing ecology and black rhino browsing ecology and mgmnt in Hluhluwe-iMfolozi Park Zululand South Africa; conslt ecologist incl conservation of the black and white rhino; author and developer of Bayesian Mark-Recapture population estimation statistical software package (Rhino); scientific/prog offr IUCN/Species Survival Cmmn African Rhino Specialist Gp; memb IUCN SSC Asian Rhino Specialist Gp, SADC Rhino and Elephant Security Gp, IUCN SSC Species Conservation Action Planning Task Force; elected expert Southern African Rhino Mgmnt Gp, consortium memb Southern African Devpt Community (SADC) regnl rhino conservation prog 1999–2006; sole prop Ecoscot Consultancy Services; memb SA Statistical Assoc; fell Darwin Initiative 2003–06; *Recreations* football, golf, cricket, jogging, gardening, cooking, listening to music, bird-watching; *Clubs* Sakabula Golf, Rampant Rhinos (cricket), Hilton Harriers (running); *Style*— Dr the Hon Richard Emslie; ✉ PO Box 1212 Hilton, Kwa-Zulu Natal 3245, South Africa (tel 00 27 33 3434065, e-mail kerynric@absamail.co.za)

EMSON, Colin Jack; s of Alfred Jack Emson (d 2002), of Ashford, Kent, and Rose Florence Jobson (d 1987); *b* 25 July 1941; *Educ* Maidstone GS; *m* 14 Sept 1974, Jennifer Claire, da of Lt-Col James Lynch, of Vancouver, Canada; 2 da (Annabel Christina b 1975, Camilla Rose b 1985), 2 s (Alexander Chase b 1976, Henry James b 1980); *Career* fndr ptnr Emson & Dudley 1966–79; chm: Robert Fraser & Partners Ltd (investment and finance gp) 1979–, Sterling Trust Ltd (investment holding company) 1988–, Number Eleven Ltd 1995–; *Recreations* polo, skiing, tennis, tobogganing; *Clubs* Turf, Cowdray Park Polo, St Moritz Toboggan; *Style*— Colin Emson, Esq; ✉ Shotters Farm, Newton Valence, nr Alton, Hampshire GU34 3RJ

ENDACOTT, Charles George; s of John Kinsman Endacott, of London, and Rita, *née* Ellul; *b* 24 September 1950; *Educ* St John's Coll Southsea; *m* 1973 (m dis 1983), Hazel, *née* Short; 1 da (Natalie b 1 Aug 1979); *Career* messenger E Allan Cooper Advertising 1967–68, studio jr J L Lakings Studio 1968–69, jr designer SF & Partner Advertising 1969–70, freelance designer and visualiser 1970–71, sole proprietor RJB Associates (design and promotions conslts) 1976–83 (fndr ptnr 1971–76), chm RJB Manpower Ltd 1979–83, md Endacott RJB Ltd 1983–89; chm RJB Group Ltd (chm/md various subsids) 1989–; dir: Pristine Products Ltd 1991–, Computer Professionals (UK) Ltd 1992–, Endacott Corner Ltd 2001–, Green Media Ltd 2003–; charity tstee Marketing Services UK - 'Promoting for Children' 1995; memb Inst of Sales Promotion; Liveryman Worshipful Co of Marketors; *Recreations* tennis, classic cars, riding, scuba, golf; *Clubs* David Lloyd, Hazelwood Golf; *Style*— Charles Endacott, Esq; ✉ Endacott Marketing Ltd, Cambridge House, Cambridge Grove, Hammersmith, London W6 0LE (tel 020 8563 0006, fax 020 8563 2889, car 07801 223082, e-mail charles@endacottmarketing.com)

ENDERBY, (Samuel) Charles; JP (1991); s of Col Samuel Enderby, DSO, MC (d 1997) and Pamela Innocence Enderby; *b* 18 September 1939; *Educ* Sandroyd Sch, Wellington, RMA Sandhurst; *m* 1973 Mary Justina, da of PW Compton, DSC; 2 da (Amelia b 1974, Verena b 1977); *Career* cmmnd 12 Royal Lancers 1959, served with 9/12 Royal Lancers 1960–84; HM The Queen's Body Guard of Yeoman of the Guard: Exon 1987, Ensign 2002, Clerk of the Cheque 2005, Lt 2006; chm Hexham Steeplechase Co Ltd 1997– (dir 1985–); High Sheriff Northumberland 2000–; *Recreations* shooting, ornithology, gardening, reading; *Clubs* Army and Navy, Pratt's; *Style*— Charles Enderby, Esq

ENFIELD, Henry Richard (Harry); s of Edward Enfield and Deirdre Enfield, of Billingshurst, W Sussex; *b* 30 May 1961; *Educ* Worth Abbey, Univ of York; *m* 22 Feb 1997, Lucy Caroline, yr da of Rae Lyster, of Layer de la Haye, Essex; *Career* writer, actor and comedian; began performing whilst at York Univ, toured UK (incl London and Edinburgh Festival) with fringe show Dusty and Dick 1983, reg appearances on Spitting Image (Channel 4) 1984 and Saturday Night Live (Channel 4, creating characters incl Stavros and Loadsamoney) 1986, writer and actor Sir Norbert Smith... A Life? (Channel 4) 1989 (Gold Rockie Banff Awards 1989, Silver Rose of Montreux 1990, Int Emmy for Popular Arts Progs 1991), own series Harry Enfield's Television Programme (BBC 2) 1990 and 1992, Men Behaving Badly (Thames) 1992, Gone to the Dogs (Central) 1993, Harry Enfield's Guide to Opera (Channel 4) 1993, Harry Enfield and Chums (BBC 1) 1994 and 1996 (Best Entertainment Series Writers Guild Awards 1995, Best Entertainment Prog RTS Awards 1997, Silver Rose of Montreux 1998), Smashie and Nicey... The End of an Era (BBC 2) 1994 (Silver Rose of Montreux 1995), Harry Enfield & Chums Christmas Special 1997, Norman Ormal (BBC) 1998, Harry Enfield's Yule Log Chums (BBC) 1998, Sermon from St Albions (Granada) 1999, Sermon from St Albions (Granada) 1999, Harry Enfield Presents Kevin's Guide to Being a Teenager (Tiger Aspect) 1999, Harry Enfield's Real Kevins (Tiger Aspect) 2000, Harry Enfield's Brand Spanking New Show (Sky One) 2000 (Satellite and Digital TV Programme of the Year Television and Radio Industry Awards 2001), Harry Enfield Presents Tim-Nice-But-Dim's Guide to Being a Bloody Nice Bloke (BBC 1) 2001, Harry Enfield Presents Wayne & Waynetta's Guide to Wedded Bliss (BBC1) 2001, We Know Where You Live (Channel 4) 2001, Celeb (BBC 1) 2002, Peter Cook Foundation Benefit Show (BBC 2) 2002; film: Kevin & Perry Go Large 1999 (Best Comedy Film Quality Street Awards 2001), Churchill: The Hollywood Years 2003, Tooth 2004; video: Harry Enfield Undressed (1997), The New Harry Enfield & Chums Video (1998), More Harry Enfield and Chums (2000); guest Desert Island Discs (BBC Radio 4) 1997; *Books* Harry Enfield and His Humorous Chums (1997), Kevin & Perry Go Large (novel based on a screenplay written with Dave Cummings, 2000), Havin' it Large - Kevin & Perry's Guide to Looking Cool and Getting Girls (2000); *Style*— Harry Enfield, Esq; ✉ c/o PBJ Management Ltd, 7 Soho Street, London W1D 3DQ (tel 020 7287 1112, fax 020 7287 1191, e-mail general@pbjmgt.co.uk, website www.pbjmgt.co.uk)

ENGEL, Matthew Lewis; s of Max David Engel, of Northampton (d 2005), and Betty Ruth, *née* Lesser (d 1998); *b* 11 June 1951; *Educ* Carmel Coll, Univ of Manchester (BA); *m* 27 Oct 1990, Hilary, da of late Laurence Davies; 1 s (Laurence Gabriel b 28 May 1992 d 2005), 1 da (Victoria Betty b 26 May 1998); *Career* reporter: Northampton Chronicle and Echo 1972–75, Reuters 1977–79; The Guardian: joined 1979, cricket corr 1982–87, feature writer, sports columnist and occasional political, foreign and war corr 1987–98, columnist 1998–2003, Washington corr 2001–03; columnist Financial Times 2004–; ed Wisden Cricketers' Almanack 1993–2000 and 2004–07; Granada Sportswriter of the Year 1985, Sports Journalist of the Year Br Press Awards 1992, shortlisted Reporter of the Year Br Press Awards 1998; *Books include* Ashes '85 (1985), The Guardian Book of Cricket (ed, 1986), Sportswriter's Eye (1989), The Sportspages Almanac (ed, 1989, 1990, 1991), Tickle The Public: a hundred years of popular newspapers (1996), Extracts from the Red Notebooks (2007), Eleven Minutes Late (2008); *Recreations* wistful thinking; *Clubs* Northamptonshire CCC (vice-pres), Nothing Writers' Dining, Cricket Writers'; *Style*— Matthew Engel, Esq; ✉ Fair Oak, Bacton, Herefordshire HR2 0AT

E

ENGEL, Natascha; MP; *b* 9 April 1967; *Career* MP (Lab) NE Derbyshire 2005–; political fund ballot co-ordinator Trade Union Co-ordinating Ctee 2005; memb: Fabian Soc, GMB, Amicus; *Style*— Mrs Natascha Engel, MP; ✉ House of Commons, London SW1A 0AA

ENGELS, Johan; s of Frederick Lodewyk Christian Engels, and Glodina Maria Johanna, *née* Uys; *Educ* Univ of Pretoria (BA); *Career* set and costume designer; 1974–79: designer The Company Market Theatre Johannesburg, over 50 prodns for Performing Arts Cncl of SA; external examiner Theatre Design Depts Univ of the Witwatersrand and Johannesburg Technicon 1985–87; AA Mutual Vita Award for Best Design: As Is, I'm A Rappaport; *Theatre* RSC: The Seagull, Tamburlaine (Olivier nomination for Best Costume Design), As You Like It, Have, Dream of People; Royal Exchange Theatre: The Idiot, She's In Your Hands; Donmar Theatre: Translations (dir Sam Mendes, *qv*), Glen Gary Glenn Ross, Electra (with Zoë Wanamaker, *qv*, transferred to Broadway); Shochiku Theatre Co Japan: Richard III, Hamlet, The Royal Hunt of The Sun; other credits incl: When We Dead Awaken (Almedia Theatre London, with Claire Bloom, *qv*), Hamlet (Companie Francis Huster Paris), various prodns for Chichester Festival incl The Visit (dir Terry Hands, *qv*); *Opera* Zurich Opera: Die Rose vom Lebesgarten, Simplicius, L'Amore dei Tre Rei; other credits incl: Hamlet (Volksoper Vienna), Simon Boccanegra (Bremen Opera), Der Ring der Nibelungen (Opera Marseille), L'Elisir D'Amor (LA Opera, Teatro Real Madrid, Geneva Opera), The Return of Ulisse in Patria (NY City Opera and Glimmerglass NY), Turandot (Saltzburg Festival 2002); *Ballet* Wiener Staatsoperballet: Beethoven V, Spartacus; Pact Ballet: The Nutcracker, Swan Lake, Romeo and Juliet; other credits incl: Cinderella (Zurich Ballet), Cinderalla (London City Ballet), Vienna New Year Concerts 1997–98 and 2001; *Films* An African Dream, The Native Who Caused All The Trouble, Othello (dir Janet Suzman, *qv*, for Channel 4); *Recreations* music, puppetry, travel; *Clubs* 2 Brydges Place; *Style*— Johan Engels, Esq; ✉ c/o Loesje Sanders, Pound Square, 1 North Hill, Woodbridge, Suffolk IP12 1HH (tel 01394 385260, fax 01394 388734)

ENGESET, Jetmund; Hon LVO (2004); s of Arne Kaare Engeset (d 1973), and Marta, *née* Birkeland (d 1999); *b* 22 July 1938; *Educ* Slemdal and Ris Skoler Oslo, Univ of Aberdeen (MB ChB, ChM); *m* 3 June 1966, Anne Graeme, da of Allan Graeme Robertson (d 1946); 2 da (Anne-Marie, Nina Katrine); *Career* sr lectr Univ of Aberdeen 1974–87, surgn to HM The Queen in Scot 1985–2004, conslt surgn Grampian Health Bd 1987–2004 (hon conslt surgn 1974–87); FRCSEd 1970, FRCS (Glasgow) 1982; *Recreations* skiing, squash, angling, gardening; *Style*— Jetmund Engeset, Esq, LVO; ✉ Pine Lodge, 315 North Deeside Road, Milltimber, Aberdeen AB13 0DL (tel 01224 733753)

ENGLAND, Neil Martin; s of Brian England, and Jean England; *b* 10 May 1954, Birmingham; *Educ* Univ of Reading (BSc); *m* 26 June 1980, Debra; 1 s (Samuel b 10 Jan 1990), 2 da (Nadya b 17 July 1993, Anastasia b 26 April 1996); *Career* vice-pres Mars Inc 1993–96, gp chief exec The Albert Fisher Gp plc 1996–98, chief exec Mindweavers Ltd 2002–02, gp commercial dir Gallaher Gp plc 2002–; non-exec dir The Eastern European Tst plc 2003–; MInstM; *Recreations* motor sport, golf; *Style*— Neil England, Esq; ✉ Gallaher Group plc, Brooklands Road, Weybridge, Surrey KT13 0QU (tel 01932 859777, fax 01932 832838, e-mail neil.england@gallaherltd.com)

ENGLANDER, Dr Peter David; s of Geoffrey Englander (d 1993), and Doris Ruth, *née* Levy; *b* 29 November 1951; *Educ* St Paul's, Univ of Manchester (BSc), MIT (Kennedy scholar, SM), Univ of London (PhD); *m* 1985, Leanda Abigail; 3 s (Simon Jonathan b 1990, Thomas Geoffrey b 1993, William Daniel b 1995); *Career* conslt Boston Consulting Gp 1977–80, dir Apax Partners Ltd 1980–; *Recreations* walking, cinema; *Style*— Dr Peter Englander; ✉ Apax Partners Worldwide LLP, 15 Portland Place, London W1B 1PT (tel 020 7872 6331, fax 020 7636 6475)

ENGLEHART, Robert Michael; QC (1986); s of G A F Englehart (d 1969), of London, and of K P Englehart, *née* Harvey (d 1973); *b* 1 October 1943; *Educ* St Edward's Sch Oxford, Trinity Coll Oxford (MA), Harvard Law Sch (LLM), Bologna Centre; *m* 2 Jan 1971, Rosalind Mary Foster, *qv*, da of Ludovic Anthony Foster (d 1990); 2 da (Alice b 1976, Lucinda b 1978), 1 s (Oliver b 1982); *Career* assistente Univ of Florence 1967–68, called to the Bar Middle Temple 1969 (bencher 1995), recorder of the Crown Court 1987–, dep judge of the High Court 1994–; chm London Common Law and Commercial Bar Assoc 1989–91, chm Jt Regulations Ctee of Inns of Court 2000–; *Books* Il Controllo Giudiziario: a Comparative Study in Civil Procedure (contrib 1968); *Recreations* shooting, cricket, windsurfing; *Clubs* Garrick, MCC; *Style*— Robert Englehart, Esq, QC; ✉ Blackstone House, Temple, London EC4Y 9BW (tel 020 7583 1770, fax 020 7822 7350, e-mail robertenglehart@blackstonechambers.com)

ENGLISH, District Judge Terence Michael; s of late John Robert English, of Edmonton, London, and Elsie Letitia, *née* Edwards; *b* 3 February 1944; *Educ* St Ignatius Coll Stamford Hill, Univ of London (LLB external); *m* 1, 23 July 1966, Ivy Joan (decd), da of Charles William Weatherley (d 1959), of Wood Green, London; 1 da (Melanie b 1967), 1 s (Andrew b 1972); m 2, 10 Sept 2001, Clare Joanne, da of late Prof David John Evans, of Llanelli, and Naldera Evans; *Career* admitted slr Supreme Court 1970; clerk to justices: Newbury, Hungerford and Lambourn (now W Berks) 1977–85, Slough and Windsor 1985–86; dist judge 1986–, chm Panel Inner London Youth Court 1989–2002 (chm Family Panel 1991–93), recorder of the Crown Court 1994–98; *Recreations* philately, classical music, art, watching sport; *Style*— District Judge English; ✉ Reading Magistrates Court, Castle Street, Reading, Berkshire RG1 7TQ

ENNIS, Catherine; da of Séamus Ennis (d 1982), of Dublin, and Margaret, *née* Glynn; *b* 20 January 1955; *Educ* Christ's Hosp Hertford, St Hugh's Coll Oxford; *m* 10 Dec 1988, John Arthur Higham, QC, *qv*, s of Frank Higham (d 1988); 2 s (Patrick b 14 Sept 1989, Edmund b 24 March 1992), 1 da (Cecily b 17 Jan 1994), 2 step da (Miranda, Charlotte), 1 step s (Christian); *Career* organist; organ scholar St Hugh's Coll Oxford 1973–76, dir of music St Marylebone Parish Church London NW1 1979–81, asst organist ChCh Cathedral Oxford 1984–86, organist St Lawrence-Jewry-next-Guildhall London EC2 1985–; prof: RAM 1982–90, Guildhall Sch of Music 1986–88; fndr ed London Organ Concerts Guide 1995–; organ tutor Trinity Coll of Music London, Shrewsbury Sch and St Giles Int Organ Sch 2002–; has given numerous concerts throughout UK and I, solo recitals at Royal Festival Hall/South Bank Centre 1985, 1988 and 2006, concert tours of USA, Scandinavia and Eastern Europe, given numerous recitals and concerto performances and presented various progs BBC Radio 3 1982–, performed at Proms; various recordings (EMI); tstee

Nicholas Danby Tst 2001–, pres Incorporated Assoc of Organists 2005– (memb Cncl 2006–); *Recreations* opera, cricket, children; *Style—* Ms Catherine Ennis; ✉ e-mail cmennis@aol.com

ENNIS, Jeff; MP; s of William Ennis, and Jean, *née* McQueen; *b* 13 November 1952; *Educ* Hemsworth GS, Redland Coll Bristol (BEd); *m* 1980, Margaret Angela; 3 s (Neil Keith, John Joseph, Michael Jeffrey); *Career* primary teacher: Wolverhampton 1976–79, Hillsborough Sch Sheffield 1979–96; MP (Lab): Barnsley E (by-election) 1996–97, Barnsley E and Mexborough 1997–; PPS to Tessa Jowell (as Min for Public Health then Min for State for Employment) 1997–; memb Educn and Skills Select Ctee 2001–, sec Br-Montserrat Gp, sec Lab Backbench Gp on Regeneration; cncllr Barnsley MBC 1980–97 (ldr 1995–96); jt chair All-Pty Racing and Bloodstock Gp; memb Co-op Pty, TGWU, Br-Irish Inter-Parliamentary Body; *Recreations* most sports especially swimming, rugby and football, caravanning; *Style—* Jeff Ennis, Esq, MP; ✉ House of Commons, London SW1A 0AA (tel 020 7219 5008, fax 020 7219 2728, e-mail ennisj@parliament.uk)

ENNISKILLEN, 7 Earl of (I 1789); Andrew John Galbraith Cole; also Baron Mountflorence (I 1760), Viscount Enniskillen (I 1776) and Baron Grinstead (UK 1815); s of 6 Earl of Enniskillen, MBE, JP (d 1989), and his 1 w, Sonia Mary, *née* Syers (d 1982); *b* 28 April 1942; *Educ* Eton; *m* 3 Oct 1964, Sarah Frances Caroline, o da of late Maj-Gen John Keith-Edwards, CBE, DSO, MC, of Nairobi; 3 da (Lady Amanda Mary b 4 May 1966, Lady Emma Frances b 14 Feb 1969, Lady Lucy Caroline b 8 Dec 1970); *Heir* cous, Berkeley Cole; *Career* late Capt Irish Guards; co dir; airline pilot; *Style—* The Rt Hon the Earl of Enniskillen

ENO, Brian Peter George St John Baptiste de la Salle; s of William Arnold Eno (d 1988), of Woodbridge, Suffolk, and Maria Alphonsine, *née* Buslot; *b* 15 May 1948; *Educ* St Mary's Convent, St Joseph's Coll, Ipswich Sch of Art, Winchester Coll of Art; *m* 1, 11 March 1967, Sarah Grenville; 1 c (Hannah b 25 July 1967); m 2, 11 Jan 1988, Anthea Norman-Taylor; 2 c (Irial b 25 Jan 1990, Darla b 5 Aug 1991); *Career* musician and prodr; visiting prof RCA 1995–; numerous lectures worldwide on matters of culture; memb Global Business Network; hon prof of new media Berlin Univ of Art; Hon DTech Univ of Plymouth; *Music* The Maxwell Demon 1969, The Scratch Orchestra 1970, The Portsmouth Sinfonia 1971–73, Roxy Music 1971–73; solo records: Here Come The Warm Jets 1974, Taking Tiger Mountain (by Strategy) 1974, Another Green World 1975, Discreet Music 1975, Before and After Science 1977, Music For Films 1978, Music for Airports 1978, On Land 1981, Thursday Afternoon 1984, Nerve Net 1992, The Shutov Assembly 1992, Neroli 1993, The Drop 1997, Another Day on Earth 2005; collaborations: No Pussyfooting (with Robert Fripp) 1972, Evening Star (with Robert Fripp) 1975, Possible Musics (with Jon Hassell) 1980, Low, Heroes and Lodger (all with David Bowie) 1978–80, The Plateaux of Mirror (with Harold Budd) 1980, My Life in The Bush of Ghosts (with David Byrne) 1980, Apollo (with Daniel Lanois and Roger Eno) 1983, The Pearl (with Harold Budd) 1984, Wrong Way Up (with John Cale) 1990, Spinner (with Jan Wobble) 1995, Drawn from Life (with J Peter Schwalm) 2001, Equatorial Stars (with Robert Fripp) 2004; selected prodns: Lucky Lief and the Longships (Bob Calvert) 1975, Are we not men? (Devo) 1978, More songs about buildings and food, Fear of Music and Remain in Light (all with Talking Heads) 1978–80, Unforgettable Fire, The Joshua Tree, Achtung Baby, Zooropa, and All That You Can't Leave Behind (all with U2) 1984–2001, Bright Red (Laurie Anderson) 1995, Outside (David Bowie) 1995; *Visual* over 70 exhibitions of video artworks in museums and galleries worldwide incl: La Forêt Museum (Tokyo) 1983, Stedelijk Museum (Amsterdam) 1984, Venice Biennale 1986, Centre D'Art (Barcelona) 1992, Circulo de Bellas Artes (Madrid) 1993, Permanent Inst Swarovski (nr Innsbruck, Austria) 1995, Russian Museum (St Petersburg) 1997, Kunsthalle (Bonn) 1998, Kiasma (Helsinki) 1999, Hayward Gallery (London) 2000, SFMOMA (San Francisco) 2001, Lyon Biennial 2005, Museum für Abgüsse Klassicher Bildwerke Munich 2005; *DVD* 77 Million Paintings 2006; *Awards* Best Producer BRIT Awards 1994, Record of the Year Grammy Awards 2001 and 2002; *Publications* Oblique Strategies (with Peter Schmidt, 1975), A Year With Swollen Appendices (1996); *Recreations* perfumery, thinking, futurology; *Style—* Brian Eno, Esq; ✉ Opal Ltd, 4 Pembridge Mews, London W11 3EQ (tel 020 7221 4933, fax 020 7727 5404)

ENRIGHT, Leo Joseph; s of Laurence James Enright (d 1978), and Mary Elizabeth (d 1998); *b* 18 March 1955; *Educ* St Fintan's HS Dublin, UCD, MacAlester Coll Minnesota; *m* 1990, Lorraine, *née* Benson; 1 s (Robert Michael b 15 April 1992); *Career* reporter Meath Chronicle Co Meath 1976–77; Radio Telefis Éireann 1977–89: presenter News Features 1977–80, correspondent Middle East 1982–83 (N America 1980–81), head of News 1983–85, correspondent London 1986–89; BBC Dublin correspondent 1989–; princ commentator Spaceflight Irish Radio and TV 1972–; Nat Radio award Investigative Reporter of the Year 1978; fell: British Interplanetary Soc 1975, World Press Inst 1981, NUJ; *Books* Encyclopedia of Space Travel and Astronomy (1979); *Recreations* tennis, walking, swimming; *Clubs* United Arts (Dublin); *Style—* Leo Enright, Esq; ✉ c/o BBC, 36 Molesworth Place, Dublin 2, Ireland (tel 00 3531 662 5500)

ENSOR, His Hon Judge George Anthony (Tony); s of George Ensor (d 1992), of Pwllheli, Gwynedd, and Phyllis, *née* Harrison (d 1997); *b* 4 November 1936; *Educ* Malvern Coll, Univ of Liverpool (LLB); *m* 14 Sept 1968, Jennifer Margaret (MB ChB), da of Dr Ronald Caile (d 1978), of Southport, Lancs; 2 da (Elizabeth b 1972, Jane b 1978); *Career* admitted slr 1961; Rutherfords (now Weightman Rutherfords): ptnr 1963–92, sr ptnr 1992–95; dep coroner (City of Liverpool) 1966–95; dep judge Crown Court 1979–83, recorder of the Crown Court 1983–95, circuit judge (Northern Circuit) 1995–, dep sr judge Sovereign Base Cyprus 2005; pt/t chm Industrial Tbnls 1975–95; dir Liverpool FC 1985–93, tstee Empire Theatre Liverpool 1986–; memb Judicial Studies Bd 1986–89; pres: Artists Club Liverpool 1976, Liverpool Law Soc 1982; govr Malvern Coll 1992–; *Recreations* golf, theatre; *Clubs* Artists (Liverpool), Formby Golf (capt 1998), Waterloo RUFC; *Style—* His Hon Judge Ensor; ✉ c/o Northern Circuit Office, 15 Quay Street, Manchester M60 9FD

ENTWISTLE, George; s of Philip Richardson Entwistle, and Wendy Patricia, *née* Firth; *b* 8 July 1962; *Educ* Silcoates Sch Wakefield, Univ of Durham (BA); *Career* BBC: prodr On the Record 1993–94, prodr Newsnight 1994–97, asst ed Newsnight 1997–99, dep ed Tomorrow's World 1999–2000, dep ed Newsnight 2000–01, ed Newsnight 2002–04, exec ed (topical arts) BBC2 and BBC4 2004–05, head of TV current affrs 2005–; *Style—* George Entwistle, Esq

ENTWISTLE, John Nicholas McAlpine; OBE (2005); s of Sir (John Nuttall) Maxwell Entwistle (d 1994), and Jean Cunliffe McAlpine, *née* Penman (d 1993); *b* 1941; *Educ* Uppingham; *m* 6 Sept 1968, Phillida Entwistle, *qv*; 1 s (Nicholas b 1970), 1 da (Louise b 1971); *Career* admitted slr 1963; asst attorney Shearman & Sterling New York 1963–64, UK rep Salzburg Seminar Scholarship 1966, ptnr Maxwell Entwistle & Byrne (solicitors) 1966–91, conslt slr Davies Wallis Foyster 1992–2002, dir Rathbone Brothers plc 1992–98; underwriting memb Lloyd's 1971–2000, gen cmmr for Income Tax 1978–83, pt/t chm Social Security Appeal Tbnls 1992–2006, memb Parole Bd 1994–2000, pt/t immigration judge 2000–; Merseyside regnl chm NW Industrial Cncl 1981–87, dir Merseyside TEC 1990–91; chm: Liverpool Chamber of Commerce and Industry 1992–94, NW Chambers of Commerce Assoc 1993–97; pres British Chambers of Commerce 1998–2000 (a dep pres 1996–98), memb Chllr of the Exchequer's Standing Ctee on Preparation for EMU 1998–2000; Home Sec's representative for appointment to the Merseyside Police Authy 1994–2000; nat vice-chm Bow Gp 1967–68, memb Liverpool City Cncl 1968–71, Parly candidate Huyton (opposed by Harold Wilson) 1970; memb Cncl Nat Fedn of Housing Assocs 1972–75, govr and dep treas Blue Coat Sch Liverpool 1971–85, pres Friends of the Nat Museums & Galleries on Merseyside 1987–90 (chm and tstee 1984–87), Merseyside rep Nat Art-Collections Fund 1985–89, memb NW Regnl Ctee Nat Tst 1992–98, tstee Nat Museums & Galleries on Merseyside 1990–97 (chm Devpt Tst 1991–96), tstee Royal Acad Tst 2006–; memb: Disciplinary Ctee Mortgage Compliance Bd 1999–2004, Cncl for Britain in Europe 1999–2004, Criminal Injuries Compensation Appeals Panel 2000–; DL Merseyside 1992–2002; *Style—* John Entwistle, Esq, OBE; ✉ Low Crag, Crook, Kendal, Cumbria LA8 8LE (tel 015395 68268, office 015395 68715, fax 015395 68769, e-mail jentwistle@onetel.net)

ENTWISTLE, Phillida Gail Sinclair; JP (Liverpool 1980); da of Geoffrey Burgess, CMG, CIE, OBE (d 1972), and Jillian Margaret Eskens, *née* Hope (d 2000); *b* 7 January 1944; *Educ* Cheltenham Ladies' Coll, Univ of London (BSc), Univ of Liverpool (PhD); *m* 6 Sept 1968, John Nicholas McAlpine Entwistle, *qv*, s of Sir (John Nuttall) Maxwell Entwistle (d 1994), of Stone Hall, Sedbergh, Cumbria; 1 s (Nicholas b 1970), 1 da (Louise b 1971); *Career* dir J Davey & Sons (Liverpool) Ltd 1983–88, gen cmmr of Inland Revenue 1985–92; memb: Mersey RHA 1987–90, Mental Health Act Cmmn 1989–94, Liverpool FHSA 1990–94; chm Furness Hosps NHS Tst 1994–98, non-exec dir NW Water (now United Utilities (Water) plc) 1996–; memb Anchor Housing Assoc 1992–96, memb Rail Users' Consultative Ctee for the NW 1994–96; govr Liverpool John Moores Univ (formerly Liverpool Poly) 1988–93, memb Cncl Lancaster Univ 1998–2006; tstee Museum of Science and Industry in Manchester 2002–; nominee Privy Cncl to Cncl of RPSGB 2001–; FRSA; *Style—* Mrs Phillida Entwistle; ✉ Low Crag, Crook, Cumbria LA8 8LE (tel 01539 568268, fax 01539 568769)

ENTWISTLE, Raymond Marvin; *b* 12 June 1944; *Educ* John Ruskin GS Surrey; *m* 23 March 1965, Barbara, *née* Hennessy; 2 s, 1 da; *Career* Lloyds Bank 1960–84 (latterly mangr Edinburgh); Adam & Co Gp plc: joined 1984, md Adam & Co plc 1991–2004, gp md 1993–2004, chm 2004–, Adam & Co Investment Management Ltd; dir: John Davidson Holdings and John Davidson (Pipes) Ltd 1990–96, I & H Brown Ltd 2002–; chm The FruitMarket Gallery 1990–2000, govr Edinburgh Coll of Art 1989–99, dir J W International plc 1995–96, dir Dunedin Smaller Companies Investment Tst plc 1998–; chm Scottish Civic Tst 2003–, memb Ctee Royal Botanic Gardens 2003–; FCIB 1992, FCIBS 2001; *Recreations* antiques, fishing, golfing, shooting, walking; *Clubs* New (Edinburgh), Duddingston Golf, Lauder Golf; *Style—* Raymond Entwistle, Esq; ✉ The Glebe, Lauder, Berwickshire TD2 6RW (tel 01578 718751); Adam & Company Group plc, 22 Charlotte Square, Edinburgh EH2 4DF (tel 0131 225 8484, fax 0131 225 5136)

EPERON, Alastair David Peter; s of Stanley Eperon, and Patricia, *née* Woodrow; *b* 17 November 1949; *Educ* Ramsden Sch for Boys Orpington; *m* 1976, Ruth, *née* Tabbenor; 2 da (Veryan b 1983, Caroline b 1988); *Career* press offr Surrey CC 1972–74, head of public affrs The Housing Corporation 1974–78, sr conslt Shandwick PR 1978–80, dir then dep md Ogilvy & Mather PR 1980–84, chief exec Ogilvy & Mather Corporate Financial 1984–86, md McAvoy Wreford Bayley 1988–89 (dir 1986), dir Valin Pollen International plc 1989–90, chief exec McAvoy Bayley 1989–91, dir of gp corporate affrs The Boots Company plc 1991–2003, fndr Eperon Consulting Ltd 2003–; chm: Zeno UK, Advsy Bd The Foundation; former: chm CBI Distributive Trades Survey Panel, dep chm British Retail Consortium; chm: East Midlands Leadership Team Business in the Community until 2003, East Midlands Business Champions; Freeman City of London; memb Guild of PR Practitioners; FIPR, FRSA 1993; *Recreations* countryside, fitness; *Clubs* Home House, Roywal Commonwealth, Walbrook; *Style—* Alastair Eperon, Esq; ✉ Eperon Consulting Limited, Yew Tree Farm, Main Street, Holwell, Leicestershire LE14 4SZ (website www.a-eperon.co.uk)

EPHSON, Martin Frederick Emmanuel; s of HE Anthony W C G Ephson, of London, and Pamela, *née* May; *b* 17 August 1956, London; *Educ* Charterhouse, Univ of Westminster (BA); *m* 9 August 1985, Eugenia, da of Dr B Collins; 1 da (Ciara b 10 July 1988), 2 s (Patrick b 3 May 1990, Ludo b 8 June 1993); *Career* in corp fin 1988–92, dir Farrow & Ball paint and wallpaper mfrs 1992– (with Tom Helme, *qv*); winner Queen's Award for Enterprise 2004; dir Farleigh House Tstees Ltd, govr Farleigh Sch; *Publications* Paint and Colour in Decoration (2003); *Recreations* playing polo, sailing; *Clubs* Tidworth Polo, Royal Cork Yacht, Cirencester Park Polo; *Style—* Martin Ephson, Esq; ✉ Poulton House, Marlborough, Wilts SN8 2LN

EPPEL, Leonard Cedric; CBE (1992); s of Dr David Eppel (d 1963), of London, and Vera, *née* Diamond (d 1973); *b* 24 June 1928; *Educ* Highgate Sch; *m* 15 July 1954, Barbara Priscilla, da of Robert Silk, of London; 1 da (Rochelle Eleanor b 7 Oct 1956), 1 s (Stuart Neil b 26 March 1959); *Career* md Silks Estates Investments Ltd 1968 (dir 1954); chm: Arrowcroft Gp plc 1969–, Albert Dock Co Ltd 1983; dir: Millwall FC 1971 (chm 1979–83), NW Tourist Bd; vice-pres Br Red Cross Soc (Merseyside); Freeman City of London, Liveryman Worshipful Co of Fletchers 1984; FVI 1962, FRICS, FRSA, FInstD 1987; *Recreations* swimming, golf; *Clubs* Carlton; *Style—* Leonard Eppel, Esq, CBE; ✉ Arrowcroft Group plc, 110 Park Street, London W1K 6AD (tel 020 7499 5432, fax 020 7493 0323, car 07860 422227)

EPSTEIN, Dr Owen; s of Dr Morris Epstein, and Nancy, *née* Frysh; *b* 12 May 1950; *Educ* Univ of the Witwatersrand (MB BCh); *m* 10 Dec 1972, June, da of D David Armist; 2 s (Daniel b 4 Aug 1976, Marc b 14 June 1979); *Career* med registrar 1977–79, clinical res fell 1979–82, lectr in medicine 1982–85, conslt and clinical postgrad tutor Royal Free Hosp London 1985–; author of several scientific publications; chm gastroenterology Royal Free Hosp; FRCP 1989, (MRCP 1976); *Style—* Dr Owen Epstein; ✉ Royal Free Hampstead NHS Trust, Pond Street, Hampstead, London NW3 2QG (tel 020 7794 0500, fax 020 7794 6614, website www.epsteingastro.demon.co.uk)

ERAUT, Prof Michael Ruarc; s of Lt-Col Ruarc Bertram Sorel Eraut (d 1987), and Frances Hurst (d 1972); *b* 15 November 1940; *Educ* Winchester, Trinity Hall Cambridge (BA, PhD); *m* 7 Aug 1964, (Mary) Cynthia, da of Michael William Wynne (d 2005), of Great Shelford; 2 s (Patrick b 10 May 1968, Christopher b 27 Aug 1971); *Career* Univ of Sussex Centre for Educnl Technol: fell 1967, sr fell 1971, dir 1973–76, reader in educn 1976–86, prof of educn 1986–2006, dir Inst of Continuing and Professional Educn 1986–91, prof emeritus 2006–; visiting prof of evaluation Univ of Illinois 1980–81 (educnl technol 1965–67); jl ed Learning in Health and Social Care; *Books* incl: Teaching and Learning: New Methods and Resources in Higher Education (1970), Analysis of Curriculum Materials (1975), Curriculum Development in Further Education (1985), Improving the Quality of YTS (1986), International Encyclopedia of Educational Technology (1989), Education and the Information Society (1991), Flexible Learning in Schools (1991), Developing Professional Knowledge and Competence (1994), Learning to Use Scientific Knowledge in Education and Practice Settings (1995), Development of Knowledge and Skill in Employment (1998), Developing the Attributes of Medical Professional Judgement and Competence (2000), Evaluation of Higher Level S/NVQs (2001), The Significance of Workplace Learning for Individuals, Groups and Organisations (jtly); *Style—* Prof Michael Eraut; ✉ 49 St Annes Crescent, Lewes, East Sussex BN7 1SD (tel 01273 475955); Education Development Building, University of Sussex, Falmer, Brighton (tel 01273 606755)

EREMIN, Prof Oleg; s of Theodore Eremin (d 1995), of Melbourne, Aust, and Maria, *née* Avramenko (d 1978); *b* 12 November 1938; *Educ* Christian Brothers Coll Melbourne, Univ of Melbourne (MB BS, MD); *m* 23 Feb 1963, Jennifer Mary, da of Ellis Charles Ching (d 1972), of Melbourne, Aust; 1 da (Katherine b 1968), 2 s (Andrew b 1972, Nicholas b 1973); *Career* asst surgn Royal Melbourne Hosp Aust 1971–72 (house offr, sr house offr, registrar 1965–71), sr registrar Combined Norwich Hosps 1972–74, sr res assoc in immunology Dept of Pathology Univ of Cambridge 1977–80 (res asst 1974–77), sr lectr and conslt surgn Edinburgh Royal Infirmary 1981–85, prof of surgery and conslt surgn Aberdeen Royal Infirmary 1985–98, conslt surgeon United Lincolnshire Hosps NHS Tst 1999–, dir of research and devpt ULH Tst 2001–; special prof Univ of Nottingham, hon professorial fell Rowett Research Inst Aberdeen 1992–98; ed Jl of RCS(Ed) 1997–2002, ed-in-chief The Surgeon 2003–; memb: Assoc of Surgns of GB and I, Surgical Research Soc, Br Assoc of Surgical Oncology, James IV Assoc of Surgns, Int Surgical Gp; hon fell Royal Coll of Surgns of Thailand 2003; FRACS, FRCSEd (memb Cncl 1994–98 and 2000–05, examiner and chm Research Bd 1996–), FMedSci; *Recreations* classical music, literature, sport; *Style*— Prof Oleg Eremin; ✉ Orchard House, 51A Washdyke Lane, Nettleham, Lincoln LN2 2PX (tel 01522 750669)

ERIAN, John; s of Dr Habib Erian (d 1976), of Cairo, and Aida, *née* Mitry; *b* 12 August 1948; *Educ* St George's Coll, Ain-Shams Med Univ Cairo (MB BCh); *m* 1, 7 July 1973, Jennifer, da of Norman Frank Felton, of Hanworth, Middx; 1 s (Michael b 1974), 2 da (Gehanne b 1976, Simonne b 1977); m 2; m 3, 25 Nov 1995, Hilary, da of George Walter Hutchings, of Leigh-on-Sea, Southend; *Career* consIt obstetrician and gynaecologist: W Cumberland Hosp 1975–79, St George's Hosp 1979–82, Queen Charlotte's Hosp and Chelsea Hosp for Women 1982–83, St Thomas' Hosp 1983, Guy's Hosp 1983–85, Farnborough Hosp Kent 1985–; clinical dir Dept of Obstetrics and Gynaecology Bromley NHS Tst 1997–, divnl dir of surgery Bromley NHS Tst 1998; chm Endoscopic Laser Fndn 1998; fndr of Bromley Dist Colposcopy Serv and Endocrine Unit and Gift Treatment, pioneered YAG laser surgery in UK as an alternative to hysterectomy, preceptor in endoscopic surgery; author of various papers on endoscopic and laser surgery in gynaecology; memb: Br Endoscopy Soc (memb Cncl 1997–), SE Gynaecological Soc, Egyptian Med Soc; MRCOG 1981, FRCOG 1993 (Merit Award 1995); *Recreations* tennis, table tennis, swimming, skiing, horse riding, travelling, theatre, music, food and wine; *Style*— John Erian, Esq; ✉ Briar Porch, Sevenoaks Road, Chelsfield Park, Orpington, Kent BR6 15E (tel 01689 851192); Farnborough Hospital, Farnborough Common, Locksbottom, Orpington, Kent (tel 01689 814094)

ERIKSSON, Sven Goran; *b* Torsby, Sweden; *Career* former footballer (defender); clubs incl: Torsby IF, Sifhalla and KB Karlskoga (all Sweden); coach/mangr 1976–; Degerfors (Sweden): asst mangr 1976, mangr 1977–78; mangr: IFK Gothenburg (Sweden) 1979–82 (Swedish Championship 1981, Swedish Cup 1979 and 1982, UEFA Cup 1982), Benfica (Portugal) 1982–84 (Portuguese Championship 1983, 1984 and 1991, Portuguese Cup 1983), AS Roma (Italy) 1984–87 (Italian Cup 1986), AC Fiorentina (Italy) 1987–89, Benfica 1989–92, Sampdoria (Italy) 1992–97 (Italian Cup 1994), SS Lazio (Italy) 1997–2000 (Italian Cup 1998, Italian Super Cup 1998, UEFA Cup Winners Cup 1999, UEFA Super Cup 1999, Italian Championship 2000); head coach England nat team 2001–06, mangr Manchester City 2007–; Coach of the Year BBC Sports Personality of the Year Awards 2001; *Style*— Sven Goran Eriksson, Esq

ERITH, Robert Felix; TD (1977), DL (Essex 1998); eld s of Felix Henry Erith, FSA (d 1991), of Ardleigh, Essex, and Barbara Penelope, *née* Hawken (d 2004); *b* 8 August 1938; *Educ* Ipswich Sch, Writtle Agric Coll; *m* 7 May 1966, Sara Kingsford Joan, da of Dr Christopher Muller (d 1990); 3 s (Charles b 1967, James, Edward (twins) b 1970); *Career* 10 Hussars: 2 Lt Serv in Aqaba Jordan and Tidworth Hants 1957–58, AVR serv in Aden, Oman, Cyprus, Hong Kong, Germany, UK 1962–79, Maj 1973; builders merchants' salesman and mgmnt trainee 1960–64: London, Washington DC, Oakland California, Perth W Aust; EB Savory Milln & Co (Milln & Robinson until 1967): bldg specialist 1966, ptnr 1969–83, sr ptnr 1983–87; chm: SBCI Savory Milln Ltd 1987–89, Swiss Bank Corporation Equities Group 1989–93; conslt UBS Warburg 1993–2002; dir Central Capital (Hldgs) 1996–, chm Crest Nicholson Pension Fund Tstees 2001–; farmer; chm Essex Environment Tst 1998–2004, vice-pres CPRE (Essex) 1998–, pres Essex Agicultural Soc 1999–2000; tstee Shakespeare Globe Tst; churchwarden Holy Innocents Lamarsh; pres Dedham Vale Soc 2003–, memb Ctee Colne-Stour Countryside Assoc; Parly candidate (Cons) Ipswich 1976–79; High Sheriff Essex 1997–98; Liveryman Worshipful Co of Builders Merchants 1987, Freeman City of London 1987; FRPSL 1994, FRSA 1995; *Books* Britain into Europe (jtly, 1962), The Role of the Monarchy (jtly, 1965), Savory Milln's Building Book (annual edns 1968–83); *Recreations* environmental pursuits, village cricket, skiing, stamp collecting, golf; *Clubs* Cavalry and Guards', Pratt's, MCC, Royal Philatelic Soc; *Style*— Robert Erith, Esq, TD, DL; ✉ Shrubs Farm, Lamarsh, Bures, Essex C08 5EA (tel 01787 227520, fax 01787 227197, mobile 078 3624 5536, e-mail bob@shrubsfarm.co.uk, website www.shrubsfarm.co.uk)

ERMISCH, Prof John; s of Elmer Ermisch (d 1986), and Frances, *née* Bertrand; *b* 1 July 1947; *Educ* Univ of Wisconsin (BS), Univ of Kansas (MA, PhD); *m* 7 May 1977, Dianne Monti; *Career* research economist US Dept of Housing and Urban Devpt 1974–76, sr research fell PSI 1976–86, sr research offr NIESR 1986–91, Bonar-McFie prof Univ of Glasgow 1991–94, prof Univ of Essex 1994–; FBA 1995; *Books* The Political Economy of Demographic Change (1983), Lone Parenthood: An Economic Analysis (1991), An Economic Analysis of the Family (2003); *Recreations* golf; *Style*— Prof John Ermisch; ✉ Institute for Social and Economic Research, University of Essex, Wivenhoe Park, Colchester, Essex CO4 3SQ (tel 01206 872335, fax 01206 873151, e-mail ermij@essex.ac.uk)

ERNE, 6 Earl of (I 1798); Henry George Victor John Crichton; JP; sat as Baron Fermanagh (UK 1876); also Baron Erne (I 1768) and Viscount Erne (I 1781); s of 5 Earl of Erne (ka 1940), and Lady Davidema (d 1995), da of 2 Earl of Lytton, KG, GCSI, GCIE, PC; *b* 9 July 1937; *Educ* Eton; *m* 1, 5 Nov 1958 (m dis 1980), Camilla Marguerite, da of late Wing Cdr Owen George Endicott Roberts; 1 s, 4 da; m 2, 1980, Mrs Anna Carin Hitchcock (*née* Bjorck); *Heir* s, Viscount Crichton; *Career* page of honour to HM King George VI 1952 and to HM The Queen 1952–54; Lt N Irish Horse 1960–68; HM Lord-Lt Co Fermanagh; *Clubs* White's, Lough Erne Yacht; *Style*— The Rt Hon the Earl of Erne; ✉ Crom Castle, Newtown Butler, Co Fermanagh (tel 028 6773 8208)

ERRERA, HE Gérard; Hon CVO; s of Paul Errera (d 1997), and Bella, *née* Montekio; *b* 30 October 1943, Brive la Gaillarde, France; *Educ* Institut d'Etudes Politiques de Paris, Ecole Nationale d'Administration; *m* 7 July 1967, Virginie, *née* Bedoya; 2 s (Philippe b 1 Dec 1969, Alexandre b 23 Oct 1986), 1 da (Emmanuelle b 10 Jan 1972); *Career* French diplomat; entered Miny of Foreign Affrs 1969, first sec Washington DC 1971–75, special advsr to min of Foreign Affrs 1975–77, political cnsllr Madrid 1977–80, special advsr to min of Foreign Affrs 1980–81, consul-gen San Francisco 1982–85, dir for int relations French Atomic Energy Cmmn and govr for France Int Atomic Energy Agency 1985–90, ambass to Conf on Disarmament Geneva 1991–95, ambass to NATO 1995–98, political dir Miny of Foreign Affrs 1998–2002, ambass to the Ct of St James's 2002–; Chevalier de la Légion d'Honneur, Officier de l'Ordre National du Mérite, Offr Order of Civil Merit (Spain), Offr Order of the White Rose (Finland); *Recreations* skiing, music; *Clubs* Travellers, Athenaeum; *Style*— HE Mr Gérard Errera, CVO; ✉ French Embassy, 58 Knightsbridge, London SW1X 7JT (tel 020 7073 1005, fax 020 7073 1003, e-mail gerard.errera@diplomatie.gouv.fr)

ERRINGTON, Col Sir Geoffrey Frederick; 2 Bt (UK 1963), of Ness, in Co Palatine of Chester; OBE (1998); s of Sir Eric Errington, 1 Bt (d 1973), and Marjorie, *née* Grant-Bennett (d 1973); *b* 15 February 1926; *Educ* Rugby, New Coll Oxford; *m* 24 Sept 1955, Diana Kathleen Forbes, da of late Edward Barry Davenport, of Edgbaston; 3 s (Robin Davenport b 1957, John Davenport, Andrew Davenport (twins) b 1959); *Heir* s, Robin Errington; *Career* Regular Army Offr The King's Regt 1945–75 (2 Lt to Col); chm Mgmnt Ctee The King's and Manchester Regts Assoc 1973–86, Col The King's Regt 1975–86; dir of personnel servs British Shipbuilders 1977–78 (conslt), employer bd memb Shipbuilding Industry Trg Board 1977–78; chm Executive Appointments Ltd 1982–90, memb Kent Consumers' Consultative Ctee Southern Water Authy 1984–89; chm: Harefield Hosp NHS Tst 1991–98, APA Community Drug and Alcohol Initiatives Ltd 1994–98 (vice-chm 1991–94), Standing Cncl of the Baronetage 2001–06 (vice-pres 2006); DG Br-Australia Soc 2006 (hon dir 1998–2006); Freeman City of London 1980; Liveryman: Worshipful Co of Coachmakers and Coach Harness Makers 1980, Worshipful Co of Broderers 1998; FRSA 1994; *Recreations* travelling and gardening; *Clubs* Boodle's, Oxford and Cambridge, Woodroffe's (chm 1987–95); *Style*— Col Sir Geoffrey Errington, Bt, OBE; ✉ Stone Hill Farm, Sellindge, Ashford, Kent TN25 6AJ; 203A Gloucester Place, London NW1 6BU

ERROLL, 24 Earl of (S 1452); Sir Merlin Sereld Victor Gilbert Hay of Erroll; 12 Bt (Baronetcy originally Moncreiffe of that Ilk, Perthshire, NS 1685); also 28 Hereditary Lord High Constable of Scotland (conferred as Great Constable of Scotland *ante* 1309 and made hereditary by charter of Robert I 1314), Lord Hay (S 1429) and Lord Slains (S 1452); Chief of the Hays; as Lord High Constable, has precedence in Scotland before all other hereditary honours after the Blood Royal; also maintains private officer-at-arms (Slains Pursuivant); s of Countess of Erroll (d 1978) by her 1 husb, Sir Iain Moncreiffe of that Ilk, 11 Bt (d 1985); his gggggf (the 18 Earl)'s w, Elizabeth FitzClarence, natural da of King William IV, whose arms he quarters debruised by a baton sinister; *b* 20 April 1948; *Educ* Eton, Trinty Coll Cambridge; *m* 8 May 1982, Isabelle, o da of Thomas Sidney Astell Hohler (*né* Hohler, assumed name and arms of Astell by Royal licence 1978, d 1989), of Wolverton Park, Basingstoke; 2 s (Harry Thomas William, Lord Hay b 8 Aug 1984, Hon Richard b 14 Dec 1990), 2 da (Lady Amelia b 23 Nov 1986, Lady Laline b 21 Dec 1987); *Heir* s, Lord Hay; *Career* mktg and trg conslt; chm: CRC Ltd, Fonem Ltd; ICT advsr; elected hereditary peer House of Lords 1999–, memb Bd Parly Office of Sci and Technol; memb Cncl: EURIM, PITCOM; memb Queen's Body Guard for Scotland (Royal Co of Archers); Lt Atholl Highlanders; Prime Warden Worshipful Co of Fishmongers 2000–01; Hon Col RMPTA 1992–97; OStJ, TEM; *Recreations* country pursuits; *Clubs* White's, Pratt's, Puffins; *Style*— The Rt Hon the Earl of Erroll; ✉ Woodbury Hall, Sandy, Bedfordshire SG19 2HR (tel 01767 650251, fax 01767 651553)

ERSKINE, (Thomas) Adrian; s of Daniel Erskine (d 1995), and Molly, *née* Balmer (d 1979); *b* 7 August 1934; *Educ* St Malachy's Coll Belfast, Queen's Univ Belfast (BSc), Imperial Coll London (DIC); *Career* civil engr Dept of Highways Ontario Canada 1957–59, structural engr Ove Arup and Partners London 1960–62, head Ulster branch BRC Engineering Co Ltd 1964–69, assoc i/c civil and structural work Belfast office Building Design Partnership 1969–78, ptnr McGladdery & Partners (consltg, civil and structural engrs) Belfast 1978–2003, conslt W J McDowell & Ptnrs Conslting Engrs 2003–; chm Jt Consultative Ctee for Bldg (NI) 1990–93; CEng, FIStructE, MICE 1962; *Recreations* squash, golf; *Clubs* Belfast Boat, Belvoir Golf, Woodvale Cricket; *Style*— Adrian Erskine, Esq; ✉ 24 Sandhurst Drive, Belfast BT9 5AY (tel 028 9029 3934); W J McDowell & Partners, Aldersgate House, 15 University Road, Belfast BT7 (tel 028 9024 5444)

ERSKINE, Barbara; da of Stuart Nigel Rose, of Beaumont-cum-Moze, and Pamela Yvonne, *née* Anding (d 1988); *b* 10 August 1944; *Educ* St George's Harpenden, Univ of Edinburgh (MA); *m*; 2 s (Adrian James Earl, Jonathan Erskine Alexander); *Career* freelance editor and journalist, short story writer, novelist; memb: Soc of Authors, The Scientific and Medical Network; *Books* Lady of Hay (1986), Kingdom of Shadows (1988), Encounters (1990), Child of the Phoenix (1992), Midnight is a Lonely Place (1994), House of Echoes (1996), Distant Voices (1996), On the Edge of Darkness (1998), Whispers in the Sand (2000), Hiding from the Light (2002), Sands of Time (2003), Daughters of Fire (2006); *Recreations* reading, growing and using herbs, exploring the past; *Style*— Mrs Barbara Erskine; ✉ c/o Blake Friedmann, Literary Agents, 122 Arlington Road, London NW1 7HP (tel 020 7284 0408)

ERSKINE, Robert Simon; s of Dr Maurice Erskine, of London, and Victoria, *née* Travers; *b* 24 April 1954; *Educ* JFS Comp Sch, Ealing Tech Coll, Kingston Poly (BA), UCL, Slade Sch of Fine Art (Higher Dip Fine Art); *m* 1984, Jo, *née* Singer; 3 s (Liam Sasher b 1989, Wyatt Lloyd b 1992, Asher Aiden b 1995); *Career* sculptor and designer specialising in direct working of bronze and stainless steel; design co-ordinator Dale Keller Design Corp USA 1978–84, numerous worldwide architectural projects in Hong Kong, Switzerland, India, Greece and England 1978–84, numerous landmark sculptures sited UK, full time professional architectural sculptor 1984–, design conslt Marks & Spencer London and Nestle UK Ltd 1998–; sculptor in residence: Caterpillar and Perkins Diesel Engine facility, Peterborough Sculpture Tst, Peterborough Green Wheel 2000; cmmnd sculptor Chartered Inst of Personnel and Devpt; visiting lectr Frink Sch of Figurative Sculpture Stoke-on-Trent; contrib: The Times, BBC Cambridge, BBC Radio 4, Tyne Tees TV, Netherlands TV, AutoLab (radio, USA), radio and national press; ARBS 1993, FRBS 1997; *Exhibitions* Nat Soc Painters and Sculptors Mall Gallery London 1977–79, Ben Uri Gallery London 1985, Int Yorkshire Sculpture Park 1986–88, Andrew Usiskin Gallery London 1989–92, Hakone Open Air Museum 1992, World Wildlife Fund Exhibition London 1992, Hannah Peschar Sculpture Garden Sussex 1994, Trade Indemnity Centre London 1994, Int Welding and Metal Working Exhibition Birmingham NEC 1994, Osterly Park London 1995, Cultural Village of Europe Holland 1999, world HQ of Pfizer Inc NY 1999 (solo exhbn); *Awards* winner maquette of excellence Hakone Int Open-Air Museum of Sculpture 1992, winner Sir Otto Beit Bronze Award RBS 1993–94, White Rhythm named most outstanding sculpture at Cultural Village of Europe in Holland 1999, public and landmark sculptures awarded status of perm public monuments by Courtauld Inst in assoc with Public Monuments and Sculptures Assoc; *Publications* The Building of SS Oriana (1995), European Village of Culture, Sculpture Symposium (1999), Public Art in Coventry (2001); People Management publication 1995–2004; *Recreations* playing jazz (trumpet), swimming every day, cycling, photography, cooking, theatre, sci and technol (reading about and going to see), fixing broken things (at home and family), reading, listening to jazz and classical music, drawing, going to the cinema, concerts, playing with the children, being on the beach, flying my big and powerful kite, looking at the clouds and sunsets, climbing hills, thinking and designing my next sculptures, watching any TV documentary about sci, archeology and design, long walks with open eyes; *Style*— Robert Erskine, Esq

ERSKINE-HILL, Prof Howard Henry; s of Capt Henry Erskine-Hill (d 1989), of Malahide, Co Dublin, and Hannah Lilian, *née* Poppleton (d 1991); *b* 19 June 1936; *Educ* Ashville Coll, Univ of Nottingham (BA, PhD), Univ of Cambridge (LittD); *Career* tutor, asst lectr then lectr in English Univ Coll Swansea 1960–69; Univ of Cambridge: lectr in English 1969–83, reader in literary history 1984–, fell Jesus Coll 1969–80, fell Pembroke Coll 1980–, prof of literary history 1994–; Olin fell Nat Humanities Center NC USA 1988–89; FBA 1985; *Books* Pope: Horatian Satires and Epistles (ed, 1964), Pope: The Dunciad (1972), The Social Milieu of Alexander Pope (1975), The Augustan Idea (1983), Swift: Gulliver's Travels (1993), Poetry and the Realm of Politics (1996), Poetry of Opposition and Revolution (1996), Alexander Pope: World and Word (ed, 1998), Alexander Pope: Selected Letters (ed, 2000); *Recreations* walking; *Clubs* Oxford and Cambridge; *Style*— Prof Howard Erskine-Hill, FBA; ✉ 194 Chesterton Road, Cambridge CB4 1NE; Pembroke College, Cambridge CB2 1RF (tel 01223 338138)

ERSKINE-HILL, Sir (Alexander) Roger; 3 Bt (UK 1945), of Quothquhan, Co Lanark; er s of Sir Robert Erskine-Hill, 2 Bt (d 1989), and Christine Alison, *née* Johnstone; *b* 15 August 1949; *Educ* Eton, Univ of Aberdeen (LLB); *m* 1 (m dis 1994), Sarah Anne Sydenham, da

E

of Dr Richard John Sydenham Clarke (d 1970); 1 da (Kirsty Rose b 1985), 1 s (Robert Benjamin b 1986); m 2, Gillian Elizabeth Borlase Mitchell, da of Mr and Mrs David Surgey; *Heir* s, Robert Erskine-Hill; *Career* dir The Hillbrooke Partnership Ltd; *Style—* Sir Roger Erskine-Hill, Bt; ✉ Les Tissanderies, 24220 Le Coux et Bigaroque, France (e-mail erskine-hill@wanadoo.fr)

ESCOTT COX, Brian Robert; QC (1974); s of George Robert Escott Cox, of Solihull; *b* 30 September 1932; *Educ* Rugby, Oriel Coll Oxford (BA); *m* 9 Aug 1969, Noelle, da of Dominique Gilormini, of Patrimonio, Corsica; 1 s (Richard b 10 Feb 1971), 1 da (Caroline b 8 Jan 1976); *Career* called to the Bar Lincoln's Inn 1954 (bencher 1985); in practice: Jr Bar 1954–74, Midland & Oxford Circuit 1954–; recorder of the Crown Court 1972–97, Lord Chllr's list of Dep High Court Judges 1979–97; *Style—* Brian Escott Cox, Esq, QC; ✉ 36 Bedford Row, London WC1R 4JH (tel 020 7421 8000, fax 020 7421 8080)

ESHUN, Ekow; *b* 27 May 1968; *Educ* Kingsbury HS, LSE (BSc); *Career* with Kiss FM 1987–88, freelance contrib 1990–93 (The Guardian, The Observer, The Face, BBC Radio 4, BBC Radio 5, BBC World Service), asst ed The Face 1993–96, ed Arena 1996, founding dir Bug Consultancy, editorial dir Tank magazine, artistic dir ICA 2005–; writer and presenter of numerous TV and radio documentaries; currently contrib to: Late Review/Newsnight Review (BBC 2), The Daily Politics, Front Row (BBC Radio 4), The Guardian, The Observer, New Statesman, Sunday Times, Wallpaper; memb: Cncl ICA 1999–2003, Bd London Arts Board 1999–, Bd Tate Members 2003–; govr Univ of Arts London 2001–; *Books* Black Gold of the Sun (2005); *Recreations* fashion design, contemporary art; *Style—* Ekow Eshun, Esq; ✉ ICA, The Mall, London SW1Y 5AH

ESIRI, Prof Margaret Miriam; da of William Evans (d 1974), and Doreen, *née* Bates (d 1994); *b* 5 October 1941; *Educ* Croydon HS GDST, St Hugh's Coll Oxford (BA, BSc, BM BCh, DM, Hilary Howarth Science Prize, Martin Wronker Prize in Med); *m* 1963, Frederick Esiri; 1 da (Henrietta b 1963), 2 s (Mark b 1964, Frederick b 1967); *Career* trainee pathologist/neuropathologist United Oxford Hosps 1973–79; Univ of Oxford: jr research fell in neuropathology 1970–73, MRC sr clinical fell 1980–85, reader 1985–96, prof of neuropathology 1996–; vice-princ St Hugh's Coll Oxford; author of over 250 peer-reviewed research papers; memb British Neuropathology Soc, sponsor Oxford branch Alzheimers Soc; FRCPath 1988 (MRCPath 1976); *Books* Viral Encephalitis: Pathology, Diagnosis and Management (with John Booss, 1986), Diagnostic Neuropathology (with D R Oppenheimer, 1989), The Neuropathology of Dementia (ed with James H Morris, 1997, 2 edn 2004), Viral Encephalitis in Humans (with John Booss, 2003); *Recreations* family, reading, theatre, walking, gardening, visiting Nigeria; *Style—* Prof Margaret Esiri; ✉ Department of Clinical Neurology, Radcliffe Infirmary, Woodstock Road, Oxford OX2 6HE (tel 01865 224403, fax 01865 224508, e-mail margaret.esiri@clneuro.ox.ac.uk)

ESLER, Gavin William James; s of William John Esler, and Georgena, *née* Knight; *b* 27 February 1953; *Educ* George Heriot's Sch Edinburgh, Univ of Kent at Canterbury (BA, DCL), Univ of Leeds (MA); *m* 3 July 1979, Patricia Margaret, da of Bernard Cyril Warner; 1 da (Charlotte Virginia b 27 May 1992), 1 s (James Conor b 22 March 1994); *Career* Thompson Newspapers grad trainee then journalist Belfast Telegraph 1975–77, reporter/presenter Spotlight BBC Northern Ireland current affrs prog 1977–81; BBC: reporter/presenter Newsnight and TV News 1982–89, Washington corr 1989–, chief N America corr 1990–97, presenter BBC News 1997–2002, presenter Newsnight and Panorama 2003–; columnist The Scotsman 1998–2005, freelance magazine and newspaper journalist; RTS Journalism Award for Newsnight Report 1987; memb White House Corrs' Assoc; Hon MA Univ of Kent at Canterbury 1995, DCL Univ of Kent 2005; Sony Gold Award for Radio 4 documentary Letters from Guantanamo 2007; FRSA; *Books* Loyalties (novel, 1990), Deep Blue (novel, 1992), The Bloodbrother (novel, 1995), The United States of Anger (non-fiction, 1997); *Recreations* skiing, squash, hill walking, backwoods camping; *Style—* Gavin Esler, Esq; ✉ Room G680, BBC Television Centre, Wood Lane, London W12 7RJ (tel 020 8743 8000, e-mail gavin.esler@bbc.co.uk)

ESMONDE, Sir Thomas Francis Grattan; 17 Bt (I 1629), of Ballynastragh, Wexford; s of His Hon Judge Sir John Henry Grattan Esmonde, 16 Bt (d 1987), and Pamela Mary, *née* Bourke; *b* 14 October 1960; *Educ* Sandford Park Sch, Trinity Coll Dublin (MD, MB BCh, BAO); *m* 26 April 1986, Pauline Loretto, 2 da of James Vincent Kearns; 1 s (Sean Vincent Grattan b 1989), 2 da (Aisling Margaret Pamela Grattan b 17 Dec 1991, Niamh Pauline Grattan b 2 May 1996); *Heir* s, Sean Esmonde; *Career* MRCPI, FRCP (MRCP); *Style—* Sir Thomas Esmonde, Bt; ✉ 6 Nutley Avenue, Donnybrook, Dublin 4, Ireland

ESPENHAHN, Peter Ian; s of Edward William Espenhahn, of E Molesey, and Barbara Mary, *née* Winmill; *b* 14 March 1944; *Educ* Westminster, Sidney Sussex Coll Cambridge (MA); *m* 10 Feb 1968, Fiona Elizabeth, da of Air Vice Marshal Brian Pashley Young, of Didmarton, Glos; 2 d (Sarah b 1971, Caroline b 1975); *Career* Deloitte Plender Griffiths London 1965–72, dir Corp Fin Dept Morgan Grenfell & Co Ltd 1983– (joined 1973); FCA; *Recreations* sailing, rugby, opera; *Style—* Peter Espenhahn, Esq; ✉ 79 Mount Ararat Road, Richmond, Surrey TW10 6PL

ESPLEN, (Sir) John Graham; 3 Bt (UK 1921), of Hardres Court, Canterbury (but does not use title); o s of Sir (William) Graham Esplen, 2 Bt (d 1989), and Aline Octavia, *née* Hedley (d 1994); *b* 4 August 1932; *Educ* Harrow, St Catharine's Coll Cambridge (BA); *Heir* s, William Esplen; *Style—* Mr John Esplen; ✉ Lauriston, Weycombe Road, Haslemere, Surrey GU27 1EL

ESSER, Robin Charles; s of Charles Esser (d 1982), and Winifred Eileen Esser (d 1972); *b* 6 May 1935; *Educ* Wheelwright GS Dewsbury, Wadham Coll Oxford (MA); *m* 1, 5 Jan 1959, Irene Shirley, *née* Clough (d 1973); 2 s (Daniel b 1962, Toby b 1963), 2 da (Sarah Jane b 1961, Rebecca b 1965); m 2, 30 May 1981, Tui, *née* France; 2 s (Jacob b 1986, Samuel b 1990); *Career* cmmnd 2 Lt KOYLI 1955, transferred General Corps 1956, Capt acting ADPR BAOR 1957, awarded GSM; Daily Express: staff reporter 1957–60, ed William Hickey Column 1962, features ed 1963, NY Bureau 1965, northern ed 1969, exec ed 1970; conslt ed Evening News 1977, exec ed Daily Express 1984–86, ed Sunday Express 1986–89, ind editorial conslt 1990–, exec managing ed Daily Mail 1998– (conslt 1997); memb Soc of Eds; *Books* The Hot Potato (1969), The Paper Chase (1971); *Recreations* lunching, reading, tennis; *Clubs* Garrick, Hurlingham; *Style—* Robin Esser, Esq; ✉ Daily Mail, 2 Derry Street, London W8 5TT

ESSEX, Sue; AM; *b* 1945; *Career* formerly: lectr of planning Univ of Wales, ldr Cardiff City Cncl, memb Countryside Cncl for Wales; memb Nat Assembly for Wales (Lab) Cardiff North, formerly min for environment, transport and planning, currently min for fin, local govt and public servs; *Style—* Ms Sue Essex, AM; ✉ The National Assembly for Wales, Cardiff Bay, Cardiff CF99 1NA (tel 029 2089 8391, fax 029 2189 8393, e-mail sue.essex@wales.gov.uk); Constituency Office, 18 Plasnewydd, Whithcurch, Cardiff CF14 1NR

ESSWOOD, Paul Lawrence Vincent; s of Alfred Walter Esswood, and Freda, *née* Garratt; *b* 6 June 1942; *Educ* West Bridgford GS Nottingham, Royal Coll of Music (Henry Blower singing prize); *m* 1, (m dis 1990); 2 s (Gabriel Peter b 1968, Michael William b 1971); m 2, 4 Aug 1990, Aimée Desirée; 1 da (Stella Jane b 1992), 1 s (Lawrence Galahad b 1993); *Career* opera, concert and recital singer (counter-tenor) specializing in Baroque period and conductor; operatic debut Univ of Calif Berkeley 1966, conducting debut Chichester Festival 2000; given performances (as singer) at venues incl: Zürich, Cologne, Stuttgart, Chicago, La Scala Milan; regular conducting work with Capella Cracoviensis and Capella Bydgostiensis (both Poland) and The Concert of Twelve (orch and choir), conducted the modern world première of Pompeo Magno by Cavalli in Varazdin Croatioa; prof of singing RCM 1977–80, prof of Baroque vocal interpretation RAM 1985–; lay vicar Westminster Abbey 1964–71; ARCM 1964, Hon RAM 1990; *Performances* as singer incl: Monteverdi operas (Zürich), Britten's A Midsummer Night's Dream (Cologne), Penderecki's Paradise Lost (La Scala), Glass's Akhnaten (Stuttgart); solo recitals incl: Purcell's Music for a While, Schumann's Dichterliebe and Liederkreis Op39, English lute songs from Songs to My Lady; counter-tenor vocalist in The Musicre Companye; *Recordings* as singer incl: all Bach Cantatas, St Matthew Passion, Christmas Oratorio, Purcell's Dido and Aeneas; recordings of Handel works incl: Brockes Passion, Jephte, Saul, Belshazzar, Rinaldo, Xerxes, Messiah, Il Pastor Fido, Britten Folk Songs and Canticle II, Abraham & Isaac; *Recreations* gardening (organic); *Style—* Paul Esswood, Esq; ✉ Jasmine Cottage, 42 Ferring Lane, Ferring, West Sussex BN12 6QT (tel and fax 01903 504480)

ESTALL, Prof Robert Charles; s of Estall John Thomas (d 1967), of London, and Hilda Lilian, *née* West (d 1976); *b* 28 September 1924; *Educ* St Mary's Coll Twickenham (Teacher's Certificate), LSE (BSc, PhD); *m* 2 April 1956, Mary (d 2004), da of Frederick Willmott (d 1988), of Exeter; 1 da (Joanna Mary b 1957), 3 s (Simon James b 1959, Martin Robert b 1961, Richard John b 1968); *Career* Petty Offr RN 1942–46; LSE: lectr in geography 1955–65, reader in econ geography of N America 1965–88, prof of geography 1988–; visiting prof Clark Univ MA 1958, res fell American Cncl of Learned Socs 1962–63, visiting prof Univ of Pittsburgh PA 1967; *Books* New England: A Study in Industrial Adjustment (1966), A Modern Geography of the United States (1976), Industrial Activity and Economic Geography (1980), Global Change and Challenge (ed with R Bennett, 1991); *Recreations* gardening, reading, walking, golf; *Style—* Prof Robert Estall; ✉ 48 The Ridings, Berrylands, Surbiton, Surrey KT5 8HQ (tel 020 8399 0430); London School of Economics and Political Science, Houghton Street, London WC2A 2AE (tel 020 7405 7686)

ESTEVE-COLL, Dame Elizabeth Anne Loosemore; DBE (1995); da of P W Kingdon, and Nora Kingdon; *b* 14 October 1938; *Educ* Darlington Girls HS, Birkbeck Coll London (BA); *m* 1960, Jose Alexander Timothy Esteve-Coll; *Career* head of learning resources Kingston Poly 1977, univ librarian Univ of Surrey 1982, keeper Nat Art Library V&A 1985, dir V&A 1988–95, vice-chllr UEA 1995–97, chllr Univ of Lincoln 2001–; tstee Sainsbury Inst for the Study of Japanese Arts and Cultures (SISJAC); freelance cultural consultancy; *Recreations* reading, music, foreign travel; *Style—* Dame Elizabeth Esteve-Coll, DBE; ✉ Coldham Hall, Tuttington, Aylsham, Norfolk NR11 6TA

ESTORICK, Michael Jacob; s of Eric Estorick (d 1993), and Salome, *née* Dessau (d 1989); *b* 24 June 1951; *Educ* Haberdashers' Aske's, Magdalene Coll Cambridge, City & Guilds of London Art Sch; *Children*; 1 s (Alexander b 1988); *Career* chm Estorick Collection of Modern Italian Art London; formerly jt chm Gerald Duckworth and Co Publishers; dir: Sevenarts Ltd, Grosvenor Gallery; book reviewer: The Tablet, Literary Review, Oldie; vice-pres Hazlitt Soc; memb Soc of Authors; hon memb 56 Group Wales; *Publications* Heirs and Graces (1981), Can't Buy Me Love (novel, 1986), What are Friends For (novel, 1990), Just Business (novel, 1996), Fortune (novel, 2001); *Recreations* real tennis (Harbour Club champion 1996), golf, reading, over-reacting; *Clubs* Savile, MCC, Buck's, Beefsteak; *Style—* Michael Estorick, Esq; ✉ c/o Estorick Collection, 39A Canonbury Square, London N1 2AN

ETHERIDGE, Hugh Charles; s of Fredan Etheridge (d 1989), and Monica, *née* Bird; *b* 1 July 1950, Weybridge, Surrey; *Educ* Bradfield College; *m* 26 Jan 1974, Jacqueline, *née* Parnell; 2 s (Tobias b 1 July 1976, Oliver b 9 Sept 1981); *Career* articled clerk Herbert Parnell 1969–73, asst mangr Peat Marwick Mitchell 1974–77, gp chief accountant Fitch Lovell plc 1977–87, finance dir Strong & Fisher Holdings plc 1987–91, finance dir Matthew Clark plc 1991–2001, finance dir Waste Recycling Group plc 2001–03, chief finance offr WRAP 2004–; non-exec dir Ashtead Group plc 2004–; FCA 1974, ACT 1981; mentor Prince's Tst; *Style—* Hugh Etheridge, Esq; ✉ WRAP, The Old Academy, 21 Horsefair, Banbury, Oxfordshire OX16 0AH (tel 01295 819935, e-mail hugh.etheridge@wrap.org.uk)

ETHERINGTON, Stuart James; s of Ronald George Etherington, of Mudeford, Dorset, and Dorothy Lillian, *née* West; *b* 26 February 1955; *Educ* Sondes Place Sch Dorking, Brunel Univ (BSc), Univ of Essex (MA), London Business Sch (MBA), SOAS Univ of London (MA); *Career* social worker 1977–79, researcher employed by housing tst 1980–83, policy advsr Br Assoc of Social Workers 1983–85, dir Good Practices in Mental Health 1985–87, chief exec RNID 1991–94 (dir of public affrs 1987–91), chief exec NCVO 1994–; visiting prof: South Bank Univ, City Univ; chm: Heritage Care 1996–2002, Civicus in Europe 1992–2000; tstee: Charity Aid Fndn (CAF) 1995–2004, English Churches Housing Tst 1999–2002, Civicus 2000–07 (treas 2004–07), Actors of Dionysus 2003–06; memb: New Deal Advsy Ctee 1997–2001, ESRC 1998–2003 (chm External Relations Ctee 1999–2003), RIIA, IISS; memb Cncl Open Univ 2002–06, memb Ct Greenwich Univ 2004–; Hon DSc Brunel Univ; FRSA; *Books* Mental Health and Housing (1984), Emergency Duty Teams (1985), Social Work and Citizenship (1987), The Sensitive Bureaucracy (1986), Worlds Apart (1990), The Essential Manager (1993); *Recreations* watching cricket and Charlton Athletic FC, reading, watching opera, film and theatre; *Clubs* Reform, Nat Liberal, Surrey CCC; *Style—* Stuart Etherington, Esq; ✉ 40 Walnut Tree Road, Greenwich, London SE10 9EU (tel 020 8305 1379); National Council for Voluntary Organisations, Regent's Wharf, 8 All Saints Street, London N1 9RL (tel 020 7713 6161, fax 020 7713 6300, e-mail stuart.etherington@ncvo-vol.org.uk)

ETHERINGTON, William (Bill); MP; *b* 17 July 1941; *Career* apprentice fitter Austin & Pickersgill Shipyard Southwick 1957–63, fitter Dawdon Colliery 1963–83; NUM: memb 1963–, branch delegate Durham Mechanics Branch 1973–83, full time official 1983–92, memb Nat Exec Ctee 1985–87, vice-pres NE Area 1988–92; tstee Mineworkers' Pension Scheme 1985–87, NUM rep to Northern Regnl TUC 1985–92, NUM delegate to TUC 1990–91; MP (Lab) Sunderland N 1992–; dep ldr Cncl of Europe and WEU Delgn 2001– (memb 1997–); sec: Miners Party Gp 1994–, APP Gp on Anti-fluoridation 1997–; vice-chair: Frame 2000–, APP Coalfield Communities Campaign 2001–; chair Northern Gp Labour MPs 2002 (vice-chair 2001); memb: Ombudsmans Select Ctee 1995–97, House of Commons Catering Ctee 1995–97, Channel Tunnel Rail Link Select Ctee 1995; former memb Exec Ctee Durham City CLP (treas Kelloe Ward 1983–88); *Recreations* fell walking, motorcycling, watching soccer, history, reading; *Style—* Bill Etherington, MP; ✉ House of Commons, London SW1A 0AA (tel 020 7219 4603)

ETTINGER, Robert Gerard Louis; s of Gerard Ettinger (d 2002), and Elizabeth, *née* Martinek (d 2004); *b* 17 August 1955, London; *Educ* Saint Nicolas Sch Northwood, Theresianische Acad Vienna, Coll St Benoit Ardouane; *m* 11 Aug 1993, Jane, *née* Gale; *Career* Mappins Jewellers Canada 1974–75, Zimmermann Co Frankfurt 1975–76, G Ettinger Ltd London 1977–; chm British Travelgoods and Accessories Assoc 2001–04; *Recreations* skiing, cycling, tennis, travel; *Clubs* Hurlingham, Ski Club of GB (memb Cncl 1981–84, chm Home Ctee 1983–86); *Style—* Robert Ettinger, Esq; ✉ G Ettinger Ltd, 215 Putney Bridge Road, London SW15 2NY (tel 020 8877 1616, fax 020 8877 1146, e-mail robert@ettinger.co.uk)

EUSTACE, Dudley Graham; s of Albert Eustace, MBE (d 1992), of Bristol, and Mary, *née* Manning (d 2004); *b* 3 July 1936; *Educ* The Cathedral Sch Bristol, Univ of Bristol (BA Econ); *m* 30 May 1964, Diane, da of Karl Zakrajsek (d 1974), of Nova Racek, Yugoslavia; 2 da (Gabriella b 1965, Chantal b 1967); *Career* actg PO RAFVR 1955–58; various appts (incl treas Canada and dir of fin UK) Alcan Aluminium Ltd of Canada 1964–87, dir of fin British Aerospace plc 1987–92, exec vice-pres Philips Electronics NV Netherlands 1992–99 (dir of fin 1992–97, vice-chm 1997–99), chm Smith & Nephew 2000–06 (dep chm

1999), chm Stork NV, non-exec chm Aegon NV; non-exec dir: Hagemeyer NV, Royal KPN NV; memb Advsy Cncl Rothschilds; vice-chm Univ of Surrey; Freeman: City of London, Worshipful Co of Chartered Accountants; FCA 1962; *Recreations* philately, gardening, reading; *Style—* Dudley Eustace, Esq; ✉ Avalon, Old Barn Lane, Churt, Surrey GU10 2NA

EUSTON, Earl of; James Oliver Charles FitzRoy; s and h of 11 Duke of Grafton, KG, DL, *qv*; *b* 13 December 1947; *Educ* Eton, Magdalene Coll Cambridge (MA); *m* 1972, Lady Clare Amabel Margaret Kerr (appeal pres Elizabeth FitzRoy Homes), da of 12 Marquess of Lothian, KCVO, DL; 4 da (Lady Louise Helen Mary b 1973, Lady Emily Clare b 1974, Lady Charlotte Rose b 1983, Lady Isobel Anne b 1985), 1 s (Henry Oliver Charles, Viscount Ipswich b 1978); *Heir* s, Viscount Ipswich; *Career* page of honour to HM The Queen 1962–63; asst dir J Henry Schroder Wagg & Co 1973–82, exec dir Enskilda Securities 1982–87; dir: Jamestown Investments Ltd 1987–91, Central Capital Holdings 1988–91, Capel-Cure Myers Capital Management 1988–96; FCA; *Clubs* Turf; *Style—* Earl of Euston; ✉ The Racing Stables, Euston, Thetford, Norfolk IP24 2QT

EVAN, Prof Gerard Ian; s of Robert Evan (*né* Robert Ekstein; d 1971), and Gwendoline, *née* Groom (d 1963); *b* 17 August 1955, London; *Educ* Forest Sch, St Peter's Coll Oxford (MA, Gibb Prize), King's Coll Cambridge (PhD, Max Perutz Prize); *m* 30 June 1984, Dr Jane Lindsay McLennan; 1 da (Tamara Jane b 9 Jan 1990), 1 s (Theodore Robert William b 26 July 1991); *Career* SERC postdoctoral research fell Dept of Microbiology and Immunology Univ of Calif San Francisco 1982–84 (MRC travelling fell 1982–83), asst memb Ludwig Inst for Cancer Research Cambridge 1984–88, fell Downing Coll Cambridge 1987–88 (research fell 1984–87), princ scientist ICRF 1988–99, Royal Soc Napier research prof UCL 1996–99, Gerson and Barbara Bass Bakar distinguished prof of cancer biology Univ of Calif San Francisco 1999–; author of 180 pubns in learned jls; fndr memb European Life Sciences Orgn 1999; memb: Biochemical Soc 1988, British Soc for Developmental Biology 1990, EMBO 1996, American Soc for Cell Biology 1999, American Assoc for Cancer Research (AACR) 2000, AAAS 2000; Pfizer Prize in Biology 1996, Joseph Steiner Prize in Cancer Research Swiss Oncological Soc 1996, Neal P Levitan chair of research Brain Tumor Soc 2004; FMedSci 1999, FRS 2004; *Recreations* hiking, music, biking; *Style—* Prof Gerard Evan; ✉ Cancer Research Institute, University of California San Francisco, Comprehensive Cancer Center, 2340 Sutter Street, Box 0875, San Francisco, CA 94143–0875, USA (tel 00 1 415 514 0438, fax 00 1 415 514 0878, e-mail gevan@cc.ucsf.edu)

EVANS, Alan Baxter; s of Arthur Llewellyn Evans (d 1947), and Ivy Geraldine, *née* Baxter (d 1954); *b* 18 May 1927; *Educ* Queen Elizabeth GS Wimborne, Exeter Coll Oxford (MA); *m* 1, 26 Nov 1949 (m dis 1964), Anne Elizabeth Gorlin; m 2, 14 Aug 1970, Janet Winifred Anne, da of Arthur Chalmers, of Woonona, NSW; 1 da (Harriet Francesca b 1971), 1 s (Jonathan Mark Arthur b 1973); *Career* Intelligence Corps 1946–48, served Italy and Austria; dir Spearing & Waldron Ltd 1955–59, mangr Du Pont UK Ltd 1959–61; dir: Evans & Co (London) Ltd 1961–70, Tyrolia Sporting Goods Ltd; dir Hall & Watts Ltd (dep chm 1971–2005); Freeman: City of London 1994, Worshipful Co of Scientific Instrument Makers 1994; FCA; *Recreations* reading, travelling; *Clubs* Oxford and Cambridge; *Style—* Alan Evans, Esq; ✉ Westwinds, Chapman Lane, Bourne End, Buckinghamshire SL8 5PA (tel 01628 529071)

EVANS, Alan William; s of Harold Evans (d 1980), of London, and Dorothy, *née* Surry (d 1999); *b* 21 February 1938; *Educ* Charterhouse, UCL (BA, PhD), Univ of Michigan; *m* 10 Aug 1964, Jill Alexandra, da of George Otto Brightwell (d 1961), of Vienna; 2 s (Christopher b 1969, Stephen b 1971); *Career* lectr Univ of Glasgow 1967–71, res offr Centre for Environmental Studies 1971–76, lectr LSE 1976–77; Univ of Reading: reader 1977–81, prof 1981–, pro-vice-chllr 1990–94, dep vice-chllr 1994–96; visiting res fell: Univ of Melbourne 1983, Australian Nat Univ 1998; Denman Lecture Univ of Cambridge 1990; other public lectures at: Tokyo 1994, Santiago de Chile 1996 and 2002, Seoul 2001, RSA 2001; socio corrispondente Societa Geographica Italiana 1994; FCA 1961, AcSS 2001; *Publications* The Economics of Residential Location (1973), Urban Economics (1985), No Room! No Room! (1988), Economics, Real Estate and the Supply of Land (2004), Economics and Planning (2004), Unaffordable Housing (jtly, 2005, Prospect Think Tank Awards Pubn of the Year), Bigger Better Faster More (jtly, 2005), Better Homes, Greener Cities (jtly, 2006), The Best Laid Plans (jtly, 2007); also author of numerous articles on the economics of cities, land and land use planning in academic and other jls; *Recreations* theatre, cinema, reading, travel; *Style—* Alan Evans, Esq; ✉ Lianda, Hill Close, Harrow on the Hill, Middlesex HA1 3PQ (tel 020 8423 0767); Centre for Spatial and Real Estate Economics, Urban and Regional Studies, University of Reading, Whiteknights, Reading, Berkshire RG6 6AW (tel 0118 378 8208, fax 0118 378 6533, e-mail a.w.evans@reading.ac.uk)

EVANS, Dame Anne Elizabeth Jane; DBE (2000); da of David Evans (d 1965), of London, and Eleanor, *née* Lewis (d 1988); *b* 20 August 1941; *Educ* RCM, Conservatoire de Genève (Thomas Beecham operatic scholarship, Boise Fndn award); *m* 1, 1962 (m dis 1981), John Heulyn Jones; m 2, 1981, John Philip Lucas; *Career* soprano; Geneva debut as Annina in La Traviata 1967, UK debut as Mimi in La Bohème 1968; subseq roles incl: Brünnhilde in Der Ring (Bayreuth Festival 1989–92, Vienna Staatsoper, Deutsche Oper Berlin, Covent Garden, etc), Isolde in Tristan und Isolde (WNO, Brussels, Berlin, Dresden), Elisabeth in Tannhäuser (Metropolitan Opera NYC, Berlin), Elsa in Lohengrin (San Francisco, Buenos Aires), Leonore in Fidelio (Metropolitan Opera NYC), Chrysothemis in Elektra (Rome, Marseilles, Geneva), Ariadne in Ariadne auf Naxos (Edinburgh Festival, 1997); also numerous roles with English National Opera and Welsh National Opera incl: Marschallin in Der Rosenkavalier, Kundry in Parsifal, Donna Anna in Don Giovanni, Empress and Dyer's Wife in Die Frau ohne Schatten; Edinburgh Festival recital 1993, soloist last night of the Proms 1997; Hon DMus Univ of Kent 2005; *Recordings* Brünnhilde in Der Ring 1991–92 (also video), Immolation Scene 1987, The Turn of the Screw 1998; *Recreations* cooking, gardening; *Style—* Dame Anne Evans, DBE; ✉ c/o Ingpen & Williams Ltd, 7 St George's Court, 131 Putney Bridge Road, London SW15 2PA (tel 020 8874 3222, fax 020 8877 3113)

EVANS, (David) Anthony; QC (1983); s of Thomas John Evans (d 1975), and May Evans, *née* Thomas (d 1962); *b* 15 March 1939; *Educ* Clifton, CCC Cambridge (BA); *m* 1974, Angela Evans, da of Clive Bewley, JP; 2 da (Serena b 17 Aug 1976, Tessa b 25 July 1978); *Career* called to the Bar Gray's Inn 1965 (bencher); practised at the Bar: Swansea 1965–84, London 1984–; recorder 1980–2002; DTI Inspector 1988–92; memb Criminal Bar Assoc; *Publications* Report to the Secretary of State for Trade and Industry on James Neill Holdings plc and other companies (1992); *Recreations* horse racing, rugby; *Clubs* Turf, MCC, Cardiff and County, Cardiff, Swansea RFC, DHO; *Style—* D Anthony Evans, Esq, QC; ✉ 9–12 Bell Yard, London WC2A 2JR (tel 020 7400 1800, fax 020 7 404 1405); Carey Hall, Rhyddings, Neath, West Glamorgan SA10 7AU (tel 01639 643859, fax 01639 630716); 8 Coleherne Mews, London SW10 9EA(tel 020 7370 1025)

EVANS, Rt Hon Sir Anthony Adney; 2 Bt (UK 1920), of Wightwick, near Wolverhampton, Co Stafford; PC (1992); s of Sir Walter Harry Evans, 1 Bt (d 1954), and Margaret Mary, *née* Dickens (d 1969); *b* 5 August 1922; *Educ* Shrewsbury, Merton Coll Oxford; *m* 1, 1 May 1948 (m dis 1957), Rita Beatrice, da of late Alfred David Kettle, of Souldern, Oxon, and formerly w of Larry Rupert Kirsch; 2 s, 1 da; m 2, 1958, Sylvia Jean; *Heir* s; *Style—* The Rt Hon Sir Anthony Evans, Bt

EVANS, Anthony Clive Varteg (Tony); s of Edward Varteg Evans (d 1978), and Doris Lilian, *née* Whitaker; *b* 11 October 1945; *Educ* De la Salle GS London, St Peter's Coll Oxford (MA), Sorbonne, UCL (MPhil); *m* 1968, Danielle Jacqueline Bégasse (d 1997); 2 s (Pascal b 11 Nov 1969, Olivier b 12 Nov 1975); *Career* teacher: Eastbourne Coll 1967–72, Winchester Coll 1972–77; head of humanities and modern languages Dulwich Coll 1977–83; headmaster: The Portsmouth GS 1983–97, KCS Wimbledon 1997–2007; chm: HMC Acad Policy Ctee 1990–94, HMC 1996 (memb 1983–), ISC Advsy Ctee 1997–2000; co-chm: HMC/GSA Univ Working Pty 1993–2002, ISC Unity Ctee 1997–2000; memb: Admiralty Interview Bd 1985–97, Nat Curriculum Cncl 1989–91, HEFCE 1999–2002; fell Winchester Coll 1997; govr: The Mall Sch 1997–2007, Sevenoaks Sch 1999–, St George's Montreux 2000–07, The Perse Sch 2003–05; FCIL 1972; *Books* Souvenirs de la Grande Guerre (1985), The Future of Modern Languages (1992); *Recreations* theatre, France, soccer; *Clubs* East India; *Style—* Tony Evans, Esq; ✉ King's College School, Southside, Wimbledon Common, London SW19 4TT (tel 020 8255 5353, fax 020 8255 5359, e-mail head.master@kcs.org.uk)

EVANS, Prof Barry George; s of William Arthur Evans (d 1984), of Dartford, Kent, and Jean Ida, *née* Lipscombe; *b* 15 October 1944; *Educ* Univ of Leeds (BSc, PhD); *m* 1 (m dis 1983), Carol Ann, *née* Gillis; 1 da (Lisa Jane b 1969), 1 s (Robert Iain Lawrie b 1971); m 2, 10 March 1984, Rhian Elizabeth Marilyn, da of Russell Lewis Jones (d 1974), of Camarthen; 1 s (Rhys David Russell b 1984), 1 da (Cerian Elizabeth Lucy b 1985); *Career* lectr, sr lectr and reader in telecommunications Univ of Essex 1968–83, Satellite Systems Conslts C&W Ltd 1976–80; Univ of Surrey: Alec Harley Reeves prof of info systems engrg 1983–, dean of Engrg Res 1999–2001, pro-vice-chllr Res and Enterprise 2001–; dir: Centre for Satellite Engineering 1990–96, Centre for Communications Systems Research 1996–, Satconsult Ltd, USEB Ltd; technical advsr to DG OFTEL 1997–2000; ed International Jl of Satellite Communications; author of over 500 papers on telecommunications and satellite systems published; memb: UK Foresight ITEC Panel, UK CCIR Ctees 5 and 8, DTI and EPSRC Link Mgmnt and SAT Ctee, Ofcom Spectrum Advsy Bd 2004; finalist McRobert award 1997; CEng, FIEE, FREng 1991, FRSA; *Books* Telecommunications Systems Design (1974), Satellite Systems Design (1988, 3 edn 1998); *Recreations* travel, wine, sport; *Style—* Prof Barry Evans, FREng; ✉ Centre for Communications Systems, University of Surrey, Guildford GU2 7XH (tel 01483 689131, fax 01483 686011, e-mail b.evans@surrey.ac.uk)

EVANS, Cerith Wyn; *b* 1958, Wales; *Educ* St Martin's Sch of Art London, RCA (MA); *Career* artist and film maker; selector Bloomberg New Contemporaries 2003; *Solo Exhibitions* incl: And Then I 'Woke Up' (London Film Makers Co-op) 1980, A Certain Sensibility (ICA Cinematheque London) 1981, Solo Project (London Film Makers Co-op) 1981 and 1983, Solo Exhibition (ICA Cinemateque London) 1989, Sense and Influence (Kijkhuis The Hague) 1990, Crossoverworkshop (HFAK Vienna) 1992, Les Visiteurs du Soir (London Film Festival) 1993, Studio Casa Grande Rome 1996, Inverse Reverse Perverse (White Cube London) 1996, Deitch Projects New York 1997, Br Sch of Rome (in collaboration with Asprey Jacques Contemporary Art Exhibitions Rome) 1998, Asprey Jacques Contemporary Art Exhibitions London 1999, "Has the film already started?" (Galerie Neu Berlin) 2000, fig-1 London 2000, Cleave.00 Art Now (Tate Britain London) 2000, Galerie Neu Berlin 2000 and 2003, Cerith Wyn Evans The Art Newspaper Project (Venice Biennale) 2001, Georg Kargl Gallery Vienna 2001, Kunsthaus Glarus 2001, Galerie Daniel Buchholz Cologne 2001, Cerith Wyn Evans Screening (Galerie Daniel Buchholz Cologne) 2002, mini MATRIX Berkeley Art Museum San Francisco 2003, Look at that picture...How does it appear to you now? Does it seem to be Persisting (White Cube London) 2003, Rabbit's Moon (Camden Arts Centre) 2004, Meanwhile Across Town (Centre Point London) 2004, The Sky is Thin as Paper Here... (Galerie Daniel Buchholz Cologne) 2004, Kunstverein Frankfurt 2004, film screening Centre Pompidou Paris 2004, Museum of Fine Arts Boston 2004, Thoughts unsaid, not forgotten... (MIT Visual Arts Center Boston) 2004, 299792458m/s (BAWAG Fndn Vienna) 2005, Once a Noun, Now a Verb (Galerie Neu Berlin) 2005; *Group Exhibitions* incl: The New Art (Tate Gallery London) 1983, Artist as Film Maker (Nat Film Theatre London) 1984, The Salon of 1984 (ICA Gallery London) 1984, The New Pluralism (Tate Gallery London) 1985, Syncronisation of the Senses (ICA Cinematheque London) 1985, The Elusive Sign (Tate Gallery London) 1987, The Melancholy Imaginary (in collaboration with Jean Mathee, London Film Makers Co-op) 1988, Degrees of Blindness (Edinburgh Film Festival) 1988, Image and Object in Current British Art (Centre Georges Pompidou Paris) 1990, Sign of the Times (MOMA Oxford) 1990, Cerith Wyn Evans and Gaylen Gerber (Wooster Gardens Gallery NY) 1992, 240 Minutes (Galerie Esther Schipper Cologne) 1992, 5th Oriel Mostyn Open Exhibition (Oriel Mostyn Llandudno) 1993, Liar (Hoxton Sq London) 1994, Flux (film screening, Minema Cinema London) 1994, Superstore Boutique (Laure Genillard Gallery London) 1994, Potato (IAS London) 1994, Future Anterior (Eigen + Art's/IIAS - Young British Artists London) 1995, Faction Video (Royal Danish Acad of Fine Arts Copenhagen) 1995, General Release: Young British Artists (Scuola di San Pasquale Venice) 1995, Stoppage (FRAC Tours) 1995, Sick (152 Brick Lane London) 1995, Kiss This (Focal Point Gallery Southend) 1996, British Artists in Rome (Studio Casagrande Rome) 1996, Against (Anthony d'Offay London) 1996, Life/Live (Musée d'Art Moderne de la Ville de Paris and Centro de Exposições do Centro Cultural de Belém Lisbon) 1996, Material Culture (Hayward Gallery London) 1997, Falseimpressions (The British Sch at Rome) 1997, Gothic (ICA Boston) 1997, A Print Portfolio from London (Atle Gehardsen Oslo) 1997, Sensation (Royal Acad of Arts London) 1997 (also at Hamburger Bahnhof Berlin 1998–99), Ray Rapp (Tz'Art & Co New York) 1998, View Four (Mary Boone New York) 1998, From the Corner of the Eye (Stedelijk Museum Amsterdam) 1998, How will we behave? (Robert Prime London) 1998, Retrace your steps: Remember Tomorrow (Sir John Soane's Museum London) 1999, Neu Gallery Berlin 1999, 54x54 (Financial Times Building London) 1999, Lost (Ikon Gallery London) 2000, The Greenhouse Effect (Serpentine Gallery London in collaboration with The Natural History Museum) 2000, The British Art Show 5 (The Scottish Nat Gallery of Modern Art Edinburgh) 2000, Out There (White Cube 2 London) 2000, There is something you should know (Die EVN Sammlung im Belvedere Vienna) 2000, Ever get the feeling you've been... (A22 Projects London) 2000, Rumours (Arc en Reve Centre d'Architecture Bordeaux) 2000, Sensitive (Le Printemps de Cahors Saint-Cloud) 2000, Diesseits und jenseits des Traums (Sigmund Freud Museum Vienna) 2001, What's Wrong (Trade Apartment London) 2001, Zusammenhänge in Biotop Kunst (Kunsthaus Muertz) 2001, Dedalic Convention (Stefan Kalmár-MAK Vienna) 2001, How do you change... (Inst of Visual Culture Cambridge) 2001, Wales - Unauthorised Versions (House of Croatian Artists Zagreb) 2001, Wir, Comawoche Film Screening (Metropolis Cinema Hamburg) 2001, My Generation 24 Hours of Video Art (Atlantis Gallery London) 2001, Gymnasion (Bregenzer Kunstverein Bregenz) 2001, There is something you should know. Die EVN Sammlung in Belvedere (Österreichische Galerie Belvedere Vienna) 2001, Yokohama 2001 International Triennale of Contemporary Art 2001, In the Freud Museum (Freud Museum London) 2002, ForwArt (Palais des Beaux-Arts Brussels) 2002, It's Only Words (Mirror Gallery London Inst) 2002, Void Archive (CCA Kitakyushu) 2002, Iconoclash. Image Wars in Science, Religion and Art (Center for Art and Media Karlsruhe) 2002, Screen Memories (Contemporary Art Centre Art Tower Mito Tokyo) 2002, My Head is on Fire but My Heart is Full of Love (Charlottenborg Museum Copenhagen) 2002, Shine (The Lowry Centre Manchester) 2002, Mirror: It's Only Words (London Coll of Printing) 2002, Edén (La Colección Jumex Mexico City) 2003, Cardinales (MARCO Vigo) 2003, The Straight or the Crooked Way (Royal Coll of Art Galleries London) 2003, Someone to Share My Life With (The Approach London) 2003, Light Works (Taka Ishii Gallery

E

Tokyo) 2003, Utopia Station (50th International Venice Biennale) 2003, Addiction (15 Micawber Street London) 2003, Independence (South London Gallery London) 2003, Galleria Lorcan O'Neill Rome 2003, Adorno (Frankfurter Kunstverein Frankfurt am Main) 2003, St Sebastian. A Splendid Readiness For Death (Kunsthalle Vienna) 2003, Wittgenstein Family Likeness (Inst of Visual Culture Cambridge) 2003, Take a Bowery: The Art and (larger than) Life of Leigh Bowery (MCA Sydney) 2003, Sans Soleil (Galerie Neu Berlin) 2004, Ulysses (Galerie Belvedere Vienna) 2004, Hidden Histories (New Art Gallery Walsall) 2004, Doubtiful Dans Les Plis Du Reel (Galerie Art & Essai Rennes) 2004, Marc Camille Chaimowicz (Angel Row Gallery Nottingham) 2004, Making Visible (Galleri Faurschou Copenhagen) 2004, Drunken Masters (Galeria Fortes Vilaça São Paulo) 2004, The Ten Commandments (Deutsches Hygiene-Museum Dresden) 2004, Black Friday: Exercise in Hermetics (Revolver Frankfurt) 2004, Eclipse (White Cube) 2004, Einleuchten (Museum der Moderne Salzburg) 2004, The Future Has a Silver Lining (Migros Museum Zurich) 2004, Trafic d'influences (Tri Postal Lille) 2004, Quodlibet (Galerie Daniel Buchholz Cologne) 2004, Utopia Station (Hans der Kunst Munich) 2004, Prince Charles Cinema London 2004, E-Flux Video Rental Store (KW Inst for Contemporary Art Berlin) 2005, I'd Rather Jack (Edinburgh) 2005, Ice Storm (Kunstverein Munich) 2005, Can Buildings Curate (AA Sch of Architecture London) 2005, Light Lab (Museoin Bolzano) 2005; *Work in Public Collections* Br Cncl London, Caldic Collection Rotterdam, ReRebaudengo, EVN Vienna, Museo de Arte Acarigua-Araure Caracas, Saatchi Collection London, Tate Gallery London, La Coleccion Jumex Mexico City, Frankfurter Kunstverein Frankfurt, Pompidou Centre Paris; *Style—* Cerith Wyn Evans, Esq; ✉ c/o White Cube, 48 Hoxton Square, London N1 6PB

EVANS, Dr Christopher Charles; s of Robert Percy (d 1974), and Nora Carson, *née* Crowther (d 1992); *b* 2 October 1941; *Educ* Wade Deacon GS Widnes, Univ of Liverpool (MB ChB, MD); *m* 5 Feb 1966, Dr Susan Evans, da of Dr Heinz Fuld, of Llanarmon-yn-Ial, Denbighshire; 2 da (Joanne b 1971, Sophie b 1975), 1 s (Matthew b 1973); *Career* sr lectr in med and hon conslt physician Univ of Liverpool 1974–78, conslt physician in gen and thoracic med Royal Liverpool Univ Hosp and Cardio-Thoracic Centre Liverpool 1978–2003 (now emeritus), clinical sub-dean Royal Liverpool Hosp 1978–88; chief MO Swiss Life, conslt MO Royal Sun Alliance plc 1978–2005, chm and pres Med Def Union 2006–; pres Liverpool Med Inst 1991–92; memb: Assoc of Physicians, Br Thoracic Soc; examiner, censor and academic vice-pres RCP London; FRCP 1979 (MRCP 1968), FRCPI (1997); *Books* Chamberlain's Symptoms and Signs in Clinical Medicine (with C M Ogilvie, 1987, 12 edn 1997); *Recreations* skiing, tennis, fell walking, watching theatre and Liverpool FC; *Clubs* XX, Artists (Liverpool), Reform; *Style—* Dr Christopher Evans; ✉ Lagom, Glendyke Road, Liverpool L18 6JR (tel 0151 724 5386, e-mail christoffe58@hotmail.com)

EVANS, Prof Sir Christopher Thomas (Chris); kt (2001), OBE (1995); s of Cyril Evans, and Jean Evans; *b* 29 November 1957; *Educ* Imperial Coll London (BSc, ARCS), Univ of Hull (PhD), DSc; *m* 1985, Judith Anne; 2 s, 2 da; *Career* postdoctoral res Univ of Michigan 1983, Alleix Inc 1984–86, Genzyme Biochemicals Ltd 1986–87, fndr and chm Merlin Ventures Ltd; fndr and dir: Enzymatix Ltd 1987–, Chiroscience plc 1992–, Celsis International plc 1992– (chm 1998–), Cerebrus Ltd 1995–; fndr, dir and chm: Toad Innovations plc 1993–, Merlin Scientific Services Ltd 1995–, Enviros Ltd 1995–, Cyclacel Ltd 1996–; dir: Microscience Ltd 1997, GEO plc, Plethora plc until 2007, Decon Sciences Ltd, Lab 21 Ltd, Derms Devpt Ltd, White Light Therapy Ltd, Energist Ltd; fndr: Merlin Fund 1996, Merlin Biosciences Fund, Finsbury Life Sciences Investment Tst (FLIT); memb PM's Cncl for Science and Technology, tstee Nat Endowment for Sci, Technol and the Arts, memb Competitiveness Cncl, ambass Nat Enterprise Campaign; former: dir BioIndustry Assoc, chm BEST Ctee EC; BVCA Cartier Vetiver Award, Henderson Meml Medal Porton Down 1997, SCI Centenary Medal 1998, RSC Interdiciplinary Medal 1999; hon prof: Univ of Manchester, Univ of Liverpool, Univ of Exeter, Univ of Bath (also fell), Imperial Coll London; hon fell: Univ of Wales Coll Cardiff 1996, Univ of Wales Swansea 1996; Hon DSc: Univ of Hull 1995, Univ of Nottingham 1995, UEA 1998, Cranfield Univ 1998; CBiol 1994, FIBiol 1994, CChem 1995, FRSC 1995, FRSA 1995, fell Acad of Med 2003, Hon FREng 2005; *Publications* author of numerous scientific papers and patents; *Recreations* rugby, gym, fly fishing, shooting, electric guitar; *Style—* Prof Sir Chris Evans, OBE; ✉ Merlin Biosciences Ltd, 33 King Street, St James's London SW1Y 6RJ (tel 020 7811 4000, fax 020 7811 4011, e-mail cevans@merlin-biosciences.com)

EVANS, Dr (William) David; s of William Harold Evans (d 1985), and Gladys Elizabeth Evans (d 1984); *b* 20 April 1949; *Educ* Haberdashers' Aske's Sch, St Catherine's Coll Oxford (MA, DPhil); *m* 1980, Elizabeth, *née* Crowe; 3 s (James William b 1982, Matthew David b 1984, Edward Michael b 1989), 1 da (Clare Elizabeth b 1986); *Career* civil servant; Dept of Energy 1974–80, first sec (sci and technol) Br Embassy Bonn 1980–83; Dept of Energy: asst sec 1984–89, chief scientist 1989–92; DTI: head Environment Div 1992–94, head Technol and Innovation Policy Div 1994–96, dir Technol and Standards 1996–98, dir Competitiveness Unit and head Central Directorate 1998–2001, dep chief-exec Small Business Serv 2001–02, dir Fin and Resource Mgmnt 2003–05, actg DG Gen Servs 2005–06, dir Innovation Mgmnt 2006–; author scientific papers in professional jls; memb: NERC 1989–92, EPSRC 1994–98, Particle Physics and Astronomy Research Cncl (PPARC) 1994–98, Senate Engrg Cncl 1996–98; FRAS 1975; *Recreations* music, reading, history of technology; *Style—* Dr David Evans; ✉ Department of Trade and Industry, 151 Buckingham Palace Road, London SW1W 9SS (tel 020 7215 1703, fax 020 7215 1340, e-mail david.evans@dti.gov.uk)

EVANS, David; *see:* Edge (The)

EVANS, David; CBE (1992); s of William Price Evans, and late Ella Mary Evans; *b* 7 December 1935; *Educ* Welwyn Garden City GS, UCL (BScEcon); *m* 1960, Susan Carter, da of late Dr John Connal; 1 s, 1 da; *Career* MAFF: joined 1959, private sec to Parly Sec (Lords) 1962–64, princ 1964, princ private sec to Mins 1970–71, asst sec 1971, seconded to Cabinet Office 1972–74, under sec 1976–80; Nat Farmers' Union: chief econ and policy advsr 1981–84, dep dir-gen 1984–85, dir-gen 1985–96; dir-gen Federation of Agricultural Co-operatives 1996–; *Style—* David Evans, Esq, CBE

EVANS, Emeritus Prof David Alan Price; s of Owen Evans (d 1978), of Liverpool, and Ellen, *née* Jones (d 1975); *b* 6 March 1927; *Educ* Univ of Liverpool (BSc, MB ChB, MSc, MD, PhD, DSc, J Hill Abram prize for med, Sir Robert Kelly,eml medal for surgery, Henry Briggs meml medal for obstetrics and gynaecology, Owen T Williams prize, N E Roberts prize, Samuels prize); *Career* Nat Serv Capt RAMC 1953–55 (active serv Japan, Singapore, Korea, Malaya); house physician and house surgn Liverpool Royal Infirmary 1951–52, Holt fell Univ of Liverpool 1952–53, SHO Broadgreen Hosp Liverpool 1955–56; med registrar: Stanley Hosp Liverpool 1956–58, Northern Hosp Liverpool 1959–60; research fell Johns Hopkins Univ 1958–59, conslt physician Royal Liverpool Hosp (formerly Royal Infirmary) and Broadgreen Hosp Liverpool 1965–83, prof Dept of Med Univ of Liverpool 1968–72 (lectr 1960–62, sr lectr 1962–68), chm and prof Dept of Med and dir Nuffield Unit of Med Genetics Univ of Liverpool 1972–83, dir of med Riyadh Al Kharj Hosp Programme 1983–99 (sr conslt physician 1999–2007), ret; visiting prof: Karolinska Univ Stockholm, Helsinki Univ, Berne Univ, Ann Arbor Univ, Johns Hopkins Univ; emeritus prof Univ of Liverpool 1994–; sci ed Saudi Med Jl 1983–93, memb Editorial Bd Int Jl of Clinical Pharmacology and Research 1980–, memb Editorial Advsy Bd Pharmacogenetics 1992–2001; memb Assoc of Physicians of GB and Ireland 1964, life memb Johns Hopkins Soc of Scholars 1972; FRCP 1968 (MRCP 1956); *Publications* Genetic Factors in Drug Therapy (1993); author of numerous articles and chapters in books on pharmacogenetics; *Style—* Emeritus Prof David A Price Evans; ✉ 28 Montclair Drive, Liverpool L18 0HA (tel 0151 722 3112, e-mail dape28mont@yahoo.com)

EVANS, Prof David Emrys; s of Evan Emrys Evans (d 1985), of Cross Hands, Carmarthenshire, and Gwynneth Mair Eurfron, *née* Owen (d 1969); *b* 14 October 1950; *Educ* Ysgol Ramadeg Dyffrun Gwendraeth, Univ of Oxford (BA, MSc, DPhil); *m* 20 Oct 1984, Pornsawan; 2 s (Emrys Wyn b 12 June 1990, Arwyn Dafydd b 15 March 1993); *Career* Dublin Inst for Advanced Studies 1975–76, Oslo Univ 1976–77, Royal Soc exchange fell Copenhagen Univ 1978, SERC res fell Univ of Newcastle upon Tyne 1979, reader Univ of Warwick 1986–87 (lectr 1979–86), prof Univ of Wales Swansea 1987–98, prof Cardiff Univ (formerly Univ of Wales Cardiff) 1998–, visiting prof Kyoto Univ Japan 1990–91; Jr Whitehead prize London Mathematical Soc 1989; memb: London Mathematical Soc, American Mathematical Soc; *Books* Dilations of Irreversible Evolutions in Algebraic Quantum Theory (with J T Lewis, 1977), Quantum Symmetries on Operator algebras (with Y Kawahigashi, 1998); *Style—* Prof David Evans; ✉ School of Mathematics, Cardiff University, Senghennydd Road, Cardiff CF24 4AG (tel 029 2087 4522, fax 029 2087 4199, e-mail evansDE@cf.ac.uk)

EVANS, Prof (John) David Gemmill; s of John Desmond Evans (d 1977), and Babette Evans (d 1985); *b* 27 August 1942; *Educ* St Edward's Sch Oxford, Queens' Coll Cambridge (BA, MA, PhD); *m* 14 Sept 1974, Rosemary, da of Gweirydd Ellis, of Chippenham; *Career* fell Sidney Sussex Coll Cambridge 1964–78, prof of logic and metaphysics Queen's Univ Belfast 1978– (dean Faculty of Arts 1986–89); memb Exec Ctee Int Fedn of Philosophical Socs, memb Exec Ctee Aristotelian Soc, memb Cncl Royal Inst of Philosophy, chm UK Nat Ctee for Philosophy, memb Conseil d'Administration AIPPh (Assoc Internationale des Professeurs de Philosophie); MRIA 1983; *Books* Aristotle's Concept of Dialectic (1977), Truth and Proof (1979), Aristotle (1987), Moral Philosophy and Contemporary Problems (1987), Teaching Philosophy on the Eve of the Twenty-First Century (1997), Proceedings of the 21st World Conference of Philosophy: Vol 4, Philosophy of Education (2006); *Recreations* mountaineering, astronomy, poker; *Style—* Prof David Evans; ✉ Philosophy Department, Queen's University, Belfast BT7 1NN (tel 028 9097 3848, fax 028 9024 7895, e-mail jdg.evans@qub.ac.uk)

EVANS, David Howard; QC (1991); s of David Hopkin Evans, of Stoneleigh, Warwicks, and Phoebe Dora, *née* Reading; *b* 27 July 1944; *Educ* The Woodlands Sch Coventry, LSE (BSc, MSc), Wadham Coll Oxford (MA); *m* 20 June 1973, Anne Celia, da of John Segall, of W London; 2 s (Oliver Anthony b 1977, Edward Alexander b 1980); *Career* called to the Bar Middle Temple 1972 (bencher 2004), practising barrister 1972–, recorder of the Crown Court 1992–; Freeman City of London, memb Worshipful Co of Pattenmakers; *Recreations* tennis, golf, reading, listening to music; *Clubs* Roehampton, Lansdowne; *Style—* David Evans, Esq, QC; ✉ 3rd Floor, Queen Elizabeth Buildings, Temple, London EC4Y 9BS (tel 020 7583 5766, fax 020 7353 0359)

EVANS, David John; *b* 23 April 1935; *Educ* Raglan Rd Sch, Tottenham Tech Coll; *m* Janice Hazel, *née* Masters; 2 s, 1 da; *Career* MP (Cons) Welwyn Hatfield 1987–97; PPS to Lord Hesketh as min for Indust at DTI 1990–91; PPS to John Redwood: as min for Corp Affrs at DTI 1991–92, as min for Local Govt and Inner Cities DOE 1992–93, as sec of state for Wales 1993–95; elected to Exec 1922 Ctee 1993–97; sec Cons Backbench Sports Ctee 1987–90; memb Select Ctee on: Members' Interests 1990, Deregulation 1995–97; treas Cons Pty 1996–97; chm: Luton Town Football & Athletic Co Ltd 1984–89 (dir 1976–90), Bradnam Enterprises Ltd 1990–95, Broadreach Gp Ltd 1990–2002; dir: Initial plc 1987–89, Trimoco plc 1987–89, Sedgwick Gp Devpt Ltd 1992–99, Marsh European Devpt Gp 1999–2002, Jardine Lloyd Thompson 2002–; fndr, chm and md Brengreen (Holdings) plc 1960–86; Freeman: City of London, Worshipful Co of Horners; Liveryman Worshipful Co of Environmental Cleaners; *Style—* David Evans, Esq

EVANS, David Mervyn; s of (Edward) Mervyn Evans, of Swansea, and Muriel Hawley, *née* Amison; *b* 18 September 1942; *Educ* Clifton, Middx Hosp Med Sch (MB BS); *m* 19 June 1971, Dr Elizabeth Cecily Evans, da of Frederick Hornung (d 1973); 1 s (Daniel b 1975), 1 da (Kate b 1976); *Career* conslt hand surgn The Hand Clinic Windsor, hon conslt hand surgn Royal Nat Orthopaedic Hosp London; hon sec Br Soc for Surgery of the Hand 1986–88 (pres 1995), chm Med Commission on Accident Prevention 1991–94, ed Jl of Hand Surgery (Br vol) 1992–95; FRCS 1969; *Recreations* music, windsurfing; *Style—* David Evans, Esq; ✉ The Hand Clinic, Oakley Green, Windsor SL4 4LH (tel 01753 831333, fax 01753 832109)

EVANS, David Morgan (Dai); s of David Morgan Evans (d 1966), and Elizabeth Margaret, *née* Massey (d 1993); *b* 1 March 1944; *Educ* King's Sch Chester, UCW (BA); *m* 1973, Sheena Gilfillan, da of James Wesley Milne; 3 da (Alexandra Elizabeth b 1976, Katherine Siân Morgan b 1978, Sarah Jane Massey b 1980); *Career* inspr Ancient Monuments (England) DOE and English Heritage 1977–92 (Wales 1969–77), gen sec Soc of Antiquaries 1992–2004, visiting prof Univ of Chester 2006–; chm Butser Ancient Farm Tst 2003–; FSA, FSA Scot, Hon MIFA; *Recreations* gardening, walking, opera, Montgomeryshire; *Style—* Dai Evans, Esq; ✉ Society of Antiquaries of London, Burlington House, Piccadilly, London W1J 0BE (tel 020 7734 0193, fax 020 7287 6967, e-mail admin@sal.org.uk)

EVANS, David Pugh; s of John David Charles Evans (d 1972), and Katherine Pugh (d 1947); *b* 20 November 1942; *Educ* Newbridge GS, Newport Coll of Art, Royal Coll of Art (RCA Silver Medal for Painting); *m* 1971 (m dis 1977), Patricia Ann, da of Kenneth Keay; *Career* artist; lectr Edinburgh Coll of Art 1965–68 and 1969–98; Granada arts fell Univ of York 1968–69; ARCA 1965, RSW 1974, RSA 1985 (ARSA 1974); *Solo Exhibitions* Univ of York 1969, Goosewell Gallery 1969, Marjorie Parr Gallery 1970, 1972 and 1974, Gilbert Parr Gallery 1977 and 1980, Fruitmarket Gallery (retrospective) 1982, Mercury Gallery 1985, Open Eye Gallery 1991 and 2005, Scottish Arts Club Edinburgh (retrospective) 2006; *Group Exhibitions* Royal Acad, Royal Scottish Acad, Soc of Scottish Artists, Univ of Stirling, Univ of York, Aberdeen Art Gallery, Dundee Art Gallery, Fine Art Soc, Royal Glasgow Inst, Richard Demarco Gallery, The Scottish Gallery, Middlesbrough Art Gallery, Kirkcaldy Art Gallery, Mercury Gallery, Galerija Fakulteta Belgrade, Compass Gallery, Royal West of England Gallery, Bath Festival of Contemporary Arts, Basle Arts Fair, British Airways Exec Lounge Edinburgh Airport (2 man) 1997, Open Eye Gallery (3 man) 1997, Thompson's Gallery London, Blythswood Gallery Glasgow 2006 and 2007, Scottish Gallery Edinburgh 2006; *Work in Collections* RA, City of Edinburgh, Royal Burgh of Arbroath, Hunterian Museum, Glasgow Art Galleries and Museums, Carlisle Art Gallery, Scottish Arts Cncl, Contemporary Arts Soc, Aberdeen Art Gallery, St Catherine's Coll Oxford, Imperial Coll London, Scottish Television, Royal Bank of Scotland, Scottish and Newcastle Breweries; *Awards* Royal Burgh of Arbroath painting prize 1971, May Marshall Brown Award RSW 1978, W G Gillies Award RSW 1983, 1986 and 1989, W J Macaulay Award RSA 1984 and 2004, Scottish Arts Club Award RSW 1993, Scottish Post Office Bd Award RSA 1994, RSW Cncl Prize RSW 1997; *Style—* David Evans, Esq, RSA; ✉ 17 Inverleith Gardens, Edinburgh EH3 5PS (tel 0131 552 2329)

EVANS, David Robert Howard; s of Rev Denys Roberts Evans (d 1988), of Oxford, and Beryl Mary, *née* Toye; *b* 27 February 1950; *Educ* Magdalen Coll Sch Oxford, Univ of Exeter (LLB), King's Coll and LSE Univ of London (LLM), Brasenose Coll Oxford (DipLaw); *m* 1, 6 Jan 1979 (m dis 1988), Gillian Mary; 1 s (Matthew Charles b 1985); m 2, 7 May 1989 m dis 2003), Janet Lea, formerly w of Amos Kollek, of Jerusalem, da of Nat T Kanarek, of New York; 1 da (Cordelia Moses Roberts b 1991); *Career* admitted slr 1976; slr: Freshfields 1975–77, British Railways Bd 1977–79, Linklaters & Paines

1980–82; ptnr: Berwin Leighton 1984–87 (slr 1982–83), D J Freeman & Co 1987–91; sr ptnr David Evans Slrs 1991–2002; md: Lox, Stock and Bagel Ltd 1992–2002, Anglo International Education Consultants Ltd 1992–, Janet's Bar 1996–2002; tstee Statute Law Tst; minister of the Gospel of Jesus Christ 2003–; Freeman City of London 1981, Liveryman Worshipful Co of Slrs 1988; memb Law Soc 1976; *Recreations* playing clarinet and piano, tennis, squash; *Style*— David Evans, Esq; ✉ 51 Drayton Gardens, London SW10 9RX (tel 020 7835 2143)

EVANS, Prof (William) Desmond; s of Bryn Gwyn Evans (d 1993), and Evelyn Evans (d 1974); *b* 7 March 1940; *Educ* Ystalyfera GS, Univ of Swansea (BSc), Univ of Oxford (DPhil); *m* 27 Aug 1966, Mari, da of Murray Richards (d 1953); 2 s (Dyfed b 1969, Owain b 1973); *Career* UC Cardiff: lectr 1964–73, sr lectr 1973–75, reader 1975–77, prof 1977–; London Maths Soc: memb 1964, editorial advsr 1977–86, ed Proceedings 1986–92, memb Cncl 1989–91; memb Editorial Bd: Jl of Inequalities and Applications 1995–, Mathematisches Nachrichten 1998–, Proceedings of the Georgian Academy of Sciences 1999–, Revista Complutense Mathematica 1999–; *Publications* Spectral Theory and Differential Equations (with D E Edmunds, 1987), Hardy Operators, Function Spaces and Embeddings (with D E Edmunds, 2004); over 120 articles on differential equations in academic jls; *Recreations* walking, tennis, music; *Clubs* Dinas Powys Tennis; *Style*— Prof Desmond Evans; ✉ School of Mathematics, Cardiff University, Senghennydd Road, Cardiff CF24 4AG (tel 029 2087 4206, fax 029 2087 4199, e-mail evanswd@cf.ac.uk)

EVANS, Prof (David) Ellis; yr s of David Evans (d 1948), and Sarah Jane, *née* Lewis; *b* 23 September 1930; *Educ* Llandeilo GS, UCW Aberystwyth, UC Swansea, Jesus Coll Oxford; *m* 1957, Sheila Mary, er da of David Thomas Jeremy, of Swansea; 2 da; *Career* former lectr, reader and prof of Welsh language and literature UC Swansea 1957–78, Jesus prof of Celtic Univ of Oxford and fell Jesus Coll 1978–96 (prof emeritus 1996–, hon fell 1997–); UC Swansea: hon fell 1985, hon prof Dept of Welsh 1990–; hon fell UCW Aberystwyth 1992, hon foreign memb American Acad of Arts and Scis 1992; Hon DLitt Univ of Wales 1993; Hon MRIA 2000; FBA 1983; *Recreations* music, flowers; *Style*— Prof Ellis Evans, FBA; ✉ 2 Price Close, Bicester, Oxfordshire OX26 4JH (tel 01869 246469)

EVANS, His Hon Fabyan Peter Leaf; s of late Peter Fabyan Evans, and Catherine Elise Evans (d 1995); *b* 10 May 1943; *Educ* Clifton; *m* 12 Sept 1967, Karen Myrtle, da of Lionel Joachim Balfour; 2 s (Nigel Henley Fabyan b 26 April 1971, Alexander Peter Sommerville b 21 Feb 1976), 1 da (Jessica Ann b 30 May 1973); *Career* called to the Bar Inner Temple 1969, recorder of the Crown Court 1985–88, circuit judge (SE Circuit) 1988–2005, resident judge Middlesex Guildhall Crown Court 1995–; chm London Criminal Justice Strategy Ctee 2000–03; *Recreations* golf, singing; *Clubs* Brooks's; *Style*— His Hon Fabyan Evans

EVANS, Gareth Robert William; QC (1994); s of David Morris John Evans, of Pontllanfraith, Gwent, and Megan, *née* Hughes (d 1964); *b* 19 January 1947; *Educ* Caerfilli GS, Univ of London (external LLB); *m* 1971, Marion, *née* Green; 1 da (Judith Ann b 1 Nov 1978), 1 s (David Glyn b 18 April 1982); *Career* called to the Bar Gray's Inn 1973; jr Midland & Oxford Circuit 1983, recorder of the Crown Court 1993–, head of chambers 2002–; *Recreations* watching rugby, reading poetry, cooking, travelling and outdoor pursuits; *Style*— Gareth Evans, QC; ✉ No 5 Chambers, Steelhouse Lane, Birmingham B4 6DR (tel 0121 606 0500, fax 0121 606 1501, e-mail ge@no5.com)

EVANS, Garry Owen; s of Derek Alwyn Evans (d 1984), and Pamela, *née* Sladden; *b* 13 February 1961; *Educ* King's Sch Canterbury, Corpus Christi Coll Cambridge (MA), Kyoto Univ; *m* 15 Dec 1985, Michiko, da of Hisami Matsuda, of Miyazaki, Japan; 2 da (Anna Sian b 1 March 1991, Maya Emily b 16 April 1994); *Career* Euromoney Publications plc: joined 1986, ed Euromoney (Japanese edn) 1987–90, ed Euromoney 1990–98; HSBC: strategist HSBC Securities (Japan) Ltd until 2003 (latterly chief strategist), head of pan-Asian equity research Corporate, Investment Banking and Markets Division 2003–; *Books* Memories of Silk and Straw (trans, by Junichi Saga, 1987); *Recreations* classical music, flying; *Style*— Garry Evans, Esq

EVANS, Garth; *Educ* Slade Sch of Art, UCL (Dip Fine Art), Manchester Regnl Coll of Art, Manchester Jr Coll of Art; *Career* artist and sculptor; visiting lectr: Central Sch of Art London 1960–65, Camberwell Sch of Art London 1960–69, St Martin's Sch of Art London 1965–79, Chelsea Sch of Art London 1978–79, Yale Sch of Art Yale Univ 1983, 1985 and 1986; visiting prof Minneapolis Coll of Art and Design 1973; visiting tutor Slade Sch of Fine Art UCL 1970–81, Goldsmiths Coll London 1978–81; visiting artist: Sculpture Dept RCA London 1970–81, Mount Holyoke Coll 1979–81, Manchester Poly 1978–83, NY Studio Sch 1988–; assoc lectr in sculpture Camberwell Sch of Art London 1971–83, lectr Faculty of Sculpture Br Sch at Rome 1978–83; memb: Fine Art Advsy Panel S Glamorgan Inst of Higher Educn 1977–79, Fine Arts Award Policy Ctee Arts Cncl of GB 1977–79, Fine Art Bd Photography Bd CNAA 1976–79, Ctee for Art and Design CNAA 1976–79; *Solo Exhibitions* Rowan Gallery London 1962, 1964, 1966, 1968, 1969, 1972, 1974, 1976, 1978 and 1980, Sch of Art and Design Gallery Sheffield 1971, Ferens Art Gallery Hull 1971, Faculty of Art and Design Gallery Leeds Poly 1971, Oriel Gallery of the Welsh Arts Cncl Cardiff 1976, Mount Holyoke Coll Art Museum S Hadley Mass 1980, Robert Elkon Gallery NY 1983, Tibor de Nagy Gallery NY 1984, HF Manes Gallery NY 1984, John Davis Gallery Akron Ohio 1986, Garth Evans Sculptures and Drawings 1979–87 (Yale Center for Br Art New Haven CT) 1988, Charles Cowles Gallery NY 1988, Compass Rose Gallery Chicago 1989, Hill Gallery Birmingham Michigan 1990, Mayor Gallery London 1991, Wrexham Museum and Art Centre Wales 1991, Sheffield Poly Art Gallery 1991, Echoes: Sculpture from 1970 and Recent Works (Paul Mellon Gallery Choate Rosemary Hall Sch Wallingford CT) 1993, Sculptural Metamorphosis (Freedman Gallery Reading PA), Watercolours (Dana Arts Centre Colgate Univ USA) 1995, Phoenix Sculptures (Opera House Gallery Earlville USA) 1995, Sculptures and Works on Paper (Korn Gallery Drew Univ USA) 1996, Watercolours (Claudia Carr Gallery NY) 1997, The 1982 (YADDO) Drawings (Marist College NY, NY Studio School, Halsey Gallery Charleston) 1997–98; *Group Exhibitions* incl: John Moores Exhibition (Liverpool) 1960, Reliefs Collages and Drawings (V&A) 1967, Drawings (MOMA NY) 1969, British Sculpture '72 (Royal Acad) 1972, The Condition of Sculpture (Hayward Gallery) 1975, David Leverett Garth Evans and Dicter Rot (Tate Gallery) 1978, Sculpture Now 1 (Gallery Wintersburger Cologne) 1983, Three Sculptors (Wolff Gallery NY) 1984, Quest - Drawings by Faculty (NY Studio Sch) 1989, Before Sculpture - British Sculptors Drawings (NY Studio Sch) 1990, Evans Saunders Tribe Tucker Turnbull (Phillips Staib Gallery NY) 1990, Newer Sculpture (Charles Cowles Gallery NY) 1990, Discourse (NY Studio Sch) 1990, Physicality (Hunter Coll City Univ NY) 1990, Summer Group (Charles Cowles Gallery NY) 1991, Sculpture in the Yard (PMW Gallery Stamford) 1992, Set A/B (Tribeca 148 Gallery NY) 1992, Millfield British 20th Century Sculpture Exhbn (Millfield Sch Somerset) 1992, Form, Shape and Vision (Schick Art Gallery NY) 1993, Summer Salon Show (Robert Morrison Gallery NY) 1993, French Ideals: French Idylls (NY Studio Sch of Drawing, Painting and Sculpture) 1993, American Academy Invitational Exhibition of Painting and Sculpture (American Acad of Arts and Letters NY) 1996, Watercolours (with Andrew Forge, Kendall Art & Design Hudson NY) 1998; *Public collections* incl: Brooklyn Museum NY, Gulbenkian Fndn Lisbon, Joseph H Hirshhorn Museum and Sculpture Garden Washington DC, Met Museum of Art NY, MOMA NY, Nat MOMA Brazil, Power Gallery of Contemporary Art Sydney, Tate Gallery London, V&A; *Awards* Newcastle Cruddas Park Sculpture Competition 1961, Gulbenkian purchase award 1964, Arts Cncl of GB sabbatical 1966, BSC fellowship 1969, Oxford Gallery purchase prize 1972, Welsh Arts Cncl purchase prize 1974, Arts Cncl of GB maj award 1975, Gtr London Arts Assoc bursary 1978, Arts Cncl of GB film bursary 1979, Br Cncl exhbns abroad grant 1979, Mount Holyoke Coll faculty award 1980, residency Yaddo Saratoga Springs NY 1982 and 1991, fell John Simon Guggenheim Meml Fndn 1986, The Marie Walsh Sharpe Art Fndn The Space Program 1992–93, Pollock-Krasner Fndn Award 1996; *Style*— Garth Evans; ✉ 287 Pulpit Rock Road, Woodstock, CT 06281, USA; c/o Lori Bookstein Fine Art, 37 West 57th Street, New York, NY 10019, USA

EVANS, Geraint; s of David Lynn Evans, and Elvira Evans; *Educ* Olchfa Sch Swansea, W Glamorgan Inst of HE, Manchester Poly (BA), Royal Acad Sch of Art (Dip Fine Art); *Career* artist; new media projects for: Jibby Beane London (Through The Looking Glass) 1997, Containership (internet project) 1998, ICA 1998, Canary Wharf 1998, LEA London 1998; work in collections: The Prudential, Br Embassy Berlin, Ferens Art Gall Hull; resident Banff Centre for the Arts Alberta 1994; visiting lectr: Univ of Tennessee 1994, Manchester Met Univ 1994–98, Liverpool John Moores Univ 1999, Univ of Lincoln 2000–01, RCA 2001, Norwich Sch of Art and Design 2002, De Montfort Univ 2002, London Coll of Fashion 2002; Br Inst Prize (printmaking) 1992 and 1993, Tooth Travel Scholarship 1993, Woo Charitable Fndn Award 2001, Berwick Gymnasium Fellowship 2002–03; *Solo Exhibitions* Univ of Tennessee 1994, Jason and Rhodes London 1998, Soho House London 1999, Anthony Wilkinson London 2000, Where Happiness Happens (Chapter Cardiff) 2001, Where Happiness Happens (Glynn Vivian Art Gallery Swansea) 2002, Centro de Arte de Salamanca Spain 2003, Berwick Gymnasium Gall 2003; *Group Exhibitions* incl: Western Exposure (Waterman's Art Centre London) 1993, London/Leipzig (Grassimuseum Leipzig) 1993, Pet Show (63 Union Street London) 1993, Whitechapel Open (Atlantis London) 1994, Oriel Mostyn Open (Mostyn Art Gallery Llandudno) 1994, Grin and Bear It (Gasworks London) 1995, John Moores 19 (Walker Art Gallery Liverpool) 1995, Wishful Thinking (Art House Lewisham) 1996, Six Monkeys (RAW London) 1996, Whitechapel Open (Whitechapel Art Gallery London) 1996, Sad (Gasworks London) 1996, Intimate (Jason and Rhodes London) 1997, Bittersweet (Whitworth Art Gallery Manchester) 1997, Sickly Sweet (Battersea Arts Centre London) 1998, Whitechapel Open (The Tannery London) 1998, London Now (Saks Fifth Avenue Arts Project NY) 1998, Asylum (Milch London) 1999, Idlewild (The Approach London) 1999, Fresh Paint (MOMA Glasgow) 1999, British Art part 2 (Diehl Vorderwuelbecke Berlin) 2000, Landscape (Barbara Gilman Miami) 2000, Record Collection (VTO London) 2001, Wales, Unauthorized Versions (The House of Croatian Artists Zagreb) 2001, On Home Ground (Oriel Mostyn, Llandudno) 2002, Art and Mountains (The Alpine Club) 2002, Dirty Pictures (The Approach London), Yes! I am a Long Way From Home (NGCA Sunderland and touring); *Style*— Geraint Evans, Esq

EVANS, Prof Gillian Rosemary; da of Arthur Raymond Evans (d 1987), of Huntley, Glos, and Gertrude Elizabeth, *née* Goodfellow (d 1980); *b* 26 October 1944, Birmingham; *Educ* King Edward VI HS for Girls Birmingham, St Anne's Coll Oxford (MA, DipEd), Univ of Reading (PhD), Univ of Oxford (DLitt), Univ of Cambridge (LittD), Middx Univ (Dip Law), Inns of Court Sch of Law; *Career* asst mistress Queen Anne's Sch Caversham 1967–72, research asst Univ of Reading 1974–78, lectr Univ of Bristol 1978–80, asst lectr rising to prof of medieval theology and intellectual history Univ of Cambridge 1980–2005; memb Cncl Univ of Cambridge 1997–2000; public policy sec Cncl for Academic Freedom and Academic Standards 1996–2003, co-fndr Oxcheps HE Mediation Serv 2004; memb Faith and Order Advsy Gp Gen Synod C of E 1985–95; ldr HEFCE-funded project improving dispute resolution in HE 2007–08; called to the Bar Gray's Inn 2002; Freeman Guild of Educators 2003; Hon DLitt Southampton Inst of HE 2001; FRHistS 1976, FRSA 1996; *Publications* incl: Anselm and Talking About God (1978), Anselm and a New Generation (1980), Old Arts and New Theology (1980), The Mind of St Bernard of Clairvaux (1983), Alan of Lille (1983), Augustine on Evil (1983), The Anselm Concordance (1984), The Logic and Language of the Bible (2 vols, 1984 and 1985), The Thought of Gregory the Great (1986), Christian Authority (ed, 1988), Problems of Authority in the Reformation Debates (1992), Philosophy and Theology in the Middle Ages (1994), The Church and the Churches (1994), Method in Ecumenical Theology (1996), The Reception of the Faith (1997), Calling Academia to Account (1998), The Medieval Epistemology of Error (1998), Discipline and Justice in the Church of England (1999), Bernard of Clairvaux (2000), Managing the Church (ed, 2000), A History of Pastoral Care (ed, 2000), The Medieval Theologians (ed, 2001), Universities and Students (jtly, 2001), Law and Theology in the Middle Ages (2002), Academics and the Real World (2002), Faith in the Medieval World (2003), A Brief History of Heresy (2003), The Medieval Theologians (ed, 2004), Inside the University of Cambridge (2004), Wyclif (2005), Belief (2006), The Church in the Early Middle Ages (2007), The Good, the Bad and the Moral Dilemma (2007), An illustrated history of Christian Europe (2007); I B Tauris History of the Christian Church (gen ed); also author of articles published in learned jls; *Recreations* painting; *Clubs* Royal Over-Seas League; *Style*— Prof G R Evans; ✉ Faculty of History, University of Cambridge, West Road, Cambridge CB3 9EF (tel and fax 01865 311427, e-mail gre1001@cam.ac.uk)

EVANS, Iain Richard; *b* 17 May 1951; *Educ* Univ of Bristol (BSc), Harvard Business Sch (MBA); *Career* sr accountant Arthur Young McClelland Moores & Co 1975–76 (joined 1972); Bain & Co: conslt 1978–80, mangr 1980–82, ptnr 1982–83; Hyder plc (formerly Welsh Water plc): non-exec dir 1989–93, exec chm 1993–96, non-exec chm 1996–98; chm LEK Consulting 1991– (fndr ptnr 1983–); FCA 1981 (ACA 1975); *Recreations* golf, fishing, tennis; *Style*— Iain Evans, Esq

EVANS, Ian Robert; s of Ellwyn Evans, and Violet, *née* Ashbridge; *b* 10 May 1950, Yorks; *Educ* Keswick Sch, Univ of Liverpool (LLB); *m* 22 Sept 1989, Victoria; 2 s (James b 13 March 1978, David b 23 Dec 1992), 4 da (Sian b 13 May 1980, Jane b 28 Feb 1986, Sally b 31 July 1994, Beth b 9 Jan 1997); *Career* admitted slr 1975; Weightmans: ptnr 1978–, sr ptnr 2000–; *Recreations* all sports, particularly rugby, soccer, cricket and sailing; *Style*— Ian Evans, Esq; ✉ Weightmans, India Buildings, Water Street, Liverpool L2 0GA (tel 0151 227 2601, fax 0151 242 7986, e-mail ian.evans@weightmans.com)

EVANS, Capt James; MBE (1992), RD (1975), DL (1978); s of Thomas Evans (d 1966), and Hilda Margaret, *née* Atkinson (d 1976); *b* 9 May 1933; *Educ* Merchiston Castle Sch Edinburgh, Univ of Newcastle upon Tyne (BSc); *m* 12 July 1958, Patricia Alexena (Pat), da of Harry Kerr (d 1973); 1 s (Ian b 1963), 2 da (Lynn b 1961, Gwen b 1967); *Career* RNR 1956–80, Hon ADC 1979–80, ret 1980; apprenticeship: Wm Weatherhead & Sons 1950–52, Swan Hunter and Whigham Richardson 1952–56; engr Yarrow-Admiralty Res Dept 1958–63, nuclear engrg certificate 1960, engr UK Atomic Energy Authy 1963–68, md Eyemouth Boat Building Co Ltd 1968–90, conslt Naval Architect 1990–2006; tech advsr Scottish Fishermen's Fedn 1993–; chm Fishing Boat Builders' Assoc 1979–90, pres Anglo Scottish Fishermen's Assoc 2006– (sec/treas 1993–2006); sec Eyemouth Port Assoc Ltd 1996–2005; Nuclear Engrg Soc Silver Medal Award for a paper on Features of Interest in Small Pressurised Water Reactors 1963, author of East Coast Fishing Boat Building (1990), a tech paper of NE Coast Inst of Engrs and Shipbuilders; chm: Berwickshire Dist Co Cncl 1980–96; Freeman of Berwick-upon-Tweed; Lord Pres Court of Deans of Guilds of Scotland 1994–95 and 2003–04; CEng, FRINA, MIMechE; Gold Cross of Merit (Poland) 1999; *Style*— Capt James Evans, MBE, RD, DL; ✉ Makore, Northburn View, Eyemouth, Berwickshire TD14 5BG (tel 01890 750701, e-mail jevans@makore.wireless.uk.com); Dundee House, Harbour Road, Eyemouth, Berwickshire TD14 5JB (tel 018907 750231, fax 01890 750701)

EVANS, Janet Charmian Christabel; da of Dr Joseph Evans (d 1981), of Bishop's Stortford, Herts, and Eileen Betty Evans-Booker, *née* Moulding (d 1989); *b* 14 December 1951; *Educ*

E

Herts & Essex HS for Girls, Somerville Coll Oxford (MA), Birkbeck Coll London (MSc); *m* 1, 1976, Robin Aaronson; m 2, 2000, Andy McLellan; *Career* civil servant; admin trainee rising to princ Dept of Employment 1975–92, head of div Dept for Culture, Media and Sport 1992–, currently head Museums, Libraries and Archives Div; *Recreations* visiting cities, food, friends, cats; *Style—* Ms Janet Evans; ✉ Department for Culture, Media and Sport, 2–4 Cockspur Street, London SW1Y 5DH (tel 020 7211 6132, fax 020 7211 6130, e-mail janet.evans@culture.gov.uk)

EVANS, Jill; MEP; da of Horace Burge, of Llwynypia, Rhondda, and Valma, *née* Yeates; *b* 8 May 1959; *Educ* Tonypandy GS, UCW Aberystwyth (BA), Poly of Wales (MPhil); *m* June 1992, Syd Morgan; *Career* res asst Poly of Wales Treforest 1981–86, admin and public affairs offr NFWI 1989–94, Wales organiser for CHILD the Nat Infertility Support Network 1997–99; cncllr: Rhonda BC 1992–95, Mid Glamorgan CC 1993–95, Rhondda Cynon Taff CBC 1995–99; memb Nat Exec Ctee Plaid Cymru; MEP (Plaid Cymru) Wales 1999–, dep pres Plaid Cymru 2003–, substitute memb Women's Rights and Gender Equality Ctee, substitute memb Ctee on Regnl Devpt, memb Ctee on the Environment, Public Health and Food Safety; chair CND Cymru; memb: CND, CHILD; *Style—* Ms Jill Evans, MEP; ✉ 23 High Street, Chancery Lane, Cardigan SA43 1HD (tel 01239 623611, fax 01239 623612, e-mail jill.evans@europarl.europe.eu)

EVANS, His Hon Judge (Maldwn) John; s of David Anthony Evans (d 1996), and Margaret, *née* Reid; *b* 11 July 1950; *Educ* Royal Hosp Sch Holbrook, Univ of Northumbria (BA); *m* 1, 17 Aug 1974, Miriam Dorothy, *née* Beaumont; 2 s (Matthew Richard b 6 Jan 1977, Daniel John b 29 Nov 1978), 1 da (Louisa Kate b 9 Aug 1980); m 2, 29 May 1989, Angela Louise, *née* Swaddle; 2 step da (Charlotte Amy b 19 May 1988, Emily Josephine b 10 April 1991), 1 step s (Lawrence Henry b 17 Sept 1989); *Career* called to the Bar 1973, barr in practice Criminal Bar Newcastle upon Tyne 1973–2005, recorder 1989–2005, head New Court Chambers Newcastle 1999–2005, circuit judge (NE Circuit) 2005–; govr Kings Sch Tynemouth, fell Woodard Corp; *Recreations* sport, rugby, cricket, squash, sailing, walking, holidays, cinema; *Clubs* Tynemouth Squash; *Style—* His Hon Judge Evans; ✉ Newcastle upon Tyne Combined Court Centre, Quayside, Newcastle upon Tyne NE1 3LA (tel 0191 201 2000)

EVANS, Prof (William) John; s of William Mervyn Evans (d 1997), and Dorothy Mary, *née* Jenkins (d 1994); *b* 23 July 1943; *Educ* Cowbridge GS, Univ of Wales Swansea (BSc, PhD, DSc); *m* 15 July 1967, Gillian Mary, da of Edwin Howard Phillips; 2 s (William Philip b 1970, Geraint Richard b 1972), 1 da (Siân Elizabeth b 1977); *Career* Nat Gas Turbine Estab (NGTE) MOD (PE): sr scientific offr 1969–79, princ scientific offr and head of mech design research 1979–85; Univ of Wales Swansea: lectr and sr lectr Dept of Materials Engrg 1985–9, reader and prof Interdisciplinary Research Centre (IRC) 1989–97, dir IRC 1997–2002, dir Rolls-Royce Univ Technol Centre 2000–, dir Welsh Devpt Agency (WDA) Centre of Excellence in Materials 2001–03, head Materials Research Centre 2003–07; visiting prof Univ of New South Wales Aust 2004–; chm WDA Materials Technol Forum for Wales 2000–07; memb Editorial Bd Jl of Fatigue of Engrg Materials and Structures; former pres S Wales Metallurgical Assoc; memb Organising Ctee: Eighth World Conf on Titanium 1995, IOM 2000 Conf; CEng, FIMMM 1994 and 2002, FREng 2002; *Publications* Titanium 95: Science and Technology (co-ed, 3 vols, 1996), Compass 2002 (co-ed, 2003); author of over 180 research pubns in scientific jls, several chapter contribs in tech books; *Recreations* photography, walking, cricket; *Style—* Prof John Evans; ✉ Materials Research Centre, School of Engineering, University of Wales Swansea, Singleton Park, Swansea SA2 8PP (tel 01792 295537, fax 01792 295693, e-mail w.j.evans@swansea.ac.uk)

EVANS, Dr (Daniel) John Owen; s of John Leslie Evans (d 1971), and Avis *née* Jones; *b* 17 November 1953; *Educ* Gowerton Boys' GS, Univ of Wales Cardiff (BMus, MA, PhD), ATCL; *Career* artistic dir Welsh Chamber Ensemble 1975–78, administrator Britten-Pears Sch 1978–80, research scholar Britten-Pears Library & Archive 1980–85, prodr Radio 3 Music Dept BBC 1985–89; artistic dir: Covent Garden Chamber Orchestra 1985–93, Volte Face Opera 1986–89; sr prodr BBC Singers 1989–92; BBC Radio: chief prodr Music Dept Radio 3 1992–93, head of Music Dept Radio 3 1993–96, head of classical music 1996–2000, head of music programming Radio 3 2000–06; currently pres and exec dir Oregon Bach Festival; juror: Int Conductors' Competition Lisbon 1995, Kondrashin Conduction Competiton 1998, BBC Cardiff Singer of the World Competition 2003 and 2005, Tost: Int Singing Competition 2004, BBC Choir of the Year 2005; chair Opera Jury Royal Philharmonic Society Awards 2000–05; chair: Concrete Circles Theatre Co 2000–05, DreamArts Theatre of the Possible 2005–07; dir The Britten Estate; tstee: Peter Pears Award 1989–92, Masterprize Composers' Competition 1997–2001, Britten-Pears Fndn 2000–07; vice-pres Welsh Music Guild; *Awards* Prix Italia 1989, Charles Heidsieck Royal Philharmonic Award for Duke Bluebeard's Castle 1989, Royal Philharmonic Award for The Art of Conducting 1994, Gold Sony Radio Award for Live from Tanglewood 1997; *Books* Benjamin Britten: Pictures from a Life 1913–76 (1978), Benjamin Britten: His Life and Operas (ed, 1982), The Britten Companion (contrib, 1984), A Britten Source Book (1987); *Recreations* theatre, musicals, travel; *Style—* Dr John Evans; ✉ Oregon Bach Festival, 1257 University of Oregon, Eugene, OR 97403, USA (tel 00 1 541 686 0736, e-mail djoevans@uoregon.edu)

EVANS, Sir John Stanley; kt (2000), QPM (1990), DL (Devon, 2000); s of William Stanley Evans (d 1970), and Doris, *née* Wooldridge (d 1994); *b* 6 August 1943; *Educ* Wade Deacon GS, Univ of Liverpool (LLB); *m* 25 Sept 1965, Beryl, da of Albert Smith (d 1976); 1 s (Mark 1967), 1 da (Lindsey 1971); *Career* Liverpool City then Merseyside Police 1960–80, asst chief constable Gtr Manchester Police 1980–84, dep chief constable Surrey Constabulary 1984–88, chief constable Devon & Cornwall Constabulary 1989–2002; pres ACPO 1999–2000, chm Police Athletic Assoc 1989–2002; ret; special security advsr FA 2004–, memb public enquiry into 1997 murder of Robert Hamill in Portadown 2005–; chm SW Regnl Cncl Prince's Tst, patron Dream-a-Way, vice-patron Exeter Leukaemia Fund (ELF) 2003–; OStJ; *Recreations* most sports (ran London Marathon in 1988 and 1989), service and charitable activities; *Clubs* Woodbury Park Golf and Country (pres 2001–); *Style—* Sir John S Evans, OStJ, QPM, DL, LLB; ✉ Woodbury Park Golf and Country Club, Woodbury Castle, Woodbury, Exeter, Devon EX5 1JJ (tel 01395 233 352)

EVANS, Jonathan Peter; MEP (Cons) Wales; s of David Evans, and Harriet Evans; *b* 2 June 1950; *Educ* Lewis Sch Pengam, Howardian HS Cardiff, Coll of Law Guildford and Lancaster Gate; *m* 24 Aug 1975, Margaret, *née* Thomas; 1 s, 2 da; *Career* slr, managing ptnr Leo Abse and Cohen slrs until 1992; MP (Cons) Brecon and Radnor 1992–97 (Parly candidate (Cons): Ebbw Vale 1974 (both gen elections), Wolverhampton NE 1979, Brecon and Radnor 1987), MEP (Cons) Wales 1999–; House of Commons: PPS to Michael Mates, MP, Min of State NI Office 1992–93, PPS to Rt Hon Sir John Wheeler, MP, Min of State 1993–94, Parly under sec DTI 1994–95 (min for corp affrs 1994–95, min for competition and consumer affrs 1995), Parly sec Lord Chancellor's Department 1995–96, Parly under sec of state Welsh Office 1996–97, former memb Welsh Affrs Select Ctee and Health Select Ctee; ldr Conservatives in European Parl 2001–; chm: Welsh Cons Parly Candidates 1985–90, Welsh Cons Policy Gp 1987–91; memb Bd Cons Pty 2002–; dir of insurance Eversheds 1997–99, conslt 1999–; dir: NFU Mutual 2000–, Country Mutual Insurance Brokers Ltd 2003–; dep chm Tai Cymru (Housing Wales) 1988–92, dep chm Wales Cncl NSPCC 1991–1994; *Recreations* rugby, music, family, reading; *Clubs* Farmers', Cardiff and County; *Style—* Jonathan Evans, Esq, MEP

EVANS, Kim; OBE (2007); da of Jon Evans, and Gwendolen, *née* McLeod; *b* 3 January 1951; *Educ* Putney HS, Univ of Warwick (BA), Univ of Leicester (MA); *Partner* David Hucker; *Career* asst ed Crafts magazine 1974–76, sub-ed and restaurant critic Harpers & Queen magazine 1976–78, researcher The South Bank Show (LWT) 1978–82; prodr/dir: Hey Good Looking (Channel 4) 1982–83, The South Bank Show (LWT) 1983–88; BBC TV: prodr 1989–92, asst head of music and arts 1992–93, head of arts and classical music 1993–99; exec dir arts Arts Cncl England 1999–2007; Huw Wheldon (BAFTA) Award for Best Arts Documentary (for 'Angela Carter's Curious Room') 1993; FRTS; *Recreations* travelling (particularly in Africa), reading, dreaming; *Style—* Miss Kim Evans, OBE

EVANS, Laurie; s of Hugh Evans (d 1997), and Greta, *née* Bryden (d 1989); *b* 10 July 1955; *Educ* Royal HS Edinburgh, Newcastle Poly, Bournemouth and Poole Coll of Art (DipAD); *m* March 1982, Lesley, da of Stanley Richardson, of Edinburgh; 2 s (James Ewan b 30 May 1983, Calum Thomas b 21 Sept 1986); *Career* photographer; Arts in Fife, freelance reportage photographer for Rock and Roll press (NME, Melody Maker), asst to Bryce Attwell, proprietor Laurie Evans Photographer 1982– (specialising in food and still life); clients incl: Boots, Sainsbury's, Nestlé, Waitrose, Tesco; magazines incl: Good Housekeeping, Homes & Gardens; winner various awards incl: Silver award Assoc of Photographers 1986, 4 Clio awards USA 1986, 1988, 1989 and 1993, Award of Excellence Communication Arts Magazine, Silver award D&AD 1990; columnist Image Magazine, contrib to over 30 cookery books; memb Assoc of Photographers (memb Cncl 1989, 1990 and 1991); *Recreations* very keen sailor, blues and jazz guitar, cycling; *Style—* Laurie Evans, Esq; ✉ Laurie Evans Photography, 11 Cameron House, 12 Castlehaven Road, London NW1 4QW (tel 020 7284 2140, e-mail laurieevans@btconnect.com, website www.laurieevans.co.uk)

EVANS, Leslie Douglas; s of Leslie Edward Evans, of St Albans, Herts, and Violet Rosina, *née* Rogerson; *b* 24 June 1945; *Educ* St Albans GS for Boys, St Albans Sch of Art, Leeds Coll of Art (DipAD), Hornsey Coll of Art (Art Teachers' Certificate); *m* 4 Sept 1965, Fionnuala Boyd, *qv*, da of Joseph Douglas Allen Boyd (d 1990); 1 s (Jack Luis b 12 Sept 1969), 1 da (Ruby Rose b 2 Dec 1971); *Career* artist; began working with Fionnuala Boyd 1968, Bi-Centennial fell USA 1977–78; artist in residence: Milton Keynes Devpt Corp 1982–84, Brunei Rainforest Project 1991–92; *Exhibitions* with Fionnuala Boyd: Angela Flowers Gallery 1972, 1974, 1977, 1979, 1980, 1982, 1984, 1986, 1988, 1990, 1992, 1994, 1996, 1998, 2000, 2002 and 2003, Park Square Gallery Leeds 1972, Boyd and Evans 1970–75 (Turnpike Gallery, Leigh) 1976, Fendrick Gallery Washington DC 1978, Graves Art Gallery Sheffield 1979, Spectro Arts Workshop Newcastle 1980, Ton Peek Utrecht 1981, A Decade of Paintings (Milton Keynes Exhibition Gallery) 1982–83, Drumcroon Art Centre Wigan 1985, Bird (Flowers East, London) 1990, English Paintings (Brendan Walter Gallery, Santa Monica) 1990, Angela Flowers (Ireland) 1990, Flowers East London 1991, Brunei Rainforest (Milton Keynes, Brunei, Malaysia & Singapore) 1993, New Rain Forest Paintings (Flowers East) 1994, Portrayal (Flowers East) 1996, Western Photographs (Flowers East) 1999, Natural Wonder (Flowers West Santa Monica) 1999 and 2001, solo show (Flowers West Santa Monica), solo show (Flowers East London) 2000, Colour in Black & White (Flowers Graphics London and Keller & Greene LA) 2003, Landmarks (Milton Keynes Gallery and Flowers Central London) 2005, Color in Black & White (Flowers NY) 2006, Boyd & Evans (Galerie d'Art Int Solana Beach CA) 2006, Looking Differently (Flowers East London) 2007; *Group Exhibitions* incl: Postcards (Angela Flowers Gallery) 1970, British Drawing 1952–72 (Angela Flowers Gallery) 1972, British Realist Show (Ikon Gallery) 1976, Aspects of Realism (Rothmans of Pall Mall, Canada) 1976–78, The Real British (Fischer Fine Art) 1981, Black and White Show (Angela Flowers Gallery) 1985, Sixteen (Angela Flowers Gallery) 1986, State of the Nation (Herbert Gallery, Coventry) 1987, Contemporary Portraits (Flowers East) 1988, The Thatcher Years (Flowers East) 1989, Picturing People - British Figurative Art since 1945 (touring exhibition Far East) 1989–90, Art '90 London (Business Design Centre) 1990, 25th Anniversary Exhibition (Flowers East) 1995, Wheels on Fire (Wolverhampton Stoke-on-Trent) 1996, Sight Lines (Honiton Festival) 1996, Contemporary British Landscape (Flowers East) 1999; *Work in Public Collections* incl: Arts Cncl of GB, Br Cncl, MOMA NY, Sheffield City Art Gallery, Wolverhampton City Art Gallery, Leeds City Art Gallery, Contemporary Art Soc, Leicester Educn Authy, Manchester City Art Gallery, Unilever plc, Tate Gallery, Williamson Art Gallery, Metropolitan Museum NY, Borough of Milton Keynes; *Awards* prizewinner Bradford Print Biennale, first prize 6 Festival Int de la Peinture Cagnes-sur-Mer; *Recreations* squash, films, friends, music, hill walking; *Style—* Leslie Evans; ✉ Boyd & Evans, Flowers East, 82 Kingsland Road, London E2 8DP (tel 020 7920 7777, e-mail gallery@flowerseast.com, website www.flowerseast.com)

EVANS, Mark; QC (1995); s of Rev Clifford Evans (d 1968), of Brynamman, and Mary, *née* Jones; *b* 21 March 1946; *Educ* Christ Coll Brecon, King's Coll London (LLB); *m* 1, (m dis); 1 s (John Clifford b 30 March 1974), 1 da (Claire Elizabeth b 1 April 1976); m 2, 2001, Carolyn Poots; *Career* called to the Bar Gray's Inn 1971, currently recorder (Western Circuit); *Clubs* Bristol Savages (chm Christ Coll Brecon OBA); *Style—* Mark Evans, Esq, QC; ✉ Grove Farm, Wapley, Chipping Sodbury, S Gloucestershire (tel 01454 312150); Queen Square Chambers, 56 Queen Square, Bristol BS1 4PR (tel 0117 921 1966, fax 0117 927 6493)

EVANS, Dr Mark Lewis; s of Rev Frank Owen Evans, of Llanelli, Carmarthenshire, and Joan, *née* Lewis (d 1978); *b* 24 March 1954; *Educ* Llanelli Boys' GS, Westfield Coll London (BA), UEA (Thomas and Elizabeth Williams scholar, PhD); *m* 27 March 1985, Reinhild, da of Helmut Weiss (d 1996), of Bückeburg, Germany; *Career* res asst Dept of Western Manuscripts Br Library 1977, lectr in history of art Univ of St Andrews 1978, asst keeper of foreign art Walker Art Gallery Liverpool 1979–84, asst keeper of fine art Nat Museum of Wales 1984–99 (actg keeper 1986–87 and 1994), sr curator of paintings V&A 2000–; dir Inventory of Public Sculpture in Wales 1998–99, expert advsr on pastels and miniatures Reviewing Ctee on the Export of Works of Art 2002–; memb: Assoc of Art Historians 1976–2003 (exec memb 1993–96, chm Museums and Galleries Sub-Ctee 2000–03), Soc of Renaissance Studies 1984– (memb Cncl 2004–), Hon Soc of Cymmrodorion 1985–, Cncl for Curators of Dutch and Flemish Art 2002–; *Publications* Catalogue of Foreign Paintings: Lady Lever Art Gallery (with E Morris, 1983), Supplementary Foreign Catalogue: Walker Art Gallery (with E Morris, 1984), Augustus John Portraits (1988), The Derek Williams Collection (1989), Twentieth Century Art in Wales (1989), Paintings from Windsor Castle (1990), Impressions of Venice from Turner to Monet (1992), The Sforza Hours (1992), The Art Gallery of the National Museum of Wales (with O Fairclough, 1993, 2 edn 1997), Das Stundenbuch der Sforza (with B Brinkmann, 1995), The Drawings of Augustus John (ed, 1996), Princes as Patrons (ed, 1998), The Romantic Tradition in British Painting 1800–1950 (2002), A Masterpiece Reconstructed: The Hours of Louis XII (ed with Thomas Kren, 2005), The Painted World: from Illumination to Abstraction (2005); numerous articles and reviews in learned jls; *Recreations* travel, cooking; *Style—* Dr Mark Evans; ✉ Word and Image Department, Victoria and Albert Museum, South Kensington, London SW7 2RL (tel 020 7942 2553, e-mail m.evans@vam.ac.uk)

EVANS, Rt Rev Michael; *see:* East Anglia, Bishop of

EVANS, Prof Michael Charles Whitmore; s of Allen Whitmore Evans, of London, and Doris, *née* Smith; *b* 24 September 1940; *Educ* King Edwards Sch Birmingham, Univ of Sheffield (BSc, PhD); *m* 28 Dec 1963, Christine Stella, da of John Marshall (d 1983); 2 s (Peter Whitmore b 1967, Nicholas John b 1969); *Career* assoc specialist Dept of Cell Physiology Univ of Calif Berkeley 1964–66, lectr in botany King's Coll London 1966–73, prof of plant chemistry UCL 1982– (reader 1973–82); contrib to numerous papers in scientific jls; chm Plant Science and Microbiology Sub-Ctee 1987–90 (memb 1985–90), memb Ctee

Biological Science Ctee SERC 1987–90; *Recreations* birdwatching, gardening; *Style*— Prof Michael Evans

EVANS, Michael Stephen James; s of William Henry Reginald Evans, of Seaford, E Sussex, and Beatrice Catherine, *née* Mottram; *b* 5 January 1945; *Educ* Christ's Hosp, QMC London (BA); *m* 1971, Robyn Nicola, da of Samuel John Wilson Coles, MBE; 3 s (Samuel b 29 Nov 1974, Christopher b 6 July 1978, James b 1 July 1980); *Career* news ed Express & Independent Loughton Essex 1969–70 (reporter E London Office 1968); Daily Express: reporter Action Line consumer column 1970–72, gen news reporter 1972–77, home affairs corr 1977–82, def and dip corr 1982–86; The Times: Whitehall corr 1986–87, def corr The Times 1987–98, def ed 1998–; vice-pres and acting pres Dip and Cwlth Writers Assoc 1985–86; memb: Defence Correspondents Assoc, Assoc of Foreign Affrs Journalists; winner of Desmond Wettern Maritime Media Award 1998; *Books* A Crack in the Dam (1978), False Arrest (1979), Great Disasters (1981), South Africa (1987), The Gulf Crisis (1988); *Recreations* cricket, tennis, golf, playing piano; *Style*— Michael Evans, Esq; ✉ The Times, 1 Pennington Street, London E98 1TA (tel 020 7782 5921, fax 020 7782 5002, e-mail michael.evans@thetimes.co.uk)

EVANS, Nicholas; s of Anthony B Evans (d 1984), and Eileen, *née* Whitehouse (d 2005); *b* 26 July 1950; *Educ* Bromsgrove Sch, St Edmund Hall Oxford (BA); *m* 1, (m dis), Jennifer, da of Ian Lyon; 2 s (Harry Hewland b 9 Jan 1980, Max b 3 Feb 1981), 1 da (Lauren b 31 March 1982); m 2, Charlotte Gordon Cumming; 1 s (Finlay b 11 Feb 2002); *Career* reporter Evening Chronicle Newcastle 1972–75, reporter then prodr Weekend World (LWT) 1975–79, ed The London Programme (LWT) 1979–82, exec prodr The South Bank Show (LWT) 1982–84, ind prodr and screenplay writer 1985–93 (winner US ACE Award for best int movie on cable (Murder by the Book) 1991), currently author; *Books* The Horse Whisperer (1995), The Loop (1998), The Smoke Jumper (2001), The Divide (2005); *Recreations* tennis, skiing, running, movies; *Style*— Nicholas Evans, Esq; ✉ c/o A P Watt, 20 John Street, London WC1N 2DR (tel 020 7405 6774)

EVANS, Nick; *b* July 1950; *Educ* Reading Sch, St John's Coll Oxford; *m*; 2 s; *Career* with MOD: joined 1971, asst private sec to sec of state for defence 1981–84, head Naval Manpower and Training Div 1984–86, head Management Consultancy Div 1986–89, head Framework Team 1989–91, head Resources and Programmes (Air) 1991–95, asst under sec (quartermaster) 1995–99, exec dir Defence Procurement Agency 1999–2000, DG (Resources) Defence Logistics Orgn 2000–02, DG Mgmnt and Orgn 2003–06, DG Resources Land Forces 2006; *Style*— Nick Evans, Esq; ✉ DeRes LF Headquarters Land Command Erskine Banacks, Room C8, Witton, Salisbury, Wiltshire SP2 0AG (tel 01722 433230, fax 01722 436328, e-mail nick.evans233@land.mod.uk)

EVANS, Nigel Martin; MP; s of late Albert Evans, of Swansea, and Betty Evans; *b* 10 November 1957; *Educ* Dynevor Sch Swansea, UC Swansea (BA); *Career* family newsagent business 1979–90; Parly candidate (Cons): Swansea W 1987, Pontypridd (by-election) 1989; MP (Cons) Ribble Valley 1992– (also contested by-election 1991); PPS to: Rt Hon David Hunt as Chllr of Duchy of Lancaster and sec of state at Office of Public Serv and Sci 1993–95, Tony Baldry, MP, *qv*, 1995–96, Rt Hon William Hague, MP, *qv*, 1996–97; oppn front bench spokesman on constitutional affrs (Wales) 1997–2001, shadow sec of state for Wales 2001–; chm All-Pty Music Gp 1992–, sec All-Pty Tourism Gp 1992–; memb: Trade and Industry Select Ctee 2003–, Welsh Select Ctee 2003–, Quadrapartite Select Ctee 2003–; former chm Swansea W Young Conservatives, former pres Swansea W Cons Assoc, chm Cons Welsh Parly Candidates Policy Gp 1990, pres Cons North West Parly Candidates Gp 1991, sec NW Cons MPs 1992–; cnclIr (Cons) Sketty Ward W Glamorgan CC 1985–91; chm Central Lancs Marie Curie Cancer Centre; campaigned for Republican Pty in NY, Florida and California US presidential elections 1980, 1984 and 1988; *Recreations* tennis, swimming, all spectator sports; *Clubs* Carlton; *Style*— Nigel Evans, Esq, MP; ✉ House of Commons, London SW1A 0AA (tel 020 7219 3000)

EVANS, Ven Patrick Alexander Sidney; *b* 28 January 1943; *Educ* Clifton, Lincoln Theol Coll; *m* 1969, Jane; 2 s, 1 da; *Career* curate: Holy Trinity Lyonsdown Barnet 1973–76, Royston 1976–78; vicar: Gt Gaddesden 1978–82, Tenterden 1982–89; rural dean West Charing 1988–89, archdeacon of Maidstone 1989–2001, archdeacon of Canterbury 2001–; dir of ordinands Diocese of Canterbury 1989–94, canon residentiary Canterbury Cathedral 2001– (hon canon 1989–); chm Pastoral Ctee, jt chm Dioceses of Canterbury and Rochester Cncl for Social Responsibility, memb Gen Synod; *Style*— The Ven the Archdeacon of Canterbury; ✉ 29 The Precincts, Canterbury, Kent CT1 2EP

EVANS, Peter Michael; s of Michael Evans (d 1976), of Chesterfield, and Fiona Mary, *née* Cassidy (d 1999); *b* 21 September 1952; *Educ* Uppingham, Univ of Oxford (MA); *m* 1, 1975 (m dis 1989), Mary-Ann, da of George Vere Howell; 1 s (Simon Michael b 9 May 1980), 1 da (Eloise Mary b 21 Sept 1981); m 2, 1992, Carol, da of Frank Longridge; 2 da (Holly Susannah, Sacha Fiona (twins) b 18 March 1995); *Career* IMI plc 1975–80 (personnel trainee, grad recruitment offr, export mktg exec), regnl mangr W Africa Wellcome plc 1980–83, int personnel exec Booker plc 1983–85, MSL International (formerly Hay-MSL) 1985–91 (conslt, regnl dir, dir), dir Whitehead Mann Ltd 1991–99, md Russell Reynolds Associates 1999–; *Style*— Peter Evans, Esq; ✉ Russell Reynolds, 24 St James's Square, London SW1Y 4HZ (tel 020 7830 8091, fax 020 7839 7370, e-mail pevans@russellreynolds.com

EVANS, Dr (Ian) Philip; OBE (1999); s of Joseph Emlyn Evans, of Ruthin, Clwyd, and Beryl, *née* Davies; *b* 2 May 1948; *Educ* Ruabon Boys' GS, Churchill Coll Cambridge (MA), Imperial Coll London (PhD, DIC); *m* 15 Jan 1972, Sandra Veronica, da of late Flying Offr Robert William Waggett, RAF (ret), of East Sheen, London; 2 s (Benjamin Joseph b 1976, Roland Mathonwy b 1978); *Career* post-doctoral fell Res Sch of Chemistry ANU 1973–75, asst master St Paul's Sch 1975–90 (head Chemistry Dept 1984–90), head master Bedford Sch 1990–; chief examiner A-level chemistry Univ of London Sch Examinations Bd 1987–90; memb: Royal Soc Sci Ctee 1990–93, School Examinations and Assessment Cncl 1991–93, School Curriculum and Assessment Authy 1993–97, Qualifications and Curriculum Authy 1997–99, chm Education Policy Bd RSC 2007– (also various ctees and working parties); memb Cncl Nat Tst 1999–2001; CChem, FRSC; *Publications* author of various papers in learned jls; *Recreations* music, cricket, poetry, wine appreciation; *Clubs* East India, Public Sch; *Style*— Dr Philip Evans, OBE; ✉ Bedford School, De Parys Avenue, Bedford MK40 2TU (tel 01234 362200, fax 01234 362283, e-mail hm@bedfordschool.org.uk)

EVANS, Dr Philip Rhys; s of James Howard Evans, and Ruby Gertrude, *née* Crouch; *b* 25 January 1946; *Educ* Shene Co GS, Guy's Hosp London (BA, MB BS), Open Univ; *Career* VSO Fiji Islands 1965–66; in gen practice: Dargaville NZ 1976–77, Leaf Rapids Canada 1977–78; princ in gen practice Bury St Edmunds 1979–; postgrad trainer in gen practice 1981–89; RCGP: memb Cncl 1985–88 and 1991–, memb Int Ctee 1987–2000, sec 1991–94, chm 1994–2000, chm UK Euro Forum 1994–96, chm Royal Coll Int Forum 1999–2001; advsr to WHO in Romania, Hungary, Czech Repub and Turkey 1991–94; memb UK Delgn to Euro Union of Gen Practitioners (UEMO) 1988–2001, UK delg Standing Ctee of Euro Doctors (CP) 1988–2001; UK rep: Int Soc of Gen Practice (SIMG) 1991–95, World Orgn of Family Doctors (WONCA) 1993–2002; hon sec Euro Soc of Gen Practice/Family Med 1995–2001, pres Euro Soc of Gen Practice/Family Med 2001–04; author of pubns on int gen practice and family med, jt ed Euro Jl of Gen Practice 1995–96; academic referee: Br Med Jl, Br Jl of Gen Practice; memb: VSO, BMA; MRCS, LRCP, DipObst RCOG, FRCGP; *Recreations* cricket, golf, history, travel, growing sweet peas; *Clubs* East India, Surrey CCC, Flempton Golf, Suffolk Hares Cricket, The Straw Boater; *Style*— Dr Philip R Evans; ✉ The Guildhall Surgery, Lower Baxter Street, Bury St Edmunds, Suffolk IP33 1ET (tel 01284 701601, fax 01284 702943, e-mail nx44@dial.pipex.com)

EVANS, Philip Wyn; CBE (2005); s of Wyndham Hubert Evans, of Tenby, Pembs, and Enid Caroline Evans; *b* 27 November 1948; *Educ* Greenhill GS Tenby, London Sch of Marine Engrg; *m* 17 Nov 1970, Jacqueline Jean, da of Malcolm C Herbert; 2 s (Mathew Giles Wyn b 1972, Daniel Charles Wyn b 1974), 3 da (Louise Elizabeth b 1982, Claire Emma Jane b 1983, Polly Anne b 1984); *Career* chm: Vox Leisure Services Ltd 1975–90, The Vox Group plc 1990–, Coastal Cottages Ltd 1992–2001, Activity Wales Ltd 1994–2001, Wales Tourist Bd 1999–2006, Tourism UK; ceo: The Vox Wine Co Ltd 1980–84, Shopper Direct Ltd 1984–88; memb Bd Br Tourism Authy; WTB/Schroeders Bank Tourism Award 1995; govr Univ of Wales; chm World Cup Amateur Golf Tournament; tstee Springboard Charitable Tst; FIMgt; *Books* Man Management and Motivation (1974); *Recreations* ocean cruising and navigation, rugby, wildlife conservation; *Style*— Philip Evans, Esq, CBE; ✉ The Vox Group plc, Waterwynch, Tenby, Pembrokeshire SA70 8TJ (tel 01834 871100, fax 01834 870025, e-mail philip@voxgroup.co.uk)

EVANS, Prof Richard John; s of Ieuan Trefor Evans, and Evelyn, *née* Jones; *b* 29 September 1947; *Educ* Jesus Coll Oxford (MA), St Antony's Coll Oxford (DPhil), UEA (LittD); *m* 1, 2 March 1976 (m dis 1993), Elin Hjaltadóttir, da of Hjalti Arnason; 1 step da (Sigridur Jónsdóttir b 1964); m 2, 17 April 2004, Christine L Corton; 2 s (Mathew b 1995, Nicholas b 1998); *Career* lectr in history Univ of Stirling 1972–76, prof of European history UEA 1983–89 (lectr 1976–83), prof of history Birkbeck Coll London 1989–98 (vice-master 1993–98, acting master 1997), prof of modern history Univ of Cambridge 1998–; fell Gonville & Caius Coll Cambridge 1998–; visiting assoc prof of European history Columbia Univ NY 1980; chair German History Soc 1989–92; Wolfson Literary Award for History 1988, William H Welch Medal of the American Assoc for the History of Med 1989, Hamburger Medaille für Kunst und Wissenschaft 1993, Fraenkel Prize for Contemporary History 1994; hon fell Jesus Coll Oxford 1998, hon fell Birkbeck Coll London 1999; FRHistS 1978, FBA 1993, FRSL 1999; *Books* The Feminist Movement in Germany 1894–1933 (1976), The Feminists (1977), Society and Politics in Wilhelmine Germany (ed, 1978), Sozialdemokratie und Frauenemanzipation im Deutschen Kaiserreich (1979), The German Family (ed with W R Lee, 1981), The German Working Class (ed, 1982), The German Peasantry (ed with W R Lee, 1986), Rethinking German History (1987), Death in Hamburg (1987), Comrades and Sisters (1987), The German Unemployed (ed with D Geary, 1987), The German Underworld (ed, 1988), Kneipengespräche im Kaiserreich (1989), In Hitler's Shadow (1989), Proletarians and Politics (1990), The German Bourgeoisie (ed with D Blackbourn, 1991), Rituals of Retribution (1996), In Defence of History (1997), Rereading German History (1997), Tales from the German Underworld (1998), Lying About Hitler (2001), The Coming of the Third Reich (2003), The Third Reich in Power (2005); *Recreations* music (piano), cooking, gardening; *Style*— Prof Richard J Evans, FBA; ✉ Gonville & Caius College, Cambridge CB2 1TA (tel 01223 332495, fax 01223 332456, e-mail rje@cam.ac.uk)

EVANS, Robert John Emlyn; MEP (Lab) London; s of Thomas Francis Evans, of Stone, Staffs, and Marjorie Gladys, *née* Macken (d 1986); *b* 23 October 1956; *Educ* County Sch Ashford Middx, Shoreditch Coll of Educn, Inst of Educn Univ of London (BEd, MA); *Career* teacher various middle schs Surrey 1978–89, headteacher Crane Jr Sch Hounslow 1990–94; MEP (Lab): London NW 1994–99 London 1999–; vice-pres Euro Parly Ctee on Citizens' Freedoms; sub-memb Euro Parly: Ctee on Culture, Youth, Educn and the Media, Delgn with countries of S Asia, Delgn to Romania; chm Chertsey and Walton CLP 1987–89, memb London Regnl Exec Lab Pty 1992–93; contested (Lab): E Berks gen election 1987, London S and Surrey E Euro election 1989, Uxbridge gen election 1992; memb GMB 1988; European Parly advsr to NUT (memb); hon Euro advsr to League Against Cruel Sports; Hon DUniv Brunel 1998; *Recreations* hockey, cricket, cycling, theatre, travel; *Clubs* Ruskin House Labour Croydon, Ashford Cricket, Ashford Hockey, Middx CC; *Style*— Robert Evans, Esq, MEP; ✉ 101 High Street, Feltham, Middlesex TW13 4HG (tel 020 8890 1818, fax 020 8890 1628, e-mail robertevansmep@btclick.com, website www.robertevansmep.net)

EVANS, Prof Robert John Weston; s of Thomas Frederic Evans (d 1992), of Cheltenham, and Margery, *née* Weston (d 1998); *b* 7 October 1943; *Educ* Dean Close Sch Cheltenham, Jesus Coll Cambridge (MA, PhD); *m* 10 May 1969, Catherine (Kati), da of Ferenc Róbert (d 1972), of Budapest; 1 s (David b 1973), 1 da (Margaret b 1979); *Career* BNC Oxford: research fell 1968–92, prof of European history 1992–97; regius prof of history Univ of Oxford 1997– (lectr 1969–90, reader 1990–92), jt ed English Historical Review 1986–95; FBA 1984; *Books* Rudolf II and his World (1984), The Making of the Habsburg Monarchy (1984), Austria, Hungary and the Habsburgs (2006); *Style*— Prof Robert Evans, FBA; ✉ Oriel College, Oxford OX1 4EW (tel 01865 276583, e-mail robert.evans@history.ox.ac.uk)

EVANS, Hon Mr Justice; Sir (David) Roderick; kt (2001); s of Thomas James Evans, of Morriston, Swansea, and Dorothy, *née* Carpenter; *b* 22 October 1946; *Educ* Bishop Gore GS Swansea, UCL (LLB, LLM); *m* 6 Nov 1971, Kathryn Rebecca, da of Leonard Thomas Lewis, of Morriston, Swansea; 3 s (Ioan b 1972, Gwion b 1974, Gruffudd b 1978), 1 da (Saran b 1976); *Career* called to the Bar Gray's Inn 1970 (bencher 2001), ad eundem Lincoln's Inn 2001; recorder of the Crown Court attached to the Wales & Chester Circuit 1987–92, QC 1989, circuit judge (Wales & Chester Circuit) 1992–99, resident judge Merthyr Tydfil Crown Court 1994–98, resident judge Swansea Crown Court 1998–99, sr circuit judge and recorder of Cardiff 1999–2001, judge of the High Court of Justice (Queen's Bench Div) 2001–, presiding judge Wales and Cheshire Circuit 2004–07, presiding judge Wales 2007–; memb Criminal Ctee Judicial Studies Bd 1998–2001; hon memb Gorsedd of Bards 2002; fell: Univ of Wales Aberystwyth 2003, Univ of Wales Swansea 2007; *Style*— The Hon Mr Justice Roderick Evans; ✉ Royal Courts of Justice, Strand, London WC2A 2LL

EVANS, Roderick Michael; s of Michael White Evans, of Monaco, and Helga Ingeborg, *née* Schneider; *b* 19 April 1962; *Educ* Millfield; *m* 7 April 1995, Ms Dawn Silver, er da of Geoffrey Richmond, of Alwoodley, Leeds; 1 s (Oliver William Roderick b 6 Nov 1996), 1 d (Isabella Daisy Florence b 27 July 1999); *Career* dir of numerous companies incl: Evans Holdings Ltd, Evans Fradley Ltd, Evans Management Ltd, Millshaw Property Co Ltd, Lansdale Developments Ltd, Deehurst Ltd; *Recreations* motorcycling, shooting, flying; *Clubs* RAC; *Style*— Roderick Evans, Esq; ✉ Evans of Leeds Ltd, Millshaw, Ring Road, Beeston, Leeds LS11 8EG (tel 0113 271 1888)

EVANS, (Jeremy) Roger; AM; s of Ronald Evans, of Rochdale, Lancs, and Doris Valentine, *née* Stanley; *b* 23 June 1964; *Educ* Laurence Jackson Sch Guisborough, Univ of Sheffield (BSc), Univ of Westminster, Inns of Court Sch of Law; *Career* various managerial roles Royal Mail 1985–95; called to the Bar Middle Temple 1997; memb Waltham Forest BC 1990–2000 (ldr Cons Gp Waltham Forest 1994–98), memb London Assembly GLA (Cons) Havering and Redbridge 2000–, memb Havering London BC 2006–; project mangr The Spring Gp 1998–2000; memb London Fire and Emergency Planning Authy; *Recreations* swimming, badminton; *Style*— Mr Roger Evans, Esq, AM; ✉ London Assembly, City Hall, Queens Walk, Southwark, London SE1 2AA (tel 020 7983 4359, fax 020 7983 4419, e-mail roger.evans@london.gov.uk)

EVANS, Roger; s of Eric Evans (d 1947), of Bristol, and Celia Mavis, *née* Roe (d 1988); *b* 28 October 1945; *Educ* Lord Wandsworth Coll; *m* Julia Margaret, da of Arthur Horace Moore Household (d 1998); 2 c (Rupert Alexander, Rebecca Grace (twins) b 14 June 1981); *Career*

gen mangr St George's Hosp 1985–90, gen mangr SW Thames RHA 1991–92, chief exec Mid Kent Healthcare Tst 1992–2000, project dir Dept of Health/Health Protection Agency 2000–06, chief exec St George's Charitable Fndn 2000–05, chief exec Haemophilia Soc 2007–; md Roger Evans & Assocs; tstee Macfarlane Tst 2007–; memb Inst of Health Care Mgmnt 1971; FRSA; *Recreations* cricket, rugby union, fine arts, 18th century music, theatre, Victorian novels; *Clubs* RSM, MCC, Gloucestershire CCC, London Wasps RFC; *Style*— Roger Evans, Esq; ✉ 36 Pepys Road, Wimbledon, London SW20 8PF (tel 020 8879 0729, e-mail rogerevans4@hotmail.com)

EVANS, Roger Kenneth; s of late Gerald Raymond Evans, and late Dr Annie Margaret Evans; *b* 18 March 1947; *Educ* Bristol GS, Trinity Hall Cambridge (MA, pres Cambridge Union); *m* 6 Oct 1973, Worshipful (Doris) June Rodgers, *qv*, da of late James Rodgers, of Co Down, NI; 2 s (Edward Arthur, Henry William); *Career* Parly candidate (Cons): Warley West Oct 1974 and 1979, Ynys Môn (Anglesey) 1987, Monmouth by-election May 1991; MP (Cons) Monmouth 1992–97, PPS to Jonathan Aitken 1994, Parly under-sec of state Dept of Social Security 1994–97; memb: Ecclesiastical Ctee of Parliament 1992–97, Welsh Affairs Select Ctee 1992–94; called to the Bar Middle Temple 1970 (ad eundum Inner Temple 1979); barr Midland Circuit 1997–, asst recorder 1998, recorder 2000–; pres Cambridge Georgian Gp 1969, chm Cambridge Univ Cons Assoc 1969; chm Prayer Book Soc 2001–06 (vice-pres 1994–2001), memb Exec Ctee Friends of Friendless Churches 1983– (chm 1998–); Freeman City of London 1976; *Recreations* gardening and architectural history; *Clubs* Carlton, Coningsby (chm 1976–77, treas 1983–87); *Style*— Roger Evans, Esq; ✉ 2 Harcourt Buildings, Temple, London EC4Y 9DB (tel 020 7353 6961, fax 020 7353 6968, e-mail revans@harcourtchambers.law.co.uk)

EVANS, Ruth Elizabeth; *b* 12 October 1957; *Educ* Camden Sch for Girls, Girton Coll Cambridge (BA); *Children* 1 da; *Career* vol Liberty 1980, dir Maternity Alliance 1981–86, dep dir then actg dir MIND 1986–89 (bd dir Minds Matter Ltd 1986–90), gen sec War on Want 1990, mgmnt conslt Dept of Health 1990–91, dir Nat Consumer Cncl 1992–99; non-exec dir: Fin Ombudsman Services 1999–2002, Liverpool Victoria Gp 1999–2002, Nationwide Bldg Soc 2002–05; memb Advsy Bd ING Direct UK 2007–; chair: Standing Advsy Gp on Consumer Involvement in NHS 1995–99, Ind Inquiry into Paediatric Cardiac Services Royal Brompton and Harefield Hospitals 1999–2001, Ind Inquiry into Drug Testing at Work 2002–04, Bar Standards Bd 2006–; dep chair Ofcom Consumer Panel 2004–; memb: Bd Nat Perinatal Epidemiology Unit 1983–86, Brook Advsy Centres 1984–87, Good Practices in Mental Health 1986–89, Ctee of Mgmnt UK Cochrane Centre 1993–95, Prevention of Professional Abuse NEtwork 1994–97, Central Research and Devpt Ctee for the NHS 1995–99, UK Round Table on Sustainable Devpt 1995–99, Acting on Complaints Advsy Bd Dept of Health 1996–97, NHS Charter Advsy Gp 1998, Expert Panel on Sustainable Devpt 1998–99, Fabian Soc Cmmn on Taxation and Citizenship 1999–2000, Panel of Ind Assessors Office of the Cmmr for Public Appts 1999–2005, Ind Review Panel on the Future Funding of the BBC 1999, Cncl Britain in Europe 1999–2002 (chair Shoppers in Europe), Human Genetics Cmmn 1999–2002, Ind Review Panel for the Advertising of Medicines 1999–2005, Medicines Cmmn 2002–03, Tbnls for Users Prog Interdepartmental Steering Gp Lord Chllr's Dept 2003–05, Governance Review Gp Law Soc 2003–05, QC Selection Panel 2005–, Customer Impact Panel Assoc of Br Insurers 2006–; lay memb GMC 1999– (chm Standards Ctee 2003–05); tstee Money Advice Tst 1994–2000 (chair Advsy Gp of UK money advice agencies); govr Camden Sch for Girls 1985–89; *Style*— Ms Ruth Evans; ✉ tel 020 7482 0420

EVANS, Sarah Hauldys; da of Wyndham Bowen Evans, and Nancy Sarah, *née* Mills; *b* 4 March 1953; *Educ* King James' GS Knaresborough, Univ of Sussex (BA), Univ of Leicester (MA), Univ of Leeds (PGCE); *m* 1989, Andrew Romanis Fowler; 1 s (Kit Wyndam Romanis b 1993); *Career* asst teacher then head of English Leeds Girls' HS 1976–84, dep head Fulneck Girls' Sch Pudsey 1986–89; head: Friends' Sch Saffron Walden 1989–96, King Edward VI High Sch for Girls Birmingham 1996–; pres Guild of Friends in Educn 1991–92, co-chair HMC/GSA Educn Ctee 2001–03, memb Exec Ctee Boarding Schs' Assoc 1990–96 (vice-chm 1995–96); SHMIS: memb Educn Ctee 1991–96, chair Educn Ctee 1992–96; non-exec dir Essex Ambulance Tst 1991–96, memb ISC teacher induction panel (ISCtip) 2003–, govr Queenswood Sch 2004–; tstee: Acad of Youth 2002–, Westhill Endowment Tst 2002–; *Recreations* the arts; *Style*— Ms Sarah Evans; ✉ 38 Amesbury Road, Moseley, Birmingham B13 8LE (tel 0121 449 4536); King Edward VI High School for Girls, Edgbaston, Park Road, Birmingham B15 2UB (tel 0121 472 1834, fax 0121 471 3808)

EVANS, Stephen Geoffrey; s of Eric Ward Evans (d 1984), and Madelane, *née* Cartledge (d 1982); *b* 23 August 1938; *Educ* Cheltenham Coll; *m* 2 June 1962, Valerie; 2 s (Nicholas b 1965, Christopher b 1967), 2 da (Harriet b 1969, Annabel b 1972); *Career* chartered surveyor; sr ptnr John Staite & Sons until 1988 (when co sold to Prudential Property Services), conslt Evans Hardy Bromwich Leamington Spa 2002–; pres Warks Valuation Tbnl 1997–; High Sheriff Warks 1995–96; surveyor to RASE 1990–2005; govr Kingsley Sch Leamington Spa 1980–2005, memb Warks Probation Ctee 1992–2000, vice-pres Leamington Spa RUFC, chm St Michael's PCC Weston-under-Wetherley, chm jt parish cncl, past chm Leamington Round Table 1973; FRICS; *Recreations* sailing, fly fishing, tennis, gardening, golf, bridge; *Style*— Stephen Evans, Esq; ✉ Glebe Cottage, Weston-under-Wetherley, Leamington Spa, Warwickshire CV33 9BY (tel 01926 632521); Evans Hardy Bromwich, Somerset House, Clarendon Place, Leamington Spa, Warwickshire CV32 5QN (tel 01926 888181, fax 01926 888018)

EVANS, HE Stephen Nicholas; CMG (2002), OBE (1994); s of Vincent Morris Evans, of Poole, Dorset, and Doris Mary Evans (d 1977); *b* 29 June 1950, Harrow, Middx; *Educ* King's Coll Taunton, Univ of Bristol (BA); *m* 29 Dec 1975, Sharon Ann, *née* Holdcroft; 2 da (Juliette b 14 April 1981, Olivia b 1 Feb 1984), 1 s (Nicholas b 20 Feb 1986); *Career* 1 Royal Tank Regt 1971–74; HM Dip Serv: FCO 1974–78, head of Chancery Hanoi 1978–80, FCO 1980–82, first sec Bangkok 1982–88, FCO 1988–90, head Political Section Ankara 1990–93, cnsllr Islamabad 1993–96, UN Special Mission to Afghanistan 1996–97, head S Asian Dept FCO 1998–2001, chargé d'affaires Kabul 2001–02, high cmmr to Sri Lanka 2002–06 (concurrently non-resident high cmmr to the Maldives), ambass to Afghanistan 2006–; *Recreations* naval and military history, golf, cycling; *Clubs* Athenaeum, Royal Colombo Golf (Sri Lanka); *Style*— HE Mr Stephen Evans, CMG, OBE; ✉ c/o Foreign & Commonwealth Office (Kabul), King Charles Street, London SW1A 2AH

EVANS, Dr Stephen Nicholas (Steve); s of William Raymond Evans, of Llanelli, and Carole Dalling, *née* White; *b* 1 December 1964; *Educ* Penyrheol Comp Sch Gorseinon, Univ of Bristol Med Sch (MB ChB), postgrad dip; *m* 5 Sept 1992, Lysette Emma, da of Michael Newman; 1 s (Joel Ieuan b 12 Sept 1999); *Career* house physician Royal Cornwall Hosp (Treliske) Truro 1988–89, house surgn Bristol Royal Infirmary 1989, MO Br Antarctic Survey 1989–91, med SHO Birmingham Heartlands Hosp 1991–94, registrar (gen and geriatric med) Jersey Gen Hosp and Southampton Gen Hosp 1995, registrar Napier Public Hosp NZ 1995–96, sr registrar (gen and geriatric med) Glenfield Gen Hosp NHS Tst and Leicester Gen Hosp NHS Tst 1997–99, locum Withybush Gen Hosp Haverfordwest 1999; Leicester Gen Hosp: conslt physician Dept of Cerebrovascular Med 1999–2002, lead clinician for emergency med 2001–02; currently conslt physician Med Specialist Gp Guernsey; memb: BMA, Br Geriatric Soc, Br Assoc of Stroke Physicians; MRCP 1994; *Publications* author of numerous papers and articles in learned jls; *Recreations* rugby, snowboarding, power kites; *Clubs* Oakham RFC; *Style*— Dr Steve Evans; ✉ c/o Medical Specialist Group, Alexandra House, Les Frieteaux, St Martin's, Guernsey GY1 3EX (tel 01481 238565, fax 01481 237782, e-mail snevans@doctors.net)

EVANS, Stuart John; s of John Redshaw Evans (d 1992), and Mabel Elizabeth, *née* Brown (d 1974); *b* 31 December 1947; *Educ* Royal GS Newcastle upon Tyne, Univ of Leeds (LLB); *m* 2 Jan 1971, Margaret Elizabeth, da of Edgar John Evans (d 1966), and Kathleen Gerardine, *née* Goulding (d 2006); 2 s (John Daniel b 1976, Thomas b 1977), 1 da (Elizabeth b 1983); *Career* articled clerk Stanley Brent & Co 1970–72, asst slr Slaughter and May 1972–79, head of corp fin Simmons & Simmons 2001– (asst slr 1979–80, ptnr 1981–); chair Tate Patrons of New Art 1997–2000, juror Turner Prize 2001, fndr (with s, John Daniel Evans) Lodeveans Collection of Contemporary Art; reader St Stephen's Church Canonbury; *Books* A Practitioner's Guide to The FSA Regulation of Investment Banking (contrib), Global Corporate Governance Guide 2004: Best Practice in the Boardroom (contrib), A Practitioner's Guide to The Financial Services Authority Listing Rules 2006/2007 (contrib); *Recreations* contemporary art; *Style*— Stuart Evans, Esq; ✉ Simmons & Simmons, CityPoint, One Ropemaker Street, London EC2Y 9SS (tel 020 7628 2020, fax 020 7628 2070)

EVANS, Timothy James (Tim); *b* 22 August 1962; *Educ* South Bank Poly, Oxford Poly (BA Arch, DipArch); *m*; 2 da; *Career* architect; Burns Guthrie and Partners 1983–84, Terry Farrell & Co 1986–89; vol work Managua Nicaragua 1989; Daryl Jackson (Aust) 1989–90; Sheppard Robson: joined 1990, ptnr 1998–, creative dir i/c design direction London and Manchester offices 2003–, ldr Sustainability Gp (formerly ldr Urban Regeneration Gp); *Style*— Tim Evans, Esq; ✉ Sheppard Robson, 77 Parkway, London NW1 7PU (tel 020 7504 1700, fax 020 7504 1701, e-mail tim.evans@sheppardrobson.com)

EVANS, Prof Timothy William; s of Philip Charles Evans, of Endcliffe, Sheffield, and Mary Elizabeth, *née* Else; *b* 29 May 1954; *Educ* High Storrs GS Sheffield, Univ of Manchester (BSc, MB ChB, MD), Univ of Sheffield (PhD, DSc), Univ of Calif San Francisco; *m* Dr Josephine Emir MacSweeney, da of Prof James MacSweeney (d 1972); 3 s (Charles James b 1990, Freddie William b 1992, Edward Christopher George b 1998), 1 da (Verity Sarah Mary b 1995); *Career* Manchester Royal Infirmary 1980, Univ of Sheffield 1981, Royal Postgraduate Med Sch 1982, Nat Heart and Lung Inst 1982, Univ of Sheffield 1982–84, Univ of Calif San Francisco 1984–85, prof of intensive care med Imperial Coll Sch of Med London, conslt in intensive care/thoracic med Royal Brompton Hosp and Westminster London 1987–, civilian conslt to HM Forces 1998–, hon conslt Royal Hosp Chelsea 2004–, academic registrar RCP 2005–, med dir Royal Brompton and Harefield NHS Tst 2005– (dep ceo 2006–); FRCP, Hon FRCA, FMedSci; *Publications* author of 5 books and over 200 chapters, invited articles and peer reviewed papers, memb Editorial Bds of 2 scientific jls; *Recreations* flying and sailing; *Clubs* RSM; *Style*— Prof Timothy Evans; ✉ Department of Anaesthesia and Intensive Care, Royal Brompton Hospital NHS Trust, Sydney Street, London SW3 6NP (tel 020 7351 8523, fax 020 7351 8524, e-mail t.evans@rbht.nhs.uk)

EVANS, Dr Trevor John; o s of late Evan Alban (John) Evans, of Market Bosworth, Leics, and Margaret Alice, *née* Hilton; *b* 14 February 1947; *Educ* King's Sch Rochester, UCL (BSc, PhD); *m* 1973, Margaret Elizabeth, da of Felix Whitham, of Anlaby, E Yorks; 3 s (Thomas b 1979, Owen b 1984, Jacob b 1988), 1 da (Jessica b 1981); *Career* chem engr; chief exec Inst of Chem Engrs 1976–2006, chief exec Ergonomics Soc 2007–; formerly: jt sec-gen Euro Fedn of Chem Engrg, dep chm Bd Engrg Cncl (UK), dir Engrg and Technol Bd (ETB), memb Bd Science Cncl; Kurnakov Meml Medal, Titanium ACHEMA Plaque; fell UCL 1997; CEng, Hon FIChemE, FCMI, FRSA, hon memb Czech Soc of Chemical Engrg 2006, hon memb European Fedn of Chemical Engrg 2007; *Recreations* the complexities of family life; *Style*— Dr T J Evans; ✉ The Bakery Cottage, 2 Rectory Lane, Market Bosworth, Nuneaton, Warwickshire CV13 0LS (e-mail tevansj@aol.com)

EVANS, Very Rev (John) Wyn; s of Ven David Eifion Evans (d 1997), and Iris Elizabeth, *née* Gravelle (d 1973); *b* 4 October 1946; *Educ* Ardwyn GS Aberystwyth, UC Cardiff (BA), St Michael's Theol Coll Llandaff (BD), Jesus Coll Oxford; *m* 1997, Diane Katherine Baker; *Career* ordained deacon 1971, priest 1972; curate St Davids Pembs 1971–72, minor canon St Davids Cathedral 1972–75, graduate student Jesus Coll Oxford 1975–77, permission to officiate Oxford Dio 1975–77, diocesan advsr on archives St Davids 1976–82, rector Llanfallteg with Castell Dwyran and Clunderwen with Henllan Amgoed and Llangan 1977–82, examining chaplain to Bishop of St Davids 1977, diocesan warden of ordinands 1978–83, diocesan dir of educn 1982–92; Trinity Coll Carmarthen: chaplain and lectr 1982–90, dean of chapel 1990–94, head Dept of Theology and Religious Studies 1991–94; St Davids Cathedral: hon canon 1988–90, canon (4th cursal) 1990–94, dean and precentor 1994–; chair St Davids Diocesan Advsy Ctee 2006–; Church in Wales: memb Rep Body 1998–2004, chm of deans 2001–, memb Cathedrals and Churches Cmmn 2001–; chm Cathedral Libraries and Archives Assoc 2001; memb: Exec Friends of Friendless Churches 1995–, Ct Nat Library of Wales 1999–, Ct Univ of Wales Cardiff 2002–; memb Gorsedd of Bards 1997; FSA 1989, FRHistS 1994; *Publications* St Davids Cathedral 1181–1981 (with Roger Worsley, 1981), contrib to various jls incl Jl of Welsh Ecclesiastical History, Carmarthen Antiquary, Diwinyddiaeth; *Recreations* reading, music, antiquities; *Clubs* Oxford and Cambridge; *Style*— The Very Rev J Wyn Evans, FSA, FRHistS; ✉ The Deanery, The Close, St Davids, Dyfed SA62 6RH (tel 01437 720202, fax 01437 721885)

EVANS, (John) Wynford; CBE; s of Gwilym Everton Evans (d 1968), of Llanelli, and Margaret Mary Elfreda, *née* Jones (d 1982); *b* 3 November 1934; *Educ* Llanelli GS, St John's Coll Cambridge (MA); *m* 20 April 1957, Sigrun, da of Gerhard and Johanna Lotte Brethfeld; 3 s (Mark, Chris, Tim); *Career* dep chm London Electricity 1977–84; chm: South Wales Electricity plc (Swalec) 1984–95, The National Grid Holding plc 1994–95, Bank of Wales 1995– (dir 1989–); dir Welsh Nat Opera 1988–93; memb Welsh Language Bd 1988–89, dep chm Prince of Wales Ctee 1989–96; tstee and dep chm Cardiff Bay Opera House Tst 1994–97; dep chm Nat Tst Ctee for Wales 1997–99, tstee Nat Botanic Garden of Wales 1998–, memb Cncl of Nat Museums and Galleries of Wales; Liveryman Welsh Livery Guild; memb Gorsedd of Bards; High Sheriff S Glamorgan 1995–96; Liveryman Worshipful Co of Tin Plate Workers; *Recreations* fly fishing, cross-country skiing, golf; *Clubs* Cardiff & County, London Welsh; *Style*— J Wynford Evans, Esq, CBE

EVANS-BEVAN, Sir Martyn Evan; 2 Bt (UK 1958), of Cadoxton-juxta-Neath, Co Glamorgan; s of Sir David Martyn Evans-Bevan, 1 Bt (d 1973), and Eira Winifred, *née* Glanley (d 2001); *b* 1 April 1932; *Educ* Uppingham; *m* 12 Oct 1957, Jennifer Jane Marion, da of Robert Hugh Stevens, of Lady Arbour, Eardisley, Herefords; 4 s (David Gawain b 1961, Richard Martyn b 1963, Thomas Rhydian b 1966, Huw Evan b 1971); *Heir* s, David Evans-Bevan; *Career* High Sheriff of Breconshire 1967–68, Freeman of City of London, Liveryman Worshipful Co of Farmers; company dir; *Clubs* Carlton; *Style*— Sir Martyn Evans-Bevan, Bt; ✉ Spring Valley, St Ouens, Jersey

EVANS-LOMBE, Hon Mr Justice; Sir Edward Christopher Evans-Lombe; only s of Vice Adm Sir Edward Evans-Lombe, KCB, JP, DL (himself gs of Rev Henry Lombe, who took the name Lombe *vice* Evans 1862 under the terms of the will of his great-uncle, Sir John Lombe, 1 Bt. Sir John was bro of Mary, Rev Henry's mother, who m Thomas Browne Evans). The surname of the Admiral's f, Alexander, became Evans Lombe following the marriage of his f with a cousin, Louisa Evans; *b* 10 April 1937; *Educ* Eton, Trinity Coll Cambridge; *m* 1964, Frances Marilyn, DL, er da of Robert Ewen Mackenzie, of Lincoln; 1 s, 3 da; *Career* served Royal Norfolk Regt 1955–57, 2 Lt; called to the Bar Inner Temple 1963 (bencher 1985); standing counsel to Dept of Trade in Bankruptcy Matters 1971, QC 1978, recorder SE Circuit 1982–93, judge of the High Court of Justice (Chancery Div)

1993–; chm Agric Land Tbnl SE Area 1983–93; *Style*— The Hon Mr Justice Evans-Lombe; ✉ Royal Courts of Justice, Strand, London WC2A 2LL

EVANS OF PARKSIDE, Baron (Life Peer UK 1997), of St Helens in the County of Merseyside; John Evans; s of James Evans (d 1937), and Margaret, *née* Robson (d 1987); *b* 19 October 1930; *Educ* Jarrow Central Sch; *m* 1959, Joan, da of Thomas Slater; 2 s, 1 da; *Career* former marine fitter and engr, memb Hebburn UDC 1962–74 (chm 1972–73, ldr 1969–74), memb S Tyneside MDC 1973–74, memb Euro Parl 1975–78 (chm Regnl Policy and Tport Ctee 1976–78); MP (Lab): Newton Feb 1974–83, St Helens N 1983–97; asst govt whip 1978–79, oppn whip 1979–80, PPS to Rt Hon Michael Foot as ldr of oppn 1980–83, memb Lab Pty NEC 1982–96, oppn front bench spokesman on employment 1983–87, chm National Lab Pty 1991–92; *Style*— The Rt Hon Lord Evans of Parkside; ✉ House of Lords, London SW1A 0PW

EVANS OF WATFORD, Baron (Life Peer UK 1998), of Chipperfield in the County of Hertfordshire; David Charles Evans; *b* 30 November 1942; *Educ* Watford Coll of Technology (City and Guilds, Edward Hunter Medal); *Career* apprentice printer, fndr and chm Centurion Press Group 1971–2002; chm: Senate Consulting Ltd, Personnel Publications Ltd, Redactive Media Gp, Indigo Publishing Ltd, Evans Mitchell Books; non-exec dir Partnership Sourcing Ltd; dir KISS 100 FM until 1992; tstee Royal Air Force Museum, dir Royal Air Force Trading Co; dir Watford Community Events, advsr West Herts Coll; hon fell Cancer Research UK; memb Worshipful Co of Marketors; FCIM, FCGI; *Style*— The Lord Evans of Watford; ✉ House of Lords, London SW1A 0PW; Senate Consulting Ltd, The Old Forge, Forge Mews, 16 Church Street, Rickmansworth, Hertfordshire WD3 1DH (tel 01923 713030, fax 01923 713040, e-mail lordevans@senateconsulting.co.uk)

EVE, Trevor John; s of Stewart Frederick Eve, of Staffordshire, and Elsie, *née* Hamer; *b* 1 July 1951; *Educ* Bromsgrove Sch, Kingston Art Coll, RADA; *m* 1 March 1980, Sharon Patricia, da of Francis Maughan, of Holland Park, London; 1 da (Alice b 6 Feb 1982), 2 s (James Jonathan (Jack) b 23 Sept 1985, George Francis b 7 March 1994); *Career* actor, producer; patron Childhope Int; prodr Projector Productions; *Theatre* incl: Children of a Lesser God (Olivier Award for best actor) 1981, The Genius (Royal Court) 1983, High Society (NT) 1986, Man Beast and Virtue (NT) 1989, The Winter's Tale (Young Vic) 1991, Inadmissible Evidence (RNT) 1993, Uncle Vanya (Albery, Olivier Award for Best Supporting Actor 1997) 1996; *Television* incl: Shoestring 1980, Jamaica Inn, A Sense of Guilt 1990, Parnell and the Englishwoman 1991, A Doll's House 1991, The Politician's Wife (Channel 4) 1995, Black Easter (Screen Two) 1995, Heat of the Sun (Carlton) 1997, Evilstreak (LWT) 1999, David Copperfield (BBC) 1999, Waking The Dead (4 series, BBC) 2000–04, Lawless (ITV) 2004, The Family Man (BBC) 2006; as prodr: Alice Through the Looking Glass (Projector/Channel 4) 1998, Cinderella (Projector/Channel 4) 1999, Twefth Night (Projector/Channel 4); *Film* incl: Hindle Wakes, Dracula, A Wreath of Roses, The Corsican Brothers, Aspen Extreme, Psychotherapy, The Knight's Tale, The Tribe, Appetite, Possession, Troy; *Recreations* golf, tennis; *Clubs* Queen's, Hurlingham, Chelsea Arts, Wentworth; *Style*— Trevor Eve, Esq; ✉ c/o ICM Ltd, Oxford House, 76 Oxford Street, London W1N 0AX (tel 020 7636 6565, fax 020 7323 0101)

EVENNETT, David Anthony; MP; s of late Norman Thomas Evennett, and Irene Evennett; *b* 3 June 1949; *Educ* Buckhurst Hill Co HS for Boys, LSE (MSc Econ); *m* 1975, Marilyn Anne, da of late Ronald Stanley Smith; 2 s (Mark, Thomas); *Career* sch teacher 1972–74; Lloyds: broker 1974–81, memb 1976–92, dir Underwriting Agency 1982–91; Parly candidate (Cons): Hackney S and Shoreditch 1979, Bexleyheath and Crayford 1997 and 2001; MP (Cons): Erith and Crayford 1983–97, Bexleyheath and Crayford 2005–; memb Select Ctee on Educn, Sci and the Arts House of Commons 1986–92; PPS: to Lady Blatch (Min of State at Dept of Educn) 1992–93, to John Redwood (Sec of State for Wales) 1993–95, to David Maclean and Lady Blatch (Mins of State at Home Office) 1995–96, to Rt Hon Gillian Shepherd (Sec of State for Educn and Employment) 1996–97; memb Select Ctee for Educn and Skills 2005, oppn whip 2005–; commercial liaison mangr for Bexley Coll 1997–2001, conslt Marsh McLennan 1998–2000, mgmnt conslt and lectr 2001–05; cncllr Redbridge BC 1974–78; *Recreations* family, reading novels and biographies, cinema, travel; *Clubs* Bexleyheath Cons; *Style*— David Evennett, Esq, MP; ✉ House of Commons, London SW1A 0AA

EVENS, Rt Rev Robert John Scott; *see:* Crediton, Bishop of

EVERALL, His Hon Judge Mark Andrew; QC (1994); s of John Dudley Everall (d 1997), of London, and Pamela, *née* Odone; *b* 30 June 1950; *Educ* Ampleforth, Lincoln Coll Oxford (MA); *m* 16 Dec 1978, (Elizabeth) Anne, da of Thomas Hugh Richard Perkins; 2 da; *Career* called to the Bar Inner Temple 1975; circuit judge (SE Circuit) 2006–; *Style*— His Hon Judge Everall, QC; ✉ 1 Hare Court, Temple, London EC4 (tel 020 7797 7070, fax 020 7797 7435, e-mail clerks@1hc.com)

EVERARD, HE John Vivian; s of William Ralph Everard, and Margaret Nora Jennifer, *née* Massey; *b* 24 November 1956; *Educ* King Edward VI Sch Lichfield, Emmanuel Coll Cambridge (William Turner Hunter bursary, MA), Peking Univ, Manchester Business Sch (MBA); *m* April 1990, Heather Ann, da of late William Starkey; *Career* HM Dip Serv; Far Eastern Dept FCO 1979–81, third sec Peking 1981–83, second sec Vienna 1983–84, Manchester Business Sch 1984–86, project conslt Metapraxis Ltd 1986–87, S America Dept FCO 1987–90, head Commercial Section Santiago 1990–93, chargé d'affaires then ambass Minsk 1993–95, OSCE Mission to Bosnia and Herzegovina 1995–96, Africa Dept (Equatorial) FCO 1996–98, political counsellor Peking 1998–2000, ambass to Uruguay 2001–05, ambass to North Korea 2006–; *Recreations* travel, cats, cycling; *Style*— HE Mr John Vivian Everard; ✉ c/o Foreign & Commonwealth Office (Pyongyang), King Charles Street, London SW1A 2AH

EVERARD, Richard Anthony Spencer; DL (Leics 1997); s of Maj Richard Peter Michael Spencer (d 1990), of Melton Mowbray, Leics, and Bettyne Ione, formerly Lady Newtown Butler (d 1989); *b* 31 March 1954; *Educ* Eton, RMA Sandhurst; *m* 9 May 1981, Caroline Anne, da of Reginald J Tower Hill, of Coggeshall, Essex; 1 da (Charlotte b 1985), 1 s (Julian b 1988); *Career* Royal Horse Gds 1st Dragoons (Blues and Royals) 1973–77, cmmnd 1973, Lt 1975; chm Everards Brewery Ltd 1988– (dir 1983–); pres Age Concern Leics; tstee: Leics Police Charitable Tst, County Air Ambulance; Dip in Company Direction IOD; High Sheriff Leics 2002–03, Vice Lord-Lt Leics 2003–; Master Worshipful Co of Brewers 2004; *Recreations* shooting, skiing, tennis, flying helicopters, motorcycling, golf; *Clubs* MCC, Eton Ramblers, The Air Squadron, Luffenham Heath Golf; *Style*— Richard Everard, Esq, DL; ✉ East Farndon Hall, Market Harborough, Leicestershire LE16 9SE; Everards Brewery Ltd, Castle Acres, Narborough, Leicestershire LE19 1BY (tel 0116 201 4307, fax 0116 281 4198)

EVERARD, Sir Robin Charles; 4 Bt (UK 1911), of Randlestown, Co Meath; s of Lt-Col Sir Nugent Henry Everard, 3 Bt (d 1984), and Frances Audrey, *née* Jesson (d 1975); *b* 5 October 1939; *Educ* Harrow, Sandhurst; *m* 28 Sept 1963, Ariel Ingrid, eldest da of Col Peter Cleasby-Thompson, MBE, MC (d 1981), of Blackhill House, Little Cressingham, Norfolk; 2 da (Catherine Mary b 1964, Victoria Frances b 1966), 1 s (Henry Peter Charles b 1970); *Heir* s, Henry Everard; *Career* three year cmmn Duke of Wellington's Regt; md P Murray-Jones Ltd 1961–75, mgmnt conslt 1975–; *Style*— Sir Robin Everard, Bt; ✉ Church Farm, Shelton, Long Stratton, Norwich NR15 2SB

EVERARD, Timothy John; CMG (1978); s of Charles Miskin Everard (d 1953), of Peterborough, and Monica Mary, *née* Barford (d 1970); *b* 22 October 1929; *Educ* Uppingham, Magdalen Coll Oxford (BA); *m* 23 July 1955, Josiane, da of Alexander Romano (d 1970), of Alexandria; 2 da (Anne-Marie b 1956, Catherine Alison b 1960), 2 s (Timothy Charles b 1958, Alexander John b 1964); *Career* Barclays Bank (Egypt, Sudan, Kenya, Zaïre) 1952–62, dir Ellis & Everard Ltd 1966–67; HM Dip Serv: first sec FO 1962–64, first sec Bangkok 1964–66, FCO 1967–68, first sec Br Political Residency Bahrain 1969–72, consul-gen and chargé d'affaires Hanoi 1972–73, cnsllr Athens 1974–78, cnsllr Paris 1978–81, min Lagos 1981–84, ambass to E Berlin 1984–88, ret; sec-gen Order of St John of Jerusalem 1988–93, tstee Dresden Tst 1994–2005; Freeman City of London 1991; AIB; KStJ 1988; *Recreations* golf, tennis; *Clubs* Reform; *Style*— Timothy Everard, Esq, CMG; ✉ Leagues, Burnt Oak, Crowborough, East Sussex TN6 3SD (tel 01892 653278)

EVEREST, Richard Anthony; s of Cecil Carlyle Everest (d 1974), of Barton on Sea, Hants, and Dorothy Helen, *née* Soldan (d 1995); *b* 26 April 1938; *Educ* Highgate Sch, ChCh Oxford (MA); *m* 9 August 1969, Brenda Anne, da of Frederick John Ralph, of Brighton, E Sussex; 2 s (Timothy b 1971, Philip b 1974); *Career* served RCS 1956–58; accountant; articled clerk Pridie Brewster and Gold 1962–66, audit sr Black Geoghegan and Till 1966–70, asst mangr Layton-Bennett Billingham and Co 1970–74, audit gp mangr Josolyne Layton-Bennett and Co 1974–79, princ mangr Arthur Young McClelland Moores and Co 1979–82, dir and sec Henry G Nicholson (Underwriting) Ltd (Lloyd's membs' agents) 1986–91, dir Bell Nicholson Henderson Ltd (Lloyd's reinsurance brokers) 1987–93 (gp chief accountant 1982–93), dir (fin and admin) UIA (Insurance) Ltd 1994–98; underwriting memb Lloyd's 1986–96; govr Townsend C of E Sch 1993– (chm 2003–); Freeman City of London 1959, memb Ct of Assts Worshipful Co of Cutlers (Freeman 1959, Master 1990); FCA 1976 (ACA 1966); *Recreations* travel, history, art, golf; *Style*— Richard Everest, Esq; ✉ 2 Palfrey Close, St Albans, Hertfordshire AL3 5RE (tel 01727 835550, e-mail randbeverest@tiscali.co.uk)

EVERETT, Charles William Vogt; s of Dr Thomas Everett (d 1976), and Ingeborg, *née* Vogt (d 1971); *b* 15 October 1949; *Educ* Bryanston, Univ of Reading; *m* 1978, Elizabeth Vanessa, *née* Ellis; 3 s; *Career* Lord Chancellor's Dept: joined 1971, asst private sec to the Lord Chancellor 1974–76, seconded to Dept of Tport 1982–84, Legal Aid Bill Div 1987–88, sec to Legal Aid Bd 1988–89, Central Unit 1990–91, head Policy and Legal Services Gp 1991–95, dir of fin and admin The Court Service 1995–99, dir of fire and emergency planning Home Office 1999–2002, dir of corp devpt and services Home Office 2002–06; chair Hastings and Rother PCT 2007–, memb Sussex Probation Bd 2007–; *Style*— Charles Everett, Esq; ✉ Hastings and Rother Primary Care Trust, Bexhill Hospital, Holliers Hill, Bethill-on-Sea, East Sussex TN40 2DZ

EVERETT, Katharine; da of Peter Everett, and Penelope Everett; *Educ* Wycombe Abbey, LMH Oxford; *m* Horacio Queiro; 1 s (Rodrigo b 1988), 1 da (Alicia b 1990); *Career* prodr BBC Science (wrote, directed and produced films incl Horizon: Iceman) 1985–92, head of commissions BBC1 1994–97, head of programming BBC Choice (launched and ran BBC's first digital entertainment channel) 1997–99, controller Interactive TV BBC 1999–2001, controller New Media BBC 2001–02, controller BBCi Development 2002–03, dir Making it Happen project BBC 2003–04, dir Change BBC 2005–; *Recreations* walking, singing, food; *Style*— Ms Katharine Everett; ✉ e-mail katharine.everett@bbc.co.uk

EVERETT, Martin Thomas; s of Dr Thomas Everett (d 1975), and Ingeborg Maria, *née* Vogt; *b* 24 September 1939; *Educ* Bryanston; *m* 14 Sept 1963, Susan Mary, da of John Peter Sworder, MC, TD (d 1987); 2 s (Oliver b 2 July 1965, George b 8 Sept 1967), 1 da (Daisy b 14 May 1975); *Career* Nat Serv 2 Lt 9/12 Royal Lancers 1959–61; Mayor Sworder and Co Ltd Wine Shippers: joined 1962, dir 1967, jt md 1974, md 1980; dir J T Davies & Sons 1995–; Freeman City of London, Liveryman Worshipful Co of Glass Sellers (memb Ct of Assts, Master 2003), Liveryman Worshipful Co of Vintners; memb Inst of Masters of Wine 1968; *Recreations* gardening, walking; *Style*— Martin Everett, Esq; ✉ Mayor Sworder & Co Ltd, 7 Aberdeen Road, Croydon, Surrey CR0 1EQ (tel 020 8686 1155, fax 020 8686 2017, e-mail martineverett.mw@btinternet.com)

EVERETT, Oliver William; CVO (1991, LVO 1980); s of Walter George Charles Everett, MC, DSO (d 1979), of Bognor Regis, W Sussex, and Gertrude Florence Rothwell, *née* Hellicar (d 1997); *b* 28 February 1943; *Educ* Felsted, Western Res Acad OH, Christ's Coll Cambridge (MA), Fletcher Sch of Law & Diplomacy Tufts Univ (MA), LSE; *m* 28 Aug 1965 (sep 2004), Theffania, da of Lt Robert Vesey Stoney (d 1944), of Rosturk Castle, Co Mayo; 2 da (Kathleen b 1966, Grania b 1969), 2 s (Toby b 1979, William b 1982); *Career* Dip Serv: first sec Br High Cmmn New Delhi 1969–73, first sec FCO 1973–78, asst private sec to HRH The Prince of Wales 1978–80, head Chancery Br Embassy Madrid 1980–81, private sec to HRH The Princess of Wales 1981–83, asst librarian Windsor Castle 1984, librarian and asst keeper of the Queen's Archives Windsor Castle 1985–2002, librarian emeritus Royal Library Windsor Castle 2002–; NADFAS lectr 2005–; *Recreations* skiing, rackets, windsurfing, baseball; *Clubs* Roxburghe; *Style*— Oliver Everett, Esq, CVO; ✉ 48 Egerton Gardens, London SW3 2BZ (tel 020 7581 3731, e-mail olivereverett@royalcollection.org.uk)

EVERETT, Rupert; *b* Norfolk; *Educ* Ampleforth, Central Sch of Speech and Drama; *Career* actor; *Theatre* incl: Waste of Time (Citizens Theatre Glasgow), Don Juan (Glasgow and London), Chinchilla (Glasgow and London), Another Country (Greenwich Theatre and Queen's Theatre), Mass Appeal (Lyric Hammersmith), Heartbreak House (Citizens Theatre Glasgow), The Vortex (Citizens Theatre Glasgow and Garrick), The Milk Train Doesn't Stop Here Anymore (Glasgow and London), Some Sunny Day (London); *Television* incl: The Far Pavilions 1994, Sherlock Holmes and the Case of the Silk Stocking 2004; *Films* incl: A Shocking Accident 1982, Princess Daisy 1983, Another Country 1984, Dance with a Stranger 1985, Arthur the King 1985, Duet for One 1986, The Gold Rimmed Glasses 1987, Hearts of Fire 1987, Chronicle of a Death Foretold 1987, The Right Hand Man 1987, Tolérance 1989, The Comfort of Strangers 1990, Inside Monkey Zetterland 1992, Remembrance of Things Fast: True Stories Visual Lies 1994, Pret-à-Porter 1994, Of Death and Love 1994, The Madness of King George 1995, Dunston Checks In 1996, My Best Friend's Wedding 1997, Shakespeare in Love 1998, B. Monkey 1998, The Next Best Thing 1999, A Midsummer Night's Dream 1999, Inspector Gadget 1999, An Ideal Husband 1999, Unconditional Love 2001, The Importance of Being Earnest 2002, To Kill a King 2003, Stage Beauty 2004, Shrek 2 2004, People 2004, A Different Loyalty 2004, Separate Lies 2005, The Chronicles of Narnia: The Lion, the Witch and the Wardrobe 2005; *Books* Hello Darling Are You Working? (1992); *Style*— Rupert Everett, Esq

EVERINGTON, Dr Anthony Herbert (Sam); OBE (1999); s of Geoffrey Everington, QC (d 1982), and Laila Everington; *b* 4 March 1957, Limpsfield, Surrey; *Educ* Inns of Court Sch of Law, Royal Free Hosp Sch of Med (MB BS); *m* 12 Sept 1987, Dr Pui-Ling Li; 1 s (Raoul b 1 April 1992), 1 da (Song-Lian b 13 Sept 1994); *Career* called to the Bar Gray's Inn 1978; cadet pilot RAF 1980–81; GP Tower Hamlets 1989–, memb Bd and chm of clinical governance Tower Hamlets PCT 2001–04; advsr to membs of shadow cabinet 1991–97; med dir and fndr GP out of hours co-op 1996–99; dep chm BMA 2004–; memb Bd Coll of Health 1998–2000, founding cmmr Cmmn for Health Improvement 1999–2004, dir Partnerships for Health UK 2002–; GP trainer 1996–; tstee: Parents Against Tobacco 1990–93, Quit 1990–94, Community Action Network 1998–2004, Stanton Guildhouse art and enterprise centre 1998–; contrib to BMJ on racism and racial discrimination; nat award from Campaign for Freedom of Information for res on racial discrimination 1995, Int Award of Excellence in Health Care The 5 Star Doctor World Family Doctors Europe 2006; memb BMA 1984, MRCGP 1989; *Recreations* family, travelling, restoring old bldgs, figure skating, boating, Norway; *Style*— Dr Sam Everington, OBE; ✉ Bromley by Bow

Health Centre, St Leonards Street, London E3 3BT (tel 020 8983 7082, e-mail sam.everington@nhs.net)

EVERITT, Prof Barry John; s of Frederick Everitt, and Winifred, *née* Tibble; *b* 19 February 1946; *Educ* SE Essex Co Technical HS, Univ of Hull (BSc), Univ of Birmingham (PhD), Univ of Cambridge (ScD); *m* 1, 1966 (m dis 1978), Valerie Sowter; 1 s (Alex Daniel b 23 Dec 1966); m 2, 1979, Jane Sterling; 1 da (Jessica Chloe b 6 May 1988); *Career* research fell Dept of Anatomy Univ of Birmingham Med Sch 1970–73, MRC travellng research fell Karolinska Institutet 1973–74; Univ of Cambridge: demonstrator Dept of Anatomy 1974–79, lectr 1979–91, reader in neuroscience Dept of Anatomy 1991–94, reader in neuroscience Dept of Experimental Psychology 1994–97, prof of behavioural neuroscience Dept of Experimental Psychology 1997–; Downing Coll Cambridge: fell 1976–2003, dir of studies in med 1978–98, master 2003–; Ciba-Geigy sr research fell Karolinska Institutet 1982–83, Soc for Neuroscience Grass lectr Univ of Texas 1997; visiting prof Univ of Calif San Francisco 2000, Sterling visiting prof Albany Medical Coll NY 2005, Swammerdam lectr Amsterdam 1999, Matarazzo lectr Univ of Oregon Portland 2005, Int Distinguished Scientist lectr Riken Inst Tokyo 2006, Dalbir Bindra lectr McGill Univ Montreal 2006, Grass Fndn Int Distinguished Scientist lectr UCLA 2006, Elsevier Lecture European Brain and Behaviour Soc 2007, lecture Int Basal Ganglia Soc 2007; pres: Br Assoc for Psychopharmacology 1992–94, Euro Brain and Behaviour Soc 1998–2000, Euro Behavioural Pharmacology Soc 2003–05; chm: Fellowships Ctee Human Frontier Sci Program Orgn 1993–95, MRC Research Studentships and Trg Awards Panel 1995–97, MRC, Neurosciences and Mental Health Bd 2001–, Nat Inst on Drug Abuse, Scientific Cnsllr 2001–; memb Scientific Advsy Bd: Astra-Zaneca 2001–04, Helsinki Neuroscience Centre 2000–, Neurogenetics & Behavious Center, John Hopkins Univ 2002–; ed-in-chief: Physiology and Behaviour 1994–98, Euro Jl of Neuroscience 1997–; reviewing ed Science 2003–; highly cited author Inst for Scientific Information (ISI); memb: Soc for Neuroscience, Euro Brain and Behaviour Soc, Br Assoc for Psychopharmacology, Euro Behavioural Pharmacological Soc, Br Neuroscience Assoc; foreign corr memb American Coll of Neuropsychopharmacology; FRS 2007; *Books* Essential Reproduction (5 edn, 2000); author of over 350 publications in scientific jls incl: Nature, Science, Nature Neurosciences, Jl of Neuroscience, Euro Jl of Neuroscience; *Recreations* opera, cricket, wine; *Style*— Prof Barry Everitt; ✉ Downing College, Cambridge CB2 1DQ (tel 01223 334806, e-mail bje10@cam.ac.uk)

EVERITT, Dom Charles Kingston (Gabriel); OSB; s of Prof (William) Norrie Everitt, FRSE, *qv*, and Katharine Elizabeth, *née* Gibson; *b* 7 January 1956; *Educ* Dundee HS, Univ of Edinburgh (MA), Balliol Coll Oxford (MA, DPhil), St Stephen's House Oxford; *Career* asst curate St Aidan and St Columba Hartlepool 1986–89; professed as a monk of Ampleforth 1991; Ampleforth Coll: asst teacher of Christian theology 1992–97, housemaster St Aidan's 1997–98, head of Christian theology 1997–2003, housemaster St Oswald's 1998–2003, third master 2001–03, headmaster 2004–; *Recreations* reading, cinema, weight training; *Style*— Dom Gabriel Everitt, OSB; ✉ Ampleforth College, York YO62 4ER (tel 01439 766800, fax 01439 788330, e-mail headmaster@ampleforth.org.uk)

EVERITT, Prof (William) Norrie; s of Charles Ernest Everitt (d 1979), of Birmingham and Sidmouth, and Elizabeth Cloudsley, *née* Ross (d 1990); *b* 10 June 1924; *Educ* Kings Norton GS Birmingham, Univ of Birmingham (BSc), Balliol Coll Oxford (MA, DPhil); *m* 25 July 1953, Katharine Elizabeth, da of Rev Dr Arthur John Howison Gibson (d 1967), of Edinburgh; 2 s (Charles Kingston (Dom Gabriel Everitt, OSB), *qv*, b 7 Jan 1956, Timothy Fraser b 25 March 1958); *Career* midshipman and Sub Lt RNVR 1944–47; Nelson Research Laboratories English Electric Co Ltd 1948–49; princ lectr in mathematics RMCS 1954–63; Baxter prof of mathematics: Univ of St Andrews 1963–67, Univ of Dundee 1967–82; emeritus prof Univ of Birmingham (Mason prof of mathematics 1982–89), visiting prof Univ of Surrey 1986–95, adjunct prof Northern Illinois Univ USA 1990–, hon prof Univ of Wales Coll of Cardiff 1994–; author of numerous pubns in mathematical periodicals; memb: Cncl London Mathematical Soc 1957–62, Br Nat Ctee for Mathematics 1972–78, Cncl and Academic Advsy Cncl Univ of Buckingham 1973–94, Educn Ctee Royal Soc of London 1978–84; memb Cncl and pres Edinburgh Mathematical Soc 1963–1966, memb Cncl and vice-pres RSE 1966–79; memb Ctee Balliol Soc 1998–2002; awarded Mathematics medal Union of Czech Mathematicians and Physicists Prague 1990; memb: Royal Soc of Sciences Sweden 1973, Acad of Letters Sci and Arts Palermo Italy 1978, Serbian Acad of Sciences and Arts 2003; FIMA 1965, FRSE 1966; *Books* Boundary Value Problems and Symplectic Algebra for Ordinary Differential and Quasi-differential Operators (with L Markus, 1998), Elliptic Partial Differential Operators and Symplectic Algebra (with L Markus, 2003), Infinate Dimensional Complex Symplectic Spaces (with L Markus, 2004), Complex Symplectic Spaces and Boundary Value Problems (with L Markus, 2006); *Recreations* music, walking, Parson Woodforde Soc; *Style*— Prof W N Everitt, FRSE; ✉ 103 Oakfield Road, Selly Park, Birmingham B29 7HW (tel 0121 471 2437, e-mail wneveritt@compuserve.com); School of Mathematics and Statistics, University of Birmingham, Edgbaston, Birmingham B15 2TT (tel 0121 414 6592 (or 6593), e-mail w.n.everitt@bham.ac.uk)

EVERITT, Richard Leslie; *b* 22 December 1948; *Educ* Univ of Southampton; *Career* BAA plc: slr 1978, dir of legal services 1988, memb bd 1990, gp strategy and compliance dir 1991; chief exec: National Air Traffic Services (NATS) 2001–04, Port of London Authy 2004–; non-exec dir Air Partner 2004–; *Style*— Richard Everitt, Esq

EVERITT-MATTHIAS, David Richard; s of Ronald Joseph Matthias (d 1996), and Kathleen Betty Matthias (d 1994); *b* 29 October 1960; *Educ* Sir Walter St Johns GS London, Ealing Coll of HE (City and Guilds); *m* 1 June 1985, Helen Mary Everitt-Matthias, *qv*, da of Peter Kingston Everitt; *Career* chef Inn on the Park London 1978–83, head chef Grand Cafe 1983–85, head chef Steamers Fish Restaurant 1985–86, head chef Fingals Restaurant Putney 1986–87, chef/co-prop (with wife, Helen) Le Champignon Sauvage Cheltenham 1987–; taken part in: The Restaurant Show London 1994–96, Hotel Olympia 1994 and 1996, Nat Restaurateurs Dinner 1995, Nat Chef of the Year Dinner 1996; TV appearances: Junior Masterchef 1996, Suprise Chefs 1996, This Morning TV 1996, Central TV 1996; memb Académie Culinaire de France; memb Sir Walter St Johns Old Boys Assoc; *Awards* Acorn Award, Midland Chef of the Year 1995 and 1996, Egon Ronay Dessert Chef of the Year 1996, Nat Chef of the Year 1996 and 1997, Michelin Star 1995, 1996, 1997, 1998 and 1999, 2 Michelin Stars 2000, 2001, 2002, 2003 and 2005, AA Guide 4 Rosettes 1997, 1998, 1999, 2000, 2001 and 2002, Roy Ackerman Guide Clover Leaf, Good Food Guide County Restaurant of the Year 2000, Egon Ronay Star and Upward Arrow, Decanter Restaurant of the Year 2001, Birmingham Plus Restaurant of the Year 2004, 2 Egon Ronay Stars 2005, Good Food Guide Restaurant of the Year 2005, Chef of the Year Cotswold Life 2005, Restaurant of the Year Square Meal 2006; *Publications* Essence: Recipes from Le Champignon Sauvage (2006); *Recreations* cricket, squash, art, jazz, reading; *Style*— David Everitt-Matthias, Esq; ✉ Le Champignon Sauvage, 24–26 Suffolk Road, Cheltenham, Gloucestershire GL50 2AQ (tel 01242 573449, fax 01242 254365, website www.lechampignonsauvage.com)

EVERITT-MATTHIAS, Helen Mary; da of Peter Everitt, of Loxwood, W Sussex, and Cynthia, *née* Frisby; *b* 25 March 1962, Sheffield; *Educ* Horsham HS for Girls, Guildford Co Coll of Technol; *m* 1 June 1985, David Everitt Matthias, *qv*, s of Ronald Joseph Matthias (d 1996); *Career* restaurateur; receptionist: Center Hotels London 1980–82, Inn on the Park London 1982–84, Cromwell Hosp London 1984–86; sec IBM Ltd 1986–87; prop (with husband, David) Le Champignon Sauvage Cheltenham 1987– (1 Michelin Star 1995, 2 Michelin Stars 2000); *Style*— Mrs Helen Everitt-Matthias; ✉ Le Champignon Sauvage, 24–28 Suffolk Road, Cheltenham, Gloucestershire GL50 2AQ (tel 01242 573449, fax 01242 254365, website www.lechampignonsauvage.com)

EVERS, Peter Lawson; s of John Henry Evers (d 1982), and Evelyn Jessica, *née* Hill (d 1997); *b* 4 January 1938; *Educ* King Edward VI GS; *m* 5 Oct 1963, Margaret Elaine, da of William Edwin Homer; 2 da (Elaine Louise b 14 Sept 1965, Alison Jane b 4 June 1967), 2 s (Jonathan, Philip Alexander (twins) b 21 March 1971); *Career* press offr J Lucas Industries 1965–67 (press and publicity asst 1959–67), publicity mangr Fafnir Bearing Co Ltd 1967–68, gp press offr John Thompson Group 1968–71, conslt John Fowler Public Relations 1971–72, ptnr and co fndr Edson Evers Public Relations 1972–99, dir and chief exec Edson Evers Communications Ltd 1980–95, UK dir PR Organisation International Ltd 1973–99 (pres 1985, 1991, 1992, 1993 and 1994), freelance PR conslt 1999–; BAIE (renamed British Assoc of Communicators in Business 1995) newspaper award winner: 1985, 1988, 1989, 1990, 1991, 1992; FIPR 1993–99 (MIPR 1969–93), memb BAIE (BACB) 1974–99, MRHS 1980; *Recreations* golf, gardening; *Clubs* Brocton Hall Golf; *Style*— Peter Evers, Esq; ✉ Peter L Evers, Freshfield House, Lower Way, Upper Longdon, Staffordshire WS15 1QG

EVERSHED, Ralph Jocelyn; s of Norman William Evershed (d 1983), and Jocelyn Slade, *née* Lyons (d 2005); *b* 16 November 1944; *Educ* St Albans Boys GS, Univ of Strathclyde (BA); *m* 6 Sept 1968, Carol Ann, da of Jerry Esmond Cullum (d 1987); 3 s (Timothy b 1973, David b 1974, John b 1982 d 1994), 2 da (Ruth b 1977, Susannah b 1980); *Career* chm Inter Varsity Press; dir: Eversheds Group Ltd 1987–2005, Woodsilk Properties Ltd 1988–; *Style*— Ralph Evershed, Esq

EVERSON, Noel Williams; s of Mervyn Cyril George Everson (d 1981), and Beryl Irene, *née* Williams; *b* 8 December 1944; *Educ* W Monmouth Sch, Middx Hosp Med Sch (MB BS), Univ of London (MS); *m* 1, 1969 (m dis 1982), Caroline Juliet Adams; 2 da (Juliet Claire b 1971, Katherine Frances Vivien b 1974); m 2, 27 June 1987, Elizabeth Mary, da of Donald Sellen; 2 da (Francesca Victoria Louise b 1990, Lucy Helen Jane b 1992); *Career* conslt surgn Leicester Royal Infirmary 1981–; memb: Assoc of Coloproctology, Assoc of Surgns; FRSM 1972, FRCS 1972; *Recreations* fly fishing; *Style*— Noel Everson, Esq; ✉ 6 Meadowcourt Road, Oadby, Leicester LE2 2PB (tel 0116 271 2512); Glenfield General Hospital, University Hospitals of Leicester NHS Trust (tel 0116 287 1471)

EVERTON, Clive Harold; s of Harold Brimley Everton (d 1996), and Alma, *née* Pugh (d 1980); *b* 7 September 1937; *Educ* Kings's Sch Worcester, UCW Cardiff (BA); *m* Valerie, *née* Teasdale; 4 da (Jane b 7 Aug 1963, Julie b 2 Sept 1965, Kate b 22 Dec 1966, Lucy b 7 Oct 1969), 1 s (Daniel b 10 April 1974); *Career* journalist, author and broadcaster; freelance broadcaster and sports writer for various pubns 1962–, specialist in snooker and billiards 1973–; ed: Billiards and Snooker magazine 1966–70, Snooker Scene 1971–; billiards and snooker corr The Guardian 1977–; snooker commentator BBC TV 1978–; billiards player; Br under 16 champion 1952, Br under 19 champion 1955, Welsh amateur champion 5 times, semi-finalist World Amateur Billiards Championship 1975 and 1977, ranked 10 in world professional ratings 1991; 6 Welsh amateur snooker caps; *Publications* Embassy Book of World Snooker (1993); author of various snooker compendiums and instructional books, co-author various biographies; *Recreations* books, films, theatre; *Style*— Clive Everton, Esq; ✉ Snooker Scene, Hayley Green Court, 130 Hagley Road, Halesowen, West Midlands B63 1DY (tel 0121 585 9188, fax 0121 585 7117, e-mail clive.everton@talk21.com)

EVERTON, Timothy Charles (Tim); s of Charles John Everton (d 1995), and Patricia Anne, *née* Sharpe; *b* 28 March 1951, Walsall; *Educ* Queen Mary's GS Walsall, Keble Coll Oxford (MA), Univ of Keele (MSc); *m* 24 July 1974, Valerie, *née* Bates; 3 da (Kate Elizabeth b 15 May 1980, Jenny Louise b 25 Jan 1982, Laura Jane b 17 June 1984); *Career* secdy sch mathematics teacher Walsall and Shrewsbury 1974–81, lectr in mathematics educn New Univ of Ulster 1981–83, lectr then sr lectr in educn Univ of Leicester 1983–92; Homerton Coll Cambridge: dep princ 1992–2001, sr tutor 1995–2001, vice-princ 2001–06; Univ of Cambridge: dean of educnl studies 2001–06, head Faculty of Educn 2002–06; treas: Br Curriculum Fndn 1991–97, Univs Cncl for the Educn of Teachers 1999–2005; *Publications* IT-INSET: Partnership in training (1989), Effective Learning: Into a new ERA (1990), 16–19 Mathematics: Problem solving (1991), 16–19: Changes in education and training (1992), 16–19 Mathematics: Handbook for teachers (1993), Mathematics for A and AS Level: Pure Mathematics (1997); *Recreations* watching sport, reading, walking, listening to jazz; *Style*— Tim Everton, Esq; ✉ 1 Seafield House, Whitby Road, Robin Hood's Bay, North Yorkshire YO22 4PB (tel 01947 880615, e-mail tce20@cam.ac.uk)

EVERY, Sir Henry John Michael; 13 Bt (E 1641), of Egginton, Derbyshire; o s of Sir John Simon Every, 12 Bt (d 1988), and his 2 w Janet Marion, *née* Page; *b* 6 April 1947; *Educ* Malvern Coll; *m* 1974, Susan Mary, eldest da of Kenneth Beaton, JP, of Eastshotte, Cambs; 3 s (Edward James Henry b 1975, Jonathan Charles Hugo b 1977, Nicholas John Simon b 1981); *Heir* s, Edward Every; *Career* ptnr Deloitte & Touche CAs Birmingham until 2001, dir Angelbourne Group plc 2001–03; pres Birmingham and W Midlands Dist Soc of CAs 1995–96 (chm Dist Trg Bd 1989–92), chm Burton Hosps NHS Tst 2003–04; memb Ctee The Birmingham Lunar Soc 1991–2003, tstee Nat Meml Arboretum 1996–2003 (conslt 2003–), patron Derby Heritage Devpt Tst 1998–, tstee Repton Fndn 2001–04, govr Repton Sch 2003–, chm Derby Cathedral Cncl 2003–; parish cncllr 1987–; memb Worshipful Co of Chartered Accountants 1998–; FCA 1970, FRSA; *Recreations* family, travel, gardening, theatre, The National Trust, supporting Nottingham Forest FC; *Style*— Sir Henry Every, Bt; ✉ Cothay, 26 Fishpond Lane, Egginton, Derby DE65 6HJ

EVES, David Charles Thomas; CB (1993); s of Harold Thomas Eves (d 1967), and Violet, *née* Edwards (d 1972); *b* 10 January 1942; *Educ* King's Sch Rochester, Univ of Durham (BA); *m* 1 Aug 1964, Valerie Ann, da of George Alexander Carter, of Pinner, Middx; 1 da (Catherine Alice b 1969); *Career* HM chief inspr of factories 1985–88, dep DG Health and Safety Exec 1989–2002; fell and hon vice-pres Inst of Occupational Safety and Health; vice-pres and sec gen Int Assoc of Labour Inspection (IALI) 1993–99, tech advsr Exec Ctee of IALI 1999–2005, hon vice-pres Nat Health and Safety Gps Cncl; assoc dir Sancroft International Ltd 2002–; *Recreations* sailing, fishing, painting, gardening, reading, music; *Clubs* Athenaeum; *Style*— David Eves, Esq, CB

EWAN, Dr Pamela Wilson; CBE (2007); da of Norman Wilson Ewan (d 1997), of Cambridge, and Frances Patterson, *née* Sellars (d 1984); *b* 23 September 1945; *Educ* Forfar Acad, Royal Free Hosp Sch of Med (MA, MB BS, DObstRCOG); *m* 15 Sept 1979, Prof Sir (David) Keith Peters, s of Lionel Herbert Peters; 2 s (James b 1980, William b 1989), 1 da (Hannah b 1982); *Career* sr lectr in clinical immunology and dir Allergy Clinic St Mary's Hosp 1980–88; Addenbrooke's Hosp 1988–: MRC clinical scientist and hon conslt in clinical immunology and allergy Univ of Cambridge Clinical Sch 1988–97, conslt in allergy and clinical immunology 1997–, dir Allergy Dept; dir of med studies Clare Hall Cambridge 1988–, assoc lectr Univ of Cambridge 1988–; pres Br Soc for Allergy and Clinical Immunology 1999–, hon sec RCP Ctee in Allergy and Clinical Immunology; memb Ctee Euro Acad of Allergy and Clinical Immunology; author of various chapters and papers in med books and scientific jls; memb: Assoc of Physicians, BSACI, BSI, MRS; FRCP, FRCPath; *Style*— Dr Pamela Ewan, CBE; ✉ 7 Chaucer Road, Cambridge CB2 2EB; Addenbrooke's Hospital, Hills Road, Cambridge CB2 2QQ (tel 01223 217777, fax 01223 216953, e-mail pamela.ewan@addenbrookes.nhs.uk)

EWARD, Paul Anthony; s of Rev Harvey Kennedy Eward (d 1969), and Delphine Eugenie Louise, *née* Pain; *b* 22 December 1942; *Educ* Radley; *m* 6 Sept 1966, Dene Kathleen, da of Geoffrey Louis Bartrip (d 1991), of Ross-on-Wye; 2 da (Sarah b 1969, Lucy b 1971); *Career* admitted slr 1967; ptnr: Slades (Newent), Orme Dykes & Yates (Ledbury)

1970–2002 (conslt 2002–); chm Newent Business & Professional Assoc 1981–83, sec PCC Ross-on-Wye 1972–88, lay co chm Ross and Archenfield Deanery Synod 1988–96 (hon treas (1980–88); memb Hereford Diocesan Synod 1988–96; memb Hereford Diocesan: Bd of Fin 1990– (and its Exec Ctee 1995–), Revenue Ctee 1985–98, Vacancy in See Ctee 1985–97, Patronage Ctee 1988–95, Benefice Buildings Ctee 1998–2002; hon jt treas Hereford DBF 1999–2002; tstee: Holts Health Centre Fund 1996–, Bishop Mascall Centre 2007–; memb: Transport Users Consultative Ctee for W England 1990–94, Rail Users' Consultative Ctee for W England 1994–2000, Rail Passenger Ctee for W England 2000–02 (vice-chm 2001–02); chm: Other Train Operating Companies sub-ctee 1999–2000, Thames Trains Jt Sub-Ctee 2000–02; Ctee Gloucestershire & Wiltshire Law Soc 1990–96; *Clubs* Gloucester Model Railway, EM Gauge Soc; *Style*— Paul Eward, Esq; ✉ Oakleigh, Gloucester Road, Ross-on-Wye, Herefordshire HR9 5NA (tel 01989 563845); Slades, 5 Broad Street, Newent, Gloucestershire GL18 1AX (e-mail paul@slades.co.uk)

EWART, John Walter Douglas; CBE (1995), DL (Northants 1993); s of Maxwell Douglas Ewart; *b* 27 January 1924; *Educ* Beaumont Coll; *m* 1, 1946, (Joan) Valerie, *née* Hoghton (d 1996); 1 da (Lavinia Anne (Mrs C G Perry) b 1947); m 2, 1997, Susannah Albinia, da of (Alfred) Drewett Chaytor (d 1977), and wid of Hon Edward Lawies Jackson (d 1982); *Career* Lt Royal Horse Gds 1942–46; md Paterson Ewart Group Ltd 1958–70; Carclo Engineering Group plc: md 1973–82, chm 1982–96; memb: Northants CC 1970–97 (ldr 1991–93), Assoc of CCs 1973–93 (ldr 1992–93); High Sheriff Northants 1977–78; *Recreations* hunting, sailing; *Clubs* Cavalry and Guards', Royal Yacht Sqdn; *Style*— John Ewart, Esq, CBE, DL; ✉ Astrop Park, Banbury, Oxfordshire OX17 3QN (tel 01295 811210, fax 01295 812034)

EWART, Sir (William) Michael; 7 Bt (UK 1887), of Glenmachan, Strandtown, Co Down, and of Glenbank, Belfast, Co Antrim; s of Sir (William) Ivan Cecil Ewart, 6 Bt, DSC (d 1995), and Pauline Chevallier, *née* Preston (d 1964); *b* 10 June 1953; *Educ* Radley; *Heir* none; *Style*— Sir Michael Ewart, Bt

EWART, Timothy John Pelham (Tim); s of John Terence Pelham Ewart (d 2003), of Woodbridge, Suffolk, and Nancy, *née* Girling (d 1990); *b* 6 February 1949; *Educ* Gresham's, Ipswich Civic Coll; *m* 3, 8 Aug 1991, Penny, da of Alan Marshall; 3 c (Jessica b 4 June 1993, Georgia b 24 Jan 1995, Holly b 4 Oct 1996); 2 c from previous m (Ben b 16 July 1977, Alice b 30 Nov 1980); *Career* newspapers 1967–74 (Bury Free Press, Leicester Mercury, Bermuda Sun), Radio 1974–77 (BBC World Service, Radio Orwell); reporter/presenter: BBC TV North (Leeds) 1977–80, Thames TV News 1980–81; ITN 1981–92: Warsaw correspondent 1983–85, Washington correspondent 1986–90, Moscow correspondent 1990–92; chief correspondent GMTV 1992 (prior to start of franchise), rejoined ITN as weekend news presenter and reporter News at Ten Focus on Britain 1992, main presenter BBC Newsroom South East Sept 1993–96; ITN: rejoined as sr reporter 1996, Africa correspondent 1998–2003, sports ed 2003–05, sr news corr 2005–; *Recreations* golf; *Clubs* Woodbridge Golf, Highgate Golf; *Style*— Tim Ewart, Esq; ✉ Independent Television News Ltd, 200 Gray's Inn Road, London WC1X 8XZ (tel 020 7833 3000)

EWER, Graham Anderson; CB (1999), CBE (1991, MBE 1983); s of Robert Christopher Ewer (d 1979), and Maud Ellie Percival, *née* Huxley (d 1992); *b* 22 September 1944; *Educ* Truro Cathedral Sch, RMAS; *m* 1969, Mary Caroline, *née* Grant; 2 da; *Career* Army: joined 1965, regtl appointments as jr offr in UK, BAOR and Middle East, Army Staff Coll 1976, staff and regtl appointments as Maj 1977–83, instr Army Staff Coll (Lt-Col) 1984–85, CO 8 Regt RCT 1985–87, Col DCOS 1 (UK) Armd Div 1988–91, Cmdt Sch of Transportation 1991–92, Col Logistic Support Secretariat 1992–93, Brig Cdr Combat Service Support Gp 1993–94, Dir Logistic Planning (Army) 1995–96, Maj-Gen and ACDS (Logistics) MOD 1996–99, ret; Col Cmdt Royal Logistics Corps 1999; chief exec Inst of Logistics and Tport 1999–2004, pres European Logistics Assoc 2004–06; FCILT, FRSA; *Publications* Blackadder's War (contrib, 1993); *Recreations* sailing (yachtsmaster offshore), military history, motoring, the theatre, cooking; *Clubs* Army and Navy; *Style*— Graham A Ewer, CB, CBE; ✉ c/o HSBC plc, 17 Boscawen Street, Truro, Cornwall TR1 2QZ

EWING, Fergus; MSP; s of Stewart Martin Ewing, and Dr Winifred Ewing, *qv*; bro of Annabelle Ewing (former MP for Perth); *b* 23 September 1957, Glasgow; *Educ* Loretto Sch Edinburgh, Univ of Glasgow (LLB); *m* Margaret Ewing (d 2006, former MSP for Moray); *Career* apprentice slr 1979–81, slr Leslie Wolfson & Co 1981–1985, ptnr Ewing & Co 1985–1999; MSP (SNP) Inverness E Nairn and Lochaber 1999–, pty spokesperson on telecommunications, transport and tourism, memb Local Govt and Transport Ctee; memb Law Soc of Scotland; *Recreations* running, jazz, playing piano; *Style*— Fergus Ewing, Esq, MSP; ✉ Highland Railhouse, Station Square, Inverness IV1 1LE (tel 01463 713004, fax 01463 710194); The Scottish Parliament, Edinburgh EH99 1SP (tel 0131 348 5731, fax 0131 348 5716, e-mail fergus.ewing.msp@scottish.parliament.uk)

EWING, Kenneth Hugh Robert; s of Hugh Wands Ewing (d 1945), of Northwood, Middx, and Agnes Jack, *née* McCance (d 1968); *b* 5 January 1927; *Educ* Merchant Taylors Sch, St John's Coll Oxford (MA); *Career* Nat Serv Flying Offr RAF 1948–50; writer and broadcaster BBC Euro Serv 1950–52; gen mangr Connaught Theatre Worthing 1952–59, md Fraser and Dunlop Scripts Ltd 1959–, pres Peters Fraser & Dunlop Group (now PFD) 1993– (jt chm 1988–93); currently dir Oliver Moon Ltd; memb Personal Managers' Assoc; *Recreations* flying (PPL), theatre, dog-walking; *Clubs* Garrick; *Style*— Kenneth Ewing, Esq; ✉ 2 Crescent Grove, London SW4; 44 Sussex Square, Brighton, East Sussex; c/o PFD, Drury House, 34–43 Russell Street, London WC2B 5HA (tel 020 7344 1000, fax 020 7836 9539)

EWING, Maria Louise; *b* 27 March 1950; *Career* soprano; Met Opera NY debut 1976 as Cherubino in The Marriage of Figaro 1976, European debut at La Scala Milan as Melisande in Pelleas et Melisande 1979, Covent Garden debut in title role in Salome 1988; worked with numerous conductors incl: James Levine, Bernard Haitink, Michael Tilson Thomas, Claudio Abbado, Semyon Bychkov, Pierre Boulez, Vladimir Askenazy, Richard Rodney Bennett, James Levine, Simon Rattle, Sir John Pritchard, Andrew Davis; given concert appearances and recitals with numerous orchs incl: City of Birmingham Symphony, Berlin Philharmonic, Bayerischer Rundfunk, Concertgebouw Orch, NY Philharmonic, Philharmonia Orch, Vienna Philharmonic, LSO, London Sinfonietta, BBC Symphony, Chicago Symphony, LA Philharmonic, Philadelphia Orch, Chamber Orch of Europe; appeared at numerous international venues incl: Lyric Opera Chicago, Washington Opera, Boston Opera, Houston Grand Opera, Barbican Hall, La Scala Milan, Le Châtalet Paris, Konzerthaus Vienna; *Roles* incl: Dorabella in Cosi fan Tutte, Susanna and Cherubino in the Marriage of Figaro, title roles in La Perichole and La Cenerentola, the Composer in Ariadne auf Naxos (Met Opera NY) 1985, title role in L'Incoronazione di Poppea (Glyndebourne) 1986, title role in Carmen (Met Opera 1986, Glyndebourne 1985, 1986 and 1987, Covent Garden 1988 and 1991, Earls Court 1988–89, Tokyo and Aust 1990, Oslo 1990), title role in Salome (LA Opera 1986, Covent Garden 1988 and 1992, Lyric Opera Chicago 1988–89, Washington Opera 1990, San Francisco Opera 1993), title role in The Merry Widow (Lyric Opera Chicago) 1986, Blanche in The Dialogues of the Carmelites (Met Opera) 1987, title role in Tosca (LA Opera 1989 and 1992, Covent Garden 1991, Seville with Placido Domingo 1991), Melisande in Pelleas et Melisande (Vienna State Opera 1991), title role in Madame Butterfly (LA Opera 1991), Dido in The Trojans (Met Opera) 1993; *Recordings* incl: Shéhérezade (with the CBSO and Simon Rattle) 1990, jazz album with the Royal Philharmonic Orch and Richard Rodney Bennett 1990, Pelleas et Melisande (with the Vienna Philharmonic Orch and Claudio Abbado) 1991, Lady Macbeth of Mtzensk (with the Bastille Opera) 1992; *Style*— Ms Maria Ewing; ✉ c/o Herbert Breslin, 119 West 57th Street, Room 1505, New York, NY 10019, USA

EWING, Dr Winifred Margaret; da of George Woodburn, and Christina Bell, *née* Anderson; *b* 10 July 1929; *Educ* Queen's Park Sr Secdy Sch, Univ of Glasgow (MA, LLB); *m* 1956, Stewart Martin Ewing; 2 s, 1 da; *Career* MP (SNP): Hamilton 1967–70, Moray and Nairn Feb 1974–79; MEP (SNP) Highlands and Islands 1979–99; MSP (SNP) Highlands and Islands 1999–2003; mother of Scottish Parliament, mother of the European Parliament; vice-pres Euro Radical Alliance 1994; pres SNP 1987–; past pres Glasgow Bar Assoc; comptroller Scottish Privileges of Veere; Freeman of Avignon 1988; Hon DUniv Open Univ, Hon LLD Univ of Glasgow 1995; *Style*— Dr Winifred Ewing; ✉ Goodwill, Miltonduff, Elgin, Moray IV30 3TL

EWINS, Prof David John; s of late Wilfred James Ewins, of Hemyock, Devon, and Patricia, *née* Goacher; *b* 25 March 1942; *Educ* Kingswood GS Bristol, Imperial Coll London (BSc, DSc), Trinity Coll Cambridge (PhD); *m* 1964 (m dis 1997), Brenda Rene, *née* Chalk; 3 da (Sally Ann b 1966, Sarah b 1968, Caroline Helene b 1971); *Career* research asst for Rolls-Royce Ltd at Univ of Cambridge 1966–67; Imperial Coll London: lectr then reader in mechanical engrg 1967–83, prof of vibration engrg 1983–, fndr Modal Testing Unit 1981, dir Centre of Vibration Engrg 1990–, pro-rector (int rels) 2001–05; Temasek prof and dir Centre for Mechanics of Microsystems Nanyang Technological Univ Singapore 1999–2001; sr lectr Chulalokorn Univ Bangkok 1968–69, maitre de conf INSA Lyon 1974–75; visiting prof: Virginia Poly and State Univ 1981, ETH Zurich 1986, Institut Nationale Polytechnique de Grenoble 1990, Nanyang Tech Univ Singapore 1994, Univ of Rome 1998; Dynamic Testing Agency: fndr 1990, chm 1990–94, pres 1995–; ptnr ICATS; conslt to: Rolls-Royce 1969–, MOD 1977–, Boeing, Ford, NASA, Intevep, Bosch, BMW, Mercedes, GM; MSEE 1970, MASME 1983, FIMechE 1982, FREng 1995, FCGI 2002, FRS 2006; *Books* Modal Testing: Theory and Practice (1984, 9 edn 1996), Modal Testing: Theory, Practice and Application (2000), Structural Dynamics @ 2000 (ed with D J Inman, 2000); *Recreations* music, hill walking, travel, good food, French; *Style*— Prof David Ewins, FRS, FREng; ✉ Imperial College of Science, Technology and Medicine, Exhibition Road, London SW7 2AZ

EWINS, Peter David; CB (2001); *b* 20 March 1943; *Educ* Imperial Coll London (BSc), Cranfield Inst of Technol (MSc); *m* Barbara; 2 s (Mark, James), 1 da (Sarah); *Career* RAE MOD (PE) Farnborough: joined 1966, various research posts rising to princ scientific offr and section head Advanced Composite Materials 1975–80, responsible for extramural prog in structural R&D 1977–80; MOD (PE) Whitehall 1980–82, sr princ scientific offr and superintendent Helicopters Div RAF Farnborough 1982–84, asst sec and head Personnel Mgmnt Div Cabinet Office 1984–87, dir Nuclear Projects MOD 1987–88, dir Admiralty Research Establishment Portsdown 1988–91; Defence Research Agency: md Maritime Div Portsdown April - Nov 1991, md Command and Maritime Systems Gp Farnborough 1991–93, md Operations 1993–94; chief scientist MOD Whitehall 1994–97, chief exec Meteorological Office 1997–2004; FRAeS, FREng 1996; *Style*— Peter Ewins, Esq, CB, FREng

EXELL, Richard Daniel; OBE (1999); s of Donald William Exell (d 1983), and Olwen Madeleine, *née* Anderson (d 1992); *b* 21 July 1956, Liverpool; *Educ* Friars Sch Bangor, Univ of Bristol (BA); *m* 16 Oct 1991, Penny Zea, *née* Bromfield; 1 da (Madeleine Zena Florence Thomasina Frederica b 22 May 1993); *Career* policy offr TUC 1990–; memb: Social Security Advsy Ctee 1997–, Disability Rights Cmmn 2000–; *Recreations* politics, the arts; *Style*— Richard Exell, Esq, OBE; ✉ Trades Union Congress, Great Russell Street, London WC1B 3LS (tel 020 7467 1319, fax 020 7467 1317, e-mail rexell@tuc.org.uk)

EXETER, Bishop of 2000–; Rt Rev Michael Laurence Langrish; s of Douglas Frank Langrish, of Southampton, and Brenda Florence, *née* Passingham; *b* 1 July 1946; *Educ* Univ of Birmingham (BSocSc, Chllr's prize, PGCE), Fitzwilliam Coll Cambridge (MA), Ridley Hall Cambridge; *m* 10 Aug 1968, Esther Vivien, da of Rev John William Rudd; 1 s (Richard Michael John b 8 Sept 1970), 2 da ((Rachel) Emma b 31 Oct 1973, Kathryn Jane b 31 Oct 1979); *Career* lectr in educn Mid-West State Coll of Educn Nigeria 1969–71, asst curate Holy Trinity Stratford-upon-Avon 1973–76, chaplain Rugby Sch 1976–81, diocesan dir of ordinands and lay min advsr, CME offr and vicar of Offchurch 1981–87, examining chaplain to the Bishop of Coventry 1982–87, team rector Rugby Team Miny 1987–93, hon canon Coventry Cathedral 1990–93; memb Gen Synod C of E 1985–93 and 1998–, chair C of E Rural Affairs Ctee 2001–; chair Melanesian Mission (UK) 2003–, tstee Christian Aid 2003–; chair Devon Strategic Partnership 2001–, memb Cncl Univ of Exeter 2001–; Hon DD: Univ of Birmingham, Univ of Exeter; *Recreations* walking, local history, reading, theatre, music, cricket; *Clubs* Athenaeum, Royal Commonwealth Soc; *Style*— The Rt Rev the Bishop of Exeter; ✉ The Palace, Exeter, Devon EX1 1HY

EXETER, 8 Marquess of (UK 1801; a previous Marquessate of Exeter was enjoyed by Henry Courtenay, Earl of Devon and gs of Edward IV, 1525–39); William Michael Anthony Cecil; also Baron Burghley (E 1571) and Earl of Exeter (E 1605; the de Reviers Earls of Devon, who enjoyed that title 1141–1262, were sometimes called Earls of Exeter), Hereditary Grand Almoner, and Lord Paramount of the Soke of Peterborough; s of 7 Marquess of Exeter (d 1988, 14 in descent from the Lord Burghley who was Elizabeth's I chief minister), and his 1 w Edith Lilian (d 1954), o da of Aurel Csanady de Telegd, of Budapest, Hungary; *b* 1 September 1935; *Educ* Eton; *m* 1, 1967 (m dis 1993), Nancy Rose, da of Lloyd Arthur Meeker; 1 s (Anthony John, Lord Burghley b 1970), 1 da (Lady Angela Kathleen b 1975); m 2, 1999, Barbara Anne, da of Eugene Magat; *Heir* s, Lord Burghley; *Career* businessman and lecturer; *Books* The Rising Tide of Change (1986), Living at the Heart of Creation (1990); *Style*— The Most Hon the Marquess of Exeter

EXMOUTH, 10 Viscount (UK 1816); Sir Paul Edward Pellew; 10 Bt (GB 1796); also Baron Exmouth (UK 1814), Marques de Olias (Spain 1625); patron of one living; s of 9 Viscount (d 1970) and Maria Luisa, Marquesa de Olias (d 1994), da of late Luis de Urquijo, Marques de Amurrio, of Madrid; *b* 8 October 1940; *Educ* Downside; *m* 1, 10 Dec 1964 (m dis 1974), Maria Krystina Garay-Marques; 1 da (Hon Patricia Sofia b 1966); m 2, 1975 (m dis 2000), Rosemary Frances, formerly w of Earl of Burford (now 14 Duke of St Albans, *qv*); 2 s (Hon Edward, Hon Alexander (twins) b 30 Oct 1978); m 3, 20 March 2002, Sarah Cameron Edgar, wid of Samuel Anthony Edgar; *Heir* s, Hon Edward Pellew; *Career* former Cross Bench Peer in House of Lords; *Style*— The Rt Hon Viscount Exmouth; ✉ e-mail paulexmouth@aol.com

EYNON, (Richard) Mark; s of late Capt Melville Victor Eynon, of Caerleon, Gwent, and Phyllis Bertha, *née* Aitken-Smith, MBE; *b* 9 November 1953; *Educ* Monmouth, Univ of Manchester (BSc), Manchester Business Sch (MBA); *m* 18 Oct 1980, Susan Elspeth, da of Dr J T D Allen, of Liverpool; *Career* vice pres Bank of America 1982–86; dir S G Warburg Securities 1986–96, chm S G Warburg Futures and Options 1992–96, md Swiss Bank Corporation (now UBS AG following merger) 1995; dir: LIFFE 1984–98, London Clearing House 1997; *Recreations* rugby, cricket; *Style*— Mark Eynon, Esq

EYRE, Prof Brian Leonard; CBE (1993); s of Leonard George Eyre (d 1988), and Mabel, *née* Rumsey (d 1984); *b* 29 November 1933; *Educ* Greenford GS, Univ of Surrey (BSc, DSc); *m* 5 June 1965, Elizabeth Caroline, da of Arthur Rackham (d 1954); 2 s (Peter John b 5 March 1966, Stephen Andrew b 22 Oct 1967); *Career* research offr CEGB 1959–62, prof of materials sci Univ of Liverpool 1979–84; UKAEA: various posts 1962–79, dir of fuel and engrg technol 1984–87, memb Bd 1987–96, dep chm 1989–96, chief exec 1990–94; dep chm AEA Technology plc 1996–97; visiting prof: Univ of Liverpool 1984–, UCL 1995–, Univ of Oxford 1997–2002; memb Cncl: Univ of Salford 1986–97, Fndn for Sci and Technol 1994–2001, Particle Physics and Astronomy Research Cncl 1996–2000, Cncl of the Central Research Labs 1998–2001 (chm 2000–2001), Royal Acad of Engrg 1996–99, Inst of Materials 1996–2000; industrial fell Wolfson Coll Oxford 1996–2001; author of over 150 scientific papers, former chm Editorial Bd Jl of Nuclear Materials; FREng 1992, FRS 2001, FIM, CEng, FInstP, CPhys; *Recreations* walking, sailing, reading; *Clubs* Athenaeum; *Style—* Prof Brian Eyre, CBE, FREng, FRS; ✉ Department of Materials, University of Oxford, Parks Road, Oxford OX1 3PH (tel 01865 273708, fax 01865 273764, e-mail brian.eyre@materials.ox.ac.uk)

EYRE, Maj John Vickers; JP (Glos 1987), DL (Glos 2000); s of Nevill Cathcart Eyre (d 1971), of Bristol, and Maud Evelyn (d 1998), *née* Truscott; *b* 30 April 1936; *Educ* Winchester; *m* 19 Oct 1974, Sarah Margaret Aline, da of Maj Geoffrey Beresford (Tim) Heywood MBE, DL, of Edgeworth, Glos; 1 da (Georgina (Mrs Crispin Daly) b 1 Jan 1977), 1 s (Charles b 8 Jan 1980); *Career* RHA 1959, 14/20 King's Hussars 1962, Staff Coll 1969, ret 1973; Royal Gloucestershire Hussars TA 1980–83 (patron 1997–); asst to chm Savoy Hotel plc 1973–75, administrator Brian Colquhoun and Ptnrs Consltg Engrs 1975–79, prop Haresfield Garden Centre 1981–86, md George Truscott Ltd 1986–2003; dist cmmr Berkeley Hunt Pony Club 1986–95, chm Berkeley Hunt 2005–; pres Community Action former County of Avon 2001–05, chm CPRE Berkeley Vale 2001–; High Sheriff Glos 2000, Vice-Lord Lt Glos 2007; *Recreations* country pursuits; *Clubs* Boodle's, Army and Navy; *Style—* Maj John Eyre, DL; ✉ Boyts Farm, Tytherington, Wotton-under-Edge, Gloucestershire GL12 8UG (tel 01454 412220, e-mail jve@talktalk.net)

EYRE, Sir Reginald Edwin; kt (1984); s of late Edwin Eyre, of Birmingham, and Mary, *née* Moseley; *b* 28 May 1924; *Educ* King Edward's Camp Hill Sch Birmingham, Emmanuel Coll Cambridge (MA); *m* 1978, Anne Clements; 1 da (Hermione Katharine b 10 Nov 1979); *Career* Midshipman and Sub Lieut RNVR 1942–45; slr 1950; sr ptnr Eyre & Co 1951–91 (conslt 1992–2002); hon conslt Poor Man's Lawyer 1948–58; contested (Cons) Birmingham Northfield 1959; chm: W Midlands Area Cons Political Centre 1960–63, Nat Advsy Ctee 1964–66; MP (Cons) Birmingham Hall Green 1965–87; oppn whip 1966–70, Lord Cmmr Treasury 1970, comptroller of HM Household 1970–72, Parly undersec of state for DOE (Housing and Planning) 1972–74, fndr chm Cons Parly Urban Affairs Ctee 1974–79, vice-chm Cons Pty responsible for Urban Areas 1975–79; Parly under sec of state for: Trade (Corporate and Consumer Affairs) 1979–82, Tport (Public Tport) 1982–84; parly rep independence ceremonies Leeward and Windward Islands 1967; ldr: Parly Delgn to Swaziland 1971, Cons Pty Delgn to People's Repub of China 1977, Parly Gp on CPA visit to Australia 1986; memb: Ctee of Selection, Environment Select Ctee; chm: Birmingham Heartlands Devpt Corp (formerly Birmingham Heartlands Ltd (East Birmingham Urban Devpt Agency)) 1987–98, Birmingham Cable Corp Ltd 1988–99; dep chm Cmmn for the New Towns 1988–92; pres Birmingham Heartlands Business Forum 2000–05; Freeman City of Birmingham 1991; Hon Dr Univ of Central England Birmingham 1997; *Publications* Hope for our Towns and Cities (1977); *Style—* Sir Reginald Eyre; ✉ c/o Eyre & Co, 1041 Stratford Road, Hall Green, Birmingham B28 8AS

EYRE, Richard Anthony; *b* 3 May 1954; *Educ* KCS Wimbledon, Lincoln Coll Oxford (MA), Harvard Business Sch (AMP); *Career* airtime buyer Benton & Bowles 1975–78, sales gp head Scottish Television 1978–79, head of media planning Benton & Bowles 1980–84 (media planner 1979–80), media dir Aspect 1984–86, media dir Bartle Bogle Hegarty 1986–91 (Media Week Agency of the Year 1990 and 1991), chief exec Capital Radio plc 1991–97, chief exec ITV 1997–99, chm and chief exec Pearson Television Ltd 2000, dir of strategy and content RTL (following merger with Pearson TV) 2000–01, non-exec chm RDF Media Holdings 2001–, chm Digital Bridges 2004–; chm Interactive Advertising Bureau 2003–; non-exec dir: Digital Bridges 2002–, Eden Project 2003–, Guardian Media Gp 2004–; advsr 19 Management Ltd; *Style—* Richard Eyre, Esq

EYRE, Sir Richard Charles Hastings; kt (1997), CBE (1992); s of Cdr Richard Galfridus Hastings Giles Eyre, RN (d 1990), and Minna Mary Jessica (d 1992), o child of Vice Adm Sir Charles William Rawson Royds, KBE, CMG, antarctic explorer Scott's 1st Lt; *b* 28 March 1943; *Educ* Sherborne, Univ of Cambridge (BA); *m* 1973, Sue Elizabeth Birtwistle, *qv*; 1 da (Lucy b 1974); *Career* theatre, television and film director; assoc dir Lyceum Theatre Edinburgh 1968–71, dir Nottingham Playhouse 1973–78, prodr Play For Today BBC TV 1978–80, dir Royal Nat Theatre 1988–97 (assoc dir 1980–86); Cameron Mackintosh visiting prof of contemporary theatre Univ of Oxford and fell St Catherine's Coll 1997; Hon DLitt: Nottingham Trent Univ 1992, South Bank Univ 1994, Univ of Liverpool 2003; Hon Dr Oxford Brookes Univ, Hon Degree Univ of Surrey 1998; hon fell: Goldsmiths Coll London 1993, KCL 1995; hon memb Guildhall 1996; Officier de l'Ordre des Arts et des Lettres (France) 1998; *Theatre* incl: Comedians 1974, Hamlet 1989, Guys and Dolls 1982 (revived 1996–97), Futurists 1986, The Changling 1988, Bartholomew Fair 1988, Voysey Inheritance 1989, Richard III 1990, Napoli Milionaria 1991, White Cameleon 1991, Night of the Iguana 1992, David Hare Trilogy 1993, Macbeth 1993, Sweet Bird of Youth 1994, Skylight (also Broadway, Wyndham's, Vaudeville 1996) 1995, La Grande Magia 1995, The Prince's Play 1996, John Gabriel Borkman 1996, Amy's View 1997 (also Broadway, Aldwych), King Lear 1997, The Invention of Love 1997, The Judas Kiss 1998, The Novice 2000, The Crucible 2002, Vincent in Brixton 2002, Mary Poppins 2005, Hedda Gabler 2006, The Reporter 2007; *Opera* incl La Traviata (Royal Opera House) 1994, Le Nozze di Figaro (Aix-en-Provence); *Television* films incl: Suddenly Last Summer 1992, The Imitation Game, Pasmore 1980, Country 1981, The Insurance Man 1986 (Tokyo Prize), Past Caring 1986, v 1988 (RTS Award), Tumbledown 1988 (Italia RAI Prize, BAFTA Award), Absence of War 1995, King Lear 1998; *Film* The Ploughman's Lunch 1983 (Evening Standard Award for Best Film), Laughterhouse 1984 (TV Prize Venice Film Festival), Iris 2001 (Humanitas Award), Stage Beauty 2003, Notes on a Scandal 2007; *Awards* incl: SWET Dir of the Year 1982, Evening Standard Best Dir 1982, STV Awards for Best Production 1969, 1970 and 1971, Sorrento Film Festival De Sica Award 1986, The Patricia Rothermere Award 1995, Olivier Award for Outstanding Achievement 1997, Critics' Circle Awards for Lifetime Achievement and Best Dir 1997, South Bank Show Award for Outstanding Achievement 1997, Dirs' Guild Award for Lifetime Achievement 1997, Evening Standard Awards for King Lear, The Invention of Love and Special Award for running the RNT 1997, Olivier Award for Best Dir 2006 (for Hedda Gabler); for King Lear: Olivier Award for Best Dir 1998, Peabody Award 1999, Eebo d'Oro Award 1998; *Books* Utopia and Other Places (autobiography, 1993), The Eyre Review: the future of lyric theatre in London (1998), Changing Stages: A Personal View of 20th Century Theatre (with Nicholas Wright, 2000), Iris (screenplay, 2002), National Service (2003); *Style—* Sir Richard Eyre, CBE; ✉ c/o Judy Daish Associates, 2 St Charles Place, London W10 6EG (tel 020 8964 8811, fax 020 8964 8966)

EYRE, Stephen John Arthur; s of Leslie James Eyre, of Solihull, and Joyce Mary, *née* Whitehouse; *b* 17 October 1957; *Educ* Solihull Sch, New Coll Oxford (MA, BCL); *m* 1 July 1989, Margaret Lynn, da of William John Goodman, of Coalville; *Career* called to the Bar Inner Temple 1981; lectr in law New Coll Oxford 1980–84, recorder 2005–; memb Bar Conduct Ctee 2006–, legal memb Mental Health Review Tbnl 2007–, dep chllr Southwell and Nottingham 2007–; memb Solihull MBC 1983–91 and 1992–96; Parly candidate (Cons): Birmingham (Hodge Hill) 1987, Strangford 1992, Stourbridge 2001, Birmingham (Hodge Hill) by-election 2004; *Recreations* gardening, reading, theatre; *Style—* Stephen Eyre, Esq; ✉ St Philips Chambers, 55 Temple Row, Birmingham B2 5LS (tel 0121 246 7000)

EYRE-TANNER, Peter Giles; *see:* Squire, Giles

EYSENCK, Prof Michael William; s of Hans Jürgen Eysenck (d 1997), of London, and Margaret Malcolm, *née* Davies (d 1986); *b* 8 February 1944; *Educ* Dulwich Coll, UCL (BA, Rosa Morison Prize for outstanding arts graduate); *m* 22 March 1975, (Mary) Christine, da of Waldemar Kabyn, of London; 2 da (Fleur Davina Ruth b 1979, Juliet Margaret Maria Alexandra b 1985), 1 s (William James Thomas b 1983); *Career* reader in psychology Birkbeck Coll London 1981–87 (lectr 1965–80), prof of psychology Royal Holloway and Bedford Coll London (now Royal Holloway Univ of London) 1987– (head of dept 1987–2005); pres Stress and Anxiety Research Soc 2006–, chm Cognitive Psychology Section Br Psychological Soc 1982–87, memb Advsy Bd Euro Soc for Cognitive Psychology; MBPsS 1965; *Books* Human Memory - Theory, Research and Individual Differences (1977), Mindwatching (with H J Eysenck, 1981), Attention and Arousal - Cognition and Performance (1982), A Handbook of Cognitive Psychology (1984), Personality and Individual Differences (with H J Eysenck, 1985), Memory - A Cognitive Approach (with G Cohen and M E Levoi, 1986), Student Learning - Research in Education and Cognitive Psychology (with J T E Richardson and D W Piper, 1987), Mindwatching - Why We Behave the Way We Do (with H J Eysenck, 1989), Happiness - Facts and Myths (1990), Cognitive Psychology - An International Review (1990), Cognitive Psychology - A Student's Handbook (with M T Keane, 1990, 5 edn 2005), Blackwell's Dictionary of Cognitive Psychology (1990), Anxiety - The Cognitive Perspective (1992), Principles of Cognitive Psychology (1994), Perspectives on Psychology (1994), Individual Differences - Normal and Abnormal (1994), Simply Psychology (1996, 2 edn 2001), Anxiety and Cognition: A Unified Theory (1997), Psychology: An Integrated Approach (1998), Psychology: A Student's Handbook (2000), Psychology for AS Level (with C.Flanagan, 2000), Psychology for A2 Level (with C.Flanagan, 2001), Key Topics in A2 Psychology (2003), Psychology: An International Perspective (2004), Fundamentals of Cognition (2007); *Recreations* tennis, travel, walking, golf, boules; *Style—* Prof Michael Eysenck; ✉ Royal Holloway, University of London, Department of Psychology, Egham Hill, Egham, Surrey TW20 0EX (tel 01784 443530, fax 01784 434347, e-mail m.eysenck@rhul.ac.uk)

EYTON, Anthony John Plowden; s of Capt John Seymour Eyton (d 1979), and Phyllis Annie, *née* Tyser (d 1929); *b* 17 May 1923; *Educ* Canford Sch, Univ of Reading, Camberwell Sch of Art (NDD); *m* 20 Aug 1960 (m dis 1986), (Frances) Mary Capell (decd); 3 da (Jane Elizabeth Phyllis, Clare Alice, Sarah Mary); *Career* served Army 1942–47; artist; Abbey Maj scholarship 1951–53, John Moores prizewinner Liverpool 1972, Worshipful Co of Grocers fellowship 1973, first prize Second Br Int Drawing Biennale 1975, retrospective S London Art Gallery 1980, Charles Woolaston award Royal Acad 1981; exhibitions: Browse and Darby 1975, 1978, 1981, 1985, 1987, 1990, 1993, 1996, 2000 and 2005, Hong Kong Imperial War Museum 1983, Austin/Desmond Fine Art 1990, A T Kearney 1997, The Prince of Wales Inst of Architecture 1998, King's Road Gallery 2002, Woodlands Art Gallery 2003; subject of book Eyton's Eye: Anthony Eyton - A Life in Painting (by Jenny Pery, 2005); RA 1986 (ARA 1976), RWS 1987, Royal Cambrian Acad 1993, memb RWA, hon memb Pastel Soc, Hon ROI; *Recreations* gardening; *Clubs* Arts; *Style—* Anthony Eyton, Esq, RA

EZRA, Baron (Life Peer UK 1983), of Horsham in the County of West Sussex; Derek Ezra; kt (1974), MBE (1945); s of late David Ezra, and Lillie Ezra; *b* 23 February 1919; *Educ* Monmouth, Magdalene Coll Cambridge (MA); *m* 1950, Julia Elizabeth, da of Thomas Wilkins, of Portsmouth, Hants; *Career* Army Serv 1939–47; memb UK Delgn to Euro Coal and Steel Community 1952–56; Nat Coal Bd: joined 1947, regnl sales mangr 1958–60, DG Marketing 1960–65, memb Bd 1965–67, dep chm 1967–71, chm 1971–82; chm Br Iron & Steel Consumers' Cncl 1983–87; dir: Redland plc 1982–89, Solvay SA 1979–89; chm: Associated Heat Services plc 1966–99, Br Inst of Mgmnt 1976–78, Energy and Technical Services Group plc 1990–99, Micropower Ltd 2000–; industrial advsr to Morgan Grenfell 1982–87; pres: Coal Industry Soc 1981–86, Inst of Trading Standards Admin 1987–92; hon fell Magdalene Coll Cambridge; Liveryman Worshipful Co of Haberdashers, Worshipful Co of Fuellers; *Style—* The Rt Hon Lord Ezra, MBE; ✉ House of Lords, London SW1A 0PW (tel 020 7219 3180)

EZZAMEL, Prof Mahmoud Azmy; s of Mahmoud Mahmoud Ezzamel (d 1975), of Egypt, and Fatima, *née* El-Shirbini (d 1992); *b* 24 October 1942; *Educ* Univ of Alexandria (BCom, MCom), Univ of Southampton (PhD); *m* 31 March 1979, Ann, da of Herbert Edgar Jackman, of Coventry; 1 s (Adam b 29 March 1983), 2 da (Nadia b 29 Jan 1985, Samia b 6 July 1988); *Career* lectr and sr lectr Univ of Southampton 1975–88, visiting assoc prof Queen's Univ Kingston Ontario Canada 1986–87, Ernst & Young prof of accounting Univ Coll Wales Aberystwyth 1988–90, Price Waterhouse prof of accounting and fin UMIST 1990–96, prof of accounting and fin Univ of Manchester 1996–99, Cardiff professorial fell Univ of Cardiff 2000–; hon prof Univ Coll Wales Aberystwyth 1991–, visiting prof Massey Univ New Zealand March 1993, visiting Scholar Queen's Univ Canada July-Aug 1994, distinguished visiting prof Instituto de Empresa Madrid 2003–; ed Accounting and Business Research; *Books* Advanced Management Accounting: An Organisational Emphasis (1987), Perspectives on Financial Control (1992), Business Unit and Divisional Performance Measurement (1992, Italian edn 1996), Changing Managers and Managing Change (1996), Local Management of Schools Iniative: The Implementation of Formula Funding in Three English LEAs (1997), New Public Sector Reforms and Institutional Change: The Local Management of Schools Initiative (1999), The Challenge of Management Accounting Change (2003), The Future Direction of UK Management Accounting Practice (2003), Governance, Directors and Boards (2005); *Recreations* volleyball, tennis; *Style—* Prof Mahmoud Ezzamel; ✉ Cardiff Business School, Cardiff University, Aberconway Building, Colum Drive, Cardiff CF10 3EU (e-mail ezzamel@cardiff.ac.uk)

F

FABER, Sir Richard Stanley; KCVO (1980), CMG (1977); of Sir Geoffrey Cust Faber (d 1961), and Enid Eleanor (d 1995); *b* 6 December 1924; *Educ* Westminster, ChCh Oxford (MA); *Career* served RNVR 1943–46; entered HM Dip Serv 1950; served: Baghdad, Paris, Abidjan, Washington; cnsllr: The Hague 1969–73, Cairo 1973–75; asst under sec of state FCO 1975–77, ambass Algiers 1977–81, ret; Liveryman Worshipful Co of Goldsmiths; FRSL 1972; *Books* Beaconsfield and Bolingbroke (1961), The Vision and the Need: Late Victorian Imperialist Aims (1966), Proper Stations: Class in Victorian Fiction (1971), French and English (1975), The Brave Courtier (Sir William Temple) (1983), High Road to England (1985), Young England (1987), A Brother's Murder (1993), A Chain of Cities (2000); *Clubs* Travellers; *Style*— Sir Richard Faber, KCVO, CMG, FRSL

FABER, His Hon Judge Trevor Martyn; s of Harry Faber (d 1986), of Edgbaston, Birmingham, and Millicent, *née* Waxman (d 1988); *b* 9 October 1946; *Educ* Clifton, Merton Coll Oxford (MA, 3 Boxing blues and capt OUABC); *m* 16 Aug 1985, Katrina Sally, da of George James Clay, of Harborne, Birmingham; *Career* called to the Bar Gray's Inn 1970; in practice Midland Circuit 1970–2001, recorder of the Crown Court 1989–2001, circuit judge (Midland Circuit) 2001–; memb Tanworth-in-Arden Assoc for the Prosecution of Felons; *Recreations* theatre, literature, sport, music, cooking; *Clubs* Vincent's (Oxford); *Style*— His Hon Judge Trevor Faber; ✉ The Crown Court, Queen Elizabeth II Law Courts, Birmingham B4 7NA

FABIANI, Linda; MSP; da of Giovanni Fabiani (d 1998), and Claire Smith; *b* 14 December 1956; *Educ* Hyndland Sch Glasgow, Napier Coll Edinburgh, Univ of Glasgow (Dip Housing Studies); *Career* admin asst Yoker Housing Assoc Glasgow 1982–85, housing offr Clydebank Housing Assoc 1985–88, devpt mangr Bute Housing Assoc 1988–94, dir East Kilbride Housing Assoc 1994–99; MSP (SNP) Scotland Central 1999–, min for Europe, External Affrs and Culture; FCIH (MCIH 1988); *Recreations* reading, folk music, culture; *Style*— Linda Fabiani, MSP; ✉ The Scottish Parliament, Edinburgh EH99 1SP (tel 0131 348 5698/9, e-mail linda.fabiani.msp@scottish.parliament.uk); The Scottish Executive, Victoria Quay, Edinburgh EH6 6QQ (tel 0131 556 8400, e-mail scottish.ministers@scotland.gsi.gov.uk)

FABRICANT, Michael Louis David; MP; s of late Isaac Nathan Fabricant, and Helen, *née* Freed; *b* 12 June 1950; *Educ* state schs, Loughborough Univ (BA), Univ of Sussex (MSc), Univs of London, Oxford and Southern Calif (DPhil); *Career* former broadcaster BBC News and Current Affrs, co-fndr and dir int broadcast and communications gp until 1992, economist and advsr on broadcasting to Home Office and various foreign govts; MP (Cons): Staffs Mid 1992–97, Lichfield 1997– (Parly candidate (Cons) South Shields 1987); PPS to Michael Jack as Fin Sec to the Treasy 1996–97; memb Nat Heritage Select Ctee 1993–96, memb Euro Scrutiny Ctee B (Trade and Industry) 1993–97, memb Culture Media & Sport Select Ctee 1997–99, memb Home Affairs Select Ctee 1999–2001, chm Info Select Ctee 2001–03, memb Culture Media and Sport Select Ctee 2001–, memb Fin and Servs Select Ctee 2001–03, memb Liaison Select Ctee 2001–03, shadow min for DTI 2002–03, shadow min for economic affrs 2003–05, sr oppn whip 2005–; jt chm: Royal Marines All-Pty Gp, Cable & Satellite Gp; lawyer and chartered electronics engr; elected to Senate Engrg Cncl 1999–, dir Engrg and Technol Bd 2002–; memb Cncl IEE; CEng, FIEE 1994; *Recreations* reading, music, fell walking, skiing, listening to the Archers; *Clubs* Rottingdean; *Style*— Michael Fabricant, Esq, MP; ✉ House of Commons, London SW1A 0AA (tel 020 7219 5022, website www.michael.fabricant.mp.co.uk)

FAGAN, Mary; JP; da of Col and Mrs G H Vere-Laurie, JP, DL, of Carlton Hall, Notts; *b* 11 September 1939; *Educ* Southover Manor; *m* Capt Christopher Tarleton Feltrim Fagan, Grenadier Gds; 2 s (Capt Christopher Hugh Fagan (d 1987), Capt James Fagan); *Career* pres: Basingstoke Male Voice Choir, ESU, Hants Cncl of Community Service, Hants Co Scouts Cncl, Hants and Isle of Wight Youth Options, Hants Voluntary Housing Soc, Hants Appeal Ctee Prince's Tst and Prince's Youth Business Tst, Hants Ctee Territorial Auxiliary and Volunteer Reserve Assoc, Winchester Assoc of Nat Tst Membs, Southern Region Ctee Winged Fellowship; vice-pres: Southern Regnl Assoc for the Blind, Assoc for the Deaf, Enham Tst, Fortune Centre of Riding Therapy, Hants and Wight Tst for Maritime Archaeology, Mary Rose Tst; tstee: Edwina Mountbatten Tst, Hants Gardens Tst, Marwell Zoological Park, New Theatre Royal; chm: Ctee Hampshire Magistrates Court, Countess of Brecknock Hospice Tst, Portsmouth Cathedral Appeal Ctee; patron: Basingstoke Ladies Choir, Hants Branch Br Red Cross, Andover Branch Cruse, Hants Co Youth Band, Hants Music Tst, Oakhaven Hospice, Rowans Hospice, Treloar Tst; vice-patron Brendoncare Fndn; govr King Edward VI Sch, chllr Univ of Winchester 2006; HM Lord-Lt Hants 1994–; Hon Col: Hampshire & Isle of Wight ACF, 457 Battery RA; Hon Capt Royal Naval Reserve; Liveryman Worshipful Co of Saddlers; Hon DLitt King Alfred's Coll 1997, Hon LLD Univ of Portsmouth 2000; DStJ (pres Cncl for Hants 1994–); *Recreations* country activities; *Style*— Mrs Mary Fagan; ✉ Deane Hill House, Deane, Basingstoke, Hampshire RG25 3AX (tel 01256 780591, fax 01256 782627)

FAGAN, Neil John; s of Lt Cdr C H Fagan, of Bucks Horn Oak, Hants, and Majorie Sadie-Jane, *née* Campbell-Bannerman; *b* 5 June 1947; *Educ* Charterhouse, Univ of Southampton (LLB); *m* 21 June 1975, Catherine, da of R J Hewitt, of Hurtmore, Surrey; 3 da (Caroline Louise b 31 Oct 1977, Felicity Clare b 1 May 1980, Emily Catherine b 20 June 1983); *Career* Lovells (formerly Lovell White Durrant and Durrant Piesse, originally Durrant Cooper and Hambling): articled clerk 1969–71, ptnr 1975–; memb Worshipful Co of Slrs; memb: Law Soc, Int Bar Assoc; *Books* Contracts of Employment (1990); *Recreations* family, swimming, sailing, gardening; *Clubs* Royal Lymington Yacht, MCC, Travellers; *Style*— Neil Fagan, Esq; ✉ Little Orchard, Farm Lane, Crondall, Farnham, Surrey GU10 5QE; Lovells, 65 Holborn Viaduct, London EC1A 2DY (tel 020 7296 2000, e-mail neilfagan@lovells.com)

FAIRBAIRN, Sir (James) Brooke; 6 Bt (UK 1869), of Ardwick, Lancs; s of Sir William Albert Fairbairn, 5 Bt (d 1972), and Christine Renée Cotton, *née* Croft; *b* 10 December 1930; *Educ* Stowe; *m* 1, 5 Nov 1960, Mary Russell (d 1992), o da of late William Russell Scott; 2 s (Robert William b 1965, George Edward b 1969), 1 da (Fiona Mary (Mrs James Gordon) b 1967); m 2, 22 Feb 1997, Rosemary Anne Victoria, da of late Edwin Henderson, FRGS; 2 step da (Amelia Sarah (Mrs Andrew Armour), Sally Georgina (Dr Sally Parnell)); *Heir* s, Robert Fairbairn; *Career* proprietor of J Brooke Fairbairn & Co Newmarket (furnishing fabric converters); vice-pres: Hants, Isle of Wight and Channel Islands Assoc for the Deaf 1979–, Barnardos 1996–99 (memb Cncl 1968–96); govr The King's Sch Ely 1995–2001; hon steward Westminster Abbey 1990–; Liveryman Worshipful Co of Weavers 1980 (Upper Bailiff 1992–93); FRSA; *Style*— Sir Brooke Fairbairn, Bt; ✉ Barkway House, Bury Road, Newmarket, Suffolk CB8 7BT (tel 01638 662733); The Railway Station, Newmarket, Suffolk CB8 9WT (tel 01638 665766, fax 01638 665124)

FAIRBAIRN, Carolyn Julie; da of David Ritchie Fairbairn, and Hon Susan Fairbairn, *née* Hill; *b* 13 December 1960; *Educ* Wycombe HS for Girls, Bryanston (scholar), Gonville & Caius Coll Cambridge (hon sr scholarship, BA), Univ of Pennsylvania (Thouron scholar, MA), INSEAD Fontainebleau (MBA); *m* 29 June 1991, Peter Harrison Chittick, s of Robert Chittick; 2 da (Emily b 25 Nov 1994, Anna b 4 May 1996), 1 s (Thomas b 18 Jan 1999); *Career* economist World Bank Washington 1984–85, fin writer The Economist 1985–87, mgmnt conslt McKinsey & Co London and Paris 1988–94, memb PM's Policy Unit 1995–97, dir of strategy BBC Worldwide 1997–99, dir of strategy BBC 2000–04, ptnr McKinsey & Co 2006–07, dir of gp devpt and strategy ITV plc 2007–; *Recreations* tennis, travel; *Style*— Carolyn Fairbairn; ✉ 24 St Thomas Street, Winchester, Hampshire SO23 9HJ

FAIRBAIRN, John Sydney; s of Sydney George Fairbairn, MC, and Angela Maude, *née* Fane; *b* 15 January 1934; *Educ* Eton, Trinity Coll Cambridge (MA); *m* 1, 1968, Mrs Camilla Fry *née* Grinling (d 2000); 1 s (John Harry b 1969), 2 da (Rose (twin) b 1969, Flora b 1972), 2 step s, 2 step da; m 2, 2001, Felicity, da of M G Ballantyne, of Montreal, and wid of 3 Baron Milford; 2 step s, 3 step da; *Career* 2 Lt 17/21 Lancers 1952–54; career with M&G Group plc (dir 1974–99 (non-exec 1989–99)); dep chm LAUTRO Ltd 1986–89, chm Central European Growth Fund plc 1994–2000; chm Unit Tst Assoc 1989–91; hon treas and memb Cncl KCL 1972–84, memb Cncl Univ of Buckingham 1987–95; memb Cncl Policy Studies Inst 1989–97; tstee: Esmée Fairbairn Fndn 1965– (chm 1988–2003), Monteverdi Tst 1991–97, Friends of Royal Pavilion Art Gallery and Museums Brighton 1993–2001, Comeback 1993–99, Dulwich Picture Gallery 1994–97; DL W Sussex 1996–2001; Hon Dr: Univ of Buckingham 1992, American Int Univ in London 2002; Hon FKC, FCA; *Style*— J S Fairbairn, Esq; ✉ The Old Vicarage, Powerstock, Dorset DT6 3TE

FAIRBAIRNS, Zoë Ann; da of John Fairbairns, and Isabel Catherine, *née* Dippie; *b* 20 December 1948; *Educ* St Catherine's Convent Sch Twickenham, Univ of St Andrews (MA), Coll of William and Mary Williamsburg VA (exchange scholarship); *Career* writer; journalist; ed Sanity 1973–74, freelance journalist 1975–; contrib: The Guardian, TES, Times Higher Educational Supplement, The Leveller, Women's Studies International Quarterley, New African, New Scientist, New Society, New Behaviour, New Statesman, Spare Rib, Time Out; poetry ed Spare Rib 1978–82; occasional contrib 1982–: Women's Review, New Internationalist, New Statesman and New Society; fiction reviewer Everywoman 1990–, contrib Sunday Times and Independent 1991–; C Day Lewis Fellowship Rutherford Sch London 1977–78; creative writing tutor: City Lit Inst London 1978–82 and 2004–, Holloway Prison 1978–82, Wandsworth Prison 1987, Silver Moon Women's Bookshop London 1987–89, Morley Coll London 1988–89; various appts London Borough of Bromley under Writers in Schs Scheme 1981–; writer in residence: Deakin Univ Geelong 1983, Sunderland Poly 1983–85, Surrey CC (working in schs and Brooklands Tech Coll) 1989; subtitler: BBC Television London 1992–93, Independent Television Facilities Centre London 1993–; Br Cncl travel grant to attend and give paper Women's Worlds - Realities and Choices Congress NY, visiting writer Dept of Creative Writing Univ of Minnesota 2003; memb Writers' Guild of GB 1985; *Publications* incl: Live as Family (1968), Down (1969), Benefits (1979, shortlisted Hawthornden prize 1980, adapted for stage 1980), Stand We At Last (1983), Here Today (1984, Fawcett Book Prize 1985), Closing (1987), Daddy's Girls (1991), Other Names (1998, shortlisted Romantic Novelists' Assoc Award 1999); Tales I Tell My Mother (contrib, 1978), Despatches From the Frontiers of the Female Mind (contrib, 1985), Voices from Arts for Labour (contrib, 1985), More Tales I Tell My Mother (contrib, 1987), The Seven Deadly Sins (contrib, 1988), Finding Courage (contrib, 1989), The Seven Cardinal Virtues (contrib, 1990), Dialogue and Difference: English into the Nineties (contrib, 1989), By The Light of The Silvery Moon (contrib, 1994), Brilliant Careers: The Virago Book of 20th Century Fiction (contrib, 2000), The Road from George Orwell - His Achievement and Legacy (contrib, 2001), Endangering Realism and Postmodernism (contrib, 2001), Saying What We Want: Women's Demands in the Feminist Seventies and Now (contrib, 2002), How Do You Pronounce Nulliparous? (2004); *Recreations* walking, reading; *Style*— Ms Zoë Fairbairns; ✉ website www.zoefairbairns.co.uk

FAIRBURN, Prof Christopher Granville; s of Ernest Alfred Fairburn, and Margaret Isabel, *née* Nicholson; *b* 20 September 1950, Belfast; *Educ* Malvern Coll, Worcester Coll Oxford (BA, BM, BCh), Univ of Edinburgh (MPhil), Univ of Oxford (DM); *m* 1979, Susan Margaret, *née* Russam; 1 s (Guy Granville b 16 Sept 1989), 1 da (Sarah Granville b 24 Jan 1992); *Career* registrar in psychiatry Royal Edinburgh Hosp 1975–78, lectr in psychiatry Univ of Edinburgh 1978–80, sr registrar in psychiatry Oxfordshire AHA 1980–81; Univ of Oxford: research psychiatrist 1981–84, Wellcome Tst sr lectr 1984–96, Wellcome princ research fell and prof of psychiatry 1996–; fell Center for Advanced Study Stanford Univ 1990–91 and 1998–99; author of 5 books on eating disorders and cognitive behaviour therapy and over 200 scientific pubns; FRCPsych 1992, FMedSci 2001; *Recreations* travelling off the beaten track; *Style*— Prof Christopher Fairburn; ✉ University Department, Warneford Hospital, Oxford OX3 7JX

FAIRCLOUGH, Geoffrey Charles; s of late John Holden Fairclough, and Kay, *née* Kear; *b* 16 October 1955; *Educ* Mount St Mary's Coll, Univ of London (BSc(Econ), external); *m* Sylvia, da of late Thomas Marshall Bird; 2 s (Alistair John b 20 April 1982, Richard Anthony b 6 Aug 1983); *Career* chartered accountant: Herring Conn Manchester 1976–80, Harry L Price Manchester 1980–83, H W Gp 1983–, Haines Watts Ltd 1992–, H W Gp Services Ltd 1992–, H W Financial Services Ltd 1992–, HWCA Ltd 2006–; FCA 1990 (ACA 1980); *Recreations* cycling, gardening and walking; *Style*— Geoffrey Fairclough, Esq; ✉ 13 St James's Square, Bath BA1 2TR; Haines Watts Ltd, Park House, Milton Park, Abingdon, Oxfordshire OX1 4RS (tel 01235 835900, e-mail gcfairclough@hwca.com)

FAIRCLOUGH, Oliver Noel Francis; s of late Arthur Basil Rowland Fairclough, and late Jean McKenzie, *née* Fraser; *Educ* Bryanston, Trinity Coll Oxford (BA), Keele Univ (MA); *Career* asst Liverpool Museum 1971–74; Birmingham Museum and Art Gallery: asst keeper of art 1975–79, dep keeper of applied art 1979–86; asst keeper of applied art Nat Museum of Wales 1986–98, keeper of art Amgueddfa Cymru - National Museum Wales

1998–; memb various arts and heritage advsy bodies and learned socs; assoc Museums Assoc 1978; *Publications* Textiles by William Morris (with E Leary, 1981), The Grand Old Mansion (1984), Companion Guide to the National Art Gallery (1993 and 1997); *Recreations* walking, travel, architectural history; *Style*— Oliver Fairclough, Esq; ✉ Tyn y Llwyn, Partishow, Crickhowell, Breconshire NP7 7LT (tel 01873 890540); Department of Art, Amgueddfa Cymru - National Museum Wales, Cathays Park, Cardiff CF10 3NP (tel 029 2057 3275, fax 029 2057 3351, e-mail oliver.fairclough@museumwales.ac.uk)

FAIREY, Michael E; *b* 17 June 1948, Louth, Lincolnshire; *Educ* King Edward VI GS Louth; *m* Patricia; 2 s (Kevin, Steven); *Career* Barclays Bank: joined 1967, ops dir Central Retail Servs Div 1986, dir i/c Barclays Card Servs 1988, sr exec i/c Barclays Direct Lending Servs 1989; TSB Gp: dir Credit Retail Div then gp credit dir and memb Gp Exec Ctee 1992, memb Bd TSB Gp plc 1993, chm UDT and Mortgage Express 1994, IT and ops dir 1996, dir Lloyds Bank plc and TSB Bank plc 1996; Lloyds TSB Gp (following merger with Lloyds Gp): memb Bd 1997–, gp dir for central servs 1997, dep gp ceo 1998–; chm Financial Servs Cncl CBI, pres Br Quality Fndn, govr European Fndn for Quality Mgmnt; chm Race for Opportunity, dir Business in the Community, non-exec dir Energy Saving Tst, tstee In Kind Direct; ACIB 1974; *Recreations* most sports, particularly soccer and tennis, most music; *Style*— Michael Fairey, Esq

FAIRFAX-LUCY, (Sir) Edmund John William Hugh Ramsay-; 6 Bt (UK 1836), of The Holmes, Roxburghshire; s of Maj Sir Brian Fulke Ramsay-Fairfax-Lucy, 5 Bt (d 1974), and Hon Alice Caroline Helen Buchan (d 1993), o da of 1 Baron Tweedsmuir, GCMG, GCVO, CH, PC; *b* 4 May 1945; *Educ* Eton, Royal Acad of Arts (Dip); *m* 1, 1974 (m dis), Sylvia, da of Graeme Ogden; m 2, 1986 (m dis 1989), Lady Lucinda Lambton, eldest da of Antony Claud Lambton (6 Earl of Durham until he disclaimed his peerage 1970); m 3, 1994, Erica, da of Warren Loane, of Crocknacrieve, Enniskillen; 2 s (Patrick Samuel Thomas Fulke b 3 April 1995, John Frederick Hugh b 12 July 1998); *Heir* s, Patrick Fairfax-Lucy; *Career* painter (chiefly of still-life and interiors), first one-man exhbn 1971; *Recreations* landscape gardening, waterworks, building; *Style*— Edmund Fairfax-Lucy; ✉ Charlecote Park, Warwick CV35 9ER

FAIRFAX OF CAMERON, 14 Lord (S 1627); Nicholas John Albert Fairfax; s of 13 Lord (d 1964; ninth in descent from the bro of the 2 Lord who defeated Prince Rupert at Marston Moor, and unc of the 3 Lord who, as C-in-C of the Parliamentarians, was the victor at Naseby, and who hired the poet, Andrew Marvell, as a tutor for his da Mary who m another poet, the 2 Duke of Buckingham); *b* 4 January 1956; *Educ* Eton, Downing Coll Cambridge; *m* 24 April 1982, Annabel, er da of late Nicholas Morriss, of Newmarket, Suffolk; 3 s (Hon Edward Nicholas Thomas b 20 Sept 1984, Hon John Frederick Anthony b 27 June 1986, Hon Rory Henry Francis b 21 May 1991); *Heir* s, Hon Edward Fairfax; *Career* dir: Sedgwick Marine & Cargo Ltd 1995–96, Aquatask Ltd 1997–2005, Sovcomflot (UK) Ltd 2005–; *Recreations* sailing, motorcycling; *Clubs* Royal Yacht Squadron; *Style*— The Rt Hon the Lord Fairfax of Cameron; ✉ 10 Orlando Road, London SW4 0LF

FAIRFIELD, Ian McLeod; CBE (1982); s of late Geoffrey Fairfield, and Inez Helen Thorneycroft Fairfield (d 1977); *b* 5 December 1919; *Educ* Monkton House Sch Cardiff, Manchester Coll of Technol; *m* 1941, Joyce Ethel (d 1999), da of Cdr Percy Fletcher, RN (d 1965); 2 s (Clive, Julian); *Career* cmmnd RNVR Electrical Branch 1940–45; engrg trainee Callenders Cables & Construction Co Ltd, area sales mangr St Helens Cable & Rubber Co 1945–51; Chemring Gp plc: sales dir 1951, md 1952, dep chm, chm and gp chief exec 1980, chm 1984, chm and gp chief exec 1985, gp chm 1985–91 (ret), dep chm 1991–94, ret; *Recreations* motor boat cruising; *Clubs* Royal Naval Sailing Assoc, Wig & Pen; *Style*— Ian Fairfield, Esq, CBE

FAIRGRIEVE, James; *Educ* Edinburgh Coll of Art (Andrew Grant jr open scholarship, DA); *Career* artist (full-time 1999–); sr lectr Sch of Drawing and Painting Edinburgh Coll of Art (ret 1998); memb 57 Gallery Assoc; RSA (ARSA 2004), RSW, SSA (past pres); *Solo Exhibitions* New 57 Gallery Edinburgh 1969 and 1971, Scottish Arts Club Edinburgh 1973, Scottish Gallery Edinburgh 1974, 1978 and 2007, Univ of Edinburgh 1975, Mercury Gallery London 1980, 1982, 1984 and 1987, Macaulay Gallery Stenton E Lothian 1983, Belgrade Acad Yugoslavia 1989, Stichill Gallery Roxburghshire 1990, London Art Fair (McLean Fine Art) 2002, Randolph Gallery Edinburgh 2004 and 2007, New Grafton Gallery London 2006; *Group Exhibitions* incl: Reeves Bi-centenary (Edinburgh Festival) 1966, Drawing and Prints Strasbourg 1967, Glasgow Inst of Fine Art 1968, Marjorie Parr Gallery London 1968, 20x57 Festival Exhibition Edinburgh 1969–72, The Edinburgh Sch (Edinburgh Festival) 1971, Richard Demarco Gallery Edinburgh 1973 and 1976, Triad Arts Centre (Bishop's Stortford) 1974, Howarth Art Gallery Accrington 1974, Howden Park Centre Livingston 1975, The Mall Galleries London 1975, Talbot Rice Art Centre Edinburgh 1975, City Art Centre Edinburgh 1975, N B Gallery 1976, Stirling Gallery 1976, Alamo Gallery London 1978, Mercury Gallery London 1978, Fine Art Soc Glasgow 1978, Gracefield Art Gallery Dumfries 1978, Basle Art Fair 1981, Pictures of Ourselves (Scottish Arts Cncl travelling exhbn) 1982, Compass Gallery Glasgow 1984 and 1996, ESU Gallery 1986, Royal Glasgow Inst 1987, Edinburgh Sch (Kingfisher Gallery) 1988, Artists Choice (Open Eye Gallery) 1989, Mercury/Scotland 1964–89 (London) 1989, State of the Art (Fine Art Soc) 1989, Scottish Painters (Fosse Gallery) 1989 and 1992, Scottish Painters (Beaux Arts Gallery, Bath Tolquhon Gallery) 1990, Arts Club Edinburgh 1990, RSW 1991, 1993, 1995 and 1996, Gillies Travel Award Exhibition (RSA annual exhbn) 1992, CD Exhibition (The Collective Gallery) 1992, Roger Billcliffe Fine Art 1993, Scottish Arts Club 1994, Fosse Gallery 1994 and 1995, Pontevedra Spain 1995, Burns Bi-centenary (Compass Gallery touring exhbn) 1996, Postcard Exhibition (Roger Billcliffe Gallery) 1996, 3 Man Show (Open Eye Gallery) 1997, Christmas Exhibition (Stenton Gallery) 1997, My Patch (Compass Gallery touring exhbn) 1997, The Big Picture Show (City Art Centre Edinburgh) 1998, Art 99 (Portland Gallery London) 1999, Frank T Sabin Gallery 2000, Fosse Gallery 2000, Compass Gallery 2000, RSW Exhbn Newport 2001, Noble-Grossart Prize Exhbn 2001, 20th Century and Modern Masters 2001, Cabinet Paintings (Compass Gallery) 2001, Art London (McLean Fine Art) 2002, Artists of Today and Tomorrow (New Grafton Gallery London) 2002, Christmas Exhibition (New Grafton Gallery London) 2002, Christmas Exhibition (McLean Fine Art) 2002, South Street Gallery St Andrews 2003, Artists of Today and Tomorrow (New Grafton Gallery London) 2003, Christmas Exhibition (Medici Gallery London) 2003, Visual Feast (Leith Gallery Edinburgh) 2004, Valentine Exhibition (Randolph Gallery Edinburgh) 2004, Affordable Art Fair (Maclean Fine Art London) 2005; *Work in Collections* HRH Prince Philip, Edinburgh City Art Centre, Scottish Arts Cncl, Lothian Regnl Schs Collection, Argyll Educn Dept, First Nat Bank of Chicago, Lillie Art Gallery, Ridderick Municipal Collection, RCP, Perth Art Gallery, Perth Art Gallery, Robert Fleming & Co, Leeds Sch Collection; *Awards* RA David Murray Landscape Award 1968, Andrew Grant travelling scholarship 1968, RSW Gillies Award 1987 and 1997, RSA Gillies Travel Award 1991, RSA Maude Gemell Hutchinson Prize 1993, RSA Macauly Award 2002; *Style*— James Fairgrieve, Esq

FAIRHAVEN, 3 Baron (UK 1961); Ailwyn Henry George Broughton; JP (S Cambridgeshire 1975), DL (Cambridgeshire and Isle of Ely 1977); s of 2 Baron (d 1973), and Hon Diana (d 1937), da of Capt Hon Coulson Fellowes (s of 2 Baron De Ramsey, JP, DL, and Lady Rosamond Spencer-Churchill, da of 7 Duke of Marlborough, KG); *b* 16 November 1936; *Educ* Eton, RMA Sandhurst; *m* 23 Sept 1960, Kathleen Patricia, er da of late Col James Henry Magill, OBE; 4 s (Hon James, Hon Huttleston Rupert (decd), Hon Charles Leander, Hon Henry Robert), 2 da (Hon Diana Cara, Hon Melanie Frances); *Heir* s, Hon James Broughton; *Career* RHG 1957–71, Maj; Vice Lord-Lt Cambridgeshire 1977–85; vice-pres: The Animal Health Tst, The Kennel Club; Kt of the White Rose (Finland) 1970, KStJ 1992 (CStJ 1983); *Recreations* gardening, cooking; *Clubs* Jockey (sr steward 1985–89), White's; *Style*— The Rt Hon the Lord Fairhaven, DL; ✉ Kirtling Tower, Cambridgeshire CB8 9PA

FAIRHEAD, Rona A; da of Douglas Andrew Haig, of Oxon, and Isabella Somerville, *née* Farmer; *b* 28 August 1961; *Educ* Yarm GS, St Catharine's Coll Cambridge (LLB, Jacobson Law Prize, Addersley Law Prize, pres Univ Law Soc), Harvard Business Sch (MBA); *m* 5 Dec 1992, Thomas Edwin, s of John Edwin Fairhead; 2 s (James Douglas Edwin b 1996, Alexander Edward Haig b 1998), 1 da (Iona Charlotte Haig b 2000); *Career* assoc conslt Bain & Co 1983–87, analyst Morgan Stanley Int 1988, mangr Bain & Co 1989–90, ind conslt British Aerospace plc 1991; Bombardier Inc/Shorts Brothers plc: joined 1991, vice-pres corp strategy and public affrs 1994–95, vice-pres UK Aerospace Servs 1995–96; ICI plc: dir of planning & acquisitions 1996–97, exec vice-pres for planning and communications 1997–98, exec vice-pres strategy and control 1998–2001 (also memb Exec Mgmnt Team); chief financial offr Pearson plc 2002–06 (dep finance dir 2001–02), chief exec FT Gp 2006–; non-exec dir: Laganside Corp Belfast 1994–2000, Harvard Business School Publishing 2002–, HSBC Holdings plc 2004–; *Recreations* skiing, flying, scuba diving, family; *Clubs* Bournemouth Flying; *Style*— Mrs Rona Fairhead

FAIRLEY, Ross; *b* 11 October 1968, Epsom, Surrey; *Educ* City of London Freemen's Sch, Univ of Leicester (LLB), Guildford Coll of Law; *Children* 3 da; *Career* slr; ptnr: Allen & Overy 2001–04 (joined as trainee), Burges Salmon LLP 2004– (co-head Environmental Law Unit and head of renewable energy 2004–); memb: Law Soc, UK Environmental Law Assoc; assoc Inst of Environmental Mgmnt and Assessment (IEMA); *Publications* Tolley's Environmental Law and Procedures Management (ed), Sweet & Maxwell's Commercial Environmental Law and Liability (contrib); *Recreations* hockey, all sport, driving an old Austin Healey Frogeye; *Style*— Ross Fairley, Esq; ✉ Burges Salmon LLP, Narrow Quay House, Narrow Quay, Bristol BS1 4AH

FAIRLIE, Andrew; s of James McGregor Fairlie, and Kay, *née* Sweeny; *b* 21 November 1963; *Educ* Perth Acad, Westminster Hotel Sch; *m* Ashley Gillian, da of William Laird; 2 da (Iona b 15 Aug 1989, Leah b 1 Oct 1996); *Career* apprentice Station Hotel Perth 1980–82, commis de cuisine Charing Cross Hotel 1982–84, chef de partie Boodles Restaurant 1984–85, stagiaire Chez Michel Guerard France June-Nov 1985, commis de cuisine tournant Hotel de Crillon Paris 1985–86, sous chef Chez Nanos Megeve 1986–87, chef de cuisine Royal Scotsman Edinburgh April-Nov 1987, stage sous chef Intercontinental Hotel Sydney 1987–88, chef de cuisine Royal Scotsman Edinburgh April-Nov 1988, chef conslt A & K Travel Kenya 1988–89, sous chef Ritz Club London 1989–90, sr sous chef Adare Manor Co Limerick 1990–91, chef de cuisine Disneyland Paris 1991–94, chef de cuisine One Devonshire Gardens Glasgow 1994–, opened own restaurant Andrew Fairlie at Gleneagles 2001; team capt Ritz Club Olympia 1990 (9 silver medals, 8 bronze medals, 4 best exhibits); memb Académie Culinaire de France 1995; *Awards* third place Robert Carrier Nat Competition 1982, winner Michel Roux scholarship 1984, Scottish Chef of the Year 1996, Michelin Star 1996, 2 Michelin Stars 2006, Hospitality Industry Trg, Lifetime Achievement Award 2006; *Recreations* hill walking, football; *Style*— Andrew Fairlie, Esq; ✉ Gleneagles Hotel, Auchterarder, Perthshire PH3 1NF (tel 01764 694267, fax 01764 694163, e-mail andrew.fairlie@gleneagles.com)

FAIRLIE-CUNINGHAME, Sir Robert Henry; 17 Bt (NS 1630), of Robertland, Ayrshire; s of Sir William Henry Fairlie-Cuninghame, 16 Bt (d 1999); *b* 19 July 1974; *m* 28 May 2005, Mary Louise, da of Capt Geoffrey Hugh Belasyse-Smith; *Style*— Sir Robert Fairlie-Cuninghame, Bt; ✉ 29A Orinoco Street, Pymble, New South Wales 2073, Australia

FAIRMAN, Dr Martin John; s of Henry Douglas Fairman, FRCS, of Bristol, and Stella Margaret, *née* Sheath; *b* 8 May 1945; *Educ* Monkton Combe Sch, London Hosp Med Coll (MB BS); *m* 12 Aug 1967, Marianne Alison Louis, da of Sqdn Ldr Roland Ernest Burton, of Limousin, France; 2 s (James b 1969, Jack b 1978), 2 da (Jocelyn b 1971, Lydia b 1980); *Career* conslt physician Pilgrim Hosp (United Lincs Hosps NHS Tst) 1979–, hon sr lectr med Leicester Univ 1979–, fell in gastroenterology Cincinnati 1976–77, med dir Pilgrim Health NHS Tst 1993–2000, med dir United Lincs Hosps NHS Tst 2000–02; FRCP; *Recreations* golf; *Style*— Dr Martin J Fairman; ✉ Skirbeck Grange, Sibsey Road, Boston, Lincolnshire (tel 01205 360743); Pilgrim Hospital, Boston, Lincolnshire (tel 01205 364801)

FAIRNEY, William; s of Thomas Fairney (d 1978), of Greenford, Middx, and Mary Evelyn, *née* Lambert; *b* 2 April 1941; *Educ* Latymer Upper Sch, Univ of Bristol (BSc); *m* 1, 1966 (m dis 1978), Barbara, *née* Wood; 2 da (Amelia Jane (Mrs Reutenauer) b 16 July 1969, Josephine Anne (Mrs Wenham) b 14 Jan 1972); m 2, 1981, Linda, da of Harold Thomas Gammage; 1 step da (Sarah Alicia Burrows (Mrs Cook) b 20 Aug 1968), 1 step s (Mark Harold Burrows b 6 Feb 1971); *Career* English Electric Co: graduate apprentice 1963–65, gen design engr 1965; CEGB: res offr 1965–74, gen design engr Generation Design and Construction Div 1974–77, electrical engrg mangr Midlands Region 1977–79, system tech engr 1979–85, dir of res 1985–86, dir of plant engrg 1986–89; National Power plc (formerly CEGB): dir of engrg and technol 1989–90, dir of engrg and project servs 1990–93, dir of projects devpt and construction 1993–95, dir of plant procurement and construction 1995–97; consulting engr 1997–2000, dir FairDiesel Ltd 2000–; visiting prof of engrg Univ of Durham 1985–, pres NW Area Assoc for Sci Educn 1988, vice-pres IEE 1993–96; chm: Power Divnl Bd IEE 1989, Professional Bd 1993–95, Centres Bd 1995–97, Year of Engrg Success (YEARCO) 1995–98; govr Chipping Sodbury Sch 2002–; FIEE 1984 (MIEE 1977), FREng 1992; *Recreations* walking, mathematics, reading, writing, flying, computing; *Style*— Prof William Fairney, FREng; ✉ Fairdiesel Ltd, 2 The Tithe Barn, Hawkesbury Upton, Badminton, South Gloucestershire GL9 1AY (tel 01454 238553, mobile 078 879 35757, e-mail william@fairney.wanadoo.co.uk)

FAIRWEATHER, Charles Philip; s of Charles Henry Fuller Fairweather (d 1979), and Doris Mary, *née* Miller (d 1995); *b* 23 November 1949, London; *Educ* Eastbourne Coll; *m* 9 July 1976, Nicola Jane, *née* McArthur; 3 s (James Robert Andrew Harland b 10 Aug 1970, Edward Charles b 29 May 1978, Henry Nicholas b 30 Jan 1982); *Career* CA 1972; Arnold Hill & Co 1967–97 (latterly ptnr), chm Bendinat Gp 1986–, dir Simon Dickinson Ltd 1993–; pres Royal Albert Hall 2001–07, dir Royal Philharmonic Orchestra 2007–; *Recreations* golf, country pursuits; *Clubs* Boodle's, MCC; *Style*— Charles Fairweather, Esq; ✉ 8 Queen Street, London W1X 7PH

FAIRWEATHER, George Rollo; s of Rollo Fairweather (d 1970), and Edith, *née* Patterson; *b* 11 October 1957; *Educ* Montrose Acad, Univ of Edinburgh (BCom); *m* 1993, Victoria, *née* Lanfear; 2 da (Natasha b 1995, Emily b 1996); *Career* Thomson McLintock & Co 1978–82, Procter & Gamble 1982–86, Dixons Gp plc 1986–94; gp fin dir: Dawson Int plc 1994–97, Elementis plc (formerly Harrisons & Crosfield plc) 1997–2002, Alliance UniChem plc 2002–2006, Alliance Boots plc 2006–; non-exec dir Mitchell & Butlers plc 2003–; MICAS 1981; *Recreations* sailing, golf, music; *Clubs* Bosham Sailing, West Surrey Golf; *Style*— George Fairweather, Esq; ✉ Alliance Boots plc, 2 The Heights, Brooklands, Weybridge, Surrey KT13 0NY (tel 01932 870581, fax 01932 870552, e-mail george.fairweather@allianceboots.com)

FAIRWEATHER, (Cyril) Paul; s of James Armstead Fairweather, of St Nicholas, Glamorgan, and Marie Francis, *née* Esnouf; *b* 26 May 1952; *Educ* Westbourne House Penarth, Marlborough (exhibitioner Worshipful Co of Salters), Fitzwilliam Coll Cambridge (MA); *m* 9 May 1981, Angela Glen, da of Lt Col Donald Duncan Burns; 1 da (Charlotte Glen b 15 Feb 1982), 1 s (Ian Charles McIntyre b 15 Aug 1985); *Career* PricewaterhouseCoopers (formerly Price Waterhouse before merger): joined London 1973, The Hague Netherlands

1977–78, London 1978–83, Windsor 1983–98, tax ptnr 1984–, ptnr in charge Thames Valley 1992–98, memb Supervisory Bd 1995–2003, London 1998–, memb Global Oversight Bd 1999–2001, business team ldr South region 2004–07; memb ICAEW; FCA 1981 (ACA 1976); *Recreations* golf, skiing, shooting, rugby, sailing; *Clubs* Cardiff and County, Royal Porthcawl Golf, Huntercombe Golf, Royal Cornwall Yacht; *Style*— Paul Fairweather, Esq; ✉ PricewaterhouseCoopers, The Atrium, 1 Harefield Road, Uxbridge UB8 1EX (tel 020 7804 8988, e-mail paul.fairweather@uk.pwc.com)

FAITH, Dr Lesley; da of Norman Faith (d 1970), of Belfast, and Estelle, *née* Sharp; *b* 30 August 1955; *Educ* Methodist Coll Belfast, Univ of St Andrews (BSc), Univ of Manchester (MB ChB); *m* (m dis); 2 da (Natasha b 1988, Nicole b 1989), 1 s (Aaron b 1991); partner, Howard Young; *Career* conslt psychiatrist: Bermuda 1986, Sydney Aust 1986–87, Stepping Hill Hosp Stockport 1987–98, Cheadle Royal Hosp Stockport 1998–; special interest in intensive care psychiatry; MRCPsych 1984; *Recreations* travel, reading; *Style*— Dr Lesley Faith; ✉ Cheadle Royal Hospital, 100 Wilmslow Road, Stockport, Cheshire SK8 3DG (tel 0161 428 9511)

FALCON, Michael Geoffrey; s of Norman Leslie Falcon (d 1996), of Church Hanborough, Oxon, and Dorothy Muriel, *née* Freeman; *b* 15 January 1941; *Educ* Tonbridge, Trinity Coll Cambridge (exhibitioner, MA, MB BChir), Guy's Hosp Med Sch London (DO); *m* 1969, Savithri, *née* Bhandary, of S India; *Career* jr hosp posts Guy's Hosp London and Royal Surrey Co Hosp Guildford 1967–70; Moorfields Eye Hosp London: resident surgical offr rising to sr resident surgical offr 1971–74, lectr Dept of Clinical Ophthalmology 1974–78; conslt ophthalmologist: Guy's Hosp 1978–81, St Thomas' Hosp London 1981–; Freeman City of London, Freeman Worshipful Co of Spectaclemakers; MRCP, FRCS 1973, FRCOphth 1990 (examiner 1992–); *Publications* author of 3 chapters in ophthalmological textbooks 1982–94 and numerous pubns on herpetic keratitis, corneal surgery, cataract surgery and glaucoma; *Recreations* mountain walking, tennis, horticulture; *Style*— Michael Falcon, Esq; ✉ 25 Wimpole Street, London W1G 8GL (tel 020 7580 7199, fax 020 7580 6855, e-mail falconeyes1@aol.com)

FALCONBRIDGE, Prof Brian William; s of James Henry Falconbridge (d 1994), of Cromer, Norfolk, and Joyce Vera Lucy Spong (d 1995); *b* 1 May 1950; *Educ* Fakenham GS, Canterbury Coll of Art, Goldsmiths Coll Sch of Art London, Slade Sch of Fine Art; *m* 1970 (m dis 1989), Elizabeth Margaret, *née* Green; 1 da (Camilla Elizabeth Vita b 9 Sept 1982), 1 s (Oliver William Merton b 9 Aug 1985); *Career* sculptor; academic: Eton 1977–81, Goldsmiths Coll London 1978–2004 (head Visual Arts Dept 1997–2002), Slade Sch of Fine Art 1979–86, Blackheath Sch of Art 1985–89, London Metropolitan Univ 2005– (head Sir John Cass Dept of Art, Media and Design 2006–); visitor The Royal Acad Schs 2007–; pt/t and visiting lectr 1974: Brighton Museum, Brighton Poly, Bristol Poly, Camberwell Sch of Art, Colchester Inst Sch of Art, Falmouth Sch of Art, Maidstone Coll of Art, Morley Coll, Norwich Sch of Art, Portsmouth Poly, Ravensbourne Coll of Art and Design, The Royal Acad Schs, Sainsbury Centre for the Visual Arts UEA; memb Visual Art Panel Eastern Arts Assoc 1983–88, memb Exec Ctee Tolly Cobbold/Eastern Arts 5th Nat Exhibition 1984–86, curator and selector A Spiritual Dimension 1986–90, Academic and Mgmnt Bds Blackheath Sch of Art 1987–89; RBS: assoc memb 1994, memb Cncl 1995–98 and 2001–03, elected fell (FRBS) 2001, elected treas 2003, elected pres (PRBS) 2004; memb City of Westminster Public Arts Advsy Panel 2006–, memb Asiatic Soc of Japan; work in several public collections; *Solo Exhibitions* House Gallery London 1977, Angela Flowers Gallery 1983, The Minories Colchester 1984, Newcastle Poly Art Gallery 1984, Arcade Gallery Harrogate 1984, Drawing Schs Gallery Eton Coll 1984, The Fermoy Centre Art Gallery King's Lynn 1986, Artist in Residence Kings' Lynn Festival (All Saints' Church with The Fermoy Centre) 1986, Artist in Residence Gaywood Park HS King's Lynn 1987, Great St Mary's Cambridge 1989, Jill George Gallery London 1990, Masterpiece Art Gallery Taipei Int Convention Centre 1996, Chappel Galleries 2002, The Fermoy Gallery King's Lynn Arts Centre 2003, Place Arte Contemporanea Caravagnolo Turin (jt exhibition) 2003, Massmaanska Kvarnen Kultucentrum Ronneby 2004; *Group Exhibitions* incl: Goldsmiths (South London Art Gallery) 1972, Royal Acad Summer Exhibition 1977, 1988, 1990, 1991, 1992, 1993, 1994, 1996, 1997, 1998, 1999, 2000, 2001, 2002, 2003, 2004 and 2005, Art for Today (Portsmouth Festival) 1979, Tolly Cobbold/Eastern Arts 3rd Nat Exhibition, Small is Beautiful (Angela Flowers Gallery) 1983, The Falconbridge Cross Highgate URC 1984, Art for Everywhere (Peterborough Museum and Art Gallery) 1985, A Spiritual Dimension (touring exhibition) 1989 and 1990, LA Art Fair (Thumb Gallery) 1989, New Icons touring exhibition 1989–90, Academicians' Choice (London Contemporary Arts and the Eye Gallery Bristol) 1990, London to Atlanta (Atlanta Thumb Gallery) 1990, Los Angeles Art Fair (Thumb Gallery) 1990, Drawing Show II (Thumb Gallery) 1990, Art 91 London (Thumb Gallery) 1990, Decouvertes - Grand Palais Paris (Jill George Gallery) 1991, Goldsmiths Coll Centenary Exhibition 1991, Los Angeles Art Fair (Jill George Gallery) 1991, 1992 and 1993, ART 92 Business Design Centre (Jill George Gallery) 1992, ARCO 1992 Madrid (Jill George Gallery) 1992, Sumida Riverside Hall Gallery Tokyo 1993, Chelsea Harbour Sculpture 1993, Artists for Romanian Orphans at Bonhams 1994, The Language of Sculpture (Collyer-Bristow Gallery London) 1995, Absolut Secret (RCA) 1996, 1997, 1998 and 1999, Secret (RCA) 2000, 2001 and 2002, London Underground (Sungkok Art Museum Seoul) 2001, Blue (Place Arte Contemporanea Cavagnolo Turin) 2002, London Underground/Taipei (Taipei Fine Arts Museum Taipei) 2002, Manufactured in the UK (Villa Boriglionne Parco Culturale 'Le Serra' Grugliasco Torino) 2003, Scultura Internazionale ad Agliè (Castle d'Agliè Associazione Piemontese Arte Torino) 2004, Salthouse 05 2005; *Awards* Walter Newrath Art History award 1972, Arts Cncl minor award 1976, Eastern Arts Assoc award 1977, Tolly Cobbold E Arts regnl prize 1981, E Vincent Harris award for mural decoration 1984, prizewinner 3 Int Exhibition of Miniature Art (Del Bello Gallery Toronto) 1988, Blackstone award Royal Acad Summer Exhibition 1991; *Clubs* Chelsea Arts; *Style*— Prof Brian Falconbridge, PRBS; ✉ Royal British Society of Sculptors, Dora House, 108 Old Brompton Road, South Kensington, London SW7 3RA (tel 020 7373 5554, fax 020 7373 8615, e-mail b.falconbridge@londonmet.ac.uk)

FALCONER, Colin; s of James Falconer, and Winnifred Falconer; *Educ* Forres Acad Moray, Duncan of Jordanstone Coll Univ of Dundee, Nottingham Trent Univ; *Career* theatre designer; prodns incl: Aladdin (costume, Scottish Ballet) 2000, The Blue Room (Minerva Theatre Chichester and West End) 2000, Hysteria (Minerva Theatre Chichester) 2000, The Merchant of Venice (RSC, London, Stratford and tour) 2001, Three Sisters (Chichester Festival Theatre) 2001, The Secret Rapture (Minerva Theatre Chichester) 2001, Twelfth Night (Liverpool Playhouse) 2001, Romeo and Juliet (Chichester Festival Theatre) 2002, The Misanthrope (Minerva Theatre Chichester) 2002, Acis and Galatea, Dido and Aeneas (RSAMD Glasgow) 2004, Madam T (Meridien Theatre Co Cork) 2005, Dominos (Theatr Genedlaethol Cymru) 2006, Endgame (Theatr Genedlaethol Cymru) 206, plunder (Watermill Theatre) 2006, Cariad Mr Bustl (Theatr Genedlaethol Cymru) 2007, Blithe Spirit (Watford Palace) 2007, Northanger Abbey (Salisbury Playhouse) 2007; *Style*— Colin Falconer, Esq; ✉ c/o Simpson Fox Associates, 52 Shaftesbury Avenue, London W1D 6LP

FALCONER, Prof Roger Alexander; s of Cyril Thomas Falconer (d 2000), of Bridgend, and Winnifred Matilda Mary, *née* Rudge (d 2004); *b* 12 December 1951; *Educ* KCL (BSc), Univ of Washington USA (MSCE), Imperial Coll London (PhD, DIC), Univ of Birmingham (DEng), Univ of London (DSc(Eng)); *m* April 1977, Nicola Jane, da of Kenneth Hayward Wonson (d 1967); 2 s (James b 30 July 1980, Simon b 19 March 1983), 1 da (Sarah b 23 June 1988); *Career* lectr Dept of Civil Engrg Univ of Birmingham 1977–86; Univ of Bradford: prof of water engrg 1987–97, head Dept of Civil and Environmental Engrg 1994–97; Halcrow prof of water mgmnt Sch of Engrg Cardiff Univ and dir Hydroenvironmental Research Centre 1997–; visiting prof: Tongji Univ Shanghai 1987–, Tianjin Univ China 2004–; memb Cncl: CIWEM 1997–2003, IAHR 2000–, ICE 2000–03, Welsh Assembly Govt Flood Risk Mgmnt Ctee 2006–; advsr to: Nat Environment Protection Agency China 1987–92, Wetland Mgmnt Project Southern California Edison USA 1992–93, BNFL 1993–94, BP Chemicals 1993–94, Environment Div US Navy 1995–96, Tianjin Municipal Government China 2000–; UN expert on Mission to Central Water and Power Research Station India 1993, expert evaluator Danish Agency for Devpt of Trade and Industry 1995, expert Malaysia v Singapore Land Reclamation Study 2004; supplier of computer models for water quality predictions to 40 water indust cos for over 100 EIA projects worldwide; recipient: Ippen Award Int Assoc for Hydraulic Research 1991, Telford Premium ICE 1994, Royal Acad of Engrg Silver Medal 1999–, Robert Carr Prize ICE 2003, Hai He Award China 2004; FCIWEM 1990, FICE 1992, FASCE 1993, FCGI 1997, FREng 1997; *Publications* edited five books, author of over 250 published academic papers in jls and conf proceedings; also lectr to over 250 instns in 17 countries on environmental water mgmnt; *Recreations* walking, music, sport, travel; *Style*— Prof Roger Falconer, FREng; ✉ School of Engineering, Cardiff University, The Parade, Cardiff CF24 3AA (tel 029 2087 4280, fax 029 2087 4939, e-mail falconerra@cardiff.ac.uk)

F

FALCONER OF THOROTON, Baron (Life Peer UK 1997), of Thoroton in the County of Nottinghamshire; Charles Leslie Falconer; PC (2003), QC (1991); s of late John Leslie Falconer, and late Anne Mansel Falconer; *b* 19 November 1951; *Educ* Trinity Coll Glenalmond, Queens' Coll Cambridge; *m* 1985, Marianna Catherine Thoroton, da of Sir David Hildyard KCMG, DFC (d 1997); 3 s, 1 da; *Career* called to the Bar Inner Temple 1974; slr-gen 1997–98, min of state Cabinet Office 1998–2001, min of state for housing and planning 2001–02, min of state Home Office 2002–03, sec of state for constitutional affrs and Lord Chllr 2003–07; sole shareholder New Millennium Experience Co with responsibility for Millennium Dome 1999–; *Style*— The Rt Hon the Lord Falconer of Thoroton

FALDO, Nicholas Alexander (Nick); MBE (1988); s of George Arthur Faldo, of Welwyn Garden City, Herts, and Joyce, *née* Smalley; *b* 18 July 1957; *Educ* Sir Fredric Osborne Sch Welwyn Garden City; *m* (m dis); 1 s (Matthew Alexander b 17 March 1989), 3 da (Natalie Lauren b 18 Sept 1986, Georgia Kate b 20 March 1993, Emma Scarlett b 28 July 2003); *Career* professional golfer, golf course designer, televised sports commentator; amateur victories: Br Youths' Open 1975, English Championship 1975; tournament victories since turning professional 1976: Skol Lager 1977, Br PGA Championship 1978, 1980 and 1981, ICL Tournament SA 1979, Haig Tournament Players' Championship 1982, French Open 1983, 1988 and 1989, Martini Int 1983, Car Care Plan Int 1983 and 1984, Lawrence Batley Int 1983, Ebel Swiss Masters 1983, Sea Pines Heritage Classic USA 1984, Spanish Open 1987, Br Open 1987, 1990 and 1992 (runner up 1993), Volvo Masters 1988, US Masters 1989, 1990 and 1996, Volvo PGA Championship 1989, Dunhill British Masters 1989, World Match-Play 1989 and 1992, Irish Open 1991, 1992 and 1993, Johnnie Walker Classic 1990 and 1993, Scandinavian Masters 1992, Euro Open 1992, Johnnie Walker World Championship 1992, Alfred Dunhill Open 1994, Million Dollar Challenge 1994, Doral-Ryder open 1995, Nissan Open 1997, World Cup 1998; England Boys rep 1974, England int 1975–, with Br team 1975; memb Ryder Cup team: 1977, 1979, 1981, 1983, 1985 (winners), 1987 (winners), 1989 (winners), 1991, 1993, 1995 (winners), and 1997 (winners), capt 2008, holds record as leading points scorer for Europe in Ryder Cup history and most appearances in the Ryder Cup; memb England team Dunhill Cup 1985, 1986, 1987 (winners), 1988, 1991 and 1993; memb Hennessy Cup team: 1978 (winners), 1980 (winners), 1982 (winners) and 1984 (capt, winners), UBS Cup 2001, 2002 and 2003; world number one for 97 weeks between 1990 and 1994; Rookie of the Year 1977, finished top Order of Merit 1983 and 1992, BBC Sports Personality of the Year 1989; *Recreations* cars, flying helicopters, photography, fishing; *Style*— Nick Faldo, Esq, MBE; ✉ info@nickfaldo.com

FALK, Fergus Antony; TD (1979); s of Leonard Solomon Falk (d 1992), and Lucy, *née* Cohen (d 1970); *b* 30 August 1941; *Educ* Uppingham, Univ of London (BSc(Econ)); *m* 5 May 1973, Vivian Dundas, da of Leonard Cockburn Dundas Irvine (d 1968), Surgn Capt RNVR, of Hove; 2 da (Harriet b 1976, Annabel b 1979), 1 s (Sebastian b 1980); *Career* dept mangr: John Lewis and Co Ltd 1959–63, C Ulysses Williams Ltd 1964–65; Deloitte & Touche: joined 1965, ptnr 1975–99, ptnr i/c forensic servs London 1985–98, nat dir forensic servs 1990–98; non-exec dir City and Hackney Teaching PCT 2002–03; treas: Islington S and Finsbury Cons Assoc 1974–76, Radwinter Branch Cons Assoc 1976–79; memb: Ct of Common Cncl 1984–95 and 1997–2002 (dep chm Fin Ctee 1998–2002); candidate (Cons) Islington Borough Election 1974; HAC: Maj 1961–80, memb Ct of Assts HAC 1975–2007 (treas 1994–96, vice-pres 1996–98); Liveryman Worshipful Co of CAs; FCA 1973 (ACA 1969), ACIArb, MAE; *Recreations* family, gardening; *Clubs* MCC, Broad Street Ward, City Livery; *Style*— Fergus Falk, Esq, TD; ✉ Brackendale House, Debden Road, Saffron Walden, Essex CB11 4AB (tel 01799 513128, e-mail fergus@brackendalehouse.co.uk)

FALK, Sarah Valerie (Mrs Marcus Flint); da of John Falk, of Radlett, Herts, and Annette Falk; *b* 1 June 1962, London; *Educ* St Albans HS, Univ of Cambridge (David Gottlieb Prize, Slaughter and May Prize, MA); *m* 23 March 1985, Marcus Flint; 1 s (Thomas b 27 Sept 1989), 1 da (Rachel b 11 Sept 1995); *Career* admitted slr 1986; ptnr Freshfields (now Freshfields Bruckhaus Deringer) 1994– (joined 1984–); *Recreations* horse riding, classical music (flautist), walking, gardening, cookery; *Style*— Ms Sarah Falk; ✉ Freshfields Bruckhaus Deringer, 65 Fleet Street, London EC4Y 1HS (tel 020 7936 4000, e-mail sarah.falk@freshfields.com)

FALKENDER, Baroness (Life Peer UK 1974), of West Haddon in the County of Northamptonshire; Marcia Matilda Falkender; CBE (1970); da of Harry Field; assumed by deed poll 1974 surname Falkender in lieu of Williams; *b* 10 March 1932; *Educ* Queen Mary Coll London (BA); *m* 1955 (m dis 1961), George Edmund Charles Williams; *Career* private sec Morgan Phillips (gen sec of Lab Pty) 1954–56, private and political sec to Rt Hon Lord Wilson of Rievaulx, formerly Rt Hon Sir Harold Wilson, KG, OBE, MP 1956–83, political columnist Mail on Sunday 1983–88; memb: BSAC 1976–, BSAC Charitable Tst 1997–; dir Peckham Building Soc 1986–91, chm Canvasback Productions 1989–91; lay govr Queen Mary & Westfield Coll London 1988–93 (lay memb External Relations Ctee 1993–96), tstee The Silver Tst 1986–; FRSA; *Books* Inside No 10 (1972), Perspective on Downing Street (1983); *Recreations* reading, film; *Style*— The Lady Falkender, CBE; ✉ House of Lords, London SW1A 0PW

FALKINER, Sir Benjamin Simon Patrick; 10 Bt (I 1778), of Annemount, Cork; s of Sir Edmond Charles Falkiner, 9 Bt (d 1997), and Janet Iris, *née* Darby; *b* 16 January 1962; *Educ* Queen Elizabeth's Boys' Sch Barnet; *m* 1998, Linda Louise, *née* Mason (d 2006); 1 s (Samuel James Matthew b 30 Aug 1993), 1 da (Alice Katharine Sally b 19 Oct 1996); *Heir* bro, Matthew Falkiner; *Career* master parts technician; *Recreations* rugby, cricket, music (drummer); *Clubs* Old Elizabethans Rugby Football, Old Elizabethans Cricket; *Style*— Sir Benjamin Falkiner, Bt; ✉ 29 Glebeland, Hatfield, Hertfordshire AL10 8AA (tel 01707 274921, e-mail benfalkiner@hotmail.com); Quickco, Stirling Way, Stirling Corner, Borehamwood, Hertfordshire WD6 2AX (tel 020 8207 3100)

FALKLAND, 15 Viscount of (S 1620); Premier Viscount of Scotland on the Roll; Lucius Edward William Plantagenet Cary; also 15 Lord Cary (S 1620); s of 14 Viscount (d 1984), and his 2 w Constance Mary, *née* Berry (d 1995); *b* 8 May 1935; *Educ* Wellington; *m* 1, 26 April 1962 (m dis 1990), Caroline Anne, da of late Lt Cdr Gerald Butler, DSC, RN; 1 s ((Lucius) Alexander Plantagenet, Master of Falkland b 1963), 2 da (Hon Samantha b 1973, Hon Lucinda b 1974) (and 1 da decd); m 2, 12 Sept 1990, Nicole, da of late Milburn Mackey; 1 s (Hon Charles b 1992); *Heir* s, Master of Falkland; *Career* 2 Lt 8 King's Royal Irish Hussars; journalist, theatrical agent, chartered shipbroker and former chief exec C T Bowring Trading (Hldgs) Ltd; memb: House of Lords Select Ctee on Overseas Trade 1984–85, Jt Select Ctee on Gambling 2003–04; dep chief whip Lib Democrats House of Lords 1988–2002, spokesman on culture, media, sport and tourism 1995–2006; elected hereditary peer under provisions of House of Lords Bill 1999; *Recreations* golf, racing, motorcycling, cinema, reading; *Clubs* Brooks's, Sunningdale Golf; *Style*— The Rt Hon the Viscount of Falkland; ✉ House of Lords, London SW1

FALL, David William; CMG (2007); *b* 10 March 1948; *Educ* St Bartholomew's GS Newbury, New Coll Oxford (MA); *m* 1973, (Margaret) Gwendolyn, *née* Richards; 3 s; *Career* retd diplomat; teacher VSO Bougainville PNG 1970–71, entered HM Dip Serv 1971, language trg Bangkok 1973–76, first sec Bangkok 1976, on loan to Cabinet Office 1977–79, first sec (Chancery) Pretoria and Cape Town 1981–85, first sec then cnsllr FCO 1985–90, dep head of mission and cnsllr (commercial) Bangkok 1990–93, dep high cmmr Canberra 1993–97, ambass to Vietnam 1997–2000, estate modernisation mangr FCO 2000–03, ambass to Thailand 2003–07 (concurrently non-resident ambass to Laos); *Style*— Mr David Fall, CMG

FALLAIZE, Prof Elizabeth; da of John Fallaize, of Staffs, and Jill, *née* Smith; *b* 3 June 1950; *Educ* Univ of Exeter (BA, MA, PhD); *m* 3 Jan 1998, Prof Alan Grafen; 1 da (Alice b 1981), 1 s (Jack b 1984); *Career* lectr in French Univ of Birmingham 1977; Univ of Oxford: fell St John's Coll 1990, lectr 1990, jr proctor 1993–94, prof of French 2002–, pro-vice-chllr (educn) 2005–; tstee Rhodes Tst 2006–; Officier dans l'Ordre des Palmes Académiques 2002; *Books* André Malraux et le monde de la nature (1975), Malraux: La Voie royale (1982), Etienne Carjat and Le Boulevard (1987), The Novels of Simone de Beauvoir (1988), Representations of Belief: Essays in honour of G V Banks (ed jtly,1991), French Women's Writing: Recent Fiction (1993), Simone de Beauvoir: A Critical Reader (1998), French Fiction in the Mitterand Years (with C Davis, 2000), The Oxford Book of French Stories (contrib, 2002); *Style*— Prof Elizabeth Fallaize; ✉ St John's College, Oxford OX1 3JP (tel 01865 277379)

FALLON, Ivan Gregory; s of Padraic Joseph Fallon (d 1974), and Dorothea, *née* Maher (d 1985); *b* 26 June 1944; *Educ* St Peter's Coll Wexford, TCD (BBS); *m* 14 Jan 1967 (m dis 1997), Susan Mary, da of Dr Robert Francis Lurring, of Kidderminster; 2 da (Tania Helen b 1967, Lara Catherine b 1970), 1 s (Padraic Robert b 1974); m 2, 1997, Elizabeth, *née* Rees-Jones; *Career* Irish Times 1964–66, Thomson Provincial Newspapers 1966–67, Daily Mirror 1967–68, Sunday Telegraph 1968–84, city ed Sunday Telegraph 1979–84, dep ed Sunday Times 1984–94, gp editorial dir Independent Group Newspapers Ltd 1994–, memb Bd Independent News & Media plc 1995–, ceo Independent News & Media (South Africa) (Pty) Ltd 1997–2002, ceo Independent News & Media (UK) Ltd 2002–; non-exec chm iTouch plc 2000–, non-exec dir N Brown Gp plc 1994–; FRSA 1989; *Books* DeLorean: The Rise and Fall of a Dream Maker (with James Srodes, 1983), Takeovers (with James Srodes, 1987), The Brothers: The Rise of Saatchi and Saatchi (1988), Billionaire: The Life and Times of Sir James Goldsmith (1991), Paperchase (1993), The Player: The Life of Tony O'Reilly (1994); *Recreations* cycling, tennis; *Clubs* Beefsteak, The Rand (Johannesburg); *Style*— Ivan Fallon, Esq

FALLON, Jane; *Career* prodr: Eastenders (BBC1) 1994, This Life (BBC) 1995 and 1996–97, Undercover Heart (BBC1), Massive Landmarks of the 20th Century (Channel 4 with Nat Theatre of Brent) 1999; exec prodr: Teachers (Channel 4) 2000–01, 2001–02, 2002–03 and 2004, 20 Things to do Before You're 30 (Channel 4) 2002–03, Single (ITV) 2002–03; *Awards* nominations for This Life (Series 1) incl: Best Drama Series BAFTA Awards, Best Drama RTS Awards, Best Drama Indie Awards; for This Life (Series 2) incl: Best Drama RTS Awards, Best Drama Indie Awards, The Indie Indie Awards, Best Drama South Bank Show Awards, Best Original Drama Serial Writers Guild, nominated Best Drama Serial BAFTA Awards; nominations for Undercover Heart incl: Best Drama Serial BAFTA Awards, Best Drama Birmingham Film & TV Festival; nominations for Teachers (Series 1) incl: Best New Drama TV Quick Awards, Best Drama Birmingham Film & TV Festival, Best Drama Series and Best New Programme Broadcast Awards; nominations for Teachers (Series 2) incl: Best Drama Series BAFTA Awards, Best Drama Series RTS Awards, Best Drama Series Monte Carlo TV Festival, Best Drama Series or Serial Broadcast Awards, Best Drama Indie Awards, Best Drama Series Banff Television Festival; for Teachers (Series 3) incl: Best TV Show Emma Awards, nomination Best Drama Series RTS Awards, nomination Best Drama Indie Awards; *Books* Getting Rid of Matthew (2007); *Style*— Ms Jane Fallon; ✉ c/o Macfarlane Chard, 33 Percy Street, London W1T 2DF (tel 020 7636 7750)

FALLON, Michael Cathel; MP; s of Martin Fallon, OBE (d 1994), and Hazel Fallon; *b* 14 May 1952; *Educ* Univ of St Andrews (MA); *m* 1986, Wendy Elizabeth, da of Peter Payne (d 2002), of Holm-on-Spalding Moor, Yorks; 2 s (Peter Martin b 1989, Timothy Bernard b 1990); *Career* advsr to Rt Hon Lord Carrington 1975–77, EEC desk offr CRD 1977–79; MP (Cons): Darlington 1983–92, Sevenoaks 1997–; PPS to Rt Hon Cecil Parkinson as sec of state for energy 1987–88, asst govt whip 1988–90, parliamentary under sec Dept of Educn and Science 1990–92, oppn spokesman on trade and industry 1997–98, oppn spokesman treasy 1998–99; co dir Quality Care Homes plc Darlington 1992–97; dir: Just Learning Ltd 1996–, International Care and Relief 1998–2003, Bannatyne Fitness Ltd 1999–2000, Just Learning Holdings 2001–, Learning Just Ltd 2001–, Just Learning Developments Ltd 2001–, Careshare Ltd 2003–, Collins Stewart Tullett plc 2004–06, Tullett Prebon plc 2006–; *Clubs* Academy; *Style*— Michael Fallon, Esq, MP; ✉ House of Commons, London SW1A 0AA (tel 020 7219 6482, fax 020 7219 6791)

FALLON, Padraic Matthew; s of Padraic Fallon (d 1974), and Dorothea, *née* Maher (d 1985); *b* 21 September 1946; *Educ* St Peter's Coll Wexford, Blackrock Coll Co Dublin, Trinity Coll Dublin (BBS, MA); *m* 8 April 1972, Gillian Elizabeth, da of Graham Hellyer, of N Humberside; 1 s (Jolyon b 1975), 3 da (Nicola b 1977, Harriet, Annabel (twins) b 1980); *Career* fin reporter: Thomson City Office London 1969–70, Daily Mirror 1970–72; City pages Daily Mail 1972–74, seconded as managing ed ME Money Beirut 1974, ed Euromoney Magazine 1974–85; Euromoney Institutional Investor plc (formerly Euromoney Publications plc): dir 1975, dep md 1982, md 1985, chief exec 1989, chm 1992–; exec dir Daily Mail and General Trust plc 1999–; memb Bd Trinity Coll Dublin Fndn; *Publications* A Hymn of the Dawn (2003); *Recreations* country sports; *Clubs* Kildare Street and Univ (overseas memb), Flyfishers', Garrick; *Style*— Padraic Fallon, Esq; ✉ Euromoney Institutional Investor plc, Nestor House, Playhouse Yard, London EC4V 5EX (tel 020 7779 8888/8556, fax 020 7779 8656)

FALLOWELL, Duncan Richard; s of Thomas Edgar Fallowell, of Finchampstead, Berks, and La Croix Valmer, France, and Celia, *née* Waller; *b* 26 September 1948; *Educ* Palmer's Sch, St Paul's, Magdalen Coll Oxford; *Career* author; *Books* Drug Tales (1979), April Ashley's Odyssey (1982), Satyrday (1986), The Underbelly (1987), To Noto (1989), One Hot Summer in St Petersburg (1994), 20th Century Characters (1994), A History of Facelifting (2003), Going As Far As I Can (2008); *Opera Libretto* Gormenghast (1998); *Style*— Duncan Fallowell, Esq; ✉ 44 Leamington Road Villas, London W11 1HT

FALLOWFIELD, Richard Gordon; s of Capt Walter Herman Gordon Fallowfield, RN (d 1954), and Elizabeth Burnett, *née* Baker (d 1956); *b* 25 January 1935; *Educ* Marlborough; *m* 21 Sept 1963, Elfrida Charlotte, da of Sir Timothy Calvert Eden, 8 Bt (d 1963); 2 s (Timothy Gordon b 1965, Nicholas John b 1967), 1 da (Laura Louise b 1974); *Career* Capt Argyll and Sutherland Highlanders 1952–54; dir: Young and Rubicam Inc 1973–80, McCann Erickson Ltd 1980–84, Grandfield Rork Collins (dep chm) 1985–91, Cardew & Co 1991–; memb IPA; *Recreations* squash, tennis, walking, reading; *Style*— Richard Fallowfield, Esq; ✉ 131 Grandison Road, London SW11 6LT; Cardew & Co, 12 Suffolk Street, London SW1Y 4HQ (tel 020 7930 0777)

FANCOURT, Dr Graham John; s of Leonard Frank Fancourt (d 1982), of Gidea Park, Essex, and Iris, *née* Anscombe (d 1994); *b* 23 February 1953; *Educ* Brentwood Sch, Univ of London (MB BS); *m* 22 July 1978, Julie Valerie, da of Leslie Tyler, of Brentwood, Essex; 1 s (Russell Graham b 20 Jan 1992); *Career* conslt physician: Glenfield Hosp, Loughborough Hosp; clinical tutor Univ of Leicester; pubns on respiratory med and physiology of ageing; memb BMA, MRCS 1977, FRCP 1994 (MRCP 1980); *Style*— Dr Graham Fancourt; ✉ University of Leicester Hospitals NHS Trust (Glenfield Hospital), Groby Road, Leicester LE39 9QD (tel 0116 256 3361, e-mail grahamfancourt@aol.com)

FANCOURT, Timothy Miles; QC (2003); s of Philip Fancourt, of Newdigate, Surrey, and Georgina Mary, *née* Brown; *b* 30 August 1964, London; *Educ* Whitgift Sch Croydon, Gonville & Caius Coll Cambridge (MA), Inns of Court Sch of Law; *m* 9 Dec 2000, Emily May Windsor; 1 da (Agatha b 23 April 2007); *Career* called to the Bar Lincoln's Inn 1987; memb Bar Cncl 1996–2001 (vice-chm Standards Ctee 2006–07); *Books* Enforceability of Landlord and Tenant Covenants (1997), Megarry's Assured Tenancies (1999 and 2006); *Recreations* cricket, classical music; *Style*— Timothy Fancourt, Esq, QC; ✉ Falcon Chambers, Falcon Court, London EC4Y 1AA (tel 020 7353 2484, fax 020 7353 1261, e-mail fancourt@falcon-chambers.com)

FANE, Andrew William Mildmay; *b* 9 August 1949; *Educ* Radley, Emmanuel Coll Cambridge (MA); *m* Clare Marx, CBE, FRCS; *Career* chief exec Whitburgh Investments Ltd 1982–92, dir and dep chm Borthwicks plc 1988–92; dep chm English Heritage 2001–04 (cmmr 1995–2004, chm Historic Buildings and Areas Advsy Ctee 1995–2001, chm London Advsy Ctee 1999–2004, chm Audit Ctee 2002–), memb Royal Cmmn on Historical Monuments of England 1999–2003; cncllr Royal Borough of Kensington and Chelsea 1987–94 (chm Planning Ctee); memb Exec Ctee National Trust 2001–05 (memb E Anglia Regnl Ctee 1994–2002); non-exec dir Gt Ormond St Hosp for Children NHS Tst 2001–, chm Special Tstees Great Ormond St Hosp Children's Charity 1999–2007 (assoc tstee 2007–), chm of govrs Framlingham Coll 2001–, memb Cncl Radley Coll 2003– (chm Fndn Bd 2002–), govr Coram Family 2005–, tstee Foundling Museum 2007–, chm Stowe House Preservation Tst 2007–; Suffolk farmer; FCA 1974; *Recreations* conservation; *Style*— Andrew W Fane, Esq; ✉ Hoo House, Hoo, Woodbridge, Suffolk; 64 Ladbroke Road, London W11 3NR (tel and fax 020 7221 2748)

FANE, Hon Julian Charles; s of 14 Earl of Westmorland (d 1948), and Diana (d 1983), da of 4 and last Baron Ribblesdale (d 1925); *b* 25 May 1927; *Educ* Harrow; *m* 1976, Gillian, yr da of John Kidston Swire (d 1983), and sis of Sir John Swire, CBE, DL, *qv*, and Sir Adrian Swire, DL, *qv*; *Career* author; FRSL 1974; *Books* incl: A Letter, Memoir in the Middle of the Journey, Gabriel Young, Tug-of-War, Hounds of Spring, Happy Endings, Revolution Island, Small Change, Morning, Best Friends, Cautionary Tales for Women, Hope Cottage, Eleanor, The Duchess of Castile, His Christmas Box, Memories of my Mother, Gentleman's Gentleman, Money Matters, The Social Comedy, Evening, Tales of Love and War, Byron's Diary, The Stepmother, The Sodbury Crucifix, Damnation, Games of Chance, The Time Diaries, According to Robin, Odd Woman Out, A Doctor's Notes, The Collected Works of Julian Fane Volumes One, Two, Three, Four and Five; *Style*— The Hon Julian Fane, FRSL; ✉ Rotten Row House, Lewes, East Sussex BN7 1TN

FANE, Peter; *Career* farmer and rural practice surveyor; dir: Br Agricultural Bureau Brussels until 1997, Eurinco Ltd, Associated Agricultural and Rural Conslts (AARC); memb: Bd Countryside Agency, Cncl Br Inst of Agricultural Conslts (BIAC), Countryside Policies Panel RICS; *Style*— Peter Fane; ✉ 6 Baker's Field, Dry Drayton, Cambridge CB3 8EG

FANNING, Aengus Aquinas; Arnold P Fanning, of Birr, Co Offaly, and Clara, *née* Connell; *b* 22 April 1947, Tralee, Co Kerry; *Educ* Tralee Christian Bros Sch, UC Cork; *m* 1, 1969, Mary, *née* O'Brien (d 1999); 3 s (Dion b 1972, Evan b 1979, Stephen b 1985); m 2, 2006, Anne Harris, *née* O'Sullivan; *Career* ed Sunday Independent (Ireland) 1984–; *Style*— Aengus Fanning, Esq; ✉ Independent House, 27–32 Talbot Street, Dublin 1 (tel 00 353 705 5333, fax 00 353 705 5770)

FANSON, David Jonathan; s of Gordon Samuel Fanson (d 1995), and Pamela Alleyne, *née* Thomas (d 2006); *b* 18 December 1954, Bristol; *Educ* Queen Elizabeth Hosp Sch Bristol, Avonhurst Sch Bristol, S Bristol Tech Coll, Bristol Poly (BA); *m* 2 March 1996, Heidi Louise, *née* Gould; 2 da (Lauren b 6 Oct 1991, Maia b 6 March 2001), 2 s (Sam b 23 Dec 1996, Josh b 3 Sept 1998); *Career* admitted slr 1985, court and police station duty slr 1987, higher court advocate (criminal) 2006; slr's clerk Trump & Ptnrs 1981–85, asst slr Rodney King 1985–86, asst slr Trump & Ptnrs 1986–87, slr then ptnr Douglas & Ptnrs 1987– (currently sr ptnr); memb Cncl Bristol Law Soc 1988–96 (memb and past chm Criminal Law Ctee), slr rep Bristol Magistrates Court User Gp; past chair: Duke of Edinburgh's Award Scheme, Bristol Support and Liaison Gp; memb Law Soc 1985; *Recreations* taekwon-do (Clifton and Henleaze Club, 4th Kup), playing bridge, family and child related activities; *Style*— David Fanson, Esq; ✉ Douglas & Partners, 116 Grosvenor Road, St Paul's, Bristol BS2 8YA (tel 0117 955 4005, fax 0117 954 0427)

FANTHORPE, Ursula Askham; CBE (2001); da of His Hon Judge Richard Fanthorpe (d 1958), and Winifrid Elsie Askham Redmore (d 1978); *b* 22 July 1929; *Educ* St Catherine's Sch Bramley, St Anne's Coll Oxford (MA), London Inst of Educn (DipEd), Univ of Swansea (Dip Sch Counselling); *Partner* Dr R V Bailey; *Career* head of English Cheltenham Ladies' Coll 1962–70 (asst mistress 1954–62), English teacher Howells Sch Llandaff 1972–73, temp clerical jobs Bristol 1973–74, clerk/receptionist Burden Neurological Hosp Bristol 1974–89; Arts Cncl writer in residence St Martin's Coll Lancaster 1983–85, freelance writer 1987–; contrib to radio and television progs, various workshops and collaborations with artists and musicians; involved with: Nat Tst, CPRE, Compassion in World Farming, Religious Soc of Friends, Poetry Soc; memb: PEN 1980, Soc of Authors 1995; Hon DLitt UWE 1995, Hon PhD Univ of Gloucestershire 2000, Hon DLitt Univ of Bath 2006; hon fell: Sarum Coll, St Anne's Coll Oxford 2003; FRSL 1988; *Awards* Soc of Authors' travelling fellowship 1986, Hawthornden fellowships 1987, 1997 and 2002, Arts Cncl Writers' Award 1994, Soc of Authors' Cholmondeley Award 1995, Queen's Gold Medal for Poetry 2003; *Books* Side Effects (1978), Standing To (1982), Voices Off (1984), A Watching Brief (1987), Neck Verse (1992), Safe as Houses (1995), Consequences (2000), Christmas Poems (2002), Queueing for the Sun (2003), Homing In (2006); anthologies: Selected Poems (1986), Penguin Modern Poets 6 (1996), Double Act (audiobook, with R V Bailey, 1997), Poetry Quartets 5 (audiobook, 1999), Collected Poems (2004); *Style*— U A Fanthorpe, CBE, FRSL; ✉ Culverhay House, Wotton-under-Edge, Gloucestershire GL12 7LS (tel and fax 01453 843105, e-mail fanthorpe_bailey@yahoo.co.uk)

FARAGE, Nigel Paul; MEP (UKIP) SE England; s of Guy Farage, and Barbara Stevens; *b* 3 April 1964; *Educ* Dulwich Coll; *m* 1, July 1988 (m dis 1997), Grainne Clare Hayes; m 2, Nov 1999, Kirsten Mehr; 2 s (Samuel b 21 Jan 1989, Thomas b 28 Nov 1991), 2 da (Victoria b 28 March 2000, Isabelle b 8 Sept 2005); *Career* commodity broker: Drexel

Burnham Lambert 1982–86, Credit Lyonnais Rouse Ltd 1986–93, REFCO Overseas Ltd 1994–2003, Natexis Metals Ltd 2003–04; MEP (UKIP) SE England 1999–, ldr UKIP 2006–, co-pres Independence and Democracy Gp; candidate UK Parl: Eastleigh (by-election) 1994, Salisbury 1997, Bexhill and Battle 2001; candidate European Parl Itchen, Test and Avon 1994; *Recreations* sea angling, 1914–18 military history, proper English pubs; *Clubs* East India; *Style*— Nigel Farage, Esq, MEP; ✉ The Old Grain Store, Church Lane, Lyminster, Littlehampton, West Sussex BN17 7QJ (tel 01903 885573, fax 01903 885574, e-mail ukipse@ukip.org)

FARAJ, Mohammed; s of Faiq Faraj (d 2006), of Baghadad, Iraq, and Hassiba Amin (d 1978); *b* 21 July 1947; *Educ* Coll of Engrg Univ of Baghdad Iraq (BSc), Inst of Planning Studies Univ of Nottingham (MA); *Career* architect; conslt firm Iraq 1968–70, James Cubitt & Ptnrs London 1973–80, conslt Design Works London 1980–; memb: ARB, RIBA 1982, RTPI 1984; *Recreations* tennis, keep fit, photography; *Style*— Mohammed Faraj, Esq; ✉ 75 Christchurch Road, Southend on Sea, Essex SS2 4JW

FARHI, (Musa) Moris; MBE (2001); *b* 1935, Ankara, Turkey; *Educ* American Coll Istanbul (BA), RADA; *m* Nina, *née* Gould; 1 step da (Rachel Sievers); *Career* author; chair Writers in Prison Ctee English PEN 1994–97, chair Writers in Prison Ctee Int PEN 1997–2000; vice-pres Int PEN 2001–; FRGS, FRSL; *Publications* author of numerous TV scripts, The Primitives (film script), From the Ashes of Thebes (stage play); novels: The Pleasure of Your Death (1972), The Last of Days (1983), Journey Through the Wilderness (1989), Children of the Rainbow (1999), Young Turk (2004); poems and short stories published in numerous anthologies and periodicals; *Style*— Moris Farhi, Esq, MBE

FARINGDON, 3 Baron (UK 1916); Sir Charles Michael Henderson; 3 Bt (UK 1902); s of Lt-Col Hon Michael Thomas Henderson (16/5 Lancers, d 1953), 2 gs of 1 Baron; suc unc 1977; *b* 3 July 1937; *Educ* Eton, Trinity Coll Cambridge (BA); *m* 30 June 1959, Sarah Caroline, o da of Maj John Marjoribanks Eskdale Askew, CBE (d 1996), and Lady Susan Alice, *née* Egerton, da of 4 Earl of Ellesmere; 3 s (Hon James b 1961, Hon Thomas b 1966, Hon Angus b 1969), 1 da (Hon Susannah b 1963); *Heir* s, Hon James Henderson; *Career* ptnr Cazenove & Co 1968–96; chm Witan Investment plc 1980–2003; a Lord-in-Waiting to HM The Queen 1998–; chm Bd of Govrs Royal Marsden Hosp 1980–85 (memb 1975–85), hon treas Nat Art-Collections Fund 1985–92, chm Royal Cmmn on the Historical Monuments of England 1994–98, cmmr English Heritage 1998–2001, chm Bd of Mgmnt Inst of Cancer Res 2001–05 (memb 1980–2000); fell Inst of Cancer Res 2000–; *Style*— The Rt Hon the Lord Faringdon; ✉ 28 Brompton Square, London SW3 2AD (fax 020 7589 0724); Buscot Park, Faringdon, Oxfordshire SN7 8BU (e-mail farbuscot@aol.com, website www.buscotpark.com)

FARLEY, Alastair Hugh; s of George Walker Farley (d 1970), of Bovinger, Essex, and Phyllis Mary, *née* Davies (d 1978); *b* 2 January 1946; *Educ* Felsted, Jesus Coll Cambridge (MA); *m* 1, 1971; 2 da (Claire Katharine b 26 Nov 1974, Joanna Helen b 22 June 1980), 1 s (Edward McMurdo b 20 Jan 1976); m 2, 1995; 2 step s (Michael Reid Winn b 23 April 1975, Peter Matthew Winn b 30 June 1978); *Career* Norton Rose: articled clerk 1968–71, admitted slr 1971, asst slr 1971–73, ptnr 1974–82; fndr ptnr Watson, Farley & Williams 1982–2001 (sr advsr 2001–); sr advsr Chandris Gp 2001–, chm Seaguard Offshore Ltd 2002–; non-exec dir: Close Brothers Gp plc 1993–2004, Opus Portfolio Ltd 2001–, Nautilus Hldgs Ltd 2006–; memb Law Soc 1971; memb Ct City of London Univ 2001–; Liveryman City of London Slrs' Co, Prime Warden Worshipful Co of Shipwrights 2003–04 (Warden 1999–2003); *Recreations* shooting, tennis, country pursuits; *Clubs* Boodle's; *Style*— Alastair Farley, Esq; ✉ Watson, Farley & Williams, 15 Appold Street, London EC2A 2HB (tel 020 7814 8000, fax 020 7814 8141, e-mail afarley@wfw.com)

FARLEY, Paul James; s of James Matthew Farley (d 1986), of Liverpool, and Thelma Irene, *née* Harris; *b* 5 June 1965; *Educ* Mabel Fletcher Tech Coll Liverpool, Chelsea Sch of Art (Christopher Head drawing scholar, BA); *m* 2006, Carole Freda Romaya; *Career* poet; writer in residence The Wordsworth Tst 2000–02, reader in poetry Lancaster Univ 2005– (lectr 2002–05); fell Royal Literary Fund 2000–02; winner Arvon/Observer Int Poetry Competition 1995, Geoffrey Dearmer Meml Prize 1997, Forward Prize for Best First Collection 1998, Sunday Times Young Writer of the Year 1999, Somerset Maugham Award 1999, Writer's Award Arts Cncl of Eng and Wales 2000, Whitbread Poetry Award 2002, Next Generation Poets 2004, Forward Prize for Best Individual Poem 2005; *Publications* The Boy from the Chemist is Here to See You (1998), The Ice Age (2002), When Louis Met George (radio play, 2003), Tramp in Flames (2006), Distant Voices, Still Lives (2006), John Clare: Poet to Poet (ed, 2007); *Recreations* photography, birding, supporting Liverpool FC; *Style*— Paul Farley, Esq; ✉ c/o Department of English and Creative Writing, Bowland College, Lancaster University, Lancaster LA1 4YW (e-mail mail@paulfarley.com); c/o Peter Straus, Rogers, Coleridge & White, 20 Powis Mews, London W11 1JN (tel 020 7221 3717)

FARMAN, Ian Glencairn Crisp; s of late Stuart C Farman, and late Joan G, *née* Wallace; *b* 27 October 1947; *Educ* Rugby, Univ of Southampton (LLB); *m* Susan Margaret, da of Maj-Gen P B Foster, RA; 4 da (Anna b 1975, Jenny b 1977, Christina b 1982, Isabel b 1984); *Career* Leslie & Godwin 1970–72; dir: MPA Ltd 1972–84, William M Mercer Ltd 1984–99, Mercer Consulting Gp Inc 1999–2002; ret; slr Supreme Court 1975–; chair of corp Chichester Coll 2004–; FRSA; *Recreations* sailing, tennis, wine, shooting; *Style*— Ian Farman, Esq; ✉ Little Meadow Cottage, Charlton, Chichester, West Sussex PO18 0HU

FARMER, Dr (Edwin) Bruce; CBE (1997); s of Edwin Bruce Farmer, and Doris Farmer; *b* 18 September 1936; *Educ* King Edward's Birmingham, Univ of Birmingham (BSc, PhD); *m* 1962, Beryl Ann; 1 da (Amanda b 1969), 1 s (Andrew b 1967); *Career* dir and gen mangr Brico Metals 1967–69; md: Brico Engineering 1970–76 (tech dir 1969–70), Wellworthy Ltd 1976–81; The Morgan Crucible Co plc: dir 1981–, gp md and chief exec 1983–97, chm 1998–2003; chm: Allied Colloids plc 1996–98, Southern Electric plc 1998, Devro plc 1998–2001, Bodycote Int plc 1999–2002, Scottish and Southern Energy plc 2000–05 (dep chm 1998–2000); dir: Scapa Gp plc 1993–99, Foreign & Colonial Smaller Companies plc 1999–; pres Inst of Materials 1999–2002, chm Mgmnt Bd IMMM 2002–04, chm Communications Bd IMMM 2006–; memb Fin Ctee Cancer Research UK; Platinum Medal IMMM 2004; Freeman City of London, Liveryman Worshipful Co of Scientific Instrument Makers; FREng, FIMMM, FRSA, CIMgt, CEng; *Recreations* music, hill walking, cricket; *Clubs* Athenaeum; *Style*— Dr Bruce Farmer, CBE, FREng; ✉ Weston House, Bracken Close, Wonersh, Surrey GU5 0QS (tel 01483 898182)

FARMER, Ian Peter; s of Brian John Farmer, and Alice Kathleen, *née* Tatchell; *b* 25 March 1962; *Educ* Univ of South Africa; *m* 1, 7 Sept 1985; 2 s (Chase Patrick b 31 Oct 1986, Kyle Leonard b 9 Aug 1989); m 2, 7 May 1994, Diane, *née* Chilangwa; 1 da (Alice Chilangwa b 24 Feb 1995), 1 s (Hugh Mutale b 12 June 1997); *Career* CA S Africa 1985; audit sr Campbell Bude Brown & Stewart South Africa 1980–85, audit sr Coopers & Lybrand London 1985–86, treasy accountant Lonrho plc 1988–89 (asst gp accountant 1986–87), regnl fin controller Lonrho Zambia Ltd 1990–95, fin dir Lonmin Platinum 1995–2000, exec dir and chief strategic offr Lonmin plc 2001–; pres Int Platinum Assoc 2005–06; Gleasons Deal of the Year South Africa 2004; *Style*— Ian Farmer, Esq; ✉ Lonmin plc, 4 Grosvenor Place, London SW1X 7YL (tel 020 7201 6029, fax 020 7201 6100, e-mail ian.farmer@lonmin.com)

FARMER, His Hon Judge (Pryce) Michael; QC (1995); s of Sarah Jane Farmer, *née* Owen; *b* 20 May 1944; *Educ* Ysgol Dyffryn Nantlle Penygroes, King's Coll London (BA); *m* 31 March 1975, Olwen Mary, da of late Rev Griffith John Roberts; 1 s (Siôn ap Mihangel b 17 July 1976), 1 da (Olwen Mair Mihangel b 1 Nov 1979); *Career* called to the Bar Gray's Inn 1972 (bencher 2005); in practice Wales & Chester Circuit 1972–, recorder of the Crown Court 1995– (jr 1991–93, asst recorder 1993–95), circuit judge (Wales & Chester Circuit) 2001–; head of Chambers Sedan House Chester 1995–96, in main practice Goldsmith Building London 1995–2001, designated family judge N Wales 2004, dep Welsh language liaison judge Wales & Chester Circuit 2004; ind chm Special Review Ctee Isle of Anglesey CC 1998–99; pt/t pres Mental Health Appeal Tbnl 2000; *Recreations* reading, gardening, music, watching rugby football; *Clubs* Reform, Clwb Rygbi yr Wyddgrug (pres 2001–05); *Style*— His Hon Judge Michael Farmer, QC; ✉ Rhyl County Court, Clwyd Street, Rhyl LL18 3LA (tel 01745 352940)

FARMER, Paul David Charles; s of David Farmer, and Ann Farmer (d 1998); *b* 8 October 1966, Oxford; *Educ* The Oratory Reading, St Peter's Coll Oxford; *m* 1993, Claire Dwyer; 2 s (Benedict b 10 Sept 1998, Thomas b 4 Jan 2003); *Career* asst dir Clerkenwell Heritage Centre 1989–90, communications mangr The Samaritans 1992–97 (press offr 1990–92), dir of public affrs Rethink 1997–2006, chief exec Mind 2006–; chair Mental Health Alliance 1999–2006; tstee: Directory of Social Change, Mental Health Providers Forum; memb BBC Appeals Advsy Ctee; *Recreations* cricket, football, film; *Style*— Paul Farmer, Esq; ✉ Mind, 15–19 Broadway, Stratford, London E15 4BQ (tel 020 8215 2262, fax 020 8522 1745, e-mail p.farmer@mind.org.uk)

FARMER, Peter; s of Kenneth Carl Farmer, and Phylis Marie Farmer (d 1973); *Career* artist and theatre designer; *Exhibitions* Redfern Gallery London 1961, Mercury Gallery London 1964, 1965, 1970 and 1973, Wright Hepburn Gallery London 1969, Lasson Gallery London 1974, 1975 and 1977, Cat Gallery Copenhagen 1975, Meredith Long Galleries Houston 1980, Royal Festival Hall 1983; *Theatre* designs incl: On a Clear Day you can see Canterbury (Stratford East) 1962, Anyone for England? (Lyric Theatre Hammersmith) 1964, The Night of the Iguana (Savoy Theatre London) 1965, The Physicists (Crest Theatre Toronto) 1965, Hayfever (Crest Theatre Toronto) 1965, Man and Superman (Vaudeville Theatre London) 1966, Kean (Globe Theatre London) 1971, Dame Edith Evans and Friends (Haymarket Theatre London) 1974, What Every Woman Knows (Albery Theatre London) 1976, A Woman of No Importance (Chichester Festival) 1981; *Ballet* Sadlers Wells Royal Ballet: The Dream 1966, Giselle 1968, Arpege 1975, Pandora 1976, Paquitta 1981, Theme & Variations 1988; London Festival Ballet: Night Shadow 1967, Les Sylphides 1967, Meadowlark 1968, Three Preludes 1972, Cinderella 1974, Bourrée Fantastique 1978, The Storm 1981, Verdi Variations 1981, That Certain Feeling 1984; London Contemporary Dance Theatre: Conversation Piece 1970, Eclipse 1970, Stages 1971, Cantabille 1971, Sky 1971, Consolations of the Rising Moon 1971, Troy Games 1974, Dressed to Kill 1974, No-Mans Land 1974, Meetings and Partings 1975, Stone Garden 1989, In Memory 1989, Metamorphoses 1989, Crescendo 1989; Washington Nat Ballet: Sleeping Beauty 1971, Graduation Ball 1973, Raymonda 1974; Houston Ballet: The Nutcracker 1972 and 1977, Coppélia 1973, Cupiditas 1981, Peer Gynt 1981, Bartok Concerto 1987, Manon 1993; New London Ballet: Othello 1974, Intimate Voices 1974, Simorge 1975, Months 1975, Soft Blue Shadows 1976, Tristan & Isolde 1979; Australian Ballet: Anna Karenina 1977, Three Musketeers 1980, Manon 1993, Butterfly 1995; Inouie Ballet Tokyo: Sleeping Beauty 1977, Coppélia 1990, Swan Lake 1995; Northern Ballet Theatre: Les Sylphides 1978, Cinderella 1979 and 1982, Faust Divertimento 1982, Brahms Love Songs 1983; Rome Opera House: Soft Blue Shadows 1979, Daydreams 1979, Faust 1979, The Nutcracker 1991; London City Ballet: Romeo & Juliet 1985, La Sylphides 1987, La Traviata 1989, Giselle 1994; Birmingham Royal Ballet: Divertimento No 15 1989, Les Sylphides 1991, Street 1994, Coppélia 1995, Birthday Offering 1995; Hong Kong Ballet: Tales of Hoffman 1991, Graduation Ball 1991, Swan Lake 1996; other credits incl: Agrionia (London Dance Theatre) 1964, Giselle (Ballet Rambert), Giselle (Stuttgart Ballet) 1966, Giselle (Cologne Opera House) 1967, Beauty and the Beast (Western Theatre Ballet) 1967, Giselle/Danse Macabre (Western Theatre Ballet) 1968, Sleeping Beauty (Cologne Opera House) 1968, Chopiana (Royal Danish Ballet) 1972, Mendelssohn Symphony (American Ballet Theatre) 1973, Sleeping Beauty (Royal Ballet) 1973, Giselle (Munich Opera House) 1974, Othello (Scottish Ballet Theatre) 1974, Running Figures (Ballet Rambert) 1975, Sleeping Beauty (Ballet Int) 1976, The Nutcracker (Ballet Int) 1976, Namoua (Stuttgart Ballet) 1976, Sleeping Beauty (Munich Staatsoper) 1976, Giselle (Dutch Nat Ballet) 1977, Giselle (Frankfurt Opera House) 1980, Konigsmark (NZ Ballet) 1980, Giselle (Rio de Janeiro) 1982, The Nutcracker (Cincinnati Ballet) 1987, The Great Gatsby (Pittsburgh Ballet Theatre) 1987 and 1996, Coppélia (Nat Ballet of Portugal) 1989, Swan Lake (Royal Winnipeg Ballet) 1989, The Nutcracker (Pittsburgh Ballet Theatre) 1990 and 1991, Winter Dreams (Royal Ballet) 1991, Manon (Vienna Ballet) 1993, Raymonde Act III (Eng Nat Ballet) 1993, The Nutcracker (Hong Kong Ballet) 1997, Swan Lake (Eng Nat Ballet) 1999, Manon (Marinsky Theatre St Petersburg) 2000, Giselle (K Ballet Japan) 2001, Giselle (Berlin Staatsoper) 2001, Swan Lake (Rio Opera House) 2001; *Style*— Peter Farmer, Esq; ✉ Flat C, 23 New Road, London E1 1HE

FARMER, Prof Richard Donald Trafford; s of Hereward Anderton Farmer (d 1987), and Kate Elizabeth Farmer (d 1986); *b* 14 September 1941; *Educ* Ashville Coll Harrogate, KCL (MB BS), Univ of Leiden (PhD); *m* 20 Nov 1965, Teresa, da of Kenneth Roland Rimer, of Beckenham, Kent; 2 s (Dominic Michael Trafford b 5 Sept 1966, Christopher Kenneth Trafford b 24 June 1968); *Career* lectr Univ of Birmingham 1971–74, sr lectr Westminster Med Sch 1974–84, Boerhaave prof Univ of Leiden 1985, sr lectr Charing Cross and Westminster Med Sch 1986, prof of community med Univ of London 1986–98 (latterly head Public Health & Primary Care Dept Imperial Coll Sch of Med Chelsea & Westminster Hosp), prof of public health Euro Inst of Health and Med Scis Univ of Surrey 1998–, prof of epidemiology Postgrad Med Sch Univ of Surrey 2000; memb Bd Int Soc for Pharmacoepidemiology; MRCS 1963, LRCP 1965, MRCGP 1968, MFCM 1979, FFPHM 1989, FFPM 2002 (MFPM 2000), FSS, FRSM; *Books* Lecture Notes on Epidemiology and Public Health Medicine (1977, 5 edn 2003), The Suicide Syndrome (1979), Epidemiology of Diseases (1982); *Style*— Prof Richard Farmer; ✉ Postgraduate Medical School, University of Surrey, Stirling House, Surrey Research Park, Surrey GU2 7DJ (tel 01483 579927)

FARMER, Robin Liempster; OBE (2002); s of Rev Alfred Victor Farmer (d 1977), of Bury St Edmunds, and Kathleen May, *née* Hand (d 1953); *b* 10 March 1933; *Educ* Radley, ChCh Oxford (MA); *Career* Nat Serv 2/Lt 1 Bn Suffolk Regt, served Malaya 1951–52, Trieste 1953; Imperial Chemical Industries: ICI (India) 1956–57, various positions ICI UK 1957–78, gen mangr Mond Div 1978–87, ICI Chemicals & Polymers Ltd 1987–91, dir ICI (China) Ltd 1982–91, associated with 3 Queen's Awards for Export; chm: Aintree Hosps NHS Tst 1991–96, Mid Cheshire NHS Tst 1996–2004; Knight Order of St Lazarus of Jerusalem 2000; *Recreations* reading, music, wines and food; *Style*— Robin L Farmer, Esq, OBE

FARMER, Sir Thomas (Tom); kt (1997), CBE (1990); s of John Farmer, and Margaret, *née* Mackie; *b* 10 July 1940, Edinburgh; *Educ* Holy Cross Acad Edinburgh; *m* 10 Sept 1966, Anne Drury, da of James Scott; 1 da (Sally Anne (Mrs Nigel Swycher) b 4 July 1967), 1 s (John Philip b 14 June 1968); *Career* sales rep 1961–64, fndr Tyre and Accessory Supplies 1964–68, dir Albany Tyre Service 1968–70, fndr md Kwik-Fit Holdings Ltd 1971–84, chm and chief-exec Kwik-Fit Holdings plc 1984–99; non-exec dir MyTravel Gp plc 1994–; chm: Duke of Edinburgh Award, Scottish Business in the Community; memb Bd: Scottish Enterprise, Investors in People; memb Ct of Regents RCS(Ed); Carnegie Medal for Philanthrophy 2005; KCSG 1997; Officier Orde van Orange-Nassau (Holland), Knight Cross Order of Merit (Poland); *Recreations* swimming, tennis, skiing; *Style*— Sir Tom Farmer, CBE

F

FARNELL, Graeme; s of Wilson Elliot Farnell (d 1998), and Mary Montgomerie Wishart, *née* Crichton (d 1987); *b* 11 July 1947; *Educ* Loughborough GS, Univ of Edinburgh (MA), London Film Sch; *m* 19 July 1969, Jennifer Gerda, da of William Holroyd Huddlestone, of Nottingham; 1 s (Paul b 1983); *Career* asst keeper Museum of E Anglian Life Stowmarket 1973–76, curator Inverness Museum and Art Gallery 1976–79, dir Scot Museums Cncl 1979–86, DG Museums Assoc 1986–89; dir: Museum Devpt Co 1989–94, IMS Publications 1994–96, Heritage Development Ltd 1996–, Heritage Business International 2005–; MIMgt, FMA, FSA Scot; *Publications* New Heritage, Heritage Retail, Heritage Restoration, Heritage 365 magazine; *Websites* HeritageBusiness.net, Heritage365.com; *Recreations* Baroque opera, contemporary music, photography; *Style*— Graeme Farnell, Esq; ✉ Heritage Development, Witan Court, 301 Upper Fourth Street, Central Milton Keynes MK9 1EH (tel 01908 395292, fax 01908 395262, e-mail info@heritage365.com)

FARNHAM, Brian Lawrence; s of Oliver Farnham (d 1991), and Florence Eunice, *née* Dear (d 2000); *b* 31 May 1938; *Educ* St Dunstan's Coll Catford, Univ of Reading (BA); *m* 1 (m dis), Jean Margaret Wallace; 3 da (Caitlin Emma b 1967, Abigail Sara b 1971, Joanna Louise b 1971); m 2, 24 May 1989, Moira Suzanne; 1 da (Alice Sophie Rose b 1986), 1 s (Harry Daniel Oliver b 1991); *Career* 2 Lt Royal Fusiliers 1957; film and TV dir; credits incl: Rock Follies (BAFTA Award 1976), My Cousin Rachel, Poirot, The Bill, I'm a Dreamer Montreal (Ewart Biggs Award), All Quiet on the Preston Front, Rosemary and Thyme; *Style*— Brian Farnham, Esq; ✉ 203 Upper Chobham Road, Camberley, Surrey GU15 1HA (tel 01276 22341 and 01276 684727, fax 01276 684727, mobile 07831 700632)

FARNISH, Christine; da of Harry Farnish, of Ipswich, and Agnes Monica, *née* Smith; *b* 21 April 1950, Ipswich; *Educ* Ipswich HS, Univ of Manchester (BSc), UCL (MSc); *m* 1, Jan 1976 (m diss); 3 s (Sam b 10 June 1976, Jack b 25 March 1978, Harry b 27 Jan 1981); m 2, March 1992, John Hayes; 1 da (Hannah b 12 June 1986); *Career* asst chief exec Cambridge City Cncl 1987–94, consumer affrs dir then dep DG Oftel 1994–98, consumer affrs dir FSA 1998–2002, ceo Nat Assoc of Pension Funds 2002–06, dir public policy Barclays 2006–; non-exec dir: ASA 2000–, OFT 2002–06; memb Advsy Bd ING Direct 2004–06; govr Pensions Policy Inst, tstee FSA Pension Scheme; former non-exec dir Papworth NHS Tst; author of numerous articles in fin services and pensions jls, magazines and newspapers; *Recreations* mountain walking, swimming, choral singing, football (Spurs); *Style*— Ms Christine Farnish; ✉ Barclays plc, 1 Churchill Place, London E14 5HP

FAROOKHI, Imtiaz; s of Mumtaz Farookhi (d 1968), and Anwar, *née* Razvi; *b* 17 January 1951; *m* (m dis 2005); 1 da (Mariam Eleanor b 16 Jan 1986), 2 s (Luke David Liaquat b 28 Jan 1988, Eden Anwar b 18 Oct 2005); *Career* CEGB 1976–79: parly branch graduate trainee then admin offr; London Borough of Camden 1979–83: sr admin offr then princ admin offr; asst chief exec London Borough of Hackney 1983–88, head of co-ordination City of Wakefield MDC 1988–89, dir of policy and admin London Borough of Southwark 1989–91, chief exec Leicester City Cncl 1991–96, chief exec National House Building Cncl 1997–; chm Strategic Forum for Construction Skills 2004–; Bd memb: Leicestershire TEC 1992–97, East Midlands Devpt 1994–96, Environment Agency 1995–97, Leicestershire Businesslink 1995–97, British Urban Regeneration Assoc 1999–, Construction Skills Cncl 2004–, SE England Devpt Agency 2004–, London Thames Gateway Urban Devpt Corp 2004–; tstee Common Purpose 2000–04; memb: FEFC 1998–2001 (memb Widening Participation Ctee 1994–97), BBA 1999–, Learning and Skills Cncl 2001–05, SEEDA 2004–; FRSA 1993; *Publications* author of various learned articles in Political Quarterly, Local Government Chronicle and Municipal Journal; *Recreations* supporting QPR, fitness, food and wine, parenting; *Style*— Imtiaz Farookhi, Esq; ✉ National House Building Council, Buildmark House, Chiltern Avenue, Amersham, Buckinghamshire HP6 5AP (tel 01494 735218, fax 01494 735293)

FARQUHAR, Sir Michael FitzRoy Henry; 7 Bt (GB 1796), of Cadogan House, Middlesex; s of Lt-Col Sir Peter Walter Farquhar, 6 Bt, DSO, OBE (d 1986), and Elizabeth Evelyn, *née* Hurt (d 1983); *b* 29 June 1938; *Educ* Eton, RAC Cirencester; *m* 29 June 1963, Veronica Geraldine, er da of Patrick Rowan Hornidge (d 1983), of Helford Passage, Cornwall; 2 s (Charles Walter FitzRoy b 21 Feb 1964, Edward Peter Henry b 6 Dec 1966); *Heir* s, Charles Farquhar; *Recreations* fishing, shooting, gardening; *Clubs* White's, Shikar; *Style*— Sir Michael Farquhar, Bt; ✉ Manor Farm, West Kington, Chippenham, Wiltshire SN14 7JG (tel 01249 782671, fax 01249 782877)

FARQUHAR, Peter Guy Powlett; s of Guy Farquhar (d 1962), and Daphne Mary Christian, *née* Henry (d 1983); *b* 13 February 1936; *Educ* Eton; *m* 1, 1961, Rosemary Anne Eaton, da of Eaton Hammond, of Wroxham, Norfolk; 2 s (Richard Charles b 7 April 1962, James Edward b 6 Dec 1963); m 2, Carolyn, da of D Graham Robertson, of Sydney, Aust; 2 s (George Peter b 29 Feb 1980, Hugh Graham b 7 June 1984), 2 da (Jane Elizabeth b 12 Dec 1982 d 1983, Alice Rose Jane b 17 Nov 1987); *Career* 2 Lt KRRC (60th Rifles); stable lad 1954–59: St Albans Stables, Woodlands and Plantation Studs Newmarket, Sledmere Stud Yorkshire, Woodlands Stud NSW Aust; asst PR offr H J Heinz Company 1959–66, md Hill & Knowlton UK Ltd 1969–79 (sr exec 1967–69), fndr and dir Ludbrook Ltd 1979–2000, md Fleishman-Hillard Europe Ltd 1987–94, chm Fleishman-Hillard UK Ltd 1987–94, memb Int Advsy Bd Fleishman-Hillard Inc 1994–97; *Recreations* racing, cartophily; *Style*— Peter Farquhar, Esq; ✉ 17 Netheravon Road, Chiswick, London W4 2NA (tel 020 8747 1829)

FARQUHAR-MUNRO, John; JP, MSP; *b* 26 August 1934; *Educ* Plockton HS, Sea Training Coll, Merchant Marine Coll Sharpness; *m* 1962, Cecilia; 1 da (Shanea Jane), 1 s (Duncan Niall); *Career* merchant marine serv 1951–61, plant fitter Kings Road Construction 1961–65, manager contracting co 1965–75, self-employed as heavy haulage, bus operator, civil engrg and quarrying contractor 1975–93, crofter 1971–97; assessor Crofters Cmmn 1977–89; dir Highland Opportunites Ltd; chair: Shipping Advsy Ctee Caledonian MacBrayne, Rail Devpt Partnership, Fishery Harbours Mgmnt, Gaelic Ctee Highland Regnl Cncl 1978–82; memb: Univ of the Highlands and Islands Fndn, Highland Cncl 1995–; past memb Electricity Consultative Cncl; local govt cncllr 1966–74, district cncllr Skye and Lochalsh 1974–90, MSP (Lib Dem) Ross, Skye & Inverness West 1999–; convenor Skye and Lochalsh DC 1984–98, chair Highland Cncl Tport Services Ctee 1995–; *Style*— John Farquhar-Munro, Esq, MSP; ✉ The Scottish Parliament, Edinburgh EH99 1SP

FARQUHARSON OF FINZEAN, Angus Durie Miller; OBE (1995), JP; s of Dr Hugo Durie Newton Miller (d 1984), and Elsie Miller, *née* Duthie (d 1995); *b* 27 March 1935; *Educ* Trinity Coll Glenalmond, Downing Coll Cambridge (MA); *m* 1 July 1961, Alison Mary Farquharson of Finzean, da of William Marshall Farquharson-Lang, CBE, 14 Laird of Finzean; 1 da (Jean b 1962), 2 s (Donald b 1963, Andrew b 1967); *Career* factor Finzean Estate; memb Cncl Scottish Landowners' Fedn 1980–88; memb Regnl Advsy Ctee Forestry Cmmn: E and N Scotland 1980–94, N Conservancy 1985–94 (chm 1993–94); memb: Nature Conservancy Cncl Ctee for Scotland 1986–91, Red Deer Cmmn 1986–92, NE Ctee Scottish Natural Heritage (SNH) 1992–94; pres Kincardine/Deeside Scouts; elder and gen tstee Church of Scotland; HM Lord-Lt Aberdeenshire 1998– (DL 1984, Vice Lord-Lt 1987–98); FRICS 1985; OStJ 2002; *Recreations* shooting, gardening, forestry, nature conservation; *Clubs* New (Edinburgh); *Style*— Angus Farquharson of Finzean, OBE, OStJ; ✉ Glenferrick Lodge, Finzean, Banchory, Aberdeenshire AB31 6NG (tel 01330 850229, fax 01330 850469)

FARQUHARSON-ROBERTS, Surgn Rear Adm Michael Atholl (Mike); CBE (2001); s of Rev Donald Arthur Farquharson-Roberts (d 2000), and Violet, *née* Crooks (d 1984); *b* 23 September 1947, Belfast; *Educ* Dorking Co GS, Westminster Hosp Sch of Med Univ of London (MB BS), KCL (MA); *m* 1974, Jean Neilsen, *née* Harding; 2 s (Guy b 1977, David b 1979), 2 da (Katherine b 1983, Megan b 1986), guardian to bro's c (Stuart b 1975, Charlotte b 1978); *Career* registrar in orthopaedic surgery Royal Naval Hosps Plymouth and Haslar then sr registrar in orthopaedics Nuffield Orthopaedic Centre Oxford, Addenbrookes Hosp Cambridge and Royal Nat Orthopaedic Hosp 1973–83, conslt in orthopaedic surgery RNH Haslar 1983, conslt advsr in orthopaedic surgery to Med DG (Naval) 1989, def conslt advsr in orthopaedic surgery to Surgn Gen 1996–2000, RCDS 2001, dir med ops (Navy) 2002–03, Surgn Rear Adm 2003, med DG (Naval) 2003–07; memb Intercollegiate Specialist Advsy Ctee in Orthopaedics 1996–2000; govr Royal Star and Garter Home; Errol Eldridge Prize 1982; accredited Jt Ctee of Higher Surgical Trg 1983; Freeman Soc of Apothecaries 2006; FRCS 1976, FBOA 1983, FRSM 2003, OStJ; *Publications* Ballistic Trauma (contrib, 1997); author of articles in learned journals; *Recreations* military history, model-making (ships); *Clubs* Army and Navy; *Style*— Surgn Rear Adm Mike Farquharson-Roberts, CBE; ✉ 45 Bury Road, Gosport, Hampshire PO12 3UE

FARR, David; *Career* dir and writer; artistic dir Gate Theatre 1995–98 (directed productions incl: Danton's Death, Leonce and Lena, Candide, The Barbarous Comedies, The Boat Plays, The Great Highway and Seven Doors), jt artistic dir Bristol Old Vic 2003–05 (directed productions incl: A Midsummer Night's Dream (TMA Award Best Dir 2003), Comedy of Errors, Paradise Lost (also writer), Loot, Twelfth Night, The Odyssey (also West Yorkshire Playhouse)), artistic dir Lyric Hammersmith 2005–; *Theatre* as dir incl: Powder Her Face (The Almeida) 1995, Snatched By the Gods (The Almeida) 1996, The Winter's Tale (Gavella Theatre Zagreb) 1998, The Taming of the Shrew (Nottingham Playhouse) 2002, Coriolanus (Swan Theatre RSC and Old Vic) 2002, Julius Caesar (Swan Theatre RSC and regional tour) 2004; as writer incl: Elton John's Glasses (Watford Palace Theatre and nat tour) 1997, Night of the Soul (RSC) 1999, The Danny Crowe Show (Bush Theatre) 2001, The Queen Must Die (Shell Connections) 2003, Great Expectations (Bristol Old Vic) 2003, The Trial (NT) 2004; as writer and dir incl: Slight Possesion 1991, Max Klapper - A Life in Pictures (The Electric Cinema) 1995, The Nativity (Young Vic Theatre) 2000, Joan of Arc's Thoughts on the English as she Burns at the Stake (RSC at the Young Vic Theatre) 2001, Crime and Punishment in Dalston (Arcola Theatre) 2002 (broadcast on BBC Radio 3), Night of the Soul (RSC at the Pit) 2002, The UN Inspector (NT) 2005; *Television* writer Spooks (several episodes, BBC) 2005–06; *Plays* The Odyssey, Crime and Punishment in Dalston, Great Expectations, Elton John's Glasses, The Nativity, Night of the Soul, The Danny Crowe Show, The UN Inspector; *Style*— David Farr, Esq; ✉ c/o PFD, Drury House, 34–43 Russell Street, London WC2B 5HA (tel 020 7344 1000, fax 020 7836 9543)

FARR, John Robert; s of Lt Col John E D Farr, MBE (d 1993), and Ank J W M, *née* Bol; *b* 16 March 1949, Kuala Lumpur, Malaya; *Educ* Beaumont Coll Univ of London (LLB); *m* 1, 21 June 1975 (m dis 1987), Caroline, *née* Masefield; 1 da (Sarah b 15 Nov 1977), 2 s (Richard b 29 Oct 1979, Timothy b 20 April 1982); m 2, 16 April 1994, Katherine S, *née* Ferris; 1 s (Henry b 2 June 1996), 1 da (Emily b 16 April 1998); *Career* admitted slr 1974; slr specialising in employment laws particularly contentious matters and corporate poaching of teams; Herbert Smith: joined Litigation Dept 1972, ptnr 1982–, fndr and head Employment Gp 1991–; commercial litigation incl Oil to Rhodesia Enquiry and the Iranian bank litigation; contrib to various pubns on employment law; memb: Law Soc 1974, Employment Lawyers Association, European Employment Lawyers Assoc, City of London Law Soc (memb Employment Law Ctee); tstee Royal Medical Benevolent Fund 2006–; Freeman City of London; *Recreations* hill walking, gardening, travel, cultural and sporting events; *Clubs* Reform, Bishopsgate Ward; Richmond FC; *Style*— John Farr, Esq; ✉ Herbert Smith, Exchange House, Primrose Street, London EC2A 2HS (tel 020 7374 8000, fax 020 7374 0888, e-mail john.farr@herbertsmith.com)

FARR, Nigel Jonathan; s of Julian Farr, and Helen Patricia, *née* Owen; *b* 27 May 1962, London; *Educ* Wimbledon Coll, Gonville & Caius Coll Cambridge (MA); *Career* admitted slr 1987; specialises in investment funds; ptnr Herbert Smith 1994– (joined 1985); *Recreations* wine, food, cinema, sport; *Style*— Nigel Farr; ✉ Herbert Smith, Exchange House, Primrose Street, London EC2A 2HS (tel 020 7466 2360, fax 020 7374 0888, e-mail nigel.farr@herbertsmith.com)

FARR, Richard Peter; s of Peter James Farr (d 1987), and Josephine Farr; *b* 8 July 1954; *Educ* Bedford Sch, Ecole de Commerce Neuchâtel, Univ of Reading (BSc); *m* 1979 (m dis 2003), Susan Jane, *née* Fairburn; *Career* surveyor Knight Frank and Rutley 1977–80, sr surveyor Richard Ellis 1980–83, assoc dir Greycoat Gp plc 1983–88, chief exec New Cavendish Estates plc 1988–90, chief exec Park Square Developments 1990–; dir: Adam Estates 1994–, The Fantastic Entertainment Co 1999–; Freeman City of London; FRICS; *Recreations* skiing, vintage Bentleys; *Style*— Richard Farr, Esq; ✉ Adams Estates Limited, 8 Oak Hill Park Mews, London NW3 7LH (tel 07776 187735, e-mail richard.farr@virgin.net)

FARR, Sue; *b* 29 February 1956; *Educ* Sheffield HS for Girls GPDST, Univ of Reading (BA); *m* 1979; *Career* graduate trainee Northern Foods plc 1977–79, sr conslt Kraushar And Eassie (KAE) Ltd (mktg consultancy) 1979–83, account dir BSB Dorland (advtg agency) 1983–85, new business devpt dir Wight Collins Rutherford Scott 1986–90, dir of corp communications Thames Television plc 1990–93 (seconded as launch mktg dir UK Gold 1992–93); BBC: head of mktg BBC Network Radio 1993–96, dir of mktg and communications BBC Broadcast 1997–99, dir of public service mktg 1999–2001; md Golin/Harris Int (London office and EMEA) 2001–02, chm Advtg and Mktg Servs Div Chime Communications plc 2003–; non-exec dir New Look plc 1994–96; tstee Historic Royal Palaces 2007–; memb Business in the Community; Mktg Soc: fell 1987, first woman chair 1991–93; memb Mktg Gp of GB (chm 1990–92), Forum UK, Women's Advtg Club of London; Advertising Woman of the Year 1998; FRSA; *Style*— Mrs Sue Farr; ✉ Chime Communications, 14 Curzon Street, London W1J 5HN (tel 020 7861 8549)

FARRAND, Prof Julian Thomas; Hon QC (1994); s of John Farrand, and E A Farrand; *b* 13 August 1935; *Educ* Portsmouth GS, Haberdashers' Aske's, UCL (Joseph Hume scholar, LLB, LLD); *m* 1, 1957 (m dis 1992), Winifred Joan, *née* Charles; 1 s, 2 da; m 2, 1992, Brenda Marjorie Hoggett (Baroness Hale of Richmond, DBE, PC (Life Peer), *qv*); *Career* slr; articled clerk to Lord Nathan at Herbert Oppenheimer, Nathan and Vandyk slrs 1957–60, slr of the Supreme Court 1960–, asst lectr then lectr King's Coll London 1960–63, lectr Univ of Sheffield 1963–65, reader in law QMC London 1965–68, prof of law Univ of Manchester 1968–84 (dean of the Faculty of Law 1970–72 and 1976–78); law cmmnr 1984–88, Insurance Ombudsman 1989–94, Pensions Ombudsman 1994–2001, visiting prof of regulatory law and policy London Met Univ 2001–06; chm: Govt Conveyancing Ctee 1984–85, Rent Assessment Panels Gtr Manchester and Lancs Area 1973–84 (vice-pres 1977–84), Supp Benefit Appeals Tribunal 1977–80, Nat Insurance Local Tbnl 1980–83, Social Security Appeal Tbnl 1983–88, Leasehold Valuation Tbnl and Rent Assessment Cncl London Rent Assessment Panel 1984–, Pensions Compensation Bd 1996–2001; memb Appeals Panel Consumer Credit Act 1974 and Estate Agents Act 1979 from licensing determinations of DG of Fair Trading; non-exec dir First Title plc 1996–2005, memb ADR Chambers (UK) Ltd 2000; hon visiting prof of law UCL 1989–2000, hon prof of law Univ of Essex 2000–, Hon LLM Univ of Manchester 1972, Hon LLD Univ of Sheffield 1990; FCIArb; *Books* Emmet On Title (ed, 1967–), Contract and Conveyance (4 edn, 1983), Love at all Risks; author of numerous articles; *Recreations* bridge, chess, wine, fiction; *Style*— Prof Julian Farrand, QC, FCIArb; ✉ 29 Morpeth Mansions, Morpeth Terrace, Westminster, London SW1P 1ET

FARRAR, David James; s of James Farrar (d 1980), of Rawdon, W Yorks, and Jessie, *née* Naylor (d 1997); *b* 3 July 1942; *Educ* Leeds GS, St Thomas' Hosp Med Sch (MB BS, MS, FRCS); *m* 25 Jan 1969, Pamela Anne, da of late Albert Sydney Allberry, MC, of Epsom, Surrey; 1 da (Charlotte b 18 April 1970), 1 s (Nicholas b 19 Nov 1976); *Career* conslt urological surgn; memb: Br Assoc Urological Surgns, Int Continence Soc, Royal Soc of Medicine; *Recreations* golf, sports history; *Style*— David Farrar, Esq; ✉ 36 Mirfield Road, Solihull, West Midlands B91 1JD (tel 0121 705 1710); 38 Harborne Road, Edgbaston, Birmingham (tel 0121 454 1390)

FARRELL, Sheriff James Aloysius; s of James Stoddart Farrell, and Harriet Louise, *née* McDonnell; *b* 14 May 1943; *Educ* St Aloysius Coll, Univ of Glasgow (MA), Univ of Dundee (LLB); *m* 1, 2 Dec 1967 (m dis 1994), Jacqueline, da of Barnett Harvey Allen (d 1967); 2 da (Suzanne b 7 April 1970, Claire Louise b 16 Oct 1973); m 2, 11 May 1996, Patricia, da of Andrew Morgan McLaren; *Career* admitted to Faculty of Advocates 1974, advocate depute 1979–83; Sheriff: Glasgow and Strathkelvin 1984–85, Dumfries and Galloway 1985–86, Lothian and Borders at Edinburgh 1986–; *Recreations* sailing, cycling, hill walking; *Style*— Sheriff James Farrell

FARRELL, Shelagh; da of Delmege Frazer-Allen (d 1981), and Mildred Anne, *née* Grigg; *b* 12 August 1947; *Educ* Notting Hill and Ealing HS, Univ of Bristol Dental Sch (BDS), Eastman Dental Hosp Univ of London (MSc); *m* 1, 2 June 1973, John Hamilton-Farrell (d 1981), s of Robert Hamilton-Farrell, CB; m 2, 22 Sept 1990, Christopher John Rutton May, s of Eric John Rutton May; 1 s (Jonathan Alexander Fraser b 15 July 1993); *Career* SHO Univ of Bristol Dental Sch 1972 (house offr 1971); in gen dental practice Frampton Cotterell 1973–95, in private dental practice Reigate 1995–; pt/t clinical lectr King's Coll Sch of Med and Dentistry London 1987–95; memb: GDC 1986–91 and 1994–2002, Standing Dental Advsy Ctee 1988–91; Royal Coll of Surgns of England: memb Bd Dental Faculty 1987–91, memb Bd Gen Dental Practitioners (UK) since its inception 1992– (vice-dean 2000–01); BDA: first woman memb Cncl 1987–90, pres Western Counties Branch 1994–95; first woman pres Br Soc for Gen Dental Surgery 1990–92; memb: Br Soc for Gen Dental Surgery, Br Soc for Restorative Dentistry, Br Soc for the Study of Prosthetic Dentistry, Br Soc of Periodontology, Bristol Medico-Legal Soc, Fédération Dentaire Internationale, Euro Prosthodontic Assoc, GDC 1986–91 and 1994–2001; St John Ambulance Bde: dep cmmr for Avon 1986–89, memb Cncl for Surrey 1995–; memb Commanderie de Bordeaux (Bristol); fell Int Coll of Dentists; FDSRCS 2004 (MGDS RCS 1980), FFGDP 2005; *Recreations* opera, singing, cooking, travel; *Style*— Mrs Shelagh Farrell; ✉ Froghole Oast House, Crockham Hill, Edenbridge, Kent TN8 6TD; Ringley Park Dental Practice, 59 Reigate Road, Reigate, Surrey RH2 0QT (tel 01737 240123, fax 01737 245704)

FARRELL, Sir Terence (Terry); kt (2001), CBE (1996, OBE 1978); s of Thomas Farrell, and Molly, *née* Maguire; *b* 12 May 1938; *Educ* St Cuthbert's GS, Univ of Newcastle Sch of Architecture (BArch), Univ of Pennsylvania Sch of Fine Arts (MArch, Master of City Planning); *m* 1, 1960, Angela Rosemarie Mallam; 2 da; m 2, 1973, Susan Hilary Aplin; 2 s, 1 da; *Career* Planning Dept: Camden New Jersey USA, Colin Buchanan & Partners 1964–65; fndr ptnr Farrell Grimshaw Partnership 1965–80; currently princ Terry Farrell & Partners; former teaching positions: Univ of Cambridge, UCL, AA London, Univ of Strathclyde, Univ of Sheffield, Univ of Pennsylvania; visiting prof Univ of Westminster 1998–; English Heritage: cmmr 1990–96, memb London Advsy Ctee, memb Royal Parks Review Group 1991–96; memb Cncl RIBA 1997–, memb Bd London First 1998–, memb Advsy Bd Royal Parks 2003, chm Central London Partnerships Walking Co-Ordination Gp 2003, memb City of Westminster Housing Cmmn; former memb: RIBA Clients Advsy Bd, RIBA Visiting Bd, RIBA Awards Panel, Historic Areas Advsy Ctee; past pres Urban Design Gp, architectural assessor for Financial Times Architectural Awards 1983, external examiner RCA; representative projects: HQ Henley Regatta, Charing Cross devpt complex London, Edinburgh int fin and conf centre, Govt HQ bldg for MI6 at Vauxhall Cross, redevelopment of The Peak Hong Kong, new Br Consulate-Gen bldg Hong Kong, Kowloon Station and Masterplan Hong Kong, Dean Art Gall Edinburgh, Int Centre for Life Newcastle upon Tyne, The Deep aquarium Hull, Greenwich Peninsular Masterplan, Home Office HQ London, Regeneration of Marylebone Euston Road London, Transportation Centre Inchon Int Airport Seoul, Univ of Newcastle Masterplan, Manchester Southern Gateway Masterplan, Univ of Manchester Masterplan; appointed Design Champion: City of Edinburgh 2004, Medway 2006; numerous lectures in UK and abroad; Hon DCL Univ of Newcastle, Hon Dr Arts Univ of Lincoln 2003; Hon FAIA 1998; MCP, ARIBA 1963, memb RTPI 1970, FCSD (formerly FSIAD) 1981, FRSA 1989, FRIAS 1996; *Publications* Urban Design Monograph (1993), The Master Architect Series: Terry Farrell (1994), Sketchbook (1998), Ten Years: Ten Cities The Work of Terry Farrell & Partners 1991–2001 (2002), Place: A Story of Modelmaking Menageries and Paper Rounds (Life and Work: Early Years to 1981, 2004); articles in: Architectural Review, Architects' Journal, L'Architecture d'Aujourd'hui, Domus, Progressive Architecture, Bauen und Wohnen, Abitare, Cree, Architectural Record, RIBA Journal, Architectural Design; *Style*— Sir Terry Farrell, CBE; ✉ Terry Farrell & Partners, 7 Hatton Street, London NW8 8PL (tel 020 7258 3433, fax 020 7723 7059, e-mail enquiries@terryfarrell.co.uk, website www.terryfarrell.com)

FARRELL, Thomas Hugh Francis; CBE (1997), TD (1969), DL (E Riding Yorks 1971 and 1995, Humberside 1974); s of Hugh Farrell (d 1959); *b* 3 February 1930; *Educ* Ampleforth, UC Hull (LLB London); *m* 2 May 1964, Hon Clodagh Mary (d 2006), yr da of 2 Baron Morris; 1 da (Sophia Mary (Mrs Marco Betti-Berutto) b 1965), 1 s (James Thomas Hugh b 1966); *Career* admitted slr 1952; cmmnd The Queen's Bays 1953–55, Lt-Col cmdg Prince of Wales's Own Yorkshire Territorials 1967–69; Sheriff of Hull 1960–61; chm: Hull Cons Fedn 1963–68, Beverley Civic Soc 1970–74; Univ of Hull: treas 1976–80, pro-chllr and chm Cncl 1980–98, pro-chllr emeritus 1998; Hon LLD Univ of Hull 1983; *Clubs* Cavalry and Guards'; *Style*— Thomas Farrell, Esq, CBE, TD, DL; ✉ 22 Wood Lane, Beverley, East Yorkshire HU17 8BS (tel 01482 869367)

FARRELLY, (Christopher) Paul; MP; s of Thomas Farrelly (d 1997), and Anne, *née* King; *b* 2 March 1962; *Educ* Wolstanton GS Newcastle-under-Lyme, Marshlands Comp Sch Newcastle-under-Lyme, St Edmund Hall Oxford (BA); *m* 19 Sept 1998, Victoria, da of David Perry; 1 s (Joe b 2 Feb 1999), 2 da (Aneira Kate b 21 Sept 2001, Octavia b 1 April 2006); *Career* mangr Corp Fin Div Barclays de Zoete Wedd Ltd 1984–90, corr Reuters 1990–95, dep city and business ed Independent on Sunday 1995–97, city ed The Observer 1997–2001; MP (Lab) Newcastle-under-Lyme 2001–, memb Culture, Media and Sport Select Ctee 2005–; memb: NUJ, MSF, Unity, Amnesty Int, Greenpeace, Liberty, Socialist Educn Assoc, Lab Pty Irish Soc; registered rep London Stock Exchange 1986; *Recreations* rugby, football, writing; *Clubs* Finchley RFC, Trentham RUFC, Commons & Lords RUFC, Holy Trinity Catholic, Halmer End Working Men's; *Style*— Paul Farrelly, Esq, MP; ✉ House of Commons, London SW1A 0AA (tel 020 7219 8391, fax 020 7219 1986, e-mail farrellyp@parliament.uk)

FARREN, Peter Stefan; *b* 16 October 1944; *Educ* Mill Hill Sch, Université de Grenoble, KCL (LLB); *m* 21 July 1973, Victoria Ann; 1 s (Ben b 11 April 1978), 2 da (Amy b 4 March 1980, Jessica b 30 Aug 1984); *Career* admitted slr 1969, William Brandt Son and Co Ltd 1973–76, Linklaters & Paines 1967–73 and 1976– (currently ptnr); memb Law Soc 1969; Freeman City of London 1979, memb Worshipful Co of Solicitors 1979; *Recreations* aviation, golf; *Style*— Peter Farren, Esq; ✉ Linklaters, One Silk Street, London EC2Y 8HQ (tel 020 7456 4752, fax 020 7456 2056, e-mail peter.farren@linklaters.com)

FARREN, Sean; s of Joseph Farren (d 1981), and Mary, *née* Cunningham (d 2000); *b* 6 September 1939; *Educ* Colaiste Mhuire Dublin, NUI (BA, HDipEd), Univ of Essex (MA), Univ of Ulster (DPhil); *m* 24 June 1967, Patricia, *née* Clarke; 3 da (Orla b 18 Aug 1968, Ciara b 30 Dec 1969, Niamh b 14 Jan 1974), 1 s (Ronan b 31 July 1976); *Career* teacher 1961–69: St Vincent's Secdy Sch Dublin, Institut Stavia Estavayer-le-Lac Switzerland, Holy Trinity Sch Sierra Leone, Catholic Teachers Trg Coll Sierra Leone; lectr and sr lectr Univ of Ulster 1970–98; elected NI Assembly 1982, memb New Ireland Forum 1983–84, memb SDLP Talks Team Brooke-Mayhew Talks 1991, elected NI Forum for Political Dialogue 1996, memb SDLP Talks Team for Castle Buildings 1996–98; MLA (SDLP) N Antrim 1998–2007, min Dept of Higher and Further Educn, Trg and Employment 1999–2001, min for Fin and Personnel 2001–02; *Books* The Politics of Irish Education 1920–65 (1995), Paths to a Settlement (co-author, 2000); *Recreations* sport, reading; *Style*— Dr Sean Farren; ✉ 30 Station Road, Portstewart BT55 7DA (tel 028 7083 3042); 37 Ann Street, Ballycastle BT54 6AN (tel 028 2076 1210, mobile 07734 473485, e-mail farren@myway.com, website www.seanfarren.com)

FARRER, David John; QC (1986); s of John Hall Farrer (d 1993), and Mary, *née* Stubbs (d 1996); *b* 15 March 1943; *Educ* Queen Elizabeth GS Barnet, Downing Coll Cambridge; *m* 29 March 1969, Hilary Jean, da of John Conway Bryson; 1 da (Emma Catherine b 22 May 1971), 2 s (Robert Edward b 20 March 1974, Thomas Andrew b 10 February 1977); *Career* called to the Bar Middle Temple 1967, recorder 1981; memb Bar Council 1987–93, chm Bar Services Ctee; chm: Parish Cncl, Rutland and Melton Liberal Soc (Parly candidate 1979 and 1983, regnl foreign affrs spokesman 1979–86); *Publications* Advice to a Suspected Abuser - Family Law Review (jtly with Rachel Langdale, 1997); *Recreations* tennis, watching rugby, listening to Sir Simon Rattle conducting Mahler, 19th century political history; *Clubs* Hamilton Tennis; *Style*— David Farrer, Esq, QC

FARRER, Sir (Charles) Matthew; GCVO (1994, KCVO 1983, CVO 1973); s of Sir (Walter) Leslie Farrer, KCVO (d 1984), and Hon Lady (Marjorie Laura) Farrer (d 1981), da of 1 Viscount Hanworth, KBE, PC; *b* 3 December 1929; *Educ* Bryanston, Balliol Coll Oxford; *m* 1962, Johanna Creszentia Maria Dorothea, da of Prof Hans-Herman Bennhold, of Tübingen, Germany; 1 s, 1 da; *Career* admitted slr 1956; ptnr Messrs Farrer & Co 1959–93; private slr to HM The Queen 1965–94; tstee Br Museum 1989–99, cmmr Royal Cmmn on Hist Manuscripts 1991–2002; memb British Library Bd 1994–2000; tstee Lambeth Palace Library 1991–2002; pres Selden Soc 2001–2003; Prime Warden Worshipful Co of Fishmongers 2007–08; *Style*— Sir Matthew Farrer, GCVO; ✉ 6 Priory Avenue, Bedford Park, London W4 1TX

FARRINGTON, Colin; s of Joseph Farrington, and Doris Farrington; *b* 12 March 1951; *Educ* Ellesmere Port Co GS for Boys, Christ's Coll Cambridge; *Partner* Paul Knott; *Career* civil servant Home Office 1972–88 (private sec to Home Sec 1974–77, on secondment HM Treasy 1980–83), dir IRRV 1988–98, DG IPR (now CIPR) 1998–; chair-elect Global Alliance for Public Relations 2006; chm of judges Cream Awards 2000–02, chm Membership Ctee City PR Guild, tstee CAM Fndn 1998–2001; chm: Cambridge Univ English Club 1970, Cambridge Univ Lab Club 1971; *Publications* Council Tax: Your Guide (1992), Business Rates: Your Guide (1993); author of numerous articles and speeches on public sector mgmnt, local govt, and PR and communications issues; *Recreations* travel, opera, whippets; *Clubs* Home House; *Style*— Colin Farrington, Esq; ✉ The Paladins, Innhams Wood, Crowborough, East Sussex TN6 1TE; The Chartered Institute of Public Relations, 32 St James's Square, London SW1Y 4JR (tel 020 7766 3333, e-mail colinf@cipr.co.uk)

FARRINGTON, Prof David Philip; OBE (2004); s of William Farrington (d 1967), of Ormskirk, Lancs, and Gladys Holden, *née* Spurr (d 1980); *b* 7 March 1944; *Educ* Ormskirk GS (state scholar), Clare Coll Cambridge (MA, PhD); *m* 30 July 1966, Sally, da of Frank Chamberlain (d 1977); 3 da (Lucy Clare b 14 April 1970, Katie Ruth b 28 March 1972, Alice Charlotte b 21 Feb 1975); *Career* research student Univ of Cambridge Psychological Lab 1966–69; Inst of Criminology Univ of Cambridge: research offr 1969–70, sr research offr 1970–74, asst dir of research 1974–76, lectr in criminology 1976–88, reader in psychological criminology 1988–92, prof of psychological criminology 1992–; visiting prof Dept of Sociology Univ of Akron 1977, visiting research worker Miny of the Solicitor Gen Ottawa 1978–79, visiting fell US Nat Inst of Justice Washington 1981, visiting scholar Nat Centre for Juvenile Justice Pittsburgh 1986, visiting fell US Bureau of Justice Statistics Washington 1995–98; memb Parole Bd for England and Wales 1984–87; memb Advsy Bd: Nat Archive of Criminal Justice Data USA 1983–93, Nat Juvenile Court Data Archive USA 1987–, UK Nat Prog on Forensic Mental Health 1999–2003 (chair 2000–03); co-chair: US Office of Juvenile Justice and Delinquency Prevention Study Gp on Serious and Violent Juvenile Offenders 1995–97, UK Dept of Health (High Security Psychiatric Servs Commissioning Bd) Network on Primary Prevention of Adult Antisocial Behaviour 1997, US Office of Juvenile Justice and Delinquency Prevention Study Gp on Very Young Offenders 1998–2000; Nat Acad of Sciences: memb Ctee on Law and Justice 1986–93, vice-chair Panel on Violence 1989–92; Br Psychological Soc: memb 1974, hon life memb Div of Forensic Psychology (chm 1983–85), memb Scientific Affairs Bd 1977–78, memb Professional Affairs Bd 1983–85, memb Cncl 1983–85, chair Bd of Examiners in Forensic Psychology 2000–03; Br Soc of Criminology: memb 1975, memb Organising Ctee 1978 and 1980–83, memb Cncl 1990–93, pres 1990–93, hon life memb 1996; American Soc of Criminology: fell 1983, Sellin-Glueck Award for int contribs to criminology 1984, memb Awards Ctee 1988–89, 1991–92 and 1993–94, memb Fells Ctee 1992–93, pres 1998–99, chair Nominations Ctee 2001–02, Sutherland Award for outstanding contribs to criminology 2002, chair Sellin-Glueck Award Ctee 2002–03; memb Bd of Dirs Int Soc of Criminology 2000–; memb AUT 1979–; Euro Assoc of Psychology and Law: memb 1991–, memb Exec Bd 1991–, pres 1997–99; memb Scientific Ctee Netherlands Inst for Study of Criminality and Law Enforcement 1995–99; pres Acad of Experimental Criminology 2001–03; Joan McCord Award Acad of Experimental Criminology 2005, Beccaria Gold Medal Criminology Soc of German-Speaking Countries 2005; FBPsS, CPsychol, FBA 1997, FMedSci 2000; *Books* Who Becomes Delinquent? (co-author, 1973), The Delinquent Way of Life (co-author, 1977), Behaviour Modification with Offenders: A Criminological Symposium (co-ed, 1979), Psychology, Law and Legal Processes (co-ed, 1979), Abnormal Offenders, Delinquency and the Criminal Justice System (co-ed, 1982), Aggression and Dangerousness (co-ed, 1985), Reactions to Crime: The Public, The Police, Courts, and Prisons (co-ed, 1985), Prediction in Criminology (co-ed, 1985), Understanding and Controlling Crime: Toward a New Research Strategy (co-author, 1986, Prize for Distinguished Scholarship Criminology Section American Sociological Assoc 1988), Human Development and Criminal Behaviour: New Ways of Advancing Knowledge (co-author, 1991), Offenders and Victims: Theory and Policy (co-ed, 1992), Integrating Individual and Ecological Aspects of Crime (co-ed, 1993), Psychological Explanations of Crime (ed, 1994), Building a Safer Society: Strategic Approaches to Crime Prevention (co-ed, 1995), Biosocial Bases of Violence (co-ed, 1997), Serious and Violent Juvenile Offenders: Risk Factors and Successful Interventions (co-ed, 1998), Antisocial Behaviour and Mental Health Problems: Explanatory Factors in Childhood and Adolescence (co-author, 1998), Evaluating Criminology and Criminal Justice (co-author, 1998), Costs and Benefits of Preventing Crime (co-ed, 2001), Child Delinquents (co-ed, 2001), Sex and Violence (co-ed, 2001), Offender Rehabilitation in Practice (co-ed, 2001), Evidence-Based Crime Prevention (co-ed, 2002), Early Prevention of Adult Antisocial Behaviour (co-ed,

2003), Integrated Developmental and Life-Course Theories of Offending (ed, 2005), Crime and Punishment in Western Countries (co-ed, 2005), Reducing Crime: The Effectiveness of Criminal Justice Interventions (co-ed, 2006), Preventing Crime: What Works for Children, Offenders, Victims and Places (co-ed, 2006), Key Issues in Criminal Career Research (co-author, 2007), Saving Children from a Life of Crime (co-author, 2007); *Style*— Prof David P Farrington, OBE, FBA; ✉ Institute of Criminology, Sedgwick Avenue, Cambridge CB3 9DT (tel 01223 335360, fax 01223 335356)

FARRINGTON, (William) Trevor; s of William Raymond Farrington, and Millicent, *née* Johnson; *b* 26 May 1941; *Educ* King's Coll Hosp Med Sch Univ of London (MB BS, FRCS); *m* 1987, Lynda Marian, *née* Ellis; *Career* former conslt otolaryngologist and head and neck surgn Central Manchester Tst, former conslt head and neck surgn Christie Hosp Tst Manchester, former hon clinical lectr in surgery Victoria Univ of Manchester; former pres: Section of Laryngology and Rhinology Royal Soc of Medicine, Manchester Surgical Soc; past memb Ct of Examiners Royal Coll of Surgns (England); *Recreations* music, literature, country pursuits; *Clubs* Carlton, Lancs CCC, Otorhinolaryngology (ORL), RSM; *Style*— Trevor Farrington, Esq; ✉ Sandilands Farm, Crowley, Northwich, Cheshire CW9 6NX (tel 01565 777462); Elm House, 2 Mauldeth Road, Withington, Manchester M20 9ND (tel 0161 434 9715, fax 0161 448 0310, e-mail wtfarrington@aol.com)

FARRON, Tim; MP; *b* 27 May 1970; *Educ* Runshaw Tertiary Coll, Univ of Newcastle; *Career* sr mangr St Martin's Coll Ambleside, Lancaster and Carlisle; cncllr (Lib Dem): S Ribble BC 1995–99, S Lakeland DC 2004–; MP (Lib Dem) Westmoreland and Lonsdale 2005– (Parly candidate (Lib Dem) Westmoreland and Lonsdale 2001); *Style*— Tim Farron, Esq, MP; ✉ House of Commons, London SW1A 0AA

FARROW, Gary; s of Leslie Bertram Farrow, and Evelyn Joyce, *née* Young; *b* 25 August 1955, Orpington, Kent; *Educ* Walsingham Sch for Boys, St Martin's Sch of Art London; *m* 4 July 2002, Jane Moore, qv; 3 da (Lauren, Ellie, Grace); *Career* shop asst One Stop Records 1973, runner Rocket Records 1974, worked with record prodr Mickie Most EMI Records 1976, Chinnichap (with Nicky Chinn and Mike Chapman) 1978, estab Gary Farrow Enterprises Media Mgmnt 1980 (worked with artists incl Elton John, Wham!, George Michael, David Bowie, Paul Young, Blondie, Duran Duran, Frankie Goes to Hollywood, Bob Geldof and Heaven 17, and managed Jonathan Ross and Paula Yates), vice-pres communications Sony Music Entertainment 1995–2004 (worked with artists incl Michael Jackson, Bruce Springsteen and Jamiroquai), estab The Corporation Gp 2005 (clients incl Sir Elton John, Sharon Osbourne, Gordon Ramsay, Jeremy Clarkson, The Old Vic and Ronnie Scott's); dep chm PR Ctee BPI; memb: BRITS Ctee, HMV Charities Ctee; patron: Elton John Aids Fndn, Music Therapy Nordoff-Robbins, Fashion Rocks; dep chm Music Industry Tst (MITS); Music Therapy Award for Outstanding Achievement 2006, Scott Piering Media Award 2006; fell Radio Acad; *Recreations* football, boxing, movies, music, art, reading; *Clubs* Morton's, Soho House, Groucho, Mark's, George; *Style*— Gary Farrow, Esq; ✉ The Corporation, 2nd Floor, 9–10 Savile Row, London W1S 3PF

FARROW, Nigel Alexander Emery; s of Arthur Hemsworth Farrow, of Bentley, Hants, and Estelle Frances, *née* Emery; *b* 24 March 1939; *Educ* Cheltenham Coll, Queens' Coll Cambridge (MA); *m* 2 Dec 1961, Susan, da of Thomas Bertram Daltry (d 1974); 3 da (Miranda b 1965, Sarah b 1967, Imogen b 1970); *Career* publisher; ed Business Mgmnt 1964–67; chm: Xerox Publishing Group Ltd 1972–82, Ginn & Co Ltd 1972–78, University Microfilms Ltd 1972–82, Information Publications International Ltd 1982–99; dir and chm: Ashgate Publishing Ltd, Connaught Training Ltd, Dartmouth Publishing Co Ltd, Gower Publishing Co Ltd, Scolar Fine Art Ltd, Lund Humphries Ltd, CDY Ltd, Mapleton International Ltd; pres: Cheltonian Soc 1988–91, Cncl Cheltenham Coll 1992–96; chm of tstees The Estelle Tst; Hon DBA; FRSA; *Books* Gower Handbook of Management (ed), The English Library (ed); author of numerous articles on business and management; *Recreations* enjoying and supporting the arts, collecting 20th century British paintings; *Clubs* Groucho; *Style*— Nigel Farrow, Esq; ✉ Dippenhall Gate, Dippenhall, Farnham, Surrey GU10 5DP; Gower House, Croft Road, Aldershot, Hampshire GU11 3HR

FARRY, Dr Stephen Anthony; MLA; s of Vincent Farry, of Bangor, and Margaret, *née* Greer; *b* 22 April 1971, Newtownards, Co Down; *Educ* Our Lady and St Patrick's Coll Belfast, Queen's Univ Belfast (BSocSc, PhD); *m* 25 July 2005, Wendy, *née* Watt; *Career* tutor Queen's Univ Belfast 1992–95, self-employed research conslt 1996–2004; Alliance Pty: pty organiser 1997–2000, policy offr 2000, gen sec 2000–07 (leave of absence as sr fell US Inst of Peace 2005–06); MLA (Alliance) N Down 2007– (Parly candidate 1998 and 2003); cncllr N Down BC 1993–, mayor N Down 2007–08 (dep mayor 2002–03); non-exec dir N Down Development Organisation Ltd 1996–2005, co sec Lagan Properties (1970) Ltd 2000–, non-exec dir Bangor and Holywood Town Centre Mgmnt Ltd 2001–; memb N Down Dist Police Partnership 2003–05, trainer/conslt Nat Democratic Inst for Int Affairs, author of articles in several jls, newspapers and magazines; *Recreations* quizzes, football, cricket, snooker, reading, travel (especially Europe and USA), international affairs; *Style*— Dr Stephen Farry, MLA; ✉ Northern Ireland Assembly, Parliament Buildings, Stormont Estate, Belfast BT4 3XX (tel 07775 687152, e-mail stephen.farry@allianceparty.org)

FARTHING, Ramon; s of Clifford Ramon George Farthing (d 1983), and Patricia Carter, of Harwich, Essex; *b* 9 February 1961; *Educ* Sir Anthony Deane Secdy Sch, Colchester Inst of HE; *m* Karen Elaine, da of John Arundel; 1 s (Kai Ramon b 6 Dec 1990), 1 da (Leila Patricia b 20 June 1995); *Career* apprentice under Chris Oakley at The Pier Restaurant 1978–80, commis chef under Sam Chalmers at Le Talbooth Restaurant Dedham 1980–83, personal chef to Earl and Countess Spencer Althorp House 1983–84, second chef to Chris Oakes The Castle Hotel Taunton 1984–86, first head chef Calcot Manor 1986–92 (Michelin Star Rating 1986–92, 1 AA Rosette for cooking 1987 rising to 3 AA Rosettes 1992, Akermann Guide Clover Leaf 1990–91, Catey Function Menu of the Year 1991), head chef and mgr Harveys Restaurant Bristol 1994–96 (head chef 1992–96) (3 AA Rosettes, Ackermann Guide Clover Leaf, County Restaurant of the Year, 1 Michelin star 1994), currently chef/patron 36 The Quay Emsworth (1 Michelin Star 1997, 3 AA Rosettes); rep chef of Br Food Festival Mandarin Hotel Jakarta Indonesia 1989; entries in Egon Ronay and The Good Food Guide; *Books* Great Fish Book (contrib), Great Pasta Book (contrib); *Recreations* music, reading cookery books; *Clubs* Caterer Acorn; *Style*— Ramon Farthing, Esq

FARTHING, Stephen Frederick Godfrey; s of Dennis Jack Farthing (d 1985), of London, and Joan Margaret, *née* Godfrey (d 2006); *b* 16 September 1950; *Educ* St Martin's Sch of Art, Royal Coll of Art, Br Sch Rome (Abbey Major scholar); *m* (m dis 2005) Joan Elizabeth, *née* Jackson; 1 da (Constance Beatrice); *Career* lectr in painting Canterbury Coll of Art 1977–79, tutor in painting Royal Coll of Art 1979–85, head Dept of Fine Art W Surrey Coll of Art and Design Farnham 1987–88 (head of painting 1985–87), artist in residence Hayward Gallery 1989; elected Ruskin master and professorial fell St Edmund Hall Oxford, exec dir NY Acad of Art 2000–04, Rootstein Hopkins prof of drawing Univ of the Arts London 2004–; tstee and chair Fine Art Faculty Br Sch at Rome 1994–2002; *Selected One Man Exhibitions* Town and Country (Edward Totah Gallery London) 1986, Mute Accomplices (MOMA Oxford (touring)) 1988, Stephen Farthing and the Leonardo Exhibition (Queen Elizabeth Hall London) 1989, Stephen Farthing at the Paco Imperial Rio De Janeiro, National Museum of Art Montevideo Uruguay, Museo de Monterray Mexico 1990, Museo de Gil Mexico 1990, The Knowledge (Nat MOMAt Kyoto) 1993, The Knowledge SE1 (The Cut Gallery London) 1995, Absolute Monarchy (Anne Berthoud Gallery London) 1996, L'Alchemie du portrait (Hôtel de la Monnaie Paris) 1997, Stephen Farthing Paintings 2000–2003 (Amagansett Applied Arts NY) 2003; *Group Exhibitions* Now for the Future (Hayward Gallery London) 1990, RA Summer Exhibition 1995–2004; *Work in Collections* Leicester City Museum, Nat Museum of Wales, Bradford Art Galleries and Museums, Government Art Collection Fund, Br Cncl, Nat Portrait Gallery; tstee The Elephant Tst 2000; RA 1998 (hon curator RA collections 1999); *Publications* An Intelligent Persons Guide to Modern Art (2000); *Style*— Stephen Farthing, Esq; ✉ The Royal Academy of Arts, Burlington House, Piccadilly, London W1J 0BD (tel 020 7300 8000)

FARZANEH, Prof Farzin; *b* 19 August 1953, Teheran, Iran; *Educ* Brighton Coll of Technol (HND), Univ of Aberdeen (BSc, MSc), Univ of Sussex (SERC studentship, DPhil); *m* Lindsay Claire, *née* Stockley; 1 da (Leili Claire b 5 July 1987), 1 s (Benjamin Bijan b 18 Dec 1993); *Career* Beit meml fell Univ of Sussex 1979–82, EMBO fell Univ of Amsterdam 1982–83, MRC fell Univ of Sussex 1983–84; King's Coll Sch of Med and Dentistry (KCSMD): 'new blood' lectr Dept of Obstetrics and Gynaecology 1985–87, sr lectr Molecular Genetics Unit Dept of Obstetrics and Gynaecology 1987–90, dir Molecular Med Unit 1990–93, head Dept of Molecular Med 1993–, awarded personal chair in Molecular Med 1996; jt holder of patents on the prevention of retroviral infection and devpt of vectors for gene therapy; recognised teacher Univ of London, KCSMD rep Univ of London Bd of Biochemistry 1988–; co-fndr and pres Int Soc for Cell and Gene Therapy of Cancer; memb Editorial Bd: Cancer Gene Therapy, Gene Therapy, Cancer Immunology Immunotherapy; FRCPath, FRSA 1997; *Publications* author of numerous original res papers in peer reviewed jls and of review articles and conf proceedings, also author of published books; *Style*— Prof Farzin Farzaneh; ✉ Department of Molecular Medicine, GKT School of Medicine, Rayne Institute, 123 Coldharbour Lane, London SE5 9NU (tel 020 7848 5901, fax 020 7733 3877, e-mail farzin.farzaneh@kcl.ac.uk)

FAST, John Claude; *b* 6 October 1949, Paris, France; *Educ* Melbourne HS, Monash Univ (BEc, Sir Charles Lowe Moot Ct Prize, LLB); *m* Jennifer; 1 da (Chloe b 5 Sept 1983), 1 s (Joshua b 20 Feb 1987); *Career* sr commercial ptnr Arnold Bloch Leibler 1976–99, vice-pres and chief legal counsel BHP Ltd 1999–2001, chief legal counsel BHP Billiton Ltd and BHP Billiton plc 2001– (also head of external affrs 2003–); memb: Takeovers Panel 2005–, Corporate Counsel Advsy Ctee Met Corporate Counsel USA; dir Medical Research Fndn for Women and Babies 1984–, chm Rotary Indigenous Aust Tertiary Scholarship Advsy Bd 2004–; memb: Law Cncl of Aust, Law Inst of Victoria, Gen Counsel 100 UK; assoc Financial Services Inst of Australasia (Finsia) 2001 (memb Markets Policy Gp); *Recreations* reading, music, art, football, walking; *Clubs* Melbourne HS Old Boys, Essendon FC, Melbourne; *Style*— John Fast, Esq; ✉ BHP Billiton, Level 28, 180 Lonsdale Street, Melbourne, Victoria 3000, Australia (tel 00 61 3 9609 3119, fax 00 61 3 9609 3204, e-mail john.c.fast@bhpbilliton.com)

FAULKNER, Amanda Jane; da of Richard George Butler Faulkner (d 1976), and Gillian Mary Josephine Hopkinson, *née* Park; *b* 5 December 1953; *Educ* St Anthony's Leweston, Canford Sch, Bournemouth Coll of Art, Ravensbourne Coll of Art, Chelsea Sch of Art; 1 s (Joseph b 21 March 1993); *Career* artist; Sch of Fine Art Chelsea Coll of Art and Design London: princ lectr in printmaking 1991–93, sr lectr in fine art 1993–; work in various public collections, selector for various awards; *Solo Exhibitions* incl: Woodlands Art Gallery Blackheath London 1983, Angela Flowers Gallery 1985–86, Big Women (Metropole Arts Centre Folkestone) 1987, Seven Deadly Sins and Recent Drawings and Prints (Flowers East London) 1988, Breaking Water (Drumcroon Arts and Educn Centre Wigan) 1989, Flowers East London 1990 and 1992, Amanda Faulkner - Recent Drawings (Manchester City Art Galleries) 1992, Amanda Faulkner - Mares' Tails Flowers East at London Fields, London 1995, Plymouth Arts Centre 1996, Amanda Faulkner - Small Mysteries (Abbot Hall Art Gallery and Museum Kendal) 1998, Amanda Faulkner - Small Mysteries (Flowers East London) 1999, Amanda Faulkner (Flowers East London) 2001, Amanda Faulkner: New Work (Flowers East London) 2002; *Group Exhibitions* incl: The Print Show (Angela Flowers Gallery London) 1983; What's New in the Arts Council Collection (touring) 1984, Double Elephant (Concourse Gallery Barbican London) 1985, The Print Show - Woodcuts and Linocuts (Angela Flowers Gallery London) 1985, Identity/Desire - Representing the Body (Scot Arts Cncl touring) 1986, Print Biennale of Liège (Musée d'Art Moderne Belgium) 1987, Mother and Child (Lefevre Gallery London) 1988, Excavations (Galerie Hubert Winter Vienna and John Hansard Gallery Southampton) 1988, New Contemporary British Painting (The Contemporary Arts Centre Cincinnati Ohio and touring) 1988, Ljubljana Print Biennale (Yugoslavia) 1989, Barbican Concourse Gallery London 1989, Angela Flowers Gallery 1990, Flowers at Moos (Gallery Moos NY) 1990, Inaugural Exhibition (Cannon Cole Gallery Chicago) 1991, European Large Formant Printmaking (Guinness Hopstore Dublin) 1991, Postmodern Prints (V&A) 1991, Images of Hope and Disquiet - Expressionism in Britain in the Nineties (Castlefield Gallery Manchester) 1992, Myth, Dream and fable (Angel Row Gallery Nottingham) 1992, New MonoPrints Amanda Faulkner and Alison Watt (Flowers East London) 1996, From the Interior (Ferens Art Gallery, Stanley Picker Gallery, Kingston Univ, Oldham Art Gallery, Univ of Brighton, Hot Bath Gallery) 1997 and also Aberystwyth Arts Centre 1998, The Body Politic (Wolverhampton Art Gallery, Derby Art Gallery) 1997, Works of Artifice: Make-Up Uncovered (Grundy Art Gallery Blackpool) 2000 and (Williamson Gallery Birkenhead) 2001, Spiritus Mundi (Flowers East London) 2004, Drawing Inspiration (Abbot Hall Museum and Gallery Kendal) 2005, After Hiroshima: Nuclear Imaginaries (Brunei Gallery SOAS and Millais Gallery Southampton Inst) 2005; *Style*— Ms Amanda Faulkner; ✉ c/o Flowers East, 82 Kingsland Road, London E2 8DP (tel 020 7920 7777, fax 020 7920 7770)

FAULKNER, David Edwart Riley; CB (1985); s of Harold Ewart Faulkner (d 1968), and Mabel, *née* Riley (d 1960); *b* 23 October 1934; *Educ* Manchester Grammar, Merchant Taylors', St John's Coll Oxford (MA); *m* 16 Sept 1961, Sheila Jean, da of James Stevenson (d 1985), of Bucks; 1 s (Martin b 1962), 1 da (Rosemary b 1965); *Career* Nat Serv RA and Intelligence Corps, 2 Lt 1957–59; Home Office: asst princ 1959, princ 1963, asst sec 1969, private sec to the Home Sec 1969, Prison Dept 1970, Police Dept 1975, asst under sec of state 1976, seconded to the Cabinet Office 1978–79, dir of operational policy Prison Dept 1980, dep under sec of state Criminal and Res and Statistical Depts 1982, princ establishment offr 1990–92; fell St John's Coll Oxford 1992–99, sr res assoc Centre for Criminological Res Univ of Oxford 1992–; memb: UN Ctee on Crime Prevention and Control 1984–91, Advsy Bd of Helsinki Inst for Crime Prevention and Control 1984–92; chm Howard League for Penal Reform 1999–2002, tstee Gilbert Murray Tst, tstee Thames Valley Partnership; *Books* Crime, State and Citizen: A Field Full of Folk (2001, 2 edn 2006); *Style*— David Faulkner, Esq, CB; ✉ Centre for Criminology, Manor Road Building, Manor Road, Oxford OX1 3UQ (tel 01865 274448, fax 01865 274445, e-mail david.faulkner@crim.ox.ac.uk)

FAULKNER OF WORCESTER, Baron (Life Peer UK 1999), of Wimbledon in the London Borough of Merton; Richard Oliver Faulkner; s of Harold Ewart Faulkner (d 1968), and Mabel, *née* Riley (d 1960); *b* 22 March 1946; *Educ* Merchant Taylors', Worcester Coll Oxford (MA); *m* 5 July 1968, Susan, da of Donald James Heyes (d 1978); 2 da (Julia b 1969, Tamsin b 1970); *Career* dep chm Citigate Westminster (formerly Westminster Communications Group) until 1999, chm Travel PR Ltd 2006–; communications advsr: Railway Trade Unions 1976–77, Bd RR 1977–98, Littlewoods 1977–, Lloyds TSB Group (formerly TSB Group) 1987–99, Interparly Union 1988–90, The Bishop at Lambeth 1990, FSA 1997–2000; acting head of communications SIB 1997; vice-chm Transport 2000 Ltd 1986–99 (vice-pres 2000–); dir Westminster Europe Ltd 1994–99, vice chm Cardiff

Millennium Stadium plc 2004– (dir 1997–2004); Parly candidate (Lab): Devizes 1970 and Feb 1974, Monmouth Oct 1974, Huddersfield West 1979; departmental liaison peer DETR 2000–01, departmental liaison peer Cabinet Office 2001–05; memb Euro Community Select Ctee Sub-Ctee B 1999–2002; sec Br-Norwegian Parly Gp 2000–, vice-chm Br-Caribbean Gp 2000–, treas Railways Parly Gp 2000–, co-chm Br Taiwan Gp 2005– (vice-chm 2001–05), sec Br-Argentine Parly Gp 2001–, jt treas Br-Danish Parly Gp 2001–, jt treas Br-Swedish Parly Gp 2001–, chm War Graves and Battlefields Heritage Parly Gp 2002–, memb Jt Scrutiny Ctee Draft Gambling Bill 2003–04, chm All-Parly Inquiry on Betting in Sport 2005–06, chm Sustainable Aviation Gp 2004–; memb Merton Borough Cncl 1971–78, communications advsr to oppn ldr and Lab Pty gen elections 1987 and 1992 (memb John Prescott's campaign team at 1997 gen election), co fndr Parly jl The House Magazine (memb Editorial Bd 2003–); Football Tst: fndr tstee 1979–83, sec 1983–86, dep chm 1986–90, first dep chm 1990–98; chm: Women's FA 1988–91, Sports Grounds Initiative 1995–2000; vice-chm Football Task Force 1997–99; memb: Sports Cncl 1986–88, Fndn for Sport and the Arts 2000–; chm Worcester Coll Oxford UK Appeal 1996–2003, memb Ct Univ of Luton; patron Roy Castle Fndn 1999– (tstee 2003–), pres Royal Soc for the Prevention of Accidents 2001–04 (vice-pres 2004–), chm Railway Heritage Committee 2004– (memb 2002–04), tstee Gamcare 2005–, tstee Nat Museum for Sci and Industry 2007–, pres Cotswold Line Promotion Gp 2007–; Friendship Medal of Diplomacy Min of Foreign Affairs Rep of China 2004; hon fell Worcester Col Oxford 2002; Hon Dr of Laws Univ of Luton 2003; *Recreations* collecting Lloyd George memorabilia, tinplate trains, watching association football, travelling by railway; *Clubs* Reform; *Style*— The Rt Hon the Lord Faulkner of Worcester; ✉ House of Lords, London SW1A 0PW (tel 020 7219 8503, fax 020 7219 1460, e-mail faulknerro@parliament.uk, website www.lordfaulkner.net)

FAULKS, Edward Peter Lawless; QC (1996); s of His Hon Peter Faulks, MC (d 1998), and Pamela, *née* Lawless (d 2003); bro of Sebastian Charles Faulks, CBE, FRSL, *qv*; *b* 19 August 1950; *Educ* Wellington, Jesus Coll Oxford (MA); *m* 1990, Catherine Frances Turner; 2 s (Leo Alexander Lawless b 8 Aug 1992, Archie Dominic b 11 Nov 1994); *Career* called to the Bar Middle Temple 1973; recorder of the Crown Court 2000–06, special advsr to DCA 2005–06; chm Professional Negligence Bar Assoc 2002–04; FCIArb; *Publications* Local Authority Liability (contributing ed 1–3 edns); *Recreations* sports, the Arts; *Clubs* Garrick; *Style*— Edward Faulks, Esq, QC; ✉ 33 Ladbroke Grove, London W11 3AY; 1 Chancery Lane, London W2A 1LF (tel 0845 634 6666, e-mail efaulks@1chancerylane.com)

FAULKS, His Hon Judge Esmond James; s of Sir Neville Major Ginner Faulks, MBE, TD (d 1985), and Bridget Marigold, *née* Bodley (d 1962); *b* 11 June 1946; *Educ* Uppingham, Sidney Sussex Coll Cambridge (Archdeacon Johnson exhibitioner, MA); *m* 12 Sept 1972, Pamela Margaret, da of William Arthur and Margaret Ives, of Almora, Rockcliffe, Kircudbright; 1 s (Sam b 17 Oct 1973), 1 da (Nicola b 6 March 1976); *Career* barr (Duke of Edinburgh scholar); recorder Crown Court 1987–93; circuit judge (North Eastern Circuit) 1993–; memb Parole Bd for England and Wales 2002; *Recreations* country pursuits; *Style*— His Hon Judge Faulks; ✉ c/o Newcastle upon Tyne Combined Court Centre, Quayside, Newcastle upon Tyne NE1 3LA

FAULKS, Sebastian Charles; CBE (2002); s of His Hon Peter Ronald Faulks, MC (d 1998), and Pamela, *née* Lawless (d 2003); bro of Edward Peter Lawless Faulks, QC, *qv*; *b* 20 April 1953; *Educ* Wellington (scholar), Emmanuel Coll Cambridge (exhibitioner, MA); *m* 1989, Veronica, *née* Youlten; 2 s (William b 1990, Arthur b 1996), 1 da (Holly b 1992); *Career* writer; ed New Fiction Soc 1978–81, reporter Daily Telegraph 1978–82, feature writer Sunday Telegraph 1983–86, literary ed The Independent 1986–89; Independent on Sunday: dep ed 1989–90, assoc ed 1990–91; columnist: The Guardian 1992–98, Evening Standard 1997–99, Mail on Sunday 1999–2000; wrote and presented Churchill's Secret Army (Channel 4) 2000, panelist The Write Stuff (BBC Radio 4) 1998–; Author of the Year British Book Awards 1995; Hon DLitt Tavistock Clinic/ Univ of E London 2007; FRSL 1995; *Books* A Trick of the Light (1984), The Girl at the Lion d'Or (1989), A Fool's Alphabet (1992), Birdsong (1993), The Fatal Englishman: Three Short Lives (1996), Charlotte Gray (1998), The Vintage Book of War Stories (ed, 1999), On Green Dolphin Street (2001), Human Traces (2005), Pistache (2006), Engleby (2007); *Recreations* tennis, wine; *Style*— Sebastian Faulks, Esq, CBE, FRSL; ✉ c/o Aitken and Stone, 18–21 Cavaye Place, London SW10 9PT; e-mail scf35@btconnect.com

FAULL, Dr Margaret Lindsay; da of Norman Augustus Faull (d 1956), of Sydney, Aust, and Myra Beryl, *née* Smith (d 2006); *b* 4 April 1946; *Educ* Fort St Girls' HS, Univ of Sydney (BA), Univ of Macquarie (MA), Univ of Sheffield (MA), Univ of Leeds (PhD); *Career* secdy sch teacher NSW Dept of Educn 1970–71, dep co archaeologist W Yorks CC 1984–85 (field archaeologist 1975–84), project mangr Thwaite Mills Industrial Museum 1985–86, dir National Coal Mining Museum for England (formerly Yorkshire Mining Museum) Caphouse Colliery 1986–; ed Soc for Landscape Studies 1979–86, chm Yorkshire Cncl for Br Archaeology 1982–84, sec Thwaite Mills Soc 1986–; non-exec dir Wakefield HA 2000–02, chm Wakefield District Med Res Ethics Ctee 2000–06, chm Leeds Central Med Res Ethics Ctee 2007–; vice-pres Cncl for Br Archaeology 2001–, chm Soc for Church Archaeology 2005–; Hon Dr Univ of Bradford, Hon Dr Univ of Huddersfield; MIFA 1983, fell ILAM 1986, affiliate Inst of Materials, Minerals and Mining 1988, FInstD 1990, FRSA 1996; *Books* Domesday Book: Yorkshire Chichester (jt ed, 1986); *Recreations* collecting African carvings, opera, cricket; *Style*— Dr Margaret Faull; ✉ 39 Eldon Terrace, Leeds Road, Wakefield, West Yorkshire WF1 3JW (tel 01924 379690, fax 01924 379690), National Coal Mining Museum, Caphouse Colliery, New Road, Overton, Wakefield, West Yorkshire WF4 4RH (tel 01924 848806, fax 01924 840694)

FAURE WALKER, Rupert Roderick; er s of Maj Roderick Edward Faure Walker (d 2002), and his 1 w, Hon Mary Chaloner (d 2003), da of 2 Baron Gisborough; *b* 9 September 1947; *Educ* Eton, Univ of Bristol (BSc); *m* 1975, Sally Anne Vivienne, da of Lt Cdr Francis John Sidebotham, RN (d 1995); 1 s (Nicholas b 1978), 2 da (Julia b 1980, Joanna b 1984); *Career* dir Samuel Montagu 1982–96, md HSBC Investment Bank 1996–; FCA; *Style*— Rupert Faure Walker, Esq; ✉ Woodhill, Danbury, Essex CM3 4AN; c/o HSBC Investment Bank, 8 Canada Square, London E14 5HQ (tel 020 7992 2101)

FAUX, (James) Christopher; s of Dr Francis Reginald Faux (d 1974), of Bolton, Lancs, and Alison Mungo, *née* Park (d 1981); *b* 11 March 1940; *Educ* Fettes, Univ of Liverpool, Univ of Glasgow; *m* 29 July 1967, Patricia Anne Lyon, da of Hugh Lyon Denson (d 1991), of Chester; 1 s (James), 2 da (Rachel, Charlotte); *Career* Liverpool Scottish TA 1960–65; conslt orthopaedic surgn Preston HA 1977–99, conslt orthopaedic surgn Wrightington Hosp Centre for Hip Surgery 1999–2003, lower limb tutor 2003–; memb: Br Hip Soc, Charnley Low Friction Soc, Liverpool Orthopaedic Circle, Sir John Charnley Tst (chm of tstees 1999–), Liverpool Med Inst; Gold Medal BOA Sydney 2004; LRCP, FBOA, FRCSGlas 1973, FRCS (ad eundum) 1997; *Recreations* boating, rugby; *Style*— Christopher Faux, Esq; ✉ New Barn Farm, Alston Lane, Longridge, Preston, Lancashire PR3 3BN (tel 01772 782333); 7 Moor Park Avenue, Preston, Lancashire PR1 6AS (tel 01772 204710, fax 01772 558705, e-mail jcfaux@nwest.net)

FAWCETT, Amelia Chilcott; CBE (2002); s of Frederick J Fawcett II, of Essex, Mass, and Betsey Chilcott Fawcett; *b* 16 September 1956, Boston, Mass; *Educ* Pingree Sch South Hamilton Mass, Wellesley Coll Mass (BA), Univ of Virginia Sch of Law (JD); *Career* called to the Bar NY 1984; Sullivan & Cromwell NY 1983–85 and Paris 1986–87; Morgan Stanley London: joined 1987, vice-pres 1990, exec dir 1992, memb European Mgmnt Ctee 1996–2006, md and chief administrative offr 1996–2002, vice-chm and chief operating offr 2002–06, sr advsr 2006–07; chair Pensions First LLP 2007–; memb Bd of Dirs: State Street Corp 2006–, Guardian Media Gp 2007–; memb Ct Bank of England 2004– (chm Audit Ctee 2005–); chm London Int Festival of Theatre 2002–, memb Cncl Univ of London 2002– (chm Audit Ctee), tstee Nat Portrait Gallery 2003– (dep chm 2005–), tstee Nat Maritime Museum Cornwall 2004–06, memb Bd Business in the Community 2005–; Prince of Wales Ambass Award 2004; Hon DIB American Univ in London 2006; memb: American Bar Assoc 1983, Guild of Int Bankers 2004; *Recreations* fly fishing, hill walking, sailing; *Clubs* Reform, Walbrook, Cradoc Golf, St Mawes Sailing; *Style*— Ms Amelia Fawcett, CBE; ✉ Pensions First LLP, 90 Long Acre, London WC2E 9RA (tel 020 7849 3496, fax 020 7225 5021, e-mail amelia@acfawcett.com)

FAWCETT, Prof James; s of Edward Fawcett, and Jane Fawcett; *b* 13 March 1950; *Educ* Westminster, Balliol Coll Oxford (BA), St Thomas' Hosp Med Sch London (MB BS); *m* 1979, Prof Kay-Tee Khaw; 1 da (Nicola b 1981), 1 s (Andrew b 1984); *Career* house physician St Thomas' Hosp London and Addenbrooke's Hosp Cambridge 1975–76, SHO St Thomas' Hosp London 1976–77, SHO Northwick Park Hosp 1977–79, scientist Nat Inst for Med Research 1979–82, asst prof Salk Inst La Jolla 1982–86, lectr Dept of Physiology Univ of Cambridge 1986–2001, prof of experimental neurology Univ of Cambridge 2001–, chm Cambridge Centre for Brain Repair 2001–; chm Scientific Ctee Int Spinal Research Tst; FRCP 2000, FMedSci 2003; *Publications* Brain Damage, Brain Repair (with Rosser and Dunnett, 2001); author of other scientific pubns on brain devpt and repair; *Recreations* sailing, bagpiping; *Clubs* Pinstriped Highlanders Pipe Band, Brancaster Staithe Sailing; *Style*— Prof James Fawcett; ✉ Cambridge University Centre for Brain Repair, Robinson Way, Cambridge CB2 2PY (tel 01223 331160, fax 01223 331174, e-mail jf108@cam.ac.uk)

FAWCETT, Tania Caroline; da of Jon Moore, of Wilts, and Adrienne Mary, *née* Parkin; *b* 4 June 1967; *Educ* Royal Naval Sch Haslemere; *m* 15 March 1987, Mark Christopher Fawcett, s of John Kroner Fawcett; 2 da (Matilda b 9 Oct 1998, Rose b 19 Sept 2000), 1 s (Frederick b 5 Mar 2005); *Career* lady clerk Office of HRH the Duke of Edinburgh 1986–88, prodn asst Anouska Hempel Couture 1988–89; Garrard & Co: asst advtg mangr 1989, advtg mangr 1992, mktg mangr 1994; Aurelia PR: account dir 1996, bd dir 1997, dep md 1998–2005; head of mktg, PR and events Candy & Candy 2006–; *Recreations* walking, skiing, relaxing with family; *Style*— Mrs Mark Fawcett; ✉ 19 Crieff Road, London SW18 2EB (tel 020 7594 4323, fax 020 7594 4801, mobile 07770 915851, e-mail tfawcett@candyandcandy.com)

FAWCUS, His Hon Simon James David; s of Gp Capt Ernest Augustus Fawcus (d 1966), and Joan Shaw (Jill), *née* Stokes; *b* 12 July 1938; *Educ* Aldenham, Trinity Hall Cambridge (BA, MA); *m* 12 March 1966, Joan Mary, da of late William John Oliphant; 4 da (Juliet Jane b 11 March 1970, Meriel Ann b 13 Dec 1972, Madeline Clare, Annabel Barbara (twins) b 22 Sept 1975), 1 s (Adrian John Oliphant b 10 April 1974); *Career* called to the Bar Gray's Inn 1961, in practice Northern Circuit 1962–85, recorder of the Crown Ct 1981–85, circuit judge (Northern Circuit) 1985–2003 (dep circuit judge 2003–); pres Cncl of Circuit Judges 1996; *Recreations* tennis, rackets, golf, music, bridge; *Clubs* MCC, Manchester Tennis and Racquet; *Style*— His Hon Simon Fawcus

FAWZI, Ahmad; *Career* lectr Cairo Univ and Inst of Strategic Studies 1968–76; ed and anchor nightly news (Egyptian television), Reuters Television: news ed, reporter, prodr, reg news ops mngr (London, Prague, Cairo and NY); press sec and chef de cabinet for wife of pres of Egypt, Jehan Sedat 1974–84; dep spokesman for sec-gen UNHQ NY 1992–96, dir UNIC 1997–; *Style*— Ahmad Fawzi, Esq

FAY, Anthony William (Tony); s of Francis Joseph Fay (d 1970), and Mary Monica, *née* Brennan (d 1986); *b* 24 August 1938; *Educ* Xaverian Coll, Univ of Birmingham (BCom, capt Br Univs Assoc Football, memb Br Olympic Squad Assoc Football); *m* 9 Oct 1963, Dr Mary Patricia Fay, da of Dr John Patrick McGovern; 3 s (Michael John b 26 Sept 1964, Paul Antony b 17 April 1966, Christopher Damian b 9 Jan 1968); *Career* Coopers and Lybrand: articled 1960–63, qualified CA 1963–64; successively mktg mangr, div md Alcan Booth Industries 1965–71, corp vice-pres Europe Data 100 Corp 1972–80, dir and chief exec trading Crest Nicholson plc 1981–88; chm: SPC International 1998–, BSS Gp plc 1999–2003 (non-exec dir 1994–99); non-exec chm: Hugh Fay Ltd 1970–88, Reynolds Med Gp Ltd 1992–2001; non-exec dir Ferraris Gp 2001–; govr St Columba's Coll 1994–2005; Liveryman Worshipful Co of Spectacle Makers; memb ICA 1963, MInstM 1970; *Recreations* golf, cricket, soccer, skiing, sailing, reading, theatre, travel; *Clubs* Ashridge Golf (capt 1992), Royal Thames Yacht, MCC, Middlesex Wanderers AFC (chm); *Style*— Tony Fay, Esq; ✉ Gatesdene House, Little Gaddesden, Hertfordshire HP4 1PB (tel 01442 842585, fax 01442 843113)

FAY, Dr Christopher Ernest; CBE (1999); *b* 4 April 1945; *Educ* Univ of Leeds (BSc, PhD); *m* 1971, Jennifer; 2 da, 1 s; *Career* Royal Dutch/Shell Group: joined 1970, various appts in Holland, Nigeria, Malaysia and Scandinavia 1971–78, devpt mangr Dansk Undergrunds Consortium Copenhagen 1978–81, tech mangr Norske Shell Exploration and Prodn Stavanger 1981–84, dir of exploration and prodn Norway 1984–86, gen mangr and chief exec Shell cos in Turkey 1986–89, md Shell UK Exploration and Prodn and an md Shell UK Ltd 1989–93, chm and chief exec Shell UK Ltd 1993–98; non-exec dir: BAA plc 1998–, Anglo-American plc 1999–, STENA Int 1999–, The Weir Gp 2001–03; non-exec chm: EXPRO Int Gp 1999–, Tuscan Energy Gp 2002–05; chm Advsy Ctee on Business and the Environment 1999–2003; pres UK Offshore Operators' Assoc 1992; CEng 1974, FRSE 1996, FREng 1996, Hon FICE 1998 (MICE 1973, FICE 1994), FEI (FInstPet 1994); *Recreations* gardening, skiing, golf, tennis; *Clubs* Sunningdale Golf, Bramley Golf; *Style*— Dr Chris Fay, CBE, FRSE, FREng; ✉ Merrifield, Links Road, Bramley, Guildford, Surrey GU5 0AL (tel 01483 893112, fax 01483 894421)

FAY, Margaret; OBE (2004); da of Oswald Allen (d 1993), and Joan, *née* Davis; *b* 21 May 1949; *Educ* South Shields GS for Girls; *m* 1, 1968 (m dis 1978), Matthew Stoker; 1 s (Graeme b 1972); m 2, 1982 (m dis 1993), Peter Fay; partner, David; *Career* Tyne Tees Television: joined as accounts clerk 1981, house services mangr properties and facilities 1984, TV prodn servs mangr 1986, controller of ops 1988, dir of ops 1995–97, md and gen mangr 1997–2003; chm One NorthEast 2003–; dir Newcastle Gateshead Initiative 1999–; non-exec dir Darlington Building Soc 2000–; govr Teesside Univ 1998–; *Recreations* entertaining advertisers at local premier league football grounds; *Style*— Mrs Margaret Fay, OBE; ✉ One NorthEast, Stella House, Goldcrest Way, Newburn Riverside, Newcastle upon Tyne NE15 8NY

FAY, Stephen Francis John; s of Gerard Fay (d 1968), and Alice, *née* Bentley (d 1969); *b* 14 August 1938; *Educ* Highgate Sch, Univ of New Brunswick Canada (BA, MA), LSE; *m* 1964, Prudence, da of Alan Butcher; 1 s (Matthew b 1967), 1 da (Susanna b 1969); *Career* journalist with: Glasgow Herald 1961–64, Sunday Times 1964–84, Independent on Sunday 1989–91; ed Business Magazine 1986–89, dep ed Independent on Sunday 1996–98, arts and cricket correspondent 1998–, ed Wisden Cricket Monthly 2001–; winner of Special Award Br Press Awards 1987 and 1989; *Publications* The Great Silver Bubble (1982), The Ring (1984), Portrait of an Old Lady (1986), Powerplay, The Life and Times of Peter Hall (1995), The Collapse of Barings (1996); *Recreations* attending plays, watching cricket, drinking wine; *Clubs* Garrick, MCC; *Style*— Stephen Fay, Esq; ✉ 5A Furlong Road, London N7 8LS (tel 020 7607 8950, fax 020 7619 9667, e-mail stephen.fay@btopenworld.com)

FAYLE, Michael John; s of late D W Fayle, of the Isle of Man; *b* 22 November 1953; *Educ* Wade Deacon GS Widnes, Douglas HS for Boys; *m* 1975, Vivien, da of late C J A Savage; 1 s (Thomas Edward b 1993); *Career* articled clerk to J G Fargher of B Sugden & Co

Chartered Accts IOM 1972–77; ptnr: J G Fargher & Co 1982–86, KPMG 1986–; chm IOM Soc of Chartered Accountants 1991; chm Friends of Manx Nat Heritage 2004; FCA 1983 (ACA 1977); *Recreations* collecting, gardening; *Style*— Michael J Fayle, Esq; ✉ Ballaqueeney Lodge, Ballaquayle Road, Douglas, Isle of Man IM2 5DD (tel 01624 675725); KPMG LLC, Heritage Court, 41 Athol Street, Douglas, Isle of Man IM1 1LA (tel 01624 681043, fax 01624 681098, e-mail mfayle@kpmg.co.im)

FAYRER, Sir John Lang Macpherson; 4 Bt (UK 1896), of Devonshire Street, St Marylebone, Co London; s of Lt-Cdr Sir Joseph Herbert Spens Fayrer, 3 Bt, DSC, RNVR (d 1976), and Helen Diana Scott, *née* Lang (d 1961); *b* 18 October 1944; *Educ* Edinburgh Acad, Univ of Strathclyde; *Heir* none; *Career* memb HCIMA; chief catering officer 1973–77, hotel night mangr and conf organiser 1977–80, clerical offr Univ of Edinburgh 1980–89, insurance broker 1989–90, research offr Moray House Inst of Educn 1991–; *Books* Child Development from Birth to Adolescence (1992), Scotplay '92: A Target for Play (ed, 1993), Scotplay '93: Providing for Play (1994); *Recreations* reading, walking, riding; *Style*— Sir John Fayrer, Bt

FAZAN, Claire; *Educ* LSE (LLB); *Career* slr specialising in clinical negligence litigation; ptnr: Bindman & Partners 1989–2003 (latterly head of clinical and personal injury), Irwin Mitchell 2003–07, Leigh Day & Co 2007–; memb Law Soc 1985 (memb Clinical Negligence Panel); *Publications* Medical Negligence Litigation, A Practitioner's Guide (co-author); *Style*— Ms Claire Fazan; ✉ Leigh Day & Co Solicitors, 25 St John's Lane, London EC1M 4LB (tel 020 7650 1200)

FAZEY, Ian Hamilton; OBE (1990); s of Albert Ronald Fazey (d 1959), of Birmingham, and Alice, *née* Livingston (d 1987); *b* 9 August 1942; *Educ* King's Norton GS Birmingham, Aston Univ (BSc); *m* 1966, Prof Cindy Sylvia Joyce Fazey, da of Horace Joseph Brookes; *Career* asst engr W Midlands Gas Bd 1964–65; The Birmingham Post 1965–69, Liverpool Daily Post 1969–71, dep ed Liverpool Echo 1972–74, md Wirral Newspapers 1974–76, gen mangr Liverpool Daily Post & Echo 1977–80, freelance journalist 1980–, retained contrib Financial Times 1981–86, northern corr Financial Times 1986–96, contrib Financial Times 1996–, conslt ed Newsco Insider 1999–2002; ed North West Business Insider 1999–2000; chm j4b plc 2000–02; conslt: OECD, UNDCP, Global Prog Against Money Laundering and UNIDO 1996–; dir: Saxon Forlags Stockholm 1985–87 (non-exec), Data TV 1988–93; chm NatWest-FT Export Excellence Forums and Awards 1993–99; chm Waterloo Residents' Assoc 2005–; Glaxo Award (science writing) 1967, commended Provincial Journalist of the Year 1967; *Books* Waterloo FC, 1882–1982 (1982, online 2004–), The How to of Small Business (1985), The Pathfinder: The Origins of the Enterprise Agency in Britain (1987), Italy's National Hatchery (1997), Attacking the Profits of Crime: Drugs, Money and Laundering (ed, 1998); *Recreations* rugby union, lurchers, gardening, cooking and eating, opera, books, active citizenship, disability rights, failing to master the 5-string banjo and Fender Stratocaster; *Clubs* Waterloo Football (rugby union), Countryside Alliance; *Style*— Ian Hamilton Fazey, Esq, OBE; ✉ 8 Beach Lawn, Waterloo, Liverpool L22 8QA (tel 0151 928 3441, e-mail ihfazey@btconnect.com)

FEARN, (Charles) Barry d'Arcy; TD (1993); s of Charles Henry Fearn (d 1982), and Gladys Lily, *née* d'Arcy Jones (d 1983); *b* 4 March 1934; *Educ* Shrewsbury, Gonville & Caius Coll Cambridge (MA, MB BChir), St Mary's Hosp Univ of London; *m* 21 April 1962, Gay Barbara Ann, da of Capt Edward Smythe (d 1940); 1 s (Giles b 1964), 3 da (Alexandra b 1967, Victoria b 1971, Jocasta b 1973); *Career* Nat Serv Capt RAMC, MO Royal Irish Fusiliers 1960, Capt RAMC (V) TAVR Regtl Surgn Kent and Co of London Yeo 1966, Maj RAMC (V) TA Regtl MO 71 YEO Signal Regt 1981; sr lectr and hon conslt orthopaedic surgn Khartoum Univ of Sudan 1969–70, sr registrar Nuffield Orthopaedic Centre Oxford 1970–72; conslt orthopaedic surgn 1972–97: Royal Sussex Co Hosp Brighton, Princess Royal Hosp Haywards Heath, Sussex Nuffield Hosp, Ashdown Hosp; chm Higher Trg Ctee in Orthopaedic Surgery SE Thames Region 1990–95, regnl advsr in orthopaedics Royal Coll of Surgns 1991–96, sr tutor SE Thames Orthopaedic Trg Prog 1998–, pt/t clinical teacher: GKT, KCL 1999–2000; fndr and dir Sussex Osteoporosis Clinic Hove 1988; Freeman City of London, Liveryman Worshipful Soc of Apothecaries; chm Sprint Fund; hon archivist Girdlestone Soc 1998; memb: Regency Soc (Brighton), Trollope Soc, RSM, Isakos; fell Br Orthopaedic Assoc, FRCS 1967, FRCSEd 1967; *Recreations* opera, the theatre, racing, travel, watching others row; *Clubs* Leander, RSM, The Arts, Oxford and Cambridge; *Style*— Barry Fearn, Esq, TD; ✉ Colwell House, Haywards Heath, West Sussex RH17 7TB

FEARN, Baron (Life Peer UK 2001), of Southport in the County of Merseyside; Ronald Cyril (Ronnie) Fearn; OBE (1985); s of James Fearn (d 1972), of Southport, and Martha Ellen, *née* Hodge (d 1995); *b* 6 February 1931; *Educ* King George V GS Southport; *m* 11 June 1955, Joyce Edna, da of John Dugan (d 1945), of Southport; 1 s (Hon Susan Lynn b 1959), 1 s (Hon Martin John b 1962); *Career* Nat Serv RN; bank official Royal Bank of Scotland plc 1947–87; MP (Lib Dem) Southport 1987–92 and 1997–2001; Lib Dem spokesman: on health and tourism 1988–89, on local govt, tport and tourism 1989–92, on tourism 1997–2001; cncllr Sefton MBC 1974–; FCIB; *Recreations* badminton, sport, athletics, drama, politics; *Style*— The Lord Fearn of Southport, OBE, FCIB

FEARNLEY, Prof Stella Marie; da of Sydney Yates (d 1993), and Mary, *née* Prime (d 2002), of Barrow on Soar, Leics; *b* 22 January 1946; *Educ* Astley GS, Univ of Leeds (BA); *m* 15 Sept 1973, Paul Douglas Fearnley, s of Raymond Fairfax Fearnley (d 1986); 2 da (Helen Mary b 31 Oct 1977, Rachel Florence b 12 Sept 1981); *Career* VSO 1968–69; Careers Res and Advsy Centre 1969–70; articled clerk Price Waterhouse 1970–73, Grant Thornton 1973–86 (audit sr rising to sr tech mangr), sr lectr Bournemouth Univ 1986–90 (asst to dir 1988–89), Grant Thornton lectr in accounting Univ of Southampton 1990–94, prof of accounting Univ of Portsmouth 1994–; memb Nat Cncl ICAEW 1991–2004; memb Professional Oversight Bd 2004–; past pres Southern Soc of Chartered Accountants; FCA 1978; *Recreations* music, theatre, walking, sailing; *Style*— Prof Stella Fearnley; ✉ Department of Accounting and Law, University of Portsmouth Business School, Richmond Building, Portland Street, Portsmouth PO1 3AH (tel 02392 848484)

FEARNLEY-WHITTINGSTALL, Hugh Christopher Edmund; s of Robert Fearnley-Whittingstall, of Glos, and Jane, *née* Lascelles; *b* 14 January 1965; *Educ* Eton, St Peter's Coll Oxford (BA); *Partner* Marie Derôme; 1 s (Oscar b 3 March 1999); *Career* writer, broadcaster, chef; sous chef River Café Hammersmith 1989, ed The Magazine 1991, assoc ed Redwood Publishing 1992–93, prodr BBC Science 1993–94 (The Maggot Mogul 1993, Sleeping It Off 1994), fndr KEO Films (with Andrew Palmer) 1996; produced/presented: A Cook on the Wild Side (Channel 4) 1996–97, Escape to River Cottage (Channel 4) 1998–99; presenter: TV Dinners (Channel 4) 1997–99, Return to River Cottage (Channel 4) 2000, River Cottage Forever (Channel 4) 2002, Treats from the Edwardian Country House (Channel 4) 2002; contrib/columnist: Independent on Sunday, Sunday Telegraph, Sunday Times, Observer, Sunday Express; patron Farmers Markets 2002, supporter and campaigner various food prodn and environmental issues especially: Friends of the Earth, Soil Assoc, Fairtrade Fndn, Dorset Wildlife Tst; Glenfiddich Award for Best Food TV Prog for A Cook on the Wild Side 1998, Glenfiddich Trophy 2002; *Books* Cuisine Bon Marché (1995), A Cook on the Wild Side (1997), Chindogu: 101 Unuseless Japanese Inventions (ed, 1997), The Very Best of TV Dinners (1999), The River Cottage Cookbook (2001), The River Cottage Year (2003), The River Cottage Meat Book (2004); *Recreations* cooking, fishing, scuba diving, vegetable gardening, charcuterie; *Style*— Hugh Fearnley-Whittingstall, Esq; ✉ c/o Anthony Topping, Greene and Heaton, 37 Goldhawk Road, London W12 8QQ (tel 020 8749 0315)

FEARON, Daniel; s of Henry Bridges Fearon (d 1995), of Maidenhead, Berks, and Alethea, *née* McKenna (d 1994); *b* 14 October 1944; *Educ* Canford; *m* 20 Feb 1971, Karen Dawn, da of Clifford M Wark (d 2005), of Toronto, Canada; 1 s (James Adrian b 1978), 1 da (Letitia Jane b 1981); *Career* Sotheby & Co 1963–69, Parke Bernet NY 1969–70, Spink & Son 1970–86; md Glendining & Co 1986–93, head of coins and medals W & F C Bonham & Sons 1993–2000, professional numismatic conslt 2000–; memb Br Numismatic Soc 1960 (memb Cncl 1986); memb Worshipful Co of Drapers 1970; FRNS 1968–2005; *Books* Catalogue of British Commemorative Medals (1984), Victorian Souvenir Medals (1986); *Style*— Daniel Fearon, Esq; ✉ 9 Coombe House Chase, New Malden, Surrey KT3 4SL (e-mail info@danielfearon.com)

FEARON, Prof Douglas Thomas; s of Henry Dana Fearon (d 1987), and Frances Hudson, *née* Eubanks (d 1995); *b* 16 October 1942; *Educ* Williams Coll Williamstown Massachusetts (BA), Johns Hopkins Univ Sch of Med Baltimore Maryland (MD); *m* 26 May 1977, Clare MacIntyre, da of Burrows J Wheless; 1 da (Elizabeth MacIntyre b 5 Feb 1982), 1 s (Thomas Henry b 22 Oct 1984); *Career* residency (internal med) Johns Hopkins Hosp Baltimore 1968–70, Maj US Army Med Corps 1970–72 (Bronze Star); Harvard Med Sch Boston: research fell in med 1972–75, instr in med 1975–76, asst prof of med 1976–79, assoc prof of med 1979–84, prof of med 1984–87; prof of med Johns Hopkins Univ and dir Grad Immunology Prog 1987–93, Wellcome Tst research prof of med Univ of Cambridge Sch of Clinical Med and princ research fell Wellcome Tst 1993–, fell Trinity Coll Cambridge; hon conslt in med Addenbrooke's Hosp Cambridge 1993–; Helen Hay Whitney Fndn research fellowship 1974–77, Merit Award Nat Insts of Health 1991, Lee C Howley Sr Prize for Arthritis Research Arthritis Fndn 1991; former memb Research Ctees Arthritis Fndn and American Heart Fndn; former memb Research Sub-ctee Arthritis and Rheumatism Cncl; currently memb Scientific Ctee Ludwig Inst for Cancer Research; author of numerous pubns in learned jls; memb Editorial Bd: Clinical and Experimental Immunology, Immunity, Science, Jl of Experimental Med; memb Exec Ctee Euro Jl of Immunology; memb: American Soc for Clinical Investigation 1979, Assoc of American Physicians 1984, Assoc of Physicians of GB and I 1994; fell American Assoc for the Advancement of Science 1990; FRCP 1994; *Recreations* tennis, golf; *Clubs* Country (Brookline, Massachusetts); *Style*— Prof Douglas Fearon; ✉ Wellcome Trust Immunology Unit, University of Cambridge School of Clinical Medicine, Hills Road, Cambridge CB2 2SP (tel 01223 330528, fax 01223 336815, e-mail dtf1000@cus.cam.ac.uk)

FEATHER, Prof John Pliny; s of Harold Renton Feather (d 1968), and Ethel May, *née* Barrett (d 1966); *b* 20 December 1947; *Educ* Heath Sch Halifax, The Queen's Coll Oxford (Hastings scholar, MA, BLitt), Univ of Cambridge (MA), Loughborough Univ (PhD); *m* 10 July 1971, Sarah, da of Rev Arthur Winnington Rees (d 1991), and Sarah Muriel Rees (d 1988); *Career* ed Scolar Press 1970–71, asst librarian Bodleian Library Oxford 1972–79, fell Darwin Coll Cambridge 1977–78, Munby fell in bibliography Univ of Cambridge 1977–78; Loughborough Univ: lectr 1979–84, sr lectr 1984–87, prof of library and info studies 1987–, head of Dept of Info and Library Studies 1989–94 and 2003–06, dean of educn and humanities 1994–96, pro-vice-chllr 1996–2000; memb numerous nat and int professional ctees; fell Library Assoc 1986, FRSA 1996; *Books* English Book Prospectuses - An Illustrated History (1984), The Provincial Book Trade in Eighteenth-Century England (1985), A Dictionary of Book History (1986), A History of British Publishing (1988, revised edn 2006), Preservation and the Management of Library Collections (1991, revised 1997), The Information Society (1994, revised 1998, 2000 and 2004), Publishing, Piracy and Politics (1994), The Wired World (with James Dearnley, 2001), Publishing: Communicating Knowledge in the 21st Century (2003); *Recreations* cookery, photography; *Clubs* Athenaeum; *Style*— Prof John Feather; ✉ Department of Information Science, Loughborough University, Leicestershire LE11 3TU (tel 01509 223058, fax 01509 223053, e-mail j.p.feather@lboro.ac.uk)

FEATHERBY, William Alan; s of Joseph Alan Featherby, of Cranleigh, Surrey, and Patricia Annie, *née* Davies; *b* 16 May 1956; *Educ* Haileybury, Trinity Coll Oxford (MA); *m* 12 April 1980, Clare Francis, da of Ian Richard Posgate, of Henley-on-Thames, Oxon; 5 s (Francis Alan b 1982, George Ian b 1986, John William b 1991, St John James Milton b 1993, William David b 1995), 5 da (Victoria Clare b 1985, Elizabeth Anne b 1988, Margaret Lucy b 1989, Eleanor Mary b 1990, Sarah Jane Webster b 1992); *Career* called to the Bar Middle Temple 1978; currently in private practice South Eastern Circuit, recorder South Eastern Circuit 2002–; *Publication* A Yorkshire Furrow (1993); *Recreations* reading, writing, opera and music, children; *Clubs* Carlton; *Style*— William Featherby, Esq; ✉ 12 King's Bench Walk, Temple, London EC4Y 7EL (tel 020 7583 0811, fax 020 7583 7228)

FEATHERSTONE, Jane; da of John Robert Featherstone, of Hemel Hempstead, and Elizabeth Ann, *née* Atherton; *b* 24 March 1969, Stirling; *Educ* Old Palace Sch Croydon, Univ of Leeds (BA); *Career* jt md Kudos Film and TV Ltd (with Stephen Garrett, *qv*); prodr: Touching Evil 1 and 2 (ITV), Sex 'n' Death (BBC2), Glasgow Kiss (BBC1); exec prodr: Pure, Spooks (MI5) 1, 2, and 3 (BBC1), Pleasureland (Channel 4), Comfortably Numb (Channel 4), Hustle 1 (BBC1), Hustle 2 (BBC1), Spooks 4 (BBC1); memb BAFTA 1996–; *Awards* incl: BAFTA nomination Best Drama Series and RTS Soc Award nomination Best Behind the Scenes Newcomer for Touching Evil 1 and 2, BAFTA nomination Best Single Film for Sex 'n' Death, various awards at festivals incl Berlin, Emden and BIFA for Pure; for Spooks (MI5) 1, 2, and 3 incl: BAFTA Award Best Drama Series, Broadcast Award Best Drama Series 2003 (nomination 2004), RTS Award Best Drama Series 2004 (nomination 2003), nomination Banff Rockie Award Best Continuing Series 2003 and 2004, nomination Indie Award Best Prodn of the Year and Best Drama, nomination BAFTA Craft Award Editing Fiction/Entertainment; *Recreations* cinema, sailing, skiing, riding; *Clubs* Soho House; *Style*— Ms Jane Featherstone; ✉ Kudos Film and TV Ltd, 12–14 Amwell Street, London EC1R 1UQ (tel 020 7812 3270)

FEATHERSTONE, Lynne Choona; MP; da of Joseph Woolf Ryness (d 1967), of London, and Gladys, *née* Schneider (d 1991); *b* 20 December 1951; *Educ* South Hampstead HS, Oxford Poly; *m* 30 April 1982 (m dis 2002), Stephen Featherstone; 2 da (Jenna Jovi b 30 Dec 1983, Cady Grace b 7 June 1989); *Career* ldr Oppn Haringey Cncl 1998–2002; memb London Assembly GLA (Lib Dem) London (list) 2000–05; MP (Lib Dem) Hornsey and Wood Green 2005–; *Publications* Marketing and Communication Techniques for Architects (1992); *Recreations* tennis, architecture, food, film; *Style*— Lynne Featherstone, MP; ✉ House of Commons, London SW1A 0PW (tel 020 7219 8401, e-mail featherstonel@parliament.uk)

FEATHERSTONE, Michael David; s of Mr L Featherstone, and Mrs N Featherstone; *b* 6 April 1951; *Educ* Whitgift Sch, St Catherine's Coll Oxford (MA); *m* 1976, Patricia Anne, da of Geoffrey French; 2 s (James b 15 Aug 1980, Tom b 30 Dec 1988), 1 da (Elizabeth b 2 Feb 1985); *Career* housemaster Radley Coll until 1990, headmaster Ryde Sch IoW 1990–97, headmaster Barnard Castle Sch 1997–2004, princ La Grand Boissière Secondary Sch Geneva 2004–; *Clubs* East India; *Style*— Michael Featherstone, Esq; ✉ La Grand Boissière, 62 route du Chêne, CH-1208, Geneva, Switzerland

FEATHERSTONE, HE Simon Mark; *b* 24 July 1958; *m* 1981, Gail Teresa, *née* Salisbury; 1 s, 2 da; *Career* diplomat; entered HM Dip Serv 1980, asst desk offr S Asian Dept FCO 1980–81, Mandarin language trg 1981–83, science and technol offr Beijing 1984–86, desk offr Falkland Islands Dept FCO 1987–88, on loan to Cabinet Office 1988–89, consul-gen Shanghai 1994–96, cnsllr (political and economic) Beijing 1996–98, head EU Dept (External) FCO 1998–2003, ambass to Switzerland 2004– (concurrently non-resident ambass to Liechtenstein); *Style*— HE Mr Simon Featherstone; ✉ c/o Foreign & Commonwealth Office (Berne), King Charles Street, London SW1A 2AH

FEAVER, William Andrew; s of Douglas Russell Feaver (d 1997), and Katherine Muriel Rose, *née* Stubbs (d 1987); *b* 1 December 1942; *Educ* St Albans Sch, Nottingham HS, Keble Coll Oxford; *m* 1, 1964, Anne Victoria Turton; m 2, 1985, Andrea Gillian Lester Rose; 6 c (Jane b 14 Oct 1964, Emily b 27 April 1966, Jessica b 20 Aug 1969, Silas b 1 Oct 1970, Dorothy b 11 May 1985, Alice b 21 Oct 1986); *Career* South Stanley Boys' Modern Sch Co Durham 1964–65, Royal GS Newcastle upon Tyne 1965–71, Univ of Newcastle upon Tyne (James Knott fell) 1971–73; art critic: Newcastle Jl 1968–73, London Magazine 1970–74, Art International 1970–74, Listener 1971–75, Sunday Times Magazine 1972–75, Vogue 1972–95, Financial Times 1974–75, Art News 1974–, The Observer 1975–98, various other pubns, radio and TV; exhibition organiser; work incl: George Cruikshank (V&A) 1974, Thirties (Hayward Gallery) 1979, Peter Moores Liverpool exhibitions 1984 and 1986, Lucian Freud (Kendal) 1996, Michael Andrews (Tate Gallery) 2001, Lucian Freud (Tate Britain) 2002, John Constable (with Lucian Freud, Grand Palais Paris) 2002, Lucian Freud (Wallace Collection) 2004, Lucian Freud (Museo Correr Venice) 2005; visiting prof Nottingham Trent Univ 1994–; memb: Art Panel Arts Cncl 1974–78, Art Ctee Nat Gallery of Wales 1991–, Academic Bd Prince of Wales Drawing Sch 2006–; tstee Ashington Gp 1989–; Critic of the Year Nat Press Awards 1983 (commended 1986); *Books* The Art of John Martin (1975), Masters of Caricature (1980), Pitman Painters (1988), James Boswell: Unofficial War Artist (2006), Lucian Freud (2007); *Recreations* painting; *Style*— William Feaver, Esq; ✉ 1 Rhodesia Road, London SW9 9EJ (020 7737 3386); Rogers Coleridge and White (Agent)

FEDDEN, (Adye) Mary; OBE (1997); da of Harry Vincent Fedden (d 1938), of Bristol, and late Ida Margaret, *née* Prichard; *b* 14 August 1915; *Educ* Badminton Sch, Slade Sch of Art (scholar); *m* 1951, Julian Otto Trevelyan (d 1988), s of Robert Trevelyan; *Career* artist; tutor: RCA 1956–64, Sir Yehudi Menuhin Sch 1964–74; *Solo Exhibitions* from 1948: Redfern Gallery London, Hamet Gallery London, New Grafton Gallery London, Christopher Hull Gallery London, Royal W of England Acad Bristol, Beaux Arts Gallery London and Bath, Bohun Gallery Henley and other provincial galleries; paintings in art galleries incl: Bristol, York, Leeds, Carlisle, Chichester, Nat Gallery of New Zealand, Univ of Cambridge, Univ of Durham, Univ of Bath, Univ of Warwick; murals incl: Festival of Britain 1951, Charing Cross Hosp, Canberra (P&O liner), schs in Bristol and London; paintings in collections of HM The Queen, HRH Prince Hassan of Jordan, Tate Gallery; pres Royal West of England Acad 1983–88; illustrated books incl: Motley the Cat (1997), The Green Man (1998), Birds (1999); subject of monograph by Mel Gooding 1995; Hon DLitt Univ of Bath 1996; RA 1992; *Recreations* reading; *Style*— Ms Mary Fedden, RA; ✉ Durham Wharf, Hammersmith Terrace, London W6 9TS (tel 020 8748 2749)

FEDER, Ami; s of Joseph Feder (d 1985), and Nicha, *née* Dornstein (d 2000); *b* 17 February 1937; *Educ* Hebrew Univ of Jerusalem, LSE; *m* 26 March 1970, Frances Annabel, da of late Michael August; 1 da (Shelley b 1972), 1 s (Ilan b 1974); *Career* Israeli Army 1956–58; called to the Bar Inner Temple 1965, and memb of Israeli Bar; currently in practice SE Circuit; memb: Hon Soc of Inner Temple, Common Law and Commercial Bar Assoc, Criminal Bar Assoc, Bar European Gp, European Criminal Bar, Justice, Int Assoc of Jewish Lawyers and Jurists; *Recreations* sport, music, theatre; *Style*— Ami Feder, Esq; ✉ 118 King Henry's Road, London NW3 3SN (tel 020 7586 4339); Chambers: The Chambers of Mr Ami Feder, Lamb Building, Temple, London EC4Y 7AS (tel 020 7797 7788, fax 020 7353 0535, e-mail afeder@lambbuilding.co.uk, website www.lambbuilding.co.uk); Office: ADAM Law Offices, The Tower - 15th Floor, 3 Daniel Frisch Street, Tel-Aviv 64731 (tel 00 972 3 607 8888, fax 00 972 3 607 8889, e-mail feder@adam-law.com)

FEDORCIO, Richard Edward (Dick); OBE (2006); s of Jan Adam Fedorcio (d 2006), of East Tilbury, Essex, and Winifred Elsie, *née* Ambler; *b* 25 March 1953; *Educ* Campion GS Hornchurch Essex, London Coll of Printing; *m* June 1982, Helen Marie, da of William Stokoe (d 1987); 1 da (Sarah b 31 July 1984), 2 s (Alex b 11 June 1987, Leo b 3 May 1990); *Career* PR offr GLC 1971–83, co info offr W Sussex CC 1983–86, dir of corp communication Kent CC 1986–94, dir of communication Electricity Assoc 1994–96, dir Westminster Advisers Ltd 1996–97, dir of public affrs and internal communication Met Police Service 1997–; IPR: chm Local Govt Gp 1985–87, Cncl memb on Educn Ctee 1988, chm Professional Practices Ctee 1989–90, pres 1992, memb Disciplinary Ctee 1997–98; FIPR 1990 (MIPR 1984), MMRS 1990, FRSA 2001, FCB 2001 (MCB 1986); *Publications* Public Relations for Local Government (1991); *Recreations* rugby, soccer, cricket, sailing, photography; *Style*— Dick Fedorcio, Esq, OBE; ✉ Metropolitan Police Service, New Scotland Yard, Broadway, London SW1H 0BG (tel 020 7230 2691, fax 020 7230 4246)

FEGGETTER, Jeremy George Weightman; TD (1986), QHS (1992), DL (1999); s of George Y Feggetter (d 2000), of Newcastle upon Tyne, and Doris, *née* Weightman (d 1997); *b* 5 May 1943; *Educ* Harrow, Univ of Durham (MB BS); *Career* sr res assoc Dept of Surgery Univ of Newcastle upon Tyne 1972–74, sr urological registrar Newcastle Gen Hosp 1975–76, sr surgical registrar Royal Victoria Infirmary Newcastle upon Tyne 1976–78 (house offr 1966–67, demonstrator in anatomy 1967–68, SHO 1968–69, registrar 1969–72), RSO St Paul's Hosp London 1978–79, conslt urologist Freeman Hosp and Wansbeck Hosp 1979–; FRCS; OStJ 1990; *Recreations* aviation, travel; *Clubs* RSM, Army and Navy; *Style*— Jeremy Feggetter, Esq, TD, DL; ✉ Department of Urology, Wansbeck General Hospital, Ashington, Northumberland NE63 9JJ (tel 01670 529310)

FEILDEN, Sir Henry Wemyss; 6 Bt (UK 1846), of Feniscowles, Lancashire; eld s of Col Wemyss Feilden, CMG (3 s of Sir William Feilden, 3 Bt, JP); suc 1 cous, Sir William Morton Buller Feilden, 5 Bt, MC, 1976; *b* 1 December 1916; *Educ* Canford Sch, King's Coll London; *m* 25 Aug 1943, Ethel May, da of late John Atkinson, of Annfield Plain, Co Durham; 2 da (Jennifer May (Mrs Graham Donald) b 1944, Anne Margaret (Mrs William Stokoe) b 1947), 1 s (Henry Rudyard b 26 Sept 1951); *Career* served in RE WWII; civil servant (ret); memb Kipling Soc; *Recreations* gardening, watching cricket; *Clubs* MCC; *Style*— Sir Henry Feilden, Bt; ✉ Little Dene, Heathfield Road, Burwash, Etchingham, East Sussex TN19 7HN (tel 01435 882205)

FEINSTEIN, Elaine Barbara; da of Isidore Cooklin (d 1974), and Fay, *née* Compton (d 1973); *b* 24 October 1930; *Educ* Wyggeston GS Leicester, Newnham Coll Cambridge; *m* 1956, Dr Arnold Feinstein (d 2002); 3 s (Adam b Feb 1957, Martin b March 1959, Joel b June 1964); *Career* poet and novelist; judge Gregory Poetry Awards Soc of Authors 1986–91, judge Heinemann Awards Royal Soc of Literature 1990, chm of judges T S Eliot Award 1994; winner Cholmondeley Award for Poetry 1990; memb Exec Ctee English Centre Int PEN 1989–; Hon DLitt Univ of Leicester 1990, Rockefeller Fndn fell at Bellagio 1998; FRSL 1980; *Novels* The Circle (1970), The Amberstone Exit (1972), The Glass Alembic (1973, US title The Crystal Garden), Children of the Rose (1975), The Ecstasy of Dr Miriam Garner (1976), The Shadow Master (1978), The Survivors (1982), The Border (1984), Mother's Girl (1988, shortlisted for LA Times Fiction Prize 1990), All You Need (1989), Loving Brecht (1992), Dreamers (1994), Lady Chatterley's Confession (1995), Dark Inheritance (2000); *Poetry* In a Green Eye (1966), The Magic Apple Tree (1971), At the Edge (1972), The Celebrants and Other Poems (1973), Some Unease and Angels - Selected Poems (1977), The Feast of Eurydice (1980), Badlands (1987), City Music (1990), Selected Poems (1994), Daylight (1997), Gold (2001), Collected Poems (2002), Collected Poems (2002), Talking to the Dead (2007); trans: The Selected Poems of Marina Tsvetayeva (1971), Three Russian Poets - Margarite Aliger, Yunna Morits and Bella Akhmadulina (1976); ed: Selected Poems of John Clare (1968), New Poetry (1988); *Biographies* Bessie Smith (1986), A Captive Lion - The Life of Marina Tsvetayeva (1987), Lawrence's Women - The Intimate Life of D H Lawrence (1993), Pushkin (1998), Ted Hughes: The Life of a Poet (2001), Anna of all the Russias: The life of Anna Akhmatova (2005); *Stories* Matters of Chance (1972), The Silent Areas (1980), New Stories (jt ed with Fay Weldon, 1979); *Television* Breath (BBC Play for Today, 1975), Lunch (dir Jon Amiel, 1981), 12–part series on The Edwardian Country Gentlewoman's Diary (1984), A Brave Face (BBC, 1985), A Passionate Woman (series on life of Marie Stopes, 1990), The Brecht Project (series on life of Bertolt Brecht); *Radio* plays: Echoes (1980), A Late Spring (1981), A Day Off (1983), Marina Tsvetayeva - A Life (1985), If I Ever Get On My Feet Again (1987), The Man in her Life (1990), Foreign Girls (1993), Winter Journey (1995), Women in Love (4 part adaptation, 1996), Book at Bedtime (10 part adaptation of Lady Chatterley's Confession,1996), Cloudberries (1999); *Recreations* theatre, music, travel, the conversation of friends; *Style*— Ms Elaine Feinstein; ✉ c/o Gill Coleridge, Rogers Coleridge & White, 20 Powis Mews, London W11 (tel 020 7221 3717, fax 020 7229 9084, e-mail gillc@rcwlitagency.demon.co.uk)

FELD, Robert Philip; s of Alfred Feld (d 1990), and Lily, *née* Green (d 1997); *b* 3 January 1953; *Educ* Brighton & Hove Sussex GS, Imperial Coll of Sci and Technol; *m* 6 March 1987, Tara Louise, da of Edward Scannell (d 1996); 2 s (Daniel Mark Joseph b 1988, Joshua Alfred b 1991); *Career* md Resort Hotels plc 1983–94, chm Aubrey Business Group 1994–96, project co-ordinator Eplon Engrg 2000–03, chief exec Aerospace and Technical Engineering 2003–; Freeman City of London; FHCIMA, FRSA; *Recreations* aviation, cricket, yachting; *Clubs* City Livery; *Style*— Robert Feld, Esq; ✉ Aubrey House, The Green, Rottingdean, Brighton BN2 7HA (tel 01273 303884, fax 01273 303884, e-mail rfeld6776@aol.com); Aerospace and Technical Engineering, Units 5 and 6, Leatherhead Industrial Estate, Station Road, Leatherhead KT22 7AL

FELDMAN, Baron (Life Peer UK 1995), of Frognal in the London Borough of Camden; Sir Basil Feldman; kt (1982); s of Philip Feldman, and Tilly Feldman; *b* 23 September 1926; *Educ* Grocers' Sch; *m* 1952, Gita, da of Albert Julius (d 1964); 2 s, 1 da; *Career* chm: Martlet Services Gp Ltd 1973–81, Solport Ltd 1980–85, Watchpost Ltd 1983–; Gtr London area Nat Union of Cons and Unionist Assocs: dep chm 1975–78, chm 1978–81, pres 1981–85, vice-pres 1985–; Nat Union of Cons and Unionist Assocs: dep chm 1982–85, chm 1985–86, vice-pres 1986–, chm Exec Ctee 1991–96 (memb 1975–98); chair Cons Conf Blackpool 1985; author of several party booklets and pamphlets; jt chm Cons Pty's Impact 80s Campaign 1982–90; memb: Policy Gp for London 1975–81 and 1984–, Nat Campaign Ctee 1976 and 1978, Advsy Ctee on Policy 1981–84, Ctee for London 1984–90, Cons Pty Bd of Treasurers 1996–, treas Cons Pty 1996–; vice-pres Gtr London Young Cons 1975–77; pres: Richmond and Barnes Cons Assoc 1976–84, Hornsey Cons Assoc 1978–82; patron Hampstead Cons Assoc 1981–86, contested GLC elections Richmond 1973; memb: GLC Housing Mgmnt Ctee 1973–77, GLC Arts Ctee 1976–81; dir Young Entrepreneurs Fund 1985–94, memb Free Enterprise Loan Soc 1977–84; chm: Better Made in Britain Campaign 1983–98 (also fndr), The Quality Mark 1987–92, Shopping Hours Reform Cncl 1988–94, Better Business Opportunities 1990–98, Festival of Arts and Culture 1994–95, London Arts Season 1993–96; membre consultatif Institutional Internat de Promotion et de Prestige Geneva (affiliated to UNESCO) 1978–93; memb: Post Office Users' Nat Cncl 1978–81, English Tourist Bd 1986–96; chm: Clothing EDC (NEDO) 1978–85, maker/user working party (NEDO) 1988–89; chm Salzburg Festival Tst 1998–2003 (vice-chm 1997–98); Silver Medal of Honour Salzburg 2003; FRSA 1987; *Books* Some Thoughts on Job Creation (for NEDO, 1984), Constituency Campaigning - a guide for Conservative Party workers; *Recreations* travel, golf, tennis, theatre, opera; *Clubs* Carlton, Garrick; *Style*— The Rt Hon Lord Feldman; ✉ House of Lords, London SW1A 0PW

FELDMAN, Prof David John; s of Alec Feldman (d 1976), and Valerie Annette, *née* Michaelson; *b* 12 July 1953, Hove, E Sussex; *Educ* Brighton Hove and Sussex GS, Exeter Coll Oxford (MA, BCL); *m* 4 Sept 1983, (Naomi) Jill, *née* Newman; 1 da (Rebecca Jane b 14 March 1985), 1 s (Jonathan Alec b 26 March 1987); *Career* Univ of Bristol: lectr in law 1976–89, reader in law 1989–92; Univ of Birmingham: Barber prof of jurisprudence 1992–2000, prof of law 2000–04; Univ of Cambridge: fell Downing Coll 2003–, Rouse Ball prof of English law 2004–, chm Faculty Bd of Law 2006–; visiting fell ANU 1989; legal advsr Jt Select Ctee on Human Rights Houses of Parl 2000–04; judge Constitutional Ct of Bosnia and Herzegovina 2002– (vice-pres 2006–); memb European Gp of Public Law Soc of Legal Scholars; memb Justice; hon bencher Lincoln's Inn 2003, academic assoc of chambers 39 Essex St; FBA 2006, FRSA; *Publications* The Law Relating to Entry, Search and Seizure (1986), Criminal Confiscation Orders: The New Law (1988), Civil Liberties and Human Rights in England and Wales (1993, 2 edn 2002), Corporate and Commercial Law: Modern Developments (jt ed, 1996), English Public Law (ed, 2004); *Recreations* music, cooking, dog walking; *Style*— Prof David Feldman; ✉ Faculty of Law, University of Cambridge, 10 West Road, Cambridge CB3 9DZ (tel 01223 330041, fax 01223 330055, e-mail djf41@cam.ac.uk)

FELDMAN, Dr Keith Stuart; s of Reuben Feldman (d 1999), and Karola, *née* Landau (d 1977); *b* 29 July 1943; *Educ* Christ's Coll Finchley, Imperial Coll of Science and Technol London (BSc, PhD); *m* 8 July 1971, Teresa Ann, da of Simon Wallace (d 2000), and, Miriam, *née* Cohen (d 1985); 1 da (Cordelia b 15 May 1979), 1 s (Alexander b 15 Dec 1981); *Career* fndr Inter-Bond Services Ltd 1969–81, sr exec Datastream International Ltd 1979–81, dir Carr Kitcat & Aitken Ltd (formerly Galloway & Pearson) 1981–93, res actuary Robert Fleming & Co Ltd 1993–98, ind consulting actuary 1999–; FIA 1976, memb Int Stock Exchange 1984, FSI; *Publications* The Zilch in General Relativity (1965), Dispersion Theory Calculations for Nucleon-Nucleon Scattering (1965), A Model to Explain Investment Trust Prices and Discounts (1977), The Gilt Edged Market Reformulated (1977), AIBD Yield Book (1979), Report on the Wilkie Stochastic Investment Model (1992), Report of the Fixed Interest Working Group (1997); *Recreations* chess, skiing; *Clubs* Argonauts; *Style*— Dr Keith Feldman; ✉ Skybreak, The Warren, Radlett, Hertfordshire WD7 7DU (tel 01923 853777, fax 01923 855657, e-mail kfeldman@onetel.com)

FELDMAN, Dr Michael Morris; s of Louis Feldman (d 1975), and Shura Miller (d 1981); *b* 3 December 1938; *Educ* King Edward VII Sch Johannesburg, UCL (BA), UCH Univ of London (MPhil); *m* 7 Jan 1960, Wendy Bankes, da of Arthur Gerald Bankes Morgan (d 1975); 2 da (Melanie Jane Bankes b 1960, Susan Rose b 1964), 1 s (Matthew Richard Bankes b 1969); *Career* house officer UCH 1966, conslt psychotherapist Bethlem Royal and Maudsley Hosp 1975–98 (registrar 1969–72), sr lectr Inst of Psychiatry 1982– (lectr 1974–75), training analyst Inst of Psycho-Analysis 1983 (assoc member 1975, full member 1981); MRCP, FRCPsych; *Books* Psychic Equilibrium and Psychic Change: Selected Papers of Betty Joseph (co-ed, 1989), The Oedipus Complex Today: Clinical Implications (jtly, 1989); *Recreations* gardening, music, photography, inland waterways; *Style*— Dr Michael Feldman; ✉ 32 Southwood Avenue, London N6 5RZ

FELDWICK, Paul; s of Cyril Eric Feldwick, of Abergavenny, Monmouthshire, and Ruby Marian, *née* Francis; *b* 25 April 1952; *Educ* Monmouth, Trinity Coll Oxford (MA), Univ of Bath (MSc); *m* 9 May 1981, Karen Millicent, da of David Rolf Thesen; 3 s (Oliver Paul b 5 June 1985, Hereward David b 2 Aug 1987, Gregory William b 20 Feb 1989); *Career* DDB London (formerly: Boase Massimi Pollitt, BMP DDB): account planner 1974–86, dep head of planning 1986–88, head of planning 1988–91, exec planning dir 1992–, worldwide brand planning dir 1999–2004, strategic learning offr DDB Univ 2005–; chm: Assoc of Qualitative Res Practitioners 1986–87, Account Planning Gp 1990–91; convenor of judges IPA Advertising Effectiveness Awards 1988–90; FIPA, fell Market Res Soc;

Books Advertising Works 5 (ed, 1990), Advertising Works 6 (ed, 1991), What is Brand Equity, Anyway? (2002); *Recreations* music, poetry; *Style—* Paul Feldwick, Esq; ✉ DDB London, 12 Bishops Bridge Road, London W2 6AA (tel 020 7258 3979, e-mail paul.feldwick@ddblondon.com)

FELL, Alison; da of Andrew Fell (d 1970), and Doris Johnstone; *b* 4 June 1944; *Educ* Kinloch Rannoch Sch, Lochmaben Sch, Lockerbie Acad, Dumfries Acad, Edinburgh Coll of Art (Dip Sculpture, post-dip scholarship and travelling scholarship); *m* 1964 (m dis), Roger Coleman, *qv*, s of Ronald Coleman; 1 s (Ivan b 1967); *Career* poet and novelist; co-fndr: The Welfare State Theatre Leeds 1969, The Women's Street Theatre Gp; journalist: Ink, Oz, Time Out; memb Spare Rib Editorial Collective 1975–79 (latterly fiction ed); writer in residence: C Day Lewis fell London Borough of Brent 1978, London Borough of Walthamstow 1981–82; tutor at writing workshops in arts centres across UK, writer in action SE Arts Kent 1985, tutor Arvon Fndn 1985–; writer in residence NSW Inst of Technol 1986, writing fell UEA 1998, Royal Literary Fund fell UCL 2002–03, res fell Middlesex Univ 2003–06, Royal Literary Fund fell Courtauld Inst 2006–; has recited at various arts venues throughout UK; subject of Whispers in the Dark (BBC TV Scotland) 1995; awarded Alice Hunt Bartlett Prize (Nat Poetry Soc) for first collections 1985; memb Greater London Arts Lit Panel 1984–86; memb: Soc of Authors, RSL; *Books* Hard Feelings (ed, 1979), The Grey Dancer (1981), Every Move You Make (1984), Truth, Dare or Promise (contrib, 1985), The Bad Box (1987), The Shining Mountain (1987, 2 edn 1988), Close Company - Stories of Mothers and Daughters (contrib, 1988), Sex and the City (contrib, 1989), Whose Cities? (contrib, 1991), Winters Tales (contrib, 1991), Mer de Glace (1991, Boardman Tasker award for mountain lit), The Pillow Boy of the Lady Onogoro (1994), The Mistress of Lilliput (1999), Tricks of Light (2003); *Poetry* Kisses for Mayakovsky (1984), The Crystal Owl (1988), Dreams, like heretics (1997), Lightyear (2005); *Plays* Mapping the Edge (jtly, performed Crucible Theatre Sheffield 2001, adapted for BBC Radio 2001); *Anthologies* The Seven Deadly Sins (ed and contrib, 1988), The Seven Cardinal Virtues (ed and contrib, 1990), Serious Hysterics (ed and contrib, 1992); poetry in anthologies: Licking The Bed Clean (1978), Bread and Roses (1979), One Foot on the Mountain (1979), Smile Smile Smile Smile (1980), Angels of Fire, Apples and Snakes, The New British Poetry, Is That The New Moon?, Anthology of Scottish Women's Poetry (1991), The Faber Book of 20th Century Scottish Verse (1992), The Faber Book of Movie Verse (1993), 20th Century Scottish Literature (2001), Red Sky at Night - Scottish Poetry (2003); stories in anthologies: Sex and the City (1992), Infidelity (1993), Bad Sex (1993), Shouting it Out (1996); *Style—* Ms Alison Fell; ✉ c/o Tony Peake, Peake Associates, 14 Grafton Crescent, London NW1 8SL (tel 020 7267 8033, fax 020 7267 4241)

FELL, Sir David; KCB (1995, CB 1990); s of Ernest Fell (d 1964), of Belfast, NI, and Jessie, *née* McCreedy (d 1981); *b* 20 January 1943; *Educ* Royal Belfast Academical Instn, Queen's Univ Belfast (BSc); *m* 22 July 1967, Sandra Jesse, da of Hubert Moore (d 1982), of Co Fermanagh, NI; 1 da (Victoria b 1972), 1 s (Nicholas b 1976); *Career* sales mangr Rank Hovis McDougall 1965–66, teacher Belfast Model Sch 1966–67, res assoc Queen's Univ Belfast 1967–69; NI civil serv: asst princ Miny of Agric 1969–72, princ Miny of Commerce 1972–77, under sec Dept of Commerce 1981–82 (asst sec 1977–81), dep chief exec Industrial Devpt Bd for NI 1982–84, perm sec Dept of Econ Devpt 1984–91; head NI Civil Serv and second perm under sec of state NI Office 1991–97; chm: Boxmore Int 1998–2000, Northern Bank Ltd 1998–2005, National Irish Bank 1999–2005, Prince's Tst NI 1999–2005, Harland & Wolff Gp plc 2001–02, Titanic Quarter Ltd 2001–04, Titanic Properties Ltd 2001–04, Goldblatt McGuigan 2005–, Chesapeake Corporation USA 2005– (dir 2000–); dir: Dunloe Ewart plc 1998–2002, Nat Aust Gp (Europe) Ltd 1998–, Fred Olsen Energy ASA 1999–2003, Clydesdale Bank plc 2005–; pro-chllr Queen's Univ Belfast 2005– (dir Fndn Bd 2003–); Hon DUniv Ulster; CIMgt, FIB; *Recreations* golf, rugby, listening to and playing music; *Clubs* Belfast Old Instonians; *Style—* Sir David Fell, KCB; ✉ The Queen's University Belfast, University Road, Belfast BT7 1NN

FELL, John Arnold; s of Charles Arthur Fell (d 1994), and Susannah, *née* Arnold (d 1978); *b* 31 August 1928; *Educ* Merchant Taylors', Pembroke Coll Oxford (MA); *m* 10 Aug 1963, Janet Eva, da of late Irvine Charles Parr, of Ottery St Mary, Devon; 2 da (Ruth Anne (Mrs Mugglestone) b 19 June 1966, Rachel Elizabeth (Mrs Ross) b 18 May 1968); *Career* admitted slr 1955; articled clerk Kimbers 1952–56; asst slr: Conquest Clare & Binns 1956–58, Hatchett Jones & Co 1958–63; Wilde Sapte: asst slr 1963–64, ptnr 1964–91, conslt 1991–; dir Moor Park (1958) Ltd; former dir: Portman Burtley Estate Co, Seymour Street Nominees Ltd; former chm: Broad St Ward Club, Queenhithe Ward Club; former dir Portman Settled Estates Ltd; Common Councilman Corp of London 1982–99; chm Tstees of Truro Fund; tstee: Royal Acad of Arts 1987–93, Housing Assoc Charitable Tst 1987–93, Lord Mayor's 800th Anniversary Awards Tst 1988, Portman Settled Estates 1995; govr: City of London Sch 1987–99 (chm Bd of Govrs 1993–96), Christ's Hosp; memb Law Soc; Freeman City of London 1980, Liveryman Worshipful Co of Gardeners 1982; *Recreations* walking, gardening, grandchildren; *Clubs* Old Merchant Taylors' Soc Guildhall, City Livery; *Style—* John Fell, Esq; ✉ Dellfield, 43 Sandy Lodge Lane, Moor Park, Northwood, Middlesex HA6 2HX (tel 01923 826508); Denton Wilde Sapte, 1 Fleet Place, London EC4M 7WS (tel 020 7246 7000, fax 020 7246 7777, telex 887793)

FELL, Richard Taylor; CVO (1996); *b* 11 November 1948; *m* 1981, Claire Peta, *née* Gates; 3 s; *Career* diplomat; entered HM Dip Serv 1971, third sec Ottawa 1972–74, second sec Saigon 1974–75, posted Vientiane 1975, second then first sec FCO 1975–79, chargé d'affaires Hanoi 1979, posted NATO Brussels 1979–83, first sec and head of Chancery Kuala Lumpur 1983–86, first sec FCO 1986–88, on secondment to industry 1988, cnsllr (commercial and economic) Ottawa 1989–93, cnsllr and dep head of mission Bangkok 1993–97, cnsllr FCO 1997–2000, consul-gen Toronto 2000–01, RCDS 2001–, high cmmr to NZ 2001–06 (concurrently non-resident high cmmr to Samoa and non-resident govr Pitcairn, Henderson, Ducie and Oeno Islands); *Style—* Richard Fell, Esq, CVO

FELL, Robert Antony (Tony); s of William Fell (d 1970), and Marie, *née* Flindt (d 1990); *b* 27 December 1932; *Educ* King's Coll Cambridge (BA); *m* 17 Dec 1993, Janis Susskind; *Career* Ibbs & Tillett 1955–56, ICI 1956–58, African Explosives and Chemical Industries 1958–63, md Hortors Printers 1968–74, fndr and conductor Johannesburg Bach Choir 1964–74, md Boosey & Hawkes Music Publishers 1974–96, dir Boosey & Hawkes plc 1977–2000; chm: The Q Gp 1996–1999, Royal Philharmonic Soc 1997–2005, Br Piano Concerto Fndn 2002–05; dir Future Talent 2007–; *Recreations* literature, all the arts, chamber music (pianist and cellist), tennis, travel, cooking, gardening; *Style—* Tony Fell, Esq

FELLNER, Eric; CBE (2005); *Educ* Cranleigh Sch, Guildhall Sch of Music and Drama; *m* (m dis), Gaby Dellal; 3 c; partner, Laura Bailey, *qv*; 1 c; *Career* prodr; co-chm (with Tim Bevan, *qv*) Working Title Films 1992–, launched Working Title 2 (with Tim Bevan) 2002; co-prodr Billy Elliot - The Musical 2005; govr BFI 2003–; 20 BAFTA Awards, 4 Academy Awards; *Film* Sid and Nancy 1986, Straight to Hell 1987, Pascali's Island 1988, The Rachel Papers 1989, Hidden Agenda 1990, Year of the Gun 1991, Liebestraum 1991, A Kiss Before Dying 1991, Wild West 1992, Frankie's House 1992, Romeo is Bleeding 1993, Posse 1993, No Worries 1993, The Hawk 1993, Four Weddings and a Funeral 1994, The Hudsucker Proxy 1994, Loch Ness 1995, Panther 1995, French Kiss 1995, Moonlight and Valentino 1995, Dead Man Walking 1995, Fargo 1996, Bean 1997, The Matchmaker 1997, The Borrowers 1997, The Hi-Lo Country 1998, Elizabeth 1998, The Big Lebowski 1998, What Rats Won't Do 1998, Notting Hill 1999, Plunkett & Macleane 1999, Oh Brother, Where Art Thou? 2000, The Man Who Cried 2000, Captain Corelli's Mandolin 2001, Bridget Jones's Diary 2001, The Man WhoWasn't There 2001, Long Time Dead 2001, 40 Days and 40 Nights 2002, Ali G Indahouse 2002, About A Boy 2002, The Guru 2002, My Little Eye 2002, The Shape of Things 2003, Thirteen 2003, Johnny English 2003, Ned Kelly 2003, The Italian Job 2003, Love Actually 2003, Shaun of the Dead 2004, Gettin' Square 2004, The Calcium Kid 2004, Thunderbirds 2004, Wimbledon 2004, Bridget Jones: The Edge of Reason 2004, The Interpreter 2005, Nanny McPhee 2005, Pride and Prejudice 2005, Mickybo & Me 2005, Sixty Six 2006, United 93 2006, Hot Stuff 2006, The Golden Age 2007, Atonement 2007, Mr Bean's Holiday 2007, Hot Fuzz 2007, Gone 2007, Smokin' Aces 2007; *Style—* Eric Fellner, Esq, CBE; ✉ Working Title Films Ltd, 76 Oxford Street, London W1D 1BS (tel 020 7307 3000)

FELLOWES, Julian Alexander (aka Kitchener-Fellowes, registered by College of Arms 1998); s of Peregrine Edward Launcelot Fellowes (d 1999), of Chipping Campden, and Olwen Mary, *née* Stuart-Jones (d 1980); *b* 17 August 1949; *Educ* Ampleforth, Magdalene Coll Cambridge (MA); *m* 28 April 1990, Emma, LVO (2000), da of Hon Charles Kitchener, ggniece of 1 Earl Kitchener of Khartoum, Lady-in-Waiting to HRH Princess Michael of Kent; 1 s (Peregrine Charles Morant Kitchener b 1991); *Career* actor, writer, lecturer and producer; chm RNIB Talking Books Appeal 2005–, vice-pres Weldman Hospicecare Tst; Paul Harris fell Rotary Club of GB; Hon DLitt Bournemouth Univ; *Theatre* West End appearances incl: Joking Apart (Globe), Present Laughter (Vaudeville), Futurists (NT); Mary Poppins (writer of book for stage musical, Prince Edward Theatre London and New Amsterdam Theatre NY, Variety Club Musical Theatre Award 2005); *Television* incl: The Greater Good (BBC), Sharpe's Regiment (Sharpe Films), Killing me Softly (BBC), Aristocrats (BBC/RTE), Monarch of the Glen (BBC); co-prodns as dir of Lionhead incl: Married Man (with LWT), Little Sir Nicholas (with BBC); writer/adaptor Little Lord Fauntleroy (BBC, winner of 1995 Int Emmy Award); writer/prodr The Prince and the Pauper (BBC, BAFTA nomination 1996); *Film* Fellow Traveller, Damage, Shadowlands, Regeneration, Tomorrow Never Dies, Place Vendôme; writer: Piccadilly Jim, Vanity Fair; writer/prodr Gosford Park (an original screenplay for Robert Altman), writer and dir Separate Lies; *Awards* New York Film Critics' Circle for Best Screenplay of 2001, Best Screenplay of 2001 National Film Circle (US), Writers' Guild Award for Best Original Screenplay of 2001, Best Screenwriter of 2001 ShoWest Distributors Award, Walpole Medal for Outstanding Achievement, Academy Award for Best Original Screenplay of 2001, Best Directorial Debut of 2005 (for Separate Lies) Nat Bd of Review; *Books* Snobs (2004); *Recreations* history, building; *Clubs* Boodle's, Annabel's; *Style—* Julian Fellowes, Esq; ✉ c/o ICM, Oxford House, 76 Oxford Street, London W1D 1BS

FELLOWES, Baron (Life Peer UK 1999), of Shotesham in the County of Norfolk; Sir Robert; GCB (1998, KCB 1991, CB 1987), GCVO (1996, KCVO 1989, LVO 1982), QSO (1999), PC (1990); s of Sir William Albemarle Fellowes, KCVO (d 1986), agent to HM at Sandringham 1936–64, and Jane Charlotte (d 1986), da of Brig-Gen Algernon Francis Holford Ferguson; bro of Thomas Fellowes, *qv*; *b* 11 December 1941; *Educ* Eton; *m* 20 April 1978, Lady (Cynthia) Jane Spencer, da of 8 Earl Spencer; 2 da (Laura Jane b 1980, Eleanor Ruth b 1985), 1 s (Alexander Robert b 1983); *Career* Lt Scots Guards 1960–63; dir Allen Harvey & Ross (discount brokers and bankers) 1968–77, private sec to HM The Queen 1990–99 (asst private sec 1977–86, dep private sec 1986–90); chm Barclays Private Banking, non-exec dir SAB Miller plc 1999–; chm Prison Reform Tst 2001–; tstee: Rhodes Tst 1999–, Winston Churchill Meml Tst 2001–, Mandela Rhodes Fndn 2003–; vice-chm Cwlth Inst 2000–, chm Voices Fndn 2004–; Liveryman Worshipful Co of Goldsmiths; *Recreations* watching cricket, golf, reading; *Clubs* White's, Pratt's, MCC; *Style—* The Rt Hon the Lord Fellowes, GCB, GCVO, QSO, PC; ✉ House of Lords, London SW1A 0PW

FELLOWES, Thomas William; s of Sir William Albemarle Fellowes, KCVO, DL (d 1986), and Jane Charlotte (d 1986), da of Brig-Gen Algernon Francis Holford Ferguson; bro of Baron Fellowes, GCB, GCVO, QSO, PC (Life Peer), *qv*; *b* 3 November 1945; *Educ* Eton; *m* 1, 1968 (m dis 1972), Caroline Moira, da of Capt D J R Ker, MC, of Portavo, Co Down; m 2, 1975, Rosamund Isobelle, da of Bernard van Cutsem (d 1975), and Lady Margaret Fortescue; 2 da (Catherine b 1977, Mary b 1978); *Career* dir Gerrard and National Discount Co Ltd 1973, dep chm Gerrard & National Holdings plc 1989–96, ret; non-exec dir: James Purdey & Sons Ltd 1991–2005, Hyperion Insurance Gp 1998–2001; chm London Discount Market Assoc 1995–97; conslt and non-exec dir Christie's International UK Ltd 1997–, conslt Julius Baer International 2002–; prop Varsearch; cmmr for Public Works Loans 1997–2001; chm of govrs Royal Hosp Sch Holbrook 1999–2003; Liveryman Worshipful Co of Ironmongers; *Clubs* Pratt's, White's, Aldeburgh Golf; *Style—* Thomas Fellowes; ✉ The Old Rectory, Barking, Ipswich, Suffolk IP6 8HH (tel and fax 01449 723060, e-mail tommy@twfellowes.f9.co.uk); Les Adrechs, Bargemon 83830, France (tel and fax 00 33 494 478168)

FELLS, Prof Ian; CBE (2000); s of Dr Henry Alexander Fells, MBE (d 1975), of Sheffield, and Clarice, *née* Rowell (d 1996); *b* 5 September 1932; *Educ* King Edward VII Sch Sheffield, Trinity Coll Cambridge (MA, PhD); *m* 17 Aug 1957, Hazel Denton, da of Donald Murgatroyd Scott, of Sheffield; 4 s (Nicholas Scott b 1959, Jonathan Wynne b 1961, Alastair Rowell b 1963, Crispin Denton b 1966); *Career* cmmnd RCS 1951, Chief Wireless Offr Br Troops in Austria 1952; lectr and dir of studies Dept of Fuel Technol and Chem Engrg Univ of Sheffield 1958–62, reader in fuel sci Univ of Durham 1962–75, prof of energy conversion Univ of Newcastle upon Tyne 1975– (public orator 1971–74), exec David Davies Inst of Int Affairs 1975–2002, pres Inst of Energy 1978–79; memb: Sci Consultative Gp BBC 1976–81, Electricity Supply Res Cncl 1979–89, Cncl for Nat Academic Awards 1988–92; dir Int Centre for Life Newcastle upon Tyne 1996–, chm New and Renewable Energy Centre Blyth 2002–05; involved with various TV series incl: Young Scientist of the Year, The Great Egg Race, Earth Year 2050, Take Nobody's Word for It, Tomorrow Tonight, QED, What If? The Lights Go Out, Horizon; Hatfield Meml Medal and Prize 1974, Beilby Meml Medal and Prize 1976, Sir Charles Parsons Meml Medal and Prize 1988, Royal Soc Faraday Medal 1993, Melchett Medal Inst of Energy 1999, Collier Medal Royal Soc 1999, Kelvin Medal Royal Philosophical Soc of Glasgow 2002; Higginson Lecture Univ of Durham 1999, Hunter Meml Lecture IEE 2000, Hawksley Meml Lecture IMechE 2001; FREng 1979, FInstE, FIChemE, FRSE 1996; *Books* UK Energy Policy Post-Privatisation (1991), Moving Ahead (1992), Energy for the Future (1995), World Energy 1923–1998 and Beyond (1998); *Recreations* sailing, cross-country skiing, energy conversation; *Clubs* Naval and Military; *Style—* Prof Ian Fells, CBE, FRSE, FREng; ✉ 29 Rectory Terrace, Newcastle upon Tyne NE3 1YB (tel and fax 0191 285 5343, e-mail ian@fellsassociates.com)

FELSTEAD, Peter John Raymond; s of Peter John William Felstead (d 1991), of E Grinstead, W Sussex, and Brenda Florence, *née* Scott (d 2007); *b* 27 October 1964, Cuckfield, Sussex; *Educ* Sackville Comp Sch E Grinstead, Univ of Manchester (BA); *m* May 1993 (m dis 2004); 2 s (Joshua William Taylor b 11 June 1995, Charles William Taylor Bradley b 15 Aug 1997); *Career* Jane's Information Gp: sub-ed and reporter Jane's Defence Weekly 1989–95, ed Jane's Intelligence Review 1997–99 (dep ed 1995–97), managing ed Security Business Unit 1999–2000, managing ed web content 2000–03, ed Jane's Defence Weekly 2003–; *Recreations* photography, films, military and aviation history, mountain biking, motorcycles; *Style—* Peter Felstead, Esq; ✉ Jane's Information Group, Sentinel House, 163 Brighton Road, Coulsdon, Surrey CR5 2YH (tel 020 8700 3707, e-mail peter.felstead@janes.com)

FELTWELL, Dr John Stewart Edmonds; s of Ray Parker Feltwell (d 1994), of Eastbourne, and Edna Mary, *née* Edmonds (d 1992); *b* 9 April 1948; *Educ* Sutton Valence, Royal Holloway Coll London (BSc, PhD), Univ of Kent at Canterbury (Dip Adult and Further

Educn), King's Coll London (Dip EC Law); *m* 21 July 1979, Carol Lynn, da of Kenneth Thomas Mellor; 1 da (Zoë Ellen Victoria b 16 March 1985), 1 s (Thomas Edgar Ray b 17 May 1989); *Career* scientist and conslt ecologist; asst biology teacher Sutton Valence Sch 1973–78; prop: Wildlife Matters (consultancy and publisher) 1978–, Garden Matters 1993–, Garden Matters and Wildlife Matters Photographic Libraries; author of 41 books on entomology and natural history for children and adults, trans into 30 languages, also numerous scientific and popular articles and reviews; tstee: Buglife - The Invertebrate Conservation Tst, Brazilian Atlantic Rainforest Tst (BART); memb Environmental Law Fndn 1997, life memb Int Dendrological Assoc; registered UK expert witness 1995–; Freeman: Worshipful Co of Poulters 1993, City of London 1994; fell Assoc of Lawyers and Legal Advsrs 1997; corp memb Inst of Environmental Mgmnt and Assessment; FRES 1970, FLS 1970, CBiol 1970, FIBiol 1993; *Books* incl: Biology and Biochemistry of the Large White (1982), Butterflies and Other Insects of Britain (1984), Discovering Doorstep Wildlife (1985), Natural History of Butterflies (1986), Naturalist's Garden (1987), Animals and Where They Live (1988, published in 27 countries), A Guide to Countryside Conservation (1989), The Story of Silk (1990), Butterflies: A Practical Guide (1990), Beekeeping: A Practical Guide (1991), Slugs, Snails and Earthworms (1991), Recycling in the School Environment (1991), Meadows: A History and Natural History (1992), Pocket Guide to European Butterflies (1992), Butterflies and Moths (Dorling-Kindersley Eyewitness series, 1993), Encyclopaedia of Butterflies of the World (1993), Butterflies and Moths, Nature Facts (1993), Bugs, Beetles and Other Insects (1993), Live Oak Splendor, Gardens Along the Mississippi (1994), Pocket Guide to North American Butterflies (1994), Butterflies of North America Folio Edition (1994), Butterflies of Europe Folio Edition (1994), The Conservation of Butterflies in Britain, past and present (1995), A Creative Step by Step Guide to Climbers and Trellis Plants (1996), Wide World of Animals (1996), Spectacular Hanging Baskets (1996), Pocket Guide of Butterflies of Britain and Europe (1998), Clematis for all Seasons (1999), Geraniums and Pelargoniums (2001), Clematis and Climbers (2003), Bumblebees (2006); *Recreations* observing nature, especially in rainforests; *Clubs* Farmers; *Style*— Dr John Feltwell; ✉ Marlham, Henley's Down, Battle, East Sussex TN33 9BN (tel 01424 830566, fax 01424 830224, e-mail john@wildlifematters.com, website www.wildlifematters.com and www.gmpix.com)

FELTWELL, Robert Leslie (Bob); s of Ray Parker Feltwell (d 1994), of Eastbourne, E Sussex, and Edna Mary, *née* Edmonds (d 1992); *b* 15 February 1944; *Educ* King Edward VI Sch Norwich, Univ of London (BSc(Econ)); *m* 22 July 1967, Christine Renée, da of Richard Henry John Rees (d 2001), of Horsham, W Sussex; 2 da (Alison Mary b 1970, Elizabeth Jane b 1972); *Career* family farm Hartfield Sussex 1962–67, grad apprentice then prodn mangr Rolls-Royce Ltd Aero Engines 1967–70, telephone prodn mangr ITT UK and Belgium 1970–76, gen mangr Western Incubators Ltd 1976–78, overseas devpt mangr Pauls International Ltd 1978–79, prodn dir Eastern Counties Farmers Ltd 1979–90, chief exec and dir Suffolk C of C, Industry and Shipping 1990–2006, elected dir Br Chambers of Commerce Ltd 1999–2004; dir: Suffolk TEC 1993–2001, Business Link for Suffolk Ltd 1995–2006, Project for a University for Suffolk Company Ltd 1997–2005, Suffolk LSC 2001–04, BLS Enterprises Ltd 2001–, Genix Holdings Ltd 2006–; treas Br C of C Execs 1993–2005, regnl sec E of England Cs of C 1993–2006, dir E of England Chambers of Commerce Ltd 1997–2006; fndr memb University for Suffolk Task Gp 1994–; ldr 35 UK Trade Missions to Brazil, Malaysia, Singapore, Hong Kong, Shanghai, South Korea, Vietnam and Thailand 1993–2005; regular broadcaster and writer on business and int trade; Freeman City of London 1993, Liveryman Worshipful Co of Poulters 1994; MIEx 1995, CCMI (MIMgt 1979); *Recreations* travel, tennis; *Clubs* Farmers, Ipswich Rotary; *Style*— Bob Feltwell, Esq; ✉ Woodfield, Bentley, Ipswich, Suffolk IP9 2DH (e-mail bobfeltwell@talk21.com)

FENBY, Jonathan Theodore Starmer; CBE; s of Charles Fenby (d 1974), and June, *née* Head; *b* 11 November 1942; *Educ* King Edward's Sch Birmingham, Westminster, New Coll Oxford (BA); *m* 1 July 1967, Renée; 1 da (Sara b 1970), 1 s (Alexander b 1972); *Career* corr bureau chief Reuters and ed Reuters World Serv 1963–77, corr The Economist France and West Germany 1982–86, home ed and asst ed The Independent 1986–88, dep ed The Guardian 1988–93 (dir 1990–95); ed: The Observer 1993–95, South China Morning Post 1995–99, Business Europe 2000–01; assoc ed Sunday Business 2000–01, co-fndr and editorial dir earlywarning.com 2004, ed-in-chief Trusted Sources 2006; memb Bd: European Journalism Centre, Belgo-Br Colloquium; contrib to Br, American, French and Japanese newspapers and magazines, broadcaster in GB, France, Switzerland, USA, Canada and the Far East; conf speaker GB, France, USA and Far East; Chevalier de l'Ordre de Merite (France); *Books* The Fall of the House of Beaverbrook (1979), Piracy and the Public (1983), The International News Services (1986), On The Brink, The Trouble With France (1998, revised edns 2002 and 2004), Comment peut-on être français? (1999), Dealing with the Dragon (2000), Generalissimo: Chiang Kai-shek and the China He Lost (2003), The Sinking of the Lancastric (2005), Alliance (2006), The Seventy Wonders of China (2007); *Style*— Jonathan Fenby, CBE; ✉ 101 Ridgmount Gardens, London WC1E 7AZ (tel 020 7323 0547, fax 020 7323 0579, e-mail jtfenby@hotmail.com)

FENDALL, Prof (Neville) Rex Edwards; s of Francis Alan Fendall (d 1967), and Ruby, *née* Matthews (d 1975); *b* 9 July 1917; *Educ* Wallingbrook, UCL and UCH (BSc, MB BS, MD, MRCS, LRCP), London Sch of Hygiene and Tropical Med (DPH); *m* 11 July 1942, Margaret Doreen, da of William Beynon (d 1917), of Pontardawe, S Wales; *Career* HM Overseas Med Serv 1944–64: Nigeria, Malaya, Singapore, Br Mil Admin Malaya 1945–46, Kenya 1948–64, dir of med servs 1962–64; Rockefeller Fndn: travelling fell 1963, memb staff 1964–67; regnl dir Population Cncl NYC 1967–71, Middlemass Hunt prof of tropical community health Liverpool Sch of Tropical Med 1971–81, emeritus prof Univ of Liverpool 1982–; visiting lectr Harvard Univ 1965–71, visiting prof of public health Boston Univ 1982– (distinguished fell Center for Int Health 1993), adjunct prof of community health sciences Univ of Calgary 1983–88; Cwlth Fndn travelling fell S Pacific 1976; conslt and advsr to numerous nat and int orgns and especially developing countries 1961–; WHO: memb Panel of Experts 1957–83, conslt SE Asia 1960; memb UK UNSCAT Delgn 1963; conslt: S Pacific Cmmn 1963, World Bank (investment survey E Africa) 1970, UNFPA (family planning prog) Arab Repub of Egypt 1972, OEO (Office of Economic Opportunity) Alaska 1972–74, Imperial Social Servs Iran (long term health planning) 1972–74, Int Devpt Res Cncl Canada (trg of health auxiliary teachers Nigeria, Malawi, Iran) 1973–75, ODA (rural health care) Pakistan Govt 1974–76, UNFPA (manpower devpt) Pakistan Govt 1974–, Mauritius Govt (health planning) 1975, Cwlth Secretariat (health manpower) Bangladesh 1976, Br Cncl (health manpower) Bangladesh 1976 and 1987, UNFPA (manpower devpt) Bangladesh 1978, WHO (health and manpower devpt) Maldives 1984, Project Hope USA (primary health care planning for displaced persons) El Salvador 1986; lead speaker Cwlth Mins of Health Conf Colombo 1974, memb Econ Devpt Advsy Panel WHO Ochocerciasis 1976–77, UK project mangr CENTO (low cost rural health care) 1976–79, India-Br Univ collaboration scheme ODA 1978–; memb: UK Delgn WHO/UNICEF (primary health care ALMA ATA) 1978, Exec Bd Cwlth Human Ecology Cncl, USA Nat Cncl for Int Health (fndr memb) 1974–85; presentation to Cwlth Min of Health Conf (paper on community approaches to health promotion and disease prevention) Aust 1989; participant speaker jt symposium Planet Earth learned socs of Canada and Queen's Univ 1991; Gold medal Migrendra Med Tst Nepal 1983; pres E African Branch Soc of Med Officers of Health; memb and patron Cwlth Human Ecology Cncl; memb: Soc of Public Health, Soc of Social Med, American Public Health Assoc, Acad of Med Physical and Natural Scis Guatemala 1986; memb BMA 1942, FFCM 1972, FFPHM; *Books* Auxiliaries in Health Care (1972), Use of Paramedicals for Primary Health Care in the Commonwealth (with J H Paxman and F M Shattock, 1979); more than 150 publications on rural health centres, med educn, epidemiology, mgmnt primary health care, planning and orgn, and ecology, with reference to developing countries; *Recreations* travel, gardening; *Clubs* Royal Cwlth Soc, Athenaeum (Liverpool); *Style*— Prof Rex Fendall; ✉ The Coach House, 48 Mill Street, Ludlow, Shropshire SY8 1BB (tel 01584 877195)

FENELEY, Mark Roger; s of Roger Charles Leslie Feneley, of Bristol, and Patricia; *b* 8 September 1961, Bristol; *Educ* Clifton (headmaster's scholarship, music scholarship, Douglas Fox Challen Gold Medal), CCC Cambridge (Smythe exhibition, Smythe scholarship, MA, MB BChir, MD), Guy's Hosp Med Sch London; *m* 1 (m dis); *m* 2, 14 July 2000, Sandra Sue Haskell, *née* Ingraham; 2 s (Ricky James b 10 Dec 1967, Anthony Scott b 28 Oct 1979), 1 da (Kim Marie b 19 May 1970); *Career* house surgn and house physician Guy's Hosp London 1987–88, demonstrator in anatomy Univ of Cambridge 1988–89, basic surgical trg posts Bart's Hosp London 1989–91, registrar (gen surgery) Ipswich Hosp 1991–92, research registrar Dept of Urology Bart's London 1992–94, sr registrar (urology) Bart's and Royal London Hosps London 1994–98, post doctoral fell James Buchanan Brady Urological Inst Johns Hopkins Hosp Baltimore MD 1998–2000, conslt urological surgn Nottingham City Hosp 2000–02, dir of postgrad med educn and clinical tutor Nottingham City Hosp 2002, conslt urological oncological surgn UCL Hosps 2003–, sr lectr in urological oncological surgery Inst of Urology UCL 2004–, hon conslt urologist UCHL NHS Fndn Tst 2004–; Hunterian prof RCS 1997; Section of Urology RSM Travelling Fellowship to USA 1997, Br Jl of Urology and Br Assoc of Urology Travelling Fellowship 1998, AstraZeneca Travelling Fellowship 2002; full memb Br Assoc of Urological Surgns, corresponding memb American Assoc of Urological Surgns; memb: Oncology Section Br Assoc of Urological Surgns, Section of Urology RSM (jr rep and elected memb Cncl 1996–98), Soc for Study of Androgen Deficiency (memb Ctee 2002–, vice-chm 2003–05, chm 2005–), Br Prostate Gp, BMA, Bristol Urological Inst, Cambridge Med Soc, European Assoc of Urology; FRCS 1991, FRSM 1994, FRCS (Urology) 1997; *Publications* numerous book chapters and articles in professional jls relating to urological oncology, prostate diseases and prostate cancer screening; *Recreations* music; *Style*— Mark Feneley, Esq; ✉ Department of Urology, University College London Hospital, Rosenheim Building, 25 Grafton Way, London WC1E 5DB (e-mail mark.feneley@uclh.org)

FENHALLS, Richard Dorian; s of Roydon Myers and Maureen Fenhalls; *b* 14 July 1943; *Educ* Hilton Coll Univ of Natal (BA), Christ's Coll Cambridge (MA, LLM); *m* 1967, Angela Sarah, *née* Allen; 1 s, 1 da; *Career* Goodricke & Son, Attorney SA 1969–70, Citibank 1970–72; sr vice-pres: Marine Midland Bank 1972–77, American Express Bank 1977–81; dep chm and chief exec Guinness Mahon & Co Ltd 1981–85, chm Henry Ansbacher & Co Ltd and chief exec Henry Ansbacher Holdings plc 1985–93, chief exec Strand Partners Ltd 1993–; *Recreations* historic car rallying; *Clubs* Royal Ocean Racing, Royal Southern Yacht (Hamble), Royal Thames Yacht, Veteran Car Club of Great Britain; *Style*— R D Fenhalls, Esq; ✉ 6 Pembridge Place, London W2 4XB; Strand Partners Limited, 26 Mount Row, London W1K 3SQ (tel 020 7409 3494, fax 020 7491 0899)

FENN, Sir Nicholas Maxted; GCMG (1995, KCMG 1989, CMG 1980); s of Rev Prof John Eric Fenn (d 1995), of Worcs, and Kathleen M, *née* Harrison (d 1999); *b* 19 February 1936; *Educ* Downs Sch, Kingswood Sch Bath, Peterhouse Cambridge (MA); *m* 1959, Susan Clare, da of Rev Dr G L Russell (d 1994), of Dorset; 2 s (Robert b 1962, Charles b 1963), 1 da (Julia b 1974); *Career* Flying Offr RAF 1954–56; HM Dip Serv; Burmese studies SOAS Univ of London 1959–60, vice-consul Mandalay 1960–61, third sec Rangoon 1961–63, asst private sec to four successive Secs of State for Foreign Affrs 1963–67, first sec and head of Chancery Br Interests Section Swiss Embassy Algiers 1967–69, first sec for public affrs UK Mission to the UN NY 1969–72, dep head successively of Sci and Technol Dept and Energy Dept FCO 1972–75, cnsllr, head of Chancery and consul-gen Peking 1975–77, RCDS 1978, head of News Dept FCO, spokesman of the FCO and press sec successively to Lord Carrington and Francis Pym 1979–82 (press sec to Lord Soames, last Governor of Southern Rhodesia (now Zimbabwe) 1979–80); ambass to: Myanmar 1982–86, Republic of Ireland 1986–91; high cmmr to Republic of India 1991–96, ret; Marie Curie Cancer Care: chief exec 1996–2000, chm 2000–06; vice-pres The Leprosy Mission 1996–2000, tstee: Sightsavers Int 1996–2005, Guide Dogs for the Blind Assoc 2002–06; Br jt chm Encounter 1997–2003; churchwarden Parish Church of St Michael and All Angels Marden 2001–06; hon fell Peterhouse Cambridge 2001; *Recreations* sailing; *Clubs* Oxford and Cambridge; *Style*— Sir Nicholas Fenn, GCMG

FENNELL, Alister Theodore (Theo); s of Alister Fennell, and Verity Fennell; *Educ* Eton (cricket XI), Byam Shaw Sch of Art; *m* 1977, Louise *née* MacGregor; 2 da (Emerald, Coco); *Career* silversmith with Edward Barnard, started own business 1975, Theo Fennell plc (jewellers with outlets worldwide); memb Ctee: Nordorff Robins Music Therapy (NRMT), Elton John Aids Fndn; *Recreations* reading, drawing, talking, golf, cricket, playing guitar, musical theatre; *Clubs* MCC, I Zingari, Chelsea Arts, Sunningdale, Saints & Sinners, Tramp; *Style*— Theo Fennell, Esq

FENNELL, Sir (John) Desmond Augustine; OBE (1982); s of Dr Augustine Joseph Fennell (d 1980), of Lincoln, and Maureen Eleanor, *née* Kidney (d 1995); *b* 17 September 1933; *Educ* Ampleforth, CCC Cambridge (MA); *m* Feb 1966, Susan Primrose, da of John Marshall Trusted (d 1979); 2 da (Alexandra b 1967, Charlotte b 1972), 1 s (Simon b 1969); *Career* Lt Grenadier Gds 1956–58; called to the Bar Inner Temple 1959 (bencher 1983); dep chm Beds Quarter Sessions 1971–72, recorder Crown Court 1972–90, QC 1974, ldr Midland & Oxford Circuit 1983–88, judge of the Court of Appeal Jersey and Court of Appeal Guernsey 1984–90, judge of the High Court (Queen's Bench Div) 1990–92, judge Employment Appeal Tbnl 1991–92; chm Gen Cncl of the Bar 1984 (memb Senate 1983, memb 1984, vice-chm 1988), inspr King's Cross Underground Fire Investigation 1987–88 (reported 1988), chm WARA (formed to oppose siting of third London airport in Bucks) 1969–90, vice-chm Wessex Area Cons 1978–80, pres Bucks Div Cons Assoc 1983–89 (chm 1976–79), pres Stoke Mandeville Burns and Reconstructive Surgery Res Tst 2002– (chm 1994–2002); *Clubs* Boodle's, Pilgrims; *Style*— Sir Desmond Fennell, OBE

FENNER, John Ronald; OBE (1997); s of Louis Finkel (d 2000), and Claire Lubkin (d 1975); *b* 7 December 1935; *Educ* Brunswick Sch Haywards Heath, Tonbridge, UCL (LLB); *m* 24 March 1963, Gillian Adelaide, da of Stanley Joshua Simmons; 2 s (Robert Matthew b 19 June 1965, Adam Edward b 28 Feb 1972), 1 da (Harriet Jane b 25 May 1967 d 1971); *Career* served articles Zeffertt Heard & Morley Lawson 1956–59, ptnr Lionel Leighton & Co 1962–70; Berwin Leighton: fndr ptnr 1970, managing ptnr 1980–84, chm 1984–90, sr ptnr 1990–94; fndr ptnr and sr ptnr Fenners 1994–2003, ptnr Maclay Murray & Spens 2003–05, sr conslt Pinsent Masons 2005–; chm: Nat Cncl for Jews in the former Soviet Union 1989–93, BURA (British Urban Regeneration Assoc) 1991–99 (tstee BURA Charitable Tst 1993–), British Friends of Israel Philarmonic Orch Fndn 1993–96, Legacy Ctee Norwood Ravenswood; tstee and dir RICS Research Fndn 2001–05; chm of appeal Nightingale House 1986–93; memb Cncl Local Investment Fund 1995–99; Freeman City of London, Master Worshipful Co of Fletchers 2002 (memb Ct of Assts); memb: Law Soc 1959, Southwestern Legal Fndn (USA) 1985, Int Bar Assoc 1985, City of London Slrs' Co (Grotius Prize 1960); *Recreations* history, theatre, opera; *Clubs* Carlton, RAC; *Style*— John Fenner, Esq, OBE; ✉ Pinsent Masons, 30 Aylesbury Street, London EC1R 0ER (tel 020 7490 4000)

F

FENTIMAN, Prof Ian Stuart; s of Harold Latter Fentiman (d 1989), and Vida Frances, *née* Jones; *b* 23 June 1945; *Educ* Trinity Sch of John Whitgift, King's Coll Hosp London (MB BS, MD, DSc); *Career* conslt surgn Guy's Hosp 1982–, prof of surgical oncology Univ of London; Arris and Gale lectr RCS 1978; LRCP, FRCS (MRCS), fell Assoc of Surgns; *Books* Detection and Treatment of Early Breast Cancer (1991, 2 edn 1998), Prevention of Breast Cancer (1993), Breast Cancer (1994), Cancer in the Elderly: Research and Treatment (1994), Atlas of Breast Examination (1997), Challenges in Breast Cancer (1999); *Style*— Prof Ian Fentiman; ✉ Academic Oncology Unit, Guy's Hospital, St Thomas Street, London SE1 9RT (tel 020 7188 4245, fax 020 7403 8381, e-mail ian.fentiman@gstt.sthames.nhs.uk)

FENTON, Prof Alexander; CBE (1986); s of Alexander Fenton (d 1960), and Annie Stirling Stronach; *b* 26 June 1929; *Educ* Turriff Acad, Univ of Aberdeen (MA), Univ of Cambridge (BA), Univ of Edinburgh (DLitt); *m* 1956, Evelyn Elizabeth, *née* Hunter; 2 da; *Career* sr asst ed Scottish Nat Dictionary 1955–59; Nat Museum of Antiquities of Scot: asst keeper 1959–75, dep keeper 1975–78, dir 1978–85; research dir Nat Museums of Scot 1985–89, dir European Ethnological Research Centre 1989–; chair of Scottish ethnology and dir School of Scottish Studies Univ of Edinburgh 1990–94; author; Hon DLitt Univ of Aberdeen 1989; FRSE 1985, FRSGS 1992, HRSA 1996 (hon prof of antiquities); *Books* incl: The Various Names of Shetland, Scottish Country Life, The Island Blackhouse, The Northern Isles: Orkney and Shetland, The Rural Architecture of Scotland, The Shape of the Past (2 vols), Wirds an' Wark 'e Seasons Roon', Country Life in Scotland, The Turra' Coo, Craiters... or twenty Buchan tales, Buchan Words and Ways; *Recreations* languages; *Clubs* New (Edinburgh); *Style*— Prof Alexander Fenton, CBE, FRSE; ✉ 132 Blackford Avenue, Edinburgh EH9 3HH (tel 0131 667 5456, e-mail alexander.fenton@btinternet.com)

FENTON, Charles Miller; OBE (1982), JP; s of Sir William Charles Fenton, MC, JP (d 1976), of Cleckheaton, W Yorks, and Margaret, *née* Hirst; *b* 24 February 1931; *Educ* Uppingham, Univ of Leeds (Dip Textile Industries); *m* 1963, Shirley Jane, da of George Arthur Windsor (d 1982), of Priestley Green, Halifax, W Yorks; 1 s, 1 da; *Career* chm Fenton Holdings Ltd, chm United Brake Ltd; High Sheriff W Yorks 1981; Hon FCGI, FTI; *Recreations* gardening, fishing; *Clubs* Carlton; *Style*— Charles Fenton, Esq, OBE; ✉ Priestley Green, Norwood Green, Halifax, West Yorkshire HX3 8RQ (tel 01422 202373)

FENTON, Maria Elizabeth Josephine; *b* 9 May 1956; *Educ* St Mary's Providence Convent, Kingston Univ, Coll of Law Guildford (BA); *Career* admitted slr of the Supreme Ct 1980; gp private banking legal advsr HSBC (Holdings) plc 1992–2007; memb: Law Soc, Sussex Law Soc; *Style*— Mrs Maria Fenton

FENTON, Dr Mark Alexander; s of Prof George Wallace Fenton (d 2000), and Dr Sylvia Fenton, *née* Hepton; *b* 20 October 1965; *Educ* Brentwood Sch, Peterhouse Cambridge (BA), Anglia Ruskin Univ (MSc, PhD); *Career* teacher Boswells Sch Chelmsford 1988–91, head of history and politics King Edward VI Sch Chelmsford 1991–97 (sr teacher 1994–97), dep head Sir Joseph Williamson's Mathematical Sch Rochester 1997–2001, headmaster Dr Challoner's GS Amersham 2001– (seconded pt/t to Br Cncl SLANT Project Trinidad and Tobago 2007–11); dir Ramsey Singers 1987–; memb Bucks Cricket Bd 2002–, chm Bucks Schs Cricket Assoc 2004–, tstee Cricket Fndn 2005–; govr Beacon Sch Chesham Bois 2005–; *Recreations* choral singing and conducting; watching, playing and coaching cricket; *Clubs* MCC; *Style*— Dr Mark Fenton; ✉ Dr Challoner's Grammar School, Chesham Road, Amersham, Buckinghamshire HP6 5HA (tel 01494 787500, fax 01494 721862, e-mail admin@challoners.com)

FENWICK, (John) Andrew; s of John James Fenwick, of London, and Muriel Gillian, *née* Hodnett; *b* 8 October 1959; *Educ* Eton, Univ of Exeter (BA), Harvard Business Sch (PMD Program); *m* 10 Sept 1994, (Fiona) Jane Morgan, da of Hubert John Watkins, of Presteigne, Powys; 4 s (Mungo b 3 Nov 1997, Theodore, Samuel, Inigo (triplets) b 18 Sept 2003); *Career* accountant Deloitte Haskins & Sells 1982–86, fin PR Broad St Assocs London 1986–87, fin ptnr and fin PR ptnr Brunswick Group LLP 1987–, dir Fenwick Ltd 1999–; govr New Kings Primary Sch Fulham 1993– (chair 1996–); tstee Royal Parks Fndn 2003–; Freeman City of London 1990, Liveryman Worshipful Co of Mercers 1992 (Freeman 1990); FCA 1995 (ACA 1985); *Recreations* travel, horticulture; *Style*— Andrew Fenwick, Esq; ✉ Brunswick Group LLP, 15 Lincoln's Inn Fields, London WC2A 3ED (tel 020 7404 5959, fax 020 7831 2823, e-mail afenwick@brunswickgroup.com)

FENWICK, Maj Charles Xtafer Sebastian; LVO (1977); s of David Fenwick (d 1982); *b* 7 April 1946; *Educ* Ampleforth; *m* 1997, Sara Elizabeth, da of late Col E Jewson, MC, DL, and Mrs Jewson, and wid of late David Nickerson; *Career* Maj, Regt Offr Grenadier Guards 1965–78, tutor to HH Sheik Maktoum Bin Rashid Al Maktoum Ruler of Dubai 1968–69, asst private sec to HRH The Duke of Edinburgh 1975–77; dir: By Pass Nurseries Ltd 1978–, By Pass Nurseries (Seeds) Ltd 1978–; chm Int Garden Centre Assoc H H (Br Gp) Ltd 1984–; md The Chelsea Gardener 1984–; *Clubs* Turf, Pratt's; *Style*— Maj Charles Fenwick, LVO; ✉ Higham Place, Higham, Suffolk CO7 6JY; 4 Ladbroke Terrace, London W11 3PG

FENWICK, Maj Justin Francis Quintus; QC (1993); s of David Fenwick (d 1982), and Maita Gwladys Joan, *née* Powys-Keck; *b* 11 September 1949; *Educ* Ampleforth, Clare Coll Cambridge (MA); *m* 21 June 1975, Marcia Mary, da of Archibald Dunn (d 1977), of Layham, Suffolk; 3 da (Corisande Mary b 1983, Rosamund Xanthe b 1985, Madeleine Isobel b 1988), 1 s (Hubert George Francis b 3 Aug 1990); *Career* Grenadier Gds 1968–81: Maj and Adj 2 Bn 1977–79, Extra Equerry to HRH The Duke of Edinburgh 1979–81; called to the Bar Inner Temple 1980 (bencher 1997); recorder 1999–, head of chambers 2000–05, dep judge of the High Court 2003–; dir: By Pass Nurseries Ltd 1982–, Bar Mutual Indemnity Fund 1998– (chm 1999); *Recreations* shooting, reading, wine; *Clubs* Garrick; *Style*— Justin Fenwick, Esq, QC; ✉ 4 New Square, Lincolns Inn, London WC2A 3RJ (tel 020 7822 2000)

FENWICK, Leonard Raymond; CBE (2000); s of Leo Stanislaws Fenwick (d 1983), of Newcastle upon Tyne, and Hilda May, *née* Downey (d 1989); *b* 10 August 1947; *Educ* West Jesmond and John Harlay Schs Newcastle upon Tyne; *m* 1969, Jacqueline; 1 da (Kate b 1982); *Career* NHS: joined 1965, various posts in health serv mgmnt in NE England and Humberside 1966–74, admin then gen mangr Freeman Hosp since 1975, chief exec Freeman Gp of Hosps NHS Tst 1990–; cncllr Tyne & Wear CC 1981–86; Freeman City of Newcastle upon Tyne, memb Worshipful Co of Shipwrights 1968, chm Stewards Ctee of Incorporated Cos and Ct of Guild of City of Newcastle upon Tyne; memb Inst of Health Servs Mgmnt 1972; *Style*— Leonard Fenwick, Esq, CBE; ✉ The Freeman Group of Hospitals, High Heaton, Newcastle upon Tyne NE7 7DN (tel 0191 284 3111, fax 0191 213 1968)

FENWICK, Mark Anthony; s of John Fenwick, of Newcastle upon Tyne, and Sheila E M, *née* Edwards; *b* 11 May 1948; *Educ* Millfield; *m* 9 Nov 1972, Margaret Kathleen, da of Col Frederick Roger Hue-Williams (d 1987), of Newbury, Berks; 1 da (Mia b 14 April 1978), 1 s (Leo b 26 Sept 1980); *Career* chm Fenwick Ltd 1997–, mangr Roger Waters 1992–; *Recreations* music, outdoor activities; *Style*— Mark Fenwick, Esq; ✉ Fenwick Ltd, New Bond Street, London W1A 3BS (tel 020 7499 7275, fax 020 7629 1186, e-mail markfenwick@mfm.demon.co.uk)

FENWICK, Dr Peter Brooke Cadogan; s of Anthony Fenwick (d 1954), of Kenya, and Betty, *née* Darling (d 1983); *b* 25 May 1935; *Educ* Stowe, Trinity Coll Cambridge (MB BChir), St Thomas' Hosp Med Sch London (DPM); *m* 18 May 1963, Elizabeth Isobel, da of Harry Nicholas Roberts (d 1985), of Bracewell, Lancs; 2 da (Annabelle Sarah Cadogan b 9 March 1964, Natasha Jane Cadogan b 13 Nov 1965), 1 s (Tristram Nicholas Cadogan b 2 Nov 1967); *Career* sr lectr Institute of Psychiatry Univ of London 1972–98, hon consIt research neurophysiologist Broadmoor Hosp 1973–; consIt neurophysiologist: Westminster Hosp 1974–77, St Thomas' Hosp 1974–89, Radcliffe Infirmary 1989–2002; consIt neuropsychiatrist Maudsley Hosp 1977–96; pres Scientific and Medical Network 2003– (chm 1986–2000); author of numerous articles on epilepsy, neurophysiology, violence, automatic behaviour; FRCPsych; *Recreations* flying, music, hill walking, trout fishing; *Style*— Dr Peter Fenwick; ✉ 42 Herne Hill, London SE24 9QP (tel 020 7738 5188)

FENWICK, Very Rev Dr Richard David; s of William Samuel and Ethel May Fenwick; *b* 3 December 1943; *Educ* Glantăf Secdy Modern Sch, Monkton House, Canton HS Cardiff, Univ of Wales Lampeter (BA, MA, PhD), Trinity Coll Dublin (MusB, MA), Fitzwilliam Coll Cambridge, Ridley Hall Cambridge; *m* 1975, Dr Jane Elizabeth Hughes; 1 s, 1 da; *Career* ordained: deacon 1968, priest 1969; asst curate: Skewen 1968–72, Penarth with Lavernock 1972–74; priest-vicar, succentor and sacrist of Rochester Cathedral 1974–78; St Paul's Cathedral: minor canon 1978–83, succentor 1979–83, warden of the Coll of Minor Canons 1981–83; vicar St Martin's Ruislip 1983–90, priest-vicar of Westminster Abbey 1983–90; Guildford Cathedral: canon residentiary and precentor 1990–97, sub-dean 1996–97; dean of Monmouth 1997–; chm Liturgical Cmmn Church in Wales; warden Guild of Church Musicians 1998–; Liveryman Worshipful Co of Musicians, Hon Liveryman and Master's Chaplain Worshipful Co of Gold and Silver Wyre Drawers; FLCM, FTCL, Hon FVCM, Hon FGCM; OStJ 2001; *Publications* contribs to various musical and theol jls; *Recreations* travel, reading, music; *Style*— The Very Rev the Dean of Monmouth; ✉ The Deanery, Stow Hill, Newport, Monmouthshire NP20 4ED (tel 01633 263338)

FENWICK, Trevor James; s of Leslie Fenwick, of London, and Mabel Alice, *née* Lee; *b* 28 February 1954; *Educ* Highgate Sch, Univ of Essex (BA); *m* Jane Seton Hindley; 3 s (James b 1987, Edward b 1989, Charles b 1991); *Career* md Euromonitor Int plc 1988– (dir 1980–), pres Euromonitor International Inc 1993–; dir Data Publishers Assoc 1997– (chm 1993–97); pres Euro Assoc of Directory and Database Publishers 2002–04; memb: Bd Confdn of Info Communication Industries, Cncl Advtg Assoc 1997–, Advsy Panel on Public Sector Information 2003–, Legal Deposit Advsy Panel 2005–; FCIM; *Style*— Trevor Fenwick, Esq; ✉ Euromonitor International plc, 60–61 Britton Street, London EC1M 5UX

FERADAY, Caroline Emma; da of Allen and Gillian Feraday; *Educ* Rochester GS, Mid Kent Coll of Higher and Further Educn; *Career* TV and radio broadcaster; presenter: Capital Radio 1995–2000, Sky One 1999–2000, Travel Deals Direct 2000–03, BBC Radio 5 Live 2001–03, LBC 97.3 2003–, GMTV, Sky Travel, Living TV; *Recreations* running, movies, travel; *Style*— Ms Caroline Feraday

FERDINAND, Rio Gavin; s of Julian Ferdinand and Janice Ferdinand; cous of Les Ferdinand (England int footballer), brother of Anton Ferdinand (professional footballer, West Ham Football Club); *b* 7 November 1978, Peckham, London; *Career* professional footballer; clubs: West Ham United 1993–2000 (first team debut 1996), Leeds United 2000–02 (transferred for then Br record fee), Manchester United 2002– (transferred for then Br record fee, winners FA Premiership 2003 and 2007, finalists FA Cup 2005 and 2007); England: 61 caps, memb World Cup squad 1998, 2002 and 2006; *Style*— Mr Rio Ferdinand; ✉ c/o Jeff Weston at SEM Group, 98 Cockfosters Road, Barnet, Herts EN4 0DP (tel 020 8447 4250)

FERGUS, Jeffrey John (Jeff); s of George M Fergus (d 1979), of Glasgow, and Catherine, *née* Fellowes; *b* 23 March 1949; *Educ* Crookson Castle Sch Glasgow, Univ of Strathclyde (BA); *m* 18 March 1989, Emily, da of Leslie Kark; 2 s (Frederick George Arthur b 1 April 1991, Charles William Merry b 26 May 1993); *Career* Leo Burnett advtg agency: joined Account Mgmnt Dept 1969, appointed to bd 1975, head of dept 1979–83, dep md 1980–83; md Grandfield Rork Collins 1983–86; Leo Burnett: md and chief exec Europe and ME 1986–94, regnl md Asia and the Pacific ops 1994–97, gp pres Europe, Africa, ME and Asia Pacific 1997–2001; dir Chartmille Roche 2005–, non-exec dir McDonald's Restaurants UK 2004–; chm Alumni Fund Bd Univ of Strathclyde 1990–94, memb Ct Univ of Strathclyde 2003–; MCIM 1980, MIPA 1982; *Clubs* Annabel's, Caledonian; *Style*— Jeff Fergus, Esq; ✉ 3 Fawcett Street, London SW10 9HN (tel 020 7352 1322, fax 020 7351 7780)

FERGUS-THOMPSON, Gordon; s of George Leonard Thompson (d 1986), of Leeds, and Constance, *née* Webb (d 2005); *b* 9 March 1952; *Educ* Temple Moor GS Leeds, Royal Manchester Coll of Music; *Career* concert pianist; debut Wigmore Hall 1976; performed as soloist with orchs incl: The Philharmonia, English Chamber Orch, City of Birmingham Symphony Orch, Royal Liverpool Philharmonic, Hallé Orch, Bournemouth Symphony Orch, BBC Symphony Orchs; regular broadcaster BBC Radio 3, toured extensively throughout Europe as recitalist and soloist with the Göteborg Symphony Orch and the Residente Orch of the Hague, also Australia, Far East, South Africa and USA; awarded Calouste Gulbenkian fellowship 1978; prof of piano Royal Coll of Music 1996–; *Recordings* incl: Complete Works of Ravel (2 Vols) 1992, Complete Works of Debussy (5 vols, winner solo instrumental section Music Retailers Assoc awards 1991) 1989, Complete Works of Scriabin (Vol 1 - Sonatas 4, 5, 9 and 10 and Studies Opus 42, winner Solo Instrumental Section MRA awards 1992) 1990, Rachmaninoff Études-Tableaux 1990, Bach transcriptions 1990, Two Rachmaninoff Sonatas 1987, Balakirev and Scriabin Sonatas 1987, Scriabin Vol 2 (Sonatas 2 and 3 and Studies Op 8) 1994, Scriabin Vol 3 (Preludes Op 2–17) 1994, Headington Piano Concerto 1997, Scriabin Vol 4 (The Complete Mazurkas) 2000, Scriabin Vol 5 (Preludes Op 22–74 and Impromptus Op 2, 7 & 10) 2001; *Recreations* art, chess, cooking, tennis, humour; *Style*— Gordon Fergus-Thompson, Esq; ✉ 12 Audley Road, London NW4 3EY (tel and fax 020 8202 5861)

FERGUSON, *see also:* Johnson-Ferguson

FERGUSON, Sir Alexander Chapman (Alex); kt (1999), CBE (1995, OBE 1984); s of Alexander Beaton Ferguson (d 1979), and Elizabeth, *née* Hardy (d 1986); *b* 31 December 1941, Glasgow; *Educ* Govan High Sr Secdy Sch; *m* 12 March 1966, Catherine Russell, da of Hugh Holding (d 1952); 3 s (Mark b 18 Sept 1968, Jason, Darren (twins) b 9 Feb 1972); *Career* football manager; player: Queen's Park 1958–60, St Johnstone 1960–64, Dunfermline Athletic 1964–67, Glasgow Rangers 1967–69, Falkirk 1969–73, Ayr United 1973–74, two Scot League caps; mangr: E Stirling 1974, St Mirren 1974–78 (First Div champions 1976–77), Aberdeen 1978–86, Scot nat team 1985–86 (asst mangr under Jock Stein 1985–86), Manchester United 1986–; honours with Aberdeen: winners Euro Cup Winners' Cup 1983, winners Super Cup 1983, Premier Div champions 1980, 1982 and 1984, winners Scot FA Cup 1982, 1983, 1984 and 1986, winners Scot League Cup 1985; honours with Manchester United: winners FA Cup 1990, 1994, 1996, 1999 and 2004, winners Charity Shield 1990, 1993, 1994, 1996, 1997, 2003 and 2007, winners Euro Cup Winners' Cup 1991, winners Super Cup 1991, winners Rumbelows Cup 1992, winners FA Premier League Championship 1993, 1994, 1996, 1997, 1999, 2000, 2001, 2003 and 2007, winners European Champions League 1999, Carling Cup 2006; Manager of the Year Scotland 1983–85, Manager of the Year England 1993–94 and 1998–99; Lifetime Achievement Award BBC Sports Personality of the Year Awards 2001; Freeman: Aberdeen 1999, Glasgow 1999, Manchester 1999; Hon MA: Univ of Salford 1996, Univ of Manchester 1997; Hon Dr jur: Robert Gordon Univ Aberdeen 1997, Univ of St Andrews 2002; Hon MSc Manchester Met and UMIST (jtly) 1998, Hon DLitt Glasgow Caledonian Univ 2001; *Books* A Light in the North (1985), Alex Ferguson - Six Years at United

(1992), Just Champion (1993), A Year in the Life (1995), A Will to Win (1997), Managing My Life (1999); *Recreations* golf, snooker; *Style*— Sir Alex Ferguson, CBE; ✉ Manchester United Football Club, Old Trafford, Manchester M16 0RA (tel 0161 868 8000, fax 0161 868 8804)

FERGUSON, Prof Allister Ian; *b* 10 December 1951; *Educ* Univ of St Andrews (BSc, PhD), Univ of Oxford (MA); *Career* visiting scholar Stanford Univ 1977–79; postdoctoral fell: Univ of St Andrews 1979–80, Univ of Oxford 1980–83; sr lectr Univ of Southampton 1987–88 (lectr 1983–87); Univ of Strathclyde: prof of photonics 1989–, tech dir Inst of Photonics 1995–, dep princ 2004; Lindemann fell 1977–79, SERC postdoctoral fell 1981–86; author of numerous pubns and chapters in books; Neil Arnott prize 1974, NPL Metrology award 1983; fndr Microlase Optical Systems Ltd; ed-in-chief JPhysD: Applied Physics 1998–2003; fell Optical Soc of America 1997; FInstP 1990, FRSE 1993, FIEEE 2000, FFCS; *Style*— Prof Allister I Ferguson, FRSE; ✉ Department of Physics, University of Strathclyde, John Anderson Building, Glasgow G4 0NG (tel 0141 548 3359, fax 0141 552 2891, e-mail a.i.ferguson@strath.ac.uk)

FERGUSON, Andrew James; s of K W E Ferguson, of Camberley, Surrey, and Sally, *née* Wragg (now Mrs Moore), of Market Harborough, Leics; *b* 22 September 1958; *Educ* St Chad's Cathedral Sch Lichfield, King's Sch Worcester, Br Sch of Osteopathy London (Dip, MSc); *m* May 1991, Louise, da of Nigel Mizen, of Dunsfold, Surrey; 2 c; *Career* in private osteopathic practice London 1980–, lectr Br Sch of Osteopathy 1982–86, osteopath to English Nat Ballet Sch 1992; memb Gen Osteopathic Cncl; *Books* Back and Neck Pain (1988); *Recreations* watching dance, gardening, writing; *Style*— Andrew Ferguson, Esq; ✉ 15 Pembridge Road, London W11 3HG (tel 020 7937 2298)

FERGUSON, Duncan George Robin; s of Dr Robert Lewis Ferguson (d 1998), and Kathleen Iris Ferguson, *née* Mackness; *b* 12 May 1942, Edinburgh; *Educ* Fettes, Trinity Coll Cambridge (MA); *m* 1966, Alison Margaret, da of James Simpson; 1 da (Sarah b 1967), 2 s (Alexander b 1969, Jason b 1971); *Career* actuarial student Bacon & Woodrow 1965–69, actuary Metropolitan Life Cape Town 1969–73, dir Int Eagle Star 1974–88, ptnr Bacon & Woodrow (latterly B&W Deloitte) 1988–2003 (sr ptnr 1994–2003); chm: Alba Life, Royal & Sun Alliance Life Holdings; non-exec dir: Halifax plc 1994–2001, Henderson Gp plc 2004–; pres Inst of Actuaries 1996–98 (memb Cncl 1989–2000), memb Cncl Int Actuarial Assoc 1996–2002; FIA 1970; *Recreations* hunting, theatre; *Style*— Duncan Ferguson, Esq

FERGUSON, George Robin Paget; s of Robert Spencer Ferguson, MVO, of Pewsey, Wilts, and Eve Mary, *née* Paget; *b* 22 March 1947; *Educ* Wellington, Univ of Bristol (BA, BArch); *m* 24 May 1969, (Aymée) Lavinia, da of Sir John Clerk, 10 Bt, of Penicuik House, Midlothian; 2 da (Alice b 1971, Corinna b 1979), 1 s (John b 1974); *Career* architect; fndr practice 1972; Ferguson Mann: ptnr 1979–87, md 1988–; fndr Acanthus Associated Architectural Practices Ltd 1986–, dir Concept Planning Group (masterplanners At Bristol harbourside project) 1991–96; dir Tobacco Factory Enterprises Ltd, dir Boats at Bristol (ferry) Ltd, fndr dir Acad of Urbanism 2005–; tstee Demos think tank 2007–; Living Landmarks Big Lottery Ctee 2006–07; creator of Bristol Brunel Mile, fndr and dir Bristol Beer Factory 2005; pres RIBA 2003–05; instigator of notion of x-listing (ugly buildings) 2004–; pres Avon Youth Assoc; tstee Br Cathedral Tst, tstee Gtr Bristol Fndn 1995–2001, patron Care & Repair; Bristol City cnclir (Lib) 1973–79, Parly candidate (Alliance) Bristol W1983–87; television and radio incl The Architecture Show 1998, Demolition (Channel 4) 2005, Building Britain (BBC 1) 2007; pres Bristol Soc of Architects 1993–94; High Sheriff Bristol 1996–97; winner RIBA, RICS and Civic Tst awards; memb Soc of Merchant Venturers 1995; Hon MA Univ of Bristol 1999, Hon PhD UWE 2003; RIBA 1972 (pres 2003–05), RWA 1997; *Books* Races Against Time (1983); *Recreations* travel, people, ideas, making things happen; *Style*— George Ferguson; ✉ Acanthus Ferguson Mann Architects, Royal Colonnade, 18 Great George Street, Bristol BS1 5RH (tel 0117 929 9293, fax 0117 929 9295, e-mail gferguson@afm-architects.co.uk, website www.afm-architects.co.uk)

FERGUSON, Gerrard Murray (Gerry); s of John Murray Ferguson (d 1976), of Tanworth in Arden, Warks, and Dorothy Maude Natalie, *née* Havill; *b* 23 July 1953, Manchester; *Educ* Abbey Sch Ashurst Wood, Epsom Coll, Univ of Birmingham (LLB); *m* 1981, Nancy Elizabeth, *née* Woodyatt; 2 s (Henry, Sam); *Career* admitted slr; articled clerk J W Ward & Son 1976–78, slr then ptnr Mowbray Woodwards 1979–89, ptnr Withy King (formerly Withy King & Lee) 1989–; claimant clinical negligence specialist; memb Action Against Medical Accidents (AvMA) Referral Panel and Law Soc Clinical Negligence Specialist Panel; memb: Legal Aid Bd, Legal Services Cmmn ctees, NHS Ind Complaints Advocacy pilots; memb Law Soc 1981; int memb American Assoc for Justice; *Recreations* motor sport photography; *Style*— Gerry Ferguson, Esq; ✉ Withy King, 5/6 Northumberland Buildings, Queen Square, Bath BA1 2JE (tel 01225 425731, fax 01225 315562, e-mail gerry.ferguson@withyking.co.uk)

FERGUSON, Brig (John) Gordon Goddard de Poulton; OBE (1984), DL (1999); s of Dr Stanley Fisher Ferguson (d 1998), and Johanna Margaret McDougall, *née* Gordon (d 1952); *b* 5 March 1943; *Educ* Downside, RMA Sandhurst, Staff Coll Camberley, NATO Def Coll Rome; *m* 5 Jan 1968, Celia Mary, da of Cdr Claudius Alexander Herdman, DL, RN, (d 1993), of Sion Mills, Co Tyrone; 2 da (Clare Joanna de Poulton (Mrs Rupert Cotterell) b 1968, Lucy Adelia de Poulton (Mrs Charles Talbot Costa Duarte) b 1970), 2 s (Edward Alexander de Poulton b 1978, Rory James de Poulton b 1980); *Career* cmmnd 1st The Queen's Dragoon Guards (QDG) 1962, helicopter pilot 1967–71, MA CinC North 1977–79, Dir Staff Army Staff Coll Camberley 1980–82, CO QDG 1982–85, Cdr Br Forces Lebanon 1983–84, ACOS G3 HQ 1 Br Corps 1985–87, Chief Policy SHAPE 1988–90, head Reinforcement Cell HQ NATO 1990–92, Dep Cmd and COS HQ S Dist Aldershot 1992–94, ACOS Ops HQ NORTH 1994–97; ADC 1995–97; conslt The Pushkin Tst 1998–2007; High Sheriff Co Tyrone 2001; FIMgt 1989; *Recreations* writing, classical music, fishing; *Style*— Brig Gordon Ferguson, OBE, DL; ✉ Braewood, Sion Mills, Co Tyrone BT82 9PY (tel and fax 028 8165 8224, e-mail gordon@braewood.freeserve.co.uk)

FERGUSON, James Gordon Dickson; s of Col James Dickson Ferguson, OBE, ERD, DL (d 1979), and Jean, *née* Gordon (d 1996); *b* 12 November 1947; *Educ* Cargilfield Sch Edinburgh, Winchester, Trinity Coll Dublin (BA); *m* 20 June 1970, Nicola Hilland, da of Walter G H Stewart; 2 s (Jim, William), 1 da (Jessica); *Career* Stewart Ivory & Co Ltd (formerly Stewart Fund Managers Ltd): joined 1970, dir 1974–, chm 1989–2000; chm: Value and Income Tst plc, The Scottish Oriental Smaller Cos Tst plc, The Monks Investment Tst plc; dir: The Independent Investment Tst plc, Edinburgh US Tracker Tst plc, Northern 3 VCT plc, Lloyds TSB Scotland plc, Lloyds TSB Fndn for Scotland; former dep chm Assoc of Investment Tst Cos; govr Gordonstoun Sch; *Recreations* country pursuits; *Clubs* New (Edinburgh); *Style*— James Ferguson, Esq; ✉ 25 Heriot Row, Edinburgh EH3 6EN

FERGUSON, Jeremy John; s of Archibald John Lindo Ferguson (d 1975), of Great Missenden, Bucks, and Ann Meryl, *née* Thomas (d 1991); *b* 12 November 1935; *Educ* Stowe; *m* 1, 19 July 1958, Josephine Mary, *née* Hitchcock (d 1995), 1 s (Paul b 1962), 1 da (Elizabeth b 1966); m 2, 21 June 1997, Gillian Marjorie Heal, *née* Stronach; *Career* ptnr: Seldon Ward & Nuttall 1960–74, Jeremy Ferguson & Co 1974–91, Chanters Barnstaple 1986–91, Chanter Ferguson Bideford & Barnstaple 1991–; dep coroner N Devon 1964–74, hon slr (memb and past pres) Bideford C of C, fndr and sec Bideford Devpt Project, pres Law Soc Motor Club, pres Devon and Exeter Law Soc 2002–03, memb Legal Aid Area Ctee, vice-pres Legal Aid Cmmn of the Fedn of European Bars 2003–04, chm Devon and Exeter Law Soc Mediation Ctee; *Recreations* motor racing, flying (PPL), civil mediation, video photography; *Style*— Jeremy Ferguson, Esq; ✉ Overskern, Churchill Way, Appledore, N Devon EX39 1PA (tel 01237 474855, e-mail jeremy.ferguson@ukonline.co.uk); 17 The Quay, Bideford, North Devon EX39 2EN (tel 01237 478751, fax 01237 470893); Bridge Chambers, Barnstaple, North Devon EX31 1HF (tel 01271 42268, e-mail jferguson@chanterferguson.co.uk)

FERGUSON, Kenneth Gordon; OBE (1990); s of late James Ferguson, of Aberdour, Fife, and late Blanche Stockdale, *née* MacDonald; *b* 17 February 1944; *Educ* Leith Acad, Heriot-Watt Univ, Napier Coll; *m* 21 Aug 1970, Jennifer Day, da of late Hugh MacTaggart Love, and late Margaret, *née* Anderson; 2 da (Amanda b 11 Aug 1971, Rebecca b 19 June 1975); *Career* chartered quantity surveyor; trainee Robert T B Gilray 1962–67; asst: Boyden and Cockrane 1967–69, City of Edinburgh Architect's Dept 1969–71, Todd and Ledson 1972–79; sr ptnr Kenneth Ferguson and Partners 1979–; vice-pres SCUA 1985–87, memb Edinburgh City Cncl 1977–92, chm Advsy Bd Commercial Unit Cardonald Coll Glasgow 1992–97; tstee dir Castles of Scotland Building Preservation Tst 1994–; incorporate CIOB 2000 (assoc CIOB 1991); FRICS 1979 (ARICS 1969); *Clubs* Scottish Arts; *Style*— Kenneth G Ferguson, Esq, OBE; ✉ Stoneheap Farm House, Stoneyburn, West Lothian EH47 8EH (tel and fax 01501 763497)

FERGUSON, Prof Mark William James; CBE (1999); s of late James Ferguson, of Marple Bridge, Cheshire, and Elanor Gwendoline, *née* McCoubrey; *b* 11 October 1955; *Educ* Coleraine Academical Inst, Queen's Univ Belfast (BSc, BDS, PhD, DMedSc); *m* (m dis); 3 da (Fleur Marcia b 9 Sept 1987, Astrid Olivia b 8 May 1991, Eanna Sorcha b 30 April 2002); *Career* Winston Churchill fell 1978, lectr in anatomy Queen's Univ Belfast 1979–84, prof of basic dental sci and head Dept of Cell and Structural Biol Univ of Manchester 1984–, dean Sch of Biological Sciences Univ of Manchester 1994–99; fndr, dir and ceo Renovo 1998–; faculty day lectr and visiting prof Univ of the Witwatersrand Johannesburg 1994; chm Health and Life Scis Panel UK Govt Technol Foresight Prog, pres Med Section BAAS, pres Craniofacial Soc, sec and pres European Tissue Repair Soc; fndr chm Manchester Biosciences Incubator 1997–99; memb: HE Cncl for Eng Basic Med and Dental Scis Panel 1996–, Scientific Ctee Br Cncl 1998–2001, Genome Valley Steering Gp 2000–, Ctee on Safety of Medicines Biologicals Sub-Gp 1999–2005; Colyer Prize RSM 1980, Alan J Davis Achievement Award American Dental Assoc 1981, Conway Medal Royal Acad of Med in Ireland 1985, Darwin lectr BAAS 1987, Distinguished Scientist Award Int Assoc for Dental Research Washington 1988, Pres's Medal BAOMS 1990, John Tomes Prize RCS 1990, Steager lectr NYU 1992, Teale lectr RCP 1994, 86th Kelvin lectr IEE 1995, JJ Pindborg Int Prize for research in oral biology 1996, Sheldon Friel Medal and lectr Euro Orthodontic Soc 1996, Broadhurst lectr Harvard Med Sch 1996, Carter Medal Soc for Human Genetics 1997, Charles Tomes lectr and Medal RCS 1998, Int Assoc for Dental Research Craniofacial Biology Award 2000, Northcroft lectr British Orthodontic Soc 2001, Lawdon-Brown lectr RCP 2002, European Sci Prize (jtly) 2002, NW Dir of the Year IOD 2006, Technol Pioneer World Economic Forum Davos 2007; Hon FFDRCSI 1990, Hon FDS (RCSEd) 1997, FMedSci 1998; *Publications* The Structure, Development and Evolution of Reptiles (1984), Crocodiles and Alligators: an Illustrated Encyclopaedic Survey by International Experts (1989), Cleft Lip and Palate: Long Term Results and Future Prospects (1990), Egg Incubation, Its Effects on Embryonic Development in Birds and Reptiles (1991), Gray's Anatomy (38 edn), The Structure, Development and Evolution of Teeth (2000); also author of over 300 papers and books on: palate devpt, wound healing, sex determination, alligators and crocodiles; *Recreations* scientific research, biology, travel, wildlife, reading, antiques; *Style*— Prof Mark Ferguson, CBE; ✉ Renovo, Manchester Incubator Building, 48 Grafton Street, Manchester M13 9XX (tel 0161 606 7222, fax 0161 606 7333, e-mail mark.ferguson@renovo.com)

FERGUSON, Nicholas Eustace Haddon; s of Capt Derrick Ferguson, RN (d 1992), of Craigard, Tighnabruaich, Argyll, and Betsy, *née* Eustace; *b* 14 October 1948; *Educ* Winchester, Univ of Edinburgh (BSc Econ), Harvard Business Sch (MBA, Baker scholar); *m* 18 Dec 1976, (Margaret) Jane Dura, da of Robert Collin, of Hook Norton, Oxon; 2 s (Alexander b 1978, Thomas b 1985), 1 da (Cornelia b 1979); *Career* venture capitalist; Schroders: joined 1980, chm Schroder Ventures Ltd 1984–2001, non-exec dir Schroders plc 2001–04, dir J Henry Schroder Wagg and Co Ltd, chief exec Schroder Ventures International Investment Trust plc, dir of several Schroder Gp cos; chm SVG Capital plc 2005– (dir 1996–); non-exec dir British Sky Broadcasting Gp plc 2004–; chm Courtauld Institute of Art, Int Students Club (C of E) Ltd; *Recreations* sailing, skiing; *Clubs* Brooks's; *Style*— Nicholas Ferguson, Esq

FERGUSON, Richard; QC; s of Wesley Ferguson (d 1972), of Derrygonnelly, Co Fermanagh, and Edith, *née* Hewitt (d 1995); *b* 22 August 1935; *Educ* Methodist Coll, Queen's Univ Belfast (LLB), Trinity Coll Dublin (BA); *m* 1 (m dis), Janet, da of Irvine Magowan, CB (d 1978), of Mount Norris, Co Armagh; 1 da (Kathrine b 1962), 3 s (Richard b 1964, William b 1966, James b 1968); m 2, Roma Felicity, da of J A Whelan, ERD (d 1997), of Belfast; 1 s (Patrick b 1987); *Career* Lt Royal Irish Fus TA 1958–61; called to the Bar Gray's Inn 1956 (bencher 1994); head of chambers, SC Republic of Ireland 1983; chm: Criminal Bar Assoc of England and Wales, Bar Cncl of England and Wales 1990–95, Mental Health Review Tbnl (NI); MP S Antrim 1968–70; FRGS; *Recreations* swimming; *Clubs* Garrick; *Style*— Richard Ferguson, Esq, QC, SC; ✉ 61 Highbury Hill, London N5 1SX (e-mail rferg77251@aol.com); Carmelite Chambers, 9 Carmelite Street, London EC4Y 0DR (tel 020 7936 6300)

FERGUSON, Dr Roger; s of Dr Alan Hudspeth Ferguson (d 1967), and Betty Fielding, *née* Willatt; *b* 23 August 1946; *Educ* City Sch Lincoln, Univ of Birmingham (MB ChB, MD); *m* 12 Jan 1974, Ruth Elizabeth, da of Prof Harold Spencer, of Willaston, Cheshire; 3 da (Sarah Helen b 1975, Jean Alison b 1976, Fiona Jane b 1978); *Career* med registrar Worcester Royal Infirmary 1970–73, res registrar Birmingham Gen Hosp 1973–75, sr med registrar Nottingham Gen Hosp and Derby Royal Infirmary 1975–79; conslt physician and gastroenterologist: Arrowe Park Hosp Wirral 1979–, BUPA Murrayfield Hosp Wirral 1980–; external professional advsr to the Health Cmmr for England (Ombudsman) 1998–; chm Mersey Region Conslts and Specialists Ctee; GMC: chm Fitness to Practice Ctee, chm Registration Appeals Panel; memb: Midland Gastroenterological Soc, Northern Gastroenterological Soc, Br Soc of Gastroenterology, Central Conslts and Specialists Ctee; former chm Wirral Wine Soc; FRCP 1987 (MRCP 1972), FRSM; *Books* Text Book of Gastroenterology (contrib, 1990 and 1993); *Recreations* swimming, golf, music, reading; *Clubs* Caldy Golf; *Style*— Dr Roger Ferguson; ✉ 89 Bidston Road, Oxton, Prenton, Wirral, Merseyside CH43 6TS (tel 0151 652 3722, fax 0151 670 9536, e-mail rferg10186@aol.com); Arrowe Park Hospital, Arrowe Park Road, Upton, Wirral CH49 5PE (tel 0151 678 5111)

FERGUSON, William James; OBE (1997), DL (Aberdeenshire); s of William Adam Fergsuon (d 1955), and Violet, *née* Wiseman; *b* 3 April 1933; *Educ* Turriff Acad, N of Scotland Coll of Agric; *m* 27 June 1961, Carroll Isobella, da of Robert Shaw McDonald Milne, of Kincardineshire; 1 s (William b 27 April 1962), 3 da (Kim b 29 May 1963, Nicola b 17 Aug 1965, Emma b 5 Aug 1968); *Career* 1 Bn Gordon Highlanders 1952–54; farmer 1954–; vice-chm Aberdeen and Dist Milk Mktg Bd 1984–94; chm: Aberdeen Milk Co Ltd 1994–99, Aberdeen Milk Servs 1995–99; dir Hannah Research Inst 1995–; memb Exec Ctee Assoc for the Protection of Rural Scotland (APRS) 1998–; chm N of Scotland Coll of Agric until 1989; vice-chm: Scottish Agric Coll until 1996, Rowett Res Inst until 1998; memb Scottish Co Life Museums Tst Ltd until 1998; Vice Lord-Lt Aberdeenshire 1998–; hon fell Scottish Agric Coll 1999; FRAgS; *Recreations* golf, skiing, field sports; *Style*—

F

William J Ferguson, Esq, OBE, DL, FRAgS; ✉ Nether Darley, Auchterless, Turriff, Aberdeenshire AB53 8LH (tel and fax 01888 511333)

FERGUSON FLATT, Rev Canon Roy Francis; s of Ray Flatt (d 1978), of Bury St Edmunds, Suffolk, and Trixie, *née* Bilner (d 1994); *b* 4 September 1947; *Educ* King Edward GS Bury St Edmunds, Scottish Sch of Librarianship Univ of Strathclyde, Coates Hall Scottish Episcopal Church Theol Coll Edinburgh; *m* 1978, Andrina Ferguson, da of Alf Ferguson (d 1999); 2 s (Andrew b 1980, Alexander b 1985); *Career* ordained: deacon 1980, priest 1981; curate St Andrews with Elie & Pittenweem (Dio of St Andrews, Dunkeld and Dunblane) 1980–82, rector of Christ Church Lochgilphead with St Columba's Kilmartin & All Saints Inveraray 1983–, dean of Argyll and the Isles 1999–2005, hon canon St John's Cathedral Oban 2006–; ecumenical relations offr C of S Presbytery of Argyll 2004–, diocesan chaplain with the deafened and hard of hearing 2006–; chm Mid Argyll Community Care Assoc; FSA Scot; *Recreations* gardening, sketching, playing solitaire on the PC; *Style*— The Rev Canon Roy Ferguson Flatt; ✉ Christ Church, Lochgilphead, Argyll PA31 8PY (tel 01546 602315, fax 01546 602519, e-mail drop.the pilot@virgin.net)

FERGUSON-SMITH, Prof Malcolm Andrew; s of Dr John Ferguson-Smith (d 1978), of Strathtay, Perthshire, and Ethel May, *née* Thorne (d 1993); *b* 5 September 1931; *Educ* Stowe, Univ of Glasgow (MB ChB); *m* 11 July 1960, Marie Eve, da of Stanislaw Franciszek Gzowski (d 1981); 3 da (Anne b 1961, Nicola b 1965, Julia b 1976), 1 s (John b 1970); *Career* prof of med genetics Univ of Glasgow 1973–87, dir West of Scot Regnl Genetics Serv 1973–87, ed-in-chief Prenatal Diagnosis 1980–2006, prof of pathology Univ of Cambridge 1987–98, hon conslt in med genetics Addenbrooke's Hosp 1987–98, dir E Anglian Regnl Genetics Serv 1987–95, emeritus fell Peterhouse Cambridge 1998– (fell 1987–98), research prof Centre for Veterinary Science Univ of Cambridge 1998–; Makdougall-Brisbane Prize Royal Soc of Edinburgh 1988; memb Neurology Bd MRC 1974–76, vice-pres Genetical Soc 1978–81; pres: Clinical Genetics Soc 1979–81, Perm Ctee Int Congress of Human Genetics 1986–91, European Soc of Human Genetics 1997, Int Soc for Prenatal Diagnosis 1998–2002, Assoc of Clinical Cytogenetics 2002–05; memb Cncl RCPath 1983–86, fndr memb Exec Ctee Human Genome Orgn 1988–92, WHO advsr in human genetics 1988–98, memb Cell Bd MRC 1989–93; Hon DSc: Strathclyde 1992, Glasgow 2002; FRCP (Glasgow) 1974, FRCPath 1978, FRSE 1978, FRS 1983, foreign memb Polish Acad of Sci 1988, FRCOG 1993, FMedSci 1998, HM Associate RCVS 2002, foreign memb Nat Acad of Med of Buenos Aires 2002; *Books* Early Prenatal Diagnosis (1983), Prenatal Diagnosis & Screening (1992), Essential Medical Genetics (5 edn, 1997); *Recreations* sailing, swimming, fishing; *Style*— Prof Malcolm Ferguson-Smith, FRS, FRSE; ✉ Department of Veterinary Medicine, University of Cambridge, Madingley Road, Cambridge CB3 0ES (tel and fax 01223 766496, e-mail maf12@cam.ac.uk, website www.vet.cam.ac.uk/genomics)

FERGUSSON, Alexander Charles Onslow; MSP; s of Lt Col the Rev Simon C D Fergusson (d 1981), of Alton Albany, Ayr, and Auriole Kathleen, *née* Hughes-Onslow; *Educ* Eton, WSAC Auchincruive; *m* 20 June 1974, Jane Merryn, da of Bertram Barthold; 3 s (Iain Alexander Onslow b 24 June 1975, Dougal George Onslow b 31 Jan 1977, Christopher David Onslow b 22 April 1986); *Career* farmer 1970–99; MSP (Cons): Scotland S 1999–2003, Galloway and Upper Nithsdale 2003–; memb: Scottish Landowners Fedn, Blackface Sheepbreeders Assoc; *Recreations* curling, rugby, folk music; *Style*— Alexander Fergusson, Esq, MSP; ✉ The Scottish Parliament, Edinburgh EH99 1SP (tel 0131 348 5636, fax 0131 348 5932, e-mail alex.fergusson.msp@scottish.parliament.uk)

FERGUSSON, Prof David; *b* 3 August 1956; *Educ* Kelvinside Acad Glasgow, Univ of Glasgow (MA), Tübingen Univ, Univ of Edinburgh (BD), Univ of Oxford (DPhil), Yale Univ; *m* Margot; 2 s (Mark, Calum); *Career* pt/t tutor Dept of Moral Philosophy Univ of Glasgow 1977, asst min St Nicholas' Church of Scotland Lanark 1983–84, assoc min St Mungo's Church of Scotland Cumbernauld 1984–86, pt/t lectr in systematic theology Univ of Glasgow 1984–86, lectr in systematic theology Univ of Edinburgh 1986–90, prof of systematic theology Univ of Aberdeen 1990–2000, prof of divinity Univ of Edinburgh 2000–; visiting lectr United Church of Japan 2002; pres Soc for the Study of Theology 2000–02 (memb Ctee 1994–97), sec Edinburgh Theological Club 1987–90; conslt ed and dir Scottish Jl of Theology 1993–, chair Editorial Bd Theology in Scotland 1993–, co-ed Eerdmans Guides to Theology series 1998–; memb Editorial Bd: Int Jl of Systematic Theology 1999–, Jl for the Study of the Christian Church 2001–; Cunningham lectr Univ of Edinburgh 1996, Bampton lectr Univ of Oxford 2001; tstee John Hope Tst 1995–; FRSE 2004; *Books* Bultmann (1992), John Macmurray: The Idea of the Personal (1992), Christ, Church and Society: Essays on John Baillie and Donald Baillie (ed, 1993), The Future of the Kirk: Theology in Scotland Occasional Paper No 2 (ed with D W D Shaw, 1997), John and Donald Baillie: Selected Devotional Writings (ed, 1997), The Cosmos and the Creator: Introduction to the Theology of Creation (1998), Community, Liberalism and Christian Ethics (1998), The Future as God's Gift: Explorations in Christian Eschatology (ed with Marcel Sarot, 2000), Northern Accents: Aberdeen Essays on Preaching (ed with Alan Main, 2001), John Macmurray: Critical Perspectives (ed with Nigel Dower, 2002), Church, State and Civil Society (2004); also author of contribs to several books; *Style*— Prof David Fergusson; ✉ New College, Mound Place, Edinburgh EH1 2LX (tel 0131 650 8912, fax 0131 650 7952, e-mail david.fergusson@ed.ac.uk)

FERGUSSON, Sir Ewen Alastair John; GCMG (1993, KCMG 1987), GCVO (1992); s of Sir Ewen MacGregor Field Fergusson (d 1974), and Winifred Evelyn Fergusson (d 1999); *b* 28 October 1932; *Educ* Rugby, Oriel Coll Oxford (MA); *m* 19 Dec 1959, Sara Carolyn, da of late Brig-Gen Lord Esmé Gordon Lennox, KCVO, CMG, DSO; 2 da (Anna b 15 June 1961, Iona b 7 May 1967), 1 s (Ewen b 30 Nov 1965); *Career* 2 Lt 60 Rifles KRRC 1954–56; Dip Serv 1956, asst private sec MOD 1957–59, Br Embassy Addis Ababa 1960, FO 1963, Br Trade Devpt Office NYC 1967, cnsllr and head of Chancery Office UK Perm Rep to Euro Communities 1972–75, private sec to Foreign and Cwlth Sec 1975–78, asst under sec state FCO 1978–82, ambass to South Africa 1982–84, dep under sec state FCO 1984–87, ambass to France 1987–92; chm: Coutts and Co 1993–99, Savoy Hotel Group 1994–98 (non-exec dir 1993–98, co-chm Int Advsy Bd 1999–2004); non-exec dir: Sun Alliance Group plc 1993–96, British Telecommunications plc 1993–99; chm of govrs Rugby Sch 1995–2002 (govr 1985–2002); tstee: Nat Gallery 1995–2002, Henry Moore Fndn 1998– (chm 2001–07); chm Govt Hospitality Wine Advsy Ctee 1993–2003, treas Saintsbury Club 2001–; played rugby for Univ of Oxford 1952–53 and Scotland (5 caps); hon fell Oriel Coll Oxford 1987; Hon LLD Univ of Aberdeen 1995; FCIB 1994; King of Arms of the Order of St Michael and St George 1996, Grand Officier Légion d'Honneur 1992; *Clubs* RAC, Beefsteak, Pratt's, Jockey (Paris); *Style*— Sir Ewen Fergusson, GCMG, GCVO; ✉ 111 Iverna Court, London W8 6TX (tel 020 7937 2240, fax 020 7938 1136, e-mail sir.ewenfergusson@btinternet.com)

FERGUSSON, HE George Duncan Raukawa; s of Brig Sir Bernard Fergusson (Baron Ballantrae, Life Peer) (d 1980), by his w Laura Margaret Grenfell (d 1979) (*see* Peerage Baron Grenfell 1976); *b* 30 September 1955; *Educ* Hereworth Sch NZ, Eton, Magdalen Coll Oxford (BA); *m* 10 Jan 1981, Margaret Sheila, da of Michael John Wookey, of Camberley, Surrey; 3 da (Laura b 1982, Alice b 1986, Elizabeth b 1991), 1 s (Alexander b 1984 d 2005); *Career* Murray & Tait Slrs 1977–78; joined NI Office 1978–, seconded to NI Dept of Commerce 1979–80, first sec Dublin 1988–91 (transferred to Dip Serv 1990), FCO London 1991–93, first sec Seoul 1994–96, head of Republic of Ireland Dept FCO 1997–99, consul-gen Boston 1999–03, on loan to Cabinet Office 2003–06, high cmmr to New Zealand 2006–; *Style*— HE Mr George Fergusson; ✉ c/o Foreign & Commonwealth Office (Wellington), King Charles Street, London SW1A 2AH

FERGUSSON, Ian Lewis Campbell; s of John Douglas Fergusson (d 1978), of London, and Alice Aleyn, *née* Maartensz (d 1968); *b* 11 April 1942; *Educ* Rugby, Univ of Cambridge (MA, MB BChir); *m* 16 Dec 1972, Marylin Susan, da of Lt-Col Guy Philip Arthur Shelley, OBE (d 1988), of Turleigh, Wilts; 1 s (Jamie b 4 Sept 1974), 3 da (Katie b 28 April 1976, Sally b 20 Feb 1980, Molly b 25 July 1982); *Career* RNR Lt-Cdr and surgn (ret 1980); conslt obstetrician and gynaecologist St Thomas' Hosp 1979–2002, conslt gynaecologist Chelsea Hosp for Women 1980–89, sr civilian gynaecologist to the RN 1982–, hon gynaecologist to St Luke's Hosp for the Clergy; tstee Tommy's - the Baby Charity; Freeman: City of London, Worshipful Soc of Apothecaries; memb BMA; FRCS 1971, FRCSEd 1971, FRCOG 1984; *Books* Records and Curiosities in Obstetrics and Gynaecology (1980); *Recreations* fishing, watercolour painting; *Clubs* MCC; *Style*— Ian Fergusson, Esq; ✉ Lister Hospital, Chelsea Bridge Road, London SW1W 8RH (tel 020 7730 1273, fax 020 7730 1275)

FERLEGER BRADES, Susan Deborah; da of Alvin Ferleger, and Beatrice, *née* Supnick; *b* 7 July 1954; *Educ* Courtauld Inst of Art (MA), Univ of Mass, Amherst/Barnard Coll Columbia Univ NY (BA, magna cum laude, Phi Beta Kappa); *m* 1979, Peter Eric Brades; 1 s (b 1989); *Career* curatorial co-ordinator Solomon R Guggenheim Museum NY 1975–79; res Whitechapel Art Gallery London 1979–80; Hayward Gallery: Arts Cncl of GB/South Bank Centre exhbn organiser 1980–88, sr exhbn organiser 1988–93 (public art prog co-ordinator 1990), dir 1996– (dep dir 1993–96), purchaser Arts Cncl Collection 1983–; memb: Visual Arts Advsy Ctee Br Cncl, South Bank Employers' Gp Public Art Gp, Visual Arts and Galleries Assoc (VAGA); patron The Nat Children's Art Awards 2001–; tstee IVAM Centro Julio Gonzalez Valencia Spain; awarded: Nat Endowment for Arts fell 1975–76, Smithsonian Inst travel grant for museum professionals 1977; ICOM; Int Ctee of Modern and Contemporary Art Museums (CIMAM); FRSA; *Style*— Ms Susan Ferleger Brades

FERMONT, Dr David Calvin; s of David Andre Fermont, of Esher, Surrey, and Edith Mary, *née* Kew; *b* 31 October 1946; *Educ* Cheltenham Coll, Middx Hosp Med Sch (MB, BS); *m* 28 Sept 1974, Linda Jane, da of Maj Geoffrey Noel Marks, of Hove, E Sussex; 1 da (Sara Louise b 7 June 1980), 1 s (James Alexander b 29 July 1983); *Career* conslt oncologist and dir Cancer Centre Mount Vernon Hosp, Northwick Park and St Marks Hosps 1983–; chm Hillingdon HA Dist Med Ctee, memb Hillingdon DHA Mgmnt Bd; med exec dir: Mount Vernon Hosp Tst, Mount Vernon and Watford Hosp NHS Tst; memb Br Inst of Radiology, FRCS, FRSM, FRCR; *Books* numerous med pubns; *Recreations* cricket; *Style*— Dr David Fermont; ✉ Great Sarratt Hall Cottage, Sarratt, Hertfordshire WD3 4PD; Cancer Centre, Mount Vernon Hospital, Northwood, Middlesex HA6 2RN (tel 01923 844231, fax 01923 844138)

FERMOR, Patrick Michael Leigh; *see:* Leigh Fermor, Patrick Michael

FERMOY, 6 Baron (I 1856); (Patrick) Maurice Burke Roche; s of 5 Baron Fermoy (d 1984), and Lavinia, *née* Pitman (who m 2, 1995, Nigel E Corbally Stourton); *b* 11 October 1967; *Educ* Eton; *m* 26 March 1998, Tessa Fiona, da of late Maj David Kayll of Briantspuddle, Dorset; 2 da (Hon Arabella Elizabeth b 18 March 1999, Hon Eliza Lavinia b 9 Nov 2000); *Heir* bro, Hon Hugh Roche; *Career* Page of Honour to HM Queen Elizabeth The Queen Mother 1982–85, former Capt The Blues and Royals; with Bass Taverns 1995–99, fndr and dir Arrow Pubs Ltd 1999; memb Cherwell DC 2000–04; *Recreations* hunting, shooting, gardening; *Clubs* Turf; *Style*— The Rt Hon Lord Fermoy; ✉ Handywater Farm, Sibford Gower, Banbury, Oxfordshire OX15 5AE (e-mail maurice@fermoy.co.uk)

FERN, Prof Dan; s of George Fern (d 1967), of Gainsborough, and Gwen Fern (d 1981); *b* 1 July 1945; *Educ* Queen Elizabeth GS Gainsborough, Manchester Coll of Art and Design, RCA; *m* 1969, Kate Fern; 2 da (Zoë b 1976, Ella b 1979), 1 s (Hugo b 1985); *Career* graphic artist; Royal Coll of Art: head of illustration 1986–, prof of illustration 1989–, head Sch of Communication Design 1993–, prof of graphic art and design 1994–; *Solo Exhibitions* Print and Collage Constructions (Curwen Gallery London) 1982, Collage, Print and Type Constructions (Curwen Gallery) 1985, Recent Work (Entrepotdok Amsterdam) 1986, Mapworks (Pentagram Gallery) 1994, Box Set (Pentagram Gallery) 1994; *Group Exhibitions* incl: Art/Work (Nat Theatre) 1979, Homage to Herge (Joan Miro Fndn Barcelona) 1984, Art Meets Science (Smiths Gallery London) 1988, Image and Object (Nat MOMA Kyoto Japan) 1990, Gate 14 (RCA) 1993, Collage (England & Co) 1993, Collage (Tate Gallery North) 2000, exhbn of original posters cmmned to mark the centenary of Henri de Toulouse-Lautrec (Centre Pompedou Paris and Stedelijk Museum Amsterdam) 2001–02, Permanent Collection V&A; clients incl: Sunday Times Magazine, Radio Times, New Scientist, Decca Records, Penguin Books, Pan Books, J Walter Thompson, Young and Rubicam, Conran Design, Michael Peters Group, Pentagram, Thames Television, Assoc of Illustrators, The Royal Court Theatre, Royal Acad London; cmmnd work incl: video on drawing (for Faber-Castell) 1993, film on Deutsche Romantik theme (for South Bank Centre and Goethe Inst) 1994, film for Harrison Birtwistle Festival (premiered South Bank) 1996; lectr and speaker various conferences and workshops; head Educn Ctee Assoc of Illustrators 1977–79, memb various jury panels; twice winner of both Gold & Silver D & AD awards; FRCA, FCSD, FRSA; *Books* Works with Paper (1990); *Recreations* opera and other performing arts, mountaineering, astronomy, cycling, collecting (books, stamps, printed ephemera); *Style*— Prof Dan Fern; ✉ 58 Muswell Road, London N10 2BE (tel 020 8883 5604); Communication, Art and Design, Royal College of Art, Kensington Gore, London SW7 (tel 020 7584 5020, fax 020 7225 1487)

FERNÁNDEZ, HE Mariano; s of Mariano Fernández (d 1999), and María Angélica, *née* Amunátegui; *b* 21 April 1945, Santiago, Chile; *Educ* Universidad Católica de Santiago, Univ of Bonn; *m* 27 June 1969, María Angélica, *née* Morales; 1 da (Magdalena b 23 Sept 1970), 2 s (Mariano b 27 Feb 1978, Cristóbal b 13 July 1983); *Career* Chilean diplomat; third sec Bonn 1971–74, exiled Bonn 1974–82 (ed magazine and chief ed news agencies), returned to Chile 1982, researcher and memb Exec Ctee Centre of Studies for Devpt 1982–90, ambass to European Community 1990–92, ambass to Italy 1992–94 (concurrently non-resident ambass to Malta), vice-min for Foreign Affrs 1994–2000, ambass to Spain 2000–02 (concurrently non-resident ambass to Andorra), ambass to the Ct of St James's 2002–06, non-resident ambass to Libya 2005–, ambass to Washington DC 2006–; pres: European-Latin American Relation Inst (IRELA) Madrid 1992–93 (vice-pres 1992), Int Cncl Latin American Centre for Relations with Europe (CELARE) Santiago 1996–98; vice-pres Italo-Latin American Inst (IILA) Rome 1994; memb Bd: Fintesa Fin Agency (Banco del Desarrollo) 1982–84, Radio Cooperativa 1982–90; memb Exec Ctee Jacques Maritain Inst Rome 1994–96; memb Political Science Assoc of Chile; memb Editorial Bd: Mensaje 1984–86, Fortin Mapocho 1986–88, Apsi 1986–89; contrib articles on int policy to magazines and jls; hon pres Chilean Assoc of Sommeliers; memb: Académie Int du Vin, Cofradía del Mérito Vitivinícola de Chile, Jurade de Saint Emilion, Commanderie de Médoc et Graves, Europaische Weinritterschaft, Slow Food; Grand Cross: Argentina, Brazil, Colombia, Ecuador, Finland, Germany, Holy See, Italy, Mexico, Panama, Peru, Spain; Grand Offr: Croatia, Germany, Sweden; *Clubs* Naval and Military, Travellers, RAC, Beefsteak; *Style*— HE Señor Mariano Fernández; ✉ Embassy of Chile, 1732 Massachusetts Avenue, NW Washington DC 20036, USA (tel 1 202 530 4115, fax 1 202 659 9634)

FERNANDO, Oswald Nihal; s of Cyril Philip Neri Fernando, and Louise, *née* Edline; *b* 22 October 1934; *Educ* Ceylon (MB BS); *m* 8 April 1961, (Susan Dulcie) Tallulah, da of Dr Charles Talbot; 3 s (Dr Hiran Chrishantha b 16 Jan 1962, Rohan Prashantha b 1 April 1963, Bimbi Shiran b 27 Feb 1967); *Career* conslt surgn Royal Free Hosp 1976– (res fell in renal transplantation 1969–70, lectr in surgery 1971–76); hon sr lectr Royal Free Hosp

Sch of Med 1976–; hon conslt surgn 1976–: Hosp of St John and St Elizabeth, Hosp for Sick Children Gt Ormond St; memb: Br Transplant Soc, RSM, Br Assoc of Urological Surgns; FRCS, FRCSEd; *Recreations* swimming, squash; *Style*— Oswald N Fernando, Esq; ✉ Renal Transplant Unit, Royal Free Hospital, Pond Street, London NW3 2QG (tel 020 7830 2882, fax 020 7830 2125, mobile 07769 682287, e-mail ossiefernando@hotmail.com or ossiefernando@yahoo.co.uk)

FERNEYHOUGH, Prof Brian John Peter; s of Frederick George Ferneyhough (d 1982), and Emily May, *née* Hopwood (d 1992); *b* 16 January 1943; *Educ* Birmingham Sch of Music, Royal Acad of Music, Royal Conservatory Amsterdam, Musikakademie Basel; *m* 19 May 1990, Stephanie Jan, *née* Hurtik; *Career* prof of composition Musikhochschule Freiburg 1973–86, composition lectr Darmstadt Summer Sch 1976–96, leader composition master class Civica Scuola di Musica di Milano 1984–87, composition teacher Royal Conservatory of The Hague 1986–87, ldr composition master class Fndn Royaumont 1990–, prof of music Univ of Calif San Diego 1987–99, William H Bonsall prof of music Stanford Univ 2000–, chair of poetics Mozarteum Salzburg 1995; memb: Jury Gaudeamus Int Composition Competition 1984 (Netherlands), Int Jury for World Music Days of Int Soc for Contemporary Music (Finland 1978, Hong Kong 1989), Akademie der Künste Berlin 1996–, Bayrische Akademie der schönen Künste 2005; Koussevitzky prize 1978, Royal Philharmonic Soc Award 1995; ARAM 1990, hon fell Birmingham Conservatoire 1996, FRAM 1998; Chevalier de l'Ordre des Arts et des Lettres (France) 1984; *Compositions* incl: Sonatas for String Quartet 1967, Transit 1975, Time and Motion Studies I-III 1974–77, La Terre est un Homme 1979, Carceri d'Invenzione 1981–86, La Chute d'Icare 1988, Fourth String Quartet 1990, Bone Alphabet, Allgebrah 1991, Terrain 1992, On Stellar Magnitudes 1994, String Trio 1995, Incipits 1996, Flurries 1997, Unsichtbare Farben 1998, Doctrine of Similarity 1999, Shadowtime 1999–2004; *Recreations* reading, wine, cats; *Style*— Prof Brian Ferneyhough; ✉ Stanford University, Department of Music, Braun Music Center, 541 Lausen Mall, Stanford, CA 94305–3076 USA (e-mail brian.ferneyhough@stanford.edu)

FERNIE, Prof Eric Campbell; CBE (1995); s of Sidney Robert Fernie (d 1988), of Johannesburg, South Africa, and Catherine Reid, *née* Forrest (d 1959); *b* 9 June 1939, Edinburgh; *Educ* Marist Brothers Coll Johannesburg, Univ of the Witwatersrand (BA); *m* 28 Nov 1964, (Margaret) Lorraine, da of John Henry French, of Norfolk; 2 da (Lyndall b 1965, Jessica b 1969), 1 s (Ivan b 1969); *Career* sr lectr UEA 1974–84; Univ of Edinburgh: Watson Gordon prof of fine art 1984–95, dean Faculty of Arts 1989–92; dir Courtauld Inst of Art 1995–2003; cmmr: English Heritage 1995–2001, Royal Cmmn on the Historical Monuments of England 1997–99; chm Ancient Monuments Bd Scotland 1989–95; pres Soc of Antiquaries of London 2004–07 (vice-pres 1992–95), vice-pres: Public Monuments and Sculpture Assoc; tstee: National Galleries of Scotland 1991–97, Heather Tst for the Arts 1997–2002, Scotland Inheritance Fund 1994–2004; memb Br Acad Corpus of Romanesque Sculpture Ctee; FSA 1973, FRSE 1993, FBA 2002; *Books* The Communar and Pitancer Rolls of Norwich Cathedral Priory (1972), The Architecture of the Anglo Saxons (1983), Medieval Architecture and its Intellectual Context (1990), An Architectural History of Norwich Cathedral (1993), Art History and its Methods (1995), The Architecture of Norman England (2000); *Style*— Prof Eric Fernie, CBE, FBA, FSA, FRSE

FERNIE, Dr (Crawford) George MacDougall; s of George Fernie (d 2000), and Joan Fisher, *née* MacDougall (d 2003); *b* 5 October 1954, Glasgow; *Educ* Hyndland Sr Secdy Sch Glasgow, Univ of Glasgow (MB, ChB, DFM, MPhil), Univ of Strathclyde (LLB); *m* 12 Oct 1984, Isobel, *née* Kerr; 1 da (Anne Fiona Eadie b 10 Aug 1970), 2 s (Keith Ian Johnson b 7 Jan 1973, Campbell Crawford b 2 Jan 1985); *Career* house offr surgical paediatrics Royal Hosp for Sick Children Glasgow 1977–78, house offr Dept of Med Raigmore Hosp Inverness 1978, SHO Dept of Neurosurgery Inst of Neurological Sci Glasgow 1978–79, SHO Dept of Obstetrics & Gynaecology Stobhill Hosp Glasgow 1979, princ in gen practice Portland Park Lanarkshire 1979–1991, pt/t GP deputising Emergency Med Serv Bellshill 1979–80, pt/t casualty offr Royal Hosp for Sick Children Glasgow 1980–81, undergrad teaching in gen practice 1980–87, GP trainer 1987–91, princ in gen practice Canonbie 1991–96; Univ of Glasgow: hon research fell in clinical forensic med 1994–97, lectr 1996–, hon sr lectr in clinical forensic med 2001–; examiner for Dip of Forensic Med for Soc of Apothecaries in London 1996–; med advsr Hamilton DC 1990–91; dep police surgn (Q Div) Strathclyde Police 1988–91, princ police surgn Annandale and Eskdale 1991–96, princ police surgn (K Div) Strathclyde Police 1996–2004, forensic med examiner Lothian & Borders Police 2004–05; memb: GP Clinical Advsy Panel Medical and Dental Defence Union of Scotland 1991–96 (med advsr 1996–), West of Scot Faculty Bd RCGP 1991–98, Cncl Scottish Medico-Legal Soc 1992–2002 and 2003–06, Tech Sub Gp to advise Strathclyde Police 1997–2004, Educn & Research Ctee Assoc of Police Surgns 1998–; Assoc of Forensic Physicians: memb Cncl 1996–2006, pres-elect 2002–04, pres 2004–06; memb Int Editorial Bd Jl of Clinical Forensic Med 2001–; BMA: memb UK Cncl 2004–06, memb Scot Cncl 2005–; memb Forensic Med Ctee 2001–04 (chm 2002–); author of various pubns incl articles and commentaries in learned jls, and chapters in Encyclopaedia of Forensic and Legal Medicine (2005); FRCGP 2004 (MRCGP 1984), fell Faculty of Forensic and Legal Medicine RCP (registrar 2006–07); *Recreations* bearded collies, reading, hill walking; *Style*— Dr George Fernie; ✉ 8 Pinegrove Gardens, Barnton, Edinburgh EH4 8DA (tel and fax 0131 317 1807, e-mail cgmf@btinternet.com); The Medical & Dental Defence Union of Scotland, Mackintosh House, 120 Blythswood Street, Glasgow G2 4EA (tel 0141 221 5858, fax 0141 228 1208, e-mail gfernie@mddus.com)

FERRAN, Prof Eilis Veronica; da of Edward Gerald Ferran, and Kathleen Mary, *née* Best; *b* 14 March 1962, Belfast; *Educ* Univ of Cambridge (BA, PhD); *m* 27 June 1992, Roderick Cantrill; 1 da (Aoife b 6 Nov 1994), 1 s (Oliver b 11 Nov 1997); *Career* admitted slr 1986; articled clerk Coward Chance 1984–86; St Catharine's Coll Cambridge: coll lectr 1986–88, fell 1987–, dir of studies 1988–, tutor 1999–2000; Univ of Cambridge: asst lectr 1988–91, lectr 1991–2000, reader in corporate and commercial law 2000–05, prof of company and securities law 2005–, co-dir Centre for Corporate and Commercial Law 2006– (asst dir 1997–99, dir 1999–2003); legal conslt: Slaughter and May 1989–2000, Herbert Smith 2003–; jt ed: Jl of Corporate Law Studies, CUP Int Corporate Law and Capital Market Regulation Series; visiting prof Univ of Hong Kong 2002, Chapman Tripp fell Univ of Victoria NZ 2004, res assoc European Corporate Governance Inst; special advsr: Parly Jt Ctee on the Draft Financial Services and Markets Bill 1999, House of Commons Select Ctee on Educn and Employment 2000–01; *Books* Guide to the Financial Services Act 1986 (jtly, 2 edn 1989), Mortgage Securitisation: Legal Aspects (1992), Company Law and Corporate Finance (1999), Boyle and Birds Company Law (jtly, 2000), Building an EU Securities Market (2004), Current Law Annotated Guide to the Companies Act 2006 (jtly, 2007); author of various chapters and articles in learned jls; *Style*— Prof Eilis Ferran; ✉ St Catharine's College, Cambridge CB2 1RL (tel 01223 338335, fax 01223 338340); Law Faculty, University of Cambridge, 10 West Road, Cambridge CB3 9DZ (tel 01223 330033, e-mail evf1000@cam.ac.uk)

FERRELL, Prof William Russell (Bill); *b* 5 March 1949, St Louis, Missouri; *Educ* St Aloysius Coll Glasgow, Univ of Glasgow (MB ChB, PhD); *Career* jr house offr posts in surgery (Southern Gen Hosp Glasgow) and med (Stirling Royal Infirmary) 1973–74, sessional clinical work 1974–, visiting res fell Dept of Orthopaedic Surgery Univ of Western Aust 1984; Univ of Glasgow: lectr in physiology 1977–89, sr lectr 1989–91, reader 1991–93, head of physiology 1993–94, head of biomedical scis 1994, reader in clinical physiology 1997–2002, prof of clinical physiology 2002–; visiting prof: Dept of Surgery Univ of Calgary 1996, Univ of Paisley 1999–; expert referee: Jl of Physiology, Experimental Physiology, Jl of Rheumatology, Br Jl of Pharmacology, Clinical Sciences, Brain, Brain Research, Annals of the Rheumatic Diseases; memb MRC Advsy Panel 1997–2005; memb: Physiological Soc 1981, BMA, Br Soc of Med and Dental Hypnosis, Euro Neuropeptide Club, Br Soc for Rheumatology; FRCPGlas 1996; *Recreations* classical music, reading, electronics, skiing, tennis, DIY; *Style*— Prof Bill Ferrell; ✉ Centre for Rheumatic Diseases, Royal Infirmary, Queen Elizabeth Building, 10 Alexandra Parade, Glasgow G31 2ER (tel 0141 211 4677, fax 0141 211 0414, e-mail w.ferrell@bio.gla.ac.uk)

FERRERS, 13 Earl (GB 1711); Sir Robert Washington Shirley; 19 Bt (E 1611), PC (1982), DL (Norfolk 1983); also Viscount Tamworth (GB 1711); s of 12 Earl Ferrers (d 1954, 17 in descent from Sir Hugh Shirley, Grand Falconer to Henry IV and victim of mistaken identity at the Battle of Shrewsbury through being accoutred as the King); 16 in descent from Sir Ralph Shirley, one of the principal commanders at Agincourt; 9 in descent from Dorothy, da of Elizabeth I's favourite, Essex, through whom Lord Ferrers descends from Edward III, hence the quartering of the arms of Fr and Eng on the Shirley escutcheon; 5 in descent from Hon Walter Shirley, yr bro of 4 Earl, the last Lord to be tried for homicide by his Peers; *b* 8 June 1929; *Educ* Winchester, Magdalene Coll Cambridge (MA); *m* 21 July 1951, Annabel Mary, da of Brig William Greenwood Carr, CVO, DSO, JP, DL (d 1982), of Ditchingham Hall, Norfolk; 2 s (Robert William Saswalo, Viscount Tamworth b 1952, Hon Andrew b 1965), 3 da (Lady Angela Ellis b 1954, Lady Sallyanne b 1957, Lady Selina Chenevière b 1958 d 1998); *Heir* s, Viscount Tamworth, *qv*; *Career* elected as (Cons) Peer in the House of Lords, pres Assoc of Cons Peers 2006–; served Coldstream Gds, Lt, Malaya; Lord-in-Waiting and govt whip Lords 1962–64 and 1971–74, oppn whip Lords 1964–67, jt-dep ldr of oppn Lords 1976–79, Parly sec Agric, Fisheries and Food 1974, min of state Agric, Fisheries and Food 1979–83, dep ldr Lords 1979–83 and 1988–97; min of state: Home Office 1988–94, DTI 1994–95, Dept of Environment 1995–97; memb: Cncl Food from Britain 1985–88, Armitage Ctee on Political Activities of Civil Servants 1976, Central Bd TSB 1977–79; tstee: E Anglian TSB 1957–75 (vice-chm 1971–75), TSB of E England 1975–79 (chm 1977–79), Central TSB Ltd 1978–79, TSB Trustcard 1978–79; dir: Economic Forestry Group plc 1985–88, Norwich Union Insurance Group 1975–79 and 1983–88, Chatham Historic Dockyard Tst 1984–88, Governing Body of Rothamsted Agric Station 1984–88; chm British Agric Export Cncl 1984–88; High Steward Norwich Cathedral 1979–; chm Royal Cmmn on Historical Monuments (England) 1984–88; fell Winchester Coll 1988–2003 (sub-warden 1998–2003); Grand Prior of the Military and Hospitaller Order of St Lazarus of Jerusalem 2002–; *Recreations* music, travel; *Clubs* Beefsteak; *Style*— The Rt Hon Earl Ferrers, PC, DL; ✉ Park Lodge, Hedenham, Norfolk NR35 2LE (tel 01508 482250, fax 01508 482332); House of Lords, London SW1A 0PW (tel 020 7219 3204)

FERRIER, Prof Robert Patton; s of William McFarlane Ferrier (d 1963), and Gwendoline Melita, *née* Edward (d 1976); *b* 4 January 1934; *Educ* Glebelands Sch, Morgan Acad, Univ of St Andrews (BSc, PhD), Univ of Cambridge (MA); *m* 2 Sept 1961, Valerie Jane, da of Samuel George Duncan (d 1986); 2 s (Hamish b 1965, Alan b 1969), 1 da (Elizabeth b 1967); *Career* sci offr UKAERE Harwell 1959–61, res assoc MIT 1961–62, asst dir of res Cavendish Lab Univ of Cambridge 1966–73 (sr asst 1962–66), guest scientist IBM Res Div San José CA 1972–73, appointed prof of nat philosophy Univ of Glasgow 1973 (currently emeritus prof); memb: local Episcopal Church, various ctees of SERC 1970–85 (sometime chm); FInstP 1964, FRSE 1977; *Recreations* tennis, gardening, reading crime novels; *Style*— Prof Robert Ferrier; ✉ Department of Physics and Astronomy, The University, Glasgow G12 8QQ (tel 0141 330 5388, 0141 339 8855, fax 0141 330 4464, telex 777070 UNIGLA)

FERRIS, Dr Elizabeth Anne Esther; da of Roy Ferris (d 1975), and Dorothy Philomena, *née* Roth (d 1990); *b* 19 November 1940; *Educ* Francis Holland Sch Clarence Gate, Middlesex Hosp Med Sch Univ of London (MB BS); *m* Julian Melzack; 1 da (Sophie b 1978); *Career* doctor and former int springboard diver; achievements as diver: represented GB 1957–64, Bronze medal Cwlth Games Cardiff 1958, Bronze medal Olympic Games Rome 1960, Gold medals springboard and highboard World Student Games Sofia 1961, Silver medal Cwlth Games Perth 1962; freelance journalist, writer and broadcaster on sport, women and sport, sports med, alternative med, health fitness 1968–; doctor specialising in: acupuncture 1972–86, autogenic trg 1980–96, sports psychology 1980–96; therapist cnsllr 1989–; research fell Dept of Nutrition KCL 1999–; fndr and life vice-pres The Olympians, vice-pres World Olympians Assoc; memb: Int Olympic Ctee Cmmn on Women and Sport, Admin Cncl of the Int Ctee for Fair Play, World Cncl for Nutrition, Fitness and Health, IAAF Workshop on Gender Verification in Sport 1990–; awarded Bronze medal of the Olympic Order by Int Olympic Ctee for work with women in sport 1980; *Books* Forty Plus (1992); *Videos* Bodyplan (1992); *Style*— Dr Elizabeth Ferris; ✉ Green Dragon House, Filkins, Lechlade, Gloucestershire GL7 3JG

FERRIS, Neil Jeremy; s of Oscar Ferris, and Benita, *née* Lewis; *b* 5 April 1955; *Educ* Brighton Hove and Sussex GS; *m* 25 Jan 1980, Jill Denise, da of William Charles Anderson, of London; 1 s (Daniel Mark); *Career* jr PR Dept EMI Records 1974; PR Dept: NEMS Records 1976, CBS Records 1977; formed The Ferret Plugging Co 1980 representing: UB40, Erasure, Depeche Mode and other major recording artists; produced TV special about Erasure for BBC 2 1988 and a documentary on Depeche Mode for BBC TV 1989; chm The Brilliant Recording Co Ltd; md: Ferret and Spanner PR 1985–95, Brilliant PR Ltd 1995–97, Ferret Music, EMI Records (UK) Ltd 1997–98, Tornado Gp plc 2002 (dir 2000–02); ceo Tornado Virtue plc 2002–03; chm Virtue Broadcasting plc 2003; artist mangr (incl Alfie Boe, opera tenor, and Polly Scattergood, singer/songwriter) 2005–07; speaker on various subjects relating to the music industry and the media; *Recreations* helicopter pilot, antiques (early oak furniture), 16th and 17th century paintings (British); *Style*— Neil Ferris, Esq

FERRIS, Paul Frederick; s of Frederick Morgan Ferris (d 1965), and Olga, *née* Boulton (d 1992); *b* 15 February 1929; *Educ* Swansea GS; *m* 1, 1953 (m dis 1995), Gloria Moreton; 1 s (Jonathan b 1955), 1 da (Virginia Ann b 1960); m 2, 1996, Mary Turnbull; *Career* journalist and author; S Wales Evening Post 1949–52, Woman's Own 1953, Observer Foreign News Serv 1953–54; *Books* incl: The City (1960), The House of Northcliffe (1971), The Detective (1976), Dylan Thomas (1977), Talk to Me About England (1979), Children of Dust (1988), Sir Huge - The Life of Huw Wheldon (1990), Sex and the British - a 20th Century History (1993), Caitlin - The Life of Caitlin Thomas (1993), The Divining Heart (1995), Dr Freud - A Life (1997), Dylan Thomas: The Biography (1999), Infidelity (1999), Dylan Thomas, New Collected Letters (2000), Cora Crane (2003); *Style*— Paul Ferris, Esq; ✉ c/o Curtis Brown Ltd, 4th Floor, Haymarket House, 28–29 Haymarket, London SW1Y 4SP (tel 020 7396 6600)

FERRY, Bryan; s of Frederick Charles Ferry (d 1984), and Mary Ann, *née* Armstrong (d 1991); *b* 26 September 1945; *Educ* Washington GS, Univ of Newcastle; *m* 26 June 1982, Lucy Margaret Mary, da of Patrick Helmore; 4 c (Otis b 1 Nov 1982, Isaac b 16 May 1985, Tara b 6 Jan 1990, Merlin b 5 Dec 1990); *Career* vocalist and fndr memb Roxy Music 1971, solo recording artist; recordings with Roxy Music: Roxy Music 1972, For Your Pleasure 1973, Stranded 1973, Country Life 1974, Siren 1975, Viva 1976, Manifesto 1979, Flesh & Blood 1980, Avalon 1982, The High Road 1983, Streetlife 1986; solo recordings: These Foolish Things 1973, Another Time Another Place 1974, Let's Stick Together 1976, In Your Mind 1977, The Bride Stripped Bare 1978, Boys and Girls 1985, Bête Noire 1987, Taxi 1993, Mamouna 1994, As Time Goes By 1999, Frantic 2002,

Dylanesque 2007; Bryan Ferry and Roxy Music Video Collection 1996; *Style—* Bryan Ferry, Esq

FERSHT, Prof Sir Alan Roy; kt (2003); s of Philip Joseph Fersht (d 1970), and Betty, *née* Mattleson (d 2003); *b* 21 April 1943; *Educ* Sir George Monoux GS, Gonville & Caius Coll Cambridge (MA, PhD); *m* 18 Aug 1966, Marilyn, da of Montague Persell (d 1973); 1 da (Naomi b 1970), 1 s (Philip b 1972); *Career* memb scientific staff MRC Laboratory of Molecular Biology Cambridge 1969–77, Wolfson res prof Royal Soc and prof of chemistry Imperial Coll London 1978–88, Herchel Smith prof of organic chemistry Univ of Cambridge 1988–, dir MRC Centre for Protein Engrg 1989; memb: EMBO 1980, Academia Europaea 1989; hon foreign memb American Acad of Arts and Scis 1988, foreign assoc Nat Acad of Sci USA; Gabor Medal of the Royal Soc 1991, Davy Medal of the Royal Soc 1998, Anfinsen Award Protein Soc 1999, Stein and Moore Award Protein Soc 2001, Bader Award American Chemical Soc 2005, Linderstrom Lang Medal 2005; Hon PhD: Univ of Uppsala 1999, Univ of Brussels 1999, Weizmann Inst 2005; fell Imperial Coll London 2004; FRS 1983; *Books* Enzyme Structure and Mechanism (1978, 1985), Structure and Mechanism in Protein Science (1998); *Recreations* chess, horology; *Style—* Prof Sir Alan Fersht, FRS; ✉ 2 Barrow Close, Cambridge CB2 2AT (tel 01223 352 963); University Chemical Laboratory, Lensfield Road, Cambridge CB2 1EW (tel 01223 336 341, fax 01223 336 445)

FESTING, Andrew Thomas; s of Field-Marshal Sir Francis Festing, GCB, DSO, DL (d 1971), of Birks, Northumberland, and Mary Cecilia, *née* Riddell (d 1992); *b* 30 November 1941; *Educ* Ampleforth, RMA Sandhurst; *m* 1968, Virginia Mary, da of Lt-Gen Sir Richard Fyffe, CBE, DSO, MC; 1 da (Charlotte b 1975); *Career* cmmnd Rifle Bde until 1968; head English Picture Dept Sotheby & Co 1977–81, full time portrait painter 1981–; commissions incl: HM The Queen, HM Queen Elizabeth The Queen Mother, The Princess Royal, Cardinal Hume, House of Lords, House of Commons, Speaker Boothroyd; RP 1992 (pres 2002–); *Recreations* hunting, shooting, fishing, gardening; *Style—* Andrew Festing, Esq, PRP; ✉ c/o Royal Society of Portrait Painters, 17 Carlton House Terrace, London SW1Y 5AH

FETHERSTONHAUGH, Guy; QC (2003); s of Theobald Fetherstonhaugh (d 1990), and Genevieve, *née* Moreau; *b* 29 January 1955, Malaya; *Educ* Stonyhurst, Univ of Bristol; *m* 23 March 1991, Alexia, *née* Lees; 1 da (Rosie b 15 June 1992), 2 s (Tom b 13 May 1994, Ned b 1 May 1996); *Career* Royal Green Jackets 1978–82; called to the Bar 1983, practising barr 1985–; *Books* Handbook of Rent Review (co-author, 2000), Commonhold (co-author, 2004); *Recreations* gardening, cycling, woodwork; *Style—* Guy Fetherstonhaugh, Esq, QC; ✉ c/o Falcon Chambers, Falcon Court, London EC4Y 1AA (tel 020 7353 2484)

FEUCHTWANGER, Antonia Mary; *see:* Cox, Antonia Mary

FEVERSHAM, 6 Baron (UK 1826; the full designation is 'Feversham of Duncombe Park'); Charles Antony Peter Duncombe; s of Col Antony John Duncombe-Anderson, TD (d 1949; gggs of 1 Baron Feversham), and Gloranna Georgina Valerie, *née* McNalty (d 1989); suc to Barony of kinsman, 3 Earl of Feversham and Viscount Helmsley (which titles became extinct 1963); *b* 3 January 1945; *Educ* Eton; *m* 1, 12 Sept 1966, Shannon (d 1976), da of late Sir Thomas Foy, CSI, CIE; 2 s (Hon Jasper b 1968, Hon Jake b 1972), 1 da (Hon Melissa b 1973); m 2, 6 Oct 1979, Pauline, da of John Aldridge, of Newark, Notts; 1 s (Hon Patrick b 1981); *Heir* s, Hon Jasper Duncombe; *Career* journalist and author; chm: Yorks Arts Assoc 1969–80, Standing Ctee of Regional Arts Assocs 1969–76, Tstees Yorks Sculpture Park 1982–2004; co-pres Arvon Foundation 1976–86; pres: Yorks Parish Cncls Assoc 1977–99, Yorks Arts Assoc 1986–91, Nat Assoc Local Cncls 1986–99; *Books* A Wolf in Tooth (1967), Great Yachts (1970); *Style—* The Rt Hon the Lord Feversham; ✉ Duncombe Park, Helmsley, York YO62 5EB (tel 01439 770213)

FEWTRELL, Nicholas Austin; s of Austin Alexander Fewtrell (d 1994), of Birmingham, and Marjorie Edna, *née* Kimberlin (d 1996); *b* 1 July 1955; *Educ* Bramcote Hills GS, QMC London (LLB); *m* 26 Nov 1983, Mahshid, da of Kazem Pouladdej (d 1998), of Tehran, Iran; 1 da (Stephanie Roxanne b 6 June 1989), 1 s (Alexander Darius b 7 June 1991); *Career* called to the Bar Inner Temple 1977; in practice Northern Circuit 1978–, recorder of the Crown Court 2003–; memb: Personal Injuries Bar Assoc, Professional Negligence Bar Assoc, Northern Circuit Cammercial Bar Assoc; *Recreations* golf, football, travel; *Clubs* Ringway Golf; *Style—* Nicholas Fewtrell, Esq; ✉ 18 St John Street, Manchester M3 4EA (tel 0161 278 1800, fax 0161 835 2051, e-mail nickfewtrell@btinternet.com)

FFOLKES, Sir Robert Francis Alexander; 7 Bt (GB 1774), of Hillington, Norfolk; OBE (1990); s of Sir (Edward John) Patrick Boschetti ffolkes, 6 Bt (d 1960); *b* 2 December 1943; *Educ* Stowe, ChCh Oxford; *Heir* none; *Career* with Save The Children Fund 1974–2003; *Style—* Sir Robert ffolkes, Bt, OBE; ✉ Coastguard House, Morston, Holt, Norfolk NR25 7BH

FFORDE, Catherine Rose (Katie); da of Michael Gordon-Cumming (d 1979), and Barbara, *née* Laub (d 1996); *b* 27 September 1952; *Educ* Assoc Arts Sch Wimbledon; *m* 1972; 2 s, 1 da; *Career* writer 1984–; former sec; prop (with husband) Narrow Boat Hotel; govr Rodborough Co Primary Sch; memb: Soc of Authors, Romantic Novelists' Assoc; *Books* Living Dangerously (1995), The Rose Revived (1996), Wild Designs (1996), Stately Pursuits (1997), Life Skills (1999), Thyme Out (2000), Artistic Licence (2001), Highland Fling (2002), Paradise Fields (2003), Restoring Grace (2004); *Recreations* gardening, singing, dogs; *Style—* Katie Fforde; ✉ c/o Press Department, Arrow, Random House, Vauxhall Bridge Road, London SW1 2SA (e-mail katiefforde@katiefforde.com)

FFRENCH, 8 Baron (I 1798); Sir Robuck John Peter Charles Mario ffrench; also Bt (I 1779); s of 7 Baron ffrench (d 1986), and Katherine Sonia, da of Maj Digby Coddington Cayley (d 1965); *b* 14 March 1956; *m* 20 June 1987, Dörthe Marie-Louise Schauer-Lixfeld, da of Capt Wilhelm Schauer, of Zürich, Switzerland, and Mrs Marie-Louise Schauer-Lixfeld, of Attymon House, Co Galway; 1 da (Hon Tara Elise Sofia Eleonora b 1993); *Style—* The Rt Hon Lord ffrench

FFYTCHE, Timothy John; LVO (1997); s of Louis E S ffytche (d 1987), of London, and Margaret Law (d 1996); *b* 11 September 1936; *Educ* Lancing, King's Coll London, St George's Hosp London (MB BS, DO); *m* 13 May 1961, Bärbl, da of Günther Fischer, of W Germany; 2 s (Dominic b 1962, Mattias b 1965); *Career* conslt ophthalmic surgn: St Thomas' Hosp London 1973–99, Moorfields Hosp 1975–2001, King Edward VII Hosp London 1980–2006, Hosp for Tropical Diseases 1988–2006, ret; surgn oculist to Royal Household 1980–99, surgn oculist to HM The Queen 1999–2001; pres Med Soc of London 2001; chm Ophthalmic Aid to Eastern Europe (OAEE); chm for Europe Int Agency for the Prevention of Blindness; author of articles and papers on retinal disease and ocular leprosy; FRCS, FRCOphth; *Recreations* fishing; *Style—* Timothy ffytche, Esq, LVO; ✉ 1 Wellington Square, London SW3 4NJ

FIDDES, Michael John Alexander; s of Alexander John Scott Fiddes, of Wrantage, Somerset, and Ann Chalcraft, *née* Forde; *b* 20 November 1959, Southsea, Hants; *Educ* Westbourne House Chichester, Marlborough, Trinity Coll Oxford (BA); *m* 18 June 1983, Julia, *née* Curry; 5 s (George b 6 Aug 1984, Edward b 31 Oct 1988, Archie b 17 Nov 1992, Hamish b 26 Nov 1994, Miles b 27 March 1998); *Career* Strutt and Parker: joined 1982, equity ptnr 1994, head Rural Div 2005; MRICS 1986; *Recreations* golf, cricket, tennis, Red Poll cows; *Clubs* Oxford and Cambridge, Flempton Golf, Felsham Farmers and Landowners; *Style—* Michael Fiddes, Esq; ✉ Hammond Hall, Drinkstone Green, Bury St Edmunds, Suffolk IP30 9TL (tel 01449 737779); Strutt and Parker, 13 Hill Street, Berkeley Square, London W1X 8DL (tel 020 7318 5192, e-mail michael.fiddes@struttandparker.co.uk)

FIDGEN, Roger Stewart; s of Eric Frank Fidgen, and Vera, *née* Clark; *b* 14 May 1946; *Educ* Sherborne; *m* 1, 10 Nov 1971 (m dis 1988), Sarah Dorothy, da of William Nevill Dashwood Lang (d 1988); 2 s (Patrick b 1973, Robert b 1976), 1 da (Joanna b 1979); m 2, 20 May 1988, Jennifer Godesen, da of Stanley Angold; *Career* Sub Lt RNR 1969–72; chartered quantity surveyor; sr ptnr Gardiner and Theobald 2000–04; non-exec chm Waterman Gp; pres Br Cncl for Offices 2002; Liveryman: Worshipful Co of Barbers, Worshipful Co of Chartered Surveyors; FRICS; *Recreations* fishing, shooting, sailing, skiing; *Clubs* Boodle's, Royal Thames Yacht, Flyfishers'; *Style—* Roger Fidgen, Esq; ✉ Wield House Farm, Upper Wield, Alresford, Hampshire SO24 9RS (tel 01420 564292)

FIDLER, Prof John Kelvin (Kel); s of Samuel Fidler (d 1974), and Barbara Warren (d 1999); *b* 11 May 1944, Doncaster; *Educ* Harrow Co Sch for Boys, King's Coll Durham (BSc), Univ of Newcastle upon Tyne (PhD); *m* 2 April 2002, Nadine; 2 step c (Leanne Cleaver b 1981, Andrew Cleaver b 1982); 2 c from previous m (Jennie b 1971, Mark b 1974); *Career* lectr, sr lectr, reader and head Dept of Electrical Engrg Univ of Essex 1969–83, prof of electronics Open Univ 1984–88, prof of electronics, head, pro-vice-chllr and dep vice-chllr Univ of York 1989–2001, vice-chllr and chief exec Univ of Northumbria at Newcastle 2001–; chair Engrg Cncl UK; FIEE 1982 (MIEE 1972), FREng 2005; *Publications* over 100 publications in learned jls and books; *Recreations* walking, dogs, DIY, cooking; *Style—* Prof Kel Fidler; ✉ University of Northumbria at Newcastle, Ellison Place, Newcastle upon Tyne NE1 8ST (tel 0191 227 4002, fax 0191 227 4417, e-mail kel.fidler@unn.ac.uk)

FIDLER, Peter John Michael; s of Dr Harry Fidler, of Bramhall, Cheshire, and Lilian, *née* Kahn; *b* 16 March 1942; *Educ* Bradford GS, St John's Coll Oxford (MA); *m* 19 July 1984, Barbara Julia Gottlieb, da of Harold Pinto, of Wembley, Middx; 1 s (David Robert b 1985), 2 step da (Clare Rachel b 1973, Katherine Anna b 1977), 1 step s (Richard Charles b 1979); *Career* admitted slr 1967; articled clerk Peacock Fisher & Finch (now Field Fisher Waterhouse) 1964–67, Coward Chance 1967–72, DJ Freeman 1972–84, ptnr Stephenson Harwood 1984–2002, conslt Pinsents 2002–04, conslt CMS Cameron McKenna LLP 2004–; memb: City of London Solicitors Co, Law Soc, City of London Law Soc; rep GB at croquet 1974; *Books* Sheldon's Practice and Law of Banking (now Sheldon and Fidler's, asst ed 1972, ed 1982), contributed chapter to Corporate Administrations and Rescue Procedures (I Fletcher, J Higham and W Trower, 2004); *Recreations* music, theatre; *Style—* Peter Fidler, Esq; ✉ 237 West Heath Road, London NW3 7UB (tel 020 8455 2247); CMS Cameron McKenna LLP, Mitre House, 160 Aldersgate Street, London 1A 4DD (tel 020 7367 3177, fax 020 7367 2000)

FIELD, Rt Hon Frank; PC (1997), MP; s of late Walter Field, and Annie Field; *b* 16 July 1942; *Educ* St Clement Danes GS, Univ of Hull; *Career* former lobbyist, memb TGWU, cncllr Hounslow 1964–68, Parly candidate (Lab) S Bucks 1966; dir Child Poverty Action Gp 1969–79, fndr and dir Low Pay Unit 1974–80; MP (Lab) Birkenhead 1979–, oppn spokesman on educn 1979–81, Parly conslt to Civil and Public Servs Assoc, front bench oppn spokesman on health and social security 1983–84, chm Select Ctee on Social Servs 1987–97; min of state for welfare reform DSS 1997–98; Hon LLD Univ of Warwick, Hon DSc Univ of Southampton; hon fell: South Bank Univ, Univ of Kent at Canterbury; *Books* Unequal Britain (1974), To Him Who Hath: A Study of Poverty And Taxation (co author, 1976), Inequality In Britain: Freedom, Welfare and The State (1981), Poverty and Politics (1982), The Minimum Wage: Its Potential And Dangers (1984), Freedom And Wealth In A Socialist Future (1987), The Politics of Paradise (1987), Losing Out: The Emergence of Britain's Underclass (1989), An Agenda for Britain (1993), Europe isn't Working (jtly, 1994), Beyond Punishment: Pathways from Workfare (jtly, 1994), Making Welfare Work (1995), How to Pay for the Future: Building a Stakeholders Welfare (1996), Stakeholder Welfare (1997), Reforming Welfare (1997), Reflections on Welfare Reform (1998), The State of Dependency, Welfare Under Labour (2000), Making Welfare Work: Reconstructing Welfare for the Millennium (2001), Universal Protected Pension: Modernising Pensions For The Millenium (report by Pensions Reform Gp, 2001), Welfare Titans: How Lloyd George and Gordon Brown Compare and Other Essays on Welfare Reform (2002), Universal Protected Pension: The Follow-Up Report (2002), Neighbours from Hell: The Politics of Behaviour (2003); as ed: 20th Century State Education (co-ed, 1971), Black Britons (co-ed, 1971), Low Pay (1973), Are Low Wages Inevitable? (1976), Education And The Urban Crisis (1976), The Conscript Army: A Study of Britain's Unemployed (1976), The Wealth Report (1979, 2 edn 1983), Policies Against Low Pay: An International Perspective (1984); *Style—* The Rt Hon Frank Field, MP; ✉ House of Commons, London SW1A 0AA (tel 020 7219 3000)

FIELD, Sir Malcolm David; kt (1991); s of Maj Stanley Herbert Raynor Field (d 1970), of Selsey, W Sussex, and Constance Frances, *née* Watson; *b* 25 August 1937; *Educ* Highgate Sch, London Business Sch; *m* 1, 1963 (m dis 1970), Jane, da of James Barrie; m 2, 1974 (m dis 1982), Anne Carolyn, *née* Churchill; 1 da (Joanna Clare b 1974); m 3, 2001, Anne Charlton; *Career* 2 Lt WG 1956–58; dir WH Smith & Son Ltd; W H Smith Group plc: dir 1974, md wholesale 1978, md retail 1978, gp md 1982–94, gp chief exec 1994–96, chm W H Smith Group (USA) Inc 1988; chm: NAAFI 1986–93 (non-exec dir 1973–93, dep chm 1985), CAA 1996–2001; chm: Sofa Workshop Ltd 1998–2002, Tube Lines Ltd 2003–06, Aricom plc 2003–; non-exec dir: MEPC plc 1989–99, Scottish & Newcastle plc 1993–99, The Stationery Office 1996–2001, Walker Greenbank 1997–2002, Evolution (formerly Beeson-Gregory) 1999–2005, Odgers 2002–, Linden Homes 2001–; non-exec memb Advsy Bd Phoenix Fund Mangrs 1992–96; policy advsr DFT (formerly DTLR) 2001–06; govr Highgate Sch (dep chm 1999–2005); CIMgt 1988; *Recreations* tennis, watching cricket, golf, collecting watercolours and modern art, re-building garden in Devon; *Clubs* Garrick, MCC; *Style—* Sir Malcolm Field; ✉ 21 Embankment Gardens, London SW3 4LH

FIELD, Mark Christopher; MP; s of Major Peter Field (d 1991), of Reading, Berks, and Ulrike, *née* Peipe; *b* 6 October 1964; *Educ* Reading Sch, St Edmund Hall Oxford (MA), Coll of Law Chester; *m* 1994, Michèle Louise, da of Raymond Acton; *Career* trainee slr Richards Butler 1988–90, slr Freshfields 1990–92, dir Kellyfield Consulting (specialist recruitment/headhunting) 1994–2001; slr of Supreme Court (non-practising); MP (Cons) Cities of London and Westminster 2001–; oppn whip 2003–04, shadow min for London 2003–05, shadow fin sec to the Treasy 2005–; sec British-German Parly Gp, sec All-Pty Gp on Venture Capital, memb Select Ctee on Lord Chllr's Dept 2003, memb Standing Ctee on Proceeds of Crime Act 2002, Enterprise Act 2002, Fin Act 2002, Licensing Act 2003, Housing Act 2004, Railways Act 2005, Finance Bill (No 3) 2005; cncllr Kensington and Chelsea BC 1994–2002; memb Advsy Bd London Sch of Commerce 2005–; Freeman City of London; *Publications* incl chapter in A Blue Tomorrow - New Visions for Modern Conservatives (2001); various articles on econs and home affairs for nat newspapers; *Recreations* sports including cricket and football, researching local history, wandering around London, avid listener to popular and rock music, browsing antique shops, travelling to interesting places with wife or Parliamentary colleagues (but rarely both at the same time!); *Clubs* City of London, Enfield Town Cons (pres), Carlton (hon memb); *Style—* Mark Field, Esq, MP; ✉ House of Commons, London SW1A 0AA (tel 020 7219 8160)

FIELD, Hon Mr Justice; Sir Richard Field; kt (2002); s of Robert Henry Field, and Ivy May, *née* Dicketts; *b* 17 April 1947; *Educ* Ottershaw Sch, Univ of Bristol (LLB), LSE (LLM); *m* 31 Aug 1968, Lynne, da of Ismay Hauskind; 2 da (Rachel Eva b 3 June 1974, Beatrice Jasmine b 17 June 1981), 2 s (Matthew Ismay b 15 Feb 1978, Thomas Richard b 26 Nov 1988); *Career* asst prof Faculty of Law Univ of Br Columbia 1969–71, lectr Hong Kong Univ 1971–73, assoc prof Faculty of Law McGill Univ Montreal 1973–77; called to the Bar Inner Temple 1977 (bencher); QC 1987, dep judge of the High Court 1998, recorder

1999, judge of the High Court of Justice (Queen's Bench Div) 2002–; *Recreations* opera, theatre, cricket, rugby football (as a spectator); *Clubs* Garrick; *Style*— The Hon Mr Justice Field; ✉ Royal Courts of Justice, Strand, London WC2A 2LL

FIELD, Prof Stephen John; s of Derek Field, of Marple, Cheshire, and Yvonne, *née* Corke; *b* 22 June 1959, Stourbridge, W Midlands; *Educ* Marple Hall GS, Univ of Birmingham (MB ChB), Univ of Dundee (MMEd); *m* 21 Oct 1992, Lynn, *née* Kennedy; 2 da (Alice Elizabeth, Helen Marie (twins) b 30 Oct 1994); *Career* regnl dir of postgrad GP educn West Midlands 1995–2001, GP princ Bellevue Med Centre Edgbaston 1997–, regnl postgrad dean West Midlands Deanery 2001–06, head of workforce and regnl postgrad dean NHS W Midlands Workforce Deanery 2006–; hon prof of med educn Univ of Warwick 2002–, hon prof of med Univ of Birmingham 2003–; memb Postgrad Med Educn and Trg Bd 2003–; chm RCGP 2007–; faculty memb Harvard Univ (Harvard Macy prog for leaders in healthcare educn); Hon Dr Univ of Staffordshire 2006; FRCGP 1997 (MRCGP 1987), ILTM 2001, FHEA 2007; *Publications* numerous pubns in med and educn jls 1994–; numerous books on med educn, med career and primary care; *Recreations* tennis, family; *Style*— Prof Stephen Field; ✉ NHS West Midlands, St Chads Court, 213 Hagley Road, Edgbaston, Birmingham B16 9RG (tel 0121 695 2383, e-mail stephen.field@westmidlands.nhs.uk)

FIELD-JOHNSON, Nicholas Anthony; s of Henry Anthony Field-Johnson (d 1988), and Magdalena, *née* von Evert (d 1971); *b* 28 March 1951; *Educ* Harrow, Univ of Oxford (MA, treas Oxford Union), Harvard Business Sch (MBA); *m* Sarah Katherine, *née* Landale; 3 s (Anthony Russell b Oct 1984, Ben Sebastian b May 1986, Oliver Nicholas b Dec 1988); *Career* corporate financier Citibank NA London 1974–78, investment advsr Atlantic Richfield Co Los Angeles 1979–82, gen mangr World Trade Bank Los Angeles 1983–85, head of M&A Dresdner Bank AG London 1986–90, dir NM Rothschild & Sons Ltd 1990–91, ceo Case International Holdings Ltd 1992–98, md (UK) Alexander Dunham & Case Capital 1998–2003, dir Robert Fraser Corporate Finance 2004–; MInstD; *Recreations* fishing, sailing, shooting, tennis, food and travel; *Clubs* Carlton, Annabel's, Pasley Tyler; *Style*— Nicholas Field-Johnson, Esq; ✉ 28 Ashchurch Park Villas, London W12 9SP (e-mail nfjuke@yahoo.com); Robert Fraser Corporate Finance (tel 020 7661 9331, website www.rfcf.net)

FIELDEN, Dr Christa Maria; da of Ludwig Robert Peix (d 1974), and Margaret Freer-Hewish, *née* von Neumann; *b* 28 June 1943; *Educ* Hampshire Co HS for Girls, Univ of London (BSc, MSc, PhD); *m* 29 Jan 1964 (m dis 1983), Christopher James Fielden; 2 s (James b 15 July 1966, William b 4 Oct 1968 d 1989); *Career* with Civil Serv 1970–74, head Computer Dept CNAA 1974–75, called to the Bar Lincoln's Inn 1982, in practice SE Circuit; FSS 1982; *Recreations* walking, cooking, dogs; *Style*— Miss Christa Fielden; ✉ 9 Woburn Court, Bernard Street, London WC1 (tel 020 7837 8752); 6 King's Bench Walk, London EC4Y 7DR (tel 020 7353 4931)

FIELDEN, Dr Jonathan Mark; s of Barry Fielden (d 1984), and Margaret, *née* Shaw; *b* 9 September 1963; *Educ* Bedford Sch, Univ of Bristol (BSc, MB ChB); *m* 29 Sept 1990, Catherine Ruth, *née* Emerson; 1 s (Alexander David); *Career* house offr Bristol Royal Infirmary 1988–89, SHO (med) Southmead Hosp and Bristol Royal Infirmary 1989–91; SHO (anaesthetics): Southmead 1991, Bath 1992–93; registrar (Bristol Anaesthetic Trg Scheme) 1993–96, provisional fell in anaesthesia St Vincent's Hosp Sydney Aust 1994–95, specialist registrar Wessex rotation 1996–98, conslt in anaesthesia and intensive care med Royal Berkshire Hosp 1998–; memb Central Consultants & Specialists Ctee 1999–; memb Cncl: BMA 1992–94 and 1996–98 (memb Jr Doctors Ctee 1986–87, 1992–94 and 1995–98), Royal Coll of Anaesthetists 1997–2001; MRCP, FRCA; *Recreations* sport, opera, hill walking, travel, healthy cynicism; *Style*— Dr Jonathan Fielden; ✉ Intensive Care Unit, Royal Berkshire Hospital, London Road, Reading RG1 5AN

FIELDING, Daryl; da of Benjamin Payne, and Muriel, *née* Matthews (d 1992); *b* 25 October 1957; *Educ* Univ of London (BSc); *m* 19 Sept 1983, Bruce John Fielding; *Career* account dir Abbott Mead Vickers 1986–89, bd dir Lowe Howard Spink 1989–96, BMP 1996–98, managing ptnr Ogilvy 1998–; memb D&AD, MIPA; *Recreations* opera, travel, scuba diving, Scotland; *Style*— Mrs Daryl Fielding; ✉ Ogilvy, 10 Cabot Square, London E14 4QB (tel 020 7345 3231, e-mail daryl.fielding@ogilvy.com)

FIELDING, David Ian; s of William Fielding, and Nora, *née* Kershaw; *b* 8 September 1948; *Educ* Central Sch of Art and Design; *Career* theatre director and designer; designer for Pet Shop Boys World Tour 1991 and the album Very; *Theatre* as dir prodns incl: Britannicus (Crucible Sheffield), The Intelligence Park (Almeida Festival), The Hypochondriacs (Citizens Glasgow), Elisabeth II (Gate), The Eve of Retirement (Gate), The New Menoza (Gate), Betrayal (Citizens Glasgow), The Park (RSC, The Pit) 1995, Back to Methuselah (RSC); design cmmns RSC incl: The Tempest, The Plain Dealer, Restoration, King Lear; other design credits incl: Scenes from an Execution (Almeida), Mother Courage (RNT) 1995; *Opera* as dir prodns for Garsington Opera incl: Capriccio, Daphne, Idomeneo, Die Ägyptische Helena, Die liebe der Danae, Intermezzo, Die schweigsame Frau; other credits incl: Elisa E Claudio (Wexford Festival Opera), Soundbites (ENO), The Turk in Itlay (ENO), Tannhäuser (Opera North), Rinaldo (Grange Park), The Turn of the Screw (Grange Park), Charodeika (Grange Park); Wexford Festival Opera design cmmns incl: Medea in Corinto, Giovanna D'Arco, Hans Heiling, La Legenda Di Sakuntala, The Turn of the Screw; design cmmns for Scottish Opera incl: Seraglio, Die Fledermaus, Rigoletto, Wozzeck, The Rise and Fall of the City of Mahagonny; designs for Welsh Nat Opera incl: The Turn of the Screw, Il Trovatore, Elektra; designs for Kent Opera incl: Ruddigore, The Marriage of Figaro, King Priam (also filmed); designs for ENO incl: Rienzi, Mazeppa, Xerxes, Simon Boccanegra, Clarissa, A Masked Ball, Don Carlos, Street Scene (co-prod Scottish Opera); other prodns incl: Der Fliegende Holländer (Royal Opera House), La Clemenza Di Tito (Glyndebourne); cmmns abroad incl: The Rake's Progress (Netherlands Opera), Werther (Nancy Opera), Iolanthe (Komische Oper Berlin), Don Carlos (San José Symphony), Idomeneo (Vienna State Opera), Jules César (Paris Opera), The Ring Cycle (New Nat Theatre Tokyo); *Recreations* bridge, crosswords, Central American archaeology, gardening; *Style*— David Fielding, Esq; ✉ c/o Harriet Cruickshank, 97 Old South Lambeth Road, London SW8 1XU (tel 020 7735 2933, fax 020 7820 1081)

FIELDING, Emma Georgina Annalies; da of John Fielding, and Sheila, *née* Brown; *Educ* RSAMD; *Career* actor; *Theatre* credits incl: Jane Eyre in Jane Eyre (Crucible Sheffield), Thomasina in Arcadia (RNT), Agnes in School for Wives (Almeida), Penthea in Broken Heart (RSC), Hermia in A Midsummer Night's Dream (RSC), Viola in Twelfth Night (RSC), Ira in 1953 (Almeida), Ellie Dunn in Heartbreak House (Almeida), Lady Teazle in The School for Scandal (RSC), Alison in Look Back in Anger (RNT), Sarah in Spinning Into Butter (Royal Court), Private Lives (Albery Theatre (Olivier Award nomination Best Supporting Actress 2002)), Isabella in Measure for Measure (RSC), Imogen in Cymbeline (RSC); *Television* credits incl: Mary Shelley in Dread Poets Society (BBC), Becky in Tell Tale Hearts (BBC), Joan in The Maitlands (BBC), Elizabeth in Drover's Gold (BBC), Isobel in Dance to the Music of Time (Dancetime), Frances in A Respectable Trade (BBC), Elizabeth Lack in Wings of Angels (BBC), Beatrice in Big Bad World (Carlton), Josie in Other People's Children (BBC), Marai in Green Eyed Monster (BBC); *Film* Frances in The Scarlet Tunic (Scarlet Films), Mary in Pandemonium (Mariner Films), DCI Pryce in Shooters (Coolbeans Films), Helga in Discovery of Heaven (Mulholland Films); *Awards* Carleton Hobbs Radio Award 1991, Ian Charleson Award (for School for Wives) 1993, London Critics' Circle Most Promising Newcomer (for Arcadia and School for Wives) 1993, Dame Peggy Ashcroft Award for Best Actress (for Twelfth Night and The Broken Heart) 1995, Theater World Award Outstanding Broadway Debut (for Private Lives); *Publications* Twelfth Night: Actors on Shakespeare (2002); *Recreations* hill walking; *Style*— Ms Emma Fielding; ✉ Sue Latimer, ARG, 4 Great Portland Street, London W1W 8PA (tel 020 7436 6400, fax 020 7436 6700)

FIELDING, Helen; *Educ* Wakefield Girls' HS, St Anne's Coll Oxford; *Career* novelist; Publishing News Br Book Awards Book of the Year 1997; *Books* Cause Celeb (1995), Bridget Jones's Diary (1996), Bridget Jones: The Edge Of Reason (1999), Olivia Joules and the Overactive Imagination (2003); *Recreations* hiking, swimming, reading, movies, salsa; *Style*— Ms Helen Fielding; ✉ c/o Viking Publicity, 375 Hudson Street, New York 10014, USA

FIELDING, Sir Leslie; KCMG (1987); o s of Percy Archer Fielding (d 1963), and Margaret, *née* Calder Horry (d 1999); *b* 29 July 1932; *Educ* Queen Elizabeth's Sch Barnet, Emmanuel Coll Cambridge (MA), SOAS Univ of London, St Antony's Coll Oxford (MA); *m* 1978, Dr Sally Patricia Joyce Fielding, FSA, da of late Robert Stanley Thomas Stibbs Harvey; 1 s, 1 da; *Career* joined Foreign Serv 1956, Tehran 1957–60, FO 1960–64, Singapore 1964, chargé d'affaires Phnom Penh 1964–66, Paris 1966–70, FCO 1970–73; transferred to European Cmmn in Brussels 1973, head of delgn Cmmn of European Communities in Japan 1978–82, DG for external rels European Cmmn in Brussels 1982–87; vice-chllr Univ of Sussex 1987–92 (memb Univ Ct 2000–), memb High Cncl European Univ Inst Florence 1988–92, chm UK Nat Curriculum Working Gp for Geography 1989–90; hon pres Univ Assoc for Contemporary European Studies 1990–2000; memb: Japan-European Community Assoc 1988–98, UK-Japan 2000 Gp 1993–2001; advsr: IBM Europe 1989–95, Panasonic Europe 1990–96; memb House of Laity Gen Synod C of E 1990–92, reader C of E 1981–2007 (emeritus 2007–, served Dioceses of Exeter, Tokyo, Gibraltar, Chichester and Hereford); hon fell: Emmanuel Coll Cambridge 1990, Sussex European Inst 1993–; Hon LLD Univ of Sussex 1992; FRSA 1989, FRGS 1991; Grand Offr of the Order of St Agatha (San Marino) 1987, Knight Cdr of the Order of the White Rose (Finland) 1988, Silver Order of Merit with Star (Austria) 1989; *Publications* Traveller's Tales (contrib, 1999), More Travellers' Tales (contrib, 2005), Before the Killing Fields: Witness to Cambodia and the Vietnam War (2007); *Recreations* living in the country; *Clubs* Travellers; *Style*— Sir Leslie Fielding, KCMG; ✉ Wild Cherry Farm, Elton, Ludlow, Shropshire, SY8 2HQ

FIENNES, Joseph Alberic; *b* 26 May 1970, Salisbury, Wilts; *Educ* Guildhall Sch of Music and Drama; *Career* actor; *Theatre* Real Classy Affair (Royal Court), Edward II (Sheffield Crucible), Love's Labour's Lost (Nat Theatre), Epitaph for George Dillon (Comedy); West End incl: The Woman in Black, A View from the Bridge, A Month in the Country; RSC incl: Son of Man, Les Enfants du Paradis, Troilus and Cressida, The Herbal Bed, As You Like It; *Television* The Vacillations of Poppy Carew 1995; *Films* Stealing Beauty 1996, Martha, Meet Frank, Daniel and Laurence 1998, Elizabeth 1998, Shakespeare in Love 1998, Forever Mine 1999, Rancid Aluminium 2000, Enemy at the Gates 2001, Dust 2001, Killing Me Softly 2001, The Great Raid 2003, Luther 2003, Leo 2003, The Merchant of Venice 2003, Sinbad: Legend of the Seven Seas 2003, Man to Man 2004, Darwin Awards 2004, Running with Scissors 2005, Goodbye Bafana 2006; *Style*— Joseph Fiennes, Esq; ✉ c/o Ken McReddie, 21 Barrett Street, London W1U 1BD (tel 020 7499 7448)

FIENNES, Ralph Nathanial; s of Mark Fiennes (d 2004), of London, and Jennifer, *née* Lash (d 1993); *b* 22 December 1962; *Educ* St Kieran's Coll Kilkenny Ireland, Bishop Wordsworth Sch Salisbury, Chelsea Sch of Art, RADA (Kendal Award, Forbes-Robertson Award, Emile Littler Award); *Career* actor; memb Br Actors' Equity Assoc; *Theatre* Twelfth Night, A Midsummer Night's Dream and Ring Round The Moon (all The Open Air Theatre) 1985, Night and Day and See How They Run (both Theatr Clwyd), Me Mam Sez, Don Quixote and Cloud Nine (all Oldham Coliseum) 1986, Romeo & Juliet and A Midsummer Night's Dream (both Open Air Theatre) 1986, Six Characters in Search of an Author, Fathers and Sons and Ting Tang Mine (all NT) 1987–88, The Plantagenets, Much Ado about Nothing, King John, The Man Who Came to Dinner, Playing with Trains, Troilus and Cressida, King Lear and Love's Labour's Lost (all RSC) 1988–91, Hamlet (Hackney Empire and Broadway) 1995 (Tony Award for Best Actor), Ivanov (Almeida) 1997, Brand (RSC) 2003, Julius Caesar (Barbican) 2005, Faith Healer (Gate Theatre Dublin and Broadway) 2006, First Love (Sydney Festival); *Films* A Dangerous Man: Lawrence After Arabia, Wuthering Heights, The Baby of Macon, The Cormorant, Schindler's List (BAFTA Award for Best Supporting Actor, London Film Critics' British Actor of the Year Award), Quiz Show, Strange Days, The English Patient, Oscar and Lucinda, The Avengers, Onegin, A Taste of Sunshine, The End of the Affair, Spider, Wallace and Gromit: The Curse of the Were-Rabbit, Harry Potter and the Goblet of Fire, The Constant Gardener (Best Actor Evening Standard British Film Awards, Best British Actor London Film Critics' Circle Awards), The White Countess, Bernard and Doris, In Bruges; *Recreations* reading; *Style*— Ralph Fiennes, Esq

FIENNES, Sir Ranulph (TWISLETON-WYKEHAM-); 3 Bt (UK 1916), of Banbury, Co Oxford; OBE (1993); s of Lt-Col Sir Ranulph Twisleton-Wykeham-Fiennes, 2 Bt, DSO (d 1943, gs of 17 Baron Saye and Sele), and Audrey Joan, *née* Newson (d 2004); *b* 7 March 1944, (posthumously); *Educ* Eton, Mons Offr Cadet Sch; *m* 1, 11 Sept 1970, Virginia Frances (d 2004), da of Thomas Pepper (d 1985); m 2, 12 March 2005, Louise Millington; 1 da (Elizabeth Grace b 2006); *Career* Capt Royal Scots Greys, Capt 22 SAS Regt 1966, Capt Sultan of Oman's Armed Forces 1968–70; exec conslt for Western Europe to Chm Occidental Petroleum Corp 1984–90; author and explorer; leader of first polar circumnavigation of earth (The Transglobe Expedition) that arrived back in UK in Sept 1982 after 3 years non-stop travel, first man (with colleague) to reach both Poles by surface travel, achieved world record for unsupported northerly travel reaching 88 degrees and 28 minutes Siberian Arctic 1990, leader of Ubar Expedition which discovered the lost city of Ubar 1992, record unsupported Polar trek of 1,272 miles in 96 days 1992–93 (also first unsupported crossing of Antarctic Continent), completed seven marathons on seven continents in seven days 2003, second in North Pole Marathon 2004, climbed North face of the Eiger 2007; *Awards* French Parachute Wings 1968, Dhofar Campaign Medal 1968, Sultan of Oman's Bravery Medal 1970, Man of the Year Award 1982, Livingstone Gold Medal Royal Scottish Geographical Soc 1983, Gold Medal NY Explorers Club 1984, Fndr's Medal RGS 1984, The Polar Medal 1984 with Bar 1995 by HM the Queen (wife was first first female recipient), ITV Award for the event of the decade 1990, Explorers Club (Br Chapter) Millennium Award for Navigation 2000, Oldie of the Year Award 2004; Hon DSc Loughborough Univ; Hon Dr: UCE 1995, Univ of Portsmouth 2000, Univ of Glasgow 2002, Univ of Sheffield 2005, Abertay 2007; *Books* Talent for Trouble (1968), Icefall in Norway (1971), The Headless Valley (1972), Where Soldiers Fear to Tread (1975), Hell on Ice (1978), To the Ends of the Earth: Transglobe Expedition 1979–82 (1983), Bothie The Polar Dog (jtly with first wife, 1984), Living Dangerously (1987), The Feather Men (1991), Atlantis of the Sands - The Search for the Lost City of Ubar (1992), Mind Over Matter (1993), The Sett (1996), Fit For Life (1998), Beyond the Limits (2000), The Secret Hunters (2002), Captain Scott (biography, 2003); *Recreations* skiing, photography; *Clubs* Guild of Vintners, Travellers (hon memb); *Style*— Sir Ranulph Fiennes, Bt, OBE

FIFE, 3 Duke of (UK 1900); James George Alexander Bannerman Carnegie; 9 Bt (NS 1663); also 12 Earl of Southesk (S 1633), Earl of Macduff (UK 1900), Lord Carnegie of Kinnaird and Leuchars (S 1616), and Baron Balinhard (UK 1869); o s of 11 Earl of Southesk, KCVO, DL (d 1992), and his 1 w, HH Princess Maud Alexandra Victoria

Georgina Bertha (d 1945; granted title of Princess, style of Highness, and special precedence immediately after all members of Royal Family bearing style of Royal Highness 1905), 2 da of 1 Duke of Fife and HRH Princess Louise (The Princess Royal), eldest da of HM King Edward VII; suc his maternal aunt, HRH Princess Arthur of Connaught, Duchess of Fife 1959; *b* 23 September 1929; *Educ* Gordonstoun, RAC Cirencester; *m* 11 Sept 1956 (m dis 1966), Hon Caroline Cecily Dewar, da of 3 Baron Forteviot, MBE, DL (d 1993); 1 da (Lady Alexandra Etherington b 1959), 1 s (David Charles, Earl of Southesk b 1961); *Heir* s, Earl of Southesk; *Career* served Malaya Campaign Scots Guards 1948–50; landowner, farmer and co dir; Amateur Boxing Assoc: pres 1959–73, vice-patron 1973; ships pres HMS Fife 1967–87; a vice-patron of Braemar Royal Highland Soc, a vice-pres British Olympic Assoc 1973–2000, ret; Freeman City of London 1954, Sr Liveryman Worshipful Co of Clothworkers 1954; *Style*— His Grace the Duke of Fife; ✉ Elsick House, Stonehaven, Kincardineshire AB39 3NT; seat: Kinnaird Castle, Brechin, Angus DD9 6TZ

FIFE, Jonathan Keith (Jon); s of Donald Ralph Fife, and Marjorie Eileen Fife; *b* 18 September 1948, Aberdeen; *Educ* Leeds Modern Sch, Lincoln Coll Oxford (BA); *m* 31 Dec 1974, Jean Margaret, *née* Northedge; 1 s (Edward James b 17 June 1978), 2 da (Katherine Alice, Rebecca Ann (twins) b 30 Jan 1981); *Career* admitted slr 1973; Waterhouse & Co: joined as trainee, slr 1973, ptnr 1978; currently sr ptnr Field Fisher Waterhouse (also head Commercial and Finance Gp); memb City of London Slrs Co; *Recreations* opera, football, golf; *Style*— Jon Fife, Esq; ✉ Field Fisher Waterhouse, 35 Vine Street, London EC3N 2AA (tel 020 7861 4170, fax 020 7488 0084, e-mail jon.fife@ffw.com)

FIGES, Eva; da of Emil Eduard Unger (d 1973), and Irma Alice, *née* Cohen (d 1991); *b* 15 April 1932; *Educ* Kingsbury Co GS, QMC London (BA); *m* John G Figes (m dis); 1 da (Catherine Jane b 1957), 1 s (Orlando Guy b 1959); *Career* writer; Guardian Fiction Prize 1967; fell QMC London 1990–; memb Soc of Authors; hon DLitt Brunel Univ 2003; *Novels* Equinox (1966), Winter Journey (1967), Konek Landing (1969), B (1972), Days (1974), Nelly's Version (1977), Waking (1981), Light (1983), The Seven Ages (1986), Ghosts (1988), The Tree of Knowledge (1990), The Tenancy (1993), The Knot (1996); *Non-fiction* Patriarchal Attitudes (1970), Tragedy and Social Evolution (1976), Little Eden (1978), Sex and Subterfuge - Women Writers to 1850 (1982), Tales of Innocence and Experience (2003); *Recreations* music, theatre, cinema, my grand-daughters; *Style*— Ms Eva Figes; ✉ Rogers, Coleridge & White Ltd, 20 Powis Mews, London W11 1JN (tel 020 7221 3717, fax 020 7229 9084)

FIGES, Prof Orlando Guy; s of John Figes (d 2003), and Eva, *née* Unger; *b* 20 November 1959, London; *Educ* Univ of Cambridge (BA, PhD); *m* 1990, Stephanie, *née* Palmer; 2 da (Lydia, Alice (twins) b 1993); *Career* Univ of Cambridge: research fell Trinity Coll 1984–87, asst lectr History Faculty 1987, coll lectr and dir of studies Trinity Coll 1988, lectr History Faculty 1987; prof of history Birkbeck Coll London 1999–; Leverhulme Tst Sr Research Fellowship 1995–96, Leverhulme Tst Institutional Grant 1999–2001, British Acad Sr Research Fellowship 2000–01; for A People's Tragedy: Wolfson Prize for History 1997, NCR Book Award 1997, WH Smith Literary Award 1997, Longman/History Today Book of the Year Award 1997, LA Times Book Prize 1997; FRSL; *Publications* V P Danilov: Rural Russia under the New Regime (trans, 1988), Peasant Russia, Civil War: The Volga Countryside in Revolution 1917–1921 (1989, 2 edn 1999), A People's Tragedy: The Russian Revolution 1891–1924 (1996), Interpreting the Russian Revolution: The Language and Symbols of 1917 (with Boris Kolonitskii, 1999), Natasha's Dance: A Cultural History of Russia (2002); also author of numerous chapters in books, articles and published lectures; *Recreations* soccer, gardening, wine; *Style*— Prof Orlando Figes; ✉ Birkbeck College, Malet Street, London WC1E 7HX (tel 020 7631 6299, e-mail orlando.figes@ntlworld.com)

FIGGIS, Sir Anthony St John Howard; KCVO (1996), CMG (1993); s of R R Figgis (d 1984), and Philippa Maria, *née* Young (d 1988); *b* 12 October 1940; *Educ* Rugby, King's Coll Cambridge; *m* 6 June 1964, Miriam Ellen (Mayella), da of Dr F C Hardt (d 1954); 1 da (Sophie b 1966), 2 s (Benedict b 1968, Oliver b 1972); *Career* HM Dip Serv: joined 1962, Belgrade 1963–65 and 1982–85, Bahrain 1968–70, Madrid 1971–74 and 1979–82, Bonn 1988–89, dir of res and analysis FCO 1989–91, Vice-Marshal of the Diplomatic Corps and an asst under sec FCO 1991–96, ambass to Austria 1996–2000, HM Marshal of the Dip Corps 2001–; pres Int Social Service (UK) 2001–; tstee Guildhall Sch Tst 2001–, govr Goodenough Coll for Overseas Grads 2004–; memb Central Cncl Royal Over-Seas League 2004– (vice-chm 2007–); Gentleman Usher of the Blue Rod Order of St Michael and St George 2002–; Freeman City of London 1996; *Recreations* family, fly fishing, tennis, music (piano); *Style*— Sir Anthony Figgis, KCVO, CMG; ✉ Clock Tower House, St James's Palace, London SW1A 1BN

FIGGURES, Lt-Gen Andrew Collingwood; CBE (1998); s of Colin Norman Figgures, and Ethel Barbara, *née* Wilks; *b* 13 November 1950; *Educ* Loughborough GS, Welbeck Coll, RMA Sandhurst, St Catharine's Coll Cambridge (MA), Open Univ (MBA); *m* 1978, Poppy Felicity Ann, *née* Ogley; 1 da; *Career* cmmnd 1970, served UK, Cyprus, BAOR, former Yugoslavia, Iraq; student: Army Staff Coll Camberley, Higher Cmd and Staff Coll, RCDS; Cdr Equipment Support Land Cmd 1995, DOR (Land)/DEC(DBE) MOD 1999–2000, capability mangr (manoeuvre) MOD 2000–03, Dep Cmdg Gen Combined Jt Task Force 7 2003–04, Master Gen of the Ordnance and tech dir Defence Procurement Agency (DPA) and Defence Logistics Orgn (DLO) 2004; Col Cmdt REME 2002–; CEng 1991, FIMechE 1992, FIET 2006, FRAeS 2006; *Clubs* Leander; *Style*— Lt-Gen Andrew Figgures, CBE; ✉ Ministry of Defence, Floor 2, Zone F, Main Building, Whitehall, London SW1A 2HB (tel 020 7218 7171, e-mail andrew.figgures944@mod.uk)

FILBY, Ian; s of Peter Filby, of Bristol, and Paquita, *née* Garrido (d 1998); *b* 27 January 1959, Finchley, London; *Educ* Queen Elizabeth's Hosp Bristol, St Catharine's Coll Cambridge (BA, Soccer blue); *m* 1 June 1991, Susan, *née* Woo; 2 da (Luisa Lara b 27 Jan 1992, Francesca Linda b 17 March 2001), 1 s (Laurence Leon b 25 Aug 1993); *Career* Boots Co plc: retail buying 1981, sales and mktg dir Fads/Homestyle 1997, dep dir trading Boots the Chemists 2001–03, commercial dir lifestyle Boots the Chemists 2003–05, exec dir beauty and lifestyle Boots the Chemists 2005–; dir Look Good Feel Better; *Recreations* golf, cricket, football, off-piste skiing, saxophone, good eating and drinking; *Clubs* Belton Woods Golf, Allington CC, Grantham Amateurs FC; *Style*— Ian Filby, Esq; ✉ Boots Co plc, Thane Road, D90 Building WF17, Nottingham NG90 1BS

FILKIN, David Shenstone; s of Brian Shenstone Filkin, of Birmingham, and Lilian Winifred, *née* Franklin (d 2004); *b* 22 November 1942; *Educ* King Edward's Sch Birmingham, UC Oxford (BA); *m* 31 Aug 1968, Angela Elizabeth, da of Geoffrey Callam (d 1974), of Woking, Surrey; 3 s (Neil b 1973, Jonathan b 1975, Matthew b 1978); *Career* BBC TV: prodr Man Alive 1964–79, exec prodr Holiday 74 1974, deviser and ed Brass Tacks 1978, ed Tomorrow's World 1979–84, ed QED 1984–91, deviser and ed Body Matters 1985–90, head of science and features 1991–94; md David Filkin Enterprises 1994–; prodr Stephen Hawking's Universe 1997; pres BBC RFC 1979–86, memb Surrey Met Rugby Football Referees Soc, memb Meteorological Office Owners Cncl 2000–; *Books* Tomorrow's World Today (1982), Bodymatters (1987), Stephen Hawking's Universe (1997); *Recreations* rugby union football coaching and refereeing, sea angling, golf, wine tasting; *Clubs* BBC RFC, Hampton Court Palace Golf (capt 2001–03), Bisley & District Sea Anglers, The Wine Soc; *Style*— David Filkin, Esq; ✉ 29 Bloomfield Road, Kingston upon Thames, Surrey KT1 2SF (tel 020 8549 3204, fax 020 8549 3204, e-mail davidsfil@aol.com)

FILKIN, Elizabeth Jill; da of John Tompkins, and Frances Trollope; *b* 24 November 1940; *Educ* Univ of Birmingham (BSocSci), Brunel Univ; *m* 2, 1974 (m dis 1994), Geoffrey Filkin, CBE, *qv*; 3 da; m 3, 1996, Michael John Honey; *Career* organiser Sparkbrook Assoc Birmingham 1961–64, res fell Anglo-Israel Assoc London and Israel 1964, lectr and researcher Univ of Birmingham 1964–68, lectr National Inst for Social Work London 1968–71 (also community worker N Southwark), community work services offr London Borough of Brent Social Services Dept 1971–75, lectr in social studies Univ of Liverpool 1975–83, chief exec National Assoc CAB 1983–88, asst chief exec London Docklands Devpt Corp 1991–92 (dir Community Servs 1988–91), The Adjudicator in The Adjudicator's Office 1993–99, Parly Cmmr for Standards 1999–2002; cmmr Audit Cmmn 1999–2004; chm HB and Senator Capital 2005–; non-exec dir: Britannia Building Soc 1992–98, Hay Management Consultants 1992–98, Logica plc 1995–99, Stanelco plc 2003–, Jarvis plc 2003–; non-exec advsr Weatherall Green & Smith 1997–99; chm ATVOD (Assoc for TV on Demand) 2004–, dep chm Regulatory Decisions Ctee FSA, chm Appts Gp RPSGB 2005–, chm Advtg Advsy Ctee 2005–; chm Rainer Fndn 2004–; chm Advsy Cncl Centre for Socio-Legal Studies Wolfson Coll Oxford 1995–2000; memb Cncl: Royal Holloway Coll London 1995–97 (dep chm Bd Govrs), Univ of E London 1997–2003; Special Award Zurich/Spectator Parly Awards 2001; Hon PhD: Brunel Univ 2002, South Bank Univ 2003; City fell Hughes Hall Cambridge 2003; *Books* The New Villagers (1969), What Community Worker Needs to Know (1974), Community Work & Caring for Children (1979), Caring for Children (1979), Women and Children First (1984); *Recreations* swimming, walking; *Style*— Elizabeth Filkin

FILKIN, Baron (Life Peer UK 1999), of Pimlico in the City of Westminster; (David) Geoffrey Nigel Filkin; CBE (1997); s of Donald Geoffrey Filkin (d 1994), and Winifred, *née* Underwood; *b* 1 July 1944; *Educ* King Edward VI GS Birmingham, Clare Coll Cambridge (MA), Univ of Manchester (DipTP); *m* 1, (m dis), Elizabeth Filkin, *qv*; 3 da (Fiona, Victoria, Beatrice); m 2, 28 May 2005, Brigitte Paupy; *Career* town planner Redditch Development Corporation 1969–72, mangr Housing Aid Centre Brent 1972–75, dir of housing and dep chief exec Merseyside Improved Housing 1975–79, dir of housing Ellesmere Port 1979–82, dir of housing Greenwich 1982–88, chief exec Reading BC 1988–91, sec Assoc of District Councils 1991–97, policy analyst and writer 1997–; Lord in Waiting (Govt whip) 2001–, Parly under sec of state Home Office 2002–03, Parly under sec of state Dept of Constitutional Affrs 2003–04, Parly under sec of state DfES 2004–05; local govt advsr to Joseph Rowntree Fndn until 2001; advsr to: Environment Ctee House of Commons until 2001, Govt of South Africa until 2001, Capgemini, NCP; non-exec dir: New Local Govt Network until 2001, Serco, Accord plc; chm: Beacon Cncl Advsy Panel 1999–2001, Parly All-Pty Business Services Gp 2000–01, Merits Ctee House of Lords, Public Serv Reform Gp, St Albans Cathedral Music Tst; fndr and chm The Parliament Choir 2001–02; memb Soc of Local Authy Chief Execs; former MRTPI; *Recreations* walking, opera, music, bird watching; *Style*— The Rt Hon the Lord Filkin, CBE; ✉ House of Lords, London SW1A 0PW (tel 020 7219 0640)

FILOCHOWSKI, (Edward) Jan; *Educ* Univ of Cambridge (MA), Univ of Newcastle upon Tyne (MA); *m* Dr Naomi Fulop; 1 s (Tom), 1 da (Kate); *Career* chief-exec Medway NHS Tst until 2002, on secondment to Royal United Hospitals Tst as chief exec 2002–03, currently peripatetic chief exec, sr magmnt adsr and tunraround specialist for NHS SE; NHS Univ fell and sr assoc Judge Business Sch Univ of Cambridge 2004–05, visiting prof Brunel Univ 2004–07; MHSM; *Style*— Jan Filochowski

FILOCHOWSKI, Julian; CMG (2004), OBE (1998); s of Tadeusz Filochowski, of Normanton, W Yorks, and Jean, *née* Royce; *b* 9 December 1947; *Educ* St Michael's Coll Leeds, Churchill Coll Cambridge (MA); *Career* Central America co-ordinator Br Volunteer Prog Guatemala City 1969–73, educn sec Catholic Inst for Int Rels (CIIR) 1973–82, dir CAFOD 1982–2003; devpt conslt 2004–; visiting fell Clare Coll Cambridge; Hon Dr of Human Rights Univ of Central America San Salvador, Hon LLD Univ of Roehampton 2006; *Books* Reflections on Puebla (jtly, 1980), Archbishop Romero - Ten Years On (1990), Opening Up: Speaking Out in the Church (jt ed, 2005); *Style*— Julian Filochowski, Esq, CMG, OBE; ✉ 57 Lyme Grove, London E9 6PX (tel and fax 020 8986 0807, mobile 07803 032430, e-mail jfilochowski@btinternet.com)

FINBOW, Roger John; s of Frederick Walter Finbow, of Sudbourne, Suffolk, and Olivia Francis, *née* Smith; *b* 13 May 1952; *Educ* Woodbridge Sch, Mansfield Coll Oxford (MA); *m* 23 May 1984, Janina Fiona (Nina), da of late John Doull; 3 da (Romy b 1985, Georgina b 1987, Isobel b 1989); *Career* Ashurst Morris Crisp (now Ashurst) London: articled clerk 1975–77, asst 1977–83 (Paris 1978–79), assoc 1983–85, ptnr 1985–; memb Ctee City Slrs Educnl Tst; memb Mansfield Coll Devpt Bd; govr Seckford Fndn, dir Ipswich Town Football Club Co Ltd, pres London Lawyers FC; *Books* UK Merger Control: Law and Practice (jtly, 1995, 2 edn 2004); *Recreations* cars, collecting model cars, keeping fit, football spectating, ballet, motorbiking; *Style*— Roger Finbow, Esq; ✉ Yew Tree House, Higham, Colchester, Essex CO7 6JZ (tel 01206 337378); Ashurst, Broadwalk House, 5 Appold Street, London EC2A 2HA (tel 020 7638 1111, fax 020 7638 1112, e-mail roger.finbow@ashurst.com)

FINCH, Alison Mary; da of Joseph Finch, and Sheila, *née* Richardson; *b* 1948; *Educ* Blackheath HS GDST, Girton Coll Cambridge (entrance scholar, BA, PhD, maj state studentship); *m* Malcolm Bowie (d 2007); 1 s, 1 da; *Career* asst lectr and lectr Dept of French Univ of Cambridge 1978–93; fell in French: Churchill Coll Cambridge 1972–93, Jesus Coll Oxford 1993–95, Merton Coll Oxford 1995–2003, Churchill Coll Cambridge 2003–; chair Sub-Faculty of French Univ of Oxford 2000–03; co-ed French Studies 2002–05; vice-master Churchill Coll Cambridge 2005–06; memb: Amnesty Int, CND; memb: Soc of French Studies 1972, memb MHRA 1974, Officier dans l'Ordre des Palmes Académiques (France) 2000; *Publications* Proust's Additions: The Making of A la Recherche du Temps Perdu (1977), Stendhal: La Chartreuse de Parme (1984), Concordance de Stendhal (1991), Women's Writing in Nineteenth-Century France (2000); numerous articles and reviews 1974–; *Recreations* singing, reading, swimming, travel, theatre; *Style*— Prof Alison Finch; ✉ Churchill College, Cambridge CB3 0DS (e-mail amf1000@cam.ac.uk)

FINCH, Prof Janet Valerie; CBE (1999), DL; da of Robert Bleakley Finch (d 1975), of Liverpool, and Evelyn Muriel, *née* Smith; *b* 13 February 1946; *Educ* Merchant Taylors' Sch for Girls, Bedford Coll London (BA), Univ of Bradford (PhD); *m* 1, 1967 (m dis 1981), Geoffrey O Spedding; m 2, 1994, David H J Morgan; *Career* research asst Dept of Anthropology Univ of Cambridge 1969–70, postgraduate research student Univ of Bradford 1970–73, lectr in sociology Endsleigh Coll of Educn Hull 1974–76; Lancaster Univ: lectr in social admin 1976–84, sr lectr 1984–88, prof of social relations 1988–, head Dept of Applied Social Science 1988–91, memb Senate 1984–87 and 1989–91, memb Academic Planning Ctee 1989–, chair Equal Opportunities Ctee 1990–93, memb Staffing Ctee 1991–93, pro-vice-chllr 1992–95; vice-chllr Keele Univ 1995–; Universities UK: memb Sutherland Ctee (Academic Standards Gp) 1988–92, pt/t secondment to the Academic Audit Unit 1990–91, memb Jt Working Party with the Br Acad on postgraduate studentships in the humanities 1991–92, chair Health Professions Ctee 1996–2000, chair Jt Equality Steering Gp 2001–07, memb Exec 2002–05, chair Health Ctee 2003–07; memb Bd Quality Assurance Agency for HE 1997–2004, memb Strategic Research Ctee HEFCE 2003–; Br Sociological Assoc: memb Nat Exec 1980–84, chair Exec 1983–84; ESRC: memb Research Centres Bd 1992–93, memb Cncl 1993–97, chair Research Grants Bd; memb Advsy Gps 1990–92: Nursing Research Unit KCL, Home Office project on Imprisonment and Family Ties Univ of Cambridge, Rowntree project on Young People and Housing Univ of Kent; memb: various Ctees CNAA 1982–92, Professoriate Standing Ctee Sheffield Poly (now Sheffield Hallam Univ) 1989–92, External Panel of Experts in Social Admin

Univ of London 1990–93, Bd Staffs Environmental Fund Ltd 2000–04, Cncl for Science and Technology 2004– (ind co-chair 2007–); chair Preston Cncl for Racial Equality 1982–86 (exec memb 1977–86), chair Bd Staffs Connexions Ltd 2002–04; tstee Nat Centre for Social Research 2002– (chair of tstees 2007–); memb N Western RHA 1992–96; non-exec dir Office for Nat Statistics 1999–; govr: Edge Hill Coll 1990–92, Sheffield Hallam Univ 1992–95, Stoke-on-Trent Sixth Form Coll 1999–2002, Manchester Met Univ 2002–; Hon DLitt UWE 1997, Hon DSc Univ of Edinburgh 2000, Hon DSc Univ of Southampton 2001, Hon DEd Univ of Lincoln 2002, Hon DEd Queen Margaret UC Edinburgh 2003; hon fell Royal Holloway Coll London 1999, hon fell Liverpool John Moores Univ 2001; AcSS 1999; *Books* Married to the Job: Wives' Incorporation in Men's Work (1983), Education as Social Policy (1984), Research and Policy: the Uses of Qualitative Methods in Social and Educational Research (1986), Family Obligations and Social Change (1989), Negotiating Family Responsibilities (with J Mason, 1993), Wills Inheritance and Families (jtly, 1996), Passing On (with J Mason, 2000); also author of numerous book chapters and of articles in refereed jls; *Style*— Prof Janet Finch, CBE, DL, AcSS; ✉ Vice-Chancellor's Office, Keele University, Staffordshire ST5 5BG

FINCH, Michael James (Mick); s of Reginald James Finch, of Chadwell Heath, Essex, and Florence Anne, *née* Selby; *b* 6 July 1957; *Educ* Ravensbourne Coll of Art (BA), RCA (MA), Terra Summer Residency (sr scholar); *Partner* Bridget Strevens; 1 da (Ella); *Career* painter; chair Fndn Parsons Sch of Design Paris 1996–98 (prof 1992–98), head of painting Kent Inst of Art and Design 1998–99, prof of fine art Ecole des Beaux-Arts de Valencienne 1999–; one man shows: Pomeroy Purdy Gallery 1990 and 1992 (curator 1988–91), Purdy Hicks Gallery 1994, Art et Patrimoine (Paris), Le Carré (Lille), Galerie é.of (Paris), Galerie Agart (France) 2004, Galerie Pitch (Paris) 2005, Gallery 33 (Berlin) 2006; included in various gp shows; paintings in collections: Peterborough City, Unilever, Burston, County NatWest, BDO Binder Hamlyn, Colas, Deutsch Bank; assoc ed Jl of the Visual Arts; regular contrib Contemporary magazine and The Burlington magazine; Unilever award 1985, Burston award 1985, Ile de France FRAC; *Clubs* Groucho; *Style*— Mick Finch, Esq; ✉ 59 Rue de Meaux, Senlis 60300, France (tel 00 33 44 60 94 20, fax 00 33 44 60 00 00, e-mail mick@mickfinch.com, website www.mickfinch.com)

FINCH, Paul Anthony; s of Ellis Finch (d 2005), and Eleanor, *née* Jones; *b* 5 October 1953, Ormskirk, Lancs; *Educ* Ormskirk GS, Univ of Newcastle upon Tyne, Coll of Law Chester; *m* 19 July 1980, Kay McDonald; *Career* admitted slr 1978; asst slr: Runnymede BC 1979–82, North Tyneside MBC 1982–86; slr Clifford Chance 1986–90, ptnr Dickinson Dees 1991– (slr 1990); memb: Law Soc 1978– (memb Planning and Environmental Ctee 1996–2006), Newcastle upon Tyne Law Soc 1990–; *Publications* Notes to Leasehold Reform Housing and Urban Development Act 1993; contrib: Rights of Way Law Review, Compass Property Law Review; *Recreations* hockey, golf, cross country skiing, squash, gardening; *Clubs* Northumbria St George's Hockey, Longhirst Hall Golf; *Style*— Paul Finch, Esq; ✉ Dickinson Dees, One Trinity Gardens, Broad Chare, Newcastle NE1 2HF (tel 0191 279 9311, fax 0191 230 8501, e-mail paul.finch@dickinson-dees.com)

FINCH, Sir Robert Gerald; kt (2005), JP (1992); s of Brig J R G Finch, OBE, and Patricia Hope, *née* Ferrar (d 1999); *b* 20 August 1944; *Educ* Felsted; *m* Patricia Ann; 2 da (Alexandra b 8 May 1975, Isabel b 8 June 1978); *Career* articled clerk Monro Pennefather & Co 1963–68; Linklaters: joined 1969 (Linklaters and Paines), ptnr 1974–, head Property Dept 1996–99; non-exec chm Liberty International 2005–; dir Int Fin Services London (IFSL) 2001; cmdt HAC 1992; Blundell Memorial lectr; memb Cncl St Paul's Cathedral 2000; tstee Morden Coll 2002; govr: Christ's Hosp 1992–, Witley Sch 1992–, Coll of Law 2000–; church cmmr 1999–; Alderman City of London, Sheriff City of London 1999–2000, HM Lt City of London 2003, Lord Mayor of the City of London 2003–04; Master Worshipful Co of Slrs 2000–01, Liveryman Worshipful Co of Innholders, Hon Liveryman Worshipful Co of Chartered Surveyors 2001, Ct Asst 2001, Hon Freeman Worshipful Co of Environmental Cleaners; memb Law Soc 1969; Hon FRICS; *Recreations* sailing, hill walking, skiing, ski mountaineering; *Clubs* Itchenor Sailing, Alpine Ski, Ski Club of Great Britain, Little Ship; *Style*— Sir Robert G Finch; ✉ Linklaters, One Silk Street, London EC2Y 8HQ

FINCH, Stephen Clark; OBE (1989); s of Frank Finch (d 1955), of Haywards Heath, and Doris, *née* Lloyd (d 1958); *b* 7 March 1929; *Educ* Ardingly, RMCS, Sch of Signals; *m* 26 April 1975, Sarah Rosemary Ann, da of Adm Sir Anthony Templer Frederick Griffith Griffin, GCB (d 1996), of Bosham; 2 da (Clare b 1977, Alice b 1980); *Career* cmmnd Royal Signals 1948, Troop Cdr BAOR 1949–50, Troop Cdr Korea 1951–52, RMCS 1953–56, Instr Sch of Signals 1956–59, Troop Cdr BAOR 1959–62, seconded Miny of Aviation 1962–64, Sqdn Cdr BAOR 1964–66, Staff Offr BAOR 1966–68, ret as Maj 1968; BP: mangr Communications Div 1968–71, gp communications mangr 1971–81, sr advsr regulatory affairs 1981–84, asst coordinator info systems 1984–89; ind conslt in IT 1989–2004; chm: Telecommunications Mangrs Assoc 1981–84 (memb 1968–, memb Exec Ctee 1971–91), Int Telecommunications Users Gp 1987–89 (memb Cncl 1981–94); memb: MMC 1985–99, Sec of State's Advsy Panel on Licensing Value Added Network Servs 1982–87, City of London Deanery Synod 1981– (lay chm 1994–), London Area Synod 1989–97, London Diocesan Synod 1994–, Bishop's Cncl and Standing Ctee 1995–, London Diocesan Advsy Ctee for the Care of Churches 1995–2006, Two Cities Area Cncl 1997– (vice-chm 2001–07), Competition Cmmn 1999–2000, City Deanery Bishop's Advsy Gp 2003–; chm Dick Lucas Tst 1999–; sec Oxford Churches Tst 1997– (memb 1996–); churchwarden St Martin Outwich; Freeman City of London 1975; FInstAM (memb Cncl 1981–84, medallist 1985), FIMgt, FCMA; *Recreations* sailing, skiing, swimming, music; *Clubs* National; *Style*— Stephen Finch, Esq, OBE; ✉ 97 Englefield Road, Canonbury, London N1 3LJ

FINCH, Stephen John; s of Harry John Finch, of New Malden, Surrey, and Evelyn Louise, *née* Baggs; *b* 28 November 1950, Carshalton, Surrey; *Educ* Raynes Park GS, Univ of London (LLB); *m* 13 Sep 1975, Leonie, *née* Spencer; 3 s (Stuart John b 9 March 1977, Matthew Edward b 19 Jan 1979, Peter Thomas b 23 Feb 1985); *Career* admitted slr 1975; articles Messrs Withers 1973–75, commercial slr Sydney 1975–76, mangr slrs office London 1976–78, asst gp slr Lloyds Bowmaker Gp 1978–82, co slr Citibank International 1982–85, ptnr Hill Bailey 1985–89, ptnr Salans 1989– (chm 2005–, head Banking and Finance Dept); former memb Legislation, E-banking and Non-Prime Finance Ctees Finance and Leasing Assoc; *Publications* Practical Commercial Precedents (contrib to Consumer Credit Section); author of articles on UK retail banking law and European law devpts for the UK finance and banking industry; *Style*— Stephen Finch, Esq; ✉ Salans, Millennium Bridge House, 2 Lambeth Hill, London EC4V 4AJ (tel 020 7429 6140, fax 020 7429 6001, e-mail sfinch@salans.com)

FINCHAM, Peter Arthur; *b* 26 July 1956; *Educ* Tonbridge, Churchill Coll Cambridge (MA); *Career* television producer; Talkback Productions: joined 1985, md 1986–2001, chief exec and jt dir of progs 2001–03; chief exec talkbackTHAMES 2003–05, controller BBC1 2005–; exec prodr: Alas Smith & Jones 1984, Bernard and the Genie 1991, The Day Today 1994, Knowing Me Knowing You with Alan Partridge 1994, They Think It's All Over 1995, Never Mind the Buzzcocks 1996, Brass Eye 1997, The 11 O'Clock Show 1998, Big Train 1998, Shooting the Past 1999, Smack the Pony 1999, Hippies 1999, Jam 2000, Da Ali G Show 2000 and 2003, Meet Ricky Gervais 2000, Too Much Sun 2000, Sword of Honour 2001, In a Land of Plenty 2001, Perfect Strangers 2001, The Armando Iannucci Shows 2001, Ali G Indahouse (feature film) 2002, Liar 2002, Bo' Selecta 2002, The Lost Prince 2003, Green Wing 2004; Indie-Vidual Award 2001; *Style*— Peter Fincham, Esq

FINDLATER, Richard Napier; s of George Richard Park Findlater (d 1963), and Rita Margaret, *née* Wade (d 1981); *b* 27 May 1947; *Educ* Pangbourne Coll, Harvard Business Sch; *m* 18 Aug 1972 (m dis 1999), Susan, da of Ronald Edmund Charlton; 2 s (Timothy Richard Park b 4 March 1975 d 2006, Simon Ian Alexander b 25 May 1978), 1 da (Harriet Leila Alexandra b 11 Sept 1987); m 2, 7 July 2001, Mairi Eastwood; *Career* Harry Price & Co CAs Eastbourne 1964–70; ptnr Ernst & Young 1976–; memb Cncl RCM 2007; ATII 1968, FCA 1970, FIMgt 1982; *Recreations* golf, paintings, food and wine; *Style*— Richard Findlater, Esq; ✉ Ernst & Young, 1 More London Place, London SE1 2AF (tel 020 7951 2000, e-mail rfindlater@uk.ey.com)

FINDLAY, Donald Russell; QC (Scot 1988); s of James Findlay (d 1980), of Edinburgh, and Mabel, *née* Muirhead (d 1985); *b* 17 March 1951; *Educ* Harris Acad Dundee, Univ of Dundee (LLB), Univ of Glasgow (MPhil); *m* 28 Aug 1982, Jennifer Edith, *née* Borrowman; *Career* lectr in law Heriot-Watt Univ Edinburgh 1975–76, advocate 1975–; past chm: Advocates Criminal Law Gp, Faculty of Advocates Criminal Practices Ctee, Think Twice Campaign; Lord Rector Univ of St Andrews (ret 1999); vice-pres Assoc for Int Cancer Research; chm Faculty Services Ltd 2003–, vice-chm Glasgow Rangers FC (resigned 1999); memb: Lothian Health Bd 1987–91, Faculty of Advocates 1975; FRSA; *Recreations* Glasgow Rangers FC, Egyptology, The Middle East, wine, malt whisky, travel, ethics, American football, Sumo; *Clubs* Royal Burgess Golfing Soc, Glasgow Rangers Bond, RAC (Glasgow); *Style*— Donald R Findlay, Esq, QC

FINDLAY, Gordon Francis George; s of Francis Gordon Findlay (d 1975), of Edinburgh, and Muriel Arras Maitland; *b* 9 February 1950; *Educ* George Watson's Coll Edinburgh, Univ of Edinburgh (BSc, MB ChB); *m* 5 April 1975, Andrea May, da of Lt Ewart Leslie Cooper, of Buxted, Surrey; 1 s (Iain b 5 Jan 1978), 2 da (Claire b 10 Oct 1980, Emma b 27 Dec 1985); *Career* conslt neurosurgeon with special interest in spinal disease Walton Hosp Liverpool 1983–; extensive pubns in jls and textbooks on spinal disease; memb Br Soc of Neurosurgeons; fndr memb: Br Cevical Spine Soc, Euro Spine Soc; FRCS 1978; *Recreations* family, golf, music; *Style*— Gordon Findlay, Esq; ✉ Walton Hospital, Department of Neurosciences, Rice Lane, Liverpool L9 1AR (tel 0151 525 3611)

FINDLAY, Richard; *Educ* Royal Scottish Acad of Music and Dramatic Art Glasgow; *m*; 3 c; *Career* work in radio and TV, English language radio station Govt of Saudi Arabia, ed English language newspaper Saudi Arabia, COI London, commercial radio London then Scotland; chief exec Scottish Radio Holdings plc and chm/dir of various subsidiary cos within the gp until 2004 (non-exec dir 2004–05), chm SMG plc 2007–; chm Iatros Ltd; currently chm of tstees RSAMD Glasgow and chm New Nat Theatre Scotland; *Recreations* sailing, music, golf; *Clubs* Scottish Arts; *Style*— Richard Findlay, Esq; ✉ National Theatre of Scotland, Atlantic Chambers, 45 Hope Street, Glasgow G2 6AF (tel 0141 221 0970, fax 041 248 7241)

FINDLAY, Richard; s of Ian Macdonald Semple Findlay, of Aberdeen, and Kathleen, *née* Lightfoot; *b* 18 December 1951, Torphins, Aberdeenshire; *Educ* Gordon Schs Huntly, Univ of Aberdeen (LLB); *Partner* Gerald McGolgan; *Career* trainee slr Wilsone & Duffus, asst slr Maclay Murray & Spens 1975–79, ptnr Ranken & Reid SSC 1979–90, ptnr Tods Murray LLP 1990–; pt/t lectr on law of film Napier Univ Edinburgh 1997–; dir: Krazy Kat Theatre Co 1984–86, Gallus Theatre Co Ltd 1996–98, Dance Base Ltd 1997–98, Lothian Gay & Lesbian Switchboard Ltd 1998–2002, Royal Lyceum Theatre Co Ltd 1999– (vice-chm 2000–), Edinburgh Music Theatre Co Ltd 1985–88, Audio Description Film Fund Ltd 2000–, The Hill Adamson 2002–, Scottish Screen 2003–07, Scottish Screen Enterprises Ltd 2003–, Luxury Edinburgh Ltd 2006–; chm Red FM Ltd 2004–05; co sec: Assoc of Integrated Media Highlands and Islands, Gay Men's Health Ltd, Edinburgh Int Jazz and Blues Festival, Moonstone Int Ltd; managing ed i2i 1995, Scotland ed Methuen Amateur Theatre Handbook; memb: Advsy Bd Screen Acad Scotland, Int Assoc of Entertainment Lawyers 1990–, BAFTA 1990– (memb Mgmnt Ctee 1998–2004), New Producers Alliance 1993–98, IBA 1993–99, Writers' Guild 1993–2002, Arts & Business Placement Scheme 1994–, Int Entertainment and Multimedia Law and Business Network 1995–, Scottish Media Lawyers Soc 1995–, Inst of Art and Law 1996–98, Theatrical Mgmnt Assoc 2000–, RTS 2003–05; tstee: Peter Darrel Tst 1996–2004, Frank Mullen Tst 2004–; *Recreations* music, theatre, opera, cinema, photography, Scottish history and culture; *Clubs* Home House (Edinburgh); *Style*— Richard Findlay, Esq; ✉ 1 Darnaway Street, Edinburgh EH3 6DW (tel 0131 226 3253, e-mail richard.findlay@hotmail.co.uk); Tods Murray LLP, Edinburgh Quay, 133 Fountainbridge, Edinburgh, EH3 9AG (tel 0131 656 2000, mobile 07814 668656, fax 0131 656 2023, e-mail richard.findlay@todsmurray.com)

FINE, Anne; OBE (2003); da of Brian Laker (d 1989), and Mary Baker; *b* 7 December 1947; *Educ* Northampton HS for Girls, Univ of Warwick (BA); *m* 3 Aug 1968 (m dis 1990), Kit Fine, s of Maurice Fine; 2 da (Ione b 3 Aug 1971, Cordelia b 26 Feb 1975); *Career* writer; memb Soc of Authors; FRSL 2003; *Awards* Scot Arts Cncl Book Award 1986, Smarties Award 1990, Guardian Children's Fiction Award 1990, Carnegie Medal 1990 and 1993, Children's Author of the Year Award Br Book Awards 1990 and 1993, Whitbread Award for a children's book 1993, Whitbread Children's Book of the Year (for The Tulip Touch) 1997, Children's Laureate 2001–03; *Books* for children incl: The Summer House Loon (1978), The Other Darker Ned (1979), The Stone Menagerie (1980), Round Behind the Icehouse (1981), The Granny Project (1983), Madame Doubtfire (1987, filmed 1993), Crummy Mummy and Me (1988), The Country Pancake (1989), Goggle-Eyes (1989, adapted for BBC), Bill's New Frock (1989), The Book of the Banshee (1991), Flour Babies (1993) Step by Wicked Step (1995), The Tulip Touch (1996), Bad Dreams (2000), Up on Cloud Nine (2002), The More, The Merrier (2003), Frozen Billy (2004), The Road of Bones (2006); books for adults: The Killjoy (1986), Taking the Devil's Advice (1990), In Cold Domain (1994), Telling Liddy (1998), All Bones and Lies (2001), Raking the Ashes (2005); *Recreations* walking, reading; *Style*— Mrs Anne Fine, OBE, FRSL; ✉ c/o David Higham Associates, 5–8 Lower John Street, Golden Square, London W1R 4HA (tel 020 7437 7888, fax 020 7437 1072)

FINE, Dr Jeffrey Howard; s of Nathan Fine, of Penylan, Cardiff, and Rebecca, *née* Levi; *b* 5 October 1955; *Educ* The Howardian HS Cardiff, Bart's Med Coll London (MB BS); *m* 1 May 1993, Kirsty Elizabeth, da of Adolf Knul, of Hilversum, Holland; 1 s (Alexander David b 27 June 1990), 1 da (Charlotte Anne b 19 May 1992); *Career* professorial registrar Acad Unit of Psychiatry Royal Free Hosp London 1981, registrar in psychological med Nat Hosp for Nervous Diseases London 1982–83, MO Home Office 1981–89, gen med practice London 1985, Euro neuroendocrine advsr Eli Lilly Pharmaceuticals Co 1986–87, private med psychiatric practice 1987–; completed London marathon 1983; freedom and key Kansas City Missouri USA 1976; MRCPsych 1984, FRSM 1987; memb: BMA 1980, Euro Assoc and Int Coll of Neuropsychopharmacology, Br Assoc of Neuropsychiatry 1988, Assoc of Independent Drs 1989; *Publications* author of papers on depression, light and obesity (Jl of Affective Disorder, 1987); *Recreations* jazz, tennis, sailing; *Clubs* Ronnie Scott's, West Heath Lawn Tennis; *Style*— Dr Jeffrey H Fine; ✉ 68 Harley Street, London W1G 7HE (tel 020 7935 3980, fax 020 7636 6262, e-mail jhfine@doctors.org.uk)

FINE, Prof Leon Gerald; s of Matthew Fine (d 1964), of Cape Town, South Africa, and Jeannette, *née* Lipshitz; *b* 16 July 1943; *Educ* Univ of Cape Town (Myer Levinson scholar, Crasnow scholar, MB BS, medals in chemistry, physiology and med, Univ Gold medal); *m* 1966, Brenda, da of Nico Sakinovsky; 2 da (Michele b 1968, Dana b 1970); *Career* Mil Serv 1971–72; asst prof of med Albert Einstein Coll of Med NY 1975–76 (fell in nephrology 1972–74, instr in med 1974–75), asst prof of med Univ of Miami 1976–78, prof of med Univ of Calif 1982–91 (assoc prof 1978–82), prof of med and head Dept of

Med UCL 1991–94, head Jt Dept of Med UCL and Royal Free Schs of Med 1994–98, head Dept of Med Royal Free and UC Med Sch 1998–, currently dean Faculty of Clinical Sciences UCL; visiting prof: Univ of Heidelberg 1988, Univ of Colorado 1989, Univ of Sheffield 1989, Univ of Minnesota 1990, Stanford Univ 1991, Univ of Manchester 1992, UC Dublin 1993; Lance Lipton visiting prof Univ of Toronto 1992; visiting res scientist: ICRF 1982, Univ of Nice 1984, UC and Middx Sch of Med 1988, MRC Mammalian Devpt Unit 1989; numerous invited lectures at nat and int meetings, author of numerous research papers and book chapters in scientific pubns; memb: Exec Ctee MRS 1991–, Res Ctee RCP 1993–; ed-in-chief Nephron; memb numerous professional socs incl: American Soc of Nephrology, Int Soc of Nephrology, American Fedn for Clinical Research, Soc for Experimental Biology and Med, American Physiological Soc, American Heart Assoc, American Assoc for the History of Med, NY Acad of Sciences, American Soc of Cell Biology, Renal Assoc, Euro Renal Assoc, Euro Dialysis and Transplantation Assoc, Assoc of Physicians of GB and Ireland (pres 1993), Assoc of American Physicians, American Soc for Clinical Investigation; fell American Coll of Physicians 1978, FMedSci 1998, FRCP 1986 (MRCP 1971), FRCP (Glasgow) 1993; *Recreations* book collecting, book binding; *Style*— Prof Leon Fine; ✉ Royal Free and University College Medical School, 5 University Street, London WC1E 6JJ (tel 020 7679 5486, fax 020 7679 5484, e-mail l.fine@ucl.ac.uk)

FINER, Dr Elliot Geoffrey; s of Reuben Finer (d 1958), and Pauline Finer; *b* 30 March 1944; *Educ* Royal GS High Wycombe, Cheadle Hulme Sch, East Barnet GS, St Catharine's Coll Cambridge (maj open scholarship, BA), UEA (MSc, PhD); *m* 1970, Viviane; 2 s (Robin b 1973, Stephen b 1975); *Career* res scientist Unilever 1968–75; Dept of Energy: joined 1975, under sec and DG Energy Efficiency Office 1988–90; dir Spiller Foods Ltd 1989–92, head Mgmnt Devpt Gp Cabinet Office 1990–92; DTI: head Enterprise Initiative Div 1992, head Chemicals and Biotechnology Div 1992–95; DG Chemical Industries Association 1996–2002; memb Cncl Royal Soc of Chemistry 2002– (hon treas 2005–); author of various scientific papers and articles; dir Vestry Ct Ltd 1998–, non-exec dir Enfield NHS PCT 2003–; Hon FEI, FRCS; *Recreations* home and family, reading, DIY, gardening, music; *Style*— Dr Elliot G Finer

FINER, Dr Nicholas; s of Sir Morris Finer (d 1974), and Edith, *née* Rubner; *b* 24 December 1949; *Educ* The Hall Sch Hampstead, Mill Hill Sch, UCL (BSc, MB BS); *m* 1 March 1975, Susan, da of Prof Charles Dent, CBE (d 1975); 3 da (Emily b 30 Nov 1976, Sarah, Louise (twins) b 2 Aug 1978); *Career* conslt physician and dir Research Dept Luton and Dunstable Hosp 1988–2002, hon conslt physician Addenbrooke's Hosp Cambridge 2002– (visiting specialist 1996–2002), visiting prof Univ of Luton 1996–2006, sr res assoc Univ of Cambridge, clinical dir Wellcome Tst Clinical Res Facility; hon conslt physician Guy's Hosp, hon sr lectr United Med and Dental Schs of Guy's and St Thomas' Hosp 1988–99 (lectr 1981–88); chm Assoc for The Study of Obesity 1993–96; FRCP 1994 (MRCP 1977); *Books* contrib: Health Consequences of Obesity (1988), Progress in Sweeteners (1989), Handbook of Sweeteners (1991), Obesity (1997), Encylopedia of Nutrition (1998), Obesity and Metabolic Disorders (2005), ABC of Obesity (2007); *Style*— Dr Nicholas Finer

FINGLETON, Dr John; s of Brendan Fingleton, of Cullenagh, Portlaoise, Ireland, and May, *née* McHugh; *b* 21 September 1965; *Educ* TCD (scholar, BA), Nuffield Coll Oxford (MPhil, DPhil); *Career* research offr Fin Markets Gp LSE 1991, lectr in economics TCD 1991–2000, chair Irish Competition Authy 2000–05, chief exec OFT 2005–; European Centre for Advanced Research in Economics Université Libre de Bruxelles 1995, visiting scholar Grad Sch of Business Univ of Chicago 1998–2000; chm Assoc of Competition Economics, UK rep Competition Ctee OECD, bd memb several jls specialising in competition policy; *Publications* Competition Policy and the Transformation of Central Europe (jtly, 1996), The Dublin Taxi Market: Re-regulate or Stay Queuing? (1998), The Economy of Ireland: Policy and Performance of a Small European Economy (contrib, 7 edn 2000); author of pubns in learned jls; *Style*— Dr John Fingleton; ✉ Office of Fair Trading, Fleetbank House, 2–6 Salisbury Square, London EC4Y 8JX (tel 020 7211 8966, e-mail ceo@oft.gsi.gov.uk)

FINGRET, His Hon Peter; s of Iser Fingret (d 1975), and Irene, *née* Jacobs (d 1979); *b* 13 September 1934; *Educ* Leeds Modern Sch, Univ of Leeds (LLB), Open Univ (BA); *m* 1, 11 Dec 1960 (m dis), June Gertrude; 1 s (Andrew b 1963), 1 da (Kathryn b 1966); m 2, 14 March 1980, Ann Lilian Mary Hollingworth; *Career* slr 1960–82; stipendiary magistrate: County of Humberside 1982–85, metropolitan 1985–92; recorder Crown Court 1987–92, circuit judge (South Eastern Circuit) 1992–2005; chm Lord Chllr's Advsy Ctee on JPs (Cities of London and Westminster) 2005–, pres Mental Health Review Tbnl 1993–, memb Parole Bd 2003–; Freeman Worshipful Co of Musicians 2002–, Freeman City of London; *Recreations* golf, music, theatre; *Clubs* Garrick, MCC, Wychwood Golf; *Style*— His Hon Peter Fingret

FINIGAN, John Patrick; s of John Joseph Finigan (d 1991), of Sale, Cheshire, and Mary Matilda Finigan (d 1983); *b* 12 November 1949; *Educ* Ushaw Coll Durham, St Bede's Coll Manchester, Cncl of Legal Educn London, Univ of Manchester, Harvard Law Sch, Fletcher Sch of Law and Diplomacy Tufts Univ; *m* 6 Dec 1976, Elizabeth, da of Joseph Liew, of Bandar Seri Begawan, Brunei; 1 s (Damien b 1980), 1 da (Emily Jane b 1982); *Career* slr; Standard Chartered Bank (UK, Germany, Brunei, Hong Kong, Indonesia and UAE) 1967–78, investment banking National Bank of Abu Dhabi 1978–82, fndr Investment Banking then branch gen mangr London Nat Bank of Kuwait 1983–95 (also founding gen mangr NKB (International) plc), gen mangr and chief exec Qatar National Bank 1995–2001, advsr to min of finance State of Qatar 2001–02, ceo National Bank of Oman (SAOG) 2002–; barr-at-law Lincoln's Inn; AIB 1970, ACIS 1973, FCIB 1980, FRSA 1988, MSI 1994; *Recreations* tennis, squash, music, literature, theatre; *Clubs* Oriental, Overseas Bankers'; *Style*— John Finigan, Esq; ✉ finiganjohn@hotmail.com

FINK, Prof George; s of John H Fink (d 1965), and Therese, *née* Weiss; *b* 13 November 1936; *Educ* Melbourne HS, Univ of Melbourne (MB BS, MD), Hertford Coll Oxford (DPhil); *m* 1959, Ann Elizabeth, da of Mark Langsam; 1 da (Naomi b 1961), 1 s (Jerome b 1965); *Career* jr and sr house offr Royal Melbourne and Alfred Hospitals Victoria Aust 1961–62, demonstrator in anatomy Monash Univ Victoria 1963–64, Nuffield Dominions demonstrator Univ of Oxford 1965–67, sr lectr in anatomy Monash Univ Victoria 1968–71, lectr Univ of Oxford 1971–80, offical fell in physiology and med Brasenose Coll Oxford 1974–80, dir MRC Brain Metabolism Unit 1980–99, hon prof Univ of Edinburgh 1984–99, vice-pres Research Pharmos Corp 1999–2003 (conslt 2003–), dir Psychiatric Neuroscience Mental Health Research Inst Aust 2003–04, dir Mental Health Research Inst Aust 2004–06 (hon prof 2007–); prosector in anatomy Univ of Melbourne 1956; Royal Soc and Israel Acad exchange fell Weizmann Inst 1979, Wolfson lectr Univ of Oxford 1982, Walter Cottman fell and visiting prof Monash Univ 1985 and 1989, first G W Harris lectr Physiological Soc Cambridge 1987, Arthur M Fishberg visiting prof The Mt Sinai Med Sch NYC 1988, visiting prof Dept of Neurobiology Rockefeller Univ 1996–; memb: Cncl of the Euro Neuroscience Assoc 1980–82 and 1994–, Mental Health Panel Wellcome Tst 1984–89, Steering Ctee Br Neuroendorcine Gp 1984–88 (tstee 1990–), Co-ordinating Ctee ESF Network on Neuroimmunomodulation 1990–92; chm External Monitoring Panel and 5 Year Review Ctee EU Biomedicine Prog, Physiological Soc, Pharmacological Soc, Anatomical Soc of GB and Ireland, Soc for Endocrinology (UK), Endocrine Soc (USA), Soc for Neuroscience (USA), Int Brain Research Orgn, Int Soc for Neuroendocrinology, European Neuroendocrine Assoc (pres 1991–95), Soc for the Study of Fertility, BMA; hon memb Br Soc for Neuroendocrinology 2005; Lifetime Achievement Award Int Soc Psychoneuroendocrinology (ISPNE) 2000; FRSE 1989, FRSA 1996, FRCPEd 1998; *Books* Neuropepides - Basic and Critical Aspects (jt ed, 1982), Neuroendocrine Molecular Biology (jt ed, 1986), Transmitter Molecules in the Brain (1987), Neuropeptides: A Methodology (jt ed, 1989), Encyclopedia of Stress (ed-in-chief, 2000, BMA Commendation for Mental Health, 2 edn 2007); author of over 360 scientific pubns, mainly on neuroendocrinology, neuroendocrine molecular biology and psychoneuroendocrinology; *Recreations* skiing; *Style*— Prof George Fink, FRSE; ✉ Mental Health Research Institute, 155 Oak Street, Parkville 3052, Victoria, Australia (tel 00 61 3 9388 1633, e-mail georgefink1@hotmail.com)

FINK, Graham Michael; s of Horace Bertram Fink, of Oxford, and Margaret May, *née* Betts; *b* 7 September 1960; *Educ* Wood Green Comp Sch Oxford, Banbury Sch of Art, Univ of Reading; *Career* French Gold Abbott advtg agency 1980–81, Collett Dickenson Pearce 1981–87, head of art WCRS 1987, gp head Saatchi & Saatchi 1987–90, creative dir Gold Greenless Trott 1990–94, commercials and music videos dir Paul Weiland Film Co 1995, fndr thefinktank 2001, creative dir M&C Saatchi 2005; winner various advtg awards for: Hamlet, Land Rover, Benson & Hedges, Met Police, Br Airways (Face commercial), Silk Cut, Red Rock Cider, Ariston, Persil; memb: Creative Circle, D&AD (memb Exec Ctee until 1998, pres 1996); RBAC, FRSA; *Style*— Graham Fink, Esq, FRSA; ✉ thefinktank, 25 Lexington Street, London W1F 1AG (e-mail graham@thefinktank.com)

FINK, Stanley; *b* 15 September 1957; *Educ* Manchester Grammar, Trinity Hall Cambridge (MA); *m* 1981, Barbara, *née* Paskin; 2 s (Alexander b 12 March 1987, Jordan b 18 May 1994), 1 da (Gabriella b 5 Sept 1989); *Career* CA Arthur Andersen 1979–82, fin planning Mars Confectionary 1982–83, vice-pres Citibank NA 1983–86; Man Group plc: joined as dir 1987, gp fin dir 1992, md asset mgmnt 1996, ceo 2000–07, non-exec dep chm 2007–, chm Strategic Investment Ctee; memb Inquiry Team Twenty-First Century Investments; chm Ctee Evelina Children's Hosp Appeal; ACA; *Recreations* golf, skiing, tennis; *Style*— Stanley Fink, Esq; ✉ Man Group plc, Sugar Quay, Lower Thames Street, London EC3R 6DU (tel 020 7285 3000, fax 020 7623 8003)

FINKELSTEIN, Prof Ludwik; OBE (1990); s of Adolf Finkelstein (d 1950), of London, and Amalia, *née* Diamantstein (d 1980); *b* 6 December 1929; *Educ* Univ of London (BSc, MSc), City Univ (DSc), Leo Baeck Coll (MA); *m* 1957, Mirjam Emma, da of Dr Alfred Wiener (d 1964), of London; 2 s (Anthony b 1959, Daniel b 1962), 1 da (Tamara b 1967); *Career* physicist Electronic Tubes Ltd 1951–52, scientist Instrument Branch Mining Res Estab NCB 1952–59; Northampton Coll London and City Univ 1959–: prof of instrument and control engrg 1970–80, prof of measurement and instrumentation 1980–96 (prof emeritus 1996–), dean Sch of Electrical Engrg and Applied Physics 1983–88, head Dept of Physics 1980–88, head Dept of Systems Sci 1974–79, co-dir Measurement and Instrumentation Centre 1970–96, dean Sch of Engrg 1988–93, pro-vice-chllr 1991–94; research fell Jewish history and thought Leo Baeck Coll 1996–; sr ptnr Finkelstein Associates 1996–; vice-pres Int Measurement Confedn 1994–97; Queen's Silver Jubilee Medal 1977, Hon DUniv St Petersburg Univ of Technol, Hon DCL City Univ; Liveryman Worshipful Co Scientific Instrument Makers; FREng 1986, FIEE, Hon FInstMC (Sir Harold Hartley Silver medal 1981), CPhys, FInstP; *Recreations* books, conversation, Jewish studies, not gardening; *Style*— Prof Ludwik Finkelstein, OBE, FREng; ✉ 9 Cheyne Walk, Hendon, London NW4 3QH (tel 020 8202 6966); City University, Northampton Square, London EC1V 0HB (tel 020 7040 8106, fax 020 7040 8568, e-mail l.finkelstein@city.ac.uk)

FINLAY, Sir David Ronald James Bell; 2 Bt (UK 1964), of Epping, Co Essex; s of Sir Graeme Bell Finlay, 1 Bt, ERD (d 1987), and June Evangeline, *née* Drake; *b* 16 November 1963; *Educ* Marlborough, Univ of Grenoble, Univ of Bristol; *m* 1998, Camilla, da of Peter Acheson, of Castlecaufield, Co Tyrone; 1 s (Tristan James Bell b 5 April 2001); *Heir* s, Tristan Finlay; *Career* KPMG Peat Marwick McLintock 1986–91, Hill Samuel Financial Services 1992–94, Gerrard Vivian Gray 1994–97, Greig Middleton 1997; Freeman City of London 1991; *Recreations* skiing, shooting, travel; *Style*— Sir David Finlay, Bt

FINLAY, (Robert) Derek; s of William Templeton Finlay (d 1972), and Phyllis, *née* Jefferies (d 1948); *b* 16 May 1932; *Educ* Kingston GS, Emmanuel Coll Cambridge (MA); *m* 1956, Una Ann, da of late David Smith Grant; 2 s (Rory, James), 1 da (Fiona); *Career* Lt Gordon Highlanders Malaya 1950–52, Capt Gordon Highlanders TA 1952–61; Mobil Oil Co UK 1955–61; McKinsey & Co Inc: assoc 1961–67, princ 1967–71, dir 1971–79; H J Heinz Co: md H J Heinz Co Ltd UK 1979–81, sr vice-pres corp devpt World HQ H J Heinz Co Pittsburgh PA 1981–93, also chief fin offr 1989–92, area vice-pres 1992–93; chm Dawson Int 1995–98 (non-exec chm 1998); chm Bd Visitors Center for Int Studies Univ of Pittsburgh 1989–93, vice-chm World Affairs Cncl of Pittsburgh 1986–93; memb: London Ctee Scottish Cncl Devpt and Industry 1975–2003, Bd US-China Business Cncl 1983–93, American Associates Cncl Templeton Coll Oxford 1985–90, US-Korea Business Cncl 1986–92, Bd Pittsburgh Public Theatre 1986–93, Bd Pittsburgh Symphony Soc 1989–92; tstee Mercy Hospital Pittsburgh 1982–93, govr Kingston GS 1997–2003; MCIM 1976–2003, FInstD, FRSA; *Recreations* tennis, rowing, walking, music, theatre; *Clubs* Caledonian, Highland Brigade, Leander, Annabel's; *Style*— Derek Finlay, Esq; ✉ The Mains of Grantully, by Aberfeldy, Perthshire PH15 2EG

FINLAY, Frank; CBE (1984); *b* 6 August 1926; *Educ* St Gregory the Great Sch Farnworth, Bolton Tech Coll, RADA (Sir James Knott scholarship); *m* Doreen, *née* Shepherd; 2 s (Stephen Francis, Daniel Joseph Laurence), 1 da (Anna Catherine (Cathy)); *Career* actor; professional debut in rep Halifax 1952; hon fell Bolton Inst 1992; Freeman City of Baltimore Maryland USA 1979; *Theatre* roles incl: The Queen and the Welshman (Edinburgh Festival, Lyric Hammersmith, two tours) 1957, Harry Kahn in Arnold Wesker's Chicken Soup with Barley (Belgrade Coventry, Royal Court), Percy Elliott in John Osborne's Epitaph for George Dillon (John Golden Theatre NY), Corporal Hill in Wesker's Chips with Everything (Royal Court and Vaudeville), Iago in Othello (with Laurence Olivier, Chichester Festival) 1963, Jesus in Dennis Potter's Son of Man (Phoenix Leicester and The Roundhouse), Bernard Link in David Mercer's After Haggerty (with RSC, Aldwych and Criterion), Peppino in Saturday Sunday Monday (Nat Theatre, Old Vic and Queen's), Freddy Malone in Plunder (first prodn at new NT South Bank), Henry VIII in Kings and Clowns (Phoenix) 1978, Filumena (Lyric and USA tour) 1978–79, Salieri in Amadeus (Her Majesty's) 1981–82, The Cherry Orchard (Haymarket) 1983, Capt Bligh in Mutiny (Piccadilly) 1985, Sir David Metcalfe QC in Jeffrey Archer's Beyond Reasonable Doubt (Queen's, Aust tour, UK tour) 1987–90, Sir Lewis Messenger in Ian Ogilvy's A Slight Hangover (Bromley and nat tour) 1991, Dr Sloper in The Heiress (Bromley and nat tour) 1992, The Woman in Black (nat tour) 1993, Captain Hook/Mr Darling in Peter Pan (Chichester Festival Theatre, Norwich and nat tour) 1994–95, Gaslight (UK tour) 1995, The Handyman (Chichester Festival Theatre and nat tour) 1999–; *Television* roles incl: Brutus in Julius Caesar, Jean Val Jean in Les Miserables, Andrew Firth in Ingmar Bergman's The Lie, title role in Dennis Potter's Casanova, title role in The Death of Adolf Hitler, Sancho Panza in Don Quixote, Voltaire in Candide, Shylock in The Merchant of Venice, Bouquet of Barbed Wire series and sequel Another Bouquet, Frank Doel in 84 Charing Cross Road, Peppino in Lord Olivier's prodn of Saturday Sunday Monday, Bridie in Dear Brutus, Arc de Triomphe, In The Secret State, The Verdict on Erebus (4 part series), Sir Arthur Conan Doyle in Encounters - The Other Side, Stalin (with Robert Duval for HBO), Mountain of Diamonds (series, 1990), Charlemagne, Lovejoy, Heartbeat, Dalgliesh, A Mind to Murder, How Do You Want Me, The Magical Legend of the Leprechauns, Longitude, The Sins, Station Jim (BBC) 2000, The Lost Prince, Eroica, Prime Suspect, Life Begins; *Films* incl: The Longest Day, The Loneliness of the Long Distance Runner, The Comedy Man, The Sandwich Man, A Study in Terror,

Othello (with Laurence Olivier, Oscar, Golden Globe and BAFTA nominations) I'll Never Forget What's 'is Name, The Deadly Bees, Inspector Clouseau, Gumshoe, Shaft in Africa, three Van der Valk films, The Three Musketeers and two sequels, The Wild Geese, Neither the Sea nor the Sand, The Thief of Baghdad, Sherlock Holmes - Murder by Decree, The Return of the Soldier, The Key (in Italy, Positano Award for Best Film, Golden Cinema Ticket Award), Jacob Marley in A Christmas Carol, Life Force, Sigmund Freud in 1919, Cthulhu Mansion, The Sparrow 1993, Limited Edition 1995, Gospa 1995, Romance and Rejection 1996, Tiré à part 1997, Stiff Upper Lips 1998, So This is Romance? 1998, Dreaming of Joseph Lees 1999, Ghosthunter 2000, For My Baby 2000, The Pianist 2001; *Awards* Man of the Year 1981; for Best Actor incl: Clarence Derwent Award (for Wesker's Chips with Everything), BAFTA Award (for The Death of Adolf Hitler and Don Quixote), TV Times Award (for Bouquet of Barbed Wire), San Sebastian Film Festival Award (for Othello); nominations for Best Actor incl: five BAFTA's and an Oscar; *Style—* Frank Finlay, Esq, CBE; ✉ c/o Ken McReddie Associates Ltd, 21 Barret Street, London W1U 1BD (tel 020 7499 7449, fax 020 7408 0886, e-mail email@kenmcreddie.com)

FINLAY, Rev Dr Hueston Edward; s of Sydney Perry Finlay, of Portlaoise, and Vera, *née* Burns; *b* 23 May 1964, Portlaoise, Ireland; *Educ* Wesley Coll Dublin, TCD (BAI, BTh, MA), Univ of Cambridge (MA), KCL (PhD); *m* 19 August 1989, Annegret; 1 da (Svea Deirdre b 6 Jan 1992), 2 s (Lars Christopher b 30 July 1996, Karsten Alexander b 24 Nov 1999); *Career* Brown & Root Ltd London 1985–86, curate St Canice's Cathedral Kilkenny 1989–92, curate Univ Church of Gt St Mary Cambridge and chaplain Girton Coll Cambridge 1992–95, dean Magdalene Coll Cambridge 1995–2004 (also tutor and affliated lectr Divinity Faculty 1996–2004), canon Coll of St George Windsor 2004–; author of various articles on philosophy and theology; *Recreations* chess, squash, fishing; *Style—* The Rev Dr Hueston Finlay; ✉ The Chapter Office, Windsor Castle, Windsor, Berkshire SL4 1NJ (tel 01753 848887, e-mail diagacht@hotmail.com)

FINLAY, Ian Gardner; s of John Gardner Finlay, of Ladybank, Fife, and Margaret Finlay, of Lothian; *Educ* Univ of St Andrews (BSc), Victoria Univ of Manchester (MB ChB); *m* 21 March 1981, Patricia Mary, *née* Whiston; 1 da (Nicola b 24 March 1984), 1 s (Euan b 20 Feb 1986); *Career* jr surgical trainee Royal Infirmary Manchester 1976–78, registrar in surgery W of Scotland Registrar Rotational Trg Scheme 1978–83, sr surgical registrar Glasgow Royal Infirmary 1983–87, clinical asst Univ of Minnesota 1985, sr registrar in colorectal surgery St Mark's Hosp London 1986, conslt colorectal surgn Dept of Coloproctology Royal Infirmary Glasgow (organised and developed dept as first unit of its type in UK) and hon sr lectr Univ of Glasgow 1987–; Patey Prize Surgical Research Soc 1982, Research Award American Soc of Colon and Rectal Surgns 1987, Audiovisual Prize Assoc of Surgns 1990, Moynihan Prize (jtly) Assoc of Surgns of GB and I 1995; memb Cncl Br Assoc of Coloproctology RSM 1991–; author of over 100 pubns incl book chapters, editorials and original articles relating to topics in coloproctology; FRCSGlas (hon treas and memb Cncl), FRCSEd 1993; *Recreations* golf, sailing, skiing, ornithology and antique furniture; *Clubs* Glasgow Golf, Glasgow Cricket, Scottish Royal Automobile; *Style—* Ian Finlay, Esq; ✉ Department of Coloproctology, Ward 61, Royal Infirmary, Glasgow G31 2ER (tel 0141 211 4084, fax 0141 211 4991)

FINLAY, Ronald Adrian; s of Harry Finlay, of London, and late Tess, *née* Matz; *b* 4 December 1956; *Educ* UCS London, St John's Coll Cambridge (MA); *m* 1992, Jennifer, *née* Strauss; 2 da; *Career* Br Market Research Bureau 1979–81, Merrill Lynch 1982–83, dir Valin Pollen Ltd 1986–90 (joined 1983); Fishburn Hedges: dir 1991–, dep chm 1999–2000, md 2000–03, ceo 2004–; sec SDP Hendon S 1984–85; memb Market Research Soc 1996 (assoc 1980); *Recreations* cycling, hill walking, tennis; *Style—* Ron Finlay, Esq; ✉ 12 Grey Close, London NW11 6QG (tel 020 8455 1367); Fishburn Hedges Ltd, 77 Kingsway, London WC2B 6SR (tel 020 7839 4321, fax 020 7242 4202, e-mail ron.finlay@fishburn-hedges.co.uk)

FINLAY OF LLANDAFF, Baroness (Life Peer UK 2001), of Llandaff in the County of South Glamorgan; Ilora Gillian Finlay; da of late Prof Charles Beaumont Benoy Downman, of New Malden, Surrey; *b* 23 February 1949; *Educ* Wimbledon HS GPDST (head girl), St Mary's Hosp Med Sch London (entrance scholarship, MB BS); *m* 1972, Andrew Yule Finlay, s of late Henry Variot Langwill Finlay; 1 s (Hon Malcolm Charles b 1976), 1 da (Hon Sarah Elise b 1978); *Career* conslt in palliative med and med dir Holme Tower Marie Curie Centre Penarth 1987–2001, conslt in palliative med and team ldr for chronic pain services Velindre NHS Tst Oncology Centre Cardiff 1993–, hon prof of palliative med Univ of Wales Coll of Med (UWCM) 1996–, vice-dean (exec) Sch of Med UWCM 1999–2004, vice-dean (postgrad) Sch of Med Cardiff Univ 2004–05; professorial assoc Dept of Med Univ of Melbourne 1996–2001, hon prof of palliative med Ulyanovsk Univ 1999–2001, visiting prof Johanna Bijtel Lehrstuhle Groningen Univ 2000–02; dir Inst of Med Ethics 2002–04; memb: Science Ctee Cancer Research UK 2002–04, Advsy Cncl on Misuse of Drugs Act Home Office 2002–, Ctee on Safety of Meds 2002–, Expert Advsy Panel Exec Meds Control Agency 2002–; non-exec dir Gwent HA 1996–2000; ed Palliative Care Today 1991–2003, memb Editorial Bd Med Humanities 2001–, sr med ed Jl of Evaluation in Clinical Practice 2002–, memb Int Editorial Bd Lancet Oncology 2002–; pres: Chartered Soc for Physiotherapy, MS Cymru, Student for Kids Int Projects (SKIP), Action on Smoking and Health (ASH) (Wales); pres RSM 2006–08, vice-pres NSPCC Cymru 2004–07; memb: Assoc for Palliative Med of GB and I, BMA, Cardiff Med Soc, European Assoc for Cancer Educn, Intractable Pain Soc, Int Assoc for the Study of Pain, Med Women's Fedn (pres 2000–02), World Soc of Pain Clinicians, Welsh Pain Soc; patron Shalom Hospice Tst; Sarah Davis Meml Tst Lecture Univ of Dublin 1998, Dame Hilda Rose Meml Lecture Med Women's Fedn 1999, Dorothy Rees Meml Lecture 2003, Annual Public Lecture Cardiff Law Sch 2003, The Cardiff Lecture 2003; Upjohn Essay Prize RCGP 1983, Silver Medal Computers in Med BMA 1992, Healthcare IT Effectiveness Award NHS Exec and NHS Staff Coll Wales 1999; sits as crossbench peer in House of Lords; memb Select Ctee: Science and Technol 2002–, Assisted Dying for the Terminally Ill Bill 2004–06, Mental Health Bill 2005–06; memb Stakeholder Bd First Great Western 2003–; vice-pres Fund for the Meml to the Women of World War II 2005–06; patron: New Bristol Symphonia Orch, Cardiff and the Vale Youth Orch; memb: Inst of Welsh Affrs, Wales Medico-Legal Soc, Royal Soc of Arts; govr Howell's Sch Llandaff GDST 2002–06; Woman into Science and Technol 1996, Welsh Woman of the Year 1996–97; Hon DSc: Univ of Glamorgan 2002, Univ of Wales 2005; hon fell: Cardiff Univ 2002, Univ of Wales Inst Cardiff; MRCS 1972, DRCOG 1974, DCH 1975, FRCGP 1992 (MRCGP 1981), FRCP 1999 (LRCP 1972, MRCP 1997), FHEA 2007 (ILTM 2001), FRSM, FRSA; *Publications* Care of the Dying - A Clinical Handbook (jtly, 1984), Cancer Patients and their Families at Home, Resource Book (jtly, 1989, 2 edn 1994), The Effective Management of Cancer Pain (jtly, 2000, 2 edn 2003), Medical Humanities (jtly, 2002), Oral Care in Advanced Disease (jtly, 2005); also author of numerous book chapters and papers in learned jls; *Style—* The Rt Hon the Lady Finlay of Llandaff; ✉ House of Lords, London SW1A 0PW (tel 020 7219 6693, e-mail finlayi@parliament.uk)

FINLAYSON, Dr Niall Diarmid Campbell; OBE (1998); s of Dr Duncan Iain Campbell Finlayson, of Edinburgh, and Helen Rita, *née* Blackney; *b* 21 April 1939; *Educ* Loretto, Univ of Edinburgh (BSc, MB ChB, PhD); *m* 12 Aug 1972, Dale Kristin, da of Dr Richmond Karl Anderson, of Chapel Hill, North Carolina, USA; 1 da (Catriona b 1973), 1 s (Iain b 1977); *Career* asst prof of med Cornell Univ Med Coll NY 1970–72, conslt physician Royal Infirmary Edinburgh 1973–2003, hon sr lectr in med Univ of Edinburgh Med Sch 1973–2003; pres Royal Coll of Physicians of Edinburgh 2001–04 (registrar 1997–99, vice-pres 1999–2000), teaching fell Univ of Edinburgh 2004–; memb: BMA, Br Soc of Gastroenterology; FRCP, FRCPEd; *Books* Diseases of the Gastro Intestinal Tract and Liver (jtly, 3 edn 1997); *Recreations* music; *Style—* Dr Niall Finlayson, OBE; ✉ 10 Queen's Crescent, Edinburgh EH9 2AZ (tel 0131 667 9369, e-mail ndc.finlayson@which.net)

FINLAYSON, Robert William (Robin); s of William Francis Finlayson (d 1988), and Isabella Forrester, *née* Knox (d 1982); *b* 16 December 1949; *Educ* Glasgow Acad, Univ of Edinburgh (LLB, BCom); *m* 22 March 1975, Jennifer Catherine, da of Thomas Nicol Dickson; 2 s (Colin Stuart b 11 Feb 1977, Andrew Graham b 17 Nov 1979), 1 da (Louise Catherine b 22 Nov 1983); *Career* apprentice Touche Ross & Co Glasgow 1972–75; Ernst & Young (formerly Arthur Young McClelland Moores): tax sr 1976–77, tax supervisor/asst mangr Glasgow 1977–79, tax ptnr Birmingham 1981–82 (tax mangr 1979–81), dir Ernst & Young Financial Management Ltd 1989–99, managing ptnr Edinburgh office 1991–99 (head of tax 1982–91, head of Entrepreneurial Services Practice 1997–99); currently dir Caledonian Heritable Investments Limited, co-fndr Longbow Capital LLP; ICAS: memb 1975, convenor Ethics Ctee and Professional Standards Bd 1991–92; *Recreations* golf, sailing, skiing, hill walking; *Clubs* Archerfield Golf Links, Murrayfield Golf, Largs Sailing; *Style—* Robin Finlayson, Esq; ✉ Longbow Capital LLP, 6A Hope Street, Edinburgh EH2 4DB

FINN, Geoffrey Stuart; *b* 23 August 1930; *Educ* Bemrose Sch Derby, Univ of London (BCom); *m* 1955, Miriam; 1 da; *Career* Joseph Sebag & Co Stockbrokers 1954–59; ptnr: W I Carr Sons & Co Stockbrokers 1959–69, Rowe & Pitman Stockbrokers 1969–86; dir S G Warburg Securities 1986–89, fin conslt Exco Int plc 1989–91; govr Bacon's City Technol Coll, memb Ct City Univ 1996–2002, hon fell Cancer Research UK; memb: Ctee City of London Friends of The Leukaemia Research Fund, Euro-Atlantic Gp, London Welsh Assoc, Anglo-Spanish Soc, Anglo-Portuguese Soc, Br-Aust Soc, Royal Soc of St George, Welsh Livery Guild, Cripplegate Ward Club (Master 1986), Broad St Ward Club, Livery Co Skills Cncl, London Youth City Livery Liaison Ctee; Liveryman: Worshipful Co of Tallow Chandlers, Worshipful Co of Chartered Secs and Admins (Master 1996–97), Worshipful Co of Musicians; FCIS, FSS, FREconS, MSI, FRSA; *Publications* contrib to several newspapers and periodicals incl: Investors Chronicle, Times, Sunday Times, Daily Telegraph, Financial Weekly, Accountancy, The Treasurer; *Recreations* music, art, bridge, cricket, travel; *Clubs* City of London, Carlton, RAC, City Livery, MCC, Middlesex CCC, Leander, Henley Regatta (memb Stewards' Enclosure), Middlesex RFU, LTA, Royal Mid-Surrey Golf, Phyllis Court; *Style—* Geoffrey Finn, Esq; ✉ 26 Rothesay Avenue, Richmond, Surrey TW10 5EA (tel 020 8878 8568, fax 020 8878 5465)

F

FINN, Johanna Elizabeth; da of Bartholomew Anthony Finn, of London, and Anna Maria, *née* Kreuth; *b* 30 August 1951; *Educ* Convent of the Sacred Heart London, UCL (BSc); *m* (m dis); 2 s (Benedict Daniel Siddle b 20 Jan 1982, Leo Dominic Siddle b 1 Oct 1984), 1 da (Chloe Anneliese Siddle b 22 June 1990); *Career* KCH London 1972–73, nat admin trainee NHS Nat Training Scheme SE Thames RHA 1973–75, asst admin Northwick Park Hosp Harrow Middx 1975–77, dep sector admin Withington Hosp S Manchester 1977–79, sector admin W Middx Univ Hosp Isleworth 1979–82, unit admin St Mary's Hosp Paddington 1982–85, acting dep dist admin Paddington & N Kensington Health Authy 1985–86; unit gen mangr: Mile End Hosp and Bethnal Green Hosp Tower Hamlets 1986–89, Community & Priority Services Tower Hamlets 1989–90; acting chief exec The Royal London and Assoc Community Services NHS Trust 1990–91, regnl dir of corp affairs NW Thames RHA 1991–93, chief exec The West Suffolk Hosps Tst 1993–2001, dir of med undergraduate clinical placements NHS Workforce Devpt Confedn (Norfolk, Suffolk, Cambs) 2001–03, mgmnt conslt 2003–; dir Suffolk TEC 1994–2001, memb Suffolk LSC 2001–; govr W Suffolk Coll 2004–; assoc memb Inst of Health Service Mangrs 1975; *Recreations* music, theatre, reading, wine and food; *Clubs* Health Chief Executives'; *Style—* Miss Johanna Finn; ✉ tel 01284 764973

FINN, (Patrick) Timothy; s of Hugh Patrick Finn (d 1983), of Laughton House, Leics, and Esther, *née* Caldwell (d 1979); *b* 20 December 1938; *Educ* Marlborough, Exeter Coll Oxford (BA, capt Univ Fencing); *m* 8 Oct 1964, Anthea Mary, *née* Fox-Male; 1 da (Emma Louise b 1966), 2 s (Jonathan Humbert, Benjamin James (twins) b 1968); *Career* mgmnt and fundraising conslt; author and playwright; md Henri Selmer & Co 1965–70, dir Genesis Programme 1979–84, employment and training conslt 1982–89, chm and md Collyer Finn Ltd 1989–; author of musicals The '45 1985, The Laughing Cavalier 1986 (with composer Simon Brown in Cambridge productions with King's Coll Sch); memb Inst of Fundraising 1989; memb: The Stambourne Singers 1968–80, The Madrigal Soc 1968–2002; churchwarden St Mary's Gedding 1989–99; *Publications* The Watney Book of Pub Games (1966), Pub Games of England (1975), Knapworth at War (1982), Knapworth Fights On (1983), Three Men (Not) in a Boat and Most of the Time Without a Dog (1984), The Laughing Cavalier (1986); *Recreations* lute playing, madrigals, fencing, snooker; *Clubs* Pot Black, Ex Tempore Cricket; *Style—* Timothy Finn, Esq; ✉ Collyer Finn Ltd, Smallwood House, Bradfield St George, Bury St Edmunds, Suffolk IP30 0AJ (tel 01449 736838, fax 01449 736310, e-mail tfinn@collyerfinn.com)

FINNEGAN, Hon Mr Justice Joseph; s of Isaac Gerald Finnegan (d 1972), of Glencree, Dublin, and Charlotte Finnegan (d 1985); *b* 1 October 1942, Dublin; *Educ* UCD (BCL, LLB); *m* 18 Sept 1968, Kathleen Monica; 3 da (Yvonne b 1969, Hazel b 1972, Charlotte b 1985), 1 s (Gerald b 1970); *Career* admitted slr 1966; practising slr 1966–78, asst sec Incorporated Law Soc of Ireland 1968–73; called to the Bar: King's Inns Dublin 1978 (bencher), Middle Temple London 1984 (bencher); practising barr 1978–99, sr counsel 1990, judge of the High Court 1999–, pres of the High Court 2001–; memb: Cncl of State, Bd Courts Serv Ireland; hon memb Dublin Slrs Bar Assoc; *Recreations* reading, music, theatre, legal history, antiquarian law books, rugby, golf, motor sport; *Clubs* Blackrock Coll RFC, Bray Golf, El Saler Golf; *Style—* The Hon Mr Justice Joseph Finnegan; ✉ The High Court, Four Courts, Dublin 7, Ireland (tel 00 353 1 888 6520, e-mail josephfinnegan@courts.ie)

FINNEGAN, Prof Ruth Hilary; OBE (2000); da of Prof Tom Finnegan (d 1964), and (Lucy) Agnes, *née* Campbell (d 1995); *b* 31 December 1933; *Educ* The Mount Sch York, Somerville Coll Oxford (BA, Dip Anthropology, BLitt), Nuffield Coll Oxford (DPhil); *m* 1963, David John Murray, s of Jowett Murray; 3 da (Rachel Clare b 1965, Kathleen Anne b 1967, Brigid Aileen b 1969); *Career* teacher Malvern Girls Coll 1956–58, lectr in social anthropology Univ Coll of Rhodesia and Nyasaland 1963–64, sr lectr in sociology Univ of Ibadan Nigeria 1967–69 (lectr 1965–67), sr lectr in comparative social instns Open Univ 1972–75 (lectr in sociology 1969–72); Univ of the South Pacific Suva Fiji: reader in sociology 1975–78, head sociology discipline 1976–78; Open Univ: sr lectr 1978–82, reader 1982–88, prof of comparative social instns 1988–99, visiting res prof social sciences 1999–, emeritus prof 2002–; visiting prof of anthropology Univ of Texas at Austin 1989; memb SSRC/ESRC Social Anthropology and Social Affrs Standing Ctees 1978–86 (vice-chm Social Affrs Ctee 1985–86), memb Cncl Br Acad 2001–04; vice-chair Governing Body SOAS Univ of London 2003–06; pres Mount Old Scholars Assoc 2003–05; jt founding ed Family and Community History (jl) 1998–2002, hon ed Man (jl of Royal Anthropological Inst) 1987–89; assoc memb Finnish Literature Soc 1989, folklore fell Finnish Acad of Sci and Letters 1991, hon memb Assoc of Social Anthropologists of the UK and the Cwlth 2002; hon fell Somerville Coll Oxford 1997; FBA 1996; *Books* Survey of the Limba people of northern Sierra Leone (1965), Limba stories and story-telling (1967), Oral literature in Africa (1970, 1976), Modes of thought. Essays on thinking in Western and non-Western societies (co-ed, 1973), Oral poetry: its nature, significance and social context (1 edn 1977, 2 edn 1992), The Penguin book of oral poetry (ed, 1978, published as A World treasury of oral poetry, 1982), Essays on Pacific literature (co-ed, 1978), Concepts of Inquiry (ed jtly, 1981), New approaches to economic life (ed jtly, 1985), Information Technology: social issues (ed jtly, 1987), Literacy and orality: studies in the technology of communication (1988), The hidden musicians: music-making in an English town (1989), Oral traditions and the verbal arts: a guide to research practices (1992), From family tree to family history (co-ed, 1994), Sources and methods for family and community historians: a handbook (co-ed, 1994), South Pacific oral traditions (co-ed, 1995), Project reports in family and community history (CD-ROM, co-ed, 1996, 1997, 1998, 1999, 2000, 2001), Tales of the City (1998), Communicating: The Multiple Modes of Human Interconnection (2002), Participating in the Knowledge Society: researchers beyond the university walls (ed, 2005); also author of articles in learned jls; *Recreations* singing in local choirs, walking; *Style*— Prof Ruth Finnegan, FBA; ✉ Faculty of Social Sciences, The Open University, Walton Hall, Milton Keynes MK7 6AA (tel 01908 654458, fax 01908 654488, e-mail r.h.finnegan@open.ac.uk)

FINNERTY, Her Hon Judge Angela; da of late Michael Finnerty, and Mary, *née* Woolfrey; *b* 22 March 1954; *Educ* Bury Convent GS, Univ of Leeds (LLB), Coll of Law London; *m* 29 July 1978, Mark England; 1 s (Thomas William England b 14 Oct 1982), 1 da (Elisabeth Louise England b 11 Oct 1984); *Career* called to the Bar Middle Temple 1976 (Harmsworth scholar); practising barr Park Lane Chambers Leeds (formerly 37 Park Square) 1977–2000; asst recorder 1994, recorder 1999, circuit judge (NE Circuit) 2000–; *Recreations* family, travel; *Style*— Her Hon Judge Finnerty; ✉ Bradford Combined Court Centre, Exchange Square, Bradford BD1 1JA (tel 01274 840274)

FINNEY, Patricia Deirdre Emöke; da of His Hon Judge Finney (d 1999), and Daisy Gizella Emöke, *née* Veszy; *b* 12 May 1958; *Educ* Henrietta Barnett Sch London, Wadham Coll Oxford (BA); *m* 28 Feb 1981, Christopher Alan Perry (d 2002), s of William J Perry; 1 da (Alexandra b 18 Dec 1987), 2 s (William b 2 Dec 1989, Luke b 7 March 1996); *Career* incl: TV reviewing The Evening Standard, sub-editing, running a medical jl, sec, freelance journalism, pt/t work in social servs, corp entertaining, selling advtg; four times runner-up Catherine Pakenham Award; memb NUJ; also writes under pseudonym P F Chisholm; *Radio plays* The Flood (R3, 1977), A Room Full of Mirrors (R4, 1988, first prize Radio Times Drama Awards); *TV plays* Biology Lessons (1986, second prize Radio Times Drama Awards); *Novels* A Shadow of Gulls (1977, David Higham Award for Best First Novel), The Crow Goddess (1978), Firedrake's Eye (1992), Unicorn's Blood (1998), Gloriana's Torch (2003); As P F Chisholm: A Famine of Horses (1994), A Season of Knives (1995), A Surfeit of Guns (1996), A Plague of Angels (1998); *Children's Books* I, Jack (2000), Jack and Police Dog Rebel (2002); *Recreations* history, making things, science, martial arts (black belt in Taekwondo); *Style*— Ms Patricia Finney

FINNIGAN, Judith (Judy); da of John Finnigan (d 1984), and Anne Finnigan; *b* 16 May 1948; *Educ* Manchester High Sch for Girls, Univ of Bristol (BA); *m* 1; 2 s (Thomas, Daniel (twins) b 2 March 1977); m 2, 21 Nov 1986; Richard Madeley, *qv*; 1 s (Jack b 19 May 1986), 1 da (Chloe b 13 July 1987); *Career* television presenter; researcher Granada TV 1971–73, reporter Anglia TV 1974–77; presenter Granada TV 1980–2001, presenter Cactus TV 2001– (Richard and Judy (Channel 4), Br Book Awards (Channel 4) 2004–); *Awards* RTS Team Award for This Morning 1994, Most Popular Daytime Programme National Television Awards 1998, 1999, 2000 and 2001; *Style*— Ms Judy Finnigan; ✉ c/o James Grant Management, 94 Strand on the Green, Chiswick, London W4 3NN (tel 020 8742 4950, fax 020 8742 4951)

FINNIS, Prof John Mitchell; s of Maurice Meredith Steriker Finnis (d 1995), of Adelaide, and Margaret McKellar, *née* Stewart; *b* 28 July 1940; *Educ* St Peter's Coll, St Mark's Coll Adelaide (LLB), Univ of Oxford (DPhil); *m* 20 June 1964, Marie Carmel, *née* McNally; 3 da (Rachel b 1965, Catherine b 1971, Maria b 1974), 3 s (John-Paul b 1967, Jerome b 1977, Edmund b 1984); *Career* assoc in law Univ of Calif Berkeley 1965–66; Univ of Oxford: fell and praelector in jurisprudence Univ Coll 1966–, Rhodes reader in laws of Br Cwlth and US 1972–89, prof of law and legal philosophy 1989–; vice-master University Coll Oxford 2001–; prof and head Law Dept Univ of Malawi 1976–78, Huber distinguished visiting prof Boston Coll 1993–94; Biolchini Family prof of law Univ of Notre Dame Indiana USA 1995–; called to the Bar Gray's Inn 1970; special advsr to Foreign Affrs Ctee of House of Commons on the role of UK Parliament in Canadian Constitution 1980–82; memb Int Theological Cmmn Vatican 1986–92; memb Pontifical Acad for Life 2001–; FBA 1990; *Books* Natural Law and Natural Rights (1980), Fundamentals of Ethics (1983), Nuclear Deterrence, Morality and Realism (1987), Commonwealth and Dependencies Halsbury's Laws of England (vol 6 1971, 2003), Moral Absolutes (1991), Aquinas: Moral, Political and Legal Theory (1998); *Style*— Prof John Finnis, FBA; ✉ University College, Oxford OX1 4BH (tel 01865 276602, e-mail john.finnis@law.ox.ac.uk)

FINSBERG, Baroness (Yvonne) Elizabeth (Yvonne Sarch); da of Albert Wright (d 1971), and Edith Abigail, *née* Bingham, of Strabane, NI (d 1997); *b* 13 November 1940; *Educ* Clarendon Sch N Wales, Trinity Coll Dublin (MA), Univ of Manchester (DMS), Univ of London (MA, DipFE); *m* 1, 1967 (m dis 1988), Michael Sarch; 2 s (Patrick b 1968, Adam b 1970); m 2, 1990, Baron Finsberg MBE, JP (Life Peer, d 1996); *Career* Home Office 1963–65, headmistress Fir Close Sch Lincs 1965–67, lectr Brunel Univ 1967–70, tutor Open Univ 1970–72, conslt James Morrell & Assocs 1972–75, independent economist and managing conslt UK and USA 1975–88, Korn/Ferry International 1988–91, fndr dir Sarch Search International (SSI) 1990–, exec search ptnr Howgate Sable & Partners London 1995–99; memb Lord Chancellor's Consultative Panel on Legal Services 2000–04; pres Bevin Boys Assoc 1996–; memb Cncl: RSA 1992–99, Int Centre for Briefing Farnham Castle 1992–99 (chm 2000–03); memb International Women's Forum; vice-pres John Grooms 1999–2001; govr Royal Sch Hampstead 1997–2000; chm Fairfax Residents' Assoc 2003; patron Cheltenham Festivals 2007; *Books* How to be Headhunted (1990), How to be Headhunted Across Europe (1992), How to be Headhunted Again and Again (1999); *Recreations* thinking, travelling, tapestry, thrillers; *Style*— Elizabeth Finsberg; ✉ The Cloth Hall, New Street, Painswick, Gloucestershire GL6 6XH (tel 01452 813707)

FIONDA, Andrew; *Educ* Trent Poly Nottingham (BA Fashion), Royal Coll of Art (MDes); *Career* fashion designer; former experience with established Br design houses incl Marks & Spencer and Alexon Internation, fndr ptnr own label Pearce Fionda (with Ren Pearce, *qv*) 1984–94, co-designer (with Ren Pearce) Pearce II Fionda collection for Designers at Debenhams 1997–; New Generation Designers of the Year (Br Fashion Awards) 1995, Newcomers Award for Export (Br Knitting and Clothing Export Cncl/Fashion Weekly) 1995, World Young Designers Award (Int Apparel Fedn Istanbul) 1996, Glamour Category Award (Br Fashion Awards) 1997; worldwide stockists incl: Liberty, Harrods, Harvey Nichols and Selfridges (UK), Saks 5th Avenue and Bergdorf Goodman (USA), Lidia Shopping (Italy), CRC (Thailand), Brown Thomas (Ireland); gp exhbns incl: Design of the Times (RCA) 1996, The Cutting Edge of British Fashion 1947–1997 (V&A) 1997; regular guest fashion critic This Morning (ITV) 2004–; *Style*— Andrew Fionda

FIREMAN, Bruce Anthony; s of Michael Fireman (d 1982), of Vinnitsa, Ukraine; *b* 14 February 1944; *Educ* Kilburn GS, Jesus Coll Cambridge (open scholar); *m* 1968, Barbara, *née* Mollett; *Career* slr 1970; chm Fireman Rose Ltd 1986–, conslt on media and communications Guinness Mahon & Co Ltd 1991–93, seconded as md London News Radio Ltd 1993–94 (non-exec dir 1994–), returned to Guinness Mahon & Co as md media and communications 1994–98; md corporate fin Investec Henderson Crosthwaite 1998–2001; dir: Newspaper Publishing plc (The Independent) 1986–93, D G Durham Group plc 1988–93, Culver Holdings plc 1991–2003, The Wyndham Motor Group plc 1998–2000, World Travel Holdings plc 2000–; chm Metrodome Group plc 2001–; arbitrator Securities and Futures Authy 1992–2003; *Clubs* Garrick; *Style*— Bruce Fireman, Esq; ✉ 1 Wood Lane, London N6 5UE (tel 020 8444 7125, fax 020 8374 6638, e-mail bfireman@sylvestermedia.com)

FIRMAN, Clive Edward; s of John Edward Firman (d 1984), of Rustington, W Sussex, and Rosaline Mary, *née* Smith (d 1995); *b* 22 May 1951; *Educ* Cranleigh Sch, Univ of London (BA), Aston Univ (MBA); *m* 1974, Wendy, da of John Gill Burrell; 1 s (Duncan Mark Edward b 4 Jan 1981), 1 da (Carolyn Mary b 16 Oct 1982); *Career* NHS: trg admin 1973–74, personnel mangr Harrow HA 1974–76, admin St George's Hosp London 1976–78, dep sector admin rising to sector admin Waltham Forest 1979–81, admin Tooting Bec Hosp 1981–86, gen mangr All Saints' Hosp Birmingham 1986–94, mgmnt conslt 1994–, md Young Options Ltd 1998–2004, dir Options Gp 2004–; memb Inst of Health Serv Mgmnt 1976, AIPM 1978, MIMgt 1986; *Recreations* voluntary work, badminton, swimming, weight training, mainly family; *Style*— Clive Firman, Esq; ✉ 49 Alderbrook Road, Solihull B91 1NR (e-mail clivefirman@hotmail.com)

FIRMAN, Ralph; *b* 20 May 1975; *Educ* Gresham's; *Career* motor racing driver; series champion Br Jr Kart 1990, 3 wins Br Sr Kart 1991, series champion Br Sr Kart 1992, champion Formula Vauxhall Jr 1993 (9 wins, 10 podiums), fourth in series Formula Vauxhall 1994, second in series Br Formula 3 Championship 1995, series champion Br Formula 3 Championship 1996, winner Macau Grand Prix 1996, competitor Formula Nippon 1997–2002 (series champion 2002), debut Formula One Grand Prix (Jordan/Ford) 2003; McLaren Autosport Young Driver of the Year 1993, Rookie of the Year F3 1994; patron Michael Matthews Fndn; *Style*— Ralph Firman, Esq; ✉ c/o 39 Park Street, London W1K 7HJ (tel 020 7495 9234, fax 020 7495 9201, website www.ralphfirman.com)

FIRTH, Colin; s of David Firth and Shirley Firth; *b* 10 September 1960, Hants; *Educ* Montgomery of Alamein Sch, Winchester, Drama Centre London; *Career* actor; *Theatre* credits incl: Bennett in Another Country (Queens) 1983, Dubedat in Doctor's Dilemma (Bromley and Guildford) 1984, Felix in The Lonely Road (Old Vic) 1985, Eben in Desire Under The Elms (Greenwich) 1987, Aston in The Caretaker 1991, Chatsky (Almeida) 1993, Walker in Three Days of Rain (Donmar Warehouse) 1999; *Television* Dutch Girls (LWT) 1984, Lost Empires (Granada) 1985–86, Tumbledown (BBC) 1987 (RTS Best Actor Award, BAFTA nomination), Out Of The Blue (BBC) 1990, Hostages (Granada) 1992, Master of the Moor (Meridian) 1993, The Deep Blue Sea (BBC) 1994, Pride and Prejudice (BBC) 1994 (Broadcasting Press Guild Award for Best Actor), The Turn of the Screw 1999, Donovan Quick 1999; *Radio* Two Planks and a Passion (BBC) 1986, The One Before The Last (BBC) 1987; *Film* Another Country 1983, Camille 1984, A Month in the Country 1986, Apartment Zero 1988, Valmont 1988, Wings of Fame 1989, Femme Fatale 1990, The Hour of the Pig 1992, Good Girls 1994, Circle of Friends 1995, The English Patient 1996, Fever Pitch 1996, My Life So Far 1997, The Secret Laughter of Women 1997, Shakespeare in Love 1998, The Secret Laughter of Women 1998, My Life So Far 1999, Blackadder Back and Forth 1999, Relative Values 2000, Londinium 2000, Bridget Jones' Diary 2001, The Importance of Being Earnest 2002, Hope Springs 2003, What a Girl Wants 2003, Girl with a Pearl Earring 2003, Love Actually 2003, Trauma 2004, Bridget Jones: The Edge of Reason 2004, Where the Truth Lies 2005; *Style*— Colin Firth, Esq; ✉ c/o ICM Ltd, Oxford House, 76 Oxford Street, London W1D 1BS (tel 020 7636 6565, fax 020 7323 0101)

FIRTH, David; s of Ivor Firth Coleman (d 1991), of Bedford, and Beatrice, *née* Jenkins (d 1990); *b* 15 March 1945; *Educ* Bedford Modern Sch, Univ of Sussex (BA), Guildhall Sch of Music and Drama; *m* 2 Jan 1969, Julia Elizabeth, da of Albert Gould; 2 s (Matthew b 24 Sept 1973, Ben b 3 March 1980); *Career* actor, writer and singer; *Theatre* incl: Notes from Underground (Garrick) 1967, RSC 1967–70, The Courier-1776 (Albery, nominated Most Promising Actor in Plays and Players Awards) 1970, Gawain and the Green Knight (Phoenix Leicester) 1972; NT 1973 incl: Macbeth, The Cherry Orchard, Measure for Measure; other credits incl: Hedda (Roundhouse) 1980, Hamlet (Piccadilly) 1982, Marilyn (Adelphi) 1983, Poppy (Adelphi) 1983, The Importance of Being Earnest (Ambassadors) 1984, The Ratepayers Iolanthe (Phoenix) 1984, Canary Blunt (Latchmere) 1985, The Metropolitan Mikado (Queen Elizabeth Hall) 1985, The Phantom of the Opera (Her Majesty's) 1986, King Lear (Old Vic) 1988, The Hunting of the Snark 1991, A Tree Grows in Brooklyn (Barbican) 1992, Jubilee (Barbican) 1992, Assassins (Donmar) 1992, Knickerbocker Holiday (Barbican) 1993, Follies (Brighton) 1993, Forty Years On (West Yorkshire Playhouse) 1994, Love Life (Barbican) 1995, Passion (Queens) 1996, The Fix (Donmar) 1997, Die Fledermaus (Arts) 1998, On A Clear Day (Barbican) 1998, Good Grief (Yvonne Arnaud, Guildford) 1998, HMS Pinafore (Royal Festival Hall) 1999, Susanna's Secret (Drill Hall) 1999, Jubilee (Her Majesty's and BBC Radio 3) 1999, Der Kuhandel (Barbican and BBC Radio 3) 2000, Journey's End (Drill Hall) 2000, Cenerentola (Music Theatre London) 2001, Cat on a Hot Tin Roof (Lyric) 2001, Relatively Speaking (Secombe Theatre Sutton) 2002, Our Song (tour) 2003, Coward and Others 2004, The Man Who... (Orange Tree Richmond) 2005, The Shell Seekers (tour) 2006, Yellow Lines (Oval House) 2007; *Television* incl: Search for the Nile, Eyeless in Gaza, Love Story, Armchair Theatre, Village Hall, Terra Firma, Love for Lydia, Wings, Raffles, Saint Joan, The Gondoliers, Nanny's Boy, Troilus and Cressida, Sorry I'm A Stranger Here Myself, Lucky Jim, Yes Minister, Drummonds, Cardtrick, Singles, One Way Out, Stay Lucky, Murder East Murder West, Poirot, Between the Lines, The Late Show, Wycliffe, Holby City, Swallow, Doctors, The Bill, Waking the Dead, Casualty, Midsomer Murders; *Film* Out on a Limb 1985, The Upside of Anger 2004; *Writing* for TV and theatre incl: Sorry I'm A Stranger Here Myself 1980, The Live Rail 1982, Canary Blunt 1985, Cause for Complaint 1986, Oblique Encounter and Sod's Law 1987, Home James 1989, Shelley 1990, Otherwise You'd Cry 1992, A Real Farce 1998, Damaged Goods 1999, The Hidden Hand 2002; *Style*— David Firth, Esq; ✉ c/o Conway van Gelder Ltd, 18–21 Jermyn Street, London SW1Y 6HP (tel 020 7287 0077, fax 020 7287 1940, e-mail mail@davidfirth.org.uk)

FIRTH, Prof David; s of Allan Firth, and Betty, *née* Bailey; *Educ* Queen Elizabeth GS Wakefield, Trinity Hall Cambridge (MA), Imperial Coll London (MSc, DIC, PhD); *Career* lectr Imperial Coll London 1986–87, asst prof Univ of Texas at Austin 1987–89, lectr and sr lectr Univ of Southampton 1989–93, sr fell in statistics for the social sciences Univ of Oxford and Nuffield Coll Oxford 1993–2003, prof Univ of Warwick 2003–; ed Jl of the Royal Statistical Soc B 1998–2001, author of numerous publications in scientific jls; chm Research Section RSS 2001–03 (hon sec 1994–96), memb Nat Statistics Methodolgy Advsy Ctee 2001–; memb RSS 1982 (Guy Medal in Bronze 1998), memb Int Statistical Inst 1998; *Recreations* water polo, wheel building; *Style*— Prof David Firth; ✉ Department of Statistics, University of Warwick, Coventry CV4 7AL (tel 024 7657 2581, fax 024 7652 4532, e-mail d.firth@warwick.ac.uk)

FIRTH, Simon Nicholas; s of Graham Alfred Firth, of Lincs, and Janice, *née* Todd; *b* 21 October 1963, Sheffield; *Educ* Nottingham HS, ChCh Oxford (MA, pres Univ Law Soc 1986), Guildford Coll of Law; *Career* admitted slr 1989; asst slr Linklaters & Paines 1989–96 (articled clerk 1987–89), ptnr Linklaters 1996– (ldr OTC (Over-the-Counter) Derivatives Practice 1996–, trainee devpt ptnr 2002–); *Books* Derivatives: Law and Practice (2003); *Style*— Simon Firth, Esq; ✉ Linklaters, One Silk Street, London EC2Y 8HQ (tel 020 7456 3764, fax 020 7456 2222, e-mail simon.firth@linklaters.com)

FIRTH, Prof William James; s of William John Flett Firth (d 1993), and Christina May Coltart, *née* Craig (d 1994); *b* 23 February 1945; *Educ* Perth Acad, Univ of Edinburgh (BSc, capt Univ hockey team), Heriot-Watt Univ (PhD); *m* 15 July 1967, Mary MacDonald, da of Charles Ramsay Anderson (d 1972), and Margaret, *née* Robertson; 2 s (Michael John Charles b 11 Feb 1973, Jonathan William b 25 Aug 1975); *Career* reader Dept of Physics Heriot-Watt Univ 1984–85 (asst lectr 1967–69, lectr 1969–82, sr lectr 1982–84), Freeland prof of natural philosophy Dept of Physics and Applied Physics Univ of Strathclyde 1985– (head of dept 1990–93 and 2001–04); visiting prof Arizona Center for Mathematical Sciences Tucson USA 1989–95; Royal Soc euro fell Univ of Heidelberg 1978–79; chm Ctee of Scottish Professors of Physics 1992–96; ed: Progress in Quantum Electronics 1984–89, Cambridge Studies in Modern Optics 1986–92; FInstP 1997 (MInstP 1972), FRSE 1989, fell Optical Soc of America 1996 (memb 1986); *Publications* author of over 200 scientific articles; *Recreations* golf, the universe and everything; *Style*— Prof William Firth, FRSE; ✉ 21 Dalhousie Terrace, Edinburgh EH10 5NE; Department of Physics, University of Strathclyde, John Anderson Building, 107 Rottenrow, Glasgow G4 0NG (tel 0141 548 3269, fax 0141 552 2891, e-mail willie@phys.strath.ac.uk)

FIRTH-BERNARD, Christopher (Chris); s of Charles George Dickenson Firth-Bernard (d 1988), and Monica Margaret, *née* Henshaw (d 1977); *b* 27 December 1954, Chichester; *Educ* Bishop Luffa Sch Chichester; *m* 4 March 1995, Ann Marie Thérèse, *née* Pochon, 3 s (Joseph Charles b 4 Jan 2002, Jack Christopher b 14 Oct 2003, Alistair Donald b 5 Oct 2005); *Career* The Mount Hotel Tettenhall Wood 1971, The Royal Hotel Bognor Regis 1972–74, The Noke Hotel St Albans 1974–76, The Grand Hotel Krasapolski Amsterdam 1976–77; chef de partie The Royal Norfolk Hotel Bognor Regis 1977–78, chef de partie The Dolphin and Anchor Hotel Chichester 1978, sous chef Avisford Park Hotel Arundel 1978–79; head chef: The Feathers Inn Wadesmill 1979–81, Green End Park Hotel Herts 1981–86, Summer Isles Hotel Achiltibuie 1986– (1 Michelin Star 1998); runner-up in the food category Scotland on Sunday Glenfiddich Spirit of Scotland Awards 1998, Scottish Chef of the Year 1998; *Recreations* photography, art, ornithology; *Style*— Chris Firth-Bernard, Esq; ✉ Summer Isles Hotel, Achiltibuie, Ross-shire IV26 2YG

FISCHEL, David Andrew; *b* 1 April 1958; *Career* Liberty International plc: joined 1985, fin dir 1988–92, md 1992–, chief exec 2001–; ACA 1983; *Style*— David Fischel

FISCHEL, Robert Gustav; QC (1998); s of Bruno Rolf Fischel (d 1977), and Sophie Kruml (d 1993); *b* 12 January 1953; *Educ* City of London Sch, Univ of London (LLB), Coll of Law; *m* 1, 1989 (m dis 1997); 1 da (Lujzka Beatrice b 3 Oct 1992); m 2, 1999, Anna Louise Landucci; 1 da (Isabella Sophie b 5 June 1999); *Career* called to the Bar Middle Temple 1975, dir Int Catering Associates Ltd 1995; Freedom of the City of London; *Recreations* skiing, tennis, fine food and wine, cooking; *Clubs* Royal Over-Seas League; *Style*—Robert Fischel, Esq, QC; ✉ 5 King's Bench Walk, Temple, London EC4Y 7DN (tel 020 7353 5638, fax 020 7353 6166)

FISCHER, Max Alfred; s of Alfred Fischer (d 1984), of Germany, and Lisa Fischer; *b* 31 August 1951; *Educ* Germany; *m* 1 Aug 1979, Susan Fischer; 2 s (Neil William b 7 Nov 1980, Daniel Alfred b 15 Sept 1982), 1 da (Selina Olive b 3 May 1988); *Career* chef; apprentice chef Lüneburg, subsequently commis chef Hotel Erbrinz 1969–72, demi chef Restaurant Nicholas Paris 1972–74, chef de partie Bell Inn Aston Clinton 1974–76, head chef Schloss Hotel Kronberg 1977–80, proprietor Fischer's Restaurant 1981–88, chef and proprietor Fischer's Baslow Hall 1989–; Michelin Star 1994–, Egon Ronay Restaurant of the Year 1995, 8 out of 10 Good Food Guide 2002, Johannsens Most Excellent UK Restaurant 2002; *Recreations* gardening; *Style*— Max Fischer, Esq; ✉ Baslow Hall Ltd, Calver Road, Baslow, Derbyshire DE45 1RR (tel 01246 583259, fax 01246 583818, website www.fischers-baslowhall.co.uk)

FISCHER, Stefanie Margaret; da of Leonhard Fischer, of Wellington NZ, and Margaret June, *née* McLeod; step da of Prof Tom Keightley Ewer, OBE (d 1997); *b* 28 February 1955; *Educ* Redland HS Bristol, Girton Coll Cambridge (MA Arch, DipArch); *Career* architect with specialist expertise in the design of bldgs for cinema and media incl works to listed buildings; ptnr Burrell Foley Associates (Burrell Foley Fischer from 1990) 1985– (joined 1982); consultancy servs to BFI and London Film & Video Devpt Agency; currently examiner in professional practice: Bartlett Sch of Architecture; past examiner: Architectural Assoc, Univ of Cambridge Sch of Architecture, De Montfort Univ; past visiting lectr and critic incl: Univ of Brighton, Univ of Cardiff, Leeds Metropolitan Univ; reg contrib to architectural and tech press, work widely published in nat and architectural press; past memb Architecture Advsy Ctee Arts Cncl of England, enabler Cmmn for Architecture and Built Environment (CABE); regnl chair RIBA Awards in Architecture: Wales 1998, Southern Region 1999, London 2000; past memb RIBA: Educn and Professional Standards Ctee, CCT Tsk Force, Appts Gp, Industry Practice Ctee; RIBA Pres's Theme Gp (client and consumer); memb ARCUK 1981, RIBA 1981, FRSA; *Recreations* opera, film, exhibitions, drama, dance, classical music, travel, literature, swimming, trekking; *Style*— Ms Stefanie Fischer; ✉ Burrell Foley Fischer LLP Architects, Unit A York Central, 70–78 York Way, London N1 9AG (tel 020 7713 5333, fax 020 7713 5444, e-mail s.fischer@bff-architects.co.uk)

FISH, Dr David John; s of George Henry Fish (d 1992), and Edith Doreen, *née* Canon; *b* 31 May 1948, Leicester; *Educ* Gateway GS Leicester, Univ of Sheffield (BSc, PhD, Mappin Medal); *m* 31 July 1976, Linda Pamela; 2 da (Hannah b 3 July 1979, Suzhannah b 26 April 1984), 1 s (Richard b 6 June 1981); *Career* regnl pres (Europe) Mars Inc 1998–2001 (memb Operating Bd 1994–2001); chm: Christian Salvesen 2003–, United Biscuits 2004–; non-exec dir Royal Mail; *Recreations* skiing, golf, tennis, soccer, cricket; *Style*—Dr David Fish; ✉ United Biscuits, Hayes Park North, Hayes End Road, Hayes, Middlesex UB4 8EE (tel 020 8234 5397)

FISH, David Thomas; QC (1997); s of Tom Fish (d 1987), and Gladys, *née* Durkin (d 1995); *b* 23 July 1949; *Educ* Ashton-under-Lyne GS, LSE (LLB); *m* 1989, Angelina Brunhilde, da of Arthur Dennett (decd); 1 s (Thomas b 8 Aug 1992), 1 da (Clementine b 20 March 1994); *Career* called to the Bar Inner Temple 1973; recorder of the Crown Court 1994–2006; non-exec chm 32 Red plc 2005–; *Recreations* horse racing, golf; *Style*— David Fish, Esq, QC; ✉ Deans Court Chambers, 24 St John Street, Manchester M3 4DF (tel 0161 214 6000)

FISH, George Marshall; OBE (1995), JP, DL (Notts 1995); s of George Frederick Fish (d 1940), of Hamilton House, and Dorothy, *née* Creswell (d 1984); *b* 26 June 1928; *Educ* Sedbergh; *m* 9 Feb 1952, Josephine Lilian, da of Joseph Sydney Plant Lowater (d 1991); 3 s (William, James, Charles); *Career* Capt RA 1946–48, Capt S Notts Hussars, 350 Heavy Regt RA (TA) 1948–52; chartered builder; chm Thomas Fish & Sons Ltd; chm and tstee Nottingham Bldg Fndn, tstee Nottingham Almshouse Charities; FCIOB, FFB; *Recreations* cricket, gardening; *Clubs* Nottingham and Notts United Services; *Style*— George Fish, Esq, OBE, JP, DL; ✉ Manor Stables, Old Main Road, Bulcote, Nottinghamshire NG14 5GU (tel 0115 931 3159, fax 0115 931 3430, e-mail gmfish@ukonline.co.uk); Office: Little Tennis Street, Nottingham (tel 0115 958 7000, fax 0115 958 6385, website www.thomasfish.co.uk)

FISH, Michael John; MBE (2004); s of Aubrey John Richard Fish (d 1970), of Eastbourne, and Dora, *née* Amos (d 1970); *b* 27 April 1944; *Educ* Eastbourne Coll, City Univ; *m* 21 Sept 1968, Susan Mary, *née* Page; 2 da (Alison Elizabeth b 9 May 1971, Nicola Katherine b 25 Nov 1975); *Career* meteorologist and sr broadcast meteorologist; Meteorological Office Gatwick Airport 1962–65, posted to Bracknell as scientific offr 1965–67; BBC Weather Centre (London Weather Centre until 1991): joined 1967, higher scientific offr 1971–89, sr scientific offr 1989–2004; first radio broadcasts 1971 (BBC), first TV broadcasts 1974; ret from Meteorological Office 2004; numerous appearances on TV and radio in various light entertainment and factual progs; famous for the 'hurricane gaffe' Oct 1987; also co-ordinator trg courses for TV weather crews in Africa, meteorological conslt for numerous pubns, advsr to govts on global warming and climate change, specialist and lectr on climate change; after dinner speaker, narrator of voice-overs and award ceremony host; patron of several charities incl Age Concern and Woodland Tst; TV Weather Presenter of the Year TRIC Awards 2004; Tie Man of the Year four times in the 1990s; Hon DSc: City Univ 1996, Univ of Exeter 2005; Freeman City of London 1997; FRMetS 1965; *Recreations* travel, wine and good food; *Style*— Michael Fish, Esq, MBE; ✉ c/o Paul Madeley, The Studios, 17 Valley Road, Bredbury, Stockport SK6 2EA (tel 0161 430 5380); e-mail michael@michael-fish.com, website www.michael-fish.comand www.fish4weather.com

FISHBURN, (John) Dudley; s of late Eskdale Fishburn and Bunting Fishburn; *b* 8 June 1946; *Educ* Eton, Harvard; *m* 1981, Victoria, da of Sir Jack Boles and step da of Lady Anne Boles (da of 12 Earl Waldegrave); 2 da (Alice b 1982, Honor b 1984), 2 s (Jack b 1985, Marcus b 1987); *Career* journalist; The Economist 1979–2003; MP (Cons) Kensington 1988–97, PPS at the Foreign and Commonwealth Office 1989–90 and the DTI 1990–93; non-exec dir: HSBC Bank plc, Household International (Chicago), Henderson Smaller Cos Tst plc, Altria Inc; int advsr TT International 1997–; govr Peabody Tst; *Clubs* Brooks's; *Style*— Dudley Fishburn, Esq; ✉ 7 Gayfere Street, London SW1P 3HN (tel 020 7976 0733)

FISHER, Andrew Charles; s of Harold Fisher, of Barbados, and Jessie, *née* Tombleson (now Mrs Stanley); *b* 22 June 1961, Aldershot; *Educ* Univ of Birmingham (BSc); *m* 15 Aug 1987, Bernadette Ann, *née* Johnson; 2 s (Christopher Andrew b 6 May 1988, Harry Lawrence b 8 May 1993); *Career* mktg mangr Unilever plc 1982–87, ptnr Coopers & Lybrand Mgmnt Consultancy 1987–91, sales and mktg dir Equitor Div Standard Chartered Bank 1991–94, md Rangeley Co Ltd 1994–97, strategic advsr NatWest Wealth Mgmnt 1997–98, gp commercial dir Coutts NatWest Gp 1998–2000, chief exec Coutts Gp 2000–02, ptnr Carlyle Gp 2002–03, chief exec CPP Gp 2003–04, chief exec Cox Insurance Holdings plc 2004–05, chm and chief exec JS & P Ltd 2004–, chm and chief exec Towry Law Gp 2006–; non-exec dir Benfield Gp Ltd 2003–; govr Sandhurst Sch; MInstD; *Recreations* skiing, golf, scuba diving, flying; *Clubs* Wentworth, Mosimann's; *Style*— Andrew Fisher, Esq

FISHER, Carol; *Educ* Univ of Birmingham (BA); *Career* prod mangr Reckitt and Colman Leisure 1978–79, brand mangr Bisto RHM Foods 1979–81, nat brand mangr and sr mktg mangr Grandmetropolitan Brewing 1982–88, mktg dir Holsten Distributors 1989–94, gen mangr mktg and commercial Courage Int 1994–95, md CLT UK Radio Sales 1996–97, strategic planning dir UK & Scandinavia CLT-UFA 1998, chief exec Central Office of Information 1999–2002, ptnr The Ingram Partnership 2003–05; memb: Women in Advtg and Communications London (WACL), Mktg Gp of GB, Nat Tst; *Recreations* long haul travel, walking; *Style*— Ms Carol Fisher

FISHER, Charles Murray; s of Kenneth John Fisher (d 1996), of Cheltenham, Glos, and Beryl Dorothy, *née* Pearman; *b* 24 December 1949; *Educ* Cheltenham Coll, St Edmund Hall Oxford, Harvard Business Sch; *m* 29 Sept 1984, Denise Ellen, *née* Williams; 2 da (Louisa Dora b 13 Dec 1985, Jasmine Diana b 24 June 1987); *Career* chm Sharpe & Fisher plc 1989–99; non-exec dir: South West Electricity plc 1990–95, Baggeridge Brick plc 1996–2005, Travis Perkins plc 2000–04, Delta plc 2000–06; chm: The Summerfield Charitable Tst 1999–, Country Homes and Gardens plc 2001–, Mowlem plc 2002–05 (non-exec dir 1993); *Recreations* tennis, travel, reading; *Clubs* MCC, Turf; *Style*— Charles Fisher, Esq; ✉ Warneford House, Sudgrove, Miserden, Gloucestershire GL6 7JD; Bayshill Estates Ltd, Buckingham House, Wellington Street, Cheltenham, Gloucestershire GL50 1XY (tel 01242 236466)

FISHER, David Paul; QC (1996); s of Percy Laurence Fisher (d 1964), and Doris Mary, *née* Western (d 2000); *b* 30 April 1949; *Educ* Felsted, Coll of Law, Inns of Court Sch of Law; *m* 1, 18 Sept 1971, Cary Maria Cicely (d 1977), da of Charles Egan Lamberton; 1 da (Clair Helen Maria b 14 Dec 1976); m 2, 7 July 1979, Diana Elizabeth, da of John Harold Dolby (d 1962); *Career* called to the Bar Gray's Inn 1973 (bencher 2003), recorder of the Crown Court 1991– (asst recorder 1987); memb: Gen Cncl of the Bar 1997–2000, Advocacy Studies Bd 1997–2001, Criminal Procedure Rule Ctee 2004–; *Recreations* travel, sport, gardening, cinema; *Style*— David Fisher, Esq, QC; ✉ 6 King's Bench Walk, Temple, London EC4Y 7DR (tel 020 7583 0410, fax 020 7353 8791)

FISHER, David Richard; s of William Horace Fisher (d 1976), and Margaret Catherine, *née* Dashper (d 1993); *b* 13 May 1947; *Educ* Reading Sch, St John's Coll Oxford (BA); *m* Sophia Josephine, da of Prof George Hibbard; 2 da (Caroline b 1979, Diana b 1982); *Career* MOD: private sec to successive RAF Mins 1973–74, on staff Naval Prog and Budget 1976–79, Defence Budget 1981–83, seconded as visiting res fell Nuffield Coll Oxford 1983–84, head of resources and progs (Air) 1984–88, seconded to FCO as defence cnsllr UK Delgn to NATO 1988–92, asst under sec of state (Systems) 1992–97, dep head Def and Overseas Secretariat Cabinet Office 1997–99, dir Def Trg Review 1999–2001, strategy dir EDS (on secondment from MOD) 2001–; memb: Mgmnt Ctee Cncl on Christian Approaches to Defence and Disarmament, Aristotelian Soc; contrib to numerous jls on defence and ethical issues; *Books* Morality and the Bomb (1985), Ethics and European Security (contrib, 1986), Just Deterrence (contrib, 1990), Some Corner of a Foreign Field (contrib, 1998), The Crescent and the Cross (contrib, 1998), The Price of Peace (contrib, 2006), Britain's Bomb: What Next? (contrib, 2006); *Recreations* philosophy and gardening; *Clubs* Nat Liberal, Commonwealth Soc, English Speaking Union; *Style*— David Fisher, Esq; ✉ EDS, Lansdowne House, Berkeley Square, London W1J 6ER (tel 020 7569 5870)

FISHER, Duncan Mark; s of Humphrey Fisher, and Helga, *née* Kricke; *b* 3 November 1961, Amman, Jordan; *Educ* Univ of Cambridge (BA, MPhil), SSEES Univ of London (MA); *m* 30 Dec 1987, Clare, *née* Warren; 2 da (Miriam b 19 Sept 1996, Abigail b 11 Nov 2000); *Career* fndr and ceo East West Environment 1989–95, fndr, ceo then tstee Travel Fndn (formerly Action for Conservation Through Tourism) 1994–, co-fndr and ceo Fathers Direct 1999–, memb Bd Equal Opportunities Cmmn 2004–; memb Amnesty Int; *Recreations* making lists, eating very good chocolate, reading to children, travelling with children; *Clubs* Chocolate; *Style*— Duncan Fisher, Esq; ✉ Fathers Direct, 9 Nevill Street, Abergavenny NP8 1BZ (tel 0845 634 1328, e-mail d.fisher@fathersdirect.com)

FISHER, Her Hon Judge Elisabeth Neill; da of Kenneth Neill Fisher (d 1995), and Lorna Charlotte Honor Fisher (d 2002); *b* 24 November 1944; *Educ* Oxford HS for Girls GDST, Girton Coll Cambridge; *Career* called to the Bar Inner Temple 1968 (bencher 2003); recorder of the Crown Court 1982–89, circuit judge (Midland Circuit) 1989–; Hon Dr UCE 1997; *Style*— Her Hon Judge Fisher; ✉ Birmingham Crown Court, 1 Newton Street, Birmingham B4 7NA (tel 0121 681 3300, fax 0121 681 3370)

FISHER, Gillian Elizabeth; da of Norman James Fisher, of Oadby, Leics, and Patricia Jean, *née* Warrington; *b* 12 March 1955; *Educ* Beauchamp Coll Oadby, Univ of Warwick (LLB), Royal Coll of Music (ARCM); *m* 11 Feb 1983, Brian Christopher Kay, *qv*, s of Noel Bancroft Kay; *Career* soprano; concert singer, mainly Baroque and Classical repertoire; professional debut Queen Elizabeth Hall 1979; has sung at numerous major venues and festivals worldwide incl: Royal Opera House Covent Garden (debut 1981), Royal Festival Hall, Barbican Hall, Edinburgh Festival (debut 1984), BBC Proms (regular soloist since debut 1985), Three Choirs Festival, Bath and York Festivals, Paris, Monte Carlo, Madrid, Vienna, Milan, Venice, Cologne, Frankfurt, Concertgebouw Amsterdam, Brussels, Oslo, New York (debut Lincoln Centre 1983, further tours 1988 and 1989), Japan and Far East (debut 1987, further tours 1989 and 1992), Australia (debut Sydney Opera House 1992); has worked with numerous major conductors incl: John Eliot Gardiner, Trevor Pinnock, Christopher Hogwood, Robert King, Roger Norrington, Ton Koopman; *Recordings* numerous incl: Purcell Complete Odes and Welcome Songs (with King's Consort under Robert King, Hyperion, 8 CDs), Pergolesi Stabat Mater (with King's Consort and Michael Chance under Robert King, Hyperion, Gramophone Critics' Choice 1988), Great Baroque Arias (with King's Consort, Pickwick, in US classical top ten for several months 1988), Handel Duets (with James Bowman and King's Consort), Purcell's The Fairy Queen (with The Sixteen under Harry Christophers, Collins Classics), Purcell's King Arthur (with Monteverdi Choir under John Eliot Gardiner, Erato), Purcell's Dioclesian and Timon of Athens (with Monteverdi Choir under Gardiner, Erato), various Handel works with London Handel Orch under Denys Darlow, Bach Cantatas (with The Sixteen under Harry Christophers), Monteverdi Vespers (with Kammerchor Stuttgart, Deutsche Harmonia Mundi); *Recreations* reading, gardening, watching cricket; *Style*— Ms Gillian Fisher

FISHER, Prof John Robert; s of John Robert Fisher, of Barrow-in-Furness, Cumbria, and Eleanor, *née* Parker; *b* 6 January 1943; *Educ* Barrow GS, UCL (BA, MPhil), Univ of Liverpool (PhD); *m* 1 Aug 1966, (Elizabeth) Ann, da of Stephen Gerard Postlethwaite, of Barrow-in-Furness, Cumbria; 3 s (David John b 27 Sept 1967, Nicholas Stephen b 10 Dec 1970, Martin Joseph b 27 Aug 1973); *Career* Univ of Liverpool: lectr 1966–75, sr lectr 1975–81, dir Inst of Latin American Studies 1983–2001, dean Faculty of Arts 1986–92, prof 1987–, pro-vice-chllr 1995–98; chm: Soc of Latin American Studies 1986–88, Anglo-Chilean Soc 1998–2000; pres Euro Assoc of Historians of Latin America 1996–99 (gen sec 1987–93), pres Int Congress of Americanists 2000– (vice-pres 1997–2000); FRHistS 1975; *Books* Government and Society in Colonial Peru (1970), Silver Mines and Silver Miners in Colonial Peru (1976), Commercial Relations between Spain and Spanish America 1778–1797 (1985), Peru (1989), Reform and Insurrection in Bourbon, New Granada and Peru (1990), Trade, War and Revolution (1992), The Economic Aspects of Spanish Imperialism in America (1997), El Perú Borbónico 1750–1824 (2000), Bourbon Peru 1750–1824 (2003); *Recreations* theatre, music, walking, gardening, travel; *Style*— Prof John Fisher; ✉ University of Liverpool, PO Box 147, Liverpool L69 3BX (tel 0151 794 3078, fax 0151 794 3080, e-mail fisher@liverpool.ac.uk)

FISHER, 3 Baron (UK 1909); John Vavasseur Fisher; DSC (1944), JP (Norfolk 1970); s of 2 Baron (d 1955, himself s of Adm of the Fleet, 1 Baron (Sir John) Fisher, GCB, OM, GCVO); *b* 24 July 1921; *Educ* Stowe, Trinity Coll Cambridge; *m* 1, 25 July 1949 (m dis 1969), Elizabeth Ann Penelope, yr da of late Maj Herbert P Holt, MC; 2 da (Hon Frances b 1951, Hon Bridget b 1956), 2 s (Hon Patrick b 1953, Hon Benjamin b 1958); m 2, 1970, Hon Rosamund Anne, da of 12 Baron Clifford of Chudleigh and formerly w of Geoffrey Forrester Fairbairn; *Heir* s, Hon Patrick Fisher; *Career* sometime Lt RNVR WWII; dir Kilverstone Latin American Zoo 1973–91; memb: Eastern Gas Bd 1961–70, E Anglian Economic Planning Cncl 1969–77; DL Norfolk 1968–82; *Style*— The Rt Hon the Lord Fisher, DSC; ✉ Marklye, Rushlake Green, Heathfield, East Sussex (tel 01435 830270)

FISHER, Jonathan Simon; QC (2003); s of Aubrey Fisher; *b* 24 February 1958; *Educ* St Dunstan's Coll, N London Poly (BA), St Catharine's Coll Cambridge (LLB); *m* 21 Dec 1980, Paula Yvonne, da of Rev Louis Goldberg (d 1988); 2 s (Benjamin b 1984, David b 1990), 2 da (Hannah b 1987, Leah b 1995); *Career* called to the Bar Gray's Inn 1980, ad eundem Inner Temple 1985; standing counsel to Inland Revenue (Central Criminal Court and London Crown Courts) 1991–2003; visiting prof Cass Business Sch City Univ London 2004–07, visiting prof LSE 2006– (visiting fell 2004–06); chm Fraud Advsy Panel Special Project Gp on Fraud Investigation and Prosecution 2006, dir and tstee Fraud Advsy Panel 2006–; chm of research Soc of Cons Lawyers 2006– (memb Exec Ctee 2005–06); memb: Steering Gp Assets Recovery Agency 2003–06, Legal Panel Accountancy Investigation and Disciplinary Bd 2005–; *Books* Pharmacy Law and Practice (co-author, 1995, 4 edn 2006), Law of Investor Protection (co-author, 1997, 2 edn 2003); *Recreations* theatre, football, arts, history, travelling; *Clubs* Carlton; *Style*— Jonathan Fisher, Esq, QC; ✉ 23 Essex Street, London WC2R 3AA (tel 020 7413 0353)

FISHER, Keith Plunket; s of Francis St George Fisher (d 1990), of Cragg, and Patricia, *née* Lyon (d 1955); *b* 28 October 1935; *Educ* Harrow; *m* 1 (m dis), Anne, da of Percy Collingwood Charleton; 1 s (Kiwa b 1966); m 2, 1986, Julia, da of Derek Pattinson, OBE; 2 s (Jeremy b 1987 d 1987, Alexander b 1989), 3 da (Poppy Frances b 1991, Xara, Kitty (twin) b 1993); *Career* ptnr Overton Shirley & Barry 1981–95; landowner Higham Estate 1990–; *Style*— Keith Fisher, Esq; ✉ Cragg, Cockermouth, Cumbria CA13 9YB (tel 01768 776277, fax 01768 776067); Sotogrande, Spain (tel 0034 956 615673)

FISHER, Kenneth John; s of Stanley Joseph Fisher (d 1983), of Dalton-in-Furness, Cumbria, and Gertrude Isabel, *née* Ridding (d 1980); *b* 26 June 1927; *Educ* Uppingham, St John's Coll Cambridge (MA, LLM, Sir Joseph Larmer award); *m* 8 May 1954, Mary Florence, da of William Isaac Towers, JP (d 1971), of Barrow-in-Furness, Cumbria; 1 da (Anne Rosemary b 24 April 1956), 1 s ((Stephen) John b 6 Oct 1957); *Career* Sub-Lt RNVR 1945–48; admitted slr 1953, formerly sr ptnr Kendall & Fisher; past chm: Agric Land Tbnl (Northern Area), Social Security Appeal Tbnl, Med Services Ctee; chm: Dalton and Dist Recreational Charity Tst, Furness Probation Support Gp; memb: Furness Hosp NHS Tst 1994–95, S Cumbria Community Health Cncl 1996–98; past memb Cumbria FHSA; past chm Area Ctee The Legal Aid Bd, clerk to Billincoat Charities and Dalton Free Sch Tstees, pres Dalton Town Band; past pres: N Lonsdale Law Assoc, N Lonsdale, Lowick and Cartmel Agric Soc, Barrow-in-Furness Branch Royal Soc of St George; fndr memb Holker Hall Garden Festival, hon life memb N Lonsdale Agric Soc; life govr ICRF; past chm Govrs of Chetwynde Sch; tstee and hon life memb Furness RUFC, life memb Dalton Cricket Club; life memb Lancs RUFC; *Recreations* rugby, cricket, skiing, gardening; *Clubs* Hawks' (Cambridge), Cambridge LX, Uppingham Rovers, Cambridge Union (life memb); *Style*— Kenneth J Fisher, Esq; ✉ Glenside House, Springfield Road, Ulverston, Cumbria LA12 0EJ (tel 01229 583437)

FISHER, Mark; MP; s of Sir Nigel Thomas Loveridge Fisher, MC (d 1996), by his 1 w, Lady Gloria Vaughan (d 1998), da of 7 Earl of Lisburne; *b* 29 October 1944; *Educ* Eton, Trinity Coll Cambridge; *m* 1971 (m dis 1999), Ghilly (Mrs Ingrid Hunt), da of late James Hoyle Geach; 2 s, 2 da; *Career* former principal Tattenhall Educn Centre; former documentary writer and film producer; memb Staffs CC 1981–85, Parly candidate (Lab) Leek 1979, MP (Lab) Stoke-on-Trent Central 1983–; memb Treasy and Civil Service Select Ctee 1983–86, opposition whip 1985–86, shadow min for arts and media 1987–92, oppn spokesman on Citizens' Charter and Open Government 1992–93, shadow min for the Arts 1993–97, Parly under-sec of state (the arts) Dept Culture, Media and Sport 1997–98; chair All-Pty Parly Gp on Indonesia 2001–; memb: BBC Gen Advsy Cncl 1987–97, Cncl Policy Studies Inst 1989–97, Panel 2000, Museums and Galleries Cmmn 1999–2000, Advsy Ctee on Acceptance in Lieu 1999–; dep pro-chllr Keele Univ 1989–97, visiting fell St Antony's Coll Oxford 2000–01; tstee: Education Extra 1992–97, Britten/Pears Fndn 1998–, Estorick Fndn 2001–; Hon FRIBA, Hon FRCA; *Books* City Centres, City Cultures (1988), Whose Cities? (ed, 1991), A New London (1992), Britain's Best Museums (2004); *Clubs* Grillions; *Style*— Mark Fisher, Esq, MP; ✉ House of Commons, London SW1A 0AA

FISHER, Rick; s of Samuel M Fisher, of Philadelphia, and Helene, *née* Korn (d 1973); *b* 19 October 1954; *Educ* Haverford HS Philadelphia, Dickinson Coll Carlisle Pennsylvania; *Career* lighting designer; chm Assoc of Lighting Designers; Bronze medal for lighting design World Stage Design Exhbn Toronto; *Theatre* RNT: Landscape with Weapon, Honour, Blue/Orange, Albert Speer, Widowers Houses, Black Snow, Peer Gynt, The Coup, An Inspector Calls (Tony Award 1994, Drama Desk Award 1994, Olivier Award nomination 1993, Ovation and Drama Circle Awards LA 1996), Pericles (Olivier Award nomination 1995), Machinal (Olivier Award 1994), What the Butler Saw, Under Milk Wood, Blinded by the Sun, The Designated Mourner, Fair Ladies at a Game of Poem Cards, Death of a Salesman, Lady in the Dark, Chips With Everything (Olivier Award 1998), Flight, Betrayal, Mother Clap's Molly House, The Winter's Tale, Jerry Springer - The Opera, Three Birds, Alighting in a Field, King Lear, Hysteria (Olivier Award 1994), Six Degrees of Separation, Bloody Poetry, Serious Money, The Old Neighbourhood (at Duke of York's) Via Dolorosa (West End and Broadway), Far Away, My Zinc Bed, A Number; RSC: Temptation, Restoration, Some Americans Abroad (also Lincoln Center NYC and Broadway), Two Shakespearean Actors, The Virtuoso, 'Tis Pity She's a Whore, Artists and Admirers, All's Well That Ends Well, The Gift of the Gorgon, Elgar's Rondo, The Broken Heart, A Russian in the Woods; other prodns incl: Moonlight (Almeida), A Walk in the Woods (Comedy Theatre), Lobby Hero, The Life of Stuff, Threepenny Opera, The Maids, Boston Marriage, Philanthropist, Old Times, Betrayal (all Donmar Warehouse), Rat in the Skull (Duke of York's), Disney's Hunchback of Notre Dame (Berlin), Billy Elliot: The Musical (Victoria Palace Theatre), Resurrection Blues (Old Vic), Tin Tin (Barbican); *Opera* incl:Betrothal in a Monastery (Glyndebourne), Fiery Angel and Turandot (both Bolshoi Moscow), A Midsummer Night's Dream (Fenice Venice), Gloriana, La Bohème, L'Étoile, Peter Grimes (Opera North), The Magic Flute (Teatro Regio, Parma), Flying Dutchman (Opera Bordeaux), La Traviata (Paris Opera), La Vestale, Verdi Requiem, The Fairy Queen, Der Freischutz, Dr Ox's Experiment, Verdi's Requiem (ENO), Musica Nel Chiostro (3 seasons, Batignano Italy), Wozzeck (ROH), 6 seasons for Santa Fe Opera; *Ballet* numerous dance pieces for The Kosh and Adventures in Motion Pictures incl Swan Lake (West End and Broadway) and Cinderella; *Recreations* cycling, travel, camping; *Style*— Rick Fisher, Esq; ✉ c/o Denis Lyne Agency, 108 Leonard Street, London EC2A 4RH (tel 020 7739 6200, fax 020 7739 4101)

FISHER, Roy; s of Walter Fisher (d 1959), of Birmingham, and Emma, *née* Jones (d 1965); *b* 11 June 1930; *Educ* Handsworth GS, Univ of Birmingham (BA, MA); *m* 1, 1953 (m dis 1987), Barbara, da of Harold Davenport Venables; 2 s (Joel b 1957, Benjamin b 1963); m 2, 1987, Joyce (d 2002), da of Arthur Holliday; *Career* lectr rising to sr lectr in English Dudley Coll of Educn 1958–63, head of Dept of English and Drama Bordesley Coll of Educn Birmingham 1963–71, lectr rising to sr lectr Keele Univ 1971–82; freelance writer, broadcaster and jazz pianist 1982–; Birmingham is What I Think With (film, 1991); Andrew Kelus Poetry prize 1969, Cholmondeley award 1980, Hamlyn award 1997; memb: Musicians' Union 1957–, Soc of Authors 1980–; Hon Poet of the City of Birmingham; Hon DLitt Keele Univ 1999; FRSL 2005; *Books* City (1961), The Ship's Orchestra (1966), Collected Poems 1968 (1968), Matrix (1971), The Cut Pages (1971), The Thing About Joe Sullivan (1978), Poems 1955–1980 (1980), A Furnace (1986), Poems 1955–1987 (1988), Birmingham River (1994), The Dow Low Drop (1996), Interviews Through Time (2000), The Long and Short of It: Poems 1955–2005 (2005); *Style*— Roy Fisher; ✉ Four Ways, Earl Sterndale, Buxton, Derbyshire SK17 0EP (tel 01298 83279)

FISHER-SMITH, Richard James; s of Derrick William Smith, of Stevenage, Herts, and Patricia, *née* Cheek; *b* 10 October 1964; *Educ* Alleyne's Boys' Sch, Stevenage Coll of Art & Design (DATEC), Berkshire Coll of Art & Design (BTEC); *m* 6 Sept 1986, Sally Josephine, da of Edward Terrence Fisher (d 1982); 1 da (Elizanell Jessica Ellen b 5 Sept 1988), 2 s (Oscar Arthur Edward James b 26 June 1991, Moses Blue Edward James b 14 Oct 1995); *Career* designer; freelance designer 1985–86; KB Design: designer 1987–89, sr designer 1989–90, sr designer Pentagram Design Ltd 1990–92; assoc dir Crescent Lodge Design Ltd 1994–97 (sr designer 1992–94); Communication Arts America Award of Excellence 1988, Int Logo and Trademark Assoc NYC Award of Excellence 1989, Art Directors' Club Award of Merit 1992; work featured in numerous jls and annuals; *Recreations* native American tradition, alternative life style, cinema, travel; *Style*— Richard Fisher-Smith, Esq; ✉ 34 Higher Street, Brixham, Devon TQ5 8HW

FISHMAN, Prof William Jack; *b* 1 April 1921; *Educ* Central Fndn GS for Boys London, LSE (BSc Econ), Univ of London (DSc Econ); *m* 1 June 1947, Doris; 2 s (Barrie Paul b 26 June 1948, Michael Ian b 8 March 1953); *Career* Home Serv and Far East Br Army 1940–46; princ Tower Hamlets Coll of Further Educn 1954–69; visiting fell Balliol Coll Oxford 1965; visiting prof: Columbia Univ NY 1967, Univ of Wisconsin Madison 1969–70; Acton Tst major research fell in history 1970–72, prof QMC London 1986– (Barnet Shine sr research fell 1972); conslt and participant BBC radio and TV and ITV progs relating to the East End (US, W German and Finnish TV), memb Ctee Toynbee Hall 1991, govr Raines Fndn Sch, former academic advsr Museum of Labour History, founding govr East End Jewish Museum; *Books* The Insurrectionists (1970), East End Jewish Radicals (1975), The Streets of East London (1979), East End 1888 (1988), East End and Docklands (with John Hall and Nicholas Breach, 1990); *Recreations* travel, reading and conducting local history tours; *Style*— Prof William Fishman; ✉ 42 Willowcourt Avenue, Kenton, Harrow, Middlesex (tel 020 8907 5166)

FISHWICK, Avril; OBE (1997), DL (Gtr Manchester 1982); da of Frank Platt Hindley (d 1966), and Charlotte Winifred, *née* Young (d 1940); *b* 30 March 1924; *Educ* Woodfield Sch, Wigan HS for Girls, Univ of Liverpool (LLB, LLM); *m* 4 Feb 1950, Thomas William Fishwick (d 1999), s of William Fishwick, of Rainford, Merseyside; 2 da (Lizbeth Joanna b 1951, Hilary Alean b 1953); *Career* FO Bletchley Park 1942–45; admitted slr 1949; ptnr Frank Platt & Fishwick 1958–94; High Sheriff Gtr Manchester 1983–84, Vice Lord-Lt Gtr Manchester 1988–98; memb Wigan and Leigh Hosp Mgmnt Ctee 1960–73, chm Wigan AHA 1973–82, memb NW RHA 1984–88; dir N Advsy Bd Nat West Bank 1984–92; memb Ct Univ of Manchester 1984–2001; pres: Wigan Branch RSPCA 1974–99, Wigan Civic Tst 1975–88, Wigan Little Theatre 1985–91, D-Day and Normandy Veterans' Assoc Wigan Branch 1997–, Friends of Drumcroon Arts Centre; Countryside Cmmn rep Groundwork Tst 1985–94, dir Environmental Research and Consultancy Unit Tidy Britain (ERCU Ltd); vice-pres Gtr Manchester Co Scout Cncl; tstee: Skelton Bounty 1985–2003, Friends of Rosie; Paul Harris fell Rotary Int; memb: RSPB, WWF; hon memb Soroptimist Int, hon assoc memb Manchester Naval Offrs Assoc; HM The Queen Mother's Birthday Award for Environmental Improvement 1996, Bronze Medal and Cert of Meritorious Serv RSPCA; Hon MA Univ of Manchester; *Recreations* countryside, natural history; *Style*— Mrs Avril Fishwick, OBE, DL; ✉ 6 Southfields, Richmond Road, Bowdon, Cheshire WA19 2TY (tel 0161 941 6660)

FISK, Prof David John; CB (1999); s of late John Howard Fisk, and Rebecca Elizabeth, *née* Haynes; *b* 9 January 1947; *Educ* Stationers' Company's Sch Hornsey, St John's Coll Cambridge (MA, ScD), Univ of Manchester (PhD); *m* 1972, Anne Thoday; 1 s, 1 da; *Career* DOE (now DETR): Building Res Estab 1972, higher sci offr 1972–73, sr sci offr 1973–75, princ sci offr 1975–78, sr princ sci offr and head Mechanical and Electrical Engrg Div 1978–84, asst sec Central Directorate of Environmental Protection 1984–87, dep chief scientist 1987–88, chief scientist 1988–, dir Environment and Int Directorate 1995–98, dir Central Strategy Directorate 1999–; visiting prof Univ of Liverpool 1988–, Royal Acad of Engrg prof of engrg for sustainable devpt Imperial Coll London; author of numerous papers on building sci, systems theory and economics; FCIBSE 1983, CEng 1983, FREng 1998; *Books* Thermal Control of Buildings (1981); *Style*— Prof David Fisk, CB; ✉ Office of the Deputy Prime Minister, Eland House, Bressenden Place, London SW1E 5DU

FISON, Sir (Richard) Guy; 4 Bt (UK 1905), of Greenholme, Burley-in-Wharfedale, West Riding of Yorkshire, DSC (1944); s of Capt Sir (William) Guy Fison, 3 Bt, MC (d 1964); *b* 9 January 1917; *Educ* Eton, New Coll Oxford; *m* 28 Feb 1952, Elyn (d 1987), da of Mogens Hartmann, of Bordeaux, and formerly wife of Count Renaud Doria; 1 s (Charles William b 1954), 1 da (Isabelle Frances b 1957); *Heir* s, Charles Fison; *Career* Lt RNVR, served Atlantic, N Sea and Channel; dir Saccone and Speed Ltd 1952–83 (sometime chm

Saccone and Speed International), non-exec dir Whitehead Mann 1982–84, chm Fine Vintage Wines plc 1986–95; pres Wine and Spirit Assoc of GB 1976–77, chm Wine Devpt Bd 1982–83, dir Wine Standards Bd 1984–87; memb Ct of Assts Worshipful Co of Vintners (Upper Warden 1982–83, Master 1983–84); Master of Wine 1954; *Style*— Sir Guy Fison, Bt, DSC; ✉ Medwins, Odiham, Hampshire RG29 1NE (tel 01256 704075)

FISZ, Anoushka; da of S Benjamin Fisz, and Ginette Fisz; *b* 1969, London; *Career* photographer; former apprentice to Plichta; *Solo Exhibitions* Galerie Pierre Nouvion Monaco 1997, Jason McCoy NYC 1998, Mayor Gallery London 1999, Eyestorm Gallery London 2001, Fiac Exhbn Paris 2003, Ikon Ltd Bergamont Statrion Santa Monica CA 2003; *Group Exhibitions* Air de Paris 1998 and 2002, Rouce Noire Presents The House (Galerie Catherine Bastide Brussels) 2003. Albertina Museum Vienna 2004; *Style*— Anoushka Fisz; ✉ c/o David Grob, Court Place Farm, Parracombe, Devon EX31 4RJ

FITCH, (John) Derek; s of John Dowson Fitch (d 1979), and Nora Fitch (d 1984); *b* 22 September 1937; *Educ* Rutherford GS Newcastle upon Tyne, Univ of Durham (BA); *m* 22 June 1963, Maureen Rose; 1 s (John Stephen b 1968); *Career* mgmnt conslt; dep chief exec Lombard North Central plc (subsid of National Westminster Bank) 1991–97; sometime: chm Lex Vehicle Leasing, chm Lex Transfleet, dir Lombard Bank; currently ptnr Fitch Delrose; *Recreations* golf, swimming (ex British record holder); *Style*— Derek Fitch, Esq; ✉ Douglas Cottage, Coombe End, Kingston upon Thames, Surrey KT2 7DQ (tel 020 8942 8009)

FITCH, Rodney Arthur; CBE (1990); s of Arthur Francis Fitch (d 1982), of London, and Ivy Fitch (d 1989); *b* 19 August 1938; *Educ* Willesden Poly, Sch of Architecture, Central Sch of Arts & Crafts, Hornsey Sch of Art; *m* 28 Aug 1965, Janet Elizabeth, da of Sir Walter Stansfield, CBE, QPM (d 1984); 4 da (Polly Jane b 27 May 1967, Emily Kate b 18 June 1968, Louisa Claire b 7 Nov 1971, Tessa Grace b 29 Oct 1974), 1 s (Edward b 18 Aug 1978); *Career* Nat Serv Pay Corps RA 1958–60; trainee designer Hickman Ltd 1956–58, Charles Kenrick Assoc 1960–62, Conran Design Group Ltd 1962–69, CDG (design conslts) Ltd 1969–71, fndr chm Fitch plc (formerly Fitch RS plc) 1971–94, the fndr dir Rodney Fitch & Co 1994–2002, dir Portland Design 2002–03, chm and ceo Fitch Woldwide (part of WPP Gp) 2003–; memb: Design Cncl 1988–94, Governing Cncl RCA 1988–94, Ct of Govrs Univ of Arts London (formerly London Inst, dep chm 1989–2005, chm Fin Ctee 1997–2004); CSD (formerly SIAD): vice-pres 1982–86, hon treas 1984–87, pres 1988–90; pres D&AD Assoc 1983; tstee V&A 1991–2001, chm Bd of Dirs V&A Enterprises 2002– (memb 1994), dir City of London Arts Festival 1996–2003, memb Mgmnt Bd Wellington Museum (Apsley House) 1996–2001; FRSA 1976, PPCSD, PPDAD 2003; *Recreations* cricket, opera, theatre, family; *Clubs* MCC, Savile, Lord's Taverners, XL; *Style*— Rodney Fitch, Esq, CBE, PPCSD, PPDAD

FITCHEW, Geoffrey Edward; CMG (1993); s of Stanley Edward Fitchew (d 1976), and Elizabeth, *née* Scott (d 1971); *b* 22 December 1939; *Educ* Uppingham, Magdalen Coll Oxford (MA), LSE (MSc); *m* 17 Sept 1966, Mary Theresa, da of Dr Joseph Patrick Spillane (d 1989); 2 s (William Owain b 1971, Benedict Wyndham b 1975); *Career* asst princ HM Treasy 1964, private sec to Perm Sec Dept of Economic Affairs 1966–67; HM Treasy: private sec to Econ Sec 1967–68, asst sec 1975, cnsllr (econ and fin) UK Perm Representation to EC 1978–80, under sec (Euro Communities Gp) 1983–85, under sec (Int Fin Gp) 1985–86; DG Directorate-General XV (Fin Instn and Company Law) EC 1986–93, dep sec Cabinet Office 1993–94; chm Building Societies Cmmn and chief registrar of Friendly Societies 1994–2002, memb Determinations Panel Pensions Regulator 2005–; vice-chm Int Cmmn on Holocaust Era Insurance Claims 1999–2003, chm Insolvency Practices Cncl 2005–; *Recreations* tennis, golf, reading, theatre, crosswords, armchair supporter Manchester Utd; *Style*— Geoffrey Fitchew, Esq, CMG

FITTALL, William Robert; s of Arthur Fittall (d 1987), and Elsie, *née* Cole; *b* 26 July 1953; *Educ* Dover GS for Boys, ChCh Oxford (MA); *m* 1978, Barbara Staples; 2 s (Jonathan b 1982, Matthew b 1984); *Career* Home Office: joined 1975, private sec to Timothy Raison as Min of State 1979–80, princ 1980; École Nationale d'Administration Paris 1980–81; Broadcasting Dept Home Office 1981–85, private sec to Home Secs Sir Leon Brittan then Douglas Hurd 1985–87, asst sec 1987, sec to Review of Parole System 1987–88, Prison Service HQ 1988–91, princ private sec to Secs of State for NI Peter Brooke then Sir Patrick Mayhew 1992–93, Police Dept Home Office 1993–95; asst under sec of state Cabinet Office 1995–97, dir Crime Reduction and Community Progs Home Office 1997–2000, assoc political dir NI Office 2000–02; sec-gen Archbishops' Cncl and Gen Synod C of E 2002–; lay reader C of E 1977–, church organist; *Recreations* playing church organs, watching sport, reading; *Style*— William Fittall, Esq; ✉ Church House, Great Smith Street, London SW1P 3NZ (tel 020 7898 1360, e-mail william.fittall@c-of-e.org.uk)

FITZ, (Cheryl) Jane; da of Cyril Albert Berwick (d 1987), and Grace, *née* Wagner; *b* 23 February 1947; *Educ* Launceston HS Tasmania, Univ of Tasmania (BSc, DipEd), Birkbeck Coll London (BSc, Alexander Silberfield Prize); *m* 26 Aug 1967, Prof John Fitz; 1 da (Emily Rose b 12 Aug 1988); *Career* teacher Sacred Heart Convent Sch Hobart Tasmania 1967–69, supply teacher Surrey CC 1970, computer programmer William Cory & Sons London 1970–71; head of chemistry: Bromley HS for Girls GPDST 1971–73, S Hampstead HS GPDST (second mistress, third mistress); headmistress Notting Hill & Ealing HS GPDST 1983–91; Howell's Sch Llandaff Cardiff GDST: headmistress 1991–2006, princ 2006–07; memb Cncl Univ of Cardiff 2005–07; Hon Freeman Worshipful Co of Drapers; FRSA 1988; *Recreations* tennis, theatre, opera, gardening; *Style*— Mrs Jane Fitz

FITZALAN HOWARD, Lord Mark; OBE (1994); 4 and yst s of 3 Baron Howard of Glossop, MBE (d 1972), and Baroness Beaumont, OBE (d 1971); *b* 28 March 1934; *Educ* Ampleforth; *m* 17 Nov 1961, Jacynth Rosemary, o da of Sir Martin Alexander Lindsay of Dowhill, 1 Bt, CBE, DSO; 2 da (Amelia b 1963, Eliza (Mrs Timothy Bell) b 1964); *Career* late Coldstream Gds; dir Robert Fleming Holdings Ltd 1971–94; memb Hon Investment Advsy Ctee Public Tst Office until 1994; chm Assoc of Investment Trust Cos 1981–83, chm Investment Ctee Univs Superannuation Scheme 1993–2002; treas Scout Assoc 1987–96; dir Hosp of St John and St Elizabeth 1997–; *Clubs* Brooks's; *Style*— Lord Mark Fitzalan Howard, OBE; ✉ 13 Campden Hill Square, London W8 7LB (tel 020 7727 0996, fax 020 7727 0492)

FITZALAN-HOWARD, Maj-Gen Lord Michael; GCVO (1981, KCVO 1971, MVO 4 Class 1952), kt SMO Malta, CB (1968), CBE (1962, MBE 1949), MC (1944), DL (Wilts 1974); 2 s of 3 Baron Howard of Glossop, MBE, and Baroness Beaumont, OBE (Barony called out of abeyance in her favour 1896); granted rank of Duke's s 1975; *b* 22 October 1916; *Educ* Ampleforth, Trinity Coll Cambridge (MA); *m* 1, Jean Marion (d 1947), da of Sir Hew Hamilton-Dalrymple, 9 Bt; 1 da; *m* 2, Jane Margaret (d 1995), yr da of Capt William Patrick Meade Newman; 4 s, 1 da; *m* 3, Victoria Winifred, wid of Maj Sir Mark Baring, KCVO, and da of late Col Reginald Edmund Maghlin Russell, CVO, CBE, DSO; *Career* served WWII, Scots Gds, Europe and Palestine, subsequently Egypt, Malaya, Germany, Maj-Gen cmdg Allied Command Europe Mobile Force (Land) 1964–66, Col The Lancashire Regt 1966–70, GOC London Dist and Maj-Gen cmdg Household Div 1968–71, Col The Queen's Lancashire Regt 1970–78, Marshal Dip Corps 1972–82; Col Life Gds 1979–99, Gold Stick to HM The Queen 1979–99; pres Cncl TAVR Assocs 1981–84 (chm 1973–81); Freeman City of London 1985; hon recorder Br Cwlth Ex Service League 1992–2001; *Clubs* Pratt's, Buck's; *Style*— Maj-Gen Lord Michael Fitzalan-Howard, GCVO, CB, CBE, MC, DL; ✉ Fovant House, Church Lane, Fovant, Salisbury, Wiltshire SP3 5LA (tel 01722 714617)

FitzGERALD, Sir Adrian James Andrew Denis; 6 Bt (UK 1880), of Valencia, Co Kerry; The 24th Knight of Kerry (first recorded use of title 1468; The Green Knight); s of Sir George FitzGerald, 5 Bt, MC, 23 Knight of Kerry (d 2001); *b* 24 June 1940; *Educ* Harrow; *Heir* cous, Anthony D FitzGerald; *Career* hotelier 1983–90; ed Monday World 1967–74; Royal Borough of Kensington and Chelsea: cncllr 1974–2002, mayor 1984–85, chm Educn and Libraries Ctee 1995–98, chm Highways & Traffic Ctee 1999–2001; dep ldr London Fire and Civil Def Authy 1989–90, pres Anglo Polish Soc 2002– (chm 1989–92), vice-chm London Chapter Irish Georgian Soc 1990–, pres Benevolent Soc of St Patrick 1997–, govr Cardinal Vaughan Meml Sch 1999– (vice-chm 2002–03, chm 2003–); Knight of Honour and Devotion in Obedience SMOM; *Clubs* Pratt's, Kildare Street and Univ, Beefsteak; *Style*— Sir Adrian FitzGerald, Bt, The Knight of Kerry; ✉ 16 Clareville Street, London SW7 5AW; Glenshelane House, Cappoquin, Co Waterford, Ireland

FITZGERALD, Christopher Francis; s of late Lt Cdr Michael Francis FitzGerald, RN, of Hove, E Sussex, and Anne Lise, *née* Winther; *b* 17 November 1945; *Educ* Downside, Lincoln Coll Oxford (MA); *m* 1, 1968 (m dis 1984), Jennifer, *née* Willis; 1 s (Matthew b 1973), 2 da (Francesca b 1975, Julia b 1978); m 2, 1986, Jill, *née* Freshwater; 2 step da (Joanna b 1978, Victoria b 1979); *Career* admitted slr 1971; Slaughter and May: ptnr 1976–95, exec ptnr fin 1986–90, partnership Bd 1986–95; gen counsel and memb Exec Dirs' Ctee NatWest Group 1995–2000, dir The Intercare Gp plc 2001–03; chm The Macfarlane Tst 2007–; dir: City Merchants High Yield Tst 2007–, Mimecast Ltd 2007–; chm Regulatory Decisions Ctee FSA 2001–04, memb Review Panel Financial Reporting Cncl 2006–; memb Fin Ctee Lincoln Coll Oxford 2003–; *Recreations* travelling, opera, theatre and concert going, appreciating fine wines; *Style*— Christopher FitzGerald, Esq; ✉ 21 Palace Gardens Terrace, London W8 4SA (tel 020 7229 2226)

FITZGERALD, Rev (Sir) Daniel Patrick; 4 Bt (UK 1903), but does not use the title; s of Sir John FitzGerald, 2 Bt, suc bro, Rev (Sir) Edward Thomas FitzGerald (3 Bt) (d 1988); *b* 28 June 1916; *Heir* cous, John FitzGerald; *Career* Roman Catholic priest; *Style*— The Rev Daniel FitzGerald; ✉ c/o J F FitzGerald, Esq, Meadowlands, Wilton Road, Cork, Ireland

FITZGERALD, Desmond John Villiers; *see:* Glin, Knight of

FITZGERALD, Michael John; s of Albert William Fitzgerald (d 1980), of West Chiltington, W Sussex, and Florence Margaret Fitzgerald, *née* Stannard (d 1981); *b* 14 May 1935; *Educ* Caterham Sch; *m* 9 June 1962, Judith-Ann, da of Dr A C Boyle, of Iping, W Sussex; 2 s (Alistair b 1964, Malcolm b 1966), 1 da (Aimee-Louise b 1970); *Career* CA; vice-pres and gen mangr Occidental International (Libya) Inc 1985–96, exec vice-pres Occidental International Oil Inc 1987–96; dir: Langham Publishing Ltd 1985–2000, Canadian Occidental North Sea Petroleum Ltd 1987–96, Hardy Exploration and Production (India) Inc 1999–2000, Mercury Oil and Gas Ltd 2001–, Kew Electrical Distributors Ltd 2002–; md OVP Associates Ltd 1996–; MInstPet, MInstD; *Recreations* golf, gardening, cricket, opera; *Clubs* West Sussex Golf, Travellers; *Style*— Michael J Fitzgerald, Esq; ✉ OVP Associates Ltd, Fir Tops, Grove Lane, West Chiltington, West Sussex RH20 2RD (tel 01798 817325, fax 01798 815597)

FITZGERALD, Niall William Arthur; KBE (2002); s of William FitzGerald (d 1972), and Doreen, *née* Chambers; *b* 13 September 1945; *Educ* St Munchins Coll Limerick, UCD (MCom); *m* 1, 2 March 1970 (m dis 2003), Monica Mary, da of John Cusack (d 1985); 1 da (Tara b 5 Dec 1973), 2 s (Colin b 30 Jan 1976, Aaron b 24 March 1982); m 2, 27 Sept 2003, Ingrid van Velzen; 1 da (Gabriella b 21 April 2001); *Career* Unilever: joined Unilever Ireland as accountant 1967, various positions with subsids Paul & Vincent, Lever Bros Ireland and W & C McDonnell, Unilever Head Office London 1972–76 (PA to fin dir 1974–76), overseas commercial offr 1976–78, commercial offr N American ops 1978–80, finance dir Unilever South Africa (Pty) Ltd 1980–82, md Van den Bergh & Jurgens (Pty) Ltd South Africa 1982–85, gp treas London 1985–86, finance dir 1986–89, main bd dir Unilever plc and Unilever NV 1987–2004, edible fats and dairy co-ordinator 1989–90, detergents co-ordinator 1991–95, vice-chm Unilever plc 1994–95, exec chm Unilever plc 1996–2004, vice-chm Unilever NV 1996–2004; non-exec chm Reuters plc 2004– (non-exec dir 2003–); non-exec dir: Bank of Ireland 1990–99, Prudential Corporation 1992–99, Merck 2000–03, Ericsson 2000–02; sr advsr Morgan Stanley, memb European Advsy Bd Blackstone, memb Advsy Bd Spencer Stuart; former chm Europe Ctee CBI, co-chm Conference Bd (US) 2003–05, co-chm Transatlantic Business Dialogue 2004–05; former memb: Kok Cmmn on the Lisbon Agenda, Accounting Standards Review Ctee, Int Policy Cncl for Agriculture and Trade; current memb: US Business Cncl, Int Business Cncl, Fndn Bd World Economic Forum; memb advsy bodies incl: Pres of S Africa's Int Investment Advsy Cncl, Int Advsy Bd Cncl on Foreign Rels, Advsy Bd Tsinghua Univ; chm of tstees Br Museum 2006–, chm Nelson Mandela Legacy Tst (UK), tstee Leverhulme Tst; pres Advertising Assoc 2000–05; FCT 1986 (former memb Cncl), FRSA; *Recreations* opera and jazz, Irish rugby, supporting Manchester United, running (slowly), playing golf (poorly), creating an exotic garden in Sussex, observing humanity; *Clubs* RAC, Wisley Golf; *Style*— Niall FitzGerald, KBE

FITZGERALD, Peter Gilbert; OBE (1993), DL (Cornwall 1999); s of P H FitzGerald (d 1995), and Hilda Elizabeth, *née* Clark; *b* 13 February 1946; *Educ* Harvey GS Folkestone; *m* 5 Dec 1970, Elizabeth Thora, da of F L Harris (d 1970), of Cornwall; 1 s (Timothy b 24 Oct 1973); *Career* chartered accountant; dir Valor Vanguard Ltd 1965–66, md FitzGerald Lighting Ltd 1980– (dir 1973–80); dir Bodmin & Wenford Railway plc 1985–; chm Cornwall Economic and Tourism Forum 1992–99; burgess Bodmin 2001–; FCA 1972; *Recreations* cycling, walking, transport; *Style*— Peter G FitzGerald, Esq, OBE, DL; ✉ FitzGerald Lighting Ltd, Normandy Way, Bodmin, Cornwall PL31 1HH (tel 01208 262200, fax 01208 73062)

FITZGERALD, Dr Richard; s of Dr Patrick Fitzgerald, of Cork, Eire, and Mary, *née* O'Donnell; *b* 14 May 1955; *Educ* Christian Brothers' Coll Cork, UC Cork NUI (MB BCh, BAO); *Career* house offr Cork Regnl Hosp 1979–81, registrar then sr registrar West Midlands Radiology Trg Scheme Birmingham 1981–86, conslt radiologist to Wolverhampton Hosps 1986–; FRCR 1985, memb BIR; *Recreations* swimming, hill walking, cinema; *Style*— Dr Richard Fitzgerald; ✉ 10 Meadway, Silvermere Park, Shifnal, Shropshire TF11 9QB (tel 01952 461729, e-mail richard.fitzgerald@talk21.com); X-Ray Department, New Cross Hospital, Wolverhampton WV10 0QP (tel 01902 307999)

FITZGERALD, Tara Anne Cassandra; da of Michael Callaby (d 1979), and Sarah Geraldine Fitzgerald; *b* 18 September 1967; *Educ* Walsingham Girls' Sch, The Drama Centre London; *m* Dec 2000, John Shahnazarian; *Career* actress; prodr A Family Man (short film); *Theatre* incl: Angela Caxton in Our Song (Apollo and Bath Theatre Royal) 1992/93, Ophelia in Hamlet (Hackney Empire and Belasco Theatre NY) 1995, Antigone 1999, Blanche Du Bois in A Streetcar Named Desire (Bristol Old Vic) 2000, Nora in A Doll's House (Birmingham Rep) 2004, Mara in Clouds (Cambridge Arts) 2004, Vera Claythorne in And Then There Were None (Gielgud Theatre) 2005–06; *Television* incl: Victoria Mordaunt in The Black Candle (Tyne Tees), Polly Cuthbertson in The Camomile Lawn (Channel 4) 1992, Dolly Stokesay in Anglo-Saxon Attitudes (Thames), The Step-daughter in Six Characters in Search of An Author (BBC 2), Catherine Pradier in Fall from Grace (SkyTV) 1994, Poppy Carew in The Vacillations of Poppy Carew (Carlton) 1994, The Tenant of Wildfell Hall 1996, Marian in The Women in White (Carlton) 1997, Beth March in Little White Lies (BBC TV) 1998, Lady Dona St Colomb in Frenchman's Creek (Carlton) 1998, Zoe in In the Name of Love (Meridian) 1999, Monica Jones in Love Again (BBC 2) 2003, Kit Ashley in The Virgin Queen (BBC) 2005, Aunt Reed in Jane Eyre (BBC) 2006, Eve Lockhart in Waking the Dead (BBC) 2006–; *Films* incl: Nancy Doyle in Hear My Song 1992, Estella Campion in Sirens 1993, Adele Rice in A Man of No

Importance 1994, Betty from Cardiff in The Englishman Who Went Up a Hill But Came Down a Mountain 1994, Gloria in Brassed Off 1995, Daisy in Conquest 1998, Snow Angel in Childhood 1997, Kris in New World Disorder 1998, Susan Whitmore in Dark Blue World 2000, Clara Salvador in Secret Passage 2001, Topaz in I Capture the Castle 2001, Mum in Five Children and It 2003; *Awards* Drama Desk Award for outstanding featured actress in a play (for Hamlet), Reims Television Festival Best Actress 1999 (for Frenchman's Creek); *Recreations* music, cinema, painting, friends, restaurants; *Clubs* Soho House; *Style—* Ms Tara FitzGerald; ✉ c/o Lindy King, PFD, Drury House, 34–43 Russell Street, London WC2B 5HA (tel 020 7344 1000, fax 020 7836 9539)

FITZHARRIS, Ven Robert Aidan; s of late John Joseph Fitzharris, and Margaret Louisa Fitzharris; *b* 19 August 1946; *Educ* St Anselm's Coll Birkenhead, Univ of Sheffield (BDS), Lincoln Theol Coll; *m* 1971, Lesley Margaret, *née* Rhind; 3 da (Rosemary, Susan, Catherine); *Career* in gen dental practice 1971–87, pt/t clinical asst Charles Clifford Dental Hosp Sheffield 1978–85; ordained: deacon 1989, priest 1990; asst curate Dinnington 1989–92, vicar of Bentley 1992–2001, substitute chaplain HMP Moorland 1992–2001, hon assoc chaplain Doncaster Royal Infirmary and Mexbrough Montague Hosp Tst 1995, area dean Adwick-le-Street 1995–2001, hon canon Sheffield Cathedral 1998, archdeacon of Doncaster 2001–; chm: Sheffied Diocesan Strategy Gp 1999–2001, Diocesan Parsonages Ctee 2001, Diocesan Bd of Educn 2001, Doncaster Minster Devpt Appeal 2005–07, Doncaster Re-Furnish Ltd 2007–; chm The Wildwood Project (Bentley) Ltd 1999–2004, Doncaster Cancer Detection Tst 2003–; *Recreations* doting on my grandson; *Style—* The Ven the Archdeacon of Doncaster; ✉ Fairview House, 14 Armthorpe Lane, Doncaster DN2 5LZ (tel 01302 352787); Office (tel 01709 309110, e-mail archdeacons.office@sheffield.anglican.org)

FITZHERBERT, Sir Richard Ranulph; 9 Bt (GB 1784), of Tissington, Derbys; o s of Rev David Henry FitzHerbert, MC (d 1976), and Charmian Hyacinthe (d 2006), da of late Samuel Ranulph Allsopp, CBE, DL; suc unc, Sir John Richard Frederick FitzHerbert, 8 Bt 1989; *b* 2 November 1963; *Educ* Eton; *m* 17 April 1993, Caroline Louise, da of Maj Patrick Shuter, of Ashbourne, Derbys; 1 s (Frederick David b 23 March 1995), 1 da (Francesca Norah b 21 April 1998); *Heir* s, Frederick FitzHerbert; *Career* pres: Derbys Community Fndn 1995–, Derbys Rural Community Cncl 1995–, Ashbourne Heritage Soc 1995–, Derbys Scouting Assoc 2004–; *Recreations* cricket, field sports, restoring family estate; *Clubs* MCC, White's, Stansted Hall CC, Parwich RBLCC, I Zingari; *Style—* Sir Richard FitzHerbert, Bt; ✉ Tissington Hall, Ashbourne, Derbyshire DE6 1RA (e-mail tisshall@dircon.co.uk)

FITZHERBERT-BROCKHOLES, Francis Joseph; eldest s of Michael John Fitzherbert-Brockholes (d 1998); *b* 18 September 1951; *Educ* Oratory Sch, CCC Oxford (MA); *m* 7 May 1983, Jennifer, da of Geoffrey George Watts, of Grassdale, Wandering, W Aust; 1 da (Susannah Louise b 23 Feb 1984), 2 s (Thomas Antony b 8 Nov 1985, George Frederick b 1 March 1988); *Career* called to the Bar 1975, admitted New York Bar 1978; in chambers Manchester 1976–77, assoc Cadwalader Wickersham & Taft 1977–78, ptnr White & Case 1985– (assoc 1978–85); *Style—* Francis Fitzherbert-Brockholes, Esq; ✉ White & Case, 5 Old Broad Street, London EC2N 1DW (tel 020 7532 1000, fax 020 7532 1001)

FITZHUGH, (Edmund Francis) Lloyd; OBE (1995), JP (Wrexham) 1990, DL (Clwyd) 1994; s of Godfrey Edmund FitzHugh (d 1985), of Plas Power, Wrexham, and Burness Grace, *née* Clemson (d 2001); *b* 2 February 1951; *Educ* Eton, Shuttleworth Agric Coll; *m* 13 Sept 1975, Pauline, *née* Davison; 2 s (Tristam Edmund b 20 March 1978, Benjamin Lloyd b 24 Jan 1981); *Career* farmer and landowner; memb Local Govt Boundary Cmmn for Wales 1995–2001, chm NE Wales NHS Tst 1999–2005; *Recreations* church music; *Style—* Lloyd FitzHugh, Esq, OBE, DL; ✉ Garden House, Plas Power, Bersham, Wrexham LL14 4LN (tel 01978 263522, fax 01978 263522)

FITZMAURICE, Kevin; s of Charles Michael Fitzmaurice, and June, *née* Ward; *b* 12 June 1963; *Educ* LAMDA (Dip Stage Mgmnt); *m* 28 July 2001, Rebecca Johnson; *Career* line prodr Almeida Theatre 1997–2001 (prodns incl: Naked, The Iceman Cometh, Plenty, Cressida, Richard II, Coriolanus), exec dir Young Vic Theatre 2001– (incl redevpt 2004–06) (prodns incl: A Raisin in the Sun, Afore Night Come, Monkey, Dr Faustus, The Daughter-in-Law, Sleeping Beauty, Simply Heavenly, Peribanez, Hobson's Choice, Romeo and Juliet, Skellig, The Skin of our Teeth, Cruel and Tender, Tintin, Love & Money, The Enchanted Pig, Vernon God Little); *Style—* Kevin Fitzmaurice, Esq; ✉ Young Vic Theatre, 66 The Cut, London SE1 8LZ (tel 020 7922 2821, fax 020 7922 2801, e-mail kevinfitzmaurice@youngvic.org)

FITZPATRICK, Frank; s of Sean Fitzpatrick, and Constance Fitzpatrick (d 1999); *b* 1 March 1958; *Educ* St Chad's Coll Wolverhampton, Lancaster Univ (BA), Inst of Educn Univ of London (PGCE), Univ of Surrey (MA), Univ of Leicester (MBA); *m* 10 June 1997, Eugenia Lisboa; 2 da (Sara b 4 May 1993, Emma b 27 June 1997); *Career* teacher of English and teacher trainer Spain, Italy and UK 1983–94; Br Cncl: dir of studies Barcelona 1994–97, dir Oporto 1997–2000, asst dir Greece 2000–02, dir Peru 2002–06, dir and cultural attaché Macedonia 2006–; *Publications* A Teacher's Guide to Practical Pronunciation (1995); various teaching and teacher training articles in educn jls incl: Modern English Teacher, Practical English Teacher, The Teacher Trainer; *Style—* Frank Fitzpatrick, Esq; ✉ British Council, Bulevar Goce Delčev 6, PO Box 562, 1000 Skopje, Republic of Macedonia (tel 00 389 2 3135 035, fax 00 389 2 3135 036, e-mail frank.fitzpatrick@britishcouncil.org.mk, website www.britishcouncil.org/macedonia)

FITZPATRICK, James (Jim); MP; s of James Fitzpatrick, of Glasgow, and Jean, *née* Stones; *b* 4 April 1952; *Educ* Holyrood Sr Secdy Glasgow; *Children* 1 s (James b 1981), 1 da (Helen b 1982); *Career* with London Fire Brigade 1974–97, memb Nat Exec Cncl Fire Brigades Union 1988–97; MP (Lab) Poplar and Canning Town 1997–; asst Govt whip 2001–02, a Lord Cmmr (Govt whip) 2002–03, vice-chamberlain HM's Household 2003–05, min for London 2005–, Parly sec ODPM 2005–06, Parly under sec of state DTI 2006–; vol agent Barking Constituency Lab Pty 1986–92, memb Exec London Lab Pty 1988–, chm Gtr London Lab Pty 1991–; govr Eastbury Comp Sch 1993–2000; awarded Fire Brigade Long Service and Good Conduct Medal; *Recreations* reading, football (West Ham United), TV and film; *Style—* Jim Fitzpatrick, Esq, MP; ✉ House of Commons, London SW1A 0AA (tel 020 7219 5085 or 020 7219 6215, fax 020 7219 2776, e-mail fitzpatrickj@parliament.uk)

FITZPATRICK, Joe; MSP; s of Joseph Kelly Fitzpatrick, and Margaret M, *née* Crabb (d 2006); *b* 1 April 1967, Dundee; *Educ* Whitfield HS, Inverness Coll of Further and Higher Educn, Univ of Abertay Dundee (BSc); *Career* asst to Shona Robison, MSP 1999–2007, cncllr Dundee City Cncl 1999–2007, asst to Stewart Hosie, MSP 2005–07, MSP (SNP) Dundee West 2007–; memb NUJ; *Style—* Joe Fitzpatrick, Esq, MSP; ✉ The Scottish Parliament, Edinburgh EH99 1SP (tel 01382 623200, fax 01382 903205, e-mail joe.fitzpatrick.msp@scottish.parliament.uk)

FITZPATRICK, Dr Kieran Thomas Joseph; s of Kieran Gerard Fitzpatrick (d 1966), of Strabane, Co Tyrone, and Margaret, *née* Ohle; *b* 23 March 1954; *Educ* Christian Brothers' GS, Omagh and St Coleman's HS Strabane, Queen's Univ Belfast (MB BCh, BAO); *m* 24 Feb 1986, Elizabeth Maureen, da of Robert McKee; 2 da (Laura Jane b 25 Feb 1987, Lucy Claire b 11 May 1990), 1 s (Andrew Kieran b 24 April 1989); *Career* jr house offr Belfast City Hosp 1979–80, SHO (anaesthetics) Belfast City Hosp 1980–81; registrar (anaesthetics): Ulster Hosp Dundonald 1981–82, Belfast City Hosp 1982–83, Coleraine Hosp 1983–85; sr registrar (anaesthetics) Royal Victoria Hosp Belfast 1985–86, sr tutor Dept of Anaesthetics Queen's Univ Belfast 1986–87, res fell Royal Belfast Hosp for Sick Children 1987–88, conslt anaesthetist Belfast City Hosp 1988–; memb: BMA 1980, Assoc of Anaesthetists of GB and I 1980, NI Soc of Anaesthetists, Anaesthetic Research Soc 1986, Obstetric Anaesthetists Assoc 1986; FFARCSI 1983; *Recreations* gardening, walking and my family; *Style—* Dr Kieran Fitzpatrick; ✉ 171 Killinchy Road, Comber, Co Down, BT23 5NE (tel 028 9754 2357, e-mail kfitzpatrick79@hotmail.com);Department of Clinical Anaesthesia, Belfast City Hospital, 97 Lisburn Road, Belfast BT9 7AB (tel 028 9032 9241 ext 2476)

FITZPATRICK, (Francis) Michael John; s of Francis Latimer FitzPatrick (d 1982), of East Bergholt, Suffolk, and Kathleen Margaret, *née* Gray (d 1997); *b* 14 July 1938; *Educ* Brentwood Sch; *m* 4 April 1964, Patricia Hilbery, OBE, da of Sir George Frederick Chaplin, CBE, DL, JP (d 1975), of Great Warley, Essex; 1 s (Richard b 1965), 1 da (Kathryn b 1967); *Career* chartered surveyor, conslt Messrs Hilbery Chaplin; Freeman City of London, Liveryman Worshipful Co of Chartered Surveyors; FRICS; *Recreations* music, travel, wine, gardening; *Clubs* Royal Over-Seas League; *Style—* Michael J FitzPatrick, Esq; ✉ Bramling House, Hop Meadow, East Bergholt, Suffolk CO7 6QR

FITZPATRICK, Nicholas David; s of Prof Reginald Jack Fitzpatrick, of Heswall, Merseyside, and Ruth, *née* Holmes; *b* 23 January 1947; *Educ* Bristol GS, Univ of Nottingham (BA); *m* 23 Aug 1969, (Patricia) Jill, da of Peter Conway Brotherton; 1 da (Paula b 14 Dec 1973), 1 s (Daniel b 12 Jan 1976); *Career* trainee analyst Friends Provident 1969–72, equity mangr Abbey Life 1972–76, equity mangr then investment mangr BR Pension Fund 1976–86, ptnr and investment specialist Bacon & Woodrow 1986–2002, global investment ldr Hewitt Assocs 2002–05, assoc BESTrustees 2006–; AMIIMR 1972, FIA 1974; *Recreations* rugby, canal boats; *Style—* Nicholas Fitzpatrick, Esq; ✉ Sommarlek, Woodhurst Park, Oxted, Surrey (tel 01883 717927, e-mail ndfitz@gmail.com)

FITZSIMONS, Prof James Thomas; s of Robert Allen Fitzsimons, FRCS, and Dr Mary Patricia Fitzsimons, *née* McKelvey; *b* 8 July 1928; *Educ* St Edmund's Coll Ware, Gonville & Caius Coll Cambridge (MB BChir, MA, PhD, MD, ScD); *m* 1961, Aude Irène Jeanne, da of Gén Jean Etienne Valluy, DSO; 2 s, 1 da; *Career* house appts Leicester Gen and Charing Cross Hosps 1954–55; Flying Offr then Flight Lt RAF Inst of Aviation Med 1955–57; Univ of Cambridge: MRC scholar Physiological Lab 1957–59, demonstrator in physiology 1959–64, lectr 1964–76, reader 1976–90, prof of med physiology 1990–95, emeritus prof 1995–; Gonville & Caius Coll Cambridge: fell 1961–, tutor 1964–72, lectr in physiology 1964–93, dir of studies in med 1978–93, pres 1997–2005; memb: Physiological Soc Ctee 1972–76 (chm 1975–76), International Union of Physiological Sciences (IUPS) Cmmn on Physiology of Food and Fluid Intake 1973–80 (chm 1979–80); Royal Soc rep British Nat Ctee for Physiological Scis 1976–80; ed Biological Reviews 1984–95; Distinguished Career Award Soc for the Study of Ingestive Behavior 1998; Hon MD Lausanne 1978; FRS 1988; *Books* The Physiology of Thirst and Sodium Appetite (1979); author of scientific papers in professional jls; *Style—* Prof James Fitzsimons, FRS; ✉ Gonville & Caius College, Cambridge CB2 1TA (tel 01223 332429, e-mail jtf10@cam.ac.uk)

FITZWALTER, Raymond Alan; s of Robert Fitzwalter (d 1997), of Bury, Lancs, and Lucy, *née* Fox (d 2000); *b* 21 February 1944; *Educ* Derby Sch, LSE (BScEcon); *m* 1, 6 Aug 1966 (m dis 1993), Mary, da of Richard Towman (d 1989), of Bury, Lancs; 2 s (Stephen Anthony b 24 Nov 1968, Matthew Paul b 11 Aug 1970), 1 da (Kathryn Anne b 16 Dec 1974); m 2, 7 May 1994, Ann Luise Nandy, da of Baron Byers (Life Peer, d 1984); *Career* Bradford Telegraph and Argus: trainee journalist 1965–67, feature writer 1967–68, dep news ed 1968–70; Granada TV: exec prodr World in Action 1986–93 (researcher 1970–75, prodr 1975–76, ed 1976–86), commissioning exec news and current affrs 1987–89, head of current affrs 1989–93, exec prodr What The Papers Say and drama documentaries 1989–93; independent prodr Ray Fitzwalter Associates Ltd 1993–; visiting fell Univ of Salford 1993–2002 (visiting prof 2002–); northern rep and memb Cncl PACT 1994–2002, chm Campaign for Quality Television 1995–; CPU scholar to Pakistan 1969, Young Journalist of the Year IPC Awards 1970 (commended 1968), BAFTA award best factual series for World in Action 1987, RTS awards for World in Action 1981, 1983 and 1985, BAFTA Desmond Davis award for outstanding creative contrib to TV 1991; FRTS 1993; *Books* Web of Corruption: The Story of John Poulson and T Dan Smith (with David Taylor, 1981); *Recreations* chess, naval history, a garden; *Style—* Raymond Fitzwalter, Esq; ✉ Ray Fitzwalter Associates, Stone Cottage, 115 Holcombe Old Road, Holcombe, Bury, Lancashire BL8 4NF (tel 01706 828054, fax 01706 821139, e-mail ray@fitzwalter.co.uk)

FITZWILLIAMS, Duncan John Lloyd; s of Charles Collinsplat Lloyd Fitzwilliams, (d 1984), of Newcastle Emlyn, Carmarthenshire, and Rosamond Muriel, *née* Hill (d 2003); *b* 24 May 1943; *Educ* Harrow, St Edmund Hall Oxford (MA); *m* 1, 1968, Hon Sarah Samuel, da of 4 Viscount Bearsted; m 2, 1978, Anna, da of Gp Capt Rex Williams, of Newton Ferrers, Devon; 2 da (Angharad, Victoria), 1 s (Logie); *Career* chm and jt fndr CASE plc 1969–88; dir: Foreign and Colonial Investment Trust plc 1973–91, Foreign and Colonial Pacific Investment Trust plc 1975–89, Anvil Petroleum plc 1975–85, Flextech Holdings plc 1976–86, Walker Greenbank plc 1977–88, Venture Link Ltd (chm) 1978–87, Henry Venture Fund II Inc (USA) 1985–, Lazard Leisure Fund 1986–94, Bespak plc 1986–2000 (Audit and Remuneration Ctee), Oakes Fitzwilliams & Co Ltd 1987–, Ozone Industries Ltd 1997–, Axa Fund Managers SA 2000–; co chm Quadrant Healthcare plc 1992–2000; memb Bd City Friends of Templeton Coll Oxford, former memb Info Technol Panel LSE; govr Harrow Sch; coracle champion of River Teifi 1956; MIIMR 1974; *Recreations* fishing, golf; *Clubs* White's, MCC, Berkshire Golf, The Brook (NY); *Style—* Duncan Fitzwilliams, Esq; ✉ Fisher's Copse House, Bradfield, Reading, Berkshire RG7 6LN (tel 0118 974 4527); Nash Fitzwilliams & Co Ltd, 7/9 St James's Street, London SW1A 1EE (tel 020 7925 1125, fax 020 7925 1026, e-mail dfitzwilliams@nashfitzwilliams.com)

FITZWILLIAMS, Richard Brathwaite Lloyd; s of Maj Robert Campbell Lloyd Fitzwilliams, TD (d 2001), and Natalie Jura Stratford, *née* Mardall (d 1965); the family has four registered Royal Descents from Ethelred II (Ethelred the Unready), Edward I (through the Howards), Edward III and Malcolm II, King of Scots, all through Richard Fitzwilliams' ggg grandmother Jane Maria, da and co-heir of Adm Richard Brathwaite; *b* 14 October 1949; *Educ* Univ of Cape Town (BA, three Lestrade scholarships); *m* 16 Nov 1981 (m dis 1995), Gillian, da of Frederick William Savill, of Blaby, Leics; *Career* worked on project for Shadow Min of Educn United Party SA 1972, Europa Publications London 1972–2001, ed Int Who's Who 1975–2001, head Fitzwilliams Assocs 2001–; PR conslt: Belgravia Gallery 2001–, Maria Andipa Gallery 2001, RSPP 2002–, Fedn of Br Artists 2002–; royal commentator, film critic, arts reviewer and contrib: CNN, Sky News, BBC News 24, ITV News, BBC World, CBC, CTV, BBC 2, BBC Wales, BBC Ulster, BBC Scotland, TalkSport, Radio 5 Live, LBC, BBC London, Radio NZ; contrib London and UK Datebook 1997–; memb: Hampstead and Highgate Cons Assoc (former memb Town and Frognal Ward Ctee, former memb Exec Cncl), YMCA; *Recreations* cinema, theatre, entertaining, shooting, travel, swimming; *Clubs* Naval and Military; *Style—* Richard B L Fitzwilliams, Esq; ✉ Fitzwilliams Associates, 84 North End Road, London NW11 7SY (tel 020 8455 7393, fax 020 8455 7393, mobile 07939 602749, e-mail richardfitzwilliams@hotmail.com)

FIVET, Edmond Charles Paul; *b* 12 February 1947; *Educ* St Marks Sch London, RCM (ARCM), Coll of St Mark & St John London (CertEd), Open Univ (pt/t BA), City Univ (pt/t MA); *m*; 1 step s; 2 c from previous m; *Career* professional freelance teacher and performer 1965–71, head of brass Surrey CC 1971–73, dir Jr Dept RCM 1983–89 (registrar 1973–82), princ Royal Welsh Coll of Music and Drama 1989–2007; external examiner for

BMus Birmingham Conservatoire 1995–98; Assoc Bd of the Royal Schs of Music: examiner 1977–92, memb Consultative Ctee 1984–86, memb Examinations Bd 1986–89; music dir Audi Jr Musician (nat competition for 12–16 year olds) 1986–97; memb: Nat Assoc of Youth Orchs 1983–84, Working Party Nat Fndn for Educnl Research LEA Instrumental Provision 1986–88, Ctee Welsh Colls of HE 1989–2007, Assoc of Euro Conservatoires 1989–2007, Conservatoires UK 1990–2007, Ctee Nat Centre for Dance and Choreography 1994–96, HE Wales 1996–2007; vice-pres Arts Cncl Richmond-upon-Thames (memb Exec Ctee 1982–86, vice-chm 1984–86), chm Richmond Music Festival 1985–94; chm Nat Yourh Arts Focus Gp 1998–2005; memb: Music Ctee Welsh Arts Cncl 1991–94, Music Ctee Cardiff Int Festival 1992–95, Arts Cncl of Wales 2000–06; tstee Millennium Stadium Charitable Tst 2002–05; FRCM 1988, FRSA, HonFBC 2005; *Recreations* golf, reading, theatre, music, current affairs; *Clubs* Aldeburgh Golf; *Style—* Edmond Fivet, Esq; ✉ Fig Tree House, 15 Church Walk, Aldeburgh, Suffolk IP15 5DU (tel 01728 454992, e-mail edmond@fivet.co.uk)

FLACK, Rt Rev John Robert; s of Edwin John Flack, of Hoddesdon, Herts, and Joan Annie, *née* Stevens; *b* 30 May 1942; *Educ* Hertford GS, Univ of Leeds (BA), Coll of the Resurrection Mirfield; *m* 5 Oct 1968, Julia Clare, da of Rev Canon Maurice Basil Slaughter; 1 da (Alison Clare b 13 Oct 1969) 1 s (Robert Alban b 22 June 1972); *Career* ordained (Ripon Cathedral): deacon 1966, priest 1967; curate: St Bartholomew Armley Leeds 1966–69, St Mary's Northampton 1969–72; vicar of Chapelthorpe 1972–81, vicar of Ripponden with Rishworth and of Barkisland with West Scammonden, concurrently chaplain of Rishworth Sch 1981–85, vicar of Brighouse 1985–92 (team rector 1988–92), rural dean of Brighouse and Elland 1986–92, hon canon of Wakefield Cathedral 1989–97, archdeacon of Pontefract 1992–97, Bishop of Huntingdon 1997–2003; dir Anglican Centre in Rome 2003–, Archbishop's representative to the Holy See 2003–; chm: Wakefield Bd of Mission 1980–94, House of Clergy Wakefield 1988–93; selector: C of E Advsy Bd of Miny 1992–, Gen Synod 1994–, C of E Central Bd of Fin 1994–; church cmmr 1995–; memb: Crigglestone CC 1973–80, Ripponden Stones CC 1981–84, Brighouse CC 1985–91; Capt Wakefield Clergy CC 1978–88; *Recreations* cricket (still playing), Mozart (writing about and speaking on); *Style—* The Rt Rev John Flack; ✉ The Anglican Centre in Rome, Palazzo Doria Pamphilj, Piazza del Collegio Romano 2, Int 7, 00186 Roma

FLACK, Mervyn Charles; s of Maj Henry George Flack (d 1978), and Marjorie, *née* Lofthouse (d 1991); *b* 30 June 1942; *Educ* Raynes Park Co GS, Northampton Coll of Advanced Technol; *m* 5 Oct 1963, Margaret Elizabeth, da of George Robert Cumnock (d 1983); 1 s (James b 3 Nov 1969), 1 da (Emma b 2 Oct 1975); *Career* asst statistician, res analyst Gillette Industries Ltd 1962–67, co statistician Marplan Ltd 1967–69, chief statistician Attwood Statistics Ltd 1969–70, dir Opinion Research Centre 1971–79, dep md Louis Harris International 1978–79 (res dir 1973–78); chm City Research Associates Ltd 1980–2000, dir Applied Research & Communications Ltd 1995–2000, chm and chief exec City Research Group plc 1990–2000, dir Yankee Delta Corp Ltd 2001–03 and 2005–, sr ptnr Mervyn Flack & Associates, dir Charterhouse Research Ltd 2004–; memb: Market Research Soc, Cncl Assoc of Br Market Research Cos 1981–84, Cncl Br Market Research Assoc 1998–99; author various articles on market research; memb Aircraft Owners and Pilots Assoc, memb Goodwood Road Racing Club; MInstD; FSS 1963, FIS 1978 (MIS 1964), MMRS; *Recreations* private pilot, food, wine; *Style—* Mervyn Flack, Esq; ✉ Mervyn Flack & Associates, Maldons, Pendell Road, Bletchingley, Surrey RH1 4QH (tel 01883 740370, e-mail mervyn@maldons.co.uk)

FLANAGAN, Andrew Henry; s of Francis Andrew Desmond Flanagan, of Glasgow, and late Martha Gilmour White, *née* Donaldson; *b* 15 March 1956; *Educ* Hillhead HS Glasgow, Univ of Glasgow (BAcc); *m* 21 March 1992, Virginia Annette, da of James Richard Alastair Walker; *Career* articled clerk Touche Ross 1976–79, audit sr Price Waterhouse 1979–81, fin mangr ITT Europe Inc 1981–86, dir of fin Europe PA Consulting Group 1986–91, gp fin dir The BIS Group Ltd 1991–93; SMG plc (formerly Scottish Television plc then Scottish Media Group plc): gp fin dir 1994–96, md 1996, currently chief exec; non-exec dir Scottish Rugby Union 2000–05; MICAS; *Recreations* golf, jogging, skiing, cinema, reading, television; *Clubs* RAC; *Style—* Andrew Flanagan, Esq

FLANAGAN, Barry; OBE; *b* 11 January 1941, Prestatyn; *Educ* Mayfield Coll, Birmingham Coll of Art and Crafts; *Career* artist; RA 1987; *Exhibitions* incl: Van Abbe Museum Eindhoven 1977, Venice Biennale 1982, Musée Nationale d'Art Moderne Paris 1983, Sculpture 1967–87 (Laing Art Gallery Newcastle upon Tyne) 1987–88, Fundación "La Caixa" Madrid 1993–94, Tate Gallery Liverpool 2000, Kunsthalle Recklinghausen 2002–03, Musee d'Art Moderne et d'Art Contemporain Nice 2002–03; *Style—* Barry Flanagan, OBE, RA; ✉ c/o Waddington Galleries, London W1S 3LT (tel 020 7851 2200, fax 020 7734 4146)

FLANAGAN, Mary; da of Martin James Flanagan (d 1981), and Mary, *née* Nesbitt (d 1977); *b* 20 May 1943; *Educ* Brandeis Univ (BA); *Career* writer; began writing 1979; works to date: Bad Girls (collection of short stories, 1984), Trust (1987), Rose Reason (1991), The Blue Woman (collection of short stories, 1994), Adèle (1997); critic for: Sunday Times, Evening Standard, New Statesman, The Independent, The Observer, The New York Times Book Review, Art Quarterly; teacher of creative writing: UEA 1995 and 1997, City Lit 2006, Birkbeck Coll London 2004–06; memb: Soc of Authors 1986, PEN (English and American) 1990; Royal Literary Fund Fellowship Univ of Leicester 2001–03; *Recreations* gardening, music, environmental activist; *Style—* Ms Mary Flanagan; ✉ c/o Bloomsbury Publishing Ltd, 38 Soho Square, London W1D 3HB

FLATHER, Gary Denis; OBE (1999), QC (1984); s of Joan Ada, *née* Walker; *b* 4 October 1937; *Educ* Oundle, Pembroke Coll Oxford; *m* Shreela (The Baroness Flather), *qv*, da of Aftab Rai; *Career* 2 Lt 1 Bn York and Lancaster Regt 1956–58, Hallamshire Bn TA 1958–61; called to the Inner Temple Bar 1962 (bencher and memb Scholarships Ctee 1995), recorder of the Crown Court 1986– (asst recorder 1983–86), dep judge of the High Court 1997–; memb Panel of Chairmen ILEA Disciplinary Tbnl 1974–90, asst Parly boundary cmmr 1982–90, inspr DTI for enquiries under Fin Servs Act 1987–88; chm (jtly): Police Disciplinary Appeal Tbnl 1987–, MOD Police Disciplinary Appeal Tbnl 1991–; legal memb Mental Health Review Tbnl 1987–; legal assessor: GMC 1987–95, Gen Dental Cncl 1987–95, RCVS 2000–; chm: Statutory Ctee Royal Pharmaceutical Soc of GB 1990–2000, Disciplinary Ctee CIM 1995, Special Educational Needs and Disability Tbnl (SENDIST) 2004–; dir Fearnehough (Bakewell) Ltd 1990–2002; escort to Mayor Royal Borough of Windsor and Maidenhead 1986–87, vice-pres Community Cncl for Berkshire 1987–2001; pres Maidenhead Rotary 1990–91; chm Bar Cncl Disability Ctee 1990–2002, memb Bar Cncl Equal Opportunities Ctee 1998–2002, hon memb of the Bar 2002; tstee: ADAPT 1995–, The Disabled Living Fndn 1997–2003; cmmr Royal Hosp Chelsea 2005–; Hon MRPharmS 2001; *Recreations* travel, music, dogs, coping with Multiple Sclerosis; *Style—* Gary Flather, Esq, OBE, QC; ✉ 4/5 Gray's Inn Square, London WC1R 5AY (tel 020 7404 5252, e-mail garyflather@yahoo.co.uk)

FLATHER, Baroness (Life Peer UK 1990), of Windsor and Maidenhead in the Royal County of Berkshire; Shreela Flather; JP (1971), DL (Berks 1994); da of Rai Bahadur Aftab Rai (d 1972), of New Delhi, and Krishna Rai (d 1989); *Educ* UCL (LLB, fell); *m* Gary Denis Flather, QC, *qv*; 2 s (Hon Paul, Hon Marcus); *Career* infant teacher ILEA 1965–67; teacher of English as foreign language: Altwood Comp Sch Maidenhead 1968–74, Broadmoor Hosp 1974–78; cnllr Royal Borough of Windsor and Maidenhead 1976–91; pres Cambs Chilterns and Thames Rent Assessment Panel, vice-pres Building Socs Assoc 1976–91; vice-chm and fndr memb Maidenhead Community Rels Cncl, vice-chm Maidenhead Volunteer Centre, vice-chm and memb Mgmnt Ctee CAB, vice-chm Estates and Amenities and Leisure Ctees Royal Borough of Windsor and Maidenhead; fndr New Star Boys' Club for Asian boys, fndr summer sch project for Asian children in Maidenhead; sec Windsor and Maidenhead Cons Gp, sec and organiser Maidenhead Ladies' Asian Club 1968–78; community rels advsr Berks Girl Guides, race rels tutor for sr police offrs' courses; memb: Lord Chllr's Legal Aid Advsy Ctee 1958–88, W Met Conciliation Ctee of Race Rels Bd 1973–78, Cons Women's Nat Ctee 1975–89, Swann Ctee (enquiry into educn of children from ethnic minority gps) 1979–85, Cmmn for Racial Equality 1980–86, Bd of Visitors Holloway Prison 1981–83, Police Complaints Bd 1982–85, HRH Duke of Edinburgh's Ctee of Enquiry into Br Housing 1984–85, Broadmoor Hosp Bd 1987–88, Berks FPC 1987–88, BBC South and East Regnl Advsy Ctee, Dist Youth and Community Ctee, UK delgn to Econ and Social Ctee EC 1987–90, Exec Ctee Anglo-Asian Cons Soc, Social Security Advsy Ctee 1987–90, Servite Houses Ctee of Mgmnt, Nat Union Exec Ctee Cons Pty 1989–90, exec ctees of Br sections Int Unions of Local Authys, LWT Prog Advsy Bd 1990–93, Select Ctee Medical Ethics 1993–94, Bar Cncl Equal Opportunities Ctee 2002–03; non-exec dir: Thames Valley Training and Enterprise 1990–93, United News and Media (Meridian Broadcasting Ltd) 1991–2001; dir: Daytime TV Ltd 1978–79, Marie Stopes Int 1996–, Cable Corp 1997–2000, Kiss and Magic FM Ltd 2000–02, Bookpower 2001–; chm: STARFM 101.6, Local Independent Radio Slough, Windsor and Maidenhead 1992–97, Ethics Ctee Broadmoor Hosp 1993–97, Alcohol Education and Research Cncl 1995–2002, Memorial Gates Tst 1998– (meml now on Constitution Hill), Club Asia 2002–; vice-chm Indo-Br Parly Gp, tstee Sir William Borlase Sch Marlow 1991–97; pres: Broadmoor League of Friends 1991–98, Berkshire Community Cncl 1991–98, Soc of Friends of the Lotus Children 1996–99, Global Money Transfer Ltd 1997–2001, Alumni Assoc of UCL 1998–2000; vice-pres: Assoc of District Cncls 1990–97, Townswomens Guilds, Servite Houses Housing Assoc, Careers Nat Assoc, Br Assoc of Counselling and Psychotherapy 1999–; vice-chm The Refugee Cncl 1991–96; patron Corona Worldwide; memb: Thames and Chilterns Tourist Bd 1987–88, Spoore Merry and Rixman Fndn, Poole's Charity, Ring's Charity, Hillingdon Hosp Tst 1990–98; UK rep on EU Advsy Cmmn on Racism and Xenophobia 1995–97; govr: Slough Coll of HE 1984–89, Cwlth Inst 1993–98; tstee: Rajiv Gandhi (UK) Fndn 1993–2001, Pan African Health Fndn 2004–; memb: Cncl of Winston Churchill Meml Tst 1993–, Cncl of St George's House Windsor Castle 1996–2002, UK Advsy Cncl Asia House, Advsy Cncl American Intercontinental Univ 2004–; lay memb UCL Cncl 2000–; Mayor Royal Borough of Windsor and Maidenhead 1986–87 (Dep Mayor 1985–86); Hon Dr Open Univ 1994; Asian of the Year Asian Who's Who 1996; FRSA 1999; *Recreations* travel, cinema; *Style—* The Baroness Flather, DL, FRSA; ✉ House of Lords, London SW1A 0PW; (fax 01628 675355)

FLAUX, Julian Martin; QC (1994); s of Louis Michael Flaux (d 2003), of Malvern, Worcs, and Maureen Elizabeth Brenda, *née* Coleman; *b* 11 May 1955; *Educ* King's Sch Worcester, Worcester Coll Oxford (MA, BCL); *m* 24 Sept 1983, Matilda Christian, da of Michael Hansard Gabb, of Canterbury, Kent; 3 s; *Career* called to the Bar Inner Temple 1978; in practice 1979–, recorder, dep judge of the High Court; *Recreations* walking, reading, opera; *Clubs* Garrick; *Style—* Julian Flaux, Esq, QC; ✉ 7 King's Bench Walk, Temple, London EC4Y 7DS (tel 020 7910 8300, fax 020 7910 8400)

FLECK, Prof Norman A; *b* 11 May 1958; *Educ* Friends' GS Lisburn, Jesus Coll Cambridge (Coll Scholar, Rex Moir Prize, Percival Prize, Baker Prize, Keller Prize, MA), Pembroke Coll Cambridge (PhD); *Career* research fell Pembroke Coll Cambridge 1983–84, visiting scholar Harvard Univ 1984–85, research fell NASA Langley 1985; Univ of Cambridge: lectr in engrg 1985–94, fell Pembroke Coll 1985–, reader in mechanics of materials 1994–97, prof of mechanics of materials 1997–, also currently head of Mechanics, Materials and Design Div Engrg Dept and dir Cambridge Centre for Micromechanics; visiting scholar Harvard Univ 1989, 1993 and 1995; memb Editorial Bd: Jl of Composites: Technology and Research, Mechanics of Composite Materials and Structures; conslt: Thomas Broadbent & Sons, Cegelec, London International Group, Weston Medical Ltd; FIM 1997, CEng 1997, FRS 2004; *Publications* author of numerous book chapters and articles in learned jls; *Style—* Prof Norman Fleck; ✉ Engineering Department, University of Cambridge, Trumpington Street, Cambridge CB2 1PZ (tel 01223 332650, fax 01223 332662, e-mail nafl@eng.cam.ac.uk)

FLECK, Richard John Hugo; s of Peter Hugo Fleck (d 1975), and Fiona Charis Elizabeth Miller; *b* 30 March 1949; *Educ* Marlborough, Univ of Southampton (LLB); *m* 1983, Mary, da of Wing Cdr Frederick Thomas Gardiner, DFC; 1 da (Sara Katherine Victoria b 10 May 1987), 1 s (Peter Frederick Hugo b 3 March 1990); *Career* ptnr Herbert Smith 1980– (joined 1971); chair Int Ethics Standards Bd for Accountants Advsy Gp 2006–; memb: Auditing Practices Ctee 1986–91, Auditing Practices Bd 1991– (chm 2003–), Financial Reporting Cncl 2004–; Freeman City of London, Liveryman Worshipful Co of Tallow Chandlers; memb Law Soc; *Recreations* sailing, real tennis, golf, rackets; *Clubs* MCC, Royal Ocean Racing, City Law, Jesters, Itchenor Sailing, Petworth House Tennis; *Style—* Richard Fleck, Esq; ✉ Slinfold Manor, Slinfold, Horsham, West Sussex RH13 0SX (tel 01403 791684); Herbert Smith, Exchange House, Primrose Street, London EC2A 2HS (tel 020 7374 8000, e-mail richard.fleck@herbertsmith.com)

FLEETWOOD, Gordon; WS (1995); s of John Edward Fleetwood, of Lossiemouth, Morayshire, and Isabel Ann, *née* Roy; *b* 3 October 1951, Elgin, Morayshire; *Educ* Elgin Academy, Univ of Edinburgh (LLB); *m* 15 Nov 1975, Jean Swanson, *née* Arthur; 2 da (Jennifer b 19 June 1981, Gillian b 18 May 1983); *Career* slr; More & Co 1977–82, Sutherland & Co 1982–86, Fleetwood & Robb 1986–2004, sole practitioner 2004–; slr-advocate 1994–; pt/t sheriff 2003–; *Recreations* curling, salmon fishing; *Style—* Gordon Fleetwood, Esq; ✉ 1 Annfield Road, Inverness IV2 3NP (tel and fax 01463 221355, e-mail gfleetwood@btinternet.com)

FLELLO, Robert; MP; *b* 14 January 1966, Birmingham; *Educ* King's Norton Boys' Sch, UCNW Bangor; *Career* Inland Revenue 1987–89, Price Waterhouse 1989–95, Arthur Andersen 1995–99, Platts Flello Ltd 1999–2004, Malachi Community Tst 2004–05, MP (Lab) Stoke-on-Trent S 2005–; cncllr (Lab) Birmingham City Cncl 2002–04, regnl organiser Lab Pty 2004–05; memb: Co-op Pty, TGWU, Amicus, Unity; *Style—* Robert Flello, Esq, MP; ✉ House of Commons, London SW1A 0AA

FLEMING, Alistair; s of James Anderson Fleming, of Glasgow, and Elizabeth Brown Davies; *b* 31 March 1944; *Educ* Univ of Strathclyde (BSc); *m* 9 July 1966, Sandra Rosemary, da of William Gillies; 2 da (Lorraine Rosalynne b 19 June 1970, Melissa Caroline b 30 April 1975), 1 s (Stuart Alexander b 4 Feb 1985); *Career* project mgmnt and engrg roles ICI Petrochemical Div UK and Aust 1965–75, project mangr Corpus Christi Petrochemicals then asst dir of engrg ICI America 1975–80, regnl mangr Western Europe Britoil Clyde Field Project 1987, gen mangr of project BP Exploration 1987–89, md of construction Eurotunnel 1990–91, dir The Weir Group plc (and subsids) 1991–96, gp chief exec Forth Ports plc 1996–; memb Scottish Cncl CBI, chm Scottish Cncl for Educn Technol; CEng, FIMechE, MInstPet, FREng 1993; *Recreations* golf; *Style—* Alistair Fleming, Esq, FREng; ✉ Forth Ports plc, Tower Place, Leith, Edinburgh EH6 7DB (tel 0131 555 8700, fax 0131 553 7462)

FLEMING, Prof Christopher Alexander; s of Brian Alexander Fleming (d 1984), and Marguerite Grace, *née* Allingham; *b* 14 August 1948; *Educ* Alleyn's Sch Dulwich, Univ of Aberdeen (BSc), Univ of Reading (PhD); *m* 17 July 1970, Christeen, da of John Louis MacLean; 1 s (Lewis Alexander b 12 Feb 1977), 1 da (Kazia Ann b 26 Sept 1980); *Career* Sir William Halcrow & Partners Ltd: grad engr UK 1970–72, site engr Port Victoria 1972, asst engr Marine Dept UK 1972–73; Univ of Reading (PhD) 1973–75; rejoined Sir

F

William Halcrow & Partners Ltd: engr Marine Dept 1975–77, section engr Mina Jebel Ali Dubai 1977–79, resident engr Jebel Ali Hotel Marine Works Dubai 1978–79, project engr Mina Jebel Ali Dubai Halcrow International Partnership 1979–80, head Maritime Computer Applications Unit UK 1980–82, conslt to KPCL Toronto 1982–84, dir of Halcrow MOE and of Halcrow-Ewbank 1983–84, dir Sir William Halcrow & Partners Ltd and dir Halcrow Offshore 1984–94, UK dir Water and Maritime Div 1984–98, chief exec Halcrow Maritime 1998–2000, chief exec Halcrow Middle East 1998–2001, gp bd dir Halcrow Gp Ltd 2000–07; visiting prof of coastal engrg: Univ of Plymouth 1994–, Univ of Strathclyde 2005–; former advsr to House of Commons Environment Ctee on Coastal Zone Protection and Planning, chm Nat Coastal Impact Modelling Ctee, chm Steering Ctee Beach Mgmnt Manual CIRIA, memb Advsy Industrial Bd Engrg Dept Univ of Plymouth; author of numerous publications in various learned jls; memb: Permanent Int Assoc of Navigation Congresses (PIANC), Int Assoc of Hydraulic Research; Hon DEng Univ of Plymouth 2006; CEng, memb Fédération Européene d'Associations Nationales d'Ingénieurs, FICE 1991 (1979), FRGS 1991, FREng 1996; *Recreations* sailing, skiing, golf, tennis; *Clubs* The Wiltshire; *Style—* Prof Christopher Fleming, FREng; ✉ Woodham House West, Bakers Road, Wroughton, Wiltshire SN4 0RP (tel 01793 813543); Halcrow Group Ltd, Burderop Park, Swindon, Wiltshire SN4 0QD (tel 01793 812479, fax 01793 816237, mobile 07710 063434, e-mail flemingca@halcrow.com)

FLEMING, Ven David; s of John Frederick Fleming, BEM (d 1976), of Norfolk, and Emma Fleming (d 1996); *b* 8 June 1937; *Educ* King Edward VII GS King's Lynn, Kelham Theol Coll; *m* 1966, Elizabeth Anne Marguerite, da of Bernard Bayleys Hughes (d 1947), of Birmingham; 3 s (Christopher b 1967, Nicholas b 1968, Matthew b 1972), 1 da (Fiona b 1970); *Career* curate St Margaret Walton on the Hill 1963–67, chaplain HM Gaynes Hall, vicar Great Staughton 1968–76, rural dean St Neots 1972–76, vicar Whittlesey 1976–85, rural dean March 1977–82, hon canon Ely Cathedral 1982–2001, archdeacon of Wisbech 1984–93, vicar Wisbech St Mary 1985–88, chaplain gen of HM prisons 1993–2001; chaplain to HM The Queen 1995–97; *Recreations* television, tennis, extolling Hunstanton; *Clubs* Whittlesey Rotary; *Style—* The Ven David Fleming; ✉ Fair Haven, 123 Wisbech Road, Littleport, Cambridgeshire CB6 1JJ (tel 01353 862498)

FLEMING, David; OBE (1997); s of Jack Fleming, of Leeds, and Doreen, *née* Wordsworth; *b* 25 December 1952; *Educ* Temple Moor GS Leeds, LSE, Univ of Leeds (BA), Univ of Leicester (MA, PhD); *Partner* Alison Jane Hastings; 4 c (Breton b 31 August 1973, Mitya b 16 July 1983, Callum b 17 June 1987, Ruby b 8 June 2001); *Career* curator: Yorkshire Museum of Farming 1981–83, Collection Servs Leeds Museums 1983–85; princ keeper of museums Hull Museums 1985–90, dir Tyne & Wear Museums 1991–2001 (asst dir 1990–91), dir Nat Museums & Galleries on Merseyside 2001–; pres Museums Assoc; tstee: Nat Football Museum, St George's Hall Liverpool; AMA 1986, FRSA 1997; *Style—* Dr David Fleming, OBE; ✉ National Museums & Galleries on Merseyside, PO Box 33, 127 Dale Street, Liverpool L69 3LA (fax 0151 478 4321)

FLEMING, Prof George; *b* 16 August 1944, Glasgow; *Educ* Univ of Strathclyde (BSc), Univ of Strathclyde/Stanford Univ (PhD); *Career* vice-pres/dir Hydrocomp International California and Glasgow 1969–77, conslt Watson Hawksley High Wycombe 1980–92; Univ of Strathclyde: lectr 1971–76, sr lectr 1976–82, reader 1982–85, vice-dean Faculty of Engrg 1984–87, personal prof 1985–86, chair prof Dept of Civil Engrg 1986–, dir Water and Environmental Mgmnt Unit 1986– (Better Environment Award for Industry RSA 1987), head Div of Water Engrg and Environmental Mgmnt 1989–2002, head Dept of Civil Engrg 1991–93, chm Mgmnt Gp David Livingstone Inst 1992–2002, md Centre for Environmental Mgmnt Studies Ltd 1993–, md Envirocentre 1996–, memb Senate 1996–2002, dir Centre for Environmental Mgmnt Res 1998–2002; visiting prof Padova Univ Italy 1980–88; conslt Clydeport Ltd (formerly Clyde Port Authy) 1987–2000, dir Scottish Consultants International 1987–91; memb: Overseas Projects Bd DTI 1991–95, Br Cncl Environment Sci & Engrg Advsy Cncl 1998–2000, Smeatonian Soc for Civil Engrs 1998–; chm: Glasgow and W of Scotland Assoc of Civil Engrs 1984–85, Cncl ICE 1985–89, Environment Ctee SERC 1985–89, Engrg Ctee Royal Acad of Engrg 1988–91, Steering Gp Telford Challenge 1998–2001, Engrgs Against Poverty 2001–, Clyde River Fndn 2000–03, ICE Cmmn on River Flood Risk Mgmnt 2001–02; pres ICE 1999–2000 (vice-pres 1996–99); non-exec dir: WRAP 2001–, Br Waterways 2001–; conslt to numerous nat and int orgns incl: UN Food and Agriculture Orgn, ILO, World Meteorological Orgn; conslt to govt agencies incl: Scottish Devpt Agency, S of Scotland Electricity Bd, Central Electricity Generating Bd; conslt to private companies incl: Babtie Shaw and Morton, Binnie and Partners, Mott MacDonald, Bovis, Wimpey Waste; significant projects incl: dams in Kenya Labuan and Brunei, Strathclyde Park Reservoir, Dinorwig Power Station Project, reservoir mgmnt in the Alps, flood control in California, Chicago and Brazil; hon memb Br Hydrological Soc 2000, fell Transport Res Fndn 2001; FICE, FREng 1987, FRSE 1992, FASCE 2000, FCIWM 2002; *Books and Publications* research pubns incl contribs to 11 books and over 200 pubns in jls; has produced 4 video documentaries and a perm exhbn; *Style—* Prof George Fleming, FRSE, FREng, FICE, FCIWM; ✉ EnviroCentre Ltd, Craighall Business Park, 8 Eagle Street, Glasgow G4 9XA (tel 0141 341 5040, e-mail gfleming@envirocentre.co.uk)

FLEMING, Grahame Ritchie; QC (Scot, 1990); s of late Ian Erskine Fleming, of Forfar, and Helen, *née* Wallace; *b* 13 February 1949; *Educ* Forfar Acad, Univ of Edinburgh (MA, LLB); *m* 23 June 1984, Mopsa Dorcas, eld da of Gerald Neil Robbins; 1 da (Leahna Damaris Robbins b 23 Aug 1985); *Career* called to the Scottish Bar 1976, standing jr counsel to the Home Office in Scotland 1986–89, sheriff of the Lothians and Borders at Linlithgow 1993–; *Recreations* travel, food, rugby; *Style—* Sheriff Grahame Fleming, QC; ✉ Advocates' Library, Parliament House, Edinburgh EH1 1RF

FLEMING, Prof Ian; s of David Alexander Fleming (d 1988), and Olwen Lloyd, *née* Jones (d 1996); *b* 4 August 1935; *Educ* King Edward VI Sch Stourbridge, Pembroke Coll Cambridge (MA, PhD, ScD); *m* 1, 3 Aug 1959 (m dis 1962), Joan, *née* Irving; m 2, 12 Nov 1965, Mary Lord Bernard; *Career* postdoctoral res Harvard Univ 1963–64; Univ of Cambridge: fell Pembroke Coll 1962–2002 (res fell 1962–64), demonstrator 1964–65, asst dir of res 1965–80, lectr 1980–86, reader in organic chemistry 1986–98, prof of organic chemistry 1998–2002, emeritus prof 2002–; RSC: memb 1962, Tilden lectr 1981, prize for organic synthesis 1983; FRS 1993; *Books* Spectroscopic Methods in Organic Chemistry (1966, 5 edn 1995), Selected Organic Syntheses (1973), Frontier Orbitals and Organic Chemical Reactions (1976), Comprehensive Organic Synthesis (jt ed, 1991), Pericyclic Reactions (1998), Science of Synthesis (ed, 2001); *Recreations* watching films, reading, music; *Style—* Prof Ian Fleming, FRS; ✉ Department of Chemistry, University of Cambridge, Lensfield Road, Cambridge CB2 1EW (tel 01223 336372, e-mail if10000@cam.ac.uk)

FLEMING, Robert (Robin); DL (Oxon 1989); s of Maj Philip Fleming (d 1971), of Barton Abbey, Oxon, and Joan Cecil, *née* Hunloke (d 1991); *b* 18 September 1932; *Educ* Eton, RMA Sandhurst; *m* 28 April 1962, Victoria Margaret, da of Frederic Howard Aykroyd (d 1978); 1 da (Joanna Kate (Mrs James King) b 19 Nov 1963), 2 s (Philip b 15 April 1965, Rory David b 5 June 1968); *Career* serv Royal Scots Greys 1951–58; joined Robert Fleming 1958, dir Robert Fleming Trustee Co Ltd 1961– (chm 1985–91), dir Robert Fleming Investment Trust Ltd 1968–2000, chm Robert Fleming Holdings Ltd 1990–97 (dir 1974–97, dep chm 1986–90), dir Glenshee Chairlift Co Ltd 1995–2004; tstee BFSS 1975–96; High Sheriff Oxon 1980; *Recreations* most country pursuits especially stalking and fishing, music especially Scottish traditional; *Style—* Robin Fleming, Esq, DL; ✉ Ely House, 37 Dover Street, London W1S 4NJ (tel 020 7409 5600, fax 020 7409 5601)

FLEMING, (Dr) Thomas Kelman (Tom); CVO (1998), OBE (1980); s of Rev Peter Fleming (d 1939), and Kate Ulla Barker (d 1932); *b* 29 June 1927; *Educ* Daniel Stewart's Coll Edinburgh; *Career* actor, writer, producer and broadcaster; co-fndr Edinburgh Gateway Co 1953–65, RSC 1962–64 (roles incl Prospero, Cymbeline, Brutus, Kent and Buckingham), fndr and dir Royal Lyceum Theatre Co 1965–66, govr Scottish Theatre Tst 1980–82, dir Scottish Theatre Company 1982–87; Edinburgh Festival prodns of: Molière, Aristophanes, Sir David Lyndsay, Sidney Goodsir Smith; The Thrie Estaites STC Warsaw 1986 (Roman Szydlowski Award); films incl: King Lear, Mary Queen of Scots, Meetings with Remarkable Men; numerous TV incl: title role Redgauntlet, Rob Roy, Jesus of Nazareth, Henry IV (parts 1 & 2), Weir of Hermiston, Reith; over 2000 broadcasts since 1944; BBC Radio commentator (royal events) 1950–; BBC TV commentator on over 300 national and state occasions incl: launch of Royal Yacht Britannia, Coronation, Silver Wedding 1972, Princess Anne's Wedding 1973, Prince of Wales's Wedding 1981, State visits to USA and Japan, Silver Jubilee 1977, The Queen Mother's 80th Birthday Celebrations 1980, The Queen's 60th Birthday 1986, Queen's Birthday Parade 1970–94, The Queen Mother's 90th Birthday Celebrations 1990 Cenotaph Service of Remembrance 1961, 1965–88 and 1994–, Installations of Archbishop of Canterbury 1975 and 1980, two Papal Inaugurations 1978, Papl visit to Great Britain 1982, Falklands Meml Serv St Paul's 1982, Gulf Meml Serv Glasgow Cathedral 1991, 50th Anniversary Battle of Alamein 1992, D Day +50 Serv Normandy 1994, VE +50 Serv St Paul's 1995, VJ +50 The Final Tribute 1995, Funeral Serv of Diana, Princess of Wales 1997; also commentator on funeral of: Duke of Gloucester, Duke of Windsor, Montgomery of Alamein, Mountbatten of Burma, King Frederick of Denmark, Marshal Tito, Princess Grace, King Olav, Cardinal Heenan, Pope John Paul I; memb: Drama Advsy Panel Br Cncl 1983–89, Lamp of Lothian Collegiate Tst 1970–95, Scottish Int Educn Tst 1996–; pres Edinburgh Sir Walter Scott Club 2000–; Hon DUniv Heriot-Watt 1984; hon memb: Royal Scottish Pipers' Soc, Saltire Soc; FRSAMD 1986; *Books* Voices Out of the Air, BBC Book of Memories (contrib), It's My Belief; also: So That Was Spring (poems), Miracle at Midnight (play), A Scottish Childhood (contrib, vol 2); *Recreations* hill walking, music; *Clubs* Royal Cwlth Soc, Scottish Arts (hon memb); *Style—* Tom Fleming, Esq, CVO, OBE; ✉ c/o PFD, Drury House, 34/43 Russell Street, London WC2B 5HA (tel 020 7344 1010)

FLESCH, Michael Charles; QC (1983); s of Carl Franz Flesch, and Ruth, *née* Seligsohn (d 1987); *b* 11 March 1940; *Educ* Gordonstoun, UCL (LLB, 1st XV rugby, 1st VI tennis); *m* 2 Aug 1972, Gail, *née* Schrire; 1 da (Dina b 1973), 1 s (Daniel b 1976); *Career* called to the Bar Gray's Inn 1963 (Lord Justice Holker sr scholarship), Bencher 1993; Bigelow teaching fell Univ of Chicago 1963–64, pt/t lectr in revenue law UCL 1965–82, practice at Revenue Bar 1966– (chm Revenue Bar Assoc 1993–95), chm Taxation and Retirement Benefits Ctee of Bar Cncl 1985–93; govr Gordonstoun Sch 1976–96; *Recreations* all forms of sport; *Clubs* Arsenal FC, MCC, Brondesbury Lawn Tennis and Cricket; *Style—* Michael Flesch, Esq, QC; ✉ Gray's Inn Chambers, Gray's Inn, London WC1R 5JA (tel 020 7242 2642, fax 020 7831 9017)

FLESHER, Timothy James; CB (2002); s of James Amos Flesher (d 1994), of Haywards Heath, and Evelyn May Flesher; *b* 25 July 1949; *Educ* Haywards Heath GS, Hertford Coll Oxford (BA); *m* 1986, Margaret, da of John McCormack; 2 da (Siobhan Rachel b 30 June 1991, Catriona Eve b 19 Nov 1999); *Career* civil servant; lectr Cambs Coll of Arts and Technol 1972–74; Home Office: joined 1974, private sec to Min of State 1977–79, sec to Prisons Bd 1979–82, private sec to PM 1982–86, head of div Immigration Dept 1981–89, head Personnel Div 1989–91, head Probation Servs Div 1991–92, dir Admin Office for Standards in Educn 1992–94, dep DG Immigration and Nationality Directorate 1994–98; dep chm and DG Corporate Services Inland Revenue 1998–2003, dep chief Defence Logistics MOD 2003–07, chief of coporate services Defence Equipment and Support MOD 2007–; *Recreations* psephology, American football; *Style—* Timothy Flesher, Esq, CB; ✉ Defence Logisitcs Organisation, Management Suite, Spur 4, Block E, DLO HQ, Ensleigh, Bath BA1 5AB (tel 01225 467 125, e-mail tim.flesher811@mod.uk)

FLETCHER, Andrew Fitzroy Stephen; QC (2006); s of late (Maj) Fitzroy Fletcher, of Castle Cary, Somerset, and Brygid, *née* Mahon; *b* 20 December 1957; *Educ* Eton, Magdalene Coll Cambridge (MA); *m* 1 Sept 1984 (m dis 1999), Felicia, da of Maj John Philip Pagan Taylor (d 1986); 2 s (Thomas b 1987, James b 1989); *Career* 2 Lt Welsh Gds 1976; called to the Bar Inner Temple 1980; Freeman City of London 1986, Liveryman Worshipful Co of Grocers 1994 (Freeman 1986); *Recreations* travel, real tennis, reading; *Clubs* Boodle's, Pratt's, MCC; *Style—* Andrew Fletcher, Esq, QC; ✉ 3 Verulam Buildings, Gray's Inn, London WC1R 5NT (tel 020 7831 8441, e-mail afletcher@3vb.com)

FLETCHER, Prof Anthony John; s of John Molyneux Fletcher (d 1986), and Isabel Clare (Delle), *née* Chenevix-Trench; *b* 24 April 1941; *Educ* Wellington, Merton Coll Oxford (MA); *m* 1, 29 July 1967 (m dis 1999), Tresna Dawn, da of Charles Henry Railton Russell; 2 s (Crispin b 1970, Dickon b 1972); m 2, 6 Sept 2006, Brenda Joan, da of Richard Burdon Knibbs; *Career* history teacher King's Coll Sch Wimbledon 1964–67, successively lectr, sr lectr then reader Dept of History Univ of Sheffield 1967–81, prof Dept of History Univ of Durham 1987–95, prof Dept of History Univ of Essex 1995–2000, dir and gen ed Victoria County History Univ of London 2001–03; Leverhulme res fell 1999–2000; pres Ecclesiastical History Soc 1996–97; vice-pres Royal Hist Soc 1997–2001; auditor HEQC 1994–97; Quality Assurance Gp (QAA) 1997–2001, (chair Hist Benchmarking Gp 1998); FRHistS; *Books* Tudor Rebellions (1967), A County Community in Peace and War: Sussex 1600–1660 (1975), The Outbreak of the English Civil War (1981), Order and Disorder in Early Modern England (ed with J Stevenson, 1985), Reform in the Provinces (1986), Religion, Culture and Society in Early Modern Britain (ed jtly, 1994), Gender, Sex and Subordination in England 1500–1800 (1995), Childhood in Question (ed with S Hussey, 1999); *Recreations* theatre, music, opera, walking, gardening; *Style—* Prof Anthony Fletcher; ✉ School House, South Newington, Banbury, Oxfordshire OX15 4JJ (tel 01295 720717)

FLETCHER, Rt Rev Colin William; *see:* Dorchester, Bishop of

FLETCHER, Duncan Andrew Gwynne; OBE (2006); s of Desmond John Hurst Fletcher (d 1979), and Mary Gwynne, *née* Auld; *b* 27 September 1948, Salisbury (now Harare), Zimbabwe (took British citizenship 2005); *m* 14 Aug 1971, Marina Patricia; 1 s (Michael Desmond b 12 March 1975), 1 da (Nicola Marina b 1 Aug 1978); *Career* cricketer; Zimbabwe 1969–84 (capt 1979–83, capt of 1983 World Cup side (man of match when Zimbabwe beat Australia), Zimbabwe Sportsman of Year 1983); formerly coach Western Province (South Africa) and Glamorgan CCC, coach England cricket team 1999–2007; *Recreations* golf; *Style—* Duncan Fletcher, Esq, OBE

FLETCHER, Giles; s of Thomas Simons Fletcher (d 1985; nephew of 1 Earl Attlee, KG, OM, CH, PC), of Nunton, Wilts, and Janet, *née* Bigg (d 1987); *b* 12 August 1936; *Educ* Marlborough; *m* 18 Jan 1964, Jennifer Marion Edith, da of Sir Eric Cecil Heygate Salmon, MC, DL (d 1946), of London; 2 s (James b 1965, Timothy b 1974), 1 da (Alice b 1967); *Career* Fletcher and Partners: ptnr 1964–76, senior ptnr 1977–2001; chm of govrs Godolphin Sch 2000–; treas: Southern Cathedrals Festival, Salisbury Cathedral Girl Choristers' Fund; tstee Charitable Tsts; churchwarden; FCA 1961; *Recreations* hill walking, English and French cathedrals and churches; *Style—* Giles Fletcher, Esq; ✉ Apple Tree House, Middle Woodford, Salisbury SP4 6NG (tel 01722 782329, e-mail gilesfletcher@ukonline.co.uk)

FLETCHER, Ian Macmillan; s of John Malcolm Fletcher, JP (d 2004), of Gourock, Scotland, and Jane Ann Cochran Fletcher (d 1980); *b* 16 February 1948; *Educ* Greenock Acad, Univ of Glasgow (LLB); *m* 15 Jan 1977, Jennifer Margaret (d 2007), da of Capt John Brown William Daly, MN (d 1972), of Glasgow; 2 da (Elizabeth Jane b 4 Aug 1978, Eleanor Kathleen b 21 Aug 1985), 1 s (Richard John Malcolm b 13 Jan 1980); *Career* admitted slr: Scotland 1971, England 1978; asst slr Richards Butler 1977–79; ptnr: MacRoberts 1980–87, Richards Butler 1987–99, Stephenson Harwood 1999–; authorised insolvency practitioner; former co sec Chilton Brothers Ltd; gen counsel and co sec NIRAH Hldgs Ltd 2007–; memb Cncl: Insolvency Lawyers Assoc Ltd 1989–2001 (past pres), Law Soc of Scotland 1992–2001 (currently convener Insolvency Slrs' Ctee), Assoc of Business Recovery Professionals (R3) 1994–2002; memb: Law Soc, Law Soc of Scotland, Soc WS, Int Bar Assoc (memb Ctee J Section on Business Law), Soc of Scottish Lawyers London (past pres), DTI Insolvency Regulation Working Party 1996–98, City of London Slrs Co (formerly vice-chm Insolvency Law Sub-Ctee); WS, LTCL, LRAM, ARCO, MInstD, FABRP; *Books* The Law and Practice of Receivership in Scotland (jtly, 1987, 3 edn 2005), Insolvency and Finance in the Transportation Industry (jtly, 1993), The Law and Practice of Corporate Administrations (jtly, 1994, 2 edn 2004), Guide to Transnational Insolvency (jt ed, 1999); *Recreations* music, golf, swimming; *Clubs* Caledonian, Gog Magog Golf (Cambridge); *Style*— Ian Fletcher, Esq, WS; ✉ 1 St Paul's Churchyard, London EC4M 8SH (tel 020 7329 4422, fax 020 7003 8464, e-mail ian.fletcher@shlegal.com or ianmfletcher@btinternet.com)

FLETCHER, Janis Richardson (Jan); OBE; *Career* entrepreneur, int property investor and developer, restaurateur, pharmaceutical and health food manufacturer and retailer; chm and financial interests in: Montpellier Estates Gp 1983–, Unique Restaurants Ltd 1984–, BHM Health Gp 1984–; memb: Women's Network 1985–, Int Businesswomen's Forum, Health Food Managers Assoc (HFMA); Veuve Clicquot Business Woman of the Year 1994, Yorkshire Woman of the Year 1995, BusinessAge Top 40 under 40 Award 1995; *Recreations* horse racing, flying, skiing and water skiing, fitness training, entertaining, business; *Style*— Ms Jan Fletcher, OBE; ✉ Montpellier Estates Group, Montpellier House, 4 Cold Bath Road, Harrogate, North Yorkshire HG2 0NQ (tel 01423 877900, fax 01423 877901)

FLETCHER, Jo(anna) Louise (GOULD-); da of Colin Adrian Gould-Fletcher, of London, and Edwina Charlotte, *née* Dean; *Educ* Queen Elizabeth's Sch Faversham; *m* 20 May 2005, Ian Charles Drury; *Career* The Whitstable Times & Kentish Observer 1978–81 (jr reporter, sr reporter, film critic); sr reporter: The Hillingdon Mirror 1981–82, The Middlesex Advertiser & Gazette 1982–83, The Ealing Gazette 1983; freelance journalist 1983–88, film critic and columnist News of the World 1991–93 (joined 1988); conslt ed: Headline Book Publishing plc 1986–88, Mandarin Books 1988–91, Pan Books 1991–94; science fiction publisher Victor Gollancz Ltd 1994–, contributing ed Science Fiction Chronicle NY 1982–; sometime guest lectr UCLA and Loyola USA, specialist tutor DipHE Univ of E London; memb: Bd World Fantasy Convention 1979–, Bd World Fantasy Awards Administration, World Horror Convention 1989–91; tstee: Horror Writers' Assoc 1989–99, Tony Godwin Memorial Tst, Richard Evans Fund; memb: NUJ 1979, Science Fiction and Fantasy Writers of America 1987; Karl Edward Wagner British Fantasy Award 1997, The World Fantasy Award 2002, GOH World Horror Convention 2002; *Books* Gaslight & Ghosts (ed, 1988), Horror At Halloween (ed, 1995), Secret City: Strange Tales of London (1997), Shadows of Light and Dark (1998); *Recreations* science fiction, ghost writing, fantasy and horror, book collecting, singing; *Style*— Ms Jo Fletcher; ✉ 24 Pearl Road, Walthamstow, London E17 4Q2 (tel 020 8521 3034, e-mail fletcherove@hotmail.com)

FLETCHER, John W S; *Educ* Uppingham, Teesside Poly (H Dip Civil and Structural Engrg); *m* 1964, Jacqueline; 2 s, 1 da; *Career* Cleveland Bridge and Engineering Company (acquired by Cementation 1968, pt of Trafalgar House 1970): joined as trainee civil engr 1959, dir 1968–75, md 1975–82, divnl md 1982; mktg and business devpt dir Kvaerner ASA (acquired Trafalgar House plc 1996) and dir various subsid cos, memb Mgmnt Bd Kvaerner ASA and chm and md Kvaerner Corporate Development Ltd until 1999; chm: GEI International plc, Gammon Construction Ltd, Heavylift Aviation Holdings Ltd, Trafalgar House Construction (India) Ltd, Foster Stockbroking Pty Ltd; currently dir: FF Financial Services Ltd, Somerley China Associates Ltd; exec vice-chm Construction Supervision Ctee Beijing 2008 Olympics Nat Stadium; *Recreations* sailing; *Style*— John W S Fletcher, CBE

FLETCHER, Prof John Walter James; s of Roy Arthur Walter Fletcher, MBE (d 1994), of Sherborne, Dorset, and Eileen Alice, *née* Beane (d 2002); *b* 23 June 1937; *Educ* Yeovil Sch, Trinity Hall Cambridge (BA, MA), Univ of Toulouse (MPhil, PhD); *m* 14 Sept 1961, Beryl Sibley, da of William Stanley Connop (d 1963), of Beckenham, Kent; 1 da (Harriet b 1972), 2 s (Hilary b 1976, Edmund b 1978); *Career* lectr in English Univ of Toulouse 1961–64, lectr in French Univ of Durham 1964–66; UEA: lectr in French 1966–68, reader in French 1968–69, prof of comparative literature 1969–89, pro-vice-chllr 1974–79, prof of European literature 1989–98, emeritus prof 1998–; hon sr res fell in French Univ of Kent 1997–; memb: Soc of Authors, Translators' Assoc; *Books* The Novels of Samuel Beckett (1964), Samuel Beckett's Art (1967), New Directions in Literature (1968), Claude Simon and Fiction Now (1975), Novel and Reader (1980), Alain Robbe-Grillet (1983), The Georgics (by Claude Simon, trans 1989, Scott Moncrieff prize for translation from French 1990), The Red Cross and the Holocaust (trans 1999), About Beckett (2003); *Recreations* food and wine, listening to Monteverdi and Schubert; *Style*— Prof John Fletcher; ✉ School of European Culture and Languages, University of Kent, Canterbury CT2 7NF (tel 01227 764000, fax 01227 823641, e-mail jwjf@kent.ac.uk)

FLETCHER, Kim Thomas; s of Jack Fletcher, and Agnes, *née* Coulthwaite; *b* 17 September 1956; *Educ* Heversham GS, Hertford Coll Oxford (BA); *m* May 1991, Sarah Sands; 1 s (Rafe b 1992), 1 da (Matilda b 1994), 1 step s (Henry Sands b 1985); *Career* journalist; The Star Sheffield 1978–81, The Sunday Times 1981–86 (Home Affairs corr, Labour corr), The Daily Telegraph 1986–87, The Sunday Telegraph 1988–98, ed Independent on Sunday 1998–99, editorial dir Hollinger Telegraph New Media 2000–03; conslt ed The Daily Telegraph 2001–03, editorial dir Telegraph Gp Ltd 2003–05; jt Reporter of the Year 1982; *Recreations* football, theatre; *Clubs* Groucho; *Style*— Kim Fletcher, Esq

FLETCHER, Malcolm Stanley; MBE (1982); s of Harold Fletcher, and Clarice Fletcher; *b* 25 February 1936; *Educ* Manchester Grammar, Univ of Manchester (BSc), Univ of London (MSc), Imperial Coll London (DIC); *m* 21 Aug 1965, Rhona Christina; 2 da (Sarah b 1966, Rachael b 1972), 1 s (Lawrence b 1968); *Career* asst site engr (Dokan Dam Iraq) Binnie, Deacon & Gourlay 1957–60, site engr (Thelwall Viaduct M6) Raymond International 1960–61, engr and site mangr G Dew & Co Contractors 1961–65, resident engr (New Jhelum Bridge Pakistan) Donovan Lee & Partners 1965–67, chm Sir William Halcrow & Partners Ltd 1991–96 (joined 1968); memb: Structural Ctee CIRIA 1979–82, Prestressed Concrete Ctee Concrete Soc 1980–84; chm Structures Steering Gp Civil Engrg Science and Engrg Res Cncl 1984–89, memb Cncl Assoc of Consulting Engrs 1988– (chm Highways Panel 1988–91); author of numerous articles in various pubns; FREng 1993, FICE; *Projects with Sir William Halcrow & Partners* chief asst engr Giuliana Bridge Libya 1968–70, resident engr Benghazi Corniche Project Libya 1970–72, sr rep Libya 1972–74; project engr: based UK 1974–77 (work incl Al Garhoud Bridge UAE, Sharjah Airport Interchange Bridge UAE and Wayaya Bridge Oman), River Orwell Bridge 1977–82, Al Kadan Bridge Yemen 1978–79, Malaysia 1980–85, Monnow Bridge Monmouth 1983–84; team ldr: Karnali Bridge Nepal 1984–85, Dartford Bridge 1986–91; project dir: Constantius Bridge Hexham 1986–87, Town Ham Viaduct Glos 1986–87, Blue Nile Bridge Ethiopia 1988–90, Thames Bridge 1988–, second Severn Bridge 1990–; memb Technical Advsy Bd Lantau Fixed Crossing Hong Kong 1991–; *Recreations* cycling; *Style*— Malcolm Fletcher, Esq, MBE, FREng; ✉ Halcrow Group Ltd, Burderop Park, Swindon SN4 0QD (tel 01793 812479, fax 01793 812089)

FLETCHER, Martin Anthony; s of Anthony Travers Nethersole Fletcher, of Brandeston, Suffolk, and Nancy Evelyn, *née* Scott (d 1994); *b* 7 July 1956; *Educ* Uppingham, Univ of Edinburgh, Univ of Pennsylvania (MA); *m* 10 Oct 1981, Catherine Jane, *née* Beney; 1 s (Barnaby Martin b 12 April 1986), 2 da (Hannah Catherine b 2 June 1984, Imogen Nancy b 26 April 1989); *Career* journalist; North Herts Gazette 1980–82, Daily Telegraph 1982–83; The Times: lobby corr 1986–89, Washington corr 1989–92, US ed 1992–; *Books* The Good Caff Guide (1980), Almost Heaven (2000); *Recreations* tennis, squash, skiing, children; *Style*— Martin Fletcher, Esq; ✉ 3236 Juniper Lane, Falls Church, VA 22044, USA (tel 00 1 703 534 2953); The Times of London, 529 14th Street, NW, Suite 1040, Washington DC 20045, USA (tel 00 1 202 347 7659)

FLETCHER, Michael; s of Richard Fletcher (d 1990), of Cardiff, and Catherine, *née* Thomas (d 1981); *b* 11 March 1945; *Educ* Whitchurch GS Cardiff, AA Sch of Arch (AADipl); *m* 1, 1969 (m dis 1982), Lesley Saunders; 1 s (Luke Fletcher b 1973), 1 da (Daisy Fletcher b 1977); m 2, 1990, Malory Massey; 1 da (Vita Massey Fletcher b 1992); *Career* architect; Farrell Grimshaw Architects 1970–72, assoc Wolff Olins design consultancy 1972–78, fndr ptnr Fletcher Priest Architects 1978–, fndr Fletcher Priest Bösl (German office) 1993–; RIBA: memb Cncl 1993–99, chm Clients Advsy Serv 1994–99, vice-chm London Region 1996, vice-pres client and consumer affrs 1997; RIBA 1972, FIMgt 1973; *Awards* Civic Tst commendation (for Babmaes St offices) 1989, Br Cncl of Offices Bldg of the Year Award and Br Inst of Facilities Mgmnt Bldg of the Year Award for Powergen offices 1996, and for Leo Burnett's offices 1997; *Recreations* water sports; *Style*— Michael Fletcher, Esq; ✉ Fletcher Priest Architects, 23 Heddon Street, London W1B 4RA (tel 020 7439 8621, fax 020 7439 8526, e-mail m.fletcher@fletcherpriest.com, website www.fletcherpriest.com)

F

FLETCHER, Sheriff Michael John; s of Walter Fletcher (d 1992), and Elizabeth, *née* Pringle (d 1986); *b* 5 December 1945; *Educ* Dundee HS, Univ of St Andrews (LLB); *m* 19 Oct 1968, Kathryn Mary, da of John Bain, and Helen *née* Gorrie; 2 s (Christopher Michael b 13 Sept 1971, Mark Richard b 11 March 1977); *Career* apprentice slr Kirk Mackie and Elliot Edinburgh 1966–68; slr (ptnr): Ross Strachan & Co Dundee 1968–88, Hendry & Fenton Dundee 1988–92, Miller Hendry Dundee 1992–94; ed Scot Civil Law Reports 1999–; sheriff: S Strathclyde Dumfries and Galloway (at Dumfries) 1994–99, Lothian and Borders (at Edinburgh) 1999–2000, Tayside Central and Fife (at Perth) 2000–; memb Sheriff Court Rules Cncl 2002–; *Publications* Delictual Damages (co-author); *Recreations* golf, gardening; *Style*— Sheriff Michael Fletcher; ✉ Sheriff Chambers, Tay Street, Perth PH2 8NL

FLETCHER, (Peter) Neil; s of Alan Fletcher, of Thurnby, Leics (d 2007), and Ruth Fletcher (d 1961); *b* 5 May 1944; *Educ* Wyggeston Boys' GS Leicester, City of Leeds Coll of Educn, Univ of London (BA), London Business Sch (MBA 1994); *m* 9 Sept 1967, Margaret Mary, da of Anthony Gerald Monaghan (d 1967); 2 s (Ben b 25 May 1971, Sam b 18 July 1974); *Career* teacher Leeds 1966–68; lectr in further educn: Leeds 1969–70, Harrow 1970–73, Merton 1973–76; educn offr (and head Educn Dept) NALGO 1991–93 (princ admin offr 1976–91), dir strategic projects UNISON 1994–95 (educn offr 1993–94), mgmnt conslt 1995–98 and 2003–; head of educn, culture and tourism Local Govt Assoc 1998–2003; cncllr London Borough of Camden 1978–86 (dep ldr 1982–84); ILEA: memb 1979–90, chm Further and Higher Educn Sub-Ctee 1981–87, ldr 1987–90; chm: Assoc of Metropolitan Authorities Educn Ctee 1987–90 (memb 1981–90), Cncl of Local Educn Authorities 1987–90; govr: Penn Sch Bucks 1985–2006, London Inst 1985–99, LSE 1990–2001; chair of govrs City Literary Inst 2003– (govr 1996–); FRSA 1989; hon fell Coll of Preceptors 1990; *Recreations* cooking, walking, theatre, cricket, football; *Clubs* Royal Over-Seas League; *Style*— Neil Fletcher, Esq; ✉ 42 Narcissus Road, London NW6 1TH (tel 020 7435 5306, mobile 07775 841427, e-mail neil.fletcher5544@ukonline.co.uk)

FLETCHER, Dr (Archibald) Peter; s of Walter Archibald Fletcher (d 1970), and Dorothy Mabel Fletcher; *b* 24 December 1930; *Educ* Kingswood Sch Bath, London Hosp Med Coll, UCL, St Mary's Hosp Med Sch, MB BS (London), PhD (London); *m* 1972, Patricia Elizabeth Samson, *née* Marr; 3 s, 2 da; *Career* sr lectr in chemical pathology St Mary's Hosp London 1967–70, head of biochemistry American Nat Red Cross 1970–73, princ med offr and med assessor to Ctee on Safety of Medicines 1977, chief scientific offr and sr princ med offr DHSS 1978, res physician Upjohn Int 1978–80, sr med offr DHSS 1978–79; currently ptnr Pharma Services International and conslt to pharmaceutical industry; ptnr Documenta Biomedica, med dir IMS International, dir PMS International Ltd; *Publications* numerous papers in scientific and med jls on: glycoproteins, physical chemistry, metabolism of blood cells, safety evaluation of new drugs; *Recreations* gardening, cooking; *Clubs* Wig and Pen, Royal Society of Medicine; *Style*— Dr Peter Fletcher

FLETCHER, Philip John; CBE (2006); s of late Alan Philip Fletcher, QC, and Annette Grace, *née* Wright; *b* 2 May 1946; *Educ* Marlborough, Trinity Coll Oxford (MA); *m* 1977, Margaret Anne, *née* Boys; 2 da (Helen b 1978 d 1989, Sarah b 1982); *Career* DOE: joined 1968, dir Central Fin 1986–89, dir (grade 3) Planning & Devpt Control 1990–93, chief exec PSA Services and Property Holdings 1993–94, dep sec (grade 2) Cities and Countryside 1994–95; receiver for Metropolitan Police District 1996–2000; DG Water Services 2000–06, chm Ofwat 2006–; memb Archbishop's Cncl C of E 2007–; *Style*— Philip Fletcher, CBE; ✉ OFWAT, Centre City Tower, 7 Hill Street, Birmingham B5 4UA (tel 0121 625 1300, fax 0121 625 1348, e-mail philip.fletcher@ofwat.gsi.gov.uk)

FLETCHER, Phillip Douglas; s of Herbert Fletcher, and Mona Fletcher; *b* 16 September 1957, Barbados; *Educ* Georgetown Univ (Bachelor of Science in Foreign Service (BSFS)), Fletcher Sch of Law and Diplomacy Tufts Univ (MA), Univ of California Berkeley (JD); *m* 1984, Elena; 1 s (Phillip b 1991), 2 da (Emily b 1995, Sarah b 1996); *Career* slr specialising in project finance; Milbank, Tweed, Hadley & McCloy LLP: assoc 1983–92, ptnr 1993–, managing ptnr Europe 1995–; *Clubs* Roehampton; *Style*— Phillip Fletcher, Esq; ✉ Milbank, Tweed, Hadley & McCloy LLP, 10 Gresham Street, London EC2V 7JD (tel 020 7615 3002, e-mail pfletcher@milbank.com)

FLETCHER, Robin Charles; s of Brian and Elaine Fletcher; *b* 11 February 1966; *Educ* Rugby, South Glamorgan Inst (NCTJ), Univ of Glamorgan (MBA), Cardiff Univ (MPhil); *Career* reporter Birmingham Post and Mail 1984–89, sr ed Midland Weekly Newspapers and ed Solihull News 1990–92; ed: Northampton Chronicle and Echo 1992–94, West Lancashire Evening Gazette 1994–95, Wales on Sunday 1996, South Wales Echo 1996–2001; communications dir Trinity Mirror Regionals 2002–03; founding dir Reflex Business Servs Ltd 2003–; dir: Northampton Mercury Co Ltd 1994, Blackpool Gazette & Herald Ltd 1994–95; Guild of Editors: memb 1993–, vice-chm Gen Purposes Ctee 1996, hon sec S Wales region 1996 and 1999 (pres 1997–98 and 1999–2001); media advsr Wales Advsy Bd Busines In the Community 2001–03; non-exec dir Williams Ross Ltd 2006–, dir Five Valleys Business Network Ltd 2007; memb Employment Support Ctee Blackpool Fylde and Wyre Soc for the Blind 1995–, memb Wales Nat Ctee Wooden Spoon Soc 1999–2000; highly commended Regional Ed of the Year Newspaper Focus Awards 1994; memb Br Assoc of Communicators in Business; hon fell Univ of Wales Inst Cardiff; FRSA 1999, MInstD; *Recreations* squash, reading, writing, country walking, piano composition; *Style*— Robin Fletcher, Esq; ✉ Reflex Business Services, Solstar House,

11 Blackwell Close, Stonehouse, Gloucestershire GL10 2HF (tel 01453 821500, e-mail robinfletcher@reflexservices.com)

FLETCHER, Prof Roger; s of Harry Fletcher (d 1942), and Alice, *née* Emms (d 1996); *b* 29 January 1939; *Educ* Huddersfield Coll, Univ of Cambridge (MA), Univ of Leeds (PhD); *m* 23 Sept 1963, Mary Marjorie, da of Charlie Taylor (d 1970), of Harrogate; 2 da (Jane Elizabeth b 17 Nov 1968, Sarah Anne b 13 Sept 1970); *Career* lectr Univ of Leeds 1963–69, princ scientific offr AERE Harwell 1969–73; Univ of Dundee: sr lectr and reader 1973–84, prof 1984–2005, emeritus prof 2005–; hon prof Univ of Edinburgh; FIMA, FRSE 1988, FRS 2003; *Books* Practical Methods of Optimization Vol I (1980), Vol 2 (1981); *Recreations* hill walking, bridge; *Style*— Prof Roger Fletcher, FRS, FRSE; ✉ Department of Mathematics, University of Dundee, Dundee DD1 4HN (tel 01382 384490, e-mail fletcher@maths.dundee.ac.uk)

FLETCHER, Susan Jane; da of late Prof Leonard Fletcher, of Bakewell, Derbys, and Joan, *née* Edmunds; *b* 3 March 1950; *m* 30 Dec 1974, Nicholas W Stuart, CB, *qv*; 1 da (Emily Fletcher b 12 Sept 1983), 1 s (Alexander Fletcher b 1 Feb 1989); *Career* managing ed Sphere Books Ltd 1979–83, publishing dir MacDonald & Co 1983–87, jt dep md Headline Book Publishing plc 1987–93, Hodder & Stoughton 1993–; *Style*— Ms Susan Fletcher; ✉ 181 Chevening Road, Queen's Park, London NW6 6DT; Hodder & Stoughton, Hodder Headline, 338 Euston Road, London NW1 3BH (tel 020 7873 6000, fax 020 7873 6024, e-mail susan.fletcher@hodder.co.uk)

FLETCHER, Winston; s of Albert Fletcher (d 1963), of London, and Bessie, *née* Miller (d 1955); *b* 15 July 1937; *Educ* Westminster City Sch, St John's Coll Cambridge (MA); *m* 14 June 1963, Jean, da of Alfred Brownston (d 1968), of Bristol; 1 da (Amelia b 1966), 1 s (Mathew b 1970 d 1996); *Career* dir Sharps Advertising 1964–69 (joined as trainee 1959), md MCR Advertising 1970; Fletcher Shelton Delaney: fndr 1974, md 1974–81, chm 1981–83; chm and chief exec Ted Bates UK 1983–85; chm: Delaney Fletcher Delaney 1985–89, Delaney Fletcher Bozell 1989–96, Bozell Europe 1989–97, Bozell UK Group 1997–99, Brook Lapping Productions 1997–2002, World Advertising Research Centre 1998–99; dir: Hemscott plc 2000–04, Delaney Lund Knox Warren & Partners 2001–05; regular author for nat business and advertising trade press; visiting prof: Lancaster Univ Mgmnt Sch, Univ of Westminster; memb Cncl Advertising Standards Authy 1986–93, chm Advertising Standards Bds of Fin 2000–; vice-pres History of Advtg Tst 2003–; chm: The Advertising Assoc 1993–97, Debating Group (Parly forum for mktg debate) 1998–2000, Knightsbridge Assoc 2004–; dir Rationalist Assoc 2007–; tstee Open Coll of the Arts 1990–95, tstee Barnado's 2000– (chm London and SE region 2002–07), dep chm Central London Training and Enterprise Cncl 1991–95; FIPA (pres 1989–91), FRSA, FCAM; *Books* The Admakers (1972), Teach Yourself Advertising (1978), Meetings, Meetings (1983), Commercial Breaks (1984), Superefficiency (1986), The Manipulators (1988), Creative People (1990), A Glittering Haze (1992), How to Capture the Advertising High Ground (1994), Advertising Advertising (1999), Tantrums & Talent (1999), Beating the 24/7 (2002), Keeping the Vision Alive (2005); *Recreations* reading, writing, arithmetic; *Clubs* Reform, Garrick, Royal Institution (memb Cncl 1997–, chm 1998–), Annabel's, Thirty (pres 1999–2000), Harry's, Groucho; *Style*— Winston Fletcher, Esq; ✉ 15 Montpelier Square, London SW7 1JU (tel 020 7584 5262); c/o ASBOF, 21 Berners Street, London W1T 3LP

FLETCHER ROGERS, Helen Susan; da of Peter Alexander Stewart (d 1995), and Jessie Mary, *née* Sykes (d 1978); *b* 24 September 1941; *Educ* Greenhead HS Huddersfield, UCL; *m* 28 Sept 1972, David Geoffrey Fletcher Rogers, s of Murray Rowland Fletcher Rogers (d 1991); 2 s (Anthony, Jonathan); *Career* called to the Bar Gray's Inn 1965; PA Thomas & Co 1964–67; Kodak Ltd 1967–99 (Euro gen counsel 1995–99), Lawyers in Business 2001–06; non-exec dir: Tropix Healthcare Ltd 2001–, Keswick Timeshare Ltd 2001–; tstee Northwick Park Inst for Medical Research 1994–2006; vice-chm Northwick Park and St Mark's Hosp NHS Trust 1992–96; memb Advsy Cncl Br Inst of Int and Comparative Law 2001–, hon treas Ctee Bar Assoc for Commerce, Finance and Industry (BACFI); MInstD; *Books* Butterworths Encyclopaedia of Forms and Precedents Vol 16a (contrib on patents and designs); Microfilm and the Law; *Recreations* walking, working, theatre, music; *Clubs* Army and Navy; *Style*— Mrs Helen Susan Fletcher Rogers; ✉ Conway House, Furlong Lane, Totternhoe, Dunstable, Bedfordshire LU6 1QR (tel and fax 01582 472300)

FLEW, Prof Antony Garrard Newton; o s of Rev Dr R Newton Flew (d 1962); *b* 11 February 1923; *Educ* Kingswood Sch, SOAS Univ of London, St John's Coll Oxford (John Locke scholar, MA), Keele Univ (DLitt); *m* 1952, Annis Ruth Harty, da of Col Frank Donnison; 2 da; *Career* prof of philosophy: Keele Univ 1954–71, Calgary Univ 1972–73, Univ of Reading 1973–82, York Univ Toronto 1983–85; distinguished research fell Social Philosophy and Policy Centre Bowling Green State Univ 1986–91; fndr memb: Cncl of Freedom Assoc, Academic Cncl Adam Smith Inst, Educn Gp of the Centre for Policy Studies; *Books incl* Hume's Philosophy of Belief (1961), God and Philosophy (1967), Crime or Disease (1973), Sociology, Equality and Education (1976), The Presumption of Atheism (1976), A Rational Animal (1978), The Politics of Procrustes (1981), Darwinian Evolution (1984), Thinking about Social Thinking (1985), David Hume: Philosopher of Moral Science (1986), The Logic of Mortality (1987), Power to the Parents (1987), Equality in Liberty and Justice (1989), Atheistic Humanism (1993), Shephard's Warning (1994), How to Think Straight (1998), Equality in Liberty and Justice (2001), Social Life and Moral Judgement (2003); *Recreations* walking, house maintenance; *Style*— Prof Antony Flew; ✉ 26 Alexandra Road, Reading, Berkshire RG1 5PD (tel 0118 926 1848)

FLIGHT, Howard Emerson; s of Bernard Thomas Flight (d 1990), of Devon, and Doris Mildred Emerson, *née* Parker (d 1999); *b* 16 June 1948; *Educ* Brentwood Sch, Magdalene Coll Cambridge (MA), Univ of Michigan Business Sch (MBA); *m* 1973, Christabel Diana Beatrice, da of Christopher Paget Norbury (d 1975), of Worcs; 3 da (Catherine b 1975, Josephine b 1986, Mary Anne b 1988), 1 s (Thomas b 1978); *Career* jt md Guiness Flight Global Asset Mgmnt 1986–98, jt chm Investec Asset Mgmnt 1998–2003; chm: Speymill Property Managers Ltd 2005–, Ferranti Ltd 2005–, CIM Investment Mgmnt Ltd 2006–, Loudwater Press Ltd 2007–; dir: Investec Asset Mgmnt 2003–, Speymill Gp plc 2005–, re-Energy Gp plc 2005–, St Helens Capital plc 2006–, Westcliff Capital 2006–, Investec Global Strategy Fund Ltd, Panmure Gordon Ltd; non-exec dir Chromogenex plc 2007–; conslt: PIMA 2000–, Kinetic Ptnrs 2005–; MP (Cons) Arundel and S Downs 1997–2005 (Parly candidate (Cons) Bermondsey and Southwark both elections 1974); shadow economic sec to Treasy 1999–2001, shadow Paymaster Gen 2001–02, shadow chief sec to the Treasy 2002–04, dep chm Cons Pty and special envoy to the City of London 2004–05; chm EIS Assoc 2005–; cmmr Guernsey Financial Services Cmmn 2005–; govr Brentwood Sch; tstee: The Elgar Fndn, Africa Research Centre; Liveryman Carpenter's Co; FRSA; *Books* All You Need to Know About Exchange Rates (jtly, 1988); *Recreations* skiing, classical music, fruit farming; *Clubs* Carlton, Pratt's, Boodle's; *Style*— Howard Flight, Esq; ✉ Investec Asset Management Ltd, 2 Gresham Street, London EC2V 7QP (tel 020 7597 2112 or 020 7222 7559, fax 020 7597 2052, e-mail howard.flight@investecmail.com or hflight@btinternet.com)

FLINT, Prof Anthony Patrick Fielding; *b* 31 August 1943; *m* 1967 (m dis 1996), Chan Mun Kwun; 2 s; *Career* research fell Depts of Physiology and Obstetrics and Gynaecology Univ of Western Ontario 1969–72, sr research biochemist Dept of Obstetrics and Gynaecology Welsh Nat Sch of Med 1972–73, lectr Nuffield Dept of Obstetrics and Gynaecology Univ of Oxford 1973–77; AFRC: sr scientific offr 1977–79, princ scientific offr 1979–85, sr princ scientific offr 1985–87, visiting scientist 1987–95; dir Inst of Zoology Univ of London 1987–93, dir of science Zoological Soc 1987–93; prof of animal physiology Univ of Nottingham 1993–; memb numerous ctees and editorial bds; author of over 240 pubns in scientific journals; Medal Soc for Endocrinology 1985, Medal of Polish Physiological Soc 1990; memb: Biochemical Soc 1967, Soc for Endocrinology 1973, Soc for the Study of Fertility 1973, Blair-Bell Research Soc 1974, Physiological Soc 1979; FIBiol 1982; *Clubs* Zoological; *Style*— Prof Anthony Flint; ✉ School of BioSciences, University of Nottingham, Sutton Bonington, Loughborough, Leicestershire LE12 5RD (e-mail anthony.flint@nottingham.ac.uk)

FLINT, Caroline Louise; MP; da of late Wendy Flint, *née* Beasley; *b* 20 September 1961; *Educ* Twickenham Girls' Sch, Richmond Tertiary Coll, UEA (BA); *m* 1, (m dis); 1 s, 1 da; m 2, Phil Cole; 1 step s; *Career* mgmnt trainee GLC/ILEA 1984–85, policy offr ILEA 1985–87, head Women's Unit NUS 1988–89, equal opportunities offr Lambeth Cncl 1989–91, welfare and staff devpt offr Lambeth Cncl 1991–93, sr researcher/political offr GMB 1994–97, MP (Lab) Don Valley 1997–; PPS: to Peter Hain, MP, *qv* (at FCO then DTI) 1999–2001, to Rt Hon Dr John Reid, MP, *qv*, 2002–03; Parly under-sec of state Home Office 2003–05, Parly under-sec of state for public health 2005–06, min of state for public health Dept of Health 2006–; chair All-Pty Parly Gp on Childcare 1997–2003; parly advsr to Police Fedn for England and Wales 1999; memb: Educn and Employment Select Ctee 1997–99, PLP Health Ctee 2005–; pres Denaby United FC; chm Working for Childcare 1991–95 (memb 1989–); govr Strand-on-the-Green Sch Chiswick 1993–97; assoc ed Renewal 1995–2000 (memb Policy Advsy Bd 2000–01); memb: Fabian Soc, GMB; *Recreations* tennis, cinema, dancing, leisure time with family and friends; *Style*— Ms Caroline Flint, MP; ✉ House of Commons, London SW1A 0AA

FLINT, Charles John Raffles; QC (1995); *Career* called to the Bar 1975, jr counsel to the Crown (common law) 1991–95; *Style*— Charles Flint, Esq, QC; ✉ Blackstone Chambers, Temple, London EC4Y 9BW

FLINT, Prof Colin David; s of Oswald George Flint (d 1981), of London, and Maud Elisabeth, *née* Hayes (d 2004); *b* 3 May 1943; *Educ* Leyton HS, Imperial Coll London (BSc, DIC, PhD, DSc); *m* 3 Aug 1968, Florence Edna, da of Charles Cowin (d 1969), of Isle of Man; 2 s (Richard Charles b 6 March 1972, Peter David b 25 July 1974); *Career* NATO postdoctoral fell Univ of Copenhagen Denmark 1967–69, prof of chemistry Birkbeck Coll London 1981– (lectr 1969–76, reader chemical spectroscopy 1976–81, head of dept 1979–86), emeritus prof of chemistry Univ of London 2003–; visiting prof: Univ of Virginia USA 1982, Univ of Chile 1985, 1987, 1991 and 1994, Tech Univ of Graz Austria 1986 and 1989, Univ of Copenhagen 1988, Univ of Padova 1991, Univ of Graz 1995 and 1996; UK co-ordinator DFID-Chiang Mai Univ Thailand Water Resource Centre Project 1988–; author of about 200 pubns in learned jls; ARCS, FRSC, CChem; *Books* Vibronic Processes in Inorganic Chemistry (ed, 1989); *Recreations* swimming, travel; *Style*— Prof Colin Flint; ✉ 34 Woolhampton Way, Chigwell Row, Essex (tel 020 8500 6373, e-mail chigwell999@hotmail.com)

FLINT, David; s of David Flint, of Glasgow, and Dorothy, *née* Jardine; *b* 7 July 1955, Glasgow; *Educ* HS of Glasgow, Univ of Glasgow (LLB, LLM), Europa Inst Univ van Amsterdam (DiplCEI); *m* 27 Oct 1979, Marie, *née* Hepburn; 2 da (Jennifer b 22 June 1983, Aimée b 19 Sept 1990); *Career* MacRoberts slrs: asst Corp and Commercial Dept 1979–84, ptnr Corp and Commercial Dept 1984–, currently head Technology Media & Communications Law Gp; memb: Nominet UK Ind Experts Panel, Jt Working Party of Scot, Eng and Northern Irish Law Socs and Bars on Competition Law 1981, Corrs Panel Computer Law and Security Report; coordinator Infobank Current Comment Business Law Review 1997; chm: European Gp Scottish Lawyers 1985–95, Intellectual Property Sub-Ctee Int Business Law American Bar Assoc; NP 1980; licensed insolvency practitioner; memb: Law Soc of Scotland 1979, Insolvency Practitioners' Assoc 1990; assoc memb American Bar Assoc; FRSA 1998, FABRP 1998; *Publications* Liquidation in Scotland (1987, 2 edn 1990), MacRoberts Scottish Liquidation Handbook (3 edn 2004), Greens Scottish E-commerce Handbook (2000, and supplements); contrib on competition law to Stair Memorial Encyclopaedia and Halsbury's Laws of England; book chapters on data protection, insolvency, employee use of internet and e-mail; articles in legal, business and trade magazines; *Recreations* reading, music; *Style*— David Flint, Esq; ✉ MacRoberts, 152 Bath Street, Glasgow G2 4TB (tel 0141 332 9988, fax 0141 332 8886, e-mail df@macroberts.com)

FLINT, Douglas Jardine; CBE (2006); s of Prof David Flint, and Dorothy, *née* Jardine; *b* 8 July 1955; *Educ* Univ of Glasgow (BAcc), Harvard Business Sch (PMD); *m* 25 May 1984, Fiona Isobel Livingstone, *née* McMillan; 2 s (Jamie Livingstone b 3 May 1989, Stuart David b 19 Jan 1991), 1 da (Catriona Lindsay b 13 Aug 1992); *Career* KPMG (formerly Peat Marwick Mitchell & Co): articled clerk 1977–80, accountant 1980–88, ptnr 1988–95; gp fin dir HSBC Holdings plc 1995–; non-exec dir BP plc 2005–; memb: ACT 1996, UK Accounting Standards Bd; CA 1980; *Recreations* golf, tennis; *Clubs* Caledonian, Rye Golf, Sloane, Denham Golf; *Style*— Douglas Flint, Esq, CBE; ✉ HSBC Holdings plc, 8 Canada Square, London E14 5HQ (tel 020 7991 2881, fax 020 7992 4872)

FLINTER, Dr Frances Anne; *née* Morgan; *b* 31 January 1959, London; *Educ* City of London Sch for Girls, Guy's Hosp Med Sch (MD, MB BS); *m* 1979, David Flinter; 2 da; *Career* various jr dr posts Guy's Hosp and Westminster Children's Hosp, conslt clinical geneticist Guy's and St Thomas' NHS Tst 1994–, sr lectr in clinical genetics KCL 1994–2006, clinical dir Children's Services and Genetics Evelina Children's Hosp Guy's and St Thomas' NHS Fndn Tst 2000–; memb Human Genetics Cmmn; author of many pubns on clinical genetics (inherited renal diseases, prenatal diagnosis and preimplantation genetic diagnosis); Elizabeth Wherry Award for research into renal disease BMA 1992; FRCP, FRCPCH; *Recreations* classical music (pianist and viola player); *Clubs* Guy's and St Thomas's Consultants'; *Style*— Dr Frances Flinter; ✉ Genetics Department, 7th Floor, New Guy's House, Guy's Hospital, London SE1 9RT (tel 020 7188 4627, e-mail frances.flinter@gstt.nhs.uk)

FLINTOFF, Andrew; MBE (2006); s of Colin Flintoff, and Susan Flintoff; *b* 6 December 1977, Preston; *m* Rachael; 1 da (Holly b 6 Sept 2004), 1 s (Corey b 8 March 2006); *Career* professional cricketer with Lancashire CCC 1995–; England: 67 test matches, 127 one-day ints, 2 Twenty20 appearances, first team debut v South Africa 1998, one-day int debut v Pakistan 1998, memb team World Cup 1999, 2003 and 2007, memb squad Twenty20 World Cup 2007, memb team touring Pakistan and Sri Lanka 2000–01, Zimbabwe, India and NZ 2001–02, Bangladesh and Sri Lanka 2003, West Indies 2004, South Africa 2004–05, Pakistan 2005, Australia 2006–07; memb winning Ashes team 2005 (Man of the Series, Compton Miller Medal); One-Day Int Player of the Year Int Cricket Cncl (ICC) Awards 2004, Player of the Year Professional Cricketers' Assoc 2004 and 2005, Player of the Year (jt winner) ICC Awards 2005, BBC Sports Personality of the Year 2005; Freeman City of Preston 2005; *Books* Being Freddie: The Story So Far (2006, Tesco Sports Book of the Year); *Style*— Andrew Flintoff, Esq, MBE; ✉ c/o The England and Wales Cricket Board, Lord's Cricket Ground, St John's Wood, London NW8 8QZ

FLÖCKINGER, Gerda; CBE (1991); da of Karl Flöckinger (d 1950), of Austria, and Anna, *née* Frankl (d 1985); *b* 8 December 1927; *Educ* Maidstone Girls' GS, Dorchester Co HS, S Hampstead HS, St Martin's Sch of Art (NDD), Central Sch of Art; *m* 1954 (m dis 1962); *Career* jewellery designer/maker, lectr and photographer; emigrated from Innsbruck to London 1938, naturalised British subject 1946; fndr course in modern jewellery Hornsey Coll of Art 1962–68; work featured in 47 books, numerous pubns, articles, leaflets and catalogues, public lecture and book in series Pioneers of Modern Craft Crafts Cncl 1995; Goldsmiths' Hall Travel Award 1956; Freeman Worshipful Co of Goldsmiths 1998; *Solo*

Exhibitions Crafts Centre London 1968, V&A 1971, City of Bristol Museum and Art Gallery 1971, Dartington Cider Press Gallery 1977, V&A 1986, Solo Showcase Exhbn Crafts Cncl Shop at V&A 1991, Electrum Gallery London 2007; *Group Exhibitions* incl: Philadelphia Museum of Art, Norway, Tokyo, Expo Osaka, Ashmolean Museum, Künstlerhaus Vienna, Schmuckmuseum Pforzheim, Nat Museum of Wales, The Netherlands, ICA 1954–64, Arnolfini Gallery Bristol 1962–73, The Observer Jewellery Exhbn (Welsh Arts Cncl touring) 1973–74, Treasures of London (Goldsmiths' Hall London) 1976–77, Diamond Story (Electrum Gallery) 1977, Objects The V&A Collects (V&A) 1978, British Women's Art (House of Commons) 1981, Sotheby's Craft Exhbn (Sotheby's London) 1988, Ornamenta (Pforzheim Germany) 1989, British Jewellery (Crafts Cncl London) 1989, Christie's Amsterdam 1990, 20th Anniversary Exhbn (Electrum Gallery) 1991, What Is Jewellery? (Crafts Cncl) 1994, British Jewellery Exhbn (Mainz) 1995, British Master Goldsmiths (Goldsmiths' Hall London) 1997, Introducing Contemporary British Jewellery (Soc of Arts & Crafts Boston) 1998, Made to Wear: Creativity in Contemporary Jewellery (Central St Martins) 1998, Contemporary Applied Arts 1998, British Gold - Italian Gold (Scottish Gallery and Graziella Grasetto Gallery Studio Milan) 1998, Jewellery Moves (Royal Scottish Museum Edinburgh) 1998, Sofa (USA) 1998–2007, The Pleasures of Peace: Craft Art and Design in Britain 1939–68 (Sainsbury Centre for Visual Arts) 1999, 25 Years of Contemporary British Craft (Crafts Cncl) 1999, Treasures of the 20th Century (Goldsmiths' Hall London) 2000, Het Versierde Ego - Het Kunstjuweel in de 20ste EEUW (Antwerp) 2000, Paper Plastics Palladium and Pearls (Lesley Craze Gallery) 2000, The Ring (Mobilia Gallery Cambridge MA, Wustum Museum Racine WI and tour) 2001–, Int Art and Design Fair NY 2003, Love Story (Goldsmiths' Hall London) 2003, Collect (V&A) 2003–07, trio exhbn with Wendy Ramshaw and David Watkins (V&A) 2006; *Work in Public Collections* City of Bristol Museum and Art Gallery, Royal Museum of Scotland Edinburgh, Goldsmiths' Hall London, Crafts Cncl London, V&A, Castle Museum Nottingham, Schmuckmuseum Pforzheim Germany, Centre Pompidou Paris (slides); work also in many private collections internationally; *Representing Galleries* Electrum Gallery London, Mobilia Gallery Cambridge MA, Clare Beck at Adrian Sassoon; *Books* incl: Jewellery Concepts and Technology (1982), The Fontana Dictionary of Modern Thought (1984), Pioneers of Modern Craft (1997), Dictionary of Women Artists (1997), Contemporary Applied Arts - 50 Years of Craft (1998), Dictionnaire International Du Bijou (1998), Crafts in Britain in the 20th Century (1999), The Ring - Design Past and Present (1999), Design Sourcebook: Jewellery (1999), 25 Years of Crafts Council Shop at the V&A (1999), Jewels and Jewellery (by Clare Philips, 2004), New Directions in Jewellery (2005); *Recordings* The National Life Story Collection British Library Sound Archive (2000); *Recreations* gardening (hybridising Iris Germanica), growing camellias, Siamese cats, pistol shooting, sewing; *Clubs* Siamese Cat, British Iris Soc; *Style—* Gerda Flöckinger, CBE; ✉ c/o Crafts Council Islington, 44A Pentonville Road, London N1 9BY; c/o Electrum Gallery, 21 South Molton Street, London W1K 5QZ

FLOOD, David Andrew; s of Frederick Joseph Alfred Flood, of Selsey, W Sussex, and June Kathleen, *née* Alexander; *b* 10 November 1955; *Educ* Royal GS Guildford, St John's Coll Oxford (MA), Clare Coll Cambridge (PGCE); *m* 26 June 1976, Alayne Priscilla, da of late Maurice Ewart Nicholas, of Farnborough, Hants; 2 da (Olivia Kathryn b 1979, Annalisa Harriet b 1989), 2 s (Christopher Nicholas b 1982, Joshua Samuel b 1986); *Career* asst organist Canterbury Cathedral 1978–86, music master King's Sch Canterbury 1978–86; organist and master of choristers: Lincoln Cathedral 1986–88, Canterbury Cathedral 1988–; organist for: enthronement of Archbishop Runcie 1980, visit of Pope John Paul II 1982; musical dir for: enthronement of Archbishop Carey 1991, Lambeth Conf 1998, enthronement of Archbishop Williams 2003; asst dir Canterbury Choral Soc 1978–85, fndr and dir Canterbury Cantata Choir 1985–86; musical dir: Lincoln Choral Soc 1986–88, Canterbury Music Club 1984–86 and 1988–, Whitstable Choral Soc 1995–, Canterbury Singers 1996–99; visiting fell St John's Coll Durham 2007; hon sr memb Darwin Coll Univ of Kent; Hon DMus Univ of Kent 2002; FRCO 1976, memb Royal Soc of Musicians 1997; Hon FGCM 2000; *Recreations* travel, motoring, DIY; *Style—* Dr David Flood; ✉ 6 The Precincts, Canterbury, Kent CT1 2EE (tel 01227 865242, fax 01227 865222, e-mail davidf@canterbury-cathedral.org)

FLOOD, Debbie; da of Edward John Flood, and Barbara Margarete, *née* Houston; *b* 27 February 1980, Harrogate, N Yorks; *Educ* Univ of Reading (BSc); *Career* amateur rower; memb Leander Club; achievements incl: Bronze medal double sculls World Junior Championships 1998, Gold medal double sculls Under 23 World Championships 1999, Gold medal single sculls Under 23 World Championships 2000, winner double sculls World Cup 2002, winner quadruple sculls World Cup 2004, Silver medal quadruple sculls Olympic Games Athens 2004; indoor rowing: jr champion British Indoor Rowing Championships 1997, jr champion World Indoor Rowing Championships 1998, under 23 champion British Indoor Rowing Championships 1999; *Style—* Miss Debbie Flood

FLOOD, Michael Donovan (Mik); s of late Gp Capt Donovan John Flood, DFC, AFC, of Wyton, and Vivien Ruth, *née* Alison; *b* 7 May 1949; *Educ* St George's Coll Weybridge, Llangefni County Sch Anglesey; *m* 1, 1975 (m dis 1989), Julie, da of Paul Ward; 1 da (Amy Louise b 8 April 1976); m 2, 2001, Ionela, da of Constantin Niculae; *Career* fndr and artistic dir Chapter Arts Centre Cardiff 1970–81, devpt dir Baltimore Theater Project 1981–82, administrator Pip Simmons Theatre Gp 1982–83, freelance prodr 1983–85; dir: Watermans Arts Centre Brentford 1985–90, Inst of Contemporary Arts 1990–97; int arts and cultural policy conslt 1997–; chm: Bd London Electronic Arts 1997–2001, The Lux Centre for Film, Video and Digital Arts 1998–2001; pres Informal European Theatre Meeting (IETM) 1998–2002; prodr: Woyzeck (open air prodn with Pip Simmons Theatre Gp) 1976, Deadwood (open air prodn with Son et Lumière Theatre Gp, Time Out award winner) 1986, Offshore Rig (open air prodn with Bow Gamelan Ensemble) 1987; dir Pip Simmons Theatre Gp 1977–81, co-fndr Nat Assoc of Arts Centres 1976; memb: Assessment Ctee West Midlands Arts Assoc 1976, Film Ctee Welsh Arts Cncl 1976–80, Exec Ctee SE Wales Arts Assoc 1980–81, Ct Royal Coll of Art 1990–97, Panel of Assessors Arts Cncl of England Arts for Everyone Lottery Fund 1997–2001, Bd European Forum for Arts and Heritage 2004–, Bd Thames Festival 2004–; awarded HRH Queen Elizabeth II Silver Jubilee Medal for outstanding services to the arts and community 1977; *Recreations* sailing, ichthyology; *Clubs* Groucho; *Style—* Mik Flood, Esq; ✉ 1 Marshall House, Dorncliffe Road, London SW6 5LF (tel 020 7736 8668, fax 020 7384 3770, e-mail mik@mikflood.com, website www.mikflood.com)

FLOOD, Thomas Oliver (Tom); CBE (2004); s of Thomas Flood (d 1988), of Newbridge, Co Kildare, and Elizabeth, *née* O'Byrne; *b* 21 May 1947; *Educ* Dominican Coll Newbridge, UCD (BA); *Partner* Paul Cornes (civil partnership, 2006); *Career* A E Herbert Ltd (machine tools) 1969–70, W S Atkins (consulting engrs) 1970–72; 3M United Kingdom plc: Market Research Dept 1972–73, mktg Industrial Products 1973–75, mktg Packaging Systems Gp 1975–77, sales mangr Strapping Systems 1977–79, sales and mktg mangr Decorative Packing 1979–82, gp mktg mangr Packaging Systems 1982–86; BTCV (formerly British Tst for Conservation Volunteers): mktg dir 1986–90, dep chief exec 1990–92, chief exec 1992–; memb: UK Biodiversity Steering Gp, Environment Advsy Task Force Gp, New Deal Taskforce, Home Office Working Gp on Barriers to Volunteering, British Citizenship 1999, Home Office Ctee on Public Liability, Home Office Ctee Governance Strategy Gp 2003, Groundwork Light Touch Review ODPM 2004, Cleaner, Safer, Greener Communities CRG 2004–; FRSA 1996, FCIM (FIMgt 1996); *Recreations* cinema, cooking, opera, theatre, walking; *Style—* Tom Flood, Esq, CBE; ✉ BTCV, 80 York Way, London N1 9AG (tel 020 7843 4298, fax 020 7278 8967, e-mail t.flood@btcv.org.uk)

FLORENCE, Prof Alexander Taylor; CBE (1994); s of Alexander Charles Gerrard Florence (d 1985), and Margaret, *née* Taylor (d 2003); *b* 9 September 1940; *Educ* Queen's Park Sch Glasgow, Univ of Glasgow (BSc, PhD), Royal Coll of Science and Technol, Univ of Strathclyde (DSc); *m* 1, 1964 (m dis 1995), Elizabeth Catherine, *née* McRae; 2 s (Graham b 1966, Alastair b 1969), 1 da (Gillian b 1972); m 2, 2000, Dr Florence Madsen, da of Bernard Madsen, of Paris; *Career* prof of pharmacy Univ of Strathclyde 1976–88 (lectr in pharmaceutical chemistry 1966–72, sr lectr 1972–76), dean Sch of Pharmacy Univ of London 1989–2006 (prof emeritus 2006–); pres European Assoc Faculties of Pharmacy 1997–2001, pres Controlled Release Soc 2002–03, vice-pres Federation Internationale Pharmaceutique 1998–2000; memb Ctee on Safety of Meds 1982–98 (chm Sub-Ctee on Chemistry Pharmacy and Standards 1989–98); Hon Dr: Hoshi Univ Tokyo 2003, Univ of Strathclyde 2004, Danish Univ of Pharmaceutical Sciences Copenhagen 2006, UEA 2007; FRSC 1977, FRSE 1987, FRPharmS 1987, FRSA 1989; *Books* Solubilization by Surface Active Agents (with P H Elworthy and C B Macfarlane, 1968), Surfactant Systems (with D Attwood, 1983), Physicochemical Principles of Pharmacy (with D Attwood, 2006); *Recreations* music, painting, writing; *Style—* Prof Alexander Florence, CBE, FRSE; ✉ Newlands, 23 North Esk Road, Edzell, Angus DD9 7TW (tel 01356 648833, e-mail ataylorflorence@aol.com); La Providence G, 7 rue Sincaire, Nice 06300, France (tel 00 33 4 93 13 03 97)

FLORENCE, Dr Peter; MBE (2005); s of Norman Florence (d 1996), and Rhoda Lewis; *b* 4 October 1964, Kingston; *Educ* Ipswich Sch, Jesus Coll Cambridge (MA), Univ de Paris-Sorbonne; *m* 12 Oct 1996, Becky Shaw; 4 s (Isaac b 25 Aug 1997, Ru b 13 Nov 2000, Morgan, Jacob (twins) b 10 March 2005); *Career* dir Hay Festival 1988– (also Hay Festival Cartagena, Hay Festival Segovia, Hay Festival California, The Orange Word London); advsr: FLIP (Festa Literaria Internacional de Parati) Brazil, Festival Literatura Mantova; Hon DLitt Univ of Glamorgan; fell Hereford Art Coll, creative fell Univ of Wales Bangor; *Recreations* family, food, walking; *Clubs* Hawks' (Cambridge), Groucho; *Style—* Dr Peter Florence, MBE; ✉ The Guardian Hay Festival, 25 Lion Street, Hay-on-Wye HR3 5AD

FLOUD, Prof Sir Roderick Castle; kt (2005); s of Bernard Francis Castle Floud (d 1967), and Ailsa, *née* Craig (d 1967); *b* 1 April 1942; *Educ* Brentwood Sch, Wadham Coll Oxford (MA), Nuffield Coll Oxford (DPhil); *m* 6 Aug 1964, Cynthia Anne, da of Col Leslie Harold Smith, OBE, of Leicester; 2 da (Lydia b 1969, Sarah b 1971); *Career* lectr in econ history: UCL 1966–69, Univ of Cambridge 1969–75; fell and tutor Emmanuel Coll Cambridge 1969–75, prof of modern history Birkbeck Coll London 1975–88, visiting prof Stanford Univ 1980–81, provost and prof London Guildhall Univ (formerly City of London Poly) 1988–2002, vice-chancellor London Metropolitan Univ (merger of London Guildhall Univ and Univ of North London) 2002–04, pres London Met Univ 2004–06 (prof emeritus 2006–); vice-pres European Univ Assoc 2005–09, chair Standing Ctee for Social Sciences European Science Fndn 2007–; memb: ESRC 1993–97, Cncl Universities UK (formerly CVCP) 1997–2005 (vice-pres 1998–2001, pres 2001–03), Tower Hamlets Coll Corp 1997–2001, London Devpt Partnership Bd 1998–2001, Cncl Gresham Coll 1998–; fell Birkbeck Coll 1995, assoc memb Nuffield Coll Oxford 2007–10; Liveryman Co of Information Technologists 2003 (Freeman 1996), Master Guild of Educators 2005–06; Hon DLitt City Univ 1999, hon fell Wadham Coll Oxford 1999, hon fell Emmanuel Coll Cambridge 2003; academician Academy for the Learned Societies in the Social Sciences (AcSS) 2000; hon DLitt Univ of Westminster 2006; FRHistS 1980, FRSA 1989, FBA 2002; *Books* An Introduction to Quantitative Methods for Historians (1973, 1979), Essays in Quantitative Economic History (ed, 1974), The British Machine Tool Industry 1850–1914 (1976), The Economic History of Britain since 1700 (co-ed, 1981, 2 edn 1994), The Power of the Past: Essays in Honour of Eric Hobsbawm (co-ed, 1984), Height, Health and History: Nutritional Status in the United Kingdom 1750–1980 (with K Wachter and A Gregory, 1990), The People and the British Economy 1830–1914 (1997), Health and Welfare during Industrialization (co-ed 1997), London Higher (co-ed, 1998), The Cambridge Economic History of Modern Britain (ed, 2003); also author of numerous articles and reviews; *Recreations* walking, skiing, theatre; *Clubs* Athenaeum; *Style—* Prof Sir Roderick Floud; ✉ Duck Bottom, 15 Flint Street, Haddenham, Buckinghamshire HP17 8AL (tel 01844 291086); London Metropolitan University, 31 Jewry Street, London EC3N 2EY (tel 020 7320 1310, fax 020 7320 1390, e-mail r.floud@londonmet.ac.uk)

FLOWER, Dr Antony John Frank (Tony); s of Frank Robert Edward Flower (d 1977), of Clyst Hydon, Devon, and Dorothy Elizabeth (d 1999), *née* Williams; *b* 2 February 1951; *Educ* Chipping Sodbury GS, Univ of Exeter (BA, MA), Univ of Leicester (PhD); *Career* graphic designer 1973–76, first gen sec Tawney Soc 1982–88, co-ordinator Argo Venture 1984–; fndr memb SDP 1981, memb Cncl for Soc Democracy 1982–83; dir: Res Inst for Econ and Social Affrs 1982–92, Argo Tst 1986–, Healthline Health Info Serv 1986–88, Health Info Tst 1987–88 (tstee 1988–90), Centre for Educnl Choice 1988–90, Environmental Concern Centre in Europe 1990–92; dir of devpt Green Alliance 1991–92; sec Ecological Studies Inst 1991–92, conslt mangr Construction Industry Environmental Forum 1992–96; chm: Inst of Community Studies 2001–05 (dep dir 1994–2005, tstee 1993–2005, sr fell), Mutual Aid Centre 2001–05 (tstee 1990–2005, dep dir 1994–2005), Young Fndn (merged Inst of Community Studies and Mutual Aid Centre) 2005–; chm: Education Extra 2001, ContinYou 2003–04; conslt: Joseph Rowntree Reform Tst Ltd 1993–2003, Family Covenant Assoc 1994–, Cambridge Female Educn Tst 1999–; GAIA: memb Cncl 1988–2000, ed Tawney Journal 1982–88; co-fndr and managing ed Samizdat magazine 1988–91; assoc: Open Coll of the Arts 1988–, Redesign Ltd 1989–94, Nicholas Lacey and Partners (architects) 1989–, IPPR 1989–95, Rocklabs (Geological Analysts) 1993–; memb Advsy Bd The Earth Centre 1990–2000; patron: Tower Hamlets Summer Univ 1995–, National Space Science Centre 1996–; FRSA; *Books* Starting to Write (with Graham Mort, 1990), The Alternative (with Ben Pimlott and Anthony Wright, 1990), Young at Eighty (ed with Geoff Dench and Kate Gavron, 1995), Guide to Pressure Groups (consultant ed, PMS, 1995), Trusting In Change (2004); *Recreations* collecting junk, making and restoring musical instruments; *Style—* Dr Tony Flower; ✉ 18 Victoria Park Square, London E2 9PF (tel 020 8980 6263, fax 020 8980 0701)

FLOWER, Prof Roderick John; s of Gp Capt Leslie Ralph Flower MBE, MM (d 1994), of Stubbington, Hants, and Audrey Ellen, *née* Eckett (d 1991); *b* 29 November 1945; *Educ* Kingwell Court Sch, Woodbridge Sch, Univ of Sheffield (BSc, Thomas Woodcock Physiology Prize), Univ of London (PhD, DSc); *m* 1994, Lindsay Joyce, da of Henry Arthur Joseph Riddell; *Career* sr scientist Dept of Prostaglandin Res Wellcome Research Labs Kent 1975–84 (memb of staff 1973–75), head Sch of Pharmacy and Pharmacology Univ of Bath 1987–89 (prof of pharmacology 1984–89), prof of biochemical pharmacology Bart's and the Royal London Sch of Med and Dentistry 1989– (head Div of Pharmacology 1998–2003); Br Pharmacological Soc: memb 1974, chm Ctee 1989–92, meeting sec 1998–2000, pres 2001–03, Sandoz Prize 1978, Gaddum Meml Lecture and Medal 1986; William Withering Lecture RCP 2003, Bayliss-Starling Prize Physiological Soc 2006; memb Biochemical Soc 1985, FMedSci 2001, fell Academia Europaea 2003; FRS 2003; *Recreations* photography, the history of pharmacology; *Style—* Prof Roderick Flower; ✉ Department of Biochemical Pharmacology, The William Harvey Research Institute, St Bartholomew's and the Royal London School of Medicine and Dentistry, Charterhouse Square, London EC1M 6BQ (tel 020 7882 6072, fax 020 7882 6076, e-mail r.j.flower@qmul.ac.uk)

FLOWERS, Angela Mary; da of Charles Geoffrey Holland (d 1974), of Ashford, Kent, and Olive Alexandra, *née* Stiby (d 1987); *b* 19 December 1932; *Educ* Westonbirt Sch, Wychwood Sch Oxford, Webber Douglas Sch of Singing & Dramatic Art (Dip); *m* 1, 1952 (m dis 1973), Adrian Flowers; 3 s (Adam b 1953, Matthew, *qv*, b 1956, Daniel b 1959), 1 da (Francesca b 1965); m 2, 2003, Robert Heller, *qv*; 1 da (Rachel Pearl b 1973); *Career* worked in stage, film and advtg until 1967, fndr Angela Flowers Gallery Lisle St 1970 (Portland Mews W1 1971–78, Tottenham Mews W1 1978–88, Richmond Rd E8 1988–2002), chm Angela Flowers Gallery plc 1989–, promotes encourages and shows the work of young emerging and established artists; Hon DUniv East London 1999; sr fell RCA 1994; *Recreations* singing, piano; *Style*— Miss Angela Flowers; ✉ Flowers East, 82 Kingsland Road, London E2 8DP (e-mail angela@flowerseast.com, website www.flowerseast.com)

FLOWERS, Baron (Life Peer UK 1979), of Queen's Gate in the City of Westminster; Brian Hilton Flowers; kt (1969); o s of late Rev Harold Joseph Flowers, of Swansea; *b* 13 September 1924; *Educ* Bishop Gore GS Swansea, Gonville & Caius Coll Cambridge (MA), Univ of Birmingham (DSc); *m* 1951, Mary Frances, er da of Sir Leonard Frederick Behrens, CBE (d 1978); 2 step s; *Career* physicist; head Theoretical Physics Div AERE Harwell 1952–58, prof of theoretical physics Univ of Manchester 1958–61, Langworthy prof of physics Univ of Manchester 1961–72, chm SRC 1967–73, rector Imperial Coll of Sci and Technol 1973–85 (fell 1972); memb Bd UKAEA 1970–80; chm: Royal Cmmn on Environmental Pollution 1973–76, Standing Cmmn on Energy and Environment 1978–81; managing tstee Nuffield Fndn 1982–98 (chm 1987–98); chm Ctee of Vice-Chllrs and Princs 1983–85; vice-chllr Univ of London 1985–90, chllr Victoria Univ of Manchester 1995–2001; chm Select Ctee on Science and Technol House of Lords 1989–93; govr Middlesex Univ 1992–2001; awarded: Rutherford medal and prize IPPS 1968, Glazebrook medal IPPS 1987, Chalmers medal Sweden 1980; MA Oxon 1956; Hon DSc: Sussex 1968, Wales 1972, Manchester 1973, Leicester 1973, Liverpool 1974, Bristol 1982, Oxford 1986 NUI 1990, Reading 1996, London 1996; Hon DEng Nova Scotia 1983, Hon ScD Dublin; Hon LLD: Dundee, Glasgow 1987, Manchester 1995; Hon DUniv Middlesex 2001; sr fell Royal Coll of Art 1983, fell Goldsmiths Coll London 1991, hon fell Royal Holloway Coll London 1996, hon fell Univ of Wales Swansea 1996; Hon FCGI 1975, Hon FIEE 1975, Hon MRIA 1976, Hon FRCP 1992, Hon FInstP 1995; FRS 1961; Offr de la Légion d'Honneur 1981; *Style*— The Rt Hon Lord Flowers, FRS; ✉ 53 Athenaeum Road, London N20 9AL (tel and fax 020 8446 5993, e-mail fofqg@clumsies.demon.co.uk)

FLOWERS, Matthew Dominic; s of Adrian John Flowers, of London, and Angela Mary Flowers, *qv*; *b* 8 October 1956; *Educ* William Ellis GS; *m* 1, 17 Feb 1985, Lindy, da of Arthur James Wesley-Smith; 1 s (Patrick b 30 Jan 1987); m 2, 19 July 1992 (m dis 2003), Huei Chjuin, da of late Et Ping Hong; 1 s (Jackson Hong Fu b 15 Jan 1995); m 3, 23 Sept 2006, Emily Jane, da of Alan Theodore Dzija; *Career* asst Angela Flowers Gallery 1975–78, mangr and keyboard player for pop group Sore Throat 1975–81, played in various other bands including Blue Zoo (Cry Boy Cry Top Twenty hit 1982, led to two appearances on Top of the Pops) 1981–83; Angela Flowers Gallery (became a plc 1989): pt/t asst 1981–83, mangr 1983–88, md 1988–; fndr: Flowers West Santa Monica 1998, Flowers Central Cork St W1 2001, Flowers New York 1000 Madison Ave NYC 2003; publisher (with ed, Mike von Joel) State of Art newspaper 2005–; govr Byam Shaw Sch of Art 1990–2000; memb: Cncl Mgmnt of Art Servs Grants 1987–92, Bradford Print Biennale Ctee 1989, Organising Ctee of London Art Fair 1989–95, Exec Soc of London Art Dealers 1993–96, Organising Ctee Miami Art Fair 1995, Patrons of New Art (Tate Gallery) 1995–99; *Recreations* music, chess, soccer; *Style*— Matthew Flowers, Esq; ✉ Flowers East, 82 Kingsland Road, London E2 8DP (tel 020 7920 7777, fax 020 7920 7770, e-mail matt@flowerseast.com)

FLOYD, Christopher David; QC (1992); s of David Floyd, journalist, and Hana, *née* Goldman; *b* 20 December 1951; *Educ* Westminster, Trinity Coll Cambridge (MA); *m* 1974, Rosalind Jane, *née* Arscott; 1 s, 2 da; *Career* called to the Bar Inner Temple 1975 (bencher 2001), head intellectual property chambers at 11 South Square Gray's Inn 1994–, asst recorder Patents Co Court 1994–2000, a dep chm Copyright Tbnl 1996–, dep High Court judge Patent Court 1999–, recorder 2000–; memb Irish Bar 1989, memb Bar Cncl Professional Conduct and Complaints Ctee 1999–2002, memb Bar Cncl 2000–04, memb Bar Cncl European Ctee 2003–04; chm Intellectual Property Bar Assoc 2000–04; writer of various articles in jls; *Recreations* cycling, walking, tennis, watching cricket, Austin Sevens; *Clubs* Garrick, Austin 7 Owners, 750 Motor; *Style*— Christopher Floyd, Esq, QC; ✉ 11 South Square, Second Floor, Gray's Inn, London WC1R 5EY (e-mail cfloyd@11southsquare.com)

FLOYD, Sir Giles Henry Charles; 7 Bt (UK 1816); s of Lt-Col Sir John Duckett Floyd, 6 Bt, TD (d 1975); *b* 27 February 1932; *Educ* Eton; *m* 1, 23 Nov 1954 (m dis 1978), Lady Gillian Moyra Katherine Cecil, da of 6 Marquess of Exeter, KCMG; 2 s (David Henry Cecil b 1956, Henry Edward Cecil b 1958); m 2, 1985, Judy Sophia, er da of late William Leonard Tregoning, CBE, of Landue, Launceston, Cornwall, and formerly w of Thomas Ernest Lane, of Tickencote Hall, Stamford; *Heir* s David Floyd; *Career* farmer; dir Burghley Estate Farms 1958–; High Sheriff of Rutland 1968; Liveryman Worshipful Co of Skinners; *Recreations* fishing; *Clubs* Turf; *Style*— Sir Giles Floyd, Bt; ✉ Tinwell Manor, Stamford, Lincolnshire PE9 3UF (tel 01780 762676)

FLOYD, Richard Eaglesfield; s of Harold Bailey Floyd (d 1999), and (Edith) Margeret, *née* Griffith (d 1954); *b* 9 June 1938; *Educ* Dean Close Sch Cheltenham; *m* 1995, Linda Ann Robinson, *née* Newnham; *Career* articled clerk Fincham Vallance & Co 1956–61 (sr clerk 1961–62 and 1964–65), insolvency administrator Cork Gully 1965–70, ptnr Floyd Nash & Co (now Richard Floyd & Co) 1971– (held appointments as administrative receiver, administrator, liquidator and tstee), conslt Baker Tilly 1997–2000; author of numerous articles on insolvency matters in specialised jls; memb Editorial Advsy Bd Insolvency Law and Practice; Freeman City of London 1985, Liveryman Worshipful Co of Basketmakers 1998; FIPA, FCA, FABRP; *Books* with I S Grier: Voluntary Liquidation and Receivership (1985, 4 edn, 1999), Personal Insolvency - A Practical Guide (1987, 3 edn 1998), Corporate Recovery: Administration Orders and Voluntary Arrangements (1995); *Recreations* poetry, mountain walking; *Style*— Richard Floyd, Esq; ✉ 29 Roseacre Garden, Chilworth, Guildford, Surrey GU4 8RQ (tel 01483 302782, fax 01483 511429, e-mail floyd@rfandw.com)

FLOYER, Cecile Anne (Ceal); da of David Cornish Floyer (d 1996), of Devon, and Gerlinde Moger, *née* Mayer; *b* 18 April 1968, Karachi, Pakistan; *Educ* Goldsmiths Coll London (BA); *Career* artist; work in public collections at MOMA San Francisco and Denver Art Museum; Philip Morris Scholarship Künstlerhaus Bethanien Berlin 1997, Paul Hamlyn Award 2002; *Selected Solo Exhibitions* Tramway Project Room Glasgow 1996, Anthony Wilkinson Fine Art London 1996, Gavin Brown's Enterprise NYC 1996, Galleria Primo Piano Rome 1996 and 1997, City Racing London 1997, Herzliya Museum of Art Tel Aviv 1997, Lisson Gallery London 1997 and 2002, Künstlerhaus Bethanien Berlin 1998, Casey Kaplan NYC 1999, Kunsthalle Bern 1999, Pinksummer Genova 2000 and 2002, Ikon Gallery Birmingham 2001, Inst of Visual Arts Milwaukee 2001, Massive Reduction (Peer Shoreditch Town Hall London) 2001, Ceal Floyer/MATRIX 192 37' 4" (Univ of Calif Berkeley Art Museum) 2001, X'rummet (Statens Museum for Kunst Copenhagen) 2002, Index (Swedish Contemporary Art Fndn Stockholm) 2002, Casey Kaplan NYC 2003, Portikus Frankfurt 2003, Kabinett füm Aktulle Bremerhaven; *Selected Group Exhibitions* Fast Surface (Chisenhale Gallery London) 1993, Fast Forward (ICA London) 1994, Making Mischief (St James's Street London) 1994, Freddy Contreras/Ceal Floyer (The Showroom London) 1995, General Release: Young British Artists at Scuola di San Pasquale (Venice Biennale) 1995, Just Do It (Cubitt Gallery London) 1995, 4th Istanbul Biennale 1995, British Art Show 4 (Manchester, Edinburgh and Cardiff) 1995, Five Artists (Frith Street Gallery London) 1995, Oporto Festival of Contemporary Art 1996, Life/Live (Musée d'Art Moderne de la Ville de Paris and Centro Cultural de Belem Lisbon) 1996–97, Snowflakes Falling on the International Dateline (Casco Utrecht) 1997, Belladonna (ICA London) 1997, Treasure Island (Centro de Art Moderna/Calouste Gulbenkian Fndn Lisbon) 1997, Sentimental Education (Cabinet Gallery London) 1997, Urban Legends - London (Staatliche Kunsthalle Baden-Baden) 1997, Belladonna, A Selection (The Minories Colchester) 1997, You Are Here (RCA London) 1997, I Luoghi Ritrovati (Centro Civico Per L'Arte Contemporanea La Grancia Serre di Rapolano Siena) 1997, Material Culture: the object in British art in the 80's and 90's (Hayward Gallery London) 1997, Projects (Irish MOMA) 1997, Pictura Britannica (Museum of Contemporary Art Sydney and tour) 1997, Genius Loci (Kunsthalle Bern) 1998, Martin Creed, Ceal Floyer, John Frankland (Delfina Studios London) 1998, Dimensions variable (Br Cncl touring exhbn) 1998, Sunday (Cabinet Gallery London) 1998, Seamless (De Appel Fndn Amsterdam) 1998, In the Meantime (Galeria Estrany-de la Moto Barcelona) 1998, Real/Life - New British Art 1998–1999 (Tochigi Prefectural Museum of Fine Arts and tour) 1998, Drawing Itself (London Inst Gallery) 1998, Recent British Art at Kunstraum (Kunstraum Innsbruck) 1998, Then and Now (Lisson Gallery London) 1998, Every Day (11th Biennale in Sydney) 1998, Malos Habitos (Soledad Lorenzo Madrid) 1998, Triennale der Kleinplastik (Stuttgart) 1998, Thinking Aloud (South Bank Centre touring exhbn) 1998, minimalisms (Akademie der Künste Berlin) 1998, Richard Wentworth & Ceal Floyer (Galerie Carlos Poy Barcelona) 1998 (Galeria Rafael Ortiz Seville 1999), Looking at Ourselves: Works by Women Artists from the Logan Collection (MOMA San Francisco) 1999, Inside Out (Overgaden - Kulturministeriets Udstillningshus for Nutidig Kunst Copenhagen) 1999, On Your Own Time (PS1 Contemporary Art Center NYC) 1999, This Other World of Ours (TV Gallery Moscow) 1999, Luminous Mischief (Yokohama Portside Gallery Kanagawa) 1999, Mirror's Edge (Bild Museet Umeå and tour) 1999, Tramway Glasgow 1999, Peace (Museum für Gegenwarts Kunst Zurich) 1999, Trace (Tate Gallery Liverpool Liverpool Biennale) 1999, From There To Here - Art From London (Konsthallen Gothenburg) 1999, Edit (Badischer Kunstverein Karlsruhe) 2000, Crossroads: Artists in Berlin (Communidad de Madrid) 2000, Quotidiana (Castello di Rivoli Turin) 2000, Drive (Govett-Brewster Art Gallery New Plymouth) 2000, Making Time: Considering Time as a Material in Contemporary Video & Film (Palm Beach ICA) 2000, Extra Ordinary (James Cohan Gallery NYC) 2000, Film/Video Works - Lisson Gallery at 9 Keane Street (Lisson Gallery London) 2000, A Shot in the Head (Lisson Gallery London) 2000, Action, we're filming (Villa Arson Nice) 2000–01, City Racing 1988–1998: a partial account (ICA London) 2001, Nothing (NGCA Sunderland and tour) 2001, Squatters #1 (Witte de With Center for Contemporary Art Rotterdam and Museu de Serralves Porto) 2001, Media Connection (Palazzo delle Esposizioni Rome) 2001, Passion (Galerie Ascan Crone Hamburg and Berlin) 2001, Loop - Alles auf Anfang (Kunsthalle der Hypo-Kulturstiftung Munich) 2001, Sunday Afternoon (303 Gallery NYC) 2002, Colour White (De La Warr Pavilion Bexhill on Sea) 2002, Liminal Space (Center for Curatorial Studies Bard Coll Annadale-on-Hudson) 2002, Tempo (MOMA NYC) 2002, Four women and one pregnant man (Galleri MGM Oslo) 2002, Invitation (Museum für Moderne Kunst Frankfurt am Main) 2002, poT (Liverpool Biennial of Contemporary Art and tour) 2002, Loop. Back to the Beginning (Contemporary Arts Center Fifth Street Space Cincinnati) 2002, 40 Jahre: Fluxus und dir Folgen (Kunstsommer Wiesbaden 2002) 2002, Spiritus (Magasin 3 Stockholm) 2003, Perfect Timeless Repetition (c/o Atle Gerhardsen Berlin) 2003, Band Wagon Jumping (Norwich Gallery) 2003, Lapdissolve (Casey Kaplan NYC) 2003, Days Like These (Tate Britain) 2003, 50th Venice Biennale (Italian Pavillion) 2003; *Public Collections* Tate Collection, Museum für Moderne Kunst Frankfurt, Contemporary Art Soc Collection; *Screenings* The Meaning of Life (Part II) (CCA Glasgow and Art Nolde Stockholm) 1996, Such is Life (Serpentine Gallery Bookshop London) 1996, Fourth Wall - Waiting (Public Art Devpt Tst in assoc with RNT London) 1999; *Style*— Ms Ceal Floyer; ✉ Lisson Gallery (London) Ltd, 67 Lisson Street, London NW1 5DA (tel 020 7724 2739, fax 020 7724 7124)

FLYNN, John Gerrard; CMG (1992); s of Thomas Flynn (d 1985), of Glasgow, and Mary Chisholm (d 1963); *b* 23 April 1937; *Educ* Univ of Glasgow (MA); *m* 10 Aug 1973, Drina Anne Coates, da of Lt Herbert Percival Coates (d 1971), of Montevideo, Uruguay; 1 s (Andrew b 1984), 1 da (Alexandra b 1985); *Career* FO: joined 1965, second sec Lusaka 1966, first sec FCO 1968, asst dir gen Canning House 1970, head of Chancery Montevideo 1971, FO 1976, chargé d'affaires Luanda 1978, cnsllr (political) Brasilia 1979, cnsllr (economic and commercial) Madrid 1982, high cmmr to Swaziland 1987–90; ambass to: Angola 1990–93, Venezuela 1993–97 (concurrently non-resident ambass Dominican Repub 1993–95); Foreign Sec's special rep Sierra Leone 1998–; *Recreations* walking, golf; *Clubs* Travellers; *Style*— John Flynn, Esq, CMG; ✉ c/o Foreign & Commonwealth Office (Sierra Leone), King Charles Street, London SW1A 2AH

FLYNN, Dr Patricia Josephine; da of Michael Joseph Flynn, of Dublin, and Mary Josephine, *née* O'Dwyer; *b* 1 April 1947; *Educ* Convent of the Sacred Heart Dublin, UC Dublin (MB BCh, BAO, DCH, DObst, DA FFARCSI); *m* 26 Sept 1987, Anthony William Goode, s of William Henry Goode, of Tynemouth, Northumberland; *Career* sr lectr in anaesthesia and dep dir Anaesthetics Unit Barts and the London Sch of Med and Dentistry 1982–2003, conslt anaesthetist Barts and the London NHS Tst; sec gen Br Acad of Forensic Scis; memb: Assoc of Dental Anaesthetists, Dental Sedation Teachers' Gp, NY Acad of Sciences, RSM, BMA; FRCA; *Recreations* antiquarian books, art, music; *Style*— Dr Patricia Flynn; ✉ Department of Anaesthesia, The Royal London Hospital, London E1 1BB (e-mail patricia.flynn@bartsandthelondon.nhs.uk)

FLYNN, Paul Phillip; MP; s of James Flynn (d 1939), and Kathleen Rosien, *née* Williams (d 1988); *b* 9 February 1935; *Educ* St Illtyd's Coll Cardiff, UC Cardiff; *m* 1, 6 Feb 1962, Ann Patricia; 1 da (Rachel Sarah b 1963 d 1979), 1 s (James Patrick b 1965); m 2, 31 Jan 1985, Lynne Samantha; *Career* chemist in steel indust 1955–81; since worked in local radio and as research asst to Euro MP Llewellyn Smith; MP (Lab) Newport W 1987–, oppn front bench spokesman on Welsh affrs May 1988–97, oppn front bench spokesman on social security Nov 1988–90; *Books* Commons Knowledge: How to be a Backbencher (1997), Baglu 'Mlaen (1998), Dragons Led by Poodles (1999); *Clubs* Ringland Labour, Pill Labour; *Style*— Paul Flynn, Esq, MP; ✉ House of Commons, London SW1A 0AA (tel 020 7219 3478, e-mail paulflynnmp@talk21.com, website paulflynnmp.co.uk)

FLYNN, Rachel Elizabeth; da of John Flynn, of Norwich, and Jennifer, *née* Bacon; *b* 28 June 1968, Norwich, Norfolk; *Educ* Norwich HS GPDST, Norwich Sch of Art, Univ of Durham (BA), Coll of Law York; *m* 11 Jan 1997, Rae Guest; *Career* trainee slr Townsends 1992–94; Taylor Vinters: slr 1994–2005, ptnr 2005–; memb: Law Soc, Employment Lawyers' Assoc, Thoroughbred Breeders' Assoc, Amateur Jockeys' Assoc; *Publications* Veterinary Notes for Horse Owners (contrib, 2002); *Recreations* horse racing, riding out, breeding racehorses; *Style*— Ms Rachel Flynn; ✉ Taylor Vinters, Merlin Place, Milton Road, Cambridge CB4 0DP (tel 01223 225168, fax 01223 423944, e-mail rachel.flynn@taylorvinters.com)

FLYNN, Roger Patrick; s of Peter Daniel Flynn, of Sidmouth, Devon, and Shirley Josephine, *née* Kent (d 1996); *b* 4 November 1962, Sidmouth, Devon; *Educ* The King's Sch Devon, Imperial Coll London (BSc); *m* 9 August 1986, Lisa Martine, *née* Eyre; 2 da (Katie Rebecca b 29 May 1990, Lucy Abigail b 19 June 1994); *Career* with Arthur Andersen & Co

1984–88, commercial dir and gp fin dir Virgin Communications (int media gp of Virgin plc) 1991–95 (corp fin exec 1988–91), gen mangr World Sales and Distribution British Airways plc 1995–98, md Prudential Retail (subsid of Prudential plc) 1998–2000, chief exec BBC Ventures Gp Ltd 2000–04, chief exec Springboard Gp Ltd 2004–; dir: Maxjet Airways Inc, SDI Media Holdings Inc, Youth Culture Television (also tstee); memb Magic Circle; memb Royal Inst of GB 1985, ACA 1988, RTS 2001; *Recreations* fitness, physics, reading, magic; *Style—* Roger Flynn, Esq; ✉ Springboard Group, St Audrey House, Doneraile Street, London SW6 6EN (tel 020 7610 6791, mobile 07736 480280, e-mail roger@springboard.uk.com)

FLYNN, Sarah Anne Judith; *see:* Markham, Sarah Anne Judith

FOAKES, Prof Reginald Anthony; s of William Warren Foakes, and Frances, *née* Poate; *b* 18 October 1923; *Educ* West Bromwich GS, Univ of Birmingham (MA, PhD); *m* 1, 1951, Barbara (d 1988), da of Harry Garratt, OBE; 2 s, 2 da; m 2, 1993, Mary (d 1996), da of Albert White; *Career* sr lectr in English Univ of Durham 1963–64 (lectr 1954–62), Cwlth Fund (Harkness) fell Yale Univ 1955–56; Univ of Kent at Canterbury: prof of English literature 1964–82, dean Faculty of Humanities 1974–77, currently emeritus prof of English and American literature; prof of English UCLA 1983; visiting prof: Univ of Toronto 1960–62, Univ of Calif Santa Barbara 1968–69, UCLA 1981; *Books* Shakespeare's King Henry VIII (ed 1957), The Romantic Assertion (1958, 1972), Henslowe's Diary (ed with R T Rickert, 1961), Coleridge on Shakespeare (1971), Marston and Tourneur (1978), Illustrations of the English Stage 1980–1642 (1985), Coleridge's Lectures 1808–1819, On Literature (ed 2 Vols, 1987), Hamlet versus Lear: Cultural Politics and Shakespeare's Art (1993), King Lear (ed 1997), Shakespeare and Violence (2003), Inventing Parents (2004); *Style—* Prof Reginald Foakes; ✉ Department of English, University of California at Los Angeles, 405 Hilgard Avenue, Los Angeles, CA 90095–1530, USA (e-mail foakes@humnet.ucla.edu)

FOALE, Marion Ann; da of Stuart Donald Foale (d 1972), and Gertrude Lillian Maud, *née* Rayner; *b* 13 March 1939; *Educ* SW Essex Tech and Sch of Art, Sch of Fashion Design RCA (DesRCA, designed Queen's Mantle for OBE); *Children* 1 da (Polly Jones b 14 Dec 1972), 1 s (Charley Jones b 25 Jan 1977); *Career* fashion designer; fndr ptnr (with Sally Tuffin) Foale and Tuffin Ltd Carnaby Street 1961–72, signed with Puritan Fashions NY for 'Youth Quake' 1965; clothes designer for films: Kaleidoscope (with Susannah York) 1966, Two for the Road (with Audrey Hepburn) 1966; fndr own label Marion Foale (predominately producing hand knitwear) 1982–; *Books* Marion Foale's Classic Knitwear (1987); *Style—* Ms Marion Foale; ✉ Foale Ltd, The Cottage, 133A Long Street, Atherstone, Warwickshire CV9 1AD (tel 01827 720333, fax 01827 720444, e-mail foale@talk21.com)

FOALE, Dr Rodney Alan; s of Maurice Spencer Foale, of Melbourne, Australia, and Lyle Gwendolin, *née* Wallace; *b* 11 September 1946; *Educ* Scotch Coll Melbourne, Univ of Melbourne Med Sch; *m* 1980, Lady Emma Cecile Gordon, er da of the Marquis of Aberdeen and Temair; 2 s (Archie Alexander b 17 Sept 1984, Jamie Alexander b 1 April 1986); *Career* St Vincent's Hosp Univ of Melbourne 1972–73, med offr Australian Himalayan Expdn through India and Kashmir 1974–75, registrar Nat Heart Hosp 1975–79, clinical res fell Harvard Univ and MIT, Massachusetts Gen Hosp 1980–82, sr registrar in cardiology Hammersmith Hosp 1982–85, conslt cardiologist and clinical dir of cardiovascular science St Mary's Hosp 1985–98, dir of surgery and cardiovascular science St Mary's Hosp Tst 1998–; hon sr lectr Hammersmith Hosp 1985–98, hon sr lectr Imperial Coll 1998–; recognised teacher Univ of London 1985–; FACC 1986, FESC 1988, FRCP 1994 (MRCP 1976); *Recreations* various indoor and outdoor pursuits; *Clubs* Flyfishers', Chelsea Arts, Shell Collectors; *Style—* Dr Rodney Foale; ✉ 66 Harley Street, London W1G 7HD (tel 020 7323 4687, fax 020 7631 5341, e-mail raf@smht-foale.co.uk)

FOCKE, His Hon Paul Everard Justus; QC (1982); s of Frederick Justus Focke (d 1959), and Muriel Focke (d 1995); *b* 14 May 1937; *Educ* Downside, Exeter Coll Oxford, Trinity Coll Dublin; *m* 13 Dec 1973, Lady Tana Focke, da of late 6 Earl of Caledon; 2 da (Diana Natasha b 1974, Victoria Justine b 1976); *Career* Nat Serv 1955–57; Capt Cheshire Yeo TA 1957–65; called to the Bar: Gray's Inn 1964 (bencher 1992), NZ 1982; QC NSW 1984; recorder of the Crown Court 1986–97, circuit judge 1997–2007; former head of chambers; dir Bar Mutual Indemnity Fund 1991–97; *Recreations* travelling, aeroplanes; *Clubs* Turf, Beefsteak, Pratt's, Cavalry and Guards'; *Style—* His Hon Paul Focke, QC

FOGDEN, Michael Ernest George (Mike); CB (1994); s of George Charles Arthur Fogden (d 1970), of Worthing, W Sussex, and Margaret May Fogden; *b* 30 May 1936; *Educ* Worthing HS; *m* 1 June 1957, (Rose) Ann, da of James Arthur Diamond (d 1983), of Morpeth, Northumberland; 3 s, 1 da; *Career* Nat Serv RAF 1956–58; Miny of Social Security 1959–67, private sec of state for Social Services 1968–70, DHSS 1971–82, Dept of Employment 1982–87; chief exec British Employment Service 1987–96; ind conslt 1997–; chm: First Division Assoc 1979–82, Public Mgmnt and Policy Assoc 1998–2003, Nat Blood Authy 1998–2005, Investigating and Discipline Bd Accounting Profession 2002–; dep chm Civil Serv Appeal Bd 1999–2006; FRSA; *Recreations* music, gardening, snooker; *Clubs* Royal Commonwealth; *Style—* Mike Fogden, Esq, CB; ✉ 59 Mayfield Avenue, Orpington, Kent BR6 0AH (tel 01689 877395, fax 01689 834354)

FOGEL, Steven Anthony; s of Joseph Gerald Fogel, JP, and Benita Rose Fogel; *b* 16 October 1951; *Educ* Carmel Coll, KCL (LLB, LLM); *m* 2 Jan 1977, Joan Selma, da of Curtis Holder (d 1972); 1 da (Frances Leah), 2 s (George Curtis, Jonathan Raphael); *Career* admitted slr 1976; sr ptnr Titmuss Sainer Dechert 1998–2000; managing ptnr (London) Dechert 2000–; memb Bd of Mgmnt Investment Property Forum 2002–; memb: Anglo American Real Property Inst, Customer Focus Ctee Br Property Fedn; dir London Jewish Cultural Centre; tstee Motivation; Freeman: City of London, Worshipful Co of Slrs; ACIArb; *Books* The Landlord and Tenant Factbook (jtly, 1992), Privity of Contract, A Practitioner's Guide (jtly, 1995, 3 edn 2000), Handbook of Rent Review (co-ed, 3 edn 2000); *Recreations* jazz, skiing, writing; *Style—* Steven Fogel, Esq; ✉ Dechert, 2 Serjeants' Inn, London EC4Y 1LT (tel 020 7583 5353, fax 020 7353 3683/2830)

FOGELMAN, Prof Ignac; s of Richard Fogelman (d 1975), and Ruth, *née* Tyras (d 1995); *b* 4 September 1948; *Educ* HS of Glasgow, Univ of Glasgow (BSc, MB ChB, MD); *m* 18 March 1974, Coral Niman, da of Harvey Norton (d 1980); 1 da (Gayle b 1974), 1 s (Richard b 1982); *Career* Guy's Hosp: conslt physician 1983–, dir Nuclear Med Dept 1988–97, dir Osteoporosis Screening and Res Unit 1988–, chm Bd of Examiners MSc in Nuclear Med 2001–; chm Specialist Advsy Ctee in Nuclear Med 1990–93, chm Densitometry Forum of the Nat Osteoporosis Soc 1999–2005; memb Bd and tstee Nat Osteoporosis Soc 1977–88 and 2002–; memb Int Skeletal Soc 1988; FRCP 1987; *Books* Bone Scanning in Clinical Practice (1987), An Atlas of Clinical Nuclear Medicine (with M Maisey, 1988), An Atlas of Planar and Spect Bone Scans (with D Collier, 1988, 2 edn with L Holder, 2000), Bone Metastases (with R Rubens, 1991), The Evaluation of Osteoporosis (with H Wahner, 1994, 2 edn with G Blake, 1999), Skeletal Nuclear Medicine (with D Collier and L Rosenthall, 1996); *Recreations* bridge, theatre, opera, food, wine, music, tennis, books, travel; *Style—* Prof Ignac Fogelman; ✉ Department of Nuclear Medicine, Guy's Hospital, St Thomas Street, London SE1 9RT (tel 020 7188 4114, fax 020 7188 4119)

FOGELMAN, Prof Kenneth Robert (Ken); s of Joseph Alfred Fogelman (d 1987), and Vera May, *née* Corrie; *b* 29 January 1945; *Educ* Ifield GS Crawley, Keele Univ (BA); *m* 26 Aug 1967, Audrey Elaine, da of Angus Corkan, of IOM (d 1992); *Career* secdy maths teacher 1966–67, research offr Sch to Univ Research Unit Nat Fndn for Educnl Research 1969–72 (research asst Section for Mathematical and Conceptual Studies 1967–69), asst dir Nat Children's Bureau 1981–85 (princ research offr 1972–81), dep dir Social Statistics Research Unit City Univ 1985–88, prof of educn Univ of Leicester 1988– (dean Faculty of Educn and Continuing Studies 1998–); fndr memb: Br Educnl Research Assoc, Social Research Assoc; memb Assoc of Child Psychiatrists and Psychologists; FBPsS 1988; *Books* Piagetian Tests for the Primary School (1970), Leaving the Sixth Form (1972), Britain's Sixteen Year Olds (1976), Growing Up in Great Britain (1983), Putting Children First (ed with I Vallender, 1988), Citizenship in Schools (1991), Developing Citizenship in the Curriculum (ed with J Edwards, 1993), Going Comprehensive in England and Wales (with A Kerckhoff, D Crook and D Reeder, 1996); *Recreations* music, travel, photography; *Style—* Prof Ken Fogelman; ✉ School of Education, University of Leicester, 21 University Road, Leicester LE1 7RF (tel 0116 252 3588, fax 0116 252 3653)

FOGLE, Benjamin Myer (Ben); s of Dr Bruce Fogle, MBE, DVM, MRCVS, and Julia Foster; *b* 3 November 1973, London; *Educ* Bryanston, Univ of Portsmouth; *m* 2 Sept 2006, Marina, *née* Hunt; *Career* TV presenter: BBC Countryfile, Animal Park, Wild in Africa, One Man and His Dog, Wild in California, Cash in the Attic, Crufts, Extreme Dreams with Ben Fogle, Through Hell and High Water, Holiday; journalist: The Telegraph, Sunday Times, Countrylife, The Guardian, NY Times, The Independent; ocean yachtmaster, RNR midshipman 1994–98, world record holder Atlantic rowing La Gomera to Antigua route (with James Cracknall, *qv*) 2005; pres Cncl for Nat Parks; ambass: WWF, Tusk; supporter: Duke of Edinburgh Awards, Hearing Dogs; FRGS; *Publications* The Tea Time Islands (2003), Offshore (2006), The Crossing (2006); *Recreations* ocean rowing, desert marathons, exploration; *Style—* Ben Fogle, Esq; ✉ c/o Arlington Enterprises Limited, 1–3 Charlotte Street, London W1T 1RD (tel 020 7580 0702, fax 020 7580 4994, e-mail hilary@arlington-enterprises.co.uk); website www.benfogle.com

FOLEY, 8 Baron (GB 1776); Adrian Gerald Foley; s of 7 Baron Foley (d 1927), and Minoru, *née* Greenstone (d 1968); *b* 9 August 1923; *m* 1, 23 Dec 1958 (m dis 1971), Patricia, da of Joseph Zoellner III, of Pasadena, California, and formerly w of Minor de Uribe Meek; 1 s (Hon Thomas Henry), 1 da (Hon Alexandra Mary); m 2, 1972, Ghislaine (d 2000), da of Cornelius Willem Dresselhuys, of The Hague, Holland, and formerly w of (1) Maj Denis James Alexander, later 6 Earl of Caledon, and (2) 4 Baron Ashcombe, *qv*; m 3, 15 Dec 2003, Hannah Anne, da of Solomon Wolfson, and formerly wife of Jack Steinberg; *Heir* s, Hon Thomas Foley; *Career* composer and pianist; *Clubs* White's; *Style—* The Rt Hon Lord Foley; ✉ c/o Marbella Club, Marbella, Malaga, Spain

FOLEY, His Hon Judge John Dominic; s of Cyril Patrick Foley (d 1972), of Bristol, and Winifred Hannah, *née* McAweeny (d 1980); *b* 17 January 1944; *Educ* St Brendan's Coll Bristol, Univ of Exeter (LLB, pres Bracton Law Soc, 1st XV rugby); *m* 1978 (m dis 1986), Helena Frances, da of Dr Kemp McGowan; 2 da (Jessica Rosalind b 23 Sept 1978, Helena Rachel b 25 Nov 1980); *Career* called to the Bar Inner Temple 1968, in practice Western Circuit 1969–, attorney-gen special prosecutor NI 1971–73, recorder of the Crown Court 1990–94 (asst recorder 1986–90), circuit judge (Western Circuit) 1994–; vice-pres Immigration Appeal Tbnl 1998–2005, memb Special Immigration Appeals Cmmn 2002–05 (investigating judge 2006–); ind arbitrator (rugby discipline) Int Rugby Bd and RFU 2006–; *Recreations* cricket, rugby, travel (especially the Caribbean), theatre, rock and blues; *Clubs* Somerset CCC, Bristol RFC, Clifton RFC, Carlton CC Barbados, Barbados Cricket Assoc; *Style—* His Hon Judge Foley

FOLEY, Lt-Gen Sir John Paul; KCB (1994, CB 1991), OBE (1979), MC (1976), DL (Herefordshire 2005); s of Maj Henry Thomas Hamilton Foley, MBE (d 1959), of Stoke Edith, Herefords, and Helen Constance Margaret, *née* Pearson (d 1985); *b* 22 April 1939; *Educ* Bradfield Coll (Mons OCS), Army Staff Coll; *m* 3 June 1972, Ann Rosamund, da of Maj John William Humphries; 2 da (Annabel b 11 July 1973, Joanna b 8 May 1976); *Career* Royal Green Jackets: Lt 1959–60, Capt 1961–69; Maj RMCS 1970–71; Cmdg Offr 3 Bn 1978–80; Brigade Maj, 51 Inf Bde Hong Kong 1974–76; Camberley: army staff course 1972–74, Lt Col dir staff 1976–78; Cmdt jr div Staff Coll Warminster 1981–82; Brig: arms dir MOD 1983–85, student RCDS 1986; chief Br mission to Soviet forces E Germany 1987–89; Maj Gen central staffs MOD 1989–92, Cdr Br Forces Hong Kong 1992–94, Col Cmdt The Light Div 1994–97, Lt-Gen central staffs MOD 1994–97, ret 1998; chief Defence Intelligence 1994–97; Lt-Govr Guernsey CI 2000–05, High Sheriff Herefords and Worcs 2006–07; Freeman City of London 1970, memb Ct of Assts Worshipful Co of Skinners 1996–2000 (Freeman 1965, Liveryman 1972); KStJ 2001; Offr Legion of Merit (USA) 1997; *Recreations* tennis, golf, walking, shooting, reading; *Clubs* Boodle's; *Style—* Lt-Gen Sir John Foley, KCB, OBE, MC, DL

FOLLAND, Nick James; s of James Charles Folland, of Ilfracombe, Devon, and Susan Rosemary Carpenter; *b* 6 October 1965, Emsworth, W Sussex; *Educ* Reading Sch, Univ of Bristol (LLB), Guildford Law Sch; *m* 15 May 1993, Emma, *née* Dunstone; 1 da (Dominique Beatrice b 11 April 1996), 1 s (Jack Charles b 5 July 1997); *Career* admitted slr: England and Wales 1993, Hong Kong 1995; slr Linklaters 1991–96, legal advsr then sr legal advsr Cable & Wireless plc 1996–2000, co sec and head of legal 365 Corporation plc 2000–01, co sec and gp legal dir Emap plc 2001–07, dir Emap Business International 2003–07, co sec and dir of governance and corporate servs Kingfisher plc 2007–; treas Br American Project 1999–2002; *Recreations* running, cycling, sailing, skiing, expedition travel; *Style—* Nick Folland, Esq

FOLLETT, (Daphne) Barbara; MP; da of late William Vernon Hubbard, and late Charlotte, *née* Goulding; *b* 25 December 1942; *Educ* Open Univ, LSE (BSc(Econ)); *m* 1, Richard Turner; 2 da (Jann b 1964, Kim b 1968); m 2, Gerald Stonestreet; m 3, Leslie Broer; 1 s (Adam b 1975); m 4, Kenneth (Ken) Follett, *qv*; 1 step s (Emanuele b 1968), 1 step da (Marie-Claire b 1973); *Career* teacher Berlitz Sch of Languages Paris 1963–64, jt mangr fruit farm South Africa 1966–77, acting regnl sec South African Inst of Race Relations 1970–71, regnl mangr Kupugani 1971–74, dir health educn projects Kupugani 1975–78, asst course organizer and lectr Centre for Int Briefing Farnham Surrey 1980–84, freelance lectr and consult 1984–92, fndr memb and dir Emily's List UK 1992–, MP (Lab) Stevenage 1997–; contested (Lab) gen elections 1983 and 1987; visiting fell Inst of Public Policy Research 1993–96; fndr memb: Women's Movement for Peace South Africa, Labour Women's Network (memb Steering Ctee 1988–); memb: The Black Sash, Fawcett Soc, Nat Alliance of Women's Orgns, Nat Women's Network, Womankind; *Recreations* film, theatre, reading, photography, Scrabble, Star Trek; *Style—* Barbara Follett, MP; ✉ Stevenage Labour Party, 4 Popple Way, Stevenage, Hertfordshire SG1 3TG (tel 01438 222 800, fax 01438 222 292); House of Commons, London SW1A 0AA (tel 020 7219 3000, e-mail barbara@barbara-follett.org.uk)

FOLLETT, Prof Sir Brian Keith; kt (1992); *b* 22 February 1939; *Educ* Bournemouth Sch, Univ of Bristol (BSc, PhD), Univ of Wales (DSc); *m* Lady (Deb) Follett; 1 da (Karen Tracy Williams b 4 June 1965), 1 s (Richard James b 1 May 1968); *Career* NIH res fell Washington State Univ 1964–65, lectr in zoology Univ of Leeds 1965–69, lectr, reader then prof of zoology Univ of Wales Bangor 1969–78, prof of zoology Univ of Bristol 1978–93, vice-chllr Univ of Warwick 1993–2001, prof of biology Univ of Oxford 2001–; chm: AHRC 2000–07, Br Library Advsy Cncl 2001–07, Teacher Trg Agency (now Trg and Devpt Agency for Schs) 2003–; chair Royal Soc investigation into scientific aspects of livestock disease epidemics 2001–03; memb: Univs Funding Cncl 1988–91, Higher Educn Funding Cncl 1991–96, AFRC 1982–88, BBSRC (formerly AFRC) 1994–2001; tstee British Museum (Natural History) 1988–99, Royal Cmmn on Environmental Pollution 2000–05; author of over 250 scientific papers published in fields of reproductive physiology and biological clocks and of various reports for Government; Hon LLD Univ of Wales 1992, Hon FLA 1997, Hon DSc Univ Tek Malaysia 1999, Hon DSc Univ of Leicester 2001, Hon LLD Univ of Calgary 2001, Hon DLitt Univ of Oxford 2002, Hon

DSc Univ of Warwick, Hon LLD Univ of St Andrews 2002, Hon DSc UEA 2004, Hon DSc Univ of London 2004; FRS 1984 (biological sec and vice-pres 1987–93); *Recreations* history; *Style*— Prof Sir Brian Follett, FRS; ✉ 120 Tiddington Road, Stratford-upon-Avon, Warwickshire CV37 5BB (tel 01289 292132); Training and Development Agency for Schools, 151 Buckingham Palace Road, London SW1W 9SZ (tel 020 7023 8814)

FOLLETT, Kenneth Martin (Ken); s of Martin Dunsford Follett, of Yatton, Somerset, and late Lavinia Cynthia, *née* Evans; *b* 5 June 1949; *Educ* Harrow Weald GS, Poole Tech Coll, UCL (BA); *m* 1, 5 Jan 1968 (m dis 1985), Mary Emma Ruth, da of Horace Henry Elson (d 1988), of Kinson, Bournemouth; 1 s (Emanuele b 13 July 1968), 1 da (Marie-Claire b 11 May 1973); m 2, 8 Nov 1985 (Daphne) Barbara Follett, MP, *qv*; *Career* journalist: S Wales Echo 1970–73, London Evening News 1973–74; dep md Everest Books 1976–77 (editorial dir 1974–76); author 1977–; pres Dyslexia Inst, chm Nat Year of Reading 1998–99, chair Reading is Fundamental (UK); Bd dir: Nat Acad of Writing; memb: Stevenage Lab Party, Arts for Lab, Liberty, Amnesty, Authors' Guild USA 1979; pres Stevenage Community Tst, tstee Nat Literary Tst, patron Stevenage Home-Start, govr Roebuck Primary Sch and Nursery; fell UCL 1995; FRSA 2000; *Books* Eye of the Needle (1978), Triple (1979), The Key to Rebecca (1980), The Man from St Petersburg (1982), On Wings of Eagles (1983), Lie Down With Lions (1986), The Pillars of the Earth (1989), Night over Water (1991), A Dangerous Fortune (1993), A Place Called Freedom (1995), The Third Twin (1996), The Hammer of Eden (1998), Code to Zero (2000), Jackdaws (2001), Hornet Flight (2002), Whiteout (2004), World Without End (2007); *Recreations* bass guitarist of Damn Right I Got the Blues; *Clubs* Groucho, Atheneum; *Style*— Ken Follett, Esq; ✉ PO Box 4, Knebworth SG3 6UT (website www.ken-follett.com)

FOLLEY, Malcolm John; s of John Trevail Folley (d 1998), of Peacehaven, E Sussex, and Rosina, *née* O'Hara (d 1975); *b* 24 April 1952; *Educ* Lewes Co GS for Boys; *m* 5 June 1976, Rachel, da of Peter Ivan Kingman; 2 da (Siân Trevail b 27 July 1987, Megan Trevail b 19 Dec 1988); *Career* sports writer; indentured Sussex Express and County Herald 1968–72; news ed: Wimpey News 1972–73, Hayter's Sports Agency 1973; sports reporter: United Newspapers (London-based) 1973–75, Daily Express 1975–82, Mail on Sunday 1982–83; tennis corr Daily Mail 1984–86, dep ed Sportsweek 1986–87, sr sports writer Daily Express 1987–92, chief sports reporter Mail on Sunday 1992– (dep sports ed 1992); highly commended Magazine Sports Writer of the Year 1986, Sports Reporter of the Year 1991, highly commended Sports News Reporter of the Year 2004; *Books* Hana: the Autobiography of Hana Mandlikova (co-author, 1989), A Time to Jump: the Authorised Biography of Jonathan Edwards (2000), Finding My Feet - The Autobiography of Jason Robinson (co-author, 2003), Borg versus McEnroe (2005), My Colourful Life, From Red to Amber (co-author with Ginger McCain, 2005); *Recreations* golf, skiing, tennis; *Style*— Malcolm Folley, Esq; ✉ Mail on Sunday, Northcliffe House, 2 Derry Street, London W8 5TS (tel 020 7938 7069, fax 020 7937 4115, e-mail malcolm.folley@mailonsunday.co.uk)

FOLWELL, Nicholas David; s of Alfred Thomas Folwell (d 1975), and Irmgard Seefeld, of Market Drayton; *b* 11 July 1953; *Educ* Spring Grove GS, Middx Royal Acad of Music, London Opera Centre; *m* 1, (m dis 1995), 31 Jan 1981, Anne-Marie, da of George Ives; 1 s (Alexander Thomas b 22 July 1981), 1 step s (Adrian Marshal Matheson-Bruce b 15 Aug 1974); m 2, 13 July 1996, Susanna, da of David Tudor Thomas; *Career* baritone; joined Welsh Nat Opera 1978, first professional role The Bosun in Billy Budd 1978; later WNO roles incl: Marchese in La Traviata 1979, Melot in Triston Und Isolde 1979, Ottone in The Coronation of Poppea 1980, Figaro in The Marriage of Figaro 1981 and 1987, Melitone in La Forza del Destino 1981, Leporello in Don Giovanni 1982, Klingsor in Parsifal 1983, Pizarro in Fidelio 1983, Alberich in Das Rheingold 1983, Schaunard in La Bohème 1984, Alberich in Siegfried and Götterdämmerung 1985; other roles incl: Beckmesser in The Mastersingers of Nuremberg (Opera North) 1985, Leporello in Don Giovanni (Opera North) 1986, The Four Villians in The Tales of Hoffmann (Scottish Opera) 1986, Tonio in Pagliacci (ENO) 1986, Alberich in Der Ring (WNO at Covent Garden) 1986, The Poacher in The Cunning Little Vixen (WNO) 1987, Father in The Seven Deadly Sins (Royal Festival Hall) 1988, Figaro in The Marriage of Figaro (Scottish Opera) 1987, Papageno in The Magic Flute (ENO) 1988, Marullo in Rigoletto (Frankfurt Opera) 1988, Alberich in Das Rheingold (Scottish Opera) 1989, Koroviev in Der Meister und Margarita (world premiere, Paris Opera) 1989, Creon and The Messenger in Oedipus Rex (Scottish Opera) 1990, Melitone in La Forza del Destino (Scottish Opera) 1990, The Poacher in The Cunning Little Vixen (Royal Opera) 1990, Pizarro in Fidelio (Glyndebourne) 1990, Figaro in Le Nozze di Figaro (Opera Zuid Holland) 1991, Mutius in Timon of Athens (ENO) 1991, Chief of Police in Lady Macbeth of Mtsensk (ENO), Falke in Die Fledermaus (ENO), Figaro in Le Nozze di Figaro (Glyndebourne) 1992, Alberich in Das Rheingold (Opera de Nantes) 1992, Ottokar in Der Freischutz (Zwingenberg) 1993, Count Laski in Le Roi Malgré Lui (Opera North) 1994, Masetto in Don Giovanni (New Israeli Opera) 1994, title role in Der Kaiser von Atlantis (Liege) 1994, title role in Blond Eckbert (ENO) 1995, Lysiart in Euryanthe (QEH) 1995, title role in Rigoletto (Opera South) 1995, The Forester in The Cunning Little Vixen (ENO) 1995, Sancho in Don Quichotte (ENO) 1996, title role in Der Fliegende Hollander (Chelsea Opera QEH) 1996, Major Mary in Die Soldaten (ENO) 1996, title role in Bluebeards Castle (QEH) 1997, The Music Master in Ariadne on Naxos (ENO) 1997, Mr van Tricasse in Dr Ox's Experiment (ENO) 1998, Alberich in Das Rheingold (Longborough Festival) 1998, The Old Man in Purgatory (Dublin) 1999, L'Elisir d'Amore (Kinsale) 1999, Hunding in Die Valküre (Longborough Festival) 1999, Scarpia in Tosca (Isle of Man) 1999, The Stranger in the Dreaming of the Bones (world premier, Dublin) 2000, Germont in La Traviata (Opera Cork) 2000, Don José in Maritana (Waterford) 2000, Sharpless in Madama Butterfly (Holland Park) 2000, Escamillo in Carmen (Cork) 2000, title role in Rigoletto (Glasgow) 2001, Forester in The Cunning Little Vixen (ENO) 2001, Méphistopélès in Faust et Hélèn (QEH) 2002, Simone Trovai in Violante (QEH) 2002, Sharpless in Madama Butterfly (ENO) 2002, Alberich and Hunding in The Ring (LFO) 2002, Don Inigo Gomez in L'Heure Espagnol (Opera Zuid) 2003, L'Horloge and Le Chat in L'Enfant et les Sortileges (Opera Zuid) 2003, Pizarro in Fideolio (Opera Holland Park) 2003, Benoit & Alcindoro in La Boheme (Opera Holland Park) 2004, Pope Clement VI in Light Passing (York and BBC Radio 3) 2004, Idraote in Armida (Channel 4) 2005, Maestro di casa, Dumas and Schmidt in Andrea Chénier (Opera Holland Park) 2005, Alberich in Siegfried (Royal Danish OPera Copenhagen) 2006, The Host in Sir John in Love (ENO) 2006, The Bosun in Billy Budd (ENO) 2006, Monterone in Rigoletto (Opera Holland Park) 2006, Antonio in The Marriage of Figaro (ENO) 2007; also numerous classical concerts in UK and abroad; ARAM; *Recordings* incl: Tristan und Isolde (as Melot), Jailer in Tosca, Klingsor in Parsifal, Rimsky-Korsakov Christmas Eve, Tchaikovsky Vakula The Smith, The Cunning Little Vixen (as the Poacher), Der Zwerg (as the Haushofmeister), Pish Tush in The Mikado, Samuel in Pirates of Penzance, also A Dream of Paradise (solo album); *Recreations* golf; *Style*— Nicholas Folwell, ARAM; ✉ e-mail n-s@nfolwell.co.uk

FONSECA, Jose Maria; da of Amador Francis Gabriel Fonseca (d 1984), of Abergavenny, Gwent, and Kathleen, *née* Jones; *b* 9 January 1944; *Educ* Sacred Heart Convent Highgate, Ursuline Convent San Sebastian Spain, Ursuline Convent St Pol de Leon Brittany, St Godric's Secretarial Coll Hampstead; *m* 1, 1975 (m dis 1982); m 2, 1985, Dick Kries; *Career* secretary, waitress, mangr of boutique, worked in model agency English Boy 1966–68, fndr Models One 1968–; *Style*— Mrs Jose Fonseca

FONTENLA-NOVOA, Manny; s of Jesus Fontenla Silver (d 1982), and Conception Novoa Gonzalez; *b* 13 May 1954, Galicia, Spain; *m* 14 Sept 1974, Lesley Ann, *née* Hughes; 3 s (Neil Anthony b 4 Sept 1976, Christopher James b 10 Feb 1978, Ross William Valentine b 3 Feb 1985), 1 da (Catherine Mary Concha b 22 Nov 1988); *Career* fndr dir Sunworld 1991–98; Thomas Cook UK & I: dep md retail 1998–2000, md retail and dep md distribution 2000–01, md tour ops 2001–03, ceo 2003–; memb Bd: Iberostar, Springboard; tstee Variety Club; *Recreations* Chelsea FC, tennis, motor racing; *Style*— Manny Fontenla-Novoa, Esq; ✉ Thomas Cook, Unit 17, Coningsby Road, Bretton, Peterborough PE3 8SB (tel 01733 417100)

FOOKES, Baroness (Life Peer UK 1997), of Plymouth in the County of Devon; Janet Evelyn Fookes; DBE (1989), DL (E Sussex 2001); da of Lewis Aylmer Fookes (d 1978), and Evelyn Margery, *née* Holmes (d 1996); *b* 21 February 1936; *Educ* Hastings and St Leonards Ladies' Coll, Hastings HS for Girls, Royal Holloway Coll London (BA); *Career* teacher 1958–70, chm Educn Ctee Hastings County Borough Cncl 1967–70 (memb 1960–61 and 1963–70); MP (Cons): Merton and Morden 1970–74, Plymouth Drake 1974–97; chm: Educn, Arts and Home Office Sub-Ctee of Expenditure Ctee 1975–79, Parly Animal Welfare Gp 1985–92, House of Lord's Refreshment Ctee 2003–; vice-chm All-Pty Mental Health Gp 1985–92 (sec 1979–85); memb: Select Ctee on Home Affrs 1983–92, Cwlth War Graves Cmmn 1987–97, Armed Services Parly Scheme 2001–; dep speaker and second dep chm of Ways and Means 1992–97 (memb Speaker's Panel of Chairmen 1976–97, dep speaker House of Lords 2003; fell Industry and Parl Tst; memb: Cncl RSPCA 1973–92 (chm 1979–81), Cncl Stonham Housing Assoc 1980–92, Cncl SSAFA - Forces Help 1980–97, Cncl of Mgmnt Coll of St Mark and St John 1989–2004; govr Kelly Coll 2002–; Hon Freeman City of Plymouth 2000; *Recreations* keep-fit exercises, swimming, theatre, gardening, yoga, scuba diving; *Style*— The Baroness Fookes, DBE, DL; ✉ House of Lords, London SW1A 0PW (tel 020 7219 5353, fax 020 7219 5979)

FOOKES, Prof Peter George; s of George Ernest James Fookes (d 1980), of Reigate, Surrey, and Ida Corina, *née* Wellby (d 1988); *b* 31 May 1933; *Educ* Reigate GS, QMC and Imperial Coll London (BSc, PhD, DSc(Eng)); *m* 1, 4 Dec 1962, Gwyneth Margaret, da of Harry William Jones, of Stratford-upon-Avon, Warks; 3 da (Jennifer Marjorie b 7 Sept 1963, Anita Janet, Rosemary Eleanor (twins) b 19 Dec 1971), 2 s (Gregory Peter Gwyn b 20 Oct 1964, Timothy David b 17 July 1968); m 2, 25 July 1987, Edna May, da of John Arthur Nix, of Surbiton, Surrey; *Career* formerly chemical/soils lab technician, co engrg geologist Binnie & Ptnrs 1960–65, lectr in engrg geology Imperial Coll London 1966–71, conslt engrg geologist in private practice 1971–; visiting prof: of geomaterials QMC London 1979–96, of geology City Univ London 1991–, of engrg geology Univ of Newcastle 1993–96; distinguished research assoc Univ of Oxford 2001; Br Geotechnical Soc Prize 1981 and 2000, William Smith Medal Geological Soc 1985, First Glossop Lectr and Medal Geological Soc 1997; ICE: Telford Premium 1981, Overseas Premium 1982 and 1992, George Stephenson Gold Medal 1990, Webb Prize 1990, Coopers Hill War Meml Medal and Prize 1992; author of over 200 published professional papers and books; memb: Geologists Assoc 1956, Br Geotechnical Soc 1963, Br Acad of Experts 1989; hon prof Univ of Birmingham 1999; Hon Dr of Science Univ of Plymouth 2005; FGS 1960, Companion ICE 1966, FIMM 1977, CEng 1977, FIGeol 1986, CGeol 1990, FREng 1991, Hon FICT 1992, FRSA 1994, Hon FRGS 2003; *Recreations* industrial archaeology, narrow boating (life memb Kennet & Avon Canal Tst), steam railways (life memb: Mid-Hants Railway Preservation Soc, The Southern Steam Tst, Swanage Railway), fell walking; *Style*— Prof Peter Fookes, FREng; ✉ tel 01962 863029, fax 01962 842317

FOOT, Michael David Kenneth Willoughby; CBE (2003); s of Kenneth Willoughby Foot (d 1980), and Ruth Joan, *née* Cornah (d 1998); *b* 16 December 1946; *Educ* Latymer Upper Sch, Pembroke Coll Cambridge (MA), Yale Univ (MA); *m* 16 Dec 1972, Michele Annette Cynthia, da of Michael Stanley Macdonald, of Kingsgate, Kent; 1 s (Anthony b 5 June 1978), 2 da (Helen b 28 Oct 1980, Joanna b 22 July 1985); *Career* Bank of England: joined 1969, mangr Gilt-Edged Div 1981, mangr Money Market Div 1983, head Foreign Exchange Div 1988–90, head Euro Div 1990–93, head of banking supervision 1993–94, dep dir supervision and surveillance 1994–96, dir of banking supervision 1996–98; md Deposit Takers and Markets Directorate FSA 1998–2004, advsr to the chm and chief exec FSA 2004–, inspr Banks and Tst Cos Bahamas 2004–07, chm Promontory Financial (UK) Ltd 2007–; UK alternate dir to IMF 1985–87; hon pres ACI (UK) 2002–04; FCIB 2002 (AIB 1973); *Recreations* church singing, chess, tennis; *Style*— Michael Foot, Esq, CBE; ✉ 14 Devonshire Square, Level 3, London EC2M 4YT (tel 020 7731 4402)

FOOT, Rt Hon Michael Mackintosh; PC (1974); 4 s of Rt Hon Isaac Foot, PC (d 1960), MP (Lib) for Bodmin 1922–24 and 1929–35, pres Lib Party Orgn 1947, and his 1 w Eva, *née* Mackintosh (d 1946); bro of Lord Caradon (d 1990) and Lord Foot (d 1999); *b* 23 July 1913; *Educ* Forres Sch, Leighton Park Sch Reading, Wadham Coll Oxford; *m* 21 Oct 1949, Jill, *née* Craigie, former w of Jeffrey Dell; *Career* pres Oxford Union 1933, ed Tribune 1948–52 and 1955–60 (md 1945–74), actg ed Evening Standard 1942, subsequently book critic, column for Daily Herald 1944–64; Parly candidate (Lab) Monmouthshire 1935; MP (Lab): Devonport 1945–55 (Parly candidate 1959), Ebbw Vale 1960–83, Blaenau Gwent 1983–92; oppn spokesman on Power and Steel Industries 1970–71, shadow ldr of House 1971–72, spokesman EEC Affairs 1972–74, sec of state Employment 1974–76, Lord Pres of the Cncl and leader House of Commons 1976–79, succeeded Rt Hon James Callaghan as ldr of Oppn 1980–Oct 1983; Freeman: City of Plymouth 1982, Borough of Blaenau Gwent 1983; hon fellow Wadham Coll Oxford; Hon LLD: Univ of Exeter 1990, Univ of Nottingham 1990; FRSL 1988; *Books* Guilty Men (with Frank Owen and Peter Howard, 1940), Armistice 1918–39 (1940), Trial of Mussolini (1943), Brendan and Beverley (1944), Still at Large (1950), Full Speed Ahead (1950), Guilty Men (with Mervyn Jones, 1957), The Pen and the Sword (1957), Parliament in Danger (1959), Aneurin Bevan Vol I 1897–1945 (1962), Vol II 1945–60 (1973), Debts of Honour (1980), Another Heart and Other Pulses (1984), Politics of Paradise (1988), The History of Mr Wells (1995), Dr Strangelove, I presume (1999); *Style*— The Rt Hon Michael Foot, FRSL

FOOT, Michael Richard Daniell; CBE (2001); s of Richard Cunningham Foot (d 1969), of Clareville Beach, NSW, and Nina, *née* Raymond (d 1970); *b* 14 December 1919; *Educ* Winchester, New Coll Oxford (MA, BLitt); *m* 1, Philippa Ruth, da of William Sydney Bence Bosanquet, DSO; m 2, Elizabeth Mary Irvine, da of Thomas Irvine King; 1 da (Sarah Rosamund Irvine b 1961), 1 s (Richard Jeffery b 1963); m 3, Mirjam Michaela, da of Prof Carl Paul Maria Romme; *Career* WWII RA rose to rank of Maj (despatches twice); taught at Univ of Oxford 1947–59, prof of modern history Univ of Manchester 1967–73, dep warden European Discussion Centre 1973–75; historian; memb: Royal Hist Soc 1958 (hon vice-pres 2001), Soc of Authors 1960; Croix de Guerre 1945, offr Order of Orange-Nassau 1990, Chevalier Legion of Honour 2005; *Publications* Gladstone and Liberalism (with J L Hammond, 1952), British Foreign Policy since 1898 (1956), Men in Uniform (1961), SOE in France (1966, 2 edn 2004), The Gladstone Diaries (volumes I and II, ed, 1968, volumes III and IV, ed with H C G Matthew, 1974), War and Society (ed, 1973), Resistance (1976), Six Faces of Courage (1978, 2 edn 2003), MI9 Escape and Evasion 1939–45 (with J M Langley, 1979), SOE: An Outline History (1984, 5 edn 2003), Holland at War against Hitler (1990), Art and War (1990), SOE in the Low Countries (2001), Oxford Companion to World War II (ed with I C B Dear, 2005); Festschrift: War, Resistance and Intelligence (ed K G Robertson, 1999); *Recreations* reading; *Clubs* Savile, Special Forces; *Style*— M R D Foot, Esq, CBE; ✉ Martins Cottage, Nuthampstead, Royston, Hertfordshire SG8 8ND; c/o Michael Sissons, PFD, Drury House, 34–43 Russell Street, London WC2B 5HA (tel 020 7344 1000, fax 020 7352 9539)

FOOT, Prof Rosemary June; da of Leslie William Foot, MBE (d 1993), and Margaret Lily Frances, *née* Fidler (d 1986); *b* 4 June 1948; *m* 27 Aug 1996, Timothy Kennedy; *Career* lectr in int relations Univ of Sussex 1978–90, prof of int relations St Antony's Coll Oxford 1996–, John Swire sr research fell in the int relations of E Asia 1990–; Fulbright/American Cncl of Learned Societies Scholar Columbia Univ NY 1981–82, visiting exchange scholar People's Univ Beijing 1986, visiting fell Center for Int Studies Princeton Univ 1997, visiting Kiriyama prof for Pacific Rim studies Univ of San Francisco 2002, visiting fell Belfer Center for Sci and Int Affrs Kennedy Sch of Govt Harvard Univ 2006, visiting S Rajaratnam prof of strategic studies Inst of Def and Strategic Studies Nanyang Technol Univ Singapore 2006; FBA 1996; *Books* The Wrong War: American Policy and the Dimensions of the Korean Conflict 1950–53 (1985), A Substitute for Victory: The Politics of Peace Making at the Korean Armistice Talks (1990), Migration: The Asian Experience (ed with Prof Judith M Brown, *qv*, 1994), The Practice of Power: US Relations with China since 1949 (1995), Hong Kong's Transitions, 1842–1997 (ed with Prof Judith M Brown, 1997), Rights Beyond Borders: The Global Community and the Struggle over Human Rights in China (2000), Order and Justice in International Relations (ed with Dr Andrew Hurrell and Prof John L Gaddis, 2003), US Hegemony and International Organizations (ed with Prof S Neil Macfarlane and Prof Michael Mastanduno, 2003), Human Rights and Counterterrorism in America's Asia Policy (2004), Does China Matter? A Reassessment (ed with Prof Barry Buzan, 2004); *Recreations* walking, music, sailing; *Style—* Prof Rosemary Foot, FBA; ✉ St Antony's College, Oxford OX2 6JF (tel 01865 432031, fax 01865 274559, e-mail rosemary.foot@sant.ox.ac.uk)

FOOTMAN, Timothy James (Tim); s of Michael Footman, and Caroline, *née* Edgeworth; *b* 7 May 1968; *Educ* Churcher's Coll Petersfield, Appleby Coll Oakville Ontario, Univ of Exeter (BA); *m* 22 Sept 2000, Boonratana Ngam-Akson; *Career* freelance journalist and editor; *Publications* The Push Guides (ed, 1994–97), Guinness World Records (ed, 1999–); contrib: The Guardian, MOJO, Time Out, Perigosto Stick; *Recreations* music of all flavours, cinema, modern art, walking the dog; *Style—* Tim Footman, Esq; ✉ Guinness World Records, 338 Euston Road, London NW1 3BD (tel 020 7891 4539, fax 020 7891 4501)

FOPP, Dr Michael Anton; s of late Sqdn-Ldr Desmond Fopp, AFC, AE, and Edna Meryl; *b* 28 October 1947; *Educ* Reading Blue Coat Sch, City Univ (MA, PhD); *m* 5 Oct 1968, Rosemary Ann, da of late V G Hodgetts, of Ashford, Kent; 1 s (Christopher Michael b 5 April 1973); *Career* Commercial and Instrument Rated pilot; keeper Battle of Britain Museum 1982–85 (dep keeper 1979–81), co sec Hendon Museums Trading Co Ltd 1981–85, visiting lectr City Univ 1984–93; dir London Tport Museum 1985–87, DG RAF Museums 1988–; chm Museum Documentation Assoc 1992–98, pres Int Assoc of Tport Museums 1992–98, vice-pres Friends of RAF Museum, London Underground Railway Soc; Freeman City of London 1980, Liveryman Guild of Air Pilots and Navigators 1987 (Warden 2006); FMA 1990, FRAeS 2001; *Publications* The Battle of Britain Museum (1981), The Bomber Command Museum (1982), Washington File (1983), The Royal Air Force Museum (1984), RAF Museum Children's Activity Book (ed, 1985), The RAF Museum (1992), High Flyers (ed, 1993), Museum and Gallery Management (1997), The Tradition is Safe (2003); author of articles published in various aviation and museum related publications; *Recreations* flying light aircraft, Chinese cookery, writing; *Clubs* RAF, Air Sqdn; *Style—* Dr Michael A Fopp; ✉ Royal Air Force Museum, Hendon, London NW9 5LL (tel 020 8205 2266)

FORBES, *see also:* Stuart-Forbes

FORBES, Anthony David Arnold William; s of Lt-Col David Walter Arthur William Forbes, MC, Coldstream Guards (ka 1943), and Diana Mary, *née* Henderson (who m 2, 6 Marquess of Exeter; he d 1981, she d 1982); *b* 15 January 1938; *Educ* Eton; *m* 1, 1962 (m dis 1973), Virginia June, yr da of Sir Leonard Ropner, 1 Bt, MC, TD (d 1977); 1 s (Jonathan David b 1964), 1 da (Susanna Jane b 1966); m 2, 1973, Belinda Mary, da of Sir Hardman Earle, 5 Bt (d 1979); *Career* Lt Coldstream Gds 1956–59; memb Stock Exchange 1965, jt sr ptnr Cazenove & Co stockbrokers 1980–94; non-exec dir: Carlton Communications plc 1994–2002, Royal Insurance Holdings plc 1994–96, Watmoughs (Holdings) plc 1994–98, Merchants Trust plc 1994–2002, Phoenix Group 1995–97, Royal & Sun Alliance Insurance Group plc 1996–2002 (dep chm 1998–2002); chm: Hosp and Homes of St Giles, Royal Choral Soc; Hon DBA De Montfort Univ 1994; FRSA; *Recreations* music, gardening; *Style—* Anthony Forbes, Esq; ✉ Wakerley Manor, Oakham, Rutland LE15 8PA (tel 01572 747549)

FORBES, Bryan; CBE (2004); *b* 22 July 1926; *Educ* West Ham Secdy Sch, RADA; *m* 1955, Nanette Newman; 2 da (Emma (m Graham Clempson), Sarah (m John Standing, *qv*)); *Career* writer, director and producer; actor 1942–60; formed Beaver Films with Richard (now Lord) Attenborough 1959; md and head of prodn ABPC Studios 1969–71, md and chief exec EMI-MGM Elstree Studios 1970–71, dir Capital Radio Ltd 1973–96; memb: Gen Advsy Cncl BBC 1966–69, BBC Schs Cncl 1971–73; pres: Beatrix Potter Soc 1982–94, Nat Youth Theatre 1984–2004, Writers Guild of GB 1988–91; Hon DLitt: Univ of London 1987, Univ of Sussex 1999; *Theatre* theatre dir incl: Macbeth (Old Vic) 1980, Star Quality (Theatre Royal Bath) 1984, Killing Jessica (Savoy) 1986, The Living Room (Royalty Theatre) 1987, One Helluva Life (tour) 2002–03; *Television* dir/prodr incl: Edith Evans I Caught Acting Like the Measles (YTV) 1973, Elton John Goodbye Norma Jean and other Things (ATV) 1973, Jessie (BBC) 1980, The Endless Game 1988; acted in: December Flower (Granada) 1984, First Among Equals (Granada) 1986; *Film* writer, dir and prodr of numerous films incl: The Angry Silence, The League of Gentlemen, Only Two Can Play, Whistle down the Wind 1961, The L Shaped Room 1962, Seance on a Wet Afternoon 1963, King Rat 1964, The Wrong Box 1965, The Whisperers 1966, Deadfall 1967, The Madwoman of Chaillot 1968, The Raging Moon 1970, The Stepford Wives 1974, The Slipper and the Rose 1975, International Velvet 1978, The Sunday Lovers 1980, Better Late than Never 1981, The Naked Face 1983; *Awards* winner of: Br Academy Award 1960, writers Guild Award (twice), Excellence in Film London Film Critics' Circle Awards 2006, BAFTA Lifetime Achievement Award 2007, numerous int awards; *Books* Truth Lies Sleeping (1950), The Distant Laughter (1972), Notes for a Life (autobiography, 1974), The Slipper and the Rose (1976), Ned's Girl (biography of Dame Edith Evans, 1977), International Velvet (1978), Familiar Strangers (1979), That Despicable Race (1980), The Rewrite Man (1983), The Endless Game (1986), A Song At Twilight (1989), A Divided Life (autobiography, 1992), The Twisted Playground (1993), Partly Cloudy (1995), Quicksand (1996), The Memory of All That (1999), The Fatal Trinity (2002), The Rules of the Game (2006); *Recreations* reading, photography, landscape gardening; *Style—* Bryan Forbes, Esq, CBE; ✉ Bryan Forbes Ltd (fax 01344 845174, e-mail endlessgame@aol.com)

FORBES, Prof Charles Douglas; s of John Forbes (d 1985), and Annie Robertson, *née* Stuart (d 1982); *b* 9 October 1938; *Educ* HS of Glasgow, Univ of Glasgow (MB ChB, MD, DSc); *m* 6 March 1965, Janette MacDonald, da of Ewan Robertson (d 1980); 2 s (John Stuart b 20 Dec 1967, Donald Alexander Ewan b 20 Sept 1971); *Career* lectr med Univ of E Africa Nairobi 1965–66, Fulbright fell American Heart Assoc 1968–70, sr lectr then reader in med Univ of Glasgow 1972–86 (lectr in therapeutics 1962–65), prof of med Univ of Dundee 1987–; author of specialist books on blood coagulation and thrombosis; FRCPG 1974, FRCPE 1976, FRCP 1978, FRSA 1990, FRSE 1992; *Recreations* gardening, walking; *Style—* Prof Charles Forbes, FRSE; ✉ East Chattan, 108 Hepburn Gardens, St Andrews, Fife KY16 9LT (tel 01334 472428)

FORBES, Colin Ames; s of John Cumming Forbes, and Kathleen Ethel Ames Forbes; *b* 6 March 1928; *Educ* Central Sch of Art and Crafts London (BA); *m* 1 (m dis), Elizabeth Hopkins; 1 da (Christine Coppe); m 2, Wendy Maria Schneider; 1 s (Aaron Forbes), 1 da (Jessica Forbes Russo); *Career* graphic design asst Herbert Spencer Studio London 1952–53, freelance graphic designer/lectr Central Sch London 1953–57, art dir Stuart Advertising London 1957–58, head Graphic Design Dept Central Sch 1958–60, freelance graphic designer 1960–62; ptnr: Fletcher Forbes Gill 1962–65, Crosby Fletcher Forbes 1965–72, Pentagram Design Ltd 1972–78, Pentragram Design Inc NY 1978–93; consulting ptnr Pentagram Design AG 1993–; chm Stanford Design Forum Stanford Calif 1988, sr critic (graphic design) Yale Sch of Art New Haven Connecticut 1989; memb: American Inst of Graphic Arts (pres 1983–84), Alliance Graphique Internationale (pres 1976–79); hon memb American Center for Design 1993; RDI 1974; *Major Design Projects* British Petroleum corp identity 1968–71, Lucas Industries corp identity 1972–79, Kodak International forms 1974, Drexel Burnham Lambert corp pubns 1979–89, ITM logo 1981, American Standard corp identity 1982, Columbia-Presbyterian Medical Center identity 1982, Nissan Motor Co logo 1982, Met Transit Authy subway station design 1982–85, Hilton International Hotels literature 1982–86, IBM corp pubns 1985 and 1990–91, 'Toray' identity 1986, Neiman Marcus identity study 1987–88, Hallmark Cards design consultancy 1989–90, Kubota Corporation identity 1989, Airco Gases retail design consultancy 1989–90, Hotel Hankyu International identity 1990; *Awards* Silver Award 4th Biennale Int Art Book Prize 1975, Pres's Award D&AD 1977, AIGA Medal American Inst of Graphic Arts 1992; *Books* Graphic Design: Visual Comparisons (jtly, 1963), A Sign Systems Manual (jtly, 1970), New Alphabets A-Z (jtly, 1973), Living by Design (jtly, 1978), Pentagram: The Compendium (jtly, 1993); *Recreations* horseback riding; *Style—* Colin Forbes; ✉ 2879 Horseshoe Road, Westfield, NC 27053, USA (tel 00 1 336 351 3941, fax 00 1 336 351 3949)

F

FORBES, Very Rev Graham John Thomson; CBE (2004); s of John Thomson Forbes (d 1986), of Edinburgh, and Doris, *née* Smith; *b* 10 June 1951; *Educ* George Heriot's Sch Edinburgh, Univ of Aberdeen (MA), Univ of Edinburgh (BD), Edinburgh Theol Coll; *m* 25 Aug 1973, Jane, da of John Tennant Miller, of Edinburgh; 3 s (Duncan, Andrew, Hamish); *Career* curate Old St Paul's Edinburgh 1976–82; provost: St Ninian's Cathedral Perth 1982–90, St Mary's Cathedral Edinburgh 1990–; non-exec dir Radio Tay 1986–90; fndr Canongate Youth Project Edinburgh, pres Lothian Assoc of Youth Clubs 1986–, HM (lay) Inspr of Constabulary for Scotland 1995–98; chm: Scottish Exec MMR Expert Gp 2001–02, Scottish Criminal Cases Review Cmmn 2002, UK Ctee on Ethical Aspects of Pandemic Influenza 2006–; dir Theological Inst of the Scottish Episcopal Church 2002–04; memb: Scottish Community Educn Cncl 1981–87, Children's Panel Advsy Ctee Tayside 1986–90, Parole Bd for Scotland 1990–95, Scottish Consumer Cncl 1995–98, GMC 1996–, Scottish Criminal Cases Review Cmmn 1998–, Clinical Standards Board for Scotland 1999–2005, Historic Buildings Cncl for Scotland 2000–02, Scottish Cncl Royal Coll of Anaesthetists 2001–04; Hon DUniv Napier; *Recreations* fly fishing, running; *Style—* The Very Rev the Provost of St Mary's Cathedral Edinburgh; ✉ 8 Lansdowne Crescent, Edinburgh EH12 5EQ (tel 0131 225 2978, fax 0131 226 1482); St Mary's Cathedral, Palmerston Place, Edinburgh EH12 5AW (tel 0131 225 6293, fax 0131 225 3181, e-mail provost@cathedral.net)

FORBES, Admiral Sir Ian Andrew; KCB (2003), CBE (1994); *b* 24 October 1946; *Educ* Eastbourne Coll; *m* 12 April 1975, Sally; 2 da; *Career* joined RN 1965; commands: HMS Kingfisher, HMS Diomede, HMS Chatham, HMS Invincible, UK Task Gp, UK Surface Fleet; Mil Advsr to High Rep in Sarajevo 1996–98, Supreme Allied Cdr Atlantic 2002–03, Dep Supreme Allied Cdr Transformation 2003–04; RAF Staff Coll Bracknell 1983, RCDS 1994; Queen's Commendation for Valuable Service 1996, US Legion of Merit 2004; memb Windsor Leadership Tst; chm Cncl Eastbourne Coll, memb Advsy Bd Occidental Univ Calif; hon citizen Norfolk Virginia; *Recreations* history, gardening, golf, tennis; *Clubs* Army and Navy; *Style—* Admiral Sir Ian Forbes, KCB, CBE; ✉ c/o Army and Navy Club, Pall Mall, London SW1Y 5JN

FORBES, James; s of Maj Donald Forbes (d 1963), of Edinburgh, and Rona Ritchie, *née* Yeats (d 1963); *b* 2 January 1923; *Educ* Christ's Hosp, Offrs Trg Sch Bangalore S India; *m* 14 Aug 1948, Alison Mary Fletcher, da of Maj George K Moffat (d 1979), of Dunblane, Perthshire; 2 s (Lindsay b 11 Oct 1953, Moray b 29 June 1962); *Career* WWII cmmnd 15 Punjab Regt 1942, transferred to Ordnance 1943, CO (Capt) Mobile Ammunition Inspection Unit 1943–44, Maj DADOS Amm GHQ (1) 1945–46, released as Hon Maj 1947; Peat Marwick Mitchell 1952–58; Schweppes plc: joined 1958, ops res mangr 1960–63, gp chief accountant and dir of subsid cos 1963–69; gp fin dir Cadbury Schweppes 1970–78 (fin advsr on formation 1969–70); Tate & Lyle: sr exec dir 1978–80, chm Pension Fund 1978–85, vice-chm 1980–84; non-exec dir: British Transport Hotels 1978–83, British Rail Investments 1980–84, Steetley plc 1984–89, Compass Hotels Ltd 1984–99, Lautro Ltd 1986–90; Forestry cmmr 1982–88; treas and chm Cncl of Almoners Christ's Hosp 1987–96 (chm Resources Ctee 1985–86); memb Highland Soc of London; FCA 1966 (memb Cncl 1971–88, treas 1984–86); *Clubs* Caledonian, Royal Commonwealth Soc; *Style—* James Forbes, Esq; ✉ 31 Rosemary Court, Church Road, Haslemere, Surrey GU27 1BH (tel 01428 652461)

FORBES, Master of; Hon Malcolm Nigel Forbes; DL (Aberdeenshire 1996); s and h of 23 Lord Forbes, KBE, *qv*; *b* 6 May 1946; *Educ* Eton, Univ of Aberdeen; *m* 1, 30 Jan 1969 (m dis 1982), Carole Jennifer Andrée, da of Norman Stanley Whitehead (d 1981), of Aberdeen; 1 s (Neil Malcolm Ross b 10 March 1970), 1 da (Joanne Carole b 23 April 1972); m 2, 15 Feb 1988, Mrs Jennifer Mary Gribbon, da of Ian Peter Whittington (d 1991), of Tunbridge Wells, Kent; *Heir* s, Neil Forbes; *Career* dir: Instock Disposables Ltd, Castle Forbes Collection Ltd; farmer and landowner; *Recreations* skiing, shooting, golf; *Clubs* Pilgrims, Eton Ramblers, XL, Scotch Malt Whisky Soc, Aboyne Golf; *Style—* The Master of Forbes, DL; ✉ Castle Forbes, Alford, Aberdeenshire AB33 8BL (tel 01975 562524, fax 01975 562898, e-mail office@castle-forbes.com)

FORBES, Neil; s of Keith Alexander Forbes, of Limoges, France, and Margaret Hannah-Crawford Forbes, *née* Mayne; *b* 7 October 1970; *Educ* Wavell Comp Sch, Farnborough Tech (City and Guilds), Perth Tech (City and Guilds); *m* 13 April 1998, Sarah, da of Douglas Stuart Grant Fowler; 2 s (Oscar Douglas b 25 July 2001, Louis Alexander b 9 April 2005); *Career* chef; experience The Waterside Inn and Le Manoir Quat'Saisons; commis chef Ballathie House, chef de partie The Peat Inn, sous chef Kinnaird, head chef Royal Scotsman train, head chef Braeval Restaurant, head chef Nairns, currently exec chef Atrium and Blue restaurants Edinburgh; guest chef Saturday Kitchen (BBC 2); *Awards* finalist Young Scottish Chef of the Year 1991, finalist Young Chef of the Year 1992, Michelin Star, 3 AA Rosettes, 5 out of 10 Good Food Guide 1999, Acorn winner 1997, Best Restaurant Edinburgh The List magazine 2004–05; *Publications* Consumables (recipe book for the Royal Scotsman train, 1996), Scotland on a Plate (contrib), Edinburgh on a Plate (contrib); *Recreations* sports cars, eating out, reading cookery books, interior design; *Clubs* Acorn; *Style—* Neil Forbes, Esq

FORBES, 22 Lord (Premier S Lordship before July 1445); Sir Nigel Ivan Forbes; KBE (1960), JP (Aberdeenshire 1955), DL (1958); s of 21 Lord Forbes (d 1953), and Lady Mabel Anson (d 1972), da of 3 Earl of Lichfield; *b* 19 February 1918; *Educ* Harrow, RMC Sandhurst; *m* 23 May 1942, Hon Rosemary Katharine Hamilton-Russell, da of 9 Viscount Boyne; 2 s, 1 da; *Heir* s, Master of Forbes, DL, *qv*; *Career* served WWII, France and Belgium (wounded), N Africa, Sicily, NW Europe Adjt Grenadier Gds, Staff Coll 1945–46, mil asst high cmmr Palestine 1947–48, Maj Grenadier Gds; representative peer for Scotland

1955–63; pres Royal Highland and Agric Soc for Scotland 1958–59; memb Inter-Parly Union Delgn to: Denmark 1956, Hungary 1965, Ethiopia 1971; memb Cwlth Parly Assoc Delgn to: Canada 1961, Pakistan 1962; min of state Scottish Office 1958–59; chm Rolawn Ltd 1975–98; chm Don Dist River Bd 1961–73; memb Bd: Scottish Nature Conservancy 1961–67, Aberdeen Milk Mktg Bd 1962–72; memb Sports Cncl for Scotland 1966–71; dep chm Tennant Caledonian Breweries Ltd 1964–74; dir: Blenheim Travel Ltd 1981–88, Grampian TV 1960–88; pres Scottish Scouts Assoc 1970–88, chm Scottish Branch Nat Playing Fields Assoc 1965–80, patron Friends of Insch Hospital 1992–; hon pres Books Abroad 1998–; *Recreations* wildlife, conservation, photography, travel; *Clubs* Army and Navy; *Style*— The Rt Hon the Lord Forbes, KBE, DL; ✉ Balforbes, Alford, Aberdeenshire AB33 8DR (tel 01975 562516, e-mail office@harthillfarms.com)

FORBES, Prof Ronald Douglas; s of William Forbes (d 1960), and Agnes Jane Campbell, *née* McIldowie (d 2004); *b* 22 March 1947; *Educ* Morrison's Acad Crieff, Edinburgh Coll of Art (DA, SED postgrad scholarship), Jordanhill Coll of Educn Glasgow; *m* 2, 1985, Sheena Henderson Bell, da of Arthur Bell; 2 da (Abigail, Susan Bell), 1 s (Ian William Lorne); *Career* artist; lectr Bell Coll Hamilton 1972–73, Leverhulme sr art fell Univ of Strathclyde 1973–74, head of painting Crawford Sch of Art Cork 1974–78, artist in residence Livingston W Lothian 1978–80, lectr Glasgow Sch of Art 1979–83, head of painting Duncan of Jordanstone Coll of Art and Design Univ of Dundee 1995–2001 (MFA prog dir 1983–95), visiting prof in fine art Univ of Abertay Dundee 2003–, Leverhulme artist-in-residence Scottish Crop Research Inst 2005–07; res Hobart Centre for the Arts Univ of Tasmania 1995; subject of numerous art catalogues; fndr Glasgow League of Artists 1971, tstee Perthshire Public Art Tst 1994–2000; prof memb SSA 1972, RSA 2005 (ARSA 1996); *Awards* first prize first Scottish Young Contemporary Exhbn 1967, RSA Guthrie Award 1979, Scottish Arts Cncl Award (for film making) 1979, Scottish Arts Cncl Studio Award Amsterdam 1980, RSA Highland Soc of London Award 1996, RSA Gillies Award (to visit India) 1999; *Solo Exhibitions* Compass Gallery Glasgow 1973, Goethe Inst Glasgow 1974, Collins Gallery Glasgow 1974, Drian Galleries London 1975, Cork Art Soc Gallery 1976 and 1978, Project Arts Centre Dublin 1976, The Lanthorn Livingston 1980, Forebank Gallery Dundee 1980, Third Eye Centre Glasgow 1980, Compass Gallery Glasgow 1983, Drian Galleries London 1984, Babbity Bowster Glasgow 1986, Seagate Gallery Dundee 1990 and 1995, Perth Museum and Art Gallery 1991, Maclaurin Art Gallery Ayr 1991, An Lanntair Gallery Stornoway 1995, Plimsoll Gallery Hobart Tasmania 1995, NS Gallery Glasgow 1996, De Keerder Kunstkamer Netherlands 1997, Zaks Gallery Chicago USA 1999, SIU Museum (Carbondale) USA 1999, VRC, DCA Dundee 2000, ROSL Galleries London and Edinburgh 2000–01, Vardy Gallery Sunderland 2001, Crawford Arts Centre St Andrews 2003, Smith Gallery and Museum Stirling 2005, Hannah Maclure Centre Univ of Abertay Dundee 2005, Hamnavoe Gallery Aberdeen 2007; *Work in Collections* incl: Arts Cncl NI, Cork Municipal Art Gallery, Dundee Museums and Art Galleries, Hunterian Gallery Glasgow, Museum Narodowego Gdansk, Smith Art Gallery Stirling (Scottish Arts Cncl Bequest), Perth Museum and Art Galleries, Ross Harper and Murphy Collection Glasgow, Univ of Strathclyde, Univ of Abertay Dundee, Rare Books Collection State Library of Qland; *Curated Exhbns* incl: Scottish Arts Cncl Touring Exhbn (Arts Cncl Belfast, Fruit Market Gallery Edinburgh, Collins Gallery Glasgow, Aberdeen Art Gallery) 1978–79, Netherlands Touring Exhbn (Hoensbruck, Roermond, Maastricht and Liege) 1983, Nature: Only and Idea (Galerie Trace Maastricht) 2002, Parallel Paths (RSA) 2006; *Films* Between Dreams (1974), She (1974), TV 74 (1974), Portfolio (1975), Behaviour Patterns (1976), Signs (1976–77), Incident (1978), Two Painters (1978), Happy Day (1979), Incident (1981), Three Artists (1982), The Illusionist (2004); *Recreations* theatre, cinema, gardening, laughing; *Clubs* Royal Over-Seas League (hon memb, London and Edinburgh); *Style*— Prof Ronald Forbes; ✉ 13 Fort Street, Dundee DD2 1BS (tel 01382 641498, e-mail ronnieforbes@blueyonder.co.uk, website www.ronald-forbes.com)

FORBES, Sandra Elizabeth Margaret (Mrs Nigel Webspers); da of Albert Forbes, of Sion Mills, Co Tyrone, and Mary, *née* Hempton; *b* 8 April 1965, Strabane, NI; *Educ* Strabane GS, Univ of Manchester (LLB), Chester Law Coll; *m* 19 Sept 2001, Nigel Websper; 2 da (Olivia, Sienna (twins) b 27 April 2005); *Career* slr; Frere Cholomeley 1989–91, Burges Salmon 1991–; *Recreations* cooking, reading, theatre; *Style*— Ms Sandra Forbes; ✉ Burges Salmon LLP, Narrow Quay House, Prince Street, Bristol BS1 4AH (tel 0117 939 2000)

FORBES, Prof Sebastian; s of Dr Watson Forbes (d 1997), and Mary Henderson, *née* Hunt (d 1997); *b* 22 May 1941; *Educ* UCS Hampstead, Royal Acad of Music, Univ of Cambridge (MA, MusD); *m* 1, 1968 (m dis 1977); 2 da (Joanna b 1971, Emily b 1974); m 2, 24 Sept 1983, Tessa Mary, da of John Brady (d 1967); 1 s (Alistair b 1984), 1 da (Nicola b 1986); *Career* prodr BBC (sound) 1964–67; lectr Univ Coll of N Wales Bangor 1968–72; Univ of Surrey: lectr 1972–, prof of music 1981–, emeritus prof 2006–; conductor incl Horniman Singers 1981–90; princ compositions incl: String Quartet No 1 (Radcliffe award 1969), Essay for Clarinet and Orchestra (1970), Death's Dominion (1971), Symphony in Two Movements (1972), Sinfonias 1 (1967, rev 1989), 2 (1978) and 3 (1990), Sonata for 21 (1975), Voices of Autumn, 8 Japanese Tanka for choir and piano (1975), Sonata for 8 (1978), Violin Fantasy No 2 (1979), Evening Canticles (Aedis Christi 1 (1980), Aedis Christi 2 (1984)), String Quartet No 3 (1981), Sonata for 17 (1987), Bristol Mass (1990), Hymn to St Etheldreda (1995), Sonata-Rondo for piano (1996), String Quartet No 4 (1996), Rawsthorne Reflections for organ (1998), String Quartet No 5 (2000), Sonata for 15 (2001), Interplay 2 for four pianists (2002), Duo for clarinet and piano (2003), Hurrah! for Brunel, cantata for young voices (2007); memb Performing Rights Soc; LRAM, ARCM, ARCO, ARAM, FRSA; *Style*— Prof Sebastian Forbes; ✉ Octave House, Boughton Hall Avenue, Send, Woking, Surrey GU23 7DF; Department of Music, University of Surrey, Guildford, Surrey GU2 7XH (tel 01483 689308, e-mail s.forbes@surrey.ac.uk, website www.sebastianforbes.com)

FORBES ADAM, Sir Christopher Eric; 3 Bt (UK 1917), of Hankelow Court, Co Chester; s of Eric Forbes Adam, CMG (2 s of Sir Frank Forbes Adam, 1 Bt, CB, CIE, JP, DL), by his w Agatha, widow of Sidney Spooner and eldest da of Reginald Walter Macan, sometime Master Univ Coll, Oxford; suc unc, Gen Sir Ronald Forbes Adam, 2 Bt, GCB, DSO, OBE, 1982; *b* 12 February 1920; *Educ* Abinger Hill Sch Surrey, privately; *m* 17 Sept 1957, Patricia Anne Wreford, yr da of John Neville Wreford Brown, of Maltings, Abberton, Colchester, Essex; 1 adopted da (Sarah Anne (Mrs Allen) b 1960); *Heir* 1 cous, Rev Timothy Forbes Adam; *Career* sometime journalist with Yorkshire Post; *Style*— Sir Christopher Forbes Adam, Bt; ✉ 46 Rawlings Street, London SW3 2LS

FORBES-LEITH OF FYVIE, Sir George Ian David; 4 Bt (UK 1923), of Jessfield, Co Midlothian; s of Sir Andrew George Forbes-Leith of Fyvie, 3 Bt (d 2000); *b* 26 May 1967; *m* 3 June 1995, Camilla Frances, eldest da of Philip Ely, of Crawley, Hants; 1 da (India Rose b 27 July 1997), 2 s (Alexander Philip George b 4 Feb 1999, Charles Ian b 4 Aug 2000); *Heir* s, Alexander Forbes-Leith; *Style*— Sir George Forbes-Leith of Fyvie, Bt; ✉ Estate Office, Fyvie, Turriff, Aberdeenshire AB53 8JS (tel 0165 1 891 246, e-mail gforbeslei@aol.com)

FORD, *see also:* St Clair-Ford

FORD, Sir Andrew Russell; 3 Bt (UK 1929), of Westerdunes, Co of East Lothian; s of Sir Henry Russell Ford, 2 Bt, TD, JP (d 1989), and Mary Elizabeth, *née* Wright (d 1997); *b* 29 June 1943; *Educ* Winchester, New Coll Oxford, Loughborough Coll of Education (DLC), London (BA external), Birmingham (MA external); *m* 8 Aug 1968, Penelope Anne, o da of Harold Edmund Relph (d 1995), of West Kirby, Wirral; 1 da (Julia Mary b 1970), 2 s (Toby Russell b 1973, David Andrew b 1984); *Heir* s, Toby Ford; *Career* schoolmaster: Blairmore Sch Aberdeenshire 1967–71, St Peter's Sch Cambridge NZ 1971–74; lectr Wiltshire Coll Chippenham 1974–2003 (head of sport and leisure 1974–96, sr lectr in English 1996–2003); *Style*— Sir Andrew Ford, Bt; ✉ 20 Coniston Road, Chippenham, Wiltshire SN14 0PX

FORD, Colin John; CBE (1993); s of John William Ford, of London, and Hélène Martha, *née* Richardson; *b* 13 May 1934; *Educ* Enfield GS, UC Oxford (MA); *m* 1, 12 Aug 1961 (m dis 1980), Margaret Elizabeth, da of Ernest Cordwell; 1 s (Richard John b 22 Nov 1970), 1 da (Clare Michaela Elizabeth b 5 Dec 1972); m 2, 7 Sept 1984, Susan Joan Frances Grayson; 1 s (Thomas Grayson b 29 March 1985); *Career* mangr and prodr Kidderminster Playhouse 1958–60, gen mangr Western Theatre Ballet 1960–62, visiting lectr in English and drama Calif State Univ at Long Beach 1962–64, dep curator Nat Film Archive 1965–72, organiser Thirtieth Anniversary Congress of Int Fedn of Film Archive London 1968, dir Cinema City exhibition 1970, prog dir London Shakespeare Film Festival 1972, keeper of film and photography Nat Portrait Gallery 1972–81, head Nat Museum of Photography, Film and TV 1982–93, dir Nat Museums and Galleries of Wales 1993–98; film Masks and Faces 1966 (BBC TV version Omnibus 1968); Hon MA Univ of Bradford 1989; *Books* An Early Victorian Album (with Sir Roy Strong, *qv*, 1974, 2 edn 1977), The Cameron Collection (1975), Oxford Companion to Film (princ contrib, 1976), Happy and Glorious: Six Reigns of Royal Photography (ed, 1977), Rediscovering Mrs Cameron (1979), People in Camera (1979), A Hundred Years Ago (with Brian Harrison, 1983), Portraits (Gallery of World Photography, 1983), André Kertész: The Manchester Collection (contrib, 1984), The Story of Popular Photography (ed, 1989), You Press the Button, We do the Rest (with Karl Steinorth, 1989), Lewis Carroll, Photographer (with Karl Steinorth, 1991), Lewis Carroll, Photographer (1998), André Kertész and the Avant Garde (1999), Julia Margaret Cameron, The Complete Photographs (2003), Julia Margaret Cameron, 19th Century Photographer of Genius (2003); *Recreations* travel, music; *Style*— Colin Ford, Esq, CBE; ✉ c/o ArtConnect, 7 Gentleman's Row, Enfield EN2 6PT (tel 020 8364 5881, e-mail colinford@blueyonder.co.uk)

FORD, Prof David Frank; s of George Ford (d 1960), of Dublin, and Phyllis Mary Elizabeth, *née* Woodman; *b* 23 January 1948; *Educ* The High Sch Dublin, Trinity Coll Dublin (fndn scholar, BA, Berkeley gold medal), St John's Coll Cambridge (scholar, MA, Naden research student, PhD), Yale Univ (Henry fell, STM); *m* 1982, Deborah Perrin, da of Rev Prof Daniel Wayne Hardy; 3 da (Rebecca Perrin b 1985, Grace b and d 1988, Rachel Mary b 1989), 1 s (Daniel George b 1991); *Career* research Tübingen Univ 1975; Univ of Birmingham: lectr in theol 1976–90, sr lectr 1990–91; Univ of Cambridge: regius prof of divinity 1991–, fell Selwyn Coll 1991–, fndn memb Trinity Coll 1991–, chm Faculty Bd of Divinity 1993–95, memb Syndicate Cambridge Univ Press 1993–, chm Centre for Advanced Religious and Theol Studies 1995–, memb Mgmnt Ctee E Asia Inst 2001–, Gomes lectr Emmanuel Coll 2003, dir Cambridge Interfaith Prog 2003–; pres Soc for the Study of Theol 1997–99; memb Center of Theol Inquiry Princeton Univ 1993–, memb Cncl of 100 Ldrs World Economic Forum West-Islamic Dialogue 2004–; visiting fell Yale Univ 1982, Donnellan lectr TCD 1984, Hollis lectr Church of S India 2002, Ebor lecture Univ of York 2006, Stephenson lectures Univ of Sheffield 2007; memb: AHRB Peer Review Coll 2005–, Ctee of Mgmnt Centre for Medical Genetics and Policy 2005–; memb Editorial Bd: Modern Theology, Scottish Jl of Theology, Teaching Theology and Religion; theol conslt Primates' Meeting Anglican Communion 2000, 2001, 2002 and 2003; church warden St Luke's Church Bristol St Birmingham 1979–84; memb: Faith and Order Advsy Gp C of E 1988–90, Bishop's Cncl Birmingham Dio 1989–91, Theol Working Gp on C of E Urban Policy 1989, Archbishop of Canterbury's Urban Theol Gp 1991–95, Cncl Ridley Hall Theol Coll 1991–, Mgmnt Ctee Soc for Scriptural Reasoning 1997–, C of E Doctrine Cmmn 1998–2003, Building Bridges Seminars (Lambeth 2002, Qatar 2003); chm Westcott House Theol Coll 1991–; memb Mgmnt Ctee Newhaven Housing Assoc 1978–84, govr Lea Mason Sch 1984–91, tstee Henry Martyn Tst 1991–; memb American Acad of Religion; Hon DD Univ of Birmingham 2000; *Books* Barth and God's Story: Biblical Narrative and the Theological Method of Karl Barth in the Church Dogmatics (1981), Jubilate: Theology in Praise (with Daniel W Hardy, 1984, 2 edn 2005), Meaning and Truth in 2 Corinthians (with F M Young, 1988), The Modern Theologians (1989, 3 edn 2005), A Long Rumour of Wisdom: Redescribing Theology (1992), The Shape of Living (1997, 2 edn 2002), Self and Salvation. Being Transformed (1999), Theology: A Very Short Introduction (1999), Christian Wisdom: Desiring God and Learning in Love (2007), Shaping Theology (2007); *Recreations* family life, ball games, poetry, drama, kayaking, walking; *Style*— Prof David Ford; ✉ Faculty of Divinity, University of Cambridge, West Road, Cambridge CB3 9BS (tel 01223 763031, fax 01223 763003)

FORD, Sir David Robert; KBE (1988, OBE 1976), LVO (1975); s of William Ewart, and Edna Ford; *b* 22 February 1935; *Educ* Tauntons Sch; *m* 1, 1958 (m dis 1987), Elspeth Anne, *née* Muckart; 2 s, 2 da; m 2, 1987, Gillian Petersen, *née* Monsarrat; *Career* Nat Serv 1953–55, reg cmmn RA 1955; regimental duty Malta 1953–58, Lt UK 1958–62, Capt Commando Regt 1962–66; active serv: Borneo 1964, Aden 1966; Staff Coll Quetta 1967, seconded to Govt of Hong Kong 1967, ret from Army as Maj 1972; dir Govt of Hong Kong Information Serv 1974–76 (dep dir 1972–74), dep sec Govt Secretariat Hong Kong 1976, under sec NI Office 1977–79, sec for information Govt of Hong Kong 1979–80, Hong Kong cmmr in London 1980–81, RCDS 1982, sec for housing Govt of Hong Kong 1985 (dir of housing 1983–84), sec for the Civil Serv 1985–86, chief sec Hong Kong 1986–93, Hong Kong cmmr London 1994–97; chm: CPRE 1998–2003, PCCW Europe 2002–, Hong Kong Soc 2003–, UK Broadband 2003–; vice-pres Rare Breeds Survival Tst 2004–; *Recreations* tennis, fishing, rearing rare breed cattle and sheep; *Style*— Sir David Ford, KBE, LVO

FORD, (James) Glyn; MEP; s of Ernest Benjamin Ford (d 1990), of Glos, and Matilda Alberta James (d 1986); *b* 28 January 1950, Gloucester; *Educ* Marling Sch Stroud, Univ of Reading (BSc), UCL (MSc); *m* 1, 1973 (m dis), Hazel Nancy, da of Hedley John Mahy (d 1969), of Guernsey; 1 da (Elise Jane b 1981); m 2, 1992, Daniela Zannelli; 1 s (Alessandro Aled b 1996); *Career* undergraduate apprentice BAC 1967–68, course tutor in oceanography Open Univ 1976–78, teaching asst UMIST 1977–78; res fell Univ of Sussex 1978–79; Univ of Manchester: res fell 1976–79, lectr 1979–80, sr res fell Prog of Policy Res in Engrg Sci and Technol 1980–84, hon visiting res fell 1984–; visiting prof Univ of Tokyo 1983; Parly candidate (Lab) Hazel Grove Gen Election 1987; MEP (Lab): Gtr Manchester East 1984–99, SW England 1999–; chm Ctee of Inquiry into Growth of Racism and Fascism in Europe for Euro Parl 1984–86, vice-chm Security and Disarmament Sub Ctee of Euro Parl 1987–89, rapporteur Ford Report Ctee of Inquiry into Racism and Xenophobia 1989–90, ldr European Parly Labour Party 1989–93 (dep ldr 1993–94), first vice-chm Socialist Gp Euro Parl 1989–93; pres: Euro Parl Chapter, Interparliamentary Cncl Against Anti-Semitism; memb: Nat Exec Ctee Lab Party 1989–93, TU Liaison Review Gp into Trade Union links 1992–93, Consultative Ctee on Racism and Xenophobia 1994–98, nat treas Anti-Nazi League 1995–; *Publications* The Future of Ocean Technology (1987), Fascist Europe (1992), Evolution of a European (1993), Changing States (1996), Making European Progress (2001); author of various articles in jls of sci and technol; *Clubs* Groucho, Soho House, Manchester Literary and Philosophical Soc; *Style*— Glyn Ford, Esq, MEP; ✉ The Bellevue Centre, 6 Bellevue Road, Cinderford, Gloucestershire GL14 2AB; European Parliament, ASP-14E169, Rue Wiertz, 1047 Brussels, Belgium

FORD, Graham; s of James Ford, GM, of Tunbridge Wells, and Muriel Betty, *née* Whitfield; *b* 8 May 1950; *Educ* St Dunstan's Coll Catford, Medway Coll of Design; *m* 4 June 1977,

Rachel Anne, da of Prof H W F Saggs; 2 s (Joseph b 1 March 1978, Oscar b 8 Feb 1989), 2 da (Charlotte b 14 May 1980, Florence b 30 Nov 1986); *Career* photographer; asst to David Davies, Bob Croxford and David Thorpe 1968–76, freelance 1977–; clients incl: Volvo, Parker Pens, Sainsbury's, Levis, BMW, Whitbread, Absolut Vodka, Land Rover, Oxfam, NSPCC, RSPCA, COI; various awards from: D&AD, Campaign, Assoc of Photographers, NY One Show, Cannes, Art Dirs' Club of Italy, Art Dirs' Club of Europe; memb: D&AD 1979, Assoc of Photographers 1979; *Books* Bill Brandt The Assemblages; *Recreations* family, sailing, photography, wine, silversmithing; *Clubs* Deben Yacht; *Style*— Graham Ford, Esq; ✉ Topfields, Fen Walk, Woodbridge, Suffolk IP12 4BH (tel 01394 383751, e-mail graham@grahamford.co.uk)

FORD, Prof Sir Hugh; kt (1975); s of Arthur Ford (d 1969), of Welwyn Garden City, Herts, and Constance Ford; *b* 16 July 1913; *Educ* Northampton Sch, Imperial Coll London (DSc, PhD); *m* 1, 1942, Wynyard Scholfield (d 1991); 2 da (Clare, Vanessa); m 2, 1993, Thelma Alys Jensen; *Career* research engr ICI 1939–42, chief engr Br Iron & Steel Fedn 1942–48; Imperial Coll London: reader and then prof of applied mechanics 1948–69, prof of mechanical engrg 1969–82 (now emeritus), head of dept 1965–78, pro-rector 1978–80; chm Sir Hugh Ford & Associates Ltd 1982– (formerly of Ford & Dain Ptnrs Ltd); tech dir: Davy Ashmore Gp 1968–71, Alfred Herbert 1972–79, Ricardo Consulting Engrg 1980–88; dir: Air Liquide UK 1970–95, International Dynamics Ltd 1982–91 (formerly RD Projects Ltd); chm Engrs Bd SERC 1970–74, memb Agric Research Cncl 1976–81; pres: IMechE 1976–77, Welding Inst 1983–85, Inst of Metals 1985–87; vice-pres Royal Acad of Engrg 1981–84; fell Imperial Coll 1983; Hon DUniv Sheffield 1984; Hon DSc: Univ of Salford, Queen's Univ Belfast, Aston Univ, Univ of Bath, Univ of Sussex; James Watt Int Gold medal 1985; Freeman: City of London, Worshipful Co of Blacksmiths, Worshipful Co of Engrs; FRS 1967, FREng 1976 (fndr fell), Hon MASME, FCGI, FICE, Hon FIMechE, Hon FIChemE, FIM; *Recreations* gardening, music, model engineering; *Clubs* Athenaeum; *Style*— Prof Sir Hugh Ford, FRS, FREng; ✉ 18 Shrewsbury House, Cheyne Walk, London SW3 5LN (tel 020 7352 4948, fax 020 7352 5320); Shamley Cottage, Shamley Green, Surrey GU5 0ST (tel 01483 898012)

FORD, Baroness (Life Peer 2006), of Cunninghame in North Ayrshire; Margaret Anne Ford; da of Edward Garland (d 1993), and Susan, *née* Townsley; *b* 16 December 1957; *Educ* St Michael's Acad Kilwinning, Univ of Glasgow (MA, MPhil); *m* 1990, David Arthur Bolger; 2 c from previous m (Michael b 14 Aug 1984, Katharine b 4 April 1986); *Career* Scottish sec BIFU 1982–87, managing conslt Price Waterhouse 1987–90, dir of personnel Scottish Homes 1990–93, md Eglinton Management Centre 1993–2002, chm Lothian Health Bd 1997–2001, fndr, dep chm and non-exec dir Goodpractice.net 2000–05 (formerly chief exec), chm English Partnerships 2002–, chm Irvine Bay Urban Regeneration Co 2006–; non-exec dir: Scottish Prison Serv 1994–98, Ofgem 2000–03, Thus Group plc 2002–05, Serco plc 2003–; memb: Industrial Tbnl Panel 1984–90, Scottish Business Forum 1997–; lay advsr HM Inspectorate of Constabulary 1993–; FRSA; *Recreations* family, golf, sports, bridge, painting, cooking, current affairs; *Style*— The Rt Hon the Lady Ford

FORD, HE Peter William; *b* 27 June 1947; *Educ* Univ of Oxford (BA); *m* 1992, Alganesh Haile Beyene; *Career* HM Dip Serv; dep high cmmr Singapore 1991–94, head Near East Dept FCO 1994–98, ambass to Bahrain 1999–2003, ambass to Syria 2003–; *Recreations* golf, cycling; *Style*— HE Mr Peter Ford; ✉ c/o Foreign & Commonwealth Office (Damascus), King Charles Street, London SW1A 2AH

FORD, Richard James Cameron; s of Bernard Thomas Ford (d 1967), of Burbage, Wilts, and Eveline Saumarez Ford (d 1952); *b* 1 February 1938; *Educ* Marlborough; *m* 27 Sept 1975, Mary Elizabeth, da of James Arthur Keevil; 3 s (James Richard Keevil b 26 July 1976, Charles John Cameron b 26 July 1978, William Bernard Saumarez b 29 May 1980); *Career* admitted slr 1961, ptnr Ford and Ford 1965, sr ptnr Ford Gunningham and Co 1970–2001, sr ptnr Wood Awdry & Ford 2002– (ptnr 2001–05, conslt 2005–); dir: Ramsbury Building Society 1984–86, West of England Building Society 1986–89, Regency and West of England Building Society 1989–90, Portman Building Society 1990; tstee Glos and Wilts Law Soc 1983– (pres 1982–83); memb Salisbury Diocesan Synod 1985–93, lay chm Pewsey Synod 1987–93; memb: Wyvern Hosp Mgmnt Ctee 1967–70, Swindon Hosp Mgmnt Ctee 1970–74, Wilts AHA 1974–82; vice-chm Swindon HA 1982–87; memb Cncl Law Soc 1992–2002, chm Wills and Equity Ctee 1992–2004; clerk to Cncl Marlborough Coll 1994–2004; *Recreations* riding, sailing; *Clubs* Royal Solent Yacht, East India and Sports; *Style*— Richard Ford, Esq; ✉ Little Estcotts, Burbage, Wiltshire SN8 3AQ; Wood Awdry & Ford, Kingsbury House, Marlborough, Wiltshire SN8 1HU (tel 01672 512265, fax 01672 514891)

FORD, Richard John; s of Arthur William Ford (d 1992), of Christchurch, Dorset, and Violet, *née* Banbury; *b* 10 April 1949; *Educ* Hove Co GS for Boys, Portsmouth Poly Sch of Architecture (BA), Poly of Central London (DipArch); *m* Janet Kathleen; 1 s (Edward Richard b 5 Feb 1984); *Career* student Portsmouth Poly and Poly of Central London 1976–80; exec creative dir responsible for all creative product Landor Associates: Europe 1984–98, New York 1998–; cmmns incl identity and environmental design for: British Airways 1984, Chase Manhattan Bank Europe 1985, Royal Jordanian Airline and Alfred Dunhill 1986, BAe and Abbey National 1987, Cepsa Petroleum Spain and Ballantyne Cashmere 1988, Emlak Bank Turkey 1989, Deutsche Shell 1990, Egnatia Bank Greece 1991, Seville Expo and Neste Petroleum Finland 1992, Lincoln Mercury USA, Telia (Swedish Telecom) and Cathay Pacific Airline 1993, Royal Mail and Delta Air Lines USA 1994, Montell (Worldwide) and KF (Swedish Co-op) 1995, Reuters (Worldwide) and Air 2000 (UK) 1996, Credit Lyonnais 1997, Shell International Petroleum and Compaq Computers (USA) 1998, Hyperion Software and Textron (USA) 1999; RIBA 1983; *Style*— Richard Ford, Esq

FORD, Timothy Graham; s of John Hamilton Ford (d 1974), of Charleston, Cornwall, and Dorothy Joyce Ford (d 1989); *b* 27 January 1945; *Educ* Bancroft's Sch, Coll of Law Lancaster Gate; *m* 4 March 1972, Marian Evelyn, da of Charles Frederick Bernard Hayward, MBE (d 2000), and Mary Evelyn Hayward (d 1995), of Wye, Kent; 2 s (Paul b 1973, Simon b 1977); *Career* Inns of Ct and City Yeo 1965–67, cmmnd RCS TA 1967, 36 Eastern Signal Regt V; admitted slr 1969, admitted slr in Ireland 1997; conslt Lester Aldridge slrs (formerly Park Nelson slrs) 1971– (managing ptnr Park Nelson slrs 1996–2001); dir Guy's and Lewisham NHS Tst 1991–93, dep chm Guy's and St Thomas' Hosps NHS Tst 1993–99, chm Guy's and St Thomas' Hosps Healthcare Services 1993–2000, special tstee Guy's Hosp 1993–2000, special tstee St Thomas' Hosp 1995–2000, tstee Guy's and St Thomas' Charitable Fndn 2000–03; chm Industrial Tbnl 1992–94 (memb 1989–92); sec-gen Nat Pawnbrokers' Assoc 1988–2006; contrib to professional press on business matters; dir Blackheath Preservation Tst 1992–2001, chm Florence Nightingale Museum Tst 1999–2005; non-exec dir of several cos; tstee: Bridget Espinosa Memorial Tst 1990–, Matthew Hodder Charitable Tst 1995–; Parly candidate (Alliance) Greenwich 1983; memb Ct and Cncl Univ of Reading 2000– (pres 2003–), memb Bd Royal Acad Schs 2003–07; Freeman: City of London 1978, City of London Slrs' Co; Liveryman Worshipful Co of Painter Stainers (memb Ct of Assts 2003–, Renter Warden 2005); memb: Law Soc 1969, Assoc of Partnership Practitioners, Inst of Assoc Mangrs; MInstD 1987, MCIArb, FICPD, FRSA; *Publications* practice manual on procedures under the Consumer Credit Act 1974 for Lending Insts, Butterworths Encyclopaedia of Forms and Precedents on partnership and lending and consumer credit (contrib), Halsbury's Laws of England (contrib and conslt ed); *Recreations* golf, cricket, music, reading (particularly Charles Dickens); *Clubs* Royal Blackheath Golf (capt 1993), Rye Golf, East India, MCC, RSA; *Style*— Timothy Ford, Esq; ✉ The Pavilion, Manorbrook, Blackheath, London SE3 9AW (tel 020 8297 2575, fax 020 8318 0031, e-mail tgford@pavilion.netkonect.co.uk); Lester Aldridge, Kildare House, 3 Dorset Rise, London EC4Y 8EN (tel 0870 224 0405, fax 020 7400 9890, e-mail timothy.ford@la-law.com)

FORD DAVIES, Oliver Robert; s of Robert Cyril Davies (d 1974), of Ealing, London, and Cicely Mary, *née* Ford (d 1990); *b* 12 August 1939; *Educ* King's Sch Canterbury, Merton Coll Oxford (DPhil, pres OUDS); *m* Jenifer Armitage, da of Edward Armitage; 1 da (Miranda Katherine b 1975); *Career* actor; lectr in history Univ of Edinburgh 1964–66; seasons at: Birmingham, Cambridge, Leicester, Oxford, Nottingham; *Theatre* 25 prodns with RSC incl: Henry IV, Henry V, Henry VI, Henry VIII, As You Like It, Coriolanus, Love's Labour's Lost, The Greeks, Troilus and Cressida, The Love Girl and The Innocent, The Forest, Measure for Measure, Waste (also Lyric 1985), The Danton Affair, Principia Scriptoriae, Merry Wives of Windsor, Jekyll and Hyde; RNT 1988–91: The Shaughraun, Hamlet, Lionel Espy in Racing Demon (Olivier Award for Actor of the Year), The Shape of the Table, The Absence of War 1993, Playing with Fire 2005, Galileo 2006, St Joan 2007; other credits incl: Bishop Talacryn in Hadrian VII (Mermaid, Haymarket) 1968–69, Tonight at Eight (Hampstead, Fortune) 1971–72, Mary Rose 1972, 1975–87, Heartbreak House (Yvonne Arnaud Guildford and Haymarket) 1992, Ivanov (Almeida) 1997, Naked (Almeida) 1998, Richard II and Coriolanus (Almeida/Gainsborough) 2000, King Lear (Almeida) 2002, Absolutely! (perhaps) (Wyndham's) 2003, King Cromwell (Orange Tree Richmond) 2003; *Television* incl: Cause Celebre, A Taste for Death, Death of a Son, A Very British Coup, Inspector Morse, The Police, The Cloning of Joanna May, Anglo-Saxon Attitudes, The Absence of War, Truth or Dare, A Royal Scandal, A Dance to the Music of Time, Kavanagh QC, David Copperfield, The Way We Live Now, Bertie and Elizabeth, Sparkling Cyanide, The Badness of King George IV, Midsomer Murders; *Film* incl: Defence of the Realm, Scandal, Paper Mask, Sense and Sensibility, Mrs Brown, Mrs Dalloway, Star Wars I and II, Johnny English, The Mother, Atonement; *Books* God Keep Lead out of Me - Shakespeare on War and Peace (jtly, 1985), Playing Lear (2003), King Cromwell (2005), Performing Shakespeare (2007); also written plays produced by Orange Tree Theatre, ATV and BBC Radio; *Recreations* music, history, carpentry; *Style*— Oliver Ford Davies, Esq; ✉ c/o Caroline Dawson Associates, 125 Gloucester Road, London SW7 4TE (tel 020 7373 3323, fax 020 7373 1110)

FORD-HUTCHINSON, Sally Mary Ann (Mrs Anthony Yeshin); da of Peter William Scott Ford-Hutchinson (d 1961), and Giuseppina Adele, *née* Leva; *b* 20 August 1950; *Educ* Holy Trinity Convent, Bristol Poly (HND, DipM), Lampeter Univ (MA); *m* 2 June 1977, Anthony David Yeshin; 2 s (Mark b 26 Dec 1979, Paul b 31 May 1983); *Career* res exec Leo Burnett Advertising Agency 1972–74, Benton & Bowles 1974–77; res mangr H J Heinz Ltd 1977–79, head Res Dept Wasey Campbell Ewald 1979–83, memb Planning Dept Grandfield Rork Collins 1983–86; DMB&B 1986–2000: dir, head Planning Dept and memb Mgmnt Ctee until 1996, a global planning dir 1996–2000; md The Thinking Shop 2000–; winner commendation IPA Advtg Effectiveness award; govr Nottingham Trent Univ, tstee Nat Cen; fell MRS; assoc MInstM; FIPA; *Recreations* opera, walking in the country, reading; *Style*— Ms Sally Ford-Hutchinson; ✉ tel 07785 290119, e-mail sally@ford-h.fsnet.co.uk

FORDE, Prof Michael Christopher; s of Michael Forde (d 1953), of Sale, Cheshire, and Mary (d 1980), *née* Murphy; *b* 15 February 1944; *Educ* De La Salle Coll Pendleton, Univ of Liverpool (BEng), Univ of Birmingham (MSc, PhD, SERC res student); *m* 1968, Edna, da of Griffith Williams; 1 s (Nicholas Simon b 1971), 1 da (Helen Louise b 1975); *Career* site civil engr Lehane Mackenzie & Shand Ltd/Christiani-Shand 1966–68; Co Surveyors Dept Cheshire CC Highway Design and Geotechnics 1968–69; Univ of Edinburgh: lectr in civil engrg 1973–84, sr lectr in civil engrg 1984–89, Carillion prof of civil engrg construction 1990–, head Inst Research in Engrg 1998–2001; memb Assessment Panel Large Structural and Building Systems prog Nat Science Fndn Washington DC 1993–2001; memb Int Standards Ctee Réunion Internationale des Laboratoires d'Essais et de Recherches sur les Matériaux et les Constructions (RILEM) MS 127 1992–; memb Ctee: American Concrete Inst ACI 228 1999– (also chair), Nat Res Cncl (USA) Transportation Research Bd AFF40, AFF40(1), AFP10–3 1998–, Euro Working Gp on Acoustic Emission 1978–, Inst Civil Engrs R&D Panel 1988–90, Inst Civil Engrs Ground Bd 1988–92, BSI No BDB/1 1989–92, BSI No B/153/1 1992–2000, Br Inst Non-Destructive Testing Res Exec Ctee 1988–96, Inst Electrical Engrs, MESIN; CEng 1973; FICE 1998, FIET 1995, FIHT 1998 (MIHT 1969), FInstNDT 1989; FREng 1999, FRSE 2006; *Publications* author of 240 papers published in scientific and learned jls; *Recreations* armchair cricketer, classic cars; *Clubs* Royal Scots; *Style*— Prof Michael Forde; ✉ University of Edinburgh, School of Engineering and Electronics, The Kings Buildings, Edinburgh EH9 3JL (tel 0131 650 5721, fax 0131 452 8596, mobile 07831 496 249, e-mail m.forde@ed.ac.uk)

FORDHAM, John Anthony; s of Lt Cdr J H Fordham, CBE (d 1967), and Ebba Fordham (d 1999); *b* 11 June 1948; *Educ* Gresham's; *m* 25 June 1974, Lynda Patricia, da of Bernard Green, of Weston-super-Mare; 2 s (Michael b 28 Dec 1979, Timothy b 3 Aug 1983); *Career* with Bowater Corporation Ltd 1973–81, head of mergers and acquisitions Hill Samuel Bank Ltd 1986–90 (joined 1981, dir 1985), md Lloyds Merchant Bank Ltd 1991–93, md Alex Brown & Sons Ltd 1993–98, md William Blair Int Ltd 1998–2000, chm Baird Int (Robert W Baird Gp Ltd) 2000–; *Recreations* running, golf, gardening; *Clubs* Royal Wimbledon Golf, Rye Golf, The Jesters, The Escorts, The Racquet (Chicago); *Style*— John Fordham, Esq; ✉ 50 Godfrey Street, Chelsea, London SW3 3SX (tel 020 7351 9508)

FORDHAM, John Michael; s of John William Fordham, and Kathleen Mary; *b* 15 December 1948; *Educ* Dulwich Coll, Gonville & Caius Coll Cambridge (MA); *m* 28 Oct 1972, Sarah Anne, da of Denis Victor Burt; 1 da (Rebecca Kate b 1977), 1 s (Benjamin John b 1979); *Career* admitted slr 1974, ptnr Stephenson Harwood 1979–, head of litigation 1995–; mediator (CEDR accredited and registered); memb: Law Soc, Ctee Commercial Litigators Forum; vice-pres Sutton CC; *Recreations* cricket and tennis (player), abstract art, jazz, twentieth century literature (observer); *Style*— John Fordham, Esq; ✉ High Trees, 31 Shirley Avenue, South Cheam, Surrey SM2 7QS (tel and fax 020 8642 1517); Stephenson Harwood, One St Paul's Churchyard, London EC2M 8SH (tel 020 7329 4422, fax 020 7606 0822, e-mail john.fordham@shlegal.com)

FORDHAM, Prof (Sigurd) Max; OBE (1994); s of Dr Michael Scott Montague Fordham (d 1995), of Jordans, Bucks, and Molly, *née* Swabey (d 1941); *b* 17 June 1933; *Educ* De Carteret Sch Jamaica, Dartington Hall Sch Totnes, Trinity Coll Cambridge (MA), Nat Coll of Heating Ventilation Refrigeration and Fan Engrg (William Nelson Haden scholar); *m* 24 Sept 1960, Thalia Aubrey, da of late Dr Reginald John Dyson; 3 s (Jason Christopher Lyle b 26 Sept 1962, Cato Michael Sigurd b 17 Nov 1964, Finn William Montague b 12 Nov 1967); *Career* Nat Serv Pilot Fleet Air Arm RN 1952–54; devpt engr Weatherfoil Heating Systems Ltd 1958–61, Ove Arup & Ptnrs Building Gp (later Arup Assocs) 1961–66, fndr Max Fordham & Ptnrs 1966– (constituted as co-op practice 1974), fndr ptnr Max Fordham Assocs 1984–, memb Max Fordham LLP 2001–; dir: Nestar Ltd 1987–2000, Panopus Printing Ltd 1987–2000, National Engineering Specification 1987–98, Max Fordham Consulting Ltd 2004–; visiting prof in building and design Univ of Bath 1990–; external examiner: Architectural Assoc 1991–97, Univ of Edinburgh 1992–94, Univ of Cambridge Sch of Architecture 1996–99; chm Working Gp for Communications for Building IT 2000, chm Res Sub Ctee for Intelligent Façades for the Centre for Window & Cladding Technol 1993–; CIBSE: accreditation panelist 1989–, memb Cncl 1993–96 and 2000–, pres 2001–02 (vice-pres 1999, pres elect 2000–01), awarded Gold Medal 1997; FCIBSE 1971 (MCIBSE 1964), FConsE (MConsE 1974), FRSA 1982, CEng 1987, Hon FRIBA 1992, FREng 1992; *Publications* A Global Strategy for Housing in the Third Milleneum - The Envelope of the House in Temperate Climates (Royal Soc, 1992), also numerous tech papers and articles; *Style—* Professor Max Fordham, OBE, FREng; ✉ Max Fordham LLP, 42/43 Gloucester Crescent, London NW1 7PE (tel 020 7267 5161, fax 020 7482 0329, e-mail max@maxfordham.com and max@maxf.co.uk)

FORDHAM, Michael John; QC (2006); s of John Skidmore Fordham, of Castle Carrock, Cumbria, and Margaret, *née* Armstrong; *b* 21 December 1964; *Educ* Spalding GS, Hertford Coll Oxford (BA, BCL, Hockey blue), Univ of Virginia Sch of Law (LLM); *m* 17 April 1993, Alison Jane, *née* Oxley; 2 da (Anna Caitlin b 19 Oct 1994, Lois Rebekah b 11 Dec 1998), 1 s (Bradley John b 7 April 1997); *Career* called to the Bar Gray's Inn 1990 (Karmel, Prince of Wales and Mould scholarships 1989); barr: 3 Gray's Inn Place 1990–94, Blackstone Chambers 1994–; counsel Burns Inquiry on hunting with dogs; coll lectr in admin law Hertford Coll Oxford; co-ed Judicial Review jl; memb: Attorney Gen's Panel of Counsel, Advsy Bd Br Inst of Int and Comparative Law; memb Admin Law Bar Assoc; Human Rights Lawyer of the Year 2005, Jr Barr of the Year Public Law 2005, Bar Pro Bono Award 2006; jr church ldr Marlborough Road Methodist Church St Albans; *Publications* Judicial Review Handbook (4 edn 2004); *Recreations* hockey; *Clubs* St Albans Hockey; *Style—* Michael Fordham, QC; ✉ Blackstone Chambers, Temple, London EC4Y 9BW (tel 020 7583 1770, fax 020 7822 7350, e-mail michaelfordham@blackstonechambers.com)

FORDY, (George) Malcolm; OBE (1997); s of George Laurence Fordy (d 1970), and Louise, *née* Birdsall (d 2002); *b* 27 August 1934; *Educ* Durham Sch; *m* 7 June 1957, Pauline, da of William Stanley Thompson, of Northallerton, N Yorks; 2 da (Susan b 1958, Sarah b 1965), 1 s (Nicholas b 1960); *Career* chm: FT Construction Gp (Holdings) Ltd (George Fordy & Son Ltd/Walter Thompson (Contractors) Ltd and associated companies), Fordy Travel Ltd; dir Bldg & Civil Engrg Holidays Scheme Mgmnt Ltd; pres Nat Fedn Bldg Trades Employers 1982–83, ldr Employers' Side Nat Jt Cncl for the Building Industry until 1997, memb Bd Construction Industry Trg Bd 1976–82 and 1985–96, chm Vocational Trg Cmmn of the Fedn de L'Industrie Europèene de la Construction 1985–94, chm Employers Gp of Building Civil Engrg and Public Works Ctee Int Labour Organisation Geneva 1992; FCIOB 1978, FCMI (FIMgt 1978); *Recreations* the countryside, travel; *Clubs* Cleveland (Middlesbrough), YCCC, ACdeM; *Style—* Malcolm Fordy, Esq, OBE; ✉ High Farm House, Ingleby Greenhow, Great Ayton, North Yorkshire TS9 6RG; FT Construction Group, Construction House, Northallerton, North Yorkshire DL7 8ED (tel 01609 780700, fax 01609 777236)

FOREMAN, Michael; s of Walter Foreman (d 1938), of Lowestoft, Suffolk, and Gladys, *née* Goddard (d 1982); *b* 21 March 1938; *Educ* Notley Road Secdy Modern, Lowestoft Sch of Art, RCA (USA scholar, MA, Silver medal); *m* 22 Dec 1980, Louise Amanda, da of Basil Gordon Phillips; 3 s (Mark b 1961, Ben b 1982, Jack b 1986); *Career* illustrator; former: art dir Playboy, King and Ambit magazines, prodr animated films in Scandinavia and for BBC; writer and illustrator of over 200 books (incl children's and travel books), regular contrib American and European magazines, held exhibitions Europe, America and Japan; awards: Aigle d'Argent at Festival International du Livre France 1972, Francis Williams Prize V&A Museum and Nat Book League 1972 and 1977, Kate Greenaway Medal 1982 and 1989, Smarties Grand Prix 1994, Graphic Prize Bologna, Kurt Maschler Award; Hon Dr Univ of Plymouth 1998; memb: AGI 1972, RDI 1986; Hon FRCA 1989; *Clubs* Chelsea Arts; *Style—* Michael Foreman, Esq

FOREMAN-PECK, Prof James Stanley; s of John Foreman-Peck (d 1984), and Muriel Joan Foreman-Peck (d 1999); *b* 19 June 1948; *Educ* Alleyn's Sch Dulwich, Univ of Essex (BA), LSE (MSc, PhD); *m* 22 June 1968, Lorraine, da of Walter Alexander McGimpsey; 1 s (Alexander b 1978), 1 da (Eleanor b 1985); *Career* economist Electricity Cncl 1971–72, lectr in econs Thames Poly 1972–79, lectr in econs Univ of Newcastle upon Tyne 1979–88, visiting assoc prof Univ of Calif 1981–82, prof of econ history Univ of Hull 1988–90, Hallsworth fell in political econ Univ of Manchester 1990–91, fell St Antony's Coll Oxford and univ lectr in econ history 1990–98, prof Welsh Economic Res Cardiff Business Sch 2002–, dir Welsh Inst for Res in Economics and Devpt 2002–; economic advsr HM Treasy 1999–2002; cncllr London Borough of Greenwich 1978–79, pres European Historical Economic Soc 1999–2001; memb: Amnesty Int, Nat Tst, Royal Econ Soc, Econ History Soc; *Books* A History of the World Economy: International Economic Relations since 1850 (1983, 2 edn 1994), European Telecommunications Organisations (ed, 1988), New Perspectives on the Late Victorian Economy (ed, 1991), Public and Private Ownership of Industry in Britain 1820–1990 (1994), The British Motor Industry (1995), Smith and Nephew in the Healthcare Industry (1995), Globalisation in History (1998), European Industrial Policy (1999); *Recreations* music, literature; *Style—* Prof James Foreman-Peck; ✉ Cardiff Business School, Cardiff CF10 3EU (tel 029 2087 6395, e-mail foreman-peckj@cardiff.ac.uk)

FORESTIER-WALKER, Sir Michael Leolin; 6 Bt (UK 1835); s of Lt-Col Alan Ivor Forestier-Walker, MBE, 7 Gurkha Rifles (ka Malaya 1954, s of Ivor Forestier-Walker, 5 s of 2 Bt) and Margaret Joan, da of Maj Henry Bennet Marcoolyn, MBE; suc kinsman, Sir Clive Radzivill Forestier-Walker, 5 Bt, 1983; *b* 24 April 1949; *Educ* Wellington, Royal Holloway Coll London (BA); *m* 16 July 1988, Elizabeth, da of Joseph Hedley, of Bellingham, Northumberland; 1 da (Chloë b 15 Jan 1990), 1 s (Joseph Alan b 2 May 1992); *Heir* s, Joseph Forestier-Walker; *Career* gen mangr The Leatherhead Theatre; *Style—* Sir Michael Forestier-Walker, Bt; ✉ Bibury, 116 Hogshill Lane, Cobham, Surrey KT11 2AW

FORFAR, Dr (John) Colin; s of Prof J O Forfar, MC, of Edinburgh, and Isobel Mary Langlands, *née* Fernback; *b* 22 November 1951; *Educ* Edinburgh Acad, Univ of Edinburgh (BSc, MD, PhD), Univ of Oxford (MA); *m* (m dis); 1 da (Katriana Louise b 1981); *Career* reader in cardiovascular med Univ of Oxford 1985–86, physician and conslt cardiologist Oxford RHA 1986–; chm Oxford Heart Centre; author of numerous med pubns; memb: Br Cardiac Soc (former local sec), Ctee on Safety of Medicines, MRS, Oxford Med Soc; FRCPE 1987, FRCP 1991; *Recreations* walking, squash; *Style—* Dr Colin Forfar; ✉ The Cullions, Elvendon Road, Goring-on-Thames, Oxfordshire RG8 0DT (tel 01491 875023); Department of Cardiology, John Radcliffe Hospital, Oxford OX3 9DU (tel 01865 220326, fax 01865 220252)

FORGE, Anna; da of Kenneth Baynton Forge (d 1976), and Rosaline, *née* Shaw (d 1984); *b* 12 May 1951, Bromley, Kent; *Educ* Bromley GS for Girls, Univ of Kent at Canterbury (BA), Coll of Law; *Family* 1 da (Beth b 22 May 1970), 1 s (Omar Ben b 27 Nov 1993); *Career* admitted slr 1982; articled clerk rising to asst head of legal servs London Borough of Southwark 1979–88, asst slr rising to ptnr Berwin Leighton 1989–99, ptnr Mayer Brown Rowe and Maw LLP 1999–2007, ptnr McGrigors LLP 2007–; CEDR accredited mediator; *Publications* Butterworth's Local Government Finance (co-author, 2000); *Recreations* ballet, travel, reading, theatre; *Style—* Miss Anna Forge; ✉ McGrigors LLP, 5 Old Bailey, London EC4M 7BA (tel 020 7054 2642, fax 020 7054 2501, e-mail anna.forge@mcgrigors.com)

FORGE, Gilly Rosamund; da of John Bliss Forge, of Cirencester, Glos, and Margaret, *née* Whitwell (d 1966); *b* 27 February 1956; *Educ* The Abbey Malvern, New Hall Boreham, Trinity Coll Dublin (LLB); *Career* milliner; former journalist, estab millinery business 1989; designers worked with incl: Jean Muir, Anouska Hempel, Caroline Charles, Amanda Wakeley; model hat range sold exclusively, diffusion range sold in major retailers throughout UK, Europe, USA and Japan, and by mail order in UK; designer to Chester Jeffries glove mfrs 1992–96; *Style—* Miss Gilly Forge

FORKER, Rev Dr William George (Wilbert); s of William Forker, of Portadown, Co Armagh, and Esther Forker; *b* 15 July 1935; *Educ* Shaftesbury House Belfast, Edgehill Coll Belfast, GFT Indiana (MBA), DMin; *m* 29 June 1959, Maureen, *née* McMullan; 1 s (Christopher Michael b 17 May 1960), 1 da (Kathryn Esther b 2 March 1963); *Career* ordained minister Methodist Church in Ireland 1961; minister Methodist Missionary Soc: Guyana 1959–62, St Vincent 1964–66, Barbados 1966–68; memb Exec Staff World Cncl of Churches 1968–72, exec vice-pres Templeton Fndn Nassau Bahamas (exec dir 1972–2000); Templeton Theological Seminary Nassau Bahamas: fndr 1985, pres 1987, chm Bd of Tstees 1989–2000; admin Templeton Prize for Progress in Religion 1972–2000; fndr and chm Tournament with a Heart Charity Golf Tournament Bahamas; memb: Advsy Bd Int Cncl of Christians and Jews 1991–, Harvard Univ Bd Centre for the Study of World Religions 1993–2000, Bd of Tstees World Parliament of Religions 1999–; Gold Medallion Int Cncl of Christians and Jews 2000; treas Lyford Cay Property Owners Assoc 1985–88; dir: Lismore Ltd Cayman Is, The Compass Fund 1994–2002, Best Investments Ltd 1997–99; FRSA 1995; *Books* The Templeton Prize (vol 1 1977, vol 4 1997), The Future Agenda (1992); *Recreations* golf, reading, philately; *Clubs* Athenaeum; *Style—* The Rev Dr Wilbert Forker; ✉ PO Box 1543, Anguilla, West Indies (tel 00 1 264 497 3025)

FORRES, 4 Baron (UK 1922); Sir Alastair Stephen Grant Williamson; 4 Bt (UK 1909); s of 3 Baron Forres (d 1978), by his 1 w, Gillian Ann Maclean, *née* Grant; *b* 16 May 1946; *Educ* Eton; *m* 2 May 1969, Margaret Ann, da of late George John Mallam, of Mullumbimby, NSW; 2 s (Hon George b 1972, Hon Guthrie b 1975); *Heir* s, Hon George Williamson; *Career* chm Agriscot Pty Ltd; dir Jaga Trading Pty Ltd; Australian rep Tattersalls; *Clubs* Australian Jockey, Tattersalls (Sydney), Sydney Turf; *Style—* The Rt Hon the Lord Forres

FORREST, Alexander (Sandy); s of William Forrest, and Mary, *née* Kirk; *b* 19 July 1953; *Educ* St John's GS, Hamilton Acad, Univ of Strathclyde (BA); *m* 4 Sept 1980, Elspeth McInnes Paton; 2 s (Alasdair, Jonathan); *Career* Strathclyde Police: joined 1974, Supt and Dep Divnl Cdr 1992–94, Chief Supt and head Traffic Dept 1994–97, Chief Supt and Divnl Cdr 1997–99; Asst Chief Constable (Scot) Br Transport Police 1999–2001, Dep Chief Constable and HM's Asst Inspr of Constabulary for Scot 2001–03, dir Cncl for Healthcare Regulatory Excellence (CHRE) 2003–07; lay memb Bar Standards Bd for Eng and Wales 2006–07; hon sec Assoc of Scot Police Supts 1994–98 (memb Police Negotiating Bd, memb Police Advsy Bd for Scot); CMILT; *Recreations* skiing; *Style—* Sandy Forrest, Esq; ✉ NHS 24, Delta House, 50 West Nile Street, Glasgow G1 2NP (tel 0141 225 0051, e-mail sandy.forrest@nhs24.scot.nhs.uk)

FORREST, Dr John Richard; CBE (2002); s of Prof John Samuel Forrest, and Ivy May Ellen, *née* Olding; *b* 21 April 1943; *Educ* KCS Wimbledon, Sidney Sussex Coll Cambridge (BA, MA), Keble Coll Oxford (DPhil); *m* 1, 8 Sept 1973 (m dis), Jane Patricia Robey, da of John Robey Leech, of Little Hockham Hall, Norfolk; 2 s (Nicholas John b 1975, Alexander Iain b 1980), 1 da (Katharine Elizabeth b 1977); m 2, Diane Martine James; *Career* UCL: lectr 1970–79, reader 1979–82, prof 1982–84; tech dir Marconi Defence Systems Ltd 1984–86, dir of engrg IBA 1986–90, chief exec National Transcommunications Ltd 1991–94, dep chm NTL Group Ltd 1994–96, chm Brewton Gp Ltd 1994–99; dir: Egan International Ltd 1994–, Loughborough Sound Images plc 1996–98, Screen plc 1996–99, Drake Automation Ltd 1996–99, Tricorder Technology plc 1997–2001, 3i Gp plc 1997–2004, Blue Wave Systems Inc 1998–2001 (chm 2000–01), Morgan Howard Int Gp Ltd 1999–2000; chm Human IT Ltd 2000–03, exec chm Cellular Design Services Ltd 2003–05; dep chm: Surrey Satellite Technology Ltd 2006–, Omniglobe Networks Ltd 2006–, System C Healthcare plc 2007– (dir 2005–); chm Advsy Bd Interregnum plc 2003–06; chm UK Govt Spectrum Mgmnt Advsy Gp 1998–2003; sr vice-pres Royal Acad of Engrg 1999–2002 (hon sec (electrical engrg) 1995–97, vice-pres 1997–99); memb Cncl Brunel Univ 1996–99, pro-chllr Univ of Surrey 2005–; Hon DSc City Univ 1992, Hon DTech Brunel Univ 1995; Hon FBKSTS 1990; FIEE 1980, FREng 1985, FRSA 1987, FRTS 1990, FInstD 1991; Chevalier de l'Ordre des Arts et des Lettres (France) 1990; *Recreations* theatre, music, reading, sailing, mountain walking; *Style—* Dr John Forrest, CBE, FREng; ✉ mobile 07785 251734, e-mail johnrforrest@aol.com

FORREST, Nigel; s of Wing Cdr Gerald Vere Forrest (d 2000), of Sydney, Aust, and Elizabeth, *née* Burnett (d 1991); *b* 12 September 1946; *Educ* Harrow, Oriel Coll Oxford (MA), INSEAD (MBA); *m* 22 Nov 1980, Julia Mary, da of Philip Nash (d 1970), of Dorking, Surrey; 1 s (Dominic b 18 April 1982), 1 da (Harriet b 9 Feb 1984); *Career* commercial technol sales mangr Rolls Royce Ltd 1972 (grad trainee 1969), mangr Lazard Bros & Co Ltd 1978 (exec 1973), dep md Nomura International plc 1989–96 (assoc md 1986, exec dir 1983, mangr 1981), sr conslt NatWest Markets 1996–98, dir Nashbrook Partners Ltd 1998–, dir Amicus Expert Witness Ltd 1999–2001; chm Fundraising Ctee Highbury Roundhouse 1978–81; MSI, FRSA; *Publications* The Channel Tunnel - Before The Decision (1973); author of five financial training books 1996; *Style—* Nigel Forrest, Esq, FRSA; ✉ Nashbrook Partners Ltd, Moor House, Arbrook Lane, Esher, Surrey KT10 9EE (tel 07768 728619)

FORREST, Paul Esme Acton; s of Richard Acton Forrest (d 1994), of Ashcott, Somerset, and Lucille Muriel, *née* Knott (d 1999); *b* 1 January 1943; *Educ* Dr Morgan's GS, Univ of Southampton; *m* 29 April 1967, Josephine Anne, da of Gp Capt John Enfield Kirk, OBE, RAF (ret), of Winscombe, N Somerset; 2 s (Richard b 1975, James b 1977), 1 da (Charlotte b 1980); *Career* admitted slr 1971, called to the Bar Gray's Inn 1979; HM coroner Dist of Avon 1992, immigration judge 2005; *Recreations* golf, fishing, jazz; *Clubs* Royal North Devon and Burnham and Berrow Golf, The Clifton, The County; *Style—* Paul Forrest, Esq; ✉ The Coroner's Court, The Courthouse, Old Weston Road, Flax Bourton BS48 1UL

FORREST, Prof (Alexander) Robert Walker; s of Alexander Muir Forrest (d 2002), of Boston, Lincs, and Rose Ellen, *née* Ringham (d 1976); *b* 5 July 1947; *Educ* Stamford Sch, Univ of Edinburgh (BSc, MB ChB), Cardiff Law Sch (LLM); *m* Wendy S Phillips, da of Ian Phillips, of Millom, Cumbria; 2 s (Michael b 1981, David b 1984); *Career* conslt chem pathologist Royal Hallamshire Hosp 1981–98; Univ of Sheffield: clinical lectr in human metabolism and clinical biochemistry 1981–98, hon lectr in forensic toxicology 1985–98, prof of forensic toxicology 1998–2005, prof of forensic chemistry 2005–; visiting prof of forensic toxicology Univ of Bradford 1996–2000; asst dep coroner S Yorks (W) 1988–91 and 1993– (dep coroner 1991–93); pres Forensic Science Soc 2005–07; memb: London Toxicology Gp, Selden Soc, Ecclesiastical Law Soc, Canon Law Soc; ed Science and Justice; FRSC 1985, FRCPE 1989, FRCPath 1992 (MRCPath 1980), FRCP 1992; *Recreations* photography, computers, books; *Clubs* Athenaeum, Crippen; *Style—* Prof Robert Forrest; ✉ 37 Marlborough Road, Sheffield S10 1DA (tel 0114 266 9769, e-mail robertforrest@mac.com); Royal Hallamshire Hospital, Sheffield S10 2JF (tel 0114 226 1002, e-mail robert.forrest@sth.nhs.uk)

FORREST, Prof (Archibald) Robin; s of Samuel Forrest (d 1982), of Edinburgh, and Agnes Dollar, *née* Robin; *b* 13 May 1943; *Educ* Daniel Stewart's Coll Edinburgh, Univ of Edinburgh (BSc), Trinity Coll Cambridge (PhD); *m* 7 April 1973, Rosemary Ann, da of Ralph Kenneth Foster (d 1983), of Grantham, Lincs; 1 s (Matthew b 1975), 1 da (Susanna b 1977); *Career* asst dir of research Computer Laboratory Cambridge Univ 1971–74 (tech offr Engrg Dept 1968–71); visiting prof: Syracuse Univ NY 1971–72, Univ of Utah 1979, Univ of São Paulo 1996; visiting expert Beijing Inst of Aeronautics and Astronautics

1979, prof of computing science UEA 1980– (reader in computing studies 1974–80), visiting scientist Xerox Palo Alto Research Centre 1982–83; hon prof Shandong Univ 2003; CEng, CMath, CSci, FBCS, FIMA 1978; *Recreations* collecting wine, reading maps; *Style*— Prof Robin Forrest; ✉ 3 Highlands, Folgate Lane, Old Costessey, Norwich NR8 5EA (tel 01603 742315); University of East Anglia, School of Computing Sciences, University Plain, Norwich NR4 7TJ (tel 01603 592605, fax 01603 593345)

FORRESTER, Prof Alexander Robert; OBE (1998); s of Robert James Forrester (d 1977), and Mary, *née* Gavin; *b* 14 November 1935; *Educ* Univ of Heriot-Watt (BSc), Univ of Aberdeen (DSc, PhD); *m* 1961, Myrna Ross, da of James Doull; 3 da (Deborah Mary b 1964, Melanie Claire b 1966, Stephanie Emma b 1969), 1 s (James Gregor b 1970); *Career* Univ of Aberdeen: asst lectr 1963–64, lectr 1964–76, sr lectr 1976–81, reader 1981–85, prof 1985–, head Dept of chemistry 1987–89, dean 1989–, vice-princ 1990–, dean and vice-princ 1995–; dir: Univ of Aberdeen research and industrial service (AURIS) 1990–, Offshore Medical Support 1992–96, Nat Collection of Industrial and Med Bacteria 1997–; memb: Cncl RSC 1987–90, Ctee of Scottish National Library 1988–93, Cncl Perkin Division 1991–94, Scottish Higher Education Funding Cncl Ctees, Ctees of Scottish Higher Education Principals (COSHEP), Cncl RSE 1998–; FRSC 1982, FRSE 1985; *Publications* Stable Organic Radicals (1968); and also author of many learned papers in academic jls; *Recreations* golf, reading, organising other people; *Clubs* Deeside Golf; *Style*— Prof Alexander Forrester, OBE, FRSE; ✉ 210 Springfield Road, Aberdeen (tel 01224 313367, fax 01224 272082); Office of the Vice-Principal, University of Aberdeen, King's College, Aberdeen AB24 3FX (tel 01224 272016, fax 01224 272082)

FORRESTER, His Hon Judge Giles Charles Fielding; s of Basil Thomas Charles Forrester (d 1981), and Diana Florence, *née* Sandeman (d 2004); *b* 18 December 1939; *Educ* Rugby, Univ of Grenoble, Trinity Coll Oxford (MA); *m* 29 Oct 1966, Georgina Elizabeth, *née* Garnett; 1 s (Edward Charles b 7 Feb 1969), 1 da (Emily Rachel b 31 Aug 1972); *Career* account exec Pritchard Wood and Partners 1962–66; called to the Bar Inner Temple 1966; in practice SE Circuit, recorder 1986, circuit judge (SE Circuit) 1986–, sr circuit judge and perm judge Central Criminal Court 1995–; judicial memb Parole Bd 2002–; memb Cncl Magistrates Assoc 1998– (pres SW London branch 2000–); memb HAC Inf Bn 1963–67 (veteran 1994–), pres HAC RFC 1994–98; Freeman City of London 1997, Liveryman Worshipful Co of Weavers 1998; FRGS 2004; *Clubs* Boodle's, Roehampton, Royal Western Yacht, St Enodoc Golf, New Zealand Golf (Weybridge); *Style*— His Hon Judge Forrester; ✉ Central Criminal Court, Old Bailey, London EC4M 7EH

FORRESTER, Helen; *b* 6 June 1919, Hoylake, Cheshire; *Educ* privately, Liverpool Evening Schs; *Career* Canadian citizen, resident Canada 1953–, author 1955–; writer in residence: Lethbridge Community Coll 1980, Edmonton Public Library 1990; contrib: Government of Alberta Heritage Magazine, book reviews Canadian Author & Bookman and Edmonton Jl; patron Chester Literature Festival (UK), Henry Marshall Tory lectr, Friends of the Univ of Alberta Annual Lectr 1992, lectr for Cunard on QE2 1996 and 1997, first lectr at Daphne Du Maurier Literary Festival Cornwall 1997; memb The Authors' Lending and Copyrights Soc Ltd London; patron Liverpool Personal Serv Soc's Major Appeal 2002–04; Hudson's Bay Beaver Award 1970 and 1977, honoured for distinguished contrib to lit and to the life of The City of Edmonton 1977, Govt of Alberta Award for Lit 1979, YWCA Woman of the Arts 1987; Hon DLitt: Univ of Liverpool 1988, Univ of Alberta 1993; *Books* Alien There Is None (novel, 1959, republished as Thursday's Child, 1985), The Latchkey Kid (novel, 1971), Twopence To Cross The Mersey (autobiography, 1974, adapted as musical, radio drama and a play for use in schools), Most Precious Employee (as June Edwards, novel, 1976), Minerva's Stepchild (autobiography, 1979, retitled Liverpool Miss 1982), Liverpool Daisy (novel, 1979), Anthology 80 (collection of Alberta writings as fiction ed, 1979), Minerva's Stepchild (1981), By The Waters of Liverpool (autobiography, 1981), The Suicide Tower (short story, 1981), Three Women of Liverpool (novel, 1984), Lime Street At Two (autobiography, 1985, Alberta Culture's Literary Award 1986), A Matter of Friendship (short story, 1986), The Moneylenders of Shahpur (novel, 1987), Yes, Mama (novel, 1987, Writers' Guild Fiction Award 1989), The Lemon Tree (novel, 1990), The Liverpool Basque (novel, 1993), Mourning Doves (novel, 1996), Madame Barbara (1999), A Cuppa Tea and an Aspirin (novel, 2003); *Recreations* reading, travel; *Clubs* Univ of Alberta Faculty, Royal Over-Seas League; *Style*— Dr Helen Forrester; ✉ c/o Ms Vivien Green, Sheil Land Associates Ltd, 52 Doughty Street, London WC1N 2LS (tel 020 7405 9351, fax 020 7831 2127, website www.helenforrester.com)

FORRESTER, Ian Stewart; QC (Scot 1988); s of Alexander Roxburgh Forrester (d 1976), of Glasgow, and Elizabeth Richardson, *née* Stewart (d 1947); *b* 13 January 1945; *Educ* Kelvinside Acad Glasgow, Univ of Glasgow (MA, LLB), Tulane Univ of Louisiana New Orleans (MCL); *m* 7 March 1981, Sandra Anne Thérèse, da of M C Keegan, of Jefferson, Louisiana; 2 s (Alexander Stewart Daigle b 24 Sept 1982, James Roxburgh b 29 May 1985); *Career* European lawyer after training in Glasgow, New Orleans, NY and Edinburgh; estab ind chambers Brussels (with Christopher Norall) 1981 (now known as White & Case), practising before Euro Cmmn and Court; admitted Faculty of Advocates 1972, admitted Bar State of NY 1977, called to the Bar (Middle Temple) 1996, admitted Bar Brussels 2000; chm: Br Cons Assoc in Belgium 1982–86; hon visiting prof in Euro law Univ of Glasgow 1991–; memb: Dean's Advsy Bd Tulane Univ Law Sch, American Bar Assoc, The Stair Soc; tstee EU Baroque Orch; elder St Andrew's Church of Scotland Brussels; *Publications* The German Civil Code (1975), The German Commercial Code (1979), author of numerous articles and chapters on EC law and policy in The Oxford Yearbook of European Law, International Antitrust Law, The European Law Review, The Common Market Law Review, Legal Issues of European Integration, European Intellectual Property Review; *Recreations* politics, wine, cooking, restoring old houses; *Clubs* Athenaeum, International Château Sainte-Anne (Brussels), Royal Yacht of Belgium; *Style*— Ian Forrester, Esq, QC; ✉ 73 Square Marie-Louise, 1000 Brussels, Belgium; 62 Rue de la Loi, 1040 Brussels, Belgium (tel 00 32 2 2191620, fax 00 32 2 2191626, e-mail iforrester@whitecase.com)

FORSTER, John Henry Knight; s of late Henry Knight Forster, MBE, of Salcombe, Devon, and Margaret Rutherford, *née* Metcalf (decd); *b* 14 February 1941; *Educ* Dean Close Cheltenham; *m* 1, 1965 (m dis 1985), Hilary; 2 da (Heidi b 7 April 1966, Hayley b 12 July 1967), 1 s (Gregory b 9 April 1969); m 2, 1986, Carol Ann, da of Arthur Lamond (decd); *Career* chm: Pool & Sons (Hartley Wintney) Ltd 1979–, Hart Retirement Developments (Southern) Ltd 1979–, Elvetham Hall Ltd 1981–2001, Hart Retirement Hldgs Ltd 1986–; dir: Color Steels Ltd 1978–2002, Kingfield Heath Ltd 1983–2004, Kaye Office Supplies Ltd 1989–2004, Kaye Enterprises Ltd 1989–, Hart Ventures Ltd 1989–, 25 St James's Place Mgmnt Ltd 1992–, St Michael's Hospice (N Hants) 1993–, Precoat Int plc 1995–2002, Albury Mill Properties Ltd 2000–; FCA 1976 (ACA 1965); *Recreations* Victorian gothic architecture; *Style*— John H K Forster, Esq; ✉ Bumblebee Cottage, Grange Lane, Hartley Wintney, Hampshire RG27 8HH (tel 01252 842381, e-mail jhkf@kaye-enterprises.co.uk); Kaye Enterprises Ltd, Oakleigh House, Hartley Wintney, Hampshire RG27 8PE (tel 01252 843773, fax 01252 842338)

FORSTER, Karen Elizabeth (KT); da of Timothy George Naylor, and Victoria Josephine, *née* Barnes-Forster; *Educ* Brighton, Hove and Sussex Sixth Form Coll, Oxford Brookes Univ (BA); *Career* rights dir Studio Editions Ltd 1993–95, rights dir Random House Ltd 1995–96, int sales dir Virgin Publishing Ltd 1996–2000, dep md Virgin Publishing Ltd 2000, md Virgin Books Ltd 2000–; MInstD 2002; *Recreations* parenting, reading, music; *Style*— Ms KT Forster; ✉ Virgin Books Ltd, Thames Wharf Studios, Rainville Road, London W6 9HA (tel 020 7386 3336, fax 020 7386 3340, mobile 07788 975779, e-mail ktforster@virgin-books.co.uk)

FORSTER, Margaret; da of Arthur Gordon Forster, and Lilian, *née* Hind; *b* 25 May 1938; *Educ* Somerville Coll Oxford; *m* 1960, (Edward) Hunter Davies, *qv*; 1 s, 2 da; *Career* author; FRSL 1974; *Books* incl: Dames's Delight (1964), Georgy Girl (1965), Elizabeth Barrett Browning (1988), Have the Men Had Enough? (1989), Daphne du Maurier (1993), Hidden Lives (1995), Shadow Baby (1996), Rich Desserts & Captain's Thin: A Family & Their Times - social history of Carr's of Carlisle 1831–1931 (1997), Precious Lives (memoir, 1998), Good Wives? Mary, Fanny, Jennie and Me, 1845–2001 (2001), Diary of an Ordinary Woman (2003), Is There Anything You Want? (2005), Keeping the World Away (2006); *Style*— Miss Margaret Forster, FRSL; ✉ 11 Boscastle Road, London NW5 1EE

FORSTER, (A) Paul; s of Alfred Forster (d 1965), of Reading, and Dorothy Forster (d 1984); *b* 19 February 1942; *Educ* Stoneham Sch Reading, Univ of Nottingham (BA); *m* 1965, Patricia, *née* Hammond; 2 da (Simone b 19 Sept 1968, Eleanor b 1 Oct 1971); *Career* mktg exec; Cadbury Schweppes plc 1962–72: gen mangr Retail CTN Stores, mktg mangr confectionary Count Line Market; ptnr Lippa Newton Ltd (advtg agency) 1972–74, KMPH Group plc 1974–77 (md PLN Partners Ltd), Saatchi & Saatchi Group plc 1977–79 (md Roe Downton Ltd); Euro RSCG (formerly Colman RSCG Group) 1979–94: md until 1988, chief exec and chm communications group of companies 1988–94; non-exec dir N Brown Group plc 1993–99, chief exec Lifetime Business Group 1994–2000, ceo Euro Customer Mgmnt Centre Dimension Data plc; chm CVC Gp 2003–; visiting prof Nottingham Business Sch and dep chm Bd of Govrs Nottingham Trent Univ 1993–; chm Bd of Tstees Prostate Cancer Charity 2004–; MCIM; *Publications* Serving Them Right (1998); *Recreations* tennis; *Clubs* Royal Commonwealth Soc; *Style*— Prof Paul Forster; ✉ tel 01494 772888, e-mail paul.forster@cvcuk.com

FORSTER, Rt Rev Peter Robert; *see:* Chester, Bishop of

FORSYTH, Alastair Elliott; s of Maj Henry Russell Forsyth (d 1941), and Marie Elaine, *née* Greensmith (d 1958); *b* 23 October 1932; *Educ* Christ's Hosp, Keble Coll Oxford (MA); *m* 1, March 1963, Kathleen Joyce Scott, da of Dr Gordon Brander, 2 s (Angus b 1963, Jamie b 1966); m 2, July 1973, Margaret Christine, da of Maj Royston Ivor Vallance, of Weasenham St Peter, Norfolk; 2 s (Alexander b 1975, John b 1978); 1 da (Arethusa b 1980); m 3, June 1997, Jacki Ashworth; 1 da (Mary b 1998); *Career* banker; dir J Henry Schroder Wagg & Co Ltd 1982–92, advsr Latin America 1992–96; hon sec South Atlantic Cncl; Orden del Libertador (Venezuela) 1996; *Recreations* writing, gardening, history; *Clubs* Sloane; *Style*— Alastair Forsyth, Esq; ✉ The Gardens, Hoxne, Eye, Suffolk IP21 5AP

F

FORSYTH, Bruce Joseph (né Forsyth-Johnson); CBE (2006, OBE 1998); s of John Frederick Forsyth-Johnson (d 1961), and Florence Ada Forsyth-Johnson (d 1957); *b* 22 February 1928; *Educ* Latimer Sch Edmonton; *m* 1, 1951 (m dis), Olivia, da of Calvert, of NI; 3 da (Debbie b 1955, Julie b 1958, Laura b 1964); m 2, 24 Dec 1973 (m dis), Anthea, da of Bernard Redfern, of Torquay; 2 da (Charlotte b 1976, Louisa b 1977); m 3, 15 Jan 1983, Wilnelia, da of Enrique Merced, of Puerto Rico; 1 s (Jonathan Joseph b 1986); *Career* entertainer and television host; *Theatre* Little Me (original Br prodn) 1964, Travelling Music Show 1978, One Man Show (Winter Garden NY 1979, Huntington Hartford Los Angeles 1979, London Palladium); numerous extensive tours UK, NZ and Aust; *Television* incl: Sunday Night at the London Palladium 1958–63, Piccadilly Spectaculars, Bruce Forsyth Show (ATV), The Generation Game (BBC, 1971–77 and 1990–94), Bruce's Big Night (LWT) 1978, Play Your Cards Right 1980–87 (ten series) and 1994–, Slingers Day (Thames) 1985–86, Hollywood or Bust 1984, You Bet! (LWT) 1987–89, Takeover Bid (BBC) 1990–91, Bruce's Guest Night (BBC) 1992–93, Bruce's Price is Right 1996; numerous specials incl: Bring on the Girls (Thames) 1976, Bruce and More Girls (Thames) 1977, Bruce Meets the Girls, The Forsyth Follies, Sammy and Bruce (with Sammy Davis Jr), The Entertainers (with Rita Moreno), The Muppet Show, The Mating Season, The Canterville Ghost; *Films* Star 1968, Can Heironymous Merkin Ever Forgive Mercy Humppe and Find True Happiness 1969, Bedknobs and Broomsticks 1971, The Seven Deadly Sins 1971, Pavlova 1984; *Awards* Daily Mirror National TV Award 1961, Variety Club Showbusiness Personality of the Year 1975, The Sun TV Personality of the Year 1976 and 1977, TV Times Favourite Male TV Personality 1975, 1976 and 1977, TV Times Favourite Game Show Host 1984, BBC TV Personality of the Year 1991, Lifetime Achievement Award for Variety 1995; *Recreations* golf, tennis; *Clubs* Tramp, Crockfords; *Style*— Bruce Forsyth, Esq, CBE; ✉ Bruce Forsyth Enterprises Ltd, Straidarran, Wentworth Drive, Virginia Water, Surrey GU25 4NY (tel and fax 01344 844056)

FORSYTH, Frederick; CBE (1997); s of Frederick William Forsyth (d 1991), and Phyllis, *née* Green (d 1989); *b* 25 August 1938, Ashford, Kent; *Educ* Tonbridge (scholar); *m* 1, 1974, Carole Ann, *née* Cunningham; 2 s (Frederick Stuart b Sept 1977, Shane Richard b June 1979); m 2, 1994 Sandra Jane (Sandy) Molloy, *née* Morris; *Career* RAF 1956–58; reporter Eastern Daily Press 1958–61, foreign corr Reuters News Agency 1961–65, reporter/corr BBC 1965–68, freelance war corr 1968–70; novelist and occasional columnist 1971–; *Publications* The Biafra Story (non-fiction, 1969), Day of the Jackal (novel, 1971), ten further novels, two novellas, two anthologies of short stories; *Recreations* scuba diving, game fishing; *Clubs* Special Forces; *Style*— Frederick Forsyth, Esq, CBE; ✉ c/o Ed Victor Limited, 6 Bayley Street, London WC1B 3HE (tel 020 7304 4100, fax 020 7304 4111)

FORSYTH, Dr Michael Graham de Jong; s of Eric Forsyth, of Wallasey, Merseyside, and Lucy Rebecca, *née* de Jong; *b* 26 November 1951; *Educ* Univ of Liverpool Sch of Architecture (BA, BArch), British Sch at Rome, Univ of Bristol (PhD); *m* 18 Sept 1975 (m dis), Vera, da of Nicos Papaxanthou, of Nicosia, Cyprus; 1 s (James b 28 Sept 1983), 2 da (Antonia b 18 Dec 1985, Henrietta b 18 March 1988); *Career* architectural practice Toronto 1976–79, res fell Univ of Bristol 1984–90 (lectr 1979–84), dir Plato Consortium Ltd Bath 1985–2002, ptnr Forsyth Chartered Architects Bath 1987–; Univ of Bath: sr visiting lectr 1996–99, MSc dir of studies in Conservation of Historic Buildings 1999–, sr lectr 1999–; awarded: Rome Scholarship in Architecture 1975, nineteenth annual ASCAP Deems Taylor award for books on music; many articles reviews and radio broadcasts; memb: Selection Board British School at Rome 1987–93, Renovations Ctee Bath Preservation Tst 1989–98, Exec Ctee Friends of Bristol Art Gallery 1985–90, Exec Ctee Friends of Victoria Art Gallery Bath 1994–97 (chm 1995–97); assessor Register for AABC 1998–; hon sec Soc of Rome Scholars 1984–89; RIBA 1979, ARCUK 1979; *Books* Buildings for Music: The Architect, the Musician, and the Listener from the Seventeenth Century to the Present Day (1985), Auditoria: Designing for the Performing Arts (1987), Bath: Pevsner Architectural Guide (2003); *Recreations* the violin, cross-country running; *Clubs* Chelsea Arts; *Style*— Dr Michael Forsyth; ✉ University of Bath, Department of Architecture and Civil Engineering, Bath BA2 7AY (tel 01225 383016, fax 01225 386691, e-mail m.forsyth@bath.ac.uk)

FORSYTH OF DRUMLEAN, Baron (Life Peer UK 1999), of Drumlean in Stirling; Michael Bruce Forsyth; kt (1997), PC (1995); s of John Tawse Forsyth, and Mary Watson; *b* 16 October 1954; *Educ* Arbroath HS, Univ of St Andrews (MA); *m* 1977, Susan Jane, da of John Bryan Clough; 1 s, 2 da; *Career* nat chm Fedn of Cons Students 1976, memb Westminster City Cncl 1978–83, MP (Cons) Stirling 1983–97; PPS to Foreign Sec 1986–87, Parly under sec of state Scottish Office 1987–90; min of state: Scottish Office 1990–92, Dept of Employment 1992–94, Home Office 1994–95; sec of state for Scotland 1995–97, memb House of Lords Ctee on Monetary Policy 1999–2001, memb Jt Ctee on Reform of the House of Lords; dir Flemings 1997–2000, vice-chm Investment Banking Europe JP Morgan 2000–01, dep chm JP Morgan UK 2001–05, sr md Evercore Ptnrs 2007– (sr advsr 2006–07); non-exec dir J&J Denham Ltd 2005–; chm Tax Reform Cmmn 2005–06; chm Scottish Cons Pty 1989–90; patron Craighalbert Centre; memb Devpt Bd Nat Portrait Gallery 2000–03; *Recreations* mountaineering, gardening, photography, astronomy, skiing; *Style—* The Rt Hon the Lord Forsyth of Drumlean, PC; ✉ House of Lords, London SW1A 0PW

FORSYTHE, Dr (John) Malcolm; s of Dr John Walter Joseph Forsythe (d 1988), and Dr Charlotte Constance Forsythe, *née* Beatty (d 1981); *b* 11 July 1936; *Educ* Repton, Guy's Med Sch London (BSc, MB BS, MRCS, DObstRCOG), Univ of N Carolina, LSHTM (MSc); *m* 1, 28 Oct 1961 (m dis 1984), Delia Kathleen, da of late Dr J K Moore; 3 da (Suzanne Delia, Nicola Kathleen (twins) b 9 July 1962, Sarah Louise b 16 May 1969), 1 s (Marcus John Malcolm b 30 Sept 1965); m 2, 27 Jan 1985, Patricia Mary Murden, *née* Barnes; *Career* house surgn Guy's 1961–62, house offr Farnborough 1962, house physician Lewisham 1962–63, GP Beckenham 1963–65, MO Birmingham Regnl Hosp Bd 1965–68, princ asst sr admin MO Wessex RHB 1968–72, dep sr admin offr SE Met RHB 1972–73 (acting sr admin offr 1973–74), area MO Kent AHA 1974–78; regnl MO SE Thames RHA 1978–89 (dir of planning 1983–89), regnl MO and dir of Public Health and Serv Devpt SE Thames RHA 1989–92, dir Inst of Public Health 1990–91, prof of public health Univ of Kent Canterbury 1992–2001, sr lectr KCH Med Sch London 1992–2006, chm SW Kent PCT 2001–04; adjunct prof St George's Univ Sch of Medicine Grenada WI 1995–; memb: Bd Public Health Laboratory Serv 1985–95, Bd of Mgmnt Horder Centre for Arthritis 1992–, BUPA Ltd 1993–, Hyde Housing Assoc 1999– (memb In Touch Bd 2006–), Chasers Charitable Tst; chm: GMC Working Party on assessment in public health med 1995–97, Horder Centre for Arthritis 1996–2000, Bd Tunbridge Wells Primary Care Gp 1998–2001; pres Epidemiology and Public Health Section RSM 1998–2000 (vice-pres 2001–02), sec Retired Fells Soc RSM 2006–; hon conslt in public health med: Camberwell HA 1992–94, King's Coll Hosp Tst 1994–; memb Editorial Bd RCP 1999–2003; tstee Sick Doctors' Tst 1996–; chm Ind Remuneration Panel Tunbridge Wells BC, Sevenoaks DC and Tonbridge and Malling BC 2001–, memb Bd Chichester Diocesan Housing Assoc 2000–; FFPHM, FRCP; *Recreations* golf, ornithology; *Clubs* RSM; *Style—* Dr Malcolm Forsythe; ✉ Buckingham House, 1 Royal Chase, Tunbridge Wells TN4 8AX

FORSYTHE, Max; *b* 2 May 1944, Staffs; *Educ* Newry GS, Belfast Coll of Art, London Coll of Printing; *m* Jane; 2 c; *Career* photographer; early career experience as art dir working at various advtg agencies incl Collett Dickenson Pearce; dir of various TV commercials and photographer (specialising in location and reportage photography for advtg indust) since 1972; campaign work for int accounts incl: Nike, Parker Pens, Bacardi, Teachers Whisky, P&O Cruises, Club Mediterranee, Bergasol, Hawaiian Tropic, Heineken, Ilford, and car mfrs Audi, Mercedes, Citroën, Range Rover, Vauxhall, BMW, Rolls Royce; numerous awards for photography in UK, USA and Europe incl: 5 Silvers (D&AD), Bronze Lion for direction (Cannes); first one-man exhbn Hamiltons Gallery London 1984; work in the collections of RPS and Nat Museum of Photography; chm Assoc of Photographers 1994; *Style—* Max Forsythe; ✉ website www.maxforsythe.com

FORTE, Hon Sir Rocco John Vincent; kt (1995); o s of Baron Forte (Life Peer); *b* 18 January 1945; *Educ* Downside, Pembroke Coll Oxford (MA); *m* 15 Feb 1986, Aliai, da of Prof Giovanni Ricci, of Rome; 2 da (Lydia Irene b 1987, Irene Alisea b 1988), 1 s (Charles Giovanni b 6 Dec 1991); *Career* former chm and chief exec Forte plc (formerly Trusthouse Forte plc) 1983–96 (chm 1993–96), currently chm and chief exec Rocco Forte Hotels; former memb: Br Tourist Authy, Grand Cncl Hotel and Catering Benevolent Assoc; Liveryman Worshipful Co of Bakers; FHCIMA, FCA, FInstD; Cavaliere di Gran Croce Order of Merit of the Italian Republic; *Recreations* golf, fishing, shooting, triathlon; *Clubs* Garrick; *Style—* The Hon Sir Rocco Forte; ✉ Rocco Forte Hotels, 70 Jermyn Street, London SW1Y 6NY (tel 020 7321 2626, fax 020 7312 2424)

FORTESCUE, 8 Earl (GB 1789); Charles Hugh Richard Fortescue; o s of 7 Earl Fortescue (d 1993), and his 1 w, Penelope Jane, *née* Henderson (d 1959); *b* 10 May 1951; *Educ* Eton; *m* 1974, Julia, er da of Air Cdre John Adam Sowrey; 3 da (Lady Alice Penelope b 8 June 1978, Lady Kate Eleanor b 25 Oct 1979, Lady Lucy Beatrice b 29 April 1983); *Heir* unc, Hon Denzil Fortescue; *Style—* The Rt Hon Earl Fortescue; ✉ House of Lords, London SW1A 0PW

FORTESCUE, Hon Seymour Henry; s of 6 Earl Fortescue, MC, TD (d 1977), and his 2 w Hon Sybil Mary (d 1985), da of 3rd Viscount Hardinge; *b* 28 May 1942; *Educ* Eton, Trinity Coll Cambridge (MA), London Business Sch (MSc); *m* 1, 25 July 1966 (m dis 1990), Julia, o da of Sir John Arthur Pilcher GCMG (d 1990); 1 da (Marissa Clare b 20 Oct 1973), 1 s (James Adrian b 15 April 1978); m 2, 23 Aug 1990, Jennifer Ann Simon; 1 da (Alexandra Kate b 10 July 1991); *Career* dir Visa International 1981–91, chief exec Barclaycard 1982–85, dir UK Retail Servs Barclays Bank plc 1987–91 (gen mangr 1985–87), dir of finance and fundraising ICRF 1991–96, chief exec Health Educn Authy 1996–99; chief exec Banking Code Standards Bd 1999–; govr Oundle Sch 1999–2003; hon treas Lepra 1986–96, chm BookPower; memb Ct of Assts Worshipful Co of Grocers (Master 1997–98); *Recreations* gardening, travel, walking, country pursuits, opera; *Style—* The Hon Seymour Fortescue; ✉ Flat 2, 28 Hyde Park Gardens, London W2 2NB (tel 020 7706 7457, fax 020 7661 9784, e-mail seymourfortescue@bcsb.org.uk); The Old School House, Denchworth, Wantage, Oxfordshire OX12 0DX (tel 01235 868592)

FORTEVIOT, 4 Baron (UK 1917); Sir John James Evelyn Dewar; 4 Bt (UK 1907); er s of 3 Baron Forteviot, MBE, DL (d 1993), and Cynthia Monica, *née* Starkie (d 1986); *b* 5 April 1938; *Educ* Eton; *m* 17 Oct 1963, Lady Elisabeth Jeronima Waldegrave (d 2002), 3 da of 12 Earl Waldegrave, KG, GCVO, TD, DL (d 1995); 3 da (Hon Mary-Emma Jeronima (The Lady Strange) b 1 June 1965, Hon Miranda Phoebe (Madame Philippe El-Khazen) b 1 March 1968, Hon Henrietta Cynthia (Hon Mrs Wateridge) b 27 Jan 1970, 1 s (Hon Alexander John Edward b 4 March 1971); *Heir* s, Hon Alexander Dewar; *Clubs* Boodle's, Royal Perth Golfing Soc; *Style—* The Rt Hon Lord Forteviot; ✉ Aberdalgie House, Perth PH2 0QD

FORTEY, Prof Richard Alan; s of Frank Allen Fortey (d 1965), and Margaret Zander Winifred, *née* Wilshin; *b* 15 February 1946; *Educ* Ealing GS for Boys, Univ of Cambridge (BA, PhD, Harkness Prize, ScD); *m* 1, 1968, Bridget Elizabeth Thomas; 1 s (Dominic b 21 Jan 1970); m 2, 1977, Jacqueline Francis; 2 da (Rebecca b 5 Oct 1978, Julia 30 Oct 1981), 1 s (Leo b 23 July 1986); *Career* sr scientific offr British Museum (Natural History) 1973–77 (jr research fell 1970–73), Howley visiting prof Memorial Univ of Newfoundland 1977–78, individual merit promotion for research distinction Natural History Museum 1986–2006 (princ scientific offr 1978–86), Collier prof in the public understanding of science and technol Univ of Bristol 2002–03, visiting prof Univ of Oxford 2000–; Lyell Medal Geological Soc 1996, Frink Medal Zoological Soc 2001, Lewis Thomas Prize Rockefeller Univ 2003, Zoological Medal Linnean Soc 2006, Michael Faraday Award Royal Soc 2006; memb: Br Mycological Soc, Geological Soc of London (pres 2007); FGS 1981, FRS 1997; *Books* Fossils, the Key to the Past (1982), The Hidden Landscape (The Natural World Book of the Year Award, 1993), Life: an unauthorised biography (1997), Trilobite! (2000), The Earth: an intimate history (2004); also author (under pseudonym) Roderick Masters' Book of Money-Making Schemes (1981); *Recreations* fungi of all sorts, humorous writing, East Anglia (especially Suffolk), beer and wine; *Style—* Prof Richard Fortey, FRS; ✉ The Natural History Museum, Cromwell Road, South Kensington, London SW7 5BD (tel 020 7942 5493, fax 020 7942 5546, e-mail raf@nhm.ac.uk)

FORTH, Dr Michael William; s of William Henry Forth (d 1990), and Gwendoline Forth (d 1994); *b* 17 August 1938; *Educ* KCL and King's Coll Hosp Med Sch (MB BS, LRCP, AKC, DPM); *m* 21 Feb 1970, Dr Margaret Foster, da of Lt Col R T Robertson, of Cape Town; 1 s (Robert William b 17 Feb 1974); *Career* conslt psychiatrist and sr lectr Royal Liverpool Hosp 1977–97; Mental Health Act cmmr 1984–86, regnl advsr in psychiatry Mersey Region 1987–91, med dir N Mersey Community Tst 1991–95, med dir W Cheshire Tst 1995–96; RCPsych: chm NW Div 1990–94, memb Cncl 1994–97, memb Ct of Electors 1994–2001 memb Mental Health Review Tbnl 1983–; memb Bd Cheadle Royal Charitable Tst 2000–03; FRCPsych 1986 (MRCPsych), MRCS; *Recreations* golf, music, crosswords; *Clubs* Royal Over-Seas League; *Style—* Dr Michael Forth; ✉ 139 Hough Green, Chester CH4 8JR (tel 01244 671845, e-mail michaelforth@hotmail.com)

FORTNUM, Rebecca; da of John Fortnum, and Eve, *née* Lomas, of London; *b* 19 September 1963; *Educ* Camden Sch for Girls London, Camberwell Sch of Arts and Crafts London, Corpus Christi Coll Oxford (BA), Univ of Newcastle upon Tyne (MA); *Children* 1 s (Marlow b 19 Sept 1999), 1 da (Stella b 2 Jan 2002); *Career* artist; fell in painting Exeter Faculty of Art Poly SW 1989–90, fell Skowhegan Sch of Painting and Sculpture ME 1991, visiting fell in painting Winchester Sch of Art 1992–93, sr lectr Painting Dept Norwich Sch of Art 1993–99, sr lectr in art Wimbledon Sch of Art 1999–2004, research fell in art Lancaster Univ 2004–, visiting artist Sch of the Art Inst Chicago 2006, sr lectr Univ of the Arts London 2006–; visiting lectr at numerous art colls and univs; author of numerous articles in art jls and nat press; *Solo Exhibitions* incl: Positions of Silence (Collective Gall Edinburgh) 1989, Wounds of Difference (Spacex Gall Exeter and Southwark Coll Gall London) 1990, Contra Diction (Winchester Gall) 1993, Smith-Jariwala Gall London 1994, Third Person (Kapil Jariwala Gall London) 1996, Solipsist (Angel Row Gall Nottingham) 2000, The Drawing Gallery London 2005, Gallery 33 Berlin 2006; *Awards incl* The Clothworkers Fndn 1987, Nuffield Fndn 1987, Northern Arts Travel award to USA 1988, Pollock-Krasner Fndn NYC 1991, British Cncl travel award to Botswana 1993, Abbey scholarship Br Sch in Rome 1997, AHRB 2004, Arts Cncl of England 2005, AHRC 2005; *Publications* Contemporary British Women Artists: in their own words (2007); *Style—* Ms Rebecca Fortnum; ✉ e-mail rebecca@elliottfortnum.co.uk

FORWOOD, Margaret Elizabeth Louise; da of Christopher Warren Forwood (d 1975), and Mona Blanche, *née* Williams (d 1978); *b* 25 March 1943; *Educ* Oswestry Girls' HS, Univ of Manchester; *Career* reporter Wolverhampton Express & Star 1964–70, TV ed and critic The Sun 1970–84; TV columnist: The People 1984–89, Daily Express 1989–2000; freelance journalist and scriptwriter 2001–; chm: Broadcasting Press Guild 1981–83, Veterans' Ctee RTS 2007–; *Books* The Real Benny Hill (1992); *Style—* Ms Margaret Forwood; ✉ e-mail mforwood@btopenworld.com

FORWOOD, Hon Judge Nicholas James; QC (1987); s of Lt-Col Harry Forwood, RA, of Cobham, Surrey, and late Wendy, *née* French-Smith; *b* 22 June 1948; *Educ* Stowe, St John's Coll Cambridge (MA); *m* 4 Dec 1971, Sally Diane, da of His Hon Judge Basil Gerrard (decd), of Knutsford, Cheshire; 3 da (Victoria b 1974, Genevra b 1976, Suzanna b 1979), 1 s (Thomas b 1990); *Career* called to the Bar Middle Temple 1970, called to the Irish Bar 1981; appointed judge Court of First Instance of the EC 1999; *Recreations* golf, opera, skiing, sailing, shooting, walking across Europe; *Clubs* Oxford and Cambridge; *Style—* The Hon Judge Nicholas Forwood; ✉ Court of First Instance of the EC, L-2925, Luxembourg (tel 00 352 4303 3562)

FORWOOD, Sir Peter Noel; 4 Bt (UK 1895), of The Priory, Gateacre, Childwall, Co Palatine of Lancaster; s of Arthur Noel Forwood (d 1959, 3 s of 1 Bt), and his 2 w, Hyacinth, *née* Pollard; suc cous, Sir Dudley Richard Forwood, 3 Bt (d 2001); *b* 15 October 1925; *Educ* Radley; *m* 1950, Roy, da of James Murphy, MBE, FRCS, LRCP, of Horsham, W Sussex; 6 da; *Career* Welsh Gds WWII; *Style—* Sir Peter Forwood, Bt; ✉ Newhouse Farm, Shillinglee, Chiddingfold, Godalming, Surrey GU8 4SZ

FOSKETT, David Robert; QC (1991); s of Robert Frederick Foskett, of Worcs, and Ruth, *née* Waddington; *b* 19 March 1949; *Educ* Warwick Sch, KCL (LLB, pres Union); *m* 11 Jan 1975, Angela Bridget, da of late Maj Gordon Jacobs, MBE; 2 da (Rosanna Marie b 14 Dec 1984, Marianne Claire b 1 Dec 1991); *Career* called to the Bar Gray's Inn 1972 (bencher 1999), in practice Common Law Bar 1972–, recorder 1995– (asst recorder 1992–95), dep judge of the High Court 1998–; memb Civil Procedure Rule Ctee 1997–2001, chm Law Reform Ctee Bar Cncl 2005–07; pres: KCL Assoc 1997–2000, Old Warwickian Assoc 2000; FCIArb; *Books* The Law and Practice of Compromise (1980, 6 edn 2005), Settlement Under the Civil Procedure Rules (1999); *Recreations* music, theatre, reading poetry and composing verse, birdwatching, cricket, golf; *Clubs* Athenaeum, MCC, Woking Golf; *Style—* David Foskett, Esq, QC; ✉ 1 Crown Office Row, Temple, London EC4Y 7HH (tel 020 7797 7500, fax 020 7797 7550)

FOSSEY, Ann; da of Reginald Fossey, and Mary Fossey; *b* 20 August 1948; *m* 3 April 1971, Hellmuth Berendt, s of Earnst Berendt; 2 s (Max b 2 July 1978, Thomas b 14 Dec 1981); *Career* dir Paul Winner Mktg Communications 1971–83, head PR Div Brompton (subsid of Lowe Howard Spink) 1983–85, currently md Good Relations (joined as head of Consumer Div 1988); memb Mktg Soc, FIPR; *Style—* Ms Ann Fossey; ✉ Good Relations, Holborn Gate, 26 Southampton Buildings, London WC2A 3PQ (tel 020 7861 3142, fax 020 7861 3131)

FOSTER, (David) Alan; s of Wilfred John Foster (d 1971), of Esher, Surrey, and Edith Mary, *née* Rowling (d 1990); *b* 13 April 1935; *Educ* Oundle, ChCh Oxford; *m* 17 Sept 1960, Jacqueline Marie, da of Charles Edward Fredrick Stowell (d 1976), of Langstone, Hants; 2 s (Mark b 1961, Richard b 1962), 2 da (Nicola b 1964, Susannah b 1971); *Career* cmmnd RA 1953–55; ptnr De Zoete & Gorton (later De Zoete & Bevan) 1963, dep chm Barclays De Zoete Wedd Asset Management Ltd 1986–88; dir Avanti Communications Gp plc; govr Christ's Hosp, memb Ctee Oundle Schs William Laxton Soc; vice-patron DSA Ro-Ro Sailing Project; Freeman City of London 1959, Master Worshipful Co of Needlemakers 1991 (Freeman 1959, memb Ct of Assts1982, Sr Warden 1990); FPMI 1988 (APMI 1976), FRSA 1992, MSI 1992; *Recreations* sailing; *Clubs* City of London, RAC; *Style—* Alan Foster, Esq; ✉ The River House, Leigh Place, Cobham, Surrey KT11 2HL (tel 01932 864249, fax 01932 867897)

FOSTER, Alison Lee Caroline (Lady Havelock-Allan); QC (2002); da of Leslie Francis Foster (d 1985), of Sussex, and Marie Ann, *née* McIntosh-Hubson; *b* 22 January 1957, Sussex; *Educ* Bexhill GS for Girls, Jesus Coll Oxford (exhibitioner, BA), Courtauld Inst of Art (MPhil), City Univ London (Dip), Inns of Ct Sch of Law; *m* 22 May 1986, Sir Mark Havelock-Allan, Bt (His Hon Judge Havelock-Allan); 2 da (Miranda Anthonia Louise b 29 July 1993, Hannah Marie Josephine b 18 Oct 1997), 1 s (Henry Caspar Francis b 6 Oct 1994); *Career* called to the Bar Inner Temple 1984 (bencher 2003); pupil then tenant 39 Essex Street Chambers 1985–, pt/t chm Mental Health Review Tbnl 2004; legal advsr Ethical Ctee Br Psychoanalytical Soc; memb: Administrative Law Bar Assoc, Assoc of Regulatory and Disciplinary Lawyers; *Recreations* painting, gardening; *Clubs* Groucho; *Style—* Miss Alison Foster, QC; ✉ 39 Essex Street, London WC2R 3AT (tel 020 7832 1111)

FOSTER, Andrew Kevin; CBE (2005); s of Kevin William Foster, of Cheshire, and Doreen Foster (d 1981); *b* 3 March 1955; *Educ* Millfield, Keble Coll Oxford (BA); *m* 1981, Sara Gillian, da of Donald Daniels; 2 da (Anna Kate b 1982, Grace Elizabeth b 1989), 1 s (Thomas Don b 1984); *Career* mktg mangr Rowntree Mackintosh 1976–81, dir Worldcrest Ltd 1981–; non-exec dir Wrighton NHS Tst 1991–92, chm West Lancs NHS Tst 1992–96, chm Wigan & Leigh NHS Tst 1996–2001, policy dir HR NHS Confederation 1995–2001, dir of HR Dept of Health 2001–06, dir of HR Blackpool, Fylde and Wyre Hosps NHS

Tst 2006–07, chief exec Wrightington and Wigan and Leigh NHS Tst 2007–; *Recreations* golf, hockey; *Style*— Andrew Foster, Esq, CBE; ✉ Wrightington and Wigan and Leigh NHS Trust, Royal Albert Edward Infirmary, The Elms, Wigan Lane, Wigan WN1 2NN (tel 01942 822196)

FOSTER, Sir Andrew William; kt (2001); s of George William Foster, and Gladys Maria Foster; *b* 29 December 1944; *Educ* Abingdon Sch, Newcastle Poly (BSc), LSE (Post Grad Dip Social Studies); *Children* 1 s, 1 da; *Career* social worker 1966–71, area social servs offr 1971–75, asst dir of social servs Haringey 1975–79; dir of social servs: Greenwich 1979–82, N Yorks 1982–87; regnl gen mangr Yorks RHA 1987–91, dep chief exec NHS Mgmnt Exec 1991–92, controller Audit Commission 1992–2003, dep chm Royal Bank of Canada 2003–, chm FE Review Gp 2003–; non-exec dir: Sports Cncl 2003–, National Express Gp plc 2004–, Nestor Healthcare Gp 2004–, Liberata 2004–, PruHealth 2005–; *Recreations* golf, walking, travel, theatre, food, wine; *Style*— Sir Andrew Foster; ✉ 269 Lauderdale Mansions, Lauderdale Road, London W9 1LZ

FOSTER, Anthony; s of Rufus Foster (d 1971), of Gravesend, Kent, and Margery Beatrice, *née* Dace (d 1978); *b* 11 April 1926; *Educ* private; piano: Anne Collins, Arthur Tracy Robson; organ: John Cook, John Webster; orchestration: Richard Arnell, Dr Gordon Jacob, CBE; LRAM, ARCO; *m* 26 July 1952, Barbara (d 1991), da of Capt Frederick William Humphreys (d 1967), of Gravesend, Kent; 1 da (Charlotte b 1958); *Career* composer; published compositions incl: Slow Waltz and Calypso (instrumental, 1968), Dona Nobis Pacem (vocal and instrumental, 1973), Jonah and the Whale (vocal and instrumental, 1974), The St Richard Evening Service (vocal, 1981), Christ The Lord is Risen Again (Easter Carol, 1982), A Child is Born (vocal, 1983), Jubilate Deo (for organ, 1985, dedicated to and first performed by Alan Thurlow Chichester Cathedral), Three Sketches for Guitar (1989), Classical Suite (for organ, 1990), The Sailor and the Maid (musical, libretto by Barbara Foster, 1991), The Blessed Virgin Mary Evening Service (vocal, 1993), Prelude - Interlude - Postlude for Organ (first performance by Jeremy Suter Carlisle Cathedral), O Jesu, King Most Wonderful (anthem), The BVM Evening Service (1993, first performance Carlisle Cathedral), Little Child (1997), Theme and Variations for Organ (1997), Anima Christi (words trans by Mary Holtby, 1998), Fête (for organ, 1998), I Love the Windows of Thy Grace (anthem, 1999), Where is This Stupendous Stranger? (Christmas carol, 2000); organ accompaniments of various hymn tunes (1992–94); incidental music for BBC prodns incl: Monty Python's Flying Circus (1970), The Wizard of Oz (1970); hon vice-pres Brighton Schs Music and Drama Assoc 1977–98; recordings incl: Christ the Lord is Risen Again (1997), Child of Heaven (1999, choir of Chichester Cathedral, dir by Alan Thurlow), Magnificat (from the Blessed Virgin Mary Evening Service, 2000, choir of Carlisle Cathedral, conducted by Jeremy Suter), Jesus is Born! (2003), The Tsunami (for unaccompanied choir, BBC cmmn, 2005); memb: Composers' Guild of GB 1961, Performing Rights Soc 1982, Br Acad of Composers & Songwriters 1999; *Recreations* cinematography; *Style*— Anthony Foster, Esq; ✉ 1 Cawley Road, Chichester, West Sussex PO19 1UZ (tel 01243 780134)

FOSTER, Brendan; MBE (1976); s of Francis Foster, and Margaret Foster; *b* 12 January 1948; *Educ* St Joseph's GS Co Durham, Univ of Sussex (BSc), Carnegie Coll Leeds (DipEd); *m* 1972, Susan Margaret, da of Kenneth Frank Alston, of Clacton, Essex; 1 s (Paul b 1977), 1 da (Catherine b 1979); *Career* sch teacher St Joseph's GS Hebburn 1970–74, recreation mangr Gateshead Metropolitan Borough Cncl 1974–81, chm Nike (UK) Ltd 1981–87 (md Nike Europe), md Nova International Ltd 1987–; former athlete; Cwlth Games medals incl: Bronze 1500m 1970, Silver 5000m 1974, Bronze 5000m 1978, Gold 10,000m 1978; Euro Championships medals incl: Bronze 1500m 1971, Gold 5000m 1974; Olympic Games Bronze medal 10,000m 1976; world record holder: 2 miles 1973, 3000m 1974; UK record holder: 10,000m 1978, 1500m, 3000m, 2 miles, 5000m; BBC commentator on athletics 1980–; chm Great North Run 1981–; Hon MEd Univ of Newcastle, Hon DLitt Univ of Sussex, fell Sunderland Poly; *Style*— Brendan Foster, Esq, MBE; ✉ Nova International, Newcastle House, Albany Court, Monarch Road, Newcastle upon Tyne NE4 7YB

FOSTER, Prof Brian; OBE (2003); *b* 4 January 1954, Crook, Co Durham; *Educ* Wolsingham Secdy Sch, Queen Elizabeth Coll London (Dillon Prize, Andrewes Prize, BSc), Univ of Oxford (MA, DPhil); *m* 1983, Sabine Margot; 2 s (Paul Kai b 1989, Mark Kristian John b 1992); *Career* research assoc: Rutherford Appleton Lab 1978–82, Imperial Coll of Science and Technol 1982–84; Univ of Bristol: lectr Dept of Physics 1984–92, PPARC advanced fell 1991–97, reader Dept of Physics 1992–96, head Particle Physics Gp 1992–2003, prof of experimental physics 1996–2003, emeritus prof 2003; prof of experimental physics Univ of Oxford 2003– (head Subdepartment of Particle Physics 2004–), professorial fell Balliol Coll Oxford 2003–; numerous positions with ZEUS experiment DESY Hamburg 1985– (incl spokesman 1999–2003), actg dir Adams Inst for Accelerator Science Univ of Oxford/Royal Holloway Univ of London 2004–05; involved with numerous cncls, ctees and panels incl: memb Particle Physics Ctee SERC 1986–90, chm Nuclear and Particle Physics Division Inst of Physics 1989–93, memb Scientific Cncl Deutsches Elektronen Synchrotron Hamburg 1999–, memb PPARC 2001– (chm Particle Physics Ctee 1996–99, co-chm Science Ctee 1996–99 (memb 2001–07)), chm European Ctee for Future Accelerators 2002–05 (and ex-officio memb Cncl CERN), European dir of global design effort for Int Linear Collider 2005–; advsr to govt oppn spokesmen on science and technol 1993–97; Special European Physical Soc Prize in Particle Physics (awarded jtly for discovery of the gluon) 1995, Research Prize Alexander von Humboldt Fndn 1999, Max Born Medal and Prize Deutsche Physikalische Gesellschaft/Inst of Physics 2003; MRI 1979, FInstP 1992, memb BAAS 1993 (recorder Physics Section 1994–97); *Publications* Topics in High Energy Particle Physics (ed, 1988), 40 Years of Particle Physics (jt ed, 1988), Electron-Positron annihilation Physics (ed, 1990); author of numerous articles in learned jls; *Recreations* football (supporter of Sunderland FC), golf, squash, cricket, skiing, climbing, walking, history, politics, biography, music, playing the violin; *Style*— Prof Brian Foster, OBE; ✉ Denys Wilkinson Building, University of Oxford, Keble Road Oxford OX1 3RH (tel 01865 273323, fax 01865 273417, e-mail b.foster@physics.ox.ac.uk); ZEUS/F1, DESY, Notkestrasse 85, 22607 Hamburg, Germany

FOSTER, Christopher Kenneth; s of Kenneth John Foster (d 1982), of Sunningdale, Berks, and Christina Dorothy, *née* Clark; *b* 5 November 1949; *Educ* Harrow HS; *Career* chm and dir Springwood Books Ltd 1975–; dir: Chase Corporation plc 1985–87, Trafalgar House plc 1988–90, Wiggins Gp plc 1993–2005, Syndicated Minerals & Resources plc 2006–; Lord of the Manor of Little Hale; *Recreations* golf, music, art; *Clubs* Sunningdale Golf, Lansdowne, Annabel's; *Style*— Christopher Foster, Esq; ✉ Springwood House, The Avenue, Ascot, Berkshire SL5 7LR (tel 01344 628753); 56 Curzon Street, Mayfair, London W1 (tel 07921 587471, e-mail christopher.foster9@btinternet.com)

FOSTER, Christopher Norman; s of Maj-Gen Norman Leslie Foster, CB, DSO (d 1995), and Joan, *née* Drury (d 1991); *b* 30 December 1946, Dublin; *Educ* Westminster; *m* 1981, Anthea Jane, *née* Sammons; 2 s (Nicholas b 9 July 1983, Piers b 18 April 1986); *Career* Cooper Bros & Co 1965–73, mangr Racing Dept then dir Weatherbys 1973–90; Jockey Club: sec 1983–90, Keeper of the Match Book 1983–, exec dir 1993–2006, conslt 2006–; vice-chm Int Fedn of Horseracing Authorities 2000–, tstee Retraining of Racehorses 2006–, dir Wincanton Racecourse 2006–; govr Westminster Sch 1990–; FCA 1979 (ACA 1969); *Recreations* racing, shooting, golf, fishing, gardening; *Clubs* MCC, St Enodoc; *Style*— Christopher Foster, Esq; ✉ The Old Vicarage, Great Durnford, Salisbury, Wiltshire SP4 6AZ (tel 01722 782773, fax 01722 782647); The Jockey Club, 151 Shaftesbury Avenue, London WC2H 8AL (tel 020 7189 3890, fax 020 7189 3899, e-mail cfoster@thejockeyclub.co.uk)

FOSTER, Rt Rev Christopher Richard James; *see:* Hertford, Bishop of

FOSTER, Donald (Don); MP; s of late Rev J A Foster, and late I E Foster; *b* 31 March 1947; *Educ* Lancaster Royal GS, Keele Univ (BA, CertEd), Univ of Bath (MEd); *m* 31 Dec 1968, Victoria Jane Dorcas, *née* Pettegree; 1 s, 1 da; *Career* science teacher Sevenoaks Sch 1969–75, science project dir Resources for Learning Devpt Unit Avon Educn Authy 1975–80, lectr in educn Univ of Bristol 1980–89, mgmnt conslt Pannell Kerr Forster 1989–92; cncllr Cabot Ward Avon CC 1981–89 (chm Educn Ctee 1987–89), Parly candidate (Alliance) Bristol E 1987, MP (Lib Dem) Bath 1992–; Lib Dem spokesman on: educn and trg 1992–94, educn and employment 1994–99, environment, tport, regions and social justice 1999–2001, tport, local govt and regions 2001–02, tport 2002–03, culture, media and sport 2003–; memb Parly Office of Sci and Technol 1992–94, memb Educn and Employment Select Ctee 1996–99; vice-chm: Nat Campaign for Nursery Educn 1993–98 (pres 1998–2001), Br Assoc for Central and Eastern Europe 1994–97; hon pres Br Youth Cncl 1993–99; hon fell Bath Coll of HE; CPhys, MInstP; *Recreations* classical music, travel, sport; *Style*— Don Foster, Esq, MP; ✉ House of Commons, London SW1A 0AA (tel 020 7219 5001, fax 020 7219 2695, constituency office tel 01225 338973, fax 01225 463630, e-mail fosterd@parliament.uk)

FOSTER, Giles Henry; s of Stanley William Foster (d 1986), and Gladys Maude, *née* Moon (d 2005); *b* 30 June 1948; *Educ* Monkton Combe Sch, Univ of York (BA), RCA (MA); *m* 28 Sept 1974, Nicole Anne, da of Alan Coates, of London; 2 s (George b 1982, William b 1987); *Career* film and TV dir; *Television* incl: Summer Solstice, Foyle's War, Bertie and Elizabeth, The Prince and the Pauper, Relative Strangers, Coming Home, Oliver's Travels, The Rector's Wife, Adam Bede, The Lilac Bus, Monster Maker, Northanger Abbey, Hotel du Lac (BAFTA Award and ACE Award), Silas Marner (co-adaptor, BAFTA nomination), Dutch Girls, The Aerodrome, Last Summer's Child, The Obelisk, five scripts by Alan Bennett (incl Talking Heads: A Lady of Letters, BAFTA nomination); *Films* incl: Devices and Desires (Grierson Award), Consuming Passions, Tree of Hands; *Clubs* Groucho; *Style*— Giles Foster, Esq; ✉ c/o Anthony Jones, PFD, Drury House, 34–43 Russell Street, London WC2B 5HA (tel 020 7344 1000, fax 020 7379 6790)

FOSTER, Jacqueline; da of Samuel Renshaw (d 1985), and Isabella, *née* Brennan (d 2001); *b* 30 December 1947; *Educ* Prescot Girls' GS; *m* (m dis 1981) Peter Laurance Foster; *Career* Cabin Services BEA/BA 1969–81 and 1985–99, area mangr Austria Horizon 1981–85; fndr memb and offr Cabin Crew '89 (Trade Union for UK Airline Crew) 1989–99; MEP (Cons) NW England 1999–2004, Cons tport spokesman 2001–04, chm Backbench Ctee of MEPs 1999–2004; aerospace conslt 2004–; *Recreations* winter sports; *Clubs* Carlton, European Aviation; *Style*— Mrs Jacqueline Foster

FOSTER, Dr James Michael Gerard; s of Dr Robert Marius Foster, and Margaret Rhona, *née* Holland; *b* 19 December 1949; *Educ* King's Sch Canterbury, St Bart's Hosp Med Coll, Univ of London (Crawford exhibition, MB BS, MRCS LRCP), Univ of Wales Coll of Med (MSc); *m* 22 Nov 1986, Felicity Patricia, da of Dr Charles Mathurin Vaillant; 2 s (Charles James Vaillant b 2 March 1989, Simon James Holland b 16 Nov 1991); *Career* extern in pediatrics Tucson Medical Centre Arizona 1973, house physician Luton and Dunstable Hosp Luton 1975, house surgn Royal Berks Hosp Reading 1975; SHO St Bart's Hosp London: in neurosurgery and cardiothoracic surgery 1976–77, in anaesthesia 1977–79; registrar in anaesthesia St George's Hosp London 1979–81; sr registrar: in anaesthesia Guy's Hosp London 1981–84, in pain med Sir Charles Gairdner Hosp Perth Western Australia 1984 (King's Fund travelling fellowship bursary); conslt: in anaesthesia and pain med St Bart's Hosp London 1985–2000, in pain med Frimley Park Hosp Surrey 2001–, in pain med King Edward VII's Hosp London; hon sr lectr St Bart's Hosp Med Coll; memb: Br Pain Soc, European Soc of Regnl Anaesthesia; FRCA, DA; *Sporting Achievements* incl: Kenya Coast Open jr tennis champion 1968, ascent of Mt Kilimanjaro Tanzania 1969, represented Dubai UAE at rugby union 1974, West Australian Marathon 1984, captain Halford Hewitt Golf Team 2000–01; *Books* Terminal Care Support Teams (contrib, 1990), Coloproctology and the Pelvic Floor (contrib, 1992), Hospital-Based Palliative Care Teams (contrib, 1998); *Recreations* golf, photography, scuba diving, skiing; *Clubs* RSM, Fountain, The Berkshire Golf (Ascot), Royal Cinque Ports Golf (Deal), Royal Ascot Golf, Royal Berkshire Racquets and Health; *Style*— Dr James Foster; ✉ Heathend Lodge, Windsor Road, Ascot, Berkshire SL5 7LQ (tel 01344 621549); Private Consulting Rooms, The Princess Grace Hospital, 42–52 Nottingham Place, London W1U 5NY (tel 020 7486 1234, fax 020 7908 2168); The Princess Margaret Hospital, Osborne Road, Windsor, Berkshire SL4 3SJ (tel 01753 743489, fax 01753 743276)

FOSTER, Joanna; CBE (2002); da of Michael Mead, OBE (d 1996), and Lesley Mead (d 1999); *b* 5 May 1939; *Educ* Benenden, Grenoble Univ France (Dip); *m* 27 May 1961, Jerome Foster, s of Cecil William Foster (d 1997); 1 s (Hugo b 1969), 1 da (Kate b 1972); *Career* sec Vogue magazine, press attachée INSEAD Fontainebleau 1975–79, dir of educn corp servs Western Psychiatric Inst and Clinic Univ of Pittsburgh 1979–81, head Youth Trg Industrial Soc London 1983–85, head Pepperell Unit Industrial Soc 1985–88, chair Equal Opportunities Cmmn 1988–93, pres EC's Advsy Ctee on Equal Opportunities 1992; chair National Work-Life Forum 1998–2001, memb Govt Advsy Ctee on Work-Life Balance 1999–2002; dir: WNO 1990–94, BT Forum (British Telecommunications plc) 1995–98; chair Lloyds TSB Fndn 1998–2003 (dep chair 1992–98); chair UK Cncl UN International Year of the Family 1993–94; former dep chm Oxford Brookes Univ (govr 1993–98); chair Pennell Initiative for Women's Health 1999–2002, chair Nuffield Orthopaedic Centre NHS Tst Oxford 2001–; memb Advsy Bd Common Purpose; pres Relate Marriage Guidance Cncl 1993–96; tstee Employment Policy Inst 1995–98; govr Birkbeck Coll 1995–98; chair Crafts Cncl 2006–; hon fell St Hilda's Coll Oxford; Hon Doctorate: Kingston Univ 1992, Oxford Brookes Univ, Univ of Essex, Univ of the West of England 1993, Univ of Strathclyde 1994, Univ of Salford 1994, Univ of Bristol 1996; *Recreations* family, food, friends; *Clubs* Reform, Forum UK; *Style*— Joanna Foster, CBE; ✉ Meadow House, Mill Street, Islip OX5 2SZ

FOSTER, His Hon Judge Jonathan Rowe; QC (1989); s of Donald Foster (d 1980), and Hilda Eaton, *née* Rowe (d 2001); *b* 20 July 1947; *Educ* Oundle, Keble Coll Oxford (exhibitioner); *m* 1978, Sarah; 4 s; *Career* called to the Bar Gray's Inn 1970 (bencher 1998); recorder of the Crown Court 1988–2004, treas Northern Circuit 1992–97, dep judge of the High Court (Family Div 1994–, Queen's Bench Div 1998–), head 18 St John Street Chambers 1998–2004, circuit judge (Northern Circuit) 2004–; memb: Criminal Injuries Compensation Bd 1995–2000, CICAP 1996–2004; govr Ryley's Sch 1990–2006; *Recreations* outdoor activities, golf, bridge; *Clubs* St James Manchester, Hale Golf, Bowdon Lawn Tennis; *Style*— His Hon Judge Jonathan Foster, QC; ✉ Manchester Crown Court, Minshull Street, Manchester M1 3FS (tel 0161 954 7500)

FOSTER, Mark Andrew; *b* 12 May 1970; *Educ* Millfield, Kelly Coll; *Career* swimmer; memb Br swimming team 1985–; 50m freestyle: Bronze medal Cwlth Games 1990, 6th Olympic Games 1992, Gold medal World Short-Course Championships 1993, Gold medal Cwlth Games 1994, 6th World Long-Course Championships 1994, 4th European Championships 1995, Gold medal European Short-Course Championships 1996, Silver medal European Championships 1997, Silver medal World Short-Course Championships 1997, Gold medal (world record 21.31 secs) European Short Course Championships 1998, Gold medal Cwlth Games 1998, Gold medal World Short-Course Championships 1999, Gold medal World Short-Course Championships 2000; 50m Butterfly: Bronze medal Cwlth Games 1986, Gold medal European Short-Course Championships 1996, Silver medal (Cwlth record 23.24 secs) European Short-Course Championships 1998, Gold medal World Short-Course Championships 1999, Gold medal World Short-Course Championships 2000, Bronze medal Cwlth Games Manchester 2002; 4x100m medley: Bronze medal European Championships 1993, Bronze medal Cwlth Games 1994, 6th European Championships 1997, Bronze medal (GB record) World Short-Course Championships 1997; 4th 4x100m freestyle European Championships 1997; Br flag bearer Cwlth Games 1998; Gt Br rep at Olympic Games: Seoul 1988, Barcelona 1992, Atlanta 1996, Sydney 2000; world record holder 50m freestyle (21.13 secs) 2001, world record holder 50m butterfly (22.87) 2001; presenter Fascination of Freestyle Swimming (video, 1997); *Style—* Mark Foster, Esq

FOSTER, Michael; MP; *Career* MP (Lab) Worcester 1997–; PPS to Margaret Hodge, MBE, MP, *qv* 2001–04, PPS to educn team 2004–05, PPS to sec of state for NI 2004–06, asst Govt whip 2006–; assoc memb CIMA; *Clubs* Worcestershire Country Cricket; *Style—* Michael Foster, MP; ✉ House of Commons, London SW1A 0AA (tel 020 7219 3000, e-mail fosterm@parliament.uk)

FOSTER, Michael Jabez; DL (E Sussex 1993), MP; s of Dorothy Foster; *b* 26 February 1946; *Educ* Hastings Secdy Boys' Sch, Hastings GS, Univ of Leicester (LLM); *m* 13 Sept 1969, Rosemary; 2 s (Damien b 15 July 1974, Luke b 30 March 1978); *Career* slr; ptnr Messrs Fynmores of Bexhill on Sea 1980–98 (conslt 1998–); MP (Lab) Hastings and Rye 1997– (Parly candidate (Lab) Hastings 1974 (twice) and 1979); PPS to: Attorney Gen 1999–2003 and 2003–05, Slr Gen 2001–03 and 2003–05; memb House of Commons Standards and Privileges Select Ctee 1997–2004, memb Work and Pensions Ctee 2005–; memb All Pty Parly: Consumer Affrs Gp (sec) 1997–, Animal Welfare Gp 1997–, Older People Gp 1997–, Fishing Gp 1997–; memb PLP: Educn and Employment Ctee 1997–, Soc Security Ctee 1997–, Treasy Ctee 1997–; cncllr: Hastings Co BC 1971–74, Hastings BC 1973–79 and 1983–87, E Sussex CC 1973–77 and 1981–97; memb: Law Soc 1980, Soc of Lab Lawyers, Christian Socialist Movement, Fabian Soc, Child Poverty Action Gp; ACIArb 1997; *Clubs* Amherst Lawn Tennis, Tigers Table Tennis, Lords and Commons Lawn Tennis, Mensa; *Style—* Michael Foster, Esq, DL, MP; ✉ House of Commons, London SW1A 0AA (tel 020 7219 1600); Constituency Office, 84 Bohemia Road, St Leonards on Sea TN37 6RN (tel 01424 460070, fax 01424 460072, e-mail mp@1066.net, website www.michaelfoster.labour.co.uk)

FOSTER, Michael Robert; s of Robert O Foster (d 1996), and Nannette, *née* Howat; *b* 6 July 1941; *Educ* Felsted, Woodberry Forest Sch Virginia USA (ESU exchange scholar), AA Sch of Arch (AADipl), Univ of Essex (MA); *m* 17 Sept 1971, Susan Rose, *née* Bolson; 3 s (Jamie b 15 Sept 1973, Tom b 15 April 1976, Marcus b 11 July 1978); *Career* architect; asst Stillman & Eastwick-Field London and Skidmore Owings & Merrill Chicago 1965–66, asst and job architect YRM Architects and Planners 1966–69, full-time teacher Dept of Arch Poly of Central London 1970–71 (pt/t 1968–70), ptnr The Tooley & Foster Partnership (architects, engrs and designers) 1971–; pt/t teacher: Environmental Design Dept Wimbledon Sch of Art and in history and contextual studies Dept of Arch Poly of Central London 1971–73, Sch of Environmental Design RCA 1973–76, Schs of Arch and 3 Dimensional Design Kingston Poly 1975–79; pt/t lectr in history of design Middx Poly fndn course 1977–79; external examiner: interior design course Sch of 3 Dimensional Design Kingston Poly 1982–84, degree course in architecture South Bank Univ 1989–93, degree and dip course in architecture Univ of Portsmouth 1999–2002, Manchester Met Sch of Architecture 2003–06; Architectural Assoc: unit master Sch of Arch 1979–83, memb Cncl 1986–93, pres 1989–91; ARCUK: memb Educn Grants Panel Bd of Educn 1975–82, memb Cncl 1992–93; sec Standing Conf of Heads of Schs of Arch 1995–2003; project ldr NVQ/SVQ in Architectural Studies level 5 1998–; RIBA architect accredited in building conservation 2004–; tstee Geffrye Museum 1990–97 (chm Friends of Geffrye Museum 1981–90); RIBA 1968, MCSD 1981, memb L'Ordre des Architectes (France) 1991; *Books* The Principles of Architecture: Style, Structure and Design (1983); occasional contrib: AA Quarterly, Architect's Jl, Town and Country Planning, The Architect, Building Design; *Recreations* sailing, painting and drawing; *Style—* Michael Foster; ✉ The Tooley & Foster Partnership, Warwick House, Palmerston Road, Buckhurst Hill, Essex IG9 5LQ (tel 020 8504 9711, fax 020 8506 1779, e-mail mfoster@tooleyfoster.com)

FOSTER, Murray Egerton; s of Maurice Foster, OBE (d 1998), of Grindleford, Derbys, and Mary, *née* Davies; *b* 17 December 1946; *Educ* Carliol Carlisle, Welsh Nat Sch of Med (BDS, MB BCh, MScD); *m* 13 July 1974, Margaret Elizabeth, da of Glynmore Jones, of Chester; 2 s (Lawrence b 1981, Richard b 1983), 1 da (Catherine b 1984); *Career* sr registrar St George's Hosp and St Thomas' Hosp 1977–80, conslt in oral maxillo-facial surgery NW Region and postgrad tutor Univ of Manchester; memb: Inst of Healthcare Mgmnt (IHM), BMA, BDA, BAOMS; FDS, FFDRCSI, FRCSEd; *Books* Dental, Oral and Maxillo-facial Surgery (jtly, 1986); *Recreations* walking, sailing, photography; *Clubs* Oral Surgery; *Style—* Murray Foster; ✉ 7 Higher Lydgate Park, Grasscroft, Saddleworth OL4 4EF (tel 01457 874196); 2 St John Street, Manchester (tel 0161 835 1149)

FOSTER, Neil William Derick; s of William Robert Brudenell Foster (d 1992), and Jean Leslie, *née* Urquhart (d 1986); bro of Richard Francis Foster, *qv*; *b* 13 March 1943; *Educ* Harrow, Aix en Provence Univ; *m* 2 Sept 1989, Anthea Caroline, da of Ian Gibson Macpherson, MC, of The Old Hall, Blofield, Norwich, Norfolk; 1 da (b 21 Nov 1992); *Career* underwriting memb Lloyd's 1971–, dir John Foster & Sons plc 1975–93, dir and past chm Norfolk Churches Tst 1976–, dir Norfolk Marketing Ltd 1985–95; gen cmmr of income tax 1992–2002 (vice-chm Dereham Div 1996); past chm: East Anglia Div Royal Forestry Soc, The Game Conservancy Norfolk, East Anglia region Timber Growers Assoc, CLA Norfolk; chm: Upper Nar Internal Drainage Bd 1993–2004 (memb 1992–), HHA East Anglia, Lexham Parish Meeting 1992–; govr Beeston Primary Sch 2001–04; High Sheriff Norfolk 1999–; Liveryman Worshipful Co of Clothworkers 1965 (4th Warden 1995, 2nd Warden 1996); *Recreations* shooting, forestry, gardening; *Clubs* Boodle's, Norfolk; *Style—* Neil Foster, Esq; ✉ Lexham Hall, King's Lynn, Norfolk PE32 2QJ (tel 01328 701 341); The Estate Office, Lexham Hall, King's Lynn, Norfolk PE32 2QJ (tel 01328 701 288, fax 01328 700 053)

FOSTER, Nigel Pearson; s of Gordon Pearson Foster (d 1985), of Wilmslow, Cheshire, and Margaret Elizabeth, *née* Bettison (d 1989); *b* 18 February 1952; *Educ* Oswestry Sch; *m* 20 May 1988, Mary Elizabeth, da of Edward Bangs; 1 da (Elizabeth Margaret b 9 June 1990), 1 s (Charlie Edward b 13 Oct 1994); *Career* Rowlinson-Broughton 1969–72, Clough Howard Richards Manchester 1972–74, prodn asst Royds Manchester 1974–76, account exec The Advertising and Marketing Organisation 1976–79, TV prodr Wasey Campbell Ewald 1980–82 (account exec 1979–80), TV prodr Foote Cone Belding 1982–84; head of TV KMP 1984–86; J Walter Thompson: TV prodr 1986–89, head of TV UK 1989–96, exec dir of TV prodn Europe 1996–; FIPA; *Style—* Nigel Foster, Esq

FOSTER, Prof Peter William; s of Percy William Foster (d 1966), and Florence Harriet, *née* Bedford (d 1976); *b* 6 December 1930; *Educ* UCL (BSc, PhD); *m* 16 Aug 1952, Elizabeth, da of Walter Goldstern, of Altrincham; 2 da (Frances M b 1956, Theresa K b 1962), 2 s (Anthony P b 1958, Andrew P b 1960); *Career* tech offr Nobel Div ICI 1954–57, assoc prof Univ of Nebraska 1957–58, res chemist E I du Pont de Nemours Inc 1958–63, mangr Du Pont International SA Geneva 1963–66, md and dir Heathcoat Yarns and Fibres and John Heathcoat 1966–82, chm Steam Storage Co Ltd 1975–98, md Universal Carbon Fibres Ltd 1982–85; UMIST (now Univ of Manchester): prof Dept of Textiles UMIST 1986–96 (emeritus prof 1996–), vice-princ 1991–94; dir Worthington plc 1999–2004; memb Textile Inst; FTI, FRSA; *Recreations* chess, theatre; *Clubs* Rotary; *Style—* Prof Peter Foster; ✉ Department of Textiles and Paper, University of Manchester, PO Box 88, Sackville Street, Manchester M60 1QD (tel 0161 200 4142, fax 0161 228 7040, e-mail peter.foster@manchester.ac.uk)

FOSTER, Richard Anthony (Tony); s of Donald Foster (d 2000), of Bishop's Stortford, Herts, and Jean Foster; *b* 2 April 1946; *Educ* King Edward VI GS Chelmsford, St Peter's Coll Birmingham, Cardiff Coll of Art; *m* 1968, Ann Margaret, da of Donald Partington (d 1987), and Joan Partington (d 1985); *Career* artist; art teacher Leicester, Cayman Is and Cornwall 1968–75, visual arts co-ord S Hill Park Arts Centre Bracknell 1976–78, visual arts offr South West Arts 1978–84, professional artist 1984–; co-fndr with Jonathan Harvey and James Lingwood of TSWA; winner Yosemite Renaissance Prize 1988, RGS Cherry Kearton Meml Medal 2002; FRGS 1993; *Solo Exhibitions* incl: Royal Watercolour Soc London 1985, Yale Center for British Art New Haven Conn 1985, Francesca Anderson Gallery Boston Mass 1985 and 1988, City of Edinburgh Art Centre 1987, Ecology Centre London 1987, Calif Acad of Sciences San Francisco 1987, Smithsonian Inst Washington DC 1989, Plymouth Arts Centre Devon 1990, Newlyn Orion Penzance 1990, Montgomery Gallery San Francisco 1990, 1993 and 1995, Bruton Gallery Bath 1992, Royal Albert Museum Exeter 1993 and 1998, Harewood House Yorks 1993, Royal Botanic Gardens Kew 1995, Sun Valley Center for the Arts & Humanities, Meyerson & Nowinski Seattle 1997 and 1999, Francesca Anderson Fine Art Lexington Mass 1997, Royal Albert Meml Museum Exeter 1998, Harewood House 1998, RGS London 1998, Montgomery Gallery San Francisco 1999, Eyre Moore Gallery Seatle 1999, World Views (retrospective), Frye Art Museum Seattle 2000 and 2003, Graham Gallery New York 2000 and 2003, Montgomery Gallery San Francisco 2001 and 2003, Nat Museum of Natural History Wyoming 2004, John Mitchell & Sons 2005; *Art Projects* incl: Travels Without a Donkey in the Cevennes (with James Ravilious) 1982, Thoreau's Country (walks and canoe journeys in New England) 1985, John Muir's High Sierra 1986–87, Exploring the Grand Canyon 1988–89, Rainforest Diaries (Costa Rica) 1991–93, Arid Lands (walks across deserts) 1993–95, Ice and Fire (series of paintings about volcanoes) 1996–98, WaterMarks (paintings of river journeys) 1998–2003, After Lewis and Clark - Explorer Artists and the American West at the Sun Valley Center for the Arts (2000) and Boise Art Museum (2001); Paint the Fire (BBC Radio 4 documentary) 1999, Escuela y Clinica Tony Foster (constructed and opened in El Chorro Honduras, 2001); 16 Days Rafting the Colorado (series of 16 paintings purchased by Denver Art Museum for their perm collection, 2002), Searching for a Bigger Subject 2005–07 (first artist to have painted all three faces of Everest and highest large-scale watercolour painted on site (3ft x 6ft at 17,400 ft), TV documentary: The Man Who Painted Everest (Sky Artsworld) 2006); *Recreations* snooker, walking, travel, scuba diving; *Style—* Tony Foster; ✉ 1 Well Street, Tywardreath Par, Cornwall PL24 2QH (tel and fax 01726 815300, website www.tony-foster.co.uk)

FOSTER, Richard Francis; s of William Robert Brudenell Foster (d 1992), of Lexham Hall, King's Lynn, and Jean Leslie, *née* Urqhuart (d 1986); bro of Neil Foster, *qv*; *b* 6 June 1945; *Educ* Harrow, Trinity Coll Oxford, Studio Simi Florence, City & Guilds of London Art Sch; *m* 1970 (m dis 1984), Hon Sarah Rachel Jane Kay-Shuttleworth (now Hon Mrs Figgins), da of 4 Baron Shuttleworth (d 1975); 2 da (Henrietta Victoria (Mrs Benjamin Stanton) b 10 Aug 1973, Georgiana Pamela b 2 May 1975), 1 s (Edward William Thomas b 7 March 1978); *Career* landscape and portrait painter; numerous public and private portrait cmmns; Lord Mayor's Award for London Landscapes 1972; Liveryman Worshipful Co of Clothworkers, Brother Art Workers' Guild; RP (vice-pres 1991–94, hon treas 2003–06); *Exhibitions* solo incl: Jocelyn Feilding Fine Art 1974, Spink & Son Venice 1978, Spink & Son India 1982, 1991 and 1997, Spink & Son Egypt 1984, Rafael Valls Ltd 1999, Partridge Fine Art 2003, Indar Pasricha Fine Art 2005; group incl: Royal Soc of Portrait Painters (annually) 1969–, Royal Acad (most years) 1972–; *Recreations* travel, country sports, family life; *Clubs* Chelsea Arts, Pratt's; *Style—* Richard Foster, Esq; ✉ Manor House, Colkirk, Fakenham, Norfolk NR21 7NW (tel 01328 864276); 5A Clareville Grove, London SW7 5AU (tel 020 7244 7164, website www.richardfoster.co.uk)

FOSTER, His Hon Judge Richard John Samuel; s of Samuel Geoffrey Foster (d 1968), and Beryl Constance, *née* Seabourne; *b* Worcester; *Educ* Bromsgrove Sch Worcs, Coll of Law Guildford; *m* 1, 10 Oct 1980, Ann, *née* Scott (d 2002); *m* 2, 5 April 2004, Susan Claire, *née* Brodie; 1 da (Charlotte Emma Scott b 15 Nov 1984), 1 step-da (Claire Georgina Emily b 13 Nov 1983), 1 step-s (James David Thomas b 11 May 1985); *Career* slr Dawson and Co 1979–81, slr Barlow Lyde and Gilbert 1981–86; Vizards: ptnr 1986–98, jt sr ptnr 1998–99; sr ptnr Vizards Oldham 1999–2002, ptnr Weightman Vizards 2002–04; recorder 1998–2004, dep High Court judge 2003–, circuit judge 2004–; memb Bd Bedfordshire Probation Serv 2006–; chm of tstees Royal Br Legion Pension Fund 2003–04; memb Law Soc 1979; *Publications* Local Authority Liability (jt ed, 3 edn 2005); *Recreations* golf and gardening; *Clubs* Reform, Berkhamsted Golf, Andratx Golf (Mallorca); *Style—* His Hon Judge Richard Foster; ✉ Luton Crown Court, 7 George Street, Luton, Bedfordshire LU1 2AA (tel 01582 522000, fax 01582 522001, e-mail hhjudge.foster@judiciary.gsi.gov.uk)

FOSTER, Robert; s of David Foster, of Ascot, and Amelia, *née* Morris; *b* 12 May 1943; *Educ* Oundle, CCC Cambridge (MA); *m* 1967, Judy, *née* Welsh; 1 s (Alan b 30 March 1976), 1 da (Joanna b 2 April 1978); *Career* electrical engr: Parkinson Cowan Ltd 1964–66, Automation Ltd 1966–71, Post Office Telecommunications 1972–77; DTI: princ 1977–84, asst sec 1984–91, dir Aerospace and Def Industries Directorate 1992–97, dir Innovation Policy and Standards 1998–2000; chief exec Competition Cmmn 2000–04; cmmr Nat Lottery Cmmn 2005–; non-exec dir: King's Coll Hosp NHS Tst, Jersey Competition Regulatory Authy; memb Advsy Cncl Oxford Capital Ptnrs; CEng, FIEE, FRAeS; *Recreations* music, squash, tennis, reading and theatre; *Style—* Robert Foster, Esq; ✉ National Lottery Commission, 101 Wigmore Street, London W1U 1QU

FOSTER, Rosalind Mary (Mrs R M Englehart); da of Ludovic Anthony Foster (d 1990), of Greatham Manor, Pulborough, W Sussex, and Pamela Margaret, *née* Wilberforce (d 1997); *b* 7 August 1947; *Educ* Cranborne Chase Sch, Lady Margaret Hall Oxford (BA); *m* 2 Jan 1971, Robert Michael Englehart, QC, *qv*, s of Gustav Axel Englehart (d 1969), of London; 2 da (Alice b 1976, Lucinda b 1978), 1 s (Oliver b 1982); *Career* called to the Bar Middle Temple 1969 (bencher 1996), recorder of the Crown Court 1987–98; legal pres Mental Health Review Tbnl; memb: Medico-Legal Soc, Assoc of Regulatory and Disciplinary Lawyers; FRSA 2002; *Publications* Learning Medicine (co-author, 2006); *Recreations* theatre, travel; *Style—* Miss Rosalind Foster; ✉ 2 Temple Gardens, The Temple, London EC4Y 9AY (tel 020 7822 1200, fax 020 7822 1300, e-mail rfoster@2templegardens.co.uk)

FOSTER, Roy William John; s of Francis Edwin Foster (d 1997), and Marjorie Florence Mary, *née* Chapman (d 1944); *b* 25 May 1930; *Educ* Rutlish Sch; *m* 6 Sept 1957, Christine Margaret, da of Albert Victor Toler (d 1972); 2 s (Nicholas Charles Roy b 23 April 1960 d 1969, Richard James b 25 March 1964); *Career* Nat Serv RAF 1953–54, cmmnd PO 1953; qualified CA 1955, ptnr Coopers & Lybrand (and predecessor firms) 1960–90; memb Cncl: CBI 1986–96, ICRF (latterly Cancer Research UK) 1998–2003; Freeman City of London; Liveryman: Worshipful Co of Painter Stainers (memb Ct of Assts), Worshipful Co of CAs; ATII 1964, FCA 1965; *Recreations* rugby and cricket watching, race horse ownership, theatre, food and wines; *Clubs* RAF, HAC, MCC, City Livery; *Style—* Roy Foster, Esq; ✉ Paddock House, 16 Paul's Place, Farm Lane, Ashtead, Surrey KT21 1HN (tel and fax 01372 270079)

FOSTER OF BISHOP AUCKLAND, Baron (Life Peer UK 2005); Derek Foster; PC (1993), DL (Co Durham 2001); s of Joseph Foster (d 1959), and Ethel, *née* Ragg (d 1982); *b* 25 June 1937; *Educ* Bede GS Sunderland, St Catherine's Coll Oxford; *m* 1972, (Florence) Anne, da of Thomas Bulmer, of Sunderland; *Career* youth and community worker 1970–73, further educn organiser 1973–74, asst dir of educn Sunderland Cncl 1974–79, chm N of England Devpt Cncl 1974–76, memb Tyne & Wear CC and Sunderland BC; MP (Lab) Bishop Auckland 1979–2005, memb House of Commons Trade & Industry Select Ctee 1980–82, additional oppn spokesman Social Security 1982, oppn whip 1982, PPS to Neil Kinnock 1983–85, oppn chief whip 1985–95, memb Shadow Cabinet 1985–97, shadow chllr of the Duchy of Lancaster 1995–97, chm House of Commons Employment Select Ctee 1997–2001, co-chm House of Commons Educn & Employment Select Ctee 1997–2001; memb: House of Commons Ecclesiatastical Ctee 1997–, House of Commons Liaison Ctee 1997–2001; exec memb Br-American Parly Gp 1997–; chm PLP: Employment Ctee 1980–81, Econ and Fin Ctee 1981–82; offr PLP 1985–95, ex-officio memb Lab Pty Nat Exec 1985–95, memb Advsy Ctee for Registration of Political Parties 1998–; hon pres Br Youth Cncl 1984–86, past vice-pres Christian Socialist Movement; chm: North Regional Information Soc Initiative 1996–2002, Pioneering Care Partnership 1997–2003, Nat Prayer Breakfast 1997–99, Manufacturing Industry Gp 1998–, Bishop Auckland Devpt Co Ltd, NE Pharmaceutical Gp, Bishop Auckland Town Forum 2002, NE e-Learning Fndn 2003; vice-chm: Youthaid 1979–85, Youth Affairs Lobby 1984–86; pres SW Durham Trainig 2003–; memb Standards and Priveledges Ctee 2003–; non-exec dir Northern Informatics 1998; memb Nat Advsy Bd Salvation Army 1995–, tstee: Auckland Castle, e-Learning Fndn 2001; memb Fabian Soc; chm Inst of Lighting Engrs 2001–; fell Industry & Parly Tst; *Recreations* brass bands, male voice choirs, soccer, cricket; *Style*— The Rt Hon Lord Foster of Bishop Auckland, PC, DL; ✉ 3 Linburn, Rickleton, Washington, Tyne & Wear NE38 9EB (tel 0191 417 1580)

FOSTER OF THAMES BANK, Baron (Life Peer UK 1999), of Reddish in the County of Greater Manchester; Sir Norman Robert Foster; OM (1997), kt (1990); s of Lilian and Robert Foster, of Manchester; *b* 1 June 1935; *Educ* Univ of Manchester Sch of Architecture (DipArch, CertTP), Yale Univ Sch of Architecture (MArch); *Career* Nat Serv RAF 1953–55; architect; fndr Foster Assocs 1967 then Foster and Partners 1996 (chm); winner of over 50 national and international competitions since 1979 for projects incl: Florence TGV Station, Hearst HQ NY, Millennium Bridge London, British Museum Great Court London, New German Parliament Reichstag Berlin, Hong Kong Int Airport Chek Lap Kok, Duisburg Inner Harbour, Lycée Fréjus France, Hongkong and Shanghai Bank HQ Hong Kong, BBC Radio Centre, Carré d'Art Nîmes, Collserola Tower Barcelona, Bilbao Metro System, King's Cross Masterplan, new wing Joslyn Art Museum Nebraska, HQ Commerzbank Frankfurt, 30 St Mary Axe London, McLaren Technol Centre, Millau Viaduct; other projects incl: GLA HQ London, Great Glass House, National Botanical Garden of Wales, Congress Hall for city of Valencia, Masterplans London, Rotterdam, Barcelona, Mallorca, Berlin, Nîmes, Cannes, Greenwich, Micro-electronic Park Duisburg, Stansted Airport London, Century Tower Tokyo, The Sackler Galleries at the Royal Acad (RIBA Building of the Year Award 1993), ITN HQ London, Crescent Wing and Sainsbury Centre Norwich, Renault Centre Swindon, Willis Faber and Dumas Ipswich; conslt architect UEA 1978–87; teacher 1967–77: London Poly, Bath Acad of Arts, Univ of Pennsylvania, AA; visiting prof Urban Research Bartlett Sch of Architecture 1998–99; over 290 major national and international awards incl: FT Industrial Architecture Award 1967, 1970, 1971, 1974, 1981, 1984 and 1993, RIBA Awards 1969, 1972, 1977, 1978, 1981, 1992, 1993, 1997, 1998,1999 and 2003, Structural Steel Award 1972, 1978, 1980, 1984, 1986, 1992 and 2000, RS Reynolds Award 1976, 1979 and 1986, International Prize for Architecture 1976 and 1980, Ambrose Congreve Award 1980, Royal Gold Medal for Architecture 1983, Civic Tst Award 1984, 1992, 1995, 1999, 2000, 2001 and 2002, Premio Compasso d'Oro Award 1987, PA Innovations Award 1988, Interiors USA Award 1988, 1992, 1993 and 1994, Kunstpreis Berlin Award 1989, BCIA Award 1989, 1991, 1992, 1993, 1997, 1998, 2000 and 2001, RIBA Tstees Medal 1990, Mies van der Rohe Pavilion Award 1991, Gold Medal French Académie de Paris, Arnold W Brunner Meml Prize NY 1992, RFAC & Sunday Times Best Building of the Year Award 1992, ICE Merit Award 1992, ISE Special Award 1992, Concrete Soc Award 1992 and 1993, BCO Award 1992, 1993 and 2001, Benedictus Award 1993, Gold Medal American Inst of Architects 1994, Bund Deutsche Architekten Award 1994, Queen's Award for Export Achievement 1995, CSD Medal for lifetime achievement in design 1997, Prince Philip Designer Prize 1997, Pritzker Architecture Prize 1999, Walpole Medal of Excellence 1999, Le Prix Europeene de l'Architectúre de la Fndn Europeene de la Culture Europa 1999, Special Prize at 4th Int Biennial of Architecture São Paulo Brazil 1999, Visual Arts Award 2000, 5th South Bank Show Award 2001, Auguste Perret Prize 2002, Praemium Imperiale (Japan) 2002, Prince Philip Designers Prize 2004; TV documentaries incl: BBC Omnibus 1981, 1995 and 1999, Anglia Enterprise 1983, BBC Late Show 1990 and 1991, Building Sites 1991, The Limit 1998, Pinnacle Europe CNN 1999, South Bank Show 2001; featured in numerous international pubns and jls; exhbns of work held in: London, NY, Paris, Cologne, Copenhagen, Bordeaux, Lyon, Nîmes, Tokyo, Berlin, Madrid, Barcelona, Milan, Venice, Florence, Hong Kong, Antwerp; work in permanent collections of MOMA NY and Centre Pompidou Paris; vice-pres AA 1974 (memb Cncl 1973), memb RIBA Visiting Bd of Educn 1971 (external examiner 1971–73); memb Cncl RCA 1981; assoc Académie Royale de Belgique, memb Ordre Français des Architectes, hon memb Bund Deutsche Architekten 1983, hon fell American Inst of Architects 1980, foreign memb Royal Acad of Fine Arts Sweden 1995, offr Order of Arts and Letters Miny of Culture France 1994, memb European Acad of Sciences and Arts 1996, foreign memb American Acad of Arts and Sciences 1996; IBM fell 1980, hon fell Kent Inst of Art and Design 1994; hon prof Univ of Buenos Aires 1997; Hon LittD UEA 1980, Hon DSc Univ of Bath 1986; Hon Dr: RCA 1991, Univ of Valencia 1992, Univ of Humberside 1992, London Inst 2001, Ben Gurion Univ of The Negev (Lifetime Achievement Award) 2001, Robert Gordon Univ 2002, Univ of Durham 2002; Hon LLD: Univ of Manchester 1993, Technical Univ of Eindhoven 1996, Univ of Oxford 1996; Hon DLit Univ of London 1996; RIBA 1965, FCSD 1975, ARA 1983, RDI 1988, Hon FREng 1995, Hon FRIAS 2000, Hon ICE 2001; Commander's Cross of the Order of Merit (Germany) 1999, Orden Pour le mérite für Wissenschaft und Künste (Germany) 2002; *Books* The Work of Foster Associates (1978), Norman Foster, Buildings and Projects, Vols 1, 2, 3, 4 (1989–90), Foster Associates (1991), Norman Foster Sketches (1991), Recent Works Foster Associates (1992), Sir Norman Foster (1997), Norman Foster, selected and current works of Foster and Partners (1997), Norman Foster - 30 Colours (1998), The Norman Foster Studio (2000), The Reichstag: The Parliament Building by Norman Foster (2000), Rebuilding the Reichstag (2000), On Foster ... Foster On (2000), Norman Foster Works 1 (2003); *Recreations* flying, skiing, running; *Style*— The Rt Hon the Lord Foster of Thames Bank, OM; ✉ Foster & Partners, Riverside Three, 22 Hester Road, London SW11 4AN (tel 020 7738 0455, fax 020 7738 1107/1108, e-mail enquiries@fosterandpartners.com)

FOULIS, Sir Iain Primrose Liston; 13 Bt (NS 1634), of Colinton, and of Ravelston but for the attainder; s of Lt-Col James Alastair Liston Foulis (d 1942, s of Lt-Col Archibald Primrose Liston-Foulis (ka 1917), 4 s of 9 Bt), and Kathleen, da of Lt-Col John Moran (d 1991) and Countess Olga de la Hogue, yr da of Marquis de la Hogue (Isle of Mauritius); *suc* kinsman, Sir Archibald Charles Liston-Foulis, 12 Bt (d 1961); Sir James Foulis, 2 Bt, was actively engaged in the wars of Scotland after the death of Charles I and was knighted during his f's lifetime; distant cous of Sir Archibald Primrose, 2 Bt of Ravelston who took arms and name of Primrose, fought with Hussars at Culloden, beheaded at Carlisle 1746, title of Ravelston and Estates forfeited; ggggs of Sir Charles Ochterlony, 2 Bt, fndr of The Gurkhas; *b* 9 August 1937; *Educ* Hodder, St Mary's Hall, Stonyhurst, Cannington Farm Inst Bridgewater; *Career* practical farming Somerset 1955; Nat Serv Argyll and Sutherland Highlanders 1957–59, Cyprus 1958; language tutor Madrid 1959–61 and 1966–83, ret; trainee exec Bank of London and S America 1962, Bank of London and Montreal Ltd Bahamas, Guatemala and Nicaragua 1963–65, sales Toronto Canada 1966; landowner 1962–; *Recreations* driving, mountain walking, country pursuits (hunting wild boar), swimming, camping, travelling, looking across the plains of Castille to the mountains; *Clubs* Friends of the Castles, Friends of the St James' Way (all in Spain); *Style*— Sir Iain Foulis, Bt; ✉ Plaza Juan Carlos 1 No 1, Portal 5–2–C, San Agustin de Guadalix, 28750 Madrid, Spain (tel and fax 00 34 91 84 18 978); Calle Universidad 28, Escalera 2, 5–D Jaca (Huesca), Spain

FOULKES, Nicholas; s of James Foulkes, and Regine, *née* Richter; *b* 2 December 1964, Aberystwyth; *Educ* Christ's Hosp, Hertford Coll Oxford; *m* 23 Sept 1989, Alexandra, *née* Holloway; 2 s (Maximilian Anton b 28 May 1996, Frederick Alexander b 9 May 1999); *Career* formerly assoc ed ES Magazine Evening Standard; author and journalist 1994–, luxury ed GQ, contributing ed Vanity Fair, columnist Newsweek, freelance contrib to Independent on Sunday, Daily Telegraph, Mail on Sunday, Spectator, Country Life and other newspapers and periodicals; Havana Man of the Year 2007; *Publications* incl: Dressed to Kill: James Bond the Suited Hero (contrib, 1996), Evening Standard Restaurant Guide (2000), Last of the Dandies: The Scandalous Life and Escapades of Count d'Orsay (2003), Marbella Club: The First Fifty Years (2005), The Bentley Miscellany (2005), The Bentley Era: The Fast and Furious Story of the Fabulous Bentley Boys (2006), Dunhill by Design (2006), Dancing into Battle: A Social History of the Battle of Waterloo (2006), The Trench Book (2007), The Carlyle (2007); *Recreations* playing backgammon, eating at Riva, visiting tailors, watchmakers and cigar factories; *Clubs* White's; *Style*— Nicholas Foulkes, Esq; ✉ c/o Luigi Bonomi Associates, 91 Great Russell Street, London WC1B 3PS (tel 020 7637 1234)

F

FOULKES, Prof (Albert) Peter; s of Henry Foulkes (d 1990), of Yorks, and Edith Cavell, *née* O'Mara (d 1989); *b* 17 October 1936; *Educ* Univ of Sheffield (BA), Univ of Cologne, Univ of Tulane (PhD); *m* 1959, (Barbara) Joy, da of William Joseph French (d 1981); 2 da (Imogen b 21 May 1960, Juliet b 26 Nov 1961); *Career* prof Stanford Univ 1965–75, prof of German Univ of Wales 1977–; Alexander Von Humboldt fell 1972; Inst of Linguists: memb Cncl 1982–89, chm Examinations Bd 1985–90, tstee 1986–90, vice-pres 1990–98; FIL 1982; *Books* The Reluctant Pessimist, Franz Kafka (1967), The Search for Literary Meaning (1975), Literature and Propaganda (1983), Tales from French Catalonia (2000); *Recreations* gardening, rambling, theatre, conjuring, photography; *Style*— Prof Peter Foulkes; ✉ Clara, Prades, 66500, France (tel 00 33 68 96 42 88, e-mail peterfoulkes@free.fr)

FOULKES, Thomas Howard Exton (Tom); s of Maj Gen Thomas H F Foulkes (d 1986), and Delphine, *née* Smith; *b* 31 August 1950; *Educ* Clifton, Sandhurst, RMCS Shrivenham (BSc), Open Univ (MBA), RCDS; *m* 14 August 1976, Sally, *née* Winter; 2 da (Emma-Jane b 23 March 1982, Kate b 13 June 1987); *Career* cmmnd RE 1971, regtl duties RE 1971–82, Defence Equipment Procurement (bridges) 1982–89, CO 28 Amphibious Engr Regt 1989–92; Defence Equipment Procurement: project mangr Gen Engr Equipment 1992–95, equipment support mangr 1995–97; RCDS 1997–98, promoted to rank of Brig 1998, project mangr CAPITAL 1998–99, dir Army Estates Orgn 1999–2002; DG ICE 2002–; sec gen Cwlth Engrs Cncl 2002–; pres Royal Engrs Assoc FC 1992–2002; memb: Public Monuments and Scuplture Assoc, Friends of Mount Athos, Smeatonian Soc of Civil Engrs; Freeman Worshipful Co of Engrs; CEng, FIMechE 1995, FICE 1996; *Publications* Monuments in Whitehall: A Walk With Heroes (series, 1985–95); author of various titles on military bridging and procurement of weapon systems 1982–98; *Recreations* skiing, cycling, gardening, studying philosophy; *Clubs* Athenaeum; *Style*— Tom Foulkes, Esq; ✉ Institution of Civil Engineers, 1 Great George Street, London SW1P 3AA (tel 020 7665 2002)

FOULKES OF CUMNOCK, Baron (Life Peer UK 2005), of Cumnock in East Ayrshire; George Foulkes; PC (2002), JP (Edinburgh 1975), MSP; s of late George Foulkes, and Jessie M A W Foulkes (decd); *b* 21 January 1942; *Educ* Keith GS, Haberdashers' Aske's, Univ of Edinburgh; *m* 1970, Elizabeth Anna, da of William Hope; 2 s, 1 da; *Career* pres: Univ of Edinburgh Students Rep Cncl 1963–64, Scottish Union of Students 1965–67; rector's assessor at Univ of Edinburgh; dir: Enterprise Youth 1968–73, Age Concern Scotland 1973–79; cncllr and bailie Edinburgh City Cncl 1970–75, chm Lothian Region Educn Ctee 1974–79, cncllr Lothian Regnl Cncl 1974–79; chm: Educn Ctee Convention of Scot Local Authorities 1976–79, Scottish Adult Literacy Agency 1977–79; MP (Lab): S Ayrshire 1979–83, Carrick, Cumnock and Doon Valley 1983–2005; MSP (Lab) Lothians 2007–; memb Commons Select Ctee on Foreign Affrs 1981–83, jt chm Commons All-Pty Pensioners' Ctee 1983–97; front bench oppn spokesman: Euro and Community Affrs 1983–85, Foreign Affrs 1985–92, Defence 1992–93, Overseas Devpt 1994–97; Parly under-sec of state for international devpt 1997–2001, min of state for Scot 2001–02; UK delegate to: Parly Assembly of Cncl of Europe, Assembly of Western European Union (WEU); memb: Exec Cwlth Parly Assoc (UK), Inter Parly Union (GB), Exec Ctee of Socialist Int (SI), Bd Britain in Europe; dir Cooperative Press Ltd 1990–97, chm John Wheatley Centre 1991–97; treas Parliamentarians for Global Action (International) 1993–97; chm Heart of Midlothian FC 2004–05; William Wilberforce Medal 1998; *Recreations* boating, supporting Heart of Midlothian FC; *Style*— The Rt Hon the Lord Foulkes of Cumnock, PC; ✉ The Scottish Parliament, Edinburgh EH99 1SP; House of Lords, London SW1A 0PW

FOULSTON, Jill Michele; da of Richard Wilbert Foulston (d 1987), and Mary Jean, *née* Northcott; *Educ* Mountain View Acad, Andrews Univ (BA), London Coll of Music (ALCM), San Francisco State Univ (MA); *Career* various editorial positions in publishing incl ed Peter Owen Ltd 1992–96, co-fndr Arcadia Books 1996, commissioning ed Virago Modern Classics 1998–2005; *Publications* The Joy of Eating (2006), The Joy of Shopping (2007); *Recreations* food, music, travel; *Style*— Ms Jill Foulston; ✉ c/o Virago Press, Brettenham House, Lancaster Place, London WC2E 7EN

FOUNTAIN, Desmond; s of Desmond Oswald Trevor Fountain (d 1976), of Calpe Alicante, Spain, and Ruth Emily, *née* Masters (d 1993); *b* 29 December 1946, Bermuda; *Educ* Whitney Inst Bermuda, Normanton Coll, Stoke-on-Trent Coll of Art, Exeter Coll of Art (DipAD), Univ of Bristol (CertEd, ATD); *m* 1, 1969 (m dis 1998), Miranda Mary Campbell, *née* Hay; 1 da (Annabel Emily Clare b 1975), 1 s (Luke Desmond Hugh b 1981); m 2, Eleonora Valerie (Luli) *née* Maunder, formerly Whitelocke; *Career* sculptor; prize for art (aged 6 years) in adult exhibition Br Cncl Sierra Leone 1953; pres Exeter Coll of Art Student's Cncl 1968, SW rep for NUS 1968; fndr Bermuda Fine Art Tst private bill passed 1982; fndr Desmond Fountain Gallery 2000; award from Miny of Cultural Affairs; Lifetime Achievment Award Govt of Bermuda 2003; FRBS 1985; *Exhibitions and Galleries*: Bermuda Soc of Arts 1958, Exe Gallery Devon 1968, Exeter City Museum and Art Gallery 1969 and 1970, Spectrum Designs Ltd Devon 1969, Univ of Bristol 1970, City Hall Bermuda (two man show) 1972, City Hall Bermuda (four man show) 1973, Country Art Gallery USA 1974, Bermuda Soc of Arts Gp Show 1974, City Hall Bermuda (three man show) 1975, Bridge House Art Gallery Bermuda (fndr Desmond Fountain) 1976, Newport USA 1976, The Int Gallery Bermuda (three man show) 1977, St George's Gallery Middx 1977, Windjammer Gallery Bermuda 1980, 1981, 1985, 1986, 1989, 1993 and 1998, Bermuda Soc of Arts Members Show 1980, Glen Gallery Canada 1981, South African Gallery London 1981, Poole Fine Art USA 1981, Boston Fine Art Inc 1981, Coach House Gallery Guernsey 1983, Sally Le Gallis Jersey 1983, Renaissance Gallery USA

1983 and 1986, Alwin Gallery Summer Exhibition London 1985, Alwin Gallery UK 1986 and 1987, RSBS USA 1986, Br Sculptors Art Centre Bermuda 1987, Art Expo LA 1987, World Congress USA 1987, The Sculpture Gallery Bermuda 1989, Pinehurst Gallery NC 1990, Hartley Hill Gallery Calif 1992–93, E S Lawrence Gallery Aspen 1993, Cavalier Galleries Stamford 1993, RSBS Chelsea Harbour 1993, L'Ortolan Sculpture Garden Berks 1993, Perry House Galleries Alexandria USA 1994, Bruton Street London 1994, Cavalier Galleries Greenwich CT, NY and Nantucket 2003, 2004 and 2005, Royall Fine Art Tunbridge Wells 2005; *Solo Exhibitions* incl: H A & E Smith Ltd Bermuda 1975, A S Cooper & Sons Gallery 1976, Hamma Galleries Bermuda 1978, Alwin Gallery London 1980, Bacardi Int 1982, Falle Fine Art Jersey 1995 and 1997, Cavalier Gallery USA 1995, Coutts Bermuda 1996; *Major Commissions* sculpture of Sir George Somers for St George's unveiled by HRH Princess Margaret 1981–84, medallions in silver, gold and platinum featuring a portrait of HRH Princess Margaret 1985, public memorial Greece 1993–94, sculpture of Mark Twain unveiled at Directors' Circle preview of Bermuda Nat Gall retrospective 1994–95, sculpture of The Spirit of Bermuda: Johnny Barnes 1997–98, Heroes of the Oz Trial UK 1997–2000, lifesize Jorgen Svendsen for Belzona in Harrogate 2002; *Recreations* sailing, boating in general, antiques, collecting art, property restoration, oenology, guitar playing, singing, composing; *Clubs* Royal Bermuda Yacht, Bermuda Boat and Canoe; *Style*— Desmond Fountain, Esq; ✉ Tangible Investments Ltd, PO Box FL 317, Flatts FL BX, Bermuda (tel 001 441 292 3955, fax 001 441 292 0355, e-mail sculpture@ibl.bm, website www.desmondfountain.com)

FOURMAN, Prof Michael Paul; s of Prof Lucien Paul Rollings Fourman (d 1968), of Leeds, and Dr Julia Mary, *née* Hunton (d 1981); *b* 12 September 1950; *Educ* Allerton Grange Sch Leeds, Univ of Bristol (BSc), Univ of Oxford (MSc, DPhil); *m* 12 Nov 1982 (m dis 2001), Jennifer Robin, da of Hector Grainger Head (d 1970), of Sydney, Aust; 1 da (Paula b 1984), 2 s (Maximillian b 1987, Robin b 1992); *Career* jr res fell Wolfson Coll Oxford 1974–78, JF Ritt asst prof of mathematics Columbia Univ NY 1976–82; Dept of Electrical and Electronic Engrg Brunel Univ: res fell 1983–86, Hirst reader in integrated circuit design 1986, prof of formal systems 1986–88; Univ of Edinburgh: prof of computer systems 1988–, head of informatics 1994–97 and 2001–, head of computer sci 1995–98; FBCS 2005; *Recreations* cooking, sailing; *Style*— Prof Michael Fourman; ✉ School of Informatics, University of Edinburgh, Appleton Tower, Crichton Street, Edinburgh EH8 9LE (tel 0131 651 3266, e-mail michael.fourman@ed.ac.uk)

FOWKE, Sir David Frederick Gustavus; 5 Bt (UK 1814), of Lowesby, Leicestershire; s of late Lt-Col Gerrard Fowke, 2 s of 3 Bt; suc unc, Sir Frederick Fowke, 4 Bt (d 1987); *b* 28 August 1950; *Educ* Cranbrook Sch Sydney, Univ of Sydney (BA); *Heir* none; *Style*— Sir David Fowke, Bt

FOWKE, Philip Francis; s of Francis Henry Villiers (d 1974), and Florence, *née* Clutton (d 2000), of Gerrards Cross; *b* 28 June 1950; *Educ* Gayhurst Sch, Downside, began piano studies with Marjorie Withers, ARAM (awarded scholarship to study piano at RAM with Gordon Green, OBE); *Career* concert pianist; Wigmore Hall debut 1974, Royal Festival Hall debut 1977, Proms debut 1979, US debut 1982; performs regularly with all leading Br orchs and for BBC Radio, toured extensively in Europe; performances incl: Lambert Piano Concerto BBC Proms 2001, Warsaw Concerto BBC Proms 2003, world première of Richard Bissell Rhapsody for Piano and Orchestra Royal Festival Hall 2003; contrib Times Literary Supplement, music magazines and obituaries for nat press; prof of piano Royal Acad of Music 1981–91, prof of piano Welsh Coll of Music and Drama 1994–95, head Keyboard Dept Trinity Coll of Music London 1995–99 (sr fell 1998); recitalist and piano tutor Dartington International Summer Sch 1996, 1997 and 2000, vice-chm European Piano Teachers' Assoc (UK), warden Performers and Composers Section ISM 2004–05; first prize Nat Fedn of Music Socs Award 1973, BBC Piano Competition 1974; Winston Churchill Fellowship 1976; FRAM; *Recordings* incl: Virtuoso Piano Transcriptions, Complete Chopin Waltzes, Chopin Sonatas Nos 2 and 3, Bliss Piano Recital, Bliss Piano Concerto (with Liverpool Philharmonic and David Atherton), Britten Scottish Ballad (with City of Birmingham Orch and Simon Rattle), Finzi Grand Fantasia and Toccata (with Liverpool Philharmonic and Richard Hickox), Rachmaninoff Piano Concerto No 2 and Rhapsody on a Theme from Paganini (with Royal Philharmonic and Yuri Temirkanov), Ravel Piano Concertos (with London Philharmonic and Serge Baudo), Saint-Saëns Carnival of Animals (with Scot Nat Orch and Sir Alexander Gibson), Tchaikovsky Piano Concertos Nos 1 and 2 (with London Philharmonic and Wilfried Boettcher), Delius Piano Concerto (with Royal Philharmonic and Norman del Mar), Hoddinott Piano Concerto No 1 (with Royal Philharmonic and Barry Wordsworth), film scores incl Warsaw Concerto (with RTE Concert Orch and Proinnsias O Duinn), Cyril Scott Piano Quartet and Quintet (with The London Piano Quartet), Alan Bush Piano Quartet (with The London Piano Quartet); *Recreations* architecture, monasticism; *Clubs* Cavendish, Royal Over-Seas League, Savage; *Style*— Philip Fowke, FRAM; ✉ e-mail philipfowke@aol.com; c/o Patrick Garvey Management (tel 0845 130 6112, e-mail patrick@patrickgarvey.com)

FOWKES, Prof Francis Gerald Reid; *b* 9 May 1946; *Educ* George Watson's Coll Edinburgh, Univ of Edinburgh Med Sch (BSc, MB ChB), Liverpool Sch of Tropical Med and Hygiene (DTM&H), London Sch of Hygiene and Tropical Med (MSc, MFCM, Littlejohn Gairdner Medal), PhD (Univ of Wales); *Career* pre-registration house offr in med Eastern Gen Hosp Edinburgh then in surgery Western Gen Infirmary Edinburgh 1970–71, SHO in paediatrics UC Ibadan Nigeria then MO Sulenkama Hosp Transkei 1971–72, SHO/registrar in gen med Aberdeen Royal Infirmary and assoc hosps 1973–74, asst prof in community and family med Univ of N Carolina USA 1974–75, lectr in gen practice Univ of Edinburgh 1975–77, trainee in community med Lothian Health Bd/London Sch of Hygiene and Tropical Med 1977–80, sr lectr in epidemiology/medical care Univ of Wales Coll of Med 1980–85, hon conslt in public health med Royal Infirmary of Edinburgh NHS Tst 1985–; Univ of Edinburgh: sr lectr in community med 1985–89, reader in epidemiology 1989–94, dir Wolfson Unit for Prevention of Peripheral Vascular Diseases 1990–, prof of epidemiology 1994– (head Dept of Public Health Scis); visiting prof Ohio State Univ 1979–80, visiting fell Rockefeller Centre for Clinical Epidemiology Univ of Newcastle NSW Aust 1982; conslt: ODA London 1985, Miny of Health Paraguay 1994; WHO conslt/advsr Div of Strengthening Health Servs Geneva 1985–94; memb: Steering Ctee Royal Soc of Med Forum on Angiology 1992–, Health Servs and Public Health Research Ctee Chief Scientist's Office Scottish Office Home and Health Dept 1995–, Peripheral Vascular Diseases Sub-Gp Scottish Office Review of Acute Hosp Servs in Scotland 1997–; numerous invited lectures at home and abroad, organiser of scientific confs, scientific referee for jl articles, book reviewer and author of original and review articles; memb: International Editorial Advsy Bd Jl of Vascular Investigation 1994–, Editorial Bd Vascular Surgery (USA) 1995–; chm Editorial Team Cochrane Collaborative Review Gp on Peripheral Vascular Diseases 1994–; membership of learned socs incl: Int Epidemiological Assoc, Soc for Social Med, Soc for Epidemiologic Research (USA), Euro Soc of Cardiology (Epidemiology and Prevention Section), Int Soc and Fedn of Cardiology (Epidemiology and Prevention Section), Euro Soc of Vascular Surgery, American Heart Assoc Cncl on Epidemiology, Int Union of Angiology, Vascular Surgns Soc of GB and I; FFPHM, FRCPEd; *Books* Epidemiology of Peripheral Vascular Disease (ed, 1991), Vascular Surgery Services (1993), The Trials and Tribulations of Vascular Surgery (ed with R M Greenhalgh, 1996); *Style*— Prof Francis Fowkes; ✉ 2 McLaren Road, Edinburgh EH9 2BH; Department of Public Health Sciences, University of Edinburgh Medical School, Teviot Place, Edinburgh EH8 9AG (tel 0131 650 3220, fax 0131 650 6904, e-mail gerryfowkes@ed.ac.uk)

FOWLDS, Derek James; s of James Witney Fowlds (d 1941), and Ketha Muriel, *née* Treacher (d 1993); *b* 2 September 1937; *Educ* Ashlyn's Sch, Watford Tech Coll, RADA; *m* 1, 1964 (m dis 1973), Wendy, *née* Tory; 2 s (James b 14 Oct 1964, Jeremy b 7 Jan 1968); m 2, 1974 (m dis 1978), Leslie, *née* Judd; *Career* actor; *Theatre* incl: The Miracle Worker, How are you Johnnie?, Spring Awakening, Chips with Everything, Child's Play, A Private Matter, Confusions, No Sex Please We're British, Run for your Wife, Billy Liar, Look Homeward Angel, Hamlet, Macbeth, Rattle of a Simple Man; *Television* incl: Play for Today, Dr Finlay's Casebook, The Villains, The Basil Brush Show, Yes Minister, Yes Prime Minister, Rules of Engagement, Die Kinder, Van der Valk, Perfect Scoundrels, Darling Buds of May, Firm Friends, Casualty, Heartbeat, The Detectives, Laughter in the House: The Story of British Sitcom, Fowlds in the Landscape, The Best British Sitcom; *Film* incl: We Joined the Navy, Tamahine, Doctor in Distress, Hot Enough for June, Tower of Evil, Hotel Paradiso, Frankenstein Created Woman, Mistress Pamela, East of Sudan, Over the Hill, After Celia, Pigeon Post; *Recreations* golf, swimming; *Clubs* Stage Golfing Soc, Bowood Golf and Country, Whitby Golf; *Style*— Derek Fowlds, Esq; ✉ c/o Caroline Dawson Associates, 125 Gloucester Road, London SW7 4TE (tel 020 7373 3323, fax 020 7373 1110, e-mail djf.2937@virgin.net)

FOWLE, (William) Michael Thomas; CBE (2000); s of William Thomas Fowle (d 1968), of Salisbury, Wilts, and Nancy, *née* Williams (d 1971); *b* 8 January 1940; *Educ* Rugby, Clare Coll Cambridge (MA); *m* 1 (m dis), Judith Anderson; m 2, Margaret Dawes; 1 da (Emma Curtis), 1 s (John), 1 step s (James Smith); *Career* KPMG: ptnr 1976–99, sr UK banking and fin ptnr 1986–90, chm KPMG Banking & Finance Group 1989–93, sr UK audit ptnr 1990–93, sr ptnr London office and SE Region 1993–98; dir: Norwich and Peterborough Building Soc 1999–2006, ICICI Bank UK Ltd 2003–, Vedanta Resources plc 2003–05; chief treas St John Ambulance 1999–2002, chair Place 2 Be 1999–, govr Sadler's Wells 1996–2003; govr Rugby Sch 1988– (chm 2002), treas The Prince's Drawing Sch 2004–; Liveryman Worshipful Co of Chartered Accountants; FCA (ACA 1965); *Recreations* collecting, boating; *Clubs* Athenaeum; *Style*— Michael Fowle, Esq, CBE; ✉ 31 Myddelton Square, London EC1Y 1RB (tel 020 7837 7906, mobile 07802 806534, e-mail michael@fowle.uk.com)

FOWLER, Alan Roy; s of Ronald James Fowler, of London, and Mary Ellen, *née* Baines (d 2004); *b* 20 September 1958, London; *Educ* London Oratory; *m* 1981, Marie-Yvonne, *née* Binsted; *Career* slr specialising in pensions law; Lovells 1987–98, Charles Russell 1998–2000, Ashursts 2000–03, head of pensions law Stevens & Bolton 2003–; memb Assoc of Pension Lawyers 1989; *Recreations* private light aviation, hill walking; *Style*— Alan Fowler, Esq; ✉ Stevens & Bolton LLP, The Billings, Guildford, Surrey GU1 4YD (tel 01483 401202, fax 01483 302254, e-mail alan.fowler@stevens-bolton.co.uk)

FOWLER, Prof Alastair David Shaw; s of David Fowler (d 1939), and Maggie, *née* Shaw (d 1978); *b* 17 August 1930; *Educ* Queens Park Sch Glasgow, Univ of Glasgow, Univ of Edinburgh (MA), Pembroke Coll Oxford, The Queen's Coll Oxford (MA, DPhil, DLitt); *m* 23 Dec 1950, Jenny Catherine, da of Ian James Simpson (d 1981), of Giffnock House, Helensburgh; 1 da (Alison b 1954), 1 s (David b 1960); *Career* jr res fell The Queen's Coll Oxford 1955–59, visiting instr Univ of Indiana 1957–58, lectr UC Swansea 1959–61, fell and tutor of English literature BNC Oxford 1962–71, regius prof of rhetoric and English literature Univ of Edinburgh 1972–84 (univ fell 1984–87); Univ of Virginia: visiting prof 1969, 1979 and 1985–90, prof of English 1990–98; visiting prof Columbia Univ 1964, memb Inst for Advanced Study Princeton 1966 and 1980, visiting fell Cncl of Humanities Princeton Univ 1974, fell Humanities Res Centre Canberra 1980, visiting fell All Souls Coll Oxford 1984, visiting prof Univ of Wales Lampeter 1996; external assessor Open Univ 1972–77; advsy ed: Word and Image 1984–91, Connotations 1990–98, New Literary History 1972–2003, English Literary Renaissance 1978–2003, Swansea Review, The Seventeenth Century 1986–2003, Translation and Literature; memb: Harrap Academic Advsy Ctee 1983–89, Scottish Arts Cncl 1972–74, Nat Printed Books Panel 1977–79, Carlyle Soc (hon vice-pres 1972), English Union Edinburgh (pres 1972), Renaissance Soc, Renaissance English Text Soc, Soc Emblem Studies, Spenser Soc, Bibliographical Soc Edinburgh, Assoc of Literary Scholars and Critics (ALSC), AUT 1971–84, Agder Akademi 2003; FBA 1974; *Books* Spenser and the Numbers of Time (1964), The Poems of John Milton (with John Carey, 1968), Triumphal Forms (1970), Conceitful Thought (1975), Catacomb Suburb (1976), From the Domain of Arnheim (1982), Kinds of Literature (1982), A History of English Literature (1987), The New Oxford Book of Seventeenth Century Verse (1991), The Country House Poem (1994), Time's Purpled Masquers (1996), Renaissance Realism (2003), How to Write (2006); *Clubs* Oxford and Cambridge; *Style*— Prof Alastair Fowler, FBA; ✉ 11 East Claremont Street, Edinburgh EH7 4HT (tel 0131 556 0366)

FOWLER, Prof Christopher Gordon; s of Gordon Fowler, of Cardiff, and Elizabeth Aled, *née* Biggs; *b* 19 March 1950; *Educ* King Alfred's GS Wantage, Middx Hosp Med Sch, Univ of London (BSc, MB BS); *m* 1, 15 Dec 1973 (m dis 1996), Dr Clare Juliet Fowler, *qv*, da of Peter Amyas Wright, of Horton-on-Studley, Oxon; 1 s (William b 9 Aug 1980), 1 da (Alice b 28 June 1977); m 2, 20 Dec 1996, Mary Jane, da of Jeffrey John Absalom, of East Horsley, Surrey; 1 da (Molly b 12 July 2001); *Career* sr lectr in urology London Hosp Med Sch 1988 (lectr 1982), conslt urologist The London Hosp and Newham Health Dist 1988, currently dean for educn Queen Mary Univ of London; author of articles and chapters on fibreoscopy, laser surgery and uro-neurology; FRCS (Urol), FRCP, FHEA; *Recreations* family; *Clubs* Y; *Style*— Prof Christopher Fowler

FOWLER, Prof Clare Juliet; da of Peter Wright, of Oxford, and Dr Jean Crum; *b* 1 July 1950; *Educ* Wycombe Abbey, Middx Hosp Med Sch (MB BS, MSc); *m* 1, 1973 (m dis 1996); 1 da (Alice Clare b 28 June 1977), 1 s (William Gordon Peter b 9 Aug 1980); m 2, 2000, Peter Bevan; *Career* sr registrar in clinical neurophysiology Middx Hosp and Nat Hosp 1984–86; conslt in clinical neurophysiology: Bart's 1987–89, Middx and UCH 1987–; conslt in uro-neurology Nat Hosp for Neurology and Neurosurgery 1987–, prof Inst of Neurology UCL 1998– (reader 1998–2001), dep med dir UCLH 1998–2001, caldicott guardian UCLH 2000–; memb: Cncl EEG Soc 1987–91, Cncl Neurology Section Standing Ctee RSM; chm: Clinical Autonomic Research Soc 1990–92 (hon sec 1986–89), SUBDIMS; hon sec Br Soc of Clinical Neurophysiology 1992–95, memb Scientific Ctee Int Continence Soc 1995–97; FRCP; *Books* Neurology of Bladder, Bowel and Sexual Dysfunction (1999); *Clubs* Athenaeum; *Style*— Prof Clare Fowler; ✉ Department of Uro-Neurology, The National Hospital for Neurology and Neurosurgery, Queen Square, London WC1N 3BG (tel 020 7837 3611, fax 020 7813 4587, e-mail cfowler@ion.ucl.ac.uk)

FOWLER, Prof Godfrey Heath; OBE (1989); s of Donald Heath Fowler (d 1985), of Wolverley, Worcs, and Dorothy, *née* Bealey (d 1987); *b* 1 October 1931; *Educ* Sebright Sch, UC Oxford (MA, BM BCh); *m* 15 Sept 1962, Sissel, da of Arnfred Vidnes (d 1983), of Oslo, Norway; 2 s (Jeremy Kristen b 1964, Adrian Dag b 1965 d 1995); *Career* GP Oxford 1959–97, professorial fell Balliol Coll 1978–97 (emeritus fell 1997–), prof of gen practice Univ of Oxford 1978–97 (emeritus prof 1997–); hon dir ICRF Gen Practice Res Unit 1986–97; Evian Award 1987, Mackenzie Medal RCGP 1991, Hippocrates Medal Euro Soc of Family Med 1998; FRCGP 1978, FRCP 1997, FFPHM 1997; *Books* Preventive Medicine in General Practice (1983), Essentials of Preventive Medicine (1984), Prevention in General Practice (1993), Prevention of Cardiovascular Disease (1996); *Recreations* skiing, mountaineering, photography; *Style*— Prof Godfrey Fowler, OBE; ✉ Orchard

House, 13 Squitchey Lane, Oxford OX2 7LD (tel 01865 558331, e-mail godfrey.fowler@balliol.ox.ac.uk)

FOWLER, Jennifer Joan; da of Russell Aubrey Fowler (d 1971), and Lucy, *née* Tobitt (d 1995); *b* 14 April 1939; *Educ* Bunbury HS, Univ of W Aust (BA, BMus, DipEd); *m* 18 Dec 1971, John Bruce, s of Maj Frederick Paterson (d 1983); 2 s (Martin b 1973, Adrian b 1976); *Career* composer; major works: Hours of the Day (for 4 singers, 2 oboes and 2 clarinets) 1968, Ravelation (for string quintet) 1971, Veni Sancte Spiritus (for 12 solo singers) 1971, Chant with Garlands (for orchestra) 1974, Voice of the Shades (for soprano, oboe, violin) 1977, When David Heard (for choir and piano) 1982, Echoes from an Antique Land (for ensemble) 1983, Lament (for baroque oboe, viol) 1988, And Ever Shall Be (for mezzo and ensemble) 1989, Reeds, Reflections (for oboe and string trio) 1990, Plainsong for Strings (for string orchestra) 1992, Lament for Dunblane (SSATB) 1996, Singing the Lost Places (for soprano and large ensemble) 1996, Eat and be Eaten (collection of songs for 6 singers) 1998–2000, Magnificat 2 (for soprano and ensemble) 2000, Spiral (for flexible ensemble) 2001, Magnificat and Nunc Dimittis (for choir and (optional) organ) 2002, Hymn for St Brigid (SATB) 2002, Apsaras Flying (for 3 recorders, cello and harpsichord) 2003, Streaming Up (for small ensemble) 2004, Towards Release (various instrumentations) 2004, Letter from haworth (for soprano and ensemble) 2005, Line Spun with Stars (trio) 2006, Threaded Stars 2 (for solo harp) 2006, Bone Dance (trombone quartet) 2006; int prizes: Acad of the Arts Berlin, Radcliffe Award of GB, Gedok Prize Mannheim, Miriam Gideon Prize USA; memb: Br Acad of Composers and Songwriters, Women in Music, SPNM, Int Alliance for Women in Music; *Recreations* literature, gardening; *Style*— Ms Jennifer Fowler; ✉ 21 Deodar Road, Putney, London SW15 2NP (e-mail 100611.2060@compuserve.com, website www.impulse-music.co.uk/fowler.htm)

FOWLER, Keith Harrison; s of late Lancelot Harrison Fowler; *b* 20 May 1934; *Educ* Aldenham; *m* 1961, Vicki Belinda, *née* Pertwee; 3 c; *Career* Lt Army Suez Canal; exec chm Edman Communications Group plc 1977–88, chief exec Cresta Corporate Services Ltd 1988–89, dir Cresta Holdings Ltd 1988–89, chief exec Euro RSCG Marketing Group Ltd 1990–95, chm Scholefield Turnbull & Partners Ltd; dir Pertwee Holdings Ltd 1982–92; chm: Blendon Communications Ltd 1991, Cousins Communications Ltd 1996–99, Willox Ambler Rodford Law Ltd 1996–, Ninah Consulting Ltd 1998–99, Empire Design Ltd 2000–; dir: Invision Microsystems Ltd 1998–99, Harrison Portfolio Ltd 1998–; dir Nat Advertising Benevolent Soc 1978–; chm Winchester House School Trust Ltd 1968–; chm Abbeyfield Soc (Great Missenden); ACIS; *Recreations* painting, classic cars, pictures; *Clubs* Arts, Lansdowne, Solus; *Style*— Keith Fowler, Esq; ✉ Corfield Cottage, Arrewig Lane, Chartridge, Chesham, Buckinghamshire HP5 2UA (tel 01494 837089, e-mail keith.fowler@arrewig.com); 21 Cedar Drive, The Causeway, London N2 0RP (tel and fax 020 8883 1688)

FOWLER, Neil Douglas; s of Arthur Vincent Fowler (d 1996), of Essex, and Helen Pauline, *née* Douglas (d 1990); *b* 18 April 1956; *Educ* Southend HS for Boys, Univ of Leicester (BA); *m* 9 June 1989, Carol Susan, da of Kenneth Sydney Eric Cherry; 1 da (Helen Christine b 28 Jan 1993), 1 step s (Maurice Christopher John Volans b 13 March 1976); *Career* trainee (later sr reporter) Leicester Mercury 1978–81, dep news ed (later asst chief sub ed) Derby Evening Telegraph 1981–84, asst to the ed (later asst ed) Lincolnshire Echo 1984–85; ed: Lincolnshire Echo 1985–87, Derby Evening Telegraph 1987–91, The Journal Newcastle upon Tyne 1991–94, The Western Mail Cardiff 1994–2002; prop Neil Fowler Communications 2002–03, ceo and publisher Toronto Sun 2003–; pres Soc of Editors 1999–2000; FRSA 1999; *Awards* newspaper industry awards: North East Newspaper of the Year 1992, Best Use of Photography 1993, highly commended Best Use of Colour 1993 and 1994, Regnl Newspaper of the Year 1994, Regnl Newspaper Ed of the Year 1994 (highly commended 1993); Daily Newspaper of the Year Welsh Press Awards 1999, 2000 and 2002, Welsh Journalist of the Year 1999; *Recreations* cricket, cinema, music of Frank Zappa; *Clubs* Essex CCC; *Style*— Neil Fowler, Esq; ✉ The Toronto Sun, 333 King Street East, Toronto, Ontario M5A 3X5, Canada (tel 1 416 947 2222, fax 1 416 947 3119, e-mail neil.fowler@tor.sunpub.com)

FOWLER, Baron (Life Peer UK 2001), of Sutton Coldfield in the County of West Midlands; Rt Hon Sir (Peter) Norman Fowler; PC (1979); s of N F Fowler (d 1964), of Chelmsford, Essex, and Katherine Fowler; *b* 2 February 1938; *Educ* King Edward VI Sch Chelmsford, Trinity Hall Cambridge; *m* 1, 1968 (m dis 1976), Linda Christmas; m 2, 1979, Fiona Poole, da of John Donald; 2 da (Hon Kate Genevieve b Nov 1981, Hon Isobel Geraldine b July 1984); *Career* with The Times 1961–70 (special corr 1962–66, home affrs 1966–70), memb Editorial Bd Crossbow 1962–69; MP (Cons): Nottingham S 1970–74, Sutton Coldfield Feb 1974–2001; PPS NI Office 1972–74, oppn spokesman Home Affrs 1974–75; chief oppn spokesman: Social Servs 1975–76, Tport 1976–79; min Tport 1979–81; sec of state: Tport 1981, Social Servs 1981–87, Employment 1987–90; special advsr to PM 1992 gen election; chm Cons Pty 1992–94, shadow sec of state for the Environment, Tport and the Regions 1997–98, shadow home sec 1998–99; dep chm Assoc of Cons Peers 2006– (memb Exec 2001–05), chm House of Lords Select Ctee on BBC Charter 2005–06; chm: Midland Ind Newspapers 1991–98, National Housebuilding Cncl 1992–98, Regnl Ind Media (publishers of the Yorkshire Post gp of newspapers) 1998–2002, Numark 1998–2006, Aggregate Industries plc 2000–06 (non-exec dir 2006–); non-exec dir: NFC plc 1990–97, Holcim 2006–; *Style*— The Rt Hon the Lord Fowler, PC

FOWLER, Richard Thomas; s of Arthur Fowler (d 1984), of Huddersfield, W Yorks, and Joan Eileen Fowler; *b* 8 September 1950; *Educ* Holme Valley GS, Loughborough Coll of Art & Design, Ravensbourne Coll of Art & Design (BA); *m* 11 Aug 1984, Jane Lesley, da of Col W P Fletcher; 1 s (Daniel John Fletcher b 6 Sept 1987), 1 da (Bryony Anne b 29 July 1990); *Career* memb design staff British Museum then display offr International Harvester Company of GB Ltd 1974–80, exhibit designer Science Museum 1980–83, head of design Nat Museum of Photography, Film and Television Bradford 1983–89, visiting designer Computer Museum Boston 1989–90, head of design Eureka! (educnl museum for children) 1990–93, fndr/designer RFA Designers 1994–; current work incl: Stockwood Discovery Centre Luton, Royal Armouries Fort Newton Project, Exeter Medieval Passages Visitor Centre; chm Museum and Exhbn Design Gp 1992–95; memb Museums Assoc; FCSD (MCSD 1983); *Recreations* drawing, morris dancing, fly fishing, vintage motorcycling; *Style*— Richard Fowler, Esq; ✉ RFA, California Works, Oxford Road, Gomersal, West Yorkshire BD19 4HQ (tel 01274 853619, fax 01274 855156, e-mail richard@rfadesigners.co.uk)

FOWLER, Sheila Patricia; da of George William Spurs (d 1975), of Sunderland, and Lillian Bean, *née* Callum (d 1986); *b* 22 April 1946; *Educ* St Anthony's GS Sunderland, Monkwearmouth Coll Sunderland, Univ of Sunderland (HNC Business Studies); *m* 1 March 1976, Richard Fowler (d 2005), s of Richard Fowler; *Career* local govt offr Sunderland BC 1962–65, industrial market research offr rising to PRO Corning Glass Co Sunderland 1965–71; PRO: Washington Devpt Corp 1971–72, N of England Devpt Cncl (Promotions) 1972–74; industrial devpt offr Cleveland CC 1974–79, PR dir Sweetman Marketing Ltd Middlesbrough 1979–82, princ Sheila P Fowler Associates 1982–; ICP Promotional Achievement Award USA 1984, 1986 and 1987; FIPR 1987 (MIPR 1971); *Recreations* golf, reading, travelling, Spanish culture; *Clubs* Hartlepool Golf, Real Club de Campo (Malaga); *Style*— Mrs Sheila Fowler; ✉ Sheila P Fowler Associates, 10 Holyrood Crescent, Hart Village, Hartlepool TS27 3BB (tel and fax 01429 272553, e-mail sheilafowlerpr@aol.com)

FOWLIE, Dr Hector Chalmers; OBE (1989); s of Hector McIntosh Fowlie (d 1954), and Agnes Blue, *née* Turner (d 1966); *b* 21 June 1929; *Educ* Harris Acad Dundee, Univ of St Andrews (MB ChB); *m* Christina Napier Morrison, da of Peter Walker (d 1967); 2 s (Stephen b 1956, Peter b 1962), 1 da (Kay b 1958); *Career* psychiatrist; formerly physician supt Royal Dundee Liff and Strathmartine Hosps Dundee, conslt psychiatrist Tayside Health Bd Dundee, chm Dundee Healthcare NHS Tst; vice-chm: Mental Welfare Cmmn for Scotland, Parole Bd for Scotland; memb Ct Univ of Abertay Dundee; hon fell Univ of Abertay Dundee; FRCPE, FRCPsych; *Style*— Dr Hector Fowlie, OBE; ✉ 21 Clepington Road, Dundee DD4 7EL (tel 01382 456926)

FOX, Dr Alan Martin; s of Sidney Nathan Fox (d 1987), and Clarice, *née* Solov (d 2000); *b* 5 July 1938; *Educ* Bancroft's Sch, QMC London (BSc, PhD, pres Union); *m* 20 June 1965, Sheila Naomi, da of Lazarus Pollard, of Bournemouth, Dorset; 2 da (Victoria Charlotte b 1968, Louise Rachel b 1971), 1 s (James Henry Paul b 1974); *Career* Miny of Aviation and Technol 1963–72 (private sec to John Stonehouse MP and Julian Snow MP 1965–67), first sec Aviation and Def Br Embassy Paris 1973–75; MOD: operational analysis studies Fin of Def Nuclear Weapons Prog 1975–78, RCDS 1979, fin control of RAF Material Requirements 1980–84, Def Intelligence Staff 1984–88, asst under sec (Ordnance) 1988–92, visiting fell Center for Int Affrs Harvard Univ 1992–93, asst under sec (Quartermaster) 1994–95, asst under sec (Export Policy and Finance) 1995–98; pt/t lectr UCL 1998–2000; administrator St Marylebone Almshouses 1998–; clerk to govrs Henrietta Barnett Sch 1999–2003, clerk to govrs Jews Free Sch 2000–02; Govt appointed memb Review Ctee for Non-Competitive Contracts 2000–07, memb London Rent Assessment Panel 1999–, memb Compliance Panel Office for Supervision of Slrs 2000–; MCIArb; *Recreations* grandchildren, bridge, chess, watching rugby and cricket; *Clubs* Surrey County Cricket; *Style*— Dr Alan Fox; ✉ 4 Woodside Avenue, London N6 4SS (e-mail amfox@btinternet.com)

F

FOX, Sir Chris; kt (2006), QPM (1997); s of Douglas Charles Fox, and Olive Eileen Fox, of Basingstoke, Hants; *b* 21 July 1949; *Educ* Robert Gordon's Coll Aberdeen, West Bridgford GS Nottingham, Loughborough Univ (BSc, Dip); *m* 1972, Carol Anne, da of Dennis Wortley, of Loughborough, Leics; 2 da (Sarah b 13 July 1975, Kathryn b 7 December 1976), 1 s (Robert b 31 July 1984); *Career* grad entry to service 1972, uniform and CID roles in Nottingham and Mansfield 1972–88, div cdr Nottingham N 1988–90, dep chief constable Warks 1994–96 (asst chief constable (ops) 1991–94), chief constable Northants 1996–2003, pres ACPO 2003–06 (first full-time pres, memb 1990–2006); lead nat police response to Jan 2005 tsunami and July 2005 terror attacks; md Chris Fox Consulting 2006–; memb Nat Police Radio and Communications project; special course 1976, senior command course 1988, top mgmnt prog 1995; tstee Endeavour; fell Univ of Northampton 2006; Companion Chartered Mgmnt Inst 2005; *Recreations* cricket (player and qualified coach), rugby (played for British Police and Nottingham RFC), inshore sailing; *Style*— Sir Chris Fox, QPM; ✉ Rowan, Mill Lane, Welford on Avon, Warwickshire CV37 8EW (tel 07714 689219, e-mail chris@thehollylodge.freeserve.co.uk)

FOX, Edward Charles Morice; OBE (2003); eld s of Maj Robin Fox, MC, Virtuti Militari (Poland), RA (d 1971), of Cuckfield, W Sussex, and Angela Muriel Darita, *née* Worthington (d 1999); bro of James Fox, *qv*, and Robert Fox, *qv*; *b* 13 April 1937; *Educ* Harrow; *m* 1, 1958 (m dis), Tracy Reed, da of late Anthony Pelissier, of Sussex; 1 da (Lucy Arabella (now Viscountess Gormanston) b 1960); m 2, Joanna David, *qv*; 1 da (Emilia Rose Elizabeth Fox , *qv*, b 31 July 1974), 1 s (Frederick Samson Robert Morice b 1989); *Career* late Coldstream Gds, 2 Lt Loyal N Lancs Regt; stage, screen and television actor 1958–; trained RADA; *Theatre* incl: Knuckle (Comedy) 1973, The Family Reunion (Vaudeville) 1979, Anyone for Denis (Whitehall) 1981, Quartermaine's Terms (Queen's) 1981, Hamlet (Young Vic) 1982, Interpreters (Queen's) 1985, Let Us Go Then You and I (Lyric) 1987, The Dance of Death (Manchester) 1987, The Admirable Crichton (Haymarket) 1988, Another Love Story (also dir, Leicester Haymarket) 1990, The Philanthropist (West End), My Fair Lady (tour) 1992, Quartermaine's Terms 1993, The Father 1995, A Letter of Resignation (Comedy and Savoy Theatres) 1997–98, The Browning Version 2000, The Twelve Pound Look 2000, The Winslow Boy (nat tour) 2002, The Old Masters (Comedy Theatre) 2004, You Never Can Tell (Garrick Theatre) 2005–06; *Television* incl: Hard Times 1977, Edward and Mrs Simpson 1978 (BAFTA Award for Best Actor 1978, TV Times Top Ten Award for Best Actor 1978–79, Br Broadcasting Press Guild TV Award for Best Actor 1978, Royal TV Soc Performance Award 1978–79), Gulliver's Travels 1995, Daniel Deronda 2002; *Film* incl: The Go-Between 1971 (Soc of Film and TV Arts Award for Best Supporting Actor, 1971), The Day of the Jackal 1973, A Doll's House 1973, Galileo 1976, The Squeeze 1977, A Bridge Too Far 1977 (BAFTA Award for Best Supporting Actor), The Duellists 1977, The Cat and the Canary 1977, Force Ten from Navarone 1978, The Mirror Crack'd 1980, Gandhi 1982, Never Say Never Again 1983, The Dresser 1983, The Bounty 1984, The Shooting Party 1985, A Month by the Lake 1996, Prince Valiant 1997, Nicholas Nickleby 2003; *Recreations* music, gardening; *Clubs* Savile; *Style*— Edward Fox, Esq, OBE

FOX, Emilia; da of Edward Fox, and Joanna David, *qqv*; *b* 1974; *Educ* Bryanston, Univ of Oxford (BA); *m* 2005, Jared Harris, s of Richard Harris (d 2002), the actor; *Career* actress; *Theatre* The Cherry Orchard 1997, Katherine Howard 1998, Good (Donmar Warehouse) 1999, Richard II 2000, Coriolanus 2000, Les Liasons Dangereuses 2003; *Television* incl: Pride and Prejudice 1995, Bright Hair 1997, Rebecca 1997, The Round Tower 1998, The Scarlet Pimpernel 1998, Bad Blood 1998, Shooting the Past 1999, David Copperfield 1999, Bad Blood 1999, Other People's Children 2000, Randall & Hopkirk (Deceased) 2000, Helen of Troy 2002, Henry VIII 2003, Silent Witness VIII 2004, Silent Witness IX 2005, The Virgin Queen 2005, Miss Marple: The Moving Finger 2005, Silent Witness 2006, Fallen Angel 2006, Born Equal 2006; *Films* The Pianist 2001, The Soul Keeper 2001, Three Blind Mice 2002, The Republic of Love 2002, The Life & Death of Peter Sellars 2003, Things to do Before You're 30 2003, The Tiger in the Snow 2004, Keeping Mum 2005, Cashback 2005, Honeymoon 2006; Tric Award for Best Newcomer, Cult TV Best Actress Award, Best Actress in Italy; *Style*— Miss Emilia Fox

FOX, Frederick Donald; LVO (1999); s of Lesley James Fox (d 1950), of Urana, NSW, Aust, and Ruby Mansfield, *née* Elliott (d 1965); *b* 2 April 1931; *Educ* St Joseph's Convent Sch Jerilderie; *Career* milliner, started in business 1962, designer for the Royal Family; pres Millinery Trades Benevolent Assoc; granted Royal Warrant to HM The Queen 1974; hon patron Australian Millinery Assoc; Freeman City of London 1989, Liveryman Worshipful Co of Feltmakers 1989; *Recreations* gardening, photography; *Style*— Frederick Fox, Esq, LVO

FOX, Lady; Hazel Mary; CMG (2006); da of John Matthew Blackwood Stuart, CIE (d 1941), and Lady (Joan Daria) Denning, *née* Elliot Taylor; *b* 22 October 1928; *Educ* Roedean, Somerville Coll Oxford (MA); *m* 1954, Rt Hon Sir Michael John Fox; 3 s, 1 da; *Career* called to the Bar 1950; Somerville Coll Oxford: lectr in law 1951–58, fell and tutor in law 1977–82, hon fell 1989–; chm: London Rent Assessment Panel 1977–97, London Leasehold Valuation Tbnl 1981–97; dir Br Inst of International and Comparative Law 1982–89, gen ed Int and Comparative Law Quarterly 1987–97; memb Home Office Departmental Ctee on Jury Serv 1963–65, chm Tower Hamlets Juvenile Ct 1968–76; JP London 1956–77; additional Bencher Lincoln's Inn 1989; assoc tenant 4/5 Gray's Inn Square WC1 1994–; memb Cncl of Legal Educn (for England and Wales) 1990–94; memb Institut de Droit International 1997; govr Summer Fields Sch 1968–98; QC (hc) 1993; *Books* International Arbitration (with J L Simpson 1959), International Economic Law and Developing States (ed, 1988 and 1992), Joint Development of Offshore Oil and Gas Vol I and II (ed, 1989 and 1990), Effecting Compliance (ed with Michael A Meyer, 1993); *Style*— Lady Fox, CMG, QC

FOX, James; s of Maj Robin Fox, MC, Virtuti Militari (Poland), RA (d 1971), of Cuckfield, W Sussex, and Angela Muriel Darita, *née* Worthington (d 1999); bro of Edward Charles Morice Fox, OBE, *qv*, and Robert Michael John Fox, *qv*; *b* 19 May 1939; *Educ* Harrow; *m* 15 Sept 1973, Mary Elizabeth, da of Maj Allan Piper, of Wadhurst, E Sussex; 4 s (Thomas b 1975, Robin b 1976, Laurence b 1978, Jack b 1985), 1 da (Lydia b 1979); *Career* actor; *Television* incl: A Question of Attribution 1991, Headhunters 1993, The Choir (BBC) 1994, The Old Curiosity Shop (Disney Channel, Cable TV) 1994, Gullivers Travels (Channel 4) 1995, Elgar's 10th Muse (Channel 4) 1995, Metropolis 2000, The Mystic Masseur 2001, The Lost World (BBC/AE TV) 2001; *Film* The Servant 1963, King Rat 1964, Thoroughly Modern Millie 1966, Performance 1969, A Passage to India 1984, The Russia House 1990, Patriot Games 1992, The Remains of the Day 1993, Anna Karenina 1997, Jinnah 1998, Micky Blue Eyes 1998, Up At The Villa 1999, Sexy Beast 2000, The Golden Bowl 2000, The Prince and Me 2004, Charlie and the Chocolate Factory 2005, Mr Lonely 2006, Suez 2007; *Books* Comeback An Actor's Direction (1983); *Recreations* Russian language experience and culture; *Style*— James Fox, Esq; ✉ c/o Peters Fraser & Dunlop, Drury House, 34–43 Russell Street, London WC2B 5HA (tel 020 7344 1010)

FOX, James George; s of George Romney Fox (d 1968), of Falmouth, Cornwall, and Barbara Muriel, *née* Twite (d 1994); *b* 14 May 1943; *Educ* Eton, Univ of Newcastle upon Tyne (BA), Univ of Pennsylvania (MBA); *m* 4 May 1974, Rebecca Jane, da of Charles Wright, of Canyon, Texas; 2 da (Rachel b 1975, Sarah b 1979), 2 s (Francis b 1977, Romney b 1981); *Career* dir: Hill Samuel Investment Management 1968–78, Falmouth Hotel plc 1981–92, Warburg Investment Management 1982–85; md: Deutsche Trust Managers 1985–2003, Deutsche Equity Income Trust plc 1991–2003, Anglo & Overseas Tst plc 1992–2003, Deutsche Latin American Companies Tst plc 1994–2004, JPMorgan American Investment Tst plc 2003–, iimia Investment Tst plc 2004–; *Recreations* sailing; *Clubs* Athenaeum; *Style*— James Fox; ✉ Trewardreva, Constantine, Falmouth, Cornwall (tel 01326 340207); 57 Andrewes House, Barbican, London EC2 (tel 020 7638 9103)

FOX, Prof Keith A A; *b* 27 August 1949; *Educ* Univ of Edinburgh (BSc, MB ChB); *Career* asst prof in internal med (cardiology) Washington Univ Sch of Med St Louis 1983–85, sr lectr in cardiology and hon conslt cardiologist Univ of Wales Coll of Med Cardiff 1985–89, currently Duke of Edinburgh prof of cardiology and head Div of Med and Radiological Sciences Univ of Edinburgh and conslt cardiologist Royal Infirmary Edinburgh; memb Editorial Bd: Heart, Coronary Artery Disease USA, Cardiology in Practice, Br Jl of Cardiology, Acute Coronary Syndromes, Cardio.net; author of numerous pubns in learned jls; memb: Cncl on Basic Sci American Heart Assoc 1984, Cncl Br Cardiac Soc 1991–94 (chm Prog Ctee 1999–2003), Cncl Br Heart Fndn 1997–2000; memb Assoc of Physicians of GB and I 1991–; Stelios Nicolaides Prize RCPEd; FRCP 1987 (MRCP 1977), FESC 1988, FMedSci 2001, FRCPEd; *Style*— Prof Keith A A Fox; ✉ Cardiovascular Research Unit, Department of Medical and Radiological Sciences, New Royal Infirmary, 49 Little France Crescent, Edinburgh EH16 4SB

FOX, Kerry Lauren; da of Thomas Albert Fox, and Margaret Doris, *née* Poole; *Educ* Hutt Valley HS NZ, NZ Drama Sch Toi Whakaari; *Career* actress; *Theatre* Gothic But Staunch (The Depot), Jism (Bats Theatre), Bloody Poetry (Circa Theatre Wellington), Cosi (Belvoir St Theatre Sydney), The Maids (Donmar Warehouse), I Am Yours (Royal Court Theatre), In Flame (New Ambassadors Theatre), Cruel and Tender (Vienna Festival, The Young Vic); *Television* Mr Wroe's Virgins, A Village Affair, Saigon Baby, The Affair (nomination Best Actress Cable Ace Awards), Deja Vu, 40, The Murder Room; *Film* incl: An Angel at My Table 1990 (Elvira Notari Award Venice Film Festival, Best Actress NZ Film Awards, Best Actress San Sebastian Film Festival), The Last Days of Chez Nous 1991, Friends 1993, The Last Tattoo 1994, Shallow Grave 1994 (Best Film Award for Acting Dinard Film Festival), Country Life 1994, The Hanging Garden 1997, Welcome to Sarajevo 1997, The Sound of One Hand Clapping 1998, Wisdom of Crocodiles 1998, To Walk With Lions 1999, The Darkest Light 1999, Fanny & Elvis 1999, Intimacy 2000 (Silver Bear for Best Actress Berlin Film Festival), The Point Men 2001, The Gathering 2002, Black and White 2002, So Close to Home 2003, Niceland 2004, Rag Tale 2005; *Style*— Ms Kerry Fox; ✉ c/o ARG Management, 4 Great Portland Street, London W1W 8PA (tel 020 7436 6400)

FOX, Prof Kim Michael; s of Lt-Col Michael Allen Fox (d 1980), of Edinburgh, and Veronica Venetia, *née* Sweeney; *b* 17 June 1948; *Educ* Fort Augustus Abbey Sch, Univ of St Andrews (MB ChB, MD); *Children* 1 s (Michael James b 6 March 1978), 1 da (India Charis b 14 Nov 1998); *Career* conslt cardiologist at The Royal Brompton Hosp; prof of clinical cardiology Imperial Coll; ed and author of textbooks in cardiology, ed Euro Heart Jl; FRCP 1988, fell Euro Soc of Cardiology (pres); *Books* Diseases of the Heart (ed, 1988, 2 edn 1996), Wolfe Atlases of Cardiology; *Style*— Prof Kim Fox; ✉ Chuffs House, Holyport, Berkshire SL6 2NA; The Royal Brompton Hospital, Sydney Street, London SW3 6NP (tel 020 7351 8626); 88 Harley Street, London W1 (tel 020 7486 4617)

FOX, Dr Liam; MP; s of William Fox, and Catherine Fox; *b* 22 September 1961; *Educ* St Brides HS East Kilbride, Univ of Glasgow (MB ChB, MRCGP); *m* Dec 2005, Dr Jesme Baird; *Career* gen practitioner, also Army MO (civilian) RAEC and divnl surgn St John Ambulance; nat vice-chm Scottish YCs 1983–84, sabbatical as guest of US State Dept studying drug abuse and Republican campaigning techniques 1985; individual speaking prize World Debating Competition Toronto 1982, best speaker's trophy Univ of Glasgow 1983; Parly candidate (Cons) Roxburgh and Berwickshire 1987, MP (Cons) Woodspring 1992–; PPS to Rt Hon Michael Howard as Home Sec 1993–94, asst Govt whip 1994–95, Lord Cmmr HM Treasy (sr Govt whip) 1995–96, Parly under-sec of state FCO 1996–97; oppn front bench spokesman on constitutional affrs (Scotland) 1997–98, oppn frontbench spokesman on constitutional affrs 1998–99, shadow sec of state for Health 1999–2003, co-chm Cons Pty 2003, shadow foreign sec 2005, shadow defence sec 2005–; memb Scottish Select Ctee 1992–93; sec Cons Backbench Health Ctee 1992–93, sec Cons West Country Members Ctee 1992–93, candidate Cons Pty leadership election 2005; *Style*— Dr Liam Fox, MP; ✉ House of Commons, London SW1A 0AA (tel 020 7219 3000)

FOX, 'Doctor' Neil Andrew Howe; s of Kenneth Roy Fox (d 2001), of Thames Ditton, Surrey, and Florence Lillian, *née* Buckley; *b* 12 June 1961; *Educ* Kingston GS, Univ of Bath (BSc); *Career* Radio Wyvern Worcester 1986–87, Radio Luxembourg 1987, presenter Pepsi Chart and Drivetime Capital FM 1993–2005 (joined 1987), host of Dr Fox's Jukebox (LWT) 1995–96, judge Pop Idol (ITV); *Awards* Smash Hits Award Sony DJ 1991, Sony Award 1993, 3 Sony Awards 1994, Sony Gold Award Broadcaster of the Year 1995, 2 World Radio Awards New York 1995, Smash Hits Pollwinner Best DJ 1993, 1994, 1997, 1998, 1999 and 2000, Sony Award 2001; *Recreations* flying helicopters, snowboarding, motorcycling, golf; *Style*— Doctor Fox; ✉ Capital Radio plc, 30 Leicester Square, London WC2H 7LA (tel 020 7766 6000, fax 020 7766 6100, website www.capitalfm.co.uk)

FOX, Richard John; s of Dennis William Fox (d 1956), of Bristol, and Winifred Joan Fox (d 1998); *b* 23 December 1943; *Educ* Cotham GS, Bristol, Univ of Wales Cardiff (BSc(Econ)); *m* Sandra Wynne; 2 c (Mark Douglas b 1970, Helen Victoria b 1971); *Career* CA; Grace Darbyshire & Todd Bristol 1965–71 (articled clerk 1965–68), Coopers & Lybrand 1971–78; ptnr: Mazars Neville Russell 1982–87 (joined 1978), KPMG 1987–93, The Learning Corporation 1993–; qualified business advsr, facilitator and corporate coach; fndr and patron Guildford Business Forum; fndr memb Guildford Chamber Choir, memb St Saviour's Church Guildford; ACA 1968; *Recreations* trekking, music especially choral, the countryside, reading; *Clubs* Glyndebourne, Royal Acad of Arts; *Style*— Richard J Fox, Esq; ✉ 35 Mountside, Guildford, Surrey GU2 4JD (e-mail rjfox@tlc.eu.com)

FOX, Prof Robert; s of Donald Fox (d 1972), and Audrey Hilda, *née* Ramsell (d 1993); *b* 7 October 1938; *Educ* Doncaster GS, Oriel Coll Oxford (MA, DPhil); *m* 20 May 1964, Catherine Mary Lilian, da of Dr Edmund Roper Power (d 1990); 3 da (Tessa b 1967, Emily b 1969, Hannah b 1972); *Career* asst master Tonbridge Sch 1961–63, Clifford Norton jr research fell The Queen's Coll Oxford 1965–66, prof of history of science Lancaster Univ 1987–88 (lectr 1966–72, sr lectr 1972–75, reader 1975–87), dir Centre de Recherche en Histoire des Sciences et des Techniques Cité des Sciences et de l'Industrie CNRS Paris 1986–88, asst dir Science Museum 1988, prof of history of science Univ of Oxford and fell Linacre Coll Oxford 1988–; pres: Br Soc of the History of Science 1980–82, Int Union for the History and Philosophy of Science 1995–97 (first vice-pres Div of History of Science 1989–93, pres Div of History of Science 1993–97), European Soc for the History of Science 2003–; FRHistS 1974, FSA 1989; Chevalier dans l'Ordre des Palmes Académiques 1998; *Books* The Caloric Theory of Gases from Lavoisier to Regnault (1971), Sadi Carnot. Réflexions sur la Puissance Motrice du Feu (1978, 1986, 1988 and 1992), The Organization of Science and Technology in France 1808–1914 (ed with G Weisz, 1980), The Culture of Science in France 1700–1900 (1992), Education, Technology and Industrial Performance in Europe 1850–1939 (ed with A Guagnini, 1993), Science, Industry and the Social Order in Post-Revolutionary France (1995), Technological Change (ed, 1996), Luxury Trades and Consumerism in Ancien Régime Paris (ed with A J Turner, 1998), Natural Dyestuffs and Industrial Culture in Europe, 1750–1880 (ed with A Nieto-Galan, 1999), Laboratories, Workshops and Sites (with A Guagnini, 2000), Thomas Harriot. An Elizabethan Man of Science (ed, 2000); *Clubs* Athenaeum; *Style*— Prof Robert Fox, FSA; ✉ Modern History Faculty, Broad Street, Oxford OX1 3BD (tel 01865 277277, fax 01865 250704)

FOX, Dr Robert McDougall (Robin); s of Sir Theodore Fortescue Fox (d 1989), and Margaret Evelyn, *née* McDougall (d 1970); *Educ* Leighton Park Sch Reading, Univ of Edinburgh (MB ChB); *m* 1969, Susan Gertrude Standerwick, da of James Clark; 1 da (Katharine b 1970), 2 s (Duncan b 1970, James b 1975); *Career* various hosp posts 1965–68; The Lancet: asst ed 1968–75, dep ed 1975–90, ed 1990–95; Euro assoc ed Circulation 1995–2004, ed Jl of the Royal Soc of Med 1996–2005; FRCPE 1991, FRCP 1996 (MRCP 1993); *Recreations* words; *Style*— Dr Robin Fox; ✉ Green House, Rotherfield, Crowborough, East Sussex TN6 3QU (tel and fax 01892 852850)

FOX, Robert Michael John; s of Maj Robin Fox, MC, Virtuti Militari (Poland), RA (d 1971), of Cuckfield, W Sussex, and Angela Muriel Darita (d 1999), *née* Worthington; bro of Edward Charles Morice Fox, OBE, *qv*, and James Fox, *qv*; *b* 25 March 1952; *Educ* Harrow; *m* 1, 26 Feb 1974 (m dis), Celestia, da of Henry Nathan Sporborg, CMG (d 1985); 2 da (Chloe Victoria b 24 May 1976, Louisa Mary b 18 July 1983), 1 s (Sam Henry b 24 June 1978); m 2, 16 Dec 1990 (m dis), Natasha Jane (actress Natasha Richardson, *qv*), da of Tony Richardson (d 1991) and Vanessa Redgrave, CBE, *qv*; m 3, 31 Jan 1996, Fiona, o da of late John Golfar; 1 s (Joseph Marlon Barnaby b 6 July 1995), 1 da (Molly Elizabeth b 24 January 1998); *Career* producer; actor When Did You Last See My Mother? (Royal Court) 1970, asst dir Royal Court Theatre 1971–73, PA to Michael White (Michael White Ltd) 1973–80, fndr Robert Fox Ltd 1980; *Theatre* prodns incl: Goose Pimples (Evening Standard Drama Desk Award for Best Comedy), Anyone for Denis?, exec prodr Another Country (Olivier Award for Best Play), Crystal Clear, The Seagull, Torch Song Trilogy, Interpreters, Orphans, J J Farr, Chess, Lettice & Lovage (Evening Standard Drama Desk Award for Best Comedy), Anything Goes, A Madhouse in Goa, Burn This, The Big Love, When She Danced, The Ride Down Mt Morgan, Vita and Virginia, Three Tall Women (Evening Standard Best Play Award), Skylight, Who's Afraid of Virgina Woolf, Master Class, Edward Albee's A Delicate Balance, Amy's View, Closer, The Judas Kiss, The Blue Room, The Boy From Oz (Australia), Little Malcolm and his Struggle Against the Eunuchs, The Lady in the Van, The Caretaker, The Breath of Life, Gypsy, The Boy From Oz, Salome: The Reading, The Pillowman, Hedda Gabler, The Vertical Hour, Frost/Nixon, The Lady from Dubuque; *Television* Oscar's Orchestra (BBC TV childrens animation series), Working with Pinter; *Film* A Month by the Lake, Iris, The Hours, Closer, Notes on a Scandal; *Style*— Robert Fox, Esq; ✉ Robert Fox Ltd, 6 Beauchamp Place, London SW3 1NG (tel 020 7584 6855, fax 020 7225 1638, e-mail robert@robertfoxltd.com)

FOX, Robert Trench (Robin); CBE (1993); s of Waldo Trench Fox (d 1954), of Penjerrick, Falmouth, Cornwall; *b* 1 January 1937; *Educ* Winchester, UC Oxford (MA); *m* 1962, Lindsay Garrett, da of Sir Donald Forsyth Anderson (d 1973); 2 da (Fenella Garrett (Mrs John Dernie) b 23 Oct 1964, Tamara Forsyth (Mrs Robert Onslow) b 24 June 1967), 2 s (Barclay Trench b 27 April 1971, Caspar Lloyd b 6 Oct 1972); *Career* dir Kleinwort Benson Ltd 1972–85, vice-chm Kleinwort Benson Group 1986–96, pres Kleinwort Benson Asia 1997–99; chm: Whiteaway Laidlaw Bank Ltd, Lombard Risk Conslts Ltd, Boyer Allan Pacific Fund, Boyer Allan Japan Fund Boyer Allan India Fund, Export Guarantees Advsy Cncl 1992–98; memb Euro Advsy Bd Credit Lyonnais 2000–05; sub-warden Winchester Coll; *Recreations* shooting, walking, sailing; *Clubs* Brooks's, Royal Cornwall Yacht; *Style*— Robin Fox, Esq, CBE; ✉ Cheriton House, Cheriton, Alresford, Hampshire SO24 0QA (tel 01962 771230, fax 01962 771824); 21st Floor, Empress State Building, 55 Lillie Road, London SW6 1TR (tel 020 7384 5006)

FOX, Ronald David (Ronnie); s of Walter Fox (d 1985), of London, and Eva, *née* Covo; *b* 27 September 1946; *Educ* Mercers Sch, City of London Sch, Lincoln Coll Oxford (MA); *m* 11 Feb 1973, Sonya Claudine, da of Shalom Birshan; 1 da (Susan b 8 July 1976), 1 s (Michael b 31 Jan 1979); *Career* admitted slr 1972; ptnr Oppenheimers 1974–88, ptnr Denton Hall 1988–89, sr ptnr Fox Williams 1989–2005, princ Fox 2006–; memb Int Bar Assoc 1984– (chm Practice Mgmnt Sub-Ctee 1995–98, vice-pres Sr Lawyers Ctee 2007–); fndr and pres Assoc of Partnership Practitioners; Law Soc: co-opted memb Completion Cheque Scheme Working Pty 1981–82, memb Standing Ctee on Co Law 1985–89, memb Cncl Membership Ctee 1990–97, memb Steering Ctee Law Mgmnt Section 1998–99, chm 1998–2001, memb Employment Law Ctee 2001–04, memb Remuneration Ctee 2005–; City of London Law Soc: memb Problems of Practice Sub-Ctee 1985–93, Working Pty (preparing evidence of City Slrs to Lady Marre's Ctee on the future of the legal profession) 1986, co-ordinator Survey on City Slrs' Attitudes to Multi-Disciplinary Practices 1987, memb Ctee 1988–2001; chm Working Pty (preparing the response of City Slrs to the Govt Green Paper on the Work and Organisation of the Legal Profession) 1989, memb Euro Employment Lawyers Assoc 1999–; nominated Star of the Year 2000 by Legal Business Magazine, Distinguished Serv award City of London Slrs' Co 1989, nominated leading partnership and employment lawyer in The Legal 500 and Chambers' Directory; Liveryman Worshipful Co of Slrs 1984 (memb Ct of Assts 1991, Jr Warden 1996, Sr Warden 1997, Master 1998); hon memb Assoc of Fells and Legal Scholars of the Centre for Int Legal Studies; *Books* Due Diligence, Disclosures and Warranties in Corporate Acquisition Practice - the United Kingdom (1988, 2 edn 1992), International Business Transactions-Service Agreements for Multinational Corporate Executives in the United Kingdom (1988), Payments on Termination of Employment (1981, 3 edn 1990), Legal Aspects of Doing Business in England & Wales (1984, 2 edn 1990), International Professional Practice - England and Wales (1992), Product Tampering in the United Kingdom (1993); also author of numerous articles on legal and management topics; *Recreations* opera, theatre, cinema, swimming, skin diving, and scuba diving, motoring and other forms of transport, management studies; *Clubs* RAC (memb Ctee 2006–);

Style— Ronnie Fox; ✉ Fox, 78 Cornhill, London EC3V 3QQ (tel 020 7618 2400, fax 020 7618 2409, mobile 07836 238436, e-mail rdfox@foxlawyers.com)

FOX-ANDREWS, (Jonathan) Mark Piers; s of His Hon Judge James Roland Blake Fox-Andrews, QC (d 2002), and (Angela) Bridget, *née* Swift (d 1991); *b* 7 May 1952; *Educ* Eton, Trinity Hall Cambridge (MA); *m* 22 Sept 1984, Rosemary Anne, da of Dennis Jenks; 2 s (Maximillian George b 28 March 1987, Alfred James b 3 Dec 1993), 2 da (Florence Rose b 14 July 1989, Constance Augusta b 26 Jan 1992); *Career* Drexel Burnham Lambert: trader 1977–80, mangr Singapore Office 1980–83, mangr Sydney Office 1984, md (Futures Ltd) London Office 1984–90; Sabre Fund Mgmnt Ltd 1990–93; md: Mees Pierson Derivatives Ltd 1993–97, ADM Investor Services Int Ltd 1998–; *Books* Futures Fund Management (1991), Derivatives Markets and Investment Management (1995); *Clubs* Garrick, Hurlingham; *Style—* Mark Fox-Andrews, Esq; ✉ 20 Cheyne Gardens, London SW3 5QT; ADM Investor Services International Ltd, 4th Floor, Millennium Bridge House, 2 Lambeth Hill, London EC4V 3TT (tel 020 7716 8012, fax 020 7294 0240, e-mail mark.fox-andrews@admisi.com)

FOX BASSETT, Nigel; s of Thomas Fox Bassett (d 1960), of London, and Catherine Adriana, *née* Wiffen (d 1960); *b* 1 November 1929; *Educ* Taunton Sch, Trinity Coll Cambridge (MA); *m* 9 Sept 1961, Patricia Anne, da of Stanley William Lambourne (d 1986), of East Horsley, Surrey; 1 da (Emma (Mrs Lines) b 19 Jan 1964), 1 s (Jonathan b 30 July 1966); *Career* Nat Serv 2 Lt RA 1949–50 (served Canal Zone Egypt with Mauritian Gds), Capt 264 (7 London) Field Regt RA TA 1950–60; admitted slr 1956, sr ptnr Clifford Chance (formerly Coward Chance) 1990–93 (articled clerk 1953, ptnr 1960); cmmr Building Societies Cmmn 1993–2000; dir: London First 1993–96, London First Centre 1995–99, London First Cncl 1999–; Br Inst of Int and Comparative Law: memb Cncl 1977–2005, memb Exec Ctee 1986–99 (chm 1986–96), hon memb 2004–, memb Advsy Bd 2005–; memb Cncl: Int Law Assoc (Br Branch) 1974–86, Int Assoc for the Protection of Industrial Property (Br Gp) 1984–89, Ctee Int Regulation of Fin Markets 1989–93, London C of C and Industry 1993–99; memb: Ctee Business Section IBA (Anti Tst, Patents and Trademarks, Securities Ctees) 1969–93, UK Govt Know How Fund Banking and Fin Mission to Poland 1989–90; chm: Intellectual Property Sub-Ctee City of London Slrs' Co 1982–87 (memb Sub-Ctee 1969–87); memb: Glyndebourne Festival Opera Soc and Kent Opera, Cncl Taunton Sch 1982–97 (pres 1994–97, hon life vice-pres 2005–), The Pilgrims of GB 1988–; vice-pres Dulwich Hockey Club, chm Old Tauntonians Sports Club until 1989, pres Kemsing Cricket Club 1994–99, memb Ctee Seaview Yacht Club 1995–2000, pres Kemsing Branch Royal British Legion 2002–; Liveryman Worshipful Co of Slrs 1960–, Freeman City of London; Law Soc Roll of Solicitors (memb Euro Gp 1969–93), Assoc Européenne d'Études Juridiques et Fiscales (UK memb) 1969–, American Bar Assoc (Futures Regulation Ctee) 1979–93; *Books* English Sections of: Branches and Subsidiaries in the European Common Market (1976), Business Law in Europe (1982 and 1990); *Recreations* shooting, cricket, art, opera; *Clubs* Garrick, MCC, Seaview Yacht; *Style—* Nigel Fox Bassett, Esq; ✉ c/o Clifford Chance, 10 Upper Bank Street, London E14 5JJ (tel 020 7006 1000, fax 020 7006 3400)

FOXALL, Colin; CBE (1995); s of Alfred George Foxall, of Chatham, Kent, and Ethel Margaret, *née* Hall; *b* 6 February 1947; *Educ* Gillingham GS; *m* m 2003, Diane Linda Price; 2 s (Ian b 1981, Neil b 1984); *Career* Dept of Trade 1974–75; NCM Credit Insurance Ltd (formerly ECGD until privatisation 1991): joined 1966, asst sec 1982–86, gp dir/under sec of insurance servs 1986–91, chief exec and md 1991–97; chief exec and md NCM Holdings (UK) Ltd, vice-chm Managing Bd NCM NV 1996–97, reinsurance and mgmnt conslt 1998–, dir Radian Asset Assurance Ltd 2003–; chm Rail Passenger Ctee Wales 2004–05, memb Br Tport Police Authy 2005–, chm Passenger Focus 2005–; advsr Benfield Gp 2007–; MIEx, FICM; *Recreations* clay pigeon shooting, farming; *Style—* Colin Foxall, CBE; ✉ Brynglas Cottage, Devauden, Chepstow NP16 6NT (tel and fax 01600 860 388, e-mail colin.foxall@credit-ins.co.uk)

FOXALL, Prof Gordon Robert; s of Gordon William Foxall (d 1978), of Birmingham, and Marion, *née* Radford; *b* 16 July 1949; *Educ* Holly Lodge Sch, Univ of Salford (BSc, MSc), Univ of Birmingham (PhD, DSocSc), Univ of Strathclyde (PhD); *m* 26 June 1971, Jean, da of William Morris, of Birmingham; 1 da (Helen b 1977); *Career* Univ of Newcastle upon Tyne 1972–79, Univ of Birmingham 1980–83, reader Cranfield Inst of Technol 1983–86; prof Univ of Strathclyde 1987–90, prof Univ of Birmingham 1990–97, distinguished research prof Univ of Wales Cardiff 1997–98, prof of consumer behaviour and hon prof of psychology Keele Univ 1998–2001, distinguished research prof Univ of Cardiff 2002–; Maynard Phelps distinguished lectr Univ of Michigan 1988–91, sabbatical visitor Balliol Coll Oxford 1993–94, visiting prof Univ of Guelph Ontario 1994, visiting prof Univ of S Aust 1994; FBPsS 1996, CPsychol 1988, fell Br Acad of Mgmnt, AcSS; *Books* Consumer Behaviour (1980), Marketing Behaviour (1981), Strategic Marketing Management (1981), Consumer Choice (1983), Corporate Innovation (1984), Consumer Psychology (1990), Consumer Psychology for Marketing (1994), Consumers in Context (1996), Marketing Psychology (1997), Consumer Behaviour Analysis (2002), Context and Cognition (2004), Understanding Consumer Choice (2005), Explaining Consumer Choice (2006); *Recreations* reading, walking; *Clubs* Reform; *Style—* Prof Gordon Foxall; ✉ 4 Ridgewood Drive, Four Oaks, Sutton Coldfield B75 6TR; University of Cardiff (tel 029 2087 4000)

FOY, Christopher (Chris); s of Whitfield Foy (d 1990), and Rachel Archbold, *née* Fawcus (d 2000); *b* 27 November 1945; *Educ* Kingswood Sch, Univ of Liverpool; *m* 14 Aug 1986, Maria da Assunção, da of late Mario da Assunção Vieira Cardoso; *Career* Unilever plc 1969–98: positions incl Personnel Div 1983–86, ops memb Res Div 1986–88, chm Lever Bros (MW) Ltd 1988–93, chm EAI Ltd 1993–97; ceo ALC plc 1998–2000, chm AEA Ltd 1998–2000, md Royal Shakespeare Co 2000–03, dir Aquifer Ltd 2004–; hon treas Univ of Warwick 2004–06; FRSA 1998; *Clubs* Reform, Muthaiga; *Style—* Chris Foy, Esq; ✉ 22–23 Gayfere Street, London SW1P 3HP (e-mail chris@voco.demon.co.uk)

FOY, John Leonard; QC (1998); s of late Leonard James Foy, and late Edith Mary, *née* Hanks, of Bucks; *b* 1 June 1946; *Educ* Dartford GS, Univ of Birmingham (LLB); *m* 1972, Colleen Patricia, *née* Austin (d 2006); 1 s (Daniel James b 25 May 1988); *Career* called to the Bar Gray's Inn 1969 (bencher 2004); recorder 2000, memb Mental Health Review Tbnl; memb: Assoc of Personal Injury Lawyers, Personal Injuries Bar Assoc, Professional Negligence Bar Assoc; *Recreations* sports, especially football, rugby and horse racing; *Style—* John Foy, Esq, QC; ✉ 9 Gough Square, London EC4A 3DG (tel 020 7832 0500, fax 020 7353 1344)

FOYLE, (William Richard) Christopher; s of (William) Richard Foyle (d 1957), and Alice (later Mrs Harrap, d 1998), da of Eugen Kun, of Vienna; the Foyles are an ancient W Country family (*see* Burke's Landed Gentry, 18 Edn, vol 3); *b* 20 January 1943; *Educ* Radley; *m* 27 July 1983, Catherine Mary, da of Rev David William Forrester Jelleyman, of Melbourn, Cambs; 1 s (Alexander b 1968), 3 da (Charlotte b 1984, Annabel b 1985, Christine b 1987); *Career* trained in publishing and bookselling in London, Tuebingen, Berlin, Helsinki and Paris; mangr W & G Foyle Ltd 1965–72, ptnr Emson & Dudley and dir Emson & Dudley Securities Ltd 1972–78, prop Christopher Foyle Aviation (Leasing) Co 1977–2003; chm: Air Foyle Ltd 1978–, Air Foyle Executive Ltd 1988–, Charters Ltd 1994–, Air Foyle Passenger Airlines Ltd 1994–, Air Foyle Holding Co Ltd 1996–, Br Cargo Airline Alliance 1998–, CityJet 1999–2000, W&G Foyle Ltd Booksellers 1999–, Air Foyle Heavylift Ltd 2001–; tstee and memb Bd International Air Cargo Assoc 1992– (pres, ceo and chm of Bd 1997–99), vice-pres Guild of Aviation Artists, chm The Air League 2006–; tstee Foyle Fndn 2006–; pres Maldon Golf Club; IFW special achievement award 1997, inducted in TIACA Air Cargo Hall of Fame 2007; Freeman City of London, Liveryman Guild of Air Pilots and Air Navigators; FRAeS 1997, FCIT 1998, FRGS 2000; *Recreations* travel, skiing, flying, reading non-fiction; *Clubs* White's, Air Squadron, Annabel's, Garrick, Soc of Bookmen, Soc of Authors, Essex; *Style—* Christopher Foyle, Esq; ✉ Foyles, 113–117 Charing Cross Road, London WC2H 0EB (tel 020 7440 1569, fax 020 7440 1566, e-mail christopher@foyles.co.uk)

FOYLE, John Lewis; s of Roland Bernard Foyle (d 1996), of Portsmouth, Hants, and Rose Vera, *née* Taylor; *b* 7 June 1948; *Educ* Portsmouth Northern GS, St John's Coll Cambridge (MA); *m* 19 Feb 1972, Patricia Mary, da of John Victor Ketteringham (d 1986), of Ruthin, Clwyd; 3 s (James b 1972, Thomas d 1978, William b 1980); *Career* sec: Inflation Accounting Steering Gp 1976–78, Jt Exchanges Ctee 1982–96, ECOFEX 1988–96; dep chief exec London Int Fin Futures Exchange 1981–, dir Assoc of Futures Brokers and Dealers 1985–91; FCA 1973; *Recreations* sport, music; *Style—* John Foyle, Esq; ✉ Brookmead, Moat Farm Chase, Chipping Hill, Witham, Essex CM8 2DE; LIFFE, Cannon Bridge House, 1 Cousin Lane, London EC4R 3XX (tel 020 7623 0444, fax 020 7588 3624)

FOZZARD, Constance; da of Albert Edward Fozzard (d 1953), and Ethel May, *née* Leibe (d 1984); *b* 10 February 1933, Mill Hill London; *Educ* Finchley Co GS, Charing Cross Hosp Medical Sch (MB BS, Preira Prize); *m* 7 May 1973, Randolph Wilbur White (d 2005); *Career* preregistration house offr Charing Cross Unit Mt Vernon Hosp 1958–59, SHO rotation Charing Cross Hosp, Women's Hosp Leeds, Queen Charlotte's Hosp and Prince of Wales Hosp 1959–61, registrar then demonstrator in anatomy Charing Cross Hosp 1962–65, resident surgical offr All Saints Hosp Chatham 1965–66, sr registrar W Middx and Charing Cross Hosp 1967–71, hon conslt gynaecologist Italian Hosp 1968–71; conslt: SW RHA 1971–92, Royal Cornwall Hosps Tst 1992–98; BMA: memb 1958, fell 1994, memb Cncl 1990–94 and 2005–, Central Conslts and Specialists Ctee 2000, Orgn Ctee, Int Ctee, Bd of Science and Educn, Bd of Medical Educn, Progress of Doctors Ctee; memb: Carrick DC 1999–, Truro City Cncl 1999– (dep mayor 2002–03, mayor 2003–04); memb: Community Health Cncl, CAB, Age Concern, Standing Ctee on Postgrad Med and Dental Educn 1988–98, S Western Obstetric and Gynaecological Soc, Br Soc for Colposcopy and Cervical Pathology, Assoc of Medical Educn in Europe, Union of European Medical Specialists (Br rep), WHO Int Network for the Control of Gynaecological Cancers, RSM, European Assoc of Gynaecologists and Obstetricians; FRCS 1967, FRCOG 1979 (MRCOG 1963); *Publications* contrib to SCOPME pubns incl: Teaching Hospital Doctors and Dentists to Teach; *Recreations* silversmithing, bookbinding, upholstery, horticulture, couture sewing; *Clubs* Women's Visiting Gynaecological; *Style—* Miss Constance Fozzard; ✉ 64 Lemon Street, Truro, Cornwall TR1 2PN (tel and fax 01872 276160, e-mail constance@cfozzard.freeserve.co.uk);Carrick District Council, Carrick House, Pydar Street, Truro, Cornwall TR1 1EB (tel 01872 224400, fax 01872 242104, e-mail cllrfozzard@carrick.gov.uk)

FRACKOWIAK, Prof Richard Stanislaus Joseph; s of Capt Joseph Frackowiak, of London, and Wanda, *née* Majewska; *b* 26 March 1950; *Educ* Latymer Upper Sch, Peterhouse Cambridge (MB BChir, MA, MD), UCL (DSc); *m* 19 Feb 1972, Christine Jeanne Françoise, da of Louis Thepot, of St Cloud, France; 1 s (Matthew), 2 da (Stephanie, Annabelle); *Career* sr lectr and hon conslt Hammersmith Hosp and Nat Hosp for Neurology and Neurosurgery 1984–94, asst dir MRC Cyclotron Unit 1988–94, prof of clinical neurology Univ of London 1991–94; dean Inst of Neurology 1998–2003, prof and head Wellcome Dept of Cognitive Neurology, dir Leopold Muller Functional Imaging Lab 1994–2003, Wellcome Tst princ research fell 1994–, currently vice-provost (special projects) UCL; adjunct prof of neurology Cornell Univ Med Sch 1992–; Sackler visiting prof Cornell Med Sch 1994, visiting prof Université Catholique de Louvain 1996–97, Geschwind visiting prof Harvard Med Sch 1999, Rogowski visiting prof Yale Med Sch; memb: Academia Europaea, Belgian Neurological Soc, Académie Royale de Medecine Belge, Canadian Neurological Soc; foreign associate Academie Nationale de Medecine, hon foreign memb Société Française de Neurologie, hon memb American Neurological Assoc; numerous named lectureships and over 300 peer reviewed publications on the subject of functional neuro imaging; Hon Dr Univ of Liège 1999; Ipsen Prize 1997, Wilhelm Feldberg Prize 1997; FRCP 1987, FMedSci 1998 (memb Cncl); *Recreations* motorcycling, travel; *Clubs* Hurlingham, Athenaeum; *Style—* Prof Richard Frackowiak; ✉ Wellcome Department of Cognitive Neurology, Institute of Neurology, 12 Queen Square, London WC1N 3AR (tel 020 7833 7458, fax 020 7813 1420, e-mail r.frackowiak@fil.ion.ucl.ac.uk)

FRADD, Dr Simon Oakley; s of Frederick Ronald Fradd, of Otford, Kent, and Beryl Grace, *née* Milledge; *b* 20 April 1950; *Educ* Sevenoaks Sch, W Kent Coll Tunbridge Wells, KCL (BSc), Westminster Med Sch London; *m* 1 May 1976 (m dis), Elizabeth Harriett, da of Norman Allen Birtwhistle; *Career* house surgn Westminster Med Sch 1977; SHO: in paediatrics Queen Mary's Roehampton 1978, in neonatology Whittington Hosp London 1979, in A/E then orthopaedics St George's Tooting 1980–81; registrar: in surgery Burton Gen Hosp Burton-on-Trent 1981–84, in urology Univ Hosp of Wales Cardiff 1984–85; GP trainee: Burton-on-Trent 1985–86, under Dr Saunders Nottingham 1986–87, Castle Donington Leics 1987; GP princ Saunders & Fradd Nottingham 1988–; chm: Hosp Doctors' Assoc 1979–82, Negotiators' Hosp Jr Staff Ctee 1986–87 (dep chm 1984–86), Jr Membs' Forum BMA 1990, Doctor Patient Partnership 1997–; dep chm Gen Practitioners Ctee of BMA 1997–; memb Med Practices Ctee 1989–93, Gen Med Servs Ctee negotiator 1993–; memb GMC 1989–; Freeman City of London 1976, Liveryman Worshipful Co of Needlemakers 1976, Liveryman Worshipful Soc of Apothecaries 1993; Hon FAMGP 1998, Hon MRCGP 2000, FRCS; *Books* Hospital Doctors' Association Guide to Your Rights (jtly, 1981), Making Sense of Partnerships (jtly, 1994), Nottingham Non-Fundholder Project, Members Reference Book RCGP (1995); *Recreations* DIY, gardening, skiing, gliding; *Style—* Dr Simon Fradd; ✉ 67 New Concordia Wharf, Mill Street, London SE7 2BB; Greenwood and Sneinton Family Medical Centre, 249 Sneinton Dale, Sneinton, Nottingham NG3 7DQ (tel 0115 948 4999, mobile 078 6069 3315)

FRAKER, Ford McKinstry; s of Harrison Shedd Fraker, and Marjorie Tomlinson Fraker (d 1987); *b* 15 July 1948; *Educ* Phillips Acad Andover Mass, Harvard Univ (BA); *m* 24 Dec 1984, Linda Margaret, da of T Hanson; 1 da (Antonia b 21 Jan 1986), 2 s (Jonathan b 2 May 1987, Charles b 29 Jan 1990); *Career* vice-pres and regnl mangr Chemical Bank (NY) Bahrain Arabian Gulf 1977–79; Saudi International Bank London: mangr Middle East 1979–82, asst gen mangr, head of gen banking 1982–85, head of credit 1985–90, head of client devpt and mktg 1990–91; dir Saudi International Bank Nassau 1987–90, princ Fraker & Co 1991–93, md Mees Pierson Investment Finance (UK) Ltd 1993–96, co-fndr and md Trinity Group 1997–; *Recreations* tennis, art, travel; *Clubs* Harvard (Boston); *Style—* Ford M Fraker

FRAME, Frank Riddell; *b* 15 February 1930; *Educ* Univ of Glasgow (MA, LLB); *m* 1958, Maureen Milligan; 1 s, 1 da; *Career* admitted slr 1954; North of Scotland Hydro-Electric Board 1955–60, UK Atomic Energy Authy 1960–68, The Weir Group plc 1968–76 (dir 1971–76); The Hongkong and Shanghai Banking Corporation Ltd: joined as gp legal advsr 1977, exec dir 1985, dep chm 1986–90; advsr to Bd HSBC Holdings plc 1990–98; dir: Edinburgh Dragon Trust plc 1994–, Northern Gas Networks Ltd 2004–; former chm: South China Morning Post Ltd, Far Eastern Economic Review Ltd, Wallem Gp Ltd; former dir: Marine Midland Banks Inc, Swire Pacific Ltd, The British Bank of the Middle East, Consolidated Press International Ltd, Securities and Futures Commission Hong Kong, Baxter International Inc; Hon DUniv Glasgow 2001; *Publications* The Law relating to Nuclear Energy (with Prof Harry Street); *Clubs* Brooks's; *Style—* Frank Frame, Esq; ✉ The Old Rectory, Bepton, Midhurst, West Sussex GU29 0HX (tel 01730 813140)

FRAME, Roger Campbell Crosbie; s of late Andrew Crosbie Frame, of Giffnock, Glasgow, and Jessie Caldwell, *née* Campbell; *b* 7 June 1949; *Educ* Glasgow Acad; *m* 10 Sept 1973, Angela Maria, da of late Louis Evaristi, of Giffnock, Glasgow; 2 s (Nicholas Roger b 1976, Mark Christopher b 1980), 1 da (Lorenza Charlotte b 1988); *Career* chartered accountant; dir: Camos Ltd, Frame & Co Management Services Ltd; treas Glasgow Gp of Artists 1983–89; sec: Royal Scottish Soc of Painters in Watercolour (RSW) 1986–99 (hon fell 1999), Glasgow Eastern Merchants and Tradesman Soc (ret 1999); chm: Int Sch of Florence 2004– (dir and govr 2003–), American Schools Abroad Inc 2004–; chm James Cusator Wards Fund (Univ of Glasgow) 1984–, offr Incorporation of Weavers of Glasgow (ret 1999); Freeman: City of Glasgow, City of London; fell Univ of Glasgow 1999; *Recreations* clay pigeon shooting, art; *Style*— Roger C C Frame, Esq; ✉ Dunglass, 56 Manse Road, Bearsden, Glasgow G61 3PN; Lungarno Della Zecca Vecchia 28, Florence, Italy

FRAME, Ronald William Sutherland; s of Alexander Frame, and Isobel, *née* Sutherland; *b* 23 May 1953; *Educ* The HS of Glasgow, Univ of Glasgow (Foulis scholarship, MA, Bradley Medal), Jesus Coll Oxford (BLitt); *Career* writer 1981–; various radio and television plays; *Awards* jt winner Betty Trask Prize 1984, Samuel Beckett Prize 1986, TV Industries Panel Most Promising Writer New to TV 1986, Saltire Prize Scottish Book of the Year 2000, Stonewall Award in Literature American Library Assoc 2003; *Television Scripts* Paris (1985), Out of Time (1987), Ghost City (1994), A Modern Man (1996), 4 Ghost Stories for Christmas (2000), Darien: Disaster in Paradise (2003), Cromwell (2003), The Two Loves of Anthony Trollope (contrib, 2004); *Radio Scripts* incl: The Lantern Bearers (1997), The Hydro (1997, second series 1998, third series 1999), Havisham (1998), Maestro (1999), Pharos (2000), Sunday at Sant' Agata (2001), Don't Look Now (adapted, 2001), Greyfriars Bobby (2002), The Servant (adapted, 2005), The Razor's Edge (adapted, 2005), A Tiger for Malgudi (adapted, 2006), The Blue Room (adapted, 2007); *Novels and Short Story Collections* Winter Journey (1984, 3 Sony Radio Award nominations 1985), Watching Mrs Gordon (1985), A Long Weekend with Marcel Proust (1986), Sandmouth People (1987), A Woman of Judah (1987), Paris: A Television Play (1987), Penelope's Hat (1989), Bluette (1990), Underwood and After (1991), Walking My Mistress in Deauville (1992), The Sun on the Wall (1994), The Lantern Bearers (1999), Permanent Violet (2002), Time in Carnbeg (2004); *Recreations* swimming, walking, gardening; *Style*— Ronald Frame, Esq; ✉ c/o Curtis Brown Ltd, Haymarket House, 28/29 Haymarket, London SW1Y 4SP (tel 020 7396 6600, fax 020 7396 0110/1, e-mail cb@curtisbrown.co.uk)

FRAMPTON, Ronald Arthur (Ron); s of Arthur John Frampton (d 1991), of Axminster, Devon, and Dorothy May, *née* Churchill (d 1995); *b* 19 October 1940; *Educ* Axe Valley Sch, Exeter Coll; *m* 30 Dec 1970, Marianne Stiegler; 1 da (Stefanie Daniela b 13 April 1972), 1 s (Magnus John b 7 Sept 1975); *Career* photographer, photographic conslt and lectr specialising in portraiture, architecture, landscape and documentary photography, acknowledged expert in fine monochrome printing; lectr in applied photography: St Clare's Coll (AEC) Devon 1992–2003, Somerset Coll of Arts and Technol 1985–; visiting lectr and tutor 1986– incl: Dillington House Coll 1995–, Urchfont Manor Coll 1992–94, Symondsbury Coll Dorset 1988–95, RPS 1993–, Univ of Bath 1995–99; reg conslt: CGLI, BIPP, RPS; dep chm Applied and Professional Adjudicating Panel (Associateship and Fellowship) RPS 1999–; elected memb Section 7 Admissions and Qualifications Bd BIPP 1993–, elected memb Applied Distinctions Adjudicating Panel (Associateship and Fellowship) RPS 1994; BIPP Peter Grugeon Meml Award for Best Fellowship Portfolio 1991, Fenton Medal RPS (hon memb); ARPS, FBIPP, FRPS 1991, FMPA 1996; *Publications* exhbn catalogues incl: Fifty Photographers (1996), Beyond the Hills (1999), A Sense of Place (2000); books: Shadows In Time - Images from the West Country (2002), Beyond the Vale - Images from the West Country (2004); RPS pubns: Gaining the RPS Associateship and Fellowship in Applied Photography, Gaining the RPS Licentiateship, The Wide Field of Applied Photography, Assessment Criteria: RPS - Associateship and Fellowship in Applied Photography; contrib: The Photographer, RPS Jl; *Recreations* landscape, ecology, ecclesiastical architecture, social history, environment and natural history; *Style*— Ron Frampton, Esq; ✉ Rose Cottage, Valley Lane, Churchill, Axminster, Devon EX13 7LZ (tel and fax 01297 33428)

FRANCE, Elizabeth Irene; CBE (2002); da of Ralph Salem, of Leicester, and Elizabeth Joan, *née* Bryan; *b* 1 February 1950; *Educ* Kibworth Beauchamp GS, UCW Aberystwyth (BSc Econ); *m* 24 July 1971, Dr Michael William France, s of Bert France (d 1976); 2 s, 1 da; *Career* Home Office: admin trainee 1971–77, princ (grade 7) 1977–86, grade 5 1986–94; Data Protection Registrar/Info Cmmr 1994–2002, telecommunications and energy supply ombudsman 2002–; memb Cmmn for the Control of Interpol Files 1998–2005; memb Aarhus Convention Compliance Ctee 2002–05; non-exec dir Serious Organised Crime Agency; memb: Ct Univ of Manchester 2002–, Cncl Univ of Wales Aberystwyth 2005–; DSc (hc) De Montfort Univ 1996, Hon DLitt Loughborough Univ 2000, Hon DLaws Univ of Bradford 2002; fell Univ of Univ of Wales Aberystwyth 2003; FRSA, FICM; *Style*— Mrs Elizabeth France, CBE; ✉ The Ombudsman Service Limited, Wilderspool Park, Greenall's Avenue, Warrington WA4 6HL (tel 01925 430049, fax 01925 430059, e-mail enquiries@tosl.org.uk, website www.otelo.org.uk and www.energy-ombudsman.org.uk)

FRANCE, Prof Peter; s of Edgar France (d 2000), of Haslemere, Surrey, and Doris Woosnam, *née* Morgan (d 1984); *b* 19 October 1935; *Educ* Bridlington Sch, Bradford GS, Magdalen Coll Oxford (MA, DPhil); *m* 30 Sept 1961, Siân Reynolds; 3 da (Katharine b 18 Aug 1962, Rose Mair, Siriol Jane (twins) b 7 Dec 1966); *Career* research fell Magdalen Coll Oxford 1960–63, successively asst lectr, lectr then reader Sch of Euro Studies Univ of Sussex 1963–80; Univ of Edinburgh: prof of French 1980–90, endowment fell 1990–2000, hon fell 2000–; pres: Int Soc for the History of Rhetoric 1993–95, British Comparative Literature Assoc 1992–98; French ed Modern Language Review 1979–85; Dr (hc) Chuvash State Univ 1996; FBA 1989, FRSE 2003; Officier de l'Ordre des Palmes Académiques 1991, Chevalier de la Légion d'Honneur 2001; *Books* Racine's Rhetoric (1965), Rhetoric and Truth in France (1972), Racine: Andromaque (1977), Diderot (1982), Poets of Modern Russia (1982), Rousseau: Confessions (1987), An Anthology of Chuvash Poetry (trans, 1991), Poetry in France (ed jtly, 1992), Politeness and its Discontents (1992), New Oxford Companion to Literature in French (ed, 1995), Oxford Guide to Literature in English Translation (ed, 2000), Mapping Lives: the Uses of Biography (ed jtly, 2002), Oxford History of Literary Translation in English (ed jtly, vol 3 2005, vol 4 2006); also translator of works by Rousseau, Diderot, Blok, Pasternak, Etkind, and Aygi; *Style*— Prof Peter France, FBA; ✉ 10 Dryden Place, Edinburgh EH9 1RP (tel 0131 667 1177)

FRANCE, Roger; s of late Harry Edmund France, and Ellen May, *née* Dark; *b* 7 January 1938; *Educ* Bedford Sch, Linacre Coll Oxford (MSc), Univ of York (scholar, MA), Imperial Coll London (scholar, DIC), Architectural Assoc (exhibitioner, AADipl), Poly of Central London (DipTP); *m* 1968 (m dis 1982), Dr Venetia Margaret King; *Career* architect and town planner; architectural asst: Schs Div Middx CC 1961–62, Maguire and Murray 1962–63; asst architect Research Gp Town Devpt Div GLC 1963–65, princ planning offr London Borough of Southwark (ldr Special Areas Gp) 1966–70, princ Roger France & Associates 1968–82; sr lectr in town planning N London Poly 1970–75, sr lectr in urban conservation Oxford Poly 1975–92 (Oxford Brookes Univ 1992–94), visiting lectr Dept of Land Economy Univ of Cambridge 1991–92, visiting scholar Univ of Cambridge Inst of Educn 1993–94, visiting lectr Dept of Town and Regnl Planning Univ of Sheffield 1996–98, visiting scholar Dept of Geography Univ of Cambridge 1999–2000, research assoc Dept of Architecture and Civil Engineering Univ of Bath 2000–03; official lectr Civic Tst 1986–90; register of expert witnesses 1995, specialist assessor Welsh Funding Cncl 1995–96, specialist advsr Design and Historic Environmental Panel RTPI 1996–; memb: Bldgs Ctee Victorian Soc 1972–86, chm annual conservation offrs' confs Univ of Oxford 1975–85, sec Inst of Religion and Medicine Oxford 1982–86, appointments advsr Oxford Diocesan Advsy Ctee 1982–87, tstee Oxford Preservation Tst 1982–90, memb Assoc for Study of Conservation of Historic Bldgs 1982–93; caseworker Cncl for Br Archaeology 1982–86, memb Educn Ctee Int Cncl of Monuments and Sites 1996–2006; fndr memb Assoc for Small Historic Towns and Villages 1989– (tstee 1991–98), fndr Research Cncl for the Historic Environment 1990–; founding memb, convenor and chm Conservation Course Dirs' Forum 1991–; memb Soc for the Protection of Ancient Buildings and Georgian Gp; hon memb: Assoc of Conservation Offrs 1984, Nat Tst for Historic Preservation of America 1985; Liveryman Worshipful Co of Chartered Architects 1994 (Master of Students 1995–2006, Warden 2006), Freeman City of London 1994, memb Coll of Readers 2000, licensed reader Church of England (Gt St Mary's Cambridge and Sidney Sussex Coll Cambridge 2003–), founding Ct memb Guild of Educators 2001 (Warden 2003); ARIBA 1964 (memb RIBA Visiting Panel 2004–05), MRTPI 1974, FRGS 1989, memb IHBC 1998, memb Inst for Learning and Teaching (ILTM) 2002, FHEA 2007; *Publications* Chester: a Study in Conservation (contrib, 1969), Look Before You Change (1985), Marston, a Case for Conservation (1988), Methods of Environmental Impact Assessment (contrib, 1995); numerous reviews and articles for pubns incl: RTPI Jl, The Planner, Context; *Recreations* music, antiques - furniture and friends; *Clubs* City Univ, New Cavendish; *Style*— Roger France, Esq; ✉ 32 Manor Place, Cambridge CB1 1LE (tel 01223 358236)

FRANCE-HAYHURST, Jeannie; da of William Smith (d 1950), of Banffshire, and Mair, *née* Davies (d 1979); *b* 20 January 1950; *Educ* Towyn GS, Univ of Wales, Inns of Court Sch of Law; *m* 1, 1978 Anthony Jamieson; 1 s (Charles b 1979); m 2, James France-Hayhurst, s of late Robert France Hayhurst; 2 da (Lucinda b 1984, Serena b 1986); *Career* called to the Bar Gray's Inn 1972, pupillage and practice 1974–78, lectr in law 1972–78, slr 1980–86, recalled to the Bar 1987, recommenced practice (Northern Circuit) 1992; vice-chm Eddisbury Conc Constituency Assoc, Parly candidate (Cons) Montgomery 1992, cncllr (Cons) Cheshire CC 2000–01; chair Women's Enterprise Network 1989–90, vice-chair Chester Cathedral Devpt Tst; *Recreations* family, friends, the countryside, music, antiques; *Style*— Ms Jeannie France-Hayhurst; ✉ India Buildings Chambers, 8th Floor, Water Street, Liverpool L2 0XG (tel 0151 243 6000, fax 0151 243 6040)

FRANCIS, Andrew James; s of Frank Sidney Francis, DFC (d 1971), of Ashtead, Surrey, and Ann, *née* Velody (d 1994); *b* 1 November 1953; *Educ* City of London Freeman's Sch, Keble Coll Oxford (MA); *m* 18 Dec 1982, Victoria Louise, da of Francis Henry Gillum-Webb (d 1972), of Weybridge, Surrey; 1 s (Hugo), 3 da (Amelia, Alexandra, Charlotte (twin with Hugo)); *Career* called to the Bar Lincoln's Inn 1977; in practice at Chancery Bar 1979–; memb: Research Ethics Ctee MOD, Advsy Ctee Law Cmmn; *Books* Restrictive Covenants and Freehold Land - A Practitioner's Guide, Rights of Light - The Modern Law (co-author), Inheritance Act Claims - Law Practice and Procedure, Contentions Probate Claims (co-author); *Style*— Andrew Francis, Esq; ✉ Serle Court, 6 New Square, Lincoln's Inn, London WC2A 3QS (tel 020 7242 6105, fax 020 7405 4004, e-mail afrancis@serlecourt.co.uk)

FRANCIS, Clare Mary; MBE (1978); da of Owen Francis, CB, and Joan St Leger, *née* Norman; *b* 17 April 1946; *Educ* Royal Ballet Sch, UCL (BSc Econ); *m* 1977 (m dis 1985), Jacques Robert Redon; 1 s (Thomas Robert Jean b 1978); *Career* writer; transatlantic singlehanded crossing 1973, first woman home Observer Singlehanded Transatlantic Race and holder women's record 1976, first woman skipper Whitbread Round The World Race 1977–78; chm Soc of Authors 1997–99, chm PLR advsy ctee 2000–03; fell UCL 1979, hon fell UMIST 1981; *Books* non-fiction: Come Hell or High Water (1977), Come Wind or Weather (1978), The Commanding Sea (1981); fiction: Night Sky (1983), Red Crystal (1985), Wolf Winter (1987), Requiem (1991), Deceit (1993), Betrayal (1995), A Dark Devotion (1997), Keep me Close (1999), A Death Divided (2001), Homeland (2004); *Recreations* opera, theatre; *Style*— Miss Clare Francis, MBE

FRANCIS, Clive; s of Raymond Francis (d 1987), of Brighton, E Sussex, and Margaret, *née* Towner; *b* 26 June 1946; *Educ* Ratton Secdy Modern Sch, RADA; *m* May 1989, Natalie, da of Martin Ogle, OBE; 1 da (Lucinda b Dec 1989), 1 s (Harry b Feb 1992); *Career* actor; caricaturist 1983–; five solo exhibitions; designer various theatre posters and book covers; *Theatre* West End incl: The Servant of Two Masters, Three, The Mating Game, Bloomsbury, The Return of A J Raffles, The Rear Column, The School for Scandal, Benefactors, The Importance of Being Earnest, Single Spies, A Small Family Business and 'Tis Pity She's a Whore (RNT), What The Butler Saw, An Absolute Turkey, Gross Indecency, Entertaining Mr Sloane, The Shakespeare Revue, The Lavender Hill Mob, Travels With My Aunt; for RSC incl: A Christmas Carol, Three Hours After Marriage, Troilus and Cressida; Chichester Festival Theatre incl: Monsieur Perichon's Travels, The Circle, Look After Lulu; *Television* incl: Poldark, Entertaining Mr Sloane, As You Like It, Masada, The Critic, A Married Man, The Far Pavilions, Yes Prime Minister, Oedipus, Adventures of Sherlock Holmes, After The War, The Rear Column, Quartermain's Terms, Old Flames, Lipstick on your Collar, The 10%ers; *Publications* Laughlines (1989), Sir John, The Many Faces of Gielgud (1994), There is Nothing Like a Dane! (1998), There is Nothing Like a Thane! (2001); adapted The Hound of the Baskervilles, Our Man in Havana and Three Men in a Boat for theatre; *Recreations* walking, exploring England, twentieth century first editions; *Clubs* Garrick; *Style*— Clive Francis, Esq; ✉ c/o Ken McReddie, 36–40 Glasshouse Street, London W1B 5DL (tel 020 7439 1456)

FRANCIS, Elizabeth Ann (Lisa); AM; da of Thomas Foelwyn Francis, and Dilys Olwen, *née* Davies; *b* 29 November 1960, London; *Educ* Ardwyn GS Aberystwyth, W London Inst of HE; *Career* mangr Queensbridge Hotel (family business) Aberystwyth 1984–2002, memb Nat Assembly for Wales (Cons) Mid and West Wales 2003–; dir Mid Wales Toursim Co 2002– (Ceredigion trade rep 2002–03); supporter N Wales Air Ambulance; *Recreations* travel, modern languages, theatre, swimming, cooking; *Clubs* Rotoract (pres); *Style*— Miss Lisa Francis, AM; ✉ National Assembly for Wales, Cardiff CF99 1NA (tel 029 2089 8286, fax 020 2089 8287, e-mail lisa.francis@wales.gov.uk)

FRANCIS, Graham John; s of Clarence William Francis, and Barbara Jean, *née* Henstridge; *b* 10 November 1945; *Educ* Univ of Manchester (BArch); *m* Irene Frances, *née* Aykroyd; 1 da (Anna b 31 Oct 1980), 1 s (William b 6 Nov 1983); *Career* project architect: GLC Housing Div 1970–72 (asst architect GLC Town Devpt 1968–69), Ahrends Burton and Koralek 1973–80; Sheppard Robson (architects, planners and interior designers) London: joined 1980, assoc 1982, ptnr i/c tech matters and managing ptnr for Commercial Gp 1984–, chm 2002–; projects incl: master planning of offices and associated activities Regent's Place London 1988, BP's architect for Britannic Tower redevelopment 1988–94, subsequently appointed architect for City Point (following name change 1996), The Helicon for London & Manchester EC2 1992–96 (RIBA Regnl Award for Architecture and Civic Tst Award commendation 1998), major refurbishment of teaching site in Regent St for Univ of Westminster 1993, masterplan/design for mfrg office facility for Motorola 1995, masterplan for First Central Park site at Park Royal 1997, new admin HQ for Toyota Great Burgh Epsom 1998, new admin HQ for Pfizer Surrey 1998; RIBA; *Recreations* tennis, squash, walking; *Clubs* Cumberland, Hampstead Cricket, Stormont; *Style*— Graham Francis, Esq; ✉ Sheppard Robson, 77 Parkway, London NW1 7PU (tel 020 7504 1700, fax 020 7504 1701, e-mail sr.mail@sheppardrobson.com)

FRANCIS, Prof Hazel; da of Harry Wright (d 1961), and Ethel Vera, *née* Bedson (d 1965); *b* 12 April 1929; *Educ* Queen Mary's HS for Girls Walsall, Girton Coll Cambridge (MA), Univ of Leeds (MA, PhD); *m* 23 May 1953, Dr Huw Wesley Stephen Francis, s of Rev Matthew Francis (d 1954), of Walsall; 3 da (Susan Margaret b 1954, Keren Mary b 1956, Hilary Ann b 1960), 2 s (Andrew Martin b 1958, Jonathan Mark b 1962); *Career* teacher Handsworth GS for Girls Birmingham 1950–53; lectr and sr lectr Sch of Educn Univ of Leeds 1973–78 (p/t lectr Dept of Psychology 1969–73), pro-dir Inst of Educn Univ of London 1985–90, prof of educnl psychology Univ of London 1978–94 (prof emeritus 1994–); author of numerous articles in relevant scientific jls; memb: Univs Cncl for the Educn of Teachers 1978–92, Br Educnl Research Assoc, Br Psychological Soc, American Educnl Research Assoc, Euro Assoc for Research on Learning and Instruction; Hon PhD Univ of Linköping Sweden 1996; CPsychol 1988, FBPsS 1980 (memb Cncl 1979–85); *Books* include: Language in Childhood (1975), Language in Teaching and Learning (1977), Learning to Read - Literate Behaviour and Orthographic Knowledge (1982), Minds of Their Own (1984), Learning to Teach: Psychology in Teacher Training (ed, 1985), The British Journal of Educational Psychology (ed, 1985–89); *Recreations* mountain walking, swimming, tennis; *Style*— Prof Hazel Francis; ✉ tel 020 8579 9589; Institute of Education, University of London, 20 Bedford Way, London WC1H 0AL (e-mail h.francis@ioe.ac.uk)

FRANCIS, Hywel; MP; *b* 6 June 1946; *Educ* Whitchurch GS, Univ of Wales Swansea (BA, PhD); *Career* policy advsr on lifelong learning DfEE 1997–2000, special advsr to Sec of State for Wales 1999–2000; MP (Lab) Aberavon 2001–, memb Welsh Affrs Ctee 2001–; fndr S Wales Miners' Library 1973, fndr Bevan Fndn, chair Welsh Congress in Support of Mining Communities 1984–86; vice-pres: Llafur (Welsh Lab History Soc), Nat Inst of Adult Continuing Educn (NIACE); memb Socialist Educn Assoc; FRSA; *Clubs* Aberavon RFC; *Style*— Hywel Francis, Esq, MP; ✉ House of Commons, London SW1A 0AA

FRANCIS, Jeremy Inglesby; s of Gordon Cedric Francis (d 1963), and Marguerite June, *née* Smith (d 2001); *b* 7 January 1951; *Educ* Wrekin Coll, Queens' Coll Cambridge (MA); *m* 30 June 1973, Susan Jane, da of late John Clark; 2 s (Matthew b 23 Aug 1978, Thomas b 10 Feb 1982), 1 da (Ellen b 7 Dec 1987); *Career* Robson Rhodes: ptnr 1982–98, ptnr in charge Cambridge office 1987–95, memb Mgmnt Bd 1989–96, nat head of tax 1993–97; Grant Thornton: ptnr 1998–, ptnr in charge Cambridge and Kettering offices 1999–2002, London head of tax 2002–; ACA 1975, CTA 1989 (John Wood medal); *Recreations* bridge, piano playing, listening to classical music, reading; *Style*— Jeremy Francis, Esq; ✉ Grant Thornton, Melton Street, Euston Square, London NW1 2EP (tel and fax 0870 991 2202, e-mail jeremy.i.francis@gtuk.com)

FRANCIS, Dr John Michael; s of William Winston Francis (d 1939), of Haverfordwest, Pembs, and Beryl Margaret, *née* Savage (d 2003); *b* 1 May 1939; *Educ* Gowerton GS, Royal Coll of Science, Imperial Coll London (BSc, ARCS, PhD, DIC); *m* 14 Sept 1963, Eileen, da of Hugh Foster Sykes (d 1977), of Whitley Bay, Northumberland; 2 da (Sarah Katherine b 1966, Rachel Victoria b 1968); *Career* R&D Dept CEGB 1963–70, first dir Soc Religion and Technol Project Church of Scot 1970–74, sr res fell in energy studies Heriot-Watt Univ 1974–76, asst sec Scottish Office 1981–84 (princ 1976–80), dir (Scotland) Nature Conservancy Cncl GB 1984–91 (memb Advsy Ctee 1974–76), chief exec Nature Conservancy Cncl for Scotland 1991–92, sr policy advsr The Scottish Office 1992–99; visiting fell Inst for Advanced Studies in the Humanities Univ of Edinburgh 1988, visiting fell Centre for Values and Social Policy Univ of Colorado at Boulder 1991; contribs to numerous professional and scientific jls; conslt (science, technol and social ethics) World Cncl of Churches Geneva 1971–83, rep UN Environment Conf Stockholm 1972; chm: Ctee on Society Religion and Technol Church of Scot 1980–94, Edinburgh Forum 1986–92; chair UK Nat Cmmn for UNESCO 2000–03, chair Sector Ctee Sustainable Devpt, Peace and Human Rights UK UNESCO 1999–2003, conslt and advsr UNESCO 2003–, dep chair UNESCO Scotland 2007–; chair/convenor UN Assoc Edinburgh 2006–; memb Cross Pty Gp on Int Devpt Scottish Parliament 1999–; memb: Oil Devpt Cncl for Scot 1973–76, Ind Cmmn on Tport 1974, Cncl Nat Tst for Scot 1984–92, Crown Estate Cmmn Advsy Ctee on Marine Fish Farming 1989–92, Scottish Universities Policy Research and Advice (SUPRA) network 1999–, Church and Nat Ctee Church of Scotland 2000–05, Exec Ctee Centre for Theology and Public Issues Univ of Edinburgh 2004–, Steering Gp Scottish Sustainable Devpt Forum 2004–; memb St Giles' Cathedral Edinburgh; chm Francis Gp conslts (Europersona (trade mark)) 1991–99, professional memb World Futures Soc Washington DC 1991–, memb Reference Gp Millennium Project UN Univ Washington DC 1992–, memb John Muir Tst, tstee RSE Scotland Fndn 2004–; hon fell Univ of Edinburgh 2000–; FRIC 1969, FRSGS 1990, FRSE 1991, FRZS Scot 1992; *Books* Scotland in Turmoil (1973), Changing Directions (jtly, 1974), The Future as an Academic Discipline (jtly, 1975), Facing up to Nuclear Power (1976), The Future of Scotland (jtly, 1977), North Sea Oil and the Environment (jtly, 1992), Democratic Contracts for Sustainable and Caring Societies (jtly, 2000); also author of review papers: Nature Conservation and the Voluntary Principle (1994), Nature Conservation and the Precautionary Principle (1996), The Reconstruction of Civil Society (1996), The Uncertainties of Nature Conservation and Environmental Protection (1997), Conserving Nature: Scotland and the Wider World (jtly, 2005); *Recreations* ecumenical travels, hill walking, theatre, writing on values and ethics; *Style*— Dr John M Francis, FRSE; ✉ 49 Gilmour Road, Newington, Edinburgh EH16 5NU (tel and fax 0131 667 3996, e-mail john.m.francis@btinternet.com)

FRANCIS, Mark Robert; s of Cecil Francis, and Lilian Louisa, *née* Richards; *b* 6 September 1962, Newtownards, Co Down; *Educ* Scabo HS Newtownards, Regent House GS Newtownards, St Martin's Sch of Art (BA), Chelsea Sch of Art (MA); *Career* artist; Grand Prize Tokyo Int Print Exhbn 1993, Irish MOMA/Glen Dimplex Artists Award 1996, Public Art Devpt Tst Mark Francis/Nicky Hurst 2004; *Solo Exhibitions* incl: Thumb Gallery London 1990, Jill George Gallery London 1992, Manchester City Art Gallery 1994, Galerie Thieme & Pohl Darmstadt 1995, Kerlin Gallery Dublin 1995, 1997, 2000 and 2003, Maureen Paley Interim Art London 1994, 1995, 1998, 2000, 2003 and 2004, Bloom Gallery Amsterdam 1996, Terra Nova - New Territories (Harewood House Leeds) 1996, Galerie Anne de Villepoix Paris 1996, 1998 and 2002, Mary Boone Gallery NY 1997 and 1999, Galerie Martina Detterer Frankfurt 1997, Kohn Turner Gallery LA 1998, Galerie Wilma Lock St Gallen 1999 and 2002, Kohji Ogura Gallery Nagoya 1999, Milton Keynes Gallery 2000, New Paintings (Galerie Reinhard Hauff Stuttgart) 2001, Michael Kohn Gallery LA 2003, Drawings (Thomas Schulte Galerie Berlin) 2003, New Paintings (Thomas Schulte Galerie Berlin) 2004, Interim Art (Maureen Paley London) 2004, New Prints (Marlborough Graphics London) 2004, Galerie Forsblom Helsinki 2005, Galerie Wilma Lock St Gallen 2005; *Group Exhibitions* incl: Summer Show (Tom Caldwell Gallery Dublin) 1983, New Contemporaries (Mall Galleries London) 1983, Stowells Trophy (Royal Acad of Arts London) 1984, Summer Show (Tom Caldwell Gallery Belfast) 1984, Athena Int Awards (Mall Galleries London) 1985, ILEA Class of 86 (Royal Festival Hall London) 1986, On The Wall Gallery Belfast 1986, Christie's New Contemporaries (RCA London) 1989, 5 Abstract Painters (Thumb Gallery London) 1989, Four Painters (New Acad Gallery London) 1990, Arco '92 (Madrid) 1992, Whitechapel Open (Whitechapel Art Gallery London) 1992, New Displays (Tate Gallery London) 1992, European Parl touring exhbn (Belfast, Edinburgh, Zürich, Brussels and London) 1992–93, Another Country (Rebecca Hossack Gallery London) 1993, Snap Shots (Eagle Gallery London) 1993, Contemporary Art at the Courtauld Inst (Courtauld Inst of Art London) 1993, Paintmarks (Kettles Yard Gallery Cambridge) 1994, Recent British Art (Richard Salmon Gallery London) 1994, The Curators Egg (Anthony Reynolds Gallery London) 1994, Mark Francis/Brad Lahore (Hervè Mikaeloff Gallery Paris) 1994, Testing the Water (Tate Gallery Liverpool) 1995, From Here (Karsten Schubert/Waddington Galleries London) 1995, Painters' Opinion (Bloom Gallery Amsterdam) 1995, Absolut Vision - New British Paintings in the 1990s (MOMA Oxford) 1996, Black Grey & White (Galerie Bugdahn und Kaimer Düsseldorf) 1996, British Abstract Art III (Flowers East Gallery London) 1996, Residue (Douglas Hyde Gallery Dublin) 1997, Beau Geste (Angles Gallery LA) 1997, Surface (Gow Langsford Gallery Auckland) 1997, Interior (Maureen Paley Interim Art London) 1997, Sensation-Young British Artists from the Saatchi Collection (Royal Acad of Arts London and Museum für Gegenwart Berlin) 1997–98, Post Naturam-nach der Natur (Stadt Münster) 1998, POSTMARK: An Abstract Effect (Site Santa Fe New Mexico) 1999, Contemporary Painters Negociate Small Truths (Blamton Museum of Art Univ of Texas) 1999, Premio Michetti (Palazzo San Domenico Museo Michetti) 2000, Shifting Ground: Fifty Years of Irish Art 1950–2000 (Irish MOMA Dublin) 2000, Wreck of Hope (The Nunnery London) 2000, Irish Art Now: From the Poetic to the Political (Chicago Cultural Center) 2000, Fluid (Wolverhampton City Art Gallery and Galerie Wilma Lock St Gallen) 2001, The Rowan Collection Contemporary British and Irish Art (Irish MOMA Dublin) 2002, Eight New Paintings (Kerlin Gallery Dublin) 2002, The Saatchi Gift (Talbot Rice Gallery Edinburgh) 2002, Prospects and Drawing Prize (Essor Project Space London) 2002, John Moores (Walker Art Gallery Liverpool) 2002 and 2003, Before and After Science (Marella Arie Contemporanea Milan) 2003, Size Matters (Arts Cncl England touring exhbn) 2005, After the Thaw (AIB Art Collection Crawford Municipal Art Gallery Cork) 2005; *Work in Collections* incl: Unilever plc, Metropolitan Museum NY, Tate Gallery London, European Parl, Manchester City Art Gallery, Contemporary Art Soc, V&A, Machida City Museum of Graphic Art Tokyo, St Peter's Coll Oxford, de Young Memorial Museum San Francisco, Irish MOMA Dublin, St Louis Museum, Ulster Museum, Saatchi Collection London, Caldic Collection Amsterdam, NatWest Gp Art Collection London, Lambert Collection Zürich, Deutsche Bank, Br Cncl, Southampton City Art Gallery, Merrill Lynch Int Bank London, Merrill Lynch & Co Inc NY, Govt Art Collection, Goldman Sachs Int; *Style*— Mark Francis, Esq; ✉ 12 Grove Park, London SE5 8LR

FRANCIS, Mary Elizabeth; CBE (2005); da of Frederick Henry George (d 1978), and Barbara Henrietta, *née* Jeffs (d 1985); *b* 24 July 1948; *Educ* James Allen's Girls' Sch, Newnham Coll Cambridge (exhibitioner, MA); *m* 24 Nov 2001, Ian Ferguson Campbell Rodger, s of Dr David Rodger; *Career* res asst All Souls Coll Oxford 1970–73; Civil Service Dept and HM Treasy 1973–90, Corp Fin Dept Hill Samuel & Co Ltd 1984–86 (on secondment), asst then fin cnsllr Br Embassy Washington DC 1990–92, econ and domestic affrs private sec to PM 1992–95, dep private sec to HM The Queen 1995–99, DG Assoc of Br Insurers 1999–2005; non-exec dir: Bank of England until 2007, Centrica plc 2004–, Aviva plc 2005–, St Modwen Properties plc 2005–; dir International Financial Services London; govr Pensions Policy Inst; memb PCC; memb Bd Almeida Theatre; *Recreations* reading, swimming, walking, theatre; *Style*— Mrs Mary Francis, CBE

FRANCIS, Matthew (né Francis Edwin Matthews); s of Ronald Leslie Matthews, OBE, and Dorothy Olive Alice, *née* Mitchell; *b* 10 January 1953; *Educ* Harrow Co Sch for Boys, UC Oxford; *Career* assoc dir Chichester Festival Theatre 1983–87, fndr dir Cut & Thrust Theatre Co 1987–89, artistic dir Greenwich Theatre 1990–98; visiting dir Univ of South Florida; memb: Br Actors' Equity 1975, BAFTA, Nat Youth Theatre Assoc, London Library; FRSA; *Theatre* prodns for Greenwich incl: The Corn is Green (with Patricia Routledge), Cyrano de Bergerac (with Edward Petherbridge), The Government Inspector (with Timothy Spall), Caesar and Cleopatra (with Alec McCowen), The Adventures of Huckleberry Finn, Side By Side By Sondheim (with Dawn French); other credits incl: Rosencrantz and Guildenstern are Dead (RNT), Fidelio (NI Opera), A Midsummer Night's Dream (Albery Theatre), Arsenic and Old Lace (Strand Theatre); *Television* prodr: Office Gossip (BBC), Gimme, Gimme, Gimme (Tiger TV, nominated Best Comedy BAFTA 2002 and Golden Globe Montreux 2002), My Dad's the Prime Minister (BBC), New Tricks (Wall to Wall) 2005–06; *Publications* adaptations incl: The Prisoner of Zenda (1994), A Tale of Two Cities (1995), Northanger Abbey (1997), David Copperfield (1998); *Recreations* French Pyrenees, gardening, cooking, theatre, films; *Style*— Matthew Francis, Esq; ✉ c/o Maureen Vincent, PFD, Drury House, 34–43 Russell Street, London WC2B 5HA (tel 020 7344 1010)

FRANCIS, Nicholas; QC (2002); s of Peter Francis (d 1973), and Jean Griffiths, *née* Beatt; *b* 22 April 1958, Penarth; *Educ* Radley, Downing Coll Cambridge (MA), Inns of Court Sch of Law; *m* 9 Sept 2000, Penny Seguss; 1 da (Joanna b 2 April 1979), 2 s (Oscar b 24 Sept 2001, Fox b 27 March 2005); *Career* called to the Bar 1981; recorder 1999– (asst recorder 1998–99); memb: Family Law Bar Assoc 1990, Int Acad of Matrimonial Lawyers 2003; *Recreations* sailing; *Clubs* Royal London Yacht, Royal Solent Yacht; *Style*— Nicholas Francis, Esq, QC; ✉ 29 Bedford Row, London WC1R 4HE (tel 020 7404 1044, e-mail nfrancis@29bedfordrow.co.uk)

FRANCIS, Penelope Julia Louise; da of Vincent Robert Paul Palmer, of Pont Royal, France, and Cynthia Ann Palmer; *b* 9 November 1959; *Educ* St Anne's Coll Sanderstead, Univ of Bristol (LLB); *m* 8 June 1985, Barry Hugh Francis, s of Stanley Francis; *Career* asst slr Beachcroft Stanleys 1984–89 (articled clerk 1982–84); Lawrence Graham: asst slr 1989–91, ptnr 1991–94, equity ptnr 1994–, formerly head Property Litigation Dept, head Property Dept 1998–2002, managing ptnr 2002–; memb Bd Centrepoint 2001–; memb Law Soc 1984; *Recreations* Middle and Far East travel, ballet, eating; *Style*— Mrs Penelope Francis; ✉ tel 020 7379 0000, e-mail penny.francis@lg-legal.com

FRANCIS, Richard Mark; s of Ralph Lawrence Francis, of Oakham, Leics, and Eileen Nellie, *née* Jenkins (d 1993); *b* 20 November 1947; *Educ* Oakham Sch, Selwyn Coll Cambridge (BA), Courtauld Inst of Art (MA); *m* 7 Oct 1976, Tamar Janine Helen, da of Donald Beazley Burchill (d 1972); 1 da (Jasmine Helen b 1979); *Career* Walker Art Gallery Liverpool 1971–72, exhibition offr Arts Cncl of GB 1973–80, asst keeper of modern collection The Tate Gallery 1980–86, curator Tate Gallery Liverpool 1986–90, independent curator and assoc curator Tate Gallery 1990–92, chief curator Museum of Contemporary Art Chicago USA 1992–; *Books* Jasper Johns (1984); *Recreations* buying books; *Style*— Richard Francis; ✉ 237 East Ontario Street, Chicago, Illinois 60611, USA

FRANCIS, Richard Maurice; s of Hugh Elvet Francis, QC (d 1986), and Emma Frances Wienholt, *née* Bowen (d 2006); *b* 28 June 1946; *Educ* Mill Hill Sch London, Univ of Durham (BA); *m* 2 Oct 1993, Victoria Adzoa, da of Godslove C Acolatse (d 2004), of Accra, Ghana; 1 da; *Career* called to the Bar Gray's Inn 1974; in practice Wales & Chester Circuit 1976–, in practice as a mediator 1996–; treas Assoc Welsh Mediators; memb: Family Bar Assoc, Personal Injuries Bar Assoc, Family Mediators Assoc; sec Cardiff Adult Christian Educn Centre Tst 1993–; Golden Cross of the Polish Republic 1985; *Books* The British Withdrawal from the Baghdad Railway Project (1973), A History of Oakley Park Church (1976); *Recreations* family, squash, listening to BBC Radios 3 and 4; *Clubs* Cardiff Squash Racquets; *Style*— Richard Francis, Esq; ✉ 9 Park Place, Cardiff CF10 3DP (tel 029 2038 2731, fax 029 2022 2542, DX 50751 CARDIFF 2); The Mediation Practice Ltd, 9 Park Place, Cardiff CF10 3DP (tel 029 2070 0131, fax 029 2070 6828)

FRANCIS, Richard Stanley (Dick); CBE (2000, OBE 1984); s of George Vincent Francis (d 1960), and Catherine Mary, *née* Thomas (d 1967); *b* 31 October 1920; *Educ* Maidenhead Co Boys' Sch; *m* Mary Margaret, *née* Brenchley (d 2000); 2 s (Merrick Ewen Douglas b 1950, Felix Richard Roger b 1953); *Career* flying offr RAF 1940–45; steeplechase jockey 1946–57 (champion jockey 1953–54, first jockey retained by HM Queen Elizabeth The

F

Queen Mother under National Hunt rules 1953–57), racing corr Sunday Express 1957–73, author 1962– (39 novels, translated into 34 languages); memb: Crime Writers' Assoc of GB, Mystery Writers' Assoc of America; Hon LHD Tufts Univ Boston 1991; FRSL; *Books* The Sport of Queens (autobiography, 1957), Dead Cert (1962), Nerve (1964), For Kicks (Crime Writers' Assoc of GB Silver Dagger, 1965), Odds Against (1965), Flying Finish (1966), Blood Sport (1967), Forfeit (Mystery Writers' of America Award, 1969), Enquiry (1969), Rat Race (1970) Bonecrack (1971), Smoke-Screen (1972), Slay-Ride (1973), Knock Down (1974), High Stakes (1975), In the Frame (1976), Risk (1977), Trial Run (1978), Reflex (1980) Whip Hand (Crime Writers' Assoc Gold Dagger, Mystery Writers' of America Award, 1980), Twice Shy (1981), Banker (1982), The Danger (1983), Proof (1984), Break In (1985), Lester - The Official Biography (1986), Bolt (1986), Hot Money (1987), The Edge (1988), Straight (1989), Great Racing Stories (jt ed, 1989), Longshot (1990), Comeback (1991), Driving Force (1992), Decider (1993), Wild Horses (1994), Come to Grief (1995, Mystery Writers' of America Award), To the Hilt (1996), 10–lb Penalty (1997), Field of Thirteen (1998), Second Wind (1999), Shattered (2000), Under Orders (2006), Dead Heat (2007); *Recreations* boating, travel; *Clubs* Tower (Fort Lauderdale), Garrick; *Style—* Dick Francis, Esq, CBE; ✉ c/o Andrew Hewson, Johnson & Alcock (Authors' Agent) Ltd, Clerkenwell House, 45/47 Clerkenwell Green, London EC1R 0HT (tel 020 7251 0125, fax 020 7251 2172)

FRANCIS, Robert Anthony; QC (1992); s of John Grimwade Francis, and Jean Isobel, *née* Wilson; *b* 4 April 1950; *Educ* Uppingham, Univ of Exeter (LLB, pres Guild of Students 1971–72); *m* 1, 1976 (m dis 2005), Catherine, da of John Georgievsky; 2 da (Anna Elizabeth b 1979, Helen Alexandra b 1981), 1 s (Nicholas John b 1985); m 2, 2007, Alison Meek, *qv*; *Career* called to the Bar Inner Temple 1973 (bencher 2002); tenant 3 Serjeants Inn Chambers 1973– (jt head of chambers 2000–), asst recorder of the Crown Court 1996–2000, recorder of the Crown Court 2000–; chm Professional Negligence Bar Assoc 2004–05; *Publications* Medical Treatment Decision and the Law (co-author, 2001); *Recreations* cricket; *Style—* Robert Francis, Esq, QC; ✉ 3 Serjeants Inn, London EC4Y 1BQ (tel 020 7427 5000, fax 020 7353 0425, e-mail rfrancis@3serjeantsinn.com)

FRANCIS, Simon James; s of Mark William Francis, and Elisabeth Ann Francis; *Educ* Univ of Exeter (BSc, England students hockey and basketball); *m* 23 May 1998, Laura Jane; 2 da (Tabitha Ann b 22 Oct 1999, Poppy Isobel b 29 July 2002); *Career* media buying/planning Zenith Media 1990–94, gp media dir Leo Burnett 1994–98, managing ptnr and planning dir then futures dir MindShare 1998–2002, dir of strategic planning OMD Europe 2002–; accounts incl: BA, Kraft, Reckitt & Colman, Kellogg's, Procter & Gamble, IBM, Nike; IPA Advtg Effectiveness Award 1995; *Recreations* fly fishing, outdoor pursuits; *Style—* Simon Francis, Esq

FRANCOIS, Mark Gino; MP; s of Reginald Francois (d 1979), of Basildon, Essex, and Anna, *née* Carloni; *b* 14 August 1965; *Educ* Nicholas Comp Basildon, Univ of Bristol (BA), KCL (MA); *m* 30 June 2000 (m dis 2006), Karen, da of Tony Thomas, Sr; *Career* cncllr Basildon DC 1991–95 (vice-chm Housing 1992–95); MP (Cons) Rayleigh 2001– (Parly candidate (Cons) Brent E 1997); oppn jr whip 2002–04, shadow economic sec to the Treasy 2004–05, shadow paymaster gen 2005–, memb Environmental Audit Ctee House of Commons 2001–05; pres Palace of Westminster Lions Club 2006–; fell Huguenot Soc of GB and I 2001–; Freeman City of London 2004; *Recreations* travel, walking, reading, history (particularly military history); *Clubs* Carlton, Rayleigh Conservative; *Style—* Mark Francois, Esq, MP; ✉ House of Commons, London SW1A 0AA (tel 020 7219 3000)

FRANCOME, John; MBE (1986); s of Norman John Francome, and Lillian Maud Francome; *b* 13 December 1952; *Educ* Park Sr HS Swindon; *m* 1976, Miriam, da of Andrew Strigner, of London; *Career* champion jockey seven times, 1138 wins (nat hunt record); racehorse trainer, commentator and author; *Books* Born Lucky (autobiography, 1985), Eavesdropper (1986), Riding High (1987), Declared Dead (1988), Bloodstock (1989), Stud Poker (1990), Stone Cold (1991), Rough Ride (1992), Outsider (1993), Break Neck (1994), Dead Ringer (1995), False Start (1996), Inside Track (2002); with James MacGregor: Eavesdropper (1986), Riding High (1988), Declared Dead (1988), Blood Stock (1989); *Recreations* tennis, music; *Style—* John Francome, Esq, MBE; ✉ c/o Channel Four Racing, Channel Four Television Corporation, 124 Horseferry Road, London SW1P 2TX

FRANK, Sir (Robert) Andrew; 4 Bt (UK 1920), of Withyham, Co Sussex; s of Sir Robert John Frank, 3 Bt (d 1987), and his 2 w Margaret Joyce, *née* Truesdale (d 1995); *b* 16 May 1964; *Educ* Eton; *m* 23 June 1990, Zoë Alia, er da of S A Hasan, of Windsor, Berks, and Pauline, *née* Davidson; *Heir* none; *Career* retailer/prodr 1986–98, event mgmnt trg conslt 1998–; *Recreations* theatre, croquet, travel; *Style—* Sir Andrew Frank, Bt; ✉ 11 Old Orchard, Shoppenhangers Road, Maidenhead, Berkshire SL6 2GW

FRANK, Dr Andrew Oliver; s of Ernest Oliver Frank (d 1993), of Haywards Heath, W Sussex, and Doris Helen Frank (d 1985); *b* 4 September 1944; *Educ* Kingswood Sch Bath, Middx Hosp Med Sch (MB BS); *m* 23 June 1973, Cynthia Mary, da of James Siviter, of Lugwardine, Herefords; 1 s (Anthony b 1979), 2 da (Christina b 1982, Julia b 1986); *Career* lectr in med Univ of Malaya 1974–76, sr registrar in med rheumatology and rehabilitation Salisbury Health Dist 1977–80; Northwick Park Hosp and Inst of Med Res: conslt physician in rehabilitation med and rheumatology 1980–, clinical dir of orthopaedics, rheumatology and rehabilitation 1990–95; conslt in rehabilitation med Disablement Servs Centre Royal Nat Orthopaedic Hosp 1997–; prof (assoc) Sch of Health Studies and Social Care Brunel Univ 1997–; Med Disability Soc (now Br Soc of Rehab Med): fndr and hon sec 1984–87, regional co-ordinator 1995–97, chm Educn Ctee 1996–99, pres 2000–02, chm Vocational Rehabilitation Working Pty 1999–2000, chair Special Interest Gp in Vocational Rehabilitation 2004–; chm NW Thames Physical Disability Advsy Gp 1992–94, regnl advsr rehabilitation med 1996–2006, clinical chair NHS Modernisation Agency Wheelchair Collaborative 2002–04, medical dir Kynixa Ltd 2007–; memb: Disability Ctee RCP 1979–87, Soc of Research into Rehabilitation 1982 (memb Cncl 1995–97 and 2000–02), N Thames Regnl Trg Ctee 1996–, SAC Rehabilitation Med 1998–99, Rehabilitation Med Ctee 2000–02, Vocational Rehabilitation Lead 2002–, Posture and Mobility Gp 2002–, Int Assoc for the Study of Pain, RSM; tstee Vocational Rehabilitation Assoc 2005– (chair Events Ctee); Hon DSc Brunel Univ 2003; FRCP 1990 (MRCP), FHEA 2007; *Books* Disabling Diseases: Physical, Environmental and Psychosocial Management (with G P Maguire, 1989), Vocational Rehabilitation: The Way Forward (2000, 2 edn 2003), Low Back Pain: Diagnosis and Management (2001), Improving Services for Wheelchair Users and their Carers: Good Practice Guide; *Recreations* bridge, family, music, walking; *Style—* Dr Andrew Frank; ✉ The Arthritis Centre, Northwick Park Hospital, Watford Road, Harrow, Middlesex HA1 3UJ (tel 020 8869 2102, fax 020 8426 4358)

FRANK, David Thomas; s of Thomas Frank (d 1984), of Robertsford, Shrewsbury, and Margaret McCrea, *née* Cowan (d 2006); *b* 29 April 1954; *Educ* Shrewsbury, Univ of Bristol (LLB); *m* 10 July 1982, Diane Lillian, da of Stephen Nash Abbott, of Farnham Common, Bucks; 1 da (Lucinda b 1986), 1 s (Charles b 1988); *Career* admitted slr 1979; Slaughter and May: asst slr 1979–86, ptnr 1986–, head of Capital Markets 1993–2001, practice ptnr 2001–; *Recreations* lawn tennis, cars, shooting; *Style—* David Frank, Esq; ✉ Slaughter and May, One Bunhill Row, London EC1Y 8YY (tel 020 7600 1200, fax 020 7090 5000, e-mail david.frank@slaughterandmay.com)

FRANK, Joanna Helen Louise; da of Sir Douglas Frank, QC, and late Sheila, *née* Beauchamp; *Educ* Oxford HS GDST, Univ of Warwick (BA); *Career* with Pan Books 1987–90, commissioning ed Random House 1990–92, editorial dir of fiction Simon & Schuster UK Ltd 1992–97, dir and agent A P Watt Literary Agency 1997–; *Recreations* walking, reading, cinema, cooking; *Clubs* Soho House; *Style—* Ms Joanna Frank; ✉ A P Watt Ltd, 20 John Street, London WC1N 2DR (tel 020 7282 3109, fax 020 7282 3412)

FRANKLAND, (Frederick) Mark; s of Hon Roger Nathaniel Frankland (d 1989), and Elizabeth Cecil, *née* Sanday (d 1968); *b* 19 April 1934; *Educ* Charterhouse, Pembroke Coll Cambridge (BA), Brown Univ USA; *Career* FO 1958–59; dep ed Time & Tide 1960–61; The Observer: Moscow corr 1962–64, Indochina corr (also for The Economist) 1967–73, Tokyo corr 1973–75, Washington corr 1975–78, Moscow corr 1982–85, East Europe corr 1987–90; winner David Holden award (Br Press Awards) 1984 and 1986; memb Soc of Authors; *Books* Khrushchev (1966), The Mother-of-Pearl Men (1985), Richard Robertovich (1987), The Sixth Continent (1987), The Patriots' Revolution (1990), Freddie the Weaver (1995), Child of my Time (1999, J R Ackerley Prize 2000), Radio Man (2002); *Recreations* travel; *Style—* Mark Frankland, Esq

FRANKLAND, Dr (Anthony) Noble; CB (1983), CBE (1976), DFC (1944); s of Edward Percy Frankland (d 1958), of Westmorland, and Maud, *née* Metcalfe-Gibson (d 1979); *b* 4 July 1922; *Educ* Sedbergh, Trinity Coll Oxford (open scholar, MA, DPhil); *m* 1, 28 Feb 1944, Diana Madeline Forvargue (d 1981), da of George Victor Tavernor (k 1928); 1 s (Arnold Edward Roger b 1951), 1 da (Linda Helga Elizabeth (Mrs Michael O'Hanlon) b 1953); m 2, 7 May 1982, Sarah Katharine, da of His Hon the late Sir David Davies, QC, and late Lady Davies (the novelist Margaret Kennedy); *Career* RAF: joined 1941, navigator Bomber Cmd 1943–45, Flt Lt 1945; narrator Air Hist Branch Air Miny 1948–51, official mil historian Cabinet Office 1951–60; dep dir of studies RIIA 1956–60, dir Imperial War Museum 1960–82 (Duxford 1976–82, HMS Belfast 1978–82); Rockefeller fell 1953, Lees Knowles lectr Trinity Coll Cambridge 1963, hist advsr Thames TV Series The World at War 1971–74; vice-chm Br Nat Ctee of Int Ctee for the Study of WWII 1976–82; memb: Cncl Morley Coll 1962–66, HMS Belfast Tst 1971–78 (vice-chm 1972–78), HMS Belfast Bd 1978–82; *Books* Documents on International Affairs for 1955, 1956 and 1957 (ed, 3 vols 1958–60), Crown of Tragedy, Nicholas II (1960), The Strategic Air Offensive Against Germany 1939–45 (4 Volumes with Sir Charles Webster, 1961), The Bombing Offensive Against Germany, Outlines and Perspectives (1965), Bomber Offensive, The Devastation of Europe (1970), The Politics and Strategy of the Second World War (jt ed series, 1974–), Decisive Battles of the Twentieth Century, Land, Sea and Air (jt ed, 1976), Prince Henry, Duke of Gloucester (1980), The Encyclopedia of Twentieth Century Warfare (gen ed, 1989), Witness of a Century, Prince Arthur, Duke of Connaught (1993), History at War, The Campaigns of an Historian (1998), The Unseen War (novel, 2007); *Clubs* Royal Over-Seas League; *Style—* Dr Noble Frankland, CB, CBE, DFC; ✉ 26/27 River View Terrace, Abingdon OX14 5AE (tel 01235 521624)

FRANKLAND-PAYNE-GALLWEY, Sir Philip; 6 Bt (UK 1812); o s of Lt-Col Lowry Philip Payne-Gallwey, OBE, MC (d 1958, ggs of 1 Bt), and Janet, *née* Payne-Gallwey; suc kinsman, Sir Reginald Frankland-Payne-Gallwey, 5 Bt, 1964; assumed by Royal Licence 1966 the additional surname of Frankland before that of Payne and Gallwey; *b* 15 March 1935; *Educ* Eton; *Heir* none; *Career* late Lt 11 Hussars; dir British Bloodstock Agency Ltd (ret 1997); *Style—* Sir Philip Frankland-Payne-Gallwey, Bt; ✉ 160 Cranmer Court, Whiteheads Grove, London SW3 3HF (tel 020 7589 4231); The Little House, Boxford, Newbury, Berkshire RG20 8DP (tel 01488 608315, fax 01488 608512)

FRANKLIN, Daniel John (Dan); s of Michael Howard Franklin, of Manningtree, Essex, and Suzanne Mary, *née* Cooper (d 1992); *b* 2 May 1949; *Educ* Bradfield, UEA (BA); *m* 29 June 1985, Lucy, da of Michael Hughes-Hallett, of Barton-on-the-Heath, Glos; 2 da (Lettice, Mary (twins) b 1 March 1990); *Career* editorial dir William Heinemann 1987, publisher Secker & Warburg 1988, publishing dir Jonathan Cape 1993–; *Style—* Dan Franklin, Esq; ✉ Jonathan Cape, 20 Vauxhall Bridge Road, London SW1V 2SA (tel 020 7840 8400, fax 020 7233 6117)

FRANKLIN, Prof Ian Maxwell; s of Edwin William Franklin, of London, and Elizabeth Joyce, *née* Kessler; *b* 6 September 1949; *Educ* Owen's Boys Sch Islington, Univ of Leeds (BSc, MB ChB), UCH Med Sch (PhD); *m* 19 July 1975 (sep 2002), Anne Christine, da of Harry Norman Bush, of Leeds; 1 s (Matthew Charles Maxwell b 1988), 1 da (Sophie Rose b 1991); *Career* MRC res fell UCH Med Sch London 1977–80, sr registrar haematology UCH and Hosp for Sick Children Gt Ormond St London 1980–82, conslt haematologist Queen Elizabeth Hosp Birmingham 1982–92, dir of haematology Central Birmingham HA 1989–91, dir Bone Marrow Transplant Unit and conslt haematologist Royal Infirmary Glasgow 1992–96 (hon conslt 1996–); prof of transfusion med Univ of Glasgow 1996–; dir Glasgow and W of Scotland Blood Transfusion Centre 1996–97, nat med and sci dir Scottish Nat Blood Transfusion Serv 1997–; Br Soc for Haematology: scientific sec 1995–98, memb Ctee 2002–05; memb: American Soc of Hematology, Assoc of Physicians of GB & Ireland; FRCP 1990 (MRCP 1977), FRCPGlas 1994, FRCPEd 1996, FRCPath (memb Cncl 2002–05); *Recreations* aerobics, triathlon, cycling, music, unpublished writing; *Style—* Prof Ian Franklin; ✉ Department of Medicine, Royal Infirmary, 10 Alexandra Parade, Glasgow G31 2ER (tel 0141 211 1202, fax 0141 2110414, e-mail i.m.franklin@clinmed.gla.ac.uk)

FRANKLIN, John Richard; s of Richard Franklin (d 2007), and Jean, *née* Pearson; *Educ* Lockyer HS, Ipswich GS, Univ of Southern Qld (BA, Dip Teaching), Univ of New England (MEd Admin); *Career* teacher Qld Educn Dept 1976–79, housemaster, OC cadet unit and head of sr sch Toowoomba GS 1980–88, teacher Sedbergh Sch 1989, teacher Marlborough Coll 1989–92, dep headmaster St Peter's Coll Adelaide 1993–98, headmaster Ardingly Coll 1998–2007, head master Christ's Hosp 2007–; memb: HMC 1998, SHA 1998; *Recreations* golf, music, theatre, cooking, travel; *Clubs* Naval, Military and Airforce Club of S Aust, East India; *Style—* John Franklin, Esq; ✉ Christ's Hospital, Horsham, West Sussex RH13 7LS (tel 01403 211293, fax 01403 211580, e-mail hmsec@christs-hospital.org.uk)

FRANKLIN, Prof Raoul Norman; CBE (1995); s of Norman George Franklin, JP (d 1977), of Auckland, NZ, and Thelma Brinley, *née* Davis (d 1981); *b* 3 June 1935; *Educ* Howick DHS, Auckland GS, Univ of Auckland (BE, BSc, ME, MSc), Univ of Oxford (DPhil, MA, DSc); *m* 1, 29 July 1961, Faith (d 2004), da of Lt-Col Harold Thomason Carew Ivens (d 1951), of Beaconsfield, Bucks; 2 s (Robert b 1965, Nicholas b 1967); m 2, 16 July 2005, Christine Penfold; *Career* Capt NZ Def Scientific Corps 1957–63, sr res fell RMCS Shrivenham 1961–63, fell Keble Coll Oxford 1963–78 (hon fell 1980), lectr in engrg sci Univ of Oxford 1966–78, vice-chllr City Univ 1978–98; visiting prof Open Univ 1998–; chm: Gen Bd of Faculties Univ of Oxford 1971–74, CVCP Health and Safety Gp 1992–98, Assessment and Qualifications Alliance 1998–2003; dir City Technol Ltd 1978–93; memb: Hebdomadal Cncl 1971–74 and 1976–78, Cncl Gresham Coll 1981–98, Sci Bd SERC 1982–85, Governing Body Ashridge Mgmnt Coll 1986–99, London Pension Fund Authy 1989–95, Associated Examining Bd 1993–98 (chm 1994–98), Cncl City & Guilds 1996–2000, Sadler's Wells Appeal Ctee 1996–; Fndn Master Guild of Educators 2001; Liveryman Worshipful Co of Curriers (Master 2002–03); Hon DCL City Univ 1999, distinguished alumnus Univ of Auckland 2004; FREng 1990; Cdr Order of Merit (Poland) 1995; *Books* Plasma Phenomena in Gas Discharges (1976), Physical Kinetics (ed 1981), Interaction of Intense Electromagnetic Fields with Plasma (ed 1981); *Recreations* walking; *Clubs* Athenaeum; *Style—* Prof Raoul Franklin, CBE, FREng; ✉ 12 Moreton Road, Oxford OX2 7AX (tel 01865 558311); Open University Oxford Research Unit (fax 01865 326322, e-mail r.n.frankin@open.ac.uk)

FRANKLIN, Prof Robin James Milroy; s of Sir Michael Franklin, KCB, CMG, of Barnet, Herts, former perm sec Dept of Trade and MAFF, and Dorothy, *née* Fraser; *b* 25 August 1962, Barnet, Herts; *Educ* Haberdashers' Aske's, RVC Univ of London (BVetMed), UCL

(BSc), Univ of Cambridge (PhD); *m* 31 July 1999, Dr Barbara Skelly; 2 s (George b 2003, Toby b 2007); *Career* Dept of Vet Med Univ of Cambridge: Wellcome Tst res fell 1991–94, Wellcome Tst res career devpt fell 1994–99, Wellcome Tst proleptic lectr 1999–2000, sr lectr in experimental neurology 2000–02, reader in experimental neurology 2002–05, prof of neuroscience 2005–; fell Pembroke Coll Cambridge 1996–; Cavanagh Prize Br Neuropathological Soc 2004; author of over 160 articles in scientific jls; MRCVS 1988, FRCPath 2007 (MRCPath 2001); *Recreations* walking, reading, birdwatching, fly fishing; *Style*— Prof Robin Franklin; ✉ Department of Veterinary Medicine, University of Cambridge, Madingley Road, Cambridge CB3 0ES

FRANKLIN, Prof Simon Colin; s of Colin Franklin, of Culham, Oxon, and Charlotte, *née* Hajnal-Konyi; *b* 11 August 1953, London; *Educ* UC Sch, King's Coll Cambridge (BA), St Antony's Coll Oxford (DPhil); *m* 24 Dec 1975, Natasha, *née* Gokova; 1 s (Andrei b 21 Feb 1979), 1 da (Marina b 29 June 1981); *Career* research fell Clare Coll Cambridge 1980–83; Dept of Slavonic Studies Univ of Cambridge: lectr in Russian 1983–99, reader in Slavonic studies 1999–2003, prof of Russian studies 2003–04, prof of Slavonic studies 2004–; chm Pushkin House Tst 2005–; Alexander Nove Prize 2003, Essa Distinguished Scholarship Award 2006; *Books* The Emergence of Rus, c750–1200 (jtly, 1996), Writing, Society and Culture in Early Rus c950–1300 (2002), National Identity in Russian Culture (jtly, 2004); *Recreations* football, theatre, gardening; *Style*— Prof Simon Franklin; ✉ Clare College, Cambridge CB2 1TL (tel 01223 333263, e-mail scf1000@cam.ac.uk)

FRANKS, Michael John Alan; s of Jacob Franks, MD (d 1976), and Janet Lilian Green (d 1978); *b* 6 May 1928; *Educ* Epsom Coll, Merton Coll Oxford (MA), Gray's Inn; *m* 1, 1962 (m dis 1978), Anne, yr da of Sir David George Home, 13 Bt; 2 da (Lucinda b 1964, Miranda b 1966); m 2, 1980, Nicola Stewart, da of Col George Harcourt Stewart Balmain (d 1962); *Career* Sub-Lt RNVR 1951–53 (Nat Service); called to the Bar Gray's Inn 1953; in practice Chancery Bar 1953–59; Royal Dutch/Shell 1959–69; dir Beaverbrook Newspapers 1969–73; chm: Clyde Paper Co 1971–76, Schwarzkopf UK 1981–86; dep chm Goodhead Gp plc 1985–91; chm: Innsite Hotel Services 1987–90, Silicon Bridge 1989–96; dir: Select Appointments plc 1987–99 (chm 1991–92); strategic conslt South & West Investments; *Publications* Limitations of Actions (1959), The Clerk of Basingstoke - A Life of Walter de Merton (2003), The Basingstoke Admiral: A Life of Sir James Lancaster (2006); *Recreations* sailing, skiing, travel; *Clubs* Royal Thames Yacht; *Style*— Michael Franks, Esq; ✉ Field House, Mapledurwell, Basingstoke, Hampshire RG25 2LU (tel 01256 464861)

FRANKS, Prof Stephen; *b* 14 September 1947; *Educ* Woodhouse GS Finchley, UCL (MB BS 1970, MD 1978); *m* 31 Aug 1972, Victoria Elizabeth, *née* Nunn; 2 s (Benjamin Paul b 8 May 1975, Joshua Jeremy b 17 Nov 1980), 1 da (Sarah Anne b 21 Jan 1977); *Career* postdoctoral res fell in endocrinology McGill Univ Montreal Canada (MRC travelling res fell, JB Collip fell) 1977–79, lectr in med Univ of Birmingham 1979–82, prof of reproductive endocrinology Imperial Coll Sch of Med at St Mary's Hosp (St Mary's Hosp Med Sch until merger) 1988– (sr lectr 1982–88); visiting prof and Griff Ross Meml lectr Nat Inst of Health Bethesda MD USA Oct 1996, Carl Gemzell lectr Univ of Uppsala Sweden 1990, Van Campenhout lectr Canadian Fertility and Andrology Soc 2002, Feldberg Prize lectr Univ of Aachen 2002, Patrick Steptoe Meml medal lectr Br Fertility Soc Glasgow 2006; ed Clinical Endocrinology 1994–96; memb: Soc for Endocrinology (memb Ctee 1989–92, ed Newsletter 1992–, gen sec 1996–, chm 1999–), BMA; Medal lectr: Clinical Endocrinology Tst 1998, Soc for Endocrinology 1999; Hon MD Univ of Uppsala Sweden 1995; FRCP 1988 (MRCP 1972), FRCOG (ad eundem) 2000, FMedSci 2000; *Publications* author of original papers and articles in refereed jls; *Recreations* music, theatre, tennis; *Style*— Prof Stephen Franks; ✉ Institute of Reproductive and Developmental Biology, Imperial College London, Hammersmith Hospital, London W12 0NN (tel 020 7594 2109/2176, e-mail s.franks@imperial.ac.uk)

FRANKS, Stephen George; s of Geoffrey Raymond Franks (d 1988), and Jean Margaret, *née* Macaree; *b* 18 September 1955; *Educ* De-Burgh Sch Epsom; *m* Sarah, da of Tony Bagnall Smith; 3 s (Archie George b 4 Oct 1986, Henry James b 14 Sept 1989, Fergus William b 25 Feb 1992); *Career* designer Lock and Petersen 1979–82; sr designer: Tayburn London 1982–83, Landsdown Euro 1983–84; ptnr and design dir Coley Porter Bell 1984–95, in own co Franks and Franks 1995–; memb D&AD 1980; FRSA 1994; *Style*— Stephen Franks, Esq; ✉ Franks and Franks, Church Farm House, Upper Wolvercote, Oxford OX2 8AH (tel 01865 310893)

FRANSMAN, Laurens Francois (Laurie); QC (2000); s of Henri Albert Fransman, of Johannesburg, South Africa, and Stanmore, London, and Hannah Lena, *née* Bernstein; *b* 4 July 1956; *Educ* King David HS, Linksfield Johannesburg, Univ of Leeds (LLB); *m* 1, 7 Aug 1977 (m dis 1985), Claire Frances, da of Prof Colin Howard Ludlow Goodman (d 1990), of Mill Hill, London; 1 s (Piers b 1980); m 2, 9 July 1994, Helena Mary, da of Leonard George Cook (d 2001), of Caterham, Surrey; 1 s (Lindsey b 1997), 1 s (Elliot b 2000); *Career* barr, author; called to the Bar Middle Temple 1979, barr-at-law 2 Garden Ct Temple 1987–; UK contrib ed Immigration Law and Practice Reporter NY 1985, memb Editorial Bd Immigration and Nationality Law and Practice 1987–, memb Editorial Bd Immigration and International Employment Law 1999–2001; Halsbury's Laws of England (4 edn): conslt in nationality law 1991 issue, co-ordinating ed and princ contributor Br Nationality, Immigration and Asylum 2002 issue; fndr Immigration Law Practitioners' Assoc 1983 (chm, memb Exec Ctee); memb: Cncl of Europe/Commission Internationale de l'Etat Civil ad hoc Ctee of Experts on Citizenship 1992, Bar Euro Gp, Administrative Law Bar Assoc, Liberty, Lawyers for Liberty; *Books* British Nationality Law and the 1981 Act (1982), Tribunals Practice and Procedure (jtly, 1985), Immigration Emergency Procedures (jtly, 1986, 2 edn 1994), Fransman's British Nationality Law (1989, 2 edn 1998), The Constitution of the United Kingdom (contrib, 1991), Strangers and Citizens (contrib, 1994), Citizenship and Nationality Status in the New Europe (contrib, 1997), Immigration, Nationality and Asylum Under the Human Rights Act 1998 (jt ed and contrib, 1999), Immigration Law and Practice (contrib, 2001), Macdonald's Immigration Law & Practice (contrib, 5 edn 2001, 6 edn 2005), Max Planck Encyclopaedia of Public International Law (contrib, 2007); *Recreations* guitar playing, history, geology, food, music, theatre; *Style*— Laurie Fransman, Esq, QC; ✉ Garden Court Chambers, 57–60 Lincoln's Inn Fields, London WC2A 3LS (tel 020 7993 7600, fax 020 7993 7700)

FRANZEN, Peter; OBE (2005); s of late Cyril Franzen, of Gerrards Cross, Bucks, and Pat, *née* Woolham; *b* 7 May 1947; *m* Kathryn; 2 s (Oliver b 5 May 1981, Samuel b 11 March 1984); *Career* reporter Buckinghamshire Advertiser; trainee sub ed Eastern Counties Newspapers 1970; ed Eastern Daily Press 1993–; memb Guild of Motoring Writers; *Recreations* gardening, sailing, motoring; *Style*— Peter Franzen, Esq, OBE; ✉ Eastern Daily Press, Prospect House, Rouen Road, Norwich NR1 1RE (tel 01603 772400, fax 01603 623872)

FRASE, (Antony) Richard Grenville; s of Flt Lt Stanislaw Frase (d 1957), and Joy, *née* Thompson; *b* 8 July 1954; *Educ* Royal GS Newcastle upon Tyne, Repton, Trinity Coll Cambridge (MA); *m* 26 May 1990, Sarah-Louise, da of John Walker, and Margaret Walker, of Château de Thury, Burgundy; 1 s (James Grenville b 8 April 1992), 1 da (Amelia b 28 Feb 1995); *Career* 2 Lt TAVR 1976–78; admitted slr 1981, asst slr Allen & Overy 1981–83 (articled 1978–80), ptnr Denton Hall 1988–93 (asst slr 1983–87), counsel MeesPierson ICS Ltd 1993–95, head of litigation Personal Investment Authy 1995–98, ptnr Dechert 2005– (of counsel 1999–2004); course co-ordinator dip in financial services law London Met Univ 2004–; seconded to SFA 1989–91; memb: SFA Derivatives Ctee 1991–92, SFA Arbitration Panel 1992–2002, Arbitration Panel London Metal Exchange 1993–2005; ACIArb 1993; *Publications* The Euromoney Guide to World Equity Markets (contrib, 1991–2000), Futures Trading, Law and Regulation (contrib, 1993), Hedge Funds Law and Regulation (contrib, 2000), Exchanges Law and Regulation (ed and contrib, 2001), Practitioner's Guide to the FSA Regulation of Designated Investment Business (contrib, 2002, 2 edn 2004), Law and Regulation of Investment Management (2004); *Recreations* neoplatonism, art, France; *Clubs* Reform, MCC; *Style*— Richard Frase, Esq; ✉ Dechert, 2 Serjeants' Inn, London EC4Y 1LT (tel 020 7583 5353)

FRASER, Sir Alasdair MacLeod; kt (2001), CB (1992), QC (1989); s of Rev Dr Donald Fraser (d 1993), and Ellen Hart McAllister (d 1986); *b* 29 September 1946; *Educ* Sullivan Upper Sch, Trinity Coll Dublin (BA, LLB), Queen's Univ Belfast (Dip Laws); *m* 8 Aug 1975, Margaret Mary, da of Dr Brian Patrick Glancy; 2 s (Andrew Ian b 1979, James Michael b 1986), 1 da (Katy Margaret b 1983); *Career* called to the Bar NI 1970 (bencher 1999); Dept of Dir of Public Prosecutions NI: court prosecutor 1973, asst dir 1974, sr asst dir 1982, dep dir 1988, dir 1989–; *Style*— Sir Alasdair Fraser, CB, QC; ✉ Belfast Chambers, 93 Chichester Street, Belfast BT1 3JR

FRASER, Andrew John; CMG (2001); s of John A Fraser (d 1999); *b* 23 October 1950; *Educ* Denstone Coll, Harvard Sch LA (ESU scholar), Univ of Sussex (BA), UCLA; *m* 1, 1976 (m dis 1987), Julia; 2 da (Sarah Alice b 12 Dec 1977, Emily Clare b 11 Nov 1979); m 2, 1996, Jane; *Career* Young & Rubicam 1972–76, md Thailand McCann Erickson 1976–80, worldwide dir of devpt (London, Hong Kong, NY) and exec vice-pres Saatchi & Saatchi Advertising 1980–92, md cdp Europe (Dentsu) 1992–94, chief exec Invest UK UKTI 1994–2000; advsr: Mitsubishi Corp 2000–, FD Int 2003–; dir ThinkLondon 2001–; pres Worldaware 2001–06; memb: Devpt Cncl Shakespeare's Globe 2000–06 (memb Tst Bd 2006–), Cncl RIIA 2006–; dir UK-Japan 21st Century Gp 2000–04; *Recreations* theatre, sports, conversation, food and wine; *Clubs* MCC, Woking Golf, RAC, V and A Cricket (best batsman 2004, 2005 and 2006); *Style*— Andrew Fraser, Esq, CMG; ✉ e-mail ajfraser@hotmail.com

FRASER, Dr Andrew Kerr; s of Sir William Kerr Fraser, GCB, FRSE, *qv*, and Lady Marion Fraser, LT, *née* Forbes; *Educ* George Watson's Coll Edinburgh, Univ of Aberdeen, Univ of Glasgow; *m* 20 April 1985, Geraldine, da of Brendan Martin, of Dublin; 3 s (Alasdair b 29 Sept 1988, Colum b 17 Feb 1990, Moray b 20 Jan 1995), 1 da (Roseanne b 25 Feb 1992); *Career* med dir Nat Servs Div Common Servs Agency NHS in Scotland Edinburgh 1993–94, dir of public health/chief admin med offr Highland Health Bd Inverness 1994–97, dep chief med offr Scottish Exec 1997–2003; Scottish Prison Service: head of health 2003–06, dir of health and care 2006–; FRCPEd 1997, FFPHM 1999, FRCPGlas 2001; *Recreations* music, mountain walking; *Style*— Dr Andrew Fraser; ✉ Scottish Prison Service, Calton House, Redheughs Rigg, Edinburgh EH12 9HW (tel 0131 224 6998, e-mail andrew.fraser@sps.gov.uk)

FRASER, Angus Robert Charles; MBE (1999); s of Donald Fraser, and Irene, *née* Tonge; *b* 8 August 1965; *Educ* Gayton HS Harrow, Orange Hill Senior HS; *Career* professional cricketer; Middlesex CCC 1984–2002 (awarded county cap 1988); England: memb tour Australia and NZ 1990–91, memb team touring West Indies 1993/94, Australia 1994/95, South Africa 1995/96, West Indies 1998 (best bowling figures 8–53 in Port of Spain), memb winning team v South Africa 1998, memb squad Emirates Trophy 1998, memb team touring Australia 1998/99, 46 test matches, 42 one-day ints, best bowling 8–53; honours with Middlesex: County Championship 1985, 1990 and 1993, Nat West Trophy 1988, Benson & Hedges Cup 1986, Nixdorf Computers Middlesex Player of the Year 1988 and 1989, one of Wisdens 5 Cricketers of the Year 1996; currently cricket writer The Independent, summariser BBC Test Match Special; qualified cricket coach; *Recreations* wine, golf, watching Liverpool FC and rugby internationals, anything in sport but racing; *Style*— Angus Fraser, Esq, MBE

FRASER, Air Cdre Anthony Walkinshaw; s of Robert Walkinshaw Fraser (d 1956), and Evelyn Elisabeth, *née* Watts (d 1955); *b* 15 March 1934; *Educ* Stowe; *m* 1 (m dis), Angela Mary Graham, da of George Richard Shaw (d 1983), of Darlington, Co Durham; 1 s (Robert), 3 da (Amanda (Hon Mrs Timothy Buxton), Antonia, Alexandra); m 2, Grania Eleanor Ruth, da of Ean Stewart-Smith, MBE, of Stanley Hall, Halstead, Essex; *Career* RAF Pilot, Instr and Staff Offr, Air Cdre 1977, Cmdt Central Flying Sch, ret 1979; ADC to HM The Queen 1977–79; dir: Society of Motor Manufacturers & Traders Ltd 1980–88, Goddard Kay Rogers (Northern) Ltd 1988–89, Nissan UK Ltd 1989–91, Enhanced Office Environments Ltd 2001–; chm and ceo: Personal Guard Sarl 1992–94, IntaNet Commercial Services Ltd 1993–95, Chlorella Products Ltd 1995–; chm: Addavita Ltd 1997–2004, Tecno Au (UK) Ltd 1998–; pres Organisation Internationale des Constructeurs d'Automobiles 1983–87; Liveryman Worshipful Co of Coachmakers & Coach Harness Makers; MIL; *Recreations* golf, shooting, fishing, languages; *Clubs* RAF, Sunningdale; *Style*— Air Cdre Anthony Fraser; ✉ 31 Grove End Road, London NW8 9LY; Chlorella Products Ltd (tel 01793 741122)

FRASER, Lady Antonia; *née* Pakenham; CBE (1999); da of 7 Earl of Longford, KG, PC (d 2001), and Elizabeth, Countess of Longford, CBE (d 2002); *b* 27 August 1932; *Educ* St Mary's Convent Ascot, LMH Oxford; *m* 1, 25 Sept 1956 (m dis 1977), Rt Hon Sir Hugh Fraser, MBE, PC, MP (d 1984), s of 16 Lord Lovat; 3 da (Rebecca (Mrs Edward Fitzgerald) b 1957, Flora Fraser, *qv*, (m Peter Soros) b 1958, Natasha (Mrs Jean Pierre Cavassoni) b 1963), 3 s (Benjamin b 1961, Damian b 1964, Orlando b 1967); m 2, 27 Nov 1980, Harold Pinter, CH, CBE, , *qv*; *Career* writer; chm: Soc of Authors 1974–75, Crimewriters' Assoc 1985–86; co-tstee Authors' Fndn 1984–; pres English PEN 1988–89; Norton Medlicott Medal Historical Assoc 2000; FRSL 2003; *Books* incl: Mary Queen of Scots (James Tait Black Memorial Prize 1969), Cromwell our chief of Men (1973), James I & VI of England and Scotland (1974), Kings and Queens of England (ed, 1975), King Charles II (1979), The Weaker Vessel (Wolfson History Award 1984), Boadicea's Chariot: The Warrior Queens (1988), Quiet as a Nun (1977), Cool Repentance (1980), The Wild Island (1978), Oxford Blood (1985), Your Royal Hostage (1987), A Splash of Red (1981, basis TV series Jemima Shore 1983), Jemima Shore's First Case (1986), The Cavalier Case (1990), Jemima Shore at the Sunny Grave (1991), The Six Wives of Henry VIII (1992), The Pleasure of Reading (ed, 1992), The Gunpowder Plot (1996, CWA Non-Fiction Dagger 1996, published in US as Faith and Treason: the story of the Gunpowder Plot, St Louis Literary Award 1996), Marie Antoinette: the journey (2001, Franco-British Soc Literary Award 2002); *Recreations* gardening (watched by cats), grandchildren; *Style*— The Lady Antonia Fraser, CBE; ✉ c/o Curtis Brown Group Ltd, 28–29 Haymarket, London SW1Y 4SP (tel 020 7396 6600, fax 020 7396 0110)

FRASER, Christopher James; MP; *Career* MP (Cons): Mid Dorset and N Poole 1997–2001, Norfolk SW 2005–; PPS to Rt Hon the Lord Strathclyde, PC (Ldr of the Oppn House of Lords) 1999–2001, memb Culture, Media & Sport Select Ctee 1997–2001, memb NI Select Ctee 2005–, vice-chm All Pty Forestry Gp 1997–2001, sec Cons Backbench Culture, Media & Sport Ctee 1997–2001, memb Parly Information Technology Ctee 1997–2001, chm Parly All-Pty Mgmnt Consultancy Gp 2000–01; memb: Inter-Parly Union 1997–, Cwlth Parly Assoc 1997–, Cncl of Europe 2005–07, Assembly WEU 2005–07; dir: Small Business Bureau until 2006, Firm Link Dorset; Freeman City of London 1992; *Style*— Christopher Fraser, Esq, MP

FRASER, Gen Sir David William; GCB (1980, KCB 1973), OBE (1962), DL (Hants 1982); er s of Brig Hon William Fraser, DSO, MC (d 1964, yst s of 18 Lord Saltoun), and Pamela Cynthia, *née* Maude (d 1975); *b* 30 December 1920; *Educ* Eton, ChCh Oxford; *m* 1, 26 Sept 1947 (m dis 1952), Anne, yr da of Brig Edward William Sturgis Balfour, CVO, DSO, OBE, MC; 1 da (Antonia Isabella (Mrs Timothy Hanbury) b 1949); m 2, 11 Oct 1957,

F

Julia Frances, yr da of Maj Cyril James Oldridge de la Hey; 2 da (Arabella (Mrs Gordon Birdwood) b 1958, Lucy (Hon Mrs Alexander Baring) b 1965), 2 s (Alexander James b 1960, Simon b 1963); *Career* WWII cmmnd Grenadier Gds 1941; served: UK and NW Europe 1939–45, Malaya 1948, Egypt 1952–54, Cyprus 1958, British Cameroons 1961, Borneo 1965; GOC 4 Div 1969–71, ACDS (Policy) MOD 1971–73, vice CGS 1973–75, Br mil rep to NATO Brussels 1975–77, Cmdt RCDS 1977–80, ADC Gen to HM The Queen 1977–80, Col The Royal Hampshire Regt 1981–87; pres Soc for Army Historical Res 1980–93; chm Treloar Tst and Governing Body Lord Mayor Treloar Coll 1982–93; Hon DLitt Univ of Reading; *Books* Alanbrooke (1982), And We Shall Shock Them (1983), The Christian Watt Papers (1983), August 1988 (1983), A Kiss for the Enemy (1985), The Killing Times (1986), The Dragon's Teeth (1987), The Seizure (1988), A Candle for Judas (1989), In Good Company (1990), Adam Hardrow (1990), Codename Mercury (1991), Adam in the Breach (1993), Knights Cross (1993), The Pain of Winning (1993), Will - a Portrait of William Douglas Home (1995), Frederick the Great (2000), Wars and Shadows (2002); *Clubs* Turf, Pratt's; *Style*— Gen Sir David Fraser, GCB, OBE, DL; ✉ Vallenders, Isington, Alton, Hampshire GU34 4PP (tel 01420 23166)

FRASER, Prof Derek; s of Jacob Fraser, of Birmingham, and Dorothy, *née* Hayes; *b* 24 July 1940; *Educ* King Edward's Camp Hill Sch Birmingham, Univ of Leeds (BA, MA, PhD); *m* 1962, Ruth, *née* Spector; 2 s (Philip Neal b 1963, Adam Jason b 1970), 1 da (Clio Lynn b 1965); *Career* sch teacher Birmingham 1962–65; sr lectr, reader then prof of modern history Univ of Bradford 1965–83, prof of English history UCLA 1982–84, HM's Inspector of Schs history and higher educn 1984–88, staff inspector for higher educn DES 1988–90; Sheffield City Poly: asst princ (on secondment), dep princ 1991–92; vice-chllr Univ of Teesside 1992–2003; Andrew W Mellon distinguished visiting prof Franklin and Marshall Coll Penn 1979; chm: Ind Football Cmmn 2001–, Standards Verification UK 2005–; memb Bd NE RDA 1998–2001; visiting prof: Univ of Vermont 1980, Stanford Univ 1981; FRHistS 1980; *Books* Urban Politics in Victorian England - The Structure of Politics in Victorian Cities (1976), Power and Authority in the Victorian City (1979), The Evolution of the British Welfare State (1984, 4 edn 2008), The Welfare State (2000); *Recreations* music, bridge, film, squash, watching football; *Style*— Prof Derek Fraser; ✉ The Independent Football Commission, Victoria Court, 82 Norton Road, Stockton-on-Tees TS18 2DE (tel 0870 060 1610, fax 0870 060 1611, e-mail derek.fraser@tees.ac.uk)

FRASER, Prof Donald Gordon; s of Dr Gordon Fraser (d 2001), and Kathleen, *née* Benson; *b* 30 October 1949, Edinburgh; *Educ* Univ of Edinburgh (BSc), Univ of Oxford (MA, DPhil); *m* 27 June 1970, Anna, *née* Fojtiková; 1 s (Andrew Gordon b 7 Dec 1971), 1 da (Elizabeth Anna b 4 Oct 1974); *Career* geologist; jr research fell Merton Coll Oxford 1974–76, asst prof in mineralogy Columbia Univ NY 1976; Univ of Oxford: lectr in geochemistry 1976–96, prof of earth sciences 1996–, chm Sub-Faculty of Earth Scis 1985–88 and 1999–2001, chm Fraser Ctee on the future structure of sci in Oxford 1988–90, chm Bd Faculty of Physical Sciences 1994–96 (vice-chm 1992–94), memb Univ Cncl 2006–, sr proctor 2008–09; governing body fell Wolfson Coll Oxford 1977–78, currently tutorial fell in geology Worcester Coll Oxford; sr visiting scientist Max-Planck Inst für Chemie Mainz 1980–81, sr research assoc CNRS Nice 1984–85, JSPS fell Inst for the Study of the Earth's Interior Misasa 1997–98, visiting assoc Div of Geological and Planetary Scis Calif Inst of Technol 1998, visiting assoc Beckman Inst Calif Inst of Technol 1998–99, Centre of Excellence research fell Inst for the Study of the Earth's Interior Misasa 2001–02; advsy ed Physics of the Earth and Planetary Interiors 1992–99; chm and md Statistical Sciences (UK) Ltd, dir Prolysis Ltd 2001–03; conslt: Shell, Chevron, Deminex Ltd, Greig Fester Ltd, Clyde Petroleum Ltd, Phillips Petroleum (Norway) Ltd; dir NATO Advanced Study Inst Thermodynamics in Geology 1976; sec European Assoc for Geochemistry 1987–89; memb: NERC ctees incl Research Grants Ctee 1986–89, Int Advsy Panel Centre of Excellence Prog Inst for the Study of the Earth's Interior Misasa 2003–, CODATA Task Gp on Geothermodynamic Data Int Cncl of Scientific Unions; UK rep Working Gp on Thermodynamics of Natural Processes Int Assoc for Geochemistry and Cosmochemistry; *Books* Elementary Thermodynamics for Geologists (with B J Wood, 1976), Thermodynamics in Geology (1977); *Recreations* skiing, climbing and trekking, golf, music; *Style*— Prof Donald Fraser; ✉ Department of Earth Sciences, University of Oxford, Parks Road, Oxford OX1 3PR

FRASER, Donald Hamilton; s of Donald Fraser (d 1964), and Dorothy Christiana, *née* Lang (d 1973); *b* 30 July 1929; *Educ* Maidenhead GS, St Martin's Sch of Art, Paris (French Govt scholarship); *m* 6 July 1954, Judith, da of Francis William Wentworth-Sheilds (d 1969); 1 da (Catherine Jane b 1955); *Career* artist; over 60 one-man exhibitions in Britain, Europe, Japan and North America; work in public collections includes: Boston Museum of Fine Arts, Albright-Knox Gallery Buffalo, Carnegie Inst Pittsburgh, Yale Univ Art Gallery, City Art Museum St Louis, Wadsworth Atheneum Hartford, Desert Art Museum Palm Springs, Smithsonian Inst Washington DC, Nat Gallery Canada, Nat Gallery Victoria Melbourne, many corp collections and Br galleries, Arts Cncl, Govt Art collection; designed Cwlth issue postage stamps 1983; tutor RCA 1958–83; vice-pres: Artists' Gen Benevolent Inst 1981– (chm 1981–86), Royal Over-Seas League 1986–; cmmr Royal Fine Art Cmmn 1986–99; hon fell RCA, hon curator RA 1992–99; tstee RA 1993–99; RA 1985 (ARA 1975); *Books* Gauguin's Vision after the Sermon (1969), Dancers (1989); *Clubs* Leander; *Style*— Donald Hamilton Fraser, Esq, RA; ✉ c/o Royal Academy of Arts, Burlington House, Piccadilly, London W1V 0DS

FRASER, Flora; da of Rt Hon Sir Hugh Fraser, MBE, PC, MP (d 1984), and The Lady Antonia Fraser, *qv*; *b* 30 October 1958; *Educ* St Paul's Girls' Sch, Wadham Coll Oxford; *m* 1, 1980 (m dis 1992), Robert Powell-Jones (d 1998); 1 da (Stella Powell-Jones b 15 May 1987); m 2, 1997, Peter Soros; 2 s (Simon Tivadar Soros b 10 March 1998, Thomas Hugh Soros b 3 May 1999); *Career* writer 1981–; tstee Nat Portrait Gallery 1999–; co-fndr: Elizabeth Longford Prize for Historical Biography 2003, Elizabeth Longford Awards for Historical Biographers 2003; *Books* Double Portrait (1983), Maud: The Diaries of Maud Berkeley (1985), Beloved Emma: The Life of Emma, Lady Hamilton (1986), The English Gentlewoman (1987), Tamgar (1990), The Unruly Queen: The Life of Queen Caroline (1996), Princesses: The Six Daughters of George III (2004); *Recreations* writing and swimming in Nantucket; *Style*— Miss Flora Fraser; ✉ c/o Georgina Capel, Capel & Land, 29 Wardour Street, London W1D 6PS (tel 020 7734 2414)

FRASER, George MacDonald; OBE (1999); s of William Fraser, of Carlisle, and Anne Struth, *née* Donaldson; *b* 2 April 1925; *Educ* Carlisle GS, Glasgow Acad; *m* 1949, Kathleen Margarette, da of George Hetherington, of Carlisle; 2 s (Simon, Nicholas), 1 da (Caroline); *Career* served Br Army 1943–47, infantryman Border Regt Burma, Lt Gordon Highlanders; journalist 1947–69, dep ed Glasgow Herald; author; FRSL; *Film Screenplays* incl: The Three Musketeers (1973), The Four Musketeers (1974), Royal Flash (1975), The Prince and the Pauper (1977), Octopussy (1983), Casanova (1987), The Return of the Musketeers (1989); *Books* the Flashman novels and various other books; *Recreations* writing, history, talking to wife; *Style*— George Fraser, Esq, OBE

FRASER, Helen Jean Sutherland; da of George Sutherland Fraser (d 1980), and Eileen Lucy, *née* Andrew; *b* 8 June 1949; *Educ* Collegiate Girls' Sch Leicester, St Anne's Coll Oxford (MA); *m* 16 April 1982, Grant James McIntyre, s of Athol McIntyre, of Cornwall; 2 da (Blanche b 1980, Marina b 1983); *Career* editorial dir William Collins 1977–87, publisher William Heinemann 1987–91, publisher Heinemann/Mandarin 1991–92, md Reed Trade Books 1996–97 (publishing dir 1992–96), md Gen Div Penguin Books (i/c Viking, Hamish Hamilton, and Michael Joseph imprints) 1997–2001, md Penguin UK 2001–; *Style*— Ms Helen Fraser; ✉ Penguin Books Ltd, 80 Strand, London WC2R 0RL (tel 020 7010 3240)

FRASER, Sir Iain Michael; 3 Bt (UK 1943), of Tain, Co Ross; s of Maj Sir James David Fraser, 2 Bt (d 1997), and (Edith) Maureen, *née* Reay; *b* 27 June 1951; *Educ* Trinity Coll Glenalmond, Univ of Edinburgh (BSc); *m* 1982 (m dis 1991), Sherylle Ann, da of Keith Gillespie, of Wellington, NZ; 1 da (Joanna Karen b 1983), 1 s (Benjamin James b 1986); *Heir* s, Benjamin Fraser; *Career* restaurant owner; *Style*— Sir Iain Fraser, Bt

FRASER, (Alexander) James (Jamie); s of Gen Sir David Fraser, GCB, OBE, DL, of Hants, and Julia, *née* De la Hey; *b* 30 June 1960, Cirencester, Glos; *Educ* Eton, RMA Sandhurst; *m* 12 April 1997, Stephanie, *née* Struthers; 3 da (Iona b 12 March 1999, Mary b 26 Sept 2000, Alice b 6 Feb 2004); *Career* cmmned Grenadier Gds 1980–89, David S Smith (Holdings) plc 1989–2001 (investor rels mangr 1992–97), dir Hamilton & Inches Ltd 2001– (md 2003–); memb Royal Co of Archers; pres Edinburgh Royal Warrant Holders; piping steward Argyllshire Gathering; MInstD; *Recreations* piping, golf, shooting; *Clubs* Pratts; *Style*— Jamie Fraser, Esq; ✉ Highwood, Craigmaddie, Milngavie, Glasgow G62 8LB (tel 0141 956 7866, e-mail ajamesfraser@aol.com)

FRASER, John Arthur; *b* 8 August 1951, Melbourne, Aust; *Educ* Monash Univ Aust (BEcon); *Career* min (economic) Aust Embassy Washington DC USA 1985–88, dep sec (economic) Aust Treasy 1990–93, dir Aust Stock Exchange 1997–2003, chm and ceo UBS Global Asset Mgmnt 2001–, memb Gp Exec Bd UBS 2002–; *Recreations* sailing, rugby; *Clubs* Oriental, Walbrook, Australian (Sydney); *Style*— John A Fraser, Esq; ✉ UBS Global Asset Management, 21 Lombard Street, London EC3V 9AH (tel 020 7901 6200)

FRASER, Murdo; MSP; *b* 1965; *Educ* Inverness Royal Acad, Univ of Aberdeen (LLB, Dip); *m* 1994, Emma Jarvis; *Career* assoc Ketchen and Stevens WS until 2001, MSP (Cons) Mid-Scotland and Fife Aug 2001– (replacement list memb); Scottish Parl: former dep spokesman on educn, Scottish Cons spokesman for enterprise and lifelong learning 2003–, dep ldr Scottish Cons 2005–, co-convenor Cross-Pty Gp on the Scottish Economy; chm Scottish Young Conservatives 1989–92, chm Young Conservatives 1991, sometime dep chm Edinburgh Central Cons Assoc, Parly candidate (Cons) E Lothian 1997 (UK Parl) and N Tayside 1999, 2003 and 2007 (Scot Parl) and 2001 (UK Parl), memb The Tuesday Club (Scottish Conservatives think tank), chm Scottish Conservatives and Churches Forum 2002–; *Publications* Defending our British Heritage (1993), Full Fiscal Freedom (1998), Scotland and the Euro (1999), The Blue Book (2006); *Recreations* hill walking, cycling, classic cars, travel, Scottish history, Rangers FC; *Style*— Murdo Fraser, Esq, MSP; ✉ The Scottish Parliament, Edinburgh EH99 1SP (tel 0131 348 5293, fax 0131 348 5934, e-mail murdo.fraser.msp@scottish.parliament.uk)

FRASER, Prof Robert W; *Educ* Univ of Adelaide (BEc), Univ of Oxford (MPhil, DPhil); *Career* prof and head Applied Economics and Business Mgmnt Section Kent Business Sch Univ of Kent; memb Editorial Bd: Jl of Agricultural Economics, Australian Jl of Agricultural and Resource Economics; *Style*— Prof Robert Fraser; ✉ Kent Business School, University of Kent, Wye Campus, Ashford, Kent TN25 5AH

FRASER, Prof Ronald Strathearn Smith (Ron); s of Allan Fraser (d 1965), and Elizabeth, *née* Smith; *b* 10 July 1944; *Educ* Univ of Edinburgh (BSc, PhD, DSc); *m* 11 April 1987, Hilary Margaret, *née* Haigh; 2 da (Rosalind Jane Strathearn b 4 Feb 1989, Eleanor Mary Haigh b 28 Aug 1990); *Career* res scientist Max-Planck Inst für Biologie Tübingen 1968–70, res fell Medical Res Cncl Dept of Zoology Univ of Edinburgh 1970–77, princ scientific offr and head Biochemistry Section Nat Vegetable Res Station Wellesbourne 1977–87; Inst of Horticultural Research: head Plant Science Div 1987–90, head of Station Inst of Horticultural Research Littlehampton 1987–96, dir of res in crop protection 1990–96; exec sec Society for General Microbiology 1996–; hon lectr: Sch of Pure and Applied Biology Univ of Wales 1980–94, Dept of Microbiology Univ of Birmingham 1981–95; hon prof Sch of Biological Scis Univ of Birmingham 1995–98; hon visiting prof Sch of Biological Sciences Univ of Manchester 2000–03; memb Soc for Gen Microbiology; FIHort 1989; *Books* Mechanisms Of Resistance To Plant Diseases (1985, 2 edn 2000), The Biochemistry Of Virus-Infected Plants (1987), Recognition and Response In Plant Virus Interactions (1990); *Recreations* hill walking, music; *Style*— Prof Ron Fraser; ✉ Society for General Microbiology, Marlborough House, Basingstoke Road, Spencers Wood, Reading, Berkshire RG7 1AG (tel 0118 988 1812, fax 0118 988 5656, e-mail r.fraser@sgm.ac.uk)

FRASER, Sheriff Simon William Hetherington; s of George MacDonald Fraser, of Baldrine, IOM, and Kathleen Margarette, *née* Hetherington; *b* 2 April 1951; *Educ* Glasgow Acad, Univ of Glasgow (LLB); *m* 7 Sept 1979, Sheena Janet, *née* Fraser; 1 da (Julie Katyana b 10 Dec 1981); *Career* apprentice slr Kerr Barrie & Duncan Slrs Glasgow 1971–73, asst slr McGrigor Donald Slrs Glasgow 1973–75, ptnr Flowers & Co Slrs Glasgow 1976–89 (asst slr 1975–76), temp sheriff 1987–89, sheriff of N Strathclyde at Dumbarton 1989–; pres Glasgow Bar Assoc 1981–82; *Recreations* watching Partick Thistle, cricket; *Clubs* Avizandum; *Style*— Sheriff Simon Fraser; ✉ Sheriff's Chambers, Sheriff Court, Church Street, Dumbarton G82 1QR (tel 01389 763266)

FRASER, Susan (Sue); *b* 15 July 1966; *Educ* Peterhead Acad, Northern Coll of Educn; *Career* int hockey player; former memb Glasgow Western Ladies Hockey Club, currently memb Bonagrass Grove Ladies Hockey Club; 162 Scottish caps, 78 GB caps 1991–; top Scottish scorer (6 goals) at Euro Championships 1991, memb GB squad Olympic Games: Barcelona 1992 (Bronze medal), Atlanta 1996 (fourth place); competed Commonwealth Games Malaysia 1998, capt Scottish squad European Cup 1999; primary sch teacher; *Recreations* golf, squash, films, music, walking, cooking, eating good food; *Style*— Miss Sue Fraser

FRASER, Prof William Duncan (Bill); s of Brian Wadsworth Fraser, of Formby, Lancs, and Susan Cochrane Fraser (d 2003); *b* 16 May 1955, Glasgow; *Educ* Allan Glen's Sch Glasgow, Univ of Glasgow (BSc, MB ChB, MD); *m* 3 Aug 1989, Aileen Agnes; 2 da (Helen Jean b 19 July 1983, Karen Susan b 5 March 1987), 1 s (Brian James b 5 July 1990); *Career* house offr Southern Gen Hosp Glasgow 1982–83, sr registrar Royal Infirmary Glasgow 1986–91 (registrar 1983–86), conslt (locum) Regina Gen Hosp Saskatchewan 1990; Royal Liverpool Univ Hosp: sr lectr 1991–98, reader and hon conslt 1998–2000, prof and hon conslt 2000–, head Metabolic Bone Disease Unit; chm: Scientific Prog Ctee Assoc of Clinical Biochemists Focus 1999, Scientific Ctee Assoc of Clinical Biochemists 1999–2003; med advsr Nat Osteoporosis Soc; ed: Jl of Endocrinology, Calcified Tissues International; author of more than 150 peer-reviewed scientific papers on bone and calcium metabolism 1986–; ACB Fndn Award 2006; FRCPath 1997 (MRCPath 1989), MRCP 1999; *Recreations* golf, guitar, violin; *Style*— Prof Bill Fraser; ✉ University Department of Clinical Chemistry, Duncan Building, Royal Liverpool University Hospital, Prescot Street, Liverpool L69 3GA (tel 0151 706 4247, fax 0151 706 5813, e-mail w.d.fraser@liv.ac.uk)

FRASER, Prof William Irvine; CBE (1998); s of Duncan Fraser (d 1979), and Muriel, *née* Macrae (d 1977); *b* 3 February 1940; *Educ* Greenock Acad, Univ of Glasgow (MB ChB, MD, DPM); *m* 1 Oct 1964, Joyce Carroll, da of Douglas Gilchrist (d 1978); 2 s (Ewen Duncan b 31 May 1966, Alan Douglas b 1 Sept 1968); *Career* physician supt and dir Fife Mental Handicap Servs 1974–78, hon sr lectr in psychology Univ of St Andrews 1973–89, pt/t sr lectr Univ of Edinburgh 1974–89, conslt psychiatrist Royal Edinburgh Hosp 1978–79, ed Journal of Intellectual Disability Research 1982–, currently prof emeritus of learning disability Univ of Wales Coll of Med; Burden Neurological Inst Prize medallist for research into mental handicap 1989, Int Assoc for Sci Study of Intellectual Disabilities Distinguished Achievement Award for Scientific Literature 1996; memb Gen

Projects Ctee Mental Health Fndn 1981–87, co-dir Welsh Centre for Learning Disability 1994–2002; pres Welsh Psychiatric Soc 2006–; FRCPsych 1978 (former chm Welsh Div), FRCPEd 2000, FMedSci 2001; *Books* Communicating with Normal and Retarded Children (with R Grieve, 1981), Caring for People with Learning Disabilities (1997), Seminars in Learning Disability (with M Kerr, 2003); *Style*— Prof William Fraser, CBE; ✉ 146 Wenallt Road, Rhiwbina, Cardiff CF4 6TQ (tel 029 2052 1343, e-mail fraser_bill@yahoo.com)

FRASER, Sir William Kerr; GCB (1984, KCB 1979, CB 1978); s of late Alexander Macmillan Fraser, and Rachel, *née* Kerr; *b* 18 March 1929; *Educ* Eastwood Sch, Univ of Glasgow (MA, LLB); *m* 1956, Marion Anne, *née* Forbes, (Lady Marion Fraser, LT); 3 s (1 of whom Dr Andrew Fraser, *qv*), 1 da; *Career* joined Scot Home Dept 1955, perm under sec of state Scot Office 1978–88 (dep sec 1975–78); princ and vice-chllr Univ of Glasgow 1988–95, chm Royal Cmmn on the Ancient and Historical Monuments of Scotland 1995–2000; chllr Univ of Glasgow 1996–2006; Hon LLD Univs of Aberdeen, Glasgow and Strathclyde; Hon Dr Univ of Edinburgh; Hon FRCP (Glasgow), FRSE 1985, Hon FRSAMD 1995; *Clubs* New (Edinburgh); *Style*— Sir William Fraser, GCB, FRSE; ✉ Broadwood, Edinburgh Road, Gifford, East Lothian EH41 4JE (tel and fax 01620 810319)

FRASER OF CARMYLLIE, Baron (Life Peer UK 1989), of Carmyllie in the District of Angus; Peter Lovat Fraser; PC (1989), QC (Scot 1982); s of Rev George Robson Fraser, of Corrennie, Edinburgh, and Helen Jean, *née* Meiklejohn; *b* 29 May 1945; *Educ* Loretto, Gonville & Caius Coll Cambridge, Univ of Edinburgh; *m* 1969, Fiona Macdonald, da of Hugh Murray Mair, of Lanark; 2 da (Hon Jane Helen Anne b 1972, Hon Catriona Elizabeth b 1981), 1 s (Hon James Murray b 1974); *Career* advocate (Scotland) 1969–; lectr in constitutional law Heriot-Watt Univ 1972–74; standing jr counsel (Scotland) to FCO 1979; contested (Cons) Aberdeen North Oct 1974; MP (Cons): Angus South 1979–83, Angus East 1983–87; PPS to George Younger (sec state Scotland) 1981–82, slr gen for Scotland 1982–89, Lord Advocate 1989–92; min of state Scottish Office 1992–95, min of state DTI 1995–97; oppn spokesman on: constitutional affrs 1997–98, trade and indust 1997–98; dep shadow ldr House of Lords 1997–98; non-exec chm JKX Oil & Gas plc 1997–; non-exec dir: ICE Futures (formerly International Petroleum Exchange) 1997–, Total Exploration & Pordn UK Ltd (formerly Total Holdings UK) 2000–, Alkane Energy; dir London Metal Exchange 1997–, chm Holyrood Strategy (Scotland) 1998–, chm Statutory Ctee Royal Pharmaceutical Soc 2000; hon bencher of Lincoln's Inn 1989; hon visiting prof of law Univ of Dundee 1985; hon pres CIArb 2001–05; *Style*— The Rt Hon Lord Fraser of Carmyllie, PC, QC; ✉ Slade House, Carmyllie by Arbroath, Angus (tel 01241 860215)

FRATER, Alexander Russell; s of Dr Alexander Smail Frater (d 1972), and Lorna Rosie, *née* Fray (d 1986); *b* 3 January 1937; *Educ* Scotch Coll Melbourne, Univ of Melbourne, Univ of Durham, Univ of Perugia; *m* 1963, Marlis, da of Erwin Pfund; 1 da (Tania Elisabeth b 1964), 1 s (Alexander John b 1969); *Career* asst ed Punch 1963–66, retained writer The New Yorker 1964–68, staff writer Daily Telegraph Magazine 1966–77, asst ed Radio Times 1977–79; The Observer: asst ed magazine 1979–84, dep ed magazine 1984–86, chief travel corr 1986–98; TV presenter: The Last African Flying Boat (BBC) 1990 (BAFTA Award for Best Single Documentary), Monsoon (BBC) 1991, In the Footsteps of Buddha (BBC) 1993; Br Press Award commendations 1982 and 1989, Br Press Award Travel Writer of the Year 1990, 1991 and 1992, Best Radio Feature Travelex Travel Writers' Awards 2000, overall winner Travelex Travel Writers' Awards 2000; *Books* Stopping-Train Britain (1983), Great Rivers Of The World (ed, 1984), Beyond The Blue Horizon (1986), Chasing The Monsoon (1990, shortlisted Thomas Cook Travel Book of the Year Award, Br Book Award, McVitie's Prize), Tales From The Torrid Zone (2004), The Balloon Factory (2007); *Recreations* books, walking; *Style*— Alexander Frater, Esq; ✉ c/o David Godwin Associates, 55 Monmouth Street, London WC2H 9DG

FRAY, Prof Derek John; s of Arthur Joseph Fray (d 2000), of London, and Doris Lilian Wilson (d 1981); *b* 26 December 1939; *Educ* Emanuel Sch, Imperial Coll London (BSc Eng, ARSM, PhD, DIC, state scholar, royal scholar), Univ of Cambridge (MA); *m* 14 Aug 1965 (m dis 2002), Mirella Christine Kathleen, da of Leslie Honey, of Thames Ditton, Surrey; 1 s (Shelton Lanning b 1972), 1 da (Justine Chloe b 1974); *Career* asst prof of metallurgy MIT 1965–68, gp ldr Res Dept Imperial Smelting Corp Ltd Avonmouth Bristol 1968–71, univ lectr Dept of Materials Sci and Metallurgy Univ of Cambridge 1971–90; Fitzwilliam Coll Cambridge: fell 1972–90, librarian 1973–74, tutorial and estates bursar 1974–86, bursar 1986–88, professorial fell 1996–; prof of mineral engrg and head Dept of Mining and Mineral Engrg Univ of Leeds 1991–96, prof of materials chemistry Dept of Materials Sci and Metallurgy Univ of Cambridge 1996– (head of dept 2001–); visiting prof Univ of Leeds 1996–; hon prof of science and technol Beijing 1995–; dir: Ion Science Ltd, Ion Science Messtechnik, Cambridge Advanced Materials Ltd, British Titanium plc, EMC Ltd, Metalysis Ltd, Camfridge Ltd, Inotec AMD Ltd; memb: Inst of Materials, Soc of Chemical Industry, AIME; hon prof Hebei Poly Univ 2006–; Sidney Gilchrist Thomas lecture 2003; MIM 1966, FIMM 1988 (memb Organizing Ctee for extraction metallurgy 1981–85 and 1987, and for pyrometallurgy 1987, memb Editorial Bd, memb Cncl), FREng 1989, FRSC 2005; *Awards* Matthey prize 1967, AIME Extractive Metallurgy Technol award 1980, Sir George Beilby medal 1981, Nuffield SERC visiting fellowship 1981, Bd of Review AIME 1985, Kroll medal and prize Inst of Metals 1987, John Phillips medal 1991, TMS Distinguished Extractive Metallurgy Lectr 2000, Billiton Medal 2001, IMM 2001, Reactive Metals Award 2002, TMS 2002, Gold Medal IMMM 2003, Armourers and Braziers' Medal and Prize Royal Soc 2003, Reactive Metals Technol Award TMS 2004; *Books* Worked Examples in Mass and Heat Transfer in Materials Technology (1983); author of over 360 papers and 160 published patents; *Recreations* sailing, reading; *Style*— Prof Derek Fray, FREng; ✉ 7 Woodlands Road, Great Shelford, Cambridge CB2 5LW (tel 01223 842296); Department of Materials Science and Metallurgy, University of Cambridge, Pembroke Street, Cambridge CB2 3QZ (tel 01223 334306, fax 01223 334567, e-mail djf25@cam.ac.uk)

FRAYLING, Prof Sir Christopher John; kt (2001); s of Maj Arthur Frederick Frayling, OBE (d 1993), and Barbara Kathleen, *née* Imhof (d 2001); *b* 25 December 1946; *Educ* Repton, Churchill Coll Cambridge (scholar, MA, PhD); *m* 1981, Helen Ann Snowdon; *Career* lectr in history Univ of Exeter 1971–72, film archivist Imperial War Museum 1972–73, lectr in history of ideas Univ of Bath 1973–79; Royal Coll of Art: prof of cultural history 1979–, pro-rector 1992–96, rector 1996–; visiting prof Shanghai Univ of Technol E China 1991; Arts Council of GB: memb Photography Panel 1983–85, chm Art Projects Ctee 1985–88, memb Cncl 1987–2000, chm Visual Arts Panel 1987–94 (dep chm 1984–87), chm Film, Video and Broadcasting Panel 1994–2000, chm Educn and Trg Panel 1996–98; chair Arts Cncl England 2004– (memb 1987–2000); V&A Museum: tstee 1983–, memb Advsy Bd 1981–83, ex officio memb Bd 1997–, memb Educn Ctee, chm Bethnal Green Museum Ctee, chm Contemporary Programme; govr BFI 1982–86 (chm Educn Ctee 1983–86); chm: Crafts Study Centre Bath 1981–2004, Free Form Arts Trust 1984–89, Design Industries Gp DTI 1999–2001, Design Gp of Liturgical Ctee 1998–2000, Design Cncl 2000–04, Royal Mint Advsy Ctee 2001–; memb: Crafts Cncl 1982–85 (chm Educn and Pubns Ctees), Nat Advsy Body Working Party on Higher Educn in the Arts 1985–88, Advsy Bd Inst of Contemporary Art, ARTEC (educn and technol gp), New Millennium Experience Co Litmus Group 1998–2000, Bd Design Museum, Arts and Humanities Research Bd 1999–2004; tstee Holburne of Menstrie Museum Bath 1983–2000; writer and presenter of numerous TV series incl: The Art of Persuasion (Channel 4) 1984, Busting the Block (Channel 4) 1986, Cinema Profiles (BBC 2) 1984–90, The Face of Tutankhamun (BBC 2) 1993, Strange Landscape - the illumination of the Middle Ages (BBC 2) 1994–95, Nightmare - the birth of horror (BBC 1) 1996–97, Hotseat (Artsworld) 2000–01; RSA Bicentennial Medal 2001, Misha Black Meml Medal 2003, Maitland Medal 2006; hon fell: Humberside Poly 1991, Kent Inst of Art and Design 1997; Hon DLitt Univ of NSW, Hon Dr Staffordshire Univ, Hon Dr UWE; Hon Dr Univ of Bath; hon RIBA 2005, life fell RSA 2006 (FRSA 1984), FCSD 1994; *Books* Napoleon Wrote Fiction (1972), The Vampyre - Lord Ruthven to Count Dracula (ed, 1977), The Schoolmaster and the Wheelwrights (1980), Spaghetti Westerns - Cowboys and Europeans from Karl May to Sergio Leone (1981), The Royal College of Art: one hundred and fifty years of art and design (1987), The BFI Companion to the Western (co-ed, 1988), Vampyres - Lord Byron to Count Dracula (1991), Beyond the Dovetail - crafts, skill and imagination (ed, 1991), Clint Eastwood - a critical biography (1992), The Face of Tutankhamun (1992), The Art Pack (with Helen Frayling, 1992), Strange Landscape (1994), Things to Come - a film classic (1995), Design of the times (with Claire Catterall, 1996), Nightmare - the birth of horror (1996), Spaghetti Westerns (rev ed, 1998 and 2005), The Royal College of Art - One Hundred Years of Art and Design (1999), Sergio Leone - something to do with death (2000), The Hound of the Baskervilles (ed, 2001), Dracula (ed, 2003), Once Upon a Time in Italy (2005), Ken Adam - the Art of Production Design (2006), Mad, Bad and Dangerous - the Image of the Scientist in Film (2006); numerous articles in learned and rather less learned journals and exhbn catalogues on aspects of Euro and American cultural history; *Recreations* finding time; *Style*— Prof Sir Christopher Frayling; ✉ Royal College of Art, Kensington Gore, London SW7 2EU (tel 020 7590 4101)

FRAYLING, Very Rev Nicholas Arthur; s of Arthur Frederick Frayling, OBE (d 1993), and Barbara Kathleen, *née* Imhof (d 2001); *b* 29 February 1944; *Educ* Repton, Univ of Exeter (BA), Cuddesdon Theol Coll; *Career* mgmnt trg retail trade 1962–64, temp probation offr (prison welfare) Inner London Probation and After-care Serv 1965–66 (pt/t 1966–71), ordained Southwark Cathedral 1971, asst curate St John's Peckham 1971–74, vicar All Saints Tooting Graveney 1974–83, chm Diocesan Advsy Ctee for Care of Churches 1980–83, canon residentiary and precentor Liverpool Cathedral 1983–87, rector of Liverpool 1987–2002, dean of Chichester 2002–; hon canon Liverpool Cathedral 1989–; chaplain: St Paul's Eye Hosp Liverpool 1987–90, Huyton Coll 1987–91, to the High Sheriff of Merseyside 1992–93, 1997–98 and 1999–2000; hon chaplain Br Nuclear Tests Veterans Assoc 1988–; chm Religious Advsy Panel BBC Radio Merseyside 1988–2002, chair Welfare Organisations Ctee Liverpool Cncl of Voluntary Service 1992–02, chm Mersey Mission to Seafarers 2000–02, chm Natural Justice 2005–; Liveryman Worshipful Co of Skinners 1980; Hon LLD Univ of Liverpool 2001; fell Liverpool John Moores Univ 2003; *Books* Pardon and Peace - a reflection on the making of peace in Ireland (1996); *Recreations* music, friends; *Clubs* Royal Cwlth Soc, Oriental; *Style*— The Very Rev the Dean of Chichester; ✉ The Deanery, Canon Lane, Chichester, West Sussex PO19 1PX (tel 01243 812494, office tel 01243 812485, fax 01243 812499, e-mail dean@chichestercathedral.org.uk)

FRAYN, Michael; s of late Thomas Allen Frayn, and late Violet Alice, *née* Lawson; *b* 8 September 1933; *Educ* Kingston GS, Emmanuel Coll Cambridge; *m* 1, 1960 (m dis 1989), Gillian, *née* Palmer; 3 da; m 2, 5 June 1993, Claire Tomalin, *qv*; *Career* author and playwright; columnist: The Guardian 1959–62 (reporter 1957–59), Observer 1962–68; recipient of numerous drama awards; hon fell Emmanuel Coll Cambridge 1985; Hon DPhil Univ of Cambridge 2001; FRSL 1969; *Stage Plays* The Two of Us 1970, The Sandboy 1971, Alphabetical Order 1975, Donkeys' Years 1976, Clouds 1976, Balmoral 1978 (new version Liberty Hall 1980), Make and Break 1980, Noises Off 1982 (film 1991), Benefactors 1984, Look Look 1990, Here 1993, Now You Know 1995, La Belle Vivette (opera) 1995, Copenhagen 1998, Alarms & Excursions 1998, Democracy 2003; *Television* plays and films incl: Jamie, On a Flying Visit 1968, Birthday 1969, Clockwise 1986, First and Last 1989, A Landing on the Sun 1994, Remember Me? 1997; documentaries incl: Second City Reports 1964, One Pair of Eyes 1968, Laurence Sterne Lived Here 1973, Imagine a City Called Berlin 1975, Vienna: The Mask of Gold 1977, Three Streets in the Country 1979, The Long Straight (Great Railway Journeys of the World) 1980, Jerusalem 1984, Prague: the Magic Lantern 1994, Budapest: Written in Water 1996; comedy series: Beyond a Joke 1972, Making Faces 1975; *Translations of Plays* incl: The Cherry Orchard, Three Sisters, The Seagull, Uncle Vanya, Wild Honey (all Chekhov), The Fruits of Enlightenment (Tolstoy), Exchange (Trifonov), Number One (Anouilh), The Sneeze (Chekhov Short Plays); *Novels* incl: The Tin Men (1965, Somerset Maugham Award), The Russian Interpreter (1966, Hawthornden Prize), Towards the End of the Morning (1967), A Very Private Life (1968), Sweet Dreams (1973), The Trick of It (1989), A Landing On The Sun (1991, Sunday Express Book of the Year Award), Now You Know (1992), Headlong (1999, shortlisted for Booker Prize 1999), Spies (2003, Whitbread Novel of the Year 2003); *Non-fiction* incl: Constructions (philosophy, 1974), Celia's Secret (with David Burke, 2000), The Human Touch: Our Part in the Creation of a Universe (2006), several volumes of collected writings and translations; *Style*— Michael Frayn; ✉ c/o Greene & Heaton Ltd, 37 Goldhawk Road, London W12 9PU (tel 020 8749 0315, fax 020 8749 0318)

FRAZER, Christopher Mark; s of Michael Leslie Frazer, of Twickenham, Middx, and Pamela Mary, *née* Stoakes; *b* 17 June 1960; *Educ* KCS Wimbledon, St John's Coll Cambridge (exhibitioner, Macaulay scholar, McMahon law student, MA, LLM, coll prizeman); *m* 20 May 1989, Victoria Margaret, da of John Peter Hess, of Chorlton-by-Backford, Cheshire; 1 s (Thomas Michael John b 19 June 1994), 1 da (Laura Charlotte Mary b 31 Aug 1996); *Career* called to the Bar Middle Temple 1983, ad eundem Inner Temple; in practice Midland, Western and SE circuits; dep district judge of the High Court and Co Court (Western Circuit) 1997–2001, recorder of the Crown Court 2000–; memb Gen Cncl of the Bar 1989–94 and 2000–, chm Bar Conf 1994, chm BARMARK panel 1999–2001; chm Editorial Bd Counsel magazine 1995–99; chm Young Barristers' Ctee of England and Wales 1991; Parly candidate (Cons) Peckham 1992, sec Soc of Cons Lawyers 1988–89 and 1998–2000; chm London West Cons Euro Constituency Cncl 1994–97; common councilman Corp of London 1986–95; Freeman City of London 1986; *Books* Thoughts for a Third Term (1987), Privatise the Prosecutors (1993); *Recreations* dinghy sailing, Classic FM, amusing my children; *Clubs* Guildhall, West Wittering Sailing; *Style*— Christopher Frazer, Esq; ✉ 2 Harcourt Buildings, Temple, London EC4Y 9DB (tel 020 7353 6961, fax 020 7353 6968)

FRAZER, Ian William; s of William George Frazer (d 1982), of Hutton, Essex, and Grace Marjorie, *née* Willis (d 1979); *b* 26 January 1933; *Educ* Framlingham Coll; *m* 3 March 1964, Priscilla, da of Capt John Daniell (ka 1943), of Kimpton, Herts; 3 da (Annabel (Mrs Alexander Dickinson) b 1965, Katharine (Mrs James Fenwick) b 1966, Henrietta b 1970); *Career* Nat Serv cmmnd The Queen's Bays (2 Dragoon Gds) 1955–57; Army Emergency Reserve 1957–64, ret Lt 1 Queen's Dragoon Gds; qualified CA 1955; CLB Littlejohn Frazer (formerly Frazer Whiting & Co): sr ptnr (formerly ptnr) 1971–98, conslt 1998–; govr: Morpeth Sch Tower Hamlets 1967–, St Mary's Sch Wantage 1984–2006; memb Chelsea Soc 1976– (hon treas 1985–2005), cmmr Royal Hosp Chelsea 2000–06; tstee: Chelsea Festival 1992– (chm 2001–), Soc for Protection of Animals Abroad (SPANA) 2000– (chm 2004–06); FCA 1955; *Recreations* music, reading, shooting, skiing; *Clubs* Cavalry and Guards' (vice-chm 1996–2002, tstee 2003–), City of London; *Style*— Ian Frazer, Esq; ✉ 6 Edith Terrace, Chelsea, London SW10 0TQ (tel 020 7352 3310); CLB Littlejohn Frazer, 1 Park Place, Canary Wharf, London E14 4HJ (tel 020 7987 5030)

FREAN, Jenny (Jennifer Margaret); da of Theodore John Farbridge (d 1984), of Lymington, Hants, and Isobel, *née* Reid Douglas (d 1988); *b* 17 April 1947; *Educ* City of London Sch for Girls, Hornsey Coll of Art (BA), Royal Coll of Art (MA); *m* 1970, Patrick Frean, s of Denis Frean, CBE; 1 da (Holly Thea b 1978); *Career* design conslt Centro Design Montefibre Milan 1974, fndr Jenny Frean Associates (textile design studio) 1975, portraitist 1984–86, fndr First Eleven Studio (textile designers) 1986; RDI 1998; *Recreations* music especially opera, all art forms, gardening; *Style*— Mrs Jenny Frean, RDI; ✉ e-mail jennyfrean@firstelevenstudio.com

FREARS, Stephen Arthur; s of Dr Russell E Frears (d 1977), of Nottingham, and Ruth M Frears (d 1971); *b* 20 June 1941; *Educ* Gresham's, Trinity Coll Cambridge (BA); *m* 1967 (m dis 1973), Mary K, *née* Wilmers; 2 s (Sam b 1972, William b 1973); partner, Anne Rothenstein; 1 s (Francis Frears b 1983), 1 da (Lola Frears b 1985); *Career* film director; pres of jury Cannes Film Festival 2007; *Films* Gumshoe 1971, Bloody Kids 1980, Going Gently 1981, Saigon 1983, Walter 1982, The Hit 1984, My Beautiful Launderette 1985, Prick up Your Ears 1986, Sammy and Rosie Get Laid 1987, Dangerous Liaisons 1989, The Grifters 1990, Accidental Hero 1992, The Snapper 1994, Mary Reilly 1995, The Van 1996, The Hi-Lo Country 1997, High Fidelity 1999, Liam 2001, Dirty Pretty Things 2002, The Deal 2003, Mrs Henderson Presents 2004, The Queen 2005; *Style*— Stephen Frears, Esq; ✉ c/o Casarotto Marsh Ltd, National House, 4th Floor, 60–66 Wardour Street, London W1V 3HP (tel 020 7287 4450, fax 020 7287 9128)

FREEBORN, David Michael; s of Herbert Aubury Freeborn (d 1976), of Whetstone, London, and May Beatrice, *née* Inwards; *b* 15 May 1950; *Educ* Christ Church Secdy Sch London, Tottenham Tech Coll, St Albans Coll of FE; *m* 25 Feb 1983, Janis, da of Roy James Lambert, of Maidstone; 1 da (Claire b 27 June 1983); *Career* chief exec Glendore Estates Ltd; Worshipful Co of Constructors; MCIOB 1972, FRICS 1983; *Recreations* golf; *Clubs* RAC; *Style*— David M Freeborn, Esq; ✉ The Old Piggery, Cornells Lane, Widdington, Essex CB11 3SP

FREEDEN, Prof Michael Stephen; s of Herbert Freeden, and Marianne Freeden; *b* 30 April 1944; *Educ* Hebrew Univ of Jerusalem (BA), Univ of Oxford (MA, DPhil); *m* 1968, Irene Gerszzon; 1 s (Jonathan Gabriel b 1969), 1 da (Daniella Leora b 1972); *Career* lectr and sr lectr Univ of Haifa 1972–77, visiting fell St Antony's Coll Oxford 1977–78; Mansfield Coll Oxford: fell and tutor 1978–, sr tutor 1982–89, professorial fell 1996–07; Univ of Oxford: chm Sub-Faculty of Politics 1991–93, prof of politics 1997–, dir Centre for Political Ideologies 2002–; founding ed Jl of Political Ideologies 1996, assoc ed Oxford DNB 1993–2004; Br Acad research readership 1989–91, ESRC professorial fellowship 2004–; FRHistS 1980; *Books* The New Liberalism: An Ideology of Social Reform (1978), Liberalism Divided: A Study in British Political Thought 1914–1939 (1986), Reappraising J A Hobson: Humanism and Welfare (ed, 1990), Rights (1991), Ideologies and Political Theory: A Conceptual Approach (1996), A Very Short Introduction to Ideology (2003), Liberal Languages (2005), The Meaning of Ideology: Cross-Disciplinary Perspectives (2007); *Recreations* second-hand book collecting, urban photography; *Style*— Prof Michael Freeden; ✉ Mansfield College, Oxford OX1 3TF (tel and fax 01865 270977, e-mail michael.freeden@mansfield.ox.ac.uk)

FREEDLAND, Michael Rodney; s of David Freedland, and Lily, *née* Mindel; *b* 18 December 1934; *Educ* Luton GS; *m* 3 July 1960, Sara, da of Abram Hockerman; 2 da (Fiona Anne b 1963, Daniela Ruth b 1964), 1 s (Jonathan Saul b 1967); *Career* journalist for local newspapers 1951–60, Daily Sketch 1960–61; freelance journalist 1961–; contrib: The Times, Sunday Telegraph, The Guardian, Economist, Spectator, The Observer, Daily Express, Sunday Express; broadcaster 1962– (progs incl You don't have to be Jewish (BBC and LBC) 1971–94 and various progs on BBC Radio 2); wrote Jolson (musical show, opened London 1995); *Books* 37 books incl: Al Jolson (1971), Irving Berlin (1973), Fred Astaire (1976), Gregory Peck (1979), The Warner Brothers (1982), Danny Kaye (1987), Leonard Bernstein (1987), Jane Fonda (1988), Dustin Hoffman (1989), Kenneth Williams (1990), André Previn (1991), Music Man (1994), Sean Connery, A Biography (1994), All The Way, A Biography of Frank Sinatra (1997), Bob Hope (1998), Bing Crosby (1998), Michael Caine (1999), Doris Day (2000), Some Like It Cool (2002), Liza with a 'Z' (2004), Dean Martin, King of the Road (2004), Confessions of a Serial Biographer (autobiography, 2005), Hollywood on Trial - McCarthyism's War on the Movies; *Recreations* reading, being with my wife and family; *Style*— Michael Freedland, Esq; ✉ Bays Hill Lodge, Barnet Lane, Elstree, Hertfordshire WD6 3QU (tel 020 8953 3000)

FREEDMAN, Cyril Winston; s of Sydney Freedman (d 1951), and Irene Rosalind, *née* Anekstein; *b* 31 August 1945; *Educ* Brighton Coll, Brighton Coll of Art and Design (Dip Graphic Art and Design); *m* 25 March 1970, Christine Mary, da of Cecil Shipman, of Swanwick, Derbys; 1 s (Mark b 1973), 1 da (Anna b 1977); *Career* chm: CWF Advertising Ltd 1971–74, Halls Homes and Gardens 1978–80 (md 1977–78, dir 1974–81); dir Pentos plc and subsidiaries 1979–81, chm Serco Ryan Ltd 1982–87, chief exec WBH Group Ltd (subsidiary of Lopex plc) 1985–88, dir Armour Automotive Products Group (subsidiary of Armour Trust plc) 1985–91; chm: Deeko plc 1988–90 (dir 1986–90), Hennell plc 1988–94, Worth Fine Fragrances plc 1992–97; dir Apax Partners & Co Ventures Ltd (formerly known as Alan Patricof Associates Ltd) 1988–95; exec chm S Daniels plc 1997–2002 (dep chm and chief exec 1995–97), non-exec chm Lloyd Maunder Ltd 2004–; dir: New Covent Garden Soup Co 1989–2002, Stead & Simpson Group 1992–; non-exec dir David Morris Int Ltd 2004–, Lighterlife UK Ltd 2005–; FInstD, MCIM; *Recreations* painting, travel, collecting fine art; *Style*— Cyril Freedman, Esq; ✉ Minety House, The Green, Minety, Malmesbury, Wiltshire SN16 9PL (tel 01666 860433, e-mail cyrilfreedman@aol.com)

FREEDMAN, Dr Danielle Beverley; *b* 28 August 1953; *Educ* Woodhouse GS London, Royal Free Hosp Sch of Med London (Winifred Ladd scholar, MB BS, Edith Peachy Phipson prize); *m* (m dis); 1 s; *Career* Royal Free Hosp London: house physician and house surgn posts 1977–78, SHO in clinical pathology 1978–79, registrar Dept of Chemical Pathology 1979–81; clinical lectr (sr registrar) Dept of Chemical Pathology Courtauld Inst of Biochemistry Middx Hosp Med Sch London 1981–84; Luton and Dunstable Hosp NHS Tst: conslt chemical pathologist and assoc physician in clinical endocrinology and metabolism 1985–, clinical dir of pathology 1990–, clinical dir of pathology and pharmacy 1993–, medical dir Luton and Dunstable Hosp 2005–; regnl postgraduate dean rep Univ of London and Univ of Cambridge; nat surveyor King's Fund Organisational Audit (Accreditation UK), nat inspr Clinical Pathology Accreditation (CPA) UK Ltd, memb Nat Working Pty for implementation of clinical guidelines; past chm Clinical Biochemistry Sub-Ctee NW Thames RHA; RCPath: chair SAC Clinical Biochemistry 2005–, former memb Cncl, memb Standing Ctee for Chemical Pathology, memb Nat Clinical Audit Ctee, RCPath rep Assoc of Clinical Biochemists Cncl, memb Standing Ctee on RCPath Academic Activities, memb Pubns Ctee, RCPath rep NHS Mgmnt Exec working with professions to develop service specifications, E Anglia rep for chemical pathology; Assoc of Clinical Biochemists: memb Scientific Ctee, sr ed Venture Pubns Gp, chm Jt Working Gp looking at near patient testing, chm Educn Ctee, Nat Ames Award and Medal for Research 1981, Prize for Clinical Audit 1992; FRCPath 1995; *Books* A Short Textbook of Chemical Pathology (ed), Clinical Chemistry (ed); numerous pubns in academic jls; *Style*— Dr Danielle Freedman; ✉ The Luton and Dunstable Hospital NHS Trust, Lewsey Road, Luton LU4 0DZ (tel 01582 497212, fax 01582 497387)

FREEDMAN, Her Hon Judge Dawn Angela; da of Julius Freedman (d 2003), and Celia, *née* Greenbaum (d 2004); *b* Watford, Herts; *Educ* Westcliff HS for Girls, UCL (LLB); *m* 5 April 1970, Neil John Shestopal; *Career* called to the Bar 1966; practising barr 1966–80, metropolitan stipendiary magistrate then district judge (criminal) 1980–91, circuit judge 1991–; *Style*— Her Hon Judge Freedman; ✉ Harrow Crown Court, Hailsham Drive, Harrow HA1 4TU (tel 020 8424 2294)

FREEDMAN, Prof Sir Lawrence David; KCMG (2003), CBE (1996); s of Lt Cdr Julius Freedman, RN (d 1987), and Myra, *née* Robinson (d 1995); *b* 7 December 1948; *Educ* Whitley Bay GS, Univ of Manchester (BA), Univ of York (BPhil), Univ of Oxford (PhD); *m* 1974, Judith Anne, da of Harry Hill, and Stella Hill; 1 s (Samuel b 1981), 1 da (Ruth b 1984); *Career* teaching asst Dept of Politics Univ of York 1971–72, res (prize) fell Nuffield Coll Oxford 1974–75, lectr in politics (pt/t) Balliol Coll Oxford 1975, research assoc IISS 1975–76, research fell on British foreign policy RIIA 1976–78, head of policy studies RIIA 1978–82, prof of war studies KCL 1982–, vice-princ (research) KCL 2003–; columnist: The Independent 1987–93, The Times 1993–2000, FT 2000–; specialist advsr House of Commons Defence Ctee 1980–97; memb: Current Affairs Advsy Gp Channel 4 1986–87, Govt and Law Ctee Economic and Social Res Cncl 1982–87, Cncl IISS 1984–92 and 1993–2002, Cncl David Davies Meml Inst 1990–95, Cncl SSEES Univ of London 1996–99, Expert Panel on Strategic Defence Review MoD 1997–98; memb Editorial Bd: Foreign Policy, Int Security, Political Quarterly, Intelligence and National Security; tstee Imperial War Museum 2001–; FKC 1992, FBA 1995; *Books* US Intelligence and the Soviet Strategic Threat (1977, reprinted with new foreword 1986), Britain and Nuclear Weapons (1980), The Evolution of Nuclear Strategy (1981, 3 edn 2003), The Troubled Alliance: Atlantic Relations in the 1980s (ed, 1983), Nuclear War and Nuclear Peace (jtly, 1983, 2 edn 1988), The Atlas of Global Strategy (1985), The Price of Peace: Living with the Nuclear Dilemma (1986), Britain and the Falklands War (1988), US Nuclear Strategy: A Reader (co-ed, 1989), Military Power in Europe: Essays in Memory of Jonathan Alford (ed, 1990), Signals of War: The Falklands Conflict of 1982 (jtly, 1990), Britain in the World (jtly, 1991), The Gulf Conflict 1990–91 (jtly, 1993), Military Intervention in European Conflicts (ed, 1994), War: A Reader (ed, 1994), Strategic Coercion (ed, 1998), The Politics of British Defence 1979–1998 (1999), Kennedy's Wars (2000), The Cold War (2001), Superterrorism (ed, 2002), Deterrence (2004), The Official History of the Falklands Campaign (2 vols, 2005); *Recreations* political cartoons, tennis; *Style*— Prof Sir Lawrence Freedman, KCMG, CBE, FBA; ✉ Principal's Office, King's College London, James Clerk Maxwell Building, 57 Waterloo Road, London SE1 8WA (tel 020 7848 3984, fax 020 7848 3457, e-mail lawrence.freedman@kcl.ac.uk)

FREEDMAN, Michael John; s of late Joseph Leopold Freedman, of London, and late Rosa Annie, *née* Bosman (d 1987); *b* 4 July 1946; *Educ* Clifton, Christ's Coll Cambridge; *m* 1973, Pamela Dawn, da of late Cyril Kay, and late Hilda Kay; 1 da (Natalie Kay b 31 Jan 1976), 1 s (Jonathan Leonard b 13 April 1979); *Career* mktg mangr Royal Angus Hotels 1965–69; mktg dir: Securadet Ltd 1969–72, Paul Kaye Studio Ltd 1972–; chm Cover Shots International 1990–2000, chm The Family Photographers Gp Ltd 2000–; memb Cncl BIPP 1989–93; FBIPP, FMPA; *Recreations* badminton, swimming, reading, walking; *Style*— Michael Freedman, Esq; ✉ Paul Kaye Studio Ltd, 80 Great Portland Street, London W1W 7NW (fax, 020 7312 1230, e-mail mf@pkstudio.demon.co.uk)

FREELAND, Chrystia; da of Donald Freeland, of Peace River, Canada, and Halyna Freeland, of Edmonton, Canada; *b* 2 August 1968; *Educ* Harvard Univ, St Antony's Coll Oxford (Rhodes scholar); *m* 4 July 1998, Graham Bowley; 2 da (Natalka b 28 Feb 2001, Halyna b 14 Jan 2005); *Career* former dep ed The Globe and Mail Toronto; FT: successively Eastern Europe corr, Moscow bureau chief, UK news ed, ed FT.com, ed Saturday edn and dep ed, currently US managing ed; Best Energy Submission Business Journalist of the Year Awards 2004; *Publications* Sale of the Century (2000); *Recreations* running; *Style*— Ms Chrystia Freeland; ✉ Financial Times, 1330 Avenue of the Americas, New York, NY 10019, USA (e-mail chrystia.freeland@ft.com, website www.ft.com)

FREELAND, James Gourlay; s of James Gourlay Freeland (d 1989), and Jessie McRobie, *née* Brown (d 1995); *b* 3 August 1936; *Educ* Haileybury and ISC, Trinity Hall Cambridge (MA); *m* 27 May 1961, Diana, da of Bryce Graham Dewsbury (d 1971); 1 s (Jeremy b 1963), 2 da (Joanna (Mrs Henry B Lloyd) b 1965, Stephanie (Mrs Algy Smith-Maxwell) b 1971); *Career* Nat Serv Royal Marines (2 Lt) 1955–57; shipbroker and dir H Clarkson & Co Ltd London 1966–91, investment banker (shipping) and dep chm First International Capital Ltd 1991–92, dir Braemar Shipbrokers Ltd London 1993–2002; pres Inst of Chartered Shipbrokers 2000–02; Liveryman Worshipful Co of Shipwrights 1963 (Prime Warden 1997–98); *Recreations* golf, shooting; *Clubs* Brooks's, Caledonian, MCC, Jesters; *Style*— James G Freeland, Esq; ✉ Staplewood, Nether Wallop, Stockbridge, Hampshire SO20 8EQ (tel 01264 781533)

FREELAND, Sir John Redvers; KCMG (1984, CMG 1973), QC (1987); o s of Clarence Redvers Freeland, and Freda, *née* Walker; *b* 16 July 1927; *Educ* Stowe, CCC Cambridge; *m* 1952, Sarah Mary, er da of late Sidney Pascoe Hayward, QC; 1 s (Nicholas b 1956), 1 da (Petra b 1959); *Career* RN 1945 and 1948–51; called to the Bar Lincoln's Inn 1952 (bencher 1985); HM Dip Serv: asst legal advsr FO 1954–63 and 1965–67, legal advsr HM Embassy Bonn 1963–65, legal cnsllr FCO 1967–70 and 1973–76, cnsllr (legal advsr) UK Mission to UN NY 1970–73, second legal advsr FCO 1976–84, legal advsr FCO 1984–87, ret; judge Arbitral Tbnl and Mixed Cmmn for the Agreement on German External Debts 1988–, judge European Court of Human Rights 1991–98; memb: Exec Ctee David Davies Meml Inst of Int Studies 1974–2001, Cncl of Mgmnt British Inst of Int and Comparative Law 1984–87, Ctee of Mgmnt Inst of Advanced Legal Studies 1984–87, US-Chile Int Cmmn of Investigation 1989–, Bd of Govrs Br Inst of Human Rights 1992–2004; *Style*— Sir John Freeland, KCMG, QC

FREELAND, Rowan Charles Bayfield; s of Col Paul Rowan Bayfield Freeland, of Lacock, Wilts, and Susanna Brigitta Elizabeth, *née* Burch; *b* 13 December 1956; *Educ* Wellington, St Catherine's Coll Oxford (BA); *m* 12 Dec 1987, Davina Alexandra Claire, da of Maj Dennis Edward Salisbury (d 1964); 3 da (Marigold Claire Salisbury b 31 Oct 1990, Constance Margaret Alexandra b 12 Nov 1992, Beatrix Emily Faith b 1 June 1995); *Career* admitted slr 1982; ptnr Simmons & Simmons 1988–; sec The Haydn-Mozart Soc 1984–; *Recreations* family, opera, gardening, reading; *Style*— Rowan Freeland, Esq; ✉ Simmons & Simmons, CityPoint, One Ropemaker Street, London EC2Y 9SS (tel 020 7628 2020, fax 020 7628 2070, e-mail rowan.freeland@simmons-simmons.com)

FREELAND, Simon Dennis Marsden; QC (2002); s of Dennis M Freeland, and Rosemary Turnbull Tarn, *née* Menzies; *b* 11 February 1956; *Educ* Malvern Coll, Univ of Manchester (LLB); *m* 12 Feb 2002, Anne Elizabeth; 1 da (Ruby Anastasia b 3 July 2004), 1 s (George Arthur Menzies b 23 March 2006); *Career* called to the Bar Gray's Inn 1978; practising barr specialising in police law, currently head of chambers 5 Essex Court; recorder 1999–; memb: Personal Injury Bar Assoc, SE Circuit Exec Ctee; *Recreations* walking, horse racing, good food and fine wine; *Style*— Simon Freeland, Esq, QC; ✉ 5 Essex Court, Temple, London EC4Y 9AH

FREEMAN, Andrew Lawrence D; s of Richard D Freeman, and Diana L, *née* Cranwell; *b* 4 March 1963; *Educ* Balliol Coll Oxford (BA), Merton Coll Oxford (sr scholar); *m* Hazel Mary Mills; 2 s (Luke Edward Freeman-Mills b 1991, Maximilian James Downing Freeman-Mills b 1993); 1 da (Georgia Beatrice Rose Freeman-Mills b 1997); *Career* Financial Times: stockmarket reporter 1988, Euromarket reporter 1989, Lex Column 1990–92; The Economist: banking corr 1992–94, American finance ed 1995–97, Euro business corr 1999–2004, dep business affrs ed 2004–; ed fin servs Economist Intelligence Unit 1997–99; *Publications* The Armoire de Fer and the French Revolution (1990), Seeing Tomorrow: Rewriting the Rules of Risk (jtly, 1998), The Risk Revolution (2000); *Style*— Andrew Freeman, Esq; ✉ The Economist, 25 St James's Street, London SW1A 1HG

FREEMAN, David Charles; s of Howard Wilfred Freeman, of Sydney, Australia, and Ruth Adair, *née* Nott; *b* 1 May 1952; *Educ* Sydney GS, Univ of Sydney (BA); *m* 1 May 1985, Marie Louise, da of (Francis) John Angel (d 1968), of Pinnaroo, Australia; 1 da (Catherine Elinor b 13 May 1989), 1 s (Lachlan John b 28 Feb 1993); *Career* opera prodr; fndr and dir: Opera Factory Sydney 1973–76, Opera Factory Zurich 1976–99, Opera Factory London 1981–98, Opera Factory Films Ltd 1991–; assoc artist ENO 1981–95; prodns incl: Monteverdi's Orfeo (ENO) 1981, Birtwistle's Punch and Judy (OFL) 1981, The Mask of Orpheus (ENO) 1986, Cosi Fan Tutte (OFL) 1986, Glass's Akhnaten (Houston, NY and London), Prokofiev's The Fiery Angel (St Petersburg, Covent Garden, Metropolitan NYC) 1992, Zimmermann's Die Soldaten (ENO) 1996, Madame Butterfly (Albert Hall) 1998; theatre: Goethe's Faust I and II (Lyric Hammersmith) 1988, adapted and directed Malory's Le Morte d'Arthur I and II (Lyric Hammersmith) 1990, The Bacchae (Xenakis' music for play) 1993, The Winter's Tale (opening season Shakespeare's Globe Theatre) 1997, Tosca (Royal Albert Hall) 1999, Carmen (Royal Albert Hall) 2002; 8 TV prodns incl: all three Mozart/da Ponte operas (viz Cosi fan Tutte, Don Giovanni and The Marriage of Figaro) for Channel Four 1989–91, Punch and Judy (Channel 4) 1992; Chevalier de l'Ordre des Arts et des Lettres (France) 1985; *Style*— David Freeman, Esq; ✉ 37 Agamemnon Road, London NW6 1EJ (e-mail freepeople@blueyonder.co.uk)

FREEMAN, Prof George Kenneth; s of Cdr John Kenneth Herbert Freeman, RN (ret), of Bath, and Jean Forbes, *née* Irving; *b* 4 August 1944; *Educ* Kingswood Sch Bath, Trinity Coll Cambridge (BChir), St Thomas' Hosp Med Sch London, Univ of Cambridge (MD); *m* 1, 1968 (m dis 1980), Marjorie Rose, *née* Downing; 1 da (Anna b 1971), 1 s (Thomas b 1973); m 2, 1982 (m dis 1997), Dr Jennifer Field; 2 s (Michael b 1983, Timothy b 1986); m 3, 1998, Dr Alison Paice Hill; *Career* house offr St Thomas' Hosp then Southampton Gen Hosp 1968–69, SHO Portsmouth Hosp, Wessex Neuro Centre Southampton, Southampton Gen Hosp then Knowle Hosp Fareham 1969–71, GP trainee Southampton 1971–72, GP Aldermoor Health Centre Southampton 1972–93, lectr then sr lectr in primary med care Univ of Southampton 1972–93 (actg head of dept 1991–93), prof of gen practice Imperial Coll London 1993–2004, pt/t GP London 1993–; Br Cncl exchange visit Univs of Utrecht and Nijmegen 1978, Janet Nash visiting fell Univ of Cincinnati Ohio 1989, visiting conslt Med Acad of St Petersburg 1999, visiting conslt Br Cncl Family Med Project Almaty Kazakhstan 2001; sec Assoc of Univ Depts of Gen Practice 1985–91; MRCP, FRCGP; *Recreations* steam railways, classical organs and their music, DIY in Victorian houses, foreign travel, child raising and support; *Style*— Prof George Freeman; ✉ Department of Primary Care and Social Medicine, Imperial College London, Charing Cross Campus, The Reynolds Building, St Dunstan's Road, London W6 8RP (tel 020 7594 3352, fax 020 7854 0854, e-mail g.freeman@imperial.ac.uk)

FREEMAN, Prof Hugh Lionel; s of late Bernard Freeman, and Dora Doris, *née* Kahn; *b* 4 August 1929; *Educ* Altrincham GS, St John's Coll Oxford (DM, MA); *m* 1957, (Sally) Joan, da of Philip Casket; 3 s, 1 da; *Career* Capt RAMC 1956–58; house surgn Manchester Royal Infirmary 1955, registrar Bethlem Royal and Maudsley Hosps 1958–60, sr registrar Littlemore Hosp Oxford 1960–61; conslt psychiatrist: Salford Royal Hosp 1961–70, Hope Hosp 1961–88; hon conslt: Salford Mental Health Tst, Univ of Manchester Sch of Med 1988–; WHO conslt: Grenada 1970, Chile 1978, Philippines 1979, Bangladesh 1981, Greece 1985; rapporteur: WHO Conf on Mental Health Servs Trieste 1984, WHO Ruanda 1985, Cncl of Europe Conf on Health in Cities 1985; ed: Br Jl of Psychiatry 1983–93 (asst ed 1978–83), Current Opinion in Psychiatry 1986–93; lectr worldwide; vice-chm MIND 1983–87; med advsr to SANE and Br False Memory Soc; hon prof Univ of Salford, hon visiting fell Green Coll Oxford; pres Section of Psychiatry RSM 2004–05; memb: Mercian Regnl Ctee Nat Tst 1986–92, Mental Health Act Cmmn 1983, Mental Health Review Tbnls, City of Manchester Historic Bldgs Panel, Home Sec's Ctee on Fear of Crime 1989, Statutory Inquiry Camden and Islington HA 1999; vice-chm Manchester Heritage Tst; corresponding fell American Psychiatric Assoc; hon memb: Chilean Soc of Psychiatry, Egyptian Psychiatric Assoc, Polish Psychiatric Assoc, Hungarian Psychiatric Assoc, Bulgarian Soc for Neurosciences; Anniversary Medal of Merit Charles Univ Prague; Freeman City of London, Liveryman Worshipful Soc of Apothecaries (ed Apothecary); Hon FRCPsych 1998 (formerly FRCPsych), FFPH; *Publications* Trends in Mental Health Services (1963), New Aspects of the Mental Health Service (jt ed, 1968), Mental Health Services in Europe (1985), Mental Health and the Environment (ed, 1985), 150 Years of British Psychiatry (jt ed, Vol I 1991, Vol II 1996), Community Psychiatry (jt ed, 1991), La Malattie del Potere (1994), A Century of Psychiatry (1999), Psychiatric Cultures Compared (jt ed, 2006); *Recreations* architecture, travel, music; *Clubs* Oxford and Cambridge; *Style*— Prof Hugh Freeman; ✉ 21 Montagu Square, London W1H 2LF (tel 020 7224 4867, fax 020 7224 6153)

FREEMAN, Michael Alexander Reykers; s of Donald George Freeman (d 1937), of Ockley, Surrey, and Florence Julia, *née* Elms (d 1962); *b* 17 November 1931; *Educ* Stowe, CCC Cambridge (open scholar, BA, MB BCh, MD, Bacon Prize), London Hosp Med Coll; *m* 1, 1951 (m dis), Elizabeth Jean; 1 da (Julianne b 5 June 1952), 1 s (Jonathan b 29 May 1954); m 2, 1959 (m dis), Janet Edith; 1 da (Emma b 18 May 1962), 1 s (Dominic b 3 April 1965); m 3, 26 Sept 1968, Patricia, da of Leslie Gill (d 1976), of Bristol; 1 s (James b 14 April 1971 d 1971), 1 da (Clare b 31 Dec 1972); *Career* clinical trg in med surgery and orthopaedic surgery London Hosp, Westminster Hosp and Middx Hosp; awarded Copeman Medal, Robert Jones Gold Medal; co-fndr and dir Biomechanics Unit Dept of Med Engrg Imperial Coll London 1966–79, sr lectr in orthopaedic surgery London Hosp Med Coll 1968–95, conslt orthopaedic surgn London Hosp 1968–95, hon conslt orthopaedic surgn Royal Hospitals Tst 1996–; visiting prof Inst of Orthopaedics and Musculo-Skeletal Science UCL 2001–; european ed-in-chief Journal of Arthroplasty 1997–2001; co-dir Bone and Joint Res Unit London Hosp Med Coll 1975; past pres: European Fedn of Nat Societies of Orthopaedics and Traumatology, Br Orthopaedic Soc, Br Hip Soc, Int Hip Soc; past memb: Bd of Govrs London Hosp, Clinical Res Bd MRC; Yeoman Worshipful Soc of Apothecaries; memb: American Academy of Orthopaedic Surgns, BOA, BES, ORS, Int Hip Soc, SICOT; Hon FRSM, FRCS; *Books* Adult Articular Cartilage (ed, 1973), The Scientific Basis of Joint Replacement (ed with S A V Swanson, 1977), Arthritis of the Knee (ed, 1980), Osteoarthritis in the Young Adult Hip (ed with D Reynolds, 1984); *Style*— Mr Michael Freeman; ✉ 79 Albert Street, London NW1 7LX (tel 020 7387 0817, fax 020 7388 5731)

FREEMAN, Prof Michael David Alan; s of Raphael Freeman, of London, and Florence, *née* Wax; *b* 25 November 1943; *Educ* Hasmonean GS Hendon, UCL (LLB, LLM); *m* 23 July 1967, Vivien Ruth, da of Sidney Brook, of Leeds; 1 da (Hilary Rachel b 1971), 1 s (Jeremy Simon Richard b 1973); *Career* called to the Bar Gray's Inn 1969; lectr in law: E London Coll of Commerce 1965–66, Univ of Leeds 1967–69 (asst lectr 1966–67); reader in law UCL 1979–84 (lectr 1969–79), prof of English law Univ of London (tenable at UCL) 1984–, fell UCL 2000–; ed: Annual Survey of Family Law 1983–95, Current Legal Problems 1992–2004, Int Jl of Children's Rights 1992–, Int Jl of Law in Context 1995–; dir of trg Nicholson Graham and Jones 1989–91; formerly govr S Hampstead HS; *Books* incl: Introduction to Jurisprudence (1 edn 1972, 5 edn 2001), The Children Act 1975 (1976), Violence in the Home (1979), Cohabitation Outside Marriage (1983), The Rights and Wrongs of Children (1983), Essays in Family Law (1986), Dealing With Domestic Violence (1987), Medicine Ethics and the Law (1988), Children, their Families and the Law (1992), The Ideologies of Children's Rights (1992), The Moral Status of Children (1997), Science in Court (1998), Law and Literature (1999), Law and Medicine (2000), Children's Rights (2004), Children, Medicine and the Law (2005), Children's Health and Children's Rights (2006), Law and Sociology (2006), The Best Interests of the Child (2007); *Recreations* opera, theatre, cricket, literature; *Clubs* Middlesex CCC; *Style*— Prof Michael Freeman; ✉ tel 020 7679 1443, fax 020 7387 9597

FREEMAN, Peter Geoffrey; *b* 12 December 1955; *Educ* St Paul's, Balliol Coll Oxford (BA); *m* 1983, Tania, *née* Bromley-Martin; 1 s, 4 da; *Career* admitted slr 1981; DJ Freeman 1979–81, co-fndr and chief exec Argent Gp 1981–1998 (non-exec dir 1998–), fndr and chm Freeman Business Information plc (formerly Freeman Publishing) 1999–; chm: Investment Property Forum, MGT plc, Puma Brandenburg; non-exec dir: Land Securities plc 2002–04, MEPC; publisher Freeman's Guide to the Property Industry; jt winner (with bro, Michael) Property Personality of the Year 1996; memb Law Soc; *Recreations* family, reading, tennis, cycling, jogging, olive oil prodn; *Style*— Peter Freeman, Esq; ✉ Argent Group plc, 5 Albany Courtyard, Piccadilly, London W1J 0HF (tel 020 7734 3721, fax 020 7734 4474)

FREEMAN, Peter John; s of Cdr John Kenneth Herbert Freeman, LVO, RN (ret), of Bath, and Jean Forbes, *née* Irving; *b* 2 October 1948; *Educ* Kingswood Sch Bath (scholar), Goethe Inst Berlin, Trinity Coll Cambridge (exhibitioner, MA), Inns of Court Sch of Law, Université Libre de Bruxelles (Licence Spéciale en Droit Européen); *m* 1972, Elizabeth Mary, da of Frank and Barbara Rogers; 2 da (Catharine b 1 Nov 1977, Sarah b 20 July 1988), 2 s (Christopher b 29 May 1979, Henry b 22 March 1983); *Career* called to the Bar 1972, requalified as slr 1977; Simmons & Simmons: joined 1973, ptnr 1978–2003, head EC and Competition Law Gp 1987–2003, managing ptnr Commercial and Trade Law Dept 1994–99; chm Competition Cmmn 2006– (dep chm 2003–06); fndr memb and former chm Regulatory Policy Inst Oxford; memb Advsy Bd: Competition Law Journal, Int Competition Law Forum, ESRC Research Centre for Competition Policy; *Publications* Butterworths Competition Law (jt gen ed 1991–2005, consulting ed 2005–), UK Competition Law Reform - a practitioner's view (RPI, 1993), The Competition Act 1998 (with Prof Richard Whish, 1999); *Recreations* naval history, music; *Clubs* Oxford and Cambridge; *Style*— Peter Freeman, Esq; ✉ Competition Commission, Victoria House, Southampton Row, London WC1B 4AD (tel 020 7271 0100, fax 020 7271 0367)

FREEMAN, Prof Raymond (Ray); s of Albert Freeman (d 1940), and Hilda Frances, *née* Bush (d 1983); *b* 6 January 1932; *Educ* Nottingham HS, Lincoln Coll Oxford (MA, DPhil, DSc); *m* 19 April 1958, Anne-Marie Cathérine, da of Philippe Pèrinet-Marquet; 3 da (Dominique b 1959, Anne b 1960, Louise b 1962), 2 s (Jean-Marc b 1964, Lawrence b 1969); *Career* ingénieur Centre d'Études Nucléaires de Saclay France 1957–59, sr sci offr Nat Physical Laboratory Teddington Middx 1959–63, mangr Nuclear Magnetic Resonance Res Varian Assoc Palo Alto California 1963–73; Univ of Oxford: fell Magdalen Coll 1973–87, lectr in physical chemistry 1973–82, Aldrichian praelector in chemistry 1982–87; Univ of Cambridge: emeritus prof of magnetic resonance, fell Jesus Coll 1988–; pres Int Soc of Magnetic Resonance 1989–92; Leverhulme medal Royal Soc 1990, Longstaff medal RSC 1999, The Queen's Medal Royal Soc 2002; Hon DSc Univ of Durham 1998; FRS 1979; *Books* A Handbook of Nuclear Magnetic Resonance (1987), Spin Choreography: Basic Steps in High Resolution NMR (1997), Magnetic Resonance in Chemistry and Medicine (2003); *Style*— Prof Ray Freeman, FRS; ✉ 29 Bentley Road, Cambridge CB2 8AW (tel 01223 323958); Jesus College, Cambridge CB5 8BL (tel 01223 339418)

FREEMAN, Richard Downing; OBE; s of John Lawrence Freeman (d 1989), of Victoria, Aust, and Phyllis Jean, *née* Walker (d 1984); *b* 28 September 1936; *Educ* Trinity GS Melbourne, Univ of Melbourne (BComm, MComm, Lacrosse blue); *m* 21 May 1960, Diana Lynne, da of Harold Thomas Cranwell; 3 s (Christopher Thomas b 7 Aug 1961, Andrew Lawrence Downing b 4 March 1963, Timothy David b 4 Dec 1965); *Career* economist; British Petroleum: joined group as jr exec BP Australia 1955, Cooper trainee BP London then BP Germany, asst aviation mangr BP Australia until 1963; lectr then sr lectr and actg prof Univ of Melbourne (concurrently economic advsr Ctee for Economic Devpt Australia) 1963–70, economic advsr then sr economic advsr HM Treay 1971–73, head of div OECD Paris 1973–84, corporate chief economist ICI plc 1984–97 (conslt 1997–98), advsr KPMG 1996–2002; review and assoc ed Economic Record 1965–70, ed OECD Economic Outlook 1976–78; CBI: memb Economic Situation Ctee 1984–92, memb Working Gps on Inflation and on Economic and Monetary Union 1990, chm Working Gp on Environmental Economic Instruments 1990–97, memb Economic Affrs Ctee 1992–96, memb Sub-Ctee on Monetary Policy 1992–93; ESRC: memb Economic Ctee 1985–88, memb Industry Economy and Environment Ctee 1988–92, memb Cncl 1993–97, chm Research Centres Bd 1994–96, chm Research Priorities Bd 1996–97; NEDO: memb Chemical Trade Ctee 1985–86, memb City and Industry Finance Ctee 1988–90; chm: Economic Appraisal Ctee Chemical Industries Assoc 1984–97, Economic Ctee CEFIC 1989–92; memb: Croham Ctee on Exchange Rates 1985–86, Cncl Soc of Business Economists 1985–97, Res Ctee RIIA 1988–91, Cncl Royal Economic Soc 1989–94, Business and Trade Bd Chemical Industries Assoc 1989–97, Innovation Advsy Bd Action Gp on Industry-City Communications 1990–91, Environmental Policy Gp ICAEW 1991–92, Innovation Advsy Bd DTI 1991–93, Cncl Inst of Fiscal Studies, Ctee Centre for Economic Policy Performance LSE, Cncl Intellectual Property Inst; fell Soc of Business Economists; *Publications* author of various articles in jls and chapters in books, incl Environmental Costs and International Competitiveness (in Green Futures for Economic Growth, ed Terry Barker and David Cope 1991), The Future of UK Manufacturing (in jl The Business Economist, Spring 1991), How the UK Economy Should Be Run in the 1990s (editorial of The Business Economist, Winter 1992); *Clubs* Woking Lawn Tennis and Croquet (pres); *Style*— Richard Freeman, Esq, OBE; ✉ Cranford, Coley Avenue, Woking, Surrey GU22 7BS (tel 01483 772247, fax 01483 831001, e-mail rdfreeman@tiscali.co.uk)

FREEMAN, Baron (Life Peer UK 1997), of Dingley in the County of Northamptonshire; Rt Hon Roger Norman Freeman; PC (1993); s of Norman and Marjorie Freeman; *b* 27 May 1942; *Educ* Whitgift Sch, Balliol Coll Oxford (MA); *m* 1969, Jennifer Margaret, *née* Watson; 1 s, 1 da; *Career* pres OUCA 1964; md Bow Publications 1968 (former memb Cncl and treas Bow Group), md Lehman Brothers 1972–83 (joined Lehman Bros US 1969); Parly candidate (Cons) Don Valley 1979, MP (Cons) 1983–97; Parly under sec of state: armed forces MOD 1986–88, Dept of Health 1988–90; min of state: for public transport Dept of Tport 1990–94, for defence procurement MOD 1994–95; Chllr of the Duchy of Lancaster and cabinet min for public serv 1995–97; currently conslt PricewaterhouseCoopers London; chm Thales plc (formerly Thomson), non-exec chm Parity Gp plc 2007–; fndr memb Hundred Gp of UK CA Fin Dirs; FCA 1978; *Publications* incl: Pensions Policy, Professional Practice, A Fair Deal for Water, Democracy in the Digital Age, All Change: British Railway Privatisation; *Recreations* sailing; *Clubs* Carlton, Kennel; *Style*— The Rt Hon the Lord Freeman, PC; ✉ House of Lords, London SW1A 0PW

FREEMANTLE, Andrew Wayne Hampshire; CBE (2007, MBE 1982); s of Lt-Col Arthur Freemantle, and Peggy Frances, *née* Wood; *b* 26 September 1944; *Educ* Framlingham Coll, RMCS, Univ of Sheffield; *m* 10 June 1972, Patricia Mary, da of Brig J H Thompson, of Wilton; 4 da (Victoria b 1974, Lucy b 1976, Emily b 1979, Gemma b 1983); *Career* cmmnd Royal Hampshire Regt 1965; served: Germany, Malaya, Borneo 1965–69; Australian Army (served Aust and S Vietnam) 1969–72; Royal Hampshire Regt: served Hong Kong, UK, NI 1972–76; Staff Coll Camberley 1978, DS at Staff Coll 1983–84, CO 1 Bn Royal Hampshire Regt Berlin and UK 1985–87 (despatches 1987), Cdr 19 Inf Bde 1987–89; ret as Brig 1990; subsequently chief exec Scottish Ambulance Serv NHS Tst

F

(former dir Scottish Ambulance Serv); RNLI: dir 1999–2001, chief exec 2001–; memb: Mensa 1989, RCDS 1990; Freeman City of London 2000; CCMI 2003; *Recreations* running, cooking; *Clubs* Army and Navy; *Style*— Andrew Freemantle, Esq, CBE; ✉ Royal National Lifeboat Institution, West Quay Road, Poole, Dorset BH15 1HZ (tel 0845 122 6999, fax 0845 126 1999)

FREER, (Joan Marian) Penelope (Mrs Terence Fuller); da of Frederick George Sinderby Freer, of Bromley, Kent, and Doris Florence, *née* Wynne; *b* 6 February 1950; *Educ* Bromley HS for Girls, Lady Margaret Hall Oxford (exhibitioner, BA, MA); *m* 1975, Terence Ronald Fuller, s of Cecil Ronald Fuller; 1 s (Timothy b 17 Dec 1980), 1 da (Emily b 17 July 1983); *Career* articled clerk Lee & Pembertons 1971–73, asst slr Nabarro Nathanson 1973–75, ptnr Freshfields 1979–96 (asst slr 1975–79); law tutor: London Metropolitan Univ 2001–, Westminster Univ 2007–; memb Law Soc; *Clubs* Reform; *Style*— Ms Penelope Freer; ✉ (tel 020 8693 3739, fax 020 8333 2151)

FREESTONE, Susan Mathilda (Sue); da of Charles Anthony Freestone, of Canada, and June Freestone (d 1991); *b* 27 March 1948; *Educ* Westdale Collegiate Sch Canada, North London Poly (BA(Eng)); *m* 1, 1966 (m dis 1978), Anthony Ashley Frank Meyer; 1 da (Sophie Mathilda Barbadee b 1972); partner, 1978–85, Donald John Macintyre, *qv*; 1 s (James Kenneth Freestone Macintyre b 1979); m 2, 1989, Vivian Louis White; *Career* bookseller 1966–69, business forecaster IBM 1969–72, ed William Heinemann 1984–1990, ed dir: Mandarin Books 1990–91, Jonathan Cape 1991; publishing dir Hutchinson 1992–; *Recreations* walking the dog; *Style*— Ms Sue Freestone; ✉ Hutchinson, Random House, 20 Vauxhall Bridge Road, London SW1V 2SA (tel 020 7840 8400, fax 020 7233 7870)

FREETH, Martin John; s of Hubert Andrew Freeth (d 1986), and Roseen Marguerite Preston (d 1991); *b* 11 November 1944; *Educ* Marlborough, Univ of Southampton (BA), RCA (MA); *m* 10 Sept 1966, Averil Mary, da of Thomas Webster Bagshaw; 2 da (Kate Sarah Jane b 19 Aug 1978, Ellen Mary b 29 Aug 1981); *Career* TV prodr and new media pioneer; with Sci & Features Dept BBC TV 1971–94, head BBC Multimedia Centre 1995–97, dir Explore-At-Bristol 1998, dep chief exec Nat Endowment for Sci, Technol and the Arts (NESTA) 1999–2001, chief exec NESTA Futurelab 2001–03; Robert F Kennedy Journalism Award (for Horizon: Finding a Voice) 1979, Br Assoc/Glaxo Sci TV Prize (for Horizon: The Spike) 1980; BAFTA: memb 1970–, founding memb Interactive Entertainment Ctee and Awards 1995–, memb Cncl 2001–03; govr Chiswick Community Sch (as Lab Pty nominee); reported on health care provision Save the Children Uganda; FRSA 2001; *Style*— Martin Freeth, Esq; ✉ 61 Sutton Lane South, Chiswick, London W4 3JJ (tel 020 8994 4824, e-mail martin@mfreeth.com, website www.mfreeth.com)

FREETH, Peter Stewart; s of Alfred William Freeth, of Fovant, Wilts; *b* 15 April 1938; *Educ* King Edward's GS Aston, Slade Sch of Fine Art London, Br Sch of Rome; *m* 5 August 1967, Mariolina, da of Prof Leonardo Meliadò, of Rome; 2 s (Dylan b 5 July 1969, Paul b 1 July 1972); *Career* artist; tutor in printmaking Royal Acad Schs 1967–; pt/t posts: Colchester Sch of Art, Camden Inst, Kingsway Coll; RE 1987, RA 1992 (ARA 1990); *Solo Exhibitions* Christopher Mendez Gallery London 1987 and 1989, Royal Acad 1991, S Maria Gradillo Ravello Italy 1997, Mary Kleinman Gallery London 1998, Bankside Gallery London 2001; *Public Collections* Br Museum, V&A, Arts Cncl, Fitzwilliam Museum, Ashmolean Museum, Govt Art Collection, Metropolitan Museum NYC, Nat Gallery Washington DC, Harvard Univ; *Awards* Prix de Rome 1960, Royal Acad Best Print Prize 1986, Wakayama Biennale Print Prize 1989, Hunting Print Prize 2002 and 2004; *Recreations* music, reading; *Style*— Peter Freeth, Esq, RA, RE; ✉ c/o The Royal Academy, London W1V 0DS

FREI, Matt; s of Peter Frei, of Baden-Baden, and Anita Frei; *b* 26 November 1963; *Educ* Westminster, St Peter's Coll Oxford (MA); *Partner* Penelope Quested; *Career* BBC Radio: disc jockey German Service 1986–87, prodr Current Affairs World Service 1987–88, reporter Jerusalem 1988–89, corr Bonn 1989–91, corr Foreign Affairs 1991–92, corr S Europe Rome 1992–; regular contrib: The Spectator, London Review of Books, Wall Street Journal; *Clubs* Gridiron (Oxford), Travellers (assoc memb); *Style*— Matt Frei, Esq; ✉ BBC Rome Bureau, la Piazza Colegio Romano, 00186 Rome, Italy

FRENCH, Dr Charles Andrew Ivey; s of Prof G S French, of Dundas, Canada, and Iris, *née* Ivey; *b* 27 April 1954, Hamilton, Canada; *Educ* Parkside HS Dundas, Univ of Wales Cardiff (BA), Inst of Archaeology Univ of London (MA, PhD); *Partner* Katarzyna Gdaniec; 2 s (Theodore b 21 Nov 1995, Hugh b 8 Dec 1998); *Career* palaeoenvironmentalist and asst dir Fenland Archaeological Tst 1983–92; Univ of Cambridge: lectr 1992–2000, sr lectr in archaeological science and head Dept of Archaeology 2000–05, reader in geoarchaeology 2006–; tstee Fenland Archaeological Tst; MIFA 1983; *Books* The South-West Fen Dyke Survey (1993), Excavation of the Deeping St Nicholas Barrow Complex (1994), Geoarchaeology in Action: Studies in soil micromorphology and landscape evolution (2003), Archaeology and Environment of the Etton Landscape (2005); *Style*— Dr Charles French; ✉ Department of Archaeology, University of Cambridge, Downing Street, Cambridge CB2 3DZ (tel 01223 333533, fax 01223 333503, e-mail caif2@cam.ac.uk)

FRENCH, Christopher; *b* 28 July 1950; *Educ* Roan GS for Boys; *Family* 1 da (Sally b 1977), 1 s (James b 1983); m, 25 June 2001, Marian Ann; *Career* Nationwide Building Society: trainee mangr 1971, branch mangr 1978, sec 1985; Nationwide Anglia Building Society: asst gen mangr 1988, gen mangr 1990, divnl dir 1991–92; chief operating offr National Home Loans plc 1993–95, chief exec Norland Capital Ltd (Kensington Mortgage Company) 1995–98; md: The Oxford Mortgage Company 1998–2004, Rosedale Mortgage Services Ltd 2003–, The Mortgage Marketing Centre 2003–; dir Lambeth Building Society 1999–2006; chm: Nationwide Building Society Staff Assoc 1980–82, Fedn of Building Society Staff Assocs 1980–81; FCIB 1978, DMS 1985, FRSA 1993; *Recreations* music, history; *Style*— Christopher French, Esq; ✉ Rosedale Mortgage Services Ltd, Tudor Cottage, The Green, East Hanney, Wantage, Oxfordshire OX12 0HQ (tel 07775 516434, e-mail chrisfrench.me@btinternet.com)

FRENCH, David; s of Capt Godfrey Alexander French, CBE, RN (d 1988), of Stoke Abbott, Dorset, and Margaret Annis, *née* Best (d 1999); *b* 20 June 1947; *Educ* Sherborne, St John's Coll Durham (BA); *m* 3 Aug 1974, Sarah Anne, da of Rt Rev Henry David Halsey, former Bishop of Carlisle; 4 s (Thomas b 1978, Alexander b 1980, William b 1983, Hal b 1993); *Career* with Nat Cncl of Social Serv 1971–74, head Social Servs Dept RNID 1974–78, dir of serv C of E Children's Soc 1978–87, ceo RELATE Nat Marriage Guidance 1987–95, conslt on Family Policy 1995–97, ceo Commonwealth Inst 1997–2002, ceo Westminster Fndn for Democracy 2003–; chm: London Corrymeela Venture 1974–76, St Albans Int Organ Festival 1985–87, The Twenty-First Century Fndn 1996–2001; memb: Governing Cncl Family Policy Studies Centre 1988–2001, Cncl UK Assoc for Int Year of the Family 1993–95, Bd ACENVO 1995–96, Cncl St Albans Cathedral 1996–2000; tstee: Charity Appointments 1984–91, British Empire and Commonwealth Museum 1999–2003, Round Table Cwlth Jl of Int Affrs 2001–; Liveryman Worshipful Co of Glaziers 1990; MIPD, MRSM, FRSA; *Recreations* challenging projects; *Style*— David French, Esq; ✉ Westminster Foundation for Democracy, 125 Pall Mall, London SW1Y 5EA (tel 020 7930 0408, fax 020 7930 0449, e-mail david@wfd.org)

FRENCH, Douglas Charles; s of Frederick Emil French, of Surrey, and late Charlotte Vera, *née* Russell; *b* 20 March 1944; *Educ* Glyn GS Epsom, St Catharine's Coll Cambridge (MA), Inns of Court Sch of Law; *m* 1978, Sue, da of late Philip Arthur Phillips; 2 s (Paul b 1982, David b 1985), 1 da (Louise b 1983); *Career* dir PW Merkle Ltd 1972–87 (exec 1966–71); called to the Bar Inner Temple 1975; Parly candidate Sheffield Attercliffe 1979, MP (Cons) Gloucester 1987–97, special advsr to Chllr of Exchequer 1982–83 (asst to Rt Hon Sir Geoffrey Howe QC, MP 1976–79), chm Westminster & City Programmes 1997– (md 1979–97); PPS to the Min of State: FCO 1988–89, ODA 1989–90, MAFF 1992–93, Local Govt and Planning 1993–94; PPS to Sec of State for Environment 1994–97; barr; chm Bow Group 1978–79; former: chm All-Pty Building Socs Gp, vice-chm All-Pty Occupational Pensions Gp, vice-chm All-Pty Central Asia Gp, sec All-Pty Insurance and Financial Servs Gp; pres: Gloucester Cons Club 1989–97, Glyn Old Boys' Assoc 2005–07; govr Glyn Technol Sch Epsom 2000– (vice-chm 2003–, chm 2006–); *Recreations* skiing, gardening, squash; *Clubs* RAC; *Style*— Douglas French, Esq; ✉ 231 Kennington Lane, London SE11 5QU (tel 020 7582 6516, fax 020 7582 7245, e-mail df@westminsterandcity.co.uk)

FRENCH, Prof Edward Alexander; s of Edward Francis French (d 1967), and Clara French (d 1982); *b* 17 October 1935; *Educ* Bemrose Sch Derby, LSE (BSc (Econ), LLB, PhD); *m* 11 Aug 1967, Lillias Margaret, da of Walter Riddoch (d 1972); 3 s (Daniel b 1974, Gregory b 1976, Steven b 1979); *Career* Nat Serv RAF 1955–57; called to the Bar Lincoln's Inn; audit examiner Dist Audit Serv 1955–59, princ (former asst princ) Home Civil Serv GPO 1963–67, lectr in accounting LSE 1967–77, prof and head of Dept of Accounting and Fin Control Univ Coll Cardiff 1977–87, prof Univ of Wales Coll of Cardiff 1987–95 (prof emeritus 1996–); pres S Wales Soc of Certified Accountants 1982–83, memb Nat Cncl Chartered Soc of Certified Accountants 1983–86; appointed by Privy Cncl to Academic Advsy Cncl Univ of Buckingham 1992–99; FCCA, FRSA; *Recreations* golf, gardening, swimming, reading; *Clubs* Radyr Golf, Cullen Golf; *Style*— Prof Edward French; ✉ 112 Pencisely Road, Llandaff, Cardiff CF5 1DQ (tel 029 2056 2599, e-mail l.m.french@amserve.net)

FRENCH, John Patrick; MBE (1981), JP (Carmarthenshire 1995); s of Francis George French (d 1985), of Sharow, Nr Ripon, and Doris Maud French; *b* 4 February 1945; *Educ* RMA Sandhurst, Army Staff Coll, Open Univ (BA); *m* 8 Feb 1986, Monica Mary Aitken; 4 s (Nicholas b 19 Nov 1970, Thomas b 9 Nov 1981, James b 1 July 1986, Edward b 16 Sept 1987), 2 da (Penny b 31 Jan 1972, Joanna b 21 Nov 1978); *Career* RCT: joined 1964, SOI Logistics MOD London 1985–88, CO 7 Tank Transporter Regt Germany 1988–90; chief exec: Dyfed Family Health Servs Authy 1990–96, Wales Tourist Bd 1996–; *Style*— John French, Esq, MBE; ✉ Wales Tourist Board, Brunel House, 2 Fitzalan Road, Cardiff CF2 1UY (tel 029 2047 5201, fax 029 2047 5320, mobile 077 7836 2565)

FRENCH, Philip Neville; s of John Wakefield French (d 1971), and Bessie, *née* Funston (d 1978); *b* 28 August 1933; *Educ* Merchant Taylors' Sch Crosby, Bristol GS, Exeter Coll Oxford (BA), Indiana Univ; *m* 31 Dec 1957, Kersti Elisabet, da of Dr Mauritz Molin, of Karlstad, Sweden; 3 s (Sean, Patrick, Karl); *Career* Nat Serv cmmnd 2 Lt Duke of Cornwall's Light Inf, seconded to The Parachute Regt 1952–54; drama critic New Statesman 1957–58, film critic London Magazine 1957–58; BBC: prodr N American Serv 1959–61, sr prodr talks and documentaries 1961–90; film critic The Observer 1978–; Hon DLitt Lancaster Univ 2006; *Books* Age of Austerity 1945–51 (jt ed, 1963), The Novelist As Innovator (ed, 1965), The Movie Moguls (1969), Westerns (1974), Three Honest Men: Edmund Wilson, Lionel Trilling, F R Leavis (1981), The Third Dimension (ed, 1983), The Press: Observed and Projected (jt ed, 1991), Malle on Malle (ed, 1992), The Faber Book of Movie Verse (jt ed, 1993), Wild Strawberries (jtly with Kersti French, 1995), Cult Movies (jtly with Karl French, 1999), Westerns and Westerns Revisited (2005); *Style*— Philip French, Esq; ✉ 62 Dartmouth Park Road, London NW5 1SN (tel 020 7485 1711); Kärne 35, 65593 Karlstad, Sweden

FRENK, Prof Carlos Silvestre; s of Silvestre Frenk, of Mexico City, and Alicia, *née* Mora; *b* 27 October 1951, Mexico City; *Educ* Univ of Mexico (BSc, Gabino Berreda medal), Univ of Cambridge (PhD); *m* 9 Dec 1978, Susan Frances, *née* Clarke; 2 s (David b 22 Oct 1985, Stephen b 31 Aug 1989); *Career* postdoctoral research fell Univ of Calif Berkeley 1981–83, asst research physicist Univ of Calif Santa Barbara 1983–85, postdoctoral research fell Univ of Sussex 1983–85; Univ of Durham: lectr in astronomy 1985–91, reader in physics 1991–93, prof of astrophysics 1993–2001, Ogden prof of fundamental physics 2001–, dir Institute for Computational Cosmology 2001–; memb SERC (later PPARC): Educn, Trg and Fellowships Panel 1990–91, Theory Grants Panel 1991–94, Astronomy and Astrophysics Ctee 1991–94, UK Dark Matter Experiment Review Panels 1991–, Bd Isaac Newton Gp of Telescopes 1994–99 (chm 1997–99), Intercouncil High Performance Computation Mgmnt Ctee 1996–97, Astronomy Ctee 1996–99, Jt Astrophysics and Particle Physics Supercomputing Panel 1996–, First and Planck Instrument Review Panel 1997 (chm); organiser and memb organising ctees of scientific confs, delivered numerous lectures at major int confs and popular science events; author of over 200 refereed and non-refereed pubns; Br Cncl fell 1976–79, Nuffield Fndn science research fell 1991–92, Sir Derman Christopherson fell Univ of Durham 1992–93, PPARC sr fell 1996–99, Leverhulme research fell 2000–01; Royal Soc Wolfson Research Merit Award 2006; FRS 2004; *Recreations* literature, ski training; *Style*— Prof Carlos Frenk; ✉ Institute for Computational Cosmology, Department of Physics, Ogden Centre for Fundamental Physics, Science Laboratories, South Road, Durham DH1 3LE (tel 0191 334 3641, fax 0191 334 3645, e-mail c.s.frenk@durham.ac.uk)

FRERIS, Marika; da of Leonard Freris, of Herts, and Delphine, *née* Squire; *b* 24 July 1962; *Educ* Loreto Coll Sch for Girls, Imperial Coll London (BSc); *Career* sr research asst Dept of Molecular Biology The Wellcome Research Labs Beckenham 1983–85, clinical research scientist Dept of Clinical Immunology and Chemotherapy The Wellcome Fndn Beckenham 1985–89; Hill & Knowlton (UK) Ltd: account dir Eurosciences 1989–91, assoc dir Eurosciences 1991–94, dir Healthcare 1994–96; md: Churchill Communications Europe 1996–98, OCC Europe 1998–2000; owner and md Galliard Healthcare Communications 2000–; memb: Amnesty Int, The Funding Network, Int Service (IS), ActionAid, Oxfam, Nat Trust, Friends of the Earth, Action on Addiction, IPR, BAJ, RCSA; MInstD; *Style*— Ms Marika Freris; ✉ Galliard Healthcare Communications, 37–41 Bedford Row, South Entrance, London WC1R 4JH (tel 020 7663 2252, fax 020 7663 2251, e-mail mfreris@galliardhealth.com)

FRESHWATER, Timothy George (Tim); s of George John Freshwater (d 1986), and Rosalie, *née* MacLauchlan (d 1987); *b* 21 October 1944; *Educ* Eastbourne Coll, Emmanuel Coll Cambridge (MA, LLB); *m* Judy, *née* Lam; *Career* Slaughter and May: joined 1967, ptnr 1975, seconded to Hong Kong office 1979–85, ptnr London (corp fin) 1985–96; Jardine Fleming Gp: joined 1996, chm 1999–2000; currently vice-chm Goldman Sachs (Asia) LLC; dir: Liu Chong Hing Bank, Pacific Century Insurance, Hong Kong Exchanges and Clearing Ltd 2000–06, Aquarius Platinum plc 2006–; pres Law Soc Hong Kong 1984–85, co-chm Jt Working Party on China of Law Soc and the Bar 1990–96; memb: Int Ctee Law Soc 1994–96, Hong Kong Panel on Takeovers and Mergers 1997–99, Securities and Futures Appeals Panel; *Books* The Practitioner's Guide to the City Code on Take-Overs and Mergers (contrib); *Style*— Tim Freshwater

FRETER, Michael Charles Franklin; s of Leslie Charles Freter, of Sidmouth, Devon, and Myra, *née* Wilkinson; *b* 29 October 1947; *Educ* Whitgift Sch, St Edmund Hall Oxford (BA); *m* 2 June 1979, Jan, da of Brian Wilson, of Ealing, London; *Career* sr brand mangr Elida Gibbs Ltd 1970–76, account dir BBDO Advertising Ltd 1976–78, exec dir McCann-Erickson Advertising Ltd 1988–94 (joined 1978), managing ptnr The Imagination Brokers 1994–96, ptnr SWK London Ltd (formerly Summerfield Wilmot Keene Ltd) 1996–; *Style*— Michael Freter, Esq; ✉ 7 Sherbrooke Way, Worcester Park, Surrey KT4 8BG

FRETWELL, Clive; s of Derek Emest Fretwell, of Yorkshire, and Doris Jean, *née* Mitchell; *b* 16 September 1961; *m* 18 Sept 1982, Julie, da of late Richard Sharrock; 2 da (Selina-Jane b 10 Oct 1984, Claire Louise b 14 Jan 1986); *Career* head chef Le Manoir aux Quat'Saisons 1986–97 (commis chef 1982–86), dir Le Petit Blanc École de Cuisine 1991–96, chef conslt Nico Central Midland Hotel Manchester 1997–98, head chef Restaurant Itsu London 1998–2001 (awarded Best Oriental Restaurant 1999–2000), exec chef and dir Blanc Brasseries 2002–; winner Boccuse d'Or Individual Gold Medal 1991 and 1993; *Recreations* cycling; *Style*— Mr C Fretwell; ✉ Blanc Brasseries, 175 Hampton Road, Twickenham TW2 5NG (tel 020 8404 0446, e-mail clive.fretwell@virgin.net)

FREUD, Anthony Peter; OBE (2006); s of Joseph Freud (d 1998), of London, and Katalin, *née* Löwi (d 1990); *b* 30 October 1957; *Educ* KCS Wimbledon, King's Coll London (LLB), Inns of Court Sch of Law; *Career* pupillage as barr 1979–80; theatre mangr Sadler's Wells Theatre 1980–84, co sec and dir of opera planning WNO 1984–92, exec prodr (opera) Philips Classics Productions (The Netherlands) 1992–94, gen dir WNO 1994–2006, gen dir and ceo Houston Grand Opera 2006–; dir National Opera Studio 1994–, chm Opera Europa 2002–; chm of jury Cardiff Singer of the World Competition 1995–; tstee NESTA 2004; memb Hon Soc of Gray's Inn 1979; hon fell Cardiff Univ 2002; *Recreations* the Arts, cooking, travel; *Style*— Anthony Freud, Esq, OBE; ✉ Houston Grand Opera, 510 Preston Street, Houston, TX 77002, USA

FREUD, Sir Clement Raphael; kt (1987); s of Ernst L Freud (d 1970), and Lucie, *née* Brasch (d 1989); bro of Lucian Freud, CH, *qv*, and gs of Prof Sigmund Freud; *b* 24 April 1924; *Educ* Dartington Hall, St Paul's; *m* Sept 1950, June Beatrice (Jill), 2 da of H W Flewett, MA; 2 da (Nicola Mary b 24 Oct 1951, Emma Vallencey, *qv*, b 25 Jan 1962), 2 s (Dominic Martin b 11 Nov 1958, Matthew Rupert, *qv*, b 2 Nov 1963); *Career* Royal Ulster Rifles 1942–47, liaison offr Int Mil Tribunal Nüremberg 1946–47; writer, broadcaster, cook, nightclub owner, amateur jockey; rector Dundee Univ 1974–80; MP (Lib): Isle of Ely 1973–1983, NE Cambs 1983–87; Lord Rector Univ of St Andrews 2002–; sponsor Official Info Bill 1978–79; MUniv Open Univ 1989; *Books* Grimble (1968), Grimble at Christmas (1973), Freud on Food (1978), Book of Hangovers (1981), Below the Belt (1983), No-One Else Has Complained (1988), The Gourmet's Tour of Great Britain and Ireland (1989), Freud Ego (2001); *Clubs* MCC, British Rail Staff Assoc, March, Groucho, Royal Ascot Racing; *Style*— Sir Clement Freud; ✉ 14 York House, Upper Montagu Street, London W1H 1FR (tel 020 7724 5432, fax 020 7724 3210)

FREUD, Emma Vallencey; da of Sir Clement Freud, *qv*, and June Beatrice (Jill), *née* Flewett; *b* 25 January 1962; *Educ* St Mary's Convent, Queen's Coll London, Univ of Bristol, Univ of London (BA); *Children* 1 da (Scarlett b 21 June 1995), 3 s (Jake b 10 June 1997, Charlie b 4 Nov 2001, Spike b 8 Dec 2003); *Career* backing singer to Mike Oldfield 1979–81, musical dir regnl theatres 1984–86, co-dir Open Air Theatre Regent's Park 1986–87; freelance journalist; memb band The Girls 1988–91, tstee Comic Relief 1993; film script ed: Four Weddings and a Funeral 1994, Notting Hill 1999, Bridget Jones's Diary 2000, Love Actually 2003; script ed The Vicar of Dibley 1995–98; assoc prodr Live 8 2005; *Television* incl: reporter Six O'Clock Show (LWT) 1986–88; host: Pillowtalk (LWT) 1987–89, The Media Show (Channel 4) 1990–91, Everyman (BBC1) 1994, Edinburgh Nights (BBC2) 1994–97, Theatreland (LWT) 1996–98, Sins of the Flesh (BBC1) 2000; *Radio* incl: reporter Loose Ends (Radio 4) 1987–, presenter The Lunchtime Programme (Radio 1) 1994; *Clubs* Electric; *Style*— Ms Emma Freud; ✉ c/o KBJ Management Ltd, 5 Soho Square, London W1V 5DE

FREUD, Esther Lea; da of Lucian Freud, OM, CH, *qv*, and Bernardine Coverley; *b* 2 May 1963; *Educ* Michael Hall Sch, Drama Centre London; *Career* writer; actress 1983–91; *Books* Hideous Kinky (1992), Peerless Flats (1993), Gaglow (1997), The Wild (2000), The Sea House (2003), Love Falls (2007); *Style*— Miss Esther Freud; ✉ c/o Georgia Garratt, A P Watt, 20 John Street, London WC1N 2DR

FREUD, Lucian; OM (1993), CH (1983); s of Ernst L Freud (d 1970), and Lucie, *née* Brasch (d 1989); bro of Sir Clement Freud, *qv*; *b* 8 December 1922; *Educ* Central Sch of Art, E Anglian Sch of Painting and Drawing; *m* 1, 1948 (m dis 1952), Kathleen Garman, da of Jacob Epstein; 2 da; m 2, 1953 (m dis 1957), Lady Caroline Maureen Blackwood, da of 4 Marquess of Dufferin and Ava; *Career* ordinary seaman SS Baltrover 1942; painter; teacher Slade Sch of Art 1948–58; visiting asst Norwich Sch of Art 1964–65; exhibitions: Lefevre Gallery 1944 and 1946, London Gallery 1947 and 1948, British Cncl and Galerie René Drouin Paris 1948, Hanover Gallery 1950 and 1952, British Cncl and Vancouver Art Coll 1951, British Cncl Venice Biennale 1954, Marlborough Fine Art 1958, 1963 and 1968, Anthony d'Offay 1972, 1978 and 1982, first retrospective (Hayward Gallery, then Bristol, Birmingham and Leeds) 1974, Nishimura Gallery Tokyo 1979, Thomas Agnew & Sons 1983, second retrospective (British Cncl, Hirshhorn Museum and Sculpture Garden, Smithsonian Inst Washington DC Sept-Nov 1987, Musée National d'Art Moderne Paris 1987–88, Hayward Gallery Feb-April 1988, Neue Nationalgalerie Berlin May-June 1988, Scottish Nat Gallery of Modern Art Edinburgh July-Oct 1988), works on paper retrospective exhibition (Ashmolean Museum Oxford May-June 1988, The Fruitmarket Gallery Edinburgh June-July 1988, Ferens Art Gallery Hull July-Aug 1988, Walker Art Gallery Liverpool Sept-Oct 1988, Royal Albert Memorial Museum Exeter Oct-Nov 1988, The Fine Arts Museum of San Francisco USA 1988, Minneapolis Inst of Art USA March-April 1989, Brooke Alexander Gallery NY May- July 1989, Cleveland Museum of Art July-Sept 1989); works in public collections: Tate Gallery, Nat Portrait Gallery, V & A Museum, Arts Cncl of GB, British Museum, British Cncl, DoE, Cecil Higgins Museum Bedford, Fitzwilliam Museum Cambridge, Nat Museum of Wales Cardiff, Scottish Nat Gallery of Modern Art Edinburgh, Hartlepool Art Gallery, Walker Art Gallery Liverpool, Univ of Liverpool, City Art Coll and Whitworth Gallery Manchester, Ashmolean Museum of Art Oxford, Harris Museum and Art Gallery Preston, Rochdale Art Gallery, Southampton Art Gallery, Queensland Art Gallery Brisbane, Art Gallery of S Australia Adelaide, Art Gallery of Western Australia Perth, Musée Nationale d'Art Moderne Pompidou Centre Paris, The Art Inst of Chicago, Beaverbrook Fndn Fredericton, Museum of Modern Art NY, Cleveland Museum of Art Ohio, Museum of Art Carnegie Inst Pittsburgh, Achenbaach Fndn for Graphic Arts ande Fine Arts Museum San Francisco, The Saint Louis Art Museum, Hirshhorn Museum and Sculpture Garden, Smithsonian Inst Washington DC; hon memb American Acad and Inst of Arts and Letters 1988; *Style*— Lucian Freud, Esq, OM, CH; ✉ c/o Matthew Marks, Matthew Marks Gallery, 523 West 24th Street, New York, NY 10011, USA

FREUD, Matthew; s of Sir Clement Freud, *qv*, and June, *née* Flewitt; *b* 2 November 1963; *Educ* Westminster, Pimlico; *m* 1 (m dis), Caroline Hutton; 2 s (George Rupert b 3 Oct 1995, Jonah Henry b 1 April 1997); m 2, Elisabeth Murdoch, *qv*, da of Rupert Murdoch; 1 da (Charlotte Emma b 17 Nov 2000), 1 s (Samson Murdoch b 13 Jan 2007); *Career* chm Freud Communications 1990–; tstee Comic Relief; *Style*— Matthew Freud, Esq; ✉ Freud Communications Ltd, 19–21 Mortimer Street, London W1T 3DX (tel 020 7580 2626, fax 020 7637 2626)

FREUDMANN, Steven; s of Max Freudmann (d 1967), and Eleanor, *née* Hughes; *b* 15 June 1949, Wrexham, Clwyd; *Educ* Grove Park GS, Kingston Univ; *m* 1971 (m dis); 1 s (Matthew b 15 Aug 1971), 1 da (Rosie b 30 Aug 1975); partner, Cristina Fernandez; 2 s (Hugo b 22 May 2002, Max b 12 Dec 2005); *Career* md Majestic Travel 1967–, chm Advantage Travel Centres 2004–, chm Seligo 2006–, dir Triton Travel Gp 2006–; dir ABTA 1991– (chm 1991–97, pres 1997–2000), chm Inst of Travel and Tourism (ITT) 2001–; ITT Odyssey Award 1999; fell ITT 1968, FTS 1998; *Recreations* all sport, gardening, mountain climbing; *Style*— Steven Freudmann, Esq; ✉ Brook House, Worthenbury, Wrexham, Clwyd LL13 0FD; Majestic Travel, St Peter's Square, Ruthin, Denbighshire LL15 1DH (tel 01824 705670, e-mail steven@itt.co.uk)

FREWER, Prof Richard John Barrett; s of Dr Edward George Frewer (d 1972), and Bridget Audrey Christina Pennefather, *née* Ford (d 1994); *b* 24 January 1942; *Educ* Shrewsbury, Gonville & Caius Coll Cambridge (MA), AA (Dip Arch); *m* 19 July 1969, Carolyn Mary, da of Thomas Arthur Butler (d 1969); 1 da (Emelye b 1971); *Career* architect Arup Assocs 1966–91 (ptnr 1977–91, conslt 1991–98); major works incl: Sir Thomas White Bldg, St John's Coll Oxford (with Sir Philip Dowson), Theatre Royal Glasgow, Liverpool Garden Festival Hall, Baburgh DC Offices Suffolk, Stockley Park Arena Heathrow; prof of architecture Univ of Bath 1991–2000; chair prof of architecture Univ of Hong Kong 2000–05; pt/t professional tenor soloist, Bach specialist, Lieder and Oratorio repertoire; RIBA, HKIA; *Recreations* painting, gardening; *Style*— Prof Richard Frewer; ✉ Alma Cottage, Charlcombe, Bath BA1 8DR (tel 01225 316485, e-mail richardfrewer@hotmail.com)

FREWIN, Jonathan Mayo; *b* 15 May 1955; *Educ* LCP; *Career* art ed Haymarket Publishers London 1976–77 and 1979–81, art dir Morgan Grampian London 1977–79, art dir PCI mgmnt consultancy New York 1981–84, prof Parsons Sch of Design New York 1984–88, pres/creative dir Frewin Shapiro Inc New York 1984–89, ptnr/creative dir ACFS Berkshire 1989–93, jt chief exec/creative dir Red Cell Glasgow 1993–; *Style*— Jonathan Frewin, Esq; ✉ Red Cell Scotland Ltd, Design House, 8 Minerva Way, Glasgow G3 8AU (tel 0141 221 6882, fax 0141 248 7965, e-mail jonathan_frewin@redcellnetwork.com)

FREYBERG, 3 Baron (UK 1951); Valerian Bernard Freyberg; o s of 2 Baron Freyberg, OBE, MC (d 1993), and Ivry Perronelle Katharine, *née* Guild; *b* 15 December 1970; *Educ* Eton, Camberwell Coll of Arts, Slade Sch of Fine Art (MA); *m* 27 April 2002, Dr Harriet Rachel, da of late John Atkinson; 1 s (Hon Joseph John b 21 March 2007); *Heir* s, Hon Joseph Freyberg; *Career* artist; memb Design Cncl 2001–04; elected hereditary crossbench peer 1999; *Recreations* beekeeping, music; *Style*— The Rt Hon the Lord Freyberg

FREYD, Michael; s of Cecil Freyd (d 1971), and Joan, *née* Woodhead (d 1960); *b* 5 June 1948; *Educ* Burnage GS Manchester, Univ of Hull (BSc); *m* 21 March 1971, Marilyn Sharon (Lyn), da of Ivor Paul Levinson (d 1960); 1 s (Mark b 29 Aug 1979), 2 da (Danielle b 14 June 1972, Elana b 7 May 1976); *Career* dep md UBS (formerly Phillips & Drew) (joined 1969, ptnr 1980–94, memb Option Ctee 1986–92), dir (with responsibility for mktg and business devpt) Prolific Objective Asset Management Ltd 1994–; memb Soc of Investment Analysts; MSI; *Recreations* golf, skiing, bridge, chess; *Style*— Michael Freyd, Esq; ✉ Prolific Objective Asset Management Ltd, Austin Friars House, 2–6 Austin Friars, London EC2N 2HE (tel 020 7628 3717)

FRICKER, His Hon (Anthony) Nigel; QC (1977); s of late Dr William Shapland Fricker, and Margaret, *née* Skinner; *b* 7 July 1937; *Educ* King's Sch Chester, Univ of Liverpool (LLB); *m* 1960, Marilynn Ann, da of late August L Martin, of Pennsylvania, USA; 2 da (Deborah b 1962, Susan b 1964), 1 s (Joseph b 1969); *Career* called to the Bar Gray's Inn 1960; prosecuting counsel to DHSS Wales & Chester Circuit (N) 1975–77, recorder of the Crown Court 1975–84, asst cmmr Boundary Cmmn Wales 1981–84, circuit judge (NE Circuit) 1984–2001 (dep circuit judge 2001–05); memb Bd Children and Family Court Advsy and Support Serv (CAFCASS) 2001; memb Mental Health Review Tbnl 2001–; pres Cncl of HM Circuit Judges 1997; *Books* Emergency Remedies in the Family Courts (gen ed and jt author, 1990, 3 edn 1997), Enforcement of Injunctions and Undertakings (jt author, 1991), The Family Court Practice (consulting ed, 1993–2002); *Style*— His Hon Nigel Fricker, QC; ✉ 6 Park Square, Leeds LS1 2LW

FRIDD, Nicholas Timothy; s of Norman Sidney Fridd, and Beryl Rosamond, *née* Phillips; *b* 21 September 1953; *Educ* Wells Blue Sch, ChCh Oxford (MA); *m* 14 Sept 1985, Fiona Bridgnell, da of Dr Keir Mackessack-Leitch; 1 da (Charlotte Mary b 11 Jan 1988), 1 s (John Bridgnell b 2 Nov 1989); *Career* called to the Bar Inner Temple 1975; *Books* Basic Practice in Courts, Tribunals and Inquiries (1989, 3 edn 2000); *Recreations* carpentry, walking disused railways; *Style*— Nicholas Fridd, Esq; ✉ Manor Farm, East Horrington, Wells, Somerset BA5 3DP (tel 01749 679832, fax 01749 679849); Albion Chambers, Broad Street, Bristol BS1 1DR (tel 0117 927 2144, fax 0117 926 2569)

FRIEDMAN, Brian Sydney; s of Roy Friedman, of London, and Denise Adele, *née* Salter; *b* 25 February 1957; *Educ* Highgate Sch, St John's Coll Cambridge (MA); *m* 1983, Frances Patricia, *née* Davey; 1 da (Emma b 24 April 1987), 1 s (Jonathan b 1 March 1989); *Career* chartered accountant; Coopers & Lybrand 1978–84, Stoy Benefit Consulting 1985–94, ptnr and global head of Human Capital Services Andersen 1994–; pres Soc of Share Scheme Practitioners 1995–; ACA 1981, FTII 1988, MIPD 1990; *Books* Effective Staff Incentives (1991), Company Car Taxation (1993), Pay and Benefits Handbook (1994), Delivering on the Promise (1998); *Recreations* children, travel, football, reading; *Style*— Brian Friedman, Esq; ✉ Andersen, 1 Surrey Street, London WC2R 2PS (tel 020 7438 2238, e-mail brian.friedman@uk.andersen.com)

FRIEDMAN, David Peter; QC (1990); s of Wilfred Emanuel Friedman (d 1973), and Rosa, *née* Lees (d 1972); *b* 1 June 1944; *Educ* Tiffin Boys' Sch, Lincoln Coll Oxford (MA, BCL); *m* 29 Oct 1972, Sara Geraldine, da of Dr Sidney Linton; *Career* called to the Bar 1968, recorder 1998–2005, bencher Inner Temple 1999; *Recreations* good food (cooked by others), reading; *Clubs* Lansdowne; *Style*— David P Friedman, Esq, QC; ✉ 4 Pump Court, Temple, London EC4Y 7AN (tel 020 7842 5555, fax 020 7583 2036)

FRIEDMAN, Maria; da of Leonard Matthew Friedman (d 1994), of Edinburgh, and Clair Llewellyn Friedman; *b* 19 March 1960; *Educ* E Barnet Comp Sch, Arts Educnl Sch Golden Lane London; *Children* 2 s (Toby Oliver Sams-Friedman b 26 Nov 1994, Alfie Olegovich Poupko Friedman b 21 July 2002); *Career* actress and singer; *Theatre* RNT incl: Ghetto (Evening Standard Award for Best Play 1990), Sunday in the Park with George (Olivier Award for Best Musical 1991), Square Rounds, Lady in The Dark 1997; other prodns incl: Blues in the Night (Donmar Warehouse, Piccadilly), April in Paris (Ambassadors) 1994, The Break of Day (Royal Court) 1995, Passion (Queen's, Olivier Award for Best Actress in a Musical 1997) 1996, Chicago (Adelphi) 1998–99, Witches of Eastwick (Theatre Royal) 2000, Maria Friedman Live One Woman Show (Ambassadors) 2002, Ragtime (Piccadilly Theatre, Olivier Award for Best Actress in a Musical 2004) 2003; *Concerts* venues incl: Barbican, Royal Festival Hall, Palladium, Drury Lane, Albert Hall, St David's Hall; By Special Arrangement (Donmar Warehouse, Olivier Awards Best Entertainment 1995), By Extra Special Arrangement (Whitehall) 1995, Henley Festival 1999, Last Night of the Proms 2002, From London to New York (Cafe Carlyle) 2003, By Special Arrangement (Cafe Carlyle) 2004; *Television* incl: Me and the Girls, Blues in the Night, Red Dwarf, Casualty, Frank Stubbs Promotes; *Film* Joseph and the Amazing Technicolour Dreamcoat; *Albums* solo recordings: Maria Friedman, Maria Friedman Live; contrib to numerous cast recordings; *Style*— Ms Maria Friedman

FRIEDMAN, Sonia; da of Leonard Friedman, and Clair Friedman; *Educ* St Christophers Letchworth, Central Sch of Speech and Drama; *Career* theatre prodr; head Mobile Prodns and Theatre for Young People RNT 1989–93, co-fndr Out of Joint Prodns (with Max Stafford-Clark, *qv*) 1993, fndr Sonia Friedman Prodns (SFP, subsid of Ambassador Theatre Gp) 2002; prodns with Out of Joint incl: The Queen and I, The Libertine, The Steward of Christendom, The Break of Day, The Positive Hour, Shopping and Fucking, Our Lady of Sligo, Blue Heart; programmed at New Ambassadors Theatre: Stones in His Pockets, Drummers, Some Explicit Polaroids, Krapp's Last Tape, Our Late Night, Al Murray the Pub Landlord, Jane Eyre, Mother Courage and Her Children, A Doll's House, The Mill on the Floss, The Vagina Monologues, One for the Road, Boston Marriage, Abigail's Party; other theatre prodns and co-prodns in the West End incl: In Celebration, Boeing-Boeing, The Dumb Waiter, Tintin, Love Song, Bent, Rock'N'Roll, 'Eh Joe, Faith Healer, The Play's the Thing, Donkey's Years, The Woman In White,

F

Celebration, Shoot the Crow, Otherwise Engaged, As You Like It, The Home Place, Whose Life is it Anyway?, By the Bog of Cats, Guantanamo: Honour Bound to Defend Freedom, Endgame, Jumpers, Calico, See You Next Tuesday, Hitchcock Blonde, Absolutely! (Perhaps), Sexual Perversity in Chicago, Ragtime, Macbeth, What the Night Is, A Day In the Death of Joe Egg (also Broadway), Afterplay, Up for Grabs, On An Average Day, Noises Off, Benefactors, Lobby Hero, Gagarin's Way, Maria Friedman, Mind Games, A Servant to Two Masters, Port Authority, Spoonface Steinberg, Speed-the-Plow, In Flame, The Mystery of Charles Dickens, The Late Middle Classes, Last Dance at Dum Dum, The Man of Mode, Road, Three Sisters, Our Country's Good, Maria Friedman by Special Arrangement; *Style—* Ms Sonia Friedman; ✉ Sonia Friedman Productions, Duke of York Theatre, 104 St Martin's Lane, London WC2N 4BG

FRIEDMANN, Julian; *b* 1944, South Africa; *Educ* Univ of York (BA), SOAS Univ of London (MA); *Career* jt md Blake Friedmann Literary Agency; ed ScriptWriter magazine 2001–; EU Media 1 project: creator and former head of studies Prog for the Int Launch of TV Series (PILOTS), UK co-ordinator European Audiovisual Entrepreneurs (EAVE) prodr trg prog; visiting lectr: Univ of Brussels, Munich Film Sch, Masterschool Drehbuch Berlin, Liverpool John Moore Univ, London Coll of Printing, RCA, Nat Film & TV Sch, Northern Sch of Film and TV Leeds (currently advsr), De Montfort Univ (also estab masters degree in TV scriptwriting); former advsr Euro Film Coll Ebeltoft Denmark; former memb: Euro Jury Emmy nominations, Jury Grierson Documentary Award; *Books* How to Make Money Scriptwriting, Writing Long-Running Television Series (ed, 2 vols); *Style—* Julian Friedmann, Esq; ✉ Blake Friedmann Literary Agency, 122 Arlington Road, London NW1 7HP (tel 020 7284 0408, fax 020 7284 0442, e-mail julian@blakefriedmann.co.uk)

FRIEDRICH, William Michael (Bill); s of William E Friedrich, and Elizabeth C, *née* Kline; *Educ* Babylon HS, Union Coll (cum laude), Columbia Law Sch (Dr Jur); *Career* assoc Thacher, Proffitt & Wood 1974–75, ptnr Shearman & Sterling 1983–95 (assoc 1975–83), gen counsel British Gas 1995–97, gen counsel BG plc 1997–2005, dep chief exec BG Gp plc 2000–; non-exec dir Royal Bank of Scotland 2006–; memb American Bar Assoc; *Recreations* field sports, riding, tennis; *Clubs* Union (NY), Mountain Lake, Tamarack (NY), Norfolk (CT); *Style—* W Friedrich, Esq; ✉ BG Group plc, 100 Thames Valley Park Drive, Reading, Berkshire RG6 1PT (tel 0118 929 3367, fax 0118 929 3327, mobile 07785 950 648, e-mail william.friedrich@bg-group.com)

FRIEL, Anna; *b* 12 July 1976, Rochdale; *Career* actress; *Theatre* Look Europe 1999, Closer 2000, Lulu 2001; *Television* incl: GBH 1991, Emmerdale 1992, Medics 1993, Brookside 1993–95, Cadfael 1996, Tales from the Crypt 1996, Our Mutual Friend 1998, The Tribe 1998, Fields of Gold 2002, Watermelon 2003, Perfect Strangers 2004, The Jury 2004; *Films* incl: The Stringer 1997, The Land Girls 1998, St Ives 1998, A Midsummer Night's Dream 1999, Rogue Trader 1999, Mad Cows 1999, Sunset Strip 2000, An Everlasting Piece 2000, The War Bride (nominee Best Actress Canadian Acad Award) 2000, Me Without You 2001, Timeline 2002; *Awards* Best Newcomer TV Quick Awards 1994, Best Actress Nat TV Awards 1995, Best Actress Smash Hits Poll Award Winner 1995, Best Supporting Actress (for Closer) Drama Desk Awards NY 1999; *Style—* Ms Anna Friel; ✉ c/o Conway van Gelder Ltd, 18–21 Jermyn Street, London SW1Y 6HP (e-mail annafriel@annafriel.com)

FRIEND, Carol Anne; da of late Leslie George Friend, of London, and Ida Margaret, *née* Earl; *b* 11 September 1949; *Educ* Tiffins Girls' GS Kingston upon Thames, St John's Coll of Further Educn Manchester (HND, DipCAM PR); *Career* dir Wyndham Public Relations 1977–80, md Pielle + Co Ltd (now PIELLE Consulting Group) 1980–, dir European Communication Partners scrl (ECP Global) 1994–, dir KioskPoint UK Ltd 1999–2001; chm Orbit Cromwell Housing Assoc 1984–86; CAM Fndn: govr 1985–92, chm 1992–94, dep chm 1994–95, vice-pres 1995–; pres IPR 1986, memb PO Users Nat Cncl 1987–90; chm London W End PO and Telecommunications Advsy Ctees 1987–2001; tstee PR Educn Tst 1989–95; previously external examiner IPR Dip; memb: London Region Cncl CBI 1990–96, Gtr London Regnl Ctee FE Funding Cncl 1995–98, Nat Cncl CBI 1995–97; awarded Sir Stephen Tallents Medal IPR for outstanding contrib to PR educn and professional standards 1993; Freeman Guild of PR Practitioners 2003– (Master 2006–07); FCIPR (FIPR 1987), FCAM 1992; *Style—* Miss Carol Friend; ✉ PIELLE Consulting Group, Museum House, 25 Museum Street, London WC1A 1PL (tel 020 7323 1587, fax 020 7631 0029)

FRIEND, Lionel; s of Norman Alfred Child Friend (d 1991), and Moya Lilian, *née* Dicks (d 2003); *b* 13 March 1945; *Educ* Royal GS High Wycombe, RCM, London Opera Centre; *m* 1969, Jane, da of Norman Edward Hyland; 1 s (Toby Thomas b 1984), 2 da (Clea Deborah b 1972, Corinne Jane b 1977); *Career* conductor WNO 1969–72, Glyndebourne Festival and Touring Opera 1969–72; 2 Kapellmeister Staatstheater Kassel Germany 1972–75; staff conductor ENO 1976–89; music dir: Nexus Opera 1981–, New Sussex Opera 1989–96; conductor-in-residence Birmingham Conservatoire 2003–; guest conductor: Philharmonia, City of Birmingham Symphony Orch, BBC Symphony Orch, Royal Ballet, Orchestre National de France, Nouvel Orchestre Philharmonique, Austrian Radio Symphony Orch, Swedish Radio Symphony Orch, Hungarian State Symphony Orch, Budapest Symphony Orch, Scot Chamber Orch, London Sinfonietta, Nash Ensemble, Opéra Nat de la Monnaie, Oper Frankfurt, LA Opera, Portland Opera, Opera Zuid; recordings incl works by Bliss, Brian, Britten, Debussy, Durkó, Colin Matthews, Anthony Milner, Payne, Poulenc, Schönberg, Souster, Stravinsky, Tavener and Turnage; *Recreations* reading, theatre; *Style—* Lionel Friend, Esq; ✉ 136 Rosendale Road, London SE21 8LG (tel and fax 020 8761 7845)

FRIEND, Mark; s of Prof John Friend, and Carol, *née* Loofe; *b* 23 November 1957; *Educ* Gonville & Caius Coll Cambridge (BA), Institut D'Etudes Européennes Brussels (Licence Spéciale en Droit Européen); *m* 19 May 1990, Margaret DeJong; 2 s; *Career* admitted slr 1982, ptnr (specialising in competition law and regulation) Allen & Overy 1990–; author of numerous contribs to legal periodicals on competition law; *Recreations* music, golf; *Clubs* RAC, Dulwich and Sydenham Hill Golf; *Style—* Mark Friend, Esq; ✉ Allen & Overy, One New Change, London EC4M 9QQ (tel 020 7330 3000, fax 020 7330 9999)

FRIEND, Prof Sir Richard Henry; kt (2003); s of John Henry Friend, and Dorothy Jean, *née* Brown; *b* 18 January 1953; *Educ* Rugby, Trinity Coll Cambridge (MA, PhD); *m* 1979, Carol Anne Maxwell, *née* Beales; 2 da (Rachel Frances b 31 July 1981, Lucy Alexandra 14 Feb 1984); *Career* res fell St John's Coll Cambridge 1977–80; Univ of Cambridge: demonstrator in physics 1980–85, lectr 1985–93, reader 1993–95, Cavendish prof of physics 1995–; visiting prof Univ of Calif Santa Barbara 1986–87, visiting fell Royal Instn London 1992–98, Mary Shepard B Upson visiting prof Cornell Univ USA 2003, Kelvin lectr IEE 2004; Nuffield Sci res fell 1992–93; chief scientist Camridge Display Technol Ltd 1997–; chief scientist and dir Plastic Logic Ltd 2000–; J V Boys prize Inst of Physics 1988, interdisciplinary award RSC 1991, Hewlett-Packard Prize European Physical Soc 1996, Rumford Medal Royal Soc 1998, Italgas Prize for Research and Technological Innovation 2001, MacRoberts Prize Royal Acad of Engrg 2002, Silver Medal Royal Acad of Engrg 2002, Faraday Medal Inst of Electrical Engrgs 2003, Gold Medal European Materials Research Soc 2003, Descartes Prize European Cmmn 2003; hon fell Trinity Coll Cambridge 2004; Hon DUniv Linköping Sweden 2000, Hon DUniv Mons Belgium 2002; FInstP 1997 (MInstP 1988), FRS 1993, FREng 2002, FIEE 2002, Hon FRSC 2004; *Publications* author of numerous papers on solid state and chemical physics in scientific journals; *Style—* Prof Sir Richard Friend, FRS; ✉ University of Cambridge, Cavendish Laboratory, Madingley Road, Cambridge CB3 OHE (tel 01223 337218, fax 01223 353397, e-mail rhf10@cam.ac.uk)

FRIEND, Tony Peter; s of H John Friend (d 1992), of Totteridge, London, and Daphne Denise, *née* Cavanagh; *b* 30 October 1954; *Educ* Highgate Sch, City of London (accountancy fndn course); *m* 25 Sept 1982, Antoinette (Toni) Julie, da of Thomas Brennan; 3 s (William Alexander Goodwin b 9 July 1988, Thomas Christopher Goodwin b 1 June 1991, John Sebastian Goodwin b 7 April 1994); *Career* Pannell Kerr Forster CAs 1974–79 (qualified 1978), Grindlay Brandts/Grindlays Bank/ANZ 1979–86; County NatWest: dir NatWest Wood Mackenzie 1986–94, dir of investment banking NatWest Markets 1995; md Ludgate Communications 1996–97; dir: Ludgate Group 1996–97, Ludgate Communications Inc 1996–97; ptnr and dir College Hill Associates 1998–; memb Nat Exec Assoc of Student Accountants 1974–79; Duke of Edinburgh Gold and Silver Awards 1971; Liveryman Worshipful Co of CAs in England and Wales; memb: Faculty of Fin and Mgmnt ICA, Investor Rels Soc; FCA, ACInstT, MSI; *Recreations* sports, travel, theatre; *Clubs* MCC (cricket and real tennis), East India and Devonshire, Old Cholmeleian Sports and Football, Totteridge Cricket; *Style—* Tony Friend, Esq; ✉ 19 Prince of Wales Drive, London SW11 4SB (tel 020 7223 0879, e-mail tony@sw11.demon.co.uk); College Hill Associates, 78 Cannon Street, London EC4N 6HH (tel 020 7457 2020, fax 020 7248 3295, e-mail tony.friend@collegehill.com)

FRIER, Prof Brian Murray; s of William Murray Frier, of Edinburgh; *Educ* George Heriot's Sch Edinburgh, Univ of Edinburgh (BSc, MB ChB, MD); *m* Isobel Margaret, da of Dr Henry Donald Wilson (d 1991), of Edinburgh; 1 da (Emily Margaret); *Career* jr med appts Edinburgh and Dundee 1972–76, research fell in diabetes and metabolism Cornell Univ 1976–77, sr med registrar Edinburgh 1978–82; conslt physician: Western Infirmary and Gartnavel Gen Hosp Glasgow 1982–87, Royal Infirmary Edinburgh 1987–; Univ of Edinburgh: former pt/t reader in medicine, currently hon prof of diabetes; author of numerous publications on diabetes and hypoglycaemia; chm Hon Advsy Panel on Diabetes and Driving (UK) 2001–, former chm Diabetes Research in Scotland (Chief Scientist Office); former govr George Heriot's Tst Edinburgh; memb: Diabetes UK (R D Lawrence lectr 1986), Assoc of Physicians GB and I, Euro Assoc for the Study of Diabetes, American Diabetes Assoc; Somogyi Award Hungarian Diabetes Assoc 2004; FRCPE 1984, FRCPG 1986; *Books* Hypoglycaemia and Diabetes: Clinical and Physiological Aspects (jt ed with B M Fisher, 1993), Hypoglycaemia in Clinical Diabetes (jt ed with B M Fisher, 1999, 2 edn 2007); *Recreations* history (ancient and modern), appreciation of the arts, sport; *Style—* Prof Brian M Frier; ✉ 100 Morningside Drive, Edinburgh EH10 5NT (tel 0131 447 1653); Royal Infirmary of Edinburgh, 51 Little France Crescent, Edinburgh EH16 4SA (tel 0131 242 1475, fax 0131 242 1485, e-mail brian.frier@luht.scot.nhs.uk)

FRIER, (Gavin Austin) Garry; s of Gavin Walter Rae Frier (d 1985), and Isabel Fraser, *née* Austin (d 1981); *b* 18 May 1953; *Educ* Hutchesons' Boys Glasgow, Univ of Strathclyde (BA); *m* 1978, Jane Carolyn, da of John Keith Burton, of Glasgow; 1 s (Stuart Austin b 1981); *Career* CA; dir County Bank Ltd (renamed County Natwest Ltd) 1985–87; chief exec: Ferrum Holdings plc 1987–94, Williams de Broë plc Edinburgh 1995–97; dir A R Brown McFarlane Ltd 1993–, dir of corp fin Charterhouse Securities Edinburgh 1997–2002, dir of corp fin ING Barings Edinburgh 2003–, chief exec Corp Governance Advsrs Ltd; MICAS 1978; *Recreations* tennis, shooting, skiing; *Clubs* New (Edinburgh); *Style—* Garry Frier, Esq; ✉ garryfrier@aol.com

FRIES, Richard James; s of Felix Theodore Fries (d 1942), Joan Mary, *née* Hickling (d 2005); *b* 7 July 1940; *Educ* Kingston GS, King's Coll Cambridge; *m* 1970, Carole Anne, da of Henry Wilson Buick; 2 da (Hannah Jane b 21 Oct 1971, Jessica Marion b 26 May 1974), 1 s (James Wilson b 31 March 1978); *Career* various positions Home Office 1965–92, Chief Charity Cmmr 1992–99, chm Bd Int Centre for Not-for-Profit Law 1999–2005, visiting fell Centre for Civil Society LSE 2000–06; *Recreations* music, chess, walking; *Style—* Richard Fries, Esq; ✉ 10 Broxash Road, London SW11 6AB (tel 020 7223 1407, e-mail rfries3340@aol.com)

FRISBY, Simon Rollo; s of Lt-Col Lionel Claud Frisby, DSO, MC (d 1936), of Basingstoke, Hants, and Angela Beryl, *née* Hoare (d 1990); *b* 23 October 1933; *Educ* Eton; *m* 29 Sept 1959, (Sara) Belinda, da of Capt William Herbert Fox (ka 1940), of Newbury, Berks, and Marjorie Ellen, *née* Ayscough (d 1992); 1 s (Richard b 1961), 2 da (Angela (Mrs Wolrige Gordon), Caroline (Mrs Henson) (twins) b 1963); *Career* Lt short serv cmmn Coldstream Guards 1952–56; C Hoare & Co Bankers 1956–57; ptnr: David A Bevan Simpson & Co 1968 (joined 1957), De Zoete & Bevan 1970–86, Barclays de Zoete Wedd 1986–90; memb London Stock Exchange 1963–93; *Recreations* fishing, gardening; *Clubs* Cavalry and Guards', MCC, Worplesdon Golf; *Style—* Simon Frisby, Esq; ✉ The Field House, Longstock, Stockbridge, Hampshire SO20 6DZ (tel 01264 810983); 59 Rosaville Road, London SW6 7BN (tel 020 7381 0918)

FRISCHMANN, Dr Wilem William; CBE; s of Lajos Frischmann (d 1944), of Hungary, and Nelly Frischmann (d 1945); *Educ* Hammersmith Coll of Art and Building, Imperial Coll of Sci and Technol (DIC), City Univ of London (PhD); *m* 1 Sept 1957, Sylvia, da of Maurice Elvey (d 1980), of Glasgow; 1 s (Richard Sandor), 1 da (Justine Elinor); *Career* CJ Pell & Partners 1956–68 (ptnr 1961–68), sr ptnr Pell Frischmann & Ptnrs 1968–, chm Pell Frischmann Group 1984–; chm Conseco International Ltd; Hon DSc City Univ 1997; FREng 1985, FCGI, FIStructE, MConsE, MASCE, MSISdeFr; *Recreations* tennis, swimming, skiing; *Clubs* Arts; *Style—* Dr Wilem Frischmann, CBE, FREng; ✉ Pell Frischmann, 5 Manchester Square, London W1A 1AU

FRITCHIE, Baroness (Life Peer UK 2005), of Gloucester in the County of Gloucestershire; Dame Irene Tordoff (Rennie) Fritchie; DBE (1996); da of Charles Fredrick Fennell (d 1975), and Eva, *née* Tordoff; *b* 29 April 1942; *Educ* Ribston Hall GS for Girls; *m* 21 Oct 1960, Don Jamie Fritchie (d 1992), s of Frederick Fritchie; 2 s (Charles Eric b 14 March 1962 d 1991, Hon Andrew Peel b 30 Sept 1965); *Career* early career experience in family hotel Royal George Birdlip, admin offr Endsleigh Insurance Brokers 1970–73, sales trg offr Trident Insurance Ltd 1973–76, head of trg confs and specialist trg advsr on women's devpt Food and Drink Industrial Trg Bd 1976–80, conslt Social Ecology Associates 1980–81, dir Transform Ltd conslts on organisational change 1981–85, The Rennie Fritchie Consultancy 1985–89, md Working Choices Ltd 1989–91, Mainstream Devpt Consultancy 1991–; vice-chair Stroud and Swindon Building Soc 1995–; cmmr for public appts 1999–2005; chair: Gloucester HA 1988–92, S Western RHA 1992–94, S and W RHA 1997–98; memb NHS Policy Bd 1994–96, chair Nat Advsy Gp on Nursing 1996, memb GMC 1996–99, pres Br Assoc of Medical Mangrs 1997–99, chair Chronic Pain Coalition 2005; Home Sec's rep on Selection Panel for Independent Membs of Police Authorities 1995–99; visiting faculty memb HSM Univ of Manchester 1994–99; non-exec bd memb Br Quality Fndn 1996; pres Winston's Wish 1996–99; memb Working Parties: on women in NHS, examining non-exec bd membership for the public sector 1996; memb: Assoc Media Literacy Gp, All-Pty Parly China Gp, All Pty Gp for Educn, All Pty Gp on Libraries and Info Mgmnt, Br-American Parly Gp; memb and dep chair Audit Advsy Ctee Scottish Public Services Ombudsman 2007–; formerly: bd memb Nat Centre for Mental Health, non-exec dir Inst of Health Servs Mgmnt Consultancy; hon visiting prof (with chair in creative leadership) Univ of York 1996–, pro-chllr Univ of Southampton 1998 (chair Cncl 1998–99); memb Editorial Bd: Revans Inst for Action Learning, Research and Practice Jl, Whitehall and Westminster World 2006; patron: Lord Mayor's Appeal 2000–01, Pied Piper Appeal 2002–; ambass Winstons Wish 2002–; memb Br and I Ombudsman Assoc 2002; fell C&G, fell Sunningdale Inst Nat Sch of Govt 2005; Hon

DPhil Univ of Southampton 1996; Hon DUniv: York 1998, Oxford Brookes 2001, Queen's Univ Belfast 2005; Hon Dr of Laws Univ of St Andrews 2002, Hon Dr Open Univ 2003, DLitt (hc) Univ of Hull 2006; CIMgt 2001; *Books* Working Choices (1988), The Business of Assertiveness (1991), Resolving Conflicts in Organisations; *Recreations* family, reading, gardening, swimming, theatre, cooking, The Archers and Coronation Street; *Style—* The Rt Hon the Baroness Fritchie, DBE; ✉ Mainstream Development, 51 St Paul's Road, Gloucester GL1 5AP (tel and fax 01452 414542); House of Lords, London SW1A 0PW

FRITH, Prof Christopher Donald (Chris); s of late Donald Alfred Frith, OBE, and late Mary Webster, *née* Tyler; *b* 16 March 1942, Cross in Hand, E Sussex; *Educ* Christ's Coll Cambridge (MA), Univ of London (Dip Abnormal Psychology, PhD); *m* 1966, Prof Uta Frith, *qv*; 2 s; *Career* research worker Dept of Psychology Inst of Psychiatry 1965–75, scientist Div of Psychiatry Clinical Research Centre MRC 1975–92, special appt MRC Cyclotron Unit Hammersmith Hosp 1992–94, currently prof in neuropsychology Wellcome Tst Centre for Neuroimaging and dep dir Leopold Müller Functional Imaging Lab UCL; Niels Bohr visiting prof Centre for Functionally Integrative Neuroscience Aarhus Univ; memb Editorial Bd Science; memb: Academia Europaea 1999, Assoc for the Scientific Study of Consciousness (pres 2001); guarantor Brain 1999–; Kenneth Craik Award St John's Coll Cambridge 1999; Hon DUniv: Paris-Lodron Salzburg 2003, York 2004; FMedSci 1999, FRS 2000, fell AAAS 2001; *Publications* The Cognitive Neuropsychology of Schizophrenia (1992, Br Psychological Soc Book Award 1996), Human Brain Function (co-author, 1997), A Very Short Introduction to Schizophrenia (co-author, 2003), The Neuroscience of Social Interaction (co-author, 2004), Making Up the Mind (2007); author of more than 300 pubns in peer-reviewed jls; *Recreations* music; *Style—* Prof Chris Frith; ✉ Wellcome Trust Centre for Neuroimaging, University College London, 12 Queen Square, London WC1N 3BG (tel 020 7833 7457, fax 020 7813 1445, e-mail cfrith@fil.ion.ucl.ac.uk)

FRITH, Mark; *b* 22 May 1970; *Educ* Gleadless Valley Sch Sheffield, Univ of East London; *Career* ed coll magazine 'Overdraft' 1989–90 (writer 1988–89); Smash Hits: writer 1990–93, features ed 1993–94, ed 1994–96; ed Sky Magazine 1996–97, ed Special Projects 1997–98, ed Heat Magazine 1999–; PPA Consumer Magazine Editor of the Year 2001 and 2002; *Publications* The Best of Smash Hits (ed, 2006); *Style—* Mark Frith, Esq; ✉ Seventh Floor, Endeavour House, 189 Shaftesbury Avenue, London WC2H 8JG

FRITH, Rt Rev Richard Michael Cokayne; *see:* Hull, Bishop of

FRITH, Prof Uta; *b* 25 May 1941; *Educ* Universität des Saarlandes Saarbrücken, Univ of London (Dip Abnormal Psychology, PhD); *m* Prof Chris Frith, *qv*; 2 s; *Career* MRC scientist 1968–2006; prof of cognitive devpt UCL 1996–2006 (emeritus prof 2006–); chartered clinical psychologist; memb: Experimental Psychology Soc, Br Neuropsychological Soc, American Psychological Soc, Soc for Neuroscience; memb Editorial Bd: Cognition, Jl of Child Psychology and Psychiatry; President's Award Br Psychological Soc 1990; Hon Dr: Univ of Göteborg Sweden 1998, Univ of St Andrews 2000, Univ of Palermo 2004, Univ of York 2004, Univ of Nottingham 2007; memb Academia Europaea 1992; FBA 2001, FMedSci 2001, FRS 2005, Hon FBPsS 2006 (FBPsS 1990); *Publications* Autism - Explaining the Enigma (2 edn 2003), Autism in History: The Case of Hugh Blair of Borgue (with Rab Houston, 2001); *Style—* Prof Uta Frith; ✉ Institute of Cognitive Neuroscience, University College London, Alexandra House, 17 Queen Square, London WC1N 3AR (tel 020 7679 1177, e-mail u.frith@ucl.ac.uk)

FRIZZELL, Edward William; CB (2000); s of Edward Frizzell (d 1987), of Bridge of Allan, and Mary McArthur, *née* Russell (d 1996); *b* 4 May 1946; *Educ* Paisley GS, Univ of Glasgow (MA); *m* 4 April 1969, Moira, da of late Alexander Calderwood; 2 s (Gregor Edward b 6 March 1973, Euan Alexander b 23 May 1980), 1 da (Karen Elizabeth b 9 Aug 1975); *Career* Scottish Milk Mktg Bd 1968–73, SCWS Ltd 1973, Scottish Cncl Devpt and Indust 1973–76, princ Dept of Agric and Fisheries for Scotland Scottish Office 1976–78, first sec Office of the UK Perm Rep to the EC FCO 1978–82; Scottish Office: asst sec Scottish Educn Dept 1982–86, Fin Div 1986–89, dir Indust Dept/Scottish Devpt Agency 1989–91, chief exec (grade 3) Scottish Prison Serv 1991–99, head (grade 2) Enterprise, Transport and Lifelong Learning Dept Scottish Exec 1999–; *Recreations* running, mountain biking, hill walking; *Clubs* Mortonhall Golf (Edinburgh); *Style—* Edward Frizzell, Esq, CB; ✉ The Scottish Executive, Enterprise and Lifelong Learning Department, Meridian Court, 5 Cadogan Street, Glasgow G2 6AT

FROGGATT, Anthony Grant (Tony); *b* 9 June 1948; *Educ* QMC (LLB), Columbia Univ NYC (MBA); *Career* with Gillette Co (USA, Asia and Aust) 1973–77 H J Heinz Aust 1978–83; International Distillers & Vinters Ltd (IDV): md Swift & Moore Aust 1983–88, chief exec Cinzano Gp 1988–92, md Northern Europe 1992–93, pres Asia Pacific 1993–95, pres Europe 1995–98; pres EMEA Seagram Spirits and Wine Gp 1999–2002, chief exec Scottish & Newcastle plc 2003–; *Style—* Tony Froggatt, Esq

FROSSARD, Sir Charles Keith; kt (1983), KBE (1992); s of Rev Edward Louis Frossard, CBE (d 1968), formerly Dean of Guernsey, and Margery Smith, *née* Latta (d 1958); *b* 18 February 1922; *Educ* Elizabeth Coll Guernsey, Univ of Caen (Bachelier en Droit); *m* 10 April 1950, Elizabeth Marguerite, da of John Edmund Leopold Martel, OBE (d 1973), of Grange Court, Guernsey; 2 da (Marguerite, Jeanne); *Career* WWII: enlisted Gordon Highlanders 1940, cmmnd IA 1941, Capt 17 Dogra Regt, seconded Tochi Scouts and Chitral Scouts, NW Frontier India 1942–46; called to the Bar Gray's Inn 1949 (hon bencher 2000), advocate of the Royal Court of Guernsey 1949; People's Dep States of Guernsey 1958, conseiller States of Guernsey 1967, slr-gen 1969, attorney-gen 1973, dep bailiff 1977, bailiff of Guernsey 1982–92, judge of Courts of Appeal of Guernsey and Jersey 1992–95; pres Indian Army Assoc 1993–, memb Cncl Br Cwlth Ex-Services League for Indian Ex-Services League; Docteur de l'Université (hc) Caen 1990; KGStJ 1987; Médaille de Vermeil Ville de Paris 1984; *Recreations* golf; *Clubs* Naval and Military; *Style—* Sir Charles Frossard, KBE; ✉ Les Lierres, Rohais, St Peter Port, Guernsey GY1 1YW (tel 01481 22076)

FROST, Alan John; s of Edward George Frost (d 1981), and Ellen Lucy, *née* Jamieson (d 1979); *b* 6 October 1944; *Educ* Stratford Co GS, Univ of Manchester (BSc); *m* 15 Dec 1973, Valerie Jean, da of Francis David Bennett; 2 s (Christopher, Patrick); *Career* investment dir Abbey Life Gp 1986–89, md Abbey Life Assurance Co Ltd 1989–98, dir Lloyds Abbey Life plc 1989–96, gp chief exec United Assurance Gp plc 1998–2000; chm: Queen Mab Consultancy Ltd 2001–04, Car Crash Line Gp plc 2002–04 (non-exec dir 2002–06), Teachers' Building Soc 2004– (non-exec dir 2001–); non-exec dir: INVESCO Pensions Ltd 2001–, NFU Mutual Insurance Co Ltd 2002–, Hamworthy plc 2004–; regular columnist in The Actuary Magazine 2002–; chm Dorset Opera 2004–; chm Bd of Govrs Bournemouth Univ 2004– (memb 2001–, dep chm 2003–04); former dir: Dorset TEC, Bournemouth Orchestras; former chm S Wessex Industrial Project Duke of Edinburgh's Award; visiting fell European Centre for Corporate Governance Bournemouth Univ; Freeman City of London 1986, Master Worshipful Co of Actuaries 2004–05 (Liveryman 1986–); FIA 1970, FIMgt 1990; *Publications* A General Introduction to Institutional Investment (with D P Hager, 1986), Debt Securities (with D P Hager, 1990), A Light Frost (2005); *Recreations* opera, genealogy; *Clubs* Reform; *Style—* Alan Frost, Esq; ✉ 20 Little Forest Road, Bournemouth, Dorset BH4 9NW (tel and fax 01202 764734, e-mail alan@alanfrost.co.uk, website www.alanfrost.co.uk)

FROST, HE David George Hamilton; CMG (2006); s of George Frost, and Margaret, *née* Murfin; *b* 21 February 1965, Derby; *Educ* St John's Coll Oxford (BA); *m* 1993, Jacqueline Elizabeth, *née* Dias; 1 da (Jennifer b 1998), 1 s (Joshua b 2000); *Career* joined FCO 1987, second sec Br High Cmmn Nicosia 1989–90, seconded to KPMG 1990–92, first sec UK perm rep to EU 1993–96, first sec UK mission to UN 1996–98, private sec to Perm Under Sec 1998–99, dep head EU Dept FCO 1999–2001, economic cnsllr Br Embassy Paris 2001–03, dir EU (internal) FCO 2003–06, ambass to Denmark 2006–; *Style—* HE Mr David Frost, CMG; ✉ British Embassy, 36–40 Kastelsvej, 2100 København Ø, Denmark (tel 00 45 3544 5200, e-mail david.frost@fco.gov.uk)

FROST, Sir David Paradine; kt (1993), OBE (1970); s of Rev Wilfred John Paradine Frost (d 1967), of Tenterden, Kent, and Maud (Monna) Evelyn, *née* Aldrich (d 1991); *b* 7 April 1939; *Educ* Gillingham GS, Wellingborough GS, Gonville & Caius Coll Cambridge (MA); *m* 1, 1981 (m dis 1982), Lynne Frederick (d 1994), widow of Peter Sellers; m 2, 19 March 1983, Lady Carina Mary Anne Gabrielle, da of 17 Duke of Norfolk, KG, GCVO, CB, CBE, MC (d 2002); 3 s (Miles Paradine b 1984, Wilfred Paradine b 1985, George Paradine b 1987); *Career* TV presenter, producer, author; chm and chief exec The David Paradine Gp of Cos 1966–, jt fndr London Weekend Television, jt fndr and dir TV-am plc 1981–93, non-exec dir West 175 Media 2000–; pres Lord's Taverners 1985, memb Cncl Wellbeing 1989–; Freeman of Louisville (Kentucky, USA) 1971; Hon LLB Emerson Coll Boston Mass USA 1970; *Television* BBC progs incl: That Was The Week That Was 1962–63, A Degree of Frost 1963 and 1973, Not So Much a Programme More a Way of Life 1964–65, The Frost Report 1966–67, Frost Over England 1967, Frost Over America 1970, Frost's Weekly 1973, The Frost Interview 1974, We British 1975–76, Forty Years of Television 1976, The Frost Programme 1977, The Guinness Book of Records Hall of Fame 1986, 1987, 1988, Breakfast With Frost 1993–2005, The Frost Interview 2005–; ITV series and progs incl: The Frost Programme 1966–67 and 1967–68, Frost on Friday 1968–69 and 1969–70, The Sir Harold Wilson Interviews 1976, The Nixon Interviews 1976–77, Frost on Sunday (TV-am) 1983–92, Through the Keyhole (ITV until 1995, Sky One 1996–) 1987–, The Frost Programme 1993–; Frost's Century (NBC Super Channel) 1995; subjects of PBS TV series Talking with David Frost incl: George and Barbara Bush, Andrew Lloyd Webber, Gen Norman Schwarzkopf, John Major, Robin Williams, Margaret Thatcher, Ted Turner, Elton John, Norman Mailer, Warren Beatty, Bill Clinton, Ross Perot, Sir John Gielgud, Dan Quayle, Al Gore, Isaac Stern, John Sununu, Sally Quinn, Peter Stone, Calvin Trillin, Clint Eastwood, F W De Klerk, Nelson Mandela, Mangosuthu Buthelezi, Boutros Boutros-Ghali, Salmon Rushdie, Lord Owen, Vladimir Zhirinovsky; *Films* prodns incl: The Rise and Rise of Michael Rimmer 1970, Charley-One-Eye 1972, Leadbelly 1974, The Slipper and the Rose 1975, James A Michener's Dynasty 1975, The Ordeal of Patty Hearst 1978, The Remarkable Mrs Sanger 1979; *Awards* Montreux Golden Rose for Frost over England 1967, RTS Silver Medal 1967, Richard Dimbleby Award 1967, Emmy Awards 1970 and 1971, Religious Heritage of America Award 1970, Albert Einstein Award Communication Arts 1971; *Books* That Was The Week That Was (1963), How to Live under Labour (1964), Talking with Frost (1967), To England With Love (1967), The Presidential Debate 1968 (1968), The Americans (1970), Whitlam and Frost (1974), I Gave them a Sword (1978), I Could Have Kicked Myself - David Frost's Book of the World's Worst Decisions (1982), Who Wants to be a Millionaire (jtly, 1983), The Mid-Atlantic Companion (jtly, 1986), The Rich Tide (jtly, 1986), The World's Shortest Books (1987), David Frost: An Autobiography Part One; *Recreations* cricket, soccer, tennis, food, wine; *Clubs* Queen's, MCC, Mark's, Annabel's, Harry's Bar, Mosimann's; *Style—* Sir David Frost, OBE

FROST, David Stuart; s of George William Stuart Frost, and Winifred Leslie, *née* Stuart; *b* 22 February 1953, Corbridge, Northumberland; *Educ* Thames Poly (BA), Poly of the South Bank (Dip); *m* June 1981, Mari, *née* Doyle; 2 da (Hannah b 11 June 1988, Sophie b 26 May 1990); *Career* economist London C of C 1976–79; Walsall C of C: dir of servs 1975–86, chief exec 1986–96; chief exec: East Mercia C of C 1996–2000, Coventry and Warks C of C 2000–02; DG Br Chambers of Commerce 2003–; chm: Enterprise Insight, Nat Cncl of Grad Entrepreneurship, Liveryman Worshipful Co of Loriners; FRSA; *Recreations* cycling, motorcycling; *Clubs* Naval and Military; *Style—* David Frost, Esq; ✉ British Chambers of Commerce, 65 Petty France, London SW1H 9EU (tel 020 7654 5800, e-mail d.frost@britishchambers.org.uk)

FROST, Derek Norton; s of John Norton Frost, of Nutley, E Sussex, and Elizabeth, *née* Gibson; *b* 24 April 1952; *Educ* Tonbridge; *Partner* since 1978, Jeremy Gordon Norman, *qv*; *Career* designer; trained under David Hicks; dir of interior design Mary Fox Linton Ltd; formed own co Derek Frost Associates Ltd 1984, ret 1997; int practice specialising in interior design/furniture design; projects include: Heaven (night club), The Kobler Centre, many residential installations; solo exhibition of furniture Leighton House 1988; currently dir various companies in leisure and property industry; yoga teacher; *Recreations* gardening, music, contemporary arts, craft, scuba diving; *Style—* Derek Frost, Esq; ✉ Derek Frost, Moreton Yard, 1 Moreton Terrace Mews North, London SW1V 2NT (tel 020 7828 1776, fax 020 7976 5059)

FROST, Ronald Edwin; s of Charles Henry Frost, and Doris, *née* Foggin; *b* 19 March 1936; *m* 19 Sept 1959, Beryl, da of Leonard Ward (d 1964), of Windsor, Berks; 1 s (Stephen Charles b 1962), 2 da (Jane Samantha b 1965, Louise Karen b 1966); *Career* chm and chief exec Hays Group Ltd 1986–89, chm Hays plc 1987–2001; dir: Hays Marine Services Ltd 1983–2001, Hays Distribution Services Ltd 1983–2001, Hays Holdings Ltd 1985–2001, Hays Personnel Services (Australia) Ltd 1987–2001, Hays Chemicals Ltd 1988–2001, Hays Commercial Services Ltd 1992–2001, Hays Overseas Holdings Ltd 1992–2001, Hays Personnel Services Holdings Ltd 1992–2001, Hays Employee Share Trust Ltd 1996–2001, Hays Pension Trustee Ltd 1996–2001; *Recreations* game shooting, sailing; *Clubs* RAC, Royal Thames Yacht, Royal CI Yacht, IOD; *Style—* Ronald Frost, Esq

FROSTICK, Raymond Charles; DL (Norfolk 1979); s of Harry Frostick (d 1965), of Hoveton, Norfolk, and Ethel Marion, *née* Preston (d 1983); *b* 18 May 1931; *Educ* Norwich Sch, CCC Cambridge (MA, LLM); *m* 27 July 1957, (Rosemary) Claire, da of Sir George Harold Banwell (d 1982), of Lincoln; 2 da (Marion b 1958, Elizabeth b 1961), 2 s (Richard b 1960, Andrew b 1963); *Career* Nat Serv RAF 1949–51; admitted slr 1957; Eversheds: ptnr 1961–94, conslt 1994–97; vice-chm R G Carter Holdings Ltd 1975–2005; UEA: memb Cncl 1972–2000, treas 1985–90, chm Cncl 1990–97, pro-chllr 1990–2002; chm: Norfolk AHA 1978–82, Norwich HA 1982–85; pres Norwich and Norfolk C of C and Industry 1985–88; cncllr: Norwich City Cncl 1966–79, Norfolk CC 1973–85 (chm 1983–84); Lord Mayor of Norwich 1976–77; pres Norwich and Norfolk Voluntary Serv 1986–99; vice-pres RELATE Nat Marriage Guidance 1990–98 (chm 1986–90), pres RELATE Norfolk and Norwich 1990–98; Hon DCL UEA 1991; memb Law Soc 1957, FRSA 1985; *Books* The Dutch Connection: Some Norfolk Maps and Their Makers (1988), The Printed Plans of Norwich 1558–1840 (2002); *Recreations* cartography, travel; *Clubs* Royal Cwlth Soc; *Style—* Raymond Frostick, Esq, DL; ✉ 425 Unthank Road, Norwich, Norfolk NR4 7QB (tel and fax 01603 452937, e-mail raymond.frostick@btinternet.com)

FROWEN, Prof Stephen Francis; s of Adolf Frowein, industrialist (d 1964), and Anne, *née* Bauer (d 1968); *b* 22 May 1923; *Educ* Univs of Cologne, Würzburg, Bonn and London (BSc, MSc); *m* 21 March 1949, Irina, da of Dr Sam Minskers, banker; 1 s (Michael b 17 Jan 1950 d 1989), 1 da (Tatiana Hosburn b 20 Sept 1955); *Career* ed The Bankers' Magazine (now Financial World) 1954–60, econ advsr Industrial and Commercial Fin Corp (now 3i) 1960–61, res offr NIESR London (concurrently pt/t lectr Univ of Westminster) 1961–62; sr lectr: Univ of Greenwich 1962–67 (concurrently pt/t lectr Univ of Birmingham 1962–63), Univ of Surrey 1967–87; special advsr UNIDO Vienna 1980–81, visiting prof Würzburg Univ 1983; prof of economics Univ of Frankfurt 1987, Bundesbank prof of monetary economics Free Univ of Berlin 1987–89, hon res fell UCL

1989–, sr res assoc Von Hügel Inst St Edmund's Coll Cambridge 1991–, hon prof Inst for German Studies Univ of Birmingham 1995–2004, fell commoner St Edmund's Coll Cambridge 1999–; contributing ed Central Banking 2000–; Commanders Cross of the Order of Merit of the Federal Republic of Germany 1993, KSG 1996; *Books* ed: Enzyklopädisches Lexikon für das Geld-, Bank- und Börsenwesen (2 vols, jtly, 1957), Economic Issues (jtly, 1957), Monetary Policy and Economic Activity in West Germany (jtly, 1977), A Framework of International Banking (1979), Controlling Industrial Economies - Essays in Honour of Christopher Thomas Saunders (1983), Business, Time and Thought - Selected Papers of G L S Shackle (1988), Unknowledge and Choice in Economics (1990), Monetary Policy and Financial Innovations in Five Industrial Countries - the UK, the USA, Germany, France and Japan (jtly, 1992), Monetary Theory and Monetary Policy - New Tracks for the 1990s (1993), Financial Decision-Making and Moral Responsibility (jtly, 1995), The German Currency Union of 1990 - A Critical Assessment (jtly, 1997), Welfare and Values: Challenging the Culture of Unconcern (jtly, 1997), Hayek: Economist and Social Philosopher - A Critical Retrospect (1997), Inside the Bundesbank (jtly, 1998), Economics as an Art of Thought (jtly, 2000), Management for Central Bankers (jtly, 2000), Financial Competition, Risk and Accountability: British and German Experiences (jtly, 2001), Economists in Discussion: The Correspondence Between G L S Shackle and Stephen F Frowen, 1951–92 (2004); author of numerous articles in learned jls and chapters in books; *Recreations* numismatics, heraldry, painting, music, reading; *Clubs* Reform, International PEN; *Style*— Prof Stephen Francis Frowen; ✉ 40 Gurney Drive, London N2 0DE (tel and fax 020 8458 0159, e-mail sfrowen@btinternet.com); Department of Economics, University College London, Gower Street, London WC1E 6BT

FRY, Dr Anthony Harold; s of Henry Fry (d 1976), and Marjorie, *née* Davies (d 1997); *b* 9 November 1942; *Educ* Highgate Sch, King's Coll Hosp (MB BS, LRCP, MRCS, MPhil, DPM); *m* 16 Nov 1974, Lynda Mary, da of Leslie Reginald Devenish, of Sussex; 3 s (Alexander b 4 June 1976, Nick b 28 April 1978, Robert b 6 Aug 1980); *Career* conslt psychiatrist; formerly recognised teacher psychiatry United Med Sch of Guy's and St Thomas' Univ of London, sr conslt physician in psychological med Guy's Hosp 1977–90, med dir Stress Mgmnt Unit London Bridge Hosp 1988–, conslt Charter Nightingale Hosp 1990–; ed Holistic Med 1984–88, med advsr Nat Marriage Guidance Cncl (Relate) 1979–90; chm Central Stress Mgmnt Ltd, chm and md Anthony Fry and Associates Ltd; memb Exec Ctee Ind Doctors' Forum 1994–, chair Ind Doctors Forum Educn Tst; memb Royal Soc of Med Colloquium on Traditional and Complementary Med 1989; Yeoman Worshipful Soc of Apothecaries; MRCPsych 1972, memb BMA 1980, FRSM; *Books* Safe Space (1987); *Recreations* travel, squash, walking, poetry; *Clubs* RAC; *Style*— Dr Anthony Fry; ✉ 129 Hemingford Road, Barnsbury, Islington, London N1 1BZ (tel 020 7609 0000); Suite 207, London Bridge Hospital, 27 Tooley Street, London SE1 (tel 020 7607 3937, fax 020 7607 3815, e-mail anthony@frydoc.demon.co.uk)

FRY, Anthony Michael; s of Denis Seymour Fry (d 2004), of Worthing, W Sussex, and Trixie, *née* Barter (d 1998); *b* 20 June 1955; *Educ* Stonyhurst, Magdalen Coll Oxford (MA, Atkinson Prize, treas Oxford Union); *m* 27 July 1985, Anne Elizabeth, da of Harry Birrell; 1 da (Sophie Alexandra b 18 April 1991), 2 s (Edward Harry Seymour b 21 Jan 1993, Hugo Benedict Cameron b 28 Nov 1996); *Career* N M Rothschild & Sons Ltd 1977–96: joined 1977, mangr International Pacific Corp Melbourne (renamed Rothschild Australia 1983) 1980–85, exec dir corp fin 1985–96; md: Barclays de Zoete Wedd 1996–97, Credit Suisse First Boston 1997–2004; head of UK investment banking Lehman Brothers 2004–; non-exec dir: Southern Water plc 1994–96, John Mowlem & Co 1998–2005, BSI 2000–04, Panel on Takeovers and Mergers 2006–; chm Opera at the Garden 1994–98, vice-chm British Lung Fndn 1990–2002; memb: Exec Bd LAMDA, Exec Bd Edinburgh Int Television Festival, Devpt Bd The Sixteen; tstee: National History Museum Development Tst 1993–98, Nat Film and TV Sch (NFTS); memb Int Advsy Bd SOAS; govr Godolphin & Latymer Sch; memb Guild of Bonnetmakers Glasgow; FRSA; *Recreations* opera, theatre, cricket; *Clubs* Cobden, Electric, Australian, Armadillos CC, Incogniti CC, The Blake, Saracens RFC, Sussex CCC, Surrey CCC, Capital; *Style*— Anthony Fry, Esq

FRY, Dominic Lawrence Charlesworth; s of Richard Noël Fry, of Lyme Regis, Dorset, and Jean Marianne, *née* Brunskill-Davies; *b* 28 August 1959; *Educ* Christ's Hosp, Faculté des Lettres Université Paul Valéry III Montpellier, Univ of North Carolina (Morehead scholar, BA); *m* 5 March 1993, Ann-Marie, *née* Finn; *Career* with various consultancies 1982–90; UK communications dir AT&T UK 1990–95, gp communications dir Eurotunnel plc 1995–96, corp rels dir J Sainsbury plc 1996–2000, corp affairs dir Scottish Power plc 2000–05, conslt Tulchan Communications 2006–; PRO Award for Excellence in Public Relations (AT&T) 1993; co-ordinator of arts sponsorship for the Almeida Theatre London 1990–95 (memb Cncl 1998–), small business mentor Prince's Youth Business Tst, head teacher and mentor; memb: ABSA, Business in the Arts Initiative, Soil Assoc; MIPR 1983; *Recreations* sailing, tennis, reading, rugby football; *Clubs* Reform; *Style*— Dominic Fry, Esq

FRY, Fiona; da of Terence Roche (d 1998), and Margaret, *née* O'Shea; *b* 17 July 1959, Cuckfield, Sussex; *Educ* Convent of the Holy Child Jesus Mayfield, Univ of Aston in Birmingham (BSc); *m* 22 Sept 1990, Christopher Fry; 3 s (Max b 8 May 1994, Henry b 8 May 1996, Arthur b 25 Jan 2001); *Career* Peat Marwick Mitchell & Co 1981–85, Arthur Young McLelland Moores & Co 1985–87, London Stock Exchange 1987–89, head of investigations FSA 1990–98, ptnr and memb UK Bd KPMG 1998–; chair of corporate sponsor recruitment Juvenile Diabetes Research Fndn 2006–07; ACA 1985; *Clubs* Chichester Yacht; *Style*— Mrs Fiona Fry; ✉ 48 Killieser Avenue, London SW2 4NT (tel 07801 494754, e-mail fiona@fryhome.com); KPMG, 8 Salisbury Square, London EC4Y 8BB

FRY, (HE) Sir Graham Holbrook; KCMG (2006); *b* 20 December 1949; *Educ* Canford Sch, BNC Oxford (BA); *m* 1994, Toyoko, *née* Komatsu; 2 s from previous m; *Career* joined HM Dip Serv 1972, third later second sec Tokyo 1975–78, seconded to DTI 1979–80, FCO 1981–83, first sec Paris 1983–87, political cnsllr Tokyo 1989–93, head Far East & Pacific Dept FCO 1993–95, dir N Asia & Pacific FCO 1995–98, high cmmr to Malaysia 1998–2001, ambass to Japan 2004–; *Recreations* bird-watching; *Style*— Sir Graham Fry, KCMG; ✉ c/o Foreign and Commonwealth Office (Tokyo), BFPO, London NW7 1PX

FRY, Jonathan Michael; s of Stephen Fry (d 1979), of London, and Gladys Yvonne, *née* Blunt (d 2001); *b* 9 August 1937; *Educ* Repton, Trinity Coll Oxford (MA); *m* 1, 21 Feb 1970 (m dis 1997), Caroline Mary, da of Col Vincent Dunkerly, DSO, JP; 4 da (Lucy b 1971, Camilla b 1973, Victoria b 1977, Sophie b 1979); m 2, 15 Dec 1999, Marilyn Diana, da of Eric Russell; *Career* account exec Pritchard Wood & Ptnrs 1961–65, account supervisor Norman Craig & Kummel 1965–66, engagement mangr McKinsey & Co 1966–72, dir and chief exec Foods Div Unigate Ltd 1972–77; Burmah Castrol plc: joined 1978, md 1990–93, chief exec 1993–98, non-exec chm 1998–2000; non-exec chm: Christian Salvesen plc 1997–2003 (non-exec dir 1995–2003, dep chm 1996–97), Elementis plc (formerly Harrisons & Crosfield plc) 1997–2004, Control Risks Gp Ltd 2000–; non-exec dep chm Northern Foods plc 1996–2002; chm: Woodborough Cons Assoc 1976–83, Beechingstoke PC 1978–91, St Francis Sch Pewsey 1984–92, Bd of Govrs Repton Sch 2003–; *Recreations* cricket, skiing, archaeology; *Clubs* MCC, Vincent's (Oxford); *Style*— Jonathan Fry, Esq; ✉ Beechingstoke Manor, Pewsey, Wiltshire SN9 6HQ

FRY, Dame Margaret Louise; DBE (1989, OBE 1982); da of Richard Reed Dawe, of Tavistock, Devon, and Ruth Dora, *née* Every (d 1968); *b* 10 March 1931; *Educ* Tavistock GS; *m* 11 April 1955, (Walter William) John Fry, s of Walter William Fry (d 1972), of Launceston, Cornwall; 3 s (Jeremy b 24 March 1957, Patrick b 17 March 1960, Robert b 12 May 1966); *Career* former Devon hockey player; memb: Cons Party 1947– (pres Torridge and W Devon Cons Assoc 1992–98 (patron 1998–)), Rail Users' Consultative Ctee 1984–96, Union of Cons and Unionist Assocs (pres Western Area 1995–), S and W RHA 1990–96, local church warden; chm: Western Area Women's Advsy Ctee 1978–81 (former memb and vice-chm 1975–78), Cons Women's Advsy Ctee 1984–87 (vice-chm 1981–82), Torridge and W Devon Cons Assoc, Nat Union of Conservative and Unionist Assocs 1990–91 (vice-chm 1987–90); chm of tstees Peninsula Med Sch 2001–04, chm Primrose Breast Care Fndn 2001–; former memb: Tavistock Cons Assoc, Tavistock Young Cons, Nat Fedn of Young Farmers Clubs; *Recreations* farming and conservation, sport; *Style*— Dame Margaret Fry, DBE; ✉ Thorne Farm, Launceston, Cornwall PL15 9SN (tel 01566 784308)

FRY, Michael Edward (Mike); JP (Manchester 1996); s of Stanley Edmund Fry, of Preston, Lancs, and Margaret, *née* Hunt; *b* 16 January 1958; *Educ* Lostock Hall Co Secdy Sch, W R Tuson Coll Preston, Univ of Newcastle upon Tyne (BA), Univ of Leeds (MA); *Career* graduate NHS admin job placements in Bath, Winchester, Newport IOW and Alton Hants 1980–82, admin St Martin's and Claverton Downs Hosps Bath 1982–84, dep admin and subsequent head of admin Freeman Gp of Hosps Newcastle upon Tyne 1984–88, unit gen mangr Christie Hosp S Manchester HA 1988–91, first chief exec Christie Hosp NHS Tst 1991–2000, first chief exec 28 St John Street Barr Chambers 2000–02, first chief exec St Johns Buildings Barr Chambers 2002–04; gen mangr Catalyst Healthcare 2004–; hon fell Univ of Manchester 1992; MIHSM; *Recreations* motor sport, football, opera; *Style*— Mike Fry, Esq; ✉ Caution Cottage, Burford Lane, Lymm, Cheshire WA13 9JN (e-mail fry1234@btinternet.com)

FRY, Nicholas Rodney Lowther; s of Rodney William Lowther Fry (d 1993), of Derby, and Mary Winifred Rosalind, *née* Ellis (d 2003); *b* 28 April 1947; *Educ* Malvern Coll, Christ's Coll Cambridge (MA); *m* 1972, Christine Sarah, da of Edmund de Chazal Rogers (d 1967), of London; 2 da (Emma b 1974, Lucy b 1981), 1 s (Jonathan b 1976); *Career* investment banker; dir S G Warburg & Co Ltd 1983–95, dir SBC Warburg 1995–96, md NatWest Corporate Advisory 1996–98, vice-chm KPMG Corporate Finance 1998–2005; non-exec dir: Brixton plc, Erinaceous Gp plc, Merrill Lynch British Smaller Companies Tst plc, Absolute Return Tst Ltd, Cliniserve Hldgs Ltd; tstee and treas Independent Age, tstee Afrikids; FICA; *Recreations* travel, music, horticulture; *Style*— Nicholas Fry, Esq

FRY, Lt-Gen Sir Robert Alan; KCB (2005), CBE (2002, MBE 1980); s of Raymond Mills Fry (d 2002), and Elizabeth, *née* Bryon; *b* 6 April 1951; *Educ* Penarth GS, Univ of Bath (BSc), KCL (MA, US Naval Inst Int Essay Prize); *m* 16 July 1977, Elizabeth, *née* Woolmore; 2 da (Katherine b 21 Dec 1979, Claire b 8 July 1984); *Career* in commerce NYC 1972–73; cmmnd Royal Marines 1973 (mentioned in despatches 1979); COS 3 Commando Bde 1989–91, CO 45 Commando Gp 1995–97, Cdr 3 Commando Bde 1999–2001, Cmdt-Gen Royal Marines 2001–02, Dep Chief Jt Ops 2002–03, DCDS (Commitments) 2003–, Dep Cmdg Gen Coalition Forces Iraq; Jt Cdr's Commendation 1992; contrib articles to jls incl RUSI Magazine and US Naval Inst Magazine; Freeman City of London, Liveryman Worshipful Co of Plaisterers; *Recreations* Welsh rugby, film, photography, walking; *Clubs* Special Forces; *Style*— Lt-Gen Sir Robert Fry, KCB, CBE

FRY, Stephen John; s of Alan John Fry, ARCS (Lt REME), of Booton, Norfolk, and Marianne Eve, *née* Newman; *b* 24 August 1957; *Educ* Uppingham, Queens' Coll Cambridge (MA); *Career* actor and writer; weekly Fry on Friday column in The Daily Telegraph 1989–91; patron: Friends for Life THT, Freeze (nuclear disarmament charity), Norwich Play House, Prisoners Abroad; memb: Amnesty Int, Comic Relief, Hysteria Tst; former rector Univ of Dundee; *Theatre* appeared with Cambridge Footlights in revue The Cellar Tapes at Edinburgh Festival 1981 (Perrier award, televised BBC 1982); Latin (Scotsman Fringe First award 1980 and Lyric Hammersmith 1983), Forty Years On (Chichester Festival and Queen's Theatre London) 1984, The Common Pursuit (Phoenix Theatre London) 1988, Look Look (Aldwych) 1990; re-wrote script for musical Me and My Girl 1984 (London, Broadway, Sydney), Homesick (West End) 1995; *Television* incl: Alfresco (Granada) 1982–84, The Young Ones (BBC) 1983, Happy Families (BBC) 1984, Saturday Night Live (Channel 4) 1986–87, Blackadder's Christmas Carol (BBC) 1988, Blackadder Goes Forth (BBC) 1989, A Bit of Fry and Laurie (4 series, BBC) 1989–94, Jeeves and Wooster (Granada) 1991–93, Stalagluft (Yorkshire) 1993, Cold Comfort Farm (BBC) 1994, Gormenghast (BBC) 1999, Surrealismo (BBC) 2001, QI (BBC) 2003, Absolute Power (BBC) 2003, Fortysomething (ITV) 2003, Tom Brown's Schooldays (ITV) 2004; *Radio* incl: Loose Ends 1986–87, Whose Line Is It Anyway? 1987, Saturday Night Fry 1987, 2004, narrator in Vanity Fair (BBC Radio 4) 2004; *Film* The Good Father, A Fish Called Wanda 1988, A Handful of Dust, Peter's Friends 1992, IQ 1995, Wilde 1997, Gosford Park 2001, Thunderpants 2002, Harry Potter and the Chamber of Secrets 2002, dir and screenwriter Bright Young Things 2003, Tooth 2004, The Life and Death of Peter Sellers 2004; *Books* The Liar (1991), Paperweight (1992), The Hippopotamus (1994), Making History (1996), Moab Is My Washpot (1997), The Stars' Tennis Balls (2000), The Ode Less Travelled (2005); *Recreations* chess, computing, dining out, light alcoholic refreshments; *Clubs* Oxford and Cambridge, Chelsea Arts, Groucho, Savile, Dorchester, Browns; *Style*— Stephen Fry, Esq; ✉ c/o Hamilton Hodell, 5th Floor, 66–68 Margaret Street, London W1W 8SR

FRYDENSON, Henry; s of Samuel Frydenson, and Barbara Frydenson; *b* 9 November 1954; *Educ* Hasmonean GS for Boys, UCL (LLB); *m* Aug 1980, Sarah, da of Samuel Reifer; 6 s (Alan, Jonathan, Martin, Sheldon, Andrew, Simon), 1 da (Deborah); *Career* admitted slr 1981; ptnr Berwin Leighton Paisner (formerly Paisner and Co) 1984–2006 (joined 1979), conslt Baker & McKenzie 2006–07, conslt Mishcon de Reya 2007–; chm Assoc of Contentious Tst and Probate Specialists (ACTAPS); memb: Soc of Tst and Estate Practitioners (STEP), Medico-Legal Soc, Trust Law Ctee, Charity Law Assoc, Public Guardianship Consultative Forum, Solicitors' Assoc of Higher Court Advocates, Law Soc; official slr and public tstee User Gp, CEDR accredited mediator; Freeman City of London 1984; *Recreations* first aid, computers; *Style*— Henry Frydenson, Esq; ✉ Mishcon de Reya Solicitors, Summit House, 12 Red Lion Square, London WC1R 4QD (tel 020 7440 7000, fax 020 7404 2376, e-mail henry.frydenson@mishcon.com)

FRYER, John Beresford; s of Reginald Arthur Fryer (d 1966), and Joyce Edith Fryer (d 1986); *b* 18 February 1945; *Educ* Chigwell Sch; *m* 1, 3 April 1971, Jennifer Margaret Glew (d 1995); 2 da (Polly Jane b 12 Dec 1976, Sally Ann b 31 March 1980); m 2, 3 Aug 1996, Gillian Holmes; 2 da (Roseanna Iris Joyce b 30 Aug 1997, Elizabeth Lily Jamie b 7 Aug 2000), 1 s (Jonathan Arthur Clive b 1 Nov 2002); *Career* sub ed and reporter: local newspapers in East London and Essex 1963–67, Daily Sketch 1967–68, London Evening Standard 1968–69; labour corr then labour ed Sunday Times 1969–82, industrial corr (formerly labour corr) BBC News 1982–97, assignments ed BBC Economic Affrs Unit 1997–99, ed Radio and New Media, Economics and Business Centre BBC News 1999–2002, head of press office and events FSA 2002–04, journalist and broadcaster 2004–; Parly candidate (Lab): Harwich 1974 (Feb and Oct), Buckingham 1979; memb Radio Acad; *Recreations* tennis, watching West Ham United FC; *Style*— John Fryer, Esq; ✉ e-mail johnberesfordfryer@yahoo.co.uk

FRYER, Martin John; s of David Ivor Fryer (d 1971), and June Laurie, *née* Bradley; *b* 3 September 1956; *Educ* Christ Church Cathedral Sch Oxford, Radley, CCC Cambridge (MA); *Career* VSO teacher Lawas Sarawak 1978–80, sponsorship asst Jacob de Vries Ltd 1981–82, VSO field co-ordinator Bangkok 1982–85; British Council: regnl offr E Europe and N Asia Dept 1986–87, asst regnl dir São Paulo 1987–90, corp planning offr London

1990–93, dir Istanbul 1993–99, head country services 1999–2001, former dir Barcelona, currently dir Argentina; *Recreations* music, reading, travel; *Style*— Martin Fryer, Esq; ✉ British Council, Marcelo T de Alvear 590, 4th Floor, C1058AAF, Buenos Aires, Argentina

FUKUDA, Haruko; OBE (2000); da of Masaru Fukuda (d 1984), and Yoko, *née* Tanaka; *b* 21 July 1946, Tokyo; *Educ* Western Jr HS Washington DC, Channing Sch London, New Hall Cambridge (MA); *Career* Atlantic Trade Study/Trade Policy Research Centre 1968–70, ODI 1970, World Bank (IBRD) Washington DC 1971, Vickers da Costa & Co Ltd 1972–74, ptnr James Capel & Co 1974–88, vice-chm Nikko Europe plc 1988–98, chief exec World Gold Cncl 1999–2002, sr advsr Lazard 1999–2004, chm Caliber Global Investment Ltd 2005–; memb Cncl Inst for Fiscal Studies; DSc (hc) City Univ 2000; FSI, memb Stock Exchange 1980; *Publications* Britain in Europe: Impact on the Third World (1973), Japan and World Trade: Years Ahead (1974); *Recreations* gardening, reading, art, cooking; *Clubs* Athenaeum; *Style*— Miss Haruko Fukuda, OBE; ✉ Flat 1, 33 Ennismore Gardens, London SW7 1AE (tel 020 7589 0406, fax 020 7584 6898); 43 St James's Place, London SW1A 1NS (tel 020 7495 8800, fax 020 7629 4010, e-mail harukofukuda@harukofukuda.com)

FULANI, Dan; *see:* Hare, John Neville

FULFORD, Hon Mr Justice; Sir Adrian Bruce Fulford; kt (2002); s of late Gerald John Fulford, and Marie Bettine, *née* Stevens; *b* 8 January 1953; *Educ* Elizabeth Coll Guernsey, Univ of Southampton (BA); *Career* housing advsr Housing Aid Centre Shelter 1974–76, called to the Bar Middle Temple 1978, in practice 1978–2002, QC 1994, recorder of the Crown Court, judge of the High Court of Justice (Queen's Bench Div) 2002–, judge at the Int Criminal Court 2003–; *Publications* A Criminal Practitioner's Guide to Judicial Review and Case Slated, UK Human Rights Reports (ed); *Recreations* tennis, golf, riding; *Clubs* Garrick, Travellers; *Style*— The Hon Mr Justice Fulford; ✉ Royal Courts of Justice, London WC2A 2LL (tel 020 7947 6000)

FULFORD, Robert Ian; s of (Howard) Bruce Fulford, of Colchester, Essex, and Mary Elizabeth, *née* Frost; *b* 26 August 1969; *Educ* Colchester Royal GS, St Aidan's Coll Durham, Univ of Essex (BSc); *Career* croquet player; World champion: 1990, 1992, 1994, 1997, 2002; Br Open Champion: 1991, 1992, 1996, 1998, 2003, 2004; President's Cup winner: 1989, 1998, 1999, 2001, 2002; NZ Open champion 1992, 2000, 2005, 2006; memb GB team winning MacRobertson Shield: 1990, 1993, 1996, 2000, 2003 (captain 2003–); ACA; *Recreations* bridge, chess, hockey, film; *Style*— Robert Fulford, Esq

FULFORD, Prof (Kenneth) William Musgrave (Bill); s of Kenneth Fulford (d 1979), and Violet Emily, *née* Robinson (d 1978); *b* 10 December 1942, Lincoln; *Educ* Aldenham Sch Herts, Univ of Cambridge, Middx Hosp Medical Sch (Burney Award), Univ of London (PhD), Univ of Oxford (DPhil); *m* 1964, Jane, *née* Bradshaw; 2 s (Charles b 8 Feb 1969, William b 28 April 1975), 1 da (Hannah b 30 Oct 1970); *Career* house offr Middx Hosp and Mt Vernon Hosp 1967–69, research registrar then sr registrar in immunology Middx Hosp 1970–74, trg rotation Inst of Psychiatry and Maudsley Hosp London 1974–77, clinical lectr Dept of Psychiatry Univ of Oxford 1977–83, research psychiatrist and hon conslt psychiatrist Univ of Oxford 1983–, prof of philosophy and mental health Univ of Warwick 1995– (estab centre of excellence for interdisciplinary field of philosophy and psychiatry), special advsr for values-based practice Dept of Health 2005–, co-dir Inst for Philosophy, Diversity and Mental Health Univ of Central Lancs 2006–, memb Faculty of Philosophy Univ of Oxford 2007–; fndr and ed Philosophy, Psychiatry & Psychology jl, lead series ed Int Perspectives in Philosophy and Psychiatry; chair Philosophy and Humanities Section and co-chair Conceptual Issues Workgroup World Psychiatric Assoc, co-chair Philosophy and Humanities Section Assoc of European Psychiatrists; fndr Int Network for Philosophy and Psychiatry; FRCPsych 1994 (MRCPsych 1976), FRCP 1999 (MRCP 1970); *Publications* incl: Moral Theory and Medical Practice (1989), In Two Minds: A Casebook of Psychiatric Ethics (co-author, 2000), Healthcare Ethics and Human Values (co-ed, 2002), Nature and Narrative: An Introduction to the New Philosophy of Psychiatry (co-ed, 2003), Whose Values? A Workbook for Values-Based Practice in Mental Health Care (2004), Oxford Textbook of Philosophy and Psychiatry (co-author, 2006); *Recreations* walking; *Style*— Prof Bill Fulford; ✉ Room A-133, The Medical School, University of Warwick, Coventry CV4 7AL (tel 024 7652 4961, fax 024 7657 3079, e-mail k.w.m.fulford@warwick.ac.uk)

FULFORD-DOBSON, Capt Michael; CVO (1999), DL (Dorset 1997), JP (1999); s of Lt Col Cyril Fulford Dobson (d 1974), of Laleham-on-Thames, and Betty Bertha, *née* Bendelack-Hudson-Barmby (d 1982); *b* 6 April 1931; *Educ* Pangbourne Coll, Royal Naval Colls Dartmouth and Greenwich; *m* 16 Dec 1966, (Elizabeth) Barbara Mary Rose, da of Maj Oswald James Tate (d 1980); 3 da (Jemima Nancy Grace (Viscountess FitzHarris) b 17 Jan 1968, Jessica Barbara Eliza b 29 April 1969, Rachel Eleanor Jane (Mrs James Burgess) b 7 Sept 1971); *Career* midshipman Korean War, CO HMS Dark Avenger 1956–57, Flag Lt Suez Operation 1956, Flag Lt to Flag offr 2 i/c Mediterranean Fleet 1956–59, Ops Offr HMS Hogue first Cod War 1959, qualified Signal Offr 1960, HMS Jaguar S Atlantic 1964–65, Cdr 1969, Br nat rep Turkish Miny of Defence 1969–71, Ops Offr UK Strategic Worldwide Communications Network 1972–74, Exec Offr RNAS Yeovilton 1976–81, Capt 1981, Sr Br Naval Offr, Asst Chief of Staff and Chief Signals Offr Allied Forces N Europe; Gentleman Usher to HM The Queen 1985–99 (Extra Gentleman Usher 1999–); chm: W Dorset General Hosps NHS Tst 1990–97, chm Dorset Tst 1991–2000; pres: Dorset Branch Cncl for the Protection of Rural England 1995–, St John Cncl for Dorset 1999–2006, Army Benevolent Fund for Dorset 1999–2006, SSAFA Forces Help for Dorset 1999–2006, Dorset Army Cadet League 1999–2006, Friends of Dorset Archives 1999–2006; vice-pres: Wessex Reserve Forces and Cadets Assoc 1999–2006, Royal Bath and West of England Soc 2001–06 (memb Cncl 2006–); dir: W Dorset Cncl on Alcohol 1986–91, In and Out Ltd 1993–96; patron: Br Red Cross Dorset Branch 1999–, Worldwide Volunteering 1994–, Dorset Yeomanry 1999–, Bridport Arts Centre 1999–, Community Fndn for Bournemouth, Dorset and Poole 2001–, Bournemouth Natural Science Soc 2002–, Anglo European Coll of Chiropatric 2003–06, Elizabeth Finn Tst in Dorset 2003–06; jt patron: Somerset and Dorset Air Ambulance Tst 1999–2006, Somerset and Dorset Sea Cadet Corps 1999–2006, Friends of Salisbury Cathedral 1999–2006; tstee: CancerCare Dorset 1998–2005, Queens Own Dorset Yeomanry & Dorset Garrison Assoc 1999–; memb Ct: Univ of Exeter 1999–2006, Univ of Southampton 1999–2006; govr Sherborne Sch 1999–2006; High Sheriff for Co of Dorset 1994–95, HM Lord-Lt Dorset 1999–2006; Hon Dr of Arts Univ of Bournemouth 2006; KStJ 1999; *Recreations* restoring historic buildings, field sports, cross country skiing; *Clubs* White's; *Style*— Capt Michael Fulford-Dobson, CVO, JP, DL, RN; ✉ Cerne Abbey, Dorset DT2 7JQ (tel and fax 01300 341284, e-mail mfd@ukonline.co.uk)

FULHAM, Suffragan Bishop of 1996–; Rt Rev John Charles Broadhurst; s of Charles Harold Broadhurst (d 1992), of St Albans, Herts, and Dorothy Sylvia, *née* Prince; *b* 20 July 1942; *Educ* Owens Sch Islington, KCL (AKC), St Boniface Coll Warminster; *m* 9 Oct 1965, Judith Margaret, *née* Randell; 2 da (Jane Elizabeth (Mrs Sanders) b 5 Oct 1967, Sarah Helena (Mrs Panteli) b 27 June 1973), 2 s (Mark John b 27 Feb 1970, Benedict Peter b 12 March 1979); *Career* ordained deacon 1966, priest 1967; asst curate St Michael-at-Bowes 1966–70, vicar St Augustine Wembley Park 1975–85 (priest-in-charge 1970–75), team rector Wood Green 1985–96; area dean: Brent 1982–85, E Haringey 1985–91; memb Gen Synod 1972–96 (memb Standing Ctee 1988–96), pro-prolocutor Convocation of Canterbury 1990–96; memb: 7th Assembly WCC Canberra 1990, Anglican Consultative Cncl 1991–96; nat chm Forward in Faith 1992–, vice-chm The Church Union; STh (by thesis) Lambeth, Hon DD Nashutah House 2003; *Publications* Quo Vaditis (ed and contrib); numerous articles; *Recreations* gardening, history, travel; *Style*— The Rt Rev the Bishop of Fulham; ✉ 26 Canonbury Park South, London N1 2FN (tel 020 7354 2334, fax 020 7354 2335, e-mail bpfulham@aol.com, website www.bishopoffulham.co.uk)

FULLER, Anthony Gerard Fleetwood; CBE (1990); 2 s of Maj Sir Gerard Fuller, 2 Bt, JP (d 1981), and his 1 w, Lady Fiona Pratt (later Countess of Normanton, d 1985), yr da of 4 Marquess Camden; *b* 4 June 1940; *Educ* Eton; *m* 19 Nov 1964, Julia Mary, er da of Lt-Col Eric Astley Cooper-Key, MBE, MC; 1 da (Camilla Fleetwood (Mrs Allan Christensen) b 16 Feb 1966), 1 s (William Gerard Fleetwood b 13 July 1968); *Career* Lt Life Gds 1959–62; Lloyd's underwriter; Fuller Smith & Turner plc (brewers): dir 1967–, md 1978–92, md and chm 1982–92, chm 1992–2007; non-exec dir Mentzendorff & Co Ltd 1992–2004; chm London region CBI 1995–97; vice-pres The Brewers of Europe 2005–07; chm: Brewers Soc 1986–89, Independent Family Brewers of Britain 1993–2005; Freeman, Liveryman and past Master Brewers' Co; *Recreations* shooting, gardening; *Style*— Anthony Fuller, Esq, CBE; ✉ Little Chalfield Manor, Melksham, Wiltshire SN12 8NN

FULLER, Sir James Henry Fleetwood; 4 Bt (UK 1910), of Neston Park, Corsham, Wiltshire; s of Maj Sir John Fuller, Bt (d 1998); *b* 1 November 1970; *Educ* Milton Abbey; *m* 22 July 2000, Ila Venetia Campbell-Mactaggart, da of Col Robin Mactaggart, and Tara Hamilton Campbell; 2 s (Archie, Harry); *Heir* s, Archie Fuller; *Career* late Capt The Life Guards 1991–98; *Style*— Sir James Fuller, Bt; ✉ Neston Park, Corsham, Wiltshire SN13 9TG

FULLER, John Leopold; s of Roy Broadbent Fuller (d 1991), and Kathleen, *née* Smith (d 1993); *b* 1 January 1937; *Educ* St Paul's, New Coll Oxford (MA, BLitt, Newdigate prize); *m* 1960, Cicely Prudence, da of Christopher Martin; 3 da (Sophie b 1961, Louisa b 1964, Emily b 1968); *Career* poet and writer; visiting lectr SUNY Buffalo NY 1962–63, asst lectr in English Univ of Manchester 1963–66, fell and tutor in English Magdalen Coll Oxford 1966–2002 (emeritus fell 2002–); Geoffrey Faber Award 1974, Cholmondeley Award, Whitbread Prize 1983, Forward Prize 1996; FRSL 1980, fell English Assoc (FAE) 2001; *Poetry* Fairground Music (1961), The Tree That Walked (1967), Cannibals and Missionaries (1972), Epistles to Several Persons (1973), The Mountain in the Sea (1975), Lies and Secrets (1979), The Illusionists (1980), Waiting for the Music (1982), The Beautiful Inventions (1983), Partingtime Hall (with James Fenton, 1987), The Grey Among the Green (1988), The Mechanical Body (1991), Stones and Fires (1996), Collected Poems (1996), Now and for a Time (2002), Ghosts (2004), The Space of Joy (2006); *Fiction* Flying to Nowhere (1983), The Adventures of Speedfall (1985), Tell It Me Again (1988), The Burning Boys (1989), Look Twice (1991), The Worm and the Star (1993), A Skin Diary (1997), The Memoirs of Laetitia Horsepole (2001), Flawed Angel (2005); *Criticism* Dramatic Works of John Gay (ed, 1983), A Reader's Guide to W H Auden (1970), The Sonnet (1972), The Chatto Book of Love Poetry (ed, 1990), W H Auden: a Commentary (1998), W H Auden: poems selected by John Fuller (2000), The Oxford Book of Sonnets (2000); *Recreations* music, chess; *Style*— John Fuller, Esq, FRSL; ✉ 4 Benson Place, Oxford OX2 6QH (tel and fax 01865 556154, e-mail john.fuller@magd.ox.ac.uk); c/o PFD, Drury House, 34–43 Russell Street, London WC2B 5HA (tel 020 7376 7676, fax 020 7352 7356)

FULLER, Martin Elliott; *b* 9 February 1943; *Educ* Mid-Warks Coll of Art, Hornsey Coll of Art; *partner* Margaret Rand (wine writer); *Career* artist; awarded Guggenheim-McKinley scholarship (American Art Workshop Italy) 1964, worked in Italy and America, now in London; work in collections incl Leamington Art Gallery and Museum; appeared on Private Passions with Michael Berkeley (BBC Radio 3) 2001; Discerning Eye Award Modern Painters Magazine 1996, Hunting Art Prize 1997; *Solo Exhibitions* incl: Midland Art Centre Birmingham 1968, Arnolfini Gallery Bristol 1968 and 1971, Centaur Gallery Bath 1969, Bristol Art Gallery 1970, Camden Art Centre London 1971, Bear Lane Gallery Oxford 1971 and 1973, Festival Gallery Bath 1973, Grabowski Gallery London 1973, Thumb Gallery London 1976 and 1979, Oxford Gallery 1983, RZA Galerie Düsseldorf 1983, Austin Desmond Fine Art 1985 and 1990, On The Wall Gallery Belfast 1987, Hendriks Gallery Dublin 1987, Retrospective curated by William Packer (Leamington Spa Art Gallery and Museum) 2001, Adam Gallery 2005, Stour Gallery 2006; *Group Exhibitions* incl: Hunterian Museum Univ of Glasgow 1997, KDK Gallery London 1997, Jonathan Clark Fine Art London (two-man show with Edward Burra) 2003, Adam Gallery London 2005, Drawing Gallery London 2006; *Commissions* incl: New Mexico 1990, Mural NY 1992/93, Times Mirror International Publishers Ltd London 1995, Dubai 1996, Chelsea and Westminster Hosp Arts Project London 1997, Railtrack Collection London 1998, Leamington Art Gallery and Museum Collection 2001, Waldorf Hotel London 2004, Radisson Hotel Cork 2005; *Recreations* jazz, modern opera, Wagner; *Clubs* Chelsea Arts, Groucho, Colony Room, Garrick, Academy, The Arts; *Style*— Martin Fuller, Esq; ✉ Studio II, 29 Blenheim Gardens, London SW2 5EU (tel 020 8678 6008, website www.martinfuller.net)

FULLER, Michael John; s of late Thomas Frederick Fuller, of Great Bookham, Surrey, and late Irene Emily, *née* Pope; *b* 20 July 1935; *Educ* Wallington GS; *m* 1, 26 March 1955 (m dis 1989), (Maureen) Rita, da of Frederick Slade; 2 s (Nicholas b 1960, Richard b 1962), 2 da (Laura, Jacqueline (twins) b 1966); m 2, 2 June 1990, Elizabeth Marion, da of Terence Townsend; 1 step s (Bruno Frost); *Career* Midland Bank plc: various positions 1952–77, gp public affairs advsr 1977–79, regnl dir Southampton 1979–81, gen mangr 1981–83, gen mangr business devpt 1983–85, UK ops dir 1985–87, dep chief exec UK banking sector 1987–89, chief exec UK banking sector 1989–90; gen mangr National Bank of Abu Dhabi 1991–92, chief exec Ahli United Bank (Bahrain) BSC(c) 1992–2002, chief exec Bank of Kuwait Middle East KSC 2003–05; FCIB, FRSA; *Recreations* reading, travelling, rough golf; *Clubs* RAF; *Style*— Michael Fuller, Esq

FULLER, Paul Malcolm; s of John Taylor Fuller (d 1997), of Billericay, Essex; *b* 4 November 1946; *Educ* Southend HS for Boys; *m* 1969, Jenifer Mary Elizabeth, da of Percy Beere (d 1955); 1 s, 2 da; *Career* accountant; fin dir: Lacrinoid Products Ltd 1973–78, TKM Foods Ltd 1978–83; ptnr Deloitte & Touche (formerly Touche Ross) 1983–99 (consulting gp ptnr 1987), md Fuller Consulting Services Ltd 1999–; MInstD; fell Chartered Inst of Mgmnt Accountants, FCMI, FCCA; *Recreations* walking, the arts; *Style*— Paul Fuller, Esq; ✉ Cameron House, 270 Noak Hill Road, Basildon, Essex SS15 4DE (tel (office) 01268 417333, fax 01268 413334, e-mail paulmfuller@msn.com)

FULLER, Paul Maurice; s of Brian Fuller, of Alvechurch, Worcs, and Linda, *née* Peters; *b* 16 February 1960, St Albans, Herts; *Educ* Elmbridge Sch Cranleigh, Radyr Comp Sch, Southbank Univ (BSc, MSc), Fire Serv Coll Moreton-in-Marsh; *m* 5 July 1979 (m dis 1994), Claire Ellen, *née* Williams; 1 da (Amy Sarah b 18 Dec 1979), 1 s (Ben Maurice b 30 March 1981); m 2, 15 March 1997, Helen Elizabeth, *née* Davey; *Career* recruit rising to station offr and advanced trg instr W Midlands Fire Service 1978–87, station cdr rising to asst divnl offr W Sussex Fire Brigade 1987–89, asst divnl offr Staffs Fire & Rescue Serv 1990–94, dep divnl cdr rising to asst chief fire offr Wilts Fire Brigade 1994–2002, chief fire offr Beds and Luton Combined Fire Authy 2002–; Chief Fire Offrs Assoc: chair Nat Procurement Bd, chair Appliance Equipment and Uniform Ctee, chair Eastern region, memb Strategy Ctee, memb Members' Sounding Bd; memb: Cncl Fire & Rescue Suppliers Assoc, Integrated Clothing Project Bd and Procurement Project Bd Nat Fire Service, Bd Firebuy, BSI ctees; sponsor Respiratory Protective Equipment Project; lead offr Eastern Region Regnl Mgmnt Bd for Common Servs Workstream; memb: Beds and Luton Chief Execs' Forum, Bedford BOOST Strategy Gp, Beds and Luton Local Resilience Forum Exec Gp; advsr Beds and Luton LGA; memb: IFireE 1984, Instn for Supervision and Mgmnt 1995; *Recreations* scuba diving, motorcycling, keep fit, walking, reading; *Style*—

Paul M Fuller, Esq; ✉ 12 Tulip Tree Close, Bromham, Bedfordshire MK43 8GH (tel 01234 824175); Chief Fire Officer, Bedfordshire and Luton Fire & Rescue Service, Southfields Road, Kempston, Bedfordshire MK42 7NR (tel 01234 845017, e-mail paul.fuller@bedsfire.com)

FULLER, Simon; *Career* with Chrysalis Music until 1985; estab 19 Entertainment 1985 (sold 2005; more than 75 UK no1 and 250 Top 40 singles and albums), brands incl 19TV, 19 Recordings, 19 Mgmnt and Popworld; mangr of artists and celebrities incl: Paul Hardcastle, Annie Lennox, Eurythmics, Spice Girls, S Club 7, S Club Juniors, Will Young, Gareth Gates, David and Victoria Beckham; prodr and creator Pop Idol (ITV) 2001 (BAFTA Award, Golden Rose of Montreux 2002), prodr American Idol (Fox Network) 2002; charity projects incl: Greenpeace, Amnesty Int, Prince's Tst; *Style—* Simon Fuller, Esq; ✉ 19 Management, Unit 32, Ransomes Dock, 35–37 Parkgate Road, London SW11 4NP

FULLER, Prof Watson; s of Edward Fuller (d 1983), of Haslingden, Lancs, and Alice, *née* Worrall (d 1991); *b* 25 February 1935; *Educ* Haslingden GS, KCL (BSc, AKC, PhD); *m* 9 Sept 1961, Shirley Ann, da of Cedric Pollack (d 1934), of London, and Vera Winifred, *née* Bowes (d 1982); 1 s (Laurence b 17 Dec 1965), 1 da (Catherine b 13 Nov 1967); *Career* scientific staff MRC 1960–63, reader in biophysics KCL 1967–73 (lectr 1963–67); Keele Univ: prof of physics 1973–2002 (emeritus prof 2002–), head Physics Dept 1973–96, dep vice-chllr 1980–83, 1984–85 and 1988–94; dir R&D for health N Staffs 1994–2002; FInstP 1974; *Style—* Prof Watson Fuller; ✉ 14 Plantation Park, Keele, Staffordshire ST5 5NA (tel 01782 627220); School of Chemistry and Physics, Keele University, Staffordshire ST5 5BG (tel 01782 583320, e-mail w.fuller@keele.ac.uk)

FULLERTON, John Skipwith; eld s of Alexander Fergus Fullerton, of E Sussex, and Elizabeth Pamela Cappa, *née* Jeans; *b* 16 January 1949; *Educ* Diocesan Coll Cape Town; *m* 1987, Lina, da of Dr George Geha; 2 da (Elizabeth Sana b 1988, Emma Jane b 1990); *Career* served: Cape Town Highlanders 1967, 1 Bn Yorks Vols (TA) 1975–77; journalist and author; Reuters: bureau chief Beirut 1984–87, ME dip corr 1988–90, bureau chief Cairo 1990–92, reported from 38 countries and covered 12 wars incl Lebanon civil war, Croatia, Bosnia, Afghanistan, Gulf War 1991; memb: Soc of Authors, CWA, Amnesty Int, Greenpeace; *Books* The Soviet Occupation of Afghanistan (non-fiction, 1984), The Monkey House (1997), A Hostile Place (2003), Give Me Death (2004); *Recreations* fishing; *Clubs* Special Forces; *Style—* John Fullerton, Esq; ✉ 185 Fentiman Road, London SW8 1JY (tel 020 7820 1688, e-mail johnsfullerton@hotmail.com)

FULTHORPE, Jonathan Mark; s of Henry Joseph Fulthorpe (d 1999), and Betty May, *née* Forshew; *b* 21 March 1949; *Educ* Sir Joseph Williamson's Mathematical Sch Rochester, UCL (LLB), Univ of London (LLM); *m* 1, 1973 (m dis 1978), Clare Elizabeth, *née* Stephenson; m 2, 1979, Carol Margaret, da of late Stanley Gordon Greenfield, of Brantford, Ontario, Canada; 1 s (James Mark Charles b 1981), 3 step da (Sarah Lynne b 1970, Jennifer Anne b 1972, Alison Claire b 1975); *Career* called to the Bar Inner Temple 1970, in practice Western circuit 1973–; fndr tstee Br Vascular Fndn 1992–; FRGS 1972; *Recreations* watching cricket, the study of geography, architecture, travel to rare places; *Clubs* Hampshire (Winchester), Hampshire CCC, Bentham, Flyfishers, Malaysian Cricket Supporters (Kuala Lumpur); *Style—* Jonathan Fulthorpe, Esq; ✉ 16 Abbotts Way, Southampton, Hampshire SO2 1QT (tel 023 80584 879); chambers: 17 Carlton Crescent, Southampton SO1 2ES (tel 023 8032 0320, fax 023 8032 0321)

FULTON, Prof (Robert) Andrew; s of late Rev Robert Morton Fulton, of Isle of Bute, Scotland, and Janet White, *née* Mackenzie; *b* 6 February 1944; *Educ* Rothesay Acad, Univ of Glasgow (MA, LLB); *m* 29 Aug 1970, Patricia Mary Crowley; 2 s (Daniel Robert b 8 Oct 1972, Edward Patrick b 8 Sept 1974), 1 da (Joanna Mary b 9 May 1979); *Career* HM Dip Serv; third sec FCO 1968, third then second sec Saigon 1968–72; first sec: Rome 1973–77, E Berlin 1978–81, FCO 1981–84; cnsllr: Oslo 1984–87, FCO 1987–89, UK Mission to UN NY 1989–92, FCO 1993–94, Washington 1995–99; chm: Advsy Bd Proudfoot Consltg 2002–, EdoMidas 2003–, nation1 2005–, GPW 2006–, Advsy Bd Huntswood 2006–, Scot N American Business Cncl; dir Scot Control Risks Gp 2002–06; int business advsr: Memex Technol 2003–, Dynamic Knowledge Corp 2005–, Armor Gp Int 2006–; visiting prof Sch of Law Univ of Glasgow 1999–; *Recreations* golf, national hunt racing, reading, cinema; *Style—* Prof Andrew Fulton; ✉ 7 Crown Road South, Glasgow G12 9DJ (tel 0141 337 3710, e-mail rafulton@7gatehouse.freeserve.co.uk)

FULTON, Rev John Oswald; s of Robert Fulton (d 1994), of Clydebank, and Margaret, *née* Wright; *b* 9 July 1953; *Educ* Clydebank HS, Univ of Glasgow (BSc, BD); *m* 1989, Margaret Paterson, da of Robert Wilson (d 1981), of Glasgow; 1 da (Ruth Janet b 6 Sept 1991); *Career* United Free Church of Scotland: ordained 1977, min Croftfoot Glasgow 1977–94, gen sec 1994–; convener Ctee on Trg for the Miny 1984–89, moderator Presbytery of Glasgow and The West 1987–88, convener Ctee on Miny and Home Affrs 1989–93, moderator Gen Assembly 2000–01; govr Hamilton Coll 2007–; *Recreations* gardening, photography, music, reading; *Style—* The Rev John Fulton; ✉ 12 Peveril Avenue, Burnside, Rutherglen, Glasgow G73 4RD (tel 0141 630 0068); United Free Church of Scotland, 11 Newton Place, Glasgow G3 7PR (tel 0141 332 3435, fax 0141 333 1973, e-mail jofulton@tiscali.co.uk)

FULTON, (Paul) Robert Anthony; s of George Alan Fulton (d 1981), and Margaret, *née* Foxton (d 2001); *b* 20 March 1951; *Educ* Nunthorpe GS York, Churchill Coll Cambridge (BA); *m* 1981, Lee Hong Tay; *Career* civil servant Home Office 1973–2003; positions incl: private sec to perm sec, dir Prison Industries and Farms 1991–96, princ fin offr 1996–2000, dir of strategy and performance 2000–02, implementation dir ARA 2002–03; vice-chair SOVA 2004–; chair DuCane Housing Assoc 2004–, chair CHAS (Central London) Ind Housing and Debt Advice Serv 2006–; *Recreations* photography, music, walking, cycling; *Style—* Robert Fulton, Esq; ✉ 1 Meadow Close, Hinchley Wood, Esher, Surrey KT10 0AY (robert@fulton-web.com)

FULTON, Lt-Gen Sir Robert Henry Gervase; KBE (2005); s of James Fulton (d 1993), and Cynthia, *née* Shaw (d 2005); *b* 21 December 1948; *Educ* Eton, UEA (BA); *m* 16 Aug 1975, Midge, *née* Free; 2 s (James b 1977, Mark b 1980); *Career* cmmnd RM 1972, 42 Commando 1973–75, 40 Commando 1976–78, instr Sch of Signals Blandford 1978–80, Army Staff Coll Camberley 1980–81, instr Jr Div Staff Coll 1981–83, 42 Commando 1983–85, SO2 Ops HQ Trg Reserves and Special Forces RM 1985–87, SO2 Commitments Dept of Cmdt Gen RM 1987–90, SO1 Directing Staff Army Staff Coll Camberley 1990–92, CO 42 Commando 1992–94, asst dir CIS Op Regts CGRM 1994–95, RCDS 1996, cmd 3 Commando Bde 1997–2001, capability mangr Information Superiority MOD 2001–03, DCDS (Equipment Capability) 2003–06; govr and C-in-C Gibraltar 2006–; memb Cncl RUSI 2003; Liveryman Worshipful Co of Haberdashers; *Recreations* playing and watching sport, military history; *Clubs* Army and Navy, MCC; *Style—* Lt-Gen Sir Robert Fulton; ✉ The Convent, Gibraltar

FURBER, (William) James; s of Frank Robert Furber, of Blackheath, London, and Anne Wilson, *née* McArthur; *b* 1 September 1954, London; *Educ* Westminster, Gonville & Caius Coll Cambridge (MA); *m* 22 Oct 1982, Rosemary Elizabeth, *née* Johnston; 1 da (Elizabeth Sarah Anne b 29 Nov 1984), 2 s (Robert William Johnston b 10 Aug 1986, Charles James Haslett b 1 Jan 1989); *Career* admitted slr 1979; Farrer & Co: joined 1976, assoc ptnr 1981–85, ptnr 1985–; slr to the Duchy of Cornwall 1994–; treas Lowtonian Soc 2003–, sec St Bartholomew's Medical Coll Tst 1996–; tstee: Leonard Cheshire Fndn 2000–06, Arvon Fndn 2000–07, Trinity Coll of Music Charitable Tst 2005–; reader C of E 1991–; memb: Law Soc 1979–, City of Westminster and Holborn Law Soc 1981– (pres 1996–97); *Publications* Encyclopedia of Forms and Precedents (Vol 36 (Sale of Land), 1990); *Recreations* golf, literature, wine, laughter; *Clubs* Athenaeum, Hawks, R&A, Royal St George's Golf, Royal West Norfolk Golf; *Style—* James Furber, Esq; ✉ Farrer & Co, 66 Lincoln's Inn Fields, London WC2A 3LH (tel 020 7242 2022, e-mail wjf@farrer.co.uk)

FURBER, (Robert) John; QC (1995); s of Frank Robert Furber, of Blackheath, London, and Anne Wilson, *née* McArthur; *b* 13 October 1949; *Educ* Westminster, Gonville & Caius Coll Cambridge (MA); *m* 16 April 1977, (Amanda) Cherry, da of Frederick Colbran Burgoyne Varney, OBE, of Blackheath, London; 1 s (Thomas b 1980), 2 da (Sophia b 1983, Olivia b 1989); *Career* called to the Bar Inner Temple 1973; chm Field Lane Fndn 2004–06; *Books* jt ed: Halsbury's Laws of England (Landlord and Tenant) (1981), Hill and Redman's Law of Landlord and Tenant (1981–2007), Halsbury's Laws of England (Compulsory Acquisition) (1996), Guide to Commonhold and Leasehold Reform Act (2002); *Recreations* literature, music, cricket; *Clubs* Buck's, Beefsteak, Pratt's; *Style—* John Furber, Esq, QC; ✉ 1 Hallgate, Blackheath Park, London SE3 9SG (tel 020 8852 7633); Wilberforce Chambers, 8 New Square, Lincoln's Inn, London WC2A 3QP (tel 020 7306 0102)

FURBER, Prof Stephen Byram; s of Benjamin Neil Furber, of Marple, Cheshire, and Margaret, *née* Schofield; *b* 21 March 1953; *Educ* Manchester Grammar, St John's Coll Cambridge (Baylis scholar, BA), Univ of Cambridge (PhD); *m* 6 Aug 1977, Valerie Margaret, da of Reginald Walter Elliott; 2 da (Alison Mary b 4 Jan 1982, Catherine Margaret b 10 April 1984); *Career* Rolls-Royce research fell Emmanuel Coll Cambridge 1978–81; princ designer BBC microcomputer hardware 1981–82; hardware design engr and design mangr Acorn Computers Ltd Cambridge 1981–90; princ hardware architect of the ARM 32-bit RISC microprocessor 1983; Univ of Manchester: ICL prof of computer engrg Dept of Computer Science 1990, head Dept of Computer Science 2001–04; dir: Manchester Informatics Ltd 1994–, Cogency Technol Inc Toronto 1997–99, Cogniscience Ltd 2000–, Transitive Technologies Ltd 2001–04, Silistix Ltd 2004–06; led research gp which developed AMULET1 won BCS Award 1995, BBC Micro and ARM both won Acorn Queen's Award for Technol, Royal Acad of Engrg Silver Medal 2003, Royal Soc Wolfson Research Merit Award 2004–09; memb PCC St Chad's Handforth (Anglican); FBCS 1997 (MBCS 1992), CEng, FREng 1999, FRS 2002, FIEE 2004, FIEEE 2005; *Publications* VLSI RISC Architecture and Organisation (1989), ARM System Architecture (1996), ARM System-on-Chip Architecture (revised edn, 2000); author of over 90 papers; *Recreations* 6 string and bass guitar (church music group); *Style—* Prof Stephen Furber, FRS, FREng; ✉ School of Computer Science, University of Manchester, Oxford Road, Manchester M13 9PL (tel 0161 275 6129, fax 0161 275 6236, e-mail steve.furber@manchester.ac.uk)

FURMANOVSKY, Jill; *b* 1953, Rhodesia; *Educ* Claremont Sch Kenton, Harrow Sch of Art, Central Sch of Art; *m*; 1 da; *Career* photographer; in-house photographer Rainbow Theatre 1972–79, freelance photo journalist 1970s and 1980s (contrib Sounds, Melody Maker, NME, Smash Hits and The Face); fndr JFA Studio 1982 (extending photography coverage to incl advtg and fashion); work featured in Sunday Times, The Observer, The Guardian, Q Magazine and others; stills photographer on films: Sister My Sister 1992, Institute Benjamenta 1993, Carrington 1994, Secret Agent 1995; official photographer to pop group Oasis; *Exhibitions* Was There Then - Oasis (touring London, Manchester, Glasgow and Europe) 1997; author of articles published in Photography Magazine 1987 and Br Journal of Photography 1990–91; *Awards* incl: Nikon Honourable Award 1984, Diamond Euro Music Photographer of the Year 1987, Ilford Award 1990, The Observer Portrait Award 1992, Kodak Gold Award 1994, Woman of the Year for the Music Industry and Related Media 1998; *Books* The Moment - 25 Years of Rock Photography (1995), Was There Then - Oasis A Photographic Journey (1997); *Style—* Ms Jill Furmanovsky; ✉ e-mail jill@rockarchive.com, website www.rockarchive.com

FURMSTON, Prof Michael Philip; TD; s of Joseph Philip Furmston (d 1987), of Chipstead, Surrey, and Phyllis, *née* Clowes (d 2004); *b* 1 May 1933; *Educ* Wellington, Exeter Coll Oxford (MA, BCL), Univ of Birmingham (LLM); *m* 26 Sept 1964, Ashley Sandra Maria, da of Edward Cope, of Cumnor, Oxon; 7 da (Rebecca b 1967, Rachel b 1969, Charlotte b 1971, Clare b 1973, Alexandra b 1975, Antonia b 1978, Olivia b 1979), 3 s (Simon b 1977, Thomas b 1981, Timothy b 1983); *Career* Nat Serv RA 1951–53, cmmnd 2 Lt 1952, TA serv 1953–78 (Maj 1966); lectr in law: Univ of Birmingham 1957–62, Queen's Univ Belfast 1962–63; fell Lincoln Coll Oxford and lectr in law 1964–78; Univ of Bristol: prof of law 1978–98, dean Faculty of Law 1980–84 and 1995–98, pro-vice-chllr 1986–89 (emeritus prof and sr research fell 1998–); bencher Gray's Inn 1989; chm Comec 1996–2000; Freeman Worshipful Co of Arbitrators; *Books* Cheshire Fifoot and Furmston's Law of Contract (ed, 8 to 15 edns, 1972–2006), A Building Contract Casebook (with V Powell-Smith, 1984, 4 edn 2006), The Law of Tort: Policies and Trends in Liability for Damage to Property and Economic Loss (ed, 1986), You and the Law (ed with V Powell-Smith, 1987), Sale and Supply of Goods (1996, 3 edn 1999), Contract Formation and Letters of Intent (1997), The Law of Contract (ed, 1999, 3 edn 2007); *Recreations* chess (rep British team in 2 correspondence olympiads), dogs, watching cricket; *Clubs* Reform, Naval and Military; *Style—* Prof Michael Furmston, TD; ✉ 5 Priory Court, Bridgewater, Somerset TA6 3NR; Faculty of Law, University of Bristol, Wills Memorial Building, Queens Road, Bristol BS8 1RJ (tel 0117 954 5301, fax 0117 922 5136)

FURNEAUX, Paul; s of James Furneaux, of Aberdeen, and Nora Mavis, *née* Davidson; *b* 2 March 1962; *Educ* Aberdeen GS, Edinburgh Coll of Art (BA, postgrad Dip), Tama Art Univ Tokyo (MA); *Partner* Ruth Hollyman; 1 da (Silvie Rose Holly Furneaux); *Career* artist; Edinburgh Coll of Art: pt/t lectr in drawing and painting 1992–96 and 2000–03, teacher Summer Sch 1992–96; first artist in residence Center for Contemporary Printmaking Norwalk CT 2003; currently artist running workshops in contemporary Japanese woodblock printing at Edinburgh Print Workshop and other nat and int venues; professional memb Soc of Scottish Artists, professional memb Aberdeen Artists Soc 1994, RSA 2007; *Solo Exhibitions* Todd Gall London 1989 and 1991, Compass Gall Glasgow 1989, Fujita Gall, Yamaguchi City Japan 1990, New Works (369 Gall Edinburgh) 1994, Colores De Un Extrano Otono (Inst of Anglo-Mexico Culture) 1995, Woodcut Prints (Lemon Tree Gall Aberdeen) 1996, Journeys on Paper - Watercolours and Woodcuts (Firth Gall Edinburgh) 1996, Woodcut Prints (Saoh and Tomos Galls Tokyo) 1999, Foyer Gall Aberdeen 2000, Genkan Gall Tokyo American Club 2001, Stone Cut Wood Cut (Royal Museum Edinburgh) 2001, Edinburgh Festival Exhbn (Firth Gall Edinburgh) 2001, Hönran Gall Falun Sweden 2002, Northern Light Gall Stockholm 2003, New Works (Center for Contemporary Printmaking CT) 2003, Blue Flowers Red Shadows (Patriot Hall Gall Edinburgh) 2005, Woodcuts (The Friends Room RSA) 2007, Woodblock Prints (Patriot Hall Gall Edinburgh) 2007; *Group Exhibitions* incl: Figure Form and Fantasy (Todd Gall) 1988, Prints from Peacock (Gulausy Gall Budapest) 1991, Made in Japan (Aberdeen Art Gall) 1991, Soc of Scottish Artists Centenary Exhibition 1991, The Spectator/Adam & Company Fifth Annual Award for Professional Artists (The Fruitmarket Gall Edinburgh and The Barbican Centre London) 1992, Art for a Fairer World (organised by Oxfam for their 50th Anniversary Art Gall and Museum Kelvingrove Glasgow, St David's Hall Cardiff and Smiths Galls Covent Garden London) 1992, An Artist's Choice (June Redfern Selects, Bohn Gall Henley-on-Thames) 1993, Thursday's Child (Robert Billcliffe Fine Art Glasgow) 1994, Gathering (Galerie Beeldspraak Amsterdam) 1995, Scottish Print Open (Glasgow Print Studio and travelling) 1996 (prizewinner), Vision of the Future Pusan Culture Centre Korea 1997, Triangle: Three British Artists in Japan Tokyo 1998, Tokyo Int Mini Print Triennial 1998, Aomori Grand Prix Competition Exhibition Aomori Museum of Art 1998, Japan Print Assoc

Annual Exhibition Tokyo Metro Museum of Art 1998, Taipei Int Print and Drawing Biennale Taiwan 1999, Connections 2000 (invited artist, RSA), Opening Exhibition (Gallery Vallmer Ljubjana Slovenia) 2001, Ink from Wood - Two Traditions (Center for Contemporary Printmaking Norwalk CT) 2003, The Directors Choice (Open Eye Gall Edinburgh) 2004, Cross Flows Five Int Artists (Shin Pu Kan Gall Kyoto) 2004, Tokyo Int Mini-print Triennial (Tama Art Univ) 2005, Urban Landscapes (Open Eye Gall Edinburgh) 2006, Crossflows (Numthong Gall Bangkok) 2006, Royal Acad Summer Exhibition 2007, Preview (Open Eye Gall) 2007; *Work in Collections* City Art Centre Edinburgh, Jean F Watson Bequest Purchase, Aberdeen Art Gall, Heriot-Watt Univ, Edinburgh Coll of Art, Royal Scottish Acad, BBC Scotland, Cornhill Hosp Aberdeen, Eastern Gen Hosp Edinburgh, Aberdeen City Library, Forester Hill Hosp Aberdeen, Art in Hosps Tst, Harry and Margery Boswell Art Collection Univ of St Andrews, Royal Scottish Museum, Univ of Edinburgh Royal Infirmary, St Andrew's House Scottish Exec, Falun city Sweden, Dalrus Region Sweden; *Awards* Royal Scottish Acad Keith Prize 1986, Edinburgh DC Spring Fling first prize for painting 1986, Young Scottish Artist of the Year 1987, Clason-Harie Bursary for Postgrad Exhibition 1987, Print Prize 1987, Largo Award Edinburgh Coll of Art, Sunday Times Scotland Mayfest Award for Visual Art 1989, Royal Over-Seas League Prize 1989, Alistair E Salvesen Art scholar 1990, Royal Scottish Acad Meyer Openheim Prize 1991, Soc of Scottish Artists J F M Purchase Prize 1991, Royal Scottish Acad Ireland Alloys Award 1994, Br Cncl travel grant to travel and exhibit in Mexico 1994, Japanese Govt (Monbusho) scholarship 1996–2000, research student and masters course in Japanese woodblock printing techniques Tama Art Univ of Tokyo 1997–2000, National Year of the Artist residency at Nat Museum of Scotland Edinburgh 2001, Dundee Contemporary Arts Technical Training Award, Aberdeen Artists Shell Expro Award, Hope Scott Assistance Grant 2003, Professional Devpt Award Scottish Arts Cncl 2003 and 2004, Shell Expro Award (Bronze) Aberdeen Artists 71 2005, Grampian Health Center Purchase Award 2005, Scottish Arts Club Award 2005, Soc of Scottish Artists Website Award 2007, RSA John Murray Thomson Award 2007; exhbn curator (contemporary Japanese woodblock print makers) Japan 2001 Edinburgh Printmakers Gallery 2001, invited artist Luboradón 2001 (international printmaking symposium and workshop) Poland 2001, artist in residence Center for Contemporary Printmaking CT 2003, artist residency for 2 months in Bjerkriem Norway; regular exhibitor RSA; *Recreations* hill walking; *Style—* Paul Furneaux, Esq; ✉ WASPS Patriot Hall Studios, Studio 108, Edinburgh; 36 Rodney Street, Edinburgh EH7 4DX (tel 0131 556 0710, e-mail mail@paulfurneaux.com, website www.paulfurneaux.com)

FURNELL, Prof James Rupert Gawayne; s of Percy Gawayne Furnell (d 1986), of London, and Margaret Katherine Aslett, *née* Wray (d 1979); *b* 20 February 1946; *Educ* Leighton Park Sch Reading, Univ of Aberdeen (MA), Univ of Glasgow (DCP), Univ of Stirling (PhD), Univ of Dundee (LLB, Dip LP); *m* 14 Sept 1974, Lesley Anne, da of John Ross, of Glasgow; 1 s (Alistair b 1976), 1 da (Rachael b 1978); *Career* clinical psychologist Royal Hosp for Sick Children Glasgow 1970–72, conslt clinical psychologist (child health 1980–98), memb Forth Valley Health Bd 1984–87; admitted Faculty of Advocates and called to Scottish Bar Parliament House Edinburgh 1993; visiting prof Caledonian Univ of Glasgow 1996–; memb Nat Consultative Ctee in Professions Allied to Med 1984–87, chm Div of Clinical Psychology Br Psychological Soc 1988–89; assoc ed Criminological and Legal Psychology 1997–2000; hon fell Univ of Edinburgh 1987–; FBPsS; *Recreations* flying, cross country skiing; *Clubs* Royal Northern and Univ (Aberdeen); *Style—* Prof James Furnell; ✉ Glensherup House, Glendevon, Perthshire (tel 01259 781234); Advocates Library, Parliament House, Edinburgh EH1 1RF (tel 0131 226 5071)

FURNELL, Stephen George; s of George Edward Furnell (d 1971), of Kettering, Northants, and Norah Delia, *née* Barritt (d 1995); *b* 30 June 1945; *Educ* Kettering GS, Cambridgeshire HS, Leicester Poly (Dip); *m* 12 Feb 1972, Maxine, da of Harry Smith (d 1989), of Edmonton, London; 2 s (Thomas b 1972, Henry b 1982); *Career* Architects Dept Leicester CC 1967, ptnr TP Bennett 1987–93 (joined 1969), fndr Furnell Associates 1993–; ARIBA 1970, MCSD 1987, FRSA 1987; *Recreations* cricket, golf, photography, painting; *Style—* Stephen Furnell, Esq

FURNESS, His Hon Judge Mark Richard; s of Sqdn Ldr Thomas Hogg Baitey Furness, (Ret), of Cardiff, and Pip, *née* Harris; *b* 28 November 1948; *Educ* Hereford Cathedral Sch, St John's Coll Cambridge (MA); *m* 27 July 1974, Margaretta, da of William Trevor Evans; 1 s (David b 21 Oct 1978), 1 da (Emma b 24 Oct 1979); *Career* called to the Bar Lincoln's Inn 1970; recorder of the Crown Court 1996–98 (asst recorder 1992–96), circuit judge 1998–; chm: Social Security Appeal Tbnl 1988–94, Disability Appeal Tbnl 1990–98; *Recreations* bridge, DIY, travel, literature, theatre, motoring; *Clubs* Cardiff & County; *Style—* His Hon Judge Furness; ✉ Newport County Court, The Concourse, Clarence House, Clarence Place, Newport NP19 7AA (tel 01633 245040, fax 01633 245041)

FURNESS, Sir Stephen Roberts; 3 Bt (UK 1913), of Tunstall Grange, West Hartlepool; s of Sir Christopher Furness, 2 Bt (d 1974, 2 cous of 2 Viscount Furness), and Violet Flower Chipchase, *née* Roberts; *b* 10 October 1933; *Educ* Charterhouse; *m* 6 April 1961, Mary, er

da of Jack Fitzroy Cann, of Cullompton, Devon; 1 s (Michael Fitzroy Roberts b 1962), 1 da (Serena Mary (Mrs Mark Searight) b 1964); *Heir* s, Michael Furness; *Career* late Lt RN, ret 1962; farmer and sporting artist (as Robin Furness); jt MFH Bedale Foxhounds 1979–87; *Recreations* hunting, racing, looking at paintings; *Style—* Sir Stephen Furness, Bt; ✉ Stanhow, Northallerton, North Yorkshire DL7 0TJ (tel 01609 748614)

FURSDON, (Edward) David; o s of Maj-Gen (Francis William) Edward Fursdon, CB, MBE (d 2007), and Joan Rosemary, *née* Worssam; succeeded uncle as owner of 700 year old Fursdon family estate in Devon 1981; *b* 20 December 1952; *Educ* Sherborne, St John's Coll Oxford (scholar, MA, Cricket blue); *m* 7 Oct 1978, Catriona Margaret, da of Geoffrey Crichton McCreath, of Berwick-upon-Tweed; 3 s (Oliver b 1980, Thomas b 1982, Charles b 1986); *Career* 6 QEO Gurkha Rifles 1972; MOD (Whitehall and UN Geneva) 1975–79, ptnr Stags auctioneers 1994–; CLA: chm Devon branch 1997–99, chm Legal and Parly Ctee 1999–2003, exec 1996– (chm 2003), dep pres 2003–05, pres 2005–; memb Regnl Ctee (Devon and Cornwall) Nat Tst 2001–04; chm Cadbury Parish Meeting 1982–; govr Blundell's Sch 1984– (chm 2000–); FRICS, FAAV; *Recreations* sport, travel; *Clubs* MCC, Vincent's (Oxford); *Style—* David Fursdon, Esq; ✉ Fursdon, Cadbury, Exeter EX5 5JS (tel 020 7235 0511)

FURSE, Clara Hedwig Frances; *Educ* St James's Sch Malvern, LSE (BSc(Econ)); *m*; 3 c; *Career* with Heinold Commodities Ltd 1979–83; Phillips & Drew/UBS: joined 1983, dir 1988–90, exec dir 1992–95, md 1995–96, global head of futures 1996–98; gp chief exec Credit Lyonnais Rouse 1998–2000, chief exec London Stock Exchange plc 2001–; LIFFE: bd dir 1990–99, dep chm 1997–99, chm Strategy Working Gp 1994–95, chm Membership and Rules Ctee 1995–97, chm Fin Ctee 1998–99; bd dir: Euroclear plc 2002–, LCH Clearnet 2004; tstee RICS 2002; *Style—* Mrs Clara Furse; ✉ London Stock Exchange plc, Paternoster Square, London EC4M 7LS

FURST, Stephen Andrew; QC (1991); *Career* called to the Bar Middle Temple 1975, recorder 1999–; *Style—* Stephen Furst, Esq, QC; ✉ Keating Chambers, 15 Essex Street, London WC2R 3AU (tel 020 7544 2600)

FURTADO, Peter Randall; s of Robert Audley Furtado (d 1992), and Marcelle Elizabeth, *née* Whitteridge (d 1992); *b* 20 May 1952; *Educ* Whitgift Sch, Oriel Coll Oxford (BA, Dip Art History); *m* 1983, Ann, *née* Swoffer; 3 da (Tamzin Eiko Swoffer b 1985, Robyn Freya b 1991, Joanna Eveline b 1991); *Career* sr ed Hamlyn Books 1977–83, freelance ed 1983–87, sr ed Equinox Books 1987–91, exec ed Andromeda Books 1991–97, ed History Today 1998–; chm Shintaido Fndn 1994–97 and 2002–, dir Int Shintaido Fedn 2004–; FRHistS 2002; *Books* managing ed: Ordnance Survey Atlas of Great Britain (1981), Illustrated History of the 20th Century (10 vols, 1989–92), Cassell Atlas of World History (1996); *Recreations* cycling, saxophone, moving meditation; *Style—* Peter Furtado, Esq; ✉ History Today, 20 Old Compton Street, London W1D 4TW (tel 020 7534 8001, fax 020 7534 8008, e-mail p.furtado@historytoday.com)

FURZE, Caroline Mary; da of John Marshall Furze (d 1992), and Mary Ann, *née* Walker; *Educ* Sherborne Sch for Girls, Trinity Coll Cambridge (BA); *Career* called to the Bar Lincoln's Inn 1992; *Publications* contrib to various legal pubns; Halsbury Law titles: Real Property (1998), Customs & Usage (1998); Atkin's Court Forms Co-ownership (2006); *Style—* Miss Caroline Furze; ✉ Wilberforce Chambers, 8 New Square, Lincoln's Inn, London WC2A 3QP (tel 020 7306 0102)

FYFE, Brig Alastair Ian Hayward; DL (Somerset 1995); s of Archibald Graham Fyfe (d 1979), of Misterton, Somerset, and Alison Amy, *née* Hayward (d 1982); *b* 21 October 1937; *Educ* Lancing, RMA Sandhurst, Staff Coll Camberley; *m* 15 Aug 1964, Deirdre Bettina, da of Air Cdre James Maitland Nicholson Pike, CB, DSO, DFC (d 1999), of Watlington, Oxon; 1 da (Nicola b 22 June 1966), 1 s (Andrew b 31 Aug 1967); *Career* cmmnd Duke of Cornwall's LI 1958, cmd 1 Bn LI 1980–82 (Adj 1968–69), mil attaché Moscow 1988–91, hon ADC to HM The Queen 1989–91, regimental sec LI (Somerset) 1991–99, Hon Col Somerset ACF 1995–2002, Dep Hon Col Rifle Volunteers 1999–2007; fell Woodard Schs Corp 1995–, vice-provost Western Div Woodard Schs 2000–04; govr: King's Hall Sch 1992–, King's Coll Taunton 1992–; High Sheriff Somerset 2006–07; *Recreations* music, walking, cricket; *Clubs* Army and Navy; *Style—* Brig Alastair Fyfe, DL

FYFE, Cameron Stuart; s of James Fyfe, of Dumfries, and Kathleen, *née* Hardman (d 1976); *b* 21 July 1954; *Educ* Dumfries Acad, Univ of Edinburgh (LLB); *m* 12 June 1995, Nuala McGrory; 2 da (Caitlin b 14 June 1996, Cara b 2 Dec 2002), 2 s (Michael b 2 May 1998, Sean b 21 June 2004), 1 step s (Mark b 17 Jan 1988); *Career* apprentice then asst slr Cornillon Craig & Co Edinburgh 1976–80; Ross Harper & Murphy: asst slr Edinburgh 1980–81, ptnr Court Dept East Kilbride 1981–89, i/c Head Office 1989–94, managing ptnr Ross Harper & Murphy 1994–; winner first Scottish case for annulment of arranged marriage; *Books* Layman's Guide to Scotland's Law (1995); *Recreations* golf, tennis, fishing, hill climbing, painting, writing, guitar; *Clubs* Hilton Park Golf, Univ of Glasgow Tennis; *Style—* Cameron Fyfe, Esq; ✉ Ross Harper & Murphy, 58 West Regent Street, Glasgow G2 2QZ (tel 0141 333 6333, fax 0141 333 6334)

F

G

GABATHULER, Prof Erwin; OBE (2001); s of Hans Gabathuler (d 1972), of NI, and Anne Lena Gabathuler, *née* Graham (d 1970); *b* 16 November 1933; *Educ* Queen's Univ Belfast (BSc, MSc), Univ of Glasgow (PhD); *m* 27 July 1962, Susan Dorothy, da of Charles Powell Jones (d 1988), of Essex; 1 da (Helen b 1964), 2 s (John b 1966, David b 1970); *Career* res fell Cornell Univ 1961–64, gp leader in res for SERC Daresbury Laboratory 1964–74; CERN Geneva: visiting scientist 1974–77 and 1991–92, head Experimental Physics Div 1978–80, dir of research 1981–83; Univ of Liverpool: prof of physics 1983–91, head of Physics Dept 1986–91 and 1996–99, Sir James Chadwick prof of physics 1991–2001, emeritus prof 2001–; author of various articles in res jls; chm Particle Physics Ctee SERC 1985–88; memb: Extended Scientific Cncl of DESY Hamburg W Germany, CNRS (IN2P3), France, Euro Physical Soc; Rutherford Medal and Prize Inst of Physics 1992; Doctoris (hc) Uppsala Univ of Sweden 1982, DSc (hc) Queen's Univ Belfast 1997; CPhys, FInstP, FRS 1990; *Recreations* swimming, walking; *Style*— Prof Erwin Gabathuler, OBE, FRS; ✉ 3 Danebank Road, Lymm, Cheshire WA13 9DQ; Physics Department, Oliver Lodge Laboratory, Oxford Street, University of Liverpool, PO Box 147, Liverpool L69 7ZE (tel 0151 794 3349, fax 0151 794 3444, e-mail erwin@hep.ph.liv.ac.uk)

GABB, Roger Michael; s of Dr Harry Gabb, MVO, ARCM (d 1995), and Helen Burnaford, *née* Mutton (d 1994); *b* 11 November 1938; *Educ* Llandaff Cathedral Choir Sch, Christ Church Choir Sch Oxford, St John's Sch Leatherhead; *m* 1966, Margaret Anne, *née* Thompson, da of Maj J Thompson, MC, of Stanley Hall; 2 s (Caspar Charles b 11 March 1970, Harry Rollo b 1 May 1972); *Career* Welsh Guards 1959–67, instructor in adventure training, mountaineering and climbing, served in special forces in N Borneo and Kenya, Borneo Service Medal 1965; joined The Distillers Co, European mangr Haig Scotch Whisky 1967–70, attended business sch in Fontainebleau France; Inver House Distillers 1970–73 (euro mangr 1973–90), Montrose Whisky Co Ltd 1980–90, fndr and chm Western Wines Ltd, owner and chm Journey's End Vineyard Cape SA, dir Barone Montalto Spa Marsala Sicily; High Sheriff Shropshire 1985; supporter St John Ambulance and local Shropshire charities; *Recreations* shooting, tennis, gardening; *Clubs* Household Brigade Yacht, Cavalry & Guards; *Style*— Roger Gabb, Esq; ✉ Woodlands Hall, Glazeley, Bridgnorth, Shropshire WV16 6AB (tel 01746 789227)

GABITASS, Jon; s of late William Gabitass, and late Nell Gabitass; *b* 25 July 1944; *Educ* Plymouth Coll, St John's Coll Oxford (Rugby blue); *m* 1967, Fiona, da of Dr Thomas Hoy; 2 da (Lindsay Jane b 15 March 1970, Rachel Fiona b 13 March 1972); *Career* English teacher Clifton Coll 1967–73; Abingdon Sch: head of English 1973–78, second master 1978–91; head master Merchant Taylors' Sch Northwood 1991–2004; *Recreations* long walks in Cornwall, theatre and art galleries, 18th and 19th century caricature, gently going to seed in the garden; *Clubs* Vincent's (Oxford), East India; *Style*— Jon Gabitass, Esq

GABRIEL, Peter; *b* 13 February 1950; *Educ* Charterhouse; *Career* rock singer and songwriter; co-fndr Genesis 1966 (with Mike Rutherford, *qv*, and Tony Banks); albums with Genesis: From Genesis to Revelation (1969), Trespass (1970), Nursery Cryme (1971), Foxtrot (1972), Genesis Live (1973), Selling England by the Pound (1973), The Lamb Lies Down on Broadway (1974); left gp to pursue solo career 1975; solo albums: Peter Gabriel I (1977), II (1978), III (1980) and IV (1982), Peter Gabriel Plays Live (1983), So (1986), Shaking the Tree (compilation, 1990), Us (1992), Up (2002); singles include: Solsbury Hill, Sledgehammer, Family Snapshot, Mercy Street, Shaking the Tree, Don't Give Up, San Jacinto, Here Comes the Flood, Red Rain, Games Without Frontiers, Shock the Monkey, I Have the Touch, Big Time, Zaar, Biko, In Your Eyes; soundtrack albums: Birdy, Passion (for Last Temptation of Christ), Long Walk Home (for Rabbit Proof Fence) 2002; Ivor Novello Lifetime Achievement Award 2007; fndr: World of Music Arts and Dance (WOMAD) 1982, Real World Group (developing projects in arts and technol) 1985, Real World Studios 1986, Real World Records 1989, Real World Multimedia 1994; launched Witness (human rights prog) 1992; CD-Rom releases: XPLORA, EVE; Hon DMus Univ of Bath 1996; *Style*— Peter Gabriel, Esq; ✉ c/o Real World Studios, Box Mill, Box, Wiltshire SN13 8PL

GABRIELYAN, HE Dr Vahe; s of Dr Vazgen Gabrielyan, of Armenia, and Dr Zhenya Kalantaryan; *b* 16 May 1965, Armenia; *Educ* Yerevan State Univ (Parouir Sevak scholar, Dip), Davidson Coll USA (Cert), Nat Acad of Scis Armenia (PhD), Diplomatic Acad of Vienna (Cert); *m* 1989, Hasmik Hovhanissyan; 2 s (Vazgen b 1990, Tigran b 1997); *Career* Armenian diplomat; assoc prof of English and land studies Yerevan State Univ 1992–2003, various posts rising to first sec Armenian Miny of Foreign Affrs 1994–98, interpreter Constitutional Ct of Armenia 1996–98, press sec to Pres of Armenia 1998–2003 (interpreter 1993–94 and 1997–2003), ambass to Ct of St James's 2003– (concurrently ambass to Repub of Ireland 2005–); author of articles and translations in newspapers, magazines and learned jls; *Recreations* reading, photography, hiking, hunting (shooting, rather than the British sense of on horseback or with hounds), travelling, DIY; *Style*— HE Dr Vahe Gabrielyan; ✉ Embassy of the Republic of Armenia, 25A Cheniston Gardens, London W8 6TG (tel 020 7938 5435, fax 020 7938 2595, e-mail ambassador@armenianembassyuk.com)

GADDUM, Anthony Henry; s of Peter William Gaddum (d 1986), of Mobberley, Cheshire, and Josephine Margaret Ferguson Wynne, *née* Roberts (d 1983); *b* 16 February 1939; *Educ* Rugby, Univ of Grenoble; *m* 7 June 1968, Hilda McIntosh, da of Rev James McIntosh Scott (d 1991); 3 s (Toby b 1971, Giles b 1973, Benedict b 1975); *Career* Nat Serv 2 Lt 13/18 Royal Hussars 1959–61; chm H T Gaddum & Co Ltd 1984–2004 (dir 1964–2004); dir: British Crepe Ltd 1976–2004, Gaddum & Wood Holdings Ltd 1991– (chm 1991–2004); nat delegate Int Silk Assoc 1979–91, delegate Euro Cmmn for the Promotion of Silk; dep vice-pres Int Silk Assoc 1991–2003, chm Silk Assoc 1995–98 (vice-chm 1998–99); author of articles on silk and genealogy; chm Clarkes & Marshalls Charity Manchester 1987–2007, hon treas The Together Tst (formerly Boys and Girls' Welfare Soc); Liveryman and memb Ct of Assts Worshipful Co of Weavers (Renter Bailiff 2005–06, Upper Bailiff 2006–07); *Recreations* genealogy, gardening, tending young trees, keeping in touch with distant cousins; *Clubs* Cavalry and Guard's; *Style*— Anthony Gaddum, Esq; ✉ Lane Ends House, Sutton Lane Ends, Macclesfield, Cheshire SK11 0DY (tel 01260 252456)

GADSBY, Dr Roger; s of Frank William Gadsby, and Nellie Irene Gadsby; *b* 2 March 1950; *Educ* King Henry VIII Sch Coventry, Univ of Birmingham Med Sch (BSc, MB ChB); *m* 19 Oct 1974, Pamela Joy, da of Clifford Raine; 1 da (Emma Elizabeth b 1 Nov 1978), 1 s (Andrew David b 6 Sept 1981); *Career* postgrad med trg Birmingham and Stoke on Trent 1974–77, trainee in gen practice 1977–79, ptnr in gen practice Nuneaton 1979–; pt/t sr lectr in gen practice Centre for Primary Healthcare Studies Univ of Warwick 1992–; memb various ctees Diabetes UK (formerly Br Diabetic Assoc); memb Cncl RCGP 1994–99 (chm Midland Faculty 1996–1999); chm of tstees Pregnancy Sickness Support; FRCGP 1992 (MRCGP); *Publications* Delivering Quality Diabetes Care in General Practice (2005); author of several chapters in textbooks and of more than 150 articles and papers about diabetes care and pregnancy sickness symptoms; *Recreations* jogging, gardening; *Style*— Dr Roger Gadsby; ✉ Redroofs Practitioners, Redroofs, 31 Coton Road, Nuneaton, Warwickshire CV11 5TW (tel 024 7635 7100, fax 024 7664 2036, e-mail rgadsby@doctors.org.uk)

GAGE, Deborah Pamela; da of late Quentin Henry Moreton Gage, and Hazel Olive, *née* Swinton-Home; *b* 26 March 1950; *Educ* Moira House Eastbourne, Study Centre of the Fine & Decorative Arts London (dip); *Career* running Antique Porcelain Co/Antique Co of New York Inc NYC 1971–78, ind dealer 17th/18th c Euro decorative arts and paintings and late 19th/early 20th c French & British pictures 1981–; non-exec dir AXA Art Insurance Ltd; treas Nat Antique & Art Dealers Assoc of America NYC 1974–78; fndr and tstee The Charleston Trust 1979–88 (opened Charleston Farmhouse Sussex, home of the artists Vanessa Bell and Duncan Grant, to public 1985); *Books* Tobacco Containers and Accessories · Their Place in Eighteenth Century European Social History (with Madeleine Marsh, 1988); *Recreations* travel, photography, riding, scuba diving, tennis; *Style*— Miss Deborah Gage; ✉ Deborah Gage (Works of Art) Ltd, 38 Old Bond Street, London W1S 4QW (tel 020 7493 3249, fax 020 7495 1352, e-mail debo@deborahgage.com)

GAGE, 8 Viscount (I 1720); Sir (Henry) Nicolas Gage; 15 Bt (E 1622); also Baron Gage of Castlebar (I 1720), and Baron Gage (GB 1790), of High Meadow, Co Gloucester; yr s of 6 Viscount Gage, KCVO (d 1982), and his 1 w, Hon Alexandra Imogen Clair Grenfell (d 1969), da of 1 Baron Desborough; suc his bro, 7 Viscount Gage (d 1993); *b* 9 April 1934; *Educ* Eton, ChCh Oxford; *m* 1974 (m dis 2002), Lady Diana Adrienne Beatty, da of 2 Earl Beatty (d 1972); 2 s (Hon Henry William b 1975, Hon David Benedict b 1977); *Heir* s, Hon Henry Gage; *Career* 2 Lt Coldstream Gds 1953; dir Firle Estate Co; *Style*— The Rt Hon the Viscount Gage; ✉ Firle Place, Lewes, East Sussex BN8 6LP (tel 01273 858535, fax 01273 858188); The Cottage, Charwelton, Daventry, Northamptonshire (tel 01327 60205)

GAGE, Rt Hon Lord Justice; Rt Hon Sir William Marcus; kt (1993), PC (2004); s of His Honour Conolly Hugh Gage, (former circuit judge d 1984), and Elinor Nancy, *née* Martyn; *b* 22 April 1938; *Educ* Repton, Sidney Sussex Coll Cambridge (MA); *m* 16 June 1962, Penelope Mary, da of Lt-Col James Jocelyn Douglas Groves, MC (d 1985); 3 s (Marcus b 1964, Timothy b 1966, Hugh b 1970); *Career* Nat Serv 1956–58, 2 Lt Irish Gds; called to the Bar Inner Temple 1963 (bencher 1991), chllr Diocese of Coventry 1980–, QC 1982, recorder of the Crown Court 1985–93, judge of the High Court of Justice (Queen's Bench Div) 1993–2004, presiding judge SE Circuit 1997–2000, Lord Justice of Appeal 2004–; chllr Diocese of Ely 1989–; memb: Criminal Injuries Compensation Bd 1987–93, Parole Bd 2001–04; *Recreations* shooting, fishing, travel; *Clubs* Beefsteak; *Style*— The Rt Hon Lord Justice Gage; ✉ Royal Courts of Justice, Strand, London WC2A 2LL

GAGGERO, John George; OBE (1981), JP (1972); s of Sir George Gaggero, OBE, JP (d 1978), of Gibraltar, and Lady Mabel, *née* Andrews-Speed (d 1986); *b* 3 March 1934; *Educ* Downside; *m* 1961, Valerie, da of John Malin, OBE, JP, of Gibraltar; 2 s (John b 12 Nov 1962, George b 4 Sept 1965), 2 da (Katrina b 23 Oct 1966, Amanda b 22 Feb 1970); *Career* Lt 12 Royal Lancers Malaya; dep chm Bland Group of Companies (incl Gibraltar Airways, Rock Hotel and Cadogan Travel) 1970–86; chm: M H Bland & Co Ltd 1986–97, M H Bland Stevedores Ltd 1990–96; hon consul for Denmark in Gibraltar 1964–98; chm Gibraltar Shipping Assoc 1993–97; CEng, MRINA; Knight (first class) Royal Order of the Dannebrog; *Recreations* boating; *Style*— John Gaggero, Esq, OBE; ✉ Cloister Building, Gibraltar (tel 00 350 79478)

GAGGERO, Joseph James; CBE (1989); s of Sir George Gaggero, OBE, JP (d 1978), of Gibraltar, and Lady Mabel, *née* Andrews-Speed (d 1986); bro of John Gaggero, OBE, JP, *qv*; *Educ* Downside; *m* 1, Nov 1958, Marilys Healing; 1 s (James b 1 Aug 1959), 1 da (Rosanne b 27 Dec 1960); m 2, July 1994, Christina Russo; *Career* chm and md of Bland Group of Companies (incl GB Airways, Gibraltar Airways, Rock Hotel, Bland Travel, Cadogan Travel and assoc cos); dir Hovertravel, founding dir Credit Suisse (Gibraltar) Ltd until 2003; hon consul gen for Sweden in Gibraltar until Dec 1995; dir Gibraltar C of C 1951–56, head Gibraltar Govt Tourist Dept 1955–59, memb Cncl of Br Travel Assoc 1958–69; chm: Hotel Assoc 1962–75, 1978 and 1986–90, Gibraltar Shipping Assoc 1970–79; pres: Gibraltar Rotarians 1973–74, Gibraltar Branch for Maritime League 1983–84, Br Moroccan Soc (London) 2005–; former chm Gibraltar Soc for Handicapped Children, Gibraltar Branch of Royal Life Saving Soc; chm Moroccan Br Business Cncl; jt patron Gibraltar Philharmonic Soc, patron Fundacion Hispano Britanica; Fndrs Medal Air League Aviation Industry 2007, memb Br Travel and Hospitality Industry Hall of Fame 2007; Freeman Guild of Air Pilots and Navigators; Cdr Order of North Star (Sweden), Knight of the Holy Sepulchre (Vatican), Cdr Royal Order of Alaoui (Morocco) 2006; *Books* Running with the Baton: A Gibraltar Family History; *Publications* Running with the Baton: A Gibraltar Family History; *Recreations* painting; *Clubs* Travellers, Valderrama Golf; *Style*— Joseph Gaggero, Esq, CBE; ✉ Cloister Building, Gibraltar (tel 00 350 78456, fax 00 350 76189)

GAIMAN, Neil Richard; s of David Bernard Gaiman, and Sheila Gaiman; *b* 10 November 1960; *Educ* Whitgift Sch, Ardingly; *m* Mary Therese, *née* McGrath; 1 s (Michael Richard b 21 July 1983), 2 da (Holly Miranda b 26 June 1985, Madeleine Rose Elvira b 28 Aug 1994); *Career* writer of modern comics, novels, TV and film scripts and songs; creator of Sandman series DC Comics, co-originator and ed The Utterly Comic Comic Relief Comic (Comic Relief 1991), creator Neverwhere (6 part TV series 1996, film script currently being prepared) BBC TV, scriptwriter Princess Mononoke (1998, film released 1999), articles in Time Out, The Sunday Times, Punch, The Observer Colour Supplement, songwriter The Flash Girls; chm Soc of Strip Illustration 1988–90; memb: Science Fiction Fndn 1988–92, Comic Art Museum Florida; dir Comic Book Legal Defense Fund; *Awards* incl: Best Graphic Novel The Eagle for Violent Cases (1988), Best Writer The Eagle of American Comics (1990), World Fantasy Award for Sandman #19 (1991), Best Writer Will Eisner Comic Indust for Sandman (1991, 1992, 1993, 1994), Best Continuing Series

Will Eisner for Sandman (1991, 1992, 1993), Best Writer Austrian Prix Vienne (1993), Best Collection Int Horror Critics' Guild for Angels and Visitations (1994), Best Int Writer Kemi (Finland) (1994), Lucca Best Writer (Italy) (1997), Best Foreign Writer Max Und Moritz (Germany) (1998), Sproing (Norway) (1998); *Books* Ghastly Beyond Belief (1985), Don't Panic (1987), Good Omens (co-author with Terry Pratchett, *qv*, 1990), Now We Are Sick (Poetry, 1991), The Golden Age (1992), Angels and Visitations (1993), The Day I Swapped My Dad For Two Goldfish (book for children, 1997), Stardust (1997), SMOKE & MIRRORS: Short Fictions and Illusions (collection of short fiction, 1998), American Gods (2001), Coraline (2002); *Publications* collections of Sandman graphic novels incl: Preludes and Nocturnes, The Doll's House, Dream Country, Season of Mists, A Game of You, Fables and Reflections, Brief Lives, World's End, The Kindly Ones, The Wake (1996); other graphic novels incl: Violent Cases (1987), Black Orchid (1988), Signal to Noise (1992, subsequently broadcast as a radio play by BBC Radio 3 1996), Death: The High Cost of Living (1993), Mr Punch (1994), Death: The Time of Your Life (1997), The Last Temptation (acknowledged inspiration for the Alice Cooper album of the same title); *Recreations* making things up, growing exotic pumpkins; *Style*— Neil Gaiman, Esq; ✉ c/o Merrilee Heifetz, Writer's House, 21 West 26th Street, New York, NY 10010, USA (tel 001 212 685 2605, fax 001 212 685 1781, e-mail heifetz@writershouse.com)

GAINFORD, 3 Baron (UK 1917); Joseph Edward Pease; s of 2 Baron Gainford, TD (d 1971), and Veronica Margaret, *née* Noble (d 1995); *b* 25 December 1921; *Educ* Eton, Gordonstoun, Open Univ (Dip Euro Humanities, BA); *m* 21 March 1953, Margaret Theophila Radcliffe, da of Henry Edmund Guise Tyndale (d 1948), of Winchester Coll, and Ruth Isabel Walcott, da of Alexander Radcliffe, of Bag Park, S Devon; 2 da (Joanna Ruth Miriam b 22 Aug 1959, Virginia Claire Margaret b 13 Oct 1960); *Heir* bro, Hon George Pease; *Career* serv WWII as Sgt RAFVR 1941–46; with: Hunting Aerosurveys Ltd 1947, Directorate of Colonial Surveys 1951, Soil Mechanics Ltd 1953, LCC 1958, GLC 1965; UK delegate to UN 1973; memb Coll Guardians Nat Shrine of Our Lady of Walsingham 1979–; memb Plaisterers' Co 1976; FRGS, RICS; *Clubs* MCC; *Style*— The Rt Hon the Lord Gainford; ✉ Swallowfield, 1 Dedmere Court, Marlow, Buckinghamshire SL7 1PL (tel 01628 484679)

GAINSBOROUGH, 5 Earl of (UK 1841); Sir Anthony Gerard Edward Noel; 7 Bt (GB 1781), JP (Leics 1974, formerly Rutland 1957); also Baron Barham (UK 1805), Viscount Campden and Baron Noel (both UK 1841); patron of two livings (but being a Roman Catholic cannot present); s of 4 Earl of Gainsborough, OBE, TD, JP (d 1927), sometime Private Chamberlain to Popes Benedict XV and Pius XI; *b* 24 October 1923; *Educ* Worth Sussex, Georgetown Maryland; *m* 23 July 1947, Mary, er da of Hon John Joseph Stourton, TD, of Miniature Hall, Wadhurst, 2 s of (24) Baron Mowbray, (25 Baron) Segrave, and (21 Baron) Stourton; 4 s, 3 da (one of whom The Lady Celestria Hales, *qv*) (and 1 da decd); *Heir* s, Viscount Campden; *Career* pres Caravan Club 1980–2002; chm Rutland CC 1970–73, pres Assoc of Dist Cncls 1974–80; memb: House of Lords All-Pty London Gp, House of Lords Horse Racing Advsy Ctee; Bailiff Grand Cross SMOM (pres Br Assoc 1968–74); Sr Past Master Worshipful Co of Gardners; Hon FICE; KStJ; *Clubs* Brooks's, Bembridge Sailing, Pratt's; *Style*— The Rt Hon the Earl of Gainsborough

GAISMAN, Jonathan Nicholas Crispin; QC (1995); o s of Peter Gaisman, of Kirdford, W Sussex; *b* 10 August 1956; *Educ* Eton, Worcester Coll Oxford (BCL, MA); *m* 24 April 1982, Teresa Mignon (Tessa), MBE (1991), eldest da of Sir John Jardine Paterson, of Norton Bavant, Wilts; 2 da (Clementine b 1986, Imogen b 1987), 1 s (Nicholas b 1989); *Career* called to the Bar Inner Temple 1979 (bencher 2004); recorder 2000– (asst recorder 1998–2000); a dir: English Chamber Orchestra and Music Soc 1992–96, Int Musicians' Seminar Prussia Cove 1994–, Streetwise Opera 2002–; FRSA 1997; *Recreations* the arts, travel, country pursuits; *Clubs* I Zingari, Beefsteak; *Style*— Jonathan Gaisman, Esq, QC; ✉ 7 King's Bench Walk, Temple, London EC4Y 7DS (tel 020 7910 8300)

GAIT, (Robert) Charles Campbell; s of Robert William Gait (d 1986), of Pembroke, and Jean, *née* Campbell (d 1981); *b* 16 July 1955; *Educ* Pembroke GS, Jesus Coll Cambridge (MA); *m* 9 Sept 1978, Anne Rose, da of Edward Nicolson, of Pembroke; 3 s (Michael Huw b 30 Sept 1984, Jonathan Edward b 25 June 1986, Nicholas Matthew b 27 July 1988); *Career* admitted slr 1980; ptnr Cameron McKenna (formerly McKenna & Co) 1985–99, currently ptnr Osborne Clarke, specialising in property devpt and investment work; memb: Law Soc, UK Chapter of FIABCI (Int Real Estate Fedn); *Recreations* sch govr, golf, rugby football, skiing; *Style*— Charles Gait, Esq; ✉ Osborne Clarke, Hillgate House, 26 Old Bailey, London EC4M 7HW (tel 020 7246 8136, fax 020 7246 8137)

GAITSKELL, Robert; QC (1994); s of Stanley Gaitskell (d 1967), and Thelma Phyllis, *née* Holmes (d 1987); *b* 19 April 1948; *Educ* Hamilton HS Zimbabwe, Univ of Cape Town (BSc(Eng)), KCL (PhD, AKC); *m* 1974, Dr Deborah Lyndall Bates; 1 da (Kezia Lyndall b 2 Nov 1983); *Career* graduate trainee Reyrolle Parsons 1971–73, engr Electricity Dept Bulawayo Zimbabwe 1973–75, electrical engr GEC (SA) 1975–76; called to the Bar Gray's Inn 1978 (bencher Gray's Inn 2003), in practice 1979–, recorder 2000– (asst recorder 1997–2000); lectr Centre of Construction Law & Mgmnt KCL 1993–2003; senator Engrg Cncl 1997–2002; vice-pres IEE 1998–2001, chm IEE/IMechE Jt Ctee on Modal Forms 2001–; past chm: Mgmnt Div IEE, Professional Gp on Engrg and the Law; legal columnist Engrg Mgmnt Jl 1993–2003; memb Ctee London Common Law and Commercial Bar Assoc 1985–2000, memb Barristers Ctee Gray's Inn 2002–03; Liveryman Worshipful Co of Engrs 1997, Liveryman Worshipful Co of Arbitrators 2002; accredited and registered mediator CEDR 1999; FIEE, CEng, FCIArb, FIMechE; *Recreations* Methodist local preacher, theatre, walking; *Style*— Dr Robert Gaitskell, QC; ✉ Keating Chambers, 15 Essex Street, London WC2R 3AA (tel 020 7544 2600, fax 020 7544 2700, e-mail rgaitskell@keatingchambers.com)

GALASKO, Prof Charles Samuel Bernard; s of David Isaac Galasko (d 1951), and Rose (d 1996); *b* 29 June 1939; *Educ* King Edward VII Sch Johannesburg, Univ of Johannesburg (MB BCh, ChM); *m* 29 Oct 1967, Carol, da of Michael Lapinsky; 1 da (Deborah b 1970), 1 s (Gavin b 1972); *Career* med trg Johannesburg Gen Hosp 1963–66, lectr Univ of the Witwatersrand 1964–66; registrar: Hammersmith Hosp 1967–69, Royal Postgrad Med Sch 1967–69; sr registrar Radcliffe Infirmary and Nuffield Orthopaedic Centre Oxford 1970–73; conslt orthopaedic surgn Hammersmith Hosp 1973–76 (dir of orthopaedic surgery), asst dir Div of Surgery Royal Postgrad Med Sch 1973–76 (dir orthopaedic surgery), prof of orthopaedic surgery Univ of Manchester 1976–2004; hon conslt orthopaedic surgn: Manchester Children's Hosp Tst 1976–2002 (Sir Arthur Sims Cwlth prof 1998), Salford Royal Hosps NHS Tst 1976–2005 (dir Educn and Trg 2003–05); contrib over 250 published articles; temp advsr World Health Authy 1981; chm Award Ctee SICOT 1984–87 and 1990–93, treas Int Assoc Olympic Med Offrs 1988–2000, memb Med Ctee British Olympic Assoc 1988–2003, vice-chm English Olympic Wrestling Assoc, chm Br Amateur Wrestling Assoc 1992–96 (vice-pres 1996–2001); pres: SIROT 1990–93 (memb Prog Ctee 1981–84, memb Exec Ctee 1981–96, prog chm 1984–87, chm Membership Ctee 1987–90), Br Orthopaedic Assoc 2000–01 (memb Cncl 1988–91, chm Acad Bd 1998–2002, vice-pres 1999–2000), Faculty of Sports and Exercise Med 2006–; vice-pres: Section of Oncology RSM 1987 (memb Cncl 1980–87), RCS 1999–2001 (memb Cncl 1991–2003, chm Trg Bd 1995–99); chm: Assoc of Profs of Orthopaedic Surgery 1983–86, Jt Ctee of Higher Surgical Trg (GB and I) 1997–2000, Intercollegiate Academic Bd of Sport and Exercise Med 2002–05; Hon MSc Univ of Manchester 1980; Hunterian prof RCS 1971, SICOT fell 1972, ABC fell 1978, Aust Cwlth fell 1982; fndr memb: Int Orthopaedic Res Soc, Metastatis Res Soc, South African Surgical Res Soc; memb Br Orthopaedic Res Soc, hon memb South African Orthopaedic Assoc, emeritus fell American Orthopaedic Assoc, hon memb American Fracture Assoc, corresponding memb Columbian Soc of Orthopaedic Surgery and Traumatology; FRCS (England), FRCSEd, FMedSci, fell Faculty of Sports and Exercise Med (FFSEM) Ireland, FFSEM UK, Hon FCMSA; *Books* Radionuclide Scintigraphy in Orthopaedics (jt ed, 1984), Principles of Fracture Management (ed, 1984), Skeletal Metastases (1986), Neuromuscular Problems in Orthopaedics (ed, 1987), Recent Developments in Orthopaedic Surgery (jt ed, 1987), Current Trends in Orthopaedic Surgery (jt ed, 1988), Imaging Techniques in Orthopaedics (jt ed, 1989); *Recreations* sport, music, theatre; *Style*— Prof Charles Galasko; ✉ 72 Gatley Road, Gatley, Cheshire SK8 4AA (tel 0161 428 0316, fax 0161 428 4558)

GALATOPOULOS, Stelios Emille; s of John Galatopoulos (d 1978), of Nicosia, Cyprus and Athens, and Maria, *née* Stylianaki (d 1948); *b* 2 August 1932; *Educ* The English Sch Nicosia, Univ of Southampton (BSc(Eng)); *Career* civil and structural engr; designer: T C Jones 1954–55, Kellogg Int Corp 1956–60; designer and head of Civil and Structural Dept Tripe and Wakeham (chartered architects) London and Cyprus for Akrotiri Strategic Base 1960–66, freelance engr 1967–72, designer Pell Frischmann 1972–75, freelance engr 1975–, lectr, concert presenter and compere; opera and music critic-journalist: Music and Musicians, Records and Recordings, Lirica nel Mondo (Italy), Opera, Musical America; broadcaster: BBC, CBC (Cyprus), RTE (Dublin) America, Germany, Austria; vice-pres Opera Italiana 1985; memb Soc of Authors 1971; *Books* Callas La Divina (1966), Italian Opera (1971), Callas Prima Donna Assoluta (1976), Maria Callas: Sacred Monster (1998), Bellini: Life, Times, Music (2002); *Recreations* opera, theatre, ballet, concerts, tennis, swimming, skiing, travel; *Style*— Stelios Galatopoulos, Esq; ✉ Flat 2, 38 Shalstone Road, London SW14 7HR (tel 020 8878 9731)

GALBRAITH, Anne; *b* 1940; *Educ* Univ of Durham (LLB); *m* 1965, John Galbraith; 1 s (b 1970), 1 da (b 1971); *Career* chm Newcastle CAB 1982–87, memb Northern RHA 1988–91, chm Royal Victoria Infirmary and Associated Hosps NHS Tst 1991–98, special tstee Newcastle Univ Hosps 1992–, tstee Rothley Tst 1994–, PM's advsr Citizens' Charter Advsy Panel 1994–97, memb Cncl on Tbnls 1997–, chair Prescription Pricing Authy; govr Prudhoe HS 1984–87; *Recreations* gardening; *Style*— Mrs Anne Galbraith

GALBRAITH, Jeremy; *b* 14 August 1966; *Educ* King's Sch Worcester, Univ of Leeds Faculty of Law (LLB); *Career* researcher to Dr Keith Hampson, MP 1988–89, conslt Market Access International 1989–95 (dep md 1994–95); md: Burson-Marsteller Public Affairs London 1995–99, Burson-Marsteller Europe Government Relations 1996–99; chief exec: Euro BKSH Govt Relations Worldwide 1999–, Burson-Marsteller Brussels 2000–07; ceo Burson-Marsteller Europe 2007; Parly candidate (Cons) Newham NE 1992; nat vice-chm Cons Friends of Israel 1990–; *Recreations* tennis, running, opera, film and restaurants; *Style*— Jeremy Galbraith, Esq; ✉ Burson-Marsteller, 37 Square de Meeus, B-1000 Brussels, Belgium (tel 00 322 743 6611, fax 00 322 733 6611, e-mail jeremy.galbraith@bm.com)

GALE, Baroness (Life Peer UK 1999), of Blaenrhondda in the County of Mid Glamorgan; Anita Gale; da of Arthut Victor Gale (decd), and Lillian Maud Gale (decd); *b* 28 November 1940; *Educ* Treherbert Secdy Modern Sch, Pontypridd Tech Coll, UC Cardiff (BSc); *m* 1959 (m dis 1983); 2 da; *Career* sewing machinist 1955–56 and 1965–69, shop asst 1956–59; joined Lab Pty 1966, former shop steward Tailors and Garment Workers Union 1967–70, women's offr and asst organiser Wales Lab Pty 1976–84, gen sec Wales Lab Pty 1984–99; sits as Lab peer in House of Lords, memb Information Ctee; jt sec Assoc Parly Gp for Animal Welfare 2001– (memb 2000–, vice-chair 2000–01); memb: All-Pty Pro-Choice Gps 1999–, Inter Parly Union 1999–, All-Pty Parly Gp on Maternity Care 2000, All-Pty Parly Gp for Children in Wales, All-Pty Parly Gp for Children, All-Pty Political Art Gp, All-Pty Gp on Smoking and Health, All-Pty Arts and Heritage Gp, British/Taiwan Parly Friendship Gp; GMB Union (Lab Organisers Branch): memb 1976–, chair Wales and SW section 1986–99, equal opportunities offr 1991–99; memb: Select Ctee on Info, Jt Ctee on Statutory Investments, Nat Ctee Lab Women's Network, Welsh Lab Women's Ctee 1999–; cmmr for Wales Women's Nat Cmmn 2004–; vice-chair: Lab Animal Welfare Soc 1999–, All-Pty Belize Gp; memb: Ramblers Assoc, British Legion (pres Treherbert and Dist branch), Emily's List, Bevan Fndn, Valleys Forward, Parkinson's Disease Soc, Nat Tst; *Recreations* walking, swimming, gardening, travel; *Style*— The Rt Hon the Lady Gale; ✉ House of Lords, London SW1A 0PW (tel 020 7219 8511, e-mail galea@parliament.uk)

GALE, Michael; QC (1979); s of Joseph Gale, and Blossom Gale; *b* 12 August 1932; *Educ* Cheltenham GS, Grocers Sch, King's Coll Cambridge (exhibitioner); *m* 1963, Joanna Stephanie Bloom; 1 s, 2 da; *Career* Royal Fus 1956–58; called to the Bar Middle Temple 1957 (Harmsworth scholar, bencher); recorder of the Crown Court 1977–97; legal assessor to: GMC, GDC, Gen Osteopathic Cncl, CIPFA; memb Gen Cncl of the Bar 1986–94, chm Review and Complaints Ctee Nat Heritage Meml Fund and Heritage Lottery Fund 1995–2001; *Books* Fraud and the plc (jtly, 1999), Guide to the Crime Sentences Act (jtly, 1997), The Criminal Justice & Police Act 2001: A Guide for Practitioners (jtly, 2001); *Recreations* arts, country pursuits; *Clubs* Oxford and Cambridge, MCC; *Style*— Michael Gale, Esq, QC; ✉ 1 Kings Bench Walk, Temple, London EC4Y 7DB (tel 020 7936 1500)

GALE, Prof Michael Denis (Mike); *Educ* Univ of Birmingham (BSc), UC Wales Aberystwyth (PhD); *Career* cytogenetics dept Plant Breeding Inst 1968–84, head cereals res dept Cambridge Lab 1988–92, head of Cambridge Lab 1992–94, John Innes Fndn emeritus fell John Innes Centre (assoc res dir 1994–2003, dir 1999); advsr Inst of Genetics Beijing 1992–, memb Consultative Gp on Int Agric Research (CGIAR) Sciences Cncl Rome 2004–, memb Int Advsy Bd Chinese Acad of Agricultural Sciences 2007–; Farrer Meml Bicentennial fell NSW Dept of Agric 1989, hon res prof Inst of Crop Germplasm Resources Acad of Science 1992–, John Innes prof UEA 2000–03, professorial fell Sch of Biological Scis 2003–; Res Medal RASE 1994, Rank Prize for Nutrition 1997, Darwin Medal Royal Soc 1998; Hon Dr: Norwegian Univ of Life Sciences 2005, Univ of Birmingham 2005; foreign memb Chinese Acad of Engrg 1999; FRS 1996; *Publications* over 300 publications in sci jls covering cereal genetics, pre-harvest sprouting, dwarfing genes, molecular markers and comparative genetics; *Style*— Prof Mike Gale, FRS; ✉ John Innes Centre, Norwich Research Park, Colney, Norwich NR4 7UH (tel 01603 450599, e-mail mike.gale@bbsrc.ac.uk)

GALE, Roger James; MP; s of Richard Byrne Gale, and Phyllis Mary, *née* Rowell (d 1948); *b* 20 August 1943; *Educ* Hardye's Sch Dorchester, Guildhall Sch of Music and Drama; *m* 1, 1964 (m dis 1967), Wendy Dawn Bowman; m 2, 1971 (m dis), Susan Sampson; 1 da (Misty); m 3, 1980, Suzy Gabrielle, da of Thomas Leopold Marks (d 1972); 2 s (Jasper, Thomas); *Career* formerly: reporter BBC Radio, prodr BBC Radio 4 Today Show, dir BBC Children's TV, prodr and dir Thames Children's TV, editor Teenage Unit Thames; Parly candidate (Cons) Birmingham Northfield (by-election) 1982, MP (Cons) Thanet N 1983–; PPS to min of state for the Armed Forces 1992–94, a vice-chm Cons Pty 2001–03; chm All-Pty Animal Welfare Gp 1992–98, pres Cons Animal Welfare Gp; fell: Indust and Parl Tst, Parl and Armed Forces Fellowship, Parl and Police Fellowship; memb Speaker's Chm Panel 1997–; special constable 2002–06; *Recreations* swimming, sailing; *Clubs* Kent CCC, Farmers', Lord's Taverners; *Style*— Roger Gale, Esq, MP; ✉ House of Commons, London SW1A 0AA (e-mail galerj@parliament.uk, website www.rogergale.co.uk)

GALEAZZI, Mara; *b* Brescia, Italy; *Educ* La Scala Milan; *Career* ballet dancer; danced with: Ashely Page Co (Scottish Ballet), Irek Mukamedov Co; princ Royal Ballet 2003– (joined 1992); *Performances* incl: Anastasia, Juliet, Lise, Firebird, Gamzatti, Tatiana, Mathilde Kschessinska, Mary Vetsera, Marie Larisch, Myrtha, Calliope, Lescaut's Mistress, Aurora

G

(Awakening pas de deux), Queen of the Dryads, The Leaves are Fading, Schnes de ballet, Agon, Thaos pas de deux, Voices of Spring, Swan Lake, Sleeping Beauty, Cinderella, My Brother, My Sisters, Song of the Earth, Fearful Symmetries, Symphonic Variations, Concerto, Raymonda Act III, The Judas Tree, Danses concertantes, Las Hermanas, Street Dancer in Don Quixote, Young Wife in La Ronde, Talisman pas de deux, Two-Part Invention, Cheating, Lying, Stealing, Tidelines, Masquerade, Hidden Variables, This House Will Burn, Les Saisons; *Style*— Ms Mara Galeazzi; ✉ c/o The Royal Ballet, Royal Opera House, Covent Garden, London WC2E 9DD

GALGANI, Franco; s of Piero Galgani, of Leghorn and Vilia Galgani; *b* 28 March 1949; *Educ* Saffi Secdy Sch Florence Italy, Florence Hotel Sch Florence (Nat Dip), Open Univ UK (BA); *m* 1, 1967 (m dis 1977), Mary Ellen, *née* McElhone; 3 s (Lorenzo b 1968, Riccardo b 1969, Giancarlo b 1971); m 2, 1981, Lynne, *née* MacDonald; 1 da (Daniela b 1983); *Career* restaurateur; industrial trg 1963–68: Alberg Ristorante L'Elba nr Grosseto Italy, Grand Hotel Florence, Hotel Iselba Island of Elba, Hotel de la Plage St Raphael France, Hotel Baglioni Florence, Grand Hotel Florence, George Hotel Keswick Eng, Hotel Parco Rimini Italy; food and beverage supervisory and mgmnt appts 1968–76: Granville Restaurant Glasgow, MacDonald Hotel (Thistle) Giffnock Glasgow, Stuart Hotel (Thistle) and Bruce Hotel (Swallow) E Kilbride Strathclyde; mangr and ptnr Balcary Bay Hotel Scot 1976–82; gen mangr: Buchanan Arms Hotel Loch Lomond Scot 1982–85, Stakis Dunkeld House Perthshire Scot 1985–86, Marine Highland Hotel Troon Ayrshire Scot 1986–91, Carlton Highland Hotel Edinburgh 1991–98; mktg dir Scottish Highland Hotels plc 1996–99; conslt and advsr to hospitality industry 1999–2001, dir of sales N Br Tst Gp 2001–03, divnl md Crerar Hotels 2003–04, mangmnt conslt 2004–; former memb: Bd of Dirs Ayrshire Tourist Bd, Cncl Ayr Coll of Further Educn, Glasgow Coll of Food Technol; former chm Edinburgh Principal Hotels Assoc; bd dir Edinburgh and Lothians Tourist Bd; Master Innholders Award 1989, Scottish Highland Hotels Group Mangr of the Year 1990; Freeman City of London; FHCIMA 1989; *Recreations* travel, theatre and classical music, outdoor pursuits with family; *Style*— Franco Galgani, Esq; ✉ 8 Newington Road, Edinburgh EH9 1QS (mobile 07788 588974, e-mail franco@galgani.co.uk)

GALIONE, Prof Antony; s of Angelo Galione, of Faulkbourne, Essex, and Margaret, *née* Cole; *b* 13 September 1963; *Educ* Felsted (Lord Butler of Saffron Walden scholar), Trinity Coll Cambridge (sr scholar, MA, PhD); *m* 22 Aug 1992, Angela Jane, da of John Clayton, and Jane Clayton, of Thorp Arch, W Yorks; *Career* Johns Hopkins Univ: Harkness fell 1989–91, Dmitri d'Arbeloff fell in biology 1990–91; Univ of Oxford: Beit meml fell for med research Dept of Pharmacology 1991–94, Hayward jr research fell Oriel Coll 1992–95, lectr in med sciences St Hilda's Coll 1993–95, Wellcome Tst career devpt fell Dept of Pharmacology 1994–97, Staines med research fell Exeter Coll 1995–98, lectr in molecular and cellular biochemistry St Catherine's Coll 1997–98, Wellcome Tst sr fell in basic biomedical science Dept of Pharmacology 1997–2005, fell and tutor in biochemical pharmacology New Coll 1998–2005, titular prof of pharmacology 2002–05, prof of pharmacology and head of dept 2006–, professorial fell Lady Margaraet Hall 2006–, extraordinary lectr in pharmacology New Coll 2006–; Herbert Rand visiting fell Marine Biological Lab Woods Hole MA 1993; memb Physiology and Pharmacology Panel Wellcome Tst 2002–05, memb Basic Science Interest Gp Wellcome Tst 2006–; ed Biochemical Jl 1997–2006, memb Editorial Bd Zygote 1998–, author of scientific papers on cell signalling in jls incl Nature, Science and Cell; memb: American Biophysical Soc 1995–, Br Marine Biological Assoc 1995–, Br Pharmacological Soc 1997–, Br Neuroscience Assoc 1997–; Novartis Prize Br Pharmacological Soc 2001; MA (by incorporation) Univ of Oxford 1992; *Recreations* Egyptology, riding, Jack Russell terriers, gardening; *Style*— Prof Antony Galione; ✉ University Department of Pharmacology, Mansfield Road, Oxford OX1 3QT (tel 01865 271633, fax 01865 271853, e-mail antony.galione@pharm.ox.ac.uk)

GALL, Henderson Alexander (Sandy); CBE (1988); s of Henderson Gall (d 1963), of Banchory, Scotland, and Jean, *née* Begg (d 1970); *b* 1 October 1927; *Educ* Glenalmond, Univ of Aberdeen (MA); *m* 11 Aug 1958, Eleanor Mary Patricia Anne, da of Michael Joseph Smyth (d 1964), of London; 3 da (Fiona Deirdre b 7 May 1959, Carlotta Maire Jean b 2 Nov 1961, Michaela Monica b 27 March 1965), 1 s (Alexander Patrick Henderson b 17 June 1960); *Career* Nat Serv RAF 1945–48; foreign corr Reuters 1953–63 (Berlin, Nairobi, Suez, Geneva, Bonn, Budapest, Johannesburg, Congo); ITN: foreign corr 1963–92 (ME, Africa, Vietnam, Far East, China, Afghanistan, Pakistan, Gulf War), newscaster 1968–90 (News at Ten 1970–90); prodr/presenter/writer of documentaries, subjects incl Cresta Run 1970 and 1985, King Hussein 1972, Afghanistan 1982, 1984 and 1986, George Adamson 1989, Richard Leakey 1995, Empty Quarter 1996, Veil of Fear (World in Action) 1996, Imran's Final Test 1997, Sandy's War (Tonight with Trevor McDonald) 2001, Afghanistan: War Without End (History Channel) 2004; freelance writer; independent TV prodr 1993–; chm Sandy Gall's Afghanistan Appeal (SGAA) 1986–; rector Univ of Aberdeen 1978–81; Sitara-i-Pakistan 1985, Lawrence of Arabia Medal RSAA 1987; Hon LLD Univ of Aberdeen 1981; *Books* Gold Scoop (1977), Chasing the Dragon (1981), Don't Worry About the Money Now (1983), Behind Russian Lines, an Afghan Journal (1983), Afghanistan: Agony of a Nation (1988), Salang (1989), George Adamson: Lord of the Lions (1991), A Year in Kuwait (1992), News from the Front (1994), The Bushmen of Southern Africa: Slaughter of the Innocent (2001); *Recreations* golf, gardening, swimming; *Clubs* Turf, Special Forces, Rye Golf, Royal St George's Golf, St Moritz Tobogganing, Travellers, Saints and Sinners; *Style*— Sandy Gall, Esq, CBE; ✉ Doubleton Oast House, Penshurst, Tonbridge, Kent TN11 8JA (fax 01892 870977); Sandy Gall's Afghanistan Appeal (SGAA), PO Box 145, Tonbridge TN11 8SA (e-mail sgaa@btinternet.com)

GALLACCIO, Anya; *b* 1963, Scotland; *Educ* Kingston Poly, Goldsmiths Coll London; *Career* artist; residencies: int artist in residence Art Pace (San Antonio TX) 1997, Sargeant Fellowship (Br Sch at Rome) 1998, Kanazawa Coll of Art 1999, 1871 Fellowship (Rothemere American Inst, Univ of Oxford and San Francisco Art Inst) 2002; Paul Hamlyn Award for Visual Artists 1999, nominated Turner Prize 2003; *Solo Exhibitions* incl: red on green (ICA London) 1992, Stephen Friedman London 1995, Keep off the grass (Serpentine Gallery Lawn London) 1997, Chasing Rainbows (Bloom Gallery Amsterdam, Delfina London) 1998, Glaschu (Tramway at Lanarkshire House Glasgow) 1999, All the rest is silence Anya Gallaccio at Sadler's Wells (Sadler's Wells London) 1999, blessed (Lehmann Maupin Gallery NY) 2001, beat (Duveen Sculpture Cmmn Tate Britain London) 2002, Turner Prize Exhibition (Tate Britain London) 2003, Ikon Birmingham 2003, Lehmann Maupin Gallery NY 2004; *Group Exhibitions* incl: Freeze (Surrey Docks London) 1988, A Group Show (Barbara Gladstone Gallery NY, Stein Gladstone Gallery NY) 1992, Pictura Britannica ART FROM BRITAIN (Museum of Contemporary Art Sydney, Art Gallery of S Aust, Te Papa Wellington) 1997, The Greenhouse Effect (Serpentine Gallery London) 2000, In Print (Br Cncl touring exhibition) 2002–03; *Work in Public Collections* incl: Br Cncl Collection London, Museum of Contemporary Art Sydney, Tate London, V&A London; *Publications* subject of: Anya Gallaccio: beat (by Mary Horlock, Heidi Reitmaier and Simon Schama) 2002, Anya Gallaccio: Chasing Rainbows (essay by Ralph Rugoff, 1999); featured in Ikon Catalogue (2003); *Style*— Ms Anya Gallaccio; ✉ c/o Lehmann Maupin, 540 West 26 Street, NY, USA (tel 00 1 212 255 2923, fax 00 1 212 255 2924)

GALLACHER, Dr Stephen John; *b* 29 May 1961; *Educ* St Aloysius' Coll Glasgow, Univ of Glasgow (MB ChB, MD); *Career* jr house offr: (med) Univ Dept of Med Glasgow Royal Infirmary 1983–84, (surgery) Dept of Surgery Duke Street Hosp Glasgow 1984; SHO/registrar (med rotation) Southern Gen Hosp Glasgow 1984–87, lectr in med Univ Dept of Med Glasgow Royal Infirmary 1990–95 (registrar in med 1987–90), consltphysician with an interest in diabetes and endocrinology Southern Gen Hosp NHS Tst 1995–; memb Cncl RCPSGlas 1993–95; FRCP (Edinburgh and Glasgow); *Publications* author of over 50 pubns in the field of metabolic bone diseases; *Style*— Dr Stephen Gallacher; ✉ Southern General Hospital NHS Trust, 1345 Govan Road, Glasgow G51 4TF (tel 0141 201 1100, fax 0141 201 1783)

GALLAGHER, Dermot Joseph; s of John Gallagher, and Barbara Gallagher; *b* 20 May 1957, Dublin; *Educ* Blessed George Napier RC Sch Banbury; *Career* football referee 1978– (professional 2001–): Southern League 1983–85, Football League 1990–92 (linesman 1985–90), Premier League 1992–, FIFA 1994–2002; matches refereed incl: World Cup U20 final Argentina v Brazil Qatar 1995, Charity Shield 1995, FA Trophy 1995, Mandela Cup Johannesburg 1995, FA Cup Final 1996, Brazilian State Play Off Final 1996, Euro 96 England 1996; *Style*— Dermot Gallagher, Esq

GALLAGHER, Edward Patrick; CBE (2001); s of Charles Henry Gallagher (d 1977), and Lucy Georgina, *née* Gardiner (d 1996); *b* 4 August 1944; *Educ* Univ of Sheffield (BEng, Dip Business Studies, Mappin medal, John Brown award); *m* 3 April 1969, Helen, da of Ronald George Wilkinson; 2 s (James Edward b 16 Feb 1975, Robert Daniel b 28 July 1977); *Career* systems analyst Vauxhall Motors 1963–68, corp planning mangr Sandoz Products Ltd 1968–70, computer servs mangr Robinson Willey Ltd 1970–71; Black and Decker: fin mangr 1971–73, prodn mangr 1973–78, dir Mktg Servs 1978–79, dir Serv and Distribution 1979–81, dir Business Analysis based USA 1981–83, dir Market and Product Devpt 1983–86; Amersham International: dir Corp Devpt 1986–88, divnl chief exec 1988–90, mfrg dir 1990–92; chief exec and memb Bd: Nat Rivers Authy 1992–95, Environment Agency 1995–2001; dir ECUS 2001–; chair: Environmental Vision 2003– (memb 2001–), Energywatch 2004–, Enviro-fresh Ltd 2004–07; vice-pres Cncl for Environmental Educn 1997–2006; chm: Health and Safety Ctee Engrg Employers Fedn 2001–04, Energy and Environment Policy Ctee IEE 2003–04 (memb 1999–2004), Pesticides Forum 2003–06, Advsy Bd Centre for Social Economic Res on Global Environment (CSERGE) 2004– (memb 2001–); memb: English Tourism Sustainability Task Force 1999–2000, Royal Acad of Engineers Sustainable Devpt Educn Working Gp 1999–2003, Cncl English Nature 2000–06, Awards Ctee Royal Acad of Engrg 2001–04; patron Environmental Industries Cmmn 2001–; civil servs cmmr 2001–06; memb Cncl Univ of Bristol 1994–97 (memb Fin Advsy Gp 1994–2000); Middlesex Univ: memb Faculty of Technology Advsy Gp 1994–97, visiting prof Business Sch and Faculty of Technol 1994–97, visiting prof Sch of Health, Biological and Environmental Sci 1997–, chair Bd of Govrs 2001–04 (govr 1994–2000, dep chm 2000–01), chm Audit Ctee 1996–2000, chm Governance Ctee 2000–01, chm Planning and Resources Ctee 2000–01; tstee: Living Again Tst, Royal Hosp for Neurodisability 1993–2003; Freeman City of London, Liveryman Worshipful Co of Water Conservators (memb Ct of Assts 1999–2001); Hon DEng Univ of Sheffield 1996; Hon DSc: Univ of Tomsk Russia 1998, Univ of Plymouth 1998, Brunel Univ; Hon DUniv Middx 2005; CEng, FIEE 1990, MRI 1992, FCIWEM 1994, FRSA 1995–2007, CIMgt 1996, FREng 1997; *Recreations* the countryside, tennis, theatre, playing the guitar; *Style*— Edward Gallagher, CBE, FREng; ✉ Energywatch, Artillery House, Artillery Row, London SW1P 1RT

GALLAGHER, Eileen; *Educ* Queen Margaret's Acad Ayr, Univ of Glasgow (MA), Univ of Wales Coll of Cardiff (NCTJ Cert); *Career* freelance journalist 1980–84 (for newspapers incl Glasgow Herald and Daily Record); Scottish Television: joined as press offr 1984, head of prog planning 1987–91, head Broadcasting Div 1991–92, concurrently i/c scheduling Children's ITV for ITV Network 1991–92, dir of broadcasting and main bd dir Scottish Television plc (now Scottish Media Group plc) 1992–94; md Broadcasting Granada/LWT 1994–96, md LWT and dep md Granada UK Broadcasting 1996–98, co-fndr and md Shed Productions 1998–, md Ginger Television 1999; non-exec dir Britt Allcroft 1998–; *Style*— Ms Eileen Gallagher

GALLAGHER, Jock James Young; s of Joseph Gallagher (d 1938), and Margaret, *née* Young (d 1984); *b* 31 March 1938; *Educ* Greenock HS; *m* 31 Dec 1970, Sheenagh Glenn, da of Richard Jones (d 1958); *Career* journalist with various newspapers 1958–66; BBC: news prodr 1966–70, head network radio 1980–89 (ed 1970–80), head special projects 1989–90; md BroadVision 1990–2003; chm The Health Independent Ltd 1999–, chm Press Freedom Network; exec dir Assoc of Br Eds 1990–99, ed British Editor 1990–99; memb: Communications Sector Ctee UK UNESCO 2000–03 (tutor and tstee Young UK Prog 2003–), WM Ctee Further Educ Funding Cncl 1997–2001, FCO Panel on Free Expression; vice-chm Kidderminster Coll 1996–2001; past pres Radio and TV Industries Club (Midlands), vice-pres Birmingham Press Club, patron Bewdley Festival; memb Fed Exec Lib Dems 2002–; past pres Wyre Forest Lib Dems, chm Lib Dems Parly Candidates Assoc 2002–05; Euro Parly candidate (Lib Dem) for Hereford and Shropshire 1994, Parly candidate (Lib Dem) Birmingham Edgbaston 1997; hon memb Soc of Editors; memb: Chartered Inst of Journalists, Radio Acad, Assoc of Euro Journalists; founding fell Inst of Contemporary Scotland (dep chair), FRSA; *Books* History of the Archers (1975), Portrait of A Lady - biography of Lady Isobel Barnett (1980), The Life And Death of Doris Archer - biography of Gwen Berryman (1981), To The Victor The Spoils (1986), Return to Ambridge (1987), Borchester Echoes (1988), The Archers Omnibus (1990), Europress (1992), Laurie Lee: A Many-coated Man (1998); also ed Who's Who in the Liberal Democrats (1998, 2000, 2002 and 2004); *Recreations* golf, reading, politics; *Clubs* National Liberal, Kidderminster Golf; *Style*— Jock Gallagher, Esq, FRSA; ✉ Home Barn, Ribbesford, Bewdley, Worcestershire DY12 2TQ (tel 01299 403110, e-mail jyg@cix.co.uk)

GALLAGHER, Noel David Thomas; s of Peggy Gallagher; er bro of Liam Gallagher, *qv*; *b* 29 May 1967, Manchester; *m* 6 June 1997 (m dis 2001), Meg Mathews; 1 da (Anaïs); *Career* former roadie The Inspiral Carpets, fndr memb (lead guitarist/backup vocals/songwriter) Oasis 1991–; albums: Definitely Maybe 1994 (entered UK charts no 1, fastest selling debut album in British history), (What's the Story) Morning Glory? 1995 (UK no 1), Be Here Now 1997 (UK no 1), The Masterplan 1998 (compilation, UK no 2), Familiar to Millions 2000 (live album, UK no 5), Heathen Chemistry 2002 (UK no 1), Don't Believe the Truth 2005 (UK no 1); top 10 UK singles incl: Live Forever (no 10), Cigarettes & Alcohol (no 7), Whatever (no 3), Some Might Say (no 1), Roll With It (no 2), Wonderwall (no 2), Don't Look Back in Anger (no 1), D'You Know What I Mean (no 1), Stand By Me (no 2), All Around the World (no 1), Go Let It Out (no 1), Who Feels Love (no 4), Sunday Morning Call (no 4), The Hindu Times (no 1), Stop Crying Your Heart Out (no 2), Little By Little/She is Love (no 2), Songbird (no 3), Lyla (no 1), The Importance of Being Idle (no 1), Let There Be Love (no 2); contrib Help (Warchild album) 1995, other contribs for artists incl The Chemical Brothers; *Awards* incl: Best New Group Brit Awards 1995, Best Group and Best Album ((What's the Story) Morning Glory?) Brit Awards 1996, Best Group and Best Song (Wonderwall) MTV Music Awards 1996, nominated Best Song (Wonderwall) Grammy Awards 1997; *Style*— Noel Gallagher; ✉ c/o Big Brother Recordings Ltd, PO Box 29479, London NW1 6GG

GALLAGHER, (Arthur) Robin; s of Hon James Albert Gallagher (d 1965), of York, and Winifred Mary, *née* Dill (d 1994); *b* 7 April 1941; *Educ* St Bede's Coll Manchester; *m* 1, 1969 (m dis 1992), 2 da (Kirsten b 8 March 1974, Kate b 1 Dec 1977); m 2, 1998, Christine Lloyd; 1 step da (Sarah Jane Lloyd, b 14 March 1979), 1 step s (Michael Midgley b 17 Feb 1970); *Career* Lt RNR 1960–66; Whinney Smith and Whinney 1963–66, Touche Ross and Co Manchester and Leeds 1966–74, Ladyship Int Gp 1974–80, Whitecroft plc

1980–81, dir Antler Property Corp plc 1981–94, md Wellholme Ltd 1988–95; dir: Towngate plc 1990–, Brigdale Ltd 1990–; chm Oakland Securities Ltd 1991–96; jt fndr Save Baguley Hall Campaign 1966; vice-pres Leeds Jr C of C 1973–75; FCA; *Publications* The Battle for Bligny Hill 6 June 1918 (2002), The Woods of Longley Old Hall (2003); *Recreations* old buildings, 17th century oak furniture; *Clubs* Army and Navy, Woodsome Hall Golf; *Style—* Robin Gallagher, Esq; ✉ Longley Old Hall, Longley, Huddersfield HD5 8LB (tel 01484 430852, mobile 07703 314282, e-mail robingallagher@debrett.net, website www.longleyoldhall.co.uk)

GALLAGHER, Stephen Kent; *b* 13 October 1954; *Educ* Eccles GS, Univ of Hull (BA); *Career* writer and director; with: Documentaries Dept Yorkshire TV, Presentation Dept Granada TV 1975; freelance writer 1980–; Northern chair Writers' Guild of GB 1994–96; novels incl: Chimera (1982), Follower (1984), Valley of Lights (1987), Oktober (1988), Down River (1989), Rain (1990), The Boat House (1991), Nightmare, With Angel (1992), Red, Red Robin (1995), White Bizango (2002), The Spirit Box (2005), The Painted Bride (2006); non fiction incl Journeyman (2000); radio plays incl: The Last Rose of Summer 1977, Hunter's Moon 1978, The Babylon Run 1979, A Resistance to Pressure 1980, The Kingston File 1987, By The River, Fontainebleau 1988, The Horn 1989, Life Line 1992; TV: Warriors' Gate (BBC) 1981, Terminus (BBC) 1984, Moving Targets (BBC) 1988, Chimera (Zenith/Anglia) 1991, Here Comes The Mirror Man (YTV) 1995, Oktober (adapted and directed for Carnival Films/LWT) 1998, The Kingdom of Bones (BBC Films) 2001, The Memory of Water (Carnival 2004), Eleventh Hour (series creator and episodes, ITV) 2005, The Cup of Silence (Carnival) 2006; *Publications* writings also incl short fiction and criticism collected in Out of his Mind (Br Fantasy Award 2004); *Style—* Stephen Gallagher, Esq; ✉ c/o The Agency, 24 Pottery Lane, Holland Park, London W11 4LZ (website www.stephengallagher.com)

GALLAGHER, William John Paul (Liam); s of Peggy Gallagher; yr bro of Noel Gallagher, *qv*; *b* 21 September 1972, Manchester; *m* 7 April 1997 (m dis 2000), Patsy Kensit; 1s (Lennon); *Career* formerly with band The Rain, fndr memb (lead vocals) Oasis 1991–; albums: Definitely Maybe 1994 (entered UK charts no 1, fastest selling debut album in British history), (What's the Story) Morning Glory? 1995 (UK no 1), Be Here Now 1997 (UK no 1), The Masterplan 1998 (compilation, UK no 2), Familiar to Millions 2000 (live album, UK no 5), Heathen Chemistry 2002 (UK no 1), Don't Believe the Truth 2005 (UK no 1); top 10 UK singles incl: Live Forever (no 10), Cigarettes & Alcohol (no 7), Whatever (no 3), Some Might Say (no 1), Roll With It (no 2), Wonderwall (no 2), Don't Look Back in Anger (no 1), D'You Know What I Mean (no 1), Stand By Me (no 2), All Around the World (no 1), Go Let It Out (no 1), Who Feels Love (no 4), Sunday Morning Call (no 4), The Hindu Times (no 1), Stop Crying Your Heart Out (no 2), Little By Little/She is Love (no 2), Songbird (no 3), Lyla (no 1), The Importance of Being Idle (no 1), Let There Be Love (no 2); contrib Help (Warchild album) 1995; *Awards* incl: Best New Group Brit Awards 1995, Best Group and Best Album ((What's the Story) Morning Glory?) Brit Awards 1996, Best Group and Best Song (Wonderwall) MTV Music Awards 1996, nominated Best Song (Wonderwall) Grammy Awards 1997; *Recreations* supporting Man City; *Style—* Liam Gallagher; ✉ c/o Big Brother Recordings Ltd, PO Box 29479, London NW1 6GG

GALLAND, Robert Brian; s of Raymond Harry Galland, and Olwyn Lilian Gladys, *née* Aston; *b* 26 December 1947; *Educ* Halesowen GS, Univ of Manchester (MB ChB, MD); *m* 21 May 1977, Janet Carmichael, da of Edward Yates (d 1982); 3 da (Emma Louise b 30 March 1979, Joanne Laura b 20 June 1980, Rebecca Jamie b 26 Dec 1985); *Career* conslt surgn Royal Berks Hosp Reading 1988–; memb Ct of Examiners RCS 1992–2000, treas Vascular Surgery Soc 2000–04; Hunterian prof RCS 2004–05; author of pubns on: vascular surgery, gastroenterology, surgical infection; FRCS 1976; *Books* Radiation Enteritis (ed with J Spencer, 1990), Clinical Problems in Vascular Surgery (ed with C A C Clyne, 1994), A Handbook of Basic Vascular Techniques (with M H Lewis, 2002), Topical Issues in Vascular Science (ed with T R Magee and M H Lewis, 2005); *Recreations* philately, reading; *Style—* Robert Galland, Esq; ✉ Little Orchard, Gardener's Lane, Upper Basildon, Berkshire RG8 8NL (tel 01491 671852); Department of Surgery, Royal Berkshire Hospital, London Road, Reading, Berkshire RG1 5AN (tel 0118 322 5111)

GALLEMORE, Michael; s of Ronald Gallemore (d 1988), of Chapel-en-le-Frith, Derbys, and Mary, *née* Slater, of Rhos-on-Sea, Colwyn Bay; *b* 3 November 1944; *Educ* Manchester Central GS; *m* 7 July 1967, Janetta Florence, da of Frank and Ada Reeves (d 1985); 1 s (Alexander Michael b 3 Nov 1974); *Career* interviewer Nat Rheumatism Survey 1961, joined Stewart & Hartleys news agency Manchester as reporter 1962, contrib various series to nat newspapers on subjects incl drugs, crime and the judicial system; Mirror Group Newspapers 1964–93: joined staff of Daily and Sunday Mirror 1964, worked as reporter, art ed, sub-ed, led attempted mgmnt buyout of MGN, managing ed (North) MGN 1985–88; The Sporting Life: managing ed 1988, ed 1989–93, md 1989–92; responsible for editorial launch of The European and Racing Times (NY), left MGN 1993; Barkers Trident Communications Corp publishers 1993–2000, commercial dir/ed Action Line magazine, Racing International, European Senior Tour and European Tour Golf Magazines and various other racing and sporting magazines; dep chm and ed-in-chief London & Edinburgh Publishing plc 1996–; ed-in-chief and md Worldwide Sporting Pubns Ltd Wimslow & Dubai 2000–; Jockey Club point-to-point course inspr 1994 (point-to-point clerk of the course); memb Br Field Sports Soc; *Books* ed: All Such Fun (by Michael Pope, 1992), A Year in Red Shirts (by Jack Berry); *Recreations* hunting, point-to-point riding, race riding, golf, rugby, soccer, cricket, tennis, squash, former semi-professional soccer and rugby league player; *Clubs* Shrigley Hall Country, Racehorse Owners' Assoc, Point-to-Point Owners' Assoc; *Style—* Michael Gallemore, Esq; ✉ Browside Farm, Stoneheads, Whaley Bridge, High Peak, Derbyshire SK23 7BB (tel 01663 732841, e-mail mikeg@sportingpublications.com); Worldwide Sporting Publications Ltd, 54 Alderley Road, Wilmslow, Cheshire SK9 1NY

GALLEWAY, William Henry; s of Major Harold Galleway, JP (d 1963), and Marjorie, *née* Frankland (d 2002); *b* 30 July 1931; *Educ* Whitby GS, Univ of Leeds (BCom); *Career* articled to M Wasley Chapman 1949; ptnr: Carlill Burkinshaw Ferguson 1963–70, Hodgson Impey (formerly Hodgson Harris) 1970–90, Price Waterhouse 1990–95; dir William Jackson & Son Ltd 1995–99 (conslt 1999–2006); pres Humberside and Dist Soc CAs 1982–83; memb Cncl ICAEW 1982–95; memb Worshipful Co of CAs 1988; FCA 1966 (ACA 1955); *Recreations* antique collecting, philately; *Clubs* Lansdowne; *Style—* William H Galleway, Esq; ✉ Streonshalh, 1 North Promenade, Whitby, North Yorkshire YO21 3JX (tel and fax 01947 602208)

GALLEY, Roy; s of Kenneth Haslam Galley, and Letitia Mary, *née* Chapman; *b* 8 December 1947; *Educ* King Edward VII GS Sheffield, Worcester Coll Oxford; *m* 1976, Helen Margaret Butcher; 1 s, 1 da; *Career* PO mangr; contested (Cons) Dewsbury 1979, MP (Cons) Halifax 1983–87; memb Social Services Select Ctee 1983–87, sec Cons Backbench Health Ctee 1983–87; memb: Calderdale Met Borough Cncl 1980–83, Marefield Parish Cncl 2006, Wealden DC 2007; chm: Kingston and Esher Health Authy 1989–93, Kingston and Richmond Health Authy 1993–98, Kingston and St George's NHS Coll of Health Studies 1993–96; Royal Mail London: dir of facilities 1992–94, dir of restructuring 1994–96, dir of operations programmes 1996–98; dir of planning Post Office Property Holdings 1998–2006; *Style—* Roy Galley, Esq

GALLIANO, John Charles; CBE (2001); s of John Joseph Galliano, of Gibraltar, and Anita, *née* Guillen; *b* 28 November 1960; *Educ* Wilson's GS Camberwell, City and East London Coll of Textiles and Art and Design, St Martin's Sch of Art; *Career* fashion designer; head of: Givenchy (Paris) 1995–96, Dior (Paris) 1996–; work on permanent display The Museum of Costume Bath 1987; British Designer of the Year (British Fashion Awards) 1987, 1994, 1995 and (jtly with Alexander McQueen, *qv*) 1997; hon fell London Inst 1997; *Style—* John Galliano, Esq, CBE

GALLIE, Prof Duncan Ian Dunbar; s of Ian Gallie, and Elsie, *née* Peers; *Educ* St Paul's (scholar), Magdalen Coll Oxford (demyship, BA), St Antony's Coll Oxford (DPhil); *m* Martine, *née* Jurdant; 2 da (Natasha, Justine); *Career* res fell Nuffield Coll Oxford 1971–73, lectr in sociology Univ of Essex 1973–79, reader in sociology Univ of Warwick 1979–85, official fell Nuffield Coll Oxford 1985–, prof of sociology Univ of Oxford 1996–; dir ESRC Social Change and Econ Life Initiative 1985–90, advsr Comité National d'Evaluation de la Recherche 1991, co-ordinator EU Employment, Unemployment and Social Exclusion Prog 1995–98; memb Scientific Ctee: Institut de Recherche sur les Sociétés Contemporaines (IRESCO) 1989–93, Institut Fédératif de Recherche sur les Économies et les Sociétés Industrielles (IFRESI) 1993–98; memb EU Advsy Gp on Social Scis and Humanities in the European Research Area 2002–; Distinguished Contribution to Scholarship Award American Sociological Assoc 1985; memb Br Sociological Assoc; FBA 1995 (vice-pres 2004–06, foreign sec 2006–); *Books* In Search of the New Working Class (1978), Social Inequality and Class Radicalism in France and Britain (1985), Restructuring the Employment Relationship (jtly, 1998), Welfare Regimes and the Experience of Unemployment (jtly, 2000), Why we need a New Welfare State (jtly, 2002), Resisting Marginalization (jtly, 2004); *Recreations* travelling, music, museum gazing; *Style—* Prof Duncan Gallie; ✉ 149 Leam Terrace, Leamington Spa, Warwickshire CV31 1DF; Nuffield College, Oxford OX1 1NF (tel 01865 278586, e-mail duncan.gallie@nuffield.ox.ac.uk)

G

GALLIE, Philip Roy (Phil); MSP; s of George Gallie, and Ivy Gallie; *b* 3 June 1939; *Educ* Dunfermline HS, Kirkcaldy Tech Coll (HNC); *m* 5 Sept 1964, Marion (d 2006), da of William Whyte; 1 s (Craig), 1 da (Kristeen); *Career* apprentice electrical fitter HM Dockyard Rosyth 1955–60, seagoing electrical engr Ben Line 1960–64, various posts in electricity supply industry 1964–92 rising from maintenance electrician through various maintenance engrg posts to mangr Galloway and Lanark Hydros and Inverkip Power Stn; MP (Cons) Ayr 1992–97 and 2001–07 (Parly candidate (Cons) Cunninghame S 1983 and Dunfermline W 1987), sec Scottish Cons Members Ctee 1992–97, former vice-chm Scottish All-Pty Housing Ctee; MSP (Cons) Scotland S 1999–2007, currently European and constitutional affrs spokesman, formerly Scottish Cons justice and home affrs spokesman; chm: Bute and N Ayrshire Cons Assoc 1978–80, Cunninghame North Cons Assoc 1986–87, Strathclyde W Cons Euro-constituency Cncl 1987–89, W of Scotland Area Cons Cncl 1990–91; vice-chm Scottish Cons and Unionist Pty 1995–97; cncllr Cunninghame DC 1980–84; business exec Scottish Enterprise 1997–98; elder Church of Scotland; MIPlantE; *Recreations* hill walking, sport, politics; *Clubs* Ayr RFC, RAFA; *Style—* Phil Gallie, Esq, MSP; ✉ 1 Wellington Square, Ayr, Strathclyde KA7 1EN (tel 01292 283439, fax 01292 280480); home: (tel 01292 619350); The Scottish Parliament, Edinburgh EH99 1SP (tel 0131 348 5665, fax 0131 348 5938, e-mail phil.gallie.msp@scottish.parliament.uk)

GALLIGAN, Prof Denis James; s of John Felix Galligan (d 1973), and Muriel Maud, *née* Johnson; *b* 4 June 1947; *Educ* Downlands Coll Toowoomba, Univ of Queensland (LLB), Univ of Oxford (MA, BCL, DCL); *m* 20 June 1972, Martha Louise, da of Alfred Lewis Martinuzzi, of Innisfail, Queensland; 1 da (Francesca Louise b 22 Feb 1975), 1 s (Finbar John b 10 Sept 1977); *Career* lectr Faculty of Law UCL 1974–76, pt/t lectr Magdalen Coll Oxford 1975, fell Jesus Coll Oxford and CUF lectr Univ of Oxford 1976–81, sr lectr Faculty of Law Univ of Melbourne 1982–84, dean Faculty of Law Univ of Southampton 1987–90 (prof 1985–93), prof of socio-legal studies and dir Centre for Socio-Legal Studies Univ of Oxford 1993–; fell Wolfson Coll Oxford; Jean Monnet prof Università degli Studi di Siena 2003–, visiting prof Central European Univ Budapest 1993–2004; pres UK Assoc for Legal and Social Philosophy 1989–91, conslt OECD Paris 1995–97; assoc ed Oxford DNB; memb Socio-Legal Studies Assoc; called to the Bar Gray's Inn, barr Supreme Court Queensland; fndn academician Acad of Social Sciences; *Books* Essays in Legal Theory (1984), Law, Rights and the Welfare State (1986), Discretionary Powers: A Legal Study of Official Discretion (1986), Procedure (1992), Administrative Law (1992), Australian Administrative Law (1993), Socio-Legal Readings in Administrative Law (1995), Socio-Legal Studies in Context (1995), Due Process and Procedural Fairness (1996), Administrative Justice in the New European Democracies (1998), Administrative Law in Central and Eastern Europe (1998), Law and Informal Practices (2003), Law in Modern Society (2006); *Recreations* reading, gardening; *Style—* Prof Denis Galligan; ✉ The Rosery, Beckley, Oxford OX3 9UU (tel and fax 01865 351281); Centre for Socio-Legal Studies, Manor Building, Oxford OX1 3UQ (tel 01865 284220, fax 01865 284221, e-mail denis.galligan@csls.ox.ac.uk); Wolfson College, Oxford OX2 6UD

GALLIMORE, Michael; s of John Gallimore (d 1998), of Surbiton, Surrey, and Rita Ida Doreen, *née* Clarke; *b* 8 March 1958; *Educ* Kingston GS, St Catharine's Coll Cambridge (MA, capt Univ Hockey Club, Hockey blue); *m* 29 July 1983, Jane Frances, da of Alfred Aspinall, of Southport, Merseyside; 1 s (William Mark b 1990), 1 da (Claire Edith b 1994); *Career* admitted slr 1983, ptnr Lovells 1988–; memb: Law Soc 1983, City of London Slrs' Co 1983; England hockey int; *Recreations* golf, hockey, theatre; *Clubs* Porters Park Golf, Ladykillers Hockey, Hawks' (Cambridge); *Style—* Michael Gallimore, Esq; ✉ Lovells, 65 Holborn Viaduct, London EC1A 2DY

GALLIMORE, Patricia Mary; da of Capt Charles Philip Gallimore, RN (d 1988), and Elizabeth St John, *née* Benn (d 1977); *b* 7 August 1944; *Educ* Hermitage House Sch Bath, Westbourne Sch Glasgow, St Margaret's Sch Sutton Coldfield, Birmingham Sch of Speech & Drama; *m* 7 April 1973, Charles Gardner, s of John Gardner; 1 s (Thomas Charles b 27 May 1977), 1 da (Harriet Mary Elizabeth b 26 July 1982); *Career* radio actress 1965–; twice memb BBC Radio Drama Co; leading roles in plays and serials incl: War and Peace, The Forsyte Saga, Wuthering Heights, Cold Comfort Farm, Waggoners Walk (BBC Radio 2) 1969–71, Pat Archer in The Archers (BBC Radio 4) 1974–; TV appearances incl: Spy-Ship (BBC), Aliens in the Family (BBC), Kinsey (BBC), Jupiter Moon (BSB); author Organic Year: A Guide to Organic Living (2000); has recorded over 150 titles for audio cassette books; winner BBC Student Radio Drama Prize (now Carleton Hobbs Award) 1965; *Recreations* swimming, reading, walking, enjoying time with friends and family; *Style—* Patricia Gallimore; ✉ c/o The Archers, BBC, The Mailbox, Birmingham B1 1RP

GALLOWAY, Alexander Kippen (Alex); s of Alexander Kippen Galloway (d 1975), and Vera Eleanor, *née* Atkinson (d 1970); *b* 29 April 1952; *Educ* Birkenhead Sch, Jesus Coll Oxford (MA); *m* 22 Sept 1973, Elaine Margaret, da of Eric Watkinson; 3 s (Richard b 21 June 1979, Peter b 21 April 1981, Charles b 19 Feb 1986); *Career* Civil Serv: Dept of the Environment 1974–98 (princ 1982, asst sec 1994), private sec to Paymaster Gen and Chllr of Duchy of Lancaster (secondment) 1982–85, memb Cabinet Office Secretariat (secondment) 1992–93, clerk of the Privy Cncl 1998–; chm of tstees Projects in Partnership; *Recreations* scuba diving, skiing, playing the cello, choral singing; *Style—* Alex Galloway, Esq; ✉ Privy Council Office, 2 Carlton Gardens, London SW1Y 5AA (tel 020 7210 1040, fax 020 7210 1072, e-mail alex.galloway@cabinet-office.x.gsi.gov.uk)

GALLOWAY, George; MP; s of George Galloway, of Dundee, and Sheila Reilly; *b* 16 August 1954; *Educ* Harris Acad; *m* 1, 1979 (m dis), Elaine, da of James Fyffe, of Dundee; 1 da (Lucy b 1982); m 2, 2000, Dr Amineh Abu-Zayyad; *Career* labourer jute & flax industry

1973, prodn worker Michelin Tyres 1973, organiser Dundee Lab Pty 1977, dir War on Want 1983; MP: (Lab) Glasgow Hillhead 1987–97, (Lab until 2003 then Respect 2004–05) Glasgow Kelvin 1997–2005, (Respect) Bethnal Green & Bow 2005–; Hilal-i-Quaid-i-Azzam decoration for servs to the movement for the restoration of democracy in Pakistan 1990, Hilal-i-Pakistan decoration for work on self-determination for Jammu and Kashmir 1996; Debater of the Year Zurich/Spectator Parly Awards 2001; appeared in Celebrity Big Brother (Channel 4) 2006; *Books* Downfall - The Ceausescus and the Romanian Revolution (jtly, 1991), I'm Not the Only One (2004), Mr Galloway Goes to Washington (2005), The Fidel Castro Handbook (2006); *Recreations* sport, films, music; *Style—* George Galloway, MP; ✉ House of Commons, London SW1 0AA

GALLOWAY, Janice; da of late James Galloway, and Janet Clark McBride (d 1982); *b* 2 December 1956; *Educ* Ardrossan Acad, Univ of Glasgow; *Children* 1 s (James b 21 Feb 1992); *Career* writer, sometime English teacher; TLS res fell British Library 1999; E M Forster Award 1994; *Books* The Trick is to Keep Breathing (1990, SAC Award, MIND/Allan Lane Award), Blood (1991, SAC Award), Foreign Parts (1994, McVitie's Prize for Scottish Writer of the Year 1994, SAC Award), Where You Find It (1996), Pipelines (with Anne Bevan, 2000), Clara (2002, Saltire Soc Scottish Book of the Year Award 2002), Boy Book See (2002), Monster (libretto, with Sally Beamish, 2002), Rosengarten (with the sculptor Anne Bevan, 2004; *Style—* Ms Janice Galloway; ✉ c/o Jonathan Cape, 20 Vauxhall Bridge Road, London SW1V 2SA; c/o Derek Johns, AP Watt Agency, 20 St John Street, London WC1N 2DR (tel 020 7405 6774, fax 020 7831 2154)

GALLOWAY, Nicholas Robert; s of Norman Patrick Robert Galloway, and Eileen, *née* Thompson; *b* 12 May 1935; *Educ* Shrewsbury, Univ of Cambridge, Univ of Edinburgh (BA, MB ChB, DO, MD); *m* 28 July 1962, Jennifer, *née* Shell; 1 da (Sarah b 15 Oct 1967), 2 s (Peter b 10 March 1969, James b 15 Jan 1978); *Career* house surgn Western Gen Hosp Edinburgh 1959–60, sr registrar Moorfields Eye Hosp 1963–65, conslt ophthalmic surgn and clinical teacher Nottingham Univ Hosp 1967–2000; master Oxford Ophthalmological Congress 1988–90; pres: Nottingham Medico Chirurgical Soc 1993–94, European Assoc for Vision and Eye Research 2005; vice-pres Int Soc for Clinical Electrophysiology of Vision; memb: BMA, Johnian Soc; FRCS, FRCOphth; *Books* Ophthalmic Electrodiagnosis (1981), Common Eye Diseases and their Management (1985, 3 edn 2005), Ophthalmology (1988); *Recreations* gardening, photography; *Clubs* RSM; *Style—* Nicholas Galloway, Esq; ✉ Queen's Medical Centre, Clifton Boulevard, Nottingham NG7 2UH (e-mail nicholas.galloway@virgin.net)

GALLOWAY, Rev Dr Peter John; OBE (1996), JP (City of London 1989); s of Henry John Galloway (d 1986), and Mary Selina, *née* Beshaw; *b* 19 July 1954; *Educ* Westminster City Sch, Univ of London (BA, PhD); *Career* ordained: deacon 1983, priest 1984; curate: St John's Wood London 1983–86, St Giles-in-the-Fields London 1986–90; vicar Emmanuel West End Hampstead London 1995– (priest-in-charge 1990–95); area dean: North Camden 2002–07, Surrogate 2006–; chm of govrs Emmanuel Sch 1990–; St John Ambulance: asst DG 1985–91, dep DG 1991–99, chm Nat Publications Ctee 1988–95; memb Lord Chancellor's Advsy Ctee 1994–2000 and 2005–, chm of the Bench 2001–04 (dep chm 2000), chm Gtr London Bench Chairmen's Forum 2004 (dep chm 2003); chm The Goldsmiths' Soc 1997– (vice-chm 1991–97); vice-chm Convocation Univ of London 1999–2003 (actg chm 2001–03), chm Univ of London Convocation Tst 2005–; memb Cncl: Goldsmiths Coll London 1993–99, Univ of London 1999–, Heythrop Coll 2006–; tstee St Gabriel's Tst 2001–04; Order of St John of Jerusalem: memb Chapter-Gen 1996–99, memb Priory of England Chapter 1999–, sub dean Priory of England 1999–; Freeman City of London 1995, Liveryman Worshipful Co of Glaziers 1997 (Freeman 1995); hon fell Goldsmiths Coll London 1999; FSA 2000; KStJ 1997 (ChStJ 1992); *Books* The Order of St Patrick 1783–1983 (1983), Henry F B Mackay (1983), Good and Faithful Servants (jtly, 1988), The Cathedrals of Ireland (1992), The Order of the British Empire (1996), Royal Service (jtly, vol 1, 1996), The Most Illustrious Order (1999), A Passionate Humility, Frederick Oakeley and the Oxford Movement (1999), The Cathedrals of Scotland (2000), The Order of St Michael and St George (2000), Companions of Honour (2002), The Order of the Bath (2006); *Recreations* reading, writing, book collecting, solitude; *Clubs* Athenaeum; *Style—* The Rev Dr Peter Galloway, OBE, FSA; ✉ The Vicarage, Lyncroft Gardens, London NW6 1JU

GALLOWAY, 13 Earl of (S 1623); Sir Randolph Keith Reginald Stewart; 12 Bt (of Corsewell S 1627 and 10 Bt of Burray S 1687); also Lord Garlies (S 1607) and Baron Stewart of Garlies (GB 1796); s of 12 Earl of Galloway, JP (d 1978); *b* 14 October 1928; *Educ* Harrow; *m* 1975, Mrs May Lily Budge (d 1999), yst da of late Andrew Miller, of Duns, Berwickshire; *Heir* kinsman, Andrew Stewart; *Style—* The Rt Hon the Earl of Galloway; ✉ Senwick House, Brighouse Bay, Borgue, Kirkcudbrightshire DT6 4TP

GALLWEY, *see:* Frankland-Payne-Gallwey

GALMICHE, Daniel Michel; s of Daniel Galmiche (d 1994), and Anne-Marie, *née* Calame; *b* 18 January 1958, Lure, France; *Educ* Lycee Hotelier de Strasbourg, Lycee Mixte de Lure; *m* (m dis); partner, Claire Marchionne; 1 s (Antoine-Daniel b 4 Feb 2000); *Career* trained with the Roux bros at Le Gavoche 1977–78; head chef: Knockinaam Lodge Hotel Portpatrick 1986–93 (1 Michelin Star 1990), The Duxton Hotel Singapore 1993–95; exec chef Penina Meridian Golf and Resort Hotel Alvor 1995–96, chef mangr Harveys Restaurant Bristol 1996–2003 (1 Michelin Star); exec chef: L'Ortolan Shinfield 2003–04 (1 Michelin Star), Cliveden House Hotel Taplow 2004– (1 Michelin Star); resident writer for Reading Evening Post Food Monthly (jt winner UK Supplement of the Year Regional Press Awards 2007); memb: Acad Culinaire of GB, World Master Chef Soc, Soil Assoc Judging Panel for Organic Food; conslt Steelite Int; TV appearances incl: The Greatest Dishes in the World (Sky), Too Many Cooks (HTV), Saturday Kitchen (BBC); Master Chef of the Year Scotland 1989; *Style—* Daniel Galmiche, Esq; ✉ Cliveden House Hotel, Taplow, Berkshire SL6 0JF (tel 01628 607149, e-mail daniel.galmiche@clivedenhouse.co.uk)

GALPIN, Rodney Desmond; s of Sir Albert James Galpin, KCVO, CBE (d 1984), and Vera Alice, *née* Tiller (d 1980); *b* 5 February 1932; *Educ* Haileybury and ISC; *m* 1956, Sylvia, da of Godfrey Craven (d 1981); 1 s (Paul), 1 da (Fenella); *Career* exec dir Bank of England 1984–88; chm: Johnson Matthey Bankers 1984–85, Standard Chartered plc 1988–93, Alpha Airports Group plc 1994–2002; dir: Cater Allen Holdings plc 1993–97, Capital Shopping Centres plc 1994–2000, Ascot Holdings plc 1995–2001; non-exec dir: Peninsular & Oriental Steam Navigation Co plc 1996–2005, Abbey National Treasury Services plc 1997–2002; chm: Independent Review Body for the Banking and Mortgage Lending Codes 1994–99, Look Ahead Housing Assoc 1994–2003; tstee Blind in Business 1991–2000; memb: Cncl Haileybury 1972–2004 (also life govr), Cncl and Fin Ctee Scout Assoc 1972–, Cncl St George's House Windsor 1995–2001; Freeman City of London; FCIB; OStJ; *Style—* Rodney Galpin, Esq; ✉ e-mail rdgalpin@aol.com

GALSWORTHY, Sir Anthony Charles; KCMG (1999, CMG 1985); s of Sir Arthur Norman Galsworthy, KCMG (d 1986), and Margaret Agnes, *née* Hiscocks (d 1973); *b* 20 December 1944; *Educ* St Paul's, CCC Cambridge (MA); *m* 30 May 1970, Jan, da of Dr A W Dawson-Grove; 1 s (Andrew b 1974), 1 da (Carolyn b 1975); *Career* Far East Dept FCO 1966–67, language student Hong Kong 1967–69, third sec (later second sec) Peking 1970–72, Rhodesia Dept FCO 1972–74, private sec to min of state 1974–77, first sec Rome 1977–81, first sec (later cnsllr and head of Chancery) Peking 1982–84, head Hong Kong Dept FCO 1984–86, princ private sec to sec of state for Foreign and Cwlth Affrs 1986–88, visiting res fell RIIA 1988–89, sr Br rep Sino-Br Jt Liaison Gp on Hong Kong 1989–93, chief of assessments staff Cabinet Office 1993–95; dep under sec of state FCO 1995–97, ambass China 1997–2002; advsr Bd Standard Chartered Bank 2002–; dir Bekaert SA 2004–; scientific assoc Nat History Museum 2001–; memb Foreign Affrs Advsy Ctee Royal Soc 2003–; tstee Wildfowl and Wetland Tst 2002–, tstee Br Tst for Ornithology 2002–06, dir Earthwatch (Europe) 2002–06; hon fell Royal Botanic Gardens Edinburgh 2001–, hon prof Kunming Inst of Botany Chinese Acad of Sciences 2002–; Order of the Lion of Finland 1975, Order of Adolph of Nassau (Luxembourg) 1976; *Recreations* ornithology, wildlife; *Clubs* Oxford and Cambridge; *Style—* Sir Anthony Galsworthy, KCMG

GALSWORTHY, (Arthur) Michael Johnstone; CVO (2002), CBE (1999), DL (Cornwall 1993); s of Sir John Edgar Galsworthy, KCVO, CMG (d 1992), of St Just-in-Roseland, Cornwall, and Jennifer Ruth, *née* Johnstone; *b* 10 April 1944; *Educ* Radley, Univ of St Andrews (MA); *m* 1, 20 June 1972, Charlotte Helena Prudence (d 1989), da of Col S M Roberts (d 1958), of Fairseat, Kent; 2 da (Olivia Victoria Jane b 4 Aug 1974, Susannah Catherine Rose b 14 Nov 1979), 1 s (Stamford Timothy John b 20 May 1976); *m* 2, 26 Oct 1991, Sarah Christian, da of Cdr Rev Peter Durnford, of St Mawes, Cornwall; 1 s (William Jack Heywood b 8 Aug 1994), 1 da (Imogen Rosdew Claire b 5 March 1996); *Career* International Harvester Corp (UK) 1967–69, English China Clays International plc 1970–81, md Hawkins Wright Associates 1981–87, dir Woodard Corporation 1983–87; chm: Trewithen Estates Management Co Ltd 1984–, Probus Garden Estate Co Ltd 1984–; local advsy dir Barclays Bank plc 1988–98; chm: Royal Cornwall Hospitals NHS Tst 1991–93, Cornwall County Playing Fields Assoc 1977–2000, Cornwall Rural Housing Assoc 1985–96, The In Pursuit of Excellence Partnership for Cornwall 1994–2000; dir Cncl for Small Industries in Rural Areas 1985–88, memb Prince of Wales' Cncl 1985–2002, tstee Rural Housing Tst 1986–91, rural devpt cmmr 1987–91, vice-pres Royal Cornwall Agric Assoc, chm Cncl Order of St John Cornwall 1995–2000; High Sheriff Cornwall 1994–95, Vice Lord-Lt Cornwall 2002–; Freeman City of London 1973, memb Ct of Assts Worshipful Co of Goldsmiths 1998 (Freeman 1973, Liveryman 1991); *Publications* In Pursuit of Excellence - a Testimony of Current Business Achievements in Cornwall (1994), The Business Journal for Cornwall (1995), A Wealth of Talent - The Craft Industry in Cornwall (1998); *Recreations* gardening, fishing, shooting; *Clubs* Brooks's, Farmers'; *Style—* Michael Galsworthy, CVO, CBE, DL; ✉ Trewithen, Grampound Road, Truro, Cornwall TR2 4DD (tel 01726 882763, fax 01726 882703)

GALTON, Prof David Jeremy; s of Maj Ernest Manuel Galton, and Cecilia, *née* Leyburn; *b* 2 May 1937; *Educ* Highgate Sch, Univ of London (MD, DSc); *m* 11 April 1967, (Gwynne) Merle; 1 da (Clare Judith b 1968), 1 s ((James) Seth b 1970); *Career* conslt physician St Bartholomew's Hosp 1971–, conslt physician i/c Moorfields Eye Hosp 1974–, prof Univ of London 1987–; chm Clinical Science 1979–81, sec Euro Atherosclerosis Soc; memb: Med Res Soc 1971, Assoc Physicians UK 1975, RSM; *Books* The Human Adipose Cell (1971), Molecular Genetics of Common Metabolic Disease (1985), Hyperlipidaemia in Practice (1991); *Recreations* skiing, sailing, music; *Style—* Prof David Galton; ✉ St Bartholomew's Hospital, West Smithfield, London EC1 (tel 020 7882 6018, fax 020 7882 6064)

GALTON, Prof Maurice James; s of James Galton (d 1948), and Olive, *née* Prendergast (d 1987); *Educ* Salesian Coll Oxford, Univ of Durham (BSc), Univ of Newcastle upon Tyne (MSc), Univ of Leeds (MEd), Univ of Leicester (PhD); *m* 19 March 1960, Pamela Jean, da of Rev Canon Albert John Bennitt (d 1985); 3 s (Simon b 1960, Giles b 1963, Matthew b 1964), 3 da (Philippa b 1968, Bridget b 1969, Su b 1977); *Career* asst master St Paul's Sch 1960–65, instr Univ of Leeds 1965–70; Univ of Leicester: lectr 1970–82, prof 1982–99, dean Faculty of Educn and Continuing Studies 1995–98; assoc dir of research Homerton Coll Cambridge 1999–; Parly candidate (Lib) Bosworth 1974–75; conslt Cncl of Europe Primary Project 1982–88, memb Primary Ctee Nat Curriculum Cncl (NCC) 1988–; memb Leicester Theatre Tst 1975–81; FRSA 1986; *Books* Inside The Primary Classroom (1980), Moving From The Primary Classroom (1984), Primary Teaching (1988), Handbook of European Primary Education (1989), Group Work in the Primary Classroom (1992), Crisis in the Primary Classroom (1994), Inside The Primary Classroom: 20 years on (1999), Transfer from the Primary Classroom 20 years on (jtly, 2002); *Recreations* golf, cricket, walking, theatre; *Style—* Prof Maurice Galton; ✉ e-mail mg266@cam.ac.uk

GALTON, Raymond Percy (Ray); OBE; s of Herbert Galton, and Christina Galton; *b* 17 July 1930; *Educ* Garth Sch Morden; *m* 1956, Tonia Phillips (d 1995); 1 s, 2 da; *Career* scriptwriter and author (in collaboration with Alan Simpson, OBE, *qv*); *Theatre* incl: Way Out In Piccadilly 1966–67, The Wind in the Sassafras Trees 1968, Albert och Herbert (Sweden) 1981; with John Antrobus: When Did You Last See Your Trousers 1987–88 (nat tour 1994), Steptoe and Son - Murder at Oil Drum Lane (Comedy Theatre and nat tour) 2006; *Radio* incl: Hancock's Half Hour 1954–59, The Frankie Howerd Show, Back with Braden, Steptoe and Son 1966–73, The Galton & Simpson Radio Playhouse 1998–99; *Television* incl: Hancock's Half Hour 1956–61, Citizen James 1961, BBC Comedy Playhouse, Steptoe and Son 1962–74, Galton and Simpson Comedy 1969, Milligan's Wake, Frankie Howerd, Clochemerle 1971, Casanova 1973, Dawson's Weekly 1975, The Galton and Simpson Playhouse 1976–77, Camilo e Filho (Portugal Steptoe) 1995, Paul Merton In Galton & Simpson's... (series) 1996 and 1997; with Johnny Speight: Spooner's Patch 1977–81, Pfeifer (Germany) 2000; with John Antrobus: Room at the Bottom 1986–87, Get Well Soon 1997; *Film* incl: The Rebel 1960, The Bargee 1963, The Wrong Arm of the Law 1964, The Spy with the Cold Nose 1966, Loot 1970, Steptoe and Son 1971, Steptoe and Son Ride Again 1973, Den Siste Fleksnes (Norway) 1974, Le Petomane 1977; with Andrew Galton: Camping (Denmark) 1990; *Awards* John Logie Baird award for outstanding contribution to TV, Writers' Guild award (twice), Guild of TV Producers and Directors 1959 Merit Awards for Scriptwriters of the Year, Screenwriters' Guild Best TV Comedy Series (for Steptoe and Son) annually 1962–65, Dutch TV Best Comedy Series (for Steptoe and Son) 1966, Screenwriters' Guild Best Comedy Screenplay (for Steptoe and Son) 1972, Banff Festival Best TV Comedy (for Room at the Bottom) 1987, Writer's Guild of GB Lifetime Achievement Award 1997, BPI Gold Disc for BBC radio collection Hancock's Half Hour 1998; *Books* Hancock (1961), Steptoe and Son (1963), The Reunion and Other Plays (1966), Hancock Scripts (1974), The Best of Hancock (1986), Hancock - The Classic Years (1987), The Best of Steptoe and Son (1988), Steptoe and Son (2002), Fifty Years of Hancock's Half Hour (2004); *Style—* Ray Galton, Esq, OBE; ✉ The Ivy House, Hampton Court, Surrey KT8 9DD (tel 020 8977 1236)

GALVIN, Jeff; s of Frank Galvin, of Southend on Sea, Essex, and Kathleen, *née* Grover; *b* 1 December 1969; *Educ* Thurrock Tech Coll (City & Guilds), Westminster Coll (Dip); *Career* chef; sous chef Chez Nico Park Lane London 1994–97, head chef Marco Pierre White at the Oak Room 1999, head chef L'Escargot 2000– (1 Michelin Star); finalist Acadamy Annual Awards of Excellence 1991; *Recreations* running, golf, cooking; *Style—* Jeff Galvin, Esq; ✉ L'Escargot, 48 Greek Street, London W1D 4EF (tel 020 7439 7474, fax 020 7437 0790)

GALWAY, 12 Viscount (I 1727); George Rupert Monckton-Arundell; CD; also Baron Killard (I 1727); s of Philip Marmaduke Monckton (d 1965), and Lavender, *née* O'Hara; suc 1 cous once removed, 11 Viscount, 1980; *b* 13 October 1922; *Educ* Victoria Coll; *m* 1944, Fiona Margaret, da of Capt W de P Taylor (d 1979), of Sooke, Br Columbia; 1 s, 3 da; *Heir* s, Hon Philip Monckton; *Career* Lt-Cdr RCN 1941–67; stockbroker 1967–83, ret; *Recreations* painting, 'birding', golfing, travelling; *Style—* The Rt Hon the Viscount Galway, CD; ✉ 787 Berkshire Drive, London, Ontario N6J 3S5, Canada

GALWAY, Sir James; kt (2001), OBE (1977); s of James Galway; *b* 8 December 1939; *Educ* Royal Coll of Music, Guildhall Sch of Music, Conservatoire National Supérieur de

Musique Paris; *m* 1; 1 s; m 2; 1 s, 2 da (twins); m 3, 1984, Jeanne Cinnante; *Career* flute-player; princ flute: London Symphony Orch 1966, Royal Philharmonic Orch 1967–69, Berlin Philharmonic Orch 1969–75; solo career 1975–, soloist/conductor 1984–, princ guest conductor London Mozart Players 1999–; records for BMG Classics and DG; Grand Prix du Disque 1976 and 1989, President's Merit Award Nat Acad of Recording, Arts and Science 2004; James Galway rose by David Austin, *qv*, displayed Chelsea Flower Show 2000; hon fell Guildhall Sch of Music 2003; Hon MA Open Univ 1979, Hon Dr Univ of St Andrews; Hon DMus: Queen's Univ Belfast 1979, New England Conservatory of Music 1980; Officier de l'Ordre des Arts et des Lettres (France) 1987; *Publications* Flute (Yehudi Menuhin Music Guide Series, 1982), James Galway - An Autobiography (1978); *Recreations* music, swimming, walking, theatre, films, TV, chess, backgammon, talking to people; *Style—* Sir James Galway, OBE; ✉ Galway Management, PO Box, 6045 Meggen, Switzerland

GAMBACCINI, Paul Matthew; s of Mario Matthew Gambaccini, of Westport, CT, and Dorothy, *née* Kiebrick; *b* 2 April 1949; *Educ* Staples HS, Dartmouth Coll (BA), UC Oxford (MA); *Career* broadcaster and music journalist; with Rolling Stone Magazine 1970–77; host: Ivor Novello Awards 1987–, Sony Radio Awards 1999–, BBC Jazz Awards 2005–, Parliamentary Jazz Awards 2005–; fundraiser: Amnesty Int, Terrence Higgins Tst; Sony Radio Awards: Best Music Broadcaster 2002 (nominated 1999, 2001 and 2006), Best Music Documentary 2003, The Gold Award 2007; *Radio* BBC Radio One 1973–86 and 1991–93, BBC Radio Four 1976–, Capital Radio 1986–91, Classic FM 1992–95 and 1998–2002, BBC Radio Three 1995–96, BBC Radio Two 1998–, Jazz FM 2003–05; *Television* incl: Omnibus (BBC 1), Pebble Mill at One (BBC 1), Summer Festivals (BBC 2), The Other Side of the Tracks (Channel 4) 1983–85, TV-am 1983–92, Television's Greatest Hits (BBC 1), GMTV 1993–96, Call My Bluff (BBC) 1998–2003, Breakfast with Frost (BBC) 2005; *Books* Guinness Book of British Hit Singles (co-ed, 10 edns), Guinness Book of British Hit Albums (co-ed, 7 edns), Radio Boy (1986), Television's Greatest Hits (1993), Love Letters (1996), Close Encounters (1998), Theatre: The Ultimate Man (co-author, 2000); *Recreations* films, theatre, British Softball Federation Hall of Fame 2007, comic books; *Style—* Paul Gambaccini; ✉ tel 020 7401 6753, fax 020 7207 6755, e-mail paulgambaccini@hotmail.com

GAMBLE, Prof Andrew Michael; s of Marcus Elkington Gamble, of Sevenoaks, Kent, and Joan, *née* Westall; *b* 15 August 1947; *Educ* Brighton Coll, Queens' Coll Cambridge (BA), Univ of Durham (MA), Gonville & Caius Coll Cambridge (PhD); *m* 15 June 1974, Christine Jennifer, da of Allan Edwin Rodway; 1 s (Thomas Simon b 7 March 1977), 2 da (Corinna Lucy b 25 Feb 1980, Sarah Eleanor b 3 August 1983); *Career* Univ of Sheffield: lectr in politics 1973–82, reader 1982–86, prof 1986–, pro-vice-chllr 1994–98; visiting prof: Univ of Kobe 1990, Univ of Hitotsubashi 1992, Univ of Chuo 1994; dir Political Econ Res Centre 1998–; Isaac Deutscher Meml Prize 1972, Mitchell Prize 1977; memb: Political Studies Assoc, Br Int Studies Assoc; jt ed: Political Quarterly, New Political Economy; FRSA 1999, FBA 2000, AcSS 2002; *Books* The Conservative Nation (1974), Britain in Decline (1981), The Free Economy and the Strong State (1988), Hayek: The Iron Cage of Liberty (1996), Politics and Fate (2000), Between Europe and America: The Future of British Politics (2003); *Recreations* music, books, walking; *Style—* Prof Andrew Gamble; ✉ Department of Politics, University of Sheffield, Sheffield S10 2TU (tel 0114 222 1651, fax 0114 273 9769)

GAMBLE, Sir David Hugh Norman; 6 Bt (UK 1897), of Windlehurst, St Helens, Co Palatine of Lancashire; s of Sir David Gamble, 5 Bt (d 1984), and Dawn Adrienne, da of late David Hugh Gittins; *b* 1 July 1966; *Heir* kinsman, Hugh Gamble; *Style—* Sir David Gamble, Bt; ✉ c/o Keinton House, Keinton Mandeville, Somerton, Somerset TA11 6DX

GAMBLE, David Martin; s of Rev Alfred Edward Gamble, of Scotland, and Yvonne, *née* Cornforth (d 1973); *b* 10 March 1953; *Educ* Soham Village Coll, Ealing Sch of Photography; *m* Lora Fox Gamble; 1 s (Zachariah Fox Gamble); *Career* photographer Observer Life Magazine 1984–; other magazines incl: Independent, Sunday Times, Telegraph, Traveller Magazine, Time-Life, Fortune (NY), Paris Match, The New Yorker Magazine, Newsweek (NY); photographic subjects incl: Martin Amis, The Dalai Lama, José Carreras, Lord (Jacob) Rothschild, Robet Altman, Alan Rickman, Karsh of Ottowa; exhibitions incl: Arles 1987 (jtly), Assoc of Photographers Gallery 1987, Kodak Euro Exhibition 1988, World Press Awards 1989, Les Portes d'Europe (Provence) 1992; winner Kodak Grande Prix Euro Award France 1987; film documentary: Faces 1989, Groucho, Portraits Exhibition London 1996; exhibition Andy Warhol House 1998; memb AFAEP; painter; pt/t artist in residence École National de la Photographie; *Recreations* watching cricket, jazz, photography; *Clubs* Groucho; *Style—* David Gamble, Esq; ✉ tel 020 7284 0757

GAMBLE, Thomas (Tom); s of Thomas Gamble (d 1987), of Stockton-on-Tees, and Dorothy, *née* Naylor (d 1986); *b* 6 February 1924; *Career* artist; served RN 1942–46; formerly sr lectr Loughborough Coll of Art and Design; Freeman City of London, Liveryman and Gold Medalist Worshipful Co of Painter/Stainers; memb Artworkers' Guild, fell Royal Watercolour Soc; *Exhibitions* incl: Royal Acad, Royal Watercolour Soc, Bankside Gallery (Sunday Times and Singer & Friedlander), Hunting Gp Prizes, Royal Festival Hall, The Arts Club, Painters Hall, Paterson's Gallery Albermarle St London, Brian Sinfield, Milne and Moller, Burlington Fine Art, Woodgates Gallery East Bergholt, American Watercolour Soc, Canadian Watercolour Soc, Exposicion Internacional de Acuarela Barcelona; *Work in Collections* incl Lloyd's of London, Middlesbrough Art Gallery, Loughborough Univ of Technol, Leics CC, Notts CC, Arts Club, Intelligence Corps and several private galleries; *Clubs* Arts; *Style—* Tom Gamble, Esq, RWS; ✉ 10 Blythe Green, East Perry, Huntingdon, Cambridgeshire PE28 0BJ (tel 01480 810468)

GAMBLING, Prof William Alexander; s of late George Alexander Gambling, of Port Talbot, and late Muriel Clara, *née* Bray; *b* 11 October 1926; *Educ* Univ of Bristol (Alfred Fry Prize, BSc, DSc), Univ of Liverpool (PhD); *m* 1, 1952 (m dis 1994), Margaret Pooley; 1 s (Paul b 1956), 2 da (Alison b 1960, Vivien b 1962); m 2, 1994, Colleen O'Neil; *Career* lectr in electric power engrg Univ of Liverpool 1950–55, NRC fell Univ of British Columbia 1955–57; Univ of Southampton: lectr, sr lectr and reader 1957–64, dean of Engrg and Applied Sci 1972–75, prof of electronics 1964–80 (head of dept 1974–79), BT prof of optical communication 1980–95, dir Optoelectronics Res Centre 1989–95; Royal Soc Kan Tong Po visiting prof and dir Optoelectronics Research Centre City Univ of Hong Kong 1996–2001; dir R&D Optoelectronics LTK Industries Ltd Hong Kong 2002–03 (conslt 2006–); industrial conslt and former co dir; visiting prof: Univ of Colorado 1966–67, Bhabha Atomic Res Centre India 1970, Univ of Osaka Japan 1977, Univ of Cape Town 1979, City Univ of Hong Kong 1995; hon prof: Wuhan Univ China 1986–, Beijing Univ of Posts and Telecommunications 1987–, Shanghai Univ 1990–, Shandong Univ China 1999–; fell Hong Kong Acad of Engrg Sciences 2000 (memb Cncl 2001–, vice-pres 2004–); hon dir Beijing Optical Fibres Inst 1987–; pres IERE 1977–78 (hon fell 1983); memb: Electronics Res Cncl 1977–80 (memb Optics and Infra-Red Ctee 1965–69 and 1974–80), Bd Cncl of Engrg Instns 1974–79, Nat Electronics Cncl 1977–78 and 1984–95, Technol Sub-Ctee of UGC 1973–83, British Nat Ctee for Radio Sci 1978–87, Engrg Working Gp Nat Advsy Bd for Local Authy HE 1982–84, Engrg Cncl 1983–88, British Nat Ctee for Int Engrg Affrs 1984–88; chm Cmmn D Int Union of Radio Sci 1984–87 (vice-chm 1981–84), chm DTI/SERC Optoelectronics Ctee 1988–91; Cncl Royal Acad of Engrg 1989–92; Selby fell Aust Acad of Sci 1982, foreign memb Polish Acad of Sci 1985; Freeman City of London 1987, Liveryman Worshipful Co of Engrs 1988; Hon Dr Universidad Politéchnica de Madrid 1994, Hon DSc Aston Univ 1995, Hon DEng Univ of Bristol 1999, Hon DSc Univ of Southampton 2005; FIERE 1964, CEng, Hon FIEE 1967, FREng 1979, FRS 1983; *Awards* Bulgin Premium IERE 1961, Rutherford Premium IERE 1964, Electronics Div Premium IEE 1976 and 1978, Oliver Lodge Premium IEE 1981, Heinrich Hertz Premium IERE 1981, J J Thomson Medal IEE 1982, Faraday Medal IEE 1983, Churchill Medal Soc of Engrs 1984 (Simms Medal 1989), Academic Enterprise Award 1982, Int Micro-Optics Award Japan 1989, Dennis Gabor Award Int Soc for Optical Engrg USA 1990, Rank Prize for Opto-Electronics UK 1991, Fndn for C & C Promotion Medal and Prize Japan 1993, Mountbatten Medal NEC 1993, J R Ewing Gold Medal ICE/Royal Soc 2002; *Publications* various papers on electronics and optical fibre communications; *Recreations* music, reading; *Clubs* Royal Over-Seas League; *Style—* Prof W A Gambling, FRS, FREng; ✉ Los Grillos MG26, Calle Carrasca 4, E-03737 JAVEA, Alicante, Spain

GAMBON, Sir Michael John; kt (1998), CBE (1990); s of Edward Gambon, and Mary Gambon; *b* 19 October 1940; *Educ* St Aloysius Sch for Boys London; *m* 1962, Anne Miller; *Career* actor; formerly engrg apprentice; Liveryman Worshipful Co of Gunmakers; Hon DLitt 2002; *Theatre* incl: first stage appearance Edwards/Mac Liammoir Dublin 1962, Nat Theatre, Old Vic 1963–67, RSC Aldwych 1970–72, Norman Conquests (Globe) 1974, Otherwise Engaged (Queen's) 1976, Just Between Ourselves (Queen's) 1977, Alice's Boys (Savoy) 1978; National Theatre: Galileo 1980 (London Theatre Critics' Best Actor Award), Betrayal 1980, Tales From Hollywood 1980, A Chorus of Disapproval 1985 (Olivier Best Comedy Performance Award), Tons of Money 1986, A View from the Bridge 1987 (Evening Standard Best Actor Award, Olivier Award, Plays and Players London Theatre Critics' Award, Variety Club Best Stage Actor Award), A Small Family Business 1987, Mountain Language 1988, Skylight (Olivier Award nomination for Best Actor 1996) 1995, Volpone (Evening Standard Best Actor Award) 1995; King Lear and Cleopatra (RSC Stratford and Barbican) 1982–83, Old Times (Haymarket) 1985, Uncle Vanya (Vaudeville) 1988, Veterans' Day (Haymarket) 1989, title role in Othello 1990, Taking Steps 1990, Man of the Moment (Globe) 1990, Tom Driberg MP in Tom and Clem (Aldwych) 1997, The Unexpected Man (Duchess) 1998, Juno and the Paycock (Dublin) 1999, Cressida (Albery) 2000, The Caretaker (Comedy Theatre, Variety Club Best Stage Actor Award) 2000, Henry IV Parts One and Two (RNT) 2005; *Television* incl: The Singing Detective 1986 (BAFTA Best Actor Award 1987), Maigret (Granada) 1991, The Entertainer (BBC) 1993, Faith (Central) 1994, Wives and Daughters (BBC) 1999 (BAFTA Best Actor Award, Royal Television Soc Best Actor Award), Longitude (Granada) 1999 (BAFTA Best Actor Award), Family Tree 2000, Endgame (Beckett on Film series) 2001, Perfect Strangers 2001, Path To War 2002, The Lost Prince 2003, Angels in America 2003; *Films* incl: The Cook, The Thief, His Wife and Her Lover 1989, The Heat of the Day 1989, Paris by Night 1989, A Dry White Season 1990, Mobsters 1990, Toys 1991, Clean Slate 1992, Indian Warrior 1993, Browning Version 1993, Two Deaths 1994, Man Of No Importance 1994, Bullet To Beijing 1994, Midnight In Moscow 1994, The Innocent Sleep 1995, Mary Reilly 1996, Nothing Personal 1996, The Gambler 1997, Sleepy Hollow 1997, Last September 1998, Dancing at Laugnasa 1998, Plunkett and Macleane 1998, The Insider 1998, End Game 1999, High Heels - Low Life 2000, Charlotte Gray 2000, Gosford Park 2001, Ali G The Movie 2000, The Actors 2002, Open Range 2003, Sylvia 2003, Harry Potter and the Prisoner of Azkaban 2004, Being Julia 2004, Sky Captain and the World of Tomorrow 2004, Layer Cake 2004; *Recreations* flying, gun collecting, clock making; *Style—* Sir Michael Gambon, CBE; ✉ c/o ICM Ltd, Oxford House, 76 Oxford Street, London W1N 0AX (tel 020 7636 6565, fax 020 7323 0101)

GAMES, Prof David Edgar; s of Alfred William Games (d 1956), and Frances Elizabeth Bell, *née* Evans; *b* 7 April 1938; *Educ* Lewis Sch Pengam, King's Coll London (BSc, PhD), Univ of Wales (DSc); *m* 28 Dec 1961, Marguerite Patricia, da of John Lee, of Newport, Gwent; 2 s (Gwilym John b 1971, Evan William b 1972); *Career* successively lectr in chemistry, sr lectr, reader then personal chair Univ of Wales Coll of Cardiff 1965–89; Univ of Wales Swansea: prof of mass spectrometry and dir of Mass Spectrometry Res Unit 1989–, head of chemistry 1996–2001; FRSC, CChem; *Recreations* swimming, walking; *Style—* Prof David Games; ✉ Mass Spectrometry Research Unit, Department of Chemistry, University of Wales Swansea, Singleton Park, Swansea SA2 8PP (tel 01792 295297, fax 01792 295747)

GAMMIE, Malcolm James; CBE (2005), QC (2002); s of Maj James Ian Gammie, MC (d 1987), of Bickley, Kent, and Florence Mary, *née* Wiggs; *b* 18 February 1951; *Educ* Edge Grove Sch Aldenham, Merchant Taylors', Sidney Sussex Coll Cambridge (MA); *m* 21 Dec 1974, Rosalind Anne, da of William James Rowe (d 1997), of Bromley, Kent; 3 da (Helen Victoria b 10 Feb 1979, Isabel Margaret Ruth b 19 Feb 1985, Catharine Alice Louise b 17 Feb 1988), 1 s (Christopher James b 18 May 1981); *Career* called to the Bar Middle Temple 1997; Linklaters & Paines: articled clerk 1973–75, slr Tax Dept 1975–78 and 1985–87, ptnr 1987–97; dep head of Tax Dept CBI 1978–79; dir: Nat Tax Office Thomson McLintock & Co 1979–84, Nat Tax Servs KMG Thomson McLintock 1984–85; ed Law and Tax Review 1982–88, contrib to Financial Times on tax matters 1983–87; memb 1987–97: Special Ctee of Tax Law Consultative Bodies, Taxation Ctee IOD, City of London Slrs Co; chm Law Soc's Revenue Law Ctee 1996–97; Inst for Fiscal Studies: memb Cncl 1985–2001, chm Capital Taxes Working Pty 1986–92, chm Exec Ctee 1991–97; Chartered Inst of Taxation: memb Cncl 1983–96, chm Tech Ctee 1990–92 and 1994–95, pres 1993–94; memb Perm Scientific Ctee Int Fiscal Assoc 1998– (vice-chm Br Branch Ctee); memb Cabinet Office: Taxation Deregulation Gp 1993–97, Fiscal Studies Working Pty Advsy Cncl on Sci & Technol 1993; Tax Law Review Ctee: memb 1994–97, research dir 1997–; London C of C and Indust: memb 1976–, memb Cncl 1989–92, chm Taxation Ctee 1989–92; dep special cmmr and pt/t chm VAT & Duties Tbnl 2002–; sec and memb Cncl Assoc of Taxation Technicians 1989–91; visiting professorial fell Centre for Commercial Law Studies QMC London, research fell Inst for Fiscal Studies 1997–, Unilever prof of int business law Leiden Univ The Netherlands 1998, visiting prof of int tax law Univ of Sydney 2000 and 2002, visiting prof of tax law LSE 2000–; memb Soc for Advanced Legal Studies 1997–; FRSA 1993; *Books* Taxation Publishing, Tax on Company Reorganisations (with Susan Ball, 1980, 2 edn 1982), Tax Strategy for Companies (1981, 3 edn 1986), Stock Relief (with D Williams, 1981), Tax Focus on Interest and Discounts (with D Williams, 1983), Tax Strategy for Directors, Executives and Employees (1983, 2 edn 1985), Land Taxation (ed, 1985–), Whiteman on Capital Gains Tax (with P Whiteman, QC, and Mark Herbert, 1988), The Process of Tax Reform in the United Kingdom (1990); Butterworths Tax Handbooks (conslt ed, 1994–); *Recreations* music, church architecture; *Style—* Malcolm Gammie, Esq, CBE, QC; ✉ Chambers of Lord Grabiner, QC, 1 Essex Court, Temple, London EC4Y 9AR (tel 020 7583 2000, fax 020 7583 0118, e-mail mgammie@compuserve.com, website www.malcolmgammie.com)

GAMMON, Philip Greenway; s of Stanley Arthur John Gammon (d 1979), of Chippenham, Wilts, and Phyllis Joyce, *née* Paul (d 1998); *b* 17 May 1940; *Educ* Chippenham GS, Royal Acad of Music (scholar), Badische Musikhochschule Karlsruhe; *m* 1963, Floretta, da of Konstantin Volovinis; 2 s (Paul Christopher b 1968, Anthony John b 1970); *Career* pianist; dep piano teacher Royal Acad of Music and Royal Scottish Acad of Music 1964, pianist Royal Ballet Covent Garden 1964–68, princ pianist Ballet For All 1968–71, pianist Royal Ballet 1971–2005 (princ pianist 1999–2005); solo pianist and conductor London Contemporary Dance 1979; tours of many countries incl Brazil, USSR, Aust, China, Japan, S Korea, Argentina and Israel; first orchestral arrangement of La Chatte Metamorphosée en Femme by Offenbach (Staatsoper Vienna, Royal Opera House Covent Garden) 1985, arrangement of MacMillan's Winter Dreams by Tchaikovsky 1991; ARCM 1968, FRAM

G

2002 (ARAM 1991); *Performances* major solo performances with Royal Ballet incl: The Four Temperaments 1973, Elite Syncopations 1974, A Month in the Country 1976, La Fin du Jour 1979, Rhapsody 1980, Return to the Strange Land 1984, Rubies 1989, Winter Dreams 1991, Ballet Imperial 1994, Duo Concertant 1995, Mr Worldly Wise 1996, Marguerite and Armand 2000, Symphonic Variations 2000, The Concert 2000; other performances as solo pianist incl: concert for 50th Anniversary of Royal Ballet (with Royal Liverpool Philharmonic Orchestra, Philharmonic Hall Liverpool) 1981, gala performance celebrating 100 years of Performing Arts (Metropolitan Opera House NY) 1984, meml serv for Sir Frederick Ashton Westminster Abbey 1988, meml serv for Dame Margot Fonteyn 1991 and for Sir Kenneth MacMillan 1993 Westminster Abbey, Symphony Hall Birmingham, Queen Elizabeth Hall (part of Sir Roger Norrington's Tchaikovsky Week-End) 1998; as conductor incl: Coppélia (Ballet for All, debut, Theatre on the Green Richmond) 1970, Royal Ballet Touring Company 1976, Sleeping Beauty (Royal Ballet, Royal Opera House debut) 1978, Royal Ballet Sch performances (Royal Opera House) 1987, 1989, 1990 and 1992, Chance to Dance ROH Educn 2002 and 2005; conducting assignments with Royal Ballet incl: Ondine 1989, The Planets 1990, The Prince of the Pagodas 1990; recent guest conducting assignments incl: Hong Kong Ballet (Grand Cultural Centre Hong Kong) 1996, Nat Ballet of Portugal (San Carlos Theatre and Centro Cultural de Belém Lisbon) 1997, Rivoli Theatre Porto 1998; *Awards* Assoc Bd Gold medal Grade 8 1954, Recital Diploma 1960, Walter MacFarren Gold medal 1961, Karlsruhe Culture prize 1962, Performer's Dip Badische Musikhochschule Karlsruhe 1963 *Recordings* incl: Elite Syncopations (Continental Record Distributors), A Month in the Country (EMI Int Classical Div), Winter Dreams (NVC Arts, Teldec Video), Marguerite et Armand (Liszt sonata DVD) 2004; presenter Music and Reminiscence (memoirs with Royal Ballet and music); *Recreations* walking, reading, holidaying in Greece; *Style*— Philip Gammon, Esq; ✉ 19 Downs Avenue, Pinner, Middlesex HA5 5AQ (tel 020 8866 3260, fax 020 8248 2906)

GAMON, Maj-Gen John Anthony; CBE (2003); s of James Davidson Gamon (d 1981), and Dorothy, *née* Radford (d 1951); *b* 13 March 1946, Swansea; *Educ* Penlan Comp Sch Swansea, Royal Dental Hosp London, Eastman Dental Inst London (MSc, BDS); *m* 1968, Mary Patricia, *née* Medicke; 1 da (Alison (Mrs Longridge) b 1 Aug 1970), 1 s (Matthew b 22 Oct 1971); *Career* cmmnd RADC 1970, Army Dental Service 1970–82, dep dir Defence Dental Services 1993–96, dir Army Dental Service 1997–2001; Defence Dental Agency: dir (clinical services) 1997–99, dir (corp devpt) 1999–2001, chief exec 2001–05; special projects offr Defence Medical Servs Dept 2005–06, ret; memb Br Soc for Gen Dental Surgery 1983– (pres 2002); chm Bucks Crimestoppers 2007–; memb English Flyfishing Assoc; friend Bach Choir, friend Aylesbury Choral Soc; MGDS RCS, DRD RCS(Ed), FInstD; *Recreations* flyfishing, furniture making, music, gardening, reading; *Clubs* Naval and Military; *Style*— Maj-Gen John Gamon, CBE; ✉ 1 Bushmead Close, Whitchurch, Aylesbury, Buckinghamshire HP22 4SH (tel 01296 640915, e-mail jagamon@gotadsl.co.uk)

GANDER, Dr Derek Reginald; s of Owen Douglas Gander (d 1965), of Shortlands, Kent, and Annie Neil (d 1985); *b* 20 September 1928; *Educ* Cathedral Sch Shanghai, prisoner Japanese camp 1942–45, Worcester GS, Middx Hosp Med Sch Univ of London (MB BS, DPM, Inorganic Chemistry prize, Walter Butcher prize); *m* 1, 1955, Phyllis Marian (d 1974), da of Joseph C Williams; 3 da (Alison Jane b 22 Sept 1957, Sarah Elizabeth b 23 July 1962, Jill Fiona b 2 July 1964), 1 s (Timothy Paul b 7 July 1960); m 2, 1979, Barbara Ann, da of Thomas L Hewitt; 1 da (Kate Eliza b 6 Feb 1981); *Career* Middx Hosp: house physician 1953, house surgn 1954, casualty offr 1955; house surgn Queen Alexandra Hosp for Children Brighton 1955, asst in gen practice London 1956, med registrar Mt Vernon Hosp 1956–59, registrar Bethlehem Royal and Maudsley Hosp 1959–62, chief asst Dept of Psychological Med St Thomas' Hosp 1962–66, sr conslt psychiatrist Queen Elizabeth II Hosp 1966–87 (sec then vice-chm, then chm Med Staff Ctee and memb E Dist Med Ctee), jtly estab Drug Addiction Clinic 1968, Br Postgrad Med Fedn tutor in psychiatry with jt responsibility for Postgrad Centre Queen Elizabeth II Hosp (lectr to student midwives), lectr NW Thames Royal HA, psychiatric conslt Herts Marriage Guidance Counselling Serv, currently conslt neuropsychiatrist in private practice; memb: Br Neuropsychiatry Assoc, UK Register of Expert Witnesses in Medico Legal Work; MRCP 1959 (memb Educn Sub-Ctee and clinical tutor), FRCPsych 1977 (MRCPsych 1971, memb RCPsych Visiting Accreditation Teams); *Recreations* music, travel, swimming, shooting, gardening; *Style*— Dr Derek Gander; ✉ 8 St Peters Close, St Albans, Hertfordshire AL1 3ES (tel 01727 850584, fax 01727 850584)

GANDON, Christopher Martin; s of late Norman Gandon, of Chiddingstone Hoath, Kent, and Sadie, *née* Evans; *b* 13 November 1945; *Educ* Penarth Co GS, Leamington Coll for Boys; *m* 6 July 1974, Christine Margaret, da of Harry Wharton; 2 s (Simon William b 10 Dec 1975, Nicholas Robert b 10 Oct 1977), 1 da (Joanna Elizabeth Edith b 19 Oct 1980); *Career* articled clerk Leech Peirson Evans & Co Coventry, chartered accountant Whinney Murray (now Ernst & Young) 1970, Rowland & Co 1971, ptnr Moores Rowland 1975–99, ptnr BDO Stoy Hayward 1999–2003, ptnr BDO Stoy Hayward LLP 2003–04, ptnr Horwath Clark Whitehill LLP 2004–; Freeman City of Coventry 1969; FCA 1979 (ACA 1969), MAE, MEWI; *Recreations* sailing, rugby football, tennis, gardening, DIY; *Clubs* Sevenoaks RFC; *Style*— Christopher Gandon, Esq; ✉ Horwath Clark Whitehill LLP, 10 Palace Avenue, Maidstone, Kent ME15 6NF (tel 01622 767676, fax 01622 691399, e-mail chris.gandon@horwath.co.uk)

GANELLIN, Prof (Charon) Robin; s of Leon Ganellin (d 1969), and Beila, *née* Cluer (d 1972); *b* 25 January 1934; *Educ* Harrow Co GS, QMC London (BSc, PhD), Univ of London (DSc); *m* 27 Dec 1956, Tamara (d 1997), da of Jacob Greene (d 1988); 1 da (Nicole b 1960), 1 s (Mark b 1963); *Career* res chemist Smith Kline & French Labs Ltd 1958–59, res assoc MIT 1960, vice-pres Smith Kline & French Research Ltd 1984–86 (vice-pres res 1980–84, dir 1978–86, head of chemistry 1962–78, medicinal chemist 1961–62); Smith Kline & French prof of medicinal chemistry UCL 1986–2003 (emeritus prof of medicinal chemistry 2003–), dir Upjohn Euro Discovery Unit UCL 1987–93; hon prof Univ of Kent 1979–89; chm Soc for Drug Res 1985–87; pres IUPAC Medicinal Chemistry 2000–01, chm IUPAC Sub Ctee of Medicinal Chemistry and Drug Devpt 2002–; Prix Charles Mentzer 1978; Royal Soc of Chemistry: Medicinal Chemistry Medal 1977, Tilden Medal 1982, Adrien Albert Medal 1999; Div of Medicinal Chemistry Award American Chemical Soc 1980, Soc Chemistry Indust Messel Medal 1988, Soc for Drug Res Award for Drug Discovery 1989, USA Nat Inventors Hall of Fame 1990, Nauta Award for Pharmacochemistry from the European Fedn for Medicinal Chemistry 2004, Pratesi Medal Medical Chemical Division Societa Chimica Italiano 2006; fell Queen Mary & Westfield Coll London 1992, foreign corresponding academician Spanish Royal Acad of Pharmacy 2006; Hon DSc Aston Univ 1995; FRSC 1968, FRS 1986; *Books* Pharmacology of Histamine Receptors (1982), Frontiers in Histamine Research (1985), Dictionary of Drugs (1990), Medicinal Chemistry (1993), Dictionary of Pharmacological Agents (1997), Analogue-based Drug Discovery (2006), Practical Studies in Medicinal Chemistry (web edn, 2007); *Recreations* music, sailing, walking, theatre; *Style*— Prof Robin Ganellin, FRS; ✉ Department of Chemistry, University College London, 20 Gordon Street, London WC1H 0AJ (tel 020 7679 4624, e-mail c.r.ganellin@ucl.ac.uk)

GANS-LARTEY, Joseph Kojo; s of Charles Botway Lartey (d 1977), of Ghana, and Felicia Adoley, *née* Gans-Boye (d 1995); *b* 28 August 1951; *Educ* Presbyterian Secdy Sch X'Borg Accra Ghana, Croydon Coll Surrey (HNC), Ealing Coll of Higher Educn (LLB), LSE (LLM); *m* 28 Oct 1978, Rosmarie, da of Harold Ramrattan (d 1987), of Trinidad and Tobago; 1 da (Josephine Annmarie Laatele b 11 Sept 1985), 1 s (Charles Andrew b 10 April 1990); *Career* sr enrolled psychiatric nurse 1978–82 (trainee 1974–76, enrolled 1976–78), sr legal asst RAC 1985–86, crown prosecutor 1986–, sr crown prosecutor 1989–, princ crown prosecutor 1990–, prosecution team ldr 1995, borough crown prosecutor 2005; memb: Hon Soc of Lincoln's Inn 1983, Bar of Trinidad and Tobago 1984; nominated a Times Lawyer of the Week 2000; *Recreations* sports, international relations, reading, writing, parenting; *Style*— Joseph Gans-Lartey, Esq; ✉ Crown Prosecution Service, Prospect West, 81 Station Road, Croydon CR0 2RD (tel 020 8662 2862, fax 020 8662 2843, e-mail ganslartey@aol.com)

GANT, Diana Jillian; da of John Edward Wakeham Scutt, and Lucy Helen Scutt; *Educ* Harrow Co GS for Girls, KCL (BD), Christ Church Coll Canterbury (PGCE); *Career* VSO New Guinea 1966–67, religious educn teacher 1973–84 (incl childcare break), head of religious studies King's Sch Worcester 1984–89, head of careers and asst head of sixth form Tonbridge GS for Girls 1989–95, dep head Norwich HS for Girls GDST 1995–2000, headmistress Mount Sch York 2001–; memb GSA 2001; active memb Anglican Church; *Recreations* gardening, reading, entertaining friends, walking, classical music; *Clubs* Univ Women's; *Style*— Mrs Diana Gant; ✉ 1 Love Lane, York YO24 1FE (tel 01904 641729); The Mount School, Dalton Terrace, York YO24 4DD (tel 01904 667508, fax 01904 667534, e-mail head@mount.n-yorks.sch.uk)

GAPES, Michael John (Mike); MP; s of Frank Gapes, and Emily Gapes; *b* 4 September 1952; *Educ* Buckhurst Hill County HS, Fitzwilliam Coll Cambridge (MA), Middx Poly; *Career* VSO teacher Swaziland 1971–72, sec Cambridge Students' Union 1973–74, chm Nat Orgn of Lab Students 1976 (vice-chm 1975); Lab Pty: nat student organiser 1977–80, research offr Int Dept 1980–88, sr int offr 1988–92; Parly candidate (Lab) Ilford N 1983, MP (Lab/Co-op Pty) Ilford S 1992–; PPS to Paul Murphy, MP, *qv*, 1997–99, PPS to Rt Hon Lord Rooker, *qv*, 2001–02; chm Foreign Affairs Select Ctee 2005– (memb 1992–97), memb Defence Select Ctee 1999–2001; chm UN Parly Gp 1997–2001; vice-chair PLP Defence Ctee 1992–94 and 1996–97, chair PLP Children and Families Ctee 1993–94; chm Westminster Fndn for Democracy 2002–05; memb: Co-op Pty, TGWU; vice-pres Ilford Football Club; memb: RIIA 1996–, Cncl RIIA 1996–99, Cncl VSO 1997–; *Recreations* spending time with my daughter, watching football, blues and jazz music; *Clubs* West Ham Supporters', Ilford and Woodford Royal Airforce Assoc; *Style*— Mike Gapes, Esq, MP; ✉ House of Commons, London SW1A 0AA (tel 020 7219 6485, fax 020 7219 0978, e-mail gapesm@parliament.uk)

GARBUTT, Graham Bernard; s of Alfred Garbutt (d 1985), and Rhoda, *née* Jones (d 2002); *b* 16 June 1947; *Educ* Univ of Bath (BSc, BArch), Univ of Sheffield (MA); *m* 15 Nov 1986, Dr Lyda Jadresić, MD, da of Prof Alfredo Jadresić; 2 da, 1 s; *Career* urban renewal co-ordinator Haringey BC 1974–80, policy and prog planning offr Hackney BC 1980–87, dir S Canning Town and Custom House Project Newham BC 1987–90, chief exec Gloucester City Cncl 1990–2001, regnl dir Govt Office for W Midlands ODPM 2001–05, ceo Countryside Agency 2005–; England rep European Assoc of State Territorial Representatives 2002–05 (pres 2004–05); visiting lectr AA Grad Sch 1976–82; *Recreations* family, visual arts, architecture, cycling, garden; *Style*— Graham Garbutt, Esq; ✉ The Countryside Agency, John Dower House, Crescent Place, Cheltenham, Gloucestershire GL50 3RA (tel 01242 533492)

GARBUTT, Nicholas Martin Antony; s of Anthony Joseph Garbutt, of Manchester, and Norah, *née* Payne; *b* 21 June 1959; *Educ* Xaverian Coll Manchester, Oriel Coll Oxford (BA, Judo half blue); *m* 3 Sept 1988, Frances, da of Francis Burscough, of Preston; *Career* journalist; reporter: Ashton-under-Lyme Reporter 1980–83, Chester Evening Leader 1983–84, Telegraph and Argus Bradford 1984; mgmnt trainee Liverpool Echo 1987–88 (reporter 1984–87), news ed Daily Post Liverpool 1988–89, asst ed Sunday Tribune Dublin 1989–90, ed The Irish News Belfast 1990–94, dep ed Belfast Telegraph 1994–96, dir of business devpt Belfast Telegraph Newspapers 1996–99, head of corp relations for Ireland Nat Australia Bank 1999, head of corp relations for Europe Nat Australia Bank 2000–02, md Asitis Consulting 2004–; *Recreations* study of Irish History and Culture, martial arts; *Style*— Nicholas Garbutt, Esq

GARDAM, David Hill; QC (1968); s of Harry Hill Gardam (d 1929), and Cecilia Clara, *née* Winkworth (d 1972); *b* 14 August 1922; *Educ* Oundle, Univ of Oxford (MA); *m* 20 April 1954, Jane Mary Gardam, FRSL, *qv*, da of William Pearson (d 1989); 2 s (Timothy David, *qv*, b 1956, Thomas Hugh b 1965), 1 da (Catharine Mary Louise b 1958); *Career* served RNVR 1941–46 (temp Lt 1945); called to the Bar Inner Temple 1949, bencher 1978–; *Recreations* painting, printmaking; *Style*— David Gardam, Esq, QC; ✉ 1 Atkin Chambers, Gray's Inn, London WC1R 5BQ (tel 020 7404 0102, fax 020 7405 7456)

GARDAM, Jane Mary; da of William Pearson (d 1988), of Coatham, N Yorkshire, and Kathleen Mary, *née* Helm (d 1988); *b* 11 July 1928; *Educ* Saltburn HS for Girls, Bedford Coll London; *m* 20 April 1954, David Hill Gardam, QC, *qv*, s of Harry Hill Gardam; 2 s (Tim, *qv*, b 1956, Thomas b 1965), 1 da (Catharine b 1958); *Career* novelist; travelling librarian Red Cross Hospital Libraries 1951, sub ed Weldon's Ladies Jl 1952, asst literary ed Time and Tide 1952–54; memb Ctee: NSPCC, PEN; HonDLitt Univ of Teesside 2002; FRSL 1976–81; *Novels* A Long Way from Verona (1971), The Summer After the Funeral (1973), Bilgewater (1977), God on the Rocks (1978), The Hollow Land (1981, Whitbread Award), Bridget and William (1981), Horse (1982), Kit (1983), Crusoe's Daughter (1985), Kit in Boots (1986), Swan (1987), Through The Doll's House Door (1987), The Queen of the Tambourine (1991, Whitbread Award), Faith Fox (1996), The Green Man (1998), The Flight of the Maidens (2001), Old Filth (2005); short stories: A Few Fair Days (1971), Black Faces, White Faces (1975, David Highams Award, Winifred Holtby Award), The Sidmouth Letters (1980), The Pangs of Love (1983, Katherine Mansfield Award 1984), Showing The Flag (1989), Going in to a Dark House (1994, PEN Silver Pen Award), Missing the Midnight (1997); *Non-Fiction* The Iron Coast (1994); *Recreations* botanical; *Clubs* Arts, PEN, University Women's; *Style*— Jane Gardam; ✉ Haven House, Sandwich, Kent CT13 9ES (tel office 01304 612680)

GARDAM, Timothy David; s of David Hill Gardam, QC, of Sandwich, and Jane Gardam, FRSL, *qqv*, *née* Pearson; *b* 14 January 1956; *Educ* Westminster, Gonville & Caius Coll Cambridge (MA); *m* Kim Scott (d 2002), da of Capt Gordon Walwyn, RN, CVO, of Warblington; 1 da; *Career* BBC: trainee 1977, prodr Newsnight 1979–82, exec prodr Timewatch 1982–85, exec prodr Bookmark 1984–85, output ed Newsnight 1985–86, dep ed Gen Election 1987, ed Panorama 1987–90, ed Newsnight 1990–93, head of weekly progs News & Current Affrs 1994–96; controller of news, current affairs and documentaries Channel 5 Broadcasting 1996–98, dir of progs Channel Four TV 1998–2002, dir of TV Channel Four 2002–03; princ St Anne's Coll Oxford 2004–, chair Reuters Inst for the Study of Journalism Univ of Oxford; non-exec dir SMG plc until 2007; dir Oxford Playhouse Tst; *Recreations* gardening, ruins; *Style*— Timothy Gardam, Esq; ✉ St Anne's College, Oxford OX2 6HS

GARDEN, Dr (David) Graeme; s of Robert Symon Garden (d 1982), of Preston, Lancs, and Janet Anne, *née* McHardy; *b* 18 February 1943; *Educ* Repton, Emmanuel Coll Cambridge (BA), King's Coll Hosp (MB BChir); *m* 1, 16 March 1968 (m dis 1981), (Mary) Elizabeth, da of Clive Wheatley Grice (d 1979); 1 s (John b 9 June 1975), 1 da (Sally b 2 April 1971); m 2, 12 Feb 1983, Emma, da of John David Valentine Williams; 1 s (Thomas b 2 Dec 1984); *Career* actor and writer; writer and performer: I'm Sorry I'll Read That Again (radio), I'm Sorry I Haven't A Clue (radio), The Goodies (TV), Do Go On (radio), The Motion Show (radio), If I Ruled the World (TV); writer for TV with Bill Oddie: Doctor In The House, Doctor At Large, The Astronauts; presenter Bodymatters BBC TV;

theatre: NT, Royal Court, Royal Exchange Manchester, Cambridge Theatre Co; author: The Magic Olympical Games (NT), Horse and Carriage (play); writer and dir trg films Video Arts; *Books* The Seventh Man (1981), The Skylighters (1987), Stovold's Mornington Crescent Almanac (2002); *Recreations* TV, fishing; *Style*— Dr Graeme Garden; ✉ c/o Emma Darrell Management, North Vale, Shire Lane, Chorleywood, Hertfordshire WD3 5NH (tel 01923 284061, fax 01923 284064)

GARDEN, Prof (Olivier) James; s of late James Garden, OBE, of Lanark, and Marguerite Marie Jeanne, *née* Vourc'h; *b* 13 November 1953; *Educ* Lanark GS, Univ of Edinburgh (BSc, MB ChB, MD); *m* 15 July 1977, Amanda Gillian, da of late Austin Merrills, OBE, of Dunbar; 1 s (Stephen James b 21 July 1988), 1 da (Katherine Laura b 13 Aug 1991); *Career* lectr in surgery Univ Dept of Surgery Glasgow Royal Infirmary 1985–88, chef de clinique Unit de Chrurgie Hepatobiliare Hôpital Paul Brousse Villejuif France 1986–87; Univ Dept of Surgery Royal Infirmary Edinburgh: sr lectr in surgery 1988–97, prof of hepatobiliary surgery 1997–2000, regius prof of clinical surgery 2000–; clinical dir Scottish Liver Transplant Unit Royal Infirmary Edinburgh 1994–, head Sch of Clinical Sciences and Community Health Univ of Edinburgh 2002–06; surgn to HM The Queen in Scotland 2004–; co sec and dir Br Jl of Surgery Soc Ltd 2003–; FRCSGlas 1981, FRCSEd 1994, FRCPEd 2003, Hon FRACS 2007; *Books* Principles and Practice of Surgical Laparoscopy (1994), Intraoperative and Laparoscopic Ultrasonography (1995), Color Atlas of Surgical Diagnosis (1995), A Companion to Specialist Surgical Practice (7 vols, 1997, 3 edn 2005), Liver Metastasis: Biology, Diagnosis and Treatment (1998), Principles and Practice of Surgery (5 edn, 2007); *Recreations* golf, skiing, food, wine; *Style*— Prof James Garden; ✉ University Department of Surgery, The Royal Infirmary, Edinburgh EH16 4SA (tel 0131 242 3614, fax 0131 242 3617, e-mail ojgarden@ed.ac.uk)

GARDEN, Ralph; s of George Garden (d 1996), and Phillippa Mary, *née* Hills; *b* 21 April 1950; *Educ* Robert Gordon's Coll Aberdeen, Univ of Aberdeen (MA); *m* 1978, Katharine Margaret, da of Patrick Linton; 2 s (Philip b 1982, David b 1986), 1 da (Kay b 1983); *Career* various positions rising to client services dir Scottish Widows 1972–96, with Govt Actuary's Dept 1997–98, chief exec Scottish Public Pensions Agency 1998–2005, head of facilities and estates Scottish Exec 2005–; FFA; *Recreations* golf, curling, hill walking; *Style*— Ralph Garden, Esq; ✉ Scottish Executive, Saughton House, Broomhouse Road, Edinburgh EH11 3XD (tel 0131 244 4261, e-mail ralph.garden@scotland.gsi.gov.uk)

GARDINER, Barry; MP; *b* 10 March 1957; *Educ* Glasgow HS, Haileybury, Univ of St Andrews, Harvard Univ (J F Kennedy scholar), Univ of Cambridge (MA); *m* 29 July 1979, Caroline, *née* Smith; 3 s, 1 da; *Career* former int company dir, MP (Lab) Brent N 1997–; PPS to Beverley Hughes, MP, *qv*, 2002–06, Parly under sec of state DEFRA 2006–; chair: All-Pty Parly Gp on Leasehold Reform, All-Pty Gp on Sports and Leisure, All-Pty Gp on Olympics, Public Accounts Select Ctee; Cambridge City Cncl: cncllr 1988–94, sometime fin chm and mayor; *Recreations* singing, playing music with children, bird watching, hill walking; *Style*— Barry Gardiner, Esq, MP; ✉ House of Commons, London SW1A 0AA (tel 020 7219 4046, e-mail gardinerb@parliament.uk, website www.barrygardiner.com)

GARDINER, David Alfred William; DL (Berks 1992); s of Neil William Gardiner (d 1973), of Burghfield Common, Berks, and Norah, *née* Clegg (d 1963); *b* 11 April 1935; *Educ* Winchester, Imperial Coll London, Harvard Business Sch; *m* 1963, Carolyn Georgina, da of Thomas Humphrey Naylor (d 1966), of Ashton, Chester; 2 s (James b 1965, Andrew b 1971), 1 da (Georgina (Mrs Charles Mullins) b 1968); *Career* Lt Grenadier Gds 1953–55; dir Huntley & Palmers Ltd and associated cos 1961–83; farmer and landowner; High Sheriff Berks 1988–89; chm Berks CLA 1989–92, pres Newbury and Royal Co of Berks Show 1993, chm Mid and W Berks Local Access Forum 2003–05; fndr-chm Green Lanes Environmental Action Movement (GLEAM) 1995–, fndr vice-chm Green Lanes Protection Gp 2005–; *Recreations* field sports; *Style*— David Gardiner, Esq, DL; ✉ The Old Rectory, Lilley, Newbury, Berkshire RG20 7HH (tel and fax 01488 638227, e-mail dawgardiner@aol.com)

GARDINER, Gavin Thomas; s of George Gardiner (d 1965), of Wellington, NZ, and Constance Gardiner (d 1991); *Educ* Wellington Coll, Univ of Otago, St Bartholomew's Hosp London; *Career* sr registrar oral surgery: Royal Dental Hosp, St George's Hosp, Royal Surrey Co Hosp Guildford; conslt oral and maxillofacial surgn 1979–: Mt Vernon Hosp, Hillingdon Hosp, Northwick Park Hosp; fell Br Assoc of Oral and Maxillofacial Surgns, FRSM; *Recreations* golf, opera, music; *Style*— Gavin Gardiner, Esq; ✉ 1 The Dell, Pinner, Middlesex HA5 3EW (tel 020 8868 2161, e-mail tigergardiner@aol.com); Department of Oral and Maxillofacial Surgery, Hillingdon Hospital, Uxbridge, Middlesex

GARDINER, Sir John Eliot; kt (1998), CBE (1990); s of Rolf Gardiner, and Marabel, *née* Hodgkin; *b* 20 April 1943; *Educ* Bryanston, King's Coll Cambridge (MA), King's Coll London; *m* 1, 1981 (m dis 1997), Elizabeth Suzanne, *née* Wilcock; 3 da; m 2, 2001, Isabella de Sabata; *Career* conductor; studied with Thurston Dart 1965–66 and Nadia Boulanger in Paris 1967–68; fndr and artistic dir: Monteverdi Choir 1964, Monteverdi Orchestra 1968, English Baroque Soloists 1978, Orchestre Révolutionnaire et Romantique 1990; youngest conductor Henry Wood Promenade concert Royal Albert Hall 1968; concert debut Wigmore Hall 1966; operatic debut: Sadler's Wells Opera London Coliseum 1969, Royal Festival Hall 1972, Royal Opera House 1973, Vienna Philharmonic 1995, Glyndebourne, London Philharmonic, London Symphony, Berlin Philharmonic 1997, Zurich Opera 1998; guest conductor with maj orchestras in: Amsterdam, Paris, Brussels, Geneva, Frankfurt, Dresden, Leipzig, London, Vienna, Berlin; US/Canadian debuts: Dallas Symphony 1981, San Francisco Symphony 1982, Carnegie Hall NY 1988, Toronto Symphony 1988, Boston Symphony 1991, Cleveland Orchestra 1992; Euro music festivals incl: Aix-en-Provence, Aldeburgh, Bath, Berlin, Edinburgh, Flanders, Holland, City of London, Lucerne, Salzburg, BBC Proms; revived works of: Purcell, Handel, Rameau (world stage première of opera Les Boréades in Aix-en-Provence 1982), Berlioz (world première of Messe Solenelle at Westminster Cathedral 1993); princ conductor: CBC Vancouver Orchestra 1980–83, NDR Symphony Orchestra Hamburg 1991–94; Opéra de Lyon: musical dir 1982–88, chef fondateur 1988; artistic dir: Göttingen Handel Festival 1981–90, Veneto Music Festival 1986; performed, recorded and broadcast Bach Cantata Pilgrimage with Monteverdi Choir and English Baroque Soloists 1999–2000; has made over 200 recordings; Hon DUniv Lumière de Lyon 1987; Commandeur de l'Ordre des Arts et des Lettres (France) 1997 (Officier 1988); hon fell King's Coll London 1992, Hon RAM 1992; *Awards* Grand Prix du Disque 1978, 1979, 1980 and 1992, Prix Caecilia 1982, 1983 and 1985, Edison award 1982, 1986, 1987, 1988, 1989, 1996 and 1997, Arturo Toscanini Music Critics award 1985 and 1986, Nat Acad of Recording Arts and Sciences nominations 1986, 1987, 1989, 1997, 2000 and 2001, Deutscher Schallplattenpreis 1986, 1994 and 1997, IRCA prize Helsinki 1987, 15 Gramophone awards incl Record of the Year 1991 and Artist of the Year 1994, Conductor of the Year Cannes Classical Music Awards 1995, Handel Halle Prize 2001, Robert Schumann Prize 2001, La Medalla Internacional Complutense Madrid Univ 2001; *Recreations* forestry, organic farming; *Style*— Sir John Eliot Gardiner, CBE; ✉ c/o Askonas Holt, Lonsdale Chambers, 27 Chancery Lane, London WC2A 1PF

GARDINER, Prof John Graham; s of William Clement Gardiner (d 2003), of Ilkley, W Yorks, and Ellen, *née* Adey (d 1976); *b* 24 May 1939; *Educ* King Edward VI GS Birmingham, Univ of Birmingham (BSc, PhD); *m* 29 Dec 1962, Sheila Joyce, da of Cecil Walter Andrews (d 1958); 2 da (Tabitha Jane b 19 July 1966, Emily Josephine 12 Dec 1972), 1 s (Benjamin John b 21 Oct 1967); *Career* pre-univ apprenticeship GEC Coventry 1957–58, Racal postdoctoral research fell Univ of Birmingham 1964–66, software engr Racal Research Ltd Tewkesbury 1966–68, sr engr Racal (Slough) Ltd 1968; Univ of Bradford: lectr 1968–72, sr lectr 1972–78, reader in electronic engrg 1978–86, chm Postgrad Sch of Info Systems Engrg 1984–88, prof of electronic engrg 1986–, head Dept of Electronic and Electrical Engrg 1993–96, dean of engrg and physical scis 1996–2002, dir Centre for Industrial Collaboration 2006–; dir: Aerial Facilities Ltd 1974–90, Nortel (Communications) Ltd 1976–96, Aerial Group Ltd 1990–97, Compec Ltd 1996–, Ventures & Consultancy Bradford Ltd 1996–2005; conslt: Telecommunications Div DTI 1987–96, EC DG XIII 1988–91 and 1994; nat co-ordinator Link Personal Communications Programme 1987–93, chm Professional Gp E8 IEE 1990–93; CEng 1971, MIERE 1971, FIEE 1984 (MIEE 1971), FREng 1994, SMIEEE 1996, FRSA 1996; *Books* Mobile Communication Systems (with J D Parsons, 1989), Personal Communication Systems (with B West, 1995); *Recreations* music - occasionally performing, but mostly, these days, listening; *Style*— Prof John Gardiner, FREng; ✉ 1 Queen's Drive Lane, Ilkley, West Yorkshire LS29 9QS (tel 01943 609581); School of Engineering, Design and Technology, University of Bradford, Richmond Road, Bradford BD7 1DP (tel 01274 234003, fax 01274 234124, mobile 07968 756477, e-mail j.g.gardiner@bradford.ac.uk)

GARDINER, John Ralph; QC (1982); *b* 28 February 1946; *Educ* Bancroft's Sch Woodford, Fitzwilliam Coll Cambridge (MA, LLM); *Career* called to the Bar Middle Temple 1968 (Harmsworth scholar, bencher); practising barr specialising in revenue law, currently head of chambers 11 New Square; supervisor in law Univ of Cambridge 1968–72; memb Bar Cncl 1982–86, treas Senate of Inns of Court and Bar Cncl 1985–86; memb Revenue Bar Assoc; *Style*— John Gardiner, Esq, QC; ✉ 11 New Square, Lincoln's Inn, London WC2A 3QB

GARDINER, Dr Julie Patricia; da of Norman Arthur Gardiner, of Warminster, Wiltshire, and Jean Margaret, *née* Driver; *b* 9 March 1958; *Educ* High Wycombe HS for Girls, Univ of Reading (BA, PhD); *m* 1, 1981 (m dis 1994), John Arthur Davies; m 2, 1998, Michael John Allen; *Career* freelance archaeologist (projects incl E Hants field survey, Cranborne Chase project, Hengistbury Head) 1983–84, asst then managing ed E Anglian Archaeology Norfolk Archaeological Unit 1984–89, managing ed Cncl for British Archaeology 1989–91, reports mangr Wessex Archaeology 1991–; dir Prehistoric Society Ltd 1991–; Prehistoric Soc: memb Cncl, ed PAST newsletter 1991–94, ed Proceedings 1994– (asst ed 1993); memb Inst of Field Archaeologists 1986 (ed Occasional Papers series 1991–93); FSA, MIFA; *Publications* Archaeology of the Mary Rose (Vols 1–5, 2003); author and ed of numerous articles and monographs incl definitive account of excavations of Stonehenge (1995); *Recreations* gardening, art, cinema, walking; *Style*— Dr Julie Gardiner, FSA; ✉ Wessex Archaeology Ltd, Portway House, Old Sarum Park, Salisbury, Wiltshire SP4 6EB (tel 01722 326867, fax 01722 337562, e-mail j.gardiner@wessexarch.co.uk)

GARDNER, *see also:* Bruce-Gardner

GARDNER, Brenda Ann Ellen; da of Michael Sweedish (d 1999), of Canada, and Flora, *née* Gibb; *b* 1 June 1947; *Educ* Univ of Saskatchewan (BA, BEd), Washington Univ; *m* 1968, (James) Douglas Gardner (d 1986), s of James Gardner; *Career* teacher USA and UK 1968–72, asst ed Penguin Books 1972–77; ed: W H Allen 1977–79, E J Arnold 1979–81, Evans 1981–83; md and chair Piccadilly Press 1983–; chair Children's Book Circle 1981–82; chair Mgmnt Ctee Castlehaven Community Assoc, memb Ctee for Ind Publishers Guild; winner Women in Publishing Pandora Award 1999; *Recreations* reading, aerobics, swimming, tennis, yoga, theatre, films; *Clubs* Groucho; *Style*— Ms Brenda Gardner; ✉ Piccadilly Press, 5 Castle Road, London NW1 8PR (tel 020 7267 4492, fax 020 7267 4493, e-mail b.gardner@piccadillypress.co.uk)

GARDNER, Brian Patrick; s of late T C Gardner, CBE, of Whittlesford, Cambs, and B T Gardner; *b* 17 July 1948; *Educ* St George's Coll Harare, Beaumont Coll, Univ of Oxford (MA, BM BCh); *m* 18 Oct 1980, Stephanie Catherine Mary, da of Dr Faller (d 1980); 5 da (Catherine b 1982, Laura b 1984, Annabelle b 1989, Edel b 1991, Felicity b 1998), 4 s (Paul b 1983, Martin b 1988, Benedict b 1994, Liam b 1996); *Career* various jr med posts 1974–79, registrar in neurosurgery Royal Victoria Hosp Belfast 1980–82, sr registrar in spinal injuries Mersey Regnl Spinal Cord Injuries Centre Southport 1982–85, conslt surgn in spinal injuries Nat Spinal Injuries Centre 1985–; memb BMA; FRCS 1980, FRCP 1995 (MRCP 1978), FRCPEd 1996; *Recreations* tennis, family, walking; *Style*— Brian Gardner, Esq; ✉ 2 Northumberland Avenue, Aylesbury, Buckinghamshire HP21 7HG (tel 01296 423420, fax 01296 424627, e-mail bgardner@eidosnet.co.uk); National Spinal Injuries Centre, Stoke Mandeville Hospital, Aylesbury, Buckinghamshire HP21 8AL

GARDNER, Christopher James Ellis; QC (1994); s of James Charles Gardner (d 1984), of Dartmouth, and Phillis May, *née* Wilkinson; *b* 6 April 1945; *Educ* Rossall Sch, Fitzwilliam Coll Cambridge (MA); *m* 1972, Arlene Sellers; 1 s (Simon James b 19 Feb 1973), 1 da (Sophie Ruth b 16 Aug 1978); *Career* called to the Bar Gray's Inn (Lord Justice Holker sr exhibitioner) 1968, legal assessor to GMC and GDC, recorder of the Crown Court 1993–, head of Lamb Chambers Middle Temple; accredited mediator, chartered arbitrator; specialist in personal injury and clinical negligence litigation; memb Common Law, Professional Negligence and International Bar Assoc; co-chair Negligence and Damages Ctee of the International Bar Assoc; fell Soc for Advanced Legal Studies, FIArb, FRSM; *Recreations* open air theatre, bell ringing, golf, cooking curries; *Style*— Christopher Gardner, Esq, QC; ✉ Lamb Chambers, Lamb Building, Temple, London EC4Y 7AS (tel 020 7797 8300, fax 020 7797 8308)

GARDNER, Prof David; OBE (1995); s of Fred Gardner (d 1990), and Mary, *née* Anderson (d 1978); *b* 11 July 1941; *Educ* St Joseph's Coll Blackpool, Loughborough Univ of Technol (BTech, DLC, DSc, cricket colours); *m* April 1964, Hazel, da of late Harold Bailey; 1 s (Anthony Paul b 6 Sept 1974), 1 da (Sarah Louise b 7 april 1977); *Career* English Electric (became BAC, British Aerospace plc since 1986, now BAE Systems 1999): joined as apprentice 1959, asst engr rising to engr Aerodynamics Dept 1965 (res into wing design of Jaguar aircraft), sr engr 1968 (leading work into afterbody/engine installation aspects of MRCA), princ devpt engr 1974 (leading Aerodynamic Team on Tornado and for devpt of air defence variant), asst chief aerodynamicist then chief flight test project engr Tornado ADV 1979, project mangr Tornado 1981, exec dir Tornado 1983, exec dir aircraft projects 1984, tech dir (Warton) Mil Aircraft Div 1986; Mil Aircraft Div (formerly British Aerospace Defence Ltd): tech dir 1992–94, dep md and dir Euro Progs 1994–97; md Progs and dep md British Aerospace Military Aircraft and Aerostructures 1997–98, engrg dir British Aerospace plc 1998–99, gp engrg dir BAE Systems 1999–2001, ret; systems engrg dir Panavia GmbH Munich 1986–94, bd dir Eurofighter Jagdflugzeug GmbH, Panavia Aircraft GmbH and SEPECAT (managing Eurofighter, Tornado and Jaguar collaborative projects) 1992–98, conslt to Eurofighter GmbH 2002–04; non-exec dir NG Bailey Org 2002–; author of numerous papers on tech subjects and on int collaborations; industrial prof Dept of Tport Technol Loughborough Univ of Technol 1991–, memb Weapon System Bd Def Scientific Advsy Cncl 1992–98, pres Preston Branch RAeS 1990–97; vice-chllr Virtual Univ 2000–01; FRAeS (Gold Medal 1995), FREng 1992, FRSA 1995; *Recreations* golf, gardening, theatre, cricket and motor racing; *Clubs* Fairhaven Golf; *Style*— Prof David Gardner, OBE, FREng

GARDNER, Dr David Alan; s of John Lawrence Gardner (d 1997), and Alice Winifred, *née* Cattermole; *b* 29 April 1938; *Educ* Minchenden Sch Southgate, Univ of Leeds; *m* 17 Sept 1966, Gillian Ann, da of Capt Edmund Patrick Flowers, of Bangor, N Wales; 4 da (Philippa b 1967, Amanda b 1969, Samantha b 1971, Jemima b 1974), 3 s (Leon b 1977, Oliver b 1980, Joshua b 1985); *Career* registrar Guy's Hosp London 1968–70, conslt pathologist Kensington Chelsea and Westminster Hosp 1973–74, conslt pathologist UCH 1974– (sr registrar 1971–73, sr lectr 1974–); chm: S Camden Pathology Ctee, NE Thames Regnl Biochemistry Ctee; memb NE Thames Regnl Scientific Ctee; FRCPath 1984 (MRCPath 1971), MRCS, LRCP; *Recreations* British campaign medals, golf; *Style*— Dr David Gardner; ✉ 200 Sandridge Road, St Albans, Hertfordshire AL1 4AL (tel 01727 862019); Department of Chemical Pathology, Windeyer Building, Cleveland Street, London W1T 4JF (tel 020 7504 9235, fax 020 7504 9496, e-mail dagardner@ntlworld.com)

GARDNER, Douglas Frank; s of Lt Ernest Frank Gardner (decd), and Mary, *née* Chattington (decd); *b* 20 December 1943; *Educ* Woolverstone Hall, Coll of Estate Mgmnt, Univ of London (BSc); *m* 5 Sept 1968, Adèle, da of Maj Charles Macmillan Alexander, 1 s (Mark b 1972), 2 da (Teresa b 1971, Amy b 1979); *Career* chief exec Properties Div Tarmac plc 1976–83; Brixton Estate plc: md 1983–93, chm 1993–2000, chm Brixton Investments Ltd and Brixton France SA; chm: Industrial Devpt Partnership II 2000–, Industrial Realisation plc 2000–, Nuffield Hospitals 2001– (govr 1995–), Halverton REIM LLP 2004– (also founding ptnr); dir: INVESCO UK Property Income Tst Ltd 2004–, Hirco plc 2006–; memb Investment Ctee European Industrial Partnership; FRICS; *Recreations* tennis; *Style*— Douglas Gardner, Esq; ✉ Halverton Real Estate Investment Management Limited, Birchin Court, 20 Birchin Lane, London EC3V 9DJ; Nuffield Hospitals, Nuffield House, 1–4 The Crescent, Surbiton, Surrey KT6 4BN

GARDNER, Douglas James; s of John Preston Gardner, of North Ferriby, E Yorks, and Elizabeth Humphrey, *née* McGinn; *b* 15 December 1961, Southampton; *Educ* South Hunsley Sch, Hull UC; *m* 7 Sept 1985, Susan Jacqueline; 2 s (Daniel Charles Douglas b 21 Sept 1987, Lewis James Matthew b 25 Sept 1990), 1 da (Amelia Claire b 26 Dec 1997); *Career* early career with Halifax, Royal Insurance and Minet Benefit Conslts, joined Thomson's Fin Planning Consts Ltd Leeds office 1988 (led mgmnt buyout 1997), ceo Thomson's Gp plc 1997–, ceo AWD plc 2001–05; dir Positive Solutions plc 2006–; memb Practitioner Panel Fin Servs Authy, dir Assoc of Ind Fin Advsrs (AIFA); MCII, MLIA; *Recreations* sports incl golf, tennis and walking, family, holidays, art, wine and food, books; *Clubs* Hessle Golf; *Style*— Douglas Gardner, Esq; ✉ Cliffe Lodge, North Cliffe, Hotham YO43 4XE (tel 07775 588835, e-mail douglas_gardner@btinternet.com)

GARDNER, John Linton; CBE (1976); s of Capt Alfred Linton Gardner, RAMC (ka 1918), of Ilfracombe, Devon, and Muriel, *née* Pullein-Thompson (d 1998); *b* 2 March 1917; *Educ* Wellington, Exeter Coll Oxford; *m* 1955, Jane Margaret Mary (d 1998), da of late Nigel James Abercrombie, of Ringmer, Lewes, E Sussex; 1 s, 2 da; *Career* composer; chief music master Repton 1939–40, on music staff Royal Opera House 1946–52, prof of harmony and composition Royal Acad of Music 1956–86; dir of music: St Paul's Girls' Sch 1962–75, Morley Coll 1965–69; dep chm Performing Rights Soc 1983–88; *Compositions incl* the opera The Moon and Sixpence, three symphonies, three string quartets, concertos for piano, oboe, trumpet, flute and organ, many large-scale choral works; *Recreations* tesseraphily; *Style*— John Gardner, Esq, CBE; ✉ 20 Firswood Avenue, Ewell, Epsom, Surrey KT19 0PR

GARDNER, Prof Julian; *b* 6 May 1940; *Educ* Balliol Coll Oxford (BA), Courtauld Inst of Art (Dip History of Art, PhD), British Sch at Rome (Rivoira Scholar); *Career* lectr Courtauld Inst of Art 1966–74; Univ of Warwick: fndn prof in the history of art 1974–2006, pro-vice-chllr 1987–91 and 1995–98, sometime memb numerous ctees and policy gps; dir AHRB Centre for the Study of Renaissance Élites and Court Cultures 2002–05; visiting research prof: Max-Planck-Gesellschaft Bibliotheca Hertziana Rome 1983–85 and 1992, Kuratorium Kunsthistorisches Institut Florence 1993–2003, Institut Nationale d' Histoire de l'Art Paris 1999–; distinguished visiting prof of mediaeval studies Univ of Calif Berkeley 2000, visiting prof Harvard Univ 2003, visiting prof Harvard Univ Center for Italian Renaissance Studies Villa e Tatti Florence 2005–06; British Library: chm Standing Ctee on Art Documentation, memb Advsy Bd Humanities and Social Scis; membre titulaire Comité Internationale d'Histoire de l'Art 1990–2000; memb Editorial Bd: Burlington Magazine, Arte Cristiana, Italian Mediaeval & Renaissance Studies, Perspective; FSA 1977; *Books* The Tomb and the Tiara. Curial tomb sculpture in Italy & Avignon 1200–1400 (1992), Patrons, Painters and Saints (1993); *Style*— Prof Julian Gardner, FSA; ✉ History of Art Department, University of Warwick, Coventry, Warwickshire CV4 7AL (tel 024 7652 8339, fax 024 7652 3006, e-mail julian.gardner@warwick.ac.uk)

GARDNER, Prof Sir Richard Lavenham; kt (2005); s of Allan Constant Gardner (d 1943), of Beare Green, Surrey, and Eileen May Alexander, *née* Clarke (d 1961); *b* 10 June 1943; *Educ* St John's Leatherhead, St Catharine's Coll Cambridge (BSc); *m* 14 Dec 1968, Wendy Joy, da of Charles Hampton Trevelyan Cresswell (d 1989), of Cobham, Surrey; 1 s (Matthew Thomas b 18 April 1985); *Career* research asst Physiological Laboratory Univ of Cambridge 1969–73, lectr Dept of Zoology Univ of Oxford 1973–77, student ChCh Oxford 1974–, Henry Dale research prof Royal Soc 1978–2003, Edward Penley Abraham research prof Royal Soc 2003–, hon dir Developmental Biology Unit ICRF 1985–96; pres Inst of Biology 2006–; ind memb Advsy Bd for the Research Cncls 1990–93; Scientific Medal Zoological Soc of London 1977, March of Dimes Prize in Developmental Biology 1999, Royal Medal Royal Soc 2001, Albert Brachet Prize Belgian Royal Acad of Sciences, Letters and Fine Arts 2004; memb Academia Europaea 1989; FRS 1979; *Recreations* sailing, painting, ornithology, gardening; *Style*— Prof Sir Richard Gardner, FRS; ✉ Department of Zoology, South Parks Road, Oxford OX1 3PS (tel 01865 281312, fax 01865 281310)

GARDNER, Dr Rita Ann Moden; CBE (2003); da of John William Gardner, of Holsworthy, N Devon, and Evelyn, *née* Moden; *b* 10 November 1955; *Educ* Huntingdon GS, UCL (BSc), Wolfson Coll Oxford (DPhil); *partner* 1982–, Dr Martin Eugene Frost; *Career* lectr in geography KCL 1979–94, dir Environmental Sci Unit and reader in environmental sci Queen Mary & Westfield Coll London 1994–96, dir and sec RGS (with Inst of Br Geographers) 1996–; sec-gen EUGEO (European Geographical Socs Cncl) 2002–; author numerous papers in academic jls; memb: Environment Advsy Panel Royal Soc, Benchmarking Steering Gp QAA (Quality and Assurance Agency of the HE Funding Cncl for Eng) 2003–07, Sci, Engrg and Environment Advsy Ctee Br Cncl 2002–07, Archives Task Force Dept for Culture Media & Sport 2002–04, Steering Gp for Humanities Specialist Schs Specialist Schs Tst 2003–, Educn and Governance Advsy Gp Br Cncl 2007–; non-political advsr on geography to Dept for Children, Schs and Families 2006–; tstee WWF-UK 2001–04; awarded Busk Medal (for contribs to geomorphology) 1995; Hon Dr: Univ of Gloucester 2003, Univ of Southampton 2004; hon fell QMC 2002; FRGS 1979; *Books* Mega-Geomorphology (1981), Landshapes (1986), Landscape in England and Wales (1994); *Recreations* contemporary architecture, gardening, travel, good food and wine; *Style*— Dr Rita Gardner, CBE; ✉ Royal Geographical Society (with IBG), 1 Kensington Gore, London SW7 2AR (tel 020 7591 3010, fax 020 7591 3011, e-mail r.gardner@rgs.org)

GARDNER, Sir Roy Alan; kt (2002); s of Roy Thomas Gardner (d 2000), and Iris Joan (d 1999); *b* 20 August 1945; *Educ* Strode's Sch Egham; *m* 1969, Carol Ann, *née* Barker; 1s, 2 da; *Career* accountant Concorde Project BAC Ltd 1963–75, fin dir Marconi Space & Defence Systems Ltd 1975–1984, fin dir Marconi Co Ltd 1984–85, exec dir STC plc 1986–91, md STC Communications plc 1989–91, chief operating offr Northern Telecom Europe Ltd 1991–92, md GEC Marconi Ltd 1992–94, exec dir British Gas plc 1994–97, chief exec Centrica plc 1997–2006; chm: Manchester United plc 2001–05 (non-exec dir 2000–05), Compass Gp 2006– (non-exec dir 2005–); non-exec dir Laporte plc 1996–2001; sr advsr Credit Suisse 2006–; pres Carers UK, chm Nat Modern Apprenticeship Task Force 2003–05, chm Apprenticeship Ambassadors Network, pres Energy Inst 2007; tstee Devpt Tst 1997–; CIMgt, FRSA, FCCA 1980, FRAeS 1992; *Recreations* golf, running; *Clubs* Annabel's, Brooks's, Mark's; *Style*— Sir Roy Gardner

GARDNER, Dr William Norman; s of Norman Charles Gardner (d 1979), of Sydney, Aust, and Ngaire Jean, *née* Dawson (d 1995); *b* 24 January 1943; *Educ* Penrith HS, Univ of Sydney (MB BS), Univ of Oxford (DPhil); *m* 1, 1971 (m dis 1974), Lydia, *née* Sinclair (d 1999); m 2, 1981, Jane Elizabeth, da of Alan Maurice Stainer (d 1990), of Kidlington, Oxon; 3 s (Timothy b 1981, Nicholas b 1985, Joseph b 1988); *Career* med house appts Sydney and Royal Adelaide Hosps 1966–68, sr house appt Brompton, London Chest and Westminster Hosps 1969–71, Wellcome grad student then MRC res offr Dept of Physiology and then Nuffield Inst Oxford 1971–80, memb Wolfson Coll Oxford until 1983, sr lectr and hon conslt physician King's Coll Sch of Med 1987–99 (lectr in med Dept of Thoracic Med 1981–87), conslt physician Eastbourne District Gen Hosp 2006–; reader and hon conslt physician GKT Sch of Medicine 1999–2004; Euro Respiratory Soc: chm Control of Breathing Gp 1993–95, head Clinical Physiology Assembly 1995–97; memb Br Thoracic Soc 1981; author of various articles on respiratory and foetal physiology, respiratory med and hyperventilation syndromes; FRCP 1991 (MRCP 1971); *Recreations* piano, sailing; *Style*— Dr William Gardner; ✉ 92 Holmdene Avenue, London SE24 9LE (tel 07710 641261, e-mail william.gardner@esht.nhs.uk)

GARDNER OF PARKES, Baroness (Life Peer UK 1981), of Southgate in Greater London, and of Parkes in the State of New South Wales and Commonwealth of Australia; (Rachel) Trixie Anne Gardner; AM, JP (N Westminster Inner London 1971); da of Hon (John Joseph) Gregory McGirr (d 1949; MLA, NSW State Govt), and late Rachel, *née* Miller; *b* 17 July 1927; *Educ* Monte Sant Angelo Coll N Sydney, Univ of Sydney (BDS); *m* 1956, Kevin Anthony Gardner (d 2007, Lord Mayor of Westminster 1987–88), s of late George Gardner, of Sydney, Australia; 3 da (Hon Sarah Louise (Hon Mrs Joiner) b 1960, Hon Rachel Trixie (Hon Mrs Pope) b 1961, Hon Joanna Mary b 1964 (Hon Mrs Everett)); *Career* dental surgeon; memb: Westminster City Cncl 1968–78, GLC Havering 1970–73, Enfield-Southgate 1977–86; Parly candidate (Cons): Blackburn 1970, N Cornwall 1974; govr National Heart Hosp 1974–90, memb Industrial Tbnl Panel for London 1974–97, Br chm European Union of Women 1978–82, nat women's vice-chm Cons Party 1978–82, UK rep on UN Status of Women Cmmn 1982–88, memb LEB 1984–90; dir: Gateway Building Society 1987–88, Woolwich Building Society 1988–93; vice-pres: Bldg Socs Assoc 1985–90, Nat House Building Cncl 1990–2002; vice-chm NE Thames RHA 1990–94, UK chm Plan International 1989–2003, chm Suzy Lamplugh Tst 1993–96, chm Royal Free Hampstead NHS Tst 1994–97; tstee Parly Advsy Cncl on Tport Safety 1992–98; House of Lords: dep speaker 1999–2002, dep chm of Ctees, memb Info Select Ctee 2003–05, memb Delegated Powers Ctee 2005–; hon vice-pres Br Legion Women's Section 2003–; memb The Cook Soc UK 1993– (chm 1996); hon fell Univ of Sydney 2005; Hon Dr Middlesex Univ 1997; *Recreations* gardening, cooking, travel, historic buildings, family life; *Style*— The Rt Hon Baroness Gardner of Parkes, AM; ✉ House of Lords, London SW1A 0PW

GARDNER-THORPE, Dr Christopher; s of Col Sir Ronald Gardner-Thorpe, GBE, TD, JP (d 1991), and Hazel Mary St George, *née* Dees; *b* 22 August 1941; *Educ* St Philip's Sch London, Beaumont Coll, St Thomas' Hosp Med Sch London (MB BS), Univ of London (MD); *m* 1 April 1967 (m dis 1988), Sheelah, da of Dr Edward Irvine (d 1993), of Exeter; 2 s (Damian, James), 3 da (Catherine, Anne, Helen); *Career* conslt neurologist SW Regnl Health Authy (duties principally Exeter, Plymouth and N Devon) 1974–, hon tutor in neurology Post Grad Med Sch Univ of Exeter 1983–90; regnl advsr in neurology RCP Assoc of Br Neurologists 1997–; fndr chm Devon and Exeter Medico-Legal Soc 1996–, pres 2004–; memb Int League Against Epilepsy 1969–, fndr memb and hon tres SW Eng Neurosciences Assoc 1981–2001, fndr memb S Eng Neurosciences Assoc, memb Res Ctee of the World Fed of Neurology 1998–, sec and treas World Fedn of Neurology Research Gp on the History of the Neurosciences 1998–; memb: Harveian Soc 1966–, SW Physicians Club 1974–, Devon and Exeter Med Soc 1974– (hon asst sec 1978–81, hon sec 1981–85, hon reporting sec 1989–98, pres-elect 1998–99, pres 1999–2000, curator 2001–), chm of tstees and memb Advsy Ctee Northcott Devon Med Fndn, memb Med Soc of London 2001–; ed various books and papers on epilepsy and other neurological topics; fndr hon med advsr Devon Sports Assoc for the Disabled 1976–, memb Northumbrian Pipers Soc 1976–; OStJ 1980, HM Lieut City of London 1981; Freeman City of London 1978, Liveryman Worshipful Co of Barbers 1980; FRSM 1968, FRCP 1985, FACP 2001, FRSA 1997; *Publications* Antiepileptic Monitoring (chief ed, 1977), James Parkinson 1755–1824 (1987), Stones Unturned (2000), The Book of Princetown (2003); ed Jl of Medical Biography, author of various papers on epilepsy and other neurological topics; *Recreations* music, travel, reading, photography, sailing, walking, medical history; *Clubs* Savile; *Style*— Dr Christopher Gardner-Thorpe; ✉ The Coach House, 1A College Road, Exeter EX1 1TE (tel 01392 433941)

GAREL-JONES, Baron (Life Peer UK 1997), of Watford in the County of Hertfordshire; Rt Hon (William Armand Thomas) Tristan Garel-Jones; PC (1992); s of Bernard Garel-Jones, of Madrid, and Meriel, *née* Williams; *b* 28 February 1941; *Educ* King's Sch Canterbury; *m* 1966, Catalina, da of Mariano Garrigues, of Madrid; 4 s, 1 da; *Career* MP (Cons) Watford 1979–97; PPS to Barney Hayhoe 1981–82, asst Govt whip 1982–83, a Lord Cmmr of the Treasy 1983–86; HM Household: vice-chamberlain 1986–87, comptroller 1987–89, treas (dep chief whip) 1989–90; min of state for Europe FCO 1990–93; md UBS Investment Bank; *Recreations* collecting books; *Style*— The Rt Hon the Lord Garel-Jones, PC; ✉ House of Lords, London SW1A 0PW

GAREY, Prof Laurence John; *b* 18 July 1941, Peterborough; *Educ* Deacon's Sch Peterborough, Univ of Nottingham (state scholarship to read modern languages), Worcester Coll Oxford (Theodore Williams scholar in anatomy, MA), Dept of Human Anatomy Univ of Oxford (MRC trg scholar, DPhil, Rolleston meml prize), St Thomas' Hosp London (clinical scholar, BM BCh (Oxon)); *m*; 2 c; *Career* Reserve Offr (Pilot) Nottingham and Oxford Univ Air Sqdns RAF 1959–63; house offr in gen med Memorial Hosp Watford 1968; Univ of Oxford: departmental demonstrator Dept of Human Anatomy 1968–71, lectr Balliol and Merton Colls 1968–72, Schorstein research fell in med sci 1970–72; Sir Henry Wellcome travelling fell and visiting prof Dept of Physiology Univ of Calif Berkeley 1972–73; Univ of Lausanne: professeur asst Inst of Anatomy 1973–76, professeur associé Inst of Anatomy 1976–87, lectr Sch of Ergotherapy 1976–87; assoc prof Dept of Anatomy Nat Univ of Singapore 1987–90; Univ of London: prof and head Dept of Anatomy (Division of Neuroscience after merger) Imperial Coll Sch of Med at Charing Cross Hosp (Charing Cross and Westminster Med Sch until merger 1997) 1990–97, vice-pres Bd of Studies in Human Anatomy and Morphology 1993–95; prof and chm of Dept of Anatomy Faculty of Medicine and Health Sciences UAE Univ Al Ain 2000; currently chair Neuroscience Programmes Network Int Brain Research Orgn; visiting fell Aust Nat Univ Canberra 1982, visiting prof Faculty of Medicine Kuwait Univ 1999; memb Editorial Bd: Biological Signals 1990–97, Jl für Hirnforschung 1992–93, Jl of Brain Research 1994–2000, Int Jl of Diabetes and Metabolism 2001–; assessor: HE Funding Cncl for Wales 1997, Quality Assurance Agency for HE 1998–2000; memb Ctee of Admin Neurobiology Research Gp Nat Cncl for Scientific Research Marseille 1979; Inst of Neurophysiology and Psychophysiology Marseille: memb Ctee of Admin 1977–81, scientific dir Dept of Cellular Neurobiology 1982–84; memb: London Ctee of Licensed Teachers of Anatomy 1990–2000 (chm 1993–2000), Panel of Examiners RCPS(Ed) 1993–98, Ct of Examiners RCS 1992–99; memb: Acad of Med of Singapore, Afro-Asia

Oceania Assoc of Anatomists (memb Int Ctee 1988–), Anatomical Soc of GB and I (vice-pres 1994–), Assoc of Profs of the Univ of Lausanne (memb Ctee 1983–87), Aust Neuroscience Soc, Br Neuropathological Soc, Child Vision Research Soc, European Biomedical Research Assoc (fndr memb), European Brain and Behaviour Soc, European Neuroscience Assoc, Hong Kong Soc of Neurosciences, Int Brain Research Orgn (treas 1983–85), Nat Postgraduate Med Coll of Nigeria, NY Acad of Scis, Physiological Soc, RSM, Singapore Neuroscience Assoc (pres 1988–90), Soc for Neuroscience, Swiss Soc of Anatomists, Histologists and Embryologists, Swiss Soc of Cellular and Molecular Biology (vice-pres 1980–82), Union of Swiss Socs of Experimental Biology; hon memb Centre for Neuroscience UCL; *Books* Plastic and Reconstructive Surgery of the Orbitopalpebral Region (jtly, 1990); translations: Neuronal Man: The Biology of Mind (1985, 2 edn 1986), The Population Alternative (1986), Localisation in the Cerebral Cortex (1994), The Paradox of Sleep: The Story of Dreaming (1999, new edn 2001); author of various scientific articles on neuroanatomy; *Style—* Prof Laurence J Garey

GARFIELD, John Samuel; s of Montagu Garfield (d 1976), of Hove, E Sussex, and Marguerite, *née* Elman (d 1983); *b* 13 February 1930; *Educ* Bradfield Coll, Emmanuel Coll Cambridge (MA, MB MChir); *m* 6 Oct 1962, Agnes Clara Teleki, da of Count Joseph Teleki de Szek (d 1985), of Pomaz, Hungary; 3 da (Stephanie b 1963, Johanna Francoise b 1965, Marie-Claire b 1969); *Career* jr specialist med RAMC 1956–58, conslt neurosurgeon 1968, hon emeritus Univ of Southampton Trust Hosps 1992–; numerous pubns on neurosurgical and medico-legal topics; former pres Soc of Br Neurological Surgns, memb Cncl Med Def Union; former chm Wessex Regnl Med Advsy Ctee; photographer; exhibitions in London, Winchester, Brussels, Ypres and Birmingham 1980–98; currently photographing musicians; FRCS 1961, FRCP 1971; *Photographic Publications* The Fallen (1990 and 2003), The Eye, the Brain and the Camera (1993), History of EANS (1995), Rehearsal (2001), Teleki Houses in Transylvania and Hungary (2004), The Garden Gallery (2006); *Clubs* Athenaeum; *Style—* John Garfield, Esq; ✉ Keyhaven, Hadrian Way, Chilworth, Southampton SO16 7HY (tel 023 8076 7674)

GARFIELD, Simon Frank; s of Herbert Sidney Garfield (d 1973), and Hella Helene, *née* Meyer (d 1979); *b* 19 March 1960; *Educ* UCS Hampstead, LSE (BSc Econ); *m* 1987, Diane, da of Rubin Samuels; 2 c; *Career* sub ed Radio Times 1981, scriptwriter radio documentaries BBC 1981–82, ed Time Out magazine 1988–89 (writer 1982–88); news feature writer: Independent and Independent on Sunday newspapers 1990–96, Observer 2001–; Guardian/NUS Student Journalist of the Year 1981, BSME Ed of the Year (Time Out) 1989, Mind Journalist of the Year 2005; *Books* Expensive Habits: The Dark Side of the Music Industry (1986), The End of Innocence: Britain in the time of AIDS (1994, Somerset Maugham Prize 1995), The Wrestling (1996), The Nation's Favourite: The True Adventures of Radio 1 (1998), Mauve (2000), The Last Journey of William Huskisson (2002), Our Hidden Lives (2004), We Are At War (2005), Private Battles (2006); *Recreations* painting, music, poker, cricket, philately, Chelsea FC; *Clubs* Two Brydges Place; *Style—* Simon Garfield, Esq; ✉ c/o PFD, Drury House, 34–43 Russell Street, London WC2B 5HA (tel 020 7344 1000, e-mail info@simongarfield.com, website www.simongarfield.com)

GARFIT, (Charles) William Aikman; s of Brian Corringham Garfit (d 1997), of Harlton, Cambridge, and Myrtle Joan, *née* Robertson Aikman (d 1945); *b* 9 October 1944; *Educ* Bradfield Coll, Cambridge Sch of Art, Byam Shaw Sch of Art (scholar, Dip ILEA Cert), Royal Acad Sch of Art (Dip); *m* 23 July 1966, Georgina Margaret, da of Sir Norman Joseph, KCVO; 2 da (Jacquelyn Jean b 1969, Penelope Mina b 1971), 1 s (Henry Charles Joseph b 1975); *Career* artist specialising in river and water landscapes; work mostly by private commission since 1994 (incl commissions in UK, Iceland, Russia, USA, Brazil, France and Austria); monthly contrib Shooting Gazette 1995–; memb: Game Shooting Ctee BASC 1991–2002, Conservation Ctee Countryside Alliance 1998–2000, Judge Ctee Purdey Award 2002–; RBA 1976; *Solo Exhibitions* incl: Waterhouse Gall London 1970, 1972 and 1974, Mall Galls London 1976, Stacey Marks Gall Eastbourne 1978, Tryon Gall London 1981, 1983, 1985, 1988 and 1991, Holland & Holland London 1994; *Awards* Laurent Perrier Award for Wild Game and Conservation Mgmnt 1988; selected for inclusion in: Shooting Times First XI Game Shots 1990, Sporting Gun Top 10 Pigeon Shots 1998, Shooting Gazette - Britain's Top Shots 1999, The Field - The 50 Best Shots 2002; European 12 Bore Hammer Gun Champion 2001; *Publications* Conservation, Development and Management of Gravel Pits for Sports and Conservation (paper, 1983), Will's Shoot (book, 1993), Will's Shoot Revisited (2005); illustrator of over 30 country sporting, shooting and conservation books and magazines; *Recreations* wood pigeon and game shooting, game and conservation management, botany, ornithology; *Style—* William Garfit, Esq; ✉ The Old Rectory, Harlton, Cambridge CB23 1ES (tel 01223 262563, fax 01223 264523)

GARLAND, Gary John Richard; s of William Garland (d 1993), and Evelyn Jobson; *b* 26 August 1958, South Shields; *Educ* Westoe Comp, South Shields Marine Coll, Newcastle Poly, Inns of Court Sch of Law; *Career* called to the Bar Inner Temple 1989; asylum support adjudicator 2000–, UN int prosecutor KFOR-Kosovo 2000–01, sr war crimes prosecutor Int Criminal Tbnl for the former Yugoslavia (ICTY) The Hague 2001–03, cmmr Ind Police Complaints Cmmn (IPCC) 2003–, dep district judge 2004–, cmmr for complaints HM Revenue and Customs 2006–; memb Bar Cncl 1991–2000; *Recreations* swimming, travel, theatre, life; *Style—* Gary Garland, Esq; ✉ 16 Fairway Court, Greenesfield, Gateshead NE8 2AY (tel 0191 477 8175, e-mail gary@gjr2005.wanadoo.co.uk); Independent Police Complaints Commission, 90 High Holborn, London WC1V 6BH (tel 020 7166 3000, fax 020 7404 0438, e-mail gary.garland@ipcc.gsi.gov.uk)

GARLAND, Nicholas Withycombe; OBE (1998); s of Thomas Ownsworth Garland, and Margaret, *née* Withycombe (d 1998); *b* 1 September 1935; *Educ* Rongotai Coll NZ, Slade Sch of Fine Art; *m* 1, 1964 (m dis 1968), Harriet Crittall; m 2, 1969 (m dis 1994), Caroline Beatrice, da of Sir Peter Medawar; 3 s (Timothy William b 1957, Alexander Medawar (Alex) b 1970, Theodore Nicholas b 1972), 1 da (Emily b 1964); m 3, 1995, Priscilla Brandchaft, *née* Roth; *Career* political cartoonist: Daily Telegraph 1966–86 and 1991–, The Independent 1986–91; *Style—* Nicholas Garland, Esq, OBE; ✉ The Daily Telegraph, 111 Buckham Palace Road, London SW1W 0DT

GARLAND, Patrick; s of Capt Ewart Garland, DFC, RFC (d 1985), of Brockenhurst, Hants, and Rosalind (d 1984), da of Herbert Granville Fell; *b* 10 April 1935; *Educ* St Mary's Coll Southampton, St Edmund Hall Oxford (MA); *m* 1980, Alexandra Bastedo; *Career* artistic dir Festival Theatre Chichester 1981–85 and 1990–94; prodr: Fanfare for Europe at Covent Garden 1975, Fanfare for Elizabeth (for HM The Queen's 60th birthday) 1986, Celebration of a Broadcaster Westminster Abbey 1987, cantata The Plague and the Moonflower for Inter-Parly Union St Paul's Cathedral, Merrie Church of St Paul's (tercentenary celebration) 1997; dir: Brief Lives, Forty Years On, Billy, Snow Goose (film), The Doll's House (film), The Secret of Sherlock Holmes (Wyndhams Theatre) 1989, Tovarich (Piccadilly) 1991, Handel's opera Ottone (for King's Consort, Royal Festival Hall London, Tokyo and Osaka Japan) 1992, Pickwick - the musical (Chichester Festival Theatre and Sadler's Wells) 1993, Vita and Virginia (The Minerva Chichester and Ambassadors) 1993, The Tempest (Regent's Park) 1996, Brief Lives 1997, The Importance of Being Oscar 1997, The Mystery of Charles Dickens (Comedy Theatre) 2000, Telling Tales (by Alan Bennett, BBC 2) 2000, Woman in Black (Old Globe San Diego and Minetta Lane Theatre NY) 2001, The Mystery of Charles Dickens (London, NY, Aust) 2002, Full Circle (by Alan Melville, starring Joan Collins, touring England) 2004; writer and dir A Room of One's Own (with Eileen Atkins as Virginia Woolf, Playhouse, Broadway and Thames TV) 1992 and (Hampstead Theatre) 2001; TV interviews: Rex Harrison 1987, Laurence Olivier 1987; organised Thanksgiving Serv for Lord Olivier (with Dean of Westminster) at Westminster Abbey 1989; hon fell St Edmund Hall Oxford 1997, Hon DLitt Univ of Southampton 1994; pres Dramatists Club 1995; *Books* Wings of the Morning (1988), Angels in the Sussex Air (1995), The Incomparable Rex (1998); *Recreations* idling in Corsica; *Clubs* Garrick; *Style—* Patrick Garland, Esq

GARLAND, Sir Patrick Neville; kt (1985); s of Frank Neville Garland (d 1984), and Marjorie, *née* Lewis (d 1972); *b* 22 July 1929; *Educ* Uppingham, Sidney Sussex Coll Cambridge (MA, LLM); *m* 1955, Jane Elizabeth, da of Harold John Bird, JP (d 1970), of Troston, Suffolk; 2 s, 1 da; *Career* called to the Bar Middle Temple 1953 (bencher 1979); asst recorder Norwich 1971, recorder of the Crown Court 1972, QC 1972, dep High Court judge 1981, judge of the High Court of Justice (Queen's Bench Div) 1985–2002; presiding judge SE Circuit 1989–94; pres: Official Referees' Bar Assoc 1985–2002 (chm 1982–85), Central Cncl of Probation Ctees 1986–2001; vice-chm Parole Bd 1989–90 (memb 1988–90); memb Worshipful Co of Clockmakers; hon fell Sidney Sussex Coll Cambridge 1991; *Recreations* gardening, shooting, industrial archaeology; *Clubs* Norfolk, Cumberland Lawn Tennis, Savage, Royal Over-Seas League; *Style—* Sir Patrick Garland; ✉ 9 Ranulf Road, London NW2 2BT (tel 020 7435 5877, fax 020 7813 2991)

GARLAND, Prof Peter Bryan; CBE (1999); s of Frederick George Garland (d 1978), and Molly Kate, *née* Jones; *b* 31 January 1934; *Educ* Hardye's Sch Dorchester, Downing Coll Cambridge (scholar, Athletics blue), KCH London (MA, MB BChir, PhD); *m* 7 Feb 1959, Ann, da of Arthur Apseley Bathurst (d 1951); 2 da (Joanna b 1961, Clare b 1962), 1 s (James b 1964); *Career* reader in biochemistry Univ of Bristol 1969–70 (lectr 1964–68), prof of biochemistry Univ of Dundee 1970–84, visiting fell Aust Nat Univ Canberra 1983, princ scientist and head of biosciences Unilever Research Colworth House Laboratory 1984–87, dir of res Amersham Int 1987–89, chief exec Inst of Cancer Research London 1989–99 (visiting fell 1999–), prof of biochemistry Univ of London 1992–99 (emeritus prof 1999–, Leverhulme emeritus fell 2000–01); author of numerous original articles on biochemistry and biophysics; visiting prof Johnson Res Fndn Philadelphia 1967–69, memb MRC 1980–84 (chm Cell Biology Disorders Bd 1980–82), memb Scientific Ctee Cancer Research Campaign 1983–92, chm Cancer Research Campaign Technology Ltd 1988–91 (dep chm 1991–96), chm Bd Cambridge Antibody Technology Ltd 1995–2004 (dir 1990–2004); Colworth Medal Biochemical Society 1970; fell UCL 1999; LLD (hc) Univ of Dundee 1990; FRSE 1977, memb EMBO 1981; *Recreations* sport, skiing, windsurfing, sailing, theatre; *Clubs* Athenaeum, Bosham Sailing; *Style—* Prof Peter B Garland, CBE, FRSE; ✉ Chester Beatty Laboratories, Fulham Road, London SW3 6JB (tel 020 7352 8133, e-mail garland@icr.ac.uk)

GARLAND, Hon Sir Victor; KBE (1981); s of Idris Victor Garland; *b* 5 May 1934; *Educ* Hale Sch, W Aust Univ (BA); *m* 1960, Lynette Jamieson; 2 s, 1 da; *Career* RAAF 1951–52; practised as chartered accountant 1958–69; memb for Curtin (Lib) Aust Fed House of Reps 1969–81; Parly and ministerial positions: min assisting the Treas 1972 and 1975–76, min for Supply 1971–72, opposition chief whip 1974–75, chm Expenditure Ctee 1976–77, min for Special Trade Representations 1977–79 (incl GATT negotiations), min for Business and Consumer Affrs 1979–80; high cmmr for Aust in the UK 1981–83; non-exec dir Prudential Corporation plc 1984–93; dir: Henderson Far East Income Trust plc 1984– (chm 1990–), Mitchell Cotts plc 1984–87, Throgmorton Trust plc 1985–2006, Govett Funds Inc 1991–2000 (pres 1997–2000), Nelson Hurst 1993–97, Fidelity Asian Values 1996– (chm 2000–), other public companies; vice-chm: South Bank Bd 1986–2000, Royal Cwlth Soc for the Blind; Freeman City of London 1982, Liveryman Worshipful Co of Tallow Chandlers, Hon Freeman Worshipful Co of Butchers; FCA; *Clubs* White's, Weld (Australia); *Style—* Hon Sir Victor Garland, KBE; ✉ Henley Road, Wargrave RG10 8HX (fax 0118 940 2245)

GARLICK, Paul Richard; QC (1996); s of Arthur Garlick (d 1978), and Dorothy Sylvia, *née* Allan; *b* 14 August 1952; *Educ* Scarisbrick Hall Sch, Univ of Liverpool (LLB); *Career* called to the Bar Middle Temple 1974, standing counsel to HM Customs & Excise 1990–96, recorder (Western Circuit) 1997–; memb Hon Soc of Middle Temple 1972; *Recreations* music, travel, walking, skiing, athletics; *Style—* Paul Garlick, Esq, QC

GARLING, Dr David John Haldane (Ben); s of Leslie Ernest Garling, and Frances Margaret, *née* Hannah; *b* 26 July 1937; *Educ* Highgate Sch, St John's Coll Cambridge (MA, PhD, ScD); *m* 30 Aug 1963, Anthea Mary Eileen, (Ann), da of George Richard Septimus Dixon, MBE (d 1983); 2 s (Hugh b 1969, Owen b 1974), 1 da (Julia b 1972); *Career* Nat Serv RA 1955–57; Univ of Cambridge: fell St John's Coll 1963– (tutor 1971–78, pres 1987–91), asst lectr 1963–64, lectr 1964–78 reader in mathematical analysis 1978–99 (emeritus reader 1999–), head Dept of Pure Maths and Mathematical Statistics 1984–91, pro-proctor 1995–96, sr proctor 1996–97, dep proctor 1997–98; London Mathematical Soc: memb 1963–, memb Cncl 1984–87 and 1995–98, meetings and memb sec 1995–98, exec sec 1998–2002; memb: Maths Ctee SERC 1981–84, Cambridge Philosophical Soc 1963–; *Books* Galois Theory (1986); *Style—* Dr Ben Garling; ✉ St John's College, Cambridge CB2 1TP (tel 01223 338600, fax 01223 337920, e-mail djg1001@hermes.cam.ac.uk)

GARMOYLE, Viscount; Hugh Sebastian Frederick Cairns; s and h of 6 Earl Cairns, CBE, *qv*; *b* 26 March 1965; *Educ* Eton, Univ of Edinburgh, London Coll of Law; *m* 19 Dec 1991, Juliet, o da of Andrew Eustace Palmer, CMG, CVO, of Little Missenden, Bucks; 1 s (Hon Oliver David Andrew b 7 March 1993), 2 da (Hon Tara Davina Amanda b 3 April 1995, Hon Harriet b 3 March 1998); *Career* Freshfields Slrs 1990–94; Cazenove & Co: joined 1994, ptnr 1999–2001, md 2001–03, md JPMorgan Cazenove 2004–; Liveryman Worshipful Co of Fishmongers; *Style—* Viscount Garmoyle; ✉ JPMorgan Cazenove, 20 Moorgate, London EC2R 6DA

GARNER, Alan; OBE (2001); s of Colin Garner (d 1983), of Cheshire, and Marjorie, *née* Greenwood Stuart (d 1997); *b* 17 October 1934; *Educ* Manchester Grammar, Magdalen Coll Oxford; *m* 1, 1956, Ann, da of Harry Cook (d 1976), of Oxford; 1 s (Adam), 2 da (Ellen, Katharine); m 2, 1972, Griselda, da of Paul Greaves (d 1986), of St Petersburg, Russia; 1 s (Joseph b 1973), 1 da (Elizabeth b 1975); *Career* author; Mil Serv Lt RA; memb Editorial Bd Detskaya Literatura Publishers Moscow; co-fndr Blackden Tst; FSA 2007; *Plays* Holly from the Bongs (1965), Lamaload (1978), Lurga Lom (1980), To Kill a King (1980), Sally Water (1982), The Keeper (1983), Pentecost (1997); *Dance Drama* The Green Mist (1970); *Libretti* The Bellybag (1971), Potter Thompson (1972), Lord Flame (1996); *Films* The Owl Service (1969), Red Shift (1978), Places and Things (1978), Images (1981, First Prize Chicago Int Film Festival), Strandloper (1992); *Books* The Weirdstone of Brisingamen (1960), The Moon of Gomrath (1963), Elidor (1965), Holly from the Bongs (1966), The Old Man of Mow (1967), The Owl Service (1967, Library Assoc Carnegie Medal 1967, Guardian Award 1968), The Hamish Hamilton Book of Goblins (1969), Red Shift (1973), The Breadhorse (1975), The Guizer (1975), The Stone Book (1976, Phoenix Award Children's Book Assoc of US 1996), Tom Fobble's Day (1977), Granny Reardun (1977), The Aimer Gate (1978), Fairy Tales of Gold (1979), The Lad of the Gad (1980), A Book of British Fairy Tales (1984), A Bag of Moonshine (1986), Jack and the Beanstalk (1992), Once Upon a Time (1993), Strandloper (1996), The Little Red Hen (1997), The Voice that Thunders (1997), The Well of the Wind (1998), Approach to the Edge (1998), Thursbitch (2003); *Recreations* work; *Clubs* The Portico Library; *Style—* Alan Garner, Esq, OBE, FSA; ✉ Blackden, Holmes Chapel, Cheshire CW4 8BY

GARNER, Dr John Angus McVicar; s of Edmund Garner (d 1998), and Catherine, *née* McVicar; *b* 4 September 1950, London; *Educ* Eltham Coll, Univ of Edinburgh (MB, ChB,

G

DCH, DRCOG); *Children* 1 da (Victoria b 21 Sept 1976), 1 s (Douglas b 5 Sept 1981); *Career* various hosp appts 1974–79, princ GP St Triduana's Medical Practice 1980– (sr ptnr 2005–); chm: Scottish GPs 1992–95, BMA Cncl Scotland 1999–2004; vice-chm Medical and Dental Defence Union of Scotland 1995–; lead assessor for performance GMC, lay observer Cncl Law Soc of Scotland; FRCGP 1995; *Recreations* photography, ponds; *Clubs* New (Edinburgh); *Style*— Dr John Garner; ✉ Idabank, Pomathorn, Penicuik EH26 8PJ (tel 01968 677870, e-mail johngarner@aol.com); St Triduana's Medical Practice, 54 Moira Park, Edinburgh EH7 6RU (tel 0131 657 3341, e-mail john.garner@lothian.scot.nhs.uk)

GARNER, Prof Paul; s of David Garner, of Liverpool, and Sylvia, *née* Card (d 1978); *b* 25 August 1955; *Educ* Spalding GS, UCL (MB BS, MD); *Career* surgical house offr UCH London 1979, med house offr Ninewells Hosp Dundee 1980; SHO: Withington Hosp Manchester 1980, N Staffs Hosp 1981, Booth Hall Hosp Manchester 1981–82; dist MO in charge Aitape PNG (VSO) 1982–84; PNG Inst of Med Research: epidemiologist Madang 1984–86, research dir Kunjingini 1986–87, offr i/c Madang 1987–88; research fell then lectr LSHTM 1988–94; Liverpool Sch of Tropical Med (LSTM): sr lectr 1994–, head Int Health Research Gp 1995–, personal chair 2001–; hon conslt in primary health care Liverpool Dist 1994–, hon research fell St George's Med Sch Grenada 1997–; co-ordinator Int Artemisinin Study Gp Secretariat 1999–; memb: MRC Physiological Med and Infections Bd 1999–2003, Ctee Royal Soc of Tropical Med 1999–, Int Grants Ctee PPP Health Care Med Tst Ltd 2000–04, MRC Audit Ctee 2002–; co-ordinating ed Cochrane Infectious Diseases Gp 1994–, section ed (infectious diseases) Clinical Evidence 1998–, specialist assoc ed Int Jl of Epidemiology 2000–, assoc ed (infectious diseases) Biomed Central 2001–; referee for jls incl BMJ and Lancet; FFPHM 2001 (MFPHM 2000); *Publications* International Co-operation in Health (jt ed, 2001); numerous articles, book reviews and other contribs to academic jls; *Recreations* running, contemporary music; *Style*— Prof Paul Garner; ✉ Liverpool School of Tropical Medicine, Pembroke Place, Liverpool L3 5QA (tel 0151 705 3201, fax 0151 705 3361, e-mail pgarner@liv.ac.uk)

GARNER, Richard Clayton; s of Eric Walter Ernest Garner (d 1981), of London, and Dorothy Bertha, *née* Taylor (d 1995); *b* 12 February 1950; *Educ* Highgate Sch, Harlow Tech Coll (NCTJ Cert); *m* 29 Oct 1985, Anne, da of George Wilkinson (d 2000); *Career* journalist; BBC News Information 1967–69, Islington and Camden Jls 1970–73, municipal corr Kent Evening Post 1973–77, educn corr then dep London ed Birmingham Evening Mail 1977–80, TES 1980–90, educn corr Daily Mirror 1990–2001, educn ed The Independent 2001–; memb NUJ 1970–; memb King's Head Theatre Club Islington; *Books* Midsummer Variations: an Anthology of Contemporary Poetry (1970); *Recreations* cricket (watching now!), going to the theatre; *Clubs* Middlesex CCC; *Style*— Richard Garner, Esq; ✉ 137 The Avenue, Hertford SG14 3DX (tel and fax 01992 583366); The Independent, 191 Marsh Wall, London E14 9RS (tel 020 7005 2880, fax 020 7005 2143, mobile 07866 544702, e-mail r.garner@independent.co.uk)

GARNER, Talitha (Tally); da of Anthony Garner, of London, and Krithia Wildfire; *b* 9 September 1977, London; *Educ* Ursuline Convent HS Wimbledon, Univ of Newcastle upon Tyne (BA), McGill Univ Montreal; *Partner* Thomas Hyde; *Career* prodr Lowe Lintas and Ptnrs 2001–02, agent representing screenwriters, dirs and film and TV rights Curtis Brown 2003– (joined as book-to-film agent 2002), jt fndr Cuba Pictures Prodn Co 2004–; *Style*— Miss Tally Garner; ✉ Curtis Brown Literary Agency, Haymarket House, 28–29 Haymarket, London SW1Y 4SP (tel 020 7393 4458, fax 020 7393 4401, e-mail tally@curtisbrown.co.uk)

GARNETT, Ven David Christopher; s of Douglas Garnett, of Elland, W Yorks, and Audrey, *née* Cragg; *b* 26 September 1945; *Educ* Giggleswick Sch, Univ of Nottingham (BA), Fitzwilliam Coll Cambridge (BLitt, MA), Westcott House Cambridge; *m* 1974, Susanne, *née* Crawford; 2 s (Christopher b 1977, Timothy b 1978); *Career* curate of Cottingham E Yorks 1969–72, chaplain, fell and tutor Selwyn Coll Cambridge and pastoral advsr Newnham Coll Cambridge 1972–77, rector of Patterdale and diocesan dir of ordinands Dio of Carlisle 1977–80, vicar of Heald Green and chaplain St Ann's Hospice Dio of Chester 1980–87, rector of Christleton and Bishop's theol advsr 1987–92, team rector of Ellesmere Port Dio of Chester 1992–96, archdeacon of Chesterfield 1996–; supporter Christian Aid; *Recreations* part time farming, poultry breeding and genetics (sec Laced Wyandotte Club), clarinet, natural history; *Style*— The Ven the Archdeacon of Chesterfield; ✉ The Old Vicarage, Baslow, Bakewell, Derbyshire DE45 1RY (tel 01246 583928, fax 01246 583949)

GARNETT, Adm Sir Ian David Graham; KCB (1998); s of Capt Ian Graham Hartt Garnett, DSC, RN (d 1996), and Barbara (d 1984); *b* 27 September 1944; *Educ* Canford Sch, BRNC Dartmouth; *m* 1973, Charlotte Mary, *née* Anderson; 1 s (b 1975), 2 da (b 1978 and 1982); *Career* joined RN 1962, appointed Lt 1967, flying trg 1968–69, HMS Hermes 814 Sqdn 1969–70, loan serv RAN 1971–72, HMS Tiger 826 Sqdn 1973–74, Warfare Offr 1974–76, Sr Pilot 820 Sqdn 1977–78, Dep Dir JMOTS 1978–80, CO HMS Amazon 1981–82, RN Staff Course 1983, Asst Dir Operational Requirements 1983–86, Capt Fourth Frigate Sqdn HMS Active 1986–88, RN Presentation Team 1988–89, Dir Operational Requirements 1989–92, Flag Offr Naval Aviation 1993–95, Dep SACLANT 1995–98, Chief of Jt Ops 1999–2001, COS SHAPE 2001–04, Commandant RCDS 2005–; chm Chatham Historic Dockyard Tst 2005–; cmmr Cwlth War Graves Cmmn 2006–; memb Fleet Air Arm Officers' Assoc; *Recreations* my family and other matters; *Clubs* Royal Navy 1765 and 1785, Army and Navy; *Style*— Sir Ian Garnett, KCB

GARNHAM, Caroline Xania; da of Edward Hatch (d 1981), of Guildford, and Elisabeth Houtman; *b* 10 October 1955; *Educ* George Abbott Sch for Girls Guildford, Univ of Exeter (BSc); *m* 1, 30 Dec 1977 (m dis 1984), Hugh Laurence Garnham, s of Jack Garnham; m 2, 9 Aug 1991 (m dis 2004), Michael Robert Little, *qv*; 1 s (Edward Charles Frank b 21 Nov 1992), 1 da (Georgia Elizabeth Medina b 10 Nov 1995); *Career* ptnr Private Capital Gp LG; memb Tech Ctee and Int Ctee of Soc of Tsts and Estates Practitioners, Law Soc; FTII; *Recreations* tennis, skiing, writing; *Style*— Ms Caroline Garnham; ✉ Flat 4, 6 Hyde Park Gardens, London W2 2LT (tel 020 7706 4320); LG, 4 More London Riverside, London SE1 2AU (tel 020 7379 0000, fax 020 7379 6854)

GARNIER, Edward Henry; QC (1995), MP; s of William d'Arcy Garnier (Col, late RA, d 1989), and Hon Mrs Garnier (*née* Hon Lavender Hyacinth de Grey); *b* 26 October 1952; *Educ* Wellington, Jesus Coll Oxford (MA); *m* 17 April 1982, Anna Caroline, da of Michael James Mellows (d 1974), of Belton House, Rutland; 1 da (Eleanor Katharine Rose b 21 Sept 1983), 2 s (George Edward b 20 July 1986, James William b 21 Jan 1991); *Career* called to the Bar Middle Temple 1976 (bencher 2001); recorder of the Crown Court 2000– (asst recorder 1998–2000); vice-pres Hemsworth Cons Assoc; contested: Wandsworth BC by-election 1984, Tooting ILEA election 1986; Parly candidate (Cons) Hemsworth W Yorks 1987, MP (Cons) Harborough 1992–; PPS to mins of state for Foreign and Cwlth Affrs: Rt Hon Alastair Goodlad 1994–95, David Davis 1994–95; PPS to Rt Hon Sir Nicholas Lyell as Attorney Gen and to Sir Derek Spencer as Slr Gen 1995–97, PPS to Rt Hon Roger Freeman as chm Duchy of Lancaster 1996–97, oppn front bench spokesman Lord Chancellor's Dept 1997–99, shadow Attorney General 1999–2001, memb Exec Ctee to the 1922 Ctee 2001–2005, shadow Home Office min 2005–; memb Home Affrs Select Ctee 1992–95, sec Cons Backbench Foreign Affrs Ctee 1992–94, jt chm All-Pty Parly Knitwear and Textile Industry Gp 1992–94, treas All-Pty Br-Netherlands Parly Gp 2001–, jt chm All-Pty Br-Italian Parly Gp 2004–06, chm All-Pty Br-Liechtenstein Parly Gp 2004–; UK election observer: Kenya 1992, Bosnia 1996; Parly fell St Antony's Coll Oxford 1996–97; *Books* Halsbury's Laws of England (contrib, 4 edn), Bearing the Standard (jtly, 1991), Facing the Future (jtly, 1993); *Recreations* cricket, shooting, opera; *Clubs* White's, Pratt's, Leicestershire CC, Vincent's (Oxford); *Style*— Edward Garnier, Esq, QC, MP; ✉ 1 Brick Court, Temple, London EC4Y 9BY (tel 020 7353 8845, fax 020 7583 9144); House of Commons, London SW1A 0AA (tel 020 7219 3000)

GARNIER, Dr Jean-Pierre; *b* 31 October 1947; *Educ* Stanford Univ (Fulbright fell, French Govt scholar, MBA, pres Small Business Club), Univ Louis Pasteur France (PhD Pharmacology); *m*; 3 c; *Career* Mil Serv Med Corp France 1974–75; Pharmaceuticals Div Schering-Plough Corporation 1975–90: various sales and mktg posts France, Switzerland and Belgium 1975–78, dir of mktg Belgium subsid 1978–80, gen mangr Danish subsid 1980–82, gen mangr Portuguese subsid 1982–83, sr dir Mktg US Domestic Div 1983–84, vice-pres Mktg US Domestic Div 1984–85, sr vice-pres and gen mangr US Domestic Div 1985–88, pres US Pharmaceuticals Products Div 1989–90; SmithKline Beecham: pres America (US and Canada) 1990–93, memb Bd SmithKline Beecham Corporation 1992–, exec vice-pres Pharmaceuticals 1993–94, chm Pharmaceuticals 1994–96, pres Pharmaceuticals and Consumer Healthcare and chief operating offr 1996–2000; ceo GlaxoSmithKline 2000–; dir United Technologies Corporation; memb French/American C of C, tstee Eisenhower Exchange Fellowships Inc, emeritus tstee Acad of Natural Scis Philadelphia; former memb Bd of Tstees Massachusetts Eye and Ear Hosp; Communicator of the Year award Int Assoc of Business Communicators 1993, Chevalier de la Légion d'Honneur 1997; *Recreations* competitive tennis and paddle player, golf, wind surfing, skiing, bridge; *Style*— Dr Jean-Pierre Garnier; ✉ GlaxoSmithKline, One Franklin Plaza, PO Box 7929, Philadelphia, PA 19101–7929, USA (tel 00 215 751 5810, fax 00 215 751 6546, e-mail jean-pierre.garnier@gsk.com)

GARNIER, Rear Adm Sir John; KCVO (1990, LVO 1965), CBE (1982); s of Rev Thomas Vernon Garnier (d 1939), and Helen Davis, *née* Stenhouse (d 1993); *b* 10 March 1934; *Educ* Berkhamsted Sch, BRNC Dartmouth; *m* 31 Dec 1966, Joanna Jane (Dodie), da of Alan Cadbury (d 1994), and Jane Cadbury, *née* Walker (d 2001); 2 s (Thomas b 1968, William b 1970), 1 da (Louisa b 1972); *Career* joined RN 1950, served HM Yacht Britannia 1956–57, HMS Tyne 1956, qualified navigation specialist 1959, Naval Equerry to HM The Queen 1962–65, cmd HMS Dundas 1968–69, Directorate of Naval Ops and Trade 1969–71, cmd HMS Minerva 1972–73, Def Policy Staff 1973–75, exec offr HMS Intrepid 1976, Asst Dir Naval Manpower Planning 1976–78, RCDS 1979, cmd HMS London 1980–81, Dir Naval Ops and Trade 1982–84, Cdre Amphibious Warfare 1985, Flag Offr Royal Yachts 1985–90, Extra Equerry to HM The Queen 1988–, Private Sec and Comptroller to HRH Princess Alexandra 1991–95; pres RNA Sherborne Branch 1997–; memb Cncl Shipwrecked Fishermen and Mariners' Royal Benevolent Soc 1996–2004; govr Sherborne Sch for Girls 1985–2004; Younger Bro of Trinity House 1974, Freeman City of London 1982; *Recreations* sailing, gardening, opera, golf, computers; *Style*— Rear Adm Sir John Garnier, KCVO, CBE; ✉ Bembury Farm, Thornford, Sherborne, Dorset DT9 6QF

GARNIER, Thomas Julian Cadbury; s of Rear Adm Sir John Garnier, KCVO, CBE, of Thornford, Dorset, and Joanna Jane (Dodie), *née* Cadbury; *b* 18 May 1968, Gibraltar; *Educ* Radley, Univ of Bristol (BSc), Univ of Oxford (PGCE); *m* 25 June 1994, Alexandra Mary, *née* Penny; 2 s (Philip b 5 Aug 2000, Peter b 28 Oct 2003); *Career* Seaman Offr RN 1987–94 (Navigating Offr HMS Brinton 1991–93); Abingdon Sch 1995–2005 (day housemaster 1998–2002, boarding housemaster 2002–05), headmaster Pangbourne Coll 2005–; memb Inst of Physics; Queen's Telescope 1988, Carl Beiss Award 1991; *Recreations* sailing, rowing, singing; *Clubs* Leander; *Style*— Thomas Garnier, Esq; ✉ Pangbourne College, Pangbourne, Reading RG8 8LA (tel 0118 984 2101, fax 0118 984 1239)

GARRAD, Charles William Wynne; s of Douglas Garrad, and Mary Ann Garrad; *Educ* Marlborough, Stourbridge Coll of Art, Cardiff Coll of Art (DipAD), Chelsea Sch of Art (HDA); *m* 1994, Mary Norden; *Career* artist, film prodn designer and dir; formerly teacher at various Br art schools; exhbns incl: Serpentine, Ikon, MCA Sydney; chm Artsadmin; *Television and Film* credits as designer incl: Amongst Women, The Englishman Who Went Up a Hill But Came Down a Mountain, The Serpent's Kiss, Paranoid, Waiting for Godot; credits as dir incl: Time Passing (BBC), That Time (Beckett on Film); *Recreations* cycling, cooking, eating; *Style*— Charles Garrad, Esq; ✉ c/o Sue Greenleaves, ICM, Oxford House, 76 Oxford Street, London W1D 1BS (tel 020 7636 6565, fax 01844 261740)

GARRATT, Prof Clifford John; s of John Taylor Garratt, and Ann, *née* Critchley; *b* 18 December 1959; *Educ* Magdalen Coll Oxford, Bart's Med Sch London; *Children* 1 da (Lucy Rebecca b 8 Sept 1994); *Career* lectr Nat Heart and Lung Inst and hon sr registrar Royal Brompton Hosp 1992–93, Br Heart Fndn int fell 1996–97, prof of cardiology Univ of Manchester 2001–, hon conslt cardiologist Manchester Royal Infirmary 2001–; treas Br Pacing and Electrophysiology Gp 1999–; Guild Burgess of Preston; fell Euro Soc of Cardiology 1999; FRCP 1997; *Publications* Mechanisms and Management of Cardiac Arrhythmias (2001); author of many other original articles relating to cardiac arrhythmias; *Recreations* fly fishing, skiing; *Style*— Prof Clifford Garratt; ✉ Manchester Heart Centre, Manchester Royal Infirmary, Oxford Road, Manchester M13 9WL (tel 0161 276 8858, fax 0161 276 4443)

GARRATT, Colin Dennis; s of Sqdn Ldr Dennis Herbert Garratt, of Uppingham, Leics, and Margaret Alice, *née* Clarke; *b* 16 April 1940; *Educ* Mill Hill Leicester; *m* 1 (m dis); m 2 (m dis), Margaret Elizabeth, *née* Grzyb; 1 s (James Daniel b 2 Aug 1987); m 3, Carol Lesley, *née* Cardwell; 1 da (Marie-Louise b 3 June 1993), 2 s (Dominion and Antaeus (twins) b 18 June 1999); *Career* photographer, author, publisher, audio visual producer and presenter; engaged in professionally documenting the last steam locomotives of the world 1969–; writer and illustrator of 60 books incl Around the World in Search of Steam (autobiography, 1987); currently dir Milepost 92 1/2 (picture library, photographers, video and multi-media producers for the railway industry); tours multi-image audio visual theatre shows based on global expeditions, launch of fine art prints of last steam locomotives 2005; latest expdns: Seward Peninsular Alaska 2000, Da Qing Shan mountains Inner Mongolia 2003–04, China and Polar Russia 2005, Bihar and Assam 2007; currently working with Indian authorities to preserve the historic Ledo Brickworks in Upper Assam; *Recreations* ornithology, politics, music, art, the appreciation of fine cigars; *Style*— Colin Garratt, Esq; ✉ Milepost 92 1/2, Newton Harcourt, Leicester LE8 9FH (tel 0116 259 2068, e-mail studio@railphotolibrary.com)

GARRATT, Sheryl; da of Frank Stephen Garratt, of Birmingham, and June Valerie, *née* Fray; *b* 29 March 1961; *Educ* Barr Beacon Comp Birmingham, UCL (BA); *m* 22 March 1994, Mark McGuire; 1 s (Liam James McGuire b 12 Feb 1996); *Career* freelance writer New Musical Express 1980–83, music ed City Limits 1983–86; freelance writer 1986–88: The Observer, The Sunday Telegraph, Honey, New York Rocker, The Face, News on Sunday, Looks; ed The Face 1989–95 (music/prodn ed 1988–89, winner Int Magazine of the Year PPA Awards 1994); freelance writer 1995–98: The Sunday Times, The Independent, The Guardian, Red, Elle and New Statesman; ed The Observer Life magazine 1998–2000, sr writer The Observer 2000–02; currently freelance; *Books* Signed Sealed and Delivered (1984), Adventures in Wonderland (1998), Bliss to be Alive - The Collected Journalism of Gavin Hills (ed, 2000); *Recreations* drinking, dancing, cooking, reading, talking; *Style*— Ms Sheryl Garratt; ✉ 52 Milton Grove, London N16 8QY (e-mail sherylg@blueyonder.co.uk)

GARRATT, Timothy George; s of George Herbert Garratt (d 1976), of Chichester, W Sussex, and Hylda Joyce, *née* Spalton (d 1958); *b* 7 September 1942; *Educ* Stowe; *m* 24 April 1965,

Vanessa Ann, da of Charles Albert Wright (d 1980), of Chichester, W Sussex; 2 s (Alastair b 1969, James b 1973); *Career* chartered surveyor; ptnr Rendells Auctioneers Valuers & Estate Agents S Devon 1976–; memb Gen Cncl RICS 1969–73; chm: Devon and Cornwall Branch RICS 1989–90, Western Counties Agric Valuers' Assoc 1993–94; memb Cncl Livestock Auctioneers' Assoc 1992–95; pres Chagford and Dist Lions Club 1984–85 and 1992–93, zone chm Lions Club Int 1985–86; FAAV 1968, FRICS 1975; *Recreations* farming, gardening, country wine making, home butchery; *Clubs* RICS Wilderness; *Style—* Timothy Garratt, Esq; ✉ Baileys Hey, Chagford, Devon TQ13 8AW (tel 01647 433396); Rock House, Chagford, Devon TQ13 8AX (01647 432277)

GARRETT, André Neil; s of Neil Garrett, of Marylebone, London, and Patricia, *née* Cainey; *b* 14 March 1972; *Educ* Beechen Cliff Sch Bath, Bath Coll of HE; *m* 2 Aug 2002, Róisín, *née* Sullivan; *Career* chef: Hunstrete House Hotel Bath 1989–91, Chez Nico Park Lane London 1991–95, Bistro Bruno 1995–96, Nico Central 1996–99, Fine Dining Room Landmark Hotel 1999–2000; Orrery Restaurant: chef 2000–02, head chef 2002–06 (Michelin Star 2003–06); head chef Galvin @ Windows London Hilton on Park Lane 2006–; Roux scholarship 2002, scholarship with Guy Savoy Paris 2003; Master of Culinary Arts (MCA) 2005; *Recreations* cycling, reading, snowboarding, eating; *Style—* André Garrett, MCA; ✉ Galvin @ Windows Restaurant, London Hilton on Park Lane, 22 Park Lane, London W1K 1BE (tel 020 7493 8000, fax 020 7208 4142, e-mail andre.garrett@hilton.co.uk)

GARRETT, Lesley; CBE (2002); *b* 10 April 1955; *Educ* Royal Acad of Music (Countess of Munster Award, Decca-Kathleen Ferrier Memorial Prize), Nat Opera Studio; *m* 1991; 1 s, 1 da; *Career* soprano; studies with Joy Mammen; princ ENO 1984–98, memb bd dir ENO 1998–; previous engagements incl: Wexford Festival, WNO, Opera North, Buxton Festival, Glyndebourne; Gramophone Award for best selling classical artist of the year 1996; FRAM; *Roles* incl: title role in Mozart's Zaide, Susanna in The Marriage of Figaro, Despina in Cosi fan Tutte, Carolina in Cimarosa's The Secret Marriage, Atalanta in Xerxes, Eurydice in Orpheus in the Underworld, Bella in Tippet's Midsummer Marriage, Musetta in La Bohème, Adele in Die Fledermaus, Rose in Kurt Weill's Street Scene, Zelrina in Don Giovanni, Dalinda in Ariodante, title role in The Cunning Little Vixen, Jenny in Kurt Weill's The Rise and Fall of the City of Mahagonny, title role in La Belle Vivette, Rosina in The Barber of Seville; *Television* Jobs for the Girls (BBC 1), Viva La Diva (BBC 2), Lesley Garrett Tonight (BBC 2); *Recordings* DIVA! A Soprano at the Movies, PriMadonna, Simple Gifts, Soprano in Red 1995, Soprano in Hollywood 1996, A Soprano Inspired 1997, Lesley Garrett 1998, I Will Wait for You 2000, Travelling Light 2001, The Singer 2002, So Deep is the Night 2003; *Recreations* watching cricket; *Style—* Ms Lesley Garrett, CBE; ✉ c/o Louise Badger, The Music Partnership, 41 Aldebert Terrace, London SW8 1BH

GARRETT, Prof Malcolm Leslie; s of Edmund Garrett (d 1992), of Northwich, Cheshire, and Edna, *née* Mullin; *b* 2 June 1956; *Educ* St Ambrose Coll Altrincham, Univ of Reading, Manchester Poly (BA), Univ of Salford (MA); *Career* fndr and design dir Assorted Images graphic design consultancy 1977–94, fndr and creative dir AMX interactive communications co 1994–2001, interactive design conslt 2002–; visiting prof: in interactive RCA, Central St Martin's Sch of Art; visiting lectr/teacher numerous univs in Europe and USA; work exhibited in solo and group shows around the world 1981–; work in permanent collection Dept of Prints and Drawings V&A; nominated Prince Philip Designers Prize 1998; Royal Designer for Industry 2000–; chm Design Week Awards 1999–2000, memb BAFTA Interactive Design Awards Ctee 1999–; memb D&AD 1997–; *Books* Duran Duran - Their Story (with Kasper de Graaf, 1982), When Cameras Go Crazy - Culture Club (with Kasper de Graaf, 1983), Interference (with Nick Rhodes, 1984), Duran Duran - The Book of Words (ed with Kasper de Graaf, 1985), More Dark Than Shark (with Brian Eno, Russell Mills and Rick Poynor, 1986), New British Graphic Designers (with Neville Brody and Peter Saville, 1991), Malcolm Garrett - Ulterior Motifs (graphic devices 1977–91) (1991), The Graphic Beat Vol 1 (1992), Sublime (1992), Graphics (1997), 100 Best Album Covers (2000); *Recreations* collecting and driving classic American cars; *Style—* Prof Malcolm Garrett

GARRETT, Stephen James; s of James Leslie Michael Peter Garrett, of Sussex, and Margot, *née* Fleischner; *b* 16 April 1957; *Educ* Westminster, Merton Coll Oxford (BA); *Career* Granada TV Manchester 1978–81, BBC TV 1982–83; freelance dir and ind prodr 1984–87, commissioning ed youth progs Channel 4 TV 1988–92, ceo Kudos Productions 1992– (with Jane Featherstone, *qv*), dir Rapture (cable channel) 1995–98; exec prodr: Rory Bremner - Who Else? (Channel 4, BAFTA Award 1994) 1994, Desperately Seeking Something, Psychos, The Magicians House (International Emmy Award 2000), Spooks 2002 (BAFTA Award for Best Drama Series, Broadcast Award); film prodr Among Giants (Fox Searchlight), exec prodr Pure 2002; memb: BAFTA, RTS, PACT; *Recreations* tennis, photography; *Clubs* Soho House, Queen's; *Style—* Stephen Garrett, Esq; ✉ Kudos Film & TV Ltd, 12–14 Amwell Street, London EC1R 1UQ ((tel 020 7812 3278, mobile 07785 770789)

GARRICK, Sir Ronald; kt (1994), CBE (1986), DL (Renfrewshire 1996); s of Thomas Garrick, and Anne, *née* MacKay; *b* 21 August 1940; *Educ* RCST Glasgow, Univ of Glasgow (BSc); *m* 1965, Janet Elizabeth Taylor Lind; 2 s, 1 da; *Career* Weir Group plc: joined G & J Weir Ltd 1962, md Weir Pumps 1981, md and chief exec 1982–99, chm 1999–2002; non-exec dir: Scottish Power plc 1992–99, Shell UK Ltd 1993–98, Bank of Scotland 2000–01, HBOS plc 2001– (dep chm 2003–); dir Devonport Management Ltd; dep chm Scottish Enterprise Bd 1991–96; memb: Scottish Cncl CBI 1982–90, Scottish Economic Cncl 1989–98, Scottish Business Forum 1998–99; memb Restrictive Practices Court 1986–96; memb Dearing Ctee of Inquiry into HE 1996–97; Univ of Strathclyde: visiting prof Mech Engrg Dept 1991–96, memb Gen Convocation 1985–96, memb Ct 1990–96; hon sec for mech engrg Royal Acad of Engrg 1991–94; Hon DUniv: Paisley 1993, Strathcylde 1994; Hon DEng Univ of Glasgow 1998; FREng (FEng 1984), FRSE 1992, FIMechE; *Style—* Sir Ronald Garrick, CBE, DL, FRSE, FREng; ✉ HBOS plc, The Mound, Edinburgh EH1 1YZ

GARROD, Lt-Gen Sir (John) Martin Carruthers; KCB (1988), CMG (1999), OBE (1980), DL (Kent, 1992); s of late Rev William Francis Garrod, and late Isobel Agnes, *née* Carruthers; *b* 29 May 1935; *Educ* Sherborne; *m* 1963, Gillian Mary, da of Lt-Col Robert Granville Parks-Smith, RM (ka 1942); 2 da (Catherine, Fenella (Mrs Mikhail Ignatiev)); *Career* Lt-Gen RM, cdr 3 Commando Bde RM 1983–84 (despatches NI 1974); ADC to HM The Queen 1983–84, COS to Cmdt Gen RM 1984–87, Cmdt Gen RM 1987–90; dep dir Maastricht Referendum Campaign 1993, memb EC Monitor Mission in Bosnia 1993–94, COS to EU Administrator of Mostar 1994–96, EU special envoy Mostar 1996–97, head Regnl Office (Mostar) of the High Representative 1997–98 (appointed a Dep High Representative 1998), UN Regnl Administrator of Mitrovica Kosovo 1999; *Recreations* portrait photography; *Clubs* East India; *Style—* Lt-Gen Sir Martin Garrod, KCB, CMG, OBE, DL; ✉ c/o Lloyds Bank, 2 High Street, Deal, Kent CT14 7AD

GARROD, Norman John; CBE (1992); s of Frank Albert Garrod (d 1965); *b* 10 July 1924; *Educ* Alleyn's Sch Dulwich; *m* 1945, Beryl Portia Betty, *née* Bastow; 2 c; *Career* served WWII, Flt Lt RAF, UK, Middle East and Far East; master printer; chm: Garrod and Lofthouse Ltd 1952–86, Theatreprint Ltd 1970–, Video Business Publications Ltd 1983–, Garrod Properties Ltd 1987–; pres Printers Charitable Corporation 1994–95 (chm 1981–94), vice-pres Variety Club of Great Britain (chief barker 1984–85); Liveryman Worshipful Co of Stationers & Newspaper Makers; *Recreations* dogs, fishing; *Clubs* Garrick, RAF; *Style—* Norman Garrod, Esq, CBE; ✉ Great Common, Big Common Lane, Bletchingley, Surrey RH1 4QE (tel 01883 743375)

GARSIDE, Gill; da of Roy Garside, of Huddersfield, West Yorkshire, and Mavis, *née* Holdsworth; *b* 23 March 1954; *Educ* Greenhead HS Huddersfield, Univ of Liverpool (BSc); *Career* editorial asst: Heyden Publishing 1976, Good Housekeeping Magazine 1977–79; press offr Tesco Stores 1979–81; account exec: VandenBurg Associates PR 1981–83, Leslie Bishop Company PR 1983–84; currently md Darwall Smith Associates Ltd PR consultancy (joined 1984); *Recreations* horse riding, walking, opera, theatre, eating out; *Style—* Ms Gill Garside; ✉ Darwall Smith Associates Ltd, 60 Ironmonger Row, London EC1V 3QR (tel 020 7553 3700, fax 020 7553 3701)

GARSIDE, Prof John; CBE (2005); *b* 9 October 1941; *Educ* Christ's Coll Finchley, UCL (state scholar, Salters' scholar, BSc(Eng), PhD, DSc(Eng)); *Career* pt/t lectr Dept of Chemical Engrg Borough Poly London 1964–66, tech offr R&D Dept Imperial Chemical Industries Ltd Agric Div Billingham 1966–69, Fulbright sr scholar and visiting prof Dept of Chemical Engrg Iowa State Univ 1976–77, reader in chemical engrg UCL 1981 (lectr 1969–81); UMIST (now Univ of Manchester): prof of chemical engrg 1982–, head of dept 1983–88 and 1990–92, vice-princ for academic devpt and external affrs 1985–87, dep princ 1986–87, pro-vice-chllr 1997–2000, vice-chllr 2000–04; Monbusho/BC visiting prof Dept of Chemical Engrg Tokyo Univ of Agric and Technol 1992; memb: Engrg and Materials Science Panel Res Corp Tst 1985–88, Engrg Bd SERC 1990–93, Cncl IChemE 1992–1997 (pres 1994–95), NW Science Cncl 2000–04; European Fedn of Chemical Engrg: UK delg 2000–, memb Working Pty on Crystallization 1990–2000 (chm 1994–2000), vice-pres 2006–; assoc ed Chemical Engrg Communications 1985–99, hon ed Trans IChemE 2000–06; fell UCL 1994; Hon LLD Univ of Manchester 2004, Hon DEng UMIST 2004; CEng 1969, FRSA 1985, FIChemE 1986, FREng 1988; *Style—* Prof John Garside, CBE, FREng; ✉ Bryham House, Askham, Penrith CA10 2PU

GARSTON, Clive Richard; s of Henry Leslie Garston (d 1978), of Manchester, and Sheila Esther, *née* Cohen; *b* 25 April 1945; *Educ* Manchester Grammar, Univ of Leeds (LLB), Coll of Law; *m* 25 Feb 1973, Racheline Raymonde, da of Jacques Sultan; 1 s (Nicholas Nathan b 15 July 1974), 1 da (Louise Anne b 22 May 1978); *Career* slr; Hall Brydon Manchester: articled clerk 1966–68, asst slr 1968–71, ptnr 1971–78; sr ptnr Halliwell Landau Manchester 1989–95 (ptnr 1978–89 and 1995–2001), sr ptnr Halliwell Landau (now Halliwells LLP) London 2001–; chm Ultimate Finance Gp plc; non-exec dep chm The Inter Care Gp plc 1990–2002; dir Ipoint Media plc; memb: Law Soc 1968, International Bar Assoc, American Bar Assoc; *Recreations* swimming, skiing, watching Manchester United and Lancashire County Cricket; *Clubs* RAC, Lancashire CCC, IOD; *Style—* Clive R Garston, Esq; ✉ 100 Howard Building, 368 Queenstown Road, London SW8 4NR (tel 020 7498 6053, 078 0235 6614); Sandy Ridge, Bollinway, Hale, Cheshire WA15 0NZ (tel 0161 904 9822); Halliwells LLP, 1 Threadneedle Street, London EC2R 8AY (tel 0870 365 8100, fax 0870 365 8101, e-mail clive.garston@halliwells.com)

GARTHWAITE, Nicholas; s of Anthony Garthwaite (d 1972), and Waveney Samuel (d 1986); *b* 26 March 1952; *Educ* Churchill Coll Cambridge (BA); *m* 2 April 1982, Caroline Catchpole Willbourne, da of Thomas Willbourne; 3 s; *Career* various posts in oil, electricity, European policy and energy efficiency divisions Dept of Energy 1973–86, managing conslt Telecommunications Gp Touche Ross Mgmnt Conslts 1986–94, dir of telecommunications Price Waterhouse Corporate Finance 1994–96, mgmnt conslt Cicero Strategy 1996–; non-exec chm Cicero Translations 1980–; Competition Cmmn (formerly Monopolies & Mergers Cmmn): memb Telecommunications Panel 1998–2007, memb Reporting Panel 2000–07; author of articles on telecommunications; memb Communications Mgmnt Assoc 1994; tstee and memb Honorary Devpt Advsy Bd Bampton Classical Opera; FRSA; *Recreations* crosswords, ballet, opera; *Style—* Nicholas Garthwaite, Esq; ✉ Cicero Strategy, 6 St Petersburgh Place, London W2 4JY (tel 020 7229 3256, e-mail nicholas.garthwaite@cicerostrategy.com)

GARTON, Dr (George) Alan; s of William Edgar Garton, DCM (d 1966), and Frances Mary Elizabeth, *née* Atkinson (d 1967); *b* 4 June 1922; *Educ* Scarborough HS, Univ of Liverpool (BSc, PhD, DSc); *m* 21 Aug 1951, Gladys Frances, da of Francis James Davison (d 1978), of Glasgow; 2 da (Prof Alison Frances b 7 Sept 1952, Dr Fiona Mary b 19 May 1955); *Career* WWII serv Miny of Supply; Johnston res and teaching fell Univ of Liverpool 1949–50; Rowett Res Inst: biochemist 1950–63, head Lipid Biochemistry Dept 1963–83, dep dir 1968–83, hon res assoc 1984–92, hon professorial fell 1992–; hon res fell Univ of Aberdeen 1987–; visiting prof of biochemistry Univ of North Carolina 1967, memb Cncl Br Nutrition Fndn 1982–2003, pres Int Conferences on Biochemistry of Lipids 1982–89, chm Br Nat Ctee for Nutritional and Food Sciences 1985–87; FRSE 1966, FRS 1978; SBStJ 1986; *Books* contributor to several multi-author books on ruminant physiology and lipid biochemistry; *Recreations* gardening, golf, philately, foreign travel; *Clubs* Farmers, Deeside Golf; *Style—* Dr Alan Garton, FRSE, FRS; ✉ 2 St Devenicks Mews, Cults, Aberdeen AB15 9LH (tel 01224 867012)

GARTON, Rt Rev John Henry; *b* 3 October 1941; *Educ* Worcester Coll Oxford (MA), Cuddesdon Theol Coll; *m* 1969, Pauline; 2 s (Stephen b 1971, Patrick b 1973); *Career* RMA Sandhurst 1960–62, cmmnd Royal Tank Regt 1962; ordained: deacon 1969, priest 1970; chaplain HM Forces 1969–73: asst chaplain Gds Depot Pirbright 1969–70, asst chaplain RMA Sandhurst 1970–72, chaplain Omagh NI 1972–73; lectr in ethics and doctrine Lincoln Theol Coll 1973–78, team rector Coventry East Team Miny 1978–86 (concurrently chm Coventry Cncl of Churches and Bishop's advsr on community rels and rels with those of other faiths), princ Ripon Coll Cuddesdon 1986–96 (concurrently vicar All Saints Church Cuddesdon), hon canon Worcester Cathedral 1987–96, bishop suffragan of Plymouth 1996–2005, hon asst bishop Oxford Dio 2006–; *Recreations* hill walking, art, literature; *Style—* The Rt Rev John Garton; ✉ 52 Clive Road, Cowley, Oxford OX4 3EL (tel 01865 771093)

GARTON ASH, Prof Timothy John; CMG (2000); s of John Garton Ash, and Lorna Garton Ash; *b* 12 July 1955; *Educ* Sherborne, Exeter Coll Oxford (BA), St Antony's Coll Oxford (MA), Free Univ W Berlin, Humboldt Univ E Berlin; *m* 1982, Danuta; 2 s (Thomas b 1984, Alexander b 1986); *Career* editorial writer on Central Euro affrs The Times 1984–86, foreign ed The Spectator 1984–90, columnist The Independent 1988–90, columnist The Guardian 2002–, regular contrib to New York Review of Books; fell: Woodrow Wilson Int Center for Scholars Washington 1986–87, St Antony's Coll Oxford 1990–, Hoover Inst Stanford Univ 2000–; prof of European studies Univ of Oxford 2004–; memb Bd of Govrs Westminster Fndn for Democracy 1992–2001; David Watt meml prize 1989, Commentator of the Year in Granada TV What the Papers Say Awards 1990, George Orwell Prize 2006; Hon DLitt Univ of St Andrews 2004; FRSA, FRHistS, FRSL; Order of Merit (Poland) 1992, memb Berlin-Brandenburg Acad of Sci 1994, Order of Merit (Germany) 1995, Imre Nagy Meml Plaque (Hungary) 1995, Premio Napoli 1995, OSCE Prize for Journalism and Democracy 1998, Order of Merit (Czech Repub) 2003; *Books* Und Willst Du Nicht Mein Bruder Sein... Die DDR heute (1981), The Polish Revolution: Solidarity (1983, 3 edn 1999, Somerset Maugham award 1984), The Uses of Adversity (1989, Prix Européen de l'Essai 1989, 3 edn 1999), We The People (1990, 2 edn 1999), In Europe's Name (1993), The File: A Personal History (1997), History of the Present: Essays, Sketches and Despatches from Europe in the 1990s (1999), Free World (2004); *Recreations* travel; *Clubs* Frontline, Institut für die Wissenschaften vom Menschen (Vienna); *Style—* Prof Timothy Garton Ash, CMG; ✉ St Antony's College, Oxford OX2 6JF

G

GARTSIDE, Edmund Travis; TD (1968), DL (Gtr Manchester 1990); s of Col J B Gartside, DSO, MC, TD, JP, DL (d 1964), and Cora Maude, *née* Baker; *b* 11 November 1933; *Educ* Winchester, Trinity Coll Cambridge (MA); *m* 1, 29 Aug 1959 (m dis 1982), Margaret Claire, *née* Nicholls; 1 s (Michael Travis b 1961), 1 da (Vanessa Perry Anne (Mrs Anderson) b 1962); m 2, 5 May 1983, Valerie Cox, da of Cyril Vowels, of Instow, Devon; *Career* Nat Serv 2 Lt RE and Lancs Fusiliers 1952–54; TA: Lancs Fusiliers (Maj) 1954–67, E Lancs Regt 1967–68; chm and md Shiloh plc (formerly Shiloh Spinners Ltd) 1966– (mgmnt trainee 1957, dir 1960, gen mangr Roy Mill 1961–65, dep chm 1963–66, md 1965); dir Oldham and Rochdale Textile Employers' Assoc 1965–2000 (pres 1971–75), memb Central Ctee Br Textile Employers' Assoc 1969–89 (pres 1976–78); pres: Eurocoton 1985–87, Cncl of Br Cotton Textiles 1989–; memb Cncl: IOD 1974–2001, Shrievalty Assoc 1996–99; High Sheriff Gtr Manchester 1995–96; memb Ct Univ of Manchester 1979–94, govr Manchester GS 1984–98; CCMI, FInstD; *Clubs* Army and Navy; *Style—* Edmund Gartside, Esq, TD, DL; ✉ Shiloh plc, Shiloh House, Lion Mill, Fitton Street, Royton, Oldham, Lancashire OL2 5JX (tel 0161 624 5641, fax 0161 627 3840)

GARVAGH, 5 Baron (I 1818); (Alexander Leopold Ivor) George Canning; s of 4 Baron Garvagh (d 1956) by his 2 w, Gladys Dora May (d 1982), da of William Bayley Parker, of Edgbaston, and widow of Lt-Col D M Dimmer, VC; *b* 6 October 1920; *Educ* Eton, Christ Church Oxford; *m* 1, 12 July 1947 (m dis 1973), Edith Christine, da of Jack H Cooper, of Worplesdon, Surrey; 1 s, 2 da; m 2, 1974, Cynthia Valerie Mary, da of Eric Ernest Falk Pretty, CMG (d 1967), of Kingswood, Surrey; *Heir* s, Hon Spencer Canning; *Career* served Indian Army WW II in Burma (despatches); accredited rep trade and industry Cayman Islands 1981–, past memb Court Worshipful Co of Painter and Stainers; MIMgt, FInstD, MIEx; *Style—* The Rt Hon the Lord Garvagh

GARVEY, Dr Conall John; *b* 9 August 1955; *Educ* NUI (MB, BCh, BAO), UC Galway (Gold medal in otorhinolaryngology, special prize in paediatrics), Newcastle Coll (Dip); *Children*; 4 c (Grainne b 15 July 1982, Darren b 3 March 1984, Fergal b 6 Nov 1985, Killian b 5 June 1988); *Career* radiologist; SHO UC Hosp Galway 1979–80, registrar then sr registrar Northwick Park Hosp & Clinical Research Centre Harrow 1980–86, hon clinical lectr in radiodiagnosis Univ of Liverpool and conslt radiologist Liverpool HA 1986–, conslt in admin charge Sefton Gen Hosp 1986–93, clinical dir of radiology Royal Liverpool Univ Hosp 1995–2001 (chm Hosp Medical Bd 1997–99), nat clinical lead for radiology NHS Modernisation Agency 2001–05; chm: Dist Med Advsy Ctee Liverpool HA 1999–2001, Radiology Network Gp Merseyside & Cheshire Cancer Network 2002–05; RCR: memb Cncl 2001–04, FRCR examiner 2001–05, treas 2005–; memb: Nat Bowel Cancer Expert Gp, Radiology Working Party (Nat Cancer Standards); Levy Prize RCR 1996; FRCR 1984; *Publications* Disorders of the Small Intestine (contrib, 1985), Complications in Diagnostic Imaging (contrib, 1987), Exercises in Diagnostic Imaging: For MRCP and other higher qualifications (co-author, 1989); numerous articles and reviews for learned jls; papers for nat and int meetings and congresses; *Style—* Dr Conall Garvey; ✉ Royal Liverpool University Hospital, Prescot Street, Liverpool L7 8XP (tel 0151 706 2915, e-mail conall.garvey@rlbuht.nhs.uk)

GARVIE, (Fiona) Jane; *b* 19 May 1956; *Educ* Westbourne Sch for Girls Glasgow, Univ of Glasgow (MA, LLB); *m* 1998, Andrew Hardie Primrose; *Career* Maclay Murray & Spens: legal apprentice 1979–81, asst slr 1981–84, seconded to Bristows, Cooke & Carpmael London 1984–85, litigation ptnr 1985–97, head Employment Law Unit 1995–97; fndr Garvie & Co (employment lawyers) 1997, ptnr and head of Employment Golds Slrs 2000–01, conslt 2001–02, chm of employment tbnls (Scotland) 2002–; Int Bar Assoc: chm Discrimination and Gender Equality Ctee 1998–2002 (vice-chm 1996–98), memb SLP Cncl 2002–04; memb: Educn and Trg Ctee Law Soc of Scotland 1996–2000, Law Soc of Scotland 1981, Law Soc 1992; *Publications* Indirect Discrimination in Managing a Legal Practice (Int Legal Practitioner, Sept 1995); *Recreations* music, reading, gardening, walking, exploring cities; *Style—* Miss Jane Garvie; ✉ Central Office of Employment Tribunals, Eagle Buildings, 215 Bothwell Street, Glasgow G2 7TS (tel 0141 204 0730)

GARVIE, Dr Wayne; s of George Garvie, of Suffolk, and Frances, *née* Passmore; *b* 9 September 1963; *Educ* Univ of Kent Canterbury (BA), Univ of Sheffield (PhD); *m* 1993, Tracey, *née* Stephenson; 2 da (Susie Lola b July 1999, Lara Honey b April 2002); *Career* Granada TV: sports researcher 1988–91, prodr 1991–96, dep dir of broadcasting 1996, dir of broadcasting 1996–98; head of entertainment and features BBC Prodn 1998–2000, head of music, entertainment and features BBC Prodn 2000–01, head Entertainment Gp BBC 2001–06, dir of content and prodn BBC Worldwide 2006–; visiting prof of media Univ of Chester; tstee: Nat Museum of Lab History, RTS; memb: RTS 1993, BAFTA; *Recreations* Ipswich Town FC, relentless child care, pottering around the garden and idleness; *Style—* Dr Wayne Garvie; ✉ BBC Worldwide, Woodlands, 80 Wood Lane, London W12 0TT (tel 020 8433 1645, e-mail wayne.garvie@bbc.co.uk)

GARWOOD, Dr Stephen John; s of Ronald David Garwood (d 1998), and Irene Gaynor, *née* Dawson; *b* 25 September 1951; *Educ* Barry Boys GS, Imperial Coll London (BSc(Eng), ACGI, PhD, DIC); *m* 20 Nov 1976, Rosemary Joy, *née* Mott; 1 da (Sophie Kate b 1 Nov 1980), 1 s (Thomas Stephen Frederick b 1 Sept 1982); *Career* Welding Inst: research engr rising to sr research engr 1976–80, section head 1980–89, head of engrg 1989–94, head of structural integrity 1994–96; tech dir RR&A 1996–98, dir of engrg and technol Rolls-Royce Marine Power 1998–2000; Rolls-Royce plc: dir of technol 2000–01, dir of materials 2001–; author of over 80 pubns in the field of structural intergrity of welded structures; Leslie Lidstone-Esab Gold Medal 1986; CEng 1981, FWeldI 1980, FIMechE 1987, FIMMM 2002, FREng 2002; *Clubs* hockey, squash, running; *Style—* Dr Stephen Garwood; ✉ Rolls-Royce plc, PO Box 31, Derby DE24 8BJ (tel 01332 245066, fax 01332 245245, mobile 07971 224926, e-mail steve.garwood@rolls-royce.com)

GASCOIGNE, (Arthur) Bamber; s of Derick (Ernest Frederick) Orby Gascoigne, TD (of the old Yorks family dating back to the 14 century, and gggs of Gen Isaac Gascoigne, whose er bro's da Frances was the Gascoigne heiress who m 2 Marquess of Salisbury, whence also the Salisbury family name of Gascoyne-Cecil) and Hon Mary (Midi) Louisa Hermione O'Neill (d 1991), sis of 3 Baron O'Neill; *b* 24 January 1935; *Educ* Eton, Magdalene Coll Cambridge; *m* 1965, Christina Mary, da of late Alfred Henry Ditchburn, CBE; *Career* author, broadcaster and publisher; Cwlth fund fell Yale 1958–59; theatre critic: Spectator 1961–63, Observer 1963–64; co-ed Theatre Notebook 1968–74, fndr St Helena Press 1977–, chm Ackermann Publishing 1981–85, co-fndr HistoryWorld 2000–; tstee: Nat Gall 1988–95, Tate Gall 1993–95; memb: Bd of Dirs Royal Opera House 1988–95, Cncl Nat Tst 1989–94; TV presenter: University Challenge 1962–87, Cinema 1964; presenter and author: The Christians 1977, Victorian Values 1987, Man and Music 1987, The Great Moghuls 1990, Connoisseur 1988; Liveryman Worshipful Co of Grocers; hon fell Magdalene Coll Cambridge 1996; FRSL 1976; *Publications* incl: Twentieth Century Drama (1962), World Theatre (1968), The Great Moghuls (1971), The Treasures and Dynasties of China (1973), The Christians (1977), Quest for the Golden Hare (1983), How to Identify Prints (1986), Encyclopedia of Britain (1993), World History, a narrative encyclopedia (2001, online at www.historyworld.net); *Style—* Bamber Gascoigne, Esq, FRSL; ✉ St Helena Terrace, Richmond, Surrey TW9 1NR

GASELEE, Nicholas Auriol Digby Charles (Nick); s of Lt-Col Auriol Stephen Gaselee, OBE (d 1987), of Tonbridge; *b* 30 January 1939; *Educ* Charterhouse; *m* 1966, Judith Mary, da of Dr Gilmer; 1 s (James b 1968), 1 da (Sarah b 1970); *Career* Life Gds 1958–63; racing trainer to HRH The Prince of Wales, trained Grand National winner Party Politics 1992; *Recreations* coursing; *Clubs* Turf; *Style—* Nick Gaselee, Esq; ✉ Saxon Cottage, Upper Lambourn, Berkshire RG16 7QN (tel 01488 71503)

GASH, Prof Norman; CBE (1988); s of Frederick Gash, MM, and Kate, *née* Hunt; *b* 16 January 1912; *Educ* Reading Sch, St John's Coll Oxford (MA, MLitt); *m* 1, 1 Aug 1935, (Ivy) Dorothy (d 1995), da of Edward Whitehorn, of Reading, Berks; 2 da (Harriet b 3 March 1944, Sarah b 30 Jan 1946); m 2, 8 March 1997, Ruth Frances Jackson, wid of B M Jackson, of Huish Episcopi, Somerset; *Career* asst lectr UCL 1936–40; Army 1940–46, Maj GS 1945; prof of modern history Univ of Leeds 1953–55, Hinkley visiting prof Johns Hopkins Univ 1962, Fords lectr Univ of Oxford 1963–64, dean Faculty of Arts Univ of St Andrews 1978–80 (lectr St Salvators Coll 1946–53, prof of history 1955–70, vice-princ 1967–71), Sir John Neale lectr UCL 1981, Swinton lectr 1989; hon fell St John's Coll Oxford 1987; Hon DLitt: Univ of Strathclyde 1984, Univ of St Andrews 1985, Univ of Southampton 1988; FRHistS 1953, FBA 1963, FRSL 1973, FRSE 1977; *Books* Politics in the Age of Peel (1953), Mr Secretary Peel (1961), Reaction and Reconstruction in English Politics 1832–1852 (1965), Sir Robert Peel (1972), Aristocracy and People 1815–1865 (1979), Lord Liverpool (1984), Pillars of Government (1986), Robert Surtees and Early Victorian Society (1993); *Recreations* gardening, swimming; *Style—* Prof Norman Gash, CBE, FRSE, FRSL, FBA; ✉ Old Gatehouse, Portway, Langport, Somerset TA10 0NQ (tel 01458 250334)

GASKELL, (Richard) Carl; s of (Henry) Brian Gaskell (d 1982), and Doris Winnifred, *née* Taylor; *b* 23 March 1948; *Educ* Gateway Sch Leicester, Univ of Newcastle upon Tyne (LLB); *m* 29 Dec 1973, Margaret Annette, da of Stanley Walter Humber; 1 s (Philip b 1975), 3 da (Victoria b 1976, Elizabeth b 1979, Gillian b 1983); *Career* called to the Bar Lincoln's Inn 1971, Midland & Oxford circuit, asst recorder of the Crown Court 1989–; chm Desford Branch Bosworth Cons Assoc; *Style—* Carl Gaskell, Esq

GASKELL, Dr Colin Simister; CBE (1987); s of James Gaskell (d 1987), of Dukinfield, Cheshire, and Carrie, *née* Simister (d 1968); *b* 19 May 1937; *Educ* Manchester Grammar, Univ of Manchester (BSc), St Edmund Hall Oxford (DPhil); *m* Aug 1961, Jill, da of A Travers Haward (d 1980), of Torquay, Devon; 1 s (John b 1970), 1 da (Sarah b 1974); *Career* tech dir Herbert Controls 1971–74, md Marconi Instruments Ltd 1979–90 (dir 1977–79), gp md The 600 Group plc 1990–97; dir St Albans Enterprise Agency; FREng 1989, FIEE (hon treas 1996–99); *Recreations* reading, theatre, walking, railways; *Style—* Dr Colin Gaskell, CBE, FREng; ✉ Sequoia Lodge, Harpenden, Hertfordshire AL5 2ND (tel and fax 01582 762821)

GASKELL, Sir Richard Kennedy Harvey; kt (1989); s of Dr Kenneth Harvey Gaskell (d 1990), of Bristol, and Jean Winsome, *née* Beaven (d 1998); *b* 17 September 1936; *Educ* Marlborough; *m* 1965, Judith (Judy), da of Roy Douglas Poland (d 1963), of Hedgerley, Bucks; 1 s (Simon Poland Harvey b 1966), 1 da (Susanna Jane b 1968); *Career* admitted slr 1960; articled to Burges Salmon Bristol 1955–60, ptnr Tucketts 1963–85 (asst slr 1960–63); Lawrence Tucketts Bristol: ptnr 1985–97, sr ptnr 1989–97, conslt 1997–; legal advsr The Laura Ashley Fndn 1988–97 (tstee 1990–97); memb: Crown Ct Rules Ctee 1977–83, Lord Justice Watkins Working Pty on Criminal Trials 1981–83, Lord Chllr's Efficiency Cmmn 1986–88 and 1989–92, Marre Ctee on Future of Legal Profession 1986–88; Law Soc: nat chm Young Slrs' Gp 1964–65, memb Cncl 1969–92; chm Contentious Business Ctee 1979–82, memb Advocacy Trg Team 1968–87 (chm 1974–87); dir Law Soc Tstees 1974–92 (chm 1982–92); Law Soc Servs Ltd 1987–89: dep vice-pres 1986–87, vice-pres 1987–88, pres 1988–89; memb: Cncl Bristol Law Soc 1965–92 (pres 1978–79), Ctee Somerset Law Soc 1969–92, Criminal Justice Consultative Cncl 1991–94, Criminal Injuries Compensation Bd 1992–2000, Criminal Injuries Compensation Appeal Panel 1996–2004; pres Assoc of S Western Law Socs 1980–81; memb: Security Service Tbnl 1989–2000, Intelligence Serv Tbnl 1994–2000, Cncl Imperial Soc of Knights Bachelor 1995– (chm 1999–2000, knight princ 2000–06), Investigatory Powers Tbnl 2001–, Professional Conduct Ctee GMC 2001–06; non-exec dir Bristol Water Holdings plc 1991–2005 (dep chm 1998); tstee Frenchay and Southmead Med Tst 1968–2000; Wildfowl and Wetlands Tst: memb Cncl 1980–92, memb Exec Ctee 1982–89, chm 1983–87, vice-pres 1992–; memb Mgmnt Ctee Bristol 5 Boys' Club 1960–66, hon cases sec Bristol branch NSPCC 1966–76, memb Ct Univ of Bristol 1973–2000; memb Cncl: Bristol Zoo 1988–2005, SS Great Britain Project 1990– (also Exec Ctee) chm 1992–2000 (vice-pres 2000–); memb Advsy Cncl Prince's Youth Business Tst 1988–2000; Hon Freeman Worshipful Co of Butchers 2002, Liveryman Worshipful Co of Farmers 2002; Hon LLD Univ of Bristol 1989, Hon LLM Bristol Poly 1989; *Style—* Sir Richard Gaskell; ✉ Grove Farm, Yatton Keynell, Chippenham, Wiltshire SN14 7BS (tel 01249 782289, fax 01249 783267)

GASKIN, Prof John Charles Addison; s of Harry James Gaskin (d 1995), of Mixbury, Oxon, and Evelyn Mary Addison Gaskin, *née* Taylor (d 1989), of Aberdeen; *b* 4 April 1936; *Educ* City of Oxford HS, Univ of Oxford (MA, BLitt), Univ of Dublin (DLitt); *m* 20 May 1972, Diana Katherine, da of Maurice Dobbin (d 1969); 1 s (Rupert John Addison b 1974), 1 da (Suzette Jane Addison b 1975); *Career* Royal Bank of Scotland 1959–61; TCD: jr dean, lectr and prof of naturalistic philosophy 1963–97, fell 1978–; hon tutor Univ of Durham 1997–; *Books* incl: Hume's Philosophy of Religion (1978, 1988), The Quest for Eternity (1984), Varieties of Unbelief (1989), The Epicurean Philosophers (1994), The Dark Companion - Ghost Stories (2001), Tale sof Twilight and Borderlands (2005); *Recreations* eating and dreaming, writing stories, old wine, gardening, walking, classical civilisation; *Clubs* Kildare St and University (Dublin), Northern Counties (Newcastle); *Style—* Prof John C A Gaskin; ✉ Crook Crossing, Netherwitton, Morpeth, Northumberland NE61 4PY; Hatfield College, Durham DH1 3RQ (fax 0191 3747472)

GASKIN, Malcolm Graeme Charles; s of Charles Augustus Gaskin (d 1981), of Blyth, Northumberland, and Jean, *née* Denton; *b* 27 February 1951; *Educ* Blyth GS, Manchester Poly, Sch of Art and Design; *m* Deborah Ann, da of Michael Loftus, of Osterley, Middx; 2 s (Jack Alexander, Lewis Ross (twins) b 1983), 1 da (Francesca Vita b 1985); *Career* art dir Leo Burnett 1973–77 (created 'Eau' campaign for Perrier); creative dir: TBWA 1977–81, Woollams Moira Gaskin O'Malley 1987–95, Osprey Park Agency 1995–96; creative dir Ford of Britain and head of art Ogilvy & Mather 1998–; advertising awards for Lego, Land Rover, CIGA, Nursing Recruitment and AIDS; pres Advertising Creative Circle; memb: Creative Circle, D&AD 1975; *Books* Design and Art Direction (1975); *Recreations* gardening, angling, hiking, art; *Clubs* Soho House; *Style—* Malcolm Gaskin, Esq; ✉ Ogilvy & Mather, 10 Cabot Square, Canary Wharf, London E14 4QB (tel 020 7345 3000)

GASS, Lady; Elizabeth Periam Acland Hood; JP (Somerset 1996); da of Hon (Arthur) John Palmer Acland-Hood, barrister (d 1964; s of 1 Baron St Audries, Barony extinct 1971), and Dr Phyllis Acland-Hood, *née* Hallett (d 2004); *b* 2 March 1940; *Educ* Cheltenham Ladies' Coll, Girton Coll Cambridge (MA); *m* 1975, Sir Michael David Irving Gass, KCMG (d 1983, sometime HM Overseas Civil Serv in W Africa, colonial sec Hong Kong, high cmmr for W Pacific, British high cmmr for New Hebrides); *Career* memb Somerset CC 1985–97, chm Exmoor National Park Ctee 1989–93, dir Avalon NHS Tst 1993–96; memb: Rail Users' Consultative Ctee for Western England 1992–99, Cncl Cheltenham Ladies' Coll 1992–2001, Wessex Regnl Ctee Nat Tst 1994–2002, Cncl Univ of Bath 1999–2002, Wells Cathedral Cncl 2004–; tstee West of England Sch for Children with Little or No Sight 1996–; cmmr English Heritage 1995–2001; pres Royal Bath and West of England Soc 2002–03; High Sheriff Somerset 1994, HM Lord-Lt Somerset 1998– (DL 1995–98, Vice Lord-Lt 1996–98); *Recreations* gardening, music, archaeology; *Style—* Lady Gass; ✉ Fairfield, Stogursey, Bridgwater, Somerset TA5 1PU (tel 01278 732251, fax 01278 732277)

GASSON, Allan; s of Maj Dr John Gasson, RAF, DSO, DFC*, FRCS, and Valerie Gasson; *b* 18 November 1955; *Educ* Diocesan Coll Cape Town, Univ of Cape Town (BSc), INSEAD (MBA); *m* Rosemary; 1 s (Benjamin), 2 da (Amy, Julia); *Career* business devpt dir BET 1985–86, chief exec United Transport Line, conslt Bain & Co 1987–90, gen mangr Beverage Div then business devpt dir EMEA Dole Food Co 1990–92, fndr and md Burlington Conslts 1993–2005, head of M&A strategy Deloitte 2005–; *Publications* Intervention Strategies of Private Equity Firms in their Portfolios (2005); *Recreations* golf, tennis, sailing, skiing, opera, theatre; *Clubs* Worplesdon Golf, Hurlingham, Royal Cape Golf, Kelvin Grove Country; *Style—* Allan Gasson, Esq; ✉ Deloitte & Touche LLP, Athene Place, 66 Shoe Lane, London EC4A 3BQ

GASSON, Andrew Peter; s of Sidney Samuel Gasson, and Elsie Gasson; *b* July 1943; *Educ* Dulwich Coll, Henry Thornton GS, City Univ; *Career* in private practice (specialising in contact lenses) 1972–; pres Contact Lens Soc 1974–75; examiner: Spectacle Makers' Co, Br Coll of Optometrists 1975–84; memb: Contact Lens Ctee BSI 1980–82, Cncl Br Contact Lens Assoc 1986; vice-chm Ophthalmic Ethics Ctee London 2003–04; lectr at numerous sci meetings; chm Br Orthokeratology Soc 1997–; chm Wilkie Collins Soc 1981–; Freeman City of London, Liveryman Worshipful Co of Spectacle Makers; fell Br Contact Lens Assoc 2001; FRGS, FRSM, FBOA, FCOptom, DCLP, FAAO, ARPS; *Books* The Contact Lens Manual (jtly, 1991, 3 edn 2003), The Good Cat Food Guide (jtly, 1992 and 2006), The Good Dog Food Guide (jtly, 1993), Wilkie Collins - an Illustrated Guide (1998), The Public Face of Wilkie Collins (jtly, 2005), Lives of Victorian Literary Figures: Wilkie Collins (jtly, 2007); *Recreations* antiquarian books, travel, photography, cricket, motoring, bridge; *Clubs* MCC, Surrey CCC; *Style—* Andrew Gasson, Esq; ✉ 6 De Walden Street, London W1G 8RL (tel 020 7224 5959, e-mail lenses@andrewgasson.co.uk); 3 Merton House, 36 Belsize Park, London NW3 4EA

GASTON, Prof (John Stanley) Hill; *b* 24 June 1952; *Educ* Royal Belfast Academical Instn, Lincoln Coll Oxford (MA), Univ of Oxford Med Sch (scholar, BM BCh), Univ of Bristol (PhD); *m*; 2 c (b 1981, b 1983); *Career* house surgn Basingstoke Dist Hosp then house physician Radcliffe Infirmary Oxford 1976, SHO in clinical haematology Royal Postgrad Med Sch London 1977, SHO in nephrology Southmead Hosp Bristol 1977–78, SHO/registrar rotation in gen med Southmead Hosp, Bristol Gen Hosp, Bristol Royal Infirmary and Torbay Dist Hosp 1978–80, Sir Michael Sobell cancer research fell Cancer Research Campaign Dept of Pathology Univ of Bristol 1980–83, hon registrar in med and rheumatology Dept of Med Bristol Royal Infirmary 1980–83, MRC travelling fell Div of Immunology Stanford Univ Med Center Calif 1984, clinical fell Div of Immunology Stanford Univ Med Sch 1985; hon conslt in rheumatology: Central Birmingham HA 1987–92, S Birmingham HA 1992–95; Univ of Birmingham: MRC research trg fell Dept of Rheumatology and hon sr registrar Dept of Med 1985–87, Wellcome sr research fell in clinical sci 1987–92, sr lectr in rheumatology 1992–94, reader in experimental rheumatology 1994–95, prof of experimental rheumatology 1995; prof of rheumatology Univ of Cambridge 1995–, fell St Edmund's Coll Cambridge; visiting fell Univ of Turku Finland 1988 (Wellcome Tst grant 1989–92); Arthritis Research Campaign: memb Research Sub-Ctee 1992–95 and 2002–, chm Fellowship Ctee 1995–2000; numerous presentations at meetings and int confs, author of published papers, reviews, editorials and book chapters; asst ed: Rheumatology; memb: Assoc of Physicians, Br Soc for Rheumatology (Michael Mason Prize 1990), Br Soc for Immunology, American Coll of Rheumatologists; FRCP, FMedSci 2001; *Style—* Prof J S Hill Gaston; ✉ University of Cambridge School of Clinical Medicine, Department of Medicine, Box 157, Level 5, Addenbrooke's Hospital, Hills Road, Cambridge CB2 2QQ (tel 01223 330161, fax 01223 330160, e-mail jshg2@medschl.cam.ac.uk)

GATENBY, Ian Cheyne; s of Lt-Col William Gatenby (d 1971), of Esher, Surrey, and Frances Alice, *née* Davies (d 1982); *b* 30 June 1942; *Educ* Royal GS Newcastle upon Tyne, Exeter Coll Oxford (MA); *m* 1, Jan 1973 (m dis 1989); 1 s (Piers b 5 Aug 1975), 1 da (Catherine b 9 April 1977); m 2, 30 April 1994, Anne Margaret, *née* Storrs; *Career* admitted slr 1968, assoc ptnr Lovell White & King 1973–77 (articled clerk then asst slr 1966–73); Cameron McKenna (formerly McKenna & Co): joined 1975, ptnr 1977–, currently sr planning ptnr; author of numerous articles on planning and rating; memb Law Soc 1988 (memb Planning Panel 1993); legal assoc RTPI 1993; *Recreations* skiing, sailing, English National Opera, gardening; *Clubs* Ski of GB, Ranelagh Sailing; *Style—* Ian Gatenby, Esq

GATENBY, John Keirl; s of Walter Edmund Gatenby, of Macclesfield, Cheshire, and Mary, *née* Keirl; *b* 26 April 1950; *Educ* Hartlepool GS, Trinity Hall Cambridge (MA, LLM); *m* 20 Sept 1975, (Thelma) Eunice, da of George Edmund Holmes, of Prestbury, Cheshire; 2 da (Amy b 1980, Joanna b 1982); *Career* admitted slr 1975, admitted barrister and slr NZ 1980; slr advocate (civil) 2003; slr Linklaters & Paines 1975–82 (articled clerk 1973–75), head Litigation Dept Withers 1983–84; Addleshaw Goddard (and predecessor firms): assoc 1984–85, ptnr 1985–, head Litigation and Dispute Resolution Gp 1991–98; occasional speaker on civil procedure, arbitration law and alternative dispute resolution, memb Bd Centre for Effective Dispute Resolution 1995–2002, co-opted memb Sub-Ctee of Independent Working Pty of Gen Cncl of the Bar and the Law Soc on Civil Justice, memb Manchester and Liverpool Mercantile Courts Users Ctee; CEDR registered mediator 1998, ADR Gp accredited mediator, panel mediator CIArb; memb: Evangelical Alliance, Nat Tst, RSPB, Law Soc, Manchester Law Soc, London Slrs' Litigation Assoc, Int Bar Assoc; MICM 1990, FCIArb 1991; *Books* Notes on Discovery and Inspection of Documents (2 edn 1975), Recovery of Money (4 edn 1976, 7 edn 1989, gen ed 8 edn 1993); *Recreations* music (play piano, bassoon, organ, clarinet), gardening, photography, computers; *Style—* John Gatenby, Esq; ✉ Addleshaw Goddard, 100 Barbirolli Square, Manchester M2 3AB (tel 0161 934 6000, fax 0161 934 6060, e-mail john.gatenby@addleshawgoddard.com)

GATES, Martin Douglas Clift; s of Douglas Hansford Ellis Gates (d 1980), and Lily Madeline, *née* Pook (d 1999); *b* 30 March 1934; *Educ* Epsom Coll; *m* 26 Sept 1964, Margaret Florence, da of William Albert George Smith; 2 s (Richard b 4 May 1966 d 1996, Andrew b 5 March 1968); *Career* Nat Serv RAF 1955–57; articled clerk EC Brown & Batts 1951–55 and 1958–59, qualified chartered accountant 1960; audit sr: Finnie Ross Welch & Co 1961–64, Peat Marwick Cassleton Elliott & Co Nigeria 1965–66, Woolley & Waldron 1966–68; ptnr: Woolley & Waldron 1969–77, Whinney Murray & Co 1977–79, Ernst & Whinney 1979–89, Ernst & Young 1989–91 (all following mergers); conslt 1991–2004; pres Hiltingbury East Cons 1996–; hon treas: Hampshire Remembers D-Day 1993–96, hon treas Rhododendron Gp RHS 2002– (sec New Forest Branch 1995–); FCA 1971; *Recreations* walking, gardening, Nat Tst, watching cricket; *Clubs* Hampshire CCC; *Style—* Martin Gates, Esq; ✉ 12 Marlborough Road, Chandlers Ford, Eastleigh, Hampshire SO53 5DH (tel 023 8025 2843)

GATES, Paul Winnett; OBE (2003); s of Harry Winnett Gates (d 1971), and Sylvia Edna Mellor (d 1969); *b* 26 April 1948; *Educ* Meols Cop HS Southport; *m* 2 Sept 1989, Elaine; 1 s (Allan b 11 Jan 1967), 1 da (Donna b 20 Feb 1971); *Career* Stirling Knitting 1965–77 (shop steward 1969–77); Nat Union of Hosiery and Knitwear Workers (NUHKW): dist offr NW 1977–82, NE dist sec 1984–90; Nat Union of Knitwear, Footwear and Apparel Traders (KFAT): nat offr 1990–94, gen sec 1994–2007; TUC: dir Partnership Inst 2000, dir Stakeholder Tstees Ltd 2001, memb Gen Cncl 2001–02; dir Skillfast-UK (Sector Skills Cncl for the Textile and Clothing Industry) 2002–; ind memb Bd DTI 2005–07; tstee Gen Fedn of Trade Unions (GFTU) 1999–2007; memb: Nat Jt Industrial Cncl for the Knitting Industries 1975–2007, Footwear Industry Jt Consultative Ctee 1991–2007, Textile Industry Health and Safety Advsy Ctee (TEXIAC) 1995–2007, Textile & Clothing Strategy Gp (TCSG) 1999–2007, Exec Int Textile, Garment and Leather Workers' Fedn (ITGLWF) 1999–2007, Exec European Trade Union Fedn for the Textile, Clothing and Leather Industries (ETUC:TCL) 1999–2007, Lab Pty, Low Pay Cmmn, Central Arbitration Ctee, Employment Trbnls Panel; dir Bolton Bury TEC (BBTEC) 1989–94, memb Duke of Edinburgh Cwlth Study Conf 1984; memb Textiles Inst 1998; *Recreations* football, cricket, gardening; *Style—* Paul Gates, Esq, OBE; ✉ 3 Channing Way, Ellistown, Leicestershire LE67 1HA (tel 01530 262197)

GATFIELD, Stephen John; s of Dennis Edward Gatfield, of Barnard Castle, Co Durham, and Hilary Marie Gatfield; *b* 2 September 1958; *Educ* Churcher's Coll Petersfield, City of London Freemans' Sch Ashtead, Univ of Bristol (BSc), IMD PED (Business Sch Mgmnt Dip); *m* 31 May 1992, Eliza, da of Dr Ronald Tepper; *Career* account planner Leo Burnett advtg 1981–84, account dir Grandfield Rork Collins 1984–85, gp account planner Saatchi & Saatchi 1985–86; StarCom (formerly Leo Burnett): bd dir 1987, head of account mgmnt 1988–90, dep md 1990–91, md 1991–96, chief exec 1992–97, md Asia/Pacific 1997–2000, chief operating offr LB Worldwide 2001–03; exec vice-pres of global ops and innovation Interpublic Gp 2004–06, exec vice-pres of network operations and strategy Interpublic Gp, ceo Lowe & Ptnrs Worldwide; memb Asia Soc; memb: IPA, IDM, MRS 1981, Strategic Planning Soc 1990; *Recreations* tennis, golf, theatre, jazz, modern art; *Clubs* RAC, IMD Alumni, Seawanhaka Yacht; *Style—* Stephen Gatfield, Esq

GATFORD, Ven Ian; s of Frederick Ernest Gatford (d 1952), and Chrissie Lilian, *née* McKeown (d 1993); *b* 15 June 1940; *Educ* Drayton Manor GS, KCL (AKC), St Boniface Coll Warminster; *m* 31 July 1965, Anne Maire, da of Peter Whitehead (d 1986); 3 da (Sarah b 24 July 1967, Delphis Charlotte b 18 Oct 1973, (Chloe) Tamsin b 5 April 1978), 1 s (Andrew b 30 Aug 1970); *Career* commercial apprentice Taylor Woodrow Ltd 1959–62, KCL 1962–67; ordained 1967, curate St Mary's Clifton Nottingham 1967–71, team vicar Holy Trinity Clifton Nottingham 1971–75, vicar St Martin's Sherwood Nottingham 1975–84, canon residentiary Derby Cathedral 1984–99 (precentor 1984–93, sub-provost 1990–93), archdeacon of Derby 1993–05; community care progs presenter BBC Radio Nottingham 1975–84, religious affrs presenter BBC Radio Derby 1984–93, chm BBC Local Advsy Bd 1998–2001; *Recreations* playing piano, hill walking, music, theatre, reading and speaking German, cycling; *Style—* The Ven Ian Gatford; ✉ 9 Poplar Nook, Allestree, Derby DE22 2DW (tel 01332 557567)

GATISS, Mark; *b* 17 October 1966; *Educ* Bretton Hall Coll, Univ of Leeds (BA); *Career* actor, writer and comedian, memb The League of Gentlemen comedy gp; Hon DLitt Univ of Huddersfield; *Theatre* A Local Show for Local People (nat tour) 2000–01, Art (Whitehall Theatre) 2002; *Television* The League of Gentlemen (BBC) 1999, 2000 and 2002, The League of Gentlemen Christmas Special (BBC) 2000, Surrealissimo (BBC) 2001, Dr Terrible's House of Horrible (BBC) 2001, Spaced (Channel 4) 2001, Nighty Night (BBC) 2004, Catterick (BBC) 2004, From Bard to Verse (BBC) 2004, Footballers' Wives (ITV) 2004, Miss Marple: Murder at the Vicarage (ITV 1) 2004, The Quartermass Experiment (BBC 4) 2005, Doctor Who: The Unquiet Dead (BBC) (writer) 2005; *Radio* The Further Adventures of Sherlock Holmes (Radio 4) 2003, Nebulous (Radio 4) 2005; *Film* Now You See Her 2001, The Cicerones 2002, Bright Young Things 2003, Sex Lives of the Potatomen 2003, Matchpoint 2005, The Hitchhiker's Guide to the Galaxy 2005, Shaun of the Dead 2004, The League of Gentlemen's Apocalypse 2005; *Awards* Perrier Award 1997, Sony Silver Award for Radio Comedy 1998, Golden Rose of Montreux 1999, BAFTA Award for Best Comedy 2000, RTS Award for Best Entertainment 2000, NME Award for Best TV Prog 2001, South Bank Show Award for Best Comedy 2003; *Books* Nightshade (1992), St Anthony's Fire (1994), The Roundheads (1997), Last of the Gaderene (1999), The Essex Files (with Jeremy Dyson, 1997), A Local Book for Local People (2000), The Vesuvius Club (2004), The Devil in Amber (2006); *Recreations* painting; *Clubs* Soho House, Vesuvius; *Style—* Mark Gatiss, Esq; ✉ c/o PBJ Management, 7 Soho Street, London W1D 3DQ (tel 020 7287 1112); ICM, 76 Oxford Street, London W1D 1BS

GATTI, Daniele; *b* 6 November 1961; *Educ* Artisit Liceo; *m* Silvia Chiesa; *Career* conductor; fndr and musical dir Stradivari (orchestra da camera) 1986–92, res conductor Pomeriffi Musicali Orchestra Milan 1986, AsLi Co 1988–89, conductor Teatro Comunale Bologna 1990–92, res conductor Accademia Nazionale di Santa Cecilia Orchestra 1993–97, princ guest conductor Royal Opera House 1994–97, music dir Royal Philharmonic Orch 1996–, music dir Teatro Comunale Bologna 1997–; conductor: Teatro alla Scala 1988, Rossini Opera Festival 1988 and 1998, Carnegie Hall NY 1990, Toronto Symphony Orch 1991, Los Angeles Philharmonic 1991, Orchestre Symphonique de Montréal 1993, Bayerische Rundfunk 1993, LSO 1993, Philadelphia Orch 1993, Cincinnati Symphony Orch 1994, Nat Symphony Orch Washington 1994, Chicago Symphony Orch 1994, 2001, San Francisco Symphony 1994, LPO 1994, White Nights Festival St Petersburg 1994, BBC Proms 1995 and 1997, New York Philharmonic 1996, 1998, 1999 and 2001, Berlin Philharmoniker 1997, Accademia di Santa Cecilia 1998, Orchestra Verdi di Milano 1998, Boston Symphony 1998 and 2001, Munich Philharmonic 1998, 2001 and 2002, Dresden Staatskapelle 1999 and 2002, Vienna State Opera 2002 and 2003, Israel Philharmonic 2002, Semperoper Dresden 2003; numerous performances with Royal Philharmonic Orch and Teatro Comunale di Bologna; tours with Royal Philharmonic Orch incl: Europe 1999, USA 1999, Germany, Italy, Spain and Belgium 2001–2002, Italy 2002, North America, Germany, Spain and Switzerland 2003–04; tours with Teatro Comunale di Bologna incl Japan 1998 and 2001; recordings on Decca and Sony Classical labels, exclusive recording with BMG Conifer; winner Int Prize Le Muse Florence 1996; *Recreations* reading, walking, football, chess; *Style—* Daniele Gatti, Esq; ✉ The Royal Philharmonic Orchestra, 16 Clerkenwell Green, London EC1R 0QT

GAUKE, David; MP; *Educ* Northgate HS, St Edmund Hall Oxford, Chester Coll of Law; *m* Rachel; 2 s (William b 2002, Robert b 2004); *Career* Parly research asst to Barry Legg MP 1993–94; slr: Richards Butler 1995–99, Macfarlanes 1999–2005; Parly candidate (Cons) Brent E 2001, MP (Cons) SW Hertfordshire 2005–; dep chair Brent E Cons Assoc 1998–2000; *Style—* David Gauke, Esq, MP; ✉ House of Commons, London SW1A 0AA (tel 020 7219 4459, fax 020 7219 4759, e-mail david@davidgauke.com, website www.davidgauke.com)

GAULTER, Andrew Martin; s of Derek Vivian Gaulter, of Chorleywood, Herts, and Edith Irene, *née* Shackleton (d 1996); *b* 4 April 1951; *Educ* Merchant Taylors', Peterhouse Cambridge (exhibitioner, BA); *m* 30 Sept 1978, Susan Jane Wright; 2 da; *Career* articled clerk Messrs Beachcrofts London, admitted slr 1976; co sec: J Henry Schroder & Co Ltd 1990– (joined 1976), Schroders plc (holding co of Schroder Group) 1990–2000, Salomon Brothers Int Ltd (now Citigroup Global Markets Ltd) 2000–; memb: Law Soc, Law Soc Commerce and Industry Gp; tstee Kidney Research UK; *Recreations* golf; *Style—* Andrew Gaulter, Esq; ✉ Citigroup Global Markets Ltd, Citigroup Centre, London E14 5LB (tel 020 7508 9524, fax 020 7508 9112)

GAUNT, Jonathan Robert; QC (1991); s of Dr Brian Gaunt, and Dr Mary Joyce Gaunt, *née* Hudson; *b* 3 November 1947; *Educ* St Peter's Coll, Radley (exhibitioner), UC Oxford (scholar, BA), Lincoln's Inn (Mansfield scholar); *m* 18 Jan 1975, Lynn Adele, da of Terence Arthur John Dennis; 1 da (Arabella b 10 April 1985); *Career* called to the Bar Lincoln's Inn 1972 (bencher), jt head of chambers, dep judge of the High Court; *Books* Halsbury's Law of England vol 27 Landlord and Tenant (ed 1981 and 1994 edns), Gale on Easements (16 edn, 1996, 17 edn 2002); *Recreations* golf, sailing; *Style—* Jonathan Gaunt, Esq, QC; ✉ Falcon Chambers, Falcon Court, London EC4Y 1AA (tel 020 7353 2484, fax 020 7353 1261, e-mail gaunt@falcon-chambers.com)

G

GAUTHIER, Alexis Pascal; s of Jean Pierre Gauthier (d 1989), and Colette Gauthier (d 1991); *b* 24 June 1973; *Educ* Avignon Hotellerie Sch; *Career* Hotel Negresco Nice 1991–93, Le Louis XV Monte Carlo 1993–96, Roussillon Restaurant 1998– (1 Michelin Star 2000–, 3 AA Rosettes 1999–, Time Out Best Vegetarian Award 2000 and 2001); *Style*— Alexis Gauthier, Esq; ⊠ Roussillon, 16 St Barnabas Street, London SW1W 8PE (tel 020 7730 5550, fax 020 7824 8617, e-mail alexis@roussillon.co.uk)

GAVAN, Peter Joseph; *b* 23 April 1951; *Educ* Knox Acad Haddington, Balliol Coll Oxford (MA); *Partner* Nicki Jane McHarg; 2 s (Alistair, Angus), 2 da (Ailsa, Isla); *Career* political journalist 1973–87, with Corp Affrs Div in the petrochemical industry 1987–89, dir issues mgmnt Burson-Marsteller 1989–92; dir corp affrs: Total (UK) 1992–95, National Grid Gp plc 1995–98, Invensys plc (BTR & SIEBE) 1998–99, Viridian Gp plc 1999–2001, Severn Trent plc 2001–; public memb (vol) Network Rail 2003–06; MCIJ, MIRS, MIPR, FRSA; *Clubs* Royal Northern and University (Aberdeen); *Style*— Peter Gavan, Esq; ⊠ Doonbrae, Blackcliffe, Welford, Warwickshire CV37 9UB (tel 01789 750039)

GAVIN, Jamila Elizabeth; da of Terence Khushal Singh, and Jessica, *née* Dean; *b* Mussoorie, India; *Educ* Notting Hill and Ealing HS, Trinity Coll of Music London (piano scholar), Paris (French Govt scholarship to study piano), Hochschule für Musik Berlin; *Career* author; studio mangr BBC Radio 1964–67, prodn asst/dir Music and Arts progs BBC 1967–71; author: The Green Factor (musical), The God at the Gate (Play for Today BBC Radio 4) 2001; memb: PEN, The Writers Guild, West of England Writers; govr Uplands Co Primary Sch Stroud; supporter: The Coram Family, North South Travel, PEN, Amnesty Int; memb Lab Pty; *Books* The Magic Orange Tree and Other Stories (1979), Double Dare and Other Stories (1982), Kamla and Kate (1983), Digital Dan (1984), Ali and the Robots (1986), Stories from the Hindu World (1986), The Hideaway (1987), Three Indian Princesses: The Stories of Savitri, Damayanti, and Sita (1987), The Singing Bowls (1989), I Want to Be an Angel (1990), Kamla and Kate Again (1991), Forbidden Clothes (1992), Deadly Friend (1994), The Demon Drummer (1994, adapted as a play, performed at Cheltenham Literary Festival 1994), Pitchou (1994, republished as Fine Feathered Friend 1996), The Temple by the Sea (1995, republished in Three Indian Goddesses, 2001), A Singer from the Desert (1996), A Fine Feathered Friend (1996), The Mango Tree (1996), Presents (1996), Who Did It? (1996), The Wormholers (1996), Grandma's Surprise (1996), Our Favourite Stories: Children Just Like Me Storybook (1997), Just Friends (1997), Out of India: An Anglo-Indian Childhood (1997), Forbidden Memories (1998), Forbidden Dreams (1998), Someone's Watching, Someone's Waiting (1998), Monkey in the Stars (1998, dramatised and performed at Polka Theatre 2000), Star Child on Clark Street (1998), Coram Boy (2001, Whitbread Children's Book of the Year 2000), The Girl who Rode on a Lion (republished in Three Indian Goddesses, 2001), Danger by Moonlight (2002), The Blood Stone (2003), Grandpa Chatterji's Third Eye (2006), Walking on my Hands, The Teenage Years (2007); contrib to various educational schemes incl: All Aboard (1995), The Lake of Stars, Grandma's Surprise and The Mango Tree (1996, Storyworlds reading scheme); Surya Trilogy: The Wheel of Surya (1992, special runner-up Guardian Children's Fiction Award 1992), The Eye of the Horse (1994, short listed Guardian Children's Fiction Award), The Track of the Wind (1997, shortlisted Guardian Children's Fiction Award); Grandpa Chatterji series: Grandpa Chatterji (1993, shortlisted Smarties Award, adapted for TV 1996), Grandpa's Indian Summer (1995); *Recreations* music, theatre, art, skiing, walking, playing the piano; *Style*— Mrs Jamila Gavin; ⊠ David Higham Associates Ltd, 5–8 Lower John Street, Golden Square, London W1F 9HA (tel 020 7437 7888, fax 020 7437 1072)

GAVIN, Kenneth George (Kent); s of George Henry Gavin (d 1970), of London, and Norah Sylvia, *née* Vine (d 1993); *b* 11 August 1939; *Educ* Tollington Park London; *m* (m dis); Thelma, *née* Diggins; 2 da (Stephanie Kim b 22 Dec 1961, Tracy June b 8 March 1963); *Career* Nat Serv RAF 1959–61; apprentice then freelance and staff photographer Keystone Press Agency, with Daily Mirror 1965–2004 (latterly chief photographer), prop Kent Gavin Associates; FRPS; *Awards* winner of over 143 incl: Br Press Photographer of the Year (four times), Royal Photographer of the Year (nine) times, Royal Photographer of the Decade (twice), World Press News Feature Photographer of the Year, Ilford News Picture of the Age 25th Anniversary Photographic Awards 1992; *Books* Flash Bang Wallop - Inside Stories of Fleet Street's Top Press Photographer, Princely Marriage (with Anthony Holden), Portraits of a Princess: Travels with Diana (2004); *Recreations* football, Arsenal FC; *Clubs* Tramp; *Style*— Kent Gavin, Esq; ⊠ Kent Gavin Associates (e-mail kent.gavin@virgin.net, website www.kentgavinassociates.com)

GAVIN, Rupert; *Career* copywriter, account dir, equity ptnr, dir of Sharps (later Saatchi & Saatchi) 1976–87, exec vice-pres Dixons US 1987–89, commercial dir Dixons Gp plc 1989–92, dep md Dixons Stores Gp 1992–94; BT plc 1994–98: dir of Information, Communications and Entertainment, dir of Multimedia Services, md Consumer Div; chief exec BBC Worldwide 1998–2004, fndr Kingdom Media 2004, chm Contender Entertainment Gp 2004–06, chief exec Odeon/UCI Cinemas Gp 2005–; dir Incidental Colman 1981–, dir Ambassador Theatre Gp 1999–, non-exec dir Virgin Mobile 2004–06; Olivier Award for Best Entertainment 1998, 1999 and 2001; FRTS; *Recreations* theatre producer, lyricist, gardener; *Style*— Rupert Gavin, Esq

GAVRON, Nicolette (Nicky); AM; da of Clayton English Coates, and Elisabet Charlotta Horstmeyer; *Educ* Worcester GS, Courtauld Inst of Art; *m* 1967 (m dis 1987), Robert Gavron (Baron Gavron, CBE (Life Peer), *qv*); 2 da; *Career* lectr Camberwell and St Martins Schs of Art; elected Archway Ward Haringey Cncl (Lab) 1986 (chair Planning, Environment and Housing Ctees); GLA: memb London Assembly (Lab) Enfield & Haringey 2000–, dep mayor 2000–03; Lab mayoral candidate 2002 (stepped down 2003); memb Cmmn for Integrated Tport 1999–2002, memb Sustainable Devpt Cmmn 2000–, memb Met Police Authy 2000–; memb Exec Greater London Arts Assoc, vice-chair London Arts Bd 1992–2000, convenor London Arts and Regeneration Gp, memb Bd London First 1999–; London Planning Advsy Ctee (LPAC): memb and ldr Lab Gp 1989–97 and 1998–2000, dep chair 1989–94, chair 1994–97 and 1998–2000; ldr Lab Gp SE Regnl Conf (SERPLAN) 1993–97, chair Local Govt Assoc (LGA) Planning Ctee 1997–99 (vice-chair 1999–2000), chair LGA Futureswork on Reforming Local Planning 1997–2002, first co vice-chair London Pride Housing Initiative, rep LPAC on London Pride Partnership and Thames Advsy Gp 1994–97, initiated and co-chair (with Lord Sheppard of London First) London Pride Waste Action Programme 1995; chair Nat Planning Forum 1999–2002, advsr Urban Task Force 1998–2000; founding tstee Jackson's Lane Community Centre 1975–, chair Broadwater Farm Community Centre 2003–, dir Broadwater Farm Enterprise Centre; Hon Dr London Guildhall Univ 2001; Hon FRIBA 2001; *Publications* London: World City Study (1992), Values Added (1997); various papers on new strategic authority for London; *Style*— Ms Nicky Gavron, AM; ⊠ London Assembly, City Hall, Queens Walk, Southwark, London SE1 2AA

GAVRON, Baron (Life Peer UK 1999), of Highgate in the London Borough of Camden; Robert Gavron; CBE (1990); s of Nathaniel Gavron, of Hampstead, London; *b* 13 September 1930; *Educ* Leighton Park Sch Reading, St Peter's Coll Oxford (MA); *m* 1, 1955, Hannah (d 1965), da of T R Fyvel, of London; 2 s (Hon Simon b 1958 d 2005, Hon Jeremy b 1961); *m* 2, 1967 (m dis 1987), Nicolette (Nicky Gavron, AM, *qv*), da of C E Coates, of Worcester; 2 da (Hon Jessica b 1968, Hon Sarah b 1970); *m* 3, 1989, Mrs Katharine Gardiner, da of His Hon Peter Macnair, of London; *Career* called to the Bar Middle Temple 1955; entered printing industry 1955; St Ives Group: fndr 1964, chm 1964–93; chm: Folio Soc Ltd 1982–, Guardian Media Group plc 1997–2000; prop Carcanet Press Ltd 1983–; chm: Open Coll of the Arts 1991–96 (tstee 1987–96), National Gallery Publications Ltd 1996–98; chm of tstees Robert Gavron Charitable Tst; dir Royal Opera House 1992–98; tstee: National Gallery 1994–2001, Scott Tst 1997–2000, IPPR 1991– (treas 1994–2000); govr LSE 1997–2002; hon fell St Peter's Coll Oxford 1992; Hon FRCA 1990, Hon FRSL 1996; *Publications* The Entrepreneurial Society (jtly, 1998); *Clubs* MCC; *Style*— The Rt Hon the Lord Gavron, CBE

GAWKRODGER, Prof David John; *Educ* King Edward's Sch Bath, Univ of Birmingham (MB ChB, MD); *Career* house physician and surgn Queen Elizabeth Hosp Birmingham 1976–77, med sr house offr and registrar N Staffordshire Hosp Centre Stoke-on-Trent 1977–81, registrar and sr registrar in dermatology Royal Infirmary Edinburgh 1981–85, lectr in dermatology Univ of Edinburgh 1985–88, conslt dermatologist Royal Hallamshire Hosp Sheffield 1988–, hon prof of dermatology Univ of Sheffield 2003–; ed Br Jl of Dermatology 1996–99 (co-ed 1994–96); hon sec Dowling Club 1987–88, referee MRC NZ; memb Br Assoc of Dermatologists; MRCP, FRCPEd, FRCP; *Books* Skin Disorders in the Elderly (contrib, 1988), Immunology (contrib, 1985, 5 edn 1997), Dermatology - An Illustrated Colour Text (1992, 3 edn 2002), Textbook of Dermatology (contrib, 6 edn 2004); *Recreations* painting, drawing; *Style*— Prof David Gawkrodger; ⊠ Department of Dermatology, Royal Hallamshire Hospital, Glossop Road, Sheffield S10 2JF (tel 0114 271 2203)

GAWLER, Dr Jeffrey; *b* 17 July 1945; *Educ* St Olave's GS London, Med Coll St Bartholomew's Hosp Univ of London (MB BS); *m* 19 Dec 1970, Janet Mary; 1 s (Robert b 12 March 1973), 3 da (Ruth b 23 Sept 1975, Susan b 4 April 1978, Sarah b 6 Oct 1980); *Career* conslt Dept of Neurology Royal London and St Bartholomew's Hosps (conslt neurologist 1976–); memb: BMA, Assoc Br Neurologists; FRCP; *Books* Neurology and Computed Tomography; *Recreations* literature, oenology, hill walking; *Style*— Dr Jeffrey Gawler; ⊠ 145 Harley Street, London W1G 6BJ (tel 020 7224 0640, fax 020 7224 0638, e-mail drjgawler@145harleystreet.co.uk); Royal London Hospital, London E1 1BB (tel 020 7377 7214, fax 020 7943 1345, e-mail jeffrey.gawler@bartsandthelondon.nhs.uk)

GAYLE, Mike; *b* 1970, Birmingham; *Career* writer and journalist; former features ed Just Seventeen and agony uncle Bliss, sometime model Benetton; contrib: FHM, More, Sky, Cosmopolitan, B Magazine, Sunday Times Style; columnist The Express; *Books* My Legendary Girlfriend (1998), Mr Commitment (1999), Turning Thirty (2000), Dinner for Two (2002), His 'n' Hers (2004); *Style*— Mike Gayle, Esq ⊠ c/o Emma Longhurst, Hodder and Stoughton, 338 Euston Road, London NW1 3BH (tel 020 7873 6102, fax 020 7873 6123)

GAYLER, Paul Michael; s of Stanley Joseph Gayler (d 1998), of Clacton-on-Sea, Essex, and Lilian May, *née* Hall (d 1993); *b* 7 July 1955; *Educ* Priory Comp Sch Dagenham, Grays Thurrock Tech Coll; *m* 30 June 1979, Anita Pauline, da of Alan Blackburn; 2 s (Lee Daniel b 24 July 1983, Ryan James b 25 April 1985), 2 da (Lauren Marie b 21 April 1987, Rosie Adele b 11 Feb 1992); *Career* chef; apprenticeship Palace Hotel Torquay 1974–75, trg Royal Garden Hotel London 1975–80, sous chef Dorchester Hotel London 1980–82; head chef: Inigo Jones Restaurant London 1982–89 (dir 1985–89), Halkin Hotel Belgravia 1990–91; exec chef Lanesborough Hotel London 1991–, conslt chef Tesco Food Stores; chm Pierre Taittinger 2000–; winner Mouton Cadet competition 1979–82, finalist Pierre Tattinger competition Paris (later Br judge), various Gold & Silver medals Germany, Switzerland, Austria and Britain, judge Roux Scholarship 1989, 1990 and 1991; holder Matrise Escoffier Assoc Culinaire Française; Master Craftsman Cookery and Food Assoc, Palmes Culinaire Assoc Culinaire Française; memb: Académie Culinaire de France, Chefs and Cooks Circle, Guild de Fromagers de France, Craft Guild of Chefs, Master Chefs of GB; hon memb of Inst of Consumer Sciences; *Books* Virtually Vegetarian (1995), Great Value Gourmet (1996), Passion for Cheese (1997), Ultimate Vegetarian (1998), Passion for Vegetables (1999), Raising the Heat (2000), Passion for Potatoes (2001), Flavours of the World (2002), Healthy Eating for your Heart (2003), Mediterranean Cook (2004), Burgers (2004), Pure Vegetarian (2006), Steak (2006), World Breads (2006), World in Bite Size (2007); *Style*— Paul Gayler, Esq; ⊠ The Lanesborough Hotel, Hyde Park Corner, London SW1X 7TA (chef's office tel 020 7333 7009, fax 020 7259 5606, e-mail pgayler@lanesborough.com, website www.paulgayler.com)

GAYMER, Janet Marion; CBE (2004); da of Ronald Frank Craddock (d 1994), of Nuneaton, Warks, and Marion Clara, *née* Stringer (d 1988); *b* 11 July 1947; *Educ* Nuneaton HS for Girls, St Hilda's Coll Oxford (MA), LSE (LLM); *m* 4 Sept 1971, John Michael Gaymer, s of Kenneth John Gaymer (d 2001), of Great Bookham, Surrey; 2 da (Helen b 1977, Natalie b 1979); *Career* admitted slr 1973; Simmons & Simmons: ptnr and head Employment Law Dept 1977–, sr ptnr 2001–06; cmmr for public appts 2006–; chm Employment Law Ctee Law Soc 1993–96 (memb 1987), former chm Employment Law Sub-Ctee City of London Law Soc 1987; fndr chm and vice-pres Employment Lawyers Assoc 1993, fndr chm and hon chm European Employment Lawyers Assoc 1998; memb Editorial Advsy Bd: Sweet & Maxwell's Encyclopaedia of Employment Law 1987, Tolley's Health and Safety at Work 1995–2006; memb: Justice Ctee Industrial Tbnls 1987, Cncl ACAS 1995–2001, Cncl Justice 1995– (also memb Exec Bd 1995–2003); memb Steering Bd Employment Tbnls Service 2001–06; chair: Employment Tbnl System Taskforce 2001–02, reconstituted Employment Tbnl System Taskforce 2003–06; memb Bd of Govrs Royal Shakespeare Co 1999; The Times Woman of Achievement in the Law Award 1997, Ptnr of the Year The Lawyer/HIFAL Award 1998; visiting law fell St Hilda's Coll Oxford 1998, hon fell St Hilda's Coll Oxford 2002–; patron: Assoc of Women Slrs, City Women's Network; Hon LLD Univ of Nottingham 2004, Hon Dr Univ of Surrey 2006; Freeman Worshipful Co of Slrs 1977; affiliate IPD, memb Law Soc; memb CIArb; FRSA; *Publications* The Employment Relationship (2001); *Recreations* watercolour painting, swimming, theatre, music, opera; *Clubs* RAF, Athenaeum, Arts; *Style*— Mrs Janet Gaymer, CBE; ⊠ Office of the Commissioner for Public Appointments, 3rd Floor, 35 Great Smith Street, London SW1P 3BQ (tel 020 7276 2603, fax 020 7276 2633, e-mail ocpa@gtnet.gov.uk)

GAZDAR, Prof Gerald James Michael; s of John Gazdar (d 1966), of Hatfield, and Kathleen, *née* Cooper (d 1993); *b* 24 February 1950; *Educ* Heath Mount Sch, Bradfield Coll, UEA (BA), Univ of Reading (MA, PhD); *Career* Univ of Sussex: lectr in linguistics 1975–80, reader in linguistics 1980–84, reader in artificial intelligence and linguistics 1984–85, prof of computational linguistics 1985–2002 (emeritus prof 2002–), dean Sch of Cognitive and Computing Scis 1988–93; fell Center for Advanced Study in the Behavioral Scis Stanford Univ 1984–85; FBA 1988–2002; *Books* Pragmatics (1979), Order, Concord and Constituency (with Klein and Pullum, 1983), Generalized Phrase Structure Grammar (with Klein, Pullum and Sag, 1985), New Horizons in Linguistics II (with Lyons, Coates and Deuchar, 1987), Natural Language Processing in the 1980s (with Franz, Osborne, Evans, 1987), Natural Language Processing in Prolog/Lisp/Pop-11 (with Mellish, 1989); *Style*— Prof Gerald Gazdar; ⊠ School of Science and Technology, University of Sussex, Brighton BN1 9QH (tel 01273 678030, fax 01273 671320)

GAZE, Dr Mark Nicholas; s of John Owen Gaze (d 1987), and May Susan, *née* Skelton (d 2000); *b* 6 February 1958; *Educ* Med Coll of St Bartholomew's Hosp Univ of London (MB BS MD); *m* 22 June 1987 (m dis 1997), Dr Janet Ann Wilson, da of Dr Henry Donald Wilson (d 1991); 1 s (Donald John b 1991); *Career* house surgn Southend Hosp Essex 1981–82, house physician St Bartholomew's Hosp London 1982; sr house offr in med: Severalls Hosp Colchester 1983, St Mary's Hosp Portsmouth 1983–85; registrar in radiation oncology Royal Infirmary and Western Gen Hosp Edinburgh 1985–87; lectr in radiation oncology: Univ of Edinburgh 1987–89, Univ of Glasgow 1989–92, sr registrar in clinical oncology Beatson Oncology Centre Glasgow 1992–93, conslt oncologist UCL

Hosps and Great Ormond Street Hosp for Children 1993–, hon sr lectr UCL and Inst of Child Health Univ of London 1993–, chm London Trg Scheme for Clinical Oncolology London Deanery 2003–, chm Radiotherapy Gp UK Children's Cancer Study Gp 2004–; chm Collegiate Membs Ctee RCPE 1989–90 (memb Cncl 1988–90); memb Bd Faculty of Clinical Oncology RCR 1997–2000, memb Jt Cncl for Clinical Oncology 1998–2004, memb Educn Bd Faculty of Clinical Oncology RCR 2006–; pres Section of Oncology RSM 2002–03 (memb Cncl 2000–); chm Medical Ctee UCL Hosps 2006–07; MRCP 1984, FRCR 1988, FRCPEd 1995, FRCP 1999; *Books* Stell and Maran's Head and Neck Surgery (4 edn, 2000), Handbook of Community Cancer Care (2003); *Style*— Dr Mark Gaze; ✉ 8 Clarkson Row, London NW1 7RA (tel 020 7387 4565, e-mail mark.gaze@blueyonder.co.uk); Department of Oncology, University College Hospital, 250 Euston Road, London NW1 2PG(tel 020 7380 9090, fax 020 7380 9055, e-mail mark.gaze@uclh.nhs.uk); 81 Harley Street, London W1G 8PP (tel 020 7299 9408, fax 020 7299 9409, e-mail mark_gaze@lineone.net)

GAZE, Nigel Raymond; s of Raymond Ernest Gaze, of Knutsford Cheshire, and Beatrice Maud, *née* Caswell; *b* 11 February 1943; *Educ* Prescot GS, Univ of Liverpool (MB ChB), Univ of London (BMus); *m* 6 Aug 1966, Heather Winifred, da of Ronald Douglas Richardson, of Leeswood, Mold, Clwyd; 3 da (Julia b 4 Aug 1967, Celia b 23 March 1970, Mary b 7 Jan 1979), 3 s (Richard b 8 April 1972, Thomas b 27 Aug 1974, Harry b 29 March 1985); *Career* conslt plastic surgn Royal Preston and Blackpool Victoria Hosps 1980–; contrib various articles on med subjects in jls; organist, accompanist and composer; musical dir Elizabethan Singers, accompanied Hutton GS Chamber Choir on the record And My Heart Shall Be There, organist Clitheroe Assoc of Church Choirs and Fishergate Baptist Church, several published compositions for organ and choir; memb: Victorian Soc, RSCM, Preston Select Vestry, CPRE, Nat Tst, Br Inst of Organ Studies, Cncl Br Assoc of Aesthetic Plastic Surgns; memb: BMA, Br Assoc Plastic Surgns, Hospital Consultants and Specialists Assoc; FRCS, FRCSEd, FRCO, FTCL, FVCM, LRAM, MBAE; *Books* Year Book of Plastic Surgery (contrib, 1981); *Recreations* collecting books and interesting junk, architecture, DIY; *Style*— Nigel Gaze, Esq; ✉ Priory House, 35 Priory Lane, Penwortham, Preston, Lancashire PR1 0AR (tel 01772 743821); Royal Preston Hospital, Sharoe Green Lane, Fulwood, Preston, Lancashire PR2 9HT (tel 01772 716565); Fulwood Hall Hospital, Midgery Lane, Fulwood, Preston, Lancashire PR2 5SX

GAZZARD, Prof Brian George; s of Edward George Gazzard, and Elizabeth, *née* Hill; *b* 4 April 1946; *Educ* Univ of Cambridge (MA, MD); *m* 18 July 1970, Joanna Alice, da of Thomas Robinson Koeller; 3 s (Simon, Nicholas, Luke); *Career* sr registrar: Liver Unit KCH 1974–76, St Bartholomew's Hosp 1976–78; conslt physician and AIDS dir Westminster and St Stephen's Hosps 1978–; memb various ctees organising res and fin for AIDS patients; FRCP; *Books* Peptic Ulcer (1988), Gastroenterological Manifestations of AIDS, Clinics in Gastroenterology (1988); *Recreations* gardening; *Style*— Prof Brian Gazzard; ✉ Old Blew House, Dulwich Common, London SE21 (tel 020 7693 1151); Chelsea and Westminster Hospital, London SW5 (tel 020 8746 8239, fax 020 8834 4240, telex 919263 VHAG)

GAZZARD, Michael John (Mike); s of Kenneth Howard Gazzard, of East Molesey, Surrey, and Nancy Campbell, *née* Lawrence; *b* 20 June 1949; *Educ* Oakham Sch, Enfield Coll of Technol (BA), City Univ London (MSc); *m* Brenda, *née* Porth; 1 da (Hannah Sascha Louise b 9 July 1991), 1 s (George Alexander Howard b 5 March 1993); *Career* Student Trg Prog Simca Cars Paris 1969–70, market analyst Chrysler Int SA London 1972–73; VAG United Kingdom (formerly VW GB Ltd): Volkswagen product mangr (cars) 1973–76, area sales mangr 1976–79, Audi product mangr 1979–83; Toyota (GB) Ltd: advtg and sales promotion mangr 1983–91, mktg ops mangr 1991–93, dir of mktg ops 1993–94, dir of corp affrs and external communications 1994–96; mktg mangr Rolls-Royce and Bentley Motor Cars Ltd 1996–97, sr exec sales & mktg Rolls-Royce Motor Cars International SA 1997, md Custom Publishing Ltd 1998–; memb Inst of Mktg 1976, FIMI 1987; *Recreations* golf, hockey, swimming, tennis, squash; *Clubs* Effingham Golf, Horsley Sports, Clandon Regis Golf; *Style*— Mike Gazzard, Esq; ✉ Fairway House, Clandon Regis, Epsom Road, West Clandon, Surrey GU4 7TT (tel 01483 225221, fax 01483 225223, e-mail mg@custompublishing.co.uk)

GEARY, Kevin; s of Frank Geary (d 1992), and Hilda, *née* Stott (d 2005); *b* 3 November 1951; *Educ* Manchester Grammar, Univ of Kent at Canterbury (BA, MA); *Children* 2 da (Kerry b 11 March 1977, Rachel b 9 June 1982); *Career* successively: ODI fell Miny of Finance Swaziland 1974–76, ptnr Coopers & Lybrand 1978–94, dir of business devpt Clifford Chance 1995–2001, currently md Cigamon Consulting Ltd; author of numerous pubns; *Recreations* tennis, squash, theatre, cinema; *Style*— Kevin Geary, Esq; ✉ Cigamon Consulting Ltd, 189 Andrewes House, Barbican, London EC2Y 8BA (tel and fax 020 7638 1323)

GEARY, Michael John; s of John Geary (d 1980), of Hemel Hempstead, Herts, and Joyce Nellie, *née* Lee; *b* 18 June 1950; *Educ* Apsley GS Hemel Hempstead, Worcester Coll Oxford (MA); *m* 4 Jan 1975 (m dis 1992), Susan Mary, da of Henry Spilman Wood (d 1989), of Turweston, Northants; 2 s (John b and d 1979, Malcolm b 1980), 1 da (Hazel b 1982); *Career* exec engr PO Telecommunications (now British Telecommunications plc) 1971–74, controller Industrial and Commercial Finance Corporation Ltd (now 3i plc) 1974–79, investment exec Charterhouse Development Ltd 1979–82, md Munford White plc 1982–85; dir: Tunstall Development Ltd 1985–86, Prudential Venture Managers Ltd 1986–92; ceo Euroventures BV 1992–98, ceo MJG Ltd 1998–; chm-elect European Venture Capital Assoc; chm PACSCOM Ltd 1999–; *Recreations* sailing, skiing; *Clubs* Royal Southern Yacht, Emsworth Sailing, Ski Club of GB; *Style*— Michael Geary, Esq

GEBBETT, Stephen Henry; s of Albert Gebbett, of Hundon, Suffolk, and Elsie Mary, *née* Kettle; *b* 24 January 1949; *Educ* Raynes Park Co GS, Univ of Wales (BSc Econ); *m* 22 Dec 1973, Linda Margaret; 1 s (Timothy Giles b 5 Oct 1976), 1 da (Kimberley Sarah b 13 May 1981); *Career* graduate trainee and assoc dir F J Lyons PR Consultancy 1970–76; Marketing Div Charles Barker (formerly Charles Baker Lyons): assoc dir 1976–79, dir 1979–86, md 1986–88, chief exec 1988–91, chm and chief exec 1991–92; dir Charles Barker BSMG (formerly Charles Barker plc) 1992–, md Charles Barker Marketing 1996–, creative dir Charles Barker BSMG Worldwide 1999–2000, sr conslt Hill and Knowlton 2000–03, dir PR Four Communications plc 2003–; FCIPR (MIPR 1976, FIPR 1998); *Recreations* squash, gardening, humour; *Style*— Stephen Gebbett, Esq; ✉ Four Communications plc, 48 Leicester Square, London WC2H 7FG (mobile 07812 149455, e-mail steve.gebbett@fourcommunications.com)

GÉBLER, Carlo Ernest; s of Ernest Gébler (d 1998), and Edna, *née* O'Brien; *b* 21 August 1954; *Educ* Bedales, Univ of York (BA), Nat Film and TV Sch; *m* Tyga; 2 da (India Rose b 1981, Georgia Madeleine b 1994), 3 s (Jack Redmond b 1987, Finn b 1990, Euan b 1998); *Career* author, script writer, film director; memb Aosdána (Eire) 1990; tutor of creative writing HM Prison Maze 1995, writer in residence HM Prison Maghaberry 1997–, Br Cncl int writing fell TCD 2004, Arts Cncl writing fell TCD 2006, lectr in creative writing Queens Univ Belfast 2007; *Publications* The Eleventh Summer (1985), August In July (1986), Work and Play (1987), Driving through Cuba: An East-West Journey (1988), The TV Genie (1989), Malachy and his Family (1989), Life of a Drum (1990), The Witch That Wasn't (1991), The Glass Curtain: Inside an Ulster Community (1991), The Cure (1994), W9 & Other Lives (1996), How to Murder a Man (1998), Frozen Out (1998), The Base (1999), Father & I (2000), Caught on a Train (2001), August '44 (2003), The Siege of Derry: A History (2005), The Bull Raid (2005), A Good Day for a Dog (2007); *Plays* How to Murder a Man (1995), The Dance of Death Parts I & II (adaptor, 1998), Ten Rounds (2002), Silhouette (2006), Henry & Harriet (2007); author of reviews, articles, short stories, travel pieces; contrib to short story collections: Travellers Tales, London Tales, 20 under 35, Winter's Tales 6, New Writing Two, Fatherhood, My Generation, New Writing 9; *Films* writer and dir: Croagh Patrick 1977, The Beneficiary 1979, Over Here 1980, Rating Notman 1981, Country & Irish 1982, Two Lives: A Portrait of Francis Stuart 1985, George Barker 1987, August in July (writer) 1990, Plain Tales from Northern Ireland 1993, Life After Death 1994, The Widow's Daughter (writer) 1995, A Little Local Difficulty 1995, Baseball in Irish History 1996, Put to the Test 1998 (winner RTS Award for Best Regnl Documentary 1999), The Suspecting Glance: Conor Cruise O'Brien 2001, Student Life 2001; *Recreations* walking, travelling, reading; *Style*— Carlo Gébler, Esq; ✉ c/o Antony Harwood, 103 Walton Street, Oxford OX2 6EB (tel 01865 559615, fax 01865 554173, e-mail ant@antonyharwood.com)

GEDDES, His Hon Judge Andrew Campbell; s of Hon Alexander Geddes, OBE, MC, TD (d 1974), and Hon Margaret, *née* Addis, of London; *b* 10 June 1943; *Educ* Stowe, ChCh Oxford (MA); *m* 1, Jacqueline Tan Bunzl; 2 s (Nicholas Campbell b 1975, Dominic Campbell b 1978); m 2, Bridget Bowring; 1 s (Leo Patrick b 1981), 1 da (Katharine Arabella b 1986); *Career* fndr Building Product Index 1968; called to the Bar Inner Temple 1972; recorder 1990–94, circuit judge (Midland Circuit) 1994–, authorised to sit as High Court judge 1995, designated civil judge Worcester Gp of Courts 1998; *Books* Product and Service Liability in the EEC (1992), Protection of Individual Rights in EC Law (1995), Public and Utility Procurement (1996); *Recreations* writing, walking, music, gardening; *Style*— His Hon Judge Andrew Geddes; ✉ c/o Courts Administrators Office, Worcester Combined Court, The Shirehall, Foregate Street, Worcester WR1 1EQ

G

GEDDES, Prof Duncan Mackay; s of Sir Reay Geddes, KBE (d 1998), and Imogen, *née* Matthey; *b* 6 January 1942; *Educ* Eton, Magdalene Coll Cambridge (MA), Westminster Med Sch (MB BS), Univ of London (MD); *m* 16 April 1968, Donatella Flaccomio Nardi Dei, da of Marchesa A Roselli del Turco Medici Tornaquinci; 2 s (Gavin b 27 Feb 1971, Acland b 3 March 1981), 1 da (Gaia b 5 April 1973); *Career* jr hosp appts Westminster, Hammersmith, Middx and Brompton Hosps 1971–78; conslt physician: London Chest Hosp 1978–87, Brompton Hosp 1978–; civilian conslt in diseases of the chest to: the Army 1988–, the Navy 1991–; dir: Finsbury Worldwide Pharmaceutical Tst 1995–, India Pharma Fund 2005–; chm Bd National Asthma Campaign 1996–2003; memb Med Advsy Bd Transgene Spa 1997–2001; Br Thoracic Soc: hon sec 1981–84, vice-pres 1999–2000, pres 2000–2001; FRCP 1982; *Books* Practical Medicine (1976), Airways Obstruction (1981), Respiratory Medicine (1990), Cystic Fibrosis (1994); author of over 250 scientific articles and invited chapters; *Recreations* tennis, golf, painting; *Clubs* Queen's, Boodle's; *Style*— Prof Duncan Geddes; ✉ Royal Brompton Hospital, Fulham Road, London SW3 6NP (tel 020 7352 8121, fax 020 7351 8999, e-mail d.geddes@rbht.nhs.uk)

GEDDES, 3 Baron (UK 1942), of Rolvenden; Euan Michael Ross Geddes; s of 2 Baron, KBE (d 1975), and Enid, *née* Butler (d 1999); *b* 3 September 1937; *Educ* Rugby, Gonville & Caius Coll Cambridge (MA), Harvard Business Sch; *m* 1, 1966, Gillian (d 1995), yr da of late William Arthur Butler, of Henley-on-Thames, Oxon; 1 da (Hon (Margaret) Clair b 1967), 1 s (Hon James George Neil b 1969); m 2, 1996, Susan Margaret, da of late George Harold Carter, of Kingswood, Surrey; *Heir* s, Hon James Geddes; *Career* Lt Cdr RNR (ret); chm: Photo Corp (UK) Ltd 1988–, Chromecastle Ltd 2000–; dir Portman Settled Estates Ltd 1977–; House of Lords: elected hereditary peer 1999–, dep speaker 2000–, chm Sub-Ctee B (Energy, Tport and Industry) 1995–99, memb Procedure Ctee 2002–05, memb Sub-Ctee B (Internal Market) 2003–, memb Liaison Ctee 2005–; treas Assoc of Conservative Peers 2000–; dir Trinity Coll of Music 1987–, chm Trinity Coll London 1992–; *Recreations* golf, music, shooting, bridge, gardening; *Clubs* Brooks's, Aldeburgh Golf, Hong Kong, Hong Kong Golf, Noble and Gentlemen's Catch; *Style*— The Lord Geddes; ✉ House of Lords, London SW1A 0PW; home (tel 020 7219 6400, fax 020 7219 5979)

GEDDES, Prof John; *Educ* Manchester Grammar, Univ of Leeds; *Career* med trg in psychiatry Sheffield, Edinburgh and Oxford, currently hon conslt psychiatrist and prof of epidemiological psychiatry Dept of Psychiatry Univ of Oxford; *Style*— Prof John Geddes; ✉ Department of Psychiatry, University of Oxford, Warneford Hospital, Oxford OX3 7JX

GEDDES, Michael Dawson; s of David Geddes, and Audrey Clinton, *née* Phillips; *b* 9 March 1944; *Educ* Sherborne, Univ of British Columbia (Goldsmiths' exhibitioner, BA); *m* 1966, Leslie Rose, *née* Webb; 2 s (b 1969 and 1971); *Career* Cranfield Inst of Technol: admin asst 1968–71, planning offr 1971–76, devpt and estates offr 1976–83, fin controller (RMCS) 1983–84; sec Ashridge (Bonar Law Meml) Trust; dir: Admin Ashridge Mgmnt Coll, Ashridge Strategic Mgmnt Centre, Ashridge Mgmnt Devpt Servs, Ashridge Mgmnt Res Gp 1984–90; chief exec: Recruitment and Assessment Servs 1990–95, Civil Serv Cmmn 1990–97; dir Milton Keynes Economic Partnership 1995–2003, vice-chm SE England Regnl Assembly 1998–2002; *Books* Project Leadership (1990), Making Public Private Partnerships Work (2005); author of numerous articles in various jls; *Recreations* golf, gardening; *Style*— Michael Geddes, Esq; ✉ 2 Tidbury Close, Woburn Sands, Milton Keynes MK17 8QW (tel 01908 282830)

GEDDES, Philip Clinton; s of David Geddes, and Audrey Clinton, *née* Phillips; *b* 26 August 1947; *Educ* Sherborne, Queens' Coll Cambridge; *m* 27 Oct 1984, Selina Valerie, da of Capt Derek Head, RNR; 3 s (David b 1985, James b 1989, Thomas Christian b 1991), 1 da (Emily Anne b 1993); *Career* gen trainee BBC 1970, prodr BBC features 1973–80, exec prodr TVS and head of sci and industry progs 1981–88; former ed Special Reports Financial Times TV; currently: chm Consilia Ltd, dir Harcourt Public Affairs, writer and conslt to business; govr Edgeborough Sch; *Books* In the Mouth of the Dragon (1981), Inside the Bank of England (1988); *Recreations* cricket; *Clubs* Ooty; *Style*— Philip Geddes, Esq; ✉ Manor Farm, Upper Wield, Alresford, Hampshire SO24 9RU (tel 01420 562361, e-mail geddesp@msn.com)

GEE, Kathryn Olive Perry (Kathy); da of Dr Eric Arthur Gee, FSA (d 1989), of York, and Olive Mary, *née* Deer (d 1992); *b* 2 July 1951; *Educ* Mill Mount GS York, Univ of Exeter (BA), Univ of Leicester (postgrad cert in mus studies); *m* 1975 (m dis 1997), Julian Elsworth Tanner; *Career* museum service dir; curator Cookworthy mus Devon and Wheal Martyn Mus Cornwall English China Clays 1973–84, freelance conslt 1983–90; dir W Midlands Regnl Museums Cncl 1990–2002, chief exec MLA W Midlands 2002–06, Volition Exec Coaching 2006–; external examiner UCL 1994–96; chair W Midlands Regnl Forum 1999–2005; memb: Ctee Area Museum Cncls 1990–2002 (dep chair 1998–2002), Midlands Fedn of Museums 1990–, Prison Servs Museum Ctee 1990–95, Assoc of Ind Museums (memb Cncl 1988–96), Exec Bd Ironbridge Gorge Museum 1994–2001, Ctee of Industry '96, Standards & Qualifications Ctee of MTI 1993–96, Working Pty on Criteria for Designation Museums & Galleries Cmmn 1996–98, DCMS Design Gp for MLAC 1999, Re:Source Working Gp on Learning Standards 2001; memb Bd, Exec and Staffing Sub-Ctee SW Area Museum Cncl 1987–90, pres SW Fedn of Museums 1987–89 memb Ctee until 1990), fndr and co-convenor Devon Fedn of Museums 1986–90; sec Feckenham Forest Local History Soc 1990–94; memb Vernacular Architecture Gp 1991–; parish cncllr 1995–2000, tstee Feckenham Village Amenity Tst 1995–2000, vice-chm Village Green Mgmnt Ctee 1995–99; author of numerous articles; Dip in corp and exec coaching 2007, NLP practitioner 2007; FMA 1986 (AMA 1976); *Publications* five for Cookworthy Museum, two for Wheal Martyn Museum, four for Nat Trust, three books on local history, Museum Projects - a handbook for volunteers (1989), The Heritage Web - structures and relationships (1993), First Principles - a framework for museum development in the West Midlands (1996), Fast Forward (2000); *Recreations* local history, travel, gardening; *Style*— Ms Kathy Gee; ✉ Volition Executive Coaching, 43 High Street, Feckenham, Redditch, Worcestershire B96 6HW (e-mail kathy.gee@volition-coaching.co.uk)

GEE, Dr Maggie Mary; da of Victor Gee, of Holt, Norfolk, and Aileen, *née* Church; *b* 2 November 1948; *Educ* Horsham HS for Girls, Somerville Coll Oxford (major open scholar, MA, BLitt), Wolverhampton Poly (PhD); *m* 1983, Nicholas Rankin; 1 da (Rosa b 1986); *Career* writer 1982–; writing fell UEA 1982, teaching fell Univ of Sussex 1996– (hon visiting fell 1986–), visiting lectr Univ of Northumbria 2000–02, visiting prof Sheffield Hallam Univ 2005–; chair RSL 2004– (memb Cncl 1999–); memb: Mgmnt Ctee Soc of Authors 1991–94, Govt Public Lending Right Ctee 2001–; judge Booker Prize 1989; Hawthornden fell 1989, Northern Arts fell 1996; FRSL 1994; *Books* Dying In Other Words (1981), The Burning Book (1983), Light Years (1985), Grace (1988), Where are the Snows (1991), Lost Children (1994), The Ice People (1998), The White Family (2002, shortlisted Orange Prize for Fiction 2002, Impac Prize for Fiction 2004), The Flood (2004), My Cleaner (2005), The Blue (2006); *Recreations* film, visual arts, walking, swimming; *Style*— Dr Maggie Gee, FRSL; ✉ c/o Society of Authors, 84 Drayton Gardens, London SW10 9SB

GEE, Stephen; s of Norman and Barbara Gee; *b* 18 February 1944; *Educ* Ardingly; *Career* Price Waterhouse CAs 1962–68, Forte plc 1968–70, Samuel Montagu & Co Ltd 1970–75, md Waterbrook Ltd 1975–82, fin dir and dep chm My Kinda Town plc 1982–97, md Wallace Clifton Ltd 1997–; dir: Ashtenne Holdings plc, English Country Inns plc; chm: Carluccio's Ltd, Henry J Beans plc; FCA; *Recreations* tennis, sailing, shooting; *Style*— Stephen Gee, Esq; ✉ Wallace Clifton Ltd, 1 Airlie Gardens, London W8 7AJ

GEE, Steven Mark; QC (1993); s of Dr Sidney Gee, of Regent's Park, London, and Dr Hilda Gee, *née* Elman; *b* 24 August 1953; *Educ* Tonbridge, BNC Oxford (open scholar, MA, Gibbs prize for law); *m* 13 June 1999, Meryll Emilie, *née* Bacri; 2 s (Alexander b 15 April 2000, Harry b 9 August 2001); *Career* called to the Bar Middle Temple (Harmsworth scholar, Senate of Inns of Court prizeman in Bar Finals) 1975, recorder and memb NY Bar, admitted Federal Courts of NY; in commercial practice, recorder, formerly standing jr counsel in export credit guarantee matters DTI, head of chambers Stone Chambers; FCIArb; *Books* Commercial Injunctions (5 edn 2004); *Recreations* marathon running; *Clubs* Serpentine Running, MCC; *Style*— Steven Gee, Esq, QC; ✉ 38 Eaton Terrace, London SW1W 8TS (tel 020 7823 4660); Stone Chambers, 4 Field Court, Gray's Inn, London WC1 (tel 020 7440 6900, fax 020 7242 0197, e-mail steven.gee@stonechambers.com)

GEE, Timothy Edward Daniel (Tim); s of Archibald Geoffrey Gee, of Northampton, and Rosemary Noel, *née* Foster; *b* 26 May 1962; *Educ* Bedford Sch, Worcester Coll Oxford (Simmons & Simmons open scholar, BA); *m* 3 July 1993, Anita Kau Heung; *Career* Baker & McKenzie: articled clerk 1984–86, based London 1986–88, Hong Kong 1989–90, Budapest 1991, ptnr (based London) 1992–, currently head Global M&A; memb Law Soc 1986, admitted slr Hong Kong 1989; *Recreations* rugby, fly fishing, wine; *Clubs* East India, Old Bedfordians, Hong Kong Football, The Flyfishers'; *Style*— Tim Gee, Esq; ✉ Baker & McKenzie, 100 New Bridge Street, London EC4V 6JA (tel 020 7919 1000, fax 020 7919 1999, e-mail timothy.gee@bakernet.com)

GEFFEN, Charles Slade Henry (Charlie); s of Bill Geffen, of Milford, Surrey, and Bridget, *née* Slade Baker; *b* 19 September 1959, London; *Educ* Harrow, Univ of Leicester (LLB); *m* 17 May 1986, Rosey, da of Peter Valder; 1 da (Becky b 22 April 1990), 3 s (Jack b 19 Feb 1992, Ben b 23 March 1994, Oliver b 10 Oct 1998); *Career* slr; ptnr Ashurst 1991–; *Style*— Charlie Geffen, Esq; ✉ Ashurst, Broadwalk House, 5 Appold Street, London EC2A 2HA (tel 020 7859 1718, e-mail charlie.geffen@ashurst.com)

GELARDI, Geoffrey Alan David; s of Albert Charles Gelardi, and Noreen, *née* Eagles; *b* 28 July 1953; *Educ* St George's Coll Weybridge Surrey; *m* 4 May 1984, Eileen Mary, da of William Sheridan; 3 da (Piera Maria b 27 Oct 1985, Georgina Maria b 28 Jan 1987, Olivia Maria b 29 April 1995); *Career* hotelier; various positions: Carlton Tower London 1970–71, Grand Hotel et Tivollier Toulouse 1971–72, London Hilton Hotel 1972–74; grad trainee prog Waldorf Astoria NYC 1974, co-ordinator of hotel opening and mangr Terrace Coffee Shop Hilton Hotel of Philadelphia 1975, asst to Food & Beverage Dir Waldorf Astoria 1976; dir of food & beverage ops: New York Statler Hilton NYC 1977, Arlington Park Hilton Chicago 1978, Resorts International Casino Hotel Atlantic City New Jersey 1979–81; resident mangr Plaza of the Americas Dallas 1981, mangr Remington Hotel Houston 1982; md Bel Air Hotel Los Angeles 1983–85, md/ptnr Sorrento Hotel Seattle 1985–90, md The Lanesborough London 1990–; *Recreations* squash, tennis, horseriding; *Clubs* RAC, Annabel's; *Style*— Geoffrey Gelardi, Esq; ✉ The Lanesborough, 1 Lanesborough Place, London SW1X 7TA

GELBER, David; s of Edward Gelber (d 1970), of Toronto, and Anna, *née* David (d 1974); *b* 10 November 1947; *Educ* Whittinghame Coll Brighton, Hebrew Univ Jerusalem (BSc), Univ of London (MSc); *m* 1, 1969 (m dis 1979), Laura Beare; 1 s (Jeremy Edward b 1973), 1 da (Amy b 1975); *m* 2, 1982, Vivienne, da of Harry Cohen, of Weybridge; *Career* Morgan Guaranty Tst 1975–76, vice-pres Citibank/Citicorp 1976–85, md (head of global swaps and foreign exchange options) Chemical Bank 1985–89, global mangr (head of swaps and options) Hong Kong Bank 1989–92, jt md James Capel Gilts Ltd 1992–94, chief operating offr Midland Global Markets, gp md Intercapital Ltd 1994–98, chief operating offr Intercapital plc 1998–2005; non-exec chm Walker Crips Weddle Beck plc 2007–; *Recreations* tennis, squash; *Clubs* RAC Cumberland Lt; *Style*— David Gelber, Esq

GELDARD, Robin John; CBE (1996); s of Cyril John Geldard (d 1984), of Thornton Dene, S Glamorgan, and Gertrude Nellie Lawrence (d 1971); *b* 9 August 1935; *Educ* Aldenham, Coll of Law; *m* 4 Sept 1965, Susan Elizabeth, da of Sir Martin Llewellyn Edwards (d 1987), of Lisvane, Cardiff; 2 s (Bruce b 1967, Michael b 1970), 1 da (Anna b 1972); *Career* recruit RM 1958, Mons Offr Cadet Sch, cmmnd RM 1959, 2 Lt Commando Trg Unit, RM rugby team 1958–60; admitted slr; ptnr then sr ptnr Edwards Geldard 1962–95, asst registrar 1980–85; dir various cos 1980–95, memb Lloyd's 1986, dir Minories Underwriting Agencies Ltd until 1998, business conslt 1998–; pres: Cardiff Incorporated C of C and Industry 1987–89, Cardiff Incorporated Law Soc 1988–89 (vice-pres 1987–88), Federated Welsh C of C 1988–94 (vice-pres 1987–88), Assoc British Chambers of Commerce 1994–96 (dep pres 1992–94); hon consul for Japan at Cardiff 1993 and 1996; *Recreations* sailing, fly fishing, music, photography; *Clubs* Naval, RYA; *Style*— Robin Geldard, Esq, CBE; ✉ Mole End, Pillory Hill, Noss Mayo, Plymouth PL8 1ED (tel and fax 01752 873094, e-mail robin@rgeldard.plus.com)

GELDER, Prof Michael Graham; s of Philip Graham Gelder (d 1972), and Alice Margaret, *née* Graham (d 1985); *b* 2 July 1929; *Educ* Bradford GS, The Queen's Coll Oxford, UCH Med Sch London; *m* 21 Aug 1954, Margaret Constance, da of Lt-Col John William Smith Anderson (d 1984); 1 s (Colin b 31 May 1960), 2 da (Fiona (Mrs Timothy Harry) b 12 Jan 1963, Nicola (Mrs Zeno Poggi) b 9 May 1964); *Career* Capt RAMC 1955–57; sr house physician Univ Coll Hosp 1957 (house physician 1955), registrar Bethlem Royal and Maudsley Hosps 1958–61, MRC fell in clinical res 1962–63; Inst of Psychiatry: lectr 1964–65, sr lectr 1965–67, vice-dean 1967–68; prof of psychiatry Univ of Oxford 1969–96 (emeritus prof 1996–), fell Merton Coll Oxford 1969–96 (emeritus fell 1996–, subwarden 1992–94); chm: Neurosciences Bd MRC 1978–79 (memb 1976–78 and 1988–91), Neurosciences Ctee Wellcome Tst 1990–95; vice-pres RCPsych 1982–84; fell Acad of Med Scis 1998; FRCP 1970, FRCPsych 1973; *Books* Psychological Aspects of Medical Practice (ed 1973), Agoraphobia: Nature and Treatment (jtly 1981), Oxford Textbook of Psychiatry (jtly 1983, 5 edn 2006), Concise Oxford Textbook of Psychiatry (jtly 1994, 3 edn 2005), New Oxford Textbook of Psychiatry (jtly 2000, Spanish edn 2003, 2 edn 2008); *Recreations* travel, reading, photography; *Style*— Prof Michael Gelder; ✉ Merton College, Oxford OX1 4JD

GELDOF, Bob; Hon KBE (1986); *b* 5 October 1951; *Educ* Blackrock Coll Dublin; *m* 1986 (m dis 1996), Paula Yates (d 2000); 3 da (Fifi Trixibelle, Peaches Honeyblossom, Pixie); 1 adopted da (Heavenly Hiraani Tigerlilly (da of Paula Yates and Michael Hutchence)); *Career* former journalist with Georgia Straight Canada, NME and Melody Maker; fndr and memb Boomtown Rats 1975–86; organiser: Live Aid 1985, Live 8 2005; chm Band Aid Tst 1985–; former co-owner Planet 24, co-fndr Ten Alps Communications 1999; fndr: Deckchair.com, WapWorld; cmmr Cmmn for Africa, campaigner against Third World debt and supporter of numerous charities incl Make Poverty History and Drop the Debt; Hon Dr of Law: Univ of Dundee 2002, UC Dublin 2004; Hon DCL: UEA 2004, Univ of Newcastle upon Tyne 2007; Hon DUniv Roehampton Univ 2007; Chavalier des Arts et des Lettres 2006; *Singles* co-writer (with Midge Ure, *qv*) Do They Know It's Christmas? (Band Aid) 1984, Do They Know It's Christmas? (Band Aid II) 1989, Do They Know It's Christmas? (Band Aid 20) 2004; *Albums* The Boomtown Rats: The Boomtown Rats 1977, Tonic for the Troops 1978, The Fine Art of Surfacing 1979, Mondo Bongo 1980, V Deep 1982, In the Long Grass 1984, The Best of The Boomtown Rats 2003; solo: Deep In the Heart of Nowhere 1986, The Vegetarians of Love 1990, The Happy Club 1992, Sex, Age & Death 2001; *Television* Grumpy Old Men (BBC) 2003, Geldof in Africa (BBC) 2005; *Film* Pink in Pink Floyd's The Wall, Harry 'Flash' Gordon in Number One (1985); *Awards* UN World Hunger Award, Irish Peace Prize, Rose d'Or Charity Award 2005, Lifetime Achievement Award Brit Awards 2005, Free Your Mind Award MTV 2005, Nobel Man of Peace Award 2005, The North-South Cncl Award 2005, Marketer of the Year Award EPM 2006, nominated 6 times for Nobel Peace Award (latest nomination 2007); *Publications* Is That It? (autobiography, 1986), Geldof in Africa (2005); *Style*— Bob Geldof, KBE; ✉ c/o Gina Nelthorpe-Cowne, Kruger Cowne Ltd, Unit 18G Chelsea Wharf, 15 Lots Road, London SW10 0QJ (tel 020 7352 2929, e-mail gina@krugercowne.com)

GEMMELL, Gavin John Norman; CBE (1998); s of late Gilbert Anderson Sloan Gemmell, of Gullane, E Lothian, and late Dorothy Maud Gemmell; *b* 7 September 1941; *Educ* George Watson's Coll; *m* 18 March 1967, Kathleen Fiona (Kate), *née* Drysdale; 2 da (Alison Fiona b 22 Aug 1969, Lynsey Jane b 4 April 1975), 1 s (John Gilbert b 9 Sept 1971); *Career* CA 1964; Baillie Gifford & Co: investment trainee 1964, ptnr 1967, ptnr i/c pension fund clients 1973, sr ptnr 1989–2001; chm: Toyo Trust Baillie Gifford Ltd 1990–2001, Scottish Widows 2002–, Gyneideas 2006–; dir: Guardian Baillie Gifford 1991–2001, Archangel Informal Investments 2001–, Lloyds TSB Group 2002–; tstee Nat Gallery of Scotland 1999–2007; chm Ct Heriot-Watt Univ 2002–; *Recreations* golf, travel; *Clubs* Gullane Golf, Hon Co of Edinburgh Golfers; *Style*— Gavin Gemmell, Esq, CBE; ✉ 14 Midmar Gardens, Edinburgh EH10 6DZ (tel 0131 466 6367, e-mail gavingemmell@blueyonder.co.uk)

GEMMELL, James Henry Fife; s of James Walter Shanks Gemmell (d 1962), and Vera McKenzie, *née* Scott (d 1990); *b* 17 May 1943; *Educ* Dunfermline HS, Univ of Edinburgh; *m* 27 Dec 1972, (Catherine) Morna Davidson, da of late John Wilson Gammie, of Elgin, Morayshire; 2 da (Caroline b 1974, Catriona b 1976); *Career* CA 1965; ptnr Fryer Whitehill and Co 1975–82; ptnr Horwath Clark Whitehill 1982–2003 (chm 1997–2002), chm Horwath Clark Whitehill Associates Ltd 1985–2003, memb Cncl Horwath International 1994–2002, chm Horwath International Europe 1996–; chm Bridford Career Mgmnt plc 1990–2000, conslt Siddall & Co Ltd 2004–, dir Pharmovation 2005–; ICAS: memb Cncl 1988–94, chm Fin and Gen Purposes Ctee 1990–94, Eng and Wales Area Ctee 1989–92, memb Discipline Ctee 1994–98; chm Flexlands Sch Educnl Tst Ltd 1988–2001; hon fell Sch of Pharmacy Univ of London (treas 2000–); MAE, FRSA; *Books* RICS Accounts Rules (1978), Insurance Brokers Accounts and Business Requirement Rules (1979), How to Value Stock (1983); *Recreations* gardening; *Clubs* Caledonian; *Style*— James Gemmell, Esq; ✉ Horwath International, St Bride's House, 10 Salisbury Square, London EC4Y 8EH (tel 020 7842 7100, fax 020 7583 1720, e-mail jgemmell@horwath.co.uk)

GEMS, Iris Pamela (Pam); da of Jim Price (d 1930), of Christchurch, Dorset, and Elsa Mabel Annetts (d 1989); *Educ* Christchurch Priory Sch, Brockenhurst GS, Univ of Manchester; *m* Sept 1949, Keith Leopold Gems, s of Leopold Frederick Gems; 2 s (Jonathan b 1952, David b 1960), 2 da (Sara b 1954, Elizabeth (Lalla) b 1965); *Career* playwright and author; memb: Dramatists' Guild (US), Writers' Guild; *Plays* Dusa, Fish, Stas and Vi (1976), Queen Christina (1977), Piaf (1978) Franz into April (1978), The Treat (1979), Pasionaria (1981), Camille (1985), The Danton Affair (1986), The Blue Angel (1991), Deborah's Daughter (1994), Marlene (1995), Stanley (1995, Evening Standard Award for Best Play 1996, Olivier Award for Best Play 1997), The Snow Palace (1998), Nelson (2005), Mrs Pat (2006); *Novels* Mrs Frampton (1989), Bon Voyage, Mrs Frampton (1990); *Recreations* gardening; *Style*— Mrs Pam Gems; ✉ c/o PFD, Drury House, 34–43 Russell Street, London WC2B 5HA

GENN, Prof Dame Hazel Gillian; DBE (2006), Hon QC (2006); da of Lionel Genn (d 2004), and Dorothy, *née* Rosen; *b* 17 March 1949, London; *Educ* Univ of Hull (BA), CNAA (LLB), Univ of London (LLD); *m* 1973, Daniel Appleby; 1 da (Beatrice Hope b 1977), 1 s (Matthew Felix b 1980); *Career* researcher: Inst of Criminology Cambridge 1972–74, Oxford Centre for Socio-Legal Studies 1974–85; successively lectr, reader, prof and head of dept Law Dept QMC London 1985–94, prof Faculty of Laws UCL 1994–; memb: Ctee on Standards in Public Life 2003–, Judicial Appts Cmmn 2006–; Hon LLD: Kingston Univ 2004, Univ of Edinburgh 2004, Univ of Leicester 2007; memb: Soc for Legal Scholars, Socio-Legal Studies Assoc; FBA 2000; *Publications* Hard Bargaining (1987), Paths to Justice (1999), Paths to Justice Scotland (2001), Tribunals for Diverse Users (2006); *Recreations* walking, music; *Clubs* Athenaeum; *Style*— Prof Dame Hazel Genn, DBE; ✉ Faculty of Laws, University College London, Bentham House, Endsleigh Gardens, London WC1H 0EG (tel 020 7679 1436, e-mail h.genn@ucl.ac.uk)

GENNARD, Prof John; s of Arthur Gennard (d 1962), of Manchester, and Vera Edith, *née* Stone (d 1980); *b* 26 April 1944; *Educ* Univ of Sheffield (BA), Univ of Manchester (MA); *m* 8 May 1976, Florence Anne, da of Daniel Russell (d 1973), of Iver Heath; 1 s (John Cooper), 1 da (Julie Anne); *Career* lectr LSE 1970–81 (res offr 1968–70), prof of industrial rels Univ of Strathclyde 1981–, dean Strathclyde Business Sch 1987–93; memb Panel of Arbitrators ACAS; FCIPD (memb Membership and Educn Ctee, nat chief examiner Employee Rels); *Books* The Reluctant Militants (1972), Financing Strikers (1977), Closed Shop in British Industry (1983), A History of the National Graphical Association (1990), A History of the Society of Graphical and Allied Trades (1995), Power and Influence in the Boardroom (2001), The Career Paths of HR Directors (2002); *Recreations* football, politics, food and drink; *Clubs* Carluke Rotary; *Style*— Prof John Gennard; ✉ 4 South Avenue, Carluke, Lanarkshire ML8 5TW (tel 01555 751361); Department of Human Resource Management, University of Strathclyde, Hills Building, Richmond Street, Glasgow G4 0GE (tel 0141 548 3999, fax 0141 552 3581, e-mail j.gennard@strath.ac.uk)

GENT, (John) David Wright; s of Pilot Offr Reginald Philip Gent, RAFVR (d 1942), and Stella Eva Wright (d 1988); *b* 25 April 1935; *Educ* Lancing; *m* 19 Aug 1970, Anne Elaine, da of John Leslie Hanson (d 1988), of Ilkley, W Yorks; *Career* admitted slr 1959; dep dir SMMT 1971–80 (legal advsr 1961–63, asst sec 1964, sec 1965–70), gen mangr Lucas Service UK Ltd 1980–82, gp PR mangr Lucas Industries plc 1982–83; dir Br Rd Fedn 1983–85, DG Retail Motor Indust Fedn (formerly Motor Agents Assoc) 1985–95, chm Motor Industry Pensions Ltd 1985–95, specialist conslt 1995–2007, dir D C Cook Holdings plc 1995–2001, co sec Whitock Mgmnt Ltd 1998–2000, dir Autofil Properties Ltd 2002–05; memb Rd Tport Indust Trg Bd 1985–91; Freeman City of London 1985, Liveryman Worshipful Co of Coach Makers and Coach Harness Makers 1985; FIMI 1985, FRSA 1995; *Recreations* gardening; *Style—* David W Gent, Esq; ✉ 44 Ursula Street, London SW11 3DW (tel 020 7228 8126); 219 High Street, Henley-in-Arden, Warwickshire B95 5BG (tel 01564 793922, e-mail david@gent44.fsnet.co.uk)

GENTLE, Mary; da of George William Gentle, of Dorset, and late Amy Mary, *née* Champion; *Educ* Bournemouth Univ (BA), Goldsmiths Coll London (MA), KCL (MA); *Career* author; computer game script and voice direction ZombieVille (1996); *Books* A Hawk in Silver (1977), Golden Witchbreed (1983), Ancient Light (1987), Scholars and Soldiers (1989), Rats and Gargoyles (1990), The Architecture of Desire (1991), Grunts! (1992), Left to His Own Devices (1994), A Secret History: The Book of Ash 1 (1999), Carthage Ascendant: The Book of Ash 2 (2000), The Wild Machines: The Book of Ash 3 (2000), Lost Burgundy: The Book of Ash 4 (2000), ASH: A Secret History (2000); as Roxanne Morgan: Dares (1995), Bets (1997), Game of Masks (1999); *Recreations* sword fighting, live role-play games; *Style—* Ms Mary Gentle

GENTLEMAN, David William; s of Tom Gentleman (d 1966), and Winifred Murgatroyd (d 1966); *b* 11 March 1930; *Educ* Hertford GS, St Albans Sch of Art, Royal Coll of Art (ARCA); *m* 1, 1953 (m dis 1966), Rosalind Dease; 1 da (Fenella); m 2, 1968, Susan, da of George Ewart Evans (d 1988), of Brooke, Norfolk; 1 s (Tom), 2 da (Sarah, Amelia); *Career* painter and designer; work incl: painting in watercolour, lithography, wood engraving, illustration, graphic design, posters, postage stamps, coins, Eleanor Cross mural designs for Charing Cross Underground Station 1979; memb: Cncl AGBI (Artists' Gen Benevolent Inst) 1970–, Alliance Graphique Internationale 1972–, Properties Ctee Nat Tst 1986–2005; RDI 1970; Hon FRIBA, Hon FRCA; *Solo Exhibitions* Watercolours (Mercury Gallery) 1970–2000, Watercolours and Designs (Royal Coll of Art) 2002, Watercolours (Fine Art Soc) 2004; *Work in Collections* Tate Gallery, V&A, British Museum, Fitzwilliam Museum, various private collections; *Books* Design in Miniature (1972), David Gentleman's Britain (1982), David Gentleman's London (1985), A Special Relationship (1987), David Gentleman's Coastline (1988), David Gentleman's Paris (1991), David Gentleman's India (1994), David Gentleman's Italy (1997), The Wood Engravings of David Gentleman (2000), Artwork (2002); illustrations for many other books; edns of lithographs (1967–2005); *Style—* David Gentleman; ✉ 25 Gloucester Crescent, London NW1 7DL (tel 020 7485 8824, fax 020 7267 4541, e-mail d@gentleman.demon.co.uk)

GENTLEMAN, Douglas de Regnéville; s of James Gentleman (d 1990), of Glasgow, and Jeanne Lucie Emma, *née* Leneveu; *b* 2 January 1954; *Educ* Hutchesons' Boys' GS Glasgow, Univ of Glasgow (BSc, MB ChB, Brunton meml prize, pres Glasgow Univ Medico-Chirurgical Soc); *m* 1984, Marjorie, da of George Armstrong (d 1998); 1 da (Emma b 12 April 1987), 1 s (Philip b 22 July 1989); *Career* jr surgical trg posts Glasgow and Manchester 1978–82, registrar then sr registrar in neurosurgery Inst of Neurological Scis Glasgow 1982–92, conslt neurosurgn Dundee Teaching Hosps NHS Tst 1992–97 (hon conslt neurosurgeon 1997–), head Dept of Surgical Neurology Univ of Dundee 1995–97, conslt in charge Centre for Brain Injury Rehabilitation Royal Victoria Hosp Dundee 1997–; memb: Scottish Cncl for Postgrad Med and Dental Educn 1983–91 (observer 1993–99), GMC 1984–2003 (chm Scottish Cncl 1993–99, chm Fitness to Practise Policy Ctee 2001–03), Dept of Health Standing Advsy Ctee on Med Manpower (Campbell Ctee) 1991–2001; chm: Scottish Head Injury Forum 2000–03 and 2007–, Scottish Devpt Ctee of Headway - the Brain Injury Assoc 2001–; vice-chm Hosp Doctors Ctee Standing Ctee of Doctors of the Euro Community 1985–88, vice-chm Scottish Intercollegiate Guidelines Network Gp on Head Injury 2006–; sec-gen Perm Working Gp of Euro Jr Hosp Doctors 1984–88, memb Jt Ctee on Higher Surgical Trg 1988–90; memb: Soc of Br Neurological Surgns, Br Trauma Soc, Int Neurotrauma Soc, Br Soc of Rehabilitation Med; memb Editorial Bd: Injury, Trauma; FRCS 1982, FRCPS 1982; *Publications* author of pubns on head injury, brain injury rehabilitation, and medical regulation; *Clubs* Reform; *Style—* Douglas de R Gentleman, Esq; ✉ 49 Clepington Road, Stobsmuir, Dundee DD4 7EL (tel 01382 462496); Centre for Brain Injury Rehabilitation, Royal Victoria Hospital, Dundee (tel 01382 423196, fax 01382 423070, e-mail douglas.gentleman@tpct.scot.nhs.uk)

GEOGHEGAN, Hon Mr Justice Hugh; s of Hon Mr Justice James Geoghegan (d 1951), of Dublin, a judge of the Supreme Court of Ireland, and Eileen, *née* Murphy (d 1980); *b* 16 May 1938, Dublin; *Educ* Clongowes Wood Coll SJ Naas, UC Dublin (BCL), King's Inns Dublin; *m* 1 Aug 1981, Hon Mrs Justice Mary Finlay Geoghegan, a judge of the High Court of Ireland; 2 da (Caren b 27 April 1982, Sarah b 26 Nov 1983), 1 s (James b 9 June 1985); *Career* called to the Bar: King's Inns Dublin 1962 (bencher 1992), Middle Temple London 1975 (bencher 2005), Inn of Court NI 1989; practising barr Midland Circuit and Dublin 1962–77, sr counsel 1977–92, judge of the High Court of Ireland 1992–2000, judge of the Supreme Court of Ireland 2000–; public serv arbitrator 1982–92; former memb: Gen Cncl Bar of Ireland, Cncl King's Inns; memb: Bd of Govrs Clongowes Wood Coll SJ Naas 1995–2002, Cncl Royal Victoria Eye and Ear Hosp Dublin 1998–; *Recreations* travel, history; *Clubs* Kildare St and Univ, Fitzwilliam Lawn Tennis; *Style—* The Hon Mr Justice Hugh Geoghegan; ✉ Supreme Court of Ireland, Four Courts, Inns Quay, Dublin 7, Ireland

GEORGALA, Prof Douglas Lindley; CBE; s of John Michael Georgala (d 1966), and Izetta Iris, *née* Smith; *b* 2 February 1934; *Educ* South African Coll Sch, Univ of Stellenbosch (BSc), Univ of Aberdeen (PhD); *m* 18 Dec 1959, Eulalia Catherina, da of George Philip Lochner (d 1962); 1 da (Jeanette b 5 March 1961), 1 s (David b 12 May 1963); *Career* res microbiologist Fishing Res Inst Univ of Cape Town 1957–60, tech memb Unilever Coordination 1973–77, head Unilever Res Colworth Laboratory 1977–86 (res microbiologist and div mangr 1960–72), industrial conslt DTI 1987–88; dir of food res Inst of Food Res AFRC 1988–94 (memb Strategy Bd); chm Advsy Ctee on Microbiological Safety of Food 1996–2004 (memb 1991–), memb Food Advsy Ctee 1989–95; external prof Univ of Leeds 1993–; memb Ownership Bd Centre for Environment, Fisheries and Agriculture Science 1997–2001, tstee World Humanity Action Tst 1999–2000; FIFST 1988; *Recreations* gardening, music; *Style—* Prof Douglas Georgala, CBE; ✉ Institute of Food Research, Norwich Research Park, Norwich NR4 7UA

GEORGE, Andrew Henry; MP; s of Reginald Hugh George, and Diana May, *née* Petherick; *b* 2 December 1958; *Educ* Helston Sch, Univ of Sussex (BA), UC Oxford (MSc); *m* 1987, Jill Elizabeth, da of William and Margery Marshall; 1 da (Morvah May b 15 Oct 1987), 1 s (Davy Tregarthen b 11 Sept 1990); *Career* rural offr Nottinghamshire Rural Community Cncl 1981–85, dep dir Cornwall Rural Community Cncl 1986–97; MP (Lib Dem) St Ives 1997–; shadow fisheries min 1997–2005, shadow disabilities min 1999–2001, PPS to Rt Hon Charles Kennedy, MP, *qv*, 2001–02, shadow sec of state for rural affrs and food 2002–05, shadow sec of state for int devpt 2005–06; vice-chair: All-Pty Parly Fisheries Gp 1997, All-Pty Parly Small Farms Gp 1998, All-Pty Euro Objective One Gp 1999, All-Pty Romany Gp, All-Pty Rugby Union Gp; memb Agriculture Select Ctee 1997–2000; pres Cncl for Racial Equality (Cornwall); memb: World Devpt Movement, Cornish Social and Economic Research Gp; pres W Cornwall Reliant Robin Owners Club; *Books* Cornwall at the Crossroads (1989), A Vision of Cornwall (1994), A View from the bottom left-hand corner: Impressions of a raw recruit through parliamentary sketches and essays 1997–2002 (2002); The Natives are Revolting Down in the Cornwall Theme Park (in Cornish Scene, 1986); also author of numerous articles and booklets on rural and Cornish themes; *Recreations* swimming, cycling, football, rugby, cricket, tennis, walking, poetry, painting/drawing, singing; *Clubs* Commons and Lords Rugby, Leedstown CC, Commons Football Team, Commons Cricket; *Style—* Andrew George, Esq, MP; ✉ House of Commons, London SW1A 0AA (tel 020 7219 4588, fax 020 7219 5572, e-mail cartera@parliament.uk); Knight's Yard, Belgravia Street, Penzance, Cornwall TR18 2EL (tel 01736 360020, fax 01736 332866, e-mail cooperu@parliament.uk)

GEORGE, Andrew Neil; s of Walter George, of Edinburgh, and Madeleine, *née* Lacey (d 1961); *b* 8 October 1952; *Educ* Royal HS Edinburgh, Univ of Edinburgh (MA); *m* 1977, Watanalak, da of Kovit Chaovieng; 1 da (Arada Caroline b 1979), 1 s (Michael Alastair b 1982); *Career* HM Dip Serv 1974–: W Africa Dept FCO 1974–75, SOAS London 1975–76, third later second sec Bangkok 1976–80, S America Dept FCO 1980–81, W Africa Dept FCO 1981–82, Perm Under-Sec's Dept FCO 1982–84, first sec Canberra 1984–88, first sec (head of Chancery) Bangkok 1988–92, Repub of Ireland Dept FCO 1993–94, Eastern Dept FCO 1994–95, Non-Proliferation Dept FCO 1995–98, ambass to Paraguay 1998–2001, cnsllr Commercial Devpt Jakarta 2002–, asst dir health and welfare 2003–06, govr of Anguilla 2006–; *Recreations* reading, golf, watching football; *Style—* Mr Andrew George

GEORGE, Brian Victor; CBE (1995); s of Victor George, of Bournemouth, Dorset, and Agnes Amelia, *née* Sweet; *b* 5 February 1936; *Educ* Southall GS, Southall Tech Coll, Brunel Coll of Advanced Technol (BTech); *m* 19 May 1962, Joan Valerie, da of John Keith Bingham; 2 s (Graham Michael b 2 Dec 1965, David Brian b 10 April 1968); *Career* welding and sheet metal worker APV (Aust) Pty Ltd 1952–54, trade and student apprentice D Napier & Sons Ltd 1954–60; NPC (W) Ltd Whetstone: engr 1960–63, section leader 1963–66, office head Boilers and Gas Circuits 1966–69, asst chief engr Mech Plant 1969–70, asst chief engr Future Systems 1970–75, chief engr Mech Plant & Systems Dept 1975–76, mangr Fast Reactors 1976–77, engr mangr designate PWR; head Nuclear Plant Design Branch CEGB GD & CD 1979–81, dir PWR CEGB GD & CD 1981–89, project and tech dir Project Mgmnt Bd PWR 1984–89; Nuclear Electric plc: chief exec PWR Project Gp 1989–92, exec dir of planning and construction 1992–94, exec dir of engrg 1994–95; gp md Marconi Marine (comprising VSEL, YSL and NNC) 1995–98, assoc dir GEC 1995–99, md Projects Marconi Electronic Systems 1999–2000, non-exec dir NNC & BNFL 2001–05; non-exec chm: Taylor Woodrow Construction, Bryant Homes 2001–04; chm Engrg Ctee, vice-pres Royal Acad of Engrg 1999–2003; Liveryman Worshipful Co of Shipwrights 1998; DTech (hc); FREng 1989, FIMechE, Hon FINucE; *Recreations* golf, bowls, DIY; *Style—* Brian George, Esq, CBE, FREng; ✉ Hollybank, 5 Danesbury Park, St Peter's Road, Malvern, Worcestershire WR14 1QA (tel 01684 578547, e-mail valandbriang@hotmail.com)

GEORGE, (William Norman) Bruce; s of Norman Macdonald George (d 1922), and Isobella Elizabeth Dunn (d 1964); *b* 3 December 1915; *Educ* Univ of Liverpool Sch of Architecture (BArch), Sch of Planning and Res for Regnl Devpt; *Career* WWII Lt RA 1940–46 (POW 1942); architect; formerly sr ptnr George/Trew/Dunn/Beckles Willson/Bowes, ret 1984; princ buildings: The Guards' Chapel 1963, Huddersfield Royal Infirmary 1966, Aberdeen Royal Infirmary 1967 and 1976, Wellington Barracks London 1984; other works at: KCH London, KCH Med Sch, Halifax Gen Hosp, New Cross Hosp Wolverhampton; served: Practice Ctee and Panel of Arbitrators RIBA, CNAA; RIBA, MRTPI, FRSA; *Books* The Architect in Practice; *Recreations* sculpture, portrait painting, music, cricket; *Style—* Bruce George, Esq; ✉ 1 Copley Dene, Wilderness Road, Chislehurst, Kent BR7 5EY (tel 020 8467 5809)

GEORGE, Rt Hon Bruce Thomas; PC (2000), MP; s of late Edgar Lewis George and Phyllis, of Mountain Ash, Glamorgan; *b* 1 June 1942; *Educ* Mountain Ash GS, UC Wales Swansea (BA), Univ of Warwick (MA); *m* 1992, Lisa Carolyn Toelle; *Career* asst lectr in politics Glamorgan Coll of Technol 1964–66, lectr in politics Manchester Poly 1968–70, sr lectr politics Birmingham Poly and pt/t tutor Open Univ 1971–74, pt/t lectr Dept of Government Univ of Essex (hon fell Arch), ed Jane's NATO Handbook 1989–92; Parly candidate (Lab) Southport 1970; MP (Lab) Walsall S 1974–; memb Select Ctee on Defence 1979–2005, chm Defence Ctee 1997–2005; former gen rapporteur Political Ctee North Atlantic Assembly, pres Parly Assembly OSCE 2002–04 (pres emeritus 2004–06, former chm First Ctee); pres Int Assoc of Business and Parl; hon advsr Royal British Legion; hon fell Univ of Wales Swansea 2001; *Publications* author and co-author of 10 books on defence and security; *Recreations* football; *Style—* The Rt Hon Bruce George, MP; ✉ 42 Wood End Road, Walsall, West Midlands WS5 3BG (tel 01922 627898); House of Commons, London SW1A 0AA (tel 020 7219 6610/4049, e-mail georgeb@parliament.uk)

GEORGE, Prof Sir Charles Frederick; kt (1998); s of William Hubert George (d 1957), and Evelyn Margaret, *née* Pryce, of Edgbaston, Birmingham; *b* 3 April 1941; *Educ* Oundle, Univ of Birmingham (BSc, MB ChB, MD); *m* 17 May 1969 (m dis 1973), Rosemary, da of late Edward Moore, JP; *Career* med registrar: Birmingham Gen Hosp 1968–69, Hammersmith Hosp London 1969–71; tutor in med and clinical pharmacology Royal Postgrad Med Sch London 1971–73; Univ of Southampton: sr lectr in med 1974–75, prof of clinical pharmacology 1975–99, dean of med 1986–90 and 1993–98; med dir Br Heart Fndn 1999–2004; pres BMA 2004–05 (currently chair Bds of Science and of Medical Educn); memb GMC (chm Educn Ctee 1994–99); chm: Jt Formulary Ctee of Br Nat Formulary 1986–2000; hon fell Faculty of Pharmaceutical Med RCP 1989; Hon DSc Univ of Birmingham 2003, Hon DM Univ of Southampton 2004, Hon DSc Univ of Leicester 2007; fndr FMedSci, FRCP 1978, FRSA 1993, FESC 2000, Hon FFPH 2004; *Books* Presystemic Drug Metabolism (with Renwick & Shand, 1982), Drug Therapy in Old Age (1998) with Woodhouse Denham and MacLennan; *Recreations* windsurfing, walking; *Style—* Prof Sir Charles George; ✉ 15 Westgate Street, Southampton SO14 2AY (tel 023 8022 9100); British Medical Association, BMA House, Tavistock Square, London WC1H 9JP

GEORGE, Charles Richard; QC (1992); s of Hugh Shaw George, CIE, IFS (d 1967), and Joan, *née* Stokes; *b* 8 June 1945; *Educ* Bradfield Coll, Magdalen Coll Oxford (MA), CCC Cambridge; *m* Joyce Tehmina, da of Rev Robert James Barnard; 2 da (Tara Sophie b 1978, Eva Jane b 1981); *Career* asst master Eton Coll 1967–72; called to the Bar: Inner Temple 1974 (bencher 2001), Irish Bar King's Inns 1995; in planning, admin and Parly law practice 1975–, recorder of the Crown Court 1997–; chllr Diocese of Southwark 1996–; memb House Cncl St Stephen's House Oxford 1999–; *Books* The Stuarts - An Age of Experiment (1973); *Recreations* tennis, history and travel; *Clubs* Athenaeum; *Style—* Charles George, Esq, QC; ✉ Ashgrove Farm, Ashgrove Road, Sevenoaks, Kent TN13 1SU; 2 Harcourt Buildings, Temple, London EC4Y 9DB (tel 020 7353 8415)

GEORGE, Baron (Life Peer UK 2004), of St Tudy in the County of Cornwall; Sir Edward Alan John (Eddie) George; GBE (2000), PC (1999); s of Alan George, and Olive Elizabeth George; *b* 11 September 1938; *Educ* Dulwich Coll, Emmanuel Coll Cambridge (MA); *m* 1962, Clarice Vanessa, *née* Williams; 1 s, 2 da; *Career* Bank of England: seconded to Bank for Int Settlements 1966–69, IMF 1972–74, dep chief cashier 1977–80, asst dir Gilt-Edged Div 1980–82, exec dir 1982–90, dep govr 1990–93, govr 1993–2003; chm G10 Governors 1999–2003; non-exec dir: Grosvenor Gp 2003–, Rothschild 2003–, Nestlé 2003–; chm Bd of Govrs Dulwich Coll 2003–; tstee: Eden Project, Cornwall Community Fndn; hon fell Emmanuel Coll 1994; hon degree: Univ of Hull 1993, Loughborough Univ of Technol 1994, City Univ 1995, London Guildhall Univ 1996, Cranfield Univ 1997, Univ of Exeter 1997, UMIST 1998, Univ of Bristol 1999, Univ of Hertfordshire 1999, Univ of Sheffield 1999, Univ of Buckingham 2000, Univ of Cambridge 2000, London Met Univ 2002, LSE 2004; Liveryman: Worshipful Co of Mercers, Worshipful Co of Grocers, Guild of Int Bankers; Hon FCIBS 2003; *Recreations* bridge, sailing; *Style—* The Rt Hon the Lord George, GBE, PC

GEORGE, Jill Findlay; da of Ronald Francis George (d 1987), and Joan Findlay, *née* Brooks (d 1987); *b* 12 September 1954; *Educ* St Margaret's Sch Bushey, Univ of Florence, Sheffield Coll of Art (BA); *Career* PR Dept V&A Museum 1972–74, antique shop N Devon 1976–77; Jill George Gallery (Thumb Gallery until 1991): joined 1978, dir 1981, co dir 1983, sole owner and dir 1986–; represented Herts in jr tennis; memb Ctee Art Business Design Centre 1989–92; memb Soc of London Art Dealers; *Recreations* theatre-going, films, music, tennis, classic car shows, croquet; *Clubs* Groucho, Chelsea Arts; *Style*— Ms Jill George; ✉ 7 West Common Way, Harpenden, Hertfordshire (tel 01582 460383); 16 Gillingham Road, London NW2 (tel 020 8450 1867); Jill George Gallery, 38 Lexington Street, Soho, London W1F 0LL (tel 020 7439 7343/7319, fax 020 7287 0478)

GEORGE, John Charles Grossmith; er s of Col Edward Harry George, OBE, WS (d 1957), and Rosa Mary, Papal Medal Benemerenti (d 1988), da of George Grossmith, OStJ, Chev de la Legion d'Honneur, Gold Cross of the Order of the Redeemer, Cross Pro Ecclesia et Pontefice; *b* 15 December 1930; *Educ* Ampleforth; *m* 13 May 1972, Margaret Mary Maria Mercedes (late sec to Garter King of Arms), Offr of Order Pro Merito Melitensi, da of Maj Edric Humphrey Weld, TD, JP (d 1969), and Maria Mercedes, da of Henry Scrope, of Danby; *Career* Lt Hertfordshire Yeo (RA, TA); College of Arms 1963–72: Earl Marshal's liaison offr with Churchill family State Funeral of Sir Winston Churchill 1965, Green Staff Offr Investiture of HRH The Prince of Wales 1969; Garioch Pursuivant to the Countess of Mar 1976–86, Kintyre Pursuivant in the Court of the Lord Lyon 1986–2000, Linlithgow Pursuivant Extraordinary in the Court of Lord Lyon 2001–05; memb Cncl: The Heraldry Soc 1976–84, The Heraldry Soc of Scotland 1986–89, The Ampleforth Soc 1990–93; co-designer Royal Wedding Stamp (Crown Agents Issue) 1981; vice-pres BBC Mastermind Club 1979–81; Col and Hon ADC to the Govr State of Kentucky USA 1991; Genealogist for Scotland for British Assoc of Order of Malta 1995–2002; FSA Scot 1975–96, FHS 1983; Freedom of Loudon County of Virginia USA 1968; Knight in Obedience SMOM 1975 (dir of ceremonies Br Assoc 1976–80), Knight of Grace and Devotion 1971, Knight of Grace Constantian Order of St George (Naples) 1982, Cdr of Order Pro Merito Melitensi 1983 (Offr 1980), KSG 2002; *Books* The Puffin Book of Flags; *Recreations* nineteenth century English operetta, musical comedy, hagiography, watching sport principally racing, rugby and golf; *Style*— J C G George, Esq, KSG; ✉ 5 Longley House, Long Street, Easingwold, N Yorkshire YO61 3HT (tel and fax 01347 824661)

GEORGE, Martin Francis; s of William Anthony George (d 1984), and Margot, *née* Cooper; *b* 1 November 1942; *Educ* Repton; *m*; 1 s (Michael David b 1973), 1 da (Alison Mary Rachel b 1975); *Career* Whitworths Holdings Ltd: mangr Animal Feeds 1964–70, dir Flour Mills 1970–80, bd dir 1980–84, jt md 1984–85, chm 1985–87, gp md 1992–97, chm 1997–; chm Leicester FC plc 1990–96 and 2002–03, former chm Mid Anglia Radio plc; pres UK Agric Supply Trade Assoc 1981–82; *Style*— Martin George, Esq; ✉ Fotheringhay Manor, Peterborough, Cambridgeshire PE8 5HZ; Whitworths Holdings Ltd, Victoria Mills, London Road, Wellingborough, Northamptonshire NN8 2DT (tel 01933 443444, fax 01933 443346)

GEORGE, Michael; s of John James George (d 1964), of Thorpe St, Andrew, Norwich, Norfolk, and Elizabeth, *née* Holmes; *b* 10 August 1950; *Educ* King's Coll Cambridge Choir Sch, Oakham Sch, RCM; *m* 15 July 1972, Julie Elizabeth Kennard (soprano), da of Stanley Kennard; 2 da (Lucy Elizabeth Sullivan b 27 May 1975, Emilie Jane b 1 Aug 1978), 1 s (Nicholas James Stanley b 19 Aug 1980); *Career* bass baritone; ranges from twelfth century to present day; has appeared at all maj festivals throughout Britain incl The Proms 1990 (4 separate concerts performing Bach, Janácek, Arvo Part and Renaissance music), The Three Choirs Festival and elsewhere with City of Birmingham Symphony, Scot Chamber and BBC Symphony Orchs; performed abroad 1990: Messiah (Italy, Spain, Poland and France), Mozart's Requiem (with Trevor Pinnock, Ottawa), Handel (California and Boston), Haydn's Creation (under Hogwood, Holland, Germany and Italy) *Recordings* incl: Carmina Burana (4 vols), Acis and Galatea, Haydn's Creation, Beethoven's Ninth Symphony, Missa Solemnis (with Hanover Band), Handel's Messiah, St John Passion (with The Sixteen), Handel's Joshua, Stravinsky's Le Rossignol (with BBC Symphony Orch), Holst's At the Boar's Head (under David Atherton), Elgar - Dream of Gerontius (EMI), Purcell - Complete Odes, Anthems & Songs (with The King's Consort, Hyperion); *Recreations* tennis, golf, food; *Clubs* Concert Golfing, Royal Mid-Surrey Golf; *Style*— Michael George, Esq; ✉ c/o IMG Artists, Lovell House, 616 Chiswick High Road, London W4 5RX (tel 020 8233 5800, fax 020 8233 5801)

GEORGE, Nicholas; s of Wallace Yewdall Evelyn George, and Joy Isabel Gilbert, *née* Hickey; *b* 1 February 1954; *Educ* Radley; *m* Lady Marsha Fitzalan Howard; *Career* articled clerk Edward Moore & Sons 1973–77, Joseph Sebag & Co 1977–79, Rowe & Pitman 1979–81; dir: WI Carr Sons & Co 1981–86, BZW Securities 1986–93, Drayton Asia Trust plc 1989–93, BZW Asia 1991–93; dir and head of SE Asian equities and emerging market securities Robert Fleming Ltd 1993–97, dir Jardine Fleming Ltd 1997, md JP Morgan 1997–2001, md HSBC Securities (head of Asian corp broking) until 2002, co-fndr and dir KGR Capital Ltd 2002–; FCA 1978, AIIMR 1980; *Recreations* shooting, fishing, travelling, gardening; *Style*— Nicholas George, Esq; ✉ KGR Capital (Europe) Ltd, 20 Grosvenor Place, London SW1X 7HN (e-mail nick.george@kgrcapital.com)

GEORGE, Terry; *b* Belfast, NI; *Career* filmmaker; *Films* incl: In the Name of the Father (writer and prodr) 1993 (nominated Oscar 1993), Some Mother's Son (writer and dir) 1996 (Young European Dir of the Year 1996), The Boxer (writer) 1997, A Bright Shining Lie (writer and dir) 1998, Hart's War (writer) 2002, Hotel Rwanda (writer, prodr and dir) 2004 (nominated Oscar 2004); *Television* The District (creator, writer and dir) 2000; *Style*— Terry George, Esq; ✉ c/o International Creative Management, 8942 Wilshire Boulevard, Beverly Hills, Los Angeles, USA, 90211 (tel 00 1 310 550 4000, fax 00 1 310 550 4100)

GEORGE, His Hon Judge William; s of William Henry George (d 1979), of Alderwasley, Derbys, and Elizabeth, *née* Ashley; *b* 28 September 1944; *Educ* Herbert Strutt GS Belper, Victoria Univ of Manchester (LLB, LLM); *m* Susan Isabel, *née* Pennington; 2 da (Elizabeth Barbara b 20 July 1977, Francesca Gordon b 18 Nov 1979); *Career* called to the Bar Lincoln's Inn 1968 (Mansfield scholar, bencher 2003); in practice Chancery Bar 1969–95, head of chambers 1985–95, standing counsel to Treasy in charity matters in Liverpool 1984–95, recorder of the Crown Court 1993–95 (asst recorder 1991), circuit judge (Northern Circuit) 1995–; chm Northern Chancery Bar Assoc 1992–94; *Recreations* contemporary British artists, military history (the American Civil War), English history, gardening; *Clubs* Athenaeum (Liverpool); *Style*— His Hon Judge George; ✉ Queen Elizabeth II Law Courts, Derby Square, Liverpool L2 1XA

GEORGE (Gilbert and George), *see:* Passmore, George

GEORGESCU, Peter; s of Valeriu Georgescu, and Lygia, *née* Bocu; *b* 9 March 1939, Bucharest, Romania; *Educ* Exeter Acad USA, Princeton Univ (BA), Stanford Business Sch (MBA); *m* 21 Aug 1965, Barbara Anne, *née* Armstrong Lipman; 1 s (Andrew b 23 March 1967); *Career* Young & Rubicam Inc: chm and ceo 1994–2000, currently chm emeritus; memb Bd: Levi's, Int Flavors & Fragrances, EMI until 2007; vice-chm NY Presbyterian Hosp, memb Cncl on Foreign Rels, memb Bd A Better Chance, memb Bd Polytechnic Univ; elected to Advtg Hall of Fame 2001; Ellis Island Medal of Honor; Hon Dr: Univ of Alabama, Cornell Coll Iowa; *Style*— Peter Georgescu, Esq; ✉ Young & Rubicam, 285 Madison Avenue, New York, NY 10017, USA (tel 00 1 212 210 3095, fax 00 1 212 210 5275, e-mail peter.georgescu@yr.com)

GEORGIADIS, Philip Andrew; s of Jack Constantine Georgiadis, and Jean Alison, *née* Tytler; *b* 6 May 1962; *Educ* KCS Wimbledon, Univ of York (BA); *m* 23 Dec 1991, Penelope, da of John Granville Brenchley; 2 da (Olivia Florence b 13 June 1992, Bella Grace b 11 Oct 2002), 1 s (Toby Alexander (twin) b 11 Oct 2002); *Career* media exec Benton & Bowles advtg agency 1984–85 (joined as trainee media buyer 1983), media exec Ray Morgan & Partners Sept-Nov 1985; WCRS: media planner/buyer 1985–87, media mangr/assoc dir 1987–89, bd dir 1989–91, media dir Esprit Media 1990–91, exec media dir 1991–94, vice-chm 1994–95; chief exec Initiative Media 1995–98, fndr ptnr Walker Media 1998–; FIPA; *Recreations* travelling, golf; *Clubs* Park, Soho House; *Style*— Philip Georgiadis, Esq; ✉ Walkermedia, Middlesex House, 34 Cleveland Street, London W1P 5FB

GERAGHTY, Barry; s of Thomas Geraghty, and Bea, *née* Monaghan; *b* 16 September 1979, Dublin; *Educ* St Michaels Sch Trim Co Meath; *partner* Paula Heaphy; 1 da (Siofra b 14 Aug 2005); *Career* jockey 1996–; races won incl: Aintree Grand Nat 2003, Champion Chase Cheltenham 2003 and 2005, Cheltenham Gold Cup 2005; 11 winners at Cheltenham Festival; Irish Champion Jump Jockey 2002 and 2004; RTE Irish Sports Personality of the Year 2003; supporter Fighting Blindness; *Recreations* golf, hunting, skiing, water skiing; *Clubs* Royal Tara Golf, Ward Union Stag Hunt; *Style*— Barry Geraghty, Esq; ✉ c/o Commonstown Stables, Moone, County Kildare, Ireland

GERARD, 5 Baron (UK 1876); Sir Anthony Robert Hugo Gerard; 17 Bt (E) 1611; s of Maj Rupert Gerard, MBE (d 1978, great nephew of 2 Baron); suc 2 cous once removed, 4 Baron Gerard (d 1992); *b* 3 December 1949; *Educ* Harvard; *m* 1976 (m dis), Kathleen, eldest da of Dr Bernard Ryan, of New York; 2 s (Hon Rupert Bernard Charles b 17 Dec 1981, Hon John Frederick William b 1986); *Heir* s, Hon Rupert Gerard; *Style*— The Rt Hon the Lord Gerard; ✉ House of Lords, London SW1A 0PW; PO Box 2308, East Hampton, NY 11937, USA

GERARD LEIGH, Col William Henry; CVO (1983), CBE (1981); s of Lt-Col J C Gerard Leigh (d 1965), of Thorpe Satchville Hall, Melton Mowbray, Leics, and Helen, *née* Goudy (d 1964); *b* 5 August 1915; *Educ* Eton, Univ of Cambridge; *m* 29 Oct 1946, (Nancy) Jean, da of Wing Cdr Sir Norman Leslie 8 Bt, CMG, CBE (d 1937); 2 da (Carolyn (Mrs Charles Benson) b 12 Nov 1947, Camilla (Mrs Hugh Seymour) b 4 July 1952), 2 s (John b 24 Jan 1949, David b 28 Aug 1958); *Career* LG: joined 1937, served ME Italy and Germany 1939–45, Lt-Col Cmdg 1953–56, Col Cmdg Household Cavalry and Silver Stick in Waiting to HM The Queen 1956–59, Gentleman Usher to HM The Queen 1967–85; chm Nat Cncl YMCA's 1974–81; *Clubs* White's; *Style*— Col W H Gerard Leigh, CVO, CBE; ✉ Crux Cottage, Kintbury, Berkshire RG17 9TN (tel 01488 658271)

GERLIS, Dr Laurence; s of Toby Gerlis, of Herts, and Sylvia, *née* Sussman; *b* 17 May 1950; *Educ* City of London Sch (scholar), Clare Coll Cambridge (scholar, MA, MB BCh, William Butler prize in med), London Hosp (scholar, DipPharmMed, paediatrics & pathology prize); *m* 1971, Pauline Benveniste; 2 da (Melanie b 1974, Sarah b 1977), 1 s (Adam b 1982); *Career* Med Unit London Hosp 1974–76, med dir Novo Laboratories 1976–82, dir of clinical res Biogen Geneva 1982–85; radio doctor Talk Radio; currently: interest in diabetes care, private GP; visiting conslt King Edward VII Hosp Port Stanley; appearances on radio and TV med progs incl: LBC, BBC, Thames, C4, Br Med TV, Talk Radio; memb Faculty Pharmaceutical Physicians 1990; MRCP; *Books* Good Clinical Practice (1987, 2 edn 1989), Biotechnology Made Simple (1989), Consumer's Guide to Prescription Medicines (1990), Thomas Cook Health Passport (1990), Consumer's Guide to Non-Prescription Medicines (1991); *Style*— Dr Laurence Gerlis; ✉ e-mail dr@gerlis.com

GERMAIN, (Dennis) Richard; s of Capt Dennis George Alfred Germain (d 1956), and Catherine Emily Violet, *née* Tickner; *b* 26 December 1945; *Educ* Mayfield Coll; *m* 7 Sept 1968, (Jadwiga) Anne Teresa, da of Zygfryd Nowinski (d 1988); 1 s (Richard b 1973), 1 da (Suzanne b 1976); *Career* called to the Bar Inner Temple 1968; memb Criminal Bar Assoc; *Recreations* cinema, photography, stamp collecting, antiques; *Style*— Richard Germain, Esq; ✉ Mander Lara, Oxford Road, Gerrards Cross, Buckinghamshire SL9 8TB (tel 01753 885775, fax 01753 891619, e-mail richardgermain@talktalk.net); 9 Bedford Row, London WC1R 4AZ (tel 020 7489 2727, fax 020 7489 2728, e-mail clerks@9bedfordrow.co.uk)

GERMAN, Michael James; OBE (1996), AM; s of Arthur Ronald German, and Molly, *née* McCarthy, of Cardiff; *b* 8 May 1945; *Educ* St Illyd's Coll Cardiff, St Mary's Coll London (Cert Ed), Open Univ (BA), UWE (DipEd Mgmnt); *m* Aug 2006, Veronica Watkins; 2 da (Sophie Gemma Ann b 26 Nov 1972, Laura Emily Jane b 27 Nov 1973); *Career* teacher 1966–91, dir European Div Welsh Jt Educn Ctee 1991–99, memb Nat Assembly for Wales (Lib Dem) South Wales East 1999–; Nat Assembly for Wales: Lib Dem ldr 1999–, Dep First Min 2000–01 and 2002–03, min for Econ Devpt 2000–01, min for Rural Devpt and Wales Abroad 2002–03; memb Cardiff City Cncl 1983–96 (Lib Dem ldr 1983–96, jt ldr of cncl 1987–91); memb Lib Dem Fed Exec 1992–; *Recreations* travel, music; *Style*— Michael German, Esq, OBE, AM; ✉ National Assembly for Wales, Cardiff Bay, Cardiff CF99 1NA (tel 029 2089 8741, fax 029 2089 8354, e-mail michael.german@wales.gov.uk)

GERRARD, David Lester; *b* 13 December 1942; *Educ* King Edward VI Sch Birmingham, Birmingham Coll of Art; *m* 6 April 1974, Catherine Robin; 2 da (Sophia Elizabeth b 22 March 1978, Charlotte Mary b 16 Oct 1980); *Career* industrial designer Robert Matthew Johnson-Marshall & Partners Edinburgh 1967–72, prod designer Pakistan Design Inst Karachi 1974–76, princ Gerrard & Medd (product, interior and furniture design consultancy) 1977–; external assessor Nat Coll of Art Lahore Pakistan 1976, visiting design lectr Dept of Architecture Nova Scotia Tech Coll Halifax 1977; memb Design for Transformation (projects in Romania and Slovakia); memb Bd Heritage Unit Robert Gordon's Univ Aberdeen 1993–; vice-pres CSD 1990–93 (chm Scottish Regn); awards: Scottish Designer of the Year 1980, Civic Trust award 1985; ASTD 1969, FCSD 1978; *Recreations* gardening, skiing, travelling, worrying; *Style*— David Gerrard, Esq; ✉ Gerrard and Medd, 18 Mayfield Terrace, Edinburgh EH9 1SA (tel 0131 667 7720, e-mail info@gerrardandmedd.co.uk)

GERRARD, Neil; MP; s of late Francis Gerrard, and Emma Gerrard; *b* 3 July 1942; *Educ* Manchester Grammar, Wadham Coll Oxford; *m* 1968 (m dis 1983); 2 s; *Career* teacher Queen Elizabeth's Sch Barnet 1965–68, lectr Hackney Coll 1968–92; Parly candidate (Lab) Chingford 1979; MP (Lab) Walthamstow 1992–; London Borough of Waltham Forest: cncllr 1973–90, ldr Lab Gp 1983–90, ldr of Cncl 1986–90; memb Bd Leyton Orient Community Sports Prog; memb GMB; *Recreations* theatre, cinema, reading, music, sport; *Style*— Neil Gerrard, Esq, MP; ✉ House of Commons, London SW1A 0AA

GERRIE, Malcolm; s of Athelstan Ross Gerrie, and Evelyn Gerrie; *Educ* various schs, Univ of Durham, Sunderland Poly (BEd); *Career* TV prodr; researcher Tyne Tees TV; creator The Tube and The White Room (both Channel 4); prodr for TV: The Brit Awards, Miss World, The Three Tenors, Glastonbury, BAFTA Film Awards; currently chief exec Initial; memb The Music Mangr' Forum Br Music Roll of Honour 2000; *Recreations* running, reading, cinema, eating, keeping fit, travel, music, music, music; *Style*— Malcolm Gerrie, Esq

GERSHON, Sir Peter Oliver; kt (2004), CBE (2000); s of Alfred Joseph Gershon (d 1970), and Gerta Gershon (d 1999); *b* 10 January 1947; *Educ* Reigate GS, Churchill Coll Cambridge (MA); *m* 17 April 1971, Eileen Elizabeth *née* Walker; 2 da (Katherine Helen b 25 Jan 1973, Jennifer Frances b 27 April 1980), 1 s (Timothy John b 29 Nov 1974); *Career* with ICL 1969–87 (memb Mgmnt Bd and dir Network Systems 1985–87); md: STC Telecommunications 1987–90, GPT Ltd 1990–94, Marconi Electronic Systems Ltd 1994–99; chief operating offr BAE Systems 1999–2000, chief exec Office of Government

Commerce 2000–04; non-exec chm: Symbian 2004–, Premier Farnell plc 2005– (non-exec dir 2004–), General Healthcare Gp Ltd 2006–; non-exec memb Treasy Mgmnt Bd, memb Advsy Bd UK Defence Acad; memb Ct and Cncl Imperial Coll 2002; Liveryman Worshipful Co of Info Technologists; Hon DTech Kingston Univ 2005; CCMI (CIMgt 1997), Hon FCIPS 2000, FREng 2001, FBCS 2005 (MBCS 1985), Hon FIEE 2005 (FIEE 1998); *Publications* Review of Civil Procurement in Central Government (1999), Independent Review of Public Sector Efficiency (2004), Independent Review of Ministerial and Royal Air Travel (2006); *Recreations* swimming, reading, theatre, skiing; *Style*— Sir Peter Gershon, CBE, FREng

GERSON, Michael Joseph; s of Maj John Leslie Gerson, TD (d 1980), and Jeanne Ida, *née* Marx (d 1981); *b* 2 November 1937; *Educ* Gresham's; *m* 28 Oct 1962, Shirley Esther, da of Alfred Simons; 3 s (Anthony, Peter, Simon); *Career* RNVR 1952–58; chm Michael Gerson Ltd 1980– (md 1961–80); chm Inst of Furniture Warehousing and Removal Indust 1968, pres Fedn Int Brussels 1982–83, dir N London TEC 1994–97; Freeman City of London 1984, Liveryman Worshipful Co of Carmen 1984; MCIT, FIFF, FMI; *Recreations* sailing; *Clubs* City Livery; *Style*— Michael Gerson, Esq

GETHIN, Maj Sir Richard Joseph St Lawrence; 10 Bt (I 1665), of Gethinsgrott, Cork; s of Lt-Col Sir Richard Patrick St Lawrence Gethin, 9 Bt (d 1988), and Fara, *née* Bartlett; *b* 29 September 1949; *Educ* Oratory, RMA Sandhurst, RMCS Shrivenham (BSc), Cranfield Inst of Technol (MSc); *m* 1974, Jacqueline Torfrida, da of Cdr David Cox, RN; 3 da (Katherine Torfrida b 1976, Rosanna Clare b 1979, Belinda Jacqueline b 1981); *Heir* cous, Antony Gethin; *Career* serv HM Forces, Maj; with Nuttall Civil Engrs; *Recreations* tennis, carpentry; *Style*— Maj Sir Richard Gethin, Bt; ✉ tel 01474 814231, e-mail rjgethin@aol.com

GETTY, Mark Harris; s of Sir Paul Getty, KBE, the philanthropist (d 2003), and Gail, *née* Harris; *b* 9 July 1960, Rome; *Educ* Taunton Sch, St Catherine's Coll Oxford (BA); *m* 16 Dec 1982, Domitilla, *née* Harding; 3 s (Alexander b 21 July 1984, Joseph b 23 Nov 1988, Julius b 25 May 1990); *Career* early career with Kidder Peabody and Hambros Bank Ltd; co-fndr and chm: Getty Investments LLC 1993–, Getty Images 1994–; chair Wisden 2003–; tstee Nat Gallery; *Recreations* reading Burke's Peerage; *Style*— Mark Getty, Esq; ✉ Getty Images, 101 Bayham Street, London NW1 0AG

GHAFFARI, Dr Kamran; s of Mir Jalil Ghaffari, of Milan, Italy, and Aschraf Ghaffari; *b* 17 July 1948; *Educ* King's Sch Ely, Univ of Milan (MD); *m* 8 Nov 1986, Farnaz, da of Mir Jafar Ghaffari-Tabrizi; *Career* sr registrar and lectr in psychiatry St Thomas' Hosp 1984–86, md and conslt psychiatrist Psychiatric and Psychological Consultant Services Ltd 1987–91, conslt i/c Eating Disorders Unit Huntercombe Manor Hosp 1991–93, conslt psychiatrist in psychotherapy Ashford Hosp 1992–2002; W Middx Univ Hosp: conslt psychiatrist in psychotherapy 1992–2006, jt dir Psychological Therapy Serv 1996–2003, head Eating Disorders Serv 1996–2003; currently head of psychological therapy servs Cardinal Clinic; also conslt psychiatrist and psychoanalyst in private practice; chm BMA Local Negotiating Ctee for Hounslow and Spelthorne Community and Mental Health NHS Tst 1993–2000; memb Assoc of Psycho-analytic Psychotherapy in the NHS; memb RMS, FRCPsych, fell Br Psycho-analytic Soc; *Recreations* theatre, bridge, chess, computer sciences; *Style*— Dr Kamran Ghaffari; ✉ The Cardinal Clinic, Oakley Green, Windsor SL4 5UL (tel 01753 869755)

GHAZAL, Prof Peter; s of George Sabah Ghazal, of Brighton, E Sussex, and Jean, *née* Chappell; *b* 21 August 1961; *Educ* Univ of Wales (BSc), Univ of Edinburgh (PhD); *m* 22 Dec 1985, Jacqueline Ann, *née* Bernklow; 1 da (Anna Lisa b 21 Oct 1992), 1 s (Andrew Peter b 14 Nov 1994); *Career* fell Nat Inst of Diabetes and Digestive and Kidney Diseases Lab of Biochemistry and Metabolism NIH Bethesda MD 1986–88; Scripps Research Inst La Jolla CA: sr research assoc Dept of Immunology 1988–90, asst prof Dept of Immunology and Dept of Neuropharmacology Div of Virology 1990–95, chair Pathogenesis Affinity Gp 1994–96, assoc prof Grad Prog in Macromolecular and Cellular Structure and Chemistry 1994–2000, assoc prof Dept of Immunology and Dept of Molecular Biology 1995–2000, adjunct prof Dept of Immunology 2000–; Univ of Edinburgh: reader Section of Med Microbiology Lab of Clinical and Molecular Virology 2000–01, fndr and dir Scottish Centre for Genomic Technology and Informatics 2000–07, prof of molecular genetics and biomedicine (personal chair) 2001–, dir of studies Faculty of Med 2001–, fndr and head Div of Pathway Medicine 2007–; lectr Grad Prog in Molecular Biology Univ of Calif San Diego 1995–97; memb Special Review Ctee: Nat Cancer Inst NIH 1992–93, Nat Inst for Neurological Disorders and Stroke NIH 1993; memb: Scientific Advsy Bd American Fndn for AIDS Research (AmFAR) 1992–, NASA review ctee for ground-based and small payload research in space life sciences 1995, US Army Med Research and Material Command (USAMRMC) review ctee for the breast cancer research prog 1996–2000, Organizing Ctee 22nd, 25th and 26th Int Herpesvirus Workshop 1997, 2000 and 2001 (also session chair), Nat Sciences and Engrg Research Cncl of Canada ad hoc review ctee 1998, Israel Science Fndn ad hoc review ctee 1999, Nat Cancer Inst NIH review panel on models for anti-cancer drug discovery 1999, Synergy Between Research in Medical Informatics, Bioinformatics and Neuorinformatics Belgian Presidency of the EU and EC 2001, Bd Faculty of 1000 2001–03, Scientific Advsy Ctee CHI- Integrated Bioinformatics: High throughtput information of pathways and biology Int Soc for Computational Biology Zurich 2002 (also session chair), Bd Connect Ltd 2002–04, Advsy Bd Bioarrays Europe 2002–, Scientific Advsy Cncl Dublin Molecular Med Centre 2002–, UK Research Cncls (UKRC) 2003, Strategy Panel BBSRC 2003–, Wellcome Tst Technology Transfer Challenge Ctee 2003–, MRC Infections and Immunity Bd 2004–, Genome Canada 2004–; founding memb Scottish Bioinformatics Forum Scottish Enterprise 2002–; co-fndr and chief scientific advsr ArrayJet Ltd 2001–, co-fndr, non-exec dir and chief scientific advsr Lab901 Ltd 2002–, co-fndr and dir Fios Genomics Ltd 2006–; sr scientific advsr Johnson & Johnson Inc 1997–2000; scientific advsr: Pharmacia Genetic Engrg Inc 1992–93, Isis Pharmaceuticals Inc 1994, Signal Pharmaceuticals Inc 1994–97, Allergan Inc 1996; assoc ed Virology 1996–2001; memb Editorial Advsy Bd: BioSilico 2002–, Target 2002–; author of numerous articles and papers in learned jls; invited panellist Science and the Parliament RSC 2001, organiser and co-chair Biochip and Functional Genomics Workshop RSE and Wellcome Tst 2002, chair and invited keynote speaker 1st European Congress on Proteomics and Protein Arrays Copenhagen 2003; scholar Leukemia Soc of America 1993–98, Beacon Award, Chllr's Award; *Recreations* sailing; *Style*— Prof Peter Ghazal; ✉ Divison of Pathway Medicine, The University of Edinburgh Medical School, Little France Crescent, Edinburgh EH16 4SB (tel 0131 242 6242, fax 0131 242 6244, e-mail p.ghazal@ed.ac.uk)

GHEE, Tony; *Educ* Univ of Adelaide (LLB); *Career* lawyer Ten Network Aust 1985–88, slr Denton Wilde Sapte 1990–94, ptnr Ashursts 1994–2003, ptnr Taylor Wessing 2003–; dir: SBS Broadcasting Networks Ltd, SBS Broadcasting (UK) Ltd; memb: Int Inst of Communications, BSAC, RTS, Br Literary Artistic Copyright Assoc, Satellite & Cable Broadcasting Gp, Australian Business in Europe; *Publications* Butterworths' Encyclopaedia of Forms and Precedents (contrib and ed of telecommunications section); *Style*— Tony Ghee, Esq; ✉ Taylor Wessing, Carmelite, 50 Victoria Embankment, Blackfriars, London EC4Y 0DX (tel 020 7300 7000, fax 020 7300 7100, e-mail t.ghee@taylorwessing.com)

GHODSE, Prof Abdol-Hamid (Hamid); Hon CBE; s of Abdol Rahim Ghods, of Iran, and Batool, *née* Daneshmand; *b* 30 April 1938; *Educ* Univ of Iran (MD), Univ of London (PhD, DPM, DSc); *m* 30 June 1973, Barbara, da of Capt William Bailin, of Tring; 2 s (Amir-Hossein b 1975, Ali-Reza b 1979), 1 da (Nassrin b 1977); *Career* Lt Iranian Health Corps 1965; subsequent postgrad trg/research psychiatrist and lectr Morgannwg Hosp Wales, Bart's and Maudsley Hosps London 1969–78, conslt St George's and St Thomas' Hosps 1978–87, prof of psychiatry of addictive behaviour St George's Hosp Med Sch 1987–2003, emeritus prof of psychiatry and int drug policy St George's Univ of London 2003–; hon conslt psychiatrist: St George's Hosp 1987–, SW London and St George's Mental Health Tst 1987–; hon conslt public health med: Merton Sutton and Wandsworth HA 1997–2002, Wandsworth Primary Care Tst 2002–; hon prof: Beijing Medical Univ 1997–, Peking Univ 2000–; visiting prof Keele Univ 2002–; dir S Thames Addiction Resource Agency for Cmmrs 1996–2004, non-exec dir Medical Cncl on Alcoholism 1996–2006, dir Int Centre for Drug Policy 2003–; RCPsych: chm Substance Misuse Section 1990–94, memb Cncl 1990–94 and 2001–, memb Ct of Electors 1993–99, vice-pres 2001–03, dir Bd of Int Affrs 2001–; pres Euro Collaborating Centres for Addiction Studies 1995–, convenor Assoc of Euro Profs of Psychiatry 1996–, chm Assoc Profs of Psychiatry (British Isles) 2002– (hon sec 1990–2002); memb: Expert Advsy Panel WHO 1979–, UN Int Narcotics Control Bd 1992– (pres 1993–95, 1997–99, 2000–02 and 2004–06), Fedn of Assocs of Clinical Profs UK 1992–, Cncl St George's Med Sch 1993–96, Subject Panel Univ of London 1993– (i/c higher degrees in psychiatry, chm 2003–), Scientific Ctee on Tobacco and Health (SCOTH) 2000–, Med Studies Ctee Univ of London 2003–; non-exec dir: Nat Clinical Assessment Authy (NCAA) 2001–05, Nat Patient Safety Agency 2005–; advsr Parly and NHS Ombudsman 2004–06; medical dir Advsy Ctee on Clinical Excellence Awards 2006–; ed International Psychiatry 2003–; inventor pupillometer for measuring Anisocoria (Euro, Canadian and US Patents with D Taylor, A Britten and G Gibson), selected by Design Cncl as a Millennium product 2000, devised Ghodse Opioid Addiction Test (GOAT) (German, French, US and UK Patents); FRCP 1992 (MRCP 1988), FRCPsych 1985 (MRCPsych 1980), FFPHM 1997 (MFPHM 1996), FRCPE 1997, FHEA 2007; *Publications* approx 300 incl: Psychoactive Drugs - Improving Prescribing Practices (1988), Drugs and Addictive Behaviour - A Guide to Treatment (1989, 3 edn 2002), Misuse of Drugs (3 edn, with P Bucknell, 1996), Young People and Substance Misuse (ed, 2004), Addiction at Work (ed, 2005); *Recreations* cycling, reading; *Clubs* Athenaeum; *Style*— Prof Hamid Ghodse; ✉ International Centre for Drug Policy, St George's University of London, Cranmer Terrace, London SW17 0RE (tel 020 8725 2624)

GHOSH, Dr Chandra; da of Prof Bhupendranath Ghosh (d 1988), and Dr Sati Ghosh (d 1992); *b* 15 June 1944; *Educ* St John's Diocesan Girls HS, Univ of Calcutta (MB BS), Univ of London (DPM); *m* 22 May 1983, Dr Norman Alexander Hindson, s of John Savage Hindson; *Career* SHO, registrar and sr registrar Univ of Liverpool, conslt psychiatrist Broadmoor Special Hosp 1988–98 (Park Lane Special Hosp 1977–87), med dir Pastoral Homes Chesterfield 1997–2001, med dir Safe Spaces Ltd; memb: Mental Health Assoc, Trans-Cultural Soc; MRCPsych 1975; *Style*— Dr Chandra Ghosh

GHOSH, Shiulie; da of Dr Salil K Ghosh, and Rose M Ghosh; *Educ* Teesside HS for Girls, St Mary's Sixth Form Coll Middlesbrough, Univ of Kent at Canterbury (BA); *m* 2001, Simon Torkington; 1 da (Maya Scarlett b 2003); *Career* BBC: prog asst Radio Cleveland 1989–90, trainee BBC News 1990–91, reporter and presenter BBC East Midlands 1991–93, reporter Countryfile 1993–95, reporter and presenter BBC Newsroom South East 1995–98; ITN: gen reporter 1998–99, home affrs corr and newscaster 1999–2002, home affrs ed and newscaster 2002–; Best TV Journalist BT Ethnic Multicultural Media Awards 2001; patron Int Care and Relief (ICR) Charity 2002–; *Recreations* scuba diving, travelling, reading; *Style*— Ms Shiulie Ghosh; ✉ ITN, 200 Gray's Inn Road, London WC1X 8XZ (tel 020 7833 3000, fax 020 7430 4302, e-mail shiulie.ghosh@itn.co.uk)

GIACHARDI, Dr David John; *b* 17 May 1948; *Educ* Watford Boys' GS, Merton Coll Oxford (open postmaster, BA), St John's Coll Oxford (DPhil); *m*; 1 da; *Career* research asst contracted to Concorde Div DTI Physical Chemistry Lab Univ of Oxford 1973–74, Boston Consulting Gp Ltd 1974–79; Courtaulds plc: joined 1979, head Policy & Planning Unit and memb Divnl Bd National Plastics Ltd 1981–82; dir: Courtaulds Fibres Ltd 1982–87; chm Courtaulds Chemicals 1986–89, dir of research and technol 1982–94, memb Main Bd 1987–98 (responsible for res and technol, human resources, health, safety and environment), memb Gp Exec 1988–98, chm Mgmnt Ctee Courtaulds Pension Fund 1991–98; dir of policy and assoc affrs Engrg Employers Fedn (EEF) 1998–2000; chief exec RSC 2000–06; memb EPSRC 1994–99, chm Sci Educn & Technol Ctee UK Chemical Industries Assoc 1988–98; FRSC; *Clubs* Oxford and Cambridge, Athenaeum, Brocket Hall Golf; *Style*— Dr David Giachardi

GIARDELLI, (Vincent Charles) Arthur; MBE (1973); s of Vincent Ausonio Elvezio Giardelli (d 1953), of Laugharne, Carmarthenshire, and Annie Alice Sophia, *née* Lutman (d 1972); *b* 11 April 1911; *Educ* Hertford Coll Oxford (MA); *m* 1, 10 April 1937 (m dis), Phillis Evelyn, da of Lt Cdr John Berry; 1 da (Judith b 1940), 1 s (Lawrence b 1942); *m* 2, 21 May 1976, Beryl Mary, da of George Trotter (d 1952), of Croydon, Surrey; *Career* fireman 1939–45, tutor then sr tutor UC Wales Aberystwyth 1958–78; artist attached to: Grosvenor Gallery London 1962–, England and Co 1999–; one man exhibitions incl: Nat Library of Wales 1963 and 2002, Manchester Coll of Art 1964, Welsh Arts Cncl 1975, Univ of Wales 1977 and 1978, Gallerie Convergence Nantes 1980, Grosvenor Gallery 1987 and 1994, England and Co 2001, MOMA Wales Ystabernacl Machynlleth 2001, Tenby Museum 2006; collections incl: Nat Library of Wales, Nat Museum of Wales, Gallery of Modern Art Dublin, Arts Cncl of GB, Welsh Arts Cncl, Musée des Beaux Arts Nantes, Nat Gallery Slovakia, Nat Gallery Prague, Tate Gallery; Br Cncl Award 1979; chm 56 Gp Wales 1958–98 (pres 1998), nat chm Assoc of Tutors in Adult Educn 1964–67, memb Calouste Gulbenkian Enquiry into economic situation of the visual artist 1977; hon fell UC Wales 1979–85; Silver Medal Czechoslovak Soc for International Relations 1985, Artist Friend of Wales Eisteddfod of Wales Silver Medal 2003; *Books* Up with the Lark (1939), The Delight of Painting (1976), The Grosvenor Gallery 1960–71 (1988), Arthur Giardelli: paintings, constructions, relief sculpture (conversations with David Shiel, 2001 and 2002); *Recreations* viola, foreign travel; *Style*— Arthur Giardelli, Esq, MBE; ✉ The Golden Plover Art Gallery, Warren, Pembroke, Dyfed SA71 5HR (tel 01646 661201)

GIBB, Prof (Arthur) Allan; OBE (1987); s of Arthur Gibb (d 1975), and Hilda, *née* Coleman (d 1977); *b* 20 November 1939; *Educ* Monkwearmouth GS Sunderland, Univ of Manchester (BA), Univ of Durham (PhD); *m* 12 Aug 1961, Joan, da of Eric Waterhouse (d 1964); 1 s (Stephen b 21 Sept 1962), 1 da (Jennie b 23 March 1965); *Career* res assoc and conslt Economist Intelligence Unit 1961–65; Univ of Durham: sr research assoc Business Research Unit 1965–67, sr research fell Business Sch 1967–70, fndr and dir Small Business Centre 1971–92, chair Fndn for SME Devpt (previously Small Business Centre) 1992–2001, currently prof emeritus of small business mgmnt; DEcon (hc) Turku Sch of Economics; *Recreations* fell walking, tennis, watching football, travel; *Style*— Prof Allan Gibb, OBE; ✉ Foundation for SME Development, Mill Hill Lane, Durham DH1 3LB (tel 0191 374 2235, fax 0191 374 1227, e-mail a.a.gibb@durham.ac.uk)

GIBB, Frances Rebecca; da of Matthew Gibb, of Islington, London, and Bettina Mary, *née* Dawson; *b* 24 February 1951; *Educ* St Margaret's Sch Bushey, UEA (BA); *m* 5 Aug 1978, Joseph Cahill, s of Col E J Cahill; 3 s (Thomas b 3 Aug 1983, James b 19 April 1985, Patrick b 8 April 1989); *Career* news res asst Visnews 1973, trainee reporter Times Higher Education Supplement 1974–78, art sales corr Daily Telegraph 1978–80; The Times: reporter 1980–82, legal affairs corr 1982–, legal ed 1999–; visiting prof Queen Mary's Coll London, govr KCS Wimbledon; *Clubs* Reform; *Style*— Ms Frances Gibb; ✉ The Times, 1 Pennington Street, London E1 9XN (tel 020 7782 5931)

G

GIBB, Sir Frank; kt (1987), CBE (1982); s of Robert Gibb (d 1932), and Violet Mary Gibb; *b* 29 June 1927; *Educ* Loughborough Coll (BSc); *m* 1, 1950, Wendy Marjorie (d 1997), da of Bernard Fowler (d 1957); 1 s, 2 da; m 2, 2000, Kirsten Harwood da of Egund A Moller (d 1956); *Career* joined Taylor Woodrow 1948, dir Taylor Woodrow International 1969–85, jt md Taylor Woodrow Construction Ltd 1970–84 (dir 1963–70, chm 1978–85, pres 1985–95), chm Taywood Santa Fe 1975–85, chm and chief exec Taylor Woodrow plc 1985–89 (jt md 1979–85, jt dep chm 1983–85); non-exec dir: Steetley plc 1990–92, Nuclear Electric 1990–94, Babcock International Group plc 1990–97, Energy Saving Tst Ltd 1992–99 (chm 1995–99), AMCO Corporation plc 1995–99, H R Wallingford Ltd 1995–; pres Fedn of Civil Engrg Contractors 1984–87 (chm 1979–80, vice-pres 1980–84), vice-pres Inst of Civil Engrs 1988–90; dir Holiday Pay Scheme and tstee Benefits Scheme Bldg and Civil Engrg Tstees 1980–83; dir British Nuclear Associates 1980–88 (chm Agrément Bd 1980–82), chm National Nuclear Corporation 1982–88; non-exec dir Fndn for the Built Environment 1999–2002; memb: Cncl CBI 1979–80 and 1985–90, Governing Body London Business Sch 1985–89; Hon DTech 1989; FICE, FREng 1980, Hon FCGI 1990; *Recreations* ornithology, gardening, walking, music; *Style*— Sir Frank Gibb, CBE, FREng; ✉ Ross Gibb Consultants, 11 Latchmoor Avenue, Gerrards Cross, Buckinghamshire SL9 8LJ

GIBB, James Robertson; RD (1983); s of David Craig Gibb (d 1971), and Mina, *née* Speirs (d 1981); *b* 19 April 1934; *Educ* Paisley GS, Univ of Glasgow (MA); *m* 21 March 1973, Elizabeth Milford, da of James Herries Henderson; 1 s (Donald James Hepburn), 1 da (Audrey Hepburn); *Career* investment mangr Scottish Amicable Life Assurance Society 1962–67 (apprentice actuary 1956–62), dir Speirs & Jeffrey Ltd 1967–99; Lt Cdr RNR (ret), FFA 1962; *Recreations* yachting, curling, skiing; *Clubs* Mudhook Yacht, R Gourock Yacht, Scottish Ski, Partick Curling; *Style*— James Gibb, Esq

GIBB, Nicolas John (Nick); MP; s of John McLean Gibb (d 1996), and Eileen Mavern Hanson Gibb; *b* 3 September 1960; *Educ* Maidstone GS, Roundhay Sch Leeds, Thornes House Sch Wakefield, Univ of Durham; *Career* tax accountant KPMG until 1997; MP (Cons) Bognor Regis and Littlehampton 1997–; shadow Treasy spokesman 1998–99, oppn Trade and Indust spokesman 1999–2001, memb Public Accounts Ctee 2001, memb Educn and Skills Select Ctee 2003–05, shadow min for schs 2005–; FCA; *Publications* Bucking the Market (1990), Maintaining Momentum (1994); *Style*— Nick Gibb, Esq, MP; ✉ House of Commons, London SW1A 0AA (tel 020 7219 6374, fax 020 7219 1395)

GIBB, Stephen John; s of Andrew Gibb, of Glasgow, and Ann M Symington, *née* Bannon; *b* 17 July 1964, Paisley; *Educ* King's Park Secdy Sch Glasgow, Univ of Glasgow (LLB, DipLP); *m* 22 Sept 1989, Christine, *née* McLintock; 1 da (Alexandra Jane), 1 s (David John); *Career* admitted slr: Scot 1988, Eng and Wales 1993; Fyfe Ireland WS (formerly Bird Semple Fyfe Ireland WS): trainee 1986–88, slr 1988–91, assoc 1991–94, ptnr 1994–99; ptnr Shepherd+Wedderburn 1999–; memb: Law Soc of Scot 1988, Law Soc of Eng and Wales 1993; MInstD; *Recreations* golf, football, reading, guitar, family taxi service; *Clubs* Murrayfield Golf; *Style*— Stephen Gibb, Esq; ✉ Kaimes Lodge, 4 Kaimes Road, Edinburgh EH12 6JS (tel 0131 334 3071, e-mail gibbsinedinburgh@hotmail.com); Shepherd+Wedderburn, Saltire Court, 20 Castle Terrace, Edinburgh EH1 2ET (tel 0131 473 5211, fax 0131 228 1222, e-mail stephen.gibb@shepwedd.co.uk)

GIBBARD, Prof Philip Leonard (Phil); s of Leonard Gibbard (d 1988), and Lorna Yvonne, *née* Lodge (d 1999); *b* 22 October 1949, Chiswick, London; *Educ* Isleworth GS, Univ of Sheffield (BSc), Darwin Coll Cambridge (PhD); *m* 19 Nov 2001, Ann Jennison; *Career* Royal Soc European exchange fell Univ of Oulu Finland 1975–76, NRC research fell Univ of Western Ontario 1976–77; Univ of Cambridge: NERC post-doctoral research assoc 1977–80, Leverhulme Tst fell 1980–82, NERC sr post-doctoral research assoc 1983–84, asst dir of research Sub-Dept of Quaternary Research Dept of Botany 1984–94, Dept of Geography univ lectr in quaternary geology 1995–2001 (fndr memb Godwin Inst of Quaternary Research), reader in quaternary palaeoenvironments 2001–05, prof of quaternary palaeoenvironments 2005–; Int Union for Quaternary Research (INQUA): corresponding memb Cmmn on Genesis of Quaternary Deposits 1978–86, jt chm Cmmn on Glaciation 1996–2003, memb Sub-Cmmn on European Quaternary Stratigraphy 1996–, sec Cmmn on Stratigraphy 1999–2003, ex-officio memb Stratigraphy and Chronology Cmmn 2003–; chm NE Atlantic Palaeoceanography and Climate Change Review Ctee NERC 1999, chair Sub-Cmmn on Quaternary Stratigraphy Int Cmmn on Stratigraphy 2002–, jt chm Anglo-French Gp Manche 1997–; memb: Int Geological Correlation Project (IGCP) 24 Ctee on Pre-Anglian Glaciation in GB 1979, CELIA/LIGA Workshop 1990, IGCP 253 End of the Pleistocene Fennoscandian Gp and Extra-Glacial Regions Gp, EC SHELF Gp 1993–97, PALTRANS Gp 1995–97, Earth Sciences Peer Review Ctee NERC 1996–99; co-ordinator BALTEEM Gp 1997–2002; Jl of Quaternary Science: book review ed 1985–89, dep ed 1988–89, ed 1990–94, asst ed 1995–96, currently memb Editorial Bd; memb Editorial Bd: Geological Magazine 1996–2006, Netherlands Jl of Geosciences 1998–, Geological Quarterly 1999–, Boreas 2000–, Jl of the Geological Society (advsy ed 2001–), Quaternaire 2002–, Bulletin de la Société Géologique de France 2004–; author of numerous chapters and articles in learned jls, book reviews, translations and websites; dosent (lectr for life) Dept of Geology Univ of Helsinki 1987, prof associé Univ de Caen-Basse Normandie 2001, chercheur associé CNRS Caen 2002, visiting prof Universität für Bodenkultur Wien 2007, prof associé Université de Caen-Basse Normandie 2007; Lyell Fund Prize Geological Soc 1999; memb: Geologists' Assoc, Geological Soc (Stratigraphy Cmmn 1995–), Quaternary Research Assoc (memb Exec Ctee 1979–81, chm Lithostratigraphy Subctee 1980, hon sec 1981–85, vice-pres 1997–2001, chair Jt Assoc Quaternary Research 2001–04), American Quaternary Assoc, Geological Soc of Finland, Deutsche Quartärvereinigung, Assoc Française pour l'Etude du Quaternaire, Lapin Tutkimus Seura, Assoc of Univ Teachers; *Books* incl: Quaternary Geology of the Vale of St Albans: Field Guide (co-ed, 1978), Pleistocene History of the Middle Thames Valley (1985), Pliocene - Middle Pleistocene of East Anglia: Field Guide (co-ed, 1988), Glacial Deposits in Great Britain and Ireland (co-ed, 1991), The Pleistocene History of the Lower Thames Valley (1994), Glacial Deposits in North-East Europe (co-ed, 1995), Stratigraphical Procedure (jtly, 2002), Extent and Chronology of Glaciation (3 Vols, co-ed, 2004), Early-Middle Pleistocene Transitions: The Land-Ocean Evidence (co-ed, 2005); *Recreations* jazz and blues music, modern architecture, art and design; *Style*— Prof Phil Gibbard; ✉ Cambridge Quaternary, Department of Geography, University of Cambridge, Downing Place, Cambridge CB2 3EN (tel 01223 333924, fax 01223 333392, e-mail plg1@cam.ac.uk)

GIBBENS, Barnaby John (Barney); OBE (1989); s of Dr Gerald Hartley Gibbens (d 1989), of Sidmouth, Devon, and Deirdre Mary, *née* Wolfe (d 1972); *b* 17 April 1935; *Educ* Winchester; *m* 1, 30 June 1960 (m dis 1990), Sally Mary, da of Geoffrey Harland Stephenson (d 1961), of Guildford; 2 da (Penelope b 1962, Virginia b 1967), 1 s (Nicolas b 1974); m 2, 26 Feb 1990, Kristina, da of Romulo de Zabala (d 1966); *Career* fndr CAP Gp (later SEMA Gp) 1962; pres Computing Servs Assoc 1975; chm: Computing Servs Industry Trg Cncl 1984–94, IT Industry Lead Body 1987–94; dir Nat Computing Centre 1987–90, memb Nat Cncl for Vocational Qualifications 1989–92, chm Skin Treatment and Research Tst (START) 1990–; dir and co sec UK Skills 1990–2001; chm: Callhaven plc 1990–92, Enterprise Systems Group Ltd 1990–96, Mercator Systems Ltd 2000–02; dir IT Industry Trg Orgn (ITITO) 1991–96, memb Nat Cncl for Educnl Technol (NCET) 1991–94; chm: IT Trg Accreditation Cncl (ITTAC) 1991–96, The Royal Tennis Court Hampton Court Palace 1994–2001; Freeman City of London 1987; Fndr Master Worshipful Co of Info Technologists 1987; hon memb City & Guilds of London Inst 1993; FBCS 1970, FCA 1972; FRSA 1993; *Recreations* golf, real tennis, photography, gardening; *Clubs* MCC (assoc), Wisley Golf; *Style*— Barney Gibbens, Esq, OBE; ✉ 12 Kings Road, Wimbledon, London SW19 8QN (tel 020 8542 3878, fax 020 8540 0581, e-mail barney.gibbens@btinternet.com)

GIBBON, Lindsay Harwin Ward (Lin); da of James Ferguson Gibbon; *b* 29 November 1949; *Educ* Glasgow Sch of Art; *Children* 1 da (Katherine Jane Harwin Gibbon McGregor b 1985); *Career* dir Randak Design Consultants Ltd 1978– (graphic designer specialising in corp literature and packaging design); memb Bd of Dirs Scottish Design 1994–98, fndr chm Scottish Design Res Forum 1994–, memb: Bd of Dirs Glasgow 1999 Festival Co Ltd 1997–, judging panel Prince Philip Prize for Design 1999, 2000 and 2001; vice-pres CSD 2001– (pres 1998–2000); FCSD 1994, FRSA 2000; *Style*— Lin Gibbon; ✉ Sorisdale, by Lanark; Randak Design Consultants Ltd, Gordon Chambers, 90 Mitchell Street, Glasgow G1 3NQ (tel 0141 221 2142, fax 0141 226 5096)

GIBBON-WILLIAMS, Andrew; s of Ivor James Williams (d 1990), of Barry, S Glamorgan, and Grace Mary, *née* Thomas; *b* 6 March 1954; *Educ* Barry Boys' GS, Edinburgh Coll of Art Univ of Edinburgh (Huntly-MacDonald Sinclair travelling scholarship, MA); *Career* artist and art critic; art critic The Sunday Times Scotland 1988–96, regnl art critic The Times 1988–97, regular contrib to BBC Arts progs; winner: Young Artist bursary Scottish Arts Cncl 1982, Warwick Arts Tst Artist award 1989; *Solo Exhibitions* 369 Gallery Edinburgh 1979, 1980, 1982 and 1986; *Group Exhibitions* incl: Scottish Painters (Chenil Gallery London) 1978, The Royal Scottish Academy 1980, Scottish Painting (Watts Gallery Phoenix) 1981, Best of 369 (St Andrews Festival) 1983, The Scottish Expression: 1983 (Freidus Ordover Gallery NYC) 1983, Peintres Contemporains Ecossais (Galerie Peinture Fraîche Paris) 1983, New Directions - British Art (Puck Building NYC) 1983, Chicago Int Art Exposition 1983–89, Int Contemporary Art Fair London 1984, Contemporary Scottish Art (Clare Hall Cambridge) 1984, Scottish Painting (Linda Durham Gallery Sante Fe) 1985, Scottish Art Since 1900 (Scottish Nat Gallery of Modern Art, Edinburgh and The Barbican Gallery, London 1989–90; *Work in Public Collections* incl: The Scottish Arts Cncl, Dundee Art Gallery, Glasgow Museums and Art Galleries, IBM UK Ltd, Philips Petroleum, Scottish Nat Gallery of Modern Art, City of Edinburgh Public Collection, The Warwick Arts Tst Collection, L&M Moneybrokers Ltd, NatWest Bank, The McDonald Corporation (USA); *Books* The Bigger Picture (1993), An American Passion (1995), Craigie: The Art of Craigie Aitchison (1996), William Roberts: An English Cubist (2005); *Recreations* travel, music, gardening; *Style*— Andrew Gibbon-Williams, Esq; ✉ e-mail agw@gibbon-williams.freeserve.co.uk

GIBBONS, Beth; *b* 4 January 1966; *Career* pop singer; lead singer and fndr memb (with Geoffrey Barrow , *qv*) Portishead 1991– (sold over 8 million albums); various press, PRS, ASCAP and IFPI awards; *Albums* Dummy (1994, Mercury Music Prize 1995), Portishead (1997), PNYC (live album, 1998), Out Of Season (solo album as Beth Gibbons & Rustin' Man, 2002); *Singles* Numb (EP, 1994), Sour Times (1994), Glory Box (1995), Cowboys (1997), All Mine (1997), Only You (1998), Over (1998), Mysteries (Beth Gibbons & Rustin' Man, 2002), Tom The Model (Beth Gibbons & Rustin Man', 2003); *Films* To Kill A Dead Man (short film, 1994), PNYC (DVD, 2000); *Style*— Ms Beth Gibbons

GIBBONS, Dr Brian J; AM; *b* 25 August 1950, Dublin; *Educ* Keadue Nat Sch, Summerhill Coll Sligo, Nat Univ of Ireland Galway (MB BCh, BAO); *Career* various hosp posts incl Univ Hosp Galway, Co Hosp Roscommon 1974–76, Calderdale GP Vocational Trg Scheme 1997–80, GP princ Blaengwynfi Port Talbot 1980–99; memb Nat Assembly for Wales (Lab) Aberavon 1999–; dep min: Health 2000–03, Economic Devpt and Tport 2003–05; min for Health and Social Servs 2005–; memb GPs Ctee UK 1990–98, sec Morgannwg Local Med Ctee 1994–99; memb BMA, memb Med Practitioners Union; FRCGP 1995; *Style*— Dr Brian Gibbons, AM; ✉ Eagle House, 2 Talbot Road, Port Talbot SA13 1DH (tel 01639 870779, e-mail brian.gibbons@wales.gov.uk)

GIBBONS, Christopher Peter; s of William Frederick Gibbons, of Holmes Chapel, Cheshire, and Hazel Doreen, *née* Flint; *b* 10 March 1949; *Educ* Manchester Grammar, Keble Coll and Wolfson Coll Oxford (MA, DPhil, BM BCh, MCh); *m* 4 July 1970, Ann Lawrence, da of George Robert White Dalgleish; 3 da (Kate b 1975, Rachel b 1978, Susannah b 1982); *Career* surgical registrar Univ Hosp of Wales 1979–82, surgical registrar Royal Hallamshire Hosp Sheffield 1982–83, clinical res fell Univ of Sheffield 1984–85, sr surgical registrar Cardiff and Swansea 1985–89, conslt gen surgn Morriston Hosp Swansea 1989– (clinical dir of surgery 1992–96), surgical tutor 1992–96, vascular advsr for Wales 2002–; author of pubns on aspects of physiology and surgery; winner NHS B Merit Award 2003; memb: BMA, Br Transplantation Soc 1985–89, Assoc of Surgns 1988, Cncl Vascular Surgical Soc of GB and I 2001–04 (memb1990), Euro Soc for Vascular Surgery 1990, Int Soc for Endovascular Surgery 1998, Vascular Access Soc 2003; FRCS 1980; *Publications* Vascular Access Simplified (co ed, 2003); *Recreations* sketching, sailing, fell walking, classical guitar; *Style*— Christopher Gibbons, Esq; ✉ Morriston Hospital, Swansea (tel 01792 702222, e-mail cp_gibbons@msn.com)

GIBBONS, Prof Gary William; s of Archibald William Stallard Gibbons, and Bertha, *née* Bunn; *b* 1 July 1946; *Educ* Purley Co GS, St Catharine's Coll Cambridge (MA, PhD); *m* 1972, Christine, da of Peter Howden; 2 s (William Peter b 1979, Charles Arthur b 9 Aug 1981); *Career* DAMTP Univ of Cambridge: lectr 1980–90, reader 1990–98, prof of theoretical physics 1998–; fell Trinity Coll Cambridge 2002–; FRS 1999; *Publications* Euclidean Quantum Gravity (with S Hawking in World Scientific, 1993); also author of numerous research papers; *Recreations* listening to music and looking at paintings; *Style*— Prof Gary Gibbons; ✉ DAMTP, University of Cambridge, CMS, Wilberforce Road, Cambridge CB3 0WA (tel 01223 337899, fax 01223 766865, e-mail gwg1@amtp.cam.ac.uk)

GIBBONS, Jeremy Stewart; QC (1995); s of Geoffrey Seed Gibbons (d 1998), of Bighton, Hants, and Rosemary Marion, *née* Stewart (d 1978); *b* 15 July 1949; *Educ* St Edward's Sch Oxford, Coll of Law Guildford; *m* 1, 1974, Mary Mercia, da of Rev Kenneth Sutton Bradley; 2 s (Edward b 16 April 1977, Tim b 13 Dec 1983), 2 da (Harriet b 21 Oct 1979 (decd), Polly b 27 March 1981); m 2, 1998, Sarah Valerie, da of Michael John Jenkins, FRICS; *Career* articled clerk 1967–71, called to the Bar Gray's Inn 1973, head of Chambers 1991–, recorder of the Crown Court 1993– (asst recorder 1989–93); *Recreations* skiing, cooking, gardening, carpentry; *Style*— Jeremy Gibbons, Esq, QC; ✉ 17 Carlton Crescent, Southampton, Hampshire SO15 2XR (tel 023 8032 0320, fax 023 8032 0321)

GIBBONS, Dr John Ernest; CBE (2000); s of John Howard Gibbons (d 1979), and Lilian Alice, *née* Shale (d 1982); *b* 20 April 1940; *Educ* Oldbury GS, Birmingham Sch of Architecture (DipArch, DipTP), Univ of Edinburgh (PhD); *m* 3 Nov 1962, Patricia, da of Eric John Mitchell, of Albany, WA; 1 s (Mark b 16 March 1963), 2 da (Carey b 20 May 1964, Ruth b 29 July 1967); *Career* lectr: Aston Univ 1964–66, Univ of Edinburgh 1969–72; Scot Devpt Dept: princ architect 1972–74 and 1976–78, superintending architect 1978–82; res scientist CSIRO Melbourne 1975; SO: dep dir bldg directorate 1982–84, dir of bldg 1984–, chief architect 1984–2005; architectural advsr to the Scottish Parly 2001–; visiting prof Mackintosh Sch of Architecture Glasgow 2000–; memb: Cncl Edinburgh Architectural Assoc 1977–80, Cncl RIAS 1977–80, Cncl ARCUK 1984–, Design Cncl 1984–88; DUniv UCE; RIBA 1964, ARIAS 1967, FSA Scot 1984, FRSA 1987; *Clubs* New (Edinburgh); *Style*— Dr John Gibbons, CBE; ✉ Crichton Ho, Pathhead, Midlothian EH37 5UX (tel 01875 320 085); The Scottish Parliament, Parliament Headquarters, Edinburgh EH99 1SP

GIBBONS, Michael Robert; s of Rev Robert Gibbons (d 1980), of Leics, and Audrey, *née* Bird; *b* 18 July 1957; *Educ* City of Leicester Boys' GS, King's Coll London (BA, AKC,

PGCE); *m* 28 July 1984, Penny, *née* Hewett; 1 s (Daniel Robert Peter b 17 May 1990), 1 da (Sarah Verity b 12 March 1993); *Career* asst master Ardingly Coll 1981–85, asst master Rugby Sch 1985–97 (housemaster 1992–97), second master Whitgift Sch 1997–2001, headmaster Queen Elizabeth GS Wakefield 2001–; memb: SHA 1997, HMC 2001; *Recreations* sport, travel, family; *Clubs* East India; *Style*— Michael Gibbons, Esq; ✉ Queen Elizabeth Grammar School, 154 Northgate, Wakefield, West Yorkshire WF1 3QX (tel 01924 373943, fax 01924 231603)

GIBBONS, Paul; s of Norman Gibbons (d 1979), of Reading, Berks, and Irene, *née* Pantlin; *b* May 1947, Reading, Berks; *m* Sept 1967, Jennifer, *née* Harwood; 1 s (Peter Joseph b 21 Oct 1987); *Career* fndr and dir: Hurst Publishing Ltd (publishers of Auto Trader magazines) 1977–99, Leaderboard Golf Ltd (owners Sandford Springs, Chart Hills and The Oxfordshire golf clubs and Dale Hill Hotel and Golf Club) 2000–; supporter: Duke of Edinburgh Award Scheme, Sparks; MInstD; *Recreations* golf, swimming, walking; *Clubs* Publishers Golf Soc; *Style*— Paul Gibbons, Esq; ✉ Leaderboard Golf Limited, Leaderboard House, Sandford Springs, Wolverton, Tadley, Hampshire RG26 5RT (tel 01635 291506, fax 01635 291501, e-mail lorrainew@leaderboardgolf.co.uk)

GIBBONS, Stephen John; s of John Gibbons, of Luton, Beds, and Wendy Patricia, *née* Luery; *b* 8 October 1956; *Educ* Bedford Modern Sch, Luton Sixth Form Coll, Dunstable Coll of FE, RCA (MA); *m* Valerie Anne, da of Michael Mercer; 1 da (Francesca Louisa b 29 Dec 1990), 1 s (Frederick Jim b 27 July 1993); *Career* graphic designer Minale Tattersfield 1982–84, ptnr The Partners 1985–96 (joined 1984), fndr ptnr Dew Gibbons 1997; recipient 2 Silver D&AD Awards for environmental graphics and signing schemes, various others from CSD/Minerva Awards, XYZ Magazine Awards, Communication Awards in the Building Industry, Donside Graphic Design and Print Awards and DBA Design Effectiveness Awards; work selected for various int awards/pubns incl: Art Dirs' Club of NY, PDC Gold Awards USA, Creativity USA, Communication Arts USA, Graphis Switzerland, Int Poster Biennale Poland; occasional design juror D&AD (memb Exec Ctee until 1998), lectr at various UK univs and seminars/confs on graphic design; external moderator BA Graphic Design Kingston Univ; *Style*— Stephen Gibbons, Esq; ✉ 49 Tabernacle Street, London EC2A 4AA (tel 020 7689 8999)

GIBBONS, Sir William Edward Doran; 9 Bt (GB 1752), of Stanwell Place, Middlesex; JP (S Westminster Inner London 1994); s of Sir John Edward Gibbons, 8 Bt (d 1982), and Mersa Wentworth, *née* Foster; *b* 13 January 1948; *Educ* Pangbourne Sch, RNC Dartmouth, Univ of Bristol (BSc), Univ of Southampton (MBA); *m* 1972, Patricia Geraldine Archer, da of Roland Archer Howse; 1 da (Joan Eleanor Maud b 1980), 1 s (Charles William Edwin b 1983); *Heir* s, Charles Gibbons; *Career* Sealink UK: asst shipping and port mangr Parkeston Quay 1979–82, serv mangr Anglo-Dutch 1982–85, mangr Harwich-Hook 1985–87, gen mangr Isle of Wight Servs 1987–90; tport and mgmnt conslt 1990–94, dir Passenger Shipping Assoc 1994–; chm Manningtree Parish Cncl 1985–87, chm Cncl of Travel and Tourism 1996–; non-exec memb IOW Dist Health Authy 1990–94; JP Portsmouth 1990–94, JP South Westminster Div Inner London Magistrates 1994–; hon MBA Univ of Southampton 1996, MCIT; *Style*— Sir William Gibbons, Bt; ✉ 5 Yarborough Road, Southsea, Hampshire PO5 3DZ

GIBBS, Antony Richard; s of Dr Antony James Gibbs (d 1993), of Cranleigh, Surrey, and Helen Margaret, *née* Leuchars; *b* 25 May 1939; *Educ* Bradfield, Byam Shaw Sch of Drawing and Painting (scholar), Kingston Sch of Art (NDD); *m* Sept 1964, Mary Jane (Janie), da of Frank Day; 1 s (Rupert Nicolas Antony b 28 April 1968), 1 da (Emily Jo b 26 July 1970); *Career* formerly: designer David Ogle Associates, product designer STC Consumer Product Div, chief stylist Radfords (Coachbuilders) Ltd, assoc TEE Design; dir Murdoch & Gibbs 1975–80; Hop Studios 1980–92 (fndr ptnr, co sec, dir), fndr Gibbs Design Partnership 1992–2005 (ret); Design Cncl Award for outstanding design 1977, BIO Industrial Design Award Yugoslavia 1977; memb: Design Cncl, Design Cncl Awards Ctee, Bursaries Judging Panel RSA; moderator BA Assessment Panel Central Sch of Art; FCSD, FRSA; *Books* Industrial Design in Engineering (jtly), Steve Hodges and his magnificent Sterling 26; *Recreations* model making, historical research; *Style*— Antony Gibbs, Esq; ✉ 6 Tarleton Gardens, Forest Hill, London SE23 3XN (tel 020 8699 4610, e-mail tony.gibbs@btinternet.com)

GIBBS, Christopher Henry; 5 and yst s of Hon Sir Geoffrey Cokayne Gibbs, KCMG (d 1975; 2 s of 1 Baron Hunsdon of Hunsdon, 4 s of 1 Baron Aldenham, JP), and Helen Margaret Gibbs, CBE, JP, *née* Leslie (d 1979); *b* 29 July 1938; *Educ* Eton, Stanbridge, Université de Poitiers; *Career* art dealer; dir Christopher Gibbs Ltd; chm J Paul Getty Jr Charitable Tst; tstee: American Friends of the National Gallery, American Sch of Tangier Morocco; *Recreations* antiquarian pursuits, gardening; *Clubs* Beefsteak, Pratt's; *Style*— Christopher Gibbs, Esq; ✉ Little Place Cottage, Clifton Hampden, Abingdon, Oxfordshire OX14 3EQ; L6 Albany, Piccadilly, London W1J 0AZ; El Foolk, 284 Rue de la Vieille Montagne, Tangiers, Morocco (e-mail secretary@christophergibbs.com)

GIBBS, David Frank; s of Frank Gerald Gibbs (d 1983), and Margaret Follit (Peggy), *née* Shaw (d 1974); *b* 30 May 1947; *Educ* Ardingly, UC Durham (BA), Emmanuel Coll Cambridge (PGCE); *m* 1984, Philippa, da of Sir Kenneth Wheare and Lady Wheare; 2 s (Matthew b 12 Sept 1990, Tom b 6 Jan 1993); *Career* asst teacher Monkton Combe Sch 1969–71, asst teacher St John's Coll Johannesburg 1972, head of economics and master i/c cricket Sherborne 1973–83, head of economics and politics Charterhouse 1983–89, housemaster Haileybury 1989–96, headmaster Chigwell Sch 1996–2007; tstee: Sherborne House Bermondsey 1984–96, Inner Cities Young People's Project 1989–2002 (chm 1999–2002); author of articles on local history; *Recreations* cricket, hockey, walking, family; *Clubs* MCC, Sussex Martlets CC; *Style*— David Gibbs, Esq

GIBBS, Marion Olive; da of Harry Norman Smith, and Olive Mabel, *née* Lewis; *Educ* Pate's GS for Girls Cheltenham, Univ of Bristol (BA, PGCE, MLitt); *Career* asst mistress City of Worcester Girls' GS 1974–76, teacher Chailey Comp Sch 1977, head of sixth form, dir of studies and head of classics Burgess Hill Sch for Girls 1977–89, head of sixth form and head of classics Haberdashers' Aske's Girls' Sch 1989–91, HM's Inspector of Schs 1992–94, headmistress James Allen's Girls' Sch 1994–; tutor Open Univ 1979–91; chm Cncl JACT 2001–04; memb: Classical Assoc (memb Cncl 1984–87 and 1995–98, jt hon sec 1989–92), Hellenic Soc (memb Cncl 1997–2000); tstee Dulwich Picture Gallery 1999–2001; FRSA 1997; *Publications* Greek Tragedy: An Introduction (1989), Two Sectors, One Purpose: Independent Schools in the System (contrib, 2002), The Teaching of Classics (contrib, 2003); *Recreations* gardening, music, drama, keeping informed about the developing world; *Style*— Mrs Marion Gibbs; ✉ James Allen's Girls' School, East Dulwich Grove, London SE22 8TE (tel 020 8693 1181, fax 020 8693 7842)

GIBBS, Hon Mr Justice; Sir Richard John Hedley Gibbs; kt (2000); s of Brian Conaway Gibbs (d 1946), Asst Dist Cmmr Colonial Admin Serv, and Mabel Joan, *née* Gatford; *b* 2 September 1941; *Educ* Oundle, Trinity Hall Cambridge (MA); *m* 26 June 1965, Janet, da of Francis Herbert Whittall, of Reigate, Surrey; 3 da (Sarah b 1966 d 1991, Susannah b 1968, Julia b 1971), 1 s (Christopher b 1979); *Career* called to the Bar Inner Temple 1965 (bencher 2000); recorder of the Crown Court 1981–90, QC 1984, circuit judge (Midland & Oxford Circuit) 1990–2000, judge of the High Court of Justice (Queen's Bench Div) 2000–, presiding judge Midland Circuit 2004–; *Style*— The Hon Mr Justice Gibbs; ✉ Royal Courts of Justice, Strand, London WC2A 2LL

GIBBS, Sir Roger Geoffrey; kt (1994); 4 s of Hon Sir Geoffrey Cokayne Gibbs, KCMG (2 s of 1 Baron Hunsdon of Hunsdon, JP, who himself was 4 s of 1 Baron Aldenham) and Hon Lady Gibbs, CBE, JP; *b* 13 October 1934; *Educ* Eton, Millfield; *Career* The Wellcome Trust 1983–99 (chm 1989–99); dir: Gerrard and National Holdings plc 1971–94 (chm 1975–89), Arsenal FC plc 1980–2006, Howard de Walden Estates Ltd 1989–2001 (chm 1993–98), The Colville Estate Ltd 1989–2003, Fleming Family & Ptnrs 2000–07 (chm 2000–03); chm: Arundel Castle Cricket Fndn 1986–97, St Paul's Cathedral Fndn 2000–; memb: Cncl Royal Nat Pension Fund for Nurses 1975–2002, Ctee MCC 1991–94, Ctee Br Museum Devpt Tst 2000–; tstee Winston Churchill Meml Tst 2001–; Liveryman Worshipful Co of Merchant Taylors; *Recreations* sport, travel; *Clubs* Boodle's, Pratt's, Swinley; *Style*— Sir Roger Gibbs

GIBBS, Stephen Cokayne; OBE (2001); 2 s of Hon Sir Geoffrey Gibbs, KCMG (d 1975), 2 s of 1 Baron Hunsdon of Hunsdon, JP, himself 4 s of 1 Baron Aldenham, JP, and Hon Lady Gibbs, CBE, JP (d 1979); *b* 18 July 1929; *Educ* Eton; *m* 1972, Lavinia Winifred, 2 da of Sir Edmund Bacon, 13 Bt, KG, KBE, TD (d 1982); 2 s, 1 da; *Career* 2 Lt KRRC, Maj QVR (TA) 1960–63 and Royal Green Jackets; dir: Charles Barker plc 1962–87, Vaux Group plc 1971–99; Nat Tst for Scotland: memb Exec Ctee 1987–97, memb Cncl 1991–96, chm Regnl Ctee Argyll, Lochaber & Western Isles 1995–2000; memb: RUCC for Scotland 1992–97, Deer Cmmn for Scot 1993–2000; chm: Isle of Arran District Salmon Fisheries Bd 1991–, Assoc of Deer Mgmnt Gps 1994–2005; *Recreations* shooting, stalking, gardening; *Clubs* Pratt's; *Style*— Stephen Gibbs, Esq, OBE; ✉ Dougarie, Isle of Arran KA27 8EB (tel 01770 840229/840259, fax 01770 840266)

GIBBS-KENNET, Peter Adrian; s of Reginald Ernest Gibbs Gibbs-Kennet, DLI (ka WWII), and Ruth, *née* Wyatt (d 1991); *Educ* Plymouth and Mannamead Coll Devon, Oriel Coll Oxford (MA, Dip Ed, Coll VIII); *m* 12 July 1968, Anna Eleanor, da of Gp Capt Hugh Llewellyn Jenkins, MD, OStJ (d 2001), and Vivienne, *née* Pawson; 1 s (Swithun Aurelian Wyatt b 6 July 1972); *Career* asst sec UCCA until 1971, academic registrar Lanchester Poly (now Coventry Univ) 1971–80, dir of educn and practice standards RIBA 1980–95; devpt conslt: AA Sch of Architecture London 2000–02, Bartlett Sch of Architecture UCL 2000–05; founding jt ed and sec Editorial Bd The Jl of Architecture (Taylor and Francis/RIBA) 1995–; memb Registration Advsy Gp and R&D Ctee RIBA 2004–; Freeman City of London 1994; FCMI 1981, FRSA 1982, Hon FRIBA 2002; *Recreations* inertia; *Clubs* Oxford and Cambridge; *Style*— Peter Gibbs-Kennet, Esq; ✉ Norwich Cottage, Bisley, Gloucestershire GL6 7AD (tel 01452 770462, e-mail dli1944@aol.com)

GIBRALTAR IN EUROPE, Bishop of 2001–; Rt Rev Dr (Douglas) Geoffrey Rowell; s of late Cecil Victor Rowell, and late Kate, *née* Hunter; *b* 13 February 1943; *Educ* Eggar's GS Alton, Winchester (Hants CC bursary), CCC Cambridge (MA, PhD, George Williams prize in liturgy), Cuddesdon Theol Coll; *Career* ordained: deacon 1968, priest 1969; asst chaplain and Hastings Rashdall student New Coll Oxford 1968–72, hon curate St Andrew's Headington 1968–71; Univ of Oxford: fell and chaplain Keble Coll 1972–94 (emeritus fell 1994–), tutor in theol Keble Coll 1976–94, univ lectr in theol 1976–94; Wiccammical canon and preb Bargham Chichester 1981–2001; bishop of Basingstoke 1994–2001; memb C of E: Liturgical Cmmn 1981–91, Doctrine Cmmn 1991–96 (conslt 1996–99, memb 1999–2003); hon dir Archbishop's Examination in Theol 1985–2002, conservator Mirfield Cert in Pastoral Theol 1988–94; chm Churches Funerals Gp 1997–; memb: Anglican-Oriental Orthodox Int Forum 1985– (Anglican co-chm 1996–), Cncl of Mgmnt St Stephen's House Oxford 1986– (chm 2004), Inter-Anglican Standing Cmmn on Ecumenical Rels 1999– (vice-chm 2002–); tstee Scott-Holland Lectureship 1979– (chm 1993–); govr: Pusey House Oxford 1979– (pres 1995–), Eggar's Sch Alton 1994–97; almoner Christ's Hosp 1979–89; visiting prof UC Chichester 1996–2003; govr SPCK 1994–94 and 1997–2003 (vice-pres 1994–); contrib to theol and historical jls; MA and DPhil (by incorporation) Univ of Oxford; Hon DD Nashotah House Wisconsin 1996, DD Univ of Oxford 1997; *Books* Hell and the Victorians (1974), Rock-Hewn Churches of Eastern Tigray (ed with B E Juel-Jensen, 1976), The Liturgy of Christian Burial (1977), The Vision Glorious (1983 and 1991), Tradition Renewed (ed, 1986), To the Church of England (ed and contrib, 1988), Confession and Absolution (ed with M Dudley and contrib, 1990), The English Religious Tradition and the Genius of Anglicanism (ed, 1992), The Oil of Gladness: Anointing in the Church (ed with M Dudley and contrib, 1993), A Speaking Life: the legacy of John Keble (contrib, 1995), From Oxford to the People: reconsidering Newman and the Oxford Movement (contrib), By Whose Authority? Newman, Manning and the Magisterium (contrib, 1996), Religious Change in Europe 1650–1914 (contrib, 1997), The History of the University of Oxford, Vol VII: Nineteenth-Century Oxford, Part 2 (contrib, 2000), Managing the Church? Order and Organization in a secular age (contrib, 2000), The Club of 'Nobody's Friends' 1800–2000 (2000), Love's Redeeming Work: The Anglican Quest for Holiness (ed with K Stevenson and R Williams, 2000), Flesh, Bone, Wood (with Julien Chilcott-Monk, 2001), Come, Lord Jesus (with Julian Chilcott-Monk, 2002), The Gestures of God (with Christine Hall, 2004), Glory Descending: Michael Ramsey and his Writings (contrib, 2005), In this Sign Conquer: A History of the Society of the Holy Cross 1855–2005 (contrib, 2006); *Style*— The Rt Rev the Bishop of Gibraltar in Europe; ✉ Bishop's Lodge, Church Road, Worth, Crawley, West Sussex RH10 7RT (tel 01293 883051, fax 01293 884479, e-mail bishop@dioceseineurope.co.uk)

GIBSON, Cdr Bryan Donald; MBE (2002); s of Donald Gibson (d 1983), of Barnston, Wirral, Cheshire, and Inez Margaret, *née* Lawrence (d 1983); *b* 21 July 1937; *Educ* Birkenhead Park GS Victoria, Univ of Manchester (BSc, MSc); *m* 1 Jan 1966, (Frances) Mary, da of Reginald Herbert Greenhalgh (d 1982), of Swinton, Lancs; 1 s (James b 1968), 1 da (Helen b 1970); *Career* cmmnd RN 1962, lectr RN Engrg Coll 1963–66; served: HMS Bulwark 1967, HMS Sultan (Nuclear Propulsion Sch) 1968–70; sr lectr Dept of Nuclear Sci and Technol RNC Greenwich 1970–72, head of materials technol RN Engrg Coll Manadon Plymouth 1973–78, ret 1978; academic sec Chartered Assoc of Certified Accountants 1978–82, sec Inst of Metallurgists 1982–84, dep sec Inst of Metals 1985–91, dir Inst of Materials 1992–96; formerly memb Ctee: CNAA, RSA, Engrg Cncl, CSTI; vice-pres Inst of Nuclear Engrs 1976–78; tstee Ironbridge Gorge Museum Devpt Tst 2005; pres Fellowship of Clerks in the City of London 2002; Freeman City of London 1984, Master Worshipful Co of Engrs 2006–07 (Liveryman 1984, Clerk 1986–2002); hon memb CGLI; FIMMM 1975, CEng 1977, FRSA 1996–2002; *Recreations* gardening, DIY; *Style*— Cdr Bryan Gibson, MBE, RN; ✉ Millers Cottage, Windmill Hill, Herstmonceux, East Sussex BN27 4RS (tel 01323 833554, e-mail bryangibson455@btinternet.com)

GIBSON, Charles; QC (2001); *b* 1960; *Educ* Wellington, Univ of Durham (BA), Univ of London (Dip Law); *m*; 4 c; *Career* called to the Bar 1984; currently memb Henderson Chambers; recorder 2001–; accredited mediator; memb: Professional Negligence Bar Assoc, Common Law and Commercial Bar Assoc; *Publications* Group Actions: Product Liability Law and Insurance; *Style*— Charles Gibson, Esq, QC; ✉ Henderson Chambers, 2 Harcourt Buildings, Temple, London EC4Y 9DB

GIBSON, His Hon Judge Charles Andrew Hamilton; s of Rev Prebendary Leslie Andrew Gibson (d 1963), of Colwall, Herefordshire, and Kathleen Anne Frances, *née* Hamilton (d 1991); *b* 9 July 1941; *Educ* Sherborne, Hertford Coll Oxford (MA); *m* 9 Aug 1969, Susan Judith, er da of Geoffrey Christopher Rowntree; 2 da (Catherine Sarah b 7 Aug 1970, Rachel Caroline b 11 Jan 1974); *Career* called to the Bar Lincoln's Inn 1966, in practice 1966–96, recorder 1991–96 (asst recorder 1987), circuit judge (SE Circuit) 1996–; memb Mental Health Review Tribunal 2002–; chm Southwark Diocesan Pastoral Ctee 1993–2003, chm Hertford Soc 2004–; *Books* Surveying Buildings (with Prof M R A Hollis 1983, 5 edn 2005); *Recreations* music, theatre, wine; *Clubs* Oxford and Cambridge; *Style*— His Hon Judge Gibson; ✉ Lambeth County Court, Cleaver Street, London SE11 4DZ (tel 020 7091 4410)

G

GIBSON, Christopher Allen Wood; QC (1995); s of Sir Ralph Brian Gibson, of London, and Ann Chapman, *née* Reuther; *b* 5 July 1953; *Educ* St Paul's, BNC Oxford (BA); *m* 4 Aug 1984, Alarys Mary Calvert, da of David Eaton, of Emsworth, Hants; 2 da (Harriet b 10 Dec 1984, Julia b 24 May 1987); *Career* called to the Bar Middle Temple 1976 (bencher 2003), recorder of the Crown Ct 2002–; memb Professional Conduct and Complaints Ctee of the Bar Cncl 1999–2002; memb Hon Soc of Middle Temple, FCIArb 1992; *Recreations* sailing, motorcycles, photography; *Clubs* Vincent's (Oxford); *Style*— Christopher Gibson; ✉ Doughty Street Chambers, 10–11 Doughty Street, London WC1N 2PL

GIBSON, Rev Sir Christopher Herbert; 4 Bt (UK 1931), of Linconia, and of Faccombe, Co Southampton; o s of Sir Christopher Herbert Gibson, 3 Bt (d 1994), and Lilian Lake, *née* Young; *b* 17 July 1948; *Heir* kinsman, Robert Gibson; *Career* ordained a Roman Catholic priest 1975; CP; *Style*— The Rev Sir Christopher Gibson, Bt, CP

GIBSON, Colin Raymond; s of Raymond Gibson, and Muriel, *née* Power (d 1992); *b* 9 February 1957; *Educ* William Hulmes GS Manchester, Nat Cncl for Trg of Journalists Coll Preston (Dip); *m* 6 June 1987, Patricia Mary, da of David Coxon; 1 da (Emma Catherine b 19 Aug 1989), 1 s (Michael Peter b 3 Aug 1993); *Career* sports writer; St Regis Newspapers Bolton (Stretford & Urmiston Jl) 1976–79, sports ed Messenger Newspapers Stockport 1979–80; sports corr: Daily Telegraph 1984 (joined 1980), Daily Mail 1984–86; chief sports writer Daily Telegraph 1986–93, sports ed Sunday Telegraph 1993–99, asst ed (sport) The Australian 1999–2001, sports ed Daily Mail 2001–2004, dir of communications FA 2004, head of communications ECB 2005–; memb: Sports Writers' Assoc of GB 1984, Football Writers' Assoc 1982; *Books* Glory, Glory Nights (1986), Football Association Publications (1990–93); *Recreations* golf, travel; *Style*— Colin Gibson, Esq; ✉ England and Wales Cricket Board, Lord's Cricket Ground, London NW8 8QZ

GIBSON, David; s of John Love Gibson (d 1984), and Patricia Ann, *née* Cowcill (d 1984); *b* 19 May 1962; *Educ* Truro Boys' Sch, Univ of Kent at Canterbury (BA), Coll of Law; *m* Marishelle, da of Donald Booth; 2 s (Angus Edmund b 16 Dec 1993, Alasdair Theodore b 9 May 1996); *Career* Alsop Wilkinson 1985–89, co sec and dir of legal affrs Rexam plc (formerly Bowater plc) 1989–; memb Law Soc 1987; *Style*— David Gibson, Esq; ✉ Rexam plc, 4 Millbank, London SW1P 3XR (tel 020 7227 4100, fax 020 7227 4139)

GIBSON, David Frank; s of Reginald James Gibson, of Warrington, Cheshire, and Emily, *née* Tanner; *b* 4 December 1946; *Educ* Boteler GS Warrington, UCL (BSc, DipArch); *m* 2 Sept 1969, Mary, da of John Greaves, of Warrington, Cheshire; 1 s (Timothy Edward Phillip b 1984), 1 da (Helen Emily Mary b 1988); *Career* architectural asst James Stirling and Ptnr 1968–70, assoc Colin St John Wilson and Ptnrs 1978–79 (architect 1971–79), studio tutor Bartlett Sch of Architecture 1979–88, Julian Harrap Architects 1981–84, assoc Alex Gordon and Partners 1985–87 (architect 1979–80), princ David Gibson Architects 1987–; chm Islington Building Preservation Tst, vice-chm Islington Soc; RIBA 1979; *Recreations* architecture, bicycle maintenance, flying; *Style*— David Gibson, Esq; ✉ 22 St George's Avenue, London N7 0HD; David Gibson Architects, 35 Britannia Row, London N1 8QH (tel 020 7226 2207, fax 020 7226 6920, e-mail mail@dgibarch.co.uk)

GIBSON, Lt-Col Edgar Matheson; MBE (1986), TD (1975), DL (1976); s of James Edgar Gibson (d 1976), and Margaret Johnston, *née* Matheson (d 2002); *b* 1 November 1934; *Educ* Kirkwall GS, Gray's Coll of Art; *m* 1960, Jean, *née* McCarrick; 2 da (Laura Margaret b 18 April 1961, Ingrid Mary b 7 Dec 1965), 2 s (Edgar James b 10 Oct 1962, Sigurd Matheson b 3 Nov 1970); *Career* Lt-Col, Nat Serv 1958–60, TA & TAVR Lovat Scouts 1961–85, Cadet Cmdt Orkney 1979–86, JSLO Orkney 1980–85; asst headmaster Kirkwall GS until 1990; ind artist 1990–; Hon Col Orkney Lovat Scouts ACF 1986–2004, Hon Sheriff Grampian Highlands and Islands 1992; examiner in higher art and design Scottish Certificate of Educn Examination Bd Dalkeith 1978–93; pres Orkney Branch SSAFA, Forces Help 1997–; chm: St Magnus Cathedral Fair 1982–2004, Northern Area Highland TAVRA 1987–93, Orkney Branch SSAFA - Forces Help and FHS 1990–97; memb Italian POW Chapel Preservation Ctee 1976– (chm 2006–); memb Orkney Health Bd 1991–99; Operation Raleigh: memb Selection Ctee 1983–91, county co-ordinator 1991–93; hon pres: Soc of Friends of St Magnus Cathedral 1994–, Orkney Craftsmen's Guild 1997–2002 (chm 1962–82); *Recreations* BA playing (old Norse game), whisky tasting; *Clubs* Highland Brigade; *Style*— Lt-Col Edgar M Gibson, MBE, TD, DL; ✉ Transcona, New Scapa Road, Kirkwall, Orkney KW15 1BN (tel 01856 872849)

GIBSON, Elspeth; *Educ* Mansfield and Notts Coll of Art and Design (BTEC); *Career* fashion designer; work experience with Zandra Rhodes 1983, womenswear designer and pattern cutter Triangle Clothing Ltd London 1984–86, designer and pattern cutter Source Clothing London 1986, designer William Hunt London 1986–87, designer Coppernob Ltd London 1987–89, head of design Monix London 1989–94; freelance designer 1994–, commissions incl Debenhams childrenswear, founded Elspeth Gibson label, opened boutique 1998, launched bath products range 1999; Br Fashion Cncl New Generation Designer of the Year 1998, Best British Designer Elle Style Awards 1999, Glamour award nominee 1999, subject of V&A exhbn 2000; *Style*— Mrs Elspeth Gibson

GIBSON, Hon Hugh Marcus Thornely; DL; eldest s of Baron Gibson (d 2004); *b* 23 June 1946; *Educ* Eton, Magdalen Coll Oxford (BA); *m* 31 March 1967, Hon Frances Towneley, da of Hon Anthony Strachey (d 1955); 2 da (Effie Dione b 1970, Amelia Mary b 1973), 1 s (Jasper Tallentyre b 1975); *Career* dir Royal Doulton plc 1983–98, md Minton Ltd 1987–99, chief exec Royal Crown Derby 1985–; Hon MUniv Derby 2004; *Recreations* National Trust, book collecting, wine, fishing; *Clubs* Reform; *Style*— Hon Hugh Gibson, DL; ✉ The Fold, Parwich, Ashbourne, Derbyshire DE6 1QL

GIBSON, Sir Ian; kt (1999), CBE (1990); s of Charles Gibson (d 1991), and Kate, *née* Hare (d 1971); *b* 1 February 1947; *Educ* Burnage GS, Univ of Manchester (BSc, vice-pres Union), London Business Sch; *m* 1969 (m dis 1985), Joy Dorothy, da of Geoffrey Musker; 2 da (Janine Victoria , *qv*, b 17 June 1972, Sarah Rachel b 15 Feb 1975); *m* 2, 1988, Susan Margaret, da of John Lawrence Wilson; 1 s (Daniel Lancelot b 2 Nov 1989); *Career* research asst ICI 1968, various industrial relations and mfrg mgmnt positions Ford Motor Co Ltd and Ford Werke AG Germany 1969–84; Nissan Motor Manufacturing (UK) Ltd: dir purchasing and prodn control 1984–87, dep md 1987–89, chief exec 1989–99; chm Nissan Yamato Engineering 1989–98, dir Nissan European Technology Centre 1990–2000, dir Nissan Motor GB 1992–2000, dir Nissan Motor Iberica SA 1996–2001, md Nissan Motor Iberica 1997–99, pres Nissan Europe NV 1999–2000 (vice-pres 1994–99), sr vice-pres Nissan Motor Co Ltd Japan 1999–2001, memb Supervisory Bd Nissan Europe NV 2000–2001; chm Trinity Mirror plc 2006–; non-exec dir: Asda Group plc 1993–99 (dep chm 1996–99), Prodrive 2002, GKN plc 2002–, Northern Rock plc 2002–, BPB plc 2002– (dep chm 2003–04, chm 2004–05); dir: Industry Forum 1997–, Centre for Life Tst 2001–; chm: Ctee NEDO, Automotive Innovation and Growth Team 2001–03; pres SMMT 1999–2000 (vice-pres 1995–99); memb Bd Tyne & Wear Development Corp until 1998; memb Ct Bank of England 1999–2004; Mensforth Gold Medal IEE 1998, Castrol IMI Gold Medal 2002; Hon DBA Univ of Sunderland 1990; FRSA 1990, CIMgt 1990, FInstP 1999; *Recreations* sailing, skiing; *Clubs* RAC; *Style*— Sir Ian Gibson, CBE; ✉ 21 Montagu Avenue, Gosforth, Newcastle upon Tyne

GIBSON, Ian; MP; *Educ* Dumfries Acad, Univ of Edinburgh; *Career* postdoctoral fell in US public health Univ of Indiana 1964, prof of genetics and zoology Univ of Washington Seattle 1964–65; UEA: sr lectr in biology 1965–91, appointed dean of biological sciences 1991, head of cancer research studies, co-fndr Francesca Gunn Lab into Leukaemia Research; MP (Lab) Norwich N 1997–; memb House of Commons Select Ctee on Science & Technol 1997– (chm 2001–05); chm: All-Pty Cancer Gp, Parly Scientific Ctee 1999–2003, All-Pty Cuba Gp 2003–; vice-chair Food & Health Forum, ME Gp; tstee Prostate Cancer Research Charity Research Tst, memb Stem Cell Fndn; *Style*— Dr Ian Gibson, MP; ✉ House of Commons, London SW1A 0AA (tel 020 7219 1100, fax 020 7219 2799); constituency office: (tel 01603 661144, fax 01603 663502, e-mail gibsoni@parliament.uk)

GIBSON, Jane; *Educ* Central Sch of Speech & Drama, École Jacques Lecoq Paris; *Career* choreographer and dir; head of movement RNT; dir of movement RSC Acad 2002–; memb Advsy Panel to Dance Res Ctee Imperial Soc of Teachers of Dancing; assoc dir Cheek By Jowl; fndr memb Common Stock Theatre Co; *Theatre* movement/choreography since 1986; for RNT incl: A Matter of Life and Death, The Pied Piper, School for Wives, Yerma, Fuente Ovejuna, Hamlet, Ghetto, Peer Gynt, The Crucible, Richard III, Piano, Wind in the Willows, Arturo Ui, Angels in America, Black Snow, Pygmalion, Uncle Vanya, Rise and Fall of Little Voice, The Recruiting Officer, Sweeney Todd, Arcadia, Perestroika, Millennium Approaches, Broken Glass, Le Cid, The Merry Wives of Windsor, Volpone, Mother Courage and Her Children, La Grande Magia, Stanley, The Prince's Play, Blue Remembered Hills, Peter Pan, The Day I Stood Still, London Cuckolds, Not About Nightingales, An Enemy of the People, Mutabilité, Flight, The Villains' Opera, Romeo and Juliet, The Cherry Orchard, Mother Clap's Molly House, Tartuffe, Mappa Mundi, The Mandate; for RSC incl: The Revenger's Tragedy, Much Ado About Nothing, The Plain Dealer, Macbeth, Don Juan, Elgar's Rondo, The School for Scandal, The Rivals, Twelfth Night; for Cheek By Jowl incl: Lady Betty, Sarah Sampson, Hamlet, Duchess of Malfi, Much Ado About Nothing, Homebody/Kabul, Twelfth Night (Moscow Theatre Assoc); other credits incl: Lear (Melbourne Theatre Co),The Merry Widow (Scottish Opera), Charlie Gorilla (Lyric Belfast), The Shaugraun (Abbey Theatre Dublin), Gawain (ROH), La Clemenza di Tito (Glyndebourne, also BBC), Emma (Cambridge Theatre Co), La Traviata (ROH), Force of Destiny and Mahagonny (ENO), Peter Pan (West Yorkshire Playhouse), The Rake's Progress (WNO), Julio Cesare (ROH), Flastaff (Salzburg), Le Noce di Figaro (Aix en Provence, Garsington), Don Giovanni (Garsington), Le Cid (Festival d'Avignon), Five Gold Rings (Almeida Theatre), Othello (Cheek by Jowl), The Importance of Being Earnest (Oxford Stage Co), Candida (Oxford Stage Co), Les Liaisons Dangereuses (Ambassadors Theatre), The Lady in the Van (Bath Theatre Royal), Blithe Spirit (Bath Theatre Royal and Savoy Theatre); as director for LAMDA credits incl: The Country Wife, Loot, The Fireraisers, The Bald Prima Donna, The Lover, Immodesty Blaize and the Adventures of Walter, Burlesque!; as co-dir with Sue Lefton credits incl: Lark Rise (Haymarket Leics and Almeida), Nana (for Shared Experience, Almeida and Mermaid), A Tale of Two Cities (Cambridge Theatre Co, Newcastle Theatre and tour), Hiawatha (Sheffield Crucible), A Working Woman (W Yorks Playhouse), Private Lives (Theatre Royal Bath), Great Expectations (RSC), The Changeling (Cheek by Jowl), Voyage Round My Father (Donmar Warehouse), Tom & Viv (Almeida) Cymbeline (Cheek by Jowl), 'Tis Pity She's a Whore (Southwark Playhouse), Our Country's Good (Liverpool Playhouse), A Midsummer Night's Dream (Sydney Theatre Co), Silverland (Lacuna Prodns), Kiss of the Spiderwoman (Donmar Warehouse); *Televison* credits incl: Far From the Madding Crowd (Granada), Tom Jones (BBC), David (TNT), Emma (ITV/A&E), Scarlett (CBS TV), Pride and Predudice (BBC, Best Choreographer nomination Emmy Awards 1996), Great Expectations (BBC), Wives and Daughters (BBC), Madame Bovary (BBC), The Russian Bride (BBC), The Scarlet Pimpernel (BBC), Lorna Doone (BBC), Love in a Cold Climate (BBC), Night and Day (BBC), Daniel Deronda (BBC), Cambridge Spies (BBC), Charles II (BBC), Reversals (ITV), The Deal (Channel 4), Mansfield Park (ITV), Persuasion (ITV), Cranford Chronicles (BBC); *Film* incl: Cousin Bette, Dracula, Sense and Sensibility, Firelight, Nancherro, Mansfield Park, Kate and Leopold, I Capture the Castle, Iris, The Girl with the Pearl Earring, Nanny McPhee, Pride and Prejudice, Elizabeth I, V for Vendetta, Perfume, The Golden Age, Atonement, Becoming Jane, Holiday, Death Defying Acts, And When Did You Last See Your Father?; *Clubs* 2 Brydges Place; *Style*— Ms Jane Gibson; ✉ for film/theatre: c/o ICM Ltd, Oxford House, 76 Oxford Street, London W1N 0AX (tel 020 7636 6565, fax 020 7323 0101); for opera: c/o Allied Artists, 42 Montpelier Square, London SW7 1JZ (tel 020 7589 6243, fax 020 7581 5269)

GIBSON, Janine Victoria; da of Sir Ian Gibson, CBE , *qv*, of Gosforth, Newcastle upon Tyne, and Joy Gibson; *b* 17 June 1972; *Educ* Walthamstow Hall Sevenoaks, St John's Coll Oxford (BA); *m* 1999, Steve Busfield; 2 da (Martha Gibson Busfield b 6 Aug 2002, Kitty Gibson Busfield b 30 March 2006); *Career* journalist; dep ed Televisual 1995–97, int ed Broadcast 1997–98, media corr The Independent 1998; The Guardian: media corr 1998–2000, media ed 2000–03, ed G3 and ed-in-chief Media Guardian 2003–06, asst ed 2006, exec ed Guardian Unlimited 2007–; memb Broadcasting Press Guild; *Publications* Guardian Media Directory (2007); *Style*— Ms Janine Gibson; ✉ The Guardian, 119 Farringdon Road, London EC1R 3ER (tel 020 7278 2332, e-mail janine.gibson@guardian.co.uk)

GIBSON, Dr John Robin; s of Norman John Gibson (d 1983), and Marie Louise Elizabeth, *née* Edwards; *b* 16 December 1949; *Educ* Eastwood HS Glasgow, Univ of Glasgow (MB ChB); *m* 25 April 1990, Sabina Silvia, da of Joachim Rosenthaler, of Basel, Switzerland; *Career* hosp MO Bulawayo 1974–77, med registrar Glasgow 1977, hon conslt dermatologist London Hosp 1983–89 (hon dermatology registrar and sr registrar 1978–82), head Dermatology Section Wellcome Res Labs Beckenham 1978–89, vice-pres of clinical res Bristol-Myers Squibb Co 1992–93 (dir 1989–90, exec dir 1990–92), sr vice-pres global devpt Allergan Inc 1993–; dir Somanta Ltd; volunteer clinical prof of dermatology: SUNY Buffalo 1992–, Univ of Calif Irvine 2001–; chm British American Business Cncl Orange County; author multiple book chapters and papers on: dermatology, therapeutics, pharmacology, allergy; Freeman City of London 1987, Liveryman Worshipful Soc of Apothecaries 1988 (Yeoman 1982); memb: BMA, BAD, AAD; MRCP, FRCPG 1987, FRSM; *Recreations* guitar playing, song writing, bridge, squash; *Style*— Dr John R Gibson; ✉ 2368 Glenneyre Street, Laguna Beach, CA 92651, USA (tel 949 376 9060); 9 Cabo Del Sol, Denia, Alicante, Spain; Global Development, Allergan Inc, 2525 Dupont Drive, PO Box 19534, Irvine, CA 92623–9534, USA (e-mail gibson_john@allergan.com)

GIBSON, Kenneth James; MSP; s of Kenneth George Gibson (d 1994), and Iris, *née* Arbuckle; *b* 8 September 1961; *Educ* Bellahouston Acad (biology and history prizes), Univ of Stirling (BA); *m* 1 June 1989, Lynda Dorothy, da of Peter Payne; 2 s (Ross Ewan Fraser b 16 Sept 1992, Lewis Duncan Callum b 13 August 1998), 1 da (Heather Kirsty Fiona b 8 July 1996); *Career* systems devpt offr Br Steel 1982–87, sponsorship advsr and visitor info mangr Glasgow Garden Festival 1987–88, pharmaceutical sales 1988–99; memb Glasgow DC 1992–96, memb Glasgow City Cncl 1995–99 (ldr of oppn 1998–99); MSP (SNP) Glasgow 1999–2003, MSP (SNP) Cunninghame North 2007–; Scot Parl: dep convenor Social Justice Ctee, memb Local Govt Ctee, convenor Cross Pty Gp on Tobacco Control, convenor Cross Pty Gp on Consumer Affrs; SNP: memb 1979–, memb NEC 1997–99 (vice-convenor Local Govt), shadow min for Local Govt 1997–2000, shadow min for Local Govt, Consumer Affrs and Urban Regeneration 2000–02, shadow min for Housing and Urban Regeneration 2002; hon patron Grandparents Apart Self-Help Gp; *Recreations* reading, theatre, cinema, opera, ballet, football and swimming; *Style*— George Lyon, Esq, MSP

GIBSON, (Alexander John) Michael; CBE (2006); s of Alexander Gibson, of Nairn, and Violet May, *née* Laughton Swanney; *b* 6 June 1952, Glasgow; *Educ* Gordonstoun, RIPHH (Cert Food Hygiene and Safety); *m* 30 Oct 1976, Susan Clare, *née* Bowser; 1 s (Jock b 12 August 1979), 1 da (Bridget b 28 Dec 1980); *Career* ptnr: Findhorn Bay Caravan Park

1973–82, Edinvale Farms 1974–, Highland American Partners 1994–98; dir Cantray Estates 1982–, md Macbeths Butchers 1985–; Food Standards Agency: memb Bd 2000–06, memb Meat Hygiene Advsy Ctee 2001–04 chair Scottish Food Advsy Ctee 2002–06; Highland Cattle Soc: memb Cncl 1977–85, sr fieldsman 1978–, panel judge 1980–, pres 1986–88 (vice-pres 1985), elite judge American Highland Cattle Assoc 1995–; Scottish Landowners Assoc: chm Agric Ctee 1995–2000, chm Highland Region 1996–99, vice-convenor 2000–02; Environmental and Rural Affairs Dept Scottish Exec: memb Rural Devpt Regulation Strategy Gp 1999–2001, monitor Agric Business Devpt Scheme 1999–2001, memb Less Favoured Area Strategy Working Gp 1999–2002, memb Agric Strategy Implementation Gp 2000–02; conslt: Johan I Hallen Butchers Gothenburg Sweden 1987–97, Swedish Cattle AB 1989–95, Falkland Islands Devpt Corp 1995–96; chair Land Use Gp Moray Firth Partnership 1977–99, food champion Health Dept Scottish Exec 2001–04 (memb Food & Health Cncl 2005–); chm: The Macaulay Land Use Research Inst 2006– (tstee 2004–06, govr 2003–06), Scottish Salmon Prodrs Orgn 2006–; memb Bd Local Better Regulation Office Cabinet Office 2007–; MICAS 1975; *Recreations* sailing, field sports, skiing; *Style*— Michael Gibson, Esq, CBE; ✉ Edinvale, Dallas, Moray IV36 2RW (tel 01343 890265, mobile 07774 234954, e-mail edinvale@lineone.net)

GIBSON, Paul Alexander; s of Wing Cdr L P Gibson (d 1954), and Betty, *née* Peveler; *b* 11 October 1941; *Educ* Kingswood Sch Bath, King's Coll London, Canterbury Sch of Architecture, Regent Street Poly Sch of Architecture; *m* 29 Aug 1969, Julia Rosemary, da of Leslie Atkinson; *Career* architect; Farrell Grimshaw Partnership 1968–69, lectr N Dakota State Univ USA 1969–70, Foster Associates 1970–72, private practice Sidell Gibson Partnership 1973–2002 (conslt 2002–); major projects incl: MEPC office buildings Frankfurt 1974, master plans Univ of Arack Iran and housing at Kermanshah Iran 1976, 25 varied housing schemes English Courtyard Assoc 1976–2001, office buildings and housing Frankfurt 1991, New Jewel House Tower of London 1993, appointed architect for Windsor Castle restoration 1994, 3 buildings at Brindley Place Birmingham 1995–2001, office building for Cazenove 2001; winner major architectural competition for Grand Buildings Trafalgar Square 1987; RIBA 1969; *Recreations* painting, music; *Style*— Paul Gibson, Esq

GIBSON, Rt Hon Sir Peter Leslie Gibson; kt (1981), PC (1993); s of Harold Leslie Gibson (d 1972), and Martha Lucy Gibson, *née* Diercking (d 1971); *b* 10 June 1934; *Educ* Malvern Coll, Worcester Coll Oxford (scholar, BA); *m* 4 Sept 1968, Katharine Mary Beatrice, *née* Hadow (d 2002); 2 s (Richard John b 1969, Nicholas Kenneth b 1972), 1 da (Annabel Martha Katharine b 1977); *Career* Nat Serv 2 Lt RA 1953–55; called to the Bar Inner Temple 1960, bencher Lincoln's Inn 1975, treas Lincoln's Inn 1996; jr counsel to the Treasy (Chancery) 1972–81, judge of the High Court of Justice (Chancery Div) 1981–93, a Lord Justice of Appeal 1993–2005; judge of Employment Appeal Tbnl 1984–86, chm Law Cmmn 1990–92; hon fell Worcester Coll Oxford; *Style*— The Rt Hon Sir Peter Gibson

GIBSON, Rob McKay; MSP; s of John Gibson, and Elsie Gibson; *b* 16 October 1945, Glasgow; *Educ* Glasgow HS, Univ of Dundee (MA), Dundee Coll of Educn (DipEd, Teaching Dip); *Partner* Dr Eleanor Roberta Scott; *Career* Invergordon Acad: teacher of geography and modern studies 1973–74, asst princ teacher of guidance 1974–77; princ teacher of guidance Alness Acad 1977–95, writer and researcher 1995–2003, MSP (SNP) Highlands and Islands 2003–; memb Environment and Rural Devpt Ctee and Public Petitions Ctee Scottish Parl; vice-pres Brittany Scotland Assoc, hon pres Kilt Society of France; *Books* The Promised Land (1974), Highland Clearances Trail (1983, new edn 2006), Toppling the Duke (1996), Plaids and Bandanas (2003); *Recreations* traditional music singer, organic gardener, hill walker, traveller; *Style*— Rob Gibson, Esq, MSP; ✉ Scottish Parliament, Edinburgh EH99 1SP (tel 0131 348 5726, e-mail rob.gibson.msp@scottish.parliament.uk); Tir Nan Oran, 8 Culcairn Road, Evanton, Rossshire IV16 9YT (tel 01349 830388, e-mail robgibson@sol.co.uk)

GIBSON, Prof Robert Edward; s of Edward Robert Ward (d 1941), of Felpham, W Sussex, and Ellen Constance Mack (d 1931), adopted s of John Gibson, and Mary, *née* Mack; *b* 12 May 1926; *Educ* Emanuel Sch, Battersea Poly, Imperial Coll London (BSc, PhD, DSc); *m* 10 Oct 1950, Elizabeth Jocelyn (d 1986), da of Donald Edward Bideleux; 2 s (Alastair Robert b 10 Oct 1952 d 1995, Jonathan Edward b 21 June 1963), 1 da (Caroline Lucy b 1 April 1957); *Career* Royal Aircraft Establishment Farnborough 1945–46, res student then asst Imperial Coll London 1948–53, sr scientific offr Building Research Station 1953–56, lectr then reader in civil engrg analysis Imperial Coll London 1956–65, reader in civil engrg then prof of engrg sci KCL 1965–83; Cwlth visiting prof Univ of Sydney 1969–70, Rankine lectr British Geotechnical Soc 1974; sr princ and dir Golder Associates 1974–94, industrial fell Wolfson Coll Oxford 1983–85, adjoint prof Univ of Colorado Boulder 1987–94, sr res fell Queen Mary & Westfield Coll London 1988–98; FREng 1984, FCGI; *Recreations* travel, listening to music; *Clubs* Athenaeum; *Style*— Prof Robert Gibson, FREng; ✉ 23 South Drive, Ferring, West Sussex BN12 5QU (tel 01903 700386, fax 01903 507122)

GIBSON, Ven Terence Allen (Terry); s of Fred William Allen Gibson, of Boston, Lincs, and Joan Hazel, *née* Bishop; *b* 23 October 1937; *Educ* Boston GS, Jesus Coll Cambridge (MA), Cuddesdon Theol Coll; *Career* curate St Chad Kirkby Liverpool 1963–66, warden Centre 63 C of E Youth Centre and vicar for Youth Work 1966–75, rector of Kirkby Liverpool 1975–84, rural dean Walton Liverpool 1979–84; archdeacon of: Suffolk 1984–87, Ipswich 1987–; *Style*— The Ven the Archdeacon of Ipswich; ✉ 99 Valley Road, Ipswich, Suffolk IP1 4NF (tel 01473 250333, fax 01473 286877)

GIBSON, Thomas Herbert; s of Clement Herbert Gibson (d 1976), of England and Argentina, and Marjorie Julia, *née* Anderson (d 1982); *b* 12 April 1943; *Educ* Eton; *m* 1966, Anthea Fiona Catherine, da of late Lt-Col G A Palmer, RE; 3 s (Miles Cosmo Archdale b 1968, Sebastian Thomas Maximilian b 1972, Benjamin Hugh George b 1973); *Career* fndr chm Thomas Gibson Fine Art Ltd 1969–96, ret, fndr Thomas Gibson Fine Art Advsy Services 1996–; *Recreations* tennis; *Style*— Thomas Gibson, Esq; ✉ Thomas Gibson Fine Art Advisory Services, 31 Bruton Street, London W1J 6QS (tel 020 7499 8572)

GIBSON, Prof Vernon Charles; *Educ* Univ of Oxford (DPhil); *Career* NATO postdoctoral fell Caltech 1984–86, lectr in inorganic chemistry Univ of Durham 1986–93, prof of chemistry Univ of Durham 1993–95; Imperial Coll London: first holder Sir Geoffrey Wilkinson chair of chemistry 1995, currently Edward Frankland BP prof of inorganic chemistry, head Catalysis and Materials Research Section; R D Haworth Medal Univ of Sheffield 1980, BP Chemicals Young Univ Lectr 1990–93, Sir Edward Frankland fell RSC 1992–93, Corday-Morgan Medal and Prize RSC 1993–94, Joseph Chatt lectr RSC 2001, Tilden lectr RSC 2004–05; FRS 2004; *Style*— Prof Vernon Gibson; ✉ Department of Chemistry, Imperial College London, South Kensington Campus, London SW7 2AZ

GIBSON, Sheriff William Erle; s of William Graham Gibson (d 1979), of Aberfeldy, and Robina Cruikshank, *née* Thomson (d 1949); *b* 30 August 1934; *Educ* Dollar Acad, Trinity Hall Cambridge (BA), Univ of Glasgow (LLB); *m* 29 Sept 1961, Anne Durie, da of late Lt Col Roy Mathieson, TD, DSO; 2 da (Fiona Jane b 3 June 1964, Clare Anne b 26 Jan 1966), 1 s (William Robert Graham b 10 Feb 1970); *Career* Nat Serv midshipman RN 1953–55; ptnr Buchanan & McIlwraith Slrs Glasgow 1961–89; sheriff S Strathclyde Dumfries & Galloway (at Hamilton) 1989–2007; *Recreations* hill walking, golf, fishing and piping; *Clubs* Glasgow Golf; *Style*— Sheriff William Gibson; ✉ 7A Briarwell Road, Milngavie, Glasgow G62 6AW

GIBSON, Hon William Knatchbull; 3 s of Baron Gibson (Life Peer, d 2004), and Elizabeth Dione, da of Hon Clive Pearson; *b* 26 August 1951; *Educ* Eton, Magdalen Coll Oxford (BA); *m* 1988, Lori Frances, o da of Herbert Mintz, of Miami, FL; 1 s (Matthew Charles b 6 Dec 1990), 1 da (Sarah Claire b 29 Aug 1992); *Career* newspaper mangr with Westminster Press (industrial rels specialist 1976–82), Sloan fell London Grad Sch of Business Studies 1983, dir of admin Financial Times 1984–86, publisher of Financial Times magazines 1986–89, md Financial Times Business Information 1989–95; chm: Westminster Press Ltd 1996–97 (also chief exec), Dowell and Associates 2000–04, Kidsactive 2000–, AYM 2002–04; dir: MQ Publications 1998–2003, Business in Focus Productions 1999–, Millbank Financial Services 2002–; memb Newspaper Panel Competition Cmmn 1999–; *Recreations* opera, shooting, skiing; *Clubs* Garrick, Sussex; *Style*— The Hon William Gibson; ✉ 46 Victoria Road, London W8 5RQ; Newhouse Farm, Balcombe, West Sussex RH17 6RB

GIBSON-BOLTON, Elaine; da of Robert William Holmes Gibson-Bolton, of Norwich, and Rosaleen Christabel, *née* Smyth; *b* 15 January 1962; *Educ* Wymondham Coll, Univ of Reading (LLB), Univ of Amsterdam (Dip), Coll of Law; *Career* admitted slr 1987; trainee slr Clifford Harris & Co 1985–87; slr: Holman Fenwick & Willan 1987–89, Freshfields 1989–93, SJ Berwin LLP 1993– (ptnr 1997–); memb: Assoc of Electricity Producers, Slrs European Gp, City of London Slrs, Competition Law Forum, Law Soc European Gp (LSEG); Competition Lawyer/Team of the Year Legal Business; memb: Law Soc 1987, Inst of Advanced Legal Studies; *Recreations* travel, theatre, film, gardening, koi; *Clubs* Century, European Aviation, Women in Media; *Style*— Ms Elaine Gibson-Bolton; ✉ SJ Berwin LLP, 10 Queen Street Place, London EC4R 1BE (tel 020 7111 2463, fax 020 7111 2000, e-mail elaine.gibson-bolton@sjberwin.com)

GIBSON HARRIS, Jeremy Miles (Jez); s of Leonard Miles Gibson Harris, and Jean Mary Royce, *née* Skinner; *b* 14 January 1960; *Educ* Shene GS, Richmond Coll, Sir John Cass Coll of Art; *m* 1994, Jayne Senft; 1 da (Eleanor Siân b 2 Aug 2000); *Career* worked in film industry 1980–; contrib special effects and animatronics on over 30 feature films; with Nick Maley's Make-Up EFX Ltd 1980, estab Crawley Creatures 1986; early animatronics work incl: The Dark Crystal 1981, Jabba the Hutt for Return of the Jedi 1982, Greystoke, Legend of Tarzan 1984; film projects incl: An American Werewolf in Paris, Blackadder Back & Forth, The Little Vampire; TV projects incl: Walking with Dinosaurs, Walking with Beasts, Sea Monsters, Primeval; jeweller and silversmith; gp exhbns incl: Jewellery Redefined, 30 Contemporary Jewellers, Period Homes and Gardens (sculpture exhbn), Oxford Artists; former rugby union player: London Welsh, Harlequins, Surrey Co; *Awards* for Walking with Dinosaurs: Team Production Award RTS Prog Awards 1999, Millennium Products award 1999, Best Documentary TRIC Awards 1999, Lead Special Effects Supervisor Primetime Emmy Awards 1999–2000; Design and Craft Innovation Award RTS Craft and Design Awards 1999–2000, Visual Effects BAFTA TV Crafts Awards 2002 and 2003; *Recreations* horse riding, kayaking, walking, travelling to exotic locations; *Style*— Jez Gibson Harris, Esq; ✉ Crawley Creatures Limited, Unit 22–23 Rabans Close, Aylesbury, Buckinghamshire HP19 8RS (tel 01296 336315, fax 01296 339590)

GIBSON OF MARKET RASEN, Baroness (Life Peer UK 2000), of Market Rasen in the County of Lincolnshire; Anne Gibson; OBE (1998); da of Harry Tasker (d 1967), of Lincs, and Jessie, *née* Roberts (d 2002); *b* 10 December 1940; *Educ* Caistor GS, Chelmsford Coll of Further Educn, Univ of Essex (BA); *m* 1, 1962 (m dis 1985), John Donald Gibson; 1 da (Rebecca Bridgid b 1964); m 2, 1988, John Bartell, s of Henry Bartell (d 1983), of Liverpool; 1 step da (Sharon Jayne b 1965); *Career* full-time organiser Lab Pty (Saffron Walden) 1965–70, researcher House Magazine (jl of Houses of Parliament) 1975–77, Party candidate (Lab) Bury St Edmunds 1979, asst/asst sec and dep head Orgn and Industrial Rels Dept TUC (with special responsibility for equal rights area of work) 1977–87; nat offr Amicus with special responsibility for: voluntary sector and equal rights section 1987–96, policy and political work 1996–2000; memb: Gen Cncl TUC 1989–2000, Dept of Employment Advsy Gp on Older Workers 1993–96, Bd Bilbao Agency 1996–2000, Trade Union Sustainable Devpt Ctee 1999–2000, Parly and Scientific Ctee; memb Lab Pty: NEC Women's Ctee 1990–98, Nat Constitutional Ctee 1997–2000, Lab Pty Policy Reform 1998–2000, Foreign and Commonwealth Affrs Gp, Home Affrs Gp, Lab Pty Defence Gp; Equal Opportunities cmmr 1991–98, Health and Safety cmmr 1996–2000; memb All-Pty Parly Gps: Adoption (sec), Brazil (vice-chair), Bullying at Work (chair), Arts and Heritage, Asthma, BBC, Breast Cancer, Children, Corporate Social Responsibility (dep chair), Insurance and Fin Servs, Latin America, Rail Freight, Safety and Health, Sex Equality, TU Gp of MPs, Rural Affrs, Food & Health Forum (treas); memb: Sub-Ctee F (social affrs, environment, educn and home affrs) Select Ctee on the EU 2001–05, Constitutional Bill Select Ctee, Lords Reform Ctee, BBC Charter Review Select Ctee 2005–06, Link Standing Ctee on Consumer Issues 2006–; chair: UMIST Research Gp on Bullying at Work 2003–05, DTI Research Gp on Bullying at Work 2004–; memb English Beef and Lamb Exec (EBLEX); pres: Yeadon Air Training Cadets 2002–, RoSPA 2004– (dep chair 2001–04); memb: Air League Cncl 2005–, Air Cadet Cncl 2006–, Fawcett Soc, Fabian Soc; *Publications* author numerous TUC and MSF Equal Opportunities Booklets incl Charter of Equal Opportunities For 1990s (1990); Disability and Employer - A Trade Union Guide (1989), Lesbian and Gay Rights in Employment (1990), Recruitment of Women Workers (1990), Part time Workers Rights (1991), Women in MSF (1991), Sexual Harassment at Work (1993), Caring - A Union Issue (1993); *Recreations* reading, theatre, knitting, embroidery; *Style*— The Rt Hon the Baroness Gibson of Market Rasen, OBE; ✉ House of Lords, London SW1A 0PW

GIBSON-SMITH, Dr Christopher (Chris); *Educ* Univ of Durham, Univ of Newcastle upon Tyne (PhD), Stanford Univ (Sloan fell); *m* Marjorie; 2 da (Emma, Sarah); *Career* BP plc: joined as exploration and production geologist 1970, chief geologist 1983, European chief exec BP Exploration 1992, chief operating offr BP Chemicals 1995, gp md 1997–2001; chm: National Air Traffic Services Ltd (NATS) 2001–05, London Stock Exchange plc 2003–, British Land Co plc 2007– (non-exec dir 2003–); non-exec dir: Lloyds TSB plc 1999–2005, Powergen 2001–02, Qatar Financial Centre Authy; formerly: memb UK Sustainability Commission, memb Sloan Advsy Bd Stanford Business Sch, memb Cncl CBI Scotland, chm Business in the Arts Scotland, chm California Marine Mammal Centre; tstee: IPPR, Arts & Business, London Business School; *Recreations* literature, music, art, skiing, sailing, golf; *Style*— Dr Chris Gibson-Smith; ✉ London Stock Exchange, 10 Paternoster Square, London EC4M 7LS

GIDDINGS, Robert; *Educ* Univ of Bristol (BA, MPhil, DipEd), Keele Univ (PhD); *Career* teacher in various schools and colleges 1961–; Fulbright Exchange prof St Louis Community Coll Florissant Valley 1975–76; emeritus prof Media Sch Bournemouth Univ 2006; author and journalist; contributor to various newspapers and jls incl The Listener, New Statesman, Observer, Tribune, New Society and The Guardian; writer and contributor to various radio and television progs incl Late Night Line Up, The Late Show, Does He Take Sugar? and Archive Hour; *Books* incl: You Should See Me in Pyjamas (autobiography, 1981), The War Poets 1914–1918 (1988), The Author, the Book and the Reader (1991), Imperial Echoes (1995), Who Was Really Who in Fiction (with Alan Bold), The Classic Serial on Television and Radio (with Keith Selby, 1999), books on Smollett, Dickens, Twain, Tolkien and cultural history, media and publishing; *Style*— Robert Giddings; ✉ c/o Watson Little Authors Agents, Lymhouse Studios, 38 Georgiana Street, London NW1 0EB (tel 020 7455 5935, e-mail robert@giddings.eclipse.co.uk)

GIDDY, Pam; da of B S Giddy, of Coventry, and N K Giddy, *née* Pabla; *b* 5 April 1967, Coventry; *Educ* Lyng Hall Girls Sch Coventry, Sidney Stringer Sch Coventry, LSE (LLB); *Career* ed Violations of Rights pamphlets for Charter 88 1990–93, ed News & Careers Cosmopolitan magazine 1993–94, prodr BBC2 Newsnight 1994–99, dir Charter 88 democratic reform gp 1999–2001, fdnr and dir POWER Inquiry 2004–; memb: Bd Joseph Rowntree Reform Trust Ltd, Content Bd Ofcom; *Recreations* swimming, reading; *Clubs* County Hall Westminster; *Style*— Ms Pam Giddy; ✉ The Power Inquiry, Southbank House, Black Prince Road, London SE1 7SJ

GIDLEY, Sandra; MP; *Educ* Eggars GS Alton, Afcent Int Sch Brunssum Netherlands, Windsor Girls Sch Hamm Germany, Univ of Bath (BPharm); *Career* pharmacist 1978–2000; MP (Lib Dem) Romsey 2000– (by-election); spokesperson for women's issues 2001–, spokesperson for older people 2003–; MRPharmS 1979; *Style*— Ms Sandra Gidley, MP; ✉ House of Commons, London SW1A 0AA (tel 020 7219 5986, fax 020 7219 2324, e-mail gidleys@parliament.uk)

GIDOOMAL, Balram (Ram); CBE (1998); *b* 23 December 1950; *Educ* Christopher Wren Sch London, Imperial Coll London (BSc); *m* Sunita Shivdasani; 2 s (Ravi b 1979, Ricki b 1983), 1 da (Nina b 1981); *Career* research analyst in mgmnt science (with Civil Service grant) Imperial Coll London 1972–75, ops research analyst Lloyds Bank International London 1976–78; Inlaks Group: dep gp chief exec Head Office France then Geneva 1978–85, UK gp chief exec London then Scotland 1985–89, non-exec vice-chm London 1988–92; currently chm Winning Communications Partnership Ltd; fndr chm: Christmas Cracker Trust 1989–2000, South Asian Concern 1991–, South Asian Development Partnership 1993–, Business Link London (South) 1995–98; dir: Christian Research Assoc 1994–96, Nat Accreditation Bd Business Links DTI 1995–2000, Business Link London 1996–98, Far Pavilions Ltd 1998–; fndr dir and vice-chair South London Trg and Enterprise Cncl (SOLOTEC) 1991–97, ldr Christian Peoples Alliance 2000–04 (candidate for London Mayor and Greater London Assembly 2000 and 2004), fndr dir and former vice-chair African Caribbean Westminster Initiative 1998–2002, patron Small Business Bureau 1996–, pres National Information Forum 2003–, vice-pres The Leprosy Mission 1999–, vice-pres The Shaftesbury Soc; dir: Epsom and St Helier NHS Tst 1999–2006 (chair Audit Ctee 2000–05), English Partnerships 2000–03 (memb Audit Ctee); chm: Business Link Nat Conference 1997, London Community Fndn 2001–03, London Sustainablility Exchange 2001–07, The Employability Forum 2003– (memb 2000–), Nat Refugee Integration Forum (Employers Subgroup) 2003–06, CityLife Industrial and Provident Soc 2005–, Henderson's Global SRI Advsy Ctee 2005– (memb 2004–); memb: Apples & Pears Res Cncl MAFF 1995–98, Bd Covent Garden Market Authy 1998–2004, Exec Ctee Assoc of Charitable Foundations 1995–98, Cabinet Office Better Regulation Task Force 1997–2002 (chair Anti Discrimination Sub-Gp 1998, chair Technol Means Business Cncl DTI 1998–2004), Cncl Britain in Europe, Advsy Ctee on Clinical Excellence Awards 2004–06, Cncl RSA 2004– (tstee 1998–2002), Home Office Immigration Nationality Database Complaints Audits Ctee 2005–, Advsy Bd Postmaster.net; business advsr for Ethnic Minorities The Prince's Tst 1991–, sec India Devpt Tst 1994–; tstee: Inst for Citizenship 2000, Timebank Charitable Tst 2001–04, Forum for the Future 2001–, Trg for Life 2001–04; memb Bd of Govrs James Allen Girls Sch 1997–2002; memb Bd Kings Coll Sch 1998–, govr The Health Fndn 2000–05; visiting prof of entrepreneurship and inner city regeneration Middx Univ, memb Ct Luton Univ; memb Cncl Bd Inst for Employment Studies; St George's Hosp Med Sch Univ of London: memb Cncl 2002– (vice-chair 2006–), memb Audit Ctee (chair 2006–), chair Estates Project Bd 2005–; crown appointee on Ct and Cncl Imperial Coll London 2002–, chair Res Ethics Ctee Imperial Coll London 2006–; hon memb Faculty of Divinity Univ of Cambridge 1997–; delivered Hansen Wessner Lecture 2000 at Saïd Business Sch Univ of Oxford; appeared on various TV and radio documentaries and progs on ethnic and business issues 1987–, subject of numerous newspaper articles; Freeman City of London, Liveryman Worshipful Co of Information Technolgists; LLD (hc) Univ of Bristol 2002, DLitt (hc) Nottingham Trent Univ 2003, Hon DUniv Middx; ARCS, FRSA; *Publications* Sari 'n' Chips (1993), Chapatis for Tea (1994), Karma 'n' Chips (1994), The Creative Manager (contrib), South Asian Development Partnership Population Report for Great Britain - The £5 billion Asian Corridor for Opportunities for TECS (with SOLOTEC), Lions Princesses, Gurus (1996), A Way of Life: Hinduism (1997), The UK Maharajahs (1997), Building on Success, The South Asian Contribution to UK Competitiveness (1997), How would Jesus vote? (2001), The British and how to deal with them: Doing Business with Britain's Ethnic Minorities (2001), Who Is My Neighbour? (2002), The Right Use of Money (contrib, 2004); Coming to Britain an Immigrant's Story (video), Songs of the Kingdom (music), Asia Worships (music); *Style*— Ram Gidoomal, Esq, CBE; ✉ 14 The Causeway, Sutton, Surrey SM2 5RS (tel 020 8661 9198, e-mail ramgidoomal@blueyonder.co.uk)

GIEDROYC, Michal Graham Dowmont (Miko); s of Michal Jan Henryk Giedroyc, of Oxford, and Rosemary Virginia Anna, *née* Cumpston; *b* 5 May 1959; *Educ* Ampleforth, New Coll Oxford (BA), Birkbeck Coll London; *m* 1 Nov 1986, Dorothee Alexandra Ulrike, da of Dr Ernst Friedrich Jung, of Bonn; 1 da (Anna Viva Magdalene b 25 Aug 1992), 2 s (Jan Tadeusz Friedrich William b 30 Oct 1994, Melchior Ernst Graham Mathias b 3 June 1996); *Career* Investment Div J Henry Schroder Wagg and Co Ltd 1980–83, vice-pres Schroder Capital Management Inc 1984–85, dir Warburg Securities 1985–95, dir Deutsche Bank AG (formerly Deutsche Morgan Grenfell) 1995–; *Recreations* jazz piano; *Style*— Miko Giedroyc, Esq; ✉ Deutsche Bank AG, Winchester House, 1 Great Winchester Street, London EC2N 2EQ (tel 020 7545 1361, fax 020 7541 1363)

GIELGUD, Maina Julia Gordon; Hon AO (1991); da of Lewis Evelyn Gielgud (d 1953), and Elisabeth Sutton (author and actress under name of Zita Gordon; d 2006); niece of Sir John Gielgud; *b* 14 January 1945; *Educ* BEPC France; *Career* ballerina with: Cuevas Co and Roland Petit Co to 1963, Grand Ballet Classique de France 1963–67; princ ballerina: Béjart Co 1967–71, Berlin 1971, London Festival Ballet 1972–76, Sadler's Wells Ballet 1976–78; freelance ballerina and guest artist 1978–82, rehearsal dir London City Ballet 1982; artistic dir: Australian Ballet 1983–96, Royal Danish Ballet March 1997–99; freelance dir guest teacher and coach 1999–, artistic assoc Houston Ballet 2003–05; creations and choreographies: Steps Notes and Squeaks (London) 1978, Petit Pas et Crac (Paris) 1979, Ghosties and Ghoulies (London City Ballet) 1982, The Sleeping Beauty (Australian Ballet) 1984, Giselle (Australian Ballet) 1986; *Style*— Miss Maina Gielgud; ✉ Stirling Court, 3 Marshall Street, London W1 (e-mail gielgud@attglobal.net)

GIEVE, Sir (Edward) John Watson; KCB (2005, CB 1999); s of David Gieve, and Susan, *née* Best; *b* 20 February 1950; *Educ* Charterhouse, New Coll Oxford (BA, BPhil); *m* 25 March 1972, Katherine Elizabeth, Vereker, da of Charles Henry Vereker; 2 s (Daniel b 6 June 1980, Matthew b 31 Aug 1982); *Career* admin trainee Dept of Employment 1974–78, princ HM Treasy 1979–84, investment controller Investors in Industry 1984–86; HM Treasy: asst sec Gen Expenditure Policy 1986–88, press sec 1988–89, princ private sec to the Chllr 1989–91, under-sec Banking Gp 1991–94, dir Budget and Public Finances 1998–99 (dep dir 1994–98), md Public Services 1999–2001, md Financial Regulation and Industry 2001; perm sec Home Office 2001–05, dep govr (financial stability) Bank of England 2006–; *Recreations* golf, football; *Clubs* Arsenal, Highgate Golf, Kyles of Bute Golf; *Style*— Sir John Gieve, KCB; ✉ Bank of England, Threadneedle Street, London EC2R 8AH

GIEVE, Katherine Elizabeth; da of Charles Vereker (d 1996), and Patricia, *née* Kastelian (d 2001); *b* 26 June 1949, Oxford; *Educ* Merchant Taylors' Sch for Girls Liverpool, St Anne's Coll Oxford (BA); *m* 25 March 1972, John Gieve; 2 s (Daniel b 6 June 1980, Matthew b 31 Aug 1982); *Career* admitted slr 1978; slr: West Hampstead Law Centre 1978–83, Wilford McBain 1983–85, Family Rights Gp 1986–88; Bindman & Ptnrs: slr 1988–91, ptnr 1991–, head Family Dept 2003–; memb: Child Protection and Family Justice Ctee Nuffield Fndn, Children Ctee Resolution, Family Justice Cncl; memb Law Soc; *Publications* Cohabitation Handbook (1981), Balancing Acts: On Being a Mother (1989); *Recreations* yoga; *Style*— Ms Katherine Gieve; ✉ Bindman & Partners, 275 Gray's Inn Road, London WC1X 8QB (tel 020 7833 4433, fax 020 7833 9792, e-mail k.gieve@bindmans.com)

GIFFORD, Andrew Graham; s of Charles Henry Pearson Gifford, OBE (d 1993), of Edinburgh, and Margaret Laetitia Gifford, MBE, *née* Lyell (d 1995); *Educ* Bedales, Univ of Edinburgh; *m* Charlotte Montrésor, da of Michael White; 4 s (Henry (Harry) Montrésor, Charles Montrésor, Peter Patrick, George Montrésor); *Career* PA to Rt Hon Sir David Steel, MP as Foreign Affrs Spokesman and Ldr of Lib Pty 1975–80 (memb Lib and SDP Ldrs' Campaign Staff 1979, 1983 and 1987 election campaigns), fndr ptnr and chief exec GJW Government Relations 1980–; fndr chm Assoc of Political Conslts 1993–2000; directorships incl: Fleming Mid Cap Investment Trust 1993–, Second London American Growth Trust 1995–, Fourth Estate (publishing co) 1984–2000, Moneyweek 2001–; advsr to Br phonographic indust 1980–2001; treas The Green Alliance; *Books* Handbook of World Development (1982); *Recreations* fishing, stalking, shooting, building; *Clubs* New, Beefsteak; *Style*— Andrew Gifford, Esq; ✉ 7 Bywater Street, London SW3 3XD; GJW at BSMG Worldwide, 110 St Martin Lane, London WC2N 4DY (tel 020 7841 5555, fax 020 7841 5777)

GIFFORD, 6 Baron (UK 1824); Anthony Maurice Gifford; QC (1982); s of 5 Baron Gifford (d 1961), and (Ellice) Margaret, *née* Allen (d 1990); *b* 1 May 1940; *Educ* Winchester, King's Coll Cambridge; *m* 1, 22 March 1965 (m dis 1988), Katherine Ann, da of Max Mundy, of Kensington, London; 1 s (Hon Thomas Adam b 1967), 1 da (Hon Polly Anna b 1969); m 2, 24 Sept 1988 (m dis 1998), Elean Roslyn, da of Bishop David Thomas, of Kingston, Jamaica; 1 da (Sheba Chanel b 1992); m 3, 11 April 1998, Tina Natalia, da of Clement Goulbourne, of Kingston, Jamaica; *Heir* s, Hon Thomas Gifford; *Career* sat as Lab Peer in House of Lords until 1999; called to the Bar Middle Temple 1962; head of chambers 2000–; chm: Broadwater Farm Inquiry 1986, Liverpool 8 Inquiry 1989; attorney at law Jamaica 1990; sr ptnr Gifford, Thompson & Bright 1991–; chm: Ctee for Freedom Mozambique, Angola and Guiné 1968–75, N Kensington Law Centre 1974–77, Legal Action Gp 1978–81, Mozambique Angola Ctee 1984; vice-chm British Defence and Aid Fund 1985; *Books* Where's the Justice (1986); *Style*— The Lord Gifford, QC; ✉ 122 Tower Street, Kingston, Jamaica (tel 00 1 876 967 0670, fax 00 1 876 967 0225, e-mail anthony.gifford@btinternet.com)

GIFFORD, Prof Paul Peerless-Dennis; s of David Arthur Gifford, of Norwich, Norfolk, and Vera Rosina, *née* Palmer; *Educ* King Edward VI Sch Norwich, Univ of Cambridge (MA), Univ of Toulouse (Lès L, Dr 3e Cycle, Dès L); *m* 20 Sept 1969, (Irma) Cynthia Mary, da of Lt-Col AFS Warwick (d 1961); 2 da (Fiona b 20 Sept 1972, Joanne b 8 May 1975), 1 s (Gregory b 27 May 1979); *Career* Buchanan chair of French Univ of St Andrews 1987–; *Books* Valéry - Le Dialogue des Choses Divines (1989), Reading Paul Valéry. Universe in Mind (1998), Voix, traces, avènement: l'écriture et son sujet (1999), Subject Matters (2000), 2000 Years (2002), Love, Desire and transcendence in Frecnh Literature: Deciphering Eros (2006), La Création en Acts (2006); *Recreations* sailing, skiing, golf, tennis; *Style*— Prof Paul Gifford; ✉ 51 Radernie Place, St Andrews, Fife KY16 8QR (tel 01334 477243); Department of French, University of St Andrews, Buchanan Building, St Andrews, Fife KY16 9PH (e-mail ppg@st-and.ac.uk)

GIFFORD, Zerbanoo; da of Bailey Irani, and Kitty Mazda; *b* 11 May 1950; *Educ* Roedean, Watford Coll of Technol, London Sch of Journalism, Open Univ (BA); *m* 14 Sept 1973, Richard David Gifford, s of David Arthur Gifford, of Norwich; 2 s (Mark Mazda b 28 Aug 1975, Alexander Justice (Wags) b 27 Feb 1979); *Career* Lib cncllr Harrow 1982–86; Parly candidate (Lib Alliance): Hertsmere 1983, Harrow East 1987; Parly candidate (Lib Dems) Hertsmere 1992; chm: Lib Pty Community Rels Panel 1985, Cmmn into Ethnic Involvement 1986; elected memb Lib Dem Federal Exec 1991–92, pres Hertsmere Lib Dems; memb Status of Women Cmmn 1987, former community affairs advsr to leader of Lib Democrats; advsr Home Sec's Race Relations Forum; former ed Libas magazine, runner-up Special Interest Magazine Ed of the Year 1988, columnist Lib Democrat News; memb Advsy Cncl The Prince's Youth Business Tst, tstee Anti-Slavery Int, dir Charities Aid Fndn India, fndr dir The ASHA Fndn, fndr ASHA Centre; Freeman City of Lincoln Nebraska; Nehru Centenary Award from Non-Resident Indians' Assoc 1989, Asian City Club Annual Award 1990, nominee Women of Europe Award 1991, Int Woman of the Year for humanitarian work 2006; fell Nat Endowment of Sci, Technol and Arts (NESTA) 2004, FRSA; *Books* The Golden Thread (1990), Dadabhai Naoroji (1992), Asian Presence in Europe (1995), Thomas Clarkson and the Campaign against Slavery (1996), Celebrating India (1998), Confessions of a Serial Womaniser (2006); *Recreations* collecting antique embroidery, meeting extraordinary people; *Style*— Mrs Zerbanoo Gifford

GIGNOUX, Peter Alan; s of Frederick Evelyn Gignoux, Jr (d 1968); *b* 17 June 1945; *Educ* St Albans Sch, The Gunnery Sch, Boston Univ, Columbia Univ; *Career* London fndr and mangr Int Energy Desk; md: Schroder Salomon Smith Barney Ltd (formerly Smith Barney Ltd then Salomon Smith Barney Ltd), Citigroup; Freeman Worshipful Co of World Traders; MInstPet; *Recreations* shooting, travelling, yacht cruising; *Clubs* Buck's, Mark's, Hurlingham, St Anthony (New York); *Style*— Peter Gignoux, Esq; ✉ 53 Carlyle Court, Chelsea Harbour, London SW10 0UQ (tel 020 7351 5094, e-mail pgignoux@compuserve.com)

GILBART, His Hon Judge Andrew James; QC (1991); s of Albert Thomas Gilbart (d 1975), of Vinehall Sch, Robertsbridge, E Sussex, and Carol, *née* Christie (d 2006); *b* 13 February 1950; *Educ* Westminster (Queen's Scholar), Trinity Hall Cambridge (MA); *m* 1, 20 Jan 1979 (m dis 2001), Morag, da of Robert Thomas Williamson (d 1990), and Agnes Buchanan Williamson; 1 s (Thomas Christie b 1980), 1 da (Ruth Alexandra b 1982); m 2, 6 Nov 2003, Paula Doone Whittell, da of Bill Fox (d 1975), and Doone Fox, of Ettington, Warks; 2 step s, 1 step da; *Career* called to the Bar Middle Temple 1972 (bencher 2000); in practice Northern Circuit and Planning and Environment Bar 1973–2004, recorder 1996–2004 (asst recorder 1992–96), head Kings Chambers Manchester and Leeds 2001–04, circuit judge (Northern Circuit) 2004–, dep High Court judge 2005–; memb: Restricted Patients Presidents Panel Mental Health Review Tbnl 2001–06, Lands Tbnl 2006–; *Recreations* history, theatre, walking, singing, computing, cooking; *Style*— His Hon Judge Andrew Gilbart, QC

GILBERT, Prof Fiona Jane; da of Dr John Knight Davidson, OBE, of Glasgow, and Edith Elizabeth, *née* McKelvie; *b* 1 May 1956; *Educ* Hutchesons' Girls' GS, Univ of Glasgow (MB ChB), Univ of Aberdeen (DMRD); *m* 4 June 1982, Martin James Gilbert, *qv*, s of James Robert Gilbert, of Aberdeen; 1 s (Jamie b 1986), 2 da (Mhairi b 1989, Kirstin b 1992); *Career* conslt radiologist 1989–96, prof of radiology Univ of Aberdeen 1996–; dir NE Scotland Breast Screening Service 1989–2000; memb BMA 1978, FRCR 1986, FRCP 1991 (MRCP 1981), FRCPE 1994; *Recreations* sailing, skiing, tennis, theatre, classical music; *Style*— Prof Fiona Gilbert; ✉ 17 Rubislaw Den North, Aberdeen AB15 4AL; Department of Radiology, Lilian Sutton Building, University of Aberdeen, Foresterhill, Aberdeen AB25 2ZD (tel 01224 559718, e-mail f.j.gilbert@abdn.ac.uk)

GILBERT, His Hon Judge Francis Humphrey Shubrick; QC (1992); s of Cdr Walter Raleigh Gilbert, RN (d 1977), of Compton Castle, S Devon, and Joan Mary Boileau, *née* Willock (d 2001); *b* 25 January 1946; *Educ* Stowe, Trinity Coll Dublin (MA); *m* 19 April 1975,

Sarah Marian, da of Col Douglas Kaye, DSO, DL (d 1996), of Brinkley Hall, Suffolk; 2 da (Emma b 11 Nov 1976, Rosella b 15 Feb 1979), 1 s (Raleigh b 28 Oct 1982); *Career* called to the Bar Lincoln's Inn 1970 (bencher 2000); recorder on Western Circuit, head of chambers Walnut House Exeter 1995–2001, circuit judge (Western Circuit) 2001–, resident judge Plymouth 2006–; pres Pegasus Club 2001; memb Devon CC 1977–85; *Recreations* sailing, shooting; *Clubs* Royal Yacht Sqdn; *Style—* His Hon Judge Gilbert, QC; ✉ The Law Courts, 10 Armada Way, Plymouth, Devon PL1 2ER

GILBERT, Baron (Life Peer UK 1997), of Dudley in the County of West Midlands; Dr John William Gilbert; PC (1978); *b* 5 April 1927; *Educ* Merchant Taylors', St John's Coll Oxford, NYU (PhD); *m* 1; 2 da (1 decd); m 2, 23 March 1963, Jean Olive, elder da of Capt William Milne Ross Skinner, The Rifle Bde (d 1979); *Career* chartered accountant (Canada); Parly candidate (Lab): Ludlow 1966, Dudley 1968; MP (Lab): Dudley 1970–74, Dudley East 1974–97; min of state (def procurement) MOD 1997–99; oppn front bench spokesman on Treasy affairs 1972–74, financial sec Treasury 1974–75, min for Transport DOE 1975–76, min of state MOD 1976–79; memb Select Ctees on: Expenditure 1970–74, Corporation Tax 1973, Defence 1979–87, Trade and Industry 1987–92; chm PLP Defence Gp 1981–83, vice-chm Lab Fin and Industry Gp 1983–91; memb Ctee on Intelligence and Security 1994–97; patron Armed Forces Parly Scheme 2003–; memb: RUSI, RIIA, IISS, Amnesty Int, GMBATU, WWF, Fabian Soc; Hon LLD Wake Forest Univ SC 1983; FRGS; *Clubs* Reform; *Style—* The Rt Hon Dr the Lord Gilbert, PC

GILBERT, Martin James; s of James Robert Gilbert, of Aberdeen, and Winifred, *née* Walker; *b* 13 July 1955; *Educ* Robert Gordon's Coll, Univ of Aberdeen (MA, LLB); *m* 4 June 1982, Prof Fiona Jane Gilbert, *qv*, da of Dr John K Davidson; 1 s (Jamie), 2 da (Mhairi, Kirstin); *Career* chartered accountant; Deloitte Haskins and Sells 1978–81, Brander and Cruickshank 1982–83; chief exec Aberdeen Asset Management plc (formerly Aberdeen Trust plc) 1991–, dir Aberdeen Development Capital plc 1986, dir Aberdeen Asian Smaller Co Investment Trust 1995, chm Aberdeen Global Income Fund 1998, chm Aberdeen Asia-Pacific Income Fund 2000; non-exec chm: Firstgroup plc 1995, Chaucer Holdings plc 1998; non-exec dir Select International Funds plc 2007–; MICAS (vice-pres 2002–03); *Recreations* golf, hockey, skiing, sailing; *Clubs* Royal and Ancient (St Andrews), Royal Aberdeen Golf, Royal Selangor Golf, Gordonians HC, Royal Northern and Univ, Deeside Golf, Wimbledon Golf, Royal Thames Yacht, Leander; *Style—* Martin Gilbert; ✉ 17 Rubislaw Den North, Aberdeen AB15 4AL; Aberdeen Asset Management plc, 10 Queens Terrace, Aberdeen AB10 1YG (tel 01224 631999)

GILBERT, Sir Martin John; kt (1995), CBE (1990); s of Peter Gilbert (d 1976), of London, and Miriam, *née* Green; *b* 25 October 1936; *Educ* Highgate Sch, Magdalen Coll Oxford (BA); *m* 1, 1964 (m dis), Helen, da of Joseph Robinson, CBE; 1 da (Natalie b 1967); m 2, 1974, Susan, da of Michael Sacher; 2 s (David b 1978, Joshua b 1982); m 3, 2005, Esther, da of Ben Goldberg; *Career* author; hon fell Merton Coll Oxford 1994– (fell 1962–94), official biographer of Sir Winston Churchill 1968–, visiting prof UCL 1995–96; DLitt Univ of Oxford; FRSL; *Publications* author of 78 historical works and atlases incl: British History Atlas (1968), American History Atlas (1968), First World War Atlas (1970), Winston S Churchill Vols 3–8 (1971–88) and Churchill Document Vols (1973–), Sir Horace Rumbold, Portrait of a Diplomat (1973), Atlas of the Holocaust (1986), The Holocaust, The Jewish Tragedy (1986), Second World War (1989), Churchill: A Life (1991), Atlas of British Charities (1993), In Search of Churchill (1994), First World War (1994), The Day the War Ended (1995), Jerusalem in the Twentieth Century (1996), The Boys, Triumph over Adversity (1996), A History of the Twentieth Century, Vol I (1997), A History of the Twentieth Century, Vol II (1998), Israel, A History (1998), A History of the Twentieth Century, Vol III (1999), Never Again, A History of the Holocaust (2000), Letters to Auntie Fori - The 5,000–Year History of the Jewish People and their Faith (2002), The Righteous, the Unsung Heroes of the Holocaust (2002), Winston Churchill's War Leadership (2004), Churchill and America (2005), Somme, The Heroism and Horror of War (2006), Will of the People, Churchill's Political Philosophy (2006), Kristallnacht, Prelude to Destruction (2006), Churchill and the Jews (2007); *Recreations* drawing maps; *Clubs* Athenaeum; *Style—* Sir Martin Gilbert, CBE, DLitt; ✉ Merton College, Oxford OX1 4JD

GILBERT, Prof (Geoffrey) Nigel; s of Geoffrey Alan Gilbert, FRS, of Birmingham, and Lilo, *née* Czigler; *b* 21 March 1950; *Educ* King Edwards Sch Birmingham, Emmanuel Coll Cambridge (exhibitioner, BA, PhD, ScD); *m* 1974, Jennifer Mary, da of Henry Roe; *Career* lectr Univ of York 1974–76; Univ of Surrey: lectr 1976–84, reader 1984–91, prof of sociology 1991–, pro-vice-chllr 1997–2005; govr Nat Inst for Econ and Social Research; Nuffield sr res fellowship 1996; vice-chm Br Sociological Assoc 1995–98, dep chm Res Priorities Bd ESRC 1997–2000; CEng 1990, FBCS 1997, FREng 1999, AcSS 2000, FRSA 2005; *Publications* Modelling Society: an introduction to loglinear analysis for social researchers (1981), Accounts and Action (with P Abell, 1983), Opening Pandora's Box: a sociological analysis of scientists discourse (with M Mulkay, 1984), Social Action and Artificial Intelligence (with C Heath, 1985), Computers and Conversation (with P Luff and D Frohlich, 1990), Fordism and Flexibility: divisions and change (with R Burrows and A Pollert, 1991), Women and Working Lives: divisions and change (with S Arber, 1991), Researching Social Life (ed, 1992, 2 edn 2001), Analyzing Tabular Data: loglinear and logistic models for social researchers (1993), Simulating Societies: the computer simulation of social phenomena (with J Doran, 1994), Artificial Societies: the computer simulation of social life (with R Conte, 1995), Perspectives on HCI: Diverse Approaches (with A F Monk, 1995), Social Science Microsimulation (with K G Troitzsch, U Mueller and J E Doran, 1996), Humans, Computers and Wizards: Studying human (simulated) computer interaction (with R C Wooffitt, N Fraser and S McGlashan, 1997), Computer Simulations in Science and Technology Studies (with P Ahrweiler, 1998), Multi-agent Systems and Agent-based Simulation (ed with J S Sichman and R Conte, 1998), Simulation for the Social Scientist (with K G Troitzsch, 1999, 2 edn 2005); also author of six other books and over 120 articles in learned jls; *Recreations* cooking; *Style—* Prof Nigel Gilbert, FREng; ✉ Department of Sociology, University of Surrey, Guildford GU2 7XH (tel 01483 689173, fax 01483 689551, e-mail n.gilbert@surrey.ac.uk)

GILBERT, Patrick Lewis William (Pat); s of Lewis Frederick Gilbert (d 1999), and Sheila May Gilbert; *b* 26 November 1965; *Educ* Cowplain Comp Sch, South Downs Coll, Middx Poly (BA); *m* 17 June 2000, Hayley Jayne, *née* Bartlett; 1 s (Luis Cosmo b 22 Jan 2002); *Career* writer; musician 1985–88, asst ed Record Collector magazine 1991–96, freelance contrib The Times and The Guardian 1997; Mojo magazine: reviews ed 1998–99, assoc ed 2000–01, ed 2001–03; appeared in film What Have You Done Today, Mervyn Day? 2005, prodr Armies for Hire (documentary, BBC World Serv); *Books* Introduction to Record Collecting (ed, 1995), Oasis '96 (1996), Mojo Collection (ed, 2003). Passion is a Fashion - The Real Story of The Clash (2004); *Recreations* golf, painting, Portsmouth FC; *Clubs* Colony Rooms; *Style—* Pat Gilbert, Esq; ✉ c/o LAW, 14 Vernon Street, London W14 0RJ (tel 020 7471 7906, e-mail pat.gilbert65@btinternet.com)

GILBERT, Pippa Beryl; da of Philip Henry Crockett, MBE, and Beryl, *née* Wright (d 1969); *b* 23 July 1955; *Educ* Abbotsholme Sch; *m* 27 Aug 2003, Robert J Gilbert; *Career* dir: County Leatherwear 1976, Hustwick Ltd 1979, Toromed Ltd 1999; md: County Leatherwear (Tinter Ltd) 1987–, County Chamois Co Ltd 1987– (dir 1980); ptnr Heart of England Antiques 1987–; dir The Coventrian Partnership Ltd 2007–; assoc memb Int Export Assoc 1978, FInstD 1991; *Recreations* sailing, antique collecting, travel; *Style—* Mrs Pippa Gilbert; ✉ Chamant Manor, Old End, Appleby Magna, Derbyshire (e-mail cchamois@aol.com)

GILBERT, Richard Simon; s of Nigel John Gilbert, of Emsworth, Hants, and Mair, *née* James; *b* 1 November 1957; *Educ* Sevenoaks Sch, Falmouth Sch of Art (BA), Wimbledon Sch of Art (BA), Chelsea Sch of Art (MA), Br Sch in Rome (Abbey Major scholar in painting), Sch of the Art Inst of Chicago (Harkness fell); *Career* self-employed fine artist; teacher Sch of Art and Design Wellington Coll Berks 1994, teacher Cheltenham Coll 2000; Barclays Postgrad Painting award 1984; *Solo Exhibitions* Recent Work (Main Gallery Warwick Arts Trust London) 1986, Recent Work (Raab Gallery London) 1988, New Work (Raab Gallery London) 1992, Touching Silence (Hereford Museum and Art Gallery) 2002, Fourteen (Leominster Priory Church) 2001; *Group Exhibitions* incl: Wet Paint (Festival Gallery Bath) 1984, CAS Market (Smiths Gallery London) 1984–87 and 1990, John Moores Fourteenth Nat Exhibition (Walker Art Gallery Liverpool) 1985, Forty European Artists (Raab Gallery) 1986, Athena Arts awards (Barbican) 1987, Art for the City (Lloyd's Building London) 1987, Fellowship Exhibition (Sch of Art, Inst of Chicago) 1989, The Landscape and the Cityscape (Raab Gallery London) 1990, Rome scholars 1980–90 (Gulbenkian Gallery RCA London) 1990, The Discerning Eye (Mall Gallery London) 1990, Six Young British Artists (Oviedo, Madrid, Barcelona) 1991–92, Royal Over-Seas League Exhibition (Rosl Houe London) 1992, CAS Market (Smiths Galleries London) 1992 and 1993, The Blue Gallery 1994 and 1995, The Beardsmore Gallery 2000 and 2002, Fine Edge 2001, Leominster 2001; *Work in Collections* Contemporary Art Soc, Victoria Art Gallery Melbourne, Arthur Andersen plc, Barclays Bank plc, Business Design Centre, Leicester Educn Authy, Lloyds Bank of Spain and South America (Madrid), Pearl Life Assurance Co London, Rosehaugh Stanhope London, Clifford Chance London and NY, National Westminster Bank London, Caja de Ahorros de Segovia, Plymouth Art Gallery, Unilever plc and in private collections; *Style—* Richard Gilbert, Esq; ✉ The Creswells, Sutton St Nicholas, Hereford HR1 3AX (tel 01432 880748)

GILBERT (Gilbert and George), *see:* Proesch, Gilbert

GILBERTSON, (Cecil) Edward Mark; s of Francis Mark Gilbertson, of Ham, Wilts, and Elizabeth Margaret, *née* Dawson; *b* 2 June 1949; *Educ* Eton; *m* 1, May 1975 (m dis 1980), Astrid Jane, da of late Lt-Col Vaughan; m 2, 3 Sept 1986, Nicola Leslie Bellairs, yr da of Maj J A B Lloyd Philipps (d 1974), of Dale Castle, Dyfed; 1 da (Georgina Charlotte Bellairs b 29 Oct 1987), 1 s (Harry Edward Bellairs b 20 Feb 1990); *Career* dir Brewin Dolphin Securities Ltd; memb Investment Ctee Rep Body The Church in Wales; FSI 1976; *Recreations* cricket, shooting, squash, tennis; *Clubs* MCC, Cardiff and County; *Style—* Edward Gilbertson, Esq; ✉ Cathedine Hill, Cathedine, Brecon, Powys LD3 7SX; Llangwarren Estate, Letterston, Dyfed SA62 5UL

GILBEY, Sir (Walter) Gavin; 4 Bt (UK 1893), of Elsenham Hall, Essex; s of Sir (Walter) Derek Gilbey, 3 Bt (d 1991), and Elizabeth Mary, *née* Campbell; *b* 14 April 1949; *Educ* Eton; *m* 1, 1980 (m dis 1984), Mary, da of late William E E Pacetti, of Florida, USA; m 2, 1984 (m dis 1992), Anna, da of Edmund Prosser, of Cheshire; *Career* pres Great British Foods Inc; also works with abused children; *Recreations* golf, travel, anthropology; *Clubs* Army and Navy, Royal Dornoch Golf; *Style—* Sir Gavin Gilbey, Bt

GILCHRIST, Clive Mace; s of John Llewellyn Gilchrist (d 1984), and Ida, *née* Mace; *b* 27 September 1950; *Educ* LSE (BSc Econ); *m* 1979, Angela Rosemary, da of Roger Watson Hagger; 2 da (Philippa Jane (Pippa) b 1985, Julia Joy b 1987); *Career* stockbroker; J & A Scrimgeour & Co 1972–75, Joseph Sebag & Co 1975–78; dep dir of investment Postel Investments Ltd 1978–87; dir: Argosy Asset Management plc 1987–91 (md Jan-May 1991), Aberdeen Asset Management plc (formerly Aberdeen Trust plc) 1991–2003; md BESTrustees plc 1992–; Nat Assoc of Pension Funds: vice-pres 1992–94, chm Investment Ctee 1990–92, vice-chm Cncl 1990–92 (memb 1988–94); Assoc of Corporate Tstees: memb Cncl 1997–2003, chm Pensions Ctee 1997–2003; FSI 1992 (MSI 1979), FRSA 1993; *Recreations* gardening, music, travel; *Style—* Clive Gilchrist, Esq; ✉ Ashleigh Grange, Westhumble, Dorking, Surrey RH5 6AY; BESTrustees plc, Five Kings House, 1 Queen Street Place, London EC4R 1QS (tel 020 7332 4100, fax 020 7332 4108, e-mail clive.gilchrist@bestrustees.co.uk)

GILCHRIST, Maj-Gen Peter; CB (2004); s of Col David Alexander Gilchrist (d 2003), and Rosemary, *née* Drewe; *b* 28 February 1952, Sidmouth, Devon; *Educ* Marlborough, RMA Sandhurst; *m* 5 Sept 1981, Sarah-Jane, da of late Lt-Col H S S Poyntz; 1 da (Joanne Elizabeth b 19 June 1983), 1 s (Alexander b 24 April 1985); *Career* troop ldr, nuclear, chemical and biological defence offr, and gunnery and intelligence offr Germany and NI 1972–76, long armour inf course 1977, gunnery instr 1978–80, ops offr and Adj 3 RTR 1980–82, Staff Coll Div 11 1983–84, Bde Maj 20 Armd Bde 1985–86, Sqdn Ldr 3 RTR Cyprus and Germany 1987–88, Mil Sec (MS) 1989, memb Directing Staff RMCS Shrivenham 1990–93, CO 1 RTR 1993–95, higher command and staff course 1996, Col Operational Requirements (OR) 1996–98, Brig PE 1998–2000, Master Gen of the Ordnance and tech dir Defence Procurement Agency 2000–04, Dep Cmdg Gen Combined Forces Cmd Afghanistan 2004–, head British Defence Staff and defence attaché Washington 2005; late Col Cmdt Royal Armd Corps, dep Col Comdt RTR; tstee Tank Museum; *Recreations* field sports, sailing, skiing, gardening; *Clubs* Army and Navy; *Style—* Maj-Gen Peter Gilchrist, CB

GILCHRIST, Roderick Munn Renshaw; s of Ronald Renshaw Gilchrist (d 1971), and Vera, *née* Ashworth (d 2003); *b* 6 December 1934; *Educ* Holt Sch Dumfriesshire, Mill Hill Sch London; *m* 19 March 1959, Patricia Frances, da of late Robert Charles Durrant; 2 s (Adam Munn Renshaw b 1959, Luke Ronald Renshaw b 1965); *Career* admitted slr, cmmr for oaths; formerly princ Bennett and Gilchrist Slrs Guildford, currently princ Renshaw Gilchrist Slrs Fleetwood and Garstang; life govr ICRF 1978–2004 (resigned), tstee and clerk to the tstees W H King Alms Houses Garstang 1982–2001; memb: Clan Maclachlan Soc (life memb), Law Soc, Heraldry Soc of Scotland; FSA Scot; *Recreations* hunting (beagle hounds), heraldry, celtic mythology; *Clubs* Old Millhillians; *Style—* Roderick Gilchrist, Esq; ✉ Sion Hill, Garstang, Lancashire PR3 1ZB (tel 01995 602389); Renshaw Gilchrist Solicitors, 9 St Peters Place, Fleetwood, Lancashire FY7 6ED (tel 01253 873569, fax 01253 777205)

GILCHRIST, Susan Georgina; da of (Robert) David Gilchrist, of West Compton, Somerset, and Constance May, *née* Hodgson; *b* 26 May 1966; *Educ* Millfield, KCL (BA, L M Faithfull prize); *Career* conslt Bain & Co 1987–90; City reporter: Mail on Sunday 1991–92, The Times 1993–95; ptnr Brunswick Group Ltd 1995– (currently sr ptnr); Specialist Writer of the Year Br Press Awards 1992; *Recreations* eating out, cinema, watching sport (particularly Liverpool FC); *Style—* Miss Susan Gilchrist; ✉ Brunswick Group Ltd, 16 Lincoln's Inn Fields, London WC2A 3ED (tel 020 7404 5959, fax 020 7831 2823, mobile 079 7498 2301, e-mail sgilchrist@brunswickgroup.com)

GILDEA, Prof Robert Nigel; s of Denis Gildea, of London, and Hazel, *née* Walsh; *b* 12 September 1952; *Educ* Merton Coll Oxford (MA), St Antony's Coll Oxford, St John's Coll Oxford (DPhil); *m* 21 March 1987, Lucy-Jean Lloyd; 2 da (Rachel b 30 Sept 1989, Georgia b 28 Dec 1991), 2 s (William b 16 Nov 1994, Adam b 28 March 1997); *Career* jr research fell St John's Coll Oxford 1976–78, lectr in history KCL 1978–79, tutor in modern history Merton Coll Oxford 1979–; Univ of Oxford: reader in modern history 1996–2002, prof of modern French history 2002–06, prof of modern history 2006–; Elie Halévy visiting prof Inst d'Etudes Politiques Paris 2000; FRHistS 1986; Chevalier dans l'Ordre des Palmes Académiques (France) 1997; *Books* Education in Provincial France: A Study of Three Departments (1983), Barricades and Borders: Europe 1800–1914 (1987, 3 edn 2003), The Past in French History (1994), France since 1945 (1996, 2 edn 2002), Marianne in Chains: In Search of the German Occupation 1940–1945 (2002, Wolfson History Prize), Surviving Hitler and Mussolini: Daily Life in Occupied Europe (2006); *Recreations* music, walking,

G

swimming, cooking, Oxford United; *Style*— Prof Robert Gildea; ✉ Worcester College, Oxford OX1 2HB (e-mail robert.gildea@history.ox.ac.uk)

GILDERNEW, Michelle; MP, MLA; *Educ* St Catherine's Coll Armagh, Univ of Ulster; *Career* Sinn Féin rep to London 1997–98, memb NI Assembly 1998– (dep chair Social Devpt Ctee 1999–2002, memb Centre Ctee 2000–02), MP (Sinn Féin) Fermanagh and S Tyrone 2001–, Sinn Féin spokesperson on enterprise, trade and investment; *Style*— Ms Michelle Gildernew, MP, MLA; ✉ House of Commons, London SW1A 0AA; Northern Ireland Assembly, Parliament Buildings, Stormont Estate, Belfast BT4 3XX

GILES, Alan James; s of Ronald Giles, of Dorset, and Christine, *née* Bastable; *b* 4 June 1954; *Educ* Blandford Sch, Merton Coll Oxford (MA), Stanford Univ (MS); *m* 22 April 1978, Gillian, da of Norman Rosser; 2 da (Claire b 12 April 1984, Nicola b 20 April 1987); *Career* The Boots Co plc: buyer 1975–78, promotions mangr 1978–80, asst merchandise controller 1980–82; WH Smith Gp plc: devpt mangr 1982–85, merchandise controller 1985–88, exec dir 1995–98; ops and devpt dir Do It All 1988–92, md Waterstone's 1993–99, chief exec HMV Gp plc 1998–2006, non-exec dir: Somerfield plc 1993–2004, Wilson Bowden 2004–, Rentokil Initial 2006–; MCIM; *Style*— Alan Giles, Esq

GILES, Prof Anthony Kent (Tony); OBE (1992); s of Harry Giles (d 1967), of Rochester, Kent, and Eva Gertrude, *née* Kent (d 1972); *b* 30 June 1928; *Educ* Sir Joseph Williamson's Mathematical Sch Rochester, Queen's Univ Belfast (BScEcon); *m* 1, 2 Jan 1954 (m dis 1985), Helen Elizabeth Margaret, da of J Charles Eaton (d 1968), of Londonderry; 3 da (Ann b 1954, Amanda b 1957, Alison b 1963), 1 s (John b 1960); m 2, 6 Aug 1987, Heather Constance, da of Frank H J Pearce (d 1987), of Durban, South Africa; 1 step s (Sean Hewson b 1971), 1 step da (Linda Hewson b 1975); *Career* PO Personnel Selection RAF 1947–49; asst agric economist and lectr Univ of Bristol 1953–59; Univ of Reading: lectr 1960–68, sr lectr 1968–83, dir Farm Mgmnt Unit 1979–91, prof of farm mgmnt and provincial agric economist 1983–93 (prof emeritus 1993–), chm Sch of Applied Mgmnt Studies 1986–91, hon res fell Rural History Centre 1994–; UK country rep Int Soc of Agric Economists 1973–87, chm UK Farm Business Survey Ctee 1975–92, nat chm Centre Mgmnt in Agric 1987–89, pres Agric Econ Soc 1988; active in Samaritans 1972–82 (dir Reading Branch 1978–80); FIMgt 1989, FIAgrM 1992; *Books* professional: Agricultural Economics 1923–73 (1973), The Farmer as Manager (1980, 2 edn 1990), Innovation and Conservation: Ernest Edward Cook and his Country Estates (jt ed, 1989), The Managers Environment (ed, 1990), Agricultural Economics at the University of Reading 1923–1993 (1993), Windows on Agricultural Economics and Farm Management (1993), See You at Oxford! A Celebration of Fifty Oxford Farming Conferences Over Sixty Years (1995), The Manager as Farmer - Wisdom from some I have known (1996), Case Studies in Agricultural and Rural Land Management (ed, 2 edn 1997), Owner, Occupier and Tennant: Reading University at Churn Farm 1969–96 (1998), A Thirty Year Gestation: The Origins, Development and Future of the Institute of Agricultural Management (1999), From 'Cow College' to Life Sciences: A Celebration of 75 Years of Reading University's Agricultural Faculty (2000); non-professional: One Hundred Years With the Clifton Rugby Football Club (princ author, 1972), About Twenty Five Years of Cricket (1983), The Publications of A K Giles, 1955–93 (1994), Never Mind the Frills - An Autobiographical Sketch (1995), The Guv'nors (1997), Not Evacuated (2002), Part of All That I Have Met: A Personal Travelogue (2005), 21 for 4 (2005), Not to Be Squandered (2007); *Recreations* watching sport (rugby and cricket), aviation, collecting books (especially early Penguins), allotment; *Clubs* Clifton Rugby Football, Penguin Collectors' Soc; *Style*— Prof Tony Giles, OBE; ✉ The Cottage, 63 Northumberland Avenue, Reading, Berkshire RG2 7PS (tel 0118 975 2763)

GILES, Ashley Fraser; MBE (2006); s of Michael Giles, and Paula Giles; *b* 19 March 1973, Chertsey, Surrey; *Educ* George Abbot Sch Guildford; *m* Stine Osland; 1 s (Anders b 2000), 1 da (Mathilde b 2002); *Career* cricketer (off spin bowler); Warwickshire CCC: joined 1992, first class debut 1993, over 150 first class appearances, winners NatWest Trophy 1993 and 1995, County Championship 1994, 1995 and 2004, Sunday League 1994, Benson & Hedges Cup 1994 and 2002; England: 54 test caps, 62 one day appearances, test debut v SA Old Trafford 1998, one day debut v Aust Oval 1997, memb squad ICC World Cup SA 2003, memb Ashes-winning team 2005; ret 2007; Wisden Cricketer of the Year 2005; Hon Citizen Droitwich Spa 2005; *Style*— Mr Ashley Giles, MBE

GILES, Brian John; s of Alfred Giles (d 1984) of Kent, and Constance, *née* Barndon (d 1996); *b* 22 September 1941; *Educ* Westlands Sittingbourne; *m* 23 Feb 1963, Shirley Jennifer; 2 da (Sarah Louise b 24 June 1965, Philippa Clare b 30 April 1969); *Career* apprentice jockey Fairlawne Racing Stables 1958–62, ed Chaseform Raceform 1963–66; Daily Mail: equestrian corr 1967, Robin Goodfellow (main tipster) 1987–2006, Gimcrack 2007–; memb: Sports Writers' Assoc, Equestrian Writers Assoc; Horse Trials Gp Award of the Year for Servs to Sport 1990, Champion Tipster of Britain (Flat Season) 1999; *Books* How to Win on the Flat, Twenty-Five Years in Showjumping - a Biography of David Broome, So You Think You Know About Horses, Behind The Stable Door, SR Direct Mail Book of Eventing (with Alan Smith); *Recreations* reading, classical music; *Style*— Brian Giles, Esq; ✉ Daily Mail, Northcliffe House, Derry Street, Kensington, London W8 (tel 020 7938 6203)

GILES, John Smart; s of Alexander Giles, of York, and Doreen, *née* Smart; *b* 30 March 1949; *Educ* Rutherford Coll Newcastle, Nunthorpe GS York; *m* 11 May 1971, Jacqueline, da of Gordon Leonard Clapham; 1 da (Claire Elizabeth b 1974); *Career* trainee/darkroom asst Westminster Press 1966–72, photographer Western Press/Yorkshire Evening Press 1972–88, staff photographer Press Association (NE) 1988–2006, chief photographer Press Association Photos 2006–; *Awards* Kodak, Fuji, Nikon, Canon Images of Life, UK Press Gazette, British Sports Cncl, Heineken Humour Awards, Whitbread Media Awards for sport, news and feature pictures, Press Gazette British Press Awards Sports Photographer 1997, BPA Photographer of the Year 2003; *Recreations* tennis, sport; *Clubs* Poppleton Tennis, Appleton Roebuck Tennis; *Style*— John Giles, Esq; ✉ The Press Association, PA News Centre, 292 Vauxhall Bridge Road, Victoria, London (tel 020 7963 7156, mob 07860 167458)

GILES, Martin Peter; s of Peter James Wickham Giles (d 1977), and Jean Winifred, *née* Smith; *b* 13 September 1964; *Educ* Wymondham Coll, Lady Margaret Hall Oxford (MA); *m* 1993, Isabelle Sylvie, da of Jacques Lescent; 1 s (Thomas b 31 Dec 1994), 1 da (Margaux b 18 April 1997); *Career* Midland Bank International 1983–85, J P Morgan 1985–86; The Economist Newspaper 1988–: banking corr 1988–89, Euro business corr 1989–93, fin ed 1994–98; publisher CFO Europe 1998–2000, dir Economist Enterprises 2000–; *Recreations* wine tasting, sport; *Style*— Martin Giles, Esq; ✉ The Economist, 25 St James's Street, London SW1A 1HG

GILES, Prof Paul David; s of Peter Brian Giles (d 2006), of Southend-on-Sea, Essex, and Mary Alice, *née* Cope; *b* 13 September 1957, London; *Educ* ChCh Oxford (MA), Univ of Oxford (DPhil); *m* 1989 (m dis 2002), Nadine, *née* Cornwall; *Career* asst/assoc prof Portland State Univ Oregon 1987–94, lectr in American studies Univ of Nottingham 1994–99, lectr in American lit Univ of Cambridge 1999–2002, reader in American lit Univ of Oxford 2002–; dir Rothermere American Inst Univ of Oxford 2003–; pres Int American Studies Assoc 2005–; memb: Br Assoc for American Studies 1985 (Arthur Miller Essay Prize 1999), Modern Language Assoc of America 1987 (William Riley Parker Essay Prize 2003); *Publications* Hart Crane: The Contexts of 'The Bridge' (1986), American Catholic Arts and Fictions: Culture, Ideology, Aesthetics (1992), Transatlantic Insurrections: British Culture and the Formation of American Literature 1730–1860 (2001), Virtual Americas: Transnational Fictions and the Transatlantic Imaginary (2002), Atlantic Republic: The American Tradition in English Literature (2006); *Recreations* soccer, cricket, classical music, opera; *Style*— Prof Paul Giles; ✉ Rothermere American Institute, University of Oxford, 1A South Parks Road, Oxford OX1 3TG (tel 01865 282710, e-mail paul.giles@rai.ox.ac.uk)

GILES, (Derryck) Peter Fitzgibbon; s of Arthur Frederick Giles, CBE (d 1960), of Knightsbridge, London, and Gladys Adelaide, *née* Hird (d 1998); *b* 17 November 1928; *Educ* Sherborne, Univ of Bristol (LLB); *Career* called to the Bar Gray's Inn 1954; Stewarts and Lloyds Ltd 1955–62, Charity Cmmn 1962–69 and 1974–84 (asst cmmr 1967), Glaxo Holdings (legal advsr) 1970–72, Soc of Authors 1973; govr BFWG Charitable Fndn (formerly Crosby Hall) 1992–98 (sec 1973, chm of govrs 1992–95); hon fell Heraldry Soc; memb: Soc of Genealogists, White Lion Soc, Norfolk Family History Soc, Charity Law Assoc; FRSA; *Recreations* heraldry, genealogy, music, reading, pipe smoking; *Clubs* Savile, New Cavendish, Norfolk (Norwich); *Style*— Peter Giles, Esq; ✉ c/o New Cavendish Club, 44 Great Cumberland Place, London W1H 8BS

GILES, William George (Bill); OBE (1995); s of Albert William George Giles, of Brislington, Bristol, and Florence Ellen Christina, *née* James; *b* 18 November 1939; *Educ* Queen Elizabeth's Sch Crediton Devon, Bristol Coll of Sci and Technol; *m* 23 Dec 1961 (m dis 1992), Eileen Myrtle, da of John Henry Lake; 1 s (Philip John b 7 Aug 1969), 1 da (Helen Mary b 15 May 1971); m 2, 7 May 1992, Patricia Maureen Stafford, da of John Mabbott; *Career* Meteorological Office 1959–72, radio broadcaster London Weather Centre 1972–75, weather presenter BBC TV 1975–80, PR offr (sr sci offr) Met Office HQ Bracknell 1980–83, head Weather Centre (princ sci offr) BBC 1990– (offr in charge 1983–90); FRMetS 1985, FRSA 1995; *Awards* Scientific Prize Paris Festival of World Broadcast Meteorology 1994; *Books* Weather Observations (1980), The Story of Weather (1990); *Recreations* gardening, golf; *Style*— Bill Giles, Esq, OBE; ✉ BBC Weather Centre, Room 2050, BBC TV Centre, Wood Lane, London W12 7RJ (tel 020 8576 7873, fax 020 8742 9432, e-mail bill@billgiles.co.uk)

GILFILLAN, Andrew Crawford; s of Robert Crawford Gilfillan (d 1995), and Joan, *née* Leslie; *b* 21 April 1952, Halifax, Yorks; *Educ* Bradford GS, Univ of Sussex (BA), Univ of Cambridge (MA); *m* 29 March 1980, Janet Elizabeth, *née* Allen; 1 s (Robert Crawford b 6 Jan 1982), 1 da (Jessica Elizabeth b 21 Nov 1986); *Career* CUP: dir educn 1995–2002, memb Press Bd 1995–, dir ELT 2002–04, md Cambridge Learning 2004–; memb Bd Educnl Publishers Cncl 1994–2002; memb Wine Soc; FRSA 2007; *Recreations* golf, walking, wine; *Clubs* Cambridge Univ Grads Centre, Brampton Park Golf; *Style*— Andrew Gilfillan, Esq; ✉ Cambridge University Press, Shaftesbury Road, Cambridge CB2 8RU (tel 01223 315052, e-mail agilfillan@cambridge.org)

GILHOOLY, John; s of Owen Gilhooly; *b* 15 August 1973, Limerick; *Educ* UC Dublin (BA); *Career* admin UC Dublin 1994–97, mangr Harrogate Int Centre 1997–99; Wigmore Hall: exec dir 1999–, artistic dir 2005–; Hon FRAM 2006; *Style*— John Gilhooly, Esq; ✉ Wigmore Hall, 36 Wigmore Street, London W1U 2BP (tel 020 7258 8265)

GILI, Katherine Montserrat; da of John Lluis Gili (d 1998), of Oxford, and Elizabeth Helen, *née* McPherson; *b* 6 April 1948; *Educ* Wychwood Sch Oxford, Bath Acad of Art (BA), St Martin's Sch of Art; *m* 1986, Robert Persey; 1 s (Harry b 1987); *Career* sculptor; art teacher: Norwich Sch of Art 1972–84, St Martin's Sch of Art 1975–84, Wimbledon Sch of Art 1979–81, The City Lit 1985–95; visiting lectr: Kingston Univ 1989–2002, Kent Inst of Art and Design 1995–2001; ptnr Rokatha creative metalwork 1997; exhibition selector for New Contemporaries 1978, Serpentine Summer Show 1979, Have you Seen Sculpture from the Body? (Tate Gallery) 1984; memb Anglo-Catalan Soc; FRBS 1999 *Solo Exhibitions* Serpentine Gallery London 1977, Salander/O'Reilly Gallery New York 1981; *Group Exhibitions* incl: MOMA Oxford 1973, Chelsea Gallery 1974, Stockwell Depot Annual exhibitions 1974–79, The Condition of Sculpture (Hayward Gallery) 1975, Silver Jubilee exhbn of contemporary British sculpture (Battersea Park) 1977, Hayward Annual (Hayward Gallery) 1979, UEA 1982, Yorkshire Sculpture Park 1983, Tate Gallery 1984, Cornerhouse Gallery Manchester 1986, Int Contemporary Arts Fair London 1986, Whitefriars Museum Coventry 1987, Centro Cultural del Conde Duque Madrid 1988, Greenwich Open Studios 1988–90 and 1992, Int Festival of Iron Cardiff 1989, Normanby County Park Scunthorpe 1990, New Art Centre Sculpture Garden at Roche Court 1991–97, South Bank Centre London 1993, Lewisham Sculpture Park Riverdale Gardens 1993–94, Charterhouse Gallery London 1994, The Living Room Gallery London 1994, Flowers East Gallery London 1995, 1998, 1999, 2001, 2002 and 2004, Mercury Gallery London 1996, Royal Acad Summer Show London 1996–97, Mount Ephraim Gardens 1997, RBS Summer Show 2000, 2001, 2002 and 2005, St Augustine's Abbey Canterbury 2003, Pride of the Valley Sculpture Park 2003–, Fe2 05 (Myles Meehan Gallery Darlington Arts Centre) 2005; *Work in Collections* incl: City of Lugano Collection, Arts Cncl, Cartwright Hall Museum Bradford, Railtrack, General Electric USA; work on loan: Gracefield Art Centre Dumfries and Galloway; *Recreations* playing tennis, walking, listening to music; *Style*— Ms Katherine Gili; ✉ 7 The Mall, Faversham, Kent ME13 8LJ (tel 01795 533235, fax 01795 520595, e-mail katherine@persey.plus.com)

GILKES, Dr Jeremy John Heming; s of Lt-Col Geoffrey Heming Gilkes, DSO, RA (d 1991), and Mary Stella, *née* Richardson (d 2001); *b* 2 December 1939; *Educ* Charterhouse, Bart's Med Coll London (MB BS), Univ of London (MD); *m* 8 July 1978, Robyn Vanessa, da of Maj Nigel Bardsley (d 1962); 2 s (Alexander, Charles), 3 step da (Emma, Sara, Katrina); *Career* conslt dermatologist: UCH 1976–95, Middx Hosp 1976–95, King Edward VII Hosp for Offrs, St Luke's Hosp for Anglican Clergy, Eastman Dental Hosp 1976–95, London Foot Hosp 1976–95; memb: Br Assoc Dermatologists, RSM; FRCP; *Clubs* Hurlingham; *Style*— Dr Jeremy J H Gilkes; ✉ 62 Wimpole Street, London W1G 8AJ (tel 020 7935 6465, fax 020 7935 5014)

GILL, A A; s of Michael Gill, of London, and Yvonne, *née* Gilan; *b* 28 June 1954; *Educ* St Christopher Sch Letchworth, St Martin's Sch of Art London, Slade Sch of Fine Art London; *Children* 1 da (Flora b 23 Dec 1991), 1 s (Hector b 30 April 1993); *Career* journalist, artist and cook; currently: TV and restaurant critic The Sunday Times; Columnist of the Year 1994, Food Writer of the Year (for work in Tatler) and Restaurant Writer of the Year (for work in The Sunday Times) Glenfiddich Awards 1996, Critic of the Year (for work in Sunday Times) British Press Awards 1997, Cover Award 1998; *Books* Sap Rising (1996), The Ivy: a restaurant and its recipes (1997), Starcrossed (1999), Le Caprice (1999); *Clubs* Chelsea Arts; *Style*— A A Gill, Esq; ✉ The Sunday Times, 1 Pennington Street, London E1 9XW (tel 020 7782 5000)

GILL, Arthur Benjamin Norman (Ben); kt (2003), CBE (1996); s of William Norman Gill (d 1978), and Annie, *née* Almack (d 1987); *b* 1 January 1950; *Educ* Barnard Castle Sch, St John's Coll Cambridge (MA); *m* Jan 1973, Carolyn, *née* Davis; 4 s (Adam Matthew b Oct 1976, Robin William b March 1978, Oliver James Norman b Dec 1980, Edward Benjamin b Jan 1983); *Career* farming teacher Uganda 1972–75, farmer 1975–, chm Westbury Dairies Ltd 2004–06, dir Hawkhills Consultancy Ltd 2004–, md The Hawk Creative Business Park 2006–, chm English Apples & Pears Ltd 2007–; non-exec dir: Countrywide Farmers plc 2004–, One Planet plc 2006–; NFU: vice-pres 1991–92, dep pres 1992–98, pres 1998–2004, chair Livestock and Wool Ctee, chair Alternative Crops Working Party, chair Long Term Strategy Gp; visiting prof Univ of Leeds 1996–; vice-pres Ctee des Organisations Professionelle Agricultures 1999–2003, pres Confedn of Euro Agric 2000–04, chm Govt Task Force on Biomass 2004–05, cmmr on rural community devpt Carnegie Tst UK 2004–07; memb: Bd FARM Africa 1991–98, Agriculture and Food Research Cncl 1991–94, BBSRC 1994–97, Food from Britain Cncl 1999–2005; govr Cncl John Innes Centre Norwich 2002–, govr Univ of Lincoln 2004–; pres Univ of Cambridge

Potato Growers Research Assoc 2004–; patron: Rural Stress Info Network, Pentalk, Farmers Overseas Action Gp, 'Plants and Us' Initiative 2004–; Hon DSc: Leeds 1997, Cranfield 2000, UWE 2002; Hon DCL UEA 2003; FRAgS; *Recreations* photography, crosswords, rowing; *Style*— Sir Ben Gill, CBE; ✉ Prospect Farm, Upper Dormington, Hereford HR1 4ED

GILL, Rt Hon Lord; Brian Gill; PC (2002); s of Thomas Gill (d 1986), of Glasgow, and Mary, *née* Robertson (d 1986); *b* 25 February 1942; *Educ* St Aloysius' Coll Glasgow, Univ of Glasgow (MA, LLB), Univ of Edinburgh (PhD); *m* 6 Sept 1969, Catherine, *née* Fox; 5 s (Brian John b 1970, Francis Damian b 1971, James Patrick b 1973, Michael Simon b 1974, Anthony Thomas b 1983), 1 da (Anne Lucy b 1978); *Career* called to the Scottish Bar 1967, Lincoln's Inn 1991 (hon bencher 2002); QC 1981, keeper Advocates Library 1987–94, senator Coll of Justice Scotland (Lord of Session) 1994, Lord Justice Clerk of Scotland and pres Second Div of the Court of Session in Scotland 2001–; chm Scottish Law Cmmn 1996–2001, dep chm Copyright Tbnl 1989–94; chm RSAMD 1999–2006; Hon LLD: Univ of Glasgow 1998, Univ of Strathclyde 2003, Univ of St Andrews 2006, Univ of Edinburgh 2007; DAcad RSAMD 2006; FRSAMD 2002, FRSE 2004; *Books* Law of Agricultural Holdings in Scotland (1982, 3 edn 1997), Scottish Planning Encyclopedia (gen ed, 1996); *Recreations* church music; *Clubs* Reform, MCC; *Style*— The Rt Hon Lord Gill; ✉ Court of Session, Parliament House, Edinburgh EH1 1RQ (tel 0131 240 6732, fax 0131 240 6704, e-mail lord.gill@scotcourts.gov.uk)

GILL, Christopher J F; RD (1971); s of late F A Gill, and late D H Gill, *née* Southan; *b* 28 October 1936; *Educ* Shrewsbury; *m* 2 July 1960, Patricia, da of late E V Greenway; 1 s (Charles b 1961), 2 da (Helen b 1963, Sarah b 1967); *Career* Lt Cdr RNR 1952–79; butcher and farmer, chm F A Gill Ltd 1968–2006; Wolverhampton BC: memb (Cons) 1965–72, chm Public Works Ctee 1967–69, chm Local Educn Authy 1969–70; MP (Cons) Ludlow 1987–2001; former vice-chm Cons European Affairs Ctee, former vice-chm Cons Agric Ctee; pres The Freedom Assoc 2007– (hon chm 2001–07); Liveryman Worshipful Co of Butchers, Freeman City of London; *Recreations* walking, sailing, skiing, golf, DIY; *Style*— Christopher Gill, Esq, RD; ✉ Billingsley Hall Farm, Bridgnorth, Shropshire WV16 6PJ (tel 01746 862345)

GILL, Rev Dr David Christopher; s of Alan Gill (d 1940), and Muriel, *née* Hodgson (d 1985); *b* 30 July 1938; *Educ* Bellevue GS Bradford, Univ of St Andrews (MB ChB), Salisbury Theol Coll, Univ of Nottingham (Dip Theol and Pastoral Studies); *Career* TA OTC 1956–61, RAMC 1961–66, 153 Highland Field Ambulance, Capt, RARO 1966–; house offr, sr house offr then registrar 1963–66 (appts at Perth Royal Infirmary, Bridge of Earn Hosp and King's Cross Hosp Dundee), medical supt and dist MO Mkomaindo Hosp Masasi Mtwara Region Tanzania 1966–72 (regnl leprosy offr 1967–72), clinical asst Herison Hosp and Yeovil Dist Hosp 1972–74, registrar then sr registrar psychiatry Knowle Hosp Fareham 1974–78, conslt psychiatrist Mapperley Hosp Nottingham 1978–2006, clinical teacher Univ of Nottingham Med Sch 1978–95, The Priory Clinic Nottingham 1993–2006 (med dir 1995–2006), ret; chm Collegiate Trainees Sub-Ctee Royal Coll of Psychiatrists 1976–78, chm Senior Med Staff Ctee Mental Illness Unit 1980–85, medical memb Mental Health Act Review Tbnl 2003–06; memb Nottingham Medico-Chirurgical Soc; memb Cncl Univ of St Andrews; ordained: deacon 1981, priest 1985, priest Russian Orthodox Church in GB 1995; priest in charge Orthodox Parish of St Aidan and St Chad Nottingham; DObstRCOG 1965, DTM&H (Liverpool) 1968, DPM 1975, FRCPsych 1986 (MRCPsych 1976); *Publications* author of papers on electro-convulsive therapy, and psychiatric aspects of paranormal and possession states; *Recreations* sailing, theatre, opera; *Clubs* RAF Yacht, Royal Yachting Assoc, Army Sailing Assoc, Naval; *Style*— The Rev Dr David Gill; ✉ 1 Malvern Court, 29 Mapperley Road, Nottingham NG3 5SS (tel 0115 962 2351, e-mail david@gill7.demon.co.uk)

GILL, Prof (Evelyn) Margaret; da of William Alexander Morrison Gill, of Edinburgh, and Eveline Elizabeth, *née* Duthie; *b* 10 January 1951, Edinburgh; *Educ* Mary Erskine Sch for Girls Edinburgh, Univ of Edinburgh (BSc), Massey Univ NZ (PhD), Open Univ (BA); *Career* researcher Grassland Research Inst 1976–89, prog mangr then dir of research Natural Resources Inst (research arm of ODA) 1989–96, chief exec Natural Resources International Ltd 1996–2000, chief exec and dir of research Macaulay Inst 2000–06, chief scientific advsr Scottish Exec Environment and Rural Affrs Dept (SEERAD) 2006–, prof of integrated land use Univ of Aberdeen 2006–; Hammond Prize Br Soc of Animal Science 1992; FRSE 2003; *Recreations* hill walking, classical music; *Style*— Prof Margaret Gill; ✉ SEERAD, Pentland House, 47 Robb's Loan, Edinburgh EH14 1TY

GILL, Neena; MEP (Lab) W Midlands; *b* 24 December 1956, Ludhiania; *Educ* Liverpool Poly (BA), London Business Sch; *Career* worked for London Borough of Ealing 1981–83, princ housing offr UK Housing Tst 1983–86, chief exec Asra Gtr London Housing Assoc 1986–90, chief exec New London Housing Gp 1990–99; dir Dalston City Challenge, chair Hackney Housing Partnership, memb Bd Hackney 2000; MEP (Lab) W Midlands 1999–; European Parl: vice-pres S Asia Delgn, Lab spokesperson Budgets Ctee, memb Industry, External Trade, Research and Energy Ctee; trade union steward 1981–83, memb Gen Ctee Constituency Lab Pty 1995–97, memb Lab NEC Ethnic Minority Taskforce; *Publications* incl: Race and Housing, Women and Housing, Standards in Housing; *Style*— Ms Neena Gill, MEP; ✉ West Midlands European Office, Terry Duffy House, Thomas Street, West Bromwich B70 6NT

GILL, Peter; OBE (1980); s of George John Gill (d 1986, union rep Spillers Flower Mill Gen Strike 1926), and Margaret Mary, *née* Browne (d 1966); *b* 7 September 1939; *Educ* St Illtyd's Coll Cardiff; *Career* dramatic author and director; actor 1957–65; directed first prodn A Collier's Friday Night at the Royal Court 1965; plays directed incl: The Local Stigmatic 1966, Crimes of Passion 1967, The Daughter-in-Law 1967 (first prize Belgrade Int Theatre Festival 1968), The Widowing of Mrs Holroyd 1968, The Duchess of Malfi 1971, Twelfth Night 1974, As You Like It 1975, The Fool 1975, The Way of the World 1992, New England 1994, Uncle Vanya 1995, A Patriot for Me 1995; assoc artistic dir Royal Court Theatre 1970–72; dir Riverside Studios 1976–80; prodns: The Cherry Orchard (own version), The Changeling 1978, Measure for Measure 1979, Julius Caesar 1980; appointed assoc dir Nat Theatre 1980–97; prodns: A Month in the Country 1981, Don Juan 1981, Major Barbara 1982, Tales from Hollywood 1983, Venice Preserv'd 1984, Fool for Love 1984, The Garden of England 1985, The Murderers 1985, Mrs Klein 1988, Juno and The Paycock 1989; dir Nat Theatre Studio 1984–90; wrote and produced: The Sleepers Den 1966 and 1969, Over Garden's Out 1969, A Provincial Life (after Chekov) 1969, Small Change 1976 and 1983, As I Lay Dying (after Faulkner) 1985, In The Blue 1985, Mean Tears 1987, Cardiff East 1996; other plays incl: Three Sisters (new version) 1997, Friendly Fire 1999, The Seagull (RSC) 1999, The York Realist 2000 (also at Royal Court 2002), Original Sin (After Wedekind) 2002; other prodns incl: Tongue of the Bird, Ellen McLauglain (Almeida) 1997, Certain Young Men (Almeida) 1999, Speed the Plow (Ambassador's) 1999, Luther (RNT) 2001, Scenes From the Big Picture (RNT) 2003, Days of Wine and Roses (Donmar), George Dillon (Comedy Theatre) 2005, The Voysey Inheritance (RNT) 2006, Look Back in Anger (Bath) 2006; *Style*— Peter Gill, Esq, OBE; ✉ c/o Casarotto Marsh Ltd, National House, 4th Floor, 60–66 Wardour Street, London W1V 3HP (tel 020 7287 4450, fax 020 7287 9128)

GILL, Robin Denys; CVO (1993); s of Thomas Henry Gill (d 1931), of Hastings, NZ, and Marjorie Mary, *née* Butler; *b* 7 October 1927; *Educ* Dulwich Coll, Brasenose Coll Oxford (MA); *m* 1, 5 Oct 1951, Mary Hope (d 1986), da of John Henry Alexander (d 1953), of Harrogate, N Yorks; 3 s (Stephen b 23 July 1953, Richard b 9 Sept 1955, Jonathan b 25 March 1957 d 1992); *m* 2, 18 Feb 1991, Denise Spencer, *née* Waterhouse; *Career* sales mangr: Van den Berghs (Unilever Ltd) 1949–54, British International Paper Ltd 1954–59; fndr and md Border TV Ltd 1960–64, md Associated TV Corporation Ltd 1964–69; chm: ITCA Ltd 1966–67, ITN Ltd 1968–70, 1970 Trust Ltd 1970–93, Yarrow Shipbuilders plc 1974–80; dir: Reed Paper Group Ltd 1970–75, Hewlett Packard 1975–92; chm: Ansvar Insurance Co Ltd 1975–98, Systems Programming Holdings 1982–88, Heidelberg Instr GmbH 1984–89, Baring Hambrecht Alpine Ltd 1986–97, Baring Communications Equity Ltd 1993–98; chm various venture capital companies; non-exec dir SD-Scicon plc 1988–91; chm Standard Industrial Trust 1970–81; memb: Ctee The Royal Family Film 1968–69, Nat Advsy Bd for Higher Educn, Visiting Ctee of RCA, Oxford Univ Appts Ctee, NW Regnl Cncl for Higher Educn, Bd IESTE (UK); memb Bd Claremont Fan Ct Sch; fndr The Royal Anniversary Tst 1990– (chm 2001–), exec chm The Queen's 40th Anniversary Celebration 1992, fndr and chm The Queen's Anniversary Prizes for Higher and Further Educn 1994–; pres The Brasenose Soc 1995–96; hon fell Brasenose Coll Oxford 2005–; *Recreations* golf, sport, music, travel, art collecting, new projects; *Clubs* Vincent's (Oxford), St George's Hill Golf, Free Foresters CC; *Style*— Robin Gill, Esq, CVO; ✉ PO Box 1, East Horsley, Surrey KT24 6RE (tel 01483 285290)

GILLAM, Sir Patrick John; kt (1998); s of Cyril Bryant Gillam (d 1978), and Mary Josephine, *née* Davis; *b* 15 April 1933; *Educ* Clapham Coll, LSE (BA); *m* 23 Nov 1963, Diana, da of Dr Francis A Echlin (d 1988); 1 da (Jane (Mrs Simon Bullivant) b 1970), 1 s (Luke b 1973); *Career* 2 Lt RA 1954–56; FO 1956–57; md The BP Co plc 1981–91 (various appts 1957–81); chm: BP Shipping Ltd 1981–88, BP Minerals Int 1982–91, BP Coal Ltd 1986–88, BP Coal Inc 1988–91, BP America Inc 1989–91, BP Oil Int 1989–91, BP Nutrition 1989–91; dir: BP New Zealand Ltd 1981–89, BP Australia Holdings Ltd 1981–89, BP South Africa (Pty) Ltd 1981–89, BP Africa Ltd 1982–88, BP Exploration Co 1983–91, BP Canada Inc 1989–92; chm: Booker Tate Ltd 1991–93, Asda Group plc 1991–96, Standard Chartered plc 1993–2003 (dep chm 1991–1993), Asia House 2003–; non-exec dir: Commercial Union plc 1991–96, Royal & Sun Alliance Insurance Group plc 1997– (chm until 2003); memb: Ct of Govrs LSE 1989–, The Cook Soc 1983, Appeal Ctee Queen Elizabeth's Fndn for the Disabled 1984–; chm ICC UK 1989–98; Freeman City of London; hon fell LSE; FRSA 1983, FInstD 1984; *Recreations* gardening, skiing, fine and decorative art; *Style*— Sir Patrick Gillam

GILLAN, Cheryl; MP; da of late Adam Mitchell Gillan, and Mona Gillan; *b* 21 April 1952; *Educ* Cheltenham Ladies' Coll, Coll of Law, Chartered Inst of Marketing; *m* 7 Dec 1985, John Coates Leeming, s of James Arthur Leeming; *Career* with Int Mgnt Gp 1977–84, dir Br Film Year 1984–86, sr mktg conslt Ernst and Young 1986–91, mktg dir Kidsons Impey 1991–93; chm Bow Gp 1987–88, European Parly candidate (Cons) Gtr Manchester Central 1989; MP (Cons) Chesham and Amersham 1992–; Parly under sec of state DfEE 1995–97; oppn frontbench spokesman on trade and industry 1997–98, oppn frontbench spokesman on foreign and Cwlth affrs 1998–2001, oppn whip 2001–03, oppn frontbench spokesman Home Office 2003–05, shadow sec of state for Wales 2005–; memb Select Ctee on: Science and Technol 1992–95, Procedures 1994–95; int treas CPA 2003–06; Liveryman Worshipful Co of Marketors; FCIM; *Recreations* golf, music, gardening; *Clubs* RAC; *Style*— Cheryl Gillan, MP; ✉ House of Commons, London SW1A 0AA

GILLARD, David Owen; s of Robert Gillard (d 1983), of Croydon, Surrey, and Winifred, *née* Owens (d 1981); *b* 8 February 1947; *Educ* Tavistock Sch Croydon; *m* 1994, Valerie Ann Miles; *Career* arts writer and critic; scriptwriter and asst dir Assoc Br Pathé 1967–70, film and theatre critic Daily Sketch 1970–71, opera critic Daily Mail 1971– (ballet critic 1971–88), instituted Drama Preview Pages in The Listener 1982, fndr ed Friends (ENO magazine) 1983–92, radio corr Radio Times 1984–91, writer My Kind of Day Radio Times 1992–2002, classical music ed Radio Times 2001–02; memb: NUJ 1963, Critics' Circle 1974, Broadcasting Press Guild 1995; *Books* Oh Brothers! (play, 1971), Beryl Grey: A Biography (1977); *Recreations* hill walking, collecting children's books and signed first editions, amateur dramatics including pantomime; *Style*— David Gillard, Esq; ✉ 1 Hambledon Court, 18 Arundel Way, Highcliffe, Dorset BH23 5DX (tel and fax 01425 275796)

GILLEN, Hon Mr Justice; Sir John Gillen; kt (1999); *b* 18 November 1947; *Educ* Methodist Coll Belfast, The Queen's Coll Oxford; *Career* called to the Bar Gray's Inn 1970; QC (NI) 1983, judge of the High Court of Justice in NI 1999–; *Style*— The Hon Mr Justice Gillen; ✉ c/o Royal Courts of Justice, Chichester Street, Belfast BT1 3JF

GILLER, Norman; *b* 18 April 1940; *Educ* Raine's Fndn GS Stepney; *m* 8 April 1961, Eileen (d 2006); 1 s (Michael), 1 da (Lisa); *Career* copy boy London Evening News 1955–56, reporter, sub ed and layout designer Boxing News 1959–61, sports ed and layout designer Stratford Express 1961–62, sports sub ed Evening Standard 1962, sports sub ed and layout designer Daily Herald 1962–64, football reporter Daily Express 1964–66 (chief football reporter 1966–74), TV sports columnist Evening News 1977–80, TV sports columnist Sunday Express 1991–97, The Judge sports column The Sun 1995–, The Silver Surfer football column FC.com 2000–; chief scripwriter Laureus World Sports Acad Awards 2002–03; numerous freelance appts 1974–; deviser many newspaper games since 1974 incl: The Name Game The Sun 1974–, Sportsword crossword The Express 1992–, Times Test Crossword in The Times 2001–06 (all games and puzzles compiled in partnership with s Michael) and two board games (Namedropper! and Tiddlythinks!); creator Petrolheads (BBC TV), script writer for This Is Your Life (scripts written for George Shearing, Richard Branson, Nigel Mansell, Jimmy Savile and many others); other TV credits incl: Stunt Challenge (ITV) 1984 and 1985, Stand and Deliver (Sky) 1995–97; writer and deviser: The Games of '48 (with Brian Moore, ITV), Eurovision Song Contest Preview 1992–93, Who's the Greatest (seven-part series, ITV); writer and deviser Ricky Tomlinson's TV Joke Shop; chief assoc to Brian Klein (On the Box Productions Ltd); co-prodr and writer of videos featuring Lawrence Dallaglio, Dickie Bird, Frankie Dettori, Gordon Ramsay, John Motson, Harry Carpenter, David Seaman and Vinnie Jones 1998–2005; also prodr and writer: Over the Moon (ITV), Frankly Bruno (Chrysalis), Football Trivial Pursuit (Telstar); PR for Joe Bugner and Frank Bruno; *Books* 77 to date; ghostwriter of numerous works with sporting personalities incl: Banks of England (with Gordon Banks), Watt's My Name (with Jim Watt), The Seventies Revisited (with Kevin Keegan), Olympic Heroes (with Brendan Foster), How to Box (with Henry Cooper), The Glory and the Grief (with George Graham), Top Ten Cricket Book (with Tom Graveney), Know What I Mean? and From Zero to Hero (with Frank Bruno), Denis Compton - the Untold Stories, While I've Still Got Lead in My Pencil (with Roy Ullyett), The Final Score (with Brian Moore); Billy Wright: A Hero For All Seasons (2002), McFootball (2003), Football and All That (2004), Football My Arse, Reading My Arse and Cheers My Arse (all with Ricky Tomlinson, 2005–07), The Great Football Quiz Book (2005); 16 books with Jimmy Greaves incl: This One's On Me, The Final (novel), The Boss (novel), The Sixties Revisited, It's A Funny Old Life, Saint and Greavsie's World Cup Special, Don't Shoot The Manager, Heroes and Entertainers (2007); other books incl: The Golden Milers, The Marathon Kings, The Olympics Handbook, This Sporting Laugh, Crown of Thorns, Mike Tyson, The Release of Power (with Reg Gutteridge), Golden Heroes (with Dennis Signy), six Carry On novels (1996), Mike Baldwin (biography, 2000), Footballing Fifties (2007); *Recreations* creating computer graphics and websites (including www.sinatra-wessex.co.uk), listening to light classics, playing banana-fingered jazz piano with SootsJazz promoter Jackie Jones, reading, travelling (34 countries to date), surfing the internet, following all major sports; *Style*— Norman Giller, Esq; ✉ PO Box 3386, Ferndown, Dorset BH22 8XT (e-mail normangiller@btinternet.com, website www.footballingfifties.co.uk)

GILLESPIE, Dr Alan Raymond; CBE (2004); s of Charles Gillespie (d 1984), and Doreen, *née* Murtagh; *b* 31 July 1950, NI; *Educ* Grosvenor HS Belfast, Univ of Cambridge (BA, PhD); *m* 27 June 1973, Ruth, *née* Milne; 1 s (Patrick b 1989), 1 da (Christianne b 1991); *Career* Citibank NA 1976–86, ptnr Goldman Sachs and Co 1986–99, chief exec Cwlth Devpt Corporation 1999–2002, chm NI Industrial Devpt Bd 1999–2001, chm Ulster Bank Gp 2001–; chm Int Finance Facility for Immunization; patron Queen's Univ of Belfast Fndn; Hon DUniv Ulster, Hon LLD Queen's Univ Belfast; *Recreations* golf, tennis, sailing; *Clubs* Wisley Golf, St George's Hill Lawn Tennis; *Style—* Dr Alan Gillespie, CBE; ✉ Ulster Bank Group, 11–16 Donegall Square East, Belfast BT1 5UB

GILLESPIE, Jonathan William James; s of J J M Gillespie, and P D, *née* Evans; *b* 6 December 1966, Luton, Beds; *Educ* Bedford Modern Sch, Selwyn Coll Cambridge (MA, PGCE); *m* 8 Aug 1992, Caroline, *née* Hotchkiss; 2 s; *Career* asst master Highgate Sch 1990–97; Fettes Coll: head of modern languages 1997–2001, housemaster Moredun House 2001–06; head master Lancing Coll 2006–; *Recreations* Highland bagpipe, hockey, cricket, hill walking; *Style—* Jonathan Gillespie, Esq; ✉ Lancing College, Lancing, West Sussex BN15 0RW (tel 01273 465802, fax 01273 464720, e-mail hmsecretary@lancing.org.uk)

GILLESPIE, (Joseph Andrew) Robert; s of John Robert Gillespie, and Honora Margaret, *née* Littlefair; *b* 14 April 1955, Nottingham; *m* 19 Sept 1987, Sally, *née* Carolyn; 3 da (Imogen b 17 Feb 1988, Isabel b 7 Feb 1996, Elizabeth b 19 April 1998); *Career* Price Waterhouse 1977–81, S G Warburg & Co Ltd 1981, head of UK investment banking SBC Warburg 1995, head of European investment banking UBS Warburg 1997; UBS Investment Bank: global head of investment banking 1999–2005, vice-chm 2005–; chm Somerset House Tstees Ltd, vice-pres Save the Children, memb Bd NSPCC; CA 1980; *Recreations* sailing, golf, shooting; *Clubs* Leander, Oriental; *Style—* Robert Gillespie, Esq; ✉ Holywell Hall, Holywell, Stamford, Lincolnshire PE9 4DL (tel 01780 410665, fax 01780 410210); UBS, 1–2 Finsbury Avenue, London EC2M 2PP (tel 020 7568 2869, fax 020 7568 1231, e-mail robert.gillespie@ubs.com)

GILLETT, (John) Anthony Cecil Walkey; s of Eric Walkey Gillett, FRSL (d 1978), and Joan, *née* Edwards (d 1956); *b* 17 March 1927; *Educ* Malvern Coll, Brasenose Coll Oxford (MA); *m* 18 Oct 1952, Jacqueline Eve, da of Philippe Leslie Caro Carrier, CBE (d 1975), of Lewes, E Sussex; 2 s (Charles b 1954, John b 1958), 1 da (Amanda b 1961); *Career* served as Lt RM 1945–47; Colonial Serv dist offr Somaliland Protectorate 1950–58, called to the Bar Inner Temple 1955, magistrate Aden (sometime acting chief justice, puisne judge and chief magistrate) 1958–63, crown counsel and asst attorney gen of Aden 1963–65, dep advocate gen Fedn of S Arabia 1965–68 (sometime acting attorney gen and advocate gen), temp legal asst Cncl on Tbnls (UK) 1968–70, legislative draftsman States of Guernsey 1970–83, stipendiary magistrate of Guernsey 1983–97; played polo for Somaliland Protectorate and Aden; hon sec Oxford University Tennis Club (Royal Tennis); *Publications* State of Aden Law Reports (1959–60), The Juvenile Court of Guernsey; *Recreations* lawn tennis, reading; *Clubs* Royal Channel Islands Yacht, MCC, Vincent's (Oxford); *Style—* Anthony Gillett, Esq; ✉ Bellieuse Farm, St Martin's, Guernsey GY4 6RW (tel 01481 236986)

GILLETT, Christopher John; yr s of Sir Robin Danvers Penrose Gillett, 2 Bt, GBE, RD; *b* 16 May 1958; *Educ* Durlston Court Sch, Pangbourne Coll, King's Coll Cambridge (choral scholar, MA), Royal Coll of Music (studied under Robert Tear and Edgar Evans), Nat Opera Studio; *m* 1984 (m dis), Julia, yr da of late W H Holmes, of Tunbridge Wells; 1 da (Tessa Holmes b 1987), 1 s (Adam Holmes b 1989); m 2, 1996, Lucy, da of H Schaufer, of Arizona USA; *Career* operatic and concert tenor; has worked with various major opera companies incl: New Sadler's Wells (over 150 performances), Royal Opera, ENO, Glyndebourne Touring Opera, Kent Opera, Music Theatre Wales, Opera Northern Ireland; Liveryman Worshipful Co of Musicians; *Performances* operatic roles incl: Ferrando in Cosi fan Tutte (Glyndebourne Touring Opera), title role in Albert Herring (Glyndebourne Touring), Roderigo in Otello (Royal Opera House Covent Garden), Dov in The Knot Garden (Covent Garden), Pang in Turandot (Covent Garden), Hermes in King Priam (with Royal Opera Co in Athens), Nooni in The Making of the Representative for Planet Eight (with ENO at the London Coliseum and in Amsterdam), St Magnus in Peter Maxwell Davies' Martyrdom of St Magnus (Music Theatre Wales), Arbace in Idomeneo (English Bach Festival), Flute in A Midsummer Night's Dream (Aix-en-Provence Festival, Teatro Regio Turin, Ravenna Festival, ENO, Rome Opera) and Lysander in the same for Netherlands Opera and New Israeli Opera, Vasek in The Bartered Bride (Opera Northern Ireland), Pysander in Ulisse (Vlaamse Opera, Netherlands Opera), Tikhon Kabanova in Katya Kabanova (Glyndebourne Touring Opera), Gigolo in Rosa (Netherlands Opera), Aschenbach in Death in Venice (Genoa); concert performances incl: Stravinsky Cantata (with La Chapelle Royale under Philippe Herreweghe in Paris and Brussels), Haydn Creation (in Madrid), Handel Messiah (with The Sixteen Choir and Orch under Harry Christophers in the Netherlands), Nyman Songs, Sounds and Sweet Airs (with Michael Nyman Band in Japan), Bach St John Passion (Symphony Hall Birmingham and King's Coll Chapel Cambridge), Britten War Requiem (Teatro Colon Buenos Aires, Stuttgart, Rotterdam, Amsterdam, Taipei), Bach's St Matthew Passion (RFH with Bach Choir), Britten Nocturne (Philadelphia Orch), Peter Grimes (LSO); *Recordings* incl: Elgar The Kingdom (with London Philharmonic under Leonard Slatkin, RCA), The Beggar's Opera (Decca), Albert Herring (Naxos), Oliver Knussen Double Bill (Deutsche Grammophon); *Style—* Christopher Gillett, Esq; ✉ 3 Woolley Street, Bradford on Avon, Wiltshire BA15 1AD (tel and fax 01225 865701, e-mail chrisgillett@tiscali.co.uk)

GILLETT, Rt Rev David Keith; *see:* Bolton, Bishop of

GILLETT, Sir Robin Danvers Penrose; 2 Bt (UK 1959), of Bassishaw Ward, City of London, GBE (1976), RD (1965); s of Sir (Sydney) Harold Gillett, 1 Bt, MC, FCA (d 1976; Lord Mayor London 1958–59), and Audrey Isabel Penrose (d 1962), da of late Capt Edgar Penrose Mark-Wardlaw; *b* 9 November 1925; *Educ* Hill Crest Sch, Pangbourne NC; *m* 1, 22 Sept 1950, Elizabeth Marion Grace (d 1997), er da of late John Findlay, JP, of Busby House, Lanarks; 2 s (Nicholas, Christopher Gillett, *qv*); m 2, 8 July 2000, Alwyne Winifred, wid of His Hon Judge Albert Edward Cox; *Heir* s, Nicholas Gillett; *Career* Canadian Pacific Steamships Ltd: cadet 1943–45, master mariner 1951–, staff cdr 1957–60; dir: Wigham Poland Home Ltd, Wigham Poland Management Services Ltd 1965–86; chm St Katharine Haven Ltd 1990–93, conslt Sedgwick Insurance Brokers 1987–89; underwriting memb Lloyd's 1965–2005, common councilman for Ward of Bassishaw 1965–69 (Alderman 1969–96), sheriff City of London 1973–74 (HM Lt 1975, Lord Mayor 1976–77); RLSS: UK pres 1979–82, dep Cwlth pres 1982–96; vice-chm PLA 1979–84, er brother Trinity House 1978 (yr brother 1973–78), fell and fndr memb Nautical Inst, tstee Nat Maritime Museum 1982–92, pres Inst of Admin Mgmnt 1980–84; vice-pres: City of London Red Cross, St John Ambulance, City of London Outward Bound Assoc, King George's Fund for Sailors 1993–; Maritime Volunteer Service: chm Fundraising & PR Ctee 1996–, vice-chm Cncl 1997, chm Cncl 1998–2001, govr 2001–; lay patron Missions to Seafarers, churchwarden St Lawrence Jewry-next-Guildhall 1969–, former tstee St Paul's Cathedral Tst; Hon Co of Master Mariners: memb 1962–, warden 1971–85, master 1979–80; Hon Cdr RNR; Gentleman Usher of the Purple Rod 1985–2000; Knight of Justice St John Ambulance; Hon DSc City of London Univ 1976 (chllr 1976–77); FRCM 1991 (memb Cncl); Offr Order of Leopard (Zaïre) 1974, Cdr Order of Dannebrog 1974, Order of Johan Sedia Mahkota (Malaysia) 1974, Grand Cross Municipal OM (Lima) 1977, Gold medal Admin Mgmnt Soc (USA) 1983; KStJ 1976; *Publications* A Fish out of Water (2001), Dogwatch Doggerel (2004); *Recreations* sailing; *Clubs* City Livery, Guildhall, City Livery Yacht (Adm), St Katharine Yacht (Adm), hon life memb Deauville Yacht; *Style—* Sir Robin Gillett, Bt, GBE, RD

GILLFORD, Lord; Patrick James Meade; o s and h of 7 Earl of Clanwilliam, *qv*; *b* 28 December 1960; *Educ* Eton, RMA Sandhurst; *m* 1989 (m dis 1992), Serena Emily, da of Lt-Col Brian Lockhart; 1 da (Hon Tamara Louise (Meade) b 1990); m 2, 1995, Cara, da of Paul de la Peña, of Elmley Castle, Pershore, Worcs; 1 s (Hon John Maximillian b 1998), 1 da (Hon Natalya Katherine Sophia b 1999); *Career* Coldstream Gds 1979–83, Hanson plc 1983–90, seconded to The Rt Hon Douglas Hurd, *qv*, 1985–86, Ian Greer Associates 1990–93, md Westminster Policy Partnership public affrs conslts 1993–96, chm The Policy Partnership 1996–; cncllr Royal Borough of Kensington and Chelsea 1990–98 (chm Traffic and Highways); dir Br Sch of Osteopathy 1997–99, chm Cleveland Bridge 2001–04, dir Polyus Gold 2006–, dir Cedar Ptnrs 2006–; fell Br American Project 1999; *Recreations* arabic, golf, skydiving, sub-aqua, helicopter flying; *Clubs* Turf, Pratt's, Mill Reef (Antigua), New Zealand Golf; *Style—* Lord Gillford; ✉ The Policy Partnership Ltd, 51 Causton Street, London SW1P 4AT (tel 020 7976 5555, fax 020 7976 5353, e-mail pgillford@policypartnership.co.uk)

GILLHAM, Ian Robert; s of William Robert Gillham (d 1987), and Hilda Ivy Gillham (d 1966); *b* 18 January 1939; *Educ* Eltham Coll, Univ of Leeds (BA); *m* 1967, Pamela Mary, da of Arthur Robert Hill; 1 s (Andrew Robert b 7 Jan 1972), 1 da (Catherine Elizabeth b 22 April 1975); *Career* BBC: scriptwriter 1966–73, organiser Italian progs 1973–75, asst head of central talks and features 1975–77, asst head of Eng World Serv 1977–84, head of prodns World Serv 1984–90, head of overseas admin 1990–94, chief advsr (Directorate) World Serv 1995–99; chm St Helena Economic Forum (UK Focus Gp) 1998–2002, exec dir Cwlth Journalists Assoc 2000–03; *Recreations* singing, reading, walking; *Style—* Ian Gillham, Esq; ✉ iangillham@yahoo.co.uk

GILLHAM, Paul Maurice; s of Gerald Albert Gillham, and Doris, *née* Kinsey; *b* 26 November 1931; *Educ* RCM, GSM (LGSM), Christ's Coll Cambridge (MA); *m* 3 Sept 1960, Jane Marion, da of Sir George Pickering (d 1982); 1 da (Carola b 7 July 1963), 2 s (Adam b 27 Dec 1965, Dan b 13 April 1968); *Career* chm: Keith Prowse Group 1970–80, St Giles Properties Ltd 1980–, Patent Developments International Ltd 1980–, Actonbarn Ltd 1983–92, Gillham Hayward Ltd 1995–; pres Accusphyg LLC (USA) 1998–; dir: Wren Underwriting Agencies Ltd 1993–97, Daisy Chain (Hair and Beauty) Ltd 1997–, Cathedral Capital plc 1997–; chm LPO Cncl 1983–87; *Recreations* playing cello and piano, walking; *Style—* Paul Gillham, Esq; ✉ Patent Developments International Ltd, Edmonds Farmhouse, Gomshall, Guildford, Surrey GU5 9LQ (tel and fax 01483 202299)

GILLIAM, Terry Vance; s of James Hall Gilliam, and Beatrice, *née* Vance; *b* 22 November 1940; *Educ* Occidental Coll (BA); *m* 1973, Maggie Weston; 1 s (Harry Thunder), 2 da (Amy Rainbow, Holly Dubois); *Career* actor, director, writer, animator; assoc ed Help! magazine 1962–64, freelance illustrator 1964–65, advertising copywriter and art dir 1966–67; exec prodr Complete Waste of Time (Monty Python CD-Rom) 1995; contrib to Spellbound Hayward Gallery 1996; visiting prof RCA 1997; govr BFI 1997–; Hon DFA: Occidental Coll 1987, RCA 1989; Hon Dr Wimbledon Sch of Art 2004; *Television* resident cartoonist We Have Ways of Making You Laugh 1968, animator Do Not Adjust Your Set 1968–69, animator, actor and co-writer Monty Python's Flying Circus 1969–76 and 1979; animator: The Marty Feldman Comedy Machine 1971–72, The Do-It-Yourself Film Animation 1974; presenter The Last Machine (BBC series) 1995; *Film* co-writer, actor and animator: And Now For Something Completely Different 1971, Monty Python and The Holy Grail 1974 (also co-dir), Monty Python's Life of Brian 1978, Monty Python Live at The Hollywood Bowl 1982, Monty Python's The Meaning of Life 1983; animator and writer The Miracle of Flight 1974; co-writer/dir: Jabberwocky 1976, Time Bandits (also prodr) 1980, Brazil 1985, The Adventures of Baron Münchhausen 1988, The Fisher King 1991, Twelve Monkeys 1995, Fear & Loathing in Las Vegas 1998, The Brothers Grimm 2005, Tideland 2005; subject of Lost in La Mancha 2002; *Albums* Monty Python's Flying Circus (jtly, 1970), Another Monty Python Record (jtly, 1971), Monty Python's Previous Record (jtly, 1972), The Monty Python Matching Tie and Handkerchief (jtly, 1973), Monty Python Live at Drury Lane (jtly, 1974), Monty Python and the Holy Grail (jtly, 1975), Monty Python Live at City Centre (jtly, 1976), The Monty Python Instant Record Collection (jtly, 1977), Monty Python's Life of Brian (jtly, 1979), Monty Python's Contractual Obligation Album (jtly, 1980), Monty Python Live at the Hollywood Bowl (jtly, 1981), Monty Python's The Meaning of Life (jtly, 1983), Monty Python The Final Rip Off (jtly, 1987), Monty Python Sings (jtly, 1989), Fear & Loathing in Las Vegas (soundtrack, produced jtly, 1998); *Books* The Cocktail People (1966), Monty Python's Big Red Book (jtly, 1977), Monty Python's Papperbok (jtly, 1977), Monty Python and The Holy Grail (jtly, 1977), Monty Python's Life of Brian (jtly, 1979), Animations of Mortality (1979), Time Bandits (jtly, 1981), Monty Python's The Meaning of Life (jtly, 1983), The Adventures of Baron Münchhausen (jtly, 1989), Monty Python's Just the Words (jtly, 1989), Not the Screenplay of Fear & Loathing in Las Vegas (jtly, 1998), Dark Knights and Holy Fools (1998), Gilliam on Gilliam (1999), The Pythons: An Autobiography (2003), Dreams & Nightmares: Terry Gilliam & The Brothers Grimm; *Recreations* sitting extremely still for indeterminate amounts of time; *Style—* Terry Gilliam, Esq; ✉ c/o Jenne Casarotto, National House 60–66 Wardour Street, London W1V 3HP (tel 020 7287 4450, fax 020 7287 9128, e-mail jenne@casarotto.uk.com)

GILLIBRAND, Sydney; CBE (1991); s of Sydney Gillibrand (d 1990), and Maud Gillibrand (d 1994); *b* 2 June 1934; *Educ* Preston GS, Harris Coll Preston, Coll of Aeronautics Cranfield (MSc); *m* 15 May 1960, Angela Ellen, da of Richard Williams (d 1982); 3 s (Paul b 1964, Simon b 1965, Jonathan b 1969); *Career* English Electric: apprentice 1950, chief stress engr 1966, works mangr Preston 1974; BAC (Preston) Ltd 1974–78 (gen mangr mfrg, special dir, dir mfrg Mil Aircraft Div); British Aerospace Aircraft Gp: dep md Warton Div 1981, divnl md Kingston/Brough Div 1983, divnl md Weybridge Div 1984; British Aerospace plc: md Civil Aircraft Div 1986–88, gp dir 1987–95, chm BAe Inc 1988–90, chm BAe (Commercial Aircraft) Ltd 1988–92, chm BAe (Dynamics) Ltd 1990–92, chm Royal Ordance plc 1990–92, chm BAe (Consultancy) Ltd 1990–95, chm BAe (Liverpool Airport) Ltd 1990–95, gp vice-chm 1992–95, ret from BAe 1995; chm TAG Aviation (UK) Ltd 1999–; non-exec dir: AMEC plc 1995– (chm 1997–2004), LucasVarity plc 1996–99, ICL plc 1996–2002, Messier Dowty Int Ltd 1998–2004, PowerGen plc 1999–2002, TAG Aviation (Holdings) SA; pres: Soc of Br Aerospace Cos 1990–91, European Association of Aerospace Industries (AECMA) 1992–95; FREng 1987, CIM 1992, Hon FRAeS 1994 (FRAeS 1975), Hon FIIE 2000; *Recreations* golf; *Style—* Sydney Gillibrand, Esq, CBE, FREng; ✉ 26A Roland Way, London SW7 3RE

GILLICK, Liam; *b* 13 April 1964; *Educ* Goldsmiths Coll London, Columbia Univ NY; *Career* artist; public cmmns incl: Fort Lauderdale airport, Home Office, Tiscali Sardinia, Rooseum Malmö, Telenor Oslo; *Solo Exhibitions* incl: 84 Diagrams (Karsten Schubert Ltd London) 1989, McNamara, Hog Bikes and GRSSPR (Air de Paris Nice) 1992, McNamara (Schipper & Krome Köln) 1994, Ibuka! (Part 2) (Kunstlerhaus Stuttgart) 1995, Ibuka! (Part 3) (Basilico Fine Arts NY) 1995, Erasmus is Late v The What If? Scenario (Schipper & Krome Berlin) 1996, The What If? Scenario (Robert Prime London) 1996, Discussion Island (Basilico Fine Arts NY) 1997, Discussion Island - A What If? Scenario Report (Kunstverein Ludwigsburg) 1997, McNamara Papers, Erasmus and Ibuka Realisations, The What If? Scenarios (Le Consortium Dijon) 1997, Reclutamento! (Emi Fontana Milan) 1997, Kunstverein Hamburg 1998, Up on the twenty-second floor (Air de Paris Paris) 1998, Big Conference Center (Orchard Gallery Derry) 1998, Robert Prime London 1998, Révision: Liam Gillick (Villa Arson Nice) 1998, When do we need more tractors? (Schipper & Krome Berlin) 1998, Kunsthaus Glarus 1999, David (Frankfurter Kunstverein Frankfurt) 1999, Rüdiger Schöttle Munich 1999 and 2002, Schipper& Krome Berlin 2000, Consultation Filter (Westfällischer Kunstverein Münster) 2000, Woody (CCA Kitakyshu) 2000, Literally No Place (Air de Paris Paris) 2000, Renovation Filter, Recent Past and Near Future (Arnolfini Bristol) 2000, Casey Kaplan NY 2000, Firststepcousinbarprize (Hauser & Wirth & Presenhuber Zurich) 2001, Corvi-Mora London 2001, Annlee You Proposes (Tate Britain London) 2001, Dedalic Convention (Salzburg Kunstverein) 2001, The Wood Way (Whitechapel Gallery London) 2002, Light Technique (Galerie Meyer Kainer Vienna) 2002, Hills and Trays and... (Schipper & Krome Berlin) 2003, ...Punctuated Everydays (Max Hetzler Berlin) 2003; *Group Exhibitions* incl: No Man's Time (CNAC Villa Arson Nice) 1991, Molteplici Culture (Folklore Museum Rome) 1992, Lying on top of a building the clouds look no nearer than they had when I was lying in the street (Monika Sprüth Köln, Esther Schipper Köln and Le Case d'Arte Milan) 1992, 12 British Artists (Barbara Gladstone and Stein Gladstone NY) 1992, Travelogue (Hochschule für Angewandte Kunst Vienna) 1992, Wonderful Life (Lisson Gallery London) 1993, Backstage (Kunstverein Hamburg) 1993, Surface de Réparations (FRAC Bourgogne Dijon) 1994, Public Domain (Centro' Santa Monica Barcelona) 1994, WM/Karaoke (Portikus Frankfurt) 1994, Lost Paradise (Kunstraum Vienna) 1994, The Institute of Cultural Anxiety (ICA London) 1994, The Moral Maze (Le Consortium Dijon) 1995, Collection fin XXème (FRAC Poitou Charentes Angouleme) 1995, Ideal Standard Summertime (Lisson Gallery London) 1995, New British Art (Museum Sztuki Lodz) 1995, Brilliant (Walker Art Center Minneapolis) 1995, Traffic (CPAC Bordeaux) 1996, Everyday Holiday (Le Magasin Grenoble) 1996, Der Umbau Raum (Kunstlerhaus Stuttgart) 1996, Nach Weimar (Landesmuseum Weimar) 1996, How Will We Behave? (Robert Prime London) 1996, Life/Live (Musée d'Art Moderne de la Ville de Paris) 1996, Such is Life (Serpentine London, Palais des Beaux Arts Brussels and Herzliya Museum of Art) 1996, Enter: audience, artist, institution (Kunstmuseum Luzern) 1997, Moment Ginza (Le Magasin Grenoble) 1997, documenta X (Kassel) 1997, Enterprise (ICA Boston) 1997, Robert Prime London 1997, Ireland and Europe (Sculptors Soc of Ireland Dublin) 1997, Hospital (Galerie Max Hetzler Berlin) 1997, Kunst...Arbeit (SudWest LB Stuttgart) 1997, Maxwell's Demon (Margo Leavin LA) 1997, Fast Forward (Kunstverein Hamburg) 1998, A to Z (The Approach London) 1998, Construction Drawings (PS1 NY) 1998, Ingelnook (Feigen Contemporary NY) 1998, Entropy (Ludwigforum Aachen) 1998, Places to Stay 4 P(rinted) M(atter) (Buro Friedrich Berlin) 1998, Weather Everything (Galerie für Zietgenössische Kunst Leipzig) 1998, Minimal-Maximal (Neues Museum Weserburg Bremen, Kunsthalle Baden-Baden and CGAC Santiago de Compostela) 1998, Dijon/Le Consortium.coll (Centre Georges Pompidou Paris) 1998, Projections (de Appel Amsterdam) 1998, 1+3+4x1 (Galerie für Zietgenössische Kunst Leipzig) 1998, Continued Investigation of the Relevance of Abstraction (Andrea Rosen Gallery NY) 1999, Laboratorium (Antwerpen Open Antwerp) 1999, Get Together/Art As Teamwork (Kunsthalle Vienna) 1999, 29th Int Film Festival Rotterdam 2000, Continuum 001 (CCA Glasgow) 2000, Media City 2000 Seoul 2000, British Art Show 5 (touring exhbn) 2000, What If/Tänk Om (Moderna Museet Stockholm) 2000, Paula Cooper Gallery NY 2000, Intelligence (Tate Britain London) 2000, Vicinato 2 (Neuggerreimschneider Berlin) 2000, Protest and Survive (Whitechapel Gallery London) 2000, Aussendienst (Kunstverein Hamburg) 2000, Casa Ideal (Museo Alejandro Otero Caracas) 2000, More Shows About Building and Food (Lisbon) 2000, Century City (Tate Modern London) 2001, There's gonna be some trouble, a whole house will need rebuilding (Rooseum Malmö) 2001, Berline Biennale (Kunst Werk Berlin) 2001, Collaborations with Parkett: 1984 to now (MOMA NY) 2001, Biennale de Lyon (Musée d'art contemporain Lyon) 2001, Beautiful Productions: Parkett (Whitechapel Gallery London) 2001, Yokohama 2001 (Yokohama Triennale) 2001, 9e Biennale de l'image en Mouvement (Centre pour l'image contemporaine Saint-Gervais Genève) 2001, Urgent Painting (Musée d'Art moderne de la ville de Paris) 2002, Passenger: The Viewer as Participant (Astrup Fearnley Museum Oslo) 2002, Do It (Museo de Arte Carrillo Gil San Angel) 2002, Art & Economy (Deichtorhallen Hamburg) 2002, Annlee You Proposes (Mamco Genève) 2002, Startkapital (K21 Dusseldorf) 2002, Inframince (Cabinet Gallery London) 2002, Happy Outsiders from Scotland and London (Zachetal Warsaw and Katowice City Gallery) 2002, The Object Sculpture (Henry Moore Inst Leeds) 2002, Without Consent (CAN Neuchatel) 2002, The Movement Began with a Scandal (Lenbachhaus Munich) 2002, Collected Contemporaries (Moderna Museet Stockholm) 2002, No Ghost Just a Shell (Kunsthalle Zurich and San Francisco MOMA) 2002, The Unique Phenomena of a Distance (Magnani London) 2002, The Galleries Show: Contemporary Art in London (Royal Acad of Arts London) 2002, Turner Prize Exhbn (Tate Britain London) 2002, This Play 31 (La Coleccion Jumex) 2002, L'image habitable - versions B, C, D, E (Mamco Genève) 2002, Ill Communication (DCA Dundee) 2003, Animations (Kunstwerk Berlin) 2003, The Air is Blue (Barragan House Mexico City) 2003, The Moderns (Castello di Rivoli Torino) 2003, Cool Luster (Collection Lambert Avignon) 2003, 25th Int Biennial of Graphic Arts Ljubljana 2003, Utopia Station (Venice Biennale) 2003; *Work in Public Collections* incl: Tate Britain London, Guggenheim NY, Fondation National d'art contemporain Paris, Arts Cncl of GB, MAK Vienna; *Style*— Liam Gillick, Esq

GILLIE, Dr Oliver John; s of John Calder Gillie, of Tynemouth, Northumberland, and Ann, *née* Philipson; *b* 31 October 1937; *Educ* Bootham Sch York, Univ of Edinburgh (BSc, PhD), Stanford Univ; *m* 3 Dec 1969 (m dis 1988), Louise, da of Col Phillip Panton; 2 da (Lucinda Kathrine b 1970, Juliet Ann b 1972); m 2, 2 Oct 1999, Jan, da of Leo Thompson; 2 s (Calder Thompson b 1994, Sholto Douglas b 1997); *Career* lectr in genetics Univ of Edinburgh 1961–65, Nat Inst for Medical Research Mill Hill 1965–68, IPC Magazines 1968–70, Haymarket Publishing 1970–72, med corr The Sunday Times 1972–86; The Independent: med ed 1986–89, special corr 1989–94; freelance journalist 1994–, fndr Health Research Forum 2004; *Books* incl: The Sunday Times Book of Body Maintenance (jtly, 1978), The Sunday Times Guide to the World's Best Food (jtly, 1981), The Sunday Times Self-Help Directory (jtly, 1982), The ABC Diet and Bodyplan (jtly, 1984), Regaining Potency (1995), Escape from Pain (1997), Food for Life (1999), Sunlight Robbery (2004), Vitamin D, Sunlight and Health (2006); *Recreations* sailing, climbing Munros; *Clubs* RSM; *Style*— Dr Oliver Gillie; ✉ 68 Whitehall Park, London N19 3TN (tel 020 7561 9677, website www.healthresearchforum.org.uk)

GILLIES, Prof William; s of Iain Gillies (d 1989), of Oban, and Mary Kyle, *née* Cathie; *b* 15 September 1942; *Educ* Oban HS, Univ of Edinburgh (MA), Univ of Oxford (MA); *m* 24 June 1972, Valerie Roselyn Anna, da of Peter John Simmons, of Edinburgh; 1 s ((John) Lachlan b 1973), 2 da (Maeve b 1974, Mairi b 1982); *Career* Dublin Inst for Advanced Studies 1969–70, prof of Celtic Univ of Edinburgh 1979– (lectr 1970–79); dir: Scottish Language Dictionaries Ltd 2001–; Hon DLitt Univ of Ulster 2006; FSA Scot 1975, FRSE 1990, FRHistS 2002; *Books* Criticism and Prose Writings of Sorley Maclean (ed, 1985), Gaelic and Scotland (ed, 1989), Survey of the Gaelic Dialects of Scotland (gen ed, 1994–97), Celtic Connections 1 (ed, 1999), Celtic Connections 2 (ed, 2005); *Style*— Prof William Gillies, FRSE; ✉ 67 Braid Avenue, Edinburgh EH10 6ED (tel 0131 447 2876); University of Edinburgh, 19–20 George Square, Edinburgh EH8 9LD (tel 0131 650 3621, fax 0131 650 3626, e-mail w.gillies@ed.ac.uk)

GILLIGAN, Andrew Paul; s of Kevin Anthony Gilligan, and Ann Elizabeth *née* Roberts; *Educ* Grey Court Sch, Richmond & Kingston Coll of FE, St John's Coll Cambridge; *Career* journalist; Cambridge Evening News 1994–95, foreign desk Sunday Telegraph 1995, def corr Sunday Telegraph 1995–99, def and dip corr Today Prog BBC Radio 4 1999–2004, currently columnist Evening Standard; MRUSI, MRAeS; *Recreations* hill walking, architecture, riding on buses; *Style*— Andrew Gilligan, Esq

GILLIGAN, Prof Christopher Aidan; s of William Christopher Gilligan (d 1995), and Kathleen Mary, *née* Doyle (d 2003); *b* 9 January 1953, New Ross, Ireland; *Educ* Keble Coll Oxford (MA), Wolfson Coll Oxford (DPhil), Univ of Cambridge (MA, ScD); *m* 21 Dec 1974, Joan Margaret, *née* Flood; 3 da (Clare Siobhan b 20 April 1978, Helen Mairead b 19 March 1984, Elizabeth Anne b 30 April 1987), 1 s (Richard Aidan John b 16 April 1980); *Career* Univ of Cambridge: demonstrator Dept of Applied Biology 1977–82, lectr Dept of Applied Biology 1982–89, lectr Dept of Plant Sciences 1989–95, fell King's Coll 1988– (professorial fell 1999), reader in mathematical biology Dept of Plant Sciences 1995–99, prof of mathematical biology Dept of Plant Sciences 1999–; visiting prof Dept of Botany and Plant Pathology Colorado State Univ 1982, research fell Rothamsted Research 1998–2006, sr research fell Royal Soc Leverhulme Tst 1998–99, professorial res fell BBSRC 2005–; memb: Cncl Nat Inst Agric Botany 1985–91, Governing Body Silsoe Res Inst 1998–2006, Cncl BBSRC 2003– (memb Strategy Bd 2005–, chm Crop Science Review 2003–04), Advsy Ctee on Forest Res Forestry Cmmn 2006–; advsr: Scottish Exec Environment and Rural Affrs Dept (SEERAD) 1998–2003, Inst Nat de la Recherche Agronomique (INRA) France 2003–05 (chair Cmmn d'Evaluation on Plant Health and Environment 2003); pres Br Soc for Plant Pathology 2001, hon fell American Phytopathological Soc 2005; FRSS 1995; *Publications* Mathematical Modelling of Crop Disease (ed, 1985); numerous articles on botanical epidemiology, modelling in biology in mathematical and biology jls; *Recreations* family, running, reading, travel; *Style*— Prof Christopher Gilligan; ✉ Department of Plant Sciences, University of Cambridge, Downing Site, Cambridge CB2 3EA (tel 01223 333900, fax 01223 333953, e-mail cag1@cam.ac.uk)

G

GILLIGAN, Timothy Joseph (Tim); OBE (1992), ERD (1989), DL (Herts 1987); s of Timothy Gilligan (d 1928), of Rosscommon, Ireland, and Mary, *née* Greevy (d 1924); *b* 18 April 1918; *Educ* Handsworth Tech Coll Birmingham; *m* 1944, Hazel (Bunty), da of William Ariel Farmer; 2 s (Simon, Peter), 2 da (Anita, Rosemary); *Career* Maj RASC WWII, served BEF France, ME and N Africa, Germany (despatches 1944 and 1945) 1939–46; exec offr (1 sec grade) FO (German Section) 1946–53; sales and mgmnt Dictaphone Co Ltd and WH Smith & Sons 1953–63; chm Pitney Bowes plc 1983–93 (joined 1963, chief exec 1967); fndr chm Conservation Fndn 1982–86; chm: The Tree Cncl 1983–85, Herts Groundwork Tst 1984–89, Shenley Park Tst 1990–98, Ridgehill Housing Assoc 1994–97; Hertsmere BC: memb 1983–91, mayor 1990–91; Hon DLitt Univ of Herts 2002; CIMgt 1983, FRSA 1977; KSG 1990; *Recreations* the countryside and environment; *Style*— Tim Gilligan, Esq, OBE, ERD, DL; ✉ The White Cottage, Mimms Lane, Shenley, Radlett, Hertfordshire WD7 9AP (tel 01923 857402, fax 01923 857307)

GILLILAND, Alan Howard; s of Wilfrid Howard Gilliland (d 1986), and Mary, *née* Miller; *b* 7 January 1949; *Educ* Bedford Sch, PCL, AA Sch of Architecture; *m* 31 Oct 1975, Pauline, *née* Howkins; 5 s (Benjamin b 30 Jan 1976, Robert b 12 Dec 1980, Alexander b 4 Feb 1983, Oliver b 29 Jan 1985, Jack b 4 June 1988), 1 da (Emily b 24 Sept 1977); *Career* press photographer Evening Despatch Darlington 1979–86; editorial graphic artist: The Northern Echo 1986, London Daily News 1986–87; Daily and Sunday Telegraph: joined 1987, head Graphics Dept 1989–2005, graphics ed 1992–2005; currently prop: Raven's Quill Ltd, Alan Gililand Graphics, Straight-Taking Photgraphy; Graphic Artist of the Year Br Press Awards 1988 and 1989 (commended 1990), Linotype Award for text and graphics (for Daily Telegraph) Newspaper Industry Awards 1990, Silver award for breaking news informational graphic Soc of News Design US 1989 (2 awards of excellence 1990, 1991, 1994, 1997, 1998 and 1999), jt winner Graphic Artist of the Year Br Press Awards 1991, highly commended Image of the Year Br Press Awards 1994, Team of the Year (for the war in Iraq) Br Press Awards 2004; *Recreations* real tennis, walking, cycling; *Style*— Alan Gilliland, Esq; ✉ Raven's Quill Limited, 63 High Street, Billingshurst, West Sussex RH14 9QP (website www.ravensquill.com); Alan Gilliland Graphics (website www.alangilliland.com); Straight-Taking Photography (website www.straight-taking.co.uk)

GILLILAND, Elsie; da of James Lauder McCully (d 1985), of Belfast, and Mary Agnes, *née* Calvert (d 1991); *b* 6 December 1937; *Educ* Richmond Lodge, Queen's Univ Belfast (LLB); *m* 22 July 1961, His Hon Judge James Andrew David Gilliland, QC; 2 s (Jeremy b 1964, Jonathan b 1967); *Career* slr in private practice; pt/t chm VAT and Duties Tbnls; *Recreations* opera, painting; *Style*— Mrs Elsie Gilliland; ✉ The Shieling, Highfield, Prestbury, Cheshire SK10 4DA (tel 01625 828029); 30 Swedish Quays, London SE16 (tel 020 7232 0144); Towns Needham, Kingsgate (2nd Floor), 51–53 South King Street, Manchester M2 6DE

GILLINGS, Ven Richard John; s of John Albert Gillings, MBE, (d 2000), and Constance Ford, *née* Weatherill (d 1991); *b* 17 September 1945; *Educ* Sale Co GS, St Chad's Coll Durham (BA, Dip Biblical Studies), Lincoln Theol Coll; *m* 22 April 1972, Kathryn Mary, da of Frank George Hill, BEM; 2 da (Elizabeth Anne b 18 Feb 1974, Chloe Amy Rose b 24 Dec 1993), 2 s (Stephen David b 28 Aug 1975, Scott Michael b 21 Nov 1988); *Career* curate St George's Altrincham 1970–75, rector St Thomas' Stockport 1977–83 (priest i/c 1975–77), priest i/c St Peter's Stockport 1978–83, rector of Birkenhead Priory 1983–93, rural dean of Birkenhead 1985–93, hon canon Chester Cathedral 1992–94, vicar St Michael and All Angels Bramhall 1993–2005, archdeacon of Macclesfield 1994–; memb Gen Synod C of E 1980–; *Recreations* Rotarian, music, cinema, railways, theatre; *Style*— The Ven the Archdeacon of Macclesfield; ✉ The Vicarage, 5 Robins Lane, Bramhall, Stockport, Cheshire SK7 2PE (tel 0161 439 2254)

GILLINGWATER, Richard; *Educ* Univ of Oxford, IMD Lausanne (MBA); *Career* formerly: corporate finance dir Kleinwort Benson, jt head global corporate finance BZW, chm European investment banking Credit Suisse First Boston; fndr chief exec Shareholder Exec Cabinet Office 2003–; chm Faber Music Ltd, dir Faber Music Holdings Ltd; non-exec dir: Kidde plc 2004–05, Qinetiq 2004–06, Tomkins plc 2005–, Debenhams plc 2006–, Scottish & Southern Energy plc 2007–, Rights Worldwide; memb Advsy Bd St Edmund Hall Oxford; *Style*— Richard Gillingwater, Esq

GILLIONS, Paul; s of William Stanley Gillions (d 1972), and Marie Lilian, *née* Crawley; *b* 15 May 1950; *Educ* St Albans GS for Boys; *m* 5 June 1976, Grace Kathleen, da of David Adam Smith, and Kathleen Iris, *née* Towers; 2 da (Jennie b 1980, Laura b 1983); *Career* int PR conslt; Burson-Marsteller Ltd: main bd dir 1987–93, dir of issues mgmnt Burson-Marsteller Europe, memb Int Bd 1992–93; sr vice-pres and dir public policy and issues mgmnt Fleishman-Hillard 1993–96, sr vice-pres int public policy Fleishman-Hillard (Europe and USA) 1996–98, int md Burson-Marsteller 1998–2000; int conslt on public policy and issues mgmnt 2001–; MInstD, MCIPR; FRSA; *Recreations* rugby, cycling, boating; *Style*— Paul Gillions, Esq; ✉ 3 Whitehurst Avenue, Hitchin, Hertfordshire SG5 1SR (tel 01462 621453, e-mail paulgillions@aol.com)

GILLMAN, Tricia; da of Dr Theodore Gillman (d 1971), of Cambridge, and Selma, *née* Cohen (d 1993); *b* 9 November 1951; *Educ* Univ of Leeds (BA), Univ of Newcastle upon Tyne (MFA); *m* 1989, Alexander Ramsay, s of Frank Raymond Faber Ramsay (d 1977); 1 s (Thomas Jesmond b 3 Jan 1990); *Career* artist; teacher: various posts 1977–83 (Newcastle Poly, Univ of Leeds, Ravensbourne Sch of Art, Lanchester Poly, Birmingham Poly, Edinburgh Sch of Art, Univ of Reading, Chelsea Sch of Art), St Martin's Sch of Art 1983–99, RCA 1988–95; *Solo Exhibitions* Parkinson Gallery Leeds 1978, Sunderland Arts Centre 1982, Arnolfini Gallery Bristol 1985, Benjamin Rhodes Gallery London 1985, 1987 and 1993, Laing Gallery Newcastle (touring) 1989–90, Gardner Centre Brighton 1994, Art

Space Gallery London 1996, Jill George Gallery London 1997, 1999 and 2002; *Group Exhibitions* incl: Northern Art Assoc Exhibition (Shipley Art Gallery and tour) 1978, St Martin's Painters (Seven Dial Gallery) 1982, Summer Show II (Serpentine Gallery) 1982, John Moores Liverpool Exhibition XIV (Walker Art Gallery) 1985, Thirty London Artists (Royal Acad of Art) 1985, Malaysian and British Exhibition Paintings and Prints (National Art Gallery, Kuala Lumpur, Singapore and Hong Kong) 1986, Britain in Vienna (Kunsthaus Vienna) 1986, London Group (RCA and tour) 1987, Summer Show (Royal Acad of Art) 1987 and 2003, John Moores Exhibition (Liverpool) 1989, Tricia Gillman and Richard Gorman: Small Paintings (Benjamin Rhodes Gallery) 1989, Homage to the Square (Flaxman Gallery) 1990, Works on Paper (Benjamin Rhodes Gallery) 1990, Forces of Nature (Manchester City Art Gallery and tour) 1990, Br Cncl and Royal Coll of Art touring exhibition of Eastern Europe 1990, Art '91 (London Contemporary Art Fair Olympia) 1991, Peter Stuyvesant Touring Exhibition (Zaragoza and Seville, Spain) 1991, The Discerning Eye (Mall Galleries) 1991, John Moores Exhibition (Liverpool) 1991, The New Patrons (Christie's London) 1992, 20th Century Women's Art (New Hall Cambridge) 1992, 3 Ways (RCA touring exhbn to Central Europe) 1992, London Group (Morley Coll London) 1992, Chicago Art Fair 1993, 3 Artists (Benjamin Rhodes Gallery) 1994, Harlech Biennale (Wales) 1994, Summer Show (RA) 1994, Harlech Biennale (Wales) 1995, Solo Show (Art Space Gallery) 1996, 20th Century Art Fair (London) 1996, 1997, 1998 and 1999, Solo Show (Gil George Gallery) 1997, Art '97 (Business Design Centre London) 1997, Hunting Group Art Prize (travelling show) 1997, Critic's Choice (New Academy Gallery) 1997, Summer Show (Royal Acad of Arts) 1997, 3x3 (Art Space Gallery) 1997, Art '98 (Business Design Centre London) 1998, Art '99 (Business Design Centre London) 1999, Santa Fe Art Fair 1999, 2K, 2K (Jill George Gallery London) 2000, Art 2000 (Business Design Centre London) 2000, 20/21 British Art Fair (RCA) 2000, Cheltenham International Drawing Exhibition 2000, Hunting Group Art Prize (RCA) 2000, Toronto International Art Fair 2000 and 2001, Palm Springs International Art Fair 2001, Art Palm Beach 2002, Art 2002 (Business Design Centre London) 2002, Roya Acad Summer Exhibition (Royal Acad of Arts London) 2003 (nominated for Delenney Prize) and 2004, Walk Gallery London 2004, Bankside Gallery London 2004; *Work in Collections* public collections: Contemporary Arts Soc, Univ of Leeds, Television South West, The Stuyvesant Fndn, Stanhope Properties plc, Herbert Art Gallery Coventry, Unilever plc; private collections in: Britain, Belgium, Holland, Japan, Thailand, USA, Italy; *Style*— Ms Tricia Gillman; ✉ c/o Jill George Gallery, 38 Lexington Street, Soho, London W1R 3HR (tel 020 7439 7319, fax 020 7287 0478)

GILLMER, Dr Michael David George; s of George Ernest Gillmer, of Pretoria, South Africa (d 1989), and (Adriana Margaretha) Janet, *née* Scholtz (d 1984); *b* 17 January 1945; *Educ* St Benedict's Sch Ealing, King's Coll Hosp (MA, MD); *m* 1, 17 Aug 1968 (m dis 1998), Janet Yvonne, da of Leslie Francis Davis (d 1987); 1 da (Charlotte Jane b 1973), 1 s (David Michael b 1978); m 2, 4 March 1999, Pauline Anne, da of Dennis William Hurley; *Career* clinical reader in obstetrics and gynaecology Nuffield Dept Univ of Oxford 1979–84, conslt obstetrician and gynaecologist John Radcliffe Hosp Oxford 1984–; author of many publications on diabetes, nutrition in pregnancy and contraception; hon memb Green Coll Oxford; memb Gynaecological Visiting Soc of GB and I; FRCOG 1984; *Books* 100 Cases For Students of Medicine (1979), Nutrition in Pregnancy (1982), 100 Case Histories in Obstetrics and Gynaecology (1991); *Recreations* scuba diving, photography, music; *Style*— Dr Michael Gillmer; ✉ Women's Centre, John Radcliffe Hospital, Headington, Oxford OX3 9DU (tel 01865 221624)

GILLON, Dr John (Jack); s of William Millar Gillon, of Shotts, and Mary, *née* Wood; *b* 24 April 1949; *Educ* Wishaw HS, Univ of Edinburgh (MB ChB, MD); *m* m 1, 2 Sept 1972 (m dis 1999), Sandria Joy, da of Alexander Headridge, of Byburn, Ecclesmachan; 1 da (Aimée b 1978), 1 s (Andrew b 1981); m 2, Dr Karen Bell, da of David Bell, of Drongan, Ayrshire; 1 da (Freya b 1996); *Career* lectr dept of med and gastro-intestinal unit Western Gen Hosp Edinburgh 1977–84, conslt Blood Transfusion Serv 1985–, clinical dir Blood Donor Serv 2005–; also chef and cookery writer; winner Observer/Mouton-Cadet Cookery Competition 1981; FRCP; *Books* Le Menu Gastronomique (1982), Chambers Scottish Food Book (1989); *Recreations* France, cycling, golf; *Style*— Dr Jack Gillon; ✉ Edinburgh and SE Scotland Blood Transfusion Service, Royal Infirmary, Lauriston Place, Edinburgh EH3 9HB (tel 0131 536 5320, fax 0131 536 5301)

GILLON, Karen MacDonald; MSP; da Edith Turnbull, *née* MacDonald; *b* 18 August 1967; *Educ* Jedburgh GS 1979–85, Univ of Birmingham 1989–91 (Certificate in Youth and Community Studies); *m* 13 March 1999, James Gillon, s of Andrew Gillon; 2 s (James, Matthew); *Career* project worker Terminal One Youth Centre 1991–94, community educn worker North Lanarkshire Cncl 1994–97, PA to Rt Hon Helen Liddell MP 1997–99, MSP (Lab) Clydesdale 1999–; *Recreations* sport, flower arranging, music, cookery; *Style*— Mrs Karen Gillon, MSP; ✉ The Scottish Parliament, Edinburgh EH99 1SP (tel 0131 348 5823, fax 0131 348 6485, e-mail karen.gillon.msp@scottish.parliament.uk)

GILLOTT, Roland Charles Graeme; s of John Arthur Gillott (d 1982), of Northwood, Middx, and Ursula Mary, *née* Bailey (d 1983); *b* 22 August 1947; *Educ* Haileybury; *m* 25 Oct 1975, (Bridget) Rae, da of Lesley Bentley Jones (d 1959), of Northwood, Middx; 2 da (Shanta b 21 April 1978, Lissa b 1 Jan 1981), 1 s (Adrian b 20 Oct 1979); *Career* admitted slr 1972, ptnr Radcliffes (now RadcliffesLeBrasseur) 1979– (managing ptnr 2004–); churchwarden St Michaels and All Angels Amersham 1991–95 and 2001–03; pres Churches on the Hill Amersham (COTHA) 2001–; Liveryman: Worshipful Co of Merchant Taylors 1979, Worshipful Co of Info Technologists 1995; memb Law Soc; *Recreations* walking, photography; *Clubs* MCC, RAC, Travellers, City Livery; *Style*— Roland Gillott, Esq; ✉ RadcliffesLeBrasseur, 5 Great College Street, Westminster, London SW1P 3SJ (tel 020 7227 7261, fax 020 7222 6208, e-mail roland.gillott@rlb-law.com)

GILMORE, David; s of David Gilmore, and Dora, *née* Baker; *b* 7 December 1945; *Educ* Alleyn's Sch Dulwich; *m* 23 Sept 1978, Fiona, da of J P R Mollison; 3 s (Charles b 1982, George b 1985, Edward b 1989); *Career* artistic director; appts incl: Watermill Theatre, Nuffield Theatre Southampton; prodns incl: Nuts (Whitehall), Daisy Pulls it Off, Lend Me a Tenor (both Globe), The Resistible Rise of Arturo Ui, Beyond Reasonable Doubt (both Queen's), The Hired Man (Astoria), Cavalcade (Chichester), Song and Dance (Sydney, Melbourne and Adelaide), Glen Garry Glenross (Brussels), Fatal Attraction (Haymarket), Mandragola (RNT), Casablanca (Whitehall), A Swell Party (Vaudeville), Radio Times (Queen's), Grease (Dominion and Australian Arena Tour), As you Like it (Chicago), Chapter Two (Queen's), Alone Together (Hong Kong and Beijing), Là Haut (Lyon and Paris), Happy Days (Olympic Superdome Sydney), Gasping (Hong Kong), The Jamie Oliver Stage Show (London and Aust), Footloose (Capitol Sydney), Hair (Berlin and Paris); *Recreations* golf, gardening; *Clubs* Garrick; *Style*— David Gilmore, Esq; ✉ 4 Wilton Crescent, Wimbledon, London SW19 3QZ (e-mail dgil2000@btopenworld.com)

GILMORE, Fiona Catherine; da of Robin (Dick) Triefus (d 1983), and Jean Margaret, *née* Herring (da of Alfred Herring, VC); *b* 7 November 1956; *Educ* Queenswood Sch Hatfield (scholar), Univ of Cambridge (MA); *m* 5 May 1979 (m dis 2004), Richard John Maurice Gilmore, s of Richard Thomas Gilmore, of Maldon, Essex; 3 s (Daniel b 1986, Alexander b 1989, Edward b 1993); *Career* Ted Bates Advertising Agency London 1977–78, Benton & Bowles Advertising Agency London 1978–84, md Michael Peters & Ptnrs 1987–90 (devpt dir 1984, mktg dir 1985), md Lewis Moberly 1990–91, fndr ptnr and ceo Springpoint (brand and corp identity positioning and design consultancy) 1991–2003, fndr ptnr and chm Acanchi 2003–; speaker CBI conf 1986; memb: CBI Vision 2010 Gp 1986–87, NEDO Maker User Working Pty 1988, Milk Mktg Bd 1988, GCSE Modern Language Working Pty 1989; govr Centre for Info on Language Teaching and Res 1987, chm Design Effectiveness Awards Scheme 1988–89; non-exec dir RSPB 1994, non-exec memb Bd United Learning Tst 2003–; advsr Lambeth Palace 1992–98, memb Cncl Water Aid 1997–2003; memb RSA; *Books* Brand Warriors (ed, 1997), CBI Growing Business Handbook (contrib, 1997), Warriors on the High Wire (2001), Brand Warriors China (2003); *Recreations* family, skiing, tennis, walking, opera; *Style*— Mrs Fiona Gilmore

GILMORE, Prof Ian Thomas; s of Dr James M Gilmore, of Clevedon, Somerset, and Jean, *née* Drummond; *b* 25 September 1946; *Educ* Royal GS Newcastle upon Tyne, King's Coll Cambridge (MA, MB BCh, MD), St Thomas' Hosp London (Beaney prize in surgery); *m* 18 Jan 1975, Hilary Elizabeth, *née* Douglas; 2 s (Alastair James b 20 March 1979, William Thomas b 15 May 1983), 1 da (Katherine Louise b 21 Jan 1981); *Career* house physician Southampton Gen Hosp 1971–72, house surgn St Thomas' Hosp 1972–73, house physician then SHO in neurology Whittington Hosp 1972–73, SHO Intensive Therapy Unit St Thomas' Hosp 1973, registrar in gen med Worthing Hosp 1973–74; St Thomas' Hosp: registrar in gen med and gastroenterology 1974–75, MRC research fell Gastrointestinal Lab and hon sr med registrar 1976–77; sr med registrar in gen med and gastroenterology Charing Cross Hosp 1978–79 and 1980, MRC travelling fell Univ of Calif San Diego 1979–80; Royal Liverpool and Broadgreen Hosps Liverpool: conslt physician and gastroenterologist 1980–, med dir 1995–98; dir of R&D Royal Liverpool Univ Hosp 1993–95; Univ of Liverpool: hon lectr Dept of Med 1980–98, chm Faculty of Med 1991–92, prof 1999–; chm Standing Liaison Ctee Mersey RHA and Univ of Liverpool 1991–94; visiting prof: Univ of Calif San Diego 1989, Univ of S Carolina 1991; memb: Cncl Br Soc of Gastroenterology 1985–88, Specialist Advsy Ctee in Gastroenterology Jt Ctee for Higher Med Trg 1988– (sec 1989–95); pres RCP 2006– (regnl advsr 1992–, memb Cncl 1993–95, registrar 1999–2004); memb: American Assoc for the Study of Liver Disease, American Gastroenterology Assoc, Assoc of Physicians of GB and I, Br Assoc for the Study of the Liver, Br Soc of Gastroenterology, Euro Assoc for the Study of the Liver, Int Assoc for the Study of the Liver, Int Hepatobiliary Pancreatic Assoc; FRCP 1985; *Books* Gastrointestinal Emergencies (ed with R Shields); author of over 100 original articles, invited reviews and chapters; *Recreations* golf, travel; *Style*— Professor Ian Gilmore; ✉ Birchways, 47 Oldfield Drive, Heswall, Wirral, Merseyside CH60 6SS (tel 0151 342 3264); Royal Liverpool University Hospital, Prescot Street, Liverpool L7 8XP (tel 0151 706 3558)

GILMORE, Margaret; da of Rev Canon Norman Gilmore (d 1996), and Barbara, *née* Elcoat; *b* 9 February 1956, Nqutu, South Africa; *Educ* N London Collegiate Sch, Westfield Coll London (BA); *m* 10 July 1993, Eamonn Matthews; 1 s (Christopher b 21 Jan 1998); *Career* reporter Kensington Post 1977–79, corr IRN 1979–84, reporter BBC NI 1984–85; corr: Newsnight 1986–89, This Week 1989–92, Panorama 1993–95, BBC News 1995–97, Environment BBC News 1997–2000, Home and Legal Affrs BBC News 2000–07; assoc fell RUSI 2007–; TV News Environment Corr of the Year Br Environment and Media Awards 1997; *Recreations* playing the piano, family and friends, supporting Reading FC; *Style*— Mrs Margaret Gilmore; ✉ c/o Knight Ayton Management, 114 St Martin's Lane, London WC2N 4BE (e-mail margaretmgilmore@aol.com)

GILMORE, Owen Jeremy Adrian (Jerry); s of Dr Owen Dermot Gilmore, of Highworth, Wilts, and Carmel, *née* Cantwell; *b* 27 December 1941; *Educ* Beaumont Coll, Bart's Med Coll London (MB BS), Univ of London (MS); *m* 1966 (m dis 1987), Hilary Ann Frances, *née* McGrudden; 4 da (Anna Benedicta Claire b 1967, Deborah Emma Frances b 1968, Katherine Laura Matilda b 1971, Natasha Olivia Polly b 1973), 2 s (Hugh Inigo Jeremy b 1969, Quentin Roderick Zebedee b 1977); 3 subseq da (Georgia Alice Louise b 1990, Octavia Phoebe Hannah b 1993, Chiara Novena Jane b 1995); *Career* conslt surgn i/c breast clinic, groin and hernia clinic 108 Harley St, conslt gen surgn Bart's London 1976–91, conslt i/c Breast Unit Bart's 1981–91, med dir Island Sports Fitness Centre Hook; Begley Prize RCS 1966, Moynihan Prize and Medal Assoc Surgns GB 1975, Hamilton Bailey Prize Int Coll Surgeons 1975, Hunterian prof RCS 1976; fell Inst of Sports Med 1995; LRCP 1966, FRCS 1971 (MRCS 1966), FRCSEd 1971; *Books* Diagnosis and Treatment of Breast Disease, Diagnosis and Treatment of Groin Injuries in Sportsmen (Gilmore's Groin); *Recreations* children, dining, travel, tennis, fishing; *Style*— Jerry Gilmore, Esq; ✉ Whitewater Mill, Hook, Hampshire RG27 9EH (tel 01256 766868, fax 01256 768747, e-mail gilmore@wwmill.co.uk); 108 Harley Street, London W1G 7ET (tel 020 7563 1234, fax 020 7563 1212, e-mail gilmore@108harleyst.co.uk)

GILMORE, Rosalind Edith Jean; CB (1995); da of Sir Robert Brown Fraser, OBE (d 1984), and Betty, *née* Harris (d 1984); *b* 23 March 1937; *Educ* King Alfred Sch London, UCL (BA), Newnham Coll Cambridge (MA); *m* 17 Feb 1962, Brian Terence Gilmore, CB, s of John Henry Gilmore; *Career* HM Treasy: appointed 1960, asst princ 1960–62, asst private sec to Chllr of Exchequer 1962–65, princ 1965, resigned to accompany husb to Washington; exec asst to Econ Dir International Bank for Reconstruction and Development 1966–67; HM Treasy: reinstated 1968, princ private sec to Paymaster Gen 1973, princ private sec to Chllr of Duchy of Lancaster 1974, asst sec 1975, head of Fin Inst Div 1977–80 (Banking Act 1979, Credits Unions Act 1979), press sec to Chllr of Exchequer 1980–82, head of Information 1980–82; gen mangr corp planning Dunlop Ltd 1982–83, dir of mktg National Girobank 1983–86, marketing conslt FI Group plc (Software) 1986–89; memb Fin Servs Act Tbnl 1986–89, full-time chm and first cmmr Building Societies Cmmn 1991–94 (dep chm 1989–91), dir SIB 1993–96, memb Regulatory Bd Lloyds of London 1995–98 (dir of regulation 1995), memb Lloyds Prudential Supervisory Gp 1998–2001; chm: Arrow Broadcasting (CLT subsid) 1994–97, Homeowners Friendly Society Ltd 1996–98; dir: Mercantile Group plc, Mercantile Credit Co Ltd, London and Manchester Group plc 1986–89, BAT Industries plc 1996–98, Zurich Financial Services AG 1998–, TU Fund Managers Ltd 2000–; IWF London: fndr memb 1983, pres 1986–89 and 2001–; vice-pres: Building Socs Assoc 1995–, Int Women's Forum 1997–2001; chm Leadership Fndn Washington DC 2005– (dir 1997–, also ex officio dir Int Women's Forum Washington DC 2005–); cmmr National Lottery 2000–02; memb: Ct Cranfield Univ (formerly Cranfield Inst of Technol) 1992–, Cncl Royal Coll of Music 1997–; dir: Opera North 1993–98, Moorfields Eye Hosp Tst 1994–2000; directing fell St George's House Windsor Castle 1986–89; fell UCL 1988, hon fell Newnham Coll Cambridge 1995 (assoc fell 1986–95); FRSA 1985, CIMgt 1992; *Publications* Mutuality for the Twenty First Century Centre for the Study of Financial Innovation (1998); *Recreations* music, reading, languages, Greece; *Style*— Mrs Rosalind Gilmore, CB; ✉ 3 Clarendon Mews, London W2 2NR (tel and fax 020 7402 8554)

GILMOUR, David Jon; CBE (2003); s of Douglas Graham Gilmour, and (Edith) Sylvia, *née* Wilson; *b* 6 March 1946; *Educ* Perse Sch for Boys, Cambridge Coll of Arts & Technol; *m*; 7 c; *Career* musician and singer; with Pink Floyd 1968–; albums with Pink Floyd incl: Atom Heart Mother (1970), Dark Side of the Moon (1973), The Wall (1979), The Final Cut (1983), A Momentary Lapse of Reason (1987), The Division Bell (1994), Pulse (1995); solo albums: David Gilmour (1978), About Face (1984), In Concert (live, 2002); *Recreations* literature, films, aviation, sailing; *Style*— David Gilmour, Esq, CBE

GILMOUR, (Hon) David Robert; s and h to btcy of Baron Gilmour of Craigmillar, PC (3 Bt, Life Peer), *qv*, *b* 14 November 1952; *Educ* Eton, Balliol Coll Oxford; *m* 1975, Sarah Anne, da of late Michael Bradstock, of Clunas, Nairn; 3 da (Rachel b 1977, Katharine b 1984, Laura b 1985), 1 s (Alexander b 1980); *Career* writer; Alistair Horne fell St Antony's Coll Oxford 1996–97; FRSL; *Books* Dispossessed: The Ordeal of The Palestinians 1917–80 (1980), Lebanon: The Fractured Country (1983), The Transformation of Spain: From Franco to the Constitutional Monarchy (1985), The Last Leopard: A Life of Giuseppe di

Lampedusa (1988), The Hungry Generations (1991), Cities of Spain (1992), Curzon (1994, Duff Cooper Prize), The Long Recessional: The Imperial Life of Rudyard Kipling (2002, Elizabeth Longford Prize), The Ruling Caste: Imperial Lives in the Victorian Raj (2005); *Style*— David Gilmour, FRSL; ✉ 27 Ann Street, Edinburgh EH4 1PL

GILMOUR, Ewen Hamilton; s of Lt Cdr Patrick Dalrymple Gilmour (d 1988), and Lorna Mary, *née* Dore; *b* 16 August 1953; *Educ* Rugby, Downing Coll Cambridge; *m* 3 June 1978, Nicola, da of Maarten Van Mesdag; 3 s (James b 27 Feb 1980, Rowallan b 3 April 1982, Fergus b 4 May 1985), 1 da (Iona b 19 Jan 1990); *Career* CA; KPMG 1974–80, Charterhouse Bank Ltd 1980–93 (dir 1987), Lloyd's of London 1993–95, Murray Lawrence Holdings plc 1995–98, chief exec Chaucer Holdings plc 2004– (dir 1998–), dep chm Lloyd's of London 2006–; FCA 1979 (ACA); *Recreations* cricket, golf, tennis; *Clubs* Invalids, I Zingari, MCC, Butterflies, Armadillos, Stragglers of Asia, Band of Brothers, City of London, Royal Wimbledon Golf; *Style*— Ewen Gilmour, Esq; ✉ 20 Arthur Road, London SW19 7DZ (tel 020 8947 6805); Chaucer Holdings plc, 9 Devonshire Square, Cutlers Gardens, London EC2M 4WL (tel 020 7397 9700, fax 020 7397 9710, e-mail ewen.gilmour@chaucerplc.com)

GILMOUR, His Hon Judge Nigel Benjamin Douglas; QC (1990); s of Benjamin Waterfall Gilmour (d 1967), and Barbara Mary, *née* Till (d 2001); *b* 21 November 1947; *Educ* Tettenhall Coll, Univ of Liverpool (LLB); *m* 1972, Isobel Ann Harborow; 2 da (Katy b 28 Feb 1977, Alison b 1 Oct 1988); *Career* called to the Bar Inner Temple 1970, recorder 1990–, circuit judge (Northern Circuit) 2000–; memb Hon Soc of Inner Temple; *Recreations* wine, gardening; *Style*— His Hon Judge Gilmour, QC; ✉ Queen Elizabeth II Law Courts, Derby Square, Liverpool L2 1XA

GILMOUR, William; s of Gordon Scott Lauder Gilmour (d 1992), and Isabella, *née* Barrowman (d 1990); *b* 26 April 1951; *Educ* Dalziel HS Motherwell, Univ of Strathclyde (BA); *m* 11 Oct 1986, Katherine Margaret, da of Francis Trevor Gatefield; 1 da (Emily Isabella Gatefield b 26 Feb 1992); *Career* trainee accountant Coopers & Lybrand 1971, CA 1974, CA Price Waterhouse Lisbon 1977–79 (LA 1975–77), mangr Audit and Special Projects (Europe) Gulf & Western Corp 1979–80, fin dir Sleepeezee 1980–83, ptnr Price Waterhouse Coopers 1983–2002, global ldr consumer packaged goods IBM 2002–; author of numerous articles on strategy, mgmnt control and IT in consumer products; MICAS 1974, ACA 1989; *Recreations* motor sport, opera, travel; *Style*— William Gilmour, Esq; ✉ IBM, 76 Upper Ground, South Bank, London SE1 9PZ (tel 020 7021 8185, e-mail bill.gilmour@uk.ibm.com)

GILMOUR OF CRAIGMILLAR, Baron (Life Peer UK 1992), of Craigmillar in the District of the City of Edinburgh; Sir Ian Hedworth John Little Gilmour; PC (1973); 3 Bt (UK 1926), of Liberton and Craigmillar, Co Midlothian; s of Sir John Little Gilmour, 2 Bt (d 1977), by his 1 w, Hon Victoria Laura, OBE, TD, *née* Cadogan (d 1991), da of Henry Arthur Cadogan, Viscount Chelsea and gda of 5 Earl Cadogan; *b* 8 July 1926; *Educ* Eton, Balliol Coll Oxford; *m* 10 July 1951, Lady Caroline Margaret Montagu Douglas Scott (d 2004), da of 8 Duke of Buccleuch and Queensberry; 4 s ((Hon) David Robert b 1952, Hon Oliver John b 1953, Hon Christopher Simon b 1956, Hon Andrew James b 1964), 1 da (Hon Jane Victoria (m Hon Peter Pleydell-Bouverie, *qv*) b 1959); *Heir* s, David Gilmour, FRSL, *qv*; *Career* late Grenadier Gds; called to the Bar 1952; ed The Spectator 1954–59; MP (Cons): Norfolk Central 1962–74, Chesham and Amersham 1974–92; Parly under sec MOD 1970–71; min of state: for defence procurement MOD 1971–72, for defence 1972–74; sec of state for defence 1974, chm Cons Research Dept 1974–75, Lord Privy Seal and dep foreign sec 1979–81; Hon Degree Univ of Essex 1995; *Books* The Body Politic (1969), Inside Right - A Study of Conservatism (1977), Britain Can Work (1983), Riot, Risings and Revolution (1992), Dancing with Dogma (1992), Whatever Happened to the Tories (1997), The Making of the Poets, Byron and Shelley (2002); *Style*— The Rt Hon Lord Gilmour of Craigmillar, PC; ✉ The Ferry House, Park Road, Old Isleworth, Middlesex TW7 6BD (tel 020 8560 6769, fax 020 8560 0709)

GILROY, Linda; MP; da of late William Jarvie, and Gwendoline, *née* Gray; *b* 19 July 1949; *Educ* Maynard Sch Exeter, Stirling HS, Univ of Edinburgh (MA), Univ of Strathclyde (postgrad secretarial dip); *m* Benny Gilroy; *Career* dep dir Age Concern Scotland 1972–79, regnl mangr Gas Consumers' Cncl 1986–96 (regnl sec 1979–86); MP (Lab/Co-op) Plymouth Sutton 1997–; memb European Select Ctee 1997–98, PPS to Rt Hon Nick Raynsford, MP, *qv* 2001–05, memb Defence Ctee, memb Science and technol Ctee, memb OSCE; memb Inst of Trading Standards Administration 1995 (assoc 1991), fndr memb Plymouth Energy Advice Centre; *Recreations* swimming, walking, keep fit; *Style*— Mrs Linda Gilroy, MP; ✉ House of Commons, London SW1A 0AA (tel 020 7219 4746, website www.lindagilroy.org.uk)

GIMBLETT, Richard; s of Frederick Gareth Robert Gimblett, of Yorks, and Margaret, *née* Cornford; *b* 7 April 1959, London; *Educ* Desborough Comp Sch Maidenhead, Jesus Coll Oxford (BA), Inns of Court Sch of Law; *m* 21 March 1987, Ruth, *née* Dyson; 1 s (Alexander James Leathley b 12 Aug 1988), 1 da (Hannah Catherine Elizabeth b 4 July 1990); *Career* called to the Bar 1982, admitted slr 1990; private practice barrister 1983–84, legal advsr CAA 1985–88, barr and slr Norton Rose 1988–94, Barlow, Lyde & Gilbert: slr 1994–1996, ptnr 1996–; memb Law Soc 1990; dir FTO Tst Fund Ltd 1994–; *Recreations* golf, hill running, reading; *Style*— Richard Gimblett, Esq; ✉ Barlow, Lyde & Gilbert, Beaufort House, 15 St Botolph Street, London EC3A 7NJ (tel 0207 643 8069, e-mail rgimblett@blg.co.uk)

GINSBERG, Dr Lionel; s of Henry Ginsberg (d 1989), of London, and Rosalind, *née* Veltman; *b* 18 April 1955; *Educ* Haberdashers' Aske's, Middx Hosp Med Sch Univ of London (BSc, PhD, MB BS, Betuel prize); *m* m 1, 8 June 1980, Dr Andrea Marguerite Cobon (d 1995), da of Herbert Frederick Cobon (d 2006); 2 da (Amelia b 16 Feb 1984, Constance May b 1 June 1989), 2 s (Louis b 12 July 1985 d 26 Nov 1985, Tobias b 11 Jan 1988); m 2, 4 April 1998, Sue, *née* Byford; *Career* MRC res student Dept of Biology as Applied to Med Middx Hosp Med Sch 1976–79, visiting specialist Nat Insts of Health Bethesda Maryland USA 1981, house physician The Middx Hosp 1982–83, house surgn N Middx Hosp 1983; SHO: in gen med (endocrinology and metabolism) Hammersmith Hosp 1983–84, in neurology The Nat Hosp Queen Square 1984; resident med offr in cardiology Nat Heart Hosp 1984–85, locum med registrar St Mary's Hosp Paddington 1985; registrar: in med (endocrinology) Hammersmith Hosp 1985, in neurology Royal Free Hosp 1985–87, in neurology The Nat Hosps 1987–88; visiting scientist Nat Insts of Health Bethesda Maryland 1988–89, clinical lectr in neurology Univ of Cambridge and hon sr registrar in neurology Addenbrooke's Hosp 1990–92, sr lectr in neurology Royal Free Hosp Sch of Med and Inst of Neurology Univ of London 1992–98, hon sr lectr in neurology Univ of London 1998–2005, campus sub-dean and assoc faculty tutor Royal Free and UC Medical Sch (Hampstead Campus) UCL 2005–; conslt neurologist: Royal Free Hosp 1992–, Princess Grace Hosp 1998–2000, King's Oak Hosp Enfield 1999–2005, Nat Hosp for Neurology and Neurosurgery Queen Square 1992–98 (hon conslt 1998–), Queen Elizabeth II Hosp Welwyn Garden City 1992–98, Chase Farm Hosp Enfield 1998–2005; memb Assoc of Br Neurologists 1992; FRCP; *Books* Lecture Notes on Neurology (1999 and 2005); also author of numerous research articles in academic jls; *Recreations* pianoforte, walking, reading; *Style*— Dr Lionel Ginsberg; ✉ Department of Clinical Neurosciences, Royal Free Hospital, Pond Street, London NW3 2QG (tel 020 7794 0500 ext 38096, e-mail lionel.ginsberg@royalfree.nhs.uk)

GINSBORG, Michael David; s of Samuel Ginsborg (d 1986), of Gerrards Cross, Bucks, and Rose, *née* Gabe (d 1996); *b* 25 April 1943; *Educ* Westminster, KCL, Central Sch of Art & Design (DipAD), Chelsea Sch of Art (Higher DipArt); *m* 1972, Rosamund (Robby), da of John Ducane Nelson; 2 da (Katharine (Teeny) b 3 Aug 1972, (Sonya) Charlotte b 2 Dec 1974); *Career* artist and educator; lectr and examiner numerous UK art schs 1979–, head of painting Ravensbourne Coll until 1984, head Sch of Fine Arts Birmingham Poly 1989–91 (course dir Masters Degree in Fine Art 1984–89); Wimbledon Sch of Art: head of fine art 1991–2000, dir of studies 2000–02, dir Centre for Drawing 2002–03; memb Register of Specialist Advsrs CNAA until 1992; specialist subject reviewer Quality Assurance Agency 1999–2000; *Solo Exhibitions* Lisson Gallery 1969, Serpentine Gallery 1973, City Museum Bolton 1976, Acme Gallery London 1980, Benjamin Rhodes Gallery 1986, 1989 and 1992, Drawing Gallery London 2005; *Group Exhibitions* incl: British Painting (Royal Acad) 1977, Recent Acquisitions (Hayward) 1978, British Art Show 1979, British Abstract Art Part 1: Painting (Flowers East) 1994, Fusion (Rhodes and Mann) 2000; *Work in Collections* Govt Art Collection, Br Cncl, Dept of the Environment, Arts Cncl of GB and in many other collections in UK, Europe and USA; cmmnd to paint St Charles' Hospital Centenary Murals 1981 and 1982, wall construction Glaxo Wellcome Medicines Research Centre Stevenage 1994; Atrium Sculpture Linklaters and Paines London 1997; *Awards* incl: first prize Univ of London Painting Competition 1963, prizewinner Cleveland Drawing Biennale 1975, Visual Arts award Greater London Arts Assoc 1976, Arts Cncl bursary 1977, Mark Rothko meml award 1979, Gold medal Florence Biennale 1997; *Style*— Michael Ginsborg; ✉ 84 Thornlaw Road, London SE27 0SA (e-mail ginsborg@thornlaw.u-net.com)

GIORDANO, Richard Vincent; KBE (1989); s of late Vincent Giordano, and Cynthia Giordano; *b* 24 March 1934, 1934, March; *Educ* Harvard Univ (BA), Columbia Univ Law Sch (LLB); *Family* 1 s, 2 da; *Career* lawyer Shearman & Sterling NYC 1959–63; Airco Inc: asst sec 1963, gp vice-pres 1967, pres and ceo 1971, chief exec 1978–79; BOC Group: dir following takeover of Airco 1978, gp md and chief exec 1979–91, chm 1985–92 and 1994–96, non-exec dir 1991–96; chm: BG plc (formerly British Gas) 1994–2000, BG Gp plc 2000–04; Grand Metropolitan plc: memb Bd 1985–97, dep chm 1991–97; non-exec dir: National Power plc (formerly CEGB) 1982–92, Georgia Pacific Corp Atlanta GA 1984–, Reuters Holdings plc 1991–94, Lucas Industries plc 1993–94; hon dr commercial sci St John's Univ 1975; hon fell London Business Sch 1994; Hon LLD Univ of Bath 1998; *Recreations* ocean sailing, tennis; *Clubs* The Links, New York Yacht, Buck's; *Style*— Sir Richard Giordano, KBE; ✉ PO Box 1598, Lakeville, CT 06039, USA

GIRLING, John Anthony (Tony); s of James William Girling, OBE, of Birchington, Kent, and Annie Doris, *née* Reeves; *b* 21 August 1943; *Educ* Tonbridge, Coll of Law Guildford; *m* 26 March 1965, Lynne, da of late Raymond Hubert Roland Davis; 1 da (Samantha Helen Dixon b 25 Nov 1968), 1 s (Richard Warwick b 19 March 1971); *Career* admitted slr 1966; Girlings: ptnr 1966–2000, chm and managing ptnr 1985–96, chm 1997–2000, conslt 2000–; pres Law Soc of England & Wales 1996–97 (memb Cncl 1980–99); High Court costs assessor 1982–; pres: Kent Law Soc 1982, Isle of Thanet Law Soc 1987, Slrs' Benevolent Assoc 1997; fndr memb Herne Bay Round Table (chm 1978), hon sec Herne Bay Branch Rotary Club 1969–72; Hon LLD Univ of Kent at Canterbury; memb Law Soc 1966, NP 1968; fell Soc for Advanced Legal Studies 1997; *Recreations* skiing, golf, travel, reading; *Clubs* Canterbury Golf; *Style*— Tony Girling, Esq; ✉ Penbourne, Millview Court, Valley Road, Barham, Canterbury, Kent CT4 6PF (tel 01227 833811, e-mail tonygirling@lineone.net); Girlings, Rose Lane, Canterbury, Kent CT1 2UG (tel 01227 768374, fax 01227 450498)

GIROUARD, Mark; s of Richard Désiré Girouard (d 1989; s of Col Sir Percy Girouard, KCMG, DSO, sometime govr N Nigeria and British E Africa Protectorates, and Mary, da of Hon Sir Richard Solomon, GCMG, KCB, KCVO), and his 1 w, Lady Blanche, *née* de la Poer Beresford, da of 6 Marquess of Waterford, KP; *b* 7 October 1931; *Educ* Ampleforth, ChCh Oxford (MA), Courtauld Inst of Art (PhD), Bartlett Sch UCL (BSc); *m* 1970, Dorothy N Dorf; 1 da; *Career* writer and architectural historian; Slade prof of fine art Univ of Oxford 1975–76; memb: Royal Fine Art Cmmn 1972–, Royal Cmmn on Hist Monuments 1976–81, Hist Bldgs Cncl 1978–84, Cncl Victorian Soc 1979– (fndr memb 1958); Hon DLitt Univ of Leicester 1982; FSA 1986, Hon FRIBA 1980; *Clubs* Beefsteak; *Style*— Mark Girouard, Esq, FSA; ✉ 35 Colville Road, London W11 2BT

GIRVAN, Rt Hon Mr Justice; Rt Hon Sir (Frederick) Paul Girvan; kt (1995), PC (2007); s of Robert Frederick Girvan (d 2000), of Holywood, Belfast, and Martha Patricia, *née* Barron (d 1989); *b* 20 October 1948; *Educ* Larne GS, Belfast Royal Acad, Clare Coll Cambridge (BA), Queen's Univ Belfast; *m* 20 July 1974, Karen Elizabeth, *née* Joyce; 1 da (Rebecca Jane b 19 March 1977), 2 s (Brian Richard b 12 Dec 1978, Peter Michael b 19 Jan 1980); *Career* called to the Bar NI 1971, called to the Inner Bar (QC) 1984, jr crown counsel (Chancery) 1981–84, judge of the High Court of Justice NI 1995–2007, chancery judge 1997–2004, a Lord Justice of Appeal NI 2007–; hon bencher Gray's Inn; chm NI Law Reform Advsy Ctee 1997–2004 (memb 1994–2004); memb Standing Advsy Ctee on Human Rights 1985–87; chllr Archdiocese of Armagh; *Recreations* reading, travel, badminton, cycling, walking, modern languages, cooking, golf; *Style*— The Rt Hon Lord Justice Girvan; ✉ The Royal Courts of Justice, Chichester Street, Belfast BT1 3JF (tel 028 903 2111)

GISBOROUGH, 3 Baron (UK 1917); Thomas Richard John Long Chaloner; s of 2 Baron Gisborough (d 1951); *b* 1 July 1927; *Educ* Eton, RAC Cirencester; *m* 26 April 1960, Shane, er da of late Sidney Arthur Newton, of London (2 s of Sir Louis Newton, 1 Bt); 2 s; *Heir* s, Hon Perry Chaloner; *Career* served Welsh Guards 16th/5th Lancers, Northumberland Hussars TA; Lt-Col Green Howards (TA); farmer and landowner; cncllr of North Riding and then Cleveland 1964–77; HM Lord-Lt Cleveland 1981–96, Lt N Yorks 1996–2001; Hon Col Cleveland Cadet Force 1981–92; memb Devpt Cmmn 1985–89; pres: Nat Ski Fedn 1985–90, N of Eng TAVRA; sometime pres Assoc Prof Foresters; JP Langbaurgh East 1981; KStJ; *Recreations* gliding, bridge, piano, tennis, painting, field sports, skiing; *Style*— The Rt Hon the Lord Gisborough; ✉ Gisborough House, Guisborough, North Yorkshire (tel 01287 630012, e-mail richargis@ic24.net)

GITSHAM, Julian Mark; s of Michael Leonard Gitsham, and Sylvia, *née* Wood; *b* 11 May 1965; *Educ* Knutsford Co HS, Oxford Poly (BA, DipArch, Dip Urban Design, Les Townshend Award, Barton Willmore Prize); *m* 31 Aug 1987, Nicola Sarah, *née* Hyde; 2 da (Honor Olivia b 22 April 1998, Phoebe Hope b 18 Sept 2000); *Career* architect; architectural asst Aldington Craig and Collinge Architects 1989–92, project architect Hants Co Architects Dept 1992–95; projects incl: Hants Record Office (RIBA Award, Civic Tst Award), Tadley Library, Hackney Community Coll (RIBA Award, Civic Tst Award), South Downs Coll, Glen House Children's Secure Unit; sr architect Portcullis House London Michael Hopkins and Partners 1996–99, ptnr Feilden Clegg Bradley Architects LLP 1999–; projects incl: housing Peabody Tst Fulham, new museum millennium project RAF Hendon, new museum devpt RAF Museum Cosford, mixed use project Mildmay Mission Hosp, Shoreditch Tabernacle Baptist Church and Peabody Tst, housing Venture Devpts Putney; Housing Design Award 1999; ARB 1990, RIBA 1990; *Recreations* waterskiing, cinema, music, mountain biking; *Clubs* Oxford Wakeboard and Ski; *Style*— Julian Gitsham, Esq; ✉ Feilden Clegg Bradley Architects LLP, Circus House, 21 Great Titchfield Street, London W1W 8BA (tel 020 7323 5737, fax 020 7323 5720, mobile 07866 595373, e-mail jmg@feildenclegg.com)

GITTINGS, (Harold) John; s of late Harold William Gittings, of Surrey, and Doris Marjorie, *née* Whiting; *b* 3 September 1947; *Educ* Duke of York's Sch Dover; *m* 22 July 1988, Andrea Mary (d 1995), da of Arnold Fisher, of Surrey; 1 step da (Tracey Andrea English b 1965), 1 step s (Jonathan Charles English b 1969); m 2, 6 July 2002, Barbara Louise, da of Nathan Lowenstein, of Johannesburg, SA; *Career* Beecham Group 1971–73, Peat

G

Marwick Mitchell Hong Kong 1973–74, N M Rothschild & Sons 1974–81, Continental Illinois Bank 1981–82, md Target Group plc 1982–85, sr md Touche Remnant & Co 1985–90; chm: Greenfield Group Ltd 1992–96, Meltemi Entertainment Ltd 1994–; ACIS 1972; *Recreations* entertaining, travel, gardening, theatre, cinema; *Style—* John Gittings, Esq; ✉ 12 Grosvenor Place, Bath BA1 6AX; Meltemi Entertainment Ltd, 10 Soho Square, London W1V 6NT (tel 020 7580 7573)

GITTUS, Prof John Henry; *b* 25 July 1930; *Educ* Univ of London (BSc, DSc), KTH Stockholm (DTech); *m* 23 May 1953, Rosemary Ann, da of John Geeves; 1 s (Michael John b 7 April 1954), 2 da (Sara Ann b 19 Aug 1956, Mary Ann b 8 Aug 1958); *Career* res worker Br Cast Iron Res Assoc 1951–56 (apprentice 1947–51), gp ldr Mond Nickel R&D Laboratories Birmingham 1956–60; UKAEA: res mangr Springfields 1960–80, head of water reactor fuel devpt 1980–81, head Atomic Energy Tech Branch Harwell 1981–83, dir of water reactor res Harwell 1981–83, dir of safety 1983–87, dir of communications 1987–89; dir gen Br Nuclear Industry Forum 1989–93 (currently conslt); fndr sr ptnr John Gittus & Associates (sci and public affrs consultancy) 1993–, sr ptnr NUSYS (nuclear conslts) Paris 1995–; working memb Lloyd's Nuclear Syndicate 1996–; conslt: Argonne Nat Laboratory Chicago 1968, Oak Ridge Nat Laboratory Tennessee 1969, ESKOM South Africa 1997–, GE Healthcare (Amersham, radio-pharmaceuticals) 1999–, Cox Insurance Holdings plc 1999–2002, Chaucer Holdings plc 2002–, NECSA South Africa 2006–; Regents prof UCLA 1990–, prof Univ of Plymouth 1997–, Royal Acad of Engrg prof 2006–; visiting prof: École Polytechnique Fédérale Lausanne Switzerland 1976, Univ of Nancy 1985; interpreter's certificate in French; FREng 1989, FIMechE, FIM, FIS, memb Mensa; *Books* Uranium (1963), Creep, Viscoelasticity and Creep-Fracture in Solids (1976), Irradiation Effects in Crystalline Solids (1980); *Recreations* old motor cars, golf, swimming; *Clubs* IOD, RSM; *Style—* Prof John Gittus, FREng; ✉ Chaucer Holdings plc, 9 Devonshire Square, Cutlers Gardens, London EC2M 4WL (tel 020 7397 9700, mobile 07775 898449, e-mail john@gittus.com)

GIVEN, Andrew Ferguson; s of Edward F Given, CMG, CVO, of Lymington, and Philida Naomi, *née* Bullwinkle; *b* 14 November 1947; *Educ* Charterhouse, Lincoln Coll Oxford; *m* 18 Sept 1971 (sep), Morwenna, da of Frederic Neil Ritchie, of Italy; 2 da (Davina, Catriona); *Career* asst to md Union Corp UK Ltd 1969–73, exec dir James Finlay Corporation 1974–75; Northern Telecom Ltd (Canada): various positions 1977–82, asst treas 1982–83, treas and controller Bell-Northern Research 1984–87, vice-pres finance Northern Telecom Europe 1987–88; gp finance controller Plessey Group plc 1988–89, gp finance dir then dep chief exec Logica plc 1990–2002; non-exec dir: Spectris plc 2001–, VT Gp plc 2002–, Spirent Communications plc until 2006; FRSA; *Recreations* sailing, photography, travel, running; *Clubs* Army and Navy; *Style—* A F Given

GIZIRIAN, Most Rev Archbishop Yeghishe; s of late Sarkis Gizirian, of Damascus, Syria, and Azniv, *née* Najarian; *b* 15 July 1925; *Educ* Damascus Syria, Seminary of the Armenian Catholicate of Cilicia Antelias Lebanon; *Career* ordained celibate priest 1947, assumed pastoral duties USA 1951–81 (served NY, Newark New Jersey, Worcester Mass, Detroit Michigan, Philadelphia Pa, Boston Mass and Toronto Canada), vicar gen Eastern Dio of America 1963–65, consecrated bishop (by His Holiness Vasken I, Catholicos and Supreme Patriarch of All Armenians) and appointed Primate of the Armenian Community in UK 1982, elevated to archbishop 1993; currently pres Cncl of Oriental Orthodox Churches in London; *Publications* numerous articles in Armenian and English periodicals on religious subjects; *Style—* The Most Rev Archibishop Yeghishe Gizirian; ✉ St Sarkis Armenian Church, Iverna Gardens, Kensington, London W8 6TP

GIZZI, Julian Anthony; s of Antonio Gizzi, and Vilma Gizzi; *b* 13 February 1957, Hove, E Sussex; *Educ* Downside, Magdalene Coll Cambridge (MA); *Career* admitted slr 1981; ptnr Beachcroft LLP (formerly Beachcroft Wansbroughs) 1986– (slr 1981–86); memb Structure and Governance Working Gp Dearing Ctee 1993; FRSA 1997; *Publications* Duties and Powers (1996), Butterworths' Law of Education (gen ed, 2000), VAT for Solicitors (3 edn, 2002); *Style—* Julian Gizzi, Esq; ✉ Beachcroft LLP, 100 Fetter Lane, London EC4A 1BN (tel 020 7242 1011, fax 020 7894 6640, e-mail jgizzi@beachcroft.co.uk)

GLADSTONE, David Arthur Steuart; CMG (1988); s of Thomas Steuart Gladstone (d 1971), and Muriel Irene Heron, *née* Day; *b* 1 April 1935; *Educ* ChCh Oxford (MA); *m* 29 July 1961, (Mary Elizabeth) April, da of Wing Cdr Patrick O'Brien Brunner (d 1966); 1 da (Perdita b 1965), 1 s (Patrick b 1969); *Career* Nat Serv 2 Lt 4 RHA 1954–56; articled to Annan Dexter & Co 1959–60; FO 1960–: Arabic language student MECAS Lebanon 1960–62, third sec political agency Bahrain 1962–63, FO 1963–65 and 1969–72, second later first sec Bonn 1965–69, first sec and head of Chancery Cairo 1972–75, political advsr BMG Berlin 1976–79, head of Western Euro Dept FCO 1979–82, consul-gen Marseilles 1983–87, high cmmr to Sri Lanka 1987–91, chargé d'affaires Ukraine 1992; fndr memb and chm the Barnsbury Assoc 1964–65, chm Homes for Barnsbury 1970–72, dir SANE 2002–; *Publications* What shall we do with the Crown Prerogative? (1998); *Recreations* domestic architecture, opera, landscape gardening; *Style—* David Gladstone, Esq, CMG; ✉ 1 Mountfort Terrace, London N1 1JJ

GLADSTONE, Sir (Erskine) William; 7 Bt (UK 1846), of Fasque and Balfour, Kincardineshire; KG (1999), JP (Clwyd 1982); s of Sir Charles Andrew Gladstone, 6 Bt (d 1968), and Isla Margaret, *née* Crum (d 1987); ggs of Rt Hon William Ewart Gladstone, PM; *b* 29 October 1925; *Educ* Eton, ChCh Oxford (MA); *m* 10 Sept 1962, Rosamund Anne, yr da of Maj Robert Alexander Hambro (d 1943), of Milton Abbey, Dorset; 2 s (Charles Angus b 1964, Robert Nicolas b 1968), 1 da (Victoria Frances (Mrs Hugo Merison) b 1967); *Heir* s, Charles Gladstone; *Career* RN 1943–46; asst master Eton 1951–61, headmaster Lancing 1961–69, chief scout of the UK and Overseas Branches 1972–82 (ret 1982); chm: World Scout Ctee 1979–81, Representative Body of the Church in Wales 1977–92, Cncl Glenalmond Coll 1982–86; DL: Flintshire 1969, Clwyd 1974; HM Lord-Lt of Clwyd 1985–2000; Hon LLD Univ of Liverpool 1998; *Style—* Sir William Gladstone, Bt, KG; ✉ Hawarden Castle, Flintshire CH5 3PB (tel 01244 520210)

GLADSTONE OF CAPENOCH, Robert Hamilton; er s of John Gladstone of Capenoch, TD (d 1977), and his 2 w, Diana Rosamond Maud Fleming, *née* Hamilton; gggs of Thomas Steuart Gladstone, JP, who acquired Capenoch 1850; *b* 17 July 1953; *Educ* Eton, Magdalene Coll Cambridge (MA); *m* 16 Jan 1982, Margaret Jane, da of Brig Berenger Colborne Bradford, DSO, MBE, MC, of Kincardine, Kincardine O'Neil, Aberdeenshire; 2 s (John, Harry (twins) b 3 March 1983), 1 da (Catharine b 13 April 1986); *Career* chartered surveyor; John Sale & Partners 1974–78, Smiths-Gore 1978–; FRICS 1989 (ARICS 1977); *Clubs* Whistle, '71; *Style—* Robert Gladstone of Capenoch; ✉ Capenoch, Thornhill, Dumfriesshire (tel 01848 330261); Smiths-Gore, 28 Castle Street, Dumfries (tel 01387 263066)

GLADWELL, David John; s of Leonard Butterworth Gladwell (d 1971), of Clayhidon Devon, and Violet Rita, *née* Lloyd-Jones (d 1977); *b* 13 March 1947, Llangynhafal, Sir Ddinbych; *Educ* Blundell's, Univ of Exeter (LLM), Queen Mary & Westfield Coll London (Dip), Univ of Greenwich (Cert); *m* 24 June 1988, Ragnhild, *née* Kuhbier; 1 step s (Olok Dominic Banerjee b 1972); *Career* J Henry Schroder Wagg Merchant bankers 1966–69, called to the Bar Gray's Inn 1972 (bencher 2004), practising barr 1972–74, Office of the Registrar of Criminal Appeals 1974–81; Lord Chllr's Dept: Private Law Div 1982–87, Int Div 1988–93, head Law Reform Div 1993–96, head Civil Justice Div 1996–99, head of sr judicial appts 1999–2001, chm Review of Criminal Immunity of the State 2001–03, head Constitutional Policy 2003, head Civil Appeals Office and Master in the Court of Appeal Civil Div 2003–; accredited mediator CEDR; chm: Working Gp on the Establishment of the Patents County Court 1986–87, Cncl of Europe Euro Ctee on Legal Co-operation 1992–93 (vice-chm 1991–92), Cncl of Europe Working Gp on Efficiency of Justice 1999–2000; sec Judicial Working Gp on Ethics 2002; memb: Editorial Advsy Panel Intellectual Property in Business 1988–92, Civil Justice Cncl 1998–2000, CEDR Advsy Cncl 1998–2000, Working Gp on a single European Patent Court 1999–2000, EU Assessment Missions to Albania and Croatia 2002 and Ukraine 2006, Exec Ctee Anglo-Russian Law Assoc 2002–, Advsy Cncl Soc for Advanced Legal Studies 2003–, European Bd Int Assoc for Ct Administration 2005–; fell Soc for Advanced Legal Studies 1999; *Publications* The Exhaustion of Intellectual Property Rights (1986), Patent Litigation (1989), The Patents County Court (1989), Are You Ready for Woolf? (1999), The Civil Justice Reforms in England and Wales (1999), Modern Litigation Culture (2000), Judicial Appointments (2001), Legal Aid in the Republic of Georgia (jtly, 2002), Legal Aid in Montenegro (jtly, 2002), Mediation and the Courts (2004), Manual of Civil Appeals (contrib ed, 2004); *Recreations* pretending not to be frightened on Crib Goch, seeking new experiences, concert and opera-going; *Clubs* Garrick; *Style—* David Gladwell, Esq; ✉ Clayhidon, Cullompton, Devon EX15 3PG

GLADWIN, Rt Rev John Warren; *see:* Chelmsford, Bishop of

GLADWYN, 2 Baron (UK 1960); Miles Alvery Gladwyn Jebb; s of 1 Baron Gladwyn, GCMG, GCVO, CB (d 1996), and Cynthia, *née* Noble (d 1990); *b* 3 March 1930; *Educ* Eton, Magdalen Coll Oxford (MA); *Heir* none; *Career* author; 2 Lt Welsh Gds, Pilot Offr RAFVR; sr mgmnt with British Airways until 1983; *Books* The Thames Valley Heritage Walk (1980), A Guide to the South Downs Way (1984), Walkers (1986), A Guide to the Thames Path (1988), East Anglia, an Anthology (1990), The Colleges of Oxford (1992), Suffolk (1995), The Diaries of Cynthia Gladwyn (1995), The Lord Lieutenants and their Deputies (2007); *Clubs* Brooks's, Beefsteak; *Style—* The Lord Gladwyn; ✉ E1 Albany, Piccadilly, London W1J 0AR

GLAISTER, Lesley Gillian; da of Leonard Oliver Richard Glaister (d 1981), and Maureen Jillian, *née* Crowley; *b* 4 October 1956; *Educ* Deben HS Felixstowe, Open Univ (BA), Univ of Sheffield (MA); *m* 1, 1976 (m dis 1984), Christopher French; 2 s (Joseph William French b 1978, Joshua James French 1981); 1 s by subsequent partner (Leo Stewart-Glaister b 1988); m 2, 1993 (m dis 1998), Dr Robert Murphy; m 3, 2001, Andrew Greig; *Career* adult educn tutor 1982–90, full time writer and teacher of creative writing 1990–; winner: Somerset Maugham Award 1991, Betty Trask Award 1991; memb Soc of Authors 1991; FRSL 1994; *Plays* Birdcalls (Crucible Theatre Sheffield) 2003; *Books* Honour Thy Father (1990), Trick-or-Treat (1991), Digging to Australia (1992), Limestone and Clay (1993), Partial Eclipse (1994), Private Parts of Women (1996), Easy Peasy (1997), Sheer Blue Bliss (1999), Now You See Me (2001), As Far As You Can Go (2004), Nina Todd Has Gone (2007); *Style—* Ms Lesley Glaister, FRSL; ✉ c/o Bill Hamilton, A M Heath & Co, 6 Warwick Court, London WC1R 5JD (tel 020 7242 2811)

GLANFIELD, Jonathan James (Joe); s of Robert Glanfield, of Exmouth, Devon, and Beverley Glanfield; *b* 6 August 1979, Sutton, Surrey; *Educ* Exmouth Community Coll; *Career* yachtsman; achievements in 470 class incl: fourth place Olympic Games Sydney 2000, Silver medal World Championships 2001, Bronze medal European Championships 2002, Silver medal Pre-Olympics Athens 2003, Silver medal Olympic Games Athens 2004, Gold medal European Championships 2004 and 2005; ranked No 1 (470 class) Int Sailing Fedn (ISAF) world rankings 2004; *Style—* Joe Glanfield, Esq

GLANUSK, 5 Baron (UK 1899); Sir Christopher Russell Bailey; 6 Bt (UK 1852), TD; only s of 4 Baron Glanusk (d 1997); *b* 18 March 1942; *Educ* Eton, Clare Coll Cambridge (BA); *m* 1974, Frances Elizabeth, da of Air Chief Marshal Sir Douglas Charles Lowe, GCB, DFC, AFC; 1 s (Hon Charles Henry b 1976), 1 da (Hon Rosemary Elizabeth b 1979); *Heir* s, Hon Charles Bailey; *Career* computer systems engr: English Electric Leo 1964–66, Ferranti 1966–78; product mktg mangr Bestobell Mobrey Ltd 1978–83, sales engr (Defence Systems) STC Telecommunications Ltd 1984–86; gen mangr: Lumenition 1986–96, Wolfram Research Europe Ltd 1997–98; memb Chobham Parish Cncl 1987–99; TA: Lt 7 Bn Cheshire Regt 1965–67, Capt 94 (Berks Yeo) Signals Sqdn 1967–76, Capt 80 (Cheshire Yeo) Signals Sqdn 1976–78, Maj HQ11 Signals Bde 1978–86; *Style—* The Rt Hon the Lord Glanusk, TD; ✉ 51 Chertsey Road, Chobham, Surrey GU24 8PD

GLANVILLE, Brian Lester; s of James Arthur Glanville (d 1960), and Florence, *née* Manches (d 1984); *b* 24 September 1931; *Educ* Charterhouse; *m* 1959, Elizabeth Pamela de Boer, da of Fritz Manasse (d 1961); 2 s (Mark, Toby), 2 da (Elizabeth, Josephine); *Career* novelist, journalist, playwright; football corr and sports columnist: The Sunday Times 1958–92, The People 1992–96, The Times 1996–98, The Sunday Times 1998–; lit advsr Bodley Head 1958–62; *Books* novels incl: Along The Arno, The Bankrupts, Diamond, The Olympian, A Roman Marriage, The Artist Type, A Second Home, The Financiers, A Cry of Crickets, The Comic, Kissing America, The Catacomb, Dictators; short story collections: A Bad Streak, The Director's Wife, The Thing He Loves, The King of Hackney Marshes, Love is Not Love; Football Memories (autobiography), Story of the World Cup, The Arsenal Stadium History, England's Football Managers, stage musical Underneath The Arches (co-author, 1981–83), A Visit to the Villa (play for stage and radio); *Style—* Brian Glanville, Esq; ✉ 160 Holland Park Avenue, London W11 4UH (tel 020 7603 6908)

GLASER, Dr Mark Gordon; s of Asher Alfred Glaser (d 1987), and Minnie, *née* Nasilewitz (d 1983); *b* 1 December 1944; *Educ* St Clement Dane's GS, Charing Cross Hosp Med Sch (MB BS, MRCS LRCP, DMRT); *Career* conslt in radiotherapy and oncology Charing Cross Hosp 1980–, hon conslt radiotherapist Hammersmith Hosp and Postgrad Med Sch 1980–, clinical teacher Univ of London 1981–, clinical dir Riverside HA Cancer Servs 1990–, dir Depts of Radiotherapy Hammersmith and Charing Cross Hosp 1994–; visiting prof Yale Univ USA 1984; author of papers on cancer and radiation therapy; memb Univ of London: Senate 1981–, Military Educn Ctee 1982–84, Central Research Fund Ctee 1982–84, Collegiate Cncl 1987–89, Academic Cncl 1989–; FFR RCSI 1977, FRCR 1978; *Recreations* walking, philosophy, comparative religion; *Clubs* Reform; *Style—* Dr Mark Glaser; ✉ Department of Radiotherapy and Oncology, Charing Cross Hospital, Fulham Palace Road, London W6 8RF (tel 020 8846 1733)

GLASGOW, Edwin John; CBE (1998), QC (1987); s of Richard Edwin Glasgow, and Mary, *née* Markby; *b* 3 August 1945; *Educ* St Joseph's Coll Ipswich, UCL; *m* 1967, Janet, *née* Coleman; 1 s (Oliver Edwin James b 17 Jan 1971), 1 da (Louise Victoria Mary b 20 March 1972); *Career* Met Police 1961–64; called to the Bar Gray's Inn 1969 (bencher 1994); barr specialising in commercial litigation, administrative and public law and public inquiries, currently memb of chambers 39 Essex St; inquiries incl: Bradford Fire, Hillsborough, Piper Alpha, Herald of Free Enterprise, Guiness DTI, Guildford Four, Alison Halford, Bloody Sunday; chm Fin Reporting Review Panel 1991–98; vice-chm Thames Ditton CC 2001–; tstee: London Opera Players, Harlequin FC (chm), Mary Glasgow Language Tst (chm); Lawyer of the Year Legal Business Awards 2005; *Recreations* music, family, France; *Clubs* RAC (steward); *Style—* Edwin Glasgow, Esq, CBE, QC; ✉ Copper Hall, Thames Ditton, Surrey KT7 0BX; Entrechaux, Vaulcluse, France; 39 Essex Street, London WC2R 3AT (tel 020 7832 1111)

GLASGOW, Archbishop of (RC) 2002–; Most Rev Mario Joseph Conti; s of Louis Conti, and Josephine Panicali; *b* 1934; *Educ* St Marie's Convent Sch Springfield Elgin, Blairs Coll Aberdeen, Pontifical Gregorian Univ Rome (STL, PhL); *Career* ordained Rome 1958, curate St Mary's Cathedral Aberdeen 1959–62, jt parish priest St Joachim's Wick and St Anne's Thurso 1962–77, Bishop of Aberdeen 1977–2002; pres/treas Scottish Catholic Int Aid Fund 1978–85, Scottish memb Episcopal Bd Int Cmmn for English in the Liturgy 1978–87; chm: Cmmn for the Pastoral Care of Migrant Workers 1978–85, Scottish

Catholic Heritage Cmmn 1980–; pres: Nat Liturgy Cmmn 1981–85, Nat Cmmn for Christian Doctrine and Unity 1985–; memb: Bishops' Jt Ctee for Bio-ethical Issues 1982–, Cncl for Promotion of Christian Unity (Rome) 1984–, Pontifical Cmmn for the Cultural Heritage of the Church (Rome) 1994–2004; convener Action of Churches Together in Scotland 1990–93; co-moderator Jt Working Gp (RC Church and WCC) 1995–2006, apostolic administrator Diocese of Paisley 2004–05; Hon DD Aberdeen 1989; FRSE 1995; Commendatore Dell'Ordine Al Merito Della Repubblica Italiana 1981, Knight Cdr of the Holy Sepulchre 1989, chaplain Sovereign Military Order of St John of Jerusalem Rhodes and Malta 1991, Conventual Chaplain Grand Cross 2001; *Style*— His Grace the Archbishop of Glasgow; ✉ Archdiocese of Glasgow Curial Offices, 196 Clyde Street, Glasgow G1 4JY

GLASGOW, 10 Earl of (S 1703); Patrick Robin Archibald Boyle; DL (Ayrshire 2000); also Lord Boyle (S 1699), Lord Boyle of Kelburn (S 1703), Baron Fairlie (UK 1897); s of Rear Adm 9 Earl of Glasgow, CB, DSC (d 1984), and his 1 wife Dorothea, only da of Sir Archibald Lyle, 2 Bt, now Dorothea, Viscountess Kelburn; *b* 30 July 1939; *Educ* Eton, Sorbonne; *m* 29 Nov 1975, Isabel Mary, da of George Douglas James; 1 s (Hon David Boyle b 1978), 1 da (Lady Alice Dorothy b 1981); *Heir* s, Hon David Boyle (does not use courtesy title of Viscount of Kelburn); *Career* Sub-Lt RNR 1960; known professionally as Patrick Boyle; asst dir Woodfall Films 1961–64, freelance asst dir 1965–68, TV documentary producer/dir Yorkshire Television 1968–70; freelance TV documentary producer/dir working for BBC, Yorkshire Television, ATV, Central and Scottish Television 1971–81; formed Kelburn Country Centre (a leisure park created from part of the family estate) 1977, currently managing Kelburn Country Centre; sits as Lib Dem in House of Lords 2004–; chm Largs Viking Festival 1981–85, dir Ayrshire and Arran Tourist Bd 1999–2000 and 2003–04; *Recreations* theatre, cinema, skiing; *Style*— The Rt Hon the Earl of Glasgow, DL; ✉ Kelburn, Fairlie, Ayrshire KA29 0BE (tel 01475 568204); Kelburn Country Centre, Fairlie, Ayrshire KA29 0BE (tel 01475 568685)

GLASGOW AND GALLOWAY, Dean of; *see:* Duncan, Very Rev Dr Gregor

GLASGOW AND GALLOWAY, Bishop of 1998–; Rt Rev Dr Idris Jones; s of Edward Eric Jones (d 1983), and Alice Gertrude, *née* Burgess (d 1964); *b* 2 April 1943; *Educ* West Bromwich GS, UC of St David Lampeter (BA), New Coll Edinburgh (LTh), NY Seminary and Urban Theol Unit (DMin); *m* 27 Oct 1973, Alison Margaret, da of Ernest Abel Williams; 2 s (Adam Edward b 4 Oct 1977, Gareth Daniel b 27 July 1979); *Career* ordained: deacon 1967, priest 1968; curate St Mary Stafford 1967–70, precentor St Paul's Cathedral Dundee 1970–73, curate i/c St Hugh Gosforth 1973–80 (team vicar 1980), chaplain St Nicholas Hosp Newcastle 1975–80, rector Montrose with Inverbervie (Brechin) 1980–89, canon St Paul's Cathedral Dundee 1983, Anglican chaplain Univ of Dundee and priest i/c Invergowrie (Brechin) 1989–92, rector Ayr with Girvan and Maybole (Glasgow and Galloway) 1992–98, pastoral dir Theol Inst 1995–98, Primus of Scottish Episcopal Church 2006–; memb Person Centred Therapy (Scotland); patron Hutcheson's Hosp, govr Hutcheson's GS 2002–; Master Incorporation of Skinners and Glovers of Glasgow, Freeman City of Glasgow; hon fell Univ of Wales Lampeter 2007; *Recreations* walking, playing piano, bird watching, golf, food and wine; *Clubs* Glasgow XIII, Western (Glasgow); *Style*— The Most Rev the Bishop of Glasgow and Galloway; ✉ Bishop's House, 25 Quadrant Road, Newlands, Glasgow G43 2QP (tel 0141 633 5877); Bishop's Office, Diocese of Glasgow and Galloway, 5 St Vincent Place, Glasgow G1 2DH (tel 0141 221 6911, fax 0141 221 6490, e-mail bishop@glasgow.anglican.org)

GLASS, Anthony Trevor; QC (1986); s of Percy Glass (d 1946); *b* 6 June 1940; *Educ* Royal Masonic Sch, Lincoln Coll Oxford (MA); *m* 30 April 1966, Deborah, da of late Dr William Wall, and late Katharine Wall, of Rocky Mount, North Carolina, USA; 1 s (James b 1969), 1 da (Emily b 1970); *Career* called to the Bar Inner Temple 1965, bencher 1995; recorder of the Crown Court 1985–2005; *Recreations* antique collecting, music; *Style*— Anthony Glass, Esq, QC; ✉ Queen Elizabeth Building, Temple, London EC4 (tel 020 7583 5766, fax 020 7353 0339)

GLASS, David Peter; s of Max Glass, of Lisbon, Portugal, and Sigrid, *née* Dressler; *b* 9 December 1957, Zurich, Switzerland; *Educ* Boundstone Comp Sch, London Sch of Contemporary Dance, Ecole Etienne Decroux Paris, Alvin Ailey Sch New York, Jean Louis Barrault Carré Sch Paris; *m* 2000, Valerie Sophie Berdaa; *Career* writer and dir 1982–; dancer and mime artist with Community Arts Theatre 1976–77, street theatre France, England and Italy 1977, began int solo career 1977; written and directed shows incl: Phoenix Dance Co, English Dance Theatre, Nottingham Playhouse, Crucible Theatre, Mime Theatre Project, Scottish Opera, Opera Circus, Scottish Chamber Orchestra, Hong Kong Symphony Orchestra, Playbox Theatre Co, Yellow Earth Theatre Co, Polka Theatre's Tate Gallery Centenary prodn; artistic dir David Glass Ensemble 1989–; David Glass Ensemble prodns incl: first adaptation of Popeye 1989, Bozo's Dead 1990, Gormenghast 1991–94, Les Enfants du Paradis 1993, The Mosquito Coast (Young Vic) 1995, Lucky (Young Vic) 1995 (also at Purcell Room 1996), first musical adaptation of La Dolce Vita 1996, Glassworks (performed internationally) 1996–98, The Lost Child Trilogy 1998–2000: The Hansel Gretel Machine, The Lost Child, The Red Thread (performed internationally), Off the Wall (UK tour) 2000, Unheimlich Spine (Riverside Studios London) 2001 2001; assoc dir feature film Beg!, movement conslt Mad and her Dad (Lyric) 1995; artistic dir Br Summer Sch of Mime, fndr and artistic dir of Southern Int Mime Festival; teacher Central Establishment of Physical Theatre, guest tutor/mentor Central Sch of Speech and Drama; memb Panel Arts Cncl; *Style*— David Glass, Esq

GLASS, Deborah Anne; da of Reuben Glass, of Melbourne, Aust, and Pauline, *née* Ritcher; *b* 15 September 1959; *Educ* Monash Univ Melbourne (BA, LLB); *m* 14 Nov 1997, Jonathan Mirsky; *Career* sr dir Hong Kong Securities and Futures Cmmn 1989–98, chief exec Investment Mgmnt Regulatory Orgn 1998–2000, memb Police Complaints Authy 2001–2004, cmmr Ind Police Complaints Cmmn 2004–; chair Kensington and Chelsea Ind Custody Visitors Panel 2002–04; *Recreations* running in the Royal Parks with my whippet; *Style*— Ms Deborah Glass; ✉ Independent Police Complaints Commission, 90 High Holborn, London WC1V 6BH (tel 020 7166 3000)

GLASS, Norman Jeffrey; CB (2000); s of Philip Glass (d 1975), and Anne, *née* Stein; *b* 31 May 1946; *Educ* Stratford Coll Dublin, Trinity Coll Dublin (BA), Univ of Amsterdam (MSc); *m* 1974, Marieanne, *née* Verger; 1 da (Anne-Sophie b 21 Oct 1978), 1 s (Jerome b 11 Oct 1980); *Career* economist: Shell-Mex & BP Co Ltd 1969–70, Economic Models Ltd 1970–72, DHSS 1975–77, HM Treasy 1977–79, Exchequer and Audit Dept 1979–81; sr economist DHSS 1981–86, asst sec Dept of Health 1986–89; chief economist: DSS 1989–92, DOE 1992–95; dep dir HM Treasy 1995–2001, chm EU Economic Policy Ctee 1999–; lectr Univ of Newcastle upon Tyne 1972–74, research scholar Int Inst for Applied Systems Analysis (IIASA) Austria 1974–75; chm: High Scope UK 2000–, Croydon Sure Start 2001–03; ceo Nat Centre for Social Research 2001–, memb Bd Countryside Agency 2003–; *Recreations* riding, choral singing, going for short walks; *Style*— Norman Glass, Esq, CB; ✉ National Centre for Social Research, 35 Northampton Square, London EC1V 0AX (tel 020 7549 9503, fax 020 7250 1524, e-mail n.glass@natcen.ac.uk)

GLASSER, Cyril; CMG (1999); s of late Phillip Glasser, and late Eva Glasser; *b* 31 January 1942; *Educ* Raine's Fndn GS, LSE (LLB, LLM); *Career* admitted slr 1967; Sheridans: ptnr 1977–2001, head Litigation Dept 1977–99, managing ptnr 1989–2001, sr ptnr 2001, conslt 2001–; Lord Chllr's Dept: special conslt Legal Aid Advsy Ctee 1974–77, memb Working Pty to Review Legal Aid Legislation 1974–77; chm Legal Aid Fin Provisions Working Pty Legal Aid Advsy Ctee 1975–77; memb: Social Science and Law Ctee SSRC 1979–83, Cncl Law Soc 1997–2001, Jt Tbnl on Barristers' Fees 1998–2001; visiting prof of law UCL 1987–; co-fndr and a dir Legal Action Gp 1972–74, memb Mgmnt Ctee Inst of Judicial Admin Univ of Birmingham 1984–, dir Law Soc Tstees Ltd 1999–2005, memb Legal Practice Course Bd 1998–2005; Bar/Law Soc: memb Jt Academic Stage Bd 2004–05, chm Common Professional Educn Bd 2004–06; tstee Legal Assistance Tst 1985–2004, memb Advsy Bd Centre of Advanced Litigation Nottingham Trent Univ 1991–2002; LSE: govr 1996–, memb Cncl 1999–2005; memb Editorial Bd: Modern Law Review 1992–, Int Jl of Evidence and Proof 1996–2002; memb Editorial Advsy Bd Litigator 1994–2001; Hon LLD London Guildhall Univ 2002; FRSA 1995, fell Inst of Advanced Legal Studies 1998; *Style*— Cyril Glasser, Esq, CMG; ✉ Sheridans, Whittington House, Alfred Place, London WC1E 7EA (tel 020 70790100)

GLASSON, Prof John; s of John Glasson, and Olive, *née* Palmer; *b* 2 April 1946; *Educ* LSE (BSc), Lancaster Univ (MA); *m* 29 June 1968, Carol; 2 da (Rebecca b 16 March 1971, Claire b 2 May 1974); *Career* economist and planner Craigavon Devpt Corp 1968–69; Sch of Planning Oxford Poly 1969–80: lectr, sr lectr, princ lectr; head Sch of Planning and dir of Impacts Assess Unit Oxford Poly (now Oxford Brookes Univ) 1980–; Oxford Brookes Univ: pro-vice-chllr Research and Consultancy 1998–2002, research dean Sch of Built Environment 2002–; founding dir Oxford Inst for Sustainable Devpt; visiting prof: Curtin Univ W Aust, Univ of S Aust; memb: UK DOE Planning Research Advsy Gp 1991–96, HEFCE Research Assessment Panel 1992, 1996 and 2001, ESRC Trg Bd 1998–2004, Strategic Planning Advsy Gp SE of Eng Regnl Assembly; dir: Oxfordshire Econ Partnership, Oxfordshire Econ Observatory; MRTPI 1971, MIMgt 1984, FRSA 1992; *Publications* Introduction to Regional Planning (1992), Towards Visitor Impact Management (1995), Introduction to Environmental Impact Assessment (1995, 3 edn 2005), Contemporary Issues in Regional Planning (2002); ed Natural and Built Environment Series 1993–; *Recreations* long distance walking, jogging, running, leisure travel, cinema, reading; *Style*— Professor John Glasson; ✉ Oxford Brookes University, Headington, Oxford OX3 0BP (tel 01865 483401, fax 01865 483559, e-mail jglasson@brookes.ac.uk); 35 Quarry Road, Headington, Oxford OX5 8NU (tel 01865 765682, fax 01865 765682)

GLASSPOOL, Frank Harry; s of Lesley William George Glasspool (d 1936), and Isobel, *née* Highfield (d 1992); *b* 14 May 1934; *Educ* Duke of York Royal Mil Sch; *m* 1, 1 April 1961 (m dis 1981), Olive, da of Charles Geddes (d 1982); 1 da (Wendy b 25 Jan 1963), 1 s (Stephen b 2 Nov 1964); m 2, 25 Feb 1984, Rosemary Esther, da of George Edward Saunders; 2 step s (Simon b 21 Dec 1963, Timothy b 7 Oct 1965), 1 step da (Juliette b 25 July 1971); *Career* sr engr Kellogg Int 1961–68, sr ptnr Glasspool & Thaiss 1968–2005 (conslt 2005–); past pres: Rotary Club Berkhamsted Bulbourne, Berkhamsted Lawn Tennis and Squash Rackets Club; CEng, FIStructE 1974, MConsE 1979; *Recreations* tennis, photography, golf; *Clubs* British Tennis Umpires Assoc, Berkhamsted Lawn Tennis & Squash Rackets, Berkhamsted Bulbourne Rotary, Mentmore Golf and Country; *Style*— Frank Glasspool, Esq; ✉ Coughtrey House, 112–116 Broad Street, Chesham, Buckinghamshire HP5 3ED (tel 01494 771314, fax 01494 791455); Barncroft, Peggs Lane, Buckland, Aylesbury, Buckinghamshire HP22 5HX (e-mail frankandrosemary@talktalk.net)

GLASSPOOL, Jonathan; s of Michael Glasspool, and Anna Glasspool; *b* 18 March 1965; *Educ* Tonbridge (music scholar), Trinity Coll Oxford (exhibitioner, BA), Univ of Bristol (MA), Warwick Business Sch (MBA); *m* 1999, Alysoun Owen; 2 da (Alice Rose b 2000, Elizabeth b 2006), 1 s (Theo b 2002); *Career* head of publishing Inst of Mgmnt 1990–93, publisher Butterworth-Heinemann Reed Elsevier plc 1993–98, appointed product dir electronic media div Bloomsbury Publishing plc 1999, currently dep md A&C Black Ltd; memb Elysian Singers London; FRSA; *Recreations* chamber music, nappy changing; *Style*— Jonathan Glasspool, Esq; ✉ A&C Black Ltd, 38 Soho Square, London W1D 3HB (tel 020 7758 0214, fax 020 7798 0222, e-mail jglasspool@acblack.com)

GLASTONBURY, Virginia; da of Rt Hon Sir Frank Cooper, GCB, CMG (d 2002), and Peggy, *née* Claxton (d 2004); *b* 25 February 1957, Bromley, Kent; *Educ* Bromley HS GPDST, Lady Margaret Hall Oxford (MA), Coll of Law; *m* 25 Oct 1980, Richard Glastonbury; 1 step s (Simon Richard b 6 Nov 1970); *Career* admitted slr 1982; specialises in PFI/PPP, property finance and general real estate; joined as articled clerk Denton Hall & Burgin 1980; Denton Hall: ptnr 1988–2000, memb Bd 1995–2000, managing ptnr UK 1999–2000; Denton Wilde Sapte (following merger): memb Bd 2000–05, managing ptnr UK 2000–02, chief exec 2002–05, ptnr 2005–; ed of various articles in pubns incl The PFI Jl; memb Law Soc; FRSA; *Recreations* cars, motor sports, travel; *Clubs* IoD (City branch); *Style*— Mrs Virginia Glastonbury; ✉ Brooklands, 4 Cardinal Close, Holbrook Lane, Chislehurst, Kent BR7 6SA (tel 020 8467 3694); Denton Wilde Sapte, One Fleet Place, London EC4M 7WS (tel 020 7320 6226, fax 020 7246 7777, e-mail virginia.glastonbury@dentonwildesapte.com)

GLAZEBROOK, Benjamin Kirkland; s of Reginald Field Glazebrook (d 1986), and late Daisy Isobel, *née* Broad; *b* 27 November 1931; *Educ* Eton, Pembroke Coll Cambridge (BA); *m* Sara Ann, *née* Kentish; 2 s (Nicholas David Kirkland, James William); *Career* PA to chm Heinemann Publishers 1958–62 (joined 1955); Constable Publishers: bought controlling interest with Donald Hyde 1962, obtained sole controlling interest 1968, merged Constable with Robinson Publishing 2000, currently chm Constable and Robinson; memb Cncl Publishers Assoc 1989–91; *Recreations* reading, salmon fishing; *Clubs* Beefsteak, Garrick; *Style*— Benjamin Glazebrook, Esq; ✉ Constable and Robinson Publishers, 3 The Lanchesters, 162 Fulham Palace Road, London W6 7ER (tel 020 8741 3663, fax 020 8748 7562)

GLAZEBROOK, (Reginald) Mark; s of Reginald Field Glazebrook (d 1986), and late Daisy Isobel, *née* Broad; *b* 25 June 1936; *Educ* Eton, Pembroke Coll Cambridge (MA), Slade Sch of Fine Art; *m* 1, 1965 (m dis 1969), Elizabeth Lea, *née* Claridge; 1 da (Lucy b 22 April 1966); m 2, 27 Sept 1974, Wanda Barbara, da of Ignacy Piotr Osinski, of Warsaw, Poland; 1 da (Bianca b 25 March 1975); *Career* Nat Serv 2 Lt Welsh Gds 1953–55; exhbn organiser Arts Cncl 1962–65, art critic London Magazine 1967–68, dir Whitechapel Art Gallery 1969–71, head of Modern British Dept Colnaghi & Co Ltd 1972–75, gallery dir San José Univ USA 1976–78; dir: Editions Alecto 1979–81, Albemarle Gallery 1986–93; writer, painter and lectr 1996–; princ exhibition catalogues written and edited: Artists and Architecture of Bedford Park 1875–1900, John Armstrong (1957), David Hockney Paintings Prints Drawings 1960–70 (1970), Edward Wadsworth Paintings Drawings and Prints (1974), John Tunnard (1977), The Seven and Five Soc (1979), Unit One, Spirit of the 30's (1984), Sean Scully (1997); contrib: The Spectator, Modern Painters, Royal Acad magazine, The Scotsman, The Independent, The Evening Standard; solo exhbn Mayor Gallery London 2000; FRSA 1971; *Recreations* cooking, walking, swimming; *Clubs* Beefsteak, Chelsea Arts, Lansdowne; *Style*— Mark Glazebrook, Esq; ✉ Flat 1, 28 Draycott Place, London SW3 2SB

GLAZEBROOK, Philip Kirkland; s of Francis Kirkland Glazebrook (d 1988), of Horsmonden, Kent, and Winifred, *née* Davison (d 1984); *b* 3 April 1937; *Educ* Eton, Trinity Coll Cambridge; *m* 5 Oct 1968 (m dis 2001), Clare Rosemary, da of Arthur Stewart Gemmell; 2 s (Augustin b 24 April 1973, Harry b 18 Dec 1980), 2 da (Olivia b 20 Jan 1976, Maisie b 3 April 1984); *Career* writer; *Fiction* Try Pleasure (1968), The Eye of the Beholder (1973), The Walled Garden (1977), Byzantine Honeymoon (1979), Captain Vinegar's Commission (1987), The Gate at the End of the World (1989), The Electric Rock Garden (2001); *Travel* Journey to Kars (1983), Journey to Khiva (1992); *Recreations* fishing; *Clubs* MCC, Travellers; *Style*— Philip Glazebrook; ✉ Richard Scott Simon, 43 Doughty Street, London WC1N 2LF (tel 020 7405 7379, fax 020 7831 2127)

G

GLAZER, Prof Anthony Michael (Mike); *Educ* Univ of St Andrews (BSc), Univ of London (PhD); *Career* postdoctoral asst rising to dir Wolfson Unit for the Sudy of Dielectric Materials Cavendish Lab Univ of Cambridge 1969–76, official fell and tutor in physics Jesus Coll Oxford 1976–, appointed lectr in physics Univ of Oxford 1976, currently prof of physics Univ of Oxford; fndr Oxford Cryosystems; pres British Crystallographic Assoc 1996; *Books* Space Groups for Solid State Scientists (with Gerald Burns, 1978, 2 edn 1990), The Structures of Crystals (1987), Statistical Mechanics: A Survival Guide (with J S Wark, 2001); *Recreations* aviation; *Style*— Prof Mike Glazer; ✉ Condensed Matter Physics, Clarendon Laboratory, Parks Road, Oxford OX1 3PU

GLAZER, Geoffrey; s of Benjamin Glazer (d 1979), of Croydon, and Dora, *née* Hornstein; *b* 11 February 1939; *Educ* Selhurst GS, St Mary's Hosp Med Sch (MB BS, MRCS, LRCP, MS); *m* Sandra Estelle, da of Bernard Lasky; 2 s (David Anthony b 1 July 1965, Simon Jonathon b 12 Oct 1968), 1 da (Debra Juliette b 7 April 1973); *Career* sr surgical registrar St Mary's Hosp London 1971–75, res fell Harvard Med Sch 1975, sr lectr in surgery St Mary's Hosp Med Sch 1976–77, conslt surgn St Mary's Hosp 1977–; Freeman: Worshipful Soc of Apothecaries 1990, City of London 1993; memb RSM 1977; FRCS, FACS; *Books* Acute Pancreatitis (1988); *Recreations* tennis, golf, dry fly fishing, travel, theatre, reading; *Clubs* MCC; *Style*— Geoffrey Glazer, Esq; ✉ 84A St John's Wood High Street, London NW8 7SH (tel 020 7483 3020, fax 020 7483 3087, e-mail g.glazer@surg.freeserve.co.uk)

GLEADELL, Colin Francis; s of Maj Gen Paul Gleadell, CB, CBE, DSO (d 1988), and Mary, *née* Montgomerie Lind (d 1994); *b* 17 December 1946; *Educ* Downside, Churchill Coll Cambridge (MA); *m* 1988, Sophie Barbara Estella, da of Ernle David Drummond Money; 1 da (Rose Montgomerie b 7 Sept 1993), 1 s (Benjamin Ernle Alexander b 23 July 1998); *Career* res Paul Mellon Fndn for Br Art 1968–71, mangr Crane Arts London 1971–73, freelance art conslt and pt/t musical dir NEMS Records 1974–78, head Modern Art Dept Bonham's Auctioneers 1979–81, freelance art conslt 1982–85, features ed Galleries Magazine 1985–97, salesroom corr Art Monthly 1986–, London corr Art Newsletter 1996–, art sales corr The Daily Telegraph 1997–; memb Advsy Ctee 20th Century Br Art Fair 1987–; conslt BBC TV: The Great Picture Chase 1990, Relative Values 1991, Eric Hebborn, Portrait of a Master Forger 1991, Sister Wendy's Grand Tour 1993; art conslt Channel 4 News 1999–; memb Int Assoc of Art Critics 1987; *Publications* numerous exhibition catalogues and articles in specialist art magazines; *Style*— Colin Gleadell, Esq; ✉ e-mail colin@glead.freeserve.co.uk

GLEAVE, Prof (Michael) Barrie; s of John Thomas Gleave (d 1959), and Mildred, *née* Darbyshire (d 1992); *b* 22 July 1936; *Educ* Roundhay Sch Leeds, Univ of Hull (BA, MA, PhD), Univ of Reading (DipEd); *m* 21 Aug 1961, Jean, da of John Marsland (d 1965); 1 da (Catherine b 1964), 1 s (Jonathan b 1966); *Career* prof of geography Fourah Bay Coll Univ of Sierra Leone 1972–74; Univ of Salford: prof of geography 1982–95, chm of dept 1983–94, research prof 1995–2000, hon research prof 2000–; treas African Studies Assoc of UK 1980–84; memb Geographical Assoc; ASA UK; FRGS with IBG; *Books* An Economic Geography of West Africa (jtly, 1971), Tropical African Development: Geographical Perspectives (ed, 1992); *Clubs* Lancs CCC; *Style*— Prof Barrie Gleave; ✉ Twin Trees Cottage, Knoll Lane, Little Hoole, Preston PR4 4TB (tel 01772 616402, fax 01772 619570, e-mail barrie.gleave@btopenworld.com); School of Environment and Life Sciences, University of Salford, Salford M5 4WT

GLEDHILL, Rt Rev Jonathan Michael; *see:* Lichfield, Bishop of

GLEDHILL, Keith Ainsworth; MBE (1994), DL (Lancs 1986); s of Norman Gledhill (d 1970), of Blackpool, and Louise, *née* Ainsworth (d 1988); *b* 28 August 1932; *Educ* Arnold Sch Blackpool; *m* 7 July 1956, Margaret Irene, da of Joseph Bramwell Burton (d 1970); 1 s (Ian C b 1958); *Career* jr offr MN 1950–54; Nat Serv RAF 1954–56; Norman Gledhill & Co Ltd 1956–65, Delta Metal Co Ltd 1965 (sr exec contract); fndr: Gledhill Water Storage Ltd 1972, Nu-Rad Ltd 1974, Thermal Sense (Energy Conservation Systems) Ltd 1979; chm Foxton Dispensary Tst, vice-chm Blackpool and Fylde Soc for the Blind, govr Skelton Bounty Tst; vice-pres: Lancs St John Cncl, Lancs Cncl Vol Youth Servs; past chm Lancs Youth Clubs Assoc, past offr Rotary Int; High Sheriff Lancs 1992, Vice Lord-Lt Lancs 2002–05; Freeman City of London, Liveryman Worshipful Co of Plumbers; FInstD 1968, MInstP 1970; KStJ; *Recreations* golf; *Clubs* Royal Lytham and St Anne's Golf, Fylde RUFC; *Style*— Keith Gledhill, Esq, MBE, DL, KStJ; ✉ Broken Hill, 35 South Park Drive, Blackpool, Lancashire FY3 9PZ (tel 01253 764462); Gledhill Water Storage Ltd, Sycamore Estate, Squires Gate, Blackpool, Lancashire FY4 3RL (tel 01253 474431, fax 01253 474456, e-mail keithg@gledhill.net)

GLEDHILL, Michael William; s of George Eric Louis Gledhill (d 1986), of Shelf, nr Halifax, W Yorks, and Sarah Jane, *née* Green (d 1979); *b* 28 October 1937; *Educ* Rishworth Sch Halifax; *m* 18 Oct 1962, Margaret, da of Cyril Ira Fletcher (d 1965), of Halifax, W Yorks; 3 s (Marc b Nov 1963, Andrew b May 1966, Jonathan b June 1969); *Career* slr; ptnr Finn, Gledhill 1962–2003 (conslt 2003–); Notary Public Halifax 1980; dir G W Estates Ltd 1968–; clerk: Waterhouse Charity Halifax 1965–2004, Tstees Abbotts Ladies Home Halifax 1967–, Mackintosh Memorial Homes 2001–04; dir Halifax Choral Soc (1817) Ltd (chm 2004–06), govr Wheelwright Charity (Rishworth Sch) 1991– (clerk 1985–91, chm 1997–2001); *Recreations* golf, gardening, rugby; *Style*— Michael W Gledhill, Esq; ✉ Post Cottage, Warley Town, Warley, Halifax HX2 7RZ (tel 01422 831890); Finn, Gledhill, 1/4 Harrison Road, Halifax HX1 2AG (tel 01422 330000, fax 01422 342604, e-mail michael.gledhill@finngledhill.co.uk)

GLEDHILL, Ruth; da of Rev Peter Gledhill, of Yr Hen Felin Pwllfanogl, LlanfairPG, Gwynedd, and Bridget Mary, *née* Rathbone; *b* 15 December 1959; *Educ* Thomas Alleyne's GS Uttoxeter, LCP (HND), Birkbeck Coll London (Cert Religious Studies); *m* 1, 1989, John Edward Stammers (m dis 1993); m 2, 1996 (m dis 2003), Andrew Daniels; 1 s (Arthur Peter Gledhill Franks b 27 Oct 2001); *Career* indentured Birmingham Post & Mail 1982–84, gen news reporter Daily Mail 1984–87; The Times: home news reporter 1987–90, religion corr 1990–, columnist At Your Service (Times Weekend) 1996–; regular radio and TV appearances on religious affrs; highly commended Templeton prize for religious reporting 1998, nominated specialist of the year UK Press Awards 2004, Andrew Cross religion writer of the year 2004; *Books* Birmingham is Not a Boring City (co-author, 1984), The Times Book of Best Sermons (ed and introduction, 1995, 1996, 1997 and 1998), At A Service Near You (1996), The Times Book of Prayers (ed, 1997); *Recreations* playing with my son, playing the guitar, reading and writing fiction; *Clubs* Reform, London Rotary; *Style*— Ms Ruth Gledhill; ✉ The Times, 1 Pennington Street, London E98 1TT (tel 020 7782 5001, fax 020 7782 5004, e-mail ruth.gledhill@thetimes.co.uk); home tel 020 8948 5871

GLEESON, Dermot James; s of Patrick Joseph Gleeson (d 2006), of Cheam, Surrey, and Margaret Mary, *née* Higgins (d 1998); *b* 5 September 1949; *Educ* Downside, Fitzwilliam Coll Cambridge (open scholarship, MA); *m* 6 Sept 1980, Rosalind Mary Catherine, da of Dr Charles Edward Moorhead (d 1953), of Chipping Campden, Glos; 1 da (Catherine b 1981), 1 s (Patrick b 1984); *Career* Cons Res Dept 1974–77 (acting dir 1979), European Cmmn (cabinet of Christopher Tugendhat) 1977–79, EEC rep of Midland Bank Brussels 1980–82; MJ Gleeson Group plc: joined 1982, chief exec 1988–1994, chm 1994–; dir: The Housing Corporation 1990–95, Construction Industry Training Bd 1995–2002; chm Major Contractors Gp 2003–05; govr BBC 2000–06, memb BBC Tst 2006–; *Clubs* Beefsteak (chm 2004–07), RAC; *Style*— Dermot Gleeson, Esq; ✉ Hook Farm, White Hart Lane, Wood Street Village, Surrey GU3 3EA (tel 01483 236210); M J Gleeson Group plc, Haredon House, London Road, North Cheam, Sutton, Surrey SM3 9BS (tel 020 8644 4321, fax 020 8644 6366)

GLEN, Hamish; *Educ* Edinburgh Acad, Univ of Aberdeen (LLB); *Career* artistic dir; asst stage mangr Traverse Theatre Co 1980–81, stage mangr Paines Plough 1981–82, fndr and dir Writers' Theatre Co 1983, trainee dir Tron Theatre/Scottish Arts Cncl 1985–87, assoc dir Tron Theatre Co 1987–89, artistic dir Winged Horse Theatre 1989–92, artistic dir Dundee Rep Theatre 1992–2003, artistic dir Belgrade Theatre 2003–, chair Fedn of Scottish Theatre 1995–2003; *Productions* Writers' Theatre Co: At It, Noonday Demons, More Happy Chickens; Tron Theatre Co: Babes in the Wood, The Tom and Sammy Show; Winged Horse Theatre: Magic Theatre, Elizabeth Gordan Quinn, Bailegangaire, The Evil Doers, American Buffalo; Dundee Rep: Who's Afraid of Virginia Woolf?, Walter, Tartuffe, Uncle Vanya, The Hypochondriak, American Buffalo, Toshie, Death and the Maiden, Bourgeois Gentilhomme, Cinderella, Hyde, A Greater Tomorrow, The Weavers, Mill Lavvies, Puss in Boots, Hansel and Gretel, Cabaret, Colquhoun and MacBryde, A Midsummer Night's Dream, A Family Affair, Abody's Aberdee, Measure for Measure, Nightflights; other credits incl: Marriage (Shared Experience) 1983, Two Way Mirror (Traverse Theatre) 1985, The Overcoat (Tron Theatre/Scottish Arts Cncl) 1985, Burning Love (Traverse Theatre) 1986, Gamblers (Tron Theatre/Traverse Theatre co-prodn) 1986, Who's Left (Swaive Kinooziers) 1986, As You Like It (Royal Lyceum Edinburgh) 1989, Le Bourgeois (Royal Lyceum Edinburgh) 1989, The Funeral (Tron Theatre/IPB Prodns) 1989, Gamblers (Lithuanian State Theatre) 1991, The Hypochondriak (Mikkeli Theatre Finland) 1994, What the Butler Saw (Tampere T Theatre) 1997, A Delicate Balance (Helsinki Theatre) 1998; *Style*— Hamish Glen, Esq; ✉ The Belgrade Theatre, Belgrade Square, Coventry CV1

GLEN, Iain Alan Sutherland; s of James Robert Glen, and Alison Helen, *née* Brown; *Educ* RADA (Bancroft Gold Medal); *Career* actor; Hon LLD Univ of Aberdeen 2004; *Theatre* incl: The Blue Room (Donmar Warehouse and Broadway, Best Actor Broadway Drama League Award, nomination Best Actor Olivier Awards), Martin Guerre (West End, nomination Best Actor in a Musical Olivier Awards), The Broken Heart (RSC), Henry V (RSC, nomination Evening Standard Awards), Here (Donmar Warehouse), Macbeth (Tron Theatre, Mayfest Award for Best Actor), King Lear (Royal Court), Coriolanus (Chichester Festival Theatre), Hamlet (Bristol Old Vic, Ian Charleson Award), Hapgood (West End), Road (Royal Court), Edward II (Royal Exchange Manchester), A Streetcar Named Desire (RNT), The Seagull (Edinburgh Fesitval), Hedda Gabler (Almeida Theatre and West End, Olivier Award for Best Revival), The Crucible (RSC, Olivier nomination for Best Actor, Olivier Award for Best Revival); *Television* incl: Will You Love Me Tomorrow, The Fear, Adam Bede, Frankie's House, Trial & Retribution, Wives & Daughters, Death of a Salesman (nomination BAFTA Awards), The Picnic, Glasgow Kiss, Anchor Me; *Film* incl: Paris By Night, Mountains of the Moon (Best Actor Evening Standard Awards), Rosencrantz and Guildenstern Are Dead, Fools of Fortune, Silent Scream (Silver Bear for Best Actor Berlin Film Festival, Michael Powell Award, Scottish BAFTA Awards), Young Americans, Tombraider, Darkness, Keeper Of My Soul, Spy Sorge, Song for a Raggy Boy, Man to Man, Tara Road, Small Engine Repairs, Resident Evil, Kingdom of Heaven, The Gift (short film, Grand Jury Prize Lille Short Film Festival, BAFTA Audience Award); *Recreations* most sports, playing guitar and piano, singing; *Style*— Iain Glen

GLEN HAIG, Dame Mary Alison; DBE (1993), (CBE 1977, MBE 1971); da of William Charles James (d 1956), and Mary Adelaide, *née* Bannochie (d 1973); *b* 12 July 1918; *Educ* Dame Alice Owen's Sch London; *Career* former int fencer and sports admin; fencing achievements: finalist Olympic Games London 1948, Gold Medal (Foil) Cwlth Games 1950 and 1954 (Bronze Medal 1958); Ladies' Amateur Fencing Union: memb Ctee 1946–, BOA rep 1948–, pres 1964–73 (vice-pres 1973–); Amateur Fencing Assoc: memb Ctee 1951–, asst hon treas 1955–56, hon sec 1956–73, pres 1973–86, hon pres 1986–; BOA: memb Exec Ctee 1972–, memb Finance & General Purposes Ctee, chm and tstee Medical Centre 1988–93; Int Olympic Ctee: British memb 1982–93, memb Medical Cmmn, hon memb 1993–; pres Cwlth Fencing Fedn 1978– (hon sec & hon treas 1950–78); Sports Cncl of GB: memb Advsy 1966–71, memb Exec 1971–82; Central Cncl for Physical Recreation: dep chm 1973–75, chm 1975–81, vice-pres 1982–; Sports Aid Fndn: fndr governor, memb Exec Ctee 1981–88, dep chm 1983–86, vice-pres 1986–; Fedn Internationale d'Escrime: Brit rep to Fedn 1972–, memb Cmmn Bàreme des Voix 1976–86, memb Cmmn Ladies' Epee 1983; pres Disability Sport England (formerly British Sports Assoc for the Disabled) 1981– (hon life pres 1991–); Disabled Sports Fndn: tstee 1979–, hon sec 1983–; King's Coll Hospital London: pupil administrator 1936–39, sec to dir 1939–41, asst dir 1941–48; gp patients servs offr: Royal National Orthopaedic Hosp 1948–73, Charing Cross Hosp 1973–74; asst district administrator South Hammersmith Health District 1975–82 (admin offr 1974–75); British Schools Exploring Soc: memb Cncl 1979–, memb Finance Ctee 1979–, vice-pres 1990–; memb: Advsy Cncl First Aid and Nursing Yeomanry 1978–, Ctee Cmmn for Prevention of Accidents to Children 1980–84, Bisham Abbey Sports Centre Ctee 1982–, Crystal Palace Sports Centre Ctee 1983–88, Prince of Wales Advsy Gp on Disability 1988–90, Rheumatic and Arthritic Cncl 1992–; chm of tstees Princess Christian Hosp 1982–94 (tstee 1981–84), tstee Charing Cross Medical Res Centre 1980–, tstee Kennedy Inst 1996–; Freeman City of London, Liveryman Worshipful Company of Glovers; *Recreations* fencing, gardening, travelling; *Clubs* East India, Lansdowne; *Style*— Dame Mary Glen Haig, DBE

GLENAMARA, Baron (Life Peer UK 1977), of Glenridding in County of Cumbria; Edward Watson Short; CH (1976), PC (1964); s of Charles and Mary Short, of Warcop, Westmorland; *b* 17 December 1912; *Educ* Bede Coll Durham (LLB); *m* 1941, Jennie, da of Thomas Sewell, of Newcastle upon Tyne; 1 s (Hon Michael Christian b 1943), 1 da (Hon Jane Bronwen (Hon Mrs Fraser) b 1945); *Career* WWII Capt DLI; sits as Labour peer in House of Lords; MP (Lab) Newcastle upon Tyne Central 1951–76, oppn whip (N) 1955–62, dep chief oppn whip 1962–64, govt chief whip (and Parly sec Treasy) 1964–66, Postmaster Gen 1966–68, sec of state Educn and Sci 1968–70, Lord President of the Cncl and Ldr of the House of Commons 1974–76, dep ldr Lab Pty 1972–76, chllr Univ of Northumbria, pres Finchale Abbey Trg Coll for Disabled, chm Cable Wireless Ltd 1976–80; Freeman City of Newcastle upon Tyne; Hon DCL Univ of Durham, Hon DCL Univ of Newcastle upon Tyne, Hon DUniv Open Univ, Hon DLitt CNAA; *Books* The Story of the Durham Light Infantry (1944), The Infantry Instructor (1946), Education in a Changing World (1971), Birth to Five (1974), I Knew My Place (1983), Whip to Wilson (1989); *Style*— The Rt Hon Lord Glenamara, CH, PC; ✉ 21 Priory Gardens, Corbridge, Northumberland (tel 0143 463 2880)

GLENARTHUR, 4 Baron (UK 1918); Sir Simon Mark Arthur; 4 Bt (UK 1903), DL (Aberdeenshire 1988); s of 3 Baron Glenarthur, OBE, DL (d 1976), by his 2 w, Margaret Risk, *née* Howie (d 1993); *b* 7 October 1944; *Educ* Eton; *m* 12 Nov 1969, Susan, yr da of Cdr Hubert Wyndham Barry, RN (d 1992), and Violet (d 1994), da of Col Sir Edward Ruggles-Brise, 1 Bt; 1 s (Hon Edward Alexander b 1973), 1 da (Hon Emily Victoria b 1975); *Heir* s, Hon Edward Arthur; *Career* served 10th Royal Hussars (PWO) (subsequently The Royal Hussars (PWO)): cmmnd 1963, Capt 1970, Maj 1973, ret; served Royal Hussars (PWO) TA 1975–80; Capt British Airways Helicopters Ltd 1976–82; dir Aberdeen & Texas Corporate Finance Ltd 1977–82, sr exec Hanson plc 1989–96 (conslt 1996–99), dep chm Hanson Pacific Ltd 1994–98; dir: The Lewis Group plc 1993–94, Whirly Bird Services Ltd 1995–2004, Millennium Chemicals Inc 1996–2004, Audax Trading (Overseas) Ltd (now Audax Global) 2003–; conslt: British Aerospace plc 1989–99, Chevron UK Ltd 1994–97, Imperial Tobacco Group plc 1996–98, Intertek Testing Services 2001–02; dir Med Defence Union 2002–06, chm St Mary's Hosp

Paddington NHS Tst 1991–98, govr Nuffield Hosps 2001–; cmmr Royal Hosp Chelsea 2001–07; sits as elected Cons peer in House of Lords, Govt whip (lord in waiting) 1982–83; Parly under sec of state: DHSS 1983–85, Home Office 1985–86; min of state: Scotland 1986–87, FCO 1987–89; pres Nat Cncl for Civil Protection 1991–2003; pres Br Helicopter Advsy Bd 2004– (chm 1992–2004) chm: Euro Helicopter Assoc 1996–2003, Int Fedn of Helicopter Assocs 1997–2004; memb Cncl The Air League 1994–, chm Nat Employer Advsy Bd for Britain's Reserve Forces 2002– (memb 1996–); Hon Col 306 Hosp Medical Support Regt (V) 2001–, Hon Air Cdre 612 (Co of Aberdeen) Sqdn RAuxAF 2004–; memb (Lt) Queen's Body Guard for Scotland (Royal Co of Archers); Liveryman Guild of Air Pilots and Air Navigators; FRAeS, FCILT; *Recreations* field sports, flying, gardening, barometers, choral singing, organ playing; *Clubs* Cavalry and Guards', Pratt's; *Style—* The Rt Hon the Lord Glenarthur, DL; ✉ PO Box 11012, Banchory, Kincardineshire AB31 6ZJ (tel 01330 844467, e-mail glenarthur@northbrae.co.uk)

GLENCONNER, 3 Baron (UK 1911); Sir Colin Christopher Paget Tennant; 4 Bt (UK 1885); s of 2 Baron Glenconner (d 1983), and his 1 w, Pamela, Baroness Glenconner; *b* 1 December 1926; *Educ* Eton, New Coll Oxford; *m* 21 April 1956, Lady Anne Veronica Coke, LVO (*see* Glenconner, Baroness); 3 s (Hon Charles Edward Pevensey b 1957 d 1996, Hon Henry Lovell b 1960 d 1990, Hon Christopher Cary b 1968), twin da (Hon May and Hon Amy b 1970); *Heir* gs, Cody Tennant; *Career* Lt Irish Gds; governing dir Tennants Estate Ltd 1967–91, chm Mustique Co 1968–87; *Style—* The Rt Hon Lord Glenconner; ✉ Beau Estate, PO Box 250, Soufriere, St Lucia, West Indies (tel 1 758 459 7864, fax 1 758 459 5057, e-mail beauestate@candur.lc)

GLENDEVON, 2 Baron (UK 1964), of Midhope, Co Linlithgow; Julian John Somerset Hope; er s of 1 Baron Glendevon, PC, ERD (d 1996), and Elizabeth Mary (d 1998), o da of late (William) Somerset Maugham, CH, FRSL; *b* 6 March 1950; *Educ* Eton, Christ Church Oxford; *Heir* bro, Hon Jonathan Hope; *Career* operatic prodr; resident prodr Welsh National Opera 1973–75; assoc prodr Glyndebourne Festival 1974–81; prodns incl: San Francisco Opera, Wexford and Edinburgh Festivals; *Style—* The Rt Hon Lord Glendevon

GLENDINNING, David Edward Hamilton; s of Dr David Glendinning, of Sleaford, Lincs, and late Kathleen Theresa, *née* Holmes; *b* 28 December 1946; *Educ* Carres GS Sleaford, UCH (BDS); *m* 1, 20 June 1971 (m dis 1974), Victoria Sorrell, da of Prof Raleigh Barcley Lucas, of Sevenoaks, Kent; m 2, 9 Oct 1976, Teresa Mary, da of Brendan James Bolger, of St Albans, Herts; 2 da (Laura b 1980, Sarah b 1982), 1 s (Andrew b 1986); *Career* house surgn UCH 1970, sr house offr in periodontology Royal Dental Hosp 1970–71, registrar Dental Dept Bart'sHosp 1972–74, sr registrar in oral surgery Manchester 1974–78, conslt oral surgn S Lincolnshire Pilgrim Hosp Boston and Grantham and Kesteven Gen Hosp 1978–; postgrad dental tutor to S Lincs 1991–; various pubns in Br and US oral surgery press; fell BAOMS 1979, FDSRCS; *Recreations* golf, sailing, old cars, racing; *Clubs* Sleaford Golf, Fakenham Raceclub; *Style—* David Glendinning, Esq; ✉ Hill House, South Rauceby, Sleaford, Lincolnshire NG34 8QQ (tel 01529 488625); Edinmore, Croc-An-Raer, North Bute, Isle of Bute PA20 0QT; Department of Oral Surgery, Pilgrim Hospital, Boston, Lincolnshire (tel 01205 64801)

GLENDINNING, (Hon) Victoria (Hon Mrs O'Sullivan); CBE (1998); er da of Baron Seebohm, TD (Life Peer, d 1990), and Evangeline (d 1990), da of His Hon Sir Gerald Berkeley Hurst, QC; *b* 23 April 1937; *Educ* St Mary's Wantage, Millfield, Somerville Coll Oxford (MA), Univ of Southampton (Dip Social Admin); *m* 1, 1958 (m dis 1981), Prof (Oliver) Nigel Valentine Glendinning; 4 s; m 2, 1982, Terence de Vere White (d 1994), s of Frederick S de Vere White; m 3, 1996, Kevin O'Sullivan; *Career* author and journalist; head Booker Prize panel 1992; pres English Centre PEN 2001 (vice-pres 2003), vice-pres RSL 2000; hon fell Somerville Coll Oxford 2004; Hon DLitt: Univ of Southampton 1994, Univ of Ulster 1995, Univ of Dublin 1995, Univ of York 2000; FRSL; *Books* A Suppressed Cry (1975), Elizabeth Bowen - Portrait of a Writer (1977), Edith Sitwell - A Unicorn among Lions (1981, Duff Cooper Award and James Tait Black Award), Vita (1983, Whitbread Biography Award), Rebecca West (1987), Hertfordshire (1989), The Grown Ups (1989), Trollope (1992, Whitbread Biography Award), Electricity (1995), Sons and Mothers (ed with Matthew Glendinning, 1996), Jonathan Swift (1998), Flight (2002), Leonard Woolf (2006); *Clubs* Athenaeum; *Style—* Victoria Glendinning; ✉ c/o David Higham Associates, 5–8 Lower John Street, London W1F 9HA (tel 020 7437 7888)

GLENDYNE, 3 Baron (UK 1922); Sir Robert Nivison; 3 Bt (UK 1914); s of 2 Baron Glendyne (d 1967); *b* 27 October 1926; *Educ* Harrow; *m* 25 April 1953, Elizabeth, yr da of Sir (Stephen) Cecil Armitage, CBE, JP, DL, of Hawksworth Manor, Notts; 1 s, 2 da; *Heir* s, Hon John Nivison; *Career* with Grenadier Gds 1944–47 (ret as Lt); sr ptnr R Nivison & Co (stockbrokers) 1967–86 (ptnr 1947–67), chm Glenfriars Unit Trust Managers Ltd 1971–93; *Clubs* City of London; *Style—* Lord Glendyne; ✉ Craigeassie By Forfar, Angus DD8 3SE

GLENN, His Hon Judge Paul Anthony; s of Sidney Glenn, of Stoke-on-Trent, and Nora, *née* Lavin (d 2006); *b* 14 September 1957, Newcastle-under-Lyme; *Educ* St Joseph's Coll Stoke-on-Trent, Univ of Liverpool (LLB); *m* 31 Aug 1985, Diane, *née* Burgess; 2 s (George Francis b 5 April 1987, Robert William b 3 Sept 1988); *Career* called to the Bar Gray's Inn 1983; clerk Cheshire Magistrates' Courts 1981–85, prosecuting slr Co Prosecuting Slrs' Office Cheshire 1985–87, sr crown prosecutor CPS Cheshire and Staffordshire 1987–90, practicing barr 1990–2004 (memb of chambers 4 Fountain Court and Citadel Chambers), recorder of the Crown Court 2001–04, circuit judge (Midland Circuit) 2004–; *Recreations* football, rugby, cricket; *Style—* His Hon Judge Glenn; ✉ c/o Stoke-on-Trent Combined Court Centre, Bethesda Street, Hanley, Stoke-on-Trent ST1 3BP

GLENNIE, Hon Lord; Angus James Scott Glennie; s of Robert Nigel Forbes Glennie, of London and Sussex, and Barbara Scott, *née* Nicoll (d 1987); *b* 3 December 1950; *Educ* Sherborne, Trinity Hall Cambridge (exhibitioner, MA); *m* 3 Oct 1981, Patricia Jean, da of His Hon Andrew James Phelan; 3 s (Alasdair Lewis Scott b 3 April 1983, Patrick James Nicoll b 27 July 1987, Pierce Nicholas Forbes b 11 Jan 1990); 1 da (Aisling Frances Robertson b 19 April 1985); *Career* called to the Bar Lincoln's Inn 1974, QC 1991; called to the Scottish Bar 1992, QC (Scot) 1998, senator Coll of Justice 2005–; memb Gibraltar Bar; farmer 1991–; assoc memb London Maritime Arbitrators' Assoc; *Recreations* sailing, real tennis, skiing; *Style—* The Hon Lord Glennie; ✉ Court of Session, Parliament House, Edinburgh EH1 1RQ

GLENNIE, Evelyn Elizabeth Ann; DBE (2007, OBE 1993); da of Herbert Arthur Glennie, of Ellon, Aberdeenshire, and Isobel Mary, *née* Howie; *b* 19 July 1965; *Educ* Ellon Acad Royal Acad of Music; further studies in Japan on Munster Tst Scholarship; *Career* solo musician (timpani and percussion); debut recital Wigmore Hall 1986, BBC Prom debut 1989; first ever solo percussion recital 1989, Last Night of the Proms 1994, other Proms appearances in 1992, 1996, 1997, 1998, 1999 and 2000; concerts with numerous orchs worldwide as percussion soloist incl: LSO, Philharmonia, London Sinfonietta, Northern Sinfonia, Eng Chamber, RTE (Dublin), Ulster Orch, BBC Scottish Symphony, Finnish Radio Symphony, Trondheim Symphony (Norway), Los Angeles Philharmonic, NY Philharmonic, Detroit Symphony, Nat Symphony (Washington), St Louis Symphony, Orchester der Deutschen Oper Berlin; concert tours of: Europe, Australia, USA, S America, Japan, Middle East, NZ, Far East, UK; composer original music for TV, radio and films; numerous concerts and recitals as a percussion soloist and Great Highland bagpiper; guest appearances and presenter on TV and radio; recordings: Bartók Sonata for Two Pianos and Percussion (with Sir Georg Solti and Murray Perahia 1987, Grammy awards 1989 and 2001), Rhythm Song (1989), Light in Darkness (1990), Last Night of the Proms 100th Season (1995), Dancin', Rebounds, Veni Veni Emmanuel, Wind in the Bamboo Grove, Drumming, Her Greatest Hits, The Music of Joseph Schwantner, Street Songs, Reflected in Brass, Shadow Behind the Iron Sun, UFO; several pieces composed for her by: John McLeod, Richard Rodney Bennett, Dominic Muldowney, James MacMillan, Geoffrey Burgon, Dave Heath, Thea Musgrave, Jonathan Harvey, Askell Masson, John Psathas, Mark Anthony Turnage; awarded: Gold Medal Shell LSO music scholarship 1984, Munster Tst scholarship 1986, Leonardo de Vinci Prize 1987, Charles Heidsieck Instrumentalist of the Year Award 1991; voted by Jr Chamber as one of ten outstanding young people in the world 1989, Scotswoman of the Decade for the 1980s; Hon DMus: Univ of Aberdeen 1991, Univ of Portsmouth 1995, Univ of Bristol 1995, Loughborough Univ 1995, Univ of Southampton, Univ of Exeter; Hon DLitt Univ of Warwick 1993, Hon LLD Univ of Dundee 1996; FRCM 1991, FRAM 1992, FRSE 2005; *Books* Good Vibrations (autobiography, 1990); *Recreations* reading, walking, music, antiques, psychology; *Style—* Dr Dame Evelyn Glennie, DBE; ✉ PO Box 6, Sawtry, Huntingdon, Cambridgeshire PE17 5WE (tel 08707 741492, fax 08707 741493, e-mail carla@evelyn.co.uk, website www.evelyn.co.uk)

GLENNY, (Alexander) Keith; s of Lt-Col Clifford Roy Glenny, TD (d 1997), of Essex, and Eileen Winifred, *née* Smith (d 1974); *b* 19 July 1946; *Educ* Charterhouse, Gonville & Caius Coll Cambridge (MA, LLM), KCL (Dip Euro Law); *m* 19 April 1975, Rachel Elizabeth, da of Rev A C Fryer, of Byfield, Northants; 2 s (Christopher b 5 Jan 1977, Matthew b 31 Oct 1986), 1 da (Anna b 24 May 1979); *Career* slr British Oxygen Co Ltd 1970–72; Hatten Asplin Glenny: slr 1972–74, ptnr 1974–88, sr ptnr 1988–; clerk Barking and Ilford United Charities and Barking Gen Charities; Freeman Worshipful Co of Poulters 1978 (Liveryman 1978, memb Ct of Assts 2001, Upper Warden 2007–08); memb Law Soc, MInstD; *Clubs* Athenaeum; *Style—* Keith Glenny, Esq; ✉ Netherfield, Powdermill Lane, Leigh, Tonbridge, Kent TN11 8PY (tel 01732 833 320); Hatten Asplin Glenny, 4 Town Quay Wharf, Abbey Road, Barking IG11 7BZ (tel 020 8591 4131, fax 020 8591 1912, e-mail kglenny@hattens.co.uk)

GLENTON, Anthony Arthur Edward; CBE (2000, MBE Mil 1983), TD (1974), DL (Northumberland, 1990); s of Lt-Col Eric Cecil Glenton (d 1978), of Gosforth, Newcastle upon Tyne, and Joan Lydia, *née* Taylor; *b* 21 March 1943; *Educ* Merchiston Castle Sch Edinburgh; *m* 8 April 1972, Caroline Ann, da of Maurice George Meade-King, of Clifton, Bristol; 1 da (Sophie b 1974), 1 s (Peter b 1977); *Career* joined TA 1961, Lt-Col 1984, cmd 101 (Northumbrian) Field Regt RA (V) 1984–86, Col 1986, dep cdr 15 Inf Bde 1986–89; ADC to HM the Queen 1987–89; TA Col advsr to GOC Eastern Dist 1990–94, chm North of England RFCA 2000–03; Hon Regtl Col 101 (Northumbrian) Regt RA (V) 2005–; sr ptnr Ryecroft Glenton Chartered Accountants Newcastle upon Tyne; chm: SSAFA - Forces Help Northumberland Branch 1989–, Newcastle Building Society 1993–98 (dir 1987–), Port of Tyne Authy 1994–2005, Charles W Taylor Ltd 1996–2003; Freeman City of London, Liveryman Worshipful Co of Chartered Accountants; FCA 1971; *Recreations* shooting, sailing, contemporary art; *Clubs* Army and Navy; *Style—* Anthony Glenton, Esq, CBE, TD, DL, FCA; ✉ Whinbank, Rothbury, Northumberland NE65 7YJ (tel 01669 620361); 32 Portland Terrace, Jesmond, Newcastle upon Tyne NE2 1QP (tel 0191 281 1292)

GLENTORAN, 3 Baron (UK 1939); Sir (Thomas) Robin Valerian Dixon; 5 Bt (UK 1903), CBE (1992, MBE 1969), DL (1979); er s of 2 Baron Glentoran, KBE, PC (d 1995), and Lady Diana Mary Wellesley (d 1984), er da of 3 Earl Cowley; *b* 21 April 1935; *Educ* Eton; *m* 1, 1959 (m dis 1975), Rona Alice Gabrielle, da of Capt George Cecil Colville, CBE, RN, of Bishop's Waltham, Hants; 3 s (Hon Daniel George b 1959, Hon Andrew Wynne Valerian b 1961, Hon Patrick Anthony b 1963); m 2, 1979 (m dis 1988), Alwyn Gillian, da of Hubert A Mason, of Donaghadee, Co Down; m 3, 1990, Mrs Margaret Anne Murphy, *née* Rainey; *Heir* s, Hon Daniel Dixon; *Career* 2 Lt Grenadier Gds 1954, Capt 1958, Maj 1966; non-exec chm Redland of NI 1996–98 (md 1972–96); opposition House of Lords spokesman: agric, fisheries and food until 2001, environment, food and rural affrs 2001–02, NI 2001–, DTI 2004–05; memb Millennium Cmmn until 2006; *Recreations* sailing, skiing; *Clubs* Royal Yacht Squadron, Royal Cruising, Irish Cruising; *Style—* The Lord Glentoran, CBE, DL; ✉ 16 Westgate Terrace, London SW10 9BJ (tel 020 7730 7190, e-mail rg@glentoran.demon.co.uk); House of Lords, London SW1A 0PW (e-mail glentoranr@parliament.uk)

GLENWRIGHT, (Harry) Donald; s of late Harry Glenwright, and Minnie Glenwright; *b* 25 June 1934; *Educ* Stockton-on-Tees Secdy Sch, Univ of Durham (BDS), Univ of Newcastle upon Tyne (MDS); *m* 29 Dec 1966, Gillian Minton, da of late Arthur Holland Thacker; 1 s (Robert b 1970), 1 da (Kate b 1973); *Career* house surgn Newcastle Dental Hosp 1957–58, Surgn Lt (D) RN 1958–61, registrar Eastman Dental Hosp 1961–63, lectr in dental surgery Univ of Birmingham 1963–66, lectr in periodontics Queen's Univ of Belfast 1966–69, Br Cncl scholar Univ of Oslo 1968, Cncl of Europe scholar Aarhus Univ and Univ of Oslo 1971, Br Cncl scholar Colombo Univ 1985; Univ of Birmingham: sr lectr in periodontology 1969–97, acting head Dept of Restorative Dentistry 1989–91, chm Bd of Undergraduate Dental Educn 1989–92, chm Dental Curriculum Devpt Ctee 1992–96, asst dir (educn) 1994–96; external examiner: Univ of Dublin 1978, Univ of London 1979–81, Univ of Manchester 1979–86, Univ of Belfast 1980–83, Univ of Leeds 1985–87, RCS 1988–93; assessor Higher Educn Funding Cncl for Wales 1996–97; specialist reviewer Quality Assurance Agency for Higher Educn 1997–98; pres: Br Soc of Periodontology 1980–81 (sr vice-pres 1991–94), Section of Odontology Birmingham Med Inst 1981–82, Conslt in Restorative Dentistry Gp 1987–96 (memb Cncl, chm 1994–96); memb: Specialist Advsy Ctee in Restorative Dentistry 1987–92, Central Ctee for Hosp Dental Servs 1988, Dental Health and Sci Ctee 1988; FDSRCS; *Recreations* gardening, reading; *Style—* Donald Glenwright, Esq; ✉ White House, Rushbrook Lane, Tanworth-in-Arden, Warwickshire B94 5HP (tel 01564 742578)

GLICK, Ian Bernard; QC (1987); s of Dr Louis Glick (d 1989), and Phyllis Esty, *née* Barnett; *b* 18 July 1948; *Educ* Bradford GS, Balliol Coll Oxford (MA, BCL); *m* 14 Dec 1986, Roxane Olivia Sarah, da of Dr R Eban, and Mrs G Levin; 3 s (Louis Daniel b 22 March 1991, Joseph Adam b 30 May 1992, Saul David b 27 Dec 1994); *Career* called to the Bar Inner Temple 1970 (bencher 1997); jr counsel in common law to the Crown 1985–87, standing counsel in export credit cases to DTI 1985–87; chm Commercial Bar Assoc (COMBAR) 1997–99; *Style—* Ian Glick, Esq, QC; ✉ 1 Essex Court, Temple, London EC4Y 9AR (tel 020 7583 2000, fax 020 7583 0118)

GLIDEWELL, Rt Hon Sir Iain Derek Laing; kt (1980), PC (1985); s of late Charles Norman Glidewell, and late Nora Glidewell; *b* 8 June 1924; *Educ* Bromsgrove Sch, Worcester Coll Oxford; *m* 1950, Hilary, da of late Clinton D Winant; 1 s, 2 da; *Career* called to the Bar 1949, QC 1969, recorder of the Crown Court 1976–80, appeal judge IOM 1979–80, judge of the High Court of Justice (Queen's Bench Div) 1980–85, memb Supreme Court Rule Ctee 1980–83, presiding judge NE Circuit 1982–85, Lord Justice of Appeal 1985–95, judge Court of Appeal of Gibraltar 1999–2003 (pres 2003–04); chm Judicial Studies Bd 1989–92; chm Panels for Examination Structure Plans: Worcs 1974, W Midlands 1975; conducted Heathrow Fourth Terminal Enquiry 1978; chm Review of the CPS 1997–98; hon fell Worcester Coll Oxford 1986; *Style—* The Rt Hon Sir Iain Glidewell; ✉ Rough Heys Farm, Henbury, Macclesfield, Cheshire SK11 9PF

GLIN, 29 Knight of (The Black Knight, Irish hereditary knighthood dating c 1300–30, though first authenticated use dates from 1424); Desmond John Villiers FitzGerald; s of 28 Knight of Glin (Desmond Windham Otho FitzGerald, d 1949), descended from John Fitz-Thomas FitzGerald (d 1261), father of three bros, The White Knight, The Knight of Glin and The Knight of Kerry; *b* 13 July 1937; *Educ* Stowe, Univ of Br Columbia, Harvard

G

Univ; *m* 1, 6 Oct 1966 (m dis 1970), Louise (Lulu) Vava Lucia Henriette, da of Alain, Marquis de la Falaise de la Coudraye, of Paris; *m* 2, 12 Aug 1970, Olda Anne, o da of Thomas Vincent Windham Willes, of London; 3 da (Catherine b 1971, Nesta b 1973, Honor b 1976); *Career* asst and dep keeper Furniture and Woodwork Dept V&A 1965–75, Irish agent Christie's 1975–, conslt 2002–; pres Irish Georgian Soc, chm and dir Irish Georgian Fndn, dir and past chm Irish Heritage Properties (formerly Historic Irish Tourist Houses Assoc), tstee Castletown Fndn; dir: Irish Architectural Archive 1972–, Irish Landmark Tst 2004–, Irish Heritage Tst 2006–; vice-pres: Stowe House Preservation Tst, Bath Preservation Tst; govr Nat Gall of Ireland 2005; author of books and numerous articles on Irish art and architecture; DLitt (hc) TCD; FSA, MRIAI 1997, hon memb RHA 2005; *Books* Ireland Observed (with Maurice Craig, 1975), Lost Demesnes (with Edward Malins, 1976), The Painters of Ireland (with Anne Crookshank, 1978), Vanishing Country Houses of Ireland (jtly, 1988), The Watercolours of Ireland (with Anne Crookshank, 1994), Ireland's Painters (with Anne Crookshank, 2002), Irish Furniture (with James Peill, 2007); *Recreations* art history; *Clubs* Brooks's, Beefsteak, Kildare St and Univ (Dublin), Dilletante; *Style*— The Knight of Glin, FSA; ✉ 52 Waterloo Road, Dublin 4 (tel 00 353 16 680 585, fax 00 353 16 680 271); Glin Castle, Co Limerick, Republic of Ireland (tel 00 353 683 4173 and 34112, fax 00 353 683 4364, e-mail knight@iol.ie)

GLOAG, Ann Heron; OBE (2004); *Career* co-fndr Stagecoach Gp 1980 (exec dir 1980–2000, non-exec dir 2000–); tstee Princess Royal Tst for Carers, bd memb Mercy Ships, non-exec dir OPTOS; Businesswoman of the Year Award, European Women in Achievement Award; *Style*— Ms Ann Gloag, OBE

GLOAG, Julian; s of John Gloag, FSA (d 1981), and Gertrude Mary, *née* Ward (d 1981); *b* 2 July 1930, London; *Educ* Rugby, Magdalene Coll Cambridge (exhibitioner, MA); *m* 1968 (m dis 1982), Danielle Haase-Dubosc; 1 s (Oliver b 1970), 1 da (Vanessa b 1974); *Career* author; awards from Centre National du Livre: Bourse d'Encouragement 1994, Année Sabbatique 1996; supporter SOS Amitiés; memb Authors' Guild USA 1963; FRSL 1970; *Novels* Our Mother's House (1963), A Sentence of Life (1966), Maundy (1969), A Woman of Character (1973), Sleeping Dogs Lie (1980), Lost and Found (1981), Blood for Blood (1985), Only Yesterday (1986), Love as a Foreign Language (1991), Le Passeur de la Nuit (1996), Chambre d'Ombre (1996); *Television Plays* Only Yesterday (1986), The Dark Room (1988); *Style*— Julian Gloag; ✉ 36 rue Gabrielle, 75018 Paris, France (tel 00 33 1 42 55 86 55)

GLOBE, His Hon Judge Henry Brian; QC (1994); s of Theodore Montague Globe (d 2007), of Liverpool, and Irene Rita, *née* Green; *b* 18 June 1949; *Educ* Liverpool Coll, Univ of Birmingham (LLB, Hockey blue); *m* 11 June 1972, Estelle, da of Irene Levin, and Israel Levin; 2 da (Danielle Rebecca (Mrs Ohana) b 5 Feb 1976, Amanda Jane (Mrs Dee) b 3 Sept 1978); *Career* called to the Bar Middle Temple 1972 (bencher 2005); jr Northern Circuit 1974; standing counsel to: Dept of Social Security 1985–94, HM Customs & Excise 1992–94; recorder 1991–2003 (asst recorder 1988–90), circuit judge (Northern Circuit) 2003– (sr circuit judge (crime) 2003–), resident judge Liverpool 2003–, hon recorder Liverpool 2003–; treas Northern Circuit 2001–03; memb: Bar Cncl 2001–03, Criminal Ctee Judicial Studies Bd 2001–05, Criminal Justice Cncl 2004–; govr King David Schs Liverpool 1979–2001, chm of govrs King David HS 1990–2000, tstee King David Fndn 2001–; *Recreations* tennis, bridge; *Style*— His Hon Judge Globe, QC; ✉ Queen Elizabeth II Law Courts, Derby Square, Liverpool L2 1XA (tel 0151 473 7373, e-mail hhjudge.globeqc@judiciary.gsi.gov.uk)

GLOCER, Thomas Henry (Tom); s of Walter Glocer (d 1973), of NY, and Ursuala, *née* Goodman; *b* 8 October 1959, NY; *Educ* Columbia Univ (BA), Yale Univ (JD); *m* 5 Aug 1988, Maarit Hannele, *née* Leso; 1 da (Mariana b 1 June 1998), 1 s (Walter b 6 Jan 2000); *Career* attorney Davis Polk and Wardwell 1984–93, Reuters Gp plc 1993– (chief exec 2001–); memb Advsy Bd: Tate Museum, Whitney Museum, Univ of Cambridge Business Sch, NYC Investment Fund; *Publications* Coney Island: A Voyage of Discovery (computer game, 1984); *Recreations* tennis, windsurfing, skiing; *Clubs* Queens Tennis; *Style*— Tom Glocer, Esq; ✉ Reuters Building, South Colonnade, Canary Wharf, London E14 5EP (tel 020 7542 7788, fax 020 7519 1210, e-mail thomas.glocer@reuters.com)

GLOSSOP, (Charles Compton) Anthony; s of Col Alfred William Compton Glossop, OBE, TD (d 1980), of Chesterfield, Derbys, and Muriel Bradbury, *née* Robinson (d 1986); *b* 24 November 1941; *Educ* Eastbourne Coll, Queens' Coll Cambridge (MA); *m* 28 June 1969, Julia Margaret Anne, da of Capt William Forrester (d 1952), of Dalton-in-Furness, Cumbria; 2 da (Clare b 5 Jan 1971, Katharine b 21 Dec 1972); *Career* admitted slr 1967; asst sec Molins Ltd 1969–72, chm St Modwen Properties plc (formerly Redman Heenan Int plc) 2004– (co sec 1972–82, dir 1976–, gp md 1982–2004, dep chm and chief exec 1998–2004); memb Worcester Civic Soc; *Recreations* walking, reading, gardening and bee-keeping; *Style*— Anthony Glossop, Esq; ✉ St Modwen Properties plc, Sir Stanley Clarke House, 7 Ridgeway, Quinton Business Park, Birmingham B32 1AF (tel 0121 222 9400, fax 0121 222 9401, mobile 07720 469158, e-mail aglossop@stmodwen.co.uk)

GLOSTER, Hon Mrs Justice; Dame Elizabeth; DBE (2004); da of Peter Gloster (d 1991), and Betty Mabel, *née* Read (d 2005); *b* 5 June 1949; *Educ* Roedean, Girton Coll Cambridge (BA); *m* 29 Oct 1973 (m dis 2005), Stanley Eric Brodie, QC, *qv*, s of Dr Abraham Brodie (d 1978); 1 da (Sophie Rebecca b 12 Sept 1978), 1 s (Samuel Rufus b 14 Jan 1981); *Career* called to the Bar 1971: Inner Temple (bencher 1992), Bermuda, Gibraltar, IOM; memb Lincoln's Inn (ad eundem) 1974, memb Panel of Jr Counsel representing DTI in co matters 1982–89, QC 1989, recorder 1995–2004 (asst recorder 1991–95), judge of the High Court of Justice (Queen's Bench Div Commercial Ct) 2004–; assoc memb (as barr) Insolvency Lawyers' Assoc 1991–2004, pt/t memb Civil Aviation Authy 1992–93, judge of the Courts of Appeal of Jersey and Guernsey (pt/t) 1994–2004; *Style*— The Hon Mrs Justice Gloster, DBE

GLOUCESTER, Dean of; *see*: Bury, Very Rev Nicholas

GLOUCESTER, Bishop of 2004–; Rt Rev Michael Francis Perham; s of Raymond Maxwell Perham (d 1992), of Dorchester, and Marcelle Winifred, *née* Barton; *b* 8 November 1947; *Educ* Hardye's Sch Dorchester, Keble Coll Oxford (open exhbn, MA), Cuddesdon Theol Coll; *m* Dr Alison Jane Grove, da of Douglas Grove; 4 da (Rachel b 1984, Anna b 1986, Sarah b 1987, Mary b 1990); *Career* curate St Mary Addington Croydon 1976–81, chaplain to the Bishop of Winchester 1981–84, team rector Oakdale Team Miny Poole 1984–92, canon residentiary and precentor Norwich Cathedral 1991–98, vice-dean of Norwich 1995–98, provost of Derby 1998–2000, dean of Derby 2000–04; sec C of E Doctrine Cmmn 1979–84; memb: C of E Liturgical Cmmn 1986–2001, Archbishops' Cmmn on Church Music 1998–92, Gen Synod C of E 1989–92 and 1993–, Cathedrals Fabric Cmmn for England 1996–2001; chm: Praxis 1990–97, Cathedrals' Liturgy Gp 1993–2001, Archbishops' Cncl 1999–2004, Church Heritage Forum 1999–2001, Business Ctee Gen Synod 2001–04,Governing Body SPCK 2006– (memb 2002–), C of E Hosp Chaplaincies Cncl 2007–; vice-chair C of E Mission and Public Affrs Cncl 2007–; pres Retired Clergy Assoc 2007–; bishop protector Soc of St Francis 2005–; pres Alcuin Club 2005–; fell Woodard Corp 2000–04; FRSCM 2002; *Publications* The Eucharist (1978), The Communion of Saints (1980), Liturgy Pastoral and Parochial (1984), Waiting for the Risen Christ (with Kenneth Stevenson, 1986), Towards Liturgy 2000 (ed, 1989), Liturgy for a New Century (ed, 1991), Welcoming the Light of Christ (with Kenneth Stevenson, 1991), Lively Sacrifice (1992), The Renewal of Common Prayer (1993), Model of Inspiration (ed, 1993), Celebrate the Christian Story (1997), The Sorrowful Way (1998), A New Handbook of Pastoral Liturgy (2000), Signs of Your Kingdom (2002), Glory in our Midst (2005); *Recreations* reading, writing, creating liturgical texts, walking in the Yorkshire dales; *Style*— The Rt Rev the Bishop of Gloucester; ✉ Bishopscourt, Pitt Street, Gloucester GL1 2BQ (tel 01452 410022 ext 271 or 01452 524598, e-mail bshpglos@glosdioc.org.uk)

GLOVER, Prof Anne; *Educ* Univ of Edinburgh, Univ of Cambridge (PhD); *Career* prof Sch of Med Sciences Univ of Aberdeen, tech dir Remedios 1999–2002; chief scientific advsr for Scotland 2006–; NERC: memb Cncl 2001–, memb Environmental Genomics Steering Ctee 2000–, memb Freshwater Sciences Peer Review Ctee 1998–2001; memb: DTI Link Biomediation Prog Steering Ctee 2001–, BBSRC Engrg and Biological Sciences Peer Review Ctee 2002–05; tstee CL:AIRE 2004; fell American Acad of Microbiology 1995, FRSE 2005; *Style*— Prof Anne Glover; ✉ College of Life Sciences and Medicine, University of Aberdeen, Foresterhill, Aberdeen AB25 2ZD

GLOVER, Anne Margaret; CBE (2006); *b* 6 February 1954; *Educ* Clare Coll Cambridge (MA), Yale Sch of Mgmnt; *Career* venture capitalist; early career with Cummins Engine, subsequently conslt and mangr Bain & Co then memb investment team Apax Partners & Co Ventures, chief operating offr Virtuality Gp plc 1993–95, fndr Calderstone Capital Ltd (advsr to IT start-up cos) 1996, co-fndr and chief exec Amadeus Capital Partners Ltd 1997–; non-exec dir Optos plc 1996–; chm BVCA 2004–05 (memb Cncl 1998–, vice-chm 2003–04); memb DTI Technology Strategy Bd; *Style*— Ms Anne Glover, CBE; ✉ Amadeus Capital Partners Limited, 16 St James's Street, London SW1A 1ER

GLOVER, Prof David Moore; *b* 28 March 1948; *Educ* Broadway Tech GS Barnsley, Fitzwilliam Coll Cambridge (BA), UCL (PhD); *Career* Damon Runyon postdoctoral res fell Stanford Univ 1972–75; Imperial Coll of Science and Technol London: lectr in biochemistry 1975–81, sr lectr 1981–83, reader in molecular genetics 1983–86, prof of molecular genetics and dir Eukaryotic Molecular Genetics Gp Cancer Research Campaign 1986–89 (jt dir 1979–86), head Dept of Biochemistry 1988–89; Univ of Dundee: prof of biochemistry 1989–92, dir Cell Cycle Genetics Gp Cancer Research Campaign 1989–, prof of molecular genetics Dept of Anatomy and Physiology 1992–99; Arthur Balfour prof of genetics Univ of Cambridge 1999–, fell Fitzwilliam Coll 2004–; chief scientist Polgen Div Cyclacel Ltd 1999–; ed Jl of Cell Science; memb Editorial Bd: Mechanisms of Development, Insect Molecular Biology; Cancer Research Campaign Career Devpt Award 1979–89; memb: EMBO 1978, Human Genome Orgn 1990; FRSE 1992; *Books* Frontiers in Molecular Biology (series ed); author of numerous scientific pubns; *Style*— Prof David M Glover, FRSE; ✉ Cancer Research UK Cell Cycle Genetics Research Group, University of Cambridge, Department of Genetics, Cambridge CB2 3EH (e-mail d.glover@gen.cam.ac.uk)

GLOVER, Edward Charles; CMG (2003), MVO (1976); s of Edward Leonard Glover (d 1994), and Mary Glover; *b* 4 March 1943; *Educ* Univ of London (BA, MPhil); *m* Dame Audrey Frances Glover, CMG; 2 da (Caroline b 21 April 1973, Charlotte b 25 Feb 1976), 2 s (Rupert b 18 Oct 1980, Crispin b 28 Jan 1983), and 1 s decd (d 1977); *Career* HM Dip Serv: SE Asian Dept FCO 1969–71, private sec to High Cmmr to Aust 1971–73, second sec Washington DC 1973–77, delgn sec and third ctee rep UK Delgn to UN Law of the Sea Conf 1978–80, on secondment to Guinness Peat Group 1980–83, Arms Control and Disarmament Dept FCO 1983–85, Br Mil Govt Berlin 1985–89, dep head Near East and N African Dept FCO 1989–91, head Mgmnt Review Staff FCO 1991–94, dep head of mission Brussels 1994–98, high cmmr to Guyana and ambass to Surinam 1998–2002, Quality and Efficiency Unit FCO 2002–03, ret; assoc conslt DFID support to the Min of Foreign Affairs Macedonia 2003–05, advsr on foreign affrs to: Iraqi Min of Foreign Affrs 2004–05, Coalition Provisional Authy Iraq 2004; assoc conslt DFID support to office of Prime Minister Kosovo 2006–07; assoc fell Centre for Caribbean Studies Univ of Warwick; chm Bd of Tstees Iwokrama Int Rainforest Centre Guyana 2005–; chm NW Norfolk Decorative and Fine Arts Soc, memb Ctee King's Lynn Preservation Tst (memb Mgmnt Bd 2003–); memb: RIIA 1969, Hakluyt Soc; *Recreations* tennis, watercolour painting, reading (biographies); *Clubs* Brooks's; *Style*— Edward Glover, Esq, CMG, MVO; ✉ Oak House, Thornham, Norfolk PE36 6LY (tel 01485 512223)

GLOVER, Eric; s of William Arthur Glover (d 1965), of Liverpool, and Margaret, *née* Walker; *b* 28 June 1935; *Educ* Liverpool Inst HS, Oriel Coll Oxford (MA); *m* 1960, Adele Diane, da of Col Cecil Geoffrey Hilliard, of Harrogate; 3 s (Ian, Paul, Jason); *Career* sec-gen Chartered Inst of Bankers 1982–94 (dir of studies 1968–82); chm Open and Distance Learning Quality Cncl 1993–98, pres Teachers and Trainers of Fin Servs 1998–; chm Intrabank Expert Witness 1997–; treas British Accreditation Cncl 1988–; hon fell Sheffield Hallam Univ; Hon MBA London Guildhall Univ; Hon FCIB, FRSA; *Recreations* golf, swimming; *Clubs* Overseas Bankers'; *Style*— Eric Glover, Esq; ✉ 12 Manor Park, Tunbridge Wells, Kent TN4 8XP (tel and fax 01892 531221)

GLOVER, Dr Jane Alison; CBE (2003); da of late Robert Finlay Glover, TD, of Malvern, Worcs, and Jean, *née* Muir, MBE; *b* 13 May 1949; *Educ* Monmouth Sch for Girls, St Hugh's Coll Oxford (MA, DPhil); *Career* conductor; musical dir Glyndebourne Touring Opera 1982–85, musical dir London Choral Soc 1983–99; artistic dir London Mozart Players 1984–91, princ conductor Huddersfield Choral Soc 1989–96, music dir Music of the Baroque (Chicago) 2002–; appeared with many orchs and opera cos incl: Glyndebourne Festival Opera 1982–, BBC Proms 1985–, ROH 1988–, ENO 1989–, Opera Australia 1996–, Glimmerglass Opera 1994–; regular broadcaster on TV and radio, regular recordings; sr research fell St Hugh's Coll Oxford 1982 (hon fell 1991); govr BBC 1990–95; NY City Opera Gen Dir's Cncl Award for Outstanding Achievement 2001; Hon DMus: Univ of Exeter 1986, Cncl for Nat Acad Awards 1991, Univ of London 1992, City Univ 1994, Univ of Glasgow 1997; Hon DUniv Open Univ 1988; Hon DLitt: Loughborough Univ of Technol 1988, Univ of Bradford 1992; memb Worshipful Co of Haberdashers; RSA 1988, FRCM 1993; *Books* Cavalli (1978), Mozart's Women (2005); *Recreations* theatre, walking, skiing; *Style*— Dr Jane Glover, CBE; ✉ c/o Askonas Holt, Lonsdale Chambers, 27 Chancery Lane, London WC2A 1PF (tel 020 7400 1700)

GLOVER, Julian Wyatt; s of (Claude) Gordon Glover (d 1975), of Arkesden, Essex, and Honor Ellen Morgan, *née* Wyatt (d 1998); *b* 27 March 1935; *Educ* St Paul's, Alleyn's Sch Dulwich, RADA; *m* 1, 1957 (m dis 1966), Dame Eileen Atkins, DBE *qv*; *m* 2, 28 Sept 1968, Isla Blair, *qv*; 1 s (Jamie Blair b 10 July 1969); *Career* actor; Nat Serv 2 Lt RASC 1954–56; started out as spear-carrier Shakespeare Meml Theatre Stratford-upon-Avon 1957; Liveryman Worshipful Co of Dyers 1956; *Theatre* incl: Aufidius in Coriolanus and Warwick in Henry VI (RSC) 1977, Habeas Corpus, Educating Rita, The Aspern Papers, Never The Sinner, title role in Henry IV Parts I and II RSC 1991–92 (winner Best Supporting Actor Olivier Award 1993), All My Sons 1992, Cyrano de Bergerac (Haymarket) 1992–93, An Inspector Calls (RNT, Aldwych) 1993–94, Chips With Everything (RNT) 1996–97, Prayers of Sherkin (Old Vic) 1997, Waiting for Godot (Peter Hall Co) 1998, Phedre and Britannicus (Albery) 1998, A Penny For a Song (Whitehall), Prospero in The Tempest (Nuffield Theatre), In Praise of Love (nat tour), title role in King Lear (Shakespeare's Globe), Macbeth (Albery), Taking Sides (nat tour) 2003–04, Galileo's Daughter (Peter Hall season Bath) 2004, The Dresser (nat tour and Duke of York's) 2004–05; theatre seasons with: RSC (Cassius and Friar Lawrence 1995–96), Prospect, The Old Vic and Nat Theatre Companies; dir Hamlet (Norwich Playhouse) 1996, Voysey Inheritance (NT) 2006, Shadowlands (Salisbury) 2007; *Television* incl: An Age of Kings, Spytrap, Z-Cars, Dombey and Son, By The Sword Divided, Wish Me Luck, Spy Trap, Cover Her Face, Warburg, Man of Influence, Darling Buds of May, Money for Nothing, Degrees of Error, Taggart, The Chief 1995, The Infiltrator, Cadfael, The Midsomer Murders, Born and Bred, Trial & Retribution, Silent Witness; *Films* incl: Tom Jones, For Your Eyes Only, The Fourth Protocol, I Was Happy Here, The Empire Strikes Back, Cry Freedom, Treasure Island, Indiana Jones and the Last Crusade, King Ralph,

Vatel, Harry Potter and the Chamber of Secrets, Two Men Went to War, Troy; *Books* Beowulf (1987 and 1995, republished 2005); *Style*— Julian Glover, Esq; ✉ c/o Conway van Gelder Ltd, 18–21 Jermyn Street, London SW1Y 6HP (tel 020 7287 0077, fax 020 7287 1940)

GLOVER, Richard Gordon Finlay; s of Robert Finlay Glover, of Malvern, Worcs, and Jean, *née* Muir; *b* 3 August 1952; *Educ* Tonbridge, Univ of Strasbourg, CCC Oxford (BA); *m* 4 Oct 1980, Teresa Anne, da of Richard Ingram Lindsell; 1 s (Thomas Finlay b 19 Jan 1984), 1 da (Alice Catherine b 31 July 1987); *Career* ICI 1974–80, Grand Metropolitan 1980–86, United Biscuits 1986–88, sr search conslt Whitehead Mann 1988–90, chief exec BSM Group plc 1997–99 (md 1990–97), md RAC Business Services 1999, chief exec ATC Group 2000–03, chief exec ATC Int Holdings 2003–; chm Haberdashers' Aske's Fndn of Academics 2004–; Liveryman Worshipful Co of Haberdashers 1977; FRSA 1993; *Recreations* Welsh rugby, cinema, squash; *Style*— Richard Glover, Esq; ✉ ATC (International Holdings) Limited, Suite 6 & 7, The Old Office Block, 16 Elmtree Road, Teddington, Middlesex TW11 8ST (tel 020 8977 8429)

GLOVER, Robert Edward; s of Ronald Glover, and Anne, *née* Richards; *b* 22 July 1936; *Educ* Bushey GS; *m* 1969 (m dis 1980); 1 da (Jessica Jane b 18 Oct 1972); *Career* photographer; trained as photogravure colour retoucher, fndr own commercial and social photography studio 1965; Portrait Photographer of the Year 1984 and 1991, Fox Talbot Award (first ever) 1996; chm Admissions and Qualifications Bd BIPP 1991–; FBIPP, FMPA, hon FDIPP; *Recreations* military history; *Clubs* MCC; *Style*— Robert Glover, Esq; ✉ Robert Glover Photography, Roundwood Farm, Near Kea, Truro, Cornwall TR3 6AS (tel 01872 864587)

GLOVER, Stephen Charles Morton; s of Prebendary John Morton Glover (d 1979), and Helen Ruth, *née* Jones (d 1984); *b* 13 January 1952; *Educ* Shrewsbury, Mansfield Coll Oxford (MA); *m* 1982, Celia Elizabeth, da of Peter Montague; 2 s (Edmund b 1983, Alexander b 1987); *Career* leader and feature writer Daily Telegraph 1978–85 (parliamentary sketch writer 1979–81), foreign ed The Independent 1986–89, ed The Independent on Sunday 1990–91, assoc ed (politics) The Evening Standard 1992–95; columnist: Daily Telegraph 1996–98, The Spectator 1996–2005, Daily Mail 1998–, The Independent 2005–; dir Newspaper Publishing plc 1986–92; *Books* Paper Dreams (1993), Secrets of the Press (ed, 1999); *Clubs* Beefsteak; *Style*— Stephen Glover, Esq

GLUCK, Malcolm; s of Harry Gluck (d 1986), of Hove, E Sussex, and Ivy, *née* Messer (d 1982); *b* 23 January 1942; *Educ* Drury Fall Sch Hornchurch, Fairkytes and Harrow Lodge public libraries; *m* 1, 1969 (m dis 1976), Marilyn Janet Day; 1 s (Ben b 1982, with Patricia Wellington); m 2, 1984 (m dis 2003), Susan Ashley; 1 da (Alexandra Ashley Harriet b 1986), 1 s (Joseph Augustus Ashley b 1989); *Career* author; oily rag Rotary Hoes Ltd 1957, apprentice Ford Motor Co 1957–60, trainee salesman Kingsland Shoes Ltd 1960, poet 1960–61, office boy Stratford East Waste Paper Mill Ltd 1961, cost clerk Hackney Springs & Screws Ltd 1961, clerk Spillers Pet Food 1961, asst to domestic supt Mile End Hosp 1961, jr sec Motor Agents Assoc 1961–62, student Watford Coll of Art 1962–63; copywriter: SH Benson (trainee) 1963, Press & Gen Publicity 1963–64, Arks Publicity 1964–65, Streets Advtg 1965, Mclaren Dunkley Friedlander 1965–66, Doyle Dane Bernbach NY (sr) 1969; copy chief Doyle Dane Bernbach London 1971–73 (copywriter 1966–69, gp head/assoc dir 1970–71), co-prop, sales dir and games developer Intellect Games Ltd 1973–75, creative dir Drakes Jarvis & Gluck Ltd 1973–75, script writer and contrib Punch 1976, conslt creative dir Pincus Vidler Arthur Fitzgerald 1976–77, dir/sr copywriter Abbott Mead Davies Vickers 1977–80, sr copywriter Collet Dickenson Pearce 1980–84, dir Olgivy & Mather 1984–85, exec creative dir Lintas 1986–88, creative dir Priestley Marin-Guzman & Gluck 1989–92; writer Superplonk wine column The Guardian 1989, publisher Adze Magazine 1992, conslt wine ed Sainsbury's Magazine 1993–2001, wine ed Cosmopolitan magazine 1995–96, wine corr The Guardian 1996–, co-prop Superplonk Online Ltd 2000–, writer Party Paupers column The Guardian 2002; compiler/presenter Vintage Classics Deutsche Grammophon 1996; presenter: Nosh & Plonk (jtly, video) 1993, Gluck Gluck Gluck (BBC 2) 1996, The World of Wine (video and DVD) 2003; involved with: CND 1957–73, Anti-Apartheid Movement 1970–92, Lab Pty Advtg Advsy Gp 1978–80; memb Circle of Wine Writers; *Awards* over 200 awards 1966–92 from D&AD, Br Advtg Film Awards, Br Creative Circle and overseas incl: Best Trade Advtg Copy 1966, Best Colour Advertisement 1967, Best Black & White Newspaper Advertisement Copy 1968, Best Newspaper Colour Advertisement 1972, Best Animated Commercial 1971, Best Travel Advtg Campaign 1979, Best Cinema Commercial 1980, Best Use of Celebrity in a TV Commercial 1982, Best Outdoor Poster 1987, Most Original Animated Commercial 1988; *Books* Superplonk (annually, 1991–), Supernosh (with Anthony Worral Thompson, *qv*, 1993), Gluck's Guide to High Street Wine (1995), Gluck on High (1996), Gluck Gluck Gluck (1996), Summerplonk (1997 and 1998), Streetplonk (1997, 1998, 1999 and 2000), The Sensational Liquid - Gluck's Guide to Wine Tasting (1999), Wine Matters - Why Water Just Won't Do (2003), New Media Language (contrib, 2003), Superplonk - The Top One Thousand (2005), Supergrub (2005), The Simple Art of Marrying Food and Wine (with Mark Hix, 2005); *Recreations* novels (European and American), poetry, music (classical and jazz piano), chess, cooking (European, Oriental), cycling, language study, London cemeteries, photography, crosswords, film, travel; *Clubs* Groucho; *Style*— Malcolm Gluck, Esq; ✉ c/o Ed Victor Limited, 6 bayley Street, Bedford Square, London W1B 3HB

GLURJIDZE, Elena; da of Levan Glurjidze, of St Petersburg, Russia, and Valentina, *née* Mikhailova; *b* 11 May 1974, Tbilisi, Georgia; *Educ* Tbilisi Choreographic Sch, Vaganova St Petersburg Acad of Russian Ballet; *m* 3 April 2004, Prince Kakhaber Abashidze; 1 s (Alexander Nicholas b 1 Oct 2004); *Career* ballerina; formerly with: Russian Ballet Co St Petersburg, St Petersburg State Academic Ballet Theatre, St Petersburg Ballet Theatre of Konstantin Tatchkin; princ dancer English Nat Ballet 2002–; roles incl: Giselle in Giselle, Kitri in Don Quixote, Aurora in Sleeping Beauty, Clara in The Nutcracker, Odette and Odile in Swan Lake, Cinderella in Cinderella, Swanild in Coppelia, Virginia in The Canterville Ghost; guest dancer World Ballet Stars Festivals Ukraine; memb Equity; Bronze medal 8th Moscow Int Competition of Ballet Artists 1997, winner 8th Paris Int Competition of Soloists 1998, Best Ptnr 7th Perm Open Competition 2002; *Recreations* growing exotic flowers, collecting pictures, visiting parks throughout Europe with my son and husband; *Style*— Mrs Elena Glurjidze; ✉ 68 St Mary Abbott's Court, Warwick Gardens, London W14 8RB (tel 020 7602 0267); c/o English National Ballet, Markova House, 39 Jay Mews, London SW7 2ES

GLYN, Sir Richard Lindsay; 10 Bt (GB 1759), of Ewell, Surrey, and 6 Bt (GB 1800), of Gaunt's House; s of Sir Richard Hamilton Glyn, OBE, TD, 9 and 5 Bt (d 1980), and Lyndsay Mary Baker; *b* 3 August 1943; *Educ* Eton; *m* 1970 (m dis 1979), Carolyn Ann, da of Roy Frank Williams (d 1979), of Pasadena, CA; 1 s (Richard Rufus Francis b 8 Jan 1971), 1 da (Eliza Jane Rose b 1975); *Heir* s, Richard Glyn; *Career* 2 Lt Royal Hampshire Regt 1962–65; Studio Orange Ltd (photography and design) 1966–71, Gaunts Estate 1972, dir Gaunt's House 1989; farmer 1976–; underwriting memb Lloyd's 1976–; co-fndr High Lea Sch 1982; fndr: Richard Glyn Foundation for Profound Learning 1995, Honeybrook County Life Centre 2002; *Style*— Sir Richard Glyn, Bt; ✉ Ashton Farmhouse, Stanbridge, Wimborne, Dorset BH21 4JD (tel 01258 840585, fax 01202 841959)

GLYNN, (Brian) David; s of William Arthur Glynn, CBE (d 1976), and Norah Haden, *née* Mottram; *b* 30 May 1940; *Educ* Epsom Coll, Guy's Hosp Dental Sch (BDS Univ of London, LDS RCS Eng, DGDP RCS Eng, represented hockey and shooting teams), Univ of Oregon Dental Sch (Newland Pedley scholar); *m* 16 May 1964, Judith Mary, da of George Charles English, CBE; 2 da (Amanda Jayne b 18 March 1968, Nicola Louise b 17 June 1970); *Career* dental surgeon; Dept of Conservation Dentistry Guy's Hosp: pt/t registrar 1967–74, pt/t jr lectr 1974–76, pt/t sr demonstrator 1976–79; in private practice 35 Devonshire Place W1 1979– (pt/t 1967–74); chm Compudent Ltd 1984–95; Fédération Dentaire Internationale: conslt Scientific Programme Ctee 1989, conslt Cmmn of Dental Practice on Computer Aided Diagnostics 1990; lectr on use of computers in gen dental practice, author of numerous papers and courses on restorative dentistry, responsible for use of closed circuit TV in teaching at Guy's Hosp (prodr various films); memb: BDA, American Dental Soc of London (sec 1972–75, pres 1992–93); fell Int Coll of Dentists 1981 (gen sec Euro section 1984–92, vice-pres 1992–93, pres 1994–95, int pres 1999 (pres-elect 1998)); *Publications* Use of Closed Circuit TV (Medical and Biological Illustration, 1973); various papers to American Dental Soc of London; *Recreations* fly fishing, skiing, sailing, tennis, flying, twin and single engine aircraft; *Clubs* Fly Fishers; *Style*— David Glynn, Esq; ✉ Glynn Setchell and Allan, 35 Devonshire Place, London W1N 1PE (tel 020 7935 3342/3, fax 020 7224 0558)

GLYNNE, Alan; s of Daniel Glynne; *b* 21 May 1941; *Educ* Univ of Edinburgh (BSc, MB ChB), RCP; *m* 21 May 1969, Barbara, da of Philip Lee; 1 s (Paul Alexander b 1970), 1 da (Kathryn Antonia b 1971); *Career* registrar in cardiology Leeds Gen Infirmary 1967–69, registrar in endocrinology and gen med Univ Dept of Med Glasgow Royal Infirmary 1969–72, sr registrar in gen med Whithington Hosp and Royal Infirmary Manchester 1972–74, dir of clinical investigation and head of clinical pharmacology Lilly Research Centre UK 1974–82, hon consult and lectr in med Guy's Hosp 1980–83, examiner RCP, currently conslt physician, pt/t conslt physician Cromwell Hosp; assoc lectr Univ of Surrey; author of various contribs to sci jls; memb: Int Diabetes Fedn, Med and Scientific Section of Br Diabetic Assoc, Br Thyroid Assoc, Chelsea Clinical Soc, Endocrine Section RSM; MRCP, FFPM; *Recreations* golf, photography; *Clubs* Coombe Hill Golf; *Style*— Dr Alan Glynne; ✉ 97 Harley Street, London W1N 1DF (tel 020 7935 5896, fax 020 7935 6617)

G

GOAD, Brig Kevin John Watson; CBE (1997); s of Maj Christopher Frederick Goad, of Portswood, Southampton, and Mary Merton, *née* Watson; *b* 8 May 1942; *Educ* Coatham Sch, Windsor Sch, RMA Sandhurst; *m* 31 July 1965, Anne Elizabeth, da of Maj Hugh Lewis Thomas; 2 da (Claire Emma b 5 Aug 1966, Annabelle Lavinia b 1 Oct 1968); *Career* cmmnd RAOC 1962, Lt 1963, Capt 1969, Staff Coll 1974, Maj 1975, Nat Def Coll Latimer 1980, Lt-Col 1980, tech weapons instr RMCS 1981–82, Col 1988, Brig 1991, Cdr Bicester Garrison/Base Ordnance Depot 1991–94, dir Base Depots 1994–95, chief exec Army Base Storage & Distribution Agency (ABSDA) 1995–97, ret 1997; ADC to HM The Queen 1995–97; served: UK, NI, Malaysia, Hong Kong, BAOR; dir projects and admin SSAFA Forces Help 1997–2000, sr conslt Advantage Technical Consulting 2000–07; MInstD 1994, FILog 1994; *Books* Brassey's Battlefield Weapons Systems and Technology Volume III (with D H J Halsey, 1982); *Recreations* water colours, military history, Arsenal FC, antiques; *Style*— Brig Kevin Goad, CBE

GOAD, Sarah Jane Frances; JP (1974); da of Uvedale Lambert, and Diana, *née* Grey (d 1944); step da of Melanie Grant Lambert, of Denver, Colorado; *b* 23 August 1940; *Educ* St Mary's Wantage; *m* 1961, Timothy Francis Goad, DL; 1 da, 2 s; *Career* dir Tilburstow Farms Co Ltd 1963–70, ptnr Lambert Farmers 1970–94; memb Surrey Magistrates' Soc 1987–93, dep chm Family Panel 1992–97; HM Lord-Lt Surrey 1997–; chm Southwark Cathedral Cncl 2000–, lay canon Southwark Cathedral 2004–; pres Yvonne Arnaud Theatre 2004–; tstee and chm: Love Walk (home for disabled) 1984–98, Surrey Care Tst 1987–97; tstee: St Mark's Fndn 1971–, Surrey History Tst 1999–, Chevening Estate 2001; govr: St Stephen's C of E Sch 1970–90, Hazelwood Sch 1979–84; DStJ 1997; *Recreations* books, buildings, arts; *Style*— Mrs Sarah Goad; ✉ Prickloves Farmhouse, South Park, Bletchingley, Surrey RH1 4NE

GOBITS, Rolph; s of Ben Gobits (d 1957), and Ruth, *née* Reinheimer; *b* 19 September 1947, The Hague, Holland; *Educ* Bournemouth & Poole Coll of Art (BA), RCA (scholar, MA, Daily Telegraph Magazine Award); *m* 1, 15 Dec 1978 (m dis 2002), Amanda, *née* Currey; 2 da (Tamara b 8 Sept 1974, Anoushka b 13 June 1981); m 2, Dec 2005, Mrs Yulia Globina; *Career* photographer; clients incl: Mercedes Benz, BMW, Audi, Volkswagen, General Motors, IBM, Apple, British Airways, TWA, Hyatt Hotels, American Express, Forte Hotel Group, AT&T, Texaco, Spalding, Bosch, Morgan Grenfell Merchant Bank, Natwest, Orient Express, Gucci, IPC Publications, French Tourist Office, Jersey Tourist Office, Scottish Tourist Office, Marconi, Granada, Red Cross, Hewlett Packard, Compaq, Mobil Oil, US Postal Services, Br Tourist Office, BT, Chrysler Corp, United Technologies in USA, Credit Suisse Gp, Royal Mail, Sotheby's, Chrystal Cruises, Guardian Newspapers; dir lensmodern.com (gallery and picture library); exhbn The Travelling Entertainers 2007; vice-chm Assoc of Photographers; *Awards* Arts Council Bursary 1974; D&AD: Silver Award for most outstanding advertising colour photograph 1979, special mention for consumer campaign 1981, Silver Award (Netherlands club) for most outstanding advertising colour photograph 1984, Silver Award for most outstanding consumer campaign 1984, Silver Award (France club) for VW campaign 1992; Campaign Press Advertising: Silver Award for best use of colour 1983, Silver Award for best media advertisement 1983, Silver Award for best travel advertisement 1985, Silver and Bronze Awards for best business advertisement 1986; Advertising Festival Gold Award for best advertisement in Europe Cannes 1992; Assoc of Photographers: Silver Award 1995, Judges Choice 2000 and 2002, Merit Award 2001; The Morton Kirschner Photography Award (Holland): Gold Award 1999, Bronze Award 2000; *Recreations* photography, reading, chess; *Style*— Rolph Gobits, Esq; ✉ Rolph Gobits Studio Ltd, The Coach House, 1 Winfrith Road, London SW18 3BE (tel 07785 292599, e-mail rolphg@aol.com)

GODBER, John; s of Harry Godber, and Dorothy, *née* Deakin; *b* 18 May 1956; *Educ* Minsthorpe HS, Bretton Hall Coll (BEd), Univ of Leeds (MA, MPhil, PhD (unfinished research thesis)); *m* 12 Sept 1993, Jane, da of Clifford Thornton; 2 da (Elizabeth b 29 Oct 1994, Martha b 10 Aug 1997); *Career* playwright and dir; former head of drama Minsthorpe HS, artistic dir Hull Truck Theatre Co 1984–; visiting prof Liverpool Hope Univ 2004, hon lectr Bretton Hall Coll 2006, prof of drama Univ of Hull; Hon DLitt: Univ of Hull 1988, Humberside and Lincolnshire Univ 1997; DUniv OU 2005; FRSA 2004; *Theatre* Cramp (NSDF) 1981, September in the Rain (Hull Truck Theatre Co) 1984, Blood Sweat and Tears (Hull Truck Theatre Co), Bouncers (London, Eur and USA, Edinburgh Fringe First Award 1984, seven Drama Critics Circle Awards, five Joseph Jefferson Awards), Up 'N' Under II, Shakers (with Jane Thornton, London, Aust and USA), Teechers (Arts Theatre London, Aust and USA), Salt of the Earth (Edinburgh Fringe First Award, Joseph Jefferson Award), On the Piste 1991, Happy Families, April in Paris 1992, The Office Party (Nottingham Playhouse nat tour) 1992, Happy Jack (Hull Truck Theatre Co and tour, Edinburgh Fringe Festival Award) 1982, Up 'N' Under (Fortune Theatre London and tour, Edinburgh Fringe First Award, Olivier Comedy of the Year Award) 1984, Passion Killers (Derby Playhouse) 1994, Lucky Sods (Hull Truck Theatre Co) 1995, Gym and Tonic (Hull Truck Theatre Co) 1996, Weekend Breaks (Hull Truck Theatre Co) 1997, It Started With a Kiss 1998, Unleashed 1999, Thick as a Brick 1999, Reunion 2002, Men of the World 2001, Screaming Blue Murder 2003, Fly Me to the Moon 2004, Going Dutch (Hull Truck Theatre Co) 2004, Wrestling Mad (Hull Truck Theatre Co) 2005, Christmas Crackers 2006, Crown Prince 2007; *Television* incl: Blood Sweat and Tears (BBC 2), The Ritz (BBC 2), The Continental (BBC Christmas Special), My Kingdom for a Horse (film for BBC) 1991, Chalkface (BBC) 1991, Bloomin Marvellous (BBC 1)

1997, Thunder Road (writer and dir, film for BBC) 2003, Thick as a Brick (film for BBC) 2005, Oddsquad (BBC) 2005 (BAFTA Best Schools Drama 2005, BAFTA Best Screenplay 2005); numerous episodes of Brookside, Crown Court and Grange Hill; *Film* Up 'N' Under (writer and dir) 1998; *Style*— John Godber, Esq; ✉ c/o Alan Brodie, Alan Brodie Representation, 6th Floor, Fairgate House, 78 New Oxford Street, London WC1A 1HB (tel 020 7079 7990, fax 020 7079 7991)

GODBOLD, Brian Leslie; OBE (2007); s of Leslie Robert Godbold (d 1970), of London, and Eileen Rosalie, *née* Hodgkinson; *b* 14 July 1943; *Educ* Elmbridge Sch Cranleigh, Walthamstow Sch of Art (NDD), RCA Fashion Sch; *Career* designer Jovi NY 1965–67, head of tailoring Wallis Shops 1967–69; head of design: Cojana 1970–74, Baccarat/Wetherall (headed team that designed BA uniform 1976) 1974–76; Marks & Spencer: exec head of design 1976–93, design dir 1993–98; dep chm Br Fashion Cncl 1997–2000 (sponsored by Marks & Spencer), non-exec dir George at Asda 2000–, strategic fashion retail and design conslt 2000–; dir Ramon Gurillo Ltd 2004–; RCA: vice-chm Cncl 2000–03 (memb 1993–2006), sr fell 2006; memb: Design Cncl 1998–2001, Advsy Bd of Fashion Merchandise Mgmnt Course Westminster Univ 1999–; photographer, exhibited Summer Open (Assoc Gallery London) 2000, one-man exhbn (Egg London) 2001; memb Br Friends of Shenkar Israel; Hon DDes: Univ of Southampton 1994, Univ of Westminster 1999; hon fell Shenkar Coll of Engrg and Design Israel 1999; FRSA, FCSD; *Recreations* antique collecting, decorating, gardening; *Style*— Brian Godbold, Esq, OBE; ✉ e-mail briangodbold43@aol.com

GODDARD, Her Hon Judge Ann Felicity; QC (1982); da of Graham Elliott Goddard (d 1973), and Margaret Louise, *née* Clark (d 1995); *b* 22 January 1936; *Educ* Grey Coat Hosp Westminster, Univ of Birmingham (LLB), Newnham Coll Cambridge (LLM); *Career* called to the Bar 1960, recorder of the Crown Court 1979–93, circuit judge (SE Circuit) 1993–; bencher Gray's Inn 1990–; memb Criminal Justice Consultative Cncl 1992–93, pres Br Acad of Forensic Sciences 1995–96; Liveryman Worshipful Co of Clockmakers 1996–, Liveryman Worshipful Co of Gardeners 2003; *Recreations* travel; *Style*— Her Hon Judge Goddard, QC; ✉ Central Criminal Court, Old Bailey, London EC4M 7EH

GODDARD, Prof John Burgess; OBE (1986); s of Burgess Goddard, of Rickmansworth, Herts, and Maud Mary, *née* Bridge (d 1970); *b* 5 August 1943; *Educ* Latymer Upper Sch, UCL (BA), LSE (PhD); *m* 24 Sept 1966, Janet Patricia, da of Stanley James Peddle (d 1956), of Rickmansworth, Herts; 2 da (Jane Elizabeth b 1 Dec 1970, Jennifer Anne b 7 Nov 1974), 1 s (David Jonathan b 4 August 1976); *Career* lectr LSE 1968–75, Leverhulme fell Univ of Lund Sweden 1974; Univ of Newcastle upon Tyne: Henry Daysh prof Regnl Devpt Studies 1975–, dir Centre of Urban and Regnl Devpt Studies 1977–, head Geography Dept 1980–87, dean Faculty of Law, Environment and Social Sciences 1994–98, pro-vice-chllr 1998–2001, dep vice-chllr 2001–, memb Senate 1981–83 and 1992–, memb Cncl 1983–86, memb Res Ctee 1984–89, memb Planning and Resources Ctee 1988–93, dir Newcastle Initiative Ltd 1988–; memb: N Econ Planning Cncl 1976–79, Exec Ctee Newcastle Common Purpose 1989–93; govr and memb Employment and Fin Ctee Univ of Northumbria at Newcastle (formerly Newcastle Poly) 1989–98; memb: Port of Tyne Authy 1990–93, Human Geography Ctee SSRC 1976–79, Editorial Bd Environment and Planning 1988–91; ed Regional Studies 1979–84; advsr: CBI Task Force on Urban Regeneration 1987–88, House of Commons Trade and Indust Select Ctee 1994–95; memb: Exec Ctee Regnl Studies Assoc 1979–84, Editorial Bd BBC Domesday Project 1985–86, Jt Ctee ESRC and Nat Sci Fndn of America on Large Scale Data Bases 1986–87; dir ESRC Prog on Info and Communication Technologies 1992–93; chm: The Assoc of Dirs of Res Centres in the Social Scis (DORCISS) 1990–97, Assoc of Research Centres in the Social Sciences (ARCISS) 1997–99, NE Regnl Ctee Community Fund 2002–06; memb: Advsy Bd of the Natural Environment and Land Use Programme 1991–95, R&D Ctee Northern RHA 1993–94, Econ Advsy Ctees, exec ctee Univ for the North East 2000–, Constitutional Forum Newcastle City Cncl 2001, Tyne & Wear C of C 1982–95, Newcastle Partnership, Tyne & Wear Sub-Regional Partnership; MIBG 1966, memb Regnl Studies Assoc 1966, FRGS 1988 (Victoria medal 1992), FRSA 1993, Fell Acad of Learned Socs in the Social Scis 2003; *Books* numerous books and pubns incl: Office Linkages and Location (1973), Office Location in Urban and Regional Development (1975), British Cities: An Analysis of Urban Change (with N A Spence, 1981), Economic Development Policies: an evaluation study of the Newcastle Metropolitan Region (with F Robinson and C Wren, 1987); *Recreations* rowing, walking; *Clubs* Northern Counties; *Style*— Prof John Goddard, OBE; ✉ University of Newcastle upon Tyne, Newcastle upon Tyne, NE1 7RU (tel 0191 222 7955, fax 0191 222 6299, e-mail john.goddard@ncl.ac.uk)

GODDARD, Rt Rev John William; *see:* Burnley, Bishop of

GODDARD, (Harold) Keith; QC (1979); s of Harold Goddard (d 1979), of Stockport, Cheshire, and Edith Goddard (d 1982); *b* 9 July 1936; *Educ* Manchester Grammar, CCC Cambridge; *m* 1, 1963 (m dis), Susan Elizabeth, yr da of late Ronald Stansfield, of Wilmslow, Cheshire; 2 s; m 2, 1983, Maria Alicja, da of Czeslaw Lazuchiewicz (d 1981), of Lodz, Poland; *Career* called to the Bar 1959; recorder of the Crown Court 1978–, head of chambers 1983–2000, dep judge of the High Court 1993–; memb Criminal Injuries Compensation Bd 1993–2001, memb Mental Health Review Tbnl 1997–; *Recreations* golf; *Clubs* Wilmslow Golf; *Style*— Keith Goddard, Esq, QC; ✉ Deans Court Chambers, 24 St John Street, Manchester M3 4DF (tel 0161 214 6000, fax 0161 214 6001, e-mail goddard@deanscourt.co.uk)

GODDARD, Martyn Stanley; s of Thomas Raymond Goddard (d 1982), and Winifred Florence, *née* Eastman (d 1998); *b* 9 October 1951; *Educ* Mandville Co Secdy Sch, Aylesbury Coll of Further Educn, Harrow Coll of Technol and Art (Dip Applied Photography); *m* Beverley Margret Ballard; 2 da (Lauren b 7 June 1985, Grace Natalie b 8 May 1990); *Career* photographer; asst to Gered Mankowitz and Denis Waugh 1975–76, freelance photographer IPC Young Magazine Group 1976–77; assignments 1977–91: Sunday Telegraph Magazine, Sunday Express Magazine, You Magazine, advtg projects (incl devpt of markets for car photography in Br and American magazines); editorial and advtg work 1991–; exhibitions incl: Blondie in Camera (Mirandy Gallery) 1978, Montserrat Studio (Lincoln Centre NY) 1979, 10 x 6 Group (Battersea Arts Centre, Neal St Gallery) 1981, Polaroid Time Zero (tour of UK) 1981, Human Views 1977–81 (J S Gallery London) 1981, National Portraits (Nat Theatre) 1983, Faces of Our Time (Nat Theatre tour) 1985, The Car (V&A) 1986, Rock'n'Roll and Speed (Exposure Gallery) 2007; Jet Media Excellence Award for Photography 1996, Hyundi Photographic Award for Motoring Photography 2002, 2004, 2005 and 2006; FBIPP; *Recreations* historic rally car driving, black and white photographic diary, mountain biking; *Clubs* Historic Rally Car; *Style*— Martyn Goddard, Esq; ✉ Martyn Goddard Photography, 5 Jeffrey's Place, London NW1 9PP (tel 07831 500477, fax 020 7485 0996, e-mail photo.mg@virgin.net)

GODDARD, Dr Peter; CBE (2002); s of Herbert Charles Goddard (d 1971), and Rosina Sarah, *née* Waite (d 1991); *b* 3 September 1945; *Educ* Emanuel Sch London, Trinity Coll Cambridge (MA, PhD, ScD); *m* 24 Aug 1968, Helen Barbara, da of Francis Fraser Ross (d 1991), of Alne, N Yorks; 1 da (Linda b 1973), 1 s (Michael b 1975); *Career* res fell Trinity Coll Cambridge 1969–73, visiting scientist CERN Geneva Switzerland 1970–72 and 1978, lectr in applied mathematics Univ of Durham 1972–74; St John's Coll Cambridge: lectr in mathematics 1975–91, fell 1975–94 and 2004–, tutor 1980–87, sr tutor 1983–87, master 1994–2004; Univ of Cambridge: univ asst lectr 1975–76, univ lectr 1976–89, reader in mathematical physics 1989–92, prof of theoretical physics 1992–2004, dep dir Isaac Newton Inst for Mathematical Sciences 1991–94, chm Local Examination Syndicate 1998–2003, memb Cncl 2000–03; dir Inst for Advanced Study Princeton 2004–; visiting prof Univ of Virginia Charlottesville 1983; govr: Berkhamsted Sch and Berkhamsted Sch for Girls 1985–96, Emanuel Sch 1992–2003, Shrewsbury Sch 1994–2003, Hills Road Sixth Form Coll Cambridge 1999–2003 (chm 2001–03); memb: Inst for Theoretical Physics Univ of Calif Santa Barbara 1986 and 1990, Inst for Advanced Study Princeton 1974 and 1988, London Mathematical Soc 1989 (pres 2002–03), Cncl Royal Soc 2000–02; Dirac medal and prize International Centre for Theoretical Physics 1997; hon fell Trinity Coll Dublin 1995; FRS 1989, FInstP 1990, FRSA 1998; *Recreations* mathematical physics, informal flower arranging, idle thought; *Style*— Dr Peter Goddard, CBE, FRS; ✉ Institute for Advanced Study, Einstein Drive, Princeton, NJ 08540, USA (tel 001 609 734 8200)

GODDARD, Philip Norman; s of Norman Goddard (d 1984), of Templecombe, Somerset, and Rose May, *née* Pitman (d 2002); *b* 28 October 1948; *Educ* Brunel Univ (BTech), Univ of Bath (MSc); *m* 1973, Elizabeth Louise; 1 da (Joanna Louise b 1979), 1 s (Edward Philip b 1982); *Career* Westland Helicopters Ltd: head of Advanced Engrg 1989–90, chief systems engr 1990–92, dir of engrg 1992–, tech dir, now conslt; MIMechE, FRAeS, FREng 1997; *Recreations* vintage cars and motorcycles, golf; *Style*— Philip Goddard, Esq, FREng; ✉ Brympton Barn, Middle Chinnock, Crewkerne, Somerset TA18 7PN (tel 01935 881948, e-mail philip45@btinternet.com)

GODDEN, (Anthony) Nicholas; s of late Tony and Molly Godden; *b* 21 February 1945; *Educ* Wellington, INSEAD; *m* 1967, Joanna Stephanie, *née* Wheeler; 2 s (James Musgrave b 1970, Peter William b 1984), 2 da (Katharine Jane b 1972, Alexandra Mary 1982); *Career* trainee accountant Ernst & Young 1963–67, fin dir Cleghorn & Harris Ltd South Africa 1967–73, chief accountant Mars Ltd 1973–75; Raychem Ltd: fin dir 1975–93, chm and md 1993–96; chm Lloyd's Superannuation Fund 1999–; memb Cncl CBI 1994–96; dir East Wilts Healthcare NHS Tst 1993–97, chm Swindon & Marlborough NHS Tst 1997–2003, chm North Bristol NHS Tst 2003–; dir Wiltshire TEC 1994–97; FCA 1967; *Recreations* sailing, gardening; *Style*— Nicholas Godden, Esq

GODDIN, Richard William; s of William Frederick Goddin (d 1967), and Audrey Joan, *née* Stearn (d 2003); *b* 17 May 1943; *Educ* Perse Sch, London Poly Univ of Westminster Sch of Mgmnt Studies (DMS, Urwick medal), Henley Mgmnt Coll; *m* 15 June 1985, Margaret Ann, da of Reginald Barlow (d 1957), and Doris, *née* Russell (d 1999); 2 s (James William b 1987, Thomas Richard Druce b 1991); *Career* sr mangr Nat West Bank plc 1977–83, treas Lombard North Central plc 1983–86, dep treas Nat West plc 1986–87; County NatWest Ltd: exec dir 1987–88, head Global Funding Gp Treasury 1989–92, md Global Money Markets 1992–97, dir BOE NatWest South Africa 1996–97, md Gp Treasury 1997–2000, md Treasury Risk Associates Ltd 2001–; dir: Ashwell Property Gp plc 2001–, Ashwell Homes (East Anglia) Ltd 2002–, Greenways Ravenswood Ltd 2004–; chm Eastern Housing Partnership Ltd 2005–; ACIB, FRSA, CMAe; *Recreations* flying, sailing, croquet, country life; *Clubs* Royal Aero, Croquet Assoc, Red Baron Flying, Whitehill Farm Aero; *Style*— Richard Goddin, Esq; ✉ Belmington Close, Meldreth, Cambridgeshire SG8 6NT (tel 01763 260061, e-mail goddin@btinternet.com)

GODFREY, Andrew Paul; s of Bernard Russel Godfrey, of Dunblane, and Carol Emma Elise, *née* Leonhardt; *b* 12 August 1953; *Educ* Morrison's Acad Crieff Perthshire, Univ of Edinburgh (BSc Econ); *m* Irene, da of Robert Simpson, MBE; 2 s (Paul Douglas b 24 Oct 1982, Stuart Mark b 22 Feb 1985); *Career* Grant Thornton: regnl managing ptnr for Scot and NI; fin advsr and auditor various cos Scotland; ACA 1977; *Recreations* golf; *Clubs* Gleneagles Golf, Dunblane Golf; *Style*— Andrew Godfrey, Esq; ✉ Faery Knowe, St Mary's Drive, Dunblane FK15; Grant Thornton, 95 Bothwell Street, Glasgow G2 7JZ (tel 0141 223 0000, fax 0141 223 0001, mobile 079 7615 5860)

GODFREY, Daniel; s of Gerald Michael and Anne Sheila Godfrey; *b* 30 June 1961; *Educ* Westminster, Univ of Manchester (BA); *m* July 1994, Frederiki, da of Iwan Perewiznyk; 3 s (Jonathan Joseph b 21 July 1981, Antony James b 14 June 1984, Benjamin David Sydney b 2 June 1997), 1 da (Mia Christina b 7 July 1987); *Career* proprietor The Sharper Image (mktg and media relations consltѕ) 1991–94, mktg dir Flemings 1994–98, DG Assoc of Investment Cos 1998–; chm Personal Finance Educn Gp 2000–03; *Recreations* raising children, watching football; *Clubs* Inst of Contemporary Arts, London Capital, IOD; *Style*— Daniel Godfrey, Esq; ✉ Association of Investment Companies, 9th Floor, 24 Chiswell Street, London EC1Y 4YY (tel 020 7282 5555, fax 020 7282 5567, e-mail daniel@theaic.co.uk)

GODFREY, (William) Edwin Martindale; s of Ernest Martindale Godfrey (d 1974), of Chesterfield, Derbys, and Anna Lol Tedde, *née* Maas; *b* 20 October 1947; *Educ* Repton, Queens' Coll Cambridge (MA); *m* 10 Sept 1977, Helen Ann, da of Dr John Arthur Clement James (d 1996), of Northfield, Birmingham; 2 s (William b 1978, Thomas b 1980), 1 da (Alice b 1983); *Career* admitted slr 1971; asst slr Norton Rose Botterell and Roche 1971–72; Simmons & Simmons: asst slr 1972–76, ptnr 1977–, head of commercial gp 1993–2002, int managing ptnr 1995–96, seconded as dep chief exec Private Fin Panel 1997, head of major projects 1998–2002; Int Bar Assoc: vice-chm Ctee on Anti Tst Law 1981–86, chm Sub-Ctee on Structure and Ethics of Business Law 1990–94 (vice-chm 1988–90), memb Standing Ctee on Professional Ethics 1990–, memb Cncl Section on Business Law 1994–98, memb Standing Ctee on Int Legal Practice 1995–2000 (chm 1997–2000), memb Standing Ctee on Multi-Disciplinary Practice 1995–; memb Advsy Bd Int and Comparative Law Center S Western Legal Fndn Dallas 1991; dir Shape London 1998–; hon legal advsr Hertford CAB until 1995; Freeman: City of London Solicitors' Co 1990, City of London 1991; memb: Law Soc 1971, City of London Law Soc 1990 (chm Commercial Law Sub-Ctee 1998–), Int Bar Assoc, Hertford Deanery Synod 1990–94; govr Abel Smith Jr Mixed Infants Sch Hertford 1992–2000; FRSA 1994; *Books* Joint Ventures in Butterworths Encyclopaedia of Forms & Precedents (ed 5 edn, 1990), Law Without Frontiers (ed, 1995), Butterworths PFI Manual (jt ed, 1998); *Style*— Edwin Godfrey, Esq; ✉ Simmons & Simmons, CityPoint, One Ropemaker Street, London EC2Y 9SS (tel 020 7628 2020, fax 020 7628 2070, telex 888562)

GODFREY, Frances Helen (Fran); da of John Leonard Thurlow Godfrey, of New Milton, Hampshire, and Joan, *née* Follebouckt; *b* 29 June 1953; *Educ* Convent of the Cross Bournemouth, PCL; *m* 1976 (m dis 1981), David Davies; *Career* trained as bi-lingual sec, sec/admin London and Bournemouth 1973–79; Two Counties Radio 1980–87: tech operator ILR Bournemouth 1980–82, commercial prodr 1982–84, presenter 1984–87; returned to admin and freelance work; announcer/newsreader BBC Radio 2 1990–; memb Equity 1984–2003; *Publications* Meditations on the Stations of the Cross, Venite, Adoremus - Advent Meditations, Thy Will Be Done - A Small Book of Prayer; *Recreations* anything creative where I can see a result, old films (especially musicals); *Style*— Miss Fran Godfrey; ✉ BBC, Broadcasting House, London W1A 1AA (tel 020 7765 4695)

GODFREY, Howard Anthony; QC (1991); s of Emanuel Godfrey (d 1991), of London, and Amy, *née* Grossman; *b* 17 August 1946; *Educ* William Ellis Sch, LSE (LLB); *m* 3 Sept 1972, Barbara, da of John Ellinger, of London; 2 s (Timothy b 1975, James b 1980); *Career* asst lectr in law Univ of Canterbury NZ 1969, pt/t tutor Dept of Law LSE 1970–72; called to the Bar Middle Temple 1970 (bencher 2004), ad eundem Inner Temple 1984; practising SE Circuit 1972–, recorder Crown Court 1992–; called to the Bar Turks and Caicos Islands 1996; fell Soc for Advanced Legal Studies 1998; *Recreations* wine and food, humour; *Style*— Howard Godfrey, Esq, QC; ✉ 2 Bedford Row, London WC1R 4BU (tel 020 7440 8888, fax 020 7242 1738)

GODFREY, Prof Patrick; s of Oliver Harcourt Godfrey, of Salisbury, Wilts, and Mary, *née* Fitzgerald (d 1987); *b* 10 March 1946; *Educ* Bishop Wordsworth Sch Salisbury, Imperial

Coll London (BSc); *m* 1970, Gertrude (Trudi) Hedwig, *née* Scott; 1 s (Daniel Sutcliffe b 1977); *Career* Sir William Halcrow and Partners Ltd 1967–2005: md (Offshore) 1987–93 (dir 1977–89), dir Halcrow-Ewbank Petroleum and Offshore Engrg Ltd 1977–93, dir 1987–2005, chm Halcrow Polymerics Ltd 1993–97, dir Geotechnics Tunnels and Transportation Div 1993–98, gp champion of partnering 1997–2001, dir Halcrow Transportation Infrastructure 1998–99, dir Halcrow Business Solutions 2000–05, dir strategic relations devpt 2001–05, dir EngD in Systems Centre Univs of Bristol and Bath 2005–; prof of systems engineering Univ of Bristol, visiting prof Civil Engrg Systems Univ of Bristol; memb: Cncl ICE 1980–83, Engrg Cncl Ctee Tech and Product Devpt 1984–91, Offshore Safety Bd 1985–92, Engrg Cncl Risk Issues Working Party 1991–93; CIOB: Author of the Year 2001, Gold Medal for Construction Mgmnt 2001; Hon DEng Univ of Bristol; FREng 1998, FICE, FEI, FCGI; *Publications* Control of Risk: CIRIA 125, Doing it Differently, Systems for Rethinking Construction, Thomas Telford; author of numerous engrg articles in learned jnls; *Recreations* sailing, gardening; *Clubs* Royal Ocean Racing; *Style—* Prof Patrick Godfrey, FREng; ✉ Systems-thinking UK, South Lodge, Bellsyew Green Road, Frant, Near Tunbridge Wells TN3 9EB (tel 01892 750554, e-mail patrick@systems-thinking.co.uk)

GODFREY, Patrick Lindesay; s of Rev Canon Frederick Godfrey (d 1984), of Swithland, Leics, and Lois Mary Gladys, *née* Turner (d 1973); *b* 15 February 1933; *Educ* Abbotsholme Sch, Central Sch of Speech and Drama; *m* 20 April 1960, Amanda Galafres Patterson Walker; 1 s (Richard Lindesay b 29 April 1961), 1 da (Kate b 12 Feb 1964); *Career* actor; Nat Serv 1951–53; *Theatre* repertory incl: Dundee, RSC London and Stratford 1970–81; credits incl: Kulyghin in Three Sisters, Mr Kenwigs in Nicholas Nickleby (Aldwych and Broadway), Friar Lawrence in Romeo and Juliet, Polonius in Hamlet (RSC tour and repertory in Stratford) 1989, Paulet in Mary Stuart (RNT) 1996; opening season at Shakespeare's Globe Theatre 1997, Captain Lewis in The Iceman Cometh (Almeida, Old Vic and Broadway), Battle Royal (RNT) 2000, Three Sisters (RNT), His Dark Materials (RNT); *Film* incl: Heat and Dust, A Room with a View, Maurice, On The Black Hill, Clockwise, The Trial, The Remains of the Day, Ever After, My Brother Tom, The Count of Monte Cristo, The Importance of Being Ernest, Oliver Twist; *Recreations* golf, restoring Islington house and house in Greece; *Clubs* Stage Golfing Soc; *Style—* Patrick Godfrey, Esq; ✉ c/o Markham & Froggatt Ltd, 4 Windmill Street, London W1T 2HZ (tel 020 7636 4412, fax 020 7637 5233)

GODFREY, Paul; s of Peter Godfrey, of Exeter, and Valerie, *née* Drake; *b* 16 September 1960; *Career* playwright, director and screenwriter; dir Perth Repertory Theatre Scotland 1983–84, Eden Court Theatre Inverness 1985–87 (estab touring co); *Plays* Inventing A New Colour (NT Studio 1987, Royal Court 1988), A Bucket of Eels 1988, Once in a While the Odd Thing Happens (RNT) 1990, The Panic (Royal Opera) 1991, The Blue Ball (RNT) 1995, Catalogue of Misunderstanding 1998, Tiananmen Square (BBC Radio) 1999, The Oldest Play 2000, Linda 2000; Trilogy of Plays from Difference Sources: The Modern Husband (ATC) 1995, The Invisible Woman (The Gate) 1996, The Candidate (Manchester Royal Exchange) 1997; Collected Plays: Volume One (1998); *Screenplays* The Best Sex of My Life (2001), A Map of the City (2004), Goodbye Hobberdy Jack! (2006), Dickens in New York (2006), Park & Ride (2006); *Awards* incl: Arts Cncl Trainee Directors bursary 1983, Arts Cncl Playwrights Award 1989, David Harlech Meml Bursary 1990, Stephen Arlen Award 1991, Arts Cncl Playwrights' Award 1992 and 1998, Wingate Scholarship 1996; *Style—* Paul Godfrey; ✉ c/o A P Watt, 20 John Street, London WC1N 2DR

GODFREY, Dr Richard Charles; s of Thomas Charles Godfrey (d 1965), of Watford, Herts, and Joan Eva, *née* Clayton; *b* 8 September 1940; *Educ* Watford GS, Peterhouse Cambridge (MA), UCL (MD); *m* 8 June 1968, Jane Catherine, da of Stanley Goodman, of Reigate, Surrey; 3 s (Thomas b 1970, Robin b 1974, Matthew b 1975), 1 da (Sarah b 1971); *Career* Univ of Southampton: lectr in med 1972–76, conslt physician 1976–2002, clinical sub-dean 1984–89; Overseas Devpt Admin prof of med Moi Univ Kenya 1991–94, health advsr Merlin 2002–; warden Farley Hosp Almshouses, organ conslt to Salisbury Diocesan Advsy Ctee; church and concert organist, music teacher; MD, FRCP, ARCO; *Recreations* squash; *Style—* Dr Richard Godfrey; ✉ The Wardenry, Farley, Salisbury SP5 1AH (tel 01722 712231); Merlin, 56–64 Leonard Street, London EC2A 4LT (tel 020 7065 0800, fax 020 7065 0801)

GODFREY-ISAACS, Laura; *b* 22 July 1964; *Educ* Kingston Poly, Brighton Poly (BA), Slade Sch of Art London, RCA (PhD); *Career* artist; sr lectr: Winchester Sch of Art, Univ of Southampton, Kent Inst of Art and Design; visiting lectr at numerous art colls incl Tate Gallery, Whitechapel Gallery, Barbican and Camden Art Centre; artist in residence: Pratt Inst Brooklyn NYC 1988–89, Tate Gallery Liverpool 1990; dir Home prodn co 1998–; public art projects with numerous galleries and museums; *Solo Exhibitions* Monima Gallery London 1987, Morgan's Gallery London 1987, Tate Gallery Liverpool 1990, Sue Williams Gallery London 1991 and 1993, John Milton Gallery London 1991, Physical Encounters (Gardner Arts Centre Univ of Sussex touring to Royal Festival Hall Galleries London) 1992, Robert Hossack Gallery London 1994, Condeso Lawler Gallery NYC 1994, John Jones Gallery London 1995; *Group Exhibitions* incl: Al Fresco Exhibition (RA) 1988, Whitechapel Open Studio Exhibition 1989, View of the New (Royal Over-Seas League London) 1991, John Moores Exhibition (Walker Art Gallery Liverpool) 1991, Roses are Red (Br Cncl touring exhbn of UK and Bulgarian artists to Polvdiv Bulgaria and London) 1991, invited artist Whitechapel Open 92, Festival International de la Peinture Cannes (Br Cncl rep artist with Saleem Arif, *qv*) 1992, Women's Art at New Hall Cambridge 1992, Somatic States (Middlesex Univ and Norwich Art Gallery) 1992, Riverside Open (Riverside Studios London) 1993, Skin (Antonio Barnola Gallery Barcelona) 1993, Wit and Excess (Sydney, Brisbane, Melbourne and Adelaide) 1994, It's a Pleasure (South Bank London) 1995, Stereo-Tip (Soros Centre for Contemporary Art Ljubljana Slovenia) 1995; *Collections* incl: Momart, New Hall, Arts Cncl of GB, Contemporary Arts Soc; *Awards* Jacob Mendelsohn scholarship 1986, McDonald fellowship from Pratt Inst NYC 1988, Boise fellowship from Slade Sch of Art London 1988, Fulbright fellowship for residency in NYC 1988, Momart fellowship for residency at Tate Gallery Liverpool 1990; *Style—* Ms Laura Godfrey-Isaacs

GODLEY, Adam; s of Samuel Jack Godley, and Gladys, *née* Gainsboro; *Educ* Rickmansworth Sch; *Career* actor; *Theatre* West End: An Inspector Calls (Westminster Theatre), June Moon (Vaudeville Theatre), The Revengers Comedies (Strand Theatre), The Wood Demon (Playhouse Theatre), The Importance of Being Earnest (Haymarket Theatre), Private Lives (Albery Theatre and Richard Rogers Theater NY, Outstanding Broadway Debut Theatre World Award), The Rivals (Albery Theatre); Royal Court Theatre: Mr Kolpert, Mouth to Mouth (nomination Best Supporting Actor Olivier Awards); Donmar Warehouse: Cabaret, The Front Page; RNT: Cleo, Camping, Emanuelle and Dick (nomination Best Supporting Actor Olivier Awards), Mr A's Amazing Maze Plays, Watch on the Rhine, Close of Play, The Pillowman, Paul, Two Thousand Years; RSC: Three Hours After the Marriage, The White Devil, The General From America, A Midsummer Night's Dream; plays at Scarborough: Eden End, The Ballroom, The Beaux Strategem, Man of the Moment, Taking Steps, Othello; other credits incl: The Critic (Royal Exchange Theatre Manchester), A Going Concern (Hampstead Theatre), Dear Charles (Guildford Theatre), Hippolytus (Gate Theatre), Zero Hour (Edinburgh Festival); *Television* Moonfleet, Class Act, Cor Blimey!, Inspector Linley Mysteries, Armadillo, Sword of Honour, Margery and Gladys, Hawking, The Young Visiters, Nuremburg; *Radio* incl: The Frederica Quartet, The School for Scandal, The Ghost Train, Birdsong, Forty Years On, Les Liaisons Dangereuses, Tess of the D'Urbevilles; *Film* Thunderpants, And Now... Ladies and Gentlemen, Bride of Ice, Around the World in 80 Days, Love Actually, Charlie and the Chocolate Factory, Nanny McPhee, Elizabeth - The Golden Age, His Dark Materials - The Golden Compass, Son of Rambow; *Style—* Adam Godley, Esq; ✉ c/o Sue Latimer, ARG, 4 Great Portland Street, London W1W 8PA (tel 020 7436 6400, fax 020 7436 6700, e-mail latimer@argtalent.com)

GODLEY, Georgina Jane (Mrs Sebastian Conran); da of Michael Godley, and Heather, *née* Couper; *b* 11 April 1955; *Educ* Putney HS, Thames Valley GS, Wimbledon Art Sch, Brighton Poly (BA), Chelsea Sch of Art (MA); *m* 16 April 1988, Sebastian Conran, s of Sir Terence Conran; 2 s (Samuel Orby Conran b 12 May 1989, Maximillian Anthony Rupert Conran b 4 April 1995); *Career* picture restorer 1978–79, menswear designer Browns London and Paris 1979, ptnr designer Crolla London 1980–85, fndr and designer own label Georgina Godley (retail outlets from London to USA and Japan, and illustrations and articles in all maj fashion pubns); currently style dir Habitat; sr lectr St Martin's Sch of Art and Sch of Fashion and Textiles RCA; *Style—* Ms Georgina Godley

GODLEY, Prof the Hon Wynne Alexander Hugh; yr s of 2 Baron Kilbracken, CB, KC (d 1950), and his 1 wife Elizabeth Helen Monteith, *née* Hamilton; *b* 2 September 1926; *Educ* Rugby, New Coll Oxford (BA), Paris Conservatoire; *m* 3 Feb 1955, Kathleen Eleanora, da of Sir Jacob Epstein, KBE, and former w of the painter Lucian Freud; 1 da (Eve b 1967); *Career* economist; economist Metal Box Ltd 1954–56, with HM Treasy 1956–70 (various posts rising to dep dir Economic Section 1967–70); Univ of Cambridge: dir Dept of Applied Economics 1970–94, fell King's Coll 1970–98 (now emeritus fell), prof of applied economics 1980–93; memb HM Treasy independent panel of economic forecasting advsrs 1992–96; visiting prof Aalborg Univ Denmark 1987–88, distinguished scholar Levy Economics Inst Bard Coll NY 1994–2001, visiting sr research fell in liquidity, flows and stocks and the macro-economy Cambridge Endowment for Research in Finance (CERF) Judge Inst of Mgmnt Studies 2002–; dir: Investing in Success Equities Ltd 1970–85, ROH 1976–86; former professional oboist, princ oboist BBC Welsh Orch 1952; *Style—* Prof the Hon Wynne Godley; ✉ Jasmine House, Cavendish, Suffolk

GODMAN, Jo; da of Frank Alfred Leonard, of Dernford Hall, Swefling, Suffolk, and Amelia Emma, *née* Day; *b* 29 May 1944; *Educ* Camden Sch for Girls, Holborn Coll of Law, Languages and Commerce; *m* 11 March 1967, Keith William Godman, s of William Christopher Godman; *Career* girl friday Chapman Raper TV commercials prodn co 1965–67, prodn asst Geoffrey Forster Associates 1967–71, prodr for Tom Bussmann of Bussmann Llewelyn 1972–80 (prodn asst 1971–72), co-fndr Patterson Godman Ltd 1980–83, md RSA Films Ltd (Ridley Scott Associates) 1983–96; fndr Godman Ltd 1997–; has produced numerous commercials winning awards at D&AD, British TV Awards, Cannes and Clio NY; *Recreations* cinema, gardening, ballet, cooking, swimming; *Clubs* Groucho, Women in Advertising, Soho House; *Style—* Jo Godman

GODMAN, Patricia (Trish); MSP; *b* 31 October 1939, Govan, Glasgow; *Educ* St Gerard's Sr Secdy Sch Glasgow, Jordanhill Coll Glasgow (CQSW); *Career* early career jobs incl bank clerk, shop asst, works cashier and latterly social worker Glasgow; MSP (Lab) W Renfrewshire 1999–; Scottish Parl: chair Local Govt Ctee 1999, currently dep presiding offr and convenor Convenors Gp; memb Cross-Pty Gp on: Learning Disability, Epilepsy, Malawi, Tracking Debt, Women; memb: Parly Bureau, Amicus, Amnesty Int, UNO, Nat Tst for Scotland, RNLI, Scottish Lab History Soc, Working Class History Soc; *Recreations* growing own vegetables, soft fruit and flowers; *Style—* Ms Trish Godman, MSP; ✉ Renfrew House, Cottage 27, Quarrier's Village, Bridge of Weir PA11 3SX (tel 01505 615337, fax 01505 690717, website www.trishgodman.com); The Scottish Parliament, Edinburgh, EH99 1SP (tel 0131 348 5837, fax 0131 348 6460, e-mail trish.godman.msp@scottish.parliament.uk)

GODSAL, Philip Caulfeild; s of Maj Philip Hugh Godsal (d 1982), of Iscoyd Park, Whitchurch, Shropshire, and Pamela Ann Delisle, *née* Caulfeild (d 2004); *b* 10 October 1945; *Educ* Eton; *m* 1, 29 Nov 1969 (m dis 1985), Lucinda Mary, da of Lt Cdr Percival Royston Dancy; 3 s (Philip Langley b 28 June 1971, Benjamin Rupert Wilmot b 17 June 1976, Thomas Henry b 3 Aug 1977), 1 da (Laura Sophie b 24 May 1973); m 2, 2 July 1986, Selina Baber, da of Thomas William Brooke-Smith (d 1991), of Canford Cliffs; 3 step da (Zoe Christina b 1974, Lucinda Selina b 1976, Christina Juliet b 1980); *Career* farmer, land agent and chartered surveyor; formerly ptnr Savills Norwich, ptnr John German Shrewsbury 1984–97, sr ptnr Carter Jonas Shrewsbury 1997–; chm Historic Houses Assoc for Wales 1989–91, chm N Wales Region Timber Growers UK 1989–91, sec Shropshire Rural Housing Assoc 1988–95; pres Iscoyd and Fenns Bank CC; Regnl Ctee National Trust: chm Mercia 2000–02, vice-chm West Midlands 2002–06; High Sheriff Clwyd 1993–94; FRICS; *Recreations* shooting, forestry, reading; *Clubs* MCC, Farmers', Lancashire CCC; *Style—* Philip Godsal, Esq; ✉ Iscoyd Park, Whitchurch, Shropshire SY13 3AT; Carter Jonas, Chartered Surveyors and Property Consultants, Black Birches, Hadnall, Shrewsbury SY4 3DH (tel 01939 210113, e-mail philip.godsal@carterjonas.uk)

GODSIFF, Roger; MP; s of late George Godsiff, and Gladys Godsiff; *b* 28 June 1937; *Educ* Catford Comp Sch; *m* Julia Brenda; 1 s, 1 da; *Career* formerly political offr APEX then sr research offr GMB; Parly candidate Birmingham Yardley 1983; MP (Lab): Birmingham Small Heath 1992–97, Birmingham Sparkbrook and Small Heath 1997–; House of Commons: chm All-Pty Kashmir Parly Gp 1992–2004, chm Br-Japanese Parly Gp 1997–; cncllr London Borough of Lewisham 1971–90 (Lab chief whip 1974–77, mayor 1977); chm Charlton Athletic Charitable Tst; *Recreations* sport, particularly football; *Clubs* Charlton Athletic Supporters', Rowley Labour; *Style—* Roger Godsiff, Esq, MP; ✉ House of Commons, London SW1A 0AA

GODSON, Anthony; *b* 1 February 1948; *m* 1977, Maryan Jane Margaret, *née* Hurst; *Career* diplomat; entered HM Dip Serv 1968, posted Bucharest 1970, third sec Jakarta 1972, private sec to High Cmmr Canberra 1976, second later first sec UKMIS NY 1983, first sec FCO 1988, dep head of mission Bucharest 1990, first sec UKMIS Geneva 1991, cnsllr then dep head of mission and consul-gen Jakarta 1998, cnsllr FCO 2002, high cmmr to Mauritius 2004–07 (concurrently non-resident ambass to Comoros); *Style—* Anthony Godson, Esq; ✉ c/o Foreign & Commonwealth Office, King Charles Street, London SW1A 2AH

GODWIN, Prof Richard John (Dick); s of John Leige Godwin (d 1992), of Nettlebed, Oxon, and Kathleen Alice, *née* Hands (d 1971); *b* 20 April 1947; *Educ* Nat Coll of Agric Engrg (BSc), Univ of Illinois (MS), Univ of Reading and Nat Coll of Agric Engrg (PhD); *m* 15 July 1975, Jill Banfield, da of J Fisher; *Career* res and teaching asst Dept of Agric Engrg Univ of Illinois 1968–70; Cranfield Univ at Silsoe (formerly Nat Coll of Agric Engrg and Silsoe Coll): res scholar 1970–73, res offr 1974–76, lectr in applied soil mechanics 1977–81, sr lectr in soil dynamics 1981–85, asst dir of R&D 1979–84, dir of res 1984–99, prof and head of agric and environmental engrg 1985–96, dean Faculty of Agric Engrg, Food Prodn and Rural Land Use 1990–93, prof and head of agric and biosystems engrg 1996–99, prof and head Inst of AgriTechnology 1999–2001, prof and ldr Engrg Gp Nat Soil Resources Inst 2001–, dir of postgrad res 2001–; pro-vice-chllr Cranfield Univ 1993–96; external examiner: Univ of the W Indies 1987–91, Harper Adams Agric Coll 1994–97, UC Dublin 1996–2000, Univ of Aberdeen, Univ of Newcastle upon Tyne, Univ of SA, Asian Inst of Technol; referee and memb Editorial Bd Jl of Agric Engrg Res 1984–; assoc ed: Jl of Terramechanics, Soil Use and Management; visiting prof: Harpur Adams Univ Coll, Honcoy prof Czech Univ of Life Sciences; pres IAgrE 1994–96; tstee Douglas Bomford Tst 1994–, memb Bd of Tstees Claas Fndn 1999–; memb Asian Assoc of Agricultural Engrs, fell American Soc of Agric Engrs 1994 (int dir 1992–94, John

Deere Medal 2005); CEng (IAgrE), Hon FIAgrE 2000, FREng 2001; *Publications* numerous articles and papers in learned jls; *Recreations* gardening, walking, DIY, photography; *Style—* Prof Dick Godwin; ✉ Cranfield University at Silsoe, Silsoe, Bedford MK45 4DT (tel 01525 863053, fax 01525 863366, e-mail r.godwin@cranfield.ac.uk)

GODWIN-AUSTEN, Dr Richard Bertram; s of R Annesley Godwin-Austen, CBE (d 1977), of Pirbright, Surrey, and Kathleen Beryl Godwin-Austen (d 1995); *b* 4 October 1935; *Educ* Charterhouse, St Thomas' London Hosp (MB BS, MD); *m* 1, 12 Aug 1961, Jennifer Jane (d 1996), da of Louis Sigismund Himely; 1 s (Jonathan Reade b 1962), 1 da (Alice Amelia b 1964); m 2, 15 Nov 1997, (Deirdre) Sally, da of Gerald Stark Toller; *Career* sr registrar Inst of Neurology Queen Sq London 1967–70, conslt neurologist Univ Hosp Nottingham 1970–98; clinical teacher (former chm) of neurological sciences Nottingham until 1998; memb Med Advsy Panel Parkinson's Disease Soc; pres Assoc of British Neurologists, vice-pres Euro Fedn of Neurological Socs, delegate to Euro Bd of Neurology, sec and treas gen World Fedn of Neurology; High Sheriff Notts 1994–95; FRCP 1976; *Books* The Parkinson's Disease Handbook (1984), Medical Aspects of Fitness to Drive (contrib, 1985), The Neurology of the Elderly (1989); *Recreations* gardening, dessert wines; *Clubs* Garrick, RSM; *Style—* Dr Richard Godwin-Austen; ✉ 15 Westgate, Southwell, Nottinghamshire NG25 0JN

GOEHR, Prof Alexander; s of Walter and Laelia Goehr; *b* 10 August 1932; *Educ* Berkhamsted Sch, Royal Manchester Coll of Music, Paris Conservatoire; *m* 1, 1954 (m dis 1971), Audrey Baker; 3 da; m 2, 1972, Anthea Staunton; 1 s; m 3, 1982, Amira Katz; *Career* composer; lectr Morley Coll 1955–57, music asst BBC 1960–67, Winston Churchill Tst fellowship 1968, composer-in-residence New England Conservatory Boston 1968–69, assoc prof of music Yale Univ 1969–70, West Riding prof of music Univ of Leeds 1971–76, prof of music and fell Trinity Hall Cambridge 1976–99 (emeritus 1999–); visiting prof Peking Conservatoire of Music 1980; artistic dir Leeds Festival 1975, memb Bd of Dirs Royal Opera House 1982–, Reith lectr BBC 1987; hon vice-pres SPNM 1983–; Hon DMus: Univ of Southampton 1973, Univ of Manchester 1989, Univ of Nottingham 1994, Univ of Siena 1999, Univ of Cambridge 2000; hon prof Beijing Central Conservatory 2001; hon memb American Acad and Inst of Arts and Letters, Hon FRMCM, Hon FRAM 1975, Hon FRNCM 1980, Hon FRCM 1981; *Style—* Prof Alexander Goehr; ✉ Trinity Hall, Cambridge CB2 1TJ

GOETZ, Michael Steven (Mike); s of Richard T Goetz (d 2004), and Nancy Feltner, *née* Worthington, of Melbourne, FL; *b* 7 August 1956, Columbus, OH; *Educ* Ohio State Univ (BA), Boston Univ Sch of Law (JD); *m* 15 Oct 1988, Dr Senah E Green; 3 s (Jonathan Richard b 12 July 1991, Christopher Robert b 26 Oct 1992, William Hunter b 1 March 1994); *Career* admitted NY State Bar 1988; slr specialising in banking; practised NY 1986–2000, ptnr White & Case LLP London 2000– (co-head Banking and Capital Markets Gp); *Style—* Mike Goetz, Esq; ✉ White & Case LLP, 5 Old Broad Street, London EC2N 1DW (tel 020 7532 1200, fax 020 7532 1001, e-mail mgoetz@whitecase.com)

GOFF, Martyn; CBE (2005, OBE 1977); s of Jacob Goff (d 1971), and Janey Goff (d 1978); *b* 7 June 1923; *Educ* Clifton; *Career* served RAF 1941–46; bookseller 1946–70; Book Tst (known as Nat Book League until 1986): dir 1970–86, chief exec 1986–88, non-exec dep chm 1991–92, chm 1992–94, vice-pres 2000–; fiction reviewer: Daily Telegraph 1975–88, Evening Standard 1988–92; chm Henry Sotheran 1988–; pres Sch Bookshop Assoc; chm: Soc of Bookmen (pres 1998–), Wingate Scholarships 1989–2003, Poetry Book Soc 1996–2000, Nat Life Story Collection (Nat Sound Archive) 1997–2003; administrator Booker Prize 1970–2006, tstee Booker Prize Fndn 2006–; Liveryman Worshipful Co of Stationers & Newspaper Makers; Hon DLitt Oxford Brookes Univ; fell Int Inst of Arts and Letters, FRSA, Hon FRSL 2002, Hon FRS 2003; *Books* novels: The Plaster Fabric, A Season with Mammon, A Sort of Peace, The Youngest Director, The Flint Inheritance, Indecent Assault, The Liberation of Rupert Bannister, Tar and Cement; music books: A Short Guide to Long Play, A Further Guide to Long Play, LP Collecting, Record Choice; others: Victorian Surrey, The Royal Pavilion, Why Conform?, Prize Writing; *Recreations* picture collecting, travel; *Clubs* Athenaeum, Savile, Groucho; *Style—* Martyn Goff, Esq, CBE; ✉ 95 Sisters Avenue, London SW11 5SW (tel 020 7228 8164)

GOFF OF CHIEVELEY, Baron (Life Peer UK 1986), of Chieveley in the Royal County of Berkshire; Sir Robert Lionel Archibald Goff; kt (1975), PC (1982); s of Lt-Col Lionel Trevor Goff, RA (d 1953), of Monk Sherborne, Hants; *b* 12 November 1926; *Educ* Eton, New Coll Oxford (MA, DCL); *m* 1953, Sarah, er da of Capt Gerald Roger Cousins, DSC, RN, of Child Okeford, Dorset; 2 da (Hon Katharine Isobel b 1959, Hon Juliet Mary Constance b 1961), 1 s (Hon Robert Thomas Alexander b 1966), and 1 s decd; *Career* served Scots Guards 1945–48; fell and tutor Lincoln Coll Oxford 1951–55; called to the Bar Inner Temple 1951 (bencher 1975); QC 1967, recorder of the Crown Court 1974–75, judge of the High Court of Justice (Queen's Bench Div) 1975–82, judge i/c Commercial List and chm Commercial Court Ctee 1979–81, Lord Justice of Appeal 1982–85, Lord of Appeal in Ordinary 1986–96, Senior Lord of Appeal in Ordinary 1996–98; hon prof of legal ethics Univ of Birmingham 1980–81; Maccabaean lectr 1983, Lionel Cohen lectr (Jerusalem) 1987, Cassell lectr (Stockholm) 1993; chm: Cncl Legal Educn 1976–82, Court Univ of London 1986–91, Br Inst of Int and Comparative Law 1986–2001 (pres 2001–), Advsy Cncl Oxford Inst of European and Comparative Law 1990–2001; pres: Chartered Inst of Arbitrators 1986–91, The Bentham Club 1986, The Holdsworth Club 1986–87; High Steward Univ of Oxford 1990–2001; Hon DLitt: City Univ, Univ of Reading; Hon LLD: Univ of Buckingham, Univ of London, Univ of Bristol; hon fell: Lincoln Coll Oxford 1983, New Coll Oxford 1986, Wolfson Coll Oxford 2001; FBA 1987; *Books* The Law of Restitution (with Prof Gareth Jones, 1966); *Style—* The Rt Hon Lord Goff of Chieveley, PC, FBA; ✉ House of Lords, London SW1A 0PW

GOFFEY, Chris Robert; s of late Sqn Ldr Peter Scott Goffey, of Worcester, and late Margaret Sydney, *née* Goffey (cousin); *b* 17 October 1945; *m* 1968 Linda Mary, *née* Nolan; 2 s (Nicholas Scott b 1971, Daniel Robert b 1974); *Career* reporter 1965–72: Ruislip Northwood Post, Bucks Advertiser, Evening Mail Slough; news ed The Autocar 1972–78, ed Motor Trader 1978–80; TV since 1980 incl: reporter and ed Wheels (Thames), presenter and co-prodr The Motor Show (Channel Four), presenter and prodr Wheeltracks (Channel Four), presenter Top Gear (BBC 2), presenter Motorweek (Granada Sky); memb: NUJ, Guild of Motoring Writers, British Actors' Equity; *Books* How to Pass the L Test, How to Buy a Good Used Car, How to Pass the Motorcycle L Test, Lucas Book of Roadside Repairs, Make the L Test Easy; *Recreations* classic cars, horse riding; *Clubs* MG Car, Citroen Owners', Traction Owners'; *Style—* Chris Goffey, Esq; ✉ Wheeltrack TV Productions, Field House, Forest Hill, Oxfordshire OX33 1EF (tel 01865 873078, fax 01865 873593, e-mail goffey@community.co.uk)

GOFFIN, Magdalen; da of Edward Ingram Watkin, author (d 1981), and Helena, *née* Shepheard (d 1972); *b* 23 July 1925, Sheringham, Norfolk; *Educ* Convent of the Sacred Heart Roehampton, St Anne's Coll Oxford (MA); *m* 27 Aug 1949, Richard Herbert Lindsay Goffin, s of Raymond Goffin; 2 da (Teresa Mary b 1955, Richenda Anne Lindsay b 1958); *Career* writer; FRSL 1980; *Publications* Objections to Roman Catholicism (contrib chapter Superstition and Credulity, 1965), The Future of Catholic Christianity (contrib chapter The Broken Pitcher, 1966), Maria Pasqua (1979), The Diaries of Absalom Watkin: A Manchester Man 1787–1861 (1993), The Watkin Path - An Approach to Belief: The Life of E I Watkin (2006); also author of reviews and articles for the New York Review of Books 1966–69; *Style—* Mrs Magdalen Goffin, FRSL

GOGGINS, Paul Gerard; MP; s of John Goggins, and Rita Goggins (d 1991); *b* 16 June 1953; *Educ* St Bede's Sch Manchester, Ushaw Coll Durham, Birmingham Poly, Manchester Poly; *m* 1977, Wyn, da of Tom Bartley (d 1991); 2 s (Matthew b 1980, Dominic b 1985), 1 da (Theresa b 1982); *Career* residential child care offr Liverpool Catholic Social Servs 1974–76, offr i/c residential children's home Wigan MBC 1976–84, project dir NCH Action for Children in Salford 1984–89, nat dir Church Action on Poverty 1989–97; MP (Lab) Wythenshawe and Sale E 1997–; PPS to Rt Hon John Denham MP, *qv*, 1998–2000, PPS to Rt Hon David Blunkett MP, *qv*, 2000–03, Parly under sec of state Home Office 2003–06, Parly under-sec of state NI Office 2006–; memb Social Security Select Ctee 1997–98; fndr chm UK Coalition Against Poverty; cnclr Salford City Cncl 1990–98; *Recreations* football (Manchester City FC), walking and music; *Style—* Paul Goggins, Esq, MP; ✉ House of Commons, London SW1A 0AA (tel 020 7219 3000); tel 0161 499 7900

GOH, Dr Beng Tin; *b* 14 May 1953; *Educ* Univ of Singapore (MB BS), Univ of London (Dip Dermatology), Soc of Apothecaries (Dip Venereology); *m* 17 Dec 1978, Dr Tiak Nyar Sim; 2 da (Po-Siann b 18 May 1983, Po-Laine b 20 Jan 1985); *Career* registrar in genitourinary med King's Coll Hosp London 1980–81, sr registrar in genitourinary med Royal London Hosp and Moorfields Eye Hosp London 1981–85, conslt genitourinary physician Barts and The London NHS Tst and Moorfields Eye Hosp London 1985–; author of papers on syphilis incl guidelines, oculo-genital infections, chlamydia and sexual health in ethnic groups; examiner Soc of Apothecaries' Dip in Genitourinary Med; hon treas: Chinese Nat Healthy Living Centre, Assoc for Genitourinary Med, E London Chinese Community Centre; FRCP, FRCPI; *Recreations* travelling, photography; *Style—* Dr Beng Tin Goh; ✉ Ambrose King Centre, The Royal London Hospital, Whitechapel, London E1 1BB (tel 020 7377 7310, fax 020 7377 7648, e-mail beng.goh@bartsandthelondon.nhs.uk); Moorfields Eye Hospital, City Road, London EC1V 2PD

GOLD, Antony; s of Ellis Neville Gold, of Liverpool, and Sonya, *née* Greene; *b* 26 August 1958; *Educ* Birkenhead Sch, Univ of Manchester (LLB), Chester Law Coll; *m* 3 Oct 1983, Sally Jane, da of late Eddie Perkin; 2 da (Clara Wendy b 21 June 1989, Martha Amanda b 27 May 1998), 1 s (Alastair b 5 March 1992); *Career* asst slr Hammelburger Marks Manchester 1983–84 (articled clerk 1980–83); Eversheds: asst slr/assoc Alexander Tatham Manchester (now part of Eversheds) 1984–88, ptnr 1988–, UK head of litigation 1993–98, head of litigation Eversheds Manchester 1995–2001, head of intellectual property Eversheds Leeds/Manchester 2001–03, head Retail Sector Gp 2005–, head of intellectual property Eversheds 2007–; acted for investors in Barlow Clowes case 1988–89, for local authorities in BCCI case 1991–92 and numerous other cases involving financial collapse, professional negligence and intellectual property; memb: Law Soc 1983, Int Arbitration Club, Int Trademark Assoc 2000; *Recreations* reading, mountaineering; *Style—* Antony Gold, Esq; ✉ Eversheds House, 70 Great Bridgewater Street, Manchester M1 5ES (tel 0161 831 8000, fax 0161 832 5337, e-mail antonygold@eversheds.com)

GOLD, David Laurence; s of Michael Gold (d 1980), and Betty, *née* Levitt; *b* 1 March 1951; *Educ* Westcliff HS, LSE (LLB); *m* 27 Aug 1978, Sharon; 1 da (Amanda b 30 March 1981), 2 s (Alexander b 23 Jan 1983, Edward b 5 Oct 1985); *Career* admitted slr 1975; Herbert Smith: ptnr 1983–, head of litigation 2003–, sr ptnr 2005–; pres Southend & Westcliff Hebrew Congregation 1997–2006; memb Ctee Br Israel Law Assoc 1997–98, memb Ctee Br Overseas Trade Gp for Israel 1998–2000; Freeman City of London Slrs' Co; memb Law Soc; *Recreations* theatre, cinema, bridge, travel, family; *Style—* David Gold, Esq; ✉ Herbert Smith, Exchange House, Primrose Street, London EC2A 2HS (tel 020 7374 8000, fax 020 7374 0888, e-mail david.gold@herbertsmith.com)

GOLD, Henry Patrick; s of Patrick Hugh Gold (d 1976), of Holland Park, London, and Agnes Bisset, *née* Crowe (d 1991); ggn of Sir Walter Gilbey, 1 Bt; *b* 11 August 1936; *Educ* Eton; *m* 1, 1966 (m dis 1998), Catherine Jane, da of Gp Capt A J Barwood, OBE; 1 s (Edward Henry b 15 June 1969), 1 da (Polly Augusta b 3 July 1972); m 2, 1998, Susan Ann Galgey, da of M W Hyde (d 1986); *Career* chartered accountant; Nat Serv Lt Royal Berks Regt 1955–57; Turquand Youngs & Co Chartered Accountants (later Turquands Barton Mayhew): articled 1957–62, mangr 1965–67, ptnr 1967–78; Royal Dutch Shell Group: head of accounting res 1978–81, dir of fin and admin Turkey 1981–84, regnl fin advsr Western Hemisphere and Africa and area co-ordinator certain S American countries 1984–88, dep gp controller 1988–91; ICAEW: memb Cncl 1980–81, chm Parly and Law Ctee 1980–81, tech dir 1991–94; chm London Soc of Chartered Accountants 1979–80, chm of tstees Int Centre for Res in Accountancy Lancaster Univ 1985–95; Accounting Standards Bd: memb Urgent Issues Task Force 1991–94, project conslt 1994–98; memb: Financial Instruments Task Force Financial Accounting Standards Bd (USA) 1989–94, Working Gp DTI Co Law Review 1999–2001; tech advsr to UK Bd membs Int Accounting Standards Ctee 1991–94, dir and hon treas Colchester and NE Essex Bldg Preservation Tst 1995–2006, hon treas Suffolk Preservation Soc and Suffolk Building Preservation Tst 1998–2006; Freeman City of London 1981, memb Ct of Assts Worshipful Co of Chartered Accountants 1995– (Liveryman 1981, Master 2007–08); FCA 1972 (ACA 1962), FRSA; *Books* British Accounting Standards - The First Ten Years (contrib, 1981); *Recreations* music (piano, cello and singing), skiing, walking, painting, ornithology, fishing; *Clubs* Oriental, MCC, Ski Club of GB (memb Cncl 1993–96); *Style—* Henry P Gold, Esq; ✉ Carlisle House, Bildeston, Suffolk IP7 7EP (tel and fax 01449 744044)

GOLD, Jacqueline; da of David Gold, and Beryl Hunt; *b* 16 July 1960; *Educ* Baston Old Sch; *m* 20 Aug 1980 (m dis 1990), Tony D'Silva; *Career* Ann Summers: joined as wages clerk 1979, launched party plan 1981, dir 1987, md and chief exec 1993–; patron Breast Cancer Campaign; Working Women Mean Business Award 1993, Gucci Business Age 40 Under 40 Award 1995, shortlisted London Entrepreneur of the Year 2001, shortlisted Nat Business Awards Entrepreneur of the Year 2003, Business Communicator of the Year 2004; *Books* Good Vibrations (autobiography, 1995); *Recreations* football, yoga; *Style—* Ms Jacqueline Gold; ✉ Ann Summers, God Group House, Godstone Road, Whyteleafe, Surrey CR3 0GG

GOLD, Murray Jonathan; s of Leonard Gold, and Suzanne Gold; *b* 1969; *Educ* Portsmouth GS, CCC Cambridge; *Career* writer and composer; memb: Writer's Guild, PRS, Mechanical Copywright Protection Soc; *Theatre* as composer incl: Hove (RNT) 1993, Transit Hotel (Battersea Arts Centre) 1995, Dr Faustus (Young Vic) 2002; as writer incl: Glue Wedding (Battersea Arts Centre), Resolution (Battersea Arts Centre), Exodus (Battersea Arts Centre), Candide (adaptation, Gate Theatre and RNT Studio) 1997, 50 Revolutions (Whitehall Theatre) 1999; *Television* composer: Vanity Fair (BBC) 1998 (Best Original Score RTS 1999, nomination Best Theme TRIC Awards 1999), Queer as Folk (Channel 4) 1999 and 2000 (nomination Best Original Score RTS 1999, nomination Best Original Music for TV BAFTA Awards 1999 and 2000), Love in the 21st Century (Channel 4) 1999, Clocking Off (Channel 4) 2000, Randall & Hopkirk (Deceased) (BBC) 2000; sometime writer Family Affairs (Channel 5); *Radio* writer Electricity (BBC Radio 3) 2000 (Best New Radio Play Soc of Authors 2001, adapted for stage Bush Theatre 2002); *Films* composer: Mojo 1997, Beautiful Creatures 2000, Wild About Harry 2000, Miranda 2002; *Recreations* music, theatre, film, pubs, cricket, football, history; *Clubs* Century; *Style—* Murray Gold, Esq; ✉ c/o Cathy King, ICM, Oxford House, 76 Oxford Street, London W1D 1BS

GOLD, Nicholas Roger; s of Rev Guy Alastair Whitmore Gold, TD, of Woodbridge, Suffolk, and Elizabeth Weldon Gold, JP, *née* Maytham; *b* 11 December 1951; *Educ* Felsted, Univ of Kent (BA), Coll of Law; *m* 23 April 1983 (m dis 2005), Laura, da of Adam Arnold-Brown, and Jane Arnold-Brown, of Salcombe, Devon; 2 da (Siena Jane b 9 Jan

1985, Elizabeth Harriet b 17 Oct 1991), 1 s (James Mortimer Fearon b 8 Oct 1987); *Career* chartered accountant Touche Ross & Co 1973–76, slr Freshfields 1977–86, md ING (formerly Baring Bros & Co Ltd) 1986–; prop The Winking Prawn (beach cafe) 1994–; memb: Cncl RADA 2003–, Bd Prince's Fndn for Integrated Health 2003–; FCA 1982 (ACA 1977); *Recreations* sailing, drawing, the arts, country pursuits, travel; *Clubs* Hurlingham, Oxford Sailing; *Style*— Nicholas Gold, Esq; ✉ 14 Northumberland Place, London W2 5BS (tel 020 7229 4773); ING, 60 London Wall, London EC2M 5TQ (tel 020 7767 1000, fax 020 7767 7222)

GOLDACRE, Prof Michael John; s of Reginald Goldacre (d 1983), and Patricia Goldacre (d 1986); *b* 3 January 1944, Melbourne, Aust; *Educ* Bec Sch London, Magdalen Coll Oxford (BA), UCH London (BM BCh); *m* 1973, Susan Maria; 4 s (Ben b 1974, Joshua b 1981, Raphael b 1983, Alexander b 1985); *Career* Univ of Oxford: clinical lectr in social and community med 1974–, dir Unit of Health-Care Epidemiology 1986–, UK Med Careers Research Gp 1993–, prof of public health 2002–; fell Magdalen Coll Oxford 1985– (tutor for grads 1993–95, dean of degrees 1993–); scientific dir SE England Public Health Observatory 2000–; author of approximately 200 papers on epidemiology, public health and health servs research in med jls; FFPH; *Style*— Prof Michael Goldacre; ✉ Department of Public Health, University of Oxford, Old Road Campus, Old Road, Oxford OX3 7LF

GOLDBERG, David Gerard; QC; s of Arthur Goldberg (d 1982), of Plymouth, and Sylvia, *née* Stone; *b* 12 August 1947; *Educ* Plymouth Coll, LSE (LLB, LLM); *m* 22 Dec 1981 (m dis 2003), Alison Ninette, da of Jack V Lunzer, of London; 1 s (Arthur b 1986), 1 da (Selina b 1984); *Career* called to the Bar Lincoln's Inn 1971 (bencher 1997), in practice at Revenue Bar; case note ed British Tax Review 1975–87, author of numerous articles on taxation and company law, chm of the tstees Surgical Workshop for Anatomical Prosection 1994–; Philip Hardman Meml Lecture 1995; *Books* An Introduction to Company Law (jtly, 1987), The Law of Partnership Taxation (jtly, 1987); *Recreations* reading, letter writing, thinking; *Style*— David Goldberg, Esq, QC; ✉ Gray's Inn Chambers, Gray's Inn, London WC1R 5JA (tel 020 7242 2642, fax 020 7831 9017, e-mail dg@taxbar.com)

GOLDBERG, Rabbi Dr David J; OBE (2004); s of Percy Selvin Goldberg (d 1981), and Frimette, *née* Yudt (d 1980); *b* 25 February 1939; *Educ* Manchester Grammar, Lincoln Coll Oxford (MA), Trinity Coll Dublin, Leo Baeck Coll London; *m* 1969, Carole-Ann, da of Sydney Marks; 1 s (Rupert Alexander Ian b 1 Feb 1974), 1 da (Emily Catherine Toby b 18 Jan 1977); *Career* rabbi Wembley and Dist Liberal Synagogue 1971–74; The Liberal Jewish Synagogue: assoc rabbi 1975–86, sr rabbi 1986–2004, emeritus rabbi 2004–; Robert Waley-Cohen travelling scholarship 1978; chm ULPS Rabbinic Conf 1983–85 and 1995–97, vice-chm Cncl of Reform and Liberal Rabbis 1984 and 1993–95, co-chm London Soc of Jews and Christians 1989–2004 (co-pres 2004–); Interfaith Gold Medallion (for outstanding contribution to interfaith understanding) 1999, Premio Iglesias (for Italian edn of To the Promised Land) 1999; DD (hc) Univ of Manchester 2000; *Books* The Jewish People (1987, new edn 1989), To the Promised Land (1996), Progressive Judaism Today (ed, 1997), Liberal Judaism: The First 100 Years (ed, 2004), The Divided Self (2006); *Recreations* fell walking, travel, watching cricket, listening to music, reading; *Style*— Rabbi Dr David J Goldberg, OBE; ✉ The Liberal Jewish Synagogue, 28 St John's Wood Road, London NW8 7HA (tel 020 7286 5181, fax 020 7266 3591, e-mail djg@bartvillas.org.uk)

GOLDBERG, Jonathan Jacob; QC (1989); s of Rabbi Dr Percy Selvin Goldberg (decd), and Frimette, *née* Yudt (decd); *b* 13 November 1947; *Educ* Manchester Grammar, Trinity Hall Cambridge (MA, LLB); *m* 7 Nov 1980 (m dis 1991), Alexis Jane, da of Sir George Martin, CBE, *qv*; 1 da (Natasha Jane Frimette b 22 Dec 1982), 1 s (Saul Percy Laurence b 22 Sept 1985); *Career* called to the Bar Middle Temple 1971, practising SE Circuit, recorder of the Crown Court 1993–; memb NY State Bar 1985, Int Presidency of the Int Assoc of Jewish Lawyers and Jurists 1999–; memb SE and Northern Circuits; *Recreations* reading, films, music, wine; *Style*— Jonathan Goldberg, QC; ✉ 30 Ely Place, London EC1N 6TD (tel 020 7400 9600, fax 020 7400 9630)

GOLDBERG, Mel; *Educ* St John's Coll Cambridge; *Career* slr specialising in sports law; fndr Douglas Goldberg & Co, currently ptnr Statham Gill Davies; chm Br Assoc for Sport and Law, memb Sport Dispute Resolution Panel of Mediators; chm Amateur Swimming Assoc; memb: Sports Ctee Variety Club of GB, Ctee Anti-Slavery Int, Ctee Sport Against Addiction; *Books* The Final Score (co-author); *Style*— Mel Goldberg, Esq; ✉ Statham Gill Davies, 54 Welbeck Street, London W1G 9XS (tel 020 7317 3210, fax 020 7487 5925)

GOLDENBERG, Philip; s of Nathan Goldenberg, OBE (d 1995), and Edith, *née* Dee; *b* 26 April 1946; *Educ* St Paul's, Pembroke Coll Oxford (MA); *m* 1, 16 Aug 1969 (m dis 1975), Dinah Mary Pye; m 2, 12 Oct 1985, Lynda Anne, *née* Benjamin; 3 s (Jonathan b 1986, Benjamin b 1990, Joshua b 1994), 1 da (Philippa b 1988); *Career* admitted slr 1972, asst slr Linklaters & Paines 1972–82, ptnr SJ Berwin 1983–2004 (asst slr 1982–83); conslt Michael Conn Goldsobel 2004–; sec Oxford Univ Lib Club 1966, pres Watford Lib Assoc 1980–81, vice-chm Home Counties Regnl Lib Pty 1976–78 and 1980–81; Lib Pty: Cncl 1975–88, Nat Exec Ctee 1977–87, Candidates Ctee 1976–85, Assembly Ctee 1985–87; Lib Dems: memb Federal Conf Ctee 1988–92, Federal Policy Ctee 1990–92, pres Woking Lib Dems 1992–94, treas SE Region 1999–2001, chair SE Region 2001–04, Panel of potential nominees for interim peerages 1999–2004, memb Federal Appeals Panel 2000– (chair 2006–), memb English Lib Dems Exec 2001–06 (vice-chair 2004–06); Parly candidate: (Lib) Eton and Slough 1974 (twice) and 1979, (Lib/SDP Alliance) Woking 1983 and 1987, (Lib Dem) Dorset and E Devon (Euro) 1994, Woking (Lib Dem) 1997; memb Woking BC 1984–92 and 2003– (chm Highways Ctee 1988–90, dep ldr Exec 2006–07, chm Overview Security Ctee 2007–); former memb Exec Ctee Wider Share Ownership Cncl, memb Cncl Electoral Reform Soc 1978–82; CBI: memb London Regnl Cncl 1989–95, memb Nat Cncl 1992–2004, memb Fin and Gen Purposes Ctee 1994–2004; RSA: legal advsr Tomorrow's Company Inquiry 1995, tstee 2004–, treas 2005–; memb: Working Party DTI Company Law Reform Project 1998–99, Federal Tst Working Party on Corporate Social Responsibility 2001–02; jt author original Constitution of the Lib Democrats 1988; advsr on formation of Lab/Lib Dem Jt Cabinet Ctee 1997, advsr on procedural provisions of Scottish Coalition Agreement 1999; memb Cncl City in Europe 2001–04; jt ed New Outlook 1974–77, memb Editorial Advsy Bd Business Law Review 1994–2004; tstee Tuberous Sclerosis Assoc 2000–; govr: Slough Coll of Higher Educn 1980–86, Annie Lawson Sch Ravenswood Village 1997–; memb Law Soc; FRSA 1992, FSALS 1997; *Books* Fair Welfare (1968), Sharing Profits (with Sir David Steel, 1986), CCH's Company Law Guide (3 edn 1990, 4 edn 1996), SJ Berwin's Business Guide to Directors' Responsibilities (2001); *Recreations* family, friends; *Clubs* National Liberal; *Style*— Cncllr Philip Goldenberg; ✉ Toad Hall, White Rose Lane, Woking, Surrey GU22 7LB (tel 01483 765377, fax 01483 764970, e-mail goldenberg@cix.co.uk); 24 Queen Anne Street, London W1G 9AX (tel 020 7291 8807, fax 020 7323 0641, e-mail philipg@mcglex.co.uk)

GOLDHILL, Flora Taylor; CBE (2007); da of Thomas Kissock (d 1981), and Flora, *née* McKenzie; *b* 13 February 1953; *Educ* Morgan Acad Dundee, Univ of Edinburgh (MA); *m* 3 June 1978, Jonathan Paul Goldhill, s of Michael Goldhill; *Career* civil servant DHSS and Dept of Health 1976–90; chief exec Human Fertilisation and Embryology Authy 1991–96; with Dept of Health 1996– (currently dir workforce capacity, analysis and HR); vice-chair Canonbury Primary Sch 1996–2003; *Recreations* family and friends, hill walking, riding, gardens; *Style*— Mrs Flora Goldhill, CBE; ✉ Department of Health, Richmond House, 79 Whitehall, London SW1 2NS (tel 020 7210 5749, fax 020 7210 5941, e-mail flora.goldhill@dh.gsi.gov.uk)

GOLDHILL, Jack Alfred; s of John Goldhill (d 1978), of London, and Sophie, *née* Hamburg (d 1973); *b* 18 September 1920; *Educ* Christ's Coll Finchley, Coll of Estate Mgmnt, Inst of Chartered Auctioneers; *m* 1, 1943, Aurelia (Rela) Freed (d 1966); 3 s (Michael b 1949, David b 1952, Simon b 1956); m 2, 1967, Grete Kohnstam; *Career* served WWII Royal Signals in France, Germany and Gold Coast 1939–46; commercial property advsr; fndr ptnr Leighton Goldhill Chartered Surveyors 1948–85; fndr and admin Jack Goldhill Charitable Tst 1974–; exhibitor of paintings Royal Acad Summer Exhibition 1983, 1988, 1989, 1991–98 and 2001–06; estab: annual bursaries for Royal Acad Sch students without grants 1981–96, The Jack Goldhill Award for Sculpture 1987–, Goldhill Prize for Drawing at the Prince's Fndn; involved (with Jewish Care) in the founding and building of the Rela Goldhill Lodge home and residential centre for young physically handicapped; fell Inst of Chartered Auctioneers 1951, FRICS 1970; *Recreations* painting, golf, keeping up with twenty-two grandchildren and great-grandchildren; *Style*— Jack Goldhill, Esq

GOLDIE, Annabel MacNicoll; DL (Renfrewshire), MSP; da of Alexander Macintosh Goldie, and Margaret MacNicoll Goldie; *Educ* Greenock Acad, Univ of Strathclyde (LLB); *Career* ptnr Donaldson Alexander Russell & Haddow Glasgow 1978–2006; MSP (Cons) West of Scotland 1999–, ldr Scottish Conservatives 2005–; dir Prince's Scottish Youth Business Tst, memb Advsy Bd West of Scotland Salvation Army; elder Church of Scotland; *Recreations* gardening, cycling, bird watching, classical music; *Style*— Annabel Goldie, DL, MSP; ✉ The Scottish Parliament, Edinburgh EH99 1SP (tel 0131 348 5662, fax 0131 348 5937, e-mail annabel.goldie.msp@scottish.parliament.uk)

GOLDIE, Ian William; *Educ* Trinity Coll Glenalmond, Jesus Coll Cambridge (MA); *m* 14 Feb 1976, Susan Kay, *née* Moore; 2 s (Stuart Douglas b 7 May 1984, Daniel Scott b 22 Oct 1987) 1 da (Emily Louise b 29 Aug 1989); *Career* ptnr Slaughter and May 1983–2005; *Recreations* golf, rugby, skiing; *Clubs* Caledonian, Royal St George's Golf, Woking Golf; *Style*— Ian Goldie, Esq; ✉ e-mail ian@thegoldies.co.uk

GOLDIE, Dr Lawrence; s of Bernard Goldie (d 1946), of Manchester, and Dora, *née* Sapper; *b* 8 September 1923; *Educ* Manchester Central GS, Univ of Manchester, Univ of Manchester Med Sch (MB ChB, MD); *m* 1, 12 July 1949, Lilian Fay (d 1991), da of Hyman Jaffa; 1 da (Helena Elspeth b 28 Sept 1954), 1 s (Boyd Stephen b 5 May 1957); m 2, Silvia Susana, da of Roberto and Sophia Oclander, of Buenos Aires, Argentina; 1 step s (Lorenzo), 1 step da (Natasha); *Career* serv WWII pilot RAF 1942–46; house offr in gen surgery Park Hosp Manchester 1953, house offr in gen surgery and med Withington Hosp Manchester 1954; sr house offr in gen psychiatry and at Geriatric Psychiatry Unit Bethlehem Royal Hosp 1955; registrar: Psychotherapy Unit (gp and individual) The Maudsley Hosp 1956, The Observation Ward (acute admissions) St Francis Hosp Dulwich London 1957, Neurosurgical Unit Guy's and Maudsley Hosps 1957, Paediatric Psychiatry Maudsley Hosp 1957; res asst in neurophysiology Dept of Clinical Neurophysiology Inst of Psychiatry 1957–61, lectr Inst of Child Health Postgrad Med Sch Hammersmith 1961–67, conslt psychiatrist Queen Mary's Hosp Carshalton 1961–74; conslt psychiatrist and conslt med psychotherapist: Inst of Laryngology and Otology Royal Nat ENT Hosp London 1966–89, The Royal Marsden Hosp 1971–89; sr lectr Inst of Obstetrics and Gynaecology The Hammersmith Hosp London 1974–89; course dir and symposium organiser Psychosexual Problems Course Inst of Obstetrics and Gynaecology 1988–95; in private practice Harley Street until 2005; formerly: hon conslt Psychiatrist Tavistock and Portman NHS Tst, dir Caring for the Bereaved and the Dying MSc course Univ of Middx/Tavistock Inst of Human Rels; memb Cncl Psychologie et Cancer Marseille France; hon memb Int Psycho-Oncology Soc; former memb: Cncl CRUSE (orgn for care of widows and widowers) 1977–91, Euro Working Gp for Psychomatic Cancer Res 1978–; med memb Steering Gp Kent Voluntary Serv Cncls' Project on Social Care of the Gravely Ill at Home 1980–81, visiting conslt on psychiatric problems St Joseph's Hospice 1982, former med advsr Cancer Link, memb Editorial Bd Medical Tribune Gp Br Jl of Sexual Med until 1989; considerable experience as teacher and lectr, author of numerous papers in learned jls; Freeman City of London 1987, Liveryman Worshipful Soc of Apothecaries 1987, memb Guild of Freemen of City of London 1988; grad memb Br Psychological Soc 1959, FRSM 1959, FRCPsych 1975, memb Acad of Experts 1993, fell Assoc of Lawyers and Legal Advsrs 1997; *Publications* Psychotherapy and the Treatment of Cancer Patients: Bearing Cancer in Mind (2005); *Recreations* serious theatre, music and art; *Clubs* RAC; *Style*— Dr Lawrence Goldie; ✉ e-mail lawrenceg@blueyonder.co.uk

GOLDING, Dr Anthony Mark Barrington; s of Dr Mark Golding (d 1954), of London, and Marian Rosalie, *née* Benjamin (d 1965); *b* 21 August 1928; *Educ* Marlborough, Univ of Cambridge (MA, MB BChir), Middx Hosp Med Sch; *m* 29 Aug 1962, (Olwen) Valery, da of Reginald Francis Orlando Bridgeman, CMG, MVO (d 1968), of Pinner, Middx; 3 da (Rosemary b 1963, Catherine b 1967, Charlotte b 1970), 1 s (Richard b 1965); *Career* RAMC 1954–56; med offr DHSS 1968–72, princ asst sr med offr SE Met RHB 1972–74, dist community physician King's Health Dist (teaching) 1974–82, dist med offr Camberwell HA 1982–86, sr conslt in community med 1986–88, hon conslt 1988–; hon sr lectr: King's Coll Hosp Med Sch, King's Coll Sch of Med & Dentistry 1977–; conslt in public health med Redbridge and Waltham Forest HA 1989–96; ed Health and Hygiene 1988–97; memb: Editorial Bd Public Health 1981–, Cncl RIPHH 1987–2005 (chm 1997–99, vice-pres 1999–), Cncl RSM 1990–92, 1993–94 and 1995–98, Cncl Section of Epidemiology and Public Health RSM 1987–2005 (pres 1990–92, vice-pres 1994–2005); tstee Sir John Golding Fund 1987–, chm of govrs Portman Early Childhood Centre 2004–06 (govr 2007–); DO 1956, MFCM 1973, FFCM 1979, FRIPHH 1983 (hon 1999), MRCOphth 1989, FFPHM 1989, FFPH 2003; *Publications* contrib to various pubns incl Public Health, Health and Hygiene, The Lancet and BMJ; *Recreations* walking; *Style*— Dr Anthony Golding; ✉ 12 Clifton Hill, London NW8 0QG (tel and fax 020 7624 0504, e-mail amb.golding@btinternet.com); Keepers, Byworth, Petworth, West Sussex

GOLDING, Dr (Harold) John; CBE (1992); s of Harold Samuel Golding (d 1990), and Dorothy Hamer (d 1991); *b* 10 September 1929; *Educ* Univ of Toronto (BA), Univ of London (MA, PhD); *Career* painter; lectr then reader in history of art Courtauld Inst Univ of London 1959–81, sr tutor Painting Sch RCA 1981–86; temp appts: Power lectr Aust 1974, Slade prof of fine art Univ of Cambridge 1978–79; FBA 1994; *One Man Exhibitions* Nishimura Gallery Tokyo 1982 and 1984, Coventry Gallery Sydney 1984, Juda Rowan Gallery London 1985, Mayor Rowan Gallery London 1988, Yale Center for British Art 1989, Mayor Gallery London 1994; *Group Exhibitions* MOMA Oxford 1971, British Painting '74 (Hayward Gallery) 1974, John Moores Exhibition (Liverpool) 1976 and 1978, British Painting 1952–77 (Royal Acad) 1977; *Works in Public Collections* incl: Tate Gallery, V&A, MOMA NY, Nat Gallery of Aust, Fitzwilliam Museum Cambridge; *Exhibitions Selected and Organised* Léger and Purist Paris (Tate Gallery) 1970, Summer Show 2 (Serpentine Gallery) 1976, Picasso's Picassos (Hayward Gallery London) 1984, Braque Still Life and Interiors (Walker Gallery Liverpool and City Art Gallery Bristol) 1990, Picasso, Sculptor-Painter (Tate Gallery) 1994, Matisse Picasso (Tate Modern) 2002; *Publications* incl: Cubism 1907–1914 (1959, new edn 1988), Visions of the Modern (1994), Paths to the Absolute (2000); *Style*— Dr John Golding, CBE, FBA; ✉ 24 Ashchurch Park Villas, London W12 9SP (tel and fax 020 8749 5221)

GOLDING, Baroness (Life Peer UK 2001), of Newcastle-under-Lyme in the County of Staffordshire; Llinos (Llin) Golding; da of Rt Hon Ness Edwards (d 1968; MP for Caerphilly 1939–68), and Elina Victoria (d 1988); *b* 21 March 1933; *Educ* Caerphilly Girls'

G

GS, Cardiff Royal Infirmary Sch of Radiography; *m* 1, June 1957 (m dis 1971), John Roland Lewis; 1 s (Hon Stephen), 2 da (Hon Caroline (Hon Mrs Hopwood), Hon Janet); *m* 2, 8 Aug 1980, John Golding (d 1999); *Career sec* Newcastle Dist Trades Cncl 1976–86, memb N Staffs DHA 1983–86; MP (Lab) Newcastle-under-Lyme 1986–2001 (by-election), W Midlands whip 1987–92; oppn frontbench spokesperson on: Social Security 1992–93, Children and the Family 1993–95, Food Agriculture and Rural Affrs 1995–97; memb Select Ctee on Culture, Media and Sport 1997–2001; chm All-Pty Parly Gp on Children, treas All-Pty Parly Gp on Racing and Bloodstock Industries; cmmr Cwlth War Graves 1993–2002; match sec Lords and Commons Fly Fishing Club, memb BBC Advsy Cncl 1989–92; chm Fishing Ctee Countryside Alliance 2005; tstee NSPCC; memb: NUPE, Soc of Radiographers; *Style—* The Rt Hon the Baroness Golding

GOLDING, Dr Richard James Arthur; s of late Arthur Bertram Golding, and Bridget Elizabeth, *née* Mahoney; *b* 13 April 1952; *Educ* Queen Elizabeth's Sch for Boys Barnet, Wadham Coll Oxford (MA, DPhil); *Career* stockbroker and investment banker 1976–; Simon and Coates 1976–81, ptnr Grieveson Grant and Co 1984–86 (joined 1981), dir Kleinwort Benson Ltd 1986–92, commercial dir Principal Fin Nomura International plc 1992–99, dir Annington Homes plc 1996–99, dir Thorn plc 1998–99, md Anthem Corporate Finance Ltd 2002–; hon chair Physics in Finance Gp Inst of Physics 2000–; FInstP, FSI, MIMA; *Clubs* Oxford and Cambridge; *Style—* Dr Richard Golding

GOLDING, Ven Simon Jefferies; CBE (2002); *b* 30 March 1946; *Educ* Bishop's Sch Poona India, HMS Conway Merchant Navy Cadet Sch, Brasted Place Coll, Lincoln Theol Coll; *m* 1968, Anne, *née* Reynolds; 1 s (Philip), 1 da (Sarah); *Career* ordained deacon 1974, priest 1975; curate St Cuthbert Wilton Cleveland 1974–77; Royal Navy: chaplain 1977–2002, various appts HMS Raleigh, HMS Invincible, BRNC Dartmouth, Hydrographic Flotilla, Clyde Submarine Base, HMS Drake (HM Naval Base Devonport) until 1997, Chaplain of the Fleet and Archdeacon for the RN 1997–2002, now emeritus; DG Naval Chaplaincy Service 2000–02; QHC 1997–2002; ex-officio memb Gen Synod C of E, former sec RN Archdeaconry Synod and the Forces Synodical Cncl; recipient C-in-C's Commendation, permission to officiate in the Diocese of Ripon and Leeds; *Recreations* naval and military history, gardening, maritime and aviation industry, railways and cricket; *Style—* The Ven Simon Golding, CBE; ✉ Arlanza, Hornby Road, Appleton Wiske, Northallerton DL6 2AF (tel 01609 881185)

GOLDINGAY, Rev Prof John Edgar; s of Edgar Charles Goldingay (d 1974), and Ada Irene, *née* Horton (d 2001); *b* 20 June 1942; *Educ* King Edward's Sch Birmingham, Keble Coll Oxford (BA), Univ of Nottingham (PhD), Lambeth (DD); *m* 28 Aug 1967, Ann Elizabeth, da of Arthur Wilson (d 1971); 2 s (Steven b 1968, Mark b 1971); *Career* ordained: deacon 1966, priest 1967; asst curate Christ Church Finchley 1966–69, princ St John's Coll Nottingham 1988–97 (lectr 1970–88), currently prof Fuller Theol Seminary Pasadena; *Books* Approaches to Old Testament Interpretation (1981), Theological Diversity and the Authority of the Old Testament (1987), Daniel (1989), Models for Scripture (1994), Models for the Interpretation of Scripture (1995), After Eating the Apricot (1996), To the Usual Suspects (1998), Men Behaving Badly (2000), Isaiah (2001), Walk On (2002), Old Testament Theology Vol 1 (2003), The Message of Isaiah 40–55 (2005), Old Testament Theology Vol 2 (2006), Psalms 1–41 (2006), Isaiah 40–55 (2006); *Recreations* The Old Testament, jazz, blues, rock music; *Style—* The Rev Prof John Goldingay; ✉ 111 South Orange Grove Boulevard, Apt 108, Pasadena, CA 91105, USA (tel 626 405 0626, fax 626 584 5251, e-mail johngold@fuller.edu)

GOLDMAN, Antony John (Tony); CB (1995); s of Sir Samuel Goldman, KCB, of Wonersh, Surrey, and step s of Patricia Hodges (d 1990); *b* 28 February 1940; *Educ* Marlborough, Peterhouse Cambridge (BA, Dip Computing); *m* 1964, Anne Rosemary, *née* Lane; 3 s (Stephen b 1965, James b 1968, Timothy b 1975); *Career* International Computers Ltd 1961–73; civil service: DOE 1973–, private sec to Sec of State for Tport 1976–78, asst sec 1977, seconded to HM Treasy 1981–83, under sec 1984, DG Civil Aviation 1996–99; special advsr to House of Lords Select Ctee on Europe 2001; pres Cncl of Eurocontrol 1998–99, vice-pres European Civil Aviation Conf 1997–99; aviation conslt 1999–; tstee Watts Gall 2004; hon CRAeS 1997; *Recreations* music, cosmology, poetry, wine; *Style—* A J Goldman, Esq, CB; ✉ Weston House, Bowcott Hill, Arford, Hampshire GU35 8DF

GOLDMAN, Ian John; s of Morris Lewis Goldman, of Liverpool, and Tina, *née* Kleinman (d 1992); *b* 28 January 1948; *Educ* Liverpool Coll, LSE (LLB); *m* 9 Sept 1970, Diane Elizabeth, JP, da of William Shipton (d 1984), of London; 3 da (Vikki b 1972, Katie b 1975, Charlotte b 1979); *Career* admitted slr 1971, princ Louis Godlove & Co 1971; dir: Commercial & Financial Investments Ltd 1972–, Goldman Investments Ltd 1972–90; sr ptnr: Godlove Pearlman 1991–96, Godloves 1996–; non-exec dir (vice-chm) Leeds Teaching Hosps NHS Tst 1998–2005; memb: Leeds Family Practitioner Ctee 1985–90, Leeds East HA 1988–90, Leeds Law Soc Ctee 1988–2002 (pres 1998–99), Nat Exec Ctee Jewish Nat Fund of GB 1981–87 (chm Leeds Dist 1981–84); vice-chm Leeds Family Health Services Authy 1990–96, chm Leeds Med Service Ctee 1985–96; hon slr Leeds Jewish Welfare Bd 1995–2005, hon life vice-pres Leeds Jewish Rep Cncl 2004– (pres 2001–04); tstee Overseas Partnering and Trg Initiative 2003–; memb Law Soc 1971; FInstD 1990; *Style—* Ian Goldman, Esq; ✉ Godloves, 8–16 Dock Street, Bridge End, Leeds LS10 1LX (tel 0113 225 8811, fax 0113 225 8844, e-mail ijgoldman@godloves.co.uk)

GOLDMAN, Prof John Michael; s of Dr Carl Heinz Goldman (d 1992), and Bertha Goldman; *b* 30 November 1938; *Educ* Westminster, Magdalen Coll Oxford (DM); *Career* prof of leukaemia biology and chm Dept of Haematology Imperial Coll Faculty of Med at Hammersmith Hosp (Royal Postgrad Med Sch until merger 1997) 1994–2004, conslt physician and haematologist Hammersmith Hosp; Fogarty Scholar Hematology Branch Nat Heart Lung and Blood Inst Nat Insts of Health Bethesda MD 2004–; med dir Anthony Nolan Bone Marrow Tst, dir Leukaemia Res Fund Centre for Adult Leukaemia Hammersmith Hosp; former pres: Euro Haematology Assoc, Int Soc for Experimental Hematology, Euro Bone Marrow Transplant Gp; sec World Marrow Donor Assoc; ed Bone Marrow Transplantation; FRCP, FRCPath, FMedSci; *Books* Leukemia (1983); *Recreations* skiing, riding; *Style—* Prof John Goldman; ✉ Imperial College London at Hammersmith Hospital, Du Cane Road, London W12 0NN

GOLDREIN, Iain Saville; QC (1997); s of Neville Clive Goldrein, CBE, of Crosby, Liverpool, and Sonia Hannah Jane, *née* Sumner; *b* 10 August 1952; *Educ* Merchant Taylors', Hebrew Univ Jerusalem, Pembroke Coll Cambridge (Squire scholar, exhibitioner, Ziegler Prize); *m* 18 May 1980, Margaret Ruth de Haas, QC, qv, da of Josef de Haas, of Finchley, London; 1 s (Alastair Phillip b 1 Oct 1982), 1 da (Alexandra Ann b 22 Feb 1985); *Career* called to the Bar Inner Temple 1975 (Duke of Edinburgh scholar); in practice London and Northern Circuit, dep head Number 7 Harrington Street Chambers, recorder of the Crown Court; memb Mental Health Review Tbnl 1999–2003; visiting prof Sir Jack Jacob chair in litigation Nottingham Trent Univ; memb Middle Temple; ed-in-chief Genetics Law Monitor 2000–02, consltg ed Practical Civil Courts Precedents; Companion Acad of Experts (BAE Register of Mediators); FSALS, FRSA; *Books* Personal Injury Litigation, Practice and Precedents (with Margaret de Haas, QC, 1985), Ship Sale and Purchase, Law and Technique (1985, ed-in-chief 2 edn, 1993, 4 edn 2003 with Clifford Chance LLB), Commercial Litigation, Pre-Emptive Remedies (with His Hon K H P Wilkinson, 1987 and 1991, with His Hon Judge Kershaw, QC, 1996, and The Rt Hon Lord Justice Jacob, 2003, int edition 2006), Butterworths' Personal Injury Litigation Service (with Margaret de Haas, QC), Pleadings: Principles and Practice (with Sir Jack Jacob, 1990), Bullen and Leake and Jacob's Precedents of Pleadings (gen ed 13 edn with Sir Jack Jacob, 1990), Structured Settlements (ed in chief with Margaret de Haas, QC, 1993 and 1997), Medical

Negligence: Cost Effective Case Management (with Margaret de Haas, QC, 1997), Insurance Disputes (co-ed, 1999, 2 edn 2003), Civil Court Practice (co-ed, annually 1999–), Personal Injury Major Claims Handling: Cost Effective Case Management (co-ed with Margaret de Haas, QC and John Frenkel, 2001); *Recreations* classical Hebrew, classical music, history, anything aeronautical, classical motor vehicles; *Clubs* Athenaeum (Liverpool); *Style—* Iain Goldrein, Esq, QC; ✉ 7 Bell Yard, London WC2A 2JR (tel 020 7831 6381, fax 020 7831 2575); Number 7, Harrington Street, Liverpool L2 7QS (tel 0151 242 0707, fax 0151 236 1120, mobile 0831 703156, e-mail goldhaas@netcomuk.co.uk)

GOLDRING, Hon Mr Justice; Sir John Bernard Goldring; kt (1999); s of Joseph Goldring (d 1980), and Marianne Goldring; *b* 9 November 1944; *Educ* Wyggeston GS Leicester, Univ of Exeter; *m* 2 Jan 1970, Wendy Margaret Lancaster, da of Ralph Lancaster Bennett (d 1980); 2 s (Jeremy b 1971, Rupert b 1974); *Career* called to the Bar Lincoln's Inn 1969 (bencher 1996), QC 1987, standing prosecuting counsel to Inland Revenue (Midland & Oxford Circuit) 1985–87, recorder Midland & Oxford Circuit 1987, dep sr judge Sovereign Base Areas Cyprus 1991, dep judge of the High Court 1995, judge Courts of Appeal Jersey and Guernsey 1998, judge of the High Court of Justice 1999–, presiding judge Midland Circuit 2002–05, cmmr Judicial Appts Cmmn 2006–; *Recreations* gardening, skiing; *Style—* The Hon Mr Justice Goldring; ✉ Royal Courts of Justice, Strand, London WC2A 2LL

GOLDSACK, His Hon Judge Alan Raymond; QC (1990); s of Raymond Frederick Goldsack, MBE (d 1985), of Hastings, and Mildred Agnes, *née* Jones (d 2000); *b* 13 June 1947; *Educ* Hastings GS, Univ of Leicester (LLB); *m* 21 Aug 1971, Christine Marion, da of Frank Leslie Clarke, MBE; 3 s (Ian b 1974, Richard b 1977, Stephen b 1980), 1 da (Tessa b 1975); *Career* called to the Bar Gray's Inn 1970 (bencher 2003), recorder 1988–94, circuit judge (NE Circuit) 1994–; sr circuit judge 2002–, hon recorder of Sheffield 2002–; *Recreations* gardening, walking; *Style—* His Hon Judge Goldsack, QC; ✉ The Old Rectory, Braithwell, Rotherham (tel 01709 812167)

GOLDSCHMIED, Marco; s of Guido Rodolfo Goldschmied, and Elinor Violet, *née* Sinnott; *b* 28 March 1944; *Educ* Rudolf Steiner Sch Milan, Liceo Manzoni Milan, William Ellis GS London, AA Sch of Architecture (Dipl), Univ of Reading (MSc); *m* 1969, Andrea, *née* Halvorsen; 4 s, 1 da; *Career* architect; assoc ptnr Piano + Rogers 1971–77; Richard Rogers Partnership: fndr ptnr 1977–84, md 1984–89; md Richard Rogers Architects Ltd London 1989–, chm River CADS Ltd, vice-pres and dir Richard Rogers Japan KK, chm Thames Wharf Studios; projects incl: masterplanning Heathrow Terminal 5 1990–, Learning Resource Centre Thames Valley Univ 1996 (RIBA Award 1998), Europier passenger terminal Heathrow 1996 (RIBA Award 1997, Br Steel Award 1997), Greenwich peninsula masterplan 1997, offices and residential Mercedes Benz Berlin 1998, Lloyd's Register of Shipping HQ London 1999, Daiwa Europe office devpt London 1999, Bordeaux Law Courts 1998, Montevetro riverside residential 1999, Millennium Dome 1999, offices and laboratories Gifu Japan 1999; teacher: AA 1971, Glasgow Sch of Art 1999; external examiner Mackintosh Sch; lectr RIBA 1981–99, also lectr at Univs incl: Darmstadt, Vienna, Manchester, Westminster, Glasgow; RIBA: chm Awards Gp, memb Cncl, memb Int Affairs Bd, memb Educn Review Gp, pres 1999–; memb: Br Cncl of Offices, ARB Cncl, ARB Euro Advsy Gp, Univ of Reading Construction Forum, Building Awards Jury 1998–99; *Books* Architecture 98 (1998), Visions of the 21st Century (ed, 2000); *Recreations* 20th century history, architecture, skiing, meditation, cooking, The Simpsons; *Style—* Marco Golschmied, Esq; ✉ Richard Rogers Partnership, Thames Wharf, Rainville Road, London W6 9HA (tel 020 7385 1235)

GOLDSMITH, Edward René David; s of Frank Benedict Hayum Goldsmith, OBE, TD (d 1967; MP (Cons) Stowmarket 1910–18), by his w Marcelle, *née* Mouiller (d 1985); er bro of Sir James Goldsmith, MEP (d 1997); *b* 8 November 1928; *Educ* Millfield, Magdalen Coll Oxford (MA); *m* 1, 1953, Gillian Marion Pretty; 1 s (Alexander), 2 da (Dido, Clio); *m* 2, 1981, Katherine Victoria, da of John Anthony James, CMG (d 1987), of Auckland, NZ; 2 s (Benedict, Zeno); *Career* author; publisher and campaigner 1970–, ed The Ecologist 1970–89; pres The Climate Initiatives Fund; tstee JMG Fndn; winner Honorary Right Livelihood Award Stockholm (known as the alternative Nobel Prize) 1991, inaugural recipient Int Forum on Globalization Annual Edward Goldsmith Lifetime Achievement Award 2007; Chevalier de la Legion d'Honneur 1991; *Books* Can Britain Survive? (ed, Tom Stacey 1971), A Blueprint for Survival (co-author 1972), The Stable Society (1977), The Social and Environmental Effects of Large Dams Vol I (with Nicholas Hildyard 1984) Vol II (co-ed, 1988) Vol III (co-ed, 1992), The Earth Report (with Nicholas Hildyard, 1988), The Great U Turn (1988), 5,000 Days to Save the Planet (with Nicholas Hildyard and others, 1990), The Way - An Ecological World-View (1992), The Case Against the Global Economy and for a turn towards the local (ed with Jerry Mander, 1996); *Clubs* Travellers' (Paris), Brooks's; *Style—* Edward Goldsmith, Esq; ✉ 9 Montague Road, Richmond, Surrey TW10 6QW

GOLDSMITH, Harvey Anthony; CBE (1996); s of Sydney Goldsmith, and Minnie Goldsmith; *b* 4 March 1946; *Educ* Christ's Coll, Brighton Coll of Technol; *m* 4 July 1971, Diana; 1 s (Jonathon b 28 July 1976); *Career* concert promoter and prodr; ptnr Big O Posters 1966–67, merged with John Smith Entertainments Ltd 1970, fndr Harvey Goldsmith Entertainments Ltd 1976, acquired Allied Entertainments Group 1984, formed Classical Productions (with Mark McCormack) 1986; staged first free open air concert Parliament Hill Fields 1968, fndr concerts Roundhouse Camden 1968, cr Crystal Palace Garden Party series 1969–72; promoter: Aida 1988, Carmen 1989, Pavarotti in the Park 1991, Tosca 1991, The 3 Tenors 1996; vice-pres: Music Users' Cncl, REACT; chm Concert Promoters Assoc, vice-chm Prince's Tst Action Mgmnt Bd; memb Bd: London Tourist Bd, Prague Heritage Fund; tstee: Band Aid, Live Aid Foundation, Royal Opera House, CST; memb Communication Gp Red Cross; Int Promoter of the Year 1994–97, Ambassador for London Judges Award 1997; *Recreations* golf; *Clubs* RAC, Hartsbourne Golf, Vale de Lobo Golf; *Style—* Harvey Goldsmith, Esq, CBE; ✉ Harvey Goldsmith Entertainments Ltd, Greenland Place, 115–123 Bayham Street, London NW1 0AG (tel 020 7482 5522, fax 020 7428 9252)

GOLDSMITH, Baron (Life Peer UK 1999), of Allerton in the County of Merseyside; Peter Henry Goldsmith; PC (2002), QC (1987); s of Sydney Elland Goldsmith, and Myra, *née* Nurick; *b* 5 January 1950; *Educ* Quarry Bank HS Liverpool, Gonville & Caius Coll Cambridge (MA), UCL (LLM); *m* Joy, *née* Elterman; 3 s (James b 1978, Jonathan b 1983, Benjamin b 1985), 1 da (Charlotte b 1981); *Career* called to the Bar Gray's Inn 1972 (bencher 1994); in practice SE Circuit, jr counsel to the Crown in Common Law 1985–87, recorder of the Crown Court 1991–, dep judge of the High Court 1994–; attorney gen 2001–07; chm Bar of England and Wales 1995; memb Gen Cncl of the Bar 1992–96 and 2001– (chm Legal Servs Ctee 1991–93, vice-chm 1994, chm Int Relations Ctee 1996); pres Bar Pro Bono Unit (chm 1995–2000) 2001–, chm Fin Reporting Review Panel 1997–2000 (memb 1995–2000), memb Advsy Bd Cambridge Centre for Commercial and Corporate law 1998–; memb Cncl Public Concern at Work 1995–99; Int Bar Assoc: chm Standing Ctee on Globalisation of Law 1995–98, chm Ctee 1 IBA Human Rights Inst 1995–98, memb Cncl 1996–, co-chm IBA Human Rights Inst 1998–2001; co-chm Twinning Ctee 1996–98; memb Exec Ctee GB-China Centre 1996–2001; PM's personal rep Convention For a European Union Charter of Fundamental Rights 1999–2000; memb Jt Select Ctee on Human Rights 2001; elected to American Law Inst 1997; Avocat Paris Bar 1997; *Style—* The Rt Hon the Lord Goldsmith, PC, QC; ✉ 9 Buckingham Gate, London SW1E 6JP (tel 020 7271 2405)

GOLDSMITH, Walter Kenneth; s of Lionel Goldsmith (d 1981), and Phoebe Goldsmith (d 2004); *b* 19 January 1938; *Educ* Merchant Taylors'; *m* 1961, Rosemary Adele, da of Joseph Salter (d 1970); 2 s, 2 da; *Career* chartered accountant Mann Judd & Co 1964–66, mgmnt conslt McLintock Mann & Whinney Murray 1964–66, with Black & Decker Ltd 1966–79 (md 1974, chief exec and European dir 1975, corp vice-pres and pres Pacific Int Ops 1976–79), dir gen IOD 1979–84, chm Korn Ferry International Ltd 1984–86 (chief exec 1984–85), gp planning and mktg dir Trusthouse Forte plc 1985–87, chm Food From Britain 1987–90; chm: Ansoll Estates Ltd 1990–98, Flying Flowers Ltd 1990–99, Betterware plc 1990–95, Beagle Holdings Ltd 1992–, Fitness First plc 1997–2003, Estates Mgmnt Ltd 2006–, Mercury Gp plc 2006–; dir: Bank Leumi (UK) plc 1984–, Isys plc 1987–97, British Food and Farming Ltd 1990–, Guiton Gp 1998–, Asite plc 1998–, Visionic Ltd 2005–, Energy Technique plc 2007–; advsr Rotch Gp 1996–; chm Governing Bd Marketing Quality Assurance 1990–; memb: Eng Tourist Bd 1982–84, Br Tourist Authy 1984–86; co-creator Festival of Food and Farming 1989 and 1992, memb Cncl Royal Agric Soc of Eng 1990–95; co-fndr Israel Diaspora Tst 1982, memb Br Overseas Trade Gp for Israel 1984– (chm 1987–91), treas Leo Baeck Coll 1987–89, chm of tstees Jewish Music Institute 2003–; Liveryman Worshipful Co of CAs in Eng and Wales 1985, Freeman City of London; FCA, FRSA; *Publications* The Winning Streak (with D Clutterbuck, 1984), The Winning Streak Workout Book (1985), The New Elite (with Berry Ritchie, 1987), The Winning Streak Mark 2 (1997); *Recreations* music, boating, painting, property; *Style—* Walter Goldsmith, Esq

GOLDSMITH, (Frank) Zac; s of Sir James Goldsmith (d 1997), and Lady Annabel Goldsmith, *née* Vane-Tempest Stewart; *b* 20 January 1975; *Educ* Eton; *m* Sheherazade, *née* Ventura-Bentley; 2 da (Uma Romaine, Thyra Amber), 1 s (James Edward); *Career* Redefining Progress (RP) San Francisco 1995–96, Int Soc for Ecology and Culture (ISEC) California, Bristol and Ladakh 1996–98 (currently associate dir), dir and ed The Ecologist 1997–; memb Bd: JMG Fndn, Fondation de Sauve, L'Association Goldsmith pour l'Environment, l'Artisanat et le Monde Rural; Beacon Prize for Philanthropy 2003, Global Green Award for Environmental Leadership 2004; *Clubs* Aspinall's, Travellers, Mark's; *Style—* Zac Goldsmith, Esq; ✉ The Ecologist Magazine, Unit 102, Lana House Studios, 116–118 Commercial Street, London E1 6NF (tel 020 7422 8100, e-mail office@2goffice.co.uk)

GOLDSPINK, Prof Geoffrey; s of James Albert Goldspink (d 1992), and Muriel, *née* Gee; *b* 2 April 1939; *Educ* Univ of Hull (BSc), Trinity Coll, Univ of Dublin (PhD, ScD), FRSC; *m* 31 Dec 1960, Barbara, da of Frederick Staniforth (d 1966); 3 s (Mark Richard b 6 Jan 1962, Paul Harvey b 28 April 1964, Andrew Jeffrey b 27 Jan 1966); *Career* prof and head of zoology Univ of Hull, visiting prof Univ of Nairobi, Agassiz visiting prof Harvard Univ, prof of anatomy and cell biology Tufts New England Med Centre Boston USA; Univ of London: fndr chair of veterinary molecular and cellular biol, dir of molecular and cellular biol RVC London, currently emeritus prof of anatomy and developmental biology and of surgery Royal Free and UC Med Sch; conslt UCL BioMedica; *Books* Growth and Differentiation of Cell in Vertebrate Tissues, Mechanics and Energetics of Animal Locomotion; *Recreations* restoration of houses of historical interest, music; *Style—* Prof Geoffrey Goldspink; ✉ Brambledene, East Common, Harpenden, Hertfordshire AL5 1DQ; The Royal Free and University College Medical School, UCL, Rowland Hill Street, London NW3 2PF (tel 020 7830 2410, fax 020 7830 2917, e-mail goldspink@rfhsm.ac.uk)

GOLDSPINK, Robert Andrew; s of late Canon R W Goldspink, of Fenstanton, Cambs, and Kathleen Edith, *née* Betts; *b* 8 August 1949; *Educ* Eltham Coll, Fitzwilliam Coll Cambridge (Squire scholar, Rebecca Flower scholar, MA, LLM); *m* 1 Sept 1973, Dr Margo Diane Dunlop, da of Roy Graham Dunlop, MBE (d 1989); 1 s (James Elliot b 1985), 1 da (Jesse Lorraine b 1991); *Career* articled clerk Wild Hewitson & Shaw Cambridge 1973–75, supervisor in constitutional legal studies Fitzwilliam and Christ's Colls Cambridge 1973–75, slr Freshfields 1975–80; Denton Hall: joined 1980, ptnr 1981–97; Morgan Lewis & Bockius LLP: ptnr 1997–, managing ptnr London 2004–; accredited mediator, lectr on legal subjects 1975–; memb: Marriot Ctee proposing revisions to English arbitration law, Jt Working Pty Gen Cncl of the Bar and the Law Soc reviewing English civil courts and court procedures 1993, Court of Appeal Mediation Steering Ctee 1997–2003, Commercial Court Users' Ctee 2003–; memb: Law Soc, City of London Law Soc, London Slrs' Litigation Assoc, Centre for Dispute Resolution; *Publications* International Commercial Fraud (co-ed); *Recreations* gardening, music; *Clubs* Cwlth; *Style—* Robert A Goldspink, Esq; ✉ Morgan, Lewis & Bockius, 2 Gresham Street, London EC2V 7PE (tel 020 7710 5500, fax 020 7710 5600, e-mail rgoldspink@morganlewis.com)

GOLDSTAUB, His Hon Judge Anthony James; QC (1992); s of Henry Goldstaub (d 1977), and Hilda Goldstaub; *b* 26 May 1949; *Educ* Highgate Sch, Univ of Nottingham (LLB); *Career* called to the Bar Middle Temple 1972, criminal and common law civil litigation 1972–2004, recorder of the Crown Court 1999–2004 (asst recorder 1994–99), circuit judge (South Eastern Circuit) 2004–; *Style—* His Hon Judge Goldstaub, QC

GOLDSTAUB, Thomas Charles; s of Werner Fritz Goldstaub, and Beate Charlotte, *née* Muller; *b* 2 September 1953; *Educ* Forest Sch; *m* 4 June 1985, Jane Hilary Elizabeth, da of Gordon Heslop Procter; 1 da (Tabitha Sophie b 11 Dec 1985), 1 s (Rollo Alexander b 16 April 1989); *Career* md Fred & Warner Ltd 1983–86 (sales and mktg dir 1979–82), special projects dir Garrard & Co 1987–88, mktg dir Mappin & Webb 1989–90, md Fintex of London 1993– (dep md 1991–93); Freeman City of London 1986, Liveryman Worshipful Co of Upholders 1986; *Books* What Do You Call A Kid (1985); *Recreations* sailing, skiing, classic cars; *Style—* Thomas Goldstaub, Esq

GOLDSTEIN, Prof Harvey; s of Jack Goldstein (d 1991), and Millicent Goldstein (d 1945); *b* 30 October 1939; *Educ* Hendon GS, Univ of Manchester (BSc), UCL (Dip Statistics); *m* 1970, Barbara, *née* Collinge; 1 s (Thomas Gregory b 1977); *Career* research asst Dept of Statistics UCL 1962–64, lectr in statistics Inst of Child Health Univ of London 1964–71, head of Statistics Section Nat Children's Bureau 1971–76, prof of statistical methods Inst of Educn Univ of London 1977–2005, prof of social statistics Univ of Bristol 2005–; jt dir WHO collaborating centre on child growth and devpt 1989–, jt dir Int Centre for Research on Assessment 1992–, assoc dir Int Sch Effectiveness and Improvement Centre 1993–; visiting lectr in biostatistics Univ of Wisconsin June-Aug 1968; visiting prof: Ontario Inst for Studies in Educn Toronto Canada July-Aug 1983 and 1986 (adjunct prof 1987–90), UEA 1992–; adjunct prof Sch of Public Health Univ of Texas Houston 1998–; memb Ed Bd Annals of Human Biology 1974–, assoc ed Jl of Educnl and Behavioural Statistics 1988–, exec ed Assessment in Educn 1993–; govr: St James' CE Primary Sch Haringey 1982–90, Tetherdown Primary Sch Haringey 1987–89; fndn govr William Ellis Sch London 1993–96; memb: Biometric Soc, Soc for the Study of Human Biology, American Statistical Assoc, Psychometric Soc, Br Educnl Research Assoc, Nat Cncl on Measurement in Educn, Int Statistical Inst 1987–; Hon DUniv Open Univ 2001; CStat, FSS (memb Cncl 1973–77 and 2000–04, Guy Medal in Silver 1998), FRSA 1991–99, FBA 1996; *Recreations* tennis, walking, cycling, playing the flute; *Style—* Prof Harvey Goldstein, FBA; ✉ Graduate School of Education, University of Bristol, Bristol BS8 1JA (e-mail h.goldstein@bristol.ac.uk)

GOLDSTEIN, Dr Michael; CBE (1997); s of Jacob Goldstein (d 1945), of London, and Sarah, *née* Goldberg (d 2001); *b* 1 May 1939; *Educ* Hackney Downs GS London, Northern Poly (BSc, PhD, DSc); *m* 5 May 1962, Janet Sandra, da of Henry Arthur Skevington (d 1979), of London; 1 s (Richard b 1968); *Career* successively lectr, sr lectr then princ lectr Poly of North London (formerly Northern Poly) 1963–73; Sheffield Poly: head Dept of Chemistry 1974–83, dean of the Faculty of Science 1979–83; vice-chllr Coventry Univ (formerly Coventry Poly) 1987–2004 (dep dir 1983–87); author of many scientific articles and several review chapters in books 1962–84 and of articles on educn and educn mktg 2004–; chm Chemistry Bd CNAA 1978–84, involved with local, regnl and nat sections of Royal Soc of Chemistry (pres Educn Div 1993–95, chm Educn and Qualifications Bd 1995–99) and various local/regnl orgns and gps, chm Cncl for the Registration of Forensic Practitioners 2005–; chm UCAS 1997–2001, memb Bd Universities and Colleges Employers Assoc (UCEA) 1994–2001, chm States of Jersey HE Devpt Gp 2005–, memb Bd Fndn Degrees Forward 2006–; chm Heist 2004–06, dep chm CV One Ltd 2002–, dir ContinYou Ltd 2003–; chm Creative Partnerships Coventry 2004–; memb Bd: Coventry, Solihull and Warwickshire Partnerships Ltd 1994–2004, The City Centre Co (Coventry) Ltd 1997–2002, Coventry and Warwickshire LSC 2001–07; non-exec dir Coventry and Warks NHS Partnership Tst 2006–; tstee Community Educn Devpt Centre 1996–2003; Hon DSc Univ of Warwick 2003; hon fell Univ of Worcester 1998; CChem, FRSC 1973 (MRSC 1967), Hon FCGI 1994; *Recreations* DIY, Coventry City FC; *Style—* Dr Michael Goldstein, CBE; ✉ 33 Frythe Close, Kenilworth, Warwickshire CV8 2SY (tel 01926 854939, e-mail michael.goldstein@btinternet.com)

GOLDSTEIN-JACKSON, Kevin Grierson; JP (Poole 1990); s of Harold Grierson Jackson (d 1992), and Winifred Miriam Emily, *née* Fellows; *b* 2 November 1946; *Educ* Univ of Reading (BA), Univ of Southampton (MPhil); *m* 6 Sept 1975, Jenny Mei Leng, da of Ufong Ng, of Malaysia; 2 da (Sing Yu b 1981, Kimberley b 1984); *Career* Staff Rels Dept London Tport 1966, Scottish Widows Pension and Life Assurance Soc 1967, prog organiser Southern TV 1970–73, asst prodr HK/TVB Hong Kong 1973, freelance writer and TV prodr 1973–75, fndr and dir Thames Valley Radio 1974–77, head of film Dhofar Region TV Serv Sultanate of Oman 1975–76, asst to head of drama Anglia TV 1977–81; TSW - Television South West: fndr controller and dir of progs 1981–85, jt md 1981–82, chief exec 1982–85; dir ITV Pubns 1981–85; dir of private cos; artist; contrib FT 1986–; govr Lilliput First Sch Poole 1988–93; Freeman City of London 1996; FRSA 1978, FIMgt 1982, FInstD 1982, FFA 1988, FRGS 1989; *Books* incl: The Right Joke for the Right Occasion (1973), Experiments with Everyday Objects (1976), Dictionary of Essential Quotations (1983), Share Millions (1989), The Public Speaker's Joke Book (1991), The Astute Private Investor (1994), Quick Quips (2002); *Recreations* writing, painting, TV, films, travel, music, walking; *Style—* Kevin Goldstein-Jackson, Esq; ✉ c/o Alcazar, 18 Martello Road, Branksome Park, Poole, Dorset BH13 7DH

GOLDSTONE, Prof Anthony Howard; *b* 13 September 1944; *Educ* Univ of Oxford (MA, BM BCh); *Career* house physician in med Chase Farm Hosp Enfield 1969, house surgn Edgware Gen Hosp 1969–70, resident clinical pathologist Guy's Hosp 1970, registrar in haematology Western Infirmary Edinburgh 1971–72 (SHO in med 1970–71), res fell in clinical immunology Cancer Research Campaign Edinburgh Royal Infirmary 1972–73, sr registrar in haematology Addenbrooke's Hosp and Dept of Haematological Med Univ of Cambridge 1973–76, postgraduate dean Sch of Med UCL 1984–87, med dir UCL Hosp NHS Tst 1992–2000; currently: conslt clinical haematologist, prof Sch of Med UCL, dir N London Cancer Network; dir Clinical Directorate in Haematology Bloomsbury District 1991–93; chm: Registry of Transplant in Lymphoma Euro Bone Marrow Transplant Gp 1984–92, Med Ctee UCH 1986–88, NE Thames Regnl Haematologists 1988–92, Working Gp Bloomsbury Haematologists 1988–92, FRCP(Edin) 1979, FRCP 1983 (MRCP 1971), FRCPath 1987 (MRCPath 1975); *Books* Leukaemia, Lymphoma and Allied Disorders (jtly, 1976), Examination Haematology (1977), Synopsis of Haematology (1983), Clinics in Haematology: Autologous Bone Marrow Transplantation (ed, 1986); author of numerous book chapters and papers in scientific jls; *Style—* Prof Anthony Goldstone; ✉ North London Cancer Network Offices, 6th Floor Rosenheim Wing, 25 Grafton Way, London WC1 (tel 020 7380 9983, fax 020 7380 9153, e-mail anthony.goldstone@uclh.nhs.uk)

GOLDSTONE, Anthony Keith; s of Myer Charles Maurice Goldstone (d 1987), and Rose, *née* Kessly (d 1987); *b* 25 July 1944; *Educ* Manchester Grammar, Royal Manchester Coll of Music; *m* 26 July 1989, Caroline Anne Clemmow, pianist, da of David Menzies Clemmow; *Career* pianist; appears as soloist, in duo with wife Caroline Clemmow and as memb various chamber ensembles; fndr Musicians of the Royal Exchange 1978; has worked with all major Br symphony orchs, performed at numerous Br and international festivals and BBC Prom concerts (incl Last Night); FRMCM 1973; *Recordings* incl: three vols of Chopin Piano Solos, Schubert Piano Solos and Schumann Piano Solos, Lyapunov Solos, Schubert Solo Masterworks Series, Beethoven Solos, Unheard Mozart, Arensky Solos, Glière Solos, Britten Resonances (piano solos by Britten and others), Parry Piano Solos on Parry's Piano, Elgar Piano Solos on Elgar's Piano, Holst and Lambert Piano Solos, Piano Music from Castle Howard, Beethoven Fourth Concerto (with RPO under Norman Del Mar), Pitfield First Concerto, Saint-Saëns Carnival of Animals (with RPO under Owain Arwel Hughes), Berkeley and Debussy Duos (with James Galway on flute), Beethoven Piano Quartets (with Cummings String Trio), Sibelius Piano Quintet (with Gabrieli String Quartet), Alkan Concerto da Camera No 2 and Bombardo-Carillon (with Morhange Ensemble and Caroline Clemmow respectively), Mendelssohn Complete Sonatas for Violin and Piano (with Yossi Zivoni), Holst Quintet for Piano and Wind and Jacob Sextet for Piano and Wind (with Elysian Wind Quintet); with w, Caroline Clemmow: A Moyzes (solos and two pianos), Holst Planets (two pianos), The Virtuoso Piano Duo (two pianos), Schubert Piano Duet Cycle, The Unauthorised Schubert Piano Duos (vols 1 and 2), Britten and McPhee (two pianos), Gál Piano Duos, Soler Double Concertos (two pianos), Russian Tableaux (solos and piano duets), Paradise Gardens (solos and piano duets), Herzogenberg (solos and piano duos), Explorations (solos and piano duos), George Lloyd Music for Two Pianos, Virtuoso Variations (various piano duets), Tchaikovsky Piano Duets, Dvořák and Mendelssohn Symphonies, Orientale, Graham Whettam (solos and piano duos), Grieg for Piano Duo, Rimsky-Korsakov Scheherazade (piano duets), Romantic Duet Sonatas, Duet Lollipops, Romantic Duet Waltzes, Romantic Duet Suites; *Recreations* antique maps, birdwatching; *Style—* Anthony Goldstone, Esq; ✉ Walcot Old Hall, Alkborough, North Lincolnshire DN15 9JT (tel 01724 720475, fax 01724 721599, e-mail akgoldstone@aol.com)

GOLDSTONE, His Hon Judge (Leonard) Clement; QC (1993); s of Maurice Goldstone (d 1980), and Maree, *née* Lewis; *b* 20 April 1949; *Educ* Manchester Grammar, Churchill Coll Cambridge (BA); *m* 20 August 1972, Vanessa, da of Donald Forster, and Muriel Forster; 3 s (Simon Lewis b 27 Dec 1973, Jonathan Andrew b 11 Oct 1976, Maurice James b 24 May 1980); *Career* called to the Bar Middle Temple 1971; recorder 1992–2002, treas Northern Circuit 1998–2001, circuit judge (Northern Circuit) 2002–; pres Mental Health Review Tbnl (restricted cases) 1999–; *Recreations* golf, bridge, theatre, music; *Clubs* Dunham Forest Golf & Country (Altrincham); *Style—* His Hon Judge Goldstone, QC

GOLDSTONE, David Joseph; s of Solomon Goldstone, and Rebecca, *née* Degotts; *b* 21 February 1929; *Educ* Dynevor Sch Swansea, LSE (LLB); *m* 21 March 1957, Cynthia, da of Walter George Easton; 1 s (Jonathan Lee b 3 Nov 1957), 2 da (Debra Ann b 24 Aug 1959, Karen Ella b 22 Oct 1964); *Career* legal practice 1955–66, chief exec Regalian Properties plc 1970–2001, dir Wales Millennium Centre 2001–06; memb: Football Assoc of Wales 1970–72, WNO 1984–89, dep chm Cncl Univ of London 2002–06, memb Ct of Govrs LSE 1985–, hon vice-pres Royal Albert Hall 2007– (memb Cncl 1998–2006); chm Coram Family 2001–06; hon fell LSE; *Recreations* family, reading, sport; *Clubs* Bath & Racquets, Lansdowne; *Style—* David Goldstone, Esq; ✉ Grosvenor Hill Court, 15 Bourdon Street, London W1E 3PX (tel 020 7499 4525)

G

GOLDSWORTHY, Andy; OBE (2000); s of Prof Fredrick Alan Goldsworthy, and Muriel, *née* Stanger; *b* 25 July 1956; *Educ* Wheatlands Secdy Modern Sch, Harrogate HS, Bradford Art Coll, Preston Poly; *m* Judith Elizabeth, da of Barry Gregson, and Audrey, *née* Jackson; 2 s (James b 8 Oct 1987, Thomas b 15 Dec 1994), 2 da (Holly b 4 April 1990, Anna b 5 Feb 1993); *Career* artist/sculptor; *Solo Exhibitions* incl: Evidence (Coracle Press Gallery London) 1985, Rain, Sun, Snow, Mist, Calm (The Henry Moore Centre for the Study of Sculpture, Leeds City Art Gallery and Northern Centre for Contemporary Art Sunderland touring) 1985, Winter Harvest (Book exhbn with John Fowles, Scottish Arts Cncl) 1987, Fabian Carlsson Gallery London 1987, Gallery Takagi Nagoya 1988, Yurakucho Asahi Gallery Tokyo and Osaka 1988, Mountain and Coast Autumn into Winter 1987 (also at Fabian Carlsson Gallery London 1988), Touching North (Anne Berthoud Gallery London and Graeme Murray Gallery Edinburgh) 1989, Black in Black (Fabian Carlsson Gallery London) 1989, Snowballs in Summer (Old Museum of Tport Glasgow) 1989, Leaves (The Natural History Museum London) 1989, Garden Mountain (Centre D'Art Contemporain Castres) 1990, Hand to Earth - Sculpture 1976–90 (retrospective exhbn touring Leeds City Art Gallery, Royal Botanic Garden Edinburgh, Stedelijke Musea Gouda and Centre D'Art Contemporain Toulouse) 1990–91, Drawings (Aline Vidal Gallery Paris) 1990–91, With Nature (Galerie Lelong NY and Chicago Arts Club) 1991, Sand Leaves (Chicago Arts Club) 1991, With Nature (Galerie Lelong NYC) 1991, Mid Winter Muster (Adelaide Festival) 1992, Verden Und Vergehen (Museum Bellerine Zurich) 1992, California Project (Haines Gallery San Francisco) 1992, Stone Sky (Galerie St Anne Brussels) 1992, Ile de Lassiuiere 1992, Flow of Earth (exhbn and film, Castlefield Gallery Manchester) 1992, Hard Earth (Turske Hue-Williams Gallery London) 1992, Australia, NZ and Japan 1993, Mid-Winter Muster (Harwood House) 1993, Wood Land (Galerie Lelong NY) 1993, Tochigi Museum of Fine Art 1993, Setagaya Museum of Fine Arts Tokyo 1994, Aline Vidal Gallery Paris 1994, Hue-Williams Fine Art London 1994, Laumeier Sculpture Park St Louis 1994, Oriel Gallery Cardiff 1994, Haines Gallery San Francisco 1994, San José Museum of Art 1995, Galerij S65 Belgium 1995, Galerie Lelong NY 1995, Musée de Digne 1995, Green on Red Gallery Dublin 1995, Tuillehouse Carlisle 1996, Margaret Harvey Gallery St Albans 1996, Michael Hue-Williams London 1996, Galerie Lelong NY 1996, Haines Gallery San Francisco 1996, Penrith Museum 1997, Musee d' Art Contemporain Montreal 1998, Galerie Lelong Paris 1998, Springer & Winckler Galerie Berlin 1998, Ingelby Gallery Edinburgh 1998, Andy Goldsworthy (Michael Hue-Williams Fine Art London) 1999, Andy Goldsworthy (Storm King Art Centre NY), Time (Barbican Centre London, Michael Hue-Williams Fine Art London) 2000, Gigne Works Hotel Scribe Paris 2000, Herbert Johnson Museum of Art Cornell Univ NY 2000, Site Santa Fe 2000, Galerie Lelong NY 2000, Time (Abbot Hall Art Gallery and Museum) 2001, Silent Spring (Gallerie Lelong Paris) 2001, Time (Springer & Winckler Galerie Berlin) 2001, Journey (Galerie S65 Aalst) 2002; *Group Exhibitions* incl: Place (Gimpel Fils Summer Show London) 1983, Sculpture in the Open Air (Yorkshire Sculpture Park) 1983, Salon D'Automne (Serpentine Gallery London) 1984, The Possibilities of Space - Fifty Years of British Sculptors' Drawings (Musee de Beaux Arts De Besançon, Kirlees Museums tour) 1987–88, Apperto 88 (Venice Biennale) 1988, Through the Looking Glass - Photographic Art in Britain 1945–1989 (Barbican Art Gallery London) 1989, Leaves (Atelier des Enfants, Centre Georges Pompidou Paris touring) 1990, Attitudes to Nature (Ile De Vassiviere) 1991, Shared Earth (Br-Russian art, UK tour) 1991, Goldsworthy and Girke (Fruitmarket Gallery Edinburgh) 1992, Galerie Lelong NY 1993, Impermanence (Alderich MOMA) 1993, Parc de la Courneuve (Paris installation) 1993, Morecambe Bay Works (Lancaster, Scott Gallery and Storey Inst) 1993, Tikon (project, Denmark) 1993, Trees (Kunstierwerkstatt Lotheringstrasse Munich) 1993, Time Machine (British Museum London) 1994; *Selected Works* Breath of Earth (San José Museum of Art) 1995, Four Stones (Galerij S65 Aalst) 1995, Black Stones, Red Pools (Galerie Lelong NY) 1995, Earth Memory (Musée de Digne les Baines) 1995, A Clearing of Arches. For The Night (Hathill Sculpture Fndn) Goodwood Sussex 1995, For the Night (Green on Red Gallery Dublin) 1995, Time Machine (Museo Egizio Turin) 1995, Vegetal (dance collaboration with Ballet Atlantique La Rochelle) 1995, clay floor installation (Glasgow MOMA) 1996, Printemps de Cahors 1996, Northern Rock Art (DLI Museum and Durham Art Gallery) 1996, Sheepfolds (Tulliehouse Carlisle) 1996, Sheepfolds (Margaret Harvey Gallery St Albans) 1996, Wood (Michael Hue-Williams Fine Art London, Galerie Lelong NY, Haines Gallery San Francisco) 1996, Andy Goldsworthy (Anchorage Museum of Art) 1996, Northern Exposure (Harris Gallery Preston) 1997, Andy Goldsworthy - Sheepfolds (Penrith Museum) 1997, Northern Lights (Mercer Art Gallery Harrogate) 1997, Obsession + Devotion (Haines Gallery) 1997, Andy Goldsworthy - Sheepfold Drawings (Egremont West Cumbria) 1998, Arch (Musée d'Art Contemporain de Montreal) 1998, Goldsworthy (Galerie Lelong Paris) 1998, Etre Nature (Foundation Cartier Paris) 1998, Installation und Photographie (Springer & Winckler Galerie Berlin) 1998, Project 8 (Total Museum Korea) 1998, Andy Goldsworthy (Staatsbosbeheer Netherlands) 1999, Arches (Plymouth Art Centre) 1999, Maison European Paris 2001; *Film* Two Autumns (ACGB/Channel 4), Flow of Earth (Granada), Rivers and Tides (Mediopolis Berlin/Skyline Edinburgh) 2000; *Publications* Rain sun snowhail mist calm (1985), Mountain and Coast Autumn into Winter (1987), Parkland (1988), Leaves (1989), Garden Mountain (1989), Touching North (1989), Andy Goldsworthy (1989), Sand Leaves (1991), Hand to Earth (1991), Ice and Snow Drawings (1992), Two Autumns (1993), Stone (1994), Black Stones, Red Pools (1995), Sheepfolds (1996), Wood (1996), Cairns (1997), Andy Goldsworthy (1998), Arch (with David Craid, 1999), Wall (2000), Time (2000); *Style*— Andy Goldsworthy, Esq, OBE; ✉ c/o Michael Hue-Williams Fine Art Ltd, 21 Cork Street, London W1X 1HB (tel 020 7434 1318, fax 020 7434 1321)

GOLDSWORTHY, Julia; MP; *b* 10 September 1978, Camborne, Cornwall; *Educ* Truro Sch, Univ of Cambridge, Daiichi Univ of Economics, Birkbeck Coll London; *Career* Parly research asst to Matthew Taylor MP, Lib Dem policy advsr educn and the economy, regeneration offr Carrick DC, MP (Lib Dem) Falmouth and Camborne 2005–; Lib Dem Treasy spokesperson 2006–; *Style*— Ms Julia Goldsworthy, MP; ✉ House of Commons, London SW1A 0AA

GOLDTHORPE, Dr John Harry; CBE (2002); s of Harry Goldthorpe (d 1989), of Great Houghton, Barnsley, and Lilian Eliza Goldthorpe (d 2002); *b* 27 May 1935; *Educ* Wath-upon-Dearne GS, UCL (BA), LSE, Univ of Cambridge (MA), Univ of Oxford (MA); *m* 1963, Rhiannon Esyllt, da of late Isaac Daniel Harry; 1 s (David Daniel Harry), 1 da (Siân Elinor); *Career* lectr Faculty of Econ and Politics Univ of Cambridge 1961–69 (fell King's Coll 1960–69), official fell Nuffield Coll Oxford 1969–2002 (emeritus fell 2002–), visiting prof Cornell Univ 2003–06; pres Int Sociological Assoc Ctee on Social Stratification 1982–85; memb Academia Europaea 1988, Br Acad assessor ESRC 1988–92, chm Social Studies Section Br Acad 1992–94; Hon Fil Dr Univ of Stockholm 1990; foreign memb Royal Swedish Acad of Sciences 2001; FBA 1984; *Books* The Affluent Worker - Industrial Attitudes and Behaviour (with David Lockwood, 1968), The Affluent Worker - Political Attitudes and Behaviour (with David Lockwood, 1968), The Affluent Worker in the Class Structure (with David Lockwood, 1969), The Social Grading of Occupations - A New Approach and Scale (with Keith Hope, 1974), Social Mobility and Class Structure in Modern Britain (2 edn, 1987), The Constant Flux - A Study of Class Mobility in Industrial Societies (with Robert Erikson, 1992), On Sociology (2000, 2 edn 2007); *Recreations* lawn tennis, bird watching, computer chess, cryptic crosswords; *Style*— Dr John Goldthorpe, CBE, FBA; ✉ 32 Leckford Road, Oxford OX2 6HX (tel 01865 556602); Nuffield College, Oxford OX1 1NF (tel 01865 278559, fax 01865 278621, e-mail john.goldthorpe@nuffield.ox.ac.uk)

GOLDWAG, Wanda Celina; *b* Rugby, Warks; *Educ* LSE (BSc); *Partner* Femi Otitoju (civil partnership, 21 Dec 2005); *Career* exec dir AIR MILES 1996–2000, chair Goldwag Empson and Otitoju Ltd 2004–; advsr Smedvig Venture Capital 2000–, non-exec chair of Precision Data Venture Ltd 2000–; non-exec dir: Challenge Consultancy 1995–, Performing Right Soc 2002–; cmmr Postcomm (Postal Servs Cmmn) 2005–; columnist Precision Marketing Magazine 2001–03; MIDM 2006; *Style*— Ms Wanda Goldwag; ✉ Postal Services Commission, Hercules House, Hercules Road, London SW1Y 5AA

GOLOMBOK, Prof Susan Esther; da of Benzion Golombok, of Glasgow, and Clara, *née* Panice; *b* 11 August 1954, Glasgow; *Educ* Univ of Glasgow (BSc), Inst of Educn Univ of London (MSc), Inst of Psychiatry Univ of London (PhD); *m* 21 Feb 1979, Prof John Rust; 1 s (Jamie Carlos b 25 March 1985); *Career* research psychologist Inst of Psychiatry Univ of London 1977–86, lectr, sr lectr, reader then prof of psychology City Univ London 1987–2005, dir Centre for Family Research and prof of family research Univ of Cambridge 2006–; tstee: Laura Ashley Fndn, One Plus One, Brazelton Fndn; memb Soc for Research in Child Devpt 1990, FRSA 2005; *Publications* Bottling it Up (jtly, 1985), Modern Psychometrics (jtly, 1989), Gender Development (jtly, 1994), Growing up in a Lesbian Family (jtly, 1997), Parenting: What Really Counts? (2000); pubns in academic jls; *Recreations* cinema, cooking, design; *Clubs* Oxford and Cambridge; *Style*— Prof Susan Golombok; ✉ Centre for Family Research, Faculty of Social and Political Sciences, University of Cambridge, Free School Lane, Cambridge CB2 3RF (tel 01223 334510, fax 01223 330574, e-mail seg42@cam.ac.uk, website www.sps.cam.ac.uk/cfr)

GOMARSALL, Andrew (Andy); MBE (2004); *b* 24 July 1974, Durham; *Career* rugby union player (scrum half); clubs: London Wasps RUFC (winners Powergen Cup 1999), Bedford RUFC (capt), currently with Gloucester RFC (winners Zurich Premiership and Powergen Cup 2003); England: 27 caps, debut v Italy 1996, winners Five Nations Championship 1996, winners Six Nations Championship 2000 and 2003 (Grand Slam 2003), ranked no 1 team in world 2003, winners World Cup Aust 2003, also represented England Schs Under 18 (capt during Grand Slam 1992); *Recreations* supporting Tottenham Hotspur FC; *Style*— Andy Gomarsall, Esq, MBE; ✉ c/o Gloucester RFC, Kingsholm, Kingsholm Road, Gloucester GL1 3AX

GOMBRICH, Prof Richard Francis; *b* 17 July 1937; *Educ* St Paul's (scholar), Magdalen Coll Oxford (Demy scholar, MA, DPhil), Harvard Univ (AM); *Career* Univ of Oxford: lectr in Sanskrit and Pali 1965–76, governing body fell Wolfson Coll 1966–76, Boden prof of Sanskrit and professorial fell Balliol Coll 1976–2004, academic dir Oxford Centre for Buddhist Studies 2003–; Benjamin Meaker visiting prof Univ of Bristol 1981–82, visiting prof École des Hautes Études en Sciences Sociales 1982, Stewart visiting fell Princeton Univ 1986–87, Numata visiting prof SOAS 2006; memb: Advsy Cncl V&A 1978–83, Theological and Religious Studies Bd Cncl for Nat Academic Awards 1983–90, Cncl Soc for S Asian Studies 1986–92, Cncl Royal Asiatic Soc 1989–90, Academia Europaea 1990–, Pubns Ctee Royal Asiatic Soc 1991–92; pres Pali Text Soc 1994–2002 (hon sec and treas 1981–94); Hon DLitt Kalyani Univ 1991, Hon DEd De Montfort Univ 1996; S C Chakraborty medal Asiatic Soc 1993; Sri Lanka Ranjana 1994, Vacaspati Tirupati 1997; *Books* Precept and Practice: Traditional Buddhism in the Rural Highlands of Ceylon (1971), The World of Buddhism: Buddhist Monks and Nuns in Society and Culture (jt ed, 1984), Theravâda Buddhism: A Social History from Ancient Benares to Modern Colombo (1988, 2 edn 2006), Buddhism Transformed: Religious Change in Sri Lanka (jtly, 1988), How Buddhism Began (1996, 2 edn 2006), Kindness and Compassion as Means to Nirvana (1998); author of over 80 articles in learned jls; *Style*— Prof Richard Gombrich; ✉ Balliol College, Oxford OX1 3BJ

GOMERSALL, Sir Stephen John; KCMG (2000, CMG); s of Harry Raymond Gomersall (d 1976), and Helen Gomersall (d 1995); *b* 17 January 1948; *Educ* Forest Sch, Queens' Coll Cambridge (MA), Stanford Univ (MA); *m* 26 Oct 1975 (m dis 2006), Lydia, da of E W Parry; 2 s (Timothy b 1978, Simon b 1980), 1 da (Emily b 1982); *Career* FCO: entered 1970, third sec (later first sec) Tokyo 1972–77, first sec Rhodesia Dept 1977–79, private sec to Lord Privy Seal 1979–82, first sec Washington 1982–86, econ cnsllr Tokyo 1986–90, head Security Policy Dept 1990–94, dep perm rep UK Mission to the UN New York 1994–98, dir of int security 1998–99, ambass to Japan 1999–2004; currently chief exec for Europe Hitachi; memb Advsy Cncl LSO; Order of the Sacred Treasure (Japan, fourth class) 1975; *Recreations* music, golf, tennis, skiing; *Style*— Sir Stephen Gomersall, KCMG; ✉ Hitachi Europe Limited, Whitebrook Park, Lower Cookham Road, Maidenhead, Berkshire SL6 8YA

GOMEZ, Jill; da of Albert Clyde Gomez, and Denise Price Denham; *b* New Amsterdam, Br Guiana; *Educ* RAM, Guildhall Sch of Music; *Career* opera and concert singer; FRAM; operatic debut with Glyndebourne Touring Opera 1968; *Opera* roles with Glyndebourne Festival Opera incl: Adina in L'Elisir d'Amore, Mélisande in Pelléas et Mélisande, title role in La Calisto, Anne Trulove in The Rake's Progress; roles with The Royal Opera incl: cr role of Flora in Tippett The Knot Garden (Covent Garden) 1970, Tytania in A Midsummer Night's Dream, Lauretta in Gianni Schicchi; roles with English Opera Gp incl: Ilia in Idomeneo, Governess in The Turn of the Screw; roles with Scottish Opera incl: Pamina in The Magic Flute, Elizabeth in Elegy for Young Lovers, the Countess in The Marriage of Figaro, Fiordiligi in Cosi fan Tutte, Anne Trulove in The Rake's Progress; other roles incl: cr role of Countess in Thea Musgrave Voice of Ariadne (Aldeburgh) 1974, title role in Thaïs (Wexford) 1974, Jenifer in The Midsummer Marriage (WNO) 1976, cr title role in William Alwyn's Miss Julie for radio 1977, Tatiana in Eugene Onegin (Kent Opera) 1977, Donna Elvira in Don Giovanni (Ludwigsburg Festival) 1978, cr title role in BBC world première of Prokofiev Maddalena 1979, Fiordiligi in Cosi Fan Tutte (Bordeaux) 1979, 8th Book of Madrigals (première, Zurich Monteverdi Festival) 1979, Violetta in La Traviata (Kent Opera at Edinburgh Festival) 1979, Cinna in Lucio Silla (Zurich) 1981, Governess in The Turn of the Screw (Geneva) 1981, Cleopatra in Giulio Cesare (Frankfurt) 1981, Teresa in Benvenuto Cellini (Berlioz Festival, Lyon) 1982, Leïla in Les Pêcheurs de Perles (Scottish Opera) 1982–83, Governess in The Turn of the Screw (ENO) 1984, Helena in A Midsummer Night's Dream (Glyndebourne 1984, Opera London 1990), Donna Anna in Don Giovanni (Frankfurt Opera 1985, Kent Opera 1988), Amyntas in Il Re Pastore (Kent Opera) 1987, cr role of the Duchess in Powder her Face (Cheltenham Festival and Almeida Theatre) 1995; *Recitals* in: France, Austria, Belgium, Netherlands, Germany, Scandinavia, Switzerland, Italy, Spain, USA; festival appearances incl: Aix-en-Provence, Spoleto, Bergen, Versailles, Flanders, Netherlands, Prague, Edinburgh and BBC Proms; *Recordings* incl: Monteverdi Vespro della Beata Vergine 1610, Handel Acis and Galatea, Ode for St Celia's Day, Tippett The Knot Garden (premiere recording), A Child of Our Time, cr title role in Alwyn's Miss Julie (premiere recording), three recital discs of French, Spanish and Mozart songs (with John Constable), Britten Quatre Chansons Françaises (premiere recording), Ravel Trois Poèmes de Mallarmé, Canteloube Chants d'Auvergne, Britten Les Illuminations, Villa Lobos Bachianas Brasileiras No 5, Samuel Barber Knoxville, Summer of 1915, Cabaret Classics with John Constable, South of the Border (...Down Mexico Way), Britten's Blues (incl songs by Cole Porter, premiere recording), cmmnd David Matthews work Cantiga - The Song of Inês de Castro (premiere recording), Mahler Seven Early Songs, A Spanish Songbook (with John Constable), cr role of Duchess in Thomas Adès Powder Her Face (premiere recording, nominated for a Grammy award 2000); *Style*— Miss Jill Gomez; ✉ 16 Milton Park, London N6 5QA

GOMEZ, Dr Joan Rae; da of Maj Charles Harold McClelland, DSO (d 1951), and Florence Gertrude Victoria, *née* Baldwin; *b* 7 October 1921; *Educ* St Paul's Girls' Sch, KCL (MB BS, DPM); *m* 1, 1943, Denis Charles Lendrum (ka 1944), s of Charles Lendrum; m 2 (m dis 1974), Dr George Gomez, s of Luis Gomez (d 1950); 4 da (Francesca b 1947, Lavinia b 1949, Vivienne b 1951, Anthea b 1953), 4 adopted s (Peter, Paul b 1952, George b 1955, Matthew b 1957), 2 adopted da (Coralie, Helena b 1964); *Career* jr pathologist W London Hosp 1946, SHO (psychiatry) St George's Hosp 1973–74, conslt psychiatrist Westminster Hosp 1982–87, hon consulting psychiatrist Chelsea and Westminster Hosp 1987–; memb Friends of The Wellcome Inst 1992–; memb: BMA 1970, Soc of Authors, Farnham Writers' Circle; FRCPsych, FRSM 1980; *Books* Living with Crohn's Disease (2000), Living with Osteoporosis (2000), Coping Successfully with Diverticulitis (2001), Coping Successfully with Menopause (2002), Ask The Dead (2002), Thyroid Problems In Women (2003), Coping with Incontinence (2003), Diet in Diverticulitis (2005), Coping with Asperger's Syndrome (2005); *Recreations* walking, theatre, reading; *Style*— Dr Joan Gomez; ✉ Natterjack, Thursley Road, Churt, Farnham, Surrey GU10 2LG (tel and fax 01428 606354, e-mail jrgomez966@aol.com)

GOMMON, Peter Nicholas; s of David Edward Gommon (d 1987), and Jean, *née* Vipond; *b* 19 December 1945; *Educ* Northampton GS, Univ of Liverpool (BArch), City of Birmingham Poly (DipLA), Univ of Central England (MA); *m* 21 July 1973, Moira Joan, da of Leonard Thomas Maguire (d 1990), of Millhouses, Sheffield; 3 s (David b 28 Dec 1974, Joseph b 7 Aug 1976 d 1986, Edward b 19 Oct 1978); *Career* architect and landscape architect; dir Ainsley Gommon Architects Ltd 1981– (winners of 25 Nat and Int Awards for community projects, landscape and architecture); external examiner Sch of Landscape Manchester Metropolitan Univ 1998–2001; memb: St Saviour PCC Oxton, St Saviour Devpt Ctee; RIBA 1975, MLI 1982, FRSA 1992; *Recreations* art, theatre, music, agriculture, motor cycling, bass player with 'Low Flier'; *Clubs* RA Yacht, RAT, TOMCC; *Style*— Peter Gommon, Esq; ✉ 12 Devon Place, Newport NP20 4NN; The Old Police Station, 15 Glynne Way, Hawarden, Flint CH5 3NS; 46 Shrewsbury Road, Oxton, Birkenhead CH43 2HZ (tel 0151 653 7204, e-mail pierregommon@btinternet.com); Ty Joseff, 6 Pen y Fron, Penmon, Ynys Môn, Gwynedd; Ainsley Gommon Architects, 1 Price Street, Birkenhead Merseyside L41 6JN (tel 0151 647 5511, fax 0151 666 2195, e-mail pgommon@ainsleygommonarchitects.co.uk, website www.ainsleygommonarchitects.co.uk)

GOMPERTZ, (Arthur John) Jeremy; QC (1988); s of Col Arthur William Bean Gompertz (d 1984), and Muriel Annie, *née* Smith (d 1991); *b* 16 October 1937; *Educ* Beaumont Coll, Trinity Coll Cambridge (MA); *Career* called to the Bar Gray's Inn 1962 (bencher 1997); head of chambers 5 Essex Court 1988–2000, recorder of the Crown Court 1987–2003; chm Mental Health Review Tbnl Panel 1994–, memb Security and Investigations Ctee Jockey Club 2001–; *Recreations* horse racing and breeding, skiing, travel; *Style*— Jeremy Gompertz, Esq, QC; ✉ 5 Essex Court, Temple, London EC4Y 9AH (tel 020 7410 2000, fax 020 7410 2010)

GONDRY, Michel; *b* 8 May 1963; *Career* music video dir London and Paris 1990– (incl clips for Bjork, Black Crowes, Rolling Stones, Radiohead, The White Stripes and Kylie), commercials dir 1995– (spots for Levi's Drugstore, Adidas, Heineken, Smirnoff, Volvo and Polaroid); awards: Gold Lion Cannes 1995, 3 Silver Awards and winner Br Advertisement of the Year D&AD 1995, Silver Award D&AD 1996, Grand Prix Clio Awards 1996, European MTV Best Director of 1996; memb D&AD; *Style*— Michel Gondry

GONSALKORALE, Dr Mahendra; s of late Edwin Gonsalkorale, of Sri Lanka, and Anula, *née* Jayanetti; *b* 27 May 1944; *Educ* Royal Coll Colombo Sri Lanka, Univ of Ceylon (MB BS, MD), Univ of Manchester (MSc); *m* 10 Dec 1977, Wendy Mary, da of Geoffrey Lock, of Thingwall, Wirral; 2 s (Gehan Richard b 1982, Roshan Edward b 1983); *Career* registrar in neurology Addenbrooke's Hosp Cambridge, conslt neurologist Gen Hosp Kandy Sri Lanka, sr registrar in geriatric med Withington Hosp Manchester, conslt physician Salford Royal Hosps NHS Tst 1980–; gp clinical dir and hon assoc lectr Salford Royal Hosps NHS Tst; pres Salford Branch Nat Parkinson's Disease Soc; currently tstee Parkinsi's Disease Soc; memb Br Geriatric Soc 1980, treas Research into Ageing NW; fndr memb Br Assoc of Continence Care; FRCP (MRCP 1975); *Recreations* snooker, badminton, walking, computing; *Style*— Dr Mahendra Gonsalkorale; ✉ Department of Healthcare for the Elderly, Hope Hospital, Stott Lane, Salford M6 8HD (tel 0161 789 7373, fax 0161 206 4044)

GONTARSKI, Steven; *Educ* Brown Univ USA (BA), Goldsmiths Coll London (MA); *Career* artist; *Solo Exhibitions* Steven Gontarski: The Unbalance of Boredom (Taché-Lévy Gallery Brussels) 2000, White Cube 2000; *Group Exhibitions* American Beauty (Brown Univ RI USA) 1994, Looking Out, Putting Out (450 Broadway Gallery NY) 1995, Imaginary Beings (Exit Art/The First World NY) 1995, Sweat (Exit Art/The First World NY) 1996, Humdrum (The Trade Apartment London) 1997, Cloth Bound (Laure Genillard Gallery London) 1998, Die Young Stay Pretty (ICA London) 1998, Neurotic Realism Part I (Saatchi Gallery London) 1999, Nurse (Johnen & Schöttle Gallery Cologne) 1999, Heart + Soul (60 Long Lane London) 1999, Din (4x4 Gallery Amsterdam) 1999, Drawing Exhbn (Taché-Lévy Gallery Brussels) 2000, Drawings (Sommer Contemporary Art Tel Aviv) 2000, Heart + Soul (Sandroni Rey Venice Calif) 2000, Hard Candy (42 Westbourne Gardens London) 2000, Hardy Candy Berlin (Galerie Wieland Berlin) 2000, Conversation (Milton Keynes Gallery) 2000, A very nice film club (Vilma Gold Gallery London) 2000, Chantal Joffe and Steven Gontarski (One in the Other London) 2001, Mind the Gap (Wetterling Gallery Stockholm) 2001, Freestyle: Werke Aus der Sammlung Boros (Museum Morsbroich Leverkusen) 2001, Jam: Tokyo-London (Barbican Gallery London) 2001, We Set Off in High Spirits (Matthew Marks Gallery NY) 2001, Friends of Mine (Gallery Muu Helsinki) 2001, Jam: Tokyo-London (Tokyo City Opera Gallery) 2002, Electric Dreams (Curve Gallery London) 2002; *Style*— Steven Gontarski, Esq; ✉ White Cube, 48 Hoxton Square, London N1 6BD; Studio (tel 020 7377 5665, fax 020 7377 5665, mobile 07958 372093, e-mail stevengontarski@aol.com)

GOOCH, Charles Albert; s of Ernest Edward Gooch; *b* 15 September 1938; *Educ* Coleman St Ward Sch London; *m* 1974, June Margaret, *née* Reardon; 2 da (Charlotte b 1976, Jessica b 1978); *Career* former chm Shaw & Marvin plc; chm: Buckland Securities Ltd, MacNiven-Cameron plc; dir: Dannimac Ltd, Four Seasons (2000) Ltd, MacNiven & Cameron Developments Ltd, Marland Properties Ltd, Paul Costelloe Collections Ltd, Signature Brands International Ltd; Liveryman Worshipful Co of Stationers and Newspaper Makers; *Style*— Charles Gooch, Esq; ✉ Buckland Securities Ltd, 28 Redchurch Street, London E2 7DP (tel 020 7739 3604, fax 020 7739 1962)

GOOCH, Graham Alan; OBE (1991); s of late Alfred Gooch, and Rose Gooch; *b* 23 July 1953; *Educ* Cannhall Sch Leytonstone, Norlington Jr HS Leytonstone, Redbridge Tech Coll; *m* 23 Oct 1976, Brenda; 3 da (Hannah, Megan, Sally); *Career* professional cricketer; Essex CCC: debut 1973, awarded county cap 1975, capt 1986–87 and 1989–94, benefit 1985, county champions 1979, 1983, 1984, 1986, 1991 and 1992, ret as player 1997, head coach 2002–05; Western Province SA winters 1982–84; England: debut 1975, 118 test matches and one day ints, capt 1988–93, highest score 333 v India Lord's 1990 (third highest test score by Englishman, also scored 123 in second innings to create record test aggregate of 456, only player to score triple century and century in same first class match), ret from Test cricket 1995; capt unofficial England team to SA 1981–82; England selector 1996–, jt mangr England A tour to Kenya and Sri Lanka 1997/98, mangr England tour to Aust 1998/99; tours: Aust 1978/79, Aust and India 1979/80, W Indies 1980/81, India and Sri Lanka 1981/82, Pakistan (incl World Cup) 1987/88, India and W Indies 1989/90, Aust 1990/91, NZ and Aust 1991/92 (incl World Cup), India and Sri Lanka 1992/93, Aust 1994/95; *Books* Out of the Wilderness (autobiography, 1988), Test of Fire (1990); *Recreations* relaxing at home; *Style*— Graham Gooch, Esq, OBE; ✉ c/o ECB, Lords Cricket Ground, London NW8 8QN

GOOCH, Sir Timothy Robert Sherlock; 13 Bt (GB 1746), of Benacre Hall, Suffolk; MBE (1970), DL (1999); s of Col Sir Robert Eric Sherlock Gooch, KCVO, DSO, JP, DL, 11 Bt (d 1978), of Benacre Hall, Suffolk, and Katharine Clervaux (d 1974), da of Maj-Gen Sir Edward Walter Clervaux Chaytor, KCMG, KCVO, CB; suc bro Sir (Richard) John Sherlock Gooch, 12 Bt (d 1999); *b* 7 December 1934; *Educ* Eton, RMA Sandhurst; *m* 17 Dec 1963, Susan Barbara Christie, da of Maj-Gen Kenneth Christie Cooper, CB, DSO, OBE (d 1981), of West End House, Donhead St Andrew, Wilts; 2 da (Lucinda Gooch, MVO b 1970, Victoria (Mrs Edward Vere Nicoll) b 1974); *Heir* cous, Brig Arthur Gooch, DL; *Career* Maj Life Gds; memb HM Body Gd of Hon Corps of Gentlemen at Arms 1986–2003; Standard Bearer 2000–03; co dir; *Clubs* White's, Cavalry and Guards'; *Style*— Sir Timothy Gooch, Bt, MBE, DL; ✉ The Cedars, Covehithe, Wrentham, Beccles, Suffolk NR34 7JW (tel 01502 675266)

GOOD, Anthony Bruton Meyrick; *b* 18 April 1933; *Educ* Felsted; *Children* 2 da; *Career* mgmnt trainee Distillers Group 1950–52, editorial asst Temple Press Ltd 1952–55, PR offr Silver City Airways (PR/marketing Br Aviation Servs Ltd) 1955–60; fndr and chm: Good Relations Gp plc 1961–89, Good Consultancy Ltd 1989–; chm: Cox & Kings Ltd 1975– (dir 1971–), Good Relations (India) Ltd 1988–, Cox & Kings (India) Ltd 1988– (dir 1980–), Flagship Gp Ltd 1999–, Miller Insurance Gp Ltd 2000–04, The Tranquil Moment Ltd 2000–07, Sage Organics Ltd 2000–, Tulip Star Hotels Ltd 2000–, Q-Link Int Ltd 2000–, Relish Events Ltd 2001–, Neutrahealth plc 2004–; dir: IM Gp Ltd 1977–, Arcadian International plc 1995–98, Care First Gp plc 1996–98, Gowrings plc 2004–05, Obento Ltd 2004–, Spank Watches plc 2007–; *Recreations* travel, reading, theatre; *Clubs* RAC; *Style*— Anthony Good, Esq; ✉ Clench House, Wootton Rivers, Marlborough, Wiltshire SN8 4NT (tel 01672 810670, fax 01672 810149); Clench Lodge, Wootton Rivers, Marlborough, Wiltshire SN8 4NT (tel 01672 810126, fax 01672 810869, e-mail tony@abmgood.demon.co.uk)

GOOD, Rev (George) Harold; OBE (1985, MBE 1970); s of Rev Robert James Good (d 1976), and Doris, *née* Allen (d 1979); *b* 27 April 1937, Londonderry, NI; *Educ* Methodist Coll Belfast, Edgehill Theol Coll Belfast, Christian Theol Seminary Indianapolis; *m* 11 Aug 1964, Clodagh Anne, da of Charles Coad, of Waterford; 3 da (Carolyn b 3 July 1965, Sharon b 18 Nov 1967, Denise b 9 May 1972), 2 s (Jonathan b 11 March 1970, Richard b 23 Aug 1972); *Career* ordained minister Methodist Church in Ireland 1962; served circuits: Co Armagh, Dublin, Waterford, Belfast, Co Down; min to youth 1st Methodist Church Warren Ohio, chaplain HMP Crumlin Rd Belfast, pt/t chaplain Belfast City Hospital, supt Belfast S Circuit; pres Methodist Church in Ireland 2001–02; dir Corrymeela Community Centre for Reconciliation 1973–78; NI supplementary benefits cmmr 1974–80, NI memb Social Security Advsy Ctee 1980–98, chair ind review of NI Cncl of Social Service 1982–83, chm Personal Social Services Advsy Ctee DHSS 1984–92, memb New Deal Task Force 1997–99, memb NI Human Rights Cmmn 1999–2004; chm NI Assoc for Care and Resettlement of Offenders 1992–2001, memb Methodist Cncl on Social Responsibility, fndr memb Healing Through Remembering project; chair Advice Services Alliance 2005–; patron: Habitat for Humanity, The Leprosy Mission; govr: Methodist Coll Belfast, Edgehill Theol Coll Belfast, Greenwood House Assessment Centre; formerly: memb Ulster TV Religious Advsy Panel, exec Relate, exec Belfast Abbeyfield Housing for Elderly, tstee and memb exec The Peace People; ind witness to decommissioning of weapons of the IRA 2005; jt recipient René Cassin Peace Award Basque Govt 2005; *Recreations* travel, painting, photography, sea angling; *Style*— The Rev Harold Good, OBE; ✉ 4 Brown's Park, Marino, Holywood, Co Down BT18 0AB (tel 028 9042 1464, e-mail harold.good@irishmethodist.org)

GOOD, Petrina Susan Maria; da of Peter Wilberforce Good, of Newmarket, Suffolk, and Pamela, *née* Davies; *b* 30 December 1966, London; *Educ* Kingston Poly (HND); *Career* Endemol UK plc: joined as freelance prodn mangr 1997, head of prodn 2003– (TV shows incl Big Brother and The Salon); *Recreations* reading, cinema, fine wines; *Style*— Ms Petrina Good; ✉ Endemol UK, Shepherds Studio Central, Charecroft Way, Shepherds Bush, London W14 0EE

GOODALL, Caroline Mary Helen; da of Capt Peter Goodall, CBE, TD (d 1995), of Wetherby, W Yorks, and Sonja Jeanne, *née* Burt; sis of Charles Peter Goodall, *qv*; *b* 22 May 1955; *Educ* Queen Ethelburga's Sch, Newnham Coll Cambridge (MA); *m* 1 Oct 1983, (Vesey) John Hill, s of Maj Vesey Michael Hill (d 1972); *Career* asst slr Slaughter and May 1980–84 (articled clerk 1978–80), ptnr Herbert Smith 1987– (asst slr 1984–87, head Corp Div 2000–05); memb Company Law Ctee Law Soc; memb American Bar Assoc; memb: Worshipful Co of Slrs, Law Soc; assoc fell Newnham Coll Cambridge; MInstD, FRSA; *Recreations* tennis, theatre, sailing, fell walking; *Clubs* Roehampton, Brancaster Staithe Sailing; *Style*— Miss Caroline Goodall; ✉ Herbert Smith, Exchange House, Primrose Street, London EC2A 2HS (tel 020 7374 8000, fax 020 7374 0888, e-mail caroline.goodall@herbertsmith.com)

GOODALL, Charles Peter; s of late Capt Peter Goodall, CBE, TD, and Sonja Jeanne, *née* Burt; bro of Caroline Mary Helen Goodall, *qv*; *b* 14 July 1950; *Educ* Sherborne, St Catharine's Coll Cambridge (MA, LLM); *Career* asst slr Slaughter and May 1976–82 (articled clerk 1974–76), ptnr Simmons & Simmons 1984–2005 (asst slr 1982–84); memb Law Soc; *Recreations* gardening, walking; *Clubs* RAC, Hawks' (Cambridge); *Style*— Charles Goodall, Esq; ✉ Simmons & Simmons, CityPoint, One Ropemaker Street, London EC2Y 9SS (tel 020 7628 2020, fax 020 7628 2070)

GOODALL, Air Marshal Sir Roderick Harvey (Rocky); KBE (2001, CBE 1990), CB (1999), AFC (1981, and Bar 1987); s of Leonard Harvey Goodall (d 2000), of Guernsey, and Muriel Doris, *née* Cooper (d 2002); *b* 19 January 1947; *Educ* Elizabeth Coll Guernsey, RAF Coll Cranwell; *m* 14 April 1973, Elizabeth Susan (Lizzie), *née* Haines; 2 da (Hannah Elizabeth b 22 July 1975, Victoria Grace b 20 April 1977); *Career* cmmnd RAF 1968, flying tours Bahrain, Brawdy, Wildenrath and Gütersloh 1970–80, RAF Staff Coll 1981; subsequent staff appts: Divnl Air Liaison Offr BOAR, Personnel Offr Air Sec's Dept and Operational Requirements MOD; cmd 16 Sqdn RAF Laarbruch 1983 (conversion to Tornado GR1), cmd RAF Brüggen 1987–89, estab and cmd RAF Detachment Bahrain 1990 (in preparation for Gulf War), dir Air Offensive MOD 1991–94, promoted Air Vice Marshal 1994, AOC No 2 Gp Germany 1994–96, COS UK Perm Jt HQ 1996–98, ldr RAF Offr Branch Structure Review Team 1998–99, promoted Air Marshal 1999, COS HQ AIRNORTH 1999–2003, ret 2004; tstee Lloyds TSB Fndn for the Channel Islands 2005; FRAeS; *Recreations* golf, photography; *Clubs* RAF (pres); *Style*— Air Marshal Sir Rocky Goodall, KBE, CB, AFC*, FRAeS; ✉ c/o Lloyds TSB, 2 Northgate, Sleaford, Lincolnshire NG34 7BL

GOODBAND, Philip Haydon; s of Philip Aubrey Goodband, of Camberley, Surrey, and Edith Emma Haydon, *née* Cooper; *b* 26 May 1944; *Educ* Strode's Sch, Dijon France, Academie Du Champagne; *m* 1; 1 da (Emily Victoria b 19 Sept 1973), 2 s (Charles Lindsey Haydon b 19 June 1976 d 1976, Henry Lindsey Charles b 24 Oct 1978); m 2, 2 Oct 2004, Ann Marie, da of Frederick Deluca, of Stockton CA; *Career* MW; Vintners scholar 1970; dir: Gilbey SA France 1972–73, Stowells of Chelsea 1981–86 (buyer 1973–80); Grants of St James's: wine buying, quality and logistics 1986–88, md Wine Div on Trade 1988–92, business devpt dir 1992–94; prop Goodband Wine Services and Consultancy 1994–; chm

G

Inst of Masters of Wine 1984–85, dir Wine Devpt Bd 1980–92, dir Wine Standards Bd UK 1999–2007; chair of judges Int Wine and Spirit Competition 2002–; tstee Wine and Spirit Trade Benevolent Soc 1986–89; lectr and broadcaster in London, Paris, Milan and San Francisco; Freeman: City of London 1972, Worshipful Co of Haberdashers 1972 (Clothed 1975); FBBI 1968; Compagnon du Beaujolais 1978, membre de L'Ordre St Etienne France 1981, Cavaleiro da Confraria do Vinho do Porto Portugal 1987, Chevalier des Coteaux de Champagne 1989, Commndeur and Conseiller d'Honneur to the Grand Conseil de Bordeaux 1996–; *Recreations* competition carriage driving, travel, tennis, theatre, food and wine; *Style—* Philip Goodband, Esq; ✉ Goodband Wine Services and Consultancy, 21 West Bank, Dorking, Surrey RH4 3DQ (tel 01306 740655, mobile 07973 119891, e-mail phg@goodband-wineservices.co.uk, www.goodband-wineservices.co.uk)

GOODBODY, Michael Ivan Andrew; s of Llewellyn Marcus Goodbody (d 1989, see Burkes Irish Family Records), of Ardclough Lodge, Straffan, Co Kildare, and Eileen Elizabeth, *née* Bourke; *b* 23 January 1942; *Educ* Kingstown Sch Dublin; *m* 9 March 1968, Susannah Elizabeth, da of Donald Guy Pearce (Capt Ayrshire Yeomanry RA, ka 1944); 2 da (Sarah b 1970, Perry b 1976), 1 s (Guy b 1972); *Career* Lt TA, 289 Parachute Battery RHA; stockbroker Smith Rice & Hill 1962–74, private client stockbroker Capel-Cure Myers 1974–88, dir: Capel-Cure Myers Capital Management Ltd 1988–98, Capel-Cure Sharp 1998–2000, Carr Sheppards Crosthwaite 2001–06; hon treas Colne Stour Countryside Assoc; MSI; *Books* The Goodbody Family of Ireland (1979); *Recreations* family history, genealogy, countryside conservation; *Style—* Michael Goodbody, Esq; ✉ The Old Rectory, Wickham St Paul's, Halstead, Essex CO9 2PJ

GOODBURN, Andrew Robert; s of Robert Goodburn, and Peggy, *née* Barrett; *b* 5 January 1947; *Educ* Harrow HS, Monkton House Sch; *m* 28 June 1969, Elizabeth Ann, da of Joseph Henry Dunn; 3 s (Giles Andrew b 11 Nov 1972, Henry Robert b 18 April 1974, Benjamin Joseph b 24 June 1978), 1 da (Anne-Marie b 19 May 1980); *Career* Peat Marwick Mitchell & Co 1964–70 (articled clerk, audit sr); Bowthorpe Holdings plc 1970–81: gen mangr Hellermann Cassettes (fin controller), fin dir Hellermann Deutsch, commercial dir Bowthorpe EMP, mktg dir Hellermann Electric; ptnr Grant Thornton 1987–91 (joined as sr mgmnt conslt 1982), head of fin consultancy Price Waterhouse (Redhill Office) 1991–93, commercial dir Ricardo Hitec 1993–94, fin dir Ricardo Aerospace 1994, fin dir Ricardo Consulting 1995–97, gp fin dir Ricardo Gp plc 1997–2007; non-exec dir Caffyns plc 2004–; FCA (ACA 1969); *Recreations* tennis, golf, travel, gardening; *Clubs* Haywards Heath Golf, Haywards Heath RFC, Royal Ashdown Forest Golf; *Style—* Andrew Goodburn, Esq; ✉ Deacons Hay, Beaconsfield Road, Chelwood Gate, East Sussex RH17 7LG (tel 01825 740225); Ricardo plc, Bridge Works, Shoreham-by-Sea, West Sussex BN43 5FG (tel 01273 455611, fax 01273 464124)

GOODCHILD, Peter Robert Edward; s of Douglas Richard Geoffrey Goodchild, MBE (d 1989), of Angmering Village, W Sussex, and Lottie May, *née* Ager (d 2000); *b* 18 August 1939; *Educ* Aldenham, St John's Coll Oxford (MA); *m* 1968, Penelope-Jane, da of Dr William Pointon-Dick (d 1956); 2 da (Abigail b 1971, Hannah b 1974); *Career* prodr Horizon BBC TV 1965–69 (winner Soc of Film and TV Arts Mullard Award for Science Broadcasting 1967, 1968 and 1969), ed Horizon BBC TV 1969–76 (winner BAFTA Award for Best Factual Series 1972 and 1974, winner Italia Prize for Factual Programmes 1973 and 1975), exec prodr drama prodns 1977–80 (including Marie Curie 1977 and Oppenheimer 1980 which both won BAFTA Awards for Best Series), prodr Bread or Blood 1980, head of science and features BBC TV 1980–84 (initiating programme QED), head of plays BBC TV 1984–89 (initiating Screen Two, Screen One and Screenplay), exec prodr and prodr Film Dept BBC 1989–94; prodr: The March 1990 (winner One World TV Premier Network award), Adam Bede 1991, Trust Me 1992, Return to Blood River 1994, Black Easter 1994 (winner Gold Award Chicago Film Festival 1996), King of Chaos 1998 (BAFTA nominee 1998); dir: Stone City Films 1995–98, Green Umbrella Features 1998–2004; pres Dunchideock Treacle Miners 2000–, vice-pres Exeter Rowing Club 2002–; CChem, FRSC; *Books* Shatterer of Worlds (the life of J Robert Oppenheimer, 1980), The Real Dr Strangelove (the life of Edward Teller, 2004); *Radio Plays* incl: The Chicago Conspiracy Trial 1993 (NY Radio Festival Gold Award 1995), Nuremberg 1996, In the Name of Security 1998, Lockerbie on Trial 2001; *Stage Plays* The Real Dr Strangelove 2006, The Great Monkey Trial (US tour) 2006; *Recreations* rowing, music, gardening; *Clubs* Groucho; *Style—* Peter Goodchild, Esq; ✉ Dunchideock House, Dunchideock, Exeter EX2 9TS (tel 01392 833535)

GOODCHILD, Tim; *Educ* Guildford Coll of Art, Wimbledon Coll of Art (Arts Cncl scholar); *Career* designer; designed costumes for opening ceremony The 2002 Commonwealth Games Manchester; *Theatre* over 70 West End prodns incl: Hadrian VII 1969, Richard II 1969, Cowardy Custard 1972, Gone with the Wind (Theatre Royal) 1972, Show Boat (Adelphi Theatre), Hans Andersen (Palladium Theatre), Pump Boys and Dinettes 1983, Bus Stop 1990, Pirandello's Henry IV 1990, Our Song 1992, Chapter Two 1996, Quartet 1999; over 20 prodns for The New Shakespeare Co incl: My Fair Lady 1979, Oklahoma (also Aust) 1980, Little Shop of Horrors 1983, Blondel 1983, Café Puccini 1986, Five Guys Named Moe (also Broadway and Aust) 1990, Hey Mr Producer 1998; for RSC prodns incl: The Taming of the Shrew 1993/94, The Relapse 1995, Zenobia 1995, Three Hours After Marriage 1996, The Merry Wives of Windsor 1996; for Chichester Festival Theatre: School for Scandal, Love for Love, Blithe Spirit, R Love J, The Royal Baccarat Scandal; other prodns incl: Antony and Cleopatra (Egyptian Nat Theatre) 1978, Cyrano de Bergerac (Stratford Ontario Festival Theatre), The Corsican Brothers (Abbey Theatre Dublin), Peter Pan (McLab Theatre Canada), Gigi (Volksoper Vienna) 1999, Lettice and Lovage (UK tour), Falstaff (Chartelet Theatre Paris), Noel Coward's Star Quality (world premiere, UK tour and West End), Taboo (Boy George musical London and Broadway), We Will Rock You (Queen tribute musical Dominion Theatre, Las Vegas, Germany, Russia, Australia, Tokyo, South Africa, Spain); *Opera* Sadler Wells Opera Co: The Mikado 1983, HMS Pinafore (also City Center NY) 1983, Gondoliers 1984; other prodns incl: La Traviata (WNO), The Mikado (Australian Opera Co), The Tales of Hoffman (Victoria State Opera Co), Mephistopheles (ENO) 1999, La Bohème (Kirov Opera), The Tales of Hoffman (Huston Grand Opera), Salome (NYC Opera), Le nozze di Figaro (LA Opera Co), La Vie Parisienne (ENO), La Traviata (Royal Danish Opera, WNO), Falstaff (Chatelet Theatre Paris), Roméo et Juliette (LA Opera), Sir John in Love (ENO), 2006, Don Carlo (LA Opera) 2006, Die Meistersinger von Nürnberg (LA Opera) 2006–07; *Ballet* numerous prodns incl: Swan Lake (Moscow National Ballet, Moscow, UK, world tour) 1988, The Look of Love (BBC2), A Simple Man (BBC2, BAFTA Award), The Fool on The Hill (Aust State Ballet and TV film), Don Quixote (Northern Ballet Theatre); *Awards* Green Room Award Best Operatic Design (for The Tales of Hoffman, Aust), Olivier Award for Best Costume Design (for The Relapse) 1997, Olivier Awards for Best Costume Design and Best Set Design (for Three Hours After Marriage) 1998; nominations incl: The Theatre LA Ovations Award for Best Set (for Five Guys Named Moe), Sammy Award (for The Fool on the Hill); *Style—* Tim Goodchild, Esq; ✉ c/o Simpson Fox Associates Ltd, 52 Shaftesbury Avenue, London W1V 7DE (tel 020 7434 9167, fax 020 7494 2887)

GOODE, Prof Anthony William; s of late William Henry Goode, of Tynemouth, and Eileen Veronica, *née* Brannan; *b* 3 August 1944; *Educ* Corby Sch, Univ of Newcastle upon Tyne Med Sch (MB BS, MD); *m* Dr Patricia Josephine, da of late Michael and Mary Flynn; *Career* surgical appts Newcastle upon Tyne teaching hosps and demonstrator anatomy Univ of Newcastle upon Tyne 1968–74, various appts Univ of London teaching hosps 1975–; clinical dir Helicopter Emergency Medical Service Royal London Hosp 1997–99; currently: prof of endocrine and metabolic surgery Univ of London, hon conslt surgn Royal London Hosp and Bart's, hon prof Dept for Biological and Med Systems Imperial Coll London, ed-in-chief Med Science and the Law; res programmes related to: nutrition, metabolism, endocrinology in surgery, role of microgravity res in future med and surgical devpt; pres Br Acad of Forensic Sciences; hon sec and treas Br Assoc Endocrine Surgns 1982–97 (fndr memb 1980); tstee Smith & Nephew Fndn 1990–; hon memb The Hunterian Soc (orator 1999); Freeman City of London 1994, Liveryman Worshipful Soc of Apothecaries 1997; memb: RSM 1972, Int Soc Surgery 1985, New York Acad Sciences 1987; fell American Coll of Surgeons 2000, FRCS 1972; *Books* contrib numerous surgical textbooks; ed-in-chief Medicine Science and the Law; *Recreations* music (especially opera), cricket, literature; *Clubs* Athenaeum, MCC, Cross Arrows CC; *Style—* Prof Anthony Goode; ✉ The Surgical Unit, The Royal London Hospital, Whitechapel, London E1 1BB (tel 020 7377 7000)

GOODE, Prof Sir Royston Miles (Roy); kt (2000), CBE (1994, OBE 1972), QC (1990); s of Samuel Goode (d 1968), of Portsmouth, Hants, and Blooma, *née* Zeid (d 1984); *b* 6 April 1933; *Educ* Highgate Sch, Univ of London (LLB, LLD); *m* 18 Oct 1964, Catherine Anne, da of Jean Marcel Rueff, and Marianne Rueff; 1 da (Naomi b 1965); *Career* Nat Serv RASC 1955–57; admitted slr 1955, ptnr Victor Mishcon & Co 1963–71 (conslt 1971–88); QMC London: prof of law 1971–73, Crowther prof of credit and commercial law 1973–89, dean Faculty of Law and head dept 1976–80; hon pres Centre Commercial Law Studies 1989– (fndr and dir 1979–89), Norton Rose prof of English law Univ of Oxford 1990–1998 (emeritus prof 1998–), fell St John's Coll Oxford 1990–98 (emeritus fell 1998–); pres Cncl Int Postgrad Law Sch Belgrade 2002–04; transferred to the Bar Inner Temple 1988 (hon bencher); chm Pension Law Review Ctee 1992–93; UK rep and memb Governing Cncl UNIDROIT Rome 1989–2003; memb Cncl Br Acad 2007–; Freeman City of London; hon fell Queen Mary & Westfield Coll London 1991; Hon DSc (Econ) Univ of London 1996, Hon LLD UEA 2003; FBA 1988, FRSA 1990; *Books* Hire-Purchase Law and Practice (2 edn 1970), Commercial Law (3 edn 2004), Proprietary Rights and Insolvency in Sales Transactions (2 edn 1989), Legal Problems of Credit and Security (3 edn 2003), Principles of Corporate Insolvency Law (3 edn 2005); *Recreations* chess, walking, browsing in bookshops; *Clubs* Reform; *Style—* Prof Sir Roy Goode, CBE, QC, FBA; ✉ 42 St John Street, Oxford OX1 2LH (tel 01865 515494, e-mail roy.goode@sjc.ox.ac.uk)

GOODENOUGH, Alan; *b* 7 December 1943; *Career* unit gen mangr Excel Bowling 1964–66, gen mangr and regnl dir Bingo and Social Clubs Rank Organisation plc 1966–71, main bd dir Pleasurama plc 1972–88, md Casinos, Hotels and Holiday Businesses and main bd dir Mecca Leisure Group plc 1988–90, fndr and chm Lyric Hotels 1990–, non-exec chm Time Line (bus and coach operator) 1990–, chief exec London Clubs International plc 1993– (brought co to UK stock market 1994); MInstD 1990; *Style—* Alan Goodenough, Esq; ✉ London Clubs International plc, 10 Brick Street, London W1Y 8HQ (tel 020 7518 0000, fax 020 7518 0174)

GOODENOUGH, Frederick Roger; DL (Oxon 1989); 3 s of Sir William Macnamara Goodenough, 1 Bt (d 1951), and Dorothea Louisa (d 1987), da of Ven the Hon Kenneth Gibbs, DD, 5 s of 1 Baron Aldenham; *b* 21 December 1927; *Educ* Eton, Magdalene Coll Cambridge (MA), Univ of Oxford (MA); *m* 15 May 1954, Marguerite June, o da of David Forbes Mackintosh, sometime headmaster of Loretto; 1 s (David b 1955), 2 da (Annabel b 1957, Victoria b 1961); *Career* RN 1946–48; joined Barclays Bank Ltd 1950; local dir Barclays Bank Ltd: Birmingham 1958–60, Reading 1960–69, Oxford 1969–87; dir: Barclays Bank UK Ltd 1971–87, Barclays International Ltd 1977–87, Barclays Bank plc 1979–89, Barclays plc 1985–89; advsy dir Barclays Bank Thames Valley Region 1988–89; memb London Ctee: Barclays Bank DCO 1966–71, Barclays Bank International Ltd 1971–80; sr ptnr Broadwell Manor Farm 1968–; curator Oxford Univ Chest 1974–93; pres Oxfordshire Rural Community Cncl 1993–98; tstee: Nuffield Med Benefaction 1968–2002 (chm 1987–2002), Nuffield Dominions Tst 1968–2002 (chm 1987–2002), Nuffield Oxford Hosps Tst 1968–2003 (chm 1982–88), Nuffield Orthopaedic Centre Tst 1978–2003 (chm 1981–2003), Oxford Preservation Tst 1980–89, Radcliffe Med Fndn 1987–98; govr: Shiplake Coll 1963–74 (chm 1966–70), Wellington Coll 1968–74, London House for Overseas Graduates (now Goodenough Coll) 1985–2006; patron Anglo-Ghanaian Society 1991–; hon fell Wolfson Coll Oxford 1995 (supernumerary fell 1989–95); High Sheriff Oxon 1987–88; FLS (memb Cncl 1968–75, treas 1970–75), FRSA, FCIB; *Recreations* shooting, fishing, photography, ornithology; *Clubs* Brooks's; *Style—* F R Goodenough, Esq, DL; ✉ Broadwell Manor, Lechlade, Gloucestershire GL7 3QS (tel 01367 860326, office tel 07836 211125, fax 01367 860046)

GOODENOUGH, Sir William McLernon; 3 Bt (UK 1943), of Broadwell and Filkins, Co Oxford; s of Sir Richard Edmund Goodenough, 2 Bt (d 1996); *b* 5 August 1954; *Educ* Stanbridge Earls; *m* 12 June 1982 (m dis), Louise Elizabeth, da of Capt Michael Ortmans, LVO, RN, of Fulham, London; 2 da (Sophie Julia b 1986, Celia Isobel b 1989), 1 s (Samuel William Hector b 11 June 1992); m 2, 10 May 2002, Delia Mary Curzon-Price; *Heir* s, Samuel Goodenough; *Career* design conslt; currently exec chm Design Bridge; Keeper of the Quaich 1998; *Recreations* shooting, fishing, stalking; *Clubs* Boodle'; *Style—* Sir William Goodenough, Bt

GOODEVE, (John) Anthony; s of Cdr Sir Charles Frederick Goodeve, OBE (d 1980), of London, and Janet Irene, *née* Wallace (d 1993); *b* 4 August 1944; *Educ* Canford Sch; *m* 30 March 2007, Elaine Day, >i<ne>ac<e>r< Langston;1 da (Claire Michelle b 29 May 1982); *Career* RNR 1963–66; Shell Mex and BP Ltd 1964–78 (latterly with Shell UK Oil), md Dupré Vermiculite Ltd 1978–79, gp mktg exec Wood Hall Building Group Ltd 1979–80, chief exec and md Grosvenor Property & Finance Ltd 1980–, md Grosvenor Investment Planning Ltd 1997–; Freeman City of London 1969, Liveryman Worshipful Co of Salters 1969 (Renter 1996, memb Ct of Assts 1998, Master 2004–05); FInstD; *Recreations* politics, boating, skiing, photography, swimming; *Clubs* IOD; *Style—* Anthony Goodeve, Esq; ✉ Highfields House, 4 Prospect Lane, West Common, Harpenden, Hertfordshire AL5 2PL

GOODEY, Felicity Margaret Sue; CBE (2001), DL (Gtr Manchester 1998); da of Henry E A Goodey (d 2001), and Susan, *née* Fong (d 2002); *b* 25 July 1949, Plymouth, Devon; *Educ* St Austell GS, St Hugh's Coll Oxford (BA); *m* 31 Aug 1973, John R Marsh; 2 s (Alexander James b 28 Oct 1980, Christopher Henry b 8 March 1985); *Career* trainee journalist rising to sr corr BBC 1971–85, self-employed with BBC contracts (presenter Radio 4 and BBC NW) and presenter and ind prodr TV documentaries 1985–99, owner and mangr Felicity Goodey & Associates 1990–98, dir Precise Communications 1998–2001; chair: Lowry Operational Co 1994–2003, Lowry Devpt Co 1994–2003, Lowry Tst 1994–2004; hon life pres The Lowry 2004–; interim chief exec mediacity:uk 2005–07; non-exec dir: Nord Anglia plc 1999–, Unique Communications Gp 2001–; chair: Cultural Consortium NW 1999–2004, NW Tourism 2003–, Central Salford Urban Regeneration Co 2004–; non-exec dir: Excellence Northwest 1993–2004, Sustainability NW 1994–98, NW Devpt Agency 1998–2002, Manchester Cwlth Games Ltd 1997–2002, Manchester C of C and Industry 1999–; memb Cncl AHRC 2003–; hon vice-pres NW Riding for the Disabled 1978–, tstee Friends of Rosie 1992–, memb Bd Going for Green 1994–98, govr Manchester GS 1994–, chair Paterson Cncl (Christie Hosp) 1996–98, chair Macmillan Day Care Hospice 1997–99, chair Smart project for First Step Tst 2005–, chair Creative Industries in Salford 2006–; Goldstone Award, Blue Circle Award; Hon LLD Univ of Manchester, Hon DLitt Manchester Met Univ, Hon DLitt Univ of Salford; hon fell: Bolton Inst, Univ of Central Lancs; Hon FRIBA 2004, FRSA 2006; *Recreations* family, theatre, opera; *Style—* Ms

Felicity Goodey, CBE, DL; ✉ Central Salford Urban Regeneration Company, Digital World Centre, No 1 Lowry Plaza, Salford Quays M50 3UB (tel 0161 601 7739, fax 0161 601 7731, e-mail felicitygoodey@centralsalford.com)

GOODFELLOW, John Graham; *b* 10 January 1947; *Educ* Allan Glen's Sch Glasgow; *Career* cashier rising to asst mangr programming Burnley Building Soc Glasgow 1964–82, asst gen mangr i/c IT National & Provincial Building Soc 1983–84; Skipton Building Society: asst gen mangr then gen mangr i/c IT and admin 1984–91, chief exec and dir 1991–; chm Business Link North Yorkshire, dir N Yorks TEC; MIDPM, FRSA; *Style*— John Goodfellow, Esq; ✉ Skipton Building Society, The Bailey, Skipton, North Yorkshire BD23 1DN (tel 01756 705000, fax 01756 705703)

GOODHARDT, Prof Gerald Joseph; s of George Goodhardt (d 1978), of London, and Miriam, *née* Simmons (d 1978); *b* 5 April 1930; *Educ* Downing Coll Cambridge (MA, DipMathStat); *m* 27 Jan 1957, Valerie Yvonne, da of Walter Goldsmith (d 1968), of Hove, E Sussex; 1 da (Catherine b 1958), 1 s (Ian b 1961); *Career* res dir Young & Rubicam Ltd 1958–65, dir Aske Research Ltd 1965–75, reader in mktg Thames Poly 1975–81; City Univ Business Sch: Sir John E Cohen prof of consumer studies 1981–95 (emeritus prof 1995–), dean 1991–92; visiting prof Kingston Univ 1996–, research conslt S Bank Univ 1996–, adjunct prof Univ of S Australia Adelaide 2000–; chm Market Res Soc 1973–74, hon sec Royal Statistical Soc 1982–88; regnl cncllr N Thames Gas Consumers Cncl 1986–95; FSS 1954, FCIM 1983, FMRS 1997 (MMRS 1958); *Books* The Television Audience (1975 and 1987); *Recreations* grandchildren; *Style*— Prof Gerald Goodhardt; ✉ 71 Eyre Court, London NW8 9TX (tel 020 77220887, e-mail gerald@goodhardt.com)

GOODHART, Prof Charles Albert Eric; CBE (1997); s of Prof Arthur Lehman Goodhart, KBE (d 1978), sometime master UC Oxford, of NY, and Cecily Agnes Mackay, *née* Carter (d 1985); *b* 23 October 1936; *Educ* Eton, Trinity Coll Cambridge (BA, Adam Smith prize), Harvard Univ (PhD); *m* 2 July 1960, Margaret Ann (Miffy), da of Prof Sir Eric Smith, KBE (d 1990), of Plymouth; 3 da (Lucy b 1963, Alice b 1968, Sophie b 1970), 1 s (William b 1965); *Career* prize fell Trinity Coll Cambridge and asst lectr Univ of Cambridge 1963–65, economic advsr Dept of Econ Affrs 1965–66, lectr LSE 1966–68, advsr on domestic monetary policy then chief econ advsr Bank of England 1968–85; Norman Sosnow prof of banking and fin LSE 1985–2002; non-exec dir Gerrard Group plc 1987–96; memb: Exchange Fund Advsy Ctee Hong Kong 1988–97, Monetary Policy Ctee Bank of England 1997–2000; advsr on financial stability to the govr Bank of England 2002–04; FBA 1990; *Books* The New York Money Market and the Finance of Trade 1900–1913 (1969), The Business of Banking 1891–1914 (1972), Money Information and Uncertainty (1973, 2 edn 1989), Monetary Theory and Practice (1984), The Evolution of Central Banks (1988), The Central Bank and the Financial System (1995); *Recreations* sheep, walking; *Style*— Prof Charles Goodhart, CBE, FBA; ✉ 27 Abbotsbury Road, London W14 8EL (tel 020 7603 5817, fax 020 7371 3664); Halford Manor, South Tawton, Okehampton, Devon EX20 2LZ (tel 01837 840354); London School of Economics and Political Science, Houghton Street, London WC2A 2AE (tel 020 7955 7555, fax 020 7242 1006)

GOODHART, Sir Robert Anthony Gordon; 4 Bt (UK 1911), of Portland Place, St Marylebone, and Holtye, Sussex; s of Sir John Gordon Goodhart, 3 Bt, FRCGP (d 1979), and (Margaret Mary) Eileen, *née* Morgan; *b* 15 December 1948; *Educ* Rugby, Univ of London, Guy's Hosp Med Sch (MB BS); *m* 1972, Kathleen Ellen, eldest da of Rev Alexander Duncan MacRae (d 1979), of Inverness; 2 s (Martin Andrew b 1974, Iain Michael b 1980), 2 da (Kim Elaine b 1977, Rachel Alice b 1987); *Heir* s, Martin Goodhart; *Career* medical practitioner 1976–; MRCGP; *Recreations* sailing, real tennis; *Style*— Sir Robert Goodhart, Bt

GOODHART, Baron (Life Peer UK 1997), of Youlbury in the County of Oxfordshire; Sir William Howard Goodhart; kt (1989), QC (1979); 2 s of Prof Arthur Lehman Goodhart, KBE (hon), QC (d 1978), and Cecily, *née* Carter; *b* 18 January 1933; *Educ* Eton, Trinity Coll Cambridge, Harvard Law Sch; *m* 21 May 1966, Hon Celia Herbert, da of 2 Baron Hemingford (d 1982); 1 s, 2 da; *Career* Nat Serv 1951–53; called to the Bar Lincoln's Inn 1957 (bencher 1986); chm Exec Ctee Justice (Br Section Int Cmmn of Jurists) 1988–94 (vice-chm 1978–88); memb: Cncl of Legal Educn 1986–92, Conveyancing Standing Ctee Law Cmmn 1987–89, Int Cmmn of Jurists 1993– (memb Exec Ctee 1995–2002, vice-pres 2002–06), Ctee on Standards in Public Life 1997–2003, Select Ctee on Delegated Powers 1998–2002, Select Ctee on the EU 1998–2001 and 2005–06, Jt Ctee on Reform of the House of Lords 2002–03; contested Kensington: SDP 1983, SDP/Alliance 1987, Lib Dem 1988; Parly candidate (Lib Dem) Oxford W and Abingdon 1992; chm: SDP Cncl Arrangements Ctee 1982–88, Lib Dem Conf Ctee 1988–91, Lib Dem Lawyers' Assoc 1988–91; memb Lib Dem Policy Ctee 1988–97; tstee Campden Charities 1975–90, chm Univ of Cambridge Ct of Discipline 1992–2001; *Style*— The Lord Goodhart, QC; ✉ House of Lords, London SW1A 0PW

GOODHEW, Prof Peter John; s of Philip Arthur Goodhew (d 1979), and Sheila Mary Goodhew; *b* 3 July 1943; *Educ* Kings Coll Sch, Univ of Birmingham (BSc, PhD, DSc); *m* 27 July 1968, Gwendoline Diane, da of Frederick Fletcher; 1 s (Robert b 1972), 1 da (Laura b 1974); *Career* prof: Univ of Surrey 1986–89 (lectr 1968, reader 1982), Dept of Engrg Univ of Liverpool 1990– (dean of engrg 1995–98, pro-vice-chllr 1998–2001, head of dept 2002–04); CEng 1978, FIM 1983, CPhys 1985, FInstP 1990, FREng 2002; *Books* Specimen Preparation in Materials Science (1972), The Operation of The Transmission Electron Microscope (1984), Specimen Preparation for TEM of Materials (1984), Thin Foil Preparation for Electron Microscopy (1985), Electron Microscopy and Analysis (1975, 3 edn 2001), Light Element Analysis in the TEM (1988), Introduction to Scanning Transmission Electron Microscopy (1998); *Recreations* wood turning, reading; *Style*— Prof Peter Goodhew; ✉ Department of Engineering, University of Liverpool, Liverpool L69 3GH (tel 0151 794 4665, e-mail goodhew@liv.ac.uk)

GOODIER, Roger Banks; s of Benjamin Bancroft Goodier (d 1967), and Ada Irene Goodier (d 1986); *b* 7 September 1944; *Educ* Moseley Hall GS Cheadle, Univ of Sheffield (LLB); *m* 20 July 1974, Denise, da of Eric and Ida Forshaw; 2 s (Benjamin b 1975, Oliver b 1978); *Career* admitted slr 1970, sr ptnr Rowley Ashworth slrs 1986–98, dep dist chm Appeals Serv 1998–2002, adjudicator Criminal Injuries Compensation Appeals Panel 2000– (chm 2002–); *Recreations* soccer, rugby, cricket, golf; *Clubs* Western (Glasgow); *Style*— Roger Goodier, Esq; ✉ CICAP, 11th Floor, Cardinal Tower, 12 Farringdon Road, London EC1M 3HS (tel 020 7549 4667)

GOODIN, His Hon Judge David Nigel; s of Nigel Robin Fyson Goodin (d 1998), and Diana, *née* Luard; *b* 31 March 1953, Cheltenham, Glos; *Educ* King's Sch Ely, Coll of Law; *m* 1993 (m dis 2003); 2 s (Mark David b 8 Dec 1994, George Luard Fyson b 6 Feb 1998); *Career* slr in private practice Suffolk 1980–2003, recorder 2000–03 (asst recorder 1996–2000), circuit judge 2003–; *Recreations* family and friends; *Style*— His Hon Judge Goodin; ✉ The Crown Court, 1 Russell Road, Ipswich, Suffolk IP1 2AG (tel 01473 228500)

GOODING, Christopher Anderson; s of late Frank L Gooding, and Maureen Gooding; *b* 27 May 1957; *Educ* St Lawrence Coll Ramsgate, Brünel Univ (LLB); *m* Natasha Miriam, da of Jafr Khajeh, of Woking; *Career* admitted slr 1981; ptnr: Clyde & Co 1985–96 (joined 1981), LeBoeuf Lamb Greene & MacRae 1996–99, Howard Kennedy 1999–; *Recreations* sailing; *Style*— Christopher Gooding, Esq; ✉ tel 020 7546 8928, fax 020 7664 4528, e-mail c.gooding@howardkennedy.com

GOODING, Mel; s of Frederick Gooding (d 1990), and Kathleen, *née* Cox; *b* 3 June 1941; *Educ* Northgate GS for Boys Ipswich, Univ of Sussex (BA, MA); *m* 1967, Esther Rhiannon Coslette, da of Ceri Richards; 2 s (Francis b 1974, Thomas b 1979); *Career* lectr in English, pedagogics and communication various London colls 1966– (notably Sidney Webb Coll of Educn 1972–80 and City of London Poly 1980–94), sr res fell Edinburgh Sch of Art 1998–2005, visiting prof Wimbledon Sch of Art 2006; contrib numerous articles to art press since 1980 incl: Arts Review, Artscribe, Flash Art, Art Monthly; contrib numerous introductions and essays to exhibition catalogues 1979–; curator of exhibitions incl: Ceri Richards (with Bryan Robertson, Tate Gallery) 1981, Ceri Richards Graphics (Nat Gallery of Wales and tour) 1979–80, Poetry into Art (UEA and Nat Library of Wales) 1982, F E McWilliam (Tate Gallery) 1989, Michael Rothenstein Retrospective (Stoke-on-Trent City Art Gallery and tour); author and publisher (with Bruce McLean) of seven artists' books 1985–90; memb Int Assoc of Art Critics; *Publications* incl: Ceri Richards Graphics (1979), F E McWilliam (1989), Michael Rothenstein The Retrospective (1989), The Phenomenon of Presence Frank Auerbach (1989), The Experience of Painting (1989), Malevich A Box (with Julian Rothenstein, 1990), Bruce McLean (1990), John Hoyland (1990), William Alsop Architect (1992), Michael Rothenstein's Boxes (1992), Patrick Heron (1994), Mary Fedden (1995), Plecnik's National and University Library of Slovenia (1997). Terry Frost: Art and Images (2000), Promenade (2001), Movements in Modern Art - Abstract Art (2001), Gillian Ayres (2001), Ceri Richards (2003), Song of the Earth (2003), John Hoyland (2006), Herman de Vries (2006), AZZ (2006); *Recreations* walking, bird watching; *Style*— Mel Gooding, Esq; ✉ 62 Castelnau, Barnes, London SW13 9EX (tel 020 8748 4434)

GOODING, Valerie Frances (Val); CBE (2002); da of Frank Gooding (d 1979), and Gladys, *née* Williamson; *b* 14 May 1950; *Educ* Leiston GS, Univ of Warwick; *m* 1986, Crawford Macdonald; 2 s (Alexander b 6 July 1987, Nicholas b 12 Aug 1989); *Career* British Airways plc: dir business units 1993–96, dir Asia Pacific 1996; BUPA: md UK 1996–98, chief exec 1998–; non-exec dir: Standard Chartered plc 2005–, J Sainsbury plc 2007–; memb: Advsy Bd Warwick Business Sch, Cncl Univ of Warwick; non-exec dir LTA; tstee Br Museum; Hon Dr Bournemouth Univ 1999; MInstD 1993, CIMgt 1998, FRSA 1998; *Recreations* tennis, theatre, travel, keeping fit, family life; *Style*— Miss Val Gooding, CBE; ✉ BUPA, 15–19 Bloomsbury Way, London WC1A 2BA (tel 020 7656 2000, e-mail goodingv@bupa.com)

G

GOODISON, Sir Nicholas Proctor; kt (1982); yr s of Edmund Harold Goodison, of Radlett, Herts, and Eileen Mary Carrington, *née* Proctor; *b* 16 May 1934; *Educ* Marlborough, King's Coll Cambridge (MA, PhD); *m* 18 June 1960, Judith Nicola, o da of Capt Robert Eustace Abel Smith (ka 1940), Grenadier Gds; 1 s, 2 da; *Career* H E Goodison & Co (later Quilter Goodison & Co, now Morgan Stanley Quilter & Co Ltd): joined 1958, ptnr 1962, chm 1975–88; chm TSB Group plc 1989–95, dep chm Lloyds TSB Group plc (following merger) 1995–2000; dir: General Accident plc 1987–95, Corus plc (formerly British Steel plc) 1989–2002 (dep chm 1993–99); chm Stock Exchange 1976–88 (memb Cncl 1968–88); pres: Int Fedn of Stock Exchanges 1985–86, Br Bankers' Assoc 1991–96, Heads, Teachers & Industry 1999–2002; vice-chm ENO 1980–98 (dir 1977–98); chm: Courtauld Inst of Art 1982–2002, Nat Art Collections Fund 1986–2002 (memb Ctee 1976–2002), Crafts Cncl 1997–2005, Retirement Income Reform Campaign 2001–, Burlington Magazine Ltd 2002–, Burlington Magazine Fndn 2002–, National Life Story Collection 2003– (tstee 2003–); tstee: Nat Heritage Meml Fund 1988–97, Harewood House Tst 1989–, Kathleen Ferrier Meml Fund; pres Furniture History Soc 1990–, hon keeper of furniture Fitzwilliam Museum Cambridge; memb: Cncl Industrial Soc 1976–2000, Royal Cmmn on Long-Term Care for the Elderly 1997–99, Further Educn Funding Cncl 1999–2001, Advsy Bd Judge Inst of Mgmnt Univ of Cambridge 1999–2002; ldr and author Goodison Review HM Treasy 2003 (report Securing the Best for our Museums: Private Giving and Government Support published 2004); govr Marlborough Coll 1981–97; Liveryman: Worshipful Co of Goldsmiths, Worshipful Co of Clockmakers; Hon DLitt: City Univ 1985, Univ of London; Hon LLD Univ of Exeter 1989, Hon DSc Aston Univ 1994, Hon DArt De Montfort Univ 1998, Hon DCL Univ of Northumbria 1999; hon fell King's Coll Cambridge, hon fell Courtauld Inst of Art; hon fell Royal Acad, sr fell RCA 1991, Hon FRIBA 1992; CIMgt, FCIB 1989 (vice-pres 1989), FBA, FSA, FRSA; Chevalier de la Legion d'Honneur 1990; *Publications* English Barometers 1680–1860 (1968, 2 edn 1977), Ormolu - The Work of Matthew Boulton (1974, revised as Matthew Boulton: Ormolu 2002), These Fragments (2005); author of many papers and articles on the history of furniture, clocks and barometers; *Recreations* history of furniture and decorative arts, opera, walking; *Clubs* Arts, Athenaeum, Beefsteak; *Style*— Sir Nicholas Goodison; ✉ PO Box 2512, London W1A 5ZP

GOODLAD, Baron (Life Peer UK 2005), of Lincoln in the County of Lincolnshire; Sir Alastair Robertson Goodlad; KCMG (1997), PC (1992); yst s of late Dr John Fordyce Robertson Goodlad, of Lincoln, and Isabel, *née* Sinclair; *b* 4 July 1943; *Educ* Marlborough, King's Coll Cambridge (MA, LLB); *m* 1968, Cecilia Barbara, 2 da of Col Richard Hurst (s of Sir Cecil Hurst, GCMG, KCB), by his w Lady Barbara, *née* Lindsay (6 da of 27 Earl of Crawford (and Earl Balcarres), KT, PC); 2 s; *Career* Parly candidate (Cons) Crewe 1970; MP (Cons): Northwich Feb 1974–83, Eddisbury 1983–99; asst Govt whip 1981–82, a Lord Cmmr of the Treasy 1982–84, jt vice-chm Cons Pty Trade Ctee 1979–81 (jt hon sec 1978–), hon sec All-Pty Heritage Gp 1979–81; memb Select Ctee Agriculture 1979–81, Parly under sec of state at Dept of Energy 1984–87; chm All-Pty Gp for Refugees 1987–89; memb Select Ctee on Televising Proceedings of the House, comptroller Her Majesty's Household and sr govt whip 1989, treas of HM Household and dep chief whip 1990–92; min of state FCO 1992–95; Parly sec to the Treasy (Govt chief whip) 1995–97, shadow int devpt sec 1997–98; high cmmr to Australia 2000–05; chm NW Area Cons Membs of Parly 1987–89, memb House of Lords Select Ctee on the Constitution 2006–; memb House of Commons bridge team in matches against Lords 1982–85, pres Water Companies Assoc 1989; *Clubs* Brooks's, Beefsteak, Pratt's; *Style*— The Rt Hon the Lord Goodlad, KCMG, PC; ✉ House of Lords, London SW1A 0PW

GOODMAN, Andrew David; s of Bernard Goodman, and Heléne, *née* Greenspan (d 1984); *b* 4 June 1956; *Educ* Queen Elizabeth's Sch Barnet, Univ of Southampton (LLB), Rushmore Univ (MBA), Birkbeck Coll London (PhD entrant); *m* 6 June 1982, Sandra Maureen, da of Charles Burney; 4 s (Adam Howard b 1986, Simon Nicholas b 1989, Sam Alexander b 1991, James Aidan Lewis b 1996); *Career* called to the Bar Inner Temple 1978; registered CEDR mediator 1992–, advocacy trainer NITA (UK) 2000, advocacy trainer Nottingham Law Sch 2001, expert UK Panel Nominet 2001–03, prof of conflict mgmnt and dispute resolution studies Rushmore Univ USA 2003–; dir XPL Professional Skills Training 2006, convenor Standing Conference of Mediation Advocates 2007, memb Civil Mediation Cncl 2007; FCIArb 2001, FInstCPD 2005, FRSA 2007; *Books* The Court Guide (1980, 19 edn 2006), The Bar Diary (1982, 1983, 1984), Gilbert and Sullivan At Law (1983), The Royal Courts of Justice Guide (1985), Gilbert and Sullivan's London (1988, 2 edn 2000), The Prison Guide (1999), The Walking Guide to Lawyer's London (2000), What's it Worth? Awards of General Damages in Non-Personal Injury Claims (2004), How Judges Decide Cases - Reading, Writing and Analysing Judgments (2005), Influencing the Judicial Mind - Effective Writing Advocacy in Practice (2006), Mediation Advocacy (2007); *Recreations* travel, music, Victorian theatre; *Style*— Andrew Goodman, Esq; ✉ 1 Chancery Lane, London WC2A 1LF (tel 0845 634 6666, fax 0845 634 6667, e-mail agoodman@1chancerylane.com)

GOODMAN, Geoffrey George; CBE (1998); s of Michael Goodman (d 1960), and Edythe, *née* Bowman (d 1976); *b* 2 July 1921; *Educ* LSE (BScEcon); *m* 1947, Margit, *née* Freudenbergova; 1 s (John Murray b 14 Feb 1949), 1 da (Karen Elizabeth Irene b 21 March 1951); *Career* RAF 1941–46; journalist, author and broadcaster; reporter: Manchester Guardian 1946–47, News Chronicle 1947–60; industrial ed and columnist:

Daily Herald 1960–64, The Sun 1964–69, Daily Mirror 1969–86 (asst ed 1976–86), ret; currently presenter and commentator various news and current affrs items for BBC and London News Radio, current affrs commentator various TV and radio progs; chm emeritus Br Journalism Review 2002– (founding ed 1989–2002), assoc fell Nuffield Coll Oxford (fell 1974–76), memb and jt author of Minority report Royal Cmmn on the Press 1974–77, head Govt Counter-Inflation Unit 1975–76; chm Hugh Cudlipp Tst 2004–; fell Soc of Ed; Descriptive Writer of the Year 1972, Gerald Barry Award for Journalism 1984–85; Hon MA Univ of Oxford; *Books* incl: The Awkward Warrior - life and times of Frank Cousins (1979), The Miners' Strike (1985), The State fo the Nation: Legacy of Aneurin Bevan (1997), From Bevan to Blair: Fifty Years Reporting from the Political Front Line (2003); *Recreations* poetry, supporting Tottenham Hotspur FC; *Clubs* Savile; *Style—* Geoffrey Goodman, Esq, CBE; ✉ c/o The Savile Club, 69 Brook Street, London W1

GOODMAN, Helen; MP; *b* 2 January 1958, Nottingham; *Educ* Lady Manners Sch Bakewell, Somerville Coll Oxford; *Career* former civil servant HM Treasy, former head of strategy The Children's Soc; MP (Lab) Bishop Auckland 2005–; memb: Amnesty Int, Christian Socialist Movement, Public Accounts Ctee 2005–07; *Style—* Ms Helen Goodman, MP; ✉ House of Commons, London SW1A 0AA

GOODMAN, Henry; twin s of late Hyman Goodman, and late Fay, *née* Tobias; *b* 23 April 1950; *Educ* CFS GS, RADA (J Barton Prize, Poel Prize, Shereck Award); *m*, Sue, *née* Parker; 1 s (Ilan b 31 Oct 1981), 1 da (Carla b 25 May 1986); *Career* teacher, director and actor; teacher and ldr various workshops incl: Guildhall Drama Sch, BADA, RNT, RNT Studio; artistic dir: Roundabout Theatre Co 1975, Peoples Space Theatre 1981; lectr in Drama and Movement Rhode Univ South Africa 1974–75; *Theatre* RNT: Roy Cohn in Angels in America, Mickey in After the Fall, Dr Baugh in Cat on a Hot Tin Roof, Steve/Les in Decadence, Beatrice and Benedick, Nathan Detroit in Guys and Dolls, Gellburg in Broken Glass (also West End); RSC: Rocky Gravo in They Shoot Horses Don't They, Kitely in Every Man in his Humour, Lefer in Henry V, Prince de Condé in The Devils, Stalin/Azhog in Redstar, Dromio of Ephesus in Comedy of Errors (Best Newcomer Olivier Awards 1983), Voltore in Volpone, Harry in The Time of Life, Stravinsky in Astonish Me, Jacques in Jacques and His Masters, Arch of Canterbury and Norfolk in Henry VIII, Klyestakov in Government Inspector, Shylock in The Merchant of Venice (Best Actor Critics Circle Awards 1999, Best Actor Olivier Awards 2000), Tartuffe in Tartuffe, Lopakhin in Cherry Orchard, Groucho Marx in Groucho, Capt Hook in Peter Pan, Richard III; West End: Buddy Fidler in City of Angels, Hal in Kvetch; Tricycle Theatre: Agent in Lady Sings the Blues, Simon in A Free Country, Goldberg in Birthday Party; other credits incl: Charles Guiteau in Assassins (Olivier Award for Best Actor in a Musical, Donmar Warehouse), Freud in Hysteria (Royal Court and Duke of Yorks, Olivier Best Actor Award nomination 1995), Billy Flynn in Chicago (Adelphi), Mark in Art (Wyndhams Theatre), Serge in Art (Royale Theatre NY), Eddie in Feelgood, Max Bialystock in The Producers (St James Theatre NY), Tevye in Fiddler on the Roof (Crucible Sheffield); dir of various plays incl: The Promise (Arbizov), Metamorphosis, Agamemnon (Best Dir Award), Decadence, Bye Bye Blues, Neighbours, Epsom Wells, Berlin Kabarett, Metropolis Kabarett, Tartuffe (Broadway); *Television* incl: Lovejoy, Rides, Spinoza, Maigret, The Gravy Train II, Zorro, El CID, Gentlemen and Players, London's Burning, This is David Lander, Bust, After the War, 99 to 1, Sherlock Holmes, The Chain, Pompei in Measure for Measure (BBC), David Siltz in Dennis Potter's Cold Lazarus (BBC/Channel 4), Xmas (TV film, Channel 4), Unfinished Business (BBC) 1997–98, Foyle's War, Murder Investigation Team, Murder in Suburbia; *Radio* Gentlemen Prefer Blondes, The Prisoner in Prisoner of Papa Stour, André Gregory in Dinner with André, David Selznik in Diaries of David Selznik, Jackson in The Nuremberg Trials, title role in Beaumarchais, defence lawyer in No2 Goering, Woody Allen in Retribution, Lavoisier in Breath of Fresh Air, Teddy in Talking Towers, Adam in East of Eden, Berlioz in Fantastic Symphony, Alan Jay Lerner Diaries, Monsieur Ibrahim (writer and performer, winner Sony Award), Les Miserables; narrator The Autograph Man (audiobook); *Film* Secret Weapon, Queen of Hearts, Son of the Pink Panther, Mary Reilly, The Saint, Private Parts, Broken Glass, Notting Hill, The Life and Death of Peter Sellers, Out on a Limb, Colour Me Kubrick; *Style—* Henry Goodman, Esq; ✉ c/o Lou Coulson Associates Ltd, 1st Floor, 37 Berwick Street, London W1F 8RS

GOODMAN, Prof John Francis Bradshaw; CBE (1995); s of Edwin Goodman (d 1979), and Amy Bradshaw, *née* Warrener (d 1989); *b* 2 August 1940; *Educ* Chesterfield Sch, LSE (BSc), Victoria Univ of Manchester (MSc), Univ of Nottingham (PhD); *m* 12 Aug 1967, Elizabeth Mary, da of Frederick William Towns (d 1993), of Romiley, Gtr Manchester; 1 da (Clare b 1970), 1 s (Richard b 1972); *Career* personnel offr Ford Motor Co 1962–64, lectr in industrial economics Univ of Nottingham 1964–69, industrial rels advsr NBPI 1969–70, sr lectr in industrial rels Univ of Manchester 1970–74; UMIST (now Univ of Manchester): Frank Thomas prof of industrial rels 1975–2002, vice-princ 1979–81, head Manchester Sch of Mgmnt 1977–79, 1986–88 and 1989–94, emeritus prof 2002–; visiting prof of industrial rels: Univ of WA 1981 and 1984, McMaster Univ 1985, Auckland Univ 1996; tstee Withington Girls Sch 1986–97 (govr 1980–92); pres: Br Univs Industrial Rels Assoc 1983–86, Manchester Industrial Rels Soc 1984–2002; chm: Professional Footballers Negotiating and Consultative Ctee 2000–, Police Arbitration Tribunal 2003–; dep chm: Wood St Mission Manchester 1986–2004, Central Arbitration Ctee 1998–; memb: Cncl ESRC 1993–97, Cncl ACAS 1987–98, Panel of Arbitrators ACAS 1980–; CCIPD 1986; *Books* Shop Stewards (1973), Rule-making and Industrial Peace (1977), Ideology and Shop-floor Industrial Relations (1980), Employment Relations in Industrial Society (1984), Unfair Dismissal Law and Employment Practice (1985), New Developments in Employee Involvement (1992), Industrial Tribunals and Workplace Disciplinary Procedures (1998); *Recreations* mountain walking (Munro-ist, 1997), football, golf; *Style—* Prof John Goodman, CBE; ✉ 2 Pott Hall, Shrigley Road, Pott Shrigley, Macclesfield, Cheshire SK10 5RT (tel 01625 572480)

GOODMAN, Jonathan Richard; s of Stanley Goodman, and Terry, *née* Asher; *Educ* St Paul's (fndn scholar), Pembroke Coll Oxford (open and closed scholarships, MA); *Career* md Bounty Books 1983–86, publisher Hamlyn Octopus 1986–90, fndr and md Carlton Books 1992–; patron Artangel; *Recreations* sport, table tennis; *Clubs* Groucho, Century; *Style—* Jonathan Goodman, Esq; ✉ Carlton Publishing Group, 20 Mortimer Street, London W1T 3JW (tel 020 7612 0406, fax 020 7612 0408, e-mail jgoodman@carltonbooks.co.uk)

GOODMAN, Margaret Beatrice (Maggie); da of John Bertram Goodman (d 1985), and Cissie Phyllis, *née* Kay (d 1952); *b* 26 November 1941; *Educ* Plymouth HS for Girls, Coll of Commerce Univ of Birmingham; *m* 1988, Dr Anthony Harold Mercer Gaze (d 2000), s of William Mercer Gaze; *Career* asst ed New Era Magazine 1960–62, Honey Magazine 1962–67 (sub ed, showbusiness ed, features ed, asst ed) asst ed rising to ed Petticoat magazine 1967–69, freelance feature writer 1969–71, dep ed Cosmopolitan 1971–79, fndr ed Company 1979–88, launch ed Hello! (with Maggie Koumi, *qv*) 1988–93, head Magazine Devpt Gp The National Magazine Company 1994–96, freelance conslt and writer 1996–, ed Home & Life 1997–2000; awards for Hello!: Consumer Magazine of the Year PPA and Media Week 1990, Magazine of the Year Br Press Circulation Awards 1991, Editors of the Year for gen interest magazine BSME 1991; memb BSME 1978–91 (chm 1982); *Books* Every Man Should Have One (jt author, 1971); *Clubs* The Groucho; *Style—* Ms Maggie Goodman; ✉ 15a Upper Park Road, London NW3 2UN (tel 020 7722 3889)

GOODMAN, Prof Martin David; s of Cyril Joshua Goodman, and Ruth, *née* Sabel; *b* 1 August 1953; *Educ* Rugby, Trinity Coll Oxford (MA, DPhil); *m* 1976, Sarah Jane, da of John Lock; 2 s (Joshua b 1982, Alexander b 1984), 2 da (Daisy b 1987, Charlotte b 1992); *Career* Kaye jr research fell Oxford Centre for Postgrad Hebrew Studies 1976–77, lectr in ancient history Univ of Birmingham 1977–86; Univ of Oxford: fell Oxford Centre for Hebrew and Jewish Studies 1986–, sr research fell St Cross Coll 1986–91, lectr in Roman history Christ Church 1988–, Hebrew Centre lectr in ancient history 1990–91, univ reader in Jewish studies and professorial fell Wolfson Coll 1991–96, prof of Jewish studies 1996–; fell Inst for Advanced Studies Hebrew Univ of Jerusalem 1993; pres Br Assoc for Jewish Studies 1995, acting pres Oxford Centre for Hebrew and Jewish Studies 1995–96 and 1999–2000; sec Euro Assoc for Jewish Studies 1994–98; review ed Jl of Roman Studies 1993–98 (ed 1999–2003), jt ed Jl of Jewish Studies 1995–99; FBA 1996; *Books* State and Society in Roman Galilee, AD 132–212 (1983, 2 edn 2000), On the Art of the Kabbalah (jt trans, 1983, 2 edn 1993), The History of the Jewish People in the Age of Jesus Christ (jt ed, 1986–87), The Ruling Class of Judaea: the origins of the Jewish revolt against Rome, AD 66–70 (1987, reprinted 1988, 1989, 1991, paperback 1993), The Essenes according to the Classical Sources (with Geza Vermes, 1989), Mission and Conversion: proselytizing in the religious history of the Roman Empire (1994), The Roman World 44 BC- AD 180 (1997), Jews in a Graeco-Roman World (ed, 1998, paperback 2004), Apologetic in the Roman World: Pagans, Jews and Christians (jt ed, 1999), Representations of Empire: Rome and the Mediterranean World (jt ed, 2002), The Oxford Handbook of Jewish Studies (ed, 2002), Judaism in the Roman World: Collected Essays (2007), Rome and Jerusalem (2007); also author of over 35 articles and 100 reviews; *Style—* Prof Martin Goodman, FBA; ✉ The Oriental Institute, University of Oxford, Pusey Lane, Oxford OX1 2LE (tel 01865 278208, fax 01865 278190)

GOODMAN, Paul Alexander Cyril; MP; s of Abel Goodman, and Irene, *née* Rubens; *b* 17 November 1959; *Educ* Cranleigh Sch, Univ of York; *m* 1999, Fiona Mary Ann Gill; 1 s; *Career* novice Quarr Abbey 1988–90, home affrs ed Catholic Herald 1991–92, ldr writer Daily Telegraph 1992, reporter Sunday Telegraph 1992–95, comment ed Daily Telegraph 1995–2001; MP (Cons) Wycombe 2001–; PPS to Rt Hon David Davis, MP, *qv*, 2001–03, shadow min for work and pensions 2003–05, shadow Treasy min and shadow min for childcare 2005–; memb: Deregulation and Regulatory Reform Select Ctee 2001–02, Work and Pensions Select Ctee 2001–05; *Style—* Paul Goodman, Esq, MP; ✉ House of Commons, London SW1A 0AA (tel 020 7219 5099)

GOODMAN, Air Cdre Philip Charles (Phil); MBE (1989); s of George John Goodman, of Bodmin, Cornwall, and Dorothy May, *née* Collins; *b* 23 April 1954, Liskeard, Cornwall; *Educ* Bodmin GS, RMCS Shrivenham (BSc); *m* 16 July 1976, Rowena Margaret, *née* Murray-Lyon; 2 da (Fiona Jane b 29 April 1979, Sarah Louise b 8 June 1980), 1 s (Thomas Philip b 13 Oct 1986); *Career* joined RAF 1972, trg RAF Coll Cranwell, RAF Finningley (Sutton Sword) and RAF Coningsby (Nicholson Trophy) 1976–78, operational F4 Phantom navigator RAF Wildenrath Germany 19(F) Sqdn 1978–81, weapons instr trg RAF Coningsby 1981, instr F4 Phantom Conversion Unit 64(F) Sqdn 1981–83, asst ops offr (US Marine Corps exchange) Air Station Beaufort South Carolina and USS Kennedy 1983–86, Sqdn Ldr 1986, Tornado F3 conversion trg RAF Coningsby 1986–87, Flt Cdr 29(F) Sqdn RAF Coningsby 1987–89, JSDC RN Coll Greenwich 1989–90, staff duties HQ Strike Command RAF High Wycombe 1990–91, Wing Cdr 1991, staff offr Operational Requirements MOD London 1991–94, OC 25(F) Sqdn RAF Leeming 1995–98, Gp Capt 1997, Asst Dir Air Ops MOD 1998–99, Detachment Cdr Ali Al Salem Kuwait 1999, Higher Command and Staff Course RAF Bracknell 2000, Station Cdr RAF Coningsby 2000–02 (ADC to HM The Queen), Air Cdre 2002, Dir Fixed Wing Ops and COS Defence Logistics Orgn RAF Wyton 2002–04, Dir Combined Air Ops Centre Al Udeid Qatar 2004, Air Attaché Br Def Staff Br Embassy Washington DC 2005–; Arthur Barratt Meml Prize 1989; FRAeS (memb Ctee Washington Branch); *Recreations* all sport; *Style—* Air Commodore Philip Goodman, MBE; ✉ 5025 Rockwood Parkway NW, Washington, DC 20016, USA (tel 00 1 202 363 8525, e-mail phil.goodman@verizon.net); British Embassy, 3100 Massachusetts Avenue NW, Washington, DC 20008, USA (tel 00 1 202 588 6828, fax 00 1 202 588 7873, e-mail phil.goodman@moduk.org)

GOODMAN, Richard Antony; s of Antony Marlow Goodman (d 1999), of Leicester, and Florence, *née* Sowry (d 1994); *b* 17 June 1952; *Educ* Dunstable GS, Selwyn Coll Cambridge (MA); *m* 14 April 1979, Julie, da of John Edwin Williams, of Chilham, Kent; 2 s (Thomas b 1982, William b 1986), 1 da (Charlotte b 1989); *Career* admitted slr 1976; ptnr: Cameron Markby Hewitt (now Cameron McKenna) 1981–2002, KLegal 2002–03, Watson Farley & Williams LLP 2003–; memb Law Soc; *Recreations* music, garden, photography; *Style—* Richard Goodman, Esq; ✉ Watson Farley & Williams LLP, 15 Appold Street, London EC2A 2HB (tel 020 7814 8164, fax 020 7814 8141)

GOODMAN, Prof Roger James; s of late Cyril Joshua Goodman, of Burnham-on-Crouch, Essex, and Ruth, *née* Sabel; *b* 26 May 1960, Burnham-on-Crouch, Essex; *Educ* Rugby, King Edward VI GS Chelmsford, Univ of Durham (BA), Univ of Oxford (DPhil); *Partner* Carolyn Joy Dodd; 2 s (Samuel John b 17 Sept 1991, Joseph James b 26 Aug 1994), 1 da (Abigail Anne b 24 Nov 1999); *Career* Nissan jr research fell in the social anthropology of Japan St Antony's Coll Oxford 1985–88, lectr Japan-Europe Industry Research Centre Imperial Coll London 1988–89, reader in Japanese studies Dept of Sociology Univ of Essex 1989–93; Univ of Oxford: lectr in the social anthropology of Japan 1993–2003, Nissan prof of modern Japanese studies 2003–; fell St Antony's Coll Oxford 1993– (actg warden 2006–07); chair Endowment Ctee Japan Fndn 1999–2006; *Books* Japan's 'International Youth': The Emergence of a New Class of Schoolchildren (1990), Ideology and Practice in Modern Japan (co-ed, 1992), Case Studies in Human Rights in Japan (co-ed, 1996), The East Asian Welfare Model: Welfare Orientalism and the State (co-ed, 1998), Children of the Japanese State: The Changing Role of Child Protection Institutions in Contemporary Japan (2000), Family and Social Policy in Japan: Anthropological Approaches (ed, 2002), Can the Japanese Reform Their Education System? (co-ed, 2003), Global Japan: The Experience of Japan's New Minorities and Overseas Communities (co-ed, 2003), The 'Big Bang' in Japanese Higher Education: The 2004 Reforms and the Dynamics of Change (co-ed, 2005); *Recreations* hockey coach; *Style—* Prof Roger Goodman; ✉ Nissan Institute of Japanese Studies, 27 Winchester Road, Oxford OX2 7NA (tel 01865 274576, fax 01865 274574, e-mail roger.goodman@nissan.ox.ac.uk)

GOODMAN, Prof Timothy Nicholas Trewin; s of J Vincent Goodman (d 1971), and Eileen M Sherwell; *b* 29 April 1947; *Educ* Judd Sch Tonbridge, St John's Coll Cambridge (open scholar, BA), Univ of Warwick (MSc), Univ of Sussex (DPhil); *m* 1 Dec 1973, Choo-Tin, da of Nam-Sang Soon; 3 c (Joy b 12 Feb 1976, Kim b 6 May 1978, Ruth b 28 Oct 1981); *Career* VSO teacher King Edward VII Sch Taiping Malaysia 1973, teacher St Andrew's Secdy Sch Singapore 1974–75, lectr Universiti Sains Malaysia 1975–79, lectr Univ of Dundee 1979–90, full prof Texas A&M Univ 1990–91, prof of applied analysis Univ of Dundee 1994– (reader 1992–94); memb Edinburgh Mathematical Soc 1979; FRSE 1997; *Publications* author of over 150 academic papers in learned jls; *Recreations* Scottish country dancing, hill walking, music; *Style—* Prof Timothy Goodman, FRSE; ✉ Department of Mathematics, The University, Dundee DD1 4HN (tel 01382 344488, fax 01382 345516, e-mail tgoodman@maths.dundee.ac.uk)

GOODRICH, David; s of William Boyle Goodrich (d 1984), of Sunderland, and Florence Bosenquet, *née* Douglas (d 1984); *b* 15 April 1941; *m* 5 June 1965, Margaret, da of Andrew Robertson Riley, of Sunderland; 1 s (John b 1981), 3 da (Helen b 1968, Kathryn b 1970, Alison b 1972); *Career* constructor RCNC MOD (Navy) 1970–80, md Br Ship Res Assoc

1980–85; British Maritime Technology Ltd: chief exec (formerly md) 1986–, dep chm 1995–97, chm 1997–; pres RINA 1999–; CEng, MBA, RCNC, FRINA; *Recreations* squash, walking; *Clubs* East India; *Style*— David Goodrich, Esq; ✉ British Maritime Technology Ltd, Orlando House, 1 Waldegrave Road, Teddington, Middlesex TW11 8LZ (tel 020 8943 5544, fax 020 8943 5347)

GOODSON, Sir Mark Weston Lassam; 3 Bt (UK 1922), of Waddeton Court, Parish of Stoke Gabriel, Co Devon; o s of Maj Alan Richard Lassam Goodson (d 1941, 2 s of 1 Bt), and Clarisse Muriel Weston, *née* Adamson; suc his uncle Sir Alfred Lassam Goodson, 2 Bt 1986; *b* 12 December 1925; *Educ* Radley, Jesus Coll Cambridge; *m* 4 May 1949, Barbara Mary Constantine, da of Surgn Capt Reginald Joseph McAuliffe Andrews, RN, of Crandel, Ferndown, Dorset; 3 da (Phylida Mary (Mrs Timothy F Wright) b 1950, Hilary Frances b 1953, Christian Mary (Mrs Christopher Collins) b 1958), 1 s (Alan Reginald b 1960); *Heir* s, Alan Goodson; *Style*— Sir Mark Goodson, Bt; ✉ Bowmont Way, Yewtree Road, Town Yetholm, Kelso TD5 8RY (tel 01573 420322, e-mail aavin@btinternet.com)

GOODSON-WICKES, Dr Charles; DL (Gtr London); s of Ian Goodson Wickes, FRCP (d 1972), of Stock Harvard, Essex, and Monica Frances Goodson-Wickes; *b* 7 November 1945; *Educ* Charterhouse, St Bartholomew's Hosp, Inner Temple; *m* 17 April 1974, Judith Amanda, da of late Cdr John Hopkinson, RN (d 1978), of Stamford, Lincs; 2 s (Edward b 1976, Henry b 1978); *Career* consulting physician, co dir and business conslt; called to the Bar 1972; house physician Addenbrooke's Hosp Cambridge 1972; Surgn Capt The Life Gds (served BAOR, NI, Cyprus) 1973–77, Silver Stick MO, Household Cavalry 1977, RARO 1977–2000, re-enlisted as Lt-Col for Gulf Campaign 1991 (served Saudi Arabia, Iraq, Kuwait); specialist physician St Bartholomew's Hosp 1977–80, conslt physician BUPA 1977–86, occupational physician 1980–94; former med advsr: Barclays Bank, RTZ, Hogg Robinson, Standard Chartered, Norwegian Directorate of Health, British Alcan, McKinsey, Christies, ltc; dir Nestor Healthcare Group plc 1993–99; currently dir: Medarc Ltd, Gyrus Group plc, Thomas Greg and Sons Ltd, and other cos; Parly candidate (Cons) Islington Central 1979, MP (Cons) Wimbledon 1987–97; PPS to Rt Hon Sir George Young, Bt, MP: as Min of State for Housing and Planning 1992–94, as Fin Sec to Treasy 1994–95, as Sec of State for Tport 1995–96; formerly: vice-chm Def Ctee and Constitutional Affrs Ctee, memb Jt Ctee Consolidation of Bills, memb Select Ctee Armed Forces Bill 1990, sec Arts and Heritage Ctee; BOC fell Industry and Parly Tst 1991; vice-chm Cons Foreign and Cwlth Cncl 1997–, patron Hansard Soc 2003–; chief exec London Playing Fields Fndn 1998– (chm 1997–98), memb London Sports Bd 2000–03; former memb: Med Advsy Ctee Industry Soc, Fitness Advsy Panel IOD, treas Dr Ian Goodson Wickes Fund for Handicapped Children 1979–88; chm Asbestos Licensing Regulations Appeals Tbnl 1982–87, chm BFSS 1994–97 (memb Public Affrs Ctee 1980–87), patron Countryside Alliance 2003– (fndr chm 1997–99); govr Highbury Grove Sch 1977–85, vice-pres Ex-Servs Mental Welfare Soc 1990–, chm The Rural Tst 1999–; *Books* The New Corruption (1984), Another Country (contrib, 1999); *Recreations* hunting, shooting, real tennis, gardening, travel, history; *Clubs* Boodle's, Pratt's, MCC; *Style*— Dr Charles Goodson-Wickes, DL; ✉ Watergate House, Bulford, Wiltshire (tel 01980 632344); 37 St James's Place, London SW1 (tel 020 7629 0981); Medarc Limited, 73 Collier Street, London N1 9BE (tel 020 7713 8685, e-mail cgw@medarc-limted .co.uk)

GOODWAY, (John) Beverley; s of Cyril Clement Goodway (d 1991), of Birmingham, and Evelyn Debora Wilding, *née* Honor (d 1983); *b* 13 August 1943; *Educ* Seaford Coll, Regent St Poly Sch of Photography; *m* 1972, Karin Anne, da of Gordon Nisbett Hope-Mason; 2 da (Pollyanna b 29 June 1974, Saskia b 4 Nov 1977); *Career* photographer; news agency Cambridge 1965, The Daily Mail 1965–67, The Times 1967, The Sun 1967–2003 (under IPC 1967–69, joined Murdoch launch 1969); Freeman City of London 1979; *Recreations* gardening, art exhibitions, opera and theatre, photography, walking, bird watching, wild flowers in Dorset; *Style*— Beverley Goodway, Esq; ✉ e-mail bandkgoodway@btinternet.com

GOODWILL, Robert; MP; *b* 31 December 1956; *Educ* Bootham Sch York, Univ of Newcastle upon Tyne (BSc); *Family* 3 c; *Career* farmer 250 acre family farm, md Mowthorpe (UK) Ltd, MEP (Cons) Yorkshire and the Humber 1999–2004 (Parly candidate: Cleveland and Richmond 1994, Yorkshire S (by election) 1998), MP (Cons) Scarborough and Whitby 2005– (Parly candidate (Cons): Redcar 1992, NW Leicestershire 1997); European Parl: memb Environment, Public Health and Consumer Policy Ctee 1999–2004, vice-chm '79 Back Bench Ctee 1999–2002, memb Delgn to Belarus, Ukraine and Moldova 1999–2004, dep ldr Cons in the the European Parl 2003–04; House of Commons: memb Select Ctee on Tport 2005–06, oppn whip 2006–; past chm: NFU Local Branch, Count Commodity Ctee; cncllr Terrington Parish Cncl 1987–99; *Recreations* cooking, eating out, languages, steam ploughing, engineering; *Style*— Robert Goodwill, Esq, MP; ✉ House of Commons, London SW1A 0AA

GOODWIN, David Pryce; eld s of Geoffrey Pryce Goodwin (d 1970), and Marjorie, *née* Perry (d 1975); *b* 10 May 1936; *Educ* Tonbridge, St Mary's Med Sch Univ of London (BSc, MB BS, MS); *m* 10 Oct 1970, Sarah Jane, da of Harold Morfee (d 1959), and Lorna, *née* Moon (d 1995); *Career* house surgn St Mary's Hosp Paddington, house surgn Hammermith Hosp, surgical registrar Edgeware Gen Hosp, sr surgical registrar St Mary's Hosp Paddington, fell in surgery Tulane Univ New Orleans 1970–71, conslt surgn Royal Berks Hosp Reading 1974–2000, ret; memb Nat Ctee Br Assoc of Surgical Oncology 1980–90 (treas 1980–88, vice-pres 1988–90), memb Editorial Bd European Jl of Surgical Oncology 1985–90; author of various pubns in med jls; curator Berks Med Heritage Centre; FRSM, FRCS 1966 (Moynihan lectr 1989), Hon FACS 1989; *Recreations* sailing, conjuring, historical medical equipment; *Clubs* Royal Southampton Yacht, Magic Circle (London); *Style*— David Goodwin, Esq; ✉ Chelsea House, 22 Parkside Road, Reading, Berkshire RG30 2DB (tel 0118 957 4633)

GOODWIN, Sir Frederick Anderson (Fred); kt (2004); s of Frederick Anderson Goodwin (d 1992), and Marylyn Marshall, *née* Mackintosh; *b* 17 August 1958; *Educ* Paisley GS, Univ of Glasgow (LLB); *m* 23 March 1990, Joyce Elizabeth, da of Norman McLean; *Career* ptnr Touche Ross 1988–95, chief exec Clydesdale Bank plc 1996–98 (dep chief exec 1995–96), dep chief exec Royal Bank of Scotland 1998–2000, gp chief exec Royal Bank of Scotland Gp plc 2000–; memb Bd Bank of China 2006–; pres Chartered Inst of Bankers in Scotland 1997, chm Prince's Tst, memb Cncl Prince's Tst; Hon DUniv Paisley 2001, Hon DUniv Glasgow 2002, Hon LLD Univ of St Andrews 2004; CA 1983, FCIBS 1996, FCIB 2002; *Recreations* cars, golf; *Style*— Sir Fred Goodwin; ✉ Royal Bank of Scotland plc, Gogarburn, Edinburgh EH12 1 (tel 0131 523 2033, fax 0131 523 5812)

GOODWIN, Prof Guy Manning; s of Kenneth Manning Goodwin (d 1974), and Constance, *née* Hudson; *b* 8 November 1947; *Educ* Manchester Grammar, Exeter Coll Oxford (MA, DPhil, BM BCh, Martin Wronker Prize in Med); *m* 1971, Philippa Catherine, *née* Georgeson; 2 da (Frances Eleanor b 28 Dec 1977, Rosalind Mary b 6 Oct 1981); *Career* scholar MRC 1968–71, fell by examination Magdalen Coll Oxford 1971–76, research assoc Univ of Washington Seattle USA 1972–74, house physician Nuffield Dept of Clinical Med Oxford 1978–79, house surgn Horton Gen Hosp Banbury 1979, SHO Professorial Unit Brompton Hosp London 1980, registrar Rotational Trg Scheme in Psychiatry Oxford 1980–83, MRC clinical trg fell and hon sr registrar MRC Clinical Pharmacology Unit Radcliffe Infirmary Oxford 1983–85, clinical lectr and hon sr registrar Univ Dept of Psychiatry Oxford 1985–86, MRC clinical scientist, hon conslt psychiatrist and hon sr lectr 1986–95, prof of psychiatry Univ of Edinburgh 1995–96, W A Handley prof of psychiatry Univ of Oxford 1996–; author of original papers in physiology, neuropharmacology and psychiatry; pres Br Assoc for Psychopharmacology 2002–2004; FRCPsych; *Recreations* football, opera and hill walking; *Style*— Prof Guy Goodwin; ✉ Department of Psychiatry, Warneford Hospital, Headington, Oxford OX3 7JX (tel 01865 226451, fax 01865 204198, e-mail guy.goodwin@psychiatry.oxford.ac.uk)

GOODWIN, Dr Neil; CBE (2007); s of James Goodwin (d 1996), of Salford, and Dorothy Goodwin (d 1986); *b* 1 March 1951; *Educ* N Salford Co Secdy Sch, London Business Sch (MBA), Manchester Business Sch (PhD); *m* 1, 1980 (m dis 1992), Sian Elizabeth Mary, *née* Holliday; 2 s (Matthew Thomas James b 17 Dec 1981, Owen David Neil b 29 March 1987); m 2, 2006, Chris Hannah; *Career* various NHS managerial positions Manchester, Liverpool and W Midlands 1969–81, St Albans 1981–84, gen mangr Central Middlesex Hosp 1985–88, gen mangr St Mary's Hosp Paddington 1988–92; chief exec: St Mary's Hosp NHS Trust 1992–94, Manchester HA 1994–2002, Gtr Manchester SHA 2002–06; dir Goodwin Hannah Ltd 2006–; advsr: EC Harris LLP, Pinsent Masons Solicitors, CHKS Ltd; visiting prof of leadership studies: Univ of Manchester, Univ of Durham; FRSA, MIMgt, CHSM 2006 (MHSM 1980, FHSM 1991); *Publications* Leadership in Healthcare: A European Perspective (2005); also book contribs and numerous articles on health services and public health leadership, hosp mgmnt incl customer care, personal devpt for chief execs and public consultations; *Recreations* music, films, Coronation Street, theatre; *Style*— Dr Neil Goodwin, CBE

GOODWIN, Vivien Catherine; da of John Crompton Kirby (d 1975), of Birmingham, UK, and Gwendoline Carole, *née* Sproston; *b* 19 June 1964; *Educ* Chaminade Coll Prep HS, Univ of Calif Santa Barbara (BFA); *m* 16 Aug 1989, Alan Goodwin, s of Alfred Stanley Goodwin; 1 da (Abigail Chelsea b 1 Feb 1996); *Career* Samuel French Ltd: asst to performing rights dir 1988–90, asst to md 1991–98, admin dir 1998–99, md 2000–; *Recreations* amateur dramatics, running, swimming, reading; *Clubs* Two Brydges, Dartford Roadrunners, Geoffrey Whitworth Theatre; *Style*— Mrs Vivien Goodwin; ✉ Samuel French Ltd, 52 Fitzroy Street, London W1T 5JR (tel 020 7255 4314, fax 020 7387 2161, mobile 07958 546896, e-mail vivien@samuelfrench-london.co.uk)

G

GOODWORTH, Simon Nicholas; s of Michael Thomas Goodworth, of Broadstone, Dorset, and Lorna Ruth, *née* Skerret; *b* 9 August 1955; *Educ* Solihull Sch W Midlands, Univ of Manchester (LLB); *m* 1991, Doris, da of Jun Yip Sew Hoy, of Outram, NZ; 2 da; *Career* admitted slr 1980; ptnr: Theodore Goddard 1986–2002 (res ptnr NY 1991), Covington & Burling 2002– (specialist in mergers and acquisitions, and in private equity funds and private equity); memb Law Soc; *Recreations* tennis, squash, theatre, music (violin, piano, guitar); *Style*— Simon N Goodworth, Esq; ✉ Covington & Burling, 265 Strand, London WC2R 1BH (tel 020 7067 2013, fax 020 7067 2222, e-mail sgoodworth@cov.com)

GOODWYN, Charles Wyndham; LVO (2002); *b* 11 March 1934; *Educ* Wellington, Univ of London (LLB); *m* 18 Aug 1962, Judith Elisabeth Ann, da of Ernest Norman Riley; 2 da (Louisa Caroline (Mrs Wainwright) b 5 June 1963, Kate Judith (Mrs Murphy) b 18 Sept 1970), 2 s (Charles James Wyndham b 11 June 1965, Edward Christopher Wyndham b 10 July 1968); *Career* Wilks Head & Eve: joined 1956, ptnr 1960, sr ptnr 1990–95, conslt 1995–97; Keeper of the Royal Philatelic Collection 1995–2002; Royal Philatelic Soc London: hon treas 1981–82, hon sec 1982, 1990 and 1999, vice-pres 1990–92, pres 1992–94, Society Medal 1994, hon fell 2000; chm Roll of Distinguished Philatelists Tst, memb Bd of Election; Gen Cmmrs of Income Tax 1956–97, chm Land Inst, tstee Montgomery Sculpture Tst; Hon FRICS (prizewinner 1958), FLI; signatory Roll of Distinguished Philatelists, FRPSL; *Recreations* golf, tennis, cricket; *Clubs* Royal Philatelic, MCC, Army and Navy; *Style*— Charles Goodwyn, Esq, LVO; ✉ Hinton House, High Street, Amersham, Buckinghamshire HP7 0EE

GOODYEAR, Charles Waterhouse (Chip); s of Charles Waterhouse Goodyear, and Linda Goodyear; *b* 18 January 1958, Connecticut USA; *Educ* Univ of Yale (BSc), Wharton Sch of Finance Univ of Pennsylvania (MBA); *m* Elizabeth Goodyear; 1 s (Charles Waterhouse b 23 Nov 1993), 1 da (Adelaide Dabezies b 14 Jan 1995); *Career* Kidder Peabody & Co: assoc 1983–85, asst vice-pres 1985–86, vice-pres 1986–89; Freeport-McMoRan: vice-pres corporate finance 1989–93, sr vice-pres and chief investment offr 1993–95, exec vice-pres and chief financial offr 1995–97; pres Goodyear Capital Corporation 1997–99; BHP Billiton: chief financial offr 1999–2001, chief devpt offr 2001–03, ceo 2003–07; memb: Int Cncl on Mining and Metals, Nat Petroleum Cncl, Business Cncl of Australia; FCPA; *Recreations* cycling, tennis, fishing, skiing; *Style*— Chip Goodyear, Esq; ✉ BHP Billiton, 180 Lonsdale St, Melbourne, Victoria 3000, Australia

GOODYER, Prof Ian Michael; s of Mark Leonard Goodyer, and Belle, *née* Warwick; *b* 2 November 1949; *Educ* Kingsbury HS, Univ of London; *m* Jane Elizabeth, da of late Frank Goodliffe Akister; 1 s (Adam b 19 Nov 1981), 1 da (Sarah b 17 April 1983); *Career* clinical posts in med, surgery and paediatrics 1974–76, postgraduate trg in psychiatry Univ of Oxford 1976–79, res fell Brown Univ RI 1979–80, sr registrar Newcastle HA 1980–83, conslt and sr lectr Univ of Manchester 1983–87, prof Univ of Cambridge 1992– (lectr 1987–92); fell Wolfson Coll Cambridge; sec-gen Int Assoc of Child Psychiatry; FRCPsych, FRCPCH, FMedSci; *Books* Life Experiences, Development and Child Psychiatry (1991), The Depressed Child Adolescent (1995, 2 edn 2001), Unipolar Depression: A Lifespan Perspective (2003), The Origins of Common Mental Illness (with D Goldberg, 2005); *Style*— Prof Ian Goodyer; ✉ Section of Developmental Psychiatry, Douglas House, 18B Trumpington Road, Cambridge CB2 2AH (tel 01223 336098, fax 01223 746122, e-mail ig104@cus.cam.ac.uk)

GOOLD, Sir George William; 8 Bt (UK 1801), of Old Court, Co Cork; s of Sir George Leonard Goold, 7 Bt (d 1997), and Joy Cecelia, *née* Cutler; *b* 25 March 1950; *m* 1973, Julie Ann, da of Leonard Powell Crack, of Whyalla; 2 s (George Leonard Powell b 1975, Jon b 1977); *Heir* s, George Goold; *Style*— Sir George Goold, Bt; ✉ PO Box 176, Woollahra, NSW 1350, Australia (tel 00 61 408 421159)

GOOLEY, Michael David William (Mike); CBE (2007); s of Denis David Gooley, and Lennie Frances May, *née* Woodward; *b* 13 October 1936, Sheffield; *Educ* St George's Coll Weybridge, RMA Sandhurst; *Family* 3 da (Katherine Mary Veronica b 1962, Jennifer Samantha b 1967, Siobhan Hilary Eila b 1975), 1 s (Tristan Patrick b 1973); m, 8 Sept 2000, Fiona Kathleen, *née* Leslie; *Career* Br Army: enlisted 1955, cmmnd 2 Lt S Staffs Regt 1956, joined 22 SAS 1958 (served Malaya and Arabian Peninsula), Adj 21 SAS 1961–63, 1 Bn Staffords 1963 (served Kenya), 22 SAS 1964 (served Malay Peninsula, Borneo and Saudi Arabia), ret 1965; mil advsr to Royalist Yemeni Army 1965–69, fndr and chm Trailfinders Ltd 1970–; fndr tstee Mike Gooley Trailfinders Charity; FInstD 1978, FRGS 1996, hon life fell RSA 2005; *Recreations* travel, aviation, wining and dining, sport; *Clubs* Special Forces (tstee 1993–2007); *Style*— Mike Gooley, Esq, CBE; ✉ Trailfinders, 9 Abingdon Road, London W8 6AH (fax 020 7937 6059, e-mail mg@trailfinders.com)

GOPAL-CHOWDHURY, Paul; *b* 1949; *Educ* Camberwell Sch of Art, Slade; *Career* artist; Boise Travelling Scholarship and French Govt Scholarship 1973–74; lectr: Chelsea Sch of Art 1973–74 (pt/t 1975–77), Fine Art Dept Univ of Leeds (pt/t) 1975–77, Byam Shaw Sch of Art (pt/t) 1975–77; Gregory fell Univ of Leeds 1975–77; artist-in-residence Gonville & Caius Coll Cambridge and Kettle's Yard Gallery Cambridge 1983–84; *Solo Exhibitions*: Art Gallery Newcastle Poly 1980, Arts Centre Folkestone 1980, Ian Birksted Gallery 1981 and 1984, Kettle's Yard Gallery Cambridge (and tour to Axiom Gallery Cheltenham and Oldham Art Gallery) 1984–85, Benjamin Rhodes Gallery 1986, 1988 and 1991, Quay Arts Centre IOW 1988; *Group Exhibitions* incl: London Gp 1971, Royal Acad Summer Exhbn (1972, 1974, 1978, invited artist 1988), Royal Soc of Oil Painters 1973, John Moores Exhbn (Liverpool) 1974, Hayward Annual 1979 and 1981, Serpentine Summer Show 3 1979, Whitechapel Open (Whitechapel Gallery) 1980 and 1983, Imperial Tobacco Portrait

Awards (Nat Portrait Gallery) 1980, 1981 and 1985, A Taste of Br Art Today (Brussels) 1981, Ian Birksted Gallery (NY) 1981, Heads (Lamont Gallery London) 1992, Royal Acad Summer Exhbn (invited artist) 1992 and 1993, Beautiful Blooms (Lamont Gallery London) 1993; *Public Collections*: Bolton Art Gallery, Chase Manhattan Bank NY, Chelmsford and Essex Museum, Contemporary Art Soc, de Beers Ltd, Doncaster Museum and Art Gallery, Newcastle Poly; 2nd prize Imperial Tobacco Portrait Award (Nat Portrait Gallery) 1982; *Publications* articles incl: My Painting (Artscribe), Painting From Life (Hayward Annual 1979 Catalogue), Portrait of the Artist (Artist's and Illustrator's Magazine 1986), Reviving the Figurative Tradition (Landscape 1987); *Style*— Paul Gopal-Chowdhury, Esq

GORDIMER, Nadine; da of Isidore Gordimer (d 1961), of Springs, South Africa, and Nan, *née* Myers (d 1973); *b* 20 November 1923; *Educ* convent sch; *m* 1, 1949 (m dis 1952), Dr Gerald Gavronsky; 1 da (Oriane Taramasco b 1950); m 2, 1954, Reinhold Cassirer, s of Hugo Cassirer (d 1920), of Berlin; 1 s (Hugo b 1955); *Career* novelist and writer; thirteen novels completed (incl: My Son's Story, The House Gun, The Pickup), nine short story collections (incl: Jump, Loot), non-fictional works incl: Writing and Being, Living In Hope & History : Notes from Our Century (1999); vice-pres Int PEN, patron Congress of South African writers; winner Nobel Prize for Literature 1991, Primo Levi Prize Italy 2002, Commonwealth Writers Award 2002; holder of fourteen honorary degrees incl: DLitt Harvard Univ 1986, DLitt Yale Univ 1986, DLitt Columbia Univ, DLitt Univ of Cambridge 1992, DLitt Univ of Oxford 1994; hon memb American Acad of Arts and Sciences, hon memb American Acad and Inst of Arts and Letters; FRSL; Commandeur de l'Ordre des Arts et des Lettres (France) 1986, Order of the Southern Cross (South Africa) 1999, Order of Friendship (Repub of Cuba) 2004; *Style*— Nadine Gordimer

GORDON, *see also:* Duff Gordon, Smith-Gordon

GORDON, Andrew Mark Ainslie; s of Robert W A Gordon, of Graveley, Cambridgeshire, and Pamela Pheby, *née* Roberts; *b* 23 January 1969, Nocton, Lincolnshire; *Educ* St Columba's Coll St Albans, Univ of Kent at Canterbury (BA); *partner* Joanna Anderson; 1 s (Hal Riley b 30 Jan 2005); *Career* jr press offr Hodder & Stoughton 1992–93; Little, Brown & Co UK: copywriter 1994–95, desk ed 1995–98, commissioning ed 1998–2000; sr ed Time Warner UK 2000–01, editorial dir Simon & Schuster UK 2001–; *Recreations* reading (occasionally for pleasure), collecting film posters; *Clubs* MCC, Century; *Style*— Andrew Gordon; ✉ Simon & Schuster UK, Africa House, 64–78 Kingsway, London WC2B 6AH

GORDON, Catherine (Kate); JP (Inner Manchester 1969); da of William Alexander Keir (d 1963), of Ayr, Scotland, and Marion Watson, *née* Prentice (d 1987); *Educ* Ayr Acad, Open Univ (BA); *m* 20 Aug 1955, (Donald) Hugh McKay Gordon, s of James Bremner Gordon, of Huntly, Aberdeenshire; 1 s (Alistair Keir b 10 Sept 1956), 1 da (Marion Louise (Mrs Livingstone Jones) b 31 July 1959); *Career* Civil Serv and PA to chm of nationalised industry 1945–56; local and met dist cncllr 1969–95, chm Trafford Ethics Ctee 1984–96; memb: Trafford HA 1976–89, Women's Nat Cmmn 1980–84, Trafford Courts Ctee 1972–88, Gtr Manchester Probation Ctee 1974–92, Cncl Nat Magistrates' Assoc 1985–92; chm Inner Manchester Magistrates 1985–89 (memb Exec 1976–92); YWCA: nat pres and chm Bd of Govrs 1980–84, govr 1970–95, delg World Cncl YWCA Forces rep (BAOR and Cyprus) 1984–96; govr: St Vincent's Jr/Infants Sch 1984–, Altrincham Girls' GS 1994–; FRSA 1980; *Recreations* music, family, friends; *Style*— Mrs Hugh Gordon; ✉ 3 West Lynn, Devisdale Road, Bowdon, Cheshire WA14 2AT (tel and fax 0161 928 6038)

GORDON, Charlie; MSP; *b* Partick, Glasgow; *m* 1; 2 s; m 2, Emma; 1 s; *Career* early career in railway industry until 1993; cncllr: Strathclyde Regnl Cncl 1987–96 (vice-convenor then convenor of roads and transport 1990–96), Glasgow CC 1995–2005 (roads convenor 1995–96, dep ldr 1997–99, ldr 1999–2005); MSP (Scottish Lab) Glasgow Cathcart 2005–; memb (all Scottish Parl): European and External Rels Ctee, Public Petitions Ctee, Cross-Party Gp on Glasgow Crossrail, Cross-Party Gp on ME; former dir: Glasgow City Mktg Bureau Ltd, Glasgow Clyde Regeneration Ltd, SECC Ltd Glasgow; non-exec dir Hampden Park Ltd; former pres Glasgow Trades Cncl; memb: Lab Party, GMB; former memb: Woodworkers' Union, Nat Union of Railwaymen/RMT (sometime branch and dist official); fell Inst of Contemporary Scotland; *Style*— Charlie Gordon, Esq, MSP; ✉ Somerville Drive, Mount Florida, Glasgow G42 9BA (tel 0141 632 8645, fax 0141 632 8645, website www.charliegordonmsp.com); The Scottish Parliament, Edinburgh EH99 1SP (e-mail charlie.gordon.msp@scottish.parliament.uk)

GORDON, Christopher James; s of (Alexander) Esmé Gordon, RSA, FRIBA (d 1993), and Betsy Ballment, *née* McCurry (d 1990); *b* 3 December 1944; *Educ* Edinburgh Acad, Univ of St Andrews (MA), Br Sch of Archaeology Athens, Poly of Central London (Dip Arts Admin); *m* 27 June 1970, Susan Merriel, da of Bonham Bazeley, DSC; 1 da (Antonia b 4 Dec 1973), 3 s (Alexander b 4 Oct 1975, Rupert b 2 Sept 1978, Adam b 24 July 1981); *Career* trainee mangr Williamson Magor & Co (tea estates) Calcutta 1967–69, asst music offr Arts Cncl of GB 1969–72, theatre and mktg mangr Hampstead Theatre 1973, sr arts offr/festival admin London Borough of Camden 1973–77, co arts offr Hampshire CC 1977–85, exec dir Cncl of Regnl Arts Assocs 1985–91, chief exec Regnl Arts Bds Services Ltd 1991–2000, freelance conslt in cultural policy and mgmnt; external examiner: MA Arts Admin Leicester Poly 1986–91, MA Euro Cultural Mgmnt Univ of Warwick 1993–96, occasional lectr 1993–, assoc fell 1998–; memb Cncl Univ of Southampton 1998–2004; visiting prof: Univ of Bologna 2002–, Univ of Turin 2004–; lectr on cultural policy: Dijon, Barcelona, Turin, Salzburg; chair Festivals Panels Gr London Arts Assoc 1976–77; memb: Nat Film & Video Forum BFI 1991–2000, Planning and Devpt Bd Arts Cncl of GB 1986–91; Southern Arts Assoc: chair General Arts, chair Festivals Panels, memb Exec Ctee, memb Gen Cncl; chair Cncl of Europe Evaluation of Cultural Policy in Latvia 1997–98, chair Advsy Bd Fondazione Fitzcarraldo Turin 1999–; hon treas Euro Forum for the Arts & Heritage (EFAH) 1996–99; vice-chair Fondation Marcel Hicter (European Dip); memb: Bd Bournmouth Orch 1982–90, Bd Nuffield Theatre Southampton; Winchester Cathedral Fabric Ctee 1996–; tstee Portsmouth Theatre Royal 1985–99, tstee and chair Hants Sculpture Tst 1987–; memb Editorial Bd Int Jl of Cultural Policy; FRSA; *Books* Cultural Policy in Italy (1995), Cultural Policy in Latvia (1997), European Perspectives on Cultural Policy (UNESCO 2001), Cultural Policy in Cyprus (2003), Gambling and Culture (2004), Cultural Policy and Social Inclusion (2004); *Recreations* travel, music, art, history; *Style*— Christopher Gordon, Esq; ✉ 28 Cornes Close, Winchester, Hampshire SO22 5DS (tel 01962 864204, e-mail christophergordon@compuserve.com)

GORDON, Prof David; s of Lawrence Gordon (d 1992), and Pattie, *née* Wood; *b* 23 February 1947, Croydon; *Educ* Magdalene Coll Cambridge (open scholar, MA, MB, BChir), Westminster Med Sch London; *m* Dr C Louise, *née* Jones; 1 da (Henrietta Katherine b 1984), 3 s (Frederick Samuel b 1986, Nathaniel Charles b 1988, Theodore William b 1990); *Career* sr lectr then hon sr lectr in medicine St Mary's Hosp Medical Sch London 1980–94 (research and academic appts 1972–80, also asst dir Medical Unit 1980–83), hon conslt physician St Mary's Hosp London 1980–94; Wellcome Tst: asst dir 1983–89, prog dir 1989–98, dir of special initiatives 1998–99; Univ of Manchester (formerly Victoria Univ of Manchester): prof of medicine 1999–, dean Faculty of Medicine, Dentistry, Nursing and Pharmacy 1999–2004, vice-pres and dean Faculty of Medical and Human Science 2004–06, vice-pres 2006–; chair Cncl of Heads of Medical Schs 2003–06, pres Assoc of Med Schs in Europe 2004–; dep chm ORPHEUS; former memb: Scottish Office Dept of Health Chief Scientist Ctee, Exec Cncl Assoc of Medical Research Charities, Research Ctee HEFCE-CVCP Task Force on Clinical Academic Careers; memb Editorial Bd Trends in Molecular Medicine; author of pubns in scientific jls incl: Lancet, BMJ, Jl of Physiology, American Jl of Physiology, Clinical Science, Molecular Medicine Today; memb: Acad of Medical Sciences (memb various ctees), Assoc of Physicians, Med Pilgrims, 1942 Club; medical referee Civil Serv 1989–94; FRCP 1989 (MRCP 1972), FMedSci 1999; *Style*— Prof David Gordon; ✉ The University of Manchester, 1.015 John Owens Building, Oxford Road, Manchester M13 9PL (tel 0161 306 3338, fax 0161 306 6051, e-mail d.gordon@man.ac.uk)

GORDON, David Michael (Dave); *b* 24 May 1951, London; *Educ* Harrow Co GS, Univ of Warwick (BA); *m* 6 Sept 1980, Barbara; 2 da (Caroline b 1 Aug 1983, Judith b 4 Oct 1985); *Career* radio studio mangr 1972–79, sr prodr Radio Sport 1983–85 (prodr 1979–83); BBC: joined as asst prodr TV Sport 1985, worked on Grandstand and Sportsnight, exec ed Grandstand 1997–2001 (asst ed 1991–97), head Major Events BBC Sport 2001–, actg dir BBC Sport 2005–; covered numerous sporting events incl: 7 Olympic Games, 5 Winter Olympics, 6 Cwlth Games, London Marathon, Great North Run, Wimbledon; winner of numerous awards incl BAFTAs; *Recreations* supporting Fulham FC, learning to play the saxophone; *Style*— Dave Gordon, Esq; ✉ Room 5060, BBC Sport, Television Centre, Wood Lane, London W12 7RJ (tel 020 8225 6233, e-mail dave.gordon@bbc.co.uk)

GORDON, David Sorrell; s of Sholom Gordon (d 1965), and Tamara (Tania) Gordon (d 1994); *b* 11 September 1941; *Educ* Clifton, Balliol Coll Oxford (BA), LSE, Harvard Business Sch (AMP); *m* 1, 1963 (m dis 1969), Enid Albagli; m 2, 1974, Maggi McCormick; 2 s; *Career* chartered accountant Thomson McLintock (now KPMG) 1965–68; The Economist: journalist 1968–78, prodn and devpt dir The Economist Newspaper Ltd 1978–81, gp chief exec The Economist Newspaper Ltd 1981–93; chief exec Independent Television News Ltd (ITN) 1993–95; business advsr 1995–96, sec Royal Acad of Arts 1996–2002, ceo and dir Milwaukee Art Museum 2002–; dir: The Financial Times Group Ltd 1983–93, Mediakey plc 1996–2001, Profile Books 1996–, Financial News 1999–2006 (chm 2001–2006), Dice Inc 2006–; chm Contemporary Art Soc 1992–98, memb Bd South Bank Centre 1986–96, govr BFI 1983–91, memb Ct of Govrs LSE 1990–2000, tstee: Tate Gallery 1993–98, Architecture Fndn 1992–2002; FCA; *Books* Newspaper Money (jtly with Fred Hirsch, 1975); *Recreations* movies, magic lanterns; *Clubs* Garrick; *Style*— David Gordon, Esq; ✉ Milwaukee Art Museum, 700 North Art Museum Drive, Milwaukee, Wisconsin 53202, USA (tel 00 1 414 224 3200, e-mail david.gordon@mam.org)

GORDON, Sir Donald; kt (2005); s of Nathan Gordon, and Sheila, *née* Shevitz; *b* 24 June 1930, Johannesburg, South Africa; *Educ* King Edward VII Sch Johannesburg; *m* 21 Jan 1958, Peggy, *née* Cowan; 2 s (Richard Michael, Graeme John), 1 da (Wendy Donna (Mrs Appelbaum)); *Career* chartered accountant (South Africa); ptnr Kessel Feinstein (Chartered Accountants) 1955–57; chair: Liberty Gp Ltd (formerly Liberty Life Assoc of Africa Ltd) 1957–99 (fndr, hon life pres 1999), Liberty Hldgs Ltd 1968–99, Liberty Investors Ltd 1971–99, Guardian Nat Insurance Co Ltd 1980–99, Liberty International plc 1981–2005 (life pres 2005), Capital and Counties plc (UK) 1982–2005, Capital Shopping Centres plc (UK) 1994–2005; dep chair: Standard Bank Gp Ltd 1979–99, Premier Gp Ltd 1983–96, South African Breweries Ltd (now SAB Miller plc) 1989–99, Beverage and Consumer Industry Holdings Ltd 1989–99, Sun Life Corporation plc (UK) 1992–95; dir: Guardbank Mgmnt Corporation Ltd 1969–99, Guardian Royal Exchange Assurance plc (UK) 1971–94, Charter Life Insurance Co Ltd 1985–99, GFSA Hldgs Ltd 1990–94; Financial Mail Businessman of the Year 1965, Sunday Times (SA) Man of the Year 1969, Financial Mail Achiever of the Century in South African Financial Services 1999, London Entrepreneur of the Year 2000, Special Entrepreneur Award for Lifetime Achievement 2001, Sunday Times (SA) Top 100 Lifetime Achievement Award 2004; Hon Dr of Economic Science Univ of the Witwatersrand 1991, Hon DCom Univ of Pretoria 2005; *Recreations* opera, ballet; *Clubs* Rand, Johannesburg Country, Plettenberg Bay Country, Houghton Golf; *Style*— Sir Donald Gordon; ✉ Liberty International plc, 40 Broadway, London SW1H 0BT (tel 020 7960 1200, fax 020 7960 1333)

GORDON, HE (Jean) Francois; CMG (1999); *b* 16 April 1953; *m* Elaine Margeret, *née* Daniel; 2 da; *Career* diplomat; entered HM Dip Serv 1979, asst desk offr EC Dept (External) FCO 1979–80, second later first sec Luanda 1981–83, first sec UK Delgn to Conf on Disarmament Geneva 1983–88, head Finance Section UN Dept FCO 1988–89, first sec (political) Nairobi 1990–92; FCO: head Lusophone Africa Section Southern African Dept 1992–94, asst head Repub of Ireland Dept 1994–95, head Drugs, Crime and Terrorism Dept 1996 (asst head 1995–96); ambass Algiers 1996–99, on secondment RCDS Algiers 2000–01, ambass to Ivory Coast 2001–04, high cmmr to Uganda 2005–; *Style*— HE Mr Francois Gordon, CMG; ✉ c/o Foreign & Commonwealth Office (Kampala), King Charles Street, London SW1A 2AH

GORDON, Sheriff Sir Gerald Henry; kt (2000), CBE (1995), QC (Scot 1972); er s of Simon Gordon (d 1982), of Glasgow, and Rebecca, *née* Bulbin (d 1956); *b* 17 June 1929; *Educ* Queen's Park Sr Secdy Sch Glasgow, Univ of Glasgow (MA, LLB, PhD), Univ of Edinburgh (LLD); *m* 1957, Marjorie (d 1996), yr da of Isaac Joseph, of Glasgow; 1 s (David), 2 da (Susan, Sarah); *Career* admitted Scots Bar 1953; Univ of Edinburgh: sr lectr 1965, head Dept of Criminal Law and Criminology 1965–72, personal prof of criminal law 1969–72, dean Faculty of Law 1970–73, prof of Scots law 1972–76, visiting prof 2000–03; Sheriff of: S Strathclyde, Dumfries and Galloway at Hamilton 1976–77, Glasgow and Strathkelvin 1978–99; temp judge Court of Session and High Court of Justiciary 1992–2004; memb Scot Criminal Cases Review Cmmn 1999–; Hon LLD Univ of Glasgow; Hon FRSE 2002; *Books* The Criminal Law of Scotland (1968, 2 edn 1978), Renton and Brown's Criminal Procedure (ed, 4 edn 1972, 5 edn 1983, 6 edn 1996); *Recreations* Jewish studies, crosswords; *Style*— Sheriff Sir Gerald Gordon, CBE, QC

GORDON, His Hon Judge (Cosmo) Gerald Maitland; s of John Kenneth Maitland Gordon, CBE (d 1967), of Farnham, Surrey, and Erica Martia, *née* Clayton-East (d 1983), of London; *b* 26 March 1945; *Educ* Eton; *m* 4 July 1973, Vanessa Maria Juliet Maxine, *née* Reilly-Morrison; 2 s (James Cosmo Alexander b 11 Oct 1975, George William Robert b 6 June 1978); *Career* called to the Bar Middle Temple 1966 (bencher 2003), recorder of the Crown Court 1986–90 (asst recorder 1982–86), circuit judge (SE Circuit) 1990–, permanent judge Central Criminal Ct 1994–; Cncl of Royal Borough of Kensington and Chelsea: memb 1971–90, chm Works and Town Planning Ctees, dep leader 1982–88, mayor 1989–90; Liveryman Merchant Taylors Co 1995; *Style*— His Hon Judge Gordon; ✉ Central Criminal Court, Old Bailey, London EC4M 7EH (tel 020 7248 3277)

GORDON, Ian; s of James Donald Gordon, of Montrose, Angus, and Winifred, *née* Thomson (d 1985); *b* 15 August 1957; *Educ* Biggar HS, Univ of Edinburgh (LLB); *m* 22 July 1988, (Mary) Angela Joan, da of Donald Macdonald, of Isle of Lewis; 1 s (James Alexander Donald b 22 April 1992), 1 da (Juliet Emily Katherine b 1 August 1994); *Career* McGrigor Donald: apprentice 1979–81, slr 1981, ptnr 1983–; memb: Law Soc of Scotland 1981, Assoc of Pension Lawyers 1986 (memb Ctee and former chm Scottish Gp); NP 1981; *Recreations* boating, getting out and about; *Style*— Ian Gordon, Esq; ✉ 25 Westbourne Gardens, Glasgow; Pacific House, 70 Wellington Street, Glasgow G2 6SB (tel 0141 248 6677, fax 0141 221 1390, e-mail ian.gordon@mcgrigors.com)

GORDON, Ian; OBE (1991), JP (Newcastle upon Tyne 1981), DL (2002); s of William Gordon (d 1984), and Elizabeth, *née* Brooks (d 1997); *b* 21 March 1939; *Educ* Carlisle GS; *m* 8 Sept 1962, Kathleen Verna, da of Ernest Francis Martin; 1 da (Lindsay Kathryn b 6 Oct 1965), 2 s (James Iain b 26 April 1968, Craig Martin b 23 Sept 1969); *Career* articled clerk N T O Reilly & Partners Carlisle 1956–61, qualified 1962; ptnr: Telfer & Co (formerly S W Telfer) 1963–70 (audit sr then mangr 1962–63), Winn & Co Newcastle (following merger) 1970–73, Tansley Witt & Co Newcastle 1973–80; sr ptnr Binder

Hamlyn (following merger) 1980–96 (memb Nat Partnership Ctee 1980–89); dir: Tyne & Wear Development Co Ltd 1985–90 and 1991–96, Signpost Europe Ltd 1989–94, Tyne & Wear Development Corp 1989–98, N Tyneside City Challenge Partnership Ltd 1993–2004, Whitley Bay Playhouse Ltd 1996–2000; N Tyneside MBC: cncllr (Cullercoats Ward) 1976–96, cncllr (St Mary's Ward) 1997–98, gp spokesman on fin 1976–80, ldr Cons Gp 1982–96 (dep ldr 1980–82); fndr memb N of England Assembly of Local Authorities 1985–90 and 1991–96 (ldr Cons Oppn Gp 1986–90 and 1991–96), chm Exec Ctee Tynemouth & Whitley Bay Cons Assoc 1988–90 (pres 1985–88, dep chm 1995–97), Parly candidate (Cons) Newcastle N 1992; memb: N Area Exec Ctee (Cons) 1988–97, Exec Ctee Nat Union 1989–90, Nat Local Govt Ctee; vice-chm Area Local Govt Ctee 1988–91 (memb 1982–98, chm 1991–97), fndr and chm N Tyneside Political Ctee 1986–96; N Soc of Chartered Accountants: memb Exec Ctee 1971–80, chm Educn, Trg and Recruitment Sub-Ctee, fndr memb and chm Fin Advice Scheme; memb: Newcastle upon Tyne Magistrates' Courts Ctee 1991–2000 (vice-chm 1997–2000), Lord Chllr's Advsy Ctee 1995–2000, Northumbria Police Authy 1995–96 and 1999–2003, Newcastle upon Tyne Cmmn of the Peace (bench dep chm 1997–2002, chm 2003–06), Northumbria Magistrates' Courts Ctee 1999–2005, Durham Bd of Studies 2000– (chm 2003–), Youth Panel and Licensing Ctee; fndr memb Northern Devpt Co, dir Cons Local Authy 1986–96; tstee and govr Netherton Park Sch; fndr tstee: Cullercoats Educn Tst, Cedarwood Tst; govr: Preston Grange Primary Sch (chm of govrs 1980–2003), N Tyneside Coll 1996–2005 (chm of govrs 1999–2003), Tyne Met Coll 2005–, John Spence Community HS; former govr: Cullercoats Primary Sch, W Moor Middle Sch, Monkhouse Primary Sch; churchwarden St Hilda's Church Marden and Preston Grange 1984–88 and 1997–99, memb Tynemouth Deanery Synod; FCA (ACA 1962); *Recreations* charity work, gardening, DIY; *Style*— Ian Gordon, Esq, OBE, DL; ✉ 6 Beach Way, Beach Road, North Shields, Tyne & Wear NE30 3ED (tel 0191 257 6879, e-mail ian.gordon1@blueyonder.co.uk)

GORDON, Ian William; *Career* with Dept of Energy 1975–81; Scottish Office: Industry Dept 1981–85, Educn Dept 1986–90, Agriculture and Fisheries Dept 1990–99; head Scotland Office 1999–2002, dir of service policy and planning Health Dept Scot Exec 2002–; *Style*— Ian Gordon, Esq; ✉ Scottish Executive Health Department, St Andrews House, Regent Road, Edinburgh EH1 3DG (tel 0131 244 1727, fax 0131 244 4015)

GORDON, John Edwin; s of Dennis Lionel Shute (d 1940); *b* 14 December 1939; *Educ* Tonbridge, Queens' Coll Cambridge; *m* 1, 1968 (m dis 1994), Monica Anne, *née* Law; 1 s, 2 da; m 2, 1994, Fay Vere Harvey Hillier; *Career* dir: Robert Fleming & Co 1974–77, Laing & Cruickshank (stockbrokers) 1978–82, Jackson Exploration Inc 1982–85; head of corporate fin: Capel-Cure Myers 1985–89, Beeson Gregory 1989–96; chm: Universal Ceramic Materials plc 1996–, Laverden Gp plc 2005–, Imprint plc 2007– (non-exec dir 2001–); non-exec dir Alizyme plc 1996–; FCA; *Recreations* fishing; *Clubs* Boodle's, Flyfishers', Hawks' (Cambridge), Leander; *Style*— John Gordon, Esq

GORDON, John Keith; s of Prof James Edward Gordon, and Theodora Mary Camilla, *née* Sinker; *b* 6 July 1940; *Educ* Marlborough, Trinity Coll Cambridge (MA), Yale Univ (Henry fell), LSE; *m* 14 Aug 1965, Elizabeth, da of Maj A J Shanks (d 1962); 2 s (Timothy Alan b 1971, Alexander Keith b 1973); *Career* Dip serv; entered FCO 1966, Budapest 1968–70, seconded to Civil Serv Coll 1970–72, FCO 1972–73, UK Mission Geneva 1973–74, head of Chancery and consul Yaoundé 1975–77 (concurrently chargé d'affaires Gabon and Central African Repub), FCO 1977–80, cultural attaché Moscow 1980–81, Office of UK Rep to EC Brussels 1982–83, UK perm delg to UNESCO Paris 1983–85, head Nuclear Energy Dept FCO 1986–88, left FCO 1990; dep and policy dir Global Environment Res Centre 1990–94; ind conslt and analyst 1994–; Parly candidate (Lib Dem) Daventry 1997; special advsr: UNED-Forum 1998–2004, Airport Watch 2004–; memb UK Nat Cmmn for UNESCO; pres Cncl for Educn in World Citizenship; *Publications* Institutions and Sustainable Development: Meeting the Challenge (with Caroline Fraser, 1991), 20/20 Vision: Britain, Germany and a New Environmental Agenda (with Tom Bigg, 1993), Canadian Round Tables (1994); author of other contributions to books, symposia and periodicals; *Recreations* walking, books, history; *Clubs* RSA, Nat Liberal; *Style*— John Gordon, Esq; ✉ Well House, Reading Road, Wallingford, Oxfordshire OX10 9HG

GORDON, Lyndall Felicity; da of Harry Louis Getz (d 1969), of Cape Town, South Africa, and Rhoda Stella Press (d 1999); *b* 1941, Cape Town, South Africa; *Educ* Good Hope Seminary Cape Town, Univ of Cape Town (BA Hons), Columbia Univ NY (PhD); *m* 1963, Prof Siamon Gordon, *qv*; 2 da (Anna b 9 Aug 1965, Olivia Jane b 26 Nov 1978); *Career* Univ of Oxford: Rhodes fell 1973–75, lectr Jesus Coll 1977–84, CUF lectr in English 1984–95, Dame Helen Gardner fell St Hilda's Coll 1984–95, sr research fell St Hilda's Coll 1995–; asst prof Columbia Univ 1975–76; Eliot meml lectr RSL 2003; memb: PEN, Virginia Woolf Soc; FRSL 2002; *Publications* Eliot's Early Years (1977, reprinted 1988, Rose Mary Shaw Prize Br Acad), Eliot's New Life (1988, Southern Arts Prize), Virginia Woolf: A Writer's Life (1984, winner James Tait Prize for Biography), Shared Lives (1992, revised edn 2005), Charlotte Brontë: A Passionate Life (1994, Cheltenham Prize for Lit), A Private Life of Henry James: Two Women and His Art (1998), T S Eliot: An Imperfect Life (single vol revised edn of Eliot's Early Years and Eliot's New Life, 1998), Vindication: A Life of Mary Wollstonecraft (2005); author of numerous essays in various pubns; *Recreations* reading, ballet; *Style*— Lyndall Gordon; ✉ St Hilda's College, Oxford OX4 1DY

GORDON, (George) Michael Winston; s of Winston Gordon, of Clonallon Rd, Warrenpoint, NI, and Marjorie Georgina Gordon; *b* 8 May 1937; *Educ* Queen's Univ Belfast (BSc, MSc), Univ of NSW (MEngSc); *m* 11 Aug 1966, Narelle Helen, da of Flt Lt Kenneth Charles Nicholl (decd), of Sydney, NSW, Aust; 3 s (Matthew b 9 Sept 1967, Nicholas b 24 May 1969, Benjamin b 8 Feb 1976); *Career* grad trainee Metropolitan Vickers 1958–60; design engr: Bristol Aircraft Co 1961–62, Amalgamated Wireless Australasia 1962–67; conslt: PA Management Consultants Aust, Singapore, Malaysia and NI 1967–76, Booz Allen and Hamilton Algeria 1976–77; dir: NI Devpt Agency 1977–80, American Monitor 1980–82, BIS London 1982–93 (chief operating offr); md LINK Training 1993–97; dir and chief operating offr The Spring Group plc (formerly CRT plc) 1994–, dir Microgen plc 1995–98; MIEE (NY), FInstD; *Style*— Michael Gordon, Esq; ✉ Kingfisher Cottage, Carr's Lane, Tattenhall, Cheshire CH3 9NT (tel 01829 770087); Shell Cottage, 3 Collingwood Street, Manly, Australia

GORDON, Prof Peter; s of Louis Gordon (d 1969), and Anne, *née* Schultz (d 1941); *b* 4 November 1927; *Educ* Univ of Birmingham (DipEd), LSE (BSc, MSc), Inst of Educn Univ of London (PhD); *m* 30 March 1958, Tessa Joan, da of Bernard Leton, of Stanmore, Middlesex; 1 da (Pauline Amanda b 24 June 1961), 1 s (David Nicholas b 12 April 1965); *Career* RAF in England and India 1945–48; teacher primary and secdy schs 1951–65, HM inspr of schs 1965–73; Inst of Educn Univ of London: lectr 1973–76, reader 1976–82, prof of history of educn 1982–93; FRHistS 1982, FSA 1991; *Books* The Victorian School Manager (1974), The Cabinet Journal of Dudley Ryder, Viscount Sandon (with Christopher Howard, 1974), Curriculum Change in the 19th and 20th Centuries (with Denis Lawton, 1978), Games and Simulations in Action (with Alec Davidson, 1978), Theory and Practice of Curriculum Studies (1978), Philosophers as Educational Reformers (with John White, 1979), Selection for Secondary Education (1980), The Study of Education: Inaugural Lectures (1980, 1988, 1995), The Red Earl: The Papers of the Fifth Earl Spencer of Althorp 1835–1910 (1981, 1986), The Study of the Curriculum (ed 1981), A Guide to English Educational Terms (with Denis Lawton, 1984), HMI (with Denis Lawton, 1987), Dictionary of British Educationists (with R Aldrich, 1989), History of Education: The Making of a Discipline (with R Szreter, 1989), Education and Policy in England in the Twentieth Century (ed 1991), Teaching the Humanities (ed 1991), The Wakes of Northamptonshire (1992), Dictionary of Education (with Denis Lawton, 1993, 2 edn 1996), International Yearbook of History Education (jt ed, 1995), A Guide to Educational Research (ed, 1996), Biographical Dictionary of North American and European Educationists (with Richard Aldrich, 1997), Royal Education: Past, Present and Future (with Denis Lawton, 1999), Politics and Society: The Journals of Lady Knightley of Fawsley 1885–1913 (1999), Dictionary of British Women's Organisations 1825–1960 (with David Doughan, 2001), International Review of History Education (jt ed, 2001), A History of Western Educational Ideas (with Denis Lawton, 2002), Dictionary of British Education (with Denis Lawton, 2003), Understanding History: Recent Research in History Education (jt ed 2005), Musical Visitors to Britain (with David Gordon, 2005), Women, Clubs and Associations in Britain (with David Doughan, 2006); *Recreations* music, architecture; *Style*— Prof Peter Gordon, FSA; ✉ Birtsmorton, 58 Waxwell Lane, Pinner, Middlesex HA5 3EN (tel 020 8868 7110); Institute of Education, University of London, 20 Bedford Way, London WC1H 0AL (tel 020 7612 6000)

GORDON, Dr Peter David; s of Sydney Gordon (d 1984), and Sarah Gordon, *née* Paskin (d 1982); *b* 25 March 1939; *Educ* Hendon County GS, Univ of Sheffield (LDS RCS), DGDP(UK); *m* 1, (m dis 1990), Ruth, *née* Summers; 2 s (Keith Michael b 20 Aug 1969, Jonathan Andrew b 6 Aug 1971); m 2, Andrea Suzanne Kon, *née* Marks; *Career* dental surgn 1964–, private gen practitioner 1970–98; house surgn Charles Clifford Dental Hosp Sheffield 1964, clinical lectr Middlesex Hosp London 1985– (pt/t dental surgn to Nursing Staff 1969–85), hon clinical conslt to: 3M 1977–79, Bayer UK 1981–; dental advsr BDA 1991–96, appointed to panel of outside advsrs to dental practition 1997–, appointed dental reference offr 1998; reg lectr in dental photography to postgrads; guest lectr: Asian Pacific Dental Congress Delhi 1987, Zoroastrian Dental Soc Bombay; lecture tour Bangkok, Kuala Lumpur, Singapore, Hong Kong 1988; memb: BDA, Alpha Omega; *Books* Dental Photography (with P Wander, 1987); *Recreations* theatre, music, bridge, swimming; *Clubs* RAC; *Style*— Dr Peter Gordon; ✉ 5 Spring Place, Windermere Avenue, London N3 3QB (tel 020 8346 4545, fax 020 8343 1621, e-mail p.d.gordon@btinternet.com)

GORDON, Richard John Francis; QC (1994); s of John Bernard Basil Gordon, of London, and Winifred Josephine, *née* Keenan; *b* 26 November 1948; *Educ* St Benedicts Sch, ChCh Oxford (MA), UCL (LLM); *m* 13 Sept 1975, Jane Belinda, da of Anthony George Lucey, of Welburn, N Yorks; 2 s (Edmund John Anthony b 17 June 1982, Adam Richard Cosby b 25 Oct 1985); *Career* called to the Bar Middle Temple 1972; ed Crown Office Digest 1988–, broadcasts and articles on admin law in legal periodicals and other pubns; Freeman City of London; FRGS, ACIArb; *Books* The Law Relating to Mobile Homes and Caravans (2 edn, 1985), Judicial Review Law and Procedure (1985); *Recreations* modern fiction, theatre, cricket; *Style*— Richard Gordon, Esq, QC; ✉ 39 Essex Street, London WC2R 3AT (tel 020 7583 1111, fax 020 7353 3978)

GORDON, HE Robert Anthony Eagleson; CMG (1999), OBE (1983); *b* 9 February 1952; *m* 1978, Pamela Jane, *née* Taylor; 2 da (Francesca b 1980, Alix b 1981), 2 s (Adam b 1985, Ollie b 1988); *Career* diplomat; entered HM Dip Serv 1973, language trg 1974–75, third then second sec Warsaw 1975–78, second then first sec (head of Chancery) Santiago 1978–83, first sec FCO 1983–87, first sec (economic) OECD Paris 1987–92, dep head of mission Warsaw 1992–95, ambass to Burma 1995–99, head of SE Asia dept FCO 1999–2003, ambass to Vietnam 2003–; *Style*— HE Mr Robert Gordon, CMG, OBE; ✉ c/o Foreign & Commonwealth Office (Hanoi), King Charles Street, London SW1A 2AH

GORDON, Maj-Gen Robert Duncan Seaton; CMG (2005), CBE (1994); s of Col Jack Gordon (d 2005), and Joan, *née* Seaton (d 1981); *b* 23 November 1950; *Educ* Wellington, St Catharine's Coll Cambridge (MA); *m* 1979, Virginia (Gina), da of Dr and Mrs William Brown of Toronto, Canada; 2 s (Seaton b 1981, Charlie b 1985); *Career* cmmnd 17/21 Lancers 1970; Army Staff Coll Shrivenham and Camberley 1982, COS 4 Armoured Bde 1983–84, Lt Col 1987, Military Asst to C in C BAOR/NORTHAG 1987–90, CO 17/21 Lancers 1990–92, Full Col 1993, Sec Chief of Staff's Ctee MOD 1993–94; Higher Cmd and Staff Course 1994; Brig 1994, Cdr 19 Mechanised Bde 1994–96, RCDS 1996, Dir Army PR 1997–99, Maj-Gen 1999, GOC 2 Div York 1999, GOC 2 Div Edinburgh 2000–02, Col Cmdt RAVC 2001–07, Force Cdr UN Mission to Ethiopia and Eritrea 2002–04, ret Army 2005; currently conslt on peacekeeping; currently md Robert Gordon Consulting Ltd; govr Edinburgh Castle 2000–02; Queen's Commendation for Valuable Service (Bosnia) 1995; MRUSI 1974; *Recreations* history, offshore sailing, countryside sports, tennis, bad golf; *Clubs* Cavalry and Guards'; *Style*— Maj-Gen Robert Gordon, CMG, CBE

GORDON, Sir Robert James; 10 Bt (NS 1706), of Afton and Earlston, Kirkcudbrightshire, probably next in remainder to the Viscountcy of Kenmure and Lordship of Lochinvar (dormant since 1872); s of Sir John Charles Gordon, 9 Bt (d 1982), and Marion, *née* Wright (d 1973); *b* 17 August 1932; *m* 1976, Helen Julia Weston, da of late John Weston Perry, of Cammeray, NSW; *Heir* none; *Style*— Sir Robert Gordon, Bt

GORDON, (Prof) Robert Patterson; s of Robert Gordon (d 1976), and Eveline, *née* Shilliday; *b* 9 November 1945; *Educ* Methodist Coll Belfast, St Catharine's Coll Cambridge (Jarrett exhibitioner and scholar, John Stewart of Rannoch Hebrew scholar, sr scholar, Bender prize, Tyrwhitt's Hebrew scholar, Mason prize, MA, PhD, LittD); *m* 1970, Helen Ruth, *née* Lyttle; 2 s ((Christopher) Graham b 17 Nov 1975, Alasdair Robert b 3 Oct 1985), 1 da ((Nicola) Claire b 19 Sept 1977); *Career* lectr in Hebrew and Semitic languages Univ of Glasgow 1970–79 (asst lectr Hebrew and Old Testament 1969–70), regius prof of Hebrew Univ of Cambridge 1995– (lectr in Old Testament 1979–95); fell: St Edmund's Coll Cambridge 1985–89, St Catharine's Coll Cambridge 1995–, Univ Preacher 1999; Macbride sermon Oxford 2000, McManis lectures Wheaton ILL 1990, Didsbury lectures Manchester 2001, Biblical Studies Lectrs Samford Univ Birmingham AL 2004; sec Int Orgn for the Study of the Old Testament 2001–04; memb: Soc for Old Testament Study (pres 2003), Br Assoc of Jewish Studies; consltg ed New Int Dictionary of Old Testament Theology and Exegesis 1997, review ed Vetus Testamentum 1998–, ed Hebrew Bible and Its Versions 2001–, memb Editorial Bd New Cambridge Bible Commentary 2003–; *Books* 1 and 2 Samuel (1984, Chinese edn 2002), 1 and 2 Samuel. A Commentary (1986, reprinted 2003), The Targum of the Minor Prophets (with K J Cathcart, 1989), Studies in the Targum to the Twelve Prophets (1994), Wisdom in Ancient Israel (jt ed, 1995), The Place is too Small for us (ed, 1995), The Old Testament in Syriac According to the Peshitta Version: Chronicles (1998), Hebrews: A New Commentary (2000), Holy Land, Holy City (2004), The Old Testament in its World (jt ed, 2005), Hebrew Bible and Ancient Versions (2006), The God of Israel (ed, 2007); *Recreations* jogging, local history (N Ireland), otopianistics; *Clubs* National, Carrickfergus Gasworks Preservation Soc; *Style*— Robert Gordon; ✉ Faculty of Oriental Studies, University of Cambridge, Sidgwick Avenue, Cambridge CB3 9DA (tel 01223 335118, fax 01223 335110, e-mail rpg1000@cam.ac.uk)

GORDON, Robert Smith Benzie; CB (2000); s of William Gladstone Gordon (d 1980), and Helen Watt, *née* Benzie (d 2003); *b* 7 November 1950; *Educ* The Gordon Schs Huntly, Univ of Aberdeen (MA); *m* 2 July 1976, Joyce Ruth, da of Stephen Cordiner; 2 da (Rachel Joyce b 19 Oct 1978, Jennifer Claire b 18 March 1984), 2 s ((Robert Stephen) Niall b 20 March 1980, David William James b 20 May 1989); *Career* Scottish Office: admin trainee 1973, various trg appointments, princ Scot Devpt Dept 1979–85, asst sec and private sec to sec of state for Scotland 1985–87, asst sec Dept of Agric and Fisheries 1987–90, asst sec mgmnt and orgn and industrial relations 1990–91, dir of admin servs 1991–, under sec 1993–97, head of Constitution Gp 1997–98, head of Scottish Exec Secretariat

G

1999–2001, head Fin and Central Servs Dept 2001–2002, chief exec Crown Office and procurator fiscal serv and head of legal and parly servs Scottish Exec 2002–04, head Justice Dept and head of legal and parly servs Scottish Exec 2004–; Warden Incorporation of Goldsmiths City of Edinburgh; *Style*— Robert Gordon, Esq, CB; ✉ Scottish Executive, St Andrew's House, Regent Road, Edinburgh EH1 3DG (tel 0131 244 2120, e-mail robert.gordon@scotland.gsi.gov.uk)

GORDON, Roderick Caryl Patrick Ramsay (Roddy); s of John Ramsay Gordon (d 1997), and Jean Carlyly, *née* Irvine; *b* 17 March 1959, Hanover, Germany; *Educ* Charterhouse, Univ of Bristol (LLB); *m* 5 Sept 1992, Katharine Elizabeth, *née* Morton; 2 s (Thomas Patrick b 25 March 1995, James Harry b 12 Sept 1997); *Career* offr 4/7 Royal Dragoon Gds 1981–84; admitted slr 1988; trainee Braby & Waller 1986–88, slr Masons 1988–1993, ptnr Robert Muckle 1993–2001, ptnr Watson Burton LLP 2001–; memb: Law Soc 1988–, Technol and Construction Slrs Assoc; MCIArb, CEDR accredited mediator; *Recreations* skiing, sailing, riding, golf; *Clubs* Cavalry and Guards'; *Style*— Roddy Gordon, Esq; ✉ Watson Burton LLP, 1 St James' Gate, Newcastle upon Tyne NE99 1YQ (tel 0191 244 4444, e-mail roddy.gordon@watsonburton.com)

GORDON, Prof Siamon; s of Jonah Gordon (d 1955), of South Africa, and Liebe, *née* Solsky (d 1988); *b* 29 April 1938; *Educ* SACS Cape Town, Univ of Cape Town (MB ChB), Rockefeller Univ (PhD); *m* April 1963, Dr Lyndall Gordon, *qv*, da of Harry Getz; 2 da (Anna b 9 Aug 1965, Olivia Jane b 26 Nov 1978); *Career* registrar Dept of Pathology Univ of Cape Town Med Sch 1963–64 (intern Dept of Med and Surgery 1962–63), res asst Wright-Fleming Inst of Microbiology St Mary's Hosp Med Sch 1964–65, asst prof and assoc physician Lab of Cellular Physiology and Immunology Rockefeller Univ 1971–76 (res assoc and asst physician Lab of Human Genetics 1965–66); Univ of Oxford: visiting scientist Dept of Biochemistry 1974–75, fell Exeter Coll 1976–, Newton-Abraham lectr in pathology 1976–91, reader in experimental pathology Sir William Dunn Sch of Pathology 1976–89, prof of cellular pathology 1989–91, Glaxo prof of cellular pathology 1991–, acting head of dept 2000–01; scholar Leukemia Soc of America Inc 1973–76 (special fell 1971), adjunct assoc prof Rockefeller Univ 1976–, Br Cncl visiting prof and lectr Hebrew Univ 1994; Friederich Sasse Award in immunology 1990, Medal of the Polish Soc of Haematology and Transfusion Med 1997; memb Editorial Bd: Jl of Cell Science 1982–90, Progress in Leukocyte Biology 1987, American Jl of Respiratory Cell and Molecular Biology 1989–91, Jl of Experimental Medicine 1993–, Jl of Leukocyte Biology 1998–2006, Immunology 2000–, Marie T Bonazinga Award Soc of Leukocyte Biology 2003; memb: Lister Scientific Advsy Ctee 1987–92, Br Soc for Immunology, Br Soc for Cell Biology, American Soc for Cell Biology, Soc for Leukocyte Biology, Henry Kunkel Soc; hon memb Assoc of Assoc of American Immunologists 2004; DSc (hc) Univ of Cape Town 2002; FMedSci 2003, FRS 2007; *Books* Macrophage Biology and Activation, Current Topics in Microbiology and Immunology (ed, 1992), Legacy of Cell Fusion (ed, 1994), Phagocytosis - The Host (V5) and Microbial Invasion (V6) Advances in Cell and Molecular Biology of Membranes and Organelles (ed, 1999), The Macrophage as Therapeutic Target (ed, 2003); author of articles in various scientific jls; *Recreations* reading, music, history; *Style*— Prof Siamon Gordon; ✉ Sir William Dunn School of Pathology, University of Oxford, South Parks Road, Oxford OX1 3RE (tel 01865 275534, fax 01865 275515, e-mail siamon.gordon@path.ox.ac.uk)

GORDON, Tanya Joan (Mrs Tanya Sarne); da of Jean-Claude Gordon, of Bayswater, London, and Daphne Thomas, *née* Tucar (d 1976); *b* 15 January 1945; *Educ* Godolphin & Latymer Sch, Univ of Sussex (BA); *m* 1969 (m dis), Michael Sarne, s of Alfred Schener; 1 s (William Gordon b 30 May 1972), 1 da (Claudia Aviva b 17 Jan 1970); *Career* model 1963–64, asst to Cultural Attaché Persian Embassy 1966–67, asst to Lit Agent Kramers 1967–68, freelance reader for Universal Film Studios 1967–68, supply teacher of history for GLC (mainly at St Martin's-in-the-Field) 1968–69, spent two years in Brazil helping husband make a film (Intimidade), working as a tour guide for Brazil Safaris and modelling 1973–75, sales dir Entrepas Ltd 1976–78, fndr Miz (fashion business) 1978–83, fndr Ghost 1984–; fndr memb Fashion Indust Action Gp, memb Br Fashion Cncl; *Recreations* cooking, tennis, acquiring property and the obvious; *Clubs* Groucho, Campden Hill Tennis; *Style*— Ms Tanya Gordon; ✉ Ghost Ltd, The Chapel, 263 Kensal Road, London W10 5DB (tel 020 8960 3121, fax 020 8960 8374)

GORDON, William John (Bill); s of Sidney Frank Gordon (d 1982), and Grace Louie, *née* Fisher; *b* 24 April 1939; *Educ* King Edward VI Sch Birmingham; *m* 17 Oct 1963, Patricia, da of Thomas Rollason; 2 s (Bruce b 1967, Lewis b 1971); *Career* Barclays Bank plc: joined 1955, asst gen mangr Barclaycard 1980–83, regnl gen mangr Central Region 1983–87, dir UK corporate servs 1987–90, gp personnel dir 1990–92, chief exec UK banking servs 1992–98, main bd dir Barclays plc and Barclays Bank plc 1995–98 (ret), chm Barclays Pension Funds Tstees Ltd 1995–; dir Britannia Building Society 1999– (dep chm 2004–); FCIB 1981 (ACIB 1959); *Recreations* bridge, golf, chess, music; *Style*— Bill Gordon, Esq; ✉ c/o Barclays plc, 54 Lombard Street, London EC3P 3AH (tel 020 7699 5000)

GORDON CUMMING, Alexander Penrose (Alastair); 7 Bt (UK 1804), of Altyre, Forres; s of Sir William Gordon Gordon Cumming, 6 Bt (d 2002); *b* 15 April 1954; *m* 20 April 1991, Louisa, er da of Edward Geoffrey Clifton-Brown, of Glastonbury, Somerset; 2 s (William b 4 April 1993, Kit b 7 May 1998), 1 da (Sophie b 2 May 1995); *Heir* s, William Gordon Cumming; *Style*— Sir Alastair Gordon Cumming, Bt

GORDON-DUFF-PENNINGTON, Patrick Thomas; OBE (1992), DL (Cumbria 1993); s of George Edward Gordon-Duff (d 1966), and Rosemary Estelle, *née* Craven; *b* 12 January 1930; *Educ* Eton, Trinity Coll Oxford (MA); *m* 1955, Phyllida Pennington, da of Sir William Pennington-Ramsden; 4 da; *Career* served Queen's Own Cameron Highlanders 1951–53; shepherd: Perthshire and Inverness-shire 1953–55, Muncaster 1955–57; student land agent Sandringham 1957–59; farmer: Dumfriesshire 1959–82, Muncaster 1969–82; Scottish NFU: memb Cncl 1972–82, pres Dumfries and Stewartry Area 1976–78, convenor Hill Farming 1976–82, vice-convenor Livestock Ctee 1976–80, hon pres 1981–83; county chm Cumbria NFU 1986, convenor Scottish Land Owners' Fedn 1988–91, md family estate Inverness-shire 1990–97; memb: Lake District Special Planning Bd 1987–93, Indust and Parly Tst 1995–; chm: Scottish Ctee Assoc of Electricity Producers 1991–96, Park Mgmnt Ctee Lake District Special Planning Bd 1989–93, Deer Cmmn for Scotland (formerly Red Deer Cmmn) 1993–98, Br Deer Soc 1999–2001; vice-pres Field Studies Cncl; *Style*— Patrick Gordon-Duff-Pennington, Esq, OBE, DL; ✉ Muncaster Castle, Ravenglass, Cumbria CA18 1RQ (tel 01229 717203, fax 01229 717010)

GORDON LENNOX, Maj-Gen Bernard Charles; CB (1986), MBE (1968); s of Lt-Gen Sir George Gordon Lennox (d 1988), and Nancy Brenda, *née* Darell (d 1993); *b* 19 September 1932; *Educ* Eton (page of honour to HM The King 1946–49), Sandhurst; *m* 1958, Sally-Rose, da of John Weston Warner (d 1981); 3 s (Edward Charles b 1961, Angus Charles b 1964, Charles Bernard b 1970); *Career* cmd 1 Bn Grenadier Gds 1974–75, GSO 1 RAF Staff Coll 1976–77, Brig 1977, Cdr Task Force H, Dep Cdr and COS SE Dist UKLF 1981–83, Maj-Gen 1982, Br Cmdt and GOC Br Sector Berlin 1983–85, sr Army memb RCDS 1986–87, Lt-Col Grenadier Gds 1989–95; dir Regions Motor Agents Assoc 1988–89; chm Guards Polo Club 1992–99; *Recreations* country sports, cricket, squash, music; *Clubs* Army and Navy, MCC; *Style*— Maj-Gen B C Gordon Lennox, CB, MBE; ✉ The Estate Office, Gordon Castle, Fochabers, Morayshire IV32 7PQ

GORDON OF STRATHBLANE, Baron (Life Peer UK 1997), of Deil's Craig in Stirling; James Stuart Gordon; CBE (1984); s of James Edward Gordon (d 1975), of Glasgow, and Elsie, *née* Riach (d 1984); *b* 17 May 1936; *Educ* St Aloysius' Coll, Univ of Glasgow (MA, winner Observer Mace and Best Individual Speaker, pres Union); *m* 1971, Margaret Anne, da of Andrew Kirkwood Stevenson (d 1968), of Glasgow; 1 da (Hon Sarah Jane b 1972), 2 s (Hon Michael Stevenson b 1974, Hon Christopher James b 1976); *Career* political ed STV 1965–73; md Radio Clyde 1973–96; chm: Scottish Radio Holdings plc (parent co) 1996–2005 (chief-exec 1991–96), Scottish Tourist Bd 1998–2001 (memb 1997–2001), RAJAR (Radio Audience Research) 2003–06; dir: Johnston Press plc 1996–2007, The Active Capital Trust plc; chm: Scottish Exhibition Centre 1983–89, Advsy Gp on Listed Sports Events on TV 1997–98; memb: Scottish Devpt Agency 1981–90, Ct Univ of Glasgow 1984–97, Ctee of Inquiry into Teachers' Pay and Conditions 1986, Ctee on Funding of the BBC 1999; tstee: National Galleries of Scotland 1998–2002, John Smith Mml Tst 1995–; Sony Award for Outstanding Services to Radio 1984, Lord Provost's Award for Public Service 1996; Hon DLitt Glasgow Caledonian Univ 1994, Hon DUniv Glasgow 1998; fell Radio Acad 1994; *Recreations* walking, skiing, genealogy; *Clubs* New (Edinburgh), Prestwick Golf; *Style*— The Lord Gordon of Strathblane, CBE; ✉ House of Lords, London SW1A 0PW (tel 020 7219 1452, fax 020 7219 1993)

GORDON-SAKER, Andrew Stephen; s of Vincent Gordon-Saker, and Gwendoline Alice, *née* Remmers; *b* 4 October 1958; *Educ* Stonyhurst, UEA (LLB); *m* 28 Sept 1985, Liza Helen Gordon-Saker, *qv*, da of William James Marle; 1 da (Francesca b 1989), 1 s (Edward b 1991); *Career* called to the Bar Middle Temple 1981; in practice 1981–2003, dep taxing master of the Supreme Court 1994–2003, costs judge 2003–; memb Eastern Region Legal Aid Area Ctee 1995–2003; cncllr London Borough of Camden 1982–86; *Style*— Andrew Gordon-Saker, Esq; ✉ Supreme Court Costs Office, Clifford's Inn, Fetter Lane, London EC4A 1DQ

GORDON-SAKER, Liza Helen; da of William James Marle, of Chislehurst, Kent, and Doreen Maud, *née* Adams; *b* 30 November 1959; *Educ* Farrington's Sch Chislehurst, UEA (LLB); *m* 28 Sept 1985, Andrew Stephen Gordon-Saker, *qv*, s of Vincent Gordon-Saker, of Norwich; 1 da (Francesca b 1989), 1 s (Edward b 1991); *Career* called to the Bar Gray's Inn 1982; in practice 1983–, dep district judge 2005–; dir Bar Mutual Indemnity Fund Ltd 1988–2002; Freeman City of London 1984; *Recreations* golf; *Style*— Mrs Liza Gordon-Saker; ✉ Fenners Chambers, 3 Madingley Road, Cambridge CB3 0EE (tel 01223 368761)

GORDON-SAKER, Paul Declan; s of Vincent Gordon-Saker (d 1992), of Norwich, and Gwendoline Alice, *née* Remmers; *b* 6 August 1944; *Educ* Stonyhurst; *m* 4 Oct 1969, Victoria May, da of James Gordon Cresswell Wood; 1 s (Steven James b 20 Jan 1971), 1 da (Nicola Clare b 20 Feb 1972); *Career* admitted slr 1970, licensed insolvency practitioner 1989; head Litigation and Insolvency Dept Alsop Wilkinson 1988–96, head Corp Recovery and Insolvency Dibb Lupton Alsop 1996–98 (ptnr 1973–99), head Restructuring and Insolvency Dept Stephenson Harwood 1999–; memb Law Soc 1970, memb Insolvency Lawyers Assoc 1990, MIPA 1991, MSPI 1992, memb American Bankruptcy Inst 1994; *Publications* Insolvency Procedure Notes (jtly with Michael Stubbs, 1987, revised edn 1991); *Recreations* theatre, opera, wine, travel; *Style*— Paul Gordon-Saker, Esq; ✉ Stephenson Harwood, One St Paul's Churchyard, London EC4M 8SH (tel 020 7329 4422, fax 020 7606 0822, e-mail paul.gordon-saker@shlegal.com)

GORDON-SMITH, Prof Edward Colin (Ted); s of Gordon John Smith (d 1938), and Valentine Strange, *née* Waddington (d 1987); *b* 26 June 1938; *Educ* Oakham Sch, Epsom Coll, Exeter Coll Oxford (BA, BSc, BM BCh), Westminster Med Sch; *m* 1967, Moira Bernadette, da of Joseph Phelan; 2 s (Duncan Joseph b 1971, James Edward b 1973); *Career* house surgn then house physician Westminster Hosp 1963–64, SHO Nuffield Dept of Med Radcliffe Infirmary Oxford 1964–65, lectr in neurology Churchill Hosp Oxford 1965–67, registrar St James' Hosp Balham 1967, registrar in haematology RPMS 1968–70, MRC clinical training fell 1970–72, reader RPMS 1982–86 (sr lectr 1972–82), prof of haematology and hon conslt St George's Hosp Med Sch London 1987–2003; res fell Metabolic Research Gp Oxford 1971; pres Euro Bone Marrow Transplant Gp 1980; ed Br Jl of Haematology 1983–86; chair: MRC Leukaemia Trials Steering Ctee 1988–2002, Nat Blood Service User Gp 1996–99; vice-pres RCPath 1996–99; chm Cncl Int Soc of Haematology 2000–04; memb: Br Soc of Haematology 1972– (pres 1994–95), Int Soc for Experimental Haematology 1984– (pres 1992), American Soc for Haematology 1987–, RSM 1980; FRCP 1978 (MRCP 1968), FRCPath 1987 (MRCPath 1985), FRCPEd, FMedSci; *Recreations* golf, gardening, music; *Style*— Prof Ted Gordon-Smith; ✉ Department of Haematology, St George's Hospital Medical School, Tooting, London SW17 0RE (tel 020 8725 5448, fax 020 8725 0245, e-mail e.gordon-smith@sghms.ac.uk)

GORDON-SMITH, William Haydn; s of Cyril Smith, ISO (d 1993), and Joyce Muriel, *née* Davies (d 2001); *b* 14 March 1944; *Educ* Richmond Hill Sch Sprotbrough, West End Co Sch Bentley, Doncaster Tech Coll; *Career* writer and local architectural historian; civil servant Ministry of Pensions & Nat Insurance 1962–89, proprietor The Lodge Gallery Cusworth Park Doncaster 1972–77, Clerk Parish Cncls of Norton and High Melton 1972–78, agent to Cusworth Estate and tstee Cusworth Church Lands 1971–; memb Doncaster Civic Tst; Lord of the Manor of Cusworth in the former W Riding of Yorkshire, Arms granted by College of Arms London 1991; *Books* Cusworth Hall (1964), Sprotbrough Hall (1966), Askern Spa (1968), Sprotbrough Colliery (1968), Cusworth Hall and the Battie-Wrightson Family (1990), Cantley Hall (1992); series of fifty illustrated articles on the Country Houses of Doncaster (1964) for Doncaster Gazette and South Yorkshire Times; *Style*— W H Gordon-Smith, Esq; ✉ 7 Christ Church Terrace, Thorne Road, Doncaster, South Yorkshire DN1 2HU (tel 07732 323903); Villa Mr Gordon, Sheikh Moussa, El Karnak, Luxor, Egypt (tel 00 20 10 655 9893); 13 Rue Kamel El Kilani, Flat 2, Alexandria, Egypt (tel 00 20 3 392 4244)

GORDON WALKER, Hon Alan Rudolf; er (twin) s of Baron Gordon-Walker, CH, PC (Life Peer, d 1980); *b* 1946; *Educ* Wellington, ChCh Oxford (MA); *m* 1976, Louise Frances Amy, da of Gen Sir Charles Henry Pepys Harington, GCB, CBE, DSO, MC; 1 s (Thomas b 1978), 1 da (Emily b 1981); *Career* former md: Hodder and Stoughton, Pan Macmillan Ltd, Cassells; chm Calder Walker Associates 1997–, publisher Politico's 2005–; *Clubs* MCC, Hurlingham; *Style*— The Hon Alan Gordon Walker

GORE, Allan Peter; QC (2003); *b* 25 August 1951, Sydney, Australia; *Educ* Purley GS for Boys, Trinity Hall Cambridge (BA, LLB), Coll of Law Chancery Lane; *m* 1981 (m dis 1998); 3 da (Rachael, Lauren, Hannah); *Career* called to the Bar Middle Temple 1978; tenant: 2 Plowden Buildings 1979–82, 5 Essex Court 1982–91, 12 King's Bench Walk 1991–; recorder 2000– (asst recorder 1999–2000); lectr then sr lectr in law Poly of the South Bank London 1975–81, instr Inns of Court Sch of Law 1986–90; memb Exec Ctee: Personal Injury Bar Assoc 1994–2003, Assoc of Personal Injury Lawyers 1995–2006 (pres 2005); ADR accredited mediator 2005; *Recreations* sport, food, travel, reading, film and theatre, music, modern art; *Style*— Allan Gore, Esq, QC; ✉ 12 King's Bench Walk, Temple, London EC4Y 7EL (tel 020 7583 0811)

GORE, Michael Balfour Gruberg; s of Dr Victor Gore (d 1985), of London, and Victoria, *née* Slavouski (d 2005); *b* 25 October 1937; *Educ* Felsted, Peterhouse Cambridge (BA); *m* 11 April 1972, Mozella (d 2005), da of Geoffrey Ransom (d 1990); 2 s (Benjamin b 1974, Daniel b 1977), 1 da (Camilla (twin) b 1977); *Career* Kemp Chatteris & Co 1959–64, dir S G Warburg & Co Ltd 1969–95 (joined 1964); chm: S G Warburg & Co (Jersey) Ltd 1979–87, Rowe & Pitman Moneybroking Ltd 1986–91, S G Warburg Group Management Ltd 1986–93, S G Warburg Asia/Pacific Ltd 1993–95; vice-chm S G Warburg Group plc (formerly Mercury International Group plc) 1991–95 (dir 1985–95, group fin dir 1986–93); dep chm Potter Warburg Ltd Melbourne 1989–95; dir Zella Gallery 1991–2001; chm Cncl Friends of Peterhouse 1996–99, memb Ctee Peterhouse Soc 1997–99; past memb Hundred

Group of Finance Directors and Senate of Bd for Chartered Accountants in Business; FCA; *Style*— Michael Gore, Esq; ✉ 19 Launceston Place, London W8 5RL (tel 020 7938 1877, fax 020 7938 1183, e-mail michaelbggore@aol.com)

GORE, Sir Nigel Hugh St George; 14 Bt (I 1622), of Magherabegg, Co Donegal; yr s of St George Richard Gore (d 1952), who was gn of 9 Bt; suc his n, Sir Richard Ralph St George Gore, 13 Bt (d 1993); *b* 23 December 1922; *m* 3 Sept 1952, Beth Allison (d 1976), da of R W Hooper; 1 da (Seonaid Beth b 1955); *Heir* cous, Hugh Gore; *Style*— Sir Nigel Gore, Bt; ✉ 5 Chelsea Court, Toowoomba, Queensland 4350, Australia

GORE-BOOTH, Sir Josslyn Henry Robert; 9 Bt (I 1760), of Artarman, Sligo; o s of Sir Angus Josslyn Gore-Booth, 8 Bt (d 1996), and Hon Rosemary Myra, *née* Vane (d 1999), da of 10 Baron Barnard, CMG, OBE, MC, TD; *b* 5 October 1950; *Educ* Eton, Balliol Coll Oxford (BA), INSEAD (MBA); *m* 1980, Jane Mary, da of Hon Sir (James) Roualeyn (Hovell-Thurlow-) Cumming-Bruce (d 2000); 2 da (Mary Georgina b 1985, Caroline Sarah b 1987); *Heir* kinsman, Julian Gore-Booth; *Career* dir Kiln Cotesworth Corporate Capital Fund plc 1993–97; patron Sacred Trinity Salford; *Recreations* shooting, cooking; *Style*— Sir Josslyn Gore-Booth, Bt; ✉ Stud Yard House, Neasham, Darlington, Co Durham DL2 1PH (tel 01325 720333)

GORE BROWNE, Alexandra Victoria (Alex); da of Anthony Giles Spencer Gore Browne , *qv*, of London, and Penelope Anne Courtenay Jones, *née* Thomson; *b* 24 August 1975; *Educ* Francis Holland Sch (scholar), Chelsea Coll of Art, Central St Martins (BA, Queens scholarship); *Career* asst Edina Ronay 1997, freelance work for Donna Karan, Gap and Warner Bros 1998–99, knit conslt for Matthew Williamson, Ghost, Joseph and Alexander McQueen (designed and made showpieces for autumn/winter 2001) 2000, consultancy alex gore browne for dcc Dawson Int 2001, fndr own label knitwear 2001; exhibited: London Designers Exhbn spring/summer 2002 and autumn/winter 2002; New Generation sponsorship by Marks and Spencer and Topshop; visiting lectr Central St Martins 2004–; *Clubs* Chelsea Arts; *Style*— Miss Alex Gore Browne; ✉ Unit E7, Cockpit Studios, Cockpit Yard, Northington Street, London WC1N 2NP (tel 020 7419 1200, fax 020 7916 2455, e-mail alex@alexgorebrowne.com, website www.alexgorebrowne.com)

GORE BROWNE, Anthony Giles Spencer; s of (John) Giles Charles Gore Browne (d 1980), of Manton, Rutland, and Pamela Helen, *née* Newton; *b* 20 April 1944; *Educ* Rannoch Sch Perthshire; *m* 1, 14 March 1970, Penelope Anne Courtenay, da of Prebendary C E Leighton Thomson, of Chelsea, London; 1 s (Edward b 1973), 1 da (Alexandra , *qv*, b 1975); *m* 2, 6 Jan 1992, (Sarah) Gay, da of F G Salway, of West Felton, Salop; 1 s (George b 1993); *Career* stockbroker 1964–; Sheppards & Co 1964–65, Sheppards & Chase 1965–73, ptnr R C Greig & Co Glasgow (London Office) 1973–82, dir Greig Middleton & Co Ltd 1986–2000 (ptnr 1982–86), dir Riverside Racquets plc 1988–93, dir client liaison Seymour Pierce Gp plc 2000–; Liveryman Worshipful Co of Fishmongers 1965, Freeman City of London 1965; MSI; *Clubs* City of London; *Style*— Anthony Gore Browne, Esq; ✉ 6 Priory Gardens, Barnes, London SW13 0JU (tel 020 8876 1531, e-mail anthonygorebrowne@amserve.com); Equity for Growth (Securities) Limited, 17 Hill Street, Mayfair, London W1J 5LJ (tel 020 7518 4344, fax 020 7409 2880, e-mail anthonygorebrown@equityforgrowth.co.uk)

GORE BROWNE, James Anthony; s of Sir Thomas Gore Browne (d 1988), and Lavinia, *née* Loyd (d 1995); *b* 26 March 1947; *Educ* Eton, Univ of Dundee (MA), Aston Univ (Dip Business Admin); *m* 16 April 1983, Jane Anne, da of Col Seton Dickson, of Symington, Ayrshire; 1 da (Marina b 19 Dec 1984); 2 s (Freddie b 21 Jan 1987, Harry b 20 April 1988); *Career* Cazenove & Co 1969–75, asst to Chm EMI Ltd 1976–79, Thames TV 1979–80, Lead Industries Group 1980–81; admitted slr 1986, fndr litigation practice Leicester 1991–2001; Parly candidate (SDP) Doncaster Central 1987, joined Lab Pty 1989 (resigned 1994), re-joined Cons Pty 1994; Liveryman Worshipful Co of Fishmongers; *Recreations* golf, studying portraiture; *Clubs* White's; *Style*— James Gore Browne, Esq; ✉ Vane House, Tugby, Leicestershire LE7 9WD (tel 0116 259 8382)

GORE-RANDALL, Philip Allan; s of Alec Albert Gore-Randall (d 1996), of Uxbridge, Middx and Joyce Margaret, *née* Gore; *b* 16 December 1952; *Educ* Merchant Taylors', UC Oxford (MA); *m* 15 Dec 1984, Prof Alison Elizabeth While, *qv*, da of Harold Arthur Armstrong While, MBE, TD (d 1983); 2 s (William b 1986, Edward b 1987); *Career* Andersen: joined 1975, ptnr 1986–2003, head London Audit and Business Advsy 1994–97, managing ptnr UK Assurance and Business Advsy 1995–97, managing ptnr Europe Assurance and Business Advsy 1996–97, UK managing ptnr 1997–2000, managing ptnr Global Operations 2001–03; chm and chief exec Aon Risk Services UK 2004–05; memb: Bd Aon UK 2004–07 (chief operating offr 2006–07), COO, HBoS; non-exec dir Int Bd Lovells; MInstPet, FCA 1978; *Recreations* classical music, good food, travel, Cotswolds; *Clubs* Vincent's (Oxford); *Style*— Philip Gore-Randall, Esq

GORELL, 4 Baron (UK 1909); Timothy John Radcliffe Barnes; s of 3 Baron Gorell, CBE, MC, (d 1963), and (Maud) Elizabeth Furse (d 1954), eld da of Alexander Radcliffe, of Bag Park, S Devon; *b* 2 August 1927; *Educ* Groton Sch Mass, Eton, New Coll Oxford; *m* 1954, Joan, da of John Collins, MC; 2 adopted da; *Heir* n, John Picton Gorell Barnes; *Career* late Lt Rifle Bde; called to the Bar 1951; sr exec Royal Dutch Shell Group 1959–84; various directorships until 1992, EEC Sub Ctee House of Lords 1987; Upper Bailiff Worshipful Co of Weavers 1977–78; *Recreations* gardening, painting; *Style*— The Rt Hon the Lord Gorell; ✉ 4 Roehampton Gate, London SW15 5JS (tel 020 8876 5522)

GORHAM, Martin Edwin; OBE (2005); s of Clifford Edwin Gorham (d 1983), and Florence Ada, *née* Wright; *b* 18 June 1947; *Educ* Buckhurst Hill Co HS, QMC London (BA); *Career* administrative trg NHS 1968–70; dep hosp sec: Scarborough Hosp 1970–72, Doncaster Royal Infirmary 1972–75; hosp administrator: Northern Gen Hosp Sheffield 1975–82, Lodge Moor Hosp Sheffield 1983; head of corp planning Newcastle HA 1983–86, unit gen mangr Norfolk and Norwich Hosps Acute Unit 1986–90, dep regnl gen mangr South West Thames RHA 1990–92, chief exec London Ambulance Serv 1992–96, dir of projects S Thames Regnl Office NHS Exec 1996–98, chief exec Nat Blood Service 1998–2005, chief exec NHS Blood and Transplant (NHSBT) 2005–; pres European Blood Alliance 2001–, tstee Princess Royal Tst For Carers 2001–06; MHSM, Dip HSM; *Recreations* walking, music, reading, gardening, travelling and the arts in general, sport (cricket and skiing); *Style*— Martin Gorham, Esq, OBE; ✉ NHS Blood and Transplant, Oak House, Reeds Crescent, Watford, Hertfordshire WD1 1QH (tel 01923 486800, mobile 07711 447265)

GORICK, (Robert) Lionel; MBE (2000); s of John Gorick (d 1989), of Llandudno, N Wales; *b* 24 February 1927; *Educ* Blackburn Tech Coll; *m* 1958, Jean Audrey, da of Frank Harwood (d 1976), of Wilpshire, nr Blackburn; 3 c; *Career* chm: Liquid Plastics Ltd 1963– (mfr of plastics-based roofing systems and fire retardant finishes, Queen's Award for Export 1982), Industrial Copolymers Ltd, Iotech Ltd; hon fell Univ of Central Lancashire 1997; *Recreations* reading, horticulture, modern music, wining and dining; *Clubs* Preston Rotary; *Style*— Lionel Gorick, Esq, MBE; ✉ The Stone House, Whittingham Lane, Broughton, Preston, Lancashire PR3 5DB (tel 01772 864872/864879); Liquid Plastics Ltd, Iotech House, Miller Street, Preston, Lancashire PR1 1EA (tel 01772 259781, fax 01772 255676, e-mail rlg@liquidplastics.co.uk)

GORING, George Ernest; OBE (1992); *b* 19 May 1938; *Educ* Cheltenham, Ecole Hoteliere Lausanne, Westminster Coll; *Career* md and prop The Goring Hotel and Manoir de Lezurec France; chm Master Innholders 1988, pres Reunion des Gastronomes 1988–90; chm London Div BHRCA 1989–92, chm Pride of Britain Hotel Consortium 1997–2000; jt master Mid Surrey Farmers' Draghounds 1993; Hotelier of the Year 1990, membre d'honneur Clefs d'Or; Liveryman Worshipful Co of Distillers; fell Tourism Soc, Master Innholder, FHCIMA; *Recreations* horseracing, hunting, the sea; *Style*— George Goring, Esq, OBE; ✉ The Goring Hotel, Beeston Place, Grosvenor Gardens, London SW1W 0JW

GORING, Lesley Susan; da of Walter Edwin Goring (d 1983), and Peggy Lambert; *b* 23 March 1950; *Educ* Northfields Sch for Girls; *Career* fashion PR conslt; PA to mangr Biba 1965–67, press offr Mr Freedom 1967–72, Lynne Franks PR 1972–75; fndr and proprietor: Goring Public Relations 1975–, Lesley Goring Fashion Show Production 1980–; *Recreations* music, social gatherings, pets; *Style*— Ms Lesley Goring; ✉ Lesley Goring Show Production, 1 The Quad, Battersea High Street, London SW11 3HX (e-mail goring@easynet.co.uk)

GORING, Sir William Burton Nigel; 13 Bt (E 1678, with precedency of 1627), of Highden, Sussex; s of Maj Frederick Yelverton Goring (d 1938, 6 s of 11 Bt), and Freda Margaret, *née* Ainsworth (d 1993); suc unc, Sir Forster Gurney Goring, 12 Bt, 1956; the Goring family is of great antiquity in Sussex and were MPs from fifteenth to the nineteenth century; *b* 21 June 1933; *Educ* Wellington, RMA Sandhurst; *m* 1, 1960 (m dis), Hon Caroline Thellusson, da of 8 Baron Rendlesham; m 2, 25 Oct 1993, Mrs Judith Rachel Walton Morison (d 1995), da of Rev Raymond John Walton Morris, OBE, of Shaftesbury, Dorset; m 3, 1998, Mrs Stephanie Bullock, da of George Carter, DFC, of Aldeburgh, Suffolk; *Heir* kinsman, Richard Goring; *Career* Lt Royal Sussex Regt; memb London Stock Exchange 1963, ptnr Quilter and Co 1976; Master Worshipful Co of Woolmen 2000–; *Recreations* social golf, bridge; *Clubs* Hurlingham; *Style*— Sir William Goring, Bt; ✉ c/o Morgan Stanley Quilter, St Helens, 1 Undershaft, London EC3A 8BB

GORLOV, Alison Mary Haymon; da of Mark Haymon (d 1992), of London, and Sylvia Theresa, *née* Rosen (d 1995), of Norwich; *b* 7 September 1951, London; *Educ* Walthamstow Hall Sevenoaks, Coll of Law London; *m* 16 Nov 1975, Peter Gorlov; 4 da (Rebecca b 1 Aug 1982, Sarah b 30 May 1984, Jessica b 2 July 1987, Naomi b 4 May 1992); *Career* admitted slr 1975; appointed Roll A Parly agent 1978; ptnr: Sherwood & Co 1978–90 (asst slr 1975), Winckworth Sherwood (following merger) 1990–; memb Law Soc, memb and past pres Soc of Parly Agents; *Recreations* reading, listening to classical music, writing, walking, history; *Style*— Mrs Alison Gorlov; ✉ 11 Queen Anne's Gate, Westminster, London SW1H 9BU; Winckworth Sherwood, 35 Great Peter Street, Westminster, London SW1P 3LR (tel 020 7593 5005, fax 020 7593 5199, e-mail agorlov@winckworths.co.uk)

GORMAN, Michael; s of Thomas Gorman (d 1977); *Educ* Univ of Liverpool (BA, PGCE), Univ of London Inst of Educn (CertEd); *m* Rosemary, da of Eric Young McDonald; *Career* teacher Farnham Coll Surrey 1974–77, football coach Bahrain Nat Side 1977–80, various coaching tasks for Football Assoc 1980–82, advtg asst Ted Bates London 1982–86, various positions rising to media dir DMB&B 1986–91, head of client servs Portland Outdoor Advertising 1992–94, media dir Saatchi & Saatchi 1994–98, European media dir Bozell Worldwide 1999–, European media dir FCB Int; author of articles for trade jls (reg contrib Media Week); *Recreations* football, cricket, golf, supporting Manchester United FC; *Clubs* RAC, Lord's Taverners; *Style*— Michael Gorman, Esq

GORMAN, Prof Neil Thomson; s of Stewart Gorman (d 1996), and Madge Isabella, *née* Thomson (d 2006); *b* 10 September 1950, Wolverhampton; *Educ* Univ of Liverpool (BVSc, Edgar Golding Prize in Anatomy, Pathology Prize, Clinical Vet Prize), Univ of Cambridge (Horserace Betting Levy Bd PhD Research Fellowship, PhD); *m* 16 Aug 1975, Susan Mary, *née* Smith; 1 da (Felicity Jane b 4 Jan 1981), 1 s (James Muir b 28 Dec 1983); *Career* postdoctoral research assoc MRC Centre Cambridge 1977–81, jr research fell Wolfson Coll Cambridge 1978–81, asst prof Dept of Med Sciences Sch of Vet Med Univ of Florida 1981–84 (concurrently asst prof Dept of Comparative and Experimental Pathology and Dept of Med Microbiology and Immunology Coll of Med), lectr in vet med and oncology Dept of Clinical Vet Med Univ of Cambridge 1984–87, tutor in vet med Christ's Coll Cambridge 1985–87, fell Wolfson Coll Cambridge 1986–87, prof of vet surgery and head Dept of Vet Surgery Glasgow Univ Vet Sch 1987–93, head of research Waltham Centre for Pet Nutrition 1993–97, vice-pres R&D Mars Petcare Europe 1997–99 (European dir of R&D 1997), vice-pres R&D (petcare) Masterfoods Europe 2000–01, global dir (science and technology platforms) Masterfoods Europe 2001–03, vice-chllr Nottingham Trent Univ 2003–; visiting prof Coll of Vet Med Michigan State Univ 1986, Evelyn Williams visiting prof Faculty of Vet Science Univ of Sydney 1988, adjunct prof Dept of Med Sciences Coll of Vet Med Univ of Florida 1987–93; hon prof Faculty of Vet Med Univ of Glasgow; memb Research Assessment Exercise for Vet Med, Agric and Food Science 2001; delivered numerous lectures and presentations worldwide; RCVS: memb Vet Nursing Ctee 1990–99 (chm 1995–99), memb Cncl 1990–, memb Educn Ctee 1991–93, memb Specialisation and FE Ctee 1995–98, chm Fin and Gen Purposes Ctee 1996–97, memb External Affrs Ctee 1996–, jr vice-pres 1996–97, pres 1997–98, sr vice-pres 1998–99, memb Advsy Ctee 2000–; Br Small Animal Vet Assoc (BSAVA): memb Scientific Ctee 1978–81, memb Educn Ctee 1986–90, memb Congress Ctee 1987–90, jr vice-pres 1990–91, pres 1992–93 (pres-elect 1991–92), sr vice-pres 1993–94; AFRC: memb Visiting Panels to BBSRC Insts 1989 and 1993, memb Agric Research Grant Ctee 1990–93, memb BBSRC Network Gp 1996–; memb Cncl Animal Welfare Cncl 1999–; memb: American Assoc of Immunologists, Br Assoc of Immunology, American Assoc of Vet Immunologists, Br Vet Cancer Soc, American Vet Cancer Soc, European Vet Cancer Soc, NY Acad of Sciences, BVA, BSAVA, Br Soc of Gen Microbiology, American Vet Med Assoc; Wellcome Tst Travel Award 1980, American Assoc of Immunologists Travel Award 1983, WHO Int Cancer Technol Transfer (ICRETT) Fellowship 1986, Diplomate American Coll of Vet Internal Med (Oncology) 1988; involved with: BioCity Nottingham Ltd, Experience Nottinghamshire; memb Ct Univ of Liverpool; FRCVS 1981 (MRCVS 1974); *Publications* Advances in Veterinary Immunology and Immunopathology (ed with F J Bourne, 1983, 2 edn 1985), Contemporary Issues on Small Animal Medicine Volume 6 - Oncology (1986), Clinical Veterinary Immunology (with R E W Halliwell, 1988), Basic and Applied Chemotherapy in Veterinary Practice (with J M Dobson, 1992), Canine Medicine and Therapeutics (ed, 1998); also author of book chapters, refereed articles and conf proceedings; *Recreations* opera, golf, sport; *Clubs* Caledonian; *Style*— Prof Neil Gorman; ✉ Nottingham Trent University, Burton Street, Nottingham NG1 4BU (tel 0115 848 6571, fax 0115 947 3523, e-mail neil.gorman@ntu.ac.uk)

GORMANSTON, 17 Viscount (I 1478, Premier Viscount of Ireland); Jenico Nicholas Dudley Preston; also Baron Gormanston (I 1365–70 and UK 1868, which latter sits as); s of 16 Viscount (ka 1940), and Pamela, *née* Hanly (whose mother was Lady Marjorie, *née* Feilding, da of 9 Earl of Denbigh); *b* 19 November 1939; *Educ* Downside; *m* 1, 1974, Eva Landzianowska (d 1984); 2 s (Hon Jenico b 1974, Hon William b 3 May 1976); m 2, 26 Nov 1997, Mrs Lucy Grenfell; *Heir* s, Hon Jenico Preston; *Career* Fine Arts; FRGS; *Clubs* Kildare St and University (Dublin); *Style*— The Rt Hon the Viscount Gormanston; ✉ 27a Ifield Road, London SW10 9AZ (tel 020 7376 3128)

GORMLEY, Antony Mark David; OBE (1997); s of Arthur John Constantine Gormley (d 1977), of Hampstead, London, and Elspeth, *née* Braüninger; bro of Brendan Gormley, MBE, *qv*; *b* 30 August 1950; *Educ* Ampleforth, Trinity Coll Cambridge (MA), Goldsmiths Coll London (BA), Slade Sch of Fine Art UCL (Higher Dip Fine Art); *m* 14 June 1980, Emelyn Victoria (Vicken), da of Maj (Ian) David Parsons, of Broxbourne, Herts; 2 s (Ivo b 16 March 1982, Guy b 17 June 1985), 1 da (Paloma b 20 July 1987); *Career* artist and sculptor; memb Arts Cncl of England 1998–; major cmmn incl Angel of the North 1997 (Civic Tst Award 2000); winner Turner Prize 1994, South Bank Art Award 1999, Br D&AD Silver Award for Illustration 2000; hon fell: Goldsmiths Coll London 1998, RIBA

G

2001, Jesus Coll Cambridge 2003, Trinity Coll Cambridge 2003; hon doctorate: Univ of Sunderland 1998, UCE 1998, Open Univ 2001, Univ of Cambridge 2003, Univ of Newcastle upon Tyne 2004; FRSA 2000, RA 2003; *Solo Exhibitions* incl: Whitechapel Art Gallery London 1981, Chapter Cardiff 1984, Salvatore Ala Gallery NY 1985, 1986, 1987, 1989 and 1991, Serpentine Gallery London 1987, Burnett Miller LA 1988, 1990 and 1992, Louisiana Museum Denmark 1989, Scot Nat Gallery of Modern Art Edinburgh 1989, Art Gallery of NSW Sydney 1989, Frith St Gallery London 1991, Shirakawa Gallery Kyoto 1991, Field (Modern Art Museum Fort Worth, Centro Cultural Arte Contemporánea Mexico City, Museum of Contemporary Art San Diego, Corcoran Gallery of Art Washington and Museum of Fine Arts Montreal) 1991–93, Body and Soul: Learning to See (Contemporary Art Centre Tokyo) 1992, Learning to Think (Br Sch Rome) 1992, European Field (Konsthall Malmö, Centrum Sztuki Wspolczesnej Zagreb, Ludwig Museum Budapest, Prague Castle, Bucharest) 1993–95, Field for the British Isles (Tate Gallery Liverpool, Irish MOMA Dublin, Oriel Mostyn Llandudno, Scot Nat Gallery of Modern Art Edinburgh, Orchard Gallery Derry, Ikon Gallery Birmingham, Nat Gallery of Wales Cardiff, Hayward Gallery London) 1993–96, Galeria Pedro Oliveira Oporto 1994, Kohji Ogura Gallery Nagoya 1995, Remise Vienna 1995, New Work (Obala Art Centar Bosnia) 1996, Inside the Inside (Galerie Xavier Hufkens Brussels) 1996, Still Moving: Works 1975–96 (retrospective touring exhbn Japan) 1996–97, Total Strangers (Koelnischer Kunstverein Cologne) 1997, Our House (Kunsthalle zu Kiel) 1997, Sculpture and Drawings (Galerie Nordenhake Stockholm) 1997, Critical Mass (Royal Acad of Arts London) 1998, Force Fields (Rupertinum Salzburg) 1998, Insiders and Other Recent Work (Galerie Xavier Hufkens Brussels) 1999, Intimate Relations (Maclaren Art Centre Ontario and Jablonka Galerie Cologne) 1999, Quantum Cloud (Millennium Dome London) 2000, Quantum Clouds and Other Work (Galerie Thaddaeus Ropac Paris) 2000, Strange Insiders (fig-1 London) 2000, Drawn (White Cube London) 2000, Insiders (New Art Centre and Sculpture Park East Winterslow) 2001, Some of the Facts (Tate Gallery St Ives) 2001, Sculpture (Centro Galego de Arte Contemporanea Santiago de Compostela) 2002, Galleria Mimmo Scognamiglio Naples 2002, Inside Australia (Lake Ballard, Menzies, Perth Int Arts Festival WA) 2002, Asian Field (Xinhuahuayuan Huajingxincheng, Guangzhou China and tour in China) 2003, Standing Matter (Galerie Thaddaeus Ropac Salzburg) 2003, Baltic Centre for Contemporary Arts Gateshead 2003, Domain Field (The Great Hall Winchester) 2004, Mass and Empathy (Fundacao Gulbenkain Lisbon) 2004; *Group Exhibitions* Objects and Sculpture (ICA London) 1981, Br Sculpture of the 20th Century (Whitechapel Art Gallery London) 1981, Venice Biennale 1982 and 1986, Biennale de São Paulo 1983, Int Survey MOMA NY 1984, British Art Now: A Subjective View (touring exhbn Japan) 1990–91, Inheritance and Transformation (Irish MOMA Dublin) 1991, Natural Order (Tate Gallery Liverpool) 1992, Images of Man (Isetan Museum of Art, Tokyo/Daimura Museum, Umeda-Osaka/Hiroshima City Museum of Contemporary Art) 1992, The Human Factor: Figurative Sculpture Reconsidered (Albuquerque Museum) 1993, HA HA: Contemporary British Art in an 18th Century Garden (Killerton Park) 1993, The Fujisankei Biennale (Hakone Open-Air Museum) 1993, From Beyond the Pale: Part One (Irish MOMA Dublin) 1994, Sculptors' Drawings from the Weltkunst Collection (Tate Gallery London) 1994, Contemporary British Art in Print (Scot Nat Gallery of Modern Art Edinburgh and Yale Center for Br Art New Haven) 1995, Glaube, Hoffnung, Liebe und Tod (Kunsthalle Vienna) 1995, Un Siècle de Sculpture Anglaise (Jeu de Paume Paris) 1996, Betong (Konsthall Malmö) 1996, A Ilha Do Tesouro (Centro de Arte Moderna Jose de Azeredo Perdigao Lisbon) 1997, L'Empreinte (Centre Georges Pompidou Paris) 1997, Material Culture: The Object in British Art of the 1980's and 90's (Hayward Gallery) 1997, Arte Urbana (Expo '98 Lisbon) 1998, Presence: Figurative Art at the End of the Century (Tate Gallery Liverpool) 1999; *Publications* La Casa Il Corpo Il Coure (Museum Moderner Kunst Stiftung Ludwig Vienna) 1999, Den Haag Sculptuure: British Sculpture of the Twentieth Century (The Hague) 1999, Reality and Desire (Fundació Joan Miro Barcelona) 1999, The Shape of the Century: 100 Years of British Sculpture (Canary Wharf London) 1999, At Home with Art (Tate Gallery London and tour) 1999, Trialogo: Guiseppe Gallo, Anthony Gormley, David Hammons (Palazzo delle Esposizione Rome) 2000, Out There (White Cube London) 2000, Vibration (Utsunomiya Museum of Art Japan) 2001, Geometrie Plus Gestus (Galerie Thaddaeus Ropac and Max-Gandolph Bibliotek Salzburg) 2001, Miroslav Balka, Anthony Gormley, Ulrich Ruckreim (Galleri Solvberget Stravanger) 2001, Time Space Motion (Galerie Thaddaeus Ropac and Max-Gandolph Bibliotek Salzburg Austria) 2002, Who Comes-Who Leaves-Who Stays (Eastern Cemetery Malmö) 2002, Blast to Freeze (Kunstmuseum Wolfsburg and tour) 2002, Self Evident: The Artist as the Subject 1969–2002 (Tate Britain London), The Nude in 20th Century Art (Kunsthalle Emden) 2002, Territoires Nomades (Landesmuseum Joanneum and Jesuit's Coll Graz and tour) 2003, Sanctuary (Gallery of Modern Art Glasgow) 2003, Blickachsen (Bad Homburg) 2003, Me & More (Kunstmuseum Luzern) 2003, Past and Present: Jewellery by 20th Century Artists (Louisa Brown Gallery) 2003, Presence - Images of Christ for the Third Millennium (Canterbury Cathedral) 2004, Off the Beaten Track: Arts Cncl Collection Explored (Longside Gallery Yorkshire Sculpture Park) 2004, Etre - Les Droits de l'Homme á Travers l'Art (Palais des Nations UN Geneva) 2004; *Collections* incl: Arts Cncl of GB, Tate Gallery, CAS, Br Cncl, Southampton Art Gallery, Neue Museum Kassel, Stadt Kassel, Walker Arts Centre Minneapolis, Leeds City Art Gallery, Irish MOMA Dublin, Louisiana Museum Denmark, Scot Nat Gallery of Modern Art Edinburgh, Moderna Museet Stockholm, Konsthall Malmö; *Recreations* sailing, skiing, walking; *Style—* Antony Gormley, Esq, OBE; ✉ 13 South Villas, London NW1 9BS (tel 020 7482 7383); 15–23 Vale Royal, London N7 9AP (tel 020 7697 2180, fax 020 7697 2188)

GORMLEY, (Paul) Brendan; MBE (2001); s of Arthur John Constantine Gormley (d 1977), and Elspeth, *née* Brauninger; bro of Antony Gormley, OBE, *qv*; *b* 2 September 1947, London; *Educ* Strasbourg Univ, Trinity Coll Cambridge (MA); *m* 14 Sept 1974, Sally Henderson; 2 s (Thomas J b 4 April 1977, Titus D b 12 July 1981), 1 da (Chloe A b 22 Feb 1979); *Career* former social worker and monk; Oxfam: country dir Niger 1976–78, regnl dir W Africa 1978–83, country dir Egypt 1983–85, positions at Oxfam HQ 1985–2000, Africa dir 1991–2000; ceo Disasters Emergency Ctee 2000–; tstee: Noel Buxton Tst, One World Broadcasting Tst; *Recreations* sailing, golf; *Style—* Brendan Gormley, Esq, MBE; ✉ Foxburrow Barn, Hailey, Witney OX29 9UH (tel 01993 773592); Disasters Emergency Committee, 15 Warren Mews, London W1T 6AZ (tel 020 7387 0200, fax 020 7387 2050, e-mail bgormley@dec.org.uk)

GORMLY, Allan Graham; CMG (2005), CBE (1991); s of William Gormly, and Christina Swinton Flockhart, *née* Arnot; *b* 18 December 1937; *Educ* Paisley GS, Univ of Glasgow; *m* 30 June 1962, Vera Margaret, da of late Alexander Grant; 1 da (Lynn Margaret b 15 Nov 1963), 1 s (Alisdair William b 10 Sept 1965); *Career* chm John Brown Engineering Ltd 1983–92, gp md John Brown plc 1983–92, chm John Brown plc 1992–94, dir Trafalgar House Construction Holdings Ltd 1986–89; Trafalgar House plc (parent co of John Brown): head Engrg Div and main bd dir 1986–92, main bd dir and gp chief exec 1992–94, non-exec dir and jt dep chm 1994–96; chm: RIGPS Properties Ltd 1994–97, Q-One Biotech Ltd 1999–2003; dir: Royal Insurance (UK) Ltd 1994–97, Bank of Scotland 1997–2001; non-exec dep chm Royal & Sun Alliance Insurance Group plc 1996–98; non-exec dir: Royal Insurance Holdings plc 1990–97 (dep chm 1992–94, chm 1994–96), Brixton plc 1994–2003 (chm 2000–03), National Grid Co plc 1994–95, BPB plc 1995–2004 (chm 1997–2004), European Capital Co Ltd 1996–2000; chm Overseas Projects Bd 1988–91, dep chm Export Guarantees Advsy Cncl 1990–92; memb: Export Guarantees Advsy Cncl 1987–92, BOTB 1988–91, Top Salaries Review Body 1990–92, Bd of Mgmnt FCO 2000–04; MICAS 1961; *Recreations* music, golf; *Style—* Allan Gormly, Esq, CMG, CBE

GORNA, Christina; da of John Gorna, of Hale, Cheshire, and Muriel Theresa Gorna; *b* 19 February 1937; *Educ* The Hollies Convent, Loreto Convent Llandudno, Univ of Manchester (LLB), Univ of Neuchâtel (Dip Swiss and Int Law), Sorbonne (Dip French Civilisation), Br Cncl scholar; *m* 6 July 1963, Ian Davies (d 1996), s of Reginald Beresford Davies, of Timperly, Cheshire; 1 da (Samantha Jane b 14 Jan 1964), 1 s (Caspar Dominick John b 11 May 1966); *Career* barr, writer, broadcaster and columnist; called to the Bar Middle Temple 1960 (Harmsworth Scholar); sr lectr Coventry Univ 1973–79, in practice specialising in criminal, family, professional negligence, licensing and media law 1980–, former head Castle Chambers Exeter, ldr Cathedral Chambers Exeter; regulator: ABIA, security industry 2003–; numerous TV and radio appearances incl: Question Time, Any Questions?, Woman's Hour, Kilroy, The Time The Place, Great Expectations, Behind the Headlines, Central Weekend, Advice Shop, The Verdict, Esther - You Are What You Wear, Points of Law, Ready Steady Cook; presenter: Careering Ahead, Experts Exported, The Flying Brief (TV series), Check it Out (consumer series); regular contrib: GMTV, UK Living, Westcountry TV, Viva Radio, Talk Radio, London Talk Radio, Gemini Radio, Channel 1, TLC, The Right Thing, Radio 5 Live, BBC Radio Sussex, Liberty Radio (legal corr), BBC Radio London (also legal corr); occasional contrib five TV, Great Lives 'Vivien Leigh' (BBC Radio 4); judge Sex in Court (series, E4), The Flying Brief (series, Channel 4); profile writer, gossip columnist, book, theatre and art reviewer, public speaker, debater and fashion model; columnist The Universe; profiled in City Magazine 1998 and Express Echo 1999; memb: SW Rent Assessment Tbnl 1999, Bd Amazonia (radical women's theatre gp) 2002–, Advsy Body Women in Prison, Prison Reform Tst, Sub-Ctee ABIA, London Ladies Ctee Cancer Research Campaign, Western Circuit, 300 Gp, Charter 88, Assoc of Women Barristers, Thomas More Soc, Assoc of Catholic Lawyers, Media Soc; hon pres Network West, chair Network Far West; FRSA 1994; *Books* Company Law, Leading Cases on Company Law, Questions and Answers on Company Law, Lies and Misdemeanours, Seize the Day (contrib); *Recreations* reading, swimming, performing and visual arts, art collecting, visiting galleries, writing, painting, clothes (especially hats); reading, writing and wrecking poetry; *Clubs* Groucho, Network; *Style—* Miss Christina Gorna; ✉ Chelsea Chambers, 10A Kempsford Gardens, London SW5 9LH (tel 020 7370 0434); The Old Warehouse, Denver Road, Topsham, Exeter, Devon EX3 0BS (tel 01392 877736); 4 Paper Buildings, Temple, London EC4Y 7EX (tel 020 7353 3366); clerk: Jan Wood (tel 01392 204259); agent: Jacque Evans (tel 020 8699 1202, mobile 07775 565101)

GORNALL, Alastair Charles; s of J I K Gornall, of Odiham, Hants, and E C Gornall, *née* Leighton; *b* 6 June 1956; *Educ* Stowe, RMA Sandhurst (RAF flying scholarship); *m* 1986, Sarah, *née* McCall; 3 c; *Career* Lt 17/21 Lancers; Business Week International NY 1979–81; md: Scope Communications 1981–90, Consolidated Communications Management Ltd 1990–2001, Madsen Gornall Ashe 2002–04; chief exec Reed Exhibitions 2004–; *Recreations* boating; *Clubs* Cavalry and Guards', Annabel's; *Style—* Alastair Gornall, Esq; ✉ Reed Exhibitions Ltd, Oriel House, 26 The Quadrant, Richmond, Surrey TW9 1DL

GORNICK, Naomi; da of Abraham Harris (d 1989), and Rachel Harris (d 1992); *Educ* Montreal Canada, Willesden Sch of Art, PCL; *m* Bruce Gornick; 1 s (Simon), 1 da (Lisa); *Career* design mgmnt conslt; assoc prof of design mgmnt; dir MA Design Strategy and Innovation Brunel Univ 1993–; advsr: Middlesex Univ, De Montfort Univ, industrial clients incl Raychem, London Underground; ed Debrett's Interior Design Collection 1988 and 1989; Chartered Soc of Designers: memb Cncl 1992–, vice-pres 1986–89, fndr chm Design Mgmnt Gp 1981–86; course ldr RCA 1989–91; memb Steering Ctee on Design Mgmnt Courses CNAA, memb Bd of Tstees Worldesign Fndn USA 1993–, chm Design Selection Ctees Design Cncl, panel judge for Design Centre Awards 1989; FCSD, FRSA; *Clubs* Chelsea Arts; *Style—* Naomi Gornick

GORRIE, Donald Cameron Easterbrook; OBE, DL; s of Robert Maclagan Gorrie (d 1970), and Sydney Grace, *née* Easterbrook (d 1977); *b* 2 April 1933; *Educ* Oundle, CCC Oxford (MA); *m* 1957, Astrid Margaret, da of Cecil Salvesen; 2 s (Robert b 1959, Euan b 1962); *Career* schoolmaster: Gordonstoun Sch 1957–60, Marlborough Coll 1960–66; dir of research then admin Scottish Lib Pty 1968–75; cncllr: Edinburgh Town Cncl 1971–75, Lothian Regional Cncl 1974–96, City of Edinburgh DC 1980–96, City of Edinburgh Cncl 1995–97; MP (Lib Dem) Edinburgh W 1997–2001, memb Lib Dem Scotland Team 1997–99; MSP (Lib Dem) Central Scotland 1999–2007; spokesman on: local govt 1999–2000, procedures 1999–2003, finance 2000–02, justice 2001–03, communities 2003–05, standards 2003–07, culture, sport, voluntary sector and older people 2003–07; convenor Procedures Ctee 2005–07; Back Bencher of the Year Herald Award 1999, Free Spirit of the Year 2001; chm Edinburgh Youth Orch 2000–03; sometime memb Bd/Ctee: Royal Lyceum Theatre, Queen's Hall Edinburgh, Edinburgh Festival, Scottish Chamber Orch, Castle Rock Housing Assoc, Lothian Assoc of Youth Clubs, Edinburgh City Youth Cafe, Diverse Attractions, Edinburgh Zoo, Corstorphine Dementia Project, Friends of Corstorphine Hill; hon pres: Edinburgh Athletic Club, Corstorphine Amateur Athletics Club, Edinburgh City Youth Cafe, Lothian Assoc of Youth Clubs; hon vice-pres Achilles Club; former Scottish record holder over 880 yards; *Recreations* reading, visiting ruins, music, theatre, opera; *Style—* Donald Gorrie, OBE, DL; ✉ 9 Garscube Terrace, Edinburgh EH12 6BW (tel 0131 337 2077)

GORRINGE, Christopher John; CBE (1999); s of Maurice Sydney William Gorringe (d 1981), of Newick, E Sussex, and Hilda Joyce, *née* Walker; *b* 13 December 1945; *Educ* Bradfield, RAC Cirencester; *m* 17 April 1976, Jennifer Mary, da of Roger Arthur Chamberlain (d 1979), of Ramsbury, Wilts; 2 da (Kim b 13 April 1978, Anna b 24 Feb 1981); *Career* asst land agent Iveagh Tstees Ltd (Guinness Family) 1968–73, chief exec All Eng Lawn Tennis and Croquet Club Wimbledon 1983–2005 (asst sec 1973–79, sec 1979–83); hon fell Univ of Roehampton 1998; ARICS 1971; *Recreations* lawn tennis; *Clubs* All England Lawn Tennis, Queen's, Jesters, Int LTC of GB, St George's Hill Lawn Tennis, Rye Lawn Tennis (pres); *Style—* Christopher Gorringe, Esq, CBE; ✉ The All England Lawn Tennis Club, Church Road, Wimbledon, London SW19 5AE (tel 020 8944 1066, fax 020 8947 3354)

GORROD, Prof John William; s of Ernest Lionel Gorrod (d 1981), and Caroline Rebecca, *née* Richardson (d 1990); *b* 11 October 1931; *Educ* Univ of London (DSc, PhD), Chelsea Coll London (Dip), Brunel Coll of Advanced Technol (HNC); *m* 3 April 1954, Doreen Mary, da of George Douglas Collins (d 1992); 1 da (Julia b 8 June 1959), 2 s (Simon b 5 April 1962, Nicholas b 16 July 1966); *Career* res fell Dept of Biochemistry Univ of Bari Italy 1964, res fell Royal Cmmn for the Exhibition of 1851 1965–67, lectr in biopharmacy Chelsea Coll London 1968–80 (reader 1980–84), prof of biopharmacy and head Chelsea Dept of Pharmacy KCL 1984–89, res prof Faculty of Life Sciences KCL 1990–97 (head of Div of Health Sciences 1988–90), prof emeritus Univ of London 1997–, prof of toxicology Univ of Essex 1997–; memb Canada Research Chairs Program Coll of Reviewers 2001–; pres Int Soc for the Study of Xenobiotics (ISSX) 2000–01; Gold medal Comenius Univ Bratislava 1991; memb: Assoc for Res in Indoor Air 1989, Air Tport Users' Ctee CAA 1990–92, Assocs for Res in Substances of Enjoyment 1990–97, Cncl Indoor Air Int 1990–98; cncllr Polstead Parish Cncl 1999–2003; corresponding memb German Pharmaceutical Soc 1985; hon fell: Pan/Hellenic Pharmaceutical Soc 1987, Turkish Pharmaceutical Assoc 1988, Bohemslovaca Pharmaceutical Soc 1991, Sch of Pharmacy Univ of London 2002; FRSC 1980, Hon MRPharmS 1982, FRCPath 1984, FKC

1996, CBiol, FIBiol; *Books* Drug Metabolism in Man (1978), Drug Toxicity (1979), Testing for Toxicity (1981), Biological Oxidation of Nitrogen in Organic Molecules (1985), Biological Oxidation of Nitrogen (1978), Metabolism of Xenobiotics (1988), Development of Drugs and Modern Medicines (1986), Molecular Basis of Human Disease (1989), Molecular Basis of Neurological Disorders and Their Treatment (1991), Nicotine and Related Tobacco Alkaloids: absorption, distribution, metabolism and excretion (1993), Analytical Determination of Nicotine and Related Compounds and Their Metabolites (ed, with Peyton Jacob III, 1999); *Recreations* reading travel and biographies; *Clubs* Athenaeum, Hillingdon Athletic; *Style*— Prof John Gorrod; ✉ The Rest Orchard, Polstead Heath, Suffolk CO6 5BG (tel 01787 211752, fax 01787 211753); Biological Sciences, University of Essex, Wivenhoe Park, Essex CO4 3SQ (tel 01206 873331, e-mail jgorr@essex.ac.uk)

GORST, Brenda Anne; *see:* Brenda Coleman

GORST, John Marcus; s of Maj James Marcus Gorst (d 1995), of Fornham All Saints, Suffolk, and Frances Gladys, *née* Espley; *b* 13 January 1944; *Educ* Culford Sch, Selwyn Coll Cambridge (MA); *m* June 1974 (m dis 1977), Marian, da of James Anthony Judge, of Glasgow; *Career* md Drayson Property Holdings Ltd 1971–, chm: Folkard and Hayward Commercial Ltd 1984–, Wild Tracks Ltd 1999–; Freeman Worshipful Co of Bakers; *Recreations* golf, shooting; *Style*— John Gorst, Esq; ✉ Folkard and Hayward Commercial Ltd, East Wing, Chippenham Park, Ely, Cambridgeshire CB7 5PT

GORST, Sir John Michael; kt (1994); s of Derek Charles Gorst; *b* 28 June 1928; *Educ* Ardingly, Corpus Christi Coll Cambridge; *m* 1954, Noël Harington, da of Austin Walker, of East Kilbride; 5 s; *Career* advertising and PR mangr Pye Ltd 1953–63, PR conslt John Gorst and Assocs Ltd 1964–; fndr 1974: Telephone Users' Assoc, Local Radio Assoc; Parly candidate (Cons): Chester-le-Street 1964, Bodmin 1966; MP (Cons) Hendon North 1970–97; memb Select Ctee: on Employment 1979–87, on Nat Heritage 1992–97; chm: Cons Back Bench Media Ctee 1988–90, All-Pty Br Mexican Gp until 1997; vice-chm All-Pty War Crimes Ctee 1988–97; chm Chadwick Associates Ltd 1997–2007; *Style*— Sir John Gorst

GORT, 9 Viscount (I 1816); Foley Robert Standish Prendergast Vereker; also Baron Kiltarton (I 1810); s of 8 Viscount Gort (d 1995), and Bettine, *née* Green; *b* 24 October 1951; *Educ* Harrow; *m* 1, 1979 (m dis 1987), Julie Denise, only da of D W Jones; m 2, 19 Oct 1991, Sharon Lyn, da of A J H Quayle; 1 s (Hon Robert Foley Prendergast b 5 April 1993), 1 da (Catherine Mary 23 Sept 1997); *Heir* s, Hon Robert Vereker; *Career* portrait photographer; *Style*— The Rt Hon the Viscount Gort; ✉ e-mail gort36@manx.net

GORTY, Peter; s of Nathan Gorty, and Bella, *née* Lancet; *b* 3 November 1944; *Educ* Owens Sch Islington, LSE (LLB); *m* 20 Sept 1970, Mariana; 1 s (Andrew), 1 da (Helen); *Career* articled clerk Gilbert Samuel & Co 1967–69, asst slr Withers 1969–70, ptnr specialising in banking and energy law Nabarro Nathanson 1972– (asst slr 1970–72); *Recreations* all sports, reading, theatre, architecture; *Style*— Peter Gorty, Esq; ✉ Nabarro Nathanson, 50 Stratton Street, London W1X 5NX (tel 020 7493 9933, fax 020 7629 7900)

GOSCHEN, Sir Edward Alexander; 4 Bt (UK 1916), of Beacon Lodge, Highcliffe, Co Southampton; s of Sir Edward Christian Goschen, 3 Bt, DSO (d 2001), and Cynthia, da of late Rt Hon Sir Alexander George Montagu Cadogan, OM, GCMG, KCB; *b* 13 March 1949; *Educ* Eton; *m* 1976, Louise Annette, da of Lt-Col Ronald Fulton Lucas Chance, MC, KRRC (d 1996), and Lady Ava, *née* Baird (d 2001), da of 1 Viscount Stonehaven and Lady (Ethel) Sidney, *née* Keith-Falconer, who was Countess of Kintore in her own right; 1 da (Charlotte Leila b 1982); *Heir* kinsman, Sebastien Goschen; *Style*— Sir Edward A Goschen, Bt; ✉ Park House, Chisbury, Marlborough, Wiltshire SN8 3JA

GOSCHEN, 4 Viscount (UK 1900); Giles John Harry Goschen; s of 3 Viscount Goschen, KBE (d 1977), and his 2 w Alvin, *née* England; *b* 16 November 1965; *m* 23 Feb 1991, Sarah, yr da of late A G Horsnail, of Clophill, Beds; 2 da (Hon Annabel Sophie Moyana b 7 July 1999, Hon Auriel Elizabeth Caroline b 9 Jan 2004), 1 s (Hon Alexander John Edward b 5 Oct 2001); *Heir* s, Hon Alexander Goschen; *Career* a Lord in Waiting to HM the Queen 1992–94; Parly under sec of state Dept of Tport 1994–97; with Investment Banking Div Deutsche Bank AG (formerly Deutsche Morgan Grenfell) 1997–2000, dir Barchester Advisory Ltd 2000–02, Korn/Ferry Int 2005–; *Style*— The Rt Hon the Viscount Goschen; ✉ House of Lords, London SW1A 0PW

GOSDEN, John Harry Martin; s of John Montague Gosden (d 1967), of Sussex, and Peggie Gosden; *b* 30 March 1951; *Educ* Eastbourne Coll, Emmanuel Coll Cambridge (MA, Athletics blue); *m* 1982, Rachel Dene Serena Hood; 2 s (Sebastian b 1983, Thaddeus b 1995), 2 da (Serena b 1985, Theodora b 1990); *Career* racehorse trainer; asst trainer: Sir Noel Murless 1974–76, Dr Vincent O'Brien 1976–77; trainer: USA 1979–88, England 1989–; achievements as trainer USA: among top ten 1982–88, leading trainer Calif meets, 8 state champions, 3 Eclipse Award winners; achievements as trainer UK: trained fastest 1000 winners in UK (incl over 125 Gp race winners), trained St Leger winner (Shantou) 1996, Derby winner (Benny the Dip) 1997, Br 1000 Guineas winner (Lahan) 2000, Eclipse Award winner (Ryafan), French 1000 Guineas (Zenda and Valentine Waltz); Sussex Martlets schoolboy cricketer 1967–68, memb Blackheath Rugby Club 1969–70, memb Br under 23 rowing squad 1973; *Recreations* opera, skiing, polo, environmental issues; *Style*— John H M Gosden, Esq; ✉ Clarehaven Stables, Bury Road, Newmarket, Suffolk CB8 7BY (tel 01638 565400, fax 01638 565401)

GOSDEN, Prof Peter Henry John Heather; s of Alfred John Gosden (d 1980), of Fittleworth, W Sussex, and Elizabeth Ann Gosden (d 1962); *b* 3 August 1927; *Educ* Midhurst GS, Emmanuel Coll Cambridge (MA), Birkbeck Coll London (PhD); *m* 2 Sept 1964, Dr (Margaret) Sheila Gosden, da of Charles Alfred Hewitt (d 1974), of Hull, E Yorks; *Career* Nat Serv RAF 1949–51; schoolmaster 1951–60; Sch of Educn Univ of Leeds: lectr 1960, sr lectr 1967, reader 1971, chm of sch 1976–80 and 1987–91, prof of history of educn 1978, pro-vice-chllr 1985–87; jt ed Jl of Educational Administration and History 1968–92; chm JMB Manchester 1988–92, academic sec Univ Cncl for Educn of Teachers 1991–97 (memb Exec 1978–91), chm Ripon and Leeds Diocesan Bd of Educn 1992–2003, pres History of Educn Soc 1993–98; memb Cncl Univ of Huddersfield 1995–2001; FRHistS 1969, FRSA 1989; *Books* incl: The Friendly Societies in England 1815–1875 (1961), Development of Educational Administration in England and Wales (1966), The Evolution of a Profession (1972), Self-Help: Voluntary Associations in Nineteenth Century Britain (1973), Education in the Second World War: a study in policy and administration (1976), The Educational System since 1944 (1983), Education Committees (with George Cooke, 1986), The North of England Education Conference 1902–1992 (1992); *Recreations* music, gardening, walking; *Clubs* National Liberal; *Style*— Prof Peter Gosden; ✉ Orchard House, Creskeld Lane, Bramhope, Leeds LS16 9ES; The University, Leeds LS2 9JT (tel 0113 343 4545, fax 0113 343 4541)

GOSFORD, 7 Earl of (I 1806); Sir Charles David Nicholas Alexander John Sparrow Acheson; 13 Bt (NS 1628); also Baron Gosford (I 1776), Viscount Gosford (I 1785), Baron Worlingham (UK 1835, sits as), and Baron Acheson of Clancairny (UK 1847); s of 6 Earl of Gosford, OBE (d 1966), by his 1 w, Francesca, er da of Francesco Cagiati, of Rome; *b* 13 July 1942; *Educ* Harrow, Byam Shaw Sch of Drawing and Painting, Royal Acad Schs; *m* 1983, Lynnette Redmond; *Heir* unc, Hon Patrick Acheson; *Career* artist; one man shows: Barry Stern Exhibition Gallery, Sydney 1983 and 1986, Von Bertouch Galleries Newcastle NSW 1983 and 1986; *Style*— The Rt Hon the Earl of Gosford

GOSLING, Christopher Spencer; DL (Essex 1995); *b* 22 August 1942; *Educ* Eton, RAC Cirencester; *m* 24 June 1967, Juliet Mary, *née* Stanton; 2 da (Venetia Rachel b 2 Oct 1969, Larissa Catherine b 9 Dec 1971), 1 s (Alexander Edward Spencer b 1 July 1975); *Career* farmer; family partnership 1964–, sole proprietor 1979–; conslt land agent and rural estate mgmnt Strutt & Parker Chelmsford 1964–98; Country Landowners' Assoc: memb Cncl 1982–88, chm Essex Branch 1983–86, memb Agricultural & Land Use Sub-Ctee 1985–88; memb Cncl Essex Agricultural Soc (Essex Show) 1981– (chm 1991–95), steward Int Pavilion Royal Show 1987–92; chm Essex Branch Game Conservancy Cncl 1983–86; memb: British Field Sports Soc, Essex Agric Assoc; High Sheriff Essex 1993–94; *Recreations* shooting, stalking, tennis, windsurfing, skiing, travel, golf; *Clubs* Beefsteak, Essex, Surveyors 1954; *Style*— Christopher Gosling, Esq, DL; ✉ Byham Hall, Great Maplestead, Halstead, Essex CO9 3AR (tel 01787 460134, fax 01787 461463, e-mail chrisgos@byhamhall.co.uk)

GOSLING, Sir (Frederick) Donald; kt (1976), KCVO (2004); *b* 2 March 1929; *m* 1959 (m dis 1988), Elizabeth Shauna, *née* Ingram; 3 s; *Career* joined RN 1944, served Med HMS Leander; jt chm Nat Car Parks Ltd 1950–98, chm Palmer & Harvey Ltd 1967–, dir Lovell Hldgs Ltd 1975–; memb Cncl of Mgmnt White Ensign Assoc 1970– (chm 1978–83, vice-pres 1983–93, pres 1993); chm Selective Employment Scheme 1976–; tstee: Fleet Air Arm Museum Yeovilton 1974–, RYA Seamanship Fndn, The Bernard Sunley Charitable Fndn; patron Submarine Meml Appeal 1978–; patron The Ark Royal Welfare Tst, vice-patron King George's Fund for Sailors 2000, chm Berkeley Square Ball Charitable Tst; younger bro Trintity House 1998; Hon Capt RNR 1993; *Clubs* Royal Yacht Squadron; *Style*— Sir Donald Gosling, KCVO

GOSLING, Paula Louise (Mrs John Hare); da of A Paul Osius (d 1986), and Sylvie, *née* Van Slembrouck (d 1986); *b* 12 October 1939; *Educ* Mackenzie HS, Wayne State Univ (BA); *m* 1, 1968 (m dis 1979), Christopher Gosling, s of Thomas Gosling; 2 da (Abigail Judith b 1970, Emily Elizabeth b 1972); m 2, 1981, John Anthony Hare, s of John Charles Hare; *Career* copywriter: Campbell-Ewald USA 1962–64, C Mitchell & Co London 1964–67, Pritchard-Wood London 1967–68, David Williams Ltd London 1968–70; copy conslt: C Mitchell & Co 1970–72, ATA Advertising Bristol 1977–79; crime writer 1979–; Arts Achievement Award Wayne State Univ 1994; Crime Writers' Assoc: memb Ctee 1984–90, chm 1988–89; memb: Soc of Authors, ALCS, Mensa; *Books* A Running Duck (1978, US title Fair Game, John Creasey Meml Award for Best First Crime Novel 1978, made into film for Japanese TV and into film Cobra and film Fair Game 1995), The Zero Trap (1979), Mind's Eye (as Ainslie Skinner 1980, US title The Harrowing), Loser's Blues (1980, US title Solo Blues), The Woman in Red (1983), Monkey Puzzle (1985, Gold Dagger Award for Best Crime Novel 1986), The Wychford Murders (1987), Hoodwink (1988), Backlash (1989), Death Penalties (1991), The Body in Blackwater Bay (1992), A Few Dying Words (1993), The Dead of Winter (1995), Death and Shadows (1999), Underneath Every Stone (2000), Ricochet (2002), Tears of the Dragon (2004); author of numerous serials and short stories incl Mr Felix (nominated Best Short Story MWA 1987); *Recreations* needlework, kite-flying; *Style*— Ms Paula Gosling; ✉ c/o Greene and Heaton Ltd, 37 Goldhawk Road, London W12 8QQ (tel 020 8749 0315, fax 020 8749 0318)

GOSLING, Prof William; s of Harold William Gosling (d 1980), of Cograve, Notts, and Aida Maisie, *née* Webb; *b* 25 September 1932; *Educ* Mundella Sch Nottingham, Imperial Coll London (BSc), Univ of Bath (DSc); *m* 5 July 1953, Patricia Mary, da of Charles Henry Best, of Rode, Somerset; 1 da (Melanie b 1954 d 2004), 2 s (Richard b 1956 d 1958, Ceri b 1959); *Career* prof of electrical engrg Univ of Wales 1966, vice-princ UC Swansea 1972, prof of electronic engrg Univ of Bath 1974, hon prof of communication engrg Univ of Southampton 1981–89, visiting prof Univ of Bath 1990–98, prof emeritus Univ of Bath 1998–; tech dir Plessey Co plc (formerly Plessey Electronic Systems Ltd) 1981–89, dir of electronic devpts Securicor Group 1990–97, dir Venture Link Investors 1991–93; pres: Euro Convention of Electrical Engrs 1977–78, Inst of Electronic and Radio Engrs 1979–80; treas Br Assoc 2002–; Freeman City of London 1980; Liveryman: Worshipful Co of Scientific Instrument Makers 1980, Worshipful Co of Engrs 1985; hon fell UMIST 1987; ARCS, FIEE 1968, FInstD 1982; *Books* Design of Engineering Systems (1962), Field Effect Electronics (1971), Radio Receivers (1986), Helmsmen and Heroes (1994), Antennas and Propagation (1998); *Recreations* music, poetry; *Clubs* Athenaeum; *Style*— Prof William Gosling; ✉ White Hart Cottage, Rode, Frome, Somerset BA11 6PA (tel 01373 830901, mobile 07710 070221, e-mail wil@gosmob.net)

GOSPER, Brett; s of Richard Kevan Gosper, of Melbourne, Aust, and Jillian Mary, *née* Galwey (d 1981); *b* 21 June 1959; *Educ* Scotch Coll Melbourne, Monash Univ Melbourne (BA); *m* 1, 1989 (m dis), Laurence, *née* Albes; 1 s (Jonathan Kevan Thomas b 24 June 1990); m 2, 1998, Elizabeth, *née* Bernsen; 1 da (Ella Jillian b 22 June 1999), 1 s (Matt William Svend b 15 March 2001); *Career* advtg exec; account exec Ogilvy & Mather Melbourne 1981–82, gp account dir Ogilvy & Mather Paris 1982–89, dir rising to dep md BDDP Paris 1989–93, fndr md BDDP Frankfurt 1993–94, chm and chief exec Euro RSCG Wnek Gosper London 1994–2003, memb Bd Euro RSCG Worldwide 1996–2003, memb Bd Media Planning Worldwide 1998–2003, chief exec McCann-Erickson NY 2003–04, pres NY Gp TWBA 2004–; *Recreations* rugby; *Clubs* Melbourne Rugby Union (Best Club Player Award 1978, 1979 and 1980, rep Victoria, Queensland and Australia), Racing Club de France (memb rugby team 1981–90, Best Club Player Award 1987, rep French Barbarians v All Blacks 1986), MCC (life memb), Castel (Paris), Melbourne Cricket; *Style*— Brett Gosper, Esq

GOSS, James Richard William; QC (1997); s of His Hon Judge W A B Goss (d 1963); *b* 12 May 1953; *Educ* Charterhouse, UC Durham (BA); *m* 1982, Dawna Elizabeth, *née* Davies; 2 s, 3 da; *Career* called to the Bar Inner Temple 1975, recorder 1994–; *Clubs* Colonsay Golf; *Style*— James Goss, QC; ✉ 6 Park Square East, Leeds LS1 2LW (tel 0113 245 9763, fax 0113 242 4395, e-mail chambers@no6.co.uk)

GOSSCHALK, His Hon Joseph Bernard; s of Lionel Samuel Gosschalk (d 1955), of London, and Johanna, *née* Lion (d 1996); *b* 27 August 1936; *Educ* East Ham GS for Boys, Magdalen Coll Oxford (MA); *m* 1973, Ruth Sandra, da of Dr Harold Jarvis; 2 da (Juliette Stella b 30 April 1975, Louise Paula b 11 June 1977); *Career* admitted Hon Soc of Gray's Inn 1956 (Lord Justice Holker jr scholarship), called to the Bar Gray's Inn 1961; head of chambers Francis Taylor Bldg Temple 1983–91, asst recorder 1983–87, recorder 1987–91, circuit judge (SE Circuit) 1991–2007; memb Hon Soc of Inner Temple 1983; *Recreations* reading, foreign travel; *Style*— His Hon Joseph Gosschalk

GOSWAMI, Prof Usha Claire; *b* 21 February 1960; *Educ* St John's Coll Oxford (BA, sr scholarship, DPhil), Inst of Educn Univ of London (PGCE); *Career* pt/t lectr in psychology Univ of Warwick 1985, actg fell for psychology St John's Coll Oxford 1985, lectr in psychology St John's Coll and Merton Coll Oxford 1986 and 1998–89, jr research fell Merton Coll Oxford 1986–87 and 1988–89, Harkness fell Univ of Illinois 1987–88, univ lectr in experimental psychology Univ of Cambridge 1990–97, prof of cognitive developmental psychology Inst of Child Health and fell Inst of Cognitive Neuroscience UCL 1997–2002, prof of educn Univ of Cambridge 2002–; fell St John's Coll Cambridge 1990–; Faculty of Educn Univ of Cambridge: memb Faculty Bd, memb Strategy Ctee, memb Research Ctee; memb: Research Steering Ctee Dept of Human Communication Sciences UCL, Bd Faculty of Social and Political Sciences Univ of Cambridge, Appointments Ctees UCL, Birkbeck Coll London, Inst of Psychology KCL and Univ of Cambridge; external examiner: Univ of Oxford, Univ of Kent at Canterbury, Univ of Burgundy, Univ of Edinburgh, Univ of Hong Kong, Univ of Newcastle, Univ of Essex; advsr Nat Curriculum Cncl for the Teaching of English 1992, conslt Nat Literacy Project 1997; UK memb Managing Ctee European Concerted Action on Learning Disorders as a Barrier to Human Devpt COST A8 1995–2000; memb: Research Grants Bd ESRC 1998–2000, Neurosciences and Mental Health Bd MRC 1999–2003, Dir's Advsy Gp Social,

G

Genetic and Developmental Psychiatry Research Centre KCL 2000–, Cross-Bd Gp MRC 2001–03, Sr Advsy Bd Nat Center for Developmental Science in the Public Interest Cornell Univ; ed Applied Psycholinguistics, reviewer for numerous pubns; memb Editorial Bd: Jl of Child Psychology and Psychiatry, Jl of Experimental Child Psychology, Developmental Science, Cognitive Development, Dyslexia, Reading Research Quarterly, Reading & Writing; reviewer: Wellcome Tst, MRC, ESRC, Nuffield Fndn, Social Sciences and Humanities Research Cncl of Canada, Australian Research Cncl; chosen speaker Br Psychology Soc Millennium Event 2001, Broadbent Lecture Br Psychology Soc Annual Conf 2003, delivered numerous invited addresses at confs and symposia worldwide; Nat Acad of Educn Spencer Fellowship 1990–92, Alexander von Humboldt Research Fellowship 1995–96; first runner-up American Psychology Assoc Outstanding Dissertation of the Year Award 1989, Br Psychology Soc Spearman Medal 1992, Norman Geschwind-Rodin Prize 1992; *Publications* Phonological Skills and Learning to Read (with P E Bryant, 1990), Analogical Reasoning in Children (1992), Cognition in Children (1998), Blackwells Handbook of Childhood Cognitive Development (ed, 2002); also author of numerous jl articles and book chapters; *Style*— Prof Usha Goswami; ✉ Faculty of Education, University of Cambridge, Shaftesbury Road, Cambridge CB2 2BX (tel 01223 369631, fax 01223 324421)

GOSWELL, Sir Brian Lawrence; kt (1991); s of Albert George Goswell (d 1971), and Florence Emily, *née* Barnett (d 1980); *b* 26 November 1935; *Educ* St David's Sch High Wycombe, Univ of Durham; *m* 1961, Deirdre Gillian, da of Harold Stones (d 1996); 2 s (Paul b 1964, Angus b 1967); *Career* served Oxford & Bucks Light Infantry 1954–57; Healey & Baker (surveyors and valuers): joined 1957, ptnr 1969, managing ptnr 1977, dep sr ptnr 1988, dep chm 1997–2001, conslt 2000–02; chm: Brent Walker Group plc 1993–97, Sunley Secure plc 1993–99, William Hill Organization Ltd 1994–97, International Security Management Group Ltd 1998–2002, ISS Group Ltd 2004–07; memb: Advsy Bd Sir Alexander Gibb & Partners 1989–95, Advsy Panel AIM Gp plc 2005–07; pres The Land Inst; past pres: ISVA, Br Cncl for Offices, American C of C London; tstee Cons and Unionist Agents' Superannuation Fund 1997–2001; memb Fulbright Advsy Bd; Liveryman Worshipful Co of Gold and Silver Wyre Drawers; FRICS, FRSA; *Recreations* shooting, horse racing, cricket, fishing; *Clubs* Carlton (vice-pres Political Ctee), City Livery, United & Cecil, MCC, Royal Green Jackets London, Leander; *Style*— Sir Brian Goswell, FRICS, FRSA; ✉ Pipers, Camley Park Drive, Pinkneys Green, Berkshire SL6 6QF (tel 01628 630768)

GOTCH, Prof Frances Margaret; da of Geoffrey Gore (d 1994), and Queenie, *née* Rawlings (d 1988); *b* 29 January 1943; *Educ* Univ of Oxford (MSc, DPhil); *m* 1 Feb 1964, Michael Gotch, s of Leonard Gotch; 3 da (Lisa Helen b 1966 d 2003, Emma Sophie b 1969, Sharon Mandy (adopted 1973) b 1960); *Career* formerly research scientist Nuffield Dept of Med then univ lectr Inst of Molecular Med Oxford, currently prof and head Dept of Immunology Imperial Coll of Science, Technol and Med Chelsea & Westminster Hosp London; author of over 100 pubns in peer reviewed jls since 1970; FRCPath; *Recreations* reading, painting, keep-fit; *Style*— Prof Frances Gotch; ✉ Department of Immunology, Imperial College of Science, Technology & Medicine, Chelsea & Westminster Hospital, 369 Fulham Road, London SW10 9NH (tel 020 8746 8257, fax 020 8746 5997, e-mail f.gotch@imperial.ac.uk)

GOTCH, Jeremy Millard Butler; s of Ralph Butler Gotch (d 1979), and Eileen Madge, *née* Millard (d 1956); *b* 6 June 1934; *Educ* Berkhamsted Sch, Jesus Coll Cambridge (MA); *m* 28 Dec 1957, Janet Phyllis, da of Eric Ralph Rich (d 1961); 2 da (Jennifer b 1960, Sarah b 1962), 1 s (Christopher b 1969); *Career* RASC 1952–54 (2 Lt 1952), ELSC RE(V) 1987–99 (Col 1997); Shell International Petroleum Co 1957–59; Traffic Services Ltd 1959–86: dir 1962, md 1968, chm 1978; md rail ops CAIB UK Ltd 1986–91, proprietor Gotch Consultancy tport conslts 1991–2005; first Br pres Union Internationale d'Associations de Propriétaires de Wagons Particuliers 1980–83 (memb 1969–91); vice-pres CIT 1990–93; chm: Assoc of Private Railway Wagon Owners 1980–91, Friends of Dulwich Picture Gallery 1981–84, The Maitland Tst 1984–2000, Int Div Private Wagon Fedn 1991–93, Motorcycle Branch Save the Children Fund 1992–95, Lord Mayor's Appeal for St John Ambulance 1995–96; chm Estates Govrs Alleyn's Coll of God's Gift 1994–96 (govr/tstee 1981–2005); govr: St Olave's & St Saviour's GS Fndn 1986–2006 (warden 2001–03), Dulwich Coll 1994–2004; sec Dulwich Sports Club 1964–73, tstee Jesus Coll Cambridge Soc 1988–2003; underwriting memb Lloyd's 1974–2003; Sheriff City of London 1993–94; memb Royal Soc of St George; Freeman City of London, Liveryman Worshipful Co of Carmen (memb Ct of Assts 1983–, Master 1996–97), Liveryman Worshipful Co of World Traders; memb Guild of Freeman City of London (Ct 1998–2003); Hon Dip London Coll of Advanced Tport Studies; FCILT, FIFP; KStJ 1997 (OStJ 1995); *Recreations* music, golf, garden; *Clubs* MCC, City Livery, United Wards, Candlewick Ward, RAC, Dulwich Sports; *Style*— Jeremy Gotch, Esq; ✉ 21 Alleyn Road, Dulwich, London SE21 8AB (tel and fax 020 8766 7999, e-mail jeremygotch@talktalk.net)

GOTO, Prof John; *Educ* Berks Coll of Art, St Martin's Sch of Art (BA); *Career* artist; pt/t lectr: Camberwell Sch of Art 1979–81, Poly of Central London 1979–87, Oxford Brookes Univ 1979–99, Ruskin Sch of Drawing & Fine Art Univ of Oxford 1987, Univ of Derby 2000–03; prof of fine art Univ of Derby 2003–; visiting lectr to numerous art colls since 1979; Br Cncl scholar: Paris 1977, Prague 1978; artist fell Girton Coll Cambridge 1988–89, vice-chm Visual Arts Panel Southern Arts Assoc 1989–90; *Solo Exhibitions* incl: Goto Photographs 1971–81 (The Photographer's Gallery) 1981, Goto Photographs 1975–83 (PPS Galerie Gundlac Hamburg) 1983, ULUV Gallery Prague (Br Cncl Exhibition) 1983, Moravian Gallery Bruno Czechoslovakia 1983 (touring Czechoslovakia and Spain 1983–85), Sites of Passage (Fischer Fine Art and Ashmolean Museum Oxford) 1986 and 1988, Terezin (Cambridge Darkroom, John Hansard Gallery Southampton, Cornerhouse Manchester and Raab Galerie Berlin) 1988–89, The Atomic Yard (Kettle's Yard Cambridge and Raab Gallery) 1993, The Scar (Benjamin Rhodes Gallery London, Manchester City Galleries and John Hansard Gallery Univ of Southampton) 1993, John Goto (touring Russia) 1994–95, The Framers' Collection (Portfolio Gallery Edinburgh) 1997, The Commissar of Space (MOMA Oxford) 1998, NPG2000 Exhibition of Cmmn Artist (Nat Portrait Gallery London) 1999, Capital Arcade (Korea, Sweden and UK tour) 1999 and 2000, High Summer (London, Edinburgh, Netherlands, Oporto and UK tour) 2001–02, Loss of Face (Tate Britain) 2002–03, Ukadia (Djanogly Art Gallery) 2003 (also at Galeria f5.6 Munich and Gallery On Seoul 2005), John Goto's New World Circus (nat tour) 2006–07, Floodscapes (Gallery On Seoul and UK tour) 2006–08; *Group Exhibitions* incl: Painting/Photography (Richard DeMarco Gallery) Edinburgh 1986, Next/Tomorrow (Kettle's Yard Cambridge) 1986, Fifteen Studios (MOMA Oxford) 1986, Romantic Visions (Camden Arts Centre) 1988, Blasphemies Ecstasies & Cries (Serpentine Gallery) 1989, Photographic Art in Britain 1945–89 (Barbican), Metamorphosis (Raab Gallery Millbank) 1989, After Auschwitz: Responses to the Holocaust in Contemporary Art (Royal Festival Hall and UK tour) 1995–96, Trade (Winterthur, Rotterdam) 2001–02, Sight Seeing (Graz) 2003, Collage (Bloomberg Space London) 2004, Identity_Factories (Mir Gallery Bucharest) 2005; *Catalogues* Shotover (1984), Terezin (1988), The Atomic Yard (1990), The Scar (1993), Commissar of Space (1998), The National Portrait Gallery: An Architectural History (2000), Ukadia (2003), Carro Electrico 104 (2005), New World Circus (2006), Floodscapes (2006); *Style*— Prof John Goto; ✉ www.johngoto.org.uk

GOTTELIER, Patrick George Campbell; s of Alfred John Dunhill Gottelier, of Penzance, Cornwall, and Freda Joan Gottelier; *b* 20 November 1951; *Educ* Birmingham Poly, Central Sch of Art (BA); *m* 3 Dec 1982, (Catherine) Jane, da of Prof Charles Lewis Foster; 2 s (Thomas Charles Morehead b 13 Feb 1988, William John de Chermont b 13 April 1991); *Career* fndr dir (with w) Artwork specialising in knitwear 1977–, estab diffusion label Artwork Blue 1990, expanded into fashion related products with ranges of toiletries and cosmetics successfully launched 1997; stockists incl Harvey Nichols and Whistles of London and numerous others worldwide, show regularly London, NY and Paris; *Recreations* photography, sailing, walking, travel, cooking; *Clubs* Chelsea Arts; *Style*— Patrick Gottelier, Esq

GOUDIE, Prof Andrew Shaw; s of William Cooper Goudie, and Mary Isobel, *née* Pulman (d 1992); bro of (Thomas) James Cooper Goudie, QC, *qv*; *b* 21 August 1945; *Educ* Dean Close Sch Cheltenham, Trinity Hall Cambridge (MA, PhD); *m* 21 March 1987, Heather Ann, da of John Viles, of Chelmsford, Essex; 2 da (Amy Louise b 7 June 1988, Alice May b 25 May 1991); *Career* Univ of Oxford: lectr in geography and fell Hertford Coll 1976–84, prof of geography 1984–, head of dept 1984–94 and 2002–03, pres Oxford Univ Devpt Prog and pro-vice-chllr 1995–97, master St Cross Coll 2003–; FRGS 1970; *Books* The Human Impact, The Nature of the Environment, Environmental Change, Geomorphological Techniques, Duricrusts, The Warm Desert Environment, Land Shapes, Discovering Landscape in England and Wales, The Prehistory and Palaeogeography of the Great Indian Desert, Chemical Sediments in Geomorphology, Climate, The Earth Transformed, Salt Weathering Hazards, Encyclopedia of Global Change, Great Warm Deserts of the World, Desert Dust in the Global System; *Recreations* old books, old records, gardening; *Clubs* Geographical; *Style*— Prof Andrew Goudie; ✉ St Cross College, Oxford OX1 3LZ (tel 01865 278490, fax 01865 278484)

GOUDIE, Dr Andrew William; s of Britton Goudie, and Joan Goudie; *b* 3 March 1955; *Educ* Queens' Coll Cambridge (Wrenbury scholar, BA Econs, MA, PhD), Open Univ (BA Maths & Stats); *m* 1978, Christine Lynne Hurley; 2 s, 2 da; *Career* Univ of Cambridge: research offr Dept of Applied Econs 1978–85, res fell Queens' Coll 1981–83, fell and dir of studies Robinson Coll 1983–85; sr econ World Bank Washington 1985–90, sr econ advsr Scottish Office 1990–95, princ econ OECD Devpt Centre Paris 1995–96, chief econ DFID 1996–99; Scottish Exec: chief econ advsr 1999–, head Financial and Central Services Dept 2003–; Hon DLitt Univ of Strathclyde 2003; FRSE; *Publications* articles in learned jls incl: Econ Jl, Jl Royal Statistical Soc Economica, Scottish Jl Political Economy; *Style*— Dr Andrew Goudie; ✉ Scottish Executive, St Andrew's House, Regent Road, Edinburgh EH1 3DG (tel 0131 244 7937, fax 0131 244 5536)

GOUDIE, (Thomas) James Cooper; QC (1984); s of William Cooper Goudie (d 1981), and Mary Isobel, *née* Pulman (d 1992); bro of Prof Andrew Shaw Goudie, *qv*; *b* 2 June 1942; *Educ* Dean Close Sch Cheltenham, LSE (LLB); *m* 30 Aug 1969, Mary Teresa (Baroness Goudie), *qv*, da of Martin Brick; 2 s (Hon Martin b 5 July 1973, Hon Alexander b 14 July 1977); *Career* slr 1966–70, called to the Bar Inner Temple 1970 (bencher 1991); SE Circuit 1970–, recorder 1985–, dep judge of the High Court (Queen's Bench Div) 1995–; chm Bar European Gp 2001–03, dep chm Info Tbnl 2000–; memb Brent Cncl 1967–78 (latterly ldr), Party candidate (Lab) Brent North 1974; past chm: Admin Law Bar Assoc, Law Reform Ctee, Bar Cncl, Soc of Labour Lawyers; govr LSE 2001–; FCIArb; *Style*— James Goudie, Esq, QC; ✉ 11 King's Bench Walk, Temple EC4Y 7EQ (tel 020 7632 8500, fax 020 7583 9123/3690)

GOUDIE, Baroness (Life Peer UK 1998), of Roundwood in the London Borough of Brent; Mary Teresa Goudie; da of Martin Brick, and Hannah Brick (d 1992); *b* 2 September 1946; *Educ* Our Lady of the Visitation Sch, Our Lady of St Anselm Sch; *m* 30 Aug 1969, James Goudie, QC, *qv*; 2 s (Hon Martin b 5 July 1973, Hon Alexander b 14 July 1977); *Career* asst dir Brent People's Housing Assoc 1977–81, sec Lab Pty Solidarity Campaign 1981–87, dir Hansard Soc 1985–89, dir House magazine 1989–90, public affrs manger World Wide Fund for Nature (UK) 1990–95, ind public affrs conslt 1995–98, strategic and mgmnt conslt 1998–; House of Lords: EC Law and Institutions Sub-Ctee 1998–2001, Procedure Ctee 2001, Finance and Staff Sub-Ctee 2002, Info Ctee 2002; memb Lab Pty 1964–, memb Lab Parly Gen Election Campaign Team 1998–2001, liaison peer for home affrs 1998–2001, vice-chair Lab Peers 2001–03; memb Brent Cncl 1971–78 (chm various ctees and also dep whip); sec Scottish Industry Forum; memb: Soc of Lab Lawyers, Fabian Soc, Industry Forum, Centre for Scottish Policy, Devpt Ctee Community Service Volunteers 1996–, Inter-Parly Union; patron: NI Voluntary Tst, National Childbirth Tst, Generation Sci Club; memb Ct Napier Univ; Hon LLD Napier Univ 2000; *Recreations* Labour Pty, family, reading, travel, food, wine, art, gardening; *Style*— The Rt Hon the Baroness Goudie; ✉ House of Lords, London SW1A 0PW (tel 020 7219 5880)

GOUGH, Sir (Charles) Brandon; kt (2002); s of Charles Richard Gough (d 1957), and Mary Evaline, *née* Goff (d 1996); *b* 8 October 1937; *Educ* Douai Sch, Jesus Coll Cambridge (MA); *m* 24 June 1961, Sarah, da of Maurice Evans Smith (d 1987); 1 s (Richard b 1962) 2 da (Lucy (Mrs Peter Harris) b 1964, Katherine (Mrs Lee Medlock) b 1967); *Career* Nat Serv Army 1956–58; Coopers & Lybrand: joined 1964, ptnr 1968–94, chm 1983–94, chm Coopers & Lybrand Europe during 1989 and 1992–94, memb Exec Ctee Coopers & Lybrand International 1982–94 (chm 1985 and 1991–92); non-exec chm: Yorkshire Water plc 1996–2000, Montanaro UK Smaller Companies Investment Tst plc 1998–2005, Montanaro European Smaller Companies plc 2000–05; non-exec dir: British Aerospace plc (govt dir) 1987–88, British Invisibles 1990–94, S G Warburg Group plc 1994–95 (dep chm 1995), De La Rue plc 1994–2004 (chm 1997–2004), National Power plc 1995–2000, George Wimpey plc 1995–99, Singer and Friedland Gp plc 1999–2005, Innogy Holdings plc 2000–02; chm Locate in Kent Ltd 2006–; chm Auditing Practices Ctee CCAB 1981–84 (memb 1976–84); memb: Accounting Standards Review (Dearing) Ctee 1987–88, Fin Reporting Cncl 1990–96, Cambridge Univ Careers Serv Syndicate 1983–86, Cncl for Industry and Higher Educn 1985–93; chm Higher Educn Funding Cncl for England 1993–97; City Univ Business Sch: memb City Advsy Panel 1980–91 (chm 1986–91), chm Fin Ctee 1988–91, chm Cncl 1992–93 (memb 1986–93); chllr UEA 2003–; chm Nat Trg Task Force working gp on The Role of Trg and Enterprise Cncls in local econ devpt 1991–92, chm Doctors' and Dentists' Pay Review Body 1993–2001; memb: Cncl of Lloyd's 1983–86 (Lloyd's Silver Medal 1986), Governing Cncl Business in the Community 1984–88, Mgmnt Cncl GB-Sasakawa Fndn 1985–96, Cncl Business in the Community 1988–94, CBI Task Force Vocational Educn and Trg 1989, UK Nat Ctee Japan-Euro Community Assoc 1989–94, Cncl Fndn for Educn Business Partnerships 1989–91, CBI Educn and Trg Affrs Ctee 1990–94, Cncl City Univ 1991–93, Cncl of Mgmnt Royal Shakespeare Theatre Tst 1991–97, President's Ctee of Business in the Community 1992–94, Cncl of The Prince of Wales Business Leaders Forum of Int Business in the Community 1992–94, Cncl London First 1993–94, Cncl Freshfields 1996–2000; tstee: Guildhall Sch Music and Drama Fndn 1989–95, Common Purpose 1989–98 (chm 1991–98), Hospice in the Weald 2003–, Canterbury Cathedral Tst Fund 2006–, Leeds Castle Fndn 2006–; Freeman: City of London 1983, Worshipful Co of Chartered Accountants 1983; Hon DSc City Univ 1994, Hon DCL UEA 2003; FCA 1974 (memb Cncl 1981–84); *Recreations* music, gardening; *Style*— Sir Brandon Gough

GOUGH, Darren; *b* 18 September 1970, Barnsley; *m* 16 Oct 1993 (m dis 2003), Anna; 2 s (Liam James b 24 Nov 1994, Brennan Kyle b 9 Dec 1997); *Career* professional cricketer; Yorkshire CCC: 1989–2004 and 2007–, awarded county cap 1993 champions CricInfo County Championship 2001, capt 2007; with Essex CCC 2004–07; England: 58 test matches (229 wickets), 151 one-day ints (first English bowler to take 200 wickets), best bowling 6–42, first one day int v New Zealand 1994, test debut v South Africa 1994, memb team touring Australia 1994–95 and 1998–99 (test hat trick Sydney 1999), memb team touring South Africa 1995–96 and 1999–2000, memb team World Cup

India/Pakistan 1995–96, memb team touring Zimbabwe and New Zealand 1996–97, memb squad Emirates Trophy 1998, memb team touring Pakistan and Sri Lanka 2000–01, memb one-day squad touring India 2002, ret test cricket 2003; memb England YC tour to Australia 1989–90; England Player of the Year 1994, 1998 and 2000, Whyte & McKay Bowler of the Year 1996, Wisden Cricketer of the Year 1999, Sheffield Sports Personality of the Year 1999, Yorkshire Personality of the Year 1999, GQ Sportsman of the Year 2001; *Style*— Darren Gough, Esq

GOUGH, Prof Douglas Owen; s of Owen Albert John Gough, of Romford, Essex, and Doris May, *née* Camera; *b* 8 February 1941; *Educ* Hackney Downs GS, St John's Coll Cambridge (MA, PhD, Strathcona award); *m* 16 Jan 1965, Rosanne Penelope, da of Prof (Charles) Thurstan Shaw; 2 da (Kim Ione May b 30 July 1966, Heidi Natasha Susan b 25 Feb 1968), 2 s (Julian John Thurstan b 29 Sept 1974, Russell Edward William b 18 Aug 1976); *Career* res assoc Jt Inst for Laboratory Astrophysics and Dept of Physics and Astrophysics Univ of Colorado 1966–67, sr postdoctoral res assoc Goddard Inst for Space Studies 1967–69; Univ of Cambridge: memb graduate staff Inst of Theoretical Astronomy 1969–73, fell Churchill Coll 1972–, lectr in astronomy and applied mathematics 1973–85, reader in astrophysics 1985–93, prof of theoretical astrophysics 1993–, dir Institute of Astronomy 1999–2004; visiting prof of physics Stanford Univ 1996–; memb Bd of Dirs Møller Centre for Continuing Educn Churchill Coll Cambridge 1992–97; astronome titulaire associé Observatoires de France 1977, SRC sr fell 1978–83, professeur associé Univ of Toulouse 1984–85, hon prof of astronomy Queen Mary & Westfield Coll London 1986–, fell Jt Inst for Laboratory Astrophysics 1986–; Sir Joseph Larmor lectr Cambridge Philosophical Soc 1988, Wernher von Braun lectr Nat Aeronautics and Space Admin 1991, Morris Loeb lectr in physics Harvard Univ 1993, Bishop lectr Columbia Univ 1996, Halley lectr Univ of Oxford 1996, R J Tayler Meml lectr RAS 2000; second prize Gravity Res Fndn 1973, James Arthur prize lectr Harvard Univ 1982, William Hopkins prize Cambridge Philosophical Soc 1984, George Ellery Hale prize American Astronomical Soc 1995, Eddington medal RAS 2002; foreign memb Royal Danish Acad of Sciences and Letters 1998; FRAS 1966, FRS 1997, FInstP 1997; Mousquetaire d'Armagnac 2001; *Books* Problems of Solar and Stellar Oscillations (ed, 1983), Seismology of the Sun and the Distant Stars (ed, 1986), Challenges to Theories of the Structure of Moderate-Mass Stars (jt ed, 1991), Models of Ordinary Astrophysical Matter (jt ed and contrib, 2004), The Scientific Legacy of Fred Hoyle (ed, 2005); author of 300 research papers in scientific jls and books; *Recreations* cooking, listening to music; *Style*— Prof Douglas Gough, FRS; ✉ 3 Oxford Road, Cambridge CB4 3PH (tel 01223 360309); Institute of Astronomy, Madingley Road, Cambridge CB3 0HA (tel 01223 337548, fax 01223 337523, e-mail douglas@ast.cam.ac.uk)

GOUGH, Ian; s of Malcolm Gough, and Sandra, *née* Carol; *b* 10 November 1976, Panteg, Wales; *Educ* Llantarnam Comp; *Career* rugby union player; formerly with Newport RFC and Pontypridd RFC, Newport Gwent Dragons 1998, Neath Swansea Ospreys 2007–; Wales: 40 caps, debut 1998, winners Six Nations Championship (Grand Slam) 2005; *Recreations* golf, scuba diving, off roading, flying, windsurfing; *Style*— Ian Gough, Esq; ✉ Newport Gwent Dragons, Rodney Parade, Rodney Road, Newport, Gwent NP19 0UU (tel 01633 670690)

GOUGH, Piers William; CBE (1998); s of late Peter Gough, and late Daphne Mary Unwin, *née* Banks; gs of Leslie Banks, the actor; *b* 24 April 1946; *Educ* Uppingham, AA Sch of Architecture (AADipl); *m* 8 June 1991, Rosemary Elaine Fosbrooke, da of Robert Bates; *Career* architect; ptnr CZWG Architects 1975–; princ works: Phillips West 2 London W2 1976, China Wharf London SE1 1988, Bermondsey CDT Building 1988, Street-Porter House London EC1 1988, The Circle London SE1 1990, Bryanston Sch, Crown Street Regeneration Project Gorbals Scotland 1991–, Westbourne Grove Public Lavatories 1993, 1–10 Summers Street Clerkenwell 1994, two Boarding Houses 1994, Soho Lofts Wardour Street London 1995, Cochrane Sq Glasgow 1995 (phase 2 1999, phase 3 1999–), Leonardo Centre 1995, 19th and 20th Century Galleries Nat Portrait Gallery London 1996, Brindleyplace Cafe Birmingham 1997, Bankside Lofts London 1999, Shuttle Street Glasgow 1999, The Glass Building Camden London 1999, Green Bridge Mile End Park 2000, Office at Edinburgh Park 2000, Tunnel Wharf Rotherhithe London 2001, Allen Jones' Studio Ledwell 2001, Samworth's Girls' Boarding House Uppingham Sch 2001, Bankside Central 2001, Suffolk Wharf at Camden Lock London 2002, Fulham Island London 2002, Ladbroke Green 2002–, Queen Elizabeth Square and Crown Street Corner Gorbials 2003–04, Regency Galleries at Nat Portrait Gallery 2003, Bling Bling Building Liverpool 2006; exhbns: Lutyens (Hayward Gallery) 1982, Gilbert (Royal Acad) 1985, CZWG 68–88 (RIBA Heinz Gallery) 1988, Soane (Royal Acad) 1999, Saved! (Hayward Gallery) 2003–04; pres AA 1995–97 (memb Cncl 1970–72 and 1991–99); memb Design Review Ctee Cmmn for Architecture and the Built Environment (CABE) 1999; cmmr English Heritage 2000–07 (memb London Advsy Ctee 1995–2003, memb Urban Panel 1999–2003); RIBA Gold Medal Panel 2000; memb GLA Cultural Strategy Gp 2000–; tstee: Chisenhale Gallery 1993–2002, Artangel 1994–2003, Kent Design Champion 2004–; Hon DUniv Middx 1999, hon fell Queen Mary Univ of London 2001; RIBA, FRSA 1992, RA 2002; *Publications* English Extremists (1988); The Shock of the Old (Channel 4); *Recreations* parties; *Clubs* Groucho; *Style*— Piers Gough; ✉ CZWG Architects LLP, 17 Bowling Green Lane, London EC1R 0QB (tel 020 7253 2523, fax 020 7250 0594, e-mail mail@czwgarchitects.co.uk)

GOUGH, 5 Viscount (UK 1849); Sir Shane Hugh Maryon Gough; 5 Bt (UK 1842); also Baron Gough of Chinkangfoo and of Maharajpore and the Sutlej (UK 1846); s of 4 Viscount Gough, MC, JP, DL (d 1951, ggs of Field Marshal 1 Viscount, KP, GCB, GCSI, PC, whose full title was Viscount Gough of Goojerat in the Punjaub and of the City of Limerick. His brilliant exploits in the two Sikh Wars resulted in the annexation of the Punjab to British India), by his w Margaretta Elizabeth (d 1977), da of Sir Spencer Maryon-Wilson, 11 Bt; *b* 26 August 1941; *Educ* Winchester; *Career* late Lt Irish Gds; stockbroker Laurence Keen & Gardner (and successor firms) 1968–97; chm: Mastiff Electronic System Ltd, Barwell plc and associate cos, Charlwood Leigh Ltd; chm: Gardners Tst for the Blind, Cecilia Charity for the Blind, Schizophrenia Research Tst; memb Assembly RNIB, tstee Spirit of Scotland, memb Cncl Fairbridge; Sr Grand Warden United Grand Lodge of England 1984–86; FRGS; Priory of Scotland, Military and Hospitaller Order of St Lazarus; *Clubs* White's, Pratt's; *Style*— The Rt Hon the Viscount Gough; ✉ Keppoch Estate Office, Strathpeffer, Ross-shire IV14 9AD (tel 01997 421224); 17 Stanhope Gardens, London SW7 5RQ; c/o John Mitchell Fine Paintings, 44 Old Bond Street, London W1S 4gb (tel 020 7491 4344, fax 020 7493 5537)

GOULD, Deborah Jane (Debby); da of Frank Cotterill (d 1981), and Lily, *née* Matthews; *b* 11 March 1960, Bedhampton, Hants; *Educ* Portsmouth GS for Girls, Univ of Portsmouth (BSc, MSc), Univ of York (Cert); *m* 13 Aug 1983 (m dis 2001), Robert Gould; 2 s (Will b 12 Jan 1988, Josh b 20 Nov 1989); partner, Stephen Evans; *Career* registered gen nurse 1981, registered midwife 1984; midwife Portsmouth NHS Tst 1984, clinical practice devpt midwife Guy's and St Thomas' Hosp Tst 1997–98, high care mangr Southampton Univ Hosps Tst 1998–2001, head of midwifery Winchester and Eastleigh Healthcare Tst 2001, conslt midwife Queen Charlotte's and Chelsea Hosps London 2001–04, actg head of midwifery and gynaecology St George's Hosp London 2004–05, head of midwifery and sr nurse for gynaecology Mayday Univ Hosp Croydon 2005–; memb Cncl Royal Coll of Midwives 2000– (dep chair 2005–; memb various ctees and working parties incl: Educn and Research Gp 2001–05, Finance and Governance Ctees 2005, Professional Policy Gp 2005–), memb NICE Topic Selection Panel for Children, Adolescence and Maternity; writer Birth Rite column Br Jl of Midwifery 2000–, author of articles in professional jls, presentations at numerous nat and int confs on midwifery and motherhood; *Style*— Miss Debby Gould; ✉ Mayday University Hospital, London Road, Croydon CR7 7YE (tel 020 8401 3000, e-mail debby.gould@mayday.nhs.uk)

GOULD, Jonathan; s of Cedric Gould (d 1956), of London, and Joan Wilson, *née* Spiers (d 1983); *b* 1 April 1952; *Educ* Hurstpierpoint Coll, Univ of Bristol (LLB); *m* 4 May 1991, Elizabeth Ann Mackie; *Career* Allen & Overy: articled 1974–76, asst slr 1976–81, ptnr 1982–2003, res ptnr Hong Kong 1988–96; gp gen counsel and dir Jardine Matheson Gp 2004–; dir: Dairy Farm Int Hldgs Ltd, Hongkong Land Ltd, Jardine Motors Gp Ltd, Jardine Pacific Gp Ltd, Mandarin Oriental Int Ltd; *Clubs* Hong Kong, Shek O; *Style*— Jonathan Gould, Esq; ✉ Jardine Matheson Ltd, 48th Floor, Jardine House, Central, Hong Kong (tel 00 852 2843 8225, fax 00 852 2845 9005)

GOULD, Jonathan Leon (Jonny); s of Robert Gould (d 2002), and Yvonne Gould; *b* 5 June 1967; *Educ* Handsworth GS Birmingham; *Career* reporter Supercall Sport 1988, sports ed Beacon Radio 1988–90, reporter BBC World Service, LBC, IRN, ITN, BFBS and BSkyB 1990–92, head of sport ITN Radio/IRN 1992–95, md Sportsmedia Broadcasting Ltd 1992–; morning sports reporter Talk Radio 1995–99; presenter: Five News and Sport 1997–2000, ITV Sport 2000–02, Football Italia (Channel 4) 2001–02, Euro Fever 2000–; touchline reporter Premiership Plus; sports columnist London Jewish News 2003–05; exec dir Inst of Sports Sponsorship; *Recreations* making hay (while the sun shines), Laurel and Hardy, Aston Villa, share speculation, property, travel, Italian, Roman and Jewish history; *Clubs* Sons of the Desert (Laurel and Hardy Appreciation Society); *Style*— Jonny Gould, Esq; ✉ Sportsmedia Broadcasting Ltd, Suite 16, Linen House, 253 Kilburn Lane, London W10 4BQ (tel 020 8964 6555, fax 07812 354742, e-mail jonny@jonnygould.com)

GOULD, Michael Philip; s of John Gould (d 1989), of Clayhall, Essex, and Amelia, *née* Cohen (d 1983); *b* 29 January 1947; *Educ* SW Essex Tech Coll; *m* 29 Aug 1971, Linda, da of Philip Keen, of Loughton, Essex; 2 da (Rosemary Julia b 1974, Jennifer Karen b 1977); *Career* CA; sr ptnr Haslers (special responsibility as head of corp fin); dir: Brontree Ltd 1982, Tametree Properties Ltd 1982; FCA, CF, ATII, MAE; *Recreations* amateur pianist, music generally, theatre, good food, skiing, travel, tennis; *Clubs* David Lloyd Tennis; *Style*— Michael P Gould, Esq; ✉ Haslers, Old Station Road, Loughton IG10 4PL (tel 020 8418 3333, fax 020 8418 3320, e-mail michael.gould@haslers.com)

G

GOULD, (John) Roger Beresford; s of John Cecil Beresford Gould (d 1978), and Dorothy, *née* Entwistle (d 2001); *b* 1 January 1940; *Educ* Bolton Sch, Merton Coll Oxford (MA); *m* 21 Sept 1968, Catherine Celia, da of William Tetlow Faulkner; 1 da (Diana b 1970), 1 s (Richard b 1973); *Career* Seton Scholl Healthcare plc: co sec 1972–99, fin dir 1974–80, dep md 1980–84, dep chm 1984–98; non-exec dir: Shiloh plc 1998–2004, Emerson Developments (Holdings) Ltd 1999–; CMI: chm Manchester Branch 1983–85 and 1999–2001, chm NW Area 1985–87, memb Nat Cncl 1984–90, vice-chm Nat Cncl 1991–97; memb Nat Cncl ICAEW 1995–2001; pres Manchester Soc of Chartered Accountants 1994–95, memb Bd of Govrs Manchester Met Univ 1995–2006, memb Oldham Local Strategic Partnership 2002–; methodist local preacher; FCA 1966, CCMI 1989 (MBIM 1971); *Recreations* theatre, golf; *Style*— Roger Gould, Esq; ✉ 4 The Park, Grasscroft, Oldham, Lancashire OL4 4ES (tel 01457 876422)

GOULD, Dr Terry Ronald; s of Sir Ronald Gould (d 1986), of Worthing, W Sussex, and Nellie Denning, *née* Fish (d 1979); *b* 11 March 1934; *Educ* Culford Sch Bury St Edmunds, KCL, St George's Hosp Med Sch (MB BS, DA, LRCP); *m* 18 June 1960, Shirley Anne, da of Robert Arthur Philip Bunce (d 1987), of Bournemouth; 2 da (Caroline Emma b 1961, Sarah Kathryn b 1970), 2 s (Simon Mark b 1962, Nicholas James b 1965); *Career* Nat Serv Lt Surgn RN 1960–63; conslt anaesthetist: Royal Dental Hosp 1968–80, Atkinson Morley's Hosp 1968–95, St George's Hosp London 1968–95 (hon conslt anaesthetist 1995–, chm Med Advsy Ctee 1976–79, hon archivist 1987–99); hon conslt anaesthetist St Luke's Nursing Home for Clergy 1968–99; Wandsworth HA: chm Dist Med Exec Ctee 1980–83 (memb 1983–85), unit gen mangr Continuing Care Unit 1985–93; sec to Special Tstees St George's Hosp London; memb: Cncl Trinity Hospice Clapham, Mgmnt Ctee Wandsworth Homes Assoc, History of Anaesthesia Soc, Assoc of Anaesthetists; DObstRCOG, MRCS, FRCA; *Books* Quality in Health Care - A Practical Guide (with H Merrett), A History of the Atkinson Morley's Hospital (with David Uttley), A Short History of St George's Hospital and the Origin of its Ward Names (with David Uttley); *Recreations* gardening, golf, reading, art, history; *Style*— Dr Terry Gould; ✉ Pendeane, 14 Chalgrove Road, Sutton, Surrey SM2 5JT (tel 020 8642 0466, e-mail tgould@blueyonder.co.uk)

GOULD, Prof Warwick; s of Leslie William Gould, and Fedora, *née* Green; *b* 7 April 1947; *Educ* Brisbane GS, Univ of Queensland (BA); *Career* Royal Holloway Univ of London (formerly Royal Holloway and Bedford New Coll London): lectr in English language and literature 1973–86, sr lectr 1986–91, reader in English literature 1991–95; research reader Br Acad 1992–94; Univ of London: memb Academic Cncl 1990–94, memb Senate 1990–94 and 2000–, memb Academic Ctee 1994–2000, memb Cncl 1995–2000 and 2002–, prof of English literature 1995–; Sch of Advanced Study Univ of London: prog dir Centre for English Studies 1997–99 (dep prog dir 1994–97), dir Inst of English Studies 1999–, dep dean 2000–03; ed Yeats Annual 1983–; Cecil Oldman Meml Medal for Bibliography and Textual Criticism Univ of Leeds 1993; FRSL 1997, FRSA 1998, FEA 1999; *Publications* Joachim of Fiore and the Myth of the Eternal Evangel (jtly, 1987, 2 edn Joachim of Fiore and the Myth of the Eternal Evangel in the Nineteenth and Twentieth Centuries 2001), The Secret Rose: Stories by W B Yeats (jt ed, 1981, 2 edn 1992), The Collected Letters of W B Yeats, Vol 2 1896–1990 (jt ed, 1997), Gioacchino da Fiore e il Mito dell'Evangelo Eterno Nella Cultura Europea (jtly, 2000), W B Yeats MythoCopies (jt ed, 2005); *Recreations* book collecting; *Style*— Prof Warwick Gould; ✉ Institute of English Studies, Senate House, Malet Street, London WC1E 7HU (tel 020 7862 8673, fax 020 7862 8720, e-mail warwick.gould@sas.ac.uk)

GOULD OF BROOKWOOD, Baron (Life Peer UK 2004), of Brookwood in the County of Surrey; Philip Gould; s of William Caleb Gould; *b* 30 March 1950; *Educ* E London Coll, Univ of Sussex, LSE (MSc), London Business Sch; *m* 1985, Gail Rebuck, CBE, *qv*, da of Gordon Woolfe Rebuck; 2 da (Hon Georgia Anne Rebuck b 1986, Hon Grace Atlanta Rebuck b 1989); *Career* dir Tinker and Partners 1979–81, fndr Brignull LeBas Gould 1981–83, mgmnt dir Doyle Dane Bernbach 1985, Philip Gould Associates 1985; visiting prof LSE; tstee Royal Parks Fndn; *Publications* The Unfinished Revolution; *Style*— The Lord Gould of Brookwood

GOULD OF POTTERNEWTON, Baroness (Life Peer UK 1993), of Leeds in the County of West Yorkshire; Joyce Brenda Gould; da of Solomon Joseph Manson; *b* 29 October 1932; *Educ* Roundhay Sch for Girls, Bradford Tech Coll; *m* 1952 (sep), Kevin Gould; 1 da (Hon Jeannette b 1953); *Career* dispensing chemist 1952–65; Labour Party: asst regnl organiser and women's offr Yorks 1969–75, asst nat agent and chief women's offr 1975–85, dir of organisation Lab Pty 1985–93, front bench spokesperson on Citizen's Charter 1993–95, oppn front bench spokesperson on women's affrs 1996–97, a Baroness in Waiting (Govt whip) 1997–98 (oppn whip 1994–97), Dept Liaison Peer to Leader of House of Lords Baroness Jay of Paddington 1998–; memb Independent Commn on Voting Systems; formerly: exec memb Women's Nat Cmmn, Lab Pty sec Nat Jt Ctee Working Women's Organisations, sec Yorks Nat Cncl of Civil Liberties, memb Ctee Campaign Against Racial Discrimination, memb Home Office Ctee on Electoral Matters, dir Maries Stopes International; pres: Br Epilepsy Assoc, Family Planning Assoc; vice-pres: Socialist Int Women 1979–85, Population Concern; dir: Diaroma Art, Studio Upstairs; chair and tstee

Mary Macarthur Holiday Homes Tst; author of numerous pamphlets on feminism, socialism and sexism; memb: Fabian Soc, Hansard Soc, Howard League, Bevan Soc, Lab Electoral Reform Soc; *Style*— The Rt Hon Baroness Gould of Potternewton; ✉ House of Lords, London SW1A 0PW

GOULDEN, Sir (Peter) John; GCMG (2001, KCMG); *Educ* King Edward VII Sch Sheffield, The Queen's Coll Oxford (BA); *m*; 1 s (b 1967), 1 da (b 1970); *Career* HM Dip Serv 1963–2001: Ankara 1963–67, second sec Hungary/Romania/Czechoslavakia desk FO 1967–69, Manila 1969–71, planning staff FO 1971–74, i/c FO's recruitment prog 1974–76, head of chancery Dublin 1976–79, asst head Defence Dept i/c NATO affrs FCO 1979–81, head Personnel Servs Dept then head News Dept and FCO spokesman 1982–84, head of chancery UK Representation to the Euro Communities Brussels 1984–87, asst under-sec of state (Defence) FCO 1988–92, ambass Ankara 1992–95, Br perm rep (with personal rank of ambass) to NATO and WEU 1995–2000; conslt to Home Office 2001–; tstee Greenwich Fndn; *Style*— Sir John Goulden, GCMG

GOULDING, Jeremy Wynne Ruthven; s of Denis Arthur Goulding (d 1979), of Nottingham, and Doreen Daphne, *née* Phizackerley; *b* 29 August 1950; *Educ* The Becket Sch Nottingham, Magdalen Coll Oxford (MA); *m* 24 Aug 1974, Isobel Mary, da of Arnold Samuel Fisher, of Worcester; 2 s (Richard b 1979, Paul b 1988), 2 da (Laura b 1983, Vanessa b 1988); *Career* asst master Abingdon Sch 1974–78, asst master Shrewsbury Sch 1978–89 (housemaster Oldham's Hall 1983–89); headmaster: Prior Park Coll 1989–96, Haberdashers' Aske's Sch 1996–2001, Shrewsbury Sch 2001–; memb: Oxford Soc, HMC; Freeman Worshipful Co of Haberdashers; *Recreations* hill walking, reading, music-making, cooking; *Style*— Jeremy Goulding, Esq; ✉ Headmaster's House, Shrewsbury School, The Schools, Shrewsbury SY3 7BA (tel 01743 280525)

GOULDING, Prof Kenneth Henry (Ken); *b* 26 September 1942; *Educ* Scarborough HS for Boys, Univ of London (external BSc, external MSc), Univ of Bradford (PhD); *m* 1962, Yvonne; 2 da (Paula Mary b 1966, Susanne b 1969); *Career* SERC res student Univ of Bradford 1964–67; pt/t lectr: Leeds Tech Coll 1964–65, Bradford Tech Coll 1965–67; Hatfield Poly: lectr 1965–68, sr lectr 1970–75, princ lectr 1975–81, dir of studies (biological scis) and head of dept 1979–85; Lancs Poly: head of dept 1985–87, actg dean of sci 1987–90, dean Faculty of Sci 1990–91; dep vice-chllr Middx Univ 1992–2005 (actg vice-chllr 1996); CNAA: memb and latterly vice-chm Life Scis Ctee 1979–91, chm Environmental Sci Review Gp 1989–91, chm Biological Scis Review Gp 1991–92; Inst of Biol: vice-chm NW Branch 1986–87 and 1989–92, chm NW Branch 1987–89, chm Working Gp on Continuing Professional Devpt 1993–96; vice-chm and memb Exec Ctee Ctee of Heads of Biology in Polytechnics 1986–88, fndr chm Deans of Sci Ctee 1989–92, Euro rep Euro Deans of Sci Ctee 1990–92; memb: Professional and Educn Ctee Biochemical Soc 1987–90, Educn Ctee Assoc for the Advancement of Br Biotechnology 1987–91, Sci Ctee Hong Kong Cncl for Accreditation 1989–92, Exec Ctee Save Br Sci 1989–92, Expert Ctee on Environmental Educn DES 1991–92 and 1996, HE Working Gp Assoc for Sci Educn 1993–95, Hendon Coll Corp 1994–99, HEQC Steering Gp on External Examiners System 1994–95, SE England Consortium for Credit Accumulation and Transfer Working Gp 1994–96, Cncl Oak Hill Theol Coll 1995–, Southgate Coll Corp 1995–2005, HEQC Task Gp on Univ Awards 1996, HEQC Working Gp on Award Titles 1996–97, Bd Upper Lee Valley Partnership 1997–2000, Univ of Wales Inst Cardiff Corp 1999–, Harrow Coll Corp 1999–, DfEE Fndn Degree Tank Gp 2000–01, Bd Univ Vocational Awards Cncl 2002–, Sport England London Educn Task Force 2002–04, Bd Fndn Degree Forward 2003–04; chair N and E London Sports Network 2000–; memb: Soc for Gen Microbiology 1965, Br Phycological Soc 1969, Freshwater Biological Assoc 1971; memb: Editorial Advsy Bd Biological Reviews 1989–99, Editorial Bd Jl of Health and Nursing Studies 1991–93; memb Bd Archive and Museum of Black Heritage 1999–2004; Hon DSc UWE, hon fell RVC 2001; CBiol 1970, FIBiol 1986 (MIBiol 1970); *Books* Biotechnology - the Biological and Microbiological Principles (jtly, 1986, German translation), Horticultural Exploitation of Recent Biological Developments (contrib and ed, 1991), Principles and Techniques of Practical Biochemistry (ed with K Wilson, 4 edn 1995, various translations); author of various book chapters and numerous pubns in academic jls; *Recreations* various sports; *Clubs* Hatfield Cricket; *Style*— Prof Ken Goulding

GOULDING, Sir (William) Lingard Walter; 4 Bt (UK 1904), of Millicent, Clane, Co Kildare, and Roebuck Hill, Dundrum, Co Dublin; er s of Sir (William) Basil Goulding, 3 Bt (d 1982), and Hon Valerie Hamilton Monckton (d 2003), o da of 1 Viscount Monckton of Brenchley; Sir Lingard is tenth in descent from William Goulding, who arrived in Ireland as a member of Oliver Cromwell's army; *b* 11 July 1940; *Educ* Winchester, Trinity Coll Dublin; *Heir* yr bro, Timothy Goulding; *Career* formerly with Conzinc Rio Tinto of Aust; former mangr Rionore; racing driver; headmaster Headfort Sch 1977– (asst master 1974–76); *Style*— Sir Lingard Goulding, Bt; ✉ Dargle Cottage, Enniskerry, Co Wicklow, Republic of Ireland

GOULDING, Sir Marrack Irvine; KCMG (1997, CMG 1983); Sir (Ernest) Irvine Goulding (d 2000), and Gladys Ethel, *née* Sennett (d 1981); *b* 2 September 1936; *Educ* St Paul's, Magdalen Coll Oxford (BA); *m* 1961, Susan Rhoda (m dis 1996), da of Air Marshal Sir John D'Albiac, KCVO, KBE, CB, DSO (d 1963); 2 s, 1 da; m 2, 1996 (m dis 2004), Catherine, da of Alexandre Pawlow (d 1997); *Career* HM Dip Serv 1959–85, served Lebanon, Kuwait, London, Libya, Egypt, London (private sec to min of state FCO, seconded Cabinet Office CPRS), Portugal, UN (NY), ambass to Angola and (concurrently but non-resident) to São Tomé and Principe 1983–85; UN Secretariat NY 1986–97: under-sec gen for peacekeeping 1986–93, under-sec gen for political affrs 1993–97; warden St Antony's Coll Oxford 1997–2006; memb Bd: Royal African Soc, Oxford Centre for Islamic Studies, Jupiter European Opportunites Tst; *Publications* Peacemonger (2002); *Recreations* travel, bird watching; *Clubs* Oxford and Cambridge; *Style*— Sir Marrack Goulding, KCMG; ✉ 11 St Gabriel's Manor, 25 Cormont Road, London SE5 9RH

GOULDING, Paul Anthony; QC (2000); s of Byron Goulding, and Audrey, *née* Lansdown; *b* 24 May 1960; *Educ* Latymer Sch Edmonton, St Edmund Hall Oxford (MA, BCL); *m* 16 June 1984, Rt Rev June Osborne, Dean of Salisbury; 1 da (Megan b 11 Jan 1990), 1 s (Tom b 16 June 1992); *Career* tutor in law St Edmund Hall Oxford 1982–84; called to the Bar Middle Temple 1984; vice-pres Employment Lawyers' Assoc 2000–04 (chm 1998–2000), memb Bd European Employment Lawyers Assoc 2001–05; *Books* European Employment Law and the UK (2001); *Recreations* football (FA coach), rugby, opera, ballet; *Clubs* Reform; *Style*— Paul Goulding, Esq, QC; ✉ Blackstone Chambers, Blackstone House, Temple, London EC4Y 9BW (tel 020 7583 1770, fax 020 7822 7350)

GOULTY, (HE) Alan Fletcher; CMG (1998); s of Anthony Edmund Rivers Goulty (d 2002), and Maisie Oliphant, *née* Stein; *b* 2 July 1947; *Educ* Bootham Sch York, CCC Oxford (MA); *m* 30 July 1983, Lillian Craig, da of Rev Dr Hendon Mason Harris Jr (d 1981), and Marjorie Elizabeth Weaver (d 2005); 1 s (Alastair Charles b 16 Dec 1970); *Career* third sec: FCO 1968–69, MECAS 1969–71, Beirut 1971–72; second sec: Khartoum 1972–75, FCO 1975–77; first sec: Cabinet Office 1977–80, Washington 1981–85, FCO 1985–87; cnsllr and head Near East and North Africa Dept FCO 1987–90, dep head of mission Cairo 1990–95, ambass to Sudan 1995–99, dir Middle East FCO 2000–02, UK special rep Sudan 2002–04, ambass to Tunisia 2004–, UK special rep Darfur 2005–06; fell Weatherhead Center for Int Affrs Harvard Univ 1999–2000; Grand Cordon du Wissam Alaouite (Morocco) 1987; *Style*— Alan Goulty, CMG; ✉ c/o Foreign & Commonwealth Office (Tunis), King Charles Street, London SW1A 2AH

GOURLAY, Gen Sir (Basil) Ian Spencer; KCB (1973), CVO (1990), OBE (1956, MBE 1948), MC (1944); s of Brig K I Gourlay, DSO, OBE, MC (d 1970), and Victoria May, *née* Oldrini (d 1986); *b* 13 November 1920; *Educ* Eastbourne Coll; *m* 1948, Natasha, da of late Col Dimitri Zinovieff, and late Princess Elisaveta Galitzine; 1 s (Michael b 1950), 1 da (Ann b 1954); *Career* cmmnd RM 1940, Capt 1949, Maj 1956, Lt-Col 1963, CO 42 Commando 1963, Col 1965, actg Brig 1966, Cdr 3 Commando Bde RM 1966, Maj-Gen 1968, Cdr Trg Gp RM 1968–71, Cmdt-Gen RM 1971–75, Lt-Gen 1971, Gen 1973, ret; vice-pres United World Colleges 1990– (DG 1975–90); *Clubs* MCC, Army and Navy; *Style*— Gen Sir Ian Gourlay, KCB, CVO, OBE, MC

GOVE, Michael; MP; *b* 26 August 1967, Edinburgh; *Educ* Robert Gordon's Coll Aberdeen, Univ of Oxford; *Career* journalist; reporter Aberdeen Press and Journal 1989, researcher and reporter Scottish Television 1990–91, reporter BBC News and Current Affrs 1991–95, journalist The Times 1995–; MP (Cons) Surrey Heath 2005–, shadow min for housing 2005–07, shadow sec of state for children, schs and families 2007–; chm Policy Exchange until 2005; *Books* Michael Portillo: The Future of the Right (1995); *Style*— Michael Gove, Esq, MP; ✉ House of Commons, London SW1A 0AA (website www.michaelgove.com)

GOVES, Andrew John (Andy); s of Arthur George Goves, MBE (d 1986), and Lois Henrietta, *née* Hudson (d 1995); *b* 10 November 1951, High Wycombe, Bucks; *Educ* Wycombe Tech HS, Univ of Buckingham (LLB), City and Guilds Inst (MCGI), Univ of Central Lancs (MSc), Univ of Coventry (MA); *m* 20 July 1982, Nicola Therese (Nikki), *née* Masters; 1 da (Samantha Jane b 17 May 1984); *Career* Bucks Fire and Rescue Service: operational firefighter and fire safety offr then sub-offr 1974–82, station offr Fire Safety and Operations 1982–86, asst divnl offr (seconded to Fire Service Coll) 1986–88, area cdr then divnl offr 1988–2000, dep chief fire offr 2000–03; chief fire offr Wiltshire Fire & Rescue Service 2003–; author of articles in industry publications; memb Cncl St John Ambulance Cncl Wiltshire 2004– (pres High Wycombe Div 2002–03); Fire Brigade Long Service and Good Conduct Medal 1994; memb: Chief Fire Offrs' Assoc, Inst of Fire Engrs 1981, Inst of Mgmnt 1987, Inst of Leadership and Mgmnt 1987, FIFireE 2007; *Recreations* owning classic MG sports cars and German Shepherd dogs; *Style*— Andy Goves, Esq; ✉ Wiltshire Fire and Rescue Service, Manor House, Potterne, Devizes, Wiltshire SN10 5PP (tel 01380 731104, fax 01380 729264)

GOVETT, (Clement) John; LVO (1990); s of Clement Charles Govett (d 1963), and Daphne Mary, *née* Norman (d 1964); *b* 26 December 1943; *Educ* St Paul's, Pembroke Coll Oxford (MA); *m* 14 June 1975, Rosalind Mary, da of Geoffrey Fawn (d 1988); 3 da (Helen b 1977, Sarah b 1978, Joanna b 1981); *Career* Price Waterhouse 1966–69, dir J Henry Schroder Wagg & Co Ltd 1980–90 (joined 1969); Schroder Investment Management Ltd: dep chief exec 1987–94, chm 1995–96; gp md asset mgmnt Schroders plc 1996–98; chm Schroder Split Fund plc 1993–2000; dir: INVESCO City & Commercial Trust plc (formerly New City & Commercial Investment Trust plc) 1993–2001, Derby Trust plc 1995–2003, Schroder Emerging Countries Fund plc 1996–2003, Schroder Ventures International Investment Tst plc 1996–2004, Peel Hotels plc 1998–; FCA; *Recreations* bridge, tennis, golf, gardening; *Clubs* Brooks's; *Style*— John Govett, Esq, LVO; ✉ 29 Marchmont Road, Richmond, Surrey TW10 6HQ (tel 020 8940 2876)

GOW, John Stobie; s of David Gow (d 1988), of Alloa, and Ann Frazer, *née* Scott (d 1984); *b* 12 April 1933; *Educ* Alloa Acad, Univ of St Andrews (BSc, PhD); *m* 29 Dec 1955, Elizabeth, da of James Henderson (d 1963), of Alloa; 3 s (Iain b 1958, Alan b 1961, Andrew b 1964); *Career* prodn mangr Chem Co of Malaysia 1966–68; ICI: research mangr Agric Div 1968–72, gen mangr Catalysts Agric Div 1972–74, research dir Organics Div 1974–79, dep chm Organics Div 1979–84, md speciality chemicals 1984–86; non-exec dir: W & J Foster Ltd 1984–93, ST&M NTO 1997–2003; sec gen Royal Soc of Chem 1986–93, sec Science Cncl 1993–2001, dir EMTA 2001–03, dir Sci, Engrg Manufacturing Technol Assoc (SEMTA) 2003–05; assessor SERC 1987–93; elder United Reformed Church; FRSE 1978, FRSC 1986, FRSA; *Style*— John Gow, Esq, FRSE; ✉ 19 Longcroft Avenue, Harpenden, Hertfordshire AL5 2RD (tel 01582 764889, e-mail jackgow@btinternet.com)

GOW, Sheriff Neil; QC (Scot 1970); s of Donald Gow, of Glasgow; *b* 24 April 1932; *Educ* Merchiston Castle Sch Edinburgh, Univ of Edinburgh, Univ of Glasgow (MA, LLB); *m* 1959, Joanna, da of Cdr S D Sutherland, of Edinburgh; 1 s; *Career* Capt Intelligence Corps (BAOR); Carnegie scholar in History of Scots Law 1956, advocate 1957–76, Standing Cncl to Miny of Soc Security (Scot) 1964–70; Parly candidate (Cons): Kircaldy Burghs 1964 and 1966, Edinburgh East 1970; Hon Sheriff Lanarkshire 1971, Sheriff S Strathclyde at Ayr 1976–2006; pres Auchinleck Boswell Soc; FSA Scot; *Books* A History of Scottish Statutes (1959), An Outline of Estate Duty in Scotland (jt ed 1970); Crime and Prejudice (Channel 4, 1993), Tests of Evidence (Radio Scotland, 1995); Documentary Class Gold Medal in NY Radio City Awards 1998; numerous articles and broadcasts on legal topics and Scottish affairs; *Recreations* golf, shooting, classic cars; *Clubs* Prestwick Golf, Western (Glasgow); *Style*— Sheriff Neil Gow, QC; ✉ Old Auchenfail Hall, by Mauchline, Ayrshire KA5 5TA

GOWAN, David John; CMG (2005); s of Prof Ivor Lyn Gowan, of Charlbury, and Gwendoline Alice, *née* Pearce; *b* 11 February 1949; *Educ* Nottingham HS, Ardwyn GS Aberystwyth, Balliol Coll Oxford (MA); *m* 10 Aug 1975, Marna Irene, da of Rhondda Williams; 2 s (Richard Vernon b 20 Sept 1978, Edward William b 29 April 1982); *Career* asst princ MOD 1970–73, Home Civil Serv 1973–75; HM Dip Serv: second sec FCO 1975–76, Russian language trg 1976–77, second then first sec Moscow 1977–80, first sec FCO 1981–85, head of Chancery and consul Brasilia 1985–88, on secondment to Cabinet Office 1988–89, asst head Soviet Dept FCO 1989–90, on secondment as cnsllr Cabinet Office 1990–91, cnsllr (commercial and Know How Fund) Moscow 1992–95, cnsllr and dep head of mission Helsinki 1995–99, cnsllr FCO 1999–2000, min Moscow 2000–03, ambass to Serbia and Montenegro 2003–06; St Antony's Coll Oxford: sr assoc memb 1999–2000, guest memb 2007–; memb: Bishop's Cncl 2007–, Synod Dio in Europe 2008–; *Publications* How the EU can help Russia (2000); *Recreations* reading, walking, travel, music, theatre; *Clubs* Athenaeum; *Style*— David Gowan, Esq, CMG; ✉ 8 Blackmore Road, Malvern, Worcestershire WR14 1QX (tel 01684 565707)

GOWAR, Martyn Christopher; s of T W Gowar (d 1987), of Ewell, Surrey, and M A Gowar, *née* Bower (d 1986); *b* 11 July 1946; *Educ* KCS Wimbledon, Magdalen Coll Oxford (MA); *m* 1971, Susan Mary, da of D B H Scotchmer; 3 s (Jonathan b 1973, Michael b 1975, Alexander b 1978); *Career* Lawrence Graham: articled clerk Lawrence Graham & Co 1967, ptnr 1973–2006, sr ptnr 1997–2002, conslt 2006–; memb: Int Ctee Soc of Tsts & Estate Practitioners (STEP), Cncl Inst of Advanced Legal Studies, Int Bar Assoc; vice-pres (Europe) Int Acad of Estate & Tst Law; taxation ed Law Soc Gazette 1979–94; frequent lectr on taxation and tst topics; clerk to the govrs Wellington Coll, clerk to the Tstees Hamlyn Tst, govr St Paul's Cathedral Sch, tstee Laura Ashley Fndn; memb Addington Soc; Liveryman Worshipful Co of Glaziers; Liveryman Worshipful Co of Tax Advsrs; MInstD, FInstT 1981 (AInstT 1976); *Publications* Butterworths Encyclopaedia of Forms & Precedents Vol 30 (ed Partnerships section), Simons Taxes (contrib); *Recreations* golf, cricket, gardening; *Clubs* MCC, Lord's Taverners, In and Out, Hankley Common Golf, Rye Golf, London Slrs' Golf Soc; *Style*— Martyn Gowar, Esq; ✉ Lawrence Graham, 4 More London Riverside, London SE1 2AU (tel 020 7379 0000, fax 020 7379 6854, e-mail martyn.gowar@lg-legal.com)

GOWDY, (David) Clive; CB (2001); s of Samuel David Gowdy (d 1977), and Eileen, *née* Porter (d 1996); *b* 27 November 1946; *Educ* Royal Belfast Academical Inst, Queen's Univ Belfast (BA, MSc); *m* 27 Oct 1973, Linda Doreen, da of Eric Anton Traub, of Belfast; 2 da (Claire b 1978, Alison b 1980); *Career* asst princ Miny of Fin 1970–73, dep princ Civil

Serv Cmmn 1973–76, sec Rowland Cmmn 1978–79, princ NI Office 1976–81, asst sec Dept of Commerce 1981–85, exec dir Industrial Devpt Bd for NI 1985–87, under sec Dept of Economic Devpt 1987–90, Dept of Health and Social Servs 1990–93, Dept of Finance and Personnel 1994–96 perm sec Dept of Health and Social Servs 1997–99, perm sec Dept Health Social Services and Public Safety 1999–2005; visiting prof Univ of Ulster; memb Bd Belfast Charitable Soc; *Recreations* tennis, golf, music, reading; *Style*— Clive Gowdy, Esq, CB; ✉ e-mail clivegowdy@hotmail.com

GOWER, David Ivon; OBE (1992); s of Richard Hallam Gower (d 1973), and Sylvia Mary, *née* Ford (d 1986); *b* 1 April 1957; *Educ* King's Sch Canterbury, UCL; *m* 18 Sept 1992, Thorunn Nash; 2 da (Alexandra Sylvia b 25 Sept 1993, Samantha Erna b 28 May 1996); *Career* former professional cricketer; Leicestershire CCC 1975–89 (capt 1984–86 and 1988–89), Hampshire CCC 1990–93 (winners NatWest Trophy 1991 and Benson & Hedges Cup 1992); England: debut 1978, 117 test caps, capt 1984–86 and 1989 (total 32 tests as capt), 114 one day int appearances, highest score 215 v Aust Edgbaston 1985, second highest scoring English player in test matches with 8,231 runs incl 18 centuries (broke Geoff Boycott's previous record v Pakistan Old Trafford 1992), ret from first class cricket 1993; dir David Gower Promotions Ltd; cricket corr Sunday Express 1993–95; joined Test Match Special team BBC (for Ashes series in Australia) 1994, memb BBC TV Cricket Commentary Team 1994–98; team capt They Think it's All Over (BBC TV) 1995–2003, presenter Sky TV International Cricket 1999–; columnist: The Sun 2000–01, The Sunday Times 2002–; Hon MA: Univ of Southampton, Loughborough Univ; *Books* David Gower: the Autobiography (with Martin Johnson, *qv*, 1992); *Recreations* tennis, skiing, Cresta run, safari; *Clubs* St Moritz Tobogganing, East India, MCC, Groucho; *Style*— David Gower, Esq, OBE; ✉ c/o Jon Holmes Media Limited, 5th Floor, Holborn Gate, 26 Southampton Buildings, London WC2A 1PQ (tel 020 7861 2550, website www.jonholmesmedia.com)

GOWER-SMITH, (Nicholas) Mark; s of Charles Samuel Smith (d 1983), of Tunbridge Wells, and Margaret Brenda, *née* Isaac; *b* 20 March 1955; *Educ* The Skinners' Sch Tunbridge Wells, City of London Poly; *m* 25 July 1987 (m dis 2005), Christine Lorraine, *née* Allan; 2 s (Charles Edward b 1989, James Andrew b 1993); *Career* CA; sr ptnr Norman Cox & Ashby 1984–; dir Grosvenor Business Services (TW) Ltd 2001–, prop Gower-Smith & Co 1984–; organist St John's Church Tunbridge Wells 1992–; Freeman City of London 1991, Liveryman Worshipful Co of Tobacco Pipe Makers and Tobacco Blenders 1991 (memb Ct of Assts 2007); FCA, FRSA; Esq in Order of St John of Jerusalem 2006; *Recreations* music, opera, heraldry, photography; *Clubs* Royal Cwlth Soc; *Style*— Mark Gower-Smith, Esq; ✉ Grosvenor Lodge, 72 Grosvenor Road, Tunbridge Wells, Kent TN1 2AZ (tel 01892 522551)

GOWERS, Andrew Richard David; s of Michael David Warren Gowers, of Haywards Heath, W Sussex, and Florence Anne Dean, *née* Sykes; *b* 19 October 1957; *Educ* Trinity Sch Croydon, Gonville & Caius Coll Cambridge (MA); *m* 1982, Finola Mary, *née* Clarke; 1 s, 1 da; *Career* Reuters: grad trainee 1980, Brussels Bureau 1981–82, Zurich corr 1982–83; Financial Times: foreign staff 1983–84, agric corr 1984–85, commodities ed 1985–87, ME ed 1987–90, features ed 1990–92, foreign ed 1992–94, dep ed 1994–97, acting ed 1997–98, ed-in-chief Financial Times Deutschland Hamburg 1998–2001, ed 2001–05; Lehman Brothers: head of corp communications, advtg and brand and mktg strategy Europe 2006–07, global co-head corp communications, mktg and brand mgmnt 2007–; columnist Sunday Times 2005–; ldr Gowers Review of Intellectual Property for HM Treasy 2005–06; jt winner Guardian/NUS Student Journalist of the Year award 1979; *Books* Behind the Myth: Yasser Arafat and the Palestinian Revolution (1990, reissued as Arafat: The Biography 1994); *Recreations* cinema, reading, opera, music of all kinds; *Style*— Andrew Gowers, Esq

GOWERS, Prof (William) Timothy; s of Patrick Gowers, of London, and Caroline Molesworth, *née* Maurice; *b* 20 November 1963; *Educ* Eton, Trinity Coll Cambridge (BA, Cert of Advanced Study in Mathematics, PhD); *m* 1988, Emily Joanna, da of Sir Keith Thomas; 2 s (John b 1992, Richard Humphrey b 1994), 1 da (Madeline Margaret b 1997); *Career* research fell Trinity Coll Cambridge 1989–93; UCL: lectr 1991–94, reader 1994–95; Univ of Cambridge: lectr 1995–98, Rouse Ball prof of mathematics 1998–; Jr Whitehead Prize (London Mathematical Soc) 1995, European Mathematical Soc Prize 1996, Fields Medal 1998; hon fell UCL 1999; FRS 1999; *Publications* various research papers in mathematical journals; *Recreations* jazz piano; *Style*— Prof Timothy Gowers; ✉ Centre for Mathematical Sciences, Wilberforce Road, Cambridge CB3 0WB (tel 01223 337973, e-mail wtg10@dpmms.cam.ac.uk)

GOWING, Nik; s of Donald James Graham Gowing (d 1969), and Prof Margaret Mary Gowing, *née* Elliott (d 1998); *b* 13 January 1951; *Educ* Latymer Upper Sch, Simon Langton GS Canterbury, Univ of Bristol (BSc); *m* 10 July 1982, Judith Wastall, da of Dr Peter Venables, of Andover, Hants; 1 da (Sarah Margaret b 21 Dec 1983), 1 s (Simon Donald Peter b 9 Feb 1987); *Career* reporter Newcastle Chronicle 1973–74, presenter-reporter Granada TV 1974–78; ITN: joined 1978, Rome corr 1979, Eastern Europe corr 1980–83, foreign affrs corr 1983–87, dip corr 1987–89, dip ed and newscaster Channel 4 News 1989–96; co-presenter The World This Week 1990–92; main presenter: BBC World TV 1996–, BBC News 1996–; conslt: in media and conflict mgmnt, Carnegie Cmmn on Prevention of Deadly Conflict 1996–97, Euro Community Humanitarian Office (ECHO) 1997–; memb: Governing Body Br Assoc for Central and Eastern Europe 1997–, Academic Cncl Wilton Park Conference Centre 1998–, Cncl RIIA 1998–2004, Strategy Ctee Project on Justice in Times of Transition 2000–, Editorial Bd Press and Politics Jl Harvard Univ; vice-chm Bd of Govrs Westminster Fndn for Democracy 1996–2005, govr Ditchley Fndn 2000–; fell Kennedy Sch of Govt Harvard Univ 1994, visiting fell Int Affairs Keele Univ; memb Exec Cncl RUSI 2005–, RIIA, RTS; *Books* The Wire (1988), The Loop (1993); *Recreations* cycling, skiing, authorship; *Style*— Nik Gowing, Esq; ✉ BBC, Room 2524, BBC TV Centre, London W12 7RJ (tel 020 8225 8137, fax 020 8287 4427, mobile 07802 877808, e-mail nik.gowing@bbc.co.uk)

GOWLAND, Robert George; s of George Fredrick Gowland (d 1978), of Enfield, Middlesex, and Meta, *née* Emck; *b* 27 January 1943; *Educ* Haileybury & ISC, RAC Cirencester (CLAS); *m* Anne Sandra, da of Douglas Markes; 1 da (Nicola Louise b 1973), 1 s (Benjamin Thomas George b 1976); *Career* Phillips International Auctioneers 1979–97, chm W & F C Bonham & Sons Ltd North of England 1998–2000, chm Bob Gowland International Golf Auctions 2000–; auctioneer and valuer of historical golfing memorabilia 1982–; hon sec Soc of Fine Art Auctioneers 1976–80 and 1981–87 (chm 1987–97), memb Br Hallmarking Cncl 1985–97; Liveryman Worshipful Co of Clockmakers; FRICS 1974 (ARICS 1966); *Recreations* restoring historic golf clubs and furniture, golf, game fishing and shooting; *Clubs* R&A, Delamere Forest; *Style*— Robert Gowland, Esq; ✉ The Stables, Claim Farm, Manley Road, Frodsham, Cheshire WA6 6HT (e-mail bob@internationalgolfauctions.com)

GOWLLAND, Robin Anthony Blantyre; s of Reginald Blantyre-Gowlland (d 1974), of London and Hawkley, Hants, and Pauline, *née* Broomfield (d 1981); *b* 6 September 1932; *Educ* RNC Dartmouth and Greenwich, IMEDE Lausanne (Dip), Harvard Business Sch (MBA); *m* 1994, Rosalie W Read, of Hackthorn, Lincs; *Career* RN 1946–62, served UK, Med, Far East and Suez Campaign 1956 (ret as Lt); mgmnt conslt and dir Egon Zehnder International 1969–92 (md UK 1969–81, chm 1981–92); dir Videotron Holdings Ltd 1985–93 (chm 1985–91), chm Robin Gowlland Consulting 1992–; md (Europe) Samanco International 1994–; dir FCCS 1989–97; chm: GLS International 1992–, BGL Associates 1992–; sr res fell Cranfield Inst of Technol 1964–66; sr conslt and ptnr Harbridge House Inc 1966–69, vice-chm London Fedn of Clubs for Young People 1976–96 (dir NABC/CYP 1986–90, dir Int Fedn), memb Cncl Christian Assoc of Business Execs (chm 1976–80 and 1986), vice-chm Inst of Business Ethics 1986–98; Downside Settlement: hon sec 1966–73, vice-chm 1973–83, chm 1983–98, pres 1998–; tstee London Playing Fields Soc 1987–97; vice-chm Friends of Westminster Cathedral 1988–98, dir InterAid 1980–; govr St Michael's Sch Bermondsey 1993–; Hon Lt-Col Alabama State Militia (USA), Hon Citizen City of Mobile (USA); FRSA, FIMgt, FInstD; KCSG, KCHS, GCLJ, GCMLJ; *Publications* various articles in mgmnt jls; *Recreations* cricket, squash, real tennis, sailing, travel, theatre, art; *Clubs* Royal Yacht Sqdn, MCC, Naval and Military, Jesters; *Style*— Robin A B Gowlland, Esq; ✉ 82 Kenyon Street, London SW6 6LB (tel 020 7381 1725) office: Swiss Centre, 10 Wardour Street, London W1V 3HG (tel 020 7851 2751, fax 020 7851 2785)

GOWRIE, 2 Earl of (UK 1945); Alexander Patrick Greysteil Hore Ruthven; PC (1984); also Baron Ruthven of Gowrie (UK 1919), Baron Gowrie (UK 1935), and Viscount Ruthven of Canberra (UK 1945); in remainder to Lordship of Ruthven of Freeland (officially recognised in the name of Ruthven by Warrant of Lord Lyon 1957); s of Maj Hon Patrick Hore Ruthven (s of 1 Earl of Gowrie, VC, GCMG, CB, DSO, PC, who was Govr Gen and C-in-C of Australia 1936–44 and 2 s of 9 Lord Ruthven of Freeland); suc gf 1955; *b* 26 November 1939, Dublin; *Educ* Eton, Balliol Coll Oxford, Harvard; *m* 1, 1962 (m dis 1974), Xandra, yr da of Col Robert Bingley, CVO, DSO, OBE; 1 s; m 2, 1974, Countess Adelheid, yst da of Count Fritz-Dietlof von der Schulenburg; *Heir* s, Viscount Ruthven of Canberra; *Career* former lectr and tutor: SUNY, Harvard, UCL; Cons whip 1971–72, lord in waiting 1972–74, oppn spokesman Economic Affrs 1974–79; min of state: Dept of Employment 1979–81, NI Office 1981–83, Privy Cncl Office (and min for the arts) 1983–84; chllr of the Duchy of Lancaster (and min for the arts) 1984–85; chm: Really Useful Group 1985–90, Sotheby's Europe 1985–94, Arts Cncl of England 1994–98, Development Securities plc 1995–99, Fine Art Fund 2002–, The Magdi Yacoub Inst 2004–; provost Royal Coll of Art 1986–94; Picasso Medal UNESCO 1998; Freeman City of London; FRSL 2003; *Books* A Postcard from Don Giovanni (1972), The Genius of British Painting (jtly, 1975), The Conservative Opportunity (jtly, 1976), Derek Hill, An Appreciation (1985), The Domino Hymn: Poems from Harefield (2005); *Recreations* book reviewing; *Clubs* Kildare Street, University (Dublin), White's, Pratt's; *Style*— The Rt Hon the Earl of Gowrie, PC; ✉ The Fine Art Fund, 2 Deanery Street, London W1X 3PA

GOYMER, His Hon Judge Andrew Alfred; s of Richard Kirby Goymer (d 1986), of Keston, Kent, and Betty Eileen, *née* Thompson; *b* 28 July 1947; *Educ* Dulwich Coll, Pembroke Coll Oxford (Hull scholar, MA); *m* 30 Sept 1972, Diana Mary, da of Robert Harry Shipway, MBE, (d 1999); 1 s (Patrick b 1977), 1 da (Eleanor b 1980); *Career* Gerald Moody entrance scholar 1968, Holker sr exhibitioner 1970, Arden Atkin and Mould prizeman 1971; called to the Bar Gray's Inn 1970, admitted to the Bar NSW Aust 1988; memb SE Circuit 1972–99, recorder of the Crown Court 1991–99 (asst recorder 1987–91), circuit judge 1999–; *Style*— His Hon Judge Andrew Goymer; ✉ 6 Pump Court, 1st Floor, Temple, London EC4Y 7AR (tel 020 7797 8400)

GOZNEY, HE Sir Richard Hugh Turton; KCMG (2006, CMG 1993); s of Thomas Leonard Gozney (d 1991), of Oxford, and Elizabeth Margaret Lilian, *née* Gardiner (d 1998); *b* 21 July 1951; *Educ* Magdalen Coll Sch Oxford, St Edmund Hall Oxford (open scholar, BA); *m* 1982, Diana Edwina, da of David Brangwyn Harvey Baird; 2 s (James b 1987, Alexander b 1990); *Career* vol teacher Rusinga Secdy Sch Kenya 1970; HM Dip Serv: joined FO 1973, third sec Jakarta 1974–78, second sec Buenos Aires 1978–81, first sec and head of Chancery Madrid 1984–88, asst private sec later private sec to Foreign Sec (Geoffrey Howe, John Major then Douglas Hurd) 1989–93, attachment to RIIA 1993, high cmmr to Swaziland 1993–96, head Security Policy Dept FCO 1996–97, chief of assessments staff Jt Intelligence Orgn 1998–2000, ambass to Indonesia 2000–04, high cmmr to Nigeria 2004–07 (concurrently non-resident ambass to Benin and Equatorial Guinea), govr and C-in-C Bermuda 2007–; *Recreations* birdwatching, walking, sailing; *Style*— HE Sir Richard Gozney, KCMG; ✉ c/o Foreign & Commonwealth Office (Hamilton), King Charles Street, London SW1A 2AH (e-mail richard.gozney@fco.gov.uk)

GRAAFF, Sir David de Villiers; 3 Bt (UK 1911), of Cape Town, Cape of Good Hope Province of Union of South Africa; s of Sir de Villiers Graaff, 2 Bt, MBE (d 1999); *b* 3 May 1940; *Educ* Diocesan Coll South Africa, Univ of Stellenbosch, Grenoble Univ, Magdalen Coll Oxford; *m* 1969, Sally, da of Robin Williams; 3 s (de Villiers b 16 July 1970, Robert b 1974, David John b 1977), 1 da (Leeza b 1973); *Heir* s, de Villiers Graaff; *Career* wine farmer, proprietor De Grendel Wines; dir: Graaff's Trust, Milnerton Estates; MP (South Africa) 1987–98, dep min of Trade & Indust and Tourism 1991–94; Hon Col Cape Garrison Artillery; *Recreations* golf; *Clubs* Cape Town, Royal Cape Golf; *Style*— Sir David Graaff, Bt; ✉ PO Box 15192, Panorama 7506 (tel 00 27 21 558 7030, fax 00 27 21 558 7031)

GRABINER, Baron (Life Peer UK 1999), of Aldwych in the City of Westminster Anthony Stephen; QC (1981); s of Ralph Grabiner (d 1985), and Freda, *née* Cohen (d 1989); *b* 21 March 1945; *Educ* Central Fndn Boys' GS London, LSE, Univ of London (LLB, LLM); *m* 18 Dec 1983, Jane Aviva, da of Dr Benjamin Portnoy, of Hale, Cheshire; 3 s (Joshua b 1986, Daniel b 1989, Samuel b 1994), 1 da (Laura Sarina b 1992); *Career* called to the Bar Lincoln's Inn 1968 (bencher 1989); standing jr counsel to the DTI Export Credits Guarantee Dept 1976–81, jr counsel to the Crown 1978–81, recorder S Eastern Circuit 1990–99, dep High Ct judge 1998–; head of chambers 1995–; non-exec chm Arcadia Gp Ltd 2002–; chm Ct of Govrs LSE 1998– (memb 1990–, vice-chm 1993–98); non-exec dir Wentworth Golf 2005–; *Books* Sutton & Shannon on Contracts (7 edn, 1970), Banking Documents in Encyclopedia of Forms and Precedents (1986), The Informal Economy (report for HM Treasury, 2000); *Recreations* golf, theatre; *Clubs* Garrick, RAC, MCC; *Style*— The Rt Hon Lord Grabiner, QC; ✉ 1 Essex Court, Temple, London EC4Y 9AR (tel 020 7583 2000, fax 020 7583 0118, e-mail agrabiner@oeclaw.co.uk)

GRABINER, Michael; s of Henry Grabiner, of London, and Renee, *née* Geller; *b* 21 August 1950; *Educ* St Albans Sch, King's Coll Cambridge (MA Econ, pres Students' Union 1972–73); *m* 30 May 1976, Jane Olivia, *née* Harris; 3 s, 1 da; *Career* joined Post Office 1973, personal asst to md Telecommunications 1976–78, London Business Sch (Sloan Programme) 1980–81; rejoined BT: dep dir of mktg 1984–85, gen mangr Northern London Dist 1985–88, gen mangr City of London Dist 1988–90, dir quality and orgn 1990–92, dir global customer serv Business Communications Div 1992–94, dir BT Europe 1994–95; former memb Bd: BT Telecommunicaciones SA Spain, VIAG InterKom Germany, Telenordia Sweden, Albacom Italy; chief exec Energis plc 1996–2001; ptnr Apax Ptnrs 2002–, chm Spectrum Strategy Consultants 2003–06, chm Synetrix Holdings Ltd 2004–06; non-exec dir: Littlewoods plc 1998–2002, Emblaze Systems 2000–05, Chelsfield plc 2002–04, Telewest Global Inc 2004–06, Tim Hellas 2005–06, Bezeq 2006–; cncllr London Borough of Brent 1978–82 (chm Devpt Ctee 1980–82), dir East London Partnership 1994–95, chm Partnership for Schools 2005–; treas Reform Synagogues of GB 2002–05, chm UK Jewish Film Festival 2004–06, chm UK Movement for Reform Judaism 2005–; Freeman City of London, memb Worshipful Co of Info Technologists; ACMA 1979; *Style*— Michael Grabiner, Esq; fax 020 8959 5020, e-mail michael.grabiner@apax.com

GRABINER, Stephen; *Educ* Manchester Business Sch (MBA); *m* 3 c; *Career* mgmnt conslt Coopers and Lybrand Assocs 1983–86; The Daily Telegraph plc: mktg dir 1986–93, dep md 1993–94, md 1994–96; exec dir Newspapers United News & Media plc 1996–98, chief exec ONdigital 1998–99; dir Apax Partners 1999–; *Style*— Stephen Grabiner, Esq; ✉ Apax Partners, 15 Portland Place, London W1B 1PT

G

GRACE, Prof John; *b* 19 September 1945; *Educ* Bletchley GS, Univ of Sheffield (BSc, PhD); *m* Elizabeth, *née* Ashworth; 2 s (Stewart, Thomas), 1 da (Josephine); *Career* Univ of Edinburgh: lectr 1970–85, reader 1985–92, prof of environmental biology 1992–, head Inst of Ecology and Resource Mgmnt 2000–02, head Inst of Atmospheric and Environmental Sci 2005–; Br Ecological Soc: memb Cncl 1983–89, co-ed Functional Ecology 1987–99, pres 2002–03; served on several ctees incl Terrestrial Life Scis Trg Ctee NERC 1986–89; section ed Encyclopaedia of Ecology and Environmental Management; memb: Soc for Experimental Biology, Int Soc for Biometeorology; delivered Africanus Horton Meml lectr Freetown Sierra Leone 1988 (among others); awarded medal Univ of Helsinki 1994, BES medal 2007; FRSE 1994, FIBiol; *Books* Plant Response to Wind (1977), Plant Atmosphere Relationships (1983); also author of over 200 book chapters and papers in refereed jls; *Recreations* gardening, bridge, outdoor pursuits; *Style—* Prof John Grace, FRSE; ✉ School of GeoSciences, University of Edinburgh, Darwin Building, Mayfield Road, Edinburgh EH9 3JU (tel 0131 650 5400, fax 0131 662 0478, e-mail jgrace@ed.ac.uk)

GRACE, John Oliver Bowman; QC (1994); s of Oliver Jelf Grace, MBE, TD, DL (d 1996), of Hollingbourne, Kent, and Marjorie Foster, *née* Bowman (d 2007); *b* 13 June 1948; *Educ* Marlborough, Univ of Southampton (LLB); *m* 1973, Carol, da of Canon Jack Roundhill; 2 s (Edward Oliver b 2 Jan 1977, George William Jack b 11 June 1980), 1 da (Eleanor Rose b 26 Nov 1983); *Career* called to the Bar Middle Temple 1973 (bencher 2001); memb: Professional Negligence Bar Assoc, London Common Law and Commercial Bar Assoc; conslt ed Lloyds Law Reports-Medical; *Recreations* gardening, music, reading, cricket, France, sailing, bricklaying, modern art; *Clubs* 4 W's, Band of Brothers Cricket, Old Stagers, Whitstable Yacht; *Style—* John Grace, Esq, QC; ✉ 3 Serjeants' Inn, London EC4Y 1BQ (tel 020 7427 5000, e-mail jgrace@3sergeantsinn.com)

GRACHVOGEL, Maria; s of Joseph George Grachvogel, of London, and Margaret Mary, *née* McHugh; *b* 11 July 1969; *Educ* Holy Family Convent Sch Enfield, St Angelas RC Sch Palmers Green; *Career* fashion designer; self-employed (with ptnr Plaze Xarizienne) 1988–90, launched Maria Grachvogel Collection 1991, first exhibited London Fashion Week 1994, first catwalk show London Fashion Week 1995; launched: G Collection at Debenhams 1997, Maria Grachvogel Couture Collection 2000, Maria Grachvogel flagship store Sloane St London 2001, Maria Grachvogel Bridal 2002; Br Apparel Export Award for Small Business 1998; *Recreations* travel, art, dance, architecture and interiors, food, cooking, entertaining; *Style—* Ms Maria Grachvogel; ✉ Maria Grachvogel Ltd, 162 Sloane Street, London SW1X 9BS (tel 020 7245 9331, fax 020 7245 9332, e-mail sales@mariagrachvogel.com)

GRADE, Michael Ian; CBE (1998); s of late Leslie Grade and n of late Lords Grade and Delfont; *b* 8 March 1943; *Educ* Stowe, St Dunstan's Coll; *m* 1, 1967 (m dis 1981), Penelope Jane, *née* Levinson; 1 s (Jonathan), 1 da (Alison); m 2, 1982 (m dis 1991), Hon Sarah Jane Lawson, *qv*, yst da of (Lt-Col) 5 Baron Burnham, JP, DL (d 1993); m 3, 1998, Francesca Mary, *née* Leahy; 1 s (Samuel); *Career* sports columnist Daily Mirror 1964–66 (trainee journalist 1960), theatrical agent Grade Organisation 1966, jt md London Management and Representation 1969–73, dir of progs and memb Bd LWT 1977–81 (dep controller of progs 1973), pres Embassy TV LA 1982–83, chm and chief operating offr The Grade Co (ind TV and motion picture prodn co) 1983–84, controller BBC1 1984–86, dir of progs BBC TV 1986–87, chief exec Channel 4 1988–97; First Leisure plc: non-exec dir 1991–97, non-exec chm 1994–97, exec chm 1997–98, chief exec 1998–99; exec chm Pinewood/Shepperton Film Studios 2000–, chm of govrs BBC 2004–06, exec chm ITV plc 2007–; non-exec chm: VCI plc 1994–98, Octopus Publishing Gp 2000–01, Hemscott.net 2000–, Camelot Gp 2002–04 (non-exec dir 2000); non-exec dir: Charlton Athletic FC plc 1997–, New Millennium Experience Co 1998–2001, Digitaloctopus 2000–01, SMG plc 2003–04; memb Cncl LAMDA 1981–, pres RTS 1995–97, chm Devpt Cncl RNT 1997–2004, chm Index on Censorship 2000–04, vice-pres BAFTA 2004–; memb Bd of Tstees Writers and Scholars Educnl Tst 2000–04; Broadcasting Press Guild Harvey Lee Award for outstanding contribution to broadcasting 1997, RTS Gold Medal 1997; *Recreations* entertainment; *Style—* Michael Grade, Esq, CBE; ✉ ITV plc, 200 Gray's Inn Road, London WC1X 8XZ

GRADON, Michael; s of late Oswald Gradon, of Cambridge, and Judy, *née* Foster (d 2005); *b* 7 April 1959, Pembury, Kent; *Educ* Haileybury, Downing Coll Cambridge (Tennis and Real Tennis blue); *m* 26 March 1983, Jill, *née* Cottrell; 2 s (Andy b 28 Dec 1989, David b 11 May 1992); *Career* P&O (The Peninsular and Oriental Steam Navigation Co) 1986–2006: joined as commercial slr 1986, head Gp Legal Dept 1991, gp legal dir 1994, co sec 1996, memb Bd 1998–2006, dir commercial and legal affrs 2002–06, chm P&O Estates 2005–06, chief exec London Gateway 2005–06; sr ind dir Modern Water 2007–; memb Ctee of Mgmnt Wimbledon Championships 2004–; *Recreations* cricket, tennis, golf; *Clubs* All England Lawn Tennis, Tandridge Golf, Hawks; *Style—* Michael Gradon, Esq

GRAEF, Roger Arthur; OBE (2006); s of Dr Irving Philip Graef (d 1978), of New York City, and Gretchen Waterman Graef (d 1984); *b* 18 April 1936; *Educ* Horace Mann Sch NY, Putney Sch VT, Harvard Univ (BA); *m* 1, 26 Nov 1971 (m dis 1985), Karen Bergemann (d 1986); 1 da (Chloe Fay b 26 Nov 1972), 1 s (Maximilian James b 26 July 1979); m 2, 26 July 1986, Susan Mary, da of Sir Brooks Richards, KCMG, DSC (d 2002), of Dorset; *Career* writer, criminologist, producer, broadcaster and director; dir 26 plays and operas USA and two dramas for CBS TV; dir Period of Adjustment (Royal Court); co-designer London Transport Bus Map, pt/t lectr Assoc Sch of Architecture; memb Bd Govrs BFI 1975–79; memb Bd: London Transport Exec 1976–79, Channel 4 1980–85; memb Cncl: ICA 1971–83, BAFTA 1976–77, Howard League for Penal Reform; chm Study Gp for Public Involvement in Planning DOE 1975–77, fndr ICA Architectural Forum, expert memb Euro Analytical Coll of Crime Prevention 1993–97, fell Mannheim Centre of Criminology LSE, News International visiting prof of broadcast media Univ of Oxford 1999–2000, visiting prof Univ of London 2000–01; special advsr Paul Hamlyn Fndn 1999–; media columnist The Times 1992–94; numerous articles in: The Sunday Times, Times, Daily Mail, Evening Standard, The Independent, The Observer, Daily Telegraph, Mail on Sunday, The Guardian, Police Review; columnist Community Care; memb Br Soc of Criminology, pres Signals Int Tst 1991–98; tstee: Koestler Award Tst 1997–, Butler Tst 1997–2001, Grierson Award Tst 1997–, Mental Health Fndn 1998–2000; patron: RAPT, Waterville Youth Club, Grassmarket Theatre, Irene Taylor Tst, Exploring Parenthood, Voice of the Child in Care, Friends United, Crime Concern (memb Bd of Tstees 2002–03); chm: Theatre de Complicité 1991–, Book Aid 1992–93, Youth Advocate Prog 2003–; memb: Devpt Control Review (Dobry Ctee) DOE 1975–77, Ctee for Control of Demolition DOE 1976, Advsy Bd Oxford Probation Studies Unit, US/UK Fulbright Cmmn 1998–, Child and Adolescent Mental Health Cmmn 1998–2000, Ind Advsy Gp Met Police 1999–, Advsy Bd John Grieve Centre 2002–, Bd of Tstees The Photographers' Gallery 2002–06, Prince's Tst Surviving Damage in Childhood Panel; James Cameron meml lectr 2007; fell BAFTA 2004; *Television* incl: The Space Between Words (BBC/KCET) 1972, A Law in the Making: Four Months Inside The Ministry (Granada) 1973, Inside The Brussels HQ (Granada) 1975, Is This the Way to Save a City? (BBC) 1976, Decision: Steel, Oil, Rates (ITV/Granada) 1976, Pleasure at Her Majesty's (Amnesty/BBC) 1977, Decision: British Communism (ITV/Granada) 1977 (RTS Award 1978), The Secret Policeman's Ball (Amnesty Int/ITV) 1978, Italy: Chain Reaction (Granada) 1979, Police (series, BBC) 1980–82 (BAFTA Award 1982), Police: Operation Carter 1981–82, Nagging Doubt (Channel 4) 1984, Comic Relief (BBC) 1985, Maybe Baby (BBC) 1985, Closing Ranks (Zenith/Central ITV) 1987, The Secret Life of the Soviet Union (Channel 4) 1990, Turning the Screws (Channel 4) 1993, Look at the State We're In (BBC) 1995, In Search of Law and Order - UK (Channel 4) 1995, Breaking the Cycle (ITV) 1996, In Search of Law and Order - USA (PBS/Channel 4) 1997–98, Keeping it in the Family (Channel 4) 1998, Masters of the Universe (Channel 4) 1999, Race Against Crime (Channel 4) 1999, The Siege of Scotland Yard (Channel 4) 1999; exec prodr: Life After Murder (BBC) 2000, Not Black and White (Channel 4) 2001, Police (BBC) 2001, September Mourning (ITV) 2002, Rail Cops (BBC) 2003 and 2004–05, Welcome to Potters Bar - A Rail Cops Special (BBC) 2003, The Truth About Potters Bar? (BBC) 2003, Who Am I Now? (BBC/BBC Scotland) 2003, Care Specials (Channel Five) 2003, Malaria: Fever Road (BBC/PBS) 2004, The Protectors (BBC) 2004, Rail Cops 2 (BBC) 2004, Who Killed PC Blakelock? (BBC) 2004, Remember the Secret Policeman's Ball? (BBC) 2004, Classroom Chaos (five) 2005, Who Killed my Child? (Channel 4) 2005; series ed: Who Is? (BBC) 1967–68, Inside Europe (ITV) 1978–79, Signals (Channel 4) 1991–92, Breaking the Rules (BBC) 1998, Who's Your Father? (Channel 4) 2000, Feltham Sings! (Channel 4/Century Films) 2002 (BAFTA Award, TV Critics' Circle Award, Cannes Festival European TV Award), Murder Blues (BBC 1) 2005, What Future for Kurt? 2005, This World: Property to Die For (BBC 2) 2006, Blood and Land (BBC 2) 2006, Potters Bar - Search for the Truth (BBC 1) 2006, My Heart Belongs to Daddy (BBC 2) 2006, Panorama: When Cops Kill (BBC) 2006, Rape on Trial 2006, Race for the Beach (BBC 2) 2007, Inside a Shari'ah Court (BBC 2) 2007, Hold Me Tight, Let Me Go (BBC 4) 2007, The Burning Season (BBC) 2007; *Internet Productions* Web Lives (itv.com) 2007; *Radio* incl: Living Dangerously (1995), The Illusion of Information (2001), Any Questions, PM, The World Tonight, Front Row, Today Programme; *Film* GM or Not? (corporate video) 2003; *Books* Talking Blues - The Police in Their Own Words (1989), Living Dangerously - Young Offenders in Their Own Words (1993), Why Restorative Justice? (2000); *Recreations* tennis, music, photography, Dorset; *Clubs* Beefsteak, Groucho, Pilgrims; *Style—* Prof Roger Graef, OBE; ✉ 72 Westbourne Park Villas, London W2 5EB (tel 020 7286 0333 or 020 7727 7868, e-mail rogerg@filmsofrecord.com)

GRAFFTEY-SMITH, John Jeremy (Jinx); s of Sir Laurence Barton Grafftey-Smith, KCMG, KBE (d 1989), and Mrs Vivien Isobel Tennant-Eyles, *née* Alderson (d 1995); bro of Roger Grafftey-Smith, *qv*; *b* 13 October 1934; *Educ* Winchester, Magdalen Coll Oxford (MA); *m* 23 Jan 1964, Lucy, da of Maj John Fletcher, MBE, of Sussex; 2 s (Alexander b 1967, Toby b 1970), 1 da (Camilla b 1968); *Career* 2 Lt Oxfordshire & Bucks LI 1953–55; banker; Samuel Montagu 1958–66, Wallace Bros 1966–76, res dir Allied Med Gp Saudi-Arabia 1977–81, London rep Nat Commercial Bank of Saudi-Arabia 1982–02 (sr advsr 2002–); sr advsr Merchant Bridge & Co Ltd; memb Guild of Int Bankers; *Recreations* golf, shooting, poetry, music, wine; *Clubs* Lansdowne, City of London, Green Jackets, Ashridge Golf, Mentmore Golf and Country, Buckingham Golf, The Benedicts' Soc; *Style—* Jinx Grafftey-Smith, Esq; ✉ Burcott Hill House, Wing, Leighton Buzzard, Bedfordshire LU7 0JU (tel 01296 682983, e-mail gsadvisory@supanet.com)

GRAFFTEY-SMITH, Roger Tilney; s of Sir Laurence Barton Grafftey-Smith, KCMG, KBE (d 1989), and Mrs Vivien Isobel Tennant-Eyles, *née* Alderson (d 1995); elder bro of Jinx Grafftey-Smith, *qv*; *b* 14 April 1931; *Educ* Winchester, Trinity Coll Oxford; *m* 28 March 1962, Jane Oriana Mary, da of Sir John Pollen, Bt (d 2003); 2 s (Simon b 1968, Max b 1974), 1 da (Selina (Mrs Charles Faircloth) b 1971); *Career* 2 Lt Queen's Bays 1949–51; md Galban Lobo (England) Ltd 1962–72; managing ptnr Grafftey-Smith & Associates Financial Conslts 1982–, chm Unilab Corporation 1985; dir: Biolytic Systems Ltd 1990–92, Decora Industries Inc 1989–2002; vice-chm N Wilts DC 1980–82; *Recreations* shooting, fishing; *Style—* Roger T Grafftey-Smith, Esq; ✉ The Dower House, Rodbourne, Malmesbury, Wiltshire SN16 0EX (tel 01666 829445, fax 01666 829447)

GRAFTON, Duchess of; (Ann) Fortune FitzRoy; GCVO (1980, DCVO 1970, CVO 1965); o da of late Capt (Evan Cadogan) Eric Smith, MC, LLD; *m* 12 Oct 1946, 11 Duke of Grafton, *qv*; 2 s, 3 da; *Career* SRCN Great Ormond St 1945, pres W Suffolk Mission to the Deaf, nat vice-pres Br Royal British Legion Women's Section 2003–; govr: Felixstowe Coll, Riddlesworth Hall; JP: Co of London 1949, Co of Suffolk 1972; memb Bd of Govrs Hosp for Sick Children Great Ormond St 1952–66; patron: Great Ormond St Nurses League, West Suffolk Relate; vice-pres Trinity Hospice (Clapham Common) 1951; lady of the bedchamber to HM The Queen 1953–66, mistress of the robes to HM The Queen 1967–; pres W Suffolk Decorative and Fine Art Soc; patron: Clarence River Historical Soc Grafton NSW Aust 1980, Guildhall String Ensemble 1988; pres Br Heart Fndn Bury St Edmunds Branch Suffolk 1992; *Style—* Her Grace the Duchess of Grafton, GCVO; ✉ Euston Hall, Thetford, Norfolk IP24 2QW (tel 01842 753282)

GRAFTON, 11 Duke of (E 1675); Hugh Denis Charles FitzRoy; KG (1976), DL (Suffolk 1973); also Earl of Euston, Viscount Ipswich and Baron Sudbury (E 1672); patron of four livings; Hereditary Ranger of Whittlebury Forest; s of 10 Duke of Grafton (d 1970), and Lady Doreen Buxton, 2 da of 1 Earl Buxton; *b* 3 April 1919; *Educ* Eton, Magdalene Coll Cambridge; *m* 12 Oct 1946, Fortune (Duchess of Grafton, GCVO, *qv*); 2 s, 3 da; *Heir* s, Earl of Euston, *qv*; *Career* Grenadier Gds ADC to Viceroy of India 1943–46; memb: Historic Buildings Cncl for England 1953–84, Historic Buildings Advsy Ctee and Churches and Cathedrals Ctee English Heritage 1984–2001, Nat Tst Properties Ctee 1981–94, Royal Fine Art Cmmn 1971–94; chm: Cathedrals Advsy Cmmn 1981–91, Architectural Heritage Fund 1976–94; chm of tstees: Historic Churches Preservation Tst 1980–97, Sir John Soane's Museum 1975–97; vice-chm of tstees Nat Portrait Gallery 1967–92; tstee: Tradescant Tst 1976–99, Buildings at Risk Tst 1986–2000; pres: Soc for the Protection of Ancient Buildings 1989–, International Students House 1972–, Br Soc of Master Glass Painters, E Anglia Tourist Bd 1973–93, Suffolk Preservation Soc 1957–96; patron: Historic Houses Assoc, Hereford Herd Book Soc; Hon DCL Univ of East Anglia 1990; *Clubs* Boodle's; *Style—* His Grace the Duke of Grafton, KG, DL; ✉ Euston Hall, Thetford, Norfolk IP24 2QW

GRAFTON-GREEN, Patrick; s of George Grafton-Green (d 1990), of London, and Brigid Anna, *née* Maxwell (d 1991); *b* 30 March 1943; *Educ* Ampleforth, Wadham Coll Oxford (MA); *m* 18 Sept 1982, Deborah Susan, da of Raymond Goodchild; 2 s (Nicholas Patrick James b 4 Nov 1983, Patrick William Peter b 18 April 1987), 2 da (Charlotte Brigid Kate b 3 Sept 1985, Lucy Anna Clare (twin) b 18 April 1987); *Career* Addleshaw Goddard (formerly Theodore Goddard): articled clerk 1966–68, staff slr 1969–73, ptnr 1973–, memb Mgmnt Ctee 1991–92 and 1997–, head Media & Sports Gp 1992–, sr ptnr 1997–2003, chm 2003–; regular speaker at confs on taxation of entertainers and businesses operating in media sector; memb Law Soc 1969; *Recreations* music, theatre, cricket, horseracing; *Clubs* MCC, Middlesex CCC; *Style—* Patrick Grafton-Green, Esq; ✉ Addleshaw Goddard, 150 Aldersgate Street, London EC1A 4EJ (tel 020 7606 8855, fax 020 7606 4390, e-mail paddygraftongreen@addleshawgoddard.com)

GRAHAM, Alan Philip; s of Aaron Goldstein (d 1981), of Edgware, Middx, and Helen, *née* Brown; *b* 4 December 1947; *Educ* Orange Hill Boys' GS; *m* Jennifer, da of Charles Phillips; 2 da (Caroline Louise b 14 Jan 1977, Lucie Vanessa b 11 April 1979); *Career* merchant banker; N M Rothschild & Sons Group: Credits Div 1967–68, money market dealer 1968–69, assigned to Manchester Branch 1969–71, Foreign Exchange and Bullion Dealing Room 1971–77, mangr 1974, md and chief exec NMR Metals Inc NY (memb Precious Metals Ctee NY Commodity Exchange) 1977–79, asst dir 1980, Int Banking Div London 1980–83, exec dir and head Banking Div N M Rothschild & Sons (CI) Limited Guernsey and dir Old Court Currency Fund Ltd 1984–88, exec dir N M Rothschild & Sons Limited 1988– (dir Treasy Div and head Treasy Admin), non-exec dir N M Rothschild & Sons (CI) Ltd, md N M Rothschild & Sons (Singapore) Ltd 1992–94;

non-exec dir SFO 2004–; chm of tstees Motor Neurone Disease Assoc, tstee WIZO UK; Freeman City of London 1977; memb Chartered Inst of Bankers 1967; *Recreations* soccer, music, theatre, tennis; *Clubs* Overseas Bankers'; *Style—* Alan Graham, Esq; ✉ N M Rothschild & Sons Ltd, New Court, St Swithin's Lane, London EC4P 4DU

GRAHAM, Sir Alexander Michael; GBE (1990), JP (City of London 1979); s of late Dr Walter Graham, and late Suzanne, *née* Simon; *b* 27 September 1938; *Educ* St Paul's; *m* 6 June 1964, Carolyn, da of Lt Col Alan Wolryche Stansfeld, MBE; 3 da; *Career* Nat Serv 1957–59, cmmnd Gordon Highlanders, TA 1959–67; Frizzell Group Ltd: joined 1957, md 1973–90, dep chm 1990–93; chm Firstcity Insurance Brokers Ltd 1993–98; underwriting memb Lloyd's 1978–98; chm: Employment Conditions Abroad Ltd 1993–2005, Euclidian plc 1994–2001, Folgate Insurance Company Ltd 1995–2001 (dir 1975–); pres British Insurance Law Assoc 1994–96, vice-pres Insurance Inst of London; Mercers' Co: Liveryman 1971–, memb Ct of Assts 1980, Master 1983–84; memb Ct of Common Cncl City of London 1978–79, alderman Ward of Queenhithe 1979–2004, pres Queenhithe Ward Club 1979–2004, Sheriff City of London 1986–87, HM Lt City of London 1989–2004, Lord Mayor of London 1990–91; Hon Freeman: Merchant Adventurers of York 1983–, Worshipful Co of Insurers 1992–; Hon Liveryman Worshipful Co of Chartered Secs and Admins 1992–; govr: Hall Sch Hampstead 1975–93, Christ's Hosp Sch 1979–2004, King Edward's Sch Whitley 1979–2004, St Paul's Girls' Sch 1980–93 and 2004–, St Paul's Sch 1980– (chair 2004–), City of London Sch 1983–85, City of London Girls' Sch 1992–95; memb Cncl Gresham Coll 1983–93, chllr City Univ 1990–91; chm of tstees: United Response 1993–2002, Morden Coll 1996– (tstee 1988–); tstee Temple Bar Tst 1992–2005, hon life memb Macmillan Cancer Relief 1993–; memb Exec Ctee Army Benevolent Fund 1991–98, chm Nat Employers Liaison Ctee for TA and Reserve Forces 1992–98; pres: Civil Serv Motoring Assoc 1993–2006, Old Pauline Club 2001–03 (formerly vice-pres); vice-pres N Herts Garden Hospice; Hon DCL City Univ 1990; Gentleman Usher of the Purple Rod Order of the Br Empire 2000; FCII 1964, FBIIBA 1967, FInstD 1975, FCIS 1990, FRSA 1980, CIMgt 1991; Commandeur l'Ordre du Tastevin 1985, Order of Wissam Alouite (Morocco) 1987, KStJ 1990 (chm Cncl Order of St John Herts 1993–2001), Grand Cross Order of Merit (Chile) 1991, Vigneron d'Honneur et Bourgeois de St Emilion 1999; *Recreations* wine, calligraphy, genealogy, music, reading, silver, bridge, sports (golf, swimming, tennis, shooting and avoiding gardening); *Clubs* Garrick, City Livery, Highland Brigade, Royal Worlington and Newmarket Golf, Mid Herts Golf; *Style—* Sir Alexander Graham, GBE; ✉ Walden Abbotts, Whitwell, Hitchin, Hertfordshire SG4 8AJ (tel and fax 01438 871997)

GRAHAM, Sir (John) Alistair; kt (2000); s of Robert Graham (d 1968), and Dorothy, *née* Horner (d 1995); *b* 6 August 1942; *Educ* Royal GS Newcastle upon Tyne; *m* 1967, Dorothy Jean, da of James Clark Wallace, of Morpeth, Northumberland; 1 da (Polly b 1972), 1 s (Richard b 1974); *Career* asst sec, asst gen sec and gen sec Civil and Public Service Assoc 1966–86, dir The Industrial Soc 1986–91, chief exec Calderdale and Kirklees Trg and Enterprise Cncl Ltd 1991–96, chief exec Leeds Trg and Enterprise Cncl 1996–2000; chm: Parades Cmmn NI 1997–2000, Police Complaints Authy 2000–04, West Yorks SHA 2002–03, British Tport Police Authy 2004–, Ctee on Standards in Public Life 2004–07 (memb 2003–), Ind Ctee for the Supervision of Standards of Telephone Info Servs (ICSTIS) 2006–; Northern and Yorks regnl cmmr NHS Appts Cmmn 2003, non-exec dir Information Cmmn; northern chm Learning and Skills Cncl Appeal Tbnl; memb: Fitness to Practice Ctee Gen Optical Cncl, Employment Appeals Tbnl; visiting prof Imperial Coll London 1982–91, visiting fell Nuffield Coll Oxford 1984–92; vice-pres Opera North; non-exec dir Durham CCC; Hon Dr Open Univ; FCIPD (FIPD 1989); *Recreations* music, theatre; *Style—* Sir Alistair Graham; ✉ Committee on Standards in Public Life, 35 Great Smith Street, London SW1P 3BQ (tel 020 7276 2595)

GRAHAM, Maj-Gen Andrew John Noble; CBE (2002); s and h of Sir John Graham, Bt, GCMG, *qv*, and Marygold, *née* Austin; *b* 21 October 1956; *Educ* Eton, Trinity Coll Cambridge (BA); *m* 7 July 1984, Susan Mary Bridget, *née* O'Riordan; 3 da (Katharine Rose b 31 July 1986, Louisa Christian b 19 April 1988, Isabella Alice b 8 Jan 1993), 1 s (James Patrick Noble b 15 March 1990); *Career* Argyll and Sutherland Highlanders (Princess Louise's): cmmnd 1979, CO 1995–97, Col of Regt 2000–06; Col Royal Regt of Scotland 2007–, Army Staff Coll Camberley 1988, Higher Command and Staff Course 1998, Cdr 3 Inf Bde 1999–2001, Dir Army Resource and Plans MOD 2001–03, DCG MNC-Iraq 2004, DG Army Recruiting and Trg 2004–07, Col Comd RAVC 2007–; Dep Col Cmdt AGC (ETS) 2006–; memb Counsel Queen's Body Guard for Scotland (Royal Co of Archers); *Recreations* piping, all sports, family, animals, reading (history, travel); *Style—* Maj-Gen Andrew Graham, CBE; ✉ c/o Home Headquarters, The Argyll and Sutherland Highlanders (Princess Louise's), The Castle, Stirling FK8 1EH

GRAHAM, Andrew Winston Mawdsley; s of Winston Graham, OBE, and Jean Mary, *née* Williamson; *b* 20 June 1942; *Educ* St Edmund Hall Oxford (MA); *m* 1970, Peggotty, da of E L Fawssett; *Career* Balliol Coll Oxford: fell and tutor in economics 1969–2001, univ lectr 1970–2001, estates bursar 1978, investment bursar 1979–83, vice-master 1988 and 1992–94, actg master 1997–2001, master 2001–; actg dir Oxford Internet Inst 2002; visiting scholar MIT and visiting fell Harvard Univ 1994; econ asst: Nat Econ Devpt Office 1964, Dept of Econ Affrs 1964–66; asst to the Econ Advsr to the Cabinet 1966–68, econ advsr to the PM 1968–69, policy advsr to the PM 1974–76; econ advsr: to the Chief Oppn Spokesman on Economic Affairs 1988–92, to the Ldr of the Lab Pty 1992–94; memb: The Wilson Ctee on the Functioning of Fin Instns 1977–80, Econs Ctee SSRC 1978–80; non-exec dir Br Tport Docks Bd 1979–82, memb Int Lab Office (ILO)/Jobs and Skills Prog for Africa (JASPA) Employment Advsy Mission to Ethiopia 1982, head Queen Elizabeth House Food Studies Gp advising the Govt of the Republic of Zambia 1984, conslt to BBC 1990–92; memb: Cncl Templeton Coll Oxford 1990–95, Econs Ctee Central European Univ 1991–, Media Advsy Ctee Inst for Public Policy 1995–98, Advsy Ctee to the Minister of Agriculture 1997–98, Bd Channel Four TV Corporation 1998–; tstee: Oxford Policy Institute 1997–, Fndn for Information Policy Research 1998–; fell Gorbachev Fndn of N America 1999–; *Publications* Government and Economies in the Postwar World (ed, 1990), Broadcasting, Society and Policy in the Multimedia Age (with Gavyn Davies, 1997); *Recreations* windsurfing; *Style—* Andrew Graham; ✉ Balliol College, Oxford OX1 3BJ

GRAHAM, Cathryn Judith; da of Kenneth Graham, and Dorothy, *née* Jefferson; *b* 28 March 1955; *Educ* Univ of Birmingham (BMus), Royal Northern Coll of Music; *Career* repetiteur and vocal coach Stockholm 1978–92 (worked with Folkoperan, Vadstena Acad, State Opera Sch, Kulturama, Norrlands Opera, Nat Touring Theatre and Dramatiska Ensemble), admin asst ENO Contemporary Opera Studio 1993, exec dir SPNM 1994–97, md London Sinfonietta 1997–2006, dir of music Br Cncl 2006–; memb: Nat Music Cncl 1994–97, Advsy Cncl Br Music Info Centre 1994–97, Bd Assoc of Br Orchs 1998–2006, Bd NMC Recordings 2000–, Bd Kings Place Music Fndn 2006–; *Recreations* theatre, visual arts, walking; *Clubs* Groucho; *Style—* Ms Cathryn Graham; ✉ British Council, 10 Spring Gardens, London SW1A 2BN (tel 020 7389 3087, fax 020 7389 3088, e-mail cathy.graham@britishcouncil.org)

GRAHAM, (Stewart) David; QC (1977); s of Lewis Graham (d 1985), of Harrogate, and Gertrude, *née* Markman (d 1989); *b* 27 February 1934; *Educ* Leeds GS, St Edmund Hall Oxford (MA, BCL); *m* 20 Dec 1959, Corinne, da of Emile Carmona (d 1984), of London; 2 da (Jeanne (Mrs Zane), Angela (Mrs Marks)); *Career* called to the Bar Middle Temple 1957 (Harmsworth scholar 1958), ret from Bar 1985, dir Coopers and Lybrand and Cork Gully 1985–92; chm: Law Party and Gen Purpose Ctee of Bd of Deputies of Br Jews 1983–88, Editorial Bd of Insolvency Intelligence 1988–94; memb: Cncl of Justice 1976–97, Insolvency Rules Advsy Ctee 1984–86; ind memb Cncl Insurance Ombudsman Bureau 1993–2001, assoc memb Br and Irish Ombudsman Assoc 1994–; editor of various works on Insolvency Law; sr visiting fell Centre for Commercial Law Studies Queen Mary & Westfield Coll London; visiting prof Faculty of Business Centre for Insolvency Law and Policy Kingston Univ 2004; memb Ctee: Stanmore Soc 2001–, Harrow Heritage Tst 2002–; FRSA 1995; *Publications* Muir Hunter on Personal Insolvency (contrib, 2002), Oxford Dictionary of National Biography (contrib, 2005); author of articles in professional jls; *Recreations* biography, travel, music, history of insolvency law; *Style—* Prof David Graham, QC; ✉ 6 Grosvenor Lodge, Dennis Lane, Stanmore, Middlesex HA7 4JE (tel 020 8954 3783)

GRAHAM, David Pottie; MBE (2003), JP, DL; s of John Armstrong Graham (d 1965), and Isabella Robertson Graham (d 1988); *b* 25 September 1937; *Educ* Dalziel HS Motherwell, Coll of Commerce Newcastle upon Tyne; *m* 18 June 1960, Jean, da of Ralph Henry Boggon; 1 da (Tracey Lynne b 10 April 1964), 1 s (Fraser John b 15 March 1966); *Career* divnl fin mangr Northumbrian Water Authy 1974–77, md Sunderland and South Shields Water Company 1988–91 (sec accountant 1978–88); chm: City Hosps Sunderland NHS Fndn Tst 1993–, Age Concern Sunderland 1982–; FCIS 1963, FCMA 1967; *Recreations* golf, hill walking, music, reading; *Style—* David Graham, Esq, MBE, JP, DL; ✉ City Hospitals Sunderland NHS Foundation Trust, Kayll Road, Sunderland, Tyne & Wear SR4 7TP (tel 0191 569 9688, fax 0191 569 9642)

GRAHAM, David Warwick; s of Peter Graham, of Edinburgh, and Maureen, *née* Ramsay; *b* 25 November 1960; *Educ* George Watson's Coll Edinburgh, Univ of Aberdeen (BA), Univ of Stirling (MBA); *m* 30 April 1993, Kirsty, *née* Gunn; 2 da (Amelia Elizabeth Lyon b 20 Jan 1999, Katherine Rae Sutherland b 5 Sept 2001); *Career* sales rep David Flatman 1983–87; Phaidon Press: sales rep 1987–91, sales mangr 1991–94, sales dir 1994–97; md: Canongate Books 2000–06, Granta 2006–; *Recreations* fishing; *Clubs* Scottish Arts; *Style—* David Graham, Esq; ✉ Granta, 2–3 Hanover Yard, Noel Road, London N1 8BE (tel 020 7704 9776)

GRAHAM, (Malcolm Gray) Douglas; DL (Shropshire 1997); s of Malcolm Graham (d 1993), of Farmcote Hall, Claverley, nr Wolverhampton, and Annie Jeanette Sankey, *née* Robinson (d 1976); *b* 18 February 1930; *Educ* Shrewsbury; *m* 18 April 1980, Sara Ann, da of William Patrick Whitelaw Anderson (d 1976), of Feckenham, Worcs; 2 step s (Colin William Edward Elwell b 12 Jan 1971, James Peter Elwell b 24 April 1973); *Career* chm: Claverley Co 1993, The Midland News Assoc Ltd 1984–, Express & Star Ltd, Shropshire Newspapers Ltd 1980–, Stars News Shops Ltd 1994–; dir Guiton Gp CI 2004; pres: Young Newspapermen's Assoc 1969, W Midlands Newspaper Soc 1973–74; chm Evening Newspaper Advtg Bureau 1978–79; *Recreations* shooting; *Style—* Douglas Graham, Esq, DL; ✉ Roughton Manor, Worfield, Bridgnorth, Shropshire WV15 5HE; Express and Star, Queen Street, Wolverhampton, West Midlands WV1 1ES (tel 01902 313131)

GRAHAM, Col Ian Derek; TD, DL (E Yorks 1974); s of Maj Ernest Frederic Graham, MBE, MC (d 1985), of Swanland, E Yorks, and Muriel, *née* Fell (d 1970); *b* 27 February 1928; *Educ* Sedbergh, UC Hull, Univ of London (LLB); *m* 1, 1954 (m dis 1984), Margaret Edwards; 3 da (Fiona Clare b 1955, Janet Elaine b 1958, Sally Anne b 1962); m 2, 1985, Betty, da of Thomas Vessey Whittaker (d 1954); *Career* cmmnd RA 1947, TA 1949–71, Lt-Col 440 LAD Regt RA (TA) 1967, Col Cmdt Humberside ACF 1971–79; admitted slr 1954; sr ptnr Graham & Rosen until 1999 (conslt 2000–05, ret); memb Cncl and Nat Exec ACF Assoc 1975–2002, vice-chm Yorks and Humberside TAVRA 1987–90; local chm Social Security Appeal Tbnl and Disability Appeal Tbnl 1970–99; *Recreations* game shooting; *Style—* Col Ian Graham, TD, DL; ✉ Kelsey Cottage, Hariff Lane, Burstwick, East Yorkshire HU12 9HU (tel 01964 622429)

GRAHAM, Sir James Bellingham; 11 Bt (E 1662), of Norton Conyers, Yorkshire; er s of Wing Cdr Sir Richard Bellingham Graham, 10 Bt, OBE, JP, DL (d 1982), and Beatrice Mary, OBE, *née* Hamilton-Spencer-Smith (d 1992); *b* 8 October 1940; *Educ* Eton, ChCh Oxford; *m* 1986, Halina, yr da of late Major Wiktor Grubert, diplomat; *Career* researcher in fine and decorative arts Cecil Higgins Museum and Art Gallery 1980–96, curator (with wife) of Norton Conyers and its collections 1996–; *Books* Cecil Higgins, Collector Extraordinary (jtly with wife, 1983), A Guide to the Cecil Higgins Museum and Art Gallery (jtly with wife, 1987), Guide to Norton Conyers(1976, several subsequent edns); contrib of exhibition reviews (jtly with wife); *Recreations* visiting museums and historic houses, travel, early science fiction; *Style—* Sir James Graham, Bt; ✉ Norton Conyers, Wath, Nr Ripon, North Yorkshire HG4 5EQ

GRAHAM, James Fergus Surtees; 7 Bt (GB 1783), of Netherby, Cumberland; s of Maj Sir Charles Spencer Richard Graham, 6 Bt (d 1997); *b* 29 July 1946; *Educ* Milton Abbey, RAC Cirencester; *m* 1975, Serena Jane, da of Ronald Frank Kershaw; 2 da (Catherine Mary b 1978, Iona Susan Alice b 1980), 1 s (Robert Charles Thomas b 19 July 1985); *Heir* s, Robert Graham; *Career* Lloyd's reinsurance broker 1969–88; *Style—* Sir James Graham, Bt; ✉ The Kennels, Longtown, Cumbria CA6 5PD (tel 01228 791262)

GRAHAM, Jefferson; MBE; *b* 24 February 1960; *Educ* Ardrossan Acad; *m* 3 May 1991, Inge Renée Van Zijll De-Jong; 1 s (Stanley b 29 Sept 1992); *Career* residential care offr Strathclyde Regnl Cncl, presenter BBC Radio Scotland Glasgow, Radio Forth Edinburgh, presenter and head of music West Sound Radio Ayr, presenter Moray Firth Radio Inverness, prodr and presenter Capital Radio London, presenter, prog controller and dep gen mangr Radio Luxembourg (Luxembourg and London), presenter and programming conslt Atlantic 252 Dublin, prog dir Red Rose Gold and Red Rose Rock FM, main bd dir and tstee Red Rose Community Tst, presenter WZZR Miami, exec prodr daytime progs and music manager BBC Radio 1; gp prog dir Independent Radio Group, channel mangr WilliamHillRadio.com, media and programming conslt and broadcaster 2003–; tutor in radio Univ of Westminster; New York Festival International Programming Award; memb: Radio Acad, Brit Award Voting Acad, Equity; Special Constable Lancs Constabulary (Inspr, divnl offr); Long Service and Good Conduct Medal, Queen's Royal Jubilee Medal; *Style—* Jefferson Graham, Esq, MBE; ✉ The Cottage, Preston Old Road, Clifton, Lancashire PR4 0ZA (tel 01772 684138, e-mail jeff.graham@jesting.com)

GRAHAM, Sir John Alexander Noble; 4 Bt (UK 1906), of Larbert; GCMG (1986, KCMG 1979, CMG 1972); s of Sir (John) Reginald Noble Graham, 3 Bt, VC, OBE (d 1980), and Rachel, *née* Sprot (d 1984); *b* 15 July 1926; *Educ* Eton, Trinity Coll Cambridge; *m* 1, 1956, Marygold Ellinor Gabrielle (Meg) (d 1991), da of Lt-Col Clive Grantham Austin, JP, DL (d 1974), and Lady Lilian Lumley, sis of 11 Earl of Scarbrough, KG, GCSI, GCVO, TD, PC; 2 s (Andrew John Noble b 1956, George Reginald Clive b 1958), 1 da (Christian Rachel (Mrs Matthew Scott Dryden) b 1961); m 2, 27 June 1992, Jane, widow of Christopher Howells; *Heir* s, Maj-Gen Andrew Graham, CBE; *Career* Army 1944–47; joined FO 1950, served Amman, Kuwait, Bahrain, Belgrade, Benghazi, and as cnsllr and head of Chancery Washington; asst private sec to Sec of State for Foreign Affrs 1954–57, private sec to Sec of State for Foreign and Cwlth Affairs 1969–72, ambass Iraq 1974–77, FCO dep under sec 1977–79 and 1980–82, ambass Iran 1979–80, ambass and UK perm rep NATO Brussels 1982–86; dir Ditchley Fndn 1987–92, chm Countrywide Workshops Charitable Trust 1992–97; Hon Air Cdre 2624 Sqdn RAuxF 1990–2001; *Recreations* outdoor activities; *Clubs* Army and Navy; *Style—* Sir John Graham, Bt, GCMG; ✉ Salisbury Place, Church Street, Shipton-under-Wychwood, Oxfordshire OX7 6BP

GRAHAM, Maj-Gen John David Carew; CB (1978), CBE (1973, OBE 1967); s of Col John Alexander Graham (d 1957), of Nettlestone, IOW, and Constance Mary, *née* Carew-Hunt (d 1987); *b* 18 January 1923; *Educ* Fernden Sch Haslemere, Cheltenham; *m* 17 Nov 1956,

G

Rosemary Elaine, da of James Basil Adamson (d 1945), of Georgetown, British Guiana; 1 s (John Christopher Malcolm b 1959), 1 da (Jacqueline Patricia Anne b 1957); *Career* cmmnd Argyll and Sutherland Highlanders 1942 (despatches), served 5 Bn The Parachute Regt 1946–49, Br Embassy Prague 1949–50, HQ Scottish Cmd 1956–58, mil asst to CINCENT Fontainebleau 1960–62, cmd 1 Bn The Parachute Regt 1964–66, instr Staff Coll Camberley 1967, Regtl Col The Parachute Regt 1968–69, Cdr Sultan's Armed Forces Oman 1970–72, Indian Nat Def Coll 1973, asst Chief of Staff HQ AFCENT 1974–76, GOC Wales 1976–78; admin Chevening Estate 1978–87; Hon Col Kent ACF 1981–88 (chm Kent ACF Ctee 1979–86), Hon Col 203 Welsh Gen Hosp, RAMC, TA 1983–89; chm St John Cncl for Kent 1978–86; memb: Cncl Royal Cwlth Soc (Barbados), Barbados Legion of Royal Cwlth Ex-Services League 1992–; CStJ; Freeman City of London 1992; Order of Oman; *Publications* Ponder Anew, Reflections on the Twentieth Century (limited edn); *Recreations* gardening, travel; *Style*— Major-General John Graham, CB, CBE; ✉ Montrose, Rendez-vous Ridge, Christ Church, Barbados, West Indies (tel 00 1 246 436 8437, fax 00 1 246 434 0609)

GRAHAM, John Malcolm; s of Malcolm Pullen Graham (d 1989), of Oxford, and Edna Stanhope, *née* Davis (d 1991); *b* 9 February 1940; *Educ* Uppingham, Pembroke Coll Oxford (MA, BM BCh), Middx Hosp; *m* 15 Jan 1966, Sandy Judy, da of Wing Cdr Eduardo Walpole Whitaker, DFC (d 1985); 1 s (Alastair b 25 April 1966), 2 da (Harriet b 9 June 1976, Emily b 17 Jan 1978); *Career* conslt ENT surgn UCH, Middx and Royal Nat Throat, Nose and Ear Hosp 1979–; ENT conslt Med Fndn for Victims of Torture 1991–, chm Med Ctee St Luke's Hosp for the Clergy London 1992–2002 (memb Cncl 2004–); fndr pres Br Assoc for Paediatric Otorhinolaryngology 1991–93, pres European Soc of Paediatric Otorhinolaryngology 2002–06, pres Section of Otology RSM 2003–04, chm Br Cochlear Implant Gp 2001–05, elected UK Cncl memb European Fedn of Otolaryngological Socs (EUFOS) 1994–2004; founding ed Cochlear Implants International 2000–; patron: Music and the Deaf, LINK Centre; Cutlers' Surgical Prize 1997, W J Harrison Prize 2003, Walter Jobson Horne Prize BMA 2005; Freeman City of London 1988, Liveryman Worshipful Soc Apothecaries; DM (Lambeth) 1998; memb: BMA, RSM; miembro correspondiente Societad del ORL de Uruguay; FRCS, FRCSE; *Publications* Ballantyne's Deafness (ed, 6 edn), Pediatric ENT (2007); author of various sci papers, contrib chapters on subjects incl: tinnitus in adults and children, cochlear implants, electric response audiometry; *Recreations* music, construction, verse; *Style*— John Graham, Esq; ✉ 150 Harley Street, London W1G 7LQ (e-mail j.graham@150harleyst.com)

GRAHAM, Sir John Moodie; 2 Bt (UK 1964), of Dromore, Co Down; s of Sir Clarence Johnston Graham, 1 Bt (d 1966); *b* 3 April 1938; *Educ* Trinity Coll Glenalmond, Queen's Univ Belfast (BSc); *m* 1970 (m dis 1982), Valerie Rosemary, da of late Frank Gill, of Belfast; 3 da (Suzanne Margaret b 1971, Alyson Rosemary b 1974, Lucy Christina b 1978); partner, David J Galway (civil partnership Jan 2006); *Heir* none; *Career* pres N Ireland Leukaemia Res Fund, dir John Graham (Dromore) Ltd, Electrical Supplies Ltd, Concrete (NI) Ltd, Ulster Quarries Ltd, G H Fieldhouse Plant (NI) Ltd; memb Lloyds 1978; ret 1983; *Style*— Sir John Graham, Bt; ✉ 1 Station Road, Holywood BT18 0BP (tel 028 9042 3390, e-mail sirjg@btinternet.com)

GRAHAM, John Strathie; s of Sir Norman Graham, CB, FRSE, and Catherine Mary, *née* Strathie; *b* 27 May 1950; *Educ* Edinburgh Acad, CCC Oxford (BA); *m* 1979, Anne, da of James Stenhouse; 1 da (Kate b 1982), 2 s (Philip b 1985, Robert b 1986); *Career* SO: joined 1972, private sec to min of state 1975–76, princ Scottish Economic Planning Dept 1976–82, asst sec 1982–83, private sec to sec of state 1983–85, under sec (local govt gp) Devpt Dept (formerly Environment Dept) 1991–96, princ fin offr 1996–98, head Environment and Rural Affrs Dept 1998–2004, chief exec Historic Scotland 2004–; *Recreations* exploring Scotland, music; *Style*— John Graham, Esq; ✉ Historic Scotland, Longmore House, Salisbury Place, Edinburgh EH9 1SH

GRAHAM, Leona; *Educ* Univ of Warwick (BA); *Career* radio presenter: Choice 102.2 Birmingham 1995, FTV London 1995, Power FM 1995–96, 96.4 The Eagle 1996–98, Surf 107.2 1998–99, Core Digital Radio 1999–2000, Virgin Radio and Virgin Radio Classic Rock 2000–; voice-over artiste: ITV, BBC, Sky; *Style*— Miss Leona Graham; ✉ Rhubarb Agency, Bakerloo Chambers, 304 Edgware Road, London W2 1DY (tel 020 7724 1300, e-mail leona@leonagraham.com, website www.leonagraham.com)

GRAHAM, (John) Michael Denning; s of William Graham (d 1962), of Glasgow, and Inez Reid (d 1988); *b* 7 September 1944; *Educ* Royal Belfast Academical Inst, Queen's Univ Belfast (LLB); *m* 25 July 1970, Christina Jeanne, da of Ronald Ernest Sinclair, of Cladyhood, NI; 2 s (David William Denning b 1974, Richard Anthony Denning b 1976); *Career* formerly sr ptnr Paterson Robertson & Graham Slrs (Glasgow, Kirkintilloch, Clydebank and Lennoxtown), currently dir of business law MacRoberts, Solicitors (Glasgow and Edinburgh); chm NHS Tbnl for Scotland, vice-chm National Appeal Panel Pharmaceutical Lists; non-exec dir John Smith & Son (Glasgow) Ltd 1988–2000; pt/t lectr and tutor Glasgow Grad Law Sch; returning offr Community Cncl Elections 1982–96, pt/t chm Rent Assessment Ctee Glasgow and West of Scotland 1983–98, dir Glasgow Slrs' Property Centre 1993–99; pt/t chm Appeals Service; non-exec dir W Glasgow Hosps Univ NHS Tst 1994–99; deacon Incorporation of Fleshers of Glasgow 1993–94; memb Law Soc of Scotland, chm: (Scotland) Int Client Counselling Competition, West of Scotland IoD; fell Caledonian Univ Glasgow (govr 1991–98); FRSA; *Recreations* tennis, skiing, golf, hang-gliding; *Clubs* Western (Glasgow); *Style*— Michael Graham, Esq; ✉ Clairmont, 11 Winton Drive, Glasgow G12 0PZ (tel 0141 334 7988, e-mail jmd.graham@ntlworld.com); Dunmhor, Lochgoilhead, Argyll; MacRoberts, Solicitors, 152 Bath Street, Glasgow (tel 0141 332 9988, fax 0141 332 8886, e-mail mike.graham@macroberts.com)

GRAHAM, Prof Neil Bonnette; s of George Henry Graham (d 1979), of Liverpool, and Constance, *née* Bonnette (d 1986); *b* 23 May 1933; *Educ* Alsop HS Liverpool, Univ of Liverpool (BSc, PhD); *m* 16 July 1955, Marjorie, da of William Edwin Royden (d 1937), of Liverpool; 1 s (Paul b 19 Sept 1957), 3 da (Kim b 7 Oct 1959, Michele b 14 May 1965, Lesley b 6 Aug 1967); *Career* res scientist Canadian Industries Ltd McMasterville PQ Canada 1956–67, gp head ICI Petrochemical and Polymer Laboratory Runcorn Cheshire 1967–73 (former assoc gp head), fndr and tech dir Polysystems Ltd Clydebank 1980–90, co-fndr and ceo Smart Tech Ltd 2000–, co-fndr and ceo Ecoco Ltd 2000–05, co-fndr and scientific dir Ocutec Ltd 2001–; res prof of chemical technol Univ of Strathclyde 1983–97 (Young prof 1973–83, prof emeritus 1997–); expert advsr on active med implants to Sec of State 1993–; memb Dept of Health Medicines Div Regulatory Advsy Ctee on Dental and Surgical Materials 1978–86; tstee: McKinnon McNeil Tst, James Clerk Maxwell Tst; memb Scot Bd of Mission Aviation Fellowship (MAF) 2000–; deacon Bearsden Baptist Church 1998–2004; holder of more than 80 patents; ALCM, CChem, CSci, FRSC, FIM, FRSE; *Recreations* walking, sailing, music; *Style*— Prof Neil Graham, FRSE; ✉ 6 Kilmardinny Grove, Bearsden, Glasgow G61 3NY (tel 0141 942 0484, e-mail 100721.314@compuserve.com)

GRAHAM, Sir Peter; KCB (1993, CB 1982), QC (1990); o s of Alderman Douglas Graham, CBE (d 1981), of Huddersfield, W Yorks, and Ena May, *née* Jackson (d 1982); f was Mayor of Huddersfield 1966–67, and Freeman of Borough 1973; family motto Verborum vi Vincimus; *b* 7 January 1934; *Educ* St Bees Sch Cumberland (scholar), St John's Coll Cambridge (scholar, MA, LLM); *m* 1, Judith Mary, da of Charles Dunbar, CB; 2 s (Ian b 1960, Alistair b 1962); m 2, Anne Silvia, da of Benjamin Arthur Garcia; m 3, Janet, da of Capt William Eric Walker, TD; *Career* Lt RNR 1952–55, served as pilot Fleet Air Arm; called to the Bar Gray's Inn 1958 (bencher 1992); Parly counsel 1972–86, second Parly counsel 1987–91, first Parly counsel 1991–94, conslt in legislative drafting 1994–; *Recreations* playing keyboards, good wines, gardens, classic cars; *Clubs* The Sette of Odd Volumes; *Style*— Sir Peter Graham, KCB, QC; ✉ Le Petit Château, La Vallette, 87190 Magnac Laval, France

GRAHAM, Dr Peter John; *b* 16 September 1943; *Educ* St Joseph's Coll Stoke-on-Trent, Univ of Liverpool (BSc, PhD); *m* 1968, Janice Head; 3 s; *Career* Miny of Technol 1969–70; DTI: joined 1970, asst private sec to Rt Hon Michael Heseltine (min for Aerospace and Shipping) 1972–73, asst sec (grade 5) Project and Export Policy Div 1982–84, asst sec Small Firms Div 1984–88; first sec (res and nuclear) UK Permanent Rep to the EC Brussels 1979–82; Health and Safety Exec 1988–95, dir (grade 3) Health Directorate 1995–99, dir Strategy and Analytical Support Directorate 1999–2003; *Recreations* gardening, travel; *Clubs* Pinnacle Sports; *Style*— Dr Peter Graham

GRAHAM, Prof Philip Jeremy; s of Jacob (Jack) Graham (d 1955), and Pauline, *née* Jacobs (d 1981); *b* 3 September 1932; *Educ* Perse Sch Cambridge, Sorbonne, Luton Tech Coll, Gonville & Caius Coll Cambridge (MA, MB BChir), UCH Med Sch London; *m* 1960, Nori, *née* Burawoy; 1 da (Anna b 11 March 1964), 2 s (Daniel b 11 March 1965, David b 4 Nov 1968); *Career* hon conslt psychiatrist: Maudsley Hosp 1966–68 (psychiatric trg 1961–64), Great Ormond St Children's Hosp 1968–94; Inst of Child Health London: prof of child psychiatry 1975–94, dean 1985–90; prof of child psychiatry (pt/t) Univ of Oslo Norway 1993–2000; affiliated lectr Dept of Psychiatry Univ of Cambridge 1994–2000; chm Nat Children's Bureau London 1994–2000; sr memb Wolfson Coll Cambridge; child psychiatry advsr to the CMO 1976–85, pres Euro Soc for Child and Adolescent Psychiatry 1987–91, vice-pres Royal Coll of Psychiatrists 1996–98 (chm Child Psychiatry Section 1974–77), chair Assoc of Child Psychology and Psychiatry; hon fell Univ of Luton 1997; memb RSM; FRCP, FRCPsych, FRCPCH; *Books* Child Psychiatry: A Developmental Approach (1991, 3 edn 1999), Cognitive Behaviour Therapy for Children and Families (ed, 1998); also author of book chapters and approx 150 articles; *Recreations* tennis, travel, reading; *Style*— Prof Philip Graham; ✉ 27 St Alban's Road, London NW5 1RG (tel 020 7485 7937, fax 020 7267 4628)

GRAHAM, Sir Ralph Stuart; 14 Bt (E 1629), of Esk, Cumberland; er s of Sir Ralph Wolfe Graham, 13 Bt (d 1988), and his 2 w, Geraldine, *née* Velour; *b* 5 November 1950; *Educ* Hofstra Univ; *m* 1, 1972, Roxanne (d 1978), da of Mrs Lovette Gurzan, of Elmont, Long Island, New York; 1 adopted s (Gabriel Lawrence b 1974); m 2, 1979, Deena Louise, da of William Robert Vandergrift, of 2903 Nemesis, Waukegan, Illinois; *Heir* bro, Robert Graham; *Career* self-employed (maintenance company); singer/songwriter (recorded three gospel albums, including Star of the Show, One by One); *Recreations* bible fellowships, performing music; *Style*— Sir Ralph Graham, Bt; ✉ 7439 Highway 70 South, Apt 270, Nashville, Tennessee 37221-1732, USA

GRAHAM, Rigby; s of Richard Alfred Graham (d 1971), of Leicester, and Helen Sutherland Downie (d 1967); *b* 2 February 1931; *Educ* Wyggeston Sch, Leicester Coll of Art & Design (Sir Jonathan North bronze and silver medals); *m* 1953, Patricia, da of Horace Dormer Green; 1 da (Eleonora b 1968); *Career* De Montfort Univ (formerly Leicester Poly): princ lectr, assoc fell 1983; *Solo Exhibitions* Gadsby Gallery Leicester 1963, 1966, 1969, 1971, 1974, 1978, 1980 and 1981, Great Yarmouth Art Gallery 1964, Mowbray Gallery Sunderland 1965, Compendium Gallery Birmingham 1966, Crescent Theatre Gallery Birmingham 1967, Kings Lynn Festival 1967, Griffin Garnett Galleries Shrewsbury 1969, St Peter Port Guernsey 1970, Pacifica Library Sharp Park California 1976, Menlo Park Civic Centre California 1976, Victoria Galleries Harrogate 1977, Retrospective Hemel Hempstead Pavilion 1977, Rawlins Art Centre Quorn 1978, Bosworth Gallery Desford 1979 and 1981, Wymondham Art Gallery 1979 and 1984, Coach House Gallery Guernsey 1981, Drew Edwards Keene Gallery 1983, Woodquay Gallery Galway 1984, Phoenix Gallery Amsterdam 1985, Artifact Gallery Leicester 1986, Bottle Kiln Gallery W Hallam 1986, David Holmes Art Gallery Peterborough 1988–94, Warwick Museum and Art Gallery 1992, Goldmark Gallery Uppingham 1987, 1989, 1991, 1992, 1994, 1997, 1999 and 2000, Navenby 1992, Bleddfa Tst Gallery Powys 1990, Manchester Poly 1990, Univ of Wales Aberystwyth 1989, Carnegie Museum Melton Mowbray 1999, Snibston Discovery Park Coalville 1999, Retrospective Exhibition New Walk Museum Leicester 1999, Manchester Metropolitan Univ 2001, Yarrow Gallery Oundle 2005, Gascoigne Gallery Harrogate 2006; *Books* The Pickworth Fragment (1966), Slieve Bingian (1968), The Casquets (1972), Ruins (with Michael Felmingham, 1972), John Piper 1973, Deserted Cornish Tin Mines (1975), String & Walnuts (1978), Seriatim (1978), Graham's Leicestershire (1980), A Broken String of Beads (1980), Sketchbook Drawings (1989), Kippers & Sawdust (1992), Cyril on the Grand Tour (1999), A Paper Snowstorm (jtly, 2005), Pennant and his Welsh Landscapes (2006); *Recreations* Italian opera, reading; *Style*— Rigby Graham, Esq; ✉ c/o Mike Goldmark, Goldmark Gallery, Uppingham, Rutland LE15 9SQ (tel 01572 821424)

GRAHAM, (George Malcolm) Roger; OBE (1987); s of William George Blampied Graham (d 1943), and Enid, *née* Townsley (d 1970); *b* 10 May 1939; *Educ* Mill Hill Sch, Fitzwilliam Coll Cambridge; *m* Irene Helen Leyden, *née* Martin; 1 s, 2 da; *Career* various appts in heavy electrical and aircraft industries 1961–62, major account mangr IBM 1965–67 (joined 1962), md ASAP Consultants Ltd 1967–69; BIS Gp Ltd: joined 1969, involved in mgmnt buy-in 1980 and sale to NYNEX Corp 1986, various positions rising to chm and chief exec until 1993; dir: Close Brothers Corporate Finance plc 1995–2001, Scottish Life Assurance Co Ltd 1999–2001; chm: Computer People plc then Delphi Gp plc 1994–96, Gresham Computing 1997–2001, Active Hotels plc, Mantix Systems Ltd, Azur Gp plc, Transversal Corp Ltd, Reevoo Ltd, Villas to Go Ltd, Skillsmarket Ltd; pres: UK Computing Servs Assoc 1981–82, European Computing Servs Assoc 1986–88; first chm World Computing Serv Indust Forum, fndr chm Computing Servs Indust Trg Cncl; govr and vice-chm Mill Hill Sch; Freeman City of London 1988; Liveryman: Worshipful Co of Glovers 1988, Worshipful Co of Information Technologists 1992 (Master 2004–05); *Books* The Handbook of Computer Management (with R B Yearsley, 1973), Information 2000 - Insights into the Coming Decades in Information Technology (1989); *Recreations* landscape gardening, opera, private flying; *Clubs* Oxford and Cambridge; *Style*— G M R Graham, Esq, OBE; ✉ Gaston House, Gaston Green, Bishop's Stortford, Hertfordshire CM22 7QS

GRAHAM, Ross; *Career* chartered accountant; dir Misys plc 1987–2003 (finance dir 1987–97, corp devpt dir 1997–); formerly ptnr Arthur Young; non-exec dir various cos incl: Wolfson Microelectronics plc, Acambis plc, Psion plc; FCA; *Style*— Ross Graham, Esq; ✉ mobile 07771 834202, fax 01608 685889, e-mail ross.graham@virgin.net

GRAHAM, Sandra Denise; da of late James Graham, of Poole, Dorset, and late Joyce N Elizabeth, *née* Botham; *Educ* Fylde Lodge HS Stockport, Manchester Poly (BA); *Career* admitted slr 1984; formerly ptnr Penningtons, currently conslt Horsey Lightly Fynn, specialist in liquor licensing and entertainment law and food law; nominated as one of ldrs in their field by Chambers and ptnrs in directory 1995–96 and 1996–97; chm Bournemouth and Dist Young Slrs' Gp 1991–92, treas Nat Young Slrs' Gp 1990–92 (Bournemouth and Dist rep 1985–92); memb: Bournemouth and Dist Law Soc (memb Gen Ctee 1990–93), Law Soc, Inst of Licensing; affiliated to Inst of Acoustics; tstee Priory House Christchurch, memb Cncl All Saints Branksome Park Parish Church; *Recreations* gardening, cake decorating (memb Br Sugarcraft Guild), sailing, music, travel; *Style*— Ms Sandra Graham

GRAHAM, Prof Stephen Douglas Nelson; s of David Douglas Nelson Graham, and Doreen Bramfit, *née* Lowerson; *b* 26 February 1965, Tynemouth; *Educ* Univ of Southampton (BSc), Univ of Newcastle upon Tyne (MPhil), Victoria Univ of Manchester (PhD); *m* 1996, Annette Marie Kearney; 2 s (Ben b 1998, Oliver b 2000); *Career* urban planner Sheffield City Cncl 1989–1992, lectr rising to prof of urban technol Univ of Newcastle upon Tyne 1992–2004, prof of human geography Univ of Durham 2004–; co-fndr Centre for Urban Technol (CUT) Univ of Newcastle upon Tyne; visiting prof: Dept of Urban Studies and Planning MIT 1999–2000, Centre for Sustainable Urban and Regnl Futures Univ of Salford 2003–04, Global Urban Research Unit Univ of Newcastle upon Tyne; conslt UN Centre for Human Settlements; Br Acad reader 2003–05; FRGS, fell IBG; *Books* Telecommunications and the City (with S Marvin, 1996), Splintering Urbanism (with S Marvin, 2001), Citta E Communicazione (with S Marvin, 2002), Cities, War and Terrorism (ed, 2004), Cybercities Reader (ed, 2004); *Recreations* cycling; *Style—* Prof Stephen Graham; ✉ Department of Geography, Science Laboratories, South Road, Durham DH1 3LE

GRAHAM, Teresa Colomba; OBE (1998); da of Albert Rea (d 1986), and Anna, *née* Mastroianni; *b* 8 March 1956; *Educ* La Sagesse Convent GS Newcastle upon Tyne, Univ of Newcastle upon Tyne (BA); *m* (m dis); *Career* Price Waterhouse CAs: Newcastle upon Tyne Office 1977–88 (qualified 1980), seconded to Govt Enterprise and Deregulation Unit 1987, London Office 1988–90 (advsr to Govt on deregulation); Baker Tilly: joined 1989, former head Business Serviced Dept, currently sr advsr, chair etc venues Salix Finance and Matrix; mentor and advsr to CW Communications, MPG, and Momentum; non-exec dir Direct Wines; advsr SME issues ICAEW; chm Regulatory Bd RICS; dep chair Govt's Better Regulation Cmmn 1997–2007, non-exec memb Steering Bd Small Business Serv DTI 2000–06, memb Small Business Cncl DTI 2003–06; former chm Educnl Policy Ctee RSA; former memb: Ctee for Smaller Entities (CASE) Accounting Standards Bd, Parly Ministerial Gp on Access Business, Advsy Ctee ONS; chm London Soc of CAs 1994–95, current chm London Entrepreneurs' Club, patron Network; govr Bromley Coll 1993–94, former dir Business Link S London; Young Accountant of the Year 1988, Outstanding Achievement Award ICEAW 2007; FCA 1992 (ACA 1982), FRSA 1993; *Recreations* opera, driving, reading; *Style—* Mrs Teresa Graham, OBE; ✉ The Mews, 9 Eccleston Square, London SW1V 1NP (tel 020 7630 6264, fax 020 7976 5518, e-mail teresa@teresagraham.co.uk)

GRAHAM, Timothy Richard (Tim); s of Herbert Maurice Graham (d 1987), and Florence Mary Warrington, *née* Winship (d 1984); *b* 23 November 1948; *m* 10 July 1976, Eileen Mary, da of George Tyner Fitzpatrick; 1 da (Lucy Mary b 24 Jan 1983), 1 s (Thomas Andrew b 15 Sept 1984); *Career* freelance photographer specialising in the Royal Family; Fox Photos 1965–70, staff photographer Daily Mail 1975–78; subjects incl: Royal Family, Heads of State, VIPs; sittings: HM The Queen and HRH Prince Philip, The Prince and Princess of Wales and Family, Princess Alice, Prince Edward, The Duke and Duchess of Gloucester and family, Prince and Princess Michael of Kent and family, Prince Albert of Monaco, Margaret Thatcher; exhibition Royal Photographs Royal Acad 1984; *Books* On the Royal Road (1984), The Prince and Princess of Wales - In Person (1985), The Prince and Princess of Wales - In Private, In Public (1986), Diana - HRH The Princess of Wales (1988), Charles and Diana - A Family Album (1991), Diana, Princess of Wales - A Tribute (1997), Dressing Diana (1998), The Royal Year, Jubilee: A Celebration of 50 Years of the Reign of Her Majesty Queen Elizabeth II; *Recreations* photography, wine, food, travel, cars, countryside, preservation of the environment and our wildlife; *Style—* Tim Graham, Esq; ✉ Tim Graham Picture Library (tel 020 7435 7693, fax 020 7431 4312, e-mail mail@timgraham.co.uk, website www.royalphotographs.com)

GRAHAM, Tony; s of David and Freda Graham; *Educ* Orange Hill GS, Univ of Kent (BA), Didsbury Coll of Educn Univ of Manchester (PGCE); *Career* teacher Central Fndn Girls' Sch London 1975–83, exchange to Olney HS Philadelphia 1983–84, head of dance and drama Haverstock Sch London 1984–86, memb ILEA Drama Advsy Team 1986–88; TAG Theatre Co: Scottish Arts Cncl assoc dir bursary 1989, artistic dir 1992; artistic dir Unicorn Theatre for Children 1997–; Edinburgh Festival Critics Prize (for Lanark) 1995, Equity/TMA Barclays Award Best Production of a Children's Play (for Tom's Midnight Garden) 2001; memb: Equity 1990–, ASSITEU 1997, Action for Children's Arts 1998–; *Recreations* reading and riding; *Style—* Tony Graham; ✉ Unicorn Theatre, 147 Tooley Street, London SE1 2HZ (tel 020 7645 0500, e-mail tony.graham@unicorntheatre.com)

GRAHAM, (Arthur) William; JP (1979), AM; s of William Douglas Graham (d 1970), and Eleanor Mary Scott, *née* Searle; *b* 18 November 1949; *Educ* Blackfriars Sch, Coll of Estate Mgmnt London; *m* 20 June 1981, Elizabeth Hannah, da of Joshua Griffiths, of Gwent; 1 s (William James b 1982), 2 da (Sarah Jane Mary b 1984, Hannah Victoria b 1987); *Career* cncllr: Gwent CC 1986–90, Newport BC 1988–2002 (ldr Cons Gp 1992–2002), Newport City Cncl 2002–; memb Nat Assembly for Wales (Cons) S Wales E 1999–; chief whip, shadow min for local govt and housing in Wales; chm Newport Harbour Cmmrs; govr Rougemont Sch Tst 1991, tstee United Reformed Church; FRICS 1974; *Recreations* breeder of pedigree Suffolk sheep, foreign travel; *Clubs* Carlton, Pall Mall; *Style—* William Graham, Esq, AM; ✉ The Volland, Lower Machen, Newport, Gwent NP1 8UY (tel 01633 440419, fax 01633 440751); National Assembly for Wales, Cardiff CF99 1NA (tel 029 2082 5111, fax 029 2089 8347, e-mail william.graham@wales.gov.uk)

GRAHAM-BROWN, James Martin Hilary; s of L H Graham-Brown, of Burton, Leics, and E C Graham-Brown, *née* Blaxland; *b* 11 July 1951; *Educ* Sevenoaks Sch, Univ of Kent (BA), Univ of Bristol (MPhil); *m* 30 Sept 1978, Susan Leslie, *née* Clarke; 2 da (Annie b 14 Dec 1985, Isobel b 15 July 1987); *Career* professional cricketer: Kent CCC 1970–76, Derbys CCC 1977–79; dep head Bournemouth Sch 1988–92, head Truro HS 1992–2000, head Royal HS Bath GDST 2000–; chief examiner English A Level Cambridge Univ Bd 1986–94; *Plays* Leaving Samson (1994), Crisis (1998), Speaking Ill of the Dead (2000), Marital Moments (2001), Redeeming Lizzie Reeve (2002), She's Gone Then (2003), You'll Never Guess What? We went to school with Tina Goddard (2004); *Recreations* writing plays, directing productions; *Style—* James Graham-Brown, Esq; ✉ The Royal High School Bath GDST, Lansdown Road, Bath BA1 5SZ (tel 01225 313877, fax 01225 465446, e-mail jgb@bat.gdst.net)

GRAHAM-BROWN, Dr Robin Alan Charles; s of Maj Lewis Hilary Graham-Brown (d 2003), of Burton on the Wolds, Leics, and Elizabeth Constance, *née* Blaxland; *b* 14 August 1949; *Educ* Sevenoaks Sch, Royal Free Hosp Sch of Med (BSc, MB BS); *m* 13 Sept 1975, Dr Margaret Marie Rose Anne Graham-Brown, da of late Dr Robert Graham; 3 s (James Robert Philip b 1980, Matthew Paul Mark b 1982, John Joseph Dominic b 1986); *Career* conslt dermatologist 1982–; Leicester Royal Infirmary, Market Harborough Hosp, Coalville Hosp, Ashby de la Zouch Hosp, BUPA Hosp Leicester; hon sr lectr Univ of Leicester Sch of Med 1993–, dep med dir Univ Hosps of Leicester 2000–; pres British Assoc of Dermatologists 2005–06 (local sec 1987–88); ed British Jl of Dermatology 2001–04; FRCP 1990 (MRCP 1976); *Books* Skin Disorders in the Elderly (1988), Lecture Notes on Dermatology (1990, 3 edn 2003), Colour Atlas and Text of Dermatology (1998); *Recreations* horse riding, cricket, opera; *Clubs* MCC, Dowling; *Style—* Dr Robin Graham-Brown; ✉ Killiecrankie, 46 Barrow Road, Burton on the Wolds, Loughborough, Leicestershire LE12 5TB (tel 01509 880558); Department of Dermatology, Leicester Royal Infirmary, Leicester LE1 5WW (tel 0116 258 5162)

GRAHAM-BRYCE, Dr Ian James; CBE (2001); s of Alexander Graham-Bryce (d 1968), and Dame Isabel Graham-Bryce, DBE, *née* Lorrain-Smith (d 1997); *b* 20 March 1937; *Educ* William Hulmes' GS, Univ of Oxford (MA, BSc, DPhil); *m* 1959, Anne Elisabeth; 1 s, 3 da; *Career* res asst Univ of Oxford 1958–61, lectr Dept of Biochemistry and Soil Science UCNW 1961–64, sr scientific offr Rothamsted Experimental Station 1964–70, sr res offr ICI Plant Protection Div Jealotts Hill Res Station Bracknell 1970–72, special lectr in pesticide chemistry Imperial Coll of Sci and Technol London 1970–72, dep dir Rothamsted Experimental Station 1975–79 (head Dept of Insecticides and Fungicides 1972–79), visiting prof Imperial Coll of Sci and Technol Univ of London 1976–79, hon lectr Univ of Strathclyde 1977–80, dir East Malling Res Station 1979–85, conslt dir Cwlth Bureau of Horticulture and Plantation Crops 1979–85, hon conslt Zoecon Corp Calif 1980–86, head Environmental Affairs Div Shell Internationale Petroleum Maatschappij BV 1986–94, princ and vice-chllr Univ of Dundee 1994–2000 (princ emeritus 2000–); hon advsr Zhejiang (Wanli) Univ China 1999–; pres: Soc of Chemical Industry 1982–84, Assoc of Applied Biologists 1988–89, Br Crop Protection Cncl 1996–2000 (hon vice-pres 2000–02), Scottish Assoc for Marine Science 2000–04 (vice-pres 2004–); chm: Agrochemical Planning Gp Int Orgn for Chem Scis in Devpt 1985–87, Environmental Cmmn Int C of C 1988–92, Working Gp on Environmental Auditing; vice-chm: Global Warming Gp Int Petroleum Industry Environmental Conservation Assoc 1988–94, Environmental Res Working Gp Industrial R&D Advsy Ctee to the Euro Communities 1988–91; memb: Br Nat Ctee for Chemistry 1982–84, Scientific Ctee Euro Chem Industry Ecology and Toxicology Centre 1988–94, UK NERC 1989–96 (chm Polar Scis and Technol Bd 1995–96), Tech Assoc Coal Indust Advsy Bd Global Warming Ctee 1989–94, Royal Cmmn on Environmental Pollution 2000–; memb Bd of Dirs: Br Cncl Educn Counselling Serv 1996–98, Quality Assurance Agency for Higher Educn (chm Scottish Advsy Ctee) 1997–98, Rothamsted Experimental Station 2000–04; govr: Long Ashton Res Station 1979–85, Imperial Coll London 1985–2000, Convener Ctee Scottish Higher Educ Principals 1998–2000; vice-pres Ctee of Vice-Chllrs and Principals (CVCP) 1999–2000; tstee East Malling Tst for Horticultural Res 1987– (chm 2001–); Br Crop Protection Cncl Medal 2000; Freeman City of London 1981, Liveryman Worshipful Co of Fruiterers 1981; Hon LLD Univ of Dundee 2001; FRSC 1981, FRSE 1996, FRSA 1996; *Books* Physical Principles of Pesticide Behaviour; *Recreations* music (especially opera), sport; *Clubs* Athenaeum; *Style—* Dr Ian Graham-Bryce, CBE, FRSE

G

GRAHAM-DIXON, Andrew Michael; s of Anthony Philip Graham-Dixon, QC, and Margaret Suzanne, *née* Villar; *b* 26 December 1960; *Educ* Westminster, ChCh Oxford (MA), Courtauld Inst; *m* 8 June 1985, Sabine Marie, *née* Pascale Tilly; 2 da (Eleanor b 1986, Florence b 1989), 1 s (Arthur b 1992); *Career* art critic The Independent 1986–98, princ art critic Sunday Telegraph 2004– (art columnist Sunday Telegraph magazine 2001–); assoc prof of history of art London Inst 1997–; BP Arts Journalist of the Year 1987 and 1988, Hawthornden Prize for Art Criticism 1991; memb Advsy Ctee Hayward Gallery 1991–96; writer and presenter: A History of British Art (6–part series, BBC2) 1996, Renaissance (6–part series, BBC2) 1999; *Books* Howard Hodgkin (1992), A History of British Art (1996), Paper Museum (1996), Renaissance (1999), In the Picture (2003); *Recreations* snooker; *Style—* Andrew Graham-Dixon, Esq; ✉ 21 Croftdown Road, London NW5 1EL

GRAHAM-DIXON, Francis; s of Michael Stuart Graham-Dixon (d 2001), and Anita, *née* Falkenstein (d 2000); *b* 21 March 1955; *Educ* Stowe, Univ of London (BA), Univ of Sussex (MA); *m* 25 July 2007, Alexandra Noble; 2 s (Freddie b 1981, Charlie b 1984), 1 da (Celia b 1989); *Career* Sotheby's London 1973–78, Record Merchandisers 1978–79, Warner Brothers 1979–80, Heiman Music 1980–81, BBC 1982–87, Francis Graham-Dixon Gallery London 1987–2003, Univ of Sussex 2006–; govr Winchester Sch of Art 1989–93; *Recreations* reading, music, real tennis; *Clubs* MCC; *Style—* Francis Graham-Dixon, Esq; ✉ Francis Graham-Dixon (e-mail f.graham-dixon@sussex.ac.uk)

GRAHAM-HALL, John; s of Leonard G Hall, of Northwood, and Betty, *née* Minns; *b* 23 November 1955; *Educ* Malvern Coll, King's Coll Cambridge (MA), RCM (Tagore Gold Medal); *m* 1990, Helen, da of John Williams; 2 da (Katharine b 31 Aug 1990, Emily b 6 Dec 1992); *Career* princ ENO; tst ENO Benevolent Fund *Major roles* incl: Britten's Albert Herring (Glyndebourne 1985–90, Royal Opera House 1989), Lysander (Sadlers Wells 1990, Aix-en-Provence 1991–92, ENO 1996, Ravenna 1995, Rone 1999), Aschenbach in Death in Venice (Glyndebourne) 1989, Vanya Kudrjas in Katya Kabanova (Glyndebourne) 1988–90, Schapkin in House of the Dead (ENO) 1997, Ferrando in Cosi fan Tutte (Opera North 1983, Vancouver 1985), Basilio in Figaro (ENO) 1991–97, Monostatos in The Magic Flute (ENO) 1995–97, Lensky in Onegin (Lyon 1984, Toronto 1990), Tanzmeister in Ariadne auf Naxos (ENO)1995, Achilles in King Priam (Antwerp) 1992, Young Man in Moses und Aron (Salzburg Festival 1996), Herod in Salome (ENO)1999, Paris in King Priam (RFH) 1999, Sylvester in The Silver Tassie (ENO) 2000, Anatole in War and Peace (ENO) 2001, Alura in Lulu (ENO) 2002; *Concerts* Schubert's Winterreise (St John Smith' Square 1997, BBC TV 1997), Honegger's Joan of Arc (BBC Proms) 1997, Carmina Burana (BBC Proms) 1998; *Recordings* Britten: Albert Herring (1985), A Midsummer's Night Dream (1990), Peter Grimes (1995, Grammy Award 1997); Orff's Carmina Burana (1987 and 1996), Janacek's Katya Kabanova (1988), Schönberg's Moses und Aron (1995); *Recreations* cookery, bridge; *Style—* John Graham-Hall, Esq; ✉ c/o Musichall, Ringmer, Lewes, East Sussex (tel 01273 814240)

GRAHAM OF EDMONTON, Baron (Life Peer UK 1983), of Edmonton in Greater London; (Thomas) Edward Graham; PC (1998); s of Thomas Edward Graham, of Newcastle upon Tyne; *b* 26 March 1925; *Educ* WEA Co-Op Coll, Open Univ (BA); *m* 1950, Margaret Golding, da of Frederick and Alice Golding, of Dagenham; 2 s (Hon Martin Nicholas b 1957, Hon Ian Stuart b 1959); *Career* various posts Co-operative Movement 1939–; memb and leader Enfield Cncl 1961–68, national sec Co-Op Party 1967–74, MP (Lab and Co-Op) Enfield Edmonton Feb 1974–83, PPS to Min of State Prices and Consumer Protection 1974–76, lord cmmr Treasury 1976–79; oppn front bench spokesman on Environment 1980–83; oppn House of Lords spokesman on Sport, Defence, N Ireland 1983; oppn whips office, oppn chief whip 1990–97, chm Lab Peers Gp; chm United Kingdom Co-operative Cncl 1997–; Hon MA 1989; pres Inst of Meat; Hon Freeman Worshipful Co of Butchers; FIMgt, FRSA; *Style—* The Rt Hon the Lord Graham of Edmonton, PC; ✉ 2 Clerks Piece, Loughton, Essex IG10 1NR (tel 020 8508 9801); House of Lords, London SW1 (tel 020 7219 6704)

GRAHAME, Christine; MSP; *b* 9 September 1944; *Educ* Boroughmuir Sr Secdy Sch, Univ of Edinburgh (MA, LLB, DipEd, DipLP, NP); *m* (m dis); 2 s (Angus b 14 Jan 1971, Niall b 1 Nov 1974); *Career* MSP (SNP) Scotland South 1999–; convenor: Justice 1 Ctee 2001–03, Health and Community Care Ctee 2003–04; shadow spokesperson Social Justice 2004–, sec Parly website; patron Scottish Heart At Risk Testing, patron Jam; memb Law Soc of Scotland 1986, memb NUJ, elected memb Royal Zoological Soc; *Recreations* malt, gardening; *Style—* Ms Christine Grahame, MSP; ✉ The Scottish Parliament, Edinburgh EH99 1SP (e-mail christinegrahame.msp@scottish.parliament.uk, website www.christinegrahame.com)

GRAHAME-SMITH, Prof David Grahame; CBE (1993); s of George Edward Smith (d 1968), Leicester, and Constance Alexandra Smith (d 1974); *b* 10 May 1933; *Educ* Wyggeston GS for Boys Leicester, St Mary's Hosp Med Sch Univ of London (MB BS, PhD), Univ of Oxford (MA); *m* 25 May 1957, Kathryn Frances, da of Dr Francis Robin Beetham (d 1985), of Leeds; 2 s (Harvey Neil b 1958, Henry Peter b 1964); *Career* Capt RAMC 1957–60; house physician Paddington Gen Hosp 1956, house surgn Battle Hosp Reading 1956–57, H A M Thompson scholar Royal Coll of Physicians 1961–62, hon med registrar Professorial Medical Unit St Mary's Hosp Paddington 1961–66 (registrar and sr registrar in medicine 1960–61), Saltwell res scholar Royal Coll of Physicians 1962–65, Wellcome

Tst res fell 1965–66, MRC travelling fell Dept of Endocrinology Vanderbilt Univ Nashville 1966–67, sr lectr and reader in clinical pharmacology and therapeutics St Mary's Hosp Med Sch Univ of London 1967–71, hon conslt physician St Mary's Hosp Paddington 1967–71, Rhodes prof of clinical pharmacology Univ of Oxford 1971–2000, hon dir MRC Unit of Clinical Pharmacology Radcliffe Infirmary Oxford 1971–93, hon conslt physician in gen internal medicine and clinical pharmacology Oxford AHA 1971–2000, fell CCC Oxford 1971–2000 (vice-pres 1998–2000), hon dir Oxford Univ/SmithKline Beecham Centre for Applied Neuropsychobiology 1989–99, tstee William Harvey Research Inst 1999–2002; visiting prof in clinical pharmacology Peking Union Med Coll Beijing 1985, conslt clinical pharmacologist to the RAF 1985–95, conslt in pharmacology to the Army 1986–98; examiner in therapeutics UK and abroad, principal examiner final BM BS Examinations Univ of Oxford 1990–94; memb: Br Nat Pharmacological Ctee 1974–79, Clinical Trials and Toxicity Sub-Ctee of Ctee on Safety of Medicines 1974–86 (memb Main Ctee 1975–86), Clinical Medicine Faculty Bd 1976–80, Res Ctee Mental Health Res Fund 1978–80, Ctee Clinical Pharmacology Section Br Pharmacological Soc 1978–81, Scientific Ctee Migraine Tst 1980–86; vice-chm Clinical Medicine Faculty Bd Univ of Oxford 1978–80, tstee Sheik Rashid Diabetes Tst Oxford 1986, chm UK Advsy Ctee on Misuse of Drugs 1988–98, pres Oxford Div BMA 1989–90; memb Cncl: Collegium Internationale Neuro-Psychopharmacologium 1988–96, Clinical Section International Union of Pharmacology 1988–92; Die Anna Monica Stiftung 2nd prize (jtly with A R Green) 1977, Paul-Martini prize in Clinical Pharmacology (jtly with J K Aronson) 1980, William Potter lectr Thomas Jefferson Univ of Philadelphia 1988, Lilly prize of the Clinical Section Br Pharmacological Soc 1995, Lifetime Achievement award Br Assoc of Psychopharmacology 2002; FRCP; *Books* Carcinoid Syndrome (1972), Oxford Textbook of Clinical Pharmacology and Drug Therapy (with JK Aronson, 1984, 3 edn 2002); *Recreations* piano; *Style—* Prof David Grahame-Smith, CBE; ✉ Romney, Lincombe Lane, Boars Hill, Oxford OX1 5DY (tel 01865 735889, e-mail david.grahame-smith@clinpharm.ox.ac.uk)

GRAINGE, Lucian Charles; s of Cecil Grainge (d 1984), and Marion Grainge (d 1994); *b* 29 February 1960; *Educ* Queen Elizabeth GS Barnet; *m* 30 June 2002, Caroline, *née* Lewis; 1 s (Elliot b 6 Nov 1993), 1 da (Alice b 7 March 2000), 1 step da (Betsy b 22 Dec 1987); *Career* creative asst MPC Artists & Mgmnt 1978, head creative dept April Music/CBS 1981 (plugger 1979), dir and gen mangr RCA Music (now BMG Music Publishing) 1982–85, A&R dir MCA UK 1985–86, md Polygram Music Publishing UK 1986–1993, md Polydor 1997–99 (gen mangr A&R and business affrs 1993–97), chm Universal Music UK 2001– (dep chm 1999–2001); dir BPI, long-standing memb Brits Ctee, co-chm Brits TV show 2004–; A&R Award Music Week Awards 1997, MD of the Year Triumph Awards 1998, Dep Chm of the Year Triumph Awards 2000; *Recreations* soccer, automobiles; *Style—* Lucian Grainge, Esq; ✉ Universal Music Group International, 364–366 Kensington High Street, London W14 8NS (tel 020 7471 5006, fax 020 7471 5391, e-mail lucian.grainge@umusic.com)

GRAMMENOS, Prof Costas Theophilos; Hon OBE (1994); s of Cdr Theophilos C Grammenos (d 1998), and Argyro, *née* Spanakos (d 1996); *b* 23 February 1944; *Educ* Third State Sch of Athens, Pantion Univ (BA), Univ of Wales (MSc), City Univ (DSc); *m* 20 Nov 1972, Anna, da of Prof Constantinos A Papadimitriou (d 1994); 1 s (Theophilos b 6 April 1975); *Career* Nat Serv Greek Navy 1968–70; Nat Bank of Greece 1962–75 (shipping fin expert, head office 1973–74); independent researcher and advsr 1977–82; Sir John Cass Business Sch City of London (formerly City Univ Business Sch): visiting prof 1982–86, fndr and head Dept of Shipping, Trade and Finance 1984–2002, prof of shipping, trade and finance 1986–, acting dean 2000, dep dean 2001–; pro-vice-chllr City Univ 1998–; fndr and chm City of London Biennial Meetings 1999–; visiting prof Univ of Antwerp 2000–; memb: Bd of Dirs Alexander S Onassis Public Benefit Fndn 1995–, BIMCO Bd of Govrs (Educn) 1995–, American Bureau of Shipping 1996–, Baltic Exchange 1997–; pres Int Assoc of Maritime Economists 1998–2002, founding tstee Inst of Marine Engrs Meml Fund 2000–; Seatrade Personality of the Year 1998; Freeman of the City of London 2000, Liveryman Worshipful Co of Shipwrights 2002; FRSA 1996; Archon Ecumenical Patriarchate of Constantinople 1994; FCIB 2004; *Books* Bank Finance for Ship Purchase (1979), The Handbook of Maritime Economics and Business (ed, 2002); author of various papers and studies on shipping finance; *Recreations* music, theatre, walking; *Clubs* Travellers; *Style—* Prof Costas Th Grammenos, OBE; ✉ Sir John Cass Business School, City of London, 106 Bunhill Row, London EC1Y 8TZ (tel 020 7477 8671, fax 020 7477 8895)

GRAMS, Gerry; *b* 29 July 1959; *Educ* Mackintosh Sch of Arch Glasgow Sch of Art (DipArch, W Sommerville Shanks legacy, Bram Stoker medal, ARIAS (Rowan Anderson Award); *Career* architectural apprentice: Murray and Manson Architects Glasgow 1980–81, McGurn Logan and Duncan Architects Glasgow 1982; architect McGurn Logan Duncan and Opfer Glasgow 1983–96 (assoc dir 1988–96), fndr ptnr Bonar & Grams Architects 1996–; projects incl: Tron Theatre, Glassford Court, private house for Robbie Coltrane, Bellgrove Cross/Graham Square housing for Molendinar Park HA, The Piping Centre Glasgow; current projects incl: Refurbishment of the Clydeway Centre Glasgow, Kelvin Square Housing Development Glasgow, Shelbourne Hotel Health Club Dublin; pt/t design tutor (fndn course) Dept of Architecture Univ of Strathclyde 1989–96; dir Workshop and Artists Studio Provision Scotland Ltd (WASPS); *Competitions* second prize Crown Street Masterplan 1990, first prize Darnley Masterplan 1991; *Exhibitions* Royal Scottish Acad Summer Exhibition 1984, For a Wee Country... (RIAS Jubilee Travelling Exhibition) 1990; *Style—* Gerry Grams, Esq; ✉ Bonar & Grams Architects, 6th Floor, 8 Elliot Place, Clydeway Skypath, Glasgow G3 8EP (tel 0141 221 4090, fax 0141 221 9290, e-mail studio@bonargrams.co.uk)

GRAN, Maurice Bernard; s of Mark Gran (d 1965), of London, and Deborah, *née* Cohen (d 1986); *b* 26 October 1949; *Educ* William Ellis GS London, UCL (BSc); *m* Carol James; 1 da (Jessica b 21 June 1985), 1 s (Thomas b 23 May 1988); *Career* mgmnt trainee Dept of Employment, various mgmnt appts Employment Services Agency 1974–80, television scriptwriter 1980–; creator and writer (with Laurence Marks, *qv*): Holding the Fort 1979–82, Roots, Shine on Harvey Moon 1982–85 and 1995, Roll Over Beethoven, Relative Strangers, The New Statesman 1987–91, Birds of a Feather 1989–99, Snakes and Ladders, So You Think You've Got Troubles, Get Back, Love Hurts 1991–93, Wall of Silence (film) 1993, Goodnight Sweetheart 1994–99, Mosley (min-series) 1997, Playing God (Stephen Joseph Theatre Scarborough) 2005, New Statesman (Trafalgar Studios London and tour) 2006–07; fndr (with Laurence Marks and Allan McKeown, *qv*) Alomo Productions 1988 (now part of Thames Talkback plc); memb Cncl BAFTA 1994–95; *Awards* Silver Medal Int Film and TV Festival NY for Relative Strangers 1985, Int Emmy for The New Statesman 1988, BAFTA Best Comedy Award for The New Statesman 1990, Mitsubishi TV Sitcom of the Year for Birds of a Feather 1991, Mitsubishi TV Drama of the Year for Love Hurts 1991, BAFTA Writer's Award (jtly with Laurence Marks) 1992; *Books* Holding the Fort (with Laurence Marks, 1981), The New Statesman Scripts (with Laurence Marks, 1992), Dorien's Diary (with Laurence Marks, 1993); *Recreations* watching football, buying clothes, fell walking; *Clubs* Groucho, Arsenal FC; *Style—* Maurice Gran, Esq

GRANARD, 10 Earl of (I 1684); Sir Peter Arthur Edward Hastings Forbes; 11 Bt (S 1628); also Viscount Granard and Baron Clanehugh (I 1675), and Baron Granard (UK 1806); er s of Hon John Forbes (d 1982), and Joan, *née* Smith; suc unc, 9 Earl of Granard, 1992; *b* 15 March 1957; *m* 1 Sept 1980, Nora Ann (Noreen), da of Robert Mitchell, of Portarlington, Co Leix; 2 s (Jonathan Peter Hastings, Viscount Forbes b 24 Dec 1981, Hon David Robert Hastings b 8 Feb 1984, Hon Edward Hastings b 13 June 1989), 1 da (Lady Lisa Ann b 2 July 1986); *Heir* s, Viscount Forbes; *Style—* The Rt Hon the Earl of Granard; ✉ Strathallan Cliff, Strathallan Road, Onchan, Isle of Man IM3 1NN

GRANATT, Mike; CB (2001); *Career* sub-ed Kent Sussex Courier 1974, press offr Dept of Employment 1979–81, press offr Home Office 1981–83, sr info offr then head of info Dept of Energy 1983–89, dir of public affrs Met Police 1989–92, dir of communication DOE 1992–95, dir of communication Home Office 1995–98; ptnr Luther Pendragon 2004–; currently DG Govt Info Communication Service (GICS) (head of Professional 1997–2001 and 2001–02, head of Civil Contingencies Secretariat 2001–02); Stephen Tallents Medal 2002; FIPR 2000; *Clubs* Savage; *Style—* Mike Granatt, CB

GRANDAGE, Michael; *b* 2 May 1962; *Educ* Humphry Davy GS Penzance, Central Sch of Speech and Drama; *Career* theatre dir; artistic dir Crucible Theatre Sheffield 1999–2005, artistic dir Donmar Warehouse 2002–; Hon DUniv: Sheffield Hallam 2002, Sheffield 2004; *Productions* Crucible Theatre Sheffield: What the Butler Saw 1997, Twelfth Night 1998, The Country Wife 2000, As You Like It 2000 (also Lyric Theatre Hammersmith; Best Dir Evening Standard Awards, Best Dir Critics Circle Awards, South Bank Show Award for Theatre), Edward II 2001, Don Juan 2001, Richard III 2002, The Tempest 2002 (also The Old Vic London), A Midsummer Night's Dream 2003, Suddenly Last Summer (also Albery Theatre London) 2004, Don Carlos 2004 (also Gielgud Theatre London, Best Dir Evening Standard Awards); Donmar Warehouse: Good 1999, Passion Play 2000 (also Comedy Theatre London; Best Dir Evening Standard Awards, Best Dir Critics Circle Awards, nomination Best Dir Olivier Awards), Merrily We Roll Along 2000–01 (3 Olivier Awards incl Best Musical, Best Dir Critics Circle Awards), Privates on Parade 2001–02 (3 nominations Olivier Awards), The Vortex 2002–03, Caligula 2003 (Best Dir Olivier Awards), After Miss Julie 2003–04, Pirandello's Henry IV 2004, Grand Hotel, the Musical 2004 (Best Musical Olivier Awards), The Wild Duck 2005 (Best Dir Critics Circle Awards), Guys and Dolls (Donmar at the Piccadilly Theatre, Best Musical Olivier Awards) 2005, The Cut 2006, Frost/Nixon 2006 (also Broadway, nomination Best Dir Tony Awards), Don Juan in Soho 2006, John Gabriel Borkman 2007, Othello 2007; Almeida Theatre: The Doctor's Dilemma 1998, The Jew of Malta 1999; Evita (Adelphi Theatre London) 2006; *Style—* Michael Grandage, Esq; ✉ Donmar Warehouse, 41 Earlham Street, London WC2H 9LY (tel 020 7845 5800, e-mail mgrandage@donmarwarehouse.com)

GRANGE, Kenneth Henry; CBE (1984); s of Harry Alfred Grange, and Hilda Gladys, *née* Long; *b* 17 July 1929; *Educ* Willesden Coll of Art; *m* 21 Sept 1984, Apryl Jacqueline, da of Deric Swift; *Career* tech illustrator RE 1947–48; architectural asst Bronek Katz & Vaughan 1949–50; designer: Gordon Bowyer 1950–52, Jack Howe & Partners 1952–58; fndr Kenneth Grange Design London 1958–72, fndr ptnr Pentagram Design Ltd 1972–; memb Bd of Dirs Shakespeare Globe Centre 1997–; winner: 10 Design Cncl Awards, Duke of Edinburgh Prize for Elegant Design 1963, CSD Gold Medal (for lifetime's achievement in design) 1996, Prince Philip's Designers Prize 2001; work represented in collections of: V&A, Design Museum London, State Museum Munich; one man shows: Kenneth Grange at the Boilerhouse V&A 1983, The Product Designs of Kenneth Grange of Pentagram XSITE Tokyo Japan 1989; juror BBC Design Awards 1996; Master Faculty of Royal Design for Industry 1985–87 (memb 1969); memb Cncl and memb Advsy Bd on Product Design Design Cncl (industrial design advsr 1971), memb Ct RCA; Hon Doctorate: RCA 1985, De Montfort Univ 1998, Univ of Staffs 1998, Open Univ 2003; Hon DUniv Heriot-Watt 1986; FCSD 1965 (pres 1987–89), RDI 1969 (Master of Faculty 1982–84); *Books* Living by Design (jtly 1977), The Compendium (jtly, 1993); *Recreations* skiing, building; *Style—* Kenneth Grange, CBE, RDI; ✉ 53 Christchurch Hill, London NW3 1LG

GRANGE, Terence; QPM (2000); s of Sidney Thomas Grange (d 1982), and Nora Elizabeth, *née* Burke (d 1993); *b* 26 September 1948; *Educ* South Bank Poly (MSc); *m* 2 Oct 1971, Patricia May, *née* Grant; 3 da (Samantha Jane b 11 Oct 1972, Louise Clare, Sarah Ann (twins) b 12 Oct 1976); *Career* enlisted Parachute Bde 1963; with Met Police 1971–88; Avon and Somerset Constabulary: Superintendent 1988, appointed head Traffic Dept 1989, Asst Chief Constable 1994–98, Asst Chief Constable (designate) 1998; Chief Constable Dyfed-Powys Police 2000–; ACPO: mem 1994, business area mangr for personal crime, portfolio holder for Child Protection and Sex Offender issues; *Publications* Rediscovering Public Services Management (contrib, 1992); *Recreations* supporter of Chelsea FC; *Clubs* Bristol Golf; *Style—* Terence Grange, Esq, QPM; ✉ Chief Constable, Dyfed-Powys Police, Dyfed-Powys Police HQ, PO Box 99, Llangunnor, Carmarthenshire SA31 2PF (tel 01267 226303, fax 01267 226310, e-mail acpo@dyfed-powys.pnn.police.uk)

GRANT, Andrew Robert; s of Walter Frank Grant (d 1984), of Southend-on-Sea, Essex, and Joan, *née* Bartram; *b* 29 April 1953; *Educ* Southend HS, CCC Cambridge (open exhbn, MA, PGCE, Cycle Racing half blue, capt Cambridge Univ Cycling Club); *m* 1977, Hilary Sheena Kerr, da of Allan Harold Charlton; 2 s (Alexander b 4 June 1985, Matthew b 21 Jan 1987); *Career* asst master Merchant Taylors' Sch Northwood 1976–83, head of English Whitgift Sch Croydon 1983–90, second master Royal GS Guildford 1990–93, headmaster St Albans Sch 1993–; HMC: memb 1993–, chm Academic Policy Ctee 2002–05 (memb 1998); co-chair HMC/GSA Educn and Academic Policy Jt Ctee 2002–05, memb Universities Sub-Ctee 2005–, chm London Div 2006–07; memb: Jt Assocs Curriculum Gp 2000–06, Tomlinson 14–19 Review Assesment Sub-Gp 2003–05, QCA 14–19 Advsy Gp 2004–06; govr: Lochinver House Sch, Abbots Hill Sch, Moorlands Sch, Beechwood Park Sch; memb SHA 1990, memb Gen Teaching Cncl 2002; FRSA 1997; *Recreations* theatre, literature, music, cycling, squash, sailing; *Clubs* Hawks' (Cambridge), East India; *Style—* Andrew Grant, Esq; ✉ St Albans School, Abbey Gateway, St Albans, Hertfordshire AL3 4HB (tel 01727 855521, fax 01727 843447, e-mail hm@st-albans-school.org.uk)

GRANT, Andrew William; DL (Worcs 2006); s of Francis Denis Grant, of Kidderminster; *b* 11 April 1945; *Educ* Belmont Abbey Hereford; *m* 1995, Beatrice Irene Helen Victoria, da of (John) Miles Huntington-Whiteley, *qv*; 2 s (Frederik Francis Thomas Augustus b 1999, Ludovic William Miles Hubertus b 2002); *Career* chartered surveyor and landowner; prop Andrew Grant estate agents and surveyors 1971–; CLA: memb Cncl 1996–, pres Worcs branch 2002–05 (vice-chm 1996–99, chm 1999–2002), chm W Midlands Regnl Ctee 2004–; hon vice-pres Worcester branch Br Red Cross; tstee: Elizabeth FitzRoy Support, Worcester and Dudley Historic Churches Assocs, St Peter, St Paul and St Elizabeth Coughton RC Church Alcester; govr St Richard's Hospice 1979–89 (patron 2006–), chm St Mary's Convent Sch 1989–99, pres Worcester Cons Assoc 2006–; High Sheriff Herefords and Worcs 2005–06; FRICS; KM 2004; *Clubs* Brooks's; *Style—* Andrew Grant, Esq, DL; ✉ Bransford Manor, Worcester WR6 5JG (tel 01886 832368)

GRANT, Hon Anne Margaret; da of Maj Sir Arthur Lindsay Grant, 11 Bt (ka 1944), and Baroness Tweedsmuir of Belhelvie (Life Peer, d 1978); *b* 1937; *Educ* Cheltenham Ladies' Coll, Lady Margaret Hall Oxford (MA); *m* 1965 (m dis 1983), Nicolas Mangriotis; 2 s (Paraskevas b 1971, Arthuros b 1974); *Career* econ conslt to OECD Paris and to Greek Govt 1962–70, dir mgmnt consultancy Athens 1975–85, mgmnt conslt (London) 1985–; dir Green Cross UK 1995–2004; non-exec dir: Plan UK 1989–, Plan International Inc 2001–; FIMgt, MCIM; *Style—* The Hon Anne Grant; ✉ 24 Amity Grove, London SW20 0LJ (tel 020 8946 9887)

GRANT, Anthony Ernest; OBE (2005); s of Ernest Grant (d 1986), of Sheffield, and Doris, *née* Hughes (d 1990); *b* 23 April 1940; *Educ* King Edward VII GS Sheffield, Keble Coll Oxford (MA); *m* 14 April 1962, Darel Avis, da of Frederick John Atkinson (d 1980), of

Sheffield; 3 da (Henrietta (Mrs Michael Flood) b 1965, Sarah (Mrs Angus Ward) b 1966, Philippa b 1969 (Mrs Richard Thompson)); *Career* Coopers & Lybrand CAs 1961–96 (head of regnl ops 1994–96); chm: Tundra Ltd 1996–, Wilton Investments Ltd 1996–2001, Dorlux Beds Ltd 1999–2002; non-exec dir: Leeds Financial Services Initiative 1993–2000 (chm 1993–94), Rocom Group Ltd 1996–2001, Leeds & Holbeck Building Soc 1996–2006, John Cotton Gp Ltd 1997–, TVision Technology Ltd 2003–; pres W Yorks CAs 1993–94, pres Leeds C of C 1996–99, chm W Yorks Employer Coalition 2000–05, dep chm Leeds Met Univ 1990–91; tstee: Thackray Medical Museum 2004–, W Yorks Police Community Tst 2006–; FCA (ACA 1965); *Clubs* Oxford and Cambridge; *Style*— Anthony Grant, Esq, OBE; ✉ 63 Old Park Road, Leeds LS8 1JB (tel 0113 266 3721, e-mail anthony.grant80@ntlworld.com)

GRANT, Charles Peter; s of Peter Forbes Grant (d 1974), and Elizabeth Ann, *née* Shirreff; *b* 9 October 1958, Oxford; *Educ* Marlborough, Univ of Cambridge, Univ of Grenoble; *Career* early career with Euromoney; The Economist: City writer 1986–89, in Brussels 1989–93, writer on British affrs London 1993–94, defence ed 1994–98; dir Centre for European Reform 1998– (fndr 1995); dir and tstee British Cncl 2002–; memb: Ctee for Russia in a United Europe, Bd Moscow Sch of Political Studies; Prix Stendhal Adelphi Fndn 1992; Chevalier de l'Ordre Nationale du Mérite (France) 2003; *Publications* Delors: Inside the House that Jacques Built (1994); author of numerous pubns and essays for Centre for European Reform; *Recreations* hill walking, music; *Clubs* Reform; *Style*— Charles Grant, Esq; ✉ Centre for European Reform, 29 Tufton Street, London, SW1P 3QL (tel 020 7233 1199, fax 020 7233 1117, e-mail charles@cer.org.uk)

GRANT, Dr Douglas; TD; s of Robert Grant (d 1959), and Ierne Grant (d 1963); *b* 6 January 1918; *Educ* George Watson's Coll; *m* 1948, Enid Whitsey, da of Raymond Whitsey Williams (d 1985); 3 s (William Neil b 1953, Richard Martin b 1955, Peter Michael b 1958); *Career* WWII Lt-Col RA (served Forth, W Africa and staff Eastern Cmd) 1939–46; Scot Widows Fund 1936–39; dir: Oliver and Boyd Ltd 1947–67, Edinburgh C of C 1952–56, New Education Ltd 1962–66, Bracken House Publications Ltd 1963–67, E & S Livingston Ltd 1963–67, Darien Press Ltd 1963–68, Sprint Productions Ltd 1963–80, R & R Clark Ltd 1963–80, Port Seton Offset Printers Ltd 1965–75, T & A Constable Ltd 1965–75, Br Journal of Educnl Psychology 1970–91, Pindar (Scot) Ltd 1986–89, Macdonald Lindsay (Printers) Ltd 1988–89; chm: Scot Journal of Theology Ltd 1948–91, Robert Cunningham & Sons Ltd 1952–76, Hunter and Foulis Ltd 1963–75, Port Seton Offset Printers Ltd 1965–75, Multi Media (AU) Services Ltd 1967–75, Church of Scot Publications Ctee 1971–76; Scot Academic Press Ltd 1969–91, Scot International Review Ltd 1970–75, The Handsel Press Ltd 1975–91, Scot Academic Press (Journals) Ltd 1976–91, Clark Constable Printers Ltd 1978–89; conslt ed: Scot Academic Press 1991–99, Dunedin Academic Press 2000–; tstee: The Lodge Tst (Natural History) 1949–85, Darling (Ogilby) Investment Tst 1955–78, Kilwarlin Tst 1964–, Esdaile Tst 1975– (chm 2001–), The Soc for the Benefit of Sons and Daughters of the Clergy of the Church of Scot 1975– (chm 2001–); memb Ctee: The Scot Cncl of Law Reporting 1947–93 and 2003–05 (conslt 1993–2003), Police Dependents' Tst (Lothian and Borders Police) 1956–95, NEDO 1968–75, Fin Bd New Coll Univ of Edinburgh 1970–, Ct Univ of Edinburgh 1972–84, Scot Arts Cncl 1975–79; pres: Edinburgh Master Printers' Assoc 1962–64, St Cuthbert's Soc of Change Ringers 1960–, Edinburgh Booksellers' Soc 1977–80, Edinburgh Amateur Angling Club 1978–80, The Charles Smith Tst 1991–; Hon DLitt Univ of St Andrews 1986; hon fell Edinburgh Geological Soc 1992; MBOU 1944, FRSE 1949, FSA Scot 1949; *Clubs* New (Edinburgh), Hon Co of Edinburgh Golfers; *Style*— Dr Douglas Grant, TD, FRSE; ✉ Flat G, The Lodge, 2 East Road, North Berwick, East Lothian EH39 4HN (tel 01620 894972)

GRANT, Hugh John Mungo; s of James Murray Grant, of Chiswick, and late Fynvola Susan, *née* MacLean; *b* 9 September 1960; *Educ* Latymer Upper Sch, New Coll Oxford (scholarship, BA); *Career* actor; began career in theatre performing Jockeys of Norfolk (written with Chris Lang & Andy Taylor); prodr Simian Films; *Films* incl: Privileged, Maurice (Best Actor Venice Film Festival 1987 (jtly with James Wilby)), White Mischief, Rowing with the Wind, The Dawning, The Bengali Night, The Lair of the White Worm, Impromptu, The Big Man, Bitter Moon, Night Train to Venice, The Remains of the Day, Sirens, Four Weddings and a Funeral (Best Actor BAFTA Awards 1995, Best Actor in a Comedy Golden Globe Awards 1995, Peter Sellers Award for Comedy Evening Standard British Film Awards 1995), An Awfully Big Adventure, Restoration, The Englishman Who Went Up a Hill But Came Down a Mountain, Nine Months, Sense & Sensibility, Extreme Measures, Notting Hill (Peter Sellers Award for Comedy Evening Standard British Film Awards 2000, Best British Actor Empire Film Awards 2000, nomination Best Actor in a Comedy Golden Globe Awards 2000), Mickey Blue Eyes, Small Time Crooks, Bridget Jones' Diary (Peter Sellers Award for Comedy Evening Standard British Film Awards 2002), About a Boy (Best British Actor Empire Film Awards 2003, Best British Actor London Critics Circle Film Awards 2003), Two Weeks Notice, Love Actually, Bridget Jones: The Edge of Reason, American Dreamz, Music and Lyrics; *Style*— Hugh Grant, Esq; ✉ c/o Sara Woodhatch, 10 Carlisle Street, London W1D 3BR (tel 020 7287 2400, fax 020 7287 2411)

GRANT, Ian David; CBE (1988); s of Alan Howison Brewster Grant (d 1974), and Florence Ogilvie, *née* Swan; *b* 28 July 1943; *Educ* Strathallan Sch, E of Scotland Coll of Agric (Dip); *m* 19 July 1968, Eileen May Louisa, da of Alexander Yule; 3 da (Catherine Louise b 10 Jan 1970, Jane Belle b 14 July 1971, Rosanne Elaine b 1 March 1974); *Career* dir East of Scotland Farmers 1976–2002, chm Copa Cereals Gp Brussels 1982–86, pres NFU Scotland 1984–90 (vice-pres 1981–84), chm Grains Gp Int Fedn of Agric Producers 1984–89; dir: Clydesdale Bank plc 1989–97, NFU Mutual Insurance Soc 1990– (dep chm 2003–), Scottish and Southern Energy plc (formerly Scottish Hydro Electric plc) 1992–2003 (dep chm 2000–03); chm Crown Estate 2002– (cmmr 1996–); chm: Scottish Tourist Bd 1990–98 (memb Bd 1988–98), Cairngorms Partnership 1998–2003, Scot Exhbn Centre Ltd 2002– (dep chm 2001, dir 1998–); memb: Cncl CBI Scotland 1984–96, Bd Br Tourist Authy 1990–98; FRAgS; *Recreations* gardening, travel, reading, music; *Clubs* Royal Smithfield (vice-pres); *Style*— Ian Grant, Esq, CBE; ✉ The Crown Estate, 16 New Burlington Place, London W1S 2HX (tel 020 7851 5002, fax 020 7851 5003)

GRANT, Prof Ian Philip; s of Harold H Grant (d 1981), and Isabella Henrietta, *née* Ornstien (d 1980); *b* 15 December 1930; *Educ* St Albans Sch, Wadham Coll Oxford (open scholar, MA, DPhil); *m* 1958, Beryl Cohen; 2 s (Paul Simon b 1960, David Michael b 1962); *Career* princ scientific offr UKAEA Aldermaston 1961–64 (sr scientific offr 1957–61); Pembroke Coll Oxford: Atlas research fell (jt appt with SRC Atlas Computer Lab) 1964–69, tutorial fell in mathematics 1969–98 (fell emeritus 1998–), actg master 1984–85; Univ of Oxford: univ lectr in mathematics 1969–90, reader in mathematical physics 1990–92, prof of mathematical physics 1992–98 (prof emeritus 1998–); visiting prof: McGill Univ Montreal 1976, Åbo Akademi Finland 1977, Inst de Fisica Univ Nacional Autónoma de México 1981; chm Oxford Synagogue and Jewish Centre 1985–2004; govr: Royal GS High Wycombe 1981–2000, St Paul's Sch London 1993–2001; memb London Mathematical Soc 1977; CMath 1992; FRAS 1966, FRS 1992, FInstP 2005; *Publications* Relativistic Quantum Theory of Atoms and Molecules (2006), author of papers in learned jls on relativistic quantum theory in atomic and molecular physics, and on radiative transfer theory in astrophysics and atmospheric science; *Recreations* walking, gardening, music, theatre-going and travel; *Style*— Prof Ian Grant, FRS; ✉ Mathematical Institute, University of Oxford, 24/29 St Giles, Oxford OX1 3LB (tel 01865 273550, fax 01865 273583, e-mail ipg@maths.ox.ac.uk)

GRANT, Dr Jane Wentworth; *Educ* Univ of Bristol (BA), Inst of Educn Univ of London (PGCE), Univ of Essex (MA, MPhil), Univ of Lagos (Cert Yoruba), Univ of Kent (PhD); *m* Neville J H Grant; 2 s, 1 da; *Career* various English teaching posts Dar-es-Salaam and England 1964–69, lectr Univ of Lagos 1971–73, educn offr/admin African Arts in Educn Project 1980–84, devpt offr Policy and Promotions Dept Nat Cncl for Voluntary Orgns 1984–89, dir Nat Alliance of Women's Orgns 1989–94, currently conslt and researcher on governance of women's orgns; non-exec dir Oxleas Mental Health Tst 2003–; reader Queen's Anniversary Prizes for Higher and Further Educn; memb: Advsy Cncl Global Fund for Women, Advsy Gp, Nat Alliance of Women's Orgns, Women's Studies Network, Int Working Gp of Women's Nat Cmmn; govr Churchfield Sch; FRSA; *Publications* author of numerous pubns on multi-cultural educn and women's issues, incl The Governance of Women's Organisations Towards Better Practice (2002); *Clubs* Commonwealth; *Style*— Dr Jane Grant; ✉ 13 Glenluce Road, Blackheath, London SE3 7SD (tel 020 8858 8489, fax 020 8293 4808, e-mail janewgrant@clara.co.uk)

GRANT, Prof John; s of John Grant, of Bedlington, and Ivy Grant; *b* 8 January 1948; *Educ* Bedlington GS, Univ of Leeds (BSc, Brodetsky prize), Univ of Newcastle upon Tyne (PhD); *m* Elizabeth, da of Robert Foster, and Ivy Foster; 2 da (Julie b 22 Nov 1972, Lara b 11 July 1974), 1 s (David b 8 May 1981); *Career* senior sci offr RAE Farnborough 1972–79; Parsons Power Generation Systems (Rolls-Royce Industrial Power Group): princ design engr 1979, chief devpt engr 1991, dir Turbine-Generator Devpt 1994, tech dir 1996–97; engrg dir Siemens Power Generation 1997–2003; visiting prof in principles of engrg design Univ of Newcastle upon Tyne; conslt memb Fossil Power Ctee Power Industries Div IMechE (ret); author of numerous tech papers in jls and conf and seminar proceedings; Alan Marsh Meml Award RAeS 1976; FIMechE 1991, FREng 1996; *Recreations* football, golf, gardening, church; *Style*— Prof John Grant, FREng; ✉ tel 01670 791836, e-mail shamels@tiscali.co.uk

GRANT, John Albert Martin; s of late Walter Grant, and Irene, *née* Smyth; *b* 13 October 1945; *Educ* Campbell Coll Belfast, Queen's Univ Belfast (BSc), Cranfield Sch of Mgmnt (MBA); *m* 1971, Corinne, da of late John Porter, and Sally Porter; 2 da (Joanna b 27 March 1974, Nicola b 9 June 1976), 1 s (James b 23 April 1979); *Career* Ford of Europe: treas 1985–87, vice-pres Business Strategy 1987–88; exec dir Corp Strategy Ford Motor Co (US) Jan-Dec 1989, exec dep chm Jaguar Ltd 1990–92; fin dir: Lucas Industries plc 1992–96, Lucas Varity plc 1996; chief exec Ascot plc 1997–2000; chm: Hasgo Group Ltd 2000–, Peter Stubs Ltd 2000–05, The Royal Automobile Club Motor Sports Assoc Ltd 2002–05, Torotrak plc 2005– (non-exec dir 1998–2005); non-exec dir: National Grid Group plc 1995–2006, Corac plc 2000–06, Royal Automobile Club Ltd 2004–, MHP SA 2006–, Melrose plc 2006–; FCT 1976; *Recreations* opera, music, theatre, motor sport, skiing; *Clubs* RAC, BRDC; *Style*— John Grant, Esq; ✉ Hasgo Group plc, The Malthouse, Manor Lane, Claverdon, Warwick CV35 8NH (tel 01926 842459, e-mail johngrant@hasgo.com)

GRANT, Prof John Paxton; s of John Dickson Grant (d 1968), and Jean Ramsay, *née* Paxton (d 1993); *b* 22 February 1944; *Educ* George Heriot's Sch, Univ of Edinburgh (LLB, Lord President Cooper prize), Univ of Pennsylvania (LLM); *m* 1983, Elaine Elizabeth, da of Eric Roy McGillvray Sutherland; *Career* lectr in public law: Univ of Aberdeen 1967–71, Univ of Dundee 1971–74; Faculty of Law Univ of Glasgow: sr lectr 1974–88, prof 1988–99, dean 1985–89 and 1992–96; prof of law Lewis and Clark Sch of Law Portland Oregon 1999–, prof emeritus Univ of Glasgow 1999–; ed The Juridical Review 1988–99; *Books* Independence and Devolution: The Legal Implications for Scotland (1976), The Impact of Marine Pollution (with Cusine, 1980), The Encyclopaedic Dictionary of International Law (with Parry, 1986), Legal Education 2000 (1989), English-Estonian Law Glossary (1993), English for Lawyers (1994), The Lockerbie Trial Briefing Handbook (1999, 2 edn 2000), The Encyclopaedic Dictionary of International Law (with Barker, 2 edn 2003), The Lockerbie Trial: A Documentary History (2004), International Law Deskbook (2005); *Recreations* walking, travelling; *Style*— Prof John Grant

GRANT, Dr John William; s of late John MacDonald Grant, and Isabella Grigor Clark, *née* Morrison; *b* 27 May 1953; *Educ* Dingwall Acad Ross & Cromarty, Univ of Aberdeen (MB ChB, MD); *m* 14 Nov 1980, Daniela, da of Hans Felix, of Bex, Switzerland; 2 da (Joanna b 1983, Marsali b 1986); *Career* registrar pathology Ninewells Hosp Dundee 1979–81, sr registrar in neuropathology and histopathology Southampton Gen Hosp 1981–86, Oberarzt Inst of Pathology Univ of Zürich Switzerland 1986–88; conslt histopathologist Addenbrooke's Hosp Cambridge 1988–, assoc lectr Univ of Cambridge 1989–, fell Emmanuel Coll Cambridge; MA Univ of Cambridge 1995; memb: BMA, Pathological Soc, Br Neuropathology Soc, Swiss Neuropathology Soc, ACP; FRCPath 1996 (MRCPath 1984); *Recreations* skiing, photography, squash; *Style*— Dr John W Grant; ✉ 243 Hinton Way, Great Shelford, Cambridge CB2 5AN; Histopathology Department, Box 235, Addenbrooke's Hospital, Hills Road, Cambridge CB2 2QQ (tel 01223 216744, fax 01223 216980, e-mail jwg21@cam.ac.uk)

GRANT, Prof Malcolm John; CBE (2003); s of Francis William Grant (d 1987), and Vera Jessica, *née* Cooke; *b* 29 November 1947; *Educ* Waitaki HS Oamaru, Univ of Otago (LLB, LLM, LLD); *m* 13 July 1974, Christine Joan, da of Thomas John Endersbee, ISO (d 1986); 2 s (Nikolas b 1976, Thomas b 1980), 1 da (Joanna b 1978); *Career* sr lectr in law (former lectr) Univ of Southampton 1972–86, prof of law UCL 1988–91 (sr lectr 1986–88), prof of land economy Univ of Cambridge 1991–2003; fell Clare Coll Cambridge 1991–, pro-vice-chllr Univ of Cambridge 2002–03; provost and pres UCL 2003–; cmmr for local govt for England 1992–2002; chm Local Govt Cmmn 1996–2002 (dep chm 1995–96), chm Agric and Environment Biotechnology Cmmn 2000–05, chm Steering Bd Nat GM Public Debate 2003–04, memb Standards Ctee GLA 2000– (chair 2004–); called to the Bar Middle Temple 1998 (bencher 2005); ed Encyclopaedia of Planning Law and Practice 1982–2005, conslt ed Encyclopaedia of Environmental Law 1993–; tstee Ditchley Fndn 2002–; govr London Business Sch 2003–, govr Royal Instn 2006–, chm Russell Gp of UK Research Univs 2006–, memb Hong Kong Univs Grants Ctee 2007–; Hon LLD Univ of Otago 2006; life hon memb NZ Resource Mgmnt Law Assoc 2000; Hon MRTPI 1994, Hon ARICS 1995; Officier dans l'Ordre Nationale de Mérite (France) 2004; *Books* Planning Law Handbook (1981), Urban Planning Law (1982, supplement 1989), Rate Capping and the Law (1984, 2 edn 1986), Permitted Development (1989, 2 edn 1996), Singapore Planning Law (1999), Environmental Court Report (2000); *Recreations* opera, gardening, forestry; *Style*— Prof Malcolm Grant, CBE; ✉ Provost's Office, University College London, Gower Street, London WC1E 6BT (tel 020 7679 7234, e-mail provost@ucl.ac.uk)

GRANT, Nicholas; s of Hugo Moore Grant (d 1987), of Edinburgh, and Cara Phyllis, *née* McMullen-Pearson (d 2007); *b* 24 March 1948; *Educ* Durham Sch, Univ of London (LLB), Univ of Warwick (MA); *m* 5 Nov 1977, Rosalind Louise, da of Winston Maynard Pipe; 1 s (Robert b 1979), 1 da (Rosemary b 1981); *Career* head of res and PR Confedn of Health Serv Employees 1972–82, dir of communications Lab Pty 1983–85, public affrs advsr to Mirror Group Newspapers 1985–89; currently: chm Mediatrack Research Ltd, chm Assoc for the Measurement and Evaluation of Communication; memb: (Lab) Lambeth BC 1978–84, West Lambeth DHA 1982–84; Parly candidate (Lab) Reigate 1979; assoc Market Res Soc, memb Int Assoc of Business Communicators; govr Clifton Coll; FCIPR; *Books* Economics of Prosperity (contrib, 1980), Political Communication for British General Election (1983); *Recreations* hill walking, history, chess, music, running; *Clubs* Reform, Westbury Harriers; *Style*— Nicholas Grant, Esq; ✉ Mediatrack Research Ltd, 1 Northumberland Avenue, London WC2N 5BW (tel 020 7430 0699, fax 020 7404 4207, e-mail ngrant@mediatrack.com)

GRANT, Prof Peter Mitchell; s of George Mitchell Grant (d 2004), of Leven, Fife, and Isobel Margaret, *née* Wilkinson (d 1973); *b* 20 June 1944; *Educ* Strathallan Sch, Heriot-Watt Univ (BSc), Univ of Edinburgh (PhD); *m* 12 Jan 1974, Marjory, da of Ness Renz (d 1991); 2 da (Lindsay Isobel b 1975, Jennifer Alison b 1977); *Career* devpt engr Plessey Company Ltd 1966–70; Univ of Edinburgh: res fell 1971–76, lectr 1976–82, reader 1982–87, prof of electronic signal processing 1987–, head Sch of Engrg and Electronics 2002–; pres European Assoc for Signal Processing 2000–02; chm Editorial Panel IEE Electronics Jl; Faraday Medal IEE 2004; Hon DEng Heriot-Watt Univ 2006; FIEE, FIEEE, FRSE 1997, FREng 1997; *Books* Adaptive Filters (1985), Digital Communications (1997), Digital Signal Processing: Concepts and Applications (1998); *Style*— Prof Peter Grant, FRSE, FREng; ✉ School of Engineering and Electronics, University of Edinburgh, King's Building, Mayfield Road, Edinburgh EH9 3JL (tel 0131 650 5569, fax 0131 650 6554, e-mail pmg@ee.ed.ac.uk)

GRANT, Richard E; *b* 5 May 1957; *Educ* Waterford-Kamthlaba Mbabane, Univ of Cape Town (BA); *m* 1 Nov 1986, Joan Washington, *qv*; 1 da (Olivia b 4 Jan 1989); *Career* actor; *Theatre* co-fndr Troupe Theatre Co Cape Town 1980–82; credits incl: Man of Mode (Orange Tree) 1983, A Midsummer Night's Dream and Merry Wives of Windsor (Regents Park) 1984, Tramway Road (Lyric Hammersmith) 1984, The Importance of Being Earnest (Aldwych) 1993, The Play What I Wrote (West End) 2002; *Television* for BBC incl: Honest Decent and True 1985, Here is the News 1988, Suddenly Last Summer 1992, Bed 1994, Karaoke (with Channel Four) 1995; A Royal Scandal 1996, The Scarlet Pimpernel 1998; *Film* incl: Withnail and I 1986, Warlock 1988, How to Get Ahead in Advertising 1988, Mountains of the Moon 1988, Killing Dad 1989, Henry and June 1989, LA Story 1990, Hudson Hawk 1990, The Player 1992, The Age of Innocence 1992, Dracula 1993, Prêt a Porter 1994, Cool Light of Day 1994, Jack & Sarah 1995, Portrait of a Lady 1995, Twelfth Night 1995, The Serpent's Kiss 1996, Food of Love 1996, Keep The Aspidistra Flying 1997, St Ives 1997, Spiceworld The Movie 1997, The Match 1998, A Christmas Carol 1999, Trial and Retribution 1999, The Little Vampire 1999, Hildegarde 2000, Gosford Park 2001, The Hound of the Baskervilles 2002, Monsieur N. 2003, Bright Young Things 2003, Tooth 2004, Colour Me Kubrick 2004, Wah-Wah 2004 (writer and dir); *Books* With Nails (1996), By Design (1998); *Recreations* scuba diving, building dolls houses, photography; *Style*— Richard E Grant, Esq; ✉ c/o ICM Ltd, Oxford House, 76 Oxford Street, London W1N 0AX (tel 020 7636 6565, fax 020 7323 0101, website www.richard-e-grant.com)

GRANT, Susan Lavinia; da of Donald Blane Grant, of Dundee, Scotland, and Lavinia Ruth, *née* Ritchie; *b* 29 January 1948; *Educ* St Leonard's Sch St Andrews Scotland, Goldsmiths Coll London; *m* 1, 1969 (m dis 1973), Charles Sharpe; m 2, 1975 (m dis 1983), Ian Woolgar; 1 da (Lavinia Unity b 1977), 1 s (Edward Rupert b 1980); *Career* res exec J Walter Thompson 1968–74, researcher BBC Publications then publicity exec BBC TV 1974–78, publicity mangr Hamlyns 1978–82, account mangr then account dir Good Relations 1982–86, fndr dir and memb Bd The Communication Group 1986–; currently fndr ptnr Grant Butler Coomber Group; MIPR; *Recreations* tennis, golf, waterskiing, Scotland, painting; *Clubs* Riverside Racquets, Panmure Golf; *Style*— Ms Susan Grant

GRANT-ADAMSON, Lesley Ann; da of late Edwin Bethuel Heycock, and Edna May, *née* Puddefoot; *b* 26 November 1942; *Educ* Dame Alice Owen Sch Islington; *m* 14 Dec 1968, Andrew Duncan Grant-Adamson; *Career* author; journalist for several trade and technical magazines and local newspapers 1960–73, staff feature writer The Guardian 1973–80, freelance writer (The Times, The Observer, The Sunday Times, The Guardian) 1980–; writer in residence Nottingham Trent Univ and E Midlands Arts 1994, Royal Literary Fund writing fell Univ of Cambridge 2001–03, teacher Writing Crime Fiction City Univ 2004, private tutor in fiction writing, project fellowship Royal Literary Fund 2004–05; writer and prodr of documentaries for Channel 4 and S4C, teaches and lectures on writing popular fiction; memb: Welsh Acad, Soc of Authors, PEN, Crime Writers' Assoc (memb Ctee 1987–90, convenor E Anglian Chapter), Royal Soc of Literature, Int Crime Writers' Assoc, Debenham Soc, Nat Assoc of Writers in Educn; *Publications* Patterns in the Dust (1985), The Face of Death (1985), Guilty Knowledge (1986), Wild Justice (1987), Threatening Eye (1988), Curse the Darkness (1990), Flynn (1991), A Life of Adventure (1992), The Dangerous Edge (1993), Dangerous Games (1994), A Season in Spain (with Andrew Grant-Adamson, 1995), Wish You Were Here (1995), Evil Acts (1996), Writing Crime and Suspense Fiction (1996), The Girl in the Case (1997), Lipstick and Lies (1998), Undertow (1999), Music to be Murdered By (2000), Domestic Crime (2002), Writing Crime Fiction (2003), Writing Practically Anything (2006); play: Blood Red; short stories in numerous anthologies and magazines, essays on crime and suspense fiction in various anthologies and magazines; *Recreations* art galleries, photography, reading much too slowly, travelling; *Clubs* English Pen, Barbara Pym Soc, East Anglian Writers, Debenham History Soc, The Debenham Soc; *Style*— Ms Lesley Grant-Adamson; ✉ 22 High Street, Debenham, Suffolk IP14 6QJ (e-mail lesley@crimefiction.co.uk, website www.crimefiction.co.uk)

GRANT OF DALVEY, Sir Patrick Alexander Benedict; 14 Bt (NS 1688), of Dalvey; Chieftain of Clan Donnachaidh Grants; s of Sir Duncan Alexander Grant of Dalvey, 13 Bt (d 1961), of Polmaily, Glen Urquhart, Inverness-shire, and Joan Penelope, *née* Cope (d 1991); *b* 5 February 1953; *Educ* Fort Augustus Abbey Sch, Univ of Glasgow (LLB); *m* 1981 (m dis 2005), Dr Carolyn Elizabeth, da of Dr John Highet, of Pollokshields, Glasgow; 2 s (Duncan Archibald Ludovic b 1982, Neil Patrick b 21 Oct 1983); *Heir* s, Duncan Grant of Dalvey; *Career* deerstalker/gamekeeper 1969–71, inshore fisherman/skipper Scottish Highlands W Coast 1971–76; chm and md Grants of Dalvey Ltd 1987–; chm The Clan Grant Museum Tst, former chm The Clan Grant Soc; winner Queen's Award for Export 1992, Highland Business Award 1995; *Recreations* deerstalking, Scottish piping; *Clubs* New (Edinburgh); *Style*— Sir Patrick Grant of Dalvey, Bt; ✉ Tomintoul House, Flichity, Farr, Inverness-shire IV1 2XD; Grants of Dalvey Ltd, Alness, Ross-shire IV17 0XT

GRANT OF MONYMUSK, Sir Archibald; 13 Bt (NS 1705), of Cullen, Co Buchan; s of Capt Sir Francis Cullen Grant, 12 Bt (d 1966, himself tenth in descent from Archibald Grant, whose f d 1553 and whose er bro John was ancestor of the Barons Strathspey), by his w Jean, only da of Capt Humphrey Tollemache, RN (s of Hon Douglas Tollemache, 8 s of 1 Baron Tollemache); *b* 2 September 1954; *Educ* Trinity Coll Glenalmond, RAC Cirencester (Dip Farm Mgmnt); *m* 31 Dec 1982, Barbara Elizabeth, eldest da of Andrew Garden Duff Forbes, of Druminnor Castle, Rhynie, Aberdeenshire, and Mrs Alison Forbes; 2 da; *Career* farmer; *Recreations* hill walking, shooting, water divining; *Clubs* Royal Northern; *Style*— Sir Archibald Grant of Monymusk, Bt; ✉ House of Monymusk, Monymusk, Inverurie AB51 7HL (tel 01467 651220, office 01467 651333, fax 01467 651250)

GRANT PETERKIN, Joanna; da of Sir Brian Young, and Fiona Marjorie, *née* Stewart (d 1997); *Educ* Downe House, Wycombe HS, Univ of Durham (BA), Univ of Oxford (PGCE); *m* Maj-Gen Peter Grant Peterkin, CB, OBE, *qv*; 1 da (Alexandra (Mrs James Burton) b 1975), 1 s (James b 1977); *Career* St Paul's Girls' Sch: teacher 1989–96, advsr on univ entrance 1996–98; head St George's Sch Ascot 1999–2005, educn conslt 2005–; govr St John's Sch Leatherhead; tstee North Foreland Lodge Tst; *Recreations* playing the piano and cello, dance, film, visiting churches, most music; *Style*— Mrs Joanna Grant Peterkin; ✉ Grange Hall, Forres Moray IV36 2TR (tel 01309 672742); 2 Parliament Street, London SW1A 2LZ (tel 020 7219 0404, e-mail joannagrantpeterkin@lineone.net)

GRANT PETERKIN, Maj-Gen (Anthony) Peter; CB (2003), OBE (1990); s of Brig James A Grant Peterkin (d 1981), and Dorothea, *née* Chapman; *b* 6 July 1947; *Educ* Ampleforth, RMA Sandhurst, Univ of Durham (BA, MSc); *m* 1974, Joanna Grant Peterkin , *qv*, da of Sir Brian Young; 1 s, 1 da; *Career* Cdr 24 Airmobile Bde 1993–94, RCDS 1995, dep mil sec 1996–98, md OSCE mission to Kosovo 1999, GOC 5 Div 2000, mil sec and chief exec Army Personnel Centre 2001–03, serjeant at arms House of Commons 2005–; chm Army Cadet Force; chm Saigon Children's Charity; *Clubs* Army and Navy; *Style*— Maj-Gen Peter Grant Peterkin, CB, OBE; ✉ Grange Hall, Forres, Morayshire IV36 2TR (tel 01309 672742, e-mail petergp@yahoo.com)

GRANT-SUTTIE, Sir James Edward; 9 Bt (NS 1702); s of Sir (George) Philip Grant-Suttie, 8 Bt (d 1997); *b* 29 May 1965; *m* 1, 10 Nov 1989 (m dis), Emma Jane, yr da of Peter Craig, of Innerwick, E Lothian; 1 s (Gregor Craig b 29 Oct 1991); m 2, 1997, Sarah Jane, da of Alan and Pearl Smale; 2 s (Andrew b 10 July 1997, David Philip b 30 March 1999); *Heir* s, Gregor Grant-Suttie; *Style*— Sir James Grant-Suttie, Bt; ✉ Sheriff Hall Farm, North Berwick, East Lothian

GRANTCHESTER, 3 Baron (UK 1953); Christopher John Suenson-Taylor; s of 2 Baron Grantchester, CBE, QC (d 1995), and Betty, *née* Moores; *b* 8 April 1951; *Educ* Winchester, LSE (BSc); *m* 1973, Jacqueline, da of Dr Leo Jaffé; 2 da (Hon Holly Rachel b 1975, Hon Hannah Robyn b 1984), 2 s (Hon Jesse David b 1977, Hon Adam Joel b 1987); *Heir* s, Hon Jesse Suenson-Taylor; *Career* dairy farmer and cattle breeder; pres Western Holstein Club 1999–2000, chm SW Cheshire Dairy Assoc; pres and dir Royal Assoc of Br Dairy Farmers 2001–; former memb Cncl Holstein Soc Exec; former memb Cncl: RASE, Cheshire Agric Soc; Supreme Dairy Female RASE 1990 and 1991; dir: Five Six (Liverpool) Ltd, Assoc of Dairy Farmers Ltd; tstee Fndn for Sport and the Arts; *Recreations* soccer; *Style*— The Rt Hon the Lord Grantchester; ✉ Lower House Farm, Back Coole Lane, Audlem, Crewe, Cheshire (tel 01270 811363)

GRANTLEY, 8 Baron (GB 1782); Richard William Brinsley Norton; s of 7 Baron Grantley, MC (d 1995), and Lady Deirdre Elisabeth Freda Hare, da of 5 Earl of Listowel; *b* 30 January 1956; *Educ* Ampleforth, New Coll Oxford (MA, pres Oxford Union); *Heir* bro, Hon Francis Norton; *Career* merchant banker; Conservative Research Dept 1977–81, cllr RBK&C 1982–86, Parly candidate (Cons) 1983, former ldr UK Independence Pty in the House of Lords; former dir Morgan Grenfell Int Ltd, dir project and export fin HSBC Bank plc 1997–2005; Knight SMOM; *Recreations* Bridge; *Clubs* White's, Pratt's; *Style*— The Rt Hon the Lord Grantley; ✉ 8 Halsey Street, London SW3 2QH

GRANVILLE, 6 Earl (UK 1833); Granville George Fergus Leveson-Gower; also Viscount Granville, of Stone Park (UK 1815), and Baron Leveson, of Stone (UK 1833); s of 5 Earl Granville, MC (d 1996), and Doon Aileen, *née* Plunket; *b* 10 September 1959; *Educ* Eton; *m* 23 May 1997, Anne, da of Bernard Topping; 2 da (Lady Rose Alice b 16 April 1998, Lady Violet May b 5 Aug 2002), 1 s (Granville George James, Lord Leveson b 22 July 1999); *Heir* s, Lord Leveson; *Career* former page of honour to HM The Queen; *Style*— The Rt Hon the Earl Granville

GRATTAN, Dr Donald Henry; CBE (1989); s of Arthur Henry Grattan (d 1980), and Edith Caroline, *née* Saltmarsh (d 1980); family of Henry Grattan, Irish PM; *b* 7 August 1926; *Educ* Harrow Co GS, KCL (BSc), Open Univ (DUniv); *m* 1950, Valmai, da of Richard Edward Morgan (d 1978); 1 s (David), 1 da (Jennifer); *Career* jr research offr TRE Great Malvern 1945–46; sr master Chiswick GS 1946–50, sr master Downer GS 1950–56; TV prodr BBC 1956–61, ed further educn BBC 1961–63, head of continuing educn BBC TV 1963–71, controller educnl broadcasting BBC TV 1971–84; chm: UDACE (Unit for Devpt of Adult Continuing Educn) 1984–91, Nat Cncl for Educnl Technol 1985–91; vice-pres Marlow Soc 2001– (chm 1993–96); memb: Cncl Open Univ 1972–84, Cncl Educnl Technol 1972–84, Advsy Cncl for Adult and Continuing Educn 1979–83, Open Univ Visiting Ctee 1987–92, Open Coll Cncl 1987–89, RTS; FRSA 1988; *Publications* Science and the Builder, Mathematics Miscellany; *Style*— Dr Donald Grattan, CBE; ✉ Delabole, 3 Gossmore Close, Marlow, Buckinghamshire SL7 1QG (tel 01628 473571)

GRATTAN, Prof Kenneth Thomas Victor; s of William Grattan (d 1983), and Sarah Jane Grattan (d 1978); *b* 9 December 1953; *Educ* Watt's Endowed Sch, Lurgan Coll Co Armagh, Queen's Univ Belfast (BSc, Dunville Scholar, PhD), City Univ (DSc); *m* 28 Sept 1979, Lesley Sharon, da of Robert George Allen (d 2003); *Career* postdoctoral research asst Dept of Physics Imperial Coll of Sci and Tech London 1978–83; City Univ London: lectr in measurement and instrumentation 1983–87, sr lectr 1987–88, reader 1988–91, prof of measurement and instrumentation 1991–, head Dept of Electrical, Electronic & Information Engrg 1991–2001, assoc dean Sch of Engrg and Mathematical Sciences 2001–06 (dep dean 2006–); ed Measurement 2001–; numerous invited lectures and talks to professional bodies and int meetings; Liveryman Worshipful Co of Scientific Instrument Makers 1995 (steward 1998–); FInstP 1992 (memb 1984), FIET (FIEE 1992, memb 1985), FInstMC 1995 (memb 1986, Callendar Medal 1992, vice-pres 1996–99, pres 2000); *Publications* Concise Encyclopedia of Measurement and Instrumentation (with L Finkelstein, 1994), Optical Fiber Sensor Technology Vols I-V (with B T Meggitt, 1995, 1997, 1999 and 2000), Fiber Optic Fluorescence Thermometry (with Z Y Zhang, 1995); also author of over 600 papers on measurement, instrumentation and optics in leading int professional jls incl Physical Review, Review of Scientific Instruments, Sensors and Actuators and IEEE Transactions; *Recreations* philately, travel, photography, church affairs; *Style*— Prof Kenneth Grattan; ✉ School of Engineering and Mathematical Sciences, City University, Northampton Square, London EC1V 0HB (tel 020 7040 8120, fax 020 7040 8568, e-mail k.t.v.grattan@city.ac.uk)

GRATWICKE, His Hon Judge Charles James Phillip; s of Maj Phillip Gratwicke (d 1993), and Maeve, *née* Power (d 1978); *b* 25 July 1951, Taunton, Somerset; *Educ* St Bernadine's Franciscan Coll Buckingham, St John's Coll Southsea, Univ of Leeds (LLB); *m* 31 Aug 1981, Jane Vivien, *née* Meyer; 2 s (James Phillip b 19 Dec 1983, Robert Charles b 1 Nov 1987), 1 da (Amy Jane b 3 Feb 1986); *Career* called to the Bar Middle Temple 1974; barr 1974–2003, asst recorder 1998–2000, recorder 2000–03, circuit judge 2003–; pt/t chm Disciplinary Ctee: Potato Mktg Bd 1988–2003, Milk Mktg Bd 1990–2000; *Recreations* long distance walks, sailing, London in all its forms, marine paintings and all things maritime; *Clubs* Nat Lib Club, Seven Seas; *Style*— His Hon Judge Gratwicke; ✉ The Crown Court, New Street, Chelmsford CM1 1EL (tel 01245 603091)

GRAVES, Prof Norman John; s of George Alfred Graves (d 1977), of Worthing, W Sussex, and Andrée Adèle Céline, *née* Carrel (d 1986); *b* 28 January 1925; *Educ* Highbury County Sch, LSE, Univ of London (BScEcon, MA, PhD); *m* 28 July 1950, Mireille Camille, da of Camille Joseph Dourguin, Croix de Guerre, of Saint Rémy de Provence (d 1991); 2 c (Francis Alan, Hélène Monica (Mrs Scott) (twins) b 26 Feb 1954); *Career* school teacher 1950–60, lectr in educn Univ of Liverpool 1961–63, prof (formerly sr lectr, reader) Inst of Educn Univ of London 1963–, prof and pro dir Inst of Educn 1984–90; pres Geographical Assoc 1979, chm World Educn Fellowship 1985–90; FRGS (awarded Victoria Medal 1993); *Books* Geography in Secondary Education (1970), Geography in Education (1975–84), Curriculum Planning in Geography (1979), The Educational Crisis (1988), New UNESCO Source Book for Geography Teaching (ed, 1982), Initial Teacher Education: Politics and Progress (ed, 1990), Learner-Managed-Learning: Practice, Theory and Policy (ed, 1993), Working for a Doctorate (1997), Education and the Environment (ed, 1998), School Textbook Research: The Case of Geography 1800–2000 (2001); *Recreations* walking, gardening, decorating; *Style*— Prof Norman Graves; ✉ Institute of Education, University of London, 20 Bedford Way, London WC1H 0AL (tel 020 7612 6000, fax 020 7612 6126, e-mail n.graves@ioe.ac.uk)

GRAVESTOCK, Peter Stanley; s of Herbert Stanley Gravestock (d 1993), and Phyllis Gwendoline, *née* Bye (d 1995); *b* 6 June 1946; *Educ* West Bromwich GS; *m* 9 Dec 1973,

Cynthia Anne, da of Maj Philip John Radford (d 1993), of Walsall, W Midlands; 1 da (Elisabeth b 1977); *Career* sr lectr West Bromwich Coll of Commerce and Technol 1971–79 (lectr 1967–71), fndr ptnr Gravestock and Owen 1974–95, dir G & O Insurance Services Ltd 1995–2004; lectr in taxation; past pres Assoc of Taxation Technicians 1995–97; treas Worshipful Co of Tax Advisers; FCA 1967, FTII 1978, ATT 1990, FRSA; *Books* Tolleys Taxwise (jtly, published annually); *Recreations* travelling, walking, reading, National Trust; *Style*— Peter Gravestock, Esq

GRAY, Adam; s of David Mackrow Gray (d 2001), and Jillan Spensley, *née* Marsh Jones; *b* 21 October 1969; *Educ* Northampton Coll of FE; *Career* chef; Four Seasons Restaurant Inn on the Park Hotel London 1989–92, Le Manoir aux Quat'Saisons Oxford 1993–94, conslt chef Coral Reef Club Barbados 1994–95, head chef The Millennium Chelsea Hotel 1997–98, head chef Coast Restaurant London 1998–99 (Time Out Best Large Restaurant Award 1998), head chef city rhodes London 2001–03 (1 Michelin Star, 2 AA Rosettes, no 1 City Restaurant Hardens Restaurant Guide), head chef Rhodes Twenty Four 2003–; *Publications* Mushrooms - Recipes from Leading Chefs (1998); *Recreations* cycling, swimming; *Style*— Adam Gray, Esq; ✉ Rhodes Twenty Four, c/o Restaurant Associates UK, 166 High Holborn, London WC1V 6TT (tel 020 7301 2000, fax 020 7301 2319)

GRAY, Alasdair James; s of Alex Gray (d 1973), and Amy, *née* Fleming (d 1952); *b* 28 December 1934; *Educ* Whitehill Secdy Sch, Glasgow Sch of Art (BA); *m* 1, 1961, Inge Sørensen; 1 s (Andrew); m 2, 1991, Morag McAlpine; *Career* pt/t art teacher and muralist 1958–62, theatrical scene painter Pavilion Vaudeville and Glasgow Citizens' Theatre 1963–64, painter and playwright 1964–76, artist recorder Peoples' Palace Glasgow (local history museum) 1977, writer in residence Univ of Glasgow 1977–80, novelist and playwright 1981–; assoc prof of creative writing Glasgow Univ 2001–03; murals in: Scottish USSR Friendship Soc, Greenhead Church of Scotland Bridgeton, Belleisle Street Synagogue Glasgow, Greenfield Church of Scotland Clarkston, Palacerigg Nature Reserve, Abbots House History Museum Dunfermline 1995, Ubiquitous Chip Restaurant Glasgow 2000, Oran Mor Leisure Centre Glasgow 2004; memb Soc of Authors; *Awards* for writing incl: Scottish Arts Cncl, Saltire Soc, Times, Guardian 1993, Whitbread 1993; *Books* Lanark: A Life in Four Books (1981), Unlikely Stories Mostly (1983), 1982 Janine (1984), The Fall of Kelvin Walker (1985), Lean Tales (with James Kelman and Agnes Owen, 1985), Saltire Self Portrait (1988), Old Negatives: 4 Verse Sequences (1989), Something Leather (1990), McGrotty and Ludmilla (1990), Why Scots Should Rule Scotland 1992 (1992), Poor Things (1992), Ten Tales Tall and True (1993), A History Maker (1994), Mavis Belfrage and Four Shorter Stories (1996), Why Scots Should Rule Scotland 1997 (1997), Working Legs: A Play for People Without Them (1997), Introduction to the Book of Jonah (1999), The Book of Prefaces (2000), Sixteen Occasional Poems (2000), A Short Survey of Classic Scottish Writing (2001), The End of Their Tethers: Thirteen Sorry Stories (2003), Old Men in Love (2007); *Recreations* liking the English; *Style*— Alasdair Gray, Esq; ✉ 2 Marchmont Terrace, Glasgow G12 9LT (website www.alasdairgray.co.uk)

GRAY, Alistair William; s of John Lambert Gray (d 1980), of St Andrews, and Agnes Roberts, *née* Pow; *b* 6 September 1948; *Educ* Madras Coll St Andrews, Univ of Edinburgh (MA); *m* 7 April 1972, Sheila Elizabeth, da of Walter Harold Rose, of Preston, Lancs; 2 da (Kathryn Julia b 1976, Nicola Elizabeth b 1978); *Career* asst mill mangr Wiggins Teape Ltd 1970–72, divnl mangr Unilever Ltd 1972–78, exec dir John Wood Group plc 1978–81, dir strategic mgmnt consltg Arthur Young 1982–87, dir of strategy PA Consulting Group 1987–91 (assoc 1991–), fndr own co Genesis Consulting 1991–; non-exec dir: Highland Distilleries plc, AorTech International plc; chm Collections Group Ltd; visiting lectr Univ of Strathclyde; chm: Scottish Inst of Sport, Devpt Ctee Euro Hockey Fedn (memb Exec); hon pres Scottish Hockey Union; Burgess of Aberdeen 1980; FInstM, ACMA, MInstD, MIMgt, FIMC, MRSH; *Books* The Managers Handbook (1986); *Recreations* hockey, golf, squash; *Clubs* Western Hockey, New Golf (St Andrews), Royal Northern and Univ; *Style*— Alistair Gray, Esq

GRAY, Bernard Peter; s of Peter Michael Gray, of Weston, Herts, and Mary Angela, *née* Murphy; *b* 6 September 1960, Redhill, Surrey; *Educ* Hitchin Boy's GS, Univ of Oxford (MA), London Business Sch; *Career* FT Gp 1989–97 (sometime columnist Lex), MOD 1997–99, United Business Media 1999–2005 (latterly ceo CMP Information), chief exec TSL Education 2005–; non-exec dir Cable & Wireless 2003–; Def Journalist of the Year RAeS 1996; *Publications* Beginners' Guide to Investment (1991 and 1993); *Recreations* motor sport, opera, cinema; *Style*— Bernard Gray, Esq; ✉ TSL Education, Admiral House, 66–68 East Smithfield, London E1 1BX

GRAY, Bryan Mark; MBE (2001), DL (Lancs 2002); s of Clifford Benjamin Gray (d 2003), and June Mary, *née* Turner (d 2007); *b* 23 June 1953; *Educ* Wath-upon-Dearne GS, Univ of York (BA); *m* 31 July 1976, Lydia, *née* Wallbridge; 3 s (Robert b 12 April 1982, Philip b 29 May 1985, Michael b 24 May 1988); *Career* various positions ICI 1974–93, chief exec Baxi Group Ltd 1993–2000 (dep chm 2000–04), chm Baxi Technologies 2001–; chm Westmorland Ltd 2005–, non exec dir Energetix Gp plc 2006–, chm Urban Splash Hotels 2006–; chm CBI NW 2000–02, chm Northwest Devpt Agency 2002–; pres Soc of Br Gas Industries 2000–01, dep pres Assoc of European Heating Industries, chm Central Heating Information Cncl until 2003; memb Bd: NW Cultural Consortium 2003–, Liverpool Culture Co 2003–; memb LSC 2004–; memb Lake District Nat Park Authy 2006–, chm Lowther Castle and Gardens Tst 2007–; pro-chllr Lancaster Univ 2003–; hon prof Univ of Nottingham 2003–; vice-pres Preston North End FC (chm 1994–2001); tstee: Nat Museums Liverpool 2004–, Nat Football Museum (fndr chm until 2001); High Sheriff Lancs 2003–04; FRSA; *Recreations* reader Dio of Liverpool, life memb Nat Tst, football; *Style*— Bryan Gray, Esq, MBE, DL; ✉ Northwest Development Agency, Renaissance House, PO Box 37, Centre Park, Warrington WA1 1XB (tel 01925 400532, fax 01925 400404, mobile 07802 950222, e-mail bryan.gray@nwda.co.uk)

GRAY, Hon Mr Justice; Sir Charles Antony St John Gray; kt (1998); s of Charles Gray (d 1982), and Catherine, *née* Hughes (d 1986); *b* 6 July 1942; *Educ* Winchester, Trinity Coll Oxford (MA); *m* 1, 7 Sept 1967 (m dis 1990), Rosalind Macleod, da of Capt R F Whinney, DSO, RN, of Lymington, Hants; 1 da (Anya Catherine Macleod b 2 Nov 1972), 1 s (Alexander Charles Macleod b 14 Dec 1974); m 2, 4 May 1995, Susan (d 1997), da of late Maj Michael Eveleigh, and formerly w of Hon Sir John Jacob Astor, MBE, ERD, DL; m 3, 5 Jan 2001, Cynthia, da of late Ralph Walford Selby; *Career* called to the Bar Lincoln's Inn 1966 (bencher 1991); in practice London, QC 1984, recorder 1990, judge of the High Court of Justice (Queen's Bench Div) 1998–; hon fell Trinity Coll Oxford 2003; *Recreations* travel, music; *Clubs* Brooks's; *Style*— The Hon Mr Justice Gray; ✉ Royal Courts of Justice, Strand, London WC2A 2LL

GRAY, Sir Charles Ireland; kt (2007), CBE (1994), JP; s of Timothy Gray (d 1971), and Janet McIntosh, *née* Brown (d 1968); *b* 25 January 1929; *Educ* Coatbridge HS; *m* 14 June 1952, Catherine Creighton, da of James Gray; 3 s (Donald b 22 March 1953, James b 30 Sept 1955, Charles b 17 Sept 1958), 2 da (Rosemary b 12 July 1960, Jacqueline b 2 Oct 1964); *Career* served BR 40 years, ret; rep Chryston Lanark CC until 1974, first Lab chm Lanark's Ninth Dist Cncl, regnl memb Chryston/Kelvin Valley 1974, first vice-convener Strathclyde (former first chm Planning and Devpt Ctee), formerly convener Educn Ctee N Lanark Cncl; memb Bd Clydeport Authy 1974–85, former memb Sec of State's Advsy Ctee for Travelling People, chm Scottish National Housing and Town Planning Cncl 1975–85, vice-chm East Kilbride Devpt Corp 1974–86 (vice-chm Planning Exchange 1976–86), chm Local Govt Int Bureau (UK) 1992–94, vice-chm Bureau of Cncl Euro Municipalities and Regions (CEMR), ldr and vice-pres UK Delgn to Euro-Ctee of Regions 1994–98; memb Bd: Scot Devpt Agency 1975–85, SECC 1986–92; COSLA: ldr Lab Gp 1988, pres 1992–94; memb: Single Market Ctee Scottish Econ Cncl 1989, Euro Consultative Cncl Local and Regnl Authys 1989; FRSA; *Recreations* politics, music and reading; *Style*— Sir Charles Gray, CBE, JP; ✉ 9 Moray Place, Chryston, Glasgow G69 (tel 0141 779 2962, fax 0141 779 3142)

GRAY, (HE) (John) Charles Rodger; CMG (2004); s of Very Rev Dr John R Gray (d 1984), of Dunblane, Perthshire, and Mrs John R Gray; *b* 12 March 1953; *Educ* HS of Glasgow, Univ of Glasgow (MA); *m* 1988, Anne-Marie Lucienne Suzanne, *née* de Dax d'Axat; 3 s (Louis b 1995, Alexander b 1997, Thomas b 2000); *Career* diplomat; entered HM Dip Serv 1974, served West African Dept FCO 1974–76, third later second sec Warsaw 1976–79, Eastern European and Soviet Dept FCO 1979–83, UK Delgn to OECD Paris 1983–87, on secondment to Cabinet Office 1987–89; FCO: dep head Central African Dept 1989, dep head Central European Dept 1989–92, head Eastern Adriatic Dept 1992–93; cnsllr and head of Chancery Jakarta 1993–96, fell Center for Int Affrs Harvard Univ 1996–97, cnsllr Washington 1997–2001; FCO: attached to Counter Terrorism Policy Dept 2001, head Middle East Dept 2002–04, Iran co-ordinator 2004–05; ambass to Morocco 2005–; *Recreations* history; *Clubs* New (Edinburgh); *Style*— Charles Gray, Esq, CMG; ✉ c/o Foreign & Commonwealth Office (Rabat), King Charles Street, London SW1A 2AH

GRAY, David; s of John Allan Gray (d 1993), of Leeds, and Vena Isabel, *née* Woods; *b* 9 January 1955; *Educ* Leeds GS, Univ of Cambridge; *m* 26 May 1984, Julie Marie, da of Anthony Sergeant; *Career* Eversheds: joined as trainee 1977, equity ptnr 1982, head of corp Leeds and Manchester 1995, head of corp and dep managing ptnr Leeds and Manchester 1998, regnl managing ptnr Leeds and Manchester 2000, managing ptnr 2003–; involved with Cares Prog; *Recreations* golf, racing, Liverpool FC; *Clubs* Alwoodley Golf, Wetherby Steeplechasing; *Style*— David Gray, Esq; ✉ Eversheds, 85 Queen Victoria Street, London EC4V 4JL (tel 020 7919 4500, fax 020 7919 4919, mobile 07721 612580, e-mail davidgray@eversheds.com)

GRAY, David John; s of James Vincent Gray (d 1989), of Liverpool, and Jeanne Winifred Veronica, *née* Lamb; *b* 2 March 1959; *Educ* Liverpool Bluecoat Sch, Univ of Bristol (BA); *m* 18 April 1962, Hilary Jane Rosemary, *née* Fletcher; 1 da (Olivia Scarlet b 22 Aug 1994); *Career* display sales exec Centaur Communications 1984–85, account mangr Pilgrim Communications 1985–87, planning dir Design in Action until 1996 (joined 1987), fndr ptnr The Creative Leap 1996–; *Recreations* mountaineering, cookery; *Style*— David Gray, Esq

GRAY, Prof Douglas; s of Emmerson Walton Gray, and Daisy Gray; *b* 17 February 1930; *Educ* Wellington Coll NZ, Victoria Univ of Wellington (MA), Univ of Oxford (MA); *m* 3 Sept 1959, Judith Claire, da of Percy Campbell; 1 s (Nicholas b 1961); *Career* asst lectr Victoria Univ of Wellington 1953–54; Univ of Oxford: lectr in English Pembroke and Lincoln Colls 1956–61, fell in English Pembroke Coll 1961–80 (emeritus fell 1980–), univ lectr in English language 1976–80, JRR Tolkien prof of English literature and language 1980–97, professorial fell Lady Margaret Hall 1980–97 (hon fell 1997–); Hon LittD Victoria Univ of Wellington 1995; FBA 1989; *Books* Themes & Images in the Medieval English Religious Lyric (1972), A Selection of Religious Lyrics (1975), Robert Henryson (1979), The Oxford Book of Late Medieval Verse and Prose (1985), Selected Poems of Robert Henryson and William Dunbar (1998), The Oxford Companion to Chaucer (2003); *Style*— Prof Douglas Gray, FBA; ✉ Lady Margaret Hall, Oxford OX2 6QA (tel 01865 274300)

GRAY, Duncan Alexander James; *b* 3 January 1968; *Educ* Robert Gordon's Coll Aberdeen, UC Oxford (BA, pres Oxford Union); *Partner* Eve Tomlinson; 2 c (Louie b 18 November 1997, Teddy b 27 July 2000); *Career* researcher GLR 1989–90 (Round at Chris's), writer Londoner's Diary Evening Standard 1991; Planet 24: devpt writer and researcher 1991–92 (Big Breakfast), researcher 1992 (The Best of The Word 2), asst prodr 1992 (The Big Breakfast End of Year Show), asst prodr 1992–93 (The Word), devpt prodr 1993, prodr 1993–94 (The Word), series prodr 1994 (Surf Potatoes), series ed 1994–95 (The Word); prodr Talk Back Productions 1995–96 (Brass Eye), creative dir Planet 24 USA 1996–97; exec prodr: Planet 24 1997–98 (The Big Breakfast), Channel Four TV Corp 1997–98 (Jo Whiley Show); controller of entertainment: Granada TV 1998–2003, Granada Content 2002–03, head of entertainment and reality programming ABC Television 2003–06, controller of entertainment ITV 2006–; *Style*— Duncan Gray, Esq; ✉ ITV plc, 200 Grays Inn Road, London WC1V 8HX

GRAY, (Edna) Eileen Mary; CBE (1997, OBE 1978); da of William Thomas Greenway (d 1957), of Reigate, Surrey, and Alice Evelyn Mary, *née* Jenkins (d 1983); *b* 25 April 1920; *Educ* St Saviour's and St Olave's GS for Girls London; *m* 24 Aug 1946, Walter Herbert Gray (d 2001), s of Walter James Gray (d 1947), of London; 1 s (Dr John Andrew Gray b 25 Nov 1947); *Career* Inspectorate Fighting Vehicles 1940–45; invited to ride abroad Br women's cycling team 1946, int delg Paris 1957, organiser first int competition for women in UK 1957, campaigner for int recognition of women in cycling and team mangr inaugural women's world championship 1958, memb Exec Ctee Br Cycling Fedn 1958–87 (chm Fin Ctee, pres), elected to Fedn International Amateur de Cyclism 1977, chm Br Sports Forum 1991, memb Manchester Olympic Bid Ctee 1991, dep cmdt British Olympic Team 1992, vice-pres BOA 1992– (vice-chm 1988–92); int official Cwlth Games Edmonton and Brisbane, special Gold award Min of Educn Taiwan; tstee London Marathon Tst; chm London Youth Games; vice-pres: Cyclists Touring Club 2000, Br Sch Cycling Assoc 2001; Royal Borough of Kingston upon Thames: cncllr 1982–98, pres Kingston Sports Cncl, Mayor 1990–91; awarded Olympic Order IOC 1993; Freeman City of London 1987, Grandmaster Hon Fraternity of Ancient Freemasons (women) and tstee of its charity; *Style*— Mrs Eileen Gray, CBE; ✉ 129 Grand Avenue, Surbiton, Surrey KT5 9HY (tel 020 8399 0068)

GRAY, George Bovill Rennie; OBE (1991); s of John Rennie Gray (d 1937), of Smeaton-Hepburn, E Lothian, and Margaret, *née* Bovill (d 1958); *b* 5 March 1920; *Educ* Clayesmore Iwerne Minster, E of Scotland Coll of Agric; *m* 30 Jan 1946, Anne Constance, da of John Robert Dale, of Auldhame, N Berwick; 4 s (John b Dec 1946, Kenneth b May 1948, Duncan b Sept 1949, Quentin b Feb 1954), 2 da (Ruth b June 1952, Joanna b Sept 1956); *Career* chm: G B R Gray Ltd (farmers) 1952–, Hanover (Scotland) Housing Assoc Ltd 1991–95; dir Moredun Scientific Ltd 1989–97; convenor Cereals Ctee NFU Scot 1955–58; dir: Scottish Soc for Res in Plant Breeding 1957–87, Animal Diseases Res Assoc Moredun 1958–93; memb: Pig Industry Devpt Authy 1958–68, Agric and Vet Sub-Ctee of UGC 1972–82, Scottish Advsy Bd Br Inst of Mgmnt 1978–90; elder Church of Scotland 1952–; tstee Scottish Soc for Crop Research; memb: Boy Scout Assoc E Lothian, Cncl Garleton Div Lothian Regnl Cncl 1974–82; FIMgt 1978; *Recreations* gardening, arboriculture; *Style*— George Gray, Esq, OBE; ✉ Smeaton-Hepburn, East Linton, East Lothian EH40 3DT (tel 01620 860275)

GRAY, Dr George Gowans; CBE (1999); *b* 21 January 1938; *Educ* Linlithgow Acad, Univ of Edinburgh (BSc), Univ of Cambridge (PhD); *Career* engr: Pratt & Whitney Canada 1960–63, RCA Ltd Canada 1963–69; researcher Univ of Cambridge 1969–71, md Serv Div RCA Ltd Sunbury-on-Thames 1974–87 (mangr 1971–74), chm Serco Group plc 1987–99, ret; non-exec dir: Misys plc 1996–2002, Regus Business Centres plc 1999–2002; chm Nat Physical Lab 1995–2002, memb PPARC 2003–05; memb Ct and Cncl Imperial Coll London 2004– (dep chm 2006–); FIMechE 1990; *Publications* contrib with K L Johnson: Journal of Sound and Vibration (1972), The Institution of Mechanical Engineers

G

Proceedings (1975); *Clubs* Oxford and Cambridge, Wentworth Golf; *Style—* Dr George Gray, CBE

GRAY, Henry Withers; s of Henry Withers Gray (d 1958), and Jean Allen, *née* Cross (d 1994); *b* 25 March 1943; *Educ* Rutherglen Acad, Univ of Glasgow (MD); *m* 5 July 1967, Mary Elizabeth, da of Angus Henry Shaw, BEM (d 1996), of Arbeadie Rd, Banchory, Aberdeenshire; 1 s (Stuart Henry b 1968), 2 da ((Elizabeth) Anne b 1970, Karen Louise b 1981); *Career* conslt physician in med and nuclear med 1977–2007, ret; FRCP 1978, FRCPG 1984, FRCR 2003; *Style—* Henry Gray, Esq; ✉ 4 Winton Park, E Kilbride, Glasgow G75 8QW (tel 01355 229525); The Department of Nuclear Medicine, The Royal Infirmary, Alexandra Parade, Glasgow (tel 0141 211 4761, fax 0141 211 4386, e-mail hwg1q@clinmed.gla.ac.uk); Student Health Service, University of Strathclyde, Livingstone Tower, 26 Richmond Street, Glasgow G1 1XH (tel 0141 548 3916, fax 0141 548 4729)

GRAY, James; MP; s of late Very Rev John R Gray, and Dr Sheila Gray; *b* 7 November 1954; *Educ* Glasgow HS, Univ of Glasgow, Christ Church Oxford; *m* Sarah; 2 s (John, William), 1 da (Olivia); *Career* mgmnt trainee P&O 1977–78, shipbroker and dept mangr Anderson Hughes Ltd 1978–84, md GNI Freight Futures Ltd 1985–92, sr mangr GNI Ltd (futures brokers) 1990–92, special advsr to Michael Howard, MP and then John Gummer, MP as secs of state for the environment 1992–95, dir Westminster Strategy Ltd (public affrs conslts) 1995–97, MP (Cons) Wiltshire N 1997– (Parly candidate Ross, Cromarty and Skye 1992); House of Commons: oppn whip 2000–01, shadow min for defence 2001–02, shadow min for environment, food and rural affairs 2002–05, shadow sec of state for Scotland 2005, memb DETR Select Ctee 1997–2000, memb DEFRA Select Ctee 2007–, vice-chm Parly Gp for Mongolia 2002–, chm Parly Gp on MS 2003–, chm Parly Gp for Army 2004–, memb Cons Defence and Security Policy Gp 2006–07; dep chm Wandsworth Tooting Cons Assoc 1994–96 (previously vice-chm and branch chm), chm Cons Rural Action Gp 2003–04; memb Baltic Exchange 1978–91 and 1997–, dir Baltic Futures Exchange 1989–91; grad RCDS 2003; vice-chm Charities Property Assoc 2001–; pres Chippenham Branch Multiple Sclerosis Soc; chm Horse and Pony Taxation Ctee 1999–2002, conslt Br Horse Ind Confedn 1999–2002, pres Assoc of Br Riding Schs 2002–; Freeman City of London; memb Ct of Assts HAC 2002–07; *Books* Financial Risk Management (1985), Futures and Options for Shipping (1987, winner Lloyd's of London Book Prize), Shipping Futures (1990), Crown in Parliament: Who Decides on Going to War (2004); *Recreations* the countryside and riding horses, British heritage and local history; *Clubs* Pratt's, Chippenham Constitutional (pres), Wootton Bassett Cons, HAC (vice-pres Saddle); *Style—* James Gray, Esq, MP; ✉ House of Commons, London SW1A 0AA (tel 020 7219 6237)

GRAY, Prof John Clinton; s of William John Gray (d 1998), and Edith Grace, *née* Tooke (d 1993); *b* 9 April 1946; *Educ* Sir Joseph Williamson's Mathematical Sch Rochester, Simon Langton GS Canterbury, Univ of Birmingham (BSc, PhD), Univ of Cambridge (MA); *m* 1971 Julia, *née* Hodgetts; 1 s (Christopher Clinton b 12 June 1977), 1 da (Stephanie Louise b 25 July 1980); *Career* univ research fell Univ of Birmingham 1970–73, research biochemist UCLA 1973–75; Univ of Cambridge: SRC fell 1975–76, demonstrator 1976–80, lectr 1980–90, reader in plant molecular biology 1990–96, prof of plant molecular biology Dept of Plant Sciences 1996–, head Dept of Plant Sciences 2003–; science research fell Nuffield Fndn 1983–84, sr research fell Royal Soc Leverhulme Tst 1991–92; non-exec dir Horticulture Research International 1997–2003; memb SERC Biological Sciences Ctee 1990–93, memb Cncl Sainsbury Lab 1999–; tstee Science and Plants for Schools (SAPS) 1991–, plant science advsr Gatsby Charitable Fndn 1996–; memb EMBO 1994–; *Publications* Ribulose Bisphosphate Carboxylase-Oxygenase (ed with R J Ellis, 1986), Plant Trichomes (ed with D L Hallahan, 2000); also author of papers in scientific jls; *Recreations* growing plants, mountains; *Clubs* Midlands Assoc of Mountaineers; *Style—* Prof John Gray; ✉ 47 Barrons Way, Comberton, Cambridge CB3 7EQ; Department of Plant Sciences, University Cambridge, Downing Street, Cambridge CB2 3EA (tel 01223 333925, fax 01223 333953, e-mail jcg2@mole.bio.cam.ac.uk); Robinson College, Grange Road, Cambridge CB3 9AN

GRAY, John F; s of Frederick Gray (d 2006), and Miriam Gray (d 1980); *b* 27 January 1944; *Educ* Thomas Richard's Tech Inst Tredegar, Coll of Distributive Trades London (DipCAM); *m* Sandra, da of D Reginald Jones; 1 da (Louise b 13 Aug 1976); *Career* successively admin offr, admin mangr and promotions mangr Methodist Assoc of Youth Clubs 1969–77 (elected hon pres 1976), launched Fundraising Dept Methodist Homes for the Aged 1977–81, dir advocacy National Children's Home 1980–90, with Princess Royal Tst for Carers 1990–91; dir corporate communications Br Red Cross 1991–2000, chm European Red Cross and Red Crescent Public Support Gp 1992–2001, vice-chm International Red Cross and Red Crescent Communications Forum 1996–2001, public affrs advsr Br Red Cross 2000–, advsr on global fundraising practices International Red Cross and Red Crescent Movement; md Stayahead Consultancy 2000–, chief exec UCL Charitable Fndn 2007–; chm London Inst of Fundraisers 1991–95, co-fndr and fell Inst of Charity Fundraising Mangrs (exec memb 1982–88, chm Int Ctee 1997–), chm European Fundraising Network 1999–2002, pres European Fundraising Assoc (EFA) 2002–05; memb: Marketing Soc of GB, American Nat Soc of Fundraising Execs, IPR Fellows Forum 1996–; memb Editorial Bd Charity Magazine 1995–98; frequent guest lectr at various fundraising and communications confs; external examiner DipPR CAM 1993–; memb Appeal Ctee Central Hall Westminster 1992–99, tstee IPR Benevolent Fund 1999–2004; pres St David's Day in London Celebration 2004–05 (vice-pres 2002–04); lay preacher Methodist Church; Freeman City of London, Liveryman Worshipful Co of Feltmakers, memb Ct Guild of PR Practitioners 2000 (Master 2004); FIPR, MIPR 1976, FRSA, FCAM 2000; *Awards* National Children's Home Order of St Christopher 1989, Br Red Cross Badge of Honour for Distinguished Service 1997, named as one of PRWeek's 100 most influential PR figures in the UK 2005, named int the PR Week Power Book as one of the most influential people in PR 2007; *Books* Organizing Special Events (co-author, 2000); *Recreations* music, theatre, travel; *Clubs* Royal Over-Seas League; *Style—* John F Gray, Esq; ✉ 47 Downside Close, Eastbourne, East Sussex BN20 8EL (tel 01323 646699, e-mail johnfgray@btconnect.com)

GRAY, John Malcolm; CBE (1996); s of Samuel Alexander Gray (d 1958), and Ellen Christina, *née* Mackay-Sim (d 1990); *b* 28 July 1934; *Educ* Strathallan Sch; *m* 1, 1966 (m dis 1979), Nicole de Fournier, da of Ellis Melville Quinn, of Tasmania; 2 da (Siobhan Laetitia Mackay b 1967, Katrina Mackay b 1970); m 2, 1984, Ursula Wee Siong Koon, da of Dato Wee Khoon Hock, of Khota Bahru, Malaysia; 1 da (Alexandra Mackay b 1985); *Career* served RAF 1952–54; Hongkong and Shanghai Banking Corporation Ltd: joined 1954, accountant Hamburg 1970–73, mangr Frankfurt 1973–75, mangr foreign exchange Hong Kong 1975–79, chief accountant 1979–81, asst gen mangr finance 1981–85, gen mangr gp finance 1985–86, exec dir finance 1986–90, dep chm 1990–92, chm and chief exec 1993–96; dir HSBC Holdings plc 1992–96; memb Hong Kong Exec Cncl 1993–95, chm Hong Kong Port Devpt Bd 1991–96, memb Airport Authy of Hong Kong 1991–96; dir: World Maritime Ltd 1985–, Harvey Nichols Group plc 1996–, Nordstrom & Thulin AB 1997–; *Recreations* golf, reading; *Clubs* Hong Kong, Royal Hong Kong Golf, Shek-O, Oriental (London); *Style—* John Gray, Esq, CBE; ✉ c/o The Hongkong and Shanghai Banking Corporation Ltd, Level 34, 1 Queen's Road, Central, Hong Kong (tel 00 852 822 1123)

GRAY, Prof John Nicholas; s of Nicholas Chatt Wardle Gray (d 1985), and Joan, *née* Bushby (d 1990); *b* 17 April 1948, South Shields, Tyne and Wear; *Educ* South Shields Grammar-Tech Sch for Boys, Exeter Coll Oxford (MA, DPhil); *m* 1988, Mieko, *née* Kawai; *Career* lectr in political theory Univ of Essex 1973–76, fell and tutor in politics Jesus Coll Oxford 1976–98, prof of politics Univ of Oxford 1996–98, prof of European thought LSE 1998–2007, emeritus prof Univ of London 2008–; visiting prof in govt Harvard Univ 1986, Olmstead visiting prof in social philosophy Yale Univ 1994; Hon DUniv Open Univ 2006; *Publications* Mill on Liberty: A Defence (1983, 2 edn 1996), Hayek on Liberty (1984, 3 edn 1998), Liberalism (1986, 2 edn 1995), Liberalisms: Essays in Political Philosophy (1989), Post-Liberalism: Studies in Political Thought (1993), Beyond the New Right: Markets, Government and the Common Culture (1993), Enlightenment's Wake: Politics and Culture at the Close of the Modern Age (1995), Isaiah Berlin (1995), Endgames: Questions in Late-Modern Political Thought (1997), Voltaire and Enlightenment (1998), False Dawn: The Delusions of Global Capitalism (1998, 3 edn 2002), Two Faces of Liberalism (2000), Straw Dogs: Thoughts on Humans and Other Animals (2002), Al Qaeda and What It Means To Be Modern (2003, 2 edn 2007), Heresies: Against Progress and Other Illusions (2004), The Political Theory of John Gray (contrib, 2007), Black Mass: Apocalyptic Religion and the Death of Utopia (2007); *Clubs* Beefsteak; *Style—* Prof John Gray; ✉ c/o Tracy Bohan, The Wylie Agency UK, 17 Bedford Square, London WC1B 3JA (tel 020 7908 5900, fax 020 7908 5901, e-mail tbohan@wylieagency.co.uk)

GRAY, Keith Sydney; *b* 19 February 1972; *Educ* The Lindsey Sch Cleethorpes; *Career* author of children's books; *Books* Creepers (1996, shortlisted Guardian Children's Fiction Award 1997), From Blood: Two Brothers (1997, nominated for Library Assoc Carnegie Medal 1998), Hunting the Cat (1997), Dead Trouble (1997), Happy (1998), The Runner (1998, winner Silver Medal Smarties' Children's Book Award 1998), £10,000 (2001), Warehouse (2002, shortlisted Guardian Children's Fiction Award 2002, shortlisted Scot Arts Cncl Book Awards 2003, winner Angus Book Award 2003), Malarkey (2003, shortlisted Book Trust Teenage Prize 2003); *Style—* Keith Gray, Esq; ✉ c/o London Independent Books, 26 Chalcot Crescent, London NW1 8YD (tel 020 7706 0486); website www.keith-gray.com

GRAY, Dr Kenneth Walter (Ken); CBE (1992); s of Robert Walter Gray (d 1994), of Bracklesham Bay, W Sussex, and Ruby May, *née* Rofe (d 1978); *b* 20 March 1939; *Educ* Blue Coat Sch Liverpool, Univ of Wales (BSc, PhD), RCDS; *m* 29 Dec 1962 (m dis 2006), Jill, da of William Hartley Henderson; 1 da (Carole Elizabeth b 1964), 2 s (Neil Kenneth b 1966, Ian Kenneth b 1968); *Career* Nat Research Cncl of Canada post-doctoral fell in magnetic resonance Univ of Br Columbia Vancouver 1963–65, researcher in semi-conductor devices and radiometry N American Rockwell Science Center California 1965–70; Royal Signals and Radar Estab (RSRE): research in devices and systems 1971, supt Solid State Physics and Devices Div 1976–79, head Physics Gp 1979–82, dep dir applied physics (CSO) RSRE/MOD 1982–84, dep dir info systems (under sec) 1984; EMI Group plc (formerly Thorn EMI plc): dir of research 1984–86, tech dir 1986–97, exec chm Thorn Software 1987–89, tech dir Thorn Security and Electronics 1991–93, md Thorn Transaction 1993–97; chm: Scipher plc 1996–2004, Ocean Blue Software 2006–, London Biofuels 2006–; non-exec dir British Steel plc 1995–99; visiting research fell Univ of Newcastle 1972–74, visiting research fell Univ of Leeds 1976–, visiting prof Univ of Nottingham 1986–; author of over 30 scientific and technical papers in learned jls; memb: Innovation Advsy Bd DTI 1988–93, SERC 1991–94, Technology Foresight Steering Gp 1992–96, HE Funding Cncl of Wales 1996–2002; Hon DSc Nottingham Trent Univ 1997; FInstP 1991, FIEE 1992, FREng 1996; *Style—* Dr Ken Gray, CBE, FREng

GRAY, Prof Kevin John; s of the late Bryce Holmes Gray, and Priscilla Margaret, *née* McCullough; *b* 23 July 1951; *Educ* Trinity Hall Cambridge (MA, PhD, LLD, Yorke prize), Univ of Oxford (DCL); *m* 1996, Susan, da of late Arthur Walter David Francis and late Helen, *née* Waggott; *Career* fell Queens' Coll Cambridge 1975–81, lectr in law Univ of Cambridge 1978–90, fell Trinity Coll Cambridge 1981–90, advocate 1986–88, research fell ANU 1990 (visiting fell 1979, 1989, 1998 and 2005–06), Drapers' prof of law Univ of London 1991–93, sr research fell St John's Coll Oxford 1993–94, prof of law Univ of Cambridge 1993–, professorial fell Trinity Coll Cambridge 1993– (dean 2006– (actg dean 2004–05)); visiting prof: Univ of Osaka 2001, Univ of NSW 2003, Univ of Stellenbosch 2005, Univ of Tasmania 2006, Nat Univ of Singapore 2006 and 2007; overseas research fell Nat Research Fndn of South Africa 2005; called to the Bar Middle Temple 1993; memb Soc of Legal Scholars 1975, assoc memb Académie Internationale de Droit Comparé 1995, memb peer review coll Arts and Humanities Research Cncl (AHRC) 2004–; jr and sr int athlete 1968–69, memb Access and Conservation Ctee Br Mountaineering Cncl 2002–; FBA 1999; *Books* Reallocation of Property on Divorce (1977), Elements of Land Law (1987, 4 edn with S F Gray 2005), Land Law (with S F Gray, 1999, 5 edn 2007); *Recreations* mountaineering and rock climbing; *Style—* Prof Kevin Gray, FBA; ✉ Trinity College, Cambridge CB2 1TQ (tel and fax 01223 314520, e-mail kjg10@cam.ac.uk)

GRAY, (Stephen) Marius; s of Basil Gray, CB, CBE (d 1989), of Long Wittenham, Oxon, and Nicolete Mary Gray, *née* Binyon (d 1997); *b* 3 August 1934; *Educ* Westminster, New Coll Oxford (MA); *m* 2 Sept 1961, Clare Anthony, da of Sir Anthony Horace Milward, CBE (d 1981); 3 da (Emma b 1962, Bridget b 1967, Jacquetta b 1971), 1 s (Theodore b 1964); *Career* Nat Serv 2 Lt RCS 1953–55; CA 1962; sr ptnr Dixon Wilson 1981–98 (ptnr 1967–81); non-exec dir: Davies Turner Ltd 1970–2002, Abingworth Management Ltd 1973–2001 (chm 1994–2001), Folkestone Ltd 1977–94, British Biotech plc 1982–99, Associated Newspapers Holdings plc 1983–, Daily Mail and General Tst plc 1985–, East German Investment Trust plc 1993–2001; chm of special tstees The London Hosp 1974–2000, govr The London Hosp Med Coll 1984–89, chm Mgmnt Ctee The King's Fund 1985–98, tstee London Library 2003–; FCA; *Clubs* Savile; *Style—* Marius Gray, Esq; ✉ 47 Maze Hill, London SE10 8XQ (fax 020 8858 0464, e-mail mariusgray@aol.com); c/o Dixon Wilson, Rotherwick House, PO Box 900, 3 Thomas More Street, London E1 9YX (tel 020 7680 8100, fax 020 7680 8101, e-mail dw@dixonwilson.co.uk)

GRAY, (H) Martin V; *Career* chief exec NatWest UK 1992–99, main bd dir National Westminster Bank plc 1993–99; memb Bd Mastercard Inc 1993–96, dir Visa Europe 1996–99; non-exec chm Evolution Gp plc 2005–; non-exec dir National Savings and Investments; *Style—* Martin Gray, Esq

GRAY, Matthew Walter; s of Matthew Dunlop Ferguson Gray (d 1982), and Eileen Mary, *née* Joyce (d 1989); *b* 18 April 1969, Elderslie, Renfrewshire; *Educ* Gryffe HS Houston, Napier Poly Edinburgh (BA); *Career* head chef Inverlochy Castle Hotel Fort William 2001– (3 AA Rosettes 2001–, 1 Michelin Star 2001–); *Style—* Matthew Gray, Esq; ✉ 4 Caledonian Apartments, Guisach Terrace, Corpach, Fort William PH33 7JN; Inverlochy Castle Hotel, Torlundy, Fort William PH33 6SN (tel 01397 702177, fax 01397 702953, e-mail info@inverlochy.co.uk)

GRAY, Lt-Gen Sir Michael Stuart; KCB (1986), OBE (1971), DL (East Riding of Yorkshire, 1996); s of Lt Cdr Frank Gray, RNVR (ka 1940); *b* 3 May 1932; *Educ* Christ's Hosp, RMA Sandhurst; *m* 1958, Juliette Antonia; 3 c; *Career* enlisted 1950, RHA, RMAS 1951, cmmnd E Yorks Regt 1952 (served Malayan Emergency 1953–56), transferred Parachute Regt 1956, Army Staff College 1963, CO 1 Para 1969–71, instr Staff Coll 1971–73 (UN SOMOC course Sweden 1972), COS HQ 1 Armoured Div BAOR 1973–75, RCDS 1976, Cdr 16 Parachute Bde 1977, Cdr 6 Field Force and COMUKMF 1977–79, Cdr Br Army Staff and Mil Attaché Washington DC (with additional responsibilities of Head Br Def Staff and Def Attaché 1980 and Mil Advsr to the Govr of Bermuda) 1979–81, GOC SW Dist 1981–83, COS HQ BAOR 1984–85, GOC SE Dist (cmd Joint Force HQ) 1985–88, ret 1988;

Hon Col 10 Para (V) 1984–90, Col Cmdt The Parachute Regt 1990–93 (dep Col Cmdt 1986–90), Hon Col 250 (Hull) Field Ambulance (V) RAMC 1991–98; chief exec Rainford Developments 1992–99; non-exec chm: June Cadman Care 1993–98, Thelma Turner Homes 1997–2001; conslt Brittany Ferries 1985–2000; defence industries advsr: Wardle Storeys plc, Irvin-GQ Parachutes Ltd (Airborne Systems) 1988–2007; Lt HM Tower of London 1995–98; chm MS&P (Rosedale) Ltd (Milburn Arms Hotel Rosedale Abbey) 2002–; pres King George's Fund for Sailors E Yorks Ctee 2000– (chm and tstee 1990–2000), chm and tstee: Airborne Assault Normandy Tst 1978–, Mil and Aerospace (Aldershot) Tst 1989–98, June Cadman Charitable Tst 1994–2000; Normandy Veterans Assoc: nat vice-pres, pres Grimsby/Leeds Branch 1989–, vice-pres Goole Branch; tstee: Airborne Forces Museum 1969–99, Airborne Forces Security Fund 1986–; pres York Branch PRA, vice-pres Tyneside Branch PRA 1990–, vice-pres Army Parachute Assoc 1988–; patron: Combined Ex Services Assoc Bridlington 1990–, Yorks Air Museum 1995–; memb Amicable Soc of Blues 1989– (pres 2007); memb Cncl BESO 2001–03 (dep patron 2003–05); chair IRVIN-GQ Museum Tst 2003–; vice-pres: The French Assoc (ASPEG) 1971–78, Beverley and Dist Civic Soc 1996–; Hon Bro The Hull Trinity House 1999–; Freeman City London 1982; FCMI, FInstD, MICFM; Officier de l'Ordre National de la Legion d'Honneur France 1994; *Recreations* military history, reading, photography, gardening; *Clubs* Army and Navy; *Style*— Lt-Gen Sir Michael Gray, KCB, OBE, DL; ✉ Endevour House, Cooper's End Road, Stanstead, Essex CM24 1SJ

GRAY, Paul Richard Charles; CB (2000); s of Rev Sidney Albert Gray (d 1981), of Thaxted, Essex, and Ina, *née* Maxey; *b* 2 August 1948; *Educ* Wyggeston Boys Sch, LSE (BSc); *m* 15 April 1972, Lynda Elsie, da of James Benjamin Braby, of Loughton, Essex; 2 s (Simon b 1978, Adam b 1980); *Career* HM Treasy 1969–77, corp planning exec Booker McConnell Ltd 1977–79; HM Treasy: princ Agric Div 1979–83, asst sec Gen Expenditure Div 1984–86, asst sec Industry and Employment Div 1987, economic affrs private sec to PM 1988–90, under sec Monetary Gp 1990–93, dir of personnel finance and support 1994–95, dir of budget and public finances 1995–98; joined DSS 1998, second perm sec and md of pensions and disability Dept of Work and Pensions 2001–04, chm HM Revenue and Customs 2006– (dep chm 2004–); non-exec dir Laing Management Ltd 1993–94; *Recreations* family, walking, Wensleydale sheep, gardening; *Style*— Paul Gray, Esq, CB

GRAY, Peter Francis; s of Rev George Francis Selby Gray; *b* 7 January 1937; *Educ* Marlborough, Trinity Coll Cambridge; *m* 1978, Fiona Bristol; 2 s (Augustus b 1979, Julius b 1981); *Career* Nat Serv Lt Royal Fus attached to 4 King's African Rifles Uganda 1956–58; with HM Foreign Serv 1963–64, SG Warburg & Co 1964–66, Cooper Brothers & Co 1966–69, Samuel Montagu & Co 1970–77, head Investment Div Crown Agents for Oversea Govts and Admins 1977–83, md Touche Remnant & Co 1983–87, dep chm The Assoc of Investment Tst Cos 1985–87; chm: Gray & Co 1987–, Nomina plc 1997–, Enhanced Zero Tst plc 1999–, Close Finsbury Eurotech Tst plc 2000–, Azuran plc 2001–; dir: Gartmore Distribution Tst plc 1993–, Graphite Enterprise Tst plc 2002–, Folio Corp Fin Ltd 1997–; FCA; *Recreations* literature and music; *Clubs* Brooks's; *Style*— Peter Gray, Esq; ✉ 1 Bradbourne Street, London SW6 3TF

GRAY, Philip Malcolm James; s of James Carter Gray (d 1932), and Lucy Venetia Emily, *née* Robson (d 1972); *b* 17 January 1927; *Educ* Eastbourne Coll, Royal Sch of Mines Univ of London (BSc); *m* 18 Aug 1949, Joan, da of Alfred Thomas Houldsworth; *Career* scientific offr AERE Harwell 1947–51, res offr Cwlth Scientific and Res Orgn Melbourne Aust 1951–55, metallurgist and devpt mangr Imperial Smelting Corporation Avonmouth UK 1955–64 (tech mangr 1964–71), chief metallurgist Non-Ferrous Div Davy Corporation London 1971–78, metallurgical conslt and ptnr Philip M J Gray and J Gray London 1978–, md Zinc Metallurgy Ltd 1992–95, tech dir The Zinc Corporation Ltd 1996–98; pres Inst of Mining and Metallurgy 1984–85 (Capper Pass award 1952 and 1955), Waverly Gold medal 1955; Freeman City of London 1984, Liveryman Worshipful Co of Engineers; ARSM, fell Aust Inst Mining and Metallurgy 1970 (memb 1952), FREng 1984, Hon FIMM 1992 (MIMM 1953, FIMM 1973); *Books* The Profitable Development of Sulphide Ore Resources (with P Loffler and G Bielstein, 1985), numerous contribs to learned pubns (1951–); *Recreations* bell ringing, opera, musical appreciation, looking at paintings, golf, cricket, travel; *Clubs* Lansdowne; *Style*— Philip Gray, Esq, FREng; ✉ 2 The Avenue, Backwell, Bristol BS48 3NB (tel 01275 464192, fax 01275 464219, e-mail philip@gray89.fsnet.co.uk)

GRAY, Richard Innes John; s of James Gray, of Falkirk, and Jean, *née* Paterson; *b* 30 November 1953, Falkirk; *Educ* Graeme HS Falkirk, Univ of Strathclyde (BSc); *m* 5 July 1975, Ann, da of George Crozier; 1 da (Lynsey Elizabeth b 26 Dec 1980), 1 s (Steven James George b 22 Nov 1986); *Career* engr; ICI: plant engr 1975–82, standards engr 1982–85, engrg mangr 1985–88; Courtaulds Chemicals: ops mangr 1988–92, site mangr 1992–95, site dir 1995–2000; site dir and dir of health, safety and environment Acetate Products Ltd 2000–07, tech dir Coventry & Solihull Waste Disposal Co Ltd 2007–; non-exec dir: Derwent Cogeneration Ltd 2002–07, Engrg and Technol Bd 2002–05; treas IMechE (E Midlands Regn) 2003– (chm 2001–03); Freeman City of London, Liveryman Worshipful Co of Engrs; CEng 1982, FIMechE 1982, affliate memb CIWM 2007; *Recreations* fitness training, travel; *Style*— Richard Gray, Esq; ✉ Coventry & Solihull Waste Disposal Co Ltd, Bar Road, Coventry CV3 4AN (tel and fax 024 7650 7423, e-mail richard.gray@cswdc.co.uk)

GRAY, Prof Richard John; s of George Ernest Gray (d 1991), and Helen, *née* Cox; *b* 5 January 1944; *Educ* Tiffin Sch, St Catharine's Coll Cambridge (open scholar, BA), Univ of Cambridge (PhD); *m* 1, 1965 (m dis), Joyce Mary, *née* Gray; 1 da (Catharine Emma b 6 April 1966), 1 s (Ben Thomas b 21 May 1972); m 2, 1990, Sheona Catherine, da of Ian Binnie; 1 da (Jessica Vivien b 7 April 1991), 1 s (Jack Ewan George b 12 March 1993); *Career* sr research scholar St Catharine's Coll Cambridge 1966–67, Harkness fell Univ of N Carolina and Univ of Calif 1967–69; Dept of Literature Univ of Essex: lectr 1969–76, sr lectr 1976–80, reader 1981–90, prof 1990–; Robert E McNair visiting prof Univ of S Carolina 1993; memb Int Cncl Centre for the Study of Southern Culture Univ of Mississippi 1979, memb Exec Ctee Br Assoc for American Studies 1990–; assoc ed Jl of American Studies 1990, ed Jl of American Studies 1997; Inaugural Eccles Centre lectr Br Library 2004, Sarah Tryphene Phillips lectr Br Acad 2005, Lamar Lectr US 2006; FBA 1993; *Books* American Verse of the Nineteenth Century (ed, 1973), American Poetry of the Twentieth Century (ed, 1976), The Literature of Memory: Modern Writers of the American South (1977), Robert Penn Warren: A Collection of Critical Essays (ed, 1980), American Fiction: New Readings (ed, 1983), Writing the South: Ideas of an American Region (1986, C Hugh Holman Award), American Poetry of the Twentieth Century (1990), The Complete Poems and Selected Essays of Edgar Allan Poe (ed, 1993), The Life of William Faulkner: A Critical Biography (1994), The Selected Poems of Edgar Allan Poe (ed, 1996), Southern Aberrations: Writers of the American South and the Problems of Regionalism (2000), Companion to the Literature and Culture of the American South (2004), A History of American Literature (2004), A Web of Words: The Great Dialogue of Southern Literature (2007), Translatlantic Exchanges: The South in Europe - Europe in the American South (ed, 2007); *Recreations* cinema, wine tasting, running, tennis, gardening, travel; *Style*— Prof Richard Gray, FBA; ✉ Berri-Dene, Anglesea Road, Wivenhoe, Colchester, Essex CO7 9JS (tel 01206 823118, e-mail richardjgray@compuserve.com); Department of Literature, University of Essex, Wivenhoe Park, Colchester, Essex CO4 3SQ (tel 01206 872590, fax 01206 873598, e-mail grayr@essex.ac.uk)

GRAY, Richard Paul; QC (1993); s of Dr J M Gray (d 1984), and Margaret Elizabeth, *née* Welsh (d 1986); *b* 1 November 1945; *Educ* Tonbridge, Univ of St Andrews (LLB); *m* April 1976, Emma Serena, da of W R C Halpin; 1 s (Jocelyn b 9 Sept 1985); *Career* called to the Bar Inner Temple 1970; *Recreations* golf, tennis, gardens; *Style*— Richard Gray, Esq, QC; ✉ 39 Essex Street, London WC2R 3AT (tel 020 7832 1111, fax 020 7353 3978)

GRAY, Ronald George; s of Henry Gray (d 1958), and Elizabeth Campbell Cowan, *née* Watson (d 1942); *b* 12 July 1929; *Educ* Royal HS Edinburgh, Univ of Edinburgh (MA); *m* 26 June 1954, Diana Ravenscroft, da of Francis Henry Houlston (d 1983); 3 da (Karen b 14 Oct 1955, Francesca b 14 Sept 1958, Fiona b 10 March 1960); *Career* trainee Unilever 1953; dir: Elida Gibbs Ltd 1967–72, Unilever Co-ordination 1973–80; chm: Elida Gibbs (Germany) 1981–84, Lever Bros Ltd 1984–91; chm: CTFA (Cosmetic Toiletry and Fragrance Assoc) 1970–72, SDIA (Soap and Detergent Industry Assoc) 1985–89; pres ISBA 1988–90, memb IBA Advertising Advsy Ctee 1985–90; govr Dulwich Estate, chm Alleyns Sch 1988–2002; FIGD 1985; *Style*— Ronald Gray, Esq; ✉ 4 Dulwich Village, London SE21 7AL (tel 020 8693 1764)

GRAY, (Clemency Anne) Rose; da of Clement Nelson Swann (d 1939), of Bedford, and Elizabeth Anne, *née* Lawrence (d 1985); *b* 28 January 1939; *Educ* Manor House Sch Guildford, Guildford Sch of Art; *m* 1961 (m dis), Michael Selby Gray; 1 s (Ossian), 2 da (Hester (Mrs Justin Guest Albert), Lucy); partner, David MacIlwaine; 1 s (Dante MacIlwaine-Gray); *Career* chef/restaurant owner; teacher of fine art London 1960–63, designer and manufacturer of paper lights and furniture 1963–68, importer of French stoves and cookers (concurrently introduced series of French creperie mobile units for pop concerts) 1969–72, dir Home Stoves Ltd (mfrg and exporting wood burning stoves) 1973–81, resided Lucca Italy 1981–85; chef: Italian restuarant within Nells nightclub NY 1985–86, River Cafe (with Ruth Rogers, *qv*) 1987–; co-fndr Cooks in Schools (charity) 2004; Italian Restaurant of the Year (The Times) 1988, Best New Restaurant (Courvoisier Best of Best Awards) 1989, Eros Awards (Evening Standard) 1994 and 1995, Michelin Star 1998, 1999, 2000, 2001, 2002 and 2003; *Books* Hot Chefs (contrib, 1992), The River Cafe Cook Book (with Ruth Rogers, 1995, Food Book of the Year Glenfiddich Awards 1996), River Cafe Cook Book 2 (with Ruth Rogers, 1997), River Cafe Cook Book Green (with Ruth Rogers, 2000), River Cafe Cook Book Easy (with Ruth Rogers, 2003); incl in Kit Chapman's Great British Chefs 2 (1995), The Italian Kitchen (to accompany television series for Channel 4); *Recreations* gardening, travelling; *Style*— Rose Gray; ✉ Flat E, No 7 Plympton Street, London NW8 8AB

GRAY, Prof Sidney John; s of Sidney George Gray (d 1978), and Mary Angeline, *née* Birch (d 1974); *b* 3 October 1942; *Educ* Bedford Modern Sch, Univ of Sydney (BEc), Lancaster Univ (PhD); *m* 23 July 1977, Hilary Fenella, da of William Leonard Jones (d 1995); 1 da (Helen b 1981), 1 s (Peter b 1985); *Career* exec: Peirce Leslie & Co Ltd UK and India 1961–67 (factory mangr 1966–67), Burns Philp & Co Ltd Aust 1967–68; tutor in accounting Univ of Sydney 1972, lectr Lancaster Univ 1974–78 (res scholar 1973–74), prof of accounting and fin Univ of Glasgow 1978–92 (head of dept 1980–87), prof of int business Univ of Warwick 1992–99, prof of int business Univ of NSW 1999–2003 (assoc dean 2002–03), prof of int business Univ of Sydney 2003– (head Sch of Business 2003–06); sec-gen Euro Accounting Assoc 1982–83, memb UK Accounting Standards Ctee 1984–87, chm Br Accounting Assoc 1987, pres Int Assoc for Accounting Educn and Res 1992–97, pres Aust and NZ Int Business Acad 2002–04; ACIS 1971, MCMI 1973, FCCA 1980, fell Acad of the Social Sciences in Australia (FASSA) 2006; *Books* Information Disclosure and the Multinational Corporation (1984), International Financial Reporting (1984), Mega-Merger Mayhem (1989), Global Accounting and Control (2001), Handbook of International Business and Management (1990), International Accounting and Multinational Enterprises (2006); *Recreations* jogging, golf; *Clubs* East India; *Style*— Prof Sidney Gray; ✉ The Old Vicarage, Elstow, Bedford MK42 9XT

GRAY, Simon James Holliday; CBE (2005); s of Dr James Davidson Gray, and Barbara Cecelia Mary, *née* Holliday; *b* 21 October 1936; *Educ* Westminster, Dalhousie Univ, Trinity Coll Cambridge (MA); *m* 1, 1965 (m dis 1997), Beryl Mary, *née* Kevern; 1 s (Ben), 1 da (Lucy); m 2, 1997, Victoria Rothschild; *Career* research student and Harper-Wood travelling student 1960, sr instr in English Univ of Br Columbia 1963–64, lectr QMC London 1965–85; author and playwright; FRSL 1985; *Stage Plays* Wise Child (1968), Sleeping Dog (1968), Dutch Uncle (1969), The Idiot (1971), Spoiled (1971), Butley (1971), Otherwise Engaged (1975, voted Best Play 1976–77 by NY Drama Critics' Circle), Plaintiffs and Defendants (1975), Two Sundays (1975), Dog Days (1976), Molly (1977), The Rear Column (1978), Close of Play (1979), Stage Struck (1979), Quartermaine's Terms (1981), The Common Pursuit (1984), Plays One (1986), Melon (1987), Hidden Laughter (and dir London and Brighton, 1990), The Holy Terror (Melon Revised) (1990), Tartuffe - An Adaptation (1990), Old Flames (1990), Cell Mates (1995), Simply Disconnected (sequel to Otherwise Engaged, 1996), Life Support (1997), Just the Three of Us (1997), The Late Middle Classes (1999), Japes (2000), Old Masters (2004); *Television Plays* After Pilkington (1987), Old Flames (1990), A Month in the Country (1990), They Never Slept (1991), Running Late (1992), Unnatural Pursuits (1993), Femme Fatale (1993); *Radio Plays* The Holy Terror (revised, 1989), The Rector's Daughter (adaption, 1992), Suffer The Little Children (1993), With A Nod and A Bow (1993); *Books* Colmain (1963), Simple People (1965), Little Portia (1967, as Hamish Reade), A Comeback for Stark (1968), An Unnatural Pursuit and Other Pieces (1985), How's That For Telling 'em Fat Lady? - A Short Life in the American Theatre (1988), Fat Chance (1995), Breaking Hearts (1997), Enter A Fox (2001), The Smoking Diaries (2004), The Year of the Jouncer (2006); *Recreations* watching cricket and soccer; *Clubs* Dramatist, Groucho; *Style*— Simon Gray, Esq, CBE; ✉ c/o Judy Daish Associates, 2 St Charles Place, London W10 6EG (tel 020 8964 8811, fax 020 8964 8966)

GRAY, Simon Talbot; s of Dr John Talbot Carmichael Gray (d 1961), of Ealing, and Doris Irene, *née* Baker; *b* 1 June 1938; *Educ* Westminster (Queen's scholar); *m* 1963, Susan, da of Felix William Grain, of Ealing; 2 s (Nicholas b 1965, Julian b 1968); *Career* chartered accountant; ptnr Smith & Williamson 1968–98; dir Yattendon Investment Trust plc; special tstee of St Bartholomew's Hosp 1982–99 (chm 1992–99); memb City & Hackney HA 1983–90; hon memb Ct of Assts Worshipful Co of Glass Sellers (Master 1978); *Recreations* yachting (yacht 'Fast Anchor'), collecting porcelain; *Clubs* Royal Lymington Yacht; *Style*— Simon Gray, Esq; ✉ Brackens, Captains Row, Lymington, Hampshire SO41 9RP (tel 01590 677101, e-mail stgray@talk21.com)

GRAY, Sir William Hume; 3 Bt (UK 1917), of Tunstall Manor, Hart, Co Durham; s of late William Talbot Gray (d 1971), s of 2 Bt, and Rosemarie Hume, *née* Elliott-Smith; suc gf, Sir William Gray, 2 Bt, 1978; Sir William Cresswell Gray, 1 Bt, was chm William Gray & Co Ltd, a memb of Lloyd's Register Ctee and fndr of the S Durham Steel and Iron Co Ltd in 1889; *b* 26 July 1955; *Educ* Eton, Poly of Central London (DipArch); *m* 1, 1984 (m dis 1998), Catherine, yst da of late John Naylor, of The Mill House, Bramley, Hants; 1 s (William John Cresswell b 1986), 2 da (Octavia b 1987, Clementine b 1990); m 2, 2001, Juliet, da of D J Jackson, of Headlam, Co Durham;1 s (Theodore James b 2007); *Heir* s, William Gray; *Career* architect William Gray Associates; High Sheriff Co Durham 1998–99; *Style*— Sir William Gray, Bt; ✉ Eggleston Hall, Eggleston, Barnard Castle, Co Durham (website www.egglestonhall.co.uk)

GRAY-CHEAPE, Hamish Leslie; JP (Warwickshire 1985), DL (Warwickshire 1990); s of Lt-Col Leslie George Gray-Cheape, MBE, JP, DL (d 1991), of Carse Gray, Forfar, Angus, and Dorothy Evelyn, *née* Thomas (d 1986); *b* 18 March 1942; *Educ* Eton; *m* 6 Oct 1965, Fiona Mariella, da of Brig Sir Harry Ripley Mackeson (d 1964, 1 Bn late Royal Scots Greys);

G

2 s (James b 1968, George b 1971); *Career* Capt Grenadier Gds 1961–71; High Sheriff of Warwickshire 1984; farmer 1972–; memb Queen's Body Guard for Scotland (Royal Co of Archers) 1972; *Style*— Hamish Gray-Cheape, JP, DL; ✉ Great Alne, Warwickshire (tel 01789 488420); Hill House, Walcote, Alcester, Warwickshire B49 6LZ

GRAYDON, Air Chief Marshal Sir Michael James; GCB (1993, KCB 1989), CBE (1984), ADC (1992); s of James Julian Graydon (d 1985), and Rita Mary, *née* Alkan (d 2006); *b* 24 October 1938; *Educ* Wycliffe Coll; *m* 25 May 1963, (Margaret) Elizabeth, da of Arthur Ronald Clark (d 1972); *Career* RAF Coll Cranwell 1957–59, QFI No 1 FTS 1960–62, No 56 Sqdn Wattisham 1963–64, 226 OCU 1965–67, Flt-Cdr No 56 Akrotiri 1967–69, RAF Staff Coll Bracknell 1970, PSO to D/CINCENT HQAFCENT 1971–73, Ops Staff MOD 1973–75, NDC Latimer 1975–76, OC No 11 Sqdn Binbrook 1977–79, MA to CDS MOD 1979–81, OC RAF Leuchars 1981–83, OC RAF Stanley FI 1983, RCDS London 1984, SASO HQ 11 Gp Bentley Priory 1985–86, ACOS Policy SHAPE Belgium 1986–89, AOC-in-C RAF Support Cmd 1989–91, AOC-in-C Strike Cmd and C-in-C UK Air Forces 1991–92, Chief of Air Staff 1992–97; chm Symbiotics Ltd, non-exec dir Thales plc; pres Battle of Britain Memorial Tst, pres Officers Assoc, chm The Air Sqdn; chm Lincs Branch ESU, vice-chm of govrs Wycliffe Coll, chm Sutton's Hosp in Charterhouse, dep chm United Church Sch Tst; memb Ctee of Mgmnt RNLI, vice-patron Air Cadet Cncl; Freeman City of London, Liveryman Guild of Air Pilots and Navigators; FRAeS; *Recreations* golf, photography; *Clubs* RAF, Royal and Ancient Golf (St Andrews); *Style*— Air Chief Marshal Sir Michael Graydon, GCB, CBE

GRAYLING, Prof Anthony Clifford; s of Henry Clifford Grayling (d 1988), and Ursula Adelaide, *née* Burns (d 1969); *b* 3 April 1949; *Educ* Univ of London (BA), Univ of Sussex (BA, MA), Univ of Oxford (DPhil); *m* 1, 1970, Gabrielle Yvonne, da of Dr Joseph Smyth, of Rottingdean, E Sussex; 1 s (Anthony Jolyon Clifford b 1971), 1 da (Georgina Evelyn Ursula b 1975); partner, Katie Hickman; 1 da (Madeleine Catherine Jennifer b 1999); *Career* lectr in philosophy St Anne's Coll Oxford 1984–91; Birkbeck Coll Univ of London: lectr 1991–98, reader in philosophy 1998–2005, prof of philosophy 2005–; visiting prof Univ of Tokyo 1998; Leverhulme Tst fell 1999, Jan Huss fell 1994 and 1996; ed Online Review, gen ed Russell series; memb Editorial Bd: Prospect magazine, Reason and Practice magazine, Russell Newsletter; columnist: The Guardian 1999–2002, The Times 2003–; cmmr Drug Testing in the Workplace Enquiry; judge Booker Prize 2003; memb Aristotelian Soc 1986– (hon sec 1992–98); FRSL, FRSA; *Books* An Introduction to Philosophical Logic (1982, 3 edn1997), The Refutation of Scepticism (1985), Berkeley: The Central Arguments (1986), Wittgenstein (1988), The Long March to the Fourth of June (with Xu You Yu, under the pseudonym Li Xiao Jun, 1991), China: A Literary Companion (with Susan Whitfield, 1993), Russell (preface, 1995), Philosophy 1: A Guide Through the Subject (introduction and ed, 1995), Philosophy 2: Further Through the Subject (introduction and ed, 1998), Moral Values (1998), The Quarrel of the Age: The Life and Times of William Hazlitt (introduction, 2000), The Meaning of Things (introduction, 2001), The Reason of Things (2002), What is Good? (2003), The Mystery of Things (2004), The Heart of Things (2005), Descartes (2005), Among the Dead Cities (2006), The Form of Things (2006), Towards the Light (2007), Against All Gods (2007), The Choice of Hercules (2007); *Recreations* opera, theatre, travel, reading, walking; *Clubs* Athenaeum, Beefsteak, Groucho; *Style*— Prof A C Grayling; ✉ Birkbeck College, University of London, 14 Gower Street, London WC1E 6DP (tel 020 7631 6377, fax 020 7631 6564, e-mail a.grayling@bbk.ac.uk)

GRAYLING, Chris; MP; s of John Grayling, of Knutsford, Cheshire, and Elizabeth, *née* Arculus; *b* 1 April 1962; *Educ* Royal GS High Wycombe, Sidney Sussex Coll Cambridge (MA); *m* 1987, Susan, da of Peter Dillistone (d 1996); 1 s, 1 da; *Career* prodr BBC News 1985–88, prodr then prog ed Business Daily Channel 4 1988–91, BBC Enterprises 1991–93; dir: Workhouse Ltd 1993–95, Charterhouse Productions 1993, SSVC Gp 1995–97; md Burson-Marsteller 1997–2001; MP (Cons) Epsom and Ewell 2001–, oppn whip 2002, shadow health min 2002–03, shadow educn min 2003–05, shadow health min 2005, shadow ldr of the House of Commons 2005, shadow sec of state for tport 2005–07, shadow sec of state for work and pensions 2007–; pres Ewell and Stoneleigh Chamber of Trade, chm Epsom Victim Support; *Publications* The Bridgewater Heritage (1984), A Land Fit for Heroes (1985), Just Another Star? Anglo-American Relations Since 1945 (co-author, 1988); *Recreations* golf, cricket, family; *Style*— Chris Grayling, Esq, MP; ✉ House of Commons, London SW1A 0AA (tel 020 7219 8226, e-mail graylingc@parliament.uk); c/o 212 Barnett Wood Lane, Ashtead, Surrey KT21 2DB (tel 01372 271036, fax 01372 270154)

GRAYSON, Edward; *Educ* Taunton's Sch Southampton, Exeter Coll Oxford; *m* 27 May 1959, (Myra) Wendy Shockett; 1 s (Harry b 26 March 1966); *Career* RAF 1943–45; called to the Bar Middle Temple 1948; uninterrupted practice in court and consultancy: Lincoln's Inn 1949–53, Temple and International 1953–; practising barrister SE Circuit; contrib: legal, sporting and nat jls, newspapers, BBC, ITV, various radio stations; contrib and conslt to Central Cncl of Physical Recreation and Sports Cncl; memb: Sports Dispute Resolution Panels, Bar Sports Law Gp; founder pres Br Assoc for Sport and Law; FRSM; *Books* Corinthians and Cricketers (1955), The Royal Baccarat Scandal (co-author, 1977, 1988), Sponsorship of Sport, Arts and Leisure (co-author, 1984), Ethics, Injuries and the Law in Sports Medicine (1999), Sport and the Law (4 edn, 2000), School Sports and the Law (2001); *Recreations* working and creative thinking about the law and sports; *Clubs* MCC, Corinthian-Casuals, Littlehampton Town FC; *Style*— Edward Grayson, Esq; ✉ 1 Brick Court, Temple, London EC4Y 9BY (tel 020 7583 6207)

GRAYSON, Sir Jeremy Brian Vincent; 5 Bt (UK 1922), of Ravenspoint, Co Anglesey; s of Brian Harrington Grayson (d 1989), and his 1 w, Sofia, *née* Buchanan; suc uncle, Sir Rupert Stanley Harrington Grayson, 4 Bt 1991; *b* 30 January 1933; *Educ* Downside; *m* 1958, Sara Mary, da of late C F Upton, of Monte Carlo; 3 s (Simon Jeremy b 1959, Paul Francis b 1965, Mark Christopher b 1968), 4 da (Caroline Mary b 1961, Anna Katherine (Mrs Christopher Turner) b 1962, Mary b and d 1964, Lucy Kate (Mrs Matthew Gosling) b 1970); *Heir* s, Simon Grayson; *Recreations* painting watercolours, walking; *Style*— Sir Jeremy Grayson, Bt

GRAZEBROOK, Adrian Michael; TD (1974); s of Brig (Tom) Neville Grazebrook, CBE, DSO (d 1967), of Sheepscombe House, Glos, and (Marion) Betty, *née* Asplin; *b* 25 March 1943; *Educ* Sherborne; *m* 22 Sept 1984, Susan Mary, da of (Frank) Geoffrey Outwin (d 2005), of Barnwood, Gloucester; *Career* cmmnd TA 1962, Lt-Col 1984–90; admitted slr 1966; ptnr Wilmot & Co 1968–; vice-pres Racehorse Owners' Assoc 1995–96, dir Br Horseracing Bd 2003–07; memb Law Soc 1966; *Recreations* racing, choral singing; *Clubs* Army and Navy, Turf; *Style*— Adrian Grazebrook, Esq, TD; ✉ The Shepherd's Cottage, Hilcot End, Ampney Crucis, Cirencester, Gloucestershire GL7 5SG (tel 01285 851507); Wilmot & Co Solicitors LLP, 38 Castle Street, Cirencester, Gloucestershire GL7 1QH (tel 01285 650551, fax 01285 654007, mobile 07831 496608)

GREATOREX, Barbara; da of Benjamin John Jackson, of Bicester, Oxon, and Millicent Clare Jackson (d 1989); *b* 11 March 1951, Bicester, Oxon; *Educ* Bicester Sch, Univ of Warwick (BSc), Univ of York (PGCE), Open Univ (MA); *Children* 2 s (Thomas Edward b 26 March 1978, Samuel John b 12 June 1979), 1 da (Sarah Ellen b 30 March 1981); *Career* sr teacher Joseph Rowntree Sch York 1984–97, dep headteacher Wolverhampton Girls' HS 1997–2002, headteacher Wallington HS for Girls 2002–; involved with RSPB; *Recreations* birding, hill walking, yoga; *Style*— Mrs Barbara Greatorex; ✉ Wallington High School for Girls, Woodcote Road, Wallington, Surrey SM6 0PH (tel 020 8647 2380, e-mail bgreatorex@suttonlea.org)

GREATOREX, Raymond Edward (Ray); s of Percy Edward Greatorex (d 1985), and Lilian Alice Greatorex (d 1986); *b* 28 May 1940; *Educ* Westcliff HS, Lewes Co GS; *m* Barbara Anne; 1 da (Joanna b 16 Sept 1974); *Career* CA 1964; ptnr: Sydenham & Co 1970, Hodgson Harris 1980, Hodgson Impey 1985, Kidsons Impey 1990; chm HLB Int 1994–99, nat managing ptnr HLB Kidsons 2000–02, exec chm Baker Tilly 2002–06; Freeman City of London, Liveryman Worshipful Co of Farriers (Master 2002–03); FCA, FRSA; *Recreations* horse racing, cricket, travelling, gardening, reading; *Clubs* East India, MCC; *Style*— Ray Greatorex; ✉ Beeches Brook, Wisborough Green, West Sussex RH14 0HP (tel 01403 700 796, e-mail ray.greatorex@bakertilly.co.uk)

GREAVES, (Ronald) John; s of Ronald Greaves, and Rose Mary, *née* Nugent; *b* 7 August 1948; *Educ* Douay Martyrs Ickenham, Central London Poly (LLB); *m* 1, 3 July 1970 (m dis 1980), Angela, da of Stanley Menze; m 2, Margaret Dorothy, da of Denis John O'Sullivan, of Lincolnshire; 1 da (Caroline Frances b 28 July 1984), 1 s (Patrick John b 30 Sept 1987); *Career* called to the Bar Middle Temple 1973; currently in practice SE Circuit, dep dist judge Magistrates Ct 1999–; Parly candidate (Lab) St Albans 1979; memb: Justice Ctee of Compensation for Wrongful Imprisonment, Criminal Bar Assoc; chm Chilterns Multiple Sclerosis Centre 2005–; *Clubs* Riverside Northwood; *Style*— John Greaves, Esq; ✉ Adams House, London Road, Rickmansworth, Hertfordshire WD3 1JT (tel and fax 01923 776878); 9–12 Bell Yard, London WC2A 2LF (tel 020 7400 1800, fax 020 7404 1405, DX LDE 390)

GREEN, Alan; s of William Green, of Belfast, and Margaret, *née* Leckey; *b* 25 June 1952, Belfast; *Educ* Methodist Coll Belfast, Queen's Univ Belfast (BA); *m* 29 March 1980, Brenda Collette; 1 da (Sarah b 14 June 1983), 1 s (Simon b 19 May 1986); *Career* football commentator, broadcaster and writer; BBC Radio: joined as news trainee London 1975, current affrs presenter and reporter on radio and TV NI, joined BBC Radio Sport 1982, currently sr football commentator and presenter 6–0–6 (BBC Radio 5 Live) and World Football (BBC World Service), rowing commentator at Olympics; currently freelance broadcaster and writer; Sony Awards: Sports Broadcaster of the Year 1997, Speech Broadcaster of the Year 2002; *Publications* The Green Line (autobiography, 2000); *Recreations* golf, travel; *Style*— Alan Green, Esq; ✉ BBC Sport (Radio), Television Centre, Wood Lane, London W12 7RJ (tel 020 8225 7035, e-mail alangreen10@compuserve.com)

GREEN, Alison Anne; da of Sam Green, CBE, of Bromley, Kent, and Lilly, *née* Pollak; *b* 18 March 1951; *Educ* Bromley HS, UCL (LLB, LLM), Univ of Louvain; *m* 20 April 1991, Thomas Francis Conlon; 1 da (Samantha Alice Green Conlon); *Career* called to the Bar Middle Temple 1974; lectr in law Univ of Surrey 1976–78; tutor in law: QMC London 1978–79, UCL 1979–81; chair Br Insurance Law Assoc 1994–96 (vice-chair 1992–94, vice-pres 1999–); vice-chair Bar Law Reform Ctee, memb Panel of Arbitrators of AIDA Reinsurance & Insurance Arbitration Soc, memb Disciplinary Panel Bar Cncl 2000–05; chm of tstees Br Insurance Law Assoc Charitable Tst; accredited mediator; *Books* Insurance Contract Law (ed advsr 1988); *Recreations* music, tennis, ballet; *Clubs* Hurlingham; *Style*— Miss Alison Green; ✉ 2 Temple Gardens, Temple, London EC4Y 9AY (tel 020 7822 1200, fax 020 7822 1300, e-mail agreen@2tg.co.uk or ali88green@aol.com)

GREEN, Sir Allan David; KCB (1991), QC (1987); s of Lionel Green (d 1991), and Irene Evelyn, *née* Abrahams (later Mrs Axelrad, d 1975); *b* 1 March 1935; *Educ* Charterhouse, St Catharine's Coll Cambridge (MA); *m* 21 Feb 1967, Eva Brita Margareta (d 1993), da of Prof Artur Attman (d 1988), of Gothenburg, Sweden; 1 s (Robin b 1969), 1 da (Susanna b 1970); *Career* served RN 1953–55; called to the Bar Inner Temple 1959; sr prosecuting counsel to the Crown Central Criminal Ct 1979–85 (jr prosecuting counsel 1977–79), recorder of the Crown Ct 1979–87, bencher 1985, first sr prosecuting counsel to the Crown 1985–87, dir of Public Prosecutions and head Crown Prosecution Serv 1987–91; non-exec dir Windsmoor plc 1986–87; *Recreations* music, studying calligraphy; *Clubs* Athenaeum; *Style*— Sir Allan Green, KCB, QC; ✉ No 2 Hare Court, Temple, London EC4Y 7BH

GREEN, Sir Andrew Fleming; KCMG (1998, CMG 1991); s of Gp Capt Joseph Henry Green, CBE (d 1970), and Beatrice Mary, *née* Bowditch (d 1997); *b* 6 August 1941; *Educ* Haileybury, Magdalene Coll Cambridge (MA); *m* 21 Sept 1968, Catherine Jane, da of Lt Cdr Peter Norton Churchill, RN (d 1940); 1 da (Diana b 1970), 1 s (Stephen b 1973); *Career* short serv cmmn Royal Greenjackets 1962–65; joined Dip Serv 1965, MECAS Lebanon 1966–68, second sec Aden 1968–70, asst political agent Abu Dhabi 1970–72; first sec: FCO 1972–77, UK Delgn OECD Paris 1977–79, FCO 1979–82; political cnsllr Washington 1982–85, consul-gen and head of Chancery Riyadh 1985–88, cnsllr FCO 1988–91, HM ambass Syria 1991–94, asst under-sec (Middle East) FCO 1994–96, HM ambass Saudi Arabia 1996–2000; chm: Migrationwatch UK 2001–, Medical Aid for Palestinians 2002–05; *Recreations* tennis, bridge; *Style*— Sir Andrew Green, KCMG; ✉ 89 St Georges Square, London SW1V 3QW (e-mail afgreen@btconnect.com)

GREEN, Andrew James (Andy); s of Phil Green (d 2001), and Judy Green (d 1996); *b* 7 September 1955; *Educ* King Edward's Sch for Boys Edgbaston, Univ of Leeds (BSc); *m* 17 Sept 1977, Alison, da of Barry Fletcher; 2 s (James Edward b 5 June 1986, Alastair Philip b 25 Nov 1993), 1 da (Alix Evelyn b 14 June 1988); *Career* chemicals sales and mktg Shell Transport & Trading 1976–84, mktg conslt Deloitte Haskins & Sells 1984–86; BT Gp: joined 1986, group strategy and devpt dir BT plc 1995–99, ceo BTopenworld 1999–2001, bd dir BT Gp plc 2001–, ceo BT Global Services (previously BT Ignite) 2001–07, ceo of gp strategy and ops 2007–; involved with Shelter Gp; *Recreations* cricket, off-road cycling, travel; *Clubs* RSA; *Style*— Andy Green, Esq; ✉ BT, 81 Newgate Street, London EC1A 7AJ (tel 020 7356 5134, fax 020 7726 8564, e-mail andy.j.green@bt.com)

GREEN, Anthony Eric Sandall; s of Frederick Sandall Green (d 1961), of London, and Marie-Madeleine (Mrs Joscelyne), *née* Dupont; *b* 30 September 1939; *Educ* Highgate Sch, Slade Sch of Fine Art (Dip Fine Art); *m* 29 July 1961, Mary Louise, da of Gordon Roberts Cozens-Walker (d 1981); 2 da (Katharine Charlotte b 1965, Lucy Rebecca b 1970); *Career* artist; Harkness fellowship USA 1967–69, fell UCL 1991–; tstee Royal Acad of Arts 2000–; over 100 one-man shows worldwide; exhbns incl Fine Art Soc 2004; featured artist at Royal Acad Summer Exhbn 2003; UK public collections: Tate, V&A, Arts Cncl of GB, Br Cncl, and others; foreign public collections: Metropolitan Museum of Art NYC, various museums in Japan and Brazil, and others; RA 1977; *Books* A Green Part of the World (with Martin Bailey, 1984); *Recreations* family, travel; *Style*— Anthony Green, Esq, RA; ✉ Mole End, 40 High Street, Little Eversden, Cambridge CB3 7HE (tel 01223 262292)

GREEN, (Michael James) Bay; s of Patrick Green, OBE, DFC, and Eileen Brenda, *née* Green; *b* 4 June 1943; *Educ* Harrow; *m* 26 Aug 1971, Ann Eila, da of James Kennedy Elliott, OBE, and Elfie Claire Temple, *née* Reed; 1 s (Edward James Patrick b 27 Nov 1973), 1 da (Caroline Eila b 6 Oct 1975); *Career* articled clerk Peat Marwick Mitchell & Co 1960–65, mangr G W Green & Sons 1965–71; Kleinwort Benson Ltd: joined 1971, dir 1978, chm and md Kleinwort Benson Australia Ltd 1981–84; head of corporate finance and md Hill Samuel Bank Ltd 1988–91; Kleinwort Benson Group plc: dir 1991–1998, head Financing and Advsy Div 1994–96, gp vice-chm 1996–98; vice-chm Dresdner Kleinwort Benson 1998–2000, vice-chm Dresdner Kleinwort 2000–; dir: RPC Gp plc 1998–, Invensys plc 2005–, Axis-Shield plc 2005–, Help the Hospices 2005–; FCA, MSI; *Recreations* opera, tennis, shooting, yachting; *Clubs* Boodle's; *Style*— Bay Green, Esq; ✉ Dresdner Kleinwort, PO Box 52715, 30 Gresham Street, London EC2P 2XY (tel 020 7623 8000, fax 020 7475 7100, e-mail bay.green@dkib.com)

GREEN, Brian Russell; QC (1997); s of Bertram Green (d 1992), and Dora, *née* Rinsler (d 2001); *b* 25 July 1956; *Educ* Ilford Co HS for Boys, St Edmund Hall Oxford (scholar, BA, BCL); *m* 2 Oct 1994, Yvonne, da of Charles Mammon; 1 s (Bertram b 1998), 1 da (Rachael b 1999); *Career* lectr in law LSE 1978–85, tutor in jurisprudence St Edmund Hall Oxford 1978–80, called to the Bar Middle Temple 1980 (Lloyd Jacob Memorial Exhibition 1980, Astbury Law Scholar 1980), in practice 1981–; memb: Revenue Law Ctee Law Soc 1994–, Assoc of Pension Lawyers, Revenue Bar Assoc, Chancery Bar Assoc, Soc of Trust & Estate Practitioners, Assoc of Contentions Tst and Probate Specialists; *Publications* author of various articles in legal periodicals; *Recreations* arts, cooking, dining, gardening, skiing, travel, walking/trekking; *Style*— Brian Green, QC; ✉ Wilberforce Chambers, 8 New Square, Lincoln's Inn, London WC2A 3QP (tel 020 7306 0102, fax 020 7306 0095, e-mail bgreen@wilberforce.co.uk)

GREEN, Prof Brynmor Hugh (Bryn); OBE (1995); s of Albert Walter Green (d 1971), and Margaret Afona, *née* Griffiths (d 1971); *b* 14 January 1941; *Educ* Dartford GS, Univ of Nottingham (BSc, PhD); *m* 14 Aug 1965, Jean, da of (Thomas) Norman Armstrong (d 1981); 2 s (David Ellis, Simon Gareth); *Career* lectr Dept of Botany Univ of Manchester 1965–67; Nature Conservancy Cncl: dep and SE regnl offr 1967–74, chief sci team 1974; Wye Coll London: lectr and sr lectr 1974–87, Sir Cyril Kleinwort prof of countryside mgmnt 1987–96, emeritus prof 1996–; memb Eng Ctee Nature Conservancy Cncl 1983–90, countryside cmmr 1984–93, chm Landscape Conservation Working Gp Int Union for the Conservation of Nature 1992–98, vice-pres Kent and Sussex Farming and Wildlife Advsy Gp 2002–, chm White Cliffs Countryside Mgmnt Project 1990–96, vice-pres Kent Wildlife Tst 2002–; Churchill fell 1999; *Books* Countryside Conservation (1981, 3 edn, 1996), The Diversion of Land (with C Potter et al, 1991), The Changing Role of the Common Agricultural Policy (with J Marsh et al, 1991), Threatened Landscapes (with W Vos et al, 2001); contrib sci papers to numerous jnls and books; *Recreations* golf, watercolour sketching, ornithology; *Style*— Prof Bryn Green, OBE; ✉ Heatherbank, 49 Brockhill Road, Saltwood, Hythe, Kent CT21 4AF (tel 01303 261093, e-mail mabr08@dial.pipex.com)

GREEN, Charles; s of Jacob Green, of Leicester, and Anna, *née* Ostersetzer; *b* 26 March 1950; *Educ* London Sch of Film Technique; *m* 28 May 1972, Toni, da of Leibish and Mania Engelberg, of Antwerp, Belgium; 1 s (Kenny b 23 Jan 1975), 2 da (Michelle b 4 June 1977, Davina b 6 Jan 1986); *Career* photographer; opened portrait studio Edgware 1978; Master Photographer of the Year Award 1985, Court of Honour Award of Excellence Professional Photographers Soc of NY USA 1986, 12 Kodak Gold Awards for tech excellence and creativity 1988–95, Gold Certificate for Achievement World Cncl of Professional Photographers 1989; exhibitions: The Forgotten People 1990, Epcot Centre Florida (portraits chosen by Professional Photographers of America) 1990–91, Leaders of GB Into the 21st Century 1995; awarded Masters and Craftsman Degree in Photography Professional Photographers of America 1991, official photographer for investitures at Buckingham Palace 1992–; Master of Electronic Imaging (MEI), Master Photographer, FASP, FBIPP 1985 (ABIPP 1983), FMPA, FRPS, FRSA; *Books* Shooting For Gold (1987), Create The Image (2004); *Style*— Charles Green; ✉ Charles Green Photography, Grosvenor House, 1 High Street, Edgware, Middlesex HA8 7TA (tel 020 7993 8093, fax 020 8952 3388, e-mail portraits@charlesgreen.com, website www.charlesgreen.com)

GREEN, Charles Frederick; s of George Frederick Green (d 1977), and late Ellen Maud Mary, *née* Brett; *b* 20 October 1930; *Educ* Harrow Co Sch; *m* 1956, Rev Elizabeth Pauline Anne Green, da of Egbert Joseph William Jackson, CB, MC (d 1975); 2 s (Nicholas b 1957, Martin b 1959), 1 da (Mary b 1963); *Career* Nat Serv Flying Offr RAF 1949–51; sec National Provincial Bank 1967–70 (joined 1946); National Westminster Bank: head of planning 1970, md Centre File 1974–76, gen mangr Financial Control Div 1982, dir 1982–89, dep gp chief exec 1986–89; chm: Multinational Affrs Panel CBI ICC 1982–87, Overseas Ctee CBI 1987–89; dir Business in the Community 1983–90 (vice-chm 1983–89), memb Cncl Policy Studies Inst 1984–97 (treas 1984–93); C of E: memb General Synod 1980–90, vice-chm Bd for Social Responsibility 1983–91 (memb 1980–93), chm Industrial and Econ Affrs Ctee 1986–93, chm Central Stewardship Ctee 1993–99; vice-chm Gloucester Diocesan Bd of Fin 1992–99; chm: County of Glos Community Fndn 1991–2000 (tstee 1991–2005), Mgmnt Ctee Glenfall House 1991–96 (chm of tstees 1996–2002); dir CAFCASH 1989–99; tstee: Small Business Research Tst 1986–96, Church Urban Fund 1987–89, Monteverdi Tst 1986–2001, Charities Aid Fndn 1989–98, Church Housing Tst 1992–2005; govr: Westonbirt Sch 1990–2003, Monkton Combe Sch 1990–96, Old Sodbury C of E Primary Sch 1992–2000; vice-chm Cheltenham and Gloucester Coll of HE (now Univ of Gloucester) 1994–2002 (memb Cncl 1993–2002); Freeman City of London 1990; FCIB, FIMgt, FRSA, Hon FLCM; *Recreations* opera, concert music, drama; *Clubs* Athenaeum, National; *Style*— Charles Green, Esq; ✉ The Old House, Parks Farm, Old Sodbury, Bristol BS37 6PX (tel 01454 311936)

GREEN, Christopher Edward Wastie (Chris); s of James Wastie Green, and Margarita, *née* Mensing; *b* 7 September 1943; *Educ* St Paul's, Oriel Coll Oxford (MA); *m* 1966, Mitzie, da of Dr Petzold; 1 da (Carol b 1969), 1 s (James b 1971); *Career* British Rail: mgmnt trainee 1965, area mangr Hull 1973, passenger ops mangr BRB 1978, regnl ops mangr Scotland 1980, dep gen mangr ScotRail 1983, gen mangr ScotRail 1984, md Network South East 1990–91 (dir 1986), md InterCity 1992–94, md ScotRail 1994–95; chief exec English Heritage March 1995–96 (cmmr July 1995–96), md (Gibb Rail) Gibb Ltd (formerly Sir Alexander Gibb & Partners) 1996–99, chief exec Virgin Trains 1999–2005; dir: Eurotunnel plc, Network Rail 2005–; pres Railway Study Assoc 1997–98, pres Railway Convalescent Homes 2002–, memb Advsy Panel Railway Heritage Tst 2003–; memb Advsy Bd Cranfield Univ 1996–99; Hon DUniv Univ of Central England 2002; Hon DBA IMC 2002; FCIT; *Recreations* canal boating, architecture, music, hill walking; *Style*— Chris Green, Esq

GREEN, Prof Christopher John Charles; OBE (1995); s of late Eric Frederick Green, and Muriel Mary, *née* Rice; *b* 3 November 1942; *Educ* Northgate GS for Boys Ipswich, Univ of Leeds (BA, PhD); *m* 3 Aug 1968, Sylvia Alice, da of Robert Buckenham, and Doris Buckenham; 2 s (Jonathan James b 13 Dec 1971, Richard Charles b 27 April 1975); *Career* lectr Enfield Coll of Technol 1971–73 (Hockerill Coll 1968–71), sr lectr Middx Poly 1973–76, head of dept Essex Coll of HE 1981–89 (Chelmer Coll of HE 1976–81), project dir Essex Centre Anglia Coll of HE 1989–91, prof of continuing and adult educn Anglia Poly Univ (formerly Anglia Poly) 1991– (dir Regnl Office 1992–); chm Four Counties Gp of HE Instns, business ldr Aimhigher: Partnerships for Progression in the East of England; sr music critic East Anglian Daily Times; artistic dir: Trianon Music Gp 1959–, Ipswich Festival 1980–83, Anglia Singers 1988–; chm: Nat Assoc of Youth Orchestras 1975–78, Chelmsford and Dist Mental Health Centre 1983–2003, Ipswich Arts Assoc 1989–; assoc fell Br Psychological Soc 1989, memb Critics Circle; FRSA; *Recreations* reading, music, theatre; *Style*— Prof Christopher Green, OBE

GREEN, Colin Henry; CBE (2005); *b* 21 October 1948; *Educ* Birkenhead Sch, Univ of Bristol (BSc); *m* Louise; 2 da, 1 s; *Career* Rolls-Royce plc: joined 1968, devpt engr 1973, subsequently gen mangr for industrial business activities in gas and oil sector, memb Bd Cooper Rolls Inc Mt Vernon USA 1981–83, exec dir GEC Rolls-Royce Ltd 1984–83, head of project European Fighter Aircraft Engine 1985–86, md Eurojet Turbo GmbH 1986–89, dir Military Engines 1989–94, md Military Aero Engines Ltd 1994–1995, exec vice-pres Business Op Indianapolis USA 1995–96, memb Bd 1996–2006, md Aerospace Gp 1996–1998, dir Ops 1998–2001, pres Defence Aerospace 2001–06; non-exec dir BAA plc 2001–; chm Aerospace Ctee DTI; pres SBAC, memb Soc of Merchant Venturers; Freeman City of London 1992, Liveryman Worshipful Co of Goldsmiths 1992; Hon DEng Univ of Bristol 1997, Hon DSc Cranfield Univ 1998; FRAeS 1990, FIMechE 1997, FREng 1998; *Recreations* vintage cars, sports, music; *Style*— Colin Green, Esq, CBE, FREng

GREEN, Colin Raymond; s of Dr Gerald Herman Green, of London, and Maisie, *née* Benkwich; *b* 16 April 1949; *Educ* Hampton GS, LSE (LLB), Coll of Law, Wujs Inst Arad Israel; *m* 1975, Hazel Ruth, *née* Lateman; 1 s (Samuel Nathan b 1983), 1 da (Hanna Judith b 1985); *Career* admitted slr 1973, asst slr Paisner & Co 1973–74 (articled clerk 1971–73), ptnr Clintons 1975–77 (asst slr 1974–75); British Telecommunications plc: legal asst The Post Office (before demerger of British Telecom) 1977–81, head of privatisation Legal Div British Telecom 1981–84, head of M&A Legal Div 1984–85, dir Commercial Dept 1985–89, slr and chief legal advsr 1989–94, chief legal advsr 1994–99, sec 1994–2002, memb Exec Ctee 1996–2002, gp commercial dir 1999–2002, dir BT Property Ltd 1991–99, tstee BT Pension Scheme 1994–2002, chm BT Telecommunications SA 2001–02; chm Hermes Group Pension Fund 2002–; dir: VIO Worldwide Ltd 1998–2001, Airtel Movil SA 1999–2001, ECI Telecom Ltd 2002–; dir CEDR 1995–99; chm Green Aid 2004–, tstee Nightingale House 2003–; chm Kingston Israel Ctee 2002–06, memb Kingston Jt Israel Appeal Ctee (former chm), memb Bd of Mgmnt Kingston Synagogue 2002–; memb Law Soc 1973; *Recreations* football, reading, theatre, walking, music (playing and composing); *Style*— Colin Green, Esq

GREEN, Damian Howard; MP; s of Howard Green, of Shiplake, Oxon, and late Audrey Edith, *née* Lyons; *b* 17 January 1956; *Educ* Reading Sch, Balliol Coll Oxford (MA, pres Oxford Union); *m* 1988, Alicia Hester Collinson, *qv*, da of late Judge Jeffreys Collinson; 2 da (Felicity b 1990, Verity b 1993); *Career* prodr/presenter Financial World Tonight BBC Radio 4 1978–82, economics scriptwriter ITN Channel 4 News 1982–84, news ed (Business News) The Times 1984–85, business ed Channel 4 News 1985–87, dep ed Business Daily Channel 4 1987–92, special advsr PM's Policy Unit 1992–94; subsequently public affrs conslt; Parly candidate (Cons) Brent E 1992; MP (Cons) Ashford 1997–; oppn front bench spokesman on educn and employment 1998–99, environment spokesman 1999–2001, shadow sec of state for Educn and Skills 2001–03, shadow sec of state for Transport 2003–04, shadow immigration min 2005–; chm Parly Mainstream 2003–; memb Select Ctee on: Culture, Media and Sport 1997–98, Procedure; vice-pres Tory Reform Gp; *Publications* ITN Budget Factbook (1984, 1985 and 1986), A Better BBC (pamphlet for Centre for Policy Studies, 1991), The Cross Media Revolution (co-author, 1995), Communities in the Countryside (Social Market Fndn, 1996), Regulating the Media in the Digital Age (1997), The Four Failures of the New Deal (Centre for Policy Studies, 1998), Restoring the Balance (Tory Reform Group, 2000), Better Learning (2002); *Recreations* cricket, football, opera, theatre; *Clubs* MCC; *Style*— Damian Green, Esq, MP; ✉ House of Commons, London SW1A 0AA (tel 020 7219 3000)

GREEN, Sir (Gregory) David; KCMG (2004, CMG 1999); s of Thomas Dixon Green, of Fulford, York, and Mabella Mary, *née* Walley; *b* 2 December 1948; *Educ* The Leys Sch Cambridge, Keswick Hall Coll of Educn Norwich, Trinity Hall Cambridge (BEd); *m* 10 Sept 1977, Corinne, da of Anthony Bernard Butler; 3 da (Hannah Mabella b 1978, Emily Corinne b 1980, Frances Ethel Rosalind b 1982); *Career* teacher of English West Pakistan (VSO) 1967–68, teacher of art/head of first year Northcliffe Comp Sch 1972–75, teacher of art/head of year Aston Comp Sch Rotherham 1975–76, dir Children's Relief Int/The Cambridge Project Save the Children 1976–79; Save the Children: staff devpt and trg offr 1979–82, dep dir of personnel 1983, dir of personnel 1983–88, dir of personnel and admin 1988–90; dir VSO 1990–99, DG British Cncl 1999–2007; memb Advsy Panel Mgmnt Devpt Unit NVCO 1985–86, memb VSO Cncl 2000–; MIPM 1987; exhibition of paintings held 1978, dir Cinderella (by Peter Maxwell Davies, Queen Elizabeth Hall) 1990; memb Laurence Olivier Award Panel 1985, tstee and memb Cncl English Stage Co 2005–; tstee Dartington Hall Tst 2006–; Freeman: City of Freetown 2004, City of London 2006; FRGS, hon fell Coll of Teachers; *Recreations* theatre, music, painting, travel; *Style*— Sir David Green, KCMG

GREEN, David John Mark; QC (2000); s of John Geoffrey Green, of Woodford Green, Essex, and Margaret Green; bro of Geoffrey Green, *qv*; *b* 8 March 1954; *Educ* Christ's Hosp, St Catharine's Coll Cambridge (MA); *m* 7 June 1980, Katherine, da of James Sharkey, of Woodford Green; 1 s (Dominic James Millican), 2 da (Clemency Alice, Leonora Isabel); *Career* Def Intelligence Staff MOD 1975–78; called to the Bar Inner Temple 1979; recorder of the Crown Court 2000–, dir Revenue and Customs Prosecution Office 2004–; Liveryman Worshipful Co of Gardeners; *Clubs* Garrick; *Style*— David Green, Esq, QC

GREEN, David William; s of William Edward Green (decd), and Joy Doris, *née* Powell; *b* 5 March 1950; *Educ* Penarth GS, Fakenham GS, King's Coll Hosp Med Sch (MB BS), Open Univ (MBA); *Career* conslt anaesthetist KCH (also chair Local Negotiating Ctee); visiting prof of regional anaesthesia Univ of Western Ontario 1987; asst prof Univ of Texas SMS at Dallas; pres Section of Anaesthesia RSM; memb: BMA, American Soc of Anaesthesiologists, Euro Acad of Anaesthesiology, Euro Soc of Anaesthesiology; MRI, FRSM, FFARCS 1977; *Books* A New Short Textbook of Anaesthetics (jtly, 1986), Anaesthesia and Perioperative Care (jtly, 1994), Fundamentals of Perioperative Management (jtly, 2003); *Recreations* classical music; *Clubs* IOD, Osler (pres); *Style*— David Green, Esq; ✉ 34 Ponsonby Terrace, London SW1P 4QA; Department of Anaesthetics, King's College Hospital, Denmark Hill, London SE5 9RS (tel 020 7346 3154/3358, e-mail david@dr-green.co.uk, website www.dr-green.co.uk)

GREEN, Prof Dennis Howard; s of Herbert Maurice Green (d 1953), and Agnes Edith, *née* Fleming; *b* 26 June 1922; *Educ* Latymer Upper Sch, Trinity Coll Cambridge (BA), Univ of Basel (DPhil); *m* 1, 15 Sept 1947, Dorothy Warren (d 2006); m 2, 17 Nov 1972, Margaret, *née* Parry (d 1997); m 3, 5 May 2001, Sarah *née* Campbell Taylor; *Career* teaching fell Trinity Coll Cambridge 1952–66 (res fell 1949–52); lectr Univ of St Andrews 1949–50; Univ of Cambridge: lectr 1950–66, prof of modern languages 1966–79, Schröder prof of German 1979–89; professorial fell Trinity Coll Cambridge 1966–; various visiting professorships in USA, Germany, Aust and NZ; hon pres Int Courtly Lit Soc; memb Wolfram-von-Eschenbach-Gesellschaft; FBA 1992; *Books* The Carolingian Lord (1965), The Millstätter Exodus (1966), Approaches to Wolfram von Eschenbach (1978), Irony in the Medieval Romance (1979), The Art of Recognition in Wolfram's Parzival (1982), Medieval Listening and Reading (1994), Language and History in the early Germanic World (1998), The Beginnings of Medieval Romance (2002), Women Readers in the Middle Ages (2007); *Recreations* walking and foreign travel; *Style*— Prof Dennis Green, FBA; ✉ Trinity College, Cambridge CB2 1TQ (tel 01223 339517)

GREEN, Geoffrey David; s of Ronald Green (d 1977), of Enfield, and Ivy May, *née* Steggles (d 1988); *b* 17 March 1946; *Educ* George Spicer Central Sch Enfield; *m* 3 April 1969, Rosmarie, da of Dominik Raber, of Affoltern Am Albis, Switzerland; 2 da (Natasha b 1970, Vanessa b 1972); *Career* dir: Bisgood 1985–, County Securities 1986–, County NatWest 1986–90, County NatWest Wood MacKenzie 1988–90; MSI 1992 (memb Stock Exchange 1970); *Recreations* cycling, gardening, travel, local history, reading; *Style*— Geoffrey Green, Esq; ✉ Hadleigh, 35 Carnaby Road, Broxbourne, Hertfordshire EN10 7EG

GREEN, Geoffrey Edward; s of Edward Bowyer Green (d 1990), of Beaconsfield, Bucks, and Clara Jane, *née* Allen (d 1972); *b* 27 March 1929; *Educ* Royal GS High Wycombe, Univ of London (LLB), Law Soc's Coll of Law; *m* 2 Jan 1954, Joy Anne, da of William Robert Willcocks (d 1963), of Beaconsfield, Bucks; 1 da (Nichola Joy (Mrs Blunt) b 1955 d 2001); *Career* admitted slr 1951, NP 1969; asst to Sir Cullum Welch, Bt, PA to Sir

G

Frank Medlicott, CBE, MP 1952–54, sole practice and ptnr in central London 1954–61, practice in Beaconsfield 1962–97; pt/t specialist law lectr 1983–94; underwriting memb Lloyd's 1972–93; memb Law Soc delgn to European Commision 1972, memb first delgn of Parly candidates (Cons) to European Parl 1973; Parly candidate (Cons) Manchester Openshaw 1974; fndr memb Central and S Middx Law Soc (former memb Cncl); memb: Soc of Cons Lawyers (memb Exec Ctee 1974–77), Law Soc, Soc of Notaries, City of London Law Soc, Berks, Bucks and Oxon Law Soc; life vice-pres Old Wycombiensian Assoc 2004; Freeman City of London 1951, Liveryman Worshipful Co of Slrs of the City of London 1974; granted armorial bearings by Coll of Arms 1986; *Recreations* reading, travel, gardening; *Style—* Geoffrey Green, Esq; ✉ Tumblers Chase, 8 Stratton Road, Beaconsfield, Buckinghamshire HP9 1HS (tel 01494 674406)

GREEN, Dr Geoffrey Frederic; s of George Hanson Green (d 1987), of Guiseley, West Yorks, and Elizabeth, *née* Kershaw; *b* 22 August 1947; *Educ* Bootham Sch York, Univ of Edinburgh (MA, PhD); *m* 25 Nov 1974, Ellen Clare, da of Edmund Favre Hughes (d 1987), of New Orleans; 1 da (Emily Anais b 31 Oct 1983), 1 s (Christopher George b 24 April 1985); *Career* T&T Clark academic publishers: publishing dir 1977–87, md 1987–2003; *Clubs* New (Edinburgh), Carlton Cricket; *Style—* Dr Geoffrey Green; ✉ 46 Dick Place, Edinburgh EH9 2JB (tel 0131 667 2028, e-mail gandegreen@btinternet.com)

GREEN, Geoffrey Stephen; s of John Geoffrey Green, of Essex, and Margaret Rowena, *née* Millican; bro of David Green, *qv*; *b* 3 September 1949; *Educ* Forest Sch, St Catharine's Coll Cambridge (MA); *m* 1 (m dis 1980), Fiona Mary Inglis; m 2, 30 Dec 1982, Sarah Charlton Chesshire, da of Wing Cdr Arthur Chesshire; 3 s (Alexander Thomas Charlton b 29 Dec 1983, Frederick Robert b 3 June 1986, Henry George Rollo b 30 July 1990); *Career* admitted slr 1975; Ashurst Morris Crisp (now Ashurst): ptnr 1979–, head of Company and Commercial Dept 1994–98, sr ptnr 1998–; *Recreations* tennis, cricket, golf; *Clubs* Hurlingham, RAC; *Style—* Geoffrey Green, Esq; ✉ Ashurst, Broadwalk House, 5 Appold Street, London EC2A 2HA (tel 020 7638 1111)

GREEN, Guy Wilfrith; s of Brig Percy William Powlett Green, CBE, DSO (d 2004), and Phyllis Margery FitzGerald, *née* May (d 1995); *b* 24 July 1947, Beaconsfield, Bucks; *Educ* Wellington, Univ of Exeter; *Career* admitted slr 1972; specialises in corp acquisitions, disposals and reorganisations, and commercial contracts; Payne Hicks Beach: articled clerk 1970–72, asst slr 1972–74, ptnr 1974–, head Company and Commercial Dept 1992–, managing ptnr 2000–; memb Law Soc 1970–; *Recreations* sport, gardening, history; *Style—* Guy Green, Esq; ✉ Woodbury, Lower Chilland Lane, Martyr Worthy, Winchester, Hampshire SO21 1EB (tel 01962 779272); Payne Hicks Beach, 10 New Square, Lincoln's Inn, London WC2A 3QG (tel 020 7465 4300, fax 020 7465 4400, e-mail ggreen@phb.co.uk)

GREEN, Prof Jennifer Clare; da of Philip Leo Bilham, and Brenda Hastings, *née* Colyer; *b* 30 December 1941; *Educ* Sutton HS, St Hugh's Coll Oxford (scholar, BA, DPhil); *m* 2 Jan 65, Malcolm Leslie Hodder Green; 2 s (Russell Philip Malcolm b 30 Jan 1969, Matthew Charles Hereward b 20 Dec 1973), 1 da (Sophie Ann Jennifer b 1 Sept 1970); *Career* Turner and Newall res fell 1966–69, fell St Hugh's Coll Oxford 1969–, prof of chemistry Univ of Oxford 1999–; chm Atalanta's Fund; FRSC; *Publications* author of 200 research papers in scientific journals; *Style—* Prof Jennifer Green; ✉ Inorganic Chemistry Laboratory, South Parks Road, Oxford OX1 3QR (tel 01865 272637)

GREEN, Jill; *b* 10 July 1959; *Educ* MSc, BA; *m* Anthony Horowitz, *qv*; 2 s (b 1989, b 1991); *Career* grad trainee rising to mktg mangr (Spain) Thomson Holidays 1980–83, account mangr Allen Brady Marsh Advtg 1983–84, account dir McCann Erickson Advtg 1984–87, sr account dir Abbott Mead Vickers Advtg Agency 1987–90; Red Rooster Films & TV Entertainment: head of children's programming rising to prodr/exec prodr 1991–95, dep md 1994–96, md 1996–98; fndr Greenlit Productions (specialising in major drama and feature films) 1998–; jury memb/chm of various TV awards incl BAFTA, RTS and int EMMYs; *Recreations* design, films, remote traveller, roller blading; *Clubs* RTS, National Film Theatre, National Geographic Society; *Style—* Mrs Jill Green; ✉ Greenlit Productions Ltd, 14/15 D'Arblay Street, London W1V 3FP (tel 020 7287 3545, fax 020 7439 6767)

GREEN, Dr John Edward; s of John Green (d 1957), and Ellen, *née* O'Dowd (d 1974); *b* 26 August 1937; *Educ* Birkenhead Inst GS, St John's Coll Cambridge (MA, PhD); *m* 12 June 1959, Gillian Mary, da of Harold Barker Jackson (d 1988); 1 da (Imogen b 1964), 1 s (John b 1966); *Career* student apprentice Bristol Aircraft Ltd 1956, tech asst De Havilland Engine Co 1959–61, dir project time and cost analysis MOD (PE) HQ 1981–84, dep head of defence staff and min-cnsllr defence equipment Br Embassy Washington 1984–85, dep dir aircraft Royal Aircraft Estab 1985–87 (aerodynamics 1964–81, head various res divs 1971–78, head Aerodynamics Dept 1978–81); Aircraft Research Association Ltd: chief exec 1988–95, chief scientist 1995–; visiting prof Coll of Aeronautics 1996–2004; Royal Aeronautical Soc: memb Cncl 1986–2000, hon treas 1992–96, vice-pres 1992–95, pres-elect 1995–96, pres 1996–97; UK rep Int Cncl of Aeronautical Sciences 1986–2000 (pres 1996–98), Cranfield Univ: memb Court 1988–, memb Cncl 1995–2005, visiting prof 1996–2004; CEng 1972, FRAeS 1978, FREng 1994, fell American Inst of Aeronautics and Astronautics (FAIAA) 1999; *Recreations* mountain walking (Munroist 1994), music; *Style—* Dr John Green, FREng; ✉ 1 Leighton Street, Woburn, Milton Keynes MK17 9PJ (tel and fax 01525 290631, e-mail greens@woburnhc.freeserve.co.uk)

GREEN, Dr John Timothy; s of Thomas Albert Green (d 1978), of Birmingham, and Joan, *née* Chamberlain; *b* 1 January 1944; *Educ* King Edward's Five Ways Sch Birmingham, Queens' Coll Cambridge (fndn scholar, MA, PhD); *m* 1985, Susan Mary, da of David Harold Shattock; 1 s (Thomas William b 16 Nov 1988); *Career* Queens' Coll Cambridge: bye fell 1970–72, dean 1972–77, tutor 1977–80, sr tutor 1977–80, fell and lectr in mathematics 1972–93, life fell 1993–; chief exec RSM 1993–96; dir Historic Properties (London) English Heritage 1997–98; sec Faculty of Med Imperial Coll of Sci, Technol & Med London 1998–2004, chief co-ordinating offr Imperial Coll London 2004–; recruitment advsr FCO 1992–99; dir: South Leicestershire Garages 1985–95, Pennant Hotels 1987–95, RSM Press Ltd 1993–96, RSM Support Services Ltd 1993–96, RSM Foundation Inc NY 1993–96; vice-chm Project Hope 1995–2001; dir Kennedy Inst of Rheumatology 1999–; tstee: Harpur Tst 1984–87, London First Medicine 1995–96; independent dir 3i plc 1996–, non-exec dir: Chadwyck-Healey Ltd 1997–99, NW London Hosps Tst 2001–, Imperial Coll Bioincubator Ltd 2004–, Burlington Danes Ltd 2004–; govr: Hills Road Sixth Form Coll Cambridge 1993–98, Perse Sch Cambridge 2001–; contrib to Jl of Fluid Mechanics and other scientific pubns; *Recreations* opera, music, fell-walking; *Style—* Dr John T Green; ✉ 40 Newton Road, Cambridge CB2 8AL (tel 01223 353756)

GREEN, Jonathon Simon; s of Arthur Green (d 1989), of London, and Salome, *née* Morris; *b* 20 April 1948; *Educ* Bedford Sch, Brasenose Coll Oxford; *Partner* Susan Ford; 2 s (Lucien b 29 Sept 1977, Gabriel b 10 May 1982); *Career* freelance journalist, broadcaster, editor and writer 1969–; *Books* Contemporary Dictionary of Quotations (1982, revsd edn 1989 and 1996), Newspeak - A Dictionary of Jargon (1983), The Dictionary of Contemporary Slang (1984, revsd edn 1993 and 1996), The Slang Thesaurus (1986), The Dictionary of Jargon (1987), Days in the Life - Voices from the English Underground 1961–71 (1988), The Encyclopedia of Censorship (1990), Them - Voices from the Immigrant Community in Contemporary Britain (1990), Neologisms - A Dictionary of Contemporary Coinages (1991), It - Sex Since the Sixties (1993), Slang Down the Ages (1994), Chasing the Sun: Dictionary Makers and the Dictionaries they Made (1996), All Dressed Up: The Sixties and the Counter-Culture (1998), The Cassell Dictionary of Slang (1998), Cassell's Rhyming Slang (2000); *Style—* Jonathon Green, Esq; ✉ c/o Lucas, Alexander, Whitley, 14 Vernon Street, London W14 0RJ (tel 020 7471 7900, fax 020 7471 7910)

GREEN, Rt Rev Dr Laurence Alexander (Laurie); *see:* Bradwell, Bishop of

GREEN, Lucinda Jane; MBE (1977); da of Maj-Gen George Erroll Prior-Palmer, CB, DSO (d 1977), by his 2 w, Lady Doreen, *née* Hope (d 1998); sis of Simon Prior-Palmer, *qv*; *b* 7 November 1953; *Educ* St Mary's Sch Wantage, Idbury Manor; *m* 1981 (m dis 1992), David Michael Green, yr s of Barry Green, of Brisbane, Aust; 1 s (Frederick b 1985), 1 da (Lissa b 1989); *Career* three day eventer; winner Badminton Horse Trials Championships 1973, 1976, 1977, 1979, 1983 and 1984, Individual Euro Championships 1975 and 1977, memb Br team Olympic Games Montreal 1976, memb Euro Championship winning team Burghley 1977, memb World Championship team Kentucky 1978, memb World Championship winning Br 3-Day Event Team Luhmühlen 1982 (also winner of individual championship), Silver medal Euro Championship Frauenfeld 1983, Team Silver medal Olympic Games LA 1984, memb winning Euro Championship team Burghley 1985; coach cross-country clinics worldwide 1989–; dir British Eventing 1997–; selector Br 3-Day Event Team 1999– (chm of selectors 2003); co-presenter of 6-part documentary Horses (Channel 4) 1986–87, presenter Rural Rides (Meridian TV) 1997–98, commentator for BBC and satellite TV; commentated on all equestrian events at Olympic Games: Barcelona (for BBC) 1992, Atlanta (for Channel 7 Aust) 1996, Sydney (for Channel 7 Aust) 2000, Athens (for Channel 7 Aust) 2004; editorial conslt Eventing magazine 1989–92, columnist Riding magazine, regular contrib Daily Telegraph; memb Cncl Sport England 1999–2003; FRSA 2000; *Books* Up, Up and Away (1978), Four Square (1980), Regal Realm (1983), Cross Country Riding (1986), The Young Rider (1993); *Clubs* Mount Kenya Safari; *Style—* Mrs Lucinda Green, MBE; ✉ The Tree House, Appleshaw, Andover, Hampshire SP11 9BS (tel 01264 771133)

GREEN, Prof Sir Malcolm; kt (2007); s of James Bisdee Malcolm Green, of Colchester, Essex, and Frances Marjorie Lois, *née* Ruffel; *b* 25 January 1942; *Educ* Charterhouse, Trinity Coll Oxford (MA, BSc, BM BCh, DM), St Thomas' Hosp Med Sch; *m* 24 April 1971, Julieta Caroline, da of William Preston (d 1978); 3 da (Nicola b 6 March 1972, Alexandra b 26 Dec 1975 d 1978, Camilla b 7 Aug 1980), 2 s (Andrew b 28 Feb 1974, Marcus b 20 June 1979); *Career* lectr in med St Thomas' Hosp 1970–74 (house physician 1968–69), Radcliffe travelling fell Univ of Oxford to Harvard Univ Med Sch 1971–73, conslt physician and conslt i/c Chest Dept Bart's 1975–87, conslt physician in chest med and sr lectr Royal Brompton Hosp 1975–2006, dean Nat Heart & Lung Inst Univ of London 1988–90, dir Br Postgrad Med Fedn 1991–96; Imperial Coll Sch of Med London: vice-princ for postgrad med 1997–2000, prof of respiratory med 1998–2006 (emeritus prof 2006–), campus dean St Mary's Campus 1997–2001; vice-princ Imperial Coll Faculty of Med London 2000–06; memb Bd: Royal Brompton Hosp 1987–90, London First Centre 1995–98, St Mary's Hosp 1997–2001, London First 1998–2003, Royal Brompton and Harefield Hosp 2001–06; head Nat Heart and Lung Inst 2000–06; acting dir research and devpt for NHS 1999; pres and chm Cncl Br Lung Fndn 1985–2001, pres United Hosps SC 1992–2001 (hon treas 1977–87), chm London Medicine 1995–2000; author of chapters, reviews and articles on gen med, respiratory med and physiology; Freeman City of London 1968, Liveryman Worshipful Soc of Apothecaries 1965; FRCP 1980 (MRCP 1970), FMedSci 2001; *Recreations* sailing, skiing; *Clubs* Royal Thames Yacht, Royal Yacht Sqdn, Itchenor Sailing, Imperial Poona Yacht; *Style—* Prof Sir Malcolm Green; ✉ 38 Lansdowne Gardens, London SW8 2EF (tel 020 7622 8286, e-mail malcolm@malcolmgreen.net)

GREEN, Prof Malcolm Leslie Hodder; s of Leslie Ernest Green (d 1946), and Ethel Sheila, *née* Hodder; *b* 16 April 1936; *Educ* Denstone Coll, Acton Tech Coll (BSc), Imperial Coll London (PhD, DIC); *m* 2 Jan 1965, Jennifer Clare, da of Philip Leo Bilham (d 1956); 3 c (Russell Philip Malcolm b 1969, Sophie Anne Jennifer b 1970, Matthew Charles Hereward b 1973); *Career* res assocs fell Imperial Coll London 1959–60, asst lectr in inorganic chemistry Univ of Cambridge 1960–63 (fell Corpus Christi Coll 1961); Univ of Oxford: septcentenary fell of inorganic chemistry Balliol Coll 1963–88, departmental demonstrator 1963, univ lectr 1965–88, vice-master Balliol Coll 1987, prof of inorganic chemistry and head of dept 1989–2003, emeritus prof 2003–, fell St Catherine's Coll; visiting prof: Univ of W Ontario 1971, École de Chimie and Institute des Substances Naturelles 1972; A P Sloan visiting prof Harvard Univ 1973, Pacific W Coast lectr in inorganic chemistry, Br Gas Royal Soc sr res fell 1979–86, Sherman Fairchild visiting scholar Caltech 1981, Karl Ziegler Gastprofessor Max Planck Inst Mulheim 1983, Hutchinson lectr Univ of Rochester 1983, Univ lectr in chem Univ of W Ontario 1984, Wuhan Univ PRC 1985, Debye lectr Cornell Univ 1985, Julius Stieglitz lectr Univ of Chicago 1986, Frontiers of Science lectr Texas A&M Univ 1987, Sir Edward Frankland prize lectr 1989, Glenn T Seaborg lectr in inorganic chemistry Univ of Calif Berkeley 1991, SE lectr in inorganic chemistry USA 1991, Walter Heiber Gastprofessor Univ of Munich 1991; conslt to: Medisense, BP, ICI; Corday-Morgan medal and prize 1974, RSC medal in Organometallic Chemistry 1986, JC Bailar medal Univ of Illinois 1983, American Chemical Soc annual award for Inorganic Chemistry 1984, Tilden prize 1982, Karl-Ziegler prize of Gesellschaft Deutscher Chemiker Germany 1992, Davy medal Royal Soc 1995, American Chemical Soc annual award for Orgonometallic Chemistry 1996, Dwyer medal Univ of NSW 1997, Sir Geoffrey Wilkinson Medal and Prize RSC 2000; hon doctorate Universidade Tecnica de Lisboa - Instituto Superior Tecnico 1996; CChem, FRSC, FRS 1985; *Recreations* family; *Style—* Prof Malcolm Green, FRS; ✉ St Catherine's College, Oxford OX1 3UJ; Inorganic Chemistry Laboratory, South Parks Road, Oxford OX1 3QR (tel 01865 272649, fax 01865 272690, e-mail malcolm.green@chem.ox.ac.uk)

GREEN, Dr Malcolm Robert; s of Frank Green (d 1970), and Margery Isabel Green (d 1997); *b* 4 January 1943; *Educ* Wyggeston GS Leicester, Magdalen Coll Oxford (MA, DPhil); *m* 18 Dec 1971, Mary Margaret, da of Leonard Charles Pratley (d 1987); 2 da (Eleanor b 1975, Sally b 1978), 1 s (Alasdair Calum b 1981); *Career* lectr in Roman history Univ of Glasgow 1967–98; memb: Corpn of Glasgow 1973–75, Strathclyde Regnl Cncl 1975–96, City of Glasgow Cncl 1996–; chm: Scottish Teachers and Lectrs Negotiating Ctee 1977–90, Nat Ctee for In-Serv Trg of Teachers 1977–86, Educn Ctee of Convention of Scottish Local Authorities 1978–90, Scottish Ctee for Staff Devpt in Educn 1987–91, Educn Ctee City of Glasgow Cncl 1995–99; Scottish cmmr MSC 1983–85, fin chm Scottish Examination Bd 1984–90; business mangr 1999–; active in community based housing assoc movement 1975–; FSQA; *Style—* Dr Malcolm Green; ✉ 46 Victoria Crescent Road, Glasgow G12 9DE (tel 0141 339 2007); City Chambers, George Square, Glasgow G2 1DU (tel 0141 287 3530, fax 0141 287 7856)

GREEN, Prof Michael Alan; s of Thomas Clifford Green (d 1987), and Anne, *née* Greaves (d 1994); *b* 26 June 1938; *Educ* Batley GS, Univ of Leeds (MB ChB), DCH, DObstRCOG, DMJ; *m* 1962, Jennifer Barbara, *née* Mencher; 2 da (Tana b 20 March 1963, Maia b 8 Nov 1964); *Career* MO Royal Flying Doctor Serv Aust 1967–68, MO forensic pathology NSW 1968–69, sr lectr in forensic pathology Univ of Leeds 1974–90 (lectr 1970–74), prof of forensic pathology Univ of Sheffield 1990–99, emeritus prof Univ of Sheffield 1999–; Royal Coll of Pathologists: chm Forensic Specialist Advsy Ctee 1992–98, memb Cncl 1995–98; pres Br Assoc of Forensic Med 1993–95; FRCPath; *Books* Clinical Toxicology (with C J Polson and M R Lee, 1984), Dealing with Death (with J B Green, 1990, 2 edn 2006), Pathology of Trauma (contrib, 1993); also numerous papers on forensic pathology since 1972; *Recreations* music, model railways, walking, motorcycle restoration; *Style—* Prof Michael Green; ✉ 5 Grosvenor Park, Allerton Hill, Leeds LS7 3QD (tel 0113 268 0825, fax 0113 268 0825, mobile 07741 010962, e-mail mike_jen_green@btopenworld.com)

GREEN, Rev Dr (Edward) Michael Bankes; s of Rev Edward Bankes Green (d 1985), and Beatrice Emily, *née* Smith (d 1980); *b* 20 August 1930; *Educ* Clifton, Exeter Coll Oxford (scholar, BA), Queens' Coll and Ridley Hall Cambridge (BA, BD, Fencing blue, Carus New Testament and Selwyn New Testament prizes), Univ of Toronto (DD); *m* 12 Sept 1957, Rosemary Wake, da of Lt-Col Charles Felix Stoehr, OBE (d 1932); 2 s (Timothy b 1960, Jonathan b 1966), 2 da (Sarah b 1962, Jenny b 1964); *Career* Nat Serv Lt RA 1953–55; ordained: deacon 1957, priest 1958; curate Holy Trinity Eastbourne 1957–60; tutor in New Testament: London Coll of Divinity 1960–69, Univ of London 1960–69, Univ of Nottingham 1969–75; canon of Coventry 1970, princ St John's Coll Nottingham 1969–75, rector St Aldate's Church Oxford 1975–86, prof of evangelism Regent Coll Vancouver 1987–92, advsr in evangelism to Archbishops of Canterbury and York 1992–2002, sr research fell Wycliffe Hall Oxford 1997–2005, co-rector Holy Trinity Church Raleigh NC 2005–; pres Christian Union Oxford 1955–57, memb Studiorum Novi Testamenti Societas 1960, conslt Lambeth Conf 1968, memb Anglican Doctrinal Cmmn 1969–75; DD (Lambeth) 1996; *Books* Called to Serve (1964), Evangelism in the Early Church (1970), I Believe in the Holy Spirit (1975), You Must Be Joking (1976), The Truth of God Incarnate (ed 1977), I Believe in Satan's Downfall (1981), To Corinth With Love (1982), Evangelism through the Local Church (1990), Who Is This Jesus? (1990), On Your Knees, My God, Good News is for Sharing, Acts for Today, New Testament Spirituality, How Can I Lead a Friend to Christ? (1995), Critical Choices (1995), Strange Intelligence (1996), Evangelism for Amateurs (1998), After Alpha (1998), Bible Reading for Amateurs (1999), Churchgoing for Amateurs (2000), The Message of Matthew (2000), Asian Tigers for Christ (2001), Adventure of Faith (2001), 30 Years that Changed the World (2002), A Prayer Journey with the Apostle Paul (2004), The Books the Church Suppressed (2005), You cannot be serious (2005), I'd like to believe, but... (2005), In Search of Spirituality (2007); *Recreations* fishing, walking, squash, gardening; *Style—* Rev Canon Dr Michael Green; ✉ 7 Little Acreage, Old Marston, Oxford OX3 0PS (tel 01865 248387, fax 01865 792083)

GREEN, Prof Michael Boris; s of Absalom Green, of London, and Genia, *née* Osherovitz; *b* 22 May 1946; *Educ* William Ellis Sch, Churchill Coll Cambridge (BA, PhD); *Career* res fell: Inst for Advanced Study Princeton NJ 1970–72, Cavendish Laboratory Cambridge 1972–77, Dept of Theoretical Physics Oxford 1977–79; Nuffield science fell 1984–86, prof Physics Dept QMC London 1985–93 (lectr 1979–85), John Humphrey Plummer prof of theoretical physics Univ of Cambridge 1993–; sr fell SERC 1986–91 (advanced fell 1977–79), distinguished Fairchild fell Caltech 1990; Maxwell medal and prize Inst of Physics 1987, Hopkins prize Cambridge Philosophical Soc 1987, Dirac medal Int Centre of Theoretical Physics 1989, Heinemann prize American Physical Soc 2002, Dirac medal and prize Inst of Physics 2004; FInstP, FRS 1989; *Books* Superstring Theory Vols 1 and 2 (with J H Schwarz and E Witten, Cambridge University Press, 1987); *Style—* Prof Michael Green, FRS; ✉ Department of Applied Mathematics and Theoretical Physics, Silver Street, Cambridge CB3 9EW (tel 01223 330884)

GREEN, Michael Philip; s of Cyril Green, and Irene, *née* Goodman; *b* 2 December 1947; *Educ* Haberdashers' Aske's; *m* 1, 12 Oct 1972 (m dis 1989), Hon Janet Frances, da of Baron Wolfson, FBA (Life Peer), *qv*; 2 da (Rebecca b 1974, Catherine b 1976); m 2, 15 June 1990, Theresa (Tessa), *née* Buckmaster; 3 s (Oliver Charles b 1992, Theodore Samuel b 1994, Jack Benjamin Maurice b 1997), 1 da (Marina Jacqueline b 2001); *Career* chm Carlton Communications plc 1983–2003; dir Tangent Industries Ltd; non-exec dir: Reuters Holdings plc 1992–99, Independent Television News Ltd, Thomson, GMTV Ltd; chm: The Media Tst, Tangent Charitable Tst; tstee Sainsbury Centre for Mental Health; *Recreations* bridge, television; *Clubs* Portland; *Style—* Michael Green, Esq

GREEN, Nicholas Nigel; QC (1998); s of John Reginald Green, of Warwickshire, and Pauline Barbara; *b* 15 October 1958; *Educ* King Edward's Camp Hill Sch Birmingham, Univ of Leicester (LLB), Univ of Toronto (LLM), Univ of Southampton (PhD); *m* 22 Sept 1990, Fiona Clare, da of Alan Lindsay Cramb (d 1997); 1 da (Natasha Victoria Green b 17 May 1992), 1 s (Alexander John Green b 18 Aug 1994); *Career* called to the Bar Inner Temple 1986 (master 2002, bencher 2003), with Brick Court Chambers; recorder of the Crown Court 2004–; memb Supplementary Panel Treasury Counsel 1997–98; lectr Univ of Southampton 1981–85, pt/t lectr UCL 1985–87; chm Bar European Gp 1999–2001, vice-chm Int Rels Ctee Bar Cncl 2000–02, memb Bar Cncl 2001–, memb Gen Mgmnt Ctee of the Bar 2001–, chm European Ctee Bar Cncl 2003–06, memb Exec Ctee Inner Temple 2003–, chm Legal Servs Ctee Bar Cncl 2006–; visiting prof of law Univ of Durham 2000–, hon prof of law Univ of Leicester; *Publications* Commercial Agreements and Competition Law: Practice and Procedures in the UK and EEC (1986, 2nd ed 1997); *Recreations* swimming (swam for England 1976 and English Univs 1978–79), family, collecting Victorian watercolours; *Style—* Nicholas Green, QC

GREEN, Dame Pauline; DBE (2003); da of Bertram William Wiltshire (d 1975), of Bracknell, Berks, and Lucy, *née* Vella; *b* 8 December 1948; *Educ* John Kelly Secdy Modern Girls' Sch, Kilburn Poly, Open Univ (BA), LSE (MSc); *m* 6 March 1971 (m dis 2003), Paul Adam Green, s of Charles Henry Green, of Southampton; 1 s (Simon Timothy b 23 April 1974), 1 da (Ruth Charlotte b 20 Oct 1976); *Career* met police offr 1969–74, subsequently asst teacher Special Educn Unit London Borough of Barnet, pt/t lectr Barnet Coll of FE 1980–85, asst Parly offr Co-operative Union (responsible for Euro affairs) 1985–89; MEP (Lab) London North 1989–99, MEP (Lab) London 1999 (lead candidate regnl list); ldr: Euro Parly Lab Pty 1993–94, Parly Gp Pty of Euro Socialists 1994–99; vice-pres Socialist International 1994–99; Lab Pty spokesperson on public health and consumer protection 1989–93, pres All-Pty Gp on Consumer Affairs 1989–94, memb Bureau of Socialist Gp 1991–; chief exec Co-operatives UK Ltd 2000–, memb Co-operative Cmmn (sponsored by PM, Tony Blair, MP, *qv*) 2000–; memb: Lab Pty NEC 1993–99, Co-operative Pty, USDAW; Grand Gold Cross with Star (Austria), Cdr of the Order of Honour (Greece), Grand Cdr of the Order of Merit (Cyprus); *Recreations* music, reading; *Style—* Dame Pauline Green; ✉ Co-operatives UK Ltd, Holyoake House, Hanover Street, Manchester M60 0AS (tel 0161 246 2939, e-mail pauline.green@cooperatives-uk.coop)

GREEN, Prof Peter James; s of Frank Arthur Green (d 1981), and Joyce Maureen, *née* Walder (d 1975); *b* 28 April 1950, Solihull; *Educ* Solihull Sch, Univ of Oxford (BA), Univ of Sheffield (MSc, PhD); *m* 25 June 1984, Elizabeth Jane Bennett, *née* Styles; 2 da (Sarah Jane (Mrs Lyall) b 1970, Katherine (Mrs Walker) b 1972); *Career* lectr in statistics Univ of Bath 1974–78, sr lectr in statistics Univ of Durham 1986–89 (lectr 1978–86); Univ of Bristol: prof of statistics 1989–, Henry Overton Wills prof of mathematics 2003–; visiting assoc prof Univ of Wisconsin 1984–85; Royal Statistical Soc: Guy Medal in Bronze 1987, Guy Medal in Silver 1999, pres 2001–03; Royal Soc Wolfson Research Merit Award 2006; FIMS 1991, CStat 2000, FRS 2003; *Publications* Nonparametric Regression and Generalised Linear Models (1994), Highly Structured Stochastic Systems (ed, 2003); author of numerous papers in academic jls; *Recreations* learning to fly, biking, running, mountains; *Style—* Prof Peter Green; ✉ School of Mathematics, University of Bristol, Bristol BS8 1TW (tel 0117 928 7967, fax 0117 928 7999, e-mail p.j.green@bristol.ac.uk)

GREEN, Prof Peter Morris; s of Arthur Green, CBE (d 1976), and Olive Emily, *née* Slaughter (d 1985); *b* 22 December 1924; *Educ* Charterhouse, Trinity Coll Cambridge (open major scholar, sr fndn scholar, res scholar, MA, PhD); *m* 1, 28 July 1951 (m dis 1975), Lalage Isobel, da of late Prof R J V Pulvertaft; 2 s (Timothy Michael b 1955, Nicholas Paul b 1958), 1 da (Sarah Francesca b 1960); m 2, 18 July 1975, Carin Margreta, da of late G N Christensen, of Saratoga, USA; *Career* WWII RAFVR 1943–47; dir of studies in classics Selwyn Coll Cambridge 1952–53, fiction critic London Daily Telegraph 1953–63, literary advsr The Bodley Head 1957–58, sr conslt ed Hodder & Stoughton 1960–63, TV critic The Listener 1961–63, film critic John London's 1961–63, emigrated to Greece as full-time writer 1963–71, lectr in Greek history and literature Coll Year in Athens Greece 1966–71 (memb Bd of Advsrs 1984–); Univ of Texas: visiting prof of classics 1971–72, prof of classics 1972–97, James R Dougherty jr centennial prof of classics 1982–97, memb numerous univ ctees and Classics Dept ctees 1974–97, emeritus prof 1997–; sr fell Nat Educn in the Humanities (NEH) 1983–84, visiting prof UCLA 1976, Mellon prof of humanities Tulane Univ 1986, visiting prof of history Univ of Iowa 1997–98, adjunct prof of classics Univ of Iowa 1998–, visiting fell and writer in residence Hellenic Studies Program Princeton Univ 2001; ed Syllecta Classica 1999–; numerous public lectures; memb Book Soc Selection Ctee 1959–62; former memb selection ctees for literary prizes: Heinemann Award, John Llewelyn Rhys Prize, WH Smith £1000 Award for Literature; Grand Prize Nat Library for Poetry USA 1997; memb: APA, AIA, Classical Assoc UK, Soc for Promotion of Hellenic Studies UK; FRSL 1956 (memb Cncl 1959–1963); *Books* The Expanding Eye (1953), Achilles His Armour (1955), Cat in Gloves (under pseudonym Denis Delaney, 1956), The Sword of Pleasure (W Heinemann award for Lit 1957), Kenneth Grahame 1859–1932: A Study of his Life, Work and Times (1959), Essays in Antiquity (1960), Habeas Corpus and Other Stories (1962), Look at the Romans (1963), The Laughter of Aphrodite (1965, reprinted 1993), Juvenal: The Sixteen Satires (trans, 1967, 3 edn 1998), Armada from Athens: The Failure of the Sicilian Expedition 415–413 BC (1970), Alexander the Great: A Biography (1970), The Year of Salamis 480–479 BC (1971, reprinted and updated as The Greco-Persian Wars, 1996), The Shadow of the Parthenon (1972), Alexander of Macedon 356–323 BC: An Historical Biography (1974, reprinted 1991), Ovid: The Erotic Poems (trans, 1982), Beyond the Wild Wood: The World of Kenneth Grahame (1982), Medium and Message Reconsidered: The Changing Functions of Classical Translation (1986), Classical Bearings: Interpreting Ancient History and Culture (1989), Alexander to Actium: The Historical Evolution of the Hellenistic Age (1990, revised reprint 1993), Hellenistic History and Culture (ed, 1993), Yannis Ritsos' The Fourth Dimension (trans, 1993), Ovid: The Poems of Exile (trans, 1994, reprinted and updated 2005), Apollonios Rhodios: The Argonautika (trans, ed and comment, 1997), From Ikaria to the Stars (2004), The Poems of Catullus: A Bilingual Edition (trans, ed and comment, 2005), Diodoros Siculus 11–12.37.1 Greek History 480–431 BC: The Alternative Version (trans, ed and comment, 2006), The Hellenistic Age: A Short History (2007), Zigzag Through the Bitter Orange Trees (trans, 2007); *Recreations* walking, chamber music, travel, avoiding urban life; *Clubs* Savile; *Style—* Prof Peter Green, FRSL; ✉ 1268 Chamberlain Drive, Iowa City, IA 52240, USA (tel 001 319 341 9805); Department of Classics, University of Iowa, Iowa City, IA 52242, USA (tel 001 319 335 2323, fax 001 319 335 3884, e-mail peter-green-1@uiowa.edu or pegreen@blue.weeg.uiowa.edu)

GREEN, Philip Ernest; s of Ernest Frederick Green, of Ashington, Dorset, and Doreen, *née* Baker; *b* 26 October 1956, Erith, Kent; *Educ* Chislehurst and Sidcup GS, Collingwood Coll Univ of Durham (BA); *m* 21 July 1979, Jane Elizabeth, *née* Ardouin; 2 s (James Edward b 7 Sept 1982, Thomas Paul b 9 April 1984); *Career* various appts Br Aerospace 1979–94; Meggitt plc: gp co sec 1994–99, gp corporate affrs dir 1999–, memb Bd 2001–; govr Queen Elizabeth's Sch Wimborne 1999–2007; FCIS 1988 (ACIS 1982); *Recreations* Southampton FC supporter; *Style—* Philip Green, Esq; ✉ Meggitt plc, Atlantic House, Aviation Park West, Bournemouth International Airport, Christchurch, Dorset BH23 6EW (tel 01202 597597, e-mail philip.green@meggitt.com)

GREEN, Philip Nevill; s of Harry Nevill Green (d 1974), and Sheila Jose, *née* Emery; *b* 12 May 1953; *Educ* Queen Mary's GS Walsall, Univ of Wales (BA), London Business Sch (MBA); *m* 27 Aug 1977, Judith Anne, *née* Rippon; 2 da (Kathryn Jane (Katie) b 12 Nov 1979, Jemma Clare b 8 Oct 1982); *Career* vice-pres Crayonne USA Inc 1977–80, md Coloroll Gp plc 1980–90, chief operating offr DHL Worldwide Express NV (Europe/Africa) 1990–99, chief operating offr Reuters Gp plc 1999–2003, ceo P&O Nedlloyd Ltd 2003–05, ceo United Utilities plc 2006–; non-exec dir: SKF Gothenberg 2000–, Lloyds TSB Group plc 2007–; tstee: Int Sch of Brussels 1993–99, Philharmonia 2000–, Missionary Aviation Fellowship (MAF) 2004–; memb Advsy Bd London Business Sch 2000; *Recreations* cricket, travel, walking, theatre, opera; *Clubs* RAC, MCC; *Style—* Philip Green, Esq; ✉ United Utilities plc, 55 Grosvenor Street, London W1K 3LJ

GREEN, Richard David; s of Bernard Green, and late Flora Amelia, *née* Wartski; *b* 25 May 1944; *Educ* Highgate Sch, The Queen's Coll Oxford (BA); *m* Jan 1994, Hazel Ann *née* Spittle; *Career* PA to Chairman/Managing Director John Wyeth & Co Ltd 1966–67; Keyser Ullman Investment Management Ltd: investment analyst 1967–68, gp economist and fund mangr 1970–72; Hill Samuel Investment Management Ltd: economist Research and Unit Trust Management 1973, instn fund mangr 1974–76, sr investment mangr 1976–77 (dir 1979); former dir Hill Samuel Investment Management (global investment) 1981, sr exec advsr/exec dir and chief investment offr Daiwa International Capital Management (UK) Ltd 1988–; memb: Soc of Business Economists, London Oil Analysts Gp, Inst of Investment Mgmnt and Res; *Recreations* travel, dog walking, charities, reading, water sports, art, theatre; *Style—* Richard Green, Esq; ✉ 45B Netherhall Gardens, Hampstead, London NW3 5RL (tel 020 7435 3497); Daiwa SB Investments (UK) Ltd, 14 St Paul's Churchyard, London EC4M 8BD (tel 020 7246 8222, fax 020 7248 1575)

GREEN, (Aylmer) Roger; s of Aylmer Green (d 1983), and Irene Cameron, *née* Hunt; *b* 15 April 1949; *Educ* Wycliffe Coll; *m* 27 July 1974, (Aud) Reidunn Teodora, da of Einar Alfred Pedersen (d 1968), of Sarpsborg, Norway; 1 da (Elizabeth b 1976), 2 s (Eric b 1978, Christian b 1988); *Career* conslt plastic surgn Mersey Regnl Plastic Surgery and Burns Centre Liverpool 1987–, clinical lectr in plastic surgery Univ of Liverpool 1987–; memb: Br Assoc of Plastic Surgns, Br Assoc of Aesthetic Plastic Surgns; LRCPI, LRCSI 1974, FRCS 1981, FRSM 1983; *Recreations* walking, skiing, fishing; *Style—* Roger Green, Esq; ✉ Mersey Regional Plastic Surgery and Burn Centre, Whiston Hospital, Prescot, Liverpool L35 5DR (tel 0151 426 1664)

GREEN, Simon Charles; s of Thomas Eric Green, of Great Longstone, Derbys, and Barbara Ann, *née* Morritt (d 1975); *b* 8 September 1961; *Educ* Worksop Coll, Aberystwyth Univ, Manchester Poly; *m* 28 April 1990, Helen Claire, da of Rodney Jameson; 1 da (Sophie Roseanna b 28 April 1991), 1 s (Sam Thomas b 13 Oct 1993); *Career* jr art dir Saatchi & Saatchi advtg 1982–86; art dir rising to gp head/bd dir: WCRS 1986–90, Still Price Lintas 1990–93; fndr ptnr Addition Marketing until 1993, jt creative/bd dir BDDH 1993–97, ptnr and jt creative dir Partners BDDH 1997–; awards: numerous from annual awards incl British TV, Campaign Press & Poster, Cannes Film Festival, NY Festival, Creative Circle, One Show, Clio, etc, 1983–; memb D&AD; *Recreations* photography, painting; *Clubs* Hogarth Health; *Style—* Simon Green, Esq

GREEN, Stephen Keith; s of Dudley Keith Green, and Dorothy Rosamund Mary, *née* Wickham; *b* 7 November 1948; *Educ* Lancing, Univ of Oxford (BA), MIT (MSc); *m* 31 July 1971, Janian Joy; 2 da (Suzannah Joy b 29 June 1974, Ruth Madalene b 16 Feb 1977); *Career* Miny of Overseas Devpt 1971–77, mgmnt conslt McKinsey & Co Inc 1977–82, Hong Kong & Shanghai Banking Corporation Ltd 1982–92; HSBC Holdings plc: gp treas 1992–98, exec dir investment banking and markets 1998–2003, gp chief exec 2003–06, gp chm 2006–; chm HSBC Investment Bank Holdings plc, chm HSBC Bank plc 2005– (dir 1995–); other HSBC directorships: The Hongkong and Shanghai Banking Corp Ltd, CCF S.A., HSBC Guyerzeller Bank AG, HSBC USA Inc., HSBC Bank USA, HSBC Private Banking Holdings (Suisse) SA, HSBC Trinkaus & Burkhardt KGaA; dir Poplar Housing and Regeneration Community Assoc 2000–, chm Int Needs UK; tstee Br Museum 2005–;

G

non-stipendiary min Anglican Church; *Books* Serving God? Serving Mammon? (1996); *Recreations* opera, European literature, walking; *Clubs* Athenaeum; *Style*— Mr Stephen Green

GREEN, Vivien; da of William Richard Green, and Violet, *née* Summers; *Career* literary agent; with: Curtis Brown Ltd 1968–71, Richard Scott Simon Ltd 1971–89, Anthony Sheil Assocs 1989–90, Sheil Land Assocs 1990–; pres Assoc of Authors' Agents; *Recreations* the company of friends; *Style*— Miss Vivien Green; ✉ Sheil Land Associates, 43 Doughty Street, London WC1N 2LH (tel 020 7405 9351, fax 020 7831 2127)

GREEN-ARMYTAGE, John McDonald (Jock); *b* 6 June 1945; *Educ* McGill Univ Montreal (BA), Columbia Univ NY (MBA); *m* 1977, Susan Rosemary, da of Lt-Col Hugh Shelley Le Messurier and Rosemary Alice Champney (maternal gda of 21 Baron Forbes and paternal ggda of Sir James Walker, 1 Bt, of Sand Hutton); 1 s (Matthew b 1978), 3 da (Anna b 1981, Camilla b 1983, Elizabeth b 1985); *Career* N M Rothschild & Sons Ltd: exec dir 1977–82, non-exec dir 1988–97; md The Guthrie Corporation 1982–88, former jt chm and chief exec Kelt Energy plc, chief exec then dep chm William Baird plc 1995–96; currently chm: Amec plc, JZ International; non-exec dir: JZ Equity Partners plc, REA Holdings plc; *Style*— Jock Green-Armytage, Esq

GREEN-PRICE, Sir Robert John; 5 Bt (UK 1874), of Norton Manor, Radnorshire; s of Capt Sir John Green-Price, 4 Bt (d 1964); *b* 22 October 1940; *Educ* Shrewsbury; *Heir* unc, Norman Green-Price, JP; *Career* landowner; Capt (ret) RCT; ADC to Govr of Bermuda 1969–72; lectr in English: Teikyo Univ 1975–82, Chiba Univ of Commerce 1982–; pt/t lectr: Keio Univ 1977–97, Waseda Univ 1986–97; guest lectr NHK Radio 1978–83, asst prof of English Chiba Univ of Commerce Japan until 1997; *Recreations* travel and relaxing at my villa in Northern Luzon, Philippines; *Style*— Sir Robert Green-Price, Bt

GREENALL, Hon Gilbert; CBE (1993); 2 s of 3 Baron Daresbury (d 1996); *b* 16 August 1954; *Educ* Eton, RMA Sandhurst, Univ of Bristol (MB ChB), INSEAD (MBA); *m* 1983, Sarah Elizabeth, er da of Ian C Mouat, of Stetchworth, Suffolk, and former w of Robert Greville Kaye Williamson; 3 s (Gilbert Edward b 1984, Frederick John b 1986, Alexander b 1988), 1 da (Amelia Frances b 1990); *Career* humanitarian relief co-ordinator: Thai/Cambodian border 1979, Karamoja Uganda 1980–81, Iran 1991, Iraq 1991; UK relief co-ordinator Northern Iraq for ODA 1991, Br Govt rep on EC/UN Mission to Baghdad and Iran/Iraq border 1991, Br Govt humanitarian relief prog for Bosnia 1992, Somalia 1993 and Angola 1993, head EC Task Force for the former Yugoslavia 1992–93, Br Govt assessment of humanitarian progs in Azerbaijan, Armenia and Georgia 1994–, Br Govt advsr on volcanic emergency Montserrat 1995, ODA advsr to GOC Multinational Div SW IFOR Bosnia 1996, Dept for Int Devpt advsr to Perm Jt Force HQ Northwood 1997; memb UN Asessment and Coordination Team (OCHA) 1997–, missions to Irian Jaya 1997, Afghanistan 1998, China 1998, Albania 1999, Kosovo 1999, East Timor 1999, Mozambique 2000, Palestinian occupied territories (West Bank and Gaza Strip) 2000, Sri Lanka 2003; DfID: advsr to Joint Task Force Sierra Leone 2000, advsr to 16 Air Assault Bde Macedonia 2001, head of mission Kabul Afghanistan 2001, humanitarian advsr Br Embassy Iraq 2004; MOD strategic review of the Balkans 2002, advsr Br Govt Post Conflict Reconstruction Unit 2005, Indian Ocean tsunami 2005, Pakistan earthquake 2005, advsr GOC UN Interim Force in Lebanon (UNIFIL) 2006; Hon MD Univ of Bristol 2006; *Recreations* flying, skiing; *Clubs* White's, St Moritz Tobogganing; *Style*— The Hon Gilbert Greenall, CBE, MD; ✉ Bromesberrow Place, Ledbury, Herefordshire HR8 1RZ

GREENAWAY, Prof David; s of David Greenaway (d 1986), and Agnes MacKechnie, *née* Parker (d 1999); *b* 20 March 1952; *Educ* Eastbank Acad Glasgow, Henry Mellish GS Nottingham; *m* (Susan) Elizabeth, da of William Hallam, of Strelley, Nottingham; 2 s (Stuart David b 1978, Daniel Christopher b 1980); *Career* lectr in econs Leicester Poly 1975–78; prof of econs: Univ of Buckingham 1986–87 (lectr sr lectr and reader 1979–86), Univ of Nottingham 1987– (pro-vice-chllr 1994–2001 and 2004–); visiting prof: Lehigh Univ Pennsylvania 1982 and 1987, Claremont Graduate Sch California 1989, 1990, 1991 and 1993; conslt: UNIDO 1983 and 1985, World Bank 1986, 1988 and 2005, Euro Cmmn 1991, GATT 1992, HM Treasy 1993, UNCTAD 1993, Asian Devpt Bank 1997, Caribbean Regional Negotiating Machinery 2000–, Dept for Tport 2003–04; jt managing ed The World Economy, assoc ed The Economic Jl; non-exec dir Nottingham Health Authy; non-exec dir QMC Hospital Tst 2001–04; govr NIESR 1995–; chm HEFC Research Assessment Panel for Economics 1999–2001 and 2005–; memb: ESRC Cncl 1997–2001, Armed Forces Pay Review Body 1998– (chm 2004–), Royal Econ Soc 1978 (memb Cncl and Exec 1991–97), Euro Econ Assoc, American Economic Assoc; fell Acad of Learning Societies for the Social Sciences 2000–; *Books* An Introduction to International Economics (1979), International Trade Policy (1983), Current Issues in International Trade (1985), The Economics of Intra Industry Trade (1986), Pioneers of Modern Economics in Britain (1989), Current Issues in Macroeconomics (1989), Economic Analysis of Regional Trading Agreements (1989), Trade and Industrial Policy in Developing Countries (1993), Macroeconomics - Theory and Policy in the UK (3 edn with G K Shaw, 1993); *Recreations* tennis, football, wine, travel, golf; *Style*— Prof David Greenaway; ✉ 238 Ruddington Lane, Wilford, Nottingham (tel 0115 914 5231), Department of Economics, University of Nottingham, University Park, Nottingham NG7 2RD (tel 0115 951 5469, e-mail david.greenaway@nottingham.ac.uk)

GREENAWAY, Sir John Michael Burdick; 3 Bt (UK 1933), of Coombe, Co Surrey; DL (Northants 2006); s of Sir Derek Burdick Greenaway, 2 Bt, CBE, TD, JP, DL (d 1994), and Sheila Beatrice, *née* Lockett; *b* 9 August 1944; *Educ* Harrow; *m* 1982, Susan Margaret, da of Henry Birch, of Tattenhall, Cheshire; 1 da (Camilla Helen b 6 July 1983), 1 s (Thomas Edward Burdick b 3 April 1985); *Heir* s, Thomas Greenaway; *Career* Lt Life Gds 1965–70; dir Daniel Greenaway & Sons Ltd 1970–79; farmer 1980–; *Recreations* skiing, tennis, riding; *Style*— Sir John Greenaway, Bt, DL; ✉ Lois Weedon House, Towcester, Northamptonshire NN12 8PJ (fax 01327 860533)

GREENBERG, Daniel Isaac; Dr Morris Greenberg, of London, and Dr Gillian Greenberg, *née* Freeman; *b* 5 September 1965; *Educ* City of London Sch, Trinity Coll Cambridge, Inns of Court Sch of Law; *m* 1988, Julia Sharon Becker; 4 c (Yisroel Meir b 1989, Avrohom Boruch b 1992, Shira Chana b 1996, Elisheva Rivka b 1999); *Career* called to the Bar 1988; legal advsr Lord Chllr's Dept 1988–91, counsel Parly Counsel Office 1991–; govr Ind Jewish Day Sch 1994–; participant in numerous Jewish communal and educational projects; *Publications* Stroud's Judicial Dictionary (7 edn 2006), Craies on Legislation (8 edn 2004); occasional articles on Jewish law in The Jewish Chronicle 1996–; *Recreations* Talmudic study, family life; *Clubs* North Hendon Adas Yisroel; *Style*— Daniel Greenberg, Esq; ✉ Office of the Parliamentary Counsel, 36 Whitehall, London SW1A 2AY

GREENBERG, Joanna Elishever Gabrielle; QC (1994); da of Ivan Marion Greenberg (d 1966), and Doris, *née* Sandground (d 1990); *Educ* Brondesbury and Kilburn HS for Girls, King's Coll London (LLB); *Career* called to the Bar Gray's Inn 1972 (bencher 2002); recorder 1995– (asst recorder 1992–95); chm Police Appeals Tbnls 1997–; *Style*— Miss Joanna Greenberg, QC; ✉ 3 Temple Gardens, Temple, London EC4Y 9AU (tel 020 7583 1155, fax 020 7353 5446, e-mail clerks@3templegardens.co.uk)

GREENBERG, Simon Marc; Benson Greenberg, and Judith, *née* Ashley; *b* 26 July 1969; *Educ* Christ's Coll Finchley, Univ of Exeter (BA), City Univ (Dip Newspaper Journalism); *Career* journalist; jr reporter Hornsey Jl 1991–92; Mail on Sunday: sports reporter, asst sports ed, dep sports ed 1992–97; sports ed Evening Standard 1997–2000, assoc ed and head of sport News of the World 2000–02, asst ed (sport) Evening Standard 2002–04, dir of communications Chelsea FC 2004–; *Awards* Br Sports Journalism Sports Reporter of the Year 1994, UK Press Gazette/Br Press Awards Sports News Reporter of the Year 1994; *Recreations* all sport, films; *Style*— Simon Greenberg; ✉ Chelsea Football Club, Stamford Bridge, Fulham Road, London SW6 1HS (tel 020 7958 2885, e-mail simon.greenberg@chelseafc.com)

GREENBURY, Toby Jonathan; s of Coleman Leonard Greenbury (d 1989), of Henley-on-Thames, Oxon, and Hannah Judith Pamela Greenbury; *b* 18 September 1951; *Educ* Clifton, UCL; *Career* asst slr Stephenson Harwood 1976–79 (articled clerk 1974–76, seconded assoc Lord Day & Lord NY 1976–77); D J Freeman: asst slr 1979–80, ptnr 1980–2001, sr ptnr 2001–03; ptnr Olswang 2003–; Freeman: City of London 1987, Worshipful Co of London Slrs 1985; memb: Law Soc, NY Bar; *Recreations* gardening, polo, riding, music; *Clubs* Hurlingham, City; *Style*— Toby Greenbury, Esq; ✉ Olswang, 90 High Holborn, London WC1V 6XX (tel 020 7067 3000, fax 020 7067 3999, e-mail toby.greenbury@olswang.com)

GREENE, Dr Alice Mary; da of Col Charles Westland Greene, Indian Med Servs, ret (d 1984), and Dr Elizabeth M Greene, *née* Rees, Capt RAMC, ret (d 2003); *b* 19 September 1952; *Educ* Wesley Coll Dublin, Trinity Coll Dublin (MB BCh, BAO, BA); *Career* Sir Patrick Dun's Hosp Dublin 1977–78, St James' Hosp 1978–79, Crumlin Children's Hosp Dublin 1980, registrar in med Royal London Homoeopathic Hosp 1982–83, GP NHS practice 1983–87, opened private practice Hampstead 1983–89, Letchworth Centre for Homoeopathic and Complementary Med 1985–91, private practice Harley St 1989–; lectr: Br Autogenic Soc, Homeopathic Physicians Teaching Gp Oxford 1991–; postgrad qualifications: DCH, DObst 1980, Family Planning Cert 1980, Dip Autogenic Psychotherapy 1988, Dip Psychosynthesis 1995, UKCP Registered Psychotherapist; MRCGP 1981, fell Br Autogenic Soc 2000 (chairwoman 1997–2000), fell Faculty of Homeopathy (FFHom) 2001 (memb 1982); *Style*— Dr Alice Greene; ✉ The Fourth Floor Flat, 86 Harley Street, London W1G 7HP (tel 020 7580 4188, fax 020 7580 6466, e-mail algreene@globalnet.co.uk, website www.dralicegreene.com)

GREENE, Graham Carleton; CBE (1986); er s of late Sir Hugh Carleton Greene; *b* 10 June 1936; *Educ* Eton, UC Oxford (MA); *m* 1, 1957 (m dis), Hon Judith Margaret, da of late Baron Gordon-Walker, CH, PC (Life Peer); m 2, 1976 (m dis 1984), Sally Georgina Horton, da of Sidney Wilfred Eaton; 1 s; *Career* merchant banking Dublin, New York and London 1957–58; publishing: Secker & Warburg Ltd 1958–62, Jonathan Cape 1962–90 (dir 1962–90, md 1966–88); dir: Chatto, Virago, Bodley Head and Jonathan Cape 1969–88 (chm 1970–88), Random House UK Ltd 1988–90, Jackdaw Publications (chm 1964–88), Cape Goliard Press 1967–88, Guinness Mahon Holdings 1968–79, Australasian Publishing Co Pty 1969–88 (chm 1978–88), Sprint Productions 1971–80, Book Reps (NZ) 1971–88 (chm 1984–88), CVBC Services Ltd (chm 1972–88), Guinness Peat Group plc 1973–87, Grantham Book Storage Ltd (chm 1974–88), Triad Paperbacks Ltd 1975–88, Chatto, Virago, Bodley Head and Jonathan Cape Australia Pty Ltd (chm 1977–88), Greene King plc 1979–2004, Statesman & Nation Publishing Co Ltd 1980–85 (chm 1981–85), Statesman Publishing Co Ltd 1980–85 (chm 1981–85), New Society (chm 1984–86), Random House Inc 1987–88, Jupiter Int Green Investment Trust plc 1989–2001, Henry Sotheran Ltd 1990–, Ed Victor Ltd 1991–, Rosemary Sandberg Ltd 1991–2002, Libra KFT (Budapest) 1991–, London Merchant Securities plc 1996–2007 (chm 2000–07), Garsington Opera Limited 1996– (chm 2006–; pres Publishers Assoc 1977–79 (memb Cncl 1969–88); memb: Book Devpt Cncl 1970–79 (dep chm 1972–73), Int Ctee Int Publishers Assoc 1977–88 (Exec Ctee 1981–88), Groupe des Editeurs de Livres de la CEE (EEC) 1977–86 (pres 1984–86), Arts Cncl Working Party Sub Ctee on Public Lending Right 1970, Paymaster Gen's Working Party on Public Lending Right 1970–72, Bd British Cncl 1977–88; chm Nat Book League 1974–76 (dep chm 1971–74), memb Gen Ctee Royal Literary Fund 1975; chm Museums and Galleries Cmmn 1991–96; British Museum: tstee 1978–2002, chm of tstees 1996–2002; vice-chm British Museum Devpt Tst 1993–2004 (chm 1986–93), pres British Museum Fndn Inc 1989–90, chm British Museum Co Ltd 1988–96, dir American Friends of British Museum 1990–2002; vice-pres GB-China Centre 1997– (chm 1986–97); memb Bd: Sainsbury Inst of Study of Japanese Arts and Culture 1999–, Stiftung Hans Arp und Sophie Taeuber-Arp 1999–; tstee Trollope Soc 1989–2004, memb Cncl Stiftung Temple Gift 2001–, chm Compton Verney House Tst 2005– (govr 1995–); Freeman City of London 1960, Liveryman Fishmongers' Co 1960; Hon DLitt Keele Univ 2002, Hon DCL UEA 2002, Hon DLitt Buckingham Univ 2004; Chevalier de l'Ordre des Arts et des Lettres (France) 1985; *Style*— Graham Greene, Esq, CBE; ✉ 6 Bayley Street, Bedford Square, London WC1B 3HE (tel 020 7304 4101, fax 020 7304 4102, e-mail grahamc.greene@virgin.net)

GREENER, Sir Anthony Armitage; kt (1999); s of William Martin Greener, and Diana Marianne, *née* Muir; *b* 26 May 1940; *m* Audrey, da of Patrick Ogilvie (d 1944); 1 da (Claire b 20 Oct 1977), 1 s (Charles b 4 May 1981); *Career* dir and gp md Dunhill Holdings plc 1974–87; Guinness plc: dir 1986–87, jt gp md 1987–91, chief exec 1992–97, chm 1993–97; jt gp chm Diageo plc (following merger with Grand Metropolitan plc) 1997–98, sole chm Diageo plc 1998–2000; chm United Distillers plc 1996–98 (md 1987–91), dep chm British Telecommunications plc 2000–06; dir: Reed International plc 1990–98, Reed Elsevier plc 1993–98, Robert Mondavi 2000–04; chm: Univ for Industry 2000–04, Qualifications and Curriculum Authy (QCA) 2002–; memb Bd: United Learning Tst 2005–, United Church Schs Tst 2005, Williams Sonoma 2007–; chair Local Governing Bd Swindon Acad 2007; *Recreations* ocean racing, skiing; *Clubs* Royal Ocean Racing, Royal Yacht Sqdn; *Style*— Sir Anthony Greener; ✉ Qualifications and Curriculum Authority, 83 Piccadilly, London W1J 8QA (tel 020 7509 5893, fax 020 7509 6975)

GREENFIELD, Dr Christopher John; s of Leonard George Greenfield (d 1991), of Oldland Common, nr Bristol, and Betty Joan, *née* Griffiths; *b* 28 December 1948; *Educ* Kingswood GS, Univ of Leeds (BA), Michigan State Univ (MA), Univ of Bristol (MEd, EdD); *m* 23 June 1984, Gillian, da of George Orme (d 1984), of Newcastle upon Tyne; 1 s (George b 1987), 1 da (Laura b 1989); *Career* researcher Rowntree Tst 1971–73, asst to Richard Wainwright MP 1974–77, teacher in Huddersfield and Bahrain 1978–82, Quaker ME sec 1982–86, headmaster Sidcot Sch 1986–97, princ Sherborne Sch Int Coll 1997–; Parly candidate: (Lib) Leeds NE 1974, (Lib) Leeds W 1979, (Lib Dem) Kingswood 2001; chm: Quaker Headteachers' Conf 1991–94, Assoc of Int Study Centres 2001–04; vice-chm: Assoc of Educnl Guardians of Int Students 2000–04, Rowntree Reform Tst 2006– (tstee 1983–); memb: Leeds CC 1973–76, W Yorks CC 1976–80, Soc of Headmasters of Ind Schs 1986, Winscombe PC 1988–97, Long Sutton PC 1997–99, Boarding Schools Assoc Exec 2006–; fell CCC Cambridge 1995–96; *Publications* White Robed Queen (1994), By Our Deeds (1997), The Bridge (ed, 2000), World Class (with P Hardaker, 2005), Schooling in England (2007); *Recreations* local history, local affairs; *Clubs* National Liberal; *Style*— Dr Christopher Greenfield; ✉ Sherborne School International College, Newell Grange, Sherborne, Dorset DT9 4EZ (tel 01935 814743, fax 01458 241191, e-mail cjgreen@jrrt.org.uk)

GREENFIELD, Jonathan (Jon); s of John Frederick Greenfield, of Hatfield, and Mary Decimer, *née* Metivier; *b* 17 April 1959; *Educ* Hatfield GS, Univ of Manchester Sch of Architecture (BA, BArch); *m* 10 Aug 1991, Margaret Mary; 1 s (Patrick Peter b 22 Sept 1992), 1 da (Rosemary Anne b 31 May 1994); *Career* architect; office jr Sir Basil Spence Partnership 1978, trg with Trevor Dannatt & Partners 1980–81; project architect Chapman Taylor Partners (shopping devpts in Stockport and Coventry), assoc dir Pentagram Design Ltd (reconstruction of Shakespeare's Globe in Southwark, campaign designs for the Rose Theatre Tst); estab Parameta Architects 1997; UNESCO travelling scholar Verona 1980, winner Mid Herts Rotary debating competition 1976; RIBA; *Books* Shakespeare's Globe Rebuilt (contrib, 1997); *Recreations* drawing and painting; *Clubs* Friends of Shakespeare's

Globe; *Style—* Jon Greenfield, Esq; ✉ The Mill House, Burnthouse Lane, Silfield, Wymondham, Norfolk NR18 9NP (tel 01953 602084)

GREENFIELD, Baroness (Life Peer UK 2001), of Ot Moor in the County of Oxfordshire; Susan Adele Greenfield; CBE (2000); da of Reginald Myer Greenfield, and Doris Margaret Winifred Greenfield; *b* 1 October 1950; *Educ* Godolphin & Latymer Sch, St Hilda's Coll Oxford (MA, DPhil); *m* 1991 (m dis 2005), Prof Peter William Atkins, *qv*; *Career* travelling scholarship to Israel 1970, MRC res scholarship Dept of Pharmacology Oxford 1973–76, Dame Catherine Fulford sr scholarship St Hugh's Coll 1974, J H Burn Tst scholarship Dept of Pharmacology Oxford 1977, MRC trg fell Lab of Physiology Oxford 1977–81, Royal Soc Study Visit Award Coll de France Paris 1978, MRC-INSERM French Exchange fell Coll de France Paris 1979–80; Univ of Oxford: jr res fell Green Coll 1981–84, tutorial fell in med Lincoln Coll 1985–, univ lectr in synaptic pharmacology 1985–, prof of pharmacology 1996–; dep dir Squibb Projects 1988–95; Gresham chair of physic Gresham Coll London 1995–98; dir Royal Instn of GB 1998– (Fullerian prof of physiology 1998–); visiting fell in neurosciences Inst La Jolla CA 1995, distinguished visiting scholar Queen's Univ Belfast 1996; Royal Instn Christmas lectr 1994 (first woman to present series); columnist Independent on Sunday 1996–98, Brain Story (series, BBC2) 2000; tstee Science Museum 1998–; chllr Heriot-Watt Univ; fell World Economic Forum 2001–; Michael Faraday Award Royal Soc 1998, Woman of Distinction of the Year Jewish Care 1998, Woman of the Year The Observer 2000; hon fell Univ of Cardiff 2000; awarded 27 Hon DScs; Hon FRCP 2000; Ordre National de la Legion d'Honneur 2003; *Books* Mindwaves (co-ed with C B Blackmore, 1987), Journey to the Centers of the Brain (with G Ferry, 1994), Journey to the Centers of the Mind (1995), The Human Mind Explained (ed, 1996), The Human Brain: A Guided Tour (1997), Brain Power (ed, 2000), Brain Story (2000), The Private Life of the Brain (2000), Tomorrow's People (2003); author of 150 published res papers; *Recreations* aerobics, travel; *Style—* The Rt Hon the Baroness Greenfield, CBE; ✉ Department of Pharmacology, Mansfield Road, Oxford OX1 3QT (tel 01865 271628, fax 01865 271853, e-mail susan.greenfield@pharm.ox.ac.uk); Royal Institution of Great Britain, 21 Albermarle Street, London W1X 4BS (tel 020 7670 2910)

GREENGROSS, Sir (David) Alan; kt (1986), DL (1986); s of Morris Philip Greengross, OBE (d 1970), and Miriam Greengross (d 1969); *b* 15 April 1929; *Educ* UC Sch, Trinity Coll Cambridge (sr scholar, MA); *m* 26 May 1959, Sally (Baroness Greengross, OBE (Life Peer), *qv*); 3 da (Gail b 1960, Joanna b 1961, Claire b 1964), 1 s (Peter b 1962); *Career* chm Memfagimal Group; dir: Indusmond Ltd, Blazy and Clement Ltd, BC Blazy and Clement Ltd, Port of London Authy 1979–84; dep traffic cmmr 1968–71; memb Holborn Borough Cncl 1957–64; memb Cncl London Borough of Camden 1965–84: chm planning and communications 1967–71, dep oppn ldr 1971–74, oppn ldr 1974–79; memb GLC 1977–86: chm Covent Garden Ctee, chm N London Area Planning Ctee, ldr Planning and Communications Policy Ctee 1979–81, dep ldr of oppn 1982–83, ldr of oppn 1983–86; visiting prof City of London Poly, chm Bloomsbury and Islington HA 1990–93, memb Bd London First; chm London Regnl Passenger Ctee 1996–2000, dep chm Rail Passengers Cncl 1999–2000, dir SW Trains 2001–; fndr memb Inst for Metropolitan Studies; govr: UC Sch 1988–, UCL 1990– (vice-chm 2003–05, hon fell); *Clubs* Hurlingham, RSM; *Style—* Sir Alan Greengross, DL; ✉ 9 Dawson Place, London W2 4TD; Batworthy on the Moor, Devon

GREENGROSS, Baroness (Life Peer UK 2000), of Notting Hill in the Royal Borough of Kensington and Chelsea; Lady Sally R; *née* Michaels; OBE (1993); *b* 29 June 1935; *Educ* Brighton & Hove HS, LSE (BA); *m* 26 May 1959, Sir Alan Greengross, *qv*; 3 da (Stephanie Gail b 24 April 1960, Joanna Louise b 31 Oct 1961, Claire Juliet b 10 Feb 1964), 1 s (Mark Peter b 6 Nov 1962); *Career* former linguist, exec in industry, lectr and researcher; vice-pres Age Concern England 2002– (asst dir 1977–82, dep dir 1982–87, DG 1987–2000), chief exec Int Longevity Centre UK 2004– (chair 2000–04); chair Experience Corps 2001–, co-chair Alliance for Health and the Future 2003–, chair Advsy Ctee English Longitudinal Study on Ageing Int Centre for Health and Soc UCL, sec-gen Eurolinkage 1981–2001, hon memb Bd of Dirs Int Fedn on Ageing, memb Bd HelpAge Int; jt chm Bd Age Concern Inst of Gerontology KCL 1987–2000, exec chair Millennium Debate of the Age 1998–2000; fndr: Age Resource, Employers' Forum on Age, Ageing Well Prog, Exchange on Ageing Law and Ethics; memb Bd Campaign for Learning 1999–, vice-chm Britain in Europe Campaign 2000–; memb: Advsy Ctee Federal Tst, Govt Task Gp on the Giving Age, Govt Task Gp on Active Ageing, Ofcom Advsy Ctee on Older and Disabled People 2004–06; pres Pensions Policy Inst 2004– (memb 2001–); patron: Action on Elder Abuse 1994–, Sheffield Inst for Studies on Ageing 1999–, Groundwork Fndn 1999–, Pennell Initiative 1999–2004, Age Concern Espana 2000–, Care and Repair England 2000–, Ransackers, Int Consortium for Intergenerational Progs; UK Woman of Europe 1990, Int Women's Forum Women That Make a Difference Award 1998; hon vice-pres Royal Soc for Promotion of Health; Hon DLitt: Univ of Ulster 1994, Brunel Univ 2002, Keele Univ 2004; Hon DUniv: Kingston and St George's, Exeter 2000, Leeds Met 2003, Open Univ 2002; FRSH 1989, FRSA 1989, Hon FIA 2000; *Books* Ageing, an Adventure in Living (ed, 1985), The Law and Vulnerable Elderly People (ed, 1986), Living, Loving and Ageing (1989), and others; *Recreations* countryside, music; *Clubs* Hurlingham, Reform; *Style—* The Rt Hon the Baroness Greengross, OBE; ✉ House of Lords, London SW1A 0PW (tel 020 7219 3000)

GREENHALGH, David Anthony; s of Rowland William Greenhalgh (d 1972), and Barbara Emily, *née* Edwards (d 1989); *b* 4 December 1943; *Educ* Sedbergh; *m* 24 May 1980, Jill Marian, da of John Donaldson (d 2001); 1 s (Thomas William Michael Iain b 26 Nov 1991); *Career* articled clerk March Pearson & Skelton Manchester 1963–68; admitted slr 1968; Linklaters: joined 1969, tax ptnr 1974–93, head of Tax Dept 1989–93, corp ptnr 1994–99; conslt: Carey Olsen 2000–03, Charles Russell LLP 2005–; dir St George's Hill Golf Club (Holdings) Ltd 2001–; memb Revenue Law Sub-Ctee City of London Law Soc 1974–91; Freeman City of London 1991; memb Law Soc 1968; *Recreations* golf, gardening; *Clubs* City of London, St George's Hill Golf, West Sussex Golf; *Style—* David Greenhalgh, Esq; ✉ Pine Close, Camp End Road, St George's Hill, Weybridge, Surrey KT13 0NU (tel 01932 862411, e-mail david.greenhalgh@cwgsy.net)

GREENHALGH, Richard; *Career* chm: Unilever UK 1998–2004, First Milk 2004–; non-exec chm CARE International UK 2004–, non-exec dir Rank Gp plc 2004–; advsr: Calor SA, All Nippon Airways; chm: Cncl for Industry and HE, Nat Coll for Sch Leadership 2000–04, Templeton Coll Oxford 2004–; memb Bd Int C of C 2000–04, memb Cncl Royal Society of Arts; CCMI 2004; *Style—* Richard Greenhalgh, Esq

GREENHALGH, Robert (Bob); s of Robert Greenhalgh (d 1994), of Lancs, and Bertha Platt (d 1980); *b* 15 March 1942; *Educ* Lancaster Royal GS, Open Univ (BA); *m* 17 July 1965, Elizabeth, da of John Richard Higdon (d 1995), of Kent; *Career* princ RNIB Nat Rehabilitation Centre 1975–83, princ of trg S Regnl Assoc for the Blind 1983–92, sr ptnr Bob Greenhalgh and Partners (t/a Iridian) 1992–94, specialist in visual disability 1994–; memb Assembly RNIB, exec memb Int Soc for Low Vision Rehabilitation and Research (ISLRR); hon chm: Mobility of the Blind Assoc 1973–76, Partially Sighted Soc 1980–88 and 1998–; hon treas Leonardo European Vision Rehabilitation Educn and Trg Assoc (LEVRETA); Freeman City of Lancaster; memb Br Assoc of Social Workers 1970; *Recreations* music, good food, writing; *Style—* Bob Greenhalgh, Esq; ✉ 43 Marine Drive, Hest Bank, Lancaster LA2 6ED (tel 01524 824878, e-mail bobgreenhalgh@btinternet.com)

GREENHALGH, Prof Roger Malcolm; s of Maj John Greenhalgh (d 1977), of IOM, and Phyllis, *née* Poynton; *b* 6 February 1941; *Educ* Ilkeston Sch, Clare Coll Cambridge (MA, MD MChir), St Thomas' Hosp; *m* 30 July 1964, Karin Maria, da of Dr Karl Gross, and Lucia, *née* Hammer; 1 s (Stephen John b 4 Sept 1967), 1 da (Christina Elizabeth b 26 June 1970); *Career* house surgn St Thomas' Hosp London 1967, lectr in surgery Bart's 1972–76; Charing Cross and Westminster Hosp Med Sch (now Imperial Coll Sch of Med since merger 1997): hon conslt surgn 1976–, sr lectr in surgery 1976–81, prof of surgery (Univ of London) 1982–, chm Dept of Surgery Charing Cross and Westminster Med Sch 1989–97, clinical dean 1991–93, dean 1993–97, head Dept of Acute and Reconstructive Surgery Imperial Coll Sch of Med 1997–, head Dept of Vascular Surgery Imperial Coll 1997–; pres of surgery Euro Union of Med Specialties 1998–2002, pres Euro Bd of Surgery 2002–; chm Med Cncl Charing Cross and Westminster Hosps 1992–93, chm Directorate of Surgery Hammersmith Hosps Tst 1993–98, chief of Vascular Service Hammersmith Hosps Tst 1998–2002; hon conslt surgn: Hammersmith Hosp Tst, Chelsea and Westminster Hosp Tst, Chelsea Royal Hosp, Queen Mary's Hosp Roehampton; Hunterian prof RCS of Eng 1980, Protem prof Brigham Hosp Harvard 1984, Boone-Powell prof Baylor Univ Dallas 1984, Hunter Sweaney prof Duke Univ North Carolina 1991, Sir Peter Freyer lectr Univ of Galway 1995, Mannick prof Brigham Hosp Harvard 1996, Scott-Heron lectr Univ of Belfast 1999, Wattie Fletcher lectr 2004, Kinmonth lectr RCS 2004; sec gen and chm Exec Ctee Assoc of Int Vascular Surgns 1982–2005, vice-pres Section of Surgery RSM 1986, pres Vascular Soc GB & I 1999–2000 (vice-pres 1998–2000) 1998–99; chm of tstees European Soc for Vascular Surgery 1987– (offr and memb Cncl 1987–93), memb Cncl Assoc of Surgns of GB and Ireland 1987–90 and 1993–, hon pres European Bd of Vascular Surgery 2005–; chm Editorial Bd European Jl of Vascular Surgery 1987–93, memb Editorial Bd Annals of Surgery; hon memb: Soc for Vascular Surgery, European Soc for Vascular Surgery, Brazilian Soc of Angiology and Vascular Surgery, Polish Surgical Soc, Hellenic Surgical Soc, Hellenic Vascular Surgical Soc, Canadian Vascular Soc, Southern Africa Vascular Surgery Soc, Mediterranean League of Vascular Surgeons, Aust Vascular Society, Swiss Vascular Soc; Liveryman: Worshipful Co of Barbers, Worshipful Soc of Apothecaries; Hon Dr (summus cum laude): Warsaw Med Acad 2003, Athens Univ 2005; ad hominem FRCS(Ed) 1999; FRCS 1971; *Books* Progress in Stroke Research (1978), Smoking and Arterial Disease (1979), Hormones and Vascular Disease (1980), Femoro Distal Bypass (1981), Extra Anatomical Bypass and Secondary Arterial Reconstruction (1982), Progress in Stroke Research 2 (1983), Vascular Surgical Techniques (1984), Diagnostic Techniques and Investigative Procedures (1985), Vascular Surgery - Issues in Current Practice (1986), Indications in Vascular Surgery (1987), Limb Salvage and Amputation in Vascular Surgery (1988), Vascular Surgical Techniques - An Atlas (2 edn 1989, 3 edn 1994, 4 edn 2001), The Cause and Management of Aneurysms (1990), The Maintenance of Arterial Reconstruction (1991), Emergency Vascular Surgery (1992), Surgery for Stroke (1993), Vascular Imaging for Surgeons (1995), The Trials and Tribulations of Vascular Surgery (1996), Clinical Surgery (ed, 1996), Inflammatory and Thrombotic Problems in Vascular Surgery (1997), Indications in Vascular and Endovascular Surgery (1998), The Durability of Vascular and Endovascular Surgery (1999), Vascular and Endovascular Opportunities (2000), The Evidence for Vascular and Endovascular Reconstruction (2002), Vascular and Endovascular Controversies (2003), Vascular and Endovascular Challenges (2004), Towards Vascular and Endovascular Consensus (2005); *Recreations* tennis, snorkelling; *Clubs* Athenaeum, Garrick; *Style—* Prof Roger Greenhalgh; ✉ 271 Sheen Lane, London SW14 8RN (tel 020 8878 1110); Department of Surgery, Charing Cross Hospital, London W6 8RF (tel 020 8846 7316, fax 020 8846 7330, e-mail r.greenhalgh@imperial.ac.uk)

GREENHILL, 3 Baron (UK 1950), of Townhead in the City of Glasgow; Malcolm Greenhill; yr s of 1 Baron Greenhill, OBE, LLD (d 1967), and Ida, *née* Goodman (d 1985); suc bro, 2 Baron Greenhill, 1989; *b* 5 May 1924; *Educ* Kelvinside Acad Glasgow, Univ of Glasgow (BSc); *Heir* none; *Career* chartered patent agent; memb UK Scientific Mission to Washington USA 1950–51, Miny of Aircraft Prodn (merged with Miny of Supply after WWII) 1944–54, UKAEA 1954–73, MOD 1973–89; *Recreations* gardening; *Style—* The Rt Hon the Lord Greenhill; ✉ 28 Gorselands, Newbury, Berkshire RG14 6PX (tel 01635 45651)

GREENING, Justine; MP; *b* 30 April 1969, Rotherham, S Yorks; *Educ* Oakwood Comp, Univ of Southampton, London Business Sch (MBA); *Career* audit mangr Price Waterhouse 1991–96, finance mangr GlaxoSmithKline 1996–2002, finance mangr Centrica plc 2002–05, MP (Cons) Putney 2005– (Parly candidate (Cons) Ealing, Acton and Shepherds Bush 2001); *Style—* Ms Justine Greening, MP; ✉ House of Commons, London SW1A 0AA

GREENISH, Damian John William; s of John William Anthony Graham Greenish (d 2000), and Sonia Petre, *née* Redfern (d 2006); *b* 20 December 1950, London; *Educ* Harrow, Univ of Warwick (BA); *m* 1, 13 Feb 1982, Bettine Mary, *née* Knudtzon; 2 s (Rupert Peter William b 7 Jan 1983, Adam Damian b 9 Feb 1985); m 2, 3 Nov 1989, Joanne Marie, *née* Paterson; 1 s (Frederick John Montrose b 20 Dec 1990), 1 da (Louisa Marie Redfern b 2 Jan 1994); *Career* admitted slr 1979; ptnr Lee & Pembertons 1980–2000, co-fndr and sr ptnr Pemberton Greenish 2000–; memb Law Soc; *Publications* Hague on Leasehold Enfranchisement (co-author, 3 edn 1999, 4 edn 2003); *Recreations* fishing, shooting, cricket; *Clubs* Armadillo Cricket, Piltdown Golf, Chelsea Arts; *Style—* Damian Greenish, Esq; ✉ Frensham House, Piltdown, East Sussex TN22 3XN (tel 01825 722291, e-mail d.greenish@tiscali.co.uk); 45 Pont Street, London SW1X 0BX (tel 020 7591 3350, fax 020 7591 3300, e-mail d.greenish@pglaw.co.uk)

GREENISH, Rear Adm Philip Duncan; CBE (2003); s of Cdr Geoffrey Greenish, OBE, RN, and late Alice Greenish; *b* September 1951; *Educ* Cheltenham Coll, Univ of Durham (BSc); *m* 1972, Wendy, *née* Midmer; 2 s, 1 da; *Career* Capt Weapon Trials and Acceptance 1992–94, MA to Chief of Defence Procurement 1994–96, RCDS 1997; dir: Operational Requirements (Sea Systems) 1997–99, Equipment Capability (Above Water Battlespace) 1999–2000; COS to C-in-C Fleet: Corp Devpt 2000–02, Support 2002–03; chief exec Royal Acad of Engrg 2003–; memb: CCLRC 2005–07, STFC 2007–; ADC to HM The Queen 1997–2000; CEng 1989, FIEE 2001; *Recreations* tennis, golf, skiing, music, gardening; *Style—* Rear Adm Philip Greenish, CBE; ✉ Royal Academy of Engineering, 29 Great Peter Street, Westminster, London SW1P 3LW

GREENLAW, Lavinia; da of Griffith John Keith Greenlaw, and Patricia Elizabeth Lindsay, *née* Mackintosh; *b* 30 July 1962, London; *Educ* Anglo-European Sch, Kingston Univ (BA), London Coll of Printing (Dip), Courtauld Inst (MA); *Children* 1 da (Georgia Elizabeth Ardizzone b 16 Nov 1987); *Career* poet and novelist; former ed and arts administrator; freelance writer, critic and broadcaster 1994–; residences incl Science Museum and Royal Festival Hall; prof of creative writing UEA 2007–; *Awards* Eric Gregory Award 1990, Arts Cncl Writers' Award 1995, Forward Prize for Single Poem 1997, Wingate Scholarship 1998, NESTA Fellowship 2000, Spycherleuk Literaturpreis 2002, Cholmondeley Award 2003, Prix du Premier Roman 2003; *Poetry* Night Photograph (1993), A World Where News Travelled Slowly (1997), Thoughts of a Night Sea (jtly, 2002), Minsk (2003); *Fiction* Mary George of Allnorthover (2001), An Irresponsible Age (2006); *Opera* Hamelin (libretto, 2003); *Non-fiction* The Importance of Music to Girls (memoir, 2007); *Opera* Minsk (2005); *Style—* Ms Lavinia Greenlaw; ✉ c/o Derek Johns, A P Watt, 20 John Street, London WC1N 2DR (tel 020 7405 6774, e-mail djohns@apwatt.co.uk)

GREENLY, Simon Stafford; s of Raymond Henry Greenly (d 2005), of Corsham, Wilts, and Brenda Margaret Agnes, *née* Stafford (d 1986); *b* 2 March 1945; *Educ* Uppingham, Univ of London (BSc); *Career* Beecham Group 1967–71; dir: Stafford Robert and Partners 1972–96, Lloyd Instruments plc 1985–87, Harlequin Financial Services 1998–2005,

Warren & Son, Snows; chm: Les Routiers 1983–90, Greenly's Management Consultants 1983–2000, ATA Selection plc 1986–88, Greenly's Holdings 1988–, GSL Systems 1991–93, Celemi UK 1993–96, Campaign for Learning 1997–2002, Leadership Alliance 1998–2001, Harlequin Leasing 1999–2000, Peter Honey Publications 2000–02, Harlequin Thoroughbred Racing 2003–04, Lucas & Greenly 2003–06, MaST International plc 2004, Winchester Capital Ptnrs 2005–; tstee: Windsor Leadership Tst 1995–2000, Bon Pere Tst 2000–; govr Meonstoke Sch; *Publications* Climate Audit (Tomorrow's Company enquiry, 1998); *Recreations* fly fishing, racing, riding, gardening, fine wine; *Clubs* RAC; *Style*— Simon Greenly, Esq

GREENO, Edward Patrick (Ted); *Educ* Cranleigh Sch, KCL; *Career* admitted slr: UK 1983, Hong Kong 1989; Herbert Smith: articled clerk 1981–83, asst slr 1983–89, ptnr 1989–; int arbitrator 2001–; memb Law Soc; MCIArb 1989; *Recreations* music, sailing, golf, Italy; *Clubs* Queen Mary Sailing; *Style*— Ted Greeno, Esq; ✉ Herbert Smith, Exchange House, Primrose Street, London EC2A 2HS (tel 020 7374 8000, fax 020 7374 0888, e-mail ted.greeno@herbertsmith.com)

GREENOUGH, Alan Edward; s of Edward Greenough (d 1987), and Nancy Dewar, *née* Houghton (d 2004); *b* 14 July 1949; *Educ* Cowley GS St Helens, Univ of Bristol (LLB); *m* 1, 1975 (m dis 1998), Sheila Mary, da of Francis Thomas Collins, of Rainhill, Merseyside; 2 da (Emma b 10 June 1978, Kate b 16 April 1980); m 2, 1999, Pamela Tracey, da of Derek Coldwell, of Ludlow, Salop; 1 da (Victoria b 3 April 2000); *Career* slr specialising in corporate finance; ptnr: Alsop Wilkinson 1979–94 (sr ptnr Manchester office 1989, sr corp fin ptnr NW 1989), Pinsent Curtis Biddle 1994–2004 (nat head of corp fin 1996–2004), White & Case 2004–06, Lovells LLP 2006– (head int private equity practice 2006–); memb Law Soc; *Recreations* rugby league, travel, cinema, most sports; *Style*— Alan Greenough, Esq; ✉ 27 Woodchester Park, Beaconsfield, Buckinghamshire HP9 2TU; Lovells LLP, Atlantic House, Holborn Viaduct, London EC1A 2FG

GREENSLADE, Prof Roy; *b* 31 December 1946, Dulwich, London; *Educ* Dagenham County HS, Univ of Sussex (BA); *Career* journalist; with Barking Advertiser 1962–66; sub ed: Lancashire Evening Telegraph 1966–67, Daily Mail Manchester 1967–69; dep chief sub ed The Sun 1969–71 and 1971–73, sub ed Daily Mirror 1971, pt/t sub ed Sunday Mirror 1975–79, news reader BBC Radio Brighton 1975–76, Daily Express and Daily Star 1979–81 (leaving as features ed), asst features ed The Sun 1981–86, managing ed (News) Sunday Times 1986–90, ed Daily Mirror 1990–91, conslt ed News International 1991, freelance 1992–, columnist The Guardian and The Observer 1996–2005, columnist Daily Telegraph 2005–; presenter Talk TV (Granada/BSkyB) 1996–97; dir: Impact Books 1993–98, Choocleus Ltd 1996–; presenter Mediumwave (BBC Radio 4); prof of journalism City Univ London 2003–; Hon DLitt Brighton 1999; *Books* Goodbye to the Working Class (1975), Maxwell's Fall (1992), Press Gang (2003); *Style*— Roy Greenslade, Esq; ✉ c/o Peters, Fraser and Dunlop, Derby House 34–43 Russell Street London WC2B 5HA (tel 020 7344 1000)

GREENSTED, Stephen; s of Leslie Bryan Greensted (d 1994), and Myra, *née* Shearsmith; *b* 6 March 1953; *Educ* Cranleigh Sch, RAF flying scholarship 1970, Keble Coll Oxford (open exhibitioner, MA); *m* 29 Sept 1976, Sally Frances, da of Prof Sir Stanley Hooker, tech dir Rolls Royce Aero Engines (d 1984); 2 da (Kate b 6 April 1982, Anna b 5 Feb 1984); *Career* advtg exec; account mangr: Hobson Bates 1974–77, Young and Rubicam 1977–79; account supr Leo Burnett 1979–84, client servs dir Gold Greenlees Trott 1984–90, gp account dir Lowe Howard-Spink 1990–94, md Woollams Moira Gaskin O'Malley 1994–95, dir Osprey Park Agency 1995–97, exec dir Euro RSCG Wnek Gosper 1997–2003, ptnr Anderson Greensted Business Strategy Consultancy 2004–; *Recreations* long-distance running; *Style*— Stephen Greensted, Esq; ✉ tel 07785 774207, e-mail results@andersongreensted.com

GREENSTOCK, Sir Jeremy Quentin; GCMG (2003, KCMG 1998, CMG 1991); s of John Wilfrid Greenstock (d 1992), of Sheepscombe, Glos, and his 1 w, Ruth Margaret, *née* Logan (d 1973); *b* 27 July 1943; *Educ* Harrow, Worcester Coll Oxford (exhibitioner, BA, Rackets blue, Tennis blue); *m* 12 April 1969, Anne Derryn Ashford Hodges, da of William Anthony Ashford Hodges, of Fritton, Norfolk; 2 da (Katherine b 1970, Alexandra b 1975), 1 s (Nicholas b 1973); *Career* asst master Eton 1966–69; HM Dip Serv: joined 1969, MECAS 1970–72, second then first sec Dubai 1970–74, private sec to HM Ambass Washington 1974–78, planning staff, personnel ops, Near E and N African Depts FCO 1978–83, commercial cnsllr Jeddah and Riyadh 1983–86, head of Chancery Paris 1987–90, asst under sec of state Western and Southern Europe FCO 1990–93, min Washington 1994–95, dep under sec Middle East and Eastern Europe FCO 1995, political dir FCO 1996–1998, UK perm rep to the UN NY and UK rep on the Security Cncl 1998–2003, UK special rep for Iraq 2003–04; dir Ditchley Fndn 2004–; non-exec dir De La Rue 2005–, special advsr BP 2004–; govr London Business Sch 2005–, tstee Int Resuce Ctee (UK) 2005–; *Recreations* reading, music, travel, sport; *Clubs* Oxford and Cambridge; *Style*— Sir Jeremy Greenstock, GCMG; ✉ The Ditchley Foundation, Ditchley Park, Enstone, Chipping Norton, Oxfordshire OX7 4ER

GREENWAY, 4 Baron (UK 1927); Sir Ambrose Charles Drexel Greenway; 4 Bt (UK 1919); s of 3 Baron (d 1975); *b* 21 May 1941; *Educ* Winchester; *m* 1985, Mrs Rosalynne Peta Schenk, da of Lt-Col Peter Geoffrey Fradgley, of Upcott Manor, Rackenford, N Devon; *Heir* bro, Hon Nigel Greenway; *Career* marine photographer and writer, chm The Marine Soc 1994–2000; pres Cruise Europe 1995, vice-pres Sail Trg Assoc 1995, pres Assoc of Sea Trg Orgns 1998; Yr Bro of Trinity House 1987; *Recreations* sailing, swimming; *Clubs* House of Lords Yacht; *Style*— The Rt Hon Lord Greenway

GREENWAY, Harry; s of late John Kenneth Greenway, and Violet Adelaide, *née* Bell; *b* 4 October 1934; *Educ* Warwick Sch, Coll of St Mark and St John London, Caen Univ; *m* 1969, Carol Elizabeth Helena, da of Maj John Robert Thomas Hooper, Metropolitan stipendiary magistrate (d 1975), and Dorinda, *née* de Courcy, of Ireland; 1 s, 2 da; *Career* former schoolmaster, chm British Atlantic Educn Ctee 1970–84; dep headmaster: Sir William Collins Sch 1971–72, Sedgehill Sch 1972–79; MP (Cons) Ealing N 1979–97; chm: All-Pty Adult Educn Ctee 1979–97, Mauritius Parly Gp 1983–97; memb Parly Select Ctee on Educn Science and Arts 1979–92, vice-chm Greater London Members 1981–87, vice-chm and hon sec Cons Parly Educn Ctee 1981–86, vice-chm Cons Pty Sports Ctee 1987–97; memb Parly Select Ctee: on Employment 1992–96, on Educn and Employment 1996–97; memb Cncl, Br Horse Soc 1973–98 (Award of Merit 1980, tstee 1998–), memb Cncl Open Univ 1981–99; pres: Nat Equine Welfare Cncl 1989–, Assoc of Br Riding Schs 1993–2003; hon vice-pres Workers' Educnl Assoc 1985–; chm Nat Prayer Breakfast 1995; currently lectr and conslt; tstee and dir The Greater London Equestrian Centres Tst Ltd; patron Teenage Cancer Tst 1994–; hockey capt House of Commons 1982–2002; hon memb Ealing Golf Club 1987–; Pres's Award Br Horse Soc 2006; Freeman City of London 1986, Liveryman Worshipful Co of Farriers; Hon DUniv Open Univ 2001; Knight Cdr's Cross of the Order of Merit Republic of Poland 1998; *Books* Adventure in the Saddle (1971), Electing to Bat (compiler, 1996); *Recreations* riding, hockey (fndr Lords and Commons Hockey Club, capt 1982–), tennis, music, cricket, skiing; *Clubs* Ski Club of GB, St Stephen's, Carlton, MCC, Middx CCC, Worcs CCC, Spencer Hockey (pres); *Style*— Harry Greenway, Esq; ✉ 64 Cambridge Street, Westminster, London SW1V 4QQ, (e-mail carolhg@globalnet.co.uk, fax 020 7976 5292)

GREENWAY, John Robert; MP; s of late Thomas William, of Northwich, Cheshire, and late Kathleen Gregory; *b* 15 February 1946; *Educ* Sir John Deane's GS Northwich; *m* 24 Aug 1974, Sylvia Ann, da of late James Francis Gant, of Whitby, N Yorks; 2 s (Stephen, Anthony), 1 da (Louise); *Career* Midland Bank 1964–65, Met Police 1965–69, insurance rep 1969–72, insurance broker 1972; MP (Cons) Ryedale 1987–; PPS to Baroness Trumpington as min of state at MAFF 1991–92; oppn front bench spokesman on home affrs (police and prisons) 1997–2000, oppn frontbench spokesman on culture, media and sport 2000–; memb Select Ctee on Home Affrs 1987–97; vice-chm All-Pty Football Ctee 1987–, chm All-Pty Insurance and Fin Servs Ctee 1992–, chm All-Pty Racing and Bloodstock Ctee 1992–97, chm All-Pty Opera Gp 1995–, sec All-Pty Media Gp 1995–; cncllr N Yorks CC 1985–87; pres York City FC; *Recreations* opera, football, racing, wine, travel; *Style*— John Greenway, Esq, MP; ✉ 11 Oak Tree Close, Strensall, North Yorkshire YO32 5TE (tel 01904 490535); 109 Town Street, Old Malton, North Yorkshire YO17 0HD (tel 01653 692023); House of Commons, London SW1A 0AA (tel 020 7219 3000)

GREENWELL, Sir Edward Bernard; 4 Bt (UK 1906), of Marden Park, Godstone, Co Surrey and Greenwell, Wolsingham, Co Durham; DL (1988); s of Capt Sir Peter McClintock Greenwell, 3 Bt, TD, DL (d 1978), and (Jean) Henrietta Rose (who m 2, Hugh Kenneth Haig, TD), da of Peter Haig Thomas and Lady Alexandra, *née* Agar, 2 da of 4 Earl of Normanton, DL; *b* 10 June 1948; *Educ* Eton, Univ of Nottingham (BSc), Cranfield Inst of Technology (MBA); *m* 1974, Sarah Louise, da of Lt-Col Philip Maitland Gore-Anley (d 1968), of Sculthorpe House, Fakenham; 3 da (Belinda Clayre b 1977, Lucy Rose b 1979, Daisy Julia b 1983), 1 s (Alexander Bernard Peter b 1987); *Heir* s, Alexander Greenwell; *Career* farmer; pres Country Land and Business Assoc 2001–03; *Clubs* Turf; *Style*— Sir Edward Greenwell, Bt, DL; ✉ Gedgrave Hall, Woodbridge, Suffolk IP12 2BX

GREENWELL, (Arthur) Jeffrey; CBE (1991), DL (Northants 1996); s of George Greenwell (d 1982), of Durham, and Kate Mary, *née* Fleming; *b* 1 August 1931; *Educ* Durham Sch, UC Oxford (MA); *m* 15 Aug 1958, Margaret Rosemary, da of Sidney David Barnard (d 1949); 2 da (Jane b 1960, Kate b 1962), 1 s (David 1964); *Career* Nat Serv RHA 1950–51; articled to Town Clerk Newcastle upon Tyne 1955–58, admitted slr 1958, law tutor Gibson and Weldon 1958–59, asst slr Birmingham Corporation 1959–61, dep clerk of the Cncl Hants CC 1967–74 (asst clerk 1964–67, asst slr 1961–64), dep clerk of the peace 1967–73, dep clerk Hants River Authy 1967–73, chief exec Northants CC 1973–96, clerk of Lieutenancy Northants 1977–96; chm: Home Office Gp on Juvenile Crime 1987, Assoc of Co Chief Executives 1993–94 (hon sec 1980–84); pres: Northants Assoc of Local Cncls 1976–96, Soc of Local Authy Chief Execs 1991 (hon sec 1984–88); independent adjudicator Office of the Dep PM 1998–; chm Northants ACRE 1998–2002, vice-chm Northants CPRE, govr UC Northampton 1989–2002, chm Central Festival Opera 1994–2004, pres Aldgate Ward Club 2008 (sr vice-pres 2007); Freeman Cities of London and Durham, Liveryman Worshipful Co of Chartered Secretaries & Administrators (master 2005–06); hon fell UC Northampton 2004; FCIS 1982 (pres 1989); *Recreations* bridge, travel, local history; *Style*— Jeffrey Greenwell, Esq, CBE, DL; ✉ 2 Hillside Way, Northampton NN3 3AW (tel and fax 01604 401858)

GREENWOOD, His Hon Judge Alan Eliezer; s of Rabbi Isaac Hans Grunewald (d 1998), and Martha Grunewald (d 1987); *b* 5 June 1947; *Educ* Hasmonean GS, UCL (LLB); *m* 15 June 1975, Naomi, *née* Ohayon; 2 s (Ilan Anthony b 20 Sept 1977, Doron Joshua b 10 Jan 1982), 1 da (Dalia Karen b 1 May 1979); *Career* called to the Bar Middle Temple 1970; asst recorder 1992–96, recorder 1996–2000, circuit judge (SE Circuit) 2000–; memb: Criminal Bar Assoc (treas 1993–97), Gen Cncl of the Bar 1993–95, United Jewish Israel Appeal (UJIA) Bench and Bar Ctee; *Recreations* five-a-side football, tennis, skiing, cycling, theatre, film, travel; *Style*— His Hon Judge Greenwood; ✉ Harrow Crown Court, Hailsham Drive, Harrow, Middlesex HA1 4TU (tel 07930 348228, e-mail hhjudge.greenwood@judiciary.gsi.gov.uk)

GREENWOOD, Maj (Arthur) Alexander; s of Dr Augustus Charles Greenwood (d 1938), of Horncastle, Lincs; cous of late Gen Sir Roland Guy, and Maj-Gen Richard Gerrard-Wright; *b* 8 March 1920; *Educ* Oakham Sch, Sidney Sussex Coll Cambridge (PhD); *m* 1, 1946 (m dis 1970), Betty Doreen, da of Brig Sidney Albert Westrop, CBE, DSO, MC (d 1979), of Brattleby, Lincs; 1 da (Jane Alexandra (Mrs Jan H Weduwer) b 12 June 1947), 1 s (Nicholas Alexander Westrop b 19 Nov 1948); m 2, 1976, Shirley Knowles Silvester, da of Wing Cdr Alec Knowles-Fitton, MBE, CC (d 1988), of Appletreewick, N Yorks, and wid of T G M Silvester; 1 da (Sara Elise Walter (*née* Silvester) b 4 Jan 1961 (adopted)); *Career* regular army, The Royal Lincs Regt 1939–59, serv WWII Norway 1940, Iceland 1940–41, India and Burma 1942–45 (despatches), ADC to Field-Marshal Sir Claude Auchinleck, GCB 1943–44, GSO 2 (Int) GHQ Middle East Land Forces 1953–54, chief instr Sch of Mil Intelligence 1954–56; memb London Stock Exchange 1963–76; co dir 1977–; dir: Allied City Share Tst plc 1964–74, Lincolnshire Chickens Ltd 1965–87; vice-pres: Reform Party of Canada 1994–95 (riding dir 1992–95 and 1999–2001), Heraldry Soc of Canada; memb: Authors Soc, Heraldry Soc, United Servs Inst, Burma Star Assoc, Soc of Genealogists; Liveryman Worshipful Co of: Pattenmakers 1965, Chartered Secretaries 1978; FCIS, FSCA, FRSA, FRGS, FREconS, FInstD; *Books* The Greenwood Tree in Three Continents (1988), Field-Marshal Auchinleck (1990), The Greenwood Family, formerly of Haddenham Bucks (1996); *Recreations* cricket, golf, shooting, genealogy; *Clubs* Carlton, Pilgrims, MCC, Union (BC); *Style*— Maj A A Greenwood; ✉ 1419 Madrona Drive, Nanoose Bay, British Columbia V9P 9C9, Canada (tel 00 1 250 468 9770 and 00 1 250 468 7476, fax 00 1 250 468 7476, e-mail shirlgrr@hotmail.com)

GREENWOOD, Brian John; s of Ronald Greenwood (d 1979), and Marianne Luise, *née* Weiss; *b* 15 April 1950; *Educ* Forest Sch, Univ of Southampton (LLB); *m* 1 July 1978, Julia Le Messurier, da of Alan Le Messurier Scott; 4 s (Jonathan Ronald b 9 April 1981, James Alan b 1 Oct 1985, Alexander Brian, Benjamin John (twins) b 5 Oct 1989), 1 da (Jacqueline Rachel b 10 April 1983); *Career* articled clerk City of Westminster 1973–76, admitted slr 1976, asst slr S Yorks CC 1976–78, asst co slr Kent CC 1980–82 (sr asst slr 1978–80), chief slr Beds CC 1982–85, ptnr and head Planning and Environmental Law Gp Norton Rose 1988– (joined 1985); visiting lectr on planning and environmental law Coll of Law 1988–93; Law Soc: exec memb Local Govt Gp 1979–85, memb Planning and Environmental Law Ctee 1989– (chm 1996–), chm Environmental Law Sub-Ctee 1995–; chm Planning and Environmental Law Sub-Ctee City of London Law Soc 1990–95; memb: CBI Environmental Protection Panel, Int Bar Assoc; Liveryman Worshipful Co of Slrs 1989 (memb of Ct 1992, Master 2003–04); FRSA; *Books* Basic Planning Law and Practice (1989), Butterworths Planning Law Encyclopaedia (1990), Butterworths Planning Law Handbook, Planning and Compensation Act 1991 (1991), Environmental Regulation and Economic Growth (contrib), Planning Law and Practice; *Recreations* family, violin, classical music, sport; *Style*— Brian Greenwood, Esq; ✉ Norton Rose, Kempson House, PO Box 570, Camomile Street, London EC3A 7AN

GREENWOOD, Prof Christopher John; CMG (2002), QC (1999); s of Capt Murray Guy Greenwood, of Lymington, Hants, and Diana Maureen, *née* Barron; *b* 12 May 1955; *Educ* Wellingborough Sch, Magdalene Coll Cambridge (MA, LLB); *m* 5 Aug 1978, Susan Anthea, da of late Geoffrey James Longbotham, and late Patricia Longbotham; 2 da (Catherine b 1982, Sarah b 1985); *Career* called to the Bar Middle Temple 1978 (bencher 2003); practising barr Essex Court Chambers; Univ of Cambridge: fell Magdalene Coll 1978–96, dir of studies in law 1982–96, tutor 1989–96, dean 1982–87, lectr Faculty of Law 1984–96 (asst lectr 1981–84); prof of int law LSE 1996–; dir of studies in public int law Hague Academy of Int Law 1989; visiting prof: West Virginia Univ 1986, Mississippi Univ 1989, Marburg Univ 1991; memb Panel of Arbitrators: Law of the Sea Convention, Int Centre for the Settlement of Investment Disputes; *Publications* jt ed Int Law Reports; articles in legal periodicals; *Recreations* politics, reading novels, walking; *Clubs* Athenaeum, Oxford and Cambridge; *Style*— Prof Christopher Greenwood, CMG, QC;

✉ Department of Law, London School of Economics and Political Science, Houghton Street, London WC2A 2AE (tel 020 7955 7250, fax 020 7955 7366, e-mail c.greenwood@lse.ac.uk); Essex Court Chambers, 24 Lincoln's Inn Fields, London WC2A 3EG (tel 020 7813 8000, fax 020 7813 8080, e-mail cgreenwood@essexcourt.net)

GREENWOOD, Jeremy John; s of Basil Procter Greenwood (d 1963), of Langham, Norfolk, and Stephanie Kathleen, *née* Davidson Houston, MBE (d 1988); *b* 30 March 1936; *Educ* Haileybury, Peterhouse Cambridge (MA); *m* 26 Oct 1963, Annabel Elizabeth Marie-Gabrielle, da of Noel Carlile (d 1945); 1 s (Simon Harry b 1966), 2 da (Elinor Rose b 1971, Gemma Charlotte b 1972); *Career* cmmnd 1st King's Dragoon Gds 1956–59; publisher; various positions with Cassell, Pergamon and Hutchinson Presses; dir Trade Div Cassell Ltd 1977–81; proprietor and md Quiller Press 1981–2002, proprietor JJG Publishing 2003–; govr Runton Hill Sch for Girls 1984–88, chm branch Arthritis Research Cncl; *Books* Sefton - Horse For Any Year (1983); *Recreations* horses, shooting, golf, tennis, theatre; *Clubs* Cavalry and Guards', Royal West Norfolk Golf, MCC; *Style—* Jeremy Greenwood, Esq; ✉ Sparrow Hall, Hindringham, Fakenham, Norfolk NR21 0DP (e-mail greenwood.quiller@btopenworld.com)

GREENWOOD, William John Heaton (Will); MBE (2004); s of John Richard Heaton Greenwood, and Susan Mary Greenwood; *b* 20 October 1972; *Educ* Sedburgh, Univ of Durham; *m*; *Career* rugby union player; clubs: Waterloo, Preston Grasshoppers, Harlequins, Leicester (Pilkington Cup winners 1997), Harlequins (rejoined 2000); England: Schools, Under 21, Students, capt A team, 55 caps, Six Nations Championship 2000, 2001 and 2003, winners World Cup Aust 2003; memb squad Br & I Lions tour SA 1997, Aust 2001 and NZ 2005; formerly with HSBC; *Recreations* golf, cricket; *Style—* Will Greenwood, Esq, MBE

GREER, Adrian; CMG (2004); s of David Smith Greer (d 1989), and Christine, *née* Dawson; *b* 26 April 1957; *Educ* Queen Mary's GS Walsall, Univ of St Andrews (MA); *m* 1985, Diana, *née* Cuddy; 3 da (Joanna b 27 Dec 1985, Sarah b 21 Sept 1987, Hazel b 7 Aug 1996), 1 s (Christopher b 25 June 1992); *Career* auditor NAO 1979–84; Br Cncl: devpt offr London 1984–85, devpt mangr Japan 1985–88, project mangr London 1988–89, chief accountant 1989–91, dir Lesotho and Swaziland 1991–93, dir Zambia 1993–96, dir Europe, Asia and Americas Devpt Services 1996–2000, dir Russia 2000–04, dir Learning, Creativity and Society 2004–; CIPFA 1984; *Recreations* running; *Style—* Adrian Greer, Esq, CMG; ✉ British Council, 10 Spring Gardens, London SW1A 2BN (e-mail adrian.greer@britishcouncil.org)

GREER, Prof Germaine; *b* 29 January 1939, Melbourne, Australia; *Educ* Star of the Sea Convent Gardenvale, Univ of Melbourne (Diocesan and Sr Govt scholar, BA), Univ of Sydney (MA), Univ of Cambridge (Cwlth scholar, PhD); *Career* broadcaster, journalist, columnist and reviewer 1972–; sr tutor in English Univ of Sydney 1963–64, asst lectr then lectr in English Univ of Warwick 1967–72, lectr throughout N America with American Program Bureau 1973–78, lectr to raise funds for Tulsa Bursary and Fellowship Scheme 1980–83, prof of modern letters Univ of Tulsa 1980–83 (visiting prof Graduate Faculty of Modern Letters 1979), dir Stump Cross Books 1988–, special lectr and unofficial fell Newnham Coll Cambridge 1989–98, prof of English and comparative literary studies Univ of Warwick 1998–2003; fndr ed Tulsa Studies in Women's Literature 1981, fndr dir Tulsa Centre for the Study of Woman's Literature; Hon Dr: Univ of Grittith 1996, Univ of York Toronto 1999, UMIST 2000; hon degree Univ of Essex 2003, Hon DLitt Anglia Poly Univ 2003, LLD (hc) Univ of Melbourne 2003, Hon DLitt Sydney Univ 2005; Centenary Medal Australian Living Treasure Nat Tst Award 2003; *Publications* The Female Eunuch (1969), The Obstacle Race: The Fortunes of Women Painters and their Work (1979), Sex and Destiny: The Politics of Human Fertility (1984), Shakespeare (1986), The Madwoman's Underclothes (selected journalism, 1986), Kissing the Rod: An Anthology of Seventeenth Century Women's Verse (ed with Susan Hastings, Jeslyn Medoff, Melinda Sansone, 1988), Daddy, We Hardly Knew You (1989, winner J R Ackerley Prize and Premio Internazionale Mondello), The Uncollected Verse of Aphra Behn (ed, 1989), The Change: Women, Ageing and the Menopause (1991), Slip-Shod Sibyls: Recognition, Rejection and The Woman Poet (1995), The Whole Woman (1999), John Wilmot, Earl of Rochester (1999), 101 Poems by 101 Women (ed, 2001), The Boy (2003), Poems for Gardeners (ed, 2003), Whitefella Jump Up The Shortest Way to Nationhood (2004), Shakespeare's Wife (2007); Stump Cross Books incl: The Uncollected Works of Aphra Behn, The Collected Works of Katherine Philips, the Matchless Orinda (3 vols), The Surviving Works of Anne Wharton; *Style—* Prof Germaine Greer; ✉ c/o Aitken Alexander Associates, 18–21 Cavaye Place, London SW10 9PT

GREER, Prof Ian Andrew; *b* 16 April 1958; *Educ* Allan Glen's Sch Glasgow, Univ of Glasgow (MB ChB, MD); *Career* SHO in obstetrics Glasgow Royal Maternity Hosp 1981–82, SHO in gynaecology Royal Infirmary 1982; Univ Dept of Med Royal Infirmary: res fell/ hon SHO 1982–83, registrar in general med, haemastasis and thrombosis 1983–85; SHO in obstetrics Glasgow Royal Maternity Hosp 1985–86, registrar in obstetrics and gynaecology Royal Maternity Hosp and Royal Infirmary 1986–87, lectr and hon sr registrar in obstetrics and gynaecology Univ of Edinburgh, Edinburgh Royal Infirmary and Simpson Meml Maternity Pavilion 1987–90 (lectr and hon sr registrar 1987), clinical res scientist and clinical conslt MRC Reproductive Biology Unit Edinburgh, hon sr lectr Dept of Obstetrics and Gynaecology Univ of Edinburgh and hon conslt obstetrician and gynaecologist Simpson Meml Maternity Pavilion 1990–91, Muirhead prof and head Dept of Obstetrics and Gynaecology Univ of Glasgow, hon conslt obstetrician Glasgow Royal Maternity Hosp and hon conslt gynaecologist Glasgow Royal Infirmary 1991–; Univ of Glasgow: regius prof 2000–, head Div of Developmental Med 2002, dep dean Faculty of Med 2003; currently dean Hull York Medical Sch; Gold Medal RCOG 1987, William Blair Bell meml lectr RCOG 1989, Bernhard Baron travelling scholar RCOG 1989, Watson Prize lectr RCPS 1990; chm Subspeciality Ctee RCOG 1995–98; memb: Soc for Gynaecologic Investigation, Gynaecological Travellers, Edinburgh Obstetric and Gynaecological Soc, Glasgow Obstetrical and Gynaecological Soc, Assoc of Profs of Obstetrics and Gynaecology (sec 1995–98), British Soc for Haemostasis and Thrombosis, BMA, Int Soc for Thrombosis and Haemostasis, Int Soc of Obstetric Medicine, MacDonald Obstetric Medicine Soc; FFFP, FRCOG, FRCPGlas, FRCPEd, FRCP, FRCPI, FMedSci, FAE, MEWI; *Books* Haemostasis and Thrombosis in Obstetrics and Gynaecology (ed, 1992), Thrombosis in Obstetrics and Gynaecology (ed, 1997), Mosby's Color Atlas and text of Obstetrics and Gynaecology (jt ed, 2000), Antenatal Disorders for the MRCOG (jtly, 2000), The Menopause in Practice (jtly, 2002), Problem-based Obstetrics and Gynaecology (jtly, 2003), Venous Thrombosis in Women, Pregnancy, the Contraceptive Pill and HRT (2003), Pregnancy: The Inside Guide (2003), Practical Obstetric Haematology (jtly, 2006), Preterm Labour (jt ed, 2006), Fertility and Conception; author of numerous medical pubns; *Style—* Prof Ian Greer; ✉ Hull York Medical School, Heslington, York YO26 4ZF

GREER, Prof (Alan) Lindsay; s of Alan Greer (d 1994), and Helena, *née* Lindsay; *b* 19 June 1955, Ballymena, Co Antrim; *Educ* Trinity Hall Cambridge (MA, PhD); *Career* Div of Applied Sciences Harvard Univ: NATO research fell 1980–81, asst prof of applied physics 1981–84; Dept of Materials Sci and Metallurgy Univ of Cambridge: sr asst in research 1984–88, lectr 1988–96, reader in microstructural kinetics 1996–2001, prof of materials sci 2001–, dep head of dept 2001–05, head of dept 2006–; Sidney Sussex Coll Cambridge: fell 1984–, tutor for grad students 1987–96, vice-master 2004–; invited prof Inst Nat Poly de Grenoble 1994, Clark Harrison distinguished visiting prof of physics Center for Materials Innovation Washington Univ St Louis MO 2005, advsy prof Chongqing Univ People's Republic of China 2005–; ed Philosophical Magazine 2003–; author of over 300 papers in materials science (rapid solidification, metallic glasses, nanocrystalline alloys, nucleation, multilayers, electromigration), ed of proceedings, author of chapters in books; Zachariasen Award Jl of Non-Crystalline Solids 1989, Light Metals Award Minerals, Metals & Materials Soc 1998, Cast Shop Technol Award Minerals, Metals & Materials Soc 1999, Cook-Ablett Award IMMM 2000, Pilkington Prize Univ of Cambridge 2000, Sr Scientist Medal Int Symposium on Metastable and Nano Materials 2000, Honda Medal Tohoku Univ 2004, Hume-Rothery Prize IMMM 2006; CEng 1981, MIMMM 1981, FRSA 1993; *Recreations* archery; *Style—* Prof Lindsay Greer; ✉ Sidney Sussex College, Cambridge CB2 3HU (tel 01223 338836, fax 01223 338884, e-mail alg13@cam.ac.uk); University of Cambridge, Dept of Materials Science & Metallurgy, Pembroke Street, Cambridge CB2 3QZ (tel 01223 334308, fax 01223 334567)

GREEY, Edward Ronald; s of Derek Edward Horace Greey (d 1979), and Irene Osborne, *née* Taylor; *b* 26 April 1939; *Educ* Malvern Coll; *m* 1 Oct 1966, Gillian Frances Rippon, da of John Sargeant Hughes, of Longthorpe, Peterborough; 3 da (Sally b 1969, Wendy b 1972, Philippa b 1976); *Career* cmmnd 16/5 Queen's Own Royal Lancers, TA Queen's Own Staffs Yeo; stockbroker and co dir; memb Birmingham Stock Exchange 1965 (chm 1975–76); dir: Gerrard (formerly Albert E Sharp), Securities Inst; non-exec chm Robinson Bros Ryders Green Ltd; guardian Birmingham Assay Office, chm Stock Exchange Midland and Western Unit 1979–95, chm Regnl Ctee Int Stock Exchange, chm London Stock Exchange Midland and Western Region, memb Governing Cncl London Stock Exchange 1985–88; govr Malvern Coll; Hon FSI; *Recreations* golf, shooting, music; *Clubs* Blackwell Golf, Royal West Norfolk Golf, Royal & Ancient Golf; *Style—* Edward Greey, Esq; ✉ Pemberley, Broad Lane, Brancaster, King's Lynn, Norfolk PE31 8AU (tel 01485 210286); Gerrard, Temple Court, 35 Bull Street, Birmingham B4 6ES (tel 0121 200 2244, fax 0121 683 7300)

GREGOR, Zdenek Jiri; s of Prof Ota Gregor, and Miroslava Gregor; *b* 27 March 1948; *Educ* Prague 7 HS, Westminster Med Sch of London; *m*; 1 s (Benjamin b 1973), 1 da (Camilla b 1977); *Career* house appts Westminster Hosp 1971–72, res surgical offr Moorfields Eye Hosp 1976–79, asst prof Univ of Southern Calif LA 1980–82, sr lectr ophthalmology Univ of London 1982–83, conslt ophthalmic surgn Moorfields Eye Hosp 1983–, numerous pubns and chapters on disorders and surgical treatment of the retina and the vitreous 1975–; memb: Oxford Ophthalmological Congress 1979, Euro Flouroscein Angiography Club 1977, Macular Soc of the US, Retina Soc of the US, Scientific Advsy Cncl, Opportunities for the Disabled; LRCP 1971, FRCS 1977, FRSM 1986 (and memb), fell Coll Ophthalmologists 1988; *Recreations* music, skiing; *Style—* Zdenek Gregor, Esq; ✉ 94 Harley Street, London W1N 1AF (tel 020 7935 0777, fax 020 7935 6860); Moorfields Eye Hospital, City Road, London EC1V 2PD (tel 020 7253 3411, fax 020 7253 4696, telex 266129)

GREGORY, Prof Alan; s of William Raymond Gregory, and Margaret Mary, *née* Richards; *b* 19 March 1954, Mountain Ash, Wales; *Educ* St Bartholomew's GS Newbury, LSE (MSc); *m* (m dis) Barbara Elaine, *née* Arnold; *Career* CA 1974; successively mgmnt trainee, accountant and mangr BR 1971–76, budgets controller Green Shield Stamps 1977, lectr SW London Coll 1977–78, sr lectr in accounting Luton Coll of HE 1978–83, sr lectr Brighton Poly 1983–86, princ lectr City of London Poly 1986–89, lectr in accounting and finance Univ of Exeter 1989–95, prof of accounting Univ of Glasgow 1995–96, prof of business studies Univ of Wales Aberystwyth 1996–97, prof of corporate finance Univ of Exeter 1997–; memb Competition Cmmn; fell CIMA 1986 (assoc 1978); *Publications* Valuing Companies (1992), Management Accounting in Hotel Companies (jtly, 1995), Cost of Capital in the UK (jtly, 1999), Recent Advances in Mergers and Acquisitions Vol 1 (ed jtly, 2000), Strategic Valuation of Companies (2 edn, 2001), Recent Advances in Mergers and Acquisitions Vol 2 (ed jtly, 2003); numerous pubns in leading jls incl: Jl of Empirical Finance, Jl of Business Finance and Accounting, European Financial Management, Jl of Accounting and Public Policy, Accounting and Business Research, Economic Jl; *Recreations* sailing, skiing; *Style—* Prof Alan Gregory; ✉ School of Business and Economics, University of Exeter, Room 214, Streatham Court, Rennes Drive, Exeter EX4 4PU (tel 01392 263220, fax 01392 262475, e-mail a.gregory@ex.ac.uk)

GREGORY, David John; s of (Newton) John Gregory, and Doris May, *née* Bennett; *b* 3 December 1942; *Educ* Loxford Sch, NE London Poly; *m* 20 Jan 1968, (Solveig) Anita, da of Artur John and Siri Niklasson, of Lerdala, Sweden; 2 da (Anna b 1971, Lisa b 1973); *Career* ptnr Keevil & Gregory Architects 1973–2004; RIBA 1972; *Style—* David Gregory, Esq; ✉ Hillcrest, The Square, Main Road, Wensley, Matlock DE4 2LS

GREGORY, David Noel; s of Charles Cope Gregory, and Caroline Ada Gregory; *b* 25 December 1944; *Educ* Hillcroft Sch London; *m* 19 Aug 1972, Angela Mary, da of Ernest James Day; 1 da (Claire Louise b 9 Feb 1975), 1 s (Daniel Mark b 24 Feb 1977); *Career* CA; articled clerk Evans Peirson & Co, gp fin controller James Walker Goldsmith & Silversmith plc; fin dir: Instore Enterprises Ltd (subsid Debenhams), Eurobrands Ltd (UK distribution co of Remy Martin & Co) 1987–90; gp fin dir: Freetraders Group Ltd 1991–95, Oxbridge Group Ltd 1995–97; md DG Corporate Services Ltd 1997–; FCA (ACA 1969), ATII 1971, FCCA 1980, MBCS 1981, JDipMA 1981, DipM 1990, MCIM 1990; *Clubs* IOD, Twickenham on Thames Rotary; *Style—* David Gregory, Esq; ✉ DG Corporate Services Ltd, 15 Orchard Rise, Richmond, Surrey TW10 5BX

GREGORY, Derek Edward; s of Edward Gregory (d 1970), of Ilkeston, and Hilda, *née* Stokeley (d 1989); *Educ* Ilkeston GS; *m* 1, 16 June 1962, Marjorie (d 1984), da of Lloyd Priest Newcastle (d 1976); 1 s (Philip Edward b 1965), 1 da (Tina Louise b 1968); m 2, 13 Dec 1986, Kate; *Career* fndr and sr ptnr Gregory Priestley & Stewart CA's Ilkeston and Long Eaton 1970–; treas Stanton by Dale CC 1958–; FCA 1961; *Recreations* golf, cricket, gardening; *Style—* Derek Gregory, Esq; ✉ Rosemary Cottage, Bowling Close, Stanton By Dale, Ilkeston, Derby (tel 0115 932 2047); Gregory Priestley & Stewart, 16 Queen Street, Ilkeston, Derbyshire (tel 0115 932 6726)

GREGORY, Rev Ian Gabriel; s of Rev Gabriel Wilson Gregory (d 1982), and Lilian, *née* Unsworth (d 1993); *b* 18 May 1933; *Educ* Pear Tree Secdy Modern Derby, Univ of Manchester (gen sec Students' Union), NCTJ (Dip Journalism); *m* 1965, Patricia Mary Elizabeth, *née* Donaldson; 2 s (Russell Gabriel b 1966, Ian James b 1969), 1 da (Rachel Frances b 1967); *Career* news ed Solihull News 1960–70, feature writer Aberdeen Express/Press & Journal 1970–71, sub ed Edinburgh Evening News 1971–72, prodr BBC Radio Derby 1972–84; congregational min: Newcastle 1984–2004, Cheadle Staffs 2004–; pres Congregational Federation 1998–99; ed Congregationalist; fndr Campaign For Courtesy 1986–; *Books* Good Manners Guide (1987), The Chair: a short guide to the conduct of meetings (2004); *Style—* The Rev Ian Gregory; ✉ 16 Grice Road, Hartshill, Stoke-on-Trent ST4 7PJ (tel 01782 614407, e-mail ian@congist.fsnet.co.uk)

GREGORY, John Frederick; s of Arthur Frederic Gregory (d 1955), of London, and Marjorie Phyllis, *née* Williams (d 1995); *b* 7 April 1935; *Educ* Ashburton HS; *m* 9 June 1956, Ethel Currie, da of Robert Burns, of Preston, Lancs; 2 da (Linda Ann b 21 May 1957, Alison Joy b 8 Dec 1960), 1 s (David Russell b 14 Nov 1965); *Career* RAF 1953–55; Capel-Cure Myers: joined 1950, ptnr 1979–85, dir 1985–89; dir: Beeson Gregory Ltd 1989–2000, Re-Org Solutions Ltd 2000–; memb Worshipful Co of Wax Chandlers; MSI (memb Stock Exchange 1972); *Recreations* music, painting, travel, memb Croydon Millenary Lodge; *Clubs* London Capital; *Style—* John Gregory, Esq; ✉ 185 Ballards Way, Croydon, Surrey CR0 5RJ (tel 020 8657 6706, e-mail john@gregory3.wanadoo.co.uk)

GREGORY, John Kennedy; s of William John Gregory, of North Tawton, Devon, and Irene Kennedy, *née* Heath; *b* 19 March 1958, Crediton, Devon; *Educ* Blundell's, Brooke Univ

Oxford (BA); *partner* Marilyn Ann Walker; 1 da (Jordan b 20 Nov 1989); *Career* mktg mangr Aust and NZ Nippon Int Containers 1980–82, gen mangr Aust, NZ and S Pacific Transamerica ICS Ltd 1982–85; Gregory Distribution: md 1985–2003, chief exec 2003–; business advsr South West Acad of Fine and Applied Art, tstee Devon Air Ambulance; MCIT 1998; *Recreations* golf, tennis, skiing; *Clubs* Exeter Golf and Country; *Style*— John Gregory, Esq; ✉ Reeds, The Retreat Drive, Topsham, Devon EX3 0LS (tel 01392 877564, e-mail johng@gdl.uk.com)

GREGORY, John Raymond; s of Raymond Gregory (d 1988), of Congleton, Cheshire, and Ivy Charlotte, *née* Bourne (d 1993); *b* 18 April 1949; *Educ* St Ambrose Coll Hale Barns, Univ of Hull; *m* 11 April 1981, Fiona Mary Kristin, da of Donald Walker (d 1997); 2 s (Gordon b 1981, Lawrence b 1984), 2 da (Victoria b 1983, Elizabeth b and d 1987); *Career* called to the Bar Middle Temple 1972, in practice 1973–; memb Chancery Bar Assoc; chm Stretford Constituency Cons Assoc 1980–82; Parly candidate (Cons) Stretford and Urmston 1997; *Recreations* swimming, archaeology, writing, painting; *Clubs* Lancashire CCC; *Style*— John Gregory, Esq; ✉ Deans Court Chambers, 24 St John Street, Manchester M3 4DF (tel 0161 214 6000, e-mail johnraymondgregory@hotmail.com)

GREGORY, Prof Kenneth John; CBE (2007); s of Frederick Arthur Gregory (d 1969), of Belper, Derbys, and Marion, *née* Yates (d 1981); *b* 23 March 1938; *Educ* Herbert Strutt Sch Belper, UCL (BSc, PhD, DSc); *m* 25 Aug 1962, Margaret (Christine), da of Lawrence Wilmot (d 1974), of Belper, Derbys; 2 da (Caroline b 1964, Sarah b 1966), 1 s (Jonathon b 1971); *Career* reader in physical geography Univ of Exeter 1972–76 (lectr 1962–72), prof Univ of Southampton 1976–92 (dean of sci 1984–87, dep vice-chllr 1988–92), warden Goldsmiths Coll London 1992–98, Leverhulme emeritus fell 1998–2001; visiting lectr Univ of New England Armidale NSW Aust 1975, distinguished visiting prof Arizona State Univ 1987, visiting prof Univ Kebangsaan Malaysia 1987; currently vice-chair Governing Body Univ of Southampton Solent; Geographical Medal Royal Scottish Geographical Soc 2000; Hon DSc: Univ of Southampton 1997, Univ of Greenwich 1997; hon fell Goldsmiths Coll 1998; fell UCL 1999; Linton Award Br Geomorphological Res Gp 1999; Freeman: City of London 1997, Worshipful Co of Goldsmiths 1997 (Liveryman 1998); FRGS 1962 (Back Award 1980, Founder's Medal 1993), CGeog 2001; *Books* Southwest England (with A H Shorter and W L D Ravenhill, 1969), Drainage Basin Form and Process (with D E Walling, 1973), River Channel Changes (ed, 1977), Geomorphological Processes (with E Derbyshire and J R Hails, 1979 and 1980), Horizons in Physical Geography (ed with M J Clark and A M Gurnell, 1988), The Nature of Physical Geography (1985), Temperate Palaeohydrology (ed with L Starkel and J B Thornes, 1989), Global Continental Palaeohydrology (ed with L Starkel and V Baker 1995), Global Continental Changes: the context of palaeohydrology (ed with J Branson and AG Brown 1996), Evaluating Teacher Quality in Higher Education (ed with R Aylett, 1996), Fluvial Geomorphology of Great Britain (ed, 1997), Palaeohydrology and Environmental Change (ed with G Benito and V R Baker, 1998), The Changing Nature of Physical Geography (2000), Palaeohydrology: Understanding Global Change (ed with G Benito, 2003), River Channel Management (with P W Downs, 2004), Physical Geography (ed 4 vols, 2005); *Recreations* gardening, travel; *Style*— Prof Kenneth Gregory, CBE; ✉ 9 Poltimore Road, Guildford, Surrey GU2 7PT (tel 01483 821123, e-mail k.j.gregory@ntlworld.com)

GREGORY, Lesley; *Educ* Charlton Park Sch Cheltenham, Somerville Coll Oxford (BA, Hockey blue), Coll of Law; *m*; 3 c; *Career* articled Courts & Co 1983; Memery Crystal: slr 1983–88, ptnr (specialising in corporate and commercial law) 1988–; non-exec dir Accumen Gp plc; memb: Law Soc, Nominated Advisors (NOMAD) Ctee Quoted Companies Alliance; *Recreations* tennis, running, golf, theatre, opera; *Style*— Ms Lesley Gregory; ✉ Memery Crystal, 44 Southampton Buildings, London WC2A 1AP (tel 020 7242 5905, fax 020 7242 2058, e-mail lgregory@memerycrystal.com)

GREGORY, Rear Adm (Alexander) Michael; OBE (1987); s of Vice Adm Sir George David Archibald Gregory, KBE, CB, DSO (d 1975), of Greymount, Alyth, Perthshire, and Florence Eve Patricia, *née* Hill; *b* 15 December 1945; *Educ* Marlborough, BRNC Dartmouth; *m* 13 June 1970, Jean Charlotte, da of Lt Cdr Gerald Robin Muir, OBE (d 1991), of Braco Castle, By Dunblane, Perthshire; 4 da (Charlotte b 1971, Katherine b 1973, Helen b 1979, Sarah b 1982); *Career* HMS Albion and HMS Aisne 1965–66, HMS Narwhale 1966–67, HMS Otter 1967–68, HMS Warspite 1968–70, HMS Courageous 1970–73, HMS Odin (based in Australia) 1973–75, i/c HMS Finwhale 1976–78, HMS Repulse 1978–80, staff of US Third Fleet Hawaii 1980–82, i/c HMS Renown 1982–85, Cdr Tenth Submarine Sqdn and i/c HMS Resolution 1985–86, Jt Servs Def Coll 1987, MOD Directorate of Naval Warfare 1987–88, i/c HMS Cumberland 1988–90, capt Tenth Submarine Sqdn 1990–92, MOD Naval Staff 1992–93, naval attaché Washington 1994–97, flag offr Scotland N England and NI 1997–2000; chief exec METCOM 2001–03, chief exec Energy Industries Cncl 2004–; memb Queen's Bodyguard for Scotland (Royal Co of Archers); *Recreations* fishing, skiing, gardening; *Style*— Rear Adm Michael Gregory, OBE

GREGORY, Dr Paul Duncan; s of Thomas Gregory, of Troon, and Elsie, *née* Millward; *b* 1 December 1954; *Educ* Marr Coll Troon, Univ of Edinburgh (BCom, PhD); *m* 21 July 1978, Catherine Margaret, da of James Campbell, of Troon; 1 s (James Alexander b 1985), 1 da (Jennifer Alison b 1987); *Career* oil analyst Wood Mackenzie & Co Ltd 1981–85, asst dir Hill Samuel 1986–87, dir County Natwest Securities 1989–92 (assoc dir 1988–89); md: Wood Mackenzie Consultants Ltd 1994–2001 (dir 1992–94), NatWest Markets 1995–98, Bankers Tst International 1998–99, Deutsche Bank 1999–2001; chief exec Wood Mackenzie Ltd 2001–; memb Scot Oil Club; MInstPet; *Books* Factors Influencing the Export Performance of the Scottish Manufacturing Sector of the Offshore Supplies Industry (1982), World Offshore Markets: Can Britain Compete? (1986); *Recreations* golf, tennis, gardening; *Clubs* Morton Hall Golf, Craigielaw Golf, Royal Burgess Golf; *Style*— Dr Paul Gregory; ✉ 25 Greenhill Gardens, Edinburgh EH10 4BL (tel 0131 447 6480); Wood Mackenzie Ltd, Kintore House, 74–77 Queen Street, Edinburgh EH2 4NS (tel 0131 243 4203, fax 0131 243 4464, e-mail paul.gregory@woodmac.com)

GREGORY, Peter William; s of William Henry Gregory, of Walton on Thames, Surrey, and Florence Mabel, *née* Peters; *b* 3 October 1934; *Educ* Surbiton GS, City & Guilds Inst, Imperial Coll London (BSc); *m* 16 Jan 1960, Angela Margaret; 1 s (Timothy b 10 March 1963), 2 da (Sarah b 14 March 1965, Susan b 22 April 1966); *Career* short serv cmmn RAF 1958–61, Flt Lt 5003 Sqdn Alb in UK; dir John Laing Construction Ltd 1984–96, chm Laing Management Ltd 1994–96 (md 1984–94), assoc dir John Laing plc 1995–96, dir Hall & Ptnrs 1996–, chm Bowey Construction Ltd 1999–; Liveryman Worshipful Co of Plumbers; CEng 1964, FRSA 1998; *Recreations* game shooting, salmon fishing, gardening, golf; *Style*— Peter W Gregory, Esq; ✉ Target House, Hexham, Northumberland NE46 4LD (tel 01434 604689, fax 01434 600806)

GREGORY, His Hon Judge Philip John; s of John Godfrey Gregory, of Alvechurch, Worcs, and Winifred, *née* Groves (d 1982); *b* 13 January 1953, Birmingham; *Educ* Moseley GS Birmingham, Pembroke Coll Oxford (MA), Inns of Court Sch of Law; *m* 14 April 1979, Deborah, *née* Lane; 2 da (Hannah b 26 Dec 1982, Elizabeth b 6 Sept 1985), 1 s (Thomas b 18 Aug 1991); *Career* called to the Bar 1975; recorder 1999–2004 (asst recorder 1997–99), circuit judge 2004–; *Recreations* tennis, golf, reading; *Style*— His Hon Judge Gregory; ✉ Birmingham Crown Court, 1 Newton Street, Birmingham B4 7NA

GREGORY, Dr Philippa; da of Arthur Percy Gregory (d 1955), of Nairobi, and Elaine, *née* Wedd (d 1983); *b* 9 January 1954; *Educ* Duncan House Sch for Girls' Clifton, Colston's Girls' Sch Bristol, Univ of Sussex (BA), Univ of Edinburgh (PhD); *m* Anthony Mason; 1 da (Victoria Elaine Chislett b 31 Jan 1982), 1 s (Adam Gregory Carter b 20 Jan 1993); *Career* work on: newspaper in Portsmouth 1972–75, prodr BBC Radio 1978–82; guest reviewer Sunday Times 1989–; *Books* Wideacre (1987), The Favoured Child (1989), Princess Florizella (1989), Meridon (1990), Florizella and the Wolves (1991), The Wise Woman (1992), Mrs Hartley and the Growth Centre (1992), Florizella and the Giant (1992), Fallen Skies (1993), The Little Pet Dragon (1994), A Respectable Trade (1995), Diggory and the Boa Conductor (1996), Perfectly Correct (1996), The Little House (1997), Earthly Joys (1998), Virgin Earth (1999), Zelda's Cut (2000), The Other Boleyn Girl (2001, Parker Pen Novel of the Year 2001), The Queen's Fool (2003), The Virgin's Lover (2004), The Constant Princess (2005); screenplays: Mrs Hartley and the Growth Centre (BBC 2, 1995), A Respectable Trade (BBC 1, 1997), The Other Boleyn Girl (BBC 2, 2003); *Style*— Dr Philippa Gregory

GREGORY, Richard John; OBE (2004); s of John Gregory, and Joan, *née* Slingsby; *b* 18 August 1954; *Educ* Danum GS Doncaster; *Career* industrial corr Morning Telegraph 1977–79, news ed Granada TV 1979–81; Yorkshire Television: news ed 1981–82, prodr 1982–84, ed Calendar 1984, head of news 1991–92, controller of regnl progs 1992–93, memb Bd 1993, dir of regnl progs 1993–95, dir of broadcasting 1995–96, md Yorkshire Television (Broadcasting) 1996–97, md Yorkshire Television 1997–2002; chair: Northern Media Sch 1996–2001, Yorkshire Initiative 1997–2000, Yorkshire Int Business Convention Ltd 1999–2003, Regional Leadership Team Yorkshire and Humber Business in the Community 2001–, Imagesound plc 2002–; dep chair Yorkshire Forward 1999–; memb: Bd Yorkshire Arts 2000–02, Cncl Inst of Employment Studies 2002–, Bd Yorkshire Cultural Consortium 2002–04; chair Yorkshire Bank 2004–; non-exec dir: Clydesdale Bank 2000–, Business in the Community Ltd 2001–, National Australia Group Europe Ltd 2004–, Sheffield Univ Enterprises Ltd 2005–; tstee dir Sheffield Galleries and Museums Tst 2002–, chair Sheffield Hallam Univ 1999–2003 (sometime govr and dep chm); *Recreations* Peak District; *Style*— Richard Gregory, Esq, OBE

GREGORY, Prof Richard Langton; CBE (1989); s of C C L Gregory (d 1969), and Patricia, *née* Gibson (d 1988); *b* 24 July 1923; *Educ* King Alfred Sch Hampstead, Downing Coll Cambridge; *m* 1, 1953 (m dis 1966); 1 s (Mark Foss Langton), 1 da (Romilly Caroline Langton); m 2, 1976 (m dis); *Career* Univ of Cambridge: res MRC Applied Psychology Res Unit 1950–53, demonstrator then lectr Dept of Psychology 1953–67, fell Corpus Christi Coll 1962–67; prof of bionics Dept of Machine Intelligence and Perception Univ of Edinburgh 1967–70 (chm 1968–70), prof of neuropsychology and dir Brain and Perception Laboratory The Med Sch Univ of Bristol 1970–88, emeritus prof Dept of Psychology Univ of Bristol; visiting prof: UCLA 1963, MIT 1964, NY Univ 1966; Freeman Worshipful Co of Spectacle Makers; hon fell: CCC Cambridge 1997, Downing Coll Cambridge 1999, Inst of Physics; FRSE 1969, FRS 1992; *Books* Recovery from Early Blindness (with Jean Wallace, 1963), Eye and Brain (1966, 5 edn 1997), The Intelligent Eye (1970), Illusion in Nature and Art (jt ed, 1973), Concepts and Mechanisms of Perception (1974), Mind in Science (1981), Oxford Companion to the Mind (1987, 2nd edn 2004), The Artful Eye (jt ed, 1995), Mirrors in Mind (1997); *Clubs* Athenaeum, Chelsea Arts; *Style*— Prof Richard Gregory, CBE, FRSE, FRS; ✉ 23 Royal York Crescent, Clifton, Bristol BS8 4JX (tel 0117 973 9701); University of Bristol, Department of Experimental Psychology, 8 Woodland Road, Clifton, Bristol BS8 1TN (tel and fax 0117 928 8461)

GREGORY-HOOD, Peter Charles Freeman; *b* 12 December 1943; *Educ* Eton, Aix-en-Provence Univ, Trinity Coll Cambridge; *m* 1966, Camilla Bethell; 3 da (b 1968, 1970 and 1973); *Career* HM Dip Serv: third sec CRO 1965, Dakar 1967, third later second sec Tel Aviv 1969, second later first sec FCO 1972, first sec (commercial) Paris 1976, first sec FCO 1981, first sec (info) New Delhi 1986, cnsllr and consul-gen Casablanca 1990–1995, dep high cmmr Colombo Sri Lanka 1995–98, ret 1999; biography (MA) Buckingham Univ 2003; *Recreations* golf, tennis, theatre, cinema; *Clubs* White's, Royal Over-Seas League, Tadmarton Heath Golf; *Style*— Peter Gregory-Hood, Esq; ✉ Loxley Hall, Loxley, Warwickshire CV35 9JP

GREGSON, Charles Henry; s of Geoffrey Gregson (d 2006), of Somerset, and Anne Gregson (d 2002); *b* 7 June 1947; *Educ* Harrow, Trinity Hall Cambridge (MA); *m* 26 Sept 1972, Caroline, *née* Blake; 2 s (Oliver b 14 Feb 1978, James b 22 June 1982); *Career* admitted slr 1972; with Clifford-Turner & Co Slrs 1970–74; United Business Media plc (formerly Mills & Allen International and MAI plc): joined 1974, md Shepperton Studios Ltd 1975–80, co sec 1976–77, chief exec MAI Money Brokers (later Garban plc) 1980–98, chm ICAP plc (formerly Garban plc) 1998–; non-exec dir Provident Financial plc 1995– (dep chm 2000–); dir Public Catalogue Fndn; *Recreations* gardening, deerstalking, racing; *Clubs* Turf; *Style*— Charles Gregson, Esq; ✉ PR Newswire Europe Ltd, 209–215 Blackfriars Road, London SE1 8NL (tel 020 7454 5144, fax 020 7454 5331, e-mail charles.gregson@prnewswire.com)

GREGSON, Edward; s of Edward Gregson (d 1978), and May Elizabeth, *née* Eaves (d 1985); *b* 23 July 1945; *Educ* Manchester Central GS, Royal Acad of Music (GRSM, LRAM, Battison Haynes, Edward Hecht and Frederick Corder Memorial Prizes (all for composition), Univ of London (BMus); *m* 1967, Susan Carole; 2 s (Mark Edward b 1968, Justin Serge b 1970); *Career* lectr in music Rachel McMillan Coll 1970–76, sr lectr then reader rising to prof of music Goldsmiths Coll London 1976–96, princ RNCM 1996–; also composer; dir: Performing Right Soc 1995–, Hallé Concerts Soc 1998–2000; govr and feoffe Chethams Sch of Music 1996–; govr Assoc Bd of RSM 1996–; tstee Nat Fndn for Youth Music 1999–2003; chm Conservatoires UK 2004–; memb: Composers' Guild of GB (vice-chm 1976–78), Assoc of Professional Composers (chm 1989–91), Br Acad of Composers and Songwriters 1992–; memb Bd Cultural Consortium for englandnorthwest 2003–04; hon prof of music Univ of Manchester 1996; Hon DMus Univ of Sunderland 1996, Hon DArts Manchester Met Univ 2003, Hon DMus Lancaster Univ 2006, Hon DUniv Univ of Central England 2007; fell Dartington Coll of Arts 1997, FRAM 1990, Hon FLCM 1998, FRNCM 1999, FRCM 2000; *Compositions* incl: Oboe Sonata 1965, Brass Quintet 1967, Music for Chamber Orchestra 1968, Horn Concerto 1971, Essay (for brass band) 1971, Tuba Concerto 1976, music for York Cycle of Mystery Plays 1976 and 1980, Connotations (for brass band) 1977, Metamorphoses 1979, Trombone Concerto 1979, The Salamander and the Moonraker (children's cantata, text by Susan Gregson) 1980, Fairground Songs (text by Susan Gregson) 1982, Trumpet Concerto 1983, Piano Sonata 1983, Contrasts - a concerto for orchestra 1983 (revised 2002), Dances and Arias (for brass band) 1984, Festivo 1985, Missa Brevis Pacem 1988, Celebration 1991, The Sword and the Crown (based on music from RSC history play prodns 1988 and 1990) 1991, Of Men and Mountains (for brass band) 1991, Blazon 1992, Clarinet Concerto 1994, Concerto for Piano and Wind 1995, The Kings Go Forth 1996, Stepping Out (for string orchestra) 1996, A Welcome Ode 1997, Three Matisse Impressions (for recorder, string orchestra, harp and percussion) 1997, And the Seven Trumpets 1998, The Dance, forever the Dance (for mezzo-soprano, choir and orchestra) 1999, Violin Concerto 2000, The Trumpets of the Angels (for brass band and organ) 2000, Occasional Fanfares (for orchestra) 2002, Romance for Treble Recorder and String Quartet 2004 (also in piano version), An Age of Kings (for brass band, male chorus, mezzo-soprano solo, harp and piano) 2004, Shadow of Paradise (oboe and percussion) 2005, Saxophone Concerto 2006, A Song for Chris (concerto for cello and chamber orchestra) 2007; *Recordings* incl: commercial recordings on the Chandos, Olympia, Doyen, Sony and Polyphonic labels, plus broadcasts on BBC TV, BBC Radio 2 and 3 and Classic FM; *Recreations* food, wine, watching sport; *Clubs* Royal Over-Seas League, Savile; *Style*— Prof Edward Gregson; ✉ Royal Northern

College of Music, 124 Oxford Road, Manchester M13 9RD (tel 0161 907 5273, fax 0161 273 8188, e-mail edward.gregson@rncm.ac.uk)

GREGSON, Baron (Life Peer UK 1975), of Stockport in Greater Manchester; John Gregson; DL (Gtr Manchester 1979); s of John Gregson; *b* 29 January 1924; *Career* Fairey Engineering Ltd: joined Stockport Base Subsidiary 1939, memb Fairey R&D team 1946, appointed to Bd 1966, md 1978–94; dir OSC Process Engineering Ltd until 1995; non-exec dir: Br Steel plc 1976–94, Fairey Group plc 1989–94, NRA 1992–95 (chm Audit Ctee 1992–95), Innvotec Ltd to 1999; pres Defence Mfrs' Assoc 1984–2001 (chm 1980–84), past vice-pres Assoc of Metropolitan Authorities; past memb House of Lords Select Ctees on Sci and Technol; pres: Parly and Scientific Ctee 1986–90, Finance and Industry Gp of Lab Party; chm: Compensation Scheme for Radiation Linked Diseases, Advsy Cncl RMCS Shrivenham 1985–99, Waste Mgmnt Industry Trg and Advsy Bd 1985–2002, Onyx Environmental Tst 1997–2003; memb Ct UMIST 1976–99; hon fell Manchester Poly 1983; Hon DUniv Open Univ, Hon DSc Aston Univ, Hon DTech Brunel Univ, Hon DSc Cranfield Univ; AMCT, Hon CIMgt, Hon FIProdE 1982, Hon FREng 1986; *Recreations* mountaineering, skiing, sailing, gardening; *Style*— The Rt Hon the Lord Gregson, DL; ✉ 12 Rosemont Road, Richmond upon Thames, Surrey TW10 6QL

GREGSON, Prof Peter John; s of Howard Davenport Gregson, and Susan Katherine, *née* Lunn; *b* 3 November 1957, Scotland; *Educ* Imperial Coll London (BSc, Bessemer Medal, PhD, Matthey Prize); *m* 13 Aug 1983, Rachael Kathleen, *née* McClaughry; 3 da (Eleanor Margaret b 18 Aug 1991, Maria Katharine b 26 July 1994, Christina Rosalind b 26 Jan 1999); *Career* Univ of Southampton 1983–2004, pres and vice-chllr Queen's Univ Belfast 2004–; non-exec dir Rolls-Royce Gp plc 2007–; memb: User Panel EPSRC 2004–07, Cncl CCLRC 2004–07; author of numerous scientific papers in learned jls on the engineering performance of aerospace materials and computational and experimental modelling of load bearing medical devices; Donald Julius Groen Prize of IMechE 1993, Rosenhain Medal and Prize Inst of Materials 1996; CEng 1986, FIMMM 1998, FREng 2001, FIEI 2004, FCGI 2006, FIAI 2007, MRIA 2007; *Recreations* opera, gardening, tennis, sailing; *Clubs* Athenaeum; *Style*— Prof Peter Gregson; ✉ Vice-Chancellor's Office, Queen's University, Belfast BT7 1NN (tel 028 9097 5134, fax 028 9033 0808, e-mail vc.office@qub.ac.uk)

GREIG, George Carron (Geordie); s of Sir Carron Greig, and Monica, *née* Stourton; *b* 16 December 1960; *Educ* Eton, St Peter's Coll Oxford (MA); *m* 1995, Kathryn Elizabeth, *née* Terry; 1 s (Jasper b 30 April 1998), 2 da (Monica, Octavia (twins) b 11 June 2000); *Career* reporter: South East London and Kentish Mercury 1981–83, Daily Mail 1984–85, Today 1985–87; The Sunday Times: reporter 1987–89, arts corr 1989–91, New York corr 1991–95, literary ed 1995–99; ed Tatler 1999–; FRSA 2006; *Books* Louis and the Prince (1999); *Clubs* White's, Colony Rooms; *Style*— Geordie Greig, Esq; ✉ Tatler Magazine, Vogue House, 1 Hanover Square, London W1R 0AD (tel 020 7499 9080)

GREIG, Dr Kenneth Muir; s of Walter Davidson Greig, of Edinburgh, and Margaret, *née* Muir (d 1997); *b* 30 March 1960; *Educ* George Heriot's Sch Edinburgh, Worcester Coll Oxford (MA), Univ of Edinburgh (PhD); *m* June 1987, Josephine Claire Berenice, da of Prof Anthony Taylor; 1 da (Matilda Louise b 13 June 1992), 1 s (Lachlan Walter b 5 Dec 1996); *Career* exploration geologist BP 1984–87; mathematics teacher and housemaster Christ's Hosp 1987–93, head of mathematics and dir of studies Dollar Acad 1993–2000, headmaster Pangbourne Coll 2000–05, rector Hutchesons' GS Glasgow 2005–; *Recreations* watching rugby, rowing, beachcombing, bagpipes; *Clubs* East India, Western; *Style*— Dr Kenneth Greig; ✉ Hutchesons' Grammar School, Beaton Road, Glasgow G41 4NW (tel 0141 423 2933, fax 0141 424 0251, e-mail rector@hutchesons.org)

GRENFELL, 3 Baron (UK 1902); Julian Pascoe Francis St Leger Grenfell; sits as Baron Grenfell of Kilvey (Life Peer UK 2000), of Kilvey, Co Swansea; s of 2 Baron Grenfell, CBE, TD (d 1976), and his 1 w, Elizabeth (gda of 1 Baron Shaughnessy); *b* 23 May 1935; *Educ* Eton, King's Coll Cambridge; *m* 1, 1961, Loretta Maria Olga Hildegarde, da of Alfredo Reali, of Florence; 1 da (Hon Isabella Sarah Frances (Hon Mrs Pianini Mazzucchetti) b 1966); m 2, 1970, Gabrielle, o da of Dr Ernst Raab, of Berlin; 2 da (Hon Katharina Elizabeth Anne (Hon Mrs O'Connor) b 1973, Hon Vanessa Julia Claire b 1976); m 3, 27 June 1987, Mrs Elizabeth Porter, of Richmond, Virginia; m 4, 28 Oct 1993, Mrs Dagmar Langbehn Debreil, da of Dr Carl Langbehn of Berlin; *Heir* first cous, Francis Grenfell; *Career* 2 Lt KRRC (60 Rifles), Capt Queen's Westminsters (TA) KRRC; World Bank: chief of info and public affrs Europe 1970, dep dir European office 1973, special rep to UNO 1974–81, special advsr 1983–87, sr advsr 1987–90, head of external affairs European Office 1990–95, sr advsr Euro Affairs 1995–, UK Delegation to Cncl of Europe Parly Assembly 1997–99, EU Select Ctee House of Lords 1999–2000, chair EU Select Ctee's Subctee on Economic, Finance and Trade Affairs 1999 and 2001–, chm EU Select Ctee 2002–, princ dep chm of Ctees 2002–, dep speaker 2002–; *Books* Margot (1984), The Gazelle (2004); *Recreations* writing; *Clubs* Royal Green Jackets; *Style*— The Rt Hon the Lord Grenfell; ✉ House of Lords, London SW1A 0PW (tel 020 7219 3601)

GRENFELL, His Hon Judge Simon Pascoe; s of Osborne Pascoe (d 1971), of Saltburn, N Yorks, and Margaret Grenfell, *née* Morris (d 1998); *b* 10 July 1942; *Educ* Fettes, Emmanuel Coll Cambridge (MA); *m* 13 April 1974, Ruth de Jersey, da of John Peter de Jersey Harvard (d 1981), of Carlton-in-Cleveland, N Yorks; 3 da (Rachel b 1975, Amelia b 1976, Philippa b 1978), 1 s (Robin b 1981); *Career* called to the Bar Gray's Inn 1965; recorder of the Crown Court 1985–92, circuit judge (NE Circuit) 1992–, designated civil judge Bradford Gp 1998–2000, designated civil judge Leeds Gp 2000–, sr circuit judge 2002–; chllr Dio of Ripon 1992– (now Dio of Ripon and Leeds); chm of govrs Ripon GS 1996–2000; Liveryman Worshipful Co of Vintners; *Recreations* music, sailing, coarse gardening; *Style*— His Hon Judge Grenfell; ✉ St John's House, Sharow Lane, Sharow, Ripon, North Yorkshire HG4 5BN (tel 01765 605771, e-mail grenfells@tiscali.co.uk)

GRENIER, David Arthur; s of Rev George A Grenier (d 1973), and Dorothy Anita, *née* Burn (d 1990); *b* 12 August 1931; *Educ* St John's Sch Leatherhead, Jesus Coll Cambridge (MA), Sorbonne; *m* 25 Aug 1959, Janet Elizabeth, da of Ralph Thompson (d 1989); 3 s (Lewis b 1962, Julian b 1968, Michael b 1969); *Career* Capel-Cure Myers Ltd: dep chm 1975–77, chm 1977–79; ptnr Scott Goff Hancock & Co 1980–82, sr ptnr Scott Goff Layton & Co 1982–86, dir Smith New Court plc 1986–88, chief exec Independent Investment Mgmnt Ltd 1989–98 (chm 1998–2001), conslt 2001–02; chm of tstees Cancer Research UK pension scheme 2003–06; Freeman City of London, Liveryman Worshipful Co of Painter Stainers; ASIP 1968, FRSA 1992; *Recreations* opera, golf; *Clubs* Oxford and Cambridge, Coningsby; *Style*— David Grenier, Esq; ✉ Horncastle, Mount Pleasant, Guildford, Surrey GU2 4HZ

GRENIER, John Allan; s of Rev George Arthur Grenier (d 1973), and Dorothy Anita *née* Burn (d 1990); *b* 2 April 1933; *Educ* St John's Sch Leatherhead Surrey; 2 c; *Career* CA 1959; ptnr Payne Stone Fraser & Co 1966–69; chm London Sch of Accountancy 1969–77; chm The HLT Group Ltd 1974–2000 (Queen's Award for Export 1982), ret; elected chm of British Mgmnt Trg Export Cncl 1985; *Clubs* RAC, IOD; *Style*— John Grenier, Esq; ✉ Casa Ninho D'Aguia, Travessa da Aldeia Nova N2, Burgau, 8650–120 Vila do Bispo, Algarve, Portugal (tel 00 351 282 697 447, e-mail grenier.john@gmail.com)

GRENVILLE, Prof John A S; s of Adolf Abraham Guhrauer (d 1960), of London, and late Charlotte, *née* Sandberg; *b* 11 January 1928; *Educ* Cambridge Tech Sch, Birkbeck Coll London, LSE (BA, PhD, Hutchinson medal); *m* 1, 1960, Betty Anne, *née* Rosenberg (d 1974); 3 s (Murray Charles b 1962, Edward Samson b 1964, George Daniel b 1966); m 2, 1975, Patricia, *née* Conway; 1 da (Annabelle Charlotte b 1979), 1 step da (Claire Georgina Carnie b 1972); *Career* gardener Peterhouse Cambridge 1945–47, lectr and reader Univ of Nottingham 1953–66, Cwlth Fund fell 1959–60, postdoctoral fell Yale Univ 1961–64, prof of int history Univ of Leeds 1966–69; Univ of Birmingham: prof of modern history and head of dept 1969–94, prof of German history 1994–96, professorial fell Inst for German Studies 1994–; visiting prof City Univ of NY and Hamburg Univ; fndr Br Univs History Film Consortium 1968; conslt: American Biographical Serv Oxford and Santa Barbara Calif 1960–90, Second German Television Service ZDF and BBC (documentary history film prodns) 1984–90; formerly: memb Cncl Royal Hist Soc, dir of films Hist Assoc; dir Leo Baeck Inst London 1987–, ed Leo Baeck Year Book 1992–; FRHistS 1960; *Books* Lord Salisbury and Foreign Policy (1964), Politics, Strategy and American Diplomacy (with G B Young, 1966), Major International Treaties 1914–1974 (1974), Europe Reshaped 1848–1878 (1976), World History of the Twentieth Century 1900–45 (1980), Major International Treaties Since 1945 (with B Wasserstein, 1987, 3 edn 2000), Collins History of the World in the Twentieth Century (1994), History of the World from the Twentieth to the Twenty-First Century (2005); *Film Documentaries* Munich Crisis (1968), End of Illusion (with Nicholas Pronay, 1970), World of the Thirties (with Dieter Franck, 1986), Another War, Another Peace 1940–60 (with Dieter Franck, 1991); *Recreations* meeting international colleagues, listening to music, ballet and opera; *Clubs* Athenaeum, Elizabethan (New Haven); *Style*— Prof John Grenville; ✉ School of History, University of Birmingham, PO Box 363, Birmingham B15 2TT (tel 0121 414 5736, fax 0121 414 3656)

GRESHAM, Prof (Geoffrey) Austin; TD; s of Thomas Michael Gresham (d 1939), of Wrexham, N Wales, and Harriet Ann, *née* Richards (d 1945); *b* 1 November 1924; *Educ* Grove Pk GS, Gonville & Caius Coll Cambridge (MA, DSc, MB BChir, MD), KCH London; *m* 1 July 1950, Gweneth Margery, da of Louis Charles Leigh (d 1983), of Cambridge; 3 s (Christopher b 1951, Andrew b 1955, Robert b 1957), 2 da (Diana b 1954, Susan b 1959); *Career* Lt and Capt RAMC 1950–52, Maj and Lt-Col RAMC (V) 1954–66; house physician KCH London 1949–50 (house surgn 1949); Univ of Cambridge: demonstrator in pathology 1953–58, fell and coll lectr (and sometime pres) Jesus Coll, sec Faculty Bd of Med 1956–61, lectr in pathology 1958–62 (sometime dep assessor to regius prof of physic and supervisor of research Students Dept of Pathology); univ morbid anatomist and histologist Addenbrooke's Hosp Cambridge 1962– (jr asst pathologist 1953, conslt pathologist 1960), Home Office pathologist to Mid Anglia 1966– (prof of morbid anatomy and histology 1973); chm MD Ctee 1996–; ed of Atherosclerosis, sci fell Zoological Soc London; hon fell Gonville & Caius Coll Cambridge 2001; FRCPath, FRCPEd 1994; *Books* A Colour Atlas of General Pathology (1971, 2 edn 1992) A Colour Atlas of Forensic Pathology (1979), Post Mortem Procedures (1979), A Colour Atlas of Wounds and Wounding (1987); *Recreations* gardening, organ playing, wine, silver; *Style*— Prof Austin Gresham, TD; ✉ 18 Rutherford Road, Cambridge CB2 8HH (tel 01223 841326); Addenbrooke's Hospital, Hills Road, Cambridge (tel 01223 217168, fax 01223 216980, e-mail gag1000@cam.ac.uk)

GRESTY, Deborah Susan; da of Alexander William Gresty, and Barbara Joan Nash, *née* Perry; *b* 3 April 1953; *Educ* Birkenhead HS, Merchant Taylors' Sch, Univ of Nottingham (BA), Oxford Centre of Mgmnt Studies; *m* Peter Warland, s of Charles Warland; *Career* magazine publisher; Thomson Publications: grad trainee 1974, advertisement sales exec Pins & Needles 1975, dep advertisement mangr Living 1977 (advertisement sales exec 1976); Slimming Magazine: advertisement mangr 1979, advertisement dir 1980, dir 1981, publisher 1982–84; publisher/dir Working Woman 1984–85; publisher: Brides and Setting Up Home 1985–90, House & Garden 1990–96, Condé Nast Traveller 1997–; bd dir Condé Nast 1993–; *Recreations* tennis, cricket, classical music, opera, theatre; *Style*— Ms Deborah Gresty; ✉ Condé Nast, Vogue House, Hanover Square, London W1R 0AD (tel 020 7499 9080)

GRESTY, Hilary Marion Bell; da of late Allan Bell Gresty, and Joy Margaret, *née* Coltham; *b* 24 February 1954; *Educ* Oxford Girls' HS, Univ of Exeter (BA), UCL (MA), Courtauld Inst London (MPhil); *Partner* Edward Macready Dickinson; 3 s (Edmund Gresty Dickinson b 12 June 1992, Arthur Gresty Dickinson b 16 Feb 1994, Roland Gresty Dickinson b 1 Feb 1997); *Career* research asst Royal Library Windsor 1977, library res asst Tate Gallery London 1978–81, curator Kettle's Yard Univ of Cambridge 1983–89, freelance writer, lectr, curator and visual arts conslt 1989–; currently dir VAGA (Visual Arts & Galleries Assoc); *Exhibitions* incl: 1965–1972 - when attitudes became form (1984), Pounds Artists (1985), C R W Nevinson (1988); progs incl work with Susan Hiller, Nan Hoover, Ron Haselden, Mary Kelly, Richard Layzell and Charlie Hooker; *Catalogues* incl: Christopher Wood - his early years (Newlyn Art Gallery, 1989), Ron Haselden (Serpentine Gallery, 1990), Alison Wilding (Newlyn Art Gallery, 1993), Other Criteria: Sculpture in 20th Century Britain (contrib, Henry Moore Inst Leeds, 2003); *Books* British Sculpture 1960–90 (contrib), Postmodern Art: theory into practice (contrib 1996); *Style*— Ms Hilary Gresty, FRSA; ✉ The Old Village School, Witcham, Ely, Cambridgeshire CB6 2LQ (tel 01353 776296, e-mail hilary@vaga.co.uk)

GRETTON, Lady; Jennifer Ann Gretton; *b* 14 June 1943, St Ives, Cornwall; *m* 3 Baron Gretton (d 1989); 1 s, 1 da; *Career* mangr Stapleford Estate 1989–; HM Lord-Lt Leics 2003– (DL Leics 2001); pres: Melton Mowbray and Dist Model Engrg Soc 1989–, Rural Community Cncl Leics and Rutland 1994, Leics Orgn for the Relief of Suffering (LOROS) 1999, Cncl St John Ambulance 2003–, E Midlands Reserve Forces and Cadets Assoc (EMRFCA) 2003–, Army Benevolent Fund Leics and Rutland Ctee 2003–; vice-pres: Cncl Leics Scouts 2003–, EMRFCA Co Ctee 2003–, Leics and Rutland Branch Magistrates Assoc 2004–; memb: Ctee Leics and Rutland CLA 1989, Student Affrs Ctee and Advsy Cncl Harlaxton Manor (Br campus of Univ of Evansville) 1989, Environment and Water Ctee CLA 1994–98; patron: Sir Frank Whittle Commemorative Gp 2003–, Royal Leics Regt Museum Appeal 2003–, Change Ashby Now (CAN) 2003–, Heart of the Nat Forest Fndn 2003–, Leics and Rutland Wildlife Tsts 2004–, Leicester City Male Voice Choir 2005–; ambassador Nat Forest 2005–; church warden All Saints Somerby 1992–95, memb Ctee Somerby PCC 1991–, memb Cncl Leicester Cathedral 2003–; patron of five parishes; restored Stapleford Miniature Railway, instigated Stapleford Steam Rally 1996; memb Oakham Sch Choral Soc; *Recreations* sport, music, steam; *Style*— The Lady Gretton; ✉ Holygate Farm, Holygate Road, Stapleford, Melton Mowbray, Leicestershire LE14 2SG (tel 01572 787540, fax 01572 787516)

GRETTON, 4 Baron (UK 1944) John Lysander Gretton; o s of 3 Baron Gretton (d 1989); *b* 17 April 1975; *Educ* Shrewsbury, RAC Cirencester; *m* Oct 2006, Sarah Elisabeth Anne Altard; *Style*— The Rt Hon Lord Gretton; ✉ Holygate Farm, Stapleford, Melton Mowbray, Leicestershire LE14 2XQ

GRETTON, Vice Adm Michael; CB (1998), CVO (2005); *b* 1946; *Educ* Ampleforth, Britannia RNC Dartmouth, Trinity Coll Oxford (MA); *m* Stephanie, *née* O'Neill; 3 da, 1 s; *Career* with RN; sometime CO HMS Bossington and HMS Ambuscade, served Directorate of Naval Plans MOD 1980–82, staff offr ops to COMASWSTRIKFOR (Commander NATO Anti-Submarine Warfare Striking Force) 1982–84, dep dir Naval Recruiting MOD 1984–86, RCDS 1987, Cabinet Office Top Mgmnt Prog 1988, successively commanded HMS Invincible then NATO Standing Naval Force Atlantic (STANAVFORLANT) 1988–91, dir Naval Staff Duties MOD 1991–93, Rear Adm 1993, COMUKTG (Commander UK Task Group) and COMASWSTRIKFOR 1993–94, Vice Adm 1994, SACLANTREPEUR (representative of Supreme Allied Commander Atlantic in Europe) 1994–98, ret; dir The Duke of Edinburgh Award 1998–; vice-pres Nautical Inst; tstee Sail Trg Assoc 1999–, pres Invincible Sea Cadet Corp Lancs; govr: St Edward's Sch Oxford, Farleigh Sch Andover, St Mary's Sch Shaftesbury; *Style*— Vice Adm Michael Gretton,

G

CB, CVO; ✉ The Duke of Edinburgh's Award, Gulliver House, Madeira Walk, Windsor, Berkshire SL4 1EU (tel 01753 727432)

GREWCOCK, Daniel Jonathan (Danny); MBE (2004); *b* 7 November 1972, Coventry, Warks; *Educ* Woodlands Sch Coventry; *Career* rugby union player (lock); clubs: Coventry RUFC, Saracens RUFC, Bath RUFC (capt); England: 57 caps, debut v Argentina 1997, winners Six Nations Championship 2001 and 2003 (Grand Slam 2003), ranked no 1 team in world 2003, winners World Cup Aust 2003; memb squad Br & I Lions tour to Aust 2001 and NZ 2005; *Recreations* Coventry FC; *Style—* Danny Grewcock, Esq, MBE

GREY, Sir Anthony Dysart; 7 Bt (UK 1814), of Fallodon, Northumberland; s of Capt Edward Elton Grey (d 1962), and Nancy, *née* Meagher; suc gf, Sir Robin Edward Dysart Grey, 6 Bt (d 1974); *b* 19 October 1949; *Educ* Guildford GS Perth (Aust); *m* 1, 1970 (m dis), Donna, da of Donald Daniels, of London; m 2, 1993, Alison Turner; 2 da (Matilda Jessie b 4 Jan 1994, Lucinda Jane b 25 Jan 1996), 1 s (Thomas Jasper b 30 April 1998); *Heir* s, Thomas Grey; *Recreations* fishing, painting; *Style—* Sir Anthony Grey, Bt; ✉ c/o 38 King's Park Road, Perth, Western Australia 6005, Australia

GREY, Dame Beryl Elizabeth; DBE (1988, CBE 1973); da of Arthur Ernest Groom (d 1983), and Annie Elizabeth, *née* Marshall (d 1952); *b* 11 June 1927; *Educ* Dame Alice Owen Girls' Sch London, Professional Madeleine Sharp Sch, Sadler's Wells Ballet Sch, de Voss Sch; *m* 15 July 1950, Dr Sven Gustav Svenson, s of Ernest Svenson (d 1967), of Heleneborg, Sweden; 1 s (Ingvar b 1954); *Career* prima ballerina; danced Swan Lake at 15, Giselle at 16, Sleeping Beauty at 19; prima ballerina Sadler's Wells later Royal Ballet 1941–57; int guest ballerina 1957–66; first Western guest artist: Bolshoi Ballet Moscow 1957, Peking Ballet 1964; appeared in film Black Swan (stereo scopic film) 1952; DG Arts Educn Schs and Teacher Trg Coll 1966–68, artistic dir London Festival Ballet (now English National Ballet) 1968–79, dir Royal Opera House Covent Garden 1999–2003; dir/prodr: Sleeping Beauty (London Festival Ballet) 1967, Swan Lake (London Festival Ballet) 1972, Giselle (West Australian Ballet) 1984 and 1986, Sleeping Beauty (Royal Swedish Ballet) 1985 and 2002; Imperial Soc of Teachers of Dancing: memb Cncl 1962–91, chm 1984–91, pres 1991–2001, elected life pres 2002; pres: Dance Cncl of Wales 1981–2004, East Grinstead Operatic Soc 1986–, Keep Fit Assoc 1992–93 (vice-pres 1968–92), Eng Nat Ballet Cos 2005; vice-pres: Royal Acad of Dancing 1980– (memb Exec Ctee 1982–89), Music Therapy Charity 1980–, Br Fedn of Music Festivals 1985–, PRO (dogs nat charity) 1991–2005, London Ballet Circle 2001–; chm Royal Ballet Benevolent Fund 1992–; vice-chm: Dance Teachers Benevolent Fund 1984–2004 (tstee 1981–2004), London Coll of Dance (govr 1966–93); vice-chm of govrs Royal Ballet Companies 1995–2002 (govr 1993–); tstee: London City Ballet 1970–92, DISCS (Diagnostic Investigation of Spinal Conditions and Sciatica) 1993–2005 (patron 2005–), Cncl for Dance Educn and Trg 1995–98 (memb Cncl 1984–98), Birmingham Royal Ballet 1995–99; patron: Frances Mary Buss Fndn 1963072, Adeline Genee Theatre 1982–90, Nature Cure Clinic 1986–, Tanya Bayona Princess Boutiatine Acad of Ballet Malta 1988–2004, Dancers Career Devpt 1988–, Benesh Inst 1988–, Language of Dance Centre 1988–, Friends of Sadler's Wells 1991–, Osteopathic Centre for Children 1992–, Furlong Research Fndn (hip replacement) 1993– (tstee 2005–), Amber Tst 1995–, Theatre Design Tst (Central St Martins Coll London) 1995–, Legat Fndn 1998–, Sussex Opera and Ballet Soc 2001–, Dance Critics Circle 2005– (also tstee), Early Dance Circle 2007–; vice-patron Br Sch of Osteopathy 1996–; govr: Dame Alice Owens Girls' Sch 1960–77, London Coll of Dance 1966–93; Imperial Award Imperial Soc of Teachers of Dancing 1987, Queen Elizabeth II Coronation Award Royal Acad of Dancing 1996, Critics Circle Dance Award for Services to Dance 2002, Imperial Soc of Teachers of Dancing Lifetime Achievement Award 2004; Hon DMus Univ of Leicester 1970, Hon DLitt City of London Univ 1974, Hon DEd CNAA 1989, Hon DLitt Univ of Buckingham 1993, Hon DMus Univ of London 1996; FISTD 1960; *Books* Red Curtain Up, Through the Bamboo Curtain, Favourite Ballet Stories (ed); *Recreations* swimming, reading, playing piano, painting; *Style—* Dame Beryl Grey, DBE; ✉ Fernhill, Forest Row, East Sussex RH18 5JE (tel and fax 01342 822539)

GREY, Prof Christopher John; s of Alan Grey (d 2005), and Madeleine, *née* Beck; *b* 5 December 1964, Sanderstead, Surrey; *Educ* Trinity Sch Croydon, Univ of Manchester (BA, PhD); *m* 11 April 1992, Nathalie, *née* Mitev; *Career* ESRC fell UMIST 1990–93, lectr then sr lectr Univ of Leeds 1993–98; Judge Business Sch Univ of Cambridge: lectr, sr lectr then reader 1999–2005, prof of organizational theory 2005–07, sr res assoc 2007–; prof of organizational behaviour Univ of Warwick 2007–; fell Wolfson Coll Cambridge 2002–; ed-in-chief Management Learning 1999–2005; chair Mgmnt Research Advsy Forum Nat Coll for Sch Leadership 2002–, memb Nat Educnl Research Forum 1999–2003; *Publications* Rethinking Management Education (1996), Making Up Accountants (1998), Essential Readings in Management Learning (2004), Studying Organizations (2005), The Oxford Reader in Critical Management Studies (2005); *Recreations* cricket, cookery; *Style—* Prof Christopher Grey; ✉ Warwick Business School, University of Warwick, Coventry CV4 7AL (tel 024 7652 2888, fax 024 7652 4656, e-mail chris.grey@wbs.ac.uk)

GREY, Ivar Andreas Robert John; s of Wing Cdr John Francis Grey, DSO, DFC (d 1962), and Caroline Maria, *née* Feichtessen (d 1958); *b* 5 December 1947, London; *Educ* Worth Sch Crawley; *m* 8 Aug 1975, Ena B, *née* Bakken; 2 da (Charlotte Natalie b 1975, Michelle Katrina b 1981), 1 s (John Francis b 1978); *Career* Peat Marwick Mitchell & Co (latterly KPMG): joined Newcastle upon Tyne office 1966, worked in London, The Hague, Copenhagen and Cardiff offices, ptnr 1981, ret 2002; non-exec dir: Finance Wales plc, Gwent Healthcare NHS Tst; memb Competition Cmmn; govr Port Regis Sch Shaftesbury; FCA 1972; *Recreations* reading, skiing, dog walking; *Style—* Ivar Grey, Esq; ✉ 1 Clos Cefn Bychan, Pentyrch, Cardiff CF15 9PF (tel and fax 029 2089 1122, e-mail ivar.grey@totalize.co.uk); c/o Competition Commission, Victoria House, Southampton Row, London WC1B 4AD

GREY, 6 Earl (UK 1806); Sir Richard Fleming George Charles Grey; 7 Bt (GB 1746); also Baron Grey of Howick (UK 1801) and Viscount Howick (UK 1806); s of Albert Grey (ggs of Adm Hon George Grey, himself 4 s of 2 Earl Grey, who was PM 1830–34); suc 2 cous twice removed 1963; *b* 5 March 1939; *Educ* Hounslow Coll, Hammersmith Coll of Bldg; *m* 1, 1966 (m dis 1974), Margaret Ann, da of Henry Bradford, of Ashburton; m 2, 1974, Stephanie Caroline, da of Donald Gaskell-Brown, of Newton Ferrers, Plymouth, and formerly w of Surgn-Cdr Neil Leicester Denham, RN; *Heir* bro, Philip Grey; *Career* chm: Academy Beverage Co Ltd, The London Cremation Co plc, Earl Grey's Wine Co Ltd; dir: Covent Garden Quality Ltd, The Countess Grey Collection Ltd, Crag Group Ltd, Earl Grey Restaurants Ltd; pres: Cost and Exec Accountants Assoc 1978, The Cremation Soc of GB; memb Liberal Pty; *Style—* The Rt Hon the Earl Grey

GREY, Robin Douglas; QC (1979); s of Dr Francis Temple Grey (d 1941), and Eglantine, *née* Ellice; *b* 23 May 1931; *Educ* Eastbourne Coll, KCL (LLB); *m* 1, 1968 (m dis 1972), Gillian, da of late Maj Esme Austin Reeves Porch; m 2, 1972 (m dis 1992), Berenice Anna, da of Dennis Wheatley (d 1985); 1 s (Julian Alexander b 2 May 1970), 1 da (Louise Katherine b 20 Aug 1973); m 3, 24 Sept 1993, Annick, da of late Henri Kerbiriou, and Lady Winskill; *Career* Nat Serv Army 1950–51; called to the Bar Gray's Inn 1957; crown counsel in Aden 1959–63 (acting attorney gen, acting registrar gen, acting sr crown counsel); in practice SE Circuit 1963–, dep circuit judge 1977–79, recorder 1979–99; head FCO Team of Legal Experts to Moscow 1993, FCO conslt to Govt of Russian Fedn 1994–; chm Police Disciplinary Appeals Tbnls 1989–, legal assessor GMC 1995–; memb: Soc of Forensic Med, Crime and Juvenile Delinquency Study Gp Centre for Policy Studies 1980, Ctee of Criminal Bar Assoc 1991–94 (chm Int Sub-Ctee 1993), advsy ctee of European Criminal Bar Assoc 2003–; co-author Professional Conduct pamphlet for Inns of Court Sch of Law; *Recreations* tennis, golf, fishing; *Clubs* Hurlingham, New Cavendish; *Style—* Robin Grey, Esq, QC; ✉ Queen Elizabeth Building, 3rd Floor, Temple, London EC4Y 9BS

GREY EGERTON, Sir (Philip) John Caledon; 15 Bt (E 1617), of Egerton and Oulton, Cheshire; s of Sir Philip Reginald Le Belward Grey Egerton, 14 Bt (d 1962); *b* 19 October 1920; *Educ* Eton; *m* 1, 1951, Margaret Voase (d 1971), eld da of late Rowland Rank, of Aldwick, W Sussex, and wid of Sqdn Ldr Robert Ullman, RAF; m 2, 1986, Frances Mary, da of late Col Robert Maximilian Rainey-Robinson, of Broadmayne, Dorset, and wid of Sqdn Ldr William Dudley Williams, DFC, RAF; *Heir* kinsman, Maj-Gen David Boswell, CB, OBE, MC; *Career* late Capt Welsh Gds; *Style—* Sir John Grey Egerton, Bt; ✉ Meadow House, West Stafford, Dorchester, Dorset DT2 8AQ

GREY OF CODNOR, 6 Baron (E 1397); Richard Henry Cornwall-Legh; DL (Cheshire 1995); o s of 5 Baron Grey of Codnor, CBE, AE, DL (in whose favour the barony, abeyant since 1497, was terminated in 1989; d 1996), and Dorothy Catherine Whitson, *née* Scott (d 1993); *b* 14 May 1936; *Educ* Stowe; *m* 1974, Joanna Storm, 7 and yst da of Sir Kenelm Henry Ernest Cayley, 10 Bt (d 1967); 3 s (Hon Richard Stephen Cayley b 1976, Hon Kenelm Michael b 1978, Hon George Henry b 1982), 1 da (Hon Caroline Philadelphia b 1983); *Heir* s, Hon Richard Cornwall-Legh; *Career* RN 1955–57 (Gen Serv Medal, Suez); landowner and dir of private cos; memb British Ski Team 1959–61 (Capt 1960–61); High Sheriff Cheshire 1993–94; *Clubs* Boodle's, MCC; *Style—* The Rt Hon the Lord Grey of Codnor, DL; ✉ High Legh House, Knutsford, Cheshire WA16 0QR

GRIBBIN, Dr John Richard; *b* 19 March 1946, Maidstone, Kent; *Educ* Maidstone GS, Univ of Sussex (BSc, MSc), Univ of Cambridge (PhD); *m* 1966, Mary, *née* Murray; 2 s (Jonathan b 1972, Benjamin b 1976); *Career* Nature magazine 1970–75, visiting fell Social Policy Research Unit 1975–78, physics conslt New Scientist 1978–98, visiting fell in astronomy Univ of Sussex 1998–; FRAS, FRMetS, FRSL, FRSA; *Non-Fiction* incl: Genesis: The origins of man and the universe (1981), In Search of Schrodinger's Cat (1984), In Search of the Double Helix (1985), In search of the Big Bang (1986), The Omega Point: The search for the missing mass, and the ultimate fate of the universe (1987), The One Per Cent Advantage (with Mary Gribbin, 1988), The Hole in the Sky (1988), Cosmic Coincidences: Dark matter, mankind and anthropic cosmology (with Martin Rees, 1989), Hothouse Earth: The Greenhouse Effect and Gaia (1990), Children of the Ice (with Mary Gribbin, 1990), Blinded by the Light: The secret life of the sun (1991), The Matter Myth (with Paul Davies, 1991), Stephen Hawking: A life in science (with Michael White, 1992), In Search of the Edge of Time: Black holes, wormholes and time machines (1992), In the Beginning: The birth of the living universe (1993), Albert Einstein: A Life in Science (with Michael White, 1993), Being Human (with Mary Gribbin, 1993), Schrodinger's Kittens and the Search for Reality (1995), Darwin: A life in science (with Michael White, 1995), Richard Feynman: A Life in Science (1997), Origins (1997), Q is for Quantum: An Encyclopedia of Particle Physics (1998), Almost Everyone's Guide to Science: The Universe, Life and Everything (1998), The Birth of Time: How Astronomers Measured the Age of the Universe (1999), What's the Big Idea? Chaos and Uncertainty (1999), Deep Space (1999), The Search for Superstrings, Symmetry, and the Theory of Everything (1999), Stardust (with Mary Gribbin, 2000), Ice Age (with Mary Gribbin, 2001), The First Chimpanzee (2001), Space: Our Final Frontier (2001), Science: A History (2002), The Science of Philip Pullman's His Dark Materials (with Mary Gribbin, 2003), The Men who Measured the Universe (with Mary Gribbin, 2004), Deep Simplicity (2004), The Fellowship: the story of a revolution (2005), The Universe: A Biography (2007); *Fiction* Double Planet (with Marcus Chown, 1988), Father to the Man (1989), Reunion (with Marcus Chown, 1991), Ragnarok (with David Compton, 1991), Innervisions (1993); *Recreations* watching cricket; *Clubs* Kent CCC; *Style—* Dr John Gribbin

GRIBBON, Angus John St George; s of Maj-Gen Nigel St George Gribbon, OBE, and Rowan Mary, *née* MacLiesh; *b* 25 December 1951; *Educ* Rugby, New Coll Oxford (MA); *m* 15 May 1976, Mary-Anne, da of Hugh Wynwel Gamon, CBE, MC, of Sevenoaks, Kent; 1 s (Edward b 1981), 2 da (Mary-Clare b 1983, Caroline b 1985); *Career* Clifford-Turner Slrs 1974–79, slr Allied-Lyons plc 1979–89, sr legal advsr Securicor plc 1989–99; dir of legal affairs Coral Eurobet 2000–01, gp legal advsr Goldshield Gp plc 2002–05, gp co sec Control Risks Gp Ltd 2005–; tstee The Scott's Project; *Recreations* tennis, skiing, the arts; *Clubs* Law Soc; *Style—* Angus Gribbon, Esq; ✉ Pedlam Brook, West Peckham, Maidstone, Kent ME18 5JS (tel 01732 851732, e-mail angusgribbon@aol.com)

GRIDLEY, 3 Baron (UK 1955); Richard David Arnold Gridley; only s of 2 Baron Gridley (d 1996), and (Edna) Leslie, *née* Wheen; *b* 22 August 1956; *Educ* Monkton Combe Sch, Portsmouth Poly, Univ of Brighton (BA); *m* 1, 1979 (m dis), Amanda J Mackenzie; m 2, 1983, Suzanne Elizabeth, *née* Ripper; 1 s (Hon Carl Richard b 5 Feb 1981), 1 da (Hon Danielle Lauren b 1983); *Career* formerly project mangr: Rush and Tompkins Gp plc, Ballast Nedam Construction UK; currently sr lectr in business and IT and travel and tourism South Downs Coll of FE; patron Care for the Wild Int; *Style—* The Rt Hon Lord Gridley

GRIEVE, Alan Thomas; CBE (2003); s of Lewis Miller Grieve (d 1963), of Stanmore, Middx, and Doris Lilian, *née* Amner (d 1975); *b* 22 January 1928; *Educ* Aldenham, Trinity Hall Cambridge (MA, LLM); *m* 1, 1957 (m dis 1971), Anne, da of Dr Lawrence Dulake, of Reigate, Surrey; 1 da (Amanda (Baroness Harlech) b 1958), 2 s (Charles b 1960, Ivan b 1962); m 2, 1971, Karen Louise, da of Michael de Sivrac Dunn (d 2000), of Honiton, Devon; 1 s (Thomas de Sivrac b 1973), 1 da (Lara b 1974); *Career* Nat Serv 2 Lt 14/20 King's Hussars, Capt City of London Yeo TA; admitted slr 1953; sr ptnr Taylor Garrett; conslt Taylor Wessing; dir: Baggeridge Brick plc 1964–2003, Stenham plc 1971–94, Medical Insurance Agency Ltd 1976–92, Reliance Resources Ltd 1978–97, Wilson Bowden plc 1993–96, Vaudeville Theatre Ltd 1993–2001, Savoy Theatre Mgmnt Ltd 1998–2004, Hereford Mappa Mundi Tstee Co Ltd 1998–, The Jerwood Space Ltd 1998–, Theatre Enterprises Ltd 2001–04, and other cos; chm The Jerwood Fndn; patron Brendoncare for the Elderly; tstee: Oakham Sch 1973–93, Br Racing Sch 1986–94; friend of RCP (memb Fin and Gen Purposes Bd 1986–92), memb Educnl Assets Bd 1988–90, hon memb Cncl Royal Court Theatre; hon Vice Cdre Sea Cadets Assoc; ambass The Samaritans 1999–; memb Law Soc; Hon FRCP 2002, Hon FTCL 2002; *Books* Purchase Tax (1958); *Recreations* performing and visual arts, country life, collecting; *Clubs* Boodle's, Baur au Lac, Hawks' (Cambridge); *Style—* Alan Grieve, Esq, CBE; ✉ Stoke Lodge, Clee Downton, Ludlow, Shropshire SY8 3EG (tel 01584 823413, fax 01584 823419); Jerwood Foundation, 22 Fitzroy Square, London W1T 6EN (tel 020 7388 6287, fax 020 7388 6289)

GRIEVE, Dominic Charles Roberts; MP; s of Percy Grieve, QC (d 1998), and Evelyn, *née* Mijouain (d 1991); *b* 24 May 1956; *Educ* Westminster, Magdalen Coll Oxford (MA), Central London Poly (Dip Law); *m* 6 Oct 1990, Caroline, da of Geoffrey Hutton; 2 s (James b 17 April 1994, Hugo b 29 Aug 1995); *Career* called to the Bar Middle Temple 1980 (bencher 2004); Parly candidate (Cons) Norwood 1987; MP (Cons) Beaconsfield 1997–; oppn frontbench spokesman for Scot 1999–2001, shadow min Home Office 2001–03, shadow attorney gen 2003–; memb Select Ctee: Statutory Instruments 1997–2001, Environmental Audit 1997–2001; memb All-Pty Waterways Gp 1997–; Legal Affrs Ctee; cncllr London Borough of Hammersmith and Fulham 1982–86, vice-chm Fulham Cons Assoc 1988–91; memb: John Muir Tst, Cncl Franco-British Soc, Luxembourg Soc, JUSTICE; lay visitor to police stations 1990–96; *Recreations* mountaineering, skiing, fell walking, travel, architecture; *Clubs* Carlton; *Style—* Dominic Grieve, Esq, MP; ✉ House of Commons, London SW1A 0AA (tel 020 7219 6220, fax 020 7219 4803)

GRIEVES, John Kerr; s of Thomas Grieves (d 1979), of Littlehampton, W Sussex, and Annie, *née* Davis (d 1976); *b* 7 November 1935; *Educ* King's Sch Worcester, Univ of Oxford (MA), Harvard Business Sch (AMP); *m* 21 Oct 1961, Ann Gorell, da of Vincent Charles Harris (d 1982), of London; 1 da (Kate b 25 May 1964), 1 s (Thomas b 11 Jan 1969); *Career* Pinsent and Co 1958–63; Freshfields: joined 1963, managing ptnr 1979, sr ptnr 1990–96; non-exec dir: British Invisibles 1992–96, Enterprise Oil plc 1996–2002, Northern Electric plc 1996–97, Barclays Private Bank 1997–, Hillsdown Holdings plc 1997–98, First Leisure Corporation plc 1998–2000 (chm), New Look Group plc 1998–2004 (chm), Esporta plc 2000–02 (chm); advsr Apax Partners 1996–99; memb Fin Reporting Review Panel; *Recreations* the arts, sport; *Clubs* Athenaeum; *Style*— John Grieves, Esq; ✉ 7 Putney Park Avenue, London SW15 5QN (tel 020 8876 1207)

GRIFFIN, Brian James; s of James Henry Griffin (d 1985), and Edith Moore; *b* 13 April 1948; *Educ* Halesowen Tech Sch, Dudley Tech Coll, Manchester Poly Sch of Photography (ONC, Dip Photography, Dip Assoc of Manchester); *m* 1, July 1980 (m dis 2001), Frances Mary, da of Morris Newman; 1 da (Layla Sky b Jan 1982), 1 s (Danz James Sky b Aug 1983); m 2, March 2003, Brynja Sverrisdottrr, da of Sverirr Thorolfson; *Career* trainee draughtsman 1964–66, trainee estimator 1966–69, photography student 1969–72, photographer 1972–90, film dir 1990–; writer and dir of short film: Claustrofoamia 1994, The Curl 1996, Xmas Steps 1998; Premi Al Llibre Fotografic award for Work (Primavera Fotografica '90 Barcelona); Hon FRPS 2006; Freeman City of Arles (France); *Books* Brian Griffin Copyright (1978), Power (1980), Open (1985), Portraits (1987), Work (1988), Brian Griffin Influences (2005), The Water People (2006), Baugur: The Movie (2006), team (2007); *Recreations* speedway racing; *Clubs* Groucho; *Style*— Brian Griffin, Esq; ✉ Flat 22, Canada Wharf, 255 Rotherhithe Street, London SE16 5ES (tel 07836 687166, website www.briangriffin.co.uk)

GRIFFIN, Christopher John (Chris); s of Peter J C Griffin; *b* 22 July 1957; *Educ* Woodhouse Grove Sch, Bradford Coll of Art and Design, Sheffield City Poly (BA); *m* 1988, Emma Victoria; 2 da (Evangeline Olivia b 1994, Sophie Georgina b 1996); *Career* Metal Box plc 1979–85, MBO of design div Metal Box plc to form Packaging Innovation Ltd (now Pi3, PIglobal) 1984, md PI Design International 1995, ceo Museum of Brand Packaging and Advtg 2003; Innovator of the Year Award Inst of Packaging 1992; dir Mktg Soc (memb 1985), FIP (memb 1980); *Publications* author of various conf proceedings covering design, research and IT; *Style*— Chris Griffin, Esq; ✉ PI, 1 Colville Mews, Lonsdale Road, London W11 2AR (tel 020 7908 0800, fax 020 7908 0950)

GRIFFIN, Prof George Edward; s of Herbert Griffin (d 1973), of Hull, and Enid Mary, *née* Borrill; *b* 27 February 1947; *Educ* Malet Lambert Sch Hull, KCL (BSc), St George's Hosp Med Sch (MB BS), Univ of Hull (PhD); *m* 15 April 1972, Daphne Joan (d 1998), da of Lionel Haylor, of Romford; 2 s (James Edward b 1978, Andrew John b 1980), 1 da (Joanna Mary b 1983); *Career* Harkness fell Harvard Univ Med Sch 1975–76; St George's Hosp Med Sch (now St George's Univ of London): house physician 1974–79, lectr 1979–83, dept head of communicable diseases 1990–, chm of med 1994–, currently vice-princ (research); Wellcome Tst: sr lectr 1983–89, reader in med 1989–92, conslt physician 1983–, prof of infectious diseases and med 1992–; sec MRS 1988–; memb: Public Health Lab Serv Bd 1995–2001, MRC (UK) Physiological Med and Infection Bd 1995–2000, Wellcome Tst Int Interest Panel 2002–05; expert advsr House of Lords Ctee Fighting Infection 2002–03; chair Advsy Ctee on Dangerous Pathogens Dept of Health/HSE/DEFRA 2005–; various pubns on pathogenesis of infection, immunological and metabolic responses to infection and vaccines; FRCP, FRCPEd, FMedSci; *Recreations* mountain walking, gardening; *Style*— Prof George Griffin; ✉ Division of Cellular and Molecular Medicine - Infectious Diseases, St George's, University of London, Tooting, London SW17 0RE (tel 020 8725 5827, fax 020 8336 0940, e-mail ggriffin@sgul.ac.uk)

GRIFFIN, Hayden; s of Robert John Griffin (d 1970), and Doreen, *née* Tuck (d 1992); *b* 23 January 1943; *Educ* Maritzburg Coll, Natal Tech Coll, Sadler's Wells Design Course; *m* 1988; Fiona, *née* Williams; 1 c (Teal b 4 Jan 1988); *Career* designer for theatre, television and film; head of design Northcott Theatre 1970–72; memb United Scenic Artists Local 829 USA; *Theatre* over 21 credits RNT incl: Madras House (Plays & Players Award for Best Design) 1977, A Fair Quarrel 1979, As You Like It 1979, The Iceman Cometh 1980, The Crucible 1980, A Map of the World 1983, King Lear 1986, After the Fall 1990; world premiere's incl: Watch It Come Down 1976, Weapons of Happiness 1976, The Woman 1978, Plenty 1978, Summer 1982, Glengarry Glen Ross 1983, Pravda 1985; RSC incl: Son of Man 1995, Comrades, Henry VIII; world premiere's incl: Duck Song, Cousin Vladimir, New England 1994; Royal Court world premiere's incl: A Mad World My Masters, Yesterday's News, Devils Island, Restoration, The Farm, The Runaway, Come Together Season, The Enoch Show, Trixie and Baba; Northcott Theatre credits incl: Guys and Dolls, Narrow Road to the Deep North, Tempest, Galileo, Julius Caesar, Caucasian Chalk Circle; world premiere's incl: Measure for Measure, Bingo, Judge Jeffrey; West End credits incl: Lennie (Criterion), All My Sons (Wyndham's), Way of the World (Chichester and Haymarket) 1984, Glengarry Glen Ross 1985, The Admirable Crichton (Lyric Theatre Royal) 1988, A Life in the Theatre 1989, The Invisible Man (Strand) 1990, A Month in the Country (Albery) 1994, Total Eclipse; world premiere Vanilla (Lyric Shaftesbury Ave) 1990; other UK world premiere's incl: The Churchill Play, Civilians, How Mad Tulloch Was Taken Away, Narrow Road to the Deep North, The Wind in the Sassafras Trees, The Gulf Between Us; numerous credits abroad incl world premiere's of A Map of the World (Sydney Theatre Co) 1982, The Day Room (Manhattan Theatre) 1987, The Knife (Joe Papp's Public Theatre) 1988; *Opera* credits incl: Jacob Lenz (Italy), Martyrdom of St Magnus (Italy), Falstaff (Los Angeles and Covent Garden), Cosi Fan Tutte (NY Metropolitan Opera) 1982, Orfeo (ENO 1983, revived 1991 & 1996), Parsifal (Covent Garden 1988, Flemish Opera Co 1991); *Ballet* with David Bintley, *qv* incl: Still Life at the Penguin Cafe (for the Royal Ballet Covent Garden 1988, Munich 1988, PACT SA 1994 (Olivier Award nomination for Outstanding Contrib to Dance 1988, also film), Hobson's Choice (Sadlers Wells Ballet, also film) 1990, Cyrano (for Royal Ballet Covent Garden) 1991, JOB (for San Francisco Ballet) 1992, Mini & Maxi (touring prod for Interpressario (Dutch Award Scheveningen Vormgevingsprÿs winner)) 1994, Far From the Madding Crowd (Birmingham Royal Ballet) 1996, Giselle (Birmingham Royal Ballet) 1999; *Television* incl: South Bank Show on Edward Bond (LWT), Six Characters in Search of an Author (BBC2/BBC Scotland); *Films* incl: Wetherby (Golden Bear Award for Best Film Berlin, 1986), Comrade Lady (short) 1989, Hope in the Year Two (Screen Two) 1993, Syrup (short, 2nd Prize at Cannes 1994, Academy nomination 1995), 1993, Painted Angels 1996, Food for Ravens 1997, Conquest 1997, Intimacy 2000 (Golden Bear Award for Best Film Berlin 2001), Out on a Limb (2004); *Recreations* scuba diving; *Style*— Hayden Griffin, Esq; ✉ c/o Marc Berlin, Berlin Associates, 14 Floral Street, London WC2E 9DH (tel 020 7836 1112, fax 020 7632 5280, e-mail haydengriffin@popmail.bta.com)

GRIFFIN, Prof James Patrick; s of Gerald Joseph Griffin (d 1961), and Catherine, *née* Noonan (d 1956); *b* 8 July 1933; *Educ* Choate Sch, Yale Univ (BA), Univ of Oxford (Rhodes scholar, sr scholar St Antony's Coll, DPhil, MA); *m* 1966, Catherine Maulde, da of Prof Hans von Halban; 1 s (Nicholas John b 1968), 1 da (Jessica Clare b 1969); *Career* Univ of Oxford: lectr ChCh 1960–66, univ lectr in philosophy 1964–90, fell and tutor in philosophy Keble Coll 1966–96, Radcliffe fell 1982–84, reader 1990–96, prof of moral philosophy 1996–2000, emeritus prof 2000–; visiting prof: Univ of Wisconsin 1970 and 1978, Univ of Santiago de Compostela 1988 and 1995, Greater Philadelphia Philosophy Consortium 1989, ITAM Mexico 1994, UNAM Mexico 1995; distinguished visiting prof Rutgers Univ NJ 2002–; adjunct prof Centre for Applied Philosphy and Public Ethics Canberra 2002–; contrib articles to philosophical jls; medal Nat Educn Cmmn Poland 1992; hon fell Keble Coll Oxford 1996; Order Diego de Losada (Venezuela) 1999; *Books* Wittgenstein's Logical Atomism (1964), Well-Being: Its Meaning, Measurement, and Moral Importance (1986), Values, Conflict and the Environment (jtly, 1989), Value Judgement: Improving Our Ethical Beliefs (1996), On Human Rights (2008); *Clubs* Oxford and Cambridge, Brooks's; *Style*— Prof James Griffin; ✉ Corpus Christi College, Oxford OX1 4JF (tel 01865 276700, fax 01865 276767)

GRIFFIN, Prof Jasper; s of Frederick William Griffin, and Constance Irene, *née* Cordwell; *b* 29 May 1937; *Educ* Christ's Hosp, Balliol Coll Oxford (MA); *m* 10 Sept 1960, Miriam Tamara, da of Leo Dressler, of NY; 3 da (Julia b 1963, Miranda b 1966, Tamara b 1969); *Career* Jackson fell Harvard Univ 1960–61; Balliol Coll Oxford: Dyson research fell 1961–63, tutorial fell 1963–90, reader 1990–92, prof of classical literature 1992–, public orator 1992–; T S Eliot lectr Univ of Kent 1984; FBA 1986; *Books* Homer on Life and Death (1980), Homer (1980), Snobs (1982), Latin Poets and Roman Life (1985), Virgil (1986), The Mirror of Myth (1986), Oxford History of the Classical World (co-ed, 1986), Homer - The Odyssey (1987), Commentary on Iliad Book 9 (1995); *Style*— Prof Jasper Griffin; ✉ 17 Staverton Road, Oxford OX2 6XH; Balliol College, Oxford (tel 01865 277782, fax 01865 277803, e-mail jasper.griffin@balliol.ox.ac.uk)

GRIFFIN, Prof John Parry; s of late David Joseph Griffin (d 1992), of Cardiff, and Phyllis May Griffin (d 1989); *b* 21 May 1938; *Educ* Howardian HS Cardiff, London Hosp Med Coll (BSc, PhD, MB BS); *m* 31 March 1962, Margaret, da of Frank Cooper (d 1975); 2 da (Jane Rachel b 1963, Ruth Catherine b 1965), 1 s (Timothy David b 1967); *Career* head of clinical res 3M Health Care 1967–71, professional head of Medicines Div Dept of Health 1971–84, hon conslt Lister Hosp 1976–; dir Assoc of Br Pharmaceutical Industry 1984–94, memb Jt Formulary Ctee Br Nat Formulary 1978–84, UK rep EEC Ctee on Proprietary Med 1976–84; Faculty of Pharmaceutical Med RCP: memb Bd 1993–, chm Bd of Examiners 1997–2003, academic registrar 2003–06; ed-in-chief Adverse Reactions and Toxicological Reviews 1991–2002; currently dir Askelepeion Ltd; visiting prof Univ of Surrey; author of over 200 pubns; Thomas Young lectr and Gold medallist St George's Hosp London 1992, Commemorative medal Faculty of Pharmaceutical Physicians RCP 2005; FRCP, FRCPath, FFPM; *Books* Iatrogenic Diseases (3 edns), Manual of Adverse Drug Interactions (5 edns), Medicines Regulation Research & Risk (2 edns), International Medicines Regulations, The Textbook of Pharmaceutical Medicine (6 edns), Regulation of Medical Products; *Style*— Prof John Griffin; ✉ Quartermans, Digswell Lane, Digswell, Welwyn, Hertfordshire AL7 1SP (tel 01438714592, e-mail jqmans5@aol.com)

GRIFFIN, Kevin Anthony; s of Patrick Anthony Griffin, of Harrow, Middx, and Patricia Barbera, *née* Squirrell; *b* 13 October 1964; *Educ* Watford Coll; *m* 2 Dec 1994, Sharon Theresa, da of Robert Gumley; 3 s (Oliver Robert b 29 March 1991, Patrick Dennis Richard b 14 Sept 1992, Thomas b 14 Sept 1994); *Career* photographer; asst to Jerry Oke, Paul Wakefield and Don McCullin 1986–89, freelance 1989–; memb Assoc of Photographers 1995; *Exhibitions* various American galleries, Hamiltons Gallery 1993; *Awards* D&AD (for best use of colour photography in advtg) 1989, Assoc of Photographers (for best colour cmmnd series) 1995; *Recreations* football, reading, cooking; *Style*— Kevin Griffin, Esq; ✉ website www.kevingriffinphoto.com

GRIFFIN, Lindsey Jane; da of Victor Wilson Riddell Smytheman (d 1998), and Vera, *née* Hopkins; *b* 19 May 1947, Edgbaston, Birmingham; *Educ* Swanshurst Girls' GS Birmingham, King Edward VI HS for Girls Birmingham, UC Cardiff (BA), Univ of York (BPhil); *m* 9 April 1977, Anthony Vivian Griffin, s of Wilfred Roger Griffin; *Career* asst teacher at various schs 1969–79, teacher Scarborough Coll 1979–91 (head of English 1979, head of sixth form 1986), lady warden and headmistress St Michael's Burton Park 1991–94, headmistress Bedgebury Sch 1995–99, headmistress Central Newcastle HS GDST 2000–05; sometime govr Arundale Sch, govr Scarborough Coll 2006; friend: Stephen Joseph Theatre, Lancing Chapel; *Recreations* singing, literature, gardening, cookery; *Style*— Mrs Lindsey Jane Griffin; ✉ e-mail l.j.griffin@freeuk.com

GRIFFIN, Patrick Charles Lake; s of late John Griffin, of Highclere, Newbury, Berks, and Helen Evelyn, da of Sir Henry Bashford, Hon Physician to King George VI, knighted for servs to med 1937; *b* 15 September 1948; *Educ* Leighton Park Sch Reading, Birmingham Sch of Architecture, Aston Univ (BSc); *m* 8 Sept 1973, Linda Dorothy, da of Reginald Mitchell (d 1955), of Yapton, W Sussex; 1 s (Thomas b 1978), 1 da (Joanna b 1980); *Career* chartered architect; chm Architectural Partnerships plc, md Sutton Griffin Architects 1973–, Inside Job Ltd 2000; received Civic Tst Award 1977, Berkshire Environmental Awards 1981, 1983, 1984, 1985, 1986, 1987 and 1988; RIBA Housing Award 1987, RIBA Southern Region Award 1999; vice-chm Berks Soc of Architects 1988; ARIBA; *Style*— Patrick Griffin, Esq; ✉ Whitewood, The Mount, Highclere, Newbury, Berkshire (tel 01635 253155); Sutton Griffin Architects, The Long Barn, Welford, Newbury, Berkshire (tel 01488 657675, fax 01488 657608)

GRIFFIN, Paul; s of Reginald Stuart Griffin, and Sylvia Mary, *née* Toyn; *b* 29 December 1955; *Educ* Humberston Fndn GS, Magdalen Coll Oxford (MA, BCL); *m* 16 April 1983, Janet Mary, da of Cecil Sidney Turner; 1 da (Leonie Sabrina b 20 May 1991), 1 s (Alexander Jake b 25 Sept 1994); *Career* called to the Bar Gray's Inn 1979, practising barr; memb Bar Cncl of England and Wales 1995–98, lay memb Practice Regulation Review Ctee ICA 1995–; memb: Ctee London Common Law and Commercial Bar Assoc 1987–98, COMBAR; *Recreations* restoring our French property, collecting furniture art books and wine, gardening, travel, skiing, music; *Style*— Paul Griffin, Esq

GRIFFIN, Prof Roger Francis; s of Ernest James Griffin (d 1959), and Dorothy Maud, *née* Brenchley (d 1992); *b* 23 August 1935, Banstead, Surrey; *Educ* Caterham Sch, St John's Coll Cambridge (major open scholar, BA, PhD, ScD); *m* 30 July 1966 (m dis 2003), Rita Elizabeth Mary, *née* Gasson; 2 s (Rupert Ivor James b 11 Jan 1971, Richard Joseph b 6 July 1977); *Career* Carnegie fell Mt Wilson Observatory Calif 1960–61, jr asst observer Cambridge Observatories 1962–65, research fell St John's Coll Cambridge 1962–65, Mr & Mrs John Jaffé research fell Royal Soc 1965–70, conslt astrophysicist to St John's Coll Cambridge 1970–72, John Couch Adams astronomer 1972–92, fell St John's Coll Cambridge 1972– (memb Cncl 1976–81, sec Cncl 1977–81), asst dir of research Inst of Astronomy Univ of Cambridge 1973–92, prof of observational astronomy Univ of Cambridge 2001–02 (reader 1992–2001); guest investigator, visiting assoc and visiting observer at several observatories in Europe and the Americas; ed The Observatory Magazine 1963–85; memb: Br Astronomical Assoc 1949, Royal Astronomical Soc 1957 (memb Cncl 1968–70 and 1988–90), Int Astronomical Union 1961 (pres Radial Velocity Cmmn 1973–76), Astronomical Soc of the Pacific 1965, Astronomical Soc of India 1983; Sir Henry Strakosch Award to visit South African observatories 1958, Jackson-Gwilt Medal and Gift Royal Astronomical Soc 1980, int conf held in honour 1991; *Publications* A Photometric Atlas of the Spectrum of Arcturus (1968), A Photometric Atlas of the Spectrum of Procyon (with R E Griffin, 1979); numerous papers in professional jls; *Recreations* joinery, running (completed London Marathon six times, 2007 time 3 hrs 39 mins 13 secs); *Clubs* Cambridge Univ Hare and Hounds; *Style*— Prof Roger Griffin; ✉ The Observatories, Madingley Road, Cambridge CB3 0HA (tel 01223 337536, fax 01223 337523)

GRIFFIN DOUGALL, Prof Beverly Elayne Smith; da of Solon Edgar Smith (d 1961), of Delhi, Louisiana, and Nina Lee, *née* Gilliland (d 2004); *b* 23 January 1930; *Educ* Baylor Univ Texas (BA, BSc), Univ of Virginia (PhD), Univ of Cambridge (Marshall scholar, PhD, ScD); *m* 1961 (m dis 1981), Dr Donald Ross Dougall (d 2005); partner, Dr Tomas Lindahl,

FRS; *Career* lectr in chemistry Mount Holyoke Coll 1958–61; Girton Coll Cambridge: research fell 1961–65, official fell/lectr in chemistry 1965–73; scientific staff MRC Lab of Molecular Biology 1968–73; ICRF London: scientific staff 1973–78, head Nucleic Acid Lab 1978–84; prof and dir Dept of Virology Royal Postgrad Med Sch 1984–96, first Denis Burkitt fell 1995–96, head Unit of Viral Oncology Division of Med Imperial Coll Sch of Med St Mary's 1997–, hon conslt Dept Genetics and Microbiology Charles Univ Prague; memb Bd of Govrs Inst of Animal Virology Pirbright 1985–88; Hon MD Univ of Göteborg Sweden; Gold medallist Charles Univ Prague 1998; *Publications* numerous book chapters, book reviews and original scientific papers/articles in academic jls; *Recreations* skiing, music, modern art, cats, gardening; *Style—* Prof Beverly Griffin Dougall; ✉ e-mail b.griffin@imperial.ac.uk

GRIFFITH, David Vaughan; *b* 14 April 1947; *Educ* Cardiff HS, Kaiser Wilhelms Gymnasium Hanover, Balliol Coll Oxford (MA); *m* 21 May 1977, Tina Frost; 1 s, 5 da; *Career* banker; with S G Warburg 1970–73, Edward Bates & Sons 1973–75, Orion Bank 1975–76, Saudi Int Bank 1976–86, exec dir Banque Paribas 1986–91, md Arbuthnot Latham & Co (formerly Aitken Hume Bank) 1992–95; dir Griffith & Partners Ltd (antiquarian bookseller) 1995–; *Recreations* hill walking, sailing; *Clubs* Royal Solent Yacht, Yarmouth Sailing; *Style—* David Griffith, Esq; ✉ Griffith & Partners, 31–35 Great Ormond Street, London WC1N 3HZ (tel 020 7430 1394)

GRIFFITH, Ven David Vaughan; s of Emmanuel Griffith (d 1969), of Bryniau, Caernarfon, Emmeline, *née* Vaughan Williams (d 1985); *b* 14 June 1936; *Educ* Caernarfon GS, St David's UC Lampeter (BA), Lichfield Theological Coll; *m* 1966, Patricia Mary, da of J T Jones; 2 da (Sarah Jane b 1968, Helen Mary b 1970); *Career* ordained priest 1963, curate Llanfairfechan 1962–66, curate Dolgellau 1966–70, rector Llanfair T H 1970–85, priest in charge Llangernyw 1977–85, vicar of Colwyn 1985–98, warden of readers 1991–99, cursal canon St Asaph Cathedral 1995–98, priest in charge Berriew and Manafon 1998–99, vicar of Berriew and rector of Manafon 1999, prebendary St Asaph Cathedral and archdeacon of Montgomery 1998–; Archdeacon Hughes Meml Prize 1965; *Books* Book of Prayers for St Asaph Diocesan Readers (ed); *Recreations* walking, climbing, boating; *Style—* The Ven the Archdeacon of Montgomery; ✉ The Vicarage, Berriew, Welshpool, Powys SY21 8PL (tel 01686 644223)

GRIFFITH, (Edward) Michael Wynne; CBE (1987), DL (Clwyd); s of Maj Humphrey Wynne Griffith, MBE (d 1986), and Phyllis Lilian Griffith, JP, *née* Theobalds; *b* 29 August 1933; *Educ* Eton, RAC; *m* 31 Oct 1959, Jill Grange, da of Maj D P G Moseley (d 1986); 3 s (Edward James Wynne b 1964 d 1994, Anthony David Wynne b 1966, Martyn b 1968 d 1969); *Career* memb ARC 1973–82, dir Regnl Advsy Bd Nat West Bank 1974–92; chm: Wales Ctee Nat Tst 1984–91, Clwyd HA 1980–90, Med and Dental Post Graduate Educn Welsh Cncl 1990–93, Countryside Cncl for Wales 1991–2000, Glan Clwyd Hosp Tst 1993–99, Cncl Univ of Wales Coll of Med 1997–2004, Conway and Denbighshire NHS Tst 1999–2000, Chm Gp HE Wales 2002– (vice-chm 2001–), Univ of Wales Audit Ctee; pres Campaign for the Protection of Rural Wales (CPRW) 2003–07; memb: Cncl Nat Tst 1988–2000, Higher Educn Fund Cncl for Wales 1992–95, Br Library Bd 1992–95, Cncl and Ct Univ of Wales 1999–; High Sheriff Denbighshire 1969, Vice Lord-Lt Clwyd 1989; FLS, FRSA; *Clubs* Boodle's; *Style—* Michael Griffith, Esq, CBE; ✉ Greenfield, Trefnant, Denbigh, Clywd LL16 5UE (tel 01745 730633, e-mail mgriffith@zoom.co.uk)

GRIFFITH, Nia; MP; *b* 4 December 1956; *Educ* Univ of Oxford, UCNW; *Career* joined Lab Pty 1981; teacher, sometime Educn advsr and Estyn Schools Inspector, head of languages Morriston Comp Swansea; MP (Lab) Llanelli 2005–; *Style—* Ms Nia Griffith, MP; ✉ House of Commons, London SW1A 0AA

GRIFFITH-JONES, David Eric; QC (2000); s of Sir Eric Griffith-Jones, KBE, CMG, QC (d 1979), and Lady (Mary) Patricia Griffith-Jones (d 2005); *b* 7 March 1953; *Educ* Marlborough, Univ of Bristol; *m* 1984, Virginia Ann Meredith, da of Sydney Brown and Annemie Brown; 2 s (Frederick Newton b 13 July 1985, Robert Peter b 18 Jan 1987), 1 da (Harriette Anna b 3 June 1991); *Career* called to the Bar Middle Temple 1975; recorder 1997– (asst recorder 1992–97), asst boundary cmmr 2000–; memb: Sports Disputes Resolution Panel 2000–, Panel of Sports Arbitrators CIArb 2002–; p/t pres Mental Health Review Tbnl 2002–, chm ICC Drugs Appeal Tbnl 2004, 2005, 2006 and 2007; memb: SE Circuit, Employment Lawyers Assoc, Employment Law Bar Assoc, Br Assoc for Sport and the Law, Bar Sports Law Gp, London Common Law and Commercial Bar Assoc; CIArb accredited mediator 2003, ACAS arbitrator 2007–; chm Appeal Ctee LTA 2004–06; FCIArb 1991; *Books* Law and the Business of Sport (1997), Sport: Law and Practice (contrib, 2003); *Recreations* sport, travel, wine; *Clubs* Falconhurst Cricket, Sevenoaks Rugby Football, Royal Cinque Ports Golf; *Style—* David Griffith-Jones, Esq, QC; ✉ Devereux Chambers, Devereux Court, London WC2R 3JH (tel 020 7353 7534, fax 0870 622 0045, e-mail griffith-jones@devchambers.co.uk)

GRIFFITH-JONES, John; s of late Mervyn Griffith-Jones, and late Joan, *née* Baker; *b* 11 May 1954; *Educ* Trinity Hall Cambridge (MA); *m* 1990, Cathryn Mary Stone; 1 s, 1 da; *Career* Peat Marwick Mitchell (now KPMG): joined 1975, ptnr corp fin 1987–2002, ceo KPMG UK 2002–06, sr ptnr KMPG UK 2006–; served TA (Royal Green Jackets) 1975–90; Liveryman Worshipful Co of Skinners; *Recreations* tennis, sailing, bridge; *Style—* John Griffith-Jones, Esq; ✉ KPMG, 8 Salisbury Square, London EC4Y 8BB (tel 020 7311 8059, fax 020 7311 8499, e-mail john.griffith-jones@kpmg.co.uk)

GRIFFITH JONES, His Hon Judge Richard Haydn; s of Wyn Griffith Jones, and Mary, *née* Alston (d 1986); *b* 29 June 1951; *Educ* Solihull Sch, Univ of Leeds; *m* 1974, Susan, *née* Hale; 1 da (Katherine b 6 Aug 1979), 3 s (David b 1 July 1982, Robert b 7 July 1986, Haydn b 16 Aug 1988); *Career* called to the Bar 1974, recorder 1994–99, circuit judge (Midland Circuit) 1999–; *Publications* Sins of the Fathers (1974); *Recreations* poultry keeping, watching association football; *Style—* His Hon Judge Griffith Jones; ✉ The Crown Court, Queen Elizabeth II Law Courts, 1 Newton Street, Birmingham B4 7NA (tel 0121 681 3000)

GRIFFITH WILLIAMS, Hon Mr Justice; Sir John; kt (2007); s of Griffith John Williams, and Alison Rundle, *née* Bennett; *b* 20 December 1944; *Educ* Kings Sch Bruton, The Queen's Coll Oxford (BA); *m* 3 April 1971, Mair, only da of Rt Hon Sir Tasker Watkins, VC, GBE, DL; 2 da (Joanna Kate b 5 June 1972, Sarah Jane b 18 May 1976); *Career* Lt Royal Welch Fus (TA) (cmmnd 1964), Welsh Volunteers (TAVR) 1967–71; called to the Bar Gray's Inn 1968 (bencher 1994); memb Wales & Chester Circuit (treas 1993–95, ldr 1996–98), recorder 1984–2000, QC 1985, dep judge of the High Court (Queen's Bench Div) 1995–2000, circuit judge 2000–07, sr circuit judge and hon recorder of Cardiff 2001–07, judge of the High Court of Justice (Queen's Bench Div) 2007–; chllr Diocese of Llandaff 1999– (dep chllr 1996–99); asst cmmr to Parly Boundary Cmmn for Wales 1994–2000; memb Bar Cncl 1990–92; fell Woodard Corp (Western Div) 1994–2002; *Recreations* golf; *Clubs* Cardiff and County, Royal Porthcawl Golf; *Style—* The Hon Mr Justice Griffith Williams; ✉ c/o Royal Courts of Justice, Strand, London WC2A 2LL

GRIFFITHS, *see also:* Norton-Griffiths

GRIFFITHS, Alan Paul; s of Emrys Mathias Griffiths, and Jane, *née* Griffiths; *b* 21 September 1953; *Educ* St Davids Sch, Jesus Coll Oxford (MA, BCL); *Career* fell and tutor in law Exeter Coll Oxford 1977–88, called to the Bar Gray's Inn 1981, practising barr; chm: MOMA Oxford 1990–2000, Oxfordshire Community Rels Cncl 1978–80; memb: Commercial Bar Assoc (memb Ctee 1992–, memb Exec 1992–95), Admin Law Bar Assoc; vice-chm Nat Ctee Child Poverty Action Gp 1987–91; memb Oxford City Cncl 1980–88 (ldr and chm Fin Ctee); *Style—* Alan Griffiths, Esq; ✉ 1 Essex Court, Temple, London EC4Y 9AR (tel 020 7583 2000, fax 020 7583 0118, e-mail agriffiths@oeclaw.co.uk)

GRIFFITHS, Bill (baptised Brian Bransom); s of William Eric Bransom Griffiths (d 1984), of Kingsbury, Middx, and Eileen Alexandra Hambleton (d 1994); *b* 20 August 1948; *Educ* Kingsbury Co GS, UCL (BA), King's Coll London (MA, PhD); *Career* poet and small press publisher (Amra Imprint), archivist Eric Mottram Collection KCL 1997–99, visiting fell Centre for Northern Studies Univ of Northumbria 2002–; poetry pubns incl: War with Windsor (1974), Tract Against the Giants (1984), Ushabtis (2001), Mud Fort (2004); works on Old English incl: Alfred's Metres of Boethius (1991), Aspects of Anglo-Saxon Magic (1996); work on dialect incl Dictionary of Nort-East Dialect (2004); *Recreations* piano, keep-fit; *Style—* Bill Griffiths, Esq; ✉ 21 Alfred Street, Seaham, Co Durham SR7 7LH (tel 0191 581 6738, website www.billygriff.co.uk)

GRIFFITHS, Courtenay; QC (1980); *b* Kingston, Jamaica; *Educ* LSE (LLB); *m* Angela; 2 s (Marcus, Adam); *Career* called to the Bar Gray's Inn (bencher); practising barr specialising in criminal justice; currently jt head Garden Court Chambers; recorder 1999–; legal asst Police Support Ctee GLC 1981–84, Revson fell City Coll City Univ NY 1984–85; previously chair: Public Affairs Ctee, Race Rels Ctee of the Bar Cncl; tstee Bernie Grant Tst; Hon LLD Leeds Met Univ; *Recreations* Liverpool FC, West Indies cricket supporter; *Style—* Courtenay Griffiths, Esq, QC; ✉ Garden Court Chambers, 57–60 Lincoln's Inn Fields, London WC2A 3LS (tel 020 7993 7754, fax 020 7993 7700)

GRIFFITHS, His Hon Judge David Laurence; s of Edward Laurence Griffiths (d 1959), and Mary Middleton, *née* Ewens, of Crewkerne, Somerset; *b* 3 August 1944; *Educ* Christ's Hosp, Jesus Coll Oxford (MA); *m* 13 March 1971, Sally, da of Canon Gerald Hollis, of Salisbury, Wilts; 4 da (Kate b 4 June 1973, Jane b 29 Jan 1975, Emily b 20 June 1977, Lucy b 5 June 1981); *Career* called to the Bar Lincoln's Inn 1967, asst recorder 1981, recorder 1985, currently circuit judge Western Circuit; *Recreations* gardening, opera, walking, rugby football, cycling; *Style—* His Hon Judge Griffiths; ✉ Winchester Combined Courts, The Law Courts, Winchester SO23 9EL (tel 01962 841212, e-mail dgriffiths@lix.compulink.co.uk)

GRIFFITHS, Prof Hugh Duncan; s of Gordon Hugh Griffiths, of Weymouth, Dorset, and Morag Gordon, *née* Nicholson; *b* 22 March 1956; *Educ* Hardye's Sch Dorchester, Keble Coll Oxford (open scholar, MA), Univ of London (PhD, DSc(Eng)); *m* 25 March 1989, Morag Shearer, da of George Muirhead Kirkwood, of Isle of Arran, Scotland; 2 da (Siân Helen b 7 March 1992, Alexandra Rose b 8 June 1993); *Career* sr scientist Plessey Electronic Systems Research 1980–81 (scientist 1978–80); Dept of Electronic and Electrical Engrg UCL: assoc research asst 1982–85, lectr 1985–90, sr lectr 1990–93, prof 1993–06, head of dept 2001–06; princ Defence Coll of Mgmnt and Technol Cranfield Univ Shrivenham 2006–; memb: PAS Bd and Technol Bd, MoD Def Scientific Advsy Cncl (DSAC) 1994–; chair Exec Ctee Campaign for Science and Engineering; hon ed IEE Proceedings on Radar, Sonar and Navigation 1994–; Liveryman Worshipful Co of Engrgs 2003; fell Inst of Acoustics 1994, FIEE 1995 (MIEE 1983), FREng 1997, FIEEE 1999; *Awards* Lord Brabazon Premium IERE (jtly) 1984, Young Scientist Award Int Union of Radio Sci 1990, AESS Radar Systems Panel Award IEEE 1996, Mountbatten Premium IEE (jtly) 1996, Maxwell Premium IEE (jtly) 1996; *Publications* Modern Antennas (jtly, 1997, 2 edn 2005), Advances in Bistatic Radar (2007), also author of over 250 pubns in jls and conf proceedings; *Recreations* food and wine, most sports; *Style—* Prof Hugh Griffiths, FREng; ✉ 34 Rochester Square, London NW1 9RZ (tel 020 7267 4009); Defence College of Management and Technology, Shrivenham, Cranfield University, Defence Academy of the United Kingdom, Wiltshire SN6 8LA (tel 01793 782 436, fax 01793 785546, e-mail h.griffiths@cranfield.ac.uk)

GRIFFITHS, Baron (Life Peer UK 1985), of Govilon in the County of Gwent; Sir (William) Hugh Griffiths; kt (1971), MC (1944), PC (1980); o s of Sir Hugh Ernest Griffiths, CBE (d 1961), and Doris Eirene, da of W H James; *b* 26 September 1923; *Educ* Charterhouse, St John's Coll Cambridge (MA); *m* 1, 1949, Evelyn, da of Col A F Krefting (d 1998); 1 s; 3 da; *m* 2, The Baroness Brigstocke (d 2004); *Career* Capt Welsh Gds 1941–46; called to the Bar Inner Temple 1949, QC 1964–70; judge: High Court of Justice (Queen's Bench Div) 1970–80, Nat Industrial Relations Court 1973–74; a Lord Justice of Appeal 1980–85, a Lord of Appeal in Ordinary 1985–93; memb Advsy Cncl on Penal Reform 1967–70, chm Tbnl of Inquiry on Ronan Point 1968, vice-chm Parole Bd 1976–77, memb Chllr's Law Reform Ctee 1976–85, chm Lord Chllr's Advsy Ctee on Legal Educn and Conduct 1991–93; pres Senate of Inns of Court and the Bar 1982–; chm Security Cmmn 1985–92; hon memb Canadian Bar Assoc 1981; hon fell: American Inst of Judicial Admin 1985, American Coll of Trail Lawyers 1988; Hon LLD: Univ of Wales 1987, De Montfort Univ 1993; hon fell St John's Coll Cambridge 1985; *Clubs* Garrick, MCC (pres 1990), Sunningdale Golf, R&A Golf (capt 1993); *Style—* The Rt Hon Lord Griffiths, MC, PC; ✉ House of Lords, London SW1A 0PW

GRIFFITHS, Dr Hugh William; s of Peter Griffiths, of Downham, Essex, and Gwyneth Margaret, *née* Roberts; *b* 20 March 1957; *Educ* Brentwood Sch, Univ of Newcastle upon Tyne (MB BS); *m* 2, 30 May 1992, Caroline, da of James Evans, of Welwyn; *Career* house offr Darlington Meml Hosp 1980–81, Newcastle Rotational Trg Scheme in psychiatry 1982–85, res registrar MRC 1985–86, sr registrar Northern Regnl Rotation 1986–88, conslt psychiatrist: St George's Hosp 1988–92, Royal Victoria Infirmary Newcastle upon Tyne 1992–94; med dir Northumberland Mental Health Tst 1994–; hon clinical lectr Univ of Newcastle upon Tyne; FRCPsych 1999 (MRCPsych 1984); *Recreations* rugby union, skiing, motor sport, photography, flying, music; *Clubs* Newcastle Aero; *Style—* Dr Hugh Griffiths; ✉ St George's Hospital, Morpeth, Northumberland (tel 01670 512121)

GRIFFITHS, John; AM; s of Albert John Griffiths (d 1982), and Hannah, *née* O'Connor, of Newport; *b* 19 December 1956; *Educ* Duffryn Comp Sch, Newport FE Coll, UC Cardiff (LLB), Bristol Poly; *m* 1978, Alison Kim, da of Donald Henry Hopkins; 2 s (Lee John b 24 Nov 1976, Neil Darren b 17 Jan 1980); *Career* lectr in FE and HE 1988–89, prodn exec 1989–90, practising slr 1990–99; memb Nat Assembly for Wales (Lab Co-op) Newport East 1999–, dep min for econ devpt 2001–03, dep min for health & social servs 2003–; memb: Health & Social Servs Ctee, Equal Opportunities Ctee; chair Objective 2 Monitoring Ctee (EU structural funds); memb: Law Soc, Workers' Educn Assoc; sch govr; *Recreations* cricket, tennis, badminton, running, reading; *Style—* John Griffiths, Esq, AM; ✉ National Assembly for Wales, Cardiff Bay, Cardiff CF99 1NA (tel 029 208 98307, fax 029 2089 8308, mobile 07786 075088, e-mail john.griffiths@wales.gov.uk)

GRIFFITHS, John Albert; s of Richard Griffiths, of Egham, Surrey, and late Katie Joan, *née* Smithers; *b* 2 December 1943; *Educ* Tiffin Boys' Sch Kingston upon Thames; *m* Peggy-Ann Marie, *née* Waite, da of late Robert Mandel, of Alberta, Canada; 2 s (James Richard b 28 Feb 1980, Charles Robert b 25 July 1984); *Career* reporter then sub ed Surrey Herald Group 1961–64, ed Blackheath Reporter 1965–66, PR offr Mannix Heavy Construction Group Calgary 1966–67, news ed The Albertan (Calgary morning newspaper) 1967–68, night ed and motoring corr Calgary Herald 1968–70; Financial Times: foreign staff 1974–76, night foreign news ed 1977, dep foreign news ed 1978–80, specialist writer on world motor industry and motor sport 1980–2000, motoring ed 2000–; memb World Land Speed Record Team (Richard Noble, Black Rock Desert Nevada 1983, 468–633 mph) and writer subsequent film (For Britain and the Hell of it), holder World Land Speed Record for a fire engine (Black Rock Desert Nevada Nov 2 1982, 130 mph); *Recreations* motor racing (as driver); *Style—* John Griffiths, Esq; ✉ Financial Times, 1 Southwark Bridge, London SE1 9HL (tel 020 7873 3000, fax 020 7873 3109, e-mail john.griffiths@ft.com)

GRIFFITHS, John Calvert; CMG (1983), QC (1972); s of Oswald Hardy Griffiths (d 1952), and Christina Flora Littlejohn; *b* 16 January 1931; *Educ* St Peter's Sch York, Emmanuel

Coll Cambridge (BA, MA); *m* 17 May 1958, Elizabeth Jessamy Jean, eld da of Prof G P Crowden, OBE (d 1967); 3 da (Amanda b 1963, Anna b 1970, Alyson b 1973); m 2, 12 Dec 2000, Marie Charlotte Biddulph; *Career* Lt RE 1949–51; called to the Bar Middle Temple 1959 (bencher 1983), Hong Kong Bar 1979; attorney gen of Hong Kong 1979–83, chm Hong Kong Law Reform Cmmn 1979–83, SC (Hong Kong) 1997; treas Bar Cncl 1987; memb: Exec Ctee Gen Cncl of Bar 1967–71, Senate Inns of Court and The Bar 1984–86 (Exec Ctee 1973–77), Cncl of Legal Educn 1983–; memb Court Hong Kong Univ 1980–84; memb: Nat Cncl of Social Service 1974–79, Gtr London CAB Exec Ctee 1978–79, Exec Ctee Prince Philip Cambridge Scholarships 1980–84; patron Matilda Hosp Charity for Handicapped Children 1981–83; Liveryman Worshipful Co of Glovers; *Recreations* fishing, first editions, gardening; *Clubs* Flyfishers', Hurlingham, Hong Kong; *Style—* John Griffiths, CMG, QC, SC

GRIFFITHS, John Charles; JP (Cardiff 1959); s of Sir Percival Griffiths, KBE (d 1992), and Kathleen, *née* Wilkes (d 1979); *b* 19 April 1934; *Educ* Uppingham, Peterhouse Cambridge (MA); *m* 1, 1956, Ann; 4 s (Timothy b 1957, Christopher b 1958, Gavin b 1961, Jonathan b 1964); m 2, 1983, Carole Jane; 1 da (Emily b 1983); *Career* Thomson Newspapers 1958–61, BBC 1961–64; exec dir Nat Extension Coll 1964–67, PR advsr Br Gas 1969–73; chm and md: MSG PR Ltd 1973–78, Rodhales Ltd 1978–, Contact PR Ltd 1981–85, Minerva Vision and Arts Channel 1983–; dep gen mangr Press Assoc 1968–69; contested (Lib): Ludlow 1964, Wanstead & Woodford 1966, Bedford (Feb and Oct) 1974; pres Lib Pty 1982–83; FLS 2005; *Books* The Survivors (1964), Afghanistan (1967), Modern Iceland (1969), The Science of Winning Squash, Three Tomorrows, Afghanistan, Key to a Continent (1980), The Queen of Spades (1983), Flashpoint Afghanistan (1987), The Third Man: The Life and Times of William Murdoch 1754–1839 (1992), Nimbus: Technology Serving the Arts (1995), Fathercare: A guide for single resident fathers (1997), Afghanistan: A History of Conflict (2001), Hostage (2003), Tea: The drink that changed the world (2007); *Recreations* reading, talking, walking, music; *Style—* John Griffiths, Esq; ✉ Pen-y-Garn, Dyffryn Crawnon, Llangynidr, Crickhowell, Powys NP8 1NU (e-mail john-minervavision@uwclub.net)

GRIFFITHS, John Egbert; s of Claude Griffiths (d 1975), of Bridgnorth, Shropshire, and Edith May, *née* Bradley; *b* 6 May 1939; *Educ* Tettenhall Coll Staffordshire (scholar), King's Coll Durham (BArch); *m* 12 Aug 1964 (m dis 1988); 2 da (Heidi Michelle b 1966, Sally Ann b 1969); *Career* architect and arbitrator; sr ptnr Mason Richards Partnership 1972–98; RIBA 1965, ACIArb 1976; Grand Offr: United Grand Lodge of Ancient Free and Accepted Masons of England, Supreme Grand Chapter of Royal Arch Masons of England; Dep Provincial Grand Master Masonic Province of Staffordshire 2005; *Books* The Evolution of a Small Town (1962); *Recreations* countryside pursuits, painting and sketching, watching rugby union football, running miniature steam trains on Welsh estate, conservation of ancient woodland and site of special scientific interest relating to bats on estate; *Clubs* Old Tettenhallians, Wolverhampton Masonic; *Style—* John Griffiths, Esq; ✉ The Fron, Glascwm, Bwlch-y-Cibau, Llanfyllin, Montgomeryshire, Powys SY22 5LU (tel and fax 01938 500204)

GRIFFITHS, John Henry Morgan; s of Sir Eldon Wylie Griffiths, and Sigrid, *née* Gante; *b* 3 December 1953; *Educ* Rugby, Emmanuel Coll Cambridge (MA); *m* 10 June 1994, Hilary R, elder da of John W Yeend, of Cheltenham, Glos; *Career* Lloyds Bank International 1975–79 (seconded to Bank of London & SA 1975–77, int mgmnt London 1977–79), Samuel Montagu & Co Ltd 1979–90 (syndications mangr 1981–83, dir and W Coast rep (USA) S M Inc 1983–87, exec dir 1986–90), dep gen mangr Nomura Bank International plc 1990–91, chief exec Lynton Bardwell Ltd 1993–; dir: Suffolk Devpt Agency 2004–, Gtr Cambridge Partnership 2004–, E of England Regnl Assembly 2004–, Newlot Farms 2004–; chm Western Suffolk LSP 2004–; cncllr St Edmundsbury BC 1997– (ldr 2003–); *Recreations* cricket, tennis, shooting; *Clubs* Lord's Taverners, Carlton; *Style—* John Griffiths, Esq; ✉ 1 West Mews, London SW1V 2DJ; Lynton Cottage, Ixworth Thorpe, Suffolk IP31 1QR (tel 01359 268881)

GRIFFITHS, Mervyn Christopher; TD (1976), DL (E Sussex 1994); s of late Rev Leonard Lewis Rees Griffiths, of Haslemere, Surrey, and Eileen Clarice, *née* Diffey; *b* 28 May 1936; *Educ* St George's Sch Windsor Castle, Uppingham, Corpus Christi Coll Cambridge (MA), Harvard Business Sch (PMD); *m* 27 April 1974, Barbara Marchant, da of late Dr (Heneage) Marchant Kelsey (d 2005), of Rudgwick, W Sussex; 1 step s (Mark Selway b 7 Feb 1964); *Career* 2 Lt 4/7 Royal Dragoon Gds 1954–56, Capt Queen's Own Warwickshire & Worcestershire Yeo 1956–68; special constable Met Police 1973–76, asst mktg mangr W & T Avery Ltd 1959–65, PR exec McLeish Associates 1965–66; Eurocard International SA Belgium: mktg mangr 1966–67, exec-vice pres NY 1967–71, md London 1971–76; dir and dep chief gen mangr: Alliance Building Society 1976–85, Alliance & Leicester Building Society (also sec) 1985–89; dir Legal & General Mortgage Services 1990–94; registrar The Med Soc of London 1991–99; exec sec: The Harveian Soc of London 1991–99, The Assurance Med Soc 1994–99; chm SE Employers Liaison Ctee for the Res Forces and vice-chm SE RFCA 1990–2002; churchwarden and treas Isfield PCC, memb Nat Centenary Appeal Ctee NSPCC 1984; govr St Bede's Sch Sussex 1983–2004; FCIM 1975; *Recreations* gardening, travel; *Style—* Mervyn Griffiths, Esq, TD, DL; ✉ The Old House, Isfield, Uckfield, East Sussex TN22 5XU (tel 01825 750446, fax 01825 750779, e-mail theoldhouse@freeuk.com)

GRIFFITHS, Nigel; MP; s of Lionel Griffiths, of Edinburgh, and Elizabeth, *née* Murray; *b* 20 May 1955; *Educ* Hawick HS, Univ of Edinburgh (MA), Moray House Coll of Educn; *m* 1979, Sally, da of Hugh McLaughlin, of Kilmarnock; *Career* joined Lab Party 1970, pres Edinburgh Univ Lab Club 1976–77; rights advsr Mental Handicap Pressure Gp 1979–87, City of Edinburgh District cncllr; MP (Lab) Edinburgh S 1987–; oppn whip 1987–89, oppn spokesman on consumer affairs 1989–97 (on trade and consumer affrs 1992–97); Parly under-sec of state DTI 1997–98, min for small business and export controls DTI 2001–06, dep ldr House of Commons 2006–07; chm: Housing Ctee, Decentralisation Ctee, Scottish Charities Kosovo Appeal 1999–, Home Energy Action Team (HEAT) New Deal Project; convenor Fin Ctee Scottish Constitutional Convention 1990; memb: Edinburgh Festival Ctee, Wester Hailes Sch Cncl 1980, Public Accounts Ctee 1999–2001; *Books* Council Housing on the point of Collapse (1982), Welfare Rights Guide (1982–86), A Guide to DHSS Claims and Appeal (1983); *Recreations* travel, hill walking, rock climbing, architecture, politics; *Style—* Mr Nigel Griffiths, MP; ✉ House of Commons, London SW1A 0AA

GRIFFITHS, Prof Paul David; *b* 30 January 1953; *Educ* St Bartholomew's Hosp Med Coll London (BSc, MB BS, MD, DSc (Med) 1995); *m* 1979, Brenda, *née* Attenborough; 3 s (Jonathon b 3 Aug 1984, Jamie b 24 May 1986, Ben b 25 Sept 1988); *Career* Fogarty int scholar Birmingham Alabama 1980–81, lectr Virology Dept St Bartholomew's Hosp 1980–82, prof Virology Dept Royal Free and Univ Coll Med Sch (formerly Royal Free Hosp Sch of Med) 1982– (currently head of dept); ed-in-chief Reviews in Med Virology, memb editorial bds of 8 other specialist jls, holder of numerous research grant awards, invited lectr at many int meetings, memb numerous ctees (local, nat and int); Ian Howat Prize in Med Microbiology 1975, Wheelwright's Prize for Paediatrics 1977, Lawrence Postgrad Research Scholarship 1979, Wellcome Award for Rapid Viral Diagnosis 1988, William Julius Mickle Fellowship 1991; memberships incl: Soc of Gen Microbiology 1982, RSM 1986, Med Research Club 1988, Euro Gp for Rapid Viral Diagnosis, Br Soc for Antimicrobial Chemotherapy, Int AIDS Soc, Int Soc for Antiviral Research; FRCPath 1995, fell American Acad of Microbiology 2003; *Publications* author of over 200 original scientific papers and over 200 book chapters and invited reviews; *Recreations* family, music, bridge; *Style—* Prof Paul D Griffiths; ✉ Department of Virology, Royal Free and University College Medical School, Royal Free Campus, Rowland Hill Street, London NW3 2PF (tel 020 7794 0500 ext 3210, fax 020 7830 2854)

GRIFFITHS, Peter Anthony; s of Albert Griffiths (d 1981), of Swansea, and Grace, *née* Cousins (d 1962); *b* 19 May 1945; *Educ* Swansea Tech Coll; *m* 29 Oct 1966, Margaret, da of Alan Harris; 2 s (Neil b 9 Oct 1969, Kevin b 17 Aug 1971); *Career* dist administrator Medway HA 1976–81, actg area administrator Kent HA 1981–82, dist gen mangr Lewisham and N Southwark HA 1984–88 (dist administrator 1982–84), regnl gen mangr SE Thames RHA 1988–89, dep chief exec Dept of Health Richmond House London 1989–91, chief exec Guy's and Lewisham NHS Tst London 1991–93, on secondment to Dept of Health 1993, chief exec Health Quality Service (in assoc with King's Fund) 2000– (dep chief exec King's Fund 1994); chm Queen Victoria NHS Fndn Tst 2005–; chm NHS Pensioners Tst; AHSM, AIMgt, memb RSA; *Recreations* golf, reading, gardening; *Style—* Peter Griffiths; ✉ Queen Victoria Hospital, Holtye Road, East Grinstead, West Sussex RH19 3DZ

GRIFFITHS, Peter Kevin; s of Denis Griffiths, of Cardiff, and Elsie Joyce, *née* Linck; *b* 15 October 1956; *Educ* Llanishen HS Cardiff, UC Cardiff (BA); *Career* studio mangr BBC 1978; prodr Radio 4: Womans Hour 1981–82, Features Dept 1982–83, presentation 1983–85, Network Features Dept Manchester 1985; sr prodr sport and ceremonial outside broadcasts Radio 2 and Radio 4 1985–90, sr prodr Features and Arts for Radio 4 and Radio 5 1990–97, prodn conslt to South African campaign using radio to offer opportunities for adult educn Johannesburg 1994–96, exec prodr BBC Features & Events Radio 1997– (led BBC Radio's coverage of the funeral of Diana, Princess of Wales (winner Sony Gold Award) and coverage of the funeral of HM Queen Elizabeth The Queen Mother), currently exec prodr responsible for Any Questions, In Touch, Loose Ends, Home Truths (winner 3 Sony Gold Awards 1999) and The Radio 4 Food and Farming Awards; memb Radio Acad; *Recreations* music, friends, tennis, books, history; *Style—* Peter Griffiths, Esq; ✉ British Broadcasting Corporation, Broadcasting House, Portland Place, London W1A 1AA (tel 020 7765 1029, fax 020 7765 5257, e-mail peter.griffiths@bbc.co.uk)

G

GRIFFITHS, (William) Robert; QC (1993); s of late William John Griffiths, of Haverfordwest, Dyfed, and Marjorie Megan, *née* Green; *b* 24 September 1948; *Educ* Haverfordwest GS, St Edmund Hall Oxford (open scholar, MA, BCL); *m* 10 March 1984, Angela May, da of Robert Victor Crawford, of Manchester; 2 da (Anna-Victoria Sophia b 7 Oct 1986, Helena Elizabeth Rose b 13 Sept 1989), 1 s (Charles William Alexander b 13 March 1991); *Career* called to the Bar Middle Temple 1974 (bencher 2004, special advocate 2004); jr counsel to the Crown (common law) 1989–93, legal practitioner New South Wales 1998–, Senior Counsel NSW 1999; memb Hon Soc of the Middle Temple; chm Test Match Grounds Consortium 1998–2001, chm First Class Forum on Line Rights Working Pty 2000–01; memb MCC: Estates Ctee 1996–2004, Working Pty on Natwest Media Centre 1997–99, Staging Agreement Working Gp 1998, Internet and e-Commerce Ctee 2000–01, Ctee and Cricket Ctee 2000–04, Indoor and Coaching sub-Ctee 2000–; Freeman City of London 1997; *Recreations* reading, collecting modern first editions, cricket (represented Welsh secondary schools at cricket and rugby), playing tennis; *Clubs* MCC (memb Ctee), Lord's Taverners; *Style—* Robert Griffiths, Esq, QC, SC; ✉ 4–5 Gray's Inn Square, Gray's Inn, London WC1R 5AY (tel 020 7404 5252, fax 020 7242 7803); Selborne-Wentworth Chambers, 174 Phillip Street, Sydney, New South Wales, Australia 2000 (tel 00 6 12 92 33 4081); Lascelles Great House, Holetown, Barbados, West Indies

GRIFFITHS, Robin John; s of David Gromweigh Morgan Griffiths, and Elizabeth Hope, *née* Limbert; *b* 15 December 1942; *Educ* Bedford Sch, Univ of Nottingham (BA); *m* 6 Jan 1968 (m dis 1995), Esme Georgina (Gina), da of Willim Hunter (d 1967); 4 s (Mark David b 24 Sept 1971, Paul Robin b 6 Sept 1974, David James b 4 Aug 1977, Andrew William b 29 Nov 1979); *Career* Phillips & Drew 1964–68, ptnr Grieveson Grant 1968–84 (formerly Carr Sebag, previously W I Carr), sr exec James Capel (latterly HSBC) 1986–2004, currently head of asset allocation Rathbones; dir MTA (Market Technicians Assoc) NY 1998; memb Ctee Int Fedn of Tech Analysts (former chm); memb Nippon Tech Analysts Assoc; author and fndr The Amateur Chartist Newsletter; sailed the Atlantic with Robin Knox Johnston setting a Br record at the time; memb: Stock Exchange 1971, FIMBRA 1987; fell Soc of Technical Analysts (former chm); *Recreations* sailing, skiing; *Style—* Robin Griffiths, Esq

GRIFFITHS, Prof Roderic Keith (Rod); CBE (2000); s of Thomas Hughes Griffiths, and Olwen Gladys Jackson Griffiths; *b* 12 April 1945; *Educ* Bristol GS, Univ of Birmingham (BSc, MB ChB, Russell Meml Prize); *m* 1, Margaret Susan Ash; 2 da (Tami, Sara), 1 s (Denzil); m 2, Lois May Parker; *Career* former basic sci research Dept of Anatomy then lectr in public health Univ of Birmingham, memb then chm Central Birmingham Community Health Cncl 1975–81, chm Assoc of Community Health Cncls for England and Wales 1979–91 (vice-chm 1977–79), dir of public health Central Birmingham 1982–90; Univ of Birmingham: prof of public health 1990–96, prof of public health practice 1996–; dir of public health W Midlands 1993–; memb CMO's Enquiry into the Public Health Function (Acheson Ctee) 1986–88; published and lectured widely on public health in the NHS; pres Faculty of Public Health 2004–; King's Fund Prize for Public Health Reports; memb Lunar Soc; FFPHM, FRCP; *Publications* Griffiths Review: Ministerial review of research framework in North Staffordshire; *Recreations* making wheel-thrown pots, skiing, surfing, very occasionally sailing; *Style—* Prof Rod Griffiths, CBE

GRIFFITHS, Prof Siân Meryl; OBE (2000); da of John Daniel Griffiths, of London, and Rosemary, *née* Quick; *b* 20 March 1952; *Educ* N London Collegiate Sch, Univ of Cambridge (MA), King's Coll Hosp Med Sch (MB BCh), Univ of London (MSc); *m* 1, 1978 (m dis 1986), Anthony Chu; 2 da (Jessica b 1979, Alexandra b 1980); m 2, 1987, Ian Wylie; 1 s (Sam b 1987); *Career* jr doctor 1977–80, trainee in public health med 1981–85, conslt in public health/dist med offr City of Hackney DHA 1985–87, conslt in public health Oxford RHA 1988–90, regnl dir of public health SW Thames RHA 1990–94, dir of public health and health policy Oxfordshire HA 1994–2001, conslt in public health med Oxford Radcliffe Hosps NHS Tst; sr fell in public health Univ of Oxford, chm Dept of Public Health and Primary Care, dir Sch of Public Health Faculty of Med Chinese Univ of Hong Kong, technical advsr of public health research Shenzhen Centre for Disease Control and Prevention 2006–09; visiting prof Oxford Brookes Univ; hon sr lectr: St George's Hosp Med Sch London 1990–94, Dept of Public Health and Primary Care Univ of Oxford 1995–; hon prof Sch of Public Health Univ of Peking, pres Faculty of Public Health Med 2001–04 (treas 1995–98, vice-pres 2000–01), memb Bd PMETB 2003–05; chair Pharmacy Healthlink 2003, co-chair Assoc of Public Health 1995–98; memb: Bd New Opportunities Fund 1998–2004, BMA, Med Women's Fedn, Bd Health Protection Agency; FFPH, FRCP, FRCS, FDSRCS; *Recreations* family, film, opera; *Clubs* Athenaeum; *Style—* Prof Siân Griffiths, OBE; ✉ 53 Plater Road, Oxford OX2 6QU; Institute of Health Sciences, Old Road, Headington, Oxford OX3 7LG (tel 01865 227174, fax 01865 227175, e-mail sian.griffiths@dphpc.ox.ac.uk); 5/F School of Public Health, Prince of Wales Hospital, Shatin, NT, Hong Kong SAR (tel 00 852 2252 8700, fax 00 852 2145 8517, e-mail siangriffiths@cuhk.edu.hk)

GRIFFITHS, Stephen Gareth (Steve); s of Dr Thomas Edwin Teasdale Griffiths (d 1984), and Kathleen Isobel Maxwell (d 1989); *b* 2 February 1949; *Educ* Ysgol Syr Thomas Jones Amlwch Ynys Môn, Churchill Coll Cambridge (BA); *m* 25 March 1978 (sep 2005), Lala Isla, da of Alfredo Isla Garcia, of Madrid; 1 s (Pablo Siôn Isla Griffiths b 20 July 1979); *Career* poet, social policy specialist; work published in many magazines incl: Stand,

Poetry Wales, Poetry Review, Literary Review, Radical Wales, Pivot (NY), Tribune, 2Plus2 (Geneva), New Welsh Review, La Traductière (Paris); poetry readings in Britain, France, Spain and USA, various BBC broadcasts; fndr memb Welsh Union of Writers 1983, memb Exec Academi Gymreig (Eng Language Section Welsh Acad) 1989–95; conslt: ODPM 2000–03, Dept of Health 2002–03; *Publications* The Green Horse (contrib, 1978), Anglesey Material (1980), Anglo-Welsh Poetry 1480–1980 (contrib, 1984), Civilised Airs (1984), Uncontrollable Fields (1990), Poetry Book Society Anthology (contrib, 1990), The Bright Field (contemporary poetry from Wales, contrib 1991), Selected Poems (1993); numerous pubns in social policy field on poverty, health inequality and supported housing for Joseph Rowntree Fndn Shelter and many local and health authorities; author of policy statements and guidance for Dept for Communities and Local Govt, Dept for Work and Pensions and Dept of Health; *Recreations* finding space and silence, eating and drinking, music, film; *Style*— Steve Griffiths; ✉ 66B Warham Road, London N4 1AT (tel 020 3213 0082)

GRIFFITHS, Trevor; s of Ernest Griffiths (d 1961), of Manchester, and Ann Veronica, *née* Connor (d 1976); *b* 4 April 1935; *Educ* St Bede's Coll Manchester, Univ of Manchester (BA); *m* 1, 13 March 1960, Janice Stansfield (d 1977); 2 da (Sian b 1965, Emma b 1967), 1 s (Joss b 1968); m 2, 6 June 1992, Gillian Cliff; *Career* playwright; work incl: The Wages of Thin (first prodn Stables Theatre Manchester 1969), The Big House (1972, BBC Radio 4 1969), Occupations (1980, Stables Theatre Manchester 1970), Lay By (jtly 1971, Traverse Theatre Edinburgh 1971), Apricots (1978, Basement Theatre London 1971), Thermidor (1978, Edinburgh Festival 1971), Sam, Sam (1972, Open Space 1972), The Party (1974, NT 1973), All Good Men and Absolute Beginners (1977, BBC TV 1974), Comedians (1976, Nottingham 1975), Through The Night and Such Impossibilities (1977, BBC TV 1975), Bill Brand (Thames TV 1976), The Cherry Orchard (new English version 1978, Nottingham Playhouse 1977), Deeds (jtly, Nottingham Playhouse 1978), Sons and Lovers (1982, BBC TV 1981), Country (1981, BBC TV 1981), Reds (with Warren Beatty, 1981), Oi For England (1982, Central TV 1982), The Last Place on Earth (Central TV 1985), published as Judgement Over The Dead 1986, Real Dreams (1987, Williamstown Theatre Festival 1984), Fatherland (1987), Collected Plays for Television (1988), Piano (1990, NT 1990), The Gulf Between Us (West Yorkshire Playhouse Leeds, 1992), Thatcher's Children (Bristol Old Vic 1993), Hope in the Year Two (1994, BBC TV 1994), Who Shall Be Happy....? (stage version of Hope in the Year Two, Belfast Festival 1995), Food for Ravens (BBC TV 1997), Camel Station (2001), These Are The Times: A Life of Thomas Paine (2005); memb: Writers' Guild of America (West), Acad of Motion Picture Arts and Sciences (AMPAS); *Recreations* chess, bridge, music, photography; *Style*— Trevor Griffiths; ✉ c/o PFD, Drury House, 34–43 Russell Street, London WC2B 5HA (tel 020 7344 1000, fax 020 7836 9539)

GRIFFITHS, Trevor Thomas; OBE (2005); s of Charles Griffiths (d 1973), of Cardiff, and Lilian, *née* Ray; *b* 3 October 1943; *Educ* Univ of Wales Cardiff (BDS, LLM, MPH), Dip Gen Dental Practice; *m* Meifis, *née* Howell; 1 s (Elis b 29 April 1980); *Career* resident house offr and SHO Morriston then Cardiff Dental Hosp 1968–70, asst lectr and hon registrar Univ of Wales Dental Sch 1970–73, dental practitioner Cardigan 1974–95; former memb and past chm: local and dist dental ctees, Welsh Dental Ctee; memb Welsh Cncl BDA, elected memb for Wales GDC 2001–04; memb: UK Interprofessional Gp (UK IPG) 2002–04, Multi-Centre Research Ethics Ctee for Wales (MREC) 2004–; tstee YCA Cardwgan Building Preservation Tst; *Recreations* Cardigan Brass Band (tuba); *Style*— Trevor Griffiths, Esq, OBE; ✉ Old Rectory, Llangoedmor, Cardigan, Ceredigion SA43 2LH (tel 01239 613699, fax 01239 613699)

GRIFFITHS, Wendy Jane; *b* 27 April 1957, Wales; *m* 23 Dec 1996, Jeremy Ross; 1 da (Katie); *Career* headmistress Tudor Hall Sch Banbury; *Style*— Miss Wendy Griffiths; ✉ Tudor Hall School, Wykham Park, Banbury, Oxfordshire OX16 9UR

GRIFFITHS, Winston James (Win); s of late Evan George Griffiths and late Rachel Elizabeth Griffiths; *b* 11 February 1943; *Educ* Brecon Boys' GS, UC Cardiff; *m* 22 Aug 1966, Elizabeth Ceri, *née* Gravell; 1 s, 1 da; *Career* teacher: Mzumbe Secdy Sch Tanzania (educn offr) 1966–68, George Dixon Boys' GS 1969–70, Barry Boys' Comprehensive Sch 1970–76; head History Dept Cowbridge Comprehensive Sch 1976–79; memb Vale of Glamorgan BC (chm Leisure Servs Ctee) 1973–76, memb St Andrew's Major Community Cncl 1974–79; MEP (Lab) South Wales 1979–89 (vice-pres Euro Parliament 1984–87), MP (Lab) Bridgend 1987–2005; memb Select Ctee on Educn, Sci and Arts 1987–90, chm PLP Educn, Arts and Sci Ctee 1988–90; an oppn spokesman on: Environment 1990–92, Educn 1992–94, Wales 1994–97; Parly under-sec of state Welsh Office 1997–98; memb Ct of Govrs Nat Museums and Galleries of Wales 1998–; House of Commons rep on the Convention on a Charter of Fundamental Rights of the EU 1999–2000; co-chair Street Children Gp 2001–, sec All-Pty Southern Africa Gp 2000–; past sec All-Pty: East African Gp, Tanzania Gp, Showman's Guild Gp; memb Panel of Chm House of Commons 2001; chm All-Pty Br Indonesia Gp 2001; chair Sierra Leone APPG; co-sec Children in Wales All-Pty Gp; sec Labour Movement For Europe 2002; *Recreations* reading, formerly running, cultivating pot plants; *Style*— Win Griffiths, Esq; ✉ 47 Nolton Street, Bridgend CF31 3AA (tel 01656 645432, fax 01656 767551)

GRIFFITHS OF BURRY PORT, Baron (Life Peer UK 2004), of Pembrey and Burry Port in the County of Dyfed; Rev Dr Leslie John Griffiths; s of Sydney John Griffiths (d 1987), and Olwen, *née* Thomas (d 1976); *b* 15 February 1942; *Educ* Univ of Wales (BA), Univ of Cambridge (MA), Univ of London (PhD); *m* 26 July 1969, Margaret, da of Alfred Rhodes (d 1989); 2 s (Hon Timothy b 24 Sept 1972, Hon Jonathan b 7 Jan 1974), 1 da (Hon Ruth b 29 Oct 1975); *Career* lectr Univ of Wales 1964–67; methodist min: Cambridge 1969–70, Haiti 1970–74 and 1977–80, Reading 1974–77, Loughton 1980–86, London 1986–91, Finchley and Hendon 1991–96, Wesley's Chapel 1996–; hon canon St Paul's Cathedral 2000, select preacher Westminster Abbey Lent 2001; pres Methodist Conf 1994; regular contribs to radio and TV broadcasting; chm: Methodist Church Caribbean and Latin American Ctee 1981–89, Churches Advsy Cncl for Local Broadcasting 1996–2000, Methodist Church Euro Reference Gp 1997–2000, Coll of Preachers 2004; memb Bd: Addiction Recovery Fndn 1987–2003, Christian Aid 1990–98, Birnbeck Housing Assoc 1993–96; memb Sir Halley Stewart Tst and tstee Art and Christianity Enquiry; tstee Central Fndn Schs 2002–; chm of govrs Southlands Coll 1997–2003; fell: Sarum Coll 2001, Sion Coll 2002, Univ of Cardiff 2005, Univ of Wales Lampeter 2006; KStJ 1989; *Books* History of Methodism in Haiti (1991), Letters Home (1995), The Aristide Factor (1997), Worship and our Diverse World (1999), Voices From the Desert (2003), World Without End? (2007); *Recreations* rugby, snooker, reading, conversation; *Clubs* The Graduate Centre (Cambridge); *Style*— The Rt Hon the Lord Griffiths of Burry Port; ✉ 49 City Road, London EC1Y 1AU (tel 020 7253 2262, fax 020 7608 3825, e-mail superintendent@wesleyschapel.org.uk)

GRIFFITHS OF FFORESTFACH, Baron (Life Peer UK 1991), of Fforestfach in the County of West Glamorgan; Brian Griffiths; s of Ivor Winston Griffiths and Phyllis Mary, *née* Morgan; *b* 27 December 1941; *Educ* Dynevor GS, LSE (BSc, MSc); *m* 18 Sept 1965, Rachel Jane, da of Howard Jones; 2 da (Hon Aeronwen Jane b 1968, Hon Owenna Mary Ruth b 1973), 1 s (Hon James Brian b 1970); *Career* lectr in economics LSE 1968–76 (asst lectr 1965–68), prof of banking and int fin City Univ 1977–85, dir Centre for Banking and Int Finance 1977–82, dean Business Sch City Univ 1982–85, visiting prof Rochester Univ USA 1972–73, prof of ethics Gresham Coll 1984–87, dir Bank of England 1984–86, head of Prime Minister's Policy Unit (Rt Hon Margaret Thatcher) 1985–90; int advsr and vice-chm Goldman Sachs (Int) 1991–; chm: Land Securities Trillium, Westminster Health Care 1998–2002, Centre for Policy Studies 1991–2000, Archbishop of Canterbury's Lambeth Tst; non-exec dir: Times Newspapers, Herman Miller, Service Master, English Welsh and Scottish Railway; chm Sch Examinations and Assessment Cncl 1991–93; *Books* The Creation of Wealth (1984), Morality and the Market Place (1989); *Clubs* Garrick; *Style*— The Rt Hon Lord Griffiths of Fforestfach; ✉ House of Lords, London SW1A 0PW

GRIGGS, His Hon Judge Jeremy David; s of Celadon Augustine Griggs, of East Brent, Somerset, and Ethel Mary (Maisie), *née* Anderson (d 1996); *b* 5 February 1945; *Educ* St Edward's Sch Oxford, Magdalene Coll Cambridge (MA); *m* 1, 1971 (m dis 1982), Wendy Anne Russell, *née* Culham; 2 s (Christopher b 1972, Tom b 1974), 1 da (Beth b 1976); m 2, 1985, Patricia Ann (the actress Patricia Maynard), da of Thomas Maynard (d 1991); 2 step da (Hannah Waterman b 1975, Julia Waterman b 1979); *Career* called to the Bar Inner Temple 1968; memb Western Circuit, recorder of the Crown Court 1990–95, circuit judge (Western Circuit) 1995–, designated civil judge for Devon and Cornwall 2006–; Bar's rep CCBE 1990–94, vice-chm Br Romanian Legal Assoc 1991–95; chm London Choral Soc 1986–90; *Publications* A South African Childhood: Biographical notes on the life of Celadon Augustine Griggs; *Recreations* playing the piano, walking on Dartmoor, beekeeping, trying to speak Greek; *Style*— His Hon Judge Griggs; ✉ Exeter Combined Court Centre, Southernhay Gardens, Exeter EX1 1UH

GRIGGS, Patrick John Spear; s of John Garson Romeril Griggs (d 1987), of Jersey, CI, and Inez Frances, *née* Cole (d 1985); *b* 9 August 1939; *Educ* Stowe, Tours Univ France, Law Soc Sch of Law London; *m* 4 April 1964, Marian Patricia, da of John Pryor Birch, of Mere, Wilts; 3 s (Simon Richard b 1967, Edward John b 1969, William Robert b 1972); *Career* slr 1963; Ince and Co: joined 1958, ptnr 1966, sr ptnr 1989–95, conslt 1995–; sec and treas Br Maritime Law Assoc 1995–2005, pres Comité Maritime Int 1997–2004, memb CMI Exec Cncl; chm Opera Rara 2004–; Freeman City of London; *Books* Limitation of Liability for Maritime Claims (jtly, 1987, 4 edn 2005); *Recreations* tennis, skiing, walking, cycling, golf; *Clubs* City of London; *Style*— Patrick Griggs, Esq, CBE; ✉ c/o Ince & Co, International House, 1 St Katherine's Way, London E1W 1UN (tel 020 7481 0010, e-mail pm.griggs@yahoo.co.uk)

GRIGGS, Roy; s of Norman Edward Griggs, CBE, of London, and Livia Lavinia, *née* Levi; *b* 26 April 1950; *Educ* Westminster, Univ of Bristol (LLB); *m* 4 Jan 1975, Anita Gwendolyn, da of Humphrey Osmond Nunes (d 1972); 4 da (Flavia b 1979, Eleanor b 1982, Cordelia b 1986, Marina b 1989); *Career* slr Norton Rose Botterell and Roche 1975–84 (seconded to Hong Kong office 1981–83), ptnr and conslt CMS Cameron McKenna LLP (formerly Cameron Markby Hewitt) 1985– (joined as slr 1984); memb City of London Slrs' Co; memb Law Soc; *Recreations* bridge, sailing, opera, skiing; *Clubs* Itchenor Sailing; *Style*— Roy Griggs, Esq; ✉ CMS Cameron McKenna LLP, Mitre House, 160 Aldersgate Street, London EC1A 4DD (tel 020 7367 2813, fax 020 7367 2000)

GRIGSON, Dr Caroline; da of Geoffrey Edward Harvey Grigson (d 1985), of Broad Town, Wilts, and Frances Franklin, *née* Galt (d 1937); *b* 7 March 1935; *Educ* Dartington Hall Sch, UCL (BSc), Inst of Archaeology Univ of London (PhD); *m* 18 Sept 1961, Colin Banks (d 2002), s of William James Banks (d 1985), of Faversham, Kent; 1 da (Frances Jenny Harriet b 1964 d 1978), 1 s (Joseph Caxton b 1967); *Career* museum curator and archaeozoologist; RCS: asst curator Odontological Museum 1973–87, Osman Hill curator Odontological Museum 1987–91, asst conservator of the museums 1991, princ curator of the museums 1996–97; author of numerous scientific papers incl many on animal remains from archaeological sites in Br and the Near E, some on the Piltdown scandal and on the life of John Hunter, FRS; fndr memb Cncl of the Int Cncl for Archaeozoology (ICAZ), memb Cncl Soc for the History of Natural History 2003–06; former memb Cncl for British Research in the Levant (CBRL), Br Inst in Amman, Br Sch of Archaeology Jerusalem, Wainwright Fund; co-organiser Fourth Int Conf in Archaeozoology Univ of London 1982; organiser Aims in Archaeozoology London Univ Inst of Archaeology 1985; former govr Kidbrooke Comp Sch; hon fell Inst of Archaeology 1996–; memb: Prehistoric Soc, Soc for the History of Natural History; C E Wallis lectr RSM 1998; FSA 1982; *Books* co-ed: Ageing and Sexing Animal Bones from Archaeological Sites (1982), Animals and Archaeology (4 vols, 1983 and 1984); Colyer's Variations and Diseases of the Teeth of Animals (co-author, 1990), The Harmony of Symbols: the Windmill Hill Causewayed Enclosure, Wiltshire (co-author, 1999); *Recreations* travelling, gardening; *Style*— Dr Caroline Grigson, FSA

GRIGSON, Hester Sophia Frances (Sophie); da of Geoffrey Edward Harvey Grigson (d 1985), of Broad Town, Wilts, and Jane, *née* McIntire (d 1990); *b* 19 June 1959; *Educ* Oxford HS, UMIST (BSc); *m* 19 June 1992 (m dis 2005), William Black, s of Brian Black; 1 da, 1 s; *Career* freelance food writer and broadcaster; cookery corr: Evening Standard 1986–93, Sunday Express Magazine 1988–91, Independent 1993–94, Sunday Times Magazine 1994–96, Independent on Sunday (restuarant reviewer) 1997–98; contrib various magazines, newspapers and radio progs incl Curious Cooks (Radio 4) 1994, columnist Waitrose Food Illustrated 2005; ptnr and contrib Food.com, chair Jane Grigson Tst, patron Oxford Children's Food Festival; memb Guild of Food Writers; *Television* for Channel 4 incl: Grow Your Greens/Eat Your Greens 1993, Travels à la Carte (with William Black) 1994, Sophie's Meat Course 1995, Taste of the Times 1997; Sophie Grigson's Herbs (BBC) 1998, Feasts for a Fiver (BBC) 1999, Sophie Grigson's Sunshine Food (BBC) 2000, Sophie's Weekends (UKTV) 2003, Grigson (UKTV) 2004; *Awards* Food Writer of the Year Restauranteur Assoc of GB 1992, Caroline Walker Award (Media) 1994, Magazine Cookery Writer of the Year Guild of Food Writers 1997, Cookery Journalist of the Year Guild of Food Writers 2001, Jacob's Creek Bronze Award for Best Hardcover Recipe Book (with William Black) 2003; *Books* Food for Friends, Sophie's Table, Sophie Grigson's Ingredients Book, The Students' Cook Book, Eat Your Greens, The Carved Angel Cook Book (with Joyce Molyneux), Travels à la Carte (with William Black), Sophie Grigson's Meat Course, Sophie Grigson's Taste of the Times (1997), Sophie Grigson's Herbs (1998), Sophie Grigson's Feasts for a Fiver (1999), Fish (with William Black, 1999), Sophie Grigson's Sunshine Food (2000), Organic (with William Black, 2001), The Complete Sophie Grigson Cookbook (2001), My Favourite Family Recipes (2003), Sophie Grigson's Country Kitchen (2003), The First-Time Cook (2004), Vegetables (2006); *Style*— Ms Sophie Grigson; ✉ c/o Deborah McKenna Ltd (tel 020 8876 0051, fax 020 8392 2462)

GRIME, Geoffrey John; s of Sqdn Ldr John Frederic Grime, DFC (d 1997), of Blackpool, Lancs, and José Thompson, *née* Bennett (d 2006); *b* 7 February 1947; *Educ* Sedbergh; *m* 19 June 1971, Margaret Joyce, da of Stanley Hamilton Russell (d 2005), of St Helier, Jersey; 1 da (Caroline b 1973), 1 s (Charles b 1975); *Career* Coopers & Lybrand: joined 1969, ptnr 1972–95, sr ptnr 1990–95; chm: Abacus Financial Services Gp Ltd 1995–99, Jersey Finance Ltd 2000–03, EFG Offshore Ltd 2006–; elected dep of St Mary (States of Jersey) 2002–05; hon treas: Jersey Arts Cncl until 1985, Br Heart Fndn Jersey until 1987, Jersey Church Schs Soc 1987–2004; Freeman: City of London 1975, Worshipful Co of Musicians 1977; FCA 1969; *Recreations* veteran and vintage cars; *Clubs* Brooks's, Victoria (Jersey), United (Jersey); *Style*— Geoffrey Grime, Esq; ✉ Pine Farm, Rue Des Landes, St Mary, Jersey JE3 3EE (tel 01534 863840)

GRIME, Mark Stephen Eastburn; QC (1987); s of Roland Thompson, and late Mary Diana, *née* Eastburn, of Morfa Nefyn; *b* 16 March 1948; *Educ* Wrekin Coll, Trinity Coll Oxford (scholar, MA); *m* 29 July 1973, Christine, da of J H A Emck, of West Wittering, W Sussex; 2 da (Eleanor b 1977, Isabel b 1981); *Career* called to the Bar Middle Temple 1970 (bencher 1997); Northern Circuit 1970–, recorder 1990–2003, recorder technol and construction 1997–2003; chm: Disciplinary Appeal Tbnl UMIST 1980–, Northern Arbitration Assoc 1994–97 (memb Cncl 1990–98), Northern Circuit Med Law Assoc 2000–02; FCIArb 1996; *Recreations* antiquarian horology, sailing; *Style*— Stephen Grime, Esq, QC; ✉ Deans Court Chambers, 24 St John Street, Manchester M3 4DF (tel 0161 214 6000, 07000 444943, fax 0161 214 6001, e-mail grime@deanscourt.co.uk)

GRIMES, Stuart Brian; s of Douglas Grimes, and Susan Grimes; *b* 4 April 1974; *Educ* Robert Gordon's Coll Aberdeen, Univ of Edinburgh (MA); *Career* professional rugby union player; clubs: 1st XV Univ of Edinburgh, Watsonians 1995–99, Newcastle Falcons 1999–; int: Scottish Univs, Scotland U21, Scotland Students World Cup, Scotland (71 caps, debut v Australia 1997, capt for 2 tests on Canada and USA tour 2002, memb squad World Cup Aust 2003); *Awards* Dist Championship 1997 (North and Midlands), champions Scot Premiership 1998 (Watsonians), winners Five Nations Championship 1999 (Scotland), winners Tetley Bitter Cup Final 2001 (Newcastle Falcons), Player of the Season 2001–02 (Newcastle Falcons); scorer Try of the Season 1999 (Scotland); *Style*— Stuart Grimes, Esq; ✉ c/o Newcastle Falcons, Kingston Park, Brunton Road, Kenton Bank Foot, Newcastle upon Tyne NE13 8AF

GRIMLEY, Very Rev Robert; *b* 26 September 1943, Derby; *Educ* Derby Sch, Christ's Coll Cambridge (MA), Wadham Coll Oxford (MA, Ellerton prizeman 1974); *m* 1968, Joan Elizabeth, *née* Platt; 2 s (Matthew, Adam), 1 da (Naomi); *Career* ordained Dio of St Albans: deacon 1968, priest 1969; asst curate Radlett, Herts 1968–72, chaplain King Edward Sch Birmingham 1972–84, vicar of St George's Edgbaston 1984–97, chaplain to High Sheriff of W Midlands 1988–89, dean of Bristol 1997–; inspr Theological Colleges for the House of Bishops 1998–, memb Church Cmmrs' Bishoprics and Cathedrals Ctee 2005–, church cmmr for England 2007–; govr: The Queen's Coll Birmingham 1974–97, Fndn of King Edward VI Birmingham 1992–97, Bristol Cathedral Sch 1997–, Kingswood Sch 1998–; tstee St Monica Tst 2005–; Hon DLitt UWE 2004; *Style*— The Very Rev the Dean of Bristol; ✉ The Deanery, 20 Charlotte Street, Bristol BS1 5PZ (tel 0117 926 4879, e-mail dean@bristol.anglican.org)

GRIMLEY EVANS, Prof Sir John; kt (1997); s of Harry Walter Grimley Evans (d 1971), of Birmingham, and Violet Prenter, *née* Walker (d 1976); *b* 17 September 1936; *Educ* King Edward's Sch Birmingham, St John's Coll Cambridge (MA, MD), Balliol Coll Oxford (MA, DM); *m* 25 March 1966, Corinne Jane, da of Leslie Bernard Cavender (d 1947), of Edenbridge, Kent; 2 s (Edmund, Piers), 1 da (Freya); *Career* res fell Med Unit Wellington NZ 1966–69, lectr London Sch of Hygiene and Tropical Med 1969–71, conslt physician Newcastle Health Authy 1971–73, prof of med (geriatrics) Univ of Newcastle upon Tyne 1973–84, prof of clinical geratology Oxford Univ 1985–2002 (fell Green Coll 1985–), conslt physician; ed Age and Ageing 1988–95; chm: Geriatric Med Ctee RCP 1985–94, Health Servs Res Ctee MRC 1989–92, Health Servs and Public Health Res Bd MRC 1992–94, Population Screening Panel 1996–2000, Ctee on Ethical Issues in Med RCP 2000–; Harveian orator 1997; vice-pres RCP 1993–95 (censor 1991–92); memb: Expert Panel on Care of the Elderly WHO 1984–, MRC 1992–95, Ctee on Medical Aspects of Food Policy Dept of Health 1992–2000 (chm 1998–2000), GMC 1994–99, Central Research & Devpt Ctee NHS Exec 1997–, National Screening Ctee 1997–2004; FSS 1970, FRCP 1976, FFPHM 1980, FMedSci 1998; *Books* Care of the Elderly (jtly, 1977), Advanced Geriatric Medicine (jtly, 1981–88), Improving the Health of Older People - A World View (jtly, 1990), Oxford Textbook of Geriatric Medicine (jtly, 1992, 2 edn 2000), Encyclopedia of Aging (jtly, 1995, 3 edn 2001); *Recreations* fly fishing, literature; *Clubs* RSM; *Style*— Prof Sir John Grimley Evans; ✉ Green College, 43 Woodstock Road, Oxford OX2 6HG

GRIMMER, Gregory Charles (Greg); *b* 13 January 1966; *Educ* Thamesmead Sch Shepperton, Torquay Boys' GS, Ealing Coll (BA); *Career* grad trainee rising to media gp manager Delaney Fletcher/Bozell 1987–91; CIA Medianetwork: sr media exec 1991, dir of press buying 1994, dir of client services 1997–98; strategic planner New PHD Gp 1998–99, managing ptnr Optimedia International Ltd 1999–; ZenithOptimedia: memb bd, commercial dir, md Zed 2005–; Media Mind Winner 1994, Media Week Magazine Face to Watch 1995, Special Award for Integration IPA Effectiveness Awards 1996, Monte Carlo TV Effectiveness Winner 1997; MIPA; *Recreations* football, cricket, skiing, tennis, cinema; *Style*— Greg Grimmer, Esq

GRIMMETT, Prof Geoffrey Richard; s of Benjamin John Grimmett, of Birmingham, and Patricia Winifred, *née* Lewis; *b* 20 December 1950; *Educ* King Edward's Sch Birmingham, Univ of Oxford (MA, MSc, DPhil), Merton Coll Oxford (postmaster); *m* 2 Sept 1986, Rosine, da of Pierre Bonay; 1 s (Hugo b 16 May 1989); *Career* IBM res fell Univ of Oxford and New Coll Oxford 1974–76, prof of mathematics Univ of Bristol 1989–92 (lectr 1976, reader 1985), prof of mathematical statistics Univ of Cambridge 1992– (dir Statistical Lab 1994–2000, head Dept of Pure Mathematics and Mathematical Statistics 2002–); visiting prof at Univs incl: Cornell, Arizona, Rome, Utah; professorial fell Churchill Coll Cambridge 1999, hon fell Inst of Actuaries 1999; memb: GB fencing team 1973–77, Olympic foil team 1976; nat under 20 foil champion 1970; *Books* Probability and Random Processes (1982, 3 edn 2001), Probability: An Introduction (1986), Percolation (1989, 2 edn 1999), One Thousand Exercises in Probability (2001), The Random-Cluster Model (2006); *Recreations* mountaineering, music; *Clubs* Climbers', Alpine; *Style*— Prof Geoffrey Grimmett; ✉ Statistical Laboratory, University of Cambridge, Wilberforce Road, Cambridge CB3 0WB (tel 01223 337958, fax 01223 337956, website www.statslab.cam.ac.uk/grg/)

GRIMOND, Hon John Jasper; er s of Baron Grimond, TD, PC (Life Peer; d 1993), by his w, Laura, *née* Bonham Carter (d 1994); *b* 1946; *Educ* Eton, Balliol Coll Oxford, Harvard Univ (Nieman fellow); *m* 1973, Kate, er da of Lt-Col Peter Fleming, OBE (d 1971), of Nettlebed, Henley-on-Thames; 3 da (Mary Jessie b 1976, Rose Clementine b 1979, Georgia Celia b 1983); *Career* The Economist: joined 1969, asst ed 1975–, Br ed 1976–79, American ed 1979–88, foreign ed 1989–2002, writer-at-large 2002–; dir Fleming American Investment Trust 1991–2000; tstee: Prison Reform Tst 1995–, Kennedy Meml Tst 2006–; Harkness fell 1974–75; *Books* The Economist Pocket Style Book (ed); *Style*— The Hon John Grimond; ✉ 49 Lansdowne Road, London W11 2LG

GRIMSBY, Bishop of 2000–; Rt Rev David Douglas James Rossdale; *b* 22 May 1953; *Educ* St John's Sch Leatherhead, KCL, Chichester Theol Coll, Westminster Coll Oxford (MA), Roehampton Inst Univ of Surrey (MSc); *m* 1982, Karen Jane, *née* Paul; 2 s (Christopher b 1986, Paul b 1989); *Career* curate St Laurance Upminster 1981–86, vicar of Moulsham St Luke 1986–90, vicar of Cookham 1990–2000, area dean of Maidenhead 1994–2000, canon ChCh Oxford 1999–2000, canon and prebendary Lincoln Cathedral 2000–; govr Wellington Coll 2004–; *Recreations* travelling, cooking; *Style*— The Rt Rev the Bishop of Grimsby; ✉ Bishop's House, Church Lane, Irby-upon-Humber, Grimsby DN37 7JR (tel 01472 371715, fax 01472 371716, e-mail rossdale@btinternet.com)

GRIMSHAW, Dr John Stuart; s of Neville Stuart Grimshaw (d 1978), and Sylvia May, *née* Taylor (d 1963); *b* 22 September 1934; *Educ* Repton, Jesus Coll Cambridge (MA), UCH Med Sch (MB BChir, DPM); *m* 12 July 1958, Anne, da of William James Vince (d 1986); 1 s (Robert b 13 March 1961), 1 da (Caroline b 14 Jan 1963); *Career* maj and sr specialist RAMC 1960–65; house physician and house surgn UCH 1959, house physician Whittington Hosp 1960, sr registrar Dept of Psychological Med St Thomas' Hosp and Knowle Hosp 1965–67, conslt psychiatrist Southampton Univ Hosps 1967–90 (emeritus conslt psychiatrist 1990–), hon clinical tutor Univ of Southampton 1973–90, chm Southampton Univ Hosps Med Exec Ctee 1977–80, chm Wessex Regnl Psychiatric Sub-Ctee 1978–81, conslt rep Dist Mgmnt Team 1978–82; approval exercise convenor RCPsych 1973–77, examiner MRCPsych 1977–81 and 1983–87; memb: Mental Health Act Cmmn 1983–89 (second opinion appointed doctor 1983–, memb Central Policy Ctee 1986–89), Mental Health Review Tbnl Southern 1990–, Nat and Regnl Trg Cmmns 1993–2003, ed Tbnl Members' Handbook 2001–02; memb Panel of Observers MRCPsych exam 1987–, external examiner Final MMed (psych) Nat Univ of Singapore 1993–95; Freeman City of London, Liveryman Worshipful Soc of Apothecaries; FRCPE 1977, FRCPsych 1977; *Recreations* history, gardening, long distance and fell walking, numismatics; *Clubs* RSM; *Style*— Dr John Grimshaw; ✉ The Orchard, Curdridge Lane, Curdridge, Southampton, Hampshire SO32 2BH (tel 01489 782525, fax 01489 798592)

GRIMSHAW, Sir Nicholas Thomas; kt (2002), CBE (1993), RA (1994); s of Thomas Cecil Grimshaw (d 1942), and Hannah Joan, *née* Dearsley; *b* 9 October 1939; *Educ* Wellington, Edinburgh Coll of Art, AA Sch of Architecture (AADipl); *m* 20 Oct 1972, Lavinia, da of John Russell, CBE, of New York; 2 da (Chloe b 1973, Isabel b 1977); *Career* chm: Nicholas Grimshaw & Ptnrs Ltd 1980–2007, Grimshaw Architects LLP 2007–; pres: AA 1999–2001, Royal Acad of Arts 2004–; major projects incl: Zurich Airport redevelopment, Channel Tunnel terminal for BR Waterloo, Br Pavilion for Expo '92 Seville, Berlin Stock Exchange, BA Combined Operation Centre Heathrow, Camden Superstore for J Sainsbury, HQ for BMW Bracknell, HQ for Igus GmbH Cologne, factory for Herman Miller Bath, Oxford Ice Rink, Gillingham Business Park for Grosvenor Devpts, res centre for Rank Xerox, printing plant for Financial Times, regional HQ for Orange Telephones, restoration of Paddington Station for Railtrack, Caixa Galicia Art Fndn A Coruña, Western Region HQ for the RAC, Euro Inst of Health and Mgmnt Studies Univ of Surrey, The Donald Danforth Plant Science Centre St Louis, The Eden Project, Millennium Point Birmingham, The New Bath Spa, Nat Space Science Centre Leicester, the grandstand at Lords for the MCC, Ijburg Bridge and Biljmer Station for high speed trains Amsterdam, New Exhibition Hall at Site of Frankfurt Fair, headquarters and assembly plant for Rolls Royce Goodwood, New East Wing for RCA London, HQ for Lloyds TSB Gresham St London, Experimental Media and Arts Centre for Rensselaer Poly Inst NY, St Botolph's office building London, HQ for KPMG Berlin, Battersea Power Station, Spencer Street Station Melbourne Aust, ExCeL London Pahse 2 Devpt, Bournemouth Winter Gardens, Garibaldi Republica (fashion and events building) Milan, Nirah (visitor destination and research centre for freshwater aquatic habitats), Adelaide Univ Project 2 Aust, Miami Science Museum, Fulton Street Station NY, Cutty Sark, Stanstead Airport masterplan for BAA, new academic building LSE, extension Queen's Museum of Art NY, Newport City Footbridge Wales; major awards and commendations incl: RIBA Awards 1975, 1978, 1980, 1983, 1986, 1989, 1990, 1991, 1994, 1995, 1999, 2001, 2002, 2003, 2004 and 2007; FT Award for Industrial Architecture 1977, 1980, 1995 and 1997, Br Construction Industry Awards 1988, 1989, 1992, 1993, 1995, 1999 and 2001, Structural Steel Design Awards 1969, 1977, 1980, 1989, 1993, 1994, 1995, 1999, 2000, 2001, 2002 and 2003, Civic Tst Award 1978, 1982, 1989, 1990, 1991, 1996 and 2003, Architectural Design Award 1974, 1982 and 1983, Royal Fine Arts Cmmn Sunday Times 1989, 1993, 1994 and 2004, BBC Design Awards finalist 1990, Business and Indust Award Certificate of Merit 1977, Euro Award for Steel Structure 1981, Constructa Preis for Industrial Architecture in Europe 1990, Quaternario Fndn Int Award 1993, Mies van der Rohe Pavilion Award for Architecture 1994; Hon DLitt; hon memb BDA, Hon FAIA, Hon FRIAS; RIBA 1967, FCSD 1969, RA 1994; *Books* Nicholas Grimshaw & Partners Ltd: Product and Process (jtly, 1988), Structure, Space and Skin: the work of Nicholas Grimshaw & Partners Ltd 1988–93 (1993), Architecture, Industry and Innovation: the work of Nicholas Grimshaw & Partners Ltd 1966–88 (jtly, 1995), Equilibrium: The Work of Nicholas Grimshaw & Partners Ltd 1993–2000 (2000); *Recreations* sailing, tennis; *Style*— Sir Nicholas Grimshaw, CBE, RA; ✉ Grimshaw Architects LLP, 57 Clerkenwell Road, London EC1M 5NG (tel 020 7291 4141, fax 020 7291 4194, e-mail emma.pearson@grimshaw-architects.com)

GRIMSTON, Neil Alexander; TD (1982); s of Flt Lt Victor Gordon Manners Grimston (d 1966), and Adeline Jean Margaret, *née* Esson (d 1992); *b* 8 September 1947; *m* 19 July 1975, Berylanne (d 2003), da of David McNaught (d 1992), of Thames Ditton, Surrey; 1 s (Alexander b 1979), 1 da (Henrietta b 1984); *Career* Private HAC 1970 (vet memb 1971–), cmmnd 2 Lt TA RCT 1971, Lt 1972, Capt 1976, cmd ind unit with BAOR 1977–82, Capt RARO 1983–2002; with Hill Samuel 1967–70, discount broker Smith St Aubyn 1970–73, discount broker Page and Gwyther Group 1973–77; Chemical Bank 1977–92: vice-pres and mangr World Insurance Gp (Asia) 1982–84, head City Instns Gp 1985–87, dir Chemical Bank Tstee Co 1986–88, vice-pres and head of Fin Instns Gp 1987–92, memb Euro Mgmnt Ctee 1991–92; ptnr The Financial Planning Gp 1992–94, dir FPG Fiscal Ltd 1992–94, sr conslt dir Telos 1993–94, gp fin dir and memb Exec Mgmnt Ctee Telos Bioinformatik AG (Lucerne) 1994–95, dir Telos Consulting Inc (USA) 1994–95, chm Isisquest Ltd 1995–96, business conslt 1992–, md Grimston & Co 1998–, dir and chief operating offr 5GM Ltd 2000–01, jt md eSecure Business Ltd 2001–04 (ceo 2003–04), md eAssure Gp 2004–07, chm Hanover Partnership Ltd 2005–, memb Advsy Panel Devonshire Corporate Finance Ltd 2005–, regnl co-ordinator Hanover Fndn 2006–; vice-chm Twickenham Cons Assoc 1969–74, cncllr (Cons) London Borough of Richmond-upon-Thames 1971–74; memb approved list of Cons Pty potential candidates for Westminster and Euro Parls 1989–93, chm Oxshott and Stoke Cons Assoc 1989–91; memb: HAC 1970–, Millennium Masters Assoc; vice-chm Westminster Adult Educn Service 2007–; Freeman City of London 1971, Liveryman Worshipful Co of Scriveners (memb Ct, Master 1999–2000); FRSA 2005; *Recreations* collecting prints, Oriental rugs, wine, photography; *Clubs* Singapore Cricket; *Style*— Neil A Grimston, Esq, TD; ✉ 27 Melcombe Court, Dorset Square, London NW1 6EP (tel 020 7262 3732, mobile 07876 741907, e-mail neil.grimston@hanoverpartnership.com)

GRIMSTON OF WESTBURY, 3 Baron (UK 1964); Sir Robert John Sylvester (Robin) Grimston; 3 Bt (UK 1952); er s of 2 Baron Grimston of Westbury (d 2003), and Hon June Mary, *née* Ponsonby, da of 5 Baron de Mauley; *b* 30 April 1951; *Educ* Eton, Univ of Reading (BSc); *m* 1984, Emily Margaret, da of Maj John Evelyn Shirley, of Ormly Hall, Ramsey, IOM; 2 da (Hon Charlotte Elgiva b 23 March 1991, Hon Philippa Margaret b 7 Oct 1995); *Career* Capt Royal Hussars (PWO) 1970–81; CA: Binder Hamlyn, Citicorp Scrimgeour Vickers Ltd, Matrix Securities Ltd; *Style*— The Lord Grimston of Westbury

GRIMSTONE, Gerald Edgar (Gerry); s of Edgar Wilfred Grimstone (d 1986), and Dorothy Yvonne, *née* Martin; *b* 27 August 1949; *Educ* Whitgift Sch, Merton Coll Oxford (MA, MSc); *m* 23 June 1973 (m dis 1995), Hon Janet Elizabeth Gudrun Suenson-Taylor, da of 2 Baron Grantchester, CBE, QC (d 1995); 1 s (Toby Stephen Gunnar b 1975), 2 da (Jenny Elizabeth May b 1979, Anna Rose Yvonne b 1982); *Career* Civil Serv 1972–86 (latterly asst sec HM Treasy); J Henry Schroder & Co Ltd: dir 1986–99, head Int Fin and Advsy Dept 1994–95, dep chm Schroder Asia Ltd, head of investment banking Asia-Pacific region 1994–97, head of investment banking North America (based in New York) 1997–98, vice-chm Schroders Investment Banking 1998–99; non-exec dir: Dairy Crest 1999–2007, Candover Investments plc 1999– (chm 2006–), Aggregate Industries 2000–04, RAF Air Command 2001–, F&C Global Smaller Companies plc 2002–07 (chm 2004–07), Standard Life 2003– (chm 2007–); advsr FCO 1999–2000; memb Horserace Totalisator Bd 1999–2006; MSI; *Clubs* Athenaeum, RAF, China, Hong Kong; *Style*— Gerry Grimstone, Esq; ✉ 34 Boscobel Place, London SW1W 9PE

GRIMTHORPE, 5 Baron (UK 1886); Sir Edward John Beckett; 9 Bt (UK 1813); s of 4 Baron Grimthorpe, OBE, DL (d 2003); *b* 20 November 1954; *Educ* Hawtreys, Harrow; *m* 20 May 1992, Mrs Carey Elisabeth McEwen, yr da of Robin Graham; 1 s (Hon Harry Maximillian b 28 April 1993); *Heir* s, Hon Harry Beckett; *Style*— The Rt Hon the Lord Grimthorpe

G

GRINYER, Clive Antony; s of Tony Grinyer, of Southampton, Hants, and Hazel Grinyer; *b* 29 July 1960; *Educ* Highcliffe Comp Sch, Brockenhurst Sixth Form Coll, Southampton Coll of Art, Central Sch of Art and Design; *m* 21 May 1988, Janis, da of late Philip Kirby; 2 s (Laurence Kirby b 16 June 1992, Miles Kirby b 3 Oct 1995); *Career* designer; Moggridge Associates UK and USA 1983–89, founding ptnr Tangerine design consultancy 1989, dir Samsung IDEO USA 1994–95, European design dir Samsung Electronics 1995–98, head of product design TAG Mclaren Audio 1998–2001, dir of design and innovation Design Cncl 2001–03, dir of customer experience Orange World 2003–06, dir of design Orange France Telecom Paris 2006–; monthly columnist Design Week magazine 2001–; memb Design Advsy Bd Br Cncl; memb Jury: Millennium Product, RSA Student Award, D&AD Awards; RSA Student Design Award 1982, Industrial Design Soc of America (IDSA) Awards for Ford car audio projects 1986, IDSA/Business Week Award for Samsung Europe products 1995; FRSA 1983, FCSD 1996; *Recreations* sailing, classic Maseratis; *Style*— Clive Grinyer, Esq; ✉ France Telecom, 6 Place d'Alleray, Paris 75015, France

GRINYER, Prof John Raymond; twin bro of Prof Peter Hugh Grinyer, *qv*; *b* 3 March 1935; *Educ* Central Park Sch East Ham, LSE (MSc); *m* 31 May 1958, Shirley Florence, da of Harry Alfred Marshall (d 1989), of Dagenham, Essex; 2 da (Julie b 1961, Sally b 1963), 1 s (Christopher b 1967); *Career* Nat Serv RAMC 1953–55; posts with LEB and Halifax Building Society 1950–56, trg as CA Martin Redhead and Co, Hope Agar and Co 1956–61, sr audit asst Kemp Chatteris and Co 1962–63, lectr Harlow Tech Coll 1963–66; sr lectr: City of London Poly 1967–71, Cranfield Sch of Mgmnt 1971–76; Univ of Dundee: prof of accountancy and business finance 1976–2000, head of dept 1976–90, dean Faculty of Law 1984–85 and 1991–93, dep princ 1997–2000, pt/t res prof 2000–06, emeritus prof 2006–; author of numerous articles in jls; chm: Assoc of Univ Teachers of Accounting 1980–81, Br Accounting Assoc 1990 (vice-chm 1989); FCA; *Recreations* golf, dinghy sailing; *Clubs* Broughty Ferry Golf, Royal Tay Yacht; *Style*— Prof John Grinyer; ✉ 81B Dundee Road, Broughty Ferry, Dundee DD5 1LZ

GRINYER, Prof Peter Hugh; s of Sydney George Grinyer (d 2005), and Grace Elizabeth, *née* Formals (d 1988); twin bro of Prof John Raymond Grinyer, *qv*; *b* 3 March 1935; *Educ* East Ham GS, Balliol Coll Oxford (BA, MA), LSE (PhD); *m* 6 Sept 1958, Sylvia Joyce, da of William James Boraston (d 1992); 2 s (Paul Andrew b 27 July 1961, Nigel James b 12 May 1964); *Career* sr mgmnt trainee Unilever Ltd 1957–59, personal asst to md (later mangr of prodn planning and stock control) E R Holloway Ltd 1959–61, asst lectr (later lectr and sr lectr) Hendon Coll of Technol 1961–64, lectr (later sr lectr and reader) Graduate Business Centre City Univ 1964–74, prof of business strategy City Univ Business Sch 1974–79; Univ of St Andrews: Esmée Fairbairn prof of economics 1979–93, chm Dept of Econs 1979–85, vice-princ 1985–87, actg princ 1986, chm Dept of Mgmnt 1987–90, emeritus prof 1993–; visiting prof Stern Sch New York Univ 1992, 1996–98, Erskine fell Univ of Canterbury NZ 1994, visiting prof Imperial Coll London 2002–; memb Business and Mgmnt Studies Sub Ctee UGC 1979–85; non-exec dir: John Brown plc 1984–86, Don & Low Holdings (formerly Don Bros Buist plc) 1985–91, Ellis & Goldstein Hldgs plc 1987–88; fndr memb Glenrothes Enterprise Tst 1983–86; chm: St Andrews Mgmnt Inst 1989–96, St Andrews Strategic Management Ltd 1989–96, McIlroy Coates Ltd 1991–95; memb: Scottish Legal Aid Bd 1992–2000, Competition Cmmn Appeals Tbnls 2000–03, Competition Appeals Tbnl 2003–; *Books* Corporate Models Today (1975, with J Wooller, 2 edn, 1978), From Private to Public (with G D Vaughan and S Birley, 1977), Turnaround (with J C Spender, 1979), Sharpbenders (with D G Mayes and P McKiernan, 1988), Organising Strategy (with Foo Check Teck, 1994); author of some 60 papers in jls; *Recreations* golf, mountain walking; *Clubs* Royal and Ancient Golf; *Style*— Prof Peter Grinyer; ✉ Aberbrothock, 60 Buchanan Gardens, St Andrews, Fife KY16 9LX (tel 01334 472966, e-mail phg@st-andrews.ac.uk)

GROBEL, His Hon Judge Peter Denis Alan Christian Joseph; s of Cyril Peter Grobel, and Kathleen, *née* Donaghy; *b* 11 August 1944; *Educ* Mount St Mary's Coll, UCL (LLB); *m* 1975, Susan, *née* Twemlow; 3 s, 1 da; *Career* called to the Bar Lincoln's Inn 1967; in practice Common Law Bar 1971–2001, recorder 1991–2001, circuit judge (SE Circuit) 2001–; chm Special Educn Needs Tbnl 1994–2000; chm of govrs St Teresa's Sch Effingham 2002; *Style*— His Hon Judge Grobel; ✉ c/o Inner London Crown Court, Sessions House, Newington Causeway, London SE1 6AZ

GROCHOLSKI, Count Alexander Luan; head of the family; hereditary title of Count confirmed in Russia 1881; er s of Count Kazimierz Adam Grocholski (d 1994), and his 1 w, Elzbieta Zofia, *née* Countess Baworowska (d 1987); suc uncle Count Stanislas Bohdan Karol Grocholski (d 2002); *b* 30 August 1949; *Educ* French Lycée London, Study Centre for the History of the Fine and Decorative Arts London; *m* 1979, Bridget Caroline, da of Capt John Hamilton Fleming (d 1971); 1 da (Katherine Rose Mary b 1980); *Career* Phillips Son & Neale Ceramics Dept 1969–73, Sotheby's Valuation Dept 1973–78; Grocholski & Co Art and Antique Valuers and Consultants 1978–; *Recreations* reading, walking; *Style*— The Count Grocholski; ✉ 27 Baalbec Road, London N5 1QN (tel 020 7226 8806)

GROCOCK, Dr Anne; *Educ* Westonbirt Sch, St Anne's Coll Oxford (MA, DPhil); *Career* Univ of Oxford Dept of Human Anatomy: departmental demonstrator 1973–79, departmental research asst 1979–80 and 1982–85, ICRF research fell 1985–89; Univ of Oxford coll lectr in anatomy and endocrinology: Worcester Coll 1976–79, Magdalen Coll 1977–80, Merton Coll 1977–80 and 1985–89, Keble Coll 1984–89, Lincoln Coll 1986–89; bursar and official fell St Antony's Coll Oxford 1990–97, exec dir RSM 1997–2006, asst registrar Univ of Oxford 2006–; dep chair Nat Museum of Science Industry 2002–06 (tstee 1996–2006, chm Audit Ctee 1997–2006); memb Def Estates Audit Ctee; Univ of Oxford: advsr to women jr membs Merton Coll 1988–89, memb SCR Merton Coll 1990–, memb Equal Opportunities Ctee 1992–95, memb Estates Bursars' Standing Ctee 1994–97, tstee Staff Pension Scheme 1994–97, memb Audit Ctee 1995–97, pres Assoc of Sr Membs St Anne's Coll 1997–2000; memb Cncl of Mgmnt Jl of Reproduction and Fertility Ltd 1977–82, chm Reproduction Research Information Services Ltd 1988–93 (memb Cncl of Mgmnt 1976–81); memb: Society for Reproduction and Fertility 1969–, Endocrine Soc 1975–, Assoc of Univ Administrators 1990–98; tstee: Oxford Soc 1995–2003, Royal Med Benevolent Fund 1998–2005, Nuffield Oxford Hosps Fund 2001– (chm 2005–); pres Westonbirt Assoc 1989–97; memb Cncl Taunton Sch 1990–2001 (chair F&GP Ctee 1992–97), govr Westonbirt Sch 1991–97, memb Ct Imperial Coll London 2001–06; MInstD 1999, FRSA 2000; *Publications* author of numerous scientific papers; *Recreations* music, opera, travel, collecting sculpture and books; *Style*— Dr Anne Grocock

GROCOTT, Baron (Life Peer UK 2001), of Telford in the County of Shropshire; Bruce Joseph Grocott; PC (2002); s of Reginald Grocott, and Helen Grocott; *b* 1 November 1940; *Educ* Univ of Leicester, Univ of Manchester; *m* 1965, Sally Barbara Kay, *née* Ridgway; 2 s (Hon John b 1970, Hon Neil b 1974); *Career* lectr in politics 1965–74, television journalist and prodr Central Television 1979–87; MP (Lab): Lichfield and Tamworth 1974–79, The Wrekin 1987–97, Telford 1997–2001; PPS to: Min for Local Govt Planning 1975–76, Min of Agric 1976–78; formerly PPS to Rt Hon Tony Blair MP, *qv* 1994–2001; Lord in Waiting (Govt whip) 2001–02, Capt HM Body Guard of Hon Corps of Gentlemen-at-Arms (chief Govt whip, House of Lords) 2002–; *Clubs* Trench Labour; *Style*— The Rt Hon the Lord Grocott, PC

GROGAN, John Timothy; MP; s of late John Martin Grogan, and late Maureen, *née* Jennings; *b* 24 February 1961; *Educ* St Michael's Coll Leeds, St John's Coll Oxford (BA, first Lab pres Oxford Univ Students' Union); *Career* communications dir Leeds City Cncl 1987–94, press offr Euro Parly Lab Party 1994–95, self employed business conf orgn Yorks 1995–97; MP (Lab) Selby 1997–; patron N Yorks and Yorks Business Forum; *Recreations* running, football (keen supporter of Bradford City FC); *Clubs* Yorkshire CCC; *Style*— John Grogan, Esq, MP; ✉ House of Commons, London SW1A 0AA; Constituency: 58 Gowthorpe, Selby, North Yorkshire YO8 4ET (tel 01757 291152, fax 01757 291153)

GROOM, Brian William Alfred; s of Fred Groom (d 1978), of Manchester, and Muriel Edith, *née* Linfoot; *b* 26 April 1955; *Educ* Manchester Grammar, Balliol Coll Oxford (BA); *m* 1980, Carola May, da of Peter Withington; 1 s (Jack Edward b 4 Oct 1984), 1 da (Elinor Rose b 6 Aug 1987); *Career* trainee reporter and sports ed Goole Times 1976–78; Financial Times: Syndication Dept 1978–79, sub ed int edn 1979–81, labour reporter and mgmnt feature writer 1981–85, UK news ed 1985–88; ed Scotland on Sunday 1994–97 (dep ed 1988–94); Financial Times: S of England corr and regions team ldr 1997–2000, political ed 2000–02, Europe Edn ed 2002–05, comment and analysis ed 2005–; Pfizer award NCTJ 1978; *Recreations* cricket, reading, hill walking, cinema; *Style*— Brian Groom, Esq; ✉ Financial Times, Number One, Southwark Bridge, London SE1 9HL (tel 020 7873 4599, fax 020 7873 3196, e-mail brian.groom@ft.com)

GROOM, Jeremy Richard; s of Peter Farrant Groom, of Walton on Thames, and Anne, *née* Dainty; *b* 2 May 1948; *Educ* King's Sch Canterbury, Lincoln Coll Oxford; *m* 9 April 1983, Jennifer, da of Sir Norman Richard Rowley Brooke, CBE (d 1989), of Cardiff; 1 da (Camilla b 1984), 1 s (Pelham b 1989); *Career* ptnr Seymour Pierce and Co 1977–87 (joined 1972), dir Seymour Pierce Butterfield Ltd 1987–94, sr divnl dir Brewin Dolphin 1994–; memb Stock Exchange 1975, FSI 2000 (MSI (Dip) 1992); *Recreations* music, theatre, real tennis, cricket; *Clubs* MCC; *Style*— Jeremy Groom, Esq; ✉ Bachelor's Mead, Horton, Devizes, Wiltshire SN10 3NB (tel 01380 860344); Brewin Dolphin, Cross Keys House, The Parade, Marlborough, Wiltshire SN8 1NE (tel 01672 519610, fax 01672 515550, e-mail jeremy.groom@brewin.co.uk)

GROOM, Michael John; s of Thomas Rowland Groom (d 1984), of Wolverhampton, and Eliza Groom (d 1971); *b* 18 July 1942; *Educ* St Chad's GS Wolverhampton, Cotton Coll; *m* 4 June 1966, Sheila Mary, da of Harold Cartwright, of Wolverhampton; 2 da (Nichola b 1971, Sally b 1975); *Career* chartered accountant; Michael Groom & Co 1971–76 and 1981–89, Tansley Witt 1976–80, Binder Hamlyn 1980–81, dir various cos, lectr in mgmnt and legislation; chm Consultative Ctee of Accountancy Bodies 2001–02, dep chm Financial Reporting Cncl; memb: ICAEW (memb Cncl 1975–2004, former treas, chm 1998–99, pres 2001–02), City Takeover Panel; Hon DBA Univ of Wolverhampton 2003; Liveryman Worshipful Co of Chartered Accountants; FCA 1964; *Books* ed/author 1975–81: Chartac Administration Manual, Chartac Accounting Manual, Chartac Auditing Manual, Chartac Taxation Manual, Chartac Accounting and Auditing Model File, Financial Management in the Professional Office, Cash Control in the Smaller Business, Budgeting and Cash Management; *Recreations* theatre, travel, food and wine, photography; *Clubs* Albert Lawn Tennis; *Style*— Michael Groom, Esq; ✉ 14 High Meadows, Compton, Wolverhampton WV6 8PH (tel 01902 753816)

GROOME, Richard Leonard; s of Leonard William Edward Groome, OBE, of London, and Patricia Yvonne, *née* Holttum; *b* 9 June 1951; *m* 10 Sept 1977, Janet Mary, da of William Edward Seckington; 1 da (Emily Sara b 2 April 1984); *Career* prodn mangr Beecham Foods Ltd 1973–76, devpt mangr then tech servs mangr Express Foods Gp 1976–86, gp planning mangr then div mangr Elliott Presco Ltd 1986–90, gen mangr prodn Muller Dairy UK Ltd 1990–92, dir UK Elliott Gp Ltd 1992–2005, chief exec Manchester Salford Trafford NHS LIFT Co 2005–; UK delg for IChemE to Int Food Gp 1984–86; non-exec dir Shropshire HA 1996–2002, treas Shropshire Rifle Assoc, clerk Westbury Parish Cncl; Freeman City of London, memb Worshipful Co of Engineers; FIChemE 1984, FRSH 2005; *Recreations* target shooting, photography, fine wines, golf; *Clubs* Farmers', Shrewsbury Rifle, Wine Share; *Style*— Richard Groome, Esq; ✉ The Brooklands, Station Road, Westbury, Shrewsbury SY5 9DA (tel 01743 884653, e-mail richard.groome@talk21.com)

GROOTENHUIS, Prof Peter; s of Johannes Christiaan Grootenhuis (d 1986), and Anna Christina van den Bergh (d 1992); *b* 31 July 1924; *Educ* Netherlands Lyceum The Hague, Imperial Coll London (BSc Eng, DIC, PhD, DScEng); *m* 7 Aug 1954, Sara Joan, da of Maj Charles Campbell Winchester, MC, RR, Royal Scots (ka 1940); 1 da (Carol Felicity b 2 June 1955), 1 s (Hugh John b 30 April 1958); *Career* apprentice rising to asst project engr Bristol Aero Engine Co 1944–46; Imperial Coll London: lectr in mech engrg 1946–59, reader in mech engrg 1959–72, prof 1972– (latterly emeritus prof), sr res fell 1989–, memb Bd of Studies of Civil and Mech Engrg 1959–89, memb Engrg Bd of Studies 1972–89, memb Governing Body Imperial Coll 1974–79; fndr Derritron Electronics Ltd 1960 (later tech dir Derritron Ltd), dir Derritron Environmental Systems Ltd 1981–84; ptnr Grootenhuis Allaway Associates (consltg engrs) 1969–92; conslt: Binnie and Partners 1962–64, Royal Armament R&D Estab 1963–64, Absorbit Ltd 1964–69, City of London Corp 1964–91, Arup Assocs 1965–67, MOD 1965–84, Esso Chemicals Ltd 1968 and 1971, Union Electrica Madrid 1976–81; memb: Special Advsy Bd in Ergonomics Univ of London 1966–89, BSI Ctees 1967–, Editorial Advsy Bd Journal of Environmental Engrg 1969–89 (chm 1974–89), jt IMechE/Dutch Working Pty on Educn 1979–81; external examiner: The Coll of Technol Dublin 1971–79, Univ of Lagos Nigeria 1972–75, Univ of Bristol 1979–81; Soc of Environmental Engrs: fndr memb 1959, fell 1964, pres 1964–67; MIM 1956–76, chm: Imperial Coll Wine Ctee 1975–89, Knightsbridge Branch Cons Pty Assoc 1974–77; pres Old Centralians 1988–89; memb Br Acoustical Soc (now Inst of Acoustics) 1965 (memb Provisional Cncl 1964–66); Freeman City of London 1984, memb Worshipful Co of Engrs 1985; AFRAeS 1950–75, FCGI 1976, FIMechE 1979 (MIMechE 1952), FREng 1982; *Publications* author of over 70 pubns in learned jls; *Recreations* gardening, sailing; *Clubs* Athenaeum; *Style*— Prof Peter Grootenhuis, FREng; ✉ Imperial College London, Department of Mechanical Engineering, Exhibition Road, London SW7 2BX (tel 020 7594 7018, fax 020 7584 1560)

GROSS, Howard Anthony; s of Harold Victor Gross (d 2005), and Pamela Alicia Tamara, *née* Rosen (d 1994); *b* 24 May 1948; *Educ* Minchenden Sch, City of London Coll; *m* 4 Nov 1973, Beverley, da of Bennett Teff, of Christchurch, Dorset; 2 da (Zoë b 1975, Amanda b 1978); *Career* chartered accountant; chief exec Gross Klein 1968–; fndr chm Hartley Computer User Gp 1979–82; chm: North London Chartered Accountants 1984–85, Heathfield Sch Parents' Assoc (GPDST) 1985–89, Solution 6 Accounts Computer User Group 1998–2000; London Soc of Chartered Accountants: elected memb 1984, hon treas 1990–93, pres 2001–02; memb Cncl ICAEW 2002–; exec ed Accountants Digest 2001–06; Freeman City of London 1990; FCA 1971, CTA 1972, FCCA 1980; *Recreations* jogging (completed London Marathon 1989), my granddaughters Charlotte and Tammy; *Style*— Howard Gross, Esq; ✉ Gross Klein, 6 Breams Buildings, London EC4A 1QL (tel 020 7242 2212, fax 020 7404 4412, e-mail howard@grossklein.com)

GROSS, John Jacob; s of Abraham and Muriel Gross; *b* 12 March 1935; *Educ* City of London Sch, Wadham Coll Oxford; *m* 1965 (m dis), Miriam Gross, *qv*, da of Kurt May; 1 s (Thomas b 1966), 1 da (Susanna b 1967); *Career* former asst lectr Univ of London, fellow King's Coll Cambridge 1962–65, literary ed New Statesman 1973, ed Times Literary Supplement 1974–81, tstee Nat Portrait Gallery 1977–84, dep chm George Weidenfeld & Nicolson Ltd 1982–83, staff writer NY Times 1983–89, theatre critic Sunday Telegraph 1990–; FRSL; *Books* The Rise and Fall of the Man of Letters (1969, Duff Cooper Meml Prize), Joyce (1971), The Oxford Book of Aphorisms (ed, 1983), Shylock: A Legend and its Legacy (1992, Heinemann Prize), The Oxford Book of Comic Verse (ed, 1994), The New Oxford Book of English Prose (ed, 1998), A Double Thread

(2001); *Style—* John Gross, Esq; ✉ Sunday Telegraph, 1 Canada Square, Canary Wharf, London E14 5DT

GROSS, Dr Michael Lester Phillip; s of Harold Victor Gross, of Southgate, and Pamela Alicia Tamar, *née* Rosen; *b* 31 March 1952; *Educ* Minchenden Sch Southgate, Sidney Sussex Coll Cambridge (MA, MB BChir, MD), The London Hosp Med Coll; *m* 30 July 1974, Jennifer Ruth, da of Lawrence Hoffman, of Edgware; 2 da (Louise b 1977, Jemma b 1981); *Career* sr resident The Nat Hosp 1983–85, sr registrar St Mary's Hosp and The Nat Hosp 1985–89, conslt neurologist Clementine Churchill Hosp, dir of neurophysiology The Clementine Churchill Harrow; former chm Div of Neurological Sci and conslt neurologist Regnl Neurological Centre Royal Surrey Co Hosp Guildford and East Surrey Hosps (memb Regnl Neurosciences Advsy Ctee), former clinical dir The Royal and East Surrey Neurology Research Unit; scientific papers and int presentations on treatment of Guillain-Barré syndrome, inflammatory polyneuropathy, experimental allergic neuritis, plasma exchange, rejection encephalopathy, migraine and headache syndromes and gen neurology topics; memb: Assoc of Br Neurologists, Euro Neurological Soc, BMA, Int Headache Soc, World Fedn of Neurology; shortlisted UK Hosp Dr of the Year 1998 and 1999; FRCP 1995; *Books* The Therapeutic Modification of Inflammatory Polyneuropathy (1987); *Recreations* bridge, tennis, photography, theatre; *Style—* Dr Michael Gross; ✉ 264 High Road, Harrow Weald, Middlesex HA3 7BB (tel 020 8861 1777, fax 020 8863 7124, e-mail drgross@neurologyclinic.co.uk); Clementine Churchill Hospital, Sudbury Hill, Harrow, Middlesex (tel 020 8872 3838, website www.neurologyclinic.co.uk); Gatwick Park Hospital, Horley, West Sussex (tel 01293 771132)

GROSS, Miriam Marianna; da of Kurt May, of Frankfurt, Germany, and Vera Hermine, *née* Freiberg; *b* 12 May 1939; *Educ* Dartington Hall Sch, St Anne's Coll Oxford (MA, DipEd); *m* 1, 1965 (m dis), John Jacob Gross, *qv*, s of Abraham Gross; 1 s (Thomas b 1966), 1 da (Susanna b 1967); m 2, 1993, Sir Geoffrey Owen; *Career* The Observer: joined as asst literary ed, dep literary ed 1964–81, woman's ed 1981–84; ed Book Choice Channel 4 1986–90, arts ed Daily and Sunday Telegraph 1986–91, literary and assoc ed Sunday Telegraph 1991–2005, freelance journalist 2005–; *Books* The World of George Orwell (1971), The World of Raymond Chandler (1976); *Recreations* painting; *Style—* Ms Miriam Gross; ✉ 24a St Petersburgh Place, London W2 4LB (tel 020 7727 2291, fax 020 7727 4591)

GROSS, Hon Mr Justice; Sir Peter Henry Gross; kt (2001); s of late Sam Lewis Gross, and Fanny Alice, *née* Cohen (d 2002); *b* 13 February 1952; *Educ* Herzlia Sch Cape Town, Univ of Cape Town (BBusSc, MBusSc, Rhodes scholar), Oriel Coll Oxford (MA, BCL, Eldon scholar); *m* 1985, Ruth Mary, *née* Cullen; 2 s (George William b 6 April 1989, Edmund Walter b 6 Aug 1992); *Career* called to the Bar Gray's Inn 1977 (bencher 2000), admitted to the Bar NSW 1986, QC 1992, recorder 1995–2001 (asst recorder 1991–95), judge of the High Court of Justice (Queen's Bench Div) 2001–, presiding judge SE Circuit 2005–; chm: London Common Law and Commercial Bar Assoc 1996–97, Educn and Trg Ctee Bar Cncl 1998–2000, Int Rels Ctee Bar Cncl 2001, Advsy Bd City Univ Inst of Law 2003–05; *Books* Legal Aid and Its Management (1976); *Recreations* jogging, cricket, sailing, cross-country skiing; *Clubs* Oxford and Cambridge; *Style—* The Hon Mr Justice Gross; ✉ Royal Courts of Justice, Strand, London WC2A 2LL

GROSS, Prof Philip John; s of Juhan Karl Gross, and Mary Jessie Alison, *née* Holmes; *b* 27 February 1952, Delabole, Cornwall; *Educ* Devonport HS Plymouth, Univ of Sussex (BA), Poly of North London (Dip Librarianship); *m* 1; 1 da (Rosemary b 20 Aug 1978), 1 s (Jonathan b 20 March 1982); m 2, 8 April 2000, Zélie, *née* Marmery; *Career* poet; early career working in publishing and libraries; writer and creative writing educator; lectr in creative studies Bath Spa Univ Coll until 2004, professor of creative writing Univ of Glamorgan 2004–; first prize National Poetry Competition 1982; *Poetry* Familiars (1983), The Ice Factory (1984), Cat's Whisker (1987), The Air Mines of Mistila (with Sylvia Kantaris, 1988), Manifold Manor (1989), The Son of the Duke of Nowhere (1991), The All-Nite Café (1993), I D (1994), Scratch City (1995), A Cast of Stones (1996), The Wasting Game (1998, shortlisted Whitbread Prize), Changes of Address (2001), Mappa Mundi (2003), The Egg of Zero (2006, shortlisted Roland Mathias Prize); *Novels* The Song of Gail and Fludd (1991), Plex (1994), The Wind Gate (1995), Transformer (1996), Psylicon Beach (1998), Facetaker (1999), Going for Stone (2002), Marginaliens (2003), The Lastling (2003), The Storm Garden (2006); *Plays* Internal Affairs (shared 1 prize BBC W of Eng playwriting competition), Rising Star (1995); *Libretti* Snail Dreaming (1997); *Clubs* Religious Soc of Friends; *Style—* Prof Philip Gross; ✉ Faculty of Humanities and Social Sciences, University of Glamorgan, Pontypridd CF37 1DL (website www.philipgross.co.uk)

GROSSART, Sir Angus McFarlane McLeod; kt (1997), CBE (1989), DL; s of William John White Grossart, JP (d 1980), and Mary Hay, *née* Gardiner (d 2000); *b* 6 April 1937; *Educ* Glasgow Acad, Univ of Glasgow (MA, LLB); *m* 1978, (Marion) Gay Kerr, *née* Dodd; 1 da (Flure b 6 Dec 1982); *Career* CA 1962; advocate Scottish Bar 1963–69, chm and md Noble Grossart Ltd (merchant bank) 1969–, chm Scottish Investment Trust plc 1974–2003; directorships incl: Edinburgh US Tracker Trust plc (formerly American Trust plc) 1973– (currently chm), Royal Bank of Scotland plc 1982–2005, Royal Bank of Scotland Group plc 1985–2005 (vice-chm 1996–2005), BP Scot Advsy Bd 1990–2005, Trinity Mirror Gp plc 1998–, Scottish & Newcastle plc 1998–; non-exec chm: Scottish Daily Record, Sunday Mail 1998–; chm of tstees Nat Galleries of Scot 1989–97, chm The Fine Art Soc 1998–, tstee and dep chm Nat Heritage Memorial Fund 1999–2005, chm Bd Nat Museums of Scotland 2006–; Livingston award Capt of Industry 1990, Walpole Medal of Excellence 2003; Hon LLD Univ of Glasgow 1985, Hon DBA Univ of Strathclyde 1998, Hon DLitt Univ of St Andrews 2004; FRSE 1998; *Recreations* golf, restoration of sixteenth century castle, decorative and applied arts; *Clubs* New (Edinburgh), Royal and Ancient (St Andrews), Hon Co of Edinburgh Golfers; *Style—* Sir Angus Grossart, CBE, LLD, DL, FRSE; ✉ Noble Grossart Ltd, 48 Queen Street, Edinburgh EH2 3NR (tel 0131 226 7011, fax 0131 226 3332)

GROSSART, Hamish McLeod; s of Kenneth William McFarlane Grossart, and Mairi, *née* Paterson; *b* 7 April 1957; *Educ* Glasgow Acad, Univ of Stirling; *m* 1, 14 May 1981 (m dis), Fiona Jean McDonald; 2 da (Mhoraig Louise b 14 March 1987, Cathleen Maire b 28 May 1989); m 2, 7 Dec 1996, Elaine Rosalind Mackenzie Simpson; 1 s (Ruairidh Sholto MacLeod b 8 Jan 1998), 1 da (Rosalind Sophie Mackenzie b 20 Nov 2000); *Career* dir Noble Grossart Ltd 1982–83 (joined 1979, responsible for corp fin), fndr dir First Northern Corporate Finance Ltd 1983–86; EFT Group plc: dir (following merger with First Northern) 1986–97, md 1987–92, chm 1992–97; chm: Quality Care Homes plc 1992–94 (dir 1994–95), Scottish Highland Hotels plc 1992–99 (dir 1991–99), Eclipse Blinds plc 1994–98, Hicking Pentecost plc 1994–98 (dir 1991–98), Royal Doulton plc 1998–2005; dep chm: Cairn Energy plc 1996– (dir 1994–), Scottish Radio Holdings 1996– (dir 1985–91 and 1993–), Indigo Vision plc 2002– (chm 1996–2002); dir: British Thornton Holdings plc 1991–94, Martin Currie Income & Growth Trust plc 1997–2005, Artemis Investment Mgmnt Ltd 1997–, Sigma Technology Group plc 2000–05, Lionheart plc 2001–04; govr Kilgraston Sch 1999–2004; *Style—* Hamish Grossart; ✉ Cairn Energy plc, 50 Lothian Road, Edinburgh EH3 9BY

GROSSMAN, Prof Ashley Barry; s of Sidney Grossman (d 1966), of London, and Rose, *née* Green; *b* 20 February 1948; *Educ* Hasmonean GS, St Catharine's Coll Cambridge (open exhibitioner), UCH Med Sch London (Atkinson scholar, BA, BSc, MB BS, MD, Belasco medal, Univ Gold medal); *m* 1, 1971 (m dis 1982), Susan, da of Dr Dennis Friedman; 1 da (Emily Priscilla Sidonie b 7 July 1978); m 2, 1984, Deborah Foster, da of John Clark; 4 da (Sophie Eleanor b 28 April 1985, Annabel Clare b 9 Oct 1986, Camilla Rose b 14 Nov 1992, Cordelia Anne b 23 Nov 1996, Elizabeth Sîan Helen b 3 Aug 2000); *Career* hon conslt Dept of Endocrinology Bart's 1986–, prof Bart's Med Coll 1993– (lectr 1982–86, sr lectr 1986–90, reader 1990–93); ed Frontiers of Hormone Research, former ed Clinical Endocrinology, memb Editorial Bd Pituitary, Functional Neurology and Jl of Clinical Endocrinology and Metabolism; pres European Neuroendocrine Assoc; elected memb Assoc of Physicians; FRCP, FMedSci; *Books* Neuroendocrinology: a Clinical Text (with Mary Forsling, 1986), Bailliere's International Clinics in Endocrinology: The Neuroendocrinology of Stress (1987), Psychoneuroendocrinology (1991), Clinical Endocrinology (ed, 1993 and 1997), Endocrinology (sr ed, 5 edn 2005); *Recreations* riding, skiing, walking, daughters; *Style—* Prof Ashley Grossman; ✉ 8 Ringwood Avenue, London N2 9NS (tel 020 8444 8918); Department of Endocrinology, St Bartholomew's Hospital, London EC1A 7BE (tel 020 7601 8343, fax 020 7601 8505, e-mail a.b.grossman@qmul.ac.uk)

GROSSMAN, Loyd Daniel Gilman; OBE (2003); s of David K Grossman (d 1982), of Boston, MA, and Helen Katherine, *née* Gilman (d 1985); *b* 16 September 1950; *Educ* Boston Univ (BA), LSE (MSc); *m* 15 June 1985, Hon Deborah Jane, da of Baron Puttnam, CBE (Life Peer), *qv*, of London (dis 2005); 2 da (Florence Grace b 1989, Constance Catherine b 1992); *Career* Harpers & Queen: design ed 1981–84, restaurant critic 1981–89 and 1991–93; contrib ed Sunday Times 1984–86; deviser/writer/presenter: Through the Keyhole (formerly ITV, now BBC) 1983–2003, Behind the Headlines (BBC) 1989–92, Master Chef (BBC) 1990–2000, The Dog's Tale (BBC) 1993, Junior Masterchef (BBC) 1994–99, Off Your Trolley (BBC) 1995, Conspicuous Consumption 1996, The World on a Plate (BBC) 1997, Loyd on Location 1999–2001, History of British Sculpture (five) 2003; memb: Bd mda (formerly Museum Document Assoc) 1998–2001, MLA (formerly Museums, Libraries and Archives Cncl then Resource: Cncl for Museums, Archives and Libraries) 1999– (chm Designation Challenge Fund 2001–03), Bd Culture Northwest: Cultural Consortium for NW England 2002– (chm 2004–); cmmr: Museums and Galleries Cmmn 1996–2000, Royal Cmmn on Historical Monuments of England 1999–2003; English Heritage: chm Museums and Collections Advsy Ctee 1997–2001, cmmr 1997–2003, memb Museum and Archives Panel 2001–03, chm Nat Blue Plaques Panel 2003–06; chm: Campaign for Museums 1995–, Museums and Galleries Month 2000 (co-chm 2001–), The 24 Hour Museum 2000–05, Public Monuments and Sculpture Assoc 2001–, Churches Conservation Tst 2007–; dep chair Liverpool Culture Co 2005–, vice-chm NW Regnl Cultural Consortium 2002–03; pres British Assoc of Friends of Museums 2005–; tstee: Museum of Science and Industry in Manchester 1999–2002, St Deiniol's Library 2003–; chm Conservation Awards 1998–2003, chm of judges Gulbenkian Prize for Museums 2004; patron: Assoc for Heritage Interpretation, Shark Tst; hon patron Hosp Caterers Assoc; vice-pres Sick Children's Tst, chm Better Hosp Food Panel NHS 2001–06, hon life memb The Dog's Tst; memb Ct of Govrs LSE 1996– (memb Cncl 2003–); FRSA, FSA, FSA Scot, FRSM; *Publications* The Social History of Rock Music (1975), Harpers & Queen Guide to London's 100 Best Restaurants (1987), The Dog's Tale (1993), Loyd Grossman's Italian Journey (1994), Courvoisier's Book of the Best (ed, 1994–96), The World on a Plate (1997), The 125 Best Recipes Ever (1998), Foodstuff (2002); articles on architecture, design and food in newspapers and magazines; *Recreations* fishing, scuba diving (PADI Divemaster), looking at buildings, tennis, chess, the Boston Red Sox, playing Gretsch and Fender guitars; *Clubs* Brooks's, Flyfishers', Hurlingham, Chelsea Arts, Lansdowne, Athenaeum (Liverpool), Artists (Liverpool); *Style—* Loyd Grossman, Esq, OBE, FSA

GROSZ, Stephen Ernest; s of Joe Emil Grosz, and Teddy Grosz; *Educ* William Ellis Sch, Clare Coll Cambridge (MA), Univ of Brussels (Licencié Spécial en Droit Européen); *Career* admitted slr 1978; ptnr Bindman & Partners 1981– (articles 1976–78); chair Human Rights Reference Gp Law Soc; memb Cncl: Justice, Br Inst of Human Rights; memb Editorial Bd: Civil Procedure, Judicial Review, Educn, Public Law and the Individual; *Publications* Human Rights: The 1998 Act and the European Convention (jtly, 2000); *Recreations* swimming, singing, cycling, theatre; *Style—* Stephen Grosz, Esq; ✉ Bindman & Partners, 275 Gray's Inn Road, London WC1X 8QB (tel 020 7833 4433, fax 020 7837 9792, e-mail s.grosz@bindmans.com)

GROTE, Dr John David; OBE (1991); s of Royal Calverton Grote (d 1996), of Sompting, W Sussex, and Fay Dorothy, *née* Judson (d 1998); *b* 5 September 1945; *Educ* Rydens Co Secdy Sch Walton on Thames, Univ of Southampton (BSc, PhD); *m* 1 (m dis), Pauline, *née* Bolton; 1 s (Matthew John b 1973), 1 da (Sarah Katherine b 1975); m 2, Barbara, da of Prof Henryk Smigielski (d 1993); 1 da (Joanna Caroline b 1981); *Career* temp lectr Maths Dept Univ of Southampton 1970–71, research fell Univ of Warwick 1971–74; Br Cncl: advsr Sci and Technol Dept 1974–75, sci offr Poland 1975–79, inspr of mgmnt servs 1979–82, dep dir Systems Dept 1982–83, sci offr Germany 1983–86, sci offr Japan 1987–91, dir Hungary 1991–96, dir Singapore 1996–2000, dir Egypt 2001–; *Style—* Dr John Grote, OBE; ✉ The British Council, 192 El Nil Street, Agouza, Cairo, Egypt

GROTRIAN, Sir (Philip) Christian Brent; 3 Bt (UK 1934), of Leighton Buzzard, Co Bedford; s of Sqdn Ldr Robert Philip Brent Grotrian (d on active service 1945, s of 1 Bt), and his 1 w, Elizabeth Mary, o da of late Maj John Hardy-Wrigley; suc unc, Sir John Appelbe Grotrian, 2 Bt (d 1984); *b* 26 March 1935; *Educ* Eton, Trinity Coll Toronto; *m* 1, 1960, Anne Isabel, da of Robert Sieger Whyte, of Toronto; 1 s ((Philip) Timothy Adam Brent b 1962); m 2, 1979, Sarah Frances, da of Reginald Harry Gale, of Montreal; 1 da (Frances Elizabeth b 1980), 1 s (John Hugh Brent b 1982); *Heir* s, Timothy Grotrian; *Style—* Sir Christian Grotrian, Bt; ✉ RR3 Mansfield, Ontario L0N 1M0, Canada (e-mail christian@cgrotrian.com); Calle Ample 2, Regencós, Gerona, Spain

GROUND, (Reginald) Patrick; QC (1981); s of Reginald Ground (d 1975), of Pinner, Middx, and Ivy Elizabeth Grace, *née* Irving (later Mrs Alan Manser, d 1992); *b* 9 August 1932; *Educ* Beckenham and Penge County GS, Lycée Gay Lussac Limoges, Selwyn Coll Cambridge (exhibitioner, MA), Magdalen Coll Oxford (MLitt); *m* 1964, Caroline, da of Col J F C Dugdale (d 1991), of London; 3 s (Andrew b 1967, Richard b 1970, Thomas b 1974), 1 da (Elizabeth b 1969); *Career* Sub Lt RNVR Med Fleet 1955–56; called to the Bar Inner Temple 1960 (Inner Temple studentship and Foster Boulton prize 1958, bencher 1987); cncllr Hammersmith BC 1968–71, chm Ctees responsible for Health and Social Servs 1969–71; MP (Cons) Feltham and Heston 1983–92, PPS to the Slr Gen 1987–92; pres OUCA 1958, chm Fulham Soc 1975–95; *Recreations* lawn tennis, sailing, theatre, forestry, travel; *Clubs* Carlton, Brooks's; *Style—* Patrick Ground, Esq, QC; ✉ 13 Ranelagh Avenue, London SW6 3PJ; 2–3 Gray's Inn Square, London WC1R 5JH (tel 020 7242 4986, e-mail pground@2–3graysinnsquare.co.uk)

GROVE, Peter Ernest; s of Ernest Grove (d 1974), and Elsie May, *née* Silver; *b* 18 November 1949; *Educ* Heathcote Sch Chingford; *m* 27 Jan 1973, Catherine Anne, da of Joseph Frederick Jolly, of Wanstead, London; 1 s (Alexander b 28 April 1979), 2 da (Elizabeth b 10 Jan 1981, Caroline b 18 Jan 1982); *Career* dep underwriter: Willis Faber Underwriting Mgmnt Ltd 1977, Lloyd's Syndicates 197/726 561 & 566 1984, Bankside Syndicates Ltd 1987; active underwriter Lloyd's Syndicates 197 & 561 1988, dir Limit plc 1998, active underwriter Lloyd's Syndicate 2999 2003, chief underwriting offr QBE European Operations 2004, dir QBE International Holdings (UK) plc 2004–; dir Minibus Plus Ltd 2005, dir British Marine Managers Ltd 2006; *Recreations* chess, reading; *Style—* Peter Grove, Esq; ✉ QBE European Operations, Plantation Place, 30 Fenchurch Street, London EC3M 3BD (tel 020 7105 4516, fax 020 7105 5020, e-mail peter.grove@qbeeurope.com)

G

GROVE, Valerie; da of Doug Smith (d 1973); *b* 11 May 1946; *Educ* Kingsbury Co GS, Girton Coll Cambridge (exhibitioner, MA); *m* 1, 1968, David Brynmor Jenkins; m 2, 1975, Trevor Charles Grove, s of Ronald Grove (d 1980); 3 da (Lucy b 1976, Emma b 1979, Victoria b 1981), 1 s (Oliver b 1983); *Career* reporter Shields Gazette 1965–66, feature writer Evening Standard 1968–87 (literary ed 1979–81 and 1984–87); columnist: Sunday Times 1987–91, The Times 1992–; *Books* Where I Was Young - Memories of London Childhoods (1977), The Compleat Woman (1987), Dear Dodie (1996), Laurie Lee: The Well-loved Stranger (1999), A Voyage Round John Mortimer (2007); *Recreations* tennis, archives; *Style*— Mrs Valerie Grove; ✉ 14 Avenue Road, Highgate, London N6 5DW (tel 020 8348 2621, fax 020 8348 5172, e-mail vgrove@dircon.co.uk)

GROVE-WHITE, Prof Robin Bernard; s of Charles William Grove-White, of Amlwch, Gwynedd, and Mary, *née* Dobbs; *b* 17 February 1941; *Educ* Uppingham, Worcester Coll Oxford (BA); *m* 1, 1970 (m dis 1974), Virginia Harriet, da of Christopher Ironside, OBE; 1 s (William b 1973); m 2, 1979, Helen Elisabeth, da of Sir Francis Graham Smith, of Henbury, Cheshire; 1 da Ruth (b 1980), 2 s (Simon b 1982, Francis b 1986); *Career* freelance writer for TV, radio, press in US, Canada and UK 1963–71, asst sec Cncl for the Protection of Rural England 1972–80 (dir 1981–87), vice-chm Cncl for National Parks; research fell Centre for Environmental Technol Imperial Coll London 1987–89, dir Centre for Study of Environmental Change Lancaster Univ 1991–2000, prof of environment and soc Lancaster Univ 2000–05 (emeritus prof 2005–); forestry cmmr 1990–98, memb Agric and Environment Biotechnology Cmmn 2000–05; chm Greenpeace UK 1996–2004; contrib to The Times, Guardian, New Scientist, Nature and numerous academic jls; *Recreations* reading, walking, cricket; *Style*— Prof Robin Grove-White; ✉ Brynddu Llanfechell, Ynys Mon LL68 0RT (tel 01407 710245)

GROVER, Derek James Langlands; CB (1999); s of Donald James Grover, of Hove, E Sussex, and Mary Barbara, *née* Langlands (d 1990); *b* 26 January 1949; *Educ* Hove Co GS for Boys, Clare Coll Cambridge (fndn scholar, MA, Grene prize); *m* 8 July 1972, Mary Katherine, da of David Yorweth Morgan, OBE (decd), of Limpsfield, Surrey; 1 s (Jonathan Richard b 1978); *Career* civil servant: Dept of Employment 1971–79, Cabinet Office 1979–81, MSC 1981–88 (head of personnel and staff trg 1986–88); DfES (formerly Dept of Employment then DfEE): under sec grade 3 1989–, dir of youth trg 1989, dir of trg strategy and standards 1989–94, dep chief exec and sr dir of ops Employment Service 1994–97, dir of employment and adult trg 1997–98, dir of skills and lifelong learning 1998–2000, dir adult learning 2000–02; NHSU: dir of devpt 2002–03, gp dir of distributed learning 2003–05; FRSA 1991, MCIPD 1993; *Recreations* music, reading, walking; *Style*— Derek Grover, Esq, CB

GROVES, Brian Arthur; s of Alfred Edward Groves (d 1990), and Winifred May, *née* Sheen (d 1996); *b* 3 July 1933; *Educ* Bishop Wordsworth Sch Salisbury; *m* 1 Aug 1955, Daphne Frances, da of Frederick Gale (d 1957); 2 da (Heather b 1956, Beverley, b 1957); *Career* journalist 1950–71, motoring ed Daily Mail 1968–71, advtg and PR dir Nissan UK Ltd 1985–88 (mktg dir 1975–85), chm David Ruskin Ltd 1988–92, md AFG Ltd 1992–94, dir Nissan UK Ltd 1994–; *Recreations* golf, flying; *Style*— Brian A Groves, Esq; ✉ Sarum, Ivy Gates, St Peter Port, Guernsey (tel 01481 727766, mobile 07781 127766)

GROVES, Philip Denys Baker; DL (Co of Hertford 1988); s of Joseph Rupert Groves (d 1958), of Watford, Herts, and Eva Lilian, *née* Baker (d 1986); *b* 9 January 1928; *Educ* Watford GS, Poly Sch of Architecture; *m* 21 June 1952, Yvonne Joyce, da of George Chapman (d 1971), of Rickmansworth; 2 s (Mark b 29 April 1957, Michael b 23 Sept 1965), 1 da (Sarah b 27 May 1961); *Career* RAF 1946–48; served: UK, Palestine, Egypt; chm Architects Co-Partnership 1980–95 (joined 1955, ptnr 1965); architect for educn and health care projects UK, ME, Far East and the Caribbean; vice-pres RIBA Cncl 1972–75 and 1978–80 (memb 1962–81), chm Bd of Educn RIBA 1974–75 and 1979–80 (memb 1962–80); chm ARCUK 1971–74 (memb Cncl 1962–80); chm: Univ of York Centre for Continuing Educn 1978–81, CPD in Construction GP 1986–96, Construction Industry Cncl 1993–96; memb Comité de Liaison des Architects du Marché Commun 1972–80; external examiner at several schools of architecture in UK and overseas; govr W Herts Coll 1993–2001; chm: Herts C of C 1985–88 (pres 1989), Herts Community Tst 1988–97 (vice-pres 1998–); dir: Herts TEC 1989–2001 (chm 1992–97), Business Link Herts 1993–2003, TEC Nat Cncl 1996–99, Herts Business Partnership 2003–; FRIBA 1968 (ARIBA 1955), FRSA 1989; *Books* Design for Health Care (jtly, 1981), Hospitals and Health Care Facilities (jtly, 1990); *Recreations* walking, reading, architecture; *Style*— Philip Groves, Esq, DL; ✉ The Dingle, Whisperwood, Loudwater, Rickmansworth, Hertfordshire WD3 4JU

GROVES, Richard Laurence; s of Wilfred Groves (d 1980), of Sheffield, and Ann Groves (d 1994); *b* 21 July 1944; *Educ* Rowlinson Secdy Sch Sheffield, Sheffield Poly (Dip Municipal Admin), Manchester Poly (Dip Mgmnt Studies), Univ of Manchester (MA); *m* 1976, Christine, da of Gerard Grady; 1 s (Jonathan b 4 Jan 1979); *Career* clerical offr Sheffield City Cncl 1961–68, admin Tport and Town Clerks Depts Manchester City Cncl 1968–73, various managerial posts Manchester Regnl Hosp Bd N Western RHA 1973–75 (regnl servs planning offr 1975–86); N Manchester Healthcare NHS Tst (formerly N Manchester HA): head of planning and admin 1986–88, unit gen mangr 1988–90, gen mangr and dep chief exec 1990–95, exec dir 1995–98; fixtures and referees sec Sheffield and District under 18 league 1996–2001, sec Hallam FC 1997–2001, gen sec Northern under 19 Alliance football league 2001–04, sec Halifax Town AFC 2002–06, head of recruitment Sheffield Wednesday FC Acad 2006–; music, plugging son's band Screaming Mimi; *Recreations* football, music, art; *Style*— Richard Groves, Esq; ✉ tel 07715 254323, website www.myspace.com/screamingmimiband

GRUDER, Jeffrey Nigel; QC (1997); of Bernard Gruder (d 1996), and Lily Gruder (d 2003); *Educ* City of London Sch, Trinity Hall Cambridge (MA); *m* 1979, Gillian Vera, *née* Hyman; 2 da (Joanna b 7 July 1982, Katherine b 26 Nov 1989), 1 s (Jonathan b 25 June 1985); *Career* called to the Bar Middle Temple 1977; *Recreations* tennis, reading, art, theatre; *Style*— Jeffrey Gruder, Esq, QC; ✉ Essex Court Chambers, 24 Lincoln's Inn Fields, London WC2A 3ED (tel 020 7583 2000, fax 020 7583 0118)

GRUEBEL-LEE, David Mark; s of Harry Gruebel-Lee (d 1959), of Johannesburg, South Africa; *b* 20 March 1933; *Educ* Parktown HS, Univ of the Witwatersrand (MB BCh); *m* 14 April 1957, Lydia Deborah (d 2002), da of Leonard Yule (d 1941), of Johannesburg, South Africa; 1 s (Leonard b 1958), 2 da (Caroline b 1961 d 1984, Elizabeth b 1969); *Career* jr appts in orthopaedic surgery: St Mary's Hosp 1960–63, The London Hosp 1963–65; sr registrar St Thomas' Hosp 1965–70, orthopaedic surgn to Albert Einstein Coll of Med Bronx NY 1967; hon conslt orthopaedic surgn Frimley Park Hosp Tst; FBOA, FRCS, FRCSEd; *Books* Disorders Of The Lumbar Spine (1978), Disorders Of The Foot (1980), Disorders Of The Hip (1983); *Recreations* sailing, photography, pottery; *Style*— David Gruebel-Lee, Esq; ✉ Woodburn, 2 Middle Bourne Lane, Farnham, Surrey GU10 3ND; Private Consulting Room, Aldershot NHS Outpatient Department, Cambridge Military Hospital, Hospital Road, Aldershot, Hampshire (e-mail david.gruebellee@btconnect.com)

GRUENBERG, Erich; OBE (1994); *b* Vienna; *Educ* Jerusalem Conservatoire; *Career* violinist; concertmaster Stockholm Philharmonic Orch 1956–58; leader: LSO 1962–65, Royal Philharmonic Orch 1972–76, London Ensemble 1975–82; prof Royal Acad of Music, formerly prof Royal Coll of Music and Guildhall Sch of Music; chm of jury Yehudi Menuhin Int Competition for Young Violinists 1997–2002, involved in int masterclasses and juries worldwide; chm of tstees Hattori Fndn for Young Musicians; played with orchs incl: all major Br orchs, Sydney Symphony, Melbourne Symphony, Hungarian State Symphony; toured in: USA, Canada, S America, Aust, Holland, Germany, Spain, Italy, Scandinavia, Switzerland, USSR, Hungary, Far East; winner Carl Flesch Int Violin Competition; cmmnd numerous new works and given first performances incl: David Morgan Violin Concerto (with the Royal Philharmonic Orch and Sir Charles Groves, Royal Festival Hall) 1975, John McCabe Violin Concerto No 2 (cmmnd, performed with the City of Birmingham Symphony Orch and Chris Seaman) 1979, John Mayer's Sangit (cmmnd, performed with Bournemouth Symphony Orch) 1980 and Ragamalika for Violin and Tambura (cmmnd, performed Cheltenham Festival) 1989, Robin Holloway's Romanza (Promenade Concert, with Simon Rattle) 1982; Hon RAM, FGSM, FRCM; *Recordings* incl: Beethoven Violin Concerto (with the Philharmonia and Jascha Horenstein), Kreisler Pieces (also with the Philharmonia), Complete Beethoven Violin and Piano Sonatas (first recording by a Br artist), various works by Bach, Stravinsky, Messiaen, Durkó, Parry, Reizenstein and Vaughan-Williams; *Style*— Erich Gruenberg, Esq, OBE; ✉ 22 Spencer Drive, Hampstead Garden Suburb, London N2 0QX (tel and fax 020 8455 4360)

GRUFFUDD, Ioan; *b* 6 October 1973, Cardiff; *Educ* RADA; *Career* actor; *Theatre* incl The Decameron (Gate Theatre), That Play Wot I Wrote (The Right Size, Wyndhams); *Television* incl: Austin, Pobol Y Cwm, William Jones, A Relative Stranger, Poldark, Hornblower (voted Best Actor in a Drama Series Biarritz Int TV Festival 1999), Great Expectations, Love in the 21st Century, Warriors, Hornblower II, Man and Boy, The Forsythe Saga, Hornblower III, Century City; *Film* incl: Wilde 1997, Titanic 1997, Solomon and Gaenor 1999, Very Annie Mary 1999, Another Life 1999, Shooters 2000, 102 Dalmations 2000, Happy Now? 2001, Black Hawk Down 2001, The Gathering 2001, This Girl's Life 2003, King Arthur 2004, Fantastic Four 2005; *Style*— Ioan Gruffudd, Esq; ✉ c/o Hamilton Hodell Ltd, 5th Floor, 66–68 Margaret Street, London W1W 8SR

GRUNDY, Rev Canon Malcolm Leslie; s of Arthur James Grundy (d 1993), and Gertrude Alice, *née* Carter (d 1995); *Educ* Sandye Place Sch, Mander Coll Bedford, King's Coll London (AKC), Open Univ (BA); *m* 1972, Wendy Elizabeth, da of Stanley Gibson (d 1977); 1 s (Stephen James b 1973); *Career* architectural asst Bedford BC 1959–63, Community Serv Vols 1963–64, King's Coll London 1964–69, curate Doncaster Parish Church 1969–72, chaplain then sr chaplain Sheffield Industrial Mission 1972–80, dir of educn and community Dio of London 1980–86, team rector of Huntingdon 1986–91, hon canon of Ely 1987–94, dir Avec 1991–94, archdeacon of Craven (Dio of Bradford) 1994–2005, canon emeritus Bradford 2005–, dir Fndn for Church Leadership 2005–; co-fndr: Edward King Inst for Miny Devpt, MODEM (chair 1999–2004); fndr ed Ministry jl 1986–; *Books* Light in the City (1990), An Unholy Conspiracy (1992), Community Work (1995), The Parchmore Partnership (ed, 1995), Management and Ministry (1996), Understanding Congregations (1998), Faith On the Way (with Peter Ball, 2000), What They Don't Teach You at Theological College (2003), What's New in Church Leadership? (2007); *Recreations* classic cars, gardening; *Style*— The Rev Canon Malcolm Grundy; ✉ 4 Portal Road, York YO26 6BQ (tel 01904 787387, e-mail director@churchleadershipfoundation.org)

GRUNDY, (James) Milton; s of Edward Kelvin Grundy (d 1958), of St Helens, Merseyside, and May Lilian, *née* Cobham (d 1980); *b* 13 June 1926; *Educ* Cowley Sch St Helens, Sedbergh, Gonville & Caius Coll Cambridge (MA); *Career* called to the Bar Inner Temple 1954, head of chambers; fndr and chm Gemini Tst for the Arts 1959–66, fndr memb and pres Int Tax Planning Assoc 1975–, fndr and chm Milton Grundy Fndn (formerly Warwick Arts Tst) 1978–, charter memb Peggy Guggenheim Collection 1980–89, chm Int Mgmnt Tst 1986–96, tstee Nat Museums and Galleries of Merseyside 1987–96; *Books* Tax and the Family Company (1956, 3 edn 1966), Offshore Business Centres (1968, 7 edn 1997), Venice (1971, 5 edn 1998), The World of International Tax Planning (1984), Mediterranean Vernacular (with V I Atroshenko, 1991), Asset Protection Trusts (with J Briggs and J Field, 3 edn 1997), Essays in International Tax Planning (2001); *Recreations* conversation; *Style*— Milton Grundy, Esq; ✉ Gray's Inn Chambers, Gray's Inn, London WC1R 5JA

GRUNDY, Stuart; s of Clifford Grundy (d 1981), of Doncaster, S Yorks, and Freda, *née* Clark; *b* 8 November 1938; *Educ* Doncaster GS, RADA; *m* 31 Aug 1963, Ann Patricia Dorothy, da of Col Harry T Stanley, MBE; 2 s (Julian Henry John b 8 Oct 1964, Simon Dominic 21 June 1967); *Career* served RAF 1956–60, announcer Br Forces Broadcasting Serv (BFBS) 1960–64, presenter/prodr Radio Luxembourg 1965–67, exec prodr BBC Radio 1 1976–92 (prodr 1967–76), exec prodr The Unique Broadcasting Company Ltd 1992–; prodn credits incl: Nelson Mandela 70th Birthday Concert, Jean Michel Jarre's Destination Docklands, Freddie Mercury Tribute Concert, Sound City concert series 1992–, Radio Acad Festival 1994–97; *Awards* incl: NY International Radio Festival Gold for Best Talk/Interview Prog 1989 (as presenter Three at 30 - Marvin Gaye), Sony Radio Award for Best Outside Broadcast 1989 (as prodr Nelson Mandela Birthday Concert), NY Int Radio Festival Silver for Best Talk/Interview Prog 1990 (as presenter In Dreams - A Tribute to Roy Orbison), Sony Radio Award for Best Popular Music Prog 1993 (as presenter Unsung Heroes), Sony Radio Award for Best Evening Music Prog 1998 (producer), Sony Radio Award Bronze for Best Music Feature 1998 (presenter and producer The Thing About Harry); *Books* Guitar Greats (with John Tobler) 1982, The Record Producers (with John Tobler) 1982; *Recreations* travel, writing, large-scale gardening; *Style*— Stuart Grundy, Esq; ✉ The Unique Broadcasting Company, 50 Lisson Street, London NW1 5DF (tel 020 7402 1011, fax 020 7402 3259)

GRUT, Lennart; *Educ* Loretto, Copenhagen Tech Univ (MSc); *Career* Folmer Anderson Associates Consltg Engineers Copenhagen 1966–68; sr engineer Ove Arup & Partners: London 1968–72, France 1972–75; md Arup France 1975–81, res and devpt dir UNITATA Bhd Malaysia 1981–83, Elga Services Pte Ltd Singapore (mgmnt conslts) 1983–86; Richard Rogers Partnership: dir, md Richard Rogers Gmbh Germany, dir Richard Rogers Japan, IT dir; *Projects* incl: Nantes and Epone shopping centres France, Marseille Airport Masterplan and extension France, Ct of Human Rights Strasbourg France, Bordeaux High Ct France, Potsdamer Platz devpt Berlin Germany, Skylight office and housing devpt Frankfurt Germany, Gifu Virtual Reality Res Centre Japan, new terminal Barajas Airport Madrid Spain, terminal 5 Heathrow Airport London; *Style*— Lennart Grut, Esq; ✉ Richard Rogers Partnership, Thames Wharf, Rainville Road, London W6 9HA

GRUZDYEV, Dmitri; s of Gennady Valyentinovich Gruzdyev, and Ludmilla Stepanovna Oulitina, of St Petersburg, Russia; *b* 27 April 1971; *Educ* Vaganova Acad of Ballet St Petersburg; *m* 1993, Sarah Victoria Arnott Gruzdeva, da of John Marshall; 1 s (Nicolas Alexander Gruzdev b 29 April 2003); *Career* ballet dancer; Kirov 1989–93; English Nat Ballet: jr soloist 1993–95, soloist 1995, sr soloist 1995, princ dancer 1997–; *Recreations* cinema, motorcars, travelling; *Style*— Dmitri Gruzdyev, Esq; ✉ English National Ballet, 39 Jay Mews, London SW7 2ES (tel 020 8581 1245, fax 020 7225 0827)

GRYK, Wesley Casimir; s of Wesley Casimir Gryk, Sr (d 2001), and Bernice Bieluch Gryk (d 1993); *b* 12 May 1949, Manchester, CT; *Educ* East Catholic HS Manchester CT, Harvard Coll (BA), Warsaw Univ (Fulbright fell), Harvard Law Sch (JD); *Partner* Dr Oliver Davis; *Career* slr; memb NYC Bar; judicial clerk to Hon Constance Baker Motley (US district judge Manhattan NY) 1975–76, with Shearman and Sterling NY and Hong Kong 1976–80, dep rep and legal advsr to UNHCR 1980–81, dep legal advsr then dep head of the research dept Int Secretariat Amnesty Int 1981–86, slr B M Birnberg and Co 1988–94, fndr and ptnr Wesley Gryk Slrs LLP 1995–; memb Cncl Law Soc; former memb Bd: Refugee Legal Centre, Redress Tst, Legal Aid Practitioners Gp; travelled extensively on int human rights missions; fndr and vol UK Lesbian and Gay Immigration Gp; *Publications* AIDS: A Guide to the Law (1990), Advising Gay and Lesbian Clients (1999), Advising Clients with HIV and AIDS (2000); *Recreations* dancing, reading, travel; *Style*—

Wesley Gryk, Esq; ✉ 4 The Lycée, 1 Stannary Street, London SE11 4AD (tel 020 7735 2444, e-mail wesley.gryk@btinternet.com); Wesley Gryk Solicitors LLP, 140 Lower Marsh, London SE1 7AE (tel 020 7401 6887, fax 020 7261 9985, mobile 07789 483812, e-mail wesley@gryklaw.com)

GRYLLS, Bear; s of Sir Michael Grylls (d 2001), and Lady Grylls; *b* 7 June 1974; *Educ* Eton, Birkbeck Coll London; *m* 2000, Shara, *née* Cannings Knight; 2 s (Jesse b 10 June 2003, Marmaduke b 6 April 2006); *Career* served E Sqdn 21 SAS Regt; youngest Br climber to reach summit of Mt Ama Dablam 1997, youngest Br climber to reach summit of Mt Everest 1998, motivational speaker, expdn ldr and TV personality 1998– (perfs incl: Oxford Union, RGS, Explorers Club, Scotland Yard, face of Sure for Men deodorant TV commercials), ldr Arnold & Son Trans Atlantic Arctic expdn 2003; nominated Boardman Tasker Mountain Literature Award 2000; ambass Prince's Tst; presenter: Escape to the Legion (series, Channel 4) 2005, Man vs Wild (series, Discovery Channel), Born Survivor: Bear Grylls (series, Channel 4); Hon Lt Cdr RN; *Books* Facing Up (2000), The Kid Who Climbed Everest (2001), Facing the Frozen Ocean (2004, shortlisted Sports Book of the Year), Born Survivor (Sunday Times Top 10 bestseller); *Recreations* climbing, sailing, martial arts, yoga, skydiving, piano and guitar, my wife Shara and our Welsh island hideaway; *Clubs* SAS Regt Assoc, Alpine, RGS; *Style*— Bear Grylls, Esq; ✉ website www.beargrylls.com

GRYLLS, Prof Vaughan Frederick; s of late Herman Francis Grylls, and late Muriel Doris, *née* Butler; *b* 10 December 1943; *Educ* Newark Magnus GS, Slade Sch of Fine Art, UCL; *m* Polly Powell, *qv*; 2 da (Sarah, Hattie), 1 s (George); *Career* lectr Univ of Reading 1970–71, lectr Homerton Coll Cambridge 1971–73, sr lectr Roehampton Inst 1974–84, prof Williams Coll Mass 1984–88, prof and dean of Sch of Art and Design Univ of Wolverhampton 1989–96, dir and chief exec Kent Inst of Art and Design 1996–2005, retired as founding chief exec Univ Coll for the Creative Arts at Canterbury, Epsom, Farnham, Maidstone and Rochester 2005 (prof emeritus 2006); chair UK Arts and Design Insts Assoc (UKADIA), chair Higher Educn Kent & Medway (HEKAM) 2000–05, dir Higher Educn and Research Opportunites (HERO) 2000–05, memb Exec Ctee Standing Conference of Principals (SCOP) 2005 (memb Mgmnt Ctee 1997–2005); memb: Rochester Cathedral Fabric Advsy Ctee 1998–, Rochester Cathedral Cncl 2001–, Rochester Cathedral Chapter 2005–; FRSA 1995; *Exhibitions* numerous since 1970 in UK, Europe and USA incl: ICA, Whitechapel, Arnolfini, Photographers' Gallery London *Public Collections* Polaroid Inc, Unilever, Pfizer, Welsh Arts Cncl, Nat Museum of Photography, Film and Television, Contemporary Arts Soc; *Clubs* Chelsea Arts; *Style*— Prof Vaughan Grylls; ✉ 46 Wilmington Square, London WC1X 0ED (tel 020 7837 1073, e-mail vaughangrylls@yahoo.co.uk); Uphousden, Westmarsh, Canterbury, Kent CT3 2LN (tel 01304 812 840)

GUARD, Howard Anthony; s of Herbert William Guard, of Seaford, E Sussex, and Lilian Maud Guard (d 1995); *b* 27 February 1946; *Educ* Ardingly, Univ of Leeds (BA); *m* 1972, Sheila Kathleen, da of Reginald Hyder; 4 s (Thomas Benjamin b 1973, Charles William b 1975, Edward Oliver b 1979, George Henry Hubert b 1982); *Career* asst dir in feature films 1968–73, prodr working in advtg industry 1973–77, fndr Howard Guard Productions (making advtg films and documentaries) 1977–; dir Eton at Work 1995; recipient of various indust awards; tstee Nat Hosp Fndn of Neurosurgery London, chm St Albans Cathedral Fabric Tst 2007, chm Sch of Film Advsy Ctee Univ of Herts 2007; High Sheriff Herts 2007–08; Freeman City of London 1995, Liveryman Worshipful Co of Barber-Surgns; *Style*— Howard Guard, Esq; ✉ Netherwylde Farm, Radlett, Hertfordshire WD7 7HS

GUBBINS, Prof David; s of Albert Edmund Gubbins (d 1964), and Joyce Lucy Gubbins (d 1994); *b* 31 May 1947; *Educ* King Edward VI GS Southampton (fndn scholar), Trinity Coll Cambridge (exhibitioner, BA), Univ of Cambridge (PhD); *m* 20 May 1972, Margaret Stella, da of James Francis McCloy; 1 s (Matthew Jonathan b 5 Aug 1975), 2 da (Katherine Joyce b 6 April 1977, Clare Margaret b 1 Sept 1981); *Career* visiting research fell Univ of Colorado 1972–73, instr in applied mathematics MIT 1973–74, postdoctoral research asst and pt/t adjunct asst prof UCLA 1974–76; Univ of Cambridge: postdoctoral research asst Dept of Geodesy and Geophysics 1976–77, sr assoc in research Dept of Geodesy and Geophysics 1977–81, fell Churchill Coll and lectr in mathematics for natural sci 1978–90, asst dir of research Dept of Earth Sci 1981–89; Univ of Leeds: prof of geophysics Dept of Earth Sci 1989–2000, head of Geophysics 1989–2000 res prof of earth sci 2000–; pres Studies of the Earth's Deep Interior 1999–2003; Cecil and Ida Green Scholar: Inst of Geophysics and Planetary Physics, Scipps Inst Oceanry 2000–2001; memb: Royal Astronomical Soc 1972–, Soc of Exploration Geophysicists 1992–; Murchison Medal Geological Soc 1999, Gold Medal Royal Astronomical Soc 2003, John Adam Fleming Medal American Geophysical Union 2004; foreign memb Norwegian Acad of Sci and Letters 2005; fell American Geophysical Union (FAGU) 1985 (memb 1972), FInstP 1996; FRS 1996; *Books* Seismology & Plate Tectonics (1990), Time Series Analysis and Inverse Theory for Geophysicists (2004); *Recreations* swimming, sailing; *Clubs* Wigtown Bay Sailing; *Style*— Prof David Gubbins, FRS; ✉ School of Earth and Environment, University of Leeds, Leeds LS2 9JT (tel 0113 343 5255, fax 0113 343 5259, e-mail gubbins@earth.leeds.ac.uk)

GUBERT, Walter Alexander; *b* 15 June 1947; *Educ* Univ of Florence (LLD), INSEAD (MBA); *m* Caroline, *née* Espagno; 2 da (Amelie b 9 Feb 1979, Elsa b 6 June 1981); *Career* J P Morgan: asst vice-pres Chemicals Analyst Paris 1973–77, vice-pres Treasy Mgmnt Advsy London 1977–81, sr vice-pres Capital Markets NY 1981–87, chief exec J P Morgan Securities Ltd London 1987–90, chm London Mgmnt Ctee 1989–92, head M&A Europe 1989–92, md and co-head Investment Banking EMEA 1992–95, sr exec EMEA 1995–97, vice-chm 1998–2000, global head Investment Banking 1998–2000, vice-chm JPMorgan Chase & Co 1998–, chm J P Morgan Investment Bank 2001–04, chm JPMorgan Chase EMEA 2004–; memb Bd of Govrs South Bank Centre 2005–; *Recreations* golf, tennis, sailing; *Clubs* Wisley, Queenwood; *Style*— Walter Gubert, Esq; ✉ JPMorgan Chase, 10 Aldermanbury, London EC2V 7RF (tel 020 7325 5087)

GUDKA, Naresh Zaverchand; s of Zaverchand Gosar, of Nairobi, Kenya, and Jiviben Zaverchand (d 1945); *b* 13 January 1942; *Educ* Duke of Gloucester Sch Nairobi, Balham and Tooting Coll of Commerce; *m* 1 April 1967, Catherine Elizabeth, da of Michael Charles Tynan (d 1951), of Limerick; 2 da (Rita Claire b 13 Feb 1968, Michelle Christine b 11 Feb 1971); *Career* articled clerk Leslie Furneaux & Co 1961–66, qualified CA 1966, Peat Marwick McLintock 1967–68, J & A Scrimgeour & Co 1968–74, Quilter Goodison & Co 1974–82, Citicorp Scrimgeour Vickers & Co 1982–89, Paribas Capital Markets Group 1989–96, Albert E Sharp 1996–98, dir English Trust Company Ltd 1998–99; FCA 1967; *Recreations* gardening, sports; *Clubs* MCC; *Style*— Naresh Gudka, Esq; ✉ 2 Aston Avenue, Kenton, Middlesex HA3 0DB (tel 020 8907 3226)

GUENIER, Robin Wyatt; s of Frank Wyatt Guenier, and Hilda Eileen Guenier; *b* 6 August 1936; *Educ* Manchester Grammar, St John's Coll Oxford (MA); *m* 1960, Mary Kate, *née* Goodsman; 3 da; *Career* Nat Serv infantry (active serv); called to the Bar Gray's Inn 1963; various legal and co sec appts, chief exec of various high-tech businesses 1960–95, dir Guenier Ltd (business consultancy) 1995–; assignments incl: chief exec Central Computer and Telecommunications Agency (IT orgn reporting to Cabinet Office), exec dir Taskforce 2000; current assignments incl chm Medix UK plc 1999–; writer and speaker on impact of computing technology on society at beginning of twenty-first century; voted IT Personality of the Year Computer Weekly 1998, Award for Outstanding Contribution to the Industry Computing Awards 1999; Liveryman Worshipful Co of Information Technologists 2003; *Recreations* the arts, the countryside, painting; *Style*— Robin Guenier, Esq; ✉ Cherry Tree Cottage, Gustard Wood, St Albans, Hertfordshire AL4 8LA (tel 01582 832110, fax 01582 832827, e-mail rg@guenier.com)

GUEST ALBERT, Revel Sarah; da of Hon Oscar Guest (d 1958), of Hereford, and Susan Kathleen, *née* Paterson (d 1982); *b* 14 September 1931; *Educ* Bedgebury Pk Sch, LSE; *m* 26 Aug 1963, Robert Alan Albert, s of James Albert, of Boston, USA; 1 s (Justin Thomas b 19 Feb 1965), 1 da (Corisande Charlotte b 10 March 1967); *Career* private sec to ldr Lib Pty (Jo Grimond) 1949–51, contested Gen Election and LCC 1951 and 1952, asst ed Time & Tide magazine 1953–55, researcher and prodr Panorama (BBC) 1961–67, bureau chief Public TV Laboratory of US 1967 and 1968, formed Transatlantic Films 1968; prodr and dir 1968–; work incl: Horse Tales, Science of Love, Extreme Body Parts, Trailblazers, The Three Gorges Dam, Treasures of the Yangtse River, Horse Tales, History's Turning Points I & II, Greek Fire, The Horse in Sport, The Monastery of Mount Sinai, A Year in the Life of Placido Domingo, Four American Composers, In Search of Paradise, Paris Lost, Feliks Topolski, Self Encounter - Man in a Fog, Bold as Brass, If It Moves Shoot It, Makin' It, Norman Mailer v Fun City USA; chm Hay on Wye Literary Festival 1997–; MRTS; *Books* Lady Charlotte - A Biography of the Nineteenth Century (1989), History's Turning Points (1995); *Recreations* horse training, gardening; *Clubs* Turf; *Style*— Mrs Revel Guest Albert; ✉ Cabalva House, Whitney-on-Wye, Hereford HR3 6EX (tel 01497 831232, fax 01497 831677, mobile 07971 807724, e-mail guest.albert@cabalva.com)

GUEST GORNALL, Anthony Richard; s of Dr Richard Guest Gornall, and Emma Mildred, *née* Jackson; *Educ* Malvern Coll, Hertford Coll Oxford; *m* 1962, Judith, *née* Redmond, da of Dr Aidan Redmond, of London; 1 da (Lucy), 1 s (Richard); *Career* Cassell & Co Publishers 1960–62, Hutchinson & Co Publishers 1962–65, co-fndr Intercontinental Literary Agency 1965; hereditary memb Preston Guild; *Recreations* golf (winner Sunningdale Fndrs Singles 1994), reading, music, gardening; *Clubs* Oxford and Cambridge, Cheshire Pitt, Sunningdale Golf; *Style*— Anthony Guest Gornall, Esq; ✉ Ridge Mount Cottage, Sunningdale, Berkshire SL5 9RW (tel 01344 623626, fax 01344 876283, e-mail anthony@ridgeascot.fsworld.co.uk); c/o Intercontinental Literary Agency, Centric House, 391 Strand, London WC2R 0LT

GUEST, Dr Ann Hutchinson; da of Robert Hare Hutchinson (d 1975), of West Redding, CT, and Delia Farley, *née* Dana (d 1989); *b* 3 November 1918; *m* 20 Jan 1962, Ivor Forbes Guest, s of Cecil Marmaduke Guest (d 1954), of Bickley, Kent; *Career* dancer in a series of successful musicals NY USA 1942–50; dance notator: Ballet Jooss 1938–39, NY City Ballet 1948–61; Dance Notation Bureau New York: fndr 1940, dir 1941–61, hon pres 1961–; fndr memb Int Cncl Kinetography Laban (pres 1985), fndr and dir Language of Dance Centre 1967–, fndr pres Language of Dance Center USA 1997–; dance reconstructor: Cachucha (Royal Ballet, Ballet for All 1967, Vienna Staatsoper 1969), Pas de Six, La Vivandière (Joffrey Ballet 1977, Sadler's Wells Royal Ballet 1982, St Petersburg State Academic Ballet 1992, Zürich Ballet 1993), L'Après-midi d'un faune (San Carlo Ballet Naples, Grands Ballets Canadiens, Juilliard Dance Ensemble 1989, Zürich Ballet 1993, Berlin Staatsoper 1996, London Royal Ballet 2000 and 2004); Hon LHD Marygrove Coll Detroit Univ 1977, Hon DHu Ohio State Univ 1987; *Books* Labanotation (1954, 1970, 2005), Your Move (1983), Dance Notation (1984), Choreo-Graphics (1989), Nijinsky's Faune Restored (1991), Advanced Labanotation (series, 1991–2003); *Recreations* photography; *Style*— Dr Ann Guest; ✉ 17 Holland Park, London W11 3TD (tel 020 7229 3780, fax 020 7792 1794)

GUEST, Prof Anthony Gordon; CBE (1989), QC (1987); s of Gordon Walter Leslie Guest (d 1982), and Alice Marjorie, *née* Hooper (d 1995), of Maidencombe, Devon; *b* 8 February 1930; *Educ* Colston's Sch Bristol, St John's Coll Oxford (MA); *Career* Lt RA (reg Army and TA) 1948–50; called to the Bar Gray's Inn 1956 (bencher 1978); memb Lord Chllr's Law Reform Ctee 1963–84, UK delg to UN Cmmn on Int Trade Law 1968–88; dean UC Oxford 1963–64 (fell and praelector 1955–65), prof of English law Univ of London 1966–97, reader in common law Cncl of Legal Educn (Inns of Court) 1967–80; visiting prof Univ of Leuven Kortrijk 2004–05; memb Bd of Govrs Rugby Sch 1968–88; FKC 1982, FCIArb 1986, FBA 1993, FRSA 2004; *Books* Anson's Law of Contract (21–26 edns, 1959–84), The Law of Hire-Purchase (1966), Chitty on Contracts (gen ed, 23–29 edns 1968–2004), Benjamin's Sale of Goods (gen ed 1–7 edns 1974–2006), Encyclopaedia of Consumer Credit (jt ed, 1975), Chalmers and Guest on Bills of Exchange (ed 14–16 edns, 1991–2005), Only Remember Me (anthology, 1993); *Clubs* Garrick; *Style*— Prof Anthony Guest, CBE, QC; ✉ 17 Ranelagh Grove, London SW1W 8PA (tel 020 7730 2799, fax 020 7259 0770, e-mail blackright@aol.com)

GUEST, Melville Richard John; OBE (2007); s of Sqdn Ldr Ernest Melville Charles Guest, DSO, DFC (d 1943), and Katherine Mary, *née* Hustler (d 1997); *b* 18 November 1943; *Educ* Rugby, Magdalen Coll Oxford (MA); *m* 23 May 1970, (Beatriz Eugenia) Jenny, da of Horacio Alberto Lopez Colombres; 4 s (Edward, Benjamin, Alexander, William); *Career* entered FCO 1966, Tokyo 1967–72, private sec to Parly Under Sec FCO 1972–75, first sec commercial Paris 1975–79, FCO 1979–80; md Lucas France SA and dir Thomson-Lucas SA 1980–85, dir Channel Tunnel Group 1985–86; commercial cnsllr Br Embassy Tokyo 1986–89, cnsllr (political) and consul-gen Stockholm 1990–93, head S Pacific Dept FCO 1993–94, head SE Asian Dept 1994–96; chief exec Asia House 1996–2002; exec dir: UK-Korea Forum for the Future 1999–2007, UK-Japan 21st Century Gp 2001–; rapporteur UK-India Round Table 2000–; memb Advsy Governing Body Ampleforth Coll 1989–96, sr advsr corporate and external affrs Imperial Coll London; *Style*— Mr Melville Guest, OBE; ✉ e-mail melvilleguest@hotmail.com

GUGGENHEIM, John Michael; s of Michael Guggenheim, and Marjorie, *née* Horsfall; *b* 26 December 1967, Wakefield, W Yorks; *Educ* Bradford GS, Univ of Hull (LLB), Chester Law Sch; *m* 6 March 1999, Alison, *née* Balding; 2 da (Isobel Grace b 8 Feb 2003, Hannah Rose b 23 April 2005); *Career* admitted slr of Supreme Court 1994; Walker Morris: joined 1992, ptnr 2000–; *Recreations* music, football, golf; *Style*— John Guggenheim, Esq; ✉ Walker Morris, Kings Court, 12 King Street, Leeds LS1 2HL

GUI, Gerald P H; s of Col George P C Gui, and Lily M F Gui; *b* 8 June 1962; *Educ* St Bees Sch Cumbria, UCL and Middx Hosp Med Sch London (MB BS, Suckling Prize in neurosciences, Univ of London Laurels), Univ of London (MS); *m* 8 Sept 1992, Corina R, da of Agustin Espinosa; 2 s (Adrian, Marcus (twins) b 26 May 2004); *Career* house surgn Whittington and Royal Northern Hosps 1986–97, house physician Queen Elizabeth II Hosp Welwyn Garden City 1987; SHO: in A&E Royal Free Hosp Med Sch London 1987–88 (also anatomy demonstrator), in cardiothoracic surgery Harefield Hosp 1988–89, in urology and gen and vascular surgery St George's Hosp London 1989–90; registrar in gen surgery: Basildon Hosp 1990–91 (with orthopaedics 1990), Bart's and Homerton Hosp 1991–92, N Middx Hosp London 1992–93; surgical res fell Professorial Surgical Unit Bart's 1993–94, lectr and sr registrar Univ Dept of Surgery St George's Hosp London 1994–96, sr registrar in gen surgery St Helier's NHS Tst Surrey 1996, conslt surgn and head Breast Diagnostic Unit Royal Marsden NHS Tst 1997–, hon sr lectr Inst of Cancer Res London 1997–, coll tutor RCS 1997–, lead clinician Cromwell Breast Centre Cromwell Hosp London 2001–; Royal Marsden NHS Tst: memb Ctee for Clinical Res, memb Appts Ctee Basic Surgical Trg; memb Teaching Faculty FRCS Course: RCS 1995–, Whipps Cross Hosp 2001–; visiting examiner: Univ of London 2001– (recognised teacher 1998–), St George's Hosp London 2001–; involved with Br Cncl Link Project for devpt of breast cancer servs in Sri Lanka 2000–; conslt advsr Marks & Spencer Health Screen Project 1998–2001, symptomatic breast cancer rep London and Thames region Br Assoc of

G

Surgical Oncology 2001–; delivered numerous oral presentations and invited lectures to symposia and learned societies; chief ed (UK) Women's Oncology Review 2001–, co-ed CME Breast Jl 2001–; memb: BMA 1986–, GMC 1986–, Surgical Res Soc 1994–, Br Assoc of Surgical Oncology 1994–, Br Oncological Assoc 1994–, Br Breast Gp 1998– (memb Membership Ctee 2001–); Surgical Res Soc Travel Award 1993, S Essex Med Educn and Res Tst Award 1993 and 1994, Surgn in Trg Medal RCS(Ed) 1994, Br Oncological Assoc Bursary 1994, RCS Fndn Inc NY Travelling Fellowship 1997 (held at Plastic and Reconstructive Surgery Unit Emory Univ Atlanta); represented Cumbria, UCL and Middx Hosp Med Sch in swimming, rep Univ of London in life saving; pres Univ of London Lifesaving Soc 1985–86 (treas 1981–85), tutor in resuscitation Essex Branch Royal Life Saving Soc 1984; friend ROH; fell Assoc of Surgns of GB and Ireland 1997 (memb 1996); FRCSEd 1990, FRCS 1991; *Publications* Breast Reconstruction: a woman's choice (contrib, 2002); numerous pubns of original work as scientific manuscripts on breast cancer diagnosis, clinical mgmnt, surgery, operative techniques and tumour biology in peer-reviewed jls; *Recreations* classical music, opera, piano, water sports; *Clubs* Royal Nautical (Santa Cruz); *Style*— Gerald Gui, Esq; ✉ Academic Surgery (Breast Unit), The Royal Marsden NHS Trust, Fulham Road, London SW3 6JJ (tel 020 7808 2783, fax 020 7808 2673), 145 Harley Street, London W1G 6BJ (tel 020 7487 5558, fax 020 7487 5559, e-mail ggui@cwcom.net)

GUILBAUD, Patrick; s of Daniel Guilbaud, and Henriette Guilbaud; *b* 22 March 1952; *Educ* Aero Spatial Pont de Levallois; *m* 10 April 1976, Sally, *née* Lloyd Owen; 1 s (Charles b 24 June 1977), 1 da (Emilie b 22 Sept 1981); *Career* chef; Hotel Moderne Caen 1969, Br Embassy Paris 1970–71, Le Doyen Paris 1972, La Maree Paris 1973, Midland Hotel Manchester 1974; chef and owner: Le Rabelais 1976–80, Restaurant Patrick Guilbaud 1981–; winner numerous Irish and European restaurant awards, incl 2 Michelin Stars; memb Restaurant Assoc of Ireland; *Recreations* golf, skiing, boating; *Clubs* Luttrellstown Castle Golf and Country, Royal Dublin Golf, Real Club de Golf Sotogrande; *Style*— Patrick Guilbaud, Esq; ✉ Restaurant Patrick Guilbaud, 21 Upper Merrion Street, Dublin 2, Ireland (tel 00 353 1676 4192, fax 00 353 1661 0052, e-mail rpguilbaud@eircom.net)

GUILD, Prof Elspeth; da of Carman Guild (d 2000), of Toronto, Canada, and Edith Ford Walker (d 1971); *b* 25 June 1954, Toronto, Canada; *Educ* Univ of Nijmegen (PhD); *Career* slr Baileys Shaw & Gillett Slrs 1989–97, ptnr Kingsley Napley Slrs 1997–; prof Law Faculty Univ of Nijmegen 2000–, visiting prof LSE 2003–; memb Cncl Justice; memb Immigration Law Practitioners Assoc; *Publications* Immigration Law in the European Community (2001), Legal Elements of European Identity: EU Citizenship and Migration Law (2004); *Style*— Prof Elspeth Guild; ✉ Kingsley Napley, Knights Quarter, 14 St John's Lane, London EC1M 4AJ (tel 020 7814 1200, fax 020 7490 2288, e-mail eguild@kingsleynapley.co.uk)

GUILD, Ivor Reginald; CBE (1985), WS; s of late Col Arthur Marjoribanks Guild, DSO, TD, DL, and Phyllis Eliza, *née* Cox; *b* 2 April 1924; *Educ* Cargilfield, Rugby, New Coll Oxford, Univ of Edinburgh; *Career* ptnr Shepherd and Wedderburn WS 1950–94, procurator fiscal of Lyon Court 1961–94, clerk to Abbey Court of Holyroodhouse 1970–79, baillie of Abbey Ct 1979–95; chm: Nat Museum of Antiquities Scotland 1981–86, Dunedin Income Growth Investment Trust plc, Dunedin Worldwide Investment Trust plc, The Edinburgh Investment Trust plc 1964–94, New Fulcrum Investment Trust 1977–2005, Scottish Oriental Smaller Companies Trust plc 1995–2005; ed Scottish Genealogist 1959–94; FRSE 1991; *Recreations* golf, genealogy; *Clubs* New (Edinburgh); *Style*— Ivor Guild, Esq, CBE, WS, FRSE; ✉ New Club, 86 Princes Street, Edinburgh EH2 2BB (home tel 0131 220 1085)

GUILD, Rear Adm Nigel Charles Forbes; CB (2003); s of William John Forbes Guild (d 1982), and Joan, *née* Innes (d 1957); *b* 9 February 1949; *Educ* Bryanston, BRNC Dartmouth, Trinity Coll Cambridge (MA), Univ of Bristol (PhD), JSDC Greenwich; *m* 10 July 1971, Felicity Jean, da of Hugh Wilson; 2 s (Allan b 17 Feb 1979, Ian b 25 June 1982); *Career* joined RN 1966; served HMS Tenby, midshipman HMS Intrepid, served HMS Hermes, dep project manager Br Underwater Test and Evaluation Centre Range MOD Kyle of Lochalsh, Weapon Engr HMS Euryalus 1982, served STANAVFORLANT, Cdr DGFMP(N) 1984, Sqdn Weapon Engr IKARA Leanders tour, HMS Beaver Armilla patrol Gulf, Staff Weapons Engr Offr Flag Offr Sea Training, Capt 1990, Mil Asst to Chief of Defence Procurement MOD, Surface Flotilla Weapons Offr Fleet Command, Chief Staff Offr (Engrg) Flag Offr Surface Flotilla, Cdre 1996, dir Combat Systems and Equipments MOD Procurement Exec 1996–98, Dir Integrated Project Teams Smart Procurement Implementation 1998, Rear Adm 2000, Exec Dir 4(XD4) Defence Procurement Agency Exec Bd and Controller of the Navy 2000–03, Sr Responsible Owner Carrier Strike and Chief Naval Engr Offr 2004–; *Recreations* village pantomime, rowing (pres RN and RM ARA); *Style*— Rear Adm Nigel Guild, CB; ✉ Ministry of Defence, Main Building, Whitehall, London SW1A 2HB

GUILDFORD, Bishop of 2004–; Rt Rev Christopher John Hill; s of Leonard Hill (d 1991), and Frances Vera, *née* Bullock; *b* 10 October 1945; *Educ* Sebright Sch, KCL (BD, MTh, Relton Prize for Theol, AKC); *m* 1976, Hilary Ann, da of Geoffrey James Whitehouse; 3 s (Vivian John b 1978, Adrian Hugh b 1982, Edmund James b 1983), 1 da (Felicity Ann b 1980); *Career* ordained: deacon 1969, priest 1970; asst curate Dio of Lichfield: St Michael Tividale 1969–73, St Nicholas Codsall 1973–74; asst chaplain to Archbishop of Canterbury for foreign rels 1974–81, Archbishop's sec for ecumenical affrs 1982–89, hon canon Canterbury Cathedral 1982–89, chaplain to HM The Queen 1987–96, canon residentiary St Paul's Cathedral 1989–96 (precentor 1990–96), bishop of Stafford 1996–2004, hon canon Lichfield Cathedral 1996–2004, Clerk of the Closet 2005–; co-sec Archbishop of Canterbury's Cmmn on Women in the Episcopate 1989–93; Anglican sec: Anglican-RC Int Cmmn (I) 1974–82 and (II) 1983–89, Anglican-Lutheran Euro Cmmn 1981–82, Anglo-German (Meissen) Conversations 1985–88, Anglo-Nordic/Baltic Cmmn 1989–92; Anglican co-chm London Soc for Jews and Christians 1991–96, Anglican chm C of E French Protestant Conversations 1994–98, Anglican co-chm Meissen Theological Conference 1999–; chm: Cathedrals' Precentors Conf 1994–96, Cncl for Christian Unity 2008– (memb 1992–97); memb: London Soc for the Study of Religion 1990–2000, Ecclesiastical Law Soc 1990– (vice-chm 1993–2002, chm 2002–), Legal Advsy Cmmn Gen Synod 1991–, Faith and Order Advsy Gp Gen Synod 1997–98 (vice-chm 1998–2007), House of Bishops and Gen Synod C of E 1999– (memb Gp on Women Bishops 2006), Working Pty on Women in the Episcopate 2001–04, Fees Advsy Cmmn Working Pty 2003, Liturgical Cmmn 2003–06, Clergy Discipline Cmmn 2003–; *Recreations* Radio 3, mountain walking, detective stories, Italian food, unaffordable wine, industrial archaeology, GWR; *Clubs* Nikaean, Athenaeum, Odd Volumes, Nobody's Friends; *Style*— The Rt Rev the Bishop of Guildford; ✉ Willow Grange, Woking Road, Guildford, Surrey GU4 7QS

GUILFORD, 10 Earl of (GB 1752) Piers Edward Brownlow North; also Baron Guilford (E 1683); patron of three livings; s of 9 Earl of Guilford, DL (d 1999); *b* 9 March 1971; *m* 26 March 1994, Michèle C, da of late Gilbert Desvaux de Marigny, of Curepipe, Mauritius, and Mrs Eric Story, of Durban, South Africa; 1 da (Tatiana Grace b 13 Sept 2000), 1 s (Frederick Edward George, Lord North b 24 June 2002); *Heir* s, Lord North; *Style*— The Rt Hon the Earl of Guilford; ✉ Waldershare Park, Dover, Kent CT15 5BA (website www.lordguilford.com)

GUILLE, Ven John Arthur; s of Arthur Leonard Guille (d 1986), of Guernsey, and Winifred Maud, *née* Lane (d 2000); *b* 21 May 1949; *Educ* Guernsey GS, Christ Church Coll Canterbury, Univ of London (CertEd), Salisbury and Wells Theological Coll, Univ of Southampton (CertTheol, BTh); *m* 10 July 1976, Susan; 2 da (Elizabeth Susan b 9 June 1981, Rose Ellen b 27 Feb 1983), 1 s (Peter John b 26 February 1987); *Career* head of religious educn: Stockbridge Co Secdy Sch 1970–72, St Sampsons Secdy Sch Guernsey 1972–73; ordained: deacon 1976, priest 1977; curate Chandlers Ford St Boniface and St Martins 1976–80; priest-in-charge: St John the Evangelist Surrey 1980–84, St Michael and All Angels Bournemouth 1983–84; vicar St John with St Michael 1984–89; chaplain: Talbot Heath Sch for Girls 1980–89, Le Monnaie Chapel 1989–99, Mitchell House/les Bourgs Hospice 1991–99, Local Scout Assoc 1994–99; rector St Andre de la Pommeraye Guernsey 1989–99, vice-dean of Guernsey 1996–99, archdeacon of Basingstoke 1999–2000, residentiary canon of Winchester Cathedral 1999–, archdeacon of Winchester 2000–; deanery vocations offr 1990–99, deanery advsr Miny of Healing and Deliverance Ministries 1990–99; chm Deanery Sunday Sch Assoc 1980–83, E Dorset Cncl of Educn 1983–86, Les Cotils Project Tst 1993–94, Sunflower Tst Bereavement Support Gp 1995–99; hon vice-pres Boys Brigade 1993–99; memb: Winchester Diocesan Cncl of Educn 1978–, Bishops Working Pty for pilgrimage walk for 1079–1979, Exec Ctee Eastleigh & District Cncl of Churches 1976–80, Exec Ctee Bournemouth Cncl of Churches 1980–85, Westcliff Christian Cncl 1985–89, Bishop's Liturgical Ctee 1983–88 (sec 1985–88), Mgmnt Ctee Old Alresford Place Diocesan and Retreat and Conference Centre 1986–89 (chm 2000–), Deanery Standing Ctee 1990–99, Standing Ctee for Winchester Dio 1999–; hosp broadcasting presenter 1977–80, vice-chm St Michaels VC Primary Sch Bournemouth 1983–89, chm St Michael's VC Primary Sch Bournemouth 1988–89, regular contrib BBC Radio Guernsey 1989–99, govr Pilgrim's Sch 1999–; memb: LEA 1990–98, Ladies Coll Bd 1992–98, Guernsey Soc 1967–, Nat Tst, La Société Guernesiaise; *Publications* A Millennium of Archdeacons (2003); *Recreations* gardening, family history; *Style*— The Ven the Archdeacon of Winchester; ✉ 9 The Close, Winchester, Hampshire SO23 9LS (tel 01962 857263, fax 01962 857242, e-mail john.guille@winchester-cathedral.org.uk)

GUILOFF, Prof Roberto Jaime; s of Angel Guiloff-Luder (d 1980), of Chile, and Blanca Eva, *née* Davis; *b* 4 March 1943; *Educ* Instituto Nacional Santiago, Univ of Chile (honour scholar, BSc, LMed Surg, MD, LPhil), LMSSA; *m* 1, 3 Feb 1968 (m dis 1997); 1 s (Claudio b 10 Nov 1968), 1 da (Carolina b 1 May 1972); m 2, 6 April 1999, Dr Heather Angus-Leppan, da of Prof P Angus-Leppan (d 2001), of Australia; 2 da (Vivien b 17 April 1999, Angelica b 27 April 2001), 1 s (David b 13 July 2002); *Career* trg in neurology Univ of Chile Hosp 1967–72, asst prof of neurology Univ of Chile 1972–74, Queen Elizabeth II scholar (Br Cncl) Nat Hosp for Nervous Diseases 1972–73; registrar in neurology: St Thomas' Hosp 1973–74, Nat Hosps 1974–76; sr registrar in neurology Nat Hosp for Nervous Diseases, Royal Free Hosp and King's Coll Hosp 1976–81; conslt neurologist: Westminster and St Stephen's Hosp 1981–89, Westminster and Charing Cross Hosps 1989–93, Charing Cross and Chelsea and Westminster Hosps 1993–; hon conslt neurologist Royal Brompton Hosp London 1993–, hon sr lectr in med (neurology) Imperial Coll Sch of Med at Charing Cross Hosp (Charing Cross and Westminster Med Sch until merger 1997) 1987–; dir: Neuromuscular Unit Charing Cross Hosp 1993–, Motor Neurone Disease Care and Research Centre Charing Cross Hosp 1994–; hon prof of neurology Univ of Chile 2006; sec for int affrs Section of Neurology RSM 1993–2001, sec and treas Motor Neurone Disease Ctee World Fedn of Neurology 1999–2005; hon sec Br Soc for Clinical Neurophysiology 1998–2000; memb: Br Soc for Clinical Neurophysiology 1979, Assoc of Br Neurologists 1981, RSM 1989, Br Peripheral Nerve Soc 2003–; pres: Section of Clinical Neurosciences RSM 2000–2001, W London Medico-Chirurgical Society 2003–2004; FRCP 1987 (MRCP); *Books* Sense Perception in Idealism and The Neurological Theory (1968), Neurological Aspects of Human Retroviruses (contrib chapter, 1992), Motor Neurone Disease (contrib chapter, 1994), Clinical Trials in Neurology (ed, 2001); *Recreations* opera, classical music, tennis, gym; *Clubs* David Lloyd; *Style*— Prof Roberto Guiloff; ✉ Charing Cross Hospital, Fulham Palace Road, London W6 8RF (tel 020 8746 8319, 020 8846 1196, fax 020 8746 8420, e-mail r.guiloff@imperial.ac.uk)

GUILOR, Ralph John; s of John Kenneth Guilor, and Ingeborg Elizabeth, *née* Bambach; *b* 1 January 1955; *Educ* Dartford GS, Portsmouth Sch of Architecture (BArch, DipArch); *m* 1, 1979 (m dis 1990); 1 da (Rachel Elizabeth b 1983), 1 s (Edward Charles b 1985); m 2, 1991 (m dis 1992); m 3, 1995; *Career* architect Ralph Guilor Architects; Civic Tst Award 1986, Cheltenham Civic Tst Award 1986, 1996, 1998, 2000, 2001, 2002 and 2004; RIBA; *Recreations* music, art, sport; *Style*— Ralph Guilor, Esq; ✉ Ralph Guilor Architects, Priory Lawn, Priory Place, Cheltenham, Gloucestershire GL52 6HG (tel 01242 251469, fax 01242 251609, e-mail ralph-guilor@supanet.com)

GUINNESS, (Cecil) Edward; CVO (1986); er s of John Cecil Guinness (d 1970, gs of Richard Samuel Guinness, whose great uncle Arthur was the founder of the family brewing firm), of Clarehaven, Parbold, Lancs; *b* 1924; *Educ* Stowe, Univ of Belfast, Sch of Brewing Birmingham; *m* 1951, Elizabeth Mary Fossett, da of George Alan Thompson (d 1971), of Albrighton Hall, nr Wolverhampton; 3 da (1 of whom decd); *Career* served WWII Offr Cadet RA (invalided out); former vice-chm Guinness Brewing Worldwide; dir: Guinness plc 1971–89 (joined as jr brewer 1945), Wolverhampton and Dudley Breweries 1964–87; chm Harp Lager 1971–87; vice-pres Brewers' Soc (chm 1985–86); chm: UK Tstees Duke of Edinburgh's Cwlth Study Cons 1971–86, Fulmer PC 1973–91 (memb Gerrards Cross with Fulmer PCC 2002–06), Licensed Trade Charities Tst 1981–92, Governing Body Dame Alice Owen's Sch Potters Bar 1981–92, Wine and Spirit Trade's Benevolent Soc 1989–90, Exec Ctee Fulmer Sports and Community Assoc 2003–04; govr and memb Exec Ctee Queen Elizabeth Fndn for Disabled People 1996– (chm Devpt Tst 1993–96); pres: Performing Arts Centre Campaign Dame Alice Owen's Sch 1997–2002, Fulmer Recreation Ground Campaign 2000–03; former pres and memb Exec Ctee Licensed Victuallers Nat Homes (vice-pres 1991–92), memb Governing Body Lister Inst of Preventive Med 1968–2001, selected as original memb Amersham Area Advsy Team Thames Valley Police Authy 1994; Hon Asst Worshipful Co of Brewers (Master 1977–78); life memb Industrial Soc; *Books* The Guinness Book of Guinness (1988); *Recreations* gardening, writing; *Style*— C Edward Guinness, Esq, CVO; ✉ Huyton Fold, Fulmer Village, Buckinghamshire SL3 6HD (tel 01753 663179)

GUINNESS, Lt Cdr Sir Howard Christian Sheldon; kt (1981), VRD (1953); s of Edward Douglas Guinness, CBE (d 1983), by his 1 w, Martha Letière, *née* Sheldon; er bro of Sir John Guinness, CB, *qv*; *b* 3 June 1932; *Educ* Eton; *m* 1958, Evadne, da of Capt Evan Gibbs, Coldstream Gds (n of 1 Baron Wraxall); 1 da (Annabel b 1959), 2 s (Christopher b 1963, Dominic b 1966); *Career* served RNR, Lt Cdr; joined S G Warburg & Co 1955, exec dir 1970–85; dir: Harris & Sheldon GP 1960–81, Quality Milk Producers 1988–, Riyad Bank Europe 1993–; dir and dep chm Youghal Carpets (Hldgs) 1972–80; chm N Hants Cons Assoc 1971–74; Wessex Cons Assoc: vice-chm 1974, chm 1975–78, treas 1978–81; dairy farmer, memb Cncl English Guernsey Cattle Assoc 1963–72; *Clubs* White's; *Style*— Lt Cdr Sir Howard Guinness, VRD; ✉ The Manor House, Glanvilles Wootton, Sherborne, Dorset DT9 5QF

GUINNESS, Jasmine; da of Patrick Guinness, and Liz, *née* Casey; *Educ* Headford Sch Kells Co Meath, St Columbas Coll Dublin, Winchester Sch of Art; *Children* 1 s; *Career* model; first job aged 9, full time aged 19; fndr and organiser Clothesline (exhbn, fashion show and auction) 2000–01; supporter of many charities; *Recreations* horse riding, tennis, reading, photography, teaching son how to play football; *Style*— Miss Jasmine Guinness

GUINNESS, Sir John Ralph Sidney; kt (1999), CB (1985); s of Edward Douglas Guinness, CBE (d 1983), by his 1 w, Martha Letière, *née* Sheldon; yr bro of Lt Cdr Sir Howard

Guinness, VRD, *qv*; *b* 23 December 1935; *Educ* Rugby, Trinity Hall Cambridge; *m* 1967, Valerie, da of Roger North, JP; 1 s, 1 da (and 1 s decd); *Career* Overseas Devpt Inst 1961–62; FO: joined 1962, Economic Relations Dept 1962–63, third sec UK Mission to UN NY 1963–64, seconded to UN Secretariat as special asst to dep under sec (later under sec Econ and Social Affrs) 1964–66, FCO 1967–69, first sec (econ) High Cmmn Ottawa 1969–72, seconded to Central Policy Review Staff (Cabinet Office) 1972–75 and 1977–79, alternate UK rep to Law of the Sea Conf 1975–77; transferred to Home Civil Serv 1980; Dept of Energy: under sec 1980–83, dep sec 1983–91, perm under sec 1991–92; chm British Nuclear Fuels plc 1992–99; chm Trinity Finance Gp Ltd 1999–2003; non-exec dir: Guinness Mahon Holdings plc 1993–99, Ocean Group plc 1993–99, Mithras Investment Trust 1994–2006; tstee Prince's Youth Business Tst 1994–2000; govr Compton Verney House Tst 2000–03; tstee: Royal Collection Tst 2001–07, Nat Maritime Museum 2005–; chm Reviewing Ctee on the Export of Works of Art 1995–2003, chair Expert Panel Heritage Lottery Fund 2005, memb Expert Panel Nat Heritage Memorial Fund 2006–; hon fell Univ of Central Lancashire 1999; *Recreations* iconography; *Clubs* Brooks's, Beefsteak; *Style*— Sir John Guinness, CB; ✉ 12 Hasker Street, London SW3 2LG (tel 020 7823 8657)

GUINNESS, Sir Kenelm Ernest Lee; 4 Bt (UK 1867), of Ashford, Co Galway; s of Kenelm Edward Lee Guinness, MBE, RNVR (d 1937), and Josephine (d 1989), da of Sir Thomas Strangman, sometime Advocate Gen in Bombay; suc unc, Sir Algernon Arthur St Lawrence Lee Guinness, 3 Bt, 1954; *b* 13 December 1928; *Educ* Eton, MIT (BSc); *m* 1961, Mrs Jane Nevin Dickson; 2 s (Kenelm Edward Lee b 1962, Sean St Lawrence Lee b 1966); *Heir* s, Kenelm Guinness; *Career* late 2 Lt RHG; engr Int Bank for Reconstruction and Devpt (World Bank) 1954–75; ind consltg engr 1975–90; memb American Soc of Civil Engrs; *Recreations* sailing; *Clubs* Cruising Club of America; *Style*— Sir Kenelm Guinness, Bt; ✉ Rich Neck, Claiborne, Maryland 21624, USA (tel and fax 00 1 410 745 5079)

GUINNESS, Lucinda Jane (Lulu); OBE (2006); da of Cdr Sir Miles James Rivett-Carnac, Bt, RN, DL, *qv*, of Martyr Worthy Manor, Hants, and April Sally, *née* Villar; *b* 29 May 1960; *Educ* Riddlesworth Hall Diss, Downe House, Queens Gate Sch London, Univ of Cape Town; *m* 11 Nov 1986, Valentine Guy Bryan Guinness, s of 3 Baron Moyne, *qv*; 1 da (Tara Victoria); *Career* handbag designer 1989–; launched career with Lulu Bag (signature briefcase design), subsequently moved into high fashion showing seasonally at The London Design Show and The Coterie NY; numerous stockists worldwide incl London, NY, Paris and Hong Kong; *Recreations* travel, reading, shopping; *Style*— Mrs Lulu Guinness, OBE

GUINNESS, Timothy Whitmore Newton (Tim); s of Capt Eustace Guinness, DSC, RN (d 1980), and Angela Beryl, *née* Hoare (d 1990); *b* 20 June 1947; *Educ* Eton, Magdalene Coll Cambridge (BSc Eng), MIT (MSc); *m* 6 June 1974, Beverley Anne, da of George Mills, of Rotherfield, E Sussex; 2 s (Edward, Harry), 2 da (Mary, Katherine); *Career* Baring Bros & Co Ltd 1970–77, Guinness Mahon & Co 1977–87 (investment dir 1982–87), chief exec Guinness Flight Global Asset Mgmnt Ltd 1987–97, chief exec Guinness Flight Hambro Asset Mgmnt Ltd 1997–98, chm Investec Guinness Flight 1998–2000, chm Investec Asset Mgmnt 2000–03, chm Guinness Atkinson Asset Mgmnt and Guinness Asset Mgmnt 2003–; dir: S R Europe Tst plc 2001–, Investec High Income Tst plc 2001–; chm: Brompton Bicycle Co Ltd 2000–, New Boathouse Capital 2001–, Atlantic Japan Growth Fund Ltd 2002–; memb Ct of Assts Worshipful Co of Grocers; *Recreations* sailing, skiing, riding, walking; *Clubs* Travellers, MCC, Royal Yacht Sqdn, City Univ; *Style*— Tim Guinness, Esq

GUINNESS ASCHAN, Marit Victoria; da of Henry Samuel Howard Guinness (d 1975), of Chelsea, London, and Alfhild Holter (d 1983); *b* London; *Educ* PNEU, art schs in Munich, Florence and Paris; *m* (m dis 1963), Carl William Aschan, s of Judge Nils Aschan (d 1966), of Stockholm, Sweden; 1 s (David), 1 da (Juliet); *Career* Nat Serv MOI 1940–45; enamellist, painter and jeweller; individual exhbns incl: Beaux Arts Gallery London 1948, Van Diemen Lilienfield Galleries NY 1949, 1955, 1957, 1959, 1962, 1966 and 1968, Leicester Galleries (the leading avant-garde art gallery of the day) 1962, 1964, 1967 and 1971, Inter Art Gallery Caracas 1973, Galleri Galtung Oslo 1974, 1981, 1984, 1990, 1991, 1993, 1994, 1996, 1998 and 2000, Galleri J Kraus Paris 1977, Roy Miles Gallery London 1979, Saga Gallery London 1990, Benney London 1996, Treasures of the 20th Century (Worshipful Co of Goldsmiths) London 2000, Tiaras (millennium exhbn, Museum of Fine Arts Boston USA) 2000; cmmns and collections in England incl: V&A, Worshipful Co of Goldsmiths London, Focal Point on the Cross for the High Altar Exeter Cathedral, J R Abbey Collection, Hugo and Reine Pitman Collection, Paul Oppé Collection, Royal Norwegian Embassy Collection, Iliffe Collection, John Studzinski Collection; in Norway: HM the late King Olav V of Norway, HM The Queen of Norway, Kunstindustrimuseet Oslo, Hans Rasmus Astrup Collection; in USA: Brooklyn Museum NY, Yale Univ Art Gallery, Nelson Gallery and Atkins Museum Kansas, New Orleans Museum of Art, North Carolina Museum of Art Raleigh, Ian Woodner Family Collection New York, Beal Fndn Collection Boston Mass, Martin and Els Wyler Collection Switzerland, Madame Jacques Koerfer Collection Switzerland, Boston Museum of Fine Arts, Arts Inst Club Chicago; work in numerous other private collections worldwide; memb Chelsea Arts Club 1967, pres Artist Enamellers 1969–90; *Books* incl: Modern Jewellery (1963), The Art of Jewellery (1968), Enamels (ed, 1983), Marit Guinness Aschan - Enamellist of Our Time (biog by Graham Hughes, 1995); *Recreations* travelling; *Clubs* Chelsea Arts; *Style*— Mrs Marit Guinness Aschan; ✉ 25 Chelsea Park Gardens, London SW3 6AF (tel 020 7352 2562); Studios 3 and 4, Moravian Close, 381 King's Road, London SW10 0LP (tel 020 7352 3790 and 020 7352 8710)

GULBENKIAN, Boghos Parsegh (Paul); s of Krikor Parsegh Gulbenkian (d 1968), of Beaulieu, Hants, and Vergine Gulbenkian (d 1965); *b* 23 March 1940; *Educ* KCS Wimbledon, LSE (LLB); *m* 1; 1 da (Vergine b 24 Nov 1968); m 2, 1 da (Sylvia b 27 July 1972); m 3, 15 Dec 1990, Jacqueline, da of late Bedros Chamlian; *Career* admitted slr 1965; ptnr Isadore Goldman 1970–89, sr ptnr Gulbenkian Harris Andonian and Isadore Goldman 1989–2005, sr ptnr Gulbenkian Andonian 2005–; asst recorder 1992–98, recorder 1998–2005; pt/t immigration adjudicator 1989–2005, immigration judge 2005–; asst cmmr to the Boundary Cmmn for England and Wales 2000–; chm Serv Mgmnt Ctee Camden CAB 1978–83, pres Holborn Law Soc 1984–85, memb Legal Aid Appeal Panel 1984–89; fndr memb: Slrs' Family Law Assoc, Immigration Law Practitioners' Assoc, Euro Immigration Lawyers' Gp (pres), Cncl of Immigration Judges; memb Int Assoc of Refugee Law Judges; hon pres: Armenian Church of St Sarkis, Apcar Tst, Benlian Tst, Essefian Tst; tstee: St Sarkis Charity Tst (hon chm 2005–), various tsts for benefit of Armenian Community; memb Law Soc 1961 (hon auditor 1988–89); hon consul (legal affairs) Embassy of the Republic of Armenia 1998–; Freeman City of London 2001; FRSA; *Recreations* music, tennis, squash, walking; *Style*— Paul Gulbenkian, Esq; ✉ Gulbenkian Andonian, Sicilian House, Sicilian Avenue, London WC1A 2QH (tel 020 7269 9590)

GULL, Prof Keith; CBE (2004); s of David Gull, and Doris, *née* Manging; *b* 29 May 1948, Middlesbrough; *Educ* Eston GS, Queen Elizabeth Coll London (BSc, PhD); *m* 1972, Dianne Hilary Leonora, *née* Elgar; 1 s (David Graeme), 1 da (Hannah Ruth); *Career* lectr, reader and prof Univ of Kent 1972–89, prof, research dean and head of dept Sch of Biological Sciences Univ of Manchester 1989–2002, Wellcome Tst princ research fell Sir William Dunn Sch of Pathology and prof of molecular microbiology Univ of Oxford 2002–, sr research fell Lincoln Coll Oxford 2002–; visiting fell Sandoz Forschungsinstitut Vienna 1978, visiting prof McArdle Lab for Cancer Research Univ of Wisconsin Madison 1982–83; chair Research Awards Advsy Ctee Leverhulme Tst, tstee Cancer Research UK; author of over 200 scientific pubns; FMedSci 1999, FRS 2003; *Recreations* fly fishing, painting; *Style*— Prof Keith Gull, CBE; ✉ Stonehaven, 6 High Street, Cumnor, Oxford OX2 9PE (tel 01865 864210); Sir William Dunn School of Pathology, University of Oxford, South Parks Road, Oxford OX1 3RE (tel 01865 285455, fax 01865 285691, e-mail keith.gull@path.ox.ac.uk)

GULL, Sir Rupert William Cameron; 5 Bt (UK 1872), of Brook Street; s of Sir Michael Swinnerton Cameron Gull, 4 Bt (d 1989), and his 1 w, Yvonne, *née* Heslop; *b* 14 July 1954; *Educ* Diocesan Coll Cape Town, Univ of Cape Town; *m* 1980, Gillian Lee, da of Robert Howard Gordon MacFarlaine; 3 da (Victoria Yvonne b 3 Oct 1984, Katie Alexandra b 9 Dec 1986, Olivia Leigh b 2 Dec 1992); *Heir* hp, cous, Angus Gull; *Clubs* Western Province Sports, Western Province Cricket, Royal Cape Golf; *Style*— Sir Rupert Gull, Bt; ✉ Harcourt Road, Claremont, Cape Town, South Africa

GULLACHSEN, Lorentz; s of Willoughby (Gus) Gullachsen, of Stratford upon Avon, and Doris, *née* Price; *b* 18 March 1951; *Educ* Birmingham Poly Sch of Photography (Dip); *m* 1982 (m dis 1991), remarried 1992 (m dis 1993), Maxine; 1 da (Laurie-Mo b 23 Nov 1983), 1 s (Jack Gustav b 19 April 1988); *Career* photographer (specialising in location advtg shooting worldwide); fndr Pictures Studio Birmingham 1974–88, working from London 1988–; numerous gp/association exhbns (incl Movers and Shakers (Birmingham Symphony Hall) 2005), has published extensively in all continents; Association of Photographers Awards incl Silver/Merits 1988–93 and Gold 1989, Gold Benson and Hedges Professional Awards 1990; memb: Assoc of Photographers 1977; *Recreations* photography; *Clubs* Birmingham Press; *Style*— Lorentz Gullachsen, Esq; ✉ The Peter Bailey Company, 2 Devonshire Mews West, London W1 (tel 020 7935 2626, fax 020 7925 7557, e-mail lorentz@gullachsen.com)

GULLAN, Richard Wilson; s of Archibald Gordon Gullan, OBE, of Rickmansworth, Herts, and (Mary) Helena, *née* Todd; *b* 22 June 1953; *Educ* Merchant Taylors', Bart's Med Coll (BSc, MB BS); *m* 28 July 1979, Christine, da of Leslie Douglas Prime, of Wimbledon, London; 2 da (Laura Jane b 1983, Helena Clare b 1988), 2 s (James Hector b 1985, Archie Charles b 1987); *Career* surgical training rotator Bart's 1979–82 (house surgn Professorial Surgical Unit 1977–78); lectr in anatomy Univ of Manchester 1978–79, neurosurgical SHO Addenbrooke's Hosp Cambridge 1982–83, supervisor in anatomy Gonville & Caius Coll Cambridge 1982–83, neurosurgical registrar Edinburgh 1983–85; neurosurgical sr registrar: Guy's Hosp 1985–87, King's Coll Hosp 1985–87, Brook Regnl Unit 1987–88; conslt neurosurgeon Regional Neuroscience Unit 1988–, hon conslt neurosurgeon Maudsley Hosp London 1988– (sr registrar 1985–87); memb: Soc of Br Neurological Surgns, BMA; fndr memb Br Cervical Spine Soc; fell: London Med Soc, Soc of Apothecaries; MRCP; FRCS 1982, FRSM; *Recreations* music (violinist), golf; *Clubs* Royal Cinque Ports Golf, Oxford and Cambridge Musical; *Style*— Richard Gullan, Esq; ✉ Regional Neuroscience Unit (Neurosurgical Offices), King's College Hospital, Denmark Hill, London SE5 9RS (tel 020 3299 3117, fax 020 3299 3280, e-mail richard.gullan@kch.nhs.uk)

GULLIVER, Ronald; s of Ronald Charles Gulliver (d 1974), and Helen Christiana Duval (d 2003); *b* 12 August 1940; *Educ* Kelvinside Acad, King Alfred's Sch, Univ of London (LLB); *m* Penelope Daphne, da of Sir Henry Lushington, Bt (d 1988); 1 s (Christopher Ronald b 5 April 1974), 1 da (Patricia Jean b 19 Jan 1976); *Career* ptnr Fryer Sutton Morris & Co Chartered Accountants 1963–65, asst tech offr ICAEW 1965–67, ptnr P A Thomas & Co Chartered Accountants 1967–70, admitted slr 1974, ptnr Nabarro Nathanson Solicitors 1974–2000; chm: Orr & Boss Ltd Management Consultants 1988–90, Forminster plc 1988–95, G Stow plc 1991–, Ron Gulliver & Co Ltd 2000–; ICAEW awards: Plender prize, Sir Harold Howitt prize, Morgan prize, certificate of merit; solicitor 1974; memb: HAC 1963–, Light Cavalry Troop HAC 1991–; Freeman City of London, Liveryman Worshipful Co of Farriers; FCA 1973 (ACA 1963); *Recreations* farming, riding, wildlife, music, travel, theatre; *Clubs* IOD, Phyllis Court; *Style*— Ronald Gulliver, Esq; ✉ c/o The Old Chapel Farm, New Mill, Eversley, Hampshire RG27 0RA

GULLIVER, Trevor; s of John Gullliver, and Eugenie Devose, *née* Barsley; *b* 29 July 1953; *Educ* Colfes Sch London, Bournemouth Colls; *Career* restaurateur and mgmnt conslt; md Mobile Merchandising Co Ltd 1977–87, md Groupe Forest Hill UK 1987–91, founding ptnr The Fire Station Waterloo 1991–94 (Evening Standard Pub of the Year), founding ptnr St John Restaurant Co Ltd (operating St John, St John Bread and Wine and HG Wines) 1993– (numerous awards incl 5 Moet et Chandon Restaurant of the Year Awards) dir Vinum Restaurants Ltd (operating Cantina Vinopolis and Wine Wharf London) and Brew Wharf Ltd 1997–; creator: Putney Bridge restaurant, Bar Blue Bankside, The Brew Wharf Borough Market; various other restaurant, food and wine directorships; judge Br Organic Food Awards, judge Br Isles Cheese Awards, int wine judge; occasional author of newspaper and magazine articles; memb Planning Ctee Covent Garden Community Assoc 1990–99; MCMI 1974; *Recreations* squash, the arts, wine, county RFU coach (Middx); *Clubs* RAC, Colony Room; *Style*— Trevor Gulliver, Esq; ✉ St John Restaurant Company Limited, 26 St John Street, London EC1M 4AY (tel 020 7553 9842, fax 020 7251 4090, e-mail tg@stjohnrestaurant.co.uk or kirsty@stjohnresaurant.com); Trevor Gulliver Consultancy (e-mail tg@trevorgulliver.com)

GUMBEL, Elizabeth-Anne; QC (1999); da of Walter Gumbel (d 1980), and Muriel Gumbel (d 1987), of London; *Educ* St Paul's Girls Sch, Wycombe Abbey, LMH Oxford (MA); *m* 1984, Michael Wainwright; 1 da (Ruth b 21 Oct 1988), 1 s (Mark b 6 Jan 1990); *Career* called to the Bar 1974; practising barrister specialising in clinical negligence and personal injury; memb Editorial Ctee Clinical Risk; memb: PNBA, PIBA, Family Law Bar Assoc; *Style*— Miss Elizabeth-Anne Gumbel, QC; ✉ Chambers of Philip Havers QC, 1 Crown Office Row, London EC4Y 7HH (tel 020 7797 7500, fax 020 7797 7550, e-mail lizanne.gumbel@1cor.com)

GUMENDE, HE António; *b* 1 January 1961; *Educ* Sch of Journalism of Mozambique (Dip Journalism), Univ of Silesia (Journalism Cert), Chartered Assoc of Certified Accountants (Dip Accounting and Fin), Nottingham Trent Business Sch (MBA), Open Univ (Dip Econ), Birkbeck Univ of London (Cert Econ); *m*; 2 c; *Career* diplomat and journalist; Mozambique News Agency: foreign desk news writer 1984–88, business and economics ed 1988–90, home ed 1988–90; business ed Southern African Economist 1992–96 (Mozambique corr 1988–90, staff writer 1990–92), ed TRANSCOM (Southern African Tport and Communication Cmmn's quarterly magazine) 1995–96, economy and fin ed Southern African Political and Economic Monthly 1996–97 (contrib 1993–96), managing ed Southern African Economist 1997, exec ed Mozambique Office Southern African Research and Documentation Centre (SARDC) 1997–2002, exec chm Mgmnt Cncl Media Coop 1997–2002; Mozambique high cmmr to UK 2002–; pt/t writing incl: ANSA (Italian news agency) 1988–90, Radio Mozambique 1990–96, Lusa (Portugese news agency) 1990–96, MediaCoop Jornalistas Associados 1992–97, A Bola (Portugese sports paper) 1995–97, Channel Africa 1995–97; shareholder and exec chm MediaCoop Jornalistas Associados SARL 1997–2002; involved with various devpt and journalism trg consultancies; *Publications* Mozambique National Human Development Report (ed, 1998, 1999, 2000 and 2003 edns); *Style*— HE Mr António Gumende; ✉ High Commission of the Republic of Mozambique, 21 Fitzroy Square, London W1T 6EL

GUMLEY, Frances; *see:* Gumley-Mason, Frances

GUMLEY-MASON, Frances Jane Miriah Katrina; da of Franc Stewart Gumley (d 1981), and Helen Teresa McNicholas (d 1987); *b* 28 January 1955; *Educ* St Augustine's Ealing, Newnham Coll Cambridge (MA); *m* 2 July 1988, Andrew Samuel Mason; 1 s (John Michael

G

b 1989), 1 da (Helena Jane b 1991); *Career* journalist, broadcaster, radio & television prodr and headmistress; Parly res 1974, braille transcriber 1975; Catholic Herald: editorial asst 1975–76, staff reporter and literary ed 1976–79, ed 1979–81; sr prodr religious broadcasting BBC 1981–88, series ed Channel 4 1988–89, acting exec prodr Religion BBC World Service 1989, guest prodr and scriptwriter BBC Radio 4 1989–95; headmistress St Augustine's Priory Ealing 1995–; Mistress of the Keys (Catholic Writers' Guild) 1982–87; *Books* with Brian Redhead: The Good Book, The Christian Centuries, The Pillars of Islam, Protestors for Paradise; Discovering Turkey (jtly); *Recreations* playing with my children's toys; *Style*— Mrs F J Gumley-Mason; ✉ St Augustine's Priory, Hillcrest Road, Ealing, London W5 2JL (tel 020 8997 2022)

GUMMER, Rt Hon John Selwyn; PC (1985), MP; s of Rev Canon Selwyn Gummer (d 1999), and (Margaret) Sybille Vera, *née* Mason (d 1993); bro of Baron Chadlington, *qv*; *b* 26 November 1939; *Educ* King's Sch Rochester, Selwyn Coll Cambridge; *m* 1977, Penelope Jane, yr da of John P Gardner; 2 s, 2 da; *Career* md EP Group of Companies 1975–80; chm: Selwyn Sancroft International 1976–81, Siemssen Hunter Ltd 1980 (dir 1973), Sancroft International 1997–, Valpak Ltd 1998–; non-exec dir Kidde 2000–05; MP (Cons): Lewisham W 1970–74, Eye Suffolk 1979–83, Suffolk Coastal 1983–; vice-chm Cons Pty 1972–74, PPS to Min of Agric 1972, govt whip 1981–83, under sec of state Employment June-Oct 1983, chm Cons Pty 1983–85, min of state: Employment 1983–84, paymaster gen 1984–85, min of state Agric Fisheries and Food 1985–88, min for Local Govt 1988–89, min Agric Fisheries and Food 1989–93, sec of state for the Environment 1993–97; memb Parly Ecclesiastical Ctee 1993–; chm: Marine Stewardship Cncl 1998–2005, International Cmmn on Sustainable Consumption 1999–2005, Assoc of Ind Financial Advsrs; memb Gen Synod C of E 1978–92, guardian of the Shrine of Our Lady of Walsingham 1983–2002; *Books* To Church with Enthusiasm (1969), The Permissive Society (1971), The Christian Calendar (1973), Faith in Politics (1987), Christianity and Conservatism (1990); *Recreations* reading, gardening, Victorian buildings; *Style*— The Rt Hon John Gummer, MP; ✉ House of Commons, London SW1A 0AA (tel 020 7219 3000)

GUNEWARDENA, Desmond Anthony Lalith (Des); s of Neville Paul Kingsley Gunewardena, of Old Coulsdon, Surrey, and Muriel G, *née* Perera; *b* 11 August 1957, Kandy, Sri Lanka; *Educ* Wimbledon Coll, Univ of Bristol (BSc); *m* Aug 1991, Elizabeth, *née* Pask; 1 da (Saskia b April 1992), 1 s (Dominic b April 1994); *Career* CA 1981; Ernst & Young 1978–1984; Heron International: head of financial planning 1984–87, finance directorships 1987–89; finance dir Conran Roche 1989–91; Conran Holdings: finance dir 1991–95, ceo 1995–2006, dep chm 2006–; chm and chief exec D&D London 2006–; non-exec dir: London First, Visit London, Individual Restaurants Gp plc; memb London Business Sch Enterprise 100; FRSA 2002; *Recreations* tennis, skiing, chess; *Style*— Des Gunewardena, Esq; ✉ D&D London, 16 Kirkby Street, London EC1N 8TJ (tel 020 7716 7800, e-mail des@danddlondon.com)

GUNN, Andrew; RD (1980); s of Andrew Gunn (d 1985), and Mary Anne Jane Murray Gunn (d 1979); *b* 6 March 1936; *Educ* Univ of Edinburgh (MB ChB); *m* 1 Dec 1962, Deirdre Elizabeth Mary, da of Edmond Richard Weld, of Kirkden House, By Letham, Angus; 3 da (Hilary Mary b 1964, Clare Elizabeth b 1966, Phillippa Jane b 1967), 1 s (Adrian Richard b 1965); *Career* RNR 1965–85, Lt Cdr; conslt surgn Tayside Health Bd, hon sr lectr Univ of Dundee, dir Iatros Ltd; pres Br Assoc of Endocrine Surgns 1988–90; FRCSEd 1962 (memb Cncl 1990–99); *Books* Exploration of the Parathyroid Glands (1988); *Style*— Mr Andrew Gunn, RD; ✉ Kirkden House, by Letham, Angus DD8 2QF (tel 01307 818296, fax 01307 819140, e-mail andrew@gunn.sol.co.uk); Iatros Ltd, Prospect 2, Dundee Technology Park, Dundee DD2 1TY (tel 01382 562111, fax 01382 561590, e-mail iatrosltd@sol.co.uk)

GUNN, Catherine Rachel (Cathy); da of late John Sinclair Gunn, of Auldearn, Nairn, and Rosemary Elizabeth, *née* Williams; *b* 28 May 1954; *Educ* St Swithun's Sch Winchester, Univ of Durham (BA), Univ of Edinburgh (Dip Business Admin), Birkbeck Coll Univ of London (MA); *m* 1994, Charles Guybon Hutson; 1 s (Rollo Guybon Hutson, b 8 Nov 1994), 1 da (Tallulah Rosemary Hutson b 4 June 1996); *Career* investment analyst Touche Remnant & Co 1976–78; fin writer: Investors Chronicle 1978–80, The Times 1980–81, freelance 1981–83; fin writer and dep ed Financial Weekly 1983–86, City ed Today 1987–91 (dep City ed 1986–87), fin ed The People 1993–99, writer, broadcaster and freelance conslt 1991–; dir ArtHut Ltd 1999–2007, devpt mangr Chicken Shed Theatre Co 2006–; FRSA; *Publications* Fraud: The Growth Industry of the Eighties (with Mihir Bose, 1989), Nightmare on Lime Street: Whatever happened to Lloyd's of London (1992 and 1993), High Street Robbery - How the Banks hold up their Customers (1993); *Recreations* reading, travel, scribbling, entertaining; *Style*— Cathy Gunn, FRSA; ✉ ArtHut Ltd, 116 Hazellville Road, London N19 3NA

GUNN, Prof John Charles; CBE (1994); s of Albert Charles Gunn (d 2003), of Charlwood, Surrey, and Lily Hilda Gunn (d 1990); *b* 6 June 1937; *Educ* Brighton, Hove and Sussex GS, Reigate GS, Univ of Birmingham (MB ChB, MD), Univ of London (DPM); *m* 1, 9 Sept 1959 (m dis 1987), Celia Ann Frances (d 1989), da of Harry Richard Willis, of Charlwood, Surrey; 1 s (Richard Charles b 10 March 1962), 1 da (Frances Margaret b 28 Sept 1964); m 2, 11 Nov 1989, Pamela Jane, da of Rev P Geoffrey Taylor, of Liverpool; *Career* house offr Queen Elizabeth Hosp Birmingham 1961–63, registrar Maudsley Hosp London 1963–67; Inst of Psychiatry: res worker and lectr 1967–71, sr lectr 1971–75, prof of forensic psychiatry 1978–2002; dir Special Hosps Res Unit 1975–78; memb Home Sec's Advsy Bd on Restricted Patients 1982–91, advsr House of Commons Social Servs Ctee 1985–86 (Ctee on Violence in Marriages 1975); chm Faculty of Forensic Psychiatry 2000–04; memb: DH/Home Office Review of Servs for Mentally Disordered Offenders (The Reed Ctee), Royal Cmmn on Criminal Justice 1991–93, Cncl RCPsych 1977–83 and 1997–2004, Ct of Electors RCPsych 2003–06, Parole Bd 2006–; FRCPsych 1980 (MRCPsych 1971), FMedSci 1999; *Books* Violence in Human Society (1973), Epileptics in Prison (1977), Psychiatric Aspects of Imprisonment (1978), Forensic Psychiatry (1993); *Recreations* walking, photography, theatre, opera, cinema; *Clubs* Athenaeum, RSM; *Style*— Prof John Gunn, CBE; ✉ PO Box 725, Bromley BR2 7WF (tel 020 8462 1751, fax 020 8462 0490, e-mail j.gunn@iop.kcl.ac.uk)

GUNN, (Anthony) William; s of William Arthur Gunn, OBE (d 1988), of Alton, Hants, and Diana Elizabeth, *née* Taylor (d 1972); *b* 21 May 1946; *Educ* Radley, Corpus Christi Coll Oxford (MA), Walter Sichel scholarship, WSET dip (Rouyer Guillet cup); *m* 6 June 1970, Amanda Marson, 3 da of Anthony Stedman Till; 2 da (Fiona Elizabeth b 10 July 1973, Rachel Georgina b 20 July 1977); *Career* Grants of St James's Ltd 1968–81: wine buyer 1977–81, buying dir Hatch Mansfield & Co; controller Wines and Spirits ASDA Stores Ltd 1981–83; Dent & Reuss Ltd (H P Bulmer plc) 1983–90; md Pol Roger Ltd 1990–; Inst of Masters of Wine: chm 1997–98; chm MW Educn and Examination Bd 1999–2002; chm: French Wines Ctee Wine & Spirit Assoc 1980–81, Champagne Agents Assoc 1993; jury memb Gault-Millau 'Olympiades of Wines' 1977, judge various nat and int wine shows; Freeman City of London 1988, Liveryman Worshipful Co of Fishmongers 1987; MW 1974; Chevalier de l'Ordre du Mérite Agricole 1983, Offr de l'Ordre des Coteaux de Champagne, Chevalier du Tastevin; *Books* contrib: Wines of the World (1981), The Wine Drinker's Handbook (1982), Which? Wine Guide (1983–86); *Recreations* fly fishing, travel, classical music and opera; *Clubs* Oxford and Cambridge; *Style*— William Gunn, Esq; ✉ The Stone Barn, Woolhope, Hereford HR1 4QR (tel 01432 860624); Pol Roger Ltd, Shelton House, 4 Coningsby Street, Hereford HR1 2DY (tel 01432 262800, fax 01432 262806, e-mail bill.gunn@polroger.co.uk)

GUNN-CAIRNS, Joyce; MBE (2004); da of John Lamb Cairns (d 1954), and Anne Gunn Nisbet (d 1994); *b* 21 October 1948; *Educ* Univ of Aberdeen (MA), Edinburgh Coll of Art (BA); *m* 1 (m dis), Allister Potter; m 2 (m dis), Rev George Shand; 2 s (Tim John b 12 July 1979, Michael David b 6 Oct 1981); partner Rev Colin Douglas; *Career* artist and portraitist; work reproduced in various exhbn catalogues; took part in Leipzig Project with Tessa Rainsford 2002; dir Exhibiting Socs of Scottish Artists; professional memb: Visual Arts Scotland 1998, Soc of Scottish Artists 2000 (memb Cncl); assoc memb Iona Community; *Exhibitions* group and solo shows incl: Art and the Female Form (Kingfisher Gallery) 1989, Scottish Nat Portrait Gallery 1991, Portraithall Gallery Edinburgh 1996, 1998, 1999, 2000 and 2002, Chessels Gallery 1997, Visual Arts Scotland (Royal Scottish Acad) 1997, 1998, 1999, 2000 and 2002, Society of Scottish Artists (Royal Scottish Acad) 1997, 1998, 1999, 2000 and 2002, SAAC (Perth Museum and Gallery) 1998, Cheltenham Open Drawing Exhbn (Kunstlerwerkstaff Bahnhof Berlin) 1998 and 1999, Portraits of Tom Scott (Scottish Nat Portrait Gallery) 1999, Royal Scottish Academy 1999 and 2000, Royal Society of Watercolour Painters (Royal Scottish Acad) 1999, 2000, 2002 and 2003, Children/Artists (Chessels Gallery) 2000, Royal Glasgow Inst (MacLellan Galleries) 2000, Writers of our time (Scottish Nat Portrait Gallery) 2000–01, Narcissus (Scottish Nat Portrait Gallery) 2001, New Acquisitions (Scottish Nat Portrait Gallery) 2001, Netherbow Arts Centre Edinburgh 2003, drawings of Prof David Daiches (Talbot Rice Gall Univ of Edinburgh) 2004, Daughters of Eve (Highland tour) 2004; *Work in Public Collections* Scottish Nat Portrait Gallery, Scottish Poetry Library, Balliol Coll Oxford, Jesus Coll Cambridge, Univ of Edinburgh; work in various private collections worldwide *Awards* Second Prize Cheltenham Open Drawing Exhbn 1998, Lily McDougall Prize Visual Arts Scotland Royal Scottish Acad 1999, Greyfriars' Painting Prize WASPS Festival Exhbn 2000; *Recreations* German literature and literature in general, going to cafés; *Style*— Mrs Joyce Gunn-Cairns, MBE; ✉ 30/1 West Pilton Gardens, Edinburgh EH4 4EG (tel 0131 332 7965, mobile 07929 925116, e-mail joycegunn@cairns01.fsnet.co.uk)

GUNNELL, Sally Jane Janet; OBE (1998, MBE 1993); da of Leslie Robert Gunnell, and Doris Rosemary, *née* Mason; *b* 29 July 1966; *m* 19 Oct 1992, Jon Bigg, s of John Bigg; 3 s (Finley b 2 June 1998, Luca b 14 Feb 2001, Marley b 16 Feb 2005); *Career* former athlete; Gold medal 100m hurdles Cwlth Games Edinburgh 1986; 400m hurdles: fifth place Olympic Games Seoul 1988 (first Briton to compete in the Olympic Games in 100m hurdles, 400m hurdles and 4x400m relay), Silver medal Euro Cup 1989, Gold medal Euro Indoor Championships 1989, Bronze medal World Cup 1989, Gold medal Cwlth Games 1990, Silver medal World Championships 1991, Gold medal Olympic Games Barcelona 1992 (also Bronze medal 4 x 400m relay), Gold medal Euro Cup 1993, Gold medal World Championships (and new world record) 1993 (also Bronze medal 4 x 400m relay), Gold medal World Cup 1994 (also Gold medal 4 x 400m relay), Gold medal Euro Championships 1994 (also Bronze medal 4 x 400m relay), Gold medal Cwlth Games 1994 (Gold medal 4 x 400m relay), ret 1997; entered Gt North Run 1999, London Marathon 2007; co-commentator (with Jeremy Guscott) Body Heat (ITV) 1994, memb athletics commentary team BBC 1999–2004, currently motivational speaker; runner-up BBC Sports Personality of the Year 1993 and 1994; *Publications* Running Tall (1994), Be Your Best (2001); *Style*— Ms Sally Gunnell, OBE; ✉ Old School Cottage, School Lane, Pyecombe, West Sussex

GUNNING, Sir Charles Theodore; 9 Bt (GB 1778), CD (1964); s of Sir Robert Charles Gunning, 8 Bt (d 1989), and Ann (Helen Nancy), *née* Hallett; *b* 19 June 1935; *Educ* Royal Roads Mil Coll BC, RN Engrg Coll, Tech Univ of Nova Scotia; *m* 1, 1969 (m dis 1982), Sarah, da of Col Patrick Arthur Easton, of Tonbridge; 1 da (Caroline Ann b 1971); m 2, 1989, Linda, da of Theodore Kachmar, of Montreal; *Heir* bro, John Gunning; *Career* Lt Cdr RCN/Canadian Armed Forces 1952–80; engrg conslt; pres Ottawa Branch Royal Cwlth Soc 1975–78, 1980–81 and 1995–96, chm Nat Cncl RCS in Canada 1990–93 (vice-chm 1980–90), dep dir (youth) 1991–; Silver Jubilee medal 1977, Golden Jubilee medal 2002; memb Professional Engrs of Ontario; PEng; *Recreations* squash, gardening, cross-country skiing, music; *Clubs* RMC of Canada, Royal Cwlth Soc; *Style*— Sir Charles Gunning, Bt, PEng, CD; ✉ 2940 McCarthy Road, Ottawa, Ontario K1V 8K6, Canada (tel 00 1 613 737 2179, e-mail cgunning@sympatico.ca)

GUNNING, Christopher; s of Alexis Lambertus Gunning (d 1962), of Cheltenham and London, and Janet Alice, *née* Bennett (d 1993); *b* 5 August 1944; *Educ* Hendon Co GS, Guildhall Sch of Music and Drama (BMus); *m* 17 June 1974, Annie Christine, da of Flt Lt Clifford William Cornwall Farrow (d 1985), of Bristol; 4 da (Olivia b 1975, Pollyanna b 1977, Verity b 1981, Chloe b 1985); *Career* composer; TV and film scores incl: Rogue Male 1975, Charlie Muffin 1979, Day of the Triffids 1981, Wilfred and Eileen 1981, Flame to the Phoenix 1982, East Lynne 1982, Children's Opera Rainbow Planet 1983, Rebel Angel 1987, Porterhouse Blue 1987 (BAFTA award for the Best Original TV Music), Agatha Christie's Poirot (BAFTA award for Best Original TV Music) 1989, When the Whales Came (Royal Premiere 1989, nominated British Film Institute Anthony Asquith award for Best Film Score 1990), Yorkshire Glory 1990, Under Suspicion 1991 (Ivor Novello award for Best Film Score), The Big Battalions 1992 (BAFTA nomination for Best TV Music), Midnight Movie 1993, The Glass Virgin 1995, The Affair 1995, All or Nothing at All, Middlemarch (BAFTA Award for Best TV Music), Karaoke and Cold Lazarus 1996 (nominated for Ivor Novello award), Rebecca 1997 (Ivor Novello Award for Best TV Score), Firelight 1997 (Ivor Novello Award for Best Film Score), The Last Train 1999, Anchor Me 2000, The Innocent 2000, Poirot 2001, Wild Africa 2001, Pollyanna 2002, The Boy David 2002, Flight of Fancy 2002, Rosemany and Thyme 2003, Five Little Pigs 2004, Death on the Nile 2004, The Hollow 2004, Sad Cypress 2004, La Mome 2006; concert works incl: Concerto for Saxophone 1998, The Lobster 1998, String Quartet 1998, Aunt Vita 2001, Piano Concerto 2001, Symphony 2002, Symphony No 2 2003, Oboe Concerto 2004, Light and Dark Music for Strings 2005, Symphony No 3 2005; ARCM, AGSM; *Books* First Book of Flute Solos, Second Book of Flute Solos, Really Easy Flute Book, Really Easy Trumpet Book, Really Easy Horn Book; *Recreations* walking, reading, horticulture; *Style*— Christopher Gunning, Esq; ✉ 24 Ranelagh Road, Ealing, London W5 5RJ

GUNNLAUGSSON, HE Sverrir Haukur; *Educ* Univ of Iceland; *m* Gudny Adalsteinsdóttir; 3 c; *Career* diplomat; joined Miny for Foreign Affrs 1970, first sec Paris 1971, chief Admin and Consular Affrs Div 1974, min-cnsllr Washington 1980 (cnsllr 1978), head Defence Div (later Defence Dept) 1983, appointed ambass 1985, perm rep to EFTA and UN Geneva 1987–89 (concurrently ambass to Egypt, Ethiopia, Kenya and Tanzania), head Dept for Foreign Trade 1989, ambass NATO 1990–94, ambass to France 1994–99 (concurrently ambass to Italy, Spain, Portugal, Cape Verde and Andorra), perm sec of state 1999, ambass to the Ct of St James's 2003– (concurrently ambass to Greece, The Netherlands, Repub of Ireland, Lebanon, Malta, Maldives, Nepal, India and Nigeria); *Style*— HE Mr Sverrir H Gunnlaugsson; ✉ Embassy of Iceland, 2A Hans Street, London SW1X 0JE

GUNSTON, Sir John Wellesley; 3 Bt (UK 1938), of Wickwar, Co Gloucester; o s of Sir Richard Wellesley Gunston, 2 Bt (d 1991), and his 2 w, Joan Elizabeth Marie, *née* Forde; *b* 25 July 1962; *Educ* Harrow, RMA Sandhurst; *m* 1 Sept 1990 (m dis 1998), Rosalind Gordon, yst da of Edward Gordon Eliott, of Bower's Mill House, nr Guildford, Surrey; 1 s (Richard St George b 3 July 1992); *Heir* s, Richard Gunston; *Career* cmmnd 1 Bn Irish Gds; chm The Rory Peck Tst and Award 1995–97, md Hard News Ltd 1998–, dir NWF Productions 1995–; memb Soc of Authors 1994; FRGS 1988, FRSAA 1995, FRAS

1998; *Clubs* Special Forces, Cavalry and Guards; *Style*— Sir John Gunston, Bt; ✉ c/o 127 Piccadilly, London W1E 6YZ

GUNSTON, Michael I; s of Daniel Denis Gunston, and Vera Constance, *née* Harris; *b* 14 January 1944; *m* Sept 1968, Judith Frances, *née* Painter; 1 da (Sarah Elizabeth b 5 Jan 1973), 1 s (Matthew Richard b 5 Dec 1974); *Career* various posts with property owing cos and gen practice firms of surveyors; dir and chief surveyor Br Land 1987–2006 (joined 1975), ret; former memb Round Table; Liveryman Worshipful Co of Gold and Silver Wyre Drawers; FRICS; *Recreations* golf, walking, motoring, travel, music, charitable and social activities; *Clubs* RAC; *Style*— Michael I Gunston, Esq; ✉ tel 023 9224 1413, e-mail michaelgunston@yahoo.co.uk

GUNSTONE, Prof Frank Denby; s of (Edwin) Leonard Gunstone (d 1981), and Adeline, *née* Benington (d 1969); *b* 27 October 1923; *Educ* Univ of Liverpool (BSc, PhD), Univ of St Andrews (DSc); *m* 20 March 1948, Eleanor Eineen, da of Sidney John Hill (d 1949); 2 s (Douglas b 1950, John b 1952), 1 da (Penny b 1958); *Career* lectr Univ of Glasgow 1946–54; Univ of St Andrews: lectr 1954–59, sr lectr 1959–65, reader 1965–70, personal prof 1971–89, hon res prof 1989–96; hon research fell Scottish Crops Research Inst 1996–; memb: Royal Soc of Chemistry 1945, Soc of Chemical Industry 1945; FRSE 1972, hon fell American Oil Chemists Soc 2000; *Books* incl: A Text-Book of Organic Chemistry (with J Read, 1958), An Introduction to the Chemistry and Biochemistry of Fatty Acids and their Glycerides (1958, 2 edn 1967), Programmes in Organic Chemistry vols 1–3, 5 and 6 (1966–74), Guidebook to Stereochemistry (1975), Lipids in Foods; Chemistry, Biochemistry and Technology (with F A Norris, 1983), The Lipid Handbook (ed with F B Padley and J L Harwood, 1986, 2 edn 1994), Critical Reports on Applied Chemistry Vol 15, Palm Oil (ed, 1987), A Lipid Glossary (with B G Herslöf, 1992, 2 edn 2000), Fatty Acid and Lipid Chemistry (1996), Lipid Technologies and Applications (with F B Padley, 1997), Lipid Synthesis and Manufacture (1999), Structured and Modified Lipids (2001), Oleochemical Manufacture and Applications (with R J Hamilton, 2001), Lipids for Functional Foods and Nutraceuticals (2003), Vegetable Oils in Food Technology (2002), Rapeseed and Canola Oil (2004), The Chemistry of Oils and Fats (2004), Modifying Lipids for use in Food (ed, 2006), The Lipid Handbook (ed with J L Harwood and A J Dijkstra, 3 edn, 2007); *Style*— Prof Frank Gunstone, FRSE; ✉ 3 Dempster Court, St Andrews, Fife KY16 9EU (tel 01334 479929, e-mail fdg1@st-and.ac.uk); Scottish Crops Research Institute, Invergowrie, Dundee DD2 5DA (tel 01382 562731, fax 01382 561442, e-mail f.gunstone@scri.sari.ac.uk)

GUNTER, John Forsyth; s of Dr Herbert Charles Gunter (d 1959), and Charlotte Rose Scott, *née* Reid (d 2000); *b* 31 October 1938; *Educ* Bryanston, Central Sch of Art and Design; *m* 19 Dec 1969, Micheline, da of late Col Maxwell S McKnight; 2 da (Jessica b 4 June 1972, Nicolette b 16 Oct 1978); *Career* theatre designer; head of Theatre Dept Central Sch of Art and Design 1974–82, head of design RNT 1988–90, assoc designer RNT 1990–; resident designer Sir Peter Hall Company: Old Vic 1997–, Picadilly Theatre 1998; FRSA 1982; *Theatre* 28 prodns Royal Court Theatre 1965–66 incl: D H Lawrence Trilogy, Saved, The Contractor, The Philanthropist, West of Suez, Inadmissible Evidence; RSC: Juno and the Paycock, All's Well that Ends Well (Broadway 1983), Mephisto 1986, Love's Labour's Lost 1993 and 1995, Christmas Carol 1994, Twelfth Night 1994, Julius Caesar 1995, Troilus and Cressida; RNT: Guys and Dolls (SWET Award Best Designer, revival 1996), The Rivals, The Beggar's Opera, Wild Honey (SWET Award Best Designer), The Government Inspector, Bay at Nice, Wrecked Eggs, The Seagull, Long Days Journey Into Night 1991, The Devil's Disciple 1994, Absolute Hell 1995, Skylight (also West End and Broadway) 1995; West End: Comedians, Stevie, The Old Country, Rose, Made in Bangkok, High Society, Mrs Klein, Secret Rapture, Piaf (Piccadilly) 1993, School for Wives 1996, Speed-The-Plow, Collected Stories 2000, Japes 2001, God Only Knows 2001, Lady Windermere's Fan 2001; Sir Peter Hall Co Repertory Season (Los Angeles USA) 1999; Macbeth (Sydney Theatre Co) 1999, Heartbreak House (Chichester) 2000, Front Page (Chichester) 2002, Mrs Warren's Profession (2002), Anything Goes (RNT, 2003), Love's Labour's Lost (RNT, 2003), Sir Peter Hall Season Bath 2003, Hamlet (Old Vic) 2004, George Dillon (Comedy Theatre) 2005, The Old Country (Trafalgar Studios) 2006, Jeffrey Barnard is Unwell (Garrick Theatre) 2006; *Opera* incl: The Greek Passion (WNO), Faust (ENO), Peter Grimes (Teatro Colon Buenos Aries), The Meistersinger (Cologne), Un Ballo in Maschera (Sydney Opera House), The Turn of the Screw (Munich), Macbeth (Leeds), Norma (Scottish Opera), Attila (Opera North) 1990, Marriage of Figaro (Salzburg Festival Opera) 1991, Madame Butterfly (Los Angeles Opera) 1991, The Flying Dutchman (Royal Opera House) 1992, West Side Story (Victoria State Opera), Figaro (Glyndebourne) 1994, Don Quixote (ENO) 1994, Don Quixote (ENO, Victoria State Opera 1995) 1994, Samson et Dalila (Opera Aust) 1996, Simon Boccanegra (Royal Opera House) 1997, Mephistopheles (ENO and Buenos Aires) 1999, Otello (Glyndebourne and Chicago) 2001, Ernani (Reisopera Netherlands) 2002, Romeo et Juliette (LA Opera) 2005, Sir John in Love (ENO) 2006, Don Carlo (LA Opera) 2006; for Sir Peter Hall Glyndebourne: Albert Herring, La Traviata 1987, Falstaff 1988, Simon Boccanegra (also Washington DC) 1998, Romeo and Juliette (LA) 2005, Peter Grimes (Salzberg) 2005; for Trevor Nunn Glyndebourne: Peter Grimes 1992, Porgy and Bess (Emmy Award 1994); *Style*— John Gunter, Esq; ✉ c/o Richard Haigh, Performing Arts, 6 Windmill Street, London W1T 2JB (tel 020 7255 1362, fax 020 7631 4631)

GUPTA, Dr Nirmal Kumar; s of Kanti Bhushan Gupta (d 1964), of Agartala, India, and Kamala, *née* Sen Gupta (d 1948); *b* 13 June 1934; *Educ* Calcutta Univ (MB BS); *m* 28 Jan 1962, Namita, da of Nibaran Chandra Das Gupta (d 1982), of Assam, India; 2 da (Chandreyi b 1967, Sharmila b 1972); *Career* Christie Hosp and Holt Radium Inst Manchester: conslt in radiotherapy and oncology 1975–88, dep dir in radiotherapy and oncology, ret 1999; visiting prof in oncology Univ National de la Plata Argentina 1998–, hon conslt IAEA and WHO, memb Sociedad Peruana de Radiologicá Lima 1982, pres The 1951 Club 1986–87; memb: Sub-Ctee on Head and Neck Cancer UK Coordinating Ctee on Cancer Res 1988–, Int Collaborative Gp on Fractionation American Coll of Radiology Philadelphia 1988–96, Cncl Faculty Bd of Radiotherapy and Oncology RCR 1988–89 (memb 1986–88), Int Cmmn on Radiation Protection 2006, Ed Bd of Nowotwory (jl of oncology, Poland) 2002–; memb Bd of Tstees Museum of Science and Industry in Manchester 1994–97; DMRT, FRCR, FFR, FRSM; *Publications* Oncology (1994), Radiotherapy and Oncology (1996); contrib: The Radiotherapy of Malignant Disease (1985 and 1990), Clinical Radiology (1987), The British Journal of Radiology (1990 and 1997), Annals, Royal Coll of Surgeons (1992), Int Jl of Radiation Oncol Biol Phys (1994 and 1995), Jl of Japanese Soc for Therapeutic Radiology and Oncology (1994), Jl of Laryngology Otology (1996), Post Graduate Doctor, Africa (1997), European Jl Nuclear Medicine (1999), Jl Cancer Res Clinical Oncology (1999), European Jl of Cancer (1999), Clinical Oncology (2001); *Recreations* tasting good food and wine; *Style*— Dr Nirmal Gupta; ✉ 12 Old Broadway, Didsbury, Manchester M20 3DF; residence tel 0161 445 6638, fax 0161 434 3462, e-mail nirmal1934@aol.com)

GUPTARA, Prabhu; *Career* univ lectr India 1970–79, mgmnt conslt and trainer 1979–95, fndr chm Prabhu Guptara Associates 1984–96, chm ADVANCE Management Training Ltd 1988–2003, gp dir Organisational Learning & Transformation Union Bank of Switzerland 1995–98, dir Orgn and Exec Devpt Wolfsberg (subsid of UBS AG) Switzerland 1999–; fndr ed Organisations and People 1994–97; prof: Int Inst for the Mgmnt of Telecommunications Univ of Fribourg Switzerland 1997–, European Inst of Purchasing Mgmnt INSEAD France 1992–95, Carlson Sch of Business Univ of Minnesota, MIT USA, Univ of St Thomas USA, Univ of Keio Japan, Univ of Sogang Korea Rotterdam Sch of Mgmnt Netherlands 1990–93; lectured at: UNCTAD, Cncl of Europe, Univ of London, Univ of Oxford, Univ of Sorbonne, Univ of Warwick, Assoc Bank Inst (Frankfurt), Henley Mgmnt Coll, Int Inst for Mgmnt Devpt (Lausanne), Sloane Sch of Business (Wharton), Int Mgmnt Assoc of Japan, Singapore Inst of Mgmnt, Keizai Koho Centre of the Keidanren Japan, Sch of Mgmnt Univ of Pennsylvania USA; contrib to Gower Handbook of Management, Gower Handbook on Quality, International Encyclopaedia of Business and Management and other reference books, as well as to numerous newspapers and magazines incl: FT, Daily Telegraph, The Times, The Guardian, The Spectator, New Statesman, Society, International Management, Jl of Japanese Trade and Industry, Training & Development (columnist); memb Cncl: Inst of Mgmnt, Int Fedn of Trg and Devpt Orgns, Assoc for Mgmnt Educn and Devpt, Ridley Hall Fndn 1998–2003; chair Career Innovation Res Gp 1998–, vice-chm Guildford Branch Inst of Trg and Devpt, judge MSC Nat Trg Awards 1988, judge Deo Gloria Award for Fiction 1990 (chm judges panel 1991 and 1992); govr Univ of Westminster (formerly Poly of Central London) 1989–92; Freeman: City of London, Worshipful Co of Info Technologists; MIMgt, MSPS, FRCS, FInstD, FIPD, FRSA; *Books* The Basic Arts of Marketing (3rd edn, 1990), Top Executives in the Global 100 Companies and their IT-Competence (1998); *Clubs* Arts Centre Group; *Style*— Prabhu S Guptara, Esq; ✉ e-mail prabhu.guptara@ubs.com

GURDON, Prof Sir John Bertrand; kt (1995); s of late W N Gurdon, DCM, of Suffolk, and late Elsie Marjorie, *née* Byass; *b* 2 October 1933; *Educ* Eton, ChCh Oxford (BA, DPhil, Beit meml fell); *m* 1964, Jean Elizabeth Margaret Curtis; 1 s, 1 da; *Career* Gosney res fell Caltech 1962; Univ of Oxford: department demonstrator Dept of Zoology 1963–64, res fell ChCh 1962–72, lectr Dept of Zoology 1965–72; visiting res fell Carnegie Inst Baltimore 1965, head Cell Biology Div MRC Laboratory of Molecular Biology Cambridge 1979–83, Fullerian prof of physiology and comparative anatomy Royal Inst 1985–91, John Humphrey Plummer prof of cell biology and chm Wellcome/CRC Inst Cambridge 1991–2001, master Magdalene Coll Cambridge 1995–2002 (hon fell 2002); fell: Churchill Coll Cambridge 1973–94, Eton Coll 1978–93; chm Co of Biologists Cambridge 2001–; govr Wellcome Tst 1995–2000; hon foreign memb: American Acad of Arts and Sciences, US Nat Acad of Sciences, Belgian Acad of Letters and Fine Arts 1984, Lombardy Acad of Sci Italy 1989, Academie des Sciences France 1990; foreign memb: American Philosophical Soc 1983, Inst of Med USA 2003; Liveryman Worshipful Co of Goldsmiths; hon fell ChCh Oxford; Hon DSc: Univ of Chicago 1978, Univ of Paris 1982, Univ of Oxford 1985, Univ of Hull 1998, Univ of Glasgow 2000; FRS 1971; *Awards* Albert Brachet Prize Belgian Royal Acad 1968, Scientific Medal Zoological Soc 1968, Feldberg Fndn Award 1975, Paul Ehrlich Award (Germany) 1977, Comfort Crookshank Award for Cancer Res 1983, William Bate Hardy Prize Cambridge Philosophical Soc 1984, Prix de Charles Leopold Mayer Acad des Scis France 1984, Ross Harrison Prize 1985, CIBA Medal Biochemical Soc 1985, Royal Medal Royal Soc 1985, Emperor Hirohito International Prize (Japan) 1987, Wolf Prize in Medicine (Israel) 1989, Jan Waldenstrom Medal 1991, Distinguished Serv Award (Miami) 1992, Jean Brachet Memorial Prize 2000, Conklin Medal 2001, Copley Medal Royal Soc 2003; *Publications* Control of Gene Expression in Animal Development (1974); author of articles in numerous scientific journals (especially on nuclear transplantation); *Recreations* tennis, skiing, horticulture, lepidoptera; *Clubs* Eagle Ski; *Style*— Prof Sir John Gurdon, FRS; ✉ Whittlesford Grove, Whittlesford, Cambridge CB2 4NZ

GURR, Prof Sarah Jane; da of Denis Coates Smith, of Lyminge, Kent, and Marie Theresa, *née* Robinson; *b* 7 May 1958, Cuckfield, Sussex; *Educ* Ashford Sch Kent, King's Sch Canterbury, ICSTM (BSc, ARCS, PhD, DIC), Univ of Oxford (MA); *m* 9 July 1983, Dr Paul Andrew Gurr; 2 da (Charlotte Lucy b 29 June 1994, Alice Eugenie b 31 Dec 1996); *Career* post doctoral research fell Univ of St Andrews 1984–89, research fell and Royal Soc univ research fell Univ of Leeds 1989–92; Univ of Oxford: fell Somerville Coll 1992–, lectr 1992–2002, reader 2002–04, prof 2004–; Royal Soc Leverhulme Tst sr research fell 2002–03, NESTA fell 2004–; dir Rothamsted Research 1999–2006; author of over 70 research papers and articles, ed of 2 books and various articles in popular press; govr: King's Sch Canterbury 1999–, Stowe Sch 2005–; Huxley medal 1998; *Recreations* wine, art, reading, plants; *Style*— Prof Sarah Gurr; ✉ Somerville College, Oxford OX2 6HD (tel 01865 275813, e-mail sarah.gurr@plants.ox.ac.uk)

GURTON, Michael John; s of Percy William Gurton, of Chelmsford, and Margaret Elsie, *née* Sargent; *b* 3 July 1950; *Educ* Chelmsford Tech HS, Chelmer Inst; *m* 10 Aug 1974, Gillian, da of Christopher Stone; 2 s (Timothy Michael b 21 March 1980, Christopher John 16 Aug 1982), 1 da (Jennifer Clare b 6 June 1989); *Career* apprentice Marconi Co Ltd 1966–71, Roff Marsh & Partners (architects) 1972–76, ptnr Purcell Miller Tritton & Partners 1989–2001 (joined 1976); chm Wakes Colne Parish Cncl; memb: Inst of Engrs & Technicians 1971, Br Inst of Architectural Technologists 1977; FFB 1988; *Recreations* fishing, shooting; *Clubs* Chappel & Wakes Colne Cricket (vice-pres); *Style*— Michael Gurton, Esq; ✉ Russets, Colchester Road, Wakes Colne, Colchester, Essex CO6 2AF; WS Atkins Consultants, Digby House, Riverside Office Centre, Causton Road, Colchester CO1 1RJ

GUTCH, Richard Evelyn; s of Sir John Gutch (d 1988), and Diana Mary, *née* Worsley; *b* 17 November 1946; *Educ* Winchester, Gonville & Caius Coll Cambridge (BA), UCL (MPhil); *m* 15 May 1971, Rosemary Anne Capel, da of John Alexander Pike; 2 s (James Alexander b 1974, Adam William b 1978); *Career* town planning posts in Camden and S Yorks 1970–76, sr lectr Planning Unit PCL 1976–80, policy co-ordinator (then asst to chief exec) London Borough of Brent 1980–85; NCVO 1985–92: head of info, then asst dir (Local Vol Action), then asst dir Resource Devpt; chief exec Arthritis Care 1992–2001, dir England and strategic progs Community Fund 2001–04, chief exec Futurebuilders England Ltd 2004–; chm then treasurer Long Term Med Conditions Alliance 1993–96, chm then vice-chm ACEVO 1995–99; MRTPI 1972–80; FRSA 1992; *Publications* incl: Getting in on the Act (NCVO, 1987), Partners or Agents? (NCVO, 1990), Contracting Lessons from the US (NCVO, 1992); *Recreations* the arts, walking, Venice, carpentry; *Style*— Richard Gutch, Esq; ✉ Futurebuilders England Ltd, 3–5 Rathbone Place, London W1T 1HJ (tel 020 7927 6344, e-mail richard.gutch@futurebuilders-england.org.uk)

GUTHRIE, James Dalglish; QC (1993); s of Ronald Dalglish Guthrie (d 1982), and Nina, *née* Llewelyn (d 1987); *b* 21 February 1950; *Educ* Harrow, Worcester Coll Oxford (BA); *m* 1981, Lucille Gay, da of Mr and Mrs Nigel Page-Roberts; 1 da (Charlotte Elizabeth b 31 July 1985), 1 s (Robert James b 17 June 1989); *Career* called to the Bar Inner Temple 1975 (bencher 2000), memb chambers 3 Hare Court (formerly 1 Crown Office Row) 1975–, recorder 1999–, head chambers 2002–; *Recreations* fishing, painting, travel; *Clubs* Turf; *Style*— James Guthrie, Esq, QC; ✉ 3 Hare Court, Temple, London EC4Y 7BJ (tel 020 7415 7800, fax 020 7415 7811, e-mail james@guthrieqc.com)

GUTHRIE, Sir Malcolm Connop; 3 Bt (UK 1936), of Brent Eleigh Hall, Co Suffolk; s of Sir Giles Connop McEacharn Guthrie, 2 Bt, OBE, DSC (d 1979), and Rhona, *née* Stileman; *b* 16 December 1942; *Educ* Millfield; *m* 1967, Victoria, da of late Douglas Willcock; 1 da (Islay Mary Welcome b 1968), 1 s (Giles Malcolm Welcome b 1972); *Heir* s, Giles Guthrie; *Career* memb Firearms Consultative Ctee 1991–94, Liveryman Worshipful Co of Gunmakers; *Recreations* competitive shooting, deer stalking, big game hunting; *Style*— Sir Malcolm Guthrie, Bt; ✉ Brent Eleigh, Belbroughton, Stourbridge, Worcestershire DY9 0DW

G

GUTHRIE, (Garth) Michael; OBE (2007); s of Henry Morton (d 1957), of Bolton, and Ann, *née* Baxter (d 1993); *b* 30 April 1941; *Educ* Isis Sch, Bolton & Blackpool Catering Coll (FHCIMA); *m* 7 Sept 1963, Joyce; 1 s (Paul b 8 May 1965), 2 da (Lynn (Mrs Dean) b 11 April 1967, Julia (Mrs Hook) b 20 Sept 1968); *Career* Mecca Leisure Group Ltd: joined as trainee mangr 1961, md catering 1969–73, md entertainment 1973–80, gp md 1980–81, chm and chief exec 1981–90; chm BrightReasons Group Ltd 1991–96, dir Welcome Break (motorway serv areas gp) 1997– (dep chm), dir Mission Capital plc 2005–; jt exec dep chm Queensborough Holdings plc 1997–2000; non-exec dir: Visual Action Holdings plc 1996–97; chm Tomorrow's People Tst 1996–2000 (dep chm 1998–2000); hon visiting fell Oxford Brookes Univ 1996–; *Recreations* skiing, reading, gardening, opera, theatre; *Style—* Michael Guthrie, Esq, OBE; ✉ Hyde Heath Farm, Hyde Heath, Buckinghamshire HP6 5RW

GUTHRIE, Peter Moir; OBE; s of William Moir Guthrie, Surrey (d 1989), and Mary Barbara, *née* McMaster (d 1991); *b* 21 February 1951; *Educ* Merchiston Castle Sch Edinburgh, Imperial Coll London (BSc, ACGI, MSc, DIC); *m* 1979, Lorna Jane, *née* Cowcher; 1 s (Oliver Moir 20 Dec 1981), 1 da (Caroline Mary b 5 April 1985); *Career* asst engr VSO Kaduna Nigeria 1974; planning engr: Turriff Taylor Tarmac Ltd (Flotta Oil Terminal Orkney Islands) 1975, Turriff Taylor Ltd (Ahwaz Iran) 1976; engrg geologist Balfour Beatty Ltd (second Dartford Tunnel Project) 1976, engr Soil Mechanics Ltd 1977–78; Scott Wilson Kirkpatrick: engr 1978–79; chartered engr 1979–80, sr chartered engr 1980–85, asst princ engr 1985–86, princ engr 1986–87, assoc (head of mktg) 1987–90, ptnr 1990–95, dir 1995–2004, Bd dir 1997–2004; prof of engrg for sustainable devpt Univ of Cambridge 2000–; author of several manuals and books; co fndr and vice-pres Red R Engineers for Disaster Relief; Hon LLD Univ of Bristol 1994; FREng 1998, FICE 1997 (MICE 1979), FCGI 1999; *Recreations* skiing, golf, tennis; *Style—* Peter Guthrie, Esq, OBE, FREng; ✉ Camrose House, 9 The Street, Old Basing, Hampshire RG24 7BW (tel 01256 352175, fax 01256 476116); Engineering Department, Cambridge University, Trumpington Street, Cambridge CB2 1PZ (e-mail pmg31@cam.ac.uk)

GUTHRIE, Robert Isles Loftus (Robin); s of Dr William Keith Chambers Guthrie (d 1981), Master of Downing Coll Cambridge, and Adele Marion, *née* Ogilvy (d 1992); *b* 27 June 1937; *Educ* Clifton, Trinity Coll Cambridge (MA), Univ of Liverpool (CertEd), LSE (MSc); *m* 1963, Sarah Julia, da of J Weltman, OBE; 2 s (Andrew b 1965, Thomas b 1970), 1 da (Clare b 1969); *Career* 2 Lt Queen's Own Cameron Highlanders 1956–58; head Cambridge House South London 1962–69, schoolteacher Kennington Sch Brixton 1964–66, social devpt offr Peterborough Devpt Corpn 1969–75, asst dir social work serv DHSS 1975–79, dir Joseph Rowntree Meml Tst 1979–88, chief charity cmmr England and Wales 1988–92, dir of social and economic affairs Cncl of Europe 1992–98; memb Arts Cncl of GB 1979–81 and 1987–88, memb UK Ctee European Cultural Fndn 2004–; chm Yorks Arts Assoc 1984–88; chm Cncl: Regnl Arts Assoc 1985–88, Univ of York 1980–94, Policy Studies Inst 1979–88; chair: York Early Music Fndn 1996–2001, Jessie's Fund 1998–, Yorks Regnl Arts Bd 2000–02, York Museums and Gallery Tst 2002–, Coll of York St John 2003–, Hans Gal Soc 2006–; memb Cncl Yorks Philosophical Soc 2000–01; tstee: Rodolfus Choir 1997– (also chair), Thalidomide Tst 1999–, York Archaeological Tst 2000–01; Hon LLD Univ of Bradford 1991; *Recreations* music, mountaineering, archaeology, travel; *Style—* Robin Guthrie, Esq; ✉ Braeside, Acomb, York YO24 4EZ (tel 01904 793130, e-mail robin@theguthries.co.uk)

GUTHRIE OF CRAIGIEBANK, Baron (Life Peer UK 2001), of Craigiebank in the City of Dundee; Gen Charles Ronald Llewelyn Guthrie; GCB (1994, KCB 1990), LVO (1977), OBE (1980); s of Ronald Dalglish Guthrie (d 1982), of Chelsea, and Nina, *née* Llewelyn (d 1987); *b* 17 November 1938; *Educ* Harrow, RMA Sandhurst; *m* 11 Sept 1971, Catherine, da of Lt-Col Claude Worrall, MVO, OBE, Coldstream Gds (d 1973), of Avon Dassett, Warks; 2 s (Hon David Charles b 21 Oct 1972, Hon Andrew James b 3 Sept 1974); *Career* cmmnd Welsh Gds 1959, served BAOR and Aden, 22 SAS Regt 1965–69, psc 1972, mil asst to Chief of Gen Staff MOD 1973–74, Bde Maj Household Div 1976–77, CO 1 Bn Welsh Gds served Berlin and NI 1977–80, Col gen staff mil ops MOD 1980–82, cmd Br Forces New Hebrides 1980, 4 Armd Bde 1982–84, Chief of Staff 1 (Br) Corps 1984–86, GOC NE Dist cmd 2 Inf Div 1986–87, Asst Chief of the Gen Staff MOD 1987–89, Cmd 1 Br Corps 1990–91, C in C BAOR 1992–94, cmd Northern Army Gp 1992–93 (NORTHAG, now disbanded), Chief of the Gen Staff 1994–97, Chief of the Defence Staff April 1997–2001; Col Cmdt Intelligence Corps 1986–95; Col Life Guards (Gold Stick) 1999–; ADC Gen to HM The Queen 1993–2001; Col Cmdt SAS Regt 2000–; pres: Army Saddle Club 1991–97, Army LTA 1991–99, Army Benevolent Fund 2002–; memb Cncl IISS; dir N M Rothschild & Sons Ltd 2001–; pres: Fedn of London Youth Clubs 2001–, Action Medical Research 2001–, Weston Spirit 2003–06; hon fell and visiting prof KCL 2001–, memb Bd Moscow Sch of Politcal Studies 2002–; Freeman City of London, Liveryman Worshipful Co of Painter-Stainers; Knight SMOM, Cdr Legion of Merit (USA) 2001; *Recreations* tennis, opera, travel; *Clubs* White's, Beefsteak, All England Lawn Tennis; *Style—* The Rt Hon the Lord Guthrie of Craigiebank, GCB, LVO, OBE; ✉ PO Box 25439, London SW1P 1AG

GUTTERIDGE, Tom Michael Gillan; s of Herbert Thomas Gutteridge (d 1972), of Tynemouth, and Ethelie, *née* Boucher; *b* 2 February 1952; *Educ* Royal GS Newcastle upon Tyne, Univ of York (BA); *m* 1, 1981 (m dis 1993), Jillian, da of Capt C Carrington Barber; 2 s (Benjamin Leo Thomas, Sam Fredric), 2 da (Rebecca Holly, Anya Romanta); m 2, 2003 (m dis 2007), Rosetta, da of Angelo Santagati (d 2004); *Career* BBC: news trainee 1973–75, dir Nationwide, Tonight and Panorama 1975–79, prodr/dir Tonight in Town 1979, prodr Harty 1980, prodr/dir A Kick up the Eighties and The Hot Shoe Show 1981, exec prodr BBC TV Music & Arts 1982–85, dir BBC coverage of Gen Election 1983; Mentorn Gp: fndr chm and chief exec 1985–2000, exec chm 2000–03; chief exec Mentorn Barraclough Carey Productions 1997–2000; non-exec chm West One Television 1991–99; jt chm Space Productions 1994–2003; dir The Television Corp plc 2000–03; broadcasting conslt Camelot plc (Nat Lottery); chief exec Fremantle Media N America 2004–05; chm Vine Media 2006–, chm Standing Stone Productions 2007–; Mentorn prodns incl: Gerry Anderson's Space Precinct, 01 for London, Challenge Anneka, Today's the Day, The Bullion Boys, The Valley, The Fall of Saigon, Star for a Night, Cancer Wars, Question Time, The Clintons, Robot Wars, Queen and Country, Paradise Hotel; Fremantle prodns incl: American Idol, The Price is Right, Family Feud; prodns as freelance dir incl: Fire & Ice (LWT) 1985, The Sleeping Beauty (Anglia) 1986; chm PACT 1993–94, memb Cncl Br Screen Advsy Cncl 1994–2004; vice-chm RTS 2000–02; tstee: Nat Film and TV Sch Fndn, Tom Gutteridge Fndn; memb BAFTA, FRTS 1996; *Awards* BAFTA Award for The Hot Shoe Show 1984, Bronze Rose of Montreux for Fire & Ice 1985, Best Dir Int Monitor Awards LA for Fire & Ice 1985, Best Prog Int Monitor Awards for Sleeping Beauty 1986, Int Emmy nomination for I Drew Roger Rabbit 1987, Bronze Rose of Montreux, Best Prog Nat Viewers and Listeners' Assoc Awards for Challenge Anneka 1991, Silver Hugo Award Chicago and NY Film Festival Bronze Medal for Passport 1994, Silver medal for Best Children's Series NY Film and TV Festival for Early Bird 1994, Int Emmy for Best Drama for The Bullion Boys 1994; *Clubs* Athenaeum, Chelsea Arts, Groucho, Century; *Style—* Tom Gutteridge, Esq; ✉ e-mail tomgutteridge@aol.com

GUY, Dr Alan James; s of James Alfred Guy (d 1967), and Florence Elizabeth, *née* Farr (d 1968); *b* 13 July 1950, Portsmouth, Hants; *Educ* Portsmouth (Southern) GS, Keble Coll Oxford; *m* 25 July 1975, Vivien Ruth, *née* Wilson; 1 s (Joseph Michael b 19 Jan 1979); *Career* Nat Army Museum: curator Dept of Weapons 1977–86, special asst to the dir 1986–88, asst dir (Collections) 1988–2000, asst dir (Admin) 2000–03, acting dir 2003–04, dir 2004–; FRHistS 1989, FRAS 1999, FSA 2001; *Books* Oeconomy and Discipline: Officership and administration in the British Army 1714–1763 (1985), Colonel Samuel Bagshawe and the Army of George II (1990), Soldiers of the Raj: The Indian Army 1660–1947 (co-author, 1997), Ashes and Blood: The British Army in South Africa 1795–1914 (co-author, 1999); *Recreations* Baroque opera and its substitutes; *Style—* Dr Alan Guy; ✉ National Army Museum, Royal Hospital Road, Chelsea, London SW3 4HT (tel 020 7730 0717, fax 020 7823 6573, e-mail aguy@national-army-museum.ac.uk)

GUY, Diana; da of Charles Stanley Eade (d 1964), of Broadstairs, Kent, and Vera Dorothy, *née* Manwaring (d 2001); *b* 27 March 1943; *Educ* Queen Anne's Sch Caversham, Lady Margaret Hall Oxford (MA); *m* 25 May 1968, (John) Robert Clare Guy, s of Wilfred Guy (d 1965), of Sydenham, London; 2 s (Jonathan b 1972, Matthew b 1975); *Career* admitted slr 1968, ptnr Theodore Goddard 1973–95, conslt 1995–2001; dep chm Competition Cmmn 2004–; memb Law Soc 1968; *Books* The EEC and Intellectual Property (with G I F Leigh, 1981); *Recreations* reading, opera, theatre; *Style—* Mrs Diana Guy

GUY, HE Frances; da of David Guy (d 1996), and Elise, *née* Hendry; *b* 1 February 1959, Edinburgh; *Educ* Univ of Aberdeen (MA), Johns Hopkins Univ Bologna (Dip), Carleton Univ Ottawa (MA); *m* 1989, Hugo G Raybaudo; 2 da (Anaide b 14 Oct 1991, Nina b 2 May 1996), 1 s (James b 5 June 1993); *Career* diplomat; joined FCO 1985, dep head of mission Addis Ababa 1997, ambass to Yemen 2001–06, head Engaging with the Islamic World Gp FCO 2004–06, ambass to Lebanon 2006–; *Recreations* running, swimming, tennis; *Clubs* Royal Cwlth Soc; *Style—* HE Ms Frances Guy; ✉ c/o Foreign and Commonwealth Office, King Charles Street, London SW1A 2AH

GUY, Dr John Alexander; *b* 16 January 1949; *Educ* Univ of Cambridge (Greene Cup Clare Coll, MA, PhD, York Prize for published work in legal history); *m* 1 (m dis 2004); 2 c; m 2, 14 May 2005, Julia Fox; *Career* research fell Selwyn Coll Cambridge 1970–73, asst keeper of public records Public Record Office London 1973–78, visiting lectr in British history Univ of Calif Berkeley 1977; Univ of Bristol: lectr in modern British history 1978–82, awarded tenure 1981, reader in British history 1982–90; John Hinkley visiting prof Johns Hopkins Univ 1990, Richard L Turner prof of humanities and prof of history Univ of Rochester 1990–92; Univ of St Andrews: prof of modern history 1992–2002, head Sch of History and Int Relations 1992–94, provost St Leonard's Coll 1994–97, vice-princ 1996–97, hon res prof 2002–; fell Clare Coll Cambridge 2003– (visiting fell 2002–03); Marc Fitch research reader British Acad 1987–89; fell Leverhulme Trust Research 1997–98; currently author, freelance presenter and historical conslt; co-ed Cambridge Studies in Early Modern British History; FRHistS 1977; *Publications* The Public Career of Sir Thomas More (1980), Tudor England (1988, paperback edn, 1990), The Reign of Elizabeth I: Court and Culture in the Last Decade (1995), The Tudor Monarchy (1997), Thomas More (2000), My Heart is My Own: The Life of Mary Queen of Scots (2004, Whitbread Biography of the Year 2004, Marsh Biography Prize 2005); also author of nine other books, 54 articles and numerous book reviews; *Recreations* opera, theatre; *Style—* Dr John Guy; ✉ Clare College, Cambridge CB2 1TL (e-mail jag64@cam.ac.uk)

GUY, Prof Keith William Arthur; s of Kenneth Leonard Guy (d 1977), of Portsmouth Co, and Margaret Olive Jesse, *née* Rose; *b* 14 December 1943; *Educ* Southern GS, Imperial Coll London (BSc, MSc, PhD, ACGI, DIC); *m* 1, 5 April 1968 (m dis 1989), Penelope Ann, da of Peter Desmond Greenyer; 3 da (Tabitha Kate b 11 Sept 1971, Victoria Rose b 31 May 1973, Hannah Roberta b 9 Sept 1976 d 30 Sept 2003); m 2, 25 May 1991, Kathryn Elizabeth, da of Dr Norman Lawrence Franklin, CBE, FRS, FEng (d 1987); *Career* Air Products plc: joined 1970, mangr Staff Engrg 1974, mangr Engrg Design 1977, mangr Process and Proposals 1983, gp mangr Engrg 1985, tech dir 1987, mktg dir 1989, business devpt dir 1995–99, dir 1999–2001; dir and sr ptnr Spiritus Group Ltd 2001, dir Webaspx Ltd 2001; chm: Process Systems Enterprise Ltd 2001, Impact Faraday Ltd, Hyradix Inc 2005–07; memb Advsy Bd Paros plc 2006–07, chm Process Integration Ltd 2007–; memb CEI 1979–83; Inst of Chem Engrs: chm London and SE Branch 1985–87, chm Engrg Practices Ctee 1989–99, chm Tech Bd 1996–2005, vice-pres 1999–2005; Royal Acad of Engrg: chm membership 1996–2000, chm President's Pro-active Gp 2001–07, memb Engrg Policy Bd 2005–; SERC (now EPSRC): appointments to Interdisciplinary Res Centre at Imperial Coll London 1989–2001, chm Process Engrg Ctee 1993–94, chm Chem Engrg Sub-Gp 1991–93, memb Clean Technol Mgmnt Ctee 1992–94; IMI (Process) STAG memb 1995–2001; memb Steering Panel Process Systems Gp Univ of Edinburgh 1992–96; external examiner: in chem engrg Univ of Bradford 1992–98, MSc int pollution mgmnt UMIST; visiting prof: Dept of Chem Engrg Univ of Bath 1994–, Imperial Coll of Science Technol and Med (ICSTM) London; memb: Res Assessment Panel (Chemical Engrg) and teaching assessment specialist assessor (Chemical Engrg) 1995–97 and 1999–2002, Chemicals Foresight Panel 1996–99, Bd Crystal Faraday Partnership 2001–05; chm: Mgmnt Bd Inst of Applied Catalysis 1996–99 (ceo 1999–), Industrial Bd Univ of Sheffield 1998–2002, Industrial Advsy Bd ICSTM London 1999–, Industrial Advsy Bd UMIST, Impact Faraday Partnership 2001–; pres Mitcham and Morden Cons Assoc 1996–99 (chm 1983–88 and 1993–95); govr and chm Fin Ctee Hatfield Sch Merton 1998–2002; Liveryman Worshipful Co of Scientific Instrument Makers 2003; CEng 1975, CSci 2004, CEnv 2005; FIChemE 1981, FREng 1988, FCGI 1998; *Publications* numerous papers and co authorships on engrg; *Recreations* bridge, politics, golf, book collecting, church, music, travel, food; *Clubs* Royal London Yacht, Island Sailing; *Style—* Prof Keith Guy, FCGI, FREng; ✉ Spiritus Consulting Ltd, Clevedon, Windsor Road, Medstead, Hampshire GU34 5EF (tel 01420 562802, fax 01420 561634, e-mail guykw@aol.com)

GUY, Richard Perran; s of Rev Wilfred Guy (d 1965), of Newlands Park, London, and Winifred Margaret Guy, *née* Hardisty (d 1988); *b* 10 May 1936; *Educ* Kingswood Sch Bath, Wadham Coll Oxford (MA); *m* 26 Sept 1981, Deborah Ann, da of Kenneth Owen, of Adlestrop, Glos; 1 s (Benjamin b 1983), 1 da (Georgina b 1986); *Career* Nat Serv 2 Lt CRMP 1955–57; ICI Ltd 1961–65, New Science Publications 1965–68; called to the Bar Inner Temple 1970; memb Hon Soc Inner Temple; *Recreations* tennis, cricket, theatre, skiing; *Clubs* RAC, MCC, Bar LTC; *Style—* Richard Guy, Esq; ✉ Godolphin Chambers, 23 Francis Street, Truro, Cornwall TR1 3DP (tel 01872 276312, fax 01872 271922)

GWENLAN, Gareth; s of Charles Aneurin Gwenlan (d 1939), and Mary, *née* Francis (d 1980); *b* 1937, Brecon; *m* 1, 1962 (m dis); 1 s (Simon); m 2, 1986 (m dis 1993), Sarah Elizabeth Fanghanel; m 3, 2000, Gail Susan Evans; *Career* television executive producer and director; actor and theatre dir 1960–64, lectr in drama and opera Royal Northern Coll of Music 1964–65, joined BBC 1965, head Comedy Dept BBC TV 1983–90, head of comedy BBC Wales 2002–; over 200 prog credits incl: Woodhouse Playhouse 1977, The Fall and Rise of Reginald Perrin 1978–80, To The Manor Born 1978–81, Butterflies 1979–81, Solo 1980, Roger Roger 1988, Waiting for God 1990–96, The Legacy of Reginald Perrin 1996, Only Fools and Horses; 2 Br Acad Awards (12 nominations); md Watson Equestrian Partnership; hon fell Royal Welsh Coll of Music and Drama 1999; FRTS 1997; *Recreations* dressage; *Clubs* Garrick; *Style—* Gareth Gwenlan, Esq; ✉ Putley Mill, Putley, Herefordshire

GWILLIAM, Kenneth Mason; s of John Gwilliam (d 1987), of Farnham, Surrey, and Marjorie, *née* Mason (d 1982); *b* 27 June 1937; *Educ* Latymer Upper Sch London, Magdalen Coll Oxford (BA); *m* 1, 1961 (m dis 1987), Jennifer Mary Bell; 2 s (David Richard b 30 Dec 1964, Michael James b 9 Jan 1967); m 2, 18 Dec 1987, Sandra, da of late John Robert; *Career* econ asst Fisons Ltd Felixstowe 1960–61, lectr in industrial economics Univ of Nottingham 1961–65, lectr in economics UEA 1965–67, prof of transport economics Univ of Leeds 1967–89, prof of the economics of transport and logistics Erasmus Univ Rotterdam 1989–93, princ transport economist Infrastructure, Water and Transport Div

World Bank 1993–2002; visiting prof of transport economics Inst for Transport Studies Univ of Leeds; dir: National Bus Company 1978–83, Yorkshire Rider 1985–87; ed Jl of Transport Economics and Policy 1977–87; specialist advsr to House of Commons Tport Ctee; FCIT; *Books* Transport and Public Policy (1964), Economics of Transport Policy (1975), Sustainable Transport: Priorities for Policy Reform (1996); *Recreations* tennis, golf, walking; *Style*— Kenneth Gwilliam, Esq

GWYNN-JONES, Peter Llewellyn; CVO (1998, LVO 1994); s of Maj Jack Llewellyn Gwynn-Jones (d 1981), of Cape Town, South Africa; stepson and ward of Lt-Col Gavin David Young (d 1978), of Long Burton, Dorset; *b* 12 March 1940; *Educ* Wellington, Trinity Coll Cambridge (MA); *Career* Bluemantle Pursuivant of Arms 1973–82, Lancaster Herald of Arms 1982–95, House Comptroller College of Arms 1982–95, Garter Principal King of Arms 1995–; Genealogist Order of the Bath 1995–, Inspr of Regimental Colours 1995–, Hon Genealogist Order of St Michael and St George 1995, Inspr RAF Badges 1996; FSA 1997; KStJ (Genealogist Order of St John) 1995; *Books* Heraldry (1993), The Art of Heraldry (1998); *Recreations* local architecture, tropical forests, wildlife conservation, fishing; *Clubs* Travellers; *Style*— Peter Gwynn-Jones, Esq, CVO, Garter Principal King of Arms; ✉ College of Arms, Queen Victoria Street, London EC4V 4BT (tel 020 7248 1188, fax 020 7248 6448, e-mail garter@college-of-arms.gov.uk); 79 Harcourt Terrace, London SW10 9JP (tel 020 7373 5859)

GWYNNE, Andrew; MP; *b* 4 June 1974; *Educ* Egerton Park Community HS, Tameside Coll, NE Wales Inst, Univ of Salford; *Career* cncllr (Lab) Tameside MBC 1996–; European co-ordinator Arlene McCarthy MEP 2000–01, research asst to Andrew Bennett MP 2000–05, MP (Lab) Denton and Reddish 2005–, PPS to Rt Hon Baroness Scotland of Asthal (as Min of State Home Office) 2005–; memb: Amicus, Co-operative Party, Christian Socialist Movement; *Style*— Andrew Gwynne, Esq, MP; ✉ House of Commons, London SW1A 0AA

GWYNNE, Haydn; da of Guy Thomas Haydn Gwynne (d 1994), and Rosamond Noelle, *née* Dobson; *Career* actress; lecturer Facoltá di Economia E Commercio Rome Univ 1983–85; *Theatre* incl: debut Susan Dunedin in His Monkey Wife (Stephen Joseph Theatre Scarborough) 1986, West End debut Billie Burke in Ziegfeld (London Palladium) 1988; other roles incl: Millamant in The Way of the World (Theatre Royal Northampton) 1990, title role in Hedda Gabler (Bolton Octagon) 1990, Lady Macbeth in Macbeth (Ludlow Festival) 1991, Oolie/Donna in City of Angels (Prince of Wales) 1993 (nomination Best Actress in a Musical Olivier Awards 1993), The Memory of Water (Hampstead) 1996, Mrs Wilkinson in Billy Elliot the Musical (Victoria Palace) 2005–06 (nomination Best Actress in a Musical Olivier Awards 2006); Manchester Royal Exchange incl: The Bluebird of Unhappiness 1987, Mrs Gaylustre in The Cabinet Minister 1988, Sylvia in The Recruiting Officer 1992; RSC incl: Olivia in Twelfth Night (Stratford, Barbican) 1994–95, Helena in A Midsummer Night's Dream (Stratford) 1994–95, Solveig/Mother Aase in Peer Gynt (Swan Stratford, Young Vic) 1994–95; *Television* incl: What Mad Pursuit (BBC) 1986, Lovejoy (BBC) 1986, Call Me Mister (BBC) 1986, The Great Writers

- Thomas Mann (LWT/Channel Four) 1987, After the War (Granada) 1987, Robyn Penrose in Nice Work (BBC) 1989, B B Miller in Time Riders (Thames) 1991, Alex in Drop the Dead Donkey (Channel Four) 1991–93 (nomination British Comedy Award and BAFTA Award), Portia in The Merchant of Venice (Channel Four) 1995, Hospital! (Channel Five) 1997, Verdict (Yorkshire) 1998, Dangerfield (BBC) 1998, Dr Joanna Graham in Peak Practice (Carlton) 1999–2000 (nominations RTS Award), Supt Susan Blake in Mersey Beat (BBC) 2001–02, Merseybeat (Best Actress RTS Awards 2002 and 2003), Emma in The Secret 2002, Midsomer Murders (ITV) 2004, Dalziel & Pascoe (BBC, Best Actress RTS Awards 2005), Absolute Power (BBC); *Film* incl: The Pleasure Principle 1990, Remember Me? 1996, The Heat of the Story 2004, These Foolish Things 2004; *Style*— Ms Haydn Gwynne; ✉ c/o Markham & Froggatt Ltd, Julian House, 4 Windmill Street, London W1P 1HF (tel 020 7636 4412, fax 020 7637 5233)

GWYNNE, Richard; s of Dr Edward Ieuan Gwynne, of Ystrad-Rhondda, Mid Glamorgan, and Mary Teresa, *née* Downey; *b* 9 March 1955; *Educ* Porth County GS, Trinity Coll Cambridge (MA); *m* 6 May 1995, Susan Mary, *née* Paton; 1 s, 1 da; *Career* admitted slr 1979, ptnr Stephenson Harwood 1986–, chm Mgmnt Ctee Fulham Legal Advice Centre 1987–91; memb Worshipful Co of Slrs; memb IBA; *Publications* International Execution Against Judgement Debtors (contrib, 1993 and subseq edns), Structuring International Contracts (contrib, 1996); *Recreations* opera, golf; *Style*— Richard Gwynne, Esq; ✉ 46 Lytton Grove, Putney, London SW15 2HE (tel 020 8788 7567, e-mail richardgwynne@tiscali.co.uk); Stephenson Harwood, One St Paul's Churchyard, London EC4M 8SH (tel 020 7329 4422, fax 020 7606 0822, e-mail richard.gwynne@shlegal.com)

GWYTHER, Christine Margery; da of Ivor George Gwyther, and Marjorie, *née* Doidge; *Educ* Pembroke Sch, UC Wales Cardiff; *Career* memb Nat Assembly for Wales (Lab) Carmarthen W and S Pembrokeshire 1999–2007; Welsh Assembly: sec for Agric and Rural Devpt 1999–2000, chair Econ Devpt Ctee; memb: RSPB, Pembrokeshire Business Club; *Recreations* walking, cooking; *Style*— Ms Christine Gwyther

GYLLENHAMMAR, Pehr Gustaf; *b* 28 April 1935, Gothenburg, Sweden; *Educ* Lund Univ (LLB), Centre d'Etudes Industrielles Geneva; *Career* md and chief exec Skandia Insurance Co 1970–83, chm and chief exec then exec chm AB Volvo 1983–93, md Lazard Frères & Co LLC 1996–2003; chm: CGU plc (latterly CGNU then Aviva plc) 1998–2005 (dep chm Commercial Union plc 1997–98), Lazard AB 1999–2003, Reuters Founder Share Co Ltd 1999–, Investment AB Kinnevik 2004–, Majid Al Futtaim Holding LLC 2004–; vice-chm Europe Rothschild 2003–; non-exec dir: Pearson plc 1983–97, Reuters Holdings plc 1984–97; fndr memb European Round Table of Industrialists, chm European Financial Services Round Table (EFR); chm London Philharmonic Tst 2006–; Hon MD Gothenburg Univ 1981, Hon DTech Brunel Univ 1987, Hon DEng Tech Univ of Nova Scotia 1988, Hon DSocSci Univ of Helsinki 1990, Hon LLD Univ of Vermont 1993, Dr of Economics (hc) Gothenburg Univ 2003, DBA (hc) Metropolitan Univ 2004; *Style*— Pehr G Gyllenhammar, Esq; ✉ Investment AB Kinnevik, 11 Bolton Street, Mayfair, London W1J 8BB

H

HAACKE, Norman Patrick von; s of Frederick and Margaret Haacke; *b* 15 March 1952; *Educ* St Joseph's Acad Blackheath, London Coll of Music (jr exhibitioner), St Catharine's Coll Cambridge (MA, MB BChir), Bart's Med Coll; *m* 17 Feb 1979, Jennifer Mary, da of Mathew Finbar Hunt (d 1986); 1 da (Georgina Alexandra Morgan b 4 Nov 1984), 1 s (Samuel James Finbar b 22 Aug 1982); *Career* house surgn Bart's 1976–77, house physician Royal Berkshire Hosp 1977, SHO Addenbrooke's 1977–78, sr registrar Royal Nat Throat, Nose and Ear Hosp 1983 (SHO 1980, registrar 1980–83), sr registrar Edinburgh Royal Infirmary 1983–87, conslt ENT surgn Southampton Univ Hosps 1987–2000, sr lectr in otolaryngology Univ of Southampton 1987–2000; currently conslt ENT surgn: Met Police Serv, Cromwell Hosp, Lister Hosp, Princess Grace Hosp, Portland Hosp for Women and Children, Wessex Nuffield Hosp, Chalybeate Hosp; med dir Wessex Regnl Hearing and Balance Centre 1987–97; examiner in fellowship Royal Coll of Surgns in Ireland; Lionel Colledge meml fell RCSE 1985–86; dir S of England Cochlear Implant Centre 1989–97; jt fndr and tstee All Hear Trust 1990–96; memb: Br Assoc of Otolaryngologists, Br Assoc for Paediatric Otorhinolaryngology, Otolaryngology Research Soc, S Western Laryngological Soc, Scottish Otolaryngological Soc, Euro Rhinologic Soc, American Rhinologic Soc, Euro Acad of Facial Plastic Surgery, BMA; FRCSI 1982, FRCS 1983, FRSM; *Publications* author of 3 chapters and over 40 papers on cochlear implantation, endoscopic sinus surgery and other aspects of ENT surgery; *Recreations* flying, sculpture and painting, music; *Style*— Norman Haacke, Esq; ✉ Chalybeate Hospital, Chalybeate Close, Tremona Road, Southampton S016 6UY (tel 023 8076 4308, fax 023 8078 5621, e-mail haacke@entfacialplastic.com); 234 Great Portland Street, London W1W 5QT (tel 020 7630 9599, fax 070 9203 9266, e-mail office@entfacialplastic.com)

HABERMAN, Prof Steven; s of Louis Haberman, of Essex, and Rita Lily, *née* Kaminsky; *b* 26 June 1951; *Educ* Ilford Co HS, Trinity Coll Cambridge (MA), City Univ (PhD, DSc); *m* 11 April 1976, Mandy Nicola Haberman, da of Arnold and Sylvia Brecker, of Herts; 1 s (Benjamin Adam b 18 Aug 1978), 2 da (Nadia Lia (twin) b 18 Aug 1978, Emily Michal b 15 Feb 1980); *Career* Prudential Assurance Co 1972–74, Govt Actuary's Dept 1977–97; City Univ: lectr Dept of Actuarial Sci 1974–79, sr lectr 1979–83, reader 1983–85, prof 1985–, dean Sch of Mathematics 1995–2002, dep dean Cass Business Sch 2002–; memb: Cncl Inst of Actuaries 1986–91 and 1993–99, Morris Review Advsy Panel 2004–05, Bd for Actuarial Standards 2006–; memb NY Acad of Sci 1995; FIA 1975, ASA 1976, FSS 1979, FRSA 1989, FIMA 1996; *Books* Pensions: The Problems of Today and Tomorrow (1987), History of Actuarial Science (1995), Modern Actuarial Theory and Practice (1999, 2 edn 2005), Actuarial Models for Disability Insurance (1999); *Recreations* walking, reading, music, cinema; *Style*— Prof Steven Haberman; ✉ Cass Business School, City University, 106 Bunhill Row, London EC1Y 8TZ (tel 020 7040 8601, fax 020 7040 8899, e-mail s.haberman@city.ac.uk)

HABGOOD, Anthony John; s of John Michael Habgood, MC, and Margaret Diana Middleton, *née* Dalby; *b* 8 November 1946; *Educ* Gresham's, Gonville & Caius Coll Cambridge (MA), Carnegie Mellon Univ Pittsburgh (MS); *m* 29 June 1974, Nancy, da of Ray Nelson Atkinson, of San Mateo, CA; 1 da (Elizabeth Ann b 21 Sept 1975), 2 s (John Alan, George Michael (twins) b 14 Nov 1979); *Career* memb Mgmnt Exec Ctee Boston Consulting Gp Inc 1979–86 (dir 1976–86), chief exec Tootal Group plc 1986–91, chief exec then chm Bunzl plc 1991–, chm Whitbread plc 2005–, chm MHC UK Ltd 2006–; non-exec dir: Geest plc 1988–93, Powergen plc 1993–2001, SVG Capital plc 1996–, National Westminster Bank plc 1998–2000, Marks & Spencer plc 2004–05; *Clubs* Royal Norfolk and Suffolk Yacht; *Style*— Anthony Habgood, Esq; ✉ Bunzl plc, 110 Park Street, London W1K 6NX (tel 020 7495 4950)

HABGOOD, Baron (Life Peer UK 1995), of Calverton in the County of Buckinghamshire; Rt Rev and Rt Hon John Stapylton Habgood; PC (1983); s of Arthur Henry Habgood, DSO, MB, BCh (d 1978), and Vera (d 1968), da of Edward Chetwynd-Stapylton (d 1938), gggs of 4 Viscount Chetwynd; *b* 23 June 1927; *Educ* Eton, King's Coll Cambridge (MA, PhD), Cuddesdon Theol Coll; *m* 7 June 1961, Rosalie Mary Anne, elder da of Edward Lansdown Boston, of Deeside, Chester; 2 da (Hon Laura Caroline (Dr Joya) b 1963, Hon Ruth Barbara (Mrs Kenyon-Slade) b 1967), 2 s (Hon Francis John Stapylton b 1964, Hon Adrian George Chetwynd b 1971); *Career* demonstrator in pharmacology Univ of Cambridge 1950–53, fell King's Coll Cambridge 1952–55; ordained: deacon 1954, priest 1955; curate of St Mary Abbots with St George's London 1954–56, vice-princ Westcott House Cambridge 1956–62, rector St John's Jedburgh 1962–67, princ Queen's Coll Birmingham 1967–73, hon canon of Birmingham Cathedral 1971–73, bishop of Durham 1973–83, Archbishop of York 1983–95, ret; hon bencher Inner Temple 2000; hon fell King's Coll Cambridge 1986; Hon DD: Univ of Durham 1975, Univ of Cambridge 1984, Univ of Aberdeen 1988, Huron Univ 1990, Univ of Hull 1991, Univ of Oxford 1996, Univ of Manchester 1996, Univ of York 1996, Univ of London 2005; *Books* Religion and Science (1964), A Working Faith (1980), Church and Nation in a Secular Age (1983), Confessions of a Conservative Liberal (1988), Making Sense (1993), Faith and Uncertainty (1997), Being a Person (1998), Varieties of Unbelief (2000), The Concept of Nature (2002); *Recreations* DIY, painting; *Clubs* Athenaeum; *Style*— The Rt Rev and Rt Hon the Lord Habgood, PC; ✉ 18 The Mount, Malton, North Yorkshire YO17 7ND

HACK, Jefferson; *b* 1971, Montevideo, Uruguay; *Educ* Pangbourne, London Coll of Printing; *Children* 1 da (Lila Grace b 29 Sept 2002, with Kate Moss, *qv*); *Career* magazine editor; Dazed & Confused: co-fndr 1991, editor 1991–2001, gp editorial dir 2001–; fndr: Another Magazine 2001, Another Man 2005; *Style*— Jefferson Hack, Esq; ✉ Dazed & Confused, 112–116 Old Street, London EC1V 9BG (tel 020 7336 0766, fax 020 7336 0966)

HACKER, Alan Ray; OBE; s of Kenneth Ray Hacker, and Sybil Blanche, *née* Cogger; *b* 30 September 1938; *Educ* Dulwich Coll, Royal Acad of Music; *m* 1 (m dis 1976), Anna Maria, *née* Sroka; 2 da (Katy, Sophie); m 2 (m dis), 1977, Karen Wynne, *née* Evans; 1 s (Alcuin); m 3, 23 Sept 1995, Margaret Shelley, *née* Lee; *Career* prof Royal Acad of Music, sr lectr Univ of York, conductor and teacher Royal Northern Coll; revived Mozart bassett clarinet in the 1960s, pioneer of authentic classical performances in England, many first modern performances of classical works in the 1970s (Haydn to Mendelssohn); operatic conductor 1986–; new prodns incl: Halström's Den Bergtagna (Sweden), Mozart's La Finta Giardiniera (England), Weir's The Vanishing Bridegroom (Scotland), Mozart's Cosi fan Tutte (Stuttgart), Monteverdi's Ulisse (Stuttgart), Handel's Julius Caesar (Halle), Bizet's Carmen (Canada), Rossini's La Cenerentola (Spain), King Arthur (Stuttgart), Alcina (Stuttgart), Saul (Berlin); conductor and clarinettist in Birtwistle's The Io Passion; fndr: York Early Music Festival (dir), York Clarion Band; memb various arts Cncl Ctees, host Br Cncl; FRAM; *Books* scores of: Mozart's Clarinet Concerto, Schumann's Fantasy Pieces (Soiréestücke); *Recreations* cooking; *Style*— Dr Alan Hacker, OBE; ✉ Hindlea, Broughton, Malton, North Yorkshire YO17 6QJ (tel and fax 01653 696163, e-mail clarionet@hackers-at-hindlea.freeserve.co.uk)

HACKER, Richard Daniel; QC (1998); s of Samuel Hacker, of London, and Lilli Paula; *b* 1954; *Educ* Haberdashers' Aske's, Downing Coll Cambridge (MA), Wiener Anspach scholar 1976, Université Libre de Bruxelles (Licencié Speciale en Droit Européen); *m* 25 March 1988, Sarah Anne, da of Richard Millar, of Bath; 1 da (Rebecca Leonora b 23 Jan 1993); *Career* called to the Bar Lincoln's Inn 1977; Hardwicke scholar 1977, Lincoln's Inn Student of the Year Prize 1977, Gray's Inn 1989; asst parly boundary cmmr 1999; chm Inquiry Into Hertforshire Parly Constituency Boundaries 2000; called to the Bar Br Virgin Islands 2003; *Recreations* travel, gastronomy, opera; *Style*— Richard Hacker, QC; ✉ 3–4 South Square, Gray's Inn, London WC1R 5HP (tel 020 7696 9900, fax 020 7696 9911)

HACKETT, Mark Christopher; *b* 13 February 1963; *Career* nat mgmnt trainee (W Midlands) Central Birmingham HA 1984–86, asst operational mangr St George's Hosp London 1986–88, business services mangr E Hosps Unit W Glamorgan 1988–90; Good Hope Hosp: dep unit gen mangr 1990–91, actg unit gen mangr 1991–93, exec dir 1993–95, dir of ops 1993–95, dir of devpt 1995; chief exec Birmingham Women's Hosp 1996–99, chief exec Royal Wolverhampton Hosps NHS Tst 1999– (formerly actg chief exec); chair: Regnl Risk Mgmnt Gp (part of Regnl Clinical Governance Framework) 1999, Wolverhampton Emergency Capacity Gp 1999–2001, Black Country Cancer Network 1999–, Wolverhampton Local Information Steering Gp 1999–; vice-chair Black Country Cardiac Network 2000–; memb: W Midlands Commnd Research Advsy Ctee 1996–2002, Expert Panel W Midlands Evidenced Based Med Union 1997–99, Dept of Health/MRC Advsy Ctee on Scientific Advances in Genetics 1998–2001, Regnl Organisational Developmental Gp 1998–2001, Chief Exec's Learning Set 1998–, Regnl Chief Execs Developmental Gp 1999–, Regnl Higher Awards Ctee 2002–, Regnl Postgrad Med Teaching Gp 2002–; reviewer and author of numerous articles in professional jls; *Recreations* sport, current affairs, my two children; *Style*— Mark Hackett, Esq; ✉ The Royal Wolverhampton Hospitals NHS Trust, New Cross Hospital, Wolverhampton, West Midlands WV10 0QP (tel 01902 307999)

HACKING, 3 Baron (UK 1945); Sir Douglas David Hacking; 3 Bt (UK 1938); s of 2 Baron Hacking (d 1971); n of Hon Lady Waller; *b* 17 April 1938; *Educ* Aldro Sch, Charterhouse, Clare Coll Cambridge (MA); *m* 1, 1965 (m dis), (Rosemary) Anne (who m subsequently, 1982, Antony Askew (decd), of Highgate, London), da of late Frank Penrose Forrest, FRCSE, of Lytchett Matravers, Dorset; 1 da (Hon Belinda Anne b 1966), 2 s (Hon Douglas Francis b 8 Aug 1968, Hon Daniel Robert b 27 May 1972); m 2, 1982, Dr Tessa Margaret Hunt, MB, MRCP, FRCA, er da of late Roland Hunt, CMG, of Whitchurch Hill, Berks; 3 s (Hon Alexander Roland Harry b 20 Jan 1984, Hon (Maxwell David) Leo b 8 July 1987, Hon Christian Eric George b 7 Dec 1989); *Heir* s, Hon Douglas Hacking; *Career* Nat Serv RN 1956–58; Lt RNR (ret); formerly sat as Lab peer in House of Lords (memb Select Ctee on Euro Community 1989–93 and 1995–99); barr 1963–76, Harmsworth Major Entrance exhibitioner and Astbury scholar Middle Temple; attorney: New York State 1975, Simpson Thacher and Bartlett New York 1975–76; slr Supreme Court of Eng & Wales 1977–99; ptnr Richards Butler 1981–94, ptnr Sonnenschein 1994–99; int arbitrator 1997–, barr 1999–, chartered arbitrator 1999–, memb Littleton Chambers 2000–; observer of Human Rights Inst of Int Bar Assoc at the trial of the Chief Justice of Gibraltar 2001; Freeman: City of London, Worshipful Co of Merchant Taylors'; Liveryman Worshipful Co of Arbitration; FCIArb 1979; *Publications* Well: Did You Get the Right Arbitrator? (2000); author of numerous articles on the law and arbitration; *Clubs* MCC, Reform; *Style*— The Rt Hon the Lord Hacking; ✉ 27 West Square, Kennington, London SE11 4SP (tel 020 7735 4400, fax 020 7735 7337); Littleton Chambers, 3 King's Bench Walk North, Temple, London EC4Y 7HR (tel 020 7797 8600, fax 020 7797 8699, e-mail clerks@littletonchambers.co.uk)

HACKNEY, Jeffrey; s of Reginald Thomas Hackney, of Stoke-on-Trent, and Mildred Anne, *née* Stanway; *b* 5 January 1941; *Educ* Newcastle HS, Wadham Coll Oxford (BA, BCL, Vinerian scholar), UCL (Churchill Jenkinson prize); *m* 27 Oct 1962, Dr Ann Christine, da of Frank Swindells; 1 s (Daniel b 3 Nov 1965), 1 da (Lucy b 2 April 1967); *Career* called to the Bar Middle Temple 1966 (Blackstone scholar, Colombos prize), pupillages with Martin Nourse (now Lord Justice Nourse) and Nicolas Browne-Wilkinson (now Lord Browne-Wilkinson); St Edmund Hall: fell and tutor in law 1964–76, librarian 1966–72, sr tutor 1972–76; Wadham Coll Oxford: fell and tutor in law 1976–, sec to Governing Body 1981–84, sr tutor 1986–88 and 2000, sub-warden 2002–03 and 2004–, actg warden 2003–04; University of Oxford: chm Law Faculty Bd 1977–79, Keeper of the Archives 1987–95, chm Libraries Bd 1988–91, Bodleian curator 1986–91, chm Gen Bd of the Faculties 1991–93, memb Hebdomadal Cncl 1991–95, chm Curators of the Sheldonian Theatre 1993–, chm Disciplinary Ct 1997–2002; *Books* Understanding Equity and Trusts (1987); *Recreations* music, theatre; *Style*— Jeffrey Hackney, Esq; ✉ 25 Barton Lane, Headington, Oxford OX3 9JW (tel 01865 61458); Wadham College, Oxford OX1 3PN (tel 01865 277918)

HACKNEY, Dr Roderick Peter (Rod); s of William Hackney, and Rose, *née* Morris; *b* 3 March 1942; *Educ* John Bright's GS Llandudno, Sch of Architecture Univ of Manchester (MA, BA, ARCH, PhD); *m* Christine (Tina); 1 s (Roan b 27 April 1982); *Career* architect Expo 1967 monorail stations Montreal Canada 1965–66, housing architect Libyan Govt Tripoli 1967–68, asst to Arne Jacobson Copenhagen 1968–71, established practice of Rod Hackney Architect in Macclesfield 1972, established a number of offices throughout the UK 1975–87, set up Castward Ltd (building and devpt) 1983, designer (with Shenzhen Sch of Architecture) 2000 Housing Scheme Shenzhen China 2002; RIBA: elected nat memb to the Cncl 1978, vice-pres 1981–83, memb 3 man delgn to USSR under Anglo-Soviet Cultural Agreement 1984, chm The Times-RIBA Community Enterprise Scheme 1985–89, pres 1987–89, memb Cncl 1991–99 and 2001–, vice-pres int affrs 1992–99, hon librarian 1998–99, tstee Br Architectural Library Tst (RIBA Library) 1998–99, chm Br Architectural Library Tst 1999–2001, chm Discipline Hearings Panel 2001–02, Discipline Ctee 2002–; UIA: elected Cncl for Gp 1 1981, memb Editorial Bd Int Architect 1983, memb Editorial Bd Jl of Architect Theory and Criticism 1988, vice-pres

1985, pres 1987–90, memb Cncl 1991–, memb Gold Medal Jury 1993, co-ordinator corp plan 1993–2001, memb Int Jury World Student Architecture Prize 1998–99, memb World Habitat Awards Advsy Gp 2003; advsr on regeneration and inner city problems in Sweden, Italy and USA 1990–, conslt BBC TV documentary series Europe by Design 1991; other TV work incl: Build Yourself A House 1974, Community Architecture 1977, BBC Omnibus 1987, Europe By Design 1991, Question Time; radio incl: The Listener 1986, Any Questions 1987, Third Ear 1990, Call to Account 1992, Woman's Hour 1992, Common Ground 1996, The Today Programme, The World at One, The Tonight Programme; conslt World Architecture Review Agency Shenzen 1992–, int advsr Centre for Int Architecture Studies Univ of Manchester Sch of Architecture 1992–; visiting prof UP6 Paris 1984, pres Young Architect World Forum Sofia 1985, pres Building Communities Int Community Architecture Conf 1986, special prof in architecture Univ of Nottingham 1987–91, lectr tour of India (sponsored by Br Cncl) 1991, advsr to Mayor of Trento 1991, lectures in Sri Lanka (sponsored by Br Cncl) 1992, juror and advsr to DVA Int Competition Netherlands 1992, memb jury Int Students Competition Beijing 1998, advsr to Mayor of City of Meridian MS (Livable Southern Communities Conf) 1992, lecture Int Biennale for Architecture BA/93 Buenos Aires 1993, lecture Univ of Shenzhen World Architecture Review Agency 1993, lecture Inst of Architects Karachi 1993, conslt speaker Livable City Conf Meridian MS1994 and 1996, speaker Biennial conf on Architecture and Children 1999, speaker Caring Communites UN HQ 1999, speaker on sustainable housing Iran 2002, advsr Centre for Human Settlements International India 1994, conslt Chapman Clarke Films (Forever England, Central TV) 1995, visiting prof Royal Danish Acad of Fine Arts Copenhagen 1995, lectr Br-American-Canadian Assocs tour USA 1995, Int Conf Writers & Intellectuals Pakistan 1995, lecture Hogeschool Mideen Brabant & IHS Netherlands 1996, lecture Acad of Architecture Rotterdam 1996, visiting prof Sunshant Sch of Art & Architecture New Delhi 1997, lectr on community architecture and people planning TV Sch for Habitat Studies New Delhi 1997, visiting prof Coll of Architecture Xian Univ 1999–; first prize: DOE Awards for Good Design in Housing 1975, St Ann's Hospice Architectural Competition 1976; Prix Int d'Architecture de l'Institut National du Logement 1979, commended RICS and The Times Conservation Awards 1980, highly commended DOE Awards 1980, commended The Civic Tst Awards 1980 and 1982, hon mention Sir Robert Matthews Award 1981, President's Award Manchester Soc for Architects 1982, commended Otis Award 1982; commendation Business Enterprise Award 1993, shortlisted Millennium Expo Competition Greenwich 1995, commended Natural Stone Award 1995, 96 citation World Habitat Awards 1995; Gold Medal: Bulgarian Inst of Architects 1983, Young Architect of the Biennale Sofia 1983; Award of Commendation Civic Tst Awards 1984, Grand Medal of the Federacion de Colegios de Arquitectos de la Republica Mexicana 1986, PA Award for Innovation in Building Design and Construction 1988, Past Pres' Medal UIA Lausanne 1998, attained ISO 9001 Certification BSI 1996; hon fell: American Inst of Architects 1988, Federacion de Colegios de Arquitectos de la Republica Mexicana 1988, United Architects of the Philippines 1988, Royal Architectural Inst of Canada 1990, Indian Inst of Architects 1990; hon memb: Consejo Superior de los Colegios de Arquitectos de España 1987, Architecture Soc of China 2003; chm of Tstees Inner City Tst 1986–96, presented the case for Int Year of Shelter for the Homeless to all Pty Confs 1986, pres Snowdonia Nat Park Soc 1987–2003; patron Llandudno Museum and Art Gallery 1988–2003, patron Dome Project Buxton 1999–2003; pres N Wales Centre of the Nat Tst 1990–; memb Advsy Ctee Int Cncl of Caring Communities NY 1998; hon memb Rural Buildings Preservation Tst 1994–2003, memb Assoc of Planning Supervisors 1996; FCIArb 1977, MCIOB 1987, FFB 1987, ARIBA 1969; *Books* The Good, The Bad and The Ugly (1990), music play (based on own work) Good Golly Miss Molly (West End, 1991), Icinquatenaire de l'Union Internationale des Architectes Paris (contrib, 1998); *Recreations* photography, butterflies, travelling, walking, outdoor pursuits, looking at buildings, speaking at conferences; *Clubs* Cwlth; *Style*— Dr Rod Hackney; ✉ St Peter's House, Windmill Street, Macclesfield, Cheshire SK11 7HS (tel 01625 431792, fax 01625 616929, e-mail mail@stpeter.demon.co.uk)

HADDACKS, HE Vice Adm Sir Paul Kenneth; KCB (2000); s of Kenneth Alexander Haddacks (d 2002), and Edith Lillian, *née* Peardon (d 1979); *b* 27 October 1946; *Educ* Kingswood Sch Bath, BRNC Dartmouth, RN Staff Coll, Staff Coll Camberley, RCDS; *m* 1970, Penny Anne, da of late Prof D Robertson; 1 s (David Paul b 1973); *Career* joined RN 1964; commanded HM Ships: Scimitar 1971–72, Cleopatra 1981–82, Naiad 1982–83, Intrepid 1986–88; Cdr 1979, instr US Naval Acad 1979–80, Capt 1984, asst dir Naval Plans 1984–86, dep dir Naval Warfare 1988–89, Cdr RN Task Force Gulf 1990, Capt of the Fleet 1991–94, Rear Adm 1994, ACOS (Policy) to SACEUR 1994–97, Vice Adm 1997, UK Mil Rep at NATO HQ 1997–2000; dir Int Mil Staff NATO HQ 2001–04, Lt Govr Isle of Man 2005–; *Recreations* family and travel; *Clubs* Army and Navy; *Style*— HE Vice Adm Sir Paul Haddacks, KCB; ✉ Government House, Isle of Man IM3 1RR

HADDAD, (Patricia) Faith; da of Lawrence Atkin (d 1987), and Letitia, *née* Green; *b* 7 November 1943; *Educ* Cleethorpes Girls' GS, Univ of Sheffield (MB ChB, MD, Dip Obstetrics); *m* 21 Feb 1972, Joseph Haddad; 1 da (Samantha Faith b 19 July 1976); *Career* pre-registration house offr Nottingham City Hosp 1967–68, pre-registration house surgn Sheffield City Gen 1968; SHO: in obstetrics and gynaecology Jessop Hosp Sheffield 1968–70, in surgery Scunthorpe Gen Hosp 1970–71; registrar in obstetrics and gynaecology Grimsby Gen Hosp 1971–72, sr med offr Hounslow and Surrey Public Health Dept 1972–75; registrar in obstetrics and gynaecology Hillingdon Hosp 1975–76, W Middx Hosp 1976–79 (acting sr registrar); assoc specialist W London Hosp and Charing Cross Hosp 1982–85 (lectr in obstetrics and gynaecology 1979–82); conslt gynaecologist: Garden Hosp London 1985–, Hosp of St John & St Elizabeth 1992–; memb: Steering Ctee Forum on Maternity and Newborn RSM, Working Pty for Change in Antenatal Care NCT 1981, Advsy Ctee on Current Fertility Royal Coll of Gynaecologists 1984–86, Advsy Ctee for First Symposium on Preconception Care 1985, Advsy Ctee for Preconception Care Symposium City Univ 1987; recognized lectr to midwives; author of numerous articles in various learned jls; Lecture of the Year prize N of England Soc for Obstetrics and Gynaecology 1970; memb: Inst of Psychosexual Med 1985, RSM, N of England Soc of Obstetrics and Gynaecology, Med Women's Fedn; FRCOG (MRCOG 1972); *Recreations* music, sport; *Style*— Mrs Faith Haddad; ✉ Tara, Trout Rise, Loudwater, Rickmansworth, Hertfordshire WD3 4JY (tel 01923 896625, fax 01923 778702); Hospital of St John and St Elizabeth, 60 Grove End Road, St John's Wood, London NW8 9NH (tel 020 7286 5126)

HADDEN, Abel Robert; s of Alan Edwin Robert Hadden (d 2003), and Carmen Clare, *née* Masters (d 1995); *b* 4 June 1953; *Educ* Westminster; *m* 1 (m dis 1984), Katherine, *née* Taylor; 1 s (Leo b 1983); m 2 (m dis 2002), Belinda, da of Dr Sir Reginald Frederick Brittain Bennett, VRD (d 2000); 1 da (Camilla b 1991); *Career* articled clerk Touche Ross 1972–75, Odhams & Gunn 1975–76, Charles Barker 1976–81, Abel Hadden Associates Ltd 1981–83, Good Relations Group/Lowe Bell Communications 1983–94, md Edelman London 1994–98, md Abel Hadden & Co 1998–2002, Bell Pottinger Communications 2003–; IPR: memb 1976, memb Consits' Gp 1979–84, memb Cncl 1981–84; CAM examiner 1984–92 (chief examiner 1988–92), memb Mktg Soc 1984; tstee The Jill Dando Fund 1999–; DipCAM 1980, FIPR 1993; *Recreations* allotment gardening, fishing, skiing, croquet; *Clubs* Hurlingham, White's, St Moritz Tobogganing, Chelsea FC; *Style*— Abel Hadden, Esq

HADDEN, Prof David Robert; s of Robert Evans Hadden (d 1978), of Portadown, and Marianne Baird, *née* Johnston; *b* 24 May 1936; *Educ* Campbell Coll, Queen's Univ Belfast (MB BCh, BAO, MD); *m* 7 April 1967, Diana Sheelah Mary, da of William Herbert Martin (d 1987), of Belfast; 1 s (Robert b 1968), 2 da (Katharine b 1970, Emily b 1971); *Career* house physician and res fell Royal Victoria Hosp Belfast 1959–62, Fulbright travelling fellowship Johns Hopkins Hosp Baltimore USA 1962–64, MRC Infantile Malnutrition Res Unit Kampala Uganda 1965–66, Dept of Experimental Med Univ of Cambridge 1966–67, conslt physician Royal Victoria Hosp Belfast 1967–2001, hon prof of endocrinology Queen's Univ of Belfast 1990–, hon conslt physician Royal Victoria Hosp Belfast 2001–; pres Ulster Med Soc 1996; chm Bd Govrs Victoria Coll Belfast 1996–2002; memb: RSM (hon sub-dean I), Assoc of Physicians of GB and I, Diabetes and Endocrinology Socs of GB and I, Europe and USA; FRCPEd 1969, FRCP 1987; *Publications* Diabetes and Pregnancy - An International Approach to Diagnosis and Management (ed, 1996); articles and chapters on diabetes and endocrinology in med lit; *Recreations* restoration and care of old houses and gardens; *Style*— Prof David Hadden; ✉ 10 Mount Pleasant, Belfast BT9 5DS (tel 028 9066 7110, fax 028 9066 7110); Regional Endocrinology and Diabetes Centre, Royal Victoria Hospital, Belfast BT12 6BA (tel 028 9063 3380, fax 028 9031 0111)

HADDEN, Frank Murray; s of James Coyne Hadden (d 2004), and Muriel Helen, *née* Anderson; *b* 14 June 1954, Dundee; *Educ* Univ of Strathclyde (BA), Univ of Leeds (PGCE); *m* 29 Dec 1978, Susan Mitchell, *née* Thomson; 2 s (Andrew Thomson b 10 Feb 1982, Scott Anderson b 1 May 1984); *Career* rugby coach; personnel asst Watson and Philip Ltd 1976–77, PE teacher Guiseley Sch 1979–83, head of PE Merchiston Castle Sch Edinburgh 1983–2000, asst coach Caledonia Reds 1997–98, head coach Edinburgh Rugby 2000–05, Scotland nat rugby coach 2005–; *Style*— Frank Hadden, Esq; ✉ Murrayfield, Edinburgh EH12 5PJ (tel 0131 346 5000, e-mail frank.hadden@sru.org.uk)

HADDINGTON, 13 Earl of (S 1619) John George Baillie-Hamilton; also Lord Binning (S 1613) and Lord Binning and Byres (S 1619); only s of 12 Earl of Haddington, KT, MC, TD (d 1986), and Sarah, *née* Cook (d 1995); *b* 21 December 1941; *Educ* Ampleforth, Trinity Coll Dublin, RAC Cirencester; *m* 1, 19 April 1975 (m dis 1981), Prudence Elizabeth, da of Andrew Rutherford Hayles, of Bowerchalke, Wilts; m 2, 8 Dec 1984, Susan Jane Antonia, da of John Heyworth, of Bradwell Grove, Burford, Oxon; 1 s (George Edmund Baldred, Lord Binning b 27 Dec 1985), 2 da (Lady Susan Moyra b 15 July 1988, Lady Isobel Joan b 16 June 1990); *Heir* s, Lord Binning; *Career* farmer, fndr Save Our Songbirds (Scot charity, website www.save-songbirds.co.uk) 1998; *Recreations* beekeeping, keeping finches, field sports, photography, racing, cerealogy, fancy fowl; *Clubs* Turf, New, Puffins, Chelsea Arts; *Style*— The Rt Hon the Earl of Haddington; ✉ Mellerstain, Gordon, Berwicks TD3 6LG (e-mail hadders@macace.net)

HADDON, Mark; *b* 1962, Northampton; *Educ* Merton Coll Oxford, Univ of Edinburgh; *m* Dr Sos Eltis; 2 s (Alfie, Zack); *Career* author, screenwriter and illustrator; formerly held pt/t positions with various orgns incl Mencap, sometime cartoonist for pubns incl The Guardian, Sunday Telegraph, New Statesman, The Spectator and Private Eye; tutor Arvon Fndn; abstract artist; *Television* credits as screenwriter incl: The Wild House (BBC) 1996, Microsoap (BBC) 1998 (Best Children's Drama RTS Awards 1998, Best Drama and Writers' Award BAFTA Children's Awards 1999), StarStreet (Carlton) 2001, Fungus the Bogeyman (adaptation, BBC) 2004; *Books* incl: The Curious Incident of the Dog in the Night-Time (2003, Whitbread Novel Award and Whitbread Book of the Year 2003, Literary Fiction Prize and Children's Book of the Year British Book Awards 2003, Booktrust Teenage Prize 2003, Guardian Children's Fiction Prize 2003); books for children incl: Gilbert's Gobstopper (1987), Toni and the Tomato Soup (1988), A Narrow Escape for Princess Sharon (1989), Titch Johnson, Almost World Champion (1993), Agent Z Meets the Masked Crusader (1993), Gridzbi Spudvetch! (1994), The Real Porky Philips (1994, shortlisted Smarties Prize 1994), Agent Z Goes Wild (1994), At Playgroup (Baby Dinosaurs series, 1994), In the Garden (Baby Dinosaurs series, 1994), At Home (Baby Dinosaurs series, 1994), On Holiday (Baby Dinosaurs series, 1994), Agent Z and the Penguin from Mars (1995, adapted for TV 1996), The Sea of Tranquility (1996), Secret Agent Handbook (1999), Agent Z and the Killer Bananas (2001), Ocean Star Express (2001), The Ice Bear's Cave (2002); *Recreations* marathon canoeing; *Style*— Mark Haddon, Esq; ✉ c/o Random House, 20 Vauxhall Bridge Road, London SW1V 2SA

HADDON-CAVE, Charles Anthony; QC (1999); s of Sir Philip Haddon-Cave, KBE, CMG (d 1999), of Tackley, Oxon, and Elizabeth, *née* Simpson; *b* 20 March 1956; *Educ* King's Sch Canterbury, Pembroke Coll Cambridge (MA); *m* 2 Aug 1980, Amanda Charlotte, da of Timothy James Law, of Godalming, Surrey; 2 da (Alexandra Charlotte b 11 Feb 1987, Florence Caroline b 8 Jan 1991); *Career* called to the Bar: Gray's Inn 1978 (bencher 2003), Hong Kong 1980; asst recorder 1998–2000, recorder 2000–; *Recreations* triathlons; *Clubs* Garrick; *Style*— Charles Haddon-Cave, Esq, QC; ✉ Quadrant Chambers, Quadrant House, 10 Fleet Street, London EC4Y 1AU (tel 020 7583 4444, fax 020 7583 4455, e-mail charles.haddon-cave@quadrantchambers.com)

HADDON-GRANT, Hugo; s of Maurice Haddon-Grant (d 1987), and Margaret Mary, *née* Cockett; *b* 28 February 1956, Melton Mowbray, Leics; *Educ* Uppingham, UEA; *m* 28 Oct 1982, Jane Ann, *née* Goldsbury; 1 s (Guy b 27 Feb 1986), 2 da (Claire b 8 Jan 1988, Sarah b 4 March 1989); *Career* chartered accountant; Thornton Baker 1978–85, The Business Exchange 1985–88, fndr and dir Cavendish Corporate Finance Ltd 1988–; FCA 1982; *Recreations* fishing, shooting, golf, photography, travel; *Style*— Hugo Haddon-Grant, Esq; ✉ Cavendish Corporate Finance Limited, 40 Portland Place, London W1B 1NB (tel 020 7908 6000, fax 020 7908 6006, e-mail hhaddongrant@cavendish.com)

HADDOW, Christopher; QC (Scot 1985); *b* 15 May 1947; *Career* admitted Faculty of Advocates 1971; *Style*— Christopher Haddow, QC; ✉ c/o Alan Moffat, Advocates Clerk, Faculty Services Ltd, Advocates' Library, Parliament House, Edinburgh EH1 1RF (tel 0131 226 5710, e-mail alan.moffat@advocates.org.uk)

HADEN-GUEST, 5 Baron (UK 1950); Christopher Haden-Guest; s of 4 Baron Haden-Guest (d 1996), and his 2 w, Jean Pauline, *née* Hindes; *b* 5 February 1948; *m* 1984, Jamie Lee Curtis, the actress, da of Tony Curtis the actor, and Janet Leigh, the actress; 1 adopted da (Anne b 1986), 1 adopted s (Thomas b 1996); *Heir* bro, Hon Nicholas Haden-Guest; *Career* actor, director, writer and humour conslt; writer of comedy for: National Lampoon (in print and for National Lampoon Radio Hour), Lily Tomlin (Emmy Award), Saturday Night Live; *Films* as as actor incl Nigel Tufnel in This is Spinal Tap 1984 (also scriptwriter); as dir incl: The Big Picture, Attack of the 50ft Woman, Waiting for Guffman, Almost Heroes, Best in Show 2000, A Mighty Wind 2003, For Your Consideration 2006; *Recreations* fly fishing; *Style*— The Rt Hon Lord Haden-Guest

HADEN-TAYLOR, Dr Anthony St John; s of Frank Pacey Haden-Taylor (d 1971), of Broughton House, Broughton Gifford, Wilts, and Enid Christine, *née* Bushnell (now Mrs Bousfield); *b* 26 March 1948; *Educ* King's Sch, Sherborne, Pacific Western Univ of Calif (BSc, MSc, PhD); *m* 15 April 1989 (m dis 2007), Hon Susan Rosemary, *née* Greenall, da of 3 Baron Daresbury (d 1996), and sis of Peter, 4 Baron Daresbury, and former w of David St C O Bruton; 2 da (Pandora Eleanor Christine b 7 Nov 1989 d 1990, Annabella Margaret Christine b 28 July 1995), 1 s (Albert Henry George b 26 Oct 1999); *Career* sr ptnr International Management Consultants SA 1970–82, chm Ashe Park Estate and Ashe Park Mineral Water Ltd 1976–83, chief exec Taylor Downs & Co 1987–91, sr ptnr The HT Partnership; chm: ReCycled Refuse International Ltd, ReCycled Refuse (Holdings) Ltd, RCR Technology Ltd, RCR Leasing Ltd, Thermsave Engrg UK Ltd, Global Marine Shipping Ltd, Global Marine Shipping (No 10), Ltd, Global Marine Shipping (No 11) Ltd, Cayman Islands Yacht Club Ltd; tstee Int Soc Security, memb Soc for the Environment; Liveryman and Freeman City of London 1982, Liveryman Worshipful Co of Basketmakers; chartered environmentalist (CEnv), memb Chartered Inst of Wastes Mgmnt (MICWM); *Recreations* polo, shooting, golf, scuba diving, tennis, skiing; *Clubs* Annabel's, La Moye Golf, Les Ormes Golf and Country, Royal Channel Islands Yacht, Cayman Islands Yacht; *Style—* Dr Anthony Haden-Taylor, CEnv, MICWM; ✉ Le Carrefour, le Rue de l'Eglise, St John, Jersey JE3 4BA (tel 01534 743416; PO Box 188, Jersey JE4 9RT (tel 01534 498123, fax 01534 498124, mobile 07797 753055 (Jersey), e-mail chairman@rcrinternational.com or ahadentaylor@gmail.com, website www.rcrinternational.com and www.rcrusa.com)

HADFIELD, Antony; s of Thomas Henry Hadfield, and Edna Hadfield; *b* 9 September 1936; *Educ* Sheffield, Brighton, Middx Poly (BA); *m* 1959, Dorothy Fay, da of Charles Edwin Osman (d 1976); 1 s (Warren b 1966); *Career* design engr Plessey 1958–62, design and project engr Metal Industries Group 1962–65, engr and mangr ESI 1965–85, chief exec and dep chm NIE plc 1985–91, md and chief exec NE plc 1991–97, dir and chief exec Teesside Power Ltd 1991–2000, chm Sovereign Exploration 1995–97, chm Northern Information Systems Ltd 1994–97, chm NEDL Ltd 1994–97, chm Northern Utility Services Ltd 1994–97, assoc P B Power Ltd 1997–2005, sr ptnr Hadfield Associates 1997–2005, dep chm BCN Data Systems Ltd 1998–2000, memb Competition Cmmn 1998–2005; former chm Power Div IEE; CEng, CCMI, FIEE, FRSA; *Recreations* mountaineering, sailing; *Clubs* Northern Counties, Royal North of Ireland Yacht; *Style—* Antony Hadfield, Esq

HADFIELD, Hon Mrs (Maureen); elder da of Baron Segal (Life Peer; d 1985), and Molly, *née* Rolo (d 1989); *b* 15 February 1935; *Educ* St Anne's Coll Oxford (MA); *m* 6 Dec 1956, Jeremy Hadfield (d 1988), s of John Hadfield; 2 s; *Career* dir Economic Assocs 1965–76, economic advsr Price Cmmn 1976–78, ptnr/proprietor Hadfield Associates 1979–, mgmnt conslt Pannell Kerr Forster Associates 1985–88, advsr UNESCO 1989–98; chm Int Consulting Economists' Assoc 1986–89; sec Oxford W and Abingdon Lib Dem Constituency Pty 2001–; *Clubs* The Groucho; *Style—* The Hon Mrs Hadfield; ✉ 2 Park Town, Oxford OX2 6SH

HADGRAFT, Prof Jonathan; s of John William Hadgraft (d 1984), and Doris, *née* Ayres (d 1996); *b* 13 December 1950; *Educ* Queen Elizabeth's Sch Barnet, UC Oxford (MA, DPhil, DSc); *m* 1, 3 May 1975 (m dis 1996), Pauline Joyce, da of Thomas Henry Bilton, of Penarth, S Glamorgan; 1 da (Eleanor Tamsin); m 2, 16 June 1997, Isobel Joyce, da of James Ednie Dow, of Nottingham; *Career* lectr in pharmaceutical chemistry Univ of Strathclyde 1977–79, lectr in pharmacy Univ of Nottingham 1979–85, prof The Welsh Sch of Pharmacy 1985–2000; prof in medway sciences and dir skin and membrane research Univ of Greenwich 2000–04, prof Sch of Pharmacy Univ of London 2004–; CChem, FRSC 1983; *Style—* Prof Jonathan Hadgraft; ✉ The School of Pharmacy, University of London, 29–39 Brunswick Square, London WC1N 1AX (e-mail jonathan.hadgraft@btinternet.com)

HADID, Zaha M; CBE (2002); *b* 1950, Baghdad; *Educ* AA Sch of Architecture (AADip, Diploma Prize 1977); *Career* architectural designer; ptnr Office for Metropolitan Architecture 1977, in sole practice 1979–; tutor AA 1977–87 (initially with Rem Koolhaas and Elia Zenghelis, latterly head of own studio), visiting design critic Harvard Graduate Sch of Design 1986 (Kenzo Tange chair 1994), visiting prof Columbia Univ 1987, Sullivan Chair Univ of Chicago Sch of Architecture; guest prof: Hochschule für Bildende Künste Hamburg, Knolton Sch of Arch Ohio; Eero Saarinen visiting prof of architectural design Yale Univ USA; holder of various master classes and lectr on architecture at venues worldwide; Special Award Royal Acad Summer Exhbn 1995, Pritzker Prize 2004; hon memb American Acad of Arts and Letters; FAIA; *Projects* incl: 59 Eaton Place London 1980 (Architectural Design Gold Medal 1982), furniture and interiors for W Bitar London 1985, design of several bldgs in Japan incl two projects in Tokyo 1988, a folly for Expo '90 Osaka and interior work for Moonsoon Restaurant Sapporo 1990, temporary structures (Folly in Osaka) 1990, Music Video Pavilion in Groningen 1990, Vitra fire station and LFone pavilion Weil am Rhein 1993–99, IBA housing scheme in Berlin 1993, Pavilion Blueprint Magazine Interbuild Birmingham 1995, the Mind Zone Millennium Dome, Greenwich London 1999, various large scale urban studies for harbour devpts in Hamburg, Bordeaux and Cologne since 1989; *Competitions* winning designs: The Peak Hong Kong 1983, Kurfürstendamm Berlin 1986, Düsseldorf Art and Media Centre project 1992–93, Cardiff Bay Opera House 1994, Thames Water/Royal Acad Habitable Bridge across The Thames 1996, Contemporary Arts Center Cincinnati 1998, Univ of N London Holloway Road Bridge 1998, Centre for Contemporary Arts Rome 1999, Bergis Ski-jump in Innsbruck Austria 1999; other entries incl: Museum Buildings Bad Deutsch Altenburg Austria Prado Reina Sofia Royal Palace Madrid, V&A Museum's Boilerhouse Gallery London, Museum of Islamic Arts Doha Qatar, Concert Halls in Copenhagen and Luxembourg, theatre for Hackney Empire London, large scale multi-functional buildings 42nd Street NYC, IIT Campus Chicago; *Exhibitions* incl: Guggenheim Museum NY 1978, AA (retropective) 1983, GA Gallery Tokyo 1985, MOMA NY (Deconstructive Architecture show) 1988, Graduate Sch of Design Harvard Univ 1995, The Waiting Room Grand Central Station NY 1995, Kunsthalle Vienna (Wish Machine exhibition) 1996, MOMA San Francisco 1997–98, Kunstmuseum Wolfsburg 2001, GA International Tokyo 2001; *Work in Perm Collections* incl: MOMA NY, MOMA San Francisco, Deutsches Architecktur Museum Frankfurt, Getty Museum LA, FRAC collection France; *Style—* Ms Zaha Hadid, CBE; ✉ Studio 9, 10 Bowling Green Lane, London EC1R 0BD (tel 020 7253 5147, fax 020 7251 8322)

HADLEE, Roger Barrington; s of Barrington William Hadlee (d 1981), of Bishop's Stortford, Herts, and Hilda Joan, *née* Newman; *b* 8 January 1935; *Educ* St Edward's Sch Oxford, Trinity Coll Oxford (MA); *m* 6 July 1960, (Alison) Jill, da of Harold Nettleton Broadley, of Folkestone, Kent; 3 da (Georgina b 1961, Caroline b 1964, Fiona b 1966); *Career* Subaltern 1 Royal Dragoons 1956–58; mktg exec: Pfizer Ltd 1958–63, Nabisco Foods 1963–65, Donald MacPherson Gp 1965–68, Br Printing Corp 1968–74 (dir Publishing Gp); fndr Royal Exchange Art Gallery 1974; *Recreations* tennis, sailing, cricket, architectural history, vintage motor rallying; *Clubs* MCC, Free Foresters, Cavalry and Guards'; *Style—* Roger Hadlee, Esq; ✉ The Abbey, Coggeshall, Essex CO6 1RD (tel 01376 561246)

HADLEY, Graham Hunter; s of Albert Leonard Hadley (d 1973), and Lorna Elizabeth, *née* Hunter (d 1997); *b* 12 April 1944; *Educ* Eltham Coll, Jesus Coll Cambridge (MA), Harvard Business Sch; *m* 1971, Lesley Mary Ann, da of Stanley Anthony Andrew Smith, of Kingston; 1 s (Andrew Hunter b 1978); *Career* Civil Service; asst princ: Miny of Aviation 1966, Miny of Technology 1968; princ: Miny of Aviation Supply 1971, Dept of Energy 1974; seconded to Civil Serv Cmmn 1976, asst sec Dept of Energy 1977, seconded to British Aerospace HQ Weybridge 1980, under sec Electricity Div Dept of Energy 1983, bd sec CEGB 1983–90; National Power plc (following privatisation of CEGB): exec dir 1990–95, md International Business Development 1992–95; non-exec dir de Havilland Aircraft Museum Tst 1990–; ind conslt and sr advsr to Nat Econ Research Assocs (NERA) 1996–2007; tstee Brewery Arts Cirencester 2006–; memb Competition Cmmn (formerly Monopolies and Mergers Cmmn) 1998–2007; *Recreations* cricket, aviation, architecture, theatre; *Clubs* London Capital; *Style—* Graham Hadley, Esq; ✉ Sundance House, Cold Aston, Cheltenham, Gloucestershire GL54 3BN

HADOW, Rupert Nigel Pendrill (Pen); s of Nigel Philip Ian Hadow, of E Sussex, and Anne Pendrill, *née* Callingham; *b* 26 February 1962; *Educ* Harrow, UCL (BA); *m* June 1995, Mary Frances, da of late Archie Nicholson; 1 s (Wilf Pendrill b 19 Oct 1998), 1 da (Freya Alice b 12 April 2002); *Career* founding dir The Polar Travel Co; promoter, organiser and professional guide numerous high Arctic and Arctic Ocean expdns incl for charitable causes and TV; polar records held: furthest N by rigid-hull inflatable from British shores (London to Taasilaq Greenland) 1989, organised first all-woman expdn to N Geographic Pole 1997, first solo unsupported expdn to N Geographic Pole from N American continent 2003, led unsupported expdn to S Geographic Pole 2004 (thereby becoming first Briton to make unsupported treks to both N and S Geographic Poles); fndr Arctic Ocean Fndn 2007; *Recreations* Dartmoor and the River Dart; *Clubs* RGS, MCC; *Style—* Pen Hadow, Esq

HAENDEL, Ida; CBE (1991); *b* 15 December 1928; *Educ* Warsaw Conservatoire (Gold Medal at age 7); *Career* violinist; began playing aged 3 1/2, studied with Carl Flesch and George Enescu in Paris, Br debut Brahm's Concerto Queen's Hall with Sir Henry Wood, gave concerts for Br and US troops and in factories WWII, has toured throughout Europe, N and S America, Scandinavia, Turkey, Israel, USSR and Far East; toured with orchs incl: London Philharmonic, BBC Symphony, English Chamber (foreign tours incl Hong Kong, China, Aust and Mexico); has played with numerous foreign orchs incl: Bayerishe Rundfunk, Berlin Philharmonic, Concertgebouw Orchestra, Israel Philharmonic, Boston Symphony, New York Philharmonic, Montreal Symphony; numerous recordings with EMI; memb Jury: Carl Flesch Competition London, Sibelius Competition Helsinki Finland, International Violin Competition Cologne; winner Sibelius medal Sibelius Soc of Finland (on 25 Anniversary of Sibelius' Death); *Books* Woman with Violin (autobiography, 1970); *Style—* Miss Ida Haendel, CBE

HAGAN, David Lloyd; s of William Hamill Hagan (d 1984), of Liverpool, and Miriam Dilys, *née* Lloyd (d 1998); *b* 21 May 1946; *Educ* Merchant Taylors' Sch Crosby, Emmanuel Coll Cambridge; *m* 5 Dec 1981, Anita Janet Shepstone, da of Lennart Pettersson, of Karlstad, Sweden; 2 s (Charles b 1 Nov 1982, Felix b 14 March 1987), 1 da (Isabel b 4 Aug 1984); *Career* chm and chief exec Marlon House Holdings Ltd 1974–83, dir Medical and Professional Software Ltd 1984–, md Tullett & Tokyo Equities Ltd 1986–91; chm: David Hagan Ltd 1986–, Trio Holdings plc 1992–2005, Neptune Energy Ltd 2004–; FCA 1970, ATII 1970, MSI; *Recreations* offshore powerboat racing (Class II World Champion 1979), boatbuilding; *Clubs* Royal Thames Yacht, Royal Lymington Yacht, The South West Shingles Yacht (Vice Cdr); *Style—* David Hagan, Esq; ✉ Eastwoods, Pitmore Lane, Sway, Lymington, Hampshire SO41 6BW

HAGDRUP, Alan; s of Sofus Vilhelm Hagdrup (d 1983), of Cheam; *b* 19 May 1932; *Educ* Epsom Coll, UCL; *m* 1958, Elizabeth, da of Lt-Col Harold Mason, OBE, TD (d 1960); 1 s, 2 da; *Career* ptnr Gouldens (slrs) 1962–69; dir: Hanson Transport Gp 1969–, Hanson plc 1974–92; memb Cncl Epsom Coll (chm 1995–2002); *Recreations* golf, skiing, bridge, music; *Clubs* Walton Heath Golf; *Style—* Alan Hagdrup, Esq; ✉ The Mill House, Borough Road, Tadworth, Surrey KT20 7TF (tel 01737 814522, fax 01737 813771)

HAGER, David Paul; s of Donald Charles Hager, of Bournemouth, Dorset, and Betty Kathleen, *née* Hewitt; *b* 7 January 1951; *Educ* Bournemouth Sch, Univ of Oxford (MA), Harvard Business Sch; *m* 10 Sept 1951, Jeanette Carolyn, da of Alan Peter Hares, of Chilbolton, Hants; 1 s (Tristram b 1984); *Career* investment advsr N M Rothschild and Sons Ltd 1972–74; Hewitt Bacon & Woodrow: joined 1975, ptnr in Investment Dept 1976–85, ptnr 1987–95, managing ptnr 1995–97, ptnr 1997–; dir County Investment Management 1985–87 (dir County Group Ltd 1986–87); Airline Tport Pilot Licence 2002; Liveryman Worshipful Co of Actuaries; FIA 1975, FPMI 1982; *Books* An Introduction to Institutional Investment (with A J Frost, 1986), Debt Securities (with A J Frost, 1990), Pension Fund Investment (with C D Lever, 1989); *Recreations* flying light aircraft; *Clubs* Oxford and Cambridge, Guild of Air Pilots and Navigators; *Style—* David Hager, Esq; ✉ tel 01372 733001, fax 01372 845046, e-mail david.hager@virgin.net

HAGERTY, William John Gell (Bill); s of William Hagerty, and Doris Julia, *née* Gell; *b* 23 April 1939; *Educ* Beal GS Ilford Essex; *m* 1, 1965 (m dis 1990), Lynda Ann, *née* Beresford; 1 s (William Daniel b 22 Jan 1970), 1 da (Faith Georgia b 5 March 1975); m 2, 1991, Elizabeth Ann Vercoe, *née* Latta; 1 s (Adam Benedict b 1 Dec 1993); *Career* local newspaper journalist 1955–58; with: Sunday Citizen, Daily Sketch, Daily Mirror 1960–67; various editorial positions The Mirror Group 1967–85, managing ed (features) Today 1986–87, ed Sunday Today 1987–88, conslt to the publisher Hola! Magazine (conslt Hello! Magazine) 1987–88, dep ed Sunday Mirror 1988–90, dep ed Daily Mirror 1990–91, ed The People 1991–92, conslt ed Tribune 1993–2004, ed British Journalism Review 2002–; theatre critic: Today 1993–95 (also film critic 1994–95), various publications 1996–2003, The Sun 2004–; *Books* Flash Bang Wallop! (with Kent Gavin, 1978), Read All About It (2003); *Recreations* watching cricket, jazz, lunch; *Clubs* Gerry's; *Style—* Bill Hagerty; ✉ Bull Cottage, 10/11 Strand on the Green, Chiswick, London W4 3PQ (tel 020 8994 4966, fax 020 8987 0206)

HAGGARD, Prof Mark Peregrine; CBE (2001); s of Capt Stephen H A Haggard (d 1943), and Morna Christian, *née* Gillespie (d 1977); *b* 26 December 1942; *Educ* Dollar Acad, Univ of Edinburgh (MA), Univ of Cambridge (PhD); *m* 22 Sept 1962, Elizabeth Gilmore, da of Thomas Jackson Houston (d 1943), of Hong Kong; 2 s (Stephen b 1963, Patrick b 1965); *Career* teaching offr and fell CCC Cambridge 1967–71, prof Queen's Univ Belfast 1971–76, dir MRC Inst Hearing Res 1977–2002, chief advsr Hearing Res Tst 1987–2002, MRC External Scientific Staff 2002–; memb Neurosciences Bd MRC 1989–93, dep chm Health Serv and Public Health Res Bd MRC 1990–93, memb HTA Commissioning Bd 1999–; fell Acoustical Soc America 1982, FMedSci 1998; *Books* Hearing Science and Hearing Disorders (with M E Lutman, 1983), British Medical Bulletin: Hearing (with E F Evans, 1987), Screening Children's Hearing (with E A Hughes, 1991), Research in the Development of Services for Hearing-Impaired People (1993); *Recreations* extreme skiing, swimming, Byzantine art; *Style—* Prof Mark Haggard, CBE

HAGGARD, Piers Inigo; s of Capt Stephen Haggard (d 1943), of London, and Morna Christian, *née* Gillespie (d 1977); *b* 18 March 1939; *Educ* Dollar Acad, Univ of Edinburgh (MA); *m* 1, Christiane, *née* Stokes; 3 da (Sarah Clemence b 1960, Claire Imogen b 1961, Rachel Lindsay b 1961), 1 s (Philip Charles Napier b 1962); m 2, Anna Maud, da of Grisha Sklovsky; 1 s (William Godfrey Abraham b 1975), 1 da ((Celia) Daisy Morna b 1978); *Career* theatre, television and film director; started as asst dir Royal Court Theatre 1960; resident dir: Dundee Repertory 1960–61, Glasgow Citizens 1961–62; asst dir Nat Theatre 1963–65, dir Ticket of Leave Man 1981; trained with BBC TV 1965; fndr The Dirs' Guild of GB and assoc organization The Dirs' and Prodrs' Rights Soc; *Television* UK prodns incl: Pennies From Heaven (UK BAFTA Award 1979) 1978, Mrs Reinhart 1981, Knockback (US ACE Award 1985) 1984, Visitors 1987, Centrepoint 1990, Heartstones 1994–95, Eskimo Day 1995, The Double (screenplay) 1996, Cold Enough for Snow 1997, Big Bad World 1999, The Hunt 2000, The Shell Seekers 2005 (Shanghai TV Festival Award 2007); USA prodns incl: Back Home (Emmy nomination, Gold Award NY Film and TV Festival) 1989, Four Eyes 1991–92, The Breakthrough 1993; *Film* incl: Wedding Night 1969, The Blood on Satan's Claw 1970, The Quatermass Conclusion (Trieste Festival Award 1980) 1979, The Fiendish Plot of Dr Fu Manchu 1980, Venom 1982, A Summer Story 1988, Conquest 1998 (best Canadian feature film Atlantic Film Festival 1998); *Recreations* politics, swimming, landscape gardening, human nature; *Style—* Piers Haggard, Esq; ✉ Piers Haggard Productions Ltd, 26 Stockwell Park Crescent, London SW9 0DE (tel 020 7733 4500, fax 020 7737 4619, e-mail haggard@onetel.com)

HAGGER, Jonathan Osborne; s of Cyril Francis Osborne Hagger (d 1957), of Loughton, Essex, and Norah Harrison, *née* Broadley (d 1981); *b* 3 February 1949; *Educ* Chigwell Sch; *m* 27 April 1974, (Carol) Anne, da of Alan David Luton, of Loughton, Essex; 2 s

(William b 1981, James b 1984); *Career* chartered accountant; Edward Moore & Sons (Chartered Accountants) 1968–72, BUPA 1972–75, Willis Faber 1976–85; gp finance dir: Bain Clarkson 1985–89, FKB Group plc 1990; chief financial offr The Grosvenor Estate 1991–; gp finance dir: Grosvenor Estate Holdings 1991–99, Grosvenor Gp Holdings 2000–03, Grosvenor Gp 2004–06; chm Realty Insurances 1994–; memb: Tax Deregulation Task Force 1996–97, American European Business Assoc 2002– (dir 2004–), Policy Ctee Inst for Family Business; chm: King Charles Music Soc 1988–2000, English Sinfonia 1995–2006; tstee Church of King Charles the Martyr 1996–; Freeman City of London 2001, Liveryman Worshipful Co of Painter Stainers 2001; ARCM 1968, FCA 1972, FCT 1993; *Recreations* organist, opera, cricket; *Style*— Jonathan Hagger, Esq; ✉ The Grosvenor Office, 70 Grosvenor Street, London W1K 3JP (tel 020 7408 0988)

HAGGETT, Stuart John; s of Wilfred Francis Haggett (d 1991), of West Kirby, Wirral, and Doreen Ada, *née* New (d 1999); *b* 11 April 1947; *Educ* Dauntsey's Sch West Lavington, Downing Coll Cambridge (MA); *m* 2 Jan 1971, (Hilary) Joy, da of Maj Albert Hammond (d 1963), of Weymouth; 2 da (Laura Louise b 26 Feb 1978, Emily Frances b 23 Sept 1979); *Career* head of modern languages and housemaster Canford Sch 1973–83, second master King's Sch Rochester 1983–88, headmaster Birkenhead Sch 1988–2003, head English Sch Nicosia 2003–; memb: SHA 1983, HMC 1988; *Recreations* sport, reading and theatre, DIY, East India; *Style*— Stuart Haggett, Esq; ✉ The English School, PO Box 23575, 1684 Nicosia, Cyprus (tel 00 357 227 99302, fax 00 357 227 99301, e-mail head@englishschool.ac.cy)

HAGMAN, Eric; CBE (2003); s of Harald Hagman (d 1989), of Fairlie, Ayrshire, and Jessie Munro, *née* Henderson; *b* 9 July 1946; *Educ* Kelvinside Acad, Univ of Glasgow; *m* 1; 2 s (Christian b 1972, Robin b 1974), 1 da (Victoria b 1978); m 2, Valerie Hagman; 2 step s (George b 1971, John b 1973); *Career* chartered accountant; trained Thomson McLintock, qualified 1969; Arthur Andersen: joined 1969, ptnr in Scot 1978, managing ptnr Glasgow 1979, regnl managing ptnr Scot 1983, chm Scotland 1998, UK sr ptnr for global markets, ret 2002; dir: British Polythene Industries plc, Celtic FC plc, Saints plc, Glen Gp plc, RCA London; past chm: Audit Practice Ctee ICAS, Technical Liaison Ctee ICAS; past memb Cncl of CBI Scotland; former dir: Scottish Enterprise, Scottish Financial Enterprise; former: pres Royal Glasgow Inst, chm RSAC, treas Police Dependents Tst, tstee Scottish Nat Galleries, memb Bd Glasgow Sch of Art; memb ICA; *Recreations* sailing, skiing, tennis, squash, art, travelling; *Clubs* Royal Scottish Motor Yacht, Clyde Corinthian Yacht; *Style*— Eric Hagman, Esq, CBE; ✉ Number Ten, 6 Mains Avenue, Giffnock, Glasgow G46 6QY (tel 0141 620 0927, e-mail eric@erichagman.com)

HAGSTON, Prof Winston Edwin; s of Thomas Hagston, and Florence Maud, *née* Kirby; *b* 30 November 1941; *Educ* Beverley GS, Imperial Coll London (BSc), Univ of Hull (PhD), Univ of London (DSc); *m* 9 Nov 1963, (Sylvia) Heather, da of Harold Robinson (d 1982), of Melbourne, York; 2 s (Winston b 19 April 1964, Paul b 21 March 1967), 1 da (Michelle b 23 March 1966); *Career* postdoctoral res fell SRC 1966–68; Dept of Physics Univ of Hull: lectr 1968–73, sr lectr 1973–80, reader in theoretical physics 1980, personal chair in theoretical physics 1986–; ARCS; *Recreations* fishing, shooting; *Style*— Prof Winston Hagston; ✉ The Wildfowlers, 7 Millbeck Close, Market Weighton, York YO43 3HT (tel 01430 873158); Department of Physics, The University, Cottingham Road, Hull HU6 7BX (tel 01482 46311 ext 5823)

HAGUE, Prof Clifford Bertram (Cliff); s of Bertram Hague (d 1979), of Manchester, and Kathleen, *née* Sedgwick (d 2004); *b* 22 August 1944; *Educ* N Manchester GS for Boys, Magdalene Coll Cambridge (BA), Univ of Manchester (DipTP); *m* 1966, Irene, *née* Williamson; 1 s (Euan b 18 Nov 1971), 3 da (Alice b 30 March 1974, Celia, Sophie (twins) b 17 April 1978); *Career* planning asst Glasgow Corporation 1968–69, School of the Built Environment at Heriot-Watt Univ: lectr Dept of Town & Country Planning 1969–73, sr lectr 1973–90, head of Sch of Planning & Housing 1990–96, prof 1995–2006 (emeritus prof 2006–); freelance provider of research, writing and trg 2006–; sec gen Cwlth Assoc of Planners 2006– (vice-pres 1996–2000, pres 2000–06); memb Int Working Pty for Euro Biennial of Towns and Town Planners 1996–; memb int jury urban planning and design competition for: the banks of the Huangpu River Shanghai 2001, 2008 Olympic Yachting Facilities at Qingdao 2003, Central Olympic Green and Forest Park 2003; Centenary Medal from Brno Tech Univ Czech Repub; UK nat contact point Euro Spatial Planning Observation Network 2001–06; MRTPI 1973 (pres 1996), FRSA 1996, AcSS 2000, MILTM 2000–06, fell HE Acad 2007–; *Books* The Development of Planning Thought: A Critical Perspective (1984), Place Identity, Participation and Planning (2005), Making Planning Work (2006), series ed RTPI Library Series; *Recreations* cricket, theatre, Manchester United; *Style*— Professor Cliff Hague; ✉ School of the Built Environment, Heriot-Watt University, Edinburgh EH14 4AS

HAGUE, Prof Sir Douglas Chalmers; kt (1981), CBE (1978); s of Laurence Hague, and Marion Hague; *b* 20 October 1926; *Educ* Moseley GS, King Edward VI HS Birmingham, Univ of Birmingham; *m* 1, 1947 (m dis 1986), Brenda Elizabeth Fereday; 2 da; m 2, 1986, Janet Mary Leach; *Career* economist (mgmnt prof, conslt, co dir); chm Manchester Industrial Relations Soc, dep chm Price Cmmn and pres NW Operational Res Gp, rapporteur to IEA 1953–78 (ed gen 1981–86), reader in political economy Univ of London 1957, Newton Chambers prof of economics Univ of Sheffield 1957–63, visiting prof of economics Duke Univ NC 1960–61, head Business Studies Dept Univ of Sheffield 1962–63, prof of applied economics Univ of Manchester 1963–65, memb Cncl Manchester Business Sch 1964–81 (prof of managerial economics 1965–81, dep dir 1978–81); visiting prof: Manchester Business Sch 1981–, Imperial Coll London 1987–91; assoc fell Templeton Coll Oxford 1984–2005 (fell 1981–84, hon fell 2005–); personal econ advsr to Rt Hon Margaret Thatcher 1967–79 (incl Gen Election 1979), advsr PM's Policy Unit 1979–83; chm: ESRC 1983–87, Oxford Strategy Network 1984–, Metapraxis Ltd 1984–90, Doctus Consulting Europe 1991–93, CRT plc 1992–93 (dir 1990–96), Professional Devpt Ctee IOD 1993–96, WIRE Ltd 1999–2000; tstee Demos 1996–2004; *Recreations* Manchester United supporter, organist of classical music (granted permission to play at Blenheim Palace); *Clubs* Athenaeum; *Style*— Prof Sir Douglas Hague, CBE; ✉ Templeton College, Oxford OX1 5NY

HAGUE, Rt Hon William Jefferson; PC (1995), MP; s of Nigel Hague, of Wentworth, S Yorks, and Stella, *née* Jefferson; *b* 26 March 1961; *Educ* Wath upon Dearne Comp Sch, Magdalen Coll Oxford (MA, pres Oxford Union), INSEAD (MBA); *m* 19 Dec 1997, Ffion, da of Emyr Jenkins, *qv*; *Career* temp special advsr to Chancellor of Exchequer 1983, mgmnt conslt McKinsey and Co 1983–88; MP (Cons) Richmond (Yorks) 1989–; PPS to Rt Hon Norman Lamont as Chancellor of the Exchequer 1990–93, under-sec of state for social security 1993–94, min of state Dept of Social Security 1994–95, sec of state for Wales 1995–97; ldr Cons Pty and ldr of HM Opposition 1997–2001, shadow foreign sec 2005–; chm Int Democrat Union 1999–2002; political and econ advsr JCB 2001–, political advsr Terra Firma Capital Partners 2002–; non-exec dir AES Engineering 2001–; *Books* William Pitt the Younger (2004, History Book of the Year Br Book Awards 2005), William Wilberforce (2007); *Style*— The Rt Hon William Hague, MP; ✉ House of Commons, London SW1A 0AA (tel 020 7219 3000)

HAHN, Prof Frank Horace; s of Dr Arnold Hahn; *b* 26 April 1925; *Educ* Bournemouth GS, LSE (BSc(Econ), PhD), Univ of Cambridge (MA); *m* 1946, Dorothy Salter; *Career* lectr in econs Univ of Birmingham 1948–58 (reader in mathematical econs 1958–60), lectr in econs Univ of Cambridge 1960–66 (fell Churchill Coll 1960–); prof of econs: LSE 1967–72, Univ of Cambridge 1972–92 (prof emeritus 1992), Univ of Siena 1989–2000; visiting prof of econs: MIT 1956–57, 1971–72 and 1982, Univ of Calif Berkeley 1959–60; fell Center for Advanced Study in Behavioural Sciences Stanford 1966–67, Taussig res prof Harvard Univ 1974, Schumpeter prof Vienna 1984, memb Workshop in Mathematical Econs Stanford Univ, memb Cncl for Scientific Policy (later Advsy Bd of Res Cncls) 1972–75; managing ed Review of Economic Studies 1965–68, asst ed Journal of Economic Theory 1971–76; pres: Econometric Soc 1968–69, Royal Economic Soc 1986–89, Section F British Assoc for the Advancement of Science 1990; Palacky Gold medal Czechoslovak Acad of Sciences 1991; Hon DSocSci Univ of Birmingham 1981, Hon DUniv Strasbourg 1984, Hon DLitt UEA 1984, Hon DSc (Econs) Univ of London 1985, Hon DUniv York 1991, Hon DLitt Univ of Leicester 1993, Hon DPhil Univ of Athens 1993, Dr (hc) Université Paris X 1999; corresponding fell American Acad of Arts and Sciences 1971, hon memb American Economic Assoc 1986, foreign assoc US Nat Acad of Sciences 1988, hon fell LSE 1989, memb Academia Europaea 1989; FBA 1975; *Books* The Theory of Interest Rates (ed with F P R Brechling, 1965), General Competitive Analysis (with K J Arrow, 1971), Readings in the Theory of Growth (ed, 1971), The Share of Wages in the National Income (1972), Money and Inflation (1982), Equilibrium and Macroeconomics (1984), Money Growth and Stability (1985), The Economics of Missing Markets Information and Games (ed, 1989), Handbook of Monetary Economics (ed with Ben Friedman, 1990), The Market: Practice and Policy (ed, 1992), Ethics and Economics (ed with F Farina and S Vannucci, 1995), A Critical Essay on Modern Macroeconomic Theory (jtly with Robert Solow, 1995), New Theories in Growth and Development (ed with Fabrizio Coricelli and Massimo di Matteo, 1998), General Equilibrium: Problems and Prospects (ed with Fabio Petri, 2003); *Style*— Prof Frank Hahn, FBA; ✉ 16 Adams Road, Cambridge CB3 9AD; Churchill College, Cambridge CB3 0DS

HAIG, 2 Earl (UK 1919); George Alexander Eugene Douglas Haig; OBE (1965), DL (Roxburghshire, Ettrick and Lauderdale 1976); also Viscount Dawick, Baron Haig (both UK 1919) and thirtieth Laird of Bemersyde Chief of the Haig family; s of Field Marshal 1 Earl Haig, KT, GCB, OM, GCVO, KCIE (d 1928), by his w, Hon Dorothy, GCStJ (d 1939), 2 da of 3 Baron Vivian; *b* 15 March 1918; *Educ* Stowe, ChCh Oxford (MA), Camberwell Sch of Arts and Crafts; *m* 1, 19 July 1956 (m dis 1981), Adrienne Thérèse, da of Derrick Morley; 1 s, 2 da; m 2, 1981, Donna Gerolama Lopez y Royo di Taurisano; *Heir* s, Viscount Dawick; *Career* Capt Royal Scots Greys M East Force 1939–42, POW 1942–45, Maj on disbandment of Home Gd; sat as Conservative Peer in House of Lords 1945–99, train bearer at Coronation of King George VI; painter; holds exhibitions at regular intervals; memb: Royal Fine Art Cmmn for Scotland 1958–61, Scottish Arts Cncl (chm Art Ctee 1969–76); tstee: Nat Galleries of Scotland 1963–73, Scottish Nat War Meml 1961–96 (chm Bd of Tstees 1983–96); pres: Border Area RBLS 1955–61, Scottish Crafts Centre 1953–74; chm: Disablement Advisory Ctee SE Scotland 1960–73, Berwickshire Civic Soc 1970–76; memb Bd of Dirs Richard DeMarco Gallery 1986–87; chm Offr's Assoc (Scottish Branch) 1977–87; pres: OA Scottish Branch 1987–92, Royal British Legion Scotland 1979–86 (nat chm 1963–66), The Earl Haig Fund Scotland 1979–86, Nat ex POW Assoc; vice-pres: Royal Blind Asylum, Scottish Nat Inst for War Blinded; DL Berwickshire 1953–76, Vice Lord-Lt Berwicks 1967–70; memb Queen's Body Guard for Scotland (Royal Co of Archers), Liveryman Worshipful Co of Mercers; ARSA 1988, FRSA; KStJ; *Publications* My Father's Son (memoir of first 30 years, 2000); *Recreations* fishing, shooting; *Clubs* New (Edinburgh), Cavalry and Guards'; *Style*— The Rt Hon the Earl Haig, OBE, DL; ✉ Bemersyde, Melrose, Roxburghshire TD6 9DP (tel 01835 822762)

HAIGH, Simon Mark; s of Philip Haigh (d 2000), and Elaine, *née* Dickinson; *b* 22 July 1964, Huddersfield; *Educ* Newsome Secdy Modern Sch, Huddersfield Tech Coll (Dip); *m* 15 Jan 2000, Joanna Elizabeth, *née* Beech; 1 s (Joshua George Philip b 9 March 2001); *Career* chef: Hambleton Hall 1988–90, Manoir aux Quat Saisons 1990–92, Inverlochy Castle 1993–2001, Seaham Hall 2001–02, Mallory Court Hotel 2002–; Michelin Star 13 years, 3 AA rosettes, 2 stars Harden Guide, 1 star Egon Ronay (Best Desserts of Scotland 1998), Caterer & Hotelkeeper 30 Under 30 Acorn Award; *Publications* recipes in: Scotland on a Plate (2001), Chefs of Distinction (2002), Children in Need (2005), Soup Kitchen (2005), Dom Perignon 1998 Vintage The Collection (2005), Glorious-Eblex (2005); *Recreations* golf, dining out, spending time with family; *Clubs* Wilmslow Golf; *Style*— Simon Haigh, Esq; ✉ Mallory Court Hotel & Restaurant, Harbury Lane, Bishops Tachbrook, Leamington Spa, Warwickshire CV33 9QB (tel 01926 330214)

HAILES, Julia Persephone; MBE (1999); da of Lt-Col John Martin Hunter Hailes, DSO (d 1995), of Stoke-sub-Hamdon, Somerset, and Marianne Carlyon, *née* Coates; *b* 23 September 1961; *Educ* St Mary's Sch Calne; *m* Edward de Courcy Bryant; 3 s (Connor Carlyon b 1 Jan 1995, Rollo Jack b 22 Nov 1996, Monty Merlin b 12 Nov 1998); *Career* Leo Burnett Advertising 1981–83; dir: SustainAbility Ltd 1987–95 (memb Cncl 1995–2006), Creative Consumer Co-operative Ltd (t/a Out of This World) 1994–2000, 5 St Lawrence Terrace Ltd 1995–, Six Fox Ltd 1996–98, Jupiter Global Green Investment Trust 2001–06; vice-chair Advsy Ctee on Consumer Products and the Environment (ACCPE) 1999–2005; writer regular monthly column for Planet Food BBC Online 2001–02; tstee Haller Fndn 2003–; memb: Cncl Global 500 Forum 1992–96, UK Eco-Labelling Bd 1992–98, Guild of Food Writers; elected to UN Global 500 Roll of Honour (for outstanding environmental achievements) 1989; dist cncllr S Somerset 1999–2003; *Books* Green Pages, The Business of Saving The World (1987), The Green Consumer Guide (1988), The Green Consumer's Supermarket Shopping Guide (1989), The Young Green Consumer Guide (1990), The Green Business Guide (1991), Holidays That Don't Cost the Earth (1992), Manual 2000 Life Choices for the Future You Want (1998), The New Foods Guide (1999), The New Green Consumer Guide (2007); *Recreations* tennis, walking, bridge; *Style*— Ms Julia Hailes, MBE; ✉ Coker Hill House, West Coker, Somerset BA22 9DG (tel 01935 864423, e-mail julia@juliahailes.com, website www.juliahailes.com and www.juliahailesblog.blogspot.com)

HAILSHAM, 3 Viscount (UK 1929); Douglas Martin Hogg; PC (1992), QC (1990), MP; also Baron Hailsham (UK 1928), of Hailsham, Co Sussex; s of Baron Hailsham of St Marylebone, KG, PC (Life Peer 1970; suc as 2 Visc Hailsham 1950, disclaimed Viscountcy 1963; d 2001); *b* 5 February 1945; *Educ* Eton, ChCh Oxford (pres Oxford Union); *m* 6 June 1968, Hon Sarah Elizabeth Mary Hogg (Baroness Hogg, *qv*); 1 da (Hon Charlotte b 26 Aug 1970), 1 s (Hon Quintin b 12 Oct 1973); *Heir* s, Hon Quintin Hogg; *Career* called to the Bar Lincoln's Inn 1968; MP (Cons): Grantham 1979–97, Sleaford and N Hykeham 1997–; PPS to Leon Brittan as chief sec to Treasury 1982–83, asst Govt whip 1983–84, Parly under sec Home Office 1986–89, min of state for Industry and Enterprise 1989–90, min of state Foreign Office 1990–95, min of Agriculture, Fisheries and Food 1995–97; *Style*— The Rt Hon Douglas Hogg, QC, MP, Viscount Hailsham; ✉ House of Commons, London SW1A 0AA

HAILSTONE, Dr (John) Donovan; s of Capt Frank Hailstone (d 1944), and Maud Eunice, *née* Greenhough; *b* 26 February 1930; *Educ* Univ of Nottingham (BSc), Univ of London (DipEd, DPM, MB BS); *m* 1, 2 Sept 1951 (m dis 1978), Pamela Margaret, da of Michael John Gray (d 1971), of Andover, Hants; 1 s (Julien John b 1965); m 2, 14 April 1979, (Beatrice) Jane; *Career* St George's Hosp London 1961–62, med resident NY and Boston 1962–63, sr registrar St Mary's Hosp London 1964–69, conslt physician in psychological med the Royal Free Hosp London 1970–, hon sr lectr Royal Free Hosp Med Sch 1970–; chm Hampstead Dist Med Ctee and Dist Mgmnt Team 1983–85, memb Hosp Advsy Serv 1989–, Lord Chllr's Med Visitor 1989–, memb Mental Health Tribunal 1990–; MRCS (LRCS 1960), FRCPsych 1983 (MRCPsych 1973); *Books* Psychiatric Illness in the Medical Profession and the Clergy (1969); *Recreations* sailing, private flying; *Clubs* Royal Ocean

H

Racing; *Style*— Dr Donovan Hailstone; ✉ Edward House, Florence Nightingale Hospital, 7 Lisson Grove, London NW1 6SH (tel 020 7535 7900, fax 020 8995 4992)

HAIN, Rt Hon Peter Gerald; PC (2001), MP; s of Walter Hain, and Adelaine Hain; *b* 16 February 1950; *Educ* QMC London (BScEcon), Univ of Sussex (MPhil); *m* 1975 (m dis), Patricia Western; 2 s; m 2, 2003, Dr Elizabeth Haywood; *Career* head of res Union of Communication Workers 1987–91 (asst res offr 1976–87), MP (Lab) Neath 1991– (Parly candidate (Lab) Putney 1983 and 1987); oppn whip 1995–96, oppn spokesman on employment 1996–97, Parly under-sec of state Welsh Office 1997–99, min of state FCO 1999–2000, min of state for Energy DTI 2001, min of state for Europe FCO 2001–02, sec of state for Wales 2002–, Ldr of the House of Commons and Pres of the Cncl 2003–05, sec of state for NI 2005–07, sec of state for work and pensions 2007–; chm Stop the Seventy Tour campaign 1969–70, nat chm Young Libs 1971–73, press offr Anti-Nazi League 1977–80; *Books* Don't Play with Apartheid (1971), Community Politics (1976), Mistaken Identity (1976), Policing the Police (ed vol I, 1978, vol II 1980), Neighbourhood Participation (1980), Crisis and Future of the Left (1980), Political Trials in Britain (1984), Political Strikes (1986), A Putney Plot? (1987), The Peking Connection (1995), Ayes to the Left (1995), Sing the Beloved Country (1996); *Recreations* soccer, cricket, rugby, motor racing, supporting Chelsea FC and Neath RFC, rock and folk music; *Clubs* Neath Rugby, Neath Working Mens', Resolven Rugby, Resolven Royal British Legion Institute, Ynysygerwn CC; *Style*— The Rt Hon Peter Hain, MP; ✉ House of Commons, London SW1A 0AA (tel 020 7219 3925); 39 Windsor Road, Neath, West Glamorgan SA11 1NB (tel 01639 630152)

HAIN, Robert Cameron; s of John MacFarlane Hain, and Beverley Jean, *née* Hendry; *b* 5 April 1953, Kingston, Ontario; *Educ* Univ of Toronto (BA), Univ of Oxford (MLitt); *m* 7 June 1991, Tracy; 2 c (Iska Simone, Kayla Cameron); *Career* vice-pres Atlantic Canada Royal Trust Corp of Canada 1988–90, vice-pres sales Royal Trust International and pres and ceo Royal Trust Bank (Switzerland) 1990–93; sr vice-pres then exec vice-pres Investors Gp Inc 1993–97, ptnr Ernst & Young 1997–98, sr vice-pres and head of global private banking CIBC Financial Gp 1998–99, global ptnr AMVESCAP plc 1999– (memb Exec Bd 2001–), pres and ceo AIM Funds Mgmnt Inc 1999–2002, ceo INVESCO UK and chm INVESCO Perpetual 2002–; memb Nat Bd Canadian Mental Health Assoc 1987–89 (chair Toronto Bd 1980–88), memb Bd Canadian Psychiatric Research Fndn 1988–90, memb Fndn Bd St Michael's Hosp Toronto 2001; dir Nat Youth Orch of Canada 1988–92, chm Winnipeg Art Gallery 1996–97, tstee Nova Scotia Coll of Art and Design 2001–04; *Recreations* sailing; *Clubs* RAC, Phyllis Court, London Capital, Leander, Granite (Toronto), St Charles Golf and Country (Winnipeg), Royal Nova Scotia Yacht Sqdn; *Style*— Robert Hain, Esq; ✉ INVESCO UK Ltd, INVESCO Park, Henley-on-Thames, Oxfordshire RG9 1HH (e-mail rob@roberthain.com)

HAINES, Prof Sir Andrew Paul; kt (2005); s of Charles George Thomas Haines, of Southall, Middx, and Lilian Emily, *née* Buck; *b* 26 February 1947; *Educ* Latymer Upper Sch, KCH Med Sch London (MB BS, MD); *m* 12 Feb 1982 (m dis 1989), June Marie Power; children, 2 s (Alexander *b* 7 Sept 1993, Adam *b* 19 Aug 1997); m 2, 14 March 1998, Dr Anita Berlin; *Career* house physician and surgn KCH 1969, SHO Nat Hosp for Nervous Diseases 1972, MO Br-Nepal Med Tst 1973, memb scientific staff MRC, Epidemiology and Med Care Unit Northwick Park Hosp 1974–86; pt/t sr lectr in gen practice: Middx Hosp Med Sch 1980–84, St Mary's Hosp Med Sch 1984–87; prof of primary health care UCL and subsequently Royal Free and Univ Coll Med Sch 1987–2000, dir London Sch of Hygiene and Tropical Med 2005– (dean 2001–); dir of R&D: NE Thames RHA (pt/t secondment) 1993–95, NHS Exec N Thames 1995–96; author of papers on med subjects incl cardiovascular prevention, alcohol, care of the elderly and environmental issues; memb: Cncl Inst of Physicians for the Prevention of Nuclear War 1982–85 (winners of Nobel Peace Prize 1985), Public Health Laboratory Serv Bd 1983–86, Cncl Pugwash Orgn for Sci and World Affrs 1987–92 (winners of Nobel Peace Prize 1996), Working Pty on Prevention RCP 1989–91, WHO/UNEP/WMO Task Gp on Health Impacts of Climate Change 1993–96, UN Intergovernmental Panel on Climate Change Working Gp 2 1993–2001, NHS Central R&D Ctee 1995–2001, Scientific Advisory Ctee Assoc of Medical Research Charities 1998–2004, London Health Cmmn 2000–, Mgmnt Ctee King's Fund 2000–06, Res Strategy Ctee Public Health Lab Serv 2001–03, Dept of Health Patient Info Advsy Gp 2001–03, Dept of Health Advsy Gp on Refugee Health Professionals 2001–03, Health Ctee Universities UK 2001–, WHO Advsy Ctee on Health Research 2004–; MRC: memb Health Servs Research Ctee 1989–92, memb Health Servs and Public Health Research Bd (chm 1996–98), memb Cncl 1996–98; vice-pres MEDACT 1992–; hon fell UCL 2006; FFPHM 1991 (MFPHM 1987), FRCGP 1991 (MRCGP 1976), FRCP (London) 1992 (MRCP 1971), fndr FMedSci 1998; *Publications* co-ed of books and author of scientific papers on topics incl: evidence-based practice, implementing research findings and environment and health; *Recreations* foreign travel, environmental and security issues; *Style*— Prof Sir Andrew Haines; ✉ London School of Hygiene and Tropical Medicine, Keppel Street, London WC1E 7HT (tel 020 7927 2278, e-mail andy.haines@lshtm.ac.uk)

HAINSWORTH, Prof Roger; s of Edward Trevor Hainsworth (d 1991), of Wakefield, W Yorks, and Constance Mary, *née* White; *b* 23 December 1938; *Educ* Queen Elizabeth GS Wakefield, Univ of Leeds (MB ChB, PhD, DSc), Cardiovascular Research Inst San Francisco; *m* 24 July 1965, Janet Ann, da of Frederick Fisher (d 1985), of Cheadle, Cheshire; 2 s (Christopher Roger *b* 1967, Jonathan Peter *b* 1968), 2 da (Caroline Ann *b* 1971, Lucy Jane *b* 1982); *Career* house offr Leeds 1963–64; Univ of Leeds: lectr in physiology 1964–69, lectr Dept of Cardiovascular Studies 1970–76, sr lectr 1976–87, reader 1987–90, prof 1990–; Br-American research fell San Francisco 1969–70, hon conslt in clinical physiology Leeds Western DHA and Leeds Eastern DHA 1979–; memb: Physiological Soc, Med Research Soc, Clinical Autonic Research Soc; author of numerous books and papers on cardiovascular physiology; *Style*— Prof Roger Hainsworth; ✉ Institute for Cardiovascular Research, University of Leeds, Leeds LS2 9JT (tel 0113 233 4820, fax 0113 233 4803, e-mail medrh@leeds.ac.uk)

HAITINK, Bernard; Hon CH (2002), Hon KBE (1977); *b* 1929; *Career* conductor; chief conductor Concertgebouw Orchestra Amsterdam 1964–88, artistic dir and princ conductor London Philharmonic Orchestra 1967–79, musical dir Glyndebourne Opera 1978–88, musical dir ROH Covent Garden 1988–2002 (debut 1977), pres London Philharmonic Orchestra 1990–, music dir European Union Youth Orch 1994–99; princ guest conductor Boston Symphony 1995–, chief conductor Dresden Staatshapelle 2002–; guest conductor: Berlin Philharmonic, Bayerische Rundfunk, Vienna Philharmonic, Concertgebouw, Salzburg Festival, Berlin Festival, re-opening of Glyndebourne Opera 1994, Tanglewood Festival, LSO 1998; conductor laureate Concertgebouw Orchestra Amsterdam 1999; numerous recordings for EMI and Philips; awarded Bruckner Medal of Honour Bruckner Soc, hon gold medal Gustav Mahler Soc 1970, Erasmus prize Holland 1991, gold medal Royal Philharmonic Soc 1991, Olivier Award for Oustanding Achievement in Opera 1996; Hon DMus Univs of Oxford and Leeds; Order of Orange (Nassau), Chevalier de l'Ordre des Arts et des Lettres (France), offr Order of the Crown (Belgium); RAM, FRCM; *Style*— Bernard Haitink, Esq, CH, KBE; ✉ c/o Askonas Holt, Lonsdale Chambers, 27 Chancery Lane, London W14 0NS (e-mail info@askonasholt.co.uk)

HAITSMA MULIER, Pieter Willem Gaspard; s of Jean Gaspard Haitsma Mulier (d 1980), of Malmesbury, Wilts, and Anna Maria Wilhelmina Jacoba Hope of Luffness, *née* Fabius; *b* 21 February 1969; *Educ* Rijks Univ Utrecht; *m* Nov 2006, HSH Princess Vanessa zu Sayn-Wittgenstein-Berleburg; *Career* Lt Netherlands Cavalry Reserve Royal Netherlands Mil Acad 1989–94; head of sales Nomura Int 1995–98, princ Oakes Fitzwilliams & Co Ltd 1998–2001, head of private placement gp ARC Assocs 2001–02, fndr and ceo Mulier Capital Ltd 2003–; memb Bd Bottletop Ltd (charity); *Recreations* sailing, skiing, tennis; *Style*— Pieter Haitsma Mulier, Esq; ✉ Luffness Castle, Aberlady EH3 0QB (tel 01875 870218); Mulier Capital Limited, 19 Eccleston Square, London SW1V 1NS (tel 020 7821 6111, fax 020 7821 5999, e-mail pieter@mulier.com)

HAJDUCKI, Andrew Michael; QC (Scot 1994); *b* 12 November 1952; *Educ* Dulwich Coll, Downing Coll Cambridge (MA); *m* 1, 1980 (m dis), Gayle Shepherd; 3 s (1 decd), 1 da; m 2, 2002, Katharine Lilli Dodd; *Career* called to the Bar Gray's Inn 1976, admitted Faculty of Advocates 1979, pt/t tutor Univ of Edinburgh 1979–81, reporter session cases 1980, temp sheriff 1987–99; safeguarder: Lothian Children's Panel 1987–96, East, West and Midlothian and City of Edinburgh 1996–97; arbiter (Scotland) Motor Insurers' Bureau Untraced Drivers' Scheme 2000–03; reporter Scottish Legal Aid Bd 1999–; candidate and agent (Lib) Scot 1978–85; FSA Scot 1990; *Publications* Scottish Civic Government Licensing Law (co-author, 1994, 2 edn 2002), Civil Jury Trials (1998), Scottish Licensing Handbook (contrib, 1999), Renton and Brown's Statutory Offences (contrib, 2000); also author of three books on railways of East Lothian and Berwickshire, author of various articles in legal jls; *Recreations* reading, travel; *Style*— Andrew Hajducki, Esq, QC; ✉ c/o Advocates' Library, Parliament House, Edinburgh EH1 1RF

HAJI-IOANNOU, Sir Stelios; kt (2006); s of Loucas Haji-Ioannou, of Athens, Greece, and Nedi Haji-Ioannou; *b* 14 February 1967; *Educ* Doucas HS Athens, LSE (BSc), City Univ (MSc); *Career* with Troodos Maritime 1989–91; fndr: Stelmar Tankers 1992, easyJet 1995, easyGroup 1998, easyInternetcafé 1999, easyCar 2000, easyValue 2000, easyMoney 2001, easyCinema 2003, easyBus 2004, easyHotel 2004, easyCruise 2004, easyPizza 2004, easyMusic 2004, easy4men 2004, easyJobs 2004, easyMobile 2005; European Communicator of the Year PR Week Awards 2000, GQ Man of the Year (entrepreneur) 2001, Ernst and Young Young Entrepreneur of the Year 2001; fndr chm Cyprus Marine Environment Protection Association (CYMEPA) 1992; hon degree Liverpool John Moores Univ; *Recreations* serial entrepreneurship; *Style*— Sir Stelios Haji-Ioannou; ✉ easyGroup, 42 Gloucester Crescent, London NW1 7DL (tel 020 7241 9000, fax 020 7482 2857, e-mail stelios@easygroup.co.uk, website www.stelios.com or www.easy.com)

HALAM, Ann; *see:* Jones, Gwyneth Ann

HALBERT, His Hon Judge Derek Rowland; s of Ronald Halbert, and Freda Mabel, *née* Impett; *b* 25 March 1948; *Educ* King's Sch Chester, Selwyn Coll Cambridge (MA), Open Univ (BA); *m* 28 Sept 1972, Heather Rose, da of late Samuel Walter Ashe; 2 da (Sarah Lucy *b* 21 Jan 1979, Elizabeth Amy *b* 17 May 1983); *Career* called to the Bar Inner Temple 1971, in practice Wales & Chester Circuit 1972–95, recorder of the Crown Court 1991–95; circuit judge: Wales & Chester Circuit 1995–2007, Northern Circuit 2007–; designated civil judge: Cheshire and N Wales 2003–06, Cheshire 2007–; *Clubs* Leander; *Style*— His Hon Judge Halbert; ✉ Chester Civil Justice Centre, Trident House, Little St John Street, Chester CH1 1SN

HALDANE OF GLENEAGLES, (James) Martin; 28th of Gleneagles; er s of James Haldane (d 1990), of Gleneagles, Auchterarder, and Joanna Margaret, *née* Thorburn; suc his kinsman, Alexander Chinnery Haldane, 27th of Gleneagles (d 1994); *b* 18 September 1941; *Educ* Winchester, Magdalen Coll Oxford; *m* 5 Oct 1968, Petronella Victoria, da of Sir Peter Scarlett, KCMG, KCVO; 1 s, 2 da; *Career* chartered accountant; ptnr: Arthur Young 1970–89, Chiene & Tait 1989–2001 (chm 1998–2001); chm: Craighead Investments plc 1982–90, Queen's Hall (Edinburgh) Ltd 1992–2001, Shires Income plc 2003– (dir 1996–), Investors Capital Trust plc 2004– (dir 1995–); dir: Northern and Scottish Bd Legal and General Assurance Soc 1984–87, Scottish Life Assurance Co 1990–2001 (dep chm 1999–2001), Wellington Members Agency Ltd 1995–96, Stace Barr Wellington Ltd 1996–97, Stace Barr Angerstein plc 1997–; chm: Scottish Philharmonic Soc 1978–85, Scottish Chamber Orchestra 1981–85; memb: Cncl Edinburgh Festival Soc 1985–89, D'Oyly Carte Opera Tst 1985–92, Cncl Nat Tst for Scotland 1992–97, Ct Univ of Stirling 1997–2005; memb Queen's Body Guard for Scotland (Royal Co of Archers) (treas 1992–2001); chm of govrs Innerpeffray Library 1994–2005; Hon DUniv Stirling 2006; FRSA; *Recreations* music, golf, shooting; *Clubs* Brooks's, New (Edinburgh), Hon Co of Edinburgh Golfers; *Style*— Martin Haldane of Gleneagles; ✉ Gleneagles, Auchterarder, Perthshire PH3 1PJ (tel 01764 682388, e-mail jmhaldane@gleneagles.org); 23 Northumberland Street, Edinburgh EH3 6LR (tel 0131 556 2924)

HALE, Charles Martin; s of Charles Sidney Hale (d 1981), and Carmen, *née* de Mora (d 2001); *b* 19 January 1936; *Educ* St Bernard's Sch NY, Culver Mil Acad, Stanford Univ (BSc), Harvard Business Sch (MBA); *m* 11 Feb 1967, Kaaren Alexis; 2 da (Melissa *b* 18 May 1971, Amanda *b* 9 Nov 1976); *Career* USN: serv USS Union, Ensign i/c Boat Gp Div 1958, Lt 1960; gen ptnr Hirsch & Co London 1963–71, md and sr offr Europe AG Becker Inc 1971–83, gen ptnr Lehman Bros Kuhn Loeb Inc 1983–84, md and head Int Div Donaldson Lufkin & Jenrette Securities Corp 1984–95, chm Donaldson Lufkin & Jenrette Int 1996–2000, vice-chm Credit Suisse First Boston (Europe) Ltd 2000–01, exec chm Polar Capital Partners 2002–; dir Innospec Corp (Nasdaq); chm UK Assoc of NY Stock Exchange Membs 1989–91; memb: Advsy Cncl Inst of United States Studies 2000–03, Chatham House US Programme Advsy Gp, Great Ormond St Hosp for Children Redevelopment Advsy Bd, The Pilgrims, Harvard Business Sch Club of London, Stanford Univ Club of GB; *Recreations* tennis, travel, opera and philately; *Clubs* Boodle's, Hurlingham, Queenwood Golf, Annabel's, Harvard (NY), Harry's Bar, Mark's, City of London, Westmoor (Nantucket); *Style*— Charles Hale, Esq; ✉ 33 Lyall Mews, London SW1X 8DJ (tel 020 7245 9916); Polar Capital Partners Ltd, 4 Matthew Parker Street, London SW1H 9NP (tel 020 7227 2700)

HALE, Julian Anthony Stuart; s of James Peter Rashleigh Hale (d 1981), and Gillian Mariette Stuart, *née* Mason; *b* 27 November 1940; *Educ* Winchester, ChCh Oxford (MA); *m* 1, 1963 (m dis 1970), Jennifer Monahan; m 2, 1971, Mary Kathleen Benét (d 1984); m 3, 1987, Helen Elizabeth Grace, da of Julian Likierman, of London; 2 da (Laura *b* 1972, Tamara *b* 1988), 1 s (Felix *b* 1990); *Career* books ed G G Harrap 1963–65, Italian prog organiser BBC External Servs 1972–73 (prodr and scriptwriter 1968–72), ed European Gazette 1973, writer 1973–; prodr BBC Radio 3 and 4 incl: In The Air, Wilko's Weekly, File On 4, Third Ear, Radio Lives 1979–94 (also presenter European Journeys); ind radio prodr 1994–; prodr Icon Books audiotapes 1996–; *Books* incl: Ceausescu's Romania (1971), Radio Power (1975), Snap Judgement (1974), Vicious Circles (1978), Midwinter Madness (1979), Black Summer (1982); *Clubs* MCC; *Style*— Julian Hale, Esq; ✉ 11 Alexander Street, London W2 5NT (tel 020 7229 0671, fax 020 7243 0001, e-mail julian.hale@alexanderstreet.demon.co.uk)

HALE OF RICHMOND, Baroness (Life Peer UK 2004), of Easby in the County of Yorkshire; Dame Brenda Marjorie Hale; DBE (1994), PC (1999); da of Cecil Frederick Hale (d 1958), and Marjorie, *née* Godfrey (d 1981); *b* 31 January 1945; *Educ* Richmond HS for Girls Yorks, Girton Coll Cambridge (MA); *m* 1, 1968 (m dis 1992), Dr (Anthony) John Christopher Hoggett, QC, *qv*, s of Christopher Hoggett (d 1989), of Grimsby; 1 da (Julia *b* 1973); m 2, 1992, Prof Julian Thomas Farrand, QC, *qv*, s of John Farrand (d 1998); *Career* Univ of Manchester: asst lectr 1966, lectr 1968, sr lectr 1976, reader 1981, prof of law 1986–89; prof of English law KCL 1989–90 (visiting prof 1990–); visiting fell Nuffield Coll Oxford 1997–2005, visitor Girton Coll Cambridge 2004– (hon fell 1996–2004); called to the Bar Gray's Inn 1969 (bencher 1994), QC 1989, asst recorder 1984–89, recorder of the Crown Court 1989–93, judge of the High Court of Justice (Family Div) 1994–99, liaison judge (Family Div) London 1997–99, Lord Justice of Appeal 1999–2004, Lord of Appeal in Ordinary 2004–; chllr Univ of Bristol 2004–; pres UK Assoc of Women Judges 2004–; law cmmr 1984–93; memb Cncl of Tribunals 1980–84; pres Nat Family Mediation 1994– (chm 1989–93), chair Mgmnt Ctee Royal Courts of Justice Advice Bureau 2002–03, memb Human Fertilisation and Embryology Authy 1990–93; jt gen ed Journal of Social Welfare Law 1978–84; managing tstee Nuffield Fndn 1987–2002; Hon LLD: Univ of Sheffield 1989, London Guildhall Univ 1996, Univ of Manchester 1997, Univ of Bristol 2002, Univ of Cambridge 2005, Univ of Hull 2006, KCL 2007, City Univ 2007, Univ of Oxford 2007, Univ of Reading 2007; Hon DUniv Essex 2005; Hon FBA 2004, Hon FRCPsych 2007; *Books* Mental Health Law (1976, 4 edn 1996), Parents and Children (1977, 4 edn 1993), The Family Law and Society - Cases and Materials (with D S Pearl, 1983, 5 edn with D S Pearl, E Cooke and P Bates 2002), Women and the Law (with S Atkins, 1984), From the Testtube to the Coffin - Choice and Regulation in Private Life (The Hamlyn Lectures, 1996); many contribs to legal texts and periodicals; *Recreations* domesticity, drama, duplicate bridge; *Clubs* Athenaeum; *Style—* The Rt Hon the Lady Hale of Richmond, DBE, PC; ✉ House of Lords, London SW1A 0PW

HALES, Antony John (Tony); s of Sidney Alfred Hales (d 1985), and Margaret Joan, *née* Wood; *b* 25 May 1948; *Educ* Repton, Univ of Bristol (BSc); *m* Linda Christine, da of Hugh Churchlow; 4 c; *Career* Cadbury Schweppes: food salesman 1969–70, asst brand mangr milk products 1970–71, brand mangr biscuits 1971–74; foods mktg mangr Cadbury Typhoo 1974–79, mktg dir Joshua Tetley & Son Ltd 1979–83, md Halls Oxford and West Brewery Co 1983–85, md Ind Coope-Taylor Walker Ltd 1985–87, retail dir Allied Breweries Ltd 1987, md Ansells Ltd 1987–89; Allied Domecq plc (Allied-Lyons plc until 1994): dir 1989–99, chief exec J Lyons & Co Ltd 1989–91, gp chief exec 1991–99; chm: Navy, Army and Air Force Institutes Ltd 2001–, Workspace Gp plc 2002–, British Waterways 2005–; non-exec dir: Hyder plc 1993–97, HSBC Bank 1994–2001, Aston Villa FC 1997–, Tempo Holdings Ltd 2000–01, David Halsall Int 2000–05, Reliance Security Gp 2001–05, Provident Financial 2006–; chm Nat Manufacturing Cncl CBI 1993–95; Freeman City of London 1986, Liveryman Worshipful Co of Brewers 1986; *Style—* Tony Hales, Esq; ✉ Belvoir House, Edstone Court, Wooton Wawen, Solihull, West Midlands B95 6DD

HALES, Lady Celestria Magdalen Mary; da of 5 Earl of Gainsborough, *qv*; *b* 27 January 1954; *Educ* St Mary's Convent Ascot, St Hilda's Coll Oxford; *m* 1 March 1990, Timothy Manville Hales, o s of late S W M Hales, MC; 1 da (Catherine Rose Mary b 11 June 1990); *Career* social ed (as Lady Celestria Noel) Jennifer's Diary in Harpers & Queen 1992–98, ed PrivatAir the Magazine 2000–; *Books* The Harpers & Queen Book of the Season (1994), Debrett's Guide to the Season (2000); *Style—* The Lady Celestria Hales; ✉ Marsh Hall, Orleton, Ludlow SY8 4HY (tel 01584 711212)

HALES, Christopher Atherstone; s of Lt-Col Herbert Marwicke Atherstone Hales (d 1956), of Turweston, Bucks, and Mary, *née* Bell (d 1970); *b* 26 August 1931; *Educ* Wellingborough, HMS Worcester; *m* 17 May 1956, Barbara Mary, da of Edwin Arthur Ryan (d 1963), of London; 4 da (Katherine b 1958, Caroline b 1959, Antonia b 1961, Marie Louise b 1964), 2 s (Julian b 1963, Adrian b 1966); *Career* MN, Midshipman to 2 Offr Blue Funnel Line 1949–58, Master Mariner 1957; called to the Bar Gray's Inn 1960, admitted slr 1964; asst slr Alsop Stevens and Co 1964 (articled clerk 1961–64); Holman Fenwick & Willan: asst slr 1965–67, ptnr 1968–92, conslt 1992–2003; dep dist judge of the High Court and County Courts 1989–2002; memb Law Soc; Freeman City of London, Liveryman Hon Co of Master Mariners; *Recreations* concert and theatregoing, history, following cricket; *Style—* Christopher Hales, Esq; ✉ Farthing Green, Elmdon, Saffron Walden, Essex CB11 4LT; 69 Bessborough Place, London SW1V 3SE

HALES, Christopher James; s of James Camille Hales (d 1968), and Genefer Enid, *née* Ratcliff; *b* 12 November 1952; *Educ* Westminster, Univ Hall (Univ of London external BA); *Career* called to the Bar Gray's Inn 1979; Treasy slr 1990–2003, lawyer Health and Safety Exec 2004–; *Recreations* composing songs, sport, art, karate, painting; *Style—* Christopher Hales, Esq; ✉ Health and Safety Executive, Rose Court, 2 Southwark Bridge, London SE1 9HS (tel 020 7717 6689, e-mail chris.hales@hse.gsi.gov.uk)

HALEY, Geoffrey Norman (Geoff); s of Norman Haley (d 1966), of Pudsey, W Yorks, and Grace Ward, *née* Cooke (d 1983); *b* 12 October 1944; *Educ* Accrington GS, Univ of London (BL), Brunel Univ and Henley Mgmnt Coll (MBA), Inst of Mktg (DipM); *m* 22 Oct 1966, Doreen Haley, da of Leslie Veitch; 1 s (Paul b 5 Sept 1974), 1 da (Julie b 24 June 1977); *Career* admitted slr 1971, dep gp legal advsr Costain Gp 1974–78, dir Costain UK 1980–86 (legal advsr 1978–86), gen mangr Costain Ventures 1986–89; ptnr: Theodore Goddard 1989–93, SJ Berwin & Co 1993–98, Arnold & Porter 1998–2000; legal advsr: Thames Barrier Consortium 1979–86, Channel Tunnel contractors Transmanche Link 1985; dir GKN Kwikform Ltd 1986–89, alternate dir Br Urban Devpt 1988–89; expert to European Cmmn; consult advsr: UNCTAD Geneva, UNIDO Vienna; chm Int Project Finance Assoc 1998–; memb: Law Soc, Soc of Construction Law, Greenlands Assoc, Ascot Round Table, Panel Euro Centre for Infrastructure Studies Rotterdam; hon prof of project finance Univ of Dundee; numerous articles in the field of construction law and private fin for transportation and infrastructure projects; Lord of the Manor of Kidderminster Burnell; MInstPet; *Books* A-Z of Boot Projects, Negotiating Infrastructure Agreements; *Recreations* swimming, cycling, walking; *Clubs* RAC; *Style—* Geoffrey Haley, Esq; ✉ Tanglewood, 39A Llanvair Drive, South Ascot, Berkshire SL5 9LW (tel 01344 627311); International Project Finance Association, Linton House, 164–180 Union Street, London SE1 0LH (tel 020 7620 1883, fax 020 7620 1886)

HALFORD, Andy; s of Frank Halford, and Norma Halford; *b* 18 March 1959, Berks; *Educ* Bedford Sch, Univ of Nottingham (BA); *m* 1984, Alison; 3 s (Matthew, Christopher, Toby); *Career* chartered accountant; Price Waterhouse Nottingham and Durban 1980–92; East Midlands Electricity plc: business devpt dir 1992–95, IT dir 1995–97, gp finance dir 1997–98; Vodafone Gp plc: chief financial offr UK 1999–2001, chief financial offr North Europe, Middle East and Africa 2001–02, chief financial offr Verizon Wireless 2002–05, gp chief financial offr 2005–; FCA; *Recreations* tennis, photography, cars, travel; *Style—* Andy Halford, Esq; ✉ Vodafone Group plc, Vodafone House, The Connection, Newbury, Berkshire RG14 2FN

HALFORD, John; s of Gordon Halford, of Bristol, and Mary, *née* Stevenson; *b* 28 May 1967, Newcastle; *Educ* Univ of Southampton (LLM, Sally Kiff Prize); *Career* admitted slr 1996; mangr and sr advsr immigration advice centre Bristol 1990–91, trainee and slr specialising in immigration cases with human rights dimension Humberside Law Centre 1992–98, slr Public Law Project 1998–2003 (currently memb Bd), ptnr Bindman & Ptnrs Solicitors 2003–; memb Mental Health and Disability Sub-Ctee and Domestic Human Rights Reference Gp Law Soc; memb: Admin Law Bar Assoc, Human Rights Lawyers' Assoc, Community Care Practitioners' Gp; *Publications* Butterworth's Health Services Law and Practice (co-author, 2001), Legal Action's Health Law Series (co-author), contrib to specialist legal pubns incl Judicial Review, Disabled Student Advisor and Legal Action; *Recreations* mountaineering, reading, music, theatre, film; *Style—* John Halford, Esq; ✉ Bindman & Partners Solicitors, 275 Gray's Inn Road, London WC1X 8QB (tel 020 7833 4433, fax 020 7837 9792, e-mail j.halford@bindmans.com)

HALFORD, Prof Stephen Edgar; s of Walter Raoul Halford (d 1976), and Jessie Margaret Edgar (d 1997); *b* 22 September 1945, Cairo, Egypt; *Educ* Rugby, Univ of Bristol (BSc, PhD); *Career* Univ of Bristol: lectr 1976–89, reader 1989–95, prof of biochemistry 1995–; author of numerous papers in scientific pubns; memb Biochemical Soc 1974– (Novartis Medal 2000); FRS 2004; *Recreations* racing, jazz; *Style—* Prof Stephen Halford; ✉ Department of Biochemistry, School of Medical Sciences, University Walk, Bristol BS8 1TD (tel 0117 928 7429, fax 0117 928 8274, e-mail s.halford@bristol.ac.uk)

HALFORD, William Timothy (Tim); s of John Halford (d 2003), of Ripon, N Yorks, and Beatrice Margery Halford (d 1959); *b* 19 February 1947; *Educ* The Leys Sch Cambridge; *m* 1969 (m dis 2000), Andrea Rosemary, da of John Henry Lee (d 1968); 3 da (Amy Katherine b 15 Dec 1971, Joanna Alice b 8 Aug 1973, Harriet Louisa b 15 Nov 1975); *Career* PR consultancy 1966–75, vice-pres of Euro public affairs Occidental Petroleum Corp 1975–84, dir group public affairs Grand Metropolitan plc 1984–92, dir group PR Trafalgar House plc 1992–94, dir group corporate affrs Standard Chartered plc 1995–2002, dir Stonehenge Public Relations Ltd 2002–07, chm True Earth Ltd 2007–; chm Crechendo Ltd 1992–; CFIPR; *Recreations* sailing, walking, theatre; *Clubs* HAC; *Style—* Tim Halford, Esq; ✉ Malt House, Llandyssil, Powys SY15 6LJ

HALIFAX, 3 Earl of (UK 1944); Sir Charles Edward Peter Neil Wood; 7 Bt (GB 1784); DL (1983); also Viscount Halifax (UK 1866), Baron Irwin (UK 1925); s of 2 Earl of Halifax (d 1980); *b* 14 March 1944; *Educ* Eton, ChCh Oxford; *m* 1976, Camilla, da of Charles Frank Johnston Younger, DSO, TD (d 1995), of Gledswood, Melrose, Roxburghshire; 1 s (James Charles, Lord Irwin b 1977), 1 da (Lady Joanna b 1980); *Heir* s, Lord Irwin; *Career* vice-chm Christie Manson & Woods; JP; High Steward of York Minster 1988; KStJ; *Style—* The Rt Hon the Earl of Halifax, KStJ, JP, DL; ✉ Garrowby, York YO41 1QD

HALL, Adrian; s of Cecil Herbert Wellington Hall, MBE (d 2003), and Jean Barbara, *née* Littlejohn; *b* 24 August 1963, Littlehampton, W Sussex; *Educ* Elgin Acad, Dorset Inst of HE; *m* 30 June 2007, Hilary Rhona Ellis; 2 s (Benjamin Daniel b 31 Jan 1990, Jacob Wellington b 2 Aug 1992); *Career* archaeologist 1981–88; Civil Serv: exec offr Dept of Employment 1991–96, higher exec offr Dept of Employment 1997–99, head of housing and regeneration Govt Office for the South East, head of multimedia resources DfES 2002–05, prog dir personalised content DfES 2005–06; dir mobile learning Steljes Ltd 2006–; memb Advsy Bd NESTA Futurelab 2002–06; *Recreations* mountain biking, cricket, travelling; *Style—* Adrian Hall, Esq; ✉ Steljes Ltd, Bagshot Manor, Green Lane, Bagshot GU19 5NL (e-mail adrian.hall@steljes.co.uk)

H

HALL, Col Alan Edmund Matticot; TD (1975), DL (London 1985); s of Maj Edmund Hall (d 1983), of Helston, Cornwall, and Norah, *née* Carrick (d 1995); *b* 7 October 1935; *Educ* Emanuel Sch, Churcher's Coll Petersfield, The GS Enfield; *m* 8 Feb 1958, Diane Mary, da of Robert William Keyte (d 1969), of Cliftonville, Kent; 2 da (Amanda b 1959, Nicola b 1962), 1 s (James b 1968); *Career* Nat Serv 1955–57, Territorial Serv RMP 1961–82; OC 44 Parachute Bde Provost Co 1965–67, OC 253 Provost Co 1969–76; appt Hon Col RMP TA 1977–82; memb Ctees Gtr London TAVRA: Exec and Fin, Gen Purpose and Fin, HQ, HQ Club (vice-chm (Army) 1992–2002)); Hon Col 36 Signal Regt 1990–2001; md: Ind Coope London 1973–77, Ind Coope Ltd 1978–80, Ind Coope East Anglia Ltd 1981–84, J & W Nicholson & Co 1984, Löwenbräu (UK) Ltd 1993–94 (dir of UK sales Löwenbräu Lager 1986–93); dir Infomatrix Ltd 1994–96; estab Alan Hall Associates 1994; dir Birchdeck Ltd 1998–2003 (chm 1998–2003); pres The Licensed Victuallers National Homes 1990, pres Soc of Past Chairmen 1991 and 1995, former pres The Percheron Horse Soc, regnl chm The Wishing Well Appeal; pres: NE London SSAFA - Forces Help and FHS, Co of Gtr London NE Scout Assoc, Ilford Div St John Ambulance, Cystic Fibrosis Holiday Fund 2000; memb NE London Nat Employers Liaison Ctee; patron: Haven House Fndn 1998–, Helen Rollason Cancer Care Appeal 2000, Abbess Adelicia Charity 2003–; vice-patron Peter May Meml Appeal; rep DL London Borough of Redbridge; chm Good Easter 2002– (parish cncllr 1999, vice-chm 2000–02); Freeman City of London 1984, Liveryman Worshipful Co of Broderers; FIMgt 1979; *Books* Seven Miles from Everywhere on the Way to Nowhere (2003); *Recreations* shooting, wood working, curry cooking, Jaguar cars; *Clubs* JDC; *Style—* Col Alan Hall, TD, DL; ✉ Pippins, Tye Green, Good Easter, Essex CM1 4SH (tel and fax 01245 231280, e-mail jaguarpippins@aol.com)

HALL, Anthony Arthur; *b* 25 May 1939; *Educ* Sir George Monoux GS Walthamstow; *m* Valerie Christine; 1 s (Graham Anthony), 2 da (Alison Lindsay, Kathryn Lorna); *Career* with Barclays Bank Ltd 1955–65, Barclays Bank DCO (Dominion Colonial & Overseas, now Barclays International) 1965–71, N M Rothschild (CI) Ltd Guernsey 1971–72, Bank of London and Montreal Nassau Bahamas 1972–73, Italian International Bank (CI) Ltd Guernsey 1974–76, md Rea Brothers (Guernsey) Ltd 1976–95 (chm 1995–96), jt ceo Rea Brothers Group plc 1988–1995, currently non-exec dir and conslt to a number of quoted investment funds; ACIB; *Recreations* flying (multi-engine instrument rated pilot), target pistol shooting, golf, chess, swimming; *Clubs* Royal Guernsey Golf; *Style—* Anthony Hall, Esq; ✉ Le Pavois, Marette de Haut, St Martin, Guernsey GY4 6JL (tel 01481 235254, fax 01481 235395, e-mail tonyhallgy@aol.com)

HALL, Anthony John; s of late Maj Percy Edwin John Hall, and late Mabel, *née* Webster; *b* 27 February 1938; *Educ* Harrogate GS, UCL (MB BS); *m* 19 Aug 1967, Avis Mary, da of Dennis John Harbour (d 1973); 2 s (Simon John Webster b 3 March 1969, Charles b 9 Sept 1970), 1 da (Julia b 26 April 1974); *Career* conslt orthopaedic surgn Chelsea and Westminster Hosp, hon conslt Royal Marsden and Queen Charlotte's Hosps 1973–, regnl advsr in orthopaedics to NW Thames RHA 1987–93; memb: Ct of Examiners RCS 1985–91, Editorial Bd International Orthopaedics 1987, Cncl Br Orthopaedic Assoc 1989–91, Int Soc of the Knee, Int Arthroscopy Assoc; sec gen Société Internationale de Chirurgie Orthopedique et de Traumatologie (SICOT); past chm NW Thames Trg Ctee in Orthopaedics, examiner for Univ of London (MB BS and MSc (Orth)), examiner fo the intercollegiate FRCS (Orth); past pres W London Medico Chirurgical Soc; FRCS; *Books* Manual of Fracture Bracing (ed, 1985), Orthopaedic Surgical Approaches (ed with C L Colton, 1991); *Recreations* sailing; *Style—* Mr Anthony Hall; ✉ 4A Durward House, 31 Kensington Court, London W8 5BH (tel 020 7937 6225); 126 Harley Street, London W1G 7JS (tel 020 7486 1096, fax 020 7224 2520, mobile 077 6851 1112, e-mail tonyhall@dircon.co.uk)

HALL, Anthony William (Tony); CBE (2006); s of Donald William Hall, and Mary Joyce, *née* Wallwork; *b* 3 March 1951; *Educ* King Edward's Sch Birmingham, Birkenhead Sch, Keble Coll Oxford (MA); *m* 6 Aug 1977, Cynthia Lesley, da of Arthur Robin Davis; 1 da (Eleanor Alice Mary b 30 Jan 1986), 1 s (William Arthur Henry b 5 June 1989); *Career* BBC TV: news trainee 1973, sr prodr World at One 1978, output ed Newsnight 1980, sr prodr Six O'Clock News 1984, ed Nine O'Clock News 1985, ed News and Elections '87 1987, dir News and Current Affrs 1990–96 (ed 1987–90), md News BBC Bd of Mgmnt 1993–96, chief exec News and Current Affrs 1996–2001; chair Theatre Royal Stratford East 2000–; Royal Opera House: exec dir 2001–, chief exec 2003–; non-exec dir: HM Customs and Excise 2002–, Univ for Industry 2003–; contrib various pubns, memb Cncl Brunel Univ 1999–2003; Liveryman Worshipful Co of Painter Stainers 1985, Freeman City of London 1988; hon visiting fell Dept of Journalism City Univ 1999; FRTS (chm 1998); *Books* King Coal - A History of The Miners (1981), Nuclear Politics (1984); *Recreations* opera, church architecture, walking; *Clubs* Reform; *Style—* Tony Hall, Esq, CBE

HALL, Prof (John) Barrie; s of John Hall (d 1980), and Kathleen, *née* Glentworth (d 1989); *b* 7 November 1937; *Educ* Watford GS, St John's Coll Cambridge (MA, PhD); *m* 1, 1962 (m dis 1991), Jennifer Anne, da of Maurice George Biggs; 1 da (Penelope Anne b 7 April 1972); m 2, 1994, Annabel Louise Ritchie; *Career* Bedford Coll London: asst lectr in Latin 1962–65, lectr in Latin 1965–74, reader in Latin 1974–87; Hildred Carlile prof of Latin Univ of London 1987–94, Hildred Carlile research prof of Latin Univ of London 1994–98 (emeritus prof 1998–); *Books* Claudian de Raptu Proserpinae (ed, 1969), Claudii Claudiani Carmina (ed, 1985), Prolegomena to Claudian (1986), John of Salisbury, Metalogicon (ed,

1991), Ovid, Tristia (ed, 1995); *Recreations* walking, opera, watching cricket; *Style*— Prof Barrie Hall

HALL, Prof Christopher; s of Victor Hall (d 2000), of Wylye, Wilts, and Doris, *née* Gregory; *b* 31 December 1944, Henley-on-Thames, Oxon; *Educ* Royal Belfast Academical Inst, Trinity Coll Oxford (MA, DPhil, DSc); *m* 1966, Sheila (d 2006), da of Thomas H McKelvey; 1 da (Liza *b* 30 May 1971), 1 s (Benjamin *b* 8 July 1973); *Career* res assoc Electrochemistry Res Centre Case Western Reserve Univ, Cleveland Ohio USA 1970–71, sr res assoc Sch of Chemical Sci UEA 1971–72, lectr in building engrg UMIST 1972–83, head Rock and Fluid Physics Dept Schlumberger Cambridge Res 1983–88, head Chemical Technol Dept Dowell Schlumberger St Etienne France 1988–90, scientific advsr Schlumberger Cambridge Res 1990–99; Univ of Edinburgh: prof of materials and dir Centre for Materials Sci and Engrg 1999–, dir of res Sch of Engrg and Electronics 2002–; visiting prof Univ of Manchester 1994–, visiting fell Princeton Univ 1998, visiting scientific advsr Schlumberger Cambridge Res 1999–, memb Ed Bd Cement and Concrete Res, sr memb Robinson Coll Cambridge 1988–, sr memb Int Union of Testing and Res Laboratories for Materials and Structures; memb: EPSRC Structural Materials Coll 1994–, EPSRC Review Panel on Scanning Probe Microscopy 1998, American Chemical Soc, Materials Res Soc, Soc of Chemical Industry; Brian Mercer Award for Innovation Royal Soc 2001; FRSC 1980, FIM 1990, CEng 1990; *Publications* Polymer Materials (1981, 2 edn 1989), Civil Engineering Materials (contrib), Water Transport in Brick, Stone and Concrete (with W D Hoff, 2002); numerous scientific papers on physical chemistry, materials sci and engrg in professional jls; *Style*— Prof Christopher Hall; ✉ 9A Church Street, Stapleford, Cambridge CB2 5DS (tel 01223 844343); Centre for Materials Science and Engineering, University of Edinburgh, Sanderson Building, The King's Buildings, Edinburgh EH9 3JL (tel 0131 650 5566, fax 0131 667 3677, e-mail christopher.hall@ed.ac.uk)

HALL, Capt Christopher John Pepler; RD (1976, Bar 1986); s of Cdr Harry John Hall, DSO, DSC*, RD (d 1994), of Salisbury, Wilts, and Kathleen Gwladys, *née* Pepler (d 1994); *b* 30 December 1940; *Educ* Marlborough, Univ of Edinburgh; *m* 1, 8 July 1967, Patricia Valerie (d 1992), da of Capt William Neil Kennedy Mellon Crawford, VRD, CA (d 1978); 5 s (Richard *b* 1969, Ian *b* 1970, David *b* 1972, Alistair, Stephen (twins) *b* 1976); *m* 2, 4 Nov 2000, Elizabeth Mary Stewart, da of Philip Ralph Scrafton, MPS, and wid of Finlay McLeay Morgan (d 1990); *Career* RNR 1960–92; Capt 1988, CO HMS Claverhouse Forth Division RNR 1983–89, Capt Mobilisation and Recruiting (Reserves) 1989–92, Hon ADC to HM The Queen 1991–92, Naval Vice-Chm Lowland RFCA 1992–2006; qualified CA 1966, Cooper Bros Mombasa 1967–68; ptnr: Davidson Smith Wighton and Crawford Edinburgh 1970–78, Turquands Barton Mayhew 1978–80, Ernst & Whinney 1980–82; md Hall Management Services Ltd 1982–93, sole prop CJP Hall CA 1989–2001; conslt to various charities 2001–; Scot Episcopal Church: convenor Finance Ctee 1991–96, diocesan sec and treas Diocese of Argyll and the Isles 1987–2001, convenor Provincial Investment Ctee 2000–06; chm Sea Cadet Assoc in Scotland 2006–; *Recreations* sailing, travel, reading, theatre; *Clubs* Royal Scots (Edinburgh), Royal Over-Seas League, RNSA, Mombasa (Kenya); *Style*— Christopher J P Hall, RD*; ✉ 31 Stirling Road, Edinburgh EH5 3JA (tel 0131 552 5991, e-mail cjph@challca.com)

HALL, Colin; s of Arthur Graham Henry Hall (d 1998), and Winifred Martha, *née* Gray (d 1979); *b* 23 April 1945; *Educ* Stationers' Company's Sch, Univ of Bristol (LLB); *m* 29 Sept 1973, Philippa Margaret, da of Hac Collinson, of Sway, Hants; 4 s (Nicholas Justin *b* 1976, Oliver Rupert *b* 1978, Giles Edward, Rupert Charles (twins) *b* 1981); *Career* HM Dip Serv 1966–68, admitted slr 1971, ptnr Slaughter and May slrs 1978–98 (joined 1969); dir The Woodland Tst 1998–; tstee The Tree Register of the British Isles 1992–; *Recreations* sailing, gardening, farming, forestry; *Style*— Colin Hall, Esq; ✉ The Oast House, West End, Frensham, Surrey GU10 3EP (tel 01252 793422, fax 01252 795263)

HALL, Daniel Charles Joseph; s of Stuart Hall, of Wilmslow, Cheshire, and Hazel, *née* Bennett; *b* 29 August 1962; *Educ* Repton, Univ of Bristol (LLB), Coll of Law London; *m* 11 May 1996, Melanie Jane; 2 s (Benjamin *b* 24 Oct 1997, Giles *b* 25 Nov 2002), 1 da (Isabel *b* 25 April 2000); *Career* slr; trainee slr Eversheds 1985–87, slr Clifford Chance 1987–92, ptnr Eversheds 1992– (head of corporate 1999–); chm Hallé Orchestra Tstees, memb regnl ctee London Stock Exchange; memb Law Soc; memb BASC; *Recreations* golf, shooting, fishing; *Style*— Daniel Hall, Esq; ✉ Brookfield Farm, Ancoats Lane, Alderley Edge, Cheshire SK9 7TT (tel 01565 872525); Eversheds, Eversheds House, 70 Great Bridgewater Street, Manchester M1 5ES (tel 0845 497 9797, fax 0845 497 8888, e-mail danielhall@eversheds.com)

HALL, Prof Sir David Michael Baldock; kt (2003); s of Ronald Hall, and Gwen, *née* Baldock; *b* 4 August 1945; *Educ* Reigate GS, St George's Med Sch (MB BS); *m* 24 Aug 1966, Susan Marianne, da of Gordon Howard Luck; 2 da (Emma *b* 1969, Vanessa *b* 1971); *Career* paediatrician Baragwanath Hosp Johannesburg 1973–76, sr registrar Charing Cross Hosp 1976–78, conslt St George's Hosp 1978–93, prof of community paediatrics Children's Hosp Sheffield 1993–2005 (emeritus prof 2005–); hon conslt: The Spastics Soc (now Scope) 1982–86, Tadworth Ct 1986–92; med advsr Assoc for All Speech-Impaired Children 1981–86; pres RCPCH (formerly Br Paediatric Assoc) 2000–03 (academic vice-pres 1994–98), fndr memb Children's Head Injury Tst, patron Scope 2003–; FRCP 1986 (MRCP 1972), FRCPCH; *Books* Health for all Children (1989, 4 edn 2003), Child Surveillance Handbook (2 edn, 1995), The Child with a Disability (2 edn, 1996); *Recreations* travel, reading, music; *Style*— Prof Sir David Hall; ✉ Storrs House Farm, Storrs Lane, Sheffield S6 6GY (tel 0114 285 3177, fax 0870 762 8445, e-mail d.hall@sheffield.ac.uk)

HALL, David Nicholas; OBE (1998); s of William Noel Hall (d 1981), of London, and Louisa Augusta, *née* Palma; *b* 19 November 1933; *Educ* London Choir Sch, Carlisle & Gregson (Jimmy's), RMA Sandhurst; *m* 28 Dec 1963, Harriet Mary Arden, da of William Lloyd McElwee, MC, TD (d 1978); 3 da (Susannah *b* 25 Feb 1965, Phillie *b* 13 April 1967, Christina *b* 17 Oct 1969); *Career* active serv Korean War 1953, cmmnd RE, served Cyprus, Congo (Zaire) and Ghana, instr RMA Sandhurst, Staff Coll, staff appt with Engr-in-Chief, Sqdn Cdr Scotland and Gibraltar, Kirkcudbright, CO RE Depot 1974–77, technical staff appt 1977–79, Record Office RE 1979–81, ret Lt-Col 1981; author of various pubns on land navigation and expdns; dir Fndn for Sci and Technol 1981–2000, liaison offr Learned Socs 1981–97, David Hall Consultancy 2000–03, sr advsr Leadership for Environment and Devpt (LEAD) Int 2001–04; chm: Young Explorers' Tst Screening 1983–93, Palestine Exploration Fund 1990–95 (hon treas 1983–90), Frederick Soddy Tst 2003– (tstee 1985–); RGS: hon foreign sec 1973–83, vice-pres 1984–87 and 1991–94, chm Expeditions and Research Ctee 1984–91, hon treas 1996–2002; memb Cncl Br Sch of Archaeology in Jerusalem 1992–94; founding pres The Desert Dining Club 1980–; tstee: Jt Servs Expdns Tst 1979–2006, Young Explorers' Tst 1990–94, Hazards Forum 1997–99, Mount Everest Fndn 2002–05; organiser and ldr: Br Expdn to Aïr Mountains (Southern Sahara) 1970, various camel journeys and scientific expdns to arid regions; RMCS Heilbronn Prize 1966, RGS Ness Award 1972; hon memb Fndn for Science and Technol 2000; FICS, FRGS (Hon FRGS 1992); *Books* contrib: Expeditions (1977), Tales from the Map Room (1993); *Recreations* exploration, fishing, wine, music; *Clubs* Athenaeum; *Style*— David Hall, Esq, OBE; ✉ East House, Mynthurst, Leigh, Surrey RH2 8RJ (tel 01293 863879, e-mail davidnhall@hotmail.com)

HALL, Prof Denis R; *b* 1 August 1942, Cardiff; *Educ* Univ of Manchester (BSc), Bart's Med Coll London (MPhil), Case Western Reserve Univ Cleveland Ohio (PhD), Edinburgh Business Sch (MBA); *m*; 2 c; *Career* graduate asst/postdoctoral fell Dept of Electrical Engrg Case Western Reserve Univ Cleveland OH 1967–71, postdoctoral research fell (Nat Acad of Scis Award) NASA Goddard Space Flight Center Greenbelt MD 1971–72, sr research scientist Avco Everett Research Lab Boston MA 1972–74 (summer visiting research scientist 1986 and 1988), princ scientific offr Royal Signals and Radar Estab MOD 1974–79, sr lectr/reader in applied laser physics Dept of Applied Physics Univ of Hull 1979–87; Heriot-Watt Univ Edinburgh: prof of optoelectronics Dept of Physics 1987–, currently asst princ (research); pt/t GS teacher in physics and physical educn 1965–67; conslt Systems Electronics Inc Cleveland OH 1969–74; MOD research contract monitor (industrial and univ contracts) 1974–79, MOD delg on Int Tech Cooperation Panel (lasers and IR systems) 1975–79, chief project scientist UK Satellite Laser Ranging Facility Royal Greenwich Observatory 1979–83; dir Laser Applications Ltd Hull 1980–86; memb: Satellite Laser Ranging Steering Ctee Astronomy, Space and Radio Bd SERC 1979–84, Quantum Electronics Bd Euro Physical Soc 1988–94, E13 Gp Ctee IEE 1993–; chm Quantum Electronics Gp Ctee Inst of Physics 1991–94 (memb 1977–81 and 1986–89); memb: Sigma Xi (elected) 1971, IEEE-LEOS 1991, Optical Soc of America; CEng, FInstP 1985 (MInstP 1974), FIEE 1986 (MIEE 1985), FRSE 1991; *Publications* author/jt author of numerous pubns in learned jls and of invited and contributed papers; *Style*— Prof Denis R Hall, FRSE; ✉ Department of Physics, Heriot-Watt University, Riccarton, Edinburgh EH14 4AS (tel 0131 451 3081)

HALL, Dinny (Mrs Brannigan); da of David Alexander Hall, of Shantock House, Bovingdon, Hertfordshire, and Susan Anne, *née* Martyr; *b* 28 April 1959; *Educ* Bourne Valley Comp, Herts Sch of Art and Design St Albans, Central Sch of Art and Design (BA); *m*; 1 s (Lorcan); *Career* jewellery designer; set up own business in Soho London 1983, launched first range of jewellery using gold and precious stones 1990, opened first shop Notting Hill 1992, second shop Chelsea 1995; clients incl Harvey Nichols, Browns, Harrods and many other prestigious stores worldwide; collections featured since 1985 in magazines incl: Vogue, Harpers & Queen, Elle, Sunday Times, Sunday Telegraph; Br Accessory Designer of the Year 1989; *Books* Creative Jewellery (1986); *Recreations* cooking, travelling, walking; *Clubs* Groucho; *Style*— Ms Dinny Hall

HALL, Edward Peter (Ed); s of Sir Peter Hall , *qv*, and Jacqueline Hall; *Educ* Bedales, Univ of Leeds, Mountview Theatre Sch; *Career* dir Propeller Theatre Co; assoc dir: Old Vic Theatre, Watermill Theatre, NT; Propeller Theatre Co prodns incl: Henry V, Twelfth Night, Comedy of Errors, Rose Rage (adaption of Henry VI part I-III, Drama Desk Broadway, Best Dir Olivier Award nomination, TMA Award), A Midsummer Night's Dream (TMA Award); RSC prodns incl: Two Gentlemen of Verona, Henry V, Julius Caesar, Tantalus (also Denver), Macbeth (Albery Theatre London), Hinge of the World (Guildford), The Constant Wife (Apollo Theatre); other prodns incl: A Funny Thing Happened on the Way to the Forum (National Theatre, Evening Standard and Olivier Award Nomination), Edmond (National Theatre), The Winter's Tale (Watermill and tour, TMA Award nomination), A Streetcar Named Desire (Roundabout Theatre NY), Once in a Lifetime (NT); dir: Safari Strife (documentary, part of Cutting Edge series Channel 4), Once in a Lifetime (Granada), Trial and Retribution: Closure (La Plante Productions, ITV); Best Dir TMA Theatre Award 1999, South Bank Show Theatre Award 2001 (for This England - The Histories); *Publications* Rose Rage; *Recreations* motorcycling, cricket, fishing; *Clubs* Steep Cricket; *Style*— Ed Hall, Esq; ✉ c/o Rebecca Blond Associates, 69A King's Road, London SW3 4NX

HALL, Sir Ernest; kt (1993), OBE (1986), DL (W Yorks 1991); s of Ernest Hall, and Mary Elizabeth Hall; *b* 19 March 1930; *Educ* Bolton Co GS, Royal Manchester Coll of Music (ARMCM, Royal Patron's Fund Prize for composition); *m* 1, 1951, June, *née* Annable (d 1994); 2 da (Virginia *b* 1959, Vivian *b* 1961), 2 s (Jeremy *b* 1962, Tom 1967); *m* 2, 1975, Sarah, *née* Wellby; 1 s (Leopold *b* 1984); *Career* pianist and composer 1954–; textile manufacturer 1961–71; fndr and chm Dean Clough enterprise educn and arts centre Halifax 1983, dep chm Eureka! Children's Museum 1989–2000; pres: Arts and Business Yorks, Yorks Youth and Music, Yorks Youth Orchestra, St Williams Fndn; vice-pres RSA 1995–99; tstee: Yorks Sculpture Park 1989–2003, Henry Moore Fndn 1996–2003; memb Design Cncl 1994–98; chllr Univ of Huddersfield 1996–2003; Albert Medal RSA 1994; Montblanc de la Culture Award 1997, ABSA Goodman Award 1997; Hon DUniv York 1986, Hon DLitt Univ of Bradford 1990, Hon DUniv Leeds Metropolitan 1996, Hon LLD Univ of Leeds 1996; Hon Dr of Arts: CNAA 1991, Univ of Lincolnshire and Humberside 1995; hon fell: Univ of Huddersfield 1989, Leeds Metropolitan Univ 1991, Univ of Central Lancashire 1996; *Recreations* gardening, art collecting, theatre, languages; *Style*— Sir Ernest Hall, OBE, DL; ✉ Dean Clough, Halifax, West Yorkshire HX3 5AX (tel 01422 250250, fax 01422 255250, e-mail sir.ernest.hall@deanclough.com)

HALL, Fiona Jane; MEP; da of Edward Cutts (d 1985), and Dorothy Cutts (d 1995); *b* 15 July 1955, Swinton, Manchester; *Educ* Worsley Wardley GS, Eccles Coll, St Hugh's Coll Oxford (BA), Oxford Poly (PGCE); *m* 24 Sept 1975 (sep), Michael Hall; 2 da (Catherine *b* 1979, Rosemary *b* 1982); *Career* pt/t teacher/tutor 1984–94, asst to Lib Dem cncllrs Newcastle upon Tyne 1994–97, press officer and researcher to Lib Dem MPs 1997–2004, MEP (Lib Dem) NE England 2004–; *Style*— Ms Fiona Hall, MEP; ✉ 55A Old Elvet, Durham DH1 3HN (tel 0191 3830119); European Parliament, Rue Wiertz, B-1047 Bruxelles, Belgium (tel 00 32 22 84 55 61, e-mail fiona.hall@europarl.europa.eu)

HALL, Prof George Martin; s of George Vincent Hall (d 1971), of Bridlington, E Yorks, and Dora Hortensia, *née* Beauchamp; *b* 14 May 1944; *Educ* King Edward VI Sch Lichfield, UCL (MB BS, PhD), Univ of London (DSc); *m* 9 Jan 1964, Marion Edith, da of Frank Gordon Burgin, MBE, of Great Missenden, Bucks; 1 da (Katherine Elizabeth *b* 1965); *Career* prof of clinical anaesthesia Royal Postgrad Med Sch Univ of London 1989–92 (sr lectr 1976–85, reader 1985–89), fndn prof of anaesthesia St George's Hosp Med Sch Univ of London 1992–; chm to British Journal of Anaesthesia; contrib research papers on anaesthesia; sec Euro Soc of Anaesthesiology 2001–05; *Recreations* cycling, jazz, supporting Staffordshire; *Clubs* Farmers'; *Style*— Prof George Hall; ✉ Department of Anaesthesia and Intensive Care Medicine, St George's Hospital Medical School, London SW17 0RE (tel 020 8725 2615, fax 020 8725 0256, e-mail ghall@sgul.ac.uk)

HALL, Gillian Mary; da of John Robert Hall (d 1990), and Mary, *née* Davison; *b* 8 November 1960, North Shields, Tyne and Wear; *Educ* Central Newcastle HS, Newnham Coll Cambridge (Squire law scholar, MA), Chester Coll of Law; *m* 7 July 1995, (John) Richard Whitaker; 1 s (Daniel George *b* 9 Jan 1997), 2 step da (Hannah Dorothy *b* 1 Aug 1986, Rhoda Constance *b* 2 Aug 1990); *Career* slr; articled clerk Lovell White & King (now Lovells) 1983–85; Watson Burton LLP: slr 1985–88, ptnr 1988–; accredited mediator; MInstD, memb Law Soc 1985; *Recreations* family, travel, cooking, literature; *Style*— Ms Gillian Hall; ✉ Watson Burton LLP, 1 St James' Gate, Newcastle upon Tyne NE99 1YQ (tel 0191 244 4444, fax 0191 244 4500, e-mail gillian.hall@watsonburton.com)

HALL, Graham Anthony; s of Kenneth Frederick Hall, of Henley-on-Thames, and Joyce Christine Edith, *née* Wallis; *b* 3 October 1957; *Educ* Trinity Sch of John Whitgift, St John's Coll Oxford (scholar, MA); *m* 14 Sept 1991, Yvette Louise-Marie, da of David Charles Ruggins; *Career* with: Hoare Govett 1980–82, County Bank 1982–85, Morgan Grenfell 1985–97; dir: Morgan Grenfell France 1990–92, Morgan Grenfell Int Ltd 1992–95, Investment Banking Div Morgan Grenfell & Co Ltd 1995–97; dir Corp Fin Div Singer & Friedlander Ltd 1997–98; conslt UBS Private Banking 1999–2005; non-exec dir Fairplace Consulting plc 1999–; *Recreations* food and wine, travel, classic cars; *Style*— Graham Hall, Esq; ✉ 9 Princes Road, London SW19 8RQ (tel and fax 020 8542 2900)

HALL, Prof Ian Philip; s of Kenneth Hall, and June, *née* Dobson; *b* 6 March 1958; *Educ* Kirkham GS, Lincoln Coll Oxford (BA, BM BCh), Univ of Nottingham (DM); *m* 23 Oct

1982, Gillian Mary, da of Samuel Wright (d 1999); 3 da (Claire Elizabeth b 3 Aug 1988, Fiona Jane b 25 Nov 1990, Sarah Louise b 18 April 1997); *Career* registrar and res fell City and Univ Hosps of Nottingham 1986–92, MRC travelling fell Univ of Pennsylvania 1992–93, sr res fell Nat Asthma Campaign 1993–98, prof of molecular med Univ of Nottingham 1998–, dir of R&D Univ Hosp of Nottingham 2001–; memb Assoc of Physicians; FRCP; *Publications* author of 107 papers and reviews on genetics of airway disease, pharmacogenetics and cell signalling; *Recreations* mountaineering, classical guitar, tennis, gardening; *Style—* Prof Ian Hall; ✉ Division of Therapeutics, University Hospital of Nottingham, Nottingham NG7 2UH (tel 0115 823 1063, fax 0115 823 1059, e-mail ian.hall@nottingham.ac.uk)

HALL, James Douglas Ellis; *b* 9 October 1954; *Educ* Edinburgh Acad, Univ of Aberdeen (MA); *m* 1980, Carol; 2 da; *Career* Accenture: joined as graduate trainee 1976, ptnr 1987, UK managing ptnr 1994–2000, currently global managing ptnr Technology and Research; memb Cmmn on Br Business and Public Policy 1995–97; tstee Save Britain's Heritage; memb Guild of Mgmnt Conslts; Freeman: City of London, Worshipful Co of Info Technologists; *Recreations* architecture and conservation; *Style—* James Hall, Esq; ✉ Accenture, 60 Queen Victoria Street, London EC4N 4TW (tel 020 7844 3822, fax 020 7844 1472, e-mail james.hall@accenture.com)

HALL, Janice Elizabeth (Jan); OBE (1996); da of John Brian Hall, and Jean, *née* Chadwick; *b* 1 June 1957; *Educ* Rutland Girls' HS, St Anne's Coll Oxford (MA); *m* Dr David Winston Costain; 1 s (Theo b 15 Feb 1996); *Career* mktg mangr Paints Div ICI 1979–83, chm and chief exec Coley Porter Bell 1983–94, Euro chief exec The GGT Group plc 1994–97, ptnr Spencer Stuart & Associates (exec search) 1997–2005, ptnr JCA Group (exec search) 2005–; sr non-exec dir First Choice Holidays plc 1994–2003; non-exec dir: Allied Maples Group Ltd 1988–91, BSM Group plc 1992–98, London First 1993–95, Veos Ltd 1998–2002; chm: Design Business Assoc 1988–90, Ashridge Coll Assoc 1990–92, DTI BOTB Small Firms Ctee 1992–96; memb: DTI Small Firms Advsy Group on the Single Market 1988–90, Southern Bd BR 1990–93, FO/DTI Br Overseas Trade Bd 1993–96, Dept of Employment TEC Assessors Ctee 1993–95, Advsy Bd Warwick Business Sch 1993–, Cmmn on Public Policy and Br Business 1995–97, President's Advsy Group on Competitiveness DTI 1997–99; memb Cncl: CSD 1988–91, IOD 1991–2005; chm Mktg Group of GB 1997–99, vice-pres Strategic Planning Soc 1995–2001; tstee Demos 1993–2000; hon prof Warwick Business Sch 1997–; FCSD 1989, FRSA 1990; *Recreations* travel, food, opera; *Style—* Ms Jan Hall, OBE; ✉ 37 St John's Wood Road, London NW8 8RA

HALL, Jerry Faye; da of John P Hall (d 1977), and Marjorie, *née* Sheffield; *b* 2 July 1956; *m* 21 Nov 1990 (sep), Sir Michael Philip (Mick) Jagger; 2 da (Elizabeth b 2 March 1984, Georgia b 12 Jan 1991), 2 s (James b 28 Aug 1985, Gabriel b 9 Dec 1997); *Career* actress and model 1973–; has been in over 100 commercials and appeared on the cover of over 150 magazines; worked for all the major designers in Paris, London, New York, Milan and Tokyo; contracts/campaigns incl: Yves Saint Laurent (Opium perfume) 1975–82, Revlon Cosmetics 1976–89, L'Oriel Hair 1979–82, Thierry Mugler (Angel perfume) 1996–98; *Theatre* Bus Stop (New Jersey) 1988 (also West End 1990), The Graduate (West End) 2000, The Vagina Monologues (West End and Austin TX) 2001, The Play What I Wrote (West End and Belfast) 2001, Picasso's Women (UK tour) 2002, Benchmark (2003), The Graduate (US tour) 2003, Les Miserables (West End) 2004, Chitty Chitty Bang Bang (West End) 2004, The Phanton of the Opera (West End) 2004, Fame (West End) 2004, Anything Goes (West End) 2004, Blood Brothers (West End) 2004; *Television* numerous appearances incl: Andy Warhol Television (host) 1985, The David Letterman Show 1984, 1985, 1987, MTV Music News 1986, She's With Me (NBC pilot) 1986, Saturday Night Live (host) 1986, Hysteria II 1989, Clive James on the 80's (co-presenter) 1989, French and Saunders 1990, Bejewelled (TVS/Disney) 1990, The Detectives 1992, Cleudo (Granada) 1993, Jerry Hall's Gurus 2004, Popetown 2004; *Radio* The Betty Grable Story (Radio 3) 1995; *Video* Let's Stick Together (Bryan Ferry) 1976, The Price of Love (Bryan Ferry) 1977, Lady Godive (Simply Red) 1989; *Films* St Germain Des Pres Après Le Guerre 1974, Willie and Phil 1978, Urban Cowboy 1979, Jack and the Beanstalk 1982, The Emperor and the Nightingale 1982, Running out of Luck 1984, Galileus Mouse 1987, Batman 1988, Princess Carabou 1994, Savage Hearts 1994, Vampire in Brooklyn 1994, Diana and Me 1996, RPM 1996, Merci Docteur Rey 2001, Tooth 2004; *Books* Tall Tales (1985); *Style—* Ms Jerry Hall; ✉ c/o ICM Models, 2 Henrietta Street, London WC2 8PS (tel 020 7557 7100); c/o ICM Acting, 76 Oxford Street, London W1D 1BS (tel 020 7636 6565)

HALL, Ven John Barrie; s of Arthur Cyril Hall, and Beatrice, *née* Clark; *b* 27 May 1941; *Educ* Salisbury and Wells Theol Coll; *m* 1963, Kay Deakin; 3 s; *Career* self-employed in garage and caravan sales until 1982; ordained: deacon 1984, priest 1985; curate St Edward Cheddleton 1984–88, vicar Rocester, then Rocester and Croxden with Hollington 1988–98, archdeacon of Salop 1998–, hon canon Lichfield Cathedral 1999; memb Gen Synod C of E 2002–; chm: Shropshire Hist Churches Tst 1998–, Lichfield Dio Child Protection 2004–, Lichfield Dio Redundant Church Uses Ctee 2004–, Lichfield Dio Pastural Ctee 2006–; *Recreations* reading, a little walking, most sports (now watching only); *Style—* The Ven the Archdeacon of Salop; ✉ Tong Vicarage, Shifnal, Shropshire TF11 8PW (tel 01902 372622, e-mail john.hall@lichfield.anglican.org)

HALL, Sir John Bernard; 3 Bt (UK 1919), of Burton Park, Sussex; s of Lt-Col Sir Douglas Montgomery Bernard Hall, 2 Bt, DSO (d 1962), and his 2 w, Ina Nancie Walton (d 1998) (who m 2, 1962, Col Peter J Bradford, DSO, MC, TD (d 1990)), o da of Col John Edward Mellor, CB, JP, DL; *b* 20 March 1932; *Educ* Eton, Trinity Coll Oxford (MA); *m* 1, 19 Oct 1957, Delia Mary (d 1997), da of Lt-Col James Archibald Innes, DSO (d 1949); 2 da (Caroline Evelyn (Mrs Martin Dixon-Ward) b 1959, Julia Nancy (Mrs Michael O'Brien) b 1965), 1 s (David Bernard b 1961); m 2, 22 Aug 1998, Diana, da of Surgn-Cdr Ernest Robert Sorley (ka 1941), and wid of Peter Antony Ravenshear; *Heir* s, David Hall; *Career* Lt Royal Fus RARO; joined J Henry Schröder & Co (later J Henry Schroder Wagg & Co Ltd) 1955 (dir 1967–73), dir Bank of America Int 1974–82, vice-pres Bank of America NT & SA 1982–90, md European Brazilian Bank 1983–89; The Nikko Bank (UK) plc: md 1990–92, chm 1992–95, advsr to the Bd 1995–96; former chm: Anglo-Colombian Soc, Assoc of British Consortium Banks; pres Met Soc for the Blind 2004–; Liveryman and memb Ct of Assts Worshipful Co of Clothworkers (Warden 1987–89, Master 1999–2000); FCIB 1976, FRGS 1988, FRSA 1989; *Recreations* travel, fishing; *Clubs* Boodle's, Lansdowne; *Style—* Sir John B Hall, Bt; ✉ Deanery Lodge, Church Walk, Hadleigh, Suffolk IP7 5ED (tel 01473 828966, fax 01473 823768, e-mail dandjhall@clara.co.uk);Inver House, Lochinver, Lairg, Sutherland IV27 4LJ (tel 01571 844349)

HALL, Sir (Frederick) John Frank; 3 Bt (UK 1923), of Grafham, Co Surrey; s of Sir Frederick Henry Hall, 2 Bt (d 1949), and Olwen Irene, *née* Collis, who subsequently m Arthur Borland Porteous; *b* 14 August 1931; *Educ* Bryanston; *m* 1, 3 April 1956 (m dis 1960), Felicity Anne, da of late Edward Rivers-Fletcher, of Norwich; m 2, 3 June 1961 (m dis 1967), Patricia Ann, da of Douglas Atkinson (d 1973), of Carlisle; 2 da (Nicola Jane b 1962, Samantha Mary b 1965); re-m 9 Nov 1967, his 1 w, Felicity Anne; 2 da (Antonia Anne b 1970, Victoria Joy b 1973); *Heir* bro, David Hall; *Career* personnel mangr Universal Pattern & Precision Engineering Co Ltd 1955–59, personnel offr The Nestlé Co Ltd 1959–63, personnel mangr SC Johnson & Sons Ltd 1963–65; The Nestlé Co Ltd: trg and mgmnt devpt mangr Nestlé UK Head Office 1965–67, gp personnel mangr Findus Ltd 1967–69; sr mangr McLintock Mann & Whinney Murray 1969–76, dir Thomson McLintock Associates 1976–87, fndr and head KPMG Career Consultancy Services 1983–93, ptnr KPMG Peat Marwick 1987–93; dir Roffey Park Inst 1978–90 (vice-chm 1983–85, chm 1985–87); *Recreations* music, collecting antique gramophone records, magic (memb The Magic Circle); *Style—* Sir John Hall, Bt; ✉ Carradale, 29 Embercourt Road, Thames Ditton, Surrey KT7 0LH (tel 020 8398 2801)

HALL, John Peirs; s of late Dr Robert Noel Hall, and late Doreen Cecilia, *née* Russell; *b* 26 June 1940; *Educ* Stowe; *m* 1965, Sarah Gillian, da of Gerard Thorpe Page; 3 s (James b 6 April 1966, Charles b 6 May 1968, Freddie b 12 May 1977); *Career* trainee Read Hurst Brown Stockbrokers 1958–65; Wontner Dolphin & Francis (became Brewin Dolphin 1974 and then Brewin Holdings plc 1994): joined 1965, md 1987, ceo 1992–; Freeman City of London 1970, memb Ct of Assts Worshipful Co of Merchant Taylors; memb IMRO, MSI (memb Stock Exchange 1965); *Recreations* breeding British White cattle, sailing, golf; *Clubs* City of London, Royal Yacht Squadron, Island Sailing, Huntercombe Golf; *Style—* John Hall, Esq; ✉ Brewin Dolphin Holdings plc, 12 Smithfield Street, London EC1A 9BD (tel 0845 213 1000, fax 0845 213 3587, e-mail john.hall@brewin.co.uk)

HALL, John Thridgould; s of Stanley Dennis Hall (d 1997), and Kathleen Joan, *née* Thridgould (d 1978); *b* 23 December 1948, Pinner, Middx; *Educ* Univ Coll Sch Hampstead, Wadham Coll Oxford (minor scholar, MA); *m* 1982, Julie Charlotte; 2 s (Christopher b 20 July 1983, David b 10 Feb 1986), 1 da (Elizabeth b 31 Aug 2000); *Career* admitted slr 1975; Wedlake Saint: joined as articled clerk, asst slr 1975–77, ptnr 1978–94; Eversheds: ptnr 1994–, head of educn 1996–2006, chm Educn Sector Gp 2006–; memb Cncl RCM, memb Ct Roehampton Univ, former govr Barnet Coll; memb Int Advsy Bd Center for Excellence in HE Law and Policy Stetson Univ FL, memb Educn Law Assoc, assoc memb Nat Assoc of Coll and Univ Attorneys; former chm London Young Slrs' Gp; former co sec: Polys and Colls Employers Forum, Colls Employers Forum; memb Law Soc, FRSA, FICPD; *Publications* Purposive Governance: An annotated guidance for further education colleges (gen ed and princ author), Law of Higher Education (conslt ed, 2006); author of many articles in the educnl press; *Recreations* walking, music, history, art, Spain; *Style—* John Hall, Esq; ✉ Eversheds, 85 Queen Victoria Street, London EC4V 4JL (tel 0845 497 4632, fax 0845 497 3770, e-mail johnhall@eversheds.com)

H

HALL, Jonathan James; s of Gordon Hall, and M Joyce, *née* Pratt; *b* 11 October 1960; *Educ* Marlborough, Univ of Bristol (BA), UCL (DipArch, MSc), KCL (MSc); *Career* architect; Building Design Partnership 1986–89, princ Allford Hall Monaghan Morris Architects LLP 1989–; clients incl: Joseph Rowntree Fndn, Peabody Tst, Derwent London, Great Portland Estates, Corporation of London, Barbican Arts Centre, Essex CC, British Cncl, Design Cncl, Centro; occasional lectr at various schs of architecture; external examiner: Sch of Architecture UCE 2001–03, De Montfort Univ 2004–; RIBA Awards for Architecture: for Poolhouse 1996, for Broadgate Club 1998, for Croydon Med Centre 1999, for Great Notley Sch and Work Learn Zone at Millennium Dome 2000, for Walsall Bus Station 2001, for Jubilee Sch and Clearwater Yard 2003, for Raines Court 2004, for Barbican Arts Centre and Unity Liverpool 2007; Royal Fine Art Cmmn Award (for Great Notley Sch), Royal Fine Art Cmmn Tst Award 2000; RIBA 1989, FCIArb 2005; *Recreations* walking, watching the occasional game of cricket; *Clubs* Surrey CC; *Style—* Jonathan Hall, Esq; ✉ Allford Hall Monaghan Morris Architects LLP, 5–23 Old Street, London EC1V 9HL (tel 020 7251 5261, fax 020 7251 5123)

HALL, Maj Gen Jonathan Michael Francis Cooper; CB (1998), OBE (1987); s of Charles Richard Hall; *b* 10 August 1944; *Educ* Taunton Sch, RMA Sandhurst; *m* 5 Oct 1968, Sarah Linda, *née* Hudson; 2 da (Candida Sarah b 1971, Rachel Katharine b 1973); *Career* cmmnd 3rd Carabiniers 1965, Staff Coll Camberley 1977, Cmd Offr Royal Scots Dragoon Guards 1984–86, Higher Cmd and Staff Course 1988, Cmd 12 Armoured Bde 1989–90, Royal Coll of Def Studies 1991, Dep Mil Sec (A) 1992–94, Dir RAC 1994–95, GOC Scotland and Govr Edinburgh Castle 1995–97; Lt Govr and cmmr Royal Hosp Chelsea 1997–2005, managing conslt Compton Fundraising Ltd 2006–, conslt Third Millennium Information (Publishers) Ltd 2006–; Hon Corps of Gentlemen at Arms 1999–; Col Cmdt: Scottish Div 1995–97, Royal Army Vet Corps 1995–2001; Col Royal Scots Dragoon Guards 1998–2003, vice-pres Royal Scots Dragoon Guards Cncl 2004–; HM's Cmmr Queen Victoria Sch Dunblane 1995–97; memb: Ethical Review Process Ctee ICL 2003–; tstee: Royal Armoured Corps War Memorial Fund 1999–, VC and GC Assoc 2004–, Army Museums Ogilby Tst 2004–; memb Sherborne Abbey Parochial Church Cncl and Deanery Synod rep 2006–; govr Taunton Sch 2007–; hon assoc memb BVA; Freeman City of London, Liveryman Worshipful Co of Farriers 2006–; FCMI (FIMgt) 1997; OStJ 1998; *Recreations* country pursuits, travel; *Clubs* Cavalry and Guards', MCC (assoc memb), Woodroffe's, Pratt's; *Style—* Maj Gen Jonathan Hall, CB, OBE; ✉ c/o Home Headquarters, The Royal Scots Dragoon Guards, Edinburgh Castle, Edinburgh EH1 2YT (tel 0131 310 5100, fax 0131 310 5101)

HALL, His Hon Judge Julian; s of Alexander Stephenson Hall (d 1995), of Bucks, and Edith Mary Partington, *née* Smith (d 1975); *b* 13 January 1939; *Educ* Eton, ChCh Oxford (MA), Trinity Coll Dublin (LLB); *m* 1, 1968 (m dis 1988), Margaret Rosalind; 1 s (Benjamin b 1971), 1 da (Rebecca b 1969); m 2, 1989, Dr Ingrid Lunt, *qv*; *Career* industrial res chemist 1961–63; called to the Bar Gray's Inn 1966 (bencher 2002); practising Northern Circuit 1966–86, recorder Crown Court 1982–86, prosecuting counsel Inland Revenue Northern Circuit 1985–86, circuit judge 1986–, res judge Northampton Crown Court 2000–02, resident judge Oxford Crown Court 2002–, hon recorder Oxford 2002–; chm Northamptonshire Family Mediation Serv 1996–2000; memb Mental Health Review Tbnl 1997–; ARCM; *Recreations* making music; *Clubs* Buxton Musical Soc, Music Camp; *Style—* His Hon Judge Julian Hall; ✉ Oxford Crown Court, St Aldate's, Oxford OX1 1TL (tel 01865 264200)

HALL, Lee; s of Peter Edward Hall, and Sylvia, *née* Rodgers; *Educ* Benfield Comp Sch Newcastle upon Tyne, Fitzwilliam Coll Cambridge (BA); *m* 2003, Beeban Kidron; 2 step c (Noah, Blaze); *Career* playwright; writer in residence: Live Theatre Newcastle upon Tyne 1997–98, RSC 1998–99; memb: BAFTA, Writers Guild of GB, Writers Guild of America, Acad of Motion Pictures; *Theatre* Mr Puntila and His Man Matti (trans, Almeida Theatre London) 1997, Cooking with Elvis (Live Theatre Newcastle upon Tyne and Whitehall Theatre London) 2000, A Servant to Two Masters (RSC at Young Vic) 2000, Billy Elliot the Musical (Victoria Palace Theatre) 2005; *Television* The Student Prince 1996; *Radio* I Luv You Jimmy Spud 1995 (Best Writing on Radio Sony Awards 1996), Spoonface Steinberg 1996 (Writers Guild Award 1997, Mental Health in the Media Award 1997); *Films* Billy Elliot 2000 (Best Screenplay Br Ind Film Awards 2000, nomination BAFTA Awards 2000, nomination Oscars 2000), Gabriel & Me 2001; *Publications* Spoonface Steinberg and Other Plays (1996), Cooking with Elvis (1999), A Servant to Two Masters (new adaptation, 2000), Pinocchio (new adaptation, 2000), Billy Elliot (screenplay, 2001), The Good Hope (new adaptation, 2001); *Recreations* buying books, sleeping and eating; *Style—* Lee Hall, Esq; ✉ c/o Judy Daish Associates, 2 St Charles Place, London W10 6EB

HALL, Mervyn Douglas; s of Matthew Douglas Hall (d 1965), of Windsor, and Maisie Eileen, *née* Allen; *b* 4 January 1949; *Educ* Windsor GS; *m* 14 April 1984, Valerie, *née* Nealson; 1 s (Nicholas James b 19 June 1974), 1 da (Suzannah Elizabeth b 27 July 1977); *Career* reporter: Windsor, Slough and Eton Express 1965–69, Shropshire Star 1969–70, Evening Post Luton 1970–73; sports ed LBC 1973–78; ITN: sports ed 1978–84, news ed 1984–89, ed Radio 1989–90, chief ed IRN 1990–93, sales dir 1993–95; int mktg mangr Reuters Media 1995–99, estab Salthouse Consultancy 1999; broadcast liasion offr All England Lawn Tennis Club; memb Cncl: RTS, Radio Acad; *Recreations* golf, reading, food and wine, rugby union; *Clubs* Reform; *Style—* Mervyn Hall, Esq

HALL, (Haddon) Michael (Mike); s of William Haddon Hall (d 1972), and Mildred, *née* Brown, of London; *b* 28 June 1945; *Educ* Aristotle Sch; *m* 1, 24 Jan 1970 (m dis 1976), Kathleen Mary, da of William Suggitt; m 2, 25 April 1981 (m dis 1986), Suzanne Marie, da of Ronald M Bell; m 3, 11 May 1989 (m dis 2002), Victoria Ann, da of Bryan John Vallas (d 1984); 1 s (Stephen b 6 Aug 1992); m 4, 19 April 2003, Maryna, da of Boris Vetrov; *Career* CA Barsham Nixon & Hamilton 1969–72 (joined as articled clerk 1961), qualified sr Stoy Hayward & Co 1972–74; Boty Cox Crawford & Ridley (merged Edward Moore & Sons 1975, which merged Rowland Nevill 1985 to become Moores Rowland, and with BDO Stoy Hayward 1999): audit mangr 1974–79, ptnr 1979–, equity ptnr 1983–2001; prop Haddon Hall 2001–; non-exec dir Croydon Business Venture Ltd 1990–96; FCA 1979 (ACA 1969); *Recreations* applied philosophy, shooting, reading science fiction, collecting collectables; *Clubs* Historical Breechloading Small-Arms Assoc (hon treas); *Style*— Mike Hall, Esq; ✉ Haddon Hall, 8 Petlands Place, Boughton Monchelsea, Maidstone, Kent ME17 4SL (tel and fax 01622 204325, car 07887 907485, e-mail hh006f6689@blueyonder.co.uk)

HALL, Prof Michael Anthony; s of Frederick Lancelot Hall (d 1982), and Eva, *née* Bridgewood-Jeffes (d 1992); *b* 7 July 1940; *Educ* Rutherford GS, Imperial Coll London (BSc, PhD, DSc); *m* 25 Aug 1964, Gillian, da of Frederick Barrone (d 1975); 1 da (Sara Jayne Barrone b 1 June 1969); *Career* Univ of Calif Riverside 1964–67, Scottish Hort Res Inst 1967–68, dir and prof Inst of Biological Sciences UCW Aberystwyth 1968–; memb Malaysian Rubber Research Devpt Bd; 150 pubns in professional jls; FIBiol, FRSA, ARCS; *Books* Plant Structure, Function and Adaptation (1976); *Recreations* skiing, music; *Style*— Prof Michael Hall; ✉ Glascoed, Piercefield Lane, Penparcau, Aberystwyth SY23 1RX (tel 01970 612465); Institute of Biological Sciences, University College of Wales, Aberystwyth SY23 3DA (tel 01970 622313, fax 01970 622350, telex 83147 VIAOR G Attn UWA, e-mail mzh@aber.ac.uk)

HALL, Michael Harold Webster; s of Dr L W Hall, of Cambridge, and Barbara, *née* Moss (d 1978); *b* 6 July 1957, Cambridge; *Educ* Cambridgeshire HS for Boys, Trinity Hall Cambridge (MA), Birkbeck Coll London (MA); *Career* ed Thames and Hudson Ltd 1982–89; Country Life: architectural writer 1989–95, architectural ed 1995–98, dep ed 1998–2004; ed Apollo 2004–; chm Activities Ctee Victorian Soc; tstee: Emery Walker Tst, Marc Fitch Fund; Essay Medal Soc of Architectural Historians of GB 1991; FSA 2003; *Publications* The English Country House, from the archives of Country Life (1994), Gothic Architecture and its Meanings 1550–1830 (ed, 2002), Waddesdon Manor (2002); *Style*— Michael Hall, Esq; ✉ Apollo, 22 Old Queen Street, London SW1H 9HP

HALL, Michael Robert; DL; s of Robert Hall (d 1980), of Cheshire, and Hannah Hall (d 2001); *b* 9 May 1942; *Educ* William Hulme's Manchester; *m* 1, 1969 (m dis 1996), Irene Mavis, da of Percy Cuthbert Archer (d 1993), of Cheshire; 1 da (Kathryn Elizabeth b 1971), 1 s (Robert Anthony b 1974); m 2, 2002, Anne Hazel, da of Gordon Cross (d 1999); 1 step s (David Charles b 1977), 1 step da (Joanna Elizabeth b 1979); *Career* dir: Selective Fin Servs Ltd 1987–, Redmill Industries Ltd 1987–, Construction Cosmetics Ltd 1988–, Chesterfield Royal Hosp 2005–; former dep vice-chllr Univ of Derby; memb Derbyshire C of C; dir LSC; Hon DUniv Derby; FCT, FCA, FCMA; *Recreations* squash, walking, sailing; *Clubs* Stakis Regency International; *Style*— Michael R Hall, Esq, DL; ✉ Derventio House, Ashford in the Water, Derbyshire DE45 1QP

HALL, Michael Thomas (Mike); MP; s of Thomas Hall (d 1996), and Veronica Hall (d 1998); *b* 20 September 1952; *Educ* St Damian's Secdy Modern Sch Ashton-under-Lyne, Ashton-under-Lyne Coll of FE, Stretford Tech Coll, Padgate Coll of HE (BEd), N Cheshire Coll, UCNW Bangor; *m* Lesley Hall; 1 s (Thomas Allen); *Career* scientific asst chemical indust 1969–73, teacher Bolton 1977–85, support teacher Halton Community Assessment Team 1985–92; ldr Warrington BC 1985–92 (cncllr 1979–93, chm Environmental Health Ctee 1981–84, chm Policy and Resources Ctee 1985–92); MP (Lab): Warrington S 1992–97, Weaver Vale 1997–; PPS to Rt Hon Ann Taylor, MP, *qv*, 1997–98, asst Govt whip 1998–2001, PPS to Rt Hon Alan Milburn, MP, *qv*, 2001–03, PPS to Rt Hon Dr John Reid, MP, *qv* 2003–05; memb: Modernisation of the House of Commons Select Ctee 1997–98, Public Accounts Ctee 1992–97, Admin Ctee 2000–01, Culture, Media and Sport Select Ctee 2005–; *Recreations* tennis, walking, cooking, reading; *Style*— Mike Hall, Esq, MP; ✉ House of Commons, London SW1A 0AA (tel 020 7219 3000, fax 01928 735250, e-mail halll@parliament.uk)

HALL, Nigel John; s of Herbert John Hall, of Chipping Sodbury, Avon, and Gwendoline Mary, *née* Olsen; *b* 30 August 1943; *Educ* Bristol GS, West of England Coll of Art (NDD), RCA (MArtRCA), Harkness fellowship to USA; *m* 1986, Manijeh Yadegar; *Career* artist; tutor RCA 1971–74, princ lectr Chelsea Sch of Art 1974–81; memb: Panel CNAA 1975–76, Faculty of Prix de Rome 1979–83; RA 2003; *Solo Exhibitions* incl: Galerie Givaudan Paris 1967, Robert Elkon Gallery NY 1974, 1977, 1979 and 1983, Annely Juda Gallery London 1978, 1981, 1985, 1987, 1991, 1996, 2000, 2003 and 2005, Galerie Maeght Paris 1981 and 1983, Staatliche Kunsthaus Baden-Baden 1982, Nishimura Gallery Tokyo 1980, 1984 and 1988, Hans Mayer Gallery Düsseldorf 1989 and 1999, Garry Anderson Gallery Sydney 1987 and 1990, Galerie Ziegler Zurich 1986, 1988 and 1995, Fondation Veranneman Belgium 1987, 1995, 1997 and 2002, Park Ryu Sook Gallery Seoul 1997, 2000 and 2005, Konstruktiv Tendens Stockholm 2000, Sculpture at Schoenthal Monastery Switzerland 2001, Galleri C Hjärne Helsingborg 2004, Galerie Scheffel Bad Homburg 2004 and 2007, Kunsthalle Mannheim 2004, Galerie Lutz und Thalmann Zurich 2006, Centre Cultural Contemporani Pelaires Palma de Mallorca 2007; *Group Exhibitions* incl: Documenta VI (Kassel) 1977, British Sculpture in the Twentieth Century (Whitechapel Gallery London) 1981, Aspects of British Art Today (Tokyo Metropolitan Museum) 1982, Carnegie International (Carnegie Inst Pittsburgh) 1982, Britannica: Thirty Years of Sculpture (Le Havre Museum of Fine Art) 1988, Blickachsen 4 (Bad Homburg) 2003, 2006 Beaufort (MOMA Ostend), Full House: Faces of a Collection (Kunsthalle Mannheim); *Commissions* Aust Nat Gallery Canberra, IBM London, Airbus Industrie Toulouse, Olympic Park Seoul, MOMA Hiroshima, British Petroleum London, Glaxo Research, Bank of America London, Bank for Int Settlements Basel; *Work in Public Collections* incl: Tate Gallery London, Musée Nat d'Art Moderne Paris, Nat Galerie Berlin, Tel Aviv Museum, Power Inst Sydney, MOMA NY; *Style*— Nigel Hall, Esq, RA; ✉ 11 Kensington Park Gardens, London W11 3HD (tel 020 7727 3162); Annely Juda Fine Art, 23 Dering Street, London W1R 9AA (tel 020 7629 7578, fax 020 7491 2139)

HALL, Nigel Ruthven; s of Ruthven Oliphant Hall (d 1983), and Dr Zaida Mary Hall, *née* Megrah; *Educ* Winchester, Balliol Coll Oxford (Frazer entrance scholarship, Periam Prize, BA, BM BCh, DM); *m* 20 April 1991, Alison Elizabeth; da of Dr Philip Kenneth Wilson, of Ipswich, Suffolk; 1 da (Emma b 2 Dec 1995), 1 s (Benjamin b 21 Feb 1998); *Career* house offr: John Radcliffe Hosp Oxford 1985–86, Royal Berks Hosp Reading 1986; SHO: UCH London 1986–86, Middx Hosp Med Sch London 1987, Guy's Hosp Rotational Scheme in Surgery London 1987–89, Royal Marsden Hosp London 1989–90; registrar NW Thames Regnl HA (Hillingdon Hosp and St Mary's Hosp Paddington) 1990–91, ICRF clinical research fell in coloproctology and hon surgical registrar Dept of Surgery Gen Infirmary at Leeds and ICRF Genetic Epidemiology Lab St James's Univ Hosp Leeds 1992–94, registrar Royal Halifax Infirmary 1994–95, sr registrar Gen Infirmary at Leeds 1995–96 and 1997–98, sr registrar Huddersfield Royal Infirmary 1996–97, clinical fell in colon and rectal surgery Univ of Minnesota Minneapolis 1998–99, conslt colorectal and gen surgn Addenbrooke's Hosp Cambridge 1999–; memb: BMA, Sections of Coloproctology and Surgery RSM, Assoc of Surgns of GB and I, Assoc of Coloproctology of GB and I, American Soc of Colon and Rectal Surgns; FRCS 1997; *Publications* numerous book chapters, reviews and articles in med jls; *Style*— Nigel Hall, Esq; ✉ Department of Surgery, Box 201, Addenbrooke's Hospital, Hills Road, Cambridge CB2 2QQ (tel 01223 586701, fax 01223 216015, e-mail nigel.r.hall@addenbrookes.nhs.uk)

HALL, Patrick; MP; *Career* MP (Lab) Bedford 1997–; *Style*— Patrick Hall, MP; ✉ House of Commons, London SW1A 0AA (tel 020 7219 3000)

HALL, Prof Sir Peter Geoffrey; kt (1998); s of Arthur Vickers Hall (d 1973), of Blackpool, and Bertha, *née* Keefe (d 1979); *b* 19 March 1932; *Educ* Blackpool GS, St Catharine's Coll Cambridge (MA, PhD); *m* 1, 7 Sept 1962 (m dis 1967), Carla Maria, da of Frank Wartenberg (d 1986); m 2, 13 Feb 1967, Magda, da of Antoni Mróz (d 1989), of Warsaw; *Career* asst lectr then lectr Birkbeck Coll London 1957–65, reader in geography LSE 1966–67, prof of geography Univ of Reading 1968–89 (emeritus prof 1989–), prof of city and regnl planning Univ of Calif 1980–92 (emeritus prof 1993–), dir Inst of Urban and Regnl Devpt 1989–92, prof of planning UCL 1992–, dir Inst of Community Studies 2001–04; memb various govt bodies incl SE Regnl Econ & Planning Cncl 1960–79; special advsr to Sec of State for the Environment 1991–94; memb Urban Task Force 1998–99; FBA 1983, FRGS; *Books* London 2000 (1963), The Containment of Urban England (1973), Europe 2000 (1977), Great Planning Disasters (1980), High-Tech America (1986), Western Sunrise (1987), Cities of Tomorrow (1988), London 2001 (1989), The Rise of the Gunbelt (1991), Technopoles of the World (1994), Cities in Civilization (1998), Urban Future 21 (2000), Working Capital (2002), The Polycentric Metropolis (2006), London Voices London Lives (2007); *Recreations* walking; *Clubs* Athenaeum, RGS; *Style*— Prof Sir Peter Hall, FBA; ✉ University College London, 22 Gordon Street, London WC1H 0QB (tel 020 8810 8723, fax 020 7679 7502, e-mail p.hall@ucl.ac.uk)

HALL, Sir Peter Reginald Frederick; kt (1977), CBE (1963); s of Reginald Edward Arthur Hall, and Grace, *née* Pamment; *b* 22 November 1930; *Educ* Perse Sch Cambridge, St Catharine's Coll Cambridge (MA); *m* 1, 1956 (m dis 1965), Leslie Caron, the actress; 1 s (Christopher), 1 da (Jennifer); m 2, 1965 (m dis 1981), Jacqueline Taylor; 1 s (Edward, *qv*), 1 da (Lucy); m 3, 1982 (m dis 1990), Maria Ewing, the mezzo-soprano; 1 da (Rebecca b 1982); m 4, 1990, Nicola (Nicki) Frei; 1 da (Emma b June 1992); *Career* director and producer of plays, films and operas; dir: Oxford Playhouse 1954–55, Arts Theatre London 1955–57; fndr Int Playwrights' Theatre 1957, md RSC 1960–68 (created the RSC as a permanent ensemble, and opened the RSC's London home at the Aldwych Theatre), co-dir RSC 1968–73, dir Nat Theatre of GB 1973–88, artistic dir Glyndebourne Festival Opera 1984–90, formed own prodn co Peter Hall Co Ltd 1988, artistic dir Old Vic 1996–; assoc prof of drama Univ of Warwick 1966–; memb Arts Cncl of GB 1969–72, fndr memb Theatre Directors' Guild of GB 1983; chllr Kingston Univ 2000–; Hon DLitt Univ of Reading 1973; Hon LittD: Univ of Liverpool 1974, Univ of Leicester 1977, Univ of Essex 1995, Univ of Cambridge 2003; Hon DUniv York 1966, Hon DUniv Cornell USA; Chevalier de l'Ordre des Arts et des Lettres (France); *Theatre* has directed over 150 major prodns in London, Stratford-upon-Avon and New York, including 19 Shakespeare plays, and the premieres of plays by Samuel Beckett, Harold Pinter, Tennessee Williams, Edward Albee, Jean Anouilh, Peter Shaffer, John Mortimer, John Whiting, Alan Ayckbourn; first prodns incl: Waiting for Godot (Arts Theatre London) 1955, Gigi 1956, Love's Labour's Lost 1956, Cat on a Hot Tin Roof 1958; RSC prodns incl: Twelfth Night 1958, 1960 and 1991, A Midsummer Night's Dream 1959 and 1963, Beckett 1961, The Collection 1962, The Wars of the Roses 1964 (televised for BBC 1965), The Homecoming 1965 and 1973, Macbeth 1967 and 1982, A Delicate Balance 1969, All's Well That Ends Well, The Gift of the Gorgon (also Wyndhams), Julius Caesar 1995; NT prodns incl: Bedroom Farce 1977, The Cherry Orchard 1978, Betrayal 1978 and 1980, The Importance of Being Earnest 1982, Yonadab 1985, Entertaining Strangers 1987, Antony and Cleopatra 1988, The Winter's Tale 1988, Cymbeline 1988, The Tempest 1988; Peter Hall Co prodns incl: Orpheus Descending (NY) 1988, The Merchant of Venice 1989, The Wild Duck (Phoenix) 1990, The Homecoming (Comedy Theatre) 1991, The Rose Tattoo (Playhouse) 1991, Tartuffe (Playhouse) 1991, Sienna Red 1992, An Ideal Husband (Globe) 1992, Four Baboons Adoring the Sun (NY) 1992, Lysistrata (Old Vic, Wyndhams) 1993, Separate Tables (Queens) 1993, Piaf (Piccadilly) 1993, An Absolute Turkey (Globe) 1993, On Approval (Playhouse) 1994, Hamlet (Gielgud Theatre) 1994, The Master Builder (Haymarket) 1995, Mind Millie for Me (Haymarket) 1996, The Oedipus Plays (Epidaurus and RNT) 1996, School for Wives 1996, A Streetcar Named Desire (Haymarket) 1997, Waste (Old Vic) 1997, The Seagull (Old Vic) 1997, Waiting For Godot (Old Vic) 1997, King Lear (Old Vic) 1997, The Misanthrope (Piccadilly) 1998, Major Barbara (Piccadilly) 1998, Filumena (Piccadilly) 1998, Kafka's Dick (Piccadilly) 1998, Amadeus (Old Vic) 1999, Measure for Measure 1999, A Midsummer Night's Dream (Ahmanson Theatre Los Angeles) 1999, Lennie (Queen's Theatre London) 1999, Amadeus (CTG/LA, Music Box NY) 1999, Cuckoos (CTG/LA) 2000, Tantalus (DCPA/Denver) 2000, Romeo and Juliet (MTA/LA) 2001, Japes (Haymarket) 2001, Tantalus (UK tour, Barbican RSC) 2001, Troilus & Cressida (TFNA/NY) 2001, Lady Windermere's Fan (Haymarket) 2002, Bacchi (NT, Epidaurus, Newcastle) 2002, Mrs Warren's Profession (Strand Theatre) 2002 (UK tour) 2003, Where There's A Will (UK tour) 2003, Betrayl (Theatre Royal Bath, UK tour) 2003, Design For Living (Theatre Royal Bath, UK tour) 2003, As You Like It (Theatre Royal Bath, UK and USA tour) 2003, Cuckoos (Barbican, Theatre Royal Bath, Happy Days (Arts Theatre London) 2003, Summer and Smoke (London) 2004, The Dresser (Duke of York's) 2005; *Operas* incl: The Magic Flute (Covent Garden) 1966, Eugene Onegin (Covent Garden) 1971, The Marriage of Figaro (Glyndebourne) 1973 and 1989, A Midsummer's Night Dream (Glyndebourne) 1981 and 1989, Macbeth (Metropolitan Opera NY) 1982, The Ring (Bayreuth) 1983, Figaro (Geneva) 1983, Carmen (Glyndebourne) 1985, Albert Herring (Glyndebourne) 1985 and 1986, (Covent Garden) 1989, Salome (LA 1986, Covent Garden 1988 and 1992, Chicago 1988), New Year (world premiere, Houston) 1989, The Magic Flute (LA) 1993, Simon Boccanegra (Glyndebourne) 1998, Midsummer Night's Dream (Glyndebourne), 2001, Othello (Glyndebourne) 2001, Othello (Chicago Lyric Opera) 2001, Albert Herring (Glyndebourne) 2002, The Marriage of Figaro (Lyric Opera of Chicago) 2003; *Films and Television* Work is a Four Letter Word 1968, A Midsummer Night's Dream 1969, Three into One Won't Go 1969, Perfect Friday 1971, The Homecoming 1973, Akenfield 1974, She's Been Away 1989, Orpheus Ascending 1991, The Camomile Lawn (Channel 4) 1991, Jacob (TNT/LUX) 1993, Never Talk to Strangers (TriStar Pictures) 1994–95, The Final Passage (Channel 4) 1995; *Awards* Tony Award: 1967 for Pinter's Homecoming, 1981 for Shaffer's Amadeus; Hamburg Univ Shakespeare Prize 1967, Standard Special Award 1979, Standard Award for Best Director 1981 and 1987, Standard Award for outstanding achievement in Opera 1981, Sidney Edwards Award for NT prodn of The Oresteia 1982, Olivier Theatre Award for lifetime achievement 1999; *Publications* The Wars of the Roses (with John Barton, 1970), translation of Ibsen's John Gabriel Borkman (with Inga-Stina Ewbank, 1975), Peter Hall's Diaries (1983), adaptation of George Orwell's Animal Farm (1986), adaptation of Ibsen's The Wild Duck (with Inga-Stina Ewbank, 1990), Making an Exhibition of Myself (autobiography, 1993), translation of Feydeau's An Absolute Turkey (with Nicki Frei, 1993), translation of Ibsen's The Master Builder (with Inga-Stina Ewbank, 1995), translation of Feydeau's L'Occupe toi d'Amelie - Mind Millie for Me (with Nicki Frei, 1996), The Necessary Theatre (1999), Exposed by the Mask (2000), Shakespeare's Advice to the Players (2003); *Clubs* Garrick, RAC; *Style*— Sir Peter Hall, CBE; ✉ Peter Hall Company, The Penthouse, 7 Leicester Place, London WC2H 7BP (tel 020 7287 7122, fax 020 7287 7123)

HALL, Peter Ruthven; s of Ruthven Oliphant Hall (d 1983), and Lady Ramsbotham, *née* Zaida Mary Megrah; *b* 16 February 1962; *Educ* Winchester, Univ of Bristol (BA), Oxford Poly (DipArch); *Career* set and costume designer; theatre conslt Theatreplan (ptnr 2004–); memb Br team Prague Quadrennial exhbn of stage design 1995 (Gold medal winners), memb Br team Prague Quadrennial exhbn of stage design 2003 (Golden Triga winners), exhibitor World Stage Design 2005 Toronto; SBTD: memb 1987–, ed newsletter 1994–2004, co sec; memb Theatre Designers' Ctee Equity; *Theatre* Love! Valour! Compassion! (Library Theatre Manchester), Long Day's Journey into Night (Theatre Royal Plymouth and Young Vic London), The Grapes of Wrath (Crucible Theatre Sheffield), Women of Troy (Gate Theatre London), Vassa Zheleznova (Gate Theatre London), The House of Bernard Alba (Oxford Playhouse); musical theatre incl: Sunset Boulevard (Sydmonton Festival), Tutankhamun (for Imagination), World Café (Edinburgh Festival), Joy to the World (for Imagination, Royal Albert Hall); *Opera* RNCM: Jenufa, Le nozze di Figaro, La Bohème, Albert Herring, Roberto Devereux; other operas incl: Der Stein der Weissen (Garsington Opera), The Turn of the Screw (Snape Maltings), Flavio (London Handel Festival), Ottone (London Handel Festival), L'Arlesiana (Holland Park Opera), Lakmé (Opera Ireland); costume designs incl: Tosca (Malmö Musiktheater), Madame Butterfly (Royal Danish Opera), The Turn of the Screw (Opera Northern Ireland), Zar und Zimmermann (Stadttheater Aachen), Don Giovanni (Vienna Kammeroper), Die Zauberflöte (Vienna Kammeroper); *Publications* Make SPACE! Design for Theatre and Alternative Spaces (with Kate Burnett, 1994), Time + Space: Design for Performance 1995–99 (with Kate Burnett, 1999), 2D>3D, Design For Theatre and Performance (with Kate Burnett, 2002); *Style*— Peter Ruthven Hall, Esq

HALL, Philip David (Phil); s of Norman Philip Hall, of Chadwell Heath, Essex, and Olive Jean Hall; *b* 8 January 1955; *Educ* Beal GS, NCTJ Course Harlow Coll; *m* Marina; 1 da (Alice), 1 s (William); *Career* reporter: Dagenham Post 1974–77, Ilford Recorder 1977–80; sub ed: Newham Recorder 1980–84, Weekend Magazine 1984–85; The People: reporter 1985–86, chief reporter 1986–89, news ed 1989–92, news ed Sunday Express 1992–93; News of the World: asst ed (features) 1993–94, dep ed 1994–95, ed 1995–2000; ed-in-chief Hello! 2001–02, editorial dir of devpt Trinity Mirror 2002–05, fndr Phil Hall Asoccs 2005–; memb PCC 1998–99 and 2002–03; memb Editors' Ctee PPA 2002–03; *Recreations* golf, cinema, theatre; *Style*— Phil Hall, Esq

HALL, Richard John Jeaffreson; s of Rev Francis James Thomas Hall (d 1991), and Patricia Musgrave, *née* Parry; *b* 31 July 1945; *Educ* Westminster, ChCh Oxford (MA); *m* 1, 25 July 1970, Wendy Jane, *née* Thomas; 1 da (Rebecca b 28 Feb 1973), 1 s (Crispian b 15 Jan 1975); m 2, 17 June 1995, Sally Frances Mary, da of Geoffrey Cass; *Career* articled Smallfield Fitzhugh Tillett 1968–71; Binder Hamlyn: joined 1971, ptnr 1978–97 (seconded to Milan Div 1979–81), head Corp Services Div 1989–91, marketing ptnr 1992–94; dir of fin Royal Opera House 1997–98; dir of fin and mgmnt services SCOPE 1998–; memb Urgent Issues Task Force of Accounting Standards Board 1991–95; FCA (ACA 1971); *Recreations* tennis, squash, Italian opera; *Clubs* Hurlingham (memb Ctee 1997–2001, chm Fin Ctee 1998–2001), Cumberland Lawn Tennis; *Style*— Richard Hall, Esq; ✉ c/o SCOPE Ltd, 6 Market Road, London N7 9PW (tel 020 7619 7100)

HALL, District Judge Richard V M; s of Geoffrey Herbert Hall, d 1977; and Mildred Hutchinson, *née* Brice (d 2006); *Educ* Bradford GS, Univ of Exeter (LLB), Coll of Law Guildford; m 1967 (m dis 1992); 3 s (Nicholas Adam John b 1 May 1968, Matthew Edward Jeremy b 20 October 1970, Richard William James b 15 March 1979); *Career* slr 1970–, lectr in law Teesside Poly 1970–71, prosecuting slr Teesside Police Authy 1971–72, ptnr Goodswens Solicitors Middlesbrough 1973–97; High Court NE Circuit: dep County Court registrar and dep district registrar 1984, district judge 1998– (dep 1990–98); hon slr Cleveland Community Relations Cncl 1973–97; memb Law Soc 1970–; *Recreations* chess (Correspondence Chess Grand Master), tennis, gardening, antiquarian chess books; *Clubs* Reform; *Style*— District Judge R V M Hall; ✉ Teesside Combined Court Centre, Russell Street, Middlesbrough TS21 2AE

HALL, Robert Stirling (Bob); s of William Smith (d 1995), and Margaret Ralston, *née* Inglesant (d 1997); *b* 2 January 1953; *Educ* Johnstone HS, Duncan of Jordanstone Art Coll (BArch); *m* Carole Ann, da of Thomas McKechnie; 1 da (Louise b 19 July 1983), 1 s (Robbie b 16 March 1985); *Career* architect; Irvine New Town Architects' Dept 1978–80; The Parr Partnership (formerly James Parr & Partners): joined 1980, assoc 1982–89 (responsible for opening Glasgow Office 1982), ptnr 1989–; projects incl: Scottish Exhbn and Conf Centre Glasgow 1985, Sun Microsystems Linlithgow 1990, Glasgow Airport stage 2 expansion 1994, NEC Semiconductors Livingston 1996, Siemens Microelectronics Newcastle 1997, Edinburgh Airport major devpt 1997; RIBA 1979, ARIAS 1979; *Recreations* badminton, golf, football; *Style*— Bob Hall, Esq

HALL, Ronald; s of John Hall (d 1960), and Amy Hall (d 1975); *b* 28 July 1934; *Educ* Dronfield GS, Pembroke Coll Cambridge (BA); *m* 1, 1956, Ruth; m 2, 1982 (m dis 2002), Christine; *Career* chief sub ed Topic Magazine 1962; Sunday Times: co-fndr Insight Team 1963, Insight ed 1964–66, asst ed 1966–68, managing ed of features 1969–77; ed Sunday Times Magazine 1978–81, jt dep ed Sunday Times 1981–82, ed Sunday Express Magazine 1982–86, associate ed London Daily News 1986–87, London ed Condé Nast Traveler New York 1987–, conslt ed Scotland on Sunday 1988–89; *Books* Scandal 63, A Study of The Profumo Affair (jtly), The Strange Voyage of Donald Crowhurst (with Nicholas Tomalin, 1970); *Recreations* chess, travel, building; *Style*— Ronald Hall, Esq

HALL, Simon Andrew Dalton; MBE (2006); s of Peter Dalton Hall, CB, of Milton Keynes, Bucks, and Stella Iris, *née* Breen; *b* 6 February 1955; *Educ* Ampleforth, St Catharine's Coll Cambridge (MA), Coll of Law; *m* 26 Aug 1978, Teresa Ann, da of John Edmund Bartleet, of Great Tey, Essex; 2 da (Rachael b 16 June 1979, Sophie b 18 March 1988), 2 s (Eddie b 8 Dec 1980, Harry b 31 March 1983); *Career* slr; articled clerk Freshfields 1977–79, seconded to Cravath Swaine & Moore 1983–84, Freshfields NY office 1984–85 (ptnr 1985–); memb: Law Soc, City of London Slrs Co; *Books* Leasing Finance (jtly, 1997), Aircraft Financing (jtly, 1998); *Style*— Simon Hall, Esq, MBE; ✉ Freshfields Bruckhaus Deringer, 65 Fleet Street, London EC4Y 1HS (tel 020 7936 4000, fax 020 7832 7001, e-mail simon.hall@freshfields.com)

HALL, Steven Richard; s of Ernest Hall, and Eva, *née* Bartle; *Educ* Bradford GS, Blackpool GS, Blackpool VI Form Coll, Univ of Leeds (BA); *Career* product manager then sales exec Macmillan Press 1978–82, area sales manager UMI 1982–88, sales dir Chadwyck-Healey Ltd 1988–96, md Chadwyck-Healey Ltd 1996–99, sr vice-pres and gen manager Chadwyck-Healey Ltd/ProQuest Information and Learning 1999–2004, jl sales and mktg dir Blackwell Publishing Ltd 2004–07, commercial dir Wiley-Blackwell 2007–; *Recreations* tennis, skiing, travel, amusing my children; *Style*— Steven Hall, Esq; ✉ Wiley-Blackwell, 9600 Garsington Road, Oxford OX4 2DQ (tel 01865 776868, fax 01865 471421, mobile 07795 978844, e-mail steven.hall@oxon.blackwellpublishing.com)

HALL, Stuart; s of Charles Duell Hall (d 1994), and Amy, *née* Boucher (d 1985); *b* 16 August 1951; *Educ* Queens' Coll Cambridge 1969–72 (MA); *m* 22 April 1977, Rosemary Florence Monica, *née* Cockshutt; 2 da (Charlotte Jane b 3 Dec 1978, Lindsay May b 7 June 1982); *Career* slr specialising in professional liability and commercial litigation; ptnr: Dawson & Co 1976–85, Barlow Lyde & Gilbert 1985–; *Recreations* tennis, swimming, fishing, rugby; *Style*— Stuart Hall, Esq; ✉ Barlow Lyde & Gilbert, Beaufort House, 15 St Botolph Street, London EC3A 7NJ (tel 020 7643 8473, e-mail shall@blg.co.uk)

HALL, Timothy Francis (Tim); s of Ronald William Hall (d 1985), and Mary, *née* Briggs; *b* 29 November 1959; *Educ* Ashburton Sch, Canterbury Coll of Art (BA), Univ of London (DipArch); *m* 30 May 1999, Elizabeth Amy, da of Jonathon Foster; 1 da (Evalina Isabelle b 18 Nov 2001), 2 s (Benjamin Jonty Ronald b 25 Sept 2003, Arthur Kenneth b 10 July 2007); *Career* architect; sr designer Officescape 1985–86, sr designer Newman Levinson 1986–90; projects incl: competition-winning scheme for new theatres, shopping centre and offices in central Milton Keynes, competition-winning scheme for housing and golf club in Bushey; Lewis + Hickey Architects 1990–93, sr architect John Outram Associates 1993–94 (projects incl Judge Inst of Mgmnt Studies Cambridge), md Lewis + Hickey Architects 1993–; work featured in Architects Jl; supporter Elizabeth Finn Tst; FRIBA 1989; *Books* Habitation au Bord de l'Eau (1994); *Recreations* tennis, swimming, photography; *Clubs* Chelsea Football; *Style*— Tim Hall, Esq; ✉ Lewis + Hickey Architects, 17 Dorset Square, London NW1 6QB (tel 020 7724 1611, fax 020 7724 2282, mobile 07702 096058, e-mail thall@lewishickey.com)

HALL, His Hon Judge Victor Edwin; s of Robert Arthur Victor James Hall (d 1978), of Selsey, W Sussex, and Gladys, *née* Fukes (d 1986); *b* 2 March 1948; *Educ* Chichester HS for Boys, Univ of Hull (LLB); *Family* 2 s (Timothy James b 24 July 1981, Matthew Peter b 16 Feb 1984); *Career* called to the Bar Inner Temple 1971; tenancy in chambers: Leicester 1972–89, London 1990–94; recorder of the Crown Ct 1988–94 (asst recorder 1983–88), asst boundary cmmr 1992–94, circuit judge (Midland & Oxford Circuit) 1994–, legal pres Mental Health Review Tbnl 1997–2004, circuit rep then treas Cncl of HM Circuit Judges 1996–2001; dir of studies Judicial Studies Bd of England and Wales 2004–; memb Inner Temple Soc; *Recreations* skiing, fell walking, sailing, cooking, music, computers, football; *Style*— His Hon Judge Hall

HALL, William Joseph (Bill); JP (Co Down 1973); s of Capt Roger Hall, MC (d 1939), and Marie Hall; *b* 1 August 1934; *Educ* Ampleforth; *m* 1964, Jennifer Mary, *née* Corbett; 1 s, 1 da; *Career* SSC Irish Gds 1952–56, with W C Pitfield & Hugh McKay (investment mgmnt co) then Shell Oil Canada 1956–62, dir own wine wholesale business, sheep farmer and commercial narcissus bulb grower 1962–90, ret; memb Lord Chllr's Advsy Ctee on JPs 1975– (chm Ards Div 1996–); High Sheriff Co Down 1983, HM Lord-Lt Co Down 1996– (DL 1975–93, Vice Lord-Lt 1993–96); NI ACF 1967–79 (Hon Maj 1980, pres NI ACFA 1999–2002, Hon Col 2003–05); pres RFCA NI 2000–05, chm Ulster Branch Irish Gds Assoc 1979–; CStJ 1997; *Recreations* field sports in general, bridge, travel abroad when time allows!; *Clubs* Down Hunt (Downpatrick), Army and Navy; *Style*— William Hall, Esq; ✉ The Mill House, Narrow Water, Warrenpoint, Co Down BT34 3LW (tel 028 4175 4904, fax 028 4175 4990, e-mail billhallmill@aol.com)

HALL-SMITH, Martin Clive William; s of (Sydney) Patrick Hall-Smith (d 2002), of Hove, E Sussex, and Angela Wilma, *née* Hall (d 1996); *b* 21 July 1948; *Educ* Eton, Univ of Edinburgh (LLB), Selwyn Coll Cambridge (MA); *m* 1983, Victoria Mary, da of John Sherwood Stephenson (d 1992), of Wylam, Northumberland; 2 da (Rose b 1985, Katharine b 1987), 1 s (Edward b 1989); *Career* called to the Bar 1972; chm Employment Tbnls 2002– (pt/t chm 1993–2002); Freeman City of London 1978, Liveryman Worshipful Co of Loriners; *Recreations* music, skiing, walking, family life; *Style*— M C W Hall-Smith, Esq

HALLETT, *see also:* Hughes Hallett

HALLETT, Prof Christine; *b* 1949; *Educ* Univ of Cambridge, Loughborough Univ (PhD); *Career* former civil servant DHSS; teaching and research posts Keele Univ and Univ of Leicester; Univ of Stirling: reader in social policy 1989–95, prof of social policy 1995–, princ and vice-chllr 2004– (formerly sr dep princ); chair Bd of Tstees UKCOSA Cncl for Int Educn; FRSE 2002; *Publications* incl: The Personal Social Services in Local Government, Interagency Co-ordination in Child Protection, Child Abuse: Aspects of Interprofessional Co-operation (with O Stevenson), Co-ordination and Child Protection: a review of the literature (with E Birchall); also author of learned articles, monographs and edited works; *Recreations* golf, walking, tennis, music; *Style*— Prof Christine Hallett; ✉ The Principal's Office, University of Stirling, Stirling FK9 4LA (tel 01786 467011, fax 01786 462087, e-mail principal@stir.ac.uk)

HALLETT, Rt Hon Lady Justice; Rt Hon Dame Heather Carol; DBE (1999), PC (2005); da of Hugh Victor Dudley Hallett, QPM (d 1991), and Doris Viola, *née* Churchill; *b* 16 December 1949; *Educ* Brockenhurst GS, St Hugh's Coll Oxford (MA); *m* 20 April 1974, Nigel Vivian Marshall Wilkinson, QC, *qv*, s of John Marshall Wilkinson (d 1993); 2 s; *Career* called to the Bar Inner Temple 1972 (bencher 1993); recorder of the Crown Court 1989, QC 1989, ldr SE Circuit 1995–97, dep judge of the High Court 1995, judge of the High Court of Justice (Queen's Bench Div) 1999–2005, presiding judge Western Circuit 2001–04, Lord Justice of Appeal 2005–; judicial appts cmmr 2006–; chm General Cncl of the Bar 1998, dir Public Affairs Bar Cncl 1993; *Recreations* theatre, music; *Style*— The Rt Hon Lady Justice Hallett, DBE

HALLETT, Jeremy Norman; s of Maj Howard Samuel Hallett (d 1979), of Stourbridge, and Majorie Winnifred, *née* Harris (d 1981); *b* 3 May 1948; *Educ* Grange Secdy Modern Sch, Bluecoat Boys' Sch Stourbridge, Bromsgrove Coll of Educn, Inst of Health Servs Mgmnt (Dip Public Admin), Harvard Business Sch; *m* 1971, Pamela Anne Stephenson; 1 s (James Dominic), 1 da (Rebecca Louise); *Career* admin asst Warley BC 1970–71 (mgmnt grad trainee 1969–70), chief admin offr Walsall Co Borough 1971–74, unit admin Walsall HA 1974–77; Kidderminster HA: dep dist gen mangr 1978–82, dist admin 1982–83, dist gen mangr 1983–87; jt chief exec Gwent Health Cmmn 1993–96 (dist gen mangr 1988–92), chief exec Wilts HA 1996–2002, assoc conslt Nat PCT Devpt Prog 2002–; memb Nat Tst; MHSM; *Recreations* family, fishing, tennis, music; *Clubs* Harvard Business; *Style*— Jeremy N Hallett, Esq; ✉ 5 Mansion Mews, Corsham, Wiltshire SN13 9BB (mobile 07971 580869, e-mail jeremy.hallett@pickmiddle.fsnet.co.uk)

HALLETT, Michael John; s of Arthur Ronald Hallett (d 1979), of Weymouth, Dorset, and Dorothy Muriel, *née* Stone (d 2004); *b* 29 April 1940; *Educ* Weymouth GS, Bournemouth Municipal Coll of Art (Dorset County Athletics colours), Manchester Poly UMIST (MPhil), Birmingham Poly (Dip History of Art and Design); *m* 1970, Carol Ann, da of Norman Maurice Flint; 1 da (Emily Jane b 22 May 1975), 1 s (William James b 11 July 1977); *Career* photographer Studio 5 1959–60; lectr in photography: Leicester Coll of Art and Design 1960–65, Bournemouth and Poole Coll of Art 1965–66; lectr then sr lectr in photographic studies Manchester Coll of Art and Design and Manchester Poly 1966–69 and 1970–75, visiting prof Sch of Photographic Arts and Scis Rochester Inst of Technol NY 1969–70; Univ of Central England in Birmingham (formerly Birmingham Poly): princ lectr Dept of Visual Communication 1975–82, head Sch of Photography 1975–78, dir BA (Hons) Graphic Design Course 1979, princ lectr Sch of Theoretical and Historical Studies in Art and Design Birmingham Inst of Art and Design 1982–97; publishing ed Article Press 1990–97; photographer, photohistorian, writer and biographer 1997–; conslt for documentary film Stefan Lorant: Man in Pictures (1997); memb: Nat Cncl Inst of Incorporated Photographers 1966–69, Associateship Panel and Fellowship Panel of History of Photography and Critical Writing Category RPS 1990–; chm Distinctions Panel Research, Educn and Application of Photography RPS 2004–; dep chm Sector 7 Admissions and Qualifications Bd BIPP 1989–98; Kodak Colour scholar Eastman Kodak Co 1964, life memb Stockport Harriers & Athletic Club 1975; memb Euro Soc for the History of Photography 1981; FRSA 1964, FRPS 1967, FBIPP 1969, MIMgt 1976, FCSD 1977; *Books* Programmed Photography (with Jack Tait, 1967), Programmed Colour Photography (1970), Worcester Cathedral: A Grand View (1987), Arts Council Independent Photography Directory (with Barry Lane, 1989), Where to Study: Photography Film Video TV (1990, 1992, 1994, 1998 and 1999), Rewriting Photographic History (1990), The Real Story of Picture Post (1994), The Worcester book (2002), Bullring: the heart of Birmingham (2003), Stefan Lorant: Godfather of Photojournalism

(2005), Seaside: Edges of England (2007); reg contrib British Journal of Photography, contrib British Journal of Photography Annual 1970–94; *Recreations* travel; *Style*— Michael Hallett, Esq; ✉ 134 Henwick Road, St John's, Worcester, WR2 5PB (tel 01905 425547, e-mail mike@michaelhallett.com)

HALLEY, Ian Alexander; s of Alexander Halley, of St Michael, Suffolk, and Betty, *née* Sheward; *b* 7 January 1957; *Educ* Dr Challoner's GS, Univ of Nottingham (BA); *m* 29 Oct 1983, Diana Mary, da of Henry Colbert; 1 da (Emily Diana b 10 April 1989), 1 s (Daniel Alexander b 5 July 1992); *Career* advtg exec; Allen Brady & Marsh 1979–86, J Walter Thompson 1986–88, Ogilvy & Mather 1988–95, dir Collett Dickenson Pearce & Partners 1995–97, gp dir McCann-Erickson Advertising 1997–2004, Euro RSCG 2004–05, md Rees Bradley Hepburn 2005–; *Recreations* football, cars, Art Deco; *Style*— Ian Halley, Esq; ✉ Rees Bradley Hepburn, Diddington Farm, Meriden, West Midlands CV7 7HQ (tel 01675 443939)

HALLGARTEN, His Hon Anthony Bernard Richard; QC; s of Siegfried Salomon (Fritz) Hallgarten (d 1991), and Friedel Liselotte, *née* Liebmann (d 1986); *b* 16 June 1937; *Educ* Merchant Taylors', Downing Coll Cambridge (BA); *m* 1, 16 Dec 1962 (m dis 1996), Katherine Anne, da of Kurt Borchard, and Ruth Borchard; da (Ruth b 1 Feb 1965, Judy b 24 Oct 1966, Emily b 26 Oct 1972), 1 s (Joseph b 22 May 1970); m 2, 12 Oct 1998, Theresa Carlson; *Career* called to the Bar Middle Temple (bencher); jr counsel 1962–78, leading counsel 1978–93, recorder 1990–93 (asst recorder 1984–90), circuit judge (SE Circuit) 1993–2004, mercantile list judge Central London Civil Trial Centre 2004–, arbitrator and mediator 20 Essex Street London; *Recreations* cricket, cycling, historical novels, visiting the Ariège; *Clubs* Garrick, MCC; *Style*— His Hon Anthony Hallgarten, QC

HALLIDAY, Charlotte Mary Irvine; da of Edward Irvine Halliday (d 1984), of St John's Wood, London, and Dorothy Lucy, *née* Hatswell (d 1986); *b* 5 September 1935; *Educ* Froebel Sch, Wester Elchies Craigellachie, Francis Holland Sch London, Royal Acad (Silver Medal for drawing); *Career* artist; keeper New English Art Club 1989–; topographical cmmns incl: Royal Hospital Chelsea 1959, Shell Centre 1957–59, head office Barclays Bank 1961–68, headquarters BP, Barbican 1964, head office Willis Faber Dumas Tower Hill and Ipswich 1978, Mowlem Nat West Tower 1980, head office Singer & Friedlander 1982, Dixons 1982–86, Royal Opera House 1984, RAC Pall Mall 1985–86, Royal Soc of Medicine 1987, United Newspapers 1989, Union Discount Co Cornhill 1990, Salisbury Cathedral 1991, Selfridges 1991, Lord's Pavilion 1994, Trinity Coll of Music 1994, The Great Hall Lincoln's Inn 1994, The Monument for Mercury Asset Management 1995, UCL 1997, The Houses of Parliament from St Thomas' Hospital 2000, St Alban's Abbey 2006; contrib to various gp exhbns and Summer Exhbns RA 1956–, 'one-man show' with Sally Hunter Fine Art 1998, Sheridan Russell Gallery 2002; memb NEAC 1961, RBA 1961–92, RWS 1976 (assoc 1971); *Awards* Lord Mayor's Art Awards 1962, 1963 and 1976, de Laszlo Medal RBA 1973, Spirit of London Awards 1978 and 1979; *Books* illustrations for Edwardian Architecture, A Biographical Dictionary (by A Stuart Gray, 1985), Fanlights - A Visual Architectural History (with A S Gray, 1990); *Recreations* amateur choral singing, walking in the Sussex Downs; *Style*— Miss Charlotte Halliday; ✉ 36a Abercorn Place, St John's Wood, London NW8 9XP (tel 020 7289 1924, fax 020 7286 7680)

HALLIDAY, Prof Ian Gibson; s of John Alexander Halliday, and Gladys, *née* Taylor; *b* 5 February 1940, Kelso, Roxburghshire; *Educ* Univ of Edinburgh (MA, MSc), Univ of Cambridge (PhD); *m* 27 July 1965, Ellenor Gardiner Hervey; 1 s (Robert Allan b 30 May 1970), 1 da (Katrina Ellenor b 31 July 1972); *Career* lectr, reader then prof Imperial Coll London 1968–93, prof and head of physics Univ of Wales Swansea 1993–98, chief exec PPARC 1998–2005, chief exec Scottish Univs Physics Alliance 2005–; pres European Science Fndn (ESF) 2006–, memb EU Research Advsy Bd (EURAB), UK delg CERN Cncl 1998–2005; author of many pubns on theoretical particle physics; FInstP; *Recreations* golf, fishing; *Style*— Prof Ian Halliday; ✉ Derwent House, Walkley Hill, Stroud, Gloucestershire GL5 3TX (tel 01453 767073, e-mail ian.halliday@e-halliday.org); School of Physics, James Clerk Maxwell Building, The Kings Buildings, West Mains Road, Edinburgh EH9 3JY

HALLIGAN, Prof Aidan William Francis; s of Michael Halligan, of Dublin, and Maureen, *née* O'Connell; *b* 17 September 1957; *Educ* Templeogue Coll Dublin, TCD (MB BCh, BAO, BA, MA, MD); *m* 1985, Carol Mary Sarah, *née* Furlong; 3 da (Molly b 20 July 1989, Becky b 23 Aug 1992, Daisy b 8 Dec 1994); *Career* sr lectr in obstetrics and gynaecology and conslt obstetrician and gynaecologist Univ of Leicester and Leicester Royal Infirmary 1994–97 (lectr 1993–94), prof of fetal maternal med Univ of Leicester and Univ Hosps of Leicester NHS Tst 1997–99, head of obstetric service Univ Hosps of Leicester 1998–99, prog trg dir obstetrics and gynaecology S Trent 1995–99, postgrad dir obstetrics and gynaecology trg Univ Hosps of Leicester NHS Tst 1995–99, ceo Elision Health Ltd 2006–, dir of educn UCL Hosp 2007–; head NHS Clinical Governance Support Team 1999–2002, dir clinical governance NHS 1999–2006, dep CMO for England 2003–05; MRCOG 1991, MRCPI 1996, FFPHM 2003, FRCOG 2004, FRCP 2004; *Recreations* reading, walking; *Style*— Prof Aidan Halligan

HALLIGAN, Liam James; s of Martin Thomas Halligan, and Evelyn, *née* Thorp; *b* 29 April 1969; *Educ* John Lyon Sch Harrow (entrance scholarship, head boy), Univ of Warwick (BSc), St Antony's Coll Oxford (MPhil, memb Isis boat race crew); *Partner* Lucy Miranda Ward; 2 da (Ailis Rosa b 5 Aug 2000, Maeve Isabella b 19 Feb 2003), 1 s (Ned Thomas b 3 Jan 2006); *Career* writer and broadcaster; econ intern IMF 1992, head of res Social Market Fndn 1993, economist Econ Miny Russian Govt 1994–95, Moscow reporter The Economist 1995–96, econ columnist Moscow Times 1995–96, political corr Financial Times 1996–98, econ corr Channel 4 News 1998–2006, econ ed Sunday Telegraph 2006–; columnist: Sunday Business 2000–01, Sunday Telegraph 2001–06, GQ Magazine 2007–; memb: Advsy Cncl Social Market Fndn, Risk Cmmn RSA, Soc of Business Economists; Wincott Fndn Business Broadcaster of the Year 1999, Industrial Soc Prog of the Year 2001, Wincott Fndn Business Prog of the Year 2002 and 2006, Workworld Prog of the Year 2002, 2003 and 2004, Bradford & Bingley Personal Fin Award 2003, Best Broadcast Story Business Journalist of the Year 2004 and 2005, Br Press Awards Business and Finance Journalist of the Year 2007, Workworld Columnist of the Year 2007, Workworld Prog of the Year 2007; *Publications* incl: Beyond Unemployment (with Robert Skidelsky, *qv*, 1993), Europe Isn't Working (with Frank Field, *qv*, MP, 1994), A Guide to Russia's Parliamentary Elections (1995), Lessons From Russia's Stabilisation Programmes (with Robert Skidelsky, 1996); author of numerous articles for Sunday Telegraph, The Economist Intelligence Unit and Wall St Jl; *Recreations* rowing, football, sailing, roller-skating, guitar; *Style*— Liam Halligan, Esq; ✉ c/o Knight Ayton, 114 St Martin's Lane, London WC2N 4BE (tel 020 7836 5333, e-mail liam.halligan@telegraph.co.uk)

HALLING, Prof Peter James; s of John Halling, of Heswall, Merseyside, and Enid Joyce, *née* Rutherford; *b* 30 March 1951; *Educ* Calday GS, Univ of Cambridge (BA), Univ of Bristol (PhD); *Career* research asst Biochemical Engrg Section UCL 1975–78, scientist Unilever Research Lab 1978–83; Univ of Strathclyde: lectr 1983–89, sr lectr 1989–90, prof 1990–; MRSC; FRSE 1996; *Recreations* orienteering; *Style*— Prof Peter Halling, FRSE; ✉ 2/2, 34 Montague Street, Glasgow G4 9HX; Department of Pure & Applied Chemistry, University of Strathclyde, Glasgow G1 1XW (tel 0141 552 4400, fax 0141 548 4822, e-mail p.j.halling@strath.ac.uk)

HALLISSEY, Michael; s of John Francis Hallissey, MBE (d 1986), and Mary, *née* Kendall; *b* 6 March 1943; *Educ* Royal GS Lancaster, Magdalen Coll Oxford (MA); *Career* chartered accountant; PricewaterhouseCoopers (formerly Price Waterhouse before merger): staff accountant 1964–68, asst mangr Melbourne 1969–70, mangr Milan 1970–71, sr mangr London 1971–74, audit ptnr London 1974–79, practice devpt ptnr UK 1979–81, strategic planning ptnr UK 1981–82, corp fin ptnr London 1982–85, head of corp fin servs UK 1985–87, head of strategic planning for world firm 1987–88, dir of strategy Price Waterhouse Europe 1988–98; visiting fell The Business Sch Imperial Coll of Sci and Technol London 1998–2003; strategic conslt specialising in mgmnt of int business principally in Germany and USA 1998–; FCA 1968, FRSA; *Books* numerous articles on corp strategy, strategic planning, mergers and acquisitions; *Recreations* politics, sailing, music, opera, good food; *Style*— Michael Hallissey, Esq; ✉ 66 Waterside Point, Albert Bridge, London SW11 4PD

HALLIWELL, Prof Neil; *b* 20 July 1948; *Educ* Univ of Liverpool (BSc, PhD); *m* 1987, Tessa Jane; 2 da (Katherine b 18 June 1990, Elisabeth b 22 Jan 1993), 1 s (Andrew b 31 July 1995); *Career* scientific offr Atomic Energy Authy 1972–74; Univ of Southampton: research fell Dept of Aeronautics 1974–77, lectr Inst of Sound and Vibration Research 1977–87 (sr lectr 1987–90); Loughborough Univ: prof of optical engrg 1990–, head Dept of Mechanical Engrg 1992–97, dean of engrg 1997–, pro-vice-chllr (research) 2001–, dep vice-chllr 2006–; author of over 200 published research papers in field of laser technol for engrg application; sr memb Laser Inst of America; UK Prize for Metrology Nat Physical Laboratory 1992, Higher Doctorate (DSc) Univ of Southampton 1992; FInstP 1990, FIMechE 1991, FREng 1996, FSPIE 1997, fell Soc of Photo-Optical and Instrumentation Engrs (USA); *Recreations* match angling; *Style*— Prof Neil Halliwell, DSc, FREng; ✉ Wolfson School of Mechanical and Manufacturing Engineering, Loughborough University, Leicestershire LE11 3TU (tel 01509 227500, fax 01509 227502, e-mail n.a.halliwell@lboro.ac.uk)

HALLOWES, Guy Rupert; s of Rupert Hallowes (d 1978), and Helen, *née* Chennells; *b* 25 August 1941, Nairobi, Kenya; *Educ* Duke of York Sch Nairobi; *m* 29 April 1967, Diana, *née* Calderwood; 1 da (Catherine b 8 Feb 1968), 3 s (Dougal b 12 Oct 1971, Kevin b 3 December 1974, Stephen b 29 Sept 1983); *Career* Nat Serv Kenya 1960; articled clerk Goddard Mellersh & Lepine London 1960–66, sr audit clerk Deloitte & Co Johannesburg 1966–68, head office accountant Bass plc London 1969–70; South African Breweries Ltd: mgmnt accountant then financial controller Beer Div 1970–78, gen mangr Kgalagadi Breweries Pty Ltd and gp gen mangr Kgalagadi Management Services Pty Ltd 1978–81, gen mangr Traditional Beer 1981–82, md Appletiser Pure Fruit Juices (Pty) Ltd 1982–85; gp mktg mangr Frozen Food Nestle Australia Ltd 1986–89; Harlequin Enterprises Limited: md Mills & Boon Pty Ltd Aust 1989–93, regnl dir Asia Pacific 1993–98, exec vice-pres overseas 1998–2002, TEC chair trg 2002–03, chair TEC 19 2003–05, md Harlequin Mills & Boon UK 2005–; FCA 1966, fell Inst of CAs in Aust; *Recreations* golf, fishing; *Clubs* Royal Mid-Surrey Golf, Cromer Golf (Sydney); *Style*— Guy Hallowes, Esq; ✉ 1 Grove Road, Barnes, London SW13 0HQ (mobile 07770 945810); Harlequin Mills & Boon Limited, Eton House, 18–24 Paradise Road, Richmond, Surrey TW9 1SR (tel 020 8288 2844, fax 020 8288 2898, e-mail guy.hallowes@hmb.co.uk)

HALLS, Andrew David; *Educ* Shenley Ct Sch Birmingham, Gonville & Caius Coll Cambridge (scholar); *Career* teacher: Chigwell Sch, Whitgift Sch, Bristol GS; dep headmaster Trinity Sch, master Magdalen Coll Sch until 2007, head master King's Coll Sch Wimbledon 2008–; *Style*— Andrew Halls, Esq; ✉ King's College School, Wimbledon SW19 4TT (tel 020 8255 5300)

HALLS-DICKERSON, Peter George; s of Woolmer George Halls-Dickerson (d 1971), of Newquay, Cornwall, and Elsie, *née* Fiddick (d 1995); *b* 29 March 1937; *Educ* Newquay Boys' GS, Wadham Coll Oxford (MA), Univ of Leeds (PGCE); *m* 29 July 1961, Ruth, da of Charles Libby; 2 da (Deborah Jayne b 1964, Nicole Clare b 1966); *Career* head of English and French Snapethorpe Sch Wakefield 1960–63, head of English and head of house Fairfax HS Bradford 1963–65, dep head The Weald Sch W Sussex 1966–70, headmaster Townfield Sch Middx 1970–74, princ Collingwood Coll Surrey 1974–95, conslt PH-D Associates 1995–2000; Cons Pty: memb Nat Union Exec Ctee 1987–, chm Nat Advsy Ctee on Educn 1991–94, first chm Nat Educn Soc 1994–95; first vice-pres CNES 1995–; memb St John Nat Schs' Ctee 1987–94, dir Surrey Crimestoppers 1993–95, pres Camberley Branch Br Heart Fndn 1994–98 (memb Br Heart Fndn Ctee on Emergency Aid 1989–94), chm Surrey Heath Duke of Edinburgh's Award Forum 1997–99, pres St John Ambulance Cadets Windle Valley 2006–; life memb NAHT 1970, memb PCC St Lawrence and St Saviour Chobham; SBStJ 1991; *Recreations* freemasonry (Provincial Grand Master Province of Middlesex Mark Master Masons 2001–), travel, speedboating; *Clubs* RYA; *Style*— Peter Halls-Dickerson, Esq; ✉ Sparrow Cottage, Sparrow Row, Chobham, Surrey GU24 8TA (tel 01276 857169)

HALSALL, Air Cdre Martin William; s of Bernard Holt Halsall, MC, of Market Harborough, Leics, and Emily Constance, *née* Sutton; *b* 10 February 1954, Melton Mowbray, Leics; *Educ* Becket Sch Nottingham, Univ of Salford; *m* 18 August 1979, Elizabeth Ann, *née* Shaw; 2 s (Matthew b 5 Jan 1982, Alexander James b 18 Oct 1983), 1 da (Amy Victoria b 22 March 1992); *Career* joined RAF 1974, pilot F4 Phantom Fighters 1976–1990 (exchange tour with JG71 'R' of the Luftwaffe 1983–86), Canadian Forces Cmd and Staff Coll Toronto 1990–91, First Offr cmdg Falkland Islands Air Wing 1995, Cdr Br Forces Italy 2000, Cdr Western Sovereign Base Area (Cyprus) and Station Cdr RAF Akrotiri 2001–03, Dep Cdr NATO Combined Air Ops Centre 3 Bodø Norway 2003–04, asst dir NATO Jt Air Power Competence Centre Kalkar Germany 2004–05; bursar Haileybury and Imperial Serv Coll 2006–; FCMI; *Recreations* golf, tennis, gardening; *Style*— Air Cdre Martin Halsall; ✉ Rose Cottage, London Road, Hertford Heath, Hertfordshire SG13 7PP (tel 01992 468579, e-mail martinhalsall@gmail.com); Haileybury, Hertfordshire SG13 7NU (tel 01992 706333, e-mail m.halsall@haileybury.com)

HALSEY, Rev Sir John Walter Brooke; 4 Bt (UK 1920), of Gaddesden, Co Hertford; s of Sir Thomas Edgar Halsey, 3 Bt, DSO (d 1970); *b* 26 December 1933; *Educ* Eton, Magdalene Coll Cambridge (BA); *Heir* kinsman, Nicholas Halsey, TD; *Career* deacon 1961, priest 1962 Diocese of York, curate Stocksbridge 1961–65, brother in Community of the Transfiguration 1965–; *Style*— Brother John Halsey; ✉ The Hermitage, 23 Manse Road, Roslin, Midlothian EH25 9LF

HALSEY, Simon Patrick; s of Louis Arthur Owen Halsey, of Kingston upon Thames, Surrey, and Evelyn Elisabeth, *née* Calder; *b* 8 March 1958; *Educ* chorister New Coll Oxford, Winchester (music scholar), King's Coll Cambridge (choral scholar), Royal Coll of Music (conducting scholar); *m* 14 June 1986, Lucy Jane, da of Norman Linsley Lunt; 1 s (Jack b 31 July 1989), 1 da (Harriet b 10 June 1992); *Career* conductor Scottish Opera-Go-Round 1980–81, dir of music Univ of Warwick 1981–88; chorus dir: CBSO 1983–, Acad of Ancient Music 1988–91, Flemish Opera Antwerp 1990–94; assoc dir Philharmonia Chorus 1986–98, music dir City of Birmingham Touring Opera 1986–2000; artistic dir: Salisbury Festival 1988–93, BBC Nat Chorus of Wales 1995–2000; princ guest conductor: Netherlands Radio Choir 1995–2002, Sydney Philharmonia Choirs 1997–2000; chief conductor: Berlin Radio Choir 2001–, Netherlands Radio Choir 2002–; principal conductor Choral Projects Northern Sinfonia of England 2005–; founding conductor European Voices 1999; has appeared as guest conductor with various major choirs and orchs incl: LSO, CBSO, English Chamber Orch, Scottish Chamber Orch, London Symphony Chorus, French, Swedish, Danish and Belgian Radio Choirs, Australian Chamber Orch, Hong Kong Philharmonic Orch; has made over 40 recordings on EMI, Chandos, Oiseau-Lyre, Harmonia Mundi, Coviello and Hyperion as chorus master and on Conifer as conductor; conslt ed Faber Music Ltd; Hon DUniv Univ of Central England 2000, Hon MA Univ of

Warwick 2007; *Recreations* architecture, food and wine, sport, English literature, travel; *Style*— Simon Halsey, Esq; ✉ Granby House, 279 High Street, Henley-in-Arden, Warwickshire B95 5BG (tel 01564 794873); c/o Catherine Gibbs, Intermusica Ltd, 16 Duncan Terrace, London N1 8BZ (tel 020 7278 5455, e-mail cpetherbridge@intermusica.co.uk)

HALSTEAD, Dr Michael Peter; s of Ronald Halstead, and Edna, *née* Calvert; *b* 10 March 1942; *Educ* Wolstanton Co GS Newcastle-under-Lyme, Gonville & Caius Coll Cambridge (state scholar, MA, PhD); *m* 1965, Christine, da of Sim Quinton; 2 s (David Edward Michael b 1968, John Simon b 1971); *Career* res fell Dept of Chemistry Univ Coll of Swansea 1967–69; Royal Dutch Shell Group: sr scientist Thornton Res Centre Shell Research Ltd Chester 1969–77, business devpt mangr Speciality Chemicals Div Shell International Chemical Co Ltd London 1977–81, planning mangr Western Regnl Orgn Shell International Petroleum Co Ltd London 1981–85; treas Univ of Cambridge 1985–93, chief exec and sec-gen Univ of Cambridge Local Examinations Syndicate 1993–2002, bursar and fell Christ's Coll Cambridge 2002–; tstee: Cambridge Cwlth Tst 1993–2002, Cambridge Overseas Tst 1993–2002, Fndn of Edward Storey 2004–; non-exec dir: CAD Centre Ltd 1987–94 (chm CAD Centre Pension Trustee Ltd 1992–98), Cambridge Water Company 1993– (chm 1995–); author of papers in scientific jls on reaction kinetics; fell Gonville & Caius Coll 1985–99; FCCA, CChem, FRSC (Investments Ctee 1989–); *Recreations* music, especially organ (ARCO), travel and walking in the Alps; *Style*— Dr Michael Halstead; ✉ 26 Newton Road, Cambridge CB2 8AL (tel 01223 327861)

HALSTEAD, Sir Ronald; kt (1985), CBE (1976); s of Richard Halstead, of Burton-in-Lonsdale, Lancs, and late Bessie, *née* Harrison; *b* 17 May 1927; *Educ* Lancaster Royal GS, Queens' Coll Cambridge; *m* 1968, Yvonne Cecile (d 1978), da of Emile de Monchaux (d 1970), of Australia; 2 s; *Career* chm Beecham Products 1967–84; Beecham Group plc: md Consumer Products 1973–84, chm and chief exec 1984–85; non-exec dir: British Steel plc 1979–94 (dep chm 1986–94), The Burmah Oil plc 1983–89, Davy Corporation plc 1986–91, Gestetner Holdings plc 1983–95, American Cyanamid Co 1986–95, Laurentian Financial Group plc 1991–95; chm: Knitting Sector Gp NEDC 1978–90, Garment and Textile Sector Gp NEDC 1991–92, Nat Coll of Food Technol 1978–83, Bd for Food Studies Univ of Reading 1978–83, Industrial Devpt Advsy Bd DTI 1985–93 (memb 1983–93), CAB Int 1995–98, Cons Foreign & Cwlth Cncl 1995–; memb Cncl and Exec Ctee Food Mfrs Fedn Inc 1966–86 (pres 1974–76); memb Cncl: CBI 1970–86, Univ of Buckingham 1973–95, Univ of Reading 1978–98, Trade Policy Res Centre 1985–89, Fndn for Science and Technology 1987–, European Policy Forum 1993–; vice-chm The Advertising Assoc 1973–81, dep chm Technol Colls Tst 1993–, dir and hon treas Centre for Policy Studies 1984–93, memb Priorities Bd for R&D in Agric and Food for MAFF 1984–87, tstee Inst of Econ Affrs 1980–93, vice-pres Chartered Inst of Mktg, pres Engineering Industries Assoc 1991–; govr: Ashridge Mgmnt Coll 1970–2006 (vice-chm 1977–2006), De Montfort Univ 1989–97; memb: Newspaper Panel Monopolies and Mergers Cmmn 1980–92, Monopolies and Mergers Cmmn 1993–99; memb Cncl and Exec Ctee Imperial Soc of Knights Bachelor 1986–2002; Hon DSc: Univ of Reading 1982, Lancaster Univ 1987; hon fell Queens' Coll Cambridge 1985; FIMgt, FRSA, FRSC, FInstM (Hon 1982), FIGD, FCIM, Hon FIFST; *Recreations* squash racquets, skiing; *Clubs* Brooks's, Athenaeum, Carlton, Royal Thames Yacht, Hurlingham; *Style*— Sir Ronald Halstead, CBE; ✉ 37 Edwardes Square, London W8 6HH (tel 020 7603 9010, fax 020 7371 2595)

HALTON, Prof David John; s of Kenneth Robert Depledge Halton (d 1985), and Margaret Alice, *née* Searle (d 1984); *b* 23 June 1949, Beckenham, Kent; *Educ* Beckenham and Penge GS for Boys, Univ of Greenwich (BA), Roehampton Inst (PGCE), Aston Univ (MSc), Univ of Leicester (EdD); *m* 25 Aug 1973, Yvonne Geneste, *née* Ambrose; 3 da (Rosalie Geneste b 18 Sept 1985, Isabelle Margaret b 22 March 1988, Megan Elizabeth b 1 Oct 1990); *Career* teacher Hurlingham Comp Sch 1973–76, lectr N Tyneside Coll of FE 1977–80, head of dept Coll for the Distributive Trades 1980–86, dean Business Sch Univ of N London 1987–90, dep rector UC Northampton 1990–99, dep vice-chllr and dep chief exec UWE 1999–2004, vice-chllr Univ of Glamorgan 2005–; chm City Acad Bristol, memb Cncl Bristol Old Vic Theatre Sch; memb Juvenile Diabetes Gp Bristol; FRSA 2003; *Publications* Theories of Education Management in Practice (1998), Pricing Toolkit for Higher Education (with KPMG, 2001); *Recreations* playing blues piano, running, ornithology; *Style*— Prof David Halton; ✉ University of Glamorgan, Pontypridd CF37 1DL (tel 01443 482001, fax 01443 482390, e-mail djhalton@glam.ac.uk)

HALUCH, (Stefan) James (Jim); s of late Stefan L Haluch, and late Elizabeth, *née* Wallace; *b* 9 March 1944; *Educ* St Mary's Acad Bathgate; *m* 25 May 1968, Joyce Vevers, da of late George S McClelland; 2 da (Helena b 1965, Shelagh b 1971), 2 s (James b 1969, Eoin b 1974); *Career* Inland Revenue 1962–65, The Scotsman Edinburgh 1965–70, business conslt and hotelier 1970–88, Sight & Sound Education Ltd 1988–91, head of mktg, head of corporate communications and assoc princ Telford Coll Edinburgh 1991–2006, business conslt Athol Consulting 2006–; chm Isle of Arran Tourist Bd 1980–83, pres Isle of Arran Licensed Trade Assoc 1983–86; former councillor: Bathgate Town Cncl, W Lothian CC; FInstSMM, FCMI, FCIPD; *Recreations* music, travel; *Style*— Jim Haluch, Esq; ✉ 11 Willow Wood Park, Cuthill Brae, West Calder, West Lothian EH55 8QE (e-mail jim.haluch@btinternet.com)

HALUSA, Dr Martin; s of Dr Arno Halusa, Austrian ambass to US (d 1979), and Constance Monro (d 1990); *b* 12 February 1955, Bangkok, Thailand; *Educ* Schule Schloss Salem, Georgetown Univ (BA), Harvard Business Sch (MBA), Univ of Innsbruck (PhD); *m* 1986 (m dis), Angelika, da of Hans-Walter Scheerbarth; 4 s (Thomas b 17 May 1987, Andreas b 18 Nov 1988, Lukas b 26 Feb 1991, Niklas b 21 June 1992); *Career* ptnr Boston Consulting Gp Munich 1979–86, dir Daniel Swarovski Corp Zurich 1986–90, co-fndr and md Apax Partners Germany 1990–2003, ceo Apax Partners Worldwide 2003–; *Recreations* mountains, art; *Style*— Dr Martin Halusa; ✉ Apax Partners Worldwide LLP, 15 Portland Place, London W1B 1PT (tel 020 7872 6300, fax 020 7636 6475, e-mail martin.halusa@apax.com)

HAM, Prof Christopher John (Chris); CBE (2004); s of Raymond Ham (d 1993), and Ann Ham (d 1993); *b* 15 May 1951, Cardiff; *Educ* Cardiff HS for Boys, Univ of Kent (BA, MPhil), Univ of Bristol (PhD); *m* 30 May 1980, Ioanna, *née* Burnell; 2 s (Alex b 6 Sept 1982, Matthew b 18 June 1989), 1 da (Jessica b 16 Dec 1985); *Career* research asst Nuffield Centre for Health Serv Studies Univ of Leeds 1975–77, lectr Sch for Advanced Urban Studies Univ of Bristol 1977–86, policy analyst King's Fund Inst and fell in health policy and mgmnt King's Fund Coll 1986–92, prof of health policy and mgmnt Health Servs Mgmnt Centre Univ of Birmingham 1992– (dir Health Servs Mgmnt Centre 1993–2000), dir (on secondment) Strategy Unit Dept of Health 2000–04; advsr to numerous orgns incl: Health Ctee House of Commons, Audit Cmmn, Nat Audit Office, Dept of Health, BDA, BMA, NHS Confedn, RCP, Demos (memb Advsy Cncl), World Bank, WHO; former vice-pres Patients' Assoc, chair Int Soc on Priorities in Health Care 1998–2000, memb Social Policy Assoc 1977–, memb bd of govrs Heart of England NHS Fndn Tsts 2005–, govr The Health Fndn 2006–, memb bd of tstees Canadian Health Services Res Fndn 2006–; ed: State of Health series Open Univ Press 1991–, Health Servs Mgmnt series Open Univ Press 1994–; memb Editorial Bd: Policy and Politics 1984–89, Br Jl of Health Care Mgmnt 1996–2000, Health Expectations 1997–; reviewer and referee for numerous professional jls; Kellogg Fndn Fellowship to Nordic Sch of Public Health Gothenburg 1986; FRSM 1993, fndr fell Acad of Med Sciences 1998, Hon FRCP 2004; *Publications* incl: Policy Making in the NHS: A Case Study of the Leeds Regional Hospital Board (1981), Health Policy in Britain (1982, 5 edn 2004), The Policy Process in the Modern Capitalist State (with M J Hill, 1984, 2 edn 1993), Managing Health Services: Health Authority Members in Search of a Role (1986), Health Check: Health Care Reforms in an International Context (with R Robinson and M Benzeval, 1990), The New NHS: Organisation and Management (1991), Management and Competition in the New NHS (1991, 2 edn 1997), Priority Setting Processes for Healthcare (with F Honigsbaum, J Calltorp and S Holmström, 1995), The NHS Guide (with S Haywood, 2 edn 1993), Priority Setting in Healthcare: Lessons for General Practice (1995), Public, Private or Community: What Next for the NHS? (1996), Health Care Reform: Learning From International Experience (ed, 1997), Tragic Choices in Health Care: The Case of Child B (with S Pickard, 1998), The Global Challenge of Health Care Rationing (ed with A Coulter, 2000), The Politics of NHS Reform 1988–97: Metaphor or Reality? (2000), Contested Decisions (with S McIver, 2000), Reasonable Rationing (ed with G Robert, 2003); numerous book chapters, articles in newspapers and refereed jls, research reports, briefing papers and conf proceedings; *Recreations* sport, music, theatre, reading, travel; *Style*— Prof Chris Ham, CBE; ✉ Health Services Management Centre, The University of Birmingham, Park House, 40 Edgbaston Park Road, Birmingham B15 2RT (tel 0121 414 3212, e-mail c.j.ham@bham.ac.uk)

HAMBLEDEN, 4 Viscount (UK 1891); William Herbert Smith; s of 3 Viscount (d 1948), and Lady Patricia Herbert, GCVO (d 1994), da of 15 Earl of Pembroke and (12 Earl of) Montgomery; *b* 2 April 1930; *Educ* Eton; *m* 1, 1955 (m dis 1988), Donna Maria Carmela Attolico di Adelfia, da of Conte Bernardo Attolico, of Rome; 5 s; m 2, 1988, Mrs Lesley Watson; *Heir* s, Hon Henry Smith; *Style*— The Rt Hon the Viscount Hambleden; ✉ Dunsaller, Thorverton, Exeter, Devon EX5 5JR

HAMBLEN, Prof David Lawrence; CBE (2001); s of Reginald John Hamblen, of Woolwich, London, and Bessie, *née* Williams; *b* 31 August 1934; *Educ* Roan Sch Greenwich, The London Hosp Med Coll (MB BS); *m* 16 Nov 1968, Gillian Frances, da of Edgar Leonard Bradley, OBE, of Bearsden, Glasgow; 2 da (Sarah Catherine b 1970, Clare Alison b 1974), 1 s (Neil Andrew b 1975); *Career* Nat Serv RAMC 16 Para Bde, Maj TA 44 Para Bde, reg army res offr 1972–89; fell in orthopaedics Harvard Med Sch, clinical and res fell Mass Gen Hosp Boston USA 1966–67, lectr in orthopaedics Univ of Oxford 1967–68, sr lectr in orthopaedic surgery Univ of Edinburgh 1968–72, prof of orthopaedic surgery Univ of Glasgow 1972–99 (emeritus prof 1999–); hon consIt orthopaedic surgn to Army in Scotland 1976–99; visiting prof National Centre for Trg and Educn in Prosthetics and Orthotics Univ of Strathclyde 1991–; sr medical ed Orthopaedics Today Int 1999–, chm Cncl of Mgmnt Jl of Bone and Jt Surgery; non-exec dir West Glasgow Hosps Univ NHS Tst 1994–97, chm Gtr Glasgow Health Bd 1997–2000; past pres Br Orthopaedic Assoc 1990–91; Hon DSc: Univ of Strathclyde 2003, Univ of Glasgow 2003; FRCS, FRCSEd, FRCSGlas; *Books* Outline of Fractures (co-author, 10 edn 1992, 11 edn 1999, 12 edn 2007), Outline of Orthopaedics (co-author, 12 edn 1995, 13 edn 2001); *Recreations* golf, music, curling; *Clubs* RSM; *Style*— Prof David Hamblen, CBE; ✉ 3 Russell Drive, Bearsden, Glasgow G61 3BB (tel 0141 942 1823, e-mail dlhortho@doctors.net.uk)

HAMBLEN, Nicholas Archibald; QC (1997); s of Derek Hamblen, and Pauline, *née* Morgan; *Educ* Westminster, St John's Coll Oxford (MA), Harvard Law Sch (LLM); *m* 1985, Kate Hamblen; 1 da (Eleanor b 1990), 1 s (Jamie b 1992); *Career* called to the Bar Lincoln's Inn 1981; specialist in commercial law especially shipping, int trade, insurance, arbitration; recorder 1999–; *Clubs* MCC, Hurlingham, Vincent's (Oxford); *Style*— Nicholas Hamblen, Esq, QC; ✉ 20 Essex Street, London WC2R 3AL (tel 020 7583 9294, fax 020 7583 1341)

HAMBLETON, Prof Kenneth George; s of George William Hambleton (d 1972), of Chesterfield, Derbys, and Gertrude Ellen, *née* Brighouse (d 1981); *b* 15 January 1937; *Educ* Chesterfield GS, Queens' Coll Cambridge (MA); *m* 4 April 1959, Glenys Patricia, da of Horace Smith, of Hayling Island, Hants; 1 s (Neil b 1963), 1 da (Lindsey b 1965); *Career* res and devpt of semiconductor materials devices and applications Servs Electronics Res Lab Herts 1958–73, res and devpt on naval radars weapon systems and computers Admty Surface Weapons Estab 1973–81 (dep dir 1981–82), dir strategic electronics MOD 1982–85, asst chief sci advsr MOD (responsible for advising on sci content of all def projects and long term res progs) 1985–86; dir gen: Air Weapons and Electronic Systems 1986–90, Aircraft 3 1990–91; prof of def engrg UCL 1991–2002 (emeritus prof 2003–); Freeman City of London 1993, Liveryman Worshipful Co of Engrs 1993; FIEE 1982, FRAeS 1993, FREng 1994; *Recreations* bridge, chess, music, computing, golf; *Clubs* 2; *Style*— Prof Kenneth Hambleton, FREng; ✉ 56 Warblington Road, Emsworth, Hampshire PO10 7HH (tel 01243 371545)

HAMBLIN, Brian James; s of Philip James Arthur Hamblin, of Orpington, and Freda Mary Hamblin; *b* 17 February 1954; *Educ* Cray Valley Tech HS, Lanchester Poly (BA); *m* 1977, Jane Karen, da of W Alan Sutherland; 2 da (Elizabeth Jane b 7 April 1983, Victoria Claire b 6 Feb 1985), 1 s (Philip James b 4 July 1987); *Career* articled clerk Warley & Warley 1975–76; PKF Leicester 1979–: asst mangr then sr audit mangr 1984–85, ptnr 1985–, managing ptnr and sr corp recovery ptnr 1986–, regnl managing ptnr for Midlands 1999–; Hon BA Coventry Poly 1976; memb Inst of Taxation 1981, MIPA 1990, MSPI 1990 (chm Midlands Region); FCA; *Recreations* playing the trumpet, badminton, golf, church steward; *Clubs* Leicester Rotary; *Style*— Brian Hamblin, Esq; ✉ PKF, Pannell House, 159 Charles Street, Leicester, Leicestershire LE1 1LD (tel 0116 250 4400, fax 0116 285 4651)

HAMBLIN, Prof Terence John (Terry); s of John Gordon Hamblin (d 1978), of Farnham, Surrey, and Gladys Marjorie, *née* Allies; *b* 12 March 1943; *Educ* Farnborough GS, Univ of Bristol (MB ChB), Univ of Southampton (DM); *m* 22 July 1967, Diane Vivienne, da of George William Lay (d 2006), of Farnham, Surrey; 2 da (Karen b 1968, Angela b 1977), 2 s (Richard b 1971, David b 1980); *Career* house physician Southmead Hosp Bristol 1967, house surgn Bristol Royal Infirmary 1968, MRC registrar in med Univ of Bristol 1970–72, sr registrar in haematology Poole Gen Hosp 1972–74, conslt haematologist Bournemouth 1974–2003, conslt haematologist KCH London 2004–; prof of immunohaematology Univ of Southampton 1987– (sr lectr in immunology 1980–87), sr examiner in pathology Univ of London 1991–99; expert advsr WHO 1981; memb: Examining Panel RCPath 1986–, Working Pty Adult Leukaemia MRC 1989–2006, Sr Advsy Ctee Haematology RCPath 1991–95, UK Coordinating Ctee for Cancer Research 1998–2002, Cncl Research Defence Soc 1998–2004, Gene Therapy Advsr Ctee 2001–, Haematology/Oncology Working Gp Nat Cancer Res Inst 2002–06; chm UKCLL Forum 2001–, sec UK MDS Forum 2003– (treas 2006–); sr ed Transfusion Sci 1985–2004, ed Leukaemia Res 1986–; pres Euro Soc of Haemapheresis 1986; vice-pres Biblical Creation Soc 1998–; hon treas Myelodysplasia Fndn 1994–; awarded Binet-Rai Medal for CLL Research 2003; FRCPath 1985 (MRCPath 1973), FRCP 1985 (MRCP 1971), FMedSci 2002; *Television* Counterblast - Of Mice and Men (BBC 2) 1998; *Books* Plasmapheresis and Plasma Exchange (1979), Immunological Investigation of Lymphoid Neoplasms (1983), Haematological Problems in the Elderly (1987), Immunotherapy of Disease (1990); over 200 medical and research papers, over 300 articles of medical journalism; *Recreations* reading theology, writing funny articles, preaching, listening to Bach, Mozart and Buddy Holly records; *Style*— Prof Terry Hamblin; ✉ 15 Queens Park, South Drive, Bournemouth BH8 9BQ (tel 01202 267156); Tenovus Research Institute, Southampton General Hospital, Shirley, Southampton SO9 4XY (tel 023 8077 7222, e-mail terjoha@aol.com)

HAMBLING, Gerald James; s of Ernest James Hambling (d 1965), and Elsie Maud, *née* Sedman (d 1971); *b* 14 June 1926; *Educ* Whitgift Middle Sch Croydon, Selhurst GS

H

Thornton Heath; *m* 23 May 1953, Margaret, da of George Speakman (d 1945); 1 da (Belinda b 18 Oct 1954), 1 s (Robert b 31 July 1957); *Career* film editor; memb: Br Guild of Film Eds 1966–, American Acad of Arts and Scis 1980–, American Cinema Eds Guild 1980–; Coldstream Gds 1944–47; asst ed J Arthur Rank Two Cities Films 1947–50; sound ed: Herbert Wilcox Films 1950–54, Alexander The Great 1954, Freud - The Passion 1962, The Servant 1964, Pretty Polly 1966, Night of the Iguana 1966, Wuthering Heights 1970; film ed: Dry Rot 1955, The Whole Truth 1956, The Story of Esther Costello 1957, Sally's Irish Rogue 1958, Left Right and Centre 1959, The Bulldog Breed 1960, She'll Have to Go 1961, The Early Bird 1963, A Stitch in Time 1965, The Intelligence Men 1967, That Riviera Touch 1968, The Magnificent Two 1969, Roger Cherrill Ltd documentaries and commercials 1971–74, Bugsy Malone 1975, Moses - The Lawgiver 1976, Midnight Express 1977 (Br Acad Award and American Acad nomination), Fame 1979 (Br and American Acad nominations, Br Guild of Film Eds Award, American Eds Guild nomination), Heartaches 1980, Shoot the Moon 1981, Pink Floyd - The Wall 1982, Another Country 1983 (Br Acad nomination), Birdy 1984 (Br Guild of Eds Award), Absolute Beginners 1985, Angel Heart 1986 (Br Guild of Eds nomination), Leonard VI 1987, Mississippi Burning 1988 (Br Acad Award), The Commitments 1991 (Br Acad Award, American Acad nomination), In The Name of the Father 1993 (American Acad nomination), The Road to Welville 1994, White Squall 1995, Evita 1996 (American Acad nomination), Angela's Ashes 1999, The Life of David Gale 2002; Career Achievement Award from American Cinema Editor's Guild 1998; ret 2003; *Recreations* horology, fishing, antiques, photography; *Style*— Gerald Hambling, Esq; ✉ Ramblers, Skirmett, Oxfordshire RG9 6TG (tel 01491 638316, fax 01491 638316, e-mail gerryhambling@aol.com)

HAMBLING, Sir (Herbert) Hugh; 3 Bt (UK 1924), of Yoxford, Co Suffolk; s of Sir (Herbert) Guy Musgrave Hambling, 2 Bt (d 1966), and Olive Margaret Gordon, *née* Carter (d 1969); *b* 3 August 1919; *Educ* Eton; *m* 1, 23 Sept 1950, Anne Page (d 1990), da of Judge Hugo Edmund Oswald (d 1932), of Seattle, USA; 1 s; m 2, 21 June 1991, Helen Seymour (d 2004), da of Donald Mackinnon, of Marida Yallock, Victoria, Australia, and widow of David Maitland Gavin; *Heir* s, Peter Hambling; *Career* RAF Training and Atlantic Ferry Cmd 1939–45; airline rep: British Airways 1956–74, Royal Brunei Airlines 1975–96; mangr Hambling & Son 1956–; *Style*— Sir Hugh Hambling, Bt; ✉ Rookery Park, Yoxford, Suffolk IP17 3HQ; 1219 Evergreen Point Road, Medina, Washington 98039, USA

HAMBLING, Maggi; OBE (1995); da of Harry Leonard Hambling (d 1998), of Hadleigh, Suffolk, and Marjorie Rose, *née* Harris (d 1988); *b* 23 October 1945; *Educ* Hadleigh Hall Sch, Amberfield Sch, Ipswich Sch of Art, Camberwell Sch of Art (DipAD Painting), Slade Sch of Fine Art (Higher Dip Fine Art), Boise travel award NY 1969; *Career* artist; first artist in residence Nat Gallery London 1980–81; Jerwood Painting Prize 1995; fell New Hall Cambridge 2003; Marsh Award for excellence in public sculpture 2005; Hon DLitt UEA 2000, hon fell Univ of the Arts London 2004; *Works in Public Collections* incl: Arts Cncl of GB, Birmingham City Art Gallery, Br Cncl, Br Museum, Christchurch Mansion Ipswich, Clare Coll Cambridge, Chelmsford and Essex Museum, Contemporary Art Soc, Eastern Arts Collection, Euro Parliament Collection, Fndn Du Musee De La Main Lausanne, GLC, Greene King Breweries, Gulbenkian Fndn, Haddo House Aberdeen, Harris Museum and Art Gallery Preston, HTV Bristol Imperial War Museum, Leics Educn Ctee, Minories Colchester, Morley Coll London, Nat Gallery, Nat Portrait Gallery, Petworth House, Rugby Museum, RAMC, Scottish Nat Gallery of Modern Art Edinburgh, Scottish Nat Portrait Gallery, Southampton Art Gallery, St Mary's Church Hadleigh Suffolk, St Mary's Coll Strawberry Hill London, St Mary's Hosp London, Tate Gallery, Unilever House London, Usher Gallery Lincoln, Whitworth Art Gallery Manchester, William Morris Sch London, Aust Nat Gallery Canberra, Hereford Cathedral, New Hall Cambridge, Yale Center for Br Art New Haven Conn, Templeton Coll Oxford, Univ of Warwick, Wakefield Art Gallery, Ashmolean Museum Oxford, Usher Gallery Lincoln, Government Art Collection, Castle Museum Norwich, Fitzwilliam Museum Cambridge, Barclay's Art Collection, Lady Margaret Hall Oxford; *Exhibitions* Hadleigh Gallery Suffolk 1967, Morley Gallery London 1973, Warehouse Gallery London 1977, Nat Gallery London 1981, Nat Portrait Gallery London and tour 1983, Serpentine Gallery London 1987, Richard Demarco Gallery Edinburgh 1988, Maclaurin Art Gallery Ayr 1988, Arnolfini Gallery Bristol and tour 1988, Bernard Jacobson Gallery London 1990, Yale Center for British Art New Haven Conn USA 1991, CCA Galleries London 1993, Northern Centre for Contemporary Art Sunderland 1993, Cornerhouse Manchester 1993, Angel Row Nottingham 1994, Christchurch Mansion Ipswich 1994, Harris Museum Preston 1994, Barbican Centre London 1994, Sculpture in Bronze Marlborough Fine Art 1996, National Portrait Gallery 1997, Yorkshire Sculpture Park 1997, Hugh Lane Gallery Dublin 1997, Monument to Oscar Wilde Adelaide Street London 1998, Good Friday Gainsborough's House Sudbury 2000, Marlborough Fine Art and Morley Gallery 2001, Very Special Brew Paintings Sotheby's 2003, North Sea Paintings Aldeburgh Festival Exhibition 2003; Scallop sculpture to celebrate Benjamin Britten Aldeburgh beach Suffolk 2003, Portraits of People and the Sea Marlborough Fine Art 2006, No Straight Lines (Fitzwilliam Museum and tour) 2007, Waves Breaking (Marlborough Graphics) 2007; *Books* Maggi and Henrietta: Drawings of Henrietta Moraes by Maggi Hambling (2001), Maggi Hambling: The Works (2006); *Clubs* Chelsea Arts; *Style*— Miss Maggi Hambling, OBE; ✉ c/o Marlborough Fine Art, 6 Albermarle Street, London W1S 4BY

HAMBRO, James Daryl; s of Jocelyn Olaf Hambro, MC (d 1994), and his 1 w, Ann Silvia, *née* Muir (d 1972); *b* 22 March 1949; *Educ* Eton, Harvard Business Sch; *m* Diana Cherry; 3 c; *Career* exec dir Hambros Bank 1972–85; md: J O Hambro Magan & Co 1988–94, J O Hambro & Co 1986–98; chm: J O Hambro Capital Management Ltd 1996–, Ashtenne Hldgs plc 1997–2005, Singer & Friedlander AIM VCT 2 2000–05, Singer & Friedlander AIM VCT 3 2005–, Hansteen Holdings plc 2005–; dir: Primary Health Properties plc 1996–, Capital Opportunities Tst 1997–2003, Enterprise Capital Tst 1997–2003; dep chm Peabody Tst 1993–2006, chm Henry Smith's Charity 2007–; *Clubs* White's, Royal West Norfolk; *Style*— James Hambro, Esq; ✉ J O Hambro Capital Management Ltd, Ryder Court, 14 Ryder Street, London SW1Y 6QB (tel 020 7747 5678, fax 020 7747 5647)

HAMBRO, Peter Charles Percival; elder s of late Lt-Col Everard B Hambro, MBE; *b* 18 January 1945; *Educ* Eton; *m* 1968, Karen Guinevere Gould, da of late Capt George Brodrick; *Career* md: Smith St Aubyn & Co Holdings until 1983, Mocatta & Goldsmid Ltd 1985–90; chm: Peter Hambro Ltd 1990–, Peter Hambro Mining plc 1994–; non-exec chm: Sundeala Ltd, Aricom plc; *Recreations* painting; *Clubs* Pratt's, White's; *Style*— Peter Hambro, Esq; ✉ Peter Hambro Limited, 11 Grosvenor Place, London SW1X 7HH

HAMBRO, (Alexander) Richard; s of Jocelyn Olaf Hambro, MC (d 1994), by his 1 w, Ann Silvia, *née* Muir (d 1972); *b* 1 October 1946; *Educ* Eton; *m* 1, 1973 (m dis 1982), Hon Charlotte, da of Baron Soames, GCMG, GCVO, CH, CBE, PC; 1 da (Clementine b 1976, bridesmaid to Lady Diana Spencer at her marriage to HRH The Prince of Wales 1981); m 2, 12 July 1984 (m dis 1992), Juliet Mary Elizabeth Grana, da of Maj Thomas Harvey and Lady Mary Harvey; m 3, 1993, Mary Christine James, *née* Briggs; *Career* dir Hambros Bank 1979– (joined 1966), pres Hambro America Inc 1975–83, co-fndr J O Hambro & Co 1986; chm: J O Hambro Investment Management Ltd, I Hennig & Co diamond brokers 1987, Wiltons (St James's) Ltd 2003–, Inst of Cancer Research 2003, Smith's Holdings Ltd 2003–, The Money Portal plc 2003–; pres Colon Cancer Concern 1997, dep pres Macmillan Cancer Relief 2001–, chm Jt Br Cancer Charities; tstee: The London Clinic 2000, Burdett Tst for Nursing; *Clubs* White's, RAC, The Brook (NY), Jockey; *Style*— Richard Hambro, Esq; ✉ Waverton House, Moreton-in-Marsh, Gloucestershire GL56 9TB

HAMBRO, Rupert Nicholas; eldest s of Jocelyn Olaf Hambro, MC (d 1994), and his 1 w, Ann Silvia, *née* Muir (d 1973); *b* 27 June 1943; *Educ* Eton, Aix-en-Provence; *m* 1970, Mary Robinson, da of late Francis Boyer; 1 s, 1 da; *Career* Peat Marwick Mitchell Co 1962–64; Hambros Bank Ltd: joined 1964, dir 1969–86, chm 1983–86; J O Hambro & Co Ltd: md 1986–94, chm 1994–99; chm: Wilton's (St James') Ltd 1987–2003, J O Hambro Magan & Co Ltd 1988–93, J O Hambro Magan Irby Holdings Ltd 1988–96, Mayflower Corporation plc 1989–2004, Fenchurch plc 1993–97, Longshot plc 1996–, J O Hambro Mansford Ltd 1998–, J O Hambro Ltd 1999–, Longshot Health and Fitness 1999–, Roland Berger & Partners Ltd 2000–03, Kapital Ventures plc 2001–06, Longshot Hotels Ltd 2001–04, Tanner Krolle Ltd 2002–, Cazenove & Loyd Ltd 2004–; dir: Hamleys plc (chm 1989–94), Anglo American Corp of SA Ltd 1981–97, Racecourse Holdings Trust 1985–94, The Telegraph plc 1984–2001 (dir Telegraph Advsy Bd 2002–03), Sedgwick Group plc 1987–92, Asset Trust plc 1987–90, Pioneer Concrete plc 1988–99, CTR plc 1990–97, KBC Peel Hunt plc 2000–03, Bank Gutmann AG 2000–, Business for Sterling 2002–, Open Europe 2006–; chm: Assoc of Int Bond Dealers 1979–82, Soc of Merchant's Trading to the Continent 1995–, Bd of Govrs Museum of London 1998–2005, Jermyn Street Assoc 2000–03, Univ of Bath in Swindon 2000–; co-chm Museum in Docklands 2003–05; chm of tstees: Garfield Weston Boys' Club Tst 1993–2000, The Silver Tst 1988–; chm: Woburn Golf and Country Club Ltd 1998–2003, The Walbrook Club Ltd 1999–2001, Third Space Gp Ltd 1999–, The Walpole Ctee Ltd 2000–05, Woburn Enterprises Ltd 2003–; hon pres Br Assoc of Adoption and Fostering 2006–; vice-patron RSBS 1997–; treas Nat Art Collection Fund 1992–2003, chm of tstees Chiswick House and Gardens Tst 2005–; Warden Worshipful Co of Goldsmiths 2006; Univ of Bath: memb Cncl, hon fell 1998–; *Recreations* golf, shooting, Marrakech; *Clubs* White's, Groucho, Walbrook, Jupiter Island (Florida); *Style*— Rupert Hambro, Esq; ✉ Rupert Hambro & Partners Ltd, 54 Jermyn Street, London SW1Y 6LX (tel 020 7292 3777, fax 020 7292 3778, e-mail rnhambro@joh.co.uk)

HAMER, (Michael Howard) Kenneth; s of Mark Hamer (d 1970), and Feodora Leonora, *née* Abrahams (d 1958); *b* 27 July 1945; *Educ* Cheltenham Coll, Sidney Sussex Coll Cambridge; *m* 20 Sept 1986, Victoria, da of Dr Thomas Walsh (d 1988); 1 da (Clara b 1989); *Career* practising barr; admitted slr 1968; called to the Bar: Inner Temple 1975, King's Inns Ireland 1998; recorder of the Crown Court 2000– (asst recorder 1991–2000); counsel for passenger gp at Southall and Ladbroke Grove rail accident inquiries 1997–2001; chair Home Office Review of Independent Membs of Police Authorities 2003–04; memb Prosecuting Panel for Conduct Ctee of the Bar 2001–; legal assessor to: GMC 2002–, Nursing and Midwifery Cncl 2004–, Gen Chiropractic Cncl 2005–; chair Appeal Ctee CIMA 2006–; memb Editorial Bd bulletin of Assoc of Regulatory and Disciplinary Lawyers; FCIArb 1999, accredited mediator 2002; *Recreations* cooking, opera, arts; *Clubs* Carlton; *Style*— Kenneth Hamer, Esq; ✉ Iford Manor, Iford, Lewes, East Sussex BN7 3EU (tel 01273 472832, fax 01273 478119); Henderson Chambers, 2 Harcourt Buildings, Temple, London EC4Y 9DB (tel 020 7583 9020, fax 020 7583 2686, e-mail khamer@hendersonchambers.co.uk)

HAMID, David; *Career* early career in mktg positions with: United Biscuits, Golden Wonder, Sony, Alfred Dunhill (latterly mktg dir Int Jewellery Division); Dixons Gp plc: joined 1986, roles incl mktg dir Supasnaps, md Dixons Financial Services, md Mastercare and gp md PC World, latterly gp chief operating offr, memb Bd 1997–2003; ceo Halfords 2003–05, ptnr Merchant Equity Ptnrs 2006–; chm MFI, Nationwide Autocentres; *Style*— David Hamid, Esq

HAMILTON, *see also:* Stirling-Hamilton

HAMILTON, Duke of ; *see:* Hamilton and Brandon

HAMILTON, Abe; s of Roberta Austin (d 1993); *b* 4 January 1962; *Educ* High Peak Coll of FE Buxton, Bournemouth & Poole Coll of Art & Design, Middx Poly; *Career* former chef; fashion designer 1986–; cmmnd by Browns to design a capsule collection for new store 1993, first show Harvey Nichols 1993, winner British Design - The New Generation category (British Fashion Awards) 1993; *Style*— Abe Hamilton, Esq; ✉ 9 Patmore House, Matthias Road, London N16 8LQ

HAMILTON, Prof (William) Allan; s of Vernon Hamilton (d 1980), and Jean Mair Murdoch Logan, *née* Hood (d 1988); *b* 4 April 1936; *Educ* Hutchesons' GS, Univ of Glasgow (BSc, PhD); *m* 1992, Evie, *née* Stewart; 2 step da (Marsali Ann Stewart b 1971, Victoria Elidh Stewart b 1974); *Career* Dept of Biochemistry Univ of Glasgow: ARC scholar 1958–60, MRC research asst 1960–61; US Public Health Serv research fell Dept of Biochemistry Univ of Illinois 1961–62, WHO research fell Dept of Phthisiology and Pneumology Univ of Brazil 1962–63, scientist Unilever Colworth House Bedford 1963–67, pt/t lectr Luton Coll of Technol 1964–65; Univ of Aberdeen: lectr Dept of Biochemistry 1967–70, sr lectr Dept of Biochemistry 1970–73, sr lectr Unit of Microbiology Dept of Biochemistry 1973–75, sr lectr and head Dept of Microbiology 1975–77, reader and head Dept of Microbiology 1977–80, prof of microbiology 1980–99, head Dept of Genetics and Microbiology 1986–88, vice-princ 1988–90; Leverhulme emeritus fell Center for Biofilm Engrg Montana State Univ 1996–97, guest prof Univ of Marburg 1998 and 2005; keynote lectures at corrosion conferences: Bahrain 1986, Knoxville 1990, Lisbon 1999; chm: Micran Ltd 1982–86, Nat Collections of Industrial and Marine Bacteria Ltd 1983–96, Aberdeen University Research and Industrial Services Ltd 1989–91 (dir 1984–97), UK Nat Cmmn for Microbiology (UKNCM) 1997–99; dir Scotland's Lighthouse Museum Ltd 2004–; Soc for Gen Microbiology: memb Cncl 1972–76 and 1985–89, memb Ctee of Cell Surfaces and Membranes Gp 1973–76, memb Editorial Bd 1981–86, treas 1992–98; treas Int Union Microbiology Soc 1999–2005; memb: Cncl Scottish Assoc for Marine Scis 1987–93 (chm Fellowship and Bursary Ctee 1990–93), Aquatic Life Scis Ctee NERC 1990–93, Biochemical Soc (Ctee of Bioenergetic Orgelle Gp 1975–81), American Soc for Microbiology; FRSE 1980 (convener Biological Sub-Ctee 1990–93, memb Cncl 1991–94), FIBiol 1983 (memb Exec Bd and Cncl 1997–2000); *Publications* incl Bacterial Energetics (SGM symposium, jtly, 1977), Microbiology (contrib, vol 39, 1985), Biofouling (contrib, vol 19, 2003), Sulphate-Reducing Bacteria (jtly, 2005); *Recreations* sailing, fly fishing, wine tasting, skiing; *Style*— Prof Allan Hamilton, FRSE; ✉ Department of Molecular and Cell Biology, Institute of Medical Services, University of Aberdeen, Aberdeen AB25 2ZD (tel 01224 555843, fax 01224 555844, e-mail w.a.hamilton@abdn.ac.uk)

HAMILTON, Andrew; s of Peter Hamilton, of Sussex, and Susie, *née* Blackwell; *b* 15 January 1950; *Educ* Univ Coll Sch, Coll of Estate Mgmnt Univ of Reading; *m* 23 July 1983, Fiona Ann, da of John Scott-Adie, of Perthshire; 2 s (Charles Scott-Adie b 1988, Malcolm Scott-Adie b 1991); *Career* dir: John D Wood SA 1975–77, Haslemere Estates plc 1985–86, Ranelagh Development Ltd 1986–95; Poundbury devpt dir Duchy of Cornwall 1991–, chm The Prince's Regeneration Tst 2004–; FRICS 1986; *Recreations* opera, conservation, France; *Clubs* RAC, Boodle's, Annabel's; *Style*— Andrew Hamilton, Esq, MVO; ✉ c/o Round Hill House, Fawley, Henley-on-Thames, Oxfordshire RG9 6HU (tel 01491 577846)

HAMILTON, Sir Andrew Caradoc; 10 Bt (NS 1646), of Silvertonhill, Lanarkshire; s of Sir (Robert Charles) Richard Caradoc Hamilton, 9 Bt (d 2001); *b* 23 September 1953; *Educ* Charterhouse, St Peter's Coll Oxford (BA); *m* 26 Oct 1984, Anthea Jane, da of Frank Huntingford, of Hindhead, Surrey; 3 da (Alice b 4 Dec 1986, Harriet b 18 March 1989, Imogen Rosie b 6 Nov 1993); *Heir* kinsman, Paul Howden; *Career* schoolmaster 1976–89; tourist attraction prop 1989–; *Recreations* cricket, real tennis, art, music, family; *Clubs*

MCC, Leamington Cricket, Leamington and Moreton Morrell Real Tennis; *Style*— Sir Andrew Hamilton, Bt

HAMILTON, His Hon Judge Andrew N R; s of Robert Bousfield Hamilton (d 1949), and Margery Wensley Iorwerth Hamilton (d 1991); *b* 7 January 1947; *Educ* Cheltenham Coll, Univ of Birmingham (LLB); *m* 17 April 1982, Isobel Louise, *née* Goode; 1 s, 1 da; *Career* called to the Bar 1970; in practice from chambers in Nottingham 1971–2001, recorder of the Crown Court 1999–2001 (asst recorder 1993–99) circuit judge (Midland Circuit) 2001–; external examiner Bar Vocational Course 1997–2000; chm Nottingham Civic Soc 1978–83, chm Nottingham Park Conservation Tst 1992–; memb Nottingham City Cncl 1973–91; Hon Alderman City of Nottingham 1991; *Books* Nottingham's Royal Castle (1976, 5 edn 1999), Nottingham's Caves (1977, 4 edn 2004); *Recreations* tennis, golf, skiing; *Clubs* Nottingham and Notts United Services; *Style*— His Hon Judge Andrew Hamilton; ✉ c/o The Crown Court, The Morledge, Derby DE1 2XE

HAMILTON, Anthony John; *Educ* Dulwich Coll, ChCh Oxford (MA, DPhil); *m* 1977 Angela Jane Lamboll, da of K C L Webb, Esq; *Career* Schroders 1969–72, Morgan Grenfell 1972–76; Wainwright Securities 1976–78, chm Fox-Pitt, Kelton Gp 1994–2003 (joined 1978); chm: AXA Equity & Law plc 1995–, AXA UK plc 2000–; non-exec dir: AXA Financial Inc (NY) 1995–, AXA (Paris) 1996–; dir Club de Golf Valderama 2006–; *Recreations* golf, country pursuits; *Clubs* Royal Ashdown Forest Golf, Royal Wimbledon Golf, Valderrama Golf (Spain), City of London, The Brook (NY); *Style*— Anthony Hamilton, Esq; ✉ AXA UK plc, 5 Old Broad Street, London EC2N 1AD (tel 020 7920 5566)

HAMILTON, Rt Hon Lord Arthur Campbell; PC (2002); s of James Whitehead Hamilton (d 1954), of Glasgow, and Isobel Walker, *née* McConnell (d 1997); *b* 10 June 1942; *Educ* Glasgow HS, Univ of Glasgow, Worcester Coll Oxford (BA), Univ of Edinburgh (LLB); *m* 12 Sept 1970, Christine Ann, da of Thomas Carlyle Croll, of St Andrews, Fife; 1 da (Miranda b 1975); *Career* memb Faculty of Advocates 1968; standing jr counsel: Scot Devpt Dept 1975–78, Bd Inland Revenue (Scot) 1978–82; QC (Scot) 1982; Advocate Depute 1982–85, judge of the Courts of Appeal of Jersey and Guernsey 1988–95, senator of the Coll of Justice 1995–2005, Lord Justice Gen of Scotland and Lord Pres of the Court of Session 2005–; pres Pensions Appeal Tbnls for Scot 1992–95; hon fell Worcester Coll Oxford 2003; *Recreations* hill walking, music, history; *Style*— The Rt Hon Lord Hamilton; ✉ 8 Heriot Row, Edinburgh EH3 6HU (tel 0131 556 4663)

HAMILTON, Caroline; da of Walter Hamilton (d 1988), and Jane, *née* Burrows; *Educ* Perse Sch for Girls Cambridge, Girton Coll Cambridge (BA, Hockey, Cricket and Athletics blues); *Career* ldr first all-women expdn to North Pole McVitie's Penguin North Pole Relay 1997, ldr first Br all-women team to ski to South Pole 2000, memb M&G Investments North Pole Expdn 2002 (becoming first all-women team to ski to both poles); motivational speaker for businesses, lectr and after-dinner speaker, film and TV financier; dir Screen Partners Gp 1993–2004, md Icebreaker Management Ltd 2004–; investment banker: HSBC Samuel Montagu 1985–98, Dresdner Kleinwort Benson 1988–92; mangr under Mental Health Act 1995–; non-exec memb Wandsworth HA 1990–95, non-exec memb Bd Threshold Housing and Support 1996–; memb Cambridge Ospreys Alumni Ctee 2000–; fell British American Project 2003–; *Books* South Pole 2000 (2000), To the Pole (2001); *Recreations* parties, travelling, sport; *Style*— Ms Caroline Hamilton

HAMILTON, David; s of C J Pilditch (d 1967), and Joyce Mary Hamilton (d 1970); *b* 10 September 1938; *m* 1, 1962 (m dis 1977), Sheila Moore; 1 da (Jane b 1963), 1 s (David b 1964); m 2, 1993, Dreena Shrager; *Career* TV and radio presenter; host of more than 12,000 radio shows and 1,000 TV shows; writer weekly column in nat football magazine whilst at school, script-writer ATV 1956 (scripted Portrait of a Star 1957); Nat Serv RAF, broadcaster Br Forces Broadcasting Serv Germany 1959; several appearances in films and maj pantomimes; hon pres Showbiz XI Football Team (memb for twenty years); *Television* continuity announcer: Tyne-Tees TV 1961, ABC TV (Manchester) 1962–68, Thames TV 1968–80; former freelance announcer several ITV stations; host of pop and sports shows, beauty contests and quizzes incl: Top of the Pops, Seaside Special, TV Times Gala Awards, Up for the Cup and All Clued Up ITV 1988–91; *Radio* first broadcast for BBC 1962, presented own daily show on Radio 1 and Radio 2 1973–86, subsequently presenter daily show for Capital Gold Radio London, currently presenter of shows on many radio stations; dir Splash FM; *Books* The Music Game (autobiography, 1986); *Recreations* tennis; *Style*— David Hamilton, Esq; ✉ e-mail mail@davidhamilton.biz, website www.davidhamilton.biz

HAMILTON, David; MP; s of David Hamilton (d 1993), and Agnes Gardner; *b* 24 October 1950; *m* 1 Aug 1969, Jean, da of James Macrae, and Mary Trench; 2 da (Shirley b 28 Sept 1971, Isla b 20 Sept 1975); *Career* coalminer Easthouses Colliery, Bilston Glen Colliery, Rufford Colliery, Notts and Monktonhall Colliery 1965–84 (NUM delegate Monktonhall Colliery 1965–85), supervisor Employment Trg Scheme Midlothian Cncl 1987–89, placement and trg offr Craigmillar Festival Soc 1989–92, chief exec Craigmillar Opportunities Tst 1992–2000, cncllr Midlothian Cncl 1995–2001; MP (Lab) Midlothian 2001–; cabinet memb for strategic services incorporating economic devpt, transportation and strategic planning 1995–2001; memb: House of Commons: Procedures Select Ctee, Broadcasting Select Ctee, Scottish Affrs Select Ctee, Defence Select Ctee, European Scrutiny Ctee, European A Standing Ctee, Exec Ctee Scottish Gp of MPs, All-Pty Non Profit Making Members Club Gp, Br American Parly Gp (BAPG), Singapore Parly Gp, Cwlth Parly Assoc (CPA), Dept for Work and Pension Select Ctee; memb: NUM 1965–; *Style*— Mr David Hamilton, MP; ✉ House of Commons, London SW1A 0AA (e-mail hamiltonda@parliament.uk, website www.davidhamiltonmp.co.uk)

HAMILTON, His Hon Judge Donald Rankin Douglas; s of Allister McNicoll Hamilton (d 1973), and Mary Glen, *née* Rankin (d 1998); *b* 15 June 1946; *Educ* Rugby, Balliol Coll Oxford (BA); *m* 11 May 1974, (Margaret) Ruth, *née* Perrens; 1 da (Sarah Margaret b 2 June 1977), 1 s (Ian Allister b 1 Nov 1979); *Career* called to the Bar Gray's Inn 1969 (Atkin scholar); pupillage 1970–71, in practice 1971–94, recorder 1991–94, head of chambers 3 Fountain Court 1993–94, circuit judge (Midland & Oxford Circuit) 1994–, designated family judge Birmingham 1996–; dir City of Birmingham Symphony Orchestra Soc Ltd 1984–99 (memb Cncl of Mgmnt of the former CBSO Friendly Soc 1974–80); *Recreations* music; *Style*— His Hon Judge Hamilton; ✉ Birmingham Family Courts, 33 Bull Street, Birmingham B4 6DS (tel 0121 681 4441, fax 0121 681 3001)

HAMILTON, Douglas (Doug); *Educ* RCA (MA); *Career* designer Rodolfo Bonetto Milan 1970, sr lectr in interior design Chelsea Sch of Art 1976–84, creative dir Wolff Olins 1995–2002 (memb MBO team 1997), currently global creative dir Hutchison Whampoa; former clients incl: Repsol, First Direct, Orange, Virgin, Goldfish, Channel 5, Go, ONDigital, Open, Sky, Odeon, Ikea, Indesit; speaker at London Business Sch and Domus Acad Italy; *Style*— Doug Hamilton, Esq

HAMILTON, Eben William; QC (1981); s of Rev John Edmund Hamilton, MC (d 1981), of Edinburgh, and Hon Lilias Hamilton, *née* Maclay (d 1966); *b* 12 June 1937; *Educ* Winchester, Trinity Coll Cambridge (MA); *m* 1985, Themy Rusi, da of Brig Rusi Bilimoria (d 1963), of Bellagio, Bombay, India; *Career* 4/7 Royal Dragoon Gds 1955–57, Fife and Forfar Yeo/Scottish Horse TA 1957–68; called to the Bar Inner Temple 1962 (bencher 1985), practising Chancery Bar 1962–, head of chambers 1990–, dep judge of the High Ct (Chancery Division) 1990–; admitted: Hong Kong Bar 1978, Singapore Bar 1982, Cayman Bar 2001; DTI inspector Atlantic Computers plc 1990–93; FRSA 1989; *Clubs* Garrick; *Style*— Eben Hamilton, Esq, QC; ✉ Chesworth House, Horsham, West Sussex RH12 1JR; 6 Stone Buildings, Lincoln's Inn, London WC2A 3XT (tel 020 7242 7650)

HAMILTON, Sir Edward Sydney; 7 Bt (GB 1776), of Marlborough House, Hampshire, and 5 Bt (UK 1819), of Trebinshun House, Brecknockshire; s of Sir (Thomas) Sydney Perceval Hamilton, 6 and 4 Bt (d 1966); *b* 14 April 1925; *Educ* Canford; *Heir* none; *Career* RE 1943–47, 1 Royal Sussex Home Guard 1953–56; *Style*— Sir Edward Hamilton, Bt; ✉ The Cottage, Fordwater Road, East Lavant, Chichester, West Sussex PO18 0AL (tel 01243 527414)

HAMILTON, Fabian; MP; *Career* MP (Lab) Leeds NE 1997–, memb Foreign Affrs Select Ctee 2001–; tstee Nat Heart Research Fund; govr Northern Sch of Contemporary Dance; *Style*— Fabian Hamilton, Esq, MP; ✉ House of Commons, London SW1A 0AA (tel 020 7219 3493, fax 020 7219 4945, e-mail fabian@leedsne.co.uk)

HAMILTON, Francis Rowan Oldfield de Courcy; s of James Percival de Courcy Hamilton (d 1995), of Watlington, Oxon, and Elizabeth Millicent (d 1991), da of Maj-Gen Sir Louis Oldfield, KBE, CB, CMG, DSO; *b* 11 February 1940; *Educ* Winchester, ChCh Oxford; *m* 22 July 1972, Catherine Rae, da of Lt Cdr William Alastair Robertson, CBE, DSC, RN (d 1998), of Gifford, E Lothian; 2 da (Antonia b 1977, Olivia b 1979), 1 s (Thomas b 1983); *Career* The Economist Intelligence Unit 1965–72 (dir Mexico Office from 1967), dir Samuel Montagu & Co Ltd 1978–86; chief of div and sr advsr Int Finance Corp Washington DC 1986–2005; chm: Melrose Arts Tst 2005–06, Borders Book Festival 2006–; dir Penicuik House Preservation Trust Ltd; *Clubs* Travellers, New (Edinburgh), Queen's; *Style*— Francis de C Hamilton, Esq; ✉ Beechwood, Melrose, Roxburghshire TD6 9SW (tel 01896 820000, fax 01896 820011)

HAMILTON, (Alexander) Gordon Kelso; s of Arthur Hamilton Kelso Hamilton (d 1996), of Weybridge, Surrey, and Elizabeth Evelyn, *née* Williams; *b* 27 August 1945; *Educ* Charterhouse, Pembroke Coll Cambridge (MA); *m* 12 July 1980, France Elisabeth Mary Colette, da of Pierre Millet (d 1998), and Elizabeth Millet (d 1984); 1 s (Edward b 1984), 1 da (Georgina b 1986); *Career* chartered accountant; ptnr: Mann Judd 1975–79, (following merger) Deloitte & Touche 1979–2006; memb Financial Reporting Review Panel 2002–; tstee Pembroke Coll Cambridge (The Valence Mary (1997) Endowment Fund) 1985–90; RNID: memb Cncl of Mgmnt 1990–92, memb Fin Ctee 1990–96, tstee 1992–96, hon treas 1993–96; dir St George's Hill Golf Club Ltd 1980–96; tstee and dir Action on Addiction 1996–2007 (hon treas 2002–07); non-exec dir: Beazley Gp plc 2006–, Barloworld Ltd 2007–; FCA; *Recreations* golf; *Clubs* Royal & Ancient, St George's Hill Golf, The Berkshire, Brooks's; *Style*— Gordon Hamilton, Esq; ✉ 51 Chelsea Square, London SW3 6LH

HAMILTON, Jeremy Ian Macaulay (Jim); s of Zachary Macaulay Hamilton (d 1986), and Pamela Lucie, *née* Robson (d 1983); *b* 6 January 1944; *Educ* Canford Sch, Univ of Bristol (LLB); *m* 12 March 1977, Janet Lorna Joanna, da of David Morrice Man (d 1957), of Alresford, Hants; 2 s (James b 1977, Kit b 1979), 1 da (Nina b 1981); *Career* slr Beaumont & Son 1969–70, asst co sec Tioxide plc 1970–73, ptnr Grieveson Grant and Co 1980–85 (joined 1973); dir Dresdner Kleinwort Investment Bank (formerly Kleinwort Benson) 1986–; memb Law Soc 1970; *Recreations* salmon and trout fishing, gardening; *Clubs* Boodle's; *Style*— Jim Hamilton, Esq; ✉ Dresdner Kleinwort Investment Bank, PO Box 52715, 30 Gresham Street, London EC2P 2XY (tel 020 7623 8000)

HAMILTON, His Hon John; s of late Cdr John Ian Hamilton, Knight SMOM, RN, of Bognor Regis, W Sussex, and Margaret Elaine, *née* Rowe (d 1959); *b* 27 January 1941; *Educ* Harrow, Hertford Coll Oxford (MA); *m* 19 Feb 1965, Patricia Ann, da of late Cedric Walter Clive Henman, of Pulham Market, Norfolk; 2 s (Mark b 1967, Rupert b 1969), 1 da (Stephanie b 1972); *Career* called to the Bar Gray's Inn 1965; recorder of the Crown Court 1983, circuit judge (SE Circuit) 1987–2006, ret; English under 18 golf int 1958, winner of Carris trophy 1958; Freeman City of London, Liveryman Worshipful Co of Merchant Taylors; Knight SMOM; *Recreations* golf, bridge, cycling, gardening; *Style*— His Hon John Hamilton

HAMILTON, (John Robert) Leslie; *b* 15 June 1952, Toronto, Canada; *Educ* Lurgan Coll NI, Queen's Univ Belfast (MB BCh, BAO); *m* Joy; 1 s (Stuart b 28 July 1981), 3 da (Suzanne b 5 Sept 1983, Carolyn b 3 July 1986, Fiona b 14 June 1988); *Career* successively: jr house offr Royal Victoria Hosp Belfast, tutor Dept of Physiology Queen's Univ Belfast, sr house offr Belfast, surgical registrar NI, sr surgical registrar Yorks RHA Leeds 1985–91 (incl one year post at Hosp for Sick Children Great Ormond Street 1988–89), conslt cardiac surgn with special interest in congenital heart disease Freeman Hosp Newcastle upon Tyne 1991–; numerous invited lectures, presentations to learned socs and published articles; chm Intercollegiate Examination Bd FRCS C-Th 2004–; memb: BMA, Soc of Cardiothoracic Surgns of GB and I (Exec Ctee), Br Congenital Cardiac Assoc, European Assoc for Cardiothoracic Surgery; FRCS 1981, FRCSEd(C-Th) 1988; *Recreations* family activities, local church; sport - ex athletics and rugby, golf, skiing, sailing (dinghy) and scuba diving; *Style*— Leslie Hamilton, Esq; ✉ Freeman Hospital, High Heaton, Newcastle upon Tyne NE7 7DN (tel 0191 213 7309, fax 0191 223 1314, e-mail leslie.hamilton@nuth.nhs.uk)

HAMILTON, Lewis; *b* 7 January 1985, Stevenage, Herts; *Career* motor racing driver; champion (with ASM F3 Dallara-Mercedes) F3 Euroseries 2005, champion (with ART Grand Prix) GP2 Series 2006, driver (with Vodafone McLaren Mercedes) Formula One 2007– (holds record for most consecutive podium finishes from debut, youngest driver to lead World Championship); grand prix victories: Canada 2007, USA 2007, Hungary 2007; *Style*— Lewis Hamilton, Esq

HAMILTON, Liam; *b* 12 August 1959; *Educ* Univ of Glasgow (MA); *Career* staff journalist STV 1981–84, with Border TV 1984–86 (ed: Answer the Question, Borderlive, Lookaround, Ten Thirty), prodr then news ed Central TV 1986–88 (credits incl: The Time The Place, Donahue in Britain, General Election coverage, Spitting Image), ed This Morning Granada TV 1988–92, ed and exec prodr GMTV 1992–95, dir of broadcasting LWT 1995–98, md LWT 1998–2000, chief operating offr Worldpop 2000–01, controller daytime ITV 2002–06, md Prospect Pictures 2006–; *Style*— Liam Hamilton, Esq

HAMILTON, Michael John; s of William E Hamilton (d 1985), of Guelph, Canada, and Jean, *née* Clark; *b* 24 October 1939; *Educ* Univ of Western Ontario (BA), Univ of Oxford (MA); *m* 20 Sept 1967, Irena, da of Albert Rudusans (d 1962); 1 s (Andrew), 3 da (Katharine, Anna, Nina); *Career* jt md Manufacturers Hanover Ltd 1969–73; exec dir: First Boston Corporation Europe Ltd 1973–78, Blyth Eastman Dillon Inc 1978–79; md Wallace Smith Trust Co Ltd 1980–91, fndr M J Hamilton & Co 1991–97, gp md Banco Finantia 1997–; dir: Midland Expressway Ltd 1992–96, Autostrade International SA 1993–94, Autostrade UK Ltd 1993–96; pres Autostrade International Equity Inc 1993–94; memb: Euro Advsy Bd Nippon Telephone and Telegraph Inc 1986–92, Bd of Mgmnt Dulles Greenway Virginia 1993–94; chm of tstees: Kempton Great Engine Tst, Guildhall Sch Tst; chm Univ of Western Ontario UK Fndn 2007–; *Recreations* tennis, opera, cottage; *Clubs* City of London; *Style*— Michael Hamilton, Esq; ✉ Finantia Securities Ltd, 11 Austin Friars, London EC2N 2HG (tel 020 7382 5200, e-mail michael.hamilton@finantia.com and mmjham16@aol.com)

HAMILTON, Prof Nigel; s of Sir Denis Hamilton (d 1988), and Olive, Lady Hamilton, *née* Wanless; *b* 16 February 1944; *Educ* Westminster, Univ of Munich, Trinity Coll Cambridge (BA, MA); m 1, 1966, Hannelore Pfeifer (d 1973); 2 s (Alexander b 1967, Sebastian b 1970); m 2, 1976 (m dis 2005), Outi Palovesi; 2 s (Nicholas b 1977, Christian b 1980); m 3, 2006, Raynel Shephard; *Career* slave Andre Deutsch Publishing House 1965–66; fndr: The Greenwich Bookshop 1966, The Biography Bookshop 1987; author,

H

lectr and broadcaster 1969–; dir British Inst of Biography 1996–2001; visiting prof Univ of Massachusetts Boston 1989–94, visiting prof of history Royal Holloway Coll London 1995–2000, prof of biography De Montfort Univ 1999–2000; jt chm BIORAMA Real Lives Centre Steering Ctee (project for a nat biographical arts centre) 1996–2000, visiting scholar George Washington Univ 2005, visiting scholar Georgetown Univ 2005; fell John W McCormack Grad Sch of Policy Studies Univ of Massachusetts Boston 2000– *Awards* Whitbread Prize for Best Biography 1981, Templer Award for Best Contrib to Mil History 1987, Blue Ribbon Award for Best Documentary (NY Film and Video Assoc) 1988; *Books* Royal Greenwich (with Olive Hamilton, 1969), The Brothers Mann, The Lives of Heinrich and Thomas Mann (1978), Monty: The Making of a General (1981), Monty: Master of the Battlefield (1983), Monty: The Field-Marshal (1986), Monty, The Man Behind the Legend (1987), JFK: Reckless Youth (1992), Monty: The Battles of Field-Marshal Bernard Montgomery (1994), The Full Monty: Montgomery of Alamein 1887–1942 (2001), Bill Clinton: An American Journey (2003), Montgomery: D-Day Commander (2007), Biography: A Brief History (2007), Bill Clinton: Mastering the Presidency (2007); *Television* writer and narrator of films incl: Monty, In Love and War (BBC TV, 1987), Frontiers, Finland and the Soviet Union (BBC TV, 1989); *Recreations* tennis; *Style*— Prof Nigel Hamilton; ✉ McCormack Graduate School of Policy Studies, UMass Boston, 100 Morrissey Blvd, Boston 02125–3393, USA (tel +1 617 287 5550, fax +1 617 287 5544, e-mail nigel.hamilton@umb.edu)

HAMILTON, Nigel James; *b* 27 March 1941; *Educ* Loretto; *m* 1966, Valerie Joan Moorwood; 1 s (James Andrew b 1968), 1 da (Fiona Allison b 1972); *Career* Graham Proom & Smith Newcastle upon Tyne 1959–64, ptnr Ernst & Young (latterly chm insolvency steering gp) 1975–2000, chm Financial Services Compensation Scheme (FSCS) 2000–; past pres Soc of Practitioners of Insolvency, past chm Insolvency Practitioners' Ctee ICAEW (memb Cncl until 1996); FCA (ACA 1965); *Recreations* rugby football, golf, boats, opera, theatre; *Style*— Nigel J Hamilton, Esq

HAMILTON, Nigel John Mawdesley; QC (1981); s of Archibald Dearman Hamilton, OBE, of 21 Briant's Piece, Hermitage, nr Newbury, Berks, and Joan Worsley, *née* Mawdesley; *b* 13 January 1938; *Educ* St Edward's Sch Oxford, Queens' Coll Cambridge (BA, MA); *m* 31 Aug 1963, Leone Morag Elizabeth, da of William Smith Gordon, CBE; 2 s (Andrew b 5 Oct 1966, William b 18 May 1970); *Career* Nat Serv 2 Lt RE; asst master: St Edward's Sch Oxford 1961–65, King's Sch Canterbury 1963–65; called to the Bar Inner Temple 1965 (bencher 1989); in practice Western Circuit; memb (Cons) Avon CC 1989–93; memb Bar Cncl 1989–93; *Recreations* fishing; *Clubs* Flyfishers'; *Style*— Nigel Hamilton, Esq, QC

HAMILTON, Peter Brian; s of late Lt-Col Brian Hamilton, and Clara Maria, *née* Ertelthaler; *b* 7 February 1941; *Educ* Beaumont Coll, Plymouth Coll of Navigation (Dip); *m* 1 (m dis); 1 s (James Drummond Alexander b 11 Sept 1977); m 2, 1979, Rosalind Mary, da of Bernard James Sanger (d 1990); 1 s (Edward Peter Willoughby b 14 Nov 1980), 1 step da (Amanda Suzanne Jerrom b 25 Aug 1970), 1 step s (Charles Lindsay Jerrom b 11 May 1973); *Career* PR exec; navigating offr Shell Tankers Ltd 1957–60, reporter and feature writer FT 1960–63, Young and Rubicam 1963–75 (exec, account dir, md), dir public affairs Gulf Oil Corporation (Europe Africa and ME) 1975–80, dir Good Relations Group plc 1980–84; md Hill & Knowlton Ltd London 1984–85, gp md/dep chm The Communication Group plc 1985–; winner of various awards for UK community affairs prog for Gulf Oil; author of various articles and essays on public relations; memb Int PR Assoc 1971, FCIPR 1998 (MIPR 1967); *Recreations* sailing, gardening, music, wine; *Clubs* Royal Cornwall Yacht; *Style*— Peter Hamilton, Esq; ✉ Quay House, 2 Tinners Walk, Port Pendennis, Falmouth, Cornwall TR11 3XZ (tel 01326 317471, e-mail peterhamilt@aol.com); The Communication Group plc, 19 Buckingham Gate, London SW1E 6LB (tel 020 7630 1411, fax 020 7931 8010, e-mail phamilton@tcg.pr.co.uk)

HAMILTON, Peter Bryan; s of Brian Hamilton, of Hythe, Hants, and Clara, *née* Marchi (d 2002); *b* 28 August 1956; *Educ* King Edward VI Sch Southampton, ChCh Oxford (MA); *m* 7 Aug 1993, Sylvie, *née* Vulliet; 2 da (Jessica b 29 Jan 1981, Anna b 14 May 1994); *Career* head of French Radley Coll 1981–89, head of modern languages Westminster Sch 1989–96 (also housemaster Wren's), headmaster King Edward VI Sch Southampton 1996–2002, headmaster Haberdashers' Aske's Boys' Sch 2002–; govr: Reddiford Sch, Lochinver House; *Recreations* skiing, hill walking, karate, canoeing, opera; *Clubs* East India; *Style*— Peter Hamilton, Esq; ✉ Haberdashers' Aske's Boys' School, Butterfly Lane, Elstree, Hertfordshire WD6 3AF (tel 020 8266 1700, fax 020 8266 1800, e-mail hm@habsboys.org.uk)

HAMILTON, Sophie; da of Rev Dr P N Hamilton (d 1989), and G M Hamilton, *née* McAndrew; *b* 14 October 1955, London; *Educ* St Mary's Sch Calne, Marlborough, Clare Coll Cambridge (BA); *m* 27 Jan 1990, Prof Peter Goldie; *Career* admitted slr 1979; articled clerk then asst slr Frere Cholmeley 1977–84, ptnr Frere Cholmeley Bischoff 1985–98 (recruitment ptnr 1985–88, trg ptnr 1988–90, head Property Dept 1989–92), ptnr Forsters 1998– (sr ptnr 2002–); memb: Law Soc, Anglo-American Real Property Inst (treas 2006–); chair Nottingham Law Sch Ltd 1991–98 (dir 1998–99), govr Nottingham Trent Univ 1991–98; chair Cheek by Jowl Theatre Co Ltd 1995– (dir 1981–), Freeman City of London, Liveryman Worshipful Co of Goldsmiths; Hon LLD Nottingham Trent Univ; *Recreations* theatre, reading, walking; *Style*— Mrs Sophie Hamilton; ✉ Forsters LLP, 31 Hill Street, London W1J 5LS (tel 020 7863 8333, fax 020 7863 8444, e-mail schamilton@forsters.co.uk)

HAMILTON, Stewart McKee; JP (Sheffield 1972); s of Ian Hamilton (d 1990), of Sheffield, and Marjorie, *née* McKee (d 1994); *b* 12 January 1937; *Educ* Oundle, King's Coll Cambridge (MA); *m* 21 July 1960, Susan Marie, da of late Ernest Lilleyman; 1 s (Bruce b 1 Nov 1962), 2 da (Madeleine b 1 Feb 1964, Tania b 29 June 1967); *Career* Nat Serv cmmnd Sub Lt RN, served Cyprus and Near East 1955–57; Rolls Royce Motors Ltd Crewe 1960–65, Tubewrights Ltd Liverpool 1965–66; T G Lilleyman & Son Ltd Sheffield: prodn dir 1966–76, md 1977–93, chm 1987–99; chm Thornton Precision Forgings Ltd Sheffield 1995–99; chm: Cncl Sheffield Cutlery Research Assoc 1980–94, Central Sheffield Univ Hosps NHS Tst 1995–99 (non-exec dir 1991–95), Sheffield Hosps Charitable Tst 2000–06; High Sheriff S Yorks 1990–91; Freeman: City of London, Worshipful Co of Cutlers in Hallamshire; CEng, FIMechE, FRSA 1995; *Recreations* walking, dry stone-walling, classical music, opera, theatre; *Style*— Stewart Hamilton, Esq; ✉ The Dairy House, Henley Manor, Crewkerne, Somerset TA18 8PQ (tel 01460 271953)

HAMILTON, Her Hon Susan; QC (1993); da of Leslie Edward Hamilton (d 1999), of Hove, E Sussex, and Olive Blossom, *née* King; *b* 30 December 1946; *Educ* Hove GS for Girls, Brighton Tech Coll; *m* 16 April 1977, Dr E P Kelly; 2 s (Thomas b 2 March 1982, Robert Eric b 16 Feb 1984); *Career* called to the Bar 1975; in practice 2 Mitre Court 1975–98, asst recorder 1993, recorder 1995, circuit judge (SE Circuit) 1998–2007; memb RHS; supporter: Barnardos, NSPCC, Nat Tst; *Books* Hamilton on Highways (1981), Halsbury's Laws: Highways vol 21 (1981 and 1995), Rating vol 39 (1982 and 1998); *Recreations* sailing, gardening, reading, music, holidays, travelling; *Clubs* Royal Southern Yacht; *Style*— Her Hon Susan Hamilton, QC; ✉ c/o Bromley County Court, College Road, Bromley, Kent BR1 3PX (e-mail shamilton@lix.compulink.co.uk)

HAMILTON, William McDonald (Bill); s of late Cdr James Hamilton, VRD, RNR, of St Andrews, Fife, Scotland, and Emily, *née* McDonald; *b* 22 September 1943; *Educ* Dundee HS, Monkwearmouth Coll Sunderland; *m* 5 Feb 1972, Gertrude Veronica, da of Michael Lee (d 1963), of Aughrim, Co Wicklow; 1 da (Claire b 1973), 1 s (David b 1980); *Career* reporter/newsreader Tyne Tees TV 1966–70, sports prodr BBC radio 1970–71, reporter/presenter Border TV 1971–73, reporter/presenter BBC TV Scotland 1973–80,

home affrs corr BBC TV News 1981–88, news and sports corr BBC TV News 1988–97, freelance corr/presenter 1997–; vice-pres Anglo-Albanian Assoc; memb Football Referees' Assoc; Paul Harris fell Rotary Int; Order of Mother Teresa (Albania); *Books* I Belong to Glasgow (1975), Albania - Who Cares? (1992); *Recreations* association football referee; *Style*— Bill Hamilton, Esq; ✉ 39 Waverley Road, St Albans, Hertfordshire AL3 5PH (tel 01727 869604, e-mail info@billhamilton.co.uk)

HAMILTON AND BRANDON, 15 and 12 Duke of (S 1643, GB 1711); Angus Alan Douglas Douglas-Hamilton; also Earl of Angus (S 1389), Earl of Arran (S 1503), Marquess of Douglas, Lord Abernethy and Jedburgh Forest (both S 1633), Marquess of Clydesdale, Earl of Arran and Cambridge, Lord Aven and Innerdale (all S 1643), Earl of Lanark, Lord Machansire and Polmont (both S 1661), Baron Dutton (GB 1711); Premier Duke in the Peerage of Scotland; Hereditary Keeper of Holyrood House; 18 Duke of Châtelherault (France 1549); eld s of 14 and 11 Duke of Hamilton and Brandon, KT, GCVO, AFC, PC (d 1973), and Lady Elizabeth Percy, OBE, DL, er da of 8 Duke of Northumberland, KG (d 1930); *b* 13 September 1938; *Educ* Eton, Balliol Coll Oxford (MA); *m* 1, 1972, Sarah Jane (d 1994), da of Sir Walter Scott, 4 Bt (d 1992); 2 da (Lady Eleanor b 1973, Lady Anne b 1976), 2 s (Alexander, Marquess of Douglas and Clydesdale b 1978, Lord John b 1979); *m* 2, 1998, Kay, da of Norman Dutch; *Heir* s, Marquess of Douglas and Clydesdale; *Career* joined RAF 1956, Flt Lt 1963, Flying Instructor 1965, Instrument Rating Examiner 1966, invalided 1967; sr commercial pilot 1968, test pilot Scottish Aviation 1970–72, authorised display pilot 1998; memb EC Sub-Ctee on Energy and Transport 1975–77; memb Queen's Body Guard for Scotland (Royal Co of Archers) 1976–; patron British Airways Pipe Band 1977–, memb Royal Scottish Pipers Soc 1977–, memb Piobaireachd Soc 1979–, memb Cancer Research Campaign 1978–; Hon Air Cdre No 2 (City of Edinburgh) Maritime HQ Unit RAuxAF 1982–93; CEng, MIMechE, KStJ 1974 (Prior for Scotland 1975–82); *Publications* Maria R (1991); *Clubs* New (Edinburgh), RAF; *Style*— Duke of Hamilton; ✉ Lennoxlove House, Haddington, East Lothian EH41 4NZ (tel 01620 828606)

HAMILTON-BURKE, Ian Douglas; s of John Douglas Burke (ka 1944), and Jean Hamilton, *née* Drane; *b* 14 October 1943; *Educ* Liverpool Coll; *m* Joan, da of Harold Planche; 2 s (James Patrick Ian, Andrew Charles Raoul), 1 da (Victoria Roisin); *Career* Poulsoms CAs 1968–86; dir Minster Executive Ltd 1978–86; ptnr: Hodgson Impey CAs 1986–90, Pannell Kerr Forster CAs 1990–91, Hamilton-Burke Dufau Ltd CAs 1991–; dir: Curtins Holdings plc 1990–2003, Curtins Gp plc 1997–2003, Westlink Gp Ltd, Blossom Street Renewal Ltd; fndn memb Liverpool Coll; TEP; FCA, FInstD; *Recreations* hockey, marathon running, fell walking; *Clubs* Liverpool Lyceum Soc; *Style*— Ian Hamilton-Burke, Esq; ✉ Bellisle, Quarry Street, Liverpool L25 6DY (tel 0151 428 3199); Hamilton-Burke Dufau, Gladstone House, 2 Church Road, Liverpool L15 9EG (tel 0151 733 0864, fax 0151 735 0370, e-mail idhb@hbdltd.com)

HAMILTON-DALRYMPLE, Sir Hew Fleetwood; 10 Bt (NS 1698), of North Berwick, Haddingtonshire; GCVO (2001, KCVO 1985, CVO 1974), JP (1987); s of Sir Hew Clifford Hamilton-Dalrymple, 9 Bt (d 1959), and Anne Dorothea Dyce Nicol, *née* Thorne (d 1979); *b* 9 April 1926; *Educ* Ampleforth; *m* 25 Sept 1954, Lady Anne-Louise Mary Keppel; 4 s (Hew Richard b 1955, John James b 1957, Robert George b 1959, William Benedict, qv, b 1965); *Heir* s, Hew Hamilton-Dalrymple; *Career* Maj Grenadier Gds, ret 1962; Queen's Body Guard for Scotland (Royal Co of Archers): Adjt 1964–85, pres Cncl 1988–96, Capt-Gen and Gold Stick for Scotland 1996–2004; dir: Scottish & Newcastle Breweries 1967–86 (vice-chm 1983–86), Scottish American Investment Co 1967–93 (chm 1985–91); HM Lord-Lt East Lothian 1987–2001 (DL 1964–87, Vice Lord-Lt 1973–87); *Clubs* Cavalry and Guards'; *Style*— Major Sir Hew Hamilton-Dalrymple, Bt, GCVO; ✉ Leuchie, North Berwick, East Lothian (tel 01620 89 2903)

HAMILTON-GRIERSON, Philip John; OBE (1994); s of Philip Francis Hamilton Grierson (d 1963), of Edinburgh, and Margaret Bartholomew (d 1969); *b* 10 October 1932; *Educ* Rugby, CCC Oxford (MA); *m* 1963, Pleasaunce Jill, da of Peter Gordon Cardew, of Somerset; 2 da (Sophie b 1964, Katherine b 1966), 1 s (Philip b 1967); *Career* PO RAF (Asst Adjutant 207 AFS); sec to Lib Pty 1962–65; dir Gallaher Ltd 1978–88, dep chm Highlands and Islands Devpt Bd 1988–91, dir Highlands and Islands Enterprise 1991–93; chm: Highland Hospice Ltd 1988–95, Northern Coll 1991–95, State Hospital Carstairs 1991–96, Raigmore NHS Tst Hosp 1997–99, Inverness Coll 2000–03; dir: Investors in People Scotland 1992–2000, AI Welders Ltd 1992–2004, Made in Scotland Ltd 1997–, UHI Millennium Project Ltd 2000–03; *Recreations* tennis, music, sailing; *Style*— Philip Hamilton-Grierson, Esq, OBE; ✉ Pitlundie, North Kessock, by Inverness IV1 3XG (tel 01463 731392, fax 01463 731729)

HAMILTON OF EPSOM, Baron (Life Peer UK 2005), of West Anstey in the County of Devon; Sir Archibald Gavin (Archie) Hamilton; kt (1994), PC (1991); yr s of 3 Baron Hamilton of Dalzell, GCVO, MC, JP (d 1990), and Rosemary Olive, *née* Coke (d 1993); *b* 30 December 1941; *Educ* Eton; *m* 14 Dec 1968, Anne, da of late Cdr Trevelyan Napier, DSC, RN; 3 da; *Career* cncllr London Borough of Kensington & Chelsea 1968–71, MP (Cons) Epsom and Ewell 1978–2001; PPS to: sec of state Energy 1979–81, sec of state Tport 1981–82; asst govt whip 1982–84, lord cmmr to the Treasy 1984–86, Parly under sec of state (Def Procurement) 1986–87, PPS to PM 1987–88, min of state (Armed Forces) Min of Defence 1988–93; chm 1922 Ctee of Cons backbench MPs 1997–2001; dir: Leafield Engineering, Jupiter Dividend and Growth Tst, New Star Global Fund, Specialised Risk Mgmnt, Specialised Investigation Servs, MSB; *Style*— The Rt Hon the Lord Hamilton of Epsom, PC

HAMILTON-SHIELD, Dr Julian Paul; *b* 26 May 1961; *Educ* Clifton, Univ of Bristol (MB ChB, MD); *m* Olivia Plunkett; 1 s (Hugo), 3 da (Antonia, Leonora, Beatrice); *Career* house offr Bristol 1985–86, SHO Bristol and Gt Ormond St Hosp London 1986–90, registrar Queen Elizabeth Hosp for Children and Gt Ormond St Hosp London 1990–92; Univ of Bristol and Bristol Royal Hosp for Children: lectr 1995–97, sr lectr in child health 1997–2006, reader 2006–; Best Practice Award ASO 2005, Clinical Excellence Award BUPA Fndn 2006; FRCP 1987, FRCPCH 1997; *Publications* numerous peer-reviewed papers on diabetes in childhood and related metabolic conditions; *Recreations* my family, sport; *Style*— Dr Julian Hamilton-Shield; ✉ Institute of Child Health, UBHT Education Centre, Upper Maudlin Street, Bristol BS2 8AE

HAMMERBECK, Brig Christopher John Anthony; CB (1991), CBE (2007); s of Sqdn Ldr Olaf Rolf William Hammerbeck (d 1988), of Frinton on Sea, Essex, and Ivy Mary, *née* Musker; *b* 14 March 1943; *Educ* Mayfield Coll; *m* 23 March 1974 (m dis 1996), Alison Mary, da of Capt John Edward Felice, VRD, JP, RNR, of Southport, Lancs; 1 s (Christian b 7 July 1976), 2 da (Lucy b 5 Oct 1977, Leonora b 26 Oct 1984); *Career* articled to firm of slrs 1961–64; cmmnd 1965, Staff Coll 1975, DAA and QMG 12 Mech Bde 1976–78, DS Army Staff Coll 1982–84, CO 2 Royal Tank Regt 1984–87, ACOS G3 HQ 1 BR Corps 1987–88, RCDS 1989, cmd 4 Armd Bde Gulf War 1990–91, dep cdr Br Forces Hong Kong 1992–94, exec dir British C of C 1994–; MIMgt 1981; *Recreations* golf, sailing, cricket, skiing, bobsleigh; *Clubs* Army and Navy, Royal Over-Seas League, Hong Kong; *Style*— Brig Christopher Hammerbeck, CB, CBE

HAMMERSLEY, Paul David; s of Phillip Tom Hammersley, of Lutterworth, Leics, and Lesley Ann, *née* Millage; *b* 22 May 1962; *Educ* Wells Cathedral Sch, Univ of Exeter (BA); *m* 13 Dec 1997, Alexandra Jane, da of Sir Greville Spratt, GBE, TD, JP, DL, qv, 2 da (Mia Theadora b 7 Nov 1998, Saskia Rose b 29 May 2000), 1 s (William Joseph b 5 November 2002); *Career* grad trainee rising to gp account dir Saatchi & Saatchi Advertising London 1984–93, exec vice-pres and gen mangr The Lowe Group NY 1993–96, md Lowe

Howard-Spink London 1996–99, ceo Lowe Lintas 1999–2001, ceo Lowe NY 2001–03, chm and chief exec DDB London 2004–05, ptnr The Red Brick Road 2006–; *Recreations* skiing, shooting; *Style—* Paul Hammersley, Esq; ✉ The Red Brick Road, 50–54 Beak Street, London W1F 9RN

HAMMERSLEY, Philip Tom; CBE (2000, OBE 1989); s of Tom Andrew Hammersley (d 1959), of Buckhurst Hill, Essex, and Winifred Alice, *née* Moyns (d 1970); *b* 10 February 1931; *Educ* Bancroft's Sch, Imperial Coll London (BSc); *m* 24 July 1954, Lesley Ann, da of Norman Stuart Millage; 2 s (Mark Andrew b 10 April 1957, Paul David b 22 May 1962), 1 da (Alison Clare b 18 May 1960); *Career* plant then design engr ICI Plastic Div 1954–65; Clarks Ltd Street Somerset: chief engr 1965–68, prodn servs mangr 1968–70, dir Children's Div 1971–79; pres Stride Rite Footwear Inc (Stride Rite Corp) Boston MA 1979–81; British Shoe Corp Ltd: factories dir 1981–85, dir responsible for mfrg, personnel and info systems 1985–87, md Freeman Hardy Willis and Trueform 1987–89, commercial dir 1989–90; non-exec chm BSS Group plc Leicester 1995–99 (non-exec dir 1991–); chm: Cncl Shoe and Allied Trades Research Assoc 1983–86, E Midlands Regnl Cncl CBI 1988–90; pres Br Footwear Mfrs Fedn 1986–87; vice-chm Leics HA 1990–92; chm: Leicester Royal Infirmary NHS Tst 1992–97, Trent Regnl Office NHS Exec 1997–99, Univ Hosps of Leicester NHS Tst 2000–06; memb Cncl Univ of Leicester 1991–2004; tstee National Space Science Centre 1997–2001 and 2006–, chm National Space Science Centre (Operations) Ltd 2001–; Freeman City of London, Liveryman Worshipful Co of Pattenmakers 1983; Hon DBA De Montfort Univ 1999; CEng, MIMechE 1961, FRSA 1993; *Clubs* MCC, East India; *Style—* Philip Hammersley, Esq, CBE; ✉ The Hollies, Wibtoft, Lutterworth, Leicestershire LE17 5BB (tel 01455 220363)

HAMMICK, Sir Stephen George; 5 Bt (UK 1834), of Cavendish Square, London; OBE (2004), DL (Dorset 1989); s of Sir George Frederick Hammick, 4 Bt (d 1964), and Mary Adeliza, *née* Welch-Thornton (d 1988); *b* 27 December 1926; *Educ* Stowe, RAC Cirencester; *m* 16 April 1953, Gillian Elizabeth, yr da of Maj Pierre Elliot Inchbald, MC (d 1959); 2 s (Paul St Vincent b 1955, Jeremy Charles b 1956), 1 da (Wendy Jane (Mrs Bob Koster) b 1960); *Heir* s, Paul Hammick; *Career* RN 1944–48, RAC Cirencester 1949–50, MFH Cattistock Hunt 1961 and 1962, CC Dorset 1958, farmer; High Sheriff Dorset 1981; vice-chm Dorset CC (chm 1988), chm Dorset Police Force; chm Cattistock Hunt; *Recreations* hunting, fishing, music; *Style—* Sir Stephen Hammick, Bt, OBE, DL; ✉ Badgers, Wraxall, Dorchester, Dorset DT2 0HN (tel 01935 83343)

HAMMON, Michael Antony; s of Arthur Stanley Hammon (d 1985), and Mary Augusta, *née* Salter (d 1993); *b* 5 March 1937; *Educ* Oundle; *m* 8 Oct 1966 (m dis 1993), Letitia Sara, da of Henry Leslie Johnson (d 1991); 2 s (Charles b 1969, George b 1973), 2 da (Sara b 1970, Elizabeth b 1972); *Career* slr and farmer; in practice Hammon Oakley; cncllr: Warwick RDC 1965–70, Warks CC 1967–81 (chm Finance, Educn and Policy and Resources Ctees, ldr of Cncl 1976–81), Coventry City Cncl 1987–96; vice-chm Warwick, Leamington and Kenilworth Cons Assoc 1970–73, lawyer memb W Midlands Rent Assessment Panel 1982–86, press and PR offr Warks Law Soc 1984–89; chm Edenhurst Court (Torquay) Ltd 1998–, dir H H Goddard Ltd; *Recreations* gardening, photography; *Clubs* Naval and Military; *Style—* Michael Hammon, Esq; ✉ Hammon Oakley, 403 Walsgrave Road, Coventry CV2 4AH (tel 024 7644 8585, fax 024 7644 1611, e-mail hammon@hammonoakleysolicitors.co.uk)

HAMMOND, Sir Anthony Hilgrove; KCB (2000, CB 1992), QC (1997); s of Col Charles William Hilgrove Hammond (d 1985), and Jessie Eugenia, *née* Francis (d 1940); *b* 27 July 1940; *Educ* Malvern, Emmanuel Coll Cambridge (open scholar, MA, LLM); *m* 29 Sept 1988, Avril, *née* Collinson; *Career* admitted slr 1965, asst slr GLC (formerly London CC) 1965–68 (articled clerk 1962–65); Home Office: legal asst 1968–70, sr legal asst 1970–74, asst legal advsr 1974–80, princ asst legal advsr to Home Office and NI Office 1980–88, dep under sec of state and legal advsr 1988–92 (legal advsr NI Office 1988–92); slr DTI 1992–97; procurator gen and Treasy slr 1997–2000; standing counsel to Gen Synod C of E 2000–; Freeman City of London 1991, Liveryman Worshipful Co of Glass Sellers 1992 (memb Ct of Assts 2000); *Recreations* bridge, music, birdwatching; *Clubs* Athenaeum; *Style—* Sir Anthony Hammond, KCB, QC; ✉ The White Cottage, Blackheath, Guildford, Surrey GV4 8RB (tel 01483 892607)

HAMMOND, Dr Brian Robert; s of Dennis Francis Hammond, of Rustington, W Sussex, and Iris Margaret Rose Hammond; *b* 28 May 1953; *Educ* Battersea GS, Anglo-Euro Coll of Chiropractic (DC, Canadian Award for Academic Distinction), Univ of Surrey (PhD); *m* 5 Nov 1975, Elizabeth-Jane, da of David Frederick Vincent Craig; 1 da (Samantha Danielle b 26 July 1978), 1 s (Daniel Michael b 29 June 1980); *Career* practising chiropractor; clinic dir Sutton Chiropractic Clinic 1975–, ed Euro Jl of Chiropractic 1976–80, govr Anglo-Euro Coll of Chiropractic 1976–80, memb Gen Cncl Euro Chiropractors' Union 1976–80, external lectr Anglo-Euro Coll of Chiropractic 1980–, external examiner CNAA 1989–92, memb Euro Cncl on Chiropractic Educn 1989–96; memb Br Chiropractic Assoc 1975– (treas 1987–89), Soc for Back Pain Res 1977–, Nat Back Pain Assoc 1977–; *Books* The Detection of Spondylolysis using Lumbar Sonography (1984); *Recreations* bridge, badminton; *Clubs* New Malden Bridge; *Style—* Dr Brian Hammond; ✉ Sutton Chiropractic Clinic, 137 Brighton Road, Sutton, Surrey SM2 5SW (tel 020 8661 1613, fax 020 8770 9517)

HAMMOND, Donald William; *b* 5 March 1948; *Educ* King's Sch Macclesfield, Lancaster Univ (BA), Manchester Business Sch (DBA); *m* 19 March 1982, Carole Isobel Hammond; *Career* T & N plc 1969–73, Citibank NA 1974–76, Banco Hispano Americano Ltd 1976–86; dir: Edington plc 1986–90, Henry Cooke Group plc 1988–90, Waterwise Technology Ltd 1993–; chm: Halton Gen Hosp Tst 1993–2000, Cheshire Community Healthcare NHS Tst 2000–02, TrusTECH 2001–; chm Fin Ctee and dep ldr London Borough of Ealing 1983–86 (cncllr 1978–86), chm Great Budworth Parish Cncl 1999–2007; chm Gt Budworth Church Restoration Tstees; various co sec roles; FInstD, FRSA; *Recreations* riding, shooting, venture capital, Bordeaux wine; *Style—* Donald Hammond, Esq; ✉ The Butts, Smithy Lane, Great Budworth, Northwich, Cheshire CW9 6HL (e-mail don@don-hammond.com)

HAMMOND, Prof Geoffrey Paul; s of Jack Hammond (d 1997), of Bognor Regis, W Sussex, and Alice Kate, *née* Elliott; *b* 3 May 1946; *Educ* South Bank Univ, Univ of Brighton, Cranfield Univ (MSc); *m* 1974, Judith Anne, da of Llewellyn Williams; 1 da (Katherine Lucy b 1976), 1 s (Benjamin David b 1978); *Career* refrigeration engineer 1963–68; design and devpt engr 1968–71; VSO lectr Uganda Tech Coll 1971–72; Dept of Applied Energy Cranfield Univ: research offr 1975, lectr 1976, sr lectr 1985, reader 1989; Univ of Bath: British Gas prof of environmental engrg 1990–94, head Sch of Architecture and Building Engrg 1992–94, prof of mechanical engrg 1995–, dir Int Centre for the Environment (ICE) 2003–; memb: Lab Pty 1974–, EPSRC/SERC panels covering the built environment, computational modelling and post grad training 1985–, Bradford on Avon Oxfam Gp 1991–, B & NES Local Agenda 21 1996–97, Environment Agency's N Wessex Area Environment Gp 1998– 2006(dep chm 2000–04, chm 2004–06); patron Bath Environment Centre 1994– (fndr tstee 1995–98); chair Combe Down Stone Mines Community Assoc 2000–02, tste and memb Cncl Wilts Wildlife Tst 2004–, chair Swindon Climate Change Action Plan Steering Gp 2005–, memb (environment rep) Swindon Strategic Partnership 2005–; Dufton Silver Medal CIBSE 1985, Willem van Gool Meml Lecture Economics and Mgmnt of Energy in Industry (ECEMEI) 3rd European Congress Estoril 2004; CEng, FIMechE 1999 (MIMechE 1973); *Publications* Contributions to professional journals and conference proceedings in the areas of energy systems and environmental sustainability and fluid flow, heat transfer and thermodynamics; *Recreations* science/science fiction, hill walking, community activities; *Clubs* Bradford on Avon Film Soc; *Style—* Prof Geoffrey Hammond; ✉ Department of Mechanical Engineering, University of Bath, Claverton Down, Bath, Avon BA2 7AY (tel 01225 386168, fax 01225 386928, e-mail ensgph@bath.ac.uk)

HAMMOND, Jane Dominica; da of Reginald Egbert Rolt Hammond (d 1967), and Nancy Mildred, *née* Hawtrey (d 1983); *b* 6 April 1934; *Educ* Queen Anne's Sch Caversham, Hampstead Secretarial Coll, CAM (Dip PR); *m* 1970, Rudolph Samuel Brown, JP (d 1986); 1 da (Louisa Catherine b 5 March 1974); *Career* secretarial work Publicity Dept BBC and latterly Press Office Swissair 1953–61, asst ed Dairy Industries 1961–64; NALGO (now UNISON): reporter Public Service (newspaper) 1964–65, Health Service PRO 1965–68; PRO St Teresa's Hosp 1968–70; sr info offr: London Borough of Hammersmith 1971–73, Community Rels Cmmn 1973–77 and its successor body Cmmn for Racial Equality 1977–78; ed Hollis PR Weekly 1978–80; chm and md Trident Public Relations Ltd 1980–2003, prop Trident Training Services 1988– (launched for client Afro Hair & Beauty annual exhbn in 1983 and ran it again in 1984 and 1985); memb Cncl IPR 1965–68, 1969–71 and 1995–97 (vice-chm Educn and Trg Ctee 1994–97, vice-chm Int Gp 2001–), chm IPRA Cncl UK 2000–02, millennium fndr memb Guild of PR Practitioners; memb PR Educators' Forum; memb Ethics Ctee and Press and PR Industrial Cncl NUJ 2004–; examiner CAM 1977–95, asst course dir annual Sr Int PR Courses 1991–96, lectr Westminster Coll 1991–, tutor PR Educn Tst (PRET) Distance Learning Prog 1991–, jt course dir annual int introductory and advanced PR courses RIPA International 1994–2003, external moderator 1995–99, course dir London Corp Trg Courses 1998–, examiner Holborn Coll 1999–2002, lectr Birkbeck Coll 1999–2000; NVQ assessor 1998–; memb Quaker Outreach London Ctee 1998–; fndr memb Women's National Cancer Control Campaign; memb NUJ, FIPR 1981 (MIPR 1968), MIPRA 1996, FCAM 2000; *Publications* contrib chapter in The Practice of Public Relations (ed S Black, 1995), Government Relations with the Public in Romania (1998); *Recreations* reading, cooking, cycling, swimming, dog (as daughter Louisa in America); *Clubs* Rotary Putney (pres 2000–01), Soc of Friends (Quakers); *Style—* Miss Jane Hammond; ✉ Trident Training Services, Suite 5, 155 Fawe Park Road, London SW15 2EG (tel and fax 020 8874 3610, e-mail trident@btconnect.com, website www.tridenttraining.co.uk)

H

HAMMOND, (John) Martin; s of Rev Canon Thomas Chatterton Hammond, Rector of Beckenham (d 1981), and Joan, *née* Cruse; *b* 15 November 1944; *Educ* Winchester, Balliol Coll Oxford; *m* 25 June 1974, Meredith Jane, da of Kenneth Wesley Shier, of Ontario, Canada; 1 s (Thomas b 1976), 1 step da (Chantal b 1970); *Career* asst master St Paul's Sch 1966–71, teacher Anargyrios Sch Spetsai Greece 1972–73, asst master Harrow Sch 1973–74, master in coll Eton Coll 1980–84 (head Classics Dept 1974–80); headmaster: City of London Sch 1984–90, Tonbridge Sch 1990–2005; *Books* Homer - The Iliad, A New Prose Translation (1987), Homer - The Odyssey (trans, 2000), The Meditations of Marcus Aurelius (trans and notes, 2006); *Style—* Martin Hammond, Esq; ✉ Shepherds' Hey, Hundon Road, Barnardiston, Haverhill, Suffolk CB9 7TJ (tel 01440 786441)

HAMMOND, Prof Norman David Curle; s of William Hammond, and Kathleen Jessie, *née* Howes; *b* 10 July 1944; *Educ* Varndean GS, Peterhouse Cambridge (Trevelyan scholar, Dip Classical Archaeology, MA, PhD, ScD); *m* 1972, Dr Jean Wilson, FSA, *qv*, da of Alan Wilson, and Beryl, *née* Wagstaff; 1 s (Gawain Jonathon Curle b 2 Dec 1975), 1 da (Deborah Julian Curle b 13 Sept 1982); *Career* Univ of Cambridge: research fell Centre of Latin American Studies 1967–71, Leverhulme research fell Centre of Latin American Studies 1972–75, research fell Fitzwilliam Coll 1973–75; sr lectr Univ of Bradford 1975–77, visiting prof of anthropology Univ of Calif Berkeley 1977; Rutgers Univ USA: visiting prof 1977–78, assoc prof 1978–84, prof of archaeology 1984–88; visiting prof Jilin Univ Changchun China 1981, Irvine chair of anthropology Calif Acad of Sciences 1984–85, Curl lectr RAI 1985, visiting prof Univ de Paris Sorbonne 1987, fell in pre-Columbian studies Dumbarton Oaks Washington 1988, assoc in Maya archaeology Peabody Museum Harvard Univ 1988–, prof of archaeology Boston Univ 1988– (chm 2005–07), visiting fell Worcester Coll Oxford 1989, academic tstee Archaeological Inst of America 1990–93, visiting fell Peterhouse Cambridge 1991 and 1996–97, visiting prof Rheinische-Wilhelms-Universität Bonn 1994, visiting fell McDonald Inst for Archaeological Research Univ of Cambridge 1997 and 2004, Rockefeller Fndn scholar 1997, visiting fell All Souls Coll Oxford 2004, visiting fell Clare Hall Cambridge 2004; Bushnell lectr Univ of Cambridge 1997, Stone lectr Archaeological Inst of America 1997–98, Brush lectr 2001, Brunswick distinguished lectr Metropolitan Museum 2001, Borowski lectr 2002, Reckitt lectr Br Acad 2006; archaeology corr The Times 1967–, memb Editorial Bds various archaeological jls in UK and USA, contrib to various scientific jls, ed Afghan Studies 1976–79, consltg ed Library of Congress (HLAS) 1977–89, archaelogy conslt Scientific American 1979–95, memb various advsy bds Belize 1987–; excavations and surveys: Libya/Tunisia 1964, Afghanistan 1966, Belize 1970– (Lubaantun 1970, Nohmul 1973–86, Cuello 1976–2002, La Milpa 1992–2002), Ecuador 1972–84; Hon Phi Beta Kappa 1989, Hon DSc Univ of Bradford 1999; FSA 1974 (memb Cncl 1996–99, Soc Medal 2001), FBA 1998; *Publications* South Asian Archaeology (ed, 1973), Mesoamerican Archaeology New Approaches (ed, 1974), Lubaantun: a Classic Maya Realm (1975), Social Process in Maya Prehistory (ed, 1977), The Archaeology of Afghanistan (ed with F R Allchin, 1978), Maya Archaeology and Ethnohistory (ed with G R Willey, 1979), Ancient Maya Civilization (1982, 5 edn 1994), Archaeology Proceedings (gen ed, 8 vols), 44th International Congress of Americanists (1983–84), Nohmul: a prehistoric Maya community in Belize - Excavations 1973–1983 (1985), Cuello: an early Maya community in Belize (1991), The Maya (2000); *Recreations* fine wine, intelligent women, opera; *Clubs* Athenaeum, Tavern (Boston); *Style—* Prof Norman Hammond, FSA, FBA; ✉ Wholeway, Harlton, Cambridge CB3 7ET (tel and fax 01223 262376); 83 Ivy Street, Apartment 32, Brookline, Massachusetts 02446–4073, USA (tel 00 1 617 739 9077, fax 00 1 617 353 6800)

HAMMOND, Philip; MP; s of Bernard Hammond, and Doris Hammond; *b* 4 December 1955; *Educ* Shenfield Sch Brentwood, UC Oxford (open scholar, MA); *m* 1991, Susan Carolyn, da of Mr and Mrs E Williams-Walker; 2 da (Amy Victoria Louise b 9 Sept 1994, Sophie Elizabeth Alice b 10 Oct 1996), 1 s (William Oliver James b 13 May 1999); *Career* asst to chm then marketing mangr Speywood Laboratories 1977–81, dir Speywood Medical Ltd 1981–83, established and ran medical equipment distribution business 1983–94 (concurrently dir various medical equipment manufacturing companies UK and Europe); dir: Castlemead Ltd 1984–2004, Castlemead Homes Ltd 1994–2004, Consort Resources Ltd 2000–03; ptnr CMA Consultants 1993–95, conslt to Govt of Malawi 1995–97; MP (Cons) Runnymede and Weybridge 1997– (Parly candidate (Cons) Newham NE 1994); memb Environment Tport and Regions Select Ctee 1997–98; oppn frontbench spokesman on: health and social servs 1998–2001, trade and industry 2001–02, local and regnl govt 2002–05; shadow chief sec to Treasy 2005, shadow sec of state for work and pensions 2005–07, shadow chief sec to the Treasy 2007–; memb Trade and Industry Select Ctee 2002; *Clubs* Carlton, Weybridge Conservative; *Style—* Philip Hammond, Esq, MP; ✉ House of Commons, London SW1A 0AA (tel 020 7219 4055, fax 020 7219 5851)

HAMMOND, His Hon Judge Simon Tristram; s of Philip Jones Hammond (d 1986), of Leicester, and Sylvia Dina, *née* Sillem (d 1988); *b* 5 January 1944; *Educ* Eastbourne Coll, Coll of Law; *m* 10 July 1976, Louise, da of Charles Duncan Weir, FRCS, MC; 2 da (Pollyann Lucy b 8 Feb 1980, Alicia Francesca b 18 Nov 1992), 1 s (Edward Charles b 2 Aug 1981); *Career* articled to Philip Jones Hammond 1962–67, admitted as slr 1967, ptnr Victor Lissack London 1970–76, ptnr Philip J Hammond & Sons Leicester 1977–93, recorder 1990–93 (asst recorder 1985–90), circuit judge (Midland & Oxford Circuit) 1993–; memb: Law Soc's Standing Ctee on Criminal Law 1982–91, Crown Court Rules Ctee 1988–93, Enforcement Sub-Ctee Home Office Review of Magistrates' Court Procedure 1989–90, Coll of Law Advsy Bd 1992; asst cmmr to Parly Boundary Cmmn for England 1992; church warden; *Recreations* riding, skiing, vegetable gardening, food and wine; *Style*— His Hon Judge Simon Hammond; ✉ Department for Constitutional Affairs, Midland Circuit Office, Priory Court, 33 Bull Street, Birmingham B4 6DW (tel 0121 681 3200)

HAMMOND, Stephen; MP; *b* 4 February 1962, Southampton; *Educ* King Edward VI Sch, QMC Univ of London; *m* 1991, Sally; 1 da (Alice); *Career* dir UK equities Dresdner Kleinwort Benson Securities 1994–98; Commerzbank Securities: joined 1998, dir pan European research 2000–; MP (Cons) Wimbledon 2005– (Parly candidate (Cons): N Warks 1997, Wimbledon 2001), shadow tport min 2005–; cncllr Merton BC 2002–06; *Style*— Stephen Hammond, Esq, MP; ✉ House of Commons, London SW1A 0AA (e-mail hammonds@parliament.uk, website www.stephenhammondmp.co.uk)

HAMMOND, Suzanna Mary; *Educ* Convent of St Clotilde Lechlade, Portsmouth Coll of FE (Dip Business Studies), Univ of Sussex/Regent St Poly (Business Communications and Journalism Degree); *m*; 3 s; *Career* account exec Good Relations Ltd 1969–72, assoc dir heading Consumer Products Div Lexington International 1975–82 (account dir 1972–75), dep md Hill & Knowlton (UK) Ltd (following merger with Lexington International) 1985–87 (dir Consumer Mktg Gp 1982–84), md Ogilvy Adams & Rinehart 1987–93, chief exec Hammond PR 1993–; *Style*— Ms Suzanna Hammond

HAMMOND, Valerie June; da of Stanley F Amas (d 1972), and Eileen M Amas (d 1995); *b* 22 October 1942; *Educ* Pendergast GS, Open Univ (BA); *m* 1982, A Knighton Berry; *Career* previously: project mangr Petroleum Industry Trg Bd, Mobil Oil, Friden Ltd, Rank Screen Servs; Roffey Park Inst: chief exec 1993–2003, chair 2003–; dir Ashridge Management Research Group 1980–93; memb Camelot Advsy Panel on Social Responsibility; dir and govr Kings Int Coll; tstee: Action Medical Research, Kingshurst Tst; memb: European Foundation for Management Development (EFMD), European Women's Management Development (EWMD); author; CIMgt, FRSA, MInstD; *Publications* Employment Potential - Issues in the Development of Women (with Ashridge team, 1980), The Computer in Personnel Work (with Edgar Wille, 1981), Tomorrow's Office Today (with David Birchall, 1981), No Barriers Here? (1982), Practical Approaches to Women's Management Development (1984), Current Research in Management (1985), Men and Women in Organisations (with Tom Boydell, 1985), INTERMAN Management Innovation Programme (1995); book chapters and jl articles from research and conferences; *Style*— Ms Valerie Hammond; ✉ Roffey Park Institute, Forest Road, Horsham, West Sussex RH12 4TB (tel 01293 854032, fax 01293 851565, e-mail val.hammond@roffeypark.com)

HAMMONDS, Peter James Scott; *b* 1 February 1954; *Educ* Douglas HS for Boys Isle of Man, Bedford Coll London (BA), LSE (MSc); *m* 27 Sept 1980, Hazel Frances; 2 da (Sophie Elizabeth b 27 June 1985, Henrietta Ellen b 21 Aug 1990); *Career* Sec and Slr's Office Central Electricity Generating Bd 1977–79; Lloyds Bank plc: joined Sec's Dept 1979, asst sec 1981–87, dep sec 1987–91, sec Lloyds Merchant Bank Ltd 1985–91; co sec National Westminster Bank plc 1991–; non-exec dir Proshare; ICSA: dep chm Co Secs' Forum, elected memb Cncl, vice-pres UK Cncl, treas and vice-pres Int Cncl, memb Int Disciplinary Tbnl, chm Admissions Ctee; assoc memb IOD (memb Professional Standards Ctee and Chartered Accreditation Bd); 3 times prizewinner for Gilbert Lectures on Banking; FRGS 1977, FCIS 1991 (ACIS 1980); *Recreations* heavy gardening; *Style*— Peter Hammonds, Esq; ✉ c/o Conister Trust plc, 16–18 Finch Road, Douglas, Isle of Man IM1 2PT

HAMNETT, Prof Andrew; s of Albert Edward Hamnett (d 1990), and Dorothy Grace, *née* Stewart (d 2000); *b* 12 November 1947; *Educ* William Hulme's GS Manchester, UC Oxford (open scholar, MA), St John's Coll Oxford (chemistry senior scholar, DPhil); *m* 2 April 1976, Suzanne Marie, da of Charles Parkin (d 1993); 3 da (Erica b 1979, Hilary, Gillian (twins) b 1981); *Career* jr research fell The Queen's Coll Oxford 1972–77, Killam research fell Univ of British Columbia 1974–76; Univ of Oxford: departmental research asst Inorganic Chemistry Lab 1977–80, lectr in inorganic chemistry 1980–89, successively fell by special election, fell then dean St Catherine's Coll 1980–89; Univ of Newcastle Upon Tyne: prof of physical chemistry 1989–2000, pro-vice-chllr 1993–97, dep vice-chllr 1997–2000; currently princ and vice-chllr Univ of Strathclyde; memb then chm Physical Chemistry Sub-Ctee SERC 1988–94, dep chm Chemistry Ctee EPSRC 1993–94; FRSC 1991, FRSA 1997, FRSE 2002; *Books* Techniques and Mechanisms in Electrochemistry (with P A Christensen, 1994), Electrochemistry (with Carl Hamann and Wolf Vielstich, 1998); *Recreations* music (organist and pianist), languages, philately; *Clubs* Athenaum, Caledonian; *Style*— Prof Andrew Hamnett; ✉ University of Strathclyde, 16 Richmond Street, Glasgow G1 1XQ (tel 0141 548 2099, fax 0141 553 1521)

HAMPDEN, 6 Viscount (UK 1884); Anthony David Brand; DL (E Sussex 1986); s of 5 Viscount Hampden (d 1975), and Hon Imogen Rhys (d 2001), da of 7 Baron Dynevor (d 1956); *b* 7 May 1937; *Educ* Eton; *m* 1, 27 Sept 1969 (m dis 1988), Cara Fiona, da of Capt Claud Proby, Irish Gds (d 1987), 2 s of Sir Richard Proby, 1 Bt, MC, JP, DL; 2 s (Hon Francis Anthony b 17 Sept 1970, Hon Jonathan Claud David Humphrey b 25 Aug 1975), 1 da (Hon Saracha Mary b 7 March 1973); m 2, 21 Oct 1993, Mrs Sally Snow, of Battersea, London, yst da of Sir Charles Jocelyn Hambro, KBE, MC (d 1963); *Heir* s, Hon Francis Brand; *Career* Lazard Brothers Co 1956–69, Hoare Govett 1970–82, land agent Glynde Estates 1984–2002; chm Govrs Emanuel Sch 1985–2004; pres Sussex branch CLA 2001– (chm 1985–88), chm SE England Regnl Ctee HHA 2001–05; *Books* Henry and Eliza, A Glimpse of Glynde; *Clubs* White's; *Style*— The Rt Hon the Viscount Hampden, DL; ✉ Glynde Place, Glynde, Lewes, East Sussex BN8 6SX (tel 01273 858337)

HAMPEL, Sir Ronald Claus; kt (1995); s of Karl Victor Hugo Hampel (d 1960), and Rutgard Emil Klothilde, *née* Hauck (d 1975); *b* 31 May 1932; *Educ* Canford Sch, CCC Cambridge (MA); *m* 11 May 1957, Jane Bristed, da of Cdr Wilfred Graham Hewson, RN, of Wellington, Somerset; 1 da (Katharine b 1958), 3 s (Andrew b 1960, Rupert b 1962, Peter b 1962); *Career* Nat Serv 2 Lt 3 RHA 1951–52; ICI plc: joined 1955, vice-pres Americas 1973–77, gen mangr Commercial Gp 1977–80, chm Paints Div 1980–83, chm Agrochemicals 1983–85, bd dir 1985–99, chief operating offr 1991–93, chief exec and dep chm 1993–95, chm 1995–99; chm United Business and Media plc 1999–2002; non-exec dir: Powell Duffryn plc 1984–89, Commercial Union 1987–95, BAE Systems plc 1989–2002, Alcoa (USA) 1995–2005, Templeton Emerging Markets Investment Tst plc 2003– (chm 2004–); memb: Br N American Ctee 1986–96 (Exec Ctee 1989), Bd American C of C 1988–91, Int Assoc for the Promotion and Protection of Private Foreign Investments (APPI), Exec Ctee European Roundtable 1995–99, Listed Cos Advsy Ctee London Stock Exchange 1995–99, Nomination Ctee New York Stock Exchange 1996–98; chm Ctee on Corp Governance 1995–98; chm of tstees Eden Project 2000–; hon fell CCC Cambridge 1996; CIMgt 1985–99; *Recreations* skiing, tennis, golf; *Clubs* All England Lawn Tennis (memb Ctee 1995–), MCC, Royal & Ancient; *Style*— Sir Ronald Hampel

HAMPSHIRE, John Harry; s of John Hampshire, and Vera Alden, *née* Windows; *b* 10 February 1941, Thurnscoe, S Yorks; *Educ* Oakwood Tech HS Rotherham, Sheffield Coll of Arts and Crafts; *m* 1, Sept 1964, Judith Ann (d 2002); 2 s (Ian Christopher b 6 Jan 1969, Paul Wesley b 12 Feb 1972); m 2, Dec 2004, Alison Mary; *Career* cricketer and umpire; former player with: Yorkshire CCC, Tasmania, Leicestershire CCC, Derbyshire CCC; England: 8 test caps, 3 one day int appearances, test debut v WI 1969; as umpire: 21 test matches, 20 one day int matches, test debut England v Aust 1989; memb Int Cricket Cncl Panel 1999–2002; *Publications* Family Argument (1982); *Recreations* golf, gardening, cooking, watching most sports; *Style*— John Hampshire, Esq; ✉ c/o English Cricket Board, Lord's Cricket Ground, London NW8 8QZ (mobile 07831 328890, e-mail jhhampshire@talk21.com)

HAMPSHIRE, Prof Michael John; CBE (1987); *b* 13 October 1939; *Educ* Heckmondwike GS, Univ of Birmingham (BSc, PhD); *m* 1962, Mavis, *née* Oakes; 1 da (Julie Louise b 1972); *Career* Univ of Salford: lectr 1964–71, sr lectr 1971–78, prof of solid state electronics 1978–83, prof of electronic info technol 1983–, chm Dept of Electronic and Electrical Engrg 1981–89, asst md Salford University Business Services (SUBS) Ltd tech conslts 1989–95; dir: SUBS Ltd 1989–98, Vertec Ltd 1991–98 (fndr chm 1981–91, co awarded N of England first prize in BTG Academic Enterprise Competition 1982), Cedeta Research Ltd 1991–92; conslt: Ferranti Semiconductors Ltd 1970–74, Volex Group plc 1977–99, Thorn EMI 1980–88; fndr chm: Mgmnt Ctee Calderdale Industrial Microelectronics Centre 1984–88, Mgmnt Ctee NW Microelectronics Awareness Prog 1986–89; chm: Mgmnt Ctee Microelectronics Awareness Scheme 1983–86, R&D Ctee Volex Group plc 1988–92; memb: SERC Nat Mgmnt Ctee for Teaching Company Scheme 1983–88, AMTEC Jt Bd of Studies 1986–88, Mgmnt Ctee Software Servs Div SUBS Ltd 1986–89; Techmart Technol Transfer Trophy 1984; author of numerous papers, theses and reports; Hon MIED 1981; FInstP 1971–2001, FIEE 1984–2001, CEng 1984, CPhys 1984, Hon FIED 2001; *Recreations* music, golf; *Style*— Prof Michael Hampshire, CBE; ✉ University of Salford Enterprises Ltd, Technology House, Lissadel Street, Salford, Manchester M6 6AP (tel 0161 257 2700, fax 0161 257 2701)

HAMPSHIRE, Susan; OBE (1995); da of George Kenneth Hampshire (d 1964), and June Hampshire (d 1967); *Educ* Hampshire Sch Knightsbridge; *m* 1, 1967 (m dis 1974), Pierre Julian Granier-Deferre; 1 s, 1 da (decd); m 2, 1981, Sir Eddie Kulukundis, OBE, *qv*; s of George Elias Kulukundis (d 1978); *Career* actress; Hon DLitt: Univ of London 1984, Univ of St Andrews 1986, Univ of Exeter 2001; Hon DEd Univ of Kingston 1994, Hon DArts Pine Manor Coll Boston USA 1994; *Theatre* incl: Express Bongo, Follow That Girl, Fairy Tales Of New York, The Ginger Man, Past Imperfect, The Sleeping Prince, She Stoops to Conquer, Peter Pan, A Doll's House, The Taming of The Shrew, Romeo and Jeanette, As You Like It, Miss Julie, The Circle, Arms and the Man, Man and Superman, Tribades, An Audience Called Edward, Crucifer of Blood, Night and Day, The Revolt, House Guest, Blithe Spirit, Married Love, A Little Night Music, The King and I, Noel and Gertie, Relative Values, Suzanna Andler, Black Chiffon, Relatively Speaking, Relative Values, The Lady in the Van, Cinderella 2005–06 and 2006–07, The Bargain 2007; *Television* incl: What Katy Did, The Andromeda Breakthrough, The Forsyte Saga 1970, Vanity Fair 1971, The First Churchills 1973, The Pallisers 1975, Dick Turpin 1980, Barchester Chronicles 1982, Leaving (2 series), Going to Pot I, II and III, Don't Tell Father, The Grand (series I & II), Coming Home, Nancherrow, Monarch of the Glen (7 series), Sparkling Cyanide; *Film* incl: During One Night, The Three Lives of Thomasina, Night Must Fall, The Fighting Prince of Donegal, Paris in August, Monte Carlo or Bust, Violent Enemy, David Copperfield, A Time For Loving, Living Free, Baffled, Malpertius, Neither The Sea Nor The Sand, Roses and Green Peppers, Bang; *Awards* winner 3 Emmy Awards for Best Actress; *Books* Susan's Story, The Maternal Instinct, Lucy Jane at the Ballet, Lucy Jane on Television, Lucy Jane and the Dancing Competition, Lucy Jane and the Russian Ballet, Trouble Free Gardening, Every Letter Counts, Easy Gardening, Rosie's First Ballet Lesson; *Recreations* gardening; *Style*— Miss Susan Hampshire, OBE; ✉ c/o Chatto & Linnit Ltd, 123A Kings Road, London SW3 4PL (tel 020 7352 7722, fax 020 7352 3450)

HAMPSON, Christopher; CBE (1994); s of Harold Ralph Hampson (d 1972), of Montreal, Canada, and Geraldine Mary, *née* Smith (d 1984); *b* 6 September 1931; *Educ* Ashbury Coll Ottawa, McGill Univ Montreal (BEng); *m* 18 Sept 1954, Joan Margaret Cassils, da of Lt-Col Arthur C Evans (d 1960), of Montreal, Canada; 3 da (Daphne Margaret (Mrs Kearns) b 1955, Sarah Anne (Mrs Clarridge) b 1958, Aimée Joan Geraldine (Mrs Pitman) b 1966), 2 s (Christopher Geoffrey b 1957, Harold Arthur b 1965); *Career* CIL Inc Canada: vice-pres and dir 1973–78, sr vice-pres and dir 1982–; md and ceo ICI Australia Ltd 1984–87, exec dir ICI plc 1987–94; non-exec chm: Yorkshire Electricity Group plc 1994–97, RMC Group plc 1996–2002 (non-exec dir 1994–2002), Br Biotech plc 1998–2002; dep chm Environment Agency 2000 (memb Bd 1995–2000); non-exec dir: SNC-Lavalin Group Inc 1993–2002, TransAlta Corporation 1994–2003, BG plc 1997–2000, Lattice Group plc 2000–02; formerly non-exec dir Costain Gp plc; CIMgt 1990; *Recreations* tennis, skiing; *Clubs* York (Toronto), Boodle's, Hurlingham; *Style*— Christopher Hampson, Esq, CBE; ✉ 77 Kensington Court, London W8 5DT (tel 020 7376 1906)

HAMPSON, Christopher; s of Geoff Hampson, and Janice, *née* Morrison; *Educ* Royal Ballet Sch; *Career* choreographer; dancer English Nat Ballet 1992–99 (jr soloist 1995); roles incl: Drosselmeyer in The Nutcracker, Paris in Romeo and Juliet, The Headmistress in Graduation Ball, lead in Square Dance; ballet master City Ballet of London 1999– (ballet master for VIVA! Tour and Wayne Sleep's Dash and Aspects of Dance tours); winner Ursula Moreton Choreographic Competition Royal Ballet Sch 1992, Best Classical Choreography Critics' Circle Awards 2002, Barclay's Theatre Award for outstanding achievement in dance 2002; hon memb Dalcroze Soc; *Choreography* for English Nat Ballet: Perpetuum Mobile 1997, Country Garden 1998, Capriol Suite 1998, Concerto Grosso 1999, Double Concerto 2001; for City Ballet of London: Coda for Three Men 1998, Dinaresade 1999, Canciones 1999; other credits incl: Notturno (for Thomas Edur and Agnes Oaks) 1998, Carnival (NY Ballet) 1999, Malcolm Arnold Dances (Elmhurst) 2000, Anniversaire (English Nat Ballet Sch) 2000, Entrées (Royal Ballet Sch and English Nat Ballet Sch) 2000, Homage to a Princess (Rojo/Kobburg) 2000, A Christmas Carol (first full-length work, Royal Festival Hall) 2000, Songs Without Words (London Studio Centre/Images of Dance) 2001, Esquisses (English Nat Ballet Sch) 2001, Saltarello (Royal NZ Ballet) 2001, Double Concerto (English Nat Ballet) 2001, A Christmas Carol (St David's Hall Cardiff) 2002, Romeo and Juliet (Royal NZ Ballet) 2002, Nutcracker (English Nat Ballet) 2002, Giselle (Nat Theatre Prague) 2004, Sinfonietta Giocosa (Atlanta Ballet) 2005, two solos for the Royal Acad of Dance Genée Int Ballet Competition 2006, Cinderella (Royal NZ Ballet) 2007, Three Dialogues (Royal Ballet Sch) 2007; *Recreations* wine, travel, theatre, reading, music; *Style*— Christopher Hampson, Esq; ✉ 36 Phoenix Court, Purchase Street, London NW1 1EL (tel 020 7388 1803)

HAMPSON, Stephen; s of Dr Frank Hampson (d 1990), of Reading, and Helen, *née* Ellis; *b* 27 October 1945; *Educ* The Leys Sch Cambridge, UC Oxford (MA, BPhil); *m* Gunilla, da of Sture Brunk; 1 da (Annika b 1975), 1 s (Nicholas b 1977); *Career* civil servant; lectr Univ of Aberdeen 1969–71, economist NEDO 1971–75, Scottish Office 1975–78, first sec FCO (New Delhi) 1978–81, Scottish Executive (formerly Scottish Office) 1981–2002; memb Cncl WWF Scotland; Hon FCIWEM; *Recreations* far away places; *Style*— Stephen Hampson, Esq; ✉ Glenelg, Park Road, Kilmacolm, Renfrewshire PA13 4EE (tel 01505 872615)

HAMPSON, Sir Stuart; kt (1998); *Educ* St John's Coll Oxford (MA); *Career* with Civil Serv 1969–82 (successively Bd of Trade, FCO, Dept of Prices and Consumer Protection and Dept of Trade); John Lewis Partnership: joined 1982, md Tyrrell & Green until 1986, memb Bd 1986, dir of research and expansion 1986–93, dep chm 1989–93, chm 1993–2007; memb Oxford Retail Gp 1987–93, a founding dep chm London First 1992–97; chm Royal Soc of Arts 1999–2001 (memb Cncl 1995–, treas 1997, dep chm 1998–99 and 2001–02), memb Royal Soc of Arts Inquiry into Tomorrow's Company, dir Centre for

Tomorrow's Company 1996–99 (chm 1998–99); pres RASE 2005–06; Hon DBA: Kingston Univ 1998, Southampton Solent Univ 2001; hon fell St John's Coll Oxford 2001; Hon FCGI 2002; *Style*— Sir Stuart Hampson

HAMPTON, Christopher James; CBE (1999); s of Bernard Patrick Hampton, and Dorothy Patience, *née* Herrington; *b* 26 January 1946; *Educ* Lancing, New Coll Oxford (MA); *m* 1971, Laura Margaret de Holesch; 2 da; *Career* res dramatist Royal Court Theatre 1968–70, freelance writer 1970–; FRSL; Officier de l'Ordre des Arts et des Lettres (France) 1997; *Plays* When Did You Last See My Mother? 1966, Total Eclipse 1968, The Philanthropist 1970 (Evening Standard Best Comedy Award, Plays and Players London Theatre Critics Best Play), Savages 1973 (Plays and Players London Theatre Critics Best Play, Los Angeles Drama Critics' Circle Award for Distinguished Playwriting 1974), Treats 1976, The Portage to San Cristobal of A H (from George Steiner) 1982, Tales from Hollywood 1982 (Standard Best Comedy Award 1983), Les Liaisons Dangereuses (from Laclos) 1985 (Plays and Players London Theatre Critics Best Play, Standard Best Play Award 1986, NY Drama Critics' Circle Best Foreign Play Award 1987, Laurence Olivier Award 1986), White Chameleon 1991, Sunset Boulevard (book and lyrics) 1993 (Tony Awards for book and lyrics 1995), Alice's Adventures Under Ground 1994, The Talking Cure 2002, Dracula (book and lyrics) 2004, Waiting for the Barbarians (opera libretto) 2005, Embers 2006, Appomattox (opera libretto) 2007; *Television* Able's Will BBC 1977, The History Man (from Malcolm Bradbury) BBC 1981, The Price of Tea 1984, Hotel du Lac (From Anita Brookner) BBC 1986 (BAFTA Best TV Film Award 1987), The Ginger Tree (from Oswald Wynd) BBC 1989; *Film* A Dolls House 1973, Tales From the Vienna Woods 1979 (Screen International Award 1980), The Honorary Consul 1983, The Good Father 1986 (Prix Italia 1988), Wolf at the Door 1986, Dangerous Liaisons 1988 (Writers Guild of America Award, BAFTA Award, Academy Award), Carrington (also dir) 1995 (Special Jury Award Cannes Film Festival 1995), Total Eclipse 1995, Mary Reilly 1996, The Secret Agent (also dir) 1996, The Quiet American 2002, Imagining Argentina 2003 (also dir), Atonement 2007; *Translations* Marya (by Isaac Babel) 1967, Uncle Vanya (by Chekhov) 1970, Hedda Gabler (by Ibsen) 1970, A Doll's House (by Ibsen) 1971, Don Juan (by Molière) 1972, Tales from the Vienna Woods (by Horváth) 1977, Don Juan Comes Back from the War (by Horváth) 1978, Ghosts (by Ibsen) 1978, The Wild Duck (by Ibsen) 1979, The Prague Trial (by Chéreau and Mnouchkine) 1980, Tartuffe (by Molière) 1983, Faith, Hope and Charity (by Horváth) 1989, Art (by Yasmina Reza) 1996 (Scott Moncrieff Prize 1997), An Enemy of the People (by Ibsen) 1997, The Unexpected Man (by Yasmina Reza) 1998, Conversations After a Burial (by Yasmina Reza) 2000, Life x 3 (by Yasmina Reza) 2000, Three Sisters (by Chekhov) 2003, The Seagull (by Chekhov) 2007; *Recreations* travel, cinema; *Clubs* Dramatists'; *Style*— Christopher Hampton, Esq, CBE, FRSL; ✉ 2 Kensington Park Gardens, London W11 3HB; c/o Casarotto Co Ltd, National House, 60–66 Wardour Street, London W1V 4ND (tel 020 7287 4450, fax 020 7287 9128)

HAMPTON, Sir (Leslie) Geoffrey; kt (1998); s of Leslie Harold Hampton, and Irene, *née* Wain; *Educ* High Arcal GS Dudley, King Alfred's Coll Winchester (CertEd), Univ of Southampton (BEd), Univ of Birmingham (MEd); *m* Christine Joyce, da of Charles Edward Bickley; 2 s (Paul Geoffrey b 29 July 1979, Ian James b 15 May 1988); *Career* teacher rising to actg dep headteacher Pensnett Sch Dudley 1974–87, dep headteacher Buckpool 1987–93, headmaster Northicote Sch Wolverhampton 1993–99; Univ of Wolverhampton: dir Leadership Centre and dean Sch of Educn 1999–, pro-vice-chllr 2006–; memb: Police Consultative Ctee 1988–93, SHA 1989–, Nat Steering Gp Basic Skills Agency 1995–2007, Bd Nat Educn Business Partnerships 2007–; Govt appointee Special Measures Action Recovery Teams (SMART Initiative) 1997, co-dir Nat Information and Communication Technologies (ICT) Research Centre DFES 2001–03; chair (govt appointee) Walsall Educn Bd 2003; assoc dir Specialist Schs Tst 2005; Hon DEd King Alfred's Coll Winchester 2003, KPMG prof of educn leadership 2005; *Publications* Transforming Northicote School - Pathfinders for Success (jtly, 2000), A Practical Guide to Teacher Professional Development (jtly, 2004); work features in Govt publications From Failure to Success (1996), Excellence in Schools (White Paper, 1997), and Trust Schools (DfES DVD, 2006); also contrib to Developing Quality Systems in Education (ed G Doherty, 1994); author of numerous articles on educn in jls; *Recreations* DIY, cycling, gardening; *Style*— Sir Geoffrey Hampton; ✉ University of Wolverhampton Executive Suite, Wulfruna Street, Wolverhampton WV1 1SB (tel 01902 518962, fax 01902 824345, e-mail g.hampton@wlv.ac.uk)

HAMPTON, 7 Baron (UK 1874); Sir John Humphrey Arnott Pakington; 7 Bt (UK 1846); s of 6 Baron (d 2003); *b* 24 December 1964; *Educ* Dyson Perrins C of E HS, Shrewsbury, Exeter Coll of Art and Design (BA); *m* 4 Oct 1996, Siena E E, yr da of Remo Caldato, of Rome; *Career* creative dir Band and Brown Communications London; *Style*— The Rt Hon the Lord Hampton; ✉ e-mail johnnie@bbpr.com

HAMPTON, Prof John Reynolds; s of Eric Albert Hampton (d 1979), of Gorleston, Norfolk, and Norah Kathleen, *née* Johnson (d 1981); *b* 8 November 1937; *Educ* Gresham's, Magdalen Coll Oxford (BA, DM, DPhil, MA, BM BCh), Radcliffe Infirmary Oxford; *m* 25 July 1964, Pamela Jean, da of Edmund Joseph Wilkins (d 1980), of Tunbridge Wells; 2 s (Christopher, Philip), 1 da (Joanna); *Career* house physician and surgn and SHO Radcliffe Infirmary 1963–64, jr lectr and lectr in med Univ of Oxford 1965–68, instr in med and jr assoc in med Harvard Univ and Peter Bent Brigham Hosp Boston 1968–69; Univ of Nottingham 1969–: lectr, sr lectr in med and hon conslt physician to Nottingham Hosps 1970–74, reader in med and conslt physician Queen's Med Centre 1974–79, prof of cardiology 1980–; sec Atherosclerosis Discussion GP 1978–81; memb: Br Cardiac Soc, Assoc of Physicians; FRCP 1975, FFPM, FESC; *Publications* author of more than 400 scientific papers; *Books* incl: Integrated Clinical Science - cardiovascular disease (1983), The ECG in practice (1986, 3 edn 2003), The ECG Made Easy (4 edn, 1992, 7 edn 2003); *Recreations* sailing; *Style*— Prof John Hampton; ✉ Cardiovascular Medicine, D Floor, S Block, Queen's Medical Centre, Nottingham NG7 2UH (tel 0115 970 9346, fax 0115 970 9384, e-mail jrhampton@doctors.net.uk)

HAMPTON, Sir Philip Roy; kt (2007); *Educ* Lincoln Coll Oxford (MA), INSEAD (MBA); *Career* CA 1978; with Coopers & Lybrand 1975–81, with Lazard Bros 1981–90, gp fin dir British Steel plc 1990–95, exec fin dir BG Group plc 1996–2000, gp fin dir BT plc 2000–02, gp fin dir Lloyds TSB Group plc 2002–04, chm J Sainsbury plc 2004–; non-exec dir Belgacom 2004–; ldr Hampton Review for HM Treasy 2004–05; *Style*— Sir Philip Hampton

HAMROUNI, Sandra Lesley; da of Vernon Carter (d 2001), and Patricia, *née* Barton; *b* 13 January 1958, Bradford, W Yorks; *Educ* Richmond Sch Yorks, Univ of Birmingham (BA), Inst of Educn Univ of London (PGCE, MA), Churchbridge Teachers' Centre (RSA Dip), CIM (Cert); *m* 29 April 1995, Lotfi Hamrouni; 2 s (Malik b 8 Feb 1997, Amir b 7 Jan 2001); *Career* English teacher: VSO Kenya 1979–81, Instituto Britannia Mexico 1981–82, Handsworth Wood Girls' Sch Birmingham 1982–83; British Cncl: English teacher Abu Dhabi 1984–86, dep dir of studies Cairo 1988–89, teaching centre mangr Tunis 1992–95, teaching centre mangr Damascus 1995–97, dir of trg and examination servs Muscat 1997–2002, teaching centre mangr Madrid 2002–04, country dir Bahrain 2004–; *Recreations* playing violin, music, opera, African and Arab literature, film, dance, running, weight training; *Clubs* Royal Over-Seas League; *Style*— Ms Sandra Hamrouni; ✉ British Council Bahrain, AMA Centre, PO Box 452, 146 Shaikh Salman Highway, Manama 356, Bahrain (tel 00 973 17261555, fax 00 973 17241272, e-mail sandra.hamrouni@britishcouncil.org.bh)

HAMWEE, Baroness (Life Peer UK 1991), of Richmond upon Thames in the London Borough of Richmond upon Thames; Sally Rachel Hamwee; AM; da of late Alec Hamwee, and late Dorothy, *née* Saunders; *b* 12 January 1947; *Educ* Manchester HS for Girls, Univ of Cambridge (MA); *Career* slr; ptnr Clintons Slrs; cncllr London Borough of Richmond-upon-Thames 1978–98 (chm Planning Ctee 1983–87); chm London Planning Advsy Ctee 1986–94; pres ALDC (Lib Dem Cncllrs' Assoc) 1995–96; memb London Assembly GLA (Lib Dem) 2000–; GLA: dep chair 2000–01, 2002–03 and 2004–05, chair 2001–02, 2003–04 and 2005–; chair London Assembly Budget Ctee 2000–; Lib Dem spokesperson in House of Lords, Office of dep Prime Minister; former memb Select Ctee on Relations between Central and Local Govt; vice-pres Town and Country Planning Assoc (former pres); former memb Cncl of Mgmnt Family Policy Studies Centre, memb Cncl of Mgmnt Refuge; legal advsr The Simon Community; chm Xfm Ltd 1996–98, former chair TCPA Inquiry 'Your Place or Mine?'; former memb: Cncl Parents for Children, Bd London First, Joseph Rowntree Fndn Inquiry, Planning For Housing; *Style*— Baroness Hamwee, AM; ✉ 101A Mortlake High Street, London SW14 8HQ

HANBURY, Benjamin; *b* 25 March 1946; *m* 31 May 1969, Moira Elizabeth, da of Sir Arthur Pilkington; 2 da (Emma Jane b 15 Dec 1970, Amanda Aline b 9 March 1973); *Career* racehorse trainer; rode over 50 winners; formerly with: Ryan Price, D L Moore, B van Cutsem; trainer's licence 1974–; horses trained incl: Kala Dancer, Batshoof, Midway Lady, Matiya; major races won: Gold Seal Oaks, General Accident 1,000 Guineas, William Hill Dewhurst Stakes, Prix Marcel Boussac, May Hill Stakes, Tattersalls Rogers Gold Cup, Prince of Wales's Stakes, Irish 1,000 Guineas; *Recreations* golf, shooting; *Style*— Benjamin Hanbury, Esq; ✉ Green Man House, Cowlinge, Newmarket, Suffolk CB8 9QA (tel 01440 820396, e-mail ben.hanbury@virgin.net)

HANBURY, Margaret Elizabeth; da of Paul Barrett Hanbury (d 1999), and late Norah, *née* Stubbs; *b* 24 November 1946; *Educ* Leweston Manor Sherborne; *m* March 1978 (m dis 1999), Guillaume de Rougemont; 1 s (Henry Paul b 14 Sept 1981); *Career* literary agent; founded own agency 1983, clients incl J G Ballard, George Alagiah, Simon Callow, Jane Glover and Katie Price; memb Assoc of Authors' Agents; *Clubs* Bembridge Sailing; *Style*— Ms Margaret Hanbury; ✉ Margaret Hanbury Literary Agency, 27 Walcot Square, London SE11 4UB (tel 020 7735 7680)

H

HANBURY-TENISON, (Airling) Robin; OBE (1981), DL (Cornwall 2003); s of Maj Gerald Evan Farquhar Tenison (d 1954), of Co Monaghan, Ireland, and Ruth Julia Marguerite, *née* Hanbury (d 2000); *b* 7 May 1936; *Educ* Eton, Magdalen Coll Oxford (MA); *m* 1, 1959, Marika (d 1982), da of Lt-Col John Montgomerie Hopkinson (d 1989), of Sussex; 1 da (Lucy b 1960), 1 s (Rupert b 1970); *m* 2, 1983, Louella Gage, da of Lt-Col George Torquil Gage Williams, of Menkee, Cornwall; 1 s (Merlin b 1985); *Career* farmer, author, explorer, environmental and human rights campaigner; pres Survival Int 1984– (chm 1969–84), memb SW Regnl Panel MAFF 1993–96, chief exec Countryside Alliance (formerly BFSS) 1995–98; pres Rain Forest Club 2001–05; RGS Patron's Medal 1979, Farmers Club Cup 1998, CLA Contribution to the Countryside Award 2000, Pio Manzù Medal Italy 2000, Mungo Park Medal Scot Royal Geographical Society 2001; Dr (hc) Univ of Mons-Hainant 1992; *Books* The Rough and The Smooth (1969), A Question of Survival (1973), A Pattern of Peoples (1975), Mulu - The Rain Forest (1980), The Yanomami (1982), Worlds Apart (1984), White Horses Over France (1985), A Ride along the Great Wall (1987), Fragile Eden (1989), Spanish Pilgrimage (1990), The Oxford Book of Exploration (1993), Jake's Escape (1996), Jake's Treasure (1998), Jake's Safari (1998), Worlds Within (2005), The Seventy Great Journeys in History (2006); *Recreations* travelling, conservation; *Clubs* Geographical, Pratt's, Travellers; *Style*— Robin Hanbury-Tenison, Esq, OBE, DL; ✉ Cabilla Manor, Cardinham, Bodmin, Cornwall PL30 4DW (tel 01208 821224, fax 01208 821267, e-mail robin@cabilla.co.uk, website www.cabilla.co.uk and www.robinsbooks.co.uk)

HANCOCK, Prof Barry William; s of George Llewellyn Hancock, of London, and Sarah Hancock (d 1973); *b* 25 January 1946; *Educ* E Barnet GS, Univ of Sheffield Med Sch (MB ChB, MD), Univ of London (DCH); *m* 5 July 1969, (Christine Diana) Helen, da of Alexander Moffatt Spray (d 1972); 1 da (Caroline b 1971), 1 s (David b 1974); *Career* medical registrar Professorial Therapeutics Unit Royal Infirmary Sheffield 1973–74, lectr in med and sr registrar Professorial Medical Unit Royal Hosp Sheffield 1974–78, hon consIt physician and oncologist Royal Hallamshire and Weston Park Hosps Sheffield 1978–88; Univ of Sheffield: sr lectr in med 1978–86, reader in med 1986–88, prof of clinical oncology 1988–, dir Supraregional Gestational Trophoblastic Tumour Serv, YCR dir Cancer Research; trial co-ordinator Br Nat Lymphoma Investigation; chm: Nat Cancer Research Inst Renal Cancer Clinical Studies Gp; pres Int Soc for the Study of Trophoblastic Disease; formerly: hon dir Trent Palliative Care Centre, divnl surgn N Derbys St John Ambulance Bde; Lord Mayor of Sheffield's Honours Award 1999, Sheffield Star Health Award 2002, Univ of Sheffield Centenary Medal 2005; MRCP 1973, FRCP (London) 1985, FRCR 1994, FRCP (Edinburgh) 1995; *Books* Assessment of Tumour Response (ed, 1982), Immunological Aspects of Cancer (jt ed, 1985), Lymphoreticular Disease (jt ed, 1985), Lecture Notes in Clinical Oncology (jtly, 1986), Cancer Care in the Community (ed, 1996), Cancer Care in the Hospital (ed, 1996), Gestational Trophoblastic Diseases (jt ed, 1997, 2 edn 2003), Malignant Lymphoma (jt ed, 2000); *Recreations* railways, photography, philately, tennis; *Style*— Prof Barry Hancock; ✉ Treetops, 253 Dobcroft Road, Ecclesall, Sheffield S11 9LG (tel 0114 235 1433); Academic Unit of Clinical Oncology, Weston Park Hospital, Whitham Road, Sheffield S10 2SJ (tel 0114 226 5000, fax 0114 226 5511, e-mail b.w.hancock@sheffield.ac.uk)

HANCOCK, Sir David John Stowell; KCB (1985); s of Alfred George Hancock (d 1955), of Beckenham, Kent, and Florence, *née* Barrow (d 1988); *b* 27 March 1934; *Educ* Whitgift Sch, Balliol Coll Oxford (MA); *m* 23 Dec 1966, Sheila Gillian (Gill), da of late Dr Even Finlay, of Walgrave, Northants; 1 s (John Farquharson b 1969), 1 da (Cordelia Jane b 1973); *Career* Nat Serv 2 Lt RTR 1953–54; BOT 1957–59; HM Treasy: joined 1959, under sec 1975–80, dep sec 1980–82; head Euro Secretariat Cabinet Office 1982–83, perm sec Dept of Educn and Science 1983–89, dir Hambros plc 1989–98, exec dir Hambros Bank Ltd 1989–98, sr advsr S G Hambros 1998–99, sr advsr Newcourt Capital 1999–2001, sr advsr Tyco Capital 2001–03; chm: Dyvell Holdings Ltd 1990–94, Combined Landfill Projects Ltd 1993–2001; dir AXA Equity and Law 1992–95; chm: UK Selection and Advsy Ctee Harkness Fellowships 1988–92 (memb 1984–92), Fndn for Young Musicians 1990–99, St Katharine and Shadwell Tst 1990–99; tstee: St Catharine's Fndn Cumberland Lodge 1989–; memb Bd: RNT 1996–2002, South Bank Bd Ltd 2000–02, SG UK Defined Benefit Pension Scheme 2003–; govr: Whitgift Sch 2000–, Br-American Drama Acad 2003–; Freeman City of London 1989; Hon LLD Poly of E London (CNAA) 1990; FRSA 1986, CCMI 1987; *Recreations* theatre, music, opera, reading, gardening; *Clubs* Athenaeum; *Style*— Sir David Hancock, KCB

HANCOCK, Prof Gus; s of Reginald Hancock, and Mary Elizabeth Hancock; *b* 17 November 1944; *Educ* Harvey GS Folkestone, Dorking Co GS, Bangor GS, Trinity Coll Dublin (Louis Claude Purser entrance scholar, fndn scholar, BA, Gold medal) Peterhouse Cambridge (res studentship, Shell Petroleum postgrad res scholar, PhD); *m*; 2 c; *Career* postdoctoral res asst Dept of Chemistry Univ of Calif San Diego 1971–73, wissenschaftlicher angestellte (perm res offr) Fakultät f Physik Universität Bielefeld 1973–76; Univ of Oxford: fell Trinity Coll 1976–, lectr in physical chemistry 1976–96, prof of chemistry 1996–, head Dept of Physical and Theoretical Chemistry 2005–; Stanford Univ: Fulbright fell 1982–83, visiting prof of chemistry 1989; ed: Research in Chemical Kinetics 1992–99, Comprehensive Chemical Kinetics 1992–99; chm Gas Kinetics Gp RSC 1988–90 (sec

1986–88); memb: Physical Chemistry Panel SERC 1990–93, Plasma and Ion Surface Engrg Panel 1990–, Structure, Bonding and Reaction Mechanisms Coll EPSRC 1995–2005, Marine and Atmospheric Sciences Panel NERC 1996–97, Atmospheric Sciences Panel NERC 1997–99, Upper Troposphere Lower Stratosphere Steering Gp NERC 1999–; Corday Morgan Medal and Prize RSC 1982, Reaction Kinetics Award RSC 1995, Japan Soc for the Promotion of Sci Fellowship 1997, 14th Italgas Prize for Sci and Technol for the Environment 2000, Polanyi Medal Gas Kinetics Gp RSC 2002; *Publications* over 150 refereed pubns in scientific literature; *Style*— Prof Gus Hancock; ✉ Physical and Theoretical Chemistry Laboratory, Oxford University, South Parks Road, Oxford OX1 3QZ (tel 01865 275439, fax 01865 275410, e-mail gus.hancock@chemistry.ox.ac.uk)

HANCOCK, Michael Thomas (Mike); CBE (1992), MP; *b* 9 April 1946; *m* 1967, Jacqueline, da of Sidney and Gwen Elliott; 1 s, 1 da; *Career* memb Bd of Dirs Drug Rehabilitation Unit Alpha Drug Clinic Droxford 1971–; memb Portsmouth City Cncl 1971– (Fratton Ward 1973–, ldr Lib Dem Gp 1989–97); Hampshire CC: memb 1973–, ldr of the oppn 1977–81 and 1989–93, ldr Lib Dem Gp 1989–97, ldr 1993–97; joined SDP 1981 (memb Nat Ctee 1984), Parly candidate (SDP) Portsmouth S 1983 (SDP/Alliance 1987), MP (SDP) Portsmouth S 1984–87, MP (Lib Dem) Portsmouth S 1997–; Lib Dem spokesman on defence 1997–; dir Daytime Club BBC 1987–90, chm Southern Branch NSPCC 1989–, dist offr for Hampshire, IOW and Channel Islands Royal Soc for Mentally Handicapped Children and Adults 1989–97; memb: Br Delgn to UN 1983–84, Bureau of the Assembly of Euro Regions 1993–96, Congress of Local and Regnl Authorities of Europe (a body of the Cncl of Europe) 1994–97; vice-pres Atlantic Arc Cmmn of the Conf of Peripheral Maritime Regions 1994; tstee: Royal Marines Museum Portsmouth, Mary Rose; dir the Beneficial Fndn Portsmouth; contrib to various jls; hon award for contrib to Anglo-German rels Homborn W Germany 1981; *Recreations* people, living life to the full; *Style*— Mike Hancock, Esq, CBE, MP; ✉ House of Commons, London SW1A 0AA (tel 020 7219 5180); office: 1A Albert Road, Southsea, Hampshire PO5 2SE (tel 023 9286 1055, fax 023 9283 0530); home: (tel 01329 287340)

HANCOCK, Paul David; QPM (2004); s of John George Hancock (d 1981), of Pinxton, Derbys, and Ellen Amelia Hancock (d 1989); *b* 26 September 1950; *Educ* Univ of Leeds (BA); *m* 23 Oct 1993, Michele Jane, da of late Stanley Albert Clayton; 2 step s (James Wetten b 16 Dec 1978, Aaron Wetten b 27 June 1980), 1 step da (Natalie Wetten (twin) b 27 June 1980); *Career* Derbys Constabulary: joined 1974, Constable rising to Supt 1974–1991 (seconded to Directing Staff Police Staff Coll Bramshill 1991–93), head Road Traffic Dept 1994, Divnl Cdr Chesterfield 1994, Asst Chief Constable (Support) 1996, Asst Chief Constable (HR) 2000; Chief Constable Beds Police 2001–06; ACPO: chair Finance Business Area, memb Millennium Co-ordinating Ctee, dir Change and Implementation Support Team 2005– (responsible for delivery of progs in Nat Community Safety Plan); *Recreations* family life, reading, collecting Jamaican stamps, supporting Nottingham Forest FC; *Style*— Paul Hancock, Esq, QPM; ✉ Association of Chief Police Officers, 25 Victoria Street, London SW1H 0EX (tel 020 7227 3434, e-mail paul.hancock@acpo.pnn.police.uk)

HANCOCK, Ven Peter; s of Kenneth Albert Hancock, of Hampshire, and Jean Margaret, *née* Crump; *b* 26 July 1955; *Educ* Price's Sch Fareham, Selwyn Coll Cambridge (MA), Oak Hill Coll Southgate (BA); *m* 1979, Elizabeth Jane, da of Cyril John Sindall; 2 da (Claire Jane b 26 March 1982, Charlotte Emma b 1 Dec 1987), 2 s (Richard Andrew b 4 Aug 1984, William Peter b 18 Dec 1989); *Career* ordained: deacon 1980, priest 1981; curate Christ Church Portsdown 1980–83, curate Radipole and Melcombe Regis Team Miny Emmanuel Church 1983–87, vicar St Wilfrid Cowplain 1987–99, rural dean of Havant 1993–98, archdeacon of Meon Dio of Portsmouth 1999–; hon canon of Portsmouth Cathedral 1997 (dir of Mission 2003–06); *Recreations* walking, swimming, skiing, third world issues, contemporary music; *Style*— The Ven the Archdeacon of the Meon; ✉ Victoria Lodge, 36 Osborn Road, Fareham, Hampshire PO16 7DS (tel 01329 280101, fax 01329 281603)

HANCOCK, Roger Markham; s of late Howard Spencer Hancock, of Oxford, and late Marjorie Helen, *née* Skelcher; *b* 4 November 1942; *Educ* Southfield Sch Oxford; *m* 14 Aug 1968, Marian Sheila, da of late Arthur Herbert Holloway, of South Tawton; 1 da (Kirsty Sheila Bevis b 14 Aug 1975), 1 s (Mark Peter Skelcher b 25 Jan 1978); *Career* articled clerk Wenn Towsend Chartered Accountants Oxford 1959–65, mgmnt accountant British Motor Corp 1965, mangr Morris & Harper Chartered Accountants 1966; Whitley Stimpson & Partners: ptnr 1967–2003, managing ptnr 1987–95, sr ptnr 1995–2003; ptnr Moores Rowland Banbury 1979–99, memb Cncl Moores Rowland Int 1985–99; chm: Morris & Harper Ltd 1997–99 (dir), Nortec Training Agency Ltd 1997–2003 (dir 1986–2003); dir S H Jones (Wine and Spirit Merchants) Ltd 2004–; pres Banbury and Dist C of C 1989–90, FCA 1967 (ACA 1965); *Recreations* theatre, music, rugby football; *Style*— Roger Hancock, Esq; ✉ Sugarswell Bungalow, Shenington, Banbury, Oxfordshire OX15 6HW (tel 01295 670368, e-mail roger@sugarswell.freeserve.co.uk)

HANCOCK, Stephen Clarence; s of Norman Harry Hancock, of Brymore, West Parade, Llandudno, Wales, and Jean Elaine, *née* Barlow; *b* 1 November 1955; *Educ* King Edward VI Lichfield, City of Stoke-on-Trent Sixth Form Coll, Univ of Sheffield (LLB); *Career* admitted slr 1980; ptnr Herbert Smith Slrs 1986– (articled clerk 1978–80, asst slr 1980–86); memb Worshipful Co of Slrs; *Style*— Stephen Hancock, Esq; ✉ Herbert Smith, Exchange House, Primrose Street, London EC2A 2HS (tel 020 7374 8000, fax 020 7496 0043)

HAND, Prof David John; s of Peter F Hand, of Lambert's Castle, Dorset, and Olive Margaret, *née* Abbott; *b* 30 June 1950, Peterborough; *Educ* Bournemouth Sch, Univ of Oxford (BA, capt Judo Team), Univ of Southampton (MSc, PhD); *m* 13 Aug 1993, Dr Shelley L Channon; 2 da (Rachel b 24 Jan 1983, Emily b 7 Feb 1986); *Career* statistician Inst of Psychiatry 1977–88, prof of statistics and head Statistics Dept Open Univ 1988–99, prof of statistics and head Statistics Section Imperial Coll London 1999–; Thomas L Saaty Prize for Applied Advances in the Math and Mgmnt Sciences 2001, Guy Medal in Silver RSS 2002; memb Int Statistical Inst 1988; FRSS 1973, CStat 1993, Hon FIA 1999, FBA 2003; *Books* Discrimination and Classification (1981), Finite Mixture Distributions (jtly, 1981), Kernel Discriminant Analysis (1982), Artificial Intelligence and Psychiatry (1985), Multivariate Analysis of Variance and Repeated Measures: a practical guide for behavioural scientists (jtly, 1987), The Statistical Consultant in Action (jt ed, 1987), Analysis of Repeated Measures (jtly, 1990), Artificial Intelligence Frontiers in Statistics (ed, 1993), AI and Computer Power (ed, 1994), A Handbook of Small Data Sets (jt ed, 1994), Elements of Statistics (jtly, 1995), Biplots (jtly, 1996), Practical Longitudinal Data Analysis (jtly, 1996), Construction and Assessment of Classification Rules (1997), Statistics in Finance (jt ed, 1998), Intelligent Data Analysis (jt ed, 1999, 2 edn 2003), Advances in Intelligent Data Analysis, IDA-99 (jt ed, 1999), Principles of Data Mining (jtly, 2001), Advances in Intelligent Data Analysis, IDA-01 (jt ed, 2001), Pattern Detection and Discovery (jt ed, 2002), Methods and Models in Statistics (jt ed, 2004), Measurement Theory and Practice (2004), Selected Statistical Papers of Sir David Cox (jt ed, 2005), Information Generation (2007); *Style*— Prof David Hand; ✉ Department of Mathematics, Imperial College, 180 Queen's Gate, London SW7 2AZ (tel 020 7594 8521, fax 020 7594 1191, e-mail d.j.hand@imperial.ac.uk)

HAND, Graham Stewart; s of Ronald Charles Hand, and Mary Fraser Hand (d 1992); *b* 3 November 1948; *Educ* Univ of Cambridge (MA); *m* 16 June 1973, Anne Mary Seton, *née* Campbell; 1 s (Nicholas b 27 Nov 1979), 1 da (Kate b 16 April 1984); *Career* with HM Forces 1969–80; joined HM Dip Serv 1980, UK Mission to UN (New York) 1981, Br Embassy Dakar 1982–85, FCO News Dept 1985–87, Br Embassy Helsinki 1987–90, Aid Policy Dept FCO/ODA 1990–92, head of human rights FCO 1992–94, dep high cmmr Lagos 1994–97, RCDS 1997, ambass to Bosnia-Herzegovina 1998–2001, chargé d'affaires Tajikistan 2002, ambass to Algeria 2002–04; chief exec British Expertise 2004–; *Publications* Human Rights in British Foreign Policy (1997), Seaford Papers; *Recreations* golf, sailing, skiing, music; *Style*— Graham Hand, Esq; ✉ British Expertise, One Westminster Palace Gardens, Artillery Row, London SW1P 1RJ (tel 020 7222 3651, e-mail gh@britishexpertise.org)

HAND, John Lester; QC (1988); s of John James Hand (d 1965), and Violet, *née* Middleton; *b* 16 June 1947; *Educ* Huddersfield New Coll, Univ of Nottingham; *m* 1, 17 Dec 1971 (m dis 1989), Helen Andrea, *née* McWatt; m 2, 6 April 1990, Lynda (Ray) Ferrigno Hand, da of Gisbert Mills (d 1985); 1 da (Theodora Isobel b 1991); *Career* called to the Bar Gray's Inn 1972 (bencher 1996), practising barrister 1972–, recorder of the Crown Court 1991–, head of chambers; legal assessor: GMC 1991–, Gen Dental Cncl 1991–; memb: Mental Health Review Tbnl, Employment Appeal Tbnl; *Recreations* computers; *Style*— John Hand, Esq, QC; ✉ 9 St John Street, Manchester M3 4DN (tel 0161 955 9000, fax 0161 955 9001, MDX 14326); Old Square Chambers, 1 Verulam Buildings, Gray's Inn, London WC1R 5LQ (tel 020 7269 3000, fax 020 7405 1387, e-mail jlh@johnhandqc.co.uk)

HANDCOCK, John Eric; CVO (2002, LVO 1991), DL (Royal Co of Berks 1986); s of Eric George Handcock (d 1979), and Gladys Ada Florence, *née* Prior (d 1997), of Windsor, Berks; *b* 7 October 1930; *Educ* Aldenham, KCL (LLB); *m* 1956, Joan Margaret, da of Wilfred Joseph Bigg, CMG (d 1983), of Swanage, Dorset; 2 s (David, Jonathan), 2 da (Sandra, Nicola); *Career* admitted slr 1954; sr ptnr Lovegrove and Durant of Windsor, Slough and Ascot (subsequently Lovegrove & Eliot of Windsor and Egham) 1966–96, conslt 1995–99; pres Berks, Bucks and Oxon Incorporated Law Soc 1979–80, dir Solicitors' Benevolent Assoc 1981–88, pt/t chm Social Security Appeals Tbnls 1992–2000; Nat Assoc of Round Tables of GB and NI: chm Thames Valley Area 1964–65, memb Nat Cncl 1966–68, nat exec convenor Rules and Special Purposes 1968–70; chm Berks Bucks and Oxon Prof Cncl 1981–82; govr: Upton House Sch Windsor 1965–99, St George's Choir Sch Windsor Castle 1975–96; capt lay stewards St George's Chapel Windsor Castle 1992– (dep capt 1977–92), tstee Prince Philip Tst for Windsor and Maidenhead 1977–2007 (hon sec 1977–2002); pres Windsor and Eton Operatic Soc 1961–, hon slr River Thames Soc 1962–2002 (life memb 1986, vice-pres 2003–06), life pres Windsor Local History Gp 2002; Paul Harris fell Rotary International 1994; Freeman City of London 1984, Liveryman Worshipful Co of Spectacle Makers 2002 (Freeman 1984); Citoyen d'Honneur de la Ville Royale de Dreux 1976; *Recreations* history, European travel, wine, books; *Style*— John E Handcock, Esq, CVO, DL; ✉ Red Deer House, Kingswood Rise, Englefield Green, Surrey TW20 0NG

HANDFORD, Rt Rev (George) Clive; CMG (2007); s of Cyril Percy Dawson Handford (d 1974), of Gedling, Notts, and Alice Ethel, *née* Bullers; *b* 17 April 1937; *Educ* Henry Mellish Sch Nottingham, Hatfield Coll Durham (BA), Queen's Coll Birmingham, Univ of Birmingham (DipTh); *m* 3 Sept 1962, (Anne Elizabeth) Jane, da of Rev Cecil Atherley; 1 da (Catherine Elizabeth b 26 Jan 1977); *Career* curate Mansfield PC 1963–66; chaplain: at Baghdad 1967, at Beirut 1967–73; res fell St Augustine's Coll Canterbury 1973, dean of St George Cathedral Jerusalem 1974–78, archdeacon in The Gulf and chaplain at Abu Dhabi and Qatar 1978–83, vicar of Kneesall with Laxton and Wellow 1983–84, rural dean of Tuxford and Norwell 1983–84, Bishop of Southwell's ecumenical offr 1983–84, archdeacon of Nottingham 1984–90, bishop of Warwick 1990–96, hon canon of Coventry 1990–96, bishop in Cyprus and The Gulf 1996–2007, pres-bishop of the Episcopal Church in Jerusalem and the Middle East 2002–07; *Recreations* bird watching, walking; *Style*— The Rt Rev George Handford, CMG

HANDFORD, Peter Thomas; MBE (1945); s of Rev Hedley William Mountenay Handford (d 1928), Vicar of Four Elms, Edenbridge, Kent, and Helen Beatrice, *née* Crosse (d 1964); *b* 21 March 1919; *Educ* Christ's Hosp; *m* 12 May 1974, Helen Margaret; 2 da (Lyn Patricia (Mrs Hedges), Pamela Anne (Mrs Kucel)), both by previous m; *Career* sound recordist; memb: Acad of Motion Picture Arts and Sciences 1986, Cinema Audio Soc (USA) 1991, Assoc of Motion Picture Sound 1993; WWII (Capt RA) serv incl 50 BEF and D Day landings 1939–46; London Film Prodns 1936–39; after war worked with various film companies before becoming freelance; responsible for sound recording on more than 60 films incl: Room at the Top, Billy Liar, Out of Africa (Academy and BAFTA Awards for sound track 1986), Murder on the Orient Express, Hope and Glory (BAFTA nomination for sound track 1987), Gorillas in the Mist (Academy nomination for sound track 1988), Dangerous Liaisons, White Hunter Black Heart, Havana; prodr Sounds of the Steam Age on records and CDs (awarded Grand Prix du Disque Paris 1964); *Books* The Sound of Railways (1980), An Autobiography of British Cinema - by the actors and film makers who made it (contrib, Methuen, 1997); *Recreations* gardening, sound recording, railway enthusiasm and travel, country pursuits; *Clubs* Academy of Motion Picture Arts and Sciences, Sloane; *Style*— Peter T Handford, Esq, MBE; ✉ c/o Casarotto Marsh Ltd, National House, 4th Floor, 60–66 Wardour Street, London W1V 3HP (tel 020 7287 4450, fax 020 7287 9128)

HANDLER, Thomas Joseph; s of Nicholas Handler (d 1958), of Budapest, Hungary, and Lily, *née* Singer (d 1986); *b* 25 May 1938; *Educ* Fort Street Boys' HS Sydney Aust, Univ of Sydney (Cwlth scholarship, BA, LLB); *m* 25 May 1970, Adrienne (d 2005), da of Alajos Marxreiter, of Szekszard, Hungary; 2 da (Rebecca Louise b 21 Dec 1974, Sophie Melinda b 15 Aug 1976); *Career* slr; WC Taylor & Scott (Sydney) 1962–65 (articled clerk 1958–61), Simmons & Simmons (London) 1965–67; Baker & McKenzie (London): joined 1967, ptnr 1973–97, admin ptnr 1975–76, 1978–79 and 1982–83, conslt 1997–99; mediator Camden Mediation Service and Centre for Dispute Reolution; tstee Environmental Law Fndn; memb: Law Soc, Br-Hungarian Fell, Highgate Soc, Highgate Literary and Scientific Instn; assoc memb: Law Soc of NSW Aust; *Publications* Regulating the European Environment (ed and contrib, 1992, 1993, 1994 and 1997); *Recreations* reading, the arts, cross-country skiing, hiking, gardening; *Style*— Thomas Handler

HANDLEY, Dr Anthony James; s of Wing Cdr Austyn James Handley, RAF (d 1985), of West Mersea, Essex, and Beryl Janet, *née* Ashling (d 1982); *b* 22 June 1942; *Educ* Kimbolton Sch, KCL, Westminster Hosp Med Sch (MB BS, MD), DipIMC RCS(Ed); *m* 3 Dec 1966, Jennifer Ann, da of Noël Lindsay Ross Kane (d 1986), of Colchester, Essex; 1 da (Juliette b 1971), 1 s (Simon b 1973); *Career* Maj RAMC (TA) 1970–94; conslt physician (cardiology) Essex Rivers Healthcare NHS Tst (formerly NE Essex HA) 1974–2002 (hon conslt physician 2003–), hon clinical tutor Charing Cross and Westminster Med Sch 1976–2002, clinical tutor Colchester Postgrad Med Centre 1980–85; chm: Resuscitation Cncl (UK) 1997–2000 (hon sec 1986–97), Basic Life Support Sub-Ctee Int Liaison Ctee on Resuscitation 2000–, Basic Life Support Sub-Ctee Resuscitation Cncl (UK) 2000–; chief med advsr RLSS (UK) 1992–, hon med offr Irish Water Safety 2000–, conslt advsr Virgin Atlantic Airways; co sec and dir Resuscitation Cncl (UK) Trading Ltd; memb: Br Cardiac Soc 1984, Editorial Bd Resuscitation; FRSM 1985, FRCP 1985; OStJ 1992; *Books* Thoracic Medicine (contrib, 1981), Life Support (ed, 1992, 4 edn 2003), Advanced Life Support (ed, 1994), ABC of Resuscitation (ed, 2003); *Recreations* swimming, music (euphonium player); *Style*— Dr Anthony J Handley; ✉ 40 Queens Road, Colchester, Essex CO3 3PB (tel 01206 562642, e-mail tony.handley@btinternet.com); professional: 55 Turner Road, Colchester, Essex CO4 5JY (tel 01206 752444)

HANDLEY, Prof Eric Walter; CBE (1983); s of Alfred Walter Handley (d 1974), and Ada Doris, *née* Cox (d 1944); *b* 12 November 1926; *Educ* King Edward's Sch Birmingham, Trinity Coll Cambridge (BA, MA); *m* 31 July 1952, Carol Margaret Handley, da of Claude Hilary Taylor (d 1966); *Career* UCL: lectr in Greek and Latin 1946–61, reader 1961–67, prof 1967–68, prof of Greek and head of dept 1968–84, hon fell 1989; Inst of Classical Studies Univ of London: dir 1967–84, sr res fell 1995–; Univ of Cambridge: regius prof of Greek 1984–94, fell Trinity Coll 1984–; prof of ancient lit Royal Acad of Arts 1990–; visiting lectr in classics Harvard Univ 1966, visiting memb Inst for Advanced Study Princeton 1971; visiting prof: Stanford Univ 1977, Univ of Melbourne 1978; sr res fell Princeton Univ 1981; chm Cncl Univ Classical Depts 1975–78 (sec 1969–70), vice-pres Union Académique Internationale 1994–97 and 1999–2000; pres: Classical Assoc 1984–85, Hellenic Soc 1993–96; Dr (hc) Univ of Athens 1995; foreign memb Societas Scientiarum Fennica 1984, hon memb Hungarian Acad of Sciences 1993, corr memb Acad Athens 1995, memb Norwegian Acad of Sci and Letters 1996, memb Academia Europaea 1988; FBA 1969 (foreign sec 1979–88), FRSA 1971, Hon RA 1990; *Books* The Telephus of Euripides (with John Rea, 1957), The Dyskolos of Menander (1965 and 1992), Relire Ménandre (with André Hurst, 1990), Aristophane (with Jan-Maarten Bremer, 1993), Images of the Greek Theatre (with Richard Green, 1995 and 2001); *Recreations* walking, travel; *Clubs* Oxford and Cambridge; *Style*— Prof Eric Handley, CBE, FBA; ✉ Trinity College, Cambridge CB2 1TQ (tel 01223 338413, fax 01223 338564)

HANDLEY, Martin Hugh; s of Dr William Richard Cecil Handley (d 1997), and Irene Jessie, *née* Edwards; *b* 8 July 1951; *Educ* Bedales, CCC Cambridge (MA); *m* 1, 6 July 1974 (m dis 2000), Anne, *née* Clayton; 1 s (David Christopher b 17 Sept 1982), 1 da (Mika Elisabeth b 24 July 1984); *Career* chorusmaster and conductor Australian Opera 1981–84, chorusmaster and conductor ENO 1984–90, head of music and conductor Royal Danish Opera 1997–99, conductor Carl Rosa Opera 2004–; presenter: BBC World Service 1985–, BBC Radio 3 1998–; guest coach: Young Artists Prog ROH 2002–, Nat Opera Studio 2006–, Royal Acad of Music 2007–; *Recreations* Weald of Kent, food, wine, travel, Oxford United FC; *Style*— Martin Handley, Esq; ✉ c/o BBC Radio 3, BBC Broadcasting House, London W1A 1AA (e-mail martin.handley@bbc.co.uk)

HANDOVER, Richard Gordon; s of Gordon Frank James (d 1991), and Hilda, *née* Dyke (d 1981); *b* 13 April 1946, South Africa; *m* 1972, Veronica Joan, da of Arthur Woodhead; 2 da (Felicity Kate b 28 Jan 1979, Alexandra Veronica b 8 Feb 1981), 1 s (James Richard Nicholas b 9 Feb 1984); *Career* WHSmith: joined 1964, md Our Price 1989, md WHSmith News 1995, memb Bd 1995–2005, gp chief exec 1997–2003, chm 2003–05; non-exec dir: Nationwide Building Soc 2000–, Royal Mail Holdings plc 2003–; chm: Educn Leadership Team Business in the Community 1999–, Adult Learning Inspectorate 2001–; *Recreations* tennis, golf, painting, running, travelling; *Style*— Richard Handover, Esq; ✉ Adult Learning Inspectorate, Spring Place, Coventry Business Park, Herald Avenue, Coventry CV5 6UB

HANDS, Donald Christopher; s of Vincent Edwin Hands (d 1989), and Marjorie Elsie, *née* Witton (d 1998); *b* 23 May 1944; *Educ* Colchester Royal GS, Southend Sch of Arch (DipArch), AA Sch of Architecture; *m* 1, 1963, Keren Margaret, *née* Steady; 1 s (Simon Christopher b 30 Nov 1964), 1 da (Kirsty Sarah b 1 June 1969); m 2, 1991, Catherine Barbara, *née* Hutton; 1 da (Amy Lotus b 3 Feb 1996); *Career* architect; Gollins Melvin Ward 1969–70: memb BOAC Terminal J F Kennedy Airport project team and Royal Opera House design team; dir Rolfe Judd 1980–99 (joined 1971, conslt 2000–): responsible for restoration and refurbishment of notable historic bldgs incl RICS Parliament Square, St Olaf House Tooley St, 49 St James St, Spencer House, St James's Place; recipient Europa Nostra Award 1994 and Civic Tst Award 1996 (for restoration of Spencer House); chm Wren Insurance Assoc 2004– (dir 1995–2002), dir LWR Consultants 2000–; RIBA 1970; *Recreations* historic sports car racing (patron Classic Team Lotus 2000–), coastal sailing, hill walking, cycling; *Clubs* Historic Sports Car (vice-chm 1995–97), Lotus; *Style*— Donald Hands, Esq; ✉ Rolfe Judd, Old Church Court, Claylands Road, The Oval, London SW8 1NZ (tel 020 7556 1533, fax 020 7556 1501, mobile 078 3152 5634, e-mail donh@rolfe-judd.co.uk)

HANDS, Greg; MP; *b* 1965, NY; *Educ* Dr Challoner's GS, Univ of Cambridge; *m* Irina; 1 da (Helena Mavis Charlotte b 12 Feb 2006); *Career* worked in banking until 1997, cncllr Hammersmith and Fulham BC 1998– (ldr Cons Gp 1999–), MP (Cons) Hammersmith and Fulham 2005–; memb: Exec Cons Way Forward (CWF), Cons Friends of Israel, Tory Green Initiative, Cons Cncllrs Assoc, Fulham and Hammersmith Historical Soc, Hammersmith and Fulham Historic Buildings Gp; govr St Thomas' RC Primary Sch; *Style*— Greg Hands, Esq, MP; ✉ House of Commons, London SW1A 0AA (website www.greghands.com)

HANDS, Guy; s of Christopher Hands, and Sally Hands; *b* 27 August 1959; *Educ* Judd Sch Tonbridge, Mansfield Coll Oxford (MA); *m* 1984, Julia Caroline, *née* Ablethorpe; 2 s, 2 da; *Career* head of Eurobond trading Goldman Sachs 1982–94 (trading 1986, head Global Asset Structuring Gp 1990), fndr and md Principal Finance Gp Nomura International plc 1994–2001, ceo Terra Firma Capital Partners Ltd 2002–; *Recreations* films, wine, fine art, photography; *Style*— Guy Hands, Esq; ✉ Terra Firma Capital Partners Limited, 2 More London Riverside, London SE1 2AP (tel 020 7015 9500)

HANDS, Philip; s of Christopher Dawson Hands, and Sally Frances, *née* Partridge; *b* 11 December 1962, Taplow, Bucks; *Educ* Judd Sch Tonbridge, Univ of Nottingham (LLB); *m* 21 Jan 1995, Samantha Dorothy, *née* Mayers; 1 s (Gage Stanley b 9 Aug 1999), 1 da (Octavia Jean b 9 Jan 2002); *Career* Beachcroft LLP (formerly Wansbroughs Willey Hargrave, then Beachcroft Wansbroughs): slr 1988–96, ptnr 1996–2007; princ Hands Law 2007–; memb: Law Soc 1988, Property Litigation Assoc 2000; *Recreations* cycling, sailing, skiing, golf; *Style*— Philip Hands, Esq; ✉ Hands Law, St Brandon's House, 29 Great George Street, Bristol BS1 5QT

HANDS, Terry; CBE (2007); *b* 9 January 1941; *Educ* Univ of Birmingham (BA), RADA; *m* 1, 1964 (m dis 1967), Josephine Barstow (now Dame Josephine Barstow, DBE, *qv*); m 2, 1974, (m dis 1980), Ludmila Mikael; 1 da (Marina); partner, 1988–96, Julia Lintott; 2 s (Sebastian, Rupert); m 3, 2002, Emma Lucia; *Career* theatre and opera director; fndr dir Liverpool Everyman Theatre 1964–66; RSC: artistic dir Theatreground (touring schs and community centres) 1966–68, assoc dir 1967, jt artistic dir 1978, chief exec 1986–91, dir emeritus 1991–; dir Clwyd Theatr Cymru 1997–; Hon DLitt, Hon PhD; hon fell: Shakespeare Inst, Welsh Coll of Music and Drama 2002, NE Wales Inst of HE; Chevalier de l'Ordre des Arts et des Lettres (France); *Theatre* dir many prodns for RSC incl: The Merry Wives of Windsor 1968 (revived 1975/76), Pericles 1969, Henry V, Henry IV Parts I and 2 (all transfered to Aldwych (centenary season Stratford)) 1975, Henry VI (all 3 parts, Stratford (1st time in entirety since Shakespeare's day, SWET Award for Dir of the Year)) 1977, As You Like It, Richard II and Richard III (the latter two completing the entire Shakespeare history cycle, begun 1975, with Alan Howard in leading roles, Stratford) 1982, Much Ado About Nothing (Stratford) 1982, Poppy (Musical of the Year), Cyrano de Bergerac (SWET Award for Best Dir, Barbican) 1983, Red Noses 1985, Singer 1989, The Seagull 1990, Tamburlaine (Evening Standard Award for Best Dir, transferred to Barbican) 1992–93, The Importance of Being Earnest (Birmingham Rep and Old Vic) 1995; for Clwyd Theatr Cymru: The Importance of Being Earnest 1997, Equus 1997, A Christmas Carol 1997, The Journey of Mary Kelly, The Norman Conquests 1998, Twelfth Night 1999, Macbeth 1999, Under Milk Wood 1999, Private Lives 2000, King Lear 2001, Bedroom Farce 2001, The Rabbit 2001, Rosencrantz and Guildenstern are Dead 2002, Betrayal 2002, Romeo and Juliet 2002, The Four Seasons 2002, Blithe Spirit 2003, The Crucible 2003, Pleasure and Repentance 2003, One Flew Over the Cuckoo's Nest 2004, Brassed Off 2004, Troilus and Cressida 2005, Chorus of Disapproval 2006, Memory 2006, Arcadia 2007; other credits incl: Richard III (Comedie Française) 1972 (Meilleur Spectacle de L'Année), Twelfth Night 1976 (Meilleur Spectacle de L'Année), Othello (Paris Opera, televised France 1978), Parsifal (Royal Opera House) 1979, Arden of Faversham (Schauspielhaus Zürich) 1992, Buffalo Bill Show (Recklinghausen) 1992, Simon Boccanegra (Bremen) 1992, Sag Mir Wo Die Blumen Sind (Berlin) 1993, Hamlet (Paris) 1994, Hadrian VII and The Visit (Chichester Festival Theatre) 1995, Merry Wives of Windsor (RNT 1995, NT Oslo 1995), The Pretenders (NT Oslo) 1996, The Seagull (NT Oslo) 1998, Macbeth (New York) 2000; conslt dir: Comedie Française 1975–80, Troilus and Cressida (Burgtheater Vienna) 1977, As You Like It (Burgtheater Vienna) 1979, Hamlet (Chicago Shakespeare Theatre) 2006; *Style*— Terry Hands, Esq, CBE; ✉ Clwyd Theatr Cymru, Mold, Flintshire CH7 1YA (tel 01352 756 331)

HANDY, Charles Brian; CBE (2000); s of Ven Brian Leslie Handy, Archdeacon of Kildare, and Joan Kathleen Herbert, *née* Scott; *b* 25 July 1932; *Educ* Bromsgrove Sch, Oriel Coll Oxford (MA), MIT (SM); *m* 5 Oct 1962, Elizabeth Ann, da of Lt-Col Rowland Fenwick Ellis Hill (d 1978); 1 da (Kate b 1966), 1 s (Scott b 1968); *Career* mktg exec Shell International Petroleum Co Ltd 1956–65, economist Charter Consolidated Co Ltd 1965–66, int faculty fell MIT 1966–67, London Business Sch 1967–95 (prof 1978–94), warden St George's House Windsor Castle 1977–81, writer and broadcaster 1981–; chm RSA 1986–88, memb CNAA 1988–91; Hon DLitt: Bristol Poly 1988, UEA, Univ of Essex 2000, Univ of Hull 2000; Hon DUniv Open Univ 1989, Hon DPhil Univ of Middlesex 1998; Hon DSc: Queen's Univ Belfast 1998, Univ of Exeter 1999; Hon DCL Univ of Durham 2000, Hon Dr Univ of Dublin 2006; hon fell: St Mary's Coll Twickenham 1999, Inst of Educn Univ of London 1999, City & Guilds 2000, Oriel Coll Oxford 2000; *Books* Understanding Organizations (1983), Future of Work (1984), Gods of Management (1985), Understanding Schools (1986), Understanding Voluntary Organizations (1988), The Age of Unreason (1989), Inside Organisations (1990), The Empty Raincoat (1994), Waiting for the Mountain to Move (1995), Beyond Certainty (1995), The Hungry Spirit (1997), The New Alchemists (1999), Thoughts for the Day (1999), The Elephant and the Flea (2001), Reinvented Lives (2002), Myself and Other Important Matters (2006), The New Philanthropists (2006); *Recreations* theatre, cooking, travel; *Style*— Charles Handy, Esq, CBE; ✉ Flat 1A, 73 Putney Hill, London SW15 3NT (tel 020 8788 1610, fax 020 8789 3821); Old Hall Cottages, Bressingham, Diss, Norfolk IP22 2AG (tel 01379 687546)

HANDY, Prof Nicholas Charles; of Kenneth George Edwards Handy (d 1995), of Swindon, Wilts, and Ada Mary, *née* Rumming; *b* 17 June 1941; *Educ* Clayesmore Sch, St Catharine's Coll Cambridge (MA, PhD, ScD); *m* 19 Aug 1967, Elizabeth Carole, da of Alfred Rennick Gates (d 1960); 2 s (Charles Paul b 1971, Julian John b 1973); *Career* Harkness fell Johns Hopkins Univ USA 1968–69; Univ of Cambridge: demonstrator 1972–77, lectr 1977–89, reader 1989–91, prof of quantum chemistry 1991–, pres St Catharine's Coll 1994–97 (fell 1965); memb Int Acad of Quantum Molecular Sci 1988; Boys-Rahman Lectr RSC 2004; Leverhulme Medal Royal Soc 2002; Dr (hc) Univ de Marne-la-Valée France 2000; FRS 1990; *Recreations* travel, gardening; *Style*— Prof Nicholas Handy, FRS; ✉ Department of Chemistry, Lensfield Road, Cambridge CB2 1EW (tel 01223 336373, fax 01223 336362, e-mail nch1@cam.ac.uk)

HANGARTNER, Dr (John) Robert Wilfred; s of John Hangartner, and Ita Patricia, *née* Brett; *b* 5 February 1955; *Educ* Merchant Taylors', Guy's Hosp Med Sch Univ of London (BSc, MB BS, MRCS, LRCP), Open Univ (MBA); *m* 1980, Jillian Mary, da of Martin Frederick Ansell; 1 da (Caroline Emma b 27 Feb 1987), 1 s (Christopher Robert b 12 May 1991); *Career* house offr gen med Lewisham Hosp 1979–80, SHO Guy's Hosp 1980–81 (house offr gen surgery 1980); St George's Hosp: SHO 1981–82, registrar (pathology) 1982–83, clinical lectr in histopathology Med Sch 1983–88; hon sr registrar SW Thames RHA 1983–88; Dept of Health: sr med offr 1988–91, sr princ med offr and divnl head 1993–97 (temp princ med offr 1991–93); CMO Guardian Health Ltd 1997–2000, sr med exec PPP Healthcare Ltd 1998–2000; princ dir Brett Cook Consulting Ltd 2001–; Guy's and St Thomas' NHS Fndn Tst: conslt pathologist (renal histopathology) 2002–, clinical dir Diagnostic and Therapeutic Services Directorate 2004, divnl dir Core Clinical Servs Div 2004–06; hon CMO Bass Healthcare Trustee Ltd 1998–2000; chm Hospital Jr Staff Ctee BMA 1984–85; former memb: Cncl BMA, Bd of Educn and Science BMA; FRSA 1994, FRCPath 1997 (MRCPath 1988); *Recreations* golf, photography, sailing; *Style*— Dr Robert Hangartner; ✉ Brett Cook Consulting Ltd, 11 Annesley Road, Blackheath, London SE3 0JX (tel 020 8319 3164, fax 020 8319 8775, e-mail rh@brettcookconsultingltd.co.uk)

HANHAM, Baroness (Life Peer UK 1999), of Kensington in the Royal Borough of Kensington and Chelsea; Joan Brownlow Hanham; CBE (1997); da of Alfred Spark, of Newcastle upon Tyne; *b* 23 September 1939; *Educ* Hillcourt Sch Dublin; *m* 1964, Dr Iain William Ferguson Hanham, s of Charles Hanham, of York; 1 s (Hon James Charles b 1971), 1 da (Hon Emma Margaret b 1973); *Style*— The Rt Hon the Baroness Hanham, CBE

HANHAM, Sir Michael William; 12 Bt (E 1667), of Wimborne, Dorsetshire, DFC (1944); o s of Patrick John Hanham (d 1965, yst s of Col Phelips Brooke Hanham, bro of 9 Bt), and his 1 w, Dulcie, *née* Daffarn, formerly Hartley (d 1979); suc his kinsman, Sir Henry Phelips Hanham, 11 Bt, 1973; *b* 31 October 1922; *Educ* Winchester; *m* 27 Feb 1954, Margaret Jane, o da of Wing-Cdr Harold Thomas, RAF; 1 da (Victoria Jane (Mrs David L Gross) b 1955), 1 s (William John Edward b 1957); *Heir* s, William Hanham; *Career* Flying Offr RAF Pathfinder Force 1944–45, actg Flt Lt India 1946; BOAC 1947–61; own garden furniture workshop 1963–74; running family estate at Wimborne 1974–; *Clubs* RAF; *Style*— Sir Michael Hanham, Bt, DFC; ✉ Deans Court, Wimborne, Dorset

HANKES, Sir Claude; KCVO (2006); *b* 8 March 1949; *Career* strategic advsr; Manufacturers Hanover 1968–72, Robert Fleming & Co Ltd 1972–77 (dir 1974–77), dep chm Leutwiler and Partners Ltd 1992–96; chm: Mgmnt Ctee Price Waterhouse and Partners 1983–89, Advsy Ctee to Jordan on Strategic Policy Matters 1993–94; interim chm Roland Berger Strategy Consultants Ltd 2003–05; advsr: to Iraq 2003, to Governing Cncl Iraq 2003–04, to Iraq on macro strategic issues 2005–, Trade Bank of Iraq 2007–; masterminded resolution to South African debt crisis 1985–86, Nobel Report 1991, testified at US Congress on UN Oil for Food scandal 2004; tstee Windsor Leadership Tst 1998– (chm 2000–07); hon memb Coll of St George Windsor Castle 2006, hon fell and life memb Cncl St George's House Windsor Castle 2006–, hon fell CCC Oxford; *Recreations* hiking, photography, surfing (Jamie Hanks); *Style*— Sir Claude Hankes, KCVO; ✉ Henry III Tower, Windsor Castle, Berkshire SL4 1NJ (tel 01367 240547, e-mail office@stanfordplace.com)

HANKEY, Dr the Hon Alexander Maurice Alers; s of 2 Baron Hankey, KCMG, KCVO (d 1996); hp of bro 3 Baron Hankey, *qv*; *b* 18 August 1947; *Educ* Rugby, Trinity Coll Cambridge, MIT (PhD), MERU (MSCI); *m* 1970 (m dis 1990), Deborah, da of Myron Benson, of Mass, USA; *Career* Greenlaw fell MIT 1969–71, Lindemann fellowship 1972–73 (held at Stanford Linear Accelerator Center), teacher of transcendental meditation 1973; Maharishi Int Univ USA: asst prof of physics 1973–74, associate prof 1974–75, prof 1975–78; prof of physics Maharishi Euro Res Univ of Switzerland and UK 1975–82, govr Age of Enlightenment 1977–, co dir Academy for the Science of Creative Intelligence Mass 1978, dean Faculty Maharishi Int Academy UK 1985–86, registrar Maharishi Univ of Natural Law North of England Campus 1986–92, exec asst to Dr Geoffrey Clements 1998–2002; memb Editorial Bd Jl of Alternative and Complementary Med 2003, memb Editorial Bd Evidence Based Complimentary and Alternative Medicine

H

(eCAM) 2004–; Leverhulme Foundation res award 1986; chm East Grinstead TM Centre 1993–, memb Exec Cncl Natural Law Party of GB 1992–2001, sec Natural Law Pty of Sussex 1994–97; *Publications* The Sun's First Rays (poems); author of numerous scientific papers and articles particularly in critical phenomena and the biophysics of complementary med; *Recreations* skiing, tennis, hiking; *Clubs* Royal Tennis; *Style*— Dr the Hon Alexander Hankey; ✉ Hethe House, Cowden, Kent TN8 7DZ (tel and fax 01342 850086, e-mail alexhank@dircon.co.uk)

HANKEY, 3 Baron (UK 1939); Donald Robin Alers Hankey; s of 2 Baron Hankey, KCMG, KCVO (d 1996), and his 1 w, Frances Bevyl, *née* Stuart-Menteth (d 1957); *b* 12 June 1938; *Educ* Rugby, UCL (Dip Arch); *m* 1, 1963 (m dis 1974), Margaretha, yr da of Cand Jur H Thorndahl, of Copenhagen, Denmark; m 2, 1974 (m dis 1994), Eileen Désirée, da of Maj-Gen Stuart Hedley Molesworth Battye, CB, of Fensacre House, Ascot, Berks; 2 da (Hon Fiona Bevyl b 1975, Hon Beatrice Eileen b 1978); m 3, 9 July 1994, June, da of late Dr Leonard Taboroff, and of Mrs Elsie Taboroff, of Palo Alto, CA; 1 s adopted (Hugh Michael Alers b 4 May 1997); *Heir* bro, Dr the Hon Alexander Hankey, *qv*; *Career* chm Intercol International 1970–72, fndr and chm Gilmore Hankey Kirke (part of GHK Gp of Cos involved in architecture, conservation, planning engrg, economics and mgmnt) 1973–2000; consltt to: nat and int agencies, local and nat govts; fndr and chm All-Pty Gp on Architecture and Planning 1997–99; pres ICOMOS (UK) 2007– (vice-chm 1997–2007), vice-chm MOD (Defence Estates Orgn) Historic Building Advsy Gp 1998–2003; memb: SPAB, EASA, ASCHB; RIBA, FRSA, FRAI; *Recreations* tennis, painting, music; *Style*— The Rt Hon the Lord Hankey; ✉ 8 Sunset Road, London SE5 8EA (tel 020 7733 0453)

HANLEY, Rt Hon Sir Jeremy James; KCMG (1997), PC (1994); s of Jimmy Hanley (d 1970), and Dinah Sheridan; *b* 17 November 1945; *Educ* Rugby; *m* 1, 1968 (m dis), Helene; 1 s (Jason b 1970); m 2, 1973, Verna, Viscountess Villiers, da of Kenneth Stott (d 1992), of Jersey; 1 s (Joel b 1974), 1 step da (Lady Sophia b 1971); *Career* CA; MP (Cons) Richmond and Barnes 1983–97 (Parly candidate (Cons) Lambeth Central (by-election) 1978 and 1979); vice-chm Cons Trade and Industry Ctee, memb House of Commons Select Ctee on Home Affrs; former memb: House of Commons Select Sub-Ctee on Race Relations and Immigration, Br-Irish Inter Parly Body; former sec All-Pty Gp for Europe; PPS to: Min of State at Privy Cncl Office, Min for Civil Serv and the Arts (Rt Hon Richard Luce, MP) 1987–90, Sec of State for the Environment (Rt Hon Christopher Patten, MP) 1990; Parly under-sec of state NI Office 1990–93 (min for Health, Social Servs and Agriculture 1990–92, min for Political Devpt, Educn and Community Relations 1992–93), min of state for Armed Forces MOD 1993–94, chm Cons Pty 1994–95, Cabinet min without portfolio 1994–95, min of state (for N Africa, ME, Indian Sub-Continent, SE Asia, Far East and Pacific, Overseas Trade) FCO 1995–97; Parly advsr Inst of CAs in England and Wales 1986–90; chm: International Trade & Investment Missions Ltd 1997–2002, AdVal Group plc 1998–2003, Brain Games Network plc 2000; non-exec dir: ITE Group plc 1998–, GTECH Hldgs Corp Inc 2001–06, consltt Lottmatica SpA 2006–, Willis Gp Holdings 2006–, Langbar Int Ltd 2006–, Blue Hackle Ltd 2006–; sr consltt Kroll Assocs 2003–04; memb: Euro Advsy Bd Credit Lyonnais 2000–05, Advsy Bd Talal Abu-Ghazaleh International 2004–05; vice-pres Br-Iranian C of C 2002–06 (chm 2000–02); memb Bd Arab-Br C of C; Freeman City of London, Master Worshipful Co of CAs 2005–06; FCA, FCIS; *Recreations* cookery, cricket, chess, languages, the arts; *Clubs* Lord's Taverners, Garrick, St Stephen's, Pilgrims; *Style*— The Rt Hon Sir Jeremy Hanley, KCMG; ✉ 6 Butts Mead, Northwood, Middlesex HA6 2TL (tel 01923 826675, fax 01923 836447)

HANLEY-BROWNE, Mark David; s of Alan Hanley-Browne, of Walton-on-Thames, Surrey, and Eileen, *née* Hankin; *b* 19 October 1961, Crawley, W Sussex; *Educ* St George's Coll Weybridge, Lady Margaret Hall Oxford (exhibitioner, MA), Homerton Coll Cambridge (PGCE); *m* 10 July 1993, Rachael, *née* Scott; *Career* asst master and biology teacher Sevenoaks Sch 1983–88, asst master and head of careers and HE Charterhouse 1988–97, dep head (pastoral) Highgate Sch 1997–2004, headmaster Emanuel Sch London 2004–; fell commoner (sabbatical) St John's Coll Cambridge 1995; memb: ASCL 1997–, HMC 2004–; memb Guild of Freemen City of London; *Recreations* writing, travel, wine appreciation; *Clubs* East India, RAF; *Style*— Mark Hanley-Browne, Esq; ✉ Emanuel School, Battersea Rise, London SW11 1HS (tel 020 8870 4171, fax 020 8877 1424, e-mail hm@emanuel.org.uk)

HANLEY-RYDER, Shirley Ann; da of late Gerard Farnworth, and late Renee Winifred, *née* Royds; *b* 2 October 1956; *Educ* Notre Dame GS Blackburn, Univ of Leicester (BSc); *m* 1, 25 June 1983 (m dis 1998), Dermot Joseph Hanley, s of Dr Donal Aloysius Hanley, and Honora Eileen, *née* O'Mahony; 3 s (Christopher Jon b 17 May 1987, William Gerard b 5 March 1990, Simon James b 22 Jan 1992); m 2, 12 Jan 2002, Stephen Albert Ryder, s of late Willaim Albert Ryder and Doris, *née* Hardy; *Career* grad trainee rising to PR account exec Octagon Marketing Consultants Ltd 1979–82, sr PR exec Byron Advertising Ltd 1982–84; QBO plc (latterly QBO Bell Pottinger Ltd): campaign mangr 1984–86, campaign dir 1986–87, associate dir 1987–89, bd dir 1989, dep md 1991–2002; fndr: The Hanley Ryder Partnership 2002, EmPower Engagement Mktg Ltd 2004; MCIPR 1988; *Recreations* tennis, travel, entertaining, family life; *Style*— Mrs Shirley Hanley-Ryder; ✉ Holmwood House, Holmwood Park, Ringwood Road, Longham, Wimborne, Dorset BH22 9AP (tel 07836 514409, e-mail shirley@hr-p.co.uk)

HANMER, Sir John Wyndham Edward; 8 Bt (GB 1774), of Hanmer, Flintshire, JP (Clwyd 1971), DL (1978); s of Lt-Col Sir (Griffin Wyndham) Edward Hanmer, 7 Bt (d 1977), by his 1 w, Aileen; *b* 27 September 1928; *Educ* Eton; *m* 1954, Audrey Melissa, eldest da of Maj Arthur Christopher John Congreve (d 1992), of the same family (which held land in Staffs from *temp* Edward II) as William Congreve, the Restoration playwright; 2 s ((Wyndham Richard) Guy b 1955, Edward Hugh b 1957); *Heir* s, Guy Hanmer; *Career* Capt late The Royal Dragoons; landowner and farmer; dir Chester Race Co 1978–2004, Ludlow Race Club Ltd 1980–2004; dir Bangor-on-Dee Races Ltd 1981–2003; High Sheriff Clwyd 1977; Lord of the Manor of Bettisfield; *Recreations* shooting, racing; *Clubs* Army and Navy; *Style*— Sir John Hanmer, Bt, DL; ✉ The Mere House, Hanmer, Whitchurch, Shropshire SY13 3DG (tel 01948 830383)

HANNA, Hon Mr Justice Michael Anthony Patrick; s of Francis Hanna (d 1987), of Belfast and Dublin, and Mary Ida, *née* Conboy (d 1999); *b* 18 July 1953, Belfast; *Educ* St MacNissi's Coll Garron Tower, TCD (BA, LLB), King's Inns Dublin; *m* 2 Jan 1981, Philomena, *née* Connolly; 4 s (Francis b 22 Feb 1982, Michael b 24 May 1983, Patrick b 1 Aug 1984, Leo b 19 Oct 1994), 1 da (Aoife Maria b 14 Oct 1988); *Career* called to the Bar King's Inns Dublin 1977 (bencher), called to the Inner Bar 1996; judge of the High Court of Ireland 2004–; *Recreations* walking, travel, golf, reading, music, cinema; *Clubs* Kildare St and Univ, Skibereen Golf, Baltimore Sailing; *Style*— The Hon Mr Justice Michael Hanna; ✉ The High Court, Four Courts, Inns Quay, Dublin 7, Ireland (tel 00 353 1 888 6000, fax 00 353 1 872 5669, e-mail michaelhanna@courts.ie)

HANNA, Robert James; CBE 1988 (OBE 1975), JP (Londonderry 1962); s of James Hanna (d 1973), of Draperstown, and Isabella Margaret, *née* Smyth (d 1978); *b* 9 May 1935; *Educ* Rainey Endowed Magherafelt Co Londonderry; *m* 1 Aug 1962, Annie Elizabeth (Betty), da of late James and Mary Faulkner, of Cookstown, Co Tyrone; 3 s (James Faulkner b 14 June 1963, (Robert) Gordon b 18 Oct 1964, (Wilfred) Sydney b 9 April 1967), 1 da (Muriel Elizabeth Margaret b 9 Dec 1969); *Career* farmer and landowner; memb: Londonderry CC 1965–73, Ulster Countryside Ctee 1965–89 (vice-chm 1968–75, chm 1975–89); Ulster Farmers' Union: pres 1972–73, hon life memb 1999; cmmr Planning Appeals Cmmn 1973–86; memb: NI Economic Cncl 1972–77, NI Agricultural Tst 1973–81, PO Users' Cncl NI 1978–81, BBC NI Agricultural Advsy Ctee 1978–84, Gen Consumer Cncl NI 1985–91 (dep chm 1991–92), NI Representative Food from Britain Advsy Ctee Home Grown Cereals Authy 1986–98, Bd NI Electricity 1991–92, NHS 50 Nat Steering Gp 1996–98 (chm Regnl Steering Gp 1996–98), Cncl Nat Assoc of Health Authorities and Tsts (now NHS Confederation) 1990–2000, Rural Devpt Cncl 1991–96, Lough Neagh Advsy Ctee 1994–2000, Moyola Valley Devpt Partnership 1994–2001, Local Govt Staff Cmmn 2001–; chm: NI Northern Health and Social Servs Bd 1989–2000, Belfast Harbour Forum 1991–97, Cncl for Nature Conservation and the Countryside 1996–2000 (dep chm 1989–96), Odyssey Tst Co Ltd 2000–; pro-chllr Univ of Ulster 1994–2002; dir Countryside Recreation NI 1999–2001, vice-pres Tree Cncl 1997–, fndr memb Ulster Tst for Nature Conservation (now the Ulster Wildlife Tst), memb Jt Nature Conservation Ctee 1996–2000, fndr and past chm Farming and Wildlife Advsy Gp NI, govr North East Inst Further & Higher Educn (NEI) 1998–, memb Probation Bd for NI 2000–; Hon DLitt Univ of Ulster 2002; FRSA 1990; *Recreations* the great outdoors, local history; *Clubs* Farmers'; *Style*— Robert J Hanna, Esq, CBE; ✉ The Oaks, 41 Tobermore Road, Draperstown, Co Londonderry BT45 7LN (tel 028 796 28278, fax 028 796 27753)

HANNAFORD, Barry William; s of Albert Edward Hannaford (d 1984), and Ethel, *née* Cesana; *b* 25 June 1953; *m* Rowena; *Career* trainee lighting engr Thorn Lighting Ltd 1970–75, lighting engr Concord Lighting Ltd 1975–76 (dep mangr 1977–80), tech offr London Borough of Greenwich 1976–77, project sales mangr Erco Lighting Ltd 1980–85, dir Lighting Design Partnership 1987–96 (assoc 1985–86), ptnr DPA Lighting Consltts 1996–; major projects incl: James Bond film set Pinewood Studios, Newport and Sequoia Lodge Disney Hotels Paris, Mercury House London, Guildhall London, Theme Park Istanbul, Adelphi Building London (exterior), Opus Sacrum (exhibition) Warsaw, refurbishment Billingsgate Market; UK rep Int Assoc of Lighting Designers; *Publications* Lighting Design (jtly, Design Cncl); *Style*— Barry Hannaford, Esq

HANNAH, Christine Margaret (Chris); da of Robert Edwin Davies (decd), of Widnes, Cheshire, and Marion, *née* Rowley; *b* 9 October 1954; *Educ* Wade Deacon GS for Girls Widnes (head girl), Inst of Personnel Mgmnt, Lancaster Univ (MA); *m* 1, 27 March 1982, Philip Stephen Hannah (decd); 1 s (Benjamin Philip), 1 da (Charlotte Faye); m 2, 7 Sept 2006, Neil Goodwin; *Career* mgmnt trainee Marks & Spencer 1973–74, mgmnt trainee Mersey RHA 1974–75, dir of personnel Halton HA 1978–88, dir of personnel Chester HA 1988–90, head of HR Mersey RHA 1990–93, chief exec S Cheshire HA 1993–96, dir of strategic devpt NW Regnl Office NHS 1996–2001, chief exec Cheshire and Merseyside Strategic HA 2002–06, chair Skills for Health (sector skills cncl UK health sector) 2004–; *Recreations* theatre, literature, political history, travel; *Style*— Ms Chris Hannah; ✉ The Old School, Windmill Lane, Preston on the Hill, Warrington, Cheshire WA4 4AZ (tel 01928 713932, fax 01928 716927, mobile 07867 538107, e-mail chris@goodwinhannah.co.uk)

HANNAH, David Stuart; s of Daniel Hannah, of Appleton, Warrington, and Phyllis, *née* Mottershead; *b* 1 January 1953; *Educ* Royal GS Lancaster, Univ of Liverpool (LLB); *m* 26 March 1977, Joanne Alison, da of James Crichton, of Minchinhampton, Glos; 1 da (Louise b 1979), 3 s (Daniel b 1981, Christopher b 1983, Michael b 1987); *Career* admitted slr 1977; tutor in law of equity and trusts Univ of Liverpool 1974–78; memb Legal Aid Area Ctee Chester 1981–, chm Educn Ctee Slrs Family Law Soc 1996–97; memb Nat Ctee SFLA 1996–97, fndr Ctee memb Br Assoc of Lawyer Mediators 1995, examiner and assessor to Law Soc Family Law Panel, memb Family Law Ctee Law Soc 1998–; Continuing Professional Devpt (CPD) assessor 1999–; *Recreations* swimming, photography, restoring classic cars; *Style*— David S Hannah, Esq; ✉ 1 Marlfield Road, Grappenhall, Warrington WA4 2JT (tel 01925 264974); 1 Victoria Road, Stockton Heath, Warrington WA4 2AL (tel 01925 261354)

HANNAH, Prof Leslie; s of Arthur Hannah (d 1969), and Marie, *née* Lancashire; *b* 15 June 1947; *Educ* Manchester Grammar, St John's Coll Oxford (MA), Nuffield Coll Oxford (DPhil); *m* 29 Dec 1984 (m dis 1998), Nuala Barbara Zahedieh, da of late Thomas Hockton, of Hove, E Sussex; 1 s (Thomas b 1988), 2 step da (Sophie b 1977, Miranda b 1981); *Career* res fell St John's Coll Oxford 1969–73, lectr in economics Univ of Essex 1973–75, lectr Univ of Cambridge 1975–78 (fell Emmanuel Coll, fin tutor 1977–78); LSE: dir Business Hist Unit 1978–88, prof 1982–97, pro-dir 1995–97, actg dir 1996–97; dean Business Sch City Univ 1997–2000; res fell Centre for Econ Policy Res London 1984–92, visiting prof Harvard Business Sch 1984–85, assoc fellow Centre for Business Strategy London Business School 1988–89, invited lectr at univs in USA Europe and Japan; dir various cos (dir NRG Victory Holdings 1987–93), dir London Economics 1992–2000 (fndr memb, subsequently specialist res consltt), chief exec Ashridge 2000–03, prof Univ of Tokyo 2004–; referee/tstee for various res funding agencies, charities and jls; memb Social Sci Res Cncl (UK) 1982–84, chm Editorial Advsy Bd Dictionary of Business Biography 1979–85; MInstD; *Books* The Rise of the Corporate Economy (1976, 2 edn 1983, Japanese edn 1987), Management Strategy and Business Development (ed, 1976), Concentration in Modern Industry: Theory, Measurement and the UK Experience (jtly, 1977), Electricity Before Nationalisation (1977), Engineers, Managers and Politicians (1982), Entrepreneurs and the Social Sciences (1984), Inventing Retirement: The Development of Occupational Pensions in Britain (1986), Electricity Privatisation and the Area Boards: the Case for 12 (jtly, 1987), Pension Asset Management: An International Perspective (ed, 1988), Barclays: The Business of Banking (jtly, 2001); *Recreations* reading, walking, talking; *Style*— Prof Leslie Hannah; ✉ 332 Lauderdale Tower, Barbican, London EC2Y 8NA (e-mail lesliehannah@hotmail.com)

HANNAN, Daniel John; MEP; s of Hugh R Hannan (d 2000), of Brighton, and Lavinia, *née* Moffat; *b* 1 September 1971; *Educ* Marlborough, Oriel Coll Oxford (MA); *m* Sara, da of Jeffrey Maynard, and Margaret Maynard; 1 da (Annabel b 2002); *Career* dir Euro Res Gp 1994–99, ldr writer Daily Telegraph 1996–, special advsr to Rt Hon Michael Howard, QC, MP, *qv*, 1997–99, MEP (Cons) SE England 1999–; *Publications* Time for a Fresh Start in Europe (1993), Britain in a Multi-Speed Europe (1994), The Challenge of the East (1996), A Guide to the Amsterdam Treaty (1997), Direct Democracy (2005); *Recreations* English poetry; *Clubs* Garrick, Carlton, Pratt's; *Style*— Daniel Hannan, Esq, MEP; ✉ 58 Keswick Road, Great Bookham, Surrey KT23 4BH (tel 01372 453678, fax 01372 453741, e-mail office@hannan.co.uk)

HANNAY, Anthony Hewitt Scott; s of Thomas Scott Hannay (d 1975), of Chorlton-by-Backford, Cheshire, and Doreen, *née* Paul (d 2006); *b* 2 May 1944; *Educ* Rugby, Univ of Liverpool (LLB); *m* 10 Oct 1970, Rosemary Susan, da of Maj Geoffrey Thomas St John Sanders, TD (d 1986), of Cirencester, Glos; 1 da (Diana b 1973), 1 s (Andrew b 1975); *Career* admitted slr 1968; ptnr: Laces & Co 1970–88, Lace Mawer 1988–93 (consltt 1993–96), Anthony Hannay (slr) 1996–99; dir Liverpool Cncl of Social Service Inc 1994–2002; consltt Bullivant Jones 2000–04; memb Mgmnt Ctee RNLI 1986–2002 (memb Cncl 2002–), chm Port and City of Liverpool Consultancy Gp RNLI (and predecessor branches) 1989–; memb: Mersey RHA 1988–90, Law Soc; *Recreations* sailing, windsurfing, waterskiing; *Clubs* Liverpool Artists; *Style*— Anthony Hannay, Esq; ✉ The Stray, School Lane, Neston CH64 7TX (tel 0151 336 8455, fax 0151 353 1755, e-mail ant@thehannays.co.uk)

HANNAY OF CHISWICK, Baron (Life Peer UK 2001), of Bedford Park in the London Borough of Ealing; David Hugh Alexander Hannay; GCMG (1995, KCMG 1986, CMG 1981), CH (2003); s of J G Hannay (d 1972), of Aston Tirrold, Oxon, and E M Hannay (d 1986), *née* Lazarus; *b* 28 September 1935; *Educ* Winchester, New Coll Oxford; *m* 1961, Gillian Rosemary, da of H Rex (d 1962), of Exmouth, Devon; 4 s (Hon Richard, Hon Philip, Hon Jonathan, Hon Alexander); *Career* 2 Lt 8 King's Royal Irish Hussars 1954–56;

HM Dip Serv: joined 1959, Tehran 1960–61, oriental sec Kabul 1961–63, Eastern Dept FO 1963–65, second then first sec UK Delgn to the EC 1965–70, first sec UK Negotiating Team with the Euro Community 1970–72, chef de cabinet to Sir Christopher Soames (vice-pres of Cmmn of Euro Community) Brussels 1973–77, head Energy Sci and Space Dept FCO 1977–79, head ME Dept FCO 1979, asst under sec of state (Euro Community) FCO 1979–84, min Washington 1984–85, ambass and UK perm rep to Euro Community 1985–90, ambass and UK permanent rep to UN and rep on Security Cncl 1990–95, ret; Br Govt special rep for Cyprus 1996–2003, PM's personal envoy to Turkey 1998, memb Cncl Britain in Europe 1999–2005, memb TANGGUH Ind Advsy Panel 2002–, memb EU Select Ctee House of Lords 2002–06, vice-chm All Party Parly Gp on the UN 2005–, vice-chm All Party Parly Gp on the EU 2006–, chm Int Advsy Bd EDHEC Business Sch 2003–, memb UN Sec-Gen's High Level Panel for Threats, Challenges and Change 2003–04, chair UN Assoc of the UK 2006–; dir Salzburg Seminar 2002–05, memb Advsy Bd Centre for European Reform 1997–, memb Advsy Bd Judge Inst of Mgmnt Univ of Cambridge 2004–; non-exec dir: Chime Communications plc 1996–2006, Aegis Gp plc 2000–03; govr Ditchley Fndn 2005–; pro-chllr Univ of Birmingham 2001–06 (memb Cncl and Ct 1999–); Hon DLitt Univ of Birmingham; hon fell New Coll Oxford; *Books* Cyprus: The Search for Solution (2004); *Recreations* photography, travel, gardening; *Clubs* Travellers; *Style*— The Rt Hon the Lord Hannay of Chiswick, GCMG, CH; ✉ 3 The Orchard, London W4 1JZ (tel 020 8987 9012)

HANNINGFIELD, Baron (Life Peer UK 1998), of Chelmsford in the County of Essex; Paul Edward Winston White; DL (Essex 1991); s of Edward Ernest William White, and Irene Joyce Gertrude, *née* Williamson; *b* 16 September 1940; *Educ* King Edward VI GS Chelmsford, Nuffield Fndn (Nuffield Scholar); *Career* chm Chelmsford Young Farmers 1962, memb Chelmsford Cons Pty Exec 1962, memb Nat Exec NFU 1965; Essex CC: cncllr 1970–, various posts incl chm of educn 1973–98, chm 1989–92, ldr 1998–; Assoc of CCs: memb 1981–97, chm Educn Ctee 1989–1993, Cons ldr 1995–97; chm: Cncl of Local Educn Authorities 1990–92, Eastern Region FEFC 1992–97, Cons Pty Local Govt Advsy Ctee 1995–98; currently: vice-chm and Cons Gp ldr Local Govt Assoc, memb Bd Cons Pty, chm Localis, memb Ct Univ of Essex, govr Brentwood Sch; *Recreations* keen botanist, current affrs, travel, food and wine; *Style*— The Rt Hon the Lord Hanningfield, DL; ✉ Pippins Place, Helmons Lane, West Hanningfield, Chelmsford, Essex CM2 8UW; Conservative Group Office, Essex County Council, County Hall, Chelmsford, Essex CM1 1LX (tel 01245 430233, fax 01245 491028)

HANRAHAN, Brian; s of Thomas Hanrahan, and Kathleen Hanrahan; *b* 22 March 1949; *Educ* St Ignatius Coll, Univ of Essex (BA); *m* 4 Jan 1986; 1 da; *Career* BBC: Far East corr 1983–85, Moscow corr 1986–89, diplomatic corr 1989–97, diplomatic ed 1997–; *Style*— Brian Hanrahan, Esq; ✉ c/o BBC TV Centre, Wood Lane, London W12 7RJ (tel 020 8743 8000)

HANRATTY, Judith Christine; OBE (2002); da of John Edward Hanratty (d 1981), and Joyce, *née* Proudfoot (d 2000), of Waikanae, NZ; *b* 16 August 1943; *Educ* Chilton St James Sch, St Hilda's Collegiate Sch NZ, Victoria Univ of Wellington NZ (LLB, LLM, LLD); *Career* barrister: High Ct of NZ 1966, Supreme Ct of Victoria Aust 1980, Inner Temple 1987; co sec BP plc until 2003; dir: BP Pension Trustees Ltd 1992–2004, London Electricity plc 1995–97, Charles Taylor Consltg plc 2000–, Partnerships UK plc 2001–05, BSI 2002–05, Partner Re 2005–; memb: Insurance Brokers' Registration Cncl (Sec of State nominee) 1993–98, Listing Authy Ctee of FSA (formerly London Stock Exchange) 1996–2003, Competition Cmmn (formerly Monopolies and Mergers Cmmn) 1997–2003, Takeover Panel 1997–2003, Cncl Lloyd's 1998– (chm Market Supervision and Review Ctee), Gas and Electricity Markets Authy 2004–; chm Cwlth Inst 2002–; chm Coll of Law 2004–05; fell Lucy Cavendish Coll Cambridge; FRSA 1994; *Recreations* golf, horticulture; *Clubs* Athenaeum, Royal Wellington, Royal Wimbledon Golf; *Style*— Miss Judith Hanratty, OBE; ✉ The Commonwealth Institute, Kensington High Street, London W8 6NQ

HANSCOMB, Christine; da of Ronald Hanscomb, and Margaret Hanscomb, of Kent; *b* 7 January 1946; *Educ* Ravensbourne Sch of Art Sunderland, Maidstone Sch of Art (BA); *m* David Versey, artist; 2 da (Crystal-Lily b 5 Nov 1976, Tara-Jade b 25 July 1984); *Career* Art Dept Vogue Magazine 1969–71, art dir Brides magazine 1971–76, art ed Vogue Magazine 1977, art dir Vogue Beauty Book 1978–81, freelance photographer 1979– (specialising in food, still life, children and underwater photography); cmmnd by all maj advtg agencies in London, Paris and Milan 1981–, and by pubns incl Vogue (London, Paris and NY), Country Living, Interiors, House and Garden, The Observer and Sunday Times; commercials dir with The Producers prodn co; *Books* English Country Style (1987); photographic illustrations for numerous cookery books incl: Madhur Jaffrey's A Taste of India, Antonio Carluccio's A Taste of Italy, Sir Terence and Lady Conran's The Cook Book, Sainsbury's The Book of Food, Nathalie Hambro's Visual Delights, Perfect Puddings, Water Babies and Aqua Yoga; *Recreations* films, music, art, deepsea scuba diving, the countryside, gardening; *Style*— Ms Christine Hanscomb; ✉ 11 Perseverance Works, 38 Kingsland Road, London E2 8DD (tel 020 7739 0132, fax 020 7729 7066, e-mail christine@christinehanscomb.co.uk, website www.christinehanscomb.co.uk)

HANSELL, Matthew Simon; s of Barry Hansell, and Hilary, *née* Tombs; *b* 15 September 1961, Birmingham; *Educ* King Edward's GS Stourbridge, UWIST Cardiff, Coll of Law Chester; *m* 17 Dec 1988, Josephine Elizabeth, *née* Marshall; 1 s (Luke b 10 Oct 1994), 1 da (Amy b 14 Nov 1997); *Career* admitted slr 1985; articled clerk Manby & Steward 1983–85, MFG Slrs 1986–87, Martineau Johnson Slrs 1988–2004 (latterly ptnr and head of Private Client Gp), ptnr Mills & Reeve 2004– (ldr National Private Client Gp 2006–); memb: Law Soc (memb Capital Taxes Ctee), Soc of Tst and Estate Practitioners (STEP); Private Client Lawyer of the Year Birmingham Law Soc 2005, UK Regnl Legal Team of the Year STEP 2006/07; *Style*— Matthew Hansell, Esq; ✉ The Barn, 23 New Wood Lane, Blakedown, Kidderminster, Worcestershire DY10 3LD (tel 01562 701238); Mills & Reeve, 78–84 Colmore Row, Birmingham B3 2AB (tel 0121 456 8297, fax 0121 456 8483, e-mail matthew.hansell@mills-reeve.com)

HANSEN, Alan David; s of John McDonald Hansen, of Clackmananshire, Scotland, and Anne Peddie, *née* Gillon; *b* 13 June 1955; *Educ* Lornshill Acad; *m* 21 June 1980, Janette, da of James Harold Rhymes; 1 s (Adam John b 29 June 1981), 1 da (Lucy Grace b 23 Aug 1984); *Career* former professional footballer; Partick Thistle 1973–77, Liverpool FC 1977–91 (621 appearances, 8 League Championships, 3 European Cups, 2 FA Cups); currently commentator and analyst Sportsnight and Match of the Day BBC TV, presenter of football documentaries; *Recreations* golf, tennis; *Clubs* Hillside Golf, Southport and Birkdale Cricket; *Style*— Alan Hansen, Esq; ✉ c/o BBC TV Sports and Events Group, Kensington House, Richmond Way, London W14 0AX

HANSEN, Brent Vivian; s of Vivian Ernest Hansen (d 1988), of Christchurch, NZ, and Noeline, *née* Eathorne; *b* 14 September 1955; *Educ* St Andrew's Coll Christchurch, Univ of Otago (BA), Canterbury Univ Christchurch (MA), Christchurch Teachers' Coll (teaching cert); *m* 30 Aug 1986, Phillipa Jennie Dann, of NZ; 1 da (Marley Harriet b 22 April 1991), 1 s (Cassidy Jake b 8 Jan 1995); *Career* TV New Zealand: floor mangr, unit mangr, prodr and dir Radio With Pictures 1982–86; MTV: news prodr 1987, dir of news 1987–88, head of prodn 1988–89, dir of programming and prodn 1989–94, pres and chief exec MTV Networks Europe 1996– (pres and creative dir 1994–), pres of creative MTV International; memb Country Music Assoc Nashville; *Recreations* rugby, collecting music; *Style*— Brent Hansen, Esq; ✉ c/o MTV Europe, Hawley Crescent, London NW1 8TT (tel 020 7284 7777, fax 020 7284 7788, e-mail hansen.brent@mtvne.com)

HANSEN, Prof Jean-Pierre; s of Georges Hansen (d 1960), and Simone Hansen-Flohr (d 1986); *b* 10 May 1942; *Educ* Athénée Grand-Ducal de Luxembourg, Université de Liège (BA), Université de Paris (PhD); *m* 22 Dec 1971, Martine, da of late Henri Béchet; 1 da (Anne-Elise Nichols b 22 June 1976); *Career* research assoc CNRS 1967–73, prof of physics Université Pierre et Marie Curie Paris 1973–86, prof of physics and head Dept of Physics Ecole Normale Supérieure de Lyon 1986–97, prof of theoretical chemistry Univ of Cambridge and fell CCC Cambridge 1997–; visiting scientist Institut Laue-Langevin Grenoble 1980–81, visiting Miller prof Univ of Calif Berkeley 1991, visiting fell Balliol Coll and Physical Chemistry Laboratory Univ of Oxford 1994–95; memb: Société Française de Physique 1969, Institut Universitaire de France 1992–97; Grand Prix de l'Etat Academy of Science (France) 1991, Prix Spécial Société Française de Physique 1998, Liquid Matter Prize European Physical Soc 2005, Rumford Medal Royal Soc 2006; FRSC 1998, FRS 2002; *Publications* Theory of Simple Liquids (monograph with I R McDonald, 1976, 3 edn 2006), Basic Concepts for Simple and Complex Liquids (monograph with J L Barrat, 2003); also author of over 250 papers in scientific jls; *Recreations* history of art, classical music, travelling around Italy; *Style*— Prof Jean-Pierre Hansen, FRS; ✉ Department of Chemistry, University of Cambridge, Lensfield Road, Cambridge CB2 1EW (tel 01223 336376, fax 01223 336362, e-mail jph32@cus.cam.ac.uk)

HANSON, Anthony David; s of William Gordon Hanson, OBE (d 1990) of Notts, and Dulce Durrant, *née* Snook (d 1996); bro of Richard Hanson, TD, *qv*; *b* 13 April 1945, Notts; *Educ* Eton, Grenoble Univ; *m* April 1968, Rosemary Patricia (Rosi), *née* Ruddle; 1 s (Christopher Jeremy Piers b 1982); *Career* wine buyer André Simon Wines Ltd and Courtenay Wines (Int) London 1970, buying dir André Simon Wines Ltd 1975–77; Haynes Hanson & Clark (wine merchants): fndr 1978, md 1979–91, buying conslt 1991–; chm Inst of Masters of Wine 1998–99; conslt: LiquorLAND and Vintage Cellars Sydney 1997–, Saulnier Blache Conslts Paris 1991–; Christie's Int Wine Dept: sr dir 2000–02, sr conslt 2002–; judge: Aust Nat Wine Show Canberra 1987, Perth Wine Show 1992, NZ Nat Wine Awards Auckland 1993, Rutherglen Wine Show 1997, Royal Sydney Wine Show 2000; speaker: Pinot Noir Conference McMinnville OR 1991, The Bordeaux Debate l'Université de Bordeaux-Talence 1999; lectr Wine Australia Melbourne 1998, currently regular lectr; current writing incl christies.com and Decanter; co-scripted and co-presented Wines of Burgundy's Côte d'Or double video 1988, Burgundy corr Microsoft On-Line Wine Guide 1995–98; chm French Wine Ctee UK Wine and Spirit Assoc 1975, memb UK Govt Hospitality Wine Ctee 1989–2006; MW 1976, FRSA; *Publications* Burgundy (1982, 2 edn 1995, winner Best Wine Book André Simon Meml Award 1995, winner 1er Cru Award 1995, runner-up Prix du Champagne Lanson 1995); *Recreations* skiing, walking, reading, fishing; *Style*— Anthony Hanson, Esq; ✉ Christie's International Wine Department, 85 Old Brompton Road, London SW7 3LD (tel 020 7226 4575, fax 020 7226 4575, mobile 07786 175570, e-mail ahanson@christies.com)

HANSON, Brian John Taylor; CBE (1996); s of Benjamin John Hanson (d 1978), of Norwood Green, Middx, and Gwendoline Ada, *née* Taylor (d 1999); *b* 23 January 1939; *Educ* Hounslow Coll, Law Soc Coll of Law, Univ of Wales (LLM); *m* 10 June 1972, Deborah Mary Hazel, da of Lt-Col Richard Stewart Palliser Dawson, OBE (d 1994), of Stowting, Kent; 2 s (James b 1973, Crispin b 1982), 3 da (Sarah b 1975, Rebecca b 1979, Alice b 1986); *Career* slr and ecclesiastical notary; slr in private practice 1963–65, slr Church Cmmrs for Eng 1965–70; Gen Synod of C of E: asst legal advsr 1970–74, legal advsr 1974–2001, registrar 1980–2001, memb Legal Advsy Cmmn 1980–2001 (sec 1970–86); legal advsr: House of Bishops 1974–2001, Archbishops' Cncl 1999–2001; registrar to the Convocation of Canterbury 1982–2001, guardian Shrine of Our Lady of Walsingham 1984–, Bishop's nominee on Chichester Diocesan Synod 1987– (chm Diocesan Bd of Patronage 1998–, chm Diocesan House of Laity and Synod, vice-pres 2001–); memb Cncl: St Luke's Hosp for the Clergy 1985–2001, The Ecclesiastical Law Soc 1987–2003, Chichester Cathedral 2000–; reviewer Cmmn for Health Improvement 2001–05, jt sec Archbishop's Panel of Reference for the Anglican Communion 2005–; memb Appeals Tribunal Healthcare Cmmn 2005–; fell Woodard Corp 1987–; govr: St Michael's Sch Burton Park 1987–94, Pusey House Oxford 1993– (vice pres 2005–), Quainton Hall Sch 1994–2005; pres Soc for the Maintenance of the Faith 1999–; Archbishop's Nominee on St Luke's Res Fndn 1998–; memb: Law Soc 1963, Canon Law Soc of GB 1980, Ecclesiastical Law Assoc 1980; Warden of the Lower Liberty St Andrew Holborn 2002–, lay canon Gibraltar Cathedral 2003–; Freeman City of London, Liveryman Worshipful Co of Glaziers and Painters of Glass; DCL (Lambeth) 2001; FRSA 1996; *Books* The Opinions of the Legal Advisory Commission (ed, 6 edn, 1985), The Canons of the Church of England (ed, 2 edn 1975, 4 edn 1986), Norwood Parish Church - A Short History (1970), Garth Moore's Introduction to English Canon Law (jtly, 3 edn, 1992), Atkin's Court Forms (ed Ecclesiastical vol, 1992, 1996, 2000); *Recreations* the family, gardening, genealogy; *Clubs* IOD; *Style*— Brian Hanson, Esq, CBE; ✉ Quarry House, Horsham Road, Steyning, West Sussex BN44 3AA (tel 01903 812214, e-mail brianhanson39@hotmail.com)

HANSON, Rt Hon David; PC (2007), MP; s of Brian Hanson, and Glenda Hanson; *b* 5 July 1957; *Educ* Verdin Comp Sch Winsford, Univ of Hull (BA, CertEd); *m* 6 Sept 1986, Margaret, *née* Mitchell; 2 s, 2 da; *Career* vice-pres Hull Univ Students' Union 1978–79, trainee Co-operative Union 1980–81, mangr Plymouth Co-operative 1981–82, various appts The Spastics Soc (now Scope) 1982–89, dir Re-Solv (Soc for Prevention of Solvent Abuse) 1989–92; MP (Lab) Delyn 1992– (also contested 1987); PPS to Chief Sec to The Treasy 1997–98, asst govt whip 1998–99, Parly under sec of state Wales 1999–2001, PPS to Rt Hon Tony Blair, MP, *qv*, 2001–05, min of state NI Office 2005–07, min of justice Dept of Justice 2007–; sec PLP Heritage Ctee 1995–97, memb Leadership Campaign Team 1995, memb Public Serv Select Ctee; Parly candidate (Lab) Eddisbury 1983, Euro Parly candidate Cheshire W 1984; cncllr: Vale Royal BC 1983–91 (chm Econ Devpt Ctee and ldr Lab Gp 1989–91), Northwich Town Cncl 1987–91; *Recreations* football, cinema, cooking; *Style*— The Rt Hon David Hanson, MP; ✉ 64 Chester Street, Flint, Flintshire (tel 01352 763159); House of Commons, London SW1A 0AA (020 7219 5064)

HANSON, Geoffrey; s of John Hanson (d 1967), of Witney, Oxon, and Grace Emily, *née* Elphick (d 1977); *b* 9 December 1939; *Educ* Eastbourne GS, Itchen GS Southampton, Trinity Coll of Music London (GTCL, LTCL, ATCL); *m* 5 Aug 1961 (m dis 1994), (Alice) Janet, MBE, da of Frank Wyatt (d 1948); *Career* conductor and composer; conductor London Ripieno Soc 1962–, prof Trinity Coll of Music London 1964–2004, conductor Square Singers of St James 1977–89; Telemann St Matthew Passion Camden Festival 1968; artistic dir East Finchley Arts Festival 1997; memb City of Westminster Arts Cncl; memb: Performing Rights Soc 1981, Incorporated Soc of Musicians 1983, Composers' Guild of GB 1983; hon fell Trinity Coll of Music London 1972; *Compositions* incl: 3 Pieces for Organ 1970, A Trilogy of Psalms for chorus and orchestra 1973, Brecon Ser 1974, concerto for piano and orchestra 1977, concerto for oboe and strings 1978, Sinfonia Amoris for soloists chorus and orchestra 1981, War! Cry War! for soloists chorus and orchestra 1986, concerto for violin and orchestra 1986, concerto for clarinet and strings 1987, concerto for viola and orchestra 1990, The Virgin Crown (opera) 1991, Te Deum (for Hanover Choir) 1993, Carols for Tring 1994, Piano Quintet 1995, Joan of Arc (opera) 1996, Concerto for Organ and Orchestra 1999, Cuthman's Journey (opera) 2000, Concerto for Flute and Strings (London Mozart Players) 2001, Requiem for Chorus, Soprano, Soloist and Organ 2002, Songs of War and Peace (Finchley Children's Music Gp) 2003,

H

Concerto for Horn and Strings (London Mozart Players) 2004, Music for Strings (London Mozart Players) 2005, Rose (Variations for Organ) 2005, Conversation Piece (Double Concerto for Violin, 'Cello and Orchestra) 2006, Piano Concerto no 2 (David Juritz, Sebastian Comberti and London Mozart Players) 2007; *Recreations* swimming, walking; *Style*— Geoffrey Hanson, Esq; ✉ 22 New Ash Close, London N2 8DQ (tel 020 84449214, e-mail geoffreyhanson@btinternet.com)

HANSON, Sir John Gilbert; KCMG (1995), CBE (1979); s of Gilbert Fretwell Hanson (d 1981), and Gladys Margaret, *née* Kay (d 1991); *b* 16 November 1938; *Educ* Manchester Grammar, Wadham Coll Oxford (MA); *m* 1962, Margaret (d 2003), da of Edward Thomas Clark, MBE, of Oxfordshire; 3 s (Mark b 1966, Paul b 1967 (decd), James b 1971); *Career* WO 1961–63; Br Cncl: Madras India 1963–66, MECAS Lebanon 1966–68, Bahrain 1968–72, London 1972–75, Tehran Iran 1975–79, London 1979–82, RCDS 1983; min (cultural affrs) Br High Cmmn New Delhi 1984–88, dep dir gen Br Cncl 1988–92, dir gen Br Cncl 1992–98; warden Green Coll Oxford 1998–2006; memb Governing Cncl SOAS 1991–99; tstee Charles Wallace (India) Tst 1998–2000; pres: Br Skin Fndn 1997–2002, Bahrain-British Fndn 1997–2005, UK Cncl for Overseas Student Affairs 1999–; Hon DLitt Oxford Brookes Univ 1995, Hon Dr Univ of Lincolnshire & Humberside 1996, Hon Dr Univ of Greenwich 1996; hon fell: Wadham Coll Oxford, Green Coll Oxford, St Edmund's Coll Cambridge; CIMgt; *Recreations* books, music, sailing, sport, travel; *Clubs* Athenaeum, MCC, Gymkhana (Madras); *Style*— Sir John Hanson, KCMG, CBE; ✉ Green College, Woodstock Road, Oxford 0X2 6HG (tel 01865 274 775, fax 01865 274 796)

HANSON, Prof Owen Jerrold; s of Lawrence Hanson-Smith (d 1972), of Cheltenham, and Edith Annette Audrey, *née* Waller (d 1995); *b* 2 January 1934; *Educ* Wallington Co GS for Boys, Univ of Cambridge (BA, MA), Univ of London (MSc), City Univ (PhD); *m* 1, 14 July 1965, Barbara Maria Teresa, da of Maj Albin Srodzinski; 2 da (Annette b 31 Aug 1967, Ilona b 9 March 1971); m 2, 16 May 1996, Lena Diane, da of R N Hall (d 1991); 1 da (Sarah b 15 Nov 1999), 1 s (Paul b 18 Jan 2001); *Career* jr technician RAF 1952–54; works metallurgist Wilkinson Sword Co Ltd 1957–60, dep mangr rising to mangr of works laboratory Gillette Industries UK Ltd 1960–64, systems analyst IBM UK Ltd 1964–70; City Univ: sr lectr 1970–89, dir Centre for Business Systems Analysis 1983–88, head Dept of Business Systems Analysis 1988–94, chair in business computing 1989–99, dir Centre for Business Systems Applications 1994–99, prof emeritus 1999–; fell Inst for the Mgmnt of Info Systems 1990–; prof of business computing and dir CBSA Middlesex Univ 1999–; *Books* Keeping Computers Under Control (ed A Chambers and O Hanson, 1975), Basic File Design (1978), Design of Computer Data Files (1982, 2 edn 1988), Essentials of Computer Data Files (1985); *Recreations* cross country running, tennis, squash; *Clubs* South London Harriers, Purley Sports; *Style*— Prof Owen Hanson; ✉ School of Computing Science, Middlesex University, Ravensfield House, The Burroughs, Hendon, London NW4 4BT (tel 020 8411 2641, fax 020 8411 2642, e-mail o.hanson@mdx.ac.uk)

HANSON, Prof Philip; s of Eric Hugh Cecil Hanson (d 1942), of London, and Doris May, *née* Ward (d 1980); *b* 16 December 1936; *Educ* Highgate Sch, Jesus Coll Cambridge (MA), Univ of Birmingham (PhD); *m* 22 Oct 1960, Evelyn, da of Sidney James Rogers (d 1968), of London; 2 s (Paul Edward b 1963, Nicholas James b 1972); *Career* Nat Serv Middx Regt and Intelligence Corps, Sgt mil interpreter (Russian); lectr in econs Univ of Exeter 1961–67, visiting prof of econs Univ of Michigan 1967–68; Univ of Birmingham 1968–: lectr, sr lectr, reader, former prof of the political economy of Russia and Eastern Europe, dir Centre for Russian & East Euro Studies, currently emeritus prof; first sec HM Embassy Moscow, sr res offr FCO 1971–72; visiting prof Univ of Michigan 1977, sr Mellon fell Harvard Univ 1986–87, economist UN Economic Cmmn for Europe Geneva 1991–92, visiting prof Kyoto Univ 2000, visiting prof Södertörns Högskola Stockholm 2004; conslt: Planecon Inc, Oxford Analytica, Radio Liberty; memb Ctee Birmingham Jazz 1978–83, memb E Europe Exec Birmingham C of C and Indust 1980–89, memb Cncl SSEES Univ of London 1990–98; assoc fell RIIA 2003–; *Books* Trade and Technology in Soviet-Western Relations (1981), The Comparative Economics of Research, Development & Innovation (with K Pavitt, 1987), Western Economic Statecraft in East-West Relations (1988), From Stagnation to Catastroika (1992), Transformation from Below (co-ed with J Gibson, 1996), Regional Economic Change in Russia (co-ed with M Bradshaw, 2000), The Rise and Fall of the Soviet Economy (2003); *Recreations* jazz, cricket; *Style*— Prof Philip Hanson; ✉ c/o CREES, University of Birmingham, Birmingham B15 2TT (tel 0121 414 6353, fax 0121 414 3423, e-mail p.hanson@bham.ac.uk)

HANSON, Richard William Durrant; TD (1969); s of William Gordon Hanson, OBE (d 1990), and Dulce Durrant Hanson (d 1996); bro of Anthony Hanson, *qv*; *b* 11 August 1935; *Educ* Eton; *m* 23 June 1961, Elizabeth Deirdre Dewar, da of late Dr A D Frazer; 2 da (Arabella (Mrs Hugh Derrick) b 1962, Georgina (Mrs Magnus Laird) b 1963), 1 s (James b 1969); *Career* 2 Lt 17/21 Lancers 1954–56, Maj Sherwood Rangers Yeo and Royal Yeo 1956–69; Hardys & Hansons plc (Kimberley Brewery Nottingham): dir 1962–, md 1973–, chm and md 1989–98, chm 1998–2004; High Sheriff Notts 1980–81; *Recreations* shooting, tennis; *Clubs* MCC, Cavalry and Guards; *Style*— Richard Hanson, Esq, TD; ✉ Budby Castle, Newark, Nottinghamshire NG22 9EU (tel 01623 822293)

HANSON, Hon Robert William; s of Baron Hanson (Life Peer, d 2004); *b* 3 October 1960; *Educ* Eton, St Peter's Coll Oxford; *Career* NM Rothschild & Sons Ltd 1983–90 (asst dir 1990), dir Hanson plc 1992–97 (assoc dir 1990–92); chm: Hanson Pacific 1994–97, Hanson Transport Gp 1996– (dir 1990–), Hanson Capital Investments Ltd 1998–, Hanson Westhouse Ltd 2006–; Liveryman Worshipful Co of Saddlers; *Recreations* hunting, shooting, tennis, golf, sailing; *Clubs* White's, Queen's, The Berkshire, The Brook (NY), Royal Thames Yacht; *Style*— The Hon Robert Hanson; ✉ Hanson Capital Investments Ltd, 2 Deanery Street, London W1K 1AU (tel 020 7647 0900, fax 020 7647 0901)

HANSON, Sir (Charles) Rupert Patrick; 4 Bt (UK 1918), of Fowey, Cornwall; s of Sir (Charles) John Hanson, 3 Bt (d 1996), and his 1 w, Patricia Helen, *née* Brind (d 2005); *b* 25 June 1945; *Educ* Eton, Central London Poly; *m* 1977, Wanda, da of Don Arturo Larrain, of Santiago, Chile; 1 s (Alexis Charles b 1978); *Heir* s, Alexis Hanson; *Career* tech, legal and commercial translator 1977–84, teacher of English as foreign language 1981–83; vol charity worker 1984–85; Inland Revenue: joined 1986, various positions in different offices, HM Inspr of Taxes Brighton 4 1993–2001, HM Inspr of Taxes Sussex Area 2001–; *Recreations* classical music, writing poetry, tennis, walking; *Style*— Sir Rupert Hanson, Bt; ✉ 125 Ditchling Road, Brighton BN1 4SE

HANWORTH, 3 Viscount (UK 1936); Sir (David) Stephen Geoffrey Pollock; 3 Bt (UK 1922); also Baron Hanworth (UK 1926); s of 2 Viscount Hanworth (d 1996), and (Isolda) Rosamond, *née* Parker; *b* 16 February 1946; *Educ* Wellington, Guildford Tech Coll, Univ of Sussex; *m* 1968, Elizabeth, da of Lawrence Vambe, of Harare, Zimbabwe; 2 da (Hon Cecile Abigail Shona b 1971, Hon Charlotte Anne Catherine b 1973); *Career* lectr Queen Mary & Westfield Coll London; *Style*— The Rt Hon the Viscount Hanworth

HARARI, Sammy; s of René David Harari, and Sandrine, *née* Olifson; *b* 4 April 1950; *Educ* Univ of Reading, Univ of Montpellier (BA); *Career* with Dunlop Ltd 1972–74, account dir Darcy Masius Benton & Bowles 1974–83, dir Yellowhammer 1983–86 (handled UK Govt first anti-heroin campaign), chief exec TBWA 1986–89 (responsible for UK Govt anti-AIDS campaign), fndr md Harari Page 1990–98, chm Travis Sully Harari Fndn 1998–99, worldwide creative dir Harari 1999– (devpt projects in Paris, London, NY and Koh Samui); MInstM, MIPA; *Style*— Sammy Harari, Esq; ✉ 1150 Park Avenue, Apartment PHD, New York, NY 10128, USA (tel 00 1 212 876 8567, e-mail sammyharari@gmail.com)

HARBERTON, 11 Viscount (I 1791); Henry Robert Pomeroy; also Baron Harberton (I 1783); s of Hon Robert Pomeroy (d 1997), and (Winifred) Anne, *née* Colegate; suc unc, 10 Viscount Harberton, 2004; *b* 23 April 1958, Hanover; *Educ* Eton, RAC Cirencester, Univ of Reading; *m* 27 Oct 1990, Caroline, da of Jeremy Grindle; 2 s (Hon Patrick Christopher b 10 May 1995, Hon Hugh William b 18 April 1997); *Heir* s, Hon Patrick Pomeroy; *Career* Portman Estate 1982–88, P&O Properties 1988–92, TEAR Fund Ghana 1993–96, Action on Disability and Devpt 1997–2005, Send A Cow 2005–; lay reader C of E; MRICS 1988; *Recreations* cycling, beekeeping; *Style*— The Rt Hon the Viscount Harberton

HARBIDGE, Ven Adrian Guy; s of John and Pat Harbidge, of Stroud, Glos; *b* 10 November 1948; *Educ* Marling Sch Stroud, St John's Coll Durham (BA), Cuddesdon Theol Coll; *m* 1975, Bridget, da of Major Colin West-Watson; 1 da (Naomi b 1979), 1 s (Colin b 1982); *Career* purser Merchant Navy 1970–73, curate Romsey Abbey 1975–80, vicar St Andrew's Bennett Rd Bournemouth 1980–86, vicar Chandler's Ford 1986–99, rural dean of Eastleigh 1993–99, archdeacon of Winchester 1999–2000, archdeacon of Bournemouth 2000–; *Books* Those Whom DDO Hath Joined Together (1996); *Recreations* landscape gardening, cycling; *Clubs* Rotary (Chandler's Ford and Itchen Valley); *Style*— The Ven the Archdeacon of Bournemouth; ✉ Glebe House, 22 Bellflower Way, Chandler's Ford, Eastleigh SO53 4HN (tel and fax 023 8026 0955, e-mail adrian.harbidge@dial.pipex.com)

HARBOR, John Liming; s of Jack Liming Harbor, of Swanage, and Isabel Katherine, *née* Lauder; *b* 11 March 1947; *Educ* Hurstpierpoint Coll; *m* 4 July 1970, Christine Elizabeth, da of John Walter De Foix Rawle; 1 da (Lucy Elizabeth b 12 May 1973), 1 s (Andrew Liming b 7 May 1979); *Career* audit supervisor London and Madrid Barton Mayhew (later merged with Ernst & Young) 1970–75, conslt to shipowners UK and Netherlands 1975–80, ptnr Bagshaws 1982–91 (joined 1980), sr insurance ptnr Moore Stephens (following merger with Bagshaws) 1991–; FCA (ACA 1970); *Recreations* golf, walking, cooking; *Style*— John Harbor, Esq; ✉ Moore Stephens, St Paul's House, 8–12 Warwick Lane, London EC4P 4BN

HARBORD, Richard Lewis; s of Lewis Walter Harbord, of Norwich, and Dorothy Florence, *née* Mobbs; *b* 30 April 1946; *Educ* Minchenden GS, Anglian Regnl Mgmnt Centre (MPhil), Henley Coll of Mgmnt (MPhil); *m* 2 May 1970, Jenny Ann, da of Herbert John Berry (d 1988); 3 s (Mark b 26 Aug 1971, Adam b 5 Oct 1975, Guy b 19 July 1984); *Career* chief exec London Borough of Richmond-upon-Thames 1988–99 (fin dir 1981–88), md London Borough of Hammersmith and Fulham 1999–2002, public sector conslt to central and local govt 2002–; dir: LDA plc, Public Sector Conslts Ltd 2002–; memb: Cncl Ratings and Valuation Assoc 1987– (pres 1994–95), Ct Univ of Surrey; chm Windlesham Community House Project, hon treas Windlesham PCC; memb IPFA 1967 (memb Cncl 2003–), memb IDPM 1968, FCCA 1981, FRVA 1982, FRSA 1990; *Recreations* family; *Style*— Richard Harbord, Esq; ✉ Gooserye, Cooper Road, Windlesham, Surrey GU20 6EA (e-mail richard@harbord.net)

HARBORNE, Peter Gale; s of late Leslie Herbert Harborne, and late Marie Mildred Edith, *née* Suckling; *b* 29 June 1945; *Educ* King Edward's Sch Birmingham, Univ of Birmingham (BCom); *m* 24 July 1976, Tessa Elizabeth Harborne, da of late Dennis Frederick Joseph Henri, of Solihull, West Midlands; 2 s (James b 1980, Alexander b 1981); *Career* Home Civil Service 1966–72, HM Dip Serv 1972, first sec Ottawa 1974–75, first sec (commercial) Mexico City 1975–78, Lloyds Bank Int 1979–81, FCO 1981–83, first sec and head of Chancery Helsinki 1983–87, counsellor and dep head of mission Budapest 1988–91, FCO 1991–95, ambass to Slovak Republic 1995–98, high cmmr to Trinidad and Tobago 1999–2004; clerk advsr European Scrutiny Ctee House of Commons 2004–; *Recreations* cricket, tennis, cross country skiing; *Clubs* MCC; *Style*— Peter Harborne, Esq

HARBOUR, Ivan; *Educ* Bartlett Sch of Architecture and Planning (UCL Environmental Design Prize); *Career* architect; YRM 1983, London Borough of Hackney 1983; Richard Rogers Partnership: joined 1985, dir 1993–; lectr: South Bank Univ, Strasbourg Univ, Univ of Melbourne, RIBA; *Projects* incl: Lloyd's of London, Reuters Data Centre, European Ct of Human Rights, Nice Masterplan, Lloyd's Register of Shipping Competition, Bordeaux Law Cts, Ile Seguin Paris Masterplan Competition, South Bank Centre Competition, VR Techno Centre Gifu Japan, Minami Yamashiro Sch Kyoto Japan, ParcBit Masterplan Mallorca, Fujita Restaurant Tokyo Japan, Electronic Arts HQ Competition, Museum of Islamic Art Quatar Competition, Madrid Airport, Nippon TV HQ Tokyo Japan, Antwerp Law Cts Competition, Nat Assembly for Wales Competition, Kyoto Retail Bldg Japan, Millennium Experience Rest Zone, Amano Laboratory Building; *Style*— Ivan Harbour, Esq; ✉ Richard Rogers Partnership, Thames Wharf, Rainville Road, London W6 9HA

HARBOUR, Malcolm John Charles; MEP (Cons) W Midlands; s of John Harbour (d 1980), and Bobby Harbour (d 1995); *b* 19 February 1947, Woking, Surrey; *Educ* Gayhurst Sch Gerrards Cross, Bedford Sch, Trinity Coll Cambridge (MA), Aston Univ (Dip Mgmnt Studies); *m* 12 July 1969, Penny, *née* Johnson; 2 da (Louise b 1974, Katy b 1977); *Career* BMC Longbridge: engrg apprentice 1967, designer and devpt engr 1969–72, product planning mangr Rover-Triumph 1972–76, project mangr Medium Cars 1976–80, dir of business planning Austin Rover 1980–82, dir of mktg 1982–84, dir of sales UK and Ireland 1984–86, dir Overseas Sales 1986–89; fndr and ptnr Harbour Wade Brown Motor Industry Conslts 1989–99, jt fndr and dir Int Car Distribution Programme (ICDP) 1993–99, non-exec dir 1999–2006, co-fndr and project dir 3 Day Car Programme 1998–99; MEP (Cons) W Midlands 1999–, Cons spokesman Internal Market, co-ordinator EPP-ED Gp, memb EPP-ED Gp Bureau; rapporteur: Motor Vehicle Fuel Tank Directive 1999, European Cmmn Personnel Reforms 2000–04, 2nd Generation Internet 2000–, Universal Service in Electronic Communications 2001, Internal Market Strategy 2003, Motor Vehicle Type Approval 2007; memb European Parl Ctees on: Internal Market and Consumer Protection, Industry, External Trade, Res and Energy, Lisbon Strategy Co-Ordination; vice-chm STOA (Scientific and Technology Options Assessment) Panel, memb Cons Delegation Bureau 1999–2002, chm Cons Technol Forum 2004–; memb Delgn to Japanese Parl; co-chm: European Forum for the Automobile in Soc 2000–, European Parl Ceramics Industry Forum 2000–; govr European Internet Fndn 2003–, dir EURIM 2004–, memb Royal Soc Int Policy Ctee 2003–; guardian Birmingham Assay Office 2007–; candidate (Cons) Euro elections 1989 and 1994, former chm Solihull Constituency, former rep Nat Union Trade and Industry Forum, former memb W Midlands Area Exec Cncl, memb Solihull Cons Assoc 1972–; CEng, MIMechE, FIMI; *Publications* Winning Tomorrow's Customers (1997), Our Vision of Europe (contrib, EPP-ED Gp, 2001), many car industry reports published by ICDP; *Recreations* choral singing, motor sport, travel, cooking; political interests: European affairs, transport, competition policy, e-commerce, telecomms, automotive indust, ceramics indust; *Style*— Malcolm Harbour, Esq, MEP; ✉ ASP 14E209, European Parliament, Rue Wiertz, B1047 Brussels (tel 322 284 5132, fax 322 284 9132, e-mail malcolm.harbour@europarl.europa.eu); UK Office, Manor Cottage, Manor Road, Solihull, West Midlands B91 2BL (tel 0121 711 3158, fax 0121 711 3159)

HARCOURT, Prof Geoffrey Colin; AO (1994); s of Kenneth Kopel Harcourt (d 1988), of Melbourne, Aust, and Marjorie Rahel, *née* Gans (d 1981); *b* 27 June 1931; *Educ* Wesley Coll Melbourne, Queen's Coll Univ of Melbourne (BCom, MCom), King's Coll Cambridge (PhD, LittD); *m* 30 July 1955, Joan Margaret, da of Edgar James Bartrop, OBE (d 1989), of Ballarat West, Victoria, Aust; 2 da (Wendy Jane b 1959, Rebecca Mary b 1968), 2 s (Robert Geoffrey b 1961, Timothy Daniel Harcourtavitz b 1965); *Career* economist; Univ of Adelaide: lectr in economics 1958–62, sr lectr 1963–65, reader 1965–67, prof (personal chair) 1967–85 (prof emeritus 1988); Univ of Cambridge: lectr in economics and politics 1964–66, fell Trinity Hall 1964–66, fell Jesus Coll 1982–98 (emeritus 1998–), lectr in economics and politics 1982–90, pres Jesus Coll 1988–89 and 1990–92, reader in the history of economic theory (ad hominem) 1990–98 (emeritus 1998–); memb Aust Labor Pty 1954–; Howard League for Penal Reform S Aust branch: sec 1959–63, vice-pres 1967–74, pres 1974–80; chm Campaign for Peace in Vietnam S Aust 1970–72, fell Acad of the Social Sciences in Aust 1971, memb Cncl Royal Economic Soc 1990–95, distinguished fell Econ Soc of Australia 1996 (life memb 2006), hon fell Queen's Coll Melbourne 1998; Hon DLitt De Montfort Univ 1997, Hon DCom Univ of Melbourne 2003, Hon Dr (hc) Univ of Freiburg Switzerland 2003, AcSS 2003, distinguished fell History of Economics Soc 2004, hon memb European Soc for the History of Economic Thought 2005; *Books* incl: Economic Activity (jtly, 1967), Capital and Growth, Selected Readings (jt ed, 1971), Some Cambridge Controversies in the Theory of Capital (1972), Theoretical Controversy and Social Significance - An Evaluation of the Cambridge Controversies (1975), The Microeconomic Foundations of Macroeconomics (ed, 1977), The Social Science Imperialists. Selected Essays (1982), Keynes and his Contemporaries (ed, 1985), Readings in the Concept and Measurement of Income (jt ed 1969, 2 edn 1986), Controversies in Political Economy. Selected Essays (1986), International Monetary Problems and Supply-side Economics. Essays in Honour of Lorie Tarshis (jt ed, 1986), On Political Economists and Modern Political Economy. Selected Essays (1992), Post-Keynesian Essays in Biography: Portraits of Twentieth Century Political Economists (1993), The Dynamics of the Wealth of Nations. Growth, Distribution and Structural Change. Essays in Honour of Luigi Pasinetti (jt ed, 1993), Markets, Madness and a Middle Way (the second Donald Horne address, 1992), Income and Employment in Theory and Practice. Essays in Honour of Athanasios Asimakopulos (jt ed, 1994), Capitalism, Socialism and Post-Keynesianism. Selected Essays (1995), A 'Second Edition' of The General Theory (2 vols, jt ed, 1997), 50 Years a Keynesian and Other Essays (2001), Selected Essays on Economic Policy (2001), L'Economie Rebelle de Joan Robinson (ed, 2001), Editing Economics: Essays in Honour of Mark Perlman (jt ed, 2002), Joan Robinson: Critical Assessments of Leading Economists (5 vols, jt ed, 2002), Capital Theory (3 vols, jt ed, 2005), The Structure of Post Keynesian Economics: Structure of Post Keynesian Economic (2006); *Recreations* cricket, running, reading, politics; *Clubs* Melbourne Cricket, S Aust Cricket; *Style*— Prof G C Harcourt, AO; ✉ 43 New Square, Cambridge CB1 1EZ (tel 01223 360833); Jesus College, Cambridge CB5 8BL

HARCOURT, Geoffrey David; JP (Oxon 1981); s of Attilio Michael Unfreid (b Brussels, changed name to Harcourt 1933, d 1968), and Barbara Kathleen, *née* Cox (d 1998); *b* 9 August 1935; *Educ* High Wycombe Tech Sch, High Wycombe Sch of Art, Royal Coll of Art (DesRCA, Silver medal for a chair design and major travelling scholarship to USA); *m* 1965, Jean Mary Vaughan, da of Hubert Pryce-Jones, JP; 1 s (William Gerard Vaughan, FRCS b 1966), 1 da (Siân Elisabeth Vaughan (Mrs Christopher Dodwell) b 1969); *Career* Nat Serv RA 1955–57; freelance designer; design office Latham, Tyler and Jensen (Chicago) then Jacob Jensen (Copenhagen) 1960–61, various jobs London 1961–62, estab own design practice producing substantial body of design work in furniture 1962–95; former clients incl: Gordon Russell Ltd, Steelcase Strafor, Ben Dawson Furniture, Gaeltarra Eireann; currently freelance designs for clients in UK and Europe incl Habitat, Hands of Wycombe and Emmemobili, Cantu, Italy; conslt to Artifort (Dutch furniture maker) 1963–96; work exhibited worldwide incl: Steidlijk Museum Amsterdam 1967 (in permanent collection), Prague Museum of Decorative Arts 1972, Science Museum 1972, Design Cncl London and Glasgow 1976 and 1981, V&A (The Eye for Industry Exhbn) 1987, The Nederlands Texteilmuseum 1988, Manchester Prize Exhbn 1988, RCA Centennial Exhbn 1995; external examiner BA Hons degree courses: Kingston Poly 1974–77, Belfast Poly 1977–81, Loughborough Coll of Art and Design 1978–81, Buckingham Coll 1982–85, Guildhall Univ 1995–98, Galway Tech Coll 1997–99, RCA 1995–98; chm Thame and Henley Magistrates' Bench, memb Lord-Lt's Advsy Ctee for Appointments to the Oxford Magistracy; chm Advsy Panel for S Oxfordshire 1997–2000 (resigned, transfer to supplemental list); Freeman City of London 1974, Liveryman Worshipful Co of Furniture Makers 1974; FCSD 1964, FRSA 1978, RDI 1978 (master 2004–05); *Recreations* golf, painting; *Clubs* Goring and Streatley Golf, Leander (assoc memb); *Style*— Geoffrey Harcourt, Esq, RDI; ✉ The Old Vicarage, Benson, Oxfordshire OX10 6SF (tel 01491 838688, e-mail geoff@harcourtgj.demon.co.uk)

HARDEN, Prof Ronald McGlashan; OBE (2003); s of Alexander Harden (d 1959), and Janet Roy, *née* McGlashan; *b* 24 December 1936; *Educ* Uddington GS, Univ of Glasgow (MB ChB, MD); *m* 4 Jan 1961, Sheila, da of James Harris (d 1956); 3 da (Susan b 28 Sept 1964, Valerie b 31 July 1966, Jennifer b 3 July 1968); *Career* res and clinical posts Western Infirmary Glasgow 1960–70, sr lectr in med Univ of Glasgow 1970–72, postgrad dean of med Univ of Dundee 1985–99 (dir centre for med educn and hon conslt physician 1972), dir Educ Devpt Unit Scottish Cncl for Postgraduate Med and Dental Educ 1999–, teaching dean Univ of Dundee Sch of Med 1994–; ed Medical Teacher and int authy on med educn with over 200 papers in scientific jls; sec/treas Assoc for Med Educn Europe, memb Exec Assoc for Study of Med Educn; FRCPGlas 1975, FRCPS Canada 1988, FRCSEd 1994; *Recreations* gardening; *Clubs* Royal Society of Medicine; *Style*— Prof Ronald Harden, OBE; ✉ Centre for Medical Education, 484 Perth Road, Dundee DD2 1LR (tel 01382 631972, fax 01382 645748)

HARDIE, Baron (Life Peer UK 1997), of Blackford in the City of Edinburgh; Andrew Rutherford Hardie; PC (1997), QC (Scot 1985); s of late Andrew Rutherford Hardie, of Alloa, and Elizabeth Currie, *née* Lowe; *b* 8 January 1946; *Educ* St Modan's HS Stirling, Univ of Edinburgh (MA, LLB); *m* 16 July 1971, Catherine Storrar, da of late David Currie Elgin, of Edinburgh; 2 s (Hon Ewan b 1975, Hon Niall b 1981), 1 da (Hon Ruth b 1977); *Career* admitted slr 1971, admitted memb Faculty of Advocates 1973; advocate depute 1979–83, standing jr counsel City of Edinburgh DC 1983–85 (sr counsel 1987–97), dean Faculty of Advocates 1994–97 (treasurer 1989–94), Lord Advocate 1997–2000, Senator Coll of Justice (Lord of Session) 2000–; convener Children in Scotland 1994–96, hon pres The Muir Soc 1994–2000; hon bencher Lincoln's Inn 1997; *Clubs* Murrayfield Golf; *Style*— The Rt Hon the Lord Hardie, PC, QC; ✉ Court of Session, Parliament House, High Street, Edinburgh EH1 1RF (tel 0131 225 2595)

HARDIE, David; WS (1982); s of John Hardie, of Gourock, Renfrewshire, and Amy Alfreda, *née* Masey; *b* 17 September 1954; *Educ* Glasgow Acad, Greenock HS, Univ of Dundee (LLB); *m* 27 Feb 1981, Fiona Mairi, da of late Dr Alexander Donaldson Willox, MBE, of W Lothian; 3 s (Iain b 1981, Stewart b 1984, Alasdair b 1989); *Career* NP 1979, currently sr corp ptnr and head of knowledge and learning Dundas & Wilson CS (ptnr 1983–); memb: Law Soc of Scot, Int Bar Assoc; *Recreations* sailing, golf, swimming, cycling, motor cycling; *Style*— David Hardie, Esq, WS; ✉ Dundas & Wilson, Saltire Court, 20 Castle Terrace, Edinburgh EH1 2EN (tel 0131 200 7345, fax 0131 228 8888, e-mail david.hardie@dundas-wilson.com)

HARDIE, Brig Donald Graeme; TD, JP; s of Graeme Hardie, BEM, of Helensburgh, and Sheila Ramsay McLennan (d 1965); *b* 23 January 1936; *Educ* Larchfield, Blairmore, Merchiston Castle Sch Edinburgh; *m* 10 Feb 1961 (m dis 1997), Rosalind Allan Ker; 2 s (Fergus Allan Graeme b 15 Sept 1962, Adam Ker b 2 June 1964); m 2, 27 Dec 1999, Sheena Roome; *Career* mgmnt trainee UTR 1956–59, F W Allan & Ker Shipbrokers 1960–61; dir: J & G Hardie & Co Ltd 1961–2000, Gilbert Plastics 1973–76, Hardie Polymers Ltd 1981–2000; md: Hardie International Sales 2000–04, Preston Stretchform 2004–; Nat Serv cmmnd 41 Field Regt RA 1954–56; TA service: 277 (A & S H) Field Regt RA 1954–66, CO G & SUOTC 1966–73, Col Lowlands 1973–76, Col DES 1976–80, Col Scot 1980–84, ACF Brig Scot 1985–87; Hon Col: 105 AD Regt RA (V) 1992–99, Glasgow & Lanarkshire ACF 1993–2000; Hon Col Commandant Royal Regiment of Artillery 2003–; chm RA Cncl for Scot 1996–2001; vice-pres: ACFA Scot 1990–99, Nat Artillery Assoc 2002–; pres until 2007: SSAFA - Forces Help Dunbartonshire, Scouts Dumbarton area, Guides Dunbartonshire, Boys Brigade Lennox & Argyll; patron: Cornerstone, Craigalbert Centre; chieftain Loch Lomond Games, pres Highland RFCA 2005–07; HM Lord-Lt Dunbartonshire 1990–2007; keeper Dumbarton Castle 1996; memb Grand Antiquity Soc; FIM; KStJ; *Recreations* shooting, fishing, skiing, sailing; *Clubs* Royal Northern & Clyde Yacht, Royal Scots; *Style*— Brig Donald Hardie, TD; ✉ Boturich Castle, by Alexandria, Dunbartonshire G83 8LX (tel 01389 757655)

HARDIE, Maj (John) Donald Morrison; OBE (1987), DL; s of Capt John David Hardie (d 1949), of Dallas, Morayshire, late Scottish Horse and Skinner's Horse, and Gertrude Louise, *née* Morrison; *b* 27 September 1928; *Educ* Beckenham GS, Univ of St Andrews (MA), Indiana Univ USA (MSc); *m* 9 Aug 1952, Sally Patricia, da of Thomas Whipple Connally (d 1928), of Atlanta, GA; 2 s (David b 1954, Robin b 1957), 1 da (Katharine b 1960); *Career* Lt 1 Bn Queen's Own Cameron Highlanders 1952–56, Maj TA Bn 1956–67; dir Wood and Hardie Ltd 1961–82; formerly dir: Bute Fabrics Ltd, McCann Erickson (Scotland) Ltd, Corporate Risk plc, Scottish Div IOD; currently dir Liberating Scots Tst; dep chm Patrons' Cncl Museum of Scotland; tstee Nat Museums of Scotland Charitable Tst 1999–; organised Yes campaign in Scotland for EEC referendum 1975; session clerk Humbie Kirk 1960–; Scottish XI (hockey) 1950–53; FRSA 1994; *Recreations* golf, shooting; *Clubs* Hon Co of Edinburgh Golfers, Royal and Ancient Golf (St Andrews), New (Edinburgh), Piedmont Driving (Atlanta), Peachtree Golf (Atlanta); *Style*— Maj Donald Hardie, OBE, DL; ✉ Chesterhill House, Humbie, E Lothian EH36 5PL (tel 01875 833648, fax 01875 833313)

HARDIE, (Reginald) George; *b* 6 December 1938; *Educ* Stockport GS; *m* 1968, Christine; 2 s, 1 da; *Career* fin controller Richard Johnson & Nephew 1969–72, jt gp md Firth Rixson plc 1989–94 (fin dir 1972), chm Harbury Group Ltd 1994–2003, chm Printing.com plc 1999–; FCA, FCT; *Recreations* golf, DIY, music, reading; *Style*— George Hardie, Esq; ✉ Printing.com plc, Chairman's Office, 1 Ladybarn Crescent, Bramhall, Stockport SK7 2EZ (tel 0161 439 8534, fax 0161 439 6356, e-mail george.hardie@printing.com)

HARDIE, Gwen Waterston; da of James Waterston Hardie, and Anne, *née* Livingston; *b* 7 January 1962; *Educ* Inverurie Acad, Edinburgh Coll of Art (BA); *Career* artist; lectr and visiting artist to various art colls incl: Glasgow, Edinburgh, Sheffield Poly, St Martin's and Royal Coll of Art, Oxford Brookes Univ, Cleveland Univ, Ottawa Univ, NY Studio School, MICA Baltimore, Bridge St Studio Center Brooklyn; *Solo Exhibitions* Paton Gallery London 1986 and 1988, Fruitmarket Gallery Edinburgh (travelling Br show) 1987, Kettle's Yard Cambridge 1988, Scottish Nat Gallery of Modern Art Edinburgh 1990, Fischer Fine Art London 1990, Annely Juda Fine Art London 1994, Talbot Rice Gallery Univ of Edinburgh 1994, Jason and Rhodes Gallery London 1996 and 1998, Peterborough Museum & Art Gallery 1997, Ogilvie & Estill Conwy Wales 1997, Beaux Art London 1999, Lindsey Brown NY 2001, Alpan Gallery Huntington 2004, Dinter Fine Art NY 2005; *Group Exhibitions* Contemporary Art for Museums - Contemporary Art Soc purchases 1982–84 (Sutton Place Guildford Surrey) 1985, Twelve British Artists (Künstlerhaus Vienna) 1986, The Human Touch (Fischer Fine Art London) 1986, Identity - Desire (Scottish Arts Cncl touring) 1986, The Self-Portrait - A Modern View (Artsite Bath) 1987, The Vigorous Imagination (Scottish Nat Gallery of Modern Art Edinburgh) 1987, The New British Painting (American touring) 1988–90, Scottish Art in the 20th Century (The Royal W of England Acad Bristol) 1991, Cabinet Paintings (Gillian Jason Gallery) 1991, Critics Choice (Bruton St Gallery) 1992, Artistic Associations (Gillian Jason Gallery) 1992, The Body Abstract - Somatic States (Quicksilver Gallery Univ of Middx) 1992, Festival Fourteen (Dunfermline Dist & City Museum) 1992, Foreground and Distances (Serpenti Galleria Rome and touring Europe) 1992–94, New Artists and Cabinet Art (both at Jason and Rhodes Gallery, London) 1995, Vigorous Imagination - 10 Years On (Scottish Gallery Edinburgh) 1997, John Moores Liverpool Exhibition (Jason and Rhodes Gallery London) 1998, 'Tech' Jason & Rhodes Gallery London 1998, Beaux Art London 1999, Quintet (Lennon Weinberg NY) 2000, Elizabeth Fndn for the Arts Studio Centre Open Studios (NY) 2000, Abstraction and Immanence (Times Square Gallery NY) 2001, Narcissus (Scottish National Gallery of Art Edinburgh) 2001, Landscape (Lindsey Brown Gallery NY) 2002, London Art Fair (Stephen Lacey Gallery) 2004, Brooklyn Artists (Alpan Gallery Huntington NY) 2005, Drawn (Dinter Fine Art NY) 2006, Closer (Alpan Gallery Huntington NY) 2006, Close (Dinter Fine Art NY) 2006; *Work in Collections* Br Cncl London, Contemporary Art Soc London, Scottish Nat Gallery of Modern Art Edinburgh, City Art Collection Edinburgh, Met Museum NYC, Gulbenkian Collection Lisbon, Scottish Arts Cncl Edinburgh, Glaxo Group Research Ltd London, Manchester Museum of Modern Art; *Recreations* travel; *Clubs* Chelsea Arts; *Style*— Ms Gwen Hardie; ✉ c/o Dinter Fine Art, 547 West 27 Street, Third Floor, New York, NY 10001, USA (website www.gwenhardie.com)

HARDIE, (Charles) Jeremy Mawdesley; CBE (1983); s of Sir Charles Hardie, CBE (d 1998); *b* 9 June 1938; *Educ* New Coll Oxford; *m* 1, 1962 (m dis 1976), Susan Chamberlain; 2 s, 2 da; m 2, 1978 (m dis 1994), Xandra, Countess of Gowrie; 1 da; m 3, 1994, Kirsteen Tait; *Career* fell and tutor in economics Keble Coll Oxford 1968–75; ptnr Dixon Wilson and Co 1975–82, Monopolies and Mergers Cmmn 1976–82 (dep chm 1980–82); National Provident Institution: dir 1972–90, dep chm 1977–80, chm 1980–90; W H Smith Group plc: non-exec dir 1988–, dep chm 1992–94, chm 1994–; chm: D P Mann Underwriting Agency 1983–99, Touch Clarity Ltd 2001–, Loch Fyne Restaurants 2002–; dir John Swire and Sons 1982–98; Parly candidate (SDP) Norwich South 1983 and 1987; memb Arts Cncl of GB 1984–86; tstee Esmée Fairbairn Charitable Tst 1972–; tstee Somerset House 2001–; FCA; *Style*— Jeremy Hardie, Esq; ✉ 13 Ainger Road, London NW3 3AR (tel 020 7722 6916)

HARDIE, Prof Philip Russell; s of late Miles Clayton Hardie, and Pauline Le Gros, *née* Clark; *b* 13 July 1952; *Educ* St Paul's, CCC Oxford (BA), Warburg Inst Univ of London (MPhil); *Partner* Susan Elizabeth Griffith; 2 s (Hugh Andrew, David Robert (twins) b 12 Aug 1989); *Career* editorial asst OED 1977–80, P S Allen jr res fell in classics CCC Oxford 1980–84, fell and coll lectr in classics Magdalene Coll Cambridge 1986–90, fell New Hall Cambridge 1990–2002, reader in Latin lit Univ of Cambridge 1998–2002, Corpus Christi prof of Latin Univ of Oxford 2002–06, sr research fell Trinity Coll Cambridge 2006–; FBA 2000; *Books* Virgil's Aeneid: Cosmos and Imperium (1986), The Epic Successors of Virgil (1993), Ovid's Poetics of Illusion (2002); *Recreations* walking, cooking; *Style*— Prof Philip Hardie; ✉ 5 Stretten Avenue, Cambridge CB4 3ES (tel 01223 513020); Trinity College, Cambridge CB2 1TQ (tel 01223 338400)

HARDIE, Sean; s of late Ven A G Hardie, and late Shelagh, *née* Jacob; *b* 4 March 1947; *Educ* Trinity Coll Glenalmond, Trinity Coll Cambridge (MA); *m* 1, 1973 (m dis 1979), Janet, *née* Hall; 1 s (William); m 2, Kerry Jolley; *Career* prodr and dir current affairs BBC TV 1969–79 (incl 24 Hours, Panorama, Midweek), prodr light entertainment BBC TV 1979–81 (incl Not the Nine O'Clock News, later Spitting Image), contract writer and dir Video Arts Ltd; prodns incl: The Signal Box (RTE) 1995, Rory Bremner - Who Else? (Channel 4) 2003; TV awards incl: BAFTA, Silver Rose Montreux, Writers' Guild, US Emmy; chair Duiske Concerts; *Books* Not!, Not the Royal Wedding (1981), Not 1982 (1982), The Last Supper (1990), Right Connections (1991), Till The Fat Lady Sings (1993),

H

Falling Off a Log (1994), Moldova (play, 2006), Burning Your Boots (play, 2007); *Recreations* reading; *Clubs* Ballytighlea Social; *Style*— Sean Hardie, Esq; ✉ Milltown, Skeoghvosteen, Co Kilkenny, Eire (tel 00 353 599 73194, e-mail hardie@iol.ie); 2 St Thomas Square, Newport, Isle of Wight PO30 1SN (tel 07796 954969)

HARDING, Prof Anthony Filmer; s of Edward Harding (d 1999) and Enid, *née* Price (d 1994); *b* 20 November 1946; *Educ* CCC Cambridge (MA, PhD); *m* 1976, Lesley Eleanor, da of Alec Forbes; 2 s (Robin Benedict b 1979, Nicholas Alexander b 1981); *Career* research asst Br Museum 1973; Univ of Durham: lectr in archaeology 1973–88, sr lectr in archaeology 1988–90, prof of archaeology 1990–2004; prof of archaeology Univ of Exeter 2004–; pres European Assoc of Archaeologists 2003–; tstee Antiquity; FSA 1981, FBA 2001; *Recreations* music, walking, gardening; *Style*— Prof Anthony Harding; ✉ Department of Archaeology, University of Exeter, Laver Building, North Park Road, Exeter EX4 4QE (tel 01392 264520, e-mail a.f.harding@exeter.ac.uk)

HARDING, Daniel; s of John and Caroline Harding, of Oxford; *b* 31 August 1975; *Career* asst to Sir Simon Rattle, *qv*, 1993–94; professional debut CBSO (won Royal Philharmonic Soc Best Debut Award) 1994; asst to Claudio Abbado Berlin Philharmonic 1995–96, youngest conductor BBC Proms conducting two programmes 1996, debut Berlin Philharmonic Berlin Festival 1996, conductor Scharoun Ensemble (incl members of Berlin Philharmonic) Salzburg Festival 1997, princ conductor Trondheim Symphony Orch Norway 1997–2000; princ guest conductor: Norrkoping Symphony Orch Sweden 1997–2003, London Symphony Orch 2007–; music dir Die Deutsche Kammerphilharmonic Bremen 1997–2003, music dir Mahler Chamber Orch 2003–, music dir Swedish Radio Orch 2007–; conducted new opera productions 1998: Don Giovanni (dir by Peter Brook Aix-en-Provence Festival with Mahler Chamber Orch, toured Lyon, Milan, Brussels and Tokyo 1998–99), Janacek's Jenufa (Katie Mitchell prodn for WNO), Aix-en-Prevence Festival (Turn of the Screw, Eugene Onegin, La Traviata, Die Zauberflöte, Le nozze di Figaro), La Scala Milan (Idomeneo, Salome); orchs conducted incl: London Philharmonic, Leipzig Gewandhausorchester, Houston Symphony Orch, Rotterdam Philharmonic, Los Angeles Philharmonic, Oslo Philharmonic, Berlin Philharmonic, Oslo Philharmonic, Frankfurt Radio Orch, Orchestre des Champs Elysees, Bayerische Staatsoper Orch, Vienna Philharmonic, Dreden Staatskapelle, Philadelphia Orch, LA Philharmonic, Chicago; *Recordings* works by Lutoslawski with soprano Solveig Kringelborn and the Norwegian Chamber Orch, works by Britten with Ian Bostridge and the Britten Sinofonia (awarded Choc de L'Annee 198), Beethoven Overtures, Brahms' Symphonies 3 and 4, with Deutsche Kammerphilharmonie, Mozart's Don Giovanni, Mahler Symphony 4 with Mahler Chamber Orch recorded live at Aix-en-Provence Festival; *Style*— Daniel Harding, Esq; ✉ c/o Askonas Holt, Lonsdale Chambers, 27 Chancery Lane, London WC2A 1PF (tel 020 7400 1700, fax 020 7400 1799, e-mail info@askonasholt.co.uk)

HARDING, Frank Alexander; s of Eric Harding (d 1981), and Elsie, *née* Alexander (d 2004); *b* 20 September 1937; *Educ* Malvern Coll, Ecole de Commerce de Neuchâtel; *m* 30 Aug 1960, Belinda Ruth; 2 s (David b 1961, Thomas b 1968), 2 da (Kate b 1963, Amanda b 1967); *Career* CA 1961, ptnr KPMG (formerly KMG Thomson McLintock) 1967–96 (joined 1955); chm: Provalis plc 1998–2006, KLM Cityhopper UK Ltd 1998–; memb Cncl: ICAS 1980–85, ICAEW 1990–93; Int Fedn of Accountants: memb Cncl (UK rep) 1987–97, pres 1997–2000; memb Exec Ctee Union of European Accountants 1983–86, memb Int Accounting Standards Advsy Cncl 1995–2000; Officier de l'Ordre National de Mérite (France); *Recreations* golf, opera, bridge; *Style*— Mr Frank Harding; ✉ 11 Pilgrim's Lane, London NW3 1SJ (tel 020 7435 3728, fax 020 7431 8689, e-mail frankaharding@btinternet.com)

HARDING, Dr Geoffrey Wright; s of Jack Harding (d 1989), of Gravesend, Kent, and Ethel Florence, *née* Wilkinson (d 1997); *Educ* KCL (LLB, AKC), Northwestern Univ Sch of Law Chicago (LLM), QMC London (PhD); *m* 7 Oct 1972, Margaret June, da of Eric Oscar Danger; 1 da (Kate Joanna b 1978), 1 s (Peter James John b 1980); *Career* Nat Serv RAF 1951–53; called to the Bar Gray's Inn 1957; asst sec FCEC 1958–60, legal advsr Br Insurance (Atomic Energy) Ctee 1960–63, exchange lawyer under Harvard Law Sch Prog Isham Lincoln and Beale Attorneys Chicago 1963–64, asst slr Joynson Hicks 1965–67, ptnr Wilde Sapte London and Brussels (specialising in banking, consumer, competition, IT and Euro Union law) 1967–94, ind legal conslt 1994–; legal advsr Competition Cmmn 2001–02; visiting prof in commercial law Univ of Greenwich 1995–98, external examiner Bd of Examiners Univ of London and UWE; business mentor The Prince's Tst, Gtr London regnl cncllr Nat Autistic Soc; patient cncllr Membership Cncl Royal Marsden NHS Fndn; Gen Electric Fndn fell Northwestern Univ Sch of Law Chicago; Freeman City of London 1986, memb Guild of Freemen of City of London; memb Law Soc; *Books* Banking Act 1987 - Current Law Annotated (1987), Encyclopaedia of Competition Law (contrib ed, 1987–2002), Consumer Credit and Consumer Hire Law (1995); *Recreations* family, mountain biking, scuba diving, trying to understand autism, avoiding domestic DIY; *Style*— Dr Geoffrey Harding; ✉ Denton Wilde Sapte, 1 Fleet Place, London EC4M 7WS (tel 020 7246 7000, fax 020 7246 7777)

HARDING, Prof Graham Frederick Anthony; s of Frederick William Harding (d 1991), of Shenstone, and Elizabeth Louise Harding (d 1991); *b* 19 March 1937; *Educ* Torquay GS, UCL (BSc), Univ of Birmingham (PhD), Aston Univ (DSc); *m* 1, 4 March 1961 (m dis 1990), Margaret; 2 da (Catherine Louise b 25 Oct 1965, Laura Jane b 14 Aug 1969); *m* 2, 20 Sept 1991, Pamela Frances, da of Peter Frederick Evans, of Solihull; 1 s (Anthony Gray b 20 May 1993); *Career* hon conslt electroencephalographer Wolverhampton AHA 1974–, hon consit neuropsychologist Birmingham AHA 1974–, hon consit clinical neurophysiologist Royal Wolverhampton Hosps Tst 1995–, hon sr research fell Med Sch Univ of Birmingham; Aston Univ: reader in neuropsychology 1973–78, head of neuropsychology unit 1969–78, prof of clinical neurophysiology 1978–2004 (emeritus prof 2004–), head of Clinical Neurophysiology Unit 1979–, head of Vision Sciences 1981–89, head of psychology and biology 1997–99; pres Br Soc for Clinical Neurophysiology (formerly Electroencephalographic Soc) 1996–99 (memb 1963–, memb Cncl 1971–75), sec Int Fedn of Clinical Neurophysiology 2001–06, dir Neurosciences Research Inst 1999–2002; memb: Ctee on Clinical Neurophysiology W Midlands RHA 1975–2004, Midland Opthalmological Soc 1985–, Int League Against Epilepsy 1983–, Int Soc for Clinical Electrophysiology of Vision 1973–2004 (vice-pres 2001–03), Birmingham Medico-Legal Soc 1992–2004; tstee Birmingham Eye Fndn 1989–2004, patron Birmingham Royal Inst for the Blind Appeal 1990–2004, patron Queen Alexandra Coll Birmingham; FRSM 1996–2004 (memb Cncl for Neurosciences 1997), Hon FRCP 2006 (Hon MRCP 1998), FBPsS, CPsychol; *Books* Photosensitive Epilepsy (1975 and 1994); over 300 chapters and papers on electroencephalography, visual evoked responses, Alzheimer's disease, psychiatry, prematurity, ophthalmology and neuromagnetism; *Recreations* railways, model railways; *Style*— Prof Graham Harding; ✉ Electro Diagnostic Centre, Greenfields, Upton Snodsbury, Worcestershire WR7 4NR (tel and fax 01905 381335, e-mail gharding@wyenet.co.uk)

HARDING, Ian John; s of Reginald Harding, of Basildon, Essex, and Sheila, *née* Felton; *b* 19 March 1964; *Educ* Nicholas Comp Basildon, Southend Coll of Technol (Design Dip, HND Graphic Design, SIAD Award); *m* 30 July 1988, Nicola, da of Antony George; 2 da (Emma b 1990, Jessica b 2001), 1 s (Joe b 1993); *Career* former creative appts: MWA Advertising, Moorgate fin advtg & mktg, FCB Impact (sr art dir), FCA (jt creative dir); founding ptnr Heresy, owner and founder The Complete Image Ltd; recipient over 78 awards across all mktg disciplines since 1992 incl: D&AD Silver Award 1993, 12 DMA Gold Awards, ISP Grand Prix, Campaign Poster Award; memb D&AD 1993 (SIAD 1984); *Recreations* gym, golf, squash, painting; *Style*— Mr Ian Harding; ✉ 43 Elmhurst Avenue, Benfleet, Essex SS7 5RY (tel 01268 565171, fax 01268 565171, e-mail ianharding@blueyonder.co.uk)

HARDING, Prof John Edmond; s of William Gordon Harding (d 1987), and Alice Eleanor Harding (d 1985); *b* 22 November 1948; *Educ* St Joseph's Coll Beulah Hill, Imperial Coll London (BSc(Eng), MSc, DIC, PhD); *m* 7 Jan 1978, Patricia Anne, da of late Henry Wigfull; 2 da (Emma Philippa b 18 Aug 1980, Laura Anne b 20 July 1982); *Career* lectr in structural engrg Imperial Coll London 1978–85 (research asst/research fell 1971–78); Univ of Surrey: prof of structural engrg 1985–, pro-vice-chllr 1991–2001, head Dept of Civil Engrg 1997–2002, dir of external academic relationships 2002–; memb US Structural Stability Research Cncl 1988–; ed Int Jl of Constructional Steel Research 1980–, hon ed Structures and Buildings proceedings Instn of Civil Engrs until 1996; memb Bd of Govrs: Farnborough Coll of Technol, NE Surrey Coll of Technol, Reigate Sixth Form Coll, St Mary's Coll Strawberry Hill, Tormead Sch Guildford, Wimbledon Sch of Art; awarded Trevithick Premium Instn of Civil Engrs 1977; CEng, FIStructE 1986 (MIStructE 1980), FICE 1993 (MICE 1989); *Books* Bridge Management - Inspection, Maintenance, Assessment and Repair (ed 3 vols, 1990, 1993 and 1996), Traversely Stiffened Girder Webs Subject to Combined Loading (1991), Constructional Steel Design - an International Guide (ed, 1992), World Developments in Constructional Steel Design (ed, 1993), Manual of Bridge Engineering (ed, 2000); also author of numerous conference papers, and contribs to learned jls; *Style*— Prof John Harding; ✉ University of Surrey, Guildford, Surrey GU2 5XH (tel 01483 689119, fax 01483 572454, e-mail j.harding@surrey.ac.uk)

HARDING, Prof John James; s of George James Harding, and Mary Edith, *née* Simmons; *b* 2 June 1938, London; *Educ* Trinity Coll Cambridge (BA), Univ of London (PhD); *m* 1962, Ruth, *née* Taylor; 2 s (Paul b 9 Nov 1969, Daniel b 20 March 1971); *Career* Nuffield Lab of Ophthalmology Univ of Oxford: sr research scientist 1986–96, reader in ophthalmology 1996–97, prof of ocular biochemistry 1997–; head of ophthalmology Univ of Oxford 2003–05; visiting prof Tangdu Hosp Fourth Military Medical Univ (FMMU) Xi'an China; memb Biochemical Soc; chm Wootton, Tackley and Dist Field Paths Gp; *Books* Cataract: Biochemistry, Epidemiology and Pharmacology (1991); *Recreations* walking, grandchildren, local history, painting; *Style*— Prof John Harding; ✉ 55 St John's Road, Tackley, Oxfordshire OX5 3AR; Nuffield Laboratory of Ophthalmology, University of Oxford, Walton Street, Oxford OX2 6AW (tel 01865 248996, fax 01865 794508, e-mail john.harding@eye.ox.ac.uk)

HARDING, Dr (Leslie) Keith; s of Leslie Charles Harding (d 1964), of West Bromwich, and Priscilla Olive, *née* Mason (d 1984); *b* 3 February 1939; *Educ* Handsworth GS, Univ of Birmingham Med Sch (BSc, MB ChB); *m* 18 Aug 1962, Carol Margaret, da of Dr Colin Starkie, of Kidderminster; 1 s (Nicholas b 1969), 1 da (Victoria b 1972); *Career* lectr in med Queen Elizabeth Hosp Birmingham, conslt in nuclear med Dudley Rd Hosp Birmingham 1982– (conslt physician in gen and nuclear med 1972–82), clinical sr lectr in med Univ of Birmingham 1982–, med dir/conslt in nuclear med City Hosp NHS Tst Birmingham 1994–2000, hon reader in med Univ of Birmingham 1999–; author of chapters on gastric emptying and bile reflux; papers on: gastro intestinal motility, the lung, radiation safety in nuclear med depts; former memb Advsy Cncl European Assoc of Nuclear Med, Int Cmmn radiological prot and sec Ctee 3, memb Article 31 Ctee (advising EC), memb Ionizing and Radiation Ctee Health and Safety Cmmn; former chm: Regnl Med Advsy Ctee, Med Exec Ctee W Birmingham Health Authy (also dep dist gen mangr), Admin of Radioactive Substances Advsy Ctee, Euro Task Gp exploring risks; past treas and pres Br Nuclear Med Soc; bailiff and fndn govr King Edward VI Schs Birmingham; chm of govrs Five Ways Sch; FRCP, FRCR, FSRP; *Recreations* music, King Edward VI School; *Clubs* Woolhope, Lunar Soc; *Style*— Dr Keith Harding; ✉ Huntroyd, 27 Manor Road North, Edgbaston, Birmingham B16 9JS (tel 0121 242 2497); Birmingham Regional Radioisotope Centre, City Hospital NHS Trust, Dudley Road, Birmingham B18 7QH (tel 0121 507 4430, fax 0121 507 5223, e-mail keith.harding@swbh.nhs.uk)

HARDING, Kerry Richard Kerwan; s of (Albert Edgar) Kerry Harding (d 1994), and Daphne Wynne, *née* Mytton (d 1988); *b* 18 January 1936; *Educ* Prior Park Coll, RMA Sandhurst; *m* 1 Aug 1970, Mary Ann, da of Alexander Badenoch (d 1965), and Midi, *née* Berger (d 1994); 4 s (Jonathan b 28 May 1971, Alexander b 20 March 1973, Richard b 9 Feb 1978, Christopher b 8 Aug 1981), 1 da (Katie b 28 Feb 1979); *Career* King's Own Yorkshire Light Infantry: Platoon Cdr Cyprus and BAOR 1956–58, Trg Offr Trg Depot 1958–60, Platoon Cdr and Co 2 i/c Malaya then intelligence offr Borneo 1961–63, instr Small Arms Wing Sch of Infantry 1963–65, 2 i/c then Co Cdr Berlin 1965–67; Adjutant 5 Bn Light Infantry (TA) 1968–70, staff offr grade III 2 Div (latterly 1 (BR) Corps) BAOR 1970–72, Co Cdr Light Infantry Trg Depot 1973–75, trg Maj 6 Bn Light Infantry 1975–77, instr/staff offr grade II Tactics Wing Royal Sch of Military Engrg 1977–78; exec sec Glass and Glazing Fedn 1978–81, sec gen Chartered Inst of Arbitrators 1986–2000 (dep sec 1981–86); memb Cncl Goring on Thames PC 1991–95 and 2003–, memb S Oxfordshire District Cncl 1999–2003, chm Goring and S Stoke Cons Branch 2003–; memb Soc of Association Execs 1978–87; MIPD 1978–2002, FCIArb 1986, FRSA 1993–2002, MInstD 1995; *Recreations* family, art, golf; *Clubs* Springs Golf; *Style*— Kerry Harding, Esq; ✉ 4 Nun's Acre, Goring on Thames, Reading, Berkshire RG8 9BE (tel 01491 873641, fax 01491 873124, e-mail mahard74@aol.com)

HARDING, Peter Leslie; s of Leslie O'Brien Harding (d 1977), and Muriel Ellen, *née* Money (d 1966); *b* 22 September 1926; *Educ* Rugby, King's Coll Cambridge; *m* 6 Nov 1954, Nina Doris, da of Charles Downing Barnard (d 1965); 1 da (Caroline b 23 March 1956), 1 s (David b 30 July 1959); *Career* Union Castle Line 1947–53, dir Alexander Howden & Co Ltd 1960–67 (joined 1953); Baltic Exchange Ltd: dir 1969–73 and 1975–83, chm 1981–83, hon life memb 2002; chm: JE Hyde & Co Ltd 1986–2000 (ptnr 1968–86), Polak Gallery Ltd 1986–2006 (ptnr 1977–86); Freeman City of London 1982, Liveryman Worshipful Co of Shipwrights 1984; FICS; *Recreations* gardening, fly fishing; *Style*— Peter Harding, Esq; ✉ Martlets, Greenways, Walton-on-the-Hill, Tadworth, Surrey KT20 7QE (tel 01737 813766)

HARDING, Philip; s of Douglas Harding, and Leonora, *née* Browne; *b* 28 April 1947; *Educ* Univ of York (BA), Wharton Business Sch; *m* 1979, Margo, da of Morris Blythman; 1 da (Laura b 1980); *Career* dep ed Nationwide 1980–81, dep ed Panorama 1981–83 (sr prodr 1978–80), ed London Plus 1984–86, asst head current affrs BBC TV 1986–87 (prodr 1972–78), ed Today BBC Radio Four 1987–93, project dir Radio Five Live, ed Five Live News Progs 1993, BBC chief political advsr 1995–96, controller Editorial Policy 1996–2001, dir English Networks and News BBC World Service 2001–07, journalist and media conslt 2007–; fell Radio Acad 1999 (memb Cncl 1995–2001), FRSA 1999; *Awards* Emmy Award for Best Documentary Who Killed Georgi Markov? (Panorama) 1980; Sony Awards: Best Current Affrs Prog 1989 (for Today), Best Response to a News Event 1989 (for Today), Best Daily News Prog 1990 (for Today), Best Response To A News Event 1990 (for Today), Best Breakfast Prog 1992 (for Today), Best Coverage Breaking News 2005 (for BBC World Service), Best News Feature 2006 (for BBC World Service); BPG Award 1992; *Recreations* thinking, walking, watching football and supporting QPR; *Style*— Philip Harding, Esq; ✉ BBC, Broadcasting House, London W1A 1AA (tel 020 7580 4468)

HARDING, Timothy John Randolph; *Career* The Peninsular & Oriental Steam Navigation Co plc: main bd dir, chm P&O Developments Ltd, md P&O Properties International Ltd, chm P&O Properties Ltd, chm Laing Property Corporation Canada, chm P&O Shopping Centres Ltd; *Style—* T J R Harding, Esq

HARDING OF PETHERTON, 2 Baron (UK 1958); John Charles Harding; o s of Field Marshal 1 Baron Harding of Petherton, GCB, CBE, DSO, MC (d 1989), and Mary, *née* Rooke (d 1983); *b* 12 February 1928; *Educ* Marlborough, Worcester Coll Oxford; *m* 20 June 1966, Harriet, da of Maj-Gen James Hare, CB, DSO (d 1970); 1 da (Hon Diana Mary b 1967), 2 s (Hon William Allan John b 1969, Hon David Richard John b 1978); *Heir* s, Hon William Harding; *Career* Maj 11 Hussars, ret 1968; farmer, ret 1991; *Style—* The Lord Harding of Petherton; ✉ Myrtle Cottage, Lamyatt, Shepton Mallet, Somerset BA4 6NP (tel 01749 812292)

HARDINGE OF PENSHURST, 4 Baron (UK 1910); Julian Alexander Hardinge; s of 3 Baron (d 1997); *b* 23 August 1945; *Educ* Eton, Trinity Coll Cambridge; *m* 1, 1972 (m dis 1993), Anthea June, da of Harold Mills West; 2 da (Frances Melanie b 1973, Sophie Jane b 1974); m 2, 2001, Ulrike, da of Heinz Adolph, of Jestetten, Germany; *Style—* The Rt Hon Lord Hardinge of Penshurst

HARDINGHAM, Adrian Charles; s of Charles Robert Hardingham (d 2004), and Dorothy Verena, *née* Yandle (d 1998); *b* 12 February 1953, Hampton, Middx; *Educ* Glyn GS Ewell, UC Oxford (open scholar, MA); *m* 21 March 1987, Jennie Amanda, da of Geoffrey Robinson (d 2006); *Career* admitted slr 1978; ptnr Ingledew Brown Bennison & Garrett 1980–89, founding ptnr Holmes Hardingham 1989– (chm 2003–); memb Law Soc; *Publications* Multimodal Transport: Avoiding Legal Problems (contrib, 1997); author of various articles in Lloyd's Maritime & Commercial Law Quarterly; *Recreations* flying (private pilot's licence); *Style—* Adrian Hardingham, Esq; ✉ Holmes Hardingham, 22–23 Great Tower Street, London EC3R 5HE (tel 020 7280 3200, fax 020 7280 3201, e-mail adrian.hardingham@hhlaw.co.uk)

HARDINGHAM, Michael; s of Edmund Arthur Hardingham, and Winifred, *née* Leeding; *b* 16 October 1939; *Educ* West House Sch, Solihull Sch, St Mary's Hosp Univ of London (MB BS); *m* 25 Sept 1982, Ellen, da of William McCafferty, of Pennsylvania, USA; 1 s (Henry b 1984), 1 da (Isabel b 1986); *Career* postgrad med trg London, Edinburgh and Sweden, trg in otorhinolaryngology St Mary's Royal Marsden Hosp, conslt ENT surgn Cheltenham Gen Hosp and Gloucestershire Royal Hosp 1974– (special interest head and neck oncology); pres Glos Div BMA 2003–04, former hon sec Br Assoc of Head and Neck Oncologists, foreign corresponding memb American Soc of Head and Neck Surgns; past pres SW Laryngolical Assoc; vice-pres Nursing Assoc of Midland Inst of Otology, past pres Midland Inst Otorhinolaryngology; contrib pubns to otolaryngolical clinics N America; FRCSEd, FRCS 1973, FRSM, fell BMA 2006; *Recreations* theatre, opera, skiing; *Style—* Michael Hardingham, Esq; ✉ Winfield Hospital, Tewkesbury Road, Gloucester GL2 9EE (tel 01452 337266, fax 01452 331200, e-mail hardinghamcheltorl@hotmail.com)

HARDMAN, Blaise Noel Anthony; s of Air Chief Marshal Sir Donald Hardman, GBE, KCB, DFC (d 1982), and Dorothy, *née* Ashcroft Thompson (d 2005); *b* 24 December 1939; *Educ* Eton; *m* 1967, Caroline Marion, da of Sir Donald Cameron of Lochiel, KT, CVO, of Inverness-shire; 4 da (Jane (Mrs Alan Parker) b 1969, Annabel b 1971 (Mrs Thomas Byng), Daisy Elizabeth b 1974 (Mrs Rollo McNally), Rosanna b 1979), 1 s (Thomas b 1977); *Career* Lt HM Forces 1959, served 13/18 Royal Hussars 1959–61, Malaya 1961, BAOR; Morgan Grenfell and Co Ltd 1962–88, (dir 1971, chm 1987); dir: P&O Steam Navigation Co 1980–83, Matthew Clark plc 1982–91, Murray Income Tst plc 1988–2004, Whiteaway Laidlaw Bank Ltd 1989–2007, Fleming Japanese Investment Tst plc 1996–2006; *Clubs* Boodle's; *Style—* Blaise Hardman, Esq; ✉ The Old Vicarage, Stapleford, Salisbury, Hampshire SP3 4LQ

HARDMAN, Ven Christine Elizabeth; da of Wynford Atkins, and Margaret Atkins; *Educ* Queen Elizabeth's Girls' GS Barnet, Univ of London (BSc), Westminster Coll Oxford (MTh); *Career* ordained: deaconess 1984, deacon 1987, priest 1994; deaconess Markyate Street 1984–88, course dir St Albans Ministerial Training Scheme (later St Albans and Oxford Ministry Course) 1988–96; vicar Holy Trinity Stevenage 1996–2001, rural dean of Stevenage 1999–2001, archdeacon of Lewisham 2001–; *Recreations* cycling, running, theatre, cinema; *Style—* The Ven the Archdeacon of Lewisham; ✉ Trinity House, 4 Chapel Court, Borough High Street, London SE1 1HW (tel 020 7939 9400)

HARDWICK, Nicholas Lionel (Nick); s of Herbert Lionel Hardwick (d 1987), and Nancy Enid, *née* Nightingale (d 1990); *b* 19 July 1957; *Educ* Epsom Coll, Univ of Hull (BA); *Children* 1 da (Sophie b 1979); *m*, Susan, *née* Heaven; 1 s (Jack b 1992); *Career* chief exec: Centrepoint 1985–95, Refugee Cncl 1995–2002; special advsr to DOE 1990, memb Social Security Advsy Ctee 1994–99; chm: Euro Cncl on Refugees and Exiles (ECRE) 1999–2003, Independent Police Complaints Commn 2003–; memb Holocaust Meml Day Steering Gp 2001–05; Hon DSSc Univ of Wolverhampton 2002; *Recreations* family; *Clubs* RSA; *Style—* Nick Hardwick; ✉ The Independent Police Complaints Commission, 6th Floor, 90 High Holborn, London WC1V 6BH (tel 020 7166 3000)

HARDWICK, Dr Peter Bernard; QHP (1992); s of Arthur William Hardwick (d 1976), of Rayleigh, Essex, and Nellie, *née* Love (d 1960); *b* 21 September 1933; *Educ* Southend-on-Sea HS for Boys, Royal Free Hosp Sch of Med London (MB BS); *m* 1, 1961 (m dis 1988), Nancy, *née* Peters; 2 da (Deborah Claire b 1962, Julia Dawn b 1964 d 1989), 2 s (Nigel Peter Arthur b 1967, Matthew James Gerald b 1969); m 2, 1998 (m dis 2003), May Rita Nemar, *née* Stephan; 1 da (Elizabeth May b 2000); *Career* conslt anaesthetist and conslt i/c clinic for pain relief Royal Free Hosp London 1969–92; Hon MO London and Schools ABA, dep dist surgn St John Ambulance London (Prince of Wales) Dist; memb Ct of Common Cncl Corp of City of London; pres Assoc of Port Health Authorities 2005–06, former chm Port Health and Environmental Services Ctee; dep chm Establishment Ctee West Ham Park (former chm Ctee of Mangrs); Liveryman: Worshipful Co of Barbers, Worshipful Soc of Apothecaries; FRCA; OStJ; *Recreations* private flying, horse riding, cricket and rugby; *Clubs* MCC, RAF; *Style—* Dr Peter Hardwick, QHP; ✉ Belmont, Point Clear Road, Point Clear, St Osyth, Essex CO16 8JW (tel 01255 822385)

HARDWICKE, 10 Earl of (GB 1754); Joseph Philip Sebastian Yorke; also Baron Hardwicke (GB 1733) and Viscount Royston (GB 1754); s of Viscount Royston (d 1973, s and h of 9 Earl, who d 1974); *b* 3 February 1971; *Heir* kinsman, Charles Yorke; *Career* dir Eagle Headhunters; *Recreations* films, music, the Caribbean Islands, wine, shooting, football, cricket, water skiing, golf; *Clubs* Wentworth; *Style—* The Rt Hon Earl of Hardwicke

HARDY, Prof Barbara Gladys; da of Maurice Nathan (d 1962), and Gladys Emily Ann, *née* Abraham (d 1992); *b* 27 June 1924; *Educ* Swansea HS for Girls, UCL (BA, MA); *m* 14 March 1946, Ernest Dawson Hardy (d 1977); 2 da (Julia b 1955, Kate b 1957); *Career* lectr English Dept Birkbeck Coll London, subsequently prof of English Royal Holloway Coll London 1965–70, prof of English literature Birkbeck Coll London 1970–89; emeritus prof Univ of London, hon prof of English UC Swansea; hon fell: Birkbeck Coll London, Royal Holloway Univ of London, Univ of Wales Swansea; pres Dickens Soc 1987–88; vice-pres Hardy Soc; fell Welsh Acad; hon memb MLA; Hon DUniv Open Univ 1981; FRSL 1997, FBA 2007; *Books* The Novels of George Eliot (1959), The Appropriate Form (1964), The Moral Art of Dickens (1970), The Exposure of Luxury: Radical Themes in Thackeray (1972), Tellers and Listeners: The Narrative Imagination (1975), A Reading of Jane Austen (1975), The Advantage of Lyric (1977), Particularities: Readings in George Eliot (1982), Charles Dickens: The Writer and His Work (1983), Forms of Feeling in Victorian Fiction (1985), Narrators and Novelists: Collected Essays (1987), Swansea Girl (1994), Henry James: The Later Writing (1996), London Lovers (1996), Shakespeare's Storytellers (1997), Thomas Hardy Imagining Imagination (2000), Dylan Thomas: An Original Language (2000), Severn Bridge: New and Selected Poems, 1965–2001 (2001, 2 edn 2002), George Eliot: A Critic's Biography (2006), The Yellow Carpet: New and Selected Poems (2006); *Recreations* learning Italian, walking, theatre, galleries; *Style—* Prof Barbara Hardy, FRSL; ✉ c/o School of English and Humanities, Birkbeck College, Malet Street, London WC1E 7HX (tel 020 7580 6622)

HARDY, David Gordon; s of Gordon Patrick Hardy, of Auchtermuchty, Fife, and Margaret Maud, *née* Cunningham; *b* 5 July 1940; *Educ* Daniel Stewart's Coll Edinburgh, Univ of Edinburgh (BSc, MB ChB), Univ of Cambridge (MA); *m* 8 Aug 1967, Maria Rosa (Rosemary), da of Johann Breu (d 1965), of Appenzell, Switzerland; 1 da (Ruth Maria b 10 Oct 1969), 1 s (James Patrick b 5 Oct 1971); *Career* Fulbright Hayes scholar Univ of Florida 1977–78, sr lectr in neurosurgery London Hosp Med Coll 1979–80, conslt neurosurgn Addenbrooke's Hosp Cambridge 1980–2005, med dir Addenbrooke's Hosp NHS Tst, supervisor in anatomy Gonville & Caius Coll Cambridge (assoc lectr faculty of clinical med); visiting conslt Norfolk and Norwich Hosp; contrib various chapters and papers on various neurosurgical and anatomical subjects; memb Section of Neurology RSM; pres Soc of Br Neurosurgeons 2002–04 (vice-pres 2001–02 and 2004–05); FRCSEd 1970, FRCS 1971, FRSM; *Recreations* gardening, walking; *Style—* David Hardy, Esq; ✉ 20 High Street, Great Wilbraham, Cambridge CB1 5JD (tel 01223 881347)

HARDY, David Malcolm; s of Roy Hardy, of Leigh-on-Sea, Essex, and late Mary, *née* Ebsworth; *b* 16 July 1955; *Educ* Westcliff HS; *m* 1, 1981 (m dis); 1 s (Matthew James Cranmer b 1985), 1 da (Joanna Louise b 1989); m 2, 1995, Marion, da of Cecil and Dorothy Brazier; *Career* Barclays Bank plc 1973–81, Barclays Merchant Bank 1981–85; London Clearing House Ltd (formerly International Commodities Clearing House Ltd): on secondment from Barclays Bank 1985–87, md 1987–95, chief exec 1995–2003; gp chief exec LCH.Clearnet Gp Ltd (following merger) 2003–; also dir: London Commodity Exchange (1986) Ltd 1991–96, International Petroleum Exchange of London Ltd 1993–99, Futures and Options Association 1993–, Inst of Fin Markets (US) 2000–; memb FSA Practitioner Panel 2001–; Freeman City of London 1995, Liveryman Worshipful Co of World Traders 1993; ACIB 1976, FCT 1992; *Recreations* golf, photography; *Style—* David Hardy, Esq; ✉ LCH.Clearnet Group Limited, Aldgate House, 33 Aldgate High Street, London EC3N 1EA (tel 020 7426 7040, fax 020 7667 7354, e-mail david.hardy@lchclearnet.com)

HARDY, Sir David William; kt (1992); s of Brig John Herbert Hardy, CBE, MC (d 1969), of Lancaster, and (Amy) Doris, *née* Bacon (d 1982); *b* 14 July 1930; *Educ* Wellington, Harvard Business Sch (AMP); *m* 11 Sept 1957, Rosemary Stratford, da of Sir Godfrey Ferdinando Stratford Collins, KCIE, CSI, OBE (d 1952); 1 da (Sarah Elizabeth b 28 May 1964), 1 s (Alexander David b 11 May 1968); *Career* 2 Lt 2 Royal Horse Artillery Germany 1953–54; with Funch Edye Co Inc 1954–64 (dir 1960–64), vice-pres fin and admin Imperial Tobacco 1964–70, HM Govt co-ordinator of advrs 1970–72, fin dir Tate and Lyle plc 1972–77; dir: Ocean Transport and Trading plc 1977–83, Waterford Wedgwood Group plc 1984–90, Paragon Group Ltd 1984–88, Total Group plc 1990–91; non-exec dir: Sturge Holdings plc 1985–95, Aberfoyle Holdings plc 1986–91, Ciba-Geigy plc 1991–96, Hanson plc 1991–2001, J Devenish plc 1991–93, James Fisher & Sons plc 1993–2004, Imperial Tobacco Group plc 1996–2001, Milner Estates plc 1999–2001, Stirling Lloyd Holdings plc, Fitzhardinge plc; chm: Ocean Inchcape Ltd 1980–83, Globe Investment Trust plc 1983–90 (dir 1976), London Park Hotels 1983–87, Docklands Light Railway 1984–87, Swan Hunter Ltd 1986–88, MGM Assurance 1986–99 (dir 1985), Leisuretime International 1988–89, Buckingham International 1989–95, London Docklands Devpt Corp 1988–92, Europa Minerals plc 1991–98, Bankers Trust Investment Management Ltd 1992–94, Burmine Ltd 1992–96, Y J Lovell Holdings plc 1994–99; dir: Sons of Gwalia Ltd 1996–98, Conrad Ritblat 1996–99; dep chm: London Regnl Tport 1984–87, The Agricultural Mortgage Corp 1985–93 (dir 1973), Colliers Capital UK 2003–; advsy dir HSBC Samuel Montagu (now HSBC Investment Bank plc) 1995–97; chm: 100 Gp of Fin Dirs 1986–88, DTI Engrg Markets Advsy Ctee 1988–90, Tport Research Fndn 1996–; memb: NEDC for Agriculture 1970–72, ECGD Advsy Cncl 1973–78, CBI Econs and Fiscal Ctee 1982–89, NACF Devpt Ctee 1990–99, Fin Ctee London Fedn of Boys' Clubs 1990–99, Industry Development Advsy Bd DTI 1991–96; co-opted Cncl ICAEW 1974–78; fndr dir: St Katherine & Shadwell Tst 1991– (vice-chm 1999–), Royal Albert Dock Tst 1992–; Nat Maritime Museum: tstee 1993–2005, dep chm 1994–95, chm 1995–2005; co-opted govr Chelsea Open Air Sch 1992–2005 (vice-chm 1993–2005); pres: Poplar, Blackwall and Dist Rowing Club 1991, Pitlochry Angling Club 1994–96; Yr Bro Trinity House; Freeman City of London; Liveryman: Worshipful Co of CA's, Worshipful Co of Shipwrights; Hon LLD Univ of Greenwich 2003; FCA, FCIT, CIMgt (chm Econs and Social Affrs Ctee 1974–78, memb Cncl 1974–79); *Recreations* fly fishing, shooting; *Clubs* Brooks's, MCC, HAC, Flyfishers', Beefsteak; *Style—* Sir David Hardy; ✉ Transport Research Foundation, Crowthorne House, Nine Mile Ride, Wokingham, Berkshire RG40 3GA (tel 01344 770081, e-mail seahardy@aol.com)

HARDY, Sir Richard Charles Chandos; 5 Bt (UK 1876), of Dunstall Hall, Co Stafford; s of Lt-Col Sir Rupert John Hardy, 4 Bt (d 1997), and Hon Diana Joan, *née* Allsopp, da of 3 Baron Hindlip; *b* 6 February 1945; *Educ* Eton; *m* 1972, Venetia Wingfield, da of Simon Wingfield Digby, TD, DL (d 1998); 4 da (Arabella Venetia Jane b 1976, Jacquetta Anne b 1977, Georgina Charlotte b 1982, Henrietta Alicia Diana b 1986); *Heir* kinsman, Gerald Hardy; *Career* insurance broker; *Recreations* hunting, point-to-pointing, racing; *Clubs* Turf; *Style—* Sir Richard Hardy, Bt; ✉ Springfield House, Gillingham, Dorset SP8 5RD

HARDY, (Timothy Sydney) Robert; CBE (1981); s of late Maj Henry Harrison Hardy, CBE, and Edith Jocelyn, *née* Dugdale; *b* 29 October 1925; *Educ* Rugby, Magdalen Coll Oxford (BA); *m* 1, 1952 (m dis), Elizabeth, da of Sir Lionel Fox, and Lady Fox; 1 s; m 2, 1961 (m dis 1986), Sally, da of Sir Neville Pearson, 2 Bt, and Dame Gladys Cooper, DBE; 2 da; *Career* actor, writer; tstee: Mary Rose Tst 1991– (conslt 1979–), WWF 1983–89; memb: Bd of Tstees Royal Armouries 1984–95, Battlefields Panel English Heritage 1993–; chm Berks Bucks and Oxon Naturalists Tst Appeal 1985–90; memb Woodmen of Arden 1982–; Hon DLitt: Univ of Reading 1990, Univ of Durham 1997, Univ of Portsmouth; Master Ct Worshipful Co Bowyers 1988–90; FSA 1996; *Theatre* early work incl: Shakespeare (Memorial Theatre) 1949–51, West End 1951–53, Old Vic Theatre 1953–54, USA 1954, 1956–58 and 1963–64 (incl Hamlet and Henry V), Shakespeare (Memorial Theatre Centenary season) 1959; later work incl: Rosmersholm (Comedy Theatre) 1960, The Rehearsal (Globe Theatre) 1961, A Severed Head (Criterion Theatre) 1963, The Constant Couple (New Theatre) 1967, I've Seen You Cut Lemons (Fortune Theatre) 1969, Habeas Corpus (Lyric Theatre) 1974, Dear Liar (Mermaid Theatre) 1982, Winnie (Victoria Palace Theatre) 1988, Body and Soul (Albery) 1992, Winston Churchill in Celui qui a dit Non (Palais des Congrès, Paris) 1999–2000; *Television* incl: David Copperfield 1956, Age of Kings 1960, Trouble-Shooters 1966–67, Elizabeth R 1970, Manhunt 1970, Edward VII 1973, All Creatures Great and Small 1978–90, Winston Churchill - The Wilderness Years 1981, Paying Guests 1986, Make and Break 1986, Churchill in The USA 1986, Hot Metal 1987–88, Northanger Abbey 1987, Sherlock Holmes 1991, Twilight of the Gods 1992, Middlemarch 1993, Gulliver's Travels 1995, Nancherrow 1998, The Tenth Kingdom 2002, Lucky Jim 2002, Bertie & Elizabeth 2002, The Falklands Play 2002, Death in Holy Orders 2002–03; author of TV documentaries: The Picardy Affair 1962, The Longbow 1972, Horses in our Blood 1977, Gordon of Khartoum 1982; *Film* incl: Torpedo Run 1956, The Spy Who Came in from the Cold, Ten Rillington Place, Young Winston, How I Won The War, Le Silencieux, La Gifle, The Far Pavilions 1983, The Shooting Party 1984, Jenny's War 1985, Paris by Night

1988, War and Remembrance 1988, A Feast at Midnight 1995, Sense and Sensibility 1995, Mrs Dalloway 1996, The Barber of Siberia 1997, The Tichborne Claimant 1997, An Ideal Husband 1998, Lucky Jim 2001, Shackleton 2001, The Gathering 2002, Harry Potter and the Chamber of Secrets 2002, Harry Potter and the Prisoner of Azkaban 2003, Harry Potter and the Goblet of Fire 2004, Harry Potter and the Order of the Phoenix 2007; *Books* Longbow (1976, 1986, 1992 and 2007), The Great War-Bow (2004); *Recreations* archery, medieval military history, bowyery; *Clubs* Buck's, Royal Toxophilite, Br Longbow; *Style*— Robert Hardy, Esq, CBE, FSA; ⊠ c/o Chatto & Linnit, 123A Kings Road, Chelsea, London SW3 4PL (tel 020 7352 7722, fax 020 7352 3450)

HARDY, Timothy (Tim); s of Robert Norman Hardy (d 1992), of Seer Green, Bucks, and Patricia Margaret May, *née* Keen (d 1985); *b* 17 February 1956; *Educ* Royal GS High Wycombe, Balliol Coll Oxford (MA); *m* 29 April 2000, Angela, *née* Spencer; *Career* admitted slr 1982; ptnr Barlow Lyde & Gilbert 1987– (slr 1982–87); Br Insurance Law Assoc: memb Ctee, chm 1996–98, vice-pres 2004–; CEDR accredited mediator 1998; memb: British Exporters' Assoc, London Slrs Litigation Assoc, Clauses Ctee Int Underwriting Assoc, Int Ctee Insurance Inst of London; charitable tstee BILA; memb Int Bar Assoc; MCII; *Publications* Reinsurance Practice and the Law (co-author, 1993); also author of various journal articles and conference papers; *Recreations* literature, theatre, sports; *Clubs* Nepotists Cricket; *Style*— Tim Hardy, Esq; ⊠ Barlow Lyde & Gilbert, Beaufort House, 15 St Botolph Street, London EC3A 7NJ (tel 020 7643 8479, fax 020 7071 9331, e-mail thardy@blg.co.uk)

HARE, Christopher Peter; s of Reginald Charles Hare (d 1980), and Mary Euphemia, *née* Lefroy (d 1988); *b* 6 November 1947; *Educ* Dover Coll; *m* (Dorothy) Jane, da of Richard Gough Dowell (d 1996), of Middleton-on-Sea, W Sussex; 1 da (Rebecca Anne b 14 Feb 1975), 2 s (Nicholas Anthony b 28 May 1977, Julian Charles b 17 Nov 1981); *Career* John Dickenson & Co 1966–68, Lyon Trail Attenborough (formerly Lyon Lohr & Sly) 1968–85; dir: Lyon Lohr Group Services 1979 (gp admin 1979–85), Lyon Lohr Int 1980; md Aberdeen Underwriting Advisers (formerly Minories Underwriting Agencies) 1997– (joined 1985, dir 1986–); dir: Hampden Agencies Ltd 1999–2001, PRO Syndicate Mgmnt 2001–05, RITC Syndicate Mgmnt Ltd 2007–; memb Lloyd's 1977–97, chm City Forum 1983 (memb 1978, memb Ctee 1980–83); govr Dover Coll 1982– (memb Cncl and Fin Ctee 1982–, vice-chm 1991–94, chm 1994–), pres Old Dovorian Club 2003– (memb 1975–96, chm 1984–90), govr Merchant Taylor Sch 1993–2005; Freeman City of London, memb Ct of Assts Worshipful Co of Merchant Taylors; *Recreations* cricket, tennis, squash, golf; *Clubs* MCC, RAC, Roehampton; *Style*— Christopher Hare, Esq; ⊠ 40 Doneraile Street, London SW6 6EP (tel and fax 020 7736 4218, e-mail chris@hare100.co.uk)

HARE, Sir David; kt (1998); s of Clifford Theodore Rippon, and Agnes Cockburn Hare; *b* 5 June 1947; *Educ* Lancing, Jesus Coll Cambridge (MA); *m* 1 (m dis), Margaret Matheson; 2 s, 1 da; *m* 2, Nicole Farhi; *Career* playwright and director; fndr Portable Theatre 1968, literary mangr and resident dramatist Royal Court Theatre 1969–71, resident dramatist Nottingham Playhouse 1973, fndr Joint Stock Theatre Gp 1975, fndr Greenpoint Films 1982, assoc dir Royal Nat Theatre 1985–; Officier de l'ordre des Art et des Lettres 1997; US/UK Bicentennial fell 1976; FRSL 1985; *Plays* writer: Slag (Royal Court and NY Shakespeare Festival 1971), The Great Exhibition (Hampstead 1972), Brassneck (also dir, Nottingham Playhouse 1973), Knuckle (Comedy Theatre 1974, televised 1989), Fanshen (ICA and Hampstead 1975, NT 1992), Teeth'n'Smiles (also dir, Royal Ct 1975, Wyndhams 1976), Plenty (also dir, NT 1978, NYC 1982, Alberry 1999), A Map of the World (NT 1983, NYC 1985), Pravda (also dir, with Howard Brenton, NT 1985), The Bay at Nice (also dir NT 1986), The Secret Rapture (NT 1988, and dir NYC & Broadway 1989), Racing Demon (NT 1990 and 1993, NYC 1995), Murmuring Judges (RNT 1992 and 1993), The Absence of War (RNT 1993, televised 1995), Skylight (RNT 1995, NYC 1996), Mother Courage (RNT, adapted, 1995), Amy's View (RNT 1997, Aldwych 1998 and Broadway 1999), The Judas Kiss (Almeida and Broadway 1998), Via Dolorosa (Royal Ct 1998, Almedia and Broadway 1999), My Zinc Bed (Royal Court 2000), The Breath of Life (Theatre Royal Haymarket 2002), The Permanent Way (NT and Out of Joint 2003), Stuff Happens (NT 2004), The Vertical Hour (Music Box Theatre NY 2006); dir: Christie in Love (Portable Theatre, 1969), Fruit (Portable Theatre, 1970), Blowjob (Portable Theatre, 1971), England's Ireland (co-dir, Portable Theatre, 1972), The Provoked Wife (Palace Watford, 1973), The Pleasure Principle (Theatre Upstairs, 1973), The Party (NT, 1974), Weapons of Happiness (NT, 1976), Devil's Island (Joint Stock, 1977), Total Eclipse (Lyric, 1981), King Lear (NT, 1986), The Designated Mourner (NT, 1996), Heartbreak House (Almeida, 1997); wrote libretto for The Knife (with Nick Bicat and Tim Rose Price, NY 1988); *Adaptations* The Rules of the Game (from Pirandello, NT 1971 and Almedia 1992), The Life of Galileo (from Brecht, Almedia 1994), Mother Courage and Her Children (from Brecht, NT 1995), Ivanov (from Chekhov, Almedia 1997, Broadway 1998), The Blue Room (from Schnitzler, Donmar and Broadway 1998, Theatre Royal Haymarket 2000), Platonov (from Chekov (Almedia 2001), The House of Bernarda Alba-Lorca (2003, NT 2005); *Television* Man Above Men (1973), Licking Hitler (also dir 1978, BAFTA Award), Dreams of Leaving (also dir 1979), Saigon - Year of the Cat (1983), Heading Home (1991), The Absence of War (1995); *Films* writer and dir: Wetherby (1985, Golden Bear Award Berlin), Paris By Night (1988), Strapless (1989); writer only: Plenty 1985, Damage (adapted from Josephine Hart novel, 1992), The Secret Rapture (1993), Via Dolorosa (also actor, 2000), The Hours (adapted from Michael Cunningham novel, 2001); as dir and prodr only: The Designated Mourner (1996); *Books* Writing Lefthanded (1991), Asking Around (1993), Acting Up (1999); *Style*— Sir David Hare, FRSL; ⊠ c/o Casarrotto Ramsay Ltd, National House, 4th Floor, 60–66 Wardour Street, London W1V 3HP (tel 020 7287 4450, fax 020 7287 9128)

HARE, John Neville; s of late Capt Lancelot Geldart Hare, MC (d 1957), and Esther Maria, *née* Whales (d 1969); *b* 11 December 1934; *Educ* St Edward's Sch Oxford; *m* 17 Sept 1966, Pippa, da of Harding McGregor Dunnett (d 2000); 3 da (Charlotte b 1968, Henrietta b 1970, Emily b 1974); *Career* Lt Oxford and Bucks LI, Royal W Africa Frontier Force 1954–55; sr dist offr Colonial Serv Northern Nigeria 1957–64; dir Macmillan Education Publishers 1966–74, author and conslt Hodder and Stoughton Publishers 1980–89; UN Environment Prog 1989–96; memb: Scientific Expdn to the Mongolian Gobi 1993 and 2005, Xinjiang Environment Protection Inst Expdn to the Gobi to survey the wild camel population 1995 and to Lop Nur 1996, 1997, 1999 and 2005; ldr Trans-Sahara Camel Expedition 2001–02, Lake Turkana 2006; fndr Wild Camel Protection Fndn 1997; Ness Award RGS 2004, Lawrence of Arabia Meml Medal 2004, Mungo Park Medal RSGS 2006; FRGS; *Books* The Lost Camels of Tartary (1998), Shadows Across the Sahara (2003) and 38 other books; *Recreations* hunting, travel, writing; *Clubs* Reform; *Style*— John Hare, Esq; ⊠ School Farm, Benenden, Kent TN17 4EU (tel 01580 241132, e-mail harecamel@aol.com)

HARE, Paul Webster; LVO (1985); s of Maurice Leslie Hare, of Leeds, and Anne Dorothy Hare; *b* 20 July 1951; *Educ* Univ of Oxford (MA); *m* 29 July 1978, Lynda Carol, da of Ian S M Henderson, CBE, GM, KPM; 3 da (Antonia b 13 Oct 1979, Victoria b 3 Aug 1982, Marina b 16 Feb 1994), 3 s (Andrew b 11 July 1984, Matthew b 16 Sept 1988, Alexander b 6 June 1991); *Career* trained as slr 1972–75, investment banker Schroders 1976–78, joined HM Dip Serv 1978; served: Brussels, Lisbon, NY, Caracas; ambass to Cuba 2001–04; visiting fell Center for Int Relations Harvard Univ 2004–; pres Baseball/Softball UK 2000–01; *Recreations* music, sport, family, writing novels; *Clubs* Rocky Point (USA); *Style*— Paul Hare, Esq, LVO; ⊠ c/o Foreign & Commonwealth Office, King Charles Street, London SW1A 2AH

HARE, Rosina Selina Alice; QC (1976); da of late William Peter Hare and Alice Catherine, *née* Holder; *m* 1971, Patrick Back, QC (d 2003); *Career* called to the Bar Middle Temple 1956, recorder 1974–98; legal memb Mental Health Review Tbnls 1983 (regnl chm South & West Mental Health Review Tbnls 1995–98); bencher Middle Temple 1986; *Recreations* fishing, golf; *Style*— Miss Rosina Hare, QC

HAREN, Patrick Hugh; *Educ* Queen's Univ Belfast; *Career* Viridian Gp plc (formerly NI Electricity plc): gp chief exec 1992–2007, dep chm 2007–; formerly dir of new business investment Electricity Supply Bd; former research fell European Centre for Nuclear Research Geneva; memb Bd Invest NI; FREng 1998; *Style*— Patrick Haren, FREng; ⊠ Viridian Group plc, Danesfort House, 120 Malone Road, Belfast BT9 5HT

HAREWOOD, 7 Earl of (UK 1812); George Henry Hubert Lascelles; KBE (1986); also Baron Harewood (GB 1796) and Viscount Lascelles (UK 1812); s of 6 Earl of Harewood, KG, GCVO, DSO, TD (d 1947), and HRH Princess Mary (The Princess Royal), CI, GCVO, GBE, RRC, TD, CD (d 1965), only da of HM King George V, see Debrett's Peerage, Royal Family section; *b* 7 February 1923; *Educ* Eton, King's Coll Cambridge; *m* 1, 29 Sept 1949 (m dis 1967; she m 2, 1973, as his 2 w, Rt Hon Jeremy Thorpe), Maria Donata Nanetta Paulina Gustava Erwina Wilhelmina (Marion), o da of late Erwin Stein; 3 s (David, Viscount Lascelles b 1950, Hon James b 1953, Hon Jeremy b 1955); *m* 2, 31 July 1967, Patricia Elizabeth, o da of Charles Tuckwell, of Sydney, and former w of (Louis) Athol Shmith (d 1990); 1 s (Hon Mark b 1964); *Heir* s, Viscount Lascelles; *Career* Capt late Grenadier Guards, serv WWII (wounded, POW); ADC to Earl of Athlone Canada 1945–46; ed Opera magazine 1950–53, asst to David Webster at The Royal Opera Covent Garden 1953–60; artistic dir: Leeds Festival 1956–74, Edinburgh Festival 1961–65, Adelaide Festival 1988, Buxton Festival; ENO: md 1972–85, chm 1986–95, pres 1995–; govr BBC 1985–87; pres: Br Bd of Film Classification 1985–96, Leeds United FC 1962–, Football Assoc 1963–72; chllr Univ of York 1963–67; Hon LLD: Univ of Leeds 1959, Univ of Aberdeen 1966; Hon DMus Univ of Hull 1962, Hon DLitt Univ of Bradford 1983, Hon DUniv York 1983; Hon RAM 1983, hon fell King's Coll Cambridge 1984, hon memb Royal Northern Coll of Music 1984; Liveryman Worshipful Co of Musicians; Austrian Great Silver Medal of Honour 1959, Lebanese Order of the Cedar 1970, Janácek Medal 1978; *Books* Kobbé's Complete Opera Book (ed), The Tongs and the Bones (memoirs 1981), The Illustrated Kobbé; *Recreations* looking at pictures, watching cricket, football, films; *Style*— The Rt Hon the Earl of Harewood, KBE; ⊠ Harewood House, Leeds LS17 9LG

HARFORD, Sir (John) Timothy; 3 Bt (UK 1934), of Falcondale, Co Cardigan; s of Lt-Col Sir George Arthur Harford, 2 Bt, OBE (d 1967), and Anstice Marion, *née* Tritton (d 1993); *b* 6 July 1932; *Educ* Harrow, Worcester Coll Oxford, Harvard Business Sch; *m* 12 May 1962, Carolyn Jane, o da of Brig Guy John de Wette Mullens, OBE (d 1981), of Weyhill, Hants; 1 da (Clare Elisabeth (Mrs Nicholas Clatworthy) b 1963), 2 s (Mark John b 1964, Simon Guy b 1966); *Heir* s, Mark Harford; *Career* dir Singer & Friedlander Ltd 1970–88; chm Wesleyan Assurance Society 1993–99; dep chm: Wolseley Gp plc 1983–97, Wagon Industrial Holdings plc 1991–98, Kwiksave Gp plc 1994–97, Sandaire Investments plc 1995–99; Liveryman Worshipful Co of Grocers; *Clubs* Boodle's; *Style*— Sir Timothy Harford, Bt; ⊠ South House, South Littleton, Evesham, Worcestershire WR11 8TJ (tel 01386 832827)

HARGRAVE, David Grant; s of late (Frank) Edward Hargrave, of Cyncoed, Cardiff, and late Margaret Constance Mabel, *née* Grant; *b* 11 April 1951; *Educ* Howardian HS Cardiff, Univ of Birmingham (BCom, MSc); *m* 13 Dec 1969, Celia, da of Harry Hawksworth (d 1963); 1 da (Emma Louise b 17 June 1970), 1 s (Neil David b 30 July 1974); *Career* actuary Duncan C Fraser & Co (later Mercer Human Resource Consulting Ltd) 1973–79; Hewitt Bacon & Woodrow (formerly TG Arthur Hargrave): ptnr 1979–95, head of employee benefits 1994–95; fndr David Hargrave Ltd 1995–; vice-chm and non-exec dir: engage Mutual Assurance (formerly Homeowners Friendly Soc Ltd) 1982–, NHP plc 1996–2001; chm Deutsche Asset Management Life & Pensions Ltd 2001–06 (non-exec dir 1998–2001); non-exec dir MetLife Assurance Ltd 2007–; sec and treas Birmingham Actuarial Soc 1979–81; Nat Assoc Pension Funds Ltd (W Midlands): treas 1982–85, sec 1985–87, chm 1987–89; tstee: Melton Medes (Fletchers) Pension Fund 1996–, Alstom Pension Scheme 1998–2005, Wiggins Teape Pension Scheme 2000–, Royal Mail Sr Executives Pension Plan 2001–, Kalamazoo Pension & Life Assurance Plan 2002–, TKM Gp Pension Scheme 2006–; FIA 1977; *Recreations* long distance running, swimming, windsurfing, rugby; *Style*— David Hargrave, Esq; ⊠ David Hargrave Ltd, Trench Hill, Painswick, Stroud, Gloucestershire GL6 6TZ (e-mail dgh@dhargrave.co.uk)

HARGRAVE, Dr Philip John; s of Edward James Anthony Hargrave (d 1963), and Doris Elsie, *née* Jackson (d 1995); *b* 21 June 1950; *Educ* Hinchley Wood Sch, Univ of Bristol (BSc), Cavendish Laboratory Univ of Cambridge (PhD); *m* 5 Oct 1985, Maureen Joyce, da of Alfred James Brook; 1 s (David John b 13 Dec 1990); *Career* Sci Research Cncl research fell Cavendish Laboratory Cambridge 1975–77; Standard Telecommunications Laboratories (STL, part of STC UK R&D Lab for ITT): joined 1977, successively research engr, sr research engr, princ research engr and sr princ research engr 1977–84, departmental mangr Adaptive Antenna Systems 1984–86, successively chief research engr, mangr tech strategy and asst dir 1986–92; Harlow Laboratories (following acquisition of STC by Nortel): dir Govt and External Progs then dir Radio and High Integrity Communications 1992–94, dir Next Generation Architecture 1994–95, dir Next Generation Products 1995–98, dir Next Generation Network Technology 1998–99, dir Next Generation Networks 1999–2000; chief scientist EMEA/Nortel 2000–06, ind conslt 2006–; visiting prof Dept of Electronic and Electrical Engrg Univ of Strathclyde 2001–; IEE: memb Professional Gp Ctee E15 (Radar, Sonar and Navigation) 1986–92 (chm 1990–92), memb Electronics Divnl Bd 1992–95, memb Schs Educn and Liaison Ctee 1993–96 and 1997–2001, chm Electronics Educn Editorial Bd 1997–; memb: Global Research Award Steering Gp Royal Acad of Engrg 1999–2002, Standing Ctee for Research and Secondment Schemes Royal Acad of Engrg 2003–, Standing Ctee for Engrg Policy Royal Acad of Engrg 2005–, Engrg and Technol Strategic Panel Br Computer Soc, Forward Looking Steering Panel Irish Cmmn for Communication Regulation (ComReg), Bd IT Telecommunications and Electronics Industry Association (INTELLECT) 2001–06, Bd EICTA (European Industry Association for Information Systems, Communication Techologies and Consumer Electronics (EICTA) 2001–05, Exec Bd UK Broadband Stakeholder Gp 2003–06; chm and sec Friends of St James the Great Thorley, vice-chair Governing Cncl Bishop's Stortford Coll; FRAS 1975, CEng 1983, CPhys 1987, FInstP 1987, FIEE 1995 (MIEE 1983), FREng 1996, CSci 2005, CITP 2007, FBCS 2007; *Publications* Observations of Cygnus A with the 5–km Radio Telescope (with Sir Martin Ryle, 1974), Design and Performance Evaluation of a Five Channel Navstar Receiver (jtly, 1982), Application of a Systolic Array to Adaptive Beamforming (jtly, 1984), A Novel Algorithm and Architecture for Adaptive Digital Beamforming (jtly, 1986), Adaptive Antennas for Modern Electronic Systems (1989), Systolic Beamforming - from Theory to Practice (1991), Next Generation Networks: Design for Reliability (2005); *Recreations* genealogy; *Style*— Dr Philip Hargrave, FREng; ⊠ 60 The Paddock, Bishop's Stortford, Hertfordshire CM23 4JW (tel 01279 657273, e-mail philip.hargrave@btinternet.com)

HARGREAVE, Dr Timothy Bruce; s of Cdr John Michael Hargreave, VRD, and Margaret Isobel Hargreave; *b* 23 March 1944; *Educ* Harrow, Univ of London (MB BS, MS); *m* 27 March 1971, Molly; 2 da (Alison Lucinda b 1972, Sophie Louise b 1976); *Career* dept of oncology Univ of Edinburgh; former: conslt urological surgn, clinical dir Surgical

Services Directorate Western General Hosp NHS Tst; corresponding memb German Urological Soc, memb Scientific and Ethical Review Gp Human Reproduction Prog WHO; former: memb Steering Ctee WHO Infertility Task Force, chm Br Andrology Soc, memb Cncl Br Assoc of Urological Surgns, sec Scot Urological Soc, pres Scottish Urological Assoc; hon memb: Hellenic Urology Soc, Columbian Urology Soc; FRCS, FRCSEd, FEB (Urol), FRCPEd; *Books* Practical Urological Endoscopy (1988), Management of Male Infertility (1990), Male Infertility (2 edn, 1994), Andrology for the Clinician (2006); *Recreations* skiing; *Style*— Dr Timothy Hargreave; ✉ BUPA, Murrayfield Hospital, Edinburgh (tel 0131 334 0363)

HARGREAVES, Andrew Raikes; s of Col and Mrs David William Hargreaves; *b* 15 May 1955; *Educ* Eton, St Edmund Hall Oxford (MA); *m* 1978, Fiona Susan, o da of Guy William Dottridge; 2 s (William b 1985, Thomas b 1986); *Career* auctioneer and valuer Christies 1977–81, exec Hill Samuel 1981–83; asst dir: Sawwa International 1983–85, Schroders 1985–87 (conslt 1987–1992); MP (Cons) Birmingham Hall Green 1987–97; former PPS to 4 FO Mins and vice-chm Cons Backbench Def Ctee; memb: House of Commons Parly Cmmr for Admin, Information Technol Select Ctee 1992–97, Armed Forces Parly Scheme RN 1994–95; UK md DaimlerChrysler Aerospace 1997–2000, UK chm Euro Aeronautics Defence and Space Co 2000–; conslt Midlands Electricity plc 1989–97; sec: back bench Urban and Inner Cities Ctee 1987–91 (chm 1992–94), Defence Ctee 1992–94 (vice-chm 1994–97); memb Bow Gp; *Recreations* fishing, gardening, walking, antiques, art; *Clubs* Boodle's; *Style*— Andrew Hargreaves, Esq

HARGREAVES, Ian Richard; s of Ronald Hargreaves (d 1988), and Edna, *née* Cheetham; *b* 18 June 1951; *Educ* Burnley GS, Altrincham GS, Queens' Coll Cambridge; *m* 1, 20 May 1972 (m dis 1991), Elizabeth Anne, da of Charles Crago, of Cornwall; 1 s (Ben b 20 Oct 1975), 1 da (Kelda b 23 June 1977); m 2, 13 Feb 1993, Adele Blakebrough; 2 da (Zola Grace b 1996, Yoko May b May 1998); *Career* Bradford & District Newspapers 1973–76, Financial Times 1976–87, dir BBC News and Current Affrs 1987–90, dep ed Financial Times 1990–94, ed The Independent 1994–95, ed New Statesman 1996–98, prof of journalism Univ of Wales Cardiff 1998–2002, dir corp and public affrs BAA plc; memb Ofcom 2003–; dir Demos; *Style*— Ian Hargreaves, Esq

HARINGTON, His Hon Judge Michael Kenneth; s of Kenneth Douglas Evelyn Herbert Harington, and Maureen Helen, *née* McCalmont; *Educ* Eton, ChCh Oxford (MA); *m* 1984, Deirdre Christine Kehoe; 1 s, 2 da; *Career* called to the Bar Inner Temple 1974; recorder 1998, circuit judge (Western Circuit) 2000–; *Recreations* golf, shooting; *Clubs* MCC; *Style*— His Hon Judge Harington; ✉ Bristol Crown Court, The Law Courts, Small Street, Bristol (tel 01179 763030)

HARINGTON, Sir Nicholas John; 14 Bt (E 1611), of Ridlington, Rutland; s of His Hon late John Charles Dundas Harington, QC (s of Sir Richard Harington, 12 Bt); suc uncle, Sir Richard Dundas Harington, 13 Bt, 1981; *b* 14 May 1942; *Educ* Eton, ChCh Oxford (MA); *Heir* bro, David Harington; *Career* called to the Bar 1969; Civil Serv 1972–2002; *Style*— Sir Nicholas Harington, Bt; ✉ The Ring o'Bells, Whitbourne, Worcester WR6 5RT

HARKIN, Marian; TD, MEP; da of James Gilmartin, and Annie Gilmartin; *b* 26 November 1953, Ballintogher, Co Sligo; *Educ* UC Dublin (BSc, HDipEd); *m* 28 July 1978, Sean Harkin (d 1996); 2 s (James 3 June 1979, John 28 July 1983); *Career* mathematics teacher Mercy Coll Sligo 1977–2002; TD (Ind) Sligo-Leitrim 2002–, MEP (Ind) N and W Ireland 2004–; European Parl: memb Ctee on Regnl Devpt, memb Delgn for Rels with Canada; chair Cncl for the West; memb: Nat Statistics Bd, Western Devpt Partnership Bd, Ulster Community Investment Tst; *Style*— Mrs Marian Harkin, TD, MEP; ✉ European Parliament, 60 rue Wiertz, B-1047 Brussels, Belgium; Office of the Houses of the Oireachtas, Leinster House, Dublin 2, Ireland

HARKNESS, Very Rev Dr James; KCVO (2005), CB (1993), OBE (1978); s of James Harkness, of Dumfries, and Jane McMorn, *née* Thomson; *b* 20 October 1935; *Educ* Dumfries Acad, Univ of Edinburgh (MA), Univ of Aberdeen (DD); *m* 1960, Elizabeth Anne, da of George Tolmie (d 1959); 1 da (Jane b 1962), 1 s (Paul b 1965); *Career* joined RAChD 1961; DACG: NI 1974–75, 4 Div 1975–78; staff chaplain HQ BAOR 1978–80, asst chaplain gen Scotland 1980–81; sr chaplain: 1 (Br) Corps 1981–82, BAOR 1982–84; dep chaplain gen 1985–86, chaplain gen 1987–95; Moderator of the Gen Assembly of the Church of Scotland 1995–96; Dean of the Chapel Royal in Scotland 1996–2006; extra chaplain to HM The Queen 1995–96 and 2006–, chaplain in ordinary to HM The Queen 1996–2006; chm Bd of Dirs Carberry 1998–2001; chm Veterans Scotland 2002–06; memb: Scottish Advsy Ctee ICRF 1995–2000, Exec Ctee Anglo Israel Assoc 1995–2001, Bd Mercy Corps Scotland 2001–; patron: Napier Univ Craighouse Appeal 1995–2000, St Mary's Music Sch Appeal 1995–2000; nat chaplain: Br Limbless Ex-Servicemen's Assoc 1995–2002, Royal Br Legion Scotland 1995–2002 (pres 2001–06); dean Order of St John in Scotland 2005–; gen tstee Church of Scotland 1996–; tstee: The Liberating Scots Tst, Scottish Nat War Meml 2003–; pres: Army Cadet Force Assoc Scotland 1996–2004, Friends of St Andrew's Jerusalem 1996–2005, Earl Haig Fund Scotland 2001–06; govr Fettes Coll 1999–; QHC 1982–95; FRSA 1992; ChStJ 1999 (OStJ 1988); *Recreations* walking, reading, watching sport; *Clubs* New (Edinburgh), Royal Scots; *Style*— The Very Rev Dr James Harkness, KCVO, CB, OBE, DD; ✉ 13 Saxe Coburg Place, Edinburgh EH3 5BR (tel 0131 343 1297)

HARLAND, Georgina Claire; da of Philip Harland, of Canterbury, Kent, and Claire, *née* Hunt; *b* 14 April 1978, Canterbury, Kent; *Educ* Benenden, Loughborough Univ (BSc); *Career* modern pentathlete; achievements as individual incl: Silver medal World Junior Championships 1997, Bronze medal World Championships 2001 and 2002, Gold medal British Championships 2002, Gold medal European Championships 2003, Gold medal World Cup Final 2003, Bronze medal Olympic Games Athens 2004; achievements in team relay events incl: Gold medal World Championships 1999, Gold medal European Championships 2000 (Silver medal 1999 and 2002); achievements in team events incl: Gold medal World Championships 2001, 2003 and 2004 (Silver medal 2000 and 2006), Gold medal European Championships 2001, 2002 and 2006 (Silver medal 2000, Bronze medal 2003); Sunday Times Student Sportswoman of the Year 2001, BBC SW Sportswoman of the Year 2003, Bath Chronicle Sportswoman of the Year 2004; *Recreations* travel, lacrosse; *Style*— Miss Georgina Harland

HARLAND, Air Marshal Sir Reginald Edward Wynyard; KBE (1974), CB (1972), AE; s of Charles Cecil Harland (d 1946); *b* 30 May 1920; *Educ* Stowe, Trinity Coll Cambridge (MA); *m* 1942, Doreen, da of William Hugh Cowie Romanis (d 1972); 2 s (Michael, David), 2 da (Diana (Mrs Hall), Sarah (Mrs Helliwell) (and 1 s Patrick, decd); *Career* joined RAF 1939, served W Med 1942–45, Air Cdre 1965, Harrier project dir Miny Technol 1967–69, idc 1969, AOC 24 Gp 1970–72, Air Vice-Marshal 1970, AO i/c E Air Support Cmd 1972, Air Marshal 1973, AOC-in-C RAF Support Cmd 1973–77; tech dir W S Atkins and Partners Epsom 1977–82, engrg and mgmnt conslt 1982–; chm Suffolk Professional Engineers 1991–96; Parly candidate (Alliance) Bury St Edmunds 1983 and 1987; chm: Suffolk Preservation Soc 1988–91, Bury St Edmunds Soc 1993–94 (pres 2004–); govr ESU 1993–2000; pres Old Stoic Soc 1999–2000; memb Cambridge Soc Cncl 1999– (chm Suffolk Branch 1998–2005); CEng, CCMI, FIMechE, FIEE, FRAeS, FRSA, FSEE (fell Soc of Environmental Engrs, pres 1974–77), Hon FAPM; *Recreations* better management, better government; *Clubs* RAF; *Style*— Air Marshal Sir Reginald E W Harland, KBE, CB, AE; ✉ 49 Crown Street, Bury St Edmunds, Suffolk IP33 1QX (tel 01284 763078, e-mail rewharland@aol.com)

HARLE, John Crofton; s of Jack Harle, and Joyce, *née* Crofton; *b* 20 September 1956; *Educ* Royal GS Newcastle upon Tyne, Royal Coll of Music (Fndn scholar, ARCM); *m* 1985, Julia Jane Eisner; 2 s; *Career* saxophonist, composer, conductor; ldr Myrha Saxophone Quartet 1977–82, formed duo with pianist John Lenehan 1979, saxophone soloist 1980–; appeared at numerous int venues incl: Carnegie Hall, South Bank Centre, BBC Proms, Germany, Switzerland, Far East; soloist Last Night of the Proms 1995 (world premiere of Sir Harrison Birtwistle's saxophone concerto Panic written for him); composer: Terror and Magnificence performed by Elvis Costello and Sarah Leonard, Little Death Machine performed by Orchestra of St John's Proms 2002; premiered Nyman Double Concerto with Julian Lloyd Webber, *qv*, James Judd, *qv*, and the Philharmonia; performer world premiere of Total Eclipse by John Tavener, *qv*, The Fall of Jerusalem by Dominic Muldowney and The Same Dog Joby Talbot 2000; conducted Film Music programme with the Winterthur Orch 2000–02; played with: LSO, English Chamber Orch, Basel Chamber Orch, London Sinfonietta, Northern Sinfonia, BBC orchs; princ saxophone London Sinfonietta 1987–, prof of saxophone Guildhall Sch of Music and Drama 1988–; composer of music for feature films (Butterfly Kiss, Breed of Heroes), TV (Love Lies Bleeding, Silent Witness, History of Britain) and advertising (Nissan, Harveys, Sony); regular broadcaster on BBC Radio, featured in One Man and his Sax BBC 2 TV 1988; EMI Classics artist 1990–; Decca recording artist 1991–; collaborations with Ute Lemper, Paul McCartney, *qv*, Willard White, the Brodsky Quartet and Lesley Garrett, *qv*; Dannreuther Concerto Prize Royal Coll of Music 1980, GLAA Young Musician 1979 and 1980, Best Artistic Achievement in a Feature Film Cannes Fim Festival 1988, RTS Award for Best Original Music 1996; FGSM 1990; *Books* John Harle's Saxophone Album (1986); *Recreations* family life, travel; *Style*— John Harle, Esq; ✉ www.johnharle.com

HARLECH, 6 Baron (UK 1876); Francis David Ormsby Gore; s of 5 Baron Harlech, PC, KCMG (d 1985), and his 1 w Sylvia (d 1967), da of late Hugh Lloyd Thomas, CMG, CVO; *b* 13 March 1954; *m* 1986 (m dis 1998), Amanda Jane, da of Alan Thomas Grieve, *qv*, of Stoke St Milborough, Salop; 1 s (Hon Jasset David Cody b 1 July 1986), 1 da (Hon Tallulah Sylvia Maria b 16 May 1988); *Heir* s, Hon Jasset Ormsby Gore; *Style*— The Rt Hon the Lord Harlech; ✉ Glyn Hall, Talsarnau, Harlech, Gwynedd LL47 6TE

HARLEN, Prof Wynne; OBE (1991); da of Arthur Mitchell, and Edith, *née* Radcliffe; *b* 12 January 1937; *Educ* Pate's GS for Girls Cheltenham, Univ of Oxford (MA), Univ of Bristol (MA, PhD); *m* 14 Aug 1958, Frank Harlen (d 1987); 1 s (Oliver b 1 Jan 1965), 1 da (Juliet b 9 July 1967); *Career* teacher Cheltenham 1958–60; lectr: St Mary's Coll Cheltenham 1960–64, Glos Coll of Art 1965–66; res fell: Univ of Bristol 1966–73, Univ of Reading 1973–77; sr res fell Univ of London 1977–84, Sidney Jones prof of sci educn Univ of Liverpool 1985–90, dir Scottish Cncl for Res in Educn 1990–99, visiting prof Univ of Bristol 1999–; pres BERA 1993–94; ed Primary Science Review 1999–2004, exec ed Assessment in Educn 1999–; chm Science Expert Group OECD/PISA Project 1998–2003; pres BA Educn section 2001–02, dir ASF project Univ of Cambridge 2003–06; chm Int Oversight Ctee IAP 2006–; memb: Sec of State's Working Gp For Devpt of the Nat Sci Curriculum, Teaching Educn Ctee CNAA until 1991, ASE, SERA, ESERA AERA, BERA, EERA; *Books* incl: Science 5 to 13: A Formative Evaluation (1975), Guides to Assessment in Education: Science (1983), Teaching and Learning Primary Science (1985, 3 edn 2000), Primary Science: Taking the Plunge (1985, revised 2001), Developing Primary Science (with S Jelly, 1989, 2 edn 1997), Environmental Science in the Primary Curriculum (with Elstgeest, 1990), The Teaching of Science (1992, 4 edn 2004), UNESCO Sourcebook for Science in the Primary School (1992), Enhancing Quality in Assessment (1994), Effective Teaching of Science: A Review of Research (1999), Setting and Streaming: A Research Review (revised, 1999), Making Progress in Primary Science (with C Macro et al, 2003), Teaching, Learning and Assessing Science 5–12 (4 edn 2006), ASE Guide to Primary Education (ed, 2006), Assessment of Learning (2007); *Recreations* listening to music, walking; *Style*— Prof Wynne Harlen, OBE; ✉ Haymount Coach House, Bridgend, Duns, Berwickshire TD11 3DJ (tel 01361 884710, e-mail wynne@torphin.freeserve.co.uk)

HARLEY, Gen Sir Alexander George Hamilton; KBE (1996, OBE 1981), CB (1991); s of late Lt-Col William Hamilton Coughtrie Harley, 1 Punjab Regt and later Royal Indian Engineers, and Eleanor Blanche, *née* Jarvis; *b* 3 May 1941; *Educ* Caterham Sch, RMA Sandhurst; *m* 12 Aug 1967, Christina Valentine, da of late Edmund Noel Butler-Cole, and Kathleen Mary, *née* Thompson; 2 s; *Career* cmmnd RA 1962; 1963–73: served 7 Para Regt RHA, instr Jr Ldrs, Staff Capt MOD, Adj; Canadian Staff Coll, Mil Asst Miny of Def 1974–75, Battery Cdr 1975–78 (despatches 1978), Directing Staff Staff Coll 1978–79, CO 19 Field Regt RA 1979–82, Col Def Staff and OPCEN Falklands War Miny of Def 1983–85, Cdr 33 Armd Bde 1985–88, Chief of Ops N Army Gp 1988–90, Asst Chief Jt Ops Overseas and Gulf War MOD 1990–93, Cdr Br Forces Cyprus and Admin of the Sovereign Base Areas 1993–95, Dep Chief of Staff Commitments and dir Jt Ops MOD 1995–97, Adjutant-Gen 1997–2000; ADC-Gen to HM The Queen 1998–2000, Master Gunner St James's Park 2001–; pres and Col Cmdt HAC 1998–2003, Col Cmdt RHA, RA; sr military advsr Thales Air Systems 2003–; hon vice-pres Combined Servs Hockey, hon vice-pres Raleigh International, patron NORDICS Hockey and Army Hockey Assoc; chm Purple International 2001–; govr King's Sch Bruton 2001–; Freeman City of London 2002, Liveryman Worshipful Co of Wheelwrights 2002; FIMgt 1982; *Recreations* country pursuits; *Clubs* Naval and Military; *Style*— Gen Sir Alexander Harley, KBE, CB; ✉ Artillery House, Artillery Centre, Larkhill, Salisbury SP4 8QT

HARLEY, Basil Hubert; s of Mervyn Ruthven Harley, JP (d 1973), of Stud Farm, Lamb Corner, Dedham, Essex, and Marion, *née* Parkinson (d 1973); *b* 17 July 1930; *Educ* Harrow, St John's Coll Oxford (MA); *m* 10 Oct 1959, Annette, da of Edgar Wolston Bertram Handsley Milne-Redhead, ISO, MBE, TD; 3 da (Jane Elizabeth b 12 Oct 1960, Emma Katherine b 7 June 1962, Harriet Susanna b 15 May 1965); *Career* Nat Serv RA 1949–50, cmmnd 2 Lt 1949, 17 Trg Regt Oswestry 1949–50, Capt TA Queen's Own Oxfords Hussars & Royal Bucks Yeo 1950–60; md Curwen Press Ltd 1964–82; dir: Curwen Prints Ltd 1970–92, Wedge Entomological Research Fndn US at Nat Museum Natural History Washington DC 1974–97; memb Exec Ctee Nat Book League 1974–78; chm Wynken de Worde Soc 1975; chm and md Harley Books Natural History Publishers (BH & A Harley Ltd) 1983–; pres Br Entomological and Natural History Soc 2003–04; Liveryman Worshipful Co of Stationers and Newspaper Makers 1973–; fell Linnean Soc 1955, fell Royal Entomological Soc 1981; *Books* Birds of the Harrow District (1949), The Curwen Press A Short History (1970), Martin Lister's English Spiders, 1678 (co-trans from Latin and co-ed, 1992), The Aurelian Legacy (co-author, 2000), Checklist of the Flora and Fauna of Wicken Fen (co-ed, 2000); *Recreations* natural history, reading; *Clubs* Oxford and Cambridge, Double Crown (pres 1996); *Style*— Basil Harley, Esq; ✉ Martins, Great Horkesley, Colchester, Essex CO6 4AH (tel 01206 271216, fax 01206 271182, e-mail harley@harleybooks.co.uk)

HARLEY, Ian; *Educ* Falkirk HS, Univ of Edinburgh (MA); *m*; 3 s; *Career* articled clerk Touche Ross & Co 1972, later in Corp Planning Dept Morgan Crucible Ltd; Abbey National plc: joined Abbey National Building Society as financial analyst 1977, SE regnl mangr Retail Ops Div 1984–86, commercial mangr for business devpt 1986, gp financial controller 1986–88, asst gen mangr fin 1988–91, fin dir retail ops 1991–92, ops dir 1992, gp treas 1992–93, memb main bd 1993–2002, gp fin dir 1993–98, chief exec 1998–2002; dir Dah Sing Financial Holdings Ltd 1998–2002; non-exec dir: Rentokil Initial plc 1999–, British Energy plc 2002–, Remploy 2004–; pres CIB 2001–02 (dep pres 2000–01); memb Ct of Govrs Whitgift Fndn 2002–, a vice-pres Nat Deaf Children's Soc; MICAS, FCA, FCIB; *Clubs* Oriental; *Style*— Ian Harley, Esq

HARLEY, Sophie Elizabeth; da of Dr Clifford Elliot Harley, and Anne Maureen, *née* Phillips; *b* 14 January 1965; *Educ* Bryanston, W Surrey Coll of Art & Design (BA), RCA (MA); *Children* 1 da (Millie Mercedes Harley Holdsworth b 31 Jan 1998); *Career* jewellery

H

designer 1990–, fndr memb The New RenaisCAnce (multi media co specialising in fashion and accessory design, display, styling and video prodn) 1991–; gp and solo exhbns incl: Taxidermy, Love and Letters (Southbank Crafts Gallery) 1990, Six of the Best (Barbican Centre) 1990, The Art Machine (McLellan Gallery Glasgow) 1990, Triennale Européenne du Bijou (Musee du Luxembourg Paris) 1990, From the Heart (Fouts & Fowler Gallery) 1991, The Evening Standard Art Machine (Barbican) 1991, Celebration of Gold (Mappin & Webb London) 1991, De Beers Diamond Showcase (David Thomas London) 1991, Four Play - The World of New RenaisCAnce (Royal Festival Hall and Parco Gallery Tokyo) 1992, Decorative Arts Today (Bonhams Knightsbridge) 1992, Court Couture 1992 (Kensington Palace) 1992, The World of New RenaisCAnce (Tokyo) 1992, Dazzle (NT) 1992, Decorative Arts Today (Bonhams Knightsbridge) 1993, Crafts in Performance (Crafts Cncl touring exhbn) 1993; New Generation catwalk show as part of London Fashion Week (with The New RenaisCAnce) 1994; cmmnd by De Beers Diamonds to make prize (18 carat yellow and white gold and diamond brooch) for King George VI and Queen Elizabeth Diamond Stakes Royal Ascot 2002; Greater London Arts Award 1992; lectr various colls of art nationwide incl RCA (actg conslt on course structure); *Style*— Ms Sophie Harley; ✉ Sophie Harley Design, Studio 109 Westbourne Studios, 242 Acklam Road, London W10 5JJ (tel 020 7430 2070, fax 020 7575 3257, mobile 07786 518436, website www.sophieharley.com)

HARLOW, Archdeacon of; *see:* Taylor, Ven Peter Flint

HARLOW, John William; s of Keith Harlow, of London, and Irene Harlow; *b* 26 July 1968; *Educ* Trinity Sch Shirley, Univ of Sussex (BA); *m* 24 Nov 1996, Lee-Anne, *née* Jordan; 1 da (Holly b 18 Jan 2001), 1 s (Jack b 23 Feb 2003); *Career* assoc dir AMV BBDO 1993–96, md Rocket (PHD Group) 1997–2000, founding ptnr Naked Communications 2000; MIPA 2001; *Recreations* writing, cooking, sailing; *Clubs* Citroën Car; *Style*— John Harlow, Esq; ✉ Naked Communications, 159–173 St John Street, London EC1V 4QJ (tel 020 7336 8084, fax 020 7336 8009, mobile 07779 623985, e-mail john@nakedcomms.com)

HARMAN, Claire Patricia; da of John Edward Harman, of the Isle of Skye, and Patricia Josephine, *née* Mullins; *b* 21 September 1957; *Educ* Farnborough Hill Convent, Univ of Manchester (BA, Samuel James Wheeler Prize); *m* 1979 (m dis 1989), Michael Norton Schmidt, s of Carl Bernhardt Schmidt; 2 s (Charles b 21 March 1980, Benedict b 19 Oct 1985), 1 da (Isabel b 12 July 1982); *Career* with Carcanet Press Manchester 1979–81, co-ordinating ed PN Review Manchester 1981–84; adjunct prof Sch of the Arts Columbia Univ 2003–; Wingate scholar 1996–98; John Llewellyn Rhys Prize 1990, Writers' Award Arts Cncl 2003; memb Soc of Authors 1990; FRSL 2006; *Books* Sylvia Townsend Warner: Collected Poems (ed, 1982), Sylvia Townsend Warner: A Biography (1989), Robert Louis Stevenson: Essays and Poems (ed, 1992), Robert Louis Stevenson: Selected Stories (ed, 1992), Sylvia Townsend Warner: Diaries (ed, 1994), Fanny Burney: A Biography (2000), Robert Louis Stevenson: A Biography (2005); *Style*— Claire Harman; ✉ c/o Elizabeth Sheinkman, Curtis Brown, Haymarket House, 28–29 Haymarket, London SW1Y 4SP (tel 020 7393 4400)

HARMAN, Rt Hon Harriet; PC (1997), QC, MP; da of Dr John Bishop Harman (d 1994), and Anna Charlotte Malcolm Spicer; *b* 20 July 1950; *Educ* St Paul's Girls' Sch, Univ of York; *m* Jack Dromey (dep gen sec TGWU); 2 s, 1 da; *Career* lawyer, memb Liberty (formerly Nat Cncl for Civil Liberties); MP (Lab): Peckham 1982–97, Camberwell and Peckham 1997–; oppn front bench spokesperson: on health and social servs 1984–89, on health 1989–92; shadow chief sec to the Treasy 1992–94; chief oppn spokesperson on: employment 1994–95, health 1995–96, social security 1996–97; sec of state for social security and min for women 1997–98, slr gen 2001–05, min of state DCA 2005–, ldr House of Commons 2007–, min for women 2007–, dep ldr Labour Pty 2007–; elected to Lab NEC 1993–; *Books* The Century Gap (1993); *Style*— The Rt Hon Harriet Harman, QC, MP; ✉ House of Commons, London SW1A 0AA

HARMAN, Sir John; kt (1997); s of John Edward Harman, of Dunvegan, Isle of Skye, and Patricia Josephine, *née* Mullins; *b* 30 July 1950, Leeds; *Educ* St George's Coll Weybridge, Univ of Manchester (BSc), Huddersfield Coll of Educn (PGCE); *m* 4 Dec 1971, Susan Elizabeth, *née* Crowther; 1 s (Christopher b 24 Dec 1974), 3 da (Ruth b 4 Feb 1977, Catherine b 20 June 1979, Alison b 14 Dec 1981); *Career* teacher of mathematics 1974–97; chm Environment Agency 2000– (memb Bd 1995–, dep chm 1999), memb Bd Energy Saving Tst 1997–; tstee Forum for the Future 2006–; chm Kirklees Stadium Devpt Ltd 1992–; cncllr W Yorks CC 1981–86, ldr Kirklees Met Cncl 1986–99, ldr Yorks and Humber Regnl Assembly 1999; chm Steering Gp Univ of Warwick Inst of Governance and Public Mgmnt 2001–, memb Bd Nat Sch of Govt 2006–; memb Advsy Cncl RSA 2006–; tstee Nat Coal Mining Museum 2004–; memb Child Poverty Action Gp; memb: RHS, RSPB; Hon DCL Univ of Huddersfield; memb Mathematical Assoc 1968, FRSA 1993, Hon FICE 2000, Hon FCIWEM 2002, Hon FIWM 2002, Hon FSE 2005; *Recreations* reading, music, gardening, Huddersfield Town AFC; *Style*— Sir John Harman; ✉ Environment Agency, 25th Floor, Millbank Tower, 21–24 Millbank, London SW1P 4XL (tel 020 7863 8720, fax 020 7863 8722, e-mail john.harman@environment-agency.gov.uk)

HARMAN, Richard Stuart; s of late Donald George Harman, and Jean Patricia, *née* Harrison; *b* 11 March 1959; *Educ* King's Sch Worcester (King's scholar), Trinity Coll Cambridge (MA), Univ of Exeter (PGCE); *m* 22 July 1989, Karin Lee, da of Rev Stanley Milton Voth; 1 da (Olivia Ruth b 13 Nov 1991); *Career* sales exec HBJ Academic Press 1981–83, asst master Marlborough Coll 1984–88, head of dept, housemaster and memb sr mgmnt team Eastbourne Coll 1988–2000, headmaster Aldenham Sch 2000–06, headmaster Uppingham Sch 2006–; memb: HMC 2000, ASCL 2000; *Recreations* sports, theatre, travel; *Style*— Richard Harman, Esq; ✉ Uppingham School, Rutland LE15 9QE (tel 01572 822216, fax 01572 822007, e-mail headmaster@uppingham.co.uk)

HARMAN, Robert Lawrence; s of Roderick Frank Harman (Gp Capt RAF, d 1994), and Katharine Lawrence, *née* Leopold; *b* 30 July 1947; *Educ* Wellington, St Catharine's Coll Cambridge (MA); *Family* 1 s (Daniel b 1976), 1 da (Antonia b 1980); *Career* currently ptnr & head Property Department Travers Smith (joined 1970); memb Law Soc; *Clubs* City of London, Royal Society of Arts; *Style*— Robert Harman, Esq; ✉ Travers Smith, 10 Snow Hill, London EC1A 2AL (tel 020 7295 3000, fax 020 7236 3728)

HARMAR-NICHOLLS, Hon Susan Frances; *see:* Nicholls, Susan

HARMER, Dr Clive Lucas; s of Cecil Norman Harmer (d 1986), and Elizabeth Mary, *née* Lucas (d 1989); *b* 18 August 1940; *Educ* Westminster Hosp Med Sch (MB BS); *m* 9 Nov 1993, Pauline Ann Cattell; 2 da from prev m (Kasha b 1968, Victoria b 1971); *Career* instr Dept of Radiation Oncology Stanford Univ Calif 1970; conslt in radiotherapy and oncology: St Luke's Hosp Guildford 1970–73, St George's Hosp London 1973–; former head Thyroid Unit Royal Marsden Hosp London, ret; memb RSM; FRCR 1968, FRCP 1992 (MRCP 1968); *Publications* author of multiple pubns on treatment of thyroid cancer and management of soft tissue sarcomas; *Recreations* wildlife photography; *Style*— Dr Clive Harmer; ✉ 19 Sydney Street, Chelsea, London SW3 6PU (e-mail cliveharmer@fsmail.net)

HARMISON, Stephen James (Steve); MBE (2006); *b* 23 October 1978, Ashington, Northumberland; *m* Hayley; 2 da (Abbie, Emily); *Career* cricketer (bowler); Durham CCC 1996–; England: 54 test caps, 46 one day appearances, 2 Twenty20 appearances, test debut v India 2002, memb winter touring squad Bangladesh 2003, one day debut v Sri Lanka Brisbane 2002, best test bowling 7–12 Sabina Park WI 2004, memb Ashes-winning team 2006, ret from one day ints 2006; ranked number 1 bowler in the world PWC Cricket Ratings Aug 2004; NBC Denis Compton Award 1998, Wisden Cricketer of the Year 2005; *Recreations* supporting Newcastle United FC; *Style*— Mr Steve Harmison, MBE; ✉ c/o England and Wales Cricket Board, Lord's Cricket Ground, St John's Wood Road, London NW8 8QZ

HARMSWORTH, Sir Hildebrand Harold; 3 Bt (UK 1922), of Freshwater Grove, Parish of Shipley, Co Sussex; s of Sir Hildebrand Alfred Beresford Harmsworth, 2 Bt (d 1977), and Elen, *née* Billenstein; *b* 5 June 1931; *Educ* Harrow, Trinity Coll Dublin; *m* 1960, Gillian Andrea, o da of William John Lewis, of Tetbury, Glos; 2 da (Claire Elen Mary b 1961, Kirsten Elizabeth Ashley b 1963), 1 s (Hildebrand Esmond Miles b 1964); *Heir* s, Hildebrand Harmsworth; *Career* garden writer; *Style*— Sir Hildebrand Harmsworth, Bt; ✉ Ewlyn Villa, 42 Leckhampton Road, Cheltenham, Gloucestershire GL53 0BB

HARMSWORTH, 3 Baron (UK 1939); Thomas Harold Raymond Harmsworth; o s of Hon Eric Beauchamp Northcliffe Harmsworth (d 1988), and Hélène Marie, *née* Dehove (d 1962); suc uncle, 2 Baron Harmsworth, 1990; *b* 20 July 1939; *Educ* Eton, ChCh Oxford; *m* 26 June 1971, Patricia Palmer, da of Michael Palmer Horsley, of Waltham House, Brough, N Humberside; 2 s (Hon Dominic Michael Eric b 18 Sept 1973, Hon Timothy Thomas John b 6 April 1979), 3 da (Hon Philomena Hélène Olivia b 10 Feb 1975, Hon Abigail Patricia Thérèse (now Mrs Valentin Stefan) b 14 June 1977, Hon Pollyanna Mary Clare b 8 Sept 1981); *Heir* s, Hon Dominic Harmsworth; *Career* Nat Serv 2 Lt Royal Horse Gds 1957–59; in the City 1962–74, Civil Serv 1974–88, publisher 1988–; chm Dr Johnson's House Gough Square London; *Publications* Gastronomic Dictionary: French-English (2003), Gastronomic Dictionary: Spanish-English (2004), Gastronomic Dictionary: Italian-English (2005); *Clubs* Carlton, Brooks's; *Style*— The Lord Harmsworth; ✉ The Old Rectory, Stoke Abbott, Beaminster, Dorset DT8 3JT

HARPER, Most Rev Alan Edwin Thomas; *see:* Armagh, Archbishop of

HARPER, Alexander James Christopher; s of late Lt-Col Alexander Forrest Harper, DSO, of W Sussex, and Rosemary Helen Margaret, *née* Hayward; *b* 16 March 1948; *Educ* Winchester; *m* 1, 1972 (m dis 1977), Peta Seccombe; 1 da (Eugénie Rose b 16 Nov 1973), 1 s (Alexander Forrest (Tom) b 17 Sept 1975); m 2, 1978 (m dis 1998), Suzy Kendall; 1 da (Elodie Lauren Geraldine b 1 July 1979); m 3, Susana Maria Tubio; 1 s (José Benito Christopher b 11 Nov 2003); *Career* sugar trader Rionda de Pass Ltd 1967–70, various posts rising to head of sugar dept Ralli Merrill Lynch 1970–74, md Lambourn (UK) Ltd 1974–75, various appointments incl int commodity trader UK, Africa and S America 1975–97, fndr Cia Minera el Desquite (brought together Brancote Holdings plc and MBP Gp of Argentina) Argentina 1996–; hon consul for Repub of Guinea 1987–; int polo player 1967–89, memb Young Eng Polo Team 1972, 1975 and 1976, Young Player of the Year 1972; *Recreations* polo, sailing, t'ai ch'i, shooting, fishing, exploring, travel in third world, writing, reading, music; *Clubs* White's, Beaufort Polo, Cowdray Park Polo, La Cañada; *Style*— Alexander Harper, Esq; ✉ Estancia Fortin Castre, Ruta 250 KM 212.50, Depto Avellaneda, Rio Negro, Argentina (tel 00 54 911 5324 2869, e-mail harperalexander@aol.com)

HARPER, David Finlay; s of Muir Harper, of Eaglesham Strathclyde, and Margaret; *b* 15 July 1956; *Educ* Kelvinside Acad Glasgow, Mackintosh Sch of Art (BArch), Univ of Glasgow (DipArch); *m* 20 July 1985 (m dis 2007), Katharine, *née* MacCarthy; 4 s (Aidan Muir b 24 April 1991, Connal David b 12 Aug 1992, Finlay Peader b 20 Oct 1996, Rory Stuart b 19 Oct 1999); *Career* architect; projects incl: St Martins Lane and the Sanderson Hotels, the Trafalgar, Butlers Wharf, the Whitefriars devpt; founding dir Harper Downie; regular contrib to many newspapers and jls; *Awards* incl: Heritage Award 1987, European Heritage Awards 1987, Electricity Cncl Awards 1988, Civil Tst Awards 1989, Patent Glazing Awards 1989, Design Week Awards 1991, 1994, 1997 and 1998, D&AD Awards 1994 and 2001, Minerva Awards 1994 and 1995, Carpenters Award 1994, Hilight Awards 1995, Br Cncl for Offices award 1998, FX Awards 2001 and 2002; RIBA 1983, RIAS 1983, FCSD 1991; *Recreations* benign exaggeration; *Clubs* Groucho; *Style*— David Harper, Esq; ✉ Harper_Downie Limited, Gate House, No 1 St John's Square, London EC1M 4DH (tel 020 7490 7674, fax 020 7490 4941, mobile 07767 348811, e-mail david.harper@harperdownie.com)

HARPER, Prof John Martin; s of Geoffrey Martin Harper, of Wednesbury, W Midlands, and Kathleen, *née* Birks; *b* 11 July 1947; *Educ* King's Coll Sch Cambridge, Clifton, Selwyn Coll Cambridge (MA), Univ of Birmingham (PhD); *m* 1, 1 July 1970 (m dis), Cynthia Margaret, da of late George Dean, of Combe Down, Bath; 3 s (Edward John b 1976, William George b 1978, Joseph Martin b 1985); m 2, 21 Dec 1991, Sally Elizabeth, da of late John Stephen Roper; *Career* lectr in music Univ of Birmingham 1974–75 and 1976–81, asst dir of music King Edward's Sch Birmingham 1975–76, fell and tutor in music Magdalen Coll Oxford (also organist and informator choristarum) 1981–90; Univ of Wales Bangor: prof of music 1991–98, research prof 1998–; Leverhulme fell 1997–98; DG Royal Sch of Church Music 1998–2007; visiting scholar Sarum Coll 2005–; dir Edington Music Festival 1971–78, dir of music St Chad's Cathedral Birmingham 1972–78, dir Int Centre for Sacred Music Studies 2008–; chm: Plainsong and Medieval Music Soc 1998–2006 (memb Cncl 1994–), Early English Organ Project 2000–05 (tstee 1999–2005); fndr dir Centre for Advanced Welsh Music Studies 1994–2003; fndr ed Welsh Music History 1996–99; Benemerenti Papal award 1978; FRCO (CHM), Hon FGCM 1996, FRSCM 2007; *Books* Orlando Gibbons: Consort Music (Musica Britannica 48, ed, 1982), The Forms and Orders of Western Liturgy (1991), Hymns for Prayer and Praise (ed, 1996), Music for Common Worship (7 vols, ed, 2000–), The Light of Life (2002), The Spirit of the Lord (2004), Psallam (ed, 2007); *Recordings* The English Carol (1984), The English Anthem (5 vols, 1990), The Victorian Carol (1990); *Recreations* walking, ecclesiastical architecture; *Style*— Prof John Harper; ✉ Bethania, Llangoed, Beaumaris, Anglesey LL58 8PH

HARPER, Joseph Charles; QC (1992); s of Frederick Charles Harper (d 1967), and Kitty, *née* Judah (d 1983); *b* 21 March 1939; *Educ* Charterhouse, LSE (BA, LLB, LLM); *m* 1984 (m dis 1994), Sylvia Helen, *née* Turner; 2 da (Helen Jane b 5 May 1987, Anna Clare b 1 April 1989); *Career* formerly lectr and head Dept of Law Kingston Poly; called to the Bar Gray's Inn (bencher); Freeman Worshipful Co of Musicians; ARCM; *Books* Hill & Redman: Law of Landlord and Tenant (ed), Halsbury's Laws: Compulsory Practice vol 8 (ed, 4 edn (and revision 2003)), Halsbury's Laws: Town and Country Planning vol 46 (2005), Encyclopedia of Planning (ed); *Recreations* playing the French horn, bibliomania; *Clubs* Garrick; *Style*— Joseph Harper, Esq, QC; ✉ Landmark Chambers, 180 Fleet Street, London EC4A 2HG (tel 020 7430 1221, fax 020 7421 6060)

HARPER, Mark; MP; *b* 1970; *Educ* Headlands Sch Swindon, Swindon Coll, BNC Oxford (MA); *Career* CA 1995; auditor KPMG 1991–95, Intel Corp 1995–2002, own chartered accountancy practice 2003–05; MP (Cons) Forest of Dean 2005– (Parly candidate (Cons) Forest of Dean 2001); South Swindon Cons Assoc: treas 1993–98, dep chair 1998; govr Newent Community Sch 2000–05; *Style*— Mark Harper, Esq, MP; ✉ House of Commons, London SW1A 0AA

HARPER, Dr Peter George; s of Frederick Charles Harper (d 1965), of Bath, and Catherine Tryphosa, *née* Judah; *b* 30 August 1945; *Educ* UCH and UCL (MB BS, LRCP); *m* 21 June 1971, Saga Margaret Elizabeth (d 1996), da of Peter Guise Tyndale; 3 s (Benjamin b 1974, Sebastian b 1976, Maximillian b 1988), 1 da (Harriet b 1980); *Career* house offr then SHO UCH and Addenbrooke's Hosp Cambridge 1969–71, SHO and med registrar St Mary's Hosp 1972–76, sr med registrar UCH 1976–82, conslt physician and med oncologist Guy's Hosp 1982–; MRC: memb Lung Cancer Ctee, memb Gynaecological Malignancies Ctee, memb Genito-Urinary Malignancies Ctee; memb: UK Central Co-ordinating Cancer Ctee, Br Prostate Gp, Hampstead Med Soc; FRCP 1987 (MRCP), MRCS; Chevalier de la Légion d'Honneur (France) 2003; *Books* numerous papers on aspects of cancer treatment; contrib chapters: The Treatment of Urological Tumours (1985), A Textbook of Unusual Tumours (1988); *Recreations* music (especially opera), walking, fly fishing, shooting; *Style*— Dr Peter Harper; ✉ London Oncology Clinic, 95 Harley Street, London W1G 6AF (tel 020 7317 2530, fax 020 7009 4230)

HARPER, Robin Charles Moreton; MSP; s of Cdr C H A Harper OBE, RN (d 2003), of Walberton, W Sussex, and Jessicca Harper (d 1992); *b* 4 August 1940; *Educ* St Marylebone GS, Elgin Acad, Univ of Aberdeen (MA), Aberdeen Teachers' Training Coll, Univ of Edinburgh (Dip); *m* 24 Sept 1994, Jenny, *née* Brown; 1 step s; *Career* teacher Braehead Sch Fife 1964–71; educn offr Kenyan govt 1968, teacher modern studies Boroughmuir HS 1972–99; MSP (Green) Lothians 1999–, co-ldr Green Gp Scottish Parly 2003–; chair Classical Guitar Soc of Edinburgh 1980–88, rector Univ of Edinburgh 2000–03, Lord Rector Univ of Aberdeen 2005–; memb: Lothian Health Cncl 1992–95, Lothian Children's Panel 1985–88, Friends of the Earth, Greenpeace, WWF, Soil Assoc, Scottish Environmental Design Assoc, CND; FRSA 1995, FEIS 1999, FRSSA 2001; *Recreations* open air, photography, music (guitar, piano), collecting jazz 78s; *Style*— Robin Charles Moreton Harper, Esq, MSP; ✉ Scottish Green Party, PO Box 14080, Edinburgh EH10 6YG (tel and fax 0131 447 1843, mobile 07957 337176, e-mail harper@ednet.co.uk)

HARPER, Rev Roger; s of Albert William Harper (d 1979), of Peel, IOM, and Joyce, *née* Griffiths (d 1990); *b* 10 January 1943; *Educ* Merchant Taylors', UMIST (BSc); *m* 26 July 1966, Joan, da of John Worthington, of Freckleton, Lancs; 2 da (Charlotte b 1967, Camilla b 1969); *Career* CA; ordained priest 1988 (diocese of Sodor and Man), chm Diocesan Bd of Fin 1984–2007; dir: Roach Bridge Holdings plc, Manx Industrial Trust 1973–; FCA; *Recreations* sailing; *Style*— Rev Roger Harper; ✉ The Barns, Strawberry Fields, Croit-e-Caley, Colby, Isle of Man IM9 4BZ; 18 St George's Street, Douglas, Isle of Man IM1 1PL (tel 01624 624945, fax 01624 617071, e-mail roger@law-man.com)

HARPER, Prof (John) Ross; CBE (1986); s of Rev Thomas Harper (d 1960), and Margaret Simpson, *née* Ross; *b* 20 March 1935; *Educ* Hutchesons' Boys' GS, Univ of Glasgow (MA, LLB); *m* 26 Sept 1963, Ursula Helga Renate, da of Hans Gathmann (d 1966), of Zimerstrasse, Darmstadt; 2 s (Robin b 1964, Michael b 1969), 1 da (Susan b 1966); *Career* slr Scotland; conslt Harper Macleod; formerly pt/t prof of law Univ of Strathclyde (now emeritus); former pres: Law Soc of Scotland, Scottish Cons and Unionist Assoc, Glasgow Bar Assoc; former chm Tory Reform Gp Scotland; former pres Int Bar Assoc 1994–96 (former chm Gen Practice Section); former chm: Mining (Scotland) Ltd, Scottish Coal Company Ltd; chm: Alarm Protection Ltd, European Scanning Centre Ltd, Scottish Biopower Ltd, Admiralty Resources NL; conslt Makanyane Safari Lodge SA; Parly candidate (Cons) Hamilton and W Renfrewshire 1970s; Hon DUniv Glasgow 2002; *Books* Practitioners' Guide to Criminal Procedure, A Guide to the Courts, The Glasgow Rape Case, Fingertip Guide to Criminal Law, Rates Reform, Devolution, New Unionism, My Client My Lord, Scotland 97, Referendums are Dangerous, Global Law in Practice; *Recreations* angling, bridge; *Clubs* Caledonian; *Style*— Prof J Ross Harper, CBE; ✉ Flat 1, 67 Cadogan Square, London SW1X 0DY (tel 020 7245 0078, e-mail jross.harper@btopenworld.com); Ca 'd'oro, 45 Gordon Street, Glasgow G1 3PE

HARPIN, Richard David; s of David Bryan Harpin, of Northumberland, and Philippa Judith, *née* Barr; *b* 10 September 1964, Huddersfield; *Educ* Royal GS Newcastle upon Tyne, Univ of York (BA), Univ of Northumbria (Dip); *m* July 1997, Kate, *née* Dawes; 1 da (Jemima b 19 June 2000), 2 s (Tom b 15 Feb 2002, William b 28 Nov 2004); *Career* fndr and owner nat mail order fishing tackle business 1981–86, fndr earring mfrg business 1984–85, brand mangr Procter and Gamble 1986–90, fndr Harpin Ltd 1988–, sr conslt Deloitte 1990–91, franchisee The Mortgage Advice Shop 1991–92, co-fndr and md Homeserve GB Ltd 1993–99, chief exec Homeserve plc 1999–; non-exec chm: Heating Components and Equipment Ltd 1998–2004, Amsys Rapid Prototyping and Tooling Limited 1999–2001; non-exec dir: Professional Properties Ltd 1990–99, Baker Tilly Consulting 1992–97, Mortgage Advice Bureau 1997–2000; presenter Graduate Enterprise Prog and Univ of Durham Business Sch 1985–86; launched nat student magazine 1988; Make It In Business Award 1984, regnl winner Livewire Business Competition 1985; memb Nat Exec Grad Industrial Soc 1986–88; *Recreations* off-piste and heliskiing, swimming, mountain biking, squash; *Style*— Richard Harpin, Esq; ✉ Homeserve plc, Cable Drive, Walsall WS2 7BN (tel 01922 659701, fax 01922 659785, e-mail richard.harpin@homeserve.com)

HARPUR, Oonagh Mary; da of Dr William Ware Harpur, of Drigg, Cumbria, and Patricia Elizabeth, *née* Coote; *b* 26 September 1953; *Educ* Keele Univ (BA); *m* 1974 (m dis 1991), Peter Edward Clamp, s of late Owen Gregory Edward Clamp; 1 da (Jennifer Sarah b 23 Nov 1978); *Career* various posts in strategy and operational research NCB 1976–85, ldr Professional Practices Consulting Gp Spicer & Oppenheim 1985–87, assoc Strategic Planning Assoc Washington DC 1987–88, princ exec Berwin Leighton 1988–94, princ tutor Centre for Law Firm Management Nottingham Law Sch 1994–; chief exec: The HUB Initiative 1997–2001, Enterprise Insight 2001–02; partnership sec Linklaters 2002–; non-exec dir Hillingdon HA 1992–96; memb IWF London, tstee Scientific and Med Network; chm The Love and Integrity in Business Network 1995–2000; FRSA; *Recreations* opera, swimming; *Style*— Ms Oonagh Harpur

HARRABIN, Roger; s of Hubert Harrabin, and Sylvia Harrabin; *Educ* King Henry VIII Sch Coventry, St Catharine's Cambridge (JCR pres); *m* Anne; 2 s (James, Hugo), 1 da (Jessica); *Career* reporter and sub ed Coventry Evening Telegraph 1976–83, freelance News of the World and Sunday Mirror 1983–84, prodr Thames TV News 1984–86, environment journalist BBC 1986–2006, environment analyst BBC 2006–; progs incl: Today, Ten O'Clock News, Panorama, Newsnight, Assignment, World at One, Costing the Earth; co-dir Cambridge Media Environment Prog; assoc press fell Wolfson Coll Cambridge, visiting fell Green Coll Oxford; *Publications* King's Fund Risk & Media report (co-author); *Recreations* family, friends, sport, architecture, Coventry City FC; *Style*— Roger Harrabin, Esq; ✉ c/o BBC, TV Centre, Wood Lane, London W12 7RJ (tel 020 8624 9644, e-mail roger.harrabin@bbc.co.uk)

HARREL, David T D; *b* 23 June 1948; *m* Julia Mary; 1 da (Rebecca b 1977), 2 s (Tom b 1979, Charlie b 1983); *Career* admitted slr 1974, asst slr then ptnr Messrs William Charles Crocker 1974–79, ptnr Messrs Burton & Ramsden 1979–82, currently sr ptnr SJ Berwin (co-fndr and ptnr 1982); tstee: Clore Duffield Fndn, John Aspinall Fndn; *Recreations* shooting, fishing, golf, tennis, music, theatre; *Style*— David Harrel, Esq; ✉ SJ Berwin, 222 Gray's Inn Road, London WC1X 8XF (tel 020 7533 2222)

HARRHY, Eiddwen Mair; *b* 14 April 1949; *Educ* St Winifred's Convent Swansea, Royal Manchester Coll of Music; *m* 23 Jan 1988, Gregory Strange; 1 da; *Career* soprano; debut: Royal Opera House Covent Garden 1974, English Nat Opera 1975; performances incl: Glyndebourne Festival, Scottish Opera, Welsh National Opera, Opera North, Teatro Colon Buenos Aires, Philharmonie St Petersburg, La Scala Milan, Amsterdam Concertgebouw, Sydney Opera House, Hong Kong, NZ, LA, BBC Promenade concerts; recordings: EMI, Harmonia Mundi, Erato, Deutsche Grammophon, Virgin Classics; prof of singing Royal Coll of Music 2001–; Imperial League of Opera Prize Gold Medal, Miriam Licette Prize; fndr convenor The Trust for Young Musicians; fell Royal Welsh Coll of Music and Drama; FRSA; *Recreations* playing golf, watching rugby in Wales, skiing; *Clubs* Friends of the Musicians' Benevolent Fund; *Style*— Miss Eiddwen Harrhy; ✉ c/o Allan Beavis, Phoenix Artists Management, 4th Floor, 6 Windmill Street, London W1P 1HF (tel 020 7636 5021, fax 020 7631 4631, e-mail allan@phoenixartists.co.uk)

HARRIES, Andy; *Career* television prodr, dir and exec prodr; scriptwriter/researcher/presenter Granada Television Manchester and London 1976–81, freelance prodr and dir 1982–92, controller of entertainment and comedy Granada Television 1994–2000 (head of comedy 1992–94), head of drama, comedy and film ITV Prodns 2000–; *Style*— Andy Harries, Esq

HARRIES, Kathryn Gwynne; da of Stanley George Harries, of St Davids, and Gwynneth Rosemary, *née* Hubbard, of Pembroke; *b* 15 February 1951; *Educ* Surbiton HS, Royal Acad of Music (jr exhibitioner, then at Sr Acad), Univ of London (BMus); *m* 30 July 1977 (m dis 1998), Christopher Charles Lane, s of Charles Victor Lane; 1 da (Victoria Jessica Gwynne b 27 Dec 1979), 1 s (William Stanley Gwynne b 21 Sept 1981); *Career* opera singer; lectr Kingston Poly 1969–82, prof Jr Dept RAM 1976–82, presenter BBC Schools TV series Music Time 1977–83, also various concerts, oratorios and recitals 1969–83; Wigmore Hall debut 1972, Royal Festival Hall debut 1977, operatic debut as a Flower Maiden in Parsifal (with WNO under Reginald Goodall) 1983; estab Coverwood Concerts Surrey 1991; Olivier Award nomination for Sieglinde and Gutrune in WNO's full Ring Cycle 1986; walked from John O'Groats to Lands End, with seven concerts and various impromptu concerts en route, to raise money for Speakability 2001; Hon DMus Kingston Univ 2001; FRAM 1991 (ARAM 1988); *Performances* incl: Leonora in Fidelio (with WNO in Liverpool 1983, Scottish Opera 1984, Teatro Colon Buenos Aires 1988, ENO 1996), Sylvie in La Colombe (Buxton Festival) 1983, Irene in Rienzi (ENO debut) 1983, Sieglinde in Die Walküre (WNO 1984, Nice Opera and Théâtre Champs Elysée 1988), Eva in Die Meistersinger (ENO) 1984, Female Chorus in The Rape of Lucretia (ENO) 1984, Adalgisa in Norma (WNO) 1985, title role in Hedda Gabler (Scottish Opera) 1985, Gutrune in Götterdämmerung (WNO 1985, Met Opera NY 1988 and 1989), Kundry in Parsifal (Met Opera debut 1986, Netherlands Opera 1990), Donna Elvira in Don Giovanni (Opera North 1986, Stuttgart debut 1992), Sieglinde and Gutrune in WNO's full Ring Cycle (Covent Garden) 1986, Senta in Der Fliegende Holländer (Scottish Opera, Paris Opera debut Palais Garnier) 1987, Donna Anna in The Stone Guest (ENO) 1987, Didon in Les Troyens (Berlioz Festival) 1987, title role in The Merry Widow (Opera North) 1988, Protaganista in Un Re in Ascolto (Covent Garden debut 1989, Opèra Bastille debut 1991), The Composer in Ariadne auf Naxos (WNO) 1989, title role in Katya Kabanova (ENO) 1989, Arianne in Arianne et Barbe Bleu (Netherlands Opera debut) 1989, Jocasta in Oedipus Rex (Los Angeles debut) 1989, Judith in Bluebeard's Castle (Scottish Opera) 1990, Didon in Les Troyens (Scottish Opera and Covent Garden 1990, La Monnaie Brussels debut 1992), title role in Cléopatre (Massenet Festival debut) 1990, Giulietta in The Tales of Hoffmann (Théâtre du Châtalet debut) 1991, Die Frau in 'Intolleranza 1960' (Stuttgart) 1992, title role in Carmen (Orange Festival debut) 1992, Principess di Bouillon in Adriana Lecouvreur (St Etienne) 1992, The Lady Macbeth of Mtensk (Stuttgart) 1995, Geschwitz in Berg's Lulu (BBC Proms) 1996, Jenufa in Kostelnika (Amsterdam, Chicago and San Francisco) 2001, Marco Polo (Netherlands Opera) 2001, title role in Herodiade (Liege) 2002, Countess Geschwitz in Berg's Lulu (BBC Proms and Glyndebourne); other roles incl: Flower Maiden and Voice from Above in Wagner's Parsifal, The Mother in Janácek's Osud, Fevronia in Rimsky-Korsakov's The Invisible City of Kitezh, Clairon (Glyndebourne and NY Met) 1998, Kundry in Parsifal (Bastille) 1997, Kostelnicka in Jenufa (Israel 1993, Amsterdam 1997, San Francisco 2001, Chicago 2000, Genoa 2003), Marie in Wozzeck (Chicago) 1993, Madame de Croisy in Poulenc's Dialogues des Carmelites (Hamburg) 2003; other credits incl: Chicago 1996, David Sawyer's From Morning to Midnight (world premiere) 2001, Waiting (Almeida Theatre) 2002, Carousel (Royal Festival Hall) 2002; *Recreations* riding and competing on own horses, reading, gardening, travelling, long-distance walking; *Clubs* Abinger Forest Riding; *Style*— Ms Kathryn Harries; ✉ c/o Ingpen & Williams Ltd, 7 St George's Court, 131 Putney Bridge Road, London SW15 2PA (tel 020 8874 3222, fax 020 8877 3113, e-mail kathrynharries@hotmail.com)

H

HARRIES OF PENTREGARTH, Baron (Life Peer UK 2006), of Pentregarth of Ceinewydd in the County of Dyfed; Rt Rev Richard Douglas Harries; s of Brig William Douglas Jameson Harries, CBE (d 1991), and Greta Miriam, da of A Bathurst Brown, MB, LRCP; *b* 2 June 1936; *Educ* Wellington, RMA Sandhurst, Selwyn Coll Cambridge (MA), Cuddesdon Theol Coll; *m* 1963, Josephine Bottomley, MA, MB BChir, DCH; 1 s, 1 da; *Career* Lt RCS 1955–58; curate Hampstead Parish Church 1963–69, chaplain Westfield Coll 1966–69, lectr Wells Theol Coll 1969–72, warden Wells, Salisbury and Wells Theol Coll 1971–72, vicar All Saints' Fulham 1972–81, dean KCL 1981–87, bishop of Oxford 1987–2006; conslt to Archbishop on Jewish Christian Relations 1986–92; chm Cncl of Christians and Jews 1992–2001 (vice-pres 2001–), chm C of E Bd of Social Responsibility 1996–2001; memb House of Lords 1993–, memb Ctee into reform of House of Lords 1999, chm House of Lords Select Ctee on Stem Cell Research 2001; chm The Johnson Soc 1988; memb Nuffield Cncl on Bioethics 2002–, pres HFEA 2002–; Sir Sigmund Sternberg award 1987; hon fell Selwyn Coll Cambridge; hon fell St Anne's Coll Oxford 2006, hon prof of theology KCL 2006; Hon DD London; Hon DUniv: Oxford Brookes, Open Univ 2006; FKC, FRSL, FMedSci 2005; *Books* Prayers of Hope (1975), Turning to Prayer (1978), Prayers of Grief and Glory (1979), Being a Christian (1981), Should Christians Support Guerrillas? (1982), The Authority of Divine Love (1983), Praying Round the Clock (1983), Seasons of the Spirit (1984), Prayer and the Pursuit of Happiness (1985), Morning has Broken (1985), Christianity and War in a Nuclear Age (1986), C S Lewis - The Man and his God (1987), The One Genius (1987), Christ has Risen (1988), Is There a Gospel for the Rich? (1992), Art and the Beauty of God (1993), The Real God (1994), Questioning Belief (1995), A Gallery of Reflections: The Nativity of Christ (1995), In the Gladness of Today (1999), God outside the Box: Why Spiritual People Object to Christianity (2002), After the Evil - Christianity and Judaism in the Shadow of the Holocaust (2003), The Passion in Art (2004), Praying the Eucharist (2004); contrib: What Hope in an Armed World (and ed, 1982), Reinhold Niebuhr and the issues of our Time (and ed, 1986), Stewards and the Mysteries of God (1975), Unholy Warfare (1983), The Cross and the Bomb (1985), Julian, Woman of our Time (1985), The Reality of God (1986), Two Cheers for Secularism (and ed, 1998), Christianity: Two Thousand Years (and ed, 2001); *Recreations* theatre, literature, sport, walking, lecturing on Swan Hellenic cruises; *Style*— The Rt Rev the Lord Harries of Pentregarth; ✉ House of Lords, London SW1A 0PW

HARRIMAN, (Joseph) William Fletcher (Bill); TD (1989); s of Flt-Lt Joseph Fletcher Harriman, MBE (d 1974), and Kathleen Harriman, *née* Robinson; *b* 27 April 1956; *Educ* Oakham Sch, Trent Poly Nottingham (BSc); *m* 25 June 1991, Janet, da of Albert Benson, of Nottingham; 2 da (Annabel b 30 May 1996, Caroline b 17 Sept 1998); *Career* S Notts Hussars Yeomanry RHA TA 1974–, troop commander 1986–88, seconded Royal Yeomanry as artillery advsr 1989–91, Army reserve 1992–2006; head of Catalogue Dept and princ valuer Weller and Dufty Auctioneers 1984–90 (conslt 1987–91), ind conslt valuer and identifier of firearms 1987–, expert witness in court cases for firearms and ballistics 1987–; head of firearms Br Assoc for Shooting and Conservation 1991– (dir 2001–); forensic ballistics Cranfield Univ 2002–; memb: Panel of Experts Antiques Roadshow, Home Office Working Gp reviewing Firearms Rules 1993–, Home Office Working Gp on Firearms Licensing by Category 1995, Home Office Working Gp Firearms Rules 1998, Home Office Working Gp Firearms Law - Guidance to the Police 2001–, Cncl Historical Breechloading Smallarms Assoc 1995–2001, Govt Firearms Consultative Ctee 1998–2004, Home Office Panel for Section 7 (3) Historic Handguns 2002–, Forensic Science Soc 2003–, Registrant Cncl for the Registration of Forensic Practitioners 2006; ed Classic Arms and Militaria 2005, columnist Shooting Times; treas Br Shooting Sports Cncl 1993–96; assoc ISVA 1982–92 (memb Fine Arts and Chattels Ctee 1991–92); MAE 1999, FSA 2006; *Books* Experts on Antiques (contrib, 1987), Tiaras,

Tallboys and Teddy Bears (contrib, 1990), Royal Armouries Yearbook 3 (contrib, 1998), Judith Miller - The Dictionary of Antiques (contrib, 2000); *Recreations* shooting, toxophily, wine, music; *Style*— Bill Harriman, Esq, TD, FSA; ✉ Pistyll Bank, Springfield Lane, Marford, Wrexham LL12 8TF (tel and fax 01244 570027, e-mail billharriman@btopenworld.com); British Association for Shooting and Conservation, Marford Mill, Rossett, Wrexham LL12 0HL (tel 01244 573010, fax 01244 573013, e-mail bill.harriman@basc.org.uk)

HARRINGTON, Jessica; da of Mary Fowler; *b* 25 February 1947, London; *Educ* Hatherop Castle Sch; *m* John Harrington; 1 s (James Lloyd), 3 da (Emma (Mrs Galway), Kate, Tara (Mrs O'Donoghue)); *Career* racehorse trainer 1991–; horses trained incl Moscow Flyer, Spirit Leader, Cork Allstar and Macs Joy; *Style*— Mrs Jessica Harrington; ✉ Commonstown Racing Stables, Moone, County Kildare, Ireland (tel 00 353 598 624153, fax 00 353 598 624292, e-mail jessicaharrington@eircom.net)

HARRINGTON, Prof (John) Malcolm; CBE (1992); s of John Roy Harrington, of Newport, Gwent, and Veda Naomi, *née* Harris; *b* 6 April 1942; *Educ* Newport HS, King's Coll, Westminster Med Sch London (BSc, MB BS, MSc, MD); *m* 20 May 1967, Madeline Mary, da of Brinley Hunter Davies (d 1971); 1 da (Kate b 27 Sept 1975); *Career* various hosp appts 1966–69, visiting scientist US Public Health Serv 1975–77, sr lectr in occupational med London Sch of Hygiene and Tropical Med 1977–80 (lectr 1969–75), fndn prof of occupational health Univ of Birmingham 1981–2001 (emeritus prof 2001–); chm Industrial Injuries Advsy Cncl 1984–96, specialist advsr House of Lords and House of Commons select ctees; vice-pres Int Cmmn on Occupational Health 1998–2003; memb: Nat Radiological Protection Bd 1992–2000, Soc of Occupational Med, Soc of Epidemiological Res, Int Epidemiology Assoc, Br Occupational Hygiene Soc; FFPH, FRCP (MRCP, LRCP), MRCS, FFOM (MFOM), FFOM(I), FACE USA, FMedSci, Hon FRSM 2004; *Books* Occupational Health (with F S Gill, 1983, 5 edn 2007), Recent Advances in Occupational Health (ed vol 2, 1984, ed vol 3, 1987), Occupational Hygiene (with K Gardiner, 3 edn 2005); Hunter's Diseases of Occupation (10 edn 2008); over 200 scientific papers published; *Recreations* music, theatre, gardening, cricket; *Clubs* Athenaeum, RSM; *Style*— Prof Malcolm Harrington, CBE; ✉ 1 The Cliff, Budleigh Salterton, Devon EX9 6JU (e-mail jmharri6@aol.com)

HARRINGTON, 11 Earl of (GB 1742); William Henry Leicester Stanhope; also Viscount Stanhope of Mahon, Baron Stanhope of Elvaston (both GB 1717), Baron Harrington (GB 1730), and Viscount Petersham (GB 1742); s of 10 Earl of Harrington, MC (d 1929, ggn of 4 Earl, inventor of the blend of snuff known as Petersham mixture, snuff being colour he used for his livery and equipage); suc kinsman, 7 and last Earl Stanhope, in the Viscountcy of Stanhope of Mahon and the Barony of Stanhope of Elvaston 1967; *b* 24 August 1922; *Educ* Eton; *m* 1, 1942 (m dis 1946), Eileen, da of Sir John Foley Grey, 8 Bt; 1 s (Charles Henry Leicester, Viscount Petersham b 1945), 2 da (Lady Jane Cameron b 1942 d 1974, Lady Avena Maxwell b 1944); m 2, 1947 (m dis 1962), Anne, da of Maj Richard Chute, of Co Limerick; 2 da (Lady Trina b 1947, Lady Sarah Barry b 1951), 1 s (Hon Steven b 1951); m 3, 1964, Priscilla, da of Hon Archibald Cubitt (5 s of 2 Baron Ashcombe); 1 s (Hon John Fitzroy b 1965), 1 da (Lady Isabella Rachel (Countess Cawdor) b 1966); *Heir* s, Viscount Petersham, *qv*; *Career* Capt RAC serv WWII; landowner; adopted Irish citizenship 1965; *Clubs* Kildare Street (Dublin); *Style*— The Rt Hon the Earl of Harrington; ✉ The Glen, Ballingarry, Co Limerick, Ireland (tel 0161 399162, fax 0161 399122)

HARRIOTT, Ainsley; s of Chester Leroy Harriott, of Manchester, and Peppy Petrona, *née* Strudwick (d 1993); *b* 28 February 1957; *Educ* Wandsworth Boys Sch, Westminster Catering Coll; *m* 3 Jan 1992, Clare Judy, da of Derek Fellows; 1 s (James Reuben b 24 June 1990), 1 da (Madeleine Joan Adaisma b 18 July 1993); *Career* trainee chef rising to commis chef Verreys Restaurant London 1975–78, demi chef de partie rising to chef tournant Strand Palace Hotel 1978–80, jr sous chef rising to sr sous chef Westbury Hotel 1980–85, chef de partie George V Paris, freelance chef and owner catering co 1985–95; head chef Long Room Lord's Cricket Ground 1985–95, head chef various ODC Cos; pres TRIC 2005–06; charity work incl: Help the Aged, Childline, Imperial Cancer Research, Children with Leukemia, Comic Relief, Barnardo's, Children in Need; *Television* presenter: Ainsley Harriott's Barbecue Bible, Can't Cook Won't Cook, Ready Steady Cook, Nat Lottery Live, Holiday Memories, Party of a Lifetime, Hidden Camera Show, Celeb Ready Steady Cook, Meals in Minutes, Ainsley's Big Cookout, Gourmet Express, 50 Things to Eat Before You Die; Television in USA incl: The Ainsley Harriot Show, The Tonight Show, Live with Regis & Kathie Lee, Rosie O'Donnell Show, Ready Set Cook; Off the Menu Now in 2 (own series, South Africa); *Awards* winner various team medals Westbury Hotel, BBC Good Food Award for Best TV/Radio Personality 1997 and 1998, TV Quick Award for Best TV Cook 1997, 1998 and 1999, Birmingham Evening Mail Readers' Award for Top TV Chef 1997, PASTA Personality of the Year 1998, Satellite TV Personality of the Year 1998, Tric Awards, UKTV Favourite TV Presenter 2003–04, Best Cookery Show Good Housekeeping Award (for Ready Steady Cook) 2005; *Books* In the Kitchen with Ainsley Harriott (1996), Ainsley Harriott's Barbecue Bible (1997), Can't Cook Won't Cook (1997), Ready Steady Cook IV (1997), Meals in Minutes (1998), Ainsley's Big Cookout (1998), Gourmet Express (2000), Low Fat Meals in Minutes (2004), Friends and Family Cookbook (2004), Ultimate Barbeque Bible (2005); *Clubs* Harbour, Soho House; *Style*— Ainsley Harriott, Esq

HARRIS, Prof Adrian Llewellyn; s of Luke Harris, and Julia, *née* Wade; *b* 10 August 1950; *Educ* Liverpool Collegiate Sch, Univ of Liverpool (BSc, MB), Univ of Oxford (DPhil); *m* 7 July 1975, Margaret Susan, da of Rev Ronald Denman; *Career* clinical scientist Clinical Pharmacology Unit MRC Oxford 1975–78, lectr in med oncology Royal Marsden Hosp London 1978–80, visiting fell ICRF London 1981, prof of clinical oncology Univ of Newcastle 1981–88, ICRF prof of medical oncology and dir of Molecular Oncology Lab Univ of Oxford 1988– (fell St Hugh's Coll); FRCP; *Recreations* swimming, walking, films and theatre; *Style*— Prof Adrian L Harris; ✉ Cancer Research UK Medical Oncology Unit, The Churchill, Oxford Radcliffe Hospital, Headington, Oxford OX3 7LJ (tel 01865 226184, fax 01865 226179)

HARRIS, 8 Baron (UK 1815), of Seringapatam and Mysore, E Indies, and of Belmont, Co Kent; Anthony Harris; o s of 7 Baron Harris (d 1996), and his 1 w, Laura Cecilia, *née* McCausland (d 1995); *b* 8 March 1942; *Educ* Eastbourne Coll; *m* 1966, Anstice (d 2007), da of Alfred Winter, of Westcliff-on-Sea, Essex; 2 da (Hon Isabel b 1973, Hon Laura b 1976); *Heir* kinsman, Cdr Antony Harris, OBE, RN; *Style*— The Rt Hon the Lord Harris

HARRIS, Prof Anthony Leonard; s of Thomas Haydn Harris (d 1967), of Cardiff, and Dora, *née* Wilkinson (d 1989); *b* 11 May 1935; *Educ* Cardiff HS, UC Wales Aberystwyth (BSc, PhD); *m* 29 Aug 1959, (Muriel) Noreen, da of Arthur Jones, of Rhondda; 1 da (Elisabeth Siân b 31 May 1964), 1 s (David Huw Mendus b 20 April 1967); *Career* geologist then princ geologist Geological Survey Edinburgh 1959–71; Univ of Liverpool 1971–: lectr, sr lectr, reader, personal chair 1987–2001, prof of geology, head Dept of Earth Scis 1987–94, dean Faculty of Science 1994–2000, emeritus prof of geology 2001–; pres: Geological Soc of London 1990–92 (hon sec 1979–82), Geological Soc of Liverpool 1989–91; C T Clough Fund and Memorial Medal Geological Soc of Edinburgh, Murchison Fund and Major John Coke Medal Geological Soc of London; FGS 1966, CGeol 1991, FRSE 1988; *Books* The Caledonides of the British Isles - reviewed (ed and contrib, 1979), The Caledonian-Appalachian Orogen (ed and contrib, 1986); *Recreations* ornithology, hill walking, gardening; *Style*— Prof Anthony Harris, FRSE; ✉ Department of Earth Sciences, University of Cardiff, Cathays Park, Cardiff CF10 3YE (tel and fax 029 2051 5608)

HARRIS, Brian Nicholas; s of Claude Harris (d 1976), and Dorothy, *née* Harris (d 1982); *b* 12 December 1931; *Educ* Coll of Estate Mgmnt London; *m* 18 March 1961, Rosalyn Marion, da of Geoffrey Alfred Caines (d 1982); 2 da (Suzanne (Mrs Richard Thompson) b 1961, Jennifer (Mrs Frederick Batt) b 1965); *Career* chartered surveyor; Richard Ellis: ptnr 1961–96, chm 1984–93; conslt C B Richard Ellis 1996–; chm: Priority Sites Ltd 2001–03, Bann System Ltd 2004–; non-exec dir EDI plc 2003–06; vice-chm: RICS Bldg Surveying Div 1976–77, RICS Continental Gp 1977–78; chm City Branch RICS 1984–85; London C of C: memb Cncl 1985–, memb Bd 1989–96, dep pres 1990–92, pres 1992–94; memb: Cncl Aust and NZ C of C (UK) 1988–2000 (chm 1996–98), Aust and NZ Trade Advsy Ctee 1988–98; first chm London Heathrow Support Gp 1993–99, chm Southern Region Assoc of Br C of Cs 1994–96, memb Bd Br C of C 1994–98 (dep pres 1996–98), memb Ct of Common Cncl Corp of London 1996– (chm Property Sub-Ctee 2002–04, memb Planning and Police Ctees 1999–04); memb London Int Ct of Arbitration Jt Consultative Ctee 1996–99; tstee Commercial Educn Tst Ctee 1990–96 (chm 2000–06); memb Bd Britain Aust Soc (chm 2002, dep chm 1999); chm Cook Soc 2001; Lay Sheriff City of London 1998–99; hon property advsr Order of St John of Jerusalem 1996–2001; memb Co of World Traders 1989–; Liveryman and memb Ct of Assts Worshipful Co of Glaziers and Painters of Glass 1975 (Upper Warden 2002, Master 2003); FRSA; *Recreations* fly fishing, gardening, golf, opera; *Clubs* Carlton, Flyfishers', City of London, MCC; *Style*— Brian Harris, Esq; ✉ Grants Paddock, Grants Lane, Limpsfield, Surrey RH8 0RQ (tel 01883 723215); C B Richard Ellis, St Martins Court, 10 Paternoster Row, London EC4M 7HD (tel 020 7182 2000, e-mail brian.harris@cbre.com)

HARRIS, His Hon Judge (Geoffrey) Charles Wesson; QC (1989); s of Geoffrey Hardy-Harris (d 1994), and Joan, *née* Wesson (d 1979); *b* 17 January 1945; *Educ* Repton, Univ of Birmingham (LLB); *m* 25 July 1970, Carol Ann, da of J D Alston, CBE, of Norfolk; 2 s (Roger, Hugh), 1 da (Kate); *Career* called to the Bar Inner Temple 1967, in practice (common law) London and Midlands 1968–93, recorder 1990–93, circuit judge (Midland & Oxford Circuit) 1993–; designated civil judge: Oxford and Northampton 1998–2001, Oxford and Thames Valley 2001–; memb: Parole Bd 1995–2000, Crown Court Rules Ctee 1997–2005, Cncl of Circuit Judges 2002–; Parly candidate (Cons) Penistone 1974; govr St Clement Danes C of E Primary Sch 1976–79; *Books* contrib current edn Halsbury's Laws of England; author of various magazine articles; *Recreations* history, stalking, skiing, architecture, travel, fireworks; *Style*— His Hon Judge Charles Harris, QC; ✉ c/o Oxford Combined Court, St Aldates, Oxford OX1 1TL

HARRIS, Prof Christopher John; s of Colin Christopher Harris, and Barbara Kay, *née* Hall; *b* 22 September 1960; *Educ* Oundle, CCC Oxford (BA), Nuffield Coll Oxford (MPhil, DPhil); *m* 1993, Qun Li; 1 s (Alexander Sheng b 26 May 1998); *Career* Univ of Oxford: prize research fell in economics Nuffield Coll 1983–84, lectr in economics 1984–94, fell Nuffield Coll 1984–94; prof of mathematical economics Univ of Cambridge 1995–, fell King's Coll Cambridge 1995–; visiting prof MIT 1990–91, Br Acad research prof 2000–03, visiting fell Princeton 2000–01 (Richard B Fisher memb Inst for Advanced Study 2001–02); *Publications* author of articles in academic journals; *Style*— Prof C J Harris; ✉ Faculty of Economics and Politics, University of Cambridge, Austin Robinson Building, Sidgwick Avenue, Cambridge CB3 9DD (tel 01223 335706, fax 01223 335475)

HARRIS, Prof Christopher John; s of George Henry Harris, BEM, and Hilda Winifred, *née* Ward; *b* 23 December 1945; *Educ* Portsmouth GS, Univ of Leicester (BSc), Univ of Oxford (MA), Univ of Southampton (PhD, DSc); *m* 10 Sept 1965, (Ruth) Joy, da of Robert Garrod (d 1986); 2 da (Caroline Louise b 1968, Kathryn Ruth b 1978), 1 s (Philip Jonathan b 1971); *Career* lectr in electronics Univ of Hull 1969–72, lectr in control engrg and maths UMIST 1972–75, lectr and fell in engrg sci Univ of Oxford and St Edmund Hall 1976–80, prof and dep chief scientist MOD 1980–84, prof and chm of sch Cranfield Inst of Technol 1984–87, prof of computational intelligence Univ of Southampton 1987–; dir Nat Research Centre in Data of Information Fusion; author of several hundred scientific papers; IEE Senior Achievement Medallist 1998, IEE Faraday Medallist 2001; CEng 1972, FIMA 1975, FIEE 1976, FREng 1996; *Books* Mathematical Modelling of Turbulent Diffusion in the Environment (1979), Stability of Linear Systems (1980), Self Tuning and Adaptive Control (1981), The Stability of Input/Output Dynamic Systems (1983), Advances in Command, Control and Communication Systems (1987), Application of Artificial Intelligence to Command and Control Systems (1988), Intelligent Control: aspects of fuzzy logic and neural nets (1993), Neurofuzzy Adaptive Modelling and Control (1994), Advances in Intelligent Control (1994), Advances and Adaptive Control (1995), Neutral Network Control of Robotic Manipulators (1998), Data Based Modelling, Control and Estimation (2002); *Recreations* gardening, sailing, fly fishing; *Style*— Emeritus Prof Christopher Harris, FREng; ✉ Department of Electronics & Computer Sciences, University of Southampton, Highfield, Southampton S017 1BJ (tel 023 8059 2748, fax 023 8059 2353, e-mail cjh@ecs.soton.ac.uk)

HARRIS, David Albert; s of Albert Edward Harris (d 1988), of Woodford Halse, Northants, and Edith Lilian, *née* Butler (d 1988); *b* 11 June 1938; *Educ* Magdalen Coll Sch Brackley, UCL (ed Sennet Univ of London student newspaper), DipCAM (PR); *m* 1965, Marjorie Ann Ney; 1 s, 1 da; *Career* editorial asst Furniture Record 1958–59, PRO Nat Union of Students 1960–62, freelance educational journalist 1962–64, on staff The Teacher (Nat Union of Teachers) 1964–66 (latterly dep ed), dep ed Focus (Consumer Cncl) 1966–67, account exec Max Redlich Ltd (PR conslts) 1967–69, info offr Consumer Cncl 1969–71, dir Braban Public Relations Ltd 1971–75, md Partnerplan Public Affairs Ltd 1975–77; dir of public affrs: The Advtg Assoc 1977–88, Market Research Soc 1988–89; dir The Hansard Soc for Parliamentary Govt 1989–98, non-exec dir Electoral Reform (Int Servs) Ltd 1999–; Lib/Lib Democrat Pty: agent for Finchley gen elections 1970 and Feb 1974, memb Finchley & Golders Green (chm 1998–2001); sometime memb Cncl CIPR (chm Govt Affrs Gp 1988–89); FCIPR 1986 (MCIPR 1972), FRSA 1994; *Recreations* watching cricket, family history, collecting political commemoratives; *Style*— David Harris, Esq; ✉ 48 Erskine Hill, Hampstead Garden Suburb, London NW11 6HG (tel 020 8455 6507, fax 020 8201 9864, e-mail da.harris@which.net)

HARRIS, David Anthony; s of Dr Samuel Harris (d 1996), and Joan, *née* Pegler; *b* 31 March 1954; *Educ* King Edward's Sch Birmingham, Univ of London (LLB); *m* 1, 7 Nov 1987, Penelope Anne (d 1998), da of Alfred Dalton, CB; 1 da (Sophie Olivia b 30 Sept 1988), 1 s (Edward Robert b 15 Dec 1991); m 2, 17 July 1999, Margaret Evelyn; *Career* admitted slr 1979; Field Fisher & Martineau 1977–82, ptnr Lovells (formerly Lovell White Durrant) 1986– (joined 1982, currently managing ptnr); memb Law Soc; Freeman Worshipful Co of Slrs; MSI; *Recreations* polo, tennis, skiing; *Style*— David Harris, Esq; ✉ Lovells, Atlantic House, Holborn Viaduct, London EC1A 2FG

HARRIS, Prof David John; CMG (1999); s of Sidney John William Harris, and Alice May, *née* Full (d 1955); *b* 3 July 1938; *Educ* Sutton HS Plymouth, KCL (LLB), LSE (LLM, PhD); *m* 15 Aug 1964, Sandra, da of Denzil Nelson, of Arcadia, California; 2 s (Mark b 20 Sept 1967, Paul b 27 March 1972); *Career* asst lectr in law Queen's Univ Belfast 1962–63; Univ of Nottingham: asst lectr in law 1963–65, lectr 1965–73, sr lectr 1973–81, prof of public int law 1981–2003, head Law Dept 1986–89, co-dir Human Rights Law Centre 1993–, emeritus prof 2003–; memb Ctee of Ind Experts Euro Social Charter 1990–96; CMG 1999; *Books* International Law - Cases and Materials (1973, 6 edn 2004), Civil Liberties - Cases and Materials (jtly, 1979, 5 edn 2001), The European Social Charter (1984, 2 edn 2000), The Law of the European Convention on Human Rights (jtly, 1995);

Recreations walking, travel; *Style—* Prof David Harris, CMG; ✉ c/o School of Law, University of Nottingham, Nottingham (tel 0115 951 5701)

HARRIS, Col David Keith; OBE (1987, MBE 1983), TD (1978), DL (Lincs 1993); s of Edwin Harris (d 1974), of Epworth, Doncaster, and Mona Doreen, *née* Sleight (d 2001); *b* 27 January 1945; *Educ* Worksop Coll, KCL (LLB); *m* 25 Jan 1975, Veronica Mary, da of Arthur Vernon Harrison (d 1983), of Finningley, S Yorks; *Career* Univ of London OTC 1963–67, cmmnd Royal Lincolnshire Regt TA 1967; served: 5 Royal Anglian 1967–78, 7 Royal Anglian 1978–80, SO2 G3 7 Field Force 1980–82, SO2 G3 49 Inf Bde 1982; cmd 7 R Anglian 1984–87, dep cdr 49 Inf Bde 1987–90, TA Col RMAS 1991–94, Dep Col The Royal Anglian Regt 1992–97; admitted slr 1969, sr ptnr HSR Law (Hayes, Son & Richmond, formerly Richmonds) 1989– (co dir); non-exec memb Doncaster HA 2000–02; Parly candidate (Cons) Bassetlaw: Oct 1974, 1979; memb Law Soc 1967; ADC 1990–93; *Recreations* rugby union, old motor cars, shooting, gardening, good food and wine; *Style—* Col David Harris, OBE, TD, DL; ✉ Green Hill House, Haxey, Doncaster, South Yorkshire DN9 2JU (tel 01427 752794); HSR Law, The Law Chambers, 8 South Parade, Doncaster, South Yorkshire DN1 2ED (tel 01302 347800, fax 01302 363466, Gainsborough tel 01427 613831, e-mail david.harris@hsrlaw.co.uk)

HARRIS, David Laurence; *b* 19 June 1944; *Educ* Liverpool GS, Coll of Law; *m* 1973, Maureen Ann, *née* Cocklin; 2 s, 1 da; *Career* admitted slr Supreme Court; Govt serv exec various appts 1963–73, ptnr Tax Law Dept Nabarro Nathanson 1973–82; Rothschild Gp 1982–; Rothschild Tst Corporation Ltd: chief exec 1987–2005, chm 2005–; exec dir N M Rothschild & Sons Limited 1987–97, chm Rothschild Tst (Bermuda) Ltd 1991; dir: Rothschild Tst Corporation Ltd 1982, Rothschild Tst Canada Inc 1989, Rothschild Tst Guernsey Ltd 1992, Rothschild Private Tst Holdings AG 1995, Rothschild Tst New Zealand Ltd 2001, Rothschild Tstee Services (Ireland) 2002, Rothschild Private Management Ltd 2003; memb: Int Tax Planning Assoc, Soc of Estate & Tst Practitioners, Inst Fiscal Studies, IBA, Law Soc; FInstT; *Recreations* sport, music, literature; *Style—* David Harris, Esq; ✉ Rothschild Trust Corporation Limited, PO Box 185, New Court, St Swithin's Lane, London EC4P 4DU (tel 020 7280 5000, fax 020 7280 5948)

HARRIS, His Hon Judge David Michael; QC (1989); s of late Maurice Harris, of Liverpool, and Doris, *née* Ellis; *b* 7 February 1943; *Educ* Liverpool Inst HS for Boys, Univ of Oxford (MA), Univ of Cambridge (PhD); *m* 16 Aug 1970, Emma Lucia, da of Dr Italo Calma, of Liverpool; 2 s (Julian b 3 July 1974, Jeremy b 9 May 1977), 1 da (Anna b 10 May 1980); *Career* asst lectr in law Univ of Manchester 1967–69, called to the Bar 1969, recorder 1988–2001 (asst recorder 1984–88), head of chambers 1988, dep judge of the High Court (Family Division) 1993, bencher Middle Temple 1997, circuit judge (Northern Circuit) 2001–; *Books* Winfield & Jolowicz on Tort (co-ed, 1971), Supplement to Bingham's The Modern Cases on Negligence (co-ed, 1985); *Recreations* arts, travel, sport; *Style—* His Hon Judge Harris, QC

HARRIS, Prof David Russell; s of Dr Herbert Melville Harris (d 1976), of Oxford, and Norah Mary, *née* Evans (d 1985); *b* 14 December 1930; *Educ* St Christopher Sch Letchworth, Univ of Oxford (MA, BLitt), Univ of Calif Berkeley (PhD); *m* 5 July 1957, Helen Margaret, da of Dr Gilbert Ingram Wilson (d 1980), of Stafford; 4 da (Sarah b 1959, Joanna b 1962, Lucy b 1964, Zoë b 1969); *Career* Nat Serv RAF 1949–50; teaching asst and instr Univ of Calif 1956–58, lectr Queen Mary Coll London 1958–64; UCL: lectr and reader 1964–79, prof of human environment Inst of Archaeology 1979–98, dir Inst of Archaeology 1989–96, prof emeritus 1998–; memb: Archaeology Ctee Museum of London 1984–93, Science and Conservation Panel English Heritage 1985–99, Dover Archaeological Advsy Bd 1989–; chm Science-Based Archaeology Ctee SERC 1989–92; pres: Prehistoric Soc 1990–94, UK Chapter Soc for Economic Botany 1995–97, Anthropology and Archaeology Section BAAS 2000–; hon fell UCL 2000; FSA 1982, FBA 2004; *Books* Plants, Animals and Man in the Outer Leeward Islands (1965), Africa in Transition (with B W Hodder, 1967), Human Ecology in Savanna Environments (1980), Foraging and Farming (with G C Hillman, 1989), Modelling Ecological Change (with K D Thomas, 1991), The Archaeology of V Gordon Childe (1994), The Origins and Spread of Agriculture and Pastoralism in Eurasia (1996), Plants for Food and Medicine (with H Prendergast, N Etkin and P Houghton, 1998); *Recreations* mountain walking, archaeo-ecological overseas travel; *Clubs* Athenaeum; *Style—* Prof David Harris, FBA; ✉ Institute of Archaeology, University College London, 31–34 Gordon Square, London WC1H 0PY (tel 020 7679 7495, fax 020 7383 2572, e-mail david.harris@ucl.ac.uk)

HARRIS, Evan; MP; s of Prof Frank Harris, CBE, and Brenda Henriette, *née* van Embden; *b* 21 October 1965; *Educ* Blue Coat Sch Liverpool, Harvard HS, Wadham Coll Oxford (BA, BM BS); *Career* hosp doctor Royal Liverpool Univ Hosp and Oxford Radcliffe Hosp 1991–94, MO (Oxford Junior Doctors Hours Task Force) 1994–97, hon registrar in public health med Oxon HA 1994–97; MP (Lib Dem) Oxford W and Abingdon 1997–; Lib Dem spokesman on health 1997–99, spokesman on HE and women's issues 1999–2001, shadow health sec 2001–03, science spokesman 2005–, memb Select Ctee on Science 2003–, memb Jt Select Ctee on Human Rights 2005–; offr All-Pty Gp on: Mental Health, Kidneys (chair), Science, Refugees, Equality, AIDS; memb BMA Med Ethics Ctee, former memb BMA Cncl; hon assoc Nat Secular Soc; *Recreations* chess, bridge, football; *Style—* Dr Evan Harris, MP; ✉ 27 Park End Street, Oxford OX1 1HU (tel 01865 245584, fax 01865 245589, e-mail harrise@parliament.uk)

HARRIS, Graham Derek; s of late Philip Henry Harris, of 16 Hardwick Rd, Folkestone, Kent, and May Dorothy, *née* Perovich; *b* 28 September 1956; *Educ* King's Sch Canterbury, Oriel Coll Oxford (MA); *m* 14 Feb 1987, Katarine Maria, da of Boris Stanislaus Brandl (d 1955), of Garstang, Lancs; 1 da (Philippa Josephine Brandl b 28 Sept 1989); *Career* slr; articled clerk Norton Rose Botterell & Roche 1979–83, admitted 1981, ptnr Richards Butler 1988–2001 (joined 1983), ptnr Thomas Cooper & Stibbard 2001–; SSC; *Style—* Graham Harris, Esq; ✉ Thomas Copper & Stibbard, Ibex House, 42–47 Minories, London EC3N 1HA (tel 020 7481 8851, fax 020 7480 6097)

HARRIS, Harry; s of Jack Harris, and Sara, *née* Cohen; *b* 30 May 1952; *Educ* Davenant Fndn GS (soccer capt), Harlow Coll; *m* (m dis); 1 s (Simon Paul b 16 Nov 1975), 1 da (Jordanna b 17 Aug 1980); *Career* journalist; Express & Independent 1971–72, North London Weekly Herald 1972–79, Newcastle Journal 1979–80, London Evening News 1980–81, Daily Mail 1981–85, The Mirror 1985–2001 (latterly chief soccer writer), Daily Express 2001–; memb: Football Writers' Assoc, Sports Writers' Assoc; Great Britain's Sports Journalist of the Year 1993, Sports Cncl's Sports Reporter of the Year (jtly) 1993, highly commended Race in the Media Awards 1993, shortlisted Br Sports Reporter of the Year 1994, runner-up GB's Sports Journalist of the Year 1996, winner of Sports Reporter of the Year British Press Awards 1998, runner up Sports Cncl's Sports Reporter of the Year 1998; Sport England: winner Sports Story of the Year 1999, highly commended Sports News Reporter of the Year 2000; *Books* incl: Spurred to Success (with Glenn Hoddle), The Inside Story (Terry Venables), Rock Bottom (with Paul Merson), Against All the Odds (with Gary Mabbutt), Macca Can (with Steve McMahon), Revelations of a Football Manager (with Terry Neill); also Bill Nicholson's autobiography (co-author), Jurgen Klinsman's Diary of a Season, Portrait of a Genius (Ruud Gullit's biography), Ruud Gullit: The Chelsea Diary, My Autobiography: Ruud Guillit, The Road to France: World Cup Masterpieces, The Fergie Factor (Alex Ferguson biography), Vialli: A Diary of His Season, Pele: The Authorised Biography; *Style—* Harry Harris, Esq

HARRIS, Hugh Christopher Emlyn; s of T E Harris, CB, CBE (d 1955), and M A Harris (d 1980); *b* 25 March 1936; *Educ* The Leys Sch Cambridge, Trinity Coll Cambridge (MA); *m* 7 Sept 1968, Pamela Susan, da of R A Woollard (d 1980); 1 da (Kate b 1970), 1 s (William b 1972); *Career* Nat Serv Lt RA 1954–56; dir: BE Services Ltd 1979–94, Houblon Nominees 1988–94, The Securities Mgmnt Tst Ltd 1988–94; Bank of England 1959–94: chief of corp servs 1984–88, assoc dir 1988–94; dir London First Global Network 1999– (gen mangr London First Centre 1995, dir of ops London First 1995–99); dep chm Cmmn for Racial Equality 1996–2000 (cmmr 1995); special advsr City and Inner London NTEC (CILNTEC) 1994–97, dir London Film Cmmn 1996–2000, dir African and Caribbean Westminster Initiative 2000–03; vice-pres Bankers Benevolent Fund 1990–; memb Cncl London Civic Forum 2001–; memb Advsy Bd Centre for Racial Equality Studies Middlesex Univ 2001–; memb Bd of Govrs Newham Coll of FE 2005–; churchwarden St Margaret Lothbury 1988–94, hon treas Kemsing Branch Royal Br Legion, chm Solefield Sch Educnl Tst Ltd 1993–2000, chm Broad St Ward Club 2002–03; memb HAC, former memb Advsy Cncl Windsor Fellowship; companion Business in the Community; Liveryman Worshipful Co of Turners; ACIB, FCIPD, FRSA; *Recreations* rugby, tennis, films, opera, ballet; *Style—* Hugh Harris, Esq; ✉ London First, 1 Hobhouse Court, Suffolk Street, London SW1Y 4HH (tel 020 7665 1570, fax 020 7665 1501, e-mail hharris@london-first.co.uk)

HARRIS, Sir Jack Wolfred Ashford; 2 Bt (UK 1932), of Bethnal Green, Co London; s of Rt Hon Sir Percy Alfred Harris, 1 Bt, DL (d 1952); *b* 23 July 1906; *Educ* Shrewsbury, Trinity Hall Cambridge (BA); *m* 1933, Patricia, da of Arthur P Penman, of Wahroonga, nr Sydney, NSW; 2 s (Christopher John Ashford b 1934, Paul Percy Ashford b 1945), 1 da (Margaret b 1939); *Heir* s, Christopher Harris; *Career* chm Bing Harris & Co NZ 1935–78 (dir 1978–82); past pres Wellington C of C; *Recreations* reading, gardening, swimming, writing; *Clubs* Wellington (NZ), Union (Sydney NSW); *Style—* Sir Jack Harris, Bt

HARRIS, Dr James Richard; s of James Derek Harris, and Valerie Olive Harris, of London; *b* 8 August 1960; *Educ* London Hosp Med Coll (MB BS, MRCGP), Inst of Aviation Med (CertAvMed); *m* 10 July 1983, Jill Elizabeth, da of Peter Charles Richards; 2 s (Edward James b 19 Dec 1986, William Peter b 10 Feb 1989), 1 da (Emily Rose b 19 March 1993); *Career* formerly: various hosp posts Chelmsford and Essex Hosp, St George's Hosp London, St Peter's Hosp Chertsey and Llandough Hosp Penarth, gen practice trainee Dinas Powis S Glamorgan; currently princ in private practice; chm: Nat Young Principals 1990–2000; memb Cncl RCGP 1991–, divnl pres BMA 1993–97; *Recreations* golf, travel; *Style—* Dr James Harris; ✉ 4 The Courtyard, Sheffield Park, East Sussex TN22 3QW (tel 01825 791341, fax 01825 791588)

HARRIS, Joanne Michèle Sylvie; da of Robert Ian Short, and Jeannette, *née* Payen; *b* 3 July 1964, Barnsley; *Educ* Wakefield Girls' HS, Barnsley Sixth Form Coll, St Catharine's Coll Cambridge (MA), Univ of Sheffield (PGCE); *m* 1988, Kevin Steven Harris; 1 da (Anouchka Fleur b 1 June 1993); *Career* writer; Hon DLitt: Univ of Huddersfield 2003, Univ of Sheffield 2004; *Books* The Evil Seed (1989), Sleep, Pale Sister (1993), Chocolat (1999, Creative Freedom Award 2000, Whittaker Gold 2001; shortlisted: Whitbread Novel of the Year Award 2000, Scripter Award 2001; film version nominated for 8 BAFTAs and 5 Oscars), Blackberry Wine (2000, winner Foreign and Int categories Salon du Livre Gourmand), Five Quarters of the Orange (2001; shortlisted: RNA Novel of the Year, Author of the Year 2002, WHSmith Award 2002), Coastliners (2002), The French Kitchen: A Cookbook (with Fran Warde, 2002), Holy Fools (2003), Jigs and Reels (2004), The French Market: A Cookbook (with Fran Warde, 2005), Gentlemen and Players (2005, shortlisted Edgar Award USA 2007), The Lollipop Shoes (2007), Runemarks (2007); *Style—* Mrs Joanne Harris; ✉ c/o Eldon House, Sharp Lane, Almondbury, Huddersfield HD5 8XL (website www.joanne-harris.co.uk)

HARRIS, Prof John Buchanan; s of John Benjamin Sargent Harris (d 1971), of Adelaide, Aust, and Mary Isobel, *née* Pratt; *b* 18 January 1940; *Educ* Tiffin Sch Kingston upon Thames, Univ of London (BPharm), Univ of Bradford (PhD); *m* 6 Sept 1965, Christine Margaret, da of Clifford Morton Holt (d 1983), of Bradford, W Yorks; 2 s (Joel b and d 1972, Jolyon Leo b 1974), 1 da (Danica Mathilde b 1981); *Career* res asst Univ of Bradford 1963–67; Univ of Newcastle: sr res asst 1967–72, princ res assoc 1972–74, sr lectr 1974–80, prof 1980–; res fell Univ of Lund Sweden 1970–71, UCLA America 1977–78, Monash Univ Melbourne Aust 1980; FIBiol, MRPharmS; *Books* Muscular Dystrophy and other Inherited Diseases of Muscle in Animals (1979), Natural Toxins (1986), Muscle Metabolism (with D M Turnbull, 1990), Medical Neurotoxicology (with P G Blain, 1999); *Recreations* reading, philately, walking; *Style—* Prof John Harris; ✉ School of School of Neurology, Neurobiology and Psychiatry, Newcastle University Medical School, Newcastle upon Tyne NE2 4HH (tel 0191 222 6648, fax 0191 222 6977, e-mail j.b.harris@ncl.ac.uk)

HARRIS, John Charles; CBE (2007), DL (S Yorks 1986); s of Sir Charles Joseph William Harris, KBE (d 1986), and Lady Emily Kyle, *née* Thompson (d 1992); *b* 25 April 1936; *Educ* Dulwich Coll (LCC scholar), Clare Coll Cambridge (MA, LLM); *m* 1 April 1961, Alison Beryl, da of Dr Kenneth Reginald Sturley, and Beryl Marion Sturley; 1 da (Susan Alison b 15 Sept 1966), 1 s (Edward John Charles b 16 June 1968); *Career* Nat Serv 2 Lt Intelligence Corps 1954–56; with UKAEA (seconded to OECD) 1959–63, Poole BC 1963–67, admitted slr 1966, dep town clerk Bournemouth CB 1971–73 (offr 1967–73); S Yorks CC 1973–86: co sec 1973–83, chief exec and co clerk 1983–86, dir SY Resid Body 1985–86, non-exec dir S Yorks Passenger Tport Exec, clerk to Lord-Lieut S Yorks 1983–86; legal, mgmnt and recruitment conslt (incl for PA Conslt Group and Daniels Bates Partnership) 1986–; exec dir: Solace International Ltd 1992–2000, Solace International (Southern Africa) Pty Ltd 1993–2000; non-exec dir Pontefract HA 1990–93; chm: Bd Northern Counties Housing Assoc 1994–2000 (memb 1990–, vice-chm 1994 and 2002–03), Bd Northern Counties (Specialised) Housing Assoc Ltd 1994–, Coal Authy 1999–2007, Audit Ctee MOD Police and Guarding Agency 2004–; ind memb Police Ctee MOD 2003–; memb Bd Guinness Partnership 2007–; memb: Rampton Special Hosp Ctee 1989–96, Arts Cncl Touring Advsy Bd 1988–92, Ctee Ackworth Gp Riding for the Disabled Assoc 1976–96; fndr memb and sec Barnsley-Rockley Rotary Club 1976–79, vice-chm and sec Friends of Opera North 1978–87; Opera North plc: memb Cncl 1979–88, memb Devpt Ctee 1987–94; tstee, dir and memb Mgmnt Cncl Homeless Int 1998–2000; dir South Africa Housing Support Network Tst 1998–2001; nat chm Soc of Co Secs 1983, Hon PRO S Yorks and Humberside Region RDA 1983–92; memb: Cncl Soc of Local Authorities Chief Exec 1984–86, RDA Nat Pubns Ctee 1988–90, W Yorks Police Authy (ind) 1994–99; tstee Housing Assocs Charitable Tst 1995–96; chm of govrs: Felkirk (formerly Ackworth Moor Top) Community Special Sch 1998–2005 (govr 1996), Wakefield Dist Community Sch (incorporating former Felkirk Community Special Sch) 2005–; jt chair Ivory Park township Johannesburg SA/Wakefield Educn Partnership 2002– (co-ordinator UK imports to community devpt 1995–); memb: Euro Movement, Law Soc; Freeman City of London 1957; FRSA 1984; *Recreations* foreign travel, opera, family and friends; *Style—* John Harris, Esq, CBE, DL; ✉ Long Lane Close, High Ackworth, Pontefract, West Yorkshire WF7 7EY (>e-mail< johnharris@coal.gov.uk, home tel 01977 795450, fax 01977 795470, mobile 07710 110407, e-mail jcharris@lineone.net)

HARRIS, John Clement; s of Norman Rees, and Leah Eastwood, *née* Clement; *b* 9 July 1936; *Educ* Seaford Coll, Petworth; *m* 19 Sept 1962, Shirley, *née* Anderson; 1 s (Jonathan b 17 May 1964); *Career* Nat Serv RAF 1955–57; own business: nursing homes 1957–62, furnishing and interior design 1962–84, commercial property devpt/mgmnt 1978–; Fedn of Small Businesses: fndr memb 1975, branch and vice-chm, region and vice-chm, nat cncllr and exec memb Bd of Dirs, policy chm, hon nat chm; chm Southern Water Consumer Consultative Ctee; dir Southern Water; *Recreations* building, walking, travelling (particularily USA); *Style*— John Harris, Esq; ✉ 21 Hastings Court, Winchelsea Gardens, Worthing, West Sussex BN11 5DD (tel 01903 609308); Federation of Small Businesses, Parliamentary Office, 2 Catherine Place, Westminster, London SW1E 6HF (tel 020 7233 7900, fax 020 7233 7899, e-mail jch@fsb.org.uk)

HARRIS, Dr John Edwin (Jack); MBE (1981); s of John Frederick Harris (d 1978), and Emily Margaret, *née* Prosser (d 1980); *b* 2 June 1932; *Educ* Larkfield GS Chepstow, Univ of Birmingham (BSc, PhD, DSc); *m* 9 June 1956, Ann, da of Peter James Foote (d 1976); 2 s (Peter b 28 March 1957, Ian b 17 May 1962), 2 da (Wendy b 3 Feb 1962, Perlita b 6 April 1966); *Career* res worker AEI John Thompson 1956–59; Berkeley Nuclear Laboratories CEGB: res offr 1959–64, section head 1964–88, univ liaison offr 1988; visiting prof of nuclear engrg Univ of Manchester 1989–, visiting prof of corrosion UMIST 1992–, visiting prof of manufacturing and materials Univ of Plymouth 1992–; memb: Bd Br Nuclear Energy Soc, Cncl British Pugwash 1996–; ed Interdisciplinary Sci Reviews 1996–2001; memb Bd of Visitors Leyhill Open Prison 1967–93; memb Jenner Museum Tst 1995–; memb St Francis & St Seraphim Tst 2002–05; hon advsr on materials for restoration of: Albert Memorial, repairs to St Paul's, roofing of Centre Court Br Museum; FIM 1974, FREng 1987, FRS 1988, FInstP 1992; *Books* Physical Metallurgy of Reactor Fuel Elements (ed), Vacancies (ed 1976), Metals of the Royal Society (with D West, 1999); *Recreations* writing popular articles on science; *Clubs* Cam Bowling (non playing memb); *Style*— Dr Jack Harris, MBE, FRS, FREng; ✉ Church Farm House, 28 Hopton Road, Upper Cam, Dursley, Gloucestershire GL11 5PB (tel 01453 543165, e-mail jack.harris@lineone.net)

HARRIS, John Eric; CBE (2005, MBE 1996); s of Jack Harris (d 1982), of Ilford, Essex, and Freda, *née* Jacobs (d 1979); *b* 29 April 1932; *Educ* Slough GS, Plaistow GS; *m* 1, 15 June 1958, Helene Hinda (d 1985), da of Aaron Coren (d 1960), of London; 1 s (Daniel Bruce b 1960), 1 da (Allyson b 1961); m 2, 10 Dec 1989, Jacqueline Maureen, da of Alfred Freeman (d 1989), of London, and wid of Philip Leigh; *Career* chm: Alba plc 1987–, Harvard International 1980–87, Bush Radio plc, Goodmans Industries Ltd, Satellite Technology Systems Ltd; md Harris Overseas Ltd 1963–82; dir: Alba France SA, Hinari Deutschland GmbH, Dirt Devil Ltd; chm and tstee Hélène Harris Meml Tst promoting res into ovarian cancer; hon memb British Gynaecological Cancer Soc; *Recreations* reading, theatre, opera; *Style*— John Harris, Esq, CBE; ✉ Alba plc, Harvard House, 14–16 Thames Road, Barking, Essex IG11 0HX (tel 020 8594 5533, fax 020 8594 9845, car 078 3187 7000)

HARRIS, Prof Jose Ferial; da of Leonard and Freda Chambers; *Educ* Univ of Cambridge (MA, PhD); *Career* research fell Nuffield Coll Oxford 1966–69, lectr LSE 1969–74 (sr lectr 1974–78); Univ of Oxford: fell St Catherine's Coll 1978–, lectr in modern history 1978–83, reader 1983–87, prof 1997–, Leverhulme research prof 1998–2002, prof of modern history 2002–, vice-master St Catherine's Coll 2003–05; Br Acad Res Readership 1989–91; memb Social History Soc, memb Past and Present Soc; FRHistS 1974, FBA 1994; *Books* Unemployment and Politics 1886–1914 (1972, 2 edn 1982), William Beveridge: a Biography (1977, 2 edn 1997), Private Lives Public Spirit 1870–1914 (1994, 2 edn 1995), Ferdinand Tönnies: Gemeinschaft und Gesellschaft (2000), Civil Society in British History (2003); *Recreations* long-distance walking, river boats, the lesser arts, family life; *Clubs* Oxford and Cambridge, Freemen; *Style*— Prof Jose Harris; ✉ 5 Belbroughton Road, Oxford OX2 6UZ; St Catherine's College, Oxford OX1 3UJ (e-mail jose.harris@stcatz.ox.ac.uk); Faculty of Modern History, Broad Street, Oxford OX1 3BD

HARRIS, Joseph Hugh; DL (1984); s of John Frederick Harris (d 1990); *b* 3 June 1932; *Educ* Harrow, RAC Cirencester (DipAg); *m* 1957, Anne, da of Brig L H McRobert (d 1981); 3 s; *Career* Lt 11 Hussars PAO; chm Cumbrian Newspapers Ltd 1987–2002 (formerly dir); farmer, landowner; memb Miny of Agric Northern Regnl Panel 1977–83; RASE: sr steward 1957–77, hon dir Royal Show 1978–82, vice-pres 1980–92, dep pres 1986–87, tstee 1992–; High Sheriff Cumbria 1976–77; chm: govrs Aysgarth Sch 1975–85, Grasmere Sports 1977–97 (dir 1997–), Penrith and Alston Magistrates Bench 1991–96; memb Cumbria Rural Devpt Cmmn 1990–; Liveryman Worshipful Co of Farmers; Vice Lord-Lt Cumbria 1994–; JP Penrith 1971–2002; *Recreations* shooting and field sports; *Style*— Joseph Harris, Esq, DL; ✉ West View, Bowscar, Penrith, Cumbria CA11 9PG (tel 01768 885661)

HARRIS, Keith Reginald; s of Reginald Harris, and Doris Lillian, *née* Smith; *b* 11 April 1953; *Educ* Buckhurst Hill Co HS, Mgmnt Sch Univ of Bradford (Elijah Hepworth Prize, BSc), Univ of Surrey (PhD); *Children* 2 da (Katherine Alexa b 4 June 1982, Francesca Alice b 30 May 1987), 1 s (Thomas Edward b 2 Sept 1993); *Career* assoc dir Orion Bank Ltd 1980 (credit analyst 1977–80); Morgan Grenfell & Co Ltd: asst director 1980–84, dir 1984–85, pres Morgan Grenfell Inc New York 1985–87; md Drexel Burnham Lambert Inc 1987–89, dir Drexel Burnham Lambert Holdings (UK) 1989–90, md Apax Partners & Co Corporate Finance Ltd (formerly MMG Patricof & Co) 1990–94, chief exec Samuel Montagu & Co Ltd and dir HSBC Investment Bank Ltd 1994–96, chief exec Investment Banking HSBC Investment Bank plc 1996–99, chm Football League 2000–02, exec chm Seymour Pierce Ltd 2003–; non-exec dir: CLS Holdings plc 1994–2007, Sports Internet 1999–, Benfield Greig 1999–, Wembley National Stadium Ltd 2001–, Halfords; *Recreations* watching Manchester United, playing tennis, crossword puzzles, music, reading; *Style*— Keith Harris, Esq

HARRIS, Prof Malcolm; *b* 8 November 1934; *Educ* Univ of Leeds Dental Sch (BChD), London Hosp Med Sch (MB BS), Univ of London (MD); *m* 10 Jan 1965; 1 s, 2 da; *Career* prof Dept of Oral Surgery and Oral Medicine Eastman Dental Hosp and UCH; visiting prof of oral and maxillofacial surgery Nat Univ of Singapore, emeritus prof UCL; Hon DSc: Univ of Athens, Univ of Malaya, Univ of Khartoum; FDSRCS (Eng), FFDRCSI, Hon FRCSEd; *Books* Oral Surgery (with G R Seward and D M McGowan, 1988), Fundamentals of Orthognathic Surgery (with I Reynolds, 1990), Clinical Oral Science (with S Meghji, 1990); *Recreations* work, painting, cooking; *Clubs* RSM; *Style*— Prof Malcolm Harris; ✉ 95 Wood Vale, London N10 3DL (tel and fax 020 8883 1379, e-mail malcolm.harris@ucl.ac.uk)

HARRIS, Malcolm Robert; *Career* Bovis Homes: joined 1974, memb Bd 1978, chief exec 1996–; non-exec dir: House Builders Fedn Ltd, Nat House Building Cncl; FCMA; *Style*— Malcolm Harris, Esq; ✉ Bovis Homes Group plc, The Manor House, North Ash Road, New Ash Green, Longfield, Kent DA3 8HQ

HARRIS, Prof Sir Martin Best; kt (2000), CBE (1992), DL; s of William Best Harris (d 1987), of Plymouth, and Betty Evelyn, *née* Martin; *b* 28 June 1944; *Educ* Devonport HS for Boys Plymouth, Queens' Coll Cambridge (MA), Univ of London (PhD); *m* 10 Sept 1966, Barbara Mary, da of Joseph Daniels (d 1971); 2 s (Robert b 1 July 1968, Paul b 13 June 1970); *Career* lectr in French linguistics Univ of Leicester 1967–72; Univ of Salford: sr lectr in French linguistics 1972–76, prof of Romance linguistics 1976–87, dean social science and arts 1978–81, pro-vice-chllr 1981–87; vice-chllr: Univ of Essex 1987–92, Univ of Manchester 1992–2004; dir Office of Fair Access DfES 2004–; memb UGC 1984–87 (chm NI sub ctee 1985–89); chm: UFC NI Ctee 1989–91, Nat Curriculum Working Party on Modern Languages 1989–90, Govrs Centre for Information on Language Teaching 1990–96, Africa Ctee CICHE 1991–93, HEFCE Review of Postgraduate Educn 1995–96 (memb Libraries Review Ctee 1992–93), Clinical Standards Advsy Gp 1996–99, DfEE Review of Univ Careers Services 2000; memb Cmmn for Health Improvement 1999–2002; dir Investment NW Trust Ltd 1998–2001, dep chair NW Devpt Agency Bd 2002– (memb 2001–), chair Manchester: Knowledge Capital 2003–; chm: CVCP 1997–99 (vice-chm 1995–97), NW Univs Assoc 1999–2001, USS (Universities Superannuation Scheme) Ltd 2006– (dir 1991–, dep chair 2004–06); govr: Parrs Wood HS 1982–87, Anglia Poly 1989–92, SOAS 1990–93, Colchester Sixth Form Coll 1987–92, European Univ Inst 1992–97, Univ of Plymouth 2004–; memb: Cncl Philological Soc 1985–92, Academia Europaea 1991–; hon fell: Queens' Coll Cambridge 1992, Bolton Inst 1996, Univ of Central Lancashire 1999; Hon LLD Queen's Univ Belfast 1992; Hon DUniv: Essex 1993, Keele 2007; Hon DLitt: Univ of Salford 1995, Manchester Met Univ 2000, Univ of Leicester 2003, Univ of Lincoln 2003, Univ of Ulster 2004, Univ of Manchester 2004, UMIST 2004; Hon FRCP 2005, Hon FRSE 2005; *Books* Evolution of French Syntax (1978), The Romance Verb (with N Vincent, 1983), The Romance Languages (with N Vincent, 1988, 2 edn 1990); *Recreations* walking, gardening, wine; *Style*— Prof Sir Martin Harris, CBE, DL; ✉ Northwest Development Agency, Renaissance House, PO Box 37, Centre Park, Warrington, Cheshire WA1 1XB (tel 01925 400100, fax 01925 400404)

HARRIS, Matthew Edwin Charles; s of Lewis Martin Harris, of Hove, E Sussex, and Gaye, *née* Lloyd; *b* 31 May 1965; *Educ* Charterhouse, Brighton & Hove Tech Coll, Ecole le Nôtre Paris; *m* 4 May 1996, Donna Lynette, da of Donald Davies; *Career* chef Geneva 1984–85, Patisserie Sch Paris 1985–86, chef Hilaire Restaurant London 1986–87, exec head chef Bibendum Restaurant London 1995– (sous chef 1987–95); *Recreations* travel, eating out, cinema, swimming; *Style*— Matthew Harris, Esq; ✉ Bibendum, Michelin House, 81 Fulham Road, London SW3 6RD (tel 020 7589 1481, fax 020 7823 7925)

HARRIS, His Hon Judge Michael Frank; s of Joseph Frank Harris (d 1982), of Bridgend, Glamorgan, and Edna, *née* Walters; *b* 11 January 1942; *Educ* St Bartholomew's GS Newbury, Merton Coll Oxford (BA); *m* 23 Aug 1969, Veronica, da of Ronald Edward Brend; 1 da (Bronwen Sarah b 13 Sept 1970), 1 s (Owen Joseph b 4 Oct 1972); *Career* called to the Bar Middle Temple 1965 (bencher 2003); recorder 1990–92, circuit judge (SE Circuit) 1992–; pres Ind Tbnl Services 1998–99, pres Appeals Service 1999–, chief social security and child support cmmr 2001–03; *Recreations* piano playing, amateur dramatics, walking, music, theatre, travel, reading; *Style*— His Hon Judge Michael Harris; ✉ 5th Floor, Fox Court, 14 Grays Inn Road, London WC1X 8HN

HARRIS, Nicholas Richard; s of Sidney George Harris, and Jean Elliott (d 1986); *b* 24 September 1941; *Educ* KHS and Nautical Coll General Botha South Africa, BRNC Dartmouth, Royal Naval Coll Greenwich, Royal Coll of Defence Studies; *m* 31 Dec 1966 (m dis 2006), Philippa Joan Harris, da of Col Donald Friswell Easten, MC, of Wormingford, Essex; 2 s (Rupert b 20 Oct 1967, Giles b 16 July 1973), 2 da (Jessica b 24 April 1971, Milly b 9 July 1983); *Career* qualified fixed wing pilot in Fleet Air Arm 1964–65; HMS Eagle 899 Sqdn (Sea Vixens) 1965–66, 766 Sqdn RNAS Yeovilton 1967–68, air warfare instr 764 Sqdn RNAS Lossiemouth 1969–70, USN VF121 and Topgun NAS Mirimar California 1971–72, HMS Devonshire 1973–74, Directorate of Naval Air Warfare MOD (Sea Harrier) 1975–76, CO 892 Sqdn (Phantoms) 1977, Air Warfare Course RAF Cranwell 1978, RN presentation team 1979, Directorate of Naval Manpower Planning MOD 1980–81, HMS Bristol (Falklands Campaign) 1982–84, Dep Sec Chief of Staff Ctee MOD 1986, Naval Attaché Rome 1987–89, Dir Mgmnt Strategy (Naval Personnel) MOD 1990–91, Asst Dir (AD1) Naval Staff MOD 1992–93, Dir Defence Staff MOD 1994–96, ret 1996; chm Farringdon Harris Group 1996–, special advsr to Guy's and St Thomas' Hosp Tst 1997–2004; dir: Bonvoyages SA 1998–, Spearhead Exhibitions (Central Europe) Ltd 1999–2000, Maiden Bower Ltd 2000–, Cyclotec Advanced Medical Technologies Inc 2001–06, Kaycom Inc 2003–05, Cyclotec International Ltd 2005–, Depro (GVB) Inc 2005–, KNG Inc 2007–; chm Sea Cadet Assoc (E Anglia) 1998–2005, special advsr to Sea Cadet Assoc 2000–05; MRUSI; *Recreations* sailing, most country pursuits, watching cricket; *Clubs* MCC, Lansdowne, Royal Naval Sailing Assoc; *Style*— Nicholas Harris, Esq; ✉ c/o Coutts & Co, 1 Cadogan Place, London SW1X 9PX (tel 020 7649 2611, e-mail nick.harris@maiden-bower.com)

HARRIS, Nick; s of Brian Harris, of London, and Susan, *née* Alexander; *b* 14 December 1965; *Educ* London Guildhall Univ (LLB); *Career* asst prodr Saatchi & Saatchi 1985–89, business and legal affrs exec EMI Records 1993–96, business and legal affrs exec Polygram Filmed Entertainment 1996–99, literary agent and company dir A P Watt Ltd 1999–; involved with: Jewish Nat Fund, ORT (orgn for rehabilitation through trg); *Recreations* garden design, art, books; *Clubs* Soho House; *Style*— Nick Harris, Esq; ✉ A P Watt Ltd, 20 John Street, London WC1N 2DR (tel 020 7282 3127, fax 020 7430 1952, e-mail nharris@apwatt.co.uk)

HARRIS, Nigel Henry; *b* 11 July 1924; *Educ* Perse Sch, Trinity Coll Cambridge and Middx Hosp (MA, MB BChir, FRCS); *m* Aug 1949, Elizabeth; *Career* Nat Serv RAF 1949–52; house surgn: Orthopaedic Dept Middx Hosp 1947, N Middx Hosp 1952–53; in charge of Casualty and registrar to Orthopaedic Dept King Edward Meml Hosp Ealing 1953–55, surgical registrar Mile End Hosp 1955–56, surgical registrar Fulham Hosp 1958–59 (orthopaedic registrar 1956–58), sr registrar Royal Nat Orthopaedic Hosp 1960 (registrar 1959–60), Euro travelling scholar 1962, conslt orthopaedic surgn to Thames Gp of Hosps 1963, conslt orthopaedic surgn to St Mary's Hosp London and the London Foot Hosp 1964–90, asst hon orthopaedic surgn to the Hosp for Sick Children Gt Ormond St 1964–87, Geigy scholar 1967, hon conslt orthopaedic surgn St Mary's Hosp (after ret from NHS 1990); currently private conslt in Orthopaedic Practice and in Medico-Legal Practice; orthopaedic surgn to: Football Assoc, Arsenal Football Club; med examiner: for Football League Underwriters, to General and Medical Legal Services; tstee Metropolitan Police Convalescent and Rehabilitation Tst; fell Animal Health Tst; memb: Br Orthopaedic Res Soc, Hosp Conslts and Specialists Assoc, Medico-Legal Soc; MCIArb; FBOA, FRSM, fell and memb Cncl Acad of Experts; *Books* Postgraduate Textbook of Clinical Orthopaedics (ed, 1984, 2 edn 1995), Medical Negligence (jt ed, 1990, 2 edn 1994, renamed Clinical Negligence, jt ed, 3 edn 2000); *Recreations* horse racing (owner), cricket; *Clubs* Oxford and Cambridge, MCC; *Style*— Nigel Harris, Esq; ✉ 14 Ashworth Road, London W9 (tel 020 7286 4725); 72 Harley Street, London W1 (tel 020 7636 9112, fax 020 7636 4015)

HARRIS, Paul Ian; s of Alexander Munsie (d 1988), and Sylvia, *née* Goodman (d 1989); *b* 13 December 1943; *Educ* Chatham House GS Ramsgate, Univ of Birmingham (LLM); *m* 21 June 1967, Margaret Eve, *née* Roer; 1 s (Keith Daniel b 1971), 1 da (Ruth Caroline b 1974); *Career* admitted slr 1969, ptnr Linklaters; dir Watford Palace Theatre; tstee World Student Drama Tst; memb: Law Soc, Slrs Benevolent Assoc; *Books* Day & Harris Unit Trusts (1974), Linklaters & Paines Unit Trusts The Law and Practice (1989); *Recreations* bridge, golf, cricket, watching football, theatre, cinema, sitting on committees; *Style*— Paul Harris, Esq; ✉ Linklaters, One Silk Street, London EC2Y 8HQ (tel 020 7456 2000, fax 020 7456 2222)

HARRIS, Prof Paul Lansley; s of late Joseph Harris, and Betty, *née* Lansley; *b* 14 May 1946; *Educ* Chippenham GS, Univ of Sussex (BA), Univ of Oxford (DPhil); *m* Pascale, da of Claude Torracinta; 3 s (Simon b 5 May 1991, Rémi b 23 Sept 1993, Louis b 9 Sept 1998); *Career* research fell: Center for Cognitive Studies Harvard Univ 1971–72, Dept of Experimental Psychology Univ of Oxford 1972–73; lectr Dept of Psychology Lancaster Univ 1973–76, reader in psychology Free Univ Amserdam 1976–79, lectr in psychology LSE 1979–81; Univ of Oxford: lectr in experimental psychology 1981–96, reader in experimental psychology 1996–98, prof of developmental psychology 1998–2001; prof of educn Harvard Univ 2001–, Victor S Thomas prof of educn Harvard Univ 2005–; fell St John's Coll Oxford 1981–2001 (emeritus fell 2001–), fell Center for Advanced Study in the Behavioural Scis Stanford 1992–93, Guggenheim fell 2005–; FBA 1998; *Books* Children and Emotion (1989), The Work of the Imagination (2000); also former ed British Jl of Developmental Psychology; *Recreations* cooking, writing; *Style*— Prof Paul Harris,

FBA; ✉ Larsen Hall, Appian Way, Cambridge, MA 02138, USA (e-mail paul_harris@gse.harvard.edu)

HARRIS, Philip Ian; s of Raymond Harris, of Hucknall, Nottinghamshire, and Cynthia, *née* Bunt; *b* 3 June 1965; *Educ* Friesland Comp Sch Sandiacre, Mansfield Coll of Art & Design (DATEC dipl), Bradford Coll of Art & Design (BA); *Career* artist; *Solo Exhibitions* Tricycle Gallery London 1990, Merz Contemporary Art London 1990 and 1992, Paintings Drawings and Etchings Woodlands Art Gallery London 1991, Ghent International Art Fair Belgium 1991, Beaux Arts Gallery London 1997; *Group Exhibitions* Works on Paper (Central Space Gallery London) 1988, The Spectator Art Award (Spink & Son London) Portobello Open (Taberncale London) 1989, BP Portrait Award Exhbn (Nat Portrait Gallery London) 1990 and 1993, 20th Century Art Fair (RCA London) 1995, Ghent Int Art Fair Belgium 1995, The Discerning Eye (Mall Galleries London) 1995, Small Picture Show (Beaux Arts London) 1996, Art 96 London Contemporary Art Fair 1996, Artists of Fame and Promise (Beaux Arts London) 1996, Art 97 London Contemporary Art Fair 1997, Re-presenting Representation - 11 (Arnot Art Museum NY) 1997, Art 98 London Contemporary Art Fair 1998, Take 3 (Beaux Arts London) 1998, 20th Century Art Fair (RCA London) 1998, Art 99 London Contemporary Art Fair 1999, Simmer (Beaux Arts London) 1999; Portrait of Sir Anthony Dowell (Nat Portrait Gallery); *Awards* BP Portrait Award 3rd Prize 1990, BP Portrait Award 1st Prize 1993; *Style—* Philip Harris, Esq; ✉ c/o Beaux Arts London, 22 Cork Street, London W1X 1HB (tel 020 7437 5799, fax 020 7437 5798)

HARRIS, Philip James; s of Philip John Harris, of Avenue Decelles, Montreal, Canada, and Violet Edna May, *née* Fretwell; *b* 4 October 1936; *Educ* Northampton Sch of Art, Watford Coll of Technol; *m* 1, 20 April 1959 (m dis 1977), Audrey Mary, da of Richard Stanley Flawn (d 1968), of Irthlingborough, Northants; 1 s (Philip Julian b 1964), 1 da (Susan Mary (Mrs Goodwin) b 1967); m 2, 21 March 1980, Esther Elizabeth, da of James Buchanan (d 1982), of Blunham, Beds; *Career* Northants Regt 1955, Parachute Regt 1955–58; active serv: Cyprus, Eoka Campaign, Suez (despatches); chief exec Reporter Newspapers Kent 1977–79, dir and gen mangr Middx Co Press 1979–83; md: B Lansdown & Sons Trowbridge 1983–87, Wessex Group of Newspapers Bath 1987–93; non-exec dir Southern and Western Press Ltd 1990–93; mangr NHS 1994–99; past pres SW Fedn of Newspaper Owners, former vice-pres Newsvendors Benevolent Inst, former memb CGLI Adjudication Ctee; HM gen cmmr of taxes 1992–, chm Bath, Barton Regis and Grumbaldsash div HM Gen Cmmrs of Taxes 2002–04, chm N Wessex Regnl Assoc Gen Cmmrs of Taxes 2002–, memb Nat Ctee Nat Assoc Gen Cmmrs of Income Tax 2002–05; memb Order of Bards, Ovates and Druids 1999–; MIIM 1979, memb Inst of Printing 1981, FIMgt 1983, MInstD 1985; *Recreations* walking, polo, rowing; *Clubs* Leander, Cirencester Park Polo; *Style—* Philip Harris, Esq; ✉ Wolery Twoo, 18 Palairet Close, Bradford-on-Avon, Wiltshire BA15 1US (tel 01225 864223, e-mail philipharris2@aol.com)

HARRIS, Prof (Ivor) Rex; s of John Fredrick Harris (d 1977), and Margaret Emily Harris (d 1980); *b* 27 July 1939; *Educ* Larkfield GS Chepstow, Univ of Birmingham (BSc, PhD, DSc); *m* Vera Winifred, da of Leslie Boylin; 2 s (Christopher John Edward b 9 June 1966, David James Andrew b 22 Aug 1968), 1 da (Margaret Jane b 13 July 1972); *Career* University of Birmingham: ICI research fell 1964–66, lectr Dept of Physical Metallurgy 1966–74, sr lectr of metallurgy and materials 1974–87, prof of materials science 1988–, head of sch of metallurgy and materials 1996–2001 (actg head 1989–90); lectr NATO Summer Sch Italy 1990, visiting lectr various univs worldwide; memb: Editorial Advsy Bd Jl of Alloys and Compounds, Int Steering Ctee Metal Hydride Conf Series; gp co-ordinator Concerted Euro Action on Magnets (CEAM), mission ldr Overseas Tech Experts Mission (OSTEM) USA 1987; chm: UK Magnetics Club 1988–90, Euro Material Research Soc (Strasbourg) 1988, Magnetism and Magnetic Materials Initiative SERC 1992–94, 13th Int Workshop on Rare Earth Magnets and their Application 1994, 8th Int Symposium on Magnetic Anisotropy and Coercivity in Rare-earth Metal Alloys 1994; memb: Metals and Magnetic Materials Ctee SERC 1991–94, EPSRC Functional Materials Coll; pres Birmingham Metallurgical Assoc 1992, Magnetics Panel Inst of Physics 1999–; foreign memb Nat Acad of Sci Ukraine 2000; Marie Curie individual fell 2000; FIM 1992, MIEEE 1992, FREng 1994, FInstP 2003; *Books* Hydrogen in Metals (ed with J P G Farr, 1976), Rare Earth Permanent Magnets (ed, 1989), Concerted European Action on Magnets (co-ed, 1989), Magnet Processing: Rare-earth Iron Permanent Magnets (contrib, 1996), Grain Boundaries: Their Character, Characterisation and Influence on Properties (co-ed, 2001); also author of over 500 scientific papers; *Style—* Prof Rex Harris, FREng; ✉ School of Metallurgy & Materials, The University of Birmingham, Edgbaston, Birmingham B15 2TT (tel 0121 414 5165, fax 0121 414 5247, e-mail i.r.harris@bham.ac.uk)

HARRIS, Eur Ing Dr Richard Peter; *b* 18 September 1941; *Educ* Univ of London (BSc), Univ of Bristol (PhD); *Career* jr engr Hants CC 1960–61, res engr Univ of Bristol 1964–67; Halcrows: engr 1967–69, sr engr 1969–70; Reed and Mallik: field engr 1970–73, construction mangr 1973–75; project mangr Halcrow-Ewbank 1975–80; Worley Engrg Ltd: sr project mangr 1980–82, ops dir 1982–84, md 1984–86; conslt Fletcher, Newell and Assocs 1986–87; Brown and Root Vickers Ltd: dir project servs 1987–88 (prev sr mangr), md 1988–90; md Brown and Root Engrg 1990–92, chief exec and md Brown and Root Skoda sro 1992–95, dir engrg and projects Brown and Root Civil and Services 1995–98; Brown and Root Services (Euro and Africa): dir of business execution 1998–99, exec dir and dep chief operating offr 2000–01; Kellogg, Brown and Root: chief engr until 2003, vice-pres Engrg Excellence, memb Exec Leadership Team 2001–03; head of Prog Mgmnt Servs NHS Nat Prog for IT 2003–04, chm Harris Mgmnt Services 2004–; md Howard Humphreys Ltd 1995–2001, shareholder exec Brown and Root N Africa, dir Aztec (Merton, Kingston and Wimbledon Training Enterprise Cncl); memb Bd: Halliburton NUS Environmental, Halliburton UK Ltd, Maj Projects Assoc, DNV-QA; visiting prof in engrg design Univ of Surrey; visiting lectr in mgmnt: Shell Int (The Hague), BP Mgmnt Coll, Henley Coll, Oxford Coll of Petroleum Studies, City Univ; presenter of numerous papers at int events and conferences 1973–; ACT Contract Law Battersea Coll of Technol, FEng, FICE, Eur Eng (FEANI); *Style—* Eur Ing Dr Richard Harris; ✉ Harris Management Services Ltd, St Catherines House, 5 Nuthatch Close, Ewshot, Farnham, Surrey GU10 5TN (tel 01252 851251, fax 01252 852198, e-mail dick@stcats.freeserve.co.uk)

HARRIS, Robert Brinley Joseph (Bob); s of William Brinley Harris, of Hunstanton, Norfolk, and Doria Katherine, *née* Dow; *b* 11 April 1946; *Educ* Northampton Trinity GS; *m* 1; 3 da (Mirelle b 23 Nov 1970, Emily b 2 Feb 1973, Charlotte b 30 Sept 1977), 2 s (Benjamin Brinley Howard b 17 Sept 1982, James David b 19 Nov 1986); m 2, 24 April 1991, Trudie Myerscough-Harris, da of Simon Myerscough-Walker; 2 s (Miles Simon b 2 June 1992, Dylan Joseph b 2 Sept 1994), 1 da (Florence Jayne b 21 May 1997); *Career* broadcaster and writer; fndr Time Out magazine 1968, commenced broadcasting BBC Radio 1 1970, presenter Old Grey Whistle Test (weekly rock show) BBC 2 1972–79, Radio Luxembourg 1975, Radio 210 1977, BBC Radio Oxford 1981, LBC London 1985, rejoined BBC Radio 1 1989–93, currently broadcasting: BBC Radio 2, BFBS; film debut Made 1971, prodr records for EMI and Atlantic 1973–74, released Best of The Test LP compilation 1991; estab ind prodn co WBBC 2005; hon fell Univ of Northampton 2007; *Books* Rock and Pop Mastermind (Orbis, 1985), Bob Harris Rockdates (Virgin, 1992); *Recreations* music, my family, watching Man Utd; *Style—* Bob Harris, Esq; ✉ c/o BBC Radio 2, London W1A 4WW (tel 020 7580 4468, e-mail bob.harris@bbc.co.uk, website www.bobharris.org)

HARRIS, Robert Dennis; s of late Dennis Harris, and Audrey, *née* Hardy; *b* 7 March 1957; *Educ* King Edward VII Sch Melton Mowbray, Selwyn Coll Cambridge (BA, chm Cambridge Fabian Soc, pres Cambridge Union); *m* 1988, Gillian, da of Sir Derek Hornby, *qv*; 2 da (Holly Miranda b 21 July 1990, Matilda Felicity b 5 Oct 1996), 2 s (Charlie Robert Nicholas b 17 April 1992, Samuel Orlando Hornby b 15 Nov 2000); *Career* res and film dir Current Affairs Dept BBC TV (progs incl Tonight, Nationwide and Panorama) 1978–81; reporter: Newsnight 1981–85, Panorama 1985–87; political ed Observer 1987–89, political reporter This Week (Thames TV) 1988–89, political columnist Sunday Times 1989–92 and 1996–97; commended Columnist of the Year Br Press Awards 1992; FRSL 1996; *Books* A Higher Form of Killing - The History of Gas and Germ Warfare (with Jeremy Paxman, 1982), Gotcha! - The Media, The Government and The Falklands Crisis (1983), The Making of Neil Kinnock (1984), Selling Hitler - The Story of the Hitler Diaries (1986, televised 1991), Good and Faithful Servant - The Unauthorised Biography of Bernard Ingham (1990), Fatherland (novel, 1992, filmed 1994), Enigma (novel, 1995, filmed 2001), Archangel (novel, 1998), Pompeii (novel, 2003), The Ghost (novel, 2007); *Style—* Robert Harris, Esq; ✉ The Old Vicarage, Kintbury, Berkshire RG17 9TR

HARRIS, Robert Frederick (Bob); s of Frederick Cecil Harris (d 1972), of Ipswich, Suffolk, and Ellen Rose Mary, *née* Damant; *b* 8 September 1943; *Educ* Northgate GS Ipswich, Kingston Coll of Art (BA); *m* 26 July 1969, Jayne Susan, da of Frederick Gibson; 1 da (Eleanor Volante Harris b 2 April 1977); *Career* art dir (advtg agencies): Collett Dickenson Pearce 1968–73, Sharps Advertising 1974–76, Geers Gross 1976–77, Marsteller 1977–78, Davidson Pearce (now BMP DDB) 1978–85; freelance photographer 1985– (various clients incl Tesco, Sainsbury, Waitrose, King & Barnes Brewery and Northern Rock Building Society); Pilots and their Favourite Aircraft (solus exhbn) Biggin Hill Aerodrome, Goodwood; Freeman City of London 1987, Liveryman Worshipful Co of Loriners 1987 (memb Ct of Assts 2002); memb Assoc of Photographers (chm 1991, 1992 and 1993, chm Awards Ctee 1992, 1993 and 1994); *Recreations* gardening, aviation; *Clubs* Aldersgate Ward; *Style—* Bob Harris, Esq; ✉ 26 Albany Park Road, Kingston upon Thames, Surrey KT2 5SW (tel 020 8546 4018)

HARRIS, Prof Robert James; s of Charles William Harris (d 1996), of Sanderstead, Surrey, and Lucy Dorothea Emily, *née* Weller (d 2000); *b* 10 March 1947; *Educ* The GS Enfield, Univ of Leeds (BA), McMaster Univ (MA), Univ of Hull (PhD); *m* 1, 23 Feb 1974 (m dis 2000), Janet Nuttall, da of James Nuttall Horne (d 1987), of Ewell, Surrey; 2 da (Ruth b 1978, Amelia b 1979), 1 s (George b 1982); m 2, 20 July 2002, Josephine Yee-kei, da of Chun-yau Tsang, of Tuen Mun, Hong Kong; *Career* probation offr Middx 1973–75; lectr: Brunel Univ 1975–77, Univ of Leicester 1977–87; Univ of Hull: prof 1987–2004, pro-vice-chllr 1993–98; asst dir Quality Assurance Agency for HE 2004–; *Books* Welfare, Power and Juvenile Justice (1987), Crime, Criminal Justice and the Probation Service (1992), Secure Accommodation in Child Care (1993), Probation Round the World (1995), Overseas Students in Higher Education (1997), Mentally Disordered Offenders (1999), Political Corruption (2003), The Politics and Economics of Drug Production on the Pakistan-Afghanistan Border (2003); *Recreations* antiquarian book collecting, travelling, talking, working; *Style—* Prof Robert Harris; ✉ 31 Sutherland Square, London SE17 3EQ (tel and fax 020 7701 6534); The Quality Assurance Agency for Higher Education, Southgate House, Gloucester GL1 1UB (tel 01452 557000, e-mail r.harris@qaa.ac.uk)

HARRIS, Robert William (Bob); s of Frank Harris (d 1992), of Birmingham, and Joan, *née* Lee (d 1995); *b* 9 November 1944; *Educ* George Dixon GS Edgbaston; *m* 1, Carol Lillian; 1 da (Zoë b 1971); m 2, Carol Ann; 2 s (Dominic b 1976, Adam b 1985); *Career* sports writer and sports ed: Birmingham Planet 1963–66, Thomson Regional Newspapers 1966–86; sports writer and chief football writer Today 1986–89, exec sports ed Sunday Mirror 1993–95 (sports ed 1989–93), ed dir and ed-in-chief Sport First 1997–99 (ed 1996–97); contrib: News of the World, Talksport, Radio Five, Skysport, BBC News 24; major events covered incl: 9 Olympic Games 1972–2004, 7 football World Cups, 8 Cwlth Games, World Athletics Championships, Wimbledon 1969–93 and 2005–06, various world title fights, cricket World Cup; *Books* No Half Measures (with Graeme Souness, 1985), Touch and Go (with Steve Coppell, 1985), More Than Somewhat (with Bruce Grobbelaar, 1986), World Cup Diary (with Bobby Robson, 1986), Bring on the Clown (with Bruce Grobbelaar, 1988), Against the Odds (with Bobby Robson, 1990), Kevin Keegan Autobiography (co-author, 1997), An Englishman Abroad (with Bobby Robson, 1998), Sweet FA (with Graham Kelly, 1999), Sir Viv (with Sir Vivian Richards, 2000), Psycho (with Stuart Pearce, 2000), Sir Garfield Sobers (co-author, 2002), Dennis Lillee: the Autobiography (2003), King John (with John Charles, 2003), The King (with Denis Law, 2003), Sir Bobby Robson: Living the Game (2003), Butcher! (with Terry Butcher, 2005), Pure Gold (with David Gold, 2006); *Style—* Bob Harris, Esq; ✉ 25 Broadheath Drive, Chislehurst, Kent BR7 6EU (tel 020 8289 3000, fax 020 8467 0735, e-mail bobharrissport@hotmail.com)

HARRIS, Prof Robin Kingsley; s of Alfred William Harris (d 1964), of Hornchurch, Essex, and Nellie, *née* Missen (d 1987); *b* 23 December 1936; *Educ* Royal Liberty GS Romford, Magdalene Coll Cambridge (MA, PhD, ScD); *m* 6 Aug 1960, Maureen Elizabeth, da of James Samuel Reardon (d 1968), of Langley, Berks; 1 s (Nigel b 1962); *Career* fell in independent res Mellon Inst Pittsburgh 1962–64; prof of chemistry UEA 1980–84 (lectr 1964–70, sr lectr 1970–73, reader 1973–80), emeritus prof of chemistry Univ of Durham 2002– (prof 1984–2002); chm Instrumentation Panel SERC 1986–89, sec-gen Int Soc of Magnetic Resonance 1986–92; author and co-author of 510 research publications; Royal Soc of Chemistry Medals: Chem Instrumentation 1985, Analytical Spectroscopy 1998; FRSC, CChem; *Books* Nuclear Magnetic Resonance Spectroscopy: A Physicochemical View (1983), Encyclopedia of Nuclear Magnetic Resonance (9 vols, jt ed-in-chief with D M Grant, 2002); *Recreations* gardening; *Style—* Prof Robin K Harris; ✉ Department of Chemistry, University of Durham, South Road, Durham DH1 3LE (tel 0191 334 2021, fax 0191 384 4737, e-mail r.k.harris@durham.ac.uk)

HARRIS, Dr Roger James; s of Sidney George Harris (ka 1940), of Northampton, and Alfreda Mabel, *née* Sibley; *b* 29 November 1937; *Educ* Northampton GS, Univ of Bristol Med Sch (MB ChB, MD); *m* 20 April 1963, Mary Jennifer Evans; 3 da (Sarah Jane b 1964, Katherine (Kate) Martha b 1980, Emmeline (Mimi) Louisa May b 1982), 1 s (Simon John b 1967); *Career* former conslt The Royal Hosps Tst Royal London Hosp, sr lectr in child health London Hosp Med Coll 1975–2002, former chair Infant and Child Nutrition Gp Tower Hamlets PCT, currently sr lectr in child health Barts and the London Sch of Medicine and Dentistry Queen Mary Coll Univ of London; author of articles on paediatrics; examiner in paediatrics for RCP and RCPCH, systems dir for human devpt module in undergraduate curriculum; FRCP 1986, FRCPCH 1997; *Recreations* theatre, opera, umpire for league cricket in Essex; *Style—* Dr Roger Harris; ✉ The Children's Department, The Royal London Hospital, Whitechapel, London E1 1BB (tel 020 7377 7799, fax 020 7377 7743, e-mail roger.harris1@btinternet.com)

HARRIS, Rolf; CBE (2006, OBE, MBE), AM; s of Cromwell Harris (d 1980), of Bassendean, WA, and Agnes Margaret Robbins (d 1994); *b* 30 March 1930, Bassendean, WA; *m* 10 March 1958, Alwen Myfanwy Hughes; 1 da; *Career* television personality, musician, songwriter and painter; work exhibited at Nat Gall London 2002, cmmned to paint portrait of Queen Elizabeth II to celebrate her 80th birthday 2005; patron PHAB, patron Children in Hosp and Animal Therapy Assoc (CHATA); Hon Dr Edith Cowan Univ Perth; hon memb RSBA; *Television* presenter: Small Time 1955, Musical Box 1959, Rolf's Walkabout, Cartoon Time, The Rolf Harris Show 1967–71, It's Rolf on Saturday OK?,

Rolf's Cartoon Club 1989–93, Animal Hospital 1994–, Cat Crazy 1995–97, Rolf! 1996, Rolf's Amazing World of Animal's 1998–2001, Rolf On Art 2001–, Rolf at the Royal Albert Hall 2003, Test Your Pet 2004, Rolf Harris' Star Portraits 2004–, The Queen by Rolf 2006, A Lifetime in Paint 2007; appearances incl: Hancock's Half Hour 1957, The Andy Williams Show 1969, This is Your Life 1995, Goodnight Sweetheart 1998; *Film* incl: Crash Drive 1959, The Little Convict 1979 (also composed musical score); *Albums* incl: Didgereely Do All That 1994, Can You Tell What it is Yet? 1997, The Definitive Rolf Harris 1998, Bootleg 1 1999, 70/30 2000, King Rolf 2001; *Singles* incl: Tie me Kangaroo Down Sport, Sun Arise, Two Little Boys, Stairway to Heaven, Fine Day; *Books* incl: Can You Tell What It Is Yet (autobiography, 2001), Rolf on Art (2002); *Style*— Rolf Harris, Esq, CBE, AM; ✉ c/o Billy Marsh Associates Ltd, 76A Grove End Road, London NW8 9ND (website www.rolfharris.com)

HARRIS, Rosemary; da of Gp Capt Stafford Berkeley Harris, DFC, AFC, RAF (d 1952), and Enid Maud, *née* Campion (d 1942); *Educ* St Helen's Sch Abingdon, All Hallows' Sch Ditchingham, RADA; *m* 1, 1960 (m dis 1967), Ellis Rabb; m 2, 1967, John Marsden Ehle; 1 da (Jennifer Anne b 1969); *Career* actress; Hon Dr: Smith Coll 1968, Wake Forest Univ 1976, North Carolina Sch of the Arts 1980; *Theatre* incl: Climate of Eden (Broadway, Theatre World Award) 1952, The Seven Year Itch (London) 1953–54, Hamlet and Uncle Vanya (NT) 1964–65, The Lion in Winter (Broadway, Tony Award) 1966, Plaza Suite (London, Evening Standard Award) 1969, The Merchant of Venice (Broadway) 1973, A Streetcar Named Desire (Broadway) 1973, All my Sons (London) 1980, Heartbreak House (London and Broadway) 1983, A Pack of Lies (Broadway) 1984, Hayfever (Broadway) 1985, Best of Friends (London) 1989, Steel Magnolias (London) 1990, Lost in Yonkers (Broadway) 1991, Arsenic and Old Lace (Chichester) 1991, Preserving Mr Panmure (Chichester) 1991, Lost in Yonkers (London) 1992, In the Summer House (Lyric Hammersmith) 1993, An Inspector Calls (Broadway) 1994, Women of Troy (RNT) 1995, A Delicate Balance (Broadway) 1996, Waiting in the Wings (Broadway) 1999, All Over (Off Broadway) 2002 (Obie Award); *Television* incl: Twelfth Night, A Tale of Two Cities, Dial M For Murder, Wuthering Heights, Notorious Woman (Emmy Award), The Holocaust (Golden Globe Award), To The Lighthouse, The Camomile Lawn, Summers Day Dream, Death of a Salesman, Belonging; *Film* incl: The Shiralee, Beau Brummel, The Boys From Brazil, The Ploughman's Lunch, Crossing Delancey, The Bridge, Tom and Viv (Academy Award nomination), Hamlet, My Life So Far, Sunshine, Blow Dry, Spiderman, Spiderman 2, Spiderman 3, Before the Devil Knows You're Dead; *Style*— Ms Rosemary Harris; ✉ c/o ICM Ltd, Oxford House, 76 Oxford Street, London W1N 0AX (tel 020 7636 6565, fax 020 7323 0101)

HARRIS, Prof Roy; s of Harry Harris (d 1978), and Emmie Jessie, *née* Oaten (d 1978); *b* 24 February 1931; *Educ* Queen Elizabeth Hosp Bristol, St Edmund Hall Oxford (MA, DPhil), SOAS Univ of London (PhD); *m* 14 July 1955, Rita Doreen, *née* Shulman; 1 da (Laura Doe b 1959); *Career* lectr Univ of Leicester 1957–60; Univ of Oxford: lectr 1960–76, fell and tutor in romance philology Keble Coll Oxford 1967–76, prof of romance languages 1976–77, prof of gen linguistics 1978–88, emeritus prof 1988; prof of English language Univ of Hong Kong 1988–91, dir d'Études Associé École Pratique des Hautes Études Paris 1991–92, fell of the univ profs and prof of modern foreign languages and literature Boston Univ 1993–95; hon fell St Edmund Hall Oxford 1987; FRSA 1986; *Books* Synonymy and Linguistic Analysis (1973), The Language-Makers (1980), The Language Myth (1981), F de Saussure, Course in General Linguistics (trans 1983), The Origin of Writing (1986), Reading Saussure (1987), The Language Machine (1987), Language, Saussure and Wittgenstein (1988), La Sémiologie de l'Ecriture (1994), Signs of Writing (1995), The Language Connection (1996), Signs, Language and Communication (1996), Introduction to Integrational Linguistics (1998), Rethinking Writing (2000), Saussure and his Interpreters (2001), The Necessity of Artspeak (2003), The Linguistics of History (2004), The Semantics of Science (2005), Definition in Theory and Practice (with C M Hutton, 2007); *Recreations* cricket, modern art and design; *Style*— Prof Roy Harris; ✉ 2 Paddox Close, Oxford OX2 7LR (tel 01865 554256)

HARRIS, Russell James; QC (2003); s of Donald Harris, and Jean, *née* Hall; *b* Tredegar, Gwent; *Educ* Heolddu Comp Sch Bargoed, St John's Coll Cambridge (MA, Larmour Award, MacMahon scholar); *m* 7 Aug 1999, Nicola, *née* Richards; 1 da (Elinor Catrin b 26 Oct 2000), 1 s (Huw Meredydd b 2 Dec 2003); *Career* barr specialising in public and planning law 1986–; memb Planning and Environment Law Assoc; *Books* Environmental Law (2000); *Recreations* rugby football, the sea around Ramsey Island St David's; *Clubs* London Welsh RFC; *Style*— Russell Harris, Esq, QC; ✉ Landmark Chambers, 180 Fleet Street, London EC4A 2HG (tel 020 7430 1221)

HARRIS, Sandra; da of C Harris (d 1991), of Perth, Aust, and Rae, *née* McPherson (d 2002); *b* 18 January 1946; *Educ* Methodist Ladies' Coll Perth; *m* 1972, Jafar Ramini, of Palestine and London; 2 s (Nidal Jafar b 1973, Tarek Jafar b 1975), 1 da (Kareema b 1982); *Career* reporter/interviewer World At One (BBC Radio 4) 1967–69; Thames TV 1969–81; reporter/interviewer Today Programme, Thames at 6 and Thames News, writer/researcher Take Two, prodr/presenter People in the News and Sandra; freelance broadcaster and writer work with Sunday Times, Channel 4 and others; Headway Publications: ed Global Business 1986–88, ed Dream Journeys (Japanese language magazine) 1992–2000, Above the Clouds (British Airways) and ed People page Highlife Magazine (British Airways) 1988–89, ed In Britain Magazine 1989–92; ed Business Life Premier Magazines 1992–2001; winner Silver award for travel writing England for Excellence Awards 1990; *Books* The Nice Girl's Handbook (1981), The Double Bed Book (1983), Venice Revisited (2003); *Recreations* playing tennis badly, dead-heading roses, behaving foolishly with my children; *Style*— Ms Sandra Harris; ✉ Sandra Harris Associates, 171 Cranley Gardens, London N10 3AG (tel 020 8444 6562, fax 020 8444 2848, e-mail sandra@highlyacclaimed.co.uk)

HARRIS, Simeon George (Sim); s of George Herbert Harris (d 1997), of Birmingham, and Kathleen Mary, *née* Bull (d 1978); *b* 26 July 1946; *Educ* Kings Norton GS Birmingham; *m* Oct 1969, Helen Patricia, da of Howard George Barlow; 2 da (Eleanor Jane b 15 July 1973, Victoria Anne b 16 June 1977); *Career* BBC: joined 1965, trained as camera and sound technician in studio, outside broadcasts and film, asst sound recordist 1967–69, news sound recordist and cameraman 1969–82, memb project team introducing electronic news gathering (ENG) to BBC 1979, held hostage for six days in London Iranian Embassy Siege until rescued by SAS 1980; ops mangr TV-am 1982–83 (from start of franchise); Central Independent Television Birmingham: head of film and ENG 1983–86, head of operational resources 1986–88, controller of resources 1988–90, controller of operations 1990–92; controller of operations and engrg Westcountry Television Plymouth 1992–94; md Racecourse Technical Services 1994–; memb RTS 1983, FBKSTS 1990; *Books* Hostage (with Chris Cramer, 1981); *Recreations* golf, sailing; *Style*— Sim Harris, Esq

HARRIS, Thomas George; KBE (2002), CMG (1995); s of Kenneth James Harris (d 1995), of Ferndown, Dorset, and Dorothy, *née* Barrett; *b* 6 February 1945; *Educ* Mercers' Sch, Haberdashers' Aske's, Gonville & Caius Coll Cambridge; *m* 21 Oct 1967, Mei-Ling, da of Kono Hwang (d 1976), of Kobe, Japan; 3 s (Ian Kenneth b 1969, Paul David b 1970, Simon Christopher b 1984); *Career* asst princ Bd of Trade 1966–68, third sec Br Embassy Tokyo 1969–71, asst private sec to Min for Aerospace 1971–72, princ Dept of Trade and Indust 1972–76, Cabinet Office 1976–78, princ private sec to Sec of State for Trade and Indust 1978–79, asst sec Civil Aviation Policy DTI 1979–83, commercial cnsllr Br Embassy Washington 1983–88, head of chancery Br High Cmmn Lagos 1988–90, Br dep high cmmr Nigeria 1990–91, head African Dept (Equatorial) FCO 1991–94, ambass Korea 1994–97, DG for Export Promotion DTI 1997–99, DG Trade and Investment in USA and HM consul-gen NY 1999–2004; vice-chm Standard Chartered Bank 2004–, non-exec dir Biocompatibles Int plc 2005–; dir Imperial War Museum, tstee Asia House; *Recreations* reading; *Style*— Sir Thomas Harris, KBE, CMG; ✉ 18 Telfords Yard, 6–8 The Highway, London E1W 2BQ (tel 020 7702 0967)

HARRIS, Tom; MP; s of Tom Harris, and Rita Ralston; *Educ* Garnock Acad Ayrshire, Napier Coll (HND Journalism); *m* 1998; *Career* trainee reporter East Kilbride News 1986–88, reporter Paisley Daily Express 1988–90, press offr Lab Pty in Scot 1990–92, press offr Strathclyde Regnl Cncl 1993–96, PR mangr E Ayrshire Cncl 1996–98, chief PR and mktg offr Strathclyde Passenger Tport Exec 1998–2001; MP (Lab) Glagow Cathcart 2001–, Parly under sec of state for transport 2006–; chair Cathcart Lab Pty 1998–2000; *Recreations* tennis, cinema, astronomy; *Style*— Tom Harris, Esq, MP; ✉ House of Commons, London SW1A 0AA (tel 020 7219 8237, e-mail tomharrismp@parliament.uk, website www.tomharris.com); Constituency Office tel 0141 649 9780

HARRIS, Valentina; da of Contessa Fiammetta Bianca Maria Sforza; *Educ* St George's English Sch Rome, Scuola di Alta Cucina Cordon Bleu Sch Rome (dips in teaching and cooking); *m* (m dis), Bob Harris, *qv*; 2 s (Ben b 17 Sept 1982, Jamie b 19 Nov 1985); *Career* authority on Italian food and food culture; reg appearances on TV and radio incl: School Dinners 1999, own TV series Italian Regional Cookery (BBC 2) 1990 (nominated Best Cookery Series Glenfiddich Awards), Cucina Valentina (two series) 2000 and 2001; contrib numerous nat newspapers and magazines, lectr/numerous live cooking demonstrations across Europe and Australasia; mangr Edible Creativity (prodn of food and beverage mktg events), opened Villa Valentina Italian cookery sch Tuscany 2000, product conslt (Italian food) Tesco plc; memb: Guild of Food Writers 1992, Int Assoc of Culinary Professionals 1993; *Books* Perfect Pasta (1984, 2 edn 1991), Pasta (1984, 2 edn 1985), Regional Italian Cookery (1986, one of series ed by Jill Norman, Glenfiddich Award 1987, 2 edn 1991), Edible Italy: A Travelling Gourmet's Guide (1988), Southern Italian Cooking (1988, 2 edn 1990), Recipes from an Italian Farmhouse (1989, nominated Best Euro Food Book James Beard Awards 1991), Valentina's Regional Italian Cookery (1990), Valentina's Italian Family Feast (1990), The Cooking of Tuscany (1992), Valentina's Complete Italian Cookery Course (1992), Instant Italian (1992), Southern Italian Cooking (1993), Simply Italian (1995), Valentina Harris Cooks Italian (1996) What Pasta, Which Sauce? (1998), Risotto! Risotto! (1998), Italia! Italia! (1999), Valentina's 4 Seasons Cookbook (2000); *Style*— Ms Valentina Harris; ✉ e-mail villaval@dircon.co.uk, website www.villavalentina.com

HARRIS OF HARINGEY, Baron (Life Peer UK 1998), of Hornsey in the London Borough of Haringey; (Jonathan) Toby Harris; s of Prof Harry Harris, FRS (d 1994), of Pennsylvania, USA, and Muriel, *née* Hargest; *b* 11 October 1953; *Educ* Haberdashers' Aske's, Trinity Coll Cambridge (BA); *m* 7 April 1979, Ann Sarah, da of Stephen Austen Herbert (d 1988); 2 s (Hon James Phillip b 1981, Hon Matthew Anthony b 1984), 1 da (Hon Francesca Rebekah Bryony Herbert b 1999); *Career* Econ Div Bank of England 1975–79, dep dir Electricity Consumers' Cncl 1983–86 (joined 1979), dir Assoc of Community Health Cncls for Eng and Wales 1987–98, chm Toby Harris Associates 1998–; cncllr (Lab) Haringey BC 1978–2002 (chm Social Servs Ctee 1982–87, ldr 1987–1999), memb London Assembly (Lab) Brent and Harrow 2000–04 (memb Mayor's Advsy Cabinet 2000–04, ldr Lab Gp 2000–04); memb Home Office Advsy Cncl on Race Rels 1993–97, memb Human Rights Act Task Force 1999–2001, chair All-Pty Parly Gp on Policing 2005–, treas Parly IT Ctee 2005–, vice-chair All-Party Parly Gp on Road Safety 2006–, memb House of Lords Select Ctee Inquiry on Personal Internet Security 2006–07; chm Univ of Cambridge Lab Club 1973, pres Cambridge Union Soc 1974, nat chm Young Fabian Gp 1976–77, chm Hornsey Lab Pty 1978, 1979 and 1980, memb Lab Pty Nat Policy Forum 1992–2004, co-opted memb Lab Pty Local Govt Policy Ctee 1993–2004; Local Govt Assoc: chm Lab Gp 1996–2004, memb Exec 1999–2004, vice-pres 2005–, memb Community Safety Panel 1997–98, memb Social Exclusion Panel 1998–99; chm: Assoc of London Authorities 1993–95 (chm Social Servs Ctee 1984–88, dep chm 1990–93), Assoc of London Govt 1995–2000, Local Govt Anti-Poverty Unit 1994–96; memb: Ctee of the Regions of the EU 1994–2002, Public Sector Advsy Cncl Anite 2005–06; jt chm London Pride Partnership 1995–98, jt chm London Waste Action 1997–2000, chm Wembley National Stadium Tst 1997–; memb: London Drug Policy Forum 1990–98, Nat Nursery Examination Bd 1992–94, Bd London First 1993–2002, Jt London Advsy Panel (Cabinet sub-ctee for London) 1996–97, London Pension Funds Authy 1998–2000, London Devpt Partnership Bd 1998–2000; special advsr Bd Transport for London 2004–; memb Met Police Ctee 1998–2000, chm Metropolitan Police Authy 2000–04, memb (representing Home Sec) Met Policy Authy 2004–, vice-pres Assoc of Police Authorities 2007– (memb Exec 2000–06); memb NHS Charter Advisors' Gp 1997–98, memb Ctee on the Med Effects of Air Pollution 1997–2002, non-exec dir London Ambulance Services NHS Tst 1998–2005; trg advsr Infolog Ltd 1998–2005, conslt Harrogate Mgmnt Centre 1998–2004, conslt advsr KPMG 1999–; dep chm AMA 1991–96 (chm Social Servs Ctee 1986–93); chm LBTC - Trg for Care 1986–94; sr assoc The King's Fund 1999–2004; dep chm Nat Fuel Poverty Forum 1981–86, pres Haringey Foster Care Assoc 1982–87, memb Exec Cncl RNIB 1993–94, memb Exec Ctee Royal Assoc for Disability and Rehabilitation 1990–93; tstee: Evening Standard Blitz Meml Appeal 1995–99, Help for Health Tst 1995–97, The Learning Agency 1996–97; govr: St Mary's Jr and Infants Schs 1978–96, Sch of St David and St Katharine 1978–96, Nat Inst for Social Work 1986–94; patron The Larches 2002–04, vice-patron Vocal Eyes 2004, vice-patron Artificial Heart Fund 2004; memb Advsy Bd The Three Faiths Forum 2003–; memb Ct Univ of Middx 1995–; Hon Dr Univ of Middlesex 1999; Freeman City of London 1998; FRSA 1993; *Books* Why Vote Labour? (with Nick Butler and Neil Kinnock, 1979), The Economics of Prosperity (contrib, 1980), Energy and Social Policy (ed with Jonathan Bradshaw, 1983), Rationing in Action (contrib, 1993), Whistleblowing in the Health Service: Accountability, Law and Professional Practice (contrib, 1994); *Style*— The Rt Hon the Lord Harris of Haringey; ✉ House of Lords, London SW1A 0PW

HARRIS OF PECKHAM, Baron (Life Peer UK 1996), of Peckham in the London Borough of Southwark; Sir Philip Charles Harris; kt (1985); s of Charles William Harris, MC, and Ruth Ellen, *née* Ward; *b* 15 September 1942; *Educ* Streatham GS; *m* 1960, Dame Pauline Norma, *née* Chumley; 3 s, 1 da; *Career* Harris Queensway plc: chm 1964–88, chief exec 1987–88; chm: Harris Ventures Ltd 1988–, C W Harris Properties Ltd 1988–97, Carpetright plc 1993– (dir 1988–93); dir Harveys Holdings plc 1986–99; non-exec dir: Fisons plc 1986–94, Great Universal Stores plc 1986–2004, Molyneux Estates plc 1990–95, Matalan 2004–; chm Guy's and Lewisham NHS Tst 1991–93, vice-chm Lewisham Hosp NHS Tst 1993–97; memb: Cncl of Govrs UMDS 1984–98 (hon fell 1992), Ct of Patrons RCOG 1984–; chm Generation Tst 1984–, dep chm Cons Pty Treasurers 1993–97; memb Br Show Jumping Assoc 1974–; Hambro Business Man of the Year 1983; Freeman City of London 1992; fell Goldsmiths Coll London 1995, hon fell Oriel Coll Oxford 1989; Hon FRCR 1992; FGCL 1995, FKC 1998; *Recreations* cricket, show jumping, tennis; *Style*— The Rt Hon Lord Harris of Peckham; ✉ Carpetright plc, Amberley House, New Road, Rainham, Essex RM13 8QN

HARRIS OF RICHMOND, Baroness (Life Peer UK 1999), of Richmond in the County of North Yorkshire; Angela Felicity Harris; DL (N Yorks) 1994; da of Rev George Henry Hamilton Richards, and Eva, *née* Lindley; *b* 4 January 1944; *Educ* Canon Slade GS Bolton, Ealing Hotel Catering Coll; *m* 1, 1965 (m dis 1974), Philip Martin Bowles; 1 s (Mark John

Hamilton Bowles); m 2, 1976, John Philip Roger Harris; *Career* memb N Yorks CC 1981–2001 (first woman chair 1991–92), chm N Yorks Police Authy 1994–2001, dep chm Assoc of Police Authorities 1997–2001, former JP N Yorks, mayor of Richmond 1993–94; pres Nat Assoc of Chaplains to the Police 2002–, vice-pres Local Govt Assoc 2002–05; patron: Lister House Br Legion, WAFE, Northern Defence Industries, Hospice Homecare; *Recreations* music, reading political biographies; *Style*— The Baroness Harris of Richmond, DL; ✉ House of Lords, London SW1A 0PW (tel 020 7219 6709)

HARRISON, Prof Alan; TD (1983, bar 1989 and 1995); s of Lt-Col John Thomas West Harrison, TD, of West Kirby, Wirral, and Mona Evelyn, *née* Gee; *b* 24 July 1944; *Educ* Rydal Sch Colwyn Bay, Welsh Nat Sch of Med Dental Sch (BDS, PhD); *m* 1, (m dis 1980), Pauline Lilian, *née* Rendell; 1 da (Jane Lorrie b 11 March 1970), 1 s (Mark Richard b 26 Aug 1973); m 2, 1 Oct 1982, Margaret Ann, da of Alan William Frost (d 1973), of Leicester; 2 da (Kathryn Ruth b 24 Feb 1984, Sally Deborah b 24 April 1985); *Career* OC 390 Field Dental Team 1971–73, CO 308 Evacuation Hosp RAMC (V) 1989–94 (2 i/c 1988–89, training offr 1984–88), CO 306 Field Hosp RAMC (V) 1994–95; lectr Dept of Restorative Dentistry Dental Sch Cardiff 1970–78, visiting asst prof Univ of S Carolina USA 1974–75, sr lectr and hon conslt Sch of Dentistry Univ of Leeds; Univ of Bristol: prof of dental care of the elderly and head Dept of Prosthodontics and Periodontology 1987–94, head Dental Sch 1990–2001, head Dept of Oral and Dental Science 1994–2001; emeritus prof 2005–; memb General Dental Cncl 1994–2003; Hon Col Cmdt RADC 1996–2001, QHDS 1996–99; hon fell Cardiff Univ 2006; fell Acad of Dental Materials 1992; FDSRCS 1971, FDSRCSE 2000 (ad hominem); *Books* Overdentures in General Dental Practice (1988), Complete Dentures - Problem Solving (1999); *Recreations* tennis, walking, DIY schemes; *Style*— Prof Alan Harrison, TD

HARRISON, HE (William) Alistair; CVO (1996); s of William K Harrison, of Newcastle upon Tyne, and (Alice) Rita Harrison; *b* 14 November 1954, Guisborough, N Yorks; *Educ* Royal GS Newcastle upon Tyne, UC Oxford, Birkbeck Coll London (Dip Economics); *m* 1, 1981 (m dis 1991), Theresa Mary, *née* Morrison; m 2, 1996, Sarah Judith, *née* Wood; 2 da (Matilda b 1999, Eliza b 2003), 1 s (Ralph (twin) b 2003); *Career* diplomat; entered HM Dip Serv 1977, desk offr NATO Section Defence Dept FCO 1977–78, Polish language trg 1978–79, third then second sec (Chancery) Warsaw 1979–82, first sec FCO 1982–84, private sec to Parly Under Sec FCO 1984–86, first sec (economic) UK Mission to UN NY 1987–92, dep head Middle East Dept FCO 1992–95, cnsllr and dep head of mission Warsaw 1995–98, seconded as foreign policy advsr European Cmmn Brussels 1998–2000, cnsllr (political) UK Mission to UN NY 2000–03, head UN Dept (later Int Orgns Dept) FCO 2003–05, high cmmr to Zambia 2005–; *Recreations* music (especially opera), mathematics (studying for Open Univ degree); *Style*— HE Mr Alistair Harrison, CVO; ✉ c/o Foreign & Commonwealth Office (Lusaka), King Charles Street, London SW1A 2AH

HARRISON, Prof Andrew; s of Prof Martin Harrison, of Keele, Staffs, and Wendy Hanford, *née* Hindle; *b* 3 October 1959; *Educ* Newcastle-under-Lyme Sch, St John's Coll Oxford (MA, DPhil, Gibbs Prize); *m* 10 Dec 1988, Alison Charlotte, *née* Ironside-Smith; 3 da (Catriona Charlotte b 10 Aug 2002, Eleanor Elizabeth b 9 Feb 2004, Rebecca Rachel b 29 Dec 2005); *Career* Fereday fell St John's Coll Oxford 1985–88, res fell McMaster Univ Canada 1988–89, Royal Soc univ research fell 1990–92; Univ of Edinburgh: lectr Chemistry Dept 1992–96, reader 1996–99, prof of solid state chemistry 1999–, dir Centre for Science at Extreme Conditions 2001–05, seconded as assoc dir Institut Laue-Langevin Grenoble 2006–; Nuffield research fell 1997–98, visiting prof Shanghai Teachers' Univ China 2002–; Eminent Scientist Award Riken Japan 2000–03; memb Sch Cncl Newcastle-under-Lyme Sch 2001–; CChem, MRSC 1995, FRSE 2002; *Publications* Fractals in Chemistry (1995); author of over 100 reports and pubns in scientific jls; *Recreations* hill walking, running, cycling on and off road, drinking British beer; *Style*— Prof Andrew Harrison; ✉ Institut Laue-Langevin, 6 rue Jules Horowitz, BP156–18042, Grenoble, France (tel 00 33 4 76 20 71 00, e-mail harrison@ill.fr)

HARRISON, Prof Brian David Walter; s of Joseph Harrison (d 1955), and Constance Jennings, *née* Horsfall (d 1994), of Lytham St Annes; *b* 24 April 1943; *Educ* Shrewsbury, St John's Coll Cambridge (MA, MB BChir), Guy's Hosp Med Sch London (LRCP, MRCS); *m* 13 July 1968, Jennifer Anne, da of Dr John Fisher Stokes, of Stoke Row, Oxfordshire; 1 s (Ben b 1970), 1 da (Nicola b 1974); *Career* house physician Guy's Hosp 1967–68, house surgn Bolingbroke Hosp London 1968–69, SHO New Cross Hosp London 1969, jr registrar cardiology and gen med Guy's Hosp 1969–70, hon clinical lectr in physiology Brompton Hosp 1971–72 (house physician 1970–71), registrar to Med Professorial Unit Westminster Hosp 1971–72, clinical lectr in physiology Brompton Hosp 1973, sr med registrar Ahmadu Bello Univ Hosp Zaria Nigeria 1973–74, lectr and sr registrar in thoracic and gen med Middlesex Hosp 1974–77; conslt physician: Norfolk and Norwich Univ Hosp 1978–2005, West Norwich Hosp 1978–2001; hon prof UEA 2005– (hon sr lectr 1997–2005); memb Cncl ASH 1983–2000 (fndr and first chm Norfolk ASH 1979); British Thoracic Soc: memb Research Ctee 1980–86, clinical coordinator Nat Pneumonia Study 1981–87, memb Educn Ctee 1986–89 and 1994–98, chm Pneumonia Standing Sub Ctee 1987–89, chm Standards of Care Ctee 1989–93, memb Cncl and Exec 1989–93 and 2002–04, coordinator confs to produce guidelines on the mgmnt of asthma in Britain 1990, 1992 and 1995, memb Manpower and Trg Ctee 1996–2003, memb Professional Standards Ctee 1999–2004 (chm 2002–04); memb Mortality and Severe Morbidity Working Gp Nat Asthma Task Force 1991–2002 (chm 1994–98); pres East Anglian Thoracic Soc 1982–84, tstee Br Lung Fndn 2001–04; FRCP 1987 (MRCP 1970), FCCP 1990, FRCPEd 1998; *Publications* author of numerous med pubns on pneumonia, smoking, asthma, pulmonary function, respiratory failure, secondary polycythemia, chronic airflow obstruction, lung biopsy, sarcoidosis; *Recreations* gardening, sailing, theatre, travel; *Clubs* Stranger's (Norwich); *Style*— Prof Brian Harrison; ✉ The White House, Church Avenue East, Norwich NR2 2AF (tel 01603 456508)

HARRISON, Prof Sir Brian Howard; kt (2005); s of Howard Harrison (d 1966), and Mary Elizabeth, *née* Savill (d 2001); *b* 9 July 1937; *Educ* Merchant Taylors' Northwood, St John's Coll Oxford (MA, DPhil); *m* 1967, Anne Victoria, da of Lawrence Greggain; *Career* Nat Serv 2 Lieut Malta Signal Sqdn 1956–58; Univ of Oxford: sr scholar St Antony's Coll 1961–64, jr res fell Nuffield Coll 1964–67, reader 1990–2000, titular prof of modern British history 1996–; CCC Oxford: tutor 1967–2000, fell 1967–2004 (emeritus fell 2004–), sr tutor 1984–86 and 1988–90, vice-pres 1992, 1993, and 1996–98; visiting prof: Univ of Michigan 1970–71, Harvard Univ 1973–74; visiting fell: Univ of Melbourne 1975, ANU 1995; ed Oxford DNB 2000–04; FRHistS 1973, FBA 2005; *Books* Drink and the Victorians (1971, 2 edn 1994), Separate Spheres: the opposition to women's suffrage in Britain (1978), Robert Lowery: Chartist and lecturer (ed with P Hollis, 1979), Peaceable Kingdom: stability and change in modern Britain (1982), A Hundred Years Ago: Britain in the 1880s in words and photographs (with C Ford, 1983), Prudent Revolutionaries: portraits of British feminists between the wars (1987), The History of the University of Oxford Vol 8: The Twentieth Century (ed and contrib, 1994), Corpuscles: a History of Corpus Christi College in the twentieth century (ed, 1994), The Transformation of British Politics 1860–1995 (1996), Civil Histories: Essays presented to Sir Keith Thomas (ed with P Burke and P Slack, and contrib, 2000); *Recreations* looking at architecture, listening to classical music; *Style*— Prof Sir Brian Harrison; ✉ Corpus Christi College, Oxford OX1 4JF (tel 01865 276700)

HARRISON, Prof Bryan Desmond; CBE (1990); s of John William Harrison (d 1963), and Norah, *née* Webster (d 1998); *b* 16 June 1931; *Educ* Whitgift Sch, Univ of Reading (Wantage scholar, BSc), Rothamsted Experimental Station Harpenden, Univ of London (PhD); *m* 13 Jan 1968, Elizabeth Ann, da of Vivian Francis Latham-Warde (d 1981); 2 s (Peter William b 1969, Robert Anthony b 1972), 1 da (Claire Janet b 1977); *Career* res scientist: Virology Section Scot Horticultural Research Inst Dundee 1954–57, Plant Pathology Dept Rothamsted Experimental Station Harpenden 1957–66; Scot Crop Research Inst Dundee (formerly Horticultural Research Inst): research scientist and head Virology Dept 1966–91, sr pso 1969, dep chief scientific offr 1981, hon research prof 1996–; Univ of Dundee: hon visiting prof 1988–91, prof of plant virology 1991–96, prof emeritus 1997–; hon prof Univ of St Andrews 1986–98, hon visiting prof Univ of Zhejiang PRC 2001–; Hon Doctorate in Agriculture and Forestry Univ of Helsinki 1990; hon memb: Assoc of Applied Biologists 1989, Soc for Gen Microbiology 1990, Phytopathological Soc of Japan 1992; foreign assoc US Nat Acad of Sciences 1998; FRSE 1979, FRS 1987; *Publications* Plant Virology: the Principles (with A J Gibbs, 1976, translated into Russian and Chinese), over 200 research papers and reviews on plant viruses; *Recreations* gardening; *Style*— Prof Bryan Harrison, CBE, FRS, FRSE; ✉ Scottish Crop Research Institute, Invergowrie, Dundee DD2 5DA (tel 01382 562731, fax 01382 562426)

HARRISON, Sir (Robert) Colin; 4 Bt (UK 1922), of Eaglescliffe, Co Durham; s of late Sir John Fowler Harrison, 2 Bt, and late Kathleen, *née* Livingston; suc bro, Sir (John) Wyndham Harrison, 3 Bt, 1955; *b* 25 May 1938; *Educ* Radley, St John's Coll Cambridge; *m* 1963, Maureen Marie, da of late E Leonard Chiverton, of Langley House, Lanchester, Co Durham; 2 da (Rachel Deborah (Mrs Waddell) b 1966, Dr Claire Grace (Mrs Caesar) b 1974), 1 s (John Wyndham Fowler b 1972); *Heir* s, John Harrison; *Career* Nat Serv cmmnd 5 Royal Northumberland Fusiliers 1957–59; general cmmr of income tax; chm Young Master Printers Nat Ctee 1972–73; *Style*— Sir Colin Harrison, Bt; ✉ Stearsby Hall, Stearsby, York YO61 4SA (tel 01347 888226)

HARRISON, Sir David; kt (1997), CBE (1990); s of Harold David Harrison (d 1987), of Exeter, Devon, and Lavinia, *née* Wilson (d 1993); *b* 3 May 1930; *Educ* Bede Sch Sunderland, Clacton Co HS, Selwyn Coll Cambridge (MA, PhD, ScD); *m* 11 Aug 1962, Sheila Rachel, da of Denis Richardson Debes, of Little Budworth, Cheshire; 2 s (Michael b 1963, Tony b 1966, d 1986), 1 da (Sarah b 1965); *Career* Nat Serv 2 Lt REME 1949; lectr Univ of Cambridge 1956–79, fell Selwyn Coll Cambridge 1957– (sr tutor 1967–79), chm of tstees Homerton Coll Cambridge 1979–, vice-chllr Univ of Keele 1979–84, vice-chllr Univ of Exeter 1984–94, master Selwyn Coll 1994–2000, dep vice-chllr Univ of Cambridge 1995–2000 (pro-vice-chllr 1997); visiting prof: Delaware Univ USA 1967, Sydney Univ Aust 1976; chm: UCCA 1984–91, Ctee of Vice-Chllrs and Princs 1991–93; pres IChemE 1991–92, former memb Engrg Cncl; chm: Governing Body Shrewsbury Sch 1989–2003, Cncl Ely Cathedral; Freeman City of London 1998, Liveryman Worshipful Co of Salters 1998 (currently dir Salters' Inst); FREng 1987, FRSC, FRIC 1961, FIChemE 1968, FRSA 1985, CIMgt 1990, FRSCM 2005; *Books* Fluidised Particles (with J F Davidson, 1963), Fluidization (with J F Davidson and R Clift, 2 edn 1985); *Recreations* music, tennis, hill walking, good food; *Clubs* Athenaeum, Oxford and Cambridge, Foundation House (Stoke-on-Trent); *Style*— Sir David Harrison, CBE, FREng; ✉ 7 Gough Way, Cambridge CB3 9LN (tel 01223 359315)

HARRISON, David; s of Robert Stanley Harrison, of Liverpool, and Jean, *née* Edmondson; *b* 9 April 1957; *Educ* Alsop Comp Sch Liverpool, Pembroke Coll Oxford (exhibitioner, BA, Football blue); *m* 17 Aug 1985, Linda Elizabeth, da of Thomas Ellis; 2 s (Matthew David b 29 Aug 1986, Alexander James b 14 Feb 1989); *Career* news, sports and feature writer Liverpool Daily Post and Echo 1980–83 (team award for coverage of Toxteth riots Nat Press Awards 1981), conslt China Daily Beijing 1983–84, asst foreign ed Daily Telegraph 1985–90 (also home and foreign news sub-ed), news ed The European 1990–91, sr reporter (home and foreign) then environment and tport ed The Observer 1991–98, environment and tport ed, war corr (Kosovo, Afghanistan and Iraq), sr corr Sunday Telegraph 1998–; Amnesty Int Press Award 1997, Paul Foot Award for Investigative Journalism 2006, shortlisted for various awards; occasional TV and radio broadcaster 1990–; conslt Thomson Fndn; conference and literary festival chair and speaker; former memb sch, regnl and coll teams in various sports, former semi-professional footballer England and France; memb NUJ 1980–; *Recreations* travel, reading, cinema, theatre, supporting Liverpool FC, swimming, playing cricket, football and tennis; *Style*— David Harrison, Esq; ✉ Sunday Telegraph, 1 Canada Square, Canary Wharf, London E14 5DT (tel 020 7538 7423, e-mail david.harrison@telegraph.co.uk)

HARRISON, Dr Edward Peter Graham (Ted); s of Rev Peter Graham Harrison (d 1998), of Bishops Lydeard, Somerset, and (Eleanor) Joan, *née* Rowland; *b* 14 April 1948; *Educ* Grenville Coll Bideford, Univ of Kent at Canterbury (BA, PhD); *m* 1968, Helen Grace, da of Ronald Percy Waters (d 1986); 1 s (David Edward Graham b 1969), 1 da (Caroline Helen b 1971); *Career* writer, broadcaster, television prodr and cartoonist; trainee journalist Kent Messenger and Evening Post 1968–72; reporter: Morgan-Grampian Magazines 1972, Southern TV 1970–73, You and Yours (BBC Radio 4) 1972–80, Sunday (Radio 4) 1972–90 (presenter 1986–88), BBC Scotland News and Current Affrs 1980–85 (also presenter), World Tonight (Radio 4) 1981–83, World at One and PM (Radio 4) 1983–87; presenter: numerous radio documentaries in Profile and Soundings series (Radio 4), Opinions (Radio 4) 1986–87, The Human Factor (ITV) 1986–92, Does he take Sugar? (Radio 4) 1991–95; series ed Ultimate Questions (ITV); dir: Redcoats (ITV), Essentials of Faith (ITV), Mosque (ITV) 2005; religious affrs corr BBC 1988–89, currently writer and ind radio and television prodr; dir Pilgrim Productions Canterbury, fndr Unst Animation Studio Shetland; Parly candidate (Lib) Bexley 1970 and Maidstone Feb 1974; exhibition of caricatures London 1977, exhibition of watercolours Oxford and Canterbury 1981; *Books* Modern Elizabethans (1977), McIndoe's Army (with Peter Williams, 1979), Marks of the Cross (1981), Commissioner Catherine (1983), Much Beloved Daughter (1985), The Durham Phenomenon (1986), Living with Kidney Failure (1990), Kriss Akabusi - On Track (1991), Elvis People (1992), Members Only (1994), Stigmata (1994), Letters to a Friend I Never Knew (1995), Disability - Rights and Wrongs (1995), Defender of the Faith (1996), Tanni (1996), Diana - Icon and Sacrifice (1998), Beyond Dying (2000), Will the Next Archbishop Please Stand Up (2002), Diana: Myth and Reality (2006); *Recreations* watercolour painting; *Clubs* Athenaeum; *Style*— Dr Ted Harrison

HARRISON, Sir Ernest Thomas; kt (1981), OBE (1972); s of late Ernest Horace Harrison, and Gertrude Rebecca, *née* Gibbons (d 1995); *b* 11 May 1926; *Educ* Trinity GS London; *m* 1960, Phyllis Brenda (Janie), *née* Knight; 3 s, 2 da; *Career* CA; Harker Holloway & Co, Voluntary Nat Savings Movement 1964–76; Racal Electronics plc: joined 1951, dir 1958, dep md 1961, chief exec 1966–92, chm 1966–; chm: Racal Telecom plc 1988–91, Vodafone plc 1991–98 (following demerger from Racal), Chubb Security plc 1992–97 (also following demerger from Racal); dir Camelot Group plc 1993–2000; chm Royal Free (formerly Ronald Raven) Cancer Research Tst 1990–; former memb Cncl Electronics Engrg Assoc and Nat Electronics Cncl; Capt of Industry (Livingston Industrial and Commercial Assoc Edinburgh) 1980, Hambro Businessman of the Year 1981, Aims of Industry Nat Free Enterprise award 1982, Br Enterprise award for Racal 1982, received The 1990 Founding Society's Centenary award by Inst of Chartered Accountants, first recipient of Mountbatten medal by National Electronics Cncl 1992; Hon DSc Cranfield Inst of Technol, Hon DUniv Surrey, Hon DSc City Univ, Hon DUniv Edinburgh; memb Worshipful Co of Scriveners; fell Royal Free Hosp Sch of Med Univ of London; memb RSA, FCA, CIERE, CIEE, CIMgt, Hon FCGI, Hon FREng; *Recreations* horse racing (owner and breeder), gardening, wild life, all sports (particularly soccer); *Clubs* Jockey; *Style—* Sir Ernest Harrison, OBE, Hon FREng

HARRISON, Frank Ronald; s of Ronald Charles Gully Harrison, of Helensburgh, Dumbartonshire, and Eva Luise Johanne, *née* Hornäffer; *b* 11 July 1962; *Educ* Eton, Oxford Poly (now Oxford Brookes Univ) (BA); *m* Caroline Elizabeth, da of Malcolm B C Ward; 1 da (Emma Louise Elizabeth b 19 Feb 1990), 2 s (William Frank Ion b 20 April 1992, Oliver Frederick Charles b 16 April 1997); *Career* media research dir/bd dir Saatchi & Saatchi Advertising 1987–91; ZenithOptimedia: dir media research 1992–94, dir worldwide media info systems 1994–95, dir worldwide strategic resources 1995–; speaker at numerous indust confs, author of various papers published on media; memb IPA/ISBA/AFVPA Working Pty on Equity Repeat Fee Agreement 1992 and 1996; memb MRS 1985 (DipMRS), FIPA 1996 (MIPA 1989), memb Mktg Soc 2000–; *Books* UK Media Yearbook (annually 1987–), UK Television Forecasts (annually 1988–), Interactive Media (1995), Television in Asia Pacific to 2000 (1995), Television in Europe to 2005 (1996), Digital Media (1997); *Recreations* music, family, travel; *Style—* Frank Harrison, Esq; ✉ Chetwode, Burchetts Green Lane, Littlewick Green, Berkshire SL6 3QW (tel 01628 829068); ZenithOptimedia, 63–65 North Wharf Road, London W2 1LA (tel 020 7298 4907, fax 020 7402 5703, e-mail frank.harrison@zenithoptimedia.co.uk)

HARRISON, Howard Michael; s of Michael Amyas Harrison, and Yvonne Betty Harrison; *Educ* Central Sch of Speech and Drama; *Career* lighting designer; *Theatre* credits incl: Nabucco (Met Opera), Il Trovatore (ROH and Teatro Real Madrid), Privates on Parade (Donmar Warehouse), Tales from Hollywood (Donmar Warehouse), To the Green Fields and Beyond (Donmar Warehouse), The Tempest (RSC), As You Like It (RSC), The Prisoners Dilemma (RSC), Finding the Sun/The Marriage Play (RNT), Look Back in Anger (RNT), Private Lives (RNT), Swan Lake (English Nat Ballet), Romeo and Juliet (English Nat Ballet), Putting it Together (Broadway), Cat on a Hot Tin Roof (West End), The Witches of Eastwick (West End), Mammia Mia (West End, Broadway, Toronto, Aust and US tour); memb Cncl of Nat Youth Theatre of GB; nomination Best Lighting Designer Olivier Awards 1998, 2000, 2001 and 2002; *Clubs* Groucho; *Style—* Howard Harrison, Esq; ✉ c/o David Watson, Simpson Fox Associates, 52 Shaftesbury Avenue, London W1D 6LP (tel 020 7434 9167)

HARRISON, John; s of John Henry Jordan (d 1995), of Grantham, Lincs, and Margaret, *née* Harrison; *b* 20 February 1944; *Educ* Silverdale Secdy Modern Sch, Sheffield Tech Coll; *m* 13 July 1968, Vivien Ann Eveline, da of Frederick Charles Hardisty (d 1988), of Brighton; 1 s (Mark b 31 July 1976); *Career* lighting designer Theatre Projects Ltd 1964–68, prodn mangr and tech dir ENO 1968–74, theatre conslt John Wyckham Associates 1975–76; tech dir: WNO 1976–88, Vancouver Opera Canada 1984–88; md Cardiff Theatrical Services Ltd 1984–88; ROH: tech dir 1989–98, admin dir 1998–2000, commercial dir 1999–2004; exec prodr Creative Entertainment Gp 2004–07; conslt Breakthru Films London 2006–, memb Tech Ctee Opera America 2004; *Recreations* travel, gardening; *Style—* John Harrison, Esq; ✉ tel and fax 020 8668 9481, e-mail harrisonjordan@btinternet.com

HARRISON, John; s of Kenneth Ridley Harrison (d 1960), of Stockton-on-Tees, and Margaret, *née* Calvert (d 1998); *b* 12 November 1944; *Educ* Grangefield GS, Univ of Sheffield (BA); *m* 4 June 1969, Patricia Alice Bridget, da of Dr Harry Raymond Alban (d 1974), of London; 2 da (Rachel b 1971, Philippa b 1973), 1 s (Joseph b 1979); *Career* articled clerk Coopers & Lybrand 1966–70, Tillotson corp planner 1970–72; Deloitte Consulting: mgmnt conslt 1972–2001, ptnr 1981–2001, ptnr i/c Corp Special Servs 1992–94, ptnr i/c Financial Institutions Consulting; chm: Portal Ltd, Erinaceous Property Maintenance Ltd; finance dir Marchpole plc; FCA 1969, FIMC 1973, FRSA 1991; *Recreations* fly fishing, skiing, sailing, shooting; *Style—* John Harrison, Esq; ✉ Goodwin Manor, Swaffham Prior, Cambridge CB5 0LG (tel 01638 742850, e-mail john.harrison@swaffham.demon.co.uk)

HARRISON, Baron (Life Peer UK 1999), of Chester in the County of Cheshire; Lyndon Henry Arthur; s of Charles William Harrison, and late Edith Harrison, *née* Johnson; *b* 28 September 1947; *Educ* Oxford Sch, Univ of Warwick (BA), Univ of Sussex (MA), Keele Univ (MA); *m* 1980, Hilary Anne, *née* Plank; 1 s (Adam b 1982), 1 da (Sara b 1985); *Career* mangr Students' Union NE Wales Inst of HE Wrexham; MEP (Lab): Cheshire W 1989–94, Cheshire W and Wirral 1994–99; Euro Parl: memb Transport and Tourism Ctee, memb Economic and Monetary Ctee, socialist spokesperson Monetary Sub-Ctee, sec European Parly Lab Pty (EPLP) 1991–94, socialist spokesperson Delegation for ASEAN and Korea, vice-pres Intergroup for Small Business, pres Tourism Intergroup; memb House of Lords Ctee: on Foreign and Security Policy 2000–04, Delegated Powers and Regulatory Reform 2003–on Social Policy and Consumer Affrs 2004–; cnclr Cheshire CC 1981–90 (formerly chm Libraries and Countryside and Tourism Ctees); *Recreations* chess, music, sport; *Style—* The Rt Hon the Lord Harrison; ✉ House of Lords, London SW1A 0PW (tel 020 7219 3000)

HARRISON, (Robert) Michael; QC (1987); s of Robert William Harrison (d 1981), and Bertha, *née* Harrison; *b* 3 November 1945; *Educ* Heckmondwike GS, Univ of Hull (LLB); *m* 20 April 1974, Jennifer, da of Edward Armstrong, of Aston, Sheffield; 1 s (Christopher Edward b 24 June 1977); *Career* called to the Bar Gray's Inn 1969, recorder of the Crown Ct 1982–, dep judge of the High Court 1997–; currently memb Park Court Chambers Leeds; *Style—* Michael Harrison, Esq, QC

HARRISON, Dr Michael; JP (Birmingham 1980); s of Frank Harrison (d 1973), of Leamington Spa, and Ruby Wilhelmina, *née* Proctor (d 1981); *b* 1 March 1939; *Educ* Leamington Coll, St Mary's Hosp Med Sch London (MB BS, LRCP, MRCS), Univ of Bristol (DPH), Open Univ (BA); *m* 23 April 1962, Ann, da of Eric Bertram Haiser (d 1963), of Leamington Spa; 2 da (Mary Jane b 1965, Susan Elizabeth b 1967); *Career* hosp med appts 1964–66, Public Health Dept City of Birmingham 1966–70, princ asst SMO Birmingham RHB 1971–74, specialist in community med West Midlands RHA 1974–76; Sandwell Health Authy: area med offr 1976–83, dist med offr 1983–88, gen mangr 1985–88; asst md and regnl dir of public health West Midlands RHA 1988–93, public health conslt 1993–96, med dir and chm Midlands Health Consultancy Network Ltd 1996–; sr clinical lectr Univ of Birmingham 1988–, visiting fell Business Sch Aston Univ 1988–, conslt advsr WHO 1989–; pres: Lichfield Sci and Engrg Soc 1991, Assoc for Industrial Archaeology 1998–99; pres Droitwich Spa Saltway Rotary Club 2001; FRSH 1978, FFPHM 1980, FIMgt 1984, LHSM 1985, FRSM 1989; SBStJ 1977; *Recreations* sailing, photography, industrial archaeology; *Clubs* RSM; *Style—* Dr Michael Harrison; ✉ 19 Sandles Close, The Ridings, Droitwich Spa WR9 8RB (tel 01905 798308, fax 01905 798307)

HARRISON, Michael Anthony; s of William Harrison (d 1981), and Gweneth Harrison (d 2001); *b* 30 April 1947; *Educ* Royal GS Newcastle upon Tyne, Aylesbury GS, Oxford Coll of Technol, Univ of Nottingham (BA); *m* 25 Aug 1973, Marie-Claude, da of Léon Victor Bouquet; 3 s (Stéphane Daniel b 5 July 1974, Frank William b 8 July 1978, John-Gabriel b 21 Jan 1986), 1 da (Laura Rachel b 20 Nov 1975); *Career* technician Tate Gallery London 1970–71; Arts Cncl of GB: regnl arts offr 1971–73, exhbn organiser 1973–77, asst dir for regnl exhbns (with South Bank Centre) 1977–90; head of fine art Winchester Sch of Art 1990–92, dir Kettle's Yard Univ of Cambridge 1992–; *Recreations* art, architecture, reading, walking; *Style—* Michael Harrison, Esq; ✉ 49 City Road, Cambridge CB1 1DP; Kettle's Yard, Castle Street, Cambridge CB3 0AQ (tel 01223 352124, fax 01223 324377, e-mail michaelharrison@kettlesyard.cam.ac.uk)

HARRISON, Sir Michael Guy Vicat; kt (1993); s of Hugh Francis Guy Harrison (d 2000), and Elizabeth Alban, *née* Jones (d 1998); *b* 28 September 1939; *Educ* Charterhouse, Trinity Hall Cambridge; *m* 1966, Judith, da of late Fernley Edward Gist; 1 da (Sarah Louise b 11 March 1970), 1 s (William Vicat b 22 July 1972); *Career* called to the Bar 1965, bencher Gray's Inn 1993; QC 1983, recorder of the Crown Court 1989–93, judge of the High Court of Justice (Queen's Bench Div) 1993–2004, dep chm Boundary Cmmn for England 1996–2004; *Recreations* tennis, sailing, fishing, walking; *Style—* Sir Michael Harrison

HARRISON, Sir Michael James Harwood; 2 Bt (UK 1961), of Bugbrooke, Co Northampton, JP (1993); s of Col Sir (James) Harwood Harrison, 1 Bt, TD (d 1980), MP (Cons) Eye 1951–79, of Hasketon, Suffolk, and Peggy Alberta Mary, *née* Stenhouse (d 1993); *b* 28 March 1936; *Educ* Rugby; *m* 1967, (Rosamund) Louise, da of Edward Buxton Clive (d 1975), of Swanmore, Hants; 2 da ((Auriol) Davina (Mrs Benet Northcote) b 1968, Priscilla Caroline (Mrs Stephen Howell) b 1971), 2 s (Edwin Michael Harwood b 1981, Tristan John b 1986); *Heir* s, Edwin Harrison; *Career* Nat Serv 17/21 Lancers 1955–56; insurance broker Lloyd's 1958–92; dir of various private cos 1980–; dep chm STA Tall Ships Ltd 1996–2000; memb Cncl Sail Training Assoc 1968–2003; Assoc of Combined Youth Clubs: vice-pres 1983–2000, chm Mgmnt Ctee 1987–95; Freeman City of London 1964, Master Worshipful Co of Mercers 1986 (Liveryman 1967); *Recreations* sailing (yacht 'Falcon'), skiing, riding, sudoku; *Clubs* Boodle's; *Style—* Sir Michael Harrison, Bt; ✉ Rise Cottage, Hasketon, nr Woodbridge, Suffolk IP13 6JA (tel 01394 382352, e-mail sirmharrison@hotmail.com)

HARRISON, (Walter) Paul; s of Walter Harrison, of Morecambe, and Margaret Hildred, *née* Buttery; *b* 19 March 1955; *Educ* Skerton Co Boys' Sch Lancaster, Univ of Lancs (OND, HNC), De Montfort Univ (BA, DipArch); *Career* architect; Cassidy & Ashton Partnership Preston 1973–75, W E Moore & Sons Leicester 1978–79, ptnr Robert Davies John West & Assocs Crawley 1987–90, md RDJW Architects Ltd 1990–; RIBA, ARCUK; *Recreations* squash, badminton, cars, horse riding; *Style—* Paul Harrison, Esq; ✉ Denholme, Crawley Road, Horsham, West Sussex (tel 01403 262224); RDJW Architects Ltd, Quoin House, 11 East Park, Crawley RH10 6AN (tel 01293 404300, fax 01293 404299, e-mail architecture@rdjwa.co.uk)

HARRISON, Paul; s of Ronald Harrison, and Maureen Harrison; *Educ* Wednesfield HS Wolverhampton, Mid Cheshire Coll of FE, Bath Coll of HE (BA); *Career* artist; in partnership with John Wood, *qv*; *Exhibitions* incl: The British Art Show 5 2000, Twenty Six (Drawing and Falling Things) (Chisenhale Gallery London) 2002, Sudden Glory (CCAC Inst Calif) 2002, Gwangju Biennale Korea 2002, Monitor: Volume One (Gagosian Gallery NY) 2002, Performing Bodies (Tate Modern London) 2002, Selected Works (MOMA NY) 2004, Art Now (Tate Britain) 2004, Irreducible (CCA Inst Calif) 2005; *Style—* Paul Harrison, Esq

HARRISON, Philip Vernon; s of Ronald Geoffrey Harrison, of Kent, and Beryl May, *née* Crisp; *b* 19 November 1952; *Educ* The Hill Sch Nuwara Eliya Sri Lanka, Worksop Coll; *m* 4 Sept 1976, Jessica Jane, da of Peter Derrick Whiteley; 1 da (Alice Maria Casuarina b 25 Dec 1985); *Career* tea buying asst Lyons Groceries Ltd 1971–73; Lyons Tetley Ltd: asst brand mangr 1973–74, product mangr 1974, new product devpt mangr 1974–79, int mktg mangr 1979–83; commercial dir Spearhead Ltd 1983–86, mktg mangr Dixons Colour Laboratories Ltd 1986–88; mktg dir: Supasnaps Ltd 1989–90 (mktg mangr 1988–89), Dixons Finance plc and Dixons Financial Services Ltd 1990–92; brand mktg dir Dixons Stores Group 1992–94, mktg dir Allied Carpets Group 1994–99, md Zalpha 1999–; *Recreations* cookery (City & Guilds 1991), sailing; *Style—* Philip Vernon Harrison, Esq

HARRISON, Philippa Mary; da of Charles Kershaw Whitfield (d 1972), and Alexina Margaret, *née* Dykes; *b* 25 November 1942; *Educ* Walthamstow Hall, Univ of Bristol (BA), Courtauld Inst; *m* July 1967 (m dis), James Fraser Harrison; *Career* jt ed-in-chief Penguin Books 1979–80, editorial dir Michael Joseph 1980–85, md and publisher Macmillan London 1986–88, md V and A Enterprises 1990–91, chief exec and publisher Little Brown & Co (UK) 1996– (md 1992–96); dir Book Tokens Ltd 1996–; pres Publishers Assoc 1998–99 (vice-pres 1997–98); memb: Bd of Book Marketing Cncl 1983–88, Literature Panel Arts Cncl 1988–92, Cncl Publishers Assoc 1995–; tstee Eric & Salome Estorick Fndn 1996–; CIMgt 1987, FRSA 1992; *Books* Publishing: The Future (contrib, 1988); *Recreations* walking, theatre, reading, the arts; *Clubs* Groucho; *Style—* Mrs Philippa Harrison; ✉ Little Brown & Co, Brettenham House, Lancaster Place, London WC2E 7EN (tel 020 7911 8002, fax 020 7911 8104)

HARRISON, Prof Robert Graham; s of Robert Graham Harrison, of Essex, and Constance May, *née* Scott; *b* 26 February 1944; *Educ* Wanstead Co HS, Univ of London (BSc, PhD); *m* Rowena Indrania; 1 s (Samuel Scott b 1972), 1 da (Sophia Victoria b 1982); *Career* research fell Univ of London/Culham Lab UKAEA 1970–72, lectr Dept of Physics Univ of Bath 1972–76; Dept of Physics Heriot-Watt Univ: lectr then sr lectr 1976–83, reader 1983–87, prof 1987–; dir of several confs and advanced workshops; FRSE 1987, FInstP; *Publications* author of over 250 pubns in int scientific jls and ed of 5 books in the fields of laser physics, nonlinear optics, chaos and complexity; *Style—* Prof Robert Harrison, FRSE; ✉ School of Engineering and Physical Sciences, Heriot-Watt University, Riccarton, Edinburgh EH14 4AS (tel 0131 449 5111, fax 0131 451 3136)

HARRISON, (Desmond) Roger Wingate; s of Maj-Gen Desmond Harrison, CB, DSO, and Kathleen, *née* Hazley; *b* 9 April 1933; *Educ* Rugby, Worcester Coll Oxford (MA), Harvard Business Sch; *m* 1965, Victoria Harrison, MVO, da of late Rear Adm John Lee-Barber; 1 s (decd), 4 da (1 decd); *Career* The Times 1957–67 (freelance writer 1955–57); The Observer: joined 1967, dir 1970–92, jt md 1977–84, chief exec 1984–87; non-exec dir: LWT Holdings plc 1976–94, Trinity Mirror plc 1991–2003, SPG Media Gp plc (formerly Sterling Publishing Group plc) 1993–2004 (chm 1993–96); dir Sableknight 1981–; dep chm Capital Radio plc 1991–2000 (dir 1975–2000); exec dir The Oak Fndn (UK) Ltd 1987–89; chm: Toynbee Hall 1989–2002, Asylum Aid 1990–97, Royal Acad of Dancing 1992–2006; govr Sadler's Wells Theatre 1984–95; *Recreations* theatre, country pursuits, tennis; *Clubs* Beefsteak, Flyfishers', Queen's; *Style—* Roger Harrison, Esq; ✉ Itchen Stoke Mill, Alresford, Hampshire SO24 0RA

HARRISON, Ronald Charles Gully; s of Ion Robinson Harrison (d 1952), of Helensburgh, Dunbartonshire, and Marie Louise, *née* Canonico (d 1977); *b* 11 June 1933; *Educ* Charterhouse, King's Coll Cambridge (MA); *m* 27 Dec 1957, Eva Luise Johanne, da of Adolf Johannes Friedrich Hornäffer; 3 s (Neal Francis Ion b 9 Dec 1960, Frank Ronald b 11 July 1962, Ivor John Anthony b 11 April 1965), 1 da (Corinna Eva Louise b 22 Sept 1966); *Career* Nat Serv 2 Lt Royal Scots Greys 1951–53; lectr in English Br Cncl Rio de Janeiro 1957–59; HM Dip Serv: entered 1960, Ibadan 1961–64, Malta 1964–67, Karachi 1967–70, FCO 1970–72, São Paulo 1972–74, Br Trade Devpt Office NY 1975–77, consul (commercial) Dallas 1977–79, FCO 1979–82, dep consul-gen Milan 1982–87, consul-gen São Paulo 1987–90, consul-gen Naples 1990–93; hon research fell Dept of Italian Univ of Glasgow 1994–; *Recreations* travelling, reading, theatre, skiing; *Style—* Ronald Harrison, Esq; ✉ Croft House, 41 George Street, Helensburgh G84 7EX (tel 01436 678250, fax 01436 679455, e-mail rcgharrison@hotmail.com)

HARRISON, Timothy David Blair (Tim); s of Blair Wilfred Wortley Harrison (d 1999), of Banwell, Avon, and Sheelagh Margurite Hildergarde, *née* Woolford (d 1972); *b* 13 December 1944; *Educ* Blundell's; *m* 2 Nov 1991, Beverley, da of George William Brindle, of Bahrain; 2 s (Blair Edward Charles b 1976, Thomas George b 1992), 1 da (Paige-Elise b 1996); *Career* UBM/MAC Group Bristol 1963–73, GKN Mills Building Services Ltd 1973–76, Norplant/Witpalm International Ltd 1976–79, Mallinson-Denny Group 1979–86 (sales and mktg dir Formwood Ltd, md Bushboard Ltd), md GA Harvey Office Furniture Ltd 1986–88, Trafalgar House Building & Civil Engineering Holdings Ltd 1988–89 (dir, sector md), gp chief exec The Company of Designers plc 1989–92; 1992–96: dir CAMAS UK Ltd (formerly part of English China Clays), md CAMAS Building Materials Ltd, pres Prefabricados de Hormigon Lurgain SA Spain, dir SMMO France; divnl md Luxfer Group Holdings plc 1996–98, md Apollo Logistics Ltd 1999–2001, divnl md Corton Gp Holdings Ltd 2001–; chm Corton Management Servs Ltd, Generation Metals Int Ltd, Norcot Engrg Ltd; Freeman City of London, memb Worshipful Co of Builders Merchants; FInstD; *Recreations* hunting, boating; *Clubs* Royal Dart Yacht; *Style—* Tim Harrison, Esq; ✉ Shiningford Farm, Carsington, Derbyshire DE4 4DD

HARRISON, Tony; s of Harry Ashton Harrison (d 1980), and Florence Horner, *née* Wilkinson (d 1976); *b* 30 April 1937; *Educ* Leeds GS, Univ of Leeds (BA); *Career* poet and dramatist; FRSL; *Television* The Oresteia (Channel 4 1982), The Big H (BBC 1984), The Mysteries (Channel 4 1985), Yan Tan Tethera (Channel 4 1986), Loving Memory (BBC 1986), V (Channel 4 1987, Royal Television Soc Award), The Blasphemers' Banquet, The Gaze of the Gorgon (1992), Black Daisies for the Bride (1993, Prix Italia 1994), A Maybe Day in Kazakhstan (1994), The Shadow of Hiroshima (Channel 4 1995), Crossings (LWT 2002); *Films* Prometheus (1999); *Books and Plays* Earthworks (1964), Aikin Mata (1965), Newcastle is Peru (1969), The Loiners (1970), The Misanthrope (1973), Phaedra Britannica (1975), The Passion (1977), Bow Down (1977), from The School of Eloquence (1978), Continuous (1981), A Kumquat for John Keats (1981), US Martial (1981), The Oresteia (1981), Selected Poems (1984), The Mysteries (1985), V (1985), Dramatic Verse 1973–85 (1985), The Fire-Gap (1985), Theatre Works 1973–85 (1986), Selected Poems (augmented edn 1987), The Trackers of Oxyrhynchus (performed ancient stadium of Delphi 1988, NT 1990), A Cold Coming - Gulf War Poems (1991), The Common Chorus (1992), The Gaze of the Gorgon and other poems (Whitbread poetry award, 1992), Square Rounds (1992), Poetry or Bust (1993), The Kaisers of Carnuntum (1995), Permanently Bard (1995), The Labourers of Herakles (1995), The Shadow of Hiroshima and other film/poems (1995), The Prince's Play (1996), Prometheus (1998), Laureate's Block and Other Poems (2000); *Collections* Tony Harrison Plays Three (1996), Tony Harrison Plays One (1999), Tony Harrison Plays Two (2002), Tony Harrison Plays Four (2002); *Style—* Tony Harrison

HARRISON-CRIPPS, William Lawrence; s of William Harrison Harrison-Cripps (d 1998), and Anne Elizabeth, *née* Graham Smith (d 1959); *b* 25 January 1950; *Educ* Marlborough; *m* 4 Nov 1977, Elizabeth Joy, da of Kenneth Henry Cornwell; 2 s (William Henry b 17 Aug 1979, Thomas Peter Seddon b 24 Oct 1987), 1 da (Alexandra Elizabeth b 9 April 1981); *Career* PricewaterhouseCoopers (formerly Price Waterhouse): articled clerk 1968–72, mangr 1976, ptnr 1982–, chm M/A Tax Servs (Europe) 1989, memb European Tax Bd and European Corp Fin Exec 1990, ptnr i/c Int Corp Tax Services Gp 1991, UK Tax Service Exec 1992, chm UK Tax Servs 1993, World Tax Service Exec 1993, managing ptnr Tax & Legal Servs EMEA 1998–2003, global markets ldr Tax and Legal Servs 2003–05, dep global ldr Tax Servs 2005–06, conslt 2006–; memb Addington Soc 1992–; FCA 1973, ATII 1975; *Books* Mergers and Acquisitions - The Complete Guide To Principles and Practice (contrib, 1986); *Recreations* flying light aircraft, sailing, photography; *Style—* William Harrison-Cripps, Esq; ✉ PricewaterhouseCoopers, 1 Embankment Place, London WC2N 6RH (tel 020 7804 3907, fax 020 7212 1498)

HARRISS, David James Bernard; s of Henry James Harriss (d 1975), and Jessie May, *née* Bright; *b* 18 April 1947; *Educ* Handsworth Tech Sch Birmingham, Architectural Assoc of Architecture (AADipl); *m* 1985, Patricia Anne; 1 da (Sarah Louise b 11 November 1987); *Career* architect; Foster Assocs 1972–75, Rock Townsend 1975–77, Michael Hopkins 1977–81; Nicholas Grimshaw & Partners Ltd (latterly Grimshaw Architects LLP): joined 1981, assoc 1983, dir 1992–2007, conslt 2007–; projects incl: R&D Facility Rank Xerox, Homebase Brentford, Gillingham Business Park, Pier 4A Heathrow, Lord's Grandstand, Terminal 1 Devpt Manchester Airport, Rolls Royce Goodwood; winner of RIBA Portfolio Prize 1970; RIBA 1974; *Books* The Pattern of Technological Innovation (1972), Building Design - Cladding Special Report (1990), Computers in Architecture (contrib chapter, 1992); *Recreations* classic cars, motor sport; *Clubs* Lotus 7, Club Lotus; *Style—* David J B Harriss, Esq; ✉ 2B The Chase, London SW4 0NH; Grimshaw Architects LLP, 57 Clerkenwell Road, London EC1M 5NG (tel 020 7291 4137, e-mail david.harriss@grimshaw-architects.com)

HARRISS-WHITE, Prof Barbara; da of Philip Beeham, and Betty, *née* Browning; *Educ* Univ of Cambridge (MA, Dip Agric Sci), Univ of Oxford (MA), UEA (PhD), Trinity Coll of Music London (ATCL); *Career* lectr Cambs Coll of Arts and Technol 1969–72, res offr Centre for S Asian Studies Univ of Cambridge 1972–77, res fell ODI London 1977–80, res fell LSHTM 1980–87; Univ of Oxford: lectr in agric econs 1987–96, special lectureship 1994–95, prof of devpt studies 1998– (reader 1996–98), fell Wolfson Coll; Directrice d'Etudes MSH Paris 2004, dir Queen Elizabeth House Oxford 2004–; Smuts lectureship Univ of Cambridge 1999; memb Cncl Devpt Studies Assoc 1987–90, 1994–97 and 2004–; chair Devpt Studies Sub-Panel Research Assessment Exercise; tstee: Action Aid 1988–94 and 1998–2005, Int Food Policy Research Inst Washnington 2006–; memb Lab Pty 1976–98; *Publications* author, co-author and ed of 40 books and major reports incl: Globalisation and Insecurity (2001), Outcast from Social Welfare: Adult Disability and Incapacity in Rural South India (2002), India Working (2003), Rural India facing the 21st Century (2004), India's Market Society (2005), Getting our Minds Around Nature (2006), Trade Liberalization and India's Informal Economy (2007); 176 published papers and chapters, 30 working papers on aspects of devpt particularly in S Asia; *Recreations* music, swimming, walking, novels, life drawing, France; *Clubs* Alpine; *Style—* Prof Barbara Harriss-White; ✉ Queen Elizabeth House, 3 Mansfield Road, Oxford OX1 3TB (tel 01865 281802, fax 01865 281801, e-mail barbara.harriss-white@qeh.ox.ac.uk)

HARRISSON, Tim; *b* 1952; *Educ* Hammersmith Coll of Art, Norwich Coll of Art (BA), Byam Shaw Sch of Fine Art, Sir John Cass Sch of Art; *Career* sculptor; *One and Two Person Exhibitions* Salisbury Art Centre 1984, The Showroom Gallery London 1986, Exhibition of Prints and Drawings (Halesworth Gallery Suffolk) 1987, South Hill Park Art Centre Bracknell 1988, The Flaxman Gallery Stoke on Trent 1988, Purdy-Hicks Gallery London 1988, Artsite Gallery Bath 1989, Recent Sculpture (New Art Centre London) 1991, Four Stone Sculptures (New Art Centre London) 1993, Winchester Cathedral 1997, Stone Works (Galerie Sebastians Kapelle Germany) 1999, New Stone Carvings (New Art Centre Roche Court) 2001; *Group Exhibitions* incl: Salisbury Library 1981, RIBA Sculpture Ct Winter Exhbn 1984, Still Life a New Life (Harris Museum Preston) 1985, Art for the Garden (Hannah Peschar Gallery Surrey) 1986–87, Coastlines (The Towner Museum Eastbourne) 1987, a winner in int art competition organised by Metro Art NYC 1987, Sculpture Open (The Minories Colchester) 1989, The Salisbury Festival 1991, The Economist Bldg Plaza London 1991, London Contemporary Art Fair 1991, Art 23 '92 Basel Switzerland 1992, Art on the Waterfront (Southampton Civic Centre) 1992; *Commissions* incl: Roche Ct Sculpture Garden 1989, The Millfield Cmmn (Millfield Sch with Artsite Gallery Bath) 1989, James Kirkham in Sussex 1989, Ivor Braka in Norfolk 1990, Russell Cotes Museum Bournemouth 1995, new terminal building Southampton Airport for BAA 1995, The Liverpool Victoria Friendly Soc Building Southampton 1996, Winchester Cathedral 1999, 'Reflection' in Epsom Coll 2000, Pegasus for Chatsworth Estate Derbys 2001, Ring for Wingfield Arts Suffolk 2002, Column I Woodford Valley Salisbury 2005; *Style—* Tim Harrisson; ✉ 4 Beckford Cottages, Hindon, Salisbury, Wiltshire SP3 6ED

HARROD, Henry Mark; s of Sir (Henry) Roy Forbes Harrod (d 1978), and Wilhelmine Margaret Eve, *née* Cresswell (d 2005); *b* 6 January 1939; *Educ* Eton, ChCh Oxford (MA); *m* 1, 1965 (m dis 1973); 2 s ((Henry) Barnaby b 1965, Huckleberry Nathaniel b 1967); m 2, 1977, Tanya Olivia Ledger, PhD, da of Dr Peter Ledger, MD (d 2003); 1 s (Hugo Roy Francis b 1979), 1 da (Horatia Mary b 1983); *Career* called to the Bar Lincoln's Inn 1963 (bencher 1991); pupil of Conrad Dehn 2 Crown Office Row Temple 1963; memb chambers of David Fenwick 46 Grainger St Newcastle upon Tyne 1964–68, chambers of Quintin Hogg 4 Paper Bldgs Temple 1968; chambers of John Brightman and others 2 New Sq Lincoln's Inn (chambers moved to 5 Stone Bldgs 1993): joined 1969, head of chambers 1990–; recorder 1993–2004 (asst recorder 1989–93), conveyancing counsel of the Court 1991–; *Clubs* Garrick; *Style—* Henry Harrod, Esq; ✉ 5 Stone Buildings, Lincoln's Inn, London WC2A 3XT (tel 020 7242 6201)

HARROP, Prof Stuart Reginald; s of Reginald Harrop, of E Yorkshire, and Valerie Mary, *née* Hotham; *b* 11 January 1956; *Educ* Beverley GS, Univ of Leeds (LLB); *m* 30 April 1983, Tracy Ann, da of Dennis Roy Green; 3 s (Lee Stuart b 11 May 1986, Joel William b 3 Feb 1990, Christian Sean b 7 Aug 1993); *Career* admitted slr 1980; slr Costain Group plc 1982–84, co slr Albright & Wilson Ltd 1984–86, ICI plc 1986–88; dir legal servs: Stock Exchange 1988–91, RSPCA 1991–96; prof of wildlife mgmnt law Univ of Kent at Canterbury 1996– (currently dep head Dept of Anthropology); tstee: Global Diversity Fndn, Kent Wildlife Tst, Gilchrist Educnl Tst; memb Law Soc; *Recreations* freelance photography (natural history); *Style—* Prof Stuart Harrop; ✉ Durrell Institute of Conservation and Ecology, Department of Anthropology, Marlowe Building, University of Kent, Canterbury, Kent CT2 7NR

HARROWBY, 7 Earl of (UK 1809); Dudley Danvers Granville Coutts Ryder; TD (1953); also Baron Harrowby (GB 1776) and Viscount Sandon (UK 1809); er s of 6 Earl of Harrowby (d 1987), and Lady Helena Blanche, *née* Coventry (d 1974), sis of 10 Earl of Coventry; *b* 20 December 1922; *Educ* Eton; *m* 1, 1949, Jeannette Rosalthé (d 1997), yr da of Capt Peter Johnston-Saint (d 1974); 1 s ((Dudley Adrian) Conroy, Viscount Sandon), 1 da (Lady Rosalthé Rundall); m 2, 2003, Janet Mary Pierette, yst da of Alan Edward Stott, JP, DL (d 1990); *Heir* s, Viscount Sandon; *Career* served WWII in NW Europe (wounded) and Far East with 59 Inf Div, 5 Para Bde, political offr India and Java 1941–45, 56 Armoured Div TA; Lt-Col RA cmdg 254 (City of London) Field Regt RA (TA) 1962–64; dir: Dinorwic Slate Quarries Co Ltd 1951–69, National Provincial Bank 1961–69, UKPI 1955–86 (dep chm 1956–64), Olympia Group 1968–73 (chm 1971–73), Powell Duffryn Group 1976–86 (chm 1981–86), Sheepbridge Engineering Ltd 1977–79; dep chm: Coutts & Co 1970–89 (md 1949), National Westminster Bank plc 1971–87 (dir 1968–87) chm: International Westminster Bank plc 1977–87, Orion Bank 1979–81, Bentley Engineering Co Ltd 1983–86, National Westminster Investment Bank 1986–87, Dowty Group plc 1986–91, The Private Bank & Trust Co Ltd 1989–92, Private Financial Holdings 1992–95; dir Saudi International Bank 1980–82 and 1985–87; chm Nat Biological Standards Bd 1973–88; memb: Ctee of Mgmnt Inst of Psychiatry 1953–73 (chm 1965–73), Trilateral Cmmn 1980–95; Bd of Govrs: Bethlem Royal and Maudsley (Postgraduate Teaching) Hosps 1955–73 (chm 1965–73), Keele Univ 1956–68, Lord Chancellor's Advsy Investment Ctee for Court of Protection 1965–77, Advsy Investment Ctee for Public Tstee 1974–77, Psychiatry Research Tst (tstee) 1982–2000, Institut Internationale d'Études Bancaires 1977–87, Kensington BC 1950–65 (chm GP Ctee 1957–59), Kensington and Chelsea BC 1965–71 (chm Finance Ctee 1968–71); govr Atlantic Inst of Int Affairs 1983–88; hon treas: Staffs Soc 1947–51, Exec Ctee London Area Conservative Assoc 1949–50, Family Welfare Assoc 1951–65, S Kensington Conservative Assoc 1953–56, Central Cncl for Care of Cripples 1953–60; mangr Fulham and Kensington Hosp Gp 1953–56, gen cmmr for Income Tax 1954–71; pres Staffordshire/Shropshire Branch Royal Soc of St George 2003; Freeman City of London 1947, Liveryman Worshipful Co of Goldsmiths 1959; Hon DSc Keele Univ 1996; CIMgt, MRIIA, Hon FRCPsych 1983; *Style—* The Rt Hon the Earl of Harrowby, TD; ✉ Apartment 20, Albert Bridge House, 127 Albert Bridge Road, London SW11 4PL (tel 020 7223 7535); Sandon Hall, Stafford ST18 0BZ (tel 01889 508338); Burnt Norton, Chipping Campden, Gloucestershire GL55 6PR (tel 01386 841488)

HARSENT, David; s of Albert Edward Harsent (d 1990), and Mary Dorothy May Harsent (d 2004); *b* 1942, Bovey Tracey, Devon; *m* 1988, Julia Watson; 1 da (Hannah b 1990); 3 c from previous m (Ysanne, Simon, Barnaby); *Career* author; distinguished writing fell Hallam Sheffield Univ 2005; Geoffrey Faber Meml Award, Cheltenham Festival Prize, two bursaries Arts Cncl, travel fellowship Soc of Authors; FRSL 2000; *Publications* poetry: Tonight's Lover (1968), Poetry Introduction 1 (contrib, 1968), A Violent Country (1969), Truce (1973), After Dark (1973), Dreams of the Dead (1977), Mister Punch (1984), Selected Poems (1989), Storybook Hero (1992), News from the Front (1993), The Sorrow of Sarajevo (trans, poems by Goran Simic, 1996), The Potted Priest (1997), Sprinting from the Graveyard (trans, poems by Goran Simic, 1997), A Bird's Idea of Flight (1998), Marriage (2002, shortlisted T S Eliot Prize and Forward Prize 2002), Legion (2005, Forward Prize 2005, shortlisted Whitbread Poetry Prize and T S Eliot Prize 2005); fiction: From an Inland Sea (1985); as ed: Savramena Britanska Poezija (poetry anthology, with Mario Susko), Another Round at the Pillars: A Festschrift for Ian Hamilton (1999), Raising the Iron: Poems for the Palace Theatre Watford (2004); music theatre: Serenade the Silkie (music by Julian Grant, 1994), Gawain (opera, music by Sir Harrison Birtwistle, *qv*, 1991), The Woman and the Hare (song cycle, music by Sir Harrison Birtwistle, 1999), When She Died (TV opera, music by Jonathan Dove, 2002), The Ring Dance of the Nazarene (music by Sir Harrison Birtwistle, 2003); *Style—* David Harsent, Esq; ✉ c/o PFD, Drury House, 34–43 Russell Street, London WC2B 5HA (tel 020 7344 1000)

HARSTON, Julian John Robert Clive; s of Lt-Col Clive Harston, ERD (d 1993), of Surrey, and Kathleen Mary, *née* Grace; *b* 20 October 1942; *Educ* King's Sch Canterbury, Univ of London (BSc); *m* 1966 (m dis 2000), Karen Howard Oake, da of Col T E Longfield (ka 1941); 1 s (Alexander b 1978); *Career* mangr Br Tourist Authy Copenhagen and Vancouver 1965–71; FCO: joined 1971, first sec/consul Hanoi 1973–74, first sec Blantyre 1975–79, first sec Lisbon 1982–84, cnsllr Harare 1984–88, cnsllr UN Geneva 1991–95; political advsr to Special Rep of Sec-Gen for former Yugoslavia 1995, dir UN Liaison Office Belgrade 1996–98, special rep of Sec-Gen and Chief of Mission Haiti 1998–99, dep special rep of Sec-Gen Bosnia and Herzegovina 1999–2001, dir Dept of Peace-Keeping NY 2001–04, dir UN Office Belgrade 2004–; *Recreations* travel, photography, Switzerland; *Clubs* East India, RAC, Gremio Literario (Lisbon), Harare, Goodwood Aero; *Style—* Julian Harston, Esq

HART, Alan; s of Reginald Thomas Hart (d 1980), of Haddenham, Bucks, and Lilian Clara, *née* Hanson (d 1992); *b* 17 April 1935; *Educ* UCS Hampstead; *m* 16 Dec 1961, Celia Mary, *née* Vine, da of Raglan Keough; 2 s (David Alan b 31 Oct 1962, Andrew Dominic b 6 May 1965), 1 da (Gabrielle Louise b 13 Nov 1975); *Career* reporter: Willesden Chronicle and Kilburn Times 1952–58, Newcastle Evening Chronicle 1958, London Evening News 1958–59; editorial asst BBC Sportsview 1959–61, TV sports prodr BBC Manchester 1962–64, ed BBC Sportsview 1965–68 (asst ed 1964–65), ed Grandstand 1968–77, head of sport BBC TV 1977–81, controller BBC 1 1981–84, special asst to DG BBC 1985, controller Int Rels BBC 1986–91, broadcasting conslt 1991–, chm Eurosport UK 1997–99 (memb Bd 1991–97), advsr to Euro Broadcasting Union on East European broadcasting 1991–93, exec dir Eurosport Consortium 1993–2005, dir Global Amg 1995–2001, dir Give Them A Sporting Chance 2003–, chm Inventure Tst 2003–07; govr S Devon Coll 2005–; FRTS; *Recreations* sport, walking, music; *Style—* Alan Hart, Esq; ✉ Cutwellwalls, Avonwick, Near South Brent, South Devon TQ10 9HA (tel 01364 72552)

H

HART, Prof (Charles) Anthony; s of Edmund Hart, of Harrogate, N Yorks, and Alice Edna, *née* Griffin; *b* 25 February 1948; *Educ* St Michael's Coll Leeds, Royal Free Hosp Sch of Med Univ of London (MB BS, BSc, PhD); *m* 26 June 1971, Jennifer Ann, da of Keith Bonnett (d 1977); 3 da (Caroline Joanne b 23 March 1975, Rachel Louise b 6 Jan 1977, Laura Jane b 5 Feb 1980); *Career* res student and hon lectr Royal Free Hosp Sch of Med 1973–76, prof and hon conslt Dept of Med Microbiology and Genito-urinary Med Univ of Liverpool 1986– (lectr 1978–82, sr lectr and hon conslt 1982–86), visiting prof Univ of Santo Tomas Manila Philippines 1987–, pres Liverpool Medical Inst 2002–03; FRSTM&H, FRCPath 1994, FRCPCH 1997; *Books* A Colour Atlas of Paediatric Infectious Diseases (with R Broadhead, 1991), A Color Atlas of Medical Microbiology (with P Shears, 1996 and 2004), Sexually Transmitted Infection and AIDS in the Tropics (with O Arya, 1998), Manual of Childhood Infections (with E G Davies, D Elliman, A Nicoll, P Rudd, 2001), Microterrors (2004); *Style—* Prof Anthony Hart; ✉ Holly Bank, 102 Barnston Road, Thingwall, Wirral L61 1AT; Department of Medical Microbiology and Genito-Urinary Medicine, University of Liverpool, PO Box 147, Liverpool L69 3BX (tel 0151 706 4381, fax 0151 706 5805, e-mail cahmm@liv.ac.uk)

HART, Hon Mr Justice; Sir Anthony Ronald Hart; kt (2005); *b* 1946; *Educ* TCD, Queen's Univ Belfast; *Career* called to the Bar: NI 1969, Gray's Inn 1975; QC (NI) 1983, recorder of Londonderry 1985–90, judge County Court 1985–2005, bencher 1995, recorder of Belfast 1997–2005, presiding judge of County Courts in NI 2002–05, judge of the High Court of Justice in NI 2005–; *Publications* A History of the King's Serjeants at Law in Ireland (2000), author of various articles on Irish legal history; *Style—* The Hon Mr Justice Hart

HART, Charles; s of George Hart, of Cookham, and Juliet, *née* Baddeley; *b* 6 June 1967; *Educ* Desborough Sch Maidenhead, Guildhall Sch of Music and Drama; *Career* lyricist; works incl: The Phantom of the Opera (musical), Aspects of Love (musical), The Vampyr (opera), The Kissing-Dance (musical), The Dreaming (musical), misc songs; *Style—* Charles Hart

HART, Sir David Michael; kt (2006), OBE (1988); *b* 27 August 1940; *Educ* Hurstpierpoint Coll; *Career* slr in private practice 1963–78, gen sec and slr Nat Assoc of Head Teachers 1978–; memb Educn/Business Partnership Team Business in the Community; memb Law Soc 1963 (Herbert Ruse prize 1962); Hon DUniv Central England; Liveryman Worshipful Co of Loriners; FRSA; *Recreations* riding, tennis, cycling, walking; *Clubs* Wig & Pen; *Style—* Sir David Hart, OBE; ✉ Whinby Cottage, Haltcliffe, Hesket Newmarket, Wigton, Cumbria CA7 8JT; National Association of Head Teachers, 1 Heath Square, Boltro Road, Haywards Heath, West Sussex RH16 1BL (tel 01444 472404, fax 01444 472405)

HART, Prof George; eld s of George Hart, of Golborne, Lancs, and Mary, *née* Britton; *b* 7 June 1951; *Educ* Boteler GS, Churchill Coll Cambridge (MA), Trinity Coll Oxford and Oxford Univ Clinical Sch (MA, BM BCh), St Peter's Coll Oxford (DM); *m* 19 Jan 1980, Dr Judy Hart, da of Alfred Alan Reynolds (d 1988), of Bognor Regis, W Sussex; 1 da (Alice b 1982), 2 s (Samuel b 1985, Joseph b 1986); *Career* jr hosp posts 1975–77; registrar: cardiology Papworth Hosp 1977–78, med Addenbrooke's Hosp 1978–79; lectr in physiology Balliol Coll Oxford 1979–80, MRC research trg fell Univ Laboratory of Physiology Oxford 1979–82, Sidney Perry jr research fell St Peter's Coll Oxford 1979–82, sr registrar in cardiology Yorkshire Regnl HA 1982–86, BHF clinical reader in cardiovascular med Univ of Oxford 1986–98, hon conslt physician and cardiologist John Radcliffe Hosp Oxford 1986–98, supernumerary fell Lady Margaret Hall Oxford 1986–98, David A Price Evans chair of med Univ of Liverpool 1998–, hon conslt physician Royal Liverpool Univ Hosp 1998–, hon research fell Lady Margaret Hall Oxford 1999–, hon conslt cardiologist Cardiothoracic Centre Liverpool 2003–; memb: Br Cardiac Soc, Physiological Soc, Soc of Expert Witnesses, Assoc of Physicians of GB and Ireland, Br Soc for Cardiovascular Research (chm 1990–93), Int Soc for Heart Research; FRCP 1990 (MRCP 1977), FACC 1999; *Recreations* photography, walking; *Style—* Prof George Hart; ✉ Division of Clinical Sciences, The Duncan Building, Daulby Street, Liverpool L69 3GA (tel 0151 706 4074, fax 0151 706 5802, e-mail g.hart@liv.ac.uk)

HART, Gerry; s of Tom Hart (d 1993), and Sylvia, *née* Robinson; *Educ* Dartford GS; *m* 31 March 1973 (sep 1997), Pamela Elizabeth; 1 da (Jane b 6 Dec 1976), 2 s (Robert Edwin b 6 Oct 1979, Jonathan William b 30 Dec 1990); *Career* tax trainee Nat West Bank 1963–66, tax mangr Temple Gothard 1970–73, gp tax asst Guthrie Corporation 1973–74, own tax practice 1980–, md The Tax Team 1994–97, head of UK ops The Tax Team (H&R Block UK Ltd) 1997–2002; fndr UK Tax Congress (held 1981–87); popular lectr in tax; memb Editorial Bd The Tax Jl; Chartered Inst of Taxation: assoc 1968, fell 1970, nat pres 1995–96, fndr chm Sussex branch; *Books* Dictionary of Taxation (Butterworths, 1983), Tolley's Tax Planning For Family Companies (1995); *Recreations* jazz, horse riding, watching most sports, travel; *Clubs* Morton's; *Style—* Gerry Hart, Esq

HART, Dr James; CBE (2007), QPM (1999); s of Lewis Hart (d 1969), and Beatrice Hart (d 1998); *b* 10 September 1947; *Educ* Wanyneflete Sch Esher, Kingston Coll, City Univ (Bramshill scholar, BSc, PhD, professors' prize for systems science); *Family* 2 s (Andrew James b 19 March 1974, Stephen John Eric b 8 Sept 1975); m, 11 June 1993, Julie, da of Alan Russell (d 1988); *Career* joined Surrey Police 1966; Met Police: transferred 1983, postings incl Heathrow Airport, Notting Hill and New Scotland Yard, Chief Supt 1989, Divnl Cdr Wandsworth 1990–94, head Diplomatic Protection Branch 1994; Surrey Police: Asst Chief Constable Support Services 1994–95, Asst Chief Constable Territorial Policing 1995–96, Asst Chief Constable Specialist Ops 1997–98; cmmr City of London Police 2002–06 (asst cmmr 1998–2002); JSDC RNC Greenwich 1990, Sr Command Course Police Staff Coll Bramshill 1992; memb Federal Bureau of Investigation (FBI) Nat Exec Inst; ACPO: memb 1994, chm Economic Crime Ctee; DSc (hc) City Univ 2004; FCMI (FIMgt 1998); *Books* Neighbourhood Policing (jtly, 1981); *Recreations* skiing, golf, walking, creating home and garden; *Clubs* Corhampton Golf; *Style—* Dr James Hart, CBE, QPM

HART, Matthew Jason; s of Colin Dennis Hart, and Susan Jean, *née* Ranson; *b* 13 July 1972; *Educ* Arts Educnl Sch London, Royal Ballet Upper Sch; *Career* dancer/choreographer and singer/actor; Royal Ballet: artist 1991–93, first artist 1993–95, soloist 1995–96; with Rambert Dance Co 1996–2000, with George Piper Dances 2001–03, freelance artist 2003–; dance analyst and expert Strictly Dance Fever (BBC1 and BBC3) 2006; *Roles* with Royal Ballet incl: The Trepak in The Nutcracker, head Fakir in La Bayadère, Bratfisch in Mayerling, Jester in Cinderella, Squirrel Nutkin in Tales of Beatrix Potter, Solo Boy in Dances Concertantes, Beggar Chief in Manon, Neopolitan Dance, lead Czardas, lead waltz in Swan Lake, 3rd movement, Symphony in C, Rhapsody, Stravinsky Violin Concerto, Les Noces, Petrouchka, Bryaxis in Daphnis and Chloë, cr role in Forsythe's Firstext, Forsythe's Steptext, Macmillans The Judas Tree; with Rambert Dance Co incl: Cruel Garden (The Poet), Four Scenes (cr role), Ghost Dances (Tie Dance, Ghost), Axioma 7, The Golden Section, Greymatter (cr role), Rooster (Rooster Man), Stream (Duet, Men's Dance), God's Plenty (cr roles), Quicksilver, No More Play, Petit Mort, Airs, August Pace; with George Piper Dances incl: Steptext, Sigue, Tangoid, Moments of Plastic Jubilation, Truely Great Thing, Red or White, Dearest Love; with ROH incl: Toad in Wind in the Willows, The Devil in The Soldier's Tale, Asyla, Anatomy of a Storyteller; with ROH2: Oswald in Ghosts, Pinocchio in Pinocchio; others incl: Sidney Cohn in On Your Toes (musical), Frank Lawson in Mrs Henderson Presents (film), Menshikov in Riot at the Rite (film, BBC2), Betrothal in a Monastery (opera, Glyndebourne) 2006, The Prince in Matthew Bourne's Swan Lake (Paris and London) 2006, Gus Fielding in Babes in Arms (musical, Chichester Festival Theatre) 2007; *Choreography* The Dream of the Cherry Blossom (Birds Gala Royal Opera House) 1991, Simple Symphony (Royal Ballet Sch) 1992, Forbidden Fruit (Royal Ballet) 1992, Solo (Royal Ballet) 1992, Street (Birmingham Royal Ballet) 1993, Fanfare (Royal Ballet) 1993, Caught Dance (Royal Ballet) 1994, Tusk (Royal Ballet) 1994, Peter and the Wolf (Royal Ballet Sch) 1995, Cinderella (London City Ballet) 1995, Sleepers (Royal Acad of Dancing 70 Anniversary) 1995, Dances with Death (Royal Ballet) 1996, Blitz (Eng Nat Ballet) 1996, Cry Baby Kreisler (Royal Ballet) 1996, Physical Propery (Jerwood Fndn) 1996, Highly Strung (RADA Gala and Royal Ballet 1997), The Golden Vanity (Royal Ballet Sch) 1998, Sonate au Chocolat (Eng Nat Ballet Sch) 1999, Revenge (solo) 1999, Girl Band (Deutche Oper Am Rhein Düsseldorf Germany) 2000, Acheron's Dream (Royal Ballet) 2000, Mulan (Hong Kong Ballet) 2001, Images of Mulan (London Studio Centre) 2002, Other Men's Wives (George Piper Dances) 2002, Meet in the Middle (K Ballet Co) 2003, Young Persons Guide to the Orchestra (London Studio Centre) 2007; *Awards* Cosmopolitan/C & A Dance Award 1988, winner Ursula Moreton Choreographic Competition 1991, winner Frederick Ashton Choreographic Award 1994, Jerwood Fndn Award for Choreographers 1996; *Recreations* singing, painting, designing, swimming, eating out, cinema, theatre; *Style—* Matthew Hart, Esq; ✉ Conway Van Gelder, 18/21 Jermyn Street, London SW1Y 6HP (tel 020 7287 0077)

HART, Norman Antony (Tony); s of Norman Chandler Hart (d 1970), and Evelyn Emma, *née* Dyke (d 1981); *b* 15 October 1925; *Educ* Clayesmore, Indian Military Acad, Maidstone Coll of Art; *m* 2 Sept 1953, Jean, da of Reginald Frederick Skingle; 1 da (Carolyn b 1957); *Career* TV presenter and artist; Indian Army 1st Gurkha Rifles 1943–47; memb 1st Gurkha Assoc 1947; *Television* former presenter Vision On, Take Hart, Hartbeat, The Artbox Bunch, Morph TV with Tony Hart, Smart Hart; *Films* prod by Video Arts: How to Lie with Statistics, The Average Chap, Man Hunt, Who Sold You This, Then?, It's All Right, It's Only a Customer, Meetings of Minds, The Balance Sheet Barrier, The Control of Working Capital, In Two Minds, When I'm Calling You, Will You Answer True?; *Awards* Society of Film and TV Arts (for Vision On) 1974, Int Children's TV Festival (for Vision On) 1972, BBC's Multi-Coloured Swap Shop Award (for Children's TV Star) 1979 and 1980, Br Acad Awards (nominated Best Children's TV Prog) 1979, BAFTA Special Lifetime Achievement Award 1998; *Books* The Young Letterer (1965), Fun with Historical Projects (1971), Fun with Picture Projects (1973), The Corporate Computer (by Norman Saunders, illustrations, 1973), Fun with Drawing (1974), Making Mosaics (1976), Fun with Art (1976), Fun with Design (1976), Make It With Hart (1979), The Art Factory (1980), Paint and Draw (1984), Art and Craft (1984), Lettercraft (1986), Small Hands Big Ideas (1988), Draw it Yourself (1989), The Tale of Billy Bouncer (1990); *Recreations* wine, building stone walls; *Style—* Tony Hart, Esq; ✉ c/o ROC Renals, 10 Heatherway, Crowthorne, Berkshire RG45 6HG

HART, Prof Oliver Simon D'Arcy; s of Philip Montagu D'Arcy Hart (d 2006), and Ruth Hart (d 2007); *b* 9 October 1948; *Educ* Univ Coll Sch, King's Coll Cambridge (BA), Univ of Warwick (MA), Princeton Univ (PhD); *m* 1974, Rita Goldberg; 2 s; *Career* lectr in economics Univ of Essex 1974–75, asst lectr then lectr in economics Univ of Cambridge 1975–81, fell Churchill Coll Cambridge 1975–81; prof of economics: LSE 1981–85 (centennial visiting prof 1997–), MIT 1985–93, Harvard Univ 1993– (Andrew E Furer prof of economics 1997–); visiting Scholar Harvard Law Sch 1987–88, Marvin Bower fell Harvard Business Sch 1988–89; memb: Coordinating Ctee Social Sci Res Cncl Econ Theory Study Gp UK 1975–79, Prog Ctee Fourth World Congress of the Econometric Soc 1980, Editorial Advsy Bd Review of Econ Studies 1975–88, Editorial Advsy Bd Cambridge Surveys of Economic Literature Cup 1984–90, Cncl Econometric Soc 1983–89 (memb Exec Ctee at large 1984–87), Nat Sci Fndn Economics Panel 1987–, Advsy Cncl Princeton Univ Economics Dept 1989–97, vice-pres American Economic Assoc 2006, pres American Law and Economics Assoc 2006–07; assoc ed: Jl of Economic Theory 1976–79, Econometrica 1984–87, Games and Economic Behaviour 1988–, Jl of Accounting Auditing and Finance 1989–; ed Review of Economic Studies 1979–83 (asst ed 1978–79), prog dir Centre for Econ Policy Res London 1983–84, res assoc Nat Bureau of Econ Res 1990–; sec-treas American Law and Economics Assoc 2004–05; Dr (hc): Free Univ of Brussels 1992, Univ of Basel 1994; fell: Econometric Soc 1979, American Acad of Arts and Scis 1988; corresponding FBA 2000; *Books* Firms, Contracts, and Financial Structure (1995); also author of numerous articles and chapters in various books; *Recreations* playing and watching tennis; *Style—* Prof Oliver Hart; ✉ Littauer 220, Department of Economics, Harvard University, Cambridge, Mass 02138, USA

HART, Prof Robert A; s of James Hart (d 1980), and Kathleen Mary Hart (d 2006); *b* 7 January 1946; *Educ* Univ of Liverpool (MA); *m*; 3 c; *Career* lectr in economics and statistics Univ of Aberdeen 1971–73 (lectr in economics 1969–71), lectr in economics Univ of Leeds 1974–75, sr lectr Univ of Strathclyde 1976–79, visiting assoc prof McMaster Univ 1979–80, sr res fell IIM Science Centre Berlin 1980–86; Univ of Stirling: prof of economics 1986–, head of dept 1986–91, head Sch of Mgmnt 1991–94; visiting res fell W E Upjohn Inst for Employment Research 1990, managing ed Scottish Jl of Political Economy 1998–; FRSE 2002; *Publications* The Economics of Non-Wage Labour Costs (1984), Working Time and Employment (1987), Employment, Unemployment and Labour Utilization (1988), Human Capital, Employment and Bargaining (with T Moutos, 1995), Work and Pay in Japan (with S Kawasaki 1999), The Economics of Overtime Working (2004); author of numerous chapters in books and articles in jls; *Recreations* reading, walking, beer drinking; *Style—* Prof Robert Hart; ✉ Department of Economics, University of Stirling, Stirling FK9 4LA (tel 01786 467471, fax 01786 67469, e-mail r.a.hart@stir.ac.uk)

HART, Stefa Belitis; da of Vladimir Georgief Daskaloff (d 1995), and Helen Brookes, *née* Bremner (d 1968); *b* 10 March 1949, Gibraltar; *Educ* Convent of the Sacred Heart Hove, Branston Coll; *m* 17 April 1974, Timothy Frederick Hart, *qv*; 3 s (Sam Kinsford, Edward George, James Harry); *Career* interior designer; sec to librarian Royal Instn 1968–69, sec to Christopher Selmes and Richard Jacobs 1969–70, asst to Marcel d'Argy Smith (as ed The Antiques Year Book) 1971–72, Galerie Altman Paris 1972–73; dir and interior designer Hambleton Hall Hotel Rutland 1980–, estab Hambleton Decorating 1988, dir and interior designer Hart's Hotel Nottingham 2003–, dir Fino's Restaurant London 2003–; chm Rutland Macmillan Cancer Support 2006–; *Recreations* painting, walking, stalking, fishing, gardening, music; *Style—* Mrs Stefa Hart

HART, Timothy Frederick (Tim); s of Louis Albert Hart (d 1977), of Dynes Hall, Halstead, Essex, and Theresa Elsie Hart (d 1994); *b* 7 December 1947; *Educ* Westminster, Jesus Coll Cambridge (MA); *m* Stefa Belitis, *qv*, da of Vladimir Daskaloff; 3 s (Samuel b Sept 1974, Edward b Aug 1976, James b March 1982); *Career* Henry Ansbacher and Co 1969–73, Lehman Brothers Inc 1974–79; purchased Hambleton Hall 1979 (opened as Country House Hotel 1980); fndr chm and chief exec Hart Hambleton plc 1986, purchased and redeveloped Ram Jam Inn 1986, opened Hart's restaurant Nottingham 1997, opened Hart's Hotel 2003; chm Br Section of Relais et Chateaux 1987–90; govr Oakham Sch 1990–; *Recreations* shooting, fishing, gastronomy, oenology, literature, gardening, watercolour painting, deer stalking, tree climbing; *Style—* Tim Hart, Esq; ✉ Hart Hambleton plc, Hambleton Hall, Hambleton, Oakham, Rutland LE15 8TH (tel 01572 756991, fax 01572 724721)

HART-DAVIS, (Peter) Duff; s of Sir Rupert Hart-Davis (d 1999), of Marske-in-Swaledale, N Yorks, and Comfort Borden, *née* Turner (d 1970); *b* 3 June 1936; *Educ* Eton, Univ of Oxford (BA); *m* 1961, Phyllida, da of Col John Barstow; 1 s (Guy b 1965), 1 da (Alice b 1963); *Career* journalist and author; graduate trainee Western Mail Cardiff 1960; Sunday Telegraph: asst to Literary Ed 1961–63, ed Close-Up (news background) team 1968–70, literary ed 1976–77, asst ed 1977–78, editorial advsr 1980–85; contrib Country Matters column The Independent 1986–2001; *Novels* The Megacull (1968), The Gold of St Matthew (1970), Spider in the Morning (1972), The Heights of Rimring (1980), Level Five (1982), Fire Falcon (1983), The Man-Eater of Jassapur (1985), Horses of War (1991); *Non-fiction* Peter Fleming (1974), Ascension (1976), Monarchs of the Glen (1978), Hitler's Games (1986), The Letters and Journals of Sir Alan Lascelles (ed 2 vols, 1986 and 1988), Armada (1988), Country Matters (1989), The House the Berrys Built (1990), Wildings: the Secret Garden of Eileen Soper (1991), Further Country Matters (1992), When the Country Went to Town (1997), Raoul Millais (1998), Fauna Britannica (2002), Audubon's Elephant (2003), Honorary Tiger (2006), King's Counsellor: Abdication and War - the Diaries of Tommy Lascelles (ed, 2006); *Recreations* opera, gardening, deer, splitting wood; *Style—* Duff Hart-Davis, Esq

HART DYKE, Sir David William; 10 Bt (E 1677), of Horeham, Sussex; s of Sir Derek William Hart Dyke, 9 Bt (d 1987), and his 1 w, Dorothy, *née* Moses; 2 Bt m Anne, da and heir of Percival Hart of Lullingstone Castle, 5 Bt unsuccessfully claimed the Barony of Brayes of which he was a co heir through the Harts 1836; *b* 5 January 1955; *Educ* Ryerson Polytechnical Inst; *Heir* unc, Guy Hart Dyke; *Style—* Sir David Hart Dyke, Bt; ✉ 28 King Street West, Apartment B14, Stoney Creek, Ontario, Canada

HART-LEVERTON, Colin Allen; QC (1979); s of Morris Hart-Leverton, of London; *b* 10 May 1936; *Educ* Stowe; *m*; 1 s (David b 1 July 1967); m 1990, Kathi, *née* Davidson; *Career* called to the Bar Middle Temple 1957, dep circuit judge 1975, attorney-at-law Turks and Caicos Islands 1976, recorder of the Crown Ct 1979; occasional radio and TV broadcasts in UK and USA; memb Taxation Inst 1957; *Recreations* table tennis, jazz; *Style—* Colin Hart-Leverton, Esq, QC; ✉ 8 King's Bench Walk, 1st Floor, Temple, London EC4Y 7DU (tel 020 7452 8900)

HART OF CHILTON, Baron (Life Peer UK 2004), of Chilton in the County of Suffolk; Garry Richard Rushby Hart; s of Dennis George Hart (d 1984), and Evelyn Mary, *née* Rushby; *b* 29 June 1940; *Educ* Northgate GS Ipswich, UCL (LLB); *m* 1, 24 March 1966 (m dis 1986), Paula Lesley, da of Leslie Shepherd; 2 s (Hon Alexander, Hon Jonathan), 1 da (Hon Kaley); m 2, 1986, Valerie Elen Mary, da of Cledwyn Wilson Davies; 2 da (Hon Sarah, Hon Stephanie (twins)); *Career* slr; ptnr Herbert Smith 1970–98 (head Property Dept 1988–98); special advsr to: Lord Chllr 1998–2003, Sec of State for Constitutional Affrs and Lord Chllr 2003–07, Sec of State for Justice 2007–; memb Building Strategy Ctee V&A 2007–; dep chm of tstees Architecture Fndn 1997–2005, tstee Almeida Theatre Islington 1997–2005 (chm 1997–2002), tstee Br Architectural Library Tst; Freeman City of London, Liveryman Worshipful Co of Slrs; fell UCL (memb Cncl 2005–); memb Law Soc 1966; FRSA, Hon FRIBA; *Books* Blundell and Dobrys Planning Applications Appeals and Proceedings (jtly, 5 edn); *Recreations* conservation, theatre, talking and travel; *Clubs* Reform, Garrick; *Style—* The Rt Hon the Lord Hart of Chilton; ✉ Selborne House, 54–60 Victoria Street, London SW1E 6QW

HARTE, Dr Michael John; s of late Harold Edward Harte, of Sussex, and late Marjorie Irene, *née* Scaife; *b* 15 August 1936; *Educ* Charterhouse, Trinity Coll Cambridge (BA), UCL (Dip Biochemical Engrg, PhD); *m* 1, 1962 (m dis); *m* 2, 1975, Mrs Mary Claire Preston, da of D J Hogan (d 1972); 4 step da (Caroline b 1962, Emma b 1964, Abigail, Lucy (twins) b 1966); *Career* chm NATO Budget Ctees 1981–83; asst under sec: Dockyard Planning Team MOD 1985, Air Personnel MOD 1987, Resources MOD 1990–93; dir gen IT Systems MOD 1994–95, currently managing conslt Greenman Enterprise; fndr and chm Wadhurst History Soc; *Publications* Wadhurst Then and Now, Victorian Wadhurst, The Day Wadhurst Changed; *Recreations* wine, Wadhurst website, weeding; *Style—* Dr Michael Harte; ✉ Greenman Farm, Wadhurst, East Sussex TN5 6LE (tel 01892 783292, e-mail harte@greenman.demon.co.uk)

HARTILL, Rosemary Jane; da of Clement Augustus Hartill (d 2001), of Salop, and Florence Margarita, *née* Ford (d 1989); *b* 11 August 1949; *Educ* Wellington Girls' HS, Univ of Bristol (BA); *Career* ed Tom Stacey Ltd 1970–73, jr ed David & Charles 1973–75, sr non-fiction ed Hamish Hamilton Children's Books 1975–76, freelance dance and book reviewer Times Education Supplement 1976–79, BBC religious affrs corr 1982–88 (reporter 1979–82), reporter Human Factor (ITV) 1988–92; presenter of progs incl: Woman's Hour (BBC Radio 4, NE editions) 1989–91, Meridian Books (BBC World Service); independent broadcaster and writer; co-fndr Voyager Television Ltd 1997, fndr Rosemary Hartill and Assoc independent radio productions 1996–; series for BBC World Service incl: Wisdom of the World 1997, Stories from the Afterlife 1998, Practical Peacemaking 1998, Just Business? 1999, Dreamtime Dreams 1999, Write Inside 2001, Healing the Wounds of War 2002; occasional presenter Something Understood (BBC Radio 4) 2004–; Sony Award nominations for: Best Radio Reporter of the Year 1988, Best Arts Feature 1990; Sandford St Martin Tst prizes 1992, 1994 and 1998 (incl personal award for outstanding contrib to religious broadcasting 1994), various other awards and nominations; dir: Ethical Investment Research and Information Service 1996–2001, Shared Interest 1997–2005; memb Bd: Nat Probation Serv Northumberland 2001–07, Northumberland Tyne & Wear SHA 2002–05; memb: Courts Bd Northumbria 2004–07, Youth Justice Bd for England and Wales 2004–; tstee Alternatives to Violence Project 1998–2001 (facilitator 1996–), memb Soc of Friends; Hon DLitt: Univ of Hull 1995, Univ of Bristol 2000; FRSA 2001; *Books* Wild Animals, Emily Brontë - Poems (ed), In Perspective, Writers Revealed, Were You There?, Florence Nightingale: Letters and Reflections (ed); *Recreations* wildlife, walking, theatre, modern art exhibitions; *Style—* Rosemary Hartill; ✉ Old Post Office, Eglingham Village, Alnwick, Northumberland NE66 2TX

HARTILL, (Edward) Theodore; OBE (2004); s of Clement Augustus Hartill (d 2001), of Salop, and Florence Margarita, *née* Ford (d 1989); *b* 23 January 1943; *Educ* Priory Sch for Boys Shrewsbury, Coll of Estate Mgmnt, Univ of London (BSc); *m* 1, 2 s (Jeremy b 1969, Richard b 1972); m 2, 1975, Gillian Ruth, da of Harold Todd (d 1963); 2 s (Andrew b 1977, Giles b 1981); *Career* joined Messrs Burd and Evans Land Agents Shrewsbury 1963; Estates Dept Legal and Gen Assurance Society 1964–73, Property Investment Dept Guardian Royal Exchange Assurance Gp 1973–85, The City Surveyor City of London Corp 1985–2008, conslt to Corderoy (int quantity surveyors and cost conslts) 2008–; visiting lectr in law of town planning and compulsory purchase Hammersmith and West London Coll of Advanced Business Studies 1968–78; RICS: memb Gen Practice Divnl Cncl 1989–97, memb Governing Cncl 1990–2004, pres Gen Practice Div 1992–93, hon treas 2000–04; Construction Industry Standing Conference (CISC): memb Steering Ctee 1992–99, chm Property Services Sub-Gp; chm Property Services Nat Trg Organisation 1999–2004; Asset Skills: chm 2003–04, vice-chm 2004–07; memb: Assoc of Chief Estates Surveyors and Property Managers in Local Govt 1988–2007 (pres 1996–97), Br Schs Exploring Soc, Cncl Univ of London 2004–; govr and tstee Coram Family 2006–; hon assoc Czech Chamber of Appraisers; hon memb Investment Property Forum; Master Worshipful Company of Chartered Surveyors 2003–04 (Liveryman 1985, memb Ct of Assts 1991–); FRICS, FRSA; *Recreations* travel, hill walking, cars and GT racing; *Style—* E T Hartill Esq, OBE; ✉ 215 Sheen Lane, East Sheen, London SW14 8LE (tel 020 8878 4494)

HARTLAND, Michael; *see:* James, Michael Leonard

HARTLEY, Dr David Fielding; s of Robert Maude Hartley (d 1980), of Hebden Bridge, W Yorks, and Sheila Ellen, *née* Crabtree (d 1977); *b* 14 September 1937; *Educ* Rydal Sch, Clare Coll Cambridge (MA, PhD); *m* 23 April 1960, Joanna Mary (d 1998), da of John Stanley Bolton (d 1988), of Halifax; 2 da (Caroline (Mrs Eatough) b 1963, Rosalind (Mrs Fell) b 1968), 1 s (Timothy b 1965); *Career* Univ of Cambridge: sr asst in res 1964–65, asst dir of res 1966–67, lectr Mathematical Laboratory 1967–70, jr res fell Churchill Coll 1964–67, dir computing serv 1970–94, fell Darwin Coll 1969–86, fell Clare Coll 1987–; chief exec UK Educn and Research Networking Assoc 1994–97, exec dir Cambridge Crystallographic Data Centre 1997–2002, steward Clare Coll Cambridge 2002–05; dir: NAG Ltd 1979–2006 (chm 1986–97), Lynxvale Ltd 1982–94, CAD Centre Ltd 1983–94; memb: Computer Bd for Univs and Res Cncls 1979–83, PM's Info Technol Advsy Panel 1981–86, BBC Sci Consultative Gp 1984–87, pres Br Computer Soc 1999–2000 (vice-pres 1984–90, dep pres 1998–99), chm Computer Conservation Soc 2007–; Freeman: City of London 1988, Co of Info Technologists 1988; FBCS 1967, CEng 1990; Medal of Merits Nicholas Copernicus Univ Poland 1984; *Style—* Dr David Hartley; ✉ Clare College, Cambridge CB2 1TL (tel 01223 333285, e-mail david.hartley@clare.cam.ac.uk)

HARTLEY, Prof Frank Robinson; DL (Beds 2005); s of Sir Frank Hartley, CBE (d 1997), and Lydia May, *née* England (d 1996); *b* 29 January 1942; *Educ* KCS Wimbledon, Magdalen Coll Oxford (MA, DPhil, DSc); *m* 12 Dec 1964, Valerie, da of George Peel (d 1984); 3 da (Susan b 1967, Judith b 1971, Elizabeth b 1974); *Career* res fell Div of Protein Chem CSIRO (Aust) 1966–69, ICI res fell and tutor in chem UCL 1969–70, lectr in chem Univ of Southampton 1970–75, princ and dean RMCS 1982–89 (prof of chem 1975–82), vice-chllr Cranfield Univ 1989–2006 (emeritus prof 2007–); chm: CIM Technology Ltd 1990–2006, CIT Holdings Ltd 1990–2006; md Cranfield Ventures Ltd 1990–2006; dir: Beds TEC 1994–96, Shuttleworth Tst 1994–97; non-exec dir: T & N plc 1989–98, Eastern Regnl Bd National Westminster Bank plc 1990–92, Kalon plc 1994–99, Kenwood Appliances plc 1995–99, Hunting-BRAE Ltd 1999–2000; special advsr to PM on Defence Systems 1988–90, memb Parly Scientific Ctee 1987– (Cncl 1992–, vice-pres 1996–98), memb Cncl IOD 2000–, memb Eastern Region Bd CBI 2000–; chm: Lorch Fndn 1995–2006, Oxon Soc of Rugby Football Referees; RFU touch judge; fell KCS Wimbledon 2003; FRSC 1977, FRSA 1988, CIMgt 1991, FRAeS 1996; *Books* Chemistry of Platinum and Palladium (1973), Elements of Organometallic Chemistry (1974), Solution Equilibria (1980), Supported Metal Complexes (1985), Chemistry of the Metal-Carbon Bond (vol 1 1983, vol 2 1984, vol 3 1985, vol 4 1987, vol 5 1989), Chemistry of Organphosphorus Compounds (vol 1 1990, vol 2 1992, vol 3 1994, vol 4 1996), Chemistry of the Platinum Group Metals (1991); *Recreations* swimming, cliff walking, reading, gardening; *Clubs* Shrivenham, IOD; *Style—* Prof Frank Hartley, DL; ✉ c/o Cranfield University, Cranfield, Bedford MK43 0AL (tel 01234 754013, e-mail f.r.perkins@cranfield.ac.uk)

H

HARTLEY, Julian Matthew Frederick; s of Max Hartley, of Bingley, W Yorks, and Rosalind, *née* Gill; *b* 24 February 1967, Keighley, W Yorks; *Educ* Bingley GS, Univ of Durham (BA, MBA), Univ of Cambridge (PGCE), Open Univ, Nuffield Inst Univ of Leeds (Cert); *m* 24 May 1997, Karina, *née* Wood; 1 da (Lydia b 22 Nov 1999), 1 s (Max Peter b 4 Oct 2002); *Career* teacher King Edward VI Sch Morpeth 1989–91, nat trainee NHS general mgmt training scheme 1991–93, planning mangr South Durham HA 1993–94, planning and mktg mangr South Tees Acute Hosps NHS Tst 1994–95, dep head of devpt Northern and Yorks regnl office NHS Exec 1995–99, asst dir planning and devpt Newcastle upon Tyne Hosps NHS Tst 1999–2000, dir of acute servs, planning and devpt North Tees and Hartlepool NHS Tst 2000–02, chief exec Tameside and Glossop PCT 2002–05, chief exec Blackpool Fylde and Wyre Hosps NHS Tst 2005–; *Recreations* collector and imbiber of fine wine, video games, performance cars, Manchester United FC, theatre, literature, film; *Style—* Julian Hartley, Esq; ✉ Blackpool Fylde and Wyre Hospitals NHS Trust, Victoria Hospital, Whinney Heys Road, Blackpool, Lancashire FY3 8NR (tel 01253 306853, fax 01253 306873, e-mail julian.hartley@bfwhospitals.nhs.uk)

HARTLEY, Prof Keith; s of W Hartley, of Leeds, and Ivy, *née* Stead; *b* 14 July 1940; *Educ* Univ of Hull (BA, PhD); *m* 12 April 1966, Winifred; 1 s (Adam b 27 Feb 1969), 2 da (Lucy b 18 Oct 1970, Cecilia b 20 July 1975); *Career* Univ of York: dir Inst for Research in Social Scis 1982–94, prof of economics 1987–, fndr dir Centre for Defence Economics 1990–; visiting prof: Univ of Illinois, Univ of Malaysia, Univ of NSW; *Books* Political Economy of NATO (1999); *Recreations* angling, football, walking, reading; *Style—* Prof Keith Hartley; ✉ Centre for Defence Economics, University of York, York YO10 5DD (tel 01904 433752, telex 01904 433759, e-mail kh2@york.ac.uk)

HARTLEY, Keith; s of Albert Hartley, MBE (d 1991), and Joan Winifred, *née* Dixson (d 1973); *b* 11 October 1956; *Educ* Chislehurst & Sidcup GS for Boys, KCL (LLB), Coll of Law; *m* 1986, Barbara Elizabeth Rundle-Smith, da of Capt Arthur Edmund Smith; 1 s (Dominic Edward b 23 Nov 1993), 1 da (Elena Joan b 28 Dec 1997); *Career* admitted slr 1982; Masons (now Pinsent Masons): articled clerk 1980–82, slr London 1982–84, Hong Kong office 1984–95 (ptnr 1986–), Leeds office 1995–; memb: Law Soc Hong Kong 1984, Inst of Arbitrators 1987, Asia Pacific Lawyers Assoc 1990; *Recreations* history, computing, family; *Style—* Keith Hartley, Esq; ✉ Pinsent Masons, 1 Park Row, Leeds LS1 5AB (tel 0113 233 8905, fax 0113 245 4285, mobile 07836 312314, e-mail keith.hartley@masons.com)

HARTMANN, Dr Reinhard Rudolf Karl; s of Walther Eduard Hartmann, of Vienna, Austria, and Gerta Emilia Stanislawa, *née* Müllner; *b* 8 April 1938; *Educ* Vienna GS, Vienna Sch of Economics (BSc and Doctorate), Univ of Vienna (Dip Translation), Southern Illinois Univ (MA); *m* 22 June 1965, Lynn, da of Kingston Vernon Warren, of Droylsden, Manchester; 1 da (Nasim b 1965), 1 s (Stefan b 1967); *Career* lectr in modern languages UMIST 1964–68, lectr in applied linguistics Univ of Nottingham 1968–74; Univ of Exeter: sr lectr in applied linguistics 1974–91, dir Language Centre 1974–92, dir Dictionary Res Centre 1984–2001, reader in applied linguistics 1991– (Sch of English 1996–2001), head Dept of Applied Linguistics 1992–96; hon prof Dept of English Univ of Birmingham 2000–, visiting prof and hon univ fell Sch of English Univ of Exeter 2001–; memb: Br Assoc for Applied Linguistics (BAAL) 1967, Euro Assoc for Lexicography (EURALEX) 1983 (fndr memb, former sec and pres, hon life memb 1994), Dictionary Soc of N America (DSNA) 1984, Asian Assoc for Lexicography (ASIALEX) 1997; FCIL 1997, FRSA 2000; *Books* Dictionary of Language and Linguistics (jtly, 1972), Contrastive Textology (1980), Lexicography Principles and Practice (ed, 1983), LEXeter '83 Proceedings (ed, 1984), The History of Lexicography (ed, 1986), Lexicography in Africa (ed, 1990), The English Language in Europe (ed, 1996), Solving Language Problems (ed, 1996), Dictionary of Lexicography (jtly, 1998 and 2001), Oxford Dictionary of National Biography (assoc ed 1998–2004), Annotated Bibliography for English Studies (assoc ed 1998–), Dictionaries in Language Learning (ed, 1999), Teaching and Researching Lexicography (2001), Lexicography - Critical Concepts (ed, 2003), Dictionaries across Cultures (2004); *Recreations* listening to music, yoga, table tennis; *Style—* Dr Reinhard Hartmann; ✉ 40 Velwell Road, Exeter EX4 4LD (e-mail r.r.k.hartmann@exeter.ac.uk)

HARTNALL, Michael James; s of late James Inglis Hartnall, of Headley Down, Hants, and late Phylis Hartnall; *b* 10 July 1942; *Educ* Ryde Sch; *m* July 1968, Pamela Hartnall; 3 da; *Career* qualified CA 1965, md Mayhew Foods plc 1987 (joined 1984), fin dir Rexam plc 1987–2003; non-exec dir: BAE Systems plc, Lonmin plc; Liveryman Worshipful Co of Butchers; FCA; *Recreations* opera, music, theatre, walking, snooker; *Clubs* Anglo Belgian; *Style—* Michael Hartnall, Esq

HARTNELL, Dr George Gordon; s of Francis George Hartnell, of Holywell Lake, Somerset, and Margaret, *née* Gordon; *b* 19 July 1952; *Educ* Abingdon Sch, Univ of Bristol (BSc, MB ChB); *Career* registrar in cardiology Harefield Hosp 1979–81, registrar and sr registrar Royal Postgrad Med Sch Hammersmith Hosp London 1983–87, formerly dir of cardiovascular and interventional radiology Beth Israel Deaconess Medical Center Boston and assoc prof Harvard Med Sch, currently head of cardiovascular and interventional radiology Baystate Medical Center and prof of radiology Tufts Univ Sch of Med; memb

Radiological Soc of North America, fell American Coll of Cardiology; MRCP 1982, FRCR 1985; *Recreations* sailing, skiing; *Style—* Dr George Hartnell; ✉ Baystate Medical Center, 759 Chestnut Street, Springfield, MA 01199, USA

HARTNETT, Angela; MBE (2007); *b* 5 September 1968; *Educ* Cambridge Poly (BA); *Career* chef; Midsummer House Cambridge 1991–93, Tamarind Cove Barbados 1993–94, Aubergine London 1994–95, L'Oranger London 1996–98, Pètrus London 1999–2001, Verre Dubai Creek Hilton 2001–02, chef and patron Angela Hartnett at The Connaught 2002– (winner Best New Restaurant BMW Square Meal Award 2003, Michelin Star 2004); *Recreations* cinema, reading, gym; *Style—* Ms Angela Hartnett, MBE; ✉ Angela Hartnett at The Connaught, Carlos Place, Mayfair, London W1K 2AL (tel 020 7592 1222, fax 020 7592 1223)

HARTOP, Barry; s of Philip William Hartop (d 1954), of Lowestoft, Suffolk, and Constance Winifred Hartop; *b* 15 August 1942; *Educ* Lowestoft GS, Univ of Durham (BSc); *m* 30 July 1966, Sandra, da of Alan Walter Swan (d 1976), of Lowestoft, Suffolk; *Career* mgmnt trainee Unilever, prodn mangr Lever Bros Ltd 1965–72, information and cost reduction mangr Unilever plc 1972–80, md Euro Business Centre Unilever plc 1980–83, chm/md Lever Industrial Ltd 1983–89, md Gestetner plc 1989–92; chief exec: Welsh Development Agency 1994–97, Millennium Central 1996–97; md Norsk Data 1997–2001, ceo Telenor Business Solutions (UK) Ltd 2001–03; chm: Hammicks Bookshops Ltd 1994–98, Locum Group 1997–2002, Reed Health Group plc 2003–05; govr Royal GS Guildford 1991–, chm Royal GS Fndn Ltd 2004–; *Recreations* keeping fit, tennis, gardening; *Clubs* County (Guildford); *Style—* Barry Hartop, Esq; ✉ Linton House, Snowdenham Links Road, Bramley, Guildford, Surrey GU5 0BX (e-mail bshartop@hotmail.com)

HARTWELL, Sir (Francis) Anthony Charles Peter; 6 Bt (UK 1805), of Dale Hall, Essex; s of Sir Brodrick William Charles Elwin Hartwell, 5 Bt (d 1993), and his 1 w, Molly Josephine, *née* Mullins; *b* 1 June 1940; *Educ* Thames Nautical Trg Coll, HMS Worcester, Cadet RNR, Univ of Southampton Sch of Navigation (Master Mariner); *m* 1968 (m dis 1989), Barbara Phyllis Rae, da of Henry Rae Green (d 1985), of Sydney, Aust; 1 s (Timothy Peter Michael Charles b 1970); *Heir* s, Timothy Hartwell; *Career* P&O/Inchcape Gp 1958–69 and 1972–75: Chief Offr/Cadet Trg Offr, Mate/Master; OCL (London) 1969–71; Cargo Supt 1975–; md Universal UKI Ltd 1999–; dir Int Diamond Drilling Ltd 1999–; Overseas Managerial Services for marine and port ops contracts; marine conslt and surveyor; memb Fedn of Aust Underwater Instructors (FAUI), MCIT, MRIN, MNI; *Recreations* scuba diving, ocean sailing, photography; *Clubs* Master Mariners (Southampton), Old Worcester's Assoc; *Style—* Sir Anthony Hartwell, Bt

HARTY, Bernard Peter; CBE (1998); s of William Harty (d 1975), and Eileen Nora, *née* Canavan; *b* 1 May 1943; *Educ* St Richard's Coll Droitwich, Ullathorne GS Coventry; *m* 12 Aug 1965, Glenys Elaine, da of Ernest Simpson (d 1969); 1 da (Sarah Jane b 1970); *Career* accountant Coventry City Cncl 1961–69; forward budget planning offr Derbys CC 1969–72, chief accountant Bradford City Cncl 1972–73, chief fin offr Bradford Met DC 1973–76, co treas Oxfordshire CC 1976–83, Chamberlain Corp of London 1983–95, md Barbican Centre 1994–95, town clerk and chamberlain Corp of London 1996–99; chm and non-exec dir Dexia Municipal Bank 1993–2000; chm: London Pension Fund Authy 1999–2001, Imerys (UK) Pension Fund 1999–, London Processing Centre Retirement and Death Benefit Scheme 2000–03, Alstom Pension Scheme 2004–05; sometime chm: Fndn for IT in Local Govt, Superannuation Investment Panel and Treasy Mgmnt Panel Chartered Inst of Public Fin Accountants; dir Gloucester Everyman Theatre; govr Cheltenham and Gloucester Coll of HE; parish cncllr Charlton Kings Cheltenham 2006–; Liveryman Worshipful Co of Tallow Chandlers, fndr memb and Hon Liveryman Worshipful Co of Information Technologists; Hon PhD London Guildhall Univ 1997; CPFA 1966; Cdr Order of Merit (France) 1996; *Recreations* National Trust, music, cricket, theatre; *Style—* Bernard Harty, Esq, CBE; ✉ e-mail bernardharty@aol.com

HARVARD TAYLOR, Nicholas; s of Paul Harvard Taylor (d 1980), and Esmèe Mary, *née* Biggs (d 1980); *b* 4 December 1952; *Educ* Haileybury and ISC; *m* Tessa Ann Harvard Taylor, JP, *née* Morris; 2 c (Jack Alfred, Katie Esmèe (twins) b 3 Oct 1989); *Career* chm and ceo Harvard Marketing Services 1981– (fndr 1979); chm: Harvard Public Relations Ltd 1982–, ChimeOnline 2001–; memb Parly Info and Technol Ctee; chm of govrs Harmondsworth Sch, memb British Red Cross Soc; Freeman City of London, Liveryman Worshipful Co of Merchant Taylors; MCIM, FRSA; *Recreations* classic cars, avoiding the ignorance of the Arts, tennis, keeping a lawn, favourite outdoor sport is the same as favourite indoor sport but with his coat on; *Clubs* Foxhills Country; *Style—* Nicholas Harvard Taylor, Esq; ✉ Kenwolde Manor, Callow Hill, Virginia Water, Surrey UB7 0AW

HARVEY, Alan James (Tim); s of Ernest Harold Harvey (d 1994), and Ida Amelia (d 1992); *b* 14 October 1936; *Educ* Hampton GS, Victoria Univ of Manchester Sch of Architecture (BArch); *m* 1956, Sheila; 1 da (Cathy b 1961), 1 s (Matthew b 1962); *Career* prodn designer: BBC Manchester 1960–64, Telefis Eirean 1964–65, BBC Scotland 1966–69, BBC London 1969–88, freelance film work 1988–; *Awards* BAFTA award for: I Claudius 1976, Bleak House 1985, Fortunes of War 1987; Emmy for: I Claudius 1976, The Pallisers 1978; RTS award for The Borgias 1981; BAFTA nominations: The Borgias 1981, Marie Curie 1982, Henry V 1990, Frankenstein 1993, Hamlet 1998; Oscar nomination Hamlet 1998; RDI 1991; *Recreations* theatre, cinema, Italian, football, reading; *Style—* Tim Harvey, Esq, RDI; ✉ c/o ICM, 76 Oxford Street, London W1N 0AX

HARVEY, Prof Andrew Charles; *b* 10 September 1947; *Educ* Leeds Modern Sch, Univ of York (BA), LSE (MSc); *Career* economist/statistician Central Bureau of Statistics Kenya 1969–71, lectr in economic and social statistics Univ of Kent 1971–77; LSE: sr lectr 1978–80, reader 1980–84, prof 1984–96; prof of econometrics Univ of Cambridge and fell Corpus Christi Coll Cambridge 1996–; fell Econometric Soc 1985, FBA 1999; *Books* The Econometric Analysis of Time Series (1981), Time Series Models (1981), Forecasting, Structural Time Series Models and the Kalman Filter (1989); *Recreations* football, opera, walking; *Style—* Prof Andrew Harvey; ✉ Corpus Christi College, Cambridge CB2 1RH (tel 01223 335228, fax 01223 335475, e-mail ach34@cam.ac.uk)

HARVEY, Prof Brian Wilberforce; s of Gerald Harvey, and Noelle, *née* Dean; *b* 17 March 1936; *Educ* Clifton, St John's Coll Cambridge (choral scholar, MA, LLM); *Career* admitted slr 1961, lectr Univ of Birmingham 1962–63, sr lectr Nigerian Law Sch 1965–67, lectr, sr lectr then prof of law Queen's Univ Belfast 1967–73; Univ of Birmingham: prof of property law 1973–98, pro-vice-chllr 1986–92, dir of Legal Office 1990–98, emeritus prof 1998–; chm: Medical and Disability Appeal Tbnls and Social Security Appeals Tbnls Birmingham 1982–99, Consumer Credit Appeals 1990–; memb Br Hallmarking Cncl 1989–91, tstee Ouseley Tst 1988–; FRSA 2005; *Books* Settlements of Land (1973), Law of Consumer Protection and Fair Trading (1978, 6 edn jtly, 2000), Law of Producing and Marketing Goods and Services (jtly, 1990), Violin Fraud (1992, 2 edn jtly, 1997), The Violin Family and its Makers in the British Isles (1995), Buying and Selling Art and Antiques - The Law (1998), Edward Heron-Allen's Journal of the Great War (ed jtly, 2002), Law of Auctions (3 edn jtly, 2006), Elgar, Vicat Cole and the Ghosts of Brinkwells (jtly, 2007); *Recreations* theological speculation, studying violins, music; *Style—* Prof Brian Harvey; ✉ c/o School of Law, The University, Birmingham B15 2TT (tel 0121 414 6282)

HARVEY, Caroline; *see:* Trollope, Joanna

HARVEY, Prof (Sir) Charles Richard Musgrave; 3 Bt (UK 1933), of Threadneedle St, City of London; does not use title; s of Sir Richard Musgrave Harvey, 2 Bt (d 1978), and Frances, *née* Lawford (d 1986); *b* 7 April 1937; *Educ* Marlborough, Pembroke Coll Cambridge; *m* 1967, Celia Vivien, da of George Henry Hodson; 1 s (Paul b 1971), 1 da (Tamara b 1977); *Heir* s, Paul Harvey; *Career* professorial fell Inst of Devpt Studies Univ of Sussex until 2002, ret; *Style—* Prof Charles Harvey

HARVEY, Prof David Robert; s of Cyril Francis Harvey (d 1971), of Orpington, Kent, and Margarita, *née* Cardew-Smith (d 1986); *b* 7 December 1936; *Educ* Dulwich Coll, Guy's Hosp Med Sch (MB BS); *Partner* Teck Ong; *Career* held jr appointments in paediatrics: Guy's Hosp, Gt Ormond St Hosp, Hammersmith Hosp; conslt paediatrician: Queen Charlotte's Maternity Hosp 1970–2002, St Charles' Hosp 1971–92, St Mary's Hosp 1987–92, Hammersmith Hosp 1992; prof of paediatrics and neonatal med Imperial Coll Sch of Med at Hammersmith Hosp (Royal Postgrad Med Sch until merger 1997) 1995–; hon sec: Neonatal Soc 1974–79, British Paediatric Assoc 1979–84, British Assoc for Perinatal Paediatrics 1983–86; James Spence Medal Royal Coll of Paediatrics and Child Health 1999; dir: Terrence Higgins Tst 1983–88, Radio Lollipop; co-chair Gay and Lesbian Assoc of Doctors and Dentists (GLADD) 1999–; Freeman of City of London, Liveryman Worshipful Soc of Apothecaries; FRCP 1976 (MRCP 1963), FRCPCH 1997; *Publications* articles on general and neonatal paediatrics and child health; A New Life (1979), New Parents (1988); *Recreations* opera, learning Chinese, using word processor; *Style—* Prof David Harvey

HARVEY, Prof David Roberton; s of Capt John Harvey (d 1983), of New Milton, Hants, and Ann, *née* Dodgson; *b* 24 October 1947; *Educ* Berkhamsted Sch, Univ of Newcastle upon Tyne (BSc), Univ of Manchester (MA, PhD); *m* 1 (m dis 1984), Cathryn, *née* Whitehead; 2 s (Daniel b 1975, James b 1977); m 2, 9 April 1985, Joan, da of John Hayward, of Ripon, N Yorks; 1 s (John b 1985); *Career* asst lectr Univ of Manchester 1972–73, sr agric economist Agriculture Canada (Ottawa) 1977–79 (agric economist 1973–76), lectr Univ of Newcastle 1979–83; prof: Univ of Reading 1984–86, Univ of Newcastle 1986– (head Dept of Agric Economics and Food Mktg 1992–97); memb Nat Ctee SDP 1983–87; pres Agricultural Economics Soc 2004; *Books* Costs of The Common Agricultural Policy (1982), The CAP and the World Economy (1 ed 1991, 2 ed 1997); *Style—* Prof David Harvey; ✉ School of Agriculture, Food and Rural Development, The University, Newcastle upon Tyne NE1 7RU (tel 0191 222 6872, fax 0191 222 6720, e-mail david.harvey@ncl.ac.uk)

HARVEY, Prof David William; s of Frederick Hercules Harvey, MBE (d 1963), and Doris Maude, *née* Morton (d 1977); *b* 31 October 1935; *Educ* Gillingham GS, St John's Coll Cambridge (MA, PhD); *Career* lectr Univ of Bristol 1961–69, prof of geography Johns Hopkins Univ Baltimore 1969–89, Halford Mackinder prof of geography Univ of Oxford 1987–93, sr res fell St Peter's Coll Oxford 1993– (fell 1987–93), prof of geography and environmental engrg GWC Whiting Sch of Engrg Johns Hopkins Univ 1993–2001, distinguished prof of anthropology City Univ of New York 2001–; fell Inst of Br Geographers, memb Assoc of American Geographers; Hon Doc: Univ of Buenes Aires 1997, Univ of Roskilde Denmark 1997, Univ of Uppsala Sweden 2000; Anders Retzius Gold medal Swedish Anthropology and Geography Soc 1989, Gill Meml Royal Geographical Soc 1972, Patron's Medal Royal Geographical Soc 1995, Vautrin Lud Int Prize in Geography 1995; *Books* Explanation in Geography (1969), Social Justice and the City (1973), The Limits to Capital (1982), The Urbanisation of Capital (1985), Consciousness & The Urban Experience (1985), The Urban Experience (1989), The Condition of Postmodernity (1989), Justice, Nature and the Geography of Difference (1996), Spaces of Hope (2000), Spaces of Captial (2001); *Style—* Prof David Harvey; ✉ PhD Program in Anthropology, The Graduate School and University Center, The City University of New York, 365 Fifth Avenue, New York, NY 10016–4309, USA (tel 212 817 7211, e-mail dharvey@gc.cuny.edu)

HARVEY, Gillian Elizabeth (Gill); da of Albert George Harvey (d 1995), and Phyllis Maria, *née* Howells; *b* 5 April 1957, Swansea; *Educ* Central St Martin's Sch of Art (BA, Queen Mary's Award for Design), RCA (MDes, Babycham Sparkle Costume Design Prize); *Partner* Adam Sweeting; *Career* fashion designer; head designer Medici Collections LIM Int Ltd 1981–92, design dir Medici 1992–; ranges incl: Decisions, Medici, Medici Sport, Gina, After Six International, Invite, Medici Casual; *Recreations* cooking, cats, opera, theatre, St Barts in hurricane season; *Style—* Miss Gill Harvey; ✉ Medici Ltd, 17–18 Margaret Street, London W1W 8RP (tel 020 7436 2882, fax 020 7436 3113, e-mail mediciltd@aol.com, websites, www.medicigroup.co.uk and www.aftersixcollection.com)

HARVEY, Guy Landor; s of Paul William Harvey, of Harrogate, N Yorks, and Elizabeth Jonet, *née* Roberts (d 2003); *b* 26 February 1951, Harpenden, Herts; *Educ* Stowe (open scholar), Trinity Coll Cambridge (BA); *m* 27 Sept 1980, Henrietta Jane Almond, *née* Gibson; 1 da (Celia b 7 Feb 1984), 1 s (George b 15 July 1987); *Career* slr Simpson Curtis Leeds 1976–96 (ptnr 1978), ptnr Dickinson Dees 1997–; dir Landor Records Ltd 2004–; memb Law Soc 1976, FRSA; *Recreations* music, arts, France, shooting; *Style—* Guy Harvey, Esq; ✉ Dickinson Dees, St Ann's Wharf, 112 Quayside, Newcastle upon Tyne NE99 1SB (tel 0191 279 9000, fax 0191 279 9100, e-mail guy.harvey@dickinson-dees.com)

HARVEY, Ian Alexander; s of Dr Alexander Harvey (d 1987), and Mona (d 2004), *née* Anderson; *b* 2 February 1945; *Educ* Cardiff HS, Univ of Cambridge (MA), Harvard Business Sch (MBA); *m* 21 Nov 1976, Dr DeAnne Julius, CBE, *qv*, da of Prof Marvin Julius, of Ames, Iowa, USA; 1 da (Megan b 1979), 1 s (Ross b 1980); *Career* apprentice mech engr Vickers Ltd 1963–69, project engr Laporte Industries 1969–73, sr loan offr World Bank 1975–82, ptnr Logan Associates Inc 1984–85, dir Process Automative and Computer Systems (PACS) 1985–92, chief exec BTG plc (formerly British Technology Group Ltd) 1985–2004; dir Primaxis Technol Ventures Inc 1999–2004, advsr NTEM Tianjin China 2005–; chm: Intellectual Property Inst 1999– (memb Bd 1998–), Intellectual Property Advsy Ctee 2001–05; memb: PM's Advsy Cncl on Sci and Technol 1989–93, Research and Mfrg Ctee CBI 1986–92, Advsy Bd Science Policy Research Unit Univ of Sussex 1988–2003, PPARC Cncl Appointments Ctee 1999–, CCMI Companions Bd 1999–, Air Products & Chemicals Inc European Advsy Cncl 1999–2005, Senate Centre for Intellectual Property Chalmers Univ Gothenberg, Advsy Bd Int Intellectual Property Inst Washington DC 2004–, Policy Ctee Cancer Research UK 2004–06, Bd London Bioscience Innovation Centre; fell Univ of Nottingham 1994, adjunct prof Tanaka Business Sch Imperial Coll London 2004–; Hon LLD Univ of Wolverhampton 2006; CCMI 1987; FRSA 1997–; *Recreations* piano, skiing, sailing, kayaking, scuba diving, mountain walking; *Style—* Ian Harvey

HARVEY, Prof Jake; *b* 3 June 1948; *Educ* Edinburgh Coll of Art (DA); *Career* sculptor; currently head of sculpture Edinburgh Coll of Art; memb: Scottish Soc of Artists 1975, Fedn of Scottish Sculptors 1983; tstee Scottish Sculpture Tst 1984–87; RSA 1989 (ARSA 1977); *Solo Exhibitions* incl: NORTH (Pier Arts Centre, Stromness Artspace and Peacock Printmakers Aberdeen) 1993, Scottish Gallery Edinburgh 1993, Retrospective (Talbot Rice Gallery Univ of Edinburgh) 1993, Recent Works (Christopher Boyd Gallery Galashiels) 1994, Ground (Crystal Gallery Japan) 1998, Residency (Iwate Art Festival Japan) 1998, The Early Imagist Works (Motherwell Heritage Centre) 1998, Nat Museum of Scotland 1999, Signifier (Art First London) 1999; *Group Exhibitions* incl: RSA Award Winners (Artspace Aberdeen) 1980, Built in Scotland (Third Eye Centre, City Arts Centre Edinburgh and Camden Arts Centre London) 1983, Putting Sculpture on the Map (Talbot Rice Art Centre) 1984, Dublin/Edinburgh (Edinburgh Coll of Art) 1985, Works on Paper (RSA Edinburgh) 1990, Scottish Art in the 20th Century (Royal W of England Acad Bristol) 1990, Scottish Scupture Open (Kildrummy Castle Aberdeen) 1991, Virtue and Vision Festival Exhbn (Nat Gallery of Scotland) 1991, William Gillies Bursary Exhbn (RSA) 1992, A Collection of Self-Portraits (Pier Art Centre Stromness) 1994, The Art of the Garden (Greywalls, Scottish Gallery) 1994, Scandex (Aberdeen Art Gallery and Norway, Sweden and Finland) 1995, Jake Harvey Sculpture (Aikwood Tower Selkirk) 1995, A Battle for Hearts and Minds (Robson Gallery Selkirk) 1995, Art First (London) 1996, Transistors (Hashimoto Art Museum Japan) 1998 (Edinburgh and Trondheim Norway 1999), Celtic Connections (Yorozu Tetsugoro Museum Japan) 1998, ECA Sculptors (Arizona State Univ and Tucson Gallery USA) 1999, Scotland's Art (Edinburgh Int Festival Exhbn) 1999, Edinburgh Artists (Odapark Sculpture Park The Netherlands and Sudbahnhoff Gallery Krefeld Germany) 2000, Marie R (Bourne Fine Art Edinburgh) 2000, Leabhar Morna Gaidhlig (Proiseact Nan Ealan) 2001; *Major Commissions* incl: Hugh McDiarmid Memorial Langholmn 1985, Charles Mackintosh Scupture Glasgow 1985, Compaq Computers Glasgow 1988, Poacher's Tree (Maclay Murray & Spens Edinburgh) 1991, Tools for the Shaman (Hunterian Museum Glasgow) 1996, Shift (granite sculpture, Aberdeen) 1999; *Public Collections* Scottish Arts Cncl, Edinburgh Museums and Galleries, Univ of Edinburgh, Contemporary Art Soc, Borders Educn Authy, Kelvingrove Museum Glasgow, Aberdeen Art Gallery, Motherwell DC, Kulturtoget Collection Lulea Sweden, Hunterian Museum Collection, Eda Garden Museum Tokyo Japan; *Awards* incl: Helen Rose Bequest 1971, Latimer award RSA 1975, Benno Schotz Sculpture prize RSA 1976, William Gillies bursary 1989; *Style—* Prof Jake Harvey, RSA

HARVEY, Prof John Kenneth; s of Cyril Frank Harvey, and Lillie Maud, *née* Sydenham; *b* 8 June 1935, London; *Educ* Christ's Coll Finchley, Imperial Coll London (BSc, PhD, DIC); *m* 14 April 1998, Priscilla May, *née* Barnardo; *Career* prof of gas dynamics Imperial Coll London 1989–, visiting prof Dept of Engrg Univ of Cambridge 2000–; research career concentrated in the field of rarefied gas dynamics and high-speed flows, also with strong interest in low-speed aerodynamics associated with road vehicle aerodynamics, atmospheric dispersion, vortex flows and experimental techniques; recognised expert in the aerodynamics of F1 cars; dir Flow Dynamics Ltd; chair of bd Tearfund 1986–90; conslt: MOD, many F1 teams, Calspan Univ of Buffalo Research Centre (CUBRC); author of 140 papers in the fields of rarefied gas dynamics, high- and low-speed aerodynamics and vehicle aerodynamics; assoc fell American Inst of Aeronautics and Astronautics, CEng 1988, FRAeS, FCGI; *Style—* Prof John Harvey; ✉ Department of Engineering, University of Cambridge, Trumpington Street, Cambridge CB2 1PZ

HARVEY, Prof Jonathan Dean; s of Gerald Harvey, and Noelle Heron, *née* Dean (d 1969); *b* 3 May 1939; *Educ* St Michael's Coll Tenbury, Repton, St John's Coll Cambridge (MA, DMus), Univ of Glasgow (PhD); *m* 24 Sept 1960, Rosaleen Marie, da of Daniel Barry (d 1949); 1 da (Anna Maria b 13 Jan 1964), 1 s (Dominic b 3 May 1967); *Career* composer; lectr Univ of Southampton 1964–77, Harkness fell Princeton Univ 1969–70; prof of music: Univ of Sussex 1980– (reader 1977–80), Stanford Univ 1995–2000; Bloch prof Univ of Calif Berkeley 1995, visiting prof Imperial Coll London 1999–2002, hon res fell Royal Coll of Music 2000–; composer in assoc with: Sinfonia 21 1996–, BBC Scottish Symphony Orch 2004–; works performed at many festivals and int centres; memb Music Advsy Panel: Br Cncl 1992–95, Arts Cncl 1995–98; Britten Award for Composition 1993, Br Acad Composer Award 2003, Royal Philharmonic Soc Award for Large-Scale Composition 2007; hon fell St John's Coll Cambridge 2003; Hon DMus: Univ of Southampton 1990, Univ of Bristol 1994, Univ of Sussex 2000; memb Academia Europaea 1989; FRCM 1994, FRSCM 2000, Hon RAM 2002; *Compositions* Persephone Dream (for orch) 1972, Inner Light (trilogy for performers and tape) 1973–77, Smiling Immortal (for chamber orch) 1977, String Quartet 1977, Veils and Melodies (for tapes) 1978, Magnificat and Nunc Dimittis (for choir and organ) 1978, Album (for wind quintet) 1978, Hymn (for choir and orch) 1979, Be(com)ing (for clarinet and piano) 1979, Concelebration (instrumental) 1979 and 1981, Mortuos Plango Vivos Voco (for tape) 1980, Passion and Resurrection (church opera) 1981, Resurrection (for double chorus and organ) 1981, Bhakti (for 15 instruments and tape) 1982, Easter Orisons (for chamber orch) 1983, The Path of Devotion (for choir and orch) 1983, Nachtlied (for soprano piano and tape) 1984, Gong-Ring (for ensemble with electronics) 1984, Song Offerings (for soprano and players) 1985, Madonna of Winter and Spring (for orch, synthesizers and electronics) 1986, Lightness and Weight (for tuba and orch) 1986, Forms of Emptiness (for choir) 1986, Tendril (for ensemble) 1987, Timepieces (for orch) 1987, From Silence (for soprano, six instruments and tape) 1988, Valley of Aosta (for 13 players) 1988, String Quartet No 2 1989, Ritual Melodies (for tape) 1990, Cello Concerto (for cello and orch) 1990, Serenade in Homage to Mozart (for wind ensemble) 1991, Fantasia (for organ) 1991, Inquest of Love (opera) 1992, Lotuses (for flute quartet) 1992, Scena (for violin and ensemble) 1992, One Evening (for voices, instruments and electronics) 1993, Advaya (for cello, keyboard and electronics) 1994, String Quartet No 3 1995, Percussion Concerto (cmmnd BBC, world première BBC Proms) 1997, Ashes Dance Back (for choir and electronics) 1997, Wheel of Emptiness (for ensemble) 1997, Tranquil Abiding (for small orch) 1998, Calling Across Time (for chamber orch) 1998, Hidden Voice 1 and 2 (for ensemble) 1999, White as Jasmine (for soprano and orch) 1999, Mothers Shall not Cry (for singers, orch and electronics) 2000, Bird Concerto with Pianosong (for piano and small orch) 2001, The Summer Cloud's Awakening (for choir and electronics) 2002, Songs of Li Po (for mezzo-soprano and ensemble) 2002, String Quartet No 4 2003, Jubilus (for viola and ensemble) 2003, Two Interludes for an Opera (for ensemble and electronics) 2004, String Trio 2004, ...towards a Pure Land (for orch) 2005, Body Mandala (for orch) 2006, Wagner Dream (opera) 2006, Sprechgesang (for oboe and ensemble) 2006; *Books* The Music of Stockhausen (1975), In Quest of Spirit (1999), Music and Inspiration (1999); *Recreations* tennis, meditation; *Style—* Prof Jonathan Harvey; ✉ c/o Faber Music, 3 Queen Square, London WC1N 3AU (fax 020 7833 7939, website www.vivosvoco.com)

HARVEY, Jonathan Paul; s of Brian Harvey, of Liverpool, and Maureen, *née* Pratt; *b* 13 June 1968; *Educ* Blue Coat Sch Liverpool, Univ of Hull (BSc); *Partner* Richard Foord; *Career* writer; special needs teacher Abbey Wood Comp London 1990–93, writer in residence Bush Theatre 1993–94; currently dir 6th Floor Ltd TV production co; memb Writers' Guild; *Awards* National Girobank/Liverpool Playhouse Young Writer of the Year 1987, Royal Court/Rank Xerox Young Writers Award 1988, George Devine Award for Babies 1993, Thames TV Bursary Award 1993, John Whiting Award for Beautiful Thing 1994, Evening Standard Most Promising Playwright for Babies 1994, London Lesbian & Gay Film Festival Best Film for Beautiful Thing 1996, Norway Film Festival Audience Award for Beautiful Thing 1996, Mike Rhodes Award for furthering the understanding of lesbian and gay life 1996, Manchester Evening News Award for Best Play for Rupert Street Lonely Hearts Club 1996, Fort Lauderdale International Film Festival President's Award Best Screenplay for Beautiful Thing 1996, GLAAD Outstanding Film Award for Beautiful Thing 1997; *Plays* The Cherry Blossom Tree (1987), Mohair (1988), Tripping and Falling (1989), Catch (1990), Lady Snogs The Blues (1991), Wildfire (1992), Babies (1993), Beautiful Thing (1993, released as film 1996), Boom Bang A Bang (1995), Rupert Street Lonely Hearts Club (1995), Swan Song (1997), Guiding Star (RNT, 1998), Hushabye Mountain (English Touring Theatre, 1999), Out in the Open (Hampstead Theatre, 2001), Closer to Heaven (Arts Theatre, 2001), Jack and the Beanstalk (Barbican, 2007); *Television* West End Girls (1993), Gimme Gimme Gimme (3 series BBC2, 1999, 2000 and 2001), Murder Most Horrid (BBC2, 1999), Birthday Girl (ITV, 2002), At Home With the Braithwaites (ITV, 2003), Margo: Life Beyond the Box (BBC 2, 2003), Coronation Street (ITV 1, 2004–), Von Trapped! (ITV 1, 2004), Charlie's Angels (BBC3), Love For Sale (BBC3), The Catherine Tate Show (BBC), Lilies (BBC); *Clubs* Soho House; *Style—* Jonathan Harvey, Esq; ✉ c/o Michael McCoy, ICM, Oxford House, 76 Oxford Street, London W1N 0AX (tel 020 7636 6565, fax 020 7323 0101)

HARVEY, Mark Andrew; s of Laurence Harvey, of Feltham, Middx, and Sheila, *née* Holland; *b* 2 September 1962, Chiswick; *Educ* Gunnersbury RC Sch for Boys, Coll of Law Guildford; *m* 24 April 1993, Karen, *née* Welton; 1 da (Rebecca Myfanwy b 11 May 1995), 1 s (Jonathan David 20 Dec 1997); *Career* slr; Owen White 1981–89, Lawford & Co 1990–94, Smith Llewellyn Partnership 1994–2001, Hugh James 2001–; tstee and vice-chm Carmarthen CAB, memb Civil Justice Cncl, UK govr American Assoc for Justice, vice-pres Cardiff Law Soc; memb Law Soc 1990; fell Inst of Legal Execs 1987; *Publications* APIL Guide to Conditional Fees (2004), Occupational Disease (contrib, 2005), APIL Personal Injury (contrib, 2006); *Recreations* wine appreciation, skiing, golf, cookery; *Style—* Mark Harvey, Esq; ✉ Hugh James, 114–116 St Mary Street, Cardiff CF10 1DY, (tel 029 2039 1174, fax 029 2066 0585, e-mail mark.harvey@hughjames.com)

HARVEY, Michael Llewellyn Tucker; QC (1982); s of Rev Victor Llewellyn Tucker Harvey, of Suffolk, and Pauline, *née* Wybrow; *b* 22 May 1943; *Educ* St John's Sch Leatherhead, Christ's Coll Cambridge (BA, LLB, MA); *m* 2 Sept 1972, Denise Madeleine, da of Leonard Walter Neary, of London; 1 s (Julian b 19 June 1976), 1 da (Alexandra b 30 June 1973); *Career* called to the Bar Gray's Inn 1966 (bencher 1991); recorder 1986; memb Review Bd Cncl of Legal Educn 1993–94, additional memb Bar Cncl 1994–; *Books* Damages (jtly, in Halsbury's Laws of England 4 edn, 1975); *Recreations* shooting, golf; *Clubs* Athenaeum, Hawks' (Cambridge); *Style—* Michael Harvey, Esq, QC

HARVEY, Nicholas (Nick); MP; s of Frederick Harvey, and Christine Harvey; *b* 3 August 1961; *Educ* Queen's Coll Taunton, Middx Poly; *Career* pres Middx Poly Students' Union 1981–82, nat vice-chm Union of Liberal Students 1981–82, communications and marketing exec Profile PR Ltd 1984–86, Dewe Rogerson Ltd 1986–91, communications conslt 1991–92; Parly candidate (Alliance) Enfield Southgate 1987, MP (Lib Dem) N Devon 1992–; Lib Dem spokesman: on Tport 1992–94, on Trade and Industry 1994–97, on English Regions 1997–99, on Health 1999–2001, on Culture, Media and Sport 2001–03, on Def 2006–; chair of campaigns and communications 1994–99; *Recreations* travel, football, walking, music; *Clubs* National Liberal; *Style—* Nick Harvey, Esq, MP; ✉ House of Commons, London SW1A 0AA

HARVEY, Prof Paul H; s of Edward Walter Harvey, of Kidderminster, Worcs, and Eileen Joan, *née* Pagett; *b* 19 January 1947; *Educ* Queen Elizabeth GS Hartlebury, Univ of York (BA, DPhil), Univ of Oxford (MA, DSc); *Children* 2 s (Joseph Edward b 2 April 1980, Benjamin Mark b 18 March 1982); *Career* lectr in biology Univ of Wales Swansea 1971–73, reader in biology Univ of Sussex 1984–85 (lectr 1973–84); Univ of Oxford: lectr in zoology 1985–89, fell and tutor in biology Merton Coll 1985–96, reader in biology 1989–96, professorial fell Jesus Coll 1996–, estab prof in zoology 1996–, head of Dept of Zoology 1998–; visiting lectr Harvard Univ 1978–79; visiting prof: Harvard Univ 1980, Univ of Washington Seattle 1982, Princeton Univ 1984–85, Imperial Coll London 1995–; sec Zoological Soc of London 2000–; Scientific medal Zoological Soc 1986, US Nat Acad of Sciences J Murray Luck Award 1997; FRS 1992 (memb Cncl 2000–02); *Books* The Comparative Method in Evolutionary Biology (with M D Pagel, 1991); *Style—* Prof Paul H Harvey, FRS; ✉ University of Oxford, Department of Zoology, South Parks Road, Oxford OX1 3PS (tel 01865 271260, fax 01865 271249, e-mail paul.harvey@zoo.ox.ac.uk)

HARVEY, Peter Derek Charles; s of Norman Charles Harvey (d 1991), and Sheila June, *née* Curtis, of Stanmore, Middx; *b* 21 December 1958; *Educ* Haberdashers' Aske's, Magdalen Coll Oxford, Guildhall Sch of Music and Drama (BP opera scholarship, Schubert Lieder prize); *m* 25 May 1985, Jean Patricia, da of John Hamilton Paterson; 2 s (William b 9 Oct 1987, Patrick b 2 May 1989); *Career* baritone; regularly appears as soloist with ensembles and choirs incl: Monteverdi Choir, London Baroque, Gabrieli Consort, Purcell Quartet, The Sixteen, The Kings Consort, Orch of the Age of Enlightenment, Yorkshire Bach Choir, La Chapelle Royale (Paris), Il Seminario Musicale (Paris), Thomanerchor (Leipzig), L'ensemble Vocal de Lausanne, Collegium Vocale (Ghent), Gulbenkian Choir and Orch (Lisbon), various symphony orchs and cathedral choirs; numerous appearances in UK and Europe, also Japan, Israel and N America; major soloist Sir John Eliot Gardiner's Bach Cantata Pilgrimage in the celebrations marking the 250 year anniversary of Bach's Death 2000; *Recordings* over fifty incl: Bach St John Passion and Cantata No 82, C P E Bach Die Auferstehung, various Purcell works incl Dido and Aeneas and Hail Bright Cecilia, Fauré Requiem, Slook in Rossini opera La Cambiale di matrimonio, Charles Wood St Mark Passion, Janácek Mass, Puccini sacred duet Vexilla Regis, Henri Pousseur Traverser la forêt, numerous works by Charpentier, Lully, Du Mont, Campra, Gilles, Rameau and Blanchard; other baroque music recordings incl: numerous Bach canatas, Zelenka Lamentations, Teixeira Te Deum, 17th Century Venetian ceremonial music, Galuppi Confiteor tibi Domine; *Recreations* not being on tour, attempting foreign languages when on tour, making and fixing things; *Style—* Peter Harvey, Esq; ✉ tel and fax 01635 255141, e-mail enquire@peterharvey.com

HARVEY, Dr Peter Kenneth Philip; s of late Philip Harvey, of London, and Leah Harvey; *b* 22 January 1942; *Educ* Emanuel Sch, Gonville & Caius Coll Cambridge (MA, MB BChir); *m* 5 June 1971, Lesley MacGregor, da of late George Henderson; 2 s (Alan b 24 May 1978, Johnny b 26 July 1980), 1 da (Zehra b 4 March 1984); *Career* successively: pre-registration posts Middx Hosp Mortimer St and Queen Elizabeth II Hosp Welwyn Garden City, post-registration house posts Middx, Brompton and Nat Heart Hosps, further studies Imperial Coll London, neurological trg Middx Hosp and Nat Hosp for Nervous Diseases Queen Sq; lately conslt neurologist: Royal Free Hampstead NHS Tst (med dir 1991–93, chm Med Advsy Ctee 1991–94, ret 1997), Chase Farm Hosp NHS Tst Enfield; currently hon and emeritus conslt neurologist Royal Free Hosp; author of articles on neurological topics incl epilepsy in various learned jls; memb: Acad of Experts, BMA, RSM (memb Section Cncl 1980–90, hon sec for overseas affrs 1985–90); FRCP; *Recreations* cooking, wining, dining, opera, France; *Style—* Dr Peter Harvey; ✉ 134 Harley Street, London W1G 7JY (tel 020 7486 8005, fax 020 7224 3905)

HARVEY, Polly Jean (PJ); *b* 9 October 1969, Corscombe, Dorset; *Career* singer/songwriter; with band PJ Harvey 1991–93, solo artist and collaborator 1993–; contrib to records by: Pascal Comelade, Nick Cave, Tricky, Sparklehorse, Giant Sand, John Parish, Josh Homme's Desert sessions; wrote songs and produced music for Marianne Faithfull; Best Songwriter and Best New Female Singer Rolling Stone magazine 1992; *Albums* Dry (1992), Rid Of Me (1993, nominated Mercury Music Prize), 4–Track Demos (1993), To Bring You My Love (1995, nominated Mercury Music Prize and 2 Grammys), Dance Hall At Louse Point (with John Parish, 1996), Is This Desire? (1998, nominated Mercury Music Prize, Grammys and Brit Awards), Stories From The City, Stories From The Sea (2000, Mercury Music Prize 2001), Uh Huh Her (2004, nominated Grammy Award), Peel Sessions (2006); *Singles* incl: Dress (1992), Sheela Na Gig (1992), 50 Foot Queenie (1993), Man-Size (1993), C'mon Billy (1995), Down By The Water (1995), Send His Love To Me (1995), That Was My Veil (1996), Good Fortune (2000), A Place Called Home (2001), This Is Love (2001), The Letter (2004); *DVD* PJ Harvey on Tour: Please Leave Quietly 2006; *Style—* Ms P J Harvey; ✉ c/o Sally-Anne McKeown, Principle Management, 30–32 Sir John Rogerson's Quay, Dublin, Ireland (tel 00 353 1 6777330, fax 00 353 1 6777276, e-mail sally@numb.ie)

HARVEY, Richard John; s of Lester Harvey, of Nailsworth, Glos, and Jean, *née* Blandford; *b* 11 July 1950; *Educ* Marling GS Stroud, Victoria Univ of Manchester (BSc); *m* 1971, Kay; 1 s (Adrian James b 9 Sept 1973), 2 da (Katherine Elizabeth b 31 Jan 1975, Jennifer Ruth Ann b 14 July 1983); *Career* mangr personal pensions Phoenix Assurance 1983–85,

H

mktg mangr Sun Alliance plc 1985–87, general mangr Sun Alliance Life NZ 1987–92, chief exec Norwich Union Holdings NZ 1992–93; Norwich Union plc (merged with CGU to become CGNU plc in 2000): gen mangr Finance Dept 1993–94, gp fin dir 1995–97, dep gp chief exec 1997–98, gp chief exec 1998–2000; Aviva plc (called CGNU plc until 2002): dep chief exec 2000–01, chief exec 2001–07; chm ABI 2003; FIA 1975; *Recreations* squash, skiing, theatre; *Style*— Richard Harvey, Esq

HARVEY, Sarah Anne; *see:* Percy-Davis, Sarah

HARVEY-JONES, Sir John Henry; kt (1985), MBE (1952); s of Mervyn Harvey-Jones, OBE, and Eileen Harvey-Jones; *b* 16 April 1924; *Educ* Tormore Sch Deal, RNC Dartmouth; *m* 1947, Mary Evelyn Atcheson, da of E F Bignell, and Mrs E Atcheson; 1 da; *Career* served RN 1937–56, submarines and naval intelligence, qualifying as German and Russian interpreter, resigned with rank of Lt Cdr; ICI: joined as work study offr 1956, dir 1973–87, dep chm 1978–82, chm 1982–87 (dep chm Heavy Organic Chemicals Div 1968, chm ICI Petrochemicals Div 1970–73); chm Parallax Enterprises Ltd 1987–97; Hon LLD: Manchester 1985, Liverpool 1986, London 1987, Cambridge 1987; Hon DUniv Surrey 1985; Hon DSc: Bradford 1986, Leicester 1986, Keele 1989, Exeter 1989; Hon DCL Newcastle upon Tyne 1988, Hon DBA (Int Mgmnt Centres) 1990, Hon DTech Loughborough 1991, hon degree Open Univ 1996; fell Smallpiece Tst 1988; sr ind fell Leicester Poly 1990, Hon FCGI (hon memb 1988); hon fell: Poly of Wales, Royal Soc of Chemistry 1985, The Inst of Chemical Engrs 1985, Liverpool John Moores Univ 1998, Chartered Inst of Purchasing and Supply; memb Soc of Chemical Industry 1978; Cdr's Cross Order of Merit FRG; *Awards* BIM Gold Medal 1985, Soc of Chemical Industry Centenary Medal 1986, Jo Hambro Br Businessman of the Year 1986, Int Assoc of Business Communicators Award of Excellence in Communication 1987, Radar Man of the Year 1987, Pipesmoker of the Year 1991, City & Guilds Insignia Award in Technol (hc), Lifetime Achievement Award Nat Business Awards 2002; *Current Appointments* vice-pres Hearing and Speech Tst 1985–, vice-pres Heaton Woods Tst 1986–, memb Royal Soc of Arts 1979– (vice-pres 1988–92); hon conslt: RUSI 1987–, Steer Orgn; vice-patron Br Polio Fellowship 1988–, hon pres Univ of Bradford MBA Alumni Assoc 1989–, vice-pres Industrial Participation Assoc 1983–, hon pres Friends of Brecon Jazz 1989–; tstee MS Research Charitable Tst 1999–; patron: Nat Canine Defence League 1990–, The Kingswood Tst, The Gordon Fndn Sixth Form Appeal, The Centre for Tomorrow's Co, Modem RN Submarine Museum Cent Appeal 1999–, Modem 1999–, Amor Fndn 2000–, Professional Contractors Gp Ltd 2000, Soc Turnaround Professionals 2001; corp patron Primrose Earth Awareness Tst 2001; hon tst memb The Andrea Adams Tst 2000–; supporter: Greyhounds UK 2000–, Campaign for Adventure 2002; hon fell Chartered Inst Purchasing and Supply 2001; *Previous Appointments* memb Tees and Hartlepool Port Authy 1970–73, chm Phillips-Imperial Petroleum 1973–75, dir ICI Americas Inc 1975–76, dir Fiber Industries Inc 1975–78, dir Grand Metropolitan 1983–94; chm: Didacticus Video Productions Ltd 1989–95, The Economist 1989–94, ProShare UK Ltd 1992–94; dep chm GPA Ltd 1989–93 (dir 1987–93); chm: Cncl Wildfowl Tst 1987–94 (vice-pres 1994–97), Book Tst Appeal Fund 1987–93; vice-pres Conseil European des Fédérations de L'Industrie Chimique (CEFIC) 1982–84, memb President's Ctee CBI 1982–87 (pres 1984–86), vice-chm Policy Studies Inst 1980–85, hon vice-pres Inst of Mktg 1982–89, memb Bd Welsh Devpt Int 1989–93; non-exec dir: Reed International plc 1975–84, Carrington Viyella Ltd 1974–79 (dir 1981–82); memb NEDO Ctee for the Chemical Industry 1980–82, memb Cncl Chemical Industries' Association Ltd 1980–82, memb NE Devpt Bd 1971–73, memb Ct Br Shippers' Cncl 1982–87, memb Cncl Br Malaysian Soc 1983–87, memb Fndn Bd Int Mgmnt Inst Geneva 1984–87, memb Cncl Youth Enterprise Scheme 1984–86, tstee the Conf Bd 1984–86, memb Int Cncl Euro Inst of Business Admin 1984–87, tstee Sci Museum 1983–87, vice-chm Great Ormond Street Redevelopment Appeal, patron Halton Chemical Industry Museum Appeal 1986; non-exec dir: Nimbus Records 1987, Burns Anderson 1987–91 (chm 1987–90), Police Fndn 1983–91 (chm of tstees 1984–88); vice-pres Newnham Coll Appeal 1987, memb Ct of Govrs Kidney Res Unit for Wales Fndn 1989–90, govr ESU 1987–91, chm Cncl St James's and The Abbey Sch Malvern 1987–93; memb Advsy Cncl Prince's Youth Business Tst 1986–99; vice-pres Tyne & Wear Fndn; patron: Cambridge Univ Young Entrepreneurs Soc 1987–91, Manpower Servs Cmmn Nat Trg Awards 1987; chllr Bradford Univ 1986–91; non-exec chm: Business Int Bd Ctee 1988–91, Trendroute Ltd 1988–91, Wider Share Ownership Cncl 1988–92; vice-chm BIM 1980–85; *Television Series* Troubleshooter 1990 and 1992, Troubleshooter Specials - Eastern Europe 1991, Troubleshooter Returns 1995, Troubleshooter Back in Business 2001; *Publications* Making it Happen, Reflections on Leadership (1987), Troubleshooter (1990), Getting it Together (1991), Troubleshooter 2 (1992), Managing to Survive, A Guide to Management Through the '90s (1993), All Together Now (1994), Troubleshooter Returns (1995); *Recreations* swimming, the countryside, cooking, contemporary literature; *Clubs* Athenaeum, Groucho, Garrick; *Style*— Sir John Harvey-Jones, MBE; ✉ c/o PO Box 18, Ross-on-Wye, Herefordshire HR9 7PH (tel 01989 567171, fax 01989 567173, e-mail carol@select-speakers.com)

HARVEY OF TASBURGH, 2 Baron (UK 1954); Sir Peter Charles Oliver Harvey; 5 Bt (UK 1868); s of 1 Baron, GCMG, GCVO, CB, (HM ambass to France 1948–54, d 1968), and Maud, da of Arthur Williams-Wynn (gn of Sir Watkin Williams-Wynn, 4 Bt); *b* 28 January 1921; *Educ* Eton, Trinity Coll Cambridge; *m* 1957, Penelope (d 1995), yr da of Lt-Col Sir William Makins, 3 Bt; 2 da (Hon Juliet (Hon Mrs Lee) b 1958, Hon Miranda b 1960); *Heir* n, Charles Harvey; *Career* served WWII RA N Africa and Italy; investment conslt Brown Shipley and Co 1978–81; formerly with: Bank of England, Binder Hamlyn & Co, Lloyds Bank International Ltd, English Transcontinental Ltd; FCA; *Clubs* Brooks's; *Style*— The Lord Harvey of Tasburgh; ✉ Crownick Woods, Restronguet, Mylor, Falmouth, Cornwall TR11 5ST

HARVEY WOOD, (Elizabeth) Harriet; OBE (1993); da of Henry Harvey Wood, OBE, FRSE (d 1977), and Lily, *née* Terry (d 2005); *b* 1 October 1934; *Educ* Cranley Sch for Girls, Univ of Edinburgh (MA, PhD); *Career* mangr Philomusica of London Orchestra 1959–66, sec Faculty of Music KCL 1966–68, head Literature Dept British Cncl 1980–94 (joined British Cncl 1973); dir The Harvill Press 1995–2002; memb: Bibliographical Soc 1970–94, English PEN 1985– (memb Exec Ctee 1994–99), Panel of Judges Booker Prize for Fiction 1992, Wingate Scholarship Ctee 1992–, Booker Prize Mgmnt Ctee 2000–03; chm Stephen Spender Meml Tst Ctee 1997–, tstee Golsoncott Fndn 1997–, tstee Asham Literary Endowment Tst 1999–; *Books* James Watson's Choice Collection of Comic and Serious Scots Poems Vol I (1977), The Percy Letters: The Correspondence of Thomas Percy and John Pinkerton (1985), James Watson's Choice Collection of Comic and Serious Scots Poems Vol II (1991), Banned Poetry (with Peter Porter, 1997), Selected Poems of William Dunbar (1999), Sightlines (with P D James, 2001), Sir Walter Scott (2006); *Recreations* reading, music, gardening, cooking; *Clubs* Oxford and Cambridge; *Style*— Miss Harriet Harvey Wood, OBE; ✉ 158 Coleherne Court, Redcliffe Gardens, London SW5 0DX (tel and fax 020 7373 2113, e-mail hhw@dircon.co.uk)

HARVIE, Patrick; s of David Harvie, of Dumbarton, and Rose, *née* Radford; *b* 18 March 1973, Dumbarton; *Educ* Dumbarton Acad, Manchester Met Univ; *Career* youth worker, sexual health project worker and devpt worker Phace Scotland 1997–2003; MSP (Green Party) Glasgow 2003–; supporter: Amnesty, CND, Friends of the Earth, Greenpeace, Humanist Soc of Scot, Nat Secular Soc; Pride Award for Lesbian Gay Bisexual and Transgender Activism 2003; Scot Politician of the Year Awards: Election Campaign of the Year 2003 (jtly), One to Watch 2004, Progress in Politics 2006 (jtly); *Recreations* science fiction, computing, food and drink; *Style*— Patrick Harvie, Esq, MSP; ✉ Room M417, Scottish Parliament, Horse Wynd, Edinburgh EH99 1SP (tel 0131 348 6363, e-mail patrick.harvie.msp@scottish.parliament.uk)

HARVIE-WATT, Sir James; 2 Bt (UK 1945), of Bathgate, Co Linlithgow; er s of Sir George Steven Harvie-Watt, 1 Bt, TD, QC (d 1989), and Jane, *née* Taylor (d 2003); *b* 25 August 1940; *Educ* Eton, ChCh Oxford (MA); *m* 28 May 1966, Roseline Gladys Virginia, da of Baron Louis de Chollet (d 1972); 1 da (Isabelle Frances b 19 March 1967), 1 s (Mark Louis b 19 Aug 1969); *Heir* s, Mark Harvie-Watt; *Career* Lt London Scottish (TA) 1959–67; with Coopers and Lybrand 1962–70, exec Br Electric Traction Co Ltd and dir of subsid cos 1970–78, md Wembley Stadium Ltd 1973–78, chm Crystal Palace Nat Sports Centre 1984–88, dir Lake & Elliot Industries Ltd 1988–93; memb: Exec Ctee London Tourist Bd 1977–80, Sports Cncl 1980–88 (vice-chm 1985–88); chm: Cannons Sports & Leisure Ltd 1990–93, Medi@Invest plc 1995–2002, Oliver & Saunders Group Ltd 1997–; dir various other cos incl: Weststar Holidays Ltd 1993–2005, Penna Consulting plc 1995– (chm 2004–05), US Smaller Companies Investment Trust plc 1998–2001, Wellington Management Portfolios (Ireland) plc 2000–02; memb Mgmnt Ctee: The Nat Coaching Fndn 1984–88, The Nat Water Sports Centre Holme Pierrepont 1985–88; memb: Sports Cncl Enquiries into Financing of Athletics in UK 1983, Karate 1986, Cncl NPFA 1985–90; dir Int Tennis Hall of Fame 1996–2005 and 2006– (chm Exec Ctee 2001–05); FCA 1975 (ACA 1965), FRSA 1978; OStJ 1964 (memb London Cncl of the Order 1975–84); *Recreations* tennis, golf, shooting, photography, philately; *Clubs* White's, Pratt's, Queen's (vice-chm 1987–90, chm 1990–93, dir 1987–2006), Swinley Forest; *Style*— Sir James Harvie-Watt, Bt; ✉ 15 Somerset Square, London W14 8EE (tel 020 7602 7353, e-mail jhw@dial.pipex.com)

HARWOOD, Prof John Leander; s of Capt Leslie James Harwood, of Tunbridge Wells, and Lt Beatrice, *née* Hutchinson; *b* 5 February 1946; *Educ* King Edward's GS Aston, Univ of Birmingham (BSc, PhD, DSc); *m* 1, 27 Aug 1967, Gail (d 1991), da of Harry Burgess (d 1968); 1 s (Nicholas James b 27 Feb 1969); m 2, 14 April 1993, Bernice Adele (d 1994), da of Brian Alfred Andrews (d 1971); m 3, 17 Sept 2000, Marilyn Joan, da of David Emrys Evans (d 1970); *Career* postdoctoral res: Univ of Calif Davis 1969–71, Univ of Leeds 1971–73; UC Cardiff: lectr 1973–80, reader 1980–84, personal chair 1984–, head of research 2001–, dep dir 2003–, head Sch of Biosciences 2004–; author of over 510 scientific pubns; guide book writer for S Wales Mountaineering Club and The Climbers Club; memb: Biochemical Soc, Phytochemical Soc, Soc of Experimental Biology; *Books* South East Wales - A Rock Climber's Guide (ed, 1977), Lipids of Plants and Microbes (1984), The Lipid Handbook (jt ed, 1986, 2 edn 1994, 3 edn 2007), Plant Membranes (jt ed, 1988), Methods in Plant Biochemistry (Vol 4, jt ed, 1990), Plant Lipid Biochemistry, Structure and Utilization (jt ed, 1990), Lipid Biochemistry (jt author, 1991, 5 edn 2002), Climbers Guide to Pembroke, 2 Vols (jt ed, 1995), Plant Lipid Biosynthesis (ed, 1998), Handbook of Olive Oil (jt ed, 2000); *Style*— Prof John Harwood; ✉ School of Biosciences, Cardiff University, Cardiff CF1 3US (tel 029 2087 4108, fax 029 2087 4116, e-mail harwood@cardiff.ac.uk)

HARWOOD, John Warwick; DL (Oxon 2001); s of late Denis George Harwood, of Dorchester, Dorset, and Winifred, *née* Hoatson; *b* 10 December 1946; *Educ* Catford Sch, Univ of Kent (BA), Univ of London (MA); *m* 1967; 1 s, 1 da; *Career* admin offr GLC 1968–73, private sec to Sir Ashley Bramall as Ldr ILEA 1973–77, asst chief exec London Borough of Hammersmith and Fulham 1979–82 (head Chief Exec's Office 1977–79); chief exec Lewisham Borough Cncl 1982–88, chief exec Oxfordshire CC 1989–2000, chief exec Learning and Skills Cncl 2000–04; clerk of the lieutenancy for Oxfordshire 1989–2001; chm CfBT Educn Tst 2004–, chief exec Food Standards Agency 2006–; dir: N Oxfordshire Business Venture Ltd 1989–97, Heart of Eng TEC (chm 1999–2001), Thames Business Advice Centre, Oxfordshire Ethnic Minorities Enterprise Developments Ltd, Thames Valley Economic Partnership 1997–98; associate fell Warwick Univ Business Sch 2004–; memb: Ct Oxford Brookes Univ, Exec Ctee Town and Country Planning Assoc 1981–89, Nat Cmmn on Future of Voluntary Sector 1995–96, Business Link Accreditation Bd 1996–2000; clerk S London Consortium 1983–89; tstee: Oxfordshire Community Fndn 1997–2003, Oxfordshire VCH Trust and Appeal 1997–; Hon MA Univ of Kent 1995; *Publications* contrib: The Renaissance of Local Government (1995), Understanding British Institutions (1998); *Recreations* walking, cooking, gardening; *Style*— John Harwood, Esq, DL; ✉ CfBT Education Trust, 60 Queen's Road, Reading, Berkshire RG1 4BS

HARWOOD, Lee; s of Wilfrid Travers Lee-Harwood (d 1969), of Chertsey, Surrey, and Grace, *née* Ladkin; *b* 6 June 1939; *Educ* St George's Coll Weybridge, QMC (BA); *m* 1 (m dis), Jenny Goodgame; 1 s (Blake b 1962); m 2 (m dis), Judith Walker; 1 s (Rafe b 1977), 1 da (Rowan b 1979); *Career* poet; chm: Nat Poetry Secretariat 1974–76, Poetry Soc London 1976–77; Poetry Fndn NY annual award 1966, Alice Hunt Bartlett prize Poetry Soc London 1976; *Publications* collections published incl: The Man with Blue Eyes (1966), The White Room (1968), Landscapes (1969), The Sinking Colony (1971), HMS Little Fox (1976), Boston-Brighton (1977), All the Wrong Notes (1981), Monster Masks (1985), Dream Quilt (1985), Rope Boy to the Rescue (1988), Crossing the Frozen River - Selected Poems (1988), In the Mists: Mountain Poems (1993), Morning Light (1998), Evening Star (2004), Collected Poems (2004), Gifts Received (2007); translations: Tristan Tzara Selected Poems (1975), Tristan Tzara - Chanson Dada: Selected Poems (1987); *Recreations* mountaineering and hill walking, the countryside; *Style*— Lee Harwood; ✉ tel 01273 733842

HARWOOD, Air Cdre Michael John; CBE (2004, MBE 1995); s of Alan Harwood (d 1984), and Mavis, *née* Thompson; *b* 29 October 1958, Buenos Aires, Argentina; *Educ* Merchant Taylors' Sch Northwood, KCL (MA); *m* 6 June 1981, Cheryl, *née* South; 2 da (Sophie b 15 July 1984, Nina b 12 Dec 1985); *Career* cmmnd RAF 1978, instr RAF Valley and RAF Chivenor 1980–84, IV(AC) Sqdn RAF Gütersloh 1984–88, Harrier trials pilot then staff offr Strike Attack Operational Evaluation Unit Boscombe Down 1988–92, OC Night then Dep OC 1(F) Sqdn RAF Wittering 1992–95, staff offr MOD PR Directorate and Perm Jt HQ 1996–98, cmd 20 Sqdn 1998–2000, Gp Capt 2000, Cdr Br Forces UK ops Southern Iraq 2000, Higher Cmd and Staff Course 2001, Station Cdr RAF Cottesmore 2001–03, Air Cdre HQ Strike Cmd RAF High Wycombe 2003–05, Asst Cmdt (Air) and Div Higher Cmd and Staff Course JSCSC Shrivenham 2005–; Arthur Barratt Meml Prize 1994; QCVSA; *Recreations* squash, reading, conversation; *Clubs* RAF; *Style*— Air Cdre Michael Harwood, CBE; ✉ Joint Services Command and Staff College, Faringdon Road, Shrivenham, Swindon, Wiltshire SN6 8TS (tel 01793 788010, fax 01793 788304, e-mail mharwood.jscsc@da.mod.uk)

HARWOOD, Richard Francis Wilson; s of Gerald Wilson Harwood, of Sutton Coldfield, and Ellen Margaret, *née* Small; *b* 7 September 1944; *Educ* Wycliffe Coll; *m* 8 Sept 1967, Kathleen Janet, da of Edward Charles Shelley; 1 s (Charles Richard Louis b 23 Oct 1973); *Career* articled to C Herbert Smith & Russell 1961–66; subsequent positions with: Thos Bourne & Co 1967, Kenneth Hayes & Co 1967–68, Deloitte & Co 1968–81; ptnr Hart Harwood 1981–98, princ Harwoods CAs 1998–; pres Birmingham and W Midlands CAs 1991–92; ICAEW: Birmingham and W Midlands rep Nat Cncl 1992–, chm Trg Standards Ctee 1995–97 (dep chm 1993–95), dep chm Educn & Trg Directorate 1995–97, chm Investigation Ctee 1999–2000 (vice-chm 1997–1999), memb Exec Ctee 2000–02, chm Professional Standards Bd 2007–, memb Bd 2007–; former dep chm of govrs Bishop Vesey's GS Sutton Coldfield (ret 1999); hon treas Quinney Hall (registered charity) 1995–, churchwarden St Mary, St Giles and All Saints Canwell 1997–2005; memb Nat Tst; Liveryman Worshipful Co of Chartered Accountants; FCA; *Recreations* gardening, music, cricket umpiring; *Style*— Richard F W Harwood, Esq; ✉ The Old Dairy, Bangley Lane,

Tamworth, Staffordshire B74 3EA (tel 0121 308 1715); Harwoods, 1 Trinity Place, Midland Drive, Sutton Coldfield B72 1TX (tel 0121 355 0901, fax 0121 355 7245, e-mail rfwh@harwoods-account.co.uk)

HARWOOD, Ronald; CBE (1999); s of Isaac Horwitz (d 1950), and Isobel, *née* Pepper (d 1985); *b* 9 November 1934; *Educ* Sea Point Boys' HS Cape Town, RADA; *m* 1959, Natasha, da of William Charles Riehle, MBE (d 1979); 1 s (Antony), 2 da (Deborah, Alexandra); *Career* actor 1953–60; writer 1960–; artistic dir Cheltenham Festival of Lit 1975; chm Writers' Guild of GB 1969; memb Lit Panel Arts Cncl of GB 1973–78; visitor in theatre Balliol Coll Oxford 1986; pres: PEN (Eng) 1989–93, PEN (Int) 1993–97 (vice-pres 1997), Royal Literary Fund 2005–; FRSL (chm 2001–04); Chevalier de l'Ordre des Arts et des Lettres (France); Hon DLitt Keele Univ *Television* presenter: Kaleidoscope (BBC) 1973, Read All About It (BBC) 1978–79, All The World's A Stage for (also writer, BBC); *Television Plays* incl: The Barber of Stamford Hill (1960), Private Potter (1961), The Guests (1972), Breakthrough at Reykjavik (1987), Countdown to War (1989); *Screenplays* incl: A High Wind in Jamaica (1965), One Day in the Life of Ivan Denisovich (1971), Evita Peron (1981), The Dresser (1983), Mandela (1987), The Browning Version (1994), Cry The Beloved Country (1995), Taking Sides (2002), The Pianist (2002, winner Academy Award 2002), The Statement (2003), Being Julia (2004), Oliver Twist (2005), The Diving Bell and the Butterfly (2007), Love in the Time of Cholera (2007); *Books* All the Same Shadows (1961), The Guilt Merchants (1963), The Girl in Melanie Klein (1969), Articles of Faith (1973), The Genoa Ferry (1976), César and Augusta (1978), Home (Jewish Quarterly Prize for Fiction, 1993); short stories: One Interior Day (adventures in the film trade 1978), New Stories 3 (ed, 1978); biography: Sir Donald Wolfit, CBE - his life and work in the unfashionable theatre (1971); essays: A Night at the Theatre (ed, 1983), The Ages of Gielgud (1984), Dear Alec (ed, 1989); others: All The World's A Stage (1984), The Faber Book of Theatre (ed, 1993); *Plays* Country Matters (1969), The Ordeal of Gilbert Pinfold (from Evelyn Waugh, 1977), A Family (1978), The Dresser (New Standard Drama Award, Drama Critics' Award, 1986), After the Lions (1982), Tramway Road (1984), The Deliberate Death of a Polish Priest (1985), Interpreters (1985), J J Farr (1987), Ivanov (from Chekov 1989), Another Time (1989), Reflected Glory (1992), Poison Pen (1993), Taking Sides (1995), The Handyman (1996), Equally Divided (1998), Quartet (1999), Mahler's Conversion (2001); *Musical Libretto* The Good Companions (1974); *Recreations* watching cricket; *Clubs* Garrick, MCC; *Style*— Ronald Harwood, Esq, CBE, FRSL; ✉ c/o Judy Daish Associates, 2 St Charles Place, London W10 6EG (tel 020 8964 8811, fax 020 8964 8966)

HARWOOD, Rosalind Jane (Ros); da of Dr John Harwood, of Wiltshire, and Frances, *née* Lee; *b* 20 May 1965, Welwyn Garden City, Herts; *Educ* Bath HS GDST, Churcher's Coll Petersfield, Univ of Birmingham (Longman professional prize, LLB), Coll of Law Guildford; *Career* slr specialising in charity law; Lee Bolton & Lee 1987–97, Speechly Bircham 1997–2000, Rollits 2001–05, ptnr Dickinson Dees 2005–; memb Law Soc 1987; FRSA 2006; *Recreations* gardening, cycling, hockey, travel; *Clubs* Lansdowne; *Style*— Ms Ros Harwood; ✉ Dickinson Dees LLP, Camden House, Prince's Wharf, Stockton-on-Tees TS17 6QY (tel 01642 631700)

HARYOTT, Richard Baskcomb; s of Reginald Arthur Haryott, OBE (d 1993), and Noreen Miller, *née* Baskcomb; *b* 28 March 1941; *Educ* The Leys Sch Cambridge, Univ of Leeds (BSc, Dorman Long Prize); *m* 1966, Virginia Mary, da of late Charles Taylor; 1 da (Josephine (Hon Mrs de Grey) b 1968), 2 s (James b 1971, Charles b 1977); *Career* Ove Arup & Partners: engr 1962–, md Arup Iran 1976–79, dir 1979–2003, dir Ove Arup Partnership (holding co) 1984–2001, dir Ove Arup Partnership Trustees Ltd 1993–, chm Ove Arup Fndn 2000–, conslt Arup Gp Ltd 2003–; major projects incl: Nat Exhibition Centre 1975, Sainsbury Wing Nat Gallery 1991, UK Pavilion Seville 1992, Glaxo Wellcome Medicines Research Labs 1995; chm Steel Construction Inst 1994–98, chm Jt Bd of Moderators 1999–2001 (dep chm 1997–99); memb: Ctee on Public Understanding of Science 1996–99, Cncl Assoc of Consulting Engrs 1997–2000; vice-pres ICE 2001–04; govr Leys Sch and St Faith's Sch Cambridge; FICE 1986, FIStructE 1993, FREng 1995, FRSA; *Publications* Integrating the Professions at the NEC Building (1976), The National Exhibition Centre (Birmingham International Arena) (jtly, 1983), Solar-Powered Pavilion (1992), The Glaxo Wellcome Medicines Research Centre (jtly, 1998), The Long Term Cost of Owning Buildings (jtly, 1998), No Innovators - No Innovation (presentation to Construction Industry Cncl, 2000), All You Need is the Best People (2001), Building Leaders of a Global Society (jtly, 2003); *Recreations* golf, tennis, family; *Style*— Richard Haryott, Esq, FREng; ✉ Wellpond Cottage, Brickendon, Hertford SG13 8NU (tel and fax 01992 511575); Ove Arup Partnership, 13 Fitzroy Street, London W1T 4BQ (tel 020 7755 3139, fax 020 7755 3675, e-mail richard.haryott@arup.com)

HASAN, (Syed) Salmaan; s of Arshad Hasan, and Waheeda Hasan; *b* 24 December 1964, London; *Educ* Univ of London (BA), City Univ Business Sch (MBA); *m* 1989, Farida, *née* Huda; 1 da (Amira b 29 Sept 1993), 2 s (Anis b 27 Jan 1997, Ismail b 25 Feb 2000); *Career* property finance Samuel Montagu & Co 1988–92, property finance IBJ London 1992–94, head of property finance Deutsche Postbank/BHF 1994–2005, chief exec Minerva plc 2005–; MInstD 2005; *Recreations* running, cinema; *Clubs* Walbrook; *Style*— Salmaan Hasan, Esq; ✉ Minerva plc, 42 Wigmore Street, London W1U 2RY (tel 020 7535 1000, fax 020 7725 0125, e-mail shasan@minervaplc.co.uk)

HASELER, Prof Stephen Michael Alan; s of Maj Cyril Percival Haseler (d 1973); *b* 9 January 1942; *Educ* Westcliff HS for Boys, LSE (BSc, PhD); *m* 24 Feb 1968, Roberta Berenice Haseler; *Career* prof of govt: London Guildhall Univ (formerly City of London Poly) 1968–, Univ of Maryland 1982–; visiting prof: Georgetown Univ Washington DC 1978, Johns Hopkins Univ 1984; chm Gen Purposes Ctee GLC 1973–75 (memb 1973–77), fndr memb SDP 1981, chm Radical Soc 1987– (fndr memb); Parly candidate (Lab): Saffron Walden 1966, Maldon 1970; hon prof Univ of Maryland 1986–; *Books* The Gaitskellites (1969), The Tragedy of Labour (1976), Eurocommunism (1978), Thatcher & The New Liberals (1989); *Clubs* IOD; *Style*— Prof Stephen Haseler; ✉ 2 Thackeray House, Ansdell Street, Kensington, London W8 (tel 020 7937 3976)

HASELHURST, Rt Hon Sir Alan Gordon Barraclough; kt (1995), PC (1999), MP; s of late John Haselhurst, and late Alyse, *née* Barraclough; *b* 23 June 1937; *Educ* Cheltenham Coll, Oriel Coll Oxford; *m* 1977, Angela, da of late John Bailey; 2 s, 1 da; *Career* MP (Cons): Middleton and Prestwich 1970–74, Saffron Walden 1977–; PPS to sec of state for Educn 1979–81; chm of tstees Community Devpt Fndn 1986–97, chm Ways and Means 1997–; dep speaker 1997–; hon sec All-Pty Parly Cricket Gp 1993–, memb Exec Ctee Essex CCC 1996–; *Publications* Occasionally Cricket, Eventually Cricket, Incidentally Cricket; *Recreations* music, gardening, watching cricket; *Style*— The Rt Hon Sir Alan Haselhurst, MP; ✉ House of Commons, London SW1A 0AA (e-mail haselhursta@parliament.uk, website www.siralanhaselhurst.net)

HASHEMI, Kambiz; s of Hussain Hashemi, of Tehran, Iran, and Aghdas, *née* Tehrani; *b* 13 August 1948; *Educ* Greenmore Coll Birmingham, Univ of Birmingham (MB ChB, MD); *m* 11 Sept 1974, Elahe, da of Dr Abbas Hashemi-Nejad, of Tehran, Iran; 1 s (Nima b 14 Nov 1978), 1 da (Neda b 14 May 1989); *Career* surgical registrar United Birmingham Hosp 1974–82, sr registrar in accident and emergency med Dudley Rd and East Birmingham Hosp 1982–85, dir of accident and emergency serv Mayday Univ Hosp 1985–, conslt in hand surgery Mayday Univ Hosp Croydon 1985–; author of numerous scientific pubns in med jls; regnl tutor in A/E med SW Thames RHA, SW Thames speciality rep to RCS; chm: Medical Cmmn for Accident Prevention, STC A/E Medicine; memb: Manpower Advsy Ctee, Bd of Examiners RCS, Dist Child Accident Prevention Gp, Academic Ctee BAEM, BMA, BAEM, BSSH, Emergency Med Res Soc, Iran Soc; FRCS, FRSM; *Books* Hazards of Forklift Truck (1989); *Recreations* squash, tennis, photography, theatre and opera; *Style*— Kambiz Hashemi, Esq; ✉ 16 Rose Walk, Purley, Surrey CR8 3LG (tel 020 8668 8127); Accident and Emergency Unit, Mayday University Hospital, Mayday Road, Thornton Heath, Surrey CR7 7YE (tel 020 8401 3000, fax 020 8401 3092)

HASKEL, Prof (the Hon) Jonathan Edward; s of Baron Haskel (Life Peer), *qv*, and Carole, *née* Lewis; *b* 1963; *Educ* Univ of Bristol (BSc), LSE (MSc, PhD); *Career* lectr Univ of Bristol 1987–88, research offr Centre for Business Strategy London Business Sch 1988–90; Queen Mary & Westfield Coll (now Queen Mary, Univ of London): joined 1990, prof 2000–, head Economics Dept 2003–; fndr and dir Centre for Research into Business Activity (CeRiBA) 2001–; visiting research scholar ANU 1995, visiting asst prof Stern Sch of Business NYU 1997, research fell Centre for Economic Policy Research, external fell Centre for Research on Globalisation and Labour Markets Univ of Nottingham, research assoc Inst for the Study of Labor (IZA) Bonn; memb Reporting Panel Competition Cmmn, visiting academic conslt HM Treasy 2000–; author of numerous articles in refereed jls and conf papers; memb Editorial Bd Economica; *Style*— Prof Jonathan Haskel; ✉ Department of Economics, Queen Mary, University of London, Mile End Road, London E1 4NS (tel 020 7882 5095, fax 020 8983 3580)

HASKEL, Baron (Life Peer UK 1993), of Higher Broughton in the County of Greater Manchester; Simon Haskel; s of Isaac Haskel, of Kaunas, Lithuania; *b* 8 October 1934; *Educ* Sedbergh, Salford Coll of Advanced Technol (BSc); *m* 1962, Carole, da of Wilbur Lewis, of New York, USA; 1 s (Hon Jonathan Edward, *qv*, b 1963), 1 da (Hon Lisa Frances b 1965); *Career* chief exec Perrotts Gp plc 1970–89 (joined Perrotts Ltd as technician 1961); sits as Lab peer in House of Lords, oppn whip 1994, front bench spokesman on trade and industry 1994–97, Lord in Waiting (Govt whip) 1997–98, liaison peer DTI 1998–2005, dep speaker and dep chm of ctees 2002–; memb Select Ctee on Science and Technol 1994–97 and 1998–; fndr memb Labour Fin and Industry Gp 1972 (sec later chm 1976–95); chm of tstees Smith Inst, pres Inst for Jewish Policy Research, tstee Israel Diaspora Tst, tstee Lord and Lady Haskel Charitable Fndn, patron Chronic Disease Research Fndn; hon pres: Environmental Industry Cmmn, Materials UK; *Style*— The Rt Hon the Lord Haskel; ✉ House of Lords, London SW1A 0PW

HASKELL, Mark John; s of John Harold Haskell, of Poole, Dorset, and Mary June, *née* Coombs; *b* 12 November 1959; *Educ* Poole GS, Univ of Warwick (BSc); *m* 1990, Jane Elizabeth, *née* Derry; *Career* chartered accountant KPMG 1981–92; md: ITV Westcountry 1997– (fin dir 1992–97), ITV West 2004–; govr Falmouth Coll of Arts 1998–2005; tstee: Frank Copplestone Tst, Devon Community Fndn; ACA 1984; FRSA; *Recreations* golf, flat-coated retrievers; *Clubs* Teignmouth Golf; *Style*— Mark Haskell, Esq; ✉ ITV Westcountry, Western Wood Way, Langage Science Park, Plymouth, Devon PL7 5BQ (tel 01752 333333, fax 01752 333444, e-mail mark.haskell@itv.com)

HASKINS, Baron (Life Peer UK 1998), of Skidby in the East Riding of Yorkshire; Christopher Robin Haskins; s of Robin Haskins, and Margaret Haskins, of Wicklow; *b* 30 May 1937; *Educ* Trinity Coll Dublin (BA); *m* 1959, Gilda, da of Alec Horsley, of Hessle, E Yorks; 3 s (Hon Paul b 1961, Hon Daniel b 1962, Hon David b 1966), 2 da (Hon Gina (Hon Mrs Hocking) b 1964, Hon Kate b 1967); *Career* with Ford Motor Co 1960–62; chm Northern Foods 1986–2002 (joined 1962), chm Better Regulation Task Force 1997–2002, chm Express Dairies plc 1998–2002, rural recovery co-ordinator 2001–, dir Nat Children's Tst for Ireland 2001–03, chm European Movement 2004–06; pro-chllr Open Univ 2004–; memb: Runnymede Tst 1989–98, Culliton Irish Industry Policy Review Gp 1991–92, Cmmn for Social Justice 1992–94, Demos 1993–2000, UK Round Table on Sustainable Devpt 1995–98, Hampel Ctee on Corp Governance 1996–97, Civil Liberties Tst 1996–2001, Bd Yorks and Humber RDA 1998–, Legal Assistance Tst 1998–2004, Lawes Agricultural Tst 1999–, Advsy Bd Nat Assoc of Citizens Advice Bureaux 2000–04, New Deal Task Force 1997–2001; Hon LLD: Univ of Hull, Univ of Dublin, Univ of Nottingham, Univ of Huddersfield; Hon DUniv: Essex, Leeds Metropolitan, Lincoln, Bradford; Hon DSc Cranfield Univ; *Recreations* writing, weekend farm relief man, cricket; *Style*— The Rt Hon the Lord Haskins; ✉ Quarryside Farm, Main Street, Skidby, Cottingham, East Yorkshire HU16 5TG (tel 01482 842692)

HASKINS, Samuel Joseph (Sam); s of Benjamin George Haskins (d 1970), and Anna Elizabeth Haskins (d 1983); *b* 11 November 1926; *Educ* Helpmekaar HS, Witwatersrand Tech Coll, London Coll of Printing; *m* 1952, Alida Elzabe, da of Stephanus Johannes van Heerden; 2 s (Ludwig b 1955, Konrad b 1963); *Career* photographer; estab: freelance advertising studio Johannesburg 1952, Haskins Studio and Haskins Press London 1968; *Exhibitions* incl: Haskins Photographs (Johannesburg) 1953, Sam Haskins (Pentax Gallery Tokyo) 1970, Haskins Posters (The Photographers Gallery) 1972, FNAC Gallery Paris 1973, The Camera Gallery Amsterdam 1974, Scandinavian Landscape (Isetan Gallery Tokyo) 1973, Photo Graphics (Nat Theatre London) 1980, Sam Haskins a Bologna (Bologna) 1984, The Best of Sam Haskins (Pentax Forum Gallery Tokyo) 1986, The Image Factor (Pentax Forum Gallery Tokyo) 1990, Remember Barcelona (Pentax Forum Gallery Tokyo, Osaka Pentax Gallery then Interkamera Prague) 1992, Hearts (Pentax Forum Tokyo, Pentax Gallery Osaka) 1993, Sam Haskins - Monochrome (Pentax Forum Gallery Tokyo, Pentax Gallery Osaka) 1996, Retrospective (Glasgow) 1997, 'Kate' (London) 1997, 'A New Era' (Focus Gallery London) 1999 (also at Pentax Forum Gallery Tokyo 1999, Pentax Gallery Osaka 2000), Image (Gallery Argus Fotokunst Berlin) 2000, Gallagher's Gallery NY 2003, Paris Photo 2004, Van Leewen Gallery Amsterdam 2005, Portraits and Other Stories (Nat Portrait Gallery Canberra) 2006; *Books* Five Girls (1962), Cowboy Kate and Other Stories (1964, Prix Nadar), November Girl (1966), African Image (1967, Silver medal Int Art Book Competition 1969), Haskins Posters (1972, Gold medal NY Art Directors' Club 1974), Photographics (1980, Kodak Book of the Year award 1980), Sam Haskins a Bologna (1984), Barcelona '92 (1991), Cowboy Kate - Director's Cut (2006); *Recreations* vintage car rallying, sculpting, joinery, painting, craft and antique collecting, horticulture; *Style*— Sam Haskins, Esq; ✉ e-mail sam@haskins.com, website www.haskins.com, blog www.samhaskinsblog.com

HASLAM, Prof David Antony; CBE (2004); *b* 4 July 1949; *Educ* Monkton Combe Sch, Univ of Birmingham Med Sch (MB ChB, DObstRCOG, DFFP); *Career* house physician Warneford Hosp Leamington Spa 1972–73, house surgn N Staffs Royal Infirmary 1973; SHO: (obstetrics) Birmingham Maternity Hosp 1973–74, (paediatrics) Birmingham Children's Hosp 1974, (psychiatry) Midland Nerve Hosp 1974–75, (gen med) Birmingham Gen Hosp 1975; trainee GP 1975–76, GP in partnership Ramsey Health Centre Huntingdon 1976–; nat clinical advsr to Healthcare Cmmn 2005–; visiting prof of primary healthcare De Montfort Univ (hon reader 1999); RCGP: memb Cncl 1987– (chm 2001–04), pres 2006–; memb Postgrad Med Educn Trg Bd (PMETB) 2003–; patron Crysis (Parents' Self Help Gp); FRCGP 1989 (MRCGP), FFPH 2003, FRCP 2004, FRSM 2004; *Books* Sleepless Children (1984), Eat it Up (1986), Travelling with Children (1987), ParentStress (1989), The Expectant Father (1990), Bulimia - A Guide for Sufferers and Their Families (1994), Your Child's Symptoms Explained (1997), Stress-free Parenting (1998); author of numerous articles and reg contrib various academic and non-academic jls, numerous appearances on local and nat radio and on TV; *Recreations* running (incl London marathon 2006), photography, skiing; *Style*— Prof David Haslam, CBE; ✉ The Health Centre, Ramsey, Huntingdon, Cambridgeshire PE26 1AQ (tel 01487 812611, fax 01487 711801, e-mail davidhaslam@hotmail.com)

H

HASLAM, Jonathan; CBE (1997); s of Arthur Haslam, and Irene Florence Haslam; *b* 2 October 1952; *Educ* Cowbridge GS, Plymouth Poly, Croydon Coll of Art and Technol, Univ of London (BSc); *m* 1982, Dawn Rachel; 2 s (James Samuel Charles b 25 July 1991, George Michael Anthony 27 July 1994); *Career* with National Westminster Bank 1975–79; information offr: COI 1979–82, DTI 1982–84; sr information offr Home Office 1984–86, dep head of information and dep press sec to sec of state Dept of Employment 1988–89 (princ information offr 1986–88), dep dir of information, dep press sec to Sec of State and head of news Home Office 1989–91, dep press sec to PM 1991–95, head of information and press sec to min for Agric, Fisheries and Food 1995, chief press sec to PM 10 Downing Street 1996–97, dir of communications Dept for Educn and Employment (DFEE) 1997, first dir of corp affrs London Metal Exchange 1997–2003, dir of gp communications Jarvis plc 2003–05; chm The Spokesmen; MIPR; *Recreations* golf, music, cinema, reading; *Style*— Jonathan Haslam, Esq, CBE

HASLAM, Prof Jonathan George; s of E A Haslam, and M M G Haslam; *b* 15 January 1951, Copthorne, Sussex; *Educ* Wellington, LSE (BSc), Trinity Coll Cambridge (MLitt); *m* 28 April 2006, Dr Karina Urbach; *Career* lectr Univ of Birmingham 1975–84, assoc prof John Hopkins Univ 1984–86; visiting assoc prof: Stanford 1986–87, Berkeley 1987–88; sr research fell King's Coll Cambridge 1988–92, Univ of Cambridge 1992– (currently prof of the history of int rels), fell CCC Cambridge 1994–; specialist advsr House of Lords EU Ctee Sub-Ctee C 2002; FRHistS 1985; *Publications* The Vices of Integrity: E H Carr, 1892–1982 (1999), No Virtue Like Necessity: Realist Thought in International Relations Since Machiavelli (2002), The Nixon Administration and the Death of Allende's Chile (2005); *Recreations* travel, languages, music; *Clubs* Athenaeum; *Style*— Prof Jonathan Haslam; ✉ Corpus Christi College, Cambridge CB2 1RH (tel 01223 338000, fax 01223 338057, e-mail jgh1001@cam.ac.uk)

HASLAM, Mark Stanley Culloden; s of Nigel Haslam (d 1994), and Daphne, *née* Low (d 1991); *b* 16 June 1957, Nairobi, Kenya; *Educ* Wellington Coll, Pembroke Coll Cambridge (MA); *m* 24 Sept 1996, Helen Fiona, *née* Lambert; 3 step s (James b 25 May 1985, Andrew b 24 March 1988, Ian b 13 Sept 1989); *Career* admitted slr 1981; Claude Hornby & Cox 1979–93, Magrath & Co 1993–97, BCL Burton Copeland 1998– (ptnr Criminal Litigation Dept); memb: Criminal Law Ctee Law Soc, Criminal Law Solicitors' Assoc; Law Soc representative Legal Services Cmmn High Costs Cases Appeal Panel, past pres London Criminal Courts Solicitors' Assoc, past chm Forces Law; *Recreations* cricket, horse racing, theatre; *Clubs* Brook CC, Sandown Park; *Style*— Mark Haslam, Esq; ✉ Brook Place, Brook Farm Road, Cobham, Surrey KT11 3AX (mobile 07976 294270); BCL Burton Copeland, 51 Lincoln's Inn Fields, London WC2A 3LZ (tel 020 7430 2277, fax 020 7430 1101, e-mail mhaslam@burtoncopeland.co.uk)

HASLAM, Simon Mark; s of Peter Haigh Haslam, of Allestree, Derby, and Elizabeth Anne, *née* Gallimore; *b* 29 May 1957; *Educ* Ecclesbourne Sch Duffield, Magdalen Coll Oxford (MA); *m* 15 May 1982, Catherine (Kate) Nina (who retains her maiden name), da of Capt Robert Kenneth Alcock, CBE, RN, of Welwyn Garden City, Herts; 2 s (Thomas b 9 July 1987, Richard Matthew b 21 July 1993), 1 da (Eleanor (twin) b 9 July 1987); *Career* Touche Ross (now Deloitte & Touche): articled clerk 1978–81, mangr 1984–86, ptnr 1986–95; currently main bd dir and chief operating offr Fidelity International Ltd; dist councillor Welwyn Hatfield 1990–2000; FCA 1991 (ACA 1981), MSI; *Books* The London Securities Markets (1990); *Recreations* choral societies, walking, reading; *Style*— Simon Haslam, Esq; ✉ Fidelity Investments, Oakhill House, 130 Tonbridge Road, Hildenborough, Kent TN11 9DZ (tel 01732 777436, fax 01732 777145)

HASLEHURST, Peter Joseph Kinder; s of Col Arthur Kinder Haslehurst, TD (d 1987), and Beatrice Elizabeth, *née* Birkinshaw (d 1998); *b* 4 March 1941; *Educ* Repton, Loughborough Univ (DLC); *m* 29 Oct 1977, Susan Marilyn, da of Mr and Mrs Geoffrey W Y Heath; 1 s (Thomas William Kinder b 22 May 1983), 2 step s (Matthew, Adam); *Career* md Wellman Mech Engrg Ltd 1969–81, chm Flexibox Int Ltd 1986–98 (chief exec 1981–86), dep chm and chief exec EIS Gp plc 1985–98; dir M&G Income Investment Tst plc 1994–2004; current chairmanships incl: Brunner Mond Gp plc 2000–, Magadi Soda Ltd Kenya 2002–, Magadi Rail Co Ltd Kenya 2002–, IMAGO at Loughborough Ltd 2003–, Luxfer plc 2006– (dir 2003–); dep chm VAI Industries UK Ltd 1999–2004 (pres emeritus 2004); memb Bd of Companions Inst of Mgmnt 1996–2002; chm Br Metalworking Plant Makers Assoc 1974 and 1980, founding chm Br Metallurgical Plant Constructors Assoc (BMPCA) 1980–81, ldr Industry Missions to E Europe and Latin America; industrial advsr to Min of State on official visit to Czechoslovakia 1978, ldr Metals Soc Team NE China 1979; memb: Jt Trade Cmmn with Czechoslovakia 1978–80, Anglo-Soviet Econ Conf 1978–88, Materials Chemicals and Vehicles Requirement Bd Dept of Industry 1981–84, Br Hydromechanics Research Assoc Cncl 1984–89, Cncl Inst of Materials 1991–2003 (vice-pres 1997–2000, hon treas 2000–03, chm Audit Ctee 2003–), Cncl Loughborough Univ 1999–, Mensa; Eisenhower fell 1980; Freeman City of London 1992, Liveryman Worshipful Co of Engrs 1993; CEng, FIMechE, FIEE, FIMMM, CCMI, FRSA; *Recreations* sailing and the countryside; *Clubs* Royal Thames Yacht (Rear Cdre 1994–96, tstee 2005–); *Style*— Peter Haslehurst, Esq; fax 01260 223731, e-mail pjkh@phtechnology.com

HASLETT, Prof Christopher; OBE (2004); s of James Haslett, of Bebington, Wirral; *b* 2 April 1953; *Educ* Wirral GS, Univ of Edinburgh (BSc, MB ChB, Ettles scholar and Leslie Gold medal); *m* Jean Margaret, da of Thomas Hale; 1 da (Kate b 29 Jan 1983), 1 s (Andrew b 4 March 1990); *Career* house physician and surgn Edinburgh Royal Infirmary 1977–78, SHO Dept of Respiratory Med City Hosp Edinburgh 1978–79, res fell and hon med registrar Eastern General Hosp Edinburgh 1980 (SHO in general med 1979–80), general med registrar Ealing Hosp and Dept of Med RPMS 1980–82, res assoc F L Bryant Jr Research Lab for the Study of the Mechanisms of Lung Disease and instr Dept of Med Nat Jewish Hosp and Research Centre/Nat Asthma Centre Denver 1982–85, sr registrar in respiratory med Dept of Med RPMS Hammersmith Hosp 1982–85, sr lectr Respiratory Div Dept of Med RPMS and conslt physician Hammersmith Hosp 1985–90, prof of respiratory med and dir of The Rayne Laboratories Univ of Edinburgh 1990–, chm Dept of Med Royal Infirmary Edinburgh 1995–98, assoc dean (research) Univ of Edinburgh 1996–, head Div of Med Sci and Community Health Edinburgh 1996–; visiting prof RPMS 1990–; sec Working Gp on Lung Injury Euro Respiratory Soc 1991–, memb Cell and Molecular Med Bd MRC 1992–, vice-chm Res Ctee Nat Asthma Campaign; Dorothy Temple Cross Award MRC 1982, George Simon Meml Fell Award Fleischner Soc 1985, sr clinical fell MRC 1986; memb: Fleischner Soc, Assoc of Physicians (memb Cncl for Scotland 1993–), Assoc of Clinical Profs, Br Thoracic Soc, MRS, American Thoracic Soc, Int Soc for Leukocyte Biology; FRCP(Edin) 1988, FRCP(London) 1991, Fndr FMedSci 1998, FRSE 2000; author of numerous medical pubns; *Style*— Prof Christopher Haslett, OBE; ✉ Respiratory Medicine Unit, Department of Medicine, The Royal Infirmary, 1 Lauriston Place, Edinburgh EH3 9YW (tel 0131 536 2263)

HASSALL, Antony David; s of Frank, and Marlene Hassall; *Educ* Britannia HS, Rewley Regis Sixth Form Coll, Open Univ; *Career* mangr J Sainsbury 1982–90; prison offr 1990–92, princ offr Feltham YOI 1993–94 (staff offr to dir of custody 1994–95), govr 5/4 Wormwood Scrubs 1995–97, team ldr Area Mangrs Support Team 1997–99, govr HMP Bullwood Hall 2002–05 (dep govr 2000–02), govr HMP Holloway 2006–; memb: Howard League, Lab Pty, Fabian Soc; *Recreations* holidays, reading, current affairs; *Style*— Antony Hassall, Esq; ✉ HMP Holloway, Parkhurst Road, London N7 0NU

HASSALL, Tom Grafton; OBE (1999); s of William Owen Hassall (d 1994), and Averil Grafton, *née* Beaves (d 1997); *b* 3 December 1943; *Educ* Dragon Sch Oxford, Lord Williams's GS Thame, CCC Oxford (BA); *m* 2 Sept 1967, Angela Rosaleen, da of Capt Oliver Goldsmith (d 1944), of Thirsk; 3 s (Oliver b 28 Nov 1968, Nicholas b 30 April 1970, Edward b 10 July 1972); *Career* asst local ed Victoria County History of Oxford 1966–67, dir Oxford Archaeological Excavation Ctee 1967–73, dir Oxford Archaeological Unit 1973–85, assoc staff tutor Dept for External Studies Univ of Oxford 1978–85, fell St Cross Coll Oxford (emeritus fell 1988–), sec Royal Cmmn on the Historical Monuments of England 1986–99, pres Int Cncl on Monuments and Sites UK 1997–2003, chm Advsy Ctee on Historic Wreck Sites 2002–; tstee Oxford Preservation Tst 1973–, chm Standing Conf of Archaeological Unit Mangrs 1980–83, pres Cncl for Br Archaeology 1983–86, chm Br Archaeological Awards 1983–87, pres Oxfordshire Architectural and Historical Soc 1984–92, chm Victoria History of Oxfordshire Tst 1997–2003, chm Kelmscott Manor Mgmnt Ctee 2000–05; Freeman City of Chester 1973; FSA 1971, MIFA 1985, Hon MIFA 1999; *Books* Oxford, The Buried City (1987); *Recreations* boating; *Clubs* Athenaeum; *Style*— Tom Hassall, Esq, OBE, FSA; ✉ Durham House, 42 Rewley Road, Oxford OX1 2RQ (tel 01865 205266)

HASSELL, Barry Frank; s of Edgar Frank Hassell (d 1990), and Rosetta Ethel, *née* Townsend; *b* 26 September 1944; *Educ* Swanscombe Co Secdy Sch, London Business Sch (LEP); *m* 29 Dec 1971, Sylvia Booth (wid); 2 step s (Stephen, Richard); *Career* various accounting and mktg appts incl periods in Scandinavia and Africa 1959–73, mgmnt conslt 1973–85, special projects exec Scope (formerly The Spastics Soc) 1980–85, chief exec The Children's Tst (formerly Tadworth Court Tst) 1983–92 (memb 1992–), dir Project Bombay 1983–88, chief exec Independent Healthcare Assoc 1992–2003, chief exec Ind Healthcare Conslts Ltd 2004–; hon sec Union of Euro Private Hosps (UEHP) 1993–97 (vice-pres 1997–2000); memb Tadworth Court Children's Hosp Appeal Fund 1984–2003; govr Nat Inst for Social Work 1998–2004; lead concordat negotiations between Ind Healthcare Assoc and Dept of Health 2000; MInstD, FCMI, FRGS; *Recreations* travel, photography, skiing; *Style*— Barry Hassell, Esq

HASSELL, Prof Michael Patrick; CBE; s of Maj Albert Marmaduke Hassell, MC, of Clench, Wilts, and Gertrude, *née* Loeser (d 1973); *b* 2 August 1942; *Educ* Whitgift Sch, Clare Coll Cambridge (MA), Oriel Coll Oxford (DPhil); *m* 1, 7 Oct 1966 (m dis), Glynis Mary Ethel, da of John Everett; 2 s (Adrian Michael b 6 Feb 1971, David Charles b 2 April 1973); m 2, Victoria Anne, da of Reginald Taylor (d 1984); 1 s (James Mark b 10 June 1986), 1 da (Kate Helen b 18 April 1988); *Career* Imperial Coll London: lectr Dept of Zoology and Applied Entomology 1970–75, reader in insect ecology Dept of Zoology and Applied Entomology 1975–79, prof of insect ecology Dept of Pure and Applied Biology 1979–, dep head Dept of Biology 1984–93, dir Silwood Park 1988– (head Dept of Biology 1993–2001), princ Faculty of Life Scis 2001–04, campus dean 2004–; tstee Natural History Museum 1999–; FRS 1986, fell Academia Europaea 1998; *Books* The Dynamics of Competition and Predation (1976), The Dynamics of Arthropod and Predator-Prey Systems (1978); *Recreations* walking, natural history, croquet; *Style*— Prof Michael Hassell, CBE, FRS; ✉ Silwood Lodge, Silwood Park, Ascot, Berkshire SL5 7PZ; Imperial College at Silwood Park, Department of Biology, Ascot, Berkshire SL5 7PY (tel 01344 294207, fax 01344 874957, e-mail m.hassell@imperial.ac.uk)

HASTE, Cate Mary; da of Eric L Haste, of Almondsbury, nr Bristol, and J Margaret, *née* Hodge; *b* 6 August 1945; *Educ* Thornbury GS Bristol, Univ of Sussex (BA), Univ of Manchester (Dip Adult Ed); *m* 1973, Baron Bragg (Life Peer), *qv*; 1 da (Hon Alice b 1977), 1 s (Hon Tom b 1980); *Career* freelance television documentary producer and director, writer and broadcaster; memb: Directors' Guild of GB 1988–, BAFTA 1995–, English PEN 1998–; *Television* The Secret War (BBC), End of Empire (Granada), Writing on the Wall (Channel 4), Munich - The Peace of Paper (Thames), Secret History - Death of a Democrat (Channel 4), The Churchills (ITV), Cold War (CNN), Millennium (CNN), Nazi Women (Channel 4), Married to the Prime Minister (Channel 4); *Books* Keep The Home Fires Burning - Propaganda in the First World War (1977), Rules of Desire - Sex in Britain WWI to the Present (1992), Nazi Women (2001), The Goldfish Bowl - Married to the Prime Minister 1955–97 (with Cherie Booth, 2004); *Recreations* reading, walking, gardening; *Style*— Ms Cate Haste; ✉ 12 Hampstead Hill Gardens, London NW3 2PL (tel 020 7794 0473)

HASTE, Prof Helen Elizabeth; da of Eric Leighton Haste (d 2000), and Joan Margaret, *née* Hodge; *b* 17 March 1943, Devizes, Wilts; *Educ* Univ of London (BA), Univ of Sussex (MPhil), Univ of Bath (PhD); *m* 1, (m dis 1978), 6 April 1963, Peter Weinreich; 1 da (Joanna Rachel b 10 Aug 1963); m 2, 30 June 1980 (m dis 1986), Paul Mosley; partner, Beverly Halstead (d 1991); *Career* Univ of Bath: lectr in psychology 1971–83, sr lectr in psychology 1983–92, reader in psychology 1992–1998, prof of psychology 1998–; Harvard Univ: assoc Center for Moral Educn 1980, visiting prof Grad Sch of Educn 1998 and 2003–; co-ordinator Moral and Social Action Interdisciplinary Colloquium 1977–2001; research dir Nestle Social Research Prog 2004–06; BAAS: pres Psychology Section 1991, vice-pres 2002–07, chair Cncl 2004–05; pres Int Soc for Political Psychology (ISPP) 2002 (memb 1981); Leverhulme research fell 2003–04, Nevitt Sanford Award ISPP 2005; FBPsS (memb 1965), FRSA 2002, hon fell BAAS 2002, AcSS 2006; *Publications* Half The Sky: An Introduction to Women's Studies (co-author, 1979), Morality in the Making: Thought, Action and Social Context (co-author, 1983), Making Sense: The Child's Construction of the World (co-author, 1987), The Development of Political Understanding (co-author, 1992), The Sexual Metaphor (1993); *Recreations* photography, playing small world; *Style*— Prof Helen Haste; ✉ 10 Belgrave Crescent, Bath BA1 5JU (tel 01225 420230, e-mail helhaste@aol.com); Department of Psychology, University of Bath, Bath BA1 5JU; Harvard Graduate School of Education, 613 Larsen Hall, Appian Way, Cambridge, MA 02138, USA (tel 00 1 617 354 1544)

HASTE, Norman David; OBE (1997); s of Jack Haste (d 1959), of Cleethorpe, Lincs, and Edith Eleanor, *née* Jarvis (d 1961); *b* 4 November 1944; *Educ* Humberstone Fndn Sch Cleethorpes, N Lindsey Tech Coll (ONC Mechanical Engrg), Royal Coll of Advanced Technol (now Univ of Salford, Associate); *Career* graduate engr rising to project mangr John Laing Construction Ltd 1966–73, section mangr Humber Bridge 1973–75, marine works mangr Littlebrook D Power Station Construction 1976–78, project mangr Long Sea Outfall Construction Gosport 1978–81, divnl chief engr Laing Civil Engineering 1981–82, contracts mangr McConnell Dowell SE Asia Singapore 1982–84, dir special projects John Laing Construction Ltd 1984–85; project dir: Civil Engrg Works Sizewell B Power Station 1985–90, Second Severn Crossing 1990–95, Terminal 5 Heathrow 1996–2002; chm Severn River Crossing plc 2000–06, chief exec Cross London Rail Links 2002–06, chief operating offr UAE Laing O'Rourke 2006–, chief exec Aldar Laing O'Rourke JV 2006–; dir Transnet South Africa 2006–; memb Cncl ICE 1994–97 and 1999–; James Prescott Joule Medal ICE 1970, Gold Medal ICE 1996, Highways and Transportation Award Instn of Highways and Transportation 1996; Hon DEng UWE 1997, Hon DSc Univ of Salford 1998; MASCE 1983, MIE Aust 1983, FICE 1984 (MICE 1970), FREng 1996, FIHT 1996; *Recreations* golf, music; *Style*— Norman Haste, Esq, OBE, FREng

HASTIE-SMITH, Rev Timothy Maybury; s of Richard Maybury Hastie-Smith, of London, and Bridget Noel, *née* Cox; *b* 8 March 1962, London; *Educ* Cranleigh Sch, Magdalene Coll Cambridge (MA), Wycliffe Hall Oxford (CertTheol); *m* 20 June 1987, Joanne Elizabeth, *née* Ide; 2 da (Emily Caroline Catherine b 7 Nov 1988, Alice Bridget Grace b 23 May 2000), 1 s (Edward Frederick Maybury b 5 Feb 1991); *Career* curate St Ebbe's Oxford 1988–91, chaplain and admissions tutor Stowe Sch 1991–98, headmaster Dean Close Cheltenham 1998–; chm HMC 2008–, chm Ind Schs Christian Alliance; govr:

Beachborough Sch, Hatherop Castle Sch, Winterfold Sch, Swanbourne House Sch, Aldro Sch; *Recreations* reading, politics, theatre, cinema, chicken husbandry; *Clubs* East India, Coningsby; *Style*— The Rev Timothy Hastie-Smith; ✉ Dean Close House, Lansdown Road, Cheltenham, Gloucestershire GL51 6QD (tel 01242 267401, e-mail headmaster@deanclose.org.uk)

HASTINGS, Christine Anne (Mrs John Gambles); da of Peter Edwards Hastings, and Anne Fauvel, *née* Picot; *b* 15 February 1956; *Educ* Whyteleafe GS; *m* 1, 5 May 1985 (m dis 1988), Lawrie Lewis; m 2, 7 June 1991, John Gambles; *Career* dir: Pact Ltd (PR Consultancy) 1980–86, Biss Lancaster plc 1986–88; founding dir (currently ptnr) Quadrangle Gp Ltd (now Fieldwork Quadrangle LLP) 1988–; FRSA; *Style*— Ms Christine Hastings; ✉ Fieldwork Quadrangle LLP, The Butlers Wharf Building, 36 Shad Thames, London SE1 2YE (tel 020 7357 9919, fax 020 7357 9773, e-mail christine.hastings@quadrangle.com)

HASTINGS, Sir Max Macdonald; kt (2002); s of Douglas Macdonald Hastings (d 1982), and Anne Scott-James (Lady Lancaster); *b* 28 December 1945; *Educ* Charterhouse (scholar), UC Oxford (exhibitioner); *m* 1, 1972 (m dis 1994), Patricia Mary, da of Tom Edmondson, of Leics; 1s (and 1 s decd), 1 da; m 2, 1999, Penny Grade; *Career* researcher Great War Series BBC TV 1963–64, reporter Evening Standard 1965–67, fell US World Press Inst 1967–68, roving corr Evening Standard 1968–70, reporter Current Affairs BBC TV 1970–73, ed Evening Standard Londoner's Diary 1976–77, columnist Daily Express 1981–83, contrib Sunday Times 1985–86; ed The Daily Telegraph 1986–95; dir: The Daily Telegraph plc 1989–95 (ed-in-chief 1990–95), Evening Standard Ltd 1996–2002, Associated Newspapers plc 1996–; ed Evening Standard 1996–2002, contrib Daily Mail 2002–; as war corr covered: Middle East, Indochina, Angola, India-Pakistan, Cyprus, Rhodesia, S Atlantic; documentaries for BBC and ITV; memb PCC 1991–92; pres CPRE 2002–07, vice-pres Game Conservancy 1992–; tstee Nat Portrait Gallery 1995–2004; Liddell-Hart lectr KCL 1994, Mountbatten lectr Univ of Edinburgh 2004; Journalist of the Year Br Press Awards 1982 (cited 1973 and 1980); What the Papers Say (Granada TV) awards: Reporter of the Year 1982, Ed of the Year 1988; Hon DLitt Univ of Leicester 1992; hon fell KCL 2004; FRHistS 1988, FRSL 1996; *Books* America 1968: The Fire This Time (1968), Ulster 1969: The Struggle for Civil Rights in Northern Ireland (1970), Montrose: The King's Champion (1977), Yoni: The Hero of Entebbe (1979), Bomber Command (1979, Somerset Maugham Prize for Non-Fiction 1980), The Battle of Britain (with Len Deighton, 1980), Das Reich (1981), The Battle for The Falklands (with Simon Jenkins, 1983, Yorkshire Post Book of the Year Award), Overlord: D-Day and the Battle for Normandy (1984, 2 edn 1989, Yorkshire Post Book of the Year Award), Victory in Europe (1985), The Oxford Book of Military Anecdotes (ed, 1985), The Korean War (1987, shortlisted NCR Prize), Outside Days (1989), Scattered Shots (1999), Going to the Wars (2000), Editor: A Memoir (2002), Armageddon (2004), Warriors (2005), Country Fair (2005), Nemesis (2007); *Recreations* shooting, fishing; *Clubs* Brooks's; *Style*— Sir Max Hastings, FRSL; ✉ Northcliffe House, 2 Derry Street, London W8 5EE; secretary (tel 01380 720894)

HASTINGS, Lady Selina Shirley; da of 16 Earl of Huntingdon (d 1990), and his 2 w, Margaret Lane (d 1994); *b* 5 March 1945; *Educ* St Paul's Girls' Sch, St Hugh's Coll Oxford (MA); *Career* writer and journalist; FRSL; *Books* incl: Nancy Mitford, Evelyn Waugh, Rosamond Lehmann; *Style*— The Lady Selina Hastings; ✉ c/o Rogers, Coleridge & White, 20 Powis Mews, London W11

HASTINGS, Steven Alan; s of Thomas Alan Hastings, OBE, of Beckenham, Kent, and Margaret Elizabeth, *née* Webber; *b* 18 September 1957; *Educ* Dulwich Coll, Univ of Bristol (BSocSci); *m* 1, 19 July 1987 (m dis 2003), Teresa Lynne Eugenie, da of John Wimbourne, of Esher, Surrey; 1 s (Thomas Magna b 1 April 1989), 2 da (Rosie Beatrice b 14 April 1991, Flora Isabella b 15 Dec 1993); m 2, 27 March 2004, Penelope Ann, da of Donald Chilvers, of Brightwell Balwdin, Oxon; 2 step da (Maria-Africa b 28 Feb 1990, Gemma Mercedes b 18 Sept 1992); *Career* planner Leagas Delaney 1980–83, planner D'Arcy McManus & Masius 1983–84, sr planner Lowe Howard-Spink 1984–88, planning dir BBDO UK Ltd 1988–91, dir The Planning Group 1991–92, managing ptnr Banks Hoggins O'Shea FCB 1992–, fndr partner isobel (advtg agency) 2003–; memb: MRS, Account Planning Gp; *Recreations* classic cars, golf, football, running; *Clubs* Serpentine Running, OAPs (sec); *Style*— Steven Hastings, Esq; ✉ 16 Beauclerc Road, London W6 0NS (mobile 07770 785445, e-mail steve@isobel.com)

HATCH, Prof David John; s of James Frederick Hatch (d 1991), of Hutton, Essex, and late Marguerite Fanny, *née* Forge; *b* 11 April 1937; *Educ* Caterham Sch, UCL (MB BS, MRCS, LRCP); *m* 4 June 1960, Rita, da of William Henry Wilkins Goulter (d 1956); 2 s (Michael b 1963, Andrew b 1969), 2 da (Susan b 1964, Jane b 1967); *Career* fell in anaesthesiology Mayo Clinic Rochester MN 1968–69, conslt in anaesthesia and respiratory measurement Hosp for Sick Children Gt Ormond St 1969–91 (chm Div of Anaesthesia 1984–87), sub dean Inst of Child Health Univ of London 1974–85, prof of paediatric anaesthesia Univ of London 1991–2004 (emeritus prof 2004–); Assoc of Paediatric Anaesthetists: hon sec 1979–86, pres 1993–95; memb Cncl: Assoc of Anaesthetists of GB and Ireland 1982–86; Royal Coll of Anaesthetists: memb Cncl 1986–98, vice-pres 1991–93, professional standards advsr 2001–; chm Assessment Ctee GMC 2004– (memb GMC 1994–2003, chm Professional Performance Ctee 1999–2004), memb RSM; FFARCS 1965, FCAnaes 1988, FRCA 1992; *Books* with Sumner: Neonatal Anaesthesia and Perioperative Care (1981, 3 edn 1995), Clinics in Anaesthesiology - Paediatric Anaesthesia (1985), Textbook of Paediatric Anaesthetic Practice (1989, 2 edn 1999); *Recreations* sailing, badminton; *Style*— Prof David Hatch; ✉ 6 Darnley Road, Woodford Green, Essex IG8 9HU (tel 020 8504 4134, fax 020 8504 1605); The Royal College of Anaesthetists, 35 Red Lion Square, London WC1R 3SG (tel 020 7092 1695, e-mail dhatch@rcoa.ac.uk)

HATCHARD, Michael Edward; s of Kenneth Edward William Hatchard (d 1997), and Diana Margaret Suzanne, *née* McMullin; *b* 21 November 1955, Wilts; *Educ* Sherborne, Univ of Reading (LLB), Coll of Law; *m* 1, Erica Bourdon Smith; m 2, Feb 1994, Pia Lucinda Bruna Lucia, *née* Gabriele; 1 s (George William Salvatore b July 1996); 1 s by Erica Bourdon Smith (Augustus Edward Percy b Sept 1991); *Career* admitted slr 1980; ptnr: Theodore Goddard 1985–94 (joined 1978), Skadden Arps Slate Meagher & Flom 1994–; contrib to various legal pubs; memb Law Soc 1980; *Recreations* fishing, collecting variously; *Clubs* Annabel's, 51, RAC; *Style*— Michael Hatchard Esq; ✉ Skadden, Arps, Slate, Meagher & Flom (UK) LLP, 40 Bank Street, Canary Wharf, London E14 5DS (tel 020 7519 7020, fax 020 7072 7020, e-mail mhatchard@skadden.com)

HATCHER, Prof (Melvyn) John; s of John Edward Hatcher (d 1960), and Lilian Florence, *née* Lepper (d 1981); *b* 7 January 1942; *Educ* Owens GS Islington London, LSE (BSc, PhD), Univ of Cambridge (LittD); *m* 16 Dec 1967, Janice Miriam, da of Herbert John Ranson; 2 da (Melissa Ann b 12 Sept 1978, Zara Sophie b 29 June 1982); *Career* research fell Inst of Historical Research Univ of London 1966–67, sr lectr in history Univ of Kent at Canterbury 1973–75 (lectr 1967–73); Univ of Cambridge: lectr in history 1976–86, reader in economic and social history 1986–95, prof of economic and social history 1995–; fell Corpus Christi Coll Cambridge 1976– (vice-master 2001–); visiting prof Univ of Colorado at Boulder USA 1975–76, visiting fell Huntington Library Calif USA 1986–87; memb SSRC Econ and Social History Ctee 1979–82; ESRC: vice-chm Econ Affrs Ctee 1982–84, memb (jtly with UGC) New Blood Ctee, dir research initiative on history of prices and incomes 1984–86, Postgrad Awards Ctee 1988–90; memb Cncl Economic History Soc 1980–; ed Economic History Review 1995–2001; FRHistS 1974, AcSS 2001; *Books* Rural Economy and Society in the Duchy of Cornwall, 1300–1500 (1970), English Tin Production and Trade before 1550 (1973), A History of British Pewter (with T C Barker, 1974), Plague, Population and the English Economy, 1348–1530 (1977), Medieval England: rural society and economic change 1086–1348 (with E Miller, 1978), The History of the British Coal Industry: Before 1700 (1993, Wadsworth Prize 1993), Medieval England: towns, commerce and crafts, 1086–1348 (with E Miller, 1995), Modelling the Middle Ages (with M Bailey, 2001); also author of book chapters and articles in learned jls; *Recreations* football, jazz; *Style*— Prof John Hatcher; ✉ Corpus Christi College, Cambridge CB2 1RH (tel 01223 338000, fax 01223 338061)

HATCHER, Mark; s of Peter Thomas Hatcher (d 1995), of Great Bookham, Surrey, and Joan Beatrice, *née* Crisp; *b* 16 October 1954; *Educ* Sutton Valence, Exeter Coll Oxford (Winter Williams law prize, MA); *m* 9 July 1988, Clare Helen, eld da of Prof Hugh Lawrence, FSA, of London; 1 da (Sophie b 13 Nov 1990); *Career* called to the Bar Middle Temple 1978 (Astbury scholar), ad eundem Lincoln's Inn; in private practice 1978–80, with Law Cmmn 1980–83, with Legislation Gp Lord Chancellor's Dept 1983–88, Courts and Legal Servs Gp 1988; mgmnt conslt Deloitte Haskins & Sells 1988–90; PricewaterhouseCoopers (formerly Coopers & Lybrand before merger 1998): head of public affrs 1990–2000, public affrs counsel Coopers & Lybrand (UK) 1996–98, memb Global Regulatory and Professional Affrs Bd 2000–03, head of public affrs consulting 2000–03; ind corp and public affrs conslt 2003–04, special advsr to Fuse PR 2003–04, dir and head of public affrs Cubitt Consulting 2004–06, dir of representation and policy Bar Cncl 2006–; rapporteur for European Services Forum 2000–; memb Advsy Bd: Centre for Corp and Public Affrs, Centre on Migration, Policy and Society Univ of Oxford 2002–; special advsr European Economic and Social Ctee 2003–05; memb Editorial Bd: Jl of Communication Mgmnt, Jl of Public Affrs; contrib to various jls; govr Sutton Valence Sch 2005–; corp fell Industry and Parl Tst 1994, Euro fell 1995; memb: Ecclesiastical Law Soc, Greenwich Soc (conservation); FRSA 1994; *Books* New Activism and the Corporate Response (with S John and S Thomson, 2003), Moving People to Deliver Services (ed A Mattoo and A Carzaniga, 2003); *Recreations* exploring churches, second-hand books, cooking; *Clubs* Reform; *Style*— Mark Hatcher, Esq; ✉ Bar Council, 289–293 High Holborn, London WC1V 7HZ (tel 020 7611 1369, fax 020 7831 9217, e-mail mhatcherdrp@barcouncil.org.uk); 41 Gloucester Circus, Greenwich, London SE10 8RY (tel 020 8293 4969, fax 020 8305 9601, mobile 07801 038389)

HATELEY, Linzi; da of Raymond William Hateley, and Margery, *née* Hammond; *b* 23 October 1970; *Educ* Wilnecote HS Tamworth, Italia Conti Acad of Theatre Arts London; *Career* actress; *Theatre* incl: title role in RSC's Carrie, Eponine in RSC's Les Miserables, Kolakola Bird in Cameron Mackintosh's Just So, narrator in Andrew Lloyd Webber's Joseph And The Amazing Technicolor Dreamcoat, Shakers - The Musical, Peter Pan, The Rise and Fall of Little Voice, Rizzo in Grease, Romance, Romance, Divorce Me Darling, Into the Woods, The Rink, Oliver, The Secret Garden, On Your Toes, Roxie Hart in Chicago, Mrs Banks in Mary Poppins, Donna in Mamma Mia; *Television* The Day The Music Died (Channel 4 documentary film), Children's Variety Performances 1992 and 1993, Brucie's Guest Night, Pebble Mill, Going Live, Children in Need, Win Lose or Draw, Des O'Connor Show; *Awards* incl: Theatre World Award for Most Promising Newcomer on Broadway 1988, Olivier Award nomination for Best Actress in a Musical/Entertainment 1992; *Recordings* Joseph (cast recording), Divorce Me Darling (cast recording), Secret Garden (cast recording), Mary Poppins (cast recording); 3 solo albums; *Style*— Ms Linzi Hateley; ✉ c/o Barry Burnett Organisation Ltd, 3 Clifford Street, London W1S 2LF (tel 020 7437 8008, fax 020 7257 3239)

HATHERTON, 8 Baron (UK 1835); Edward Charles Littleton; only s of Mervyn Cecil Littleton (d 1970), gs of 3 Baron, by his w, Margaret Ann, da of Frank Sheehy; *b* 24 May 1950; *m* 1974, Hilda Maria, da of Rodolfo Robert, of San José, Costa Rica; 2 da (Hon Melissa Ann b 1975, Hon Valerie Ann b 1981), 1 s (Hon Thomas Edward b 1977); *Heir* s, Hon Thomas Littleton; *Style*— The Rt Hon Lord Hatherton; ✉ PO Box 3358, San José, Costa Rica

HATHORN, (Alexander) Michael; s of Douglas Stuart Hathorn, and Elizabeth, *née* Snowdon; *b* 5 June 1948; *Educ* Stranraer HS Sedbergh; *m* 14 Oct 1972, Deborah Christian, da of Hamish Gordon Farquhar; 2 s (Iain Fergus b 30 April 1977, Andrew Alexander b 4 Aug 1984), 1 da (Emma Louise b 4 Sept 1979); *Career* ptnr Scott-Moncrieff, CAs (formerly Scott-Moncrieff Thomson & Shiells) 1974– (apprentice 1967–72); dir: Scott-Moncrieff Life & Pensions Ltd 1993–, Scott-Moncrieff Consultants Ltd 1993–, Baillie Gifford Shin Nippon plc 1994– (chm 1999–), Companies House 2001–; chm Moore Stephens UK Ltd 1989–, ptnr Moore Stephens London 2003–; accountant to the Village XIII Commonwealth Games 1986; assoc dir (Fin) Edinburgh International Festival 1989–90; chm: Local Authy (Scotland) Accounts Advsy Ctee 1991–93, LASAAC/CIPFA Jt Ctee 1992–94; dir Edinburgh Academy; memb ASB Public Sector and Not-for-Profit Ctee 1994–; hon treas and tstee Age Concern Scotland 1988–, hon treas Alcohol Focus Scotland; UK rep Public Sector Ctee Int Fedn of Accountants; memb: CIPFA 1993 (Capital Accounting Gp 1991–93, Tech Ctee 1995–2002, chair Accounting and Auditing Standards Panel), ICAS 1972 (chm Members Services Ctee 1990–99, chm Public Sector Ctee 1995–2001, memb Cncl 1999–, sr vice-pres 2003–); *Recreations* golf, curling, music, visual arts; *Clubs* New (Edinburgh), Lismore RFC, Hon Co of Golfers; *Style*— Michael Hathorn, Esq; ✉ Moore Stephens, St Paul's House, Warwick Lane, London EC2P 4BN (tel 020 7248 4499, e-mail mike.hathorn@moorestephens.com)

HATOUM, Mona; da of Joseph Salim Hatoum, MBE (d 1986), of Beirut, and Claire Indrawes Eid; *b* 11 February 1952; *Educ* Beirut UC, The Byam Shaw Sch of Art (Leverhulme Tst Fund bursary), Slade Sch of Art London; *Career* artist; Gtr London Arts Assoc grant 1982, Arts Cncl of GB bursary 1985; artist-in-residence: Western Front Art Center Vancouver 1984 and 1988, Chisenhale Dance Space London 1986–87, Capp Street Project San Francisco 1996; pt/t lectr St Martin's Sch of Art 1986–89, visual arts advsr Gtr London Arts 1986–88, sr fell in fine art Cardiff Inst of HE 1989–92, pt/t lectr Jan Van Eyck Akademie Maastricht 1992–97; nominated for Turner Prize 1995; awarded hon fell Dartington Coll of Arts 1997; *Important Works* incl: The Light at the End (installation work with electric heating elements in the collection of Arts Cncl of GB) 1989, Light Sentence (installation work with wire-mesh lockers and moving lightbulb in the collection of FNAC Paris) 1993, Corps Étranger (video projection inside a cylindrical structure in the collection of Centre Georges Pompidou); *Exhibitions* incl: The British Art Show (McLellan Galleries Glasgow and tour) 1990, Pour la Suite du Monde (Musée d'Art Contemporair de Montréal) 1992, Arnolfini Gallery Bristol 1993, Centre Georges Pompidou (solo exhbn) 1994, Sense and Sensibility: Women Artists and Minimalism in the Nineties (MOMA NY) 1994, Cocido y Crudo (Centro de Arte Reina Sofia Madrid) 1994/95, Heart of Darkness (Kröller Müller Holland) 1994/95, Corps Étranger (Venice Biennale) 1995, Rites of Passage: Art for the End of the Century (Tate Art Gallery) 1995, 4th International Istanbul Biennial 1995, The British Sch at Rome (solo exhbn) 1995, Distemper: Dissonant Themes in the Art of the 1990s (Hirshhorn Museum and Sculpture Garden Washington) 1996, Life/Live la Scène artistique au Royaume-Uni en 1996, de nouvelles aventures (Musée d'art moderne de la Ville de Paris) 1996, A Quality of Light (St Ives Cornwall) 1997, De-Genderism: détruire dit-elle/il (Setagaya Art Museum Tokyo) 1997, Chicago Museum of Contemporary Art (solo exhbn) 1997, The New Museum of Contemporary Art NY (solo exhbn) 1997, Sensation (Royal Academy of Art London) 1997, MOMA Oxford (solo exhbn) 1998; *Style*— Ms Mona Hatoum

HATT, Paul William David; s of William Oliver Hatt (d 1989), and Henrietta, *née* McGregor; *b* 21 November 1949; *Educ* Sir Joseph Williamson's Sch Rochester, Lincoln Coll Oxford (scholar, MA, PGCE), Nat Defence Coll; *m* 1975, Cecilia Anne, *née* Freeman; 2 s (James b 1978, Robert b 1980), 2 da (Mary b 1983, Elinor b 1985); *Career* MOD: joined 1973, princ 1980–85, on secondment to FCO as first sec UK Delgn to NATO 1985–89, asst sec 1990, head Defence Lands 1990–92, dir Proliferation and Arms Control Secretariat 1992–97, head Resources and Progs (Army) 1997–98, asst under sec 1998; command sec RAF Logistics Command 1998–2000, command sec to Second Sea Lord and C-in-C Naval Home Command and asst under sec of state (Naval personnel) MOD 2001–06; sec Royal Hosp Chelsea 2007–; fell Center for Int Affrs Harvard Univ 2000–01; *Recreations* sedentary pursuits, incl family, literature and music; *Style*— P W D Hatt, Esq; ✉ The Royal Hospital Chelsea, Royal Hospital Road, London SW3 4SR

HATT-COOK, Mark Edward; OBE (1996), RD (and Bar); s of Lt-Col John Edward Hatt-Cook, MC (d 1999), of Stoke Farthing, Wilts, and Lavender Helen, *née* Covernton; *b* 18 December 1942; *Educ* Bradfield Coll; *m* 18 Oct 1969, Susan Georgina, da of Lt-Col Ronald John Henry Kaulback, OBE (d 1995), of Hoarwithy, Herefords; 2 da (Catherine Emma b 13 Aug 1974, Georgina Alice b 13 June 1977); *Career* cmmnd RMR 1963, 45 Commando S Arabia 1963 (active serv), 42 Commando Malaysia 1969, 41 Commando N Ireland 1970, qualified Arctic survival instr 1980, TAVR staff course Camberley 1981, USMC staff course Quantico 1984, Lt-Col CO RMR City of London 1990–92, RMR Col 1992–95; chm City RFCA 1999–2002; vice-chm: Eastern Wessex TAVRA 1991–99, Cncl TAVRA 1992–95, Gtr London RFCA 1998–2007; Lord Mayor's Marshal 1980–; ADC to HM The Queen 1992–95; HM Cmmr of Lieutenancy for City of London 1999; articled with Hunters and with Bischoffs, admitted slr 1970, asst slr Deacons Hong Kong, ptnr Wilsons Salisbury (sr ptnr 1997–2002); memb regnl Br Olympic Ctee 1988, pres Salisbury Slrs Assoc 1989; tstee Salisbury Museum 1998–, pres Salisbury Sea Cadets 2001, chm Ulysses Tst 1999–2006, chm RFCA Pension Fund 2001; Freeman City of London 1981, Liveryman Worshipful Co of Turners 1995; memb Law Soc; *Recreations* shooting, skiing, sailing, numismatics, deer management; *Clubs* Army and Navy; *Style*— Col Mark Hatt-Cook, OBE, RD*; ✉ Mascalls, Broadchalke, Salisbury, Wiltshire (tel 01722 780480); Steynings House, Salisbury, Wiltshire (tel 01722 412412, e-mail mhc@wilsonslaw.com)

HATTERSLEY, Prof (William) Martin; s of Col Sidney Martin Hattersley, MC, MD, late RAMC (ka 1943), and Vera, *née* Blackbourn (d 1962); *b* 31 March 1928; *Educ* Marlborough, Univ of London (BSc); *m* 1, 1 Sept 1951 (m dis 1982), Shena Mary, da of Sydney Drummond Anderson (d 1961); 3 da (Susan Mary (Mrs Boyce) b 13 Jan 1955, Clare Helen (Mrs Papavergos) b 6 June 1956, Diana Rosine (Mrs Warner) b 5 Nov 1957); m 2, 1 Oct 1982, May Ling, da of Wee Bin Chye (d 1949), of Singapore; *Career* probationary 2 Lt RM 1946, Lt RM 1948, resigned cmmn 1950, elected memb HAC 1988; Gerald Eve & Co (chartered surveyors): improver 1950–54, tech asst 1954–58, ptnr 1958, responsible for all overseas assignments 1962–86, responsible for Brussels Office 1975–83; chief resident valuation offr Kuala Lumpur Municipal Cncl 1959–61; City Univ: prof and head of Dept of Property Valuation and Mgmnt 1985–91, visiting prof 1991–95, prof emeritus 1996; memb: RNLI, Lavant Valley Decorative and Fine Arts Soc, Emsworth Maritime and Historical Tst, Chichester Canal Soc; friend of: Chichester Festival Theatre, National Maritime Museum, Yvonne Arnaud Theatre, National Library of Wales; pres: BSc Estate Mgmnt Club 1970, Rating Surveyors' Assoc 1978; Freeman: City of London 1950, Co of Waterman and Lighterman 1992; Liveryman: Worshipful Co of Skinners 1963, Worshipful Co of Chartered Surveyors 1977; FIABCI (Int Real Estate Fedn) Medaille d'Honor for Leadership of Professional Standards Ctee (France 1986), hon fell of SBV Univ of Amsterdam 1991; FRICS 1963, FISM 1968, FSVA 1971, FIABCI 1973; memb: RNSA 1946, RYA, IRRV 1986; ACIArb 1990; *Books* Valuation: Principles into Practice (contrib 1992); *Recreations* sailing; *Clubs* Army and Navy, City Livery; *Style*— Prof Martin Hattersley; ✉ 62 King George Gardens, Chichester, West Sussex PO19 6LE (tel 01243 774775)

HATTERSLEY, Baron (Life Peer UK 1997), of Sparkbrook in the County of West Midlands; Rt Hon Roy Sydney George Hattersley; PC (1975); s of late Frederick Hattersley, and Enid Hattersley (Lord Mayor Sheffield 1981–82, d 2001); *b* 28 December 1932; *Educ* Sheffield City GS, Univ of Hull (BScEcon); *m* 1956, Edith Mary (Molly), da of Michael Loughran; *Career* joined Lab Pty 1949, memb Sheffield City Cncl 1957–65, Parly candidate (Lab) Sutton Coldfield 1959; MP (Lab) Birmingham Sparkbrook 1964–97, PPS to Min of Pensions and Nat Insurance 1964–67, jt Parly sec of state for employment and productivity 1967–69, min of defence for admin 1969–70; oppn spokesman on: defence 1972, educn and science 1972–74; min of state FCO 1974–76, sec of state for prices and consumer protection 1976–79; chief oppn spokesman on: environment 1979–80, home affairs 1981–83, Treasy and econ affairs 1983–87, home affairs 1987–92; dep ldr Lab Pty Oct 1983–1992; pres Local Govt Gp for Europe 1998–; journalist; named columnist of the year What the Papers Say (Granada TV) 1982; *Books* Nelson (1974), Goodbye to Yorkshire (essays, 1976), Politics Apart (1982), Press Gang (1983), A Yorkshire Boyhood (1983), Choose Freedom - The Future for Democratic Socialism (1987), Economic Priorities for a Labour Government (1987), The Maker's Mark (novel, 1990), In That Quiet Earth (novel, 1991), Skylark's Song (novel, 1993), Who Goes Home? Scenes from a Political Life (1995), Fifty Years On: A Prejudiced History of Britain Since The War (1997), Buster's Diaries: As told to Roy Hattersley (1998), John Wesley: A Brand from the Burning (2002); *Recreations* writing, watching football and cricket; *Style*— The Rt Hon Lord Hattersley, PC; ✉ House of Lords, London SW1A 0PW

HATTERSLEY-SMITH, Dr Geoffrey Francis; s of Maj Wilfred Hattersley-Smith DSO, RA (d 1968), of Cranbrook, Kent, and Ethel, *née* Willcocks (d 1937); *b* 22 April 1923, London; *Educ* Winchester (scholar), New Coll Oxford (scholar, MA, DPhil); *m* 12 May 1955, Maria, *née* Kefallinou; 2 da (Kara Mary b 31 Jan 1959, Fiona Anastasia b 12 Sept 1964); *Career* RN (Sub Lt RNVR) 1942–45 (incl N Atlantic, Russian convoys, Normandy (D-Day), Norway, E Indies Fleet (Japanese surrender Singapore), Br and USSR war medals); base ldr Falkland Is Dependencies Survey 1948–50, expeditions incl Beaufort Sea, Yukon Mountains, Rocky Mountains and Cornwallis Is Defence Research Bd Ottawa 1951–52, i/c Defence Research Bd ops N Ellesmere Is 1953–72, sec Antarctic Place Names Ctee Br Antarctic Survey 1973–89; memb: UK Antarctic Place Names Ctee, UK Polar Medal Assessment Ctee, Editorial Ctee Polar Record; Fndr's Gold Medal RGS 1966, Polar Medal (Antartic and Artic Clasp); commemorated in Cape Hattersley-Smith (Black Coast, Antarctic Peninsula); FRSC 1971, FRGS 1973; *Publications* incl: North of Latitude Eighty (1974), The Norwegian with Scott (ed, 1974), History of Place-Names in the Falkland Islands Dependencies (1980), ...in the British Antarctic Territory (1991), Geographical Names in Ellesmere Island (1998); author of 40 scientific papers and hundreds of papers, obituaries and reviews in Arctic, Polar Record, Daily Telegraph and British Antarctic Survey Bulletin; *Recreations* polar, naval and local history; *Clubs* Arctic (pres 1976), Antarctic, Geographical; *Style*— Dr Geoffrey Hattersley-Smith; ✉ The Crossways, Cranbrook, Kent TN17 2AG (tel 01580 712865)

HATTON, David William; QC (1996); s of Thomas William Hatton, of Bolton, and Margery, *née* Greenhalgh; *b* 29 May 1953; *Educ* Bolton Sch, Univ of Bristol (LLB); *m* 1994, Janet Elizabeth, da of Terence Bossons; 1 da (Charlotte Rose b 6 Nov 1995), 1 s (David Jack Terence b 14 Sept 1997); *Career* called to the Bar Gray's Inn 1976, recorder of the Crown Court 1995–, bencher 2005–; *Recreations* music, history, cooking, dining; *Clubs* Bolton Wanderers FC; *Style*— David W Hatton, Esq, QC

HATTON, Humphry; s of Dr Joseph Hatton, and Gwyneth Hatton; *b* 18 January 1962; *Educ* St Edward's Sch Oxford, Imperial Coll London (BSc, ARSM); *m* Ruth; 1 s (Thomas), 1 da (Lucy); *Career* ptnr i/c forensic and dispute servs Deloitte 2000–; FCA 1988; *Recreations* rowing, wine and food, music, tennis; *Clubs* Univ of London Tyrian, Leander, Crabtree, Bantham Sailing; *Style*— Humphry Hatton, Esq; ✉ Deloitte & Touche LLP, Stonecutter Court, 1 Stonecutter Street, London EC4A 4TR

HATTON, Richard John (Ricky); MBE (2007); s of Raymond Hatton, of Gee Cross, Hyde, and Carol, *née* Slann; *b* 6 October 1978, Stockport; *Educ* Hattersley Comp Hyde; *Children* 1 s (Campbell b 9 Jan 2001); *Career* professional boxer; ABA Champion 1997, Bronze medalist World Boxing Games 1997, WBU Light Welterweight World Champion 2001, IBF and WBA Light Welterweight World Champion 2005, WBA Welterweight World Champion 2006, IBF and IBO Light Welterweight World Champion 2007; memb British Boxing Bd of Control; British Boxer of the Year 2003 and 2005, American Boxing Writers' Fighter of the Year 2005; patron: Genesis Breast Cancer Charity, Manchester Kids Charity; *Books* Ricky Hatton, The Hitman: My Story (2006); *Recreations* boxing, football; *Style*— Ricky Hatton, Esq, MBE; ✉ c/o Paul Speak, PO Box 76, Manchester M26 3YW (tel 07932 001309, fax 0161 723 4862, e-mail speak3536@aol.com)

HAUGHEY, Edward Enda; *see*: Lord Ballyedmond, OBE

HAUGHEY, William; OBE (2003); s of Thomas Haughey, and Margaret, *née* Morton; *b* 2 July 1956, Glasgow; *Educ* Holyrood Sr Secdy Sch Glasgow, Springburn Coll Glasgow (C&G); *m* 30 Sept 1978, Susan, *née* Moore; 1 s (Kenneth b 17 April 1980); *Career* engrg supervisor Turner Refrigeration Ltd 1973–83, head of engrg in UAE UTS Carrier 1983–85, jt owner and md (with Susan Haughey) City Refrigeration Hldgs (UK) Ltd 1985–; chm: Scottish Enterprise Glasgow, Asset Skills; non-exec dir: Dunedin Enterprise Tst, Glasgow Culture and Leisure; charter memb Duke of Edinburgh Awards Scheme, memb Growth Fund Panel Prince's Scottish Youth Business Tst, patron CSV; Entrepreneur of the Year Entrepreneurial Exchange 2000 (finalist 1999), Business to Business section and Masterclass winner Ernst & Young Awards 2000, Refrigeration Industry Business of the Year 2000, Lanarkshire Business of the Year 2002, Business Man of the Year Award Insider Pubns 2003, Bighearted Business Person of the Year 2004, Excellence in Public Service Award 2004, Business Award Great Scot 2005, Awards Sunday Mail 2005; Loving Cup from Lord Provost of Glasgow for charity work 2001, St Mungo Prize for distinguished serv to the City of Glasgow 2007; Hon DTech Glasgow Caledonian Univ 2005; *Recreations* golf, reading, football; *Clubs* Celtic FC (ambass); *Style*— William Haughey, Esq, OBE, DTech; ✉ City Refrigeration Holdings (UK) Ltd, 38 Southcroft Road, Rutherglen, Glasgow G73 1UG (tel 0141 613 6107, fax 0141 647 7184, e-mail willie.haughey@city-holdings.co.uk)

HAUSER, Dr Hermann Maria; Hon CBE (2001); s of Hermann Hauser (d 1979), and Gerti Hauser; *b* 23 October 1948, Vienna; *Educ* Vienna Univ (MA), Univ of Cambridge (PhD); *Career* co-fndr and later chm Acorn Computers 1978 (led devpt of Acorn system 1 and Acorn ATOM, and BBC Basic and BBC Micro Computer), fndr dir IQ (Bio) 1982, vice-pres research Olivetti 1986, fndr dir Harlequin 1986, fndr dir IXI Ltd 1987, co-fndr Active Book Co 1988, co-chm and chief technical offr EO Incorporated 1991, fndr dir Vocalis 1992, fndr dir SynGenix 1993, fndr dir Advanced Displays Ltd 1993, fndr dir Electronic Share Infomation Ltd 1993, fndr and chm Advanced Telecommunications Modules Ltd (now Virata Corp) 1993, fndr Net Products Ltd 1996, fndr NetChannel 1996, co-fndr Amadeus Capital Ptnrs Ltd 1997, co-fndr Cambridge Network Ltd 1998; memb: Esprit Advsy Bd 1986, Foresight Panel 1994, Cncl for Science and Technol 2004; Computer Personality of the Year 1984; Hon Dr: Univ of Bath 1990, Loughborough Univ 1998, Anglia Poly Univ 2001; hon fell King's Coll Cambridge 1999; FInstP 1998, FREng 2002; *Style*— Dr Hermann Hauser, CBE; ✉ Amadeus Capital Partners Ltd, Mount Pleasant House, 2 Mount Pleasant, Cambridge CB3 0RN (tel 01223 707000, fax 01223 707070, e-mail hhauser@amadeuscapital.com)

HAVARD, Dai; MP; s of Edward (Ted) Havard (d 1989), and Eileen Havard (d 2006); *b* 7 February 1950, Quakers Yard, Merthyr Tydfil; *Educ* Secdy Modern Treharris, Grammar Tech Quakers Yard, Edwardsville Comp Afon Taf, St Peter's Coll Birmingham (CertEd), Univ of Warwick (MA); *m* 1986 (sep), Julia Watts; *Career* MSF: studies tutor 1971–75, researcher 1975–79, educn 1975–82, official 1988–, delgn ldr, Wales sec; MP (Lab) Merthyr Tydfil and Rhymney 2001–, memb Deregulation and Reform Ctee 2001–, memb Regulatory Reform Select Ctee 2001–, memb Defence Select Ctee 2003–; memb Armed Forces Parly Scheme 2001–02 (attached to Army); memb: Co-operative Pty 1996–, Constituency Lab Pty 2001–, Jt Policy Ctee Wales Lab Pty 2001–, MSF Section AMICUS, Merthyr Tydfil Credit Union; *Publications* contrib to academic pubns on trade union and economic devpt; *Recreations* hill walking, horse riding, bird watching, Commons and Lords Rugby Team; *Clubs* Aberfan Social and Democratic; *Style*— Dai Havard, Esq, MP; ✉ House of Commons, London SW1A 0AA

HAVARD, Dr John David Jayne; CBE (1989); s of Dr Arthur William Havard (d 1964), of Lowestoft, Suffolk, and Ursula Jayne Vernon, *née* Humphrey (d 1990); *b* 5 May 1924; *Educ* Malvern Coll, Jesus Coll Cambridge (MA, MD, LLM), Middx Hosp Med Sch; *m* 1, Sept 1950 (m dis 1982), Margaret Lucy, da of Albert Lumsden Collis, OBE (d 1963), of Wimbledon, London; 2 s (Jeremy Michael Jayne b 18 April 1952, Richard William b 27 Jan 1954), 1 da (Amanda b 12 May 1956); m 2, July 1982, Audrey Anne, da of Rear Adm Laurence Boutwood, CB, OBE (d 1982), of Tideford, Cornwall; *Career* Nat Serv Actg Sqdn Ldr RAF Med Serv 1950–52; called to the Bar Middle Temple 1954; house physician Professorial Med Unit Middx Hosp 1950, GP Lowestoft 1952–58, sec E Suffolk LMC 1956–58; staff BMA 1958–89, sec BMA 1979–89; former dep chm Staff Side Whitley Cncl (Health Servs), chm Sci Ctee Int Driver Behaviour Res Assoc 1969–94, pres Br Acad of Forensic Sciences 1985, hon sec Cwlth Med Assoc 1986–2001, chm Cwlth Med Tst 2001–05; memb: GMC 1989–94, President's Advsy Bd Med Protection Soc 1991–96, Clinical Res Ethical Ctee RCGP 1991–96; tstee Orchid Cancer Appeal 1998–2002; sec Int Ctee on Alcohol, Drugs and Traffic Safety 1962–70; Stevens medal RSM 1989, lectr Green Coll Oxford 1989, Widmark award Int Ctee on Alcohol, Drugs and Traffic Safety Chicago 1989, Gold medal for Distinguished Merit BMA 1990, Safety and Health Hall of Fame Int USA 1994; Hon FRCGP 1997, FRCP; *Books* Detection of Secret Homicide (Cambridge Studies in Criminology Vol XI, 1960), Medical Negligence: The Mounting Dilemma (1989), author of chapters in text books on subjects incl legal med, alcohol and drugs; *Recreations* country walks; *Clubs* Oxford and Cambridge, Achilles; *Style*— Dr John Havard, CBE; ✉ 1 Wilton Square, London N1 3DL (tel 020 7359 2802, fax 020 7354 9690, e-mail johnhavard@lineone.net); Myrtle Cottage, Tideford, Saltash, Cornwall PL12 5HW

HAVARD, (Michael) Robin; s of Capt Cyril Havard, of St Nicholas, Cardiff, and Elizabeth Mary Morgan Havard, JP, *née* Williams; *b* 7 May 1957; *Educ* Epsom Coll, UC Cardiff (BSc); *m* 4 Dec 1982, Ann, da of Kenneth John Evans (d 1976); 2 da (Abigail Tanya b 31 May 1987, Clare Elizabeth Orla b 7 April 1990); *Career* slr; ptnr: Loosemore 1981–83, Watkin Jones & Co 1984–85, Morgan Bruce 1985–98, Morgan Cole 1998– (chm 2003–); pt/t chm Employment Tbnls Eng and Wales; memb Law Soc 1981; *Recreations* watching rugby, sailing, golf, cycling; *Clubs* Bridgend, London Welsh, Swansea, Newport, Glamorgan County, WRU Presidents XV; *Style*— Robin Havard, Esq

HAVELOCK-ALLAN, His Hon Judge; Sir (Anthony) Mark David; 5 Bt (UK 1858), of Lucknow; QC (1993); s of Sir Anthony James Allan Havelock-Allan, 4 Bt (d 2003), and Valerie Babette Louise Hobson (d 1998) (later married to John Profumo, CBE (d 2006)); *b* 4 April 1951; *Educ* Eton, Univ of Durham (BA), Trinity Coll Cambridge (LLB, Dip Int Law); *m* 1, 1976 (m dis 1984), Lucy Clare; yr da of Alexander Plantagenet Mitchell-Innes; m 2, 1986, Alison Lee Caroline, da of Leslie Francis Foster; 2 da (Miranda Antonia Louise b 29 July 1993, Hannah Marie Josephine b 18 Oct 1997), 1 s (Henry Caspar Francis

(Harry) b 6 Oct 1994); *Heir* s, Harry Havelock-Allan; *Career* called to the Bar Inner Temple 1974 (bencher 1995); recorder of the Crown Court 1997–2001 (asst recorder 1993–97), sr circuit judge (Bristol Mercantile Court) 2001–; FCIArb 1991; *Recreations* salmon fishing, foreign travel; *Clubs* Garrick, RAC; *Style*— His Hon Judge Havelock-Allan, QC; ✉ The Law Courts, Small Street, Bristol BS1 1DA (tel 0117 910 6706, fax 0117 910 6727)

HAVENHAND, Martin; *Educ* Sheffield Hallam Univ (MSc, DMS); *Family* 3 c; *Career* formerly: asst chief offr with S Yorks Met CC, dir of leisure and environment Trafford MBC, chief exec Bassetlaw DC; chief exec Yorkshire Forward 1999–, currently chm NAMTEC (Nat Metals Technol Centre); memb IOD; FISRM, FRSA; *Recreations* golf, gardening, reading; *Style*— Martin Havenhand, Esq; ✉ NAMTEC, Swinden House, Moorgate Road, Rotherham S60 3AR

HAVERS, Hon Nigel Allan; yr s of Baron Havers, PC, QC (Life Peer, d 1992), and Carol Elizabeth, *née* Lay (now Mrs Charles Hughesdon); *b* 6 November 1951; *m* 1, 1974 (m dis 1989), Carolyn Gillian, da of Vincent Cox; 1 da (Katharine b 1977); m 2, 1989, Mrs Polly Bloomfield (d 2004); *Career* actor; *Theatre* incl: Importance of Being Earnest, Ricochet, Art, See You Next Tuesday, Rebecca; *Television* incl: A Horseman Riding By, Upstairs Downstairs, Nancy Astor, Strangers and Brothers, Don't Wait Up, The Charmer, A Perfect Hero, Sleepers, The Good Guys, The Heart Surgeon; *Film* incl: Chariots of Fire, A Passage to India, Burke and Wills, The Whistle Blower, Empire of the Sun, Farewell to the King, Burning Season, Paradise Lost; *Recreations* keeping fit, reading, gardening; *Clubs* Garrick; *Style*— The Hon Nigel Havers

HAVERS, Hon Philip Nigel; QC (1995); er s of Baron Havers, PC, QC (Life Peer, d 1992), and Carol Elizabeth, *née* Lay (now Mrs Charles Hughesdon); *b* 16 June 1950; *Educ* Eton, CCC Cambridge; *m* 20 March 1976, Patricia Frances, *née* Searle; *Career* called to the Bar Inner Temple 1974; *Books* An Introduction to Human Rights and the Common Law (jt ed); *Recreations* tennis, music; *Clubs* Garrick; *Style*— The Hon Philip Havers, QC; ✉ 1 Crown Office Row, Temple, London EC4Y 7HH (tel 020 7797 7500, fax 020 7797 7550, e-mail philip.havers@1cor.com)

HAVERY, His Hon Richard Orbell; QC (1980); s of Joseph Horton Havery (d 1994), of Blackheath, London, and W Chiltington, and Constance Eleanor, *née* Orbell (d 1987); *b* 7 February 1934; *Educ* St Paul's, Magdalen Coll Oxford (MA); *Career* called to the Bar Middle Temple 1962 (bencher 1989), recorder of the Crown Court 1986–93 (asst recorder 1982–86), circuit judge and official referee 1993–98, judge Technol and Construction Court 1998–2007; *Books* Kemp and Kemp The Quantum of Damages (jt ed 3 edn, 1967); *Recreations* music, croquet, steam locomotives; *Clubs* Garrick, Hurlingham, Athenaeum; *Style*— His Hon Richard Havery, QC; ✉ Technology and Construction Court, St Dunstan's House, 133–137 Fetter Lane, London EC4A 1HD (tel 020 7947 7429)

HAVILLE, Robert William; s of James Haville (d 1983), and Eileen Haville; *b* 27 July 1955; *Educ* Marlborough GS, Lancaster Univ (BA), Univ of Bradford (MBA); *m* 18 Oct 1980, Hazel Dawn, da of George Burke, of London; 2 da (Rosalind b 1986, Sarah b 1990), 2 s (James b 1988, Ralph b 1995); *Career* fin analyst Kimberley Clark 1976–77; investment analyst: McAnally Montgomery 1978–81, James Capel 1982–87, Morgan Stanley 1988–91, Smith New Court/Merrill Lynch 1991–99, West LB Panmure 1999–2002, College Hill Associates 2003–04, Financial Dynamics 2005–07, Town End Consits 2007–; non-exec chm TLC Europe Ltd; memb Assoc of Business Graduates (AMBA); MSI, MIRS; *Clubs* RAC; *Style*— Robert Haville, Esq

HAW, Brandon; s of Ken Haw, and Brenda Haw; *b* 7 September 1960; *Educ* Brighton, Hove & Sussex GS for Boys, Bartlett Sch of Arch and Environmental Studies UCL (BSc), Sch of Arch Princeton Univ (MArch); *Partner* Pritanjan Kaler; 2 c (Marlon b 19 Oct 1992, Bonner b 5 Dec 1994); *Career* architect; NYC USA 1982–87; HOK then Skidmore Owings and Merrill NYC 1985–87; sr ptnr Foster and Partners London 1987–; sponsor: WWF, Khairabad Eye Hosp India; RIBA 1990, ARB 1990; *Recreations* 20th Century art and design, painting and sculpture; *Clubs* Soho House; *Style*— Brandon Haw, Esq; ✉ Foster and Partners, 22 Hester Road, London SW11 4AN (tel 020 7738 0455, fax 020 7738 8612/1107, e-mail bhaw@fosterandpartners.com)

HAW, Jonathan Stopford; s of Denis Stopford Haw (d 1979), of Sidcup, Kent, and Elisabeth Mary Dorothy, *née* Mack (d 1998); *b* 16 March 1945; *Educ* Radley, Keble Coll Oxford (MA), Coll of Law; *m* 20 Dec 1969, Hélène Lucie, da of Louis Lacuve, Chevalier de l'Ordre National du Mérite, of Perpignan, France; 1 s (Alexander b 1973), 1 da (Katherine b 1976); *Career* slr; Slaughter and May: ptnr 1977–2002, first ptnr NY 1984–87, exec ptnr 1996–2001; dep chm Coll of Law 2005–; Juvenile Diabetes Research Fndn: dir 1990–99 and 2003–, chm 1996–99, memb Int Lay Review Ctee 2004–; tstee Mary Kinross Charitable Tst 2003–; Freeman City of London 1970, Upper Warden Worshipful Co of Armourers and Brasiers 2007–08; *Recreations* gardening, art, wine; *Clubs* Leander; *Style*— Jonathan S Haw, Esq

HAWARDEN, 9 Viscount (I 1793); Sir (Robert) Connan Wyndham Leslie Maude; 11 Bt (I 1705); also Baron de Montalt (I 1785); er s of 8 Viscount Hawarden (d 1991), and Susannah Caroline Hyde, *née* Gardner; *b* 23 May 1961; *Educ* St Edmund's Sch Canterbury, RAC Cirencester; *m* 8 April 1995, Judith Anne, yst da of John Bates, of Shepherdswell, Kent; 1 s (Hon Varian John Connan Eustace b 1 Sept 1997), 2 da (Hon Izetta Clementine b 21 Oct 1999, Avery Joan Constance Elita b 24 Feb 2002); *Heir* s, Hon Varian Maude; *Career* farming and interactive distribution; *Recreations* shooting, motorcycling, riding, skiing, animal husbandry; *Style*— The Rt Hon the Viscount Hawarden; ✉ Great Bossington Farm House, Adisham, Canterbury, Kent CT3 3LN

HAWES, Ven Arthur John; s of late John Beadnell Hawes, of Cumnor, Oxford, and Sylvia Mary Lilian, *née* Taylor; *b* 31 August 1943; *Educ* City of Oxford HS for Boys, Chichester Theol Coll, Richmond Fellowship Coll (Cert Human Rels), Univ of Birmingham (Dip Pastoral Studies, Dip Liturgy and Architecture), UEA (BA); *m* 1969, Melanie Gay, da of John Harris, and late Gay Harris; 1 da (Emma (Mrs Matthew Morrall) b 13 July 1971), 1 s (Luke John b 6 June 1973); *Career* curate St John the Baptist Kidderminster 1968–72, priest-in-charge St Richard Droitwich 1972–76, rector of Alderford with Attlebridge and Swannington 1976–92, chaplain Hellesdon and David Rice Hosps and Yare Clinic 1976–92, rural dean of Sparham 1981–91, canon of Norwich Cathedral 1988–95, chm Norwich Diocesan Bd for Social Responsibility 1990–95, rector St Faith's Gaywood King's Lynn 1992–95, archdeacon of Lincoln and canon and prebendary of Lincoln Cathedral 1995–; memb: Gen Synod of the C of E 2000–, Mission and Public Affairs Cncl 2000–; Mental Health Act cmmr for England and Wales 1986–94, chm E Midlands Regnl Devpt Centre 2003–05; non-exec dir S Lincs Healthcare NHS Tst 1998–2001, non-exec dir Lincs Partnership NHS Tst 2002–06, memb NHS Confederation Mental Health Policy Ctee 2003, vice-chm Nat Forum for Spirituality and Mental Health 2006, Mental Health Act advsr Lincs Partnership Tst 2006, patron Nat Assoc for Mental Health (MIND), pres Purfleet Tst, pres Lincs Rural Housing Assoc; *Recreations* golf, theatre, music; *Clubs* Sleaford Golf; *Style*— The Ven the Archdeacon of Lincoln; ✉ Archdeacon's House, Northfield Road, Quarrington, Sleaford, Lincolnshire NG34 8RT (tel 01529 304348, fax 01529 304354, mobile 07803 249834, e-mail archdeacon.lincoln@lincoln.anglican.org)

HAWKE, 11 Baron (GB 1776); Edward George Hawke; TD; o s of 10 Baron Hawke (d 1992), and his 2 w, Georgette Margaret, *née* Davidson; *b* 25 January 1950; *Educ* Eton; *m* 4 Sept 1993, Bronwen M, da of William James, BVMS, MRCVS; 1 s (Hon William Martin Theodore b 1995), 1 da (Hon Alice Julia b 8 Feb 1999); *Heir* s, Hon William Hawke; *Career* 1 Bn Coldstream Gds 1970–73, The Queen's Own Yeomanry 1973–93, Hon Col Cheshire Yeomanry 1998–2005; dir Lambert Smith Hampton (Manchester) 1987–; FRICS; *Style*— The Rt Hon the Lord Hawke, TD

HAWKER, Ven Alan Fort; s of Albert Hawker (d 1975), of Woodford Green, Essex, and Florence Lilian, *née* Fort (d 1978); *b* 23 March 1944; *Educ* Buckhurst Hill Co HS, Univ of Hull (BA), Clifton Theol Coll (DipTh); *m* 13 April 1968, Jeanette Dorothy, da of Maurice Law; 3 da (Ruth Elizabeth b 29 March 1969, Nicola Margaret b 30 Oct 1970, Fiona Anne b 28 Dec 1972), 1 s (Ian Alan b 27 Jan 1975); *Career* asst curate St Leonard and St Mary Bootle Merseyside 1968–71, asst curate i/c St Paul Fazakerley Liverpool 1971–73, vicar St Paul Goose Green Wigan 1973–81, team rector St Mary Southgate Crawley 1981–98, canon of Chichester and preb of Bury 1991–98, archdeacon of Swindon and canon of Bristol Cathedral 1998–99, archdeacon of Malmesbury and canon of Bristol Cathedral 1999–; proctor in convocation and memb Gen Synod C of E 1990– (memb Standing and Policy Ctees 1995–98, memb Business and Legislative Ctees 2000–), chair Working Pty on Reform of Clergy Discipline 1994–2004, memb Clergy Discipline Cmmn 2004–; vice-chair Cncl Univ of Gloucestershire 2004–; tstee Willows Counselling Serv 2000–; memb: Clinical Theol Assoc 1973, CEDR 1997; *Publications* Under Authority; *Recreations* reading, music, theatre, eating out, walking, model railways; *Style*— The Ven the Archdeacon of Malmesbury; ✉ Church Paddock, Church Lane, Kington Langley, Chippenham, Wiltshire SN15 5NR (tel 01249 750085, fax 01249 750086, e-mail alan.hawker@bristol5.gotadsl.co.uk)

HAWKER, Eur Ing Geoffrey Fort; TD; *b* 20 December 1929; *Educ* Univ of London (BSc Eng); *m*; 2 da; *Career* Nat Serv Royal Engrs 1951–52; chartered civil engr 1956; called to the Bar Gray's Inn 1970; with: Aston Construction Co 1945–50, Sir William Halcrow & Ptnrs 1953–59, Mitchel Construction Co 1960–61, Rendel Palmer & Tritton 1961–63, Chadwick, O'Heocha and Assocs 1963–64; in practice as: engrg consIt 1964–, arbitrator 1970–; head of barristers' chambers 1990–2003; formerly: pres Soc of Construction Arbitrators, memb Cncl ICE (chm Arbitration Advsy Bd), memb Cncl CIArb; memb: Soc of Construction Law, Int Bar Assoc, Dispute Review Bd Fndn USA, Adjudication Soc; Liveryman: Worshipful Co of Arbitrators, Worshipful Co of Engrs; FREng 1988, FICE, CEng, FIEI, FIStructE, FConsE, MSocIS (France), FCIArb, fell Soc of Maritime Adjudicators; *Books* A Guide to Commercial Arbitration under the 1979 Act (with R Gibson-Jarvis, 1980), The ICE Arbitration Practice (with Uff and Timms, 1986), The ICE Conditions of Contract for Minor Works - A User's Guide and Commentary (with G Cottam, 1992); *Style*— Eur Ing Geoffrey Hawker, TD, FREng

HAWKER, Graham Alfred; CBE (1999), DL (Gwent 1998); s of Alfred Hawker, and Sarah Rebecca, *née* Bowen; *b* 12 May 1947; *Educ* Bedwellty GS; *m* April 1967, Sandra Ann Evans; 1 s, 1 da; *Career* trainee accountant Caerphilly DC 1964–66; Abercarn DC: accountant 1966–67, chief accountant 1967–68, dep treas 1968–70; chief auditor Taf Fechan Water Bd 1970–74; Welsh Water Authy: audit mangr 1974–78, div fin mangr 1978–84, chief accountant 1984–86, dir planning and devpt 1986–87, dir fin 1987–89; Welsh Water plc (later Hyder plc): dir fin 1989–91, gp md 1991–93, chief exec 1993–2000; chief exec Welsh Devpt Agency 2000–04; a dir Bank of England 1998–2000; chm: Dwr Cymru Ltd 1993–2000, Hyder Consulting (formerly Acer) 1993–2000, Swalec 1996–2000; memb CBI Cncl for Wales 1994–97; chm Business in the Community (BITC) Wales 1994–2000, New Deal Task Force Advsy Ctee (Wales) 1997–98, memb New Deal Advsy Ctee (UK) 1997–98; memb Prince of Wales Review Ctee on Queen's Awards 1999; Prince of Wales Ambassador's Award for Corp Social Responsibility 1999; Hon Dr Univ of Glamorgan 1996, hon fell Univ of Wales Cardiff 1999; CIPFA 1969, FCCA 1981, CIMgt, FRSA; *Recreations* family, walking, wine; *Clubs* Abergavenny Rugby (pres); *Style*— Graham Hawker, Esq, CBE, DL

HAWKES, Prof David John; s of Roy Hawkes, of Teignmouth, Devon, and Joyce, *née* Davey; *b* 16 January 1953; *Educ* Portsmouth GS, ChCh Oxford (BA, Keasbey Bursary, Allen Award), Univ of Birmingham (MSc), Univ of Surrey (PhD); *m* 8 July 1978, Elizabeth Anne, da of John Nicholson; 2 da (Sarah Joanne b 20 August 1983, Rosie Louise b 12 Oct 1986); *Career* basic grade physicist in nuclear med Southampton Gen Hosp 1976–78, research assoc Univ of Surrey and Royal Marsden Hosp 1978–81, WHO consIt in medical physics and nuclear medicine Philippines 1982; St George's Hosp London: sr physicist 1981–84, princ physicist and head of imaging section Dept of Medical Physics and Bio-Engrg 1984–88; reader in radiological scis UMDS 1993–98 (sr lectr 1988–93); KCL: scientific tutor 1992–2004, couse co-ordinator 1998–2004, prof in computational imaging sci 1998–2004, chm Div of Imaging Scis 2002–04, memb Sch of Med Research Ctee 2002–04, memb Sch of Med Mgmnt Bd 2002–04, memb Sch of Med Space Ctee 2002–04, memb GKT Research Ctee 2003–04; hon consIt physicist Guy's and St Thomas' NHS Tst 1998–2004; UCL: prof of computational imaging sci 2005–, dir Centre of Medical Image Computing 2005–; dir Med Images and Signals IRC 2003– (memb Bd 2001–), track chair World Congress in Med Physics Sydney 2003; chm: MIUA'99 (Medical Image Understanding and Analysis conf), EPSRC Panel in Healthcare Engrg 2001 and 2002; memb: Panel Natural Scis and Engrg Research Cncl (NSERC, Canada) 2001, Int Sci Advsy Bd OCF Medical Imaging Consortium Canada 2001 and 2002, Dept of Health Technols Devpt Panel 2002; visiting lectr Univ of Surrey 1982–94, teacher and memb Bd of Medical Physics, Biophysics and Bioengineering Univ of London 1988–, occasional lectr South Bank Univ and Charterhouse Sch of Radiography (now City Univ); external examiner: Univ of Aberdeen 1993–2002, Univ of Manchester 1999–2002; memb editorial bd of numerous jls, chm and invited speaker at numerous int confs; Royal Soc visiting fell Montreal Neurological Inst Canada 1991, visiting prof Johns Hopkins Univ USA 1999; tstee Mayneord Philip Tst 1999–2002; memb: Br Machine Vision Assoc (BMVA), Br Inst of Radiology (BIR), American Assoc of Physics in Medicine (AAPM); business fell London Technol Network London Business Sch 2003–; FREng 1992, memb Inst of Physics and Engrg in Medicine (IPEM) 1993, FInstP 1997, CPhys 1997; *Style*— Prof David Hawkes

HAWKES, Prof John Gregory; OBE (1994); s of Charles William Hawkes (d 1964), and Gertrude Maude, *née* Chappell (d 1970); *b* 27 June 1915; *Educ* Cheltenham GS, Christ's Coll Cambridge (MA, PhD, ScD); *m* 20 Dec 1941, Ellen Barbara (d 2005), da of Charles Henry Leather (d 1954); 2 da (Phillada Daphne (Dr Collins) b 1944, Stephanie Katherine (Mrs Hazeldine) b 1946), 2 s (Anthony Christopher b 1950, Peter Geoffrey b 1950); *Career* Cwlth Bureau of Plant Breeding and Genetics 1939–48, dir Colombian Miny of Agric Res Station 1948–52; Univ of Birmingham: lectr and sr lectr in botany 1952–61, prof of plant taxonomy 1961–67, prof and head Plant Biology Dept 1967–82, emeritus prof of plant biology 1982; plant collecting expdns in Mexico, Central and South America 1939, 1949–50, 1958, 1964, 1965, 1966, 1971, 1974, 1980 and 1981; hon prof Vavilov Inst for Plant Genetic Resources St Petersburg; hon life memb: Euro Assoc for Research in Plant Breeding 1989, Potato Assoc of America 1989; FLS 1945 (pres 1991–94), FIBiol 1976; *Books* incl: Reproductive Biology and Taxonomy of Vascular Plants (ed, 1966), Chemotaxonomy and Serotaxonomy (ed, 1968), The Potatoes of Argentina, Brazil, Paraguay and Uruguay (jtly, 1969), A Computer-Mapped Flora (jtly, 1971), Crop Genetic Resources for Today and Tomorrow (jt ed, 1975), Conservation and Agriculture (ed, 1978), The Biology and Taxonomy of the Solanaceae (jt ed, 1979), The Diversity of Crop Plants (1983), A Bibliography of Crop Genetic Resources (jt ed, 1983), Revised Edition of Salaman's History and Social Influence of the Potato (ed, 1985), The Potatoes of Bolivia (jtly, 1989), The Potato - Evolution, Biodiversity and Genetic Resources (1990), Plant Genetic Resources of Ethiopia (jt ed, 1991), Genetic Conservation of World Crops (ed, 1991), Solanaceae III - Taxonomy, Chemistry, Evolution (jt ed, 1991), Vavilov Lectures,

H

Collecta Clusiana 4 (ed A T Sabo, BioTar series, 1994), The History of the Rose (1995), Plant Genetic Conservation: The In Situ Approach (jt ed, 1997), The Ex Situ Conservation of Plant Genetic Resources (jt ed, 2000), Hunting the Wild Potato in the South American Andes (2004); *Recreations* gardening, travel; *Style*— Prof John Hawkes, OBE

HAWKES, (Henry) William; s of late William Neville Hawkes, of Honington, Warks, and Marjorie Elsie, *née* Jackson; *b* 4 December 1939; *Educ* Uppingham, Univ of Cambridge (MA, DipArch); *m* 22 Oct 1966, Hester Elizabeth, da of David Foster Gretton (d 1967); 3 da (Harriet b 1967, Polly b 1969, Olivia b 1972); *Career* architect, in practice Hawkes Edwards and Cave; dir Stoneleigh Abbey Preservation Tst 1980–97, chm Coventry Diocesan Advsy Ctee 1986–2006, memb Georgian Gp Exec Ctee 1985–2002, tstee Coventry and Warwickshire Historic Churches Tst 1986–, memb Ctee Cncl for the Care of Churches 1991–2001, exec tstee The Shakespeare Birthplace Tst 1992–, memb Fabric Advsy Ctee and chm Tech Gp St George's Chapel Windsor 1998–, vice-chm Advsy Bd for Redundant Churches 2001–; author of various publications on 18th Century Gothic Revival; ARIBA 1967; *Recreations* hand printing, cycling, architectural history; *Style*— William Hawkes, Esq, FSA; ✉ 20 Broad Street, Stratford-upon-Avon, Warwickshire (tel 01789 266415); Hawkes Edwards and Cave, 1 Old Town, Stratford-upon-Avon, Warwickshire (tel 01789 298877)

HAWKESFORD, John Ernest; s of Ernest Hawkesford (d 1965), of Rushwick, Worcs, and Sarah Elizabeth, *née* Jones (d 1992); *b* 29 November 1946; *Educ* Warwick Sch, UC Med Sch London; *m* 29 June 1974, Barbara, da of Alexander Howe, of Gateshead, Tyne & Wear; 3 da (Abigail Lisa b 1976, Julia Marie b 1979, Rachel Chloe b 1989); *Career* registrar in oral maxillofacial surgery Stoke Mandeville Hosp Bucks 1973–76, sr registrar in oral maxillofacial surgery W of Scotland Plastic Surgery Unit Canniesburn Hosp Bearsden Glasgow, hon clinical lectr in oral surgery and oral med Univ of Glasgow 1976–79, hon clinical teacher in oral and maxillofacial surgery Univ of Newcastle upon Tyne 1979–; conslt in oral maxillofacial surgery 1979–: Newcastle HA (teaching), Northern RHA, (latterly) Newcastle upon Tyne Hosps NHS Tst (clinical dir of oral and maxillofacial surgery 1991–95); chm Specialist Sub-Ctee Dentistry Northern Regnl Med Ctee 1987–95, chm Regnl Ctee for Hosp Dental Servs 1990–96, memb Northern Regnl Med Ctee 1987–95, memb Central Ctee for Hosp Dental Services 2000–04; pres BDA Hosp Gp 1993–94 (vice-chm 2000–), pres N of England Odontological Soc 2001–02, tstee BDA Benevolent Fund 2000–04; memb: BDA, RSM, Br Assoc of Oral Maxillofacial Surgery, Oral Surgery Club of GB (pres 2006–07), Euro Assoc for Cranio-Maxillofacial Surgery; *Books* Maxillofacial and Dental Emergencies (1994); *Recreations* squash, skiing, swimming; *Style*— Mr John Hawkesford; ✉ The Quarry, 31 Batt House Road, Stocksfield, Northumberland NE43 7RA (tel 01661 842338); Catherine Cookson Maxillo Facial Surgery Department, Newcastle General Hospital, Westgate Road, Newcastle upon Tyne NE4 6BE (tel 0191 273 8811 ext 22204, fax 0191 226 0752, e-mail john@hawkesford.onyxnet.co.uk)

HAWKESWORTH, His Hon Judge (Thomas) Simon Ashwell; QC (1982); s of Charles Peter Elmhirst Hawkesworth (d 1990), and Felicity, *née* Ashwell (d 2004); *b* 15 November 1943; *Educ* Rugby, The Queen's Coll Oxford (MA); *m* 1, 1970 (m dis 1989), Jennifer, da of Dr Thomas Lewis (d 1944); 2 s (Thomas b 1973, Edward b 1978); m 2, 1990, Dr May Bamber; 2 s (Henry, Charles (twins) b 1992); *Career* called to the Bar Gray's Inn 1967 (bencher 1990); recorder of the Crown Court 1982–99, circuit judge (NE Circuit) 1999–; *Style*— His Hon Judge Hawkesworth, QC; ✉ Leeds Combined Court Centre, Oxford Row, Leeds LS1 3BG

HAWKHEAD, Anthony Gerard (Tony); CBE (2003); s of Harry Cheltenham, and Mary, *née* Geary; *b* 7 October 1957, Bedford; *Educ* Whitefriars Sch Cheltenham; *m* 31 Aug 1981, Marion, *née* Small; 1 da (Laura b 19 April 1988), 1 s (James b 13 Feb 1991 d 1991); *Career* MOD 1978–87, Inner Cities Unit DTI 1987–88, leader Govt Task Force N Peckham 1988–89, head of business and econ devpt LDDC 1989–91, chief exec E London Partnership 1991–96, chief exec Groundwork 1996–; tstee: Youthworks 1996–, Groundworks Wales 2001–; MInstD; *Recreations* sport, music, wine, France; *Clubs* Mandarins' CC, Olton and West Warks Sports; *Style*— Tony Hawkhead, Esq, CBE; ✉ Groundwork UK, Lockside, 5 Scotland Street, Birmingham B1 2RR (tel 0121 236 8565 fax 0121 236 7356, e-mail info@groundwork.org.uk)

HAWKINS, Andrew John; s of Austen Ralph Hawkins, of Bournemouth, and May, *née* O'Donnell; *b* 24 September 1958; *Educ* Bedford Modern Sch, Lancaster Univ (BA), Kellogg Graduate Sch of Mgmnt Northwestern Univ Evanston (MBA); *m* 16 Nov 1990, Karen, da of Gerald Edward Pursey; 2 s (Jack b 2 May 1992, Ned b 14 Sept 1994), 1 da (Martha (twin) b 14 Sept 1994); *Career* graduate trainee Ogilvy and Mather advtg 1982, account dir Publicis 1985 (account mangr 1983); GGK London: joined Bd 1988, dep md Jan 1990, md Nov 1990–93, jt chm and ceo 1993–95; md Doner Cardwell Hawkins 1995–; *Recreations* water-skiing, running, movies; *Style*— Andrew Hawkins, Esq; ✉ 23 Westmoreland Road, London SW13 9RZ (tel 020 8748 4465); Doner Cardwell Hawkins, 26–34 Emerald Street, London WC1N 3QA (tel 020 7734 0511, fax 020 7287 5310)

HAWKINS, Prof Anthony Donald; CBE (2000); s of Kenneth St David Hawkins, and Marjorie, *née* Jackson; *b* 25 March 1942; *Educ* Poole GS, Univ of Bristol (BSc, PhD); *m* 31 July 1966, Susan Mary; 1 s (David Andrew b 23 Feb 1973); *Career* dir of Fisheries Res Scotland 1987–2002, chief scientific offr SO 1987–2002, prof Univ of Aberdeen 2002–; chair North Sea Cmmn Fisheries Partnership 2001–; md Loughine Ltd 2002–; FRSE 1988; *Recreations* whippet racing; *Style*— Prof Anthony Hawkins, CBE, FRSE; ✉ Kincraig, Blairs, Aberdeen AB1 5YT (tel 01224 868984, e-mail a.hawkins@btconnect.com)

HAWKINS, Prof Denis Frank; s of Frank Reginald Hawkins (d 1970), and Elsie Anne May, *née* Sallis (d 1986); *b* 4 April 1929; *Educ* Alleyn's Sch Dulwich, UCL, UCH (BSc, MB BS, PhD, DSc); *m* 10 July 1957, Joan Dorothy Vera, da of Walter James Taynton (d 1949); 2 da (Valerie Joan b 1958, Susan Pauline b 1966 d 1995), 2 s (Robert James b and d 1960, Richard Frank b 1961 d 2003); *Career* prof and chm of obstetrics and gynaecology Boston Univ 1965–68, conslt obstetrician and gynaecologist Hammersmith Hosp 1968–99; emeritus prof of obstetric therapeutics Univ of London 1989– (lectr 1961–65, sr lectr 1968–74, reader 1974–79, prof 1979–89); ed Jl of Obstetrics and Gynaecology 1980–95 (consltg ed 1995–2001); memb: BMA, Br Pharmacological Soc, Italian Soc for Perinatal Med, American Soc of Pharmacology and Experimental Therapeutics; Freeman City of London 1985, Liveryman Worshipful Soc of Apothecaries 1987; FACOG 1966, FRCOG 1970 (DObstRCOG 1957, MRCOG 1962); *Books* Obstetric Therapeutics (1974), The Intrauterine Device (1977), Human Fertility Control (1979), Gynaecological Therapeutics (1981), Drugs and Pregnancy (1983, 2 edn 1987), Drug Treatment in Obstetrics (1983, 2 edn 1991), Perinatal Medicine (1986), Advances in Perinatal Medicine (1988), Diabetes and Pregnancy (1989), Progress in Perinatal Medicine (1990), Recent Advances in Perinatal Medicine (1993, 2 edn 1999), Prescribing Drugs in Pregnancy (2000); *Recreations* Arabian primitive rock carvings, Greek archaeology; *Clubs* Savage; *Style*— Prof Denis Hawkins; ✉ Blundel Lodge, Blundel Lane, Stoke D'Abernon, Cobham, Surrey KT11 2SP (tel 01372 843073)

HAWKINS, Dr (Thomas) Desmond; s of Thomas Hawkins (d 1985), of Co Cork, and Helen, *née* Laing (d 1960); *b* 22 May 1923; *Educ* Alleyne's Sch, St Mary's Hosp Med Sch (exhibitioner, MB BS), Manchester Univ Med Sch (DMRD), Univ of Cambridge (MA, MPhil); *m* 26 April 1947, Margaret Frances, da of Kenneth Archibald Blair; 1 da (Bryony Jane b 22 Sept 1949 (decd)), 3 s (Martin Thomas b 18 Oct 1951, Patrick Francis b 14 June 1957, Richard Oliver b 11 July 1962); *Career* student house offr Park Prewett (Mil) Hospital 1944, British Red Cross (famine relief) Belsen Germany 1945; MO RAF 1946–49, med registrar St Mary's Hosp 1949–50, SHO (paediatrics) W Middx Hosp 1951–52, GP Brill Bucks 1952–54, SHO (diagnostic radiology) Radcliffe Infirmary Oxford 1955, registrar and sr registrar (diagnostic radiology) Manchester Royal Infirmary 1955–60, visiting fell Stockholm and Göteborg Sweden 1960–61, conslt radiologist (neuroradiology) Addenbrooke's Hosp Cambridge 1960–88, assoc lectr Univ of Cambridge 1976–88, memb St John's Coll Cambridge 1976–, clinical dean Sch of Clinical Med 1979–84, pres Hughes Hall Cambridge 1989–94 (hon fell 1994–); author of papers on pathophysiology of the cerebral circulation, interventional neuroradiology and palaeopathology; fndr memb: Euro Soc of Neuroradiology 1969–, Br Soc of Neuroradiology 1970– (pres 1986–88), Assoc of Med Deans in Europe 1980–84; FRSM, FRCR, FRCP; *Books* Roads to Radiology (jtly, 1983), Textbook of Radiological Diagnosis (contrib, 1984), The Drainage of Wilbraham, Fulbourn and Teversham Fens (1990, 2 edn 2000), The Wilbrahams 1894–1994 (jtly, 1994); *Recreations* landscape history, gardening, cycling; *Clubs* Hawks' (Cambridge); *Style*— Dr Desmond Hawkins; ✉ Greyfriars, Church Green, Little Wilbraham, Cambridge CB21 5LE (tel 01223 811219); Hughes Hall, Mortimer Road, Cambridge CB1 2EW (tel 01223 334893, fax 01223 311179, e-mail tdhawkins@doctors.net.uk)

HAWKINS, Keith John; *b* 19 November 1947; *m* 1 (m dis 1985), 23 April 1977, Linda Claire; 1 s (Richard b 1979), 1 da (Philippa b 1982); m 2, 30 Aug 1991, Anthea Frances Hedley; *Career* admitted slr 1974; ptnr Dutton Gregory; memb Law Soc 1974; *Style*— Keith Hawkins, Esq; ✉ St Just, Red Lane, West Tytherley, Salisbury, Wiltshire SP5 1NY (tel 01794 340689); Dutton Gregory, Trussell House, 23 St Peter Street, Winchester, Hampshire SO23 8BT (tel 01962 844333, fax 01962 863582, e-mail k.hawkins@duttongregory.co.uk)

HAWKINS, Prof Keith Owen; s of (Lewis) Cyril Hawkins (d 1989), and (Lillian) Grace Hawkins (d 1974); *b* 8 September 1941; *Educ* Univ of Birmingham (LLB), Univ of Cambridge (Dip Criminology, MA, PhD), Univ of Oxford (MA, DPhil); *m* 1 July 1978, Susan Jillian, *née* Lock; 3 s (Alexander James Owen b 3 May 1981, Nicholas Guy Lewis b 9 Feb 1984, Edmund Charles Stuart b 28 Sept 1985); *Career* W M Tapp research fell Gonville & Caius Coll Cambridge 1970–73; Centre for Socio-Legal Studies Univ of Oxford: research fell 1972–75, sr research fell 1975–93, dep dir 1985–93, actg dir 1999; Univ of Oxford: research fell Wolfson Coll 1972–93, tutorial fell Oriel Coll 1993–2006 (tutor for graduates 2001–06, emeritus 2006–), research assoc Centre for Criminological Research 2002–, prof of law and society; visiting prof: Law Sch Univ of Texas at Austin 1985, Coll of Law Ohio State Univ 1989; visiting fell: Nat Inst of Justice US Dept of Justice 1979–80, Gonville & Caius Coll Cambridge 1987–88; Ford Fndn fell Columbia Law Sch NY 1967–68, Inter-Univ Cncl visiting lectr Univ of Singapore 1973, Rockefeller Fndn collaborative residency Bellagio 2000; delivered papers at legal confs and symposia worldwide; memb: Parole Bd for England and Wales 1977–79 and 1983–86, Research Ctee American Bar Fndn 1986–, Socio-Legal Task Force Campaign for Oxford 1990–93, Research Ctee on the Sociology of Law Int Sociological Soc; memb Advsy Ctee: Centre for Law, Policy and Social Science Ohio State Univ, Mannheim Centre for Criminal Justice and Criminal Justice Policy LSE; US Law and Society Assoc: memb Bd of Tstees 1981–84, memb 25th Anniversary Prog Ctee 1988–89, memb Didactic Workshops Ctee 1998–99; founding co-ed Law in Social Context Univ of Pennsylvania Press 1984–93, ed Law and Policy 1987–2006 (memb Editorial Bd 1981–83, memb Sr Editorial Bd 1983–86), gen ed Oxford Socio-Legal Studies OUP (formerly Macmillan) 1993– (memb Editorial Bd 1979–93); memb Editorial Bd: Law and Society Review 1982–83, Jl of Financial Regulation and Compliance 1988–95, The Justice System Jl; reviewer for numerous jls incl: Br Jl of Criminology, Jl of Law and Society, Justice Quarterly, Law and Policy, Oxford Jl of Legal Studies; memb: US Law and Society Assoc, UK Socio-Legal Studies Assoc; *Publications* Psychology, Law and Legal Processes (co-ed, 1979), Enforcing Regulation: policy and practice (co-ed, 1984), Environment and Enforcement. Regulation and the social definition of pollution (1984, reprinted 1993), Making Regulatory Policy (co-ed, 1989), The Uses of Discretion (ed, 1992), The Regulation of Occupational Health and Safety: a socio-legal perspective (1993), Law as Last Resort: prosecution decision-making in a regulatory agency (2002, Herbert Jacob Prize American Law and Society Assoc 2003); author of numerous essays, monographs and papers; *Recreations* music, wine, food, sport, travel; *Style*— Prof Keith Hawkins; ✉ Oriel College, Oxford OX1 4EW (tel 01865 276555, e-mail keith.hawkins@oriel.ox.ac.uk)

HAWKINS, Peter John; s of Derek Gilbert, of Ariège, France, and Harriet Joanne, *née* Mercier; *b* 20 June 1944; *Educ* private tutors, Hawtreys, Eton, Univ of Oxford (MA); *Career* dir Christies 1973–2003, md Christies Monaco (Monte Carlo) sale room 1987–89; Freeman City of London, Liveryman Worshipful Co of Gunmakers; *Recreations* shooting, driving collectors' cars; *Clubs* Turf, Carlton House Terrace; *Style*— Peter Hawkins, Esq; ✉ 20 Ennismore Gardens, London SW7 1AA

HAWKINS, His Hon Judge Richard Graeme; QC (1984); s of late Denis William Hawkins, of Frinton-on-Sea, Essex, and Norah Mary Hawkins, *née* Beckingsale; *b* 23 February 1941; *Educ* Hendon County Sch, UCL (LLB); *m* 1969, Anne Elizabeth, da of late Dr Glyn Charles Edwards, of Bournemouth, Dorset; 1 da (Victoria b 1972), 1 s (Benjamin b 1975); *Career* called to the Bar Gray's Inn 1963 (bencher 2003); in practice SE Circuit, recorder of the Crown Court 1985, circuit judge (SE Circuit) 1989–; Liveryman Worshipful Co of Curriers; *Recreations* sailing; *Clubs* Royal Thames Yacht; *Style*— His Hon Judge Hawkins, QC; ✉ Central Criminal Court, City of London, London EC4M 7EH

HAWKINS, Richard Ingpen Shayle; s of Vice Adm Sir Raymond Hawkins, KCB (d 1987), and Rosalind Constance Lucy, *née* Ingpen (d 1990); *b* 20 June 1944; *Educ* Bedford Sch; *m* 26 July 1969, Amanda Louise, da of Rear Adm E F Gueritz, CB, OBE, DSC, of Salisbury, Wilts; 2 s (William b 1973, George b 1976); *Career* cmmnd 2 Lt RM 1962, Lt 42 Commando Far East 1964–65, 43 Commando UK 1965–66, 45 Commando Aden and UK 1967–69, Capt 40 Commando Far East 1970–71, GSO3 HQ Commando Forces 1971–73, Adj RMR Tyne 1973–75, Army Staff Coll Camberley 1976, Co Cdr 45 Commando UK 1977–78, Maj Instr Sch of Inf 1978–80, GSO2 Dept of Cmdt Gen RM MOD 1980–82, ret 1982; insurance broking 1982–; md Marsh Inc 1999–2001; dir: Bowring Marsh & McLennan Ltd 1994–97, Marsh UK Ltd 1997–2001, AIG 2002–04; *Recreations* sailing, field sports, cross country skiing; *Clubs* Royal Yacht Sqdn, Boodle's; *Style*— Richard Hawkins, Esq; ✉ The Old Forge, Upton, Andover, Hampshire SP11 OJS (tel 01264 736269)

HAWKINS, Prof Robert Edward; *b* 10 November 1955; *Educ* Trinity Coll Cambridge (open and sr scholar, MA Maths 1981, MB 1981), UCH London (MB BS 1984, Magrath and Fellowes Gold Medal 1984), MRC Lab of Molecular Biology Cambridge (PhD 1992); *Career* actuarial trainee Prudential Assurance Co 1977–79; house offr: in gen surgery Basingstoke Dist Hosp 1984–85, in med with oncology and haematology UCH London 1985; SHO: rotation in gen med Whittington Hosp London 1985–86, in thoracic med Brompton Hosp London 1986–87, in med oncology and radiotherapy Royal Marsden Hosp London 1987; St George's Hosp med registrar rotation: registrar in gen med and endocrinology St Helier Hosp Carshalton 1987–88, registrar in med oncology/haematology and palliative care Royal Marsden Hosp 1988–89; MRC recombinant DNA trg fellowship MRC Lab of Molecular Biology Cambridge 1989–92; MRC Centre and Addenbrooke's Hosp Cambridge: CRC sr clinical research fell and hon sr registrar in med oncology 1992–94, CRC sr clinical research fell and hon conslt in med oncology 1994–96; prof and head Dept of Oncology Univ of Bristol 1996–98, hon conslt in med oncology Bristol Oncology Centre 1996–98, CRC prof and dir of med oncology Univ of Manchester 1998–, hon conslt in med oncology Christie Hosp NHS Tst

1998–, head Cancer Studies Univ of Manchester 1998–2004; co-ordinator EU project www.attack-cancer.org 2005–; memb NHS and CRC R&D Ctee; conslt to Biotech; clinical ed Br Jl of Cancer 1997–2005; author of numerous articles in learned jls, invited lectures at home and abroad; FRCP 1999 (MRCP 1987); *Style*— Prof R E Hawkins; ✉ Paterson Institute of Cancer Research, Wilmslow Road, Manchester M20 4BX (tel 0161 446 3208, fax 0161 446 3269, e-mail rhawkins@picr.man.ac.uk)

HAWKINS, Dr Stanley Arthur; s of Canon John Henry Hawkins, of Dublin; *b* 2 March 1948; *Educ* Belfast Royal Acad, Queen's Univ Belfast (BSc, MB BCh, BAO); *Career* registrar rising to sr registrar NI Neurology Serv 1974–79, res registrar Nat Hosp Queen Sq London 1979–81, conslt neurologist and sr lectr Queen's Univ Belfast and Royal Victoria Hosp Belfast 1981–97, conslt neurologist and reader in neurology Queen's Univ Belfast 1997–; visiting prof UCLA 1984; pres Ulster Med Soc 2005–06; former chair Res Ctee Multiple Sclerosis (MS) Ireland, memb Scientist Panel on Neuroimmunology Euro Fedn of Neurological Socs 1996–2005; Euro Ctee on Treatment and Res in Multiple Sclerosis (ECTRIMS): memb Cncl 1996–, memb Scientific Organising Ctee Basel 1999, Toulouse 2000, Dublin 2001 and Vienna 2004; session chair World Fedn of Neurology Delhi 1989, chair scientific session Int Fedn of Multiple Sclerosis Socs Dublin 1990, delivered numerous lectures in Europe and USA; memb Int Editorial Bd Multiple Sclerosis Clinical and Laboratory Research 1994–; FRCP 1990 (MRCP 1975); *Publications* over 80 full papers in peer-review jls; articles reviewed for numerous jls; *Recreations* gardening (memb Nat Tst Open Gardens Scheme); *Style*— Dr Stanley Hawkins; ✉ Queen's University, Belfast BT12 6BJ (tel 028 9024 0503, fax 028 9032 9899)

HAWKSLEY, John Richard; s of Richard Walter Benson Hawksley (d 1976), and Jean Lilley, of Norwich; *b* 11 March 1942; *Educ* Haileybury; *m* 9 March 1968, Jane, da of Col Hugh Pettigrew; 2 s (Benjamin b 26 Nov 1968, David b 23 April 1971), 1 da (Victoria b 11 Dec 1973); *Career* qualified chartered accountant 1965; PricewaterhouseCoopers (formerly Deloitte Haskins & Sells, then Coopers & Lybrand before merger): ptnr 1975–99, ptnr i/c Reading 1981–85, ptnr i/c Birmingham 1986–90, regnl ptnr i/c Midland Region 1987–95, ptnr i/c Birmingham Coopers & Lybrand (following merger) 1990–95; chm: Amelca plc 2000–03, T + L Ltd 2002–, Tom Aikens Restaurant, Tom Aikens Ltd 2006–, Tea (F&C) Ltd 2006–; dep chm DTI Business Action Team 1989–94; dir: Public Arts Cmmn Agency 1988–2000 (chm 1988–93), Newtown and South Aston City Challenge Ltd 1992–95, Birmingham Hippodrome Theatre Tst 1993–2006, Acad for Youth Ltd 1997–2001, 3 E's Enterprises Ltd 1998–2004, The Coal Authy 2000–; pres Cncl Birmingham C of C and Industry 1995–96 (vice-pres 1993–95), memb Cncl W Midlands CBI 1991–97, memb Business Link Accreditation Bd 1996–99; govr City Technol Coll Kingshurst 1988–2002; FCA (ACA 1965), FRSA; *Recreations* travel, cricket, golf, skiing, watching all sport, opera, theatre, music; *Clubs* MCC, Stratford Oaks and Sheringham Golf; *Style*— John Hawksley, Esq; ✉ 25 Beach Road, Mundesley, Norfolk NR11 8BQ

HAWKSWORTH, Prof David Leslie; CBE (1996); *b* 5 June 1946; *Educ* Univ of Leicester (BSc, PhD, DSc); *m* 1, 1968, Madeleine Una, *née* Ford; 1s, 1 da; m 2, 1999 (sep 2004), Patricia Ann, *née* Ford; *Career* mycologist Cwlth Mycological Inst Kew 1969–81 (princ taxonomist 1980–81), scientific asst to exec dir Cwlth Agric Bureaux Farnham Royal Slough 1981–83, dir Int Mycological Inst Kew and Egham 1983–97, dir MycoNova 1998–; Universidad Complutense de Madrid: visiting prof 2000–01, Ramón y Cajal res prof 2001–06, prof contractado doctorado indefinado 2006–; hon research assoc Natural History Museum London 2006–; memb Cncl (Govt appointee) English Nature 1996–99; visiting prof: Univ of Reading 1984–, Univ of Kent 1990–, Univ of London 1992–; chm: Int Cmmn on the Taxonomy of Fungi 1982–2002, Int Cmmn on Bionomenclature 1995–; pres Br Lichen Soc 1986–87 (memb 1964–), pres Br Mycological Soc 1990 (memb 1969–), pres Int Union of Biological Sciences 1994–97, hon pres Int Mycological Assoc 1994– (sec gen 1977–90, pres 1990–94); Int Assoc for Plant Taxonomy: memb 1967–, memb Ctee for Fungi 1981–93, memb Gen Ctee 1987–, memb Editorial Ctee 1987–, Admin Finances 1993–99; Systematics Assoc: memb 1969–, treas 1972–81, ed-in-chief 1981–84 and 1986, memb Cncl 1970–72 and 1986–95; ed: The Lichenologist 1970–90, Mycopathologia 1984–87, Plant Systematics and Evolution 1986–98, Systema Ascomycetum 1986–98, Mycosystema 1986–, Mycological Research 1999– (sr ed 2000–), Biodiversity and Conservation (ed-in-chief 2006–, memb Editorial Bd 1991–2005); memb Editorial Bd: Field Studies 1975–80, Nat History Book Reviews 1976–80, Plant Pathology 1985–91, Cryptogamic Botany 1988–90, Fungal Diversity 1999–, Taxon 2006–; memb: Field Studies Cncl 1965–, Int Assoc for Lichenology 1967– (awarded Acharius Medal 2002), Botany Sub-Ctee Royal Soc Nat Ctee for Biology 1975–82, Tropical Agric Assoc 1982–98, Ct Univ of Surrey 1983–98, Ruislip Woods Mgmnt Advsy Gp 1983–2001, American Phytopathological Soc 1986–98, Exec Bd World Fedn of Culture Collections 1988–96, Standing Ctee on Nomenclature Int Union of Biological Scis 1988–94, Int Relations Ctee Royal Soc 1994–95; Dr (hc) Univ of Umeå 1996; hon memb: Società Lichenologica Italiana 1989, Ukrainian Botanical Soc 1992, Mycological Soc of America 1994, Latin American Mycological Assoc 1996, Br Mycological Soc (Centenary fell) 1996, Br Lichen Soc 1997, Japanese Soc for Lichenology 2002; author of numerous books, articles, papers and book reviews in learned jls mainly on fungi (incl lichens), biological diversity and bionomenclature; FLS 1969 (Bicentenary Medal 1978, vice-pres 1985–88), FIBiol 1982, FRSA 1997; *Recreations* lichenology, natural history, museums, walking, history of biology; *Style*— Prof David L Hawksworth, CBE; ✉ Milford House, The Mead, Ashtead, Surrey KT21 2LZ (tel 01372 272087, e-mail myconova@terra.es)

HAWLEY, Prof Christine Elizabeth; da of John and Margaret Hawley; *b* 3 August 1949, Shrewsbury; *Educ* City of London Sch for Girls, AA Sch of Arch London (AADipl); *m* 1974, Clyde Watson; 1 da (Lucy b 1982), 2 s (Samuel b 1984, Joseph b 1991); *Career* asst R&D Unit Dept of the Environment 1972; asst architect: Renton Howard Wood and Levin Architects London 1972–73, De Soissons Partnership London 1974–77, YRM (Yorke Rosenberg and Madell) London 1977, Pearson International London 1978; ptnr Cook and Hawley Architects London 1974–; unit master AA Sch of Architecture London 1980–88 (tutor 1979–80), head Univ of E London (formerly Poly of E London) Sch of Architecture 1987–93; prof of architectural studies Bartlett Sch of Architecture UCL 1993–, dean Bartlett Faculty of the Built Environment UCL 1999–; visiting prof: Western Aust Inst of Technol Perth 1985, Oslo Sch of Architecture 1987, Tech Univ Vienna 1993 and 1996–97; Hyde prof Lincoln Univ Nebraska 1987; lectures at numerous instns at home and abroad incl: Rhode Island Sch of Design 1978, AA 1979–87, Berkeley Calif 1980–91, Aarhus Sch of Architecture 1985–93, UCLA 1993, Hong Kong Univ 1994, RIBA 1995, UCL (inaugural lecture) 1996; subject of numerous articles in architectural/design pubns; Br Cncl Award Rome 1977, Yamagiwa Art Fndn Award Tokyo 1979, Br Cncl Award Helsinki and Stockholm 1980; ARCUK 1978, RIBA 1982, FRSA 1983; *Projects* incl: limited int competition for social housing and exhbn centre W Berlin 1991, Stadel Acad Frankfurt 1992, competition in Lower Austria for a museum, belvedere, external amphitheatre and gallery 1993, participation of urban devpt forum on int workshops and symposium Hamburg 1993, Strathclyde Visions Centre Glasgow 1993, Elbberg Offices Hamburg 1993, Kitagata social housing Gifu 1994–, Shanghai planning study for social housing 1996; *Exhibitions* incl: Graham Fndn Chicago (Three Architects) 1982, Manspace London and NY 1982, Aedes Gallery Berlin 1994 and 1995, Venice Biennale 1996, Sagacho Gallery Tokyo 1997; *Recreations* swimming, reading, badminton; *Style*— Prof Christine Hawley; ✉ The Bartlett School of Architecture, University College London, 22 Gordon Street, London WC1H 0QB (tel 020 7380 7504, fax 020 7380 7453, e-mail c.hawley@ucl.ac.uk)

HAWLEY, Sir Donald Frederick; KCMG (1978, CMG 1970), MBE (1955); s of Frederick George Hawley (d 1973), of Little Gaddesden, Herts, and Gertrude Elizabeth, *née* Hills; *b* 22 May 1921; *Educ* Radley, New Coll Oxford (MA); *m* 1964, Ruth Morwenna Graham, da of Rev Pery Graham Howes (d 1964), of Charmouth, Dorset; 1 s, 3 da; *Career* served WWII Capt RA; Sudan Govt and Sudan Judiciary 1944–55; called to the Bar Inner Temple 1951; Dip Serv 1956–81: ambass to Oman 1971–75, asst under sec of state 1975–77, high cmmr to Malaysia 1977–81; dir Ewbank & Partners 1981–82, chm Ewbank Preece Ltd 1982–86 (special advsr 1986–96); memb London Advsy Ctee Hongkong and Shanghai Banking Corp 1981–91; chm: The Centre for Br Teachers 1987–91, Confedn of Br SE Asian Socs 1988–95, Sudan Govt Br Pensioners Assoc 1992–, The Sir William Luce Meml Fund 1996–; vice-pres: Anglo-Omani Soc 1981–, Royal Soc for Asian Affairs (chm 1994); pres Sudan Defence Force Dinner Club 1995–, pres Bath Branch Royal Cwlth Soc 1997–, sr vice-pres Br Malaysian Soc (chm 1983–95), memb Cncl RGS 1985–87; govr ESU 1989–95; memb Ct Univ of Reading 1994– (memb Cncl 1981, pres 1987–94); Hon DLitt Univ of Reading 1994, Hon DCL Univ of Durham 1997; *Books* Handbook for Registrars of Marriage and Ministers of Religion (Sudan Govt, 1963), Courtesies in the Trucial States (1965), The Trucial States (1971), Oman and its Renaissance (1977, new edn 1995), Courtesies in the Gulf Area (1978), Manners and Correct Form in the Middle East (1984, 2 edn 1996), Sandtracks in the Sudan (1995), Sudan Canterbury Tales (ed, 1999), Desert Wind and Tropic Storm (2000), Khartoum Perspectives (ed, 2001), The Emirates: Witness to a Metamorphosis (2007); *Recreations* tennis, gardening, travel; *Clubs* Travellers, Beefsteak; *Style*— Sir Donald Hawley, KCMG, MBE; ✉ Cheverell Place, Little Cheverell, Devizes, Wiltshire SN10 4JJ (tel 01380 813322)

HAWLEY, James Appleton; TD (1968), JP (Staffs 1969); s of John James Hawley (d 1968), of Longdon Green, Staffs, and Ethel Mary Hawley, JP (d 1999); *b* 28 March 1937; *Educ* Uppingham, St Edmund Hall Oxford (MA); *m* 8 April 1961, Susan Anne Marie, da of Alan Edward Stott, JP, DL, of Armitage, Staffs; 2 da (Catherine Marie (Mrs Taylor) b 1963, Jane Rachel (Mrs Lane Fox) b 1968), 1 s (Charles John b 1965); *Career* 2 Lt S Staffs Regt 1955–57, Nat Serv Cyprus, TA 2 Lt to Maj Staffs Yeo 1957–69; called to the Bar Middle Temple 1961; chm: John James Hawley Ltd 1961–98, J W Wilkinson & Co Ltd 1970–98; dir Stafford Railway Bldg Soc 1985–2003; High Sheriff Staffs 1976–77, HM Lord-Lt Staffs 1993– (DL 1978–93); vice-pres W Midlands RFCA; pres: Walsall Soc for Blind 1992– (chm 1977–92) Staffs Scouts; pres Staffs and Birmingham Agricultural Soc 2004–05; chm Cncl Lichfield Cathedral; tstee Armed Forces Meml; patron, pres and tstee of many orgns in Staffs; Freeman City of London 1987, Liveryman Worshipful Co of Saddlers 1988; Hon Dr Staffordshire Univ 2003; KStJ 1993; *Recreations* family, Staffordshire and outdoor pursuits; *Clubs* Oxford and Cambridge; *Style*— James Hawley, Esq, TD; ✉ Lieutenancy Office, County Buildings, Martin Street, Stafford ST16 2LH (tel 01785 276805, fax 01785 214139)

H

HAWLEY, Peter Edward; s of Albert Edward Hawley (d 1962), of Leicester, and Winifred, *née* Skinner (d 1992); *b* 20 July 1938; *Educ* Wyggeston Sch, Magdalene Coll Cambridge (MA, LLB); *m* 19 Sept 1964, (Mary) Tanya, da of John Ounsted, of Appletree Cottage, Woodgreen Common, Fordingbridge, Hants; 1 da (Sasha Louise b 26 Aug 1967); *Career* Nat Serv, Sgt (RAEC) attached 99 Gurkha Inf Bde Johore Malaya 1957–59; admitted slr 1967; Walker Martineau: articled clerk 1964–67, asst slr 1967–69, ptnr 1970–2000, managing ptnr 1983–91, sr ptnr 1998–2000; ptnr Penningtons 2000–03; chm: Multilaw Multinational Assoc of Ind Law Firms 1998–2000, Heligan Devpt Ltd 1992–, Pentewan Sands Ltd 2005–; Freeman City of London 1989, Freeman Worshipful Co of Slrs 1988; *Recreations* hogging shade; *Clubs* Royal Over-Seas League; *Style*— Peter Hawley, Esq; ✉ 3 Whitchurch House, Whitchurch on Thames, Reading, Berkshire RG8 7EP (e-mail peterhawley@btopenworld.com)

HAWLEY, Dr Robert; CBE (1997); s of William Hawley (d 1960), and Eva, *née* Dawson; *b* 23 July 1936; *Educ* Wallasey GS, Wallasey Tech Coll, Birkenhead Tech Coll, King's Coll Durham (BSc, PhD), Univ of Newcastle upon Tyne (DSc); *m* 1, 1962 (m dis), Valerie, da of Colin Clarke; 1 da (Fiona Jane b 10 Dec 1966), 1 s (Nicholas Richard b 30 July 1968); m 2, 2002, Pamela Elizabeth, da of John Neesham; *Career* C A Parsons: head of research team 1961–64, electrical designer Generators 1964–66, dep chief generator engr 1966–70, dir and chief electrical engr 1973–74 (chief electrical engr 1970–73), dir of prodn and engrg 1974–76; NEI plc: md NEI Parsons Ltd (following t/o of C A Parsons) 1976–84, md Power Engineering Gp 1984–88, dir 1984–88, md Ops 1989–92; chm Engrg Cncl 1999–2002; chief exec: Rolls-Royce 1992 (main bd dir 1989–92), Nuclear Electric plc 1992–96, British Energy plc 1995–97; non-exec chm: Rotork plc 1996–98, INBIS plc 1997–2000, Taylor Woodrow plc 1999–, Rocktron 2001–; non-exec dir: W S Atkins plc 1994–97, Colt Telecommunications plc 1998–, Tricorder Technology plc 1997–2001, Rutland Tst plc 2000–; conslt SEMA 1994–96; chm Hawley Ctee on Corp Governance and Information Mgmnt 1993–98; pres IEE 1996–97; chm Engrg Cncl 1998–2002; memb Cncl Fellowship of Engrg (now Royal Acad of Engrg) 1981–84; author of numerous scientific papers; C A Parsons meml lectr IEE and Royal Soc 1977, Hunter meml lectr IEE 1990, Blackadder lectr NE Coast Instn of Engrs and Shipbuilders 1992, Wilson Campbell meml lectr 1994, Bowden lectr 1994, John Collier lectr 1997; IEE Achievement Medal 1989; pres Energy Industries Club 1989–91; memb Boat and Shoreworks Ctee RNLI 1992–97; chm Anglo-Korean Soc 2002– (pres 2002); memb Ct Univ of Newcastle upon Tyne 1979–, chm Cncl Univ of Durham 1997–2002, memb Ct Loughborough Univ 2003; Freeman City of London, Master Worshipful Co of Engrgs 2005–06; Hon DSc: Univ of Durham 1996, City Univ 1998, Cranfield Univ 2002; Hon DEng: South Bank Univ 1997, UWE 1997, Univ of Newcastle upon Tyne 2002, UMIST 2002; Hon DTech: Staffordshire Univ 2000, Univ of Abertay 2001, Robert Gordon Univ 2002; Hon DUniv Surrey Univ; hon fell Inst of Nuclear Engrs 1994, hon fell Liverpool John Moores Univ 2002; fell City and Guilds of London Inst 2003; FIEE 1970, FInstP 1970, FREng 1979, FIMechE 1987, FRSE 1997, Hon FIEE 2003, Hon FIIE 2003, FCGI 2003, Hon FIET 2006; Order of Diplomatic Serv Gwanghwa Medal Korea 1999; *Recreations* gardening, philately; *Clubs* Athenaeum, New (Edinburgh); *Style*— Dr Robert Hawley, CBE, DSc, FREng, FRSE

HAWORTH, Baron (Life Peer UK 2004), of Fisherfield in Ross and Cromarty; Alan Robert Haworth; s of John Haworth (d 1991), and Hilma, *née* Westhead (d 1990); *b* 26 April 1948, Blackburn, Lancs; *Educ* Blackburn Tech and GS, Univ of St Andrews, Barking Regnl Coll of Technol (BSc); *m* 1991, Maggie Rae; *Career* N E London Poly: registrar Faculty of Art & Design 1972–73, asst to Dir of Course Devpt 1973–75; PLP: ctee offr 1975–85, sr ctee offr 1985–92, sec 1992–2004; memb: John Muir Tst, Ramblers Assoc, Munro Soc, Scottish Wild Land Gp, Mountain Bothies Assoc; *Publications* Men Who Made Labour (co-ed, 2006); *Recreations* hill walking, mountaineering (completion of the Munros 2001), foreign travel; *Style*— The Lord Haworth; ✉ House of Lords, London SW1A 0PW (e-mail hawartha@parliament.uk)

HAWORTH, Jane Victoria, *née* Wright; da of Peter Donald Wright (decd), and Barbera Anne, *née* Haworth; *b* 8 April 1964; *Educ* White Lodge, Royal Ballet Sch; *Career* ballerina; English Nat Ballet (formerly London Festival Ballet): joined 1983, sr soloist 1990–, artistic co-ordinator 2002–; *Performances* princ and soloist roles incl: title roles in La Sylphide and Carmen, Sugar Plum Fairy in The Nutcracker, Teresina in Napoli, Olga/Tsarina in Anastasia, Prelude and Waltz in Les Sylphides, Persian Princess in Prince Igor, Good Girl in Graduation Ball, Flower Festival pas de deux, Pink Lady in Sanguine Fan, Livia in Romeo and Juliet, Polyhymnia in Apollo, Fairy Godmother and Winter Fairy in Cinderella, Pas de Deux in Petrouchka Variations, Dawn in Coppélia, first solo in

Raymonda, second solo in La Bayadere, Pas de Quatre, Pas de Trois and Lead Swans in Swan Lake; created roles: Woman in Stranger I Came, Symphony in 3, Countess in Sleeping Beauty, Cook in Alice in Wonderland, Stepmother in Cinderella, Batilde in Giselle, Lady Capulet in Romeo and Juliet, Clara's Mother in The Nutcracker; guest appearance in La Sylphide (with Peter Shaufuss, Vienna State Opera Ballet) 1990; character roles incl: Queen in Swan Lake, Lady Capulet and Nurse in Romeo and Juliet, Berthe in Giselle, Queen and Countess in Sleeping Beauty; *Television* Young Indiana Chronicles 1992, Live and Kicking 1995, Boxing Academy 2004, Don't Just Dream It 2005; *Recreations* horse riding, gardening, collecting antiques; *Style—* Miss Jane Haworth; ✉ c/o English National Ballet, Markova House, 39 Jay Mews, London SW7 2ES (tel 020 7581 1245, fax 020 7225 0827, e-mail jane.haworth@ballet.org.uk)

HAWORTH, Dr (John) Martin; s of Reginald Haworth (d 1989), of Oswaldtwistle, Lancs, and Hilda, *née* Barnes; *b* 22 January 1949, Oswaldtwistle, Lancs; *Educ* Accrington GS, London Sch of Theology (BD), Univ of Birmingham (MA, PhD), Univ of Warwick (MEd); *m* 1973, Brenda; 2 da (Emma Louisa, Charlotte Clare); *Career* religious educn teacher Plymstock Sch Plymouth 1973–77, head of sixth form and head of religious educn Coundon Ct Sch Coventry 1977–85, dep head Wisewood Sch Sheffield 1985–90, head master Wallington Co GS 1990–; MInstD 1991, FRSA 1992; *Recreations* karate, fitness, theatre, opera, church; *Style—* Dr Martin Haworth; ✉ Wallington County Grammar School, Croydon Road, Wallington, Surrey SM6 7PH (tel 020 8647 2235, fax 020 8254 7921, e-mail mhaworth@suttonlea.org)

HAWORTH, Nigel; s of Harry Haworth (d 2001), and Constance, *née* Southern; *b* 11 July 1958; *Educ* St Christopher's C of E Secdy Mod, Accrington & Rossendale Coll of FE; *m* 2006, Katherine, *née* Brooks; 1 da (Keeley Emma b 20 May 1985), 1 s (Kirk James b 26 July 1987); *Career* chef; lectr in catering Accrington & Rossendale Coll 1981–84; chef Northcote Manor (one Michelin star) 1984–; Egon Ronay Chef of the Year 1995, winner Wedgwood Chef & Potter Top 100 Chefs 2000; memb Acad of Culinary Arts, former memb Master Chefs of GB; sponsor: Lady Taverners, NSPCC; Prince Philip Medal C&G; hon prof Lancaster and Morecombe Coll; *Recreations* running, squash, football, scuba diving, mushroom picking; *Clubs* Blackburn Rovers 500, Fullwood Sub Aqua; *Style—* Nigel Haworth, Esq; ✉ Northcote Manor, Northcote Road, Langho, Blackburn, Lancashire BB6 8BE (tel 01254 240555, fax 01254 246568, mobile 07787 537824, e-mail admin@northcotemanor.com)

HAWORTH, Sir Philip; 3 Bt (UK 1911), of Dunham Massey, Co Chester; s of Sir (Arthur) Geoffrey Haworth, 2 Bt (d 1987); *b* 17 January 1927; *Educ* Dauntsey's Sch West Lavington, Univ of Reading (BSc); *m* 1951, Joan Helen, da of late Stanley Percival Clark, of Ipswich; 4 s (Christopher b 1951, Mark b 1956, Simon Nicholas b 1961, Adam Ewart b 1964), 1 da (Penelope Jane b 1953); *Heir* s, Christopher Haworth; *Career* agriculture; chm Bd Buxton Festival 1994–99; *Recreations* music, ornithology, sculpture; *Clubs* Farmers'; *Style—* Sir Philip Haworth, Bt; ✉ Free Green Farm, Over Peover, Knutsford, Cheshire WA16 9QX

HAWORTH, Richard Anthony; s of George Ralph Haworth (d 1995), and Joan Kershaw, *née* Taylor; *b* 3 September 1955; *Educ* Oundle, Univ of Leeds (LLB); *m* 18 March 1994, Sara Kay, da of Dr Ian Smith; 1 s (George Frederick b 1 Jan 1996); *Career* called to the Bar Inner Temple 1978; in practice Northern Circuit; jr counsel Crown Provincial Panel; *Recreations* shooting, salmon fishing, growing sweet peas, stalking, working gundogs; *Clubs* East India, Yorkshire Flyfishers'; *Style—* Richard Haworth, Esq; ✉ 15 Winckley Square, Preston, Lancashire (tel 01772 252828, fax 01772 258520, e-mail richard.haworth@virgin.net)

HAWTON, Prof Keith Edward; s of Lesley William Hawton (d 1988), and Eliza, *née* Davies (d 1999); *b* 23 December 1942, Barnet, Herts; *Educ* Univ of Cambridge (MB BChir, MA), Univ of Oxford (DM, DSc); *m* 1978, Joan; 2 da (Jane b 17 May 1981, Katherine b 1 Oct 1983); *Career* trg in psychiatry 1969–74, research psychiatrist 1974–76; Dept of Psychiatry Univ of Oxford: lectr 1976–79, clinical tutor 1979–84, prof of psychiatry 1996–, dir Centre for Suicide Research; dean Green Coll Oxford (governing body fell 1985–); conslt psychiatrist Oxfordshire Mental Healthcare Tst 1984–; Erwin Stengel Research Award Int Assoc for Suicide Prevention 1995, Louis I Dublin Award American Assoc of Suicidology 2001, Research Award American Fndn for Suicide Prevention 2002; FRCPsych 1972; *Books* Attempted Suicide: A Practical Guide to its Nature and Management (with José Catalán, 1982), Sex Therapy: A Practical Guide (1985), Suicide and Attempted Suicide among Children and Adolescents (1986), Cognitive Behaviour Therapy for Psychiatric Problems: A Practical Guide (1989), Dilemmas and Difficulties in the Management of Psychiatric Patients (ed with Philip Cowen, 1990), Practical Problems in Clinical Psychiatry (ed with Philip Cowen, 1992), Suicide and Stress in Farmers (1998), The International Handbook of Suicide and Attempted Suicide (ed with Kees van Heeringen, 2000), Deliberate Self-Harm in Adolescence (with Claudine Fox, 2004), Prevention and Treatment of Suicidal Behaviour: From Science to Practice (ed, 2005), By Their Own Young Hand: Deliberate Self-Harm and Suicidal Ideas in Adolescents (with Karen Rodham, 2006); *Recreations* golf, fishing, cricket, wine; *Style—* Prof Keith Hawton; ✉ Centre for Suicide Research, Warneford Hospital, Oxford OX3 7JX (e-mail keith.hawton@psych.ox.ac.uk)

HAY, Alexander Douglas; s of Lt-Col George Harold Hay, DSO (d 1967), and Patricia Mary, *née* Hugonin (d 1998); *b* 2 August 1948; *Educ* Rugby, Univ of Edinburgh (BSc); *m* 20 Jan 1973, Aline Mary, da of Robert Rankine Macdougall; 1 s (Robert Alexander b 29 July 1976), 1 da (Caroline Laura b 9 July 1978); *Career* ptnr Greaves West & Ayre CAs Berwick-upon-Tweed 1978–2005 (joined 1975); chm: Scottish Episcopal Church Widows & Orphans Fund Corp Ltd 1980–89, Roxburgh & Berwickshire Cons & Unionist Assoc 1989–92, Berwickshire Housing Assoc 1994–2000; MICAS 1975; *Recreations* golf; *Clubs* Hon Co Edinburgh Golfers; *Style—* Alexander Hay, Esq; ✉ Duns Castle, Duns, Berwickwshire (tel 01361 883211)

HAY, David John MacKenzie; s of Ian Gordon McHattie Hay, of Inverness, and Ishbel Jean Hay, *née* MacKenzie; *b* 30 June 1952; *Educ* Inverness Royal Acad, Univ of Edinburgh (MA), Magdalene Coll Cambridge (MA, LLM); *Career* called to the Bar Inner Temple 1977, joined Butterworth & Co (Publishers) Ltd 1979, managing ed Atkin's Encyclopaedia of Court Forms 1984–85, ed R&D 1985–86, managing ed Electronic Forms Publishing 1986–88; gen ed: Halsbury's Laws of England (reissue) 1995–96 (ed 1989–96), Words and Phrases Legally Defined 1993–, Halsbury's Laws of Hong Kong 1995–, Major Works Butterworths Asia 1996–; *Recreations* music, enjoying the countryside, reading, travel; *Style—* David Hay, Esq; ✉ The Cottage, School Lane, Barley, Royston, Hertfordshire SG8 8JZ; E3–02–4 Pantai Hill Park Phase 1, Jalan Pantai Dalam, 59200 Kuala Lumpur Malaysia; Malayan Law Journal Sdn Bhd, 3 Floor, Wisma Bandar, No 18 Jalan Tuanku Abdul Rahman, 50100 Kuala Lumpur, Malaysia (tel 00 60 3 291 7273, fax 00 60 3 291 6471)

HAY, Elizabeth Joyce (Jocelyn); CBE (2005, MBE 1999); da of William George Board (d 1951), and Olive Price Jones (d 1962); *b* 30 July 1927; *Educ* Open Univ (BA); *m* 26 Aug 1950, William Andrew Hunter Hay, TD (decd), s of Sheriff J C E Hay, CBE, MC, TD, DL (d 1975); 2 da (Penelope Jill b 1960, Rosemary Anne b 1961); *Career* freelance writer and broadcaster 1954–83; work incl: Forces Broadcasting Serv, Woman's Hour BBC Radio 2 and 4; head Press and PR Dept Girl Guides Assoc, Cwlth HQ 1973–78, fndr and dir London Media Workshops 1978–94, fndr and chm Voice of the Listener and Viewer 1983–, tstee and former chm The Voice of the Listener Tst 1987–, tstee Mediawise 2003–; memb: Steering Ctee Info Soc Forum, Directorate for Enterprise and Info Soc of the EC 1997–2001; examiner CAM Dip in PR Exams 1985–2002; memb Soc of Authors; Elizabeth R Award for an outstanding contribution to public service broadcasting Commonwealth Broadcasting Assoc 1999, European Woman of Achievement Award (Humanitarian Category) Br Section European Union of Women 2007; FRSA; *Recreations* ancient history and art; *Style—* Mrs Jocelyn Hay, CBE; ✉ 101 Kings Drive, Gravesend, Kent DA12 5BQ (tel 01474 564676)

HAY, Prof Frank Charles; s of Edward Frank Hay, of London, and Doris Irene, *née* Webber; *b* 8 October 1944; *Educ* Sir George Monoux GS, Brunel Univ (BTech), Univ of London (PhD); *m* 2 Aug 1969, Frances Margaret, da of Prof George Baron; 1 da (Rebecca b 28 March 1974), 1 s (Thomas b 9 Feb 1977); *Career* Middx Hosp Med Sch: res assoc 1972–77, lectr in immunology 1977–78, sr lectr 1978–84, reader 1984–89; currently prof Centre for Medical and Healthcare Educn St George's Univ of London (chm Div of Immunology 1989, head Dept of Cellular and Molecular Scis 1991, vice-princ 1993); memb: Br Soc for Immunology 1970, Royal Soc of Med 1982, Biochemical Soc 1991; *Books* Practical Immunology (3 edn, 1989); *Recreations* swimming, mountain walking; *Style—* Prof Frank Hay

HAY, Ian Wood; s of John William Hay (d 1977), of Harwich, Essex, and Winifred May, *née* Fox (d 1975); *b* 25 January 1940; *Educ* Colchester Sch of Art (NDD), RCA; *m* 26 March 1968, Teresa Mary, da of Stanislav Antoni Sliski, of Harwich, Essex; 2 s (James b 1978, Rupert b 1982); *Career* artist known for pastel paintings of London and The Thames; visiting lectr: St Martin's Sch of Art 1963–77, Norwich Sch of Art 1971–75; sr lectr in drawing Sch of Art Colchester Inst 1978–2001 (sch gall named The Hay Gallery in his honour); RCA prize for landscape painting 1963; many one man and group shows in Essex and London in The Minories and Phoenix Art Gallery; works in private and public collections incl: Guildhall Art Gallery, Sheffield Art Gallery, Doncaster City Art Gallery, Univ of Essex; chm of selectors Colchester Art Soc 2002–; memb North Countryman's Club Colchester 2002–; ARCA (1963); *Recreations* travel; *Style—* Ian Hay, Esq; ✉ 32 Tall Trees, Mile End, Colchester, Essex CO4 5DU (tel 01206 852510)

HAY, Lady Olga; *see:* Maitland, Lady Olga

HAY, Peter Laurence; s of Norman Leslie Stephen Hay (d 1979); *b* 7 March 1950; *Educ* St Paul's, Brunel Univ; *m* 1, 19 July 1985 (m dis 1992), Perdita Sarah Amanda Lucie Rogers; m 2, 29 Aug 1996, Caroline Mary Buchanan-Jones; *Career* chm: Norman Hay plc 1977–, Plasticraft Ltd 1987–, Advanceaction Ltd 1987–99, Montgomery Plating Co Ltd 1988–, Norman Hay International Ltd 1988–, Plasplate Ltd 1988–, Armourcote East Kilbride Ltd 1988–, Armourcote Suface Treatments Ltd 1988–, Surface Technology plc 1989–, Lew-Ways Ltd 1998–2000; *Recreations* flying helicopters; *Style—* Peter Hay, Esq; ✉ Windlesham Grange, Kennel Lane, Windlesham, Surrey GU20 6AA (tel 01276 472980, fax 01276 476139); Norman Hay plc, Godiva Place, Coventry CV1 5PN (tel 024 7622 9373, fax 024 7622 4420, e-mail plhay@aol.com)

HAY, Peter Rossant; s of Vincent Hay, and Marie Winifred, *née* Chase; *b* 11 October 1948; *Educ* Clifton Coll; *m* 14 April 1973, Christine Maria; 1 da (Nicola Marie b 8 March 1975), 2 s (Alexander William Rossant b 11 Feb 1978, James Vincent Rossant b 10 Aug 1985); *Career* admitted slr 1973; ptnr: Penningtons 1973–92, Perry Hay & Co 1993– (formerly Peter Hay & Associates); hon slr The Royal Scot Corp 1985–; chm Richmond Athletic Association Ltd 1986–91; non-exec dir: Meat Trade Suppliers plc 1988–89, West London TEC 1996–97, London Scottish Rugby Ltd 1996–98; vice-pres Richmond C of C 1994–98; govr and vice-chm Corp of Richmond-upon-Thames Coll 1999–2005; tstee Richmond Parish Lands Charity 2005–; memb Law Soc; FRSA; *Recreations* golf, skiing, swimming, ex-rugby and rowing; *Clubs* City of London, Caledonian, Sunningdale; *Style—* Peter R Hay, Esq; ✉ Perry Hay & Co, 25 The Green, Richmond, Surrey TW9 1LY (tel 020 8332 7532, fax 020 8948 8013, e-mail peterhay@perryhay.co.uk)

HAY, Robin William Patrick Hamilton; s of William Reginald Hay (d 1975), of Nottingham, and (Mary Constance) Dora, *née* Bray; *b* 1 November 1939; *Educ* Eltham Coll, Selwyn Coll Cambridge (MA, LLB); *m* 18 April 1969, Lady Olga Maitland, *qv*, er da of 17 Earl of Lauderdale, *qv*; 2 s (Alastair b 18 Aug 1972, Fergus b 22 April 1981), 1 da (Camilla b 25 June 1975); *Career* called to the Bar Inner Temple 1964, recorder of Crown Court 1985–2005; legal assessor GMC 2002–, chm Appeal Panel Postgrad Medical and Education and Training Bd 2005–, legal advsr Faculty and Inst of Actuaries 2006–, legal advsr Royal Pharmaceutical Soc Statutory Ctees 2006–, legal assessor Nursing and Midwifery Cncl 2007–; ILEA candidate (Cons) Islington S and Finsbury 1986, chm Nat Musicians Symphony Orch 1990–2001; *Recreations* gastronomy, church tasting, choral singing; *Clubs* Garrick; *Style—* Robin Hay, Esq; ✉ Lamb Chambers, Lamb Building, Temple, London EC4Y 7AS (tel 020 7797 8300, fax 020 7797 8308, e-mail robinhay@lambchambers.co.uk)

HAY, Prof Roderick James; s of Kenneth Stuart Hay (d 1992), and Margery Geidt, *née* Winterbotham (d 1983); *b* 13 April 1947; *Educ* Wellington, Merton Coll Oxford, Guy's Hosp Med Sch London (MA, BM BCh, DM); *m* 18 August 1973, Delyth, *née* Price; 2 da (Lucy Arianwen b 6 March 1976, Harriet Alexandra b 20 August 1979); *Career* former registrar Guy's Hosp, lectr, sr lectr then reader LSHTM 1977–89, Mary Dunhill prof of cutaneous med GKT 1989–2002 (dean for external affrs 1995–2002), dean and clinical dir St John's Inst of Dermatology St Thomas' Hosp 1996–2002, dir Centre for Caribbean Med (UK) 1997–2002, head Sch of Med and Dentistry Queen's Univ Belfast 2005– (dean Faculty of Med and Health Sciences 2002–05); Dowling orator 1989, Avery Chan meml lectr 1997; pres: St John's Dermatology Soc, Br Soc for Med Mycology, Euro Confedn for Med Mycology, Br Assoc of Dermatologists 2001; non-exec dir EHSSB, chm Int Fndn for Dermatology; FRCP 1984, FRCPath 1992, FMedSci 2000; *Recreations* music, gardening, walking; *Style—* Prof Roderick Hay; ✉ School of Medicine and Dentistry, Queens University Belfast, 71 University, Belfast BT7 1NN (tel 028 9097 2186, e-mail r.hay@qub.ac.uk)

HAY, Sir Ronald Frederick Hamilton; 12 Bt (NS 1703), of Alderston; o s of Sir Ronald Nelson Hay, 11 Bt (d 1988), and Rita, *née* Munyard; *b* 1941; *m* 1978, Kathleen, da of John Thake; 2 s (Alexander James b 1979, Anthony Ronald b 1984), 1 da (Sarah Jane b 1981); *Heir* s, Alexander Hay; *Style—* Sir Ronald Hay, Bt

HAYCOCKS, Richard John; s of Roy Terence Haycocks (d 1988), of Wilts, and Barbara Alice, *née* Rons; *b* 8 June 1949; *Educ* City of Westminster Coll, Dartford GS; *m* 30 June 1986, Myra Anne, da of Alan Douglas Kinghorn; 2 s (Thomas Richard Henry b 20 May 1987, James Richard John b 20 Aug 1990); *Career* Allfields 1969–74, Deloitte Haskins & Sells 1974–80, dir Baker Energy Holdings Ltd (part of Baker Hughes) 1980–83; Ernst & Young: joined 1984, ptnr 1989, ptnr corp fin 1990–2001; ptnr Baker Tilly 2002–06, dir Consensus Business Gp 2007–; Liveryman Worshipful Co of Coachmakers and Coach Harness Makers; FCA (ACA 1971), MSI; *Clubs* RAC; *Style—* Richard Haycocks, Esq; ✉ tel 020 7355 7944, e-mail richardhaycocks@hotmail.com

HAYDAY, Terence John (Terry); s of John Alfred Hayday (d 1978), and Annie Dorothy Hayday (d 2004); *b* 23 June 1947; *Educ* Hampton GS, Univ of Sussex (BA), City Univ (MBA); *m* 9 June 1973, Susan Pamela, da of Gordon Grenville Dean (d 1997); 2 s (Nicholas b 1977, Christopher b 1979), 1 da (Annabel b 1987); *Career* Lloyd's broker Leslie & Godwin Ltd 1965–67, Lloyd's underwriting asst R W Sturge & Co 1967–69, reinsurance underwriter Slater Walker Insurance Co Ltd 1972–76; Holmes Hayday (Underwriting Agencies) Ltd (formerly Holmes Kingsley Carritt Ltd): dep Lloyd's underwriter and dir 1976–79, md 1980–88, chm 1988–92; active underwriter Lloyd's Syndicate 694 1980–91, dir and chief exec Sturge Holdings plc (which acquired Holmes Hayday in 1990) 1991–94, co sec and dir Owen & Wilby Underwriting Agency Ltd 1995–99, co sec Gerling

Corporate Capital Ltd 1998–99, dir and compliance offr Gerling at Lloyd's Ltd (which acquired Owen & Wilby Underwriting Agency in 1999) 1999–2003, co sec Gerling UK Ltd 2002–03, tech exec Lloyd's Market Assoc 2004–; chm Optimum Consultants Ltd 1994–, non-exec chm Pembroke Managing Agency Ltd 2007–; memb sr mgmnt team GIS UK (German Industiral Insurer); dir: Highgate Managing Agencies Ltd 1994–96, Apex Professional Education Programme at Lloyd's 1995–98, Mitchell McLure Ltd 1995–, Pembroke JV Ltd 2007–; non-exec dir: Newman & Stuchbery Ltd 1988–93, LIMNET Bd (London Insurance Market Network) 1992–; vice-pres Insurance Inst of London; Distinguished Serv Medal CII 2004, Pres's Award Insurance Inst of London 2007; FCII 1976; *Recreations* sailing, rugby, theatre, literature; *Clubs* Lloyd's Yacht, Twickenham Yacht; *Style*— Terry Hayday, Esq; ✉ Lloyd's Market Association, Suite 358, One Lime Street, London EC3M 7DQ (tel 020 7327 3333, fax 020 7327 4443, e-mail terry.hayday@lmalloyds.com)

HAYDEN, Prof Jacqueline (Jacky); da of Robert Leslie James Hayden, of Majorca, Spain, and Dorothy Blanche, *née* Cowell (d 1986); *b* 4 December 1950; *Educ* Croydon HS, KCL, St George's Hosp Med Sch (MB BS, LRCP, DCH, DRCOG); *m* 11 Dec 1976, Edward Milne Dunbar, s of David Milne Dunbar; 2 s (Alexander James b 10 July 1980, Benjamin David b 20 Jan 1984); *Career* pre-registration house offr: St James's Hosp Balham London 1974, Ashford Hosp Middx 1975; SHO in thoracic med Churchill Hosp Oxford 1975–76, gen practice trg scheme Oxford 1976–79, princ in gen practice Unsworth Med Centre Bury Lancs 1979–, dean of postgrad med studies Univ of Manchester 1997– (assoc advsr in gen practice 1990–91, regional advsr in gen practice 1991–96), civil conslt in general practice RAF 1998–; memb: Cncl RCGP 1985– (chm NW England Bd 1994–96), Jt Ctee on Postgraduate Trg for Gen Practice 1986–, Armed Servs Gen Practice Approval Bd 1992–, Chief Med Offr's Working Pty on Specialist Trg 1993–94; chm Ctee of Regional Advsrs in Gen Practice in England 1994–97; MRCS; FRCP, FRCGP; *Books* A Guide for New Principals (1996); contrib: The Medical Annual (1987), Practice Information Booklets (1987), The Practice Receptionist (1989), Change and Teamwork in Primary Care (1993), The Child Surveillance Handbook (1994), Professional Development in General Practice (series ed, 1990–99); *Recreations* my family, the house and garden; *Style*— Prof Jacky Hayden; ✉ 12 Mercers Road, Heywood, Lancashire OL10 2NP (tel 01706 625470, fax 01706 627593, e-mail jackyhayden@aol.com); Department of Postgraduate Medicine, Gateway House, Piccadilly South, Manchester M60 7LP (tel 0161 237 2104, fax 0161 237 2108)

HAYDEN, Paul Leslie; s of Leslie Hayden (d 1985), and Jean, *née* Brown (d 1977); *b* 12 May 1960, Birmingham; *Educ* Univ of Central Lancs (MSc), Coventry Univ (MA); *m* 26 Oct 1991, Tina, *née* Hawkes; 3 s (Phillip b 1983, Christopher b 1987, Adam b 1988); *Career* firefighter rising to station offr West Midlands Fire Serv 1978–91, asst divnl offr Fire Serv Coll 1991–93, asst divnl offr rising to asst chief offr Suffolk Fire Service 1993–2002, dep chief fire offr Norfolk Fire Serv 2002–05, chief fire offr and ceo Hereford and Worcester Fire and Rescue Serv 2005–; advsr to Local Govt Assoc, lead on environment and inland water rescue Chief Fire Offrs Assoc; Fire Serv Long Serv Medal 1998; MIFireE 1991; *Publications* A Uniform Approach (Audit Cmmn report, 2000); *Recreations* classic car restoration; *Style*— Paul Hayden, Esq; ✉ Hereford and Worcester Fire and Rescue Service, 2 Kings Court, Charles Hastings Way, Worcester WR5 1JR (tel 01905 368201, e-mail phayden@hwfire.org.uk)

HAYDEN, Richard Michael; s of Richard Taylor Hayden, and Cecelia Hayden; *b* 31 July 1945; *Educ* Georgetown Univ (BA), Wharton Grad Sch of Business (MBA); *m* 1978, Susan Margolies; 1 s, 1 da; *Career* Goldman Sachs & Co: assoc 1969–73, vice-pres 1973–80, ptnr/md 1980–98; Goldman Sachs International: dep chm 1995–98, vice-chm 1999; ptnr and chm GSC Partners Europe Ltd 2000–; memb Bd: Compton & Knowles 1988–2000, Cortefiel SA 1994–96, Abbey National Gp 1999–2004, Perry Capital 2002–04, Cofra Holding AG 2003–, Deutsche Börse 2005–; *Recreations* golf, tennis; *Clubs* Queenwood, RAC, Queen's, Hurlingham, Links (NYC), Union (NYC), River (NYC); *Style*— Mr Richard Hayden; ✉ GSC Partners Europe Ltd, 68 Pall Mall, London SW1Y 5ES (tel 020 7968 3600)

HAYES, Brian; *b* 17 December 1937; *Family* 1 s; *Career* broadcaster; memb NUJ; *Radio* announcer 6KG Kalgoorlie Australia 1955–60, presenter Breakfast Show Perth, fndr (prog controller and chief presenter) Local Radio Station 6TZ-CI Bunbury, prodr and presenter (phone-ins, news and documentaries) Morning Talk Radio 6IX Perth; Capital Radio London: prodr talk progs 1973–74, presenter Open Line 1974–75; presenter: morning phone-in show LBC Radio 1976–90, late night phone-in GLR 1990, Breakfast Show Radio 2 1992, Breakfast Show London News Talk 1994–95, Hayes Over Britain Radio 2 1992–98; Not Today Thank You (BBC Radio 4) 2006; *Television* incl: Sunday Sunday (LWT), Out of Order (ITV), VIP (BSB), Right to Reply (Channel 4) 1989–90, For Greater Good (BBC), Prime Suspect (Granada), Between the Lines (BBC), The Chief (Anglia), Rules of Engagement (YTV), Pty Conf coverage (BBC) 1995; *Awards* incl: Independent Radio Personality of the Year Variety Club Award 1980, Best Phone-in Prog Rediffusion/Radio Month Award 1981, commendation Local Radio Personality category Sony Special Award 1985, Outstanding Contrib to the Devpt of Radio Sony Special Award 1987, memb Sony Roll of Honour Sony Radio Awards 1988, Best Phone-in Show (for Hayes Over Britain) Sony Radio Awards 1993, Service to the Community Award (jtly) Sony Radio Awards, Sony News Award 2000 (for Late Night Live); *Recreations* theatre, opera, cinema, television, literature; *Style*— Brian Hayes, Esq; ✉ c/o Jacquie Drewe, Curtis Brown Group Ltd, 28–29 Haymarket, London SW1Y 4SP (tel 020 7393 4400)

HAYES, Sir Brian David; GCB (1988, KCB 1980, CB 1976); s of Charles Wilfred Hayes (d 1958); *b* 5 May 1929; *Educ* Norwich Sch, CCC Cambridge (MA, PhD); *m* 1958, Audrey, da of Edward Mortimer Jenkins (d 1973); 1 da (Catherine b 1962), 1 s (Edward b 1963); *Career* 2 Lt RASC Home Cmd 1948–49; civil servant; perm sec: MAFF 1979–83, Dept of Industry 1983 (jt perm sec 1983–85), DTI 1985–89; dir: Guardian Royal Exchange plc 1989–99, Tate and Lyle plc 1989–98; advsy dir Unilever plc 1990–99; Lloyd's members' ombudsman 1994–; *Recreations* reading, opera, ballet; *Style*— Sir Brian Hayes, GCB; ✉ Office of the Lloyd's Members' Ombudsman, G5/86, 1 Lime Street, London EC3M 7HA

HAYES, John Forbes Raymond; s of (George) Forbes Raymond Hayes (d 1995), of Brocastle, Mid Glamorgan, and Jean Hayes, OBE, *née* Cory (d 2007); *b* 21 October 1948; *Educ* Harrow, Trinity Hall Cambridge (MA); *m* 1 May 1976, Nicola Anne, da of Brian Thomas Reilly (d 1988); 4 s (Charles, Hugh, Matthew, Benjamin); *Career* mgmnt conslt; PricewaterhouseCoopers: accounting articles 1971, conslt 1980, dir Nigerian firm 1982–84, ptnr UK firm 1986–2002, chm UK Investment Gp 1990; ptnr IBM Business Consulting Services Europe 2002–; memb Fin Ctee RUSI 1999–2005 (memb Cncl 1999–2003); govr Harrow Sch 2000–, govr John Lyon Sch 2005; Freeman City of London 1970, memb Worshipful Co of Tin Plate Workers 1970 (Master 1992); FCA 1980 (ACA 1975); *Recreations* music, sailing, golf; *Clubs* Leander; *Style*— John Hayes, Esq; ✉ Wood End, Beech Lane, Jordans, Buckinghamshire HP9 2SZ (tel 01494 872419); IBM United Kingdom Ltd, 76/78 Upper Ground, South Bank, London SE1 9PZ (tel 020 7021 8758, mobile 07710 045150)

HAYES, John Henry; MP; *b* 23 June 1958; *Educ* Colfe's GS, Univ of Nottingham (BA, PGCE); *m* 12 July 1997, Susan, *née* Hopewell; *Career* dir The Database (Nottingham) Ltd 1986–99; cncllr Nottingham CC 1985–98 (party spokesman on educn 1988–96); MP (Cons) S Holland and The Deepings 1997– (Parly candidate (Cons) Derbyshire NE 1987 and 1992); vice-chm Cons Pty 1999–2000, actg head Political Section Office of the Ldr of the Oppn 2000, frontbench spokesman on educn and employment 2001, oppn pairing whip 2001–02, shadow min for agriculture and fisheries 2002–03, shadow min for housing and planning 2003–05, shadow min for tport 2005, shadow min for vocational educn and skills 2005–; memb: Agriculture Select Ctee 1997–99, Educn Employment Select Ctee 1998–99, Admin Select Ctee 2001–, Ctee of the Selection 2001–02; vice-chm Cons Backbench Educn Ctee 1997–99, jt chm All-Pty Disablement Gp 1998–, sec All-Pty Acquired Brain Injury Ctee; author of various articles and pamphlets; adjunct assoc prof Richmond the American Int Univ in London 2002–; chm: Univ of Nottingham Cons Assoc, E Midlands Regnl Cons Students; former chm Young Conservatives; memb: Countryside Alliance, countryside NFU, SPUC; vice-chm Br Caribbean Assoc; patron Headway Cambs; *Recreations* the arts (particularly English painting, poetry and prose), good wine and food, many sports (incl darts), studying history, making jam, antiques, architecture and aesthetics; *Clubs* Carlton, Spalding Spalding Gentleman's Soc (Lincs); *Style*— John Hayes, Esq, MP; ✉ House of Commons, London SW1A 0AA (tel 020 7219 3000, e-mail hcinfo@parliament.uk)

HAYES, Josephine Mary (Jo); da of Reginald Francis Hayes, DFC (d 1977), and Eileen, *née* Bass; *b* 26 June 1955; *Educ* Colchester Co HS for Girls, Lady Margaret Hall Oxford, City Univ (Dip Law), Yale Law Sch (alumni fell, LLM); *Career* called to the Bar 1980; chair Assoc of Women Barristers 1996–98; memb SDP 1983–87, fndr memb Lib Dems 1987–; *Clubs* Reform; *Style*— Miss Jo Hayes; ✉ 5 Cathedral Mansions, London SW1V 1BP (tel 020 7828 4578); Gough Square Chambers, 6–7 Gough Square, London EC4A 3DE (tel 020 7353 0924, e-mail josephine.hayes@goughsq.co.uk)

HAYES, Malcolm Lionel Fitzroy; s of Vice Adm Sir John Hayes, KCB, OBE (d 1998), and Hon Rosalind Mary Finlay (d 2002); *b* 22 August 1951; *Educ* St George's Sch Windsor, Eton, Univ of St Andrews, Univ of Edinburgh (BMus, Tovey Prize for Composition); *Career* formerly involved in weaving indust Lewis Outer Hebrides until 1981; music critic: The Times 1985–86, The Sunday Telegraph 1986–89, The Daily Telegraph 1989–95; contrib 1982–: Tempo, The Independent, Musical Times, The Listener, Classical Music, Opera Now, BBC Music Magazine, Classic FM Magazine, BBC Radio 4, BBC Radio 3, BBC World Service, Classic FM; memb Critics' Circle 1988–; compositions incl: 3 Songs on Chinese Poems (1972), Cantata for flute and chamber group (1983), Into the Night for unaccompanied choir (1984), Stabat Mater (2001), Odysseus remembers (2004); *Books* New Music 88 (co-ed, 1988), Anton von Webern (1995), 20th Century Music (2001), Selected Letters of William Walton (ed, 2002); *Recreations* skiing, photography; *Clubs* Surrey CCC; *Style*— Malcolm Hayes, Esq; ✉ e-mail malcolmhayes@btinternet.com

HAYES, Michael Anthony; s of Brian George Gerard Hayes (d 1983), of Wimbledon and Dorking, Surrey, and June Louise, *née* Wenner (d 1967); *b* 10 January 1943; *Educ* Wimbledon Coll, UC Oxford (MA); *m* 5 June 1971, Jacqueline Mary, da of Peter Kenneth Judd; 2 s (Dominic b 11 Aug 1972, William b 13 Feb 1978), 1 da (Victoria b 25 April 1974); *Career* admitted slr 1968; Macfarlanes: joined 1966 ptnr 1974–2004, head Tax and Fin Planning Dept 1991–2000; with Maitland Group 2004–; memb: Ctee City of London Law Soc 1978–92 (Distinguished Service award 1987), Law Soc and its Wills and Equity Ctee, Mgmnt Ctee City of London CAB 1982–2004 (chm 1985–88); tstee Ind Age (Royal UK Beneficent Assoc) 2004–; *Recreations* narrowboating, wine; *Clubs* Garrick, RAC, Roehampton; *Style*— Michael Hayes, Esq

HAYES, Roger Peter; s of Peter Hall, and Patricia Mary, *née* Lacey; *b* 15 February 1945; *Educ* Isleworth GS, Univ of London, Univ of Southern Calif (BSc, MA); *m* 15 Feb 1974, Margaret Jean Hayes; 1 s (Nicolas Alexander b 25 Nov 1983); *Career* corr Reuters Paris 1967–72, dir and vice-pres Burson Marsteller 1972–79, PA Management Consultants 1979–83, dir of corp communications Thorn EMI plc 1985–88, dir IT World 1985–, chm Hayes Macleod International and Investor Corporate Communications 1988–91, non-exec dir Echo Communications Research Gp 1989–; pres Int PR Assoc 1997; vice-pres Public Affrs and Govt Rels Ford of Europe 1991–93, DG British Nuclear Industry Forum 1993–97, dir Int Inst of Communications 1998–2003; sr cnsllr APCO Worldwide; memb Bd of Regents Potomac Inst Washington DC; assoc Euro Centre for Public Affrs; FIPRA 1987, FIPR 1988 (memb emeritus 2006); *Books* Corporate Revolution (jtly, 1986), Experts in Action (jtly, 1988), Systematic Networking (1996); *Recreations* tennis, travel, movies and music; *Clubs* Reform, Hurlingham; *Style*— Roger Hayes, Esq; ✉ 75 Ellerby Street, London SW6 6EL (tel 020 7731 1255, e-mail roger_p_hayes@yahoo.co.uk)

HAYES, Dr William; s of Robert Hayes (d 1986), and Eileen, *née* Tobin (d 1985); *b* 12 November 1930; *Educ* UC Dublin (BSc, PhD), Univ of Oxford (MA, DPhil); *m* 28 Aug 1962, Joan Mary (d 1996), da of John Ferriss (d 1986); 1 da (Julia b 1970), 2 s (Robert b 1973, Stephen b 1974); *Career* official fell and tutor in physics St John's Coll Oxford 1960–78, 1851 overseas scholar 1955–57, sr fell American Nat Sci Fndn Purdue Univ 1963–64, visiting prof Univ of Illinois 1971, princ bursar St John's Coll Oxford 1977–87, dir and head Clarendon Lab Oxford 1985–87, pres St John's Coll Oxford 1987–2001, pro-vice-chllr Univ of Oxford 1990–2001, delg of OUP 1991–2001, chm of curators Oxford Univ Chest 1992–2000, currently sr research fell Clarendon Lab Oxford; hon fell St John's Coll Oxford 2001; Hon DSc: Nat Univ of Ireland 1988, Purdue Univ 1996; Hon MRIA 1998; *Books* Scattering of Light by Crystals (with R Loudon, 1978), Defects and Defect Processes in Non-Metallic Solids (with A M Stoneham, 1985); *Recreations* walking, reading, listening to music; *Style*— Dr William Hayes; ✉ St Johns College, Oxford OX1 3JP (tel 01865 277300, e-mail w.hayes1@physics.ox.ac.uk)

HAYES, William (Billy); s of William Hayes, and Margaret, *née* Ellis; *b* 8 June 1953; *Educ* St Swithins RC Sch, Univ of Liverpool (Dip); *m* 1995, Dian Lee; 1 s (Niall William b 7 Feb 2000), 1 da (Melissa Clare b 15 April 2002); *Career* former welder JJ Howards Fabrication Steel then John West Foods; joined Post Office 1974; Communication Workers Union: memb 1974–, former positions incl magazine ed, TUC youth conf delg, union conf delg and branch sec, memb Nat Exec 1992–, nat offr 1992–2001, gen sec 2001–; memb Lab Pty, memb Lab Pty Policy Forum, memb Lab Campaign for Electoral Reform, regular delg to Lab Pty Conf; memb: Greenpeace, Gen Cncl TUC; vol Simon Community; *Publications* All Around the World (1998); *Recreations* films, books, music, Liverpool FC; *Style*— Billy Hayes, Esq; ✉ Communication Workers Union, 150 The Broadway, Wimbledon, London SW19 1RX (tel 020 8971 7251, fax 020 8971 7430, e-mail bhayes@cwu.org)

HAYHOE, Baron (Life Peer UK 1992), of Isleworth in the London Borough of Hounslow; Rt Hon Sir Bernard John (Barney) Hayhoe; kt (1987), PC (1985); s of late Frank Stanley Hayhoe and Catherine Hayhoe; *b* 8 August 1925; *Educ* Borough Poly; *m* 1962, Anne Gascoigne, da of late Bernard W Thornton; 2 s (Hon Crispin Bernard Gascoigne b 1963, Hon Dominic Adam Scott b 1965), 1 da (Hon Sarah Anne Sherwood b 1967); *Career* MP (Cons): Heston and Isleworth 1970–74, Hounslow Brentford and Isleworth 1974–83, Brentford and Isleworth 1983–92; CRD 1965–70, PPS to Lord Pres of the Cncl and Ldr of the Commons 1972–74, additional oppn spokesman on Employment 1974–79, Parly under sec Def (Army) 1979–81; min of state: CSD 1981, Treasy 1981–85, for Health 1985–86; chm Guy's and St Thomas' NHS Tst 1993–95; CEng, FIMechE; *Clubs* Garrick; *Style*— The Rt Hon Lord Hayhoe, PC; ✉ 20 Wool Road, London SW20 0HW (tel 020 8947 0037)

HAYLE, Michael Philip (Mike); *b* 27 July 1959; *Educ* Royal GS Newcastle upon Tyne, Magdalene Coll Cambridge (MA), Manchester Business Sch (MBA); *Career* various posts incl roles with Bombadier Inc and The Cadogan Gp, md Specialist Aviation Services Ltd, chief exec ABRO 2001–; CEng 1985, MIEE 1985, Eur Ing 1989, MCMI (MIMgt 1992),

H

MCIM 1999, FRAeS 2000, FIMechE 2003; *Style—* Mike Hayle, Esq; ✉ ABRO, Monxton Road, Andover, Hampshire SP11 8HT (tel 01264 383148, fax 01264 383280)

HAYLER, Clive Reginald; s of Reginald Hayler (d 1985), and Dorothy Edith Hayler (d 2001); *b* 11 August 1955; *Educ* Steyning GS, Univ of Liverpool (BSc), Univ of Exeter; *m* Heather Jayne, da of Derek John Roberts (d 2002); 2 s (Richard Mark b 1984, Christopher James b 1985); *Career* mktg mangr Beckman RIIC Ltd 1979–83 (UK Sales Person of the Year 1981); md: Hawksley & Sons Ltd 1985–91 (gen mangr 1983–85), Marco Scientific Ltd 1991–98; dir AIS Cleanroom Products Ltd 1998–2000; md Primarius Ltd 2000–; memb Ctee: BSI Cleanroom Standards Working Gp, UK/Ireland Chapter of Parental Drug Assoc (chm Biotech Gp), Soc of Environmental Engrgs; memb: Int Soc for Pharmaceutical Engrg, Inst of Environmental Sciences and Technol, Int Soc for Cellular Therapy, Br Fertility Soc, S2C2; FInstD, CBiol, FSEE, MPS; *Recreations* running, surfing, martial arts, tropical horticulture, travel; *Clubs* IOD, HMC; *Style—* Clive Hayler, Esq; ✉ Primarius Ltd, 66 Roman Road, Steyning, West Sussex BN44 3FN (e-mail chayler@primarius.co.uk)

HAYLOCK, John Mervyn; s of Dr Sydney John Haylock, FRCS, LRCP (d 1939), of Southbourne, Dorset, and Winifred Margaret, *née* Baker (d 1955); *b* 22 September 1918; *Educ* Aldenham, Institut de Touraine Tours (Dip), Grenoble Univ, Pembroke Coll Cambridge; *Career* WWII: cmmnd Hampshire Regt 1940, served ME and Greece; writer; English instructor: Primary Teachers Trg Coll Baghdad, Coll of Commerce & Economics Baghdad 1948–56, Waseda Univ Tokyo 1958–60 and 1962–65; prof of English Rikkyo Univ Tokyo 1975–84; author of short stories in Blackwoods Magazine, London Magazine, Winter Tales and others; FRSL 1995; Ordre de Leopold II 1947, Croix de Guerre (Belge) 1947; *Novels* See You Again (1963), It's All Your Fault (1964), One Hot Summer in Kyoto (1980), A Touch of the Orient (1990), Uneasy Relations (1993), Doubtful Partners (1998), Body of Contention (1999), Loose Connections (2003), Sex Gets in the Way (2005); *Non-Fiction* New Babylon - A Portrait of Iraq (with Desmond Stewart, 1956), Eastern Exchange, Memoirs of People and Places (1997); *Translations from the French* Robert de Montesquiou - A Prince of the Nineties (with Francis King, by Philippe Jullian, 1967), Flight into Egypt (by Philippe Jullian, 1968); *Recreations* travel, swimming, collecting Oriental porcelain, reading, listening to music; *Clubs* Oriental; *Style—* John Haylock, Esq, FRSL; ✉ Flat 28, 15 Grand Avenue, Hove, East Sussex BN3 2NG (tel 01273 325472)

HAYMAN, Andrew (Andy); CBE (2006), QPM (2004); *Career* joined Essex Police 1978, Cdr Drugs Directorate Met Police 1998, Dep Asst Cmmr Met Police 2001 (ldr Anti-Corruption Branch), Chief Constable Norfolk Constabulary 2002–05, Asst Cmmr Met Police 2005– (Specialist Ops); *Style—* Andy Hayman, Esq, CBE, QPM; ✉ Metropolitan Police Service, New Scotland Yard, Broadway, London SW1H 0BG

HAYMAN, Baroness (Life Peer UK 1995), of Dartmouth Park in the London Borough of Camden; Helene Valerie Hayman; PC (2000); da of Maurice Middleweek (decd); *b* 26 March 1949; *Educ* Wolverhampton Girls' HS, Newnham Coll Cambridge (MA, pres Cambridge Union); *m* 1974, Martin Hayman, *qv*, s of Ronald Hayman (decd); 4 s (Hon Ben b 1976, Hon Joseph b 1980, Hon Jacob b 1982, Hon David b 1985); *Career* worked successively with SHELTER (nat campaign for homeless), Camden Social Servs Dept then Nat Cncl for One Parent Families (dep dir) 1969–74, MP (Lab) Welwyn and Hatfield 1974–79, fndr memb Maternity Alliance and broadcaster 1979–85, vice-chm Bloomsbury HA 1985–92, chm Bloomsbury and Islington DHA 1992, chm Whittington Hosp NHS Tst 1992–97, chm Cancer Research UK 2001–04; sat as Lab peer House of Lords 1995–2006, Parly under-sec of state DETR 1997–98, Parly under-sec of state Dept of Health 1998–99, min of state MAFF 1999–2001, Lord Speaker House of Lords 2006–; chair Human Tissue Authy 2005–06, memb Human Fertilisation and Embryology Authy 2005–06; former lay memb UCL Cncl; former chair of govrs Brookfield Sch; tstee Royal Botanic Gardens Kew 2002–06; *Style—* The Rt Hon the Baroness Hayman, PC; ✉ House of Lords, London SW1A 0PW

HAYMAN, Martin Heathcote; *b* 20 December 1942; *Educ* Highgate Sch, Univ of Cambridge (MA); *m* 1974, Baroness Hayman, PC (Life Peer), *qv*; 4 s (Hon Ben, Hon Joseph, Hon Jacob, Hon David); *Career* slr 1964–69; successively co slr: Plessey Co, ITT and Pullman Kellogg; sec and chief legal advsr Cadbury Schweppes 1985–88 (chief legal advsr 1978–85), gp sec and head of gp legal servs Standard Chartered Bank 1988–2000; chm Mediation UK 2001–03; non-exec dir Fin Objects plc 2002–; advsr and former chm Community Partnership Prog Africa Region Standard Chartered Bank, memb Bd of Tstees Care Int UK 2002–; former memb Bd CEDR; former chair of govrs William Ellis Sch NW London; winner In-House Banking/Finance Lawyer of the Year Award 1995; *Recreations* family; *Style—* Mr Martin Hayman; ✉ 12 Brookfield Park, London NW5 1ER (tel 020 7482 5094, e-mail martinhayman@yahoo.co.uk)

HAYMAN, Prof Walter Kurt; s of Prof Franz Samuel Haymann (d 1947), of Cologne, Germany, and Ruth Matilde Therese, *née* Hensel (d 1979); *b* 6 January 1926; *Educ* Gordonstoun, St John's Coll Cambridge (BA, MA, ScD); *m* 1, 20 Sept 1947, Margaret Riley (d 1994), da of Thomas William Crann (d 1978), of New Earswick, N Yorks; 3 da (Daphne Ruth b 1949, Anne Carolyn b 1951, Gillian Sheila b 1956); m 2, 11 May 1995, Waficka Katifi (d 2001); m 3, 21 April 2007, Marie Patricia Jennings, *qv*; *Career* lectr Univ of Newcastle upon Tyne 1947, fell St John's Coll Cambridge 1947–50, reader in mathematics Univ of Exeter 1953–56 (lectr 1947–53), dean Royal Coll of Sci Imperial Coll London 1978–81 (first prof of pure mathematics 1956–85), pt/t prof Univ of York 1985–93 (prof emeritus 1993), sr research fell Imperial Coll London 1995–; fndr with Mrs Hayman Br Mathematic Olympiad; memb: Cncl of Royal Soc 1962–63, Finnish Acad of Arts and Scis 1978, Bavarian Acad 1982, Accademia Dei Lincei (Rome) 1985, London Mathematical Soc (de Morgan Medal 1995), Cambridge Philosophical Soc, Cncl for Assisting Refugee Academics; Hon DSc: Exeter 1981, Birmingham 1985, Uppsala Sweden 1992, Giessen Germany 1992, Nat Univ of Ireland Dublin 1997; FRS 1956, FIC 1989; *Books* Multivalent Functions (1958, 2 edn 1994), Meromorphic Functions (1964), Research Problems in Function Theory (1967), Subharmonic Functions (vol 1 with P B Kennedy, 1976, vol 2 1989); *Recreations* music, travel, television; *Style—* Prof W K Hayman, FRS; ✉ Department of Mathematics, Imperial College London, Huxley Building, 180 Queen's Gate, London SW7 2AZ (tel 020 7594 8536, fax 020 7594 8517)

HAYMAN-JOYCE, James Leslie; s of Maj Thomas F Hayman-Joyce, RA (d 1946), and Betty Christine, *née* Bruford (d 1995); *b* 12 May 1945; *Educ* Radley, RAC Cirencester; *m* 3 March 1973, Charlotte Alexandra Mary, da of J P Crump, DFC (d 1998); 2 s (Thomas Leslie b 12 April 1981, Simon Patrick b 10 Nov 1983); *Career* chartered surveyor; ptnr Blinkhorn & Co 1983–88, dir Sandoes Nationwide Anglia Estate Agents 1988–91, princ Hayman-Joyce Chartered Surveyors 1991–; FRICS 1970; *Style—* James Hayman-Joyce, Esq; ✉ Bakers Farmhouse, Barton-on-the-Heath, Moreton-in-Marsh, Gloucestershire GL56 0PN (tel 01608 674291, fax 01608 674170, e-mail hj@haymanjoyce.co.uk); High Street, Moreton-in-Marsh, Gloucestershire GL56 0AX (tel 01608 651188, fax 01608 650030)

HAYMAN-JOYCE, Lt-Gen Sir Robert John; KCB (1996), CBE (1989, OBE 1979), DL (Monmouthshire 1996); s of Maj Thomas Fancourt Hayman-Joyce (d 1946), and Betty Christine, *née* Bruford; *b* 16 October 1940; *Educ* Radley, Magdalene Coll Cambridge (MA); *m* 19 Oct 1968, Diana, da of Maj Neil Livingstone-Bussell (d 2005), of Sydling St Nicholas, Dorset; 2 s (Richard Livingstone b 21 Oct 1973, Alexander Robert b 11 Dec 1976); *Career* cmmnd 11 Hussars (PAO) 1963, Cmd Royal Hussars (PWO) 1980–82, Cdr RAC BAOR 1983–85, Dep Cmdt RMCS 1987, Dir UK Tank Prog 1988, DG Fighting Vehicles MOD(PE) 1989, DG Land Fighting Systems MOD (PE) 1990–92, Dir Royal Armoured Corps 1992–94, Mil Sec 1994–95, Master Gen of the Ordnance 1995–98, dep chief of def procurement (Ops) 1997–98; Col Cmdt Royal Armoured Corps 1995–99; non-exec dir Alvis plc 1999–2004; non-exec chm Raytheon Systems Ltd 2000–; Col The Royal Yeomanry 2002–; chm: tstees Tank Museum 1995–2002, Monmouthshire Hunt 1998–2002; patron: Retired Offrs Assoc 2000–, Soc for Welfare of Horses and Ponies 2003–; Hon DSc Cranfield Univ 1998; FCIPS 1997; *Recreations* skiing, horses, reading, music; *Clubs* Cavalry and Guards', Leander; *Style—* Sir Robert Hayman-Joyce, KCB, CBE, DL; ✉ Ty Isha, Mamhilad, Pontypool, Gwent NP4 0JE (tel 01495 785507, fax 01495 785428, e-mail robert@frengis.demon.co.uk)

HAYNES, Anthony Robert; s of Robert Haynes (d 1976), and Joan, *née* Harris; *b* 10 October 1959, Farnborough, Kent; *Educ* Trinity Coll Cambridge (MA, PGCE), Univ of Malta (Cert), Open Univ (Cert); *m* 1985, Karen, *née* Turner; 1 da (Frances Rachel b 3 March 1993), 2 s (Jonty Gower b 29 Dec 1994, Simon Walcott b 22 Dec 2000); *Career* various teaching jobs 1983–96; Continuum International Publishing Gp Ltd: commissioning ed 1999–2002, editorial dir 2002–03, publishing dir 2003–06; ptnr The Professional and Higher Partnership 2006–; visiting prof Beijing Normal Univ 2005–; *Publications* Writing Successful Textbooks (2001), 100 Ideas for Lesson Planning (2007), 100 Ideas for Teaching Writing (2007); *Recreations* beach-hutting; *Clubs* Army and Navy; *Style—* Anthony Haynes, Esq; ✉ c/o The Professional and Higher Partnership, 4 The Links, Cambridge Road, Newmarket, Suffolk CB8 0TG (tel 01638 663456, e-mail anthony@professionalandhigher.com)

HAYNES, Derek Leslie; s of Frederick Leslie Haynes, North Walsham, Norfolk, and Doreen Florence, *née* Saville; *b* 13 June 1950; *Educ* Dagenham Co HS; *m* Julie Iris, da of Iris Maskell; 1 s (Kieren Stephen b 20 Jan 1992); *Career* qualified CA 1975; articled clerk Rowley, Pemberton, Roberts 1968–74, mangr Deloitte Haskins & Sells 1974–80; Clark Whitehill: sr audit mangr 1980–82, tech ptnr 1982–92; ptnr and head of audit Mazars & Guerard 1993–98, ptnr Mazars Neville Russell 1998–2002, dep gp fin dir Pinnacle Insurance plc 2002–05, principle KPMG 2005–; memb ICAEW: Nat Tech Advsy Ctee (dep chm), Insurance Industry Sub Ctee; memb Worshipful Co of Insurers 2002; Freedom of The City of London 1985, memb Worshipful Co of Glass Sellers of London 1985; FCA; *Recreations* classic cars, steam railways, motorcycling, cricket, rugby, motor racing, music; *Style—* Derek L Haynes, Esq; ✉ Pine Lodge, Gimingham Road, Trimingham, Norfolk NR11 8HP (tel 01263 833902); KPMG LLP, 1 Canada Square, London E14 5AG (tel 020 7311 6075, fax 020 7311 5861)

HAYNES, John Harold; OBE (1995); *b* 25 March 1938; *Educ* Sutton Valence; *m* Annette Constance; 3 s (John b 1967, Marc b 1968, Christopher b 1972); *Career* wrote and published first book 1956, ret from RAF as Flt-Lt 1967 to take up full-time publishing, having founded J H Haynes and Co 1960; chm Haynes Publishing Gp plc; dir: J H Haynes and Co Ltd 1960–, Haynes Publications Inc (USA) 1974, GT Foulis and Co Ltd 1977–, Haynes Developments Ltd 1979–, J H Haynes (Overseas) Ltd 1979–, John H Haynes Developments Inc (USA) 1979–, Oxford Illustrated Press Ltd 1981–, Gentry Books Ltd, Camway Autographics Ltd 1984–, Oxford Publishing Co 1988–, Patrick Stephens Ltd 1990–; *Recreations* cycling, walking, veteran and vintage cars, reading; *Clubs* Southern Milestone Motor (pres), Guild of Motoring Writers; *Style—* John H Haynes, Esq, OBE; ✉ Haynes Publishing Group plc, Sparkford, Somerset BA22 7JJ (tel 01963 440635, e-mail smackinnon@haynes.co.uk); 861 Lawrence Drive, Newbury Park, Ca 91320, USA (tel 00 1 818 889 5400)

HAYNES, Keith Anthony; s of Ernest Haynes (d 1996), and Mary, *née* McElroy (d 1980); *b* 2 March 1958; *Educ* St Peter's GS, Univ of Hull (LLB), Manchester Poly (MSc); *m* 3 Sept 1986, Louise Mary, *née* Jackson; *Career* gen mangr Booth Hall Children's Hosp 1984–87, gen mangr Maternity and Paediatric Servs Gtr Glasgow Health Bd 1988–90; chief exec: Liverpool Obstetric and Gynaecology Servs NHS Tst 1990–94, Royal Liverpool Univ Hosp Tst 1994–95; Med Protection Soc: gen mangr Clinical Negligence Scheme for NHS Tsts 1995–98, dir MPS Risk Consulting 1998–; memb Bd Family Housing Assoc Manchester 1997–2002, visiting sr lectr Dept of Health Sciences Univ of York 1999–2005; hon fell Faculty of Med Univ of Manchester 2003–, hon sr lectr Faculty of Med Univ of Leeds 2006–; MHSM; *Recreations* walking, political biography, fine wine; *Style—* Keith Haynes, Esq; ✉ Medical Protection Society, Granary Wharf House, Leeds LS11 5PY (tel 0113 241 0706, fax 0113 241 0710, e-mail keith.haynes@mps.org.uk)

HAYNES, Lawrence John (Lawrie); s of Donald H Haynes, of Eastoft, Lincs, and Irene, *née* Langford; *b* 6 December 1952; *Educ* North Axholme Comp Sch Crowle, Stevenson Coll of FE, Heriot-Watt Univ (BA); *m* Carol Anne, *née* Nelson; 1 da (Liberty Rose b 26 Aug 1981), 2 step da (Natasha Jane b 15 March 1969, Victoria Louise b 21 July 1970); *Career* apprentice RAF (Halton) 1968–71, RAF Sqdn Serv 1971–78, Stevenson Coll 1978–79, Heriot-Watt Univ 1979–83, contracts offr rising to contracts exec British Aerospace (Space Systems) Ltd 1983–88, legal dir then md Microtel Communications Ltd (now Orange) 1988–91, projects dir British Aerospace plc 1991–94, chief exec Highways Agency 1994–99, md Lattice Group Telecommunications 2000–02, ceo British Nuclear Gp and memb Bd BNFL plc 2003–07, ceo White Young Green plc 2007–; tstee RAF Benevolent Fund 2006; FRSA 1994, FIHT 1995, FCIT 1997; *Recreations* sailing, cricket, skiing; *Style—* Lawrie Haynes, Esq

HAYNES, Timothy Hugh Penzer; s of Denzil Barry Penzer Haynes (d 1992), of Hampton-in-Arden, and Felicia Ann, *née* Nettlefold; *b* 2 April 1955; *Educ* Shrewsbury, Univ of Reading (BA), Pembroke Coll Cambridge (PGCE); *m* 1987, Charlotte Geraldine Mary, *née* Southall; 2 s (Theo Robert Penzer b 12 May 1994, Joseph Edward Penzer b 4 Dec 1995); *Career* stockbroker 1979–80; teacher: Queen Elizabeth's GS Blackburn 1980, Hampton Sch 1980–82; St Paul's Sch: teacher 1982–88, undermaster 1988–92, surmaster 1992–95; headmaster: Monmouth Sch 1995–2005, Tonbridge Sch 2005–; *Style—* Tim Haynes, Esq; ✉ Tonbridge School, Tonbridge, Kent TN9 1JP (tel 01732 365555)

HAYTER, Dr Dianne; da of Flt Lt Alec Bristow Hayter (d 1972), and Nancy, *née* Evans (d 1959); *b* 7 September 1949; *Educ* Penrhos Coll, Aylesbury HS, Trevelyan Coll Durham (BA), Queen Mary Univ of London (PhD); *m* Prof Anthony David Caplin; *Career* research asst GMWU 1970–72, research offr European Trade Union Confedn Brussels 1973, research offr Trade Union Advsy Ctee to OECD Paris 1973–74, gen sec Fabian Soc 1976–82 (asst gen sec 1974–76), journalist Channel 4's A Week in Politics 1982–83, dir Alcohol Concern 1983–90, chief exec EPLP 1990–96, dir corp affrs Wellcome Trust 1996–99, chief exec Pelican Centre 1999–2001; memb: Royal Cmmn on Criminal Procedure 1978–81, Exec Ctee NCVO 1987–90, Financial Services Consumer Panel 2001–05 (vice-chm), Bd Nat Consumer Cncl 2001–, Bd Nat Patient Safety Agency 2001–04, Determinations Panel Pension Regulator 2005–, Bd of Actuarial Standards Financial Reporting Cncl 2006–, Insolvency Practices Cncl 2006–; chair Consumer Panel Bar Standards Bd 2006–; memb: London Lab Party Exec 1976–82, Exec Ctee Fabian Soc 1986–95 (chair 1992–93), Lab Party Nat Constitutional Ctee 1987–98, Lab Party NEC 1998– (vice-chair 2006–07, chair 2007–08); JP Inner London 1976–90; *Publications* Fightback! (2005), Men Who Made Labour (co-ed, 2006); *Style—* Dr Dianne Hayter; ✉ 80 Leverton Street, London NW5 2NY (e-mail d.hayter@btinternet.com)

HAYTER, Sir Paul David Grenville; KCB (2007), LVO (1992); s of Rev Canon Michael George Hayter, and Katherine Patricia, *née* Schofield; *b* 4 November 1942; *Educ* Eton (King's scholar), ChCh Oxford (MA); *m* 1973, Hon Deborah Gervaise, da of Baron Maude of Stratford-upon-Avon; 2 s, 1 da; *Career* House of Lords: clerk Parliament Office 1964, seconded as private sec to Ldr of the House and Chief Whip 1974–77, clerk of ctees 1977, princ clerk of ctees 1985–90, reading clerk 1991–97, princ fin offr 1991–94, clerk of legislation 1994–2003, clerk asst 1997–2003, clerk of the Parliaments 2003–; sec Assoc of Lord-Lieuts 1977–91; *Recreations* music, gardening, botanising, local history, archery, painting; *Style*— Sir Paul Hayter, KCB, LVO; ✉ Walnut House, Charlton, Banbury, Oxfordshire OX17 3DR; House of Lords, London SW1A 0PW

HAYTER, Peter Reginald; s of Reginald James Hayter (d 1994), of Bushey, Herts and Lucy Gertrude Gray (d 2004); *b* 13 March 1959; *Educ* Aldenham, Goldsmiths Coll London (BA); *m* 28 Nov 1987, Mary Ann, da of late Geoffrey William Hamlyn; 1 s (Maximilian Geoffrey Reginald Hamlyn b 28 Dec 1990), 1 da (Sophie Grace b 9 July 1995); *Career* actor Greatest Show on Legs 1977–78; journalist; Hayter's Sports Reporting Agency 1982–86 (office boy, jr reporter, reporter, managing ed), football corr Sportsweek Magazine 1986–87, freelance writer 1987–88 (football diarist, writer and cricket writer Independent, football writer Observer, features ed Allsport Photographic), editorial prodr Running Late (Channel 4 sports discussion prog) 1988, cricket corr Mail on Sunday 1989–; *Books* Visions of Sport (1988), The Ashes - Highlights since 1948 (with BBC Test Match Special Team, 1989), Cricket Heroes (1990), Great Tests Recalled (1991), England v West Indies - Highlights since 1948 (with BBC Test Match Special Team, 1991), Botham - My Autobiography (Don't Tell Kath) (with Ian Botham, 1994), The Botham Report (with Ian Botham, 1997), Postcards from The Beach (with Phil Tufnell, 1998), Tufnell - My Autobiography (What Now?) (with Phil Tufnell, 1999), Botham's Century - My 100 great cricketing characters (with Ian Botham, 2001), Ashes Victory (with the England cricket team, 2005); *Video* Botham Hits Back (interview, 1992); *Recreations* cricket, theatre, cinema, hard liquor; *Clubs* MCC, The Cricketers Club of London, Stanmore Cricket, Elvino's Cricket, Incogniti Cricket, Fleet St Strollers Cricket, Bunbury's Cricket; *Style*— Peter Hayter, Esq; ✉ The Mail on Sunday, Northcliffe House, Derry Street, London W8 5TS (e-mail peter.hayter@mailonsunday.co.uk)

HAYTER, 4 Baron (UK 1927); Sir (George) William Michael Chubb; 4 Bt (UK 1909); s of 3 Baron Hayter, KCVO, CBE (d 2003), and Elizabeth Anne, *née* Rumbold; *b* 9 October 1943; *Educ* Marlborough, Univ of Nottingham (BSc); *m* 8 Jan 1983, Waltraud, yr da of J Flackl, of Sydney, Aust; 1 s (Hon Thomas Frederik Flackl Chubb b 23 July 1986); *Heir* s, Hon Thomas Frederik Flackl Chubb; *Career* md Chubb Malaysia 1972–79, md Chubb Aust 1979–82, dir Business Devpt Chubb plc 1982–89, dir William Chubb Associates 1991–; Liveryman Worshipful Co of Weavers (Upper Bailiff 1999); *Style*— The Rt Hon the Lord Hayter; ✉ Rookery Cottage, Monk Sherborne, Hampshire RG26 5HS

HAYTHORNTHWAITE, Richard Neil; s of Christopher Haythornthwaite (d 1984), and Angela, *née* Painter (d 1967); *b* 17 December 1956, Chatham, Kent; *Educ* Colston's Sch Bristol, Queen's Coll Oxford (MA), MIT (SM); *m* 7 April 1979, Janeen, *née* Dennis; 1 s (Alisdair b 27 Sept 1981), 1 da (Sophia b 21 May 1986); *Career* Br Petroleum 1975–95, commercial dir Premier Oil 1995–97, gp ceo Blue Circle Industries 1999–2001 (ceo Europe and Asia 1997–99), ceo Invensys plc 2001–05, md Star Capital Partners 2006–, chm Mastercard 2006–; non-exec dir ICI 2001–; chm: Better Regulation Cmmn, Almeida Theatre, Corp Advsy Gp Tate Gallery; memb Bd Br Cncl; *Recreations* arts, cycling, flying; *Clubs* RAC; *Style*— Richard Haythornthwaite, Esq; ✉ Star Capital Partners, 6th Floor, 33 Cavendish Square, London W1G 0PW (tel 020 7016 8500, fax 020 7016 8501, e-mail rhaythornthwaite@star-capital.com)

HAYTON, Brian John; s of John Edward Hayton, of Ardrossan, Ayrshire, and Williamina Boden Cairns, *née* Tipper; *b* 1 May 1953; *Educ* Ardrossan Acad, Univ of Glasgow (MA), Univ of London (Dip), Museums Assoc (Dip), Univ of Bradford (MBA), CIM (DipM); *m* 23 July 1976, Fiona Mary-Ellen, da of John Murray Innes; 1 da (Pamela Jane b 21 July 1979), 1 s (Ian Brian b 8 June 1981); *Career* volunteer N Ayrshire Museum 1967–74, trainee Glasgow Museums and Art Galleries 1975–78, dist curator Moray DC 1978–80, dep dir NW Museums and Art Gallery Serv 1981–87 (asst dir 1980–81), county museum offr N Yorks Co Cncl 1987–95, museum advsr ACC 1990–95, dir Compton Verney House Tst 1996–98, project dir Nat Railway Museum 1998–2000; museum conslt 1998–2000; Kingston upon Hull City Cncl: head of museums 2000–03, head of cultural services 2003–06, head of cultural, leisure and sports services 2006–; pres NW Fedn of Museums and Art Galls 1987–88, pres elect Midlands Fedn of Museums and Art Galls 1997; chm: Soc of County Museum Officers 1994–95, Museums Benevolent Fund 2000–; dir Humber Sports Partnership 2006–, hon treas Museums Assoc 1996–2002; tstee: Beecroft Bequest 1996–2002, Trevor Walden Tst 2000–; memb: Registration Ctee Museums and Galleries Cmmn 1992–2000, Museums Assoc Cncl 1996–2002 and 2003–; chm MA Pension Fund 2001–; Chartered Marketer; FMA 1988, FRSA 1996, FCIM 2006 (MCIM 1998); *Recreations* walking, swimming, exploring towns; *Style*— Brian J Hayton, Esq; ✉ Ferens Art Gallery, Queen Victoria Square, Hull HU1 3RA (tel 01482 613900, e-mail brian.hayton@hullcc.gov.uk)

HAYTON, Hon Mr Justice David John; s of Flt Lt Arthur Hayton (d 2001), and Beatrice, *née* Thompson (d 1999); *b* 13 July 1944; *Educ* Royal GS Newcastle upon Tyne, Univ of Newcastle upon Tyne (LLB), Jesus Coll Cambridge (MA, LLD); *m* 17 March 1979, Linda Patricia, da of James David Rae (d 1974); 1 s (John James b 28 July 1990); *Career* called to the Bar Inner Temple 1968; in practice Lincoln's Inn 1970–2005, recorder Co Court 1984–2000, acting justice Supreme Court of the Bahamas 2000–01, justice of Caribbean Ct of Justice Trinidad 2005–; lectr Univ of Sheffield 1968–69 (asst lectr 1966–68), fell Jesus Coll Cambridge 1973–87, prof of law KCL 1987–2005 (dean Faculty of Law 1988–90); head of UK delgn to Hague Conf On Private Int Law 1988 (1984), dep chm English Trust Law Ctee 1994–2005; memb Law Panel for Higher Education Funding Cncl Research Assessment Exercise 2001; coach Cambridge RFC I XV 1980–83; *Publications* books: Registered Land (1973, 3 edn 1981), Cases and Commentary on Law of Trusts (6 edn 1975, 11 edn 2001), Law of Trusts and Trustees (13 edn 1979, 16 edn 2003, 17 edn 2007), Law of Trusts (1989, 4 edn 2003), European Succession Laws (1991, 2 edn 2002), Modern International Developments in Trust Law (1999), Extending the Boundaries of Trusts and Similar Ring-Fenced Funds (2002); author of Hayton Report on Financial Services and Trust Law for SIB and IMRO (1990); *Recreations* playing tennis, watching rugby, health club; *Clubs* Royal Cwlth, MCC, Athenaeum; *Style*— Hon Mr Justice David Hayton; ✉ 22 Fondes Amandes, St Anns, Port of Spain, Trinidad and Tobago (tel 00 868 629 4245, e-mail linda.hayton@tstt.net.tt)

HAYTON, Philip John; s of Rev Austin Hayton, of Mansfield, Notts, and Jennie Margaret Violet, *née* Errington; *b* 2 November 1947; *Educ* Fyling Hall Sch Robin Hood's Bay; *m* 22 Dec 1972, Thelma Susan, da of James Gant; 1 s (James b 1980), 1 da (Julia Elizabeth b 1988); *Career* various former posts incl: teacher in Jordan, foundry worker, lavatory assembler, valet, doughnut salesman; pirate radio disc jockey and advertising salesman 1967, reporter and prodr BBC Radio Leeds 1968–71; BBC TV: reporter and presenter Look North Leeds 1971–74, nat news reporter (covering Belfast, Beirut, Iranian Revolution, Ugandan War, Cod War and Rhodesian War) 1974–80, South Africa corr (also covering Argentina during Falklands War) 1980–83, reporter and newscaster (One, Six and Nine O'Clock News) 1983–93, presenter NorthWest Tonight and Great British Quiz (BBC) 1993–95, newscaster BBC World TV 1995–, newscaster BBC News 24 1998–2005; *Recreations* sailing, theatre, walking, restaurants; *Style*— Philip Hayton, Esq; ✉ e-mail hayton@talk21.com

HAYWARD, Sir Jack Arnold; kt (1986), OBE (1968); s of late Sir Charles Hayward, CBE, and Hilda, *née* Arnold; *b* 14 June 1923; *Educ* Stowe; *m* 1948, Jean Mary, *née* Forder; 2 s, 1 da; *Career* RAF 1941–46 (flying trg in Florida, active service pilot in SE Asia, demobilized as Flt Lt); served South Africa Branch Rotary Hoes Ltd until 1950 (joined 1947), fndr USA ops Firth Cleveland gp of cos 1951, joined Grand Bahama Port Authority Ltd 1956, chm Grand Bahama Development Co Ltd and Freeport Commercial and Industrial Ltd 1976–; chm Wolverhampton Wanderers FC until 2003; pres: Lundy Field Soc, Wolverhampton Wanderers FC; vice-pres: SS Great Britain Project, Wildfowl and Wetlands Tst; hon life vice pres Maritime Tst 1971, Paul Harris fell (Rotary) 1983; Hon LLD Exeter 1971; Hon DBA Wolverhampton 1994; William Booth award Salvation Army 1987; *Recreations* promoting British endeavours (mainly in sport), watching cricket, amateur dramatics, preserving the British landscape, keeping all things bright, beautiful and British; *Clubs* MCC, Pratt's, RAF, RAC; *Style*— Sir Jack Hayward, OBE; ✉ Seashell Lane, PO Box F-40099, Freeport, Grand Bahama Island, Bahamas (tel 00 1 242 352 5165)

HAYWARD, Prof Jack Ernest Shalom; s of Menachem Hayward (d 1961), of Vancouver, Canada, and Stella, *née* Isaac (d 1959); *Educ* Horsley Hall, LSE (BSc, PhD); *m* 10 Dec 1965, Margaret Joy, da of Harold Clow Glenn (d 1985), of Adelaide, Aust; 1 da (Clare b 1971), 1 s (Alan b 1973); *Career* Nat Serv flying offr RAF 1956–58; asst lectr and lectr Univ of Sheffield 1959–63, lectr and sr lectr Keele Univ 1963–73, sr research fell Nuffield Coll Oxford 1968–69, prof of politics Univ of Hull 1973–92, dir Oxford Univ European Studies Inst and professorial fell St Antony's Coll 1993–98, research prof Univ of Hull 1999–; visiting prof: Univ of Paris III 1979–80, Inst d'Études Politiques Paris 1990–91; vice-pres Political Studies Assoc of the UK 1981– (chm 1975–77, pres 1979–81); Award for Lifetime Achievement in Political Studies 2003; FBA 1990; Chevalier de l'Ordre Nat du Mérite (France) 1980, Chevalier de la Légion d'Honneur (France) 1996; *Books* Private Interests and Public Policy, The Experience of the French Economic and Social Council (1966), The One and Indivisible French Republic (1973), Planning Politics and Public Policy: The British French and Italian Experience (jtly, 1975), Planning in Europe (jtly, 1978), State and Society in Contemporary Europe (jtly, 1979), The Political Science of British Politics (jtly, 1986), The State and the Market Economy: Industrial Patriotism and Economic Intervention in France (1986), Developments in French Politics (jtly, 1990 and 1994), After the French Revolution: Six Critics of Democracy and Nationalism (1991), De Gaulle to Mitterrand (1993), Industrial Enterprise and European Integration (1995), Governing the New Europe (jtly, 1995), The Crisis of Representation in Europe (1995), Elitism, Populism and European Politics (1996), The British Study of Politics in the Twentieth Century (jtly, 1999), Developments in French Politics (jtly, 2001), Governing from the Centre (jtly, 2002), Governing Europe (jtly, 2003), Fragmented France: Two Centuries of Disputed Identity (2007); *Recreations* music, books, walking; *Clubs* Royal Commonwealth Soc; *Style*— Prof Jack Hayward; ✉ Politics Department, University of Hull, Hull HU6 7RX (tel 01482 465903, fax 01482 466208)

H

HAYWARD, Paul; s of Dennis Hayward, and Shirley Hayward; *Educ* Ringmer Comp Sch, Eastbourne Coll of FE, Univ of Bristol (BA); *Children* 1 s (Lewis b 27 Nov 1995), 1 da (Martha b 7 Feb 1999); *Career* journalist; chief reporter Racing Post, racing corr The Independent, chief sports feature writer Daily Telegraph, chief sports writer Daily Telegraph, chief sports writer The Guardian, chief sports writer Daily Telegraph until 2005, columnist Daily Mail 2005–; Sports Cncl Sports Writers' Assoc Br Sports Journalist of the Year 1996, Sky Sports Writer of the Year 1997, 1999 and 2001, Br Press Awards Sports Writer of the Year 2002 and 2003; *Recreations* post-war American fiction, tennis, Brighton and Hove Albion, the South Downs, the National Trust; *Style*— Paul Hayward, Esq

HAYWARD, Peter Allan; s of Peter Hayward (d 1953), and Anne, *née* Jackson (d 1975); *b* 27 March 1932; *Educ* Haileybury, Trinity Coll Cambridge (MA); *m* 13 March 1954, Elizabeth Layton, da of John Layton Smith (d 1976); 1 da (Pandora b 1962); *Career* Nat Serv 2 Lt RA 1952; called to the Bar Lincoln's Inn 1958 (Cassell scholar); practised at Patent Bar 1958–68, lectr UCL 1959–60, fell and tutor in jurisprudence St Peter's Coll Oxford 1968–99 (vice-master 1992–94, emeritus fell 1999–), fndr and first dir Oxford Intellectual Property Research Centre 1990–98; memb: Gen Bd of Faculties Univ of Oxford 1980–85, Holborn BC 1962–66; *Books* Halsbury's Laws of England (3 edn), Trade Marks and Designs (contrib, 1962), Annual Survey of Commonwealth Law (contrib, 1970–73), Reports of Patent Cases (ed, 1970–74), Hayward's Patent Cases 1600–1883 (11 vols, 1988); *Style*— Peter Hayward, Esq; ✉ 52 The Cloisters, Pegasus Grange, White House Road, Oxford OX1 4QQ (tel 01865 248102); St Peter's College, Oxford OX1 2DL

HAYWARD, His Hon Judge Richard Michael; s of George Michael Hayward (d 1993), of Winchelsea, E Sussex, and Esmé Mary Florence, *née* Howard (d 1985); *b* 12 July 1946; *Educ* Highgate Sch, Inns of Court Sch of Law; *m* 1969, Laura Louise, da of E M Buchan; 2 s (Nicholas Richard b 20 Feb 1971, Anthony Pascoe b 17 Oct 1972), 1 da (Emily Alexandra b 23 Sept 1977); *Career* called to the Bar Middle Temple 1969, recorder 1994–96 (asst recorder 1990), circuit judge (SE Circuit) 1996–; *Recreations* golf, painting, gardening, horses; *Clubs* Rye Golf; *Style*— His Hon Judge Hayward; ✉ Lewes Combined Court, High Street, Lewes, East Sussex BN7 1YB

HAYWARD, Robert Antony; OBE (1991); s of late Ralph Hayward, of Eynsham, Oxon, and Mary Patricia, *née* Franklin; *b* 11 March 1949; *Educ* Maidenhead GS, Univ of Rhodesia (BSc); *Career* vice-chm Nat Young Cons 1976–77, cncllr Coventry City Cncl 1976–78, MP (Cons) Kingswood 1983–92; PPS: to under sec of state for Trade and Industry 1985–87, to min for Industry 1986–87, to sec of state for Transport 1987–92; memb Select Ctee on Energy 1983–85, jt sec Back Bench Aviation Ctee 1991–92; co-fndr and jt co-ordinator Gulf Support Gp 1990–91; DG Br Soft Drinks Assoc 1993–99, chief exec Br Beer and Pub Assoc 1999–; chm CBI Trade Assoc Forum 2007–; dir Stonewall 1997–2003; pres Kingscross Steelers RFC 1999–2003; *Recreations* former national level rugby official, psephology; *Style*— Robert Hayward, Esq, OBE; ✉ 11 Grosvenor Park, London SE5 0NQ; British Beer & Pub Association, Market Towers, 1 Nine Elms Lane, London SW8 5NQ (tel 020 7627 9162, fax 020 7627 9179, e-mail rhayward@beerandpub.com, website www.beerandpub.com)

HAYWARD SMITH, His Hon Judge Rodger; QC (1988); s of late Frederick Ernest Smith, and late Heather Hayward, *née* Rodgers, of Ingatestone, Essex; *b* 25 February 1943; *Educ* Brentwood Sch, St Edmund Hall Oxford (MA); *m* 4 Jan 1975, (Gillian) Sheila, *née* Johnson; 1 s (Richard b 1976), 1 da (Jane b 1978); *Career* called to the Bar Gray's Inn 1967, recorder 1986–2002 (asst recorder 1981–86), dep High Ct judge 1990–2002, circuit judge (SE Circuit) 2002–; legal assessor GMC 2000–02; *Publications* Jackson's Matrimonial Finance and Taxation (jt ed, 5, 6 and 7 edns); author of various articles on family law; *Style*— His Hon Judge Hayward Smith, QC; ✉ Chelmsford Crown Court, New Street, Chelmsford, Essex CM1 1EL

HAYWOOD, Sir Harold; KCVO (1988), OBE (1974), DL (1983); s of Harold Haywood (d 1988), of Burton-on-Trent, Staffs, and Lillian, *née* Barratt (d 1929); *b* 30 September 1923; *Educ* Guild Sch Burton-on-Trent, Westhill Coll Birmingham, Ecumenical Inst Geneva; *m* Jan 1944, Amy, da of Charles William Richardson (d 1955), of Burton-on-Trent, Staffs; 3 s; *Career* RN 1943, med discharge; organiser St John's Clubland Sheffield 1948–51, lectr Westhill Coll of Educn 1951–53, regnl organiser Methodist Youth Dept Birmingham and vice-pres Methodist Assoc of Youth Clubs 1954–55, nat tutor King George VI leadership course 1955–57, educn offr Nat Assoc of Mixed Clubs and Girls' Clubs 1957–77, dir of trg Nat Assoc of Youth Clubs 1966–74, gen sec Educn Interchange Cncl 1974–78, dir Royal Jubilee and Prince's Tsts 1978–88, nat chm YMCA 1989–92 (vice-pres 1992–); visiting fell Inst of Technol Melbourne 1987; vice-chm Br Nat Ctee World Assembly of Youth 1964–66, chm Gen and Liberal Studies Dept Dacorum Coll of Further Educn 1965–69 (also vice-chm of govrs), memb Univ of Leeds Inst of Educn res project on Carnegie Community Sch 1966–74, external examiner Roehampton Inst and Rolle and St Luke's Colls Univ of Exeter 1969–74, memb Cresset Neighbourhood Mgmnt Bd 1971–74, gen sec Educational Interchange Cncl and memb Advsy Ctee on Exchange Br

Cncl 1974–78, memb Bd Anglo Austrian Soc 1974–81, govr Bell Educational Tst Cambridge until 1990; memb: Home Sec's Advsy Cncl on the Misuse of Drugs 1970–75, Sec of State for Educn's Nat Advsy Cncl for the Youth Serv 1985–88, Bd Nat Youth Theatre 1987–90, BBC Gen Advsy Cncl 1988–93; chm BBC IBA Central Appeals Advsy Ctee 1988–93, vice-pres Cwlth Youth Exchange Cncl 1988–, tstee and chm Advsy Cncl Charities Aid Fndn 1989–97, tstee Children in Need Tst 1989–93; chm: Assoc of Charitable Fndns 1989–93, The Help Tst 1992–96, Action Aid 1994–96; pres Kids Int UK 1995–, vice-pres Derbyshire Community Fndn 1996–, patron Univ of Derby Multi-Faith Project 1999–; pres Oakwood Branch Royal Br Legion 1999–; FRSA 1985; *Books* A Role for Voluntary Work (1970), Partnership with the Young (1979); *Recreations* the garden, books; *Clubs* Athenaeum, Civil Service; *Style*— Sir Harold Haywood, KCVO, OBE, DL

HAYWOOD, HE Nigel Robert; CVO (2006); s of Leslie Haywood (d 1965), and Peggy, *née* Webb; *b* 17 March 1955, Betchworth, Surrey; *Educ* Truro Sch, New Coll Oxford (MA, MPhil); *m* 1979, (Mary) Louise, da of Robert Smith (d 2007), of Whimple, Devon; 3 s (Christopher b 1984, Thomas b 1985, Peter b 1991); *Career* Lt RAEC 1977–80; entered HM Dip Serv 1983, second later first sec Budapest 1985–89, FCO 1989–92, dep consul-gen Johannesburg 1992–96, cnsllr and dep head of delgn UK Delgn to OSCE Vienna 1996–2000, FCO 2000–03, ambass to Estonia 2003–07; hon pres Golden Scale Club 2002– (memb 1983–); Bard of the Cornish Gorseth 1977; memb Philological Soc 1981; MIL 1988; *Publications* The One That Got Away (contrib, 1991); various articles in the angling press; *Recreations* fishing (especially saltwater fly fishing), running; *Clubs* Oxford and Cambridge, Falmouth Sports; *Style*— HE Mr Nigel Haywood, CVO; ✉ c/o Foreign & Commonwealth Office (Tallinn), King Charles Street, London SW1A 2AH (e-mail nigelhaywood@hot.ee)

HAYWOOD, Roger; s of Maj George Haywood, of Norwich, and Ethel Florence, *née* Reynolds; *b* 24 July 1939; *Educ* Westcliff Sch; *m* 30 June 1962, Sandra Leonora, da of George Yenson (d 1972); 2 da (Sarah b 1963, Laura b 1971), 2 s (Ian b 1965, Mark b 1966); *Career* mktg positions with Dunlop, Dexion and in various advertising agencies, Euro PR mangr Air Products 1970–72; md: Haywood Hood & Associates Ltd 1972–75, Tibbenham Group 1975–82; chm: Roger Haywood Associates Ltd 1982–92, Worldcom Inc 1989–91, Kestrel Communications Ltd 1992–2001; chief exec Issues Analysis Ltd 2001–; pres Inst of PR 1991; chm: Chartered Inst of Mktg 1992, Worldcom Europe 1997–98, PR Standards Cncl 1998–; vice-chm PR Conslts Assoc 1982–92; Freeman City of London, memb Worshipful Co of Marketers; FCIM, ABC, FCAM, FIPR, FRSA; *Books* All About Public Relations (1985, 3 edn 1994), Managing Your Reputation (1994), Public Relations for Marketing Professionals (1997); *Recreations* economics, the media, motoring, music, politics and sport; *Clubs* Reform, Capital; *Style*— Roger Haywood, Esq; ✉ 34 The Cloisters, Folgate Street, London E1 6EB (tel and fax 020 7247 4670); Barron Lodge Farm, Happisburgh, Norfolk NR12 0QZ (tel 01692 651494, fax 01692 651573); Issues analysis Ltd, 24 Lime Street, London EC3M 7HR (tel 020 7648 8600, fax 020 7648 8601, e-mail r.haywood@issuesanalysis.com)

HAYWOOD, Timothy Paul (Tim); s of Ron Haywood, of Walsall, West Midlands, and Marilyn, *née* Farmer; *b* 2 June 1963, Walsall, West Midlands; *Educ* Queen Mary's GS Walsall, St Edmund Hall Oxford (MA); *m* 7 June 1986, Bev, *née* Bird; 1 s (Chris b 8 Sept 1990), 1 da (Katie b 9 April 1992); *Career* Arthur Andersen & Co 1985–91, Williams Holdings 1991–97 (finance dir of subsids Larch Lap and Swish), chief financial offr Hagemeyer UK Ltd 1997–2003, finance dir St Modwen Properties plc 2003–; treas and tstee Areley Kings Village Hall 1999–2005; FCA; *Recreations* rowing, gardening; *Clubs* Stourport Boat; *Style*— Tim Haywood, Esq; ✉ St Modwen Properties plc, 7 Ridgeway, Quinton Business Park, Birmingham B32 1AF (tel 0121 222 9400, e-mail thaywood@stmodwen.co.uk)

HAZEEL, Francis Ida McCulloch; s of late Capt Harry Hazeel, of Dunoon, Argyllshire, and late Eliane, *née* Parascou, of Chelsea; *b* 13 February 1945; *Educ* George Watson's Coll Edinburgh, King's Sch Canterbury, Pembroke Coll Oxford (Cleobury scholar); *m* 1985, Carolyn Robin, da of late Hon Robin Warrender; 2 s (Jamie, Geordie); *Career* successively asst mangr Charterhouse Japhet, mangr Spencer Thornton Brussels, mangr corp fin and export credits Nordic Bank, mangr property and project fin Banque Indosuez London, gen mangr Aareal Bank (formerly DePfa Bank) London branch 1993–2004; pres Assoc of Property Bankers 1994–95; former chm Export Credits Ctee Foreign Banks Assoc; dir Thistle II Ltd; dir Asset & Infrastructure Mgmnt Solutions Ltd (AIMS), dir Wolsey Residential Finance plc; govr, sr fell and visiting prof De Montfort Univ Leicester 1997–2004; memb: Advsy Bd Royal Acad of Arts Tst 1986–98, Sadlers Wells Appeal Ctee, Keats-Shelley Memorial Assoc Devpt Gp; tstee: Public Arts Devpt Tst, Our Right to Read 2005–07, Guild of Educators Tst Fund, Friends of Round Square UK; Freeman Guild of Educators; Knight Order of St Maurice and St Lazarus; *Recreations* art, opera, architecture; *Style*— Francis Hazeel, Esq; ✉ AIMS, Epic House, 4 Barling Way, Nuneaton CV10 7RH (tel 024 7679 6900, mobile 07770 466109, e-mail fh@aimsltd.co.uk)

HAZELL, Peter Frank; s of Frank Henry Hazell (d 1977), and Kathleen, *née* Rowland; *b* 4 August 1948, Kent; *Educ* Hertford Coll Oxford (MA, MPhil); *m* 11 Aug 1972, Maureen Pamela, *née* Church; 1 da (Lucy Alexandra b 11 April 1979), 1 s (Rupert Peter James b 4 Sept 1983); *Career* econs asst Home Office 1971–72; Deloitte Haskins & Sells: conslt, mangr then ptnr Mgmnt Consultancy Div and memb Mgmnt Ctee 1972–85, nat corp fin ptnr 1985–89; Coopers & Lybrand (following merger): ptnr 1989–91, seconded as business strategy dir Nat Grid Co 1991–92, memb Partnership Bd 1992–98, head of ops London Central 1992–94, managing ptnr London office 1994–96, memb Mgmnt Ctee 1994–98, managing ptnr HR 1996–98, managing ptnr audit practice 1996–98; UK managing ptnr PricewaterhouseCoopers (following merger) 1998–2000, chm Argent Gp plc 2001–; non-exec dir: UK Coal plc 2003–, Smith & Williamson Holdings 2004–, BRIT Insur Holdings plc 2004–; memb Competition Cmmn 2002–, memb Cncl and chm Audit Ctee NERC 2004–; *Recreations* opera, ballet, theatre, cinema, hill walking, all sports (especially cricket and rugby), reading; *Clubs* MCC; *Style*— Peter Hazell, Esq; ✉ Argent Group plc, 5 Albany Courtyard, Piccadilly, London W1V 9RB

HAZELL, Prof Robert John Davidge; CBE (2006); s of Peter Hazell, of Cheltenham, Glos, and Elizabeth Complin, *née* Fowler; *b* 30 April 1948; *Educ* Eton, Wadham Coll Oxford (MA); *m* 27 June 1981, Alison Sophia Mordaunt, da of Arthur Hubert Mordaunt Richards (d 1982); 2 s (Alexander Robert Mordaunt b 5 May 1982, Jonathan William Joshua b 4 Jan 1985); *Career* barr 1973–75; numerous depts of Home Office 1975–89, Nuffield and Leverhulme travelling fellowship to study freedom of info in Aust, Canada and NZ 1986–87, dir Nuffield Fndn 1989–95, dir Constitution Unit UCL 1995–, prof of govt and the constitution UCL 1998–; magistrate 1978–96; vice-chm Assoc of Charitable Fndns 1990–92; tstee Citizenship Fndn 1991–2000; vice-chm Ind Cmmn to Review Britain's Experience of PR 2002–03; memb: Cncl JUSTICE 1995, Cncl Hansard Soc 1997 (vice-chm Cmmn on Scrutiny Role of Parliament 2000–01); FRSA 1991; *Books* Conspiracy and Civil Liberties (1974), The Bar on Trial (1978), Constitutional Futures (1999), The State and the Nations: the first year of devolution in the United Kingdom (ed, 2000), The State and the Nations: the third year of devolution in the United Kingdom (ed, 2003), Devolution, Law Making and the Constitution (ed, 2005), The English Question (ed, 2006); *Recreations* opera, badgers, bird watching, canoeing; *Style*— Prof Robert Hazell, CBE; ✉ 94 Constantine Road, London NW3 2LS (tel 020 7267 4881); Constitution Unit, School of Public Policy, University College London, 29 Tavistock Square, London WC1H 9QU (tel 020 7679 4977, fax 020 7679 4978, e-mail constitution@ucl.ac.uk)

HAZLEHURST, Dr (George) Cameron Lee; s of George Henry Hazlehurst (d 1985), and Eileen Leonie, *née* Carmody (d 2001); *b* 12 October 1941, Harrogate, N Yorks; *Educ* Footscray HS, Melbourne HS, Univ of Melbourne (BA), Balliol Coll and Nuffield Coll Oxford (DPhil); *m* 2, 7 May 1983, Dr Kayleen M Hazlehurst, *née* Morrison; 3 c from previous m (David b 1969, Peter b 1972, Jane b 1974); *Career* jr research fell Nuffield Coll Oxford 1968–70, The Queen's Coll Oxford 1970–72, sr fell Research Sch of Social Sciences ANU 1988–92 (fell 1972–88), fndn prof and head Sch of Humanities Queensland Univ of Technol 1992–97, adjunct prof of govt Hawke Inst Univ of South Australia 2002–05, adjunct prof Humanities Research Centre ANU 2006–; asst sec Dept of Urban and Regnl Devpt 1973–75, first asst sec Dept of Communications 1984–86, nat campaign dir AIDS Educn and Info 1988–89, chm NSW Pesticides Implementation Ctee 2000–04, memb NSW Radiation Advsy Cncl 2005–; md Flaxton Mill House 1997–; FRHistS 1971, FRSL 1973; *Publications* Politicians at War (1971), Menzies Observed (1979), Gordon Chalk (1987), A Liberal Chronicle (ed with Christine Woodland, 1995), A Guide to the Papers of British Cabinet Ministers 1900–1964 (with Sally Whitehead and Christine Woodland, 1996), Gangs & Youth Subcultures (ed with Kayleen Hazlehurst, 1998), Public Sector Ethics Resource Series (CD-ROMs, with Howard Whitton, 1999); *Recreations* watching television, cricket, soccer; *Clubs* Univ House (Canberra); *Style*— Dr Cameron Hazlehurst; ✉ PO Box 60, Mapleton, Queensland 4560, Australia (tel 00 61 7 5445 7708, e-mail cameron.hazlehurst@gmail.com)

HAZLEMAN, Dr Brian Leslie; s of Eric Edward Hazleman (d 1981), of Reading, Berks, and Gladys Marjorie, *née* Wells; *b* 4 March 1942; *Educ* Leighton Park Sch, London Hosp Univ of London (MB BS), Univ of Cambridge (MA); *m* 29 Jan 1972, Ruth Margaret, da of Douglas Eynon, of Bristol; 3 da (Anna b 1973, Christina b 1976, Sarah b 1983); *Career* London Hosp 1966–71: house physician and surgn 1966–67, registrar rheumatology 1968–69, registrar med 1969–71; sr registrar med and rheumatology: Radcliffe Infirmary Oxford 1971–73, Nuffield Orthopaedic Hosp 1971–73; conslt physician: Addenbrooke's Hosp Cambridge 1973–, Newmarket Hosp 1973–; hon conslt Strangeways Res Laboratory Cambridge 1973–94, dir Rheumatology Res Unit Cambridge 1975–, assoc lectr Univ of Cambridge 1975– (fell Corpus Christi Coll 1982–); pres Br Soc for Rheumatology 1998–2001 (memb Cncl 1995–98); civilian advsr to the Army on Rheumatology 2000–; memb Editorial Bd: Jl of Orthopaedic Rheumatology, Jl of Inflammo Pharmacology; Begley prize RCS 1965, Margaret Holyrode prize Heberden Soc 1975; Heberden Roundsman Br Soc for Rheumathology 1993; FRCP 1980; *Books* The Sclera and Systemic Disorders (1976, 2 edn 2004), Rheumatoid Arthritis Pathology and Pharmacology (1976), The Shoulder Joint (1989), Polymyalgia Rheumatica and Giant Cell Arteritis (1992), Rheumatology Examination and Injection Techniques (1992, 2 edn 1998), Soft Tissue Rheumatology (2004); author of over 300 scientific articles, reviews and chapters; *Recreations* sailing, photography, golf; *Clubs* Aldeburgh Yacht, Aldeburgh Golf; *Style*— Dr Brian L Hazleman; ✉ Church End House, Weston Colville, Cambridgeshire CB1 5PE (tel 01223 290 543); Department of Rheumatology, Addenbrooke's Hospital, Hills Road, Cambridge (tel 01223 217457, fax 01223 217838, e-mail brian.hazleman@addenbrookes.nhs.uk)

HAZLERIGG, 3 Baron (UK 1945); Sir Arthur Grey Hazlerigg; 15 Bt (E 1622); s of 2 Baron (d 2002); *b* 5 May 1951; *m* 1, 1986 (m dis 1998), Laura, eld da of Sir William Dugdale, 2 Bt; 1 s (Hon (Arthur) William Grey b 13 May 1987), 3 da (Hon Eliza Patricia, Hon Amelia Frances (twins) b 1989, Hon Viola Camilla Alice b 1 July 1993); m 2, 1999, Mrs Shan Chichester, *née* McIndoe; *Heir* s, Hon (Arthur) William Hazlerigg; *Clubs* Leicester Tigers Old Players, MCC; *Style*— The Rt Hon the Lord Hazlerigg; ✉ Noseley Hall, Billesdon, Leicestershire LE7 9EH (tel 01162 596606, fax 01142 596 989, e-mail arthur@noseley.demon.co.uk)

HAZLEWOOD, Gerald Alan (Gerry); OBE (1986); s of Richard Hazlewood, of Okanagan Centre, BC, Canada, and Lilian May, *née* Lofts; *b* 25 July 1939; *Educ* Royal GS High Wycombe; *m* 6 Sept 1961, Toni Gay, da of Sqdn Ldr Edward John Lisle, of Mundaring, Western Australia; 2 da (Christina b 1967, Helen b 1965), 1 s (Daniel b 1979); *Career* chm: Westwood Engineering Ltd 1986–90 (dir 1967–86), Westwood Automation Ltd 1990–; *Recreations* golf; *Style*— Gerry Hazlewood, Esq, OBE

HAZOU, Kyra K; *née* Kreshik; *b* 13 December 1956; *Career* md and European gen counsel Salomon Bros 1985–99, md and EMEA regnl gen counsel Salomon Smith Barney/Citibank 1999–2000; non-exec dir FSA 2001–07; *Style*— Mrs Kyra Hazou

HAZZARD, Charles Walker; s of Frank Hazzard, of Droitwich, and Margaret, *née* Harris (d 1980); *Educ* Bournville Sch of Art and Design, Glos Coll of Arts and Technol (BA), Sir Henry Doulton Sch of Sculpture 1988–90, London Art Sch (postgrad higher dip); *Career* sculptor; Bro Art Workers Guild 1996–, memb Art and Architecture Soc 1998–; Grants for Individuals Award Arts Cncl 2003 and 2007, Wellcome Tst People Award 2005, Emley Fndn Art Award 2007; fell Henry Moore Fndn (sponsored fell in sculpture at Loughbrough Univ Sch of Art and Design) 1996–99, FRBS 1998 (ARBS 1992–98, memb Cncl 1994–97); *Selected Exhibitions* The London Gp Barbican London 1992, Whitechapel Open Atlantis Gall London 1994, Royal West of England Acad Autumn Show 1994, Royal West of England Acad 2nd Sculpture 1996, Loughborough Univ 1999, Woodlands Art Gall London 1999, touring solo exhbn 2001–; selected commissions incl: portraits, wooden assemblies; *Style*— Charles Hazzard, Esq; ✉ 6 Clydesdale Road, Droitwich, Worcestershire WR9 7SA (e-mail c.w.hazzard@charleswalkerhazzard.com, website www.charleswalkerhazzard.com)

HAZZARD, (Lawrence) Gordon; s of Frederick Hazzard, and Minnie Hazzard; *b* 1925; *Educ* Waverley GS Birmingham; *m* 1, 1956 (m dis), Margery Elizabeth Charles; 1 da (Clare); m 2, 1985 (m dis), Miyuki Sedohara; *Career* served WWII, RAF 1943–47; gp md MK Electric Holdings until 1980; dep chm then chm Grosvenor Gp plc 1981–86; chm: Gordon Hazzard Ltd Business Advsrs 1980–2005, Wigfalls plc 1981–88, HB Electronic Components plc 1983–85, Toby Lane Ltd 1984–89, Waingate Insurance Ltd 1985–88, Green Park Health Care plc 1989–94, Opera Hldgs Ltd 1992–2004, Fleet International plc 1994–99, Fleet Electronics 1996–99, DataNet Gp plc 2000–; former: pres London Handel Festival, dep pres Br Electric and Allied Mfrs Assoc, vice-chm EIEMA, memb Cncl and Industrial Policy Ctee CBI, memb Bd ASTA; memb Japan-Br Soc of Hiroshima; CIMgt, FInstD; *Recreations* music; *Clubs* Annabel's, George; *Style*— Gordon Hazzard, Esq; ✉ 5 Balfour Place, Mayfair, London W1K 2AU (tel 020 7408 0626, e-mail hazzard@btclick.com)

HB, Sarah (*née* Sarah HB Mastronardi); da of Giovanni Mastronardi, and Susan, *née* Hill; *Educ* The Study Wimbledon, Chelsea Art Sch; *Children* 2 s (Harry Wingate b 26 Oct 1998, Archie Wingate b 24 Jan 2003); *Career* DJ; runner Thames News 1985–87, ed Avatar Films 1987–88, ed Worldwide Pictures 1988–90; DJ: Kiss FM 1990–98, Galaxy 1998–99, BBC Radio 1 1999–; columnist Blues and Soul magazine 1992–95; *Recreations* music, art, walking, travel, horses, gardening, festivals, cars; *Style*— Ms Sarah HB; ✉ c/o Guy Wingate, Paradise Productions Ltd, PO Box 999, London NW3 1SQ (tel and fax 020 7435 4444)

HEAD, His Hon Judge John Philip Trevelyan; s of Walter Raleigh Trevelyan Head (d 1996), and Rosemary Constance Beatrice, *née* Borwick; *b* 6 July 1953, Bombay; *Educ* Marlborough, Merton Coll Oxford (MA, Hockey blue), Univ of Virginia (LLM, Fulbright scholar, univ grad fell); *m* 26 March 1983, Erica Lesley, *née* Cox; 1 da (Eleanor Beatrice b 29 Sept 1985), 1 s (Lawrence James Trevelyan b 31 July 1989); *Career* called to the Bar Middle Temple 1976; recorder 2000–04 (asst recorder 1996–2000), circuit judge 2004–; memb Hon Artillery Co 1978–85; *Recreations* travel, books; *Clubs* Saville, Sette of Odd

Volumes; *Style*— His Hon Judge Head; ✉ The Crown Court, 90 Wellington Street, Leicester LE1 6HG

HEAD, Peter; OBE (1998); s of Robert Cyril Head (d 1974), and Vera Alice, *née* Kent; *b* 27 February 1947; *Educ* Tiffin Sch Kingston upon Thames, Imperial Coll London (BSc); *m* 1970, Susan, da of Edmund East; 1 s (Andre *b* 3 Feb 1975), 1 da (Melody *b* 30 Oct 1976); *Career* engr: Geo Wimpey & Co 1965–66, Freeman Fox & Partners 1969–80; Maunsell Group: sr engr 1980–84, assoc 1985–89, tech dir 1989–93, dir 1993–95, md 1995–97, chief exec 1997–2001; also dir Maunsell Structural Plastics Ltd 1983–97; corp devpt dir FaberMaunsell / AECOM 2001–04, dir ARUP 2004–; maj projects incl: Avonmouth Bridge Bristol 1970–74, Friarton Bridge Perth 1975–78, Myton Bridge Hull 1973–79, Second Severn Crossing 1984–96, Aberfeldy Bridge (world's first major advanced composite bridge) 1992, Kap Shui Mun Bridge Hong Kong 1993–97, Bonds Mill Bridge (world's first advanced composite road bridge) 1994, Rion-Antiron Bridge Greece 1998–2004, Tsing Lung Bridge Hong Kong 2000–03, Dongtan Eco-city Shanghai 2005–; inventor of the advanced composite construction system and the SPACES bridge concept; cmmr GLA Sustainable Devpt Cmmn 2003–, ICE Waste Mgmnt Bd 2003–, chm SCI 2003–06; author and deliverer of numerous papers UK and overseas; FICE 1977, FIHT 1981, FIStructE 1983, FREng 1996, FCGI 2001, FRSA 2006; *Awards* John Howard Structural Challenge Award SE ICE 1984, Gold Medal BPF Congress 1986 and 1990, Premier Gold Award Plastics and Rubber Weekly Awards for Excellence in Design 1993, Personal Award for Best Presentation and Best Paper Euro Pultrusion Technol Assoc 1994, Royal Acad of Engrg Silver Medal for Outstanding Contrib to Br Engrg 1995, Prince Philip Award for Polymers in the Serv of Mankind 1996, Coopers Hill Meml Prize ICE 1997, laureate IABSE Award of Merit for Outstanding Contrib to Structural Engrg 1998 (first Br engr to receive honour since 1979), Telford Medal ICE 2005; *Recreations* gardening, painting, hill walking; *Style*— Peter Head, Esq, OBE, FREng; ✉ ARUP, 13 Fitzroy Street, London W1T 4BQ (tel 020 7755 4121, fax 020 7755 4008, e-mail peter.head@arup.com)

HEAD, 2 Viscount (UK 1960); Richard Antony Head; s of 1 Viscount Head, GCMG, CBE, MC, PC (d 1983), and Lady Dorothea Louise (d 1987), da of 9 Earl of Shaftesbury, KP, PC, GCVO, CBE; *b* 27 February 1937; *Educ* Eton, RMA Sandhurst; *m* 1974, Alicia Brigid, da of Julian John William Salmond, of Tetbury, Glos; 2 s (Hon Henry Julian *b* 30 March 1980, Hon George Richard *b* 20 July 1982), 1 da (Hon Sarah Georgiana *b* 26 Nov 1984); *Heir* s, Hon Henry Head; *Career* served The Life Guards 1957–66, ret Capt; trainer of racehorses 1968–83; farmer; *Recreations* shooting, golf; *Clubs* White's; *Style*— The Rt Hon the Viscount Head; ✉ Throope Manor, Bishopstone, Salisbury, Wiltshire SP5 4BA (tel 01722 718318)

HEAD, Sarah Daphne (Sally); da of Richard George Head, of Helston, Cornwall, and Daphne Grace, *née* Henderson; *b* 20 February 1951; *Educ* Ancaster House Sussex, St Maurs Convent Weybridge; *m* 25 Sept 1975 (m dis 1987), Francis Vincent Keating, s of Bryan Keating; *Career* Sally Head Poetry Corner Radio London 1969, story ed of Warner Bros (Europe) 1972–75, script ed BBC and Thames TV 1976–84; prodr BBC Drama 1984–88: First Born, Marksman, Life and Loves of a She Devil, Breaking Up, The Detective, Inside Out; head then controller of drama Granada TV 1988–95 (credits incl Prime Suspect, Cracker and Band of Gold), controller of drama London Weekend Television 1995–97 (credits incl Jane Eyre and Tess of D'Urbervilles); fndr Sally Head Productions 1997– (prodr Four Fathers, Plastic Man, The Cry, The Mayor of Casterbridge, Tipping the Velvet, Fingersmith); *Recreations* gardening sailing, theatre, pubs, ceramic painting; *Clubs* Helford River Sailing, Strand-on-the-Green Sailing; *Style*— Miss Sally Head; ✉ The Dutch House, 60 Strand-on-the-Green, Chiswick, London W4 3PE (tel 020 8994 8650); Sally Head Productions Ltd, Twickenham Film Studios, The Barons, St Margarets Twickenham, Middlesex TW1 2AW (tel 020 8607 8730, fax 020 8607 8964, e-mail sally@shpl.demon.co.uk)

HEADFORT, 7 Marquess of (I 1800); Sir Thomas Michael Ronald Christopher Taylour; 10 Bt (I 1704); also Baron Headfort (I 1760), Viscount Headfort (I 1762), Earl of Bective (I 1766), and Baron Kenlis (UK 1831, which sits as); s of 6 Marquess of Headfort (d 2005); *b* 10 February 1959; *Educ* Harrow, RAC Cirencester; *m* 17 Oct 1987, Susan Jane, da of Charles Anthony Vandervell (d 1987), of Burnham, Bucks; 2 s (Thomas Rupert Charles Christopher, Earl of Bective *b* 18 June 1989, Hon Henry James Anthony Christopher *b* 18 April 1991), 2 da (Lady Natasha Jane Rosanagh *b* 6 May 1997, Lady Alexandra Susan Katherine *b* 8 June 1998); *Heir* s, Earl of Bective; *Career* co-dir Bective Leslie Marsh Ltd (formerly Bective Davidson Ltd Independent Property Conslts); *Style*— The Most Hon the Marquess of Headfort; ✉ Bective Leslie Marsh Ltd, One Cadogan Street, London SW3 2PP (tel 020 7589 6677, fax 020 7589 9692)

HEAL, Prof (Barbara) Jane; da of William Calvert Kneale, and Martha Hurst; *Educ* Oxford HS for Girls, New Hall Cambridge (BA), Newnham Coll Cambridge (MA, PhD); *Career* Sarah Smithson Res Fell Newnham Coll Cambridge 1971–74; Harkness Fell Cwlth Fund of NY, visiting fell Princeton Univ and Univ of Calif Berkeley 1974–76; lectr in philosophy Univ of Newcastle upon Tyne 1976–86; Univ of Cambridge: asst lectr 1986, lectr 1991, reader 1996, prof of philosophy 1999, fell St John's Coll 1986, pres St John's Coll 1999–2003; FBA 1997; *Books* Fact and Meaning (1989), Mind, Reason and Imagination (2003); *Style*— Prof Jane Heal; ✉ St John's College, Cambridge CB2 1TP (tel 01223 338668, fax 01223 337720, e-mail bjh1000@cam.ac.uk)

HEAL, Jeremy Philip Winteringham; s of Philip William Dunstan Heal (d 1997), and Elizabeth, *née* Winteringham (d 1995); *b* 18 September 1942; *Educ* Marlborough (scholar), Queens' Coll Cambridge (MA, LLM), Coll of Law; *m* 22 Oct 1971, Joanna Sylvia, *née* Bromley-Martin; 3 da (Robin Mary, Charlotte Mary, Bibi Doyle), 1 s (Dominic Philip); *Career* business mangr Cambridge Footlights 1963–64; admitted slr 1967; slr specialising in tax, tsts, estate planning, private client, agric and devpt; ptnr: E Edwards Son and Noice 1969–70, Turner Martin and Symes (later Eversheds) 1970–88, Howes Percival 1988– (currently head Property and Estates); author of articles in pubns incl: Taxation, Farmers Weekly, Private Client Business; tstee Mrs L D Rope Third Charitable Settlement 1986–; memb: Law Soc 1987, Soc of Tst and Estate Practitioners (chm Norfolk and Norwich branch), Agricultural Law Assoc, Royal Norfolk Agicultural Assoc, Country Land and Business Assoc; ACIArb; *Recreations* music, sailing, gliding, playing tenor saxophone; *Clubs* Eastern Opera (chm); *Style*— Jeremy Heal, Esq; ✉ Pearces Farm, Blo Norton Road, South Lopham, Diss, Norfolk IP22 2HT (tel 01379 687311, fax 01379 687445, e-mail jeremyheal@aol.com); Howes Percival, The Guildyard, 51 Colegate, Norwich NR3 1DD (tel 01603 762103, fax 01603 766212, e-mail jeremy.heal@howespercival.com)

HEAL, Sylvia Lloyd; JP (Surrey 1973), MP; da of John Lloyd Fox (d 1974), of Ewloe, N Wales, and Ruby, *née* Hughes (d 2005); *b* 20 July 1942; *Educ* Elfed Secdy Modern, Coleg Harlech, UC Wales Swansea (BSc); *m* 1965, Keith Heal, s of Cecil Heal; 1 da (Joanne Siân Lloyd *b* 14 Sept 1970), 1 s (Gareth Aneurin *b* 12 Aug 1973); *Career* med records clerk Chester Royal Infirmary 1957–63; social worker: Dept of Employment 1968–70, Health Serv and Dept of Employment 1983–90; MP (Lab): Staffs Mid 1990–92, Halesowen and Rowley Regis 1997–; memb Select Ctee on Educn and Sci 1990–91, Lab spokesperson on health and women's issues 1991–92, PPS to sec of state for Defence 1997–2000, dep speaker and first dep chm Ways and Means 2000–, memb Parly Ctee 1997–2000; worker Young Carers Devpt Carers Nat Assoc 1992–97; memb: Cncl Advtg Standards Authy 1992–97, GMB, UK Delegation to NATO Parly Assoc 1997–2000, ACTSA (Anti Apartheid Soc); fell Univ of Wales; *Recreations* walking, male voice choirs, theatres;

Style— Mrs Sylvia Heal, MP; ✉ House of Commons, London SW1A 0AA (tel 020 7219 3000)

HEALD, Oliver; MP; s of John Anthony Heald (d 2000), of Dore, and Joyce, *née* Pemberton; *b* 15 December 1954; *Educ* Reading Sch, Pembroke Coll Cambridge (MA); *m* 18 Aug 1979, Christine Janice, da of Eric Arthur Whittle (d 1980), of Eastbourne; 2 da (Sarah *b* 1985, Victoria *b* 1989), 1 s (William *b* 1987); *Career* called to the Bar Middle Temple 1977, practised SE Circuit; MP (Cons): Herts N 1992–97, Herts NE 1997–; PPS: to Rt Hon Sir Peter Lloyd, MP 1994, to Rt Hon William Waldegrave, MP 1994–95; Parly under-sec of state DSS 1995–97; oppn whip 1997–2000, shadow police min 2000–01, oppn frontbench spokesman on health 2001–02, shadow min for work and pensions 2002–03, shadow ldr of the House of Commons 2003–05, shadow sec of state for constitutional affrs 2004–, shadow chllr of the Duchy of Lancaster 2005–; memb: Employment Select Ctee 1992–94, Admin Select Ctee 1998–2000, Modernisation Ctee 2003–05; vice-chm Backbench Employment Ctee 1992–94; sponsor Private Members Bill Insurance Companies (Reserves) Act 1995; patron Southwark and Bermondsey Cons Assoc; *Recreations* travel, gardening, sports; *Style*— Oliver Heald, Esq, MP; ✉ House of Commons, London SW1A 0AA

HEALD, Prof Richard John; OBE (1998); s of late John Eric Heald, and late Muriel Heald; *b* 11 May 1936; *Educ* Berkhamsted Sch, Gonville & Caius Coll Cambridge, Guy's Hosp Med Sch (MA, MB MChir); *Children* 3 da (Sara, Lucy, Anna); *Career* ships surgn Union Castle Line; conslt surgn Basingstoke Dist Hosp, currently prof of surgery North Hampshire Hosp and surgical dir Pelican Cancer Fndn; author of books and papers on surgery of rectal cancer; former vice-pres RCS, pres Sections of Surgery and Coloproctology RSM, pres Assoc of Coloproctology of GB; Hon DUniv Linköping Sweden, hon prof Univ of Leiden Holland, hon prof Univ of Belgrade; FRCS, FRCSEd, Hon FRSM; hon fell Surgical Assocs of: Austria, France, Germany, Sweden, Switzerland; *Recreations* sailing; *Style*— Prof Richard Heald, OBE

HEALD, Timothy Villiers; s of Col Villiers Archer John Heald, CVO, DSO, MBE, MC (d 1972), of Wilts, and Catherine Eleanor Jean, *née* Vaughan; *b* 28 January 1944; *Educ* Sherborne, Balliol Coll Oxford (MA); *m* 1, 1968 (m dis 1999), Alison Martina, da of Norman Alexander Leslie, of Bucks; 2 da (Emma *b* 1970, Lucy *b* 1973), 2 s (Alexander *b* 1971, Tristram *b* 1977); *m* 2, Penelope, *née* Byrne; *Career* author; contrib to various newspapers and magazines, writer Atticus Column Sunday Times 1965–67; features ed: Town Magazine 1967, Daily Express 1967–72; assoc ed Weekend Magazine Toronto 1977–78, thriller reviewer The Times 1983–89, Pendennis (The Observer) 1990; visiting fell: Jane Franklin Hall Univ of Tasmania 1997 and 1999, St John's Coll Univ of Sydney 2007; guest speaker QE2 1998–, writer in residence Univ of South Aust 2001; founding pres Real Tennis Club of Cornwall; FRSL 2000; *Books* Simon Bognor Mystery Novels (1973–, televised by Thames TV), Networks (1983), Class Distinctions (1984), Red Herrings (1985), The Character of Cricket (1986), Brought to Book (1988), The Newest London Spy (ed, 1988), The Rigby File (ed, 1989), Business Unusual (1989), 150 Years of The Royal Warrant and Its Holders (by appt, 1989), My Lord's (ed, 1990), A Classic English Crime (ed, 1990), The Duke: A Portrait of Prince Philip (1991), Honourable Estates: The English and Their Country Houses (1992), Barbara Cartland - A Life of Love (1994), Denis - The Authorised Biography of the Incomparable Compton (1994), Brian Johnston - The Authorised Biography, A Classic Christmas Crime (ed, 1995), Beating Retreat - Hong Kong under the Last Governor (1997), Stop Press (1998), A Peerage for Trade: A History of the Royal Warrant (2001), The Best After-Dinner Stories (ed, 2003), Village Cricket (2004), Death and the Visiting Fellow (2004), Death and the D'Urbervilles (2005), Denis Compton: The Life of a Sporting Hero (2006), Princess Margaret: A Life Unravelled (2007), A Death on the Ocean Wave (2007); *Recreations* real tennis, spectator sports, lunch; *Clubs* MCC, Royal Tennis, Crime Writers' Assoc (chm 1987–88), PEN (int co-ordinator Writers-in-Prison Ctee 1986–89), Soc of Authors, Groucho, Royal Fowey Yacht, Detection, Frontline, Fowey Cricket (pres 2007–); *Style*— Timothy Heald, Esq, FRSL; ✉ 66 The Esplanade, Fowey, Cornwall PL23 1JA (tel 01726 832781, fax 01726 833246, e-mail tim@timheald.com, website www.timheald.co.uk)

HEALE, Simon John Newton; s of James Newton Heale (d 1999), and Ruth Elizabeth, *née* Max; *b* 27 April 1953; *Educ* Winchester, Oriel Coll Oxford (exhibitioner, BA); *m* 16 Oct 1982, Catriona Jean, da of Lt-Gen Sir Robin Carnegie, KCB, OBE, DL; 1 s (James Newton *b* 16 Aug 1985), 2 da (Charlotte Esme Serena *b* 17 May 1987, Anna Frances *b* 15 April 1989); *Career* Price Waterhouse 1975–79; Swire Gp: joined 1979, fin dir Swire Japan 1982–85, pres Ocean Routes Inc 1985–88, gen mangr cargo Cathay Pacific 1988–90, chief operating offr Dragon Air 1990–94, dep md Cathay Pacific 1994–97; Jardine Fleming Ltd: gp fin dir 1997–99, chief operating offr 1999–2001; chief exec London Metal Exchange 2001–06, dir London Clearing House 2001–06, chief exec China Now 2007–; non-exec dir: Morgan Crucible Co 2005–, Panmure Gordon & Co plc 2007–, Kazakhmys plc 2007–; dir Hong Kong Tourism Assoc 1994–97, chm Jt Cncl of the Tourism Industry Hong Kong 1995–97; Aviation Week and Space Technology Laurel Award 1993; ACA 1978; *Recreations* travel, reading, walking labradors; *Clubs* Hong Kong; *Style*— Simon Heale, Esq

HEALEY, Baron (Life Peer UK 1992), of Riddlesden in the County of West Yorkshire; Denis Winston Healey; CH (1979), MBE (1945), PC (1964); s of William Healey, of Keighley, W Yorks; *b* 30 August 1917; *Educ* Bradford GS, Balliol Coll Oxford; *m* 1945, Edna May, da of Edward Edmunds, of Coleford, Glos; 2 da (Hon Jenifer Clare (Hon Mrs Copsey) *b* 12 April 1948, Hon Cressida *b* 27 July 1954), 1 s (Hon Timothy Blair *b* 5 June 1949); *Career* MP (Lab): Leeds SE 1952–55, Leeds E 1955–92; sec Int Dept Lab Pty 1946–52, memb shadow cabinet PLP 1959, sec of state for def 1964–70, oppn spokesman on foreign and Cwlth affrs 1971, shadow chllr 1972–74, chllr of the exchequer 1974–79, dep ldr Lab Pty 1981–83, shadow foreign sec 1981–87; memb Exec Fabian Soc 1954–61; pres Birkbeck Coll 1993; Freeman City of Leeds 1991; hon fell Balliol Coll Oxford 1980, Hon DLitt Univ of Bradford 1983, Hon LLD Univ of Sussex 1989; FRSL; Grand Cross Order of Merit (Germany) 1979; *Books* The Curtain Falls (1951), New Fabian Essays (1952), Neutralism (1955), Fabian International Essays (1956), A Neutral Belt in Europe (1958), NATO and American Security (1959), The Race Against the H Bomb (1960), Labour Britain and the World (1963), Healey's Eye (photographs, 1980), Labour and a World Society (1985), Beyond Nuclear Deterrence (1986), The Time of My Life (autobiography, 1989), When Shrimps Learn to Whistle (1990), My Secret Planet (1992), Denis Healey's Yorkshire Dales (1995), Healey's World (2002); *Style*— The Rt Hon Lord Healey, CH, MBE, PC; ✉ House of Lords, London SW1A 0PW

HEALEY, John; MP; *Career* MP (Lab) Wentworth 1997–; PPS to Chancellor of the Exchequer 1999–2001, Parly under-sec of state Dept of Educn and Skills 2001–02, economic sec to HM Treasy 2002–05, financial sec to HM Treasy 2005–; *Style*— John Healey, Esq, MP; ✉ House of Commons, London SW1A 0AA

HEALEY, Dr Norman John; s of Dr Ronald Jack Healey, of Launceston, Cornwall, and Monica Mary Patricia Healey, JP, *née* Gibbins (d 1995); *b* 2 September 1940; *Educ* Mount House Sch Tavistock, Epsom Coll, Guy's Hosp Med Sch London (Kitchener scholarship 1959, MRCS, LRCP, DA, DObstRCOG, 1st XV Rugby); *m* 24 June 1978, Maureen Anne, da of Clarence Meadows Brock; 3 da (Rebecca Jane *b* 10 Feb 1980, Alicia June, Nicola Joy (twins) *b* 13 Sept 1981); *Career* Surgn Lt RN 1965–71; RN Hosp Haslar: Dept of Orthopaedics 1966, Dept of Anaesthetics 1967, HMS Albion serv in Far East 1968–69, RM Depot Deal 1970–71; SHO Obstetrics and Gynaecology Royal Bucks Hosp Aylesbury 1972, London Coll of Osteopathic Med 1973–74; clinical asst Dept of Rheumatology and

Rehabilitation St Mary's Hosp London 1975–82; full time private practice as registered med osteopath and specialist in musculo-skeletal med 1975–; hon conslt St Luke's Hosp London 1987–; hon sec Br Osteopathic Assoc 1976–82, memb Cncl Br Assoc of Manipulative Med 1980–83; MRO 1975, FLCOM 1979, FRSM 1985, ND 1994; memb: Br Soc for Rheumatology 1982, Br Inst of Musculoskeletal Med 1992, Br Naturopathic Assoc 1994; *Recreations* seaside, music hall, flowers; *Clubs* Royal Western Yacht; *Style*— Dr Norman Healey; ✉ Honorary Consultant Physician, 86 Harley Street, London W1G 7HP (tel 020 7255 1424, website www.healeyclinic.co.uk)

HEALEY, Prof Patsy; OBE (1999); da of Prof C T Ingold, CMG, of Benson, Oxon, and L M Ingold, *née* Kemp; *b* 1 January 1940; *Educ* Walthamstow Hall Sevenoaks, UCL (BA), LSE (PhD), Regents St Poly (DipTP), Univ of Wales (DipEd); *m* 1, 25 June 1961, Dr Ian Nevill Healey (d 1972), s of Douglas Healey (d 1978); m 2, 9 July 1977, David Reiach Hunter (d 1979), s of David Reiach (d 1919); *Career* sch teacher 1962–65, planning offr London Borough of Lewisham GLC 1965–69, sr res fell LSE 1970–72, lectr in planning Kingston Poly 1969–70 and 1972–74, lectr then head of dept and dean Oxford Poly 1974–87; Univ of Newcastle upon Tyne: prof and head of Dept of Town and Country Planning 1988–92, prof and dir Centre for Research in European Urban Environments 1992–2002, emeritus prof 2002–; memb: various ctees CNAA 1976–81, Cncl and various ctees RTPI 1987–92, various ctees ESRC, Bd Tyne & Wear Devpt Corp 1998, JRF Housing and Neighbourhoods Ctee 1999–2003, RTPI Knowledge and Res Ctee 2003–; pres Assoc of European Schs of Planning 1994–96; *Books* Professional Ideals and Planning Practice (with J Underwood, 1979), Planning Theory - Prospects for the 1980s (ed with G McDougall and M Thomas, 1982), Local Plans in British Land Use Planning (1983), Land Policy: Problems and Alternatives (ed with S M Barrett, 1985), A Political Economy of Land (with A Gilbert, 1985), Land Use Planning and the Mediation of Urban Change (with P F McNamara, M J Elson and A J Doak, 1988), Land and Property Development in a Changing Context (ed with R Nabarro, 1990), Dilemmas of Planning Practice (with H Thomas, 1991), Rebuilding the City (with S Davoudi, M O'Toole, S Tavsanoglu and D Usher, 1992), Managing the City (with S Cameron, S Davoudi and S Graham, 1995), Collaborative Planning (1997), Making Strategic Spatial Plans (with A Khakee, A Motte and B Needham, 1997), Planning, Governance and Spatial Strategy in Britain (with G Vigar, A Hull and S Davoudi, 2000), Urban Governance, Institutional Capacity and Social Milieux (jtly, 2002); *Recreations* reading, walking, gardening, swimming, travelling; *Style*— Prof Patsy Healey, OBE; ✉ School of Architecture, Planning and Landscape, University of Newcastle upon Tyne, Newcastle upon Tyne NE1 7RU (tel 0191 222 8810, fax 0191 222 5709, telex UNINEW 953654)

HEALY, Francis (Fran); *b* 23 July 1973, Stafford; *Educ* Holyrood Secdy Sch Glasgow, Glasgow Sch of Art; *Career* lead singer Travis; *Albums* Good Feeling 1997, The Man Who 1999 (UK no 1, biggest selling album in the UK by a Br gp 1999), The Invisible Band 2001 (UK no 1), 12 Memories 2003; *Singles* All I Want To Do Is Rock 1996, U16 Girls 1997, Tied To The 90's 1997, Happy 1997, More Than Us 1998, Writing To Reach You 1999, Driftwood 1999, Why Does It Always Rain On Me? 1999, Turn 1999, Coming Around 2000, Sing 2001, Side 2001, Flowers In The Window 2002, Re-Offender 2003, The Beautiful Occupation 2003, Love Will Come Through 2004; *Videos* More Than Us: Live In Glasgow 2001, At The Palace 2004; *Awards* Best Br Gp and Best Br Album (for The Man Who) Brit Awards 2000, Best Songwriter and Best Contemporary Song (for Why Does It Always Rain On Me?) Ivor Novello Awards 2000, Best Br Gp Brit Awards 2002; *Style*— Fran Healy, Esq; ✉ c/o Helter Skelter, The Plaza, 535 Kings Road, London SW10 0SZ (tel 020 7376 8501); website www.travisonline.com

HEALY, Prof Thomas Edward John; s of Thomas Healy (d 1977), and Gladys May, *née* Paulger (d 1998); *b* 11 December 1935; *Educ* Guy's Hosp Med Sch Univ of London; *m* 3 Nov 1966, Lesley Edwina; 3 da (Maria b 23 March 1968, Michaela b 8 Dec 1970, Laura b 28 Jan 1975), 1 s (Thomas b 19 April 1979); *Career* conslt anaesthetist and conslt i/c intensive care Nottingham 1971– (planned and commissioned Intensive Care Unit for opening of Queens Medical Centre Nottingham 1978), reader in anaesthesia Univ of Nottingham 1974, prof of anaesthesia Univ of Manchester 1981–97 (chm Sch of Surgical Scis 1992–94); visiting prof Univs of Arizona (Tuscon and Phoenix), Michigan, Philadelphia and Vancouver; memb S Manchester DHA 1981–87; ed Monographs in Anaesthesiology, ed-in-chief European Jl of Anaesthesiology 1995–2000, author of over 200 published papers; expert witness in court cases UK and Canada for the Crown, GMC, defendants and claimants; memb Cncl: Assoc of Anaesthetists 1973–76, Anaesthetic Research Soc Cncl 1978–80, RSM (hon sec 1986–88, pres Section of Anaesthetics 1996–97), Royal Coll of Anaesthetists 1989–97 (chm Professional Standards Ctee 1994–97), Postgrad Medical Fellowship 1990–94; memb Advsy Bd Medical Litigation 1999–; memb Bd of Govrs Linacre Centre for Health Care Ethics 1999–2005; Freeman: Worshipful Soc of Apothecaries, City of London; academician and memb of Senate and Exec Ctee European Acad of Anaesthesiology, hon memb Romanian Soc of Anaesthesiology 1995–2000, special visitor Shanghai Univ; FRCA; *Books* Aids to Anaesthesia Book 1: Basic Science, Aids to Anaesthesia Book 2: Clinical Practice, Anaesthesia for Day Case Surgery, A Practice of Anaesthesia (6 edn, 1st Prize BMA Book Competition, 7 edn 2003), Encylcopedia of Forensic Medicine (contrib, 2005), Medicine for Lawyers (contrib, 2005); *Recreations* cycling, reading; *Style*— Prof Thomas Healy, MD, FRCA

HEANEY, Kevin; s of Patrick Heaney, and Carol Hicks; *b* 20 March 1963, London; *m* 17 Feb 2001, Marina; 1 s (Sean b 8 Jan 2002), 1 da (Grace b 5 June 2004); *Career* owner cornishhomes.co.uk; chm and owner Truro City FC; Cornwall memb Panel Prince's Tst, memb Panel Lord Lt's Tst Fund for Youth; *Recreations* football, international travel; *Style*— Kevin Heaney, Esq; ✉ 9 Heron Way, Newham Industrial Estate, Truro, Cornwall TR1 2XN (tel 01872 278000, fax 01872 240840, e-mail enquiries@cornishhomes.co.uk)

HEANEY, Prof Seamus Justin; *b* 13 April 1939; *Educ* St Columb's Coll Derry, Queen's Univ Belfast (BA); *m* 1965, Marie, *née* Devlin; 3 c; *Career* formerly on staff St Joseph's Coll of Educn, lectr English Dept Queen's Univ 1966–72, freelance writer 1972–75, teacher Carysfort Coll 1975, Boylston prof of rhetoric Harvard Univ 1984–96, prof of poetry Univ of Oxford 1989–94; visiting prof Univ of Calif 1970–71; Somerset Maugham Award 1968, Denis Devlin Award 1973, American Irish Fndn Literary Award 1973, Duff Cooper Meml Prize 1975, W H Smith Annual Award 1976, Nobel Prize for Literature 1995; memb Aosdána; CLit 1991; *Books* Eleven Poems (1965), Death of a Naturalist (1966), Door into the Dark (1969), Wintering Out (1972), North (1975), Field Work (1979), Preoccupations: Selected Prose 1968–1978 (1980), Selected Poems 1965–1975 (1980), The Rattle Bag (ed with Ted Hughes, 1982), Sweeney Astray (1984), Station Island (1984), The Haw Lantern (1987, Whitbread Award 1987), The Government of the Tongue (1988), New Selected Poems 1966–1987 (1990), The Cure at Troy - A Version of Sophocles' Philoctetes (1990), Seeing Things (1991), Sweeney's Flight (1992), The Redress of Poetry (1995), Laments (trans with Stanislaw Baranczak, 1995), The Spirit Level (1996, Whitbread Book of the Year Award 1997), The School Bag (ed with Ted Hughes, 1997), Opened Ground Poems 1966–96 (1998), Beowulf, A New Translation (1999, also Faber Poetry Cassette (with Tom Paulin, 1983)), Electric Light (2001), Finders Keepers: Selected Prose 1971–2001 (2002), The Burial at Thebes - A Version of Sophocles' Antigone (2004), District and Circle (2006, T S Eliot Prize 2007); *Style*— Prof Seamus Heaney; ✉ c/o Publicity Department, Faber & Faber, 3 Queen Square, London WC1N 3AU (tel 020 7465 0045, fax 020 7465 0034)

HEAPS, Christopher Seymour; s of Capt Christopher Robert Milner Heaps, TD (d 1962), and Peggy Margaret Catherine, *née* Mill (d 1984); *b* 15 November 1942; *Educ* Dorking GS, Univ of Exeter (LLB); *m* 14 March 1970, Ann Mary, da of Capt Peter Dudley Frederick Mays (d 1994), of Dorking; 2 da (Grace b 1973, Elizabeth b 1975); *Career* admitted slr 1967; ptnr Eversheds (formerly Jaques & Lewis) 1971–96 (conslt 1996–98); traffic cmmr Western Traffic Area 1997–2000, traffic cmmr South Eastern and Metropolitan Area 2000–07; dir Porterbrook Leasing Co Ltd 2000–02, dir UK Bus Driver of the Year Assoc Ltd 2004–; pres Holborn Law Soc 1983–84, memb Cncl Law Soc 1985–97, memb Cncl on Tbnls 1991–97; chm Law Soc: Planning & Environmental Law Ctee 1988–91 and 1995–96, Adjudication and Appeals Ctee (Slrs' Complaints Bureau) 1992–95; memb: Transport Users' Consultative Ctee for London 1981–84, London Regnl Passengers Ctee 1984–92 (dep chm 1985–92), Advsy Panel Railway Heritage Tst 1985–; chm Railway Study Assoc 1997–2003; chm Dorking Round Table 1978–79, pres Dorking Deepdene Rotary Club 1986–87; memb Cncl of Mgmnt PDSA 1996– (dep chm 2007–); hon steward Helston Furry Dance 1996–; Liveryman Worshipful Co of Curriers 1976 (Master 1997–98), Liveryman Worshipful Co of Coachmakers and Coach Harness Makers 1985; FCIT 1996 (MCIT 1988); *Books* London Transport Railways Album (1978), Western Region in the 1960's (1981), This is Southern Region Central Division (1982), BR Diary 1968–1977 (1988); *Recreations* transport and transport history; *Style*— Christopher Heaps, Esq; ✉ Pinecroft, Ridgeway Road, Dorking, Surrey RH4 3AP (tel 01306 881752, fax 01306 876756, e-mail heaps@waitrose.com); 33 Wendron Street, Helston, Cornwall TR13 8PT

HEARING, Roger; s of Terence Hearing, and Margaret, *née* Standley; *Educ* Hardye's Sch Dorchester, Downing Coll Cambridge (MA), City Univ (Dip Journalism); *m* 1994, Emma, *née* Garfit; 1 da, 1 s; *Career* reporter Birmingham Post 1984–87, corr BBC World Serv Zambia 1988–89, reporter and presenter The World at One (BBC Radio 4) 1990–93, reporter Newsnight (BBC 2) 1993, E Africa corr BBC 1993–96, presenter The World Tonight (BBC Radio 4/BBC World Serv) 1998–; *Recreations* genealogy, walking, fishing (unsuccessfully); *Style*— Roger Hearing, Esq; ✉ Room 3084, BBC, Bush House, Aldwych, London (tel 020 7240 3456, mobile 07939 176801, e-mail roger.hearing@bbc.co.uk)

HEARLEY, Timothy Michael; s of Maurice James Goodwin Hearley, CBE (d 1975); *b* 10 March 1942; *Educ* Malvern Coll, Lincoln Coll Oxford (MA); *m* 1966, Pauline Muriel, *née* Dunn; 3 s (Philip Michael b 1967, James Paul b 1970, Richard Matthew b 1973); *Career* currently chm: Rolfe & Nolan plc, Securitex Investments Ltd, Vail Corporation Ltd, Virgin Cars UK Ltd, C4 Group Ltd, Vicorp Group Ltd, Binns & Co PR Ltd; currently dir: Nyne plc, Green Cone Ltd, Oakdene Homes plc; AIIMR, MSI; *Recreations* tennis, piano, ballet, theatre; *Clubs* Fox; *Style*— Timothy Hearley, Esq; ✉ Rush Leys, 4 Birds Hill Rise, Oxshott, Surrey KT22 0SW (tel 01372 842506); Vail Corporation Ltd, 58 Grosvenor Street, London W1K 3JB (tel 020 7240 6090, fax 020 7240 6091)

HEARN, Andrew; *b* 23 July 1957; *Educ* UC Sch London, St John's Coll Oxford (BA); *m* Sarah; 3 s (Luke, Adam, Matthew); *Career* Dechert: articled clerk (qualified 1982), litigation ptnr and slr-advocate (Higher Courts Civil) 1986–, specialising in intellectual property, defamation and gen commercial litigation; recorder London and South Eastern Circuit; accredited mediator CEDR and mediator World Intellectual Property Orgn; former memb Litigation Sub-Ctee City of London Law Soc; author of various pubns and articles in the press; memb: City of London Law Co, Law Soc; FCIArb; *Recreations* skiing, the arts, trying to keep fit; *Clubs* Campden Hill Lawn Tennis, Old Gowers; *Style*— Andrew Hearn, Esq; ✉ Dechert, 2 Serjeants' Inn, London EC4Y 1LT (tel 020 7583 5353, fax 020 7353 3683, e-mail andrew.hearn@dechert.com)

HEARN, Donald Peter; s of Lt-Col Peter James Hearn, and Anita Margaret Hearn; *b* 2 November 1947; *Educ* Clifton, Selwyn Coll Cambridge; *m* 21 July 1973, Rachel Mary Arnold; 2 da (Emma b 1975, Sarah b 1977); *Career* Ernst & Young 1969–79, gp fin controller Saga Holidays 1979–83, chief fin offr Lee Valley Water Co 1983–86, sec RHS 1989–2001 (fin dir 1986, hon fell 2001–), bursar and fell Clare Coll Cambridge 2001–, dir Fitzwilliam Museum Enterprises 2003–, memb Audit Ctee Univ of Cambridge 2003–, tstee Cambridge Botanic Garden 2003–, tstee and treasr Chelsea Physic Garden 2003–; Gen Cmmr of Taxes 1991–, memb Fin Gen Purposes Ctee Royal Postgrad Med Sch 1991–97; tstee Cambridge Univ Staff Pension Scheme 2002– (chm Investments Ctee 2002–), govr Woldingham Sch 1990–93, memb Ct Imperial Coll London 1998–2005 (chm Audit Ctee 1996–2005, chm House Ctee 1999–2001, govr 2001–05); memb Selwyn Coll Assoc Ctee 1997–2001; *Style*— Donald Hearn, Esq; ✉ Clare College, Cambridge CB2 1TL

HEARN, Prof John Patrick; s of Lt-Col Hugh Patrick Hearn, and Cynthia Ellen, *née* Nicholson; *b* 24 February 1943; *Educ* Crusaders Sch Headley, St Mary's Sch Nairobi, UC Dublin (MSc, BSc), Australian Nat Univ (PhD); *m* 30 Sept 1967, Margaret Ruth Patricia, *née* McNair; 4 s (Shaun Robin b 1968, Bruce Edward b 1973, Adrian Hugh b 1975, Nicholas Gordon b 1984), 1 da (Karina Anne b 1970); *Career* lectr in zoology Strathmore Coll Nairobi 1967–69, research scholar Dept of Zoology Aust Nat Univ Canberra 1969–72, scientist MRC Reproductive Biology Unit Univ of Edinburgh 1972–79 (hon fell 1974–79), conslt scientist WHO Geneva 1978–79, visiting prof in reproductive biology Dept of Biology UCL 1979–94; Zoological Soc of London: dir Wellcome Laboratories of Comparative Physiology 1979–80, dir of science 1980–87, dir Inst of Zoology 1980–87; dir MRC/AFRC Comparative Physiology Research Gp 1983–89, dep sec AFRC 1987–90, prof Dept of Physiology Univ of Wisconsin Med Sch 1990–96, dir Wisconsin Regnl Primate Research Center 1990–96, sr scientist WHO Research Prog in Reproductive Health Geneva 1996–98, dir Research Sch of Biological Sciences Aust Nat Univ Canberra 1998–2001; dep vice-chllr (research) Aust Nat Univ Canberra 2001–04, dep vice-chllr Univ of Sydney 2004–; Bolliger Award Australian Mammal Soc 1972, Scientific Medal Zoological Soc of London 1983, Osman Hill Medal Primate Soc of GB 1986, Aust Centenary Medal 2003; memb: American Soc of Primatology, Brazilian Soc of Primatology, Soc for Reproductive Biology (chm 2000–04), Soc for the Study of Fertility, Int Primatological Soc (pres 1984–88); scientific fell Zoological Soc of London; *Publications* ed: Reproduction in New World Primates (1983), Advances in Animal Conservation (1985), Reproduction and Disease in Captive and Wild Animals (1988), Conservation of Primate Species Studied in Biomedical Research (1994); *Recreations* swimming, running, conservation; *Clubs* Athenaeum; *Style*— Prof John Hearn; ✉ The Quadrangle, University of Sydney, NSW 2006, Australia (tel and fax 00 612 9351 4461, e-mail j.hearn@vcc.usyd.ed.au)

HEARNDEN, Dr Arthur George; OBE (1990); s of Hugh William Hearnden (d 1985), of Bangor, Co Down, and Violet May, *née* Frazer (d 1971); *b* 15 December 1931; *Educ* Methodist Coll Belfast, Christ's Coll Cambridge (MA), Wadham Coll Oxford (DPhil); *m* 25 August 1962, Josephine Honor, da of Joseph Cuthbert McNeill; 1 s (Barney Hugh b 11 June 1963), 2 da (Katharine Louisa (Mrs Farrow) b 21 Nov 1964, Anna Mary (Mrs Hummerston) b 4 Jan 1968); *Career* former schoolmaster and univ lectr; sec Standing Conf on Univ Entrance 1975–84, gen sec ISC 1985–97, memb Sch Exams and Assessment Cncl 1988–91, memb Funding Agency for Schs 1994–97, memb Press Complaints Cmmn 1999–2005; pres Ind Schs Assoc 1997–2002, vice-pres Cncl of Br Ind Schs in the Euro Communities 1997–; chm: Worldwide Volunteering for Young People 1995–2000, HSBC Bursary Fund 1998–2002, The Hall Sch Charitable Tst 1998–; *Books* Paths to University (1973), Education in the Two Germanies (1974), Education, Culture and Politics in West Germany (1974), The British in Germany (ed, 1978), Red Robert, A Life of Robert Birley

(1984); *Recreations* family, hill walking, theatre; *Clubs* Athenaeum; *Style*— Dr Arthur Hearnden, OBE; ✉ Hethe House, Hethe, Bicester, Oxfordshire OX27 8ES (tel 01869 277985, fax 01869 278445, mobile 07702 408155, e-mail arthurandjo@clara.co.uk)

HEARNE, Sir Graham James; kt (1998), CBE (1990); s of Frank Hearne, and Emily, *née* Shakespeare; *b* 23 November 1937; *Educ* George Dixon GS Birmingham; *m* 1961, Carol Jean, *née* Brown; 1 s, 3 da; *Career* admitted slr 1959, Pinsent & Co Slrs 1959–63, attorney NYC Fried Frank Harris Shriver & Jacobson 1963–66, Herbert Smith & Co Slrs 1966–67, Industrial Reorganisation Corp 1967–68, N M Rothschild & Sons Ltd 1968–77, fin dir Courtaulds Ltd 1977–81, chief exec Tricentrol plc 1981–83, gp md Carless Capel & Leonard plc 1983–84, chief exec Enterprise Oil plc 1984–91 (chm 1991–2002), non-exec chm: Novar plc (formerly Caradon plc) 1999–2005, Catlin Gp Ltd 2003–, Stratic Energy Corp 2005–; dep chm: Gallaher plc 1997–, Wellstream plc 2003–, Rowan Cos Inc 2004–; non-exec dir N M Rothschild & Sons Ltd 1977–, Invensys plc 1997–2003, Braemar Seascope Gp plc 1999– (chm 2002); High Sheriff Gtr London 1995; *Clubs* Reform, MCC, Brooks's; *Style*— Sir Graham Hearne, CBE; ✉ 5 Crescent Place, London SW3 2EA

HEARNE, Dr John Michael; s of Reginald Hearne (d 1974), of Ipplepen, Devon, and Mary Rachel, *née* Rees (d 2001); *b* 19 September 1937; *Educ* Torquay GS, St Luke's Coll Exeter, UC Wales Aberystwyth (BMus, MMus), Univ of Wales (DMus); *m* 6 July 1974, Margaret Gillespie, da of Archibald Jarvie (d 2006), of Glasgow; *Career* teacher Tónlistarskóli Borgarfjardar (Rural Music Sch) Iceland 1968–69, lectr Aberdeen Coll of Educn 1970–87; composer, singer (bass-baritone) and conductor; compositions incl: Piano Sonata 1968, Piano Trio 1981, Songs and Choral Music, String Quartet 1971, Triduum (Festival Oratorio) 1982, Channel Firing 1979, The Four Horsemen (brass, percussion) 1985, Trumpet Concerto (BBC Cmmn) 1990, Laetatus Sum for Chorus (jt winner Gregynog Composers Award of Wales 1992), De Profundis for wind band (Aberdeen University Quincentenary cmmn) 1995, A Legend of Margaret for Sch Choirs and Ensemble (St Margaret's Sch Aberdeen cmmn for 150th anniversary) 1996, Quintet for Alto Saxophone and String Quartet 1997, Solemn and Strange Music for piano duet (winner Gregynog Composers' Award for Wales 1998) 1998, Into Uncharted Seas overture for orch (Dundee Orch Soc cmmn for centenary of launch of RRS Discovery) 2001, The Ben cantata for soloists, choirs and orch (Gordon Forum for the Arts Cmmn) 2001; performances incl: reader in Sincerely Edvard Grieg (compilation of Grieg's letters, songs, piano music), regular concert appearances in Scotland; conductor: Stonehaven and Dist Choral Soc 1989–, Inverurie Choral Soc 1998–2003; self publishing Longship Music; chm: Gordon Forum for the Arts 1991–94, Scot Music Advsy Ctee BBC 1986–90; memb Bd Enterprise Music Scotland 2006–; dist cncllr (E Scotland) Inc Soc of Musicians 1992–98; warden Performers & Composers Section Inc Soc Musicians 1999–2000; memb: Exec Ctee Composers' Guild of GB 1994–98, Bd Nat Youth Choir of Scotland 1996–2003; *Recreations* classic motoring - 1954 Daimler Conquest Roadster; *Style*— Dr John Hearne; ✉ Longship Music, Smidskot, Fawells, Keithhall, Inverurie AB51 0LN (tel and fax 01651 882274, website www.impulse-music.co.uk/hearne.htm)

HEARNE, Peter Ambrose; s of Dr Arthur Ambrose Hearne (d 1976), and Helen Mackay, *née* Noble (d 1981); *b* 14 November 1927; *Educ* Tunstall Sch Sunderland, Sherborne, Loughborough Coll (DLC), Coll of Aeronautics Cranfield (MSc), MIT USA; *m* 19 April 1952, Georgina Gordon; da of Alexander Gordon Guthrie (d 1986); 3 s (Patrick Gordon b 7 June 1956, Mark Alexander b 3 Feb 1958, Charles Peter Garrett b 24 May 1962); *Career* aerodynamicist Saunders Roe IOW 1946–47, ops devpt engr BOAC 1949–54, helicopter project engr BEA 1954–58, asst gen mangr Guided Flight Group Elliott Bros 1960–65 (mangr Guided Weapons Div 1959), dir and gen mangr Elliott Flight Automation (subsequently GEC Avionics) 1965–86, md GEC Avionics 1986–87; GEC Marconi: asst md 1987–90, pres US Ops 1990–92; chm GEC Marconi Avionics 1992–93, dir of civil aviation GEC Marconi 1993–94; aerospace conslt 1994–; pres: Royal Aeronautical Soc 1980, Cranfield Soc 1979–87; vice-chm Br Gliding Assoc 1997 (vice-pres 1999); FREng 1984, Hon FRAeS 1990, FRIN 2000; *Recreations* mountain soaring, model railways; *Clubs* RAF, Surrey and Hants Gliding, Aero Club Alpin, Southwold Sailing; *Style*— Peter Hearne, Esq, FREng; ✉ The Limes, Wateringbury, Kent ME18 5NY (tel 01622 812385, e-mail peter.hearne@homecall.co.uk)

HEARSE, Prof David James; s of James Read Hearse (d 1974), of Holt, Wilts, and Irene Annetta, *née* Nokes (d 1982); *b* 3 July 1943; *Educ* John Willmott GS, Univ of Wales (BSc, PhD, DSc); *Career* instr in pharmacology New York Univ Med Centre 1968–70, res fell Br Heart Fndn Imperial Coll London 1970–76, hon sr lectr St Thomas' Hosp Med Sch 1976–86, prof of cardiovascular biochemistry United Med and Dental Schs Guy's Hosp and St Thomas' Hosp, currently dir cardiovascular research The Rayne Inst St Thomas' Hosp; author of 8 books and over 500 scientific papers in areas of res into heart disease; fell American Coll of Cardiology 1980; memb: RSM, Br Cardiac Soc; *Recreations* furniture, house restoration, photography, carpentry; *Clubs* RSM; *Style*— Prof David Hearse; ✉ Director Cardiovascular Research, The Rayne Institute, St Thomas' Hospital, London SE1 7EH (tel 020 7928 9292)

HEATH, Prof Anthony Francis; s of Ronald John Heath (decd), of Bampton, Oxon, and Cicely Florence, *née* Roberts; *b* 15 December 1942; *Educ* Merchant Taylors', Trinity Coll Cambridge (sr scholar, BA, Cross-Country half blue); *m* Mary-Jane, da of David Lionel Pearce; 2 s (Oliver Francis b 17 Oct 1975, Ralph Francis b 18 April 1987), 1 da (Eleanor b 13 Nov 1984); *Career* asst lectr Univ of Cambridge 1968–70; Univ of Oxford: lectr and fell Jesus Coll 1970–87, fell Nuffield Coll 1987–, prof of sociology 1999–; jt dir Centre for Research into Elections and Social Trends 1994–; FRSS, FBA 1992; *Books* Rational Choice and Social Exchange (1976), Origins and Destinations (with A Halsey and J Ridge, 1980), Social Mobility (1981), How Britain Votes (with R Jowell and J Curtice, 1985), Understanding Political Change (jtly, 1991), Labour's Last Chance? (with Jowell and Curtice, 1994), Ireland North and South (with Breen and Whelan, 1999), The Rise of New Labour (with Jowell and Curtice, 2001); *Recreations* running, climbing, piano; *Clubs* Achilles; *Style*— Prof Anthony Heath, FBA; ✉ Nuffield College, Oxford OX1 1NF (tel 01865 278543, fax 01865 278557, e-mail anthony.heath@nuf.ox.ac.uk)

HEATH, Christopher John; s of Lt-Gen Sir Lewis Macclesfield Heath (d 1954), of Bath, and Katherine Margaret, *née* Lonergan (d 1984); *b* 26 September 1946; *Educ* Ampleforth; *m* 14 June 1979, Margaret Joan, da of Col Richard Arthur Wiggin, TD, JP, DL (d 1977), of Ombersley, Worcs; 1 s (William Henry Christopher b 29 April 1983); *Career* commercial asst ICI 1964–69; sales exec George Henderson & Co 1969–75; ptnr Henderson Crosthwaite & Co 1975–84; ceo Baring Securities Ltd 1984–93, dir Baring Bros & Co Ltd 1986–93, dir Barings plc 1992–93; fndr investment bank Caspian Securities Ltd 1995, joined as md Optima Fund Mgmnt NY 1998; FSI, memb SFA; *Recreations* fishing; *Clubs* Boodle's, Pratt's, Turf, The Brook (NY); *Style*— Christopher Heath, Esq; ✉ 230 East 67th Street, New York, NY 10065, USA

HEATH, David Arthur; s of Richard Arthur Heath, of Chesterfield, Derbys, and Gladys Heath (d 1998); *b* 6 September 1946; *Educ* Chesterfield Boys' GS, Glos Coll of Art and Design (DipArch), RIBA; *m* 27 June 1973, Angela Mary, da of James Joseph Niall Hardy (d 1988), and Una, *née* Hanley (d 1993); 2 s (Richard b 1978, John b 1980); *Career* architect; ptnr Heath Avery Partnership 1980–2002, dir Heath Avery Architect Ltd 2002–, tstee Heath Family Properties 1986, memb Cotswold Dist Cncl Architects Panel 1988–; Cheltenham Civic Award 1987, 1989, 1992, 2002 and 2006 (commendations 1986, 1987, 2001 and 2002), Epsom & Ewell Award for Outstanding Conservation 1993, Malvern Hills District Cncl Conservations Design Award (commendation 1999); *Books* Accommodating Technology in Schools (co-author, 1990); *Recreations* motor racing, music, walking, reading; *Clubs* Alfa Romeo Owners; *Style*— David Heath, Esq; ✉ 11A The Verneys, Old Bath Road, Cheltenham, Gloucestershire (tel 01242 242066); 3 Bath Mews, Bath Parade, Cheltenham, Gloucestershire (tel 01242 529169, fax 224069, e-mail architects@heath-avery.co.uk)

HEATH, David William St John; CBE (1989), MP; s of Eric William Heath, of Street, Somerset, and Pamela Joan, *née* Bennett; *b* 16 March 1954; *Educ* Millfield, St John's Coll Oxford (MA), City Univ; *m* 15 May 1987, Caroline Marie Therese, da of Harry Page Netherton, of Alicante, Spain; 1 da (Bethany b 31 March 1988), 1 s (Thomas b 2 May 1991); *Career* optician; memb Somerset CC 1985–97 (ldr 1985–89), Nat Exec Lib Pty 1986–87, Fed Exec Lib Democrats 1989–92 and 1994–96, Audit Cmmn 1995–97; vice-chm and ldr Lib Democrats Assoc of CCs 1994–97; chm Avon & Somerset Police Authy 1993–96 (dep chm 1996–97), vice-chm Ctee of Local Police Authorities 1995–97; MP (Lib Dem) Somerton and Frome 1997–; Lib Dem spokesman on: European affrs 1997–98, foreign affrs 1997–99, agric, rural affrs and fisheries 1999–2001, work and pensions 2001–02, science 2001–04, constitutional affrs 2002–06, Home Office 2002–05, Cabinet Office 2006–; shadow to Ldr of the House 2005–; memb Foreign Affrs Select Ctee 1997–; Parly conslt to Worldwide Fund for Nature 1990; head of fund raising Nat Meningitis Tst 1992–93; *Recreations* rugby football, cricket, pig breeding; *Clubs* Nat Lib; *Style*— David Heath, Esq, CBE, MP; ✉ 34 The Yard, Witham Friary, Frome, Somerset BA11 5HF; House of Commons, London SW1A 0AA (tel 020 7219 6245)

HEATH, (Barrie) Duncan; s of Sir Barrie Heath (d 1988), and Joy Heath (d 1980); *b* 30 June 1946, Leamington Spa, Warks; *Educ* St Peters Court Sch Broadstairs, Wrekin Coll; *m* (m dis 1989) Hilary Dwyer; 1 s (Daniel), 1 da (Laura); *Career* agent William Morris 1970–72, chm Duncan Heath Associates 1972–88, chm ICM (International Creative Management, incorporating Duncan Heath Assocs) 1988– (led MBO from US owners 2002); supporter of various animal charities; memb BAFTA 1984; *Recreations* sailing, horse racing, motorbikes, ballroom dancing; *Clubs* Royal London Yacht, RAC, Hurlingham; *Style*— Duncan Heath, Esq; ✉ ICM, Oxford House, 76 Oxford Street, London W1D 1BS (tel 020 7636, fax 020 7323 0101, e-mail duncanheath@icmlondon.co.uk)

HEATH, His Hon Judge Michael John; s of Norman Heath (d 2006), of Grimsby, Lincs, and Dorothy, *née* Fryman (d 2000); *b* 12 June 1948; *Educ* Wintringham GS Grimsby, Univ of Leeds (LLB); *m* 5 Aug 1972, Heather, *née* Croft; 2 s (John Alexander b 1 June 1978, Duncan Robert b 6 Nov 1981); *Career* ptnr RAC Symes & Co 1977–95 (asst slr 1975–77), dep dist judge 1987–95, recorder 1993–95 (asst recorder 1989–93), circuit judge (Midland Circuit) 1995–, ethnic minorities liaison judge for Lincs 1995–, youth justice liaison judge for Lincs 2000–, magistrates' liaison judge for Lincs 2000–, hon recorder City of Lincoln 2000–, resident judge Lincoln Crown Court 2000–; memb: Lincs Courts Bd 2004–06, Lincs Probation Bd 2004–06; FCIArb 1993; *Recreations* strolling; *Style*— His Hon Judge Heath; ✉ Lincoln Combined Court Centre, 360 High Street, Lincoln LN5 7RL (tel 01522 883000)

HEATH, Stephen Christopher; s of George Albert Heath, of Knottingley, W Yorks, and Patricia Anne, *née* Miller (d 1989); *b* 18 April 1959; *Educ* Knottingley HS, Wakefield Coll of Art, Teesside Poly (BA), Leicester Poly (MA); *m* 31 May 2001, Trisha Andee Theodore-Heath, *née* Theodore; *Career* commercial design conslt; site mangr Space Planning and Coordinated Environmental Services Ltd (Spaces) 1985–86 (designer/planner 1983–85), assoc David Leon Partnership 1989–94 (joined 1986, design team ldr 1988–94), design assoc BDG/McColl 1994–96, dir and princ conslt Special Projects Bureau 1996–, dir and company sec HxR Special Projects 1999, sr ptnr SPB3 2002–04; work covers the professions, professional instns, healthcare, science and technol, financial instns; clients incl: Unilever Research Ltd, Borax Consolidated Ltd, National Trust, V&A, Russell Reynolds Associates Inc, BMW (GB) Ltd; FCSD 1993; *Recreations* fitness training, travelling, writing; *Style*— Stephen Heath, Esq

HEATH-BROWN, Prof David Rodney (Roger); s of Basil Heath-Brown, of Welwyn Garden City, Herts, and Phyllis Joan, *née* Watson; *b* 12 October 1952; *Educ* Welwyn Garden City GS, Trinity Coll Cambridge (BA, PhD, Smith's essay prize); *m* 11 July 1992, Ann Louise, da of William Sharpley; 2 da (Jennifer Louisa b 5 Oct 1993, Clare Eleanor b 24 June 1997); *Career* research fell Trinity Coll Cambridge 1977–79; Univ of Oxford: tutor in pure mathematics Magdalen Coll 1979–98; reader in pure mathematics 1990–98, prof of pure mathematics 1999–, professorial fell Worcester Coll 1999–; corresponding memb Göttingen Acad of Science 1999–; memb London Mathematical Soc 1979 (Jr Berwick Prize 1981, Sr Berwick Prize 1996); FRS 1993; *Recreations* British field botany, gardening, bridge; *Style*— Prof Roger Heath-Brown, FRS; ✉ Mathematical Institute, 24–29 St Giles', Oxford OX1 3LB (tel 01865 273535, e-mail rhb@maths.ox.ac.uk)

HEATH-WELCH, Anne; da of L R Welch, of Houston, Texas, and late Le Noir Rabb; *Educ* Centenary Coll of Louisiana USA (BMus), Univ of Texas at Austin (MM), Vienna Conservatory of Music; *Career* princ ENO 1995–98; *Roles* Minnie in La Fanciulla del West (WNO), title role in Tosca (WNO and ENO), title role in Madam Butterfly (ENO), title role in Turandot (ENO), title role in Manon Lescaut (Kentish Opera Gp), Mimi in La Bohème, Iphigenie in Iphigenie en Tauride (WNO), Foreign Princess in Rusalka (ENO), Leonore in Fidelio (ENO), Brangaene in Tristan und Isolde (Scottish Opera), Sieglinde, Freia and Gutruene in Der Ring (reduced version for Pocket Opera Nurenberg), title role in Aida (Nonsuch Opera & Kentish Opera Gp), Violetta in La Traviata, Lady Macbeth in Macbeth (WNO), Leonora in La Forza del Destino (ENO), Santuzza in Cavalleria Rusticana (Kentish Opera Gp), Tatyana in Eugene Onegin (Kentish Opera Gp), Laura in La Gioconda (Hull), Erste Dame in Magic Flute (ENO), Donna Elvira in Don Giovanni (ENO), Minnie in La Fanciulla Del West (Opera Zuid Maastricht), Amelia in Un Ballo in Maschera (Opera Zuid Maastricht); *Recreations* gardening; *Style*— Ms Anne Heath-Welch; ✉ e-mail anneheathwelch@hotmail.com

HEATHCOAT-AMORY, Rt Hon David Philip; PC (1996), MP; s of Brig Roderick Heathcoat-Amory (d 1998), and Sonia (d 1999), da of Capt Edward Conyngham Denison, MVO, RN; half-bro of Michael Heathcoat-Amory, *qv*; *b* 21 March 1949; *Educ* Eton, ChCh Oxford (MA); *m* 1978, Linda Adams; 1 s (and 1 s decd), 1 da; *Career* CA, asst fin dir Br Technol Gp 1980–83; Parly candidate (Cons) Brent S 1979, MP (Cons) Wells 1983–; PPS to Home Sec 1987–88, asst whip 1988–89; Parly under sec of state: DOE 1989–90, Dept of Energy 1990–92; treas HM Household (dep chief whip) 1992–93, min of state Foreign Office 1993–94, Paymaster Gen 1994–96 (resigned), shadow chief sec to the Treasy 1997–2000, shadow sec of state DTI 2000–01, Cons Pty delg EU Convention on the Future of Europe 2002; a non-exec dir: London & Devonshire Tst Ltd 1983–, Lowman Mfrg Co Ltd 1983–; FCA; *Recreations* walking, talking; *Style*— The Rt Hon David Heathcoat-Amory, MP; ✉ House of Commons, London SW1A 0AA

HEATHCOAT AMORY, Sir Ian; 6 Bt (UK 1874), of Knightshayes Court, Tiverton, Devon; DL (Devon 1981); s of Lt-Col Sir William Heathcoat-Amory, 5 Bt, DSO (d 1982), and Margaret (d 1997), da of Col Sir Arthur Doyle, 4 Bt, JP (d 1948); *b* 3 February 1942; *Educ* Eton; *m* 1972, (Frances) Louise, da of late (Jocelyn Francis) Brian Pomeroy (gggs of 4 Viscount Harberton); 4 s (William Francis b 1975, Harry James b 1977, Patrick Thomas b 1979, Benjamin David b 1983); *Heir* s, William Heathcoat-Amory; *Style*— Sir Ian Heathcoat Amory, Bt, DL; ✉ Calverleigh Court, Tiverton, Devon EX16 8BB

HEATHCOAT AMORY, (Ian) Mark; *see:* Amory, Mark

HEATHCOAT-AMORY, Michael FitzGerald; only s of Maj Edgar Heathcoat-Amory, by his w Sonia (d 1999), da of Capt Edward Conyngham Denison, MVO, RN; half-bro of David Heathcoat-Amory, MP, *qv*; *b* 2 October 1941; *Educ* Eton, ChCh Oxford; *m* 1, 1965 (m dis 1970), Harriet Mary Sheila, da of Lt-Gen Sir Archibald Nye, GCSI, GCMG, GCIE, KCB, KBE, MC (d 1967); 1 s (Edward b 1967); m 2, 1975, Arabella, da of late Raimund von

Hofmannstahl, and formerly w of Piers von Westenholz; 2 da (Lucy b 1977, Jessica b 1979); *Career* chm London & Devonshire Trust Ltd; md Jupiter Asset Management Ltd 1986–2000; dir: Jupiter Global Green Investment Trust plc, Jupiter Enhanced Income Investment Trust plc, Jupiter Primadona Growth Trust plc, Aurora Investment Trust plc; High Sheriff Devon 1985–86; farmer; *Recreations* field sports, collecting oak trees, talking politics; *Clubs* White's, Pratt's; *Style*— Michael Heathcoat-Amory, Esq; ✉ Chevithorne Barton, Tiverton, Devon EX16 7QB; 2 Montrose Court, London SW7 2QH

HEATHCOTE, Brig Sir Gilbert Simon; 9 Bt (GB 1733), of London, CBE (Mil 1964, MBE 1945); s of Lt-Col Robert Evelyn Manners Heathcote, DSO (d 1969), of Manton Hall, Rutland (gggs of Sir Gilbert Heathcote, 3 Bt, MP, who was gs of Sir Gilbert Heathcote, 1 Bt, one of the originators of the Bank of England and Lord Mayor of London 1711, also bro of Samuel, ancestor of Heathcote, Bt of Hursley), and Edith Millicent Heathcote (d 1977); suc kinsman, 3 Earl of Ancaster, 8 Bt, KCVO, TD, JP, DL, who d 1983; *b* 21 September 1913; *Educ* Eton; *m* 1, 1939 (m dis 1984), Patricia Margaret, da of Brig James Leslie, MC, of Sway, Hants; 1 s (Mark Simon Robert b 1941), 1 da (Joanna b 1947); m 2, 1984, Ann, da of Wing Cdr J A Hatton, and widow of Brig James Frederick Charles Mellor, DSO, OBE; *Heir* s, Mark Heathcote, OBE; *Career* 2 Lt RA 1933, served WWII NW Europe, Lt-Col 1953, Brig 1960, COS Mid E Cmd 1962–64, Brig RA Scottish Cmd 1964–66, ret 1966; *Recreations* travel, writing; *Clubs* Garrick, Army and Navy; *Style*— Brig Sir Gilbert S Heathcote, Bt, CBE; ✉ The Coach House, Tillington, Petworth, West Sussex GU28 0RA

HEATHCOTE, Sir Michael Perryman; 11 Bt (GB 1733), of Hursley, Hampshire; s of Sir Leonard Vyvyan Heathcote, 10 Bt (d 1963); in remainder to the Earldom of Macclesfield; *b* 7 August 1927; *Educ* Winchester, Clare Coll Cambridge; *m* 2 June 1956, Victoria, da of Cdr James Edward Rickards Wilford, RD, RNR, of Ackland Cottage, Shirley Holms, Lymington, Hants; 2 s (Timothy Gilbert b 1957, George Benjamin b 1965), 1 da ((Harriet) Louise (Mrs C Felstead) b 1962); *Heir* s, Timothy Heathcote; *Career* 2 Lt 9 Lancers; farmer 1951–; *Style*— Sir Michael Heathcote, Bt; ✉ Warborne Farm, Boldre, Lymington, Hampshire SO41 5QD (tel 01590 673478)

HEATHCOTE, Paul; s of Ken Heathcote, of Bolton, Lancs, and Brenda, *née* Walsh; *b* 3 October 1960; *Educ* Turton HS Bromley Cross Bolton, Bolton Catering Coll; *Career* chef/restaurateur; apprenticeship Holdsworth House Halifax 1979–80, Hotel Sternen Bern Switzerland 1980–81, Sharrow Bay Hotel Ullswater 1981–83, The Connaught Mayfair London 1983–85, Le Manoir aux Quat'Saisons Oxford 1985–87, Broughton Park Hotel Preston 1987–90, chef/prop Paul Heathcote's Restaurant Preston 1990–, prop Heathcote's Brasserie 1995–, prop Simply Heathcote's 1996–, fndr Heathcote's Sch of Excellence 1997–; 1 Egon Ronay star 1990, 1 Michelin star 1990, Good Food Guide Co Restaurant of Year 1990, Catey Newcomer of Year 1992, 2 Michelin stars 1994, Egon Ronay Chef of Year 1994, 2 Egon Ronay stars 1994, 4/5 Good Food Guide (Paul Heathcote's Restaurant) 1996 and 1997, Good Food Guide Lancashire Newcomer Restaurant of the Year (Heathcote's Brasserie) 1996, Catey Restaurateur of the Year 1997; hon fell: Univ of Lancs 1995, Bolton Inst 2001; *Style*— Paul Heathcote, Esq; ✉ Paul Heathcote's Restaurant, 104–106 Higher Road, Longridge, Preston, Lancashire PR3 3SY (tel 01772 784969, fax 01772 785713, e-mail longridge@heathcotes.co.uk)

HEATHERINGTON, Stuart; JP (1998); s of Harold Heatherington (d 1992), and Olive Watson, *née* Marr; *b* 25 September 1949; *Educ* Dame Allan's Boys' Sch Newcastle upon Tyne, Univ of Wales Aberystwyth (BSc), Univ of Durham (MSc), Open Univ (BA); *m* 1980, Pauline Elizabeth, da of John Alderson Holt (d 1983); 1 da (Rachel Anne b 18 Sept 1984); *Career* princ mathematician Durham County Cncl 1971–83, major shareholder and tech dir Moss Systems Ltd 1983–97, dir Euromoss BV 1991–97, jt md Euromoss GMBH 1995–97, chm Worthing Priority Care NHS Tst 1998–2000, chm Worthing and Southlands Hosps NHS Tst 2000–06 (non-exec dir 1998); lay memb: GMC 2003–, GOC 2007–; involved with: Tyneside Samaritans 1972–83 (dir 1981–83), British Red Cross 1997–98; FIMA 1981, MBCS 1983, CEng 1983, CMath 1993, CSc 2005; *Recreations* art history, running; *Style*— Stuart Heatherington, Esq; ✉ 3 The Gables, Nightingale Lane, Storrington, West Sussex RH20 4TB (tel 01903 740840)

HEATHERWICK, Thomas Alexander; s of Hugh Heatherwick, and Stefany, *née* Tomalin; *b* 17 February 1970; *Career* designer; estab Heatherwick Studio 1994–; visiting lectr: Chelsea Sch of Art and Design 1999, Manchester Met Univ 2000, RCA 2000 and 2002, Bartlett Sch of Architecture 2001, Kingston Univ 2001; master plans Barking Town Centre for Barking & Dagenham Cncl 2000, artist conslt St Hellier Waterfront for Jersey Govt 2000, conslt Milton Keynes Cncl 2001; architectural projects incl: pavilion for Hat Hill Fndn Sussex 1992, gazebo for Sir Terence Conran, *qv*, 1994, sitooterie for English Heritage Northumberland 2003, kiosk for Royal Borough of Kensington and Chelsea, info box for Milton Keynes City Cncl, temple for Shingon-Shu Sect Kagoshima Japan, cultural centre for St Francis Initiative Hereford, Longchamp world flagship store NY, Pacific Place Hong Kong, East Beach café Littlehampton, business units Aberystwyth; sculpture projects incl: Harvey Nichols Autumn Intrusion 1997, Guastavino's for Sir Terence Conran NY 2000, B of the Bang for Manchester City Cncl (the UK's tallest sculpture) 2004, Bleigiessen for The Wellcome Tst London 2004; infrastructure projects incl: Paternoster Vents for MEC / Stanhope plc Paternoster Square London 2002, King's Cross Glass Bridge, Rolling Bridge for Paddington Basin Devpts Ltd London 2004; planning and urban design projects incl: Arts Cncl 2002, Blue Carpet for Newcastle City Cncl 2002, Milton Keynes (lead artist for the city 2004–05), Edgeware Road, Guy's Approaches Guy's Hosp London; *Awards* Edward Marshall Prize 1994, Crafts Cncl Setting-up Award 1995, Gold D&AD Awards 1998 (Silver 2003), Sustainable Furniture Competition Earth Centre Doncaster 2000, Design Week Awards 2001, Paviors Award for Excellence 2002, Bombay Sapphire Awards 2003 and 2004, International Footbridge Awards 2005, Structural Steel Design Awards 2005, Walpole Award for Design 2005, Art and Work Awards 2006; *Style*— Thomas Heatherwick, Esq; ✉ Heatherwick Studio, Willing House, 356–364 Grays Inn Road, London WC1X 8BH (tel 020 7833 8800, fax 020 7833 8400, e-mail mail@heatherwick.com)

HEATLEY, Dr (Richard) Val; s of Walter Russell Heatley, of Bridport, Dorset, and Constance Marjorie, *née* Davis; *b* 11 October 1947; *Educ* Latymer Upper Sch, Welsh Nat Sch of Med (MB BCh, MD); *m* 5 May 1979, Ruth Mary, da of William Elderkin, of Leics; 2 da (Kirsteen Ruth b 1980, Francine Mary b 1982), 2 s (Richard Piers b 1986, Matthew Connel b 1988); *Career* clinical fell Sr Res Dept of Med Univ of McMaster Hamilton Ontario 1978–80, sr lectr in med WNSM and conslt physician Univ Hosp of Wales 1981–82, sr lectr in med Univ of Leeds 1982–, conslt physician and gastroenterologist St James's Univ Hosp Leeds 1982–; ed Int Jl of Gastroenterology; memb: Br Soc of Gastroenterology and Immunology, Bd Aliment Pharmacology and Therapeutics, Ctee on Gastroenterology RCP; FRCP; *Books* The Helicobacter pylori Handbook (1998), Clinical Economics in Gastroenterology (1999), Dyspepsia: The Clinical Consequences (2000), Medicine and Myths (2003); *Recreations* children, music, travel, walking; *Style*— Dr Val Heatley; ✉ Department of Medicine, St James's University Hospital, Leeds LS9 7TF (tel 0113 243 3144)

HEATON, *see also:* Henniker-Heaton

HEATON, Frances Anne; da of John Ferris Whidborne (d 1985), and Marjorie Annie, *née* Maltby (d 1989); *b* 11 August 1944; *Educ* Queen Anne's Sch Caversham, Trinity Coll Dublin (BA, LLB); *m* 26 April 1969, Martin Christopher Crispin Heaton; 2 s (Mark Christopher Francis b 14 April 1972, Andrew John Ralph b 9 Nov 1974); *Career* called to the Bar Inner Temple 1967; Dept of Econ Affrs 1967–70, HM Treasy 1970–80 (seconded S G Warburg & Co Ltd 1977–79), dir of corp fin Lazard Brothers & Co Ltd 1986–2001 (joined 1980); non-exec dir: W S Atkins 1990–2003 (dep chm 1996–2003), Commercial Union 1994–98, Elementis plc (formerly Harrisons & Crosfield) 1994–99, BUPA 1998–2001, Worldpay Ltd 2000–02, Legal & General Gp plc 2001–, AWG plc 2002–, Jupiter Primadona Growth Tst 2005–; DG Takeovers and Mergers Panel 1992–94, memb Ct Bank of England 1993–2001, memb Ctee on Standards in Public Life 1998–2003; *Recreations* riding, gardening, bridge; *Style*— Mrs Frances Heaton

HEATON, Mark Frederick; s of Peter Heaton (d 1965), and Rachael, *née* Frampton; *b* 20 December 1951; *m* 1, 24 July 1976 (m dis 1986), Lorna, da of Col Ralph Stewart-Wilson, MC; 2 s (Henry Peter Frederick b 14 April 1980, Oliver James Stewart b 12 Jan 1983); m 2, 18 March 1988, Naomi Claire Helen Heaton, *qv*, da of Dr Boaz Antony Jarrett; *Career* landowner in Glos; Leo Burnett Advertising Ltd (1972–); chm London Central Portfolio Ltd 1999–; memb: CLA, Countryside Alliance, Racehorse Owners' Assoc, Lloyd's, BASC, Game Conservancy Tst; *Recreations* horse racing, skiing, shooting, golf; *Clubs* White's, MCC, Turf, Sloane, Frilford Heath, Annabel's, Cricketers'; *Style*— Mark Heaton, Esq; ✉ Ampney St Mary Manor, Cirencester, Gloucestershire GL7 5SP (tel 0128585 1321)

HEATON, Naomi Claire Helen; da of Dr Boaz Antony Jarrett (d 2003), of Chiswick, London, and Patricia Evelyn, *née* White; *b* 11 September 1955; *Educ* Walthamstow Hall Sch for Girls, St Hilda's Coll Oxford (BA); *m* 18 March 1988, Mark Frederick Heaton, *qv*; *Career* Leo Burnett Advertising 1977–82; main bd dir: Saatchi & Saatchi Advertising 1984 (joined 1982), Young & Rubicam 1985–86; chief exec London Central Portfolio Ltd (specialists in residential investment asset mgmnt, estab 1989) 1999– (md 1994–99); *Recreations* skiing, country pursuits; *Clubs* Boodle's, Sloane, Cricketers; *Style*— Mrs Mark Heaton; ✉ Ampney St Mary Manor, Cirencester, Gloucestershire GL7 5SP; 116 Seymour Place, London W1H 1NW (tel 020 7723 1733, fax 020 7724 1744, e-mail naomi.heaton@londoncentralportfolio.com, website www.londoncentralportfolio.com)

HEATON-ARMSTRONG, Anthony Eustace John; s of William Henry Dunamace Heaton-Armstrong, of Berks, and Idonea, *née* Chance; *b* 27 September 1950; *Educ* Ampleforth, Univ of Bristol (LLB); *m* 1, 10 Feb 1973 (m dis 1977), Susan, *née* Allnutt; m 2, 20 May 1982, Anne Frances, da of late Ethel Rigbo; 1 s (John William b 15 Feb 1983), 2 da (Eleanor b 8 May 1985, Celestine b 3 Sept 1988); *Career* called to the Bar Gray's Inn 1973, in practice 1973–; expert on police evidence, Int Cmmn of Jurists' observer at trials overseas involving alleged human rights abuses, memb team appointed by Home Office to conduct fundamental review of death certification and Coronial Inquest systems 2001–03; tstee Aldo Tst; *Books* Confession Evidence (with David Wolchover, 1996), Analysing Witness Testimony (with Eric Shepherd and David Wolchover, 1999), Witness Testimony: Psychological, Investigative and Evidential Perspectives (with Eric Shepherd, Gisli Gudjonsson and David Wolchover, 2006); also author of numerous legal articles in learned jls; *Recreations* prisoners' welfare, gardening, dry fly fishing, wildlife and the countryside; *Clubs* Garrick; *Style*— Anthony Heaton-Armstrong, Esq; ✉ 9–12 Bell Yard, London WC2A 2JR (tel 020 7400 1800, fax 020 7404 1405, e-mail anthony@heaton-armstrong.freeserve.co.uk)

HEATON-HARRIS, Chris; MEP; s of David Barry Heaton-Harris, of Esher, Surrey, and Ann Geraldine, *née* Cox; *b* 28 November 1967; *Educ* Tiffin Boys GS, Wolverhampton Poly; *m* 30 June 1990, Jayne Yvonne, da of Gregory Harold Spencer Carlow; 2 da (Megan Elizabeth Tate b 5 May 1996, Tess Alexandra Jayne b 1 April 2000); *Career* MEP (Cons) E Midlands 1999–; Parly candidate (Cons) Leicester S 1997 and 2004 (by-election); memb various Euro Parl Ctees; sabbatical Wolverhampton Poly Students' Union; *Recreations* Grade 5 soccer referee; *Style*— Chris Heaton-Harris, Esq, MEP; ✉ Conservative Office, 23 Queen Street, Market Rasen, Lincolnshire LN8 3EN (tel 0845 234 0059 or 01673 849585, e-mail cheaton@europarl.eu.int)

HEBER-PERCY, Algernon Eustace Hugh; JP; s of Brig Algernon George William Heber-Percy, DSO (d 1961), of Hodnet Hall, and Daphne Wilma Kenyon, *née* Parker Bowles; *b* 2 January 1944; *Educ* Harrow; *m* 6 July 1966, Hon Margaret Jane, *née* Lever, yst da of 3 Viscount Leverhulme, KG, TD; 3 da (Emily Jane b 19 Feb 1969, Lucy Ann b 29 Dec 1970, Sophie Daphne b 22 Jan 1979), 1 s ((Algernon) Thomas Lever b 29 Jan 1984); *Career* Lt Grenadier Gds 1962–66; farmer; memb Exec Ctee and chm Mercia Regnl Ctee Nat Tst 1990–99, memb Heart of England Historic Houses Assoc, tstee Nat Gardens Scheme; govr Shrewsbury Sch 2004; Hon Col 5 LI (Shropshire and Herefordshire Regt) 1998–99, Hon Col (W Midlands Regt) 1999–; High Sheriff Shropshire 1987, HM Lord-Lt Shropshire 1996– (DL 1986, Vice Lord-Lt 1990); *Recreations* gardening, country sports; *Clubs* Cavalry and Guards'; *Style*— Algernon Heber-Percy, Esq; ✉ Hodnet Hall, Hodnet, Market Drayton, Shropshire TF9 3NN (tel 01630 685202)

HEDDEN, Robert; s of Frederick Hedden (d 1982), of Okehampton, Devon, and Winifred Elizabeth, *née* Trenaman (d 1996); *b* 22 February 1948; *Educ* Okehampton GS, KCL (LLB, AKC); *m* 10 Sept 1977 (m dis 1996), Jean Mary, da of Walter John Worboyes (d 1982), of London; 1 da (Rachel Louise), 1 s (Oliver Michael Ward); partner, Mustakeem Shariff (civil partnership 7 July 2007), of Penang, Malaysia; *Career* admitted slr 1972 (Clifford's Inn prizeman), ptnr Herbert Smith 1980–93 (conslt 1993–94), gp slr Freshwater Group of Companies 1993–; memb: Ctee Br-Polish Legal Assoc 1989–93, Planning and Environmental Law Sub-Ctee City of London Law Soc 1991–93; memb Law Soc; assoc memb Dirs' Guild of GB 1990–96; Freeman City of London, Liveryman Worshipful Co of Slrs; *Recreations* theatre, music, tennis, skiing, powerboating, swimming, homes in Ibiza and Malaysia and other travel; *Clubs* Athenaeum, Royal Yachting Assoc; *Style*— Robert Hedden, Esq; ✉ Freshwater House, 158–162 Shaftesbury Avenue, London WC2H 8HR (tel 020 7836 1555, fax 020 7240 9770)

HEDGECOE, Prof John; s of William Alec Hedgecoe (d 1983), of Great Dunmow, Essex, and Kathleen Alice, *née* Don (d 1981); *b* 24 March 1937; *Educ* Gulval Village Sch, Guildford Sch of Art, Epsom Sch of Art, Ruskin Coll Oxford, RCA (Dr RCA); *m* 1, 3 Oct 1959 (m dis 1994), Julia, da of Sidney Mardon (d 1971), of Bishop's Stortford, Herts; 2 s (Sebastian John b 1961, Auberon Henry b 1968), 1 da (Imogen Dolly Alice b 1964); m 2, 1 Dec 2001, Jennifer, da of Col and Mrs Donald Hogg, of Kelso, Scotland; *Career* photographer; Nat Serv RAF SAC 1955–56; staff photographer Queen magazine 1957–72; freelance for most int magazines 1958– (Sunday Times and The Observer 1960–70); RCA: fndr Photography Sch 1965, reader and head Photography Dept 1965–74, fell 1973, prof of photography 1975, fndr Audio/Visual Dept 1980, fndr Holography Unit 1982, managing tstee 1983, pro-rector until 1993, sr fell 1992, prof emeritus 1995; advsr English Heritage 1995; definitive portrait of HM The Queen for Br and Aust postage stamps 1966, photographer The Arts Multi-Projection Br Exhibition Expo Japan Show 1970, visiting prof Norwegian Nat TV Sch Oslo 1985; dir: John Hedgecoe Ltd 1965–95, Perennial Pictures Ltd 1980–90; md Lion & Unicorn Press Ltd 1986–94; illustrator of numerous books 1958–, contributor to numerous radio broadcasts; TV: Tonight (Aust) 1967, Folio (Anglia TV) 1980, eight programmes on photography (Channel 4) 1983 (repeated 1984), Winners (Channel 4) 1984, Light and Form (US Cable TV) 1985; exhibitions incl: Nat Portrait Gallery 2000, Sainsbury Centre Visual Arts Norwich 2000, RCA 2000, Guildford House Gallery 2001, Christchurch Gallery Ipswich 2001, Westcliffe Gallery Sheringham 2002, Milton Gallery St Pauls Sch London 2005, also in London, Sydney, Toronto, Detroit, Edinburgh, Venice and Prague; work in collections incl: V&A, Museum Art Gallery of Ontario, Nat Portrait Gallery, Citibank London, Henry Moore Fndn, MOMA NY, Leeds City Art Gallery; govr W Surrey Coll of Art 1975–80 (memb

Acad Advsy Bd 1975–80), memb Photographic Bd CNAA 1976–78, acad govr Richmond Coll London; laureate and medal for achievement in photography (Czechoslovakian Govt) 1989, awarded Lente y Pluma de Plata prize for photography (Mexican Govt) 2002; fell Indian International Photographic Soc, FRSA; *Books* Henry Moore (1968, prize best art book world-wide 1969), Kevin Crossley-Holland Book of Norfolk Poems (jtly 1970), Photography, Material and Methods (jtly 1971–74 edns), Henry Moore Energy in Space (1973), The Book of Photography (1976), Handbook of Photographic Techniques (1977, 2 edn 1982), The Art of Colour Photography (1978, Kodak Book Prize), Possession (1978), The Pocket Book of Photography (1979), Introductory Photography Course (1979), Master Classes in Photography: Children and Child Portraiture (1980), Poems of Thomas Hardy (illustrated 1981), Poems of Robert Burns (illustrated), The Book of Advanced Photography (1982), What a Picture! (1983), The Photographer's Work Book (1983), Aesthetics of Nude Photography (1984), The Workbook of Photo Techniques (1984, 2 edn 1997), The Workbook of Darkroom Techniques (1984, 2 edn 1997), Pocket Book of Travel and Holiday Photography (1986), Henry Moore: His Ideas, Inspirations and Life as an Artist (1986), The Three Dimensional Pop-up Photography Book (with A L Rowse, 1986), Shakespeare's Land (1986), Photographers Manual of Creative Ideas (1986), Portrait Photography (with A L Rowse, 1987), Rowse's Cornwall (1987), Practical Book of Landscape Photography (1988), Hedgecoe on Photography (1988), Hedgecoe on Video (1989), The Complete Guide to Photography (1990, 2 edn 2004), The Complete Guide to Video Photography (1992), The Art of Ceramics and Zillij (1992), The New Book of Photography (1994, 2 edn 2004), The Complete Guide to Black and White Photography (1994), John Hedgecoe's New Book of Photography (1995), John Hedgecoe's Video Basics (1995), Breakfast with Dolly (1996), John Hedgecoe's Figure and Form (1996), Introductory Photography Course (1996), Hedgecoe on Photography (CD-Rom), Spirit of the Garden (1997), England's World Heritage (1997), A Monumental Vision: The Sculpture of Henry Moore (1998), Art of Colour (1998), 35mm Handbook, Portraits, Photographing your Children (2000), How to take Great Photographs (2001), Photographing Your Baby (2002), Holiday Photography (2003), The New Manual of Photography (2003); *Recreations* sculpture, building, gardening; *Clubs* Arts; *Style*— Prof John Hedgecoe; ✉ c/o Dorling Kindersley, 80 Strand, London WC2R 0RL

HEDGER, John Clive; CB (1998); s of Leslie John Keith Hedger, and Iris, *née* Freidlos; *b* 17 December 1942; *Educ* The Quirister Sch Winchester, Victoria Coll Jersey, Univ of Sussex (MA); *m* 1966, Jean Ann, *née* Felstead; 2 s, 1 da; *Career* Department for Educn and Employment (formerly DES then Dept for Educn): joined 1966, asst private sec 1970–74, sec Ctee of Enquiry on Educn of the Handicapped 1974–76, head of schs branch and under sec 1988–92, dep sec 1992–95; dir of operations Dept for Educn and Employment 1995–2000; assoc Fin and Educn Services 2000–, chm Skills Cncl for Lifelong Learning 2004–06; tstee Rathbone; memb Cncl Radley Coll 1998–2007; *Recreations* coarse sailing, coarse acting, walking; *Clubs* Royal Over-Seas League; *Style*— John Hedger, Esq, CB; ✉ Poultons, Cookham, Berkshire SL6 9HW (tel 01628 524146, e-mail jhedger1@btconnect.com)

HEDGES, Dr Anthony John; s of Sidney George Hedges (d 1974), and Mary, *née* Dixon; *b* 5 March 1931; *Educ* Bicester GS, Keble Coll Oxford (MA, BMus, DipEd); *m* 28 Aug 1957, (Delia) Joy, da of Maj Albert Marsden (d 1971); 2 da (Fiona b 25 Feb 1959, Deborah b 4 March 1961), 2 s (Nicholas b 28 Oct 1964, Simon b 10 May 1966); *Career* Nat Serv Royal Signals Band 1955–57; teacher and lectr Royal Scottish Acad of Music 1957–63; Univ of Hull: lectr 1963, sr lectr 1968, reader in composition 1978–95; princ compositions incl: orchestral: Comedy Overture 1962 (revised 1967), Overture Oct '62 1962 (revised 1968), Variations on a Theme of Rameau 1969, Festival Dances 1976, Four Breton Sketches 1980, Sinfonia Concertante 1980, Scenes from the Humber 1981, Symphony 1 1972–73, A Cleveland Overture 1984, Concertino for Horn and String Orchestra 1987, Sinfonia Giovanile 1991, Symphony 2 1998; choral: Epithalamium 1969, Psalm 104 1973, The Temple of Solomon 1979, I Sing the Birth (Canticles for Christmas) 1985, I'll Make Me a World 1990, The Lamp of Liberty 2006; chamber music: String Quartets 1970 and 1990, Piano Trio 1977, Flute Trios 1985 and 1989, Clarinet Quintet 1988; Sonatas for Piano 1974, Flute 1989, Cello 1982, Viola 1982, Wind Quintet 1984, Bassoon Quintet 1991, Piano Quartet 1992, Piano Duets 1993, Cello Suite 1993; opera: Shadows in the Sun 1976; musical: Minotaur 1978; miscellaneous: anthems, partsongs music for TV, film and stage, complete archive in Hull Central Library; memb Cncl The Composers' Guild of GB (memb Exec Ctee 1969–73 and 1977–81, chm 1972–73); memb: Cncl Central Music Library Westminster 1970–91, SPNM Cncl 1974–81; memb Music Panels: Yorkshire Arts 1974–75, Lincs and Humberside Arts 1975–78; memb Music Bd CNNA 1974–77; Hon DMus Univ of Hull 1977; LRAM; *Books* Basic Tonal Harmony (1988), An Introduction to Counterpoint (1988); also made many recordings on LP and CD; *Recreations* reading, playing chamber music; *Style*— Dr Anthony Hedges; ✉ Malt Shovel Cottage, 76 Walkergate, Beverley, East Yorkshire HU17 9ER (tel 01482 860580, e-mail ahedges@westfieldmusic.karoo.co.uk, website www.westfieldmusic.karoo.net)

HEDGES, Neil Francis; s of Kenneth Francis Chevalier, of Walmer, Kent, and Peggy, *née* Best; *b* 12 December 1956; *Educ* Watford Boys' GS, Univ of Sheffield (BA); *m* 19 Sept 1981, Katherine Anne, da of Trevor Noel Louis, of Bushey Heath, Herts; 2 da (Frances b 13 Feb 1986, Alexandra b 18 March 1989); *Career* md Valin Pollen Ltd 1988–90 (asst md 1985, account exec 1980), co-fndr and chm Fishburn Hedges (formerly Fishburn Hedges Boys Williams); *Recreations* music, cinema, walking, family; *Style*— Neil Hedges, Esq

HEDLEY, Hon Mr Justice; Sir Mark Hedley; kt (2001); s of late Peter Hedley, of Windsor, and late Eve, *née* Morley; *b* 23 August 1946; *Educ* Framlingham Coll, Univ of Liverpool (LLB); *m* 14 April 1973, Erica Rosemary, da of late John Capel Britton, of Ashbourne; 3 s (Michael b 1975, Steven b 1981, Peter b 1982), 1 da (Anna b 1978); *Career* called to the Bar Gray's Inn 1969 (bencher 2002); recorder of the Crown Court 1988; circuit judge (Northern Circuit) 1992–2002, judge of the High Court of Justice (Family Div) 2002–; reader C of E; chllr Diocese of Liverpool 2002–; Hon LLD Univ of Liverpool 2003, hon fell Liverpool John Moores Univ 2005; *Recreations* cricket, railways; *Style*— The Hon Mr Justice Hedley; ✉ Royal Courts of Justice, Strand, London WC2A 2LL

HEDLEY LEWIS, Vincent Richard; s of John Hedley Lewis (d 1976), of Birkholme Manor, Corby Glen, Lincs, and Sheelagh Alice Valentine, *née* De Paravicini (d 1990); *b* 24 May 1941; *Educ* Wellesley House, Harrow; *m* 17 June 1978, Penelope Ann, da of A C Hobson, MC; 3 da (Selena Priscilla b 27 Sept 1980, Melissa Sheelagh b 12 Sept 1982, Amanda Jane b 28 Jan 1985); *Career* articled to H R Crouch, Crouch Chapman & Co 1960–68, CA 1966; ptnr Agribusiness Div Deloitte & Touche 1968–2000; memb: Lincolnshire Jt Devpt Ctee 1981–97, Econ Advsy Panel Rural Devpt Cmmn 1989–99, Country Landowners' Cncl 1994–2003; dir: Peterborough Devpt Agency 1987–94, NIAB Ltd 2000–07, JSR Farms Ltd 2000–, Oxford Farming Conference 2007–; chm Farmacy plc 2000–; farmer of 1700 acres Corby Glen Lincs; chm CLA Game Fair Bd 2005–; govr Harper Adams Univ 2000–07; memb SCGB (Gold medallist), ran London Marathon 1989; *Books* Contract Farming (1976); *Recreations* cricket, skiing, tennis, golf, shooting; *Clubs* Farmers', MCC, Free Foresters Cricket, Luffenham Heath Golf, Lincolnshire; *Style*— Vincent Hedley Lewis, Esq; ✉ Birkholme Manor, Corby Glen, Grantham, Lincolnshire NG33 4LF (tel 01476 550255, car 07836 759553, e-mail vincent.hedleylewis@farmline.com)

HEDLEY-MILLER, Rosalind; da of Roger Latham Hedley-Miller (d 2004), and Dame Mary Elizabeth Hedley-Miller, DCVO, CB; *b* 25 November 1954; *Educ* St Paul's Girls' Sch, St Hugh's Coll Oxford (MA), Harvard Univ; *Career* Investment Dept J Henry Schroder

Wagg & Co Ltd 1977–79; Dresdner Kleinwort: Corp Fin Dept 1979–, dir 1987–, jt head Corp Fin Dept 1994–96, gp dir 1996–2001, vice-chm 2001–; non-exec dir: Bejam Group plc 1987–88, TV-am plc 1990–93; memb: Fin Ctee Oxford University Press 1995–, Industrial Devpt Advsy Bd DTI 1997–2005; Rhodes Tstee 1999–; *Recreations* music, bridge, golf; *Style*— Miss Rosalind Hedley-Miller; ✉ 48 Elms Road, London SW4 9EX; Dresdner Kleinwort, 30 Gresham Street, London EC2P 2XY (tel 020 7623 8000)

HEDWORTH, (Alan) Toby; QC (1996); s of John William Swaddle Hedworth (d 1998), and Margaret Ena, *née* Dodds (d 2004); *b* 23 April 1952; *Educ* King's Sch Tynemouth, Royal GS Newcastle upon Tyne, St Catharine's Coll Cambridge (MA); *m* 12 Dec 1987, Kathleen Mary, da of Gordon Luke; 2 da (Anna Charlotte Pettinger b 2 July 1979, Alice Lucinda Marie b 6 May 1989); *Career* called to the Bar Inner Temple 1975; recorder 1995– (asst recorder 1991), head of chambers Trinity Chambers Newcastle upon Tyne 1999–; memb Criminal Bar Assoc; vice-chm Northumberland & Newcastle Soc; *Recreations* Newcastle United FC, English Lake District, motoring, the built environment; *Clubs* Northern Counties (Newcastle upon Tyne); *Style*— Toby Hedworth, Esq, QC; ✉ Trinity Chambers, The Custom House, Quayside, Newcastle upon Tyne NE1 3DE (tel 0191 232 1927, fax 0191 232 7975)

HEFFER, Simon James; s of James Heffer (d 1971), of Woodham Ferrers, Essex, and Joyce Mary, *née* Clements; *b* 18 July 1960; *Educ* King Edward VI Sch Chelmsford, Corpus Christi Coll Cambridge (MA); *m* 31 July 1987, Diana Caroline, da of Sqdn Ldr P A Clee, of Marlow, Bucks; 2 s (James William Frederick b 3 Sept 1993, Charles Hubert John b 5 July 1996); *Career* med journalist 1983–85, freelance journalist 1985–86; Daily Telegraph: leader writer 1986–91, dep political corr 1987–88, political sketch writer 1988–91, political columnist 1990–91; dep ed: The Spectator 1991–94, Daily Telegraph 1994–95; columnist: Evening Standard 1991–93, Daily Mail 1993–94 and 1995–2005; assoc ed Daily Telegraph 2005–; memb Bd Britten Sinfonia; *Books* A Century of County Cricket (ed, 1990), A Tory Seer (jt ed with C Moore, 1989), Moral Desperado: a Life of Thomas Carlyle (1995), Power and Place: The Political Consequences of King Edward VII (1998), Like the Roman: The Life of Enoch Powell (1998), Nor Shall My Sword: The Reinvention of England (1999), Vaughan Williams (2000), Great British Speeches (ed, 2007); *Recreations* cricket, music, ecclesiology, bibliophily, my wife and children; *Clubs* Beefsteak, Garrick, MCC; *Style*— Simon Heffer, Esq; ✉ The Daily Telegraph, 111 Buckingham Palace Road, London SW1W 0DT

HEFFERNAN, John Francis; *b* 1 September 1927; *Educ* Gunnersbury GS, Univ of London (BCom); *m* 19 July 1952, Veronica, da of Dr John Laing; 2 da (Maureen, Catherine); *Career* called to the Bar Inner Temple 1954; fin journalist Daily Express then Evening Standard, chm and princ shareholder City Press newspaper 1965–75, city ed United Provincial Newspapers Ltd 1965–93 (incl Yorkshire Post 1985–94); memb Assoc of Regnl City Eds (currently hon sec); pres City Livery Club 1997–98 (vice-pres 1996–97); Worshipful Co of Basketmakers: Liveryman 1965, Jr Warden 1995, Prime Warden 1996; *Style*— John Heffernan, Esq; ✉ 1 Fern Dene, top of Templewood, off Cleveland Road, Ealing, London W13 8AN (tel 020 8997 6868, e-mail john.heffernan@virgin.net)

HEFFERNAN, Patrick Benedict; s of Dr Daniel Anthony Heffernan (d 2000), of Reading, Berks, and Margaret, *née* Donovan (d 1996); *b* 17 March 1948; *Educ* Wimbledon Coll, Jesus Coll Cambridge (MA); *m* 5 May 1973, Elizabeth, da of Robert Essery (d 1966), of Huddersfield and Melbourne; 2 s (Thomas b 1984, Rory Patrick b 1993), 1 da (Miranda b 1987); *Career* slr 1974; ptnr: Clyde & Co 1988–97, Mishcon de Reya 1997–99, Halliwell Landau 1999–2002, Orchard Brayton Graham LLP 2002–; Liveryman Worshipful Company of Farriers (1994); *Recreations* Times crossword, sport, reading; *Style*— Patrick Heffernan, Esq; ✉ 3 Cholmeley Crescent, Highgate, London N6 5EZ; Orchard Brayton Graham LLP, 24 Britton Street, London EC1M 5UA (tel 0870 874 7477, fax 0870 874 7577, e-mail patrick.heffernan@obglaw.com)

HEGARTY, Sir John Kevin; kt (2007); *Career* jr art dir Benton and Bowles 1965, briefly with John Collings & Ptnrs; Cramer Saatchi (later Saatchi & Saatchi): joined 1967, founding shareholder Saatchi & Saatchi 1970, dep creative dir 1971–73; TBWA London: co-fndr 1973, creative dir 1973–82; Bartle Bogle Hegarty (BBH): fndr 1982, currently worldwide creative dir and chm; Hon Dr Univ of Middx 2006; *Awards* Campaign Agency of Year for TBWA 1980; for BBH: Campaign Agency of Year 2003, 2004 and 2005, Cannes Advtg Festival Agency of Year 1993 and 1994; 2 Gold and 6 Silver D&AD Awards, Cannes Golds and Silvers, Br TV Gold and Silvers, D&AD President's Award for outstanding achievement in advtg industry, inducted into One Club Creative Hall of Fame (US) 2005, Lifetime Achievement Award Clio Awards 2005; *Style*— Sir John Hegarty; ✉ Bartle Bogle Hegarty, 60 Kingly Street, London W1B 5DS (tel 020 7734 1677, fax 020 7437 3666)

HEGGESSEY, Lorraine; *Career* jr reporter Acton Gazette 1978–79; BBC TV: news trainee 1979–81, news sub-ed 1981–82, asst prodr Current Affrs Dept (Newsnight, Panorama, 60 Minutes) 1982–83, prodr Current Affrs Dept (60 Minutes, Panorama) 1983–86; prodr Thames TV (This Week) 1986–90; Channel 4 TV: dep ed Hard News 1990–91, prodr and reporter Dispatches 1991, prodr As It Happens 1991; BBC TV: ed Biteback 1991, series prodr The Underworld 1992–94, exec prodr (Minders, Animal Hospital Live, States of Mind) 1994, exec prodr Animal Hospital 1994–96, series ed QED 1994–96, exec prodr The Human Body 1996–97, head of Children's Progs 1997–99, dir of programmes BBC Productions 1999–2000, jt dir BBC Factual and Learning 2000, controller BBC1 2000–05, chief exec talkback THAMES 2005–; *Style*— Ms Lorraine Heggessey

HEGLEY, John Richard; s of René Hegley, and Joan, *née* Harris; *b* 1 October 1953, Islington, London; *Educ* Univ of Bradford (BSc); *Children* 1 da (Isabella b 1995); *Career* performance poet; began career in children's theatre with Interaction and Soapbox 1980 then at Comedy Store 1981 and John Peel sessions with The Popticians 1983–84 (previously employed as bus conductor); numerous tours; regular presenter BBC Radio 4; performed in The Pyjama Game (musical) 1999; Hon Dr of Arts Univ of Luton 2000; *Poetry* Poems for Pleasure (1989), Glad to Wear Glasses (1990), Can I Come Down Now, Dad? (1991), Five Sugars Please (1993), Saint and Blurry (audio recording, poetry and songs, 1993), These Were Your Father's (1994), Love Cuts (1995), The Family Pack (collection, 1996), Beyond Our Kennel (1998), Dog (2000), My Dog is a Carrot (for children, 2002), The Sound of Paint Drying (2003); *Clubs* Islington Folk; *Style*— John Hegley, Esq; ✉ c/o Will Darlow, Torika Management, 74 Clarenwell Road EC1M 5QA (tel 020 7336 7868)

HEIGL, Peter Richard; *b* 21 February 1943; *m* Sally, *née* Lupton; 3 s (Thomas James b 1971, Jonathan William b 1973, Paul Alexander b 1977), 1 da (Phillipa Jane b 1982); *Career* entered FCO 1974; second sec (commercial) Kuala Lumpur 1974–77, second sec (admin) Accra 1978–81, S Asian Dept 1981–84, first sec (commercial) Riyadh 1984–87, dep consul-gen Jeddah 1987–89, ME Dept 1989–91, dep head of mission Khartoum 1991–94, chargé d'affaires Phnom Penh 1994, dep head of mission Kathmandu 1994–99, UK high cmmr Nassau 1999–2003, resident dep high cmmr Tarawa Kiribati 2004–; *Style*— Peter Heigl, Esq; ✉ c/o Foreign & Commonwealth Office (Tarawa), King Charles Street, London SW1A 2AH

HEILBRON, Hilary Nora Burstein; QC (1987); da of Dr Nathaniel Burstein, and Dame Rose Heilbron, DBE; *b* 2 January 1949; *Educ* Huyton Coll, LMH Oxford (MA); *Career* called to the Bar: Gray's Inn 1971 (bencher 1995), NSW Aust 1996 (SC 1997); dep chm City Disputes Panel, DTI inspr into the affairs of Blue Arrow plc 1989; chm: Jt Ctee on Civil Cts Gen Cncl of the Bar and Law Soc, London Common Law and Commercial Bar Assoc 1992–93; memb: Gen Cncl of the Bar 1991–98, Advsy Cncl CEDR; vice-chm Marshall Aid Commemoration Cmmn 1998–2002; fell Soc for Advanced Legal Studies 1996–2002;

H

Style— Hilary Heilbron, QC; ✉ Brick Court Chambers, 7–8 Essex Street, London WC2R 3LD (tel 020 7379 3550, fax 020 7379 3558)

HEIN, Prof Jotun John; *b* 19 July 1956, Denmark; *Educ* Aarhus Univ; *Career* grad asst Aarhus Univ 1981–84, visiting assoc Nat Inst of Environmental Health Sciences (NIEHS) NC 1985–87, conslt Harvard Med Sch 1987, research assoc Inst of Mathematics Univ of Southern Calif 1987–1988, post-doctoral fell Center for Molecular Genetics Univ of Calif San Diego 1988–89, visiting appt Univ of Washington Seattle 1989, post-doctoral work Centre Recherche Mathematiquee Montreal 1989–90, Japanese Soc for the Promotion of Sci fell Nat Inst of Genetics Mishima and Japanese DNA Database 1990–91; Aarhus Univ: sr stipend 1991–, assoc prof 1994–, dir Bioinformatics Research Centre 2001–; prof of bioinformatics Dept of Statistics Univ of Oxford 2001–; invited stay Newton Inst for Mathematical Sciences Cambridge 1998, Erskine Award to stay at Dept of Mathematics Massey Univ Christchurch 1999; assoc ed Genetics 2001–03, author of numerous articles and reviews in learned jls; memb Royal Soc of Sci Denmark; *Style—* Prof Jotun Hein; ✉ Department of Statistics, University of Oxford, 1 South Parks Road, Oxford OX1 3TG (tel 01865 281886, fax 01865 281239)

HEINDORFF, Michael; *b* 1949; *Educ* Art Coll and Univ of Braunschweig, Royal Coll of Art London; *Career* artist; teacher RCA London 1980–99; work in the collections of: RCA, Univ of Liverpool, V&A, Vicaria di Santiago de Chile, Herzog Anton Ulrich-Museum Braunschweig, State of Niedersachsen Germany, Arts Cncl of GB, The Br Cncl, Bank of America LA, Security Pacific Bank LA, MOMA NY, The Bank of Montreal London, Bradford Municipal Museum, Green Coll Oxford, Imperial War Museum, Nat Gallery Washington USA; *Solo Exhibitions* Galerie Axiom Cologne 1977, Bernard Jacobson Gallery London 1978–1992, Bernard Jacobson Gallery NY 1983–89, Bernard Jacobson Gallery LA 1981, 1982 and 1984, Jacobson/Hochman Gallery NY 1981 and 1982, Mathildenhöhe Darmstadt Germany 1983, Villa Massimo Rome 1984, Northern Centre for Contemporary Art Sunderland 1987, Royal Coll of Art 1993 and 1995, NORD/LB Galerie (Braunschweig) 1998, NORD/LB Forum (Dessau) 1998, Schlossmuseum (Furstenberg) 1998, touring show of drawings (museums in northern Germany) 1999–2001, Guildhall Art Gallery 2002, Deutsche Bank London 2003; *Group Exhibitions* incl: John Moore's Liverpool Exhibition 1976, Air Gallery 1977, Royal Coll of Art London (Annual Exhibitions) 1977, Whitechapel Art Gallery London 1979, Serpentine Gallery London (Summer show 1) 1980, Anne Berthand Gallery London 1981, Herzog Anton Ulrich-Museum Braunschweig 1981 and 2004, Bradford Print Biennale 1982, Paton Gallery London (Alternative Tate) 1982, Ashmolean Museum Oxford (Innovations in Contemporary Printmaking) 1982, Third Biennale of European Graphic Art Baden-Baden 1983, Bruecke Museum Berlin 1984, MOMA NY 1984, Univ of Maryland USA 1985, Bank of America San Francisco 1985, V&A Museum London 1986, Sunderland Arts Centre & Laing Art Gallery Newcastle 1987, Royal Acad of Arts London 1988–, RCA 150th Anniversary Show 1988, Imperial War Museum London (On Commission) 1989, Nat Gallery Washington USA 1989, Bernard Jacobson Gallery London 1990 and 1991, Flowers East Gallery London 1992, 1994, 1997 and 1998, Royal Acad Summer Exhibition 1995, V&A Museum London 1996, Museum of London 1997 and 2001; *Awards*: German Nat Scholarship Fndn scholar 1972–76, DAAD scholarship for London 1976–77, John Moore's Liverpool award 1976, State of Niedersachsen scholarship 1980, Schmidt-Rotluff prize 1981, Rome prize Villa Massimo 1981; hon fell RCA; *Clubs* Chelsea Arts (life memb); *Style—* Michael Heindorff, Esq; ✉ e-mail heindorff@aol.com

HELLAWELL, Keith; QPM (1990); s of Douglas Hellawell (d 1986), and Ada Alice, *née* Battye; *b* 18 May 1942; *Educ* Kirkburton Secdy Modern Sch, Dewsbury Tech Coll, Barnsley Coll of Mining, Univ of London (LLB), Cranfield Inst of Technol (MSc); *m* 1963, Brenda, da of late Percy Hey; 2 da (Samantha Louise b 26 Sept 1965, Alexandra Jane b 18 May 1967), 1 s (Charles Justin Spencer b 17 May 1970); *Career* Huddersfield Borough Police: joined 1962, Sgt 1965, Inspr 1967; W Yorks Police (later W Yorks Metropolitan Police): joined 1968, Chief Inspr 1972, Supt 1975, Chief Supt 1979, Asst Chief Constable 1983; Dep Chief Constable Humberside 1985–90, Chief Constable Cleveland Constabulary 1990–93, Chief Constable W Yorks Police 1993–97; UK Anti-Drugs co-ordinator 1998–2001, Govt advsr on int drug issues 2001–02; non-exec dir: Evans plc 1998–, Universal Vehicles Gp plc 2001, Catapult Presentations plc 2001, Dalkia plc 2002; non-exec chm: Sterience Ltd 2003, Howells Assocs 2005; memb Bd of Tstees NSPCC; non-exec dir Huddersfield Giants (rugby league); newspaper columnist and broadcaster; Dr (hc): Leeds Metropolitan Univ 1997, Bradford Univ 1998, Huddersfield Univ 1998; Officer Brother StJ 1995; *Books* The Outsider (autobiography, 2002); *Recreations* reading, design, gardening, sport; *Style—* Dr Keith Hellawell, QPM

HELLER, Lawrance (Laurie); *b* 14 April 1934; *Educ* Battersea GS, Sidney Sussex Coll Cambridge (scholar, MA); *m* Lilian Patricia Heller; 1 da (Charlotte b 9 April 1964); *Career* articled Silkin & Silkin 1956–59, jr ptnr Titmuss Sainer & Webb 1962–63 (asst slr 1959–62), ptnr Leighton & Co 1964–70, a fndr and sr ptnr Berwin Leighton (now Berwin Leighton Paisner) 1970–; *Books* Practical Commercial Precedents (contrib, 1987), Commercial Property Development Precedents (gen ed and maj contrib, 1993); *Recreations* teaching law, writing articles, skiing, gardening; *Style—* Laurie Heller, Esq; ✉ Berwin Leighton Paisner, Adelaide House, London Bridge, London EC4R 9HA (tel 020 7760 1000, fax 020 7760 1111)

HELLER, Michael Aron; s of Simon Heller (d 1989), of Harrogate, N Yorks, and Nettie, *née* Gordon (d 1997); *b* 15 July 1936; *Educ* Harrogate GS, St Catharine's Coll Cambridge (MA); *m* 1965, Morven, da of Dr Julius Livingstone; 2 s (John b 1966, Andrew b 1968), 1 da (Nicola b 1981); *Career* chm: London & Associated Properties plc, Bisichi Mining plc, Electronic Data Processing plc; dep chm Centre for Policy Studies; FCA; *Recreations* opera, walking, collecting twentieth century art; *Clubs* RAC; *Style—* Michael Heller, Esq; ✉ London & Associated Properties plc, Carlton House, St James's Square, London SW1Y 4JH (tel 020 7415 5000)

HELLER, Robert Gordon Barry; s of late Norman Joseph Heller, and Helen, *née* Flatto; *b* 10 June 1932; *Educ* Christ's Hosp, Jesus Coll Cambridge (BA); *m* 1, 8 Jan 1955, Lois Ruth, da of Michael Malnick; 1 s (Matthew Jonathan b 1960), 2 da (Jane Charlotte b 1962, Kate Elizabeth b 1965); m 2, 10 June 2003, Angela Mary Flowers, *qv*; 1 da (Rachel Pearl b 1973); *Career* 2 Lt RASC 1950–52; industrial corr (later diary ed and US corr) Financial Times 1955–63, business ed Observer 1963–65, ed (later ed-in-chief and editorial dir) Management Today 1965–87, editorial dir Haymarket Publishing 1978–85; chm and dir: Heller Arts, Heller Mgmnt; dir Angela Flowers Gallery plc 1970–; *Books* Superman, Can you Trust your Bank? (with Norris Willatt), The European Revenge (with Norris Willatt), The Naked Investor, The Common Millionaire, The Once and Future Manager, The Business of Winning, The Business of Success, The Naked Market, The Pocket Manager, The New Naked Manager, The State of Industry, The Supermanagers, The Supermarketers, The Age of the Common Millionaire, Unique Success Proposition, The Decision Makers, The Best of Robert Heller, Culture Shock, The Super Chiefs, The Quality Makers, The Fate of IBM, The Leadership Imperative, The Naked Manager for the 90s, The Way to Win (with Will Carling), In Search of European Excellence, Essential Managers Manual, Goldfinger, Roads to Success (Business Masterminds), The Fusion Manager, The Seven Summits of Success (with Rebecca Stephens); *Recreations* art, food and wine, books, music, exercise; *Style—* Mr Robert Heller; ✉ Angela Flowers Gallery plc, 21 Cork Street, London W1S 3LZ (tel 020 7439 7766, e-mail heller@dircon.co.uk)

HELLICAR, Michael William; s of Jonathan Ernest Hellicar (d 1991), of London, and Eileen May, *née* Williams (d 1983); *b* 3 April 1941; *m* 1962, June Betty, da of Charles Edward Pitcher; 3 da (Nicola Jane b 24 May 1965, Justine Louise b 28 July 1966, Charlotte Laura b 18 April 1979); *Career* journalist; apprentice reporter South London Observer 1956–60, asst news ed and feature writer New Musical Express 1960–63, news ed Rave Magazine 1963–64, feature writer Daily Sketch 1964–67; Daily Mirror: feature and leader writer 1967–72, ed Inside Page 1972–73, features ed 1973–76, sr writer 1976–81; asst ed Daily Star 1989– (chief feature writer 1982–89); chief critic: World's Greatest Restaurants Monthly 1991–, First Class Air Travel Monthly 1993–; *Recreations* causing trouble, whingeing; *Style—* Michael Hellicar, Esq; ✉ Daily Star, Express Newspapers plc, Ludgate House, 245 Blackfriars Road, London SE1 9UX (tel 020 7928 8000, fax 020 7922 7962)

HELLIKER, Adam Andrew Alexander; s of Maurice William Helliker, DFC, AFC (d 1984), and Jane Olivia, *née* Blunt (d 2005); *b* 13 September 1958; *Educ* King's Sch Bruton, Somerset Coll of Arts and Technol; *m* 2003, Lucy Alice Elizabeth, da of John Naylor; 1 da (Marina b 24 May 2006); *Career* reporter: Western Times Co Ltd 1978–81, Daily Mail 1981–86; dep diary ed: Daily Mail 1986–98, Mail on Sunday 1988–98; diary ed Sunday Telegraph 1998–2002; diary ed Mail on Sunday 2002–04, columnist Sunday Express 2004–; special corr McCalls magazine (USA) 1996–; contrib to several nat magazines; vice-chm London Diarists' Club; Freeman: City of London 1989, Worshipful Co of Wheelwrights 1989; memb Royal Soc of Lit; FRGS, FRSA; *Books* The Debrett Season (ed, 1981), The English Season (contrib, 1988); *Recreations* shooting, collecting leather luggage; *Clubs* Carlton, St James's, Mosimann's, Morton's, RAC, Hurlingham, Century; *Style—* Adam Helliker, Esq; ✉ Sunday Express, 10 Lower Thames Street, London EC3R 6EN (tel 08715 202 750, e-mail adamhelliker@aol.com)

HELLMAN, Louis Mario; MBE (1993); s of late Mario Biselli, and Monalda, *née* Caraffi; *b* 19 March 1936; *Educ* Cardinal Vaughan GS, William Ellis GS, UCL (BArch), Ecole des Beaux-Arts Paris; *m* Maria Anna, da of late Sabin Popkiewicz; 1 da (Katherine Monalda b 31 Aug 1963), 1 s (Nicholas Sabin b 5 Sept 1964); *Career* architect; work incl: Spastics Soc (now Scope), GLC, YRM; cartoonist Architects Jl 1967–92 and 1997–, Building Design 1992–97, Design Week 1995–; cartoons published in: The Observer, Sunday Times, The Guardian, Evening Standard, Architectural Review, Design Week, Punch, Private Eye; lectr: UK, USA, Australia; Exhibitions incl: AA 1979, Interbuild 1991, RIBA 1989–, Sir John Soane's Museum 2000, Barcelona 2001, Shrewsbury 2006; subject of biography - Seven Ages of the Architect: The Very Best of Louis Hellman 1967–92 (1991); memb: Assoc of Architect Artists, ARB, Br Cartoonists' Assoc, Cartoonists' Club of GB; Hon Dr Oxford Brookes Univ 2002; *Publications* A Is for Architect (1974), All Hellman Breaks Loose (1980), Architecture for Beginners (1986), Archi-têtes (1999), Do it with an Architect (1999), Architecture A to Z: A Rough Guide (2001); author of numerous articles in architectural magazines; *Recreations* music, cinema, travel, art; *Style—* Dr Louis Hellman, MBE; ✉ tel 020 8992 8318, e-mail info@louishellman.co.uk, website www.louishellman.co.uk

HELME, Patrick Ian (Tom); s of Anthony Helme, and Pauline, *née* Lancaster; *b* 17 January 1956; *Educ* Charterhouse, Brighton Coll of Art, UEA (BA); *m* 9 Aug 1984, Hon Mirabel Guinness, da of 2 Baron Moyne (d 1992); 3 da (Alice Mirabel b 15 May 1987, Tyga Elizabeth b 12 Feb 1990, Lily Pauline b 17 March 1994), 1 s (Toby Antony b 17 July 1992); *Career* apprentice (with restorer and decorator John Sutcliffe) 1978–80, studied restoration Soc for the Preservation of New England Antiquities 1980, asst to David Mlinaric 1981, co-fndr Silvergate Papers 1982, fndr interior design business 1982–91, official advsr on decoration National Trust 1991–98 (advsr 1982–91), organised and originated National Trust Paints (jtly with The National Trust Enterprises Ltd and Farrow & Ball Ltd) 1991, dir Farrow & Ball Ltd mfrs of paint and wallpaper 1992– (with Martin Ephson, *qv*); interior design projects 1982– incl: HM Ambassadors' residences (in The Hague, Rome, Cairo, Paris, Prague and Lisbon), Hoares Bank, Linton Park plc, King's Lynn Town Hall, Duncombe Park, Ashridge Mgmnt Coll, Madame Tussauds, Luton Hoo, St John's Coll Cambridge, Brooks's Club, Magdalen Coll Oxford, John Murray Publishers Ltd, Wadham Coll Oxford, The Medical Soc; winner Queen's Award 2004; *Publications* Paint and Colour in Decoration (2003); *Recreations* salmon fishing; *Clubs* Tedworth Hunt, Piscatorial Soc, Georgian Gp; *Style—* Tom Helme, Esq; ✉ Farrow & Ball Ltd, Uddens Estate, Wimbourne, Dorset BH21 7NL (tel 01202 876151, fax 01202 870197, mobile 07780 660217, e-mail headoffice@farrow-ball.com)

HELMER, Roger; MEP; *Educ* King Edward VI GS Southampton (state scholarship), Churchill Coll Cambridge (MA); *m* Sara; 3 c; *Career* MEP (Cons) E Midlands 1999–; md Donisthorpe & Co Ltd 1996–98; formerly mktg and mgmnt roles with Procter & Gamble, Nat Semiconductor, United Distillers; vice-chm Br C of C Seoul 1992–93, memb Bd Euro Chamber Seoul 1992–93; memb: Countryside Alliance, NFU, Lutyens Tst; *Style—* Roger Helmer, Esq, MEP; ✉ 11 Central Park, Leicester Road, Lutterworth, Leicestershire LE17 4PN (tel 01455 558447)

HELMS, Prof Peter Joseph; s of Joseph Helms (d 1966), and Eileen Dorothea, *née* Macfarlane, of Geelong, Aust; *b* 26 June 1947; *Educ* Wimbledon Coll, Royal Free Hosp Sch of Med London (MB BS), Univ of London (PhD); *m* 7 Nov 1970, Kathleen Mary, da of Reginald Woodward; 3 da (Rachel Anne b 19 March 1973, Joanna Catherine b 23 April 1974, Laura Jane b 1 Oct 1980), 1 s (Matthew John b 12 May 1977); *Career* house offr posts Royal Free Hosp, London Hosp, Royal Brompton Hosp, Hammersmith Hosp and Hosp for Sick Children Great Ormond St 1973–76, lectr Charing Cross Hosp 1977–78, research fell Inst of Child Health and Cardiothoracic Inst Univ of London 1978–83, sr lectr Inst of Child Health London 1983–92, prof of child health and head of dept Univ of Aberdeen 1992–; Donald Patterson Prize Br Paediatric Assoc 1983; FRCPEd 1992, FRCPCH 1996; *Publications* over 200 scientific pubns and book chapters on paediatric respiratory health and disease and child health education; co-ed on paediatric undergraduate and postgraduate texts; *Recreations* hill walking, music; *Style—* Prof Peter Helms; ✉ Department of Child Health, University of Aberdeen, Foresterhill, Aberdeen AB25 2ZD (tel 01224 552471, fax 01224 663658, e-mail p.j.helms@abdn.ac.uk)

HELPS, Dominic David Wycliffe; s of Dr (Edmund) Peter Wycliffe Helps, of Coleshill, Bucks, and Heather, *née* Hood; *b* 8 July 1956, London; *Educ* Radley, Downing Coll Cambridge (scholar, BA, CPE); *m* 2005, Serena Elizabeth Chandler, *née* Cobley; *Career* staff writer Management Today and Engineering Today 1978–79, articled clerk then asst slr Linklaters & Paines 1980–84, sr asst slr Lovell White and King (latterly LWD then Lovells) 1984–96, ptnr Shadbolt & Co 1996–; co-ed Construction Law Jl, regular contrib of articles to Building magazine and various construction law pubns; sec Technol and Construction Slrs Assoc (T&CSA), chm Law Courts Branch Arbitration Club; memb: Soc of Construction Law 1980–, Law Soc 1982–; *Recreations* sports (especially football and cricket), gardening, reading (literature, history, arts); *Style—* Dominic Helps, Esq; ✉ South Court, Kinnersley Manor, Reigate Road, Sidlow, Surrey RH2 8QJ (tel 01293 784359); Shadbolt & Co, Chatham Court, Lesbourne Road, Reigate, Surrey RH2 7LD (tel 01737 226277, fax 01737 226165, e-mail dominic_helps@shadboltlaw.com)

HELSBY, Richard John Stephens (Rick); s of John Michael Helsby (d 1972), and Margaret Stella, *née* Andrews; *b* 10 January 1949; *Educ* Magdalen Coll Sch Oxford, Univ of Warwick (BA), Univ of Oxford (DipEd); *Children* 4 s (James b 1968, Nathan b 1972, William b 1986, Joseph 1993); *Career* HM inspr of Taxes Oxford 1972–78, sr inspr of Taxes Inland Revenue Enquiry Branch 1978–84, sr tax mangr Deloitte Haskins & Sells 1984–87; PricewaterhouseCoopers (formerly Coopers & Lybrand before merger): nat ptnr Fraud and Investigations Gp 1987–93, ptnr in charge Forensic Accountancy 1993–2000, head Forensic Invesitgations (Europe, Middle East and Africa) 2000–; *Books* Trouble with the Taxman (1985), Offshore Survival (with Jim McMahon, Bernard McCarthy 1988); *Recreations* squash, football, theatre, cinema, snooker; *Style*— Rick Helsby, Esq; ✉ PricewaterhouseCoopers, Plumtree Court, London EC4A 4HT (tel 020 7583 5000)

HELY HUTCHINSON, Hon Timothy Mark; 2 s of 8 Earl of Donoughmore, *qv*; *b* 26 October 1953; *Educ* Eton, Univ of Oxford; *Career* md: Macdonald & Co (Publishers) Ltd 1982–86, Headline Book Publishing plc 1986–93; gp chief exec Hodder Headline Ltd 1993–, chm WHSmith News Ltd 2001–04, chief exec Hachette Livre UK Ltd 2004–; dir: WHSmith Gp plc 1999–2004, Inflexion plc 2000–03; *Clubs* Groucho; *Style*— The Hon Timothy Hely Hutchinson; ✉ Hodder Headline Ltd, 338 Euston Road, London NW1 3BH (tel 020 7873 6000, fax 020 7873 6012)

HELYAR, Mark Andrew Jonathan; s of Barry Robert Helyar (d 2004), and Constance, *née* West; *b* 15 March 1968, Guernsey; *Educ* Elizabeth Coll Guernsey, UEA (BSc), Nottingham Trent Univ (PGDL), Univ of Caen (Cert); *m* 3 June 1995, Amanda Jayne, *née* Cash; 2 da (Natascha May b 2 Sept 1996, Aimee Adele b 10 June 2000); *Career* called to the Bar: Gray's Inn 2000, Guernsey 2001; NP Guernsey; States of Guernsey Civil Service 1991–96, Babbe le Pelley Tostevin Advocates 1996–2006 (ptnr 2003–06), managing ptnr Bedell Cristin Guernsey and ptnr Bedell Gp 2006–; sec Condor Gp, chm Culture Guernsey; memb Performing Rights Soc; *Recreations* golf, scuba, motor sport; *Clubs* Guernsey Sporting; *Style*— Mark Helyar, Esq; ✉ Bedell Group, 3rd Floor, La Plaiderie House, La Plaiderie, St Peter Port, Guernsey GY1 1ND (tel 01481 812812, fax 01481 812813, e-mail mark.helyar@bedellgroup.com)

HEMBLADE, Christopher Mark Andrew; s of late Bernard Hemblade, of Sussex, and Jennie, *née* Howard; *b* 1 May 1970; *Educ* Cardinal Newman Sch, KCL (BA), Central St Martin's Sch of Art (MA); *Career* freelance journalist: Arena, The Face, ID, Interview, BBC Radio, The Observer and The Guardian 1994–96; ed Student Guide Time Out 1994–96, London ed Marie Claire 1994–97, asst ed Empire Magazine 1996–98, ed Sky Magazine 1998–99, sr ed Scene Magazine 1999, features ed Time Out Magazine 2000–04 (latterly actg ed, nominated (entertainment category) BSME Awards 2004), currently exec ed Elle magazine; memb Panel Opinion Leader Research 2003–07; *Recreations* theatre, film, travel, yoga; *Clubs* Century; *Style*— Christopher Hemblade, Esq

HEMINGFORD, 3 Baron (UK 1943), of Watford, Co Hertford; (Dennis) Nicholas Herbert; s of 2 Baron Hemingford (d 1982), and Elizabeth McClare, *née* Clark (d 1979); *b* 25 July 1934; *Educ* Oundle, Clare Coll Cambridge (MA); *m* 8 Nov 1958, Jennifer Mary Toresen, OBE, DL, o da of Frederick William Bailey (d 1986), of Harrogate, N Yorks; 3 da (Hon Elizabeth Frances Toresen (Hon Mrs Witt) b 1963, Hon Caroline Mary Louise b 1964, Hon Alice Christine Emma (Hon Mrs McManus) b 1968), 1 s (Hon Christopher Dennis Charles b 1973); *Heir* s, Hon Christopher Herbert; *Career* known professionally as Nicholas Herbert; journalist Reuters Ltd London and Washington DC 1956–61; joined The Times 1961: asst Washington correspondent 1961–65, Middle East correspondent 1965–69, dep features ed 1969–70; ed Cambridge Evening News 1970–74, dep chief exec Westminster Press 1992–95 (editorial dir 1974–92), pres Guild of Br Newspaper Editors 1980–81 (vice-pres 1979–80); hon sec Assoc of British Editors 1985–94; chm East Anglia Regnl Ctee Nat Tst 1990–2000; pres Huntingdonshire Family History Soc 1985; dir and tstee Arts 2000 East 1996–98, tstee Ely Cathedral Restoration Tst 1993–; memb: Cncl Europa Nostra 1999–2005, Culture Ctee UK Cmmn for UNESCO 2000–04, Cncl Friends of the Br Library 2005–; Liveryman Worshipful Co of Grocers 1975; FRSA; *Recreations* genealogy, Victorian military history, opera-going; *Clubs* Royal Commonwealth Society, Civil Service; *Style*— The Rt Hon the Lord Hemingford; ✉ The Old Rectory, Hemingford Abbots, Huntingdon, Cambridgeshire PE28 9AN (tel 01480 466234, fax 01480 380275, e-mail nickh@britishlibrary.net)

HEMINGWAY, Ann Elizabeth; CBE (2003); da of Robert Cherrill (d 1973), and (Nora) Betty, *née* Kingsley (d 1967); *b* 17 July 1947, Beckenham, Kent; *m* 9 Sept 1981, Anthony John Hemingway (d 2002); *Career* lectr Flour Advsy Bureau 1968–1970, jr posts SE Gas Bd (Home Service) 1970–73; British Gas Trading Ltd (formerly British Gas plc): regnl chief home service advsr SE Region 1973–77, project mangr HQ 1977–78, marketing devpt mangr NW Region 1978–88, IT mangr NE Region 1988–89, dir of personnel British Gas Wales 1989–91, project mangr IS Personnel Policy Devpt 1991–92, dir of personnel NW Region 1992–93, HR leader and memb Devpt Strategy Team 1993–94, business dir Public Gas Supply 1994–96, head of sales Home Energy 1996–99; memb Bd and chm Advsy Ctee Wales Food Standards Agency 2000–06; Driver Vehicle Licence Agency: memb Advsy Bd 1993–2002, chm Audit Ctee 2003–05 (memb 1997–2003); Dept for Tport: non-exec memb Driver and Vehicle Operators Strategic Review 1998–2003, memb Bd DVO 2003–, memb Bd 2003–; memb: Cncl CBI Wales 1994–98, Bd Business in the Community in Wales 1994–98, Advsy Bd Cardiff Common Purpose 1995–98, Bd and Audit Ctee Strategic Rail Authy 2000–02, Advsy Bd Highways Agency 2002–05, Bd Local Better Regulation Office Cabinet Office 2007–; tstee Sports Aid Wales 1994–2000, chm Steering Gp Opportunity 2000 in Wales 1995–99, ind assessor Nat Assembly for Wales 1997–2002; dir Uskbridge Mgmnt Co Ltd 1999– (sec 1996–99); FCIPD, FCIM (DipM); *Recreations* walking, cookery, entertaining; *Style*— Mrs Ann Hemingway, CBE

HEMINGWAY, Gerardine Mary; da of Thomas Kenneth Astin, and Mary Patricia Astin; *b* 1961, Padiham, Lancs; *Educ* Univ of Plymouth (DDes); *m* Wayne Andrew Hemingway , *qv*, s of Chief Billy Two Rivers; 2 s (Jack b 1986, Beck b 1997), 2 da (Tilly b 1987, Corey b 1990); *Career* designer; co-fndr (with husband) Red or Dead 1982 (winner Street Style category British Fashion Cncl Awards 1996, 1997 and 1998); prop hemingway design (interior, product and building design consultancy) 2000–; building design: Home 1997, Workplace offices 2000, mass-market housing estate for George Wimpey Homes, new wing for IoD; projects incl: carpet design for Milliken, wall coverings for Graham and Brown; *Recreations* gardening, cooking, travelling; *Style*— Mrs Gerardine Hemingway

HEMINGWAY, Michael Patrick; s of John Allman Hemingway, and Helen Bridget Barbara, *née* Prowse; *b* 28 August 1951; *Educ* Oundle; *m* 17 Dec 1977, Annamaria, da of John David Fitness; 2 s (Jay Matthew John Allman b 15 May 1980, Toby Michael Christopher Allman b 28 May 1983); *Career* account mangr Leo Burnett advtg agency 1976 (joined Invoice Control Dept 1975), account dir Michael Bungey and Partners 1977–82, Collett Dickenson Pearce 1982–85; bd dir: Boase Massimi Pollitt 1985–88, DDB Needham 1989; Grey Communications Group: joined as bd dir 1989, vice-chm Grey London 1991, subsequently sr vice-pres Grey Europe, currently exec vice-pres Grey International (i/c Mars Confectionery); *Recreations* watching sport, travel, popular music; *Clubs* Tramp; *Style*— Michael Hemingway, Esq; ✉ Grey International, 215–227 Great Portland Street, London W1N 5HD (tel 020 7636 3399)

HEMINGWAY, Wayne Andrew; MBE (2006); s of Chief Billy Two Rivers (chief of Khanawake Tribe (Mohawk) Quebec), and Maureen, *née* Hemingway; *b* 19 January 1961; *Educ* Queen Elizabeth's GS Blackburn, UCL (BSc); *m* Gerardine Mary Hemingway , *qv*, da of Ken Astin; 2 s (Jack b 22 June 1986, Beck b 11 June 1997), 2 da (Tilly b 23 July 1987, Corey b Aug 1990); *Career* fashion designer; Red or Dead: founded as design co retailing from Camden Market stall 1982, entered jt venture with Pentland Gp plc 1996, currently non-exec chm, winners of Street Style Category British Fashion Awards 1995, 1996 and 1997; md Dr Martens Clothing 1992–94; dir Br Fashion Cncl 1999–; designer Hemingway Design (projects incl IoD club, George Wimpey Homes devpt); chm Building for Life; prof of built environment Univ of Northumbria 2004; regular speaker to housing industry on housing and urban regeneration, and to fashion colls and footwear assocs on shoe, clothing and interior design; work shown in numerous exhibitions of Br design incl: Boymans Museum Rotterdam, Orange County California, V&A London; second place Young Business Person of the Year 1990; Hon MA Surrey Inst 2002, Hon DDes Univ of Wolverhampton 2005; *Recreations* football, cricket, tennis; *Style*— Wayne Hemingway, Esq, MBE; ✉ Hemingway Design, 15 Wembley Park Drive, Wembley, Middlesex HA9 8HD (tel 020 8903 1074, fax 020 8903 1076, e-mail info@hemingwaydesign.co.uk)

HEMMING, John; MP; *Educ* King Edwards Sch Edgbaston, Magdalen Coll Oxford (MA); *Career* fndr John Hemming & Co (now JHC plc) 1983, fndr MarketNet 1994, fndr Music Mercia Int (MMI) 1997, fndr The Purchasing Agency (SafeSimple.com) 2000, fndr Phoenix Consortium 2000; cncllr (Lib Dem) South Yeardley City Cncl 1990–, ldr Birmingham City Cncl Lib Dem Gp; Parly candidate (Lib Dem): Birmingham Hall Green 1983, Birmingham Yardley 1992, 1997 and 2001; MP (Lib Dem) Birmingham Yardley 2005–; *Style*— John Hemming, Esq, MP; ✉ House of Commons, London SW1A 0AA

HEMMING, Dr John Henry; CMG (1994); s of Lt-Col Henry Harold Hemming, OBE, MC (d 1977), of London, and Alice Louisa, OBE, *née* Weaver (d 1994); *b* 5 January 1935; *Educ* Eton, McGill Univ Montreal, Univ of Oxford (MA, DLitt); *m* 19 Jan 1979, Sukie Mary, da of Brig Michael J Babington-Smith, CBE (d 1984), and Lady Jean Babington-Smith; 1 s (Henry Sebastian b 1979), 1 da (Beatrice Margaret Louisa b 1981); *Career* charity dir Royal Geographical Soc 1975–96; publisher; jt chm: Hemming Gp Ltd (formerly Municipal Jl Ltd) 1976– (dir 1962, dep chm 1967–76); chm: Brintex Ltd 1979– (md 1962–71), Newman Books Ltd 1979–; ldr Maracá Rainforest Project Brazil 1987–89; fndr tstee and sponsor Survival Int; memb Cncl/Ctee: Br Cncl 1992–2002, Anglo-Brazilian Soc, John Ellerman Fndn, Rainforest Fndn, Earth Love Fund, Gilchrist Educnl Tst, Pro Natura Int, Hakluyt Soc, Global Diversity Fndn, Cusichaca Tst, Museum of Empire & Cwlth Tst, Earthwatch Tst; chm: Anglo-Peruvian Soc, Green Card Tst; dep chm LEPRA; Pitman Literary Prize 1971, Christopher Medal NY 1972, Founders Medal RGS 1990, Mungo Park Medal Royal Scottish Geographical Soc 1988, Washburn Medal Boston Museum of Sci 1990; Rolex Award for Enterprise citation 1988, Explorers' Club NY citation of merit 1997; Hon DUniv: Univ of Warwick 1989, Univ of Stirling 1991; hon fell Magdalen Coll Oxford 2004; Orden al Mérito (Peru) 1987, hon corresponding memb Academia Nacional de Historia Venezuela, special award Instituto Nacional de Cultura Peru 1996, Ordem do Cruzeiro do Sul (Brazil) 1998; *Books* The Conquest of the Incas (1970), Tribes of the Amazon Basin in Brazil (1973), Red Gold (1978), The Search for El Dorado (1978), Machu Picchu (1981), Monuments of the Incas (1982), Change in the Amazon Basin (1985), Amazon Frontier (1987), Maracá (1988), Roraima, Brazil's northernmost frontier (1990), The Rainforest Edge (1993), The Golden Age of Discovery (1998), Die If You Must (2003), The Amazon Story (2008); *Recreations* writing, travel; *Clubs* Beefsteak (chm), Boodle's, Geographical; *Style*— Dr John Hemming, CMG; ✉ 10 Edwardes Square, London W8 6HE (tel 020 7602 6697); Hemming Group Ltd, 32 Vauxhall Bridge Road, London SW1V 2SS

HEMMING, Lindy; da of Alan Hemming (d 1983), of Crug-y-Bar, Dyfed, and Jean, *née* Alexander; *b* 21 August 1948; *Educ* RADA; *m* Bob Starrett; 1 da (Alexandra Grace b 30 Jan 1969), 1 s (Daniel Grace b 16 Nov 1974); *Career* costume designer for theatre and film 1972–; memb: Soc Br Theatre Designers, Acad of Motion Pictures, Film Designers Guild; *Theatre* Hampstead Theatre Club 1974–79: Abigail's Party, Ecstasy, The Elephant Man, Uncle Vanya, Clouds; RSC 1978–84: Juno and the Paycock, Mother Courage, All's Well That Ends Well; NT: Death of a Salesman, Schweyk in the Second World War, Pravda, A View from the Bridge, A Small Family Business, Waiting for Godot; West End theatre: Donkeys Years, Brighton Beach Memoirs, Steel Magnolias, Clouds, Chorus of Disapproval, King (musical) 1990, Revengers Comedies 1991; *Film* incl: Wetherby, 84 Charing Cross Road, Abigail's Party, My Beautiful Laundrette, High Hopes, Meantime, Queen of Hearts, The Krays, Life is Sweet, Hear My Song, Blame it on the Bellboy, Naked, Four Weddings and a Funeral, Funnybones, GoldenEye (Bond 17), Blood and Wine, The Brave, Tomorrow Never Dies (Bond 18), The Rise and Fall of Little Voice, Topsy Turvy (Academy Award 2000), The World is Not Enough (Bond 19), The Man Who Cried, Tomb Raider, Harry Potter and the Chamber of Secrets, Die Another Day (Bond 20), Tombraider II, Batman, The Intimidation Game; *Recreations* walking, eating, drinking coffee, watching people; *Style*— Ms Lindy Hemming; ✉ 8 Bewdley Street, London N1 1HB

HEMMINK, Wilhelmus Hubertus Matheus Maria (Wim); s of late Matheus Hemmink, and late Maria Hemmink Van Den Brink; *Educ* Fashion Dept Koninklijke Academie voor Beeldende Kunst S'Gravenhage, Rotterdamse Snijschool, Rundshau, Constance Wilbaut's Sch Amsterdam, Chambre Syndicale de la Couture Parisienne; *Career* fashion designer; recipient Cotton Inst award Holland, subsequent experience with Madeleine de Rauch (haute couture house) Paris, Kay Selig Inc NY, Michael of Carlos Place (couture house) London; latterly estab own label Wim Hemmink (retailed worldwide and with extensive private clientele); *Style*— Wim Hemmink, Esq; ✉ 106 Crawford Street, London W1H 2HY (tel 020 7935 1755, fax 020 7224 0573)

HEMPHILL, 5 Baron (UK 1906); Peter Patrick Fitzroy Martyn Martyn-Hemphill; assumed the additional surname of Martyn by deed poll of 1959; s of 4 Baron (d 1957); *b* 5 September 1928; *Educ* Downside, BNC Oxford (MA); *m* 1952, Olivia, da of Major Robert Ruttledge, MC, of Co Mayo, and sis of Lady Edward FitzRoy (herself da-in-law of 10 Duke of Grafton); 1 s, 2 da; *Heir* s, Hon Charles Martyn-Hemphill; *Career* memb Turf Club and former sr steward; memb Irish Nat Hunt Steeplechase Ctee and former sr steward, chm Galway Race Ctee 1990–; Cross of Order of Merit, Order of Malta; *Clubs* White's, Irish Cruising, RIAC; *Style*— The Rt Hon the Lord Hemphill; ✉ Dunkellin, Kiltulla, Co Galway, Ireland (tel 00 353 91848002, fax 00 353 91848174, e-mail hemphill@eircom.net)

HEMPLING, Dr Stephen Michael; s of Dr Henry Hempling (d 1992), and Sylvia, *née* Bergman; *b* 23 November 1944, Manchester; *Educ* Manchester Grammar, Univ of Manchester (MB, ChB), Cardiff Univ (LLM); *m* 21 Oct 1973, Henrietta, *née* Barton; 1 da (Dr Melissa Charlotte Hempling b 17 Jan 1975), 1 s (Dr Marc Warren Hempling b 7 Jan 1977); *Career* GP Woking 1972–84, med advsr pharmaceutical industry 1984–85, GP Brighton 1986–97, expert in clinical forensic med 1997– (pt/t 1978–97); expert in clinical forensic med, police surgn Surrey, London and Sussex 1972–91, hon lectr in forensic med Guys Hosp Med Sch 1978; author of case reports and articles in learned jls; memb Cncl RSM (also memb Forensic and Legal Med Section Cncl); memb: Br Acad of Forensic Sci, Expert Witness Inst, Faculty of Forensic and Legal Medicine RCP; assoc memb: Assoc of Police Surgns (memb Cncl 1983–86 and 1986–92), Soc of Drs in Law; MRCS 1968, LRCP 1968, DObstRCOG 1972, DMJ 1977; FRSM; *Clubs* Brighton & Hove Soirée, Rotary; *Style*— Dr Stephen Hempling; ✉ 28 Tongdean Avenue, Hove, East Sussex BN3 6TN (tel 01273 555382, fax 01273 556093, e-mail shempling2@aol.com)

HEMSLEY, Michael Stuart; s of Alan Fraser Hemsley, of Totton, Hants, and Janet Enid, *née* Taylor; *b* 13 July 1957; *Educ* Beverley Boys' Sch New Malden, Salisbury Coll of Art; *m* 30 May 1981, Catherine Bernadette Hemsley, da of Thomas Oswald O'Keeffe; 2 s (Thomas Joseph b 26 Sept 1986, Robert Michael b 19 Oct 1988); *Career* professional photographer; Colt International Ltd Havant: trainee Photographic Dept 1974, photographed industrial sites for advtg and promotional use until 1981; industrial and commercial photographer Walter Gardiner Photography Worthing 1981–; photographic assignments in UK and abroad incl: magazine illustration, corporate video, report and accounts, public relations, managerial portraits; current specialisms incl: 3D imaging, advertising photography, book illustration, digital imaging technology; Bausch and

H

Lomb Young Photographer of the Year 1982, Ilford Photographer of the Year 1985 and 1989 (highly commended 1992), Peter Grugeon Award for best fellowship application 1986, BIPP Gold Award 1996, 2004 and 2006; FBIPP 1986; *Books* Digital Photography (author and illustrator, 2006); *Style*— Michael Hemsley, Esq; ✉ 17 Maltravers Drive, Littlehampton, West Sussex BN17 5EY (tel 0844 800 2990, e-mail mike@wgphoto.co.uk, website www.wgphoto.co.uk)

HENCKE, David Robert; s of late Charles Ewald Hencke, of London, and Enid, *née* Rose; *b* 26 April 1947; *Educ* Tulse Hill Comp Sch, Univ of Warwick (BA); *m* 5 July 1969, Margaret Mary, da of late Laurie Langrick; 1 da (Anne Margaret b 14 Aug 1979); *Career* jr reporter Northamptonshire Evening Telegraph 1968–71; reporter: Western Mail 1971–73, Times Higher Educational Supplement 1973–76; The Guardian: reporter 1976–79, planning corr 1979–81, social servs corr 1981–86, Westminster corr 1986–; memb Ld Chllr's Advsy Gp on Implementing Freedom of Information; Reporter of the Year: E Midlands Allied Press 1971, Br Press Awards 1989 (specialist writer of the year 1981) and 1993 (reporter of the year), Journalist of the Year What the Papers Say 1994, Scoop of the Year (Peter Mandelson's Home Loan) What The Papers Say 1998, London Press Club Scoop of the Year Award 1998, Best Environmental Campaign Br Environment and Media Awards 2001; dir Brown Envelope TV Ltd 2000–; FRSA; *Books* Colleges in Crisis (1976), The Blair's and their Court (jtly, 2004); *Recreations* theatre, walking, gardening, cooking, riding; *Style*— David Hencke, Esq; ✉ The Guardian, 119 Farringdon Road, London EC1R 3ER (tel 020 7278 2332 or 020 7219 6769 (Westminster office), fax 020 7222 1321, e-mail david.hencke@guardian.co.uk)

HENDERSON, Alan Brodie; yr s of Neil Brodie Henderson (d 1982), of Buntingford, Herts, and Conn, *née* Madden (d 1979); *b* 30 July 1933; *Educ* Eton; *m* 1, 25 April 1956 (m dis), Antonia, only da of James McMullen, of 63 Eaton Square, London; 2 s (Bryan Brodie b 1960, Gavin Brodie b 1963), 1 da (Kerena Brodie b 1958); m 2, 9 June 1969, Fiona Douglas, er da of Maj Thomas Douglas Pilkington of Reay; 2 s (David Brodie b 1970, Thomas Brodie b 1976); m 3, 30 Sept 1992, Hon Diana Cara, da of 3 Baron Fairhaven, *qv*; *Career* Capt Welsh Gds 1952–59; with James Capel stockbrokers 1959–63, md Henderson Administration Ltd 1965–77 (joined 1963), chm Henderson Unit Trust Co Ltd 1974–77; dir: Mackay Shields Financial Corporation NY 1974–77, Schlesinger Investment Management Services Ltd 1977–81; md Schlesinger Trust Managers Ltd 1979–81; non-exec chm: Newmarket Venture Capital plc 1972–90, Ranger Oil (UK) Ltd 1982– (chm 1995–), Aberdeen New Thai Investment Trust plc until 2005, Aberdeen New Dawn Investment Trust plc, Aberdeen Emerging Economies Investment Trust plc, Forum Energy plc; non-exec dir: Energy Capital Investment Company plc, Global Energy Development plc, Public Service Properties Investments Ltd 2007–; *Clubs* White's, City of London; *Style*— Alan Henderson, Esq

HENDERSON, Charles Edward; CB (1992); s of David Henderson (d 1972), and Georgiana Leggatt, *née* Mackie (d 2000); *b* 19 September 1939; *Educ* Charterhouse, Univ of Cambridge; *m* 1966, Rachel, da of Dr A S Hall, of Bucks; 1 da (Catherine b 1970), 1 s (Luke b 1971); *Career* asst investment sec Equity and Law Life Assurance Soc Ltd 1966–70, princ Export Credits Guarantee Dept DTI 1971–73; Dept of Energy: princ 1974–75, asst sec 1976–82, head Atomic Energy Div 1982–84, head Oil Div 1984–85, princ estab and fin offr 1985–88; head Office of Arts and Libraries 1989–92, dep sec DTI 1992–96, chm Total Holdings UK and Total Exploration and Production UK 1998–2005; memb Competition Commn 1998–; pres Soc for Underwater Technol 1999–2001, pres Inst of Petroleum 2000–02; FIA; *Recreations* music (listening and playing), golf, reading, mountain walking; *Style*— Charles Henderson, Esq, CB; ✉ 17 Sydney House, Woodstock Road, London W4 1DP

HENDERSON, (George) Clifford McLaren; s of Robert McLaren Henderson (d 1962), and Stella, *née* Walter (d 1996); *b* 7 February 1938; *Educ* Bembridge Sch IOW; *Career* trainee Sotheby & Co 1955–57, Nat Service RAF 1957–59, Union Int (Vestey Gp) 1959–61, Phillips Auctioneers 1962–70; dir: Frank Partridge 1972–77, Stair and Co New York 1977–79; antiques conslt 1979–88, exec dir Partridge Fine Arts plc 1988–2001; Freeman The Guild of Arts Scholars, Dealers and Collectors; *Recreations* music, swimming, theatre, bridge; *Clubs* Brooks's; *Style*— Clifford Henderson, Esq; ✉ 18 Lochmore House, Ebury Street, London SW1W 9JX (tel 020 7730 2725); The Vine House, 38 Roedean Crescent, Roedean, East Sussex BN2 5RH (tel 01273 671072)

HENDERSON, Douglas John (Doug); MP; s of John Henderson, and Joan, *née* Bryson; *b* 9 June 1949; *Educ* Waid Acad, Central Coll Glasgow, Univ of Strathclyde (BA); *m* 1, 1974 (m dis), Janet Margaret, da of Robert Graham (d 1984), of Scotland; 1 s (Keir John b 1986), 1 da (Ella b 2000); m 2, 2002, Geraldine, *née* Daly; *Career* apprentice Rolls Royce Glasgow 1966–68, Trade Union organiser (GMWU later GMB) 1973–87, MP (Lab) Newcastle upon Tyne N 1978–, memb Exec Scottish Cncl Lab Pty 1979–87 (chm 1984–85), memb NEDO Sector Working Pty 1981–84; oppn spokesman on: industry 1988–92, local govt 1992–94, public servs 1994–95, home affairs 1995–97; min of state: FCO 1997–98, MOD 1998–99; chair Northern Gp of Lab MPs 2000–01, chair GMB Parly Gp 2002–, sec All Party Athletics Gp 2002–, memb Cncl of Europe and WEU 2005–; *Recreations* athletics, mountaineering; *Clubs* Lemington Labour, Newburn Meml, Dinnington, Cambuslang Harriers, Elswick Harriers, Desperados Climbing; *Style*— Doug Henderson, Esq, MP; ✉ House of Commons, London SW1A 0AA (tel 020 7219 5017 and 0191 286 2024)

HENDERSON, Douglas Lindsay; s of Capt Arthur Henderson, of Sydney, Australia, and Sheila Lindsay, *née* Russel; *b* 17 December 1947; *Educ* Univ of New England (BA), Univ of NSW Australia (MBA, PhD); *m* 20 Jan 1970, Marilyn Gail, da of Ronald Clifford (d 1982), of Sydney, Australia; 3 s (Angus Arthur Lindsay b 1975, Duncan Ronald Alan b 1978, Stuart b 1987); *Career* lectr Univ of NSW Aust 1972–74; vice-pres Bank of America NT & SA 1974–83, first vice-pres and dir Swiss Bank Corporation 1983–89, dir Europacific Corporate Finance Ltd 1991–; memb Graduate Business Assoc; ACIB, MSI; *Clubs* Royal Over-Seas League; *Style*— Douglas Henderson, Esq; ✉ Europacific Corporate Finance Ltd, 5 Fredericks Place, London EC2R 8AB (tel 020 7600 1940)

HENDERSON, Gavin Douglas; CBE (2004); s of Magnus Reginald Henderson (d 1975), and Sybil Nancy, *née* Horton, of Brighton; *b* 3 February 1948; *Educ* Brighton Coll (music and art scholar), Brighton Coll of Art, Kingston Coll of Art (BA), Slade Sch of Fine Art (Goldsmith's travelling scholarship to USA); *m* 1, 1973, Jane Williams; m 2, 1984, Carole Becker; 2 s (Piers b 1980, Caspar b 1985); m 3, 1992, Mary Jane Walsh; *Career* artistic dir: Crawley Festival 1972–73, York Festival and Mystery Plays 1973–76; chief exec Philharmonia Orch 1975–79, dir South Hill Park Arts Centre and fndr Wilde Theatre Bracknell 1979–85, artistic dir Brighton Festival 1984–94, princ Trinity Coll of Music 1994–; dir Dartington Int Summer Sch 1985–; chm: Music Panel Arts Cncl of England 1994–, Brighton Youth Orch 1998–, Nat Fndn for Youth Music 1998–, Regency Soc of Brighton and Hove 2000–; pres Nat Piers Soc, pres Bournemouth Festival, vice-pres Euro Festivals Assoc, vice-pres Br Arts Festivals Assoc (chm 1992–99); memb Bd Corps of Army Music 2001–; tstee West Pier Tst 2000–; patron: Chiddingly Festival, A Very Moving Festival, Farnham Maltings; chm Arts Worldwide; memb: Musicians' Union 1964, ISM 1994, RSM 1996; Liveryman Worshipful Co of Musicians 1996, Freeman City of London 1997; FRSA; *Recreations* cooking seafood, baroque trumpet, vintage motoring; *Clubs* Garrick, Savile, Royal Over-Seas League (hon memb); *Style*— Gavin Henderson, Esq, CBE; ✉ Trinity College of Music, 11–13 Mandeville Place, London W1M 6AQ (tel 020 7935 5773, fax 020 7935 5069)

HENDERSON, Giles Ian; CBE (1992); s of Charles David Henderson (d 1980), of Henfield, W Sussex, and Joan, *née* Firmin (d 1994); *b* 20 April 1942; *Educ* Michaelhouse Natal, Univ of the Witwatersrand (BA), Magdalen Coll Oxford (sr Mackinnon scholar, MA, BCL); *m* 21 Aug 1971, Lynne, da of Charles William Fyfield, OBE (d 1997), of Alnmouth, Northumberland; 2 s (Mark b 1974, Simon b 1975), 1 da (Clare b 1978); *Career* memb Law Faculty Univ of Calif Berkeley (Fulbright Award 1966–67); admitted slr 1970, sr ptnr Slaughter and May 1993–2001 (ptnr 1975–2001); master Pembroke Coll Oxford 2001–, chm Conf of Oxford Colls 2007–; memb: Hampel Ctee on Corp Governance, Fin Reporting Cncl 1998–2001, chm Law Gp UK/China Forum 1997–2000; non-exec dir: Land Securities plc 2000–02, The Standard Life Assurance Co 2001–03; chm Nuffield Medical Tst 2003–, dir Cumberland Lodge 2007–; *Recreations* sport, opera, ballet; *Style*— Giles Henderson, Esq, CBE; ✉ The Master's Lodgings, Pembroke College, Oxford OX1 1DW (tel 01865 276403)

HENDERSON, Prof Graham; s of Thomas Henderson, and Elizabeth Henderson (d 1989); *b* 23 August 1952, Newcastle upon Tyne; *Educ* Heaton GS Newcastle upon Tyne, Lanchester Poly (BSc), City Univ London (MSc), Nene Coll Northampton (FE Teachers' Cert); *m* 15 Dec 1987, Joan, *née* Younger; 1 da (Nicola b 22 March 1981), 2 s (Robert b 26 June 1986, Michael b 4 Aug 1988); *Career* lectr Nene Coll Northampton 1975–79, lectr rising to princ lectr Newcastle Business Sch Northumbria Univ 1980–89, asst dir Newcastle Business Sch Northumbria Univ 1989–97, dir Sunderland Business Sch Univ of Sunderland 1997–99, vice-chllr Univ of Teesside 2003– (dep vice-chllr 1999–2003); dir Univs Vocational Awards Cncl 2002; memb: Jt Costing and Pricing Steering Gp HEFCE 2002, HEFCE Teaching Fund Method Review Sounding Bd; exec memb Campaign for Mainstream Univs; chair: Univs for the NE Bd, Regnl Cncl of the NE Higher Skills Network; dir Middlesbrough Town Centre Co 2003, exec memb NE C of C; memb: Corp Bd Darlington Coll of Technol 1999, NE Assembly 2003, Tees Valley Partnership Bd 2003, CBI Regnl Cncl; tstee: Captain Cook Birthplace Tst 2003, Trincomalee Tst 2003; *Recreations* rugby union (coach and club chm of mini and jr rugby), football (spectator), walking, bridge; *Style*— Prof Graham Henderson; ✉ University of Teesside, Middlesbrough, Tees Valley TS1 3BA (tel 01642 342002, fax 01642 342000, e-mail graham.henderson@tees.ac.uk)

HENDERSON, Henry Merton (Harry); s of John Ronald Henderson, CVO, OBE, and Katherine Sarah, *née* Beckwith-Smith (d 1972); *b* 25 April 1952; *Educ* Eton; *m* 4 Feb 1977, Sarah Charlotte Margaret, *née* Lowther; 1 s (Harry Oliver b 24 March 1979), 1 da (Katie Sarah b 7 April 1981); *Career* ptnr Cazenove & Co 1982–, (md Cazenove Fund Mgmnt Ltd 1996–2000, md Cazenove Private Health Services 2000–02); dir: Updown Investment Co plc 1984–2000, Witan Investment Co plc 1988–; High Sheriff Berkshire 2007–08; MSI; *Recreations* skiing, shooting, squash, golf; *Clubs* White's; *Style*— Harry Henderson, Esq; ✉ West Woodhay House, Newbury, Berkshire RG20 0BS

HENDERSON, Hugh Peter; s of Dr Peter Wallace Henderson (d 1984), and Dr Stella Dolores Henderson (d 2006); *b* 23 October 1945; *Educ* Radley, St Catharine's Coll Cambridge, St Thomas' Hosp (MB BChir); *m* 11 Dec 1971, Elizabeth Anne Lynette, da of Hon Mr Justice Arthur Douglas Davidson (d 1977), of Johannesburg, South Africa; 1 da (Fiona Elizabeth b 1984); *Career* trg as plastic surgn 1975–82, conslt plastic surgn 1982–; author of articles in plastic surgery on subjects incl: thermography, hypospadias, palate fistulae, anti-drooling operation, use of turbinates as graft material; former chm: Research and Educn Sub-Ctee Br Assoc of Plastic Surgns, Leicester Royal Infirmary Pressure Sore Working Party; memb Cncl Br Assoc of Aesthetic Plastic Surgns; FRCS 1975; *Books* Questions and Answers in General Surgery, Questions and Answers in Surgery for Students; *Style*— Hugh Henderson, Esq; ✉ Nether Hall, Snows Lane, Keyham, Leicestershire LE7 9JS (tel 01162 595214, e-mail hugh.h@home.gb.com); The Bupa Hospital, Gartree Road, Oadby, Leicester LE2 2FF (tel 0116 265 3043, fax 0116 265 3600)

HENDERSON, Iain Stirling; s of Michael Henderson, of Lamberhurst, Kent, and Anita, *née* Skidmore; *b* 2 August 1965, Oxted, Surrey; *Educ* Tonbridge, CCC Cambridge (open exhibitioner, Adam Fox exhibitioner, Manners scholar, BA); *m* Heloise, *née* Stevenson (sep); 2 s (Max b 23 March 1997, Charlie b 6 Nov 1999); *Career* Accenture (UK) Ltd (formerly Arthur Andersen and Andersen Consulting): joined 1988, assoc ptnr 1998, ptnr 2000–, head UK Delivery Centre 2002–, head UK Solutions Workforce 2002–, memb Bd Accenture UK and I 2003–, head UK People Advocates 2004–06, md Systems Integration & Technol UK and I 2005–, memb CEO Advsy Cncl 2006–; Accenture sponsor Inst of Electronics and Technol, alliance ptnr Microsoft/Avanade UK; changemaker Working Families; FBCS 2006; *Recreations* guitarist in band (Uncle Keith's Disco Champion), guitar collector, my children; *Style*— Iain Henderson, Esq; ✉ Accenture (UK) Ltd, 1 Plantation Place, 30 Fenchurch Street, London EC3M 3BD (tel 020 7844 2689, e-mail iain.henderson@accenture.com)

HENDERSON, Ian James; CBE (2001); s of Robert Henderson, and Sheila, *née* Macpherson; *Educ* Coll of Estate Mgmnt London (BSc); *Career* Land Securities Group plc: joined 1971, exec dir 1987, gp chief exec 1997–2004; chm New West End Co, non-exec chm Dawnay Day Treveria 2005–; non-exec dir: Liberty International 2005–, Evans Property Group 2006–; pres Br Property Fedn 2002–03, vice-chm Central and Cecil Housing Tst, chm Devpt Tst for the Renewal of the Buildings of St-Martin-in-the-Fields 2004–; tstee Nat History Museum 2005–, memb Cncl Royal Albert Hall 2005–. memb President's Ctee London First, cmmr Cwlth War Graves Cmmn; govr Dolphin Square Charitable Fndn 2005–; FRICS; *Style*— Ian Henderson, Esq, CBE

HENDERSON, Ian Ramsay; s of David Hope Henderson (d 1977), of New Galloway, Kirkcudbrightshire, and Eleanora A Henderson, *née* Spence (d 2006); *Educ* Eton, Univ of Edinburgh (MA, LLB); *m* 28 Oct 1978, Virginia Theresa, da of Lt-Col John E B Freeman (d 1986), and Lady Winefride Freeman, of Buxhall Vale, Suffolk; 3 s (Alexander b 1982, Charles b 1984, George b 1987); *Career* Peat Marwick Mitchell & Co 1972–76, Morgan Grenfell & Co 1977–82; md Wardley Marine International Investment Management Ltd 1985 (dir 1982), dir Wardley Investment Services International Ltd 1987–91, dir Fleming Investment Management Ltd 1991–2001, md JP Morgan Fleming Asset Management Ltd 2006– (vice-pres (investments) 2001–); FCA 1980 (ACA 1975), MSI 1992; *Recreations* golf, tennis; *Clubs* Brooks's, St James's; *Style*— Ian Henderson, Esq; ✉ 20 Westbourne Park Road, London W2 5PH (e-mail hendeir@hotmail.com); JP Morgan Fleming Asset Management Ltd, Finsbury Dials, 20 Finsbury Street, London EC2V 9AQ (tel 020 7742 8591)

HENDERSON, (William) James Carlaw; s of James Henderson, of Kelso, Roxburghshire, and Nan Stark, *née* Fergusson (d 1984); *b* 26 September 1948; *Educ* George Heriot's Sch Edinburgh, Univ of Edinburgh (LLB); *Career* apprentice Patrick & James WS Edinburgh 1971–73, asst Wallace & Guthrie WS Edinburgh 1973–74; ptnr: Allan McDougall & Co SSC Edinburgh 1976–83 (asst 1974–76), Brodies WS Edinburgh 1983–2003; speaker Federalism and Regional Policy (Moscow Sch of Political Studies seminar): Altai Russia July 1996, Pskov Russia June 1997; curator: Chris J Fergusson, A Dumfries and Galloway Artist (retrospective exhbn) Kirkcudbright 2001, Dumfries Arts Festival 2002, Whithorn Priory 2002; govr Edinburgh Coll of Art 1996–98, memb Bd Edinburgh Printmakers Workshop 2001–06, memb Edinburgh Ctee RSGS 2003–, memb Scottish Ctee TARS 2005–; tstee Mendelssohn on Mull Festival 2003–, memb Bd Family Mediation Lothian 2005; hon life memb Soc of Scottish Artists 2005 (sec 1980–83, memb 1983), memb Soc of Writers to the Signet 1981; FRGS 1992; *Publications* Chris J Fergusson, 1876–1957: A Dumfries and Galloway Artist (2001); *Recreations* sailing, hill walking, skiing, the arts; *Clubs* Royal Highland Yacht, Edinburgh Sports, Scottish Arts; *Style*— James Henderson,

Esq; ✉ 11 Inverleith Place, Edinburgh EH3 5QE (tel 0131 552 7518); Drimmie Cottage, Bridge of Cally, Perthshire PH10 7JS

HENDERSON, Hon Mr Justice; Hon Sir Launcelot Dinadan James; kt (2007); er s of late Baron Henderson of Brompton (Life Peer), and Susan Mary, *née* Dartford; *b* 20 November 1951; *Educ* Westminster, Balliol Coll Oxford; *m* 1989, Elaine Elizabeth, er da of late Kenneth Frank Webb, of Dringhouses, York; 2 s (Peter George Galahad b 12 Aug 1990, Arthur Frank Gabriel b 18 Feb 1994), 1 da (Matilda Jane b 29 Aug 1992); *Career* called to the Bar Lincoln's Inn 1977 (bencher 2004); appointed standing jr counsel Chancery to the Inland Revenue 1987, standing jr counsel to Inland Revenue 1991–95, QC 1995, judge of the High Court of Justice (Chancery Div) 2007– (dep High Ct judge 2001); fell All Souls Coll Oxford 1974–81 and 1982–89; tstee Samuel Courtauld Tst 2005; *Recreations* botany, art, music, books; *Style*— The Hon Mr Justice Henderson; ✉ c/o Royal Courts of Justice, Strand, London WC2A 2LL

HENDERSON, Mark; s of Gordon Henderson, of Mansfield, and Margaret Eileen, *née* Moakes; *b* 26 September 1957; *Educ* Sherwood Hall Tech GS Mansfield; *Children* 2 s (Sam b 8 Nov 1993, Charlie b 1 Aug 1995); *Career* lighting designer; started career as lighting technician Newark Notts 1975; subsequently chief electrician for: Kent Opera, English Music Theatre, London Contemporary Dance, Sadler's Wells, Opera North; *Theatre* has lit over 50 West End shows incl: Grease, Follies, Girlfriends, Mutiny, Kiss me Kate, Carmen Jones, Becket, The Merchant of Venice, A Patriot for Me, The Dresser, Gasping, Heartbreak House, No Man's Land, The Deep Blue Sea, Rowan Atkinson in Revue, Home, St Joan, Neville's Island, Indian Ink, Design for Living, Passion; RNT prodns incl: The Shaugraun, Cat on a Hot Tin Roof (also Broadway), Hamlet, The Changeling, Racing Demon, Long Day's Journey into Night, Napoli Millionaria, Murmuring Judges, Pygmalion, The Absence of War, The Birthday Party, Les Parent Terribles (Indiscretions, Broadway) Sweet Bird of Youth, Le Cid, Absolute Hell, La Grande Magia, A Little Night Music, John Gabriel Borkman, Oedipus Plays, The Cripple of Inishmaan, Marat/Sade, Amy's View, Copenhagen, Antony and Cleopatra; RSC prodns incl: Macbeth, The Tempest, Kiss Me Kate, Measure for Measure, General from America; Almeida prodns incl: The Deep Blue Sea, Rules of the Game, No Man's Land, Life of Galileo, Hamlet, Tartuffe, Britannicus, Judas Kiss, Naked, Iceman Cometh; other prodns incl: Hamlet (Broadway), Rowan Atkinson Tours (Aust, NZ, USA), The Seagull (Old Vic); *Opera* numerous prodns incl: The Merry Widow (New Sadler's Wells), Werther (Opera de Nancy), The Flying Dutchman (Royal Opera), The Makropulos Case (Glyndebourne Festival Opera), Tosca (Welsh Nat Opera), Anna Karenina (ENO); *Dance* prodns incl: Agora, Shadows in the Sun (both London Contemporary Dance Theatre), Swan of Tuonela (Sadler's Wells Royal Ballet), Quicksilver (Rambert Dance Co); for Royal Ballet: The Tales of Beatrix Potter, The Planets, Don Quixote, The Judas Tree, Daphnis and Chloë; *Films* incl: The Tall Guy (Working Title Prodn), Under Milk Wood (Imagination Entertainment), Rowan Atkinson in Boston USA; *Other Work* Madame Tussaud's: 200 Years Exhibition, Garden Party Exhibition, Spirit of London Dark Ride, Rock Circus Entrance, Planetarium Foyer, Royal Court redevelopment; *Awards* incl: Olivier Award for Lighting Designer of the Year 1992, Olivier Award for Best Lighting Designer 1995, Tony Award nomination Best Lighting Designer 1995, Olivier Award nomination for Best Lighting Designer 1996; *Style*— Mark Henderson, Esq; ✉ c/o PBJ Management Ltd, 5 Soho Square, London W1V 5DE (tel 020 7287 1112, fax 020 7287 1448)

HENDERSON, Mark Ian; s of Ian Sidney Campbell Henderson (d 1954), and Patricia Joyce, *née* Muers (d 1989); *b* 10 April 1947; *Educ* Stowe, CLP (BA); *m* 1970, Ann (d 2002), da of Albert Edwin Reed (d 1982); 1 da (Johanna b 1976), 1 s (James b 1978); *Career* md RCB International Ltd 1987–89; dir: Hill Samuel Pensions Investment Management 1981–87 (md 1986–87), Mpalanganga Estates (Malawi) 1983–2003, Hill Samuel Asset Management 1984–87, Hill Samuel Investment Management 1985–87, Touche Remnant 1989–93, Clerical Medical Investment Gp 1993–96; managing ptnr Solutions in Investment 1996–2006; Liveryman Worshipful Co of Curriers; ASIP, MSI; *Publications* numerous articles on investment mgmnt; *Recreations* running, music, bonsai trees, scuba diving; *Clubs* Cwlth; *Style*— Mark Henderson, Esq; ✉ 18 Clifton Place, London W2 2SW (tel 020 7402 8262, e-mail mark_henderson@lineone.net)

HENDERSON, Mary Katharine; *Educ* Berkhamsted Sch for Girls, Univ of St Andrews (MA), Univ of Durham (PGCE); *Career* modern languages teacher (French and German) and housemistress Cheltenham Ladies' Coll 1980–92, modern languages teacher Warminster Sch 1992–96 (conductor sch choir); Westonbirt Sch: head of modern languages 1996–99, headmistress 1999–, conductor staff choir; dir Bath Mozart Festival; tstee Tetbury Hosp; memb Paragon Singers of Bath, soprano renaissance gp and St Andrews chorus; capt lacrosse team Univ of St Andrews, memb home Scots team 1973–75; memb: PCC, SHA; FRSA; *Recreations* singing, golf, travelling, hill walking, Scottish country dancing; *Clubs* Univ Women's; *Style*— Mrs Mary Henderson; ✉ Westonbirt School, Tetbury, Gloucestershire GL8 8QG (tel 01666 880333, fax 01666 880364, e-mail head@westonbirt.gloucs.sch.uk)

HENDERSON, Michael John Glidden; s of William Glidden Henderson (d 1946), and Aileen Judith, *née* Malloy (d 1996); *b* 19 August 1938; *Educ* St Benedict's Sch Ealing; *m* 29 Sept 1965, Stephanie Maria, da of John Dyer, of Hampton Court, Surrey; 4 s (Nicholas b 1966, Simon b 1968, Angus b 1972, Giles b 1976); *Career* chm and chief exec Cookson Group plc 1978–90; chm Henderson Crosthwaite Ltd 1995–2000, exec vice-chm Quexco Inc (USA) 2002; dir: Guinness Mahon Holdings plc 1988–2000, Cyril Sweett Ltd 1998, Eco-Bat Technolgies plc 1999–2002, Wisley Golf Club plc 2002 (dep chm 2003), Ronar Services Ltd, Three Counties Financial Mgmnt Services Ltd, Pennymead Sports Ground Ltd; memb DTI Innovation Advsy Bd 1998–2003; tstee Natural History Museum Devpt Tst 1990–2000; govr: St George's Coll Weybridge 1990 (chm Fin and Gen Purposes Ctee 1991–, dep chm 2002), Cranmore Sch West Horsley 1991 (dep chm 1998, chm Fin and Gen Purposes Ctee 1992–), St Teresa's Convent Effingham 2002– (chm Fin and Gen Purposes Ctee 2002–); FCA 1961, FRSA 1989; Knight of the Holy Sepulchre 2005; *Recreations* tennis, golf; *Clubs* MCC, Wisley Golf, Horsley Sports, Queen's, Thurlestone Golf, Salcombe Yacht; *Style*— Michael Henderson, Esq; ✉ Langdale, Woodland Drive, East Horsley, Surrey KT24 5AN (tel 01483 283844, office 01483 284464, e-mail mike.henderson3@btopenworld.com)

HENDERSON, Sir (John) Nicholas; GCMG (1977, KCMG 1972, CMG 1965), KCVO (1991); s of Prof Sir Hubert Henderson; *b* 1 April 1919; *Educ* Stowe, Hertford Coll Oxford; *m* 1951, Mary Barber, *née* Cawadias (d 2004); 1 da (Alexandra (Countess of Drogheda)); *Career* private sec to Foreign Sec 1963–65, min Madrid 1965–69; ambass: Poland 1969–72, W Germany 1972–75, France 1975–79, USA (Washington) 1979–82; dir: M and G Reinsurance 1982–89, Foreign and Colonial Investment Trust plc 1982–89, Hambros plc 1983–89, Tarmac plc 1983–92, F and C Eurotrust plc 1984–, Sotheby's 1989–; chm: Channel Tunnel Gp 1985–86, Fuel Tech NV; Lord Warden of the Stannaries, Keeper of the Privy Seal of the Duchy of Cornwall, vice-chm of the Prince of Wales Cncl 1985–90; tstee Nat Gallery 1985–89; hon fell Hertford Coll Oxford 1975, Hon DCL Univ of Oxford; *Books* Prince Eugen of Savoy (biography), The Birth of NATO (1982), The Private Office (1984), Channels and Tunnels (1987), Mandarin (1994), Old Friends and Modern Instances (2000), The Private Office Revisited (2001); *Recreations* gardening; *Clubs* Brooks's, Pratt's; *Style*— Sir Nicholas Henderson, GCMG, KCVO; ✉ 6 Fairholt Street, London SW7 1EG (tel 020 7589 4291)

HENDERSON, Nicholas John; s of John Ronald Henderson, CVO, OBE, of Newbury, Berks, and Katherine Sarah, *née* Beckwith-Smith (d 1972); *b* 10 December 1950; *Educ* Eton; *m* 10 June 1978, Diana Amanda, da of John Thorne; 3 da (Sarah Lucy b 5 Dec 1981, Tessa Jane b 8 Dec 1983, Camilla Penny b 3 Nov 1987); *Career* national hunt racehorse trainer; asst trainer to Fred Winter 1973–78, amateur rider 1970–78 (rode 75 winners incl The Imperial Cup Sandown and Liverpool Foxhunters); trainer 1978–; trained over 1000 winners incl See You Then (3 Champion Hurdles 1985, 1986, 1987), Brown Windsor (Whitbread Gold Cup), The Tsarevich (16 races and 2nd place in Grand National), Zongalero (won Mandarin Chase and 2nd place in Grand National), First Bout, Alone Success Katarino (Daily Express Triumph Hurdle), Remittance Man (Champion Chase); leading nat hunt trainer 1986–87 and 1987–88, Piper Heidsieck trainer of the Year 1986, 1987 and 1988; *Recreations* golf, shooting; *Style*— Nicholas Henderson, Esq; ✉ Seven Barrows, Lambourn, Hungerford, Berkshire RG17 8UH (tel 01488 72259, fax 01488 72596)

HENDERSON, Prof Paul; CBE (2003); s of Thomas William Henderson (d 1988), and Dorothy Violet, *née* Marriner; *b* 7 November 1940; *Educ* KCS Wimbledon, Univ of London (BSc), Univ of Oxford (DPhil); *m* Aug 1966, Elizabeth Kathryn, da of William Albert Ankerson; 1 s (Gideon Mark b 29 July 1968), 1 da (Laura Kate b 19 Jan 1972); *Career* asst lectr in chemistry Univ of Glasgow 1966–67, lectr in geochemistry Chelsea Coll London 1968–76; Br Museum (Natural History): head Rock and Mineral Chemistry Div 1977–87, dep keeper of Mineralogy Natural History Museum (name change) 1987–89, keeper of Mineralogy 1989–95, also assoc dir for Earth Scis 1992–95, dir of Sci 1995–2003; UCL: visiting prof in mineral scis 1990–98, hon prof 1998–; Muséum National d'Histoire Naturelle Paris: memb Sci Advsy Ctee 2000–01, memb Conseil Scientifique 2003–06; pres Mineralogical Soc of GB and Ireland 1989–91, vice-pres Geological Soc London 2002–; tstee Horniman Museum and Public Park Tst 2004–; Fourmarier Medal Belgian Geological Soc 1989; FGS 1990, chartered geologist; *Books* Inorganic Geochemistry (1982), Rare Earth Element Geochemistry (1984); *Recreations* history, music, Paris, wine; *Style*— Prof Paul Henderson, CBE; ✉ 4 Linden Avenue, Maidenhead, Berkshire SL6 6HB (e-mail p.henderson@btinternet.com)

HENDERSON, Dr Richard; *b* 19 July 1945; *Educ* Hawick HS and Boroughmuir Secdy Sch, Univ of Edinburgh (Isaac Newton scholar, Neil Arnott scholar, BSc), Univ of Cambridge (MRC scholar, PhD); *Career* research staff MRC Lab of Molecular Biology Cambridge 1969–70, Helen Hay Whitney postdoctoral fell Yale Univ 1970–73; MRC Lab of Molecular Biology Cambridge: research staff 1973–79, sr research staff 1979–84, special appts grade research staff 1984–86, jt head Div of Structural Studies 1986–95, dep dir 1995–96, dir 1996–2006; fell Darwin Coll Cambridge 1982–, hon fell Corpus Christi Coll Cambridge 2003–; memb EMBO 1981; William Bate Hardy Prize Cambridge Philosophical Soc 1978, Ernst-Ruska Prize for electron microscopy 1980, Rosenstiel Award 1991, Louis Jeantet Award 1993, Gregori Aminoff Award 1999; foreign assoc Nat Acad of Scis USA 1998; FRS 1983; *Style*— Dr Richard Henderson, FRS; ✉ MRC Laboratory of Molecular Biology, Hills Road, Cambridge CB2 2QH (tel 01223 402215, fax 01223 213556, e-mail rh15@mrc-lmb.cam.ac.uk)

HENDERSON, Maj Sir Richard Yates; KCVO (2006), TD (1966), JP; s of late John Wishart Henderson, and late Dorothy, *née* Yates; *b* 7 July 1931; *Educ* Rugby, Hertford Coll Oxford (BA), Univ of Glasgow (LLB); *m* 1957, Frances Elizabeth Chrystal; 2 s, 1 da; *Career* Nat Serv: Royal Scots Greys 1950–52, Ayrshire Yeomanry 1953–69; conslt Mitchells Roberton Slrs 1990–92 (ptnr 1958–90); tstee TSB Glasgow 1966–74, dir West of Scotland TSB 1974–83; HM Lord-Lt Ayrshire and Arran 1991–2006 (DL 1970–90); Ensign Queen's Body Guard for Scotland (Royal Co of Archers), Hon Col Ayrshire Yeomanry Sqdn Scottish Yeomanry 1992–97, hon sheriff S Strathclyde, Dumfries and Galloway at Ayr 1997, pres Lowlands TAVRA 1996–2000; *Recreations* shooting, tennis, golf; *Clubs* Western (Glasgow); *Style*— Maj Sir Richard Henderson, KCVO, TD; ✉ Blairston, by Ayr KA7 4EF (tel 01292 441601)

HENDERSON, Roger Anthony; QC (1980); s of Dr Peter Wallace Henderson (d 1984), and Dr Stella Dolores, *née* Morton (d 2006); *b* 21 April 1943; *Educ* Radley, St Catharine's Coll Cambridge; *m* 1968, Catherine Margaret; 3 da (Camilla (Mrs William Gray Muir), Antonia (Mrs Andrew Dalmahoy), Venetia); *Career* called to the Bar Inner Temple 1964 (bencher 1985); recorder 1983–, dep judge of the High Court 1987–, head of chambers; pres Br Acad of Forensic Sci 1986; chm: Public Affrs Ctee of the Bar 1989 and 1990, Special Ctee of St Peter's Hosps Gp 1989–92, Civil Serv Arbitration Tbnl 1994–; chm Ctee Assoc of Regulatory Disciplinary Lawyers 2003–; chm London Hosp Med Coll 1993–95 (govr 1989–95); hon fell Queen Mary Univ of London; *Recreations* fly fishing, gardening, shooting; *Clubs* Boodle's; *Style*— R A Henderson, Esq, QC; ✉ 9 Brunswick Gardens, London W8 4AS (tel 020 7727 3980); 2 Harcourt Buildings, Temple, London EC4Y 9DB (tel 020 7583 9020, fax 020 7583 2686, e-mail rhenderson@hendersonchambers.co.uk); Holbury Mill, Lockerley, Hampshire SO51 0JR

HENDERSON-STEWART, Sir David James; 2 Bt (UK 1957), of Callumshill, Co Perth; s of Sir James Henderson-Stewart, 1 Bt, MP (d 1961); *b* 3 July 1941; *Educ* Eton, Trinity Coll Oxford; *m* 1972, Anne, da of Count Serge de Pahlen; 3 s (David b 1973, Nicolas b 1974, André b 1976), 1 da (Nathalie b 1981); *Heir* s, David Henderson-Stewart; *Style*— Sir David Henderson-Stewart, Bt; ✉ 90 Oxford Gardens, London W10 (tel 020 8960 1278)

HENDRICK, Prof David John; *b* 18 October 1941, Reading, Berks; *Educ* Maidstone GS, Guy's Hosp Med Sch London (pre-clinical entrance scholar, MB BS, MD), McGill Univ Montreal (MSc); *m* Alex Margaret; 2 da (Vicki, Shona); *Career* house physician (gen med and cardiology) and house surgn Guy's Hosp 1966–67, SHO (neurology) Royal Victoria Infirmary Newcastle upon Tyne 1968, jr med registrar Guy's Hosp 1968, med registrar Greenwich Hosp and clinical asst Brompton Hosp 1968–70, sr med registrar Sydney Hosp 1970–72, research asst (clinical immunology) Brompton Hosp 1972–73, sr registar (chest and gen med) Churchill Hosp and Radcliffe Infirmary Oxford 1973–76, asst prof of pulmonary and internal med West Virginia Univ Morgantown 1976–79, assoc prof of pulmonary and internal med Tulane Univ New Orleans 1979–82, conslt physician (chest and gen med) and head Dept of Respiratory Med Newcastle Gen Hosp 1982–94, conslt physician (respiratory and gen med) Royal Victoria Infirmary NHS Tst 1994– (head Dept of Respiratory Med 1994–98), sabbatical year McGill Univ Montreal 1998–99; Univ of Newcastle upon Tyne Med Sch: hon lectr then hon sr lectr 1982–97, sr lectr then prof of occupational respiratory med 1997–; memb: Ctee on Thoracic Med RCP 1988–92, Steering Ctee SWORD (Surveillance of Work-related and Occupational Respiratory Diseases) Project 1988–, Grants Ctee Br Lung Fndn 1991–95, Med Appeals Tbnl 1992–, Advsy Gp on Respiratory Sensitizers Dept of Employment 1993–96, Nat Asthma Taskforce Mortality and Severe Morbidity Working Gp 1994–98, Grants Ctee North of England Cancer Research Campaign 1996–98; memb Editorial Bd Thorax 1988–91, co-ordinating ed Thorax - Year in Review Annual Supplement 1994–98; MRCS 1966, FRCP 1985 (LRCP 1966, MRCP 1969), FFOM 1994; *Publications* Occupational Disorders of the Lung: recognition, management and prevention (jt ed, 2002); jl articles and book chapters chiefly related to asthma, allergic alveolitis, and occupational diseases of the lung; *Recreations* family, coarse golfing, even coarser sailing; *Style*— Prof David Hendrick; ✉ Department of Respiratory Medicine, Royal Victoria Infirmary, Queen Victoria Road, Newcastle upon Tyne NE1 4LP (tel 0191 282 0143, fax 0191 282 0112, e-mail d.j.hendrick@ncl.ac.uk)

HENDRICK, Mark; MP; *b* 2 November 1958; *Educ* Univ of Manchester (MSc, CertEd), Liverpool Poly (BSc); *Career* design engr for six years SERC (Daresbury Lab); Lab Pty: memb 1982–, memb (and former branch sec) Salford Co-op Pty 1984–1994, chm Weaste and Seedley Branch 1987–94, chm Eccles Constituency 1990–94; MEP (Lab Co-op) Lancashire Central 1994–99; Euro Parly Lab Pty spokesperson on economic and

H

monetary affrs, memb Euro Parl Economic and Monetary Affrs Ctee, sec NW Gp of Lab MEPs 1994–98; MP (Lab Co-op) Preston (by-election) 2000–; memb Salford City Cncl 1987–95 (served on Policy, Planning, Educn Ctees and Management Services Ctee (vice-chm)); alternate dir representing City of Salford Manchester Airport plc 1985–94; memb GMB; *Style—* Mark Hendrick, Esq, MP; ✉ Constituency Office, 6 Sedgwick Street, Preston PR1 1TP (tel 01772 883575, fax 01772 887188, e-mail hendrick@prestonlabour.fsnet.co.uk)

HENDRICKS, Rt Rev Paul Joseph; s of Gerald St Alban Hendricks, of Southampton, and Grace Rose, *née* Deacon (d 1994); *b* 18 March 1956, Beckenham, Kent; *Educ* St Mary's RC GS Sidcup, CCC Oxford (MA), English Coll Rome and Gregorian Univ Rome (BTh, MPhil); *Career* microwave engr GEC Hirst Research Centre Wembley 1977–79; ordained: deacon Rome 1983, priest Orpington 1984; asst priest St Boniface Parish Tooting 1985–89, philosophy lectr and bursar St John's Seminary Wonersh 1989–99, parish priest Our Lady of Sorrows Peckham 1999–2006, auxiliary bishop (RC) SW Area Archdiocese of Southwark 2006–; govr: Inform, Catholic Truth Soc; memb Jane Austen Soc; *Recreations* walking, reading, sailing; *Style—* The Rt Rev Paul Hendricks; ✉ 95 Carshalton Road, Sutton SM1 4LL; Archbishop's House, 150 St George's Rd, Southwark, London SE1 6HX (tel 020 8643 8007, e-mail p.hendricks@btinternet.com)

HENDRY, Charles; MP; s of late Charles W R Hendry, and Peggy Hendry; *b* 6 May 1959; *Educ* Rugby, Univ of Edinburgh (BComm); *m* 20 July 1995, Sallie A Moores, yr da of Stuart Smith; 2 s (Charles Stuart Benjamin b 3 Sept 1996, James William Ruairidh b 13 May 1998); *Career* account dir Ogilvy & Mather PR Ltd then assoc dir Burson-Marsteller Ltd PR conslts 1982–88; political advsr: to Rt Hon John Moore MP as sec of state for Social Servs 1988, to Rt Hon Tony Newton MP as min for Trade and Industry then sec of state for Social Security 1988–90; MP (Cons): High Peak 1992–97, Wealden 2001– (Parly candidate (Cons): Clackmannan 1983, Mansfield 1987); PPS: to Rt Hon William Hague, MP, *qv*, as min for Disabled People 1994–95, to Rt Hon Gillian Shephard, DL, *qv*, as sec of state for Educn 1995; COS Office of the Ldr of the Oppn 1997, oppn pairing whip 2001–02, shadow min for Young People 2002–05, dep chm Cons Pty 2003–05 (vice-chm 1995–97), shadow min for Industry and Enterprise 2005–; chm All-Pty Parly Gp on Homelessness 1992–95, memb Culture, Media and Sport Select Ctee 2004; sec Cons Backbench: Social Security Ctee 1992–94, Inner Cities and Urban Affairs Ctee 1994–95; sec E Midlands Cons MPs 1992–97; head of business liaison Cons Pty 1997–99; The Agenda Gp Ltd: chief exec 1999–2001, dir 1999–2005, non-exec chm 2001–05; pres Edinburgh Univ Cons Assoc 1979–80, vice-chm Scot Fedn of Cons Students 1980–81, vice-chm Battersea Cons Assoc 1981–83; tstee Drive for Youth 1989–99, hon pres Br Youth Cncl 1992–97, patron The Big Issue Fndn 1997– (tstee 1996–97); non-exec dir IncrediBull Ideas Ltd 2003–04; *Recreations* tennis, skiing; *Style—* Charles Hendry, Esq, MP; ✉ House of Commons, London SW1A 0AA (tel 020 7219 3000, e-mail hendryc@parliament.uk)

HENDRY, Prof David Forbes; s of Robert Ernest Hendry, of Fortrose, and Catherine Elizabeth, *née* Mackenzie; *b* 6 March 1944; *Educ* Glasgow HS, Univ of Aberdeen (MA), LSE (MSc, PhD); *m* 7 Oct 1966, Evelyn Rosemary, da of Rev John Vass (d 1974), of Aberdeen; 1 da (Vivien Louise b 1977); *Career* LSE: lectr 1969–73, reader 1973–77, prof of economics 1977–81; Univ of Oxford: prof of economics 1982–, fell Nuffield Coll 1982–, Leverhulme personal research prof 1995–2000, chm Economics Dept 2001–07, ESRC professorial fell 2003–06; visiting prof: Yale Univ 1975, Univ of Calif Berkeley 1976, Catholic Univ of Louvain-la-Neuve 1980, Univ of Calif San Diego 1981 and 1989–90; special advsr House of Commons Select Ctee on the Treasy and Civil Serv 1979–80 and 1991, memb Academic Panel of HM Treasy 1976–89, chm Research Assessment Panel in Economics 1995–96; Royal Economic Soc: pres 1992–95, hon vice-pres 1995–; pres Section F BAAS 1999–2000; foreign hon memb: American Econ Assoc 1991, American Acad of Arts and Sciences 1994; Guy medal in Bronze of the Royal Statistical Soc 1986; chartered statistician 1992; Hon LLD Univ of Aberdeen 1987, Hon DSc Univ of Nottingham 1998, Hon DPhil Norwegian Univ of Sci and Technol, Hon Dr Univ of St Gallen, Hon LLD Univ of St Andrews 2002, Hon DPhil Univ of Lund 2006; hon fell Int Inst of Forecasters 2001; fell Econometric Soc 1976, FBA 1987, FRSE 2002; *Books* Econometrics and Quantitative Economics (with K F Wallis, 1984), Pc-Give: An Interactive Econometric Modelling System (1989, with J A Doornik 1992, 1994, 1997, 2001 and 2006), Pc-Naive: An Interactive Program for Monte Carlo Experimentation in Econometrics (with A J Neale and N R Ericsson, 1991, with J A Doornik 2001 and 2006), Econometrics: Alchemy or Science (1993, 2 edn 2000), Cointegration, Error Correction and the Econometric Analysis of Non-stationary Data (with A Banerjee, J J Dolado and J W Galbraith, 1993), Dynamic Econometrics (1995), The Foundations of Econometric Analysis (with M S Morgan, 1995), Forecasting Economic Time Series (with M P Clements, 1998), Forecasting Non-stationary Economic Time Series (with M P Clements, 1999), Understanding Economic Forecasts (with N R Ericsson, 2001), Automatic Econometric Model Selection Using PcGets (with H M Krolzig, 2001), Companion to Economic Forecasting (with M P Clements, 2002), General to Specific Modelling (ed with J Campos and N R Ericsson, 2005); *Recreations* golf; *Style—* Prof David F Hendry, FBA, FRSE; ✉ 26 Northmoor Road, Oxford OX2 6UR (tel 01865 515588); Nuffield College, Oxford OX1 1NF (tel 01865 278587, fax 01865 278621)

HENDRY, Diana Lois; da of Leslie Gordon McConomy (d 1964), and Amelia, *née* Kesler (d 1993); *b* 2 October 1941; *Educ* W Kirby Co GS for Girls, Filton Tech Coll, Univ of Bristol (BA, MLitt), privately (LLCM); *m* 1965 (m dis 1981), George Alexander Forbes Hendry; 1 s (Hamish b 1966), 1 da (Kate b 1970); *Career* reporter/feature writer The Western Mail Cardiff 1960–65, freelance journalist and writer 1965–; Eng teacher Clifton Coll 1987–90, tutor Bristol Poly 1987–93, tutor in lit Open Univ 1990–91, tutor in creative writing Univ of Bristol 1995–97, writer in residence Dumfries and Galloway Royal Infirmary 1997–98; first prize Stroud Int Poetry Competition 1976, second prize Peterloo Poetry Competition 1993 (third prize 1991), Whitbread Award (for children's novel) 1991, first prize Housman Soc Poetry Competition 1996, Scottish Arts Cncl Children's Book Award 2001; memb Soc of Authors 1987, memb PEN 1993; *Books* incl: Fiona Finds Her Tongue (1985, short-listed Smartie Award), Double Vision (1990), Harvey Angell (1991), Peterloo Preview 3 (1993), Making Blue (Peterloo Poets) (1995), The Awesome Bird (1995), Harvey Angell and the Ghost Child (1997), Minders (1998), Harvey Angell Beats Time (2000), Borderers (Peterloo Poets, 2001), You Can't Kiss It Better (2003), Twelve Lilts: Psalms and Responses (2003), Sparks (with Tom Pow, 2005); numerous poems published in leading jls and anthologies; contrib book reviews The Spectator; *Recreations* playing the piano; *Style—* Diana Hendry; ✉ c/o Jenny Brown Associates, 33 Arglye Place, Edinburgh EH9 1JT (e-mail jenny-brown@blueyonder.co.uk)

HENDRY, Gerry; s of James Hendry (d 1995), and Phaneulina, *née* Webster (d 2000); *b* 5 May 1948, Leeds; *Educ* Fraserburgh Acad, Buchan Coll, Univ of Leeds; *m* 1, 1973 (m dis); 1 s (Craig b 18 July 1973), 1 da (Emma b 7 Nov 1975); m 2, 1993, Geraldine, *née* Hamer; 2 da (Alexandra b 4 Oct 1996, Antonia b 13 Nov 1997); *Career* engr Consolidated Pneumatic 1968, civil servant MOD 1970–, joined Prison Serv as prison offr Northallerton 1980, past positions incl head of residence, head of regimes, head of security, head of personnel and planning, head of secretariat and dep govr, govr Shrewsbury Prison 2005–; memb Hambleton DC 1978, dep mayor Northallerton 1979, Northallerton parish cncllr; involved with UN Mission in Kosovo (UNMIK) as head of team evacuating refugees from Macedonia and Albania during Kosovo Conflict; supporter NE Aid to Orphans Lithuania; memb Inst of Mgmnt 1994; *Recreations* golf, folk music, freemasonry; *Clubs* Brancepeth Golf; *Style—* Gerry Hendry, Esq; ✉ HMP Shrewsbury, The Dana, Shrewsbury SY1 2HR (tel 01743 273101, fax 01743 273002, e-mail gerry.hendry@hmps.gsi.gov.uk)

HENDRY, James David (Jim); MBE (2007); s of Alexander Hendry (d 1986), of Perth, and Ethel, *née* Stephen (d 1990); *b* 10 October 1939; *Educ* Perth Sr Acad; *m* 1 Sept 1969, Georgina, da of Edwin John Adkins (d 1989), of Wibarston, Leics; *Career* housing offr: Perth Town Cncl 1955–61, Glenrothes Devpt Corp 1961–65; dist housing offr Corby Devpt Corp 1965–76, sr housing offr Corby Town Cncl 1976–79; Br Cycling Fedn: offr and coach nat team mangr 1969–79, dir of racing 1979–85, dir of coaching devpt 1985–87, chief exec 1987–97, gen sec 1997–2005; conslt on anti-doping 2006–; club div and nat offr Scottish Cyclists' Union 1956–62; memb: Nat Assoc of Sports Coaches 1979, Soc of Assoc Execs 1988; *Books* BCF Training Manual (1987), Take Up Cycle Racing (1989); *Recreations* cycling, sea fishing; *Style—* Jim Hendry, Esq, MBE; ✉ British Cycling Federation, Stuart Street, Manchester M11 4DQ (tel 0870 871 2000, fax 0870 871 2001, e-mail jimhendry@britishcycling.org.uk)

HENDRY, Stephen Gordon; MBE (1994); s of Gordon John Hendry, of Edinburgh, and Irene Agnes, *née* Anthony; *b* 13 January 1969; *Educ* Inverkeithing HS; *m* 30 June 1995, Amanda Elizabeth; 1 s (Blaine Thomas b 2 Oct 1996); *Career* professional snooker player 1985–; winner Grand Prix 1987, 1990, 1991 and 1995, world doubles champion 1987 and 1991, Australian Masters champion 1987, Br Open champion 1988, 1991 and 1999, NZ Masters champion 1988, Scottish champion 1986, 1987 and 1988, Benson & Hedges Masters champion 1989, 1990, 1991, 1992, 1993, 1996, 1997 and 1999, Asian champion 1989 and 1990, Regal Masters champion 1989, 1990 and 1995, Dubai Classic champion 1989, 1990 and 1993, UK champion 1989, 1990, 1994, 1995 and 1996, Embassy world champion 1990, 1992, 1993, 1994, 1995, 1996 and 1999 (setting new record), Matchroom League champion 1991–92, 1993–94, 1994–95 and 2000; winner: Hong Kong 555 Classic 1991, India Masters 1991, Benson & Hedges Irish Masters 1992, Canal+ Challenge 1992, Regal Welsh Open 1992, 1997 and 2003, European Open 1993, 1994 and 2001, International Open 1993 and 1997, Liverpool Victoria Charity Challenge 1995 and 1997, World Cup 1996, Thailand Masters 1998, Malta Grand Prix 1998 and 2001, Liverpool Victoria Champions' Cup 1999, Regal Scottish Open 1999, Nations Cup 2001; holds record for most major titles won in a season (9 in 1991–92); memb Lord's Taverners Scotland; *Recreations* golf, music; *Style—* Stephen Hendry, Esq, MBE; ✉ c/o 110Sport Ltd, Kerse Road, Stirling FK7 7SG (tel 01786 462634, fax 01786 450068, e-mail mail@110sport.com)

HENDY, John; QC (1987); s of late Jack Hendy, of Penzance, and Mary, *née* Best; *b* 11 April 1948; *Educ* Univ of London (LLB), Queen's Univ Belfast (LLM); *Career* memb Hon Soc of Gray's Inn 1966; called to the Bar 1972 (bencher 1995), admitted to the Bar NSW 1998; visiting prof King's Coll Sch of Law 1999–; chm Inst Employment Rights 1989–, chair Employment Law Bar Assoc 2003–05; sr cmmr Int Cmmn on Labour Rights 2000–; fell Inst of Advanced Legal Studies; ACIArb 1989; FRSM; *Books* Munkman's Employers' Liability (co-author, 13 edn 2001); *Style—* John Hendy, Esq, QC; ✉ 1 Verulam Buildings, Gray's Inn, London WC1R 5LQ (tel 020 7269 0300, fax 020 7405 1387, e-mail hendyqc@oldsquarechambers.co.uk)

HENIG, Baroness (Life Peer UK 2004), of Lancaster in the County of Lancashire; Ruth Beatrice Henig; CBE (2000), JP (1984), DL (Lancs 2002); da of Kurt Munzer, of Leicester; *b* 10 November 1943, Leicester; *Educ* Bedford Coll London, Univ of London, Lancaster Univ (PhD); *m* 1, 1966 (m dis 1993), Stanley Henig, s of Sir Mark Henig (d 1978), of Leicester; 2 s (Hon Simon Anthony b 1969, Hon Harold David b 1972); m 2, 1994, Jack Johnstone; *Career* Lancaster Univ: lectr History Dept 1968–93, sr lectr 1993–, dean of arts and humanities 1997–2000; elected cncllr Lancaster E Lancs CC 1981; chair: Lancs Police Authy 1995–2005, Nat Assoc of Police Authorities 1997–2005, Security Industry Authy 2007–; memb: Lawrence Steering Gp Home Office 2000–05, Nat Criminal Justice Bd 2002–2005; chair Bd Duke's Playhouse Lancaster; *Books* The League of Nations (1973), Versailles and After (1984), Origins of the Second World War (1985), Origins of the First World War (1989), The Weimar Republic (1998), Women and Political Power (with Simon Henig, 2000), Modern Europe, 1870–1945 (with Chris Culpin, 1997); *Recreations* fell walking, bridge, gardening, wine appreciation; *Clubs* Lancaster Bridge; *Style—* The Rt Hon the Lady Henig, CBE, DL; ✉ Roeburn House, Main Street, Wray, Lancaster LA2 8QD (tel 01524 221280, mobile 07768 526210, e-mail ruthhenig@aol.com)

HENKE, Malcolm; s of Donald Henke, of Spain, and Berry, *née* Entwisle (d 2003); *b* 27 January 1959, Coventry, West Midlands; *Educ* Holy Trinity Sch Crawley; *partner* Jane Hall; 4 da (Alexis, Ashley, Lydia, India), 1 s (Oliver); *Career* slr: Hextall Erskine & Co 1977–90, Davies Arnold Cooper 1990–2000, Barlow Lyde & Gilbert 2000–02, Greenwoods 2002–; memb Master of the Rolls Working Party on Structured Settlements, memb Clinical Disputes Forum; *Recreations* golf, motor racing; *Style—* Malcolm Henke, Esq; ✉ Ridgeway, Station Road, Woldingham, Surrey CR3 7DA; The Old Post Office, Shepton Montague, Wincanton, Somerset BA9 8JW; Greenwoods, 18 Bedford Square, London WC1B 3JA (tel 020 7323 4632, e-mail mch@greenwoods-law.co.uk)

HENLEY, Darren Richard; *Educ* St Edmund's Sch Canterbury, Univ of Hull (BA); *Career* freelance radio journalist for stations incl Invicta, LBC, IRN, Classic FM and BBC GLR 1989–92, sr broadcast journalist ITN Radio 1992–95; Classic FM: prog ed Classic Newsnight 1995–96, news mangr 1996–99, news and prog mangr 1999–2000, managing ed 2000–04, station mangr 2004–; md Classic FM and theJazz 2006–; memb: Bd of Judges and Advsrs NY Int Radio Festival 2001–; UN Gold medal 2000, Gold medal Arts and Culture Catgory NY Int Radio Festival 2000, UK Station of the Year Song Radio Acad Awards 2007, Gold medal Best Music Prog NY Int Radio Festival 2007, Chm's Award Arqiva Commercial Radio Awards 2007; dir Bd Canterbury Festival and Theatre Tst 2001–, memb SE Regnl Cncl Arts Cncl England 2002–05, memb Founder Partners Bd The Beacon Fellowship 2003–, tstee Future Talent 2006–; FRSA 1998; *Publications* The Classic FM Pocket Book of Music (2003), The Classic FM Pocket Book of Quotes (2004), The Story of Classical Music (audio, 2004, Best Original Audio Book American Audio Publishers Awards, Radio Times Readers' Choice Award Br Spoken Word Awards 2005, nominated Grammy Award 2005), The Classic FM Pocket Book of Trivia (2004), Aled - The Autobiography (with Aled Jones, 2005), Classic Ephemera (2005), Famous Composers (audio, 2005, Best Original Audio Book Audio Publishers Awards 2006), G4 - The Official Book (2005), The Classic FM Friendly Guide to Mozart (2005), The Classic FM Friendly Guide to Beethoven (with John Suchet, 2006), The Classic FM Friendly Guide to Music (2006), More Famous Composers (2007), The Classic FM Friendly Guide to Elgar (2007), Hayley Westenra - In Her Own Voice (with Hayley Westenra); *Recreations* horse racing, classical music, food; *Style—* Darren Henley, Esq; ✉ Classic FM, 30 Leicester Square, London WC2H 7LA (tel 020 7343 9000, fax 020 7344 2703, e-mail darren.henley@classicfm.com)

HENLEY, Prof Jeremy Martin; s of Brian Henley, and Brenda Mavis Gillette, *née* Colley; *b* 10 September 1958, Worcester; *Educ* Queen Elizabeth's GS Hartlebury, Aston Univ (BSc), KCL (PhD); *m* 1984, Kathrin Jean, *née* Garvey; 2 s (Samuel Edward, Benjamin Seth), 1 da (Sophie Annabelle); *Career* Cornell Univ 1984–86, MRC Cambridge 1986–89, Univ of Birmingham 1990–94, Univ of Bristol 1995– (currently head Dept of Anatomy and asst dir MRC Centre for Synaptic Plasticity); sabbatical Kyoto Univ 1996; *Recreations* building stone walls, reading, travel; *Style—* Prof Jeremy Henley; ✉ MRC Centre for Synaptic Plasticity, Department of Anatomy, School of Medical Sciences, Bristol BS8 1TD (tel 0117 954 6449, fax 0117 929 1687, e-mail j.m.henley@bris.ac.uk)

HENLEY, 8 Baron (I 1799); Oliver Michael Robert Eden; also (and sits as) Baron Northington (UK 1885); s of 7 Baron (d 1977) by his 2 w Nancy, da of late S Walton, of Gilsland, Cumbria; *b* 22 November 1953; *Educ* Clifton, Univ of Durham; *m* 11 Oct 1984, Caroline Patricia, da of late A G Sharp, of Mackney, Oxon; 3 s (Hon John Michael Oliver b 30 June 1988, Hon Patrick Francis b 23 Nov 1993, Hon Edward Andrew b 16 July 1996), 1 da (Hon Elizabeth Caroline b 26 Feb 1991); *Heir* s, Hon John Eden; *Career* sits as Cons in House of Lords; called to the Bar Middle Temple 1977; memb Cumbria CC 1986–89, chm Penrith and The Border Cons Assoc 1987–89 (pres 1989–94); Lord in Waiting 1989; Parly under sec of state: Dept of Social Security 1989–93, Dept of Employment 1993–94, MOD 1994–95; min of state Dept for Education and Employment 1995–97, oppn spokesman on home affrs House of Lords 1997–98, oppn chief whip House of Lords 1998–2001; *Clubs* Brooks's, Pratt's; *Style—* The Rt Hon the Lord Henley; ✉ Scaleby Castle, Carlisle, Cumbria CA6 4LN

HENMAN, Tim; OBE (2004); *b* 6 September 1974; *m* Lucy; 2 da (Rose Elizabeth b 2002, Olivia Susan b 2004); *Career* tennis player; turned professional 1993, highest ATP Tour ranking no 4 in the world 2004; semi-finalist: Wimbledon Championships 1998, 1999 and 2001, French Open 2004, US Open 2004; Silver medal men's doubles (with Neil Broad) Olympic Games Atlanta 1996; winner: Br Nat Championships 1995, 1996 and 1997, (singles and doubles) Seoul ATP Challenger 1995, Reunion ATP Challenger 1995, Sydney Int ATP Tour Event 1997, President's Cup Tashkent 1997 and 1998, Swiss Indoor Championships Basle 1998, CA Trophy Vienna 2000, Samsung Open Brighton 2000, Copenhagen Open 2001, Australian Hardcourt Championships Adelaide 2002, Legg Mason Classic Washington 2003, BNP Paribas Masters Paris 2003; memb Br Davis Cup Team 1995–2007; ret 2007; voted 2nd in BBC Sports Personality of the Year 1997; *Style—* Tim Henman, Esq, OBE; ✉ c/o IMG, The Pier House, Strand on the Green, Chiswick, London W4 3NN (tel 020 8233 5000)

HENNESSY, Prof Peter John; s of William Gerald Hennessy (d 2001), and Edith, *née* Wood-Johnson (d 1986); *b* 28 March 1947; *Educ* Marling Sch Stroud, St John's Coll Cambridge (BA, PhD), LSE, Harvard Univ; *m* 14 June 1969, Enid Mary, *née* Candler; 2 da (Cecily b 1976, Polly b 1979); *Career* lobby corr Financial Times 1976, reporter Br Section The Economist 1982; The Times: reporter Higher Educn Supplement 1972–74, reporter 1974–76, Whitehall corr 1976–82, ldr writer 1982–84; columnist: New Statesman 1986–87, Whitehall Watch The Independent 1987–91, Director Magazine 1989–93; presenter Analysis BBC Radio Four 1986–92; dir and columnist The Tablet 2003–; co fndr and co dir Inst of Contemporary Br History 1986–89 (memb Bd 1989–98, hon fell 1995–2003), ptnr Intellectual R&D 1990–, prof of contemporary history Queen Mary & Westfield Coll London 1992–2000, Gresham prof of rhetoric Gresham Coll 1994–97 (fell 1997–), Attlee prof of contemporary British history Queen Mary Univ of London 2001–; visiting prof of govt Univ of Strathclyde 1989–, visiting scholar Griffith Univ Brisbane 1991; memb Cncl Policy Studies Inst 1992–97; visiting fell: Policy Studies Inst 1986–92, Dept of Politics Univ of Reading 1988–94, Politics Dept Univ of Nottingham 1989–94, RIPA 1989–92; hon res fell Birkbeck Coll London 1990–91; chair Advsy Ctee Inst of Contemporary British History 2001–03, memb Advsy Ctee Sharman Inquiry into Parly Audit and Accountability 2000–01; govr Ditchley Fndn 2001–, chm Kennedy Meml Tst 1995–2000, tstee Attlee Fndn 1986–98, tstee Geffrye Museum 2001–; Hon DLitt: UWE 1995, Univ of Westminster 1996, Kingston Univ 1998; hon fell LSE 2000; FRSA 1992, FRHistS 1993 (vice-pres 1996–2000), FBA 2003; *Books* States of Emergency (jtly, 1983), Sources Close to the Prime Minister (jtly, 1984), What the Papers Never Said (1985), Cabinet (1986), Ruling Performance (jt ed, 1987), Whitehall (1989), Never Again - Britain 1945–51 (1992, Duff Cooper prize 1993, NCR award for non-fiction 1993), The Hidden Wiring - Unearthing the British Constitution (1995), Muddling Through - Power, Politics and the Quality of Government in Post War Britain (1996), The Prime Minister: The Office and its Holders Since 1945 (2000), The Secret State: Whitehall and the Cold War (2002); *Recreations* watching West Ham, listening to music; *Clubs* Savile, Attlee Meml Runners; *Style—* Prof Peter Hennessy; ✉ Department of History, Queen Mary, University of London, Mile End Road, London E1 4NS (tel 020 7882 5016)

HENNIKER, Sir Adrian Chandos; 9 Bt (UK 1813), of Newton Hall, Essex; s of Brig Sir Mark Chandos Auberon Henniker, 8 Bt, CBE, DSO, MC (d 1991), and Kathleen Denys, *née* Anderson (d 1998); *b* 18 October 1946; *Educ* Marlborough; *m* 1971, Ann, da of Stuart Britton, of Llandaff, Cardiff; 2 da (Victoria Louise, Holly Georgina (twins) b 1976); *Heir* none; *Style—* Sir Adrian Henniker, Bt; ✉ The Coach House, Llwydu, Abergavenny, Gwent NP7 7HG

HENNIKER-HEATON, Sir Yvo Robert; 4 Bt (UK 1912), of Mundarrah Towers, Sydney, Aust; s of Wing Cdr Sir (John Victor) Peregrine Henniker-Heaton, 3 Bt (d 1971); *b* 24 April 1954; *m* 1978, Freda, da of Brian Jones, of Broughton Astley, Leics; 1 da (Julia Sermonda b 1987), 1 s (Alastair John b 1990); *Heir* s, Alastair Henniker-Heaton; *Career* memb NW Leics DC 1987–95; chm Kegworth Cons Assoc 1986–89 and 1991–94; govr Ashby Willesley Sch 1995–; chm CEA Computer Security Technical Ctee 1993–95; MIIA; *Publications* Corporate Computer Insurances (1990); *Recreations* walking, writing, public speaking, travel, squash; *Style—* Sir Yvo Henniker-Heaton, Bt

HENNING, Matthew Clive Cunningham; s of Matthew Henning (d 1982), of Co Londonderry, and Olivia Mary, *née* Cunningham (d 1990); *b* 4 January 1934; *Educ* St Andrew's Coll Dublin, Coll of Architecture Oxford (DipArch); *m* 27 Sept 1972, Vivien Margaret, da of David Ernest Walker (d 1971), of Armagh; 1 s (Daniel Clive Walker b 1978), 1 da (Kate Louise b 1982); *Career* conslt architect in private practice; princ architect for the Southern Educn and Library Bd 1966–78; memb Southern Health and Social Services Cncl; ARIBA, MRIAI, memb Royal Soc of Ulster Architects; *Recreations* Golf; *Clubs* Portadown Golf, Tandragee Golf, Bushfoot Golf, County (Armagh), City (Armagh); *Style—* Matthew C C Henning, Esq; ✉ Carraboo, Upper Church Lane, Portadown, Craigavon, Co Armagh BT63 5JE (tel 028 3833 3066); Bawnmore, Castlerock, Coleraine, Co Londonderry BT51 4RA; Clive Henning Architects, 4 Carleton Street, Portadown, Co Armagh BT62 3EN (tel 028 3833 8811, fax 028 3833 0567, e-mail charc@btinternet.com)

HENRIQUES, Hon Mr Justice; Sir Richard Henry Quixano Henriques; kt (2000); s of Cecil Quixano Henriques (d 2001), of Thornton, Cleveleys, and Doreen Mary Henriques (d 1965); *b* 27 October 1943; *Educ* Bradfield, Worcester Coll Oxford (BA); *m* 14 July 1979, Joan Hilary (Toni), da of Maj Percy Sheard Senior (d 1947); 1 s (Daniel b 1981), 1 step s (David b 1970); *Career* called to the Bar Inner Temple 1967 (bencher 1994); recorder of the Crown Ct 1983, QC 1986, memb Gen Cncl of the Bar 1993–98, memb Northern Circuit Exec Ctee 1993–98, ldr of Northern Circuit 1996–98, judge of the High Court Queen's Bench Div 2000–, presiding judge NE Circuit 2001–04; memb Cncl Rossall Sch 1986–96; *Style—* The Hon Mr Justice Henriques; ✉ Royal Courts of Justice, Strand, London WC2A 2LL

HENRY, Anthony Patrick Joseph; s of Patrick Joseph Henry (d 1944), of Nottingham, and Helen Alethea, *née* Green; *b* 19 April 1939; *Educ* Epsom Coll Surrey, St Thomas' Hosp Med Sch London (MB BS); *m* 1973, Patricia Mary, da of Kenneth Spiby, of Packington, nr Ashby De La Zouch, Leics; 2 s (Joseph Patrick b 1974, George Michael b 1981), 1 da (Sarah Louise b 1977); *Career* TA Artists Rifles 21 SAS 1959–61; lectr in anatomy Univ of Alberta Canada 1966–67, res in surgery Durban South Africa 1968–70, sr registrar in orthopaedics Nottingham 1972–76, conslt orthopaedic surgn Derby 1976–; lectr in anatomy Derby Sch of Occupational Therapy 1974–88; examiner in surgery Br Assoc of Occupational Therapists 1976–88, pres Naughton-Dunn Club (orthopaedic club of the Midlands) 1993–94, pres Br Orthopaedic Foot Surgery Soc 1998; memb Int Ed Bd Foot and Ankle Surgery 1996–; govr St Wynstans Sch Repton 1980–86; memb BMA 1963; author of numerous papers in orthopaedic jls; FRCS 1971, FBOA 1976 (memb Cncl 2000–); *Recreations* sailing, tennis, cricket; *Style—* Anthony Henry, Esq; ✉ Four Winds, Wagon Lane, Bretby, Derbyshire DE15 0QF (tel 01283 217358); Orthopaedic Department, Derbyshire Royal Infirmary, Derby DE1 2QY (tel 01332 347141)

HENRY, Clare; da of Walter Price Jenkinson (d 1989), and Marjorie Amy, *née* Bratley (d 1997); *b* 21 February 1947; *Educ* Queen Elizabeth GS, Univ of Reading (BA); *Children* 1 s (Damian b 25 Dec 1969), 1 da (Zara b 29 Nov 1976); m, 2 Mar 2002, Phillip A Bruno, of New York; *Career* researcher Paul Mellon Fndn of Br Art 1968–70, art critic The Herald 1980–2000, art critic FT NY 2000–, ed-at-large State of Art USA 2005–; Scot ed: Artline 1984–90, Arts Review 1984–93, Scottish TV 1984–87; arts contrib: Sculpture Magazine 1999–, ARTNews 1999–, The Scotsman 2000–, The Herald, The Art Newspaper and BBC radio and TV; contrib to various magazines and exhbn catalogues incl: Victoria Crowe 1999, Hugh O'Donnell 203, Patricai Leighton 2004, RT Houben 2005; exhbn curator: New Scottish Prints (NY) 1983, London's Serpentine Summer Show 1985, Artists at Work (Edinburgh Festival) 1986, The Vigorous Imagination (Nat Gallery of Scot, Edinburgh Festival) 1987, Scotland at the Venice Biennale 1990, Critics Choice London 1992, Critics Choice Glasgow 1994, Glasgow Sch of Art Choice 1994, Illinois Women Artists Nat Museum of Women Washington 2000, Illinois Millennium Artists 2004; tstee Scot Sculpture Tst 1986–89; memb: Glasgow Print Studio 1973–80 (also chm), NUJ, AICA, Visiting Arts Br Cncl; fndr memb: SALVO, Glasgow Print Studio; FRSA; *Clubs* Chelsea Arts; *Style—* Clare Henry; ✉ c/o Financial Times, 1 Southwark Bridge, London SE1 9HL

HENRY, Julie; da of Mrs A M Hood, of Cambridge; *b* 1959, Cambridge; *Educ* N Herts Coll, London Coll of Fashion, Mornington Centre Art Fndn, Central St Martins Sch of Art (BA); *Partner* Jim Chynoweth; 1 da (Emma); *Career* artist; *Solo Exhibitions* Anthony Wilkinson Gallery London 2000 and 2003, Impressions Gallery York 2002, BCA Gallery Bedford 2003, Millais Gallery Southampton 2004, Metroploe Gallery Folkstone 2004, Northern Gallery Sunderland 2004, Presentation Gallery Vancouver 2005, Great Eastern Hotel London 2006; *Group Exhibitions* Six British Artists (Ars Locus Gallery Tokyo)) 1996, Zone Multi-media Festival (Maidstone Kent) 1996, Arts Alive Festival (Dorking) 1997, WorldCup 98, The Final (London Printworks Tst) 1998, Volcano Festival (The Oval House London) 1998, Going Down (Croydon Clocktower 1998, Edinburgh City Gallery 1999, Oldham Museum and Gallery 2000, Dynamo Kiev 2001), My Eyes My Eyes (Milch Gallery London, The Silo Greenwich) 1998, New Contemporaries 99 (South London Gallery, Exchange Flags Liverpool) 1999, The Fantastic Recurrence of Certain Situations: Recent British Art and Photography (Sala de Exposiciones del Canal de Isabel II Madrid) 2001, Record Collection (VTO Gallery London) 2001, Sport in der zeitgenossischen Kunst (Kunsthalle Nurnberg) 2001, Tirana Biennale (Tirana Nat Gallery) 2001, Predator (KX auf Kampnagel Hamburg) 2001, Sense of Wonder (Herzliya Museum of Art Israel) 2001, Cornerhouse Gallery Manchester 2002, Galeria Arsenal Blalystok Poland 2002, Velan Centre for Contemporary Arts Torino 2002, Intervention (John Hansard Gallery Southampton) 2003, Strangers (Int Centre of Photography) 2003, Somewhere Better Than This Place (Contemporary Arts Centre Cincinnati) 2003, Sport in Art (The Israel Museum Jeruslaem, Contemporary Arts Centre Cincinnati) 2004, Brittania Works (Br Cncl Athens) 2004, Going Down (John Hansard Gallery Southampton) 2004, Divine Heroes (Minoritten Galerien Graz) 2004, Belgrade Biennale (Galerija Zvomo) 2004, Ready Steady Go (Three Colts Gallery London) 2004, Only a Game (Impressions Gallery York) 2004, Upon Further Review (Hunters Gallery NY) 2005, Star Star (Contemporary Arts Center Cincinnati) 2005, Episode (Temporary Contemporary London) 2005, Celebrations (Pumphouse Gallery London) 2005, Rundlederwelten (Martin Gropius Bau Berlin) 2005, X (Millais Gallery Southampton) 2006, You'll Never Walk Alone (OK Centre for Contemporary Art Austia) 2006, The Beautiful Game: Contemporary ARt and Fütbol (Brooklyn Inst of Contemporary Art) 2006, Human Game (Stazione Leopolda Florence) 2006; *Publications* Dyed In The Wool: Julie Hendry (2004); *Recreations* Liverpool FC supporter, keen breakdancer; *Style—* Ms Julie Henry; ✉ c/o Anthony Wilkinson Gallery, 242 Cambridge Heath Road, London E2 9DA (tel 020 8980 2662, fax 020 8980 0028, website www.anthonywilkinsongallery.co.uk)

HENRY, Keith Nicholas; s of Kenneth George Henry (d 1999), and Barbara, *née* Benns (d 1989); *b* 3 March 1945; *Educ* Bedford Sch, Univ of London (BSc), Univ of Birmingham (MSc); *m* 1974, Susan Mary, da of Roy Horsburgh; 2 da (Lucy Elizabeth b 1976, Claire Suzanne b 1978); *Career* engr mangr Brown & Root de France SA 1975–77, md Far East area Brown & Root (Singapore) Ltd 1977–80; Brown & Root (UK) Ltd: sr mangr 1980–83, chief engr 1983–85, commercial dir 1985–87; md Brown & Root Vickers Ltd 1987–89, pres Brown & Root Marine 1989–90; chief exec: Brown & Root Ltd 1990–95, National Power plc 1995–99, Kvaerner E&C plc 2000–03; chm Burren Energy plc 2006– (non-exec dir 2005–), dep chm Petrojarl ASA 2003–06; non-exec dir: Enterprise Oil plc 1995–2002, Emerald Energy plc 2004–, South-East Water Ltd 2005–; memb Cncl DERA 1992–2001; FREng, FICE; *Recreations* shooting, sailing, golf; *Clubs* RAC, IOD; *Style—* Keith Henry, Esq, FREng

HENRY, Lenny; CBE (1999); *b* 29 August 1958; *m* Dawn French; *Career* comedian and actor; numerous tours incl Loud! 1994, Australia 1995, Large! (Aust) 1998, Large'99 (UK) 1999, Have You Seen This Man (UK) 2001; Monaco Red Cross Award, TRIC Award for BBC Personality of the Year 1993; *Television* incl: New Faces (debut), Tiswas, Three of a Kind (BBC) 1981–83, The Lenny Henry Show, Alive and Kicking (BBC) 1991 (Golden Nymph Award), Bernard & the Genie (BBC) 1991, In Dreams (BBC) 1992, The Real McCoy (BBC) 1992, Gareth Blackstock in Chef (3 series, BBC), Lenny Hunts the Funk (South Bank Special), New Soul Nation (Channel 4), White Goods (ITV) 1994, Funky Black Shorts 1994, The Lenny Henry Show (BBC) 1995, Comic Relief 1996–, Lenny Go Home (Channel 4) 1996, host The British Academy Awards 1997, Lenny's Big Amazon Adventure (BBC) 1997, Lenny Goes to Town (BBC) 1998, Ian George in Hope & Glory (BBC) 1999, The Man 1999, Lenny Henry in Pieces Christmas Special 2000, Lenny Henry in Pieces Special 2001 (Golden Rose of Montreux 2001), Lenny Henry in Pieces (series) 2002 and 2003, Little Robots (BBC) 2003, Lenny Henry: This is My Life (BBC) 2003; *Films* incl: True Identity (Touchstone/Disney) 1991; *Video* Lenny Henry Live and Unleashed 1989, Lenny Henry Live and Loud 1994; *Books* The Quest for the Big Woof (1991), Charlie and the Big Chill (children's book, 1995); *Style—* Lenny Henry, Esq, CBE; ✉ c/o PBJ Management Ltd, 7 Soho Street, London W1D 3DQ (tel 020 7287 1112, fax 020 7287 1191, e-mail general@pbjmgt.co.uk)

HENRY, Michael Meldrum; s of Cdre J M Henry, of Prinsted, Hants, and Helen Muriel, *née* Davies (d 1971); *b* 19 August 1946; *Educ* Steyning GS, Univ of London (MB BS); *m* 3 Aug 1981, Christine Mary, da of Alfred Douglas Parkyn (d 1985); *Career* lector to Trinity Coll Cambridge and lectr in surgery Cambridge Univ 1976–78, Hunterian prof RCS 1980, conslt surgn Royal Marsden Hosp and Chelsea and Westminster Hosp, sr lectr Academic Surgical Unit UCL; hon conslt surgn: St Mark's Hosp for Diseases of Colon and Rectum London, Nat Hosp for Nervous Diseases London; Freeman Worshipful Soc of Apothecaries; memb: BMA, RSM; FRCS; *Books* Coloproctology & The Pelvic Floor (1985), Surgery of Prolapse & Incontinence (1988), Clinical Surgery (2001), The Pelvic Floor (2001); *Recreations* modern history, opera; *Clubs* Athenaeum; *Style—* Michael Henry, Esq; ✉ 26 Langham Mansions, Earls Court Square, London SW5 9UJ (tel 020 7370 7551)

HENRY, Richard Charles; TD (1976); s of John Richard Henry, OBE, JP (d 1993), and Blanche Catherine, *née* Barrett; *b* 26 February 1941; *Educ* Sherborne; *m* 15 April 1976,

Judy Ann Massey; 1 s (Charles b 1977), 3 da (Belinda b 1979, Jane b 1979, Margaret b 1983); *Career* articled Deloittes 1960; fin dir and sec Press Association 1984–96, gp fin dir Nation Media Gp 1996–2004, gp fin dir Credit Reference Bureau 2004–; Capt HAC (TA) 1961–76; memb Ct of Assts HAC 1975–96 (treas 1990–93, vice-pres 1994–96); steward Jockey Club of Kenya 1998–; memb Bd Kenya Hosp Assoc 1999–2005; Freeman City of London 1986, Liveryman Worshipful Co of Barbers 1989; FCA 1966; *Recreations* racing, bridge, fishing; *Clubs* Army and Navy, Muthaiga; *Style—* Richard Henry, Esq, TD; ✉ PO Box 16526, Muthaiga, Nairobi 00620, Kenya

HENRY, Stephen James Bartholomew (Steve); s of John Keith Maxwell Henry (d 1979), and Jose Isobel Prendergast, *née* Bartholomew (d 1975); *b* 21 September 1955; *Educ* Cranleigh Sch, St Catherine's Coll Oxford (BA, Shelley-Mills prize); *m* 18 Oct 1986, Angela Marie, da of Michael Coates; 2 da (Sophia Dominique Marie b 19 Nov 1989, Bryony Christabel b 24 Dec 1992); *Career* copywriter: Crawfords 1979–81, Gold Greenlees Trott 1981–85; copywriter and creative gp head Wight Collins Rutherford Scott 1985–87, fndr and creative ptnr HHCL and Partners (formerly Howell Henry Chaldecott Lury) 1987–2004, chm HHCL/Red Cell 2004–06, exec creative dir TBWA/London 2006–; agency of year Campaign magazine 1989 and 1993, agency of the decade Campaign magazine 2000, winner of awards for various advertising campaigns; FIPA; *Recreations* swimming, reading, writing, being with my daughters; *Style—* Steve Henry, Esq; ✉ HHCL/Red Cell, Kent House, 14–17 Market Place, Great Titchfield Street, London W1N 7AJ (tel 020 7436 3333, fax 020 7436 2677)

HENRY, Susie Elizabeth Jane; da of Brian Glynn Henry, of Bere House, Pangbourne, Berks, and Elizabeth Jean, *née* Craig; *b* 24 June 1951; *Educ* Wycombe Abbey, Winchester Coll of Art, Goldsmiths' Coll of Art (DipAD); *m* 1 1975 (m dis 1988), Michael Richard Graham Gilmore, s of Richard Gilmore; m 2 1989, Alexander Denis Field, s of late Denis Alfred Field; 2 s (Rory Alexander Ernest Field b 1984, Angus James Alfred Field b 1990), 1 da (Sarah-Rose Elizabeth Mathilde Gilmore b 1979); *Career* copywriter: Maisey Mukerjee Russell 1972–74, French Gold Abbott Kenyon and Eckhart 1974–76, Cogent Elliott London 1976–78; sr writer Doyle Dane Bernbach 1978–80; Waldron Allen Henry & Thompson: founding ptnr, jt creative dir 1980, dir Miller & Leeves WAHT and BST Ltd since mergers 1990 and 1992; sr copywriter and memb Bd K Advertising (formerly KHBB) 1993–97, Bd dir Saatchi & Saatchi 1997–; best known campaign 'We won't make a drama out of a crisis' for Commercial Union; other award winning campaigns incl: COI drink-drive and child safety, Cheltenham & Gloucester, Bob Martin's, Welsh Devpt Agency; major awards: 5 Silver D&AD Awards, 3 Gold and 5 Silver BTA Awards, Best Financial Advertisement Campaign Press Awards 1980, 1988 and 1994, Cannes Silver Lion, Clio Gold Award, etc; memb D&AD Assoc; *Recreations* family, cooking, Italian opera, walking, Scotland; *Clubs* Academy; *Style—* Ms Susie Henry; ✉ Saatchi & Saatchi Ltd, 80 Charlotte Street, London W1A 1AQ (tel 020 7636 5060)

HENSHALL, John Mark; s of John Henshall (d 1996), of Stockport, and Margaret Winifred, *née* Passmore (d 1989); *b* 6 January 1942; *Educ* Queen Elizabeth GS Wakefield, Stockport GS; *m* 21 Sept 1979 (m dis 2003), Paulien, da of Dr Pieter Roorda (d 1991), of Haarlem, Netherlands, and Jeanette Pauline, *née* Volkmaars; 2 da (Annelies b 11 Jan 1981, Martien b 13 July 1984), 1 s (John Pieter b 12 May 1987); *Career* BBC cameraman and lighting 1961–76; dir of photography and lighting in film and TV 1978–, dir Electronic Photo-Imaging 1993–; conslt, writer and lectr on digital imaging - photography without film 1991–; memb Ctee Soc of TV Lighting Dirs 1986–93; Guild of TV Cameramen: vice-chm 1974–78, hon life memb 1978, hon fell 1984; memb Cncl RPS 1988–94 (chm Film and Video Associateship and Fellowship Distinctions Ctee 1992–); BIPP: chm Admissions and Qualifications in motion picture, TV, video and electronic imaging, memb Cncl 1986–94, pres 1991–92; Br Imaging and Photographic Assoc: memb Cncl 1991–97, chm Digital Imaging Ctee 1993–98; FRGS 1967, FRPS 1985, FBIPP 1985; *Books* Dealers in Coins (1969), Sir H George Fordham, Cartobibliographer (1969), Photographic Qualifications for Professionals (1992 and 1997), Wedding and Portrait Photography (co-author, 2003); ed Digital Imaging Plus; contributing ed digital imaging The Photographer; author of numerous articles on digital imaging, photography, film and TV; *Recreations* freelance philosopher; *Style—* John Henshall, Esq; ✉ Electronic Photo-Imaging, 68 High Street, Stanford in the Vale, Oxfordshire SN7 8NL (tel 01367 710191, e-mail john@epi-centre.com, website www.epi-centre.com)

HENSHALL, Keith Rodney; s of Bernard Henry Henshall, and Doris Lilian Henshall, of London; *b* 15 August 1947; *Educ* Henry Thornton Sch London, Univ of Manchester (LLB, MBA); *m* 9 Dec 1967, Maureen, da of George Pascoe; 1 s (Carl Matthew b 10 July 1968), 1 da (Sharon Marie b 9 Sept 1970); *Career* md Charles Barker Public Relations Ltd 1985–88; chm: The Henshall Centre Ltd 1988–, Cutting Edge Software Ltd 1988–, One Clear Voice Ltd 1997–; IPR: memb Nat Cncl 1984–89, nat educn chm 1988 and 1989, pres-elect 1994, pres 1995; founding external examiner to PR degrees Bournemouth and Stirling Univs, fndr chm Professional Advsy Ctee to PR masters degree Manchester Metropolitan Univ; MIPR 1984, FInstD 1986; *Recreations* basketball; *Style—* Keith Henshall, Esq

HENSHALL, Ruthie; da of David Henshall, of Stutton, Suffolk, and Gloria Diana Mary, *née* Wilson; *b* 7 March 1967; *Educ* Bullerswood GS Chislehurst, Laine Theatre Arts Coll Epsom; *Career* actress and singer; Theatregoers Award for Most Popular Musical Actress of the Last 21 Years; FRSA; *Theatre* work incl: Mitzi in the Pied Piper of Hamlyn (Churchill Theatre Bromley) 1985, Ethel Dobbs in Fainettes (Bromley) 1985, lead role in Celluloid City, Dandini in Cinderella (Aldershot) 1986, Maggie in A Chorus Line (nat tour) 1987, Jemima/Demeter/Grizabella/Griddlebone in Cats (New London Theatre) 1987–89, Ellen in Miss Saigon (Theatre Royal London) 1989–90, Aphra in Children of Eden (The Prince Edward Theatre) 1990–91, season at Chichester Festival Theatre 1991 and 1997, Ellen in Miss Saigon (NY) 2001; singer and dancer: Mack and Mabel (charity performance for Theatre Royal), Fantine in Les Miserables, Polly Baker in Crazy for You (Prince Edward) 1993 (Olivier nomination for Best Actress in a Musical), Amalia Balash in She Loves Me (Savoy Theatre) 1995 (Olivier Award for Best Acress in a Musical), Nancy in Oliver! (London Palladium) 1996, Polly in Divorce Me Darling (Chichester Festival Theatre) 1997, Roxie Hart in Chicago (Adelphi Theatre) 1997 (Olivier nomination for Best Actress in a Musical), Zigfield Follies 1936 (New York City Centre), Velma Kelly in Chicago (Shubert Theatre NY) 1999, Putting it Together (NY) 1999, Peggy Sue in Peggy Sue Got Married (Shaftesbury Theatre) 2001 (Olivier nomination for Best Actress in a Musical), Velma Kelly in Chicago (West End) 2003, The Woman in White (Palace Theatre) 2005, The Other Woman (Ensemble Studio Theatre NYC); other credits incl: singer in Andrew Lloyd Webber's concert in Spain for Expo 92, Ruthie Henshall in Concert (Royal Festival Hall), opening solo performance Olivier Awards 1994, solo concert Crazy for Musicals (nat tour) 1997, solo appearance Hey Mr Producer! (tribute to Cameron Mackintosh, Lyceum Theatre) 1998; *Television* Law and Order 2000, Mysteries of 71st Street 2000, The Sound of Musicals (BBC 1); *Recordings* original London cast albums of: Miss Saigon (also sang role of Ellen on int recording), Children of Eden, Crazy for You, She Loves Me, Chicago, Fantine in 10th anniversary concert of Les Miserables (Royal Albert Hall) 1996 (also on video); solo albums: Love is Here to Stay, Ruthie Henshall Sings Gershwin, The Ruthie Henshall Album, Pilgrim; *Style—* Ms Ruthie Henshall

HENSHALL, (Alastair) Scott; s of Nigel Henshall, and Mavis *née* Smith; *b* 15 November 1975, York; *Educ* Scorton Boys Sch, Richmond Assumption Sch, Univ of Northumbria (BA, British Fashion Cncl Best Womenswear Award 1997); *Career* Scott Henshall main line 1998–, Revisitation by Scott Henshall Japan 1999–, creative dir Mulberry 2000–02, Core Jeans by Scott Henshall 2006–; Vidal Sassoon London Fashion Week Award for cutting edge talent 2001; ambass: Prince's Tst 2002–, Happy Hearts Fndn 2005–; *Recreations* travelling, painting, living life to the full; *Style—* Scott Henshall, Esq; ✉ c/o Firas Kamourieh, Gorland, 29 Portland Place, London W1Q 1QB (tel 020 7878 8600, fax 020 7878 8650, e-mail firas@gorland.co.uk)

HENSHAW, Hugh Nigel; s of Harold Henshaw (d 1955), of Rottingdean, E Sussex, and Evelyn Louise, *née* Henshaw; *b* 28 September 1935; *Educ* Sherborne; *m* 29 March 1980, Anne Victoria Helen, da of Henry Thomas Hamilton Foley, MBE, JP (d 1959), of Stoke Edith Park, Hereford; 1 da (Katharine b 1981), 1 s (Thomas b 1983); *Career* Nat Serv 2 Lt 2 RHA 1954–55, TA Capt HAC 1956–60; admitted slr 1961; Clifford Turner, Freshfields; ptnr: Lovell White & King 1968–88 (former memb), Lovell White Durrant 1988–96, conslt Farrer & Co 1996–98; chm: Will Charitable Tst 1989–2006, Will Woodlands 1994–; memb Law Soc 1961; *Recreations* conservation, reading; *Clubs* HAC, Hurlingham; *Style—* Hugh Henshaw, Esq; ✉ 3 Fernshaw Close, London SW10 0TA (tel 020 7352 9524)

HENSMAN, Hon Mrs ((Mary) Sheila); *née* Wakefield; OBE (1992); da of 1 Baron Wakefield of Kendal (d 1983), and Rowena Doris, *née* Lewis (d 1981); *b* 29 April 1922; *Educ* Francis Holland Sch, Downe House; *m* 6 July 1945, Brig Richard Frank Bradshaw Hensman, CBE (d 1988), s of Capt Melvill Hensman, DSO, RN (d 1967), of Bordon, Hants; 1 s (Peter Richard Wavell b 30 Aug 1948), 1 da (Suzannah Mary b 9 Feb 1953 d 2006); *Career* dir: Battlefields (Holdings) Ltd, Lake District Estates Co Ltd, Ullswater Navigation & Transit Co Ltd, Ravenglass & Eskdale Railway Co Ltd; pres: DHO Ski Club 1975–80, Ladies Ski Club 1987–90, Cumbria Tourist Bd 1996–2004 (chm 1990–96); *Recreations* skiing, walking, gardening; *Clubs* Lansdowne, Ski Club of GB; *Style—* The Hon Mrs Hensman, OBE; ✉ Lindum Holme, Stricklandgate, Kendal, Cumbria LA9 4QG (tel 01539 725093, fax 01539 732048)

HENSON, Brian David; s of late James Maury (Jim) Henson, of New York and London, and Jane Anne Nebel Henson; *b* 3 November 1963; *Educ* Phillips Acad Andover Mass, Univ of Colorado; *m* Nov 1990, Ellis Flyte; *Career* film and TV prodr, dir and puppeteer; pres Jim Henson Productions; special effects technician and performer The Great Muppet Caper 1981 and The Muppets Take Manhattan 1983, performer of Jack Pumpkinhead in Return to Oz 1984, princ performer and performer co-ordinator Labyrinth 1984–85, princ performer Little Shop of Horrors 1986, princ performance co-ordinator Storyteller (TV series) 1987, dir Mother Goose Stories (TV) 1988, exec prodr Dinosaurs (TV series) 1991–93, dir and prodr The Muppet Christmas Carol 1993; memb: SAG, AFTRA, Equity (UK), ACTT; *Recreations* skiing, squash, cars, dogs, travelling; *Style—* Brian Henson, Esq; ✉ Manor Cottage, The Vale of Health, Hampstead, London NW3 1BB (tel and fax 020 7431 7550)

HENSON, Michael Brian; s of Patrick Henson, and Irene Henson; *b* 3 May 1961; *Educ* Collyers Sch Horsham, Univ of Sheffield (BMus), Univ of Leicester (MPhil), scholarship to study in Vienna; *m* 1993, Helen; 1 s (Luke), 1 da (Corinne); *Career* research fell Huddersfield Poly 1985–88, educn and community dir Bournemouth Orchestras 1988–92, chief exec Ulster Orch 1992–99, md Bournemouth Symphony Orchestra 1999–; memb Bd of Assoc of British Orchestras, memb Bd of Sonorities Contemporary Music Festival of NI; *Books* Musical Awareness (with G Pratt, OUP), Proceedings of Musical Awareness (ed); also author of 20 articles; *Style—* Michael Henson, Esq; ✉ Bournemouth Symphony Orchestra, 2 Seldown Lane, Poole Dorset BH15 1UF

HENSON, Nicholas Victor Leslie (Nicky); s of Leslie Lincoln Henson, and Billie Dell, *née* Collins; *b* 12 May 1945; *Educ* St Bede's Eastbourne, Charterhouse, RADA; *m* 1, 1968 (m dis 1975), Una Stubbs; 2 s (Christian b 25 Dec 1971, Joe b 18 Sept 1973); m 2, 1 Aug 1986, Marguerite Ann Porter, *qv*; 1 s (Keaton b 24 March 1988); *Career* actor; former popular song writer incl 3 year writing contract with The Shadows and Cliff Richard, fndr memb Young Vic Co 1970; *Theatre* incl: All Square (Vaudeville) 1963, Camelot (Drury Lane) 1964, Passion Flower Hotel (Prince of Wales) 1965, London Laughs (Palladium) 1966, Canterbury Tales (Phoenix) 1968, The Ride Across Lake Constance (Hampstead and Mayfair) 1973, Hamlet (Greenwich) 1973, Mind Your Head (Shaw) 1973, A Midsummer Night's Dream (Open Air) 1973, Taming of the Shrew (Shaw) 1973, Cinderella (Casino) 1973, Mardi Gras (Prince of Wales) 1976, Rookery Nook (Her Majesty's) 1979, Noises Off (Lyric and Savoy) 1982, The Relapse (Lyric) 1983, Sufficient Carbohydrate (Hampstead and Albery) 1983, Journeys End (Whitehall) 1988, Ivanov (Strand) 1989, Much Ado About Nothing (Strand) 1989, Three Sisters (Royal Court) 1990, Reflected Glory (Vaudeville) 1992, An Ideal Husband (Globe, Broadway and Australia) 1993, Rage (Bush) 1994, Enter the Guardsman (Donmar) 1997, Alarms and Excursions (Gielgud) 1998, Passion Play (Donmar at Comedy) 2000, Frame 312 (Donmar) 2002, Jumpers (Piccadilly London and Broadway NY) 2004; Young Vic incl: Waiting for Godot, Scapino, The Soldier's Tale, She Stoops to Conquer, Measure for Measure, Oedipus, Wakefield Nativity Plays, Romeo and Juliet, The Maids, Deathwatch, Look Back in Anger, Rosencrantz and Guildenstern are Dead, Charley's Aunt; NT incl: The Cherry Orchard, Macbeth, The Women, The Double Dealer, A Fair Quarrel, The Browning Version, Harlequinade, The Provok'd Wife, The Elephant Man, Mandragola, Long Time Gone; RSC incl: Man and Superman 1977, As You Like It 1985–86, The Merry Wives of Windsor 1985–86, Twelfth Night 2005; *Television* incl: A Midsummer Night's Dream, Absurd Person Singular, Seasons Greetings, Love After Lunch, Thin Air, Startrap 1988, Inspector Morse 1988, Boon 1989, After Henry 1990, The Upper Hand 1990, The Green Man 1990, The Healer 1994, Preston Front 1994, Shine On Harvey Moon 1994, Blue Dove 2001, NCS Manhunt 2002; *Film* appearances in over 30 incl: There's A Girl in My Soup, Witch Finder General, Tom Jones, Number One of The Street Service, Vera Drake, Syriana; *Recreations* snooker; *Style—* Nicky Henson, Esq; ✉ c/o Richard Stone Partnership, 2 Henrietta Street, London WC2E 8PS (tel 020 7497 0849, fax 020 7497 0869)

HENTON, Roger Gordon; s of (William) Gordon Henton (d 1990), of Lincoln, and Pamela, *née* Evans (d 1983); *b* 2 August 1940; *Educ* Bedford Sch; *m* 25 June 1966 (m dis 1999), Susan Eleanor, da of John Richmond Edwards; 1 da (Isabel b 1970), 1 s (Thomas b 1972); *Career* Streets & Co CAs Lincoln 1959–64, Coopers & Lybrand Geneva 1965–67, PA to md AAH plc Lincoln 1968–72, dir Camamile Assocs Lincoln 1973–77, fndr and sr ptnr Henton & Peycke CAs Leeds 1978–93, princ Roger Henton & Co Chartered Accountants 1993–, fin dir LD Group plc 1993–2003, mangr Euro Defi EEIG accountants network 1994–97, dir Outside the Box plc 2000–03; govr Leeds Coll of Art and Design 1999–; tstee The Second World War Experience Centre 1998–; FCA (ACA 1964); *Recreations* golf; *Clubs* RAC, Scarcroft Golf; *Style—* Roger Henton, Esq; ✉ St Andrews House, Leeds LS3 1LF (tel 0113 246 7900, fax 0113 246 9200, mobile 078 3674 2200, e-mail roger@hentons.com)

HENWOOD, John Philip; MBE (1998); s of Snowdon William Henwood (d 1980), and Amy Doris, *née* Stickley (d 1979); *b* 27 August 1945; *Educ* St Lawrence Sch Jersey, Victoria Coll Jersey; *Career* Channel Television: joined as trainee 1962, cameraman, studio mangr, ops supervisor and head of prog planning and presentation, dep ops mangr, estab Commercial Prodn Unit, head of news and features 1977, prog controller, dir of progs, md 1987–2000; chm: Byerley Ltd 1999–, Jersey Telecom Ltd 2002–; dir: Jersey Finance Ltd 2001–, Flying Brands Ltd 2007–, Kleinwort Benson Channel Islands Ltd; memb Horserace Writers' Assoc, past pres Jersey Race Club; pres Jersey CIM; tstee Durrell Wildlife Conservation Tst 2006–; MInstD (pres Jersey Branch (chm 2001–02)); *Recreations* horseracing and thoroughbreds, writing, painting, reading, skiing, motoring; *Clubs*

Channel Islands Racing and Hunt, Victoria, MG Owners; *Style*— John Henwood, MBE; ✉ e-mail john.henwood@jerseymail.co.uk

HENWOOD, Roderick Waldemar Lisle (Rod); s of Noel Gordon Lisle Henwood (d 1972), and Daphne Muirhead, *née* Schroeder; *b* 29 November 1963; *Educ* Dollar Acad, Univ of Geneva, New Coll Oxford (BA); *m* 22 June 1996, Amanda Penelope, da of Michael Stacey, of Blakedown, Worcs; *Career* controller of prog business affrs Central Independent TV plc 1988–90; Central Broadcasting: dir of legal and business affrs 1990–93, dir of broadcasting 1993–94, md 1994–96; md Fox Kids 1997–99, fndr dir Prism Entertainment Ltd 1999–2001 (non-exec dir 2001–), dir of TV NTL 2001–02, chief exec PTV 2003–; *Recreations* tennis, running; *Style*— Rod Henwood, Esq

HENZE, Hans Werner; *b* 1926; *Career* composer; studied under Wolfgang Fortner 1946–48 then Rene Leibowitz; fndr Montepulciano Cantiere 1976, composition teacher Cologne Acad of Music 1980–, artistic dir Accademia Filarmonica Romana 1981–83, fndr Munich Int Festival of New Music Theatre 1988, dir Gütersloh Henze Summer Acad 1989, first int chair of composition RAM, composer-in-residence Aldeburgh Festival 1996; pres Contemporary Opera Studio ENO 1996; subject of major festival by BBC Barbican 1991; compositions incl: Boulevard Solitude 1953, König Hirsch 1952–55, Der Prinz von Homburg 1958, Elegy for Young Lovers 1959–61, Novae de Infinito Laudes 1962, Los Caprichos 1963, Der Junge Lord 1964, The Bassarids 1965, The Raft of the Medusa 1968, El Cimarron 1970, Voices 1973, Orpheus 1978, The English Cat 1980–83, Le Miracle de la Rose 1981, Seventh Symphony 1983–84, Das Verratene Meer 1986–90, Requiem 1990–92, Eighth Symphony 1993 (performed by CBSO under Sir Simon Rattle BBC Proms 1995), Ninth Symphony (premiered by Berlin Philharmonic Orchestra 1996), Venus and Adonis 1995, Three Pieces for Orchestra (UK premiere BBC Proms 1996), Second Sonata for Strings (UK premiere BBC Proms 1997), Trio in three movements 1998, Scorribanda Sinfonica 2001, L'Heure Bleue 2001; hon memb: Deutsche Oper Berlin, American Acad and Inst of Arts and Letters; hon fell RNCM 1998; *Awards* incl: Siemens Prize 1990, Apollo d'Oro 1990, Cannes Classical Award for Best Living Composer 2001; *Style*— Hans Werner Henze, Esq; ✉ Chester Music, 8/9 Frith Street, London W1B 3JB (website www.chesternovello.com)

HEPBURN, Robin; *b* 28 January 1961; *Educ* Milton Abbey, Arnewood Sch, Brockenhurst Coll; *m* 1989, Emma; 2 s, 3 da; *Career* with Barclays Bank plc 1979–88, assoc dir Dewe Rogerson Ltd 1988–94, dir Shandwick Consultants 1994–96, chief exec Ludgate Communications 1996–2001, fndr Waughton 2002; warden St Mary Woolnoth Church London, memb Parish Clerks Co; Freeman City of London; ACIB, MIPR; *Recreations* choral music, piano, organ, gardening; *Style*— Robin Hepburn, Esq; ✉ Waughton, 20 Ironmonger Lane, London EC2V 8EP (tel 020 7796 9999, fax 020 7726 2938)

HEPBURN, Stephen; MP; s of late Peter Hepburn, and Margaret, *née* Pollock; *b* 6 December 1959; *Educ* Springfield Comp Jarrow, Univ of Newcastle upon Tyne (BA); *Career* dep ldr S Tyneside Cncl 1990–97 (cncllr 1985–97); MP (Lab) Jarrow 1997–, chair All-Pty Shipbuilding Shiprepair Gp, memb NI Affrs Select Ctee; chm Tyne & Wear Pensions Cmmn 1989–97; memb Union of Construction, Allied Trades and Technicians (UCATT); *Recreations* sport, music; *Clubs* Neon Social (CIU), Iona Catholic, Jarrovians RFC, Jarrow FC; *Style*— Stephen Hepburn, Esq, MP; ✉ 38 Stirling Avenue, Jarrow, Tyne & Wear NE32 4JT; House of Commons, London SW1A 0AA (tel 020 7219 4134, fax 020 7219 1111)

HEPHER, Michael Leslie; s of Leslie Hepher, and Edna Hepher; *b* 17 January 1944; *Educ* Kingston GS; *m* 1971 (m dis 2004), Janice Morton; 2 da (Kelly b 1973, Erin b 1975), 1 s (Daniel b 1980); *Career* former chm and chief exec Lloyds Abbey Life plc, former dir Lloyds Bank, former pres and chief exec Maritime Life Assurance Co of Canada; gp md British Telecommunications plc until 1995, chm and chief exec Charterhouse plc 1996–98; non-exec chm TeleCity 2000–05, chm Lane, Clark and Peacock LLP 2003–05, non-exec chm Cardpoint plc 2005–06; non-exec dir: Kingfisher plc 1997–, Canada Life 1999–, Catlin Gp Ltd 2003–, Great West Life Co 2006–; memb Int Advsy Cncl CGI Gp 2004–; Liveryman Worshipful Co of Actuaries; FIA, FCIA, ASA, FLIA; *Recreations* golf, reading; *Style*— Michael Hepher, Esq; ✉ 54 Jermyn Street, London SW1Y 6LX (tel 020 7292 3792, e-mail michael.hepher@btconnect.com)

HEPPELL, John; MP; s of late Robert Heppell, and late Helen Heppell; *b* 3 November 1948; *Educ* Rutherford GS, SE Northumberland Tech Coll, Ashington Tech Coll; *m* Eileen Golding; 2 s, 1 da; *Career* fitter NCB 1964–70, with various cos Nottingham 1970–75, workshop supervisor BR 1978–89 (diesel fitter 1975–78); Notts CC: cncllr 1981–92, asst Lab whip 1982, vice-chm Environment Ctee 1983, chm Resources Ctee 1986, chm Equal Opportunities Ctee, dep ldr 1989–92; MP (Lab) Nottingham E 1992–; PPS to: Lord Privy Seal 1997–98, John Prescott as Dep PM 1998–2001; a Lord Cmmr to HM Treasy (Govt whip) 2001–06, Vice-Chamberlain of HM Household (Govt whip) 2006–; vice-chm Lab Pty Tport Ctee 1992–97; sec All-Pty Gp Kashmir 1992–97, treas All-Pty Gp Breast Cancer 1995–2001; memb All-Pty Gp: Head Injuries 1995–97, Home Safety 1995–2001; chm: E Midlands Airport 1985, Gtr Nottingham LRT Bd 1990–92; *Recreations* walking, reading; *Style*— John Heppell, Esq, MP; ✉ 9 Trinity Square, Nottingham NG1 4AF (tel 0115 947 4132, fax 0115 947 2029, e-mail johnheppellmp@yahoo.co.uk); House of Commons, London SW1A 0AA

HEPPELL, (Thomas) Strachan; CB (1986); s of Leslie Thomas Davidson Heppell, and Doris Abbey, *née* Potts; *b* 15 August 1935; *Educ* Acklam Hall GS Middlesbrough, The Queen's Coll Oxford (BA); *m* 1963, Felicity Ann, da of Lt-Col Richard Bernard Rice (ka 1943); 2 s (Jeremy Strachan b 1965, Martin Richard b 1967); *Career* princ Nat Assistance Bd 1963 (asst princ 1958); DHSS: asst sec 1973, under sec 1979, dep sec 1983, conslt 1995–2000; chm: Mgmnt Bd Euro Medicines Evaluation Agency 1994–2000, Family Fund Tst 1997–2003; memb Broadcasting Standards Cmmn 1996–2003, expert memb Fairness Cmmn Office of Communications (Ofcom) 2003–, memb Advsy Bd Institut des Sciences de la Santé 2004–, chair Audit Advsy Ctee European Medicines Agency 2004–, chair European Inst for Health 2006–; *Recreations* gardening, travelling; *Style*— Strachan Heppell, CB; ✉ European Medicines Agency, 7 Westferry Circus, London E14 4HB

HEPPLE, Prof Sir Bob Alexander; kt (2004), Hon QC (1996); s of Alexander Hepple (d 1983), of Canterbury, and Josephine, *née* Zwarenstein (d 1992); *b* 11 August 1934; *Educ* Univ of the Witwatersrand (BA, LLB), Univ of Cambridge (LLD, MA); *m* 1, 1960 (m dis 1993), Shirley Rona, da of Morris Goldsmith (d 1972), of London; 1 da (Brenda (Mrs Henson) b 7 July 1961), 1 s (Paul Alexander b 11 Dec 1962); m 2, 1994, Mary Coussey, da of Rev Stanley Dowding; *Career* practising attorney Johannesburg 1958, lectr in law Univ of the Witwatersrand 1959–62, practising advocate Johannesburg 1962–63, called to the Bar Gray's Inn 1966 (bencher 1996), practising barr 1972–; lectr in law Univ of Nottingham 1966–68, fell Clare Coll and lectr law Cambridge 1968–76, prof of comparative social and labour law Univ of Kent 1976–77, chm Industrial Tbnls England and Wales 1977–82 (pt/t chm 1974–77 and 1982–93); UCL: prof of English law 1982–93, dean Faculty of Laws and head Dept of Laws 1989–93; master Clare Coll Cambridge 1993–2003 (emeritus master 2003–), prof of law Univ of Cambridge 1995–2001 (emeritus prof 2001–); chm Univ of Cambridge: Local Exams Syndicate 1994–97, Septemviri 1995–98 and 2002–03, Cncl 1998–99; chm Managers Smuts Meml Fund 1994–2003; chair European Roma Rights Centre 2001–07, judge UN Administrative Tbnl 2007–, chm Appointing Authy for Phase 1 Ethics Ctees 2007–; memb: Cmmn for Racial Equality 1986–90, Tbnls Ctee Judicial Studies Bd 1988–93, Lord Chllr's Advsy Ctee on Legal Educn and Conduct 1994–99, Legal Services Consultative Panel 2000–01, Nuffield Cncl on Bioethics 2000– (chm 2003–07), Bd Int Centre for Protection of Human Rights 2005–, Bd Equal Rights Tst 2006–; tstee Canon Collins Educnl Tst for South Africa 1990–; Leverhulme emeritus fell 2003–05, Nuffield Fndn New Career Devt Fellowship (with Dr J Browne) 2003–06; Hon LLD: Univ of the Witwatersrand 1996, UCL 2005, Univ of Cape Town 2006; hon prof Univ of Cape Town 1999–2005; FBA 2003; *Publications* Independent Review of Anti-Discrimination Legislation (with M Coussey, 2000), Labour Laws and Global Trade (2005), Rights at Work (Hamlyn Lectrs 2005); numerous books and articles on labour law and industrial relations, race relations and discrimination and legal obligations in general; *Recreations* theatre, music, reading, walking, gardening; *Style*— Prof Sir Bob Hepple, QC, FBA; ✉ Clare College, Queens' Road, Cambridge CB3 9AJ (tel 01223 333200)

HEPWORTH, David; s of Ernest Hepworth (d 1981), of Ossett, W Yorks, and Sarah Marjorie, *née* Rollinson; *b* 27 July 1950; *Educ* Queen Elizabeth GS Wakefield, Trent Park Coll of Educn Barnet (BEd); *m* 5 Sept 1979, Alyson, da of Ronald Elliott, of Hove, E Sussex; 2 da (Clare b 1982, Imogen b 1992), 1 s (Henry b 1987); *Career* freelance journalist 1975–79; presenter: The Old Grey Whistle Test (later just Whistle Test, BBC TV) 1980–86, BBC Radio GLR; ed: Smash Hits 1980–82, Just Seventeen 1983–85; editorial dir Emap Metro 1984–94, former editorial dir Emap Consumer Magazines (launched Q 1985, Empire 1988, Mojo 1997, Heat 1999), co-fndr Development Hell Ltd 2002 (launched Word magazine 2003); contrib Front Row BBC Radio 4; Periodical Publishers' Assoc: Ed of the Year 1985, Writer of the Year 1988; Mark Boxer Award British Soc of Magazine Editors 1993; *Books* The Secret History of Entertainment (2004); *Recreations* books, tennis, music; *Style*— David Hepworth, Esq; ✉ Development Hell Ltd, 90–92 Pentonville Road, London N1 9HS (tel 020 7520 8625, e-mail mail@davidhepworth.com, website www.davidhepworth.com)

HEPWORTH, Vivien; da of William Cecil Hepworth, OBE (d 1993), of Leigh, Kent, and Emmie, *née* Turner; *b* 9 March 1953; *Educ* Beaverwood Girls' Sch, Univ of Manchester (BA); *m* 29 May 1976, Ian Michael Jones, s of Derek Jones; 2 s (Samuel Martin b 16 Aug 1983, William Max b 4 Aug 1986); *Career* reporter Croydon Advertiser Series 1974–76; Northcliffe Newspapers: gen news and features writer 1976–78, lobby corr 1978–87; maternity leave 1987–88; Grayling Group of Companies: dir Westminster Strategy (public affrs subsid) 1989–97 (joined 1988), dir Grayling Holding Bd 1991–97, dir Grayling (PR consultancy) 1994–97; dir of marketing St Piers Nat Centre for Children with Severe Epilepsy 1997–2000, advsr Nat Centre for Young People with Epilepsy (NCYPE) 2000–; chief exec: Westminster Strategy 2002–, Grayling Political Strategy 2003–; non-exec dir Surrey and Sussex Healthcare Tst 1999– (vice-chm 1999–2000, chm 2000–02); fndr Nystagmus Network (visual impairment charity) 1984 (hon pres 1991–); tstee: Prince's Fndn 2001–, St Barnabas Coll 2005– (vice-chm 2007–); lay memb PCC 2001–; *Recreations* music, painting, not gardening; *Style*— Miss Vivien Hepworth; ✉ Grayling Political Strategy, 1 Bedford Avenue, London WC1B 3AU (tel 020 7255 5444, fax 020 7255 5454, e-mail vivien.hepworth@uk.grayling.com)

HERBERT, Rt Rev Christopher William; *see:* St Albans, Bishop of

HERBERT, 19 Baron (E 1461); David John Seyfried Herbert; s of Capt John Beeton Seyfried, of Warks, and Lady Cathleen Blanche Lily Hudson, *née* Eliot (d 1994); suc on termination of abeyance 2002; assumed the additional surname of Herbert; *b* 3 March 1952, London; *Educ* Harrow; *m* 1, 29 Aug 1975, Jane Angela, *née* Bishop; 1 s (Dr the Hon Oliver Richard b 17 June 1976), 1 da (Hon Charlotte Sophia Caroline b 27 Oct 1977); m 2, 24 May 2003, Sarah Victoria Fergusson; 1 s (Oscar James b 27 Nov 2004); *Career* dir David Seyfried Ltd; *Style*— The Lord Herbert; ✉ David Seyfried Ltd, 1/5 Chelsea Harbour Design Centre, London SW10 0XE (tel 020 7823 3848, fax 020 7823 3221, e-mail info@davidseyfried.com)

HERBERT, Prof David Thomas; s of Trevor John Herbert (d 1992), of Rhondda, and (Winifred) Megan, *née* Pearce (d 1990); *b* 24 December 1935; *Educ* Rhondda Co GS, Univ of Wales (BA, DipEd, DLitt), Univ of Birmingham (PhD); *m* 30 Dec 1968, Tonwen, da of Thomas Maddock (d 1953); 1 s (David Aled b 1971), 1 da (Nia Wyn b 1973); *Career* Nat Serv RAF 1954–56; lectr Keele Univ 1963–65; Univ of Wales Swansea: lectr 1965–73, sr lectr 1973–77, reader 1977–80, prof of geography 1980–2003, dean 1981–84, vice-princ 1986–89, sr pro-vice-chllr 1995–2003, emeritus prof 2003–; visiting prof: Univ of Toronto 1965, Univ of Manitoba 1967, Univ of York Ontario 1969, Univ of Leuven 1973, Univ of Colorado 1979, Univ of Oklahoma 1980, Univ of Sudan 1982, Univ of Warsaw 1987 (1985), Univ of Calgary 1989 and 1999; Killam visiting scholar Calgary 1992; memb: Inst of Br Geographers (formerly on Cncl), Geographical Assoc, Gen Dental Cncl, Sports Cncl for Wales, Pembrokeshire Coast Nat Park, Welsh Jt Educn Ctee; former memb SSRC, chm Swansea Crime Prevention Panel; pres: Br Assoc for the Advancement of Science (Section E) 1994, Research Assessment Panel (Geography) 1994–96; *Books* incl: Urban Geography - A Social Perspective (1972), Geography and the Urban Environment (ed with R J Johnston, 1978–), Social Problems and the City (ed with D M Smith, 1979), Geography of Urban Crime (1982), Cities in Space - City as Place (with C J Thomas, 1982, new edn 1997), Heritage Sites - Strategies for Marketing and Development (jtly, 1989), Communities Within Cities (with W K D Davies, 1993), Crime, Policing and Place (ed, 1993), Heritage, Tourism and Society (ed, 1995), Unifying Geography: Common Heritage, Shared Future (ed with John Matthews, 2004), Geography: A Very Short Introduction (with John Matthews, 2008); *Recreations* tennis, golf, fishing, skiing, reading, music; *Style*— Prof David Herbert; ✉ Department of Geography, University of Wales, Swansea SA2 8PD (tel 01792 295229, telex 48358 UCSWAN G, fax 01792 295955, e-mail d.t.herbert@swansea.ac.uk)

HERBERT, Ivor; s of Sir Edward Herbert, OBE (d 1963), and Lady Sybil, *née* Davis (d 1989); *b* 20 August 1925; *Educ* Eton, Trinity Coll Cambridge (MA); *m* 1, 1950 (m dis), Jennifer, da of D R McBean, MC; 1 s (Nicholas b 13 April 1954; m Serena, da of Maj Sir Hamish Forbes, Bt, MBE, MC); m 2 (m dis), Gilly, da of Dr Peter Steele-Perkins; 2 da (Kate b 20 Sept 1970, Jane b 11 March 1972); *Career* served Capt Coldstream Gds 1944–47 (seconded to Intelligence Germany 1945–47); PA to Chm then asst md Charterhouse Finance Corporation 1949–54, columnist Evening News Associated Newspapers 1954–70, racing corr and features columnist Sunday Express 1970–80, racing ed and main travel writer Mail on Sunday 1980–2002; ptnr: Bradenham Wines 1970–, Equus Productions 1974–; trained Nat Hunt racehorses 1947–62 (winner Cheltenham Gold Cup with Linwell 1957); scriptwriter and playwright: The Great St Trinian's Train Robbery, Night of the Blue Demands; TV documentaries incl: Odds Against, Stewards' Enquiry, Classic Touch and The Queen's Horses; chm Bradenham Parish Cncl 1966–; memb: Soc of Authors, Writers' Guild; *Books* 27 incl: Arkle, Red Rum, The Winter Kings, Winter's Tale, The Diamond Diggers, Riding Through My Life (with HRH The Princess Royal), Vincent O'Brien; novels incl: The Filly, Revolting Behaviour; *Recreations* tennis, travel; *Clubs* Turf; *Style*— Ivor Herbert, Esq; ✉ The Old Rectory, Bradenham, High Wycombe, Buckinghamshire HP14 4HD (tel 01494 563310, fax 01494 564504)

HERBERT, James; s of H Herbert, of London, and Catherine, *née* Riley; *b* 8 April 1943; *Educ* Our Lady of the Assumption Sch Bethnal Green, St Aloysius Coll Highgate, Hornsey Coll of Art Highgate; *m* August 1967, Eileen; 3 da (Kerry Jo b 22 July 1968, Emma Jane b 21 April 1972, Casey Lee b 31 Oct 1983); *Career* author; typographer John Collings Advertising 1962, successively art dir, gp head then assoc dir Charles Barker Advertising 1965–77; *Films* The Rats, The Survivor, Fluke (1995), Haunted (1995); *Books* The Rats (1974), The Fog (1975), The Survivor (1976, Avoriaz Grand Prix for Literature Fantastique 1977), Fluke (1977), The Spear (1978), Lair (1979), The Dark (1980), The Jonah (1981), Shrine (1983), Domain (1984), Moon (1985), The Magic Cottage (1986), Sepulchre (1987), Haunted (1988), Creed (1990), Portent (1992), James Herbert: by Horror

H

Haunted (ed by Stephen Jones, 1992), James Herbert's Dark Places (photographs by Paul Barkshire, 1993), The City (graphic novel, illustrated by Ian Miller, 1993), The Ghosts of Sleath (1993), '48 (1996), Others (1999), Once (2001), Nobody True (2003), James Herbert: Terror in the Dark (2003), The Secret of Crickley Hall (2006); *Recreations* guitar, piano, painting, book design, swimming, wildlife conservation; *Style—* James Herbert, Esq; ✉ c/o David Higham Associates, 5–8 Lower John Street, Golden Square, London W1R 4HA (tel 020 7437 7888, fax 020 7437 1072)

HERBERT, Dr Jeffrey William; *b* 21 July 1942; *Educ* Loughborough Univ (DTech), Cranfield Business Sch; *m*; 2 da, 1 s; *Career* grad trainee rising to mfrg dir Perkins Engines Ltd/Massey Ferguson Gp Ltd 1965–76, md Rover Triumph Cars Ltd 1976–81, md GEC Diesels Ltd 1981–85; Charter plc: exec dir industry 1985–89, chief exec 1990–96, chm 1996–2001; chm: Cape plc 1985–96, Anderson Group plc 1987–95, Esab AB 1994–2001, British South Africa Co 1996–2001, Howden Gp plc 1997–2001, Claverham Ltd 1998–2000, Concentric Gp plc 1999–; dep chm House of Fraser plc 2001–06; non-exec dir: Vickers plc 1991– (dep chm 1997–2000), M&G Recovery Investment Trust plc 1992–2002, F T Everard & Sons 2002–, Tendring Hundred Water Services Ltd 2003–; memb Cncl Royal Acad of Engrg 1995– (hon treas 1997–2003); dir Thrombosis Research Inst 2005–; memb Worshipful Co of Wheelwrights; CEng, FIMechE, MIEE, MIMfgE, MInstD, MIMgt, FREng 1993; *Style—* Dr Jeffrey Herbert, FREng

HERBERT, Prof Joe; s of Dr Benjamin Herbert (d 1972), of Birmingham, and Elizabeth, *née* Leek (d 1983); *b* 8 April 1936; *Educ* Bromsgrove Sch, Univ of Birmingham (scholar, BSc, MB ChB), Univ of London (PhD); *m* 1980, Rachel Meller; 2 s (Daniel Meller-Herbert b 21 Jan 1982, Oliver Meller-Herbert b 15 Dec 1983); *Career* Gonville & Caius Coll Cambridge: fell 1976, dir of studies in med 1993; Univ of Cambridge: reader in neuroendocrinology Dept of Anatomy 1987, dir of trg 1992, dir of res, prof of neuroscience 1999–, dir of trg Dept of Clinical Neuroscience; *Publications* The Minder Brain (2007); papers in learned jls on reproduction, stress, brain function and depression; *Style—* Prof Joe Herbert; ✉ Department of Physiology, Development and Neuroscience, Downing Street, Cambridge CB2 3DY (tel 01223 333749, 01223 333789, e-mail jh24@cam.ac.uk)

HERBERT, John Anthony; s of Rev Canon Frank Selwood Herbert (d 1978), of Nuneaton, Warks, and Joan Mary Walcot Herbert, *née* Burton (d 1976); *b* 10 September 1939; *Educ* Dean Close Sch Cheltenham, Univ of Exeter; *m* 2 Aug 1962, Michelle, da of Nigel Forbes Dennis, of Malta; 2 da (Rebecca b 1964, Tamsin b 1968); *Career* over 300 films and documentaries to credit, on archaeological, military trg and historical subjects (clients incl: Saudi Arabian TV, MOD, oil industry), chief exec Tabard Productions; ed: Qaryat Al Fau 1981, Al Rabadhah 1984, books of archaeological excavations; contrib articles on Arabian archaeology to Illustrated London News; numerous awards for film and video prodn 1990–2003; FRGS; *Style—* John A Herbert, Esq; ✉ Manor Cottage, Buscot, Oxfordshire SN7 8DA (tel 01367 252294, e-mail johnherbert@tabard.co.uk)

HERBERT, John Paul (Johnny); s of Robert Ernest Trevor Herbert, and Georgina Jane Herbert; *b* 25 June 1964; *Educ* Forest Lodge Comp Sch; *m* 10 Dec 1990, Rebecca May, da of Michael Francis and Pauline Ann Cross; 2 da (Chloe Ann b 31 Jan 1990, Aimelia Jane b 21 July 1992); *Career* motor racing driver; go-karts: began racing aged 10, memb Br team 1978–82, Br jr champion 1979, Br sr champion 1982; Formula Ford 1600 1983–85 (Formula Ford Festival winner 1985), Formula Ford 2000 and Formula 3 1986, Br Formula 3 champion 1987, Formula 3000 1988 (won first race then injured in crash at Brands Hatch), Formula 3000 Japan 1990–91 (winner Le Mans with Mazda 1991); Formula One: Benetton 1989 (fourth in debut race Brazil), Lotus 1991–94, Benetton 1995, Sauber team 1996–98, Jaguar (formerly Stewart-Ford) 1999–2000 (winner British Grand Prix 1995, Italian Grand Prix 1995 and European Grand Prix, 1st win for Stewart); devpt driver Arrows F1 Team; driver: Le Mans 24 hour 2001 (Champion Racing), 2002 (Audi Works, second place), 2003 (Bentley, second place), 2004 (Audi Works, second place) and 2007 (Aston Martin), Road Atlanta USA 2001, American Le Mans Series 2002, 2003 (Champion Racing, second place) and 2007 (Porsche), Sebring 12 hour 2002 (winner), 2003 (Bentley, third place) and 2004 (Audi, third place), Sears Point USA 2002 (second place), Elms at Monza (Audi works team, winner), Speedcar series Asia 2007; Formula One career: 130 races, 3 wins; Cellnet Award 1986; PR mangr MFI Formula One team 2005–06; *Recreations* golf; *Style—* Johnny Herbert, Esq; ✉ c/o Mark Perkins, 31 Avenue Princesse Grace, Monaco 98000 (tel 00 377 97 700525, fax 00 377 93 305159, e-mail csm@csm.mc)

HERBERT, Mark Jeremy; QC (1995); s of Kenneth Faulkner Herbert (d 1993), of Winchester, and Kathleen Ellis, *née* Robertson; *b* 12 November 1948; *Educ* Lancing, KCL (BA); *m* 1977, Shulanjini Shiranikha, da of Dr Sefton Pullenayegum (decd); *Career* called to the Bar Lincoln's Inn 1974 (bencher 2004), in practice Chancery Bar 1975–; mediator 2002; *Books* Whiteman on Capital Gains Tax (contrib, 1988), Drafting and Variation of Wills (1989); *Recreations* bell-ringing, theatre, travel; *Style—* Mark Herbert, Esq, QC; ✉ 5 Stone Buildings, Lincoln's Inn, London WC2A 3XT (tel 020 7242 6201, fax 020 7831 8102, e-mail mherbert@5sblaw.com)

HERBERT, Mary Therese; da of James Ewart Herbert (d 1984), and Anne Josephine, *née* Blee; *b* 30 March 1954, Omagh, Co Tyrone; *Educ* Univ of Leeds (BSc); *Partner* Prof Julian Anthony Pearce; 1 s (Simon Alexander b 9 Aug 1992); *Career* admitted slr 1988; Ingledew Botterell 1988–90, ptnr Eversheds LLP 1993– (slr 1990–93); memb Law Soc 1988; FFB 2002; *Recreations* art, gardening; *Style—* Ms Mary Herbert; ✉ Eversheds LLP, 1 Callaghan Square, Cardiff CF10 5BT (tel 029 2047 7905, e-mail maryherbert@eversheds.com)

HERBERT, Nicholas; *see:* Hemingford, 3 Baron

HERBERT, Nick; MP; *b* 1963; *Educ* Haileybury, Magdalene Coll Cambridge (MA); *Career* dir political affrs Br Field Sports Soc 1992–96 (co-fndr Countryside Movement), chief exec Business for Sterling 1998–2000 (fndr 'No' Campaign), dir Reform 2002–05, MP (Cons) Arundel and S Downs 2005– (Parly candidate (Cons) Berwick upon Tweed 1997), shadow min for police reform 2005–07, shadow sec of state for justice 2007–; co-chm All Pty Parly Gp on Global TB 2006–; frequent radio and TV appearances, author of articles for The Times, Sunday Times, Daily Telegraph and The Spectator; *Style—* Nick Herbert, MP; ✉ House of Commons, London SW1A 0AA (tel 020 7219 4080, fax 020 7219 1295); Constituency Office tel 01903 816880, fax 01903 810348, e-mail nick@nickherbert.com, website www.nickherbert.com

HERBERT, Peter George; s of George Frederick Herbert (d 1974), of London, and Ellen Alice, *née* Reed (d 1980); *b* 11 June 1926; *Educ* Dulwich Coll, Rossall Sch, Royal Coll of Music (scholarship); *m* 1, 1951, (m dis 1977), Pip, *née* Harkell; 2 s (Leigh Seaton b 1953, Robin Harkell Seaton b 1960), 1 da (Jennifer Reed b 1958); m 2, 1978, Susan Alison, da of Dr Gilbert Edward Hicks; 2 da (Joanna Kate b 1980, Nicola Jane b 1982); *Career* served Royal Fusiliers & Royal Sussex Regt 1944–48; trg in family hotel business then Austria & France 1948–50; md: Gore Hotel & Elizabethan Rooms London 1950–67, The Yard Arm Club Westminster 1963–67; chm Gravetye Manor Hotel East Grinstead W Sussex 1958–2004; Br Branch Relais et Chateaux: chm 1978–82, memb Exec Ctee 1983–88; fell HCIMA 1960; Chevalier du Tastevin 1958, Cdr d'honneur de la Commanderie du Bontemps de Medoc et des Graves 1996; *Recreations* sailing, game fishing, opera (Glyndebourne), gardening; *Style—* Peter Herbert, Esq; ✉ The Moat, Gravetye, East Grinstead, West Sussex RH19 4LJ

HERBERTSON, (Robert) Ian; yr s of Robert Hopkirk Herbertson (d 1969), and Winifred Rose, *née* Rawlinson (d 1994); *b* 30 December 1953; *Educ* Selhurst GS, Birkbeck Coll London (BA), Univ of East London (MA); *m* 22 March 1985 (m dis 2001), Joanna Hazel, da of Reginald Bernard North, of Gwent; 3 da (Rebecca Elizabeth b 1987, Emma Louise b 1990, Amy Ellen b 1992); *Career* Bank of England: joined 1985, an audit mangr 1990–92, official Banking Supervision 1992–93, Legal Unit 1993, Monetary and Fin Statistics Div 1994–96, Business Fin Div 1996–97, head of IT Audit 1997–99, dep head Internal Audit 1999–2003; head of risk and compliance VocaLink Ltd (formerly BACS Ltd) 2003–; dir Claridge Press 1987–88; memb: Convocation Univ of London 1984, Ctee Ct of Electors Birkbeck Coll London 1987–90; chm IIA Professional Issues Gp 2000–02, chm Bd of Tstees Voca Final Salary Scheme, chair G10 Central Banks IT Audit Gp 2002–03; Freeman of City of London, Liveryman Worshipful Co of Chartered Secs and Admins; memb: Lithic Studies Soc (memb Ctee 2000–, treas 2002–), Cambridge Antiquarian Soc, Prehistoric Soc, Royal Archeological Inst; author of articles on archaeology; CDipAF 1985, FIAP (Inst of Analysts and Programmers) 1986–92, FCIS 1995 (ACIS 1991), fell Royal Statistical Soc 1995, FIIA 2000 (MIIA 1998), memb Inst of Risk Mgmnt (MIRM) 2004, fell Royal Anthropological Inst 2006, memb NY Acad of Science 2006; *Recreations* philosophy, prehistoric archaeology, palaeoanthropology, literature; *Clubs* City Univ; *Style—* Ian Herbertson, Esq; ✉ 18 Weir Close, Buckden, Cambridgeshire PE19 5TH (tel 01480 810929, e-mail ianherbertson@aol.com); 5 Swanfield, Northway, Rickmansworth, Hertfordshire WD3 1EN (tel 01923 776550); Voca Ltd, Drake House, Three Rivers Court, Homestead Road, Rickmansworth, Hertfordshire WD3 1FX (tel 0870 920 8045, fax 0870 920 8712, e-mail ian.herbertson@bacs.co.uk)

HERD, Christopher John (Chris); s of Robin Herd, CBE, and Eve Herd; *b* 19 June 1967; *Educ* Abingdon Sch, Aston Univ (BSc); *Career* WCRS: grad trainee 1990–91, account mangr 1991–93, account dir 1993–95; account dir Leagas Delaney 1995–97; WCRS: gp dir 1997–2001, head of e-brands 2000–01; md Bates UK 2001–; nominated as a "face to watch" Campaign magazine 1995; *Recreations* golf (handicap 4, competed in English Amateur Golf Championship 1987), skiing, Oxford United FC; *Style—* Chris Herd, Esq; ✉ Bates UK, 121–141 Westbourne Terrace, London W2 6JR (tel 020 7262 5077, fax 020 7706 4997)

HERDAN, Bernard Laurence; CB (2007); s of Gustav Herdan (d 1969), and Innes, *née* Jackson; *b* 23 November 1947; *Educ* Univ of Cambridge (MA), Univ of Bath (Dip Mgmnt); *m* 1971, Janet Elizabeth, *née* Hughes; 2 da (Charlotte Lucy b 13 May 1974, Emma Jane b 10 March 1976 d 27 Oct 1988); *Career* gp ldr Space Systems Div Br Aerospace 1969–73, prog mangr Euro Space Agency The Netherlands 1973–84, divisional mangr BIS-Macintosh 1984–85, md Defence Technol Enterprises Ltd (DTE) 1985–1990, dir of commercial services Met Office 1990–95, chief exec Driving Standards Agency 1995–99, chief exec Passport and Records Agency 1999–2003, chief exec UK Passport Service 2003–06, exec dir of service delivery Identity and Passport Serv 2006–; non-exec dir: Lazards Defence Fund Ltd 1988–90, MIKROS Corp New Jersey 1989–91, JRA Aerospace 1990–2003; conslt Renaissance Venture Capital Fund 1989–91; bd advsr: BSB 1986–89, Scott Instruments Texas 1989–91; dep chm Bedford Hosp NHS Tst 2005–; MInstD, CEng, MIEE; *Publications* conceived quarterly jl Space Communications (ed-in-chief until 1987, currently ed emeritus); *Recreations* horse riding, skiing, foreign travel, theatre, the Arts; *Style—* Bernard Herdan, Esq, CB; ✉ Identity and Passport Service, Globe House, 89 Eccleston Square, London SW1V 1PN (tel 020 7901 2400, fax 020 7901 2425, e-mail bernard.herdan@ips.gsi.gov.uk)

HERDMAN, Dr John Macmillan; s of William Morrison Herdman (d 1975), of Edinburgh, and Catherine, *née* Macmillan (d 1991); *b* 20 July 1941; *Educ* Merchiston Castle Sch Edinburgh, Magdalene Coll Cambridge (MA, PhD); *m* 1, 30 July 1983 (m dis 1993), Dolina, da of Angus Maclennan (d 1950), of Marvig, Isle of Lewis; m 2, 17 Aug 2002, Mary Ellen Watson, da of late JGR Robertson, of Cupar, Fife; *Career* writer; awarded Scottish Arts Cncl bursaries 1976, 1982, 1998 and 2004, creative writing fell Univ of Edinburgh 1977–79, winner book awards 1978 and 1993, Hawthornden Writer's fellowship 1989 and 1995, William Soutar Writer's fellowship 1990–91, writer in residence Champlain Coll Trent Univ Canada 1998; *Books* Descent (1968), A Truth Lover (1973), Clapperton (1974), Pagan's Pilgrimage (1978), Stories Short and Tall (1979), Voice without Restraint: Bob Dylan's Lyrics and their Background (1982), Three Novellas (1987), The Double in Nineteenth Century Fiction (1990), Imelda and Other Stories (1993), Ghostwriting (1996), Cruising: A Play (1997), Poets, Pubs, Polls and Pillar-Boxes (1999), Four Tales (2000), The Sinister Cabaret (2001), Triptych (2004), My Wife's Lovers (2007); *Recreations* reading, walking, listening to music, medieval church history; *Style—* Dr John Herdman; ✉ Roselea, Bridge of Tilt, Pitlochry PH18 5SX

HEREFORD, Bishop of 2004–; Rt Rev Anthony Martin Priddis; s of John Edward Priddis (d 1982), and Joan Priddis (d 1999); *b* 15 March 1948; *Educ* Watford Boys' GS, CCC Cambridge (MA), Cuddesdon Theol Coll, New Coll Oxford (DipTheol, MA (by incorporation)); *m* 28 July 1973, Kathy; 2 s (Michael b 7 July 1975, James b 16 Aug 1977), 1 da (Sarah b 25 March 1981); *Career* ordained: deacon 1972, priest 1973; asst curate St Edward's New Addington 1972–75, coll chaplain ChCh Oxford 1975–80, team vicar St John's High Wycombe 1980–86, rector of Amersham 1986–96, rural dean of Amersham 1992–96, bishop of Warwick 1996–2004; hon canon of Christ Church 1995; chm Rural Bishops' Panel 2006–, memb C of E Centeral Safeguarding Liaison Gp 2002–; tstee and chm Amersham United Charities 1986–96, chm governing bodies of 2 schs 1986–96, fndr memb Bd Chilterns Hundred Housing Assoc 1988–92, tstee Coventry Relate 2001–04, co-chm Family Life and Marriage Educn (FLAME) Network 2003–06 (tstee 2001–06), memb W Midlands Cultural Consortium 2002–05; hon fell Faculty of A&E Med 2004– (lay memb Bd 2002–), fell Coll of Emergency Medicine; *Books* The Study of Spirituality (contrib, 1986); *Recreations* walking, gardening, sport (including golf), music, reading; *Clubs* Farmers'; *Style—* The Rt Rev the Bishop of Hereford; ✉ The Bishop's House, Hereford HR4 9BN (tel 01432 271355, fax 01432 373346, e-mail bishop@hereford.anglican.org)

HEREFORD, Archdeacon of; *see:* Colmer, Ven Malcolm John

HEREFORD, 19 Viscount (E 1550); Sir (Charles) Robin de Bohun Devereux; 16 Bt (E 1611); Premier Viscount in the Peerage of England; s of 18 Viscount Hereford (d 2004), and Susan Mary, *née* Godley; *b* 11 August 1975, London; *Educ* Stowe, UEA (BA); *Heir* bro, Hon Edward Devereux; *Career* gen valuer Bonhams Auctioneers 1998–, dir Valuations 2007–; *Recreations* fishing, rollerblading, the arts, food and wine; *Clubs* White's; *Style—* The Rt Hon the Viscount Hereford; ✉ 8 Vauxhall Bridge Road, London SW1V 2SD

HERFORD, (Richard) Henry; s of Philip Henry Herford (d 1982), of Glasgow, and Elisabeth Jean, *née* Hawkins; *b* 24 February 1947; *Educ* Trinity Coll Glenalmond, King's Coll Cambridge, Univ of York, Royal Manchester Coll of Music; *m* 14 Feb 1982, Jane Lindsay, da of Peter John; 2 s (Thomas Hal b 31 Oct 1982, John Peter b 19 Jan 1985), 1 da (Alice Jane b 5 March 1988); *Career* opera and concert singer; performances incl operas with Covent Garden, Glyndebourne, Scottish Opera and throughout Europe, concerts, recitals, broadcasts and recordings throughout Britain, Europe and the USA, and in Canada, S America and Hong Kong; co-fndr and dir Abingdon Summer Sch for Solo Singers 1998–; tutor Sch of Vocal Studies: Royal Northern Coll of Music 1994–, Guildhall Sch of Music 1998, Royal Coll of Music 1998–, Birmingham Conservatoire 1998–; examiner and adjudicator in all principal British conservatoires; Curtis Gold Medal for singing Royal Northern Coll of Music 1976, Benson and Hedges Gold Award 1980, first prize Int American Music Competition 1982; *Recordings* incl: Rameau Castor et Pollux (Erato), Bridge The Christmas Rose (Pearl), Handel Messiah (excerpts, Contour), Peter Dickinson Dylan Thomas Song Cycle (Conifer), Britten A Midsummer Night's Dream (Virgin) Charles Ives Song Recital I and II (Unicorn-Kanchana, Music Retailers' Assoc Record of the Year), Charles Ives songs with instrumental ensemble (Ensemble Modern, EMI), George Lloyd Iernin (Albany), Stravinsky Pulcinella (Naxos), Edward Gregson Missa Brevis Pacem, Handel Israel in Egypt (Decca), John Joubert The Instant Moment (BIRC), Arthur Bliss: Complete Songs (Hyperion), Sir John Manduell: Renaissance Songs (ASC); *Recreations* family, house restoration, chamber music (cello), reading, walking; *Style—* Henry Herford; ✉ Pencots, Northmoor, Oxfordshire OX29 5AX (tel and fax 01865 300884, e-mail the.herfords@btinternet.com)

HERHOLDT, Frank Devilliers; s of Albrecht Johan Devilliers Herholdt, of Cape Town, South Africa, and Frances, *née* Robberts (d 1992); *b* 6 October 1945; *Educ* Parktown Boys' HS, Johannesburg Sch of Art; *m* 1, Verona Somers (m dis 1981); m 2, July 1999 (m dis 2005), Susan, *née* Rowlands; 1 s (Zacharias Devilliers b 23 Oct 2006); *Career* photographer; asst to Lynton Stephenson Johannesburg SA 1967–68, in-house photographer Forsyth Advertising 1969–71, in own studio Johannesburg 1971–75, freelance photographer in London and Europe assisting various photographers incl Art Kane 1976–83, in own studio London 1983–; memb: Assoc of Photographers, Dirs' Guild of GB; *Awards* numerous awards incl several Communication Arts USA, Assoc of Photographers and London Photographic awards; Grand Prix Cannes Advtg Award (for website www.frankherholdt.com); *Recreations* cooking, eating and travelling; *Style—* Frank Herholdt, Esq; ✉ 15 Gascoigne Place, London E2 7LY (e-mail info@frankherholdt.com)

HERITAGE, Robert Charles; CBE (1980); s of Charles John Heritage, and Daisy May, *née* Clay; *b* 2 November 1927; *Educ* King Edward's GS Birmingham, Birmingham Coll of Art and Industrial Design, RCA Furniture Sch (MDes); *m* 4 April 1953, Dorothy, da of William Shaw; 2 s (Paul Robert b 1956, Michael Justin Lawrence b 1965), 1 da (Rachael Francesca b 1958); *Career* design conslt in private practice 1953–; prof of furniture design RCA 1974–85; Br Aluminium Design award 1966; 12 Cncl of Industrial Design awards for furniture, products and lighting; Bundespreise for lighting products 1972; Liveryman Worshipful Co of Furniture Makers; RDI 1963, hon fell RCA, FRSA, FCSD; *Recreations* salmon fishing, tennis; *Style—* Robert Heritage, Esq, CBE

HERMAN, Daniel James; s of Kenneth Joseph Herman (d 2006), and Miroslava, *née* Radić; *b* 12 August 1974, Manchester; *Educ* Bury GS for Boys, Univ of Warwick (LLB), Coll of Law Chester (DipLP); *m* 2 July 2005, Rebecca, *née* Such; *Career* slr; Graham Leigh Pfeffer & Co 1996–98, Kingsford Stacey Blackwell 1998–2000, Stewarts Slrs 2000– (ptnr 2003–); memb Law Soc 1999; *Recreations* football, tennis, relaxing in Croatia; *Style—* Daniel Herman, Esq; ✉ Stewarts Solicitors, St Paul's House, 23 Park Square South, Leeds LS1 2ND (tel 0113 222 0022, fax 0113 222 0044, e-mail dherman@stewartslaw.com)

HERMAN, Dr Stephen Sydney; s of Maurice Herman (d 1975), and Deborah, *née* Dutkevitch (d 1980); *b* 7 July 1942; *Educ* Central Foundation Boys GS, King's Coll London, St George's Hosp Med Sch (MB BS); *m* 21 June 1966, Yvette Hannah, da of Isaac Solomons (d 1964); 1 s (Simon b 13 March 1969), 2 da (Rachel b 31 July 1970, Ruth b 5 May 1973); *Career* hon conslt paediatrician Royal National Orthopaedic Hosp, conslt paediatrician Central Middx Hosp 1974–93; memb: Neonatal Soc 1972; FRCP 1981, FRCPCH 1997; *Recreations* amateur radio (call sign M0SSH); *Style—* Dr Stephen Herman; ✉ Barbary House, California Lane, Bushey Heath, Hertfordshire WD23 1EX (tel 020 8950 0534, fax 020 8950 0130, e-mail stephen_herman@hotmail.com)

HERMER, Richard; *b* 1968; *Career* called to the Bar 1993; practising barr specialising in human rights and tort law, currently memb Doughty Street Chambers; human rights practitioner in residence Columbia Univ NY 2000–; *Style—* Richard Hermer; ✉ Doughty Street Chambers, 10–11 Doughty Street, London WC1N 2PL

HERMON, Lady; Sylvia; MP; da of Samuel Robert Paisley, and Mary Eileen, *née* McMinn (d 1959); *b* 11 August 1955, Co Tyrone; *Educ* Dungannon HS for Girls, Univ of Aberystwyth (LLB); *m* Sir John Charles Hermon; 2 s (Robert Paisley b 21 Oct 1989, Thomas Rowan b 11 April 1992); *Career* lectr in law Queen's Univ Belfast 1978–88; MP (UUP) Down N 2001–; UUP spokesman on home affrs House of Commons; memb N Down UU Assoc; chm N Down Support Gp Marie Curie Cancer Care, memb Friends of Bangor Community Hosp; *Publications* incl: A Guide to European Community Law in Northern Ireland, The Response to the Patten Report; *Recreations* ornithology, swimming and fitness training, letter writing; *Style—* Lady Hermon, MP; ✉ House of Commons, London SW1A 0AA

HERMON-TAYLOR, Prof John; s of Hermon Taylor (d 2001), of Bosham, W Sussex, and Marie Amelie, *née* Pearson (d 1981); *b* 16 October 1936; *Educ* Harrow, St John's Coll Cambridge (BA, MB BChir, MChir), The London Hosp Med Coll; *m* 18 Sept 1971, Eleanor Ann, da of Dr Willard S Pheteplace (d 1985), of Davenport, Iowa; 1 da (Amy Caroline b 1975), 1 s (Peter Maxwell b 1979); *Career* various NHS and univ trg posts in surgery 1963–68, MRC travelling fell in gastrointestinal physiology Mayo Clinic USA 1968–69, reader in surgery The London Hosp Med Coll 1971–76 (sr lectr 1970–71), prof and chm of surgery St George's Hosp Med Sch 1976–2002 (emeritus 2002–), conslt in gen surgery RN 1989–2002, author of numerous scientific and med res articles; memb: Cncl Assoc of Surgeons of GB and Ireland 1980–83, Clinical Panel The Wellcome Tst 1985–88, Cncl Action Research 1988–97, Scientific Ctee Br Digestive Fndn 1991–94, Health Servs Research and Clinical Epidemiology Ctee The Wellcome Tst 1996–2001, Working Gp on Paratuberculosis and Crohn's disease Animal Sci and Animal Health Ctee EC; winner: The Times Newspaper/Barclays Bank Innovator of the Year award 1988, Hallett prize; FRCS 1963; *Recreations* sailing, fishing, shooting; *Style—* Prof John Hermon-Taylor; ✉ 11 Parkside Avenue, Wimbledon, London SW19 5ES; Department of Surgery, St George's University of London, Cranmer Terrace, London SW17 0RE (tel 020 8767 7631, fax 020 8725 3594, e-mail jhermon@sgul.ac.uk)

HERMSEN, (Adriaan) John; s of Adriaan Marinus Christiaan Hermsen (d 1982), of Broadway, Worcs, and Margaret, *née* Stanley (d 1989); *b* 20 August 1933; *Educ* Salvatorian Sch, Royal West of England Acad Sch of Architecture, KCL (MSc); *m* 23 March 1963, Jean Russell, da of Charles Herbert Simmonds (d 1971), of Durban, South Africa; 2 s ((Adriaan) Keir b 1968, Mark Christian Piers b 1971); *Career* Howard Lobb & Partners 1956–57, Richard Sheppard Robson & Partners 1957–59, R D Russell & Partners 1961–62, Douglas Stephen & Partners 1962–64, Nat Building Agency 1964–71, ptnr and dir Ahrends Burton & Koralek 1974–97 (joined 1971), architect arbitrator and expert witness 1997–2006; rep Miny Housing & Local Govt on Br Standard Ctee 3921 1969–71; chair Architects' Law Forum RIBA 1995–97 (pres 1997–2005), memb President's Ctee on Arbitration RIBA 1999–2005; chm Joint Contracts Tbnl Ltd (JCT) Conslts Coll (ACE, RIBA & RICS) 1998–99; FRIBA 1969 (ARIBA 1962), FCIArb 1993 (ACIArb 1984), MAE 1992; *Recreations* construction law, walking and sailing; *Style—* John Hermsen, Esq; ✉ 18 Frogmore Close, Hughenden Valley, High Wycombe, Buckinghamshire HP14 4LN (tel 01494 562260, fax 01494 565744, e-mail john.hermsen@member.riba.org)

HERON, David Leslie Norton; s of late Edward Wallace Heron, and Eunice Cecilia, *née* Mott; *b* 5 October 1941; *Educ* Christ's Coll Finchley; *m* 25 July 1965, Margaret Ann, *née* Berry, da of Leonard Kenneth Berry; 3 s (Simon Alexander b 6 Sept 1968, Daniel Mark b 17 April 1970, Luke Nicholas b 20 Sept 1978), 1 da (Kathryn Alice b 29 Dec 1973); *Career* trainee chartered accountant 1957–59; James Capel & Co: accountant asst 1959–61, investment analyst asst 1961–66, stockbroker 1966–, fund mgmnt 1966–68, institutional sales 1968–72 and 1976–83, head of Far East sales 1972–76, head of derivatives 1983–94, dir 1987–94; head of derivatives Smith New Court 1994, dep chm LIFFE 1992–94; chm: Premier Radio 1995–, CCP Ltd (magazine publishing); tstee Mildmay Hospital; *Recreations* tennis, active church member; *Style—* David L N Heron, Esq; ✉ 71 Grasmere Road, Muswell Hill, London N10 2DH

HERON, Prof Kenneth Harry (Ken); s of Wilfred Heron (d 1993), of Blackburn, Lancs, and Jennie, *née* Newby (d 1998); *b* 2 May 1943; *Educ* Queen Elizabeth's GS Blackburn, Univ of Bristol (BSc), Univ of Southampton (external PhD); *m* 1 April 1967, Patricia Ann, *née* Milnes; 1 s (Dale Robert b 15 May 1971), 1 da (Heidi Denise b 6 May 1973); *Career* Royal Aircraft Estab Farnborough (later DRA and DERA, now QinetiQ): research scientist 1964–, appointed PSO 1976, sr fell 1998–; inventor flat panel loudspeaker; visiting prof Imperial Coll London 1996; awarded first DERA Prize for the Exploitation of Science 1999; FREng 2001; *Publications* over 20 papers and over 150 internal reports in the fields of structural acoustics and dynamics; *Style—* Prof Ken Heron; ✉ QinetiQ, Cody Technology Park, Farnborough, Hampshire GU14 0LX (tel 01252 395289, e-mail khheron@qinetiq.com)

HERON, Sir Michael Gilbert (Mike); kt (1996); s of Gilbert Thwaites Heron (d 1962), and Olive Lilian, *née* Steele; *b* 22 October 1934; *Educ* St Joseph's Acad Blackheath, New Coll Oxford (MA); *m* 16 Aug 1958, Celia Veronica Mary, da of Capt Clarence Hunter (d 1960); 2 s (Jonathan, Damian), 2 da (Louise, Annette); *Career* Lt RA 1953–55; dir BOCM Silcock 1971–76, chm Batchelors Foods Ltd 1976–82, dep co-ordinator Food and Drinks Co-ordination Unilever 1982–86, dir Main Bd Unilever plc and NV 1986–92, chm The Post Office 1993–98; chm Cncl of St George's Hosp Med Sch 1992–2000; chm Cncl of Industry and Higher Educn 1998–2004; memb Armed Forces Pay Review Bd 1981 and 1982; dep chm Business in the Community 1990–95 (chm Educn Business Partnerships), chm NCVQ 1993–97, patron Nat Trg Awards 1993 and 1994; *Recreations* very keen sportsman in the past, now a viewer; *Style—* Sir Mike Heron; ✉ 43 Albion Gate, Albion Street, London W2 2LG

HERON-MAXWELL, Sir Nigel Mellor; 10 Bt (NS 1683), of Springkell, Dumfriesshire; s of Sir Patrick Ivor Heron-Maxwell, 9 Bt (d 1982), sr male rep of the Maxwells of Pollock and the Clydesdale Maxwells, and (Dorothy) Geraldine Emma, *née* Mellor (d 2001); *b* 30 January 1944; *Educ* Milton Abbey; *m* 1972, Mary Elizabeth Angela, o da of William Ewing, of Co Donegal; 1 s (David Mellor b 1975), 1 da (Claire Louise b 1977); *Heir* s, David Heron-Maxwell; *Career* navigation apprentice London and Overseas Freighters Ltd 1961–65, navigation offr Royal Fleet Aux Service 1966–76, flying instr 1976–80; commercial pilot 1980–83; asst data controller SmithKline & French Research Ltd 1983–85, analyst/programmer SmithKline & French Laboratories Ltd 1985–89; SmithKline Beecham Pharmaceuticals: analyst/programmer 1989–94, planning and scheduling co-ordinator 1994–96; admissions administrator Univ of Hertfordshire 1999–; *Style—* Sir Nigel Heron-Maxwell, Bt; ✉ 50 Watlington Road, Old Harlow, Essex CM17 0DY (tel 01279 301669)

HERRIES OF TERREGLES, Lady (14 holder of S Lordship 1490); Lady Anne Elizabeth; *née* Fitzalan Howard; eldest da of 16 Duke of Norfolk, KG, GCVO, GBE, TD, PC (d 1975, when the Dukedom and all other honours save the Lordship passed to his kinsman, 17 Duke of Norfolk (d 2002); the late Duke's mother was Lady Herries of Terregles *suo jure* following the death of her f, the 11 Lord), and Lavinia, Duchess of Norfolk, LG, CBE (d 1995); *b* 12 June 1938; *m* 1985, as his 2 w, Baron Tonbridge, CBE (Life Peer, d 2000); *Heir* sis, Lady Mary Mumford; *Career* racehorse trainer; *Style—* The Rt Hon the Lady Herries of Terregles; ✉ Angmering Park, Littlehampton, West Sussex BN16 4EX (tel 01903 871421)

HERRING, Timothy Stephen; s of Cdr Philip Maurice Herring, RNVR (d 1982), and Flora Pepita Herring (d 1985); *b* 25 May 1936; *Educ* Bishop's Stortford Coll; *m* 22 April 1960, Cathleen Elizabeth, da of Thomas Stephen Nevin (d 1972); 2 s (Stephen Ashley b 26 Nov 1960, Andrew Philip b 15 March 1963); *Career* Lamson Engineering 1956–66; proprietor: Julie's Restaurant 1969–, Portobello Hotel 1970–, Ark Restaurant USA 1983–93; yachtsman; winner: Britannia Cup, Queen's Cup, Queen Victoria Cup; Freeman City of London 1961, Prime Warden Worshipful Co of Blacksmiths 1997–98 (memb 1961), Liveryman Worshipful Co of Turners; *Recreations* yachting; *Clubs* Royal Burnham Yacht, Royal Thames Yacht; *Style—* Timothy Herring, Esq; ✉ 133 Portland Road, London W11 4LW (tel 020 7727 2776); Quaycote, Burnham-on-Crouch, Essex CM0 8AS

HERRINGTON, Timothy John (Tim); s of John Herrington, of Basingstoke, Hants, and Barbara Jean Margaret, *née* Toon (d 1996); *b* 22 April 1954; *Educ* Queen Mary's GS Basingstoke, Univ of Bristol (LLB); *m* 20 Feb 1982, Kathleen Mary, da of Peter Loy Chetwynd Pigott, of Bulawayo, Zimbabwe; 1 s (James b 1987); *Career* admitted slr 1978; ptnr: Coward Chance 1985–87 (joined 1976), Clifford Chance 1987–2005; chm: Law Soc Standing Ctee on Co Law 1996–99 (memb 1988–2004), Investment Funds Ctee Int Bar Assoc 2000–02, Regulatory Decisions Ctee Financial Servs Authy 2005–; memb Advsy Bd Financial Servs Lawyers' Assoc 2007–; Freeman: City of London 1977, Worshipful Co of Slrs 1985; memb Law Soc; *Books* Life After Big Bang (contrib, 1987), Insider Dealing in Europe (contrib, 1994), Law Making, Law Finding and Law Shaping (contrib, 1997), Capital Guide to Offshore Funds (contrib, 1999), Legal Aspects of Investment Management (contrib, 1999); *Recreations* cricket, travel, walking, gardening, numismatics, wine, English countryside; *Clubs* Hampshire CCC, National Liberal; *Style—* Tim Herrington, Esq; ✉ Financial Services Authority, 25 The North Colonnade, London E14 5HS (tel 020 7066 3420, fax 020 7066 3421, e-mail tim.herrington@fsa.gov.uk)

HERSCHELL, 3 Baron (UK 1886); Rognvald Richard Farrer; s of 2 Baron, GCVO (d 1929), and Vera (d 1961), da of Sir Arthur Nicolson, 10 Bt; *b* 13 September 1923; *Educ* Eton; *m* 1 May 1948, Lady Heather Mary Margaret Legge, o da of 8 Earl of Dartmouth; 1 da; *Heir* none; *Career* page of honour to King George V, King Edward VIII and King George VI 1935–39; Capt Coldstream Gds (ret), served WWII 1942–45; *Style—* The Rt Hon the Lord Herschell; ✉ Westfield House, Ardington, Wantage, Oxfordshire OX12 8PN (tel 01235 833224)

HERSEY, David Kenneth; s of Charles Kenneth Hersey, and Ella, *née* Morgan; *b* 30 November 1939; *Educ* Oberlin Coll; *m* 1, 1962 (m dis 1967), Ellen Diamond; m 2, 1967 (m dis 1972), Juliet Case; 1 da (Miranda Louise b 1969); m 3, 25 Sept 1976, Demetra, da of Demetrius Maraslis; 1 s (Demetri Alexander b 1978), 1 da (Ellen Katherine b 1980); *Career* lighting designer; fndr DHA Lighting, lighting conslt NT 1974–84, chm Assoc of Lighting Designers 1984–86; West End and Broadway prodns incl: Oliver, Piaf, Cyrano, Miss Saigon, Baker's Wife, Les Miserables, Cats, Starlight Express, Chess, Metropolis, Song and Dance, The Little Shop of Horrors, Evita, Nicholas Nickleby, Merrily We Roll Along, Burning Blue, The Glass Menagerie, Martin Guerre, Jesus Christ Superstar, Oklahoma!; RNT prodns incl: Bartholomew Fair, Ghetto, Guys and Dolls 1996, Enemy of the People 1997, Peter Pan 1997, Oklahoma! 1998, My Fair Lady 2001, South Pacific 2001, The Coast of Utopia 2002, Anything Goes 2002; many prodns for RSC; numerous operas and ballets incl: Royal Opera House, ENO, Ballet Rambert, London Contemporary Dance, Scot Ballet, Glyndebourne, Birmingham Royal Ballet; *Awards* for Miss Saigon: Drama Desk Award 1991; for Les Miserables: Tony Award 1987, Los Angeles Drama Critics' Circle Award 1988, Dora Mavor Moore Award 1989; for Cats Tony Award 1983, Drama Desk Award 1983, Dora Mavor Moore Award 1984; for Evita: Los Angeles Drama Critics' Circle Award 1979, Tony Award 1980; Olivier Award for Best Lighting Designer 1996; *Recreations* sailing (Millennium Odyssey Round the World Yacht Rally 1998–2000); *Style—* David Hersey, Esq; ✉ DHA Lighting Ltd, 289–302 Waterloo Road, London SE1 8RQ (tel 020 7771 2900, fax 020 7771 2901)

HERSOV, Gregory Adam (Greg); s of Dr Lionel Hersov, and Zoe, *née* Menell; *b* 4 May 1956; *Educ* Bryanston, Mansfield Coll Oxford (MA); *Career* theatre dir; Thames TV regnl dirs trainee Redgrave Theatre Farnham 1976–78, involved with Royal Exchange Theatre 1979– (artistic dir 1987–); *Theatre* Royal Exchange prodns incl: The Tempest, King Lear,

H

One Flew Over the Cuckoo's Nest, Blues for Mister Charlie, All My Sons, Death of a Salesman, The Crucible, Ghosts, A Doll's House, The Alchemist, The Beggar's Opera, Look Back in Anger, The Homecoming, Venice Preserv'd, The Voysey Inheritance, Uncle Vanya, The Seagull; Royal Exchange on tour prodns: Romeo and Juliet, A View From the Bridge (TMA Best Dir); premieres: Prize Night, Woundings, Behind Heaven, Winding the Ball, Misfits; other credits incl: Les Blancs (co-dir European premiere), Animal Crackers (Royal Exchange, Barbican Int Festival and West End), Look Back in Anger (RNT); *Style*— Greg Hersov, Esq; ✉ Royal Exchange Theatre, St Ann's Square, Manchester M2 7DH (tel 0161 615 6704, fax 0161 832 0881, e-mail greg.hersov@royalexchange.co.uk)

HERTFORD, Archdeacon of; *see:* Jones, Ven Trevor Pryce

HERTFORD, Bishop of 2001–; Rt Rev Christopher Richard James Foster; *b* 1953; *Educ* UC Durham (BA), Univ of Manchester (MA(Econ)), Trinity Hall Cambridge (MA), Westcott House Cambridge; *m* 1, 1982, Julia Marie, *née* Jones (d 2001); 1 s (Richard Edward Joseph b 1983), 1 da (Miriam Laura Elizabeth b 1985); m 2, 2006, Sally Elizabeth, *née* Davenport; *Career* lectr in economics Univ of Durham 1976–77; ordained: deacon 1980, priest 1981; asst curate Tettenhall Regis Team Miny Wolverhampton 1980–82, chaplain Wadham Coll Oxford 1982–86, asst priest Univ Church of St Mary the Virgin with St Cross and St Peter in the East Oxford 1982–86, vicar Christ Church Southgate 1986–94, Continuing Ministerial Educn (CME) dir Edmonton Episcopal Area 1988–94, sub dean and residentiary canon Cathedral and Abbey Church of St Alban 1994–2001; *Style*— The Rt Rev the Bishop of Hertford; ✉ Hertford House, Abbey Mill Lane, St Albans, Hertfordshire AL3 4HE (tel 01727 866420, fax 01727 811426, e-mail bishophertford@stalbans.anglican.org)

HERTFORD, 9 Marquess of (GB 1793); Henry Jocelyn Seymour; also Lord Conway, Baron Conway of Ragley (E 1703), Baron Conway of Killultagh (I 1712), Viscount Beauchamp, Earl of Hertford (both GB 1750), and Earl of Yarmouth (GB 1793); patron of 3 livings; s of 8 Marquess (d 1997); *b* 6 July 1958; *Educ* Harrow, RAC Cirencester; *m* 15 Dec 1990, Beatriz, da of Jorge Karam, of Copacabana, Brazil; 2 da (Lady Gabriella Helen b 23 April 1992, Lady Antonia Louisa b 24 July 1998), 2 s (William Francis, Earl of Yarmouth b 2 Nov 1993, Lord Edward George b 24 Jan 1995); *Heir* s, Earl of Yarmouth; *Style*— The Most Hon the Marquess of Hertford; ✉ Ragley Hall, Alcester, Warwickshire B49 5NJ (tel 01789 762090, fax 01789 764791, e-mail lordhertford@ragleyhall.com)

HERVEY-BATHURST, Sir (Frederick) John Charles Gordon; 7 Bt (UK 1818), of Lainston, Hants; s of Sir Frederick Peter Methuen Hervey-Bathurst, 6 Bt (d 1995), and his 1 w, Maureen Gladys Diana, *née* Gordon; *b* 23 April 1934; *Educ* Eton, Trinity Coll Cambridge (MA); *m* 1957, Caroline Myrtle, da of Sir William Randle Starkey, 2 Bt; 2 da (Louisa Caroline (Lady Portal) b 1959, Sophia Selina Irene (Mrs Henry Colthurst) b 1961), 1 s (Frederick William John b 1965); *Heir* s, Frederick Hervey-Bathurst; *Career* Lt Grenadier Gds (Reserve); former dir Lazard Bros and Co Ltd, ret; *Style*— Sir John Hervey-Bathurst, Bt

HERXHEIMER, Dr Andrew; s of Herbert G J Herxheimer (d 1985), of London, and Ilse M, *née* König (d 1980); *b* 4 November 1925; *Educ* Highgate Sch, St Thomas' Hosp Med Sch (MB, BS); *m* 1, 4 March 1960 (m dis 1974), Susan Jane, da of Harry Collier (d 1983), of London; 2 da (Charlotte b 1961, Sophie b 1963); m 2, 24 March 1983, Dr Christine Herxheimer, da of Willrecht Bernecker (d 1942), of Stuttgart, Germany; *Career* lectr and sr lectr in pharmacology London Hosp Med Coll 1959–76, sr lectr in clinical pharmacology Charing Cross Med Sch/Charing Cross and Westminster Med Sch 1976–91, extraordinary prof of clinical pharmacology Univ of Groningen Netherlands 1968–77; ed Drug and Therapeutics Bulletin 1963–92; conslt UK Cochrane Centre NHS R&D Prog Oxford 1992–95, chm Int Soc of Drug Bulletins 1986–96, editorial advsr La revue Prescrire Paris 1997–99; founding memb DIPEx project Univ of Oxford (www.dipex.org); memb Cncl Ethical Investment Research Service 1996–2000; emeritus fell UK Cochrane Centre 1996–; memb: Br Pharmacological Soc 1960–, Health Action Int 1981, European Assoc of Science Eds 1994, Medicines Labelling Group 2000; Georg Klemperer Medal Berlin Aerztekammer 2007; FRCP 1977; *Books* Drugs and Sensory Functions (ed, 1968), Side Effects of Drugs (jt ed, 1972), Pharmaceuticals and Health Policy (jt ed, 1981), Nausea and Vomiting (conslt ed, 2000), Evidence-based Dermatology (co-ed, 2003, 2 edn 2007); author of papers in scientific jls; *Recreations* reading, travel; *Style*— Dr Andrew Herxheimer; ✉ 9 Park Crescent, London N3 2NL (tel 020 8346 5470, fax 020 8346 0407)

HERZBERG, Henry Joseph; s of Georges Herzberg (d 1989), and Nancibel, *née* Joseph; *b* 7 October 1943; *Educ* Ashburton Secdy Sch, Selhurst GS, Architectural Assoc London, RIBA (AADipl); *m* 6 Aug 1976, Kate, da of Thomas Bampton, 1 s (Joseph Daniel b 4 July 1977), 3 da (Chloe Zylpha b 18 Feb 1972, Anna Zimena b 12 Sept 1973, Rachel Henrietta b 4 April 1982); *Career* architect; in professional practice Ahrends, Burton and Koralek 1966–67; site architect: Sir Robert McAlpine Ltd 1969–71, Wates Ltd 1971–72; Lethaby and Bannister Fletcher scholar Soc for the Protection of Ancient Buildings 1972; project architect Wimpey Ltd 1973–75, Ahrends Burton Koralek 1975; bldg ed Architects Journal 1975–77; architect (work includes): Colin St John Wilson & Ptnrs (The Br Library Euston) 1977–79, YRM (Central Med Stores and Laundry Bahrain) 1979–80; Chapman Taylor Partners: architect 1980– (Ridings Wakefield), assoc 1983–86 (The Poplars Supermarket and District Centre Stevenage, Orchard Square Fargate Sheffield), ptnr 1986– (refurbishment of The Octagon High Wycombe, Lakeside Thurrock, Priory Park Merton, Vicarage Field Barking, Peacocks Woking, Royal Victoria Place Tunbridge Wells, South Terminal Departure Lounge Gatwick, refurbishment of Brunel Centre Swindon), currently sr ptnr; ARIBA 1970; memb: AA 1970, Soc for the Protection of Ancient Buildings 1971, Victorian Soc, Georgian Soc, Wind and Windmill Soc; *Style*— Henry Herzberg, Esq; ✉ Chapman Taylor Partners, 96 Kensington High Street, London W8 4SG

HERZBERG, Prof Joseph Larry; s of Adolf Heinrich Herzberg, of London, and Pearl, *née* Mesh; *b* 10 May 1953; *Educ* Carmel Coll, Hasmonean Sch, The London Hosp Med Coll (BSc, MB BS, MPhil); *m* 13 Feb 1977, Helene Ruth, da of Harry Gordon, of London; 1 s (Laurence b 1982); *Career* SHO and registrar in pyschiatry London Hosp 1980–84 (house physician 1979–80); sr registrar in psychiatry: St Mary's Hosp London 1984–85, The Bethlem Royal and Maudsley Hosps London 1986–87; conslt psychogeriatrician Lewisham & Guy's Mental Health and NHS Tst (formerly Guy's Hosp) and sr lectr UMDS Guy's Campus 1987–96; conslt old age psychiatrist The Royal London Hosp (Mile End), assoc med dir E London and City Mental Health Tst, assoc dean of postgrad med London Postgrad Med and Dental Educn (LPMDE) Univ of London 1996–, NHS prof of postgraduate medical educn Barts and the London Sch of Med and Dentistry and Queen Mary Univ of London 2006– (hon reader in postgraduate medical educn 2002–06); author of various scientific papers on: social psychiatry, neuropsychiatry, psychogeriatrics, audit and med educn; former memb Exec Assoc for the Study of Medical Education ASME (RCPsych representative, treas 2002–06); Worshipful Soc of Apothecaries, memb Ct of Assts Guild of Freemen of the City of London; FRSM, FRCPsych 1995 (MRCPsych 1983); *Recreations* music (particularly opera), theatre, travel; *Style*— Prof Joseph Herzberg; ✉ 3 Ashley Gardens, Ambrosden Avenue, Westminster, London SW1P 1QD; Royal London Hospital (Mile End), Bancroft Road, London E1 4DG (tel 020 7377 7000, e-mail jherzberg@londondeanery.ac.uk)

HESELTINE, Baron (Life Peer UK 2001), of Thenford in the County of Northamptonshire; Michael Ray Dibdin Heseltine; CH (1997), PC (1979); s of late Col R D Heseltine, of Swansea, Glamorgan; *b* 21 March 1933; *Educ* Shrewsbury, Pembroke Coll Oxford (BA, pres Oxford Union); *m* 1962, Anne Harding Williams; 1 s, 2 da; *Career* Nat Serv cmmnd Welsh Gds 1959; Parly candidate (Cons): Gower 1959, Coventry North 1964; MP (Cons): Tavistock 1966–74, Henley 1974–2001; dir Bow Publications 1961–65, chm Haymarket Press 1966–70; vice-chm Cons Parly Tport Ctee 1968, oppn spokesman on Tport 1969, Parly sec Miny of Tport June-Oct 1970, Parly under-sec for the Environment 1970–72, min for Aerospace and Shipping DTI 1972–74, oppn spokesman on Indust 1974–76, oppn spokesman on the Environment 1976–79, sec of state for the Environment 1979–83, sec of state for Defence 1983–86 (resigned over Westland affair), contested leadership of Cons Party Nov 1990, sec of state for the Environment Nov 1990–92, pres Bd of Trade (sec of state for Trade and Industry) 1992–95, dep PM 1995–97; pres: Assoc of Cons Clubs 1978, Nat Young Conservatives 1982–84 (vice-pres 1978), Quoted Companies Alliance 2000–; chm: UK-China Forum 1998–, Haymarket Group plc 1999–; memb Cncl Zoological Soc of London 1987–90; hon fell Pembroke Coll Oxford 1986, hon fell UC Swansea 2001; Hon LLD Univ of Liverpool 1990, Hon DBA Luton Univ 2003; *Publications* Reviving the Inner Cities (1983), Where There's A Will (1987), The Challenge of Europe, Can Britain Win? (1989), Life in the Jungle (autobiography, 2000); *Clubs* Carlton; *Style*— The Rt Hon the Lord Heseltine, CH, PC

HESELTINE, Richard Mark Horsley; s of late Edwin Oswald Heseltine, and Penelope Horsley, *née* Robinson; *b* 3 October 1945; *Educ* Winchester, New Coll Oxford (MA), Wharton Sch Univ of Pennsylvania (MBA); *m* 1976, Joanna Elisabeth, da of late Ronald C Symonds, CB; 2 da (Catherine b 1978, Emma b 1981); *Career* Corp Fin Dept Morgan Grenfell 1969–71, dir Croda International plc 1981–97 (exec 1971–80); non-exec dir The Smaller Companies Investment Trust plc; cncllr London Borough of Islington (SDP) 1986–90 and (Lib Dem) 1998–, chm Planning Ctee; govr: Cripplegate Fndn, Sadler's Wells, City Univ; *Recreations* yacht racing; *Clubs* Reform, Oxford and Cambridge Sailing Soc, Royal Western Yacht; *Style*— Richard Heseltine, Esq; ✉ 28 Gibson Square, London N1 0RD (tel 020 7359 0702)

HESFORD, Stephen; MP; s of Bernard Hesford, of Lymm, Cheshire, and Nellie, *née* Haworth; *b* 27 May 1957; *Educ* Univ of Bradford (BSc), Poly of Central London (Dip Law); *m* 21 July 1984, Elizabeth Anne, da of late Dudley Henshall, of Bramhall, Cheshire; 2 s (John b 1986, David b 1988); *Career* called to the Bar Gray's Inn 1981; MP (Lab) Wirral W 1997– (Parly candidate Suffolk S 1992), PPS to Baroness Amos (as Ldr House of Lords) 2005–; memb: Fabian Soc, Lab Pty; *Recreations* cricket, politics, antiquarian books, biographies; *Clubs* Lancashire CCC (life memb); *Style*— Stephen Hesford, Esq, MP; ✉ House of Commons, London SW1A 0AA (tel 020 7219 3000, fax 020 7219 4953)

HESKETH, Ven Ron D; CB (2004), QHC (2001); *b* 1947, Broughty Ferry, Angus; *Educ* King David Sch Liverpool, Univ of Durham (BA), Univ of Cambridge, Univ of Cardiff (Dip Pastoral Studies), Open Univ; *m* Vera; 1 s (Richard), 1 da (Fiona); *Career* ordained 1971; curate Holy Trinity Church Southport 1971–73; asst chaplain: Mersey Mission to Seamen 1973–75, RAF Coll Cranwell 1975–76; chaplain: RAF Odiham 1976–78, RAF Finningley 1978–80, RAF(H) Wegberg 1980–82, sMOD 1982–85, RAF Akrotiri 1985–88, RAF Lyneham 1988–91, RAF Locking 1991–93, RAF(H) Wroughton 1993–95; Anglican chaplain HQ AFCENT 1995–98, cmd chaplain HQLC 1998–99, dir (policy and plans) HQPTC 1999–2001, Chaplain in Chief RAF 2001–; memb Gen Synod C of E; *Recreations* theatre, travel, books (old and new), stamps (definitely old), wine, Jaguar and Alfa Romeo cars, being a grandfather; *Style*— The Ven R D Hesketh, CB, QHC; ✉ Ministry of Defence, Chaplaincy Services (RAF), RAF Innsworth, Gloucester GL3 1EZ (tel 01452 712612, fax 01452 510828)

HESKETH, 3 Baron (UK 1935); Sir Thomas Alexander Fermor-Hesketh; 10 Bt (GB 1761), KBE (1997), PC (1991); s of 2 Baron Hesketh (d 1955), and Dowager Lady Hesketh; *b* 28 October 1950; *Educ* Ampleforth; *m* 1977, Hon Claire, da of 3 Baron Manton; 1 s, 2 da; *Heir* s, Hon Frederick Fermor-Hesketh; *Career* a govt whip House of Lords 1986–91, Parly under sec of state DOE 1989–90, min of state DTI 1990–91, Capt Hon Corps of Gentlemen-at-Arms (govt chief whip House of Lords) 1991–93; exec chm British Mediterranean Airways 1994–; non-exec dir: Babcock International Gp plc 1993– (dep chm 1996–), British Aerospace plc 1993–; Hon FSE 1979; *Clubs* Turf, White's, Beefsteak; *Style*— The Rt Hon the Lord Hesketh, KBE, PC; ✉ Easton Neston, Towcester, Northamptonshire NN12 7HS (tel 01327 350969, fax 01327 358534)

HESKIA, Samantha; da of Mansour Heskia, and Patricia Heskia; *Educ* Francis Holland Sch, Chelsea Sch of Art; *Career* designer; Ofner Associates 1991–93 (projects incl Boeing 757 private aircraft); set up own accessories business 1995, collection designer Debenhams plc 1999–; work featured in The Handbag by Carmel Allen (1999); asst art dir on British films incl Second Best and Princess Caraboo 1993–2003; costume asst: Love Actually 2003, Ferrero Rocher commercial; patron Gilda's Club, patron Red Cross; memb Guild of Master Craftsmen 1998; *Recreations* playing the piano, Far Eastern travel, tennis, yoga; *Style*— Miss Samantha Heskia; ✉ 53A Moreton Street, London SW1V 2NY (tel 020 7931 7604, e-mail enq@samanthaheskia.co.uk, website www.samanthaheskia.com)

HESLOP, Martin Sydney; QC (1995); s of Sydney Heslop, and Patricia Mary, *née* Day; *b* 6 August 1948; *Educ* St George's Coll Weybridge, Univ of Bristol; *m* 11 March 1994, Aurea Jane (Jenny), *née* Boyle; *Career* called to the Bar Lincoln's Inn 1972, first jr Treasy counsel Central Criminal Court 1992 (jr Treasy counsel 1987), sr Treasy counsel Central Criminal Court and recorder of the Crown Court 1993– (asst recorder 1989–93); *Recreations* sailing, travel, photography, swimming, wine and food, sport generally; *Clubs* Royal London Yacht, Bar Yacht; *Style*— Martin Heslop, Esq, QC; ✉ 2 Hare Court, Temple, London EC4Y 7BE (tel 020 7353 5324, fax 020 7353 0667)

HESLOP, Sean Martin; s of Roy Heslop (d 1990), and Eileen Carroll; *b* 31 October 1967, Huntingdon, Cambs; *Educ* Neale Wade Community Coll March, Queens' Coll Cambridge (MA), KCL (PGCE), Inst of Educn London (MA), London Leadership Centre (NPQH); *m* 6 Aug 2005, Céline Gagnon; *Career* English teacher Queen Elizabeth's Sch Barnet 1994–97, head of English St Olave's GS Orpington 1997–2000, dep head Ravens Wood Sch Bromley 2000–04, headteacher Tiffin Sch Kingston upon Thames 2004–; research assoc Nat Coll of Sch Leadership; *Publications* The Challenge of Change: The effect on knowledge capital and social capital in times of turbulence (2005); *Recreations* walking, reading, wine; *Style*— Sean Heslop, Esq; ✉ Tiffin School, Queen Elizabeth Road, Kingston upon Thames, Surrey KT2 6RL

HESS, Nigel John; s of John Hess, of Weston-super-Mare, Somerset, and Sheila, *née* Merrick; *b* 22 July 1953; *Educ* Weston-super-Mare GS for Boys, St Catharine's Coll Cambridge (MA); *m* 1996, Lisa Claire, da of Raymond Telford; 1 da (Alice Elizabeth b 31 Aug 1990); *Career* composer for TV, theatre and film; music scores for TV incl: A Woman of Substance, Vanity Fair, Campion, Summer's Lease (TV and Radio Industries Club Award for Best TV Theme), Testament (Novello Award for Best TV Theme), Titmuss Regained, Maigret, Wycliffe, Just William, Dangerfield, Hetty Wainthropp Investigates (Novello Award for Best TV Theme); film scores incl Ladies in Lavender (nominated Classical Brit Award 2005); co-music dir and house composer RSC 1981–85; contrib music scores to 20 RSC prodns incl: Troilus and Cressida, Much Ado About Nothing, Julius Caesar, Cyrano de Bergerac (NY Drama Desk Award for Outstanding Music in a Play on Broadway), Comedy of Errors, Hamlet, Love's Labour's Lost, Othello, The Winter's Tale, The Swan Down Gloves, A Christmas Carol, Twelfth Night; West End prodns incl The Secret of Sherlock Holmes; composer many chamber vocal and orchestral pieces incl Piano Concerto (cmmnd by HRH The Prince of Wales); commercial recordings incl: TV Themes (television compilation), The Winds of Power (works for Symphonic Wind

Band), Chameleon (MRA award for Best MOR Album); *Recreations* travel and photography; *Clubs* Br Acad of Composers and Songwriters; *Style*— Nigel Hess, Esq; ✉ c/o Bucks Music Ltd, 11 Uxbridge Street, London W8 7TQ (tel 020 7221 4275, fax 020 7229 6893, e-mail nigel@myramusic.co.uk)

HESSAYON, Dr David Gerald; OBE (2007); s of Jack Hessayon (d 1958), and Lena Hessayon (d 1933); *b* 13 February 1928; *Educ* Univ of Leeds, Univ of Manchester; *m* 1951, Joan Parker (d 2001), da of Weeden T Gray, of USA; 2 da; *Career* chm: Turbair 1970–93, Pan Britannica Industries Ltd 1972–93, pbi Publications 1988–93, Expert Publications 1988–, Hessayon Books Ltd 1993–; dir Orion Publishing Group 1992–93; chm Br Agrochemicals Assoc 1980–81; Lifetime Achievement Trophy Nat British Book Awards 1992, Veitch Gold Meml Medal RHS 1992, Lifetime Achievement Award Garden Writers Guild 2005; vice-patron Royal Nat Rose Soc, hon vice-pres Capel Manor; Freeman City of London, memb Worshipful Co of Gardeners; *Books* The Tree and Shrub Expert, The Armchair Book of the Garden, The Indoor Plant Spotter, The Garden Expert, The Home Expert, The Gold Plated House Plant Expert, Rose Jotter, House Plant Jotter, Vegetable Jotter, Be Your Own Greenhouse Expert, The Bio Friendly Gardening Guide, The Fruit Expert, The House Plant Expert, The Garden DIY Expert, The Rock and Water Garden Expert, The Greenhouse Expert, The Flowering Shrub Expert, The Flower Arranging Expert, The Container Expert, The Bulb Expert, The Easy-care Gardening Expert, The Bedding Plant Expert, The Rose Expert, The Lawn Expert, The Vegetable and Herb Expert, The Evergreen Expert, The Flower Expert, The Pocket Flower Expert, The Pocket Tree and Shrub Expert, The Pocket Garden Troubles Expert, The Pocket House Plant Expert, The Pocket Vegetable Expert, The Home DIY Expert, The Garden Revival Expert, The House Plant Expert: Book Two, The Pest and Weed Expert; *Recreations* Times crossword, river cruising; *Style*— Dr David Hessayon, OBE; ✉ c/o Transworld Publishers Ltd, 61–63 Uxbridge Road, London W5 5SA (tel 020 8579 2652, fax 020 8231 6666)

HESTER, Stephen A M; *b* 14 December 1960; *Educ* Univ of Oxford (MA); *Career* Credit Suisse First Boston: joined 1982, co-head European Investment Banking 1993–96, memb Exec Bd 1996, chief financial offr 1996–2000, head Fixed Invome Div 2000–01; Abbey National plc: finance dir 2002–03, chief operating offr 2003–04; ceo British Land Company plc 2004–; *Style*— Stephen Hester, Esq

HETHERINGTON, John William; s of John Albert Hetherington, of Doncaster, S Yorks, and Eva Mary, *née* Reed; *b* 9 July 1951; *Educ* Sir Percy Jackson GS Doncaster, Univ of Birmingham Med Sch (MB ChB); *m* 9 Jan 1991, Kim, *née* Dawes; *Career* house surgn Birmingham Gen Hosp 1974–75, house physician Dudley Rd Hosp Birmingham 1975, SHO (orthopaedics) Nottingham Gen Hosp 1975–76 (concurrently anatomy demonstrator Nottingham Med Sch), surgical trg scheme United Birmingham Hosps 1976–81, registrar in paediatric urology Alder Hay Children's Hosp Liverpool 1981–92, univ tutor in urology St James's Univ Hosp Leeds 1982–85, research fell in prostate cancer Unit for Cancer Research Univ of Leeds 1985–86, sr registrar in urology St Mary's Hosp London 1986–87, lectr and sr registrar in urology Charing Cross Hosp London 1987–88, sr registrar in urology Royal Marsden Hosp London 1988–89, conslt and head Dept of Urology Castle Hill Hosp Cottingham 1989– (clinical co-ordinator for urology 1993–); chm: Yorks Urological Cancer Research Gp 1991–95, Humber & East Coast Urology Cancer Network; memb: Genito-Urinary Gp European Orgn for the Research and Treatment of Cancer (EORTC) 1989–, MRC Superficial Bladder Cancer Working Pty 1991–2001, Yorks Urology Trg Ctee 1992–2001, Med Advsy Gp Yorkshire Cancer Orgn 1995–2000, Scientific Ctee Br Prostate Gp 1996–2002; author of numerous articles in urological jls; cmmnd RAMC (TA) 202 Gen Hosp Birmingham 1978–1992; memb: BMA, Br Prostate Gp 1985, EORTC 1989; FRCS 1979, FRCSEd 1979; *Recreations* fell walking, photography; *Style*— John Hetherington, Esq; ✉ Department of Urology, Castle Hill Hospital, Cottingham, East Yorkshire HU16 5JQ (tel 01482 860412, fax 01482 860130)

HETTIARATCHY, Dr Pearl Daisy Jebaranee; OBE (2002); da of Solomon Vinnasitamby Muttiah (d 1952), and Grace Constance Manonmanie, *née* Sittampalam (d 1977); *b* 4 February 1942; *Educ* Holy Family Convent Bambalipittya Sri Lanka, Univ of Colombo Sri Lanka (MB BS), Univ of London (DPM); *m* 2 Jan 1967, Dr Sidney Walter Hettiaratchy, s of Cornelius Peter Hettiaratchy; 2 da (Ashanti Suvendrini (Mrs Dickson) b 25 Jan 1968, Chemaine Natasha (Mrs Bravery) b 25 May 1975), 1 s (Dr Shehan Peter Hettiaratchy b 5 Nov 1969); *Career* pre-registration Kandy Gen Hosp Sri Lanka 1965–66, women's med offr Akurana Sri Lanka 1966–68; conslt psychiatrist (old age psychiatry): St James' Hosp Portsmouth 1975–84 (trg in psychiatry 1968–75), Winchester and Eastleigh Healthcare NHS Tst (formerly Winchester DHA) 1984–2001, W Hampshire Tst 2001–02 (now emeritus); clinical teacher Univ of Southampton 1985–2002, memb Exec Ctee Age Concern Hampshire 1985–93, Mental Health Act cmmr (Sec of State appt) 1989–98, second opinion appt dr (Sec of State appt) 1989–2003 and 2005–; hon conslt St Luke's Hosp for the Clergy London 1990–2003, selector Med Faculty Univ of Southampton 1990–94, conslt advsr Samaritans Winchester and Dist Branch 1990–2002; RCPsych: memb Special Ctee on Unethical Psychiatric Practice 1990–94, vice-pres 1995–97, memb Mental Health Law Sub-Ctee 2000–01, College rep for Southern Region for High Awards 1999–2001; assoc memb GMC 2003– (screener for conduct and performance, memb Overseas Review Bd, Ctee on Professional Performance, and Race Equality and Diversity Ctee, elected memb 1994–2003); memb Mental Health Review Tbnl (Lord Chllr's appt) 1994–; vice patron BASE (Br Assoc for Services to the Elderly) 2006–; postgrad dean's rep Wessex Deanery 2002–07; memb: BMA, Southern Region Awards Ctee 1997–2000; Hon FRCPsych 2003 (FRCPsych 1986, MRCPsych 1972); *Publications* Care in the Community (contrib chapter, 1982), Psychotherapy Supporting the Carers of Mentally Ill People (contrib chapter, 1992), International Review of Psychiatry (contrib chapter, 1993), Clinical Governance in Mental Health and Learning Disabilities, a practical guide (contrib chapter, 2005); *Recreations* gardening, religious music, spending time with my children and grandchildren; *Style*— Dr Pearl Hettiaratchy, OBE, FRCPsych; ✉ Robin's Hill, 2 Oliver's Battery Road North, Winchester, Hampshire SO22 4JA (tel 01962 861287, e-mail pearlhet@globalnet.co.uk)

HEUMANN, Andreas Carl Manuel; s of Rainer Heumann; *b* 17 April 1946, Germany; *Educ* Switzerland; *m* Philippa Ramsay; 1 da (Marina b 11 Aug 1992); *Career* photographer; early career as apprentice block-maker and printer, subsequent fashion assignments for Stern, Vogue, Twen, Harpers, etc London, currently serving advtg indust; one-man exhbns incl: Photographers Gallery London, Hamiltons Gallery London, Special Photographers Co London, Assoc of Photographers Gallery London, K61 Gallerie Amsterdam, Royal Photographic Soc Bath; awards incl: Gold (Art Dirs Club of NY) 1988, Silver (Art Dirs Club of Switzerland) 1990, Silver (Art Dirs Club of France) 1990, Gold and 5 Silvers (Campaign Press Awards) 1991, 6 Golds, 6 Silvers and 16 Merits (Assoc of Photographers) since 1983 (judge 1990 Awards), Fine Art Photography category winner (World Image Awards USA) 1992, Gold for best advtg picture (Art Dir Club Italy) 1993, merit award (New York Art Directors Club) 1994, Agfa Picture of the Year award 1994, finalist (John Kobal portrait award) 1995, Gold & Silver Award Cannes Advertising Festival 1998; work in the collections of V&A, Kodak's Museum of Photography Rochester USA, and in numerous private collections; *Style*— Andreas Heumann, Esq; ✉ Unit 2F, Woodstock Studios, 36 Woodstock Grove, London W12 8LE (website www.andreas-heumann.com)

HEUVEL, Christopher John; s of Desmond John Heuvel, of Lower Earley, and Joan Margaret, *née* Hooper; *b* 22 October 1953; *Educ* Douai Sch Woolhampton, Univ of Newcastle upon Tyne (BA, BArch), Poly of Central London (DipTP), Huddersfield Poly (CertEd), Anglia Poly Univ (DMS, MBA); *m* 7 March 1986, Diana Crystal, da of James William Joseph Collis (d 1981), of Ipswich; 1 s (Benjamin b 1985), 1 da (Beatrice b 1986); *Career* architect and planning conslt; princ in one-man private practice 1980–98, princ architect Carter Design Gp 1999–2004, assoc LSI Architects LLP 2005–; sr lectr in environmental science City Coll Norwich 1985–98; memb Cncl RIBA; FRSA 1994; *Recreations* the arts, landscape; *Clubs* RIBA, Norfolk Punt; *Style*— Christopher J Heuvel, Esq; ✉ Chris Heuvel Architect, 9 Earlham Road, Norwich NR2 3RA (tel 01603 629746, e-mail bircham.house@btinternet.com)

HEWER, Prof Richard Langton; s of Dr Christopher Langton Hewer (d 1986), of London, and Doris Phoebe, *née* Champney (d 1978); *b* 29 March 1930; *Educ* St Lawrence Coll Ramsgate, Bart's Univ of London (MB BS); *m* 21 June 1958, Jane Ann, da of Robert Wotherspoon, of St Helens, Lancs; 2 da (Marian Jane b 19 April 1961, Sarah Ann b 21 Jan 1965), 1 s (Simon Christopher b 9 Nov 1962); *Career* Nat Serv, RAF; chief asst Professorial Neurology Unit Oxford 1965–68, conslt neurologist Bristol 1968–95; Univ of Bristol: prof of neurology 1990–, sr research fell Dept of Social Med 1995–; fndr chm: Friedreich's Ataxia Gp 1963–75, Bristol Stroke Fndn 1983–; fndr and dir Experimental Stroke Res Unit 1975, sec and chm RCP Disability Ctee 1978–92, chm Bristol Stroke Fndn 1981–, memb Cncl Assoc of Br Neurologists 1987–91 (1981–84), chm Assoc of Br Neurologists' Serv (Policy) Ctee 1983–, sec Working Gp on Physical Disability RCP 1986, chm Med Disability Soc 1986–88, pres Bristol Medico-Chirurgical Soc 1990–91; memb: World Fedn of Neurology, Med Disability Soc, Soc for Res in Rehabilitation, Chest Heart and Stroke Assoc; FRSM, FRCP; *Books* Stroke - A Critical Approach to Diagnosis Treatment and Management (jtly, 1985), Stroke - A Guide to Recovery (with D T Wade, 1986), Modern Medicine (ed, 1975, 1979, 1983), The Oxford Companion to the Mind (1987), Rehabilitation of the Physically Disabled Adults (1988), More Dilemmas in the Management of the Neurological Patient (1987), The Management of Motor Neurone Disease (1987), The Stroke Recovery Plan (with D T Wade, 1996); *Recreations* sailing, walking; *Style*— Prof Richard Langton Hewer; ✉ Three Gables, Valley Road, Leigh Woods, Bristol BS8 3PZ (tel 0117 973 2110, fax 0117 973 0071, e-mail litfieldhouse@dial.pipex.com, website www.tdla.co.uk/langtonhewer)

HEWINS, John Francis; s of late John Hewins, and Gladys Maud, *née* Van Mierlo; *b* 19 March 1936; *Educ* Mount St Mary's Coll; *m* 20 Oct 1964, Valerie, da of late John Fife Mortimer; 2 da (Natalie Brigid b 2 May 1966, Frances Camille b 2 Jan 1968), 1 s (Dominic John b 12 July 1969); *Career* Nat Serv; student apprentice Davy United 1953, md Davy McKee Sheffield 1988 (sales dir 1977, gen mangr 1983, md 1983–90); exec vice-chm S York Supertram 1992–94; dir Hallamshire Investments 1990–95, chm Mechtech International 1992–95, dir Eurolube AB; chm and md: Ernest H Hill Ltd, Nesthill Ltd, Watsons, Name Plates Ltd; Freeman Cutlers' Co in Hallamshire; FRSA; *Recreations* garden, mediocre tennis, remote trekking, walking, sailing; *Style*— John Hewins, Esq; ✉ The Homestead, Nether Shatton, Bamford, Hope Valley, Derbyshire S33 0BG (tel 01433 651201, e-mail john.hewins@hillpumps.com or john@hewins.net)

HEWISH, Prof Antony; s of Ernest William Hewish (d 1975), and Francis Grace Lanyon, *née* Pinch (d 1970); *b* 11 May 1924; *Educ* King's Coll Taunton, Gonville & Caius Coll Cambridge (MA, PhD); *m* 19 Aug 1950, Marjorie Elizabeth Catherine, da of Edgar Richards (d 1954); 1 da (Jennifer b 1954 d 2004), 1 s (Nicholas b 1956); *Career* RAE Farnborough 1943–46; Univ of Cambridge: res fell Gonville & Caius Coll 1952–54 (hon fell 1976–), asst dir of res 1954–62, fell Churchill Coll 1961–, lectr in physics 1962–69, reader 1969–71, prof of radioastronomy 1971–89 (now emeritus prof); discovered pulsars (with S J Bell-Burnell) 1967; Nobel Prize for Physics (with M Ryle) 1974, Hughes medal Royal Soc 1974; prof of astronomy Royal Instn 1977–81, dir Mullard Radio Astronomy Observatory 1982–87; churchwarden Kingston Parish Church Cambridge; Hon DSc: Univ of Leicester 1976, Univ of Exeter 1977, Univ of Manchester 1989, Santa Maria Univ Brazil 1989, Univ of Cambridge 1996, Univ of Malaysia 1997; foreign hon memb American Acad of Arts and Scis, foreign fell Indian Nat Sci Acad 1982, hon fell Tata Inst of Fundamental Sci Bombay 1996, hon fell Inst of Electronics and Telecommunication Engrs Delhi 1985; hon citizen Kwangju S Korea 1995; memb: Belgian Royal Acad 1990, Academia Europaea 1993; FRS 1968; *Publications* author of numerous papers in scientific jls; *Recreations* music, cliff walking, gardening; *Style*— Prof Antony Hewish, FRS; ✉ Pryor's Cottage, Field Road, Kingston, Cambridge CB23 7NQ (tel 01223 262657); Cavendish Laboratory, Madingley Road, Cambridge CB3 0HE (tel 01223 337299, fax 01223 354599, e-mail ah120@mrao.cam.ac.uk)

HEWITT, Anthony Ronald; s of Ronald Berwick Hewitt (d 1995), and Phyllis Lavina, *née* Tammadge (d 1992); *b* 9 May 1949; *Educ* St Albans GS, BRNC Dartmouth, RNC Greenwich, Open Univ (BA); *m* 11 Nov 1978 (m dis 2001), Felicity Heather, da of Roy Chalice Orford, CBE, of Budleigh Salterton, Devon; 2 s (Richard b 1980, Edward b 1987), 2 da (Penelope b 1981, Deborah b 1984); *Career* cmmnd serv RN 1968–88: Robert Roxburgh prize 1971, Ronald Megaw prize 1972, submarine cmdg offr's course 1979, submarine tactics and weapons gp 1981–83, exec offr HMS Churchill 1980, HMS Revenge 1983–86, Directorate of Naval Warfare MOD 1986–88; sec Cable Authy 1989–90, dep sec Ind TV Cmmn 1991–96, dep dir cable Ind TV Cmmn 1996–2001, dir IOM Communications Cmmn 2001–; conslt advsr Cncl of Europe Directorate of Human Rights (media legislation) 1999–; ICSA Ralph Bell prize 1989; Freeman City of London 1992, Liveryman Worshipful Co of Chartered Secs and Administrators; MCMI (MIMgt 1988), FCIS 1990; *Publications* Telecommunications Law (contrib, 1997); author of various articles on broadcasting and telecommunications in professional jls; *Recreations* music, gardening, walking, kite flying; *Clubs* IOM Yacht, Erin Arts; *Style*— Anthony Hewitt, Esq; ✉ Communications Commission, Salisbury House, Victoria Street, Douglas, Isle of Man IM1 2LW (tel 01624 677022, fax 01624 626499, e-mail anthony.hewitt@cc.gov.im)

HEWITT, Charles Edward James; s of Sir Nicholas Hewitt, 3 Bt, *qv*, and Pamela, *née* Hunt; *Educ* Rugby (received Sword of Honour as CCF senior cadet, 1st XV), Kingston Business Sch; *m* 18 May 2002, Alison Brown; *Career* account mangr Riley Advtg 1993–96; Pen & Sword Books Ltd: publishing mangr 1996–98, chief exec 1998–99, md 1999–; dir Tours With Experts Ltd 2000–; memb Young Newspaper Persons Executives Assoc (YNA) 1996; MInstD 1999; *Recreations* pigeon racing, Barnsley FC supporter; *Style*— Charles Hewitt, Esq; ✉ Rose Cottage, Huttons Ambo, York YO60 7HF; Pen & Sword Books Ltd, 47 Church Street, Barnsley, South Yorkshire S70 2AS (tel 01226 734222, fax 01226 734438, e-mail charles@pen-and-sword.co.uk)

HEWITT, Christopher; s of His Hon Harold Hewitt, of Corbridge, Northumberland, and Doris Mary, *née* Smith (d 2002); *b* 16 September 1947, Darlington, N Yorks; *Educ* Sedburgh, Univ of Newcastle upon Tyne (LLB); *m* 1, 1972; 2 s (Benjamin b 3 Sept 1978, Jonathan b 22 April 1982); m 2, 22 Oct 2005, Annette Marilyn, *née* Robson; *Career* admitted slr 1971; slr and ptnr in family firm 1973–87; Ward Hadaway: ptnr 1987–2004, conslt 2004–, head Countryside Farms and Estates Unit; advsr Central Assoc of Agric Valuers; *Recreations* hunting, the countryside; *Clubs* Northern Counties; *Style*— Christopher Hewitt, Esq; ✉ Brockley Hall, Longframlington, Northumberland NE65 8JG (tel 01665 570944); Ward Hadaway, Sandgate House, 102 Quayside, Newcastle upon Tyne NE1 3DX (tel 0191 402 4262, fax 0191 204 4110, e-mail christopher.hewitt@wardhadaway.com)

HEWITT, Ewan Christian; s of Dr Rupert Conrad Hewitt (d 1981), of Glenbeigh, Frinton-on-Sea, Essex, and Gladys Muriel, *née* Christian (d 1967); *b* 13 April 1928; *Educ* Wellington, Gonville & Caius Coll Cambridge (MA), Manchester Business Sch; *m* 1, 25

July 1959 (m dis 1973), Gaylor Margaret Joyce, da of Henry Fraeke, of Westerham, Kent; m 2, 14 Dec 1973, Susan Mary, da of Donald James Maclachlan, of Hull, E Yorks; 2 da (Annabel Elizabeth Christina b 16 Sept 1974, Lucinda Katherine Mary b 11 March 1977); *Career* Nat Serv Royal Engrs 1946–48; apprentice Davy Paxman & Co Ltd Colchester 1949; Davy & United Engineering Co Ltd Sheffield: apprentice 1952–54, sales engr 1954–56, contract mangr Durgapur Steelworks Project 1956–57, sr sales engr 1957–59, liaison engr Pittsburgh PA 1959–60, asst chief engr Proposals 1961–64, tech sales mangr 1964–67, tech asst to MD 1967–68; tech dir: Davy Construction Co Sheffield 1971–72 (mangr tech services 1968–71), Davy Ashmore Ltd Stockton-on-Tees 1972–73, Davy-Loewy Ltd 1973–80, Davy McKee Ltd 1980–88 (dir tech mktg 1988–93); engrg conslt 1993–; Metals Soc/Inst of Materials: memb Engrg Ctee 1974–85, memb Iron and Steel Ctee 1975–98, memb Cncl 1981–87, memb Rolling Ctee 1989–2002; memb: Assoc of Iron and Steel Engrs USA 1959, Iron and Steel Inst Inst of Materials 1973; FIMechE 1976 (MIMechE 1954), FREng 1989; *Recreations* photography, fly fishing, bridge, gardening, walking, jazz record collection; *Style*— Ewan Hewitt, Esq, FREng; ✉ Orchard Close, East Street, Martock, Somerset TA12 6NF (tel 01935 822968)

HEWITT, Gavin James; s of Rev Thomas Hewitt (d 1964), and Daffodil Anne, *née* Thorne; *Educ* St John's Sch Leatherhead, Univ of Durham (BA); *m* 1972, Sally Jane, da of Norman Lacey; 1 da (Rebecca Jane b 1978), 1 s (Daniel James b 1980); *Career* reporter BBC TV News 1976–81, corr The Journal (CBC Canada) and documentary maker McNeil-Lehrer Newshour USA 1981–84, corr Panorama (BBC1) 1985–98, special corr BBC News 1999–; *Awards* Broadcast Award 2001, RTS Award 2002; *Books* Terry Waite and Oliver North (1991); *Style*— Gavin Hewitt, Esq; ✉ BBC Television Centre (e-mail gavin.hewitt@bbc.co.uk)

HEWITT, Gavin Wallace; CMG (1995); s of Rev George Burrill Hewitt, TD, FEIS (d 1976), and Elisabeth Murray, *née* Wallace (d 1976); *b* 19 October 1944; *Educ* George Watson's Coll Edinburgh, Univ of Edinburgh (MA); *m* 6 Oct 1973, Heather Mary, da of Trevor Shaw Clayton, of Whaley Bridge, Derbys; 2 da (Claire Rebecca b 20 March 1975, Mary Elisabeth Courtney b 29 Sept 1979), 2 s (Alexander Francis Reid b 3 Nov 1977, Peter James Clayton b 26 Jan 1982); *Career* asst princ Miny of Tport 1967–70, second sec UK delegation to the Euro Communities Brussels 1970–72, first sec Br High Cmmn Canberra 1973–78, first sec and head of Chancery Br Embassy Belgrade 1981–84, dep permanent rep UK mission UN Geneva 1987–92, cnsllr FCO 1992–94; ambass: Croatia 1994–97, Finland 1997–2000, Belgium 2001–03; chief exec Scotch Whisky Assoc 2003–, dir Spirits Energy Efficiency Co 2003–; memb: CBI Trade Assoc Cncl, Scottish Cncl for Devpt and Industry; vice-chm Bd of Govrs Geneva English Sch 1989–92, patron Br Sch of Brussels 2001–03; *Style*— Gavin Hewitt, Esq, CMG; ✉ The Scotch Whisky Association, 20 Atholl Crescent, Edinburgh EH3 8HF (tel 0131 222 9200, fax 0131 222 9203, e-mail ghewitt@swa.org.uk)

HEWITT, Prof Geoffrey Frederick (Geoff); s of Frederick Hewitt (d 1961), and Elaine, *née* Ellam (d 1975); *b* 3 January 1934; *Educ* Boteler GS, UMIST (BScTech, PhD); *m* 11 Aug 1956, Shirley Hodges, da of Stanley Foulds; 2 da (Karen Louise b 4 April 1958, Alison Jane b 29 Oct 1959); *Career* scientist UKAEA Harwell 1957–90 (div head 1976); fndr and head Heat Transfer and Fluid Flow Service 1968–82; pres: Heat Transfer Soc 1977 and 2000, Inst of Chem Engrs 1989; Courtaulds prof of chem engrg Imperial Coll London 1985–99 (emeritus prof 1999–); foreign assoc US Nat Acad of Engrg 1998; Hon DSc Univ of Louvain, Hon DEng Heriot-Watt Univ 1995, Hon DEng UMIST 1998; FIChemE, FRSC, FIMechE, FCGI, FREng 1985, FRS 1989; *Awards* Donald Q Kern award American Inst of Chem Engrs 1981; Int Centre for Heat and Mass Transfer: fellowship award 1982, Cncl medal Inst of Chem Engrs 1984, Luikov Medal 1996, Arnold Greene Medal Inst of Chem Engrs 2000; Max Jacob award American Soc of Mechanical Engrs 1994, Nusselt-Reynolds Prize 1997; *Books* Annular Two-Phase Flow (with N S Hall Taylor, 1970), Measurement of Two-Phase Flow Parameters (1978), Two-Phase Flow and Heat Transfer in the Power and Process Industries (with J G Collier, A E Bergles, J M Delhaye and F Mayinger, 1981), Introduction to Nuclear Power (with J G Collier, 1987), Process Heat Transfer (with G L Shires and T R Bott, 1994), Encyclopedia of Heat and Mass Transfer (1998); *Recreations* music, bridge; *Style*— Prof Geoffrey Hewitt, FRS, FREng; ✉ Department of Chemical Engineering, Imperial College London, Prince Consort Road, London SW7 2BY (tel 020 7594 5562, fax 020 7594 5564, e-mail g.hewitt@imperial.ac.uk)

HEWITT, Prof (Brian) George; s of Thomas Douglas Hewitt (d 1991), and Joan, *née* Cousins (d 1991); *b* 11 November 1949; *Educ* Doncaster GS for Boys, St John's Coll Cambridge (open Henry Arthur Thomas scholarship, John Stewart of Rannoch univ scholarship, coll Graves' Prize, MA, Warr classical studentship, Dip Linguistics, PhD, Br Cncl exchange postgrad (to Tbilisi), Marjory Wardrop scholarship); *m* 1976, Zaira Kiazimovna, *née* Khiba; 2 c (Amra Shukia b 18 Nov 1977, Gunda Amza-Natia b 2 Sept 1984); *Career* lectr in linguistics Univ of Hull 1981–88; SOAS Univ of London: lectr in linguistics and Caucasian languages 1988–92, reader in Caucasian languages 1992–96, prof of Caucasian languages 1996–; first pres Societas Caucasologica Europaea 1986–88 and 1988–90, memb Philological Soc 1973–; memb Bd of Mgmnt Marjory Wardrop Fund 1983–; one-time tstee: North Caucasus Tst (NCT), Med Aid and Relief for the Children of Chechnya (MARCCH); memb Writers' Union of Abkhazia 2003; hon memb: Int Circassian Acad of Sciences 1997, Acad of Sciences of Abkhazia 1997; hon prof Abkhazia State Univ 1995; FBA 1997; *Books* Lingua Descriptive Studies 2: Abkhaz (1979), Typology of Subordination in Georgian and Abkhaz (1987), Georgian - A Learner's Grammar (1995, 2 edn 2005), Structural Reference Grammar of Georgian (1995), A Georgian Reader (1996), An Abkhaz Newspaper Reader (with Zaira Khiba, 1998), The Abkhazians - A Handbook (ed, 1998), The Languages of the Caucasus - Scope for Study and Survival (1998), Introduction to the Study of the Languages of the Caucasus (2004), Abkhaz Folk-tales (2005); *Recreations* classical music, growing fuchsias; *Style*— Prof George Hewitt; ✉ School of Oriental and African Studies, Thornhaugh Street, Russell Square, London WC1H 0XG (tel 020 7898 4332, fax 020 7436 3859, e-mail gh2@soas.ac.uk)

HEWITT, Prof Godfrey Matthew; s of Horace John Hewitt (d 1997), of Hereford and Worcester, and Violet May, *née* Hann (d 1989); *b* 10 January 1940; *Educ* Worcester Cathedral King's Sch, Univ of Birmingham (BSc, PhD, DSc); *m* 23 June 1963 (m dis 1982), Elizabeth June, da of Ivor Cecil Shattock, of Taunton, Somerset; 3 s (Daniel John b 14 July 1965, Matthew Alexander b 27 March 1967, James Justin b 20 May 1968); *Career* Fulbright fell Univ of Calif 1965–66; visiting fell: Gulbenkian Fndn Lisbon 1970, ANU Canberra 1973–74, Univ of Hawaii 1979; prof UEA 1988– (lectr 1966–75, reader 1975–88); visiting prof Univ of Rome 1999, hon prof Chinese Acad of Sci 2001–; numerous pubns in learned sci jls; Prize for Molecular Ecology 2005, Nature-NESTA Award for Creative Mentoring in Science 2006; memb: SERC Ctee, NERC Ctee, EC Biotech Ctee, Genetical Soc, Soc Study of Evolution, Euro Soc of Evolution (pres 1998–); FIBiol 1975, FRES 1980, FLS 1987; *Books* Animal Cytogenetics-Grasshoppers and Crickets (1979), Insect Cytogenetics (1981), Molecular Techniques in Taxonomy (1991), Genes in Ecology (1991); *Recreations* alpine hiking, jazz, running, poetry, cooking; *Style*— Prof Godfrey Hewitt; ✉ 25 Camberley Road, Norwich NR4 6SJ (tel 01603 458142); School of Biological Sciences, University of East Anglia, Norwich NR4 7TJ (tel 01603 456161, fax 01603 592250, e-mail g.hewitt@uea.ac.uk)

HEWITT, Jamie Neil Terry; s of Peart Derek Hewitt, and Leanne, *née* Vallely; *b* 3 January 1959; *Educ* Rugby, City of London Poly (BA); *m* Roslyn Joyce, da of Thomas Russell Lennon; 2 da (Eleanor Joy b 21 July 1990, Madeleine Victoria b 3 Oct 1998), 1 s (Harry Moutray b 6 March 1992); *Career* articled clerk Peat Marwick Mitchell CAs 1980–83, co sec Zetland Advertising Ltd 1983–86, chief accountant Conran Design Group Ltd 1986–88; fin dir: Brewer Jones Ltd 1988–89, Butterfield Day Devito Hockney Ltd 1989–95, Collett Dickenson Pearce & Partners Ltd advtg agency 1995–97, McCann-Erickson Advertising Ltd 1997–2000, Hat Pin plc 2001–2003, WCRS Ltd 2003–04, M&C Saatchi UK 2004–; ACA 1983; *Recreations* rugby, running, dogs, riding in Richmond Park; *Style*— Jamie Hewitt, Esq; ✉ M&C Saatchi Ltd, 36 Golden Square, London W1F 9EE (tel 020 7543 4500)

HEWITT, Jeffrey Lindsay; s of Enoch Reginald Hewitt, of Stoke-on-Trent, Staffs, and Brenda Elizabeth, *née* Mason; *b* 6 September 1947; *Educ* Longton Sixth Form Coll Stoke-on-Trent, St Catherine's Coll Oxford (MA, Gibbs prize), Stanford Univ (MBA); *m* 6 July 1968, Pauline Margaret, da of Reginald Rezin; 1 s (Richard Lindsay b 11 Jan 1975), 1 da (Karen Faye b 9 March 1977); *Career* with: Arthur Andersen & Co 1969–72, The Boston Consulting Gp 1974–80; strategy dir Coats Viyella plc 1980–90, fin dir Unitech plc 1990–96, dep chm and fin dir Electrocomponents plc 1996–2005; chm Plasmon plc 2006–, dep chm Dialight plc 2001–; non-exec dir: Cookson Gp plc 2005–, John Lewis Partnership 2005–, TDG plc 2006–, Whatman plc 2007–; memb Industrial Devpt Advsy Bd 1985–95; memb Advsy Bd: Oxford Philomusica, Saïd Business Sch Univ of Oxford; ICAEW Gold Medal 1972; memb Ct of Assts Worshipful Co of Glovers; FCA 1974; *Recreations* theatre, concerts, tennis, antique maps; *Clubs* Royal Over-Seas League; *Style*— Jeffrey Hewitt, Esq; ✉ Palo Alto, 6 College Way, Northwood, Middlesex HA6 2BL (tel 01923 821190, fax 01923 821190, mobile 07767 887186)

HEWITT, Michael Geoffrey; s of Geoffrey Hewitt, of Bradmore, Wolverhampton, and Edna, *née* Sharples; *b* 6 September 1962; *Educ* Wolverhampton Sch, Univ of Stirling (BA); *m* 21 April 1990, Sara da of Ian Bryant; 1 s (Max b 17 April 1994), 2 da (Susanna b 21 May 1996, Matilda b 7 Jan 2000); *Career* ed The Publisher 1987–89, ed Journalist's Week 1989–91; Haymarket Publishing: ed Marketing 1993–96, publisher Marketing 1998–2000, Planning 1998–, new media dir Haymarket Business Publications Ltd 2000–03; publishing dir: World Business 2003–, Management Today 2003–; Freeman City of London 1993, Liveryman Worshipful Co of Stationers and Newspapermakers 1994; *Recreations* travel, books, military history, food; *Clubs* Arts, Royal Over-Seas League; *Style*— Michael Hewitt, Esq; ✉ Haymarket Business Publications Ltd, 174 Hammersmith Road, London W6 7JP (tel 020 7413 4270, fax 020 7413 4504)

HEWITT, Sir Nicholas Charles Joseph; 3 Bt (UK 1921), of Barnsley, West Riding, Co York; s of Maj Sir Joseph Hewitt, 2 Bt (d 1973), and Marguerite, *née* Burgess; *b* 12 November 1947; *m* 1969, Pamela Margaret, da of Geoffrey J M Hunt, TD, of Scalby, Scarborough; 2 s (Charles Edward James b 1970, Michael Joseph b 1973), 1 da (Victoria Alexandra Margaret b 1978); *Heir* s, Charles Hewitt; *Style*— Sir Nicholas Hewitt, Bt; ✉ Colswayn House, Huttons Ambo, York YO60 7HJ

HEWITT, Patricia Hope; PC (2001), MP; da of Sir (Cyrus) Lenox Simson Hewitt, OBE, of Sydney, Aust, and (Alison) Hope Hewitt; *b* 2 December 1948; *Educ* Girls' GS Canberra, Aust Nat Univ Canberra, Newnham Coll Cambridge (MA), Univ of Sydney (AMusA); *m* 1, 8 Aug 1970 (m dis 1978), (David) Julian Gibson-Watt, s of Baron Gibson-Watt (Life Peer, d 2002); m 2, 17 Dec 1981, His Hon Judge William Jack Birtles, *qv*, s of William George Birtles (d 1976), of Shepperton, Middx; 1 da (Alexandra b 1986), 1 s (Nicholas b 1988); *Career* gen sec NCCL 1974–83, policy coordinator to Ldr of the Opposition 1988–89 (press and broadcasting sec 1983–88), dep dir and sr res fell Inst for Public Policy Research 1989–94, dir of research Andersen Consulting (now Accenture) 1994–97; MP (Lab) Leicester W 1997–; economic sec to the Treasy 1998–99, min of state for e-commerce and small business DTI 1999–2001, sec of state for trade and industry 2001–05, sec of state for health 2005–07; assoc Newnham Coll Cambridge 1989–97, visiting fell Nuffield Coll Oxford; tstee Inst for Public Policy Research 1995–98; memb: Bd Int League for Human Rights 1979–1997, Sec of State's Advsy Ctee on the Employment of Women 1977–83, vice-chm Bd Br Cncl 1997–98; dep chair Cmmn for Social Justice 1992–94; Parly candidate Leicester East 1983; FRSA; *Books* The Abuse of Power: Civil Liberties in the United Kingdom (1983), Your Second Baby (with Wendy Rose-Neil, 1990), About Time: The Revolution in Work and Family Life (1993); *Recreations* gardening, music, theatre, cooking; *Style*— The Rt Hon Patricia Hewitt, MP; ✉ 1 Grand Floor Front, 5 Frog Island, Leicester LE3 5AG (tel 0116 251 6160, fax 0116 251 0482); House of Commons, London SW1A 0AA (e-mail hewittph@parliament.uk)

HEWITT, Dr Penelope Boulton; da of Leslie Frank Hewitt (d 1967), of Belmont, Surrey, and Beryl Boulton (d 1978); *b* 23 July 1938; *Educ* Sutton HS GPDST, Guy's Hosp, Univ of London (MB BS); *Career* res anaesthetist Guy's Hosp 1962–63; registrar in anaesthetics 1963–67: Nat Hosp for Nervous Diseases Queen Square London, St Mary's Hosp, Guy's Hosp; Guy's Hosp: sr registrar 1967–72, conslt anaesthetist 1972–2001, hon sr lectr in anaesthetics 1992–, emeritus conslt anaesthetist 2001–; recognised teacher in anaesthetics Univ of London 1974–2001; approved lectr: Central Midwives Bd 1979–83, English Nat Bd 1983–2001, combined Guy's and St Thomas' Hosp Schs of Midwifery, King's Coll 1994–2001; anaesthetics tutor Faculty of Anaesthetists RCS Guy's Hosp 1980–87, regnl assessor in anaesthetics for confidential enquiries into maternal deaths SE Thames Region Dept of Health 1981–2000, hon sec and treas SE Thames Soc of Anaesthetists 1984–87 (pres 1991–93), anaesthetic assessor confidential enquiry into perioperative deaths Nuffield Prov Hosp Tst 1985–87, examiner for fellowship examination of the Royal Coll of Anaesthetists 1986–97, examiner for European Dip in Anaesthesia and Intensive Care 1992–2003, chm OSCE Working Pty Royal Coll of Anaesthetists 1994–96, memb Cncl Anaesthetics Section RSM (hon sec 1987–89, pres elect 1996–97, pres 1997–98, immediate past pres 1998–99, vice-pres 1999–2002, membership offr 2001–04), hon life memb Assoc of Dental Anaesthetists 2002– (hon asst sec and ed of proceedings 1989–92, hon sec 1992–95, pres 1995–97), memb Cncl European Soc of Anaesthesiology 2005–06; examiner GMC 1997–; assoc ed European Jl of Anaesthesiology 2000–04; senator European Acad of Anaesthesiology 2001–05; hon memb Anaesthetic Research Soc 2002–; LRCP, MRCS, FFARCS (FRCA) 1966; *Books* Emergency Anaesthesia (1986, 2 edn 1998); *Recreations* golf, gardening; *Clubs* The Addington Golf; *Style*— Dr Penelope B Hewitt; ✉ Hillcrest, 150 Burdon Lane, Cheam, Sutton, Surrey SM2 7DQ (tel 020 8642 2993)

HEWITT, Peter John; s of Charles Rowland Hewitt (d 1993), and Eunice, *née* Nixon; *b* 17 November 1951; *Educ* Barnard Castle Sch, Univ of Leeds (BA, MA); *m* (sep), Joan, *née* Coventry; 3 da (Laura b 26 March 1978, Anna b 29 July 1980, Kate b 23 Jan 1984); *Career* Inter-Action Trust 1976–77, arts offr N Tyneside BC 1977–82; Northern Arts 1982–97: community arts and gen arts offr, asst dir Local Devpt, dep dir, chief exec 1992–97; corp affrs dir Tees HA 1997–98, chief exec Arts Cncl of England (latterly Arts Cncl England) 1998–; *Recreations* the arts, walking, Middlesbrough FC; *Style*— Peter Hewitt, Esq; ✉ Arts Council England, 14 Great Peter Street, London SW1P 3NQ (tel 020 7333 0100)

HEWITT, Peter William Hughes (Pete); s of David Claud Hughes Hewitt (d 1981), and Eileen Winifred, *née* Chambers; *b* 9 October 1962, Brighton, E Sussex; *Educ* Christ's Hosp, London Coll of Printing, Nat Film Sch; *m* 14 June 1994, Sophie Jane, da of George Ringrose (d 2003); 3 da (Molly Rose b 18 March 1992, Elsie Rose b 5 March 1996, Dora Unity Rose b 1 Jan 2001); *Career* filmmaker; feature films incl: Bill and Ted's Bogus Journey 1991, Tom and Huck 1995, The Borrowers 1997, Whatever Happened to Harold Smith 1999, Thunderpants 2001, Garfield 2004, Zoom 2006; TV incl: Wild Palms (miniseries, ABC US) 1992, Princess of Thieves (ABC US) 2000; BAFTA Award for Best Short Film (for The Candy Show) 1990; *Style*— Pete Hewitt; ✉ c/o MacCorkindale,

Alonso and Holton, PO Box 2398, London W1G 9WZ (tel 020 7636 1888, fax 020 7636 2888)

HEWLETT, David; *b* 2 October 1954; *Career* lecteur d'Anglais Univ of Montpellier 1978–80, regnl examiner Languedoc-Rousillon Univ of Cambridge 1978–80, researcher and lectr Univ of Cambridge 1981–86; with Dept of Social Security 1986–87, dep mangr Benefits Office Stoke Newington 1987–88, with Dept of Health 1988–90, head Family Health Servs Mgmnt Unit Dept of Health 1990–91; NHS Exec: head NHS Performance Mgmnt Central Unit 1991–93, head GP Fundholding and Prescribing 1993–95, head NHS Purchasing and Commissioning 1995–97, head NHS Quality Strategy 1997, head Health Servs Branch 1 1997–2000, head Specialist Health Servs 2000–; *Recreations* current affairs, modern lit, modern art, motorcycling; *Style*— David Hewlett, Esq; ✉ Specialist Health Services, Department of Health, Wellington House, 133–155 Waterloo Road, London SE1 8UG

HEWLETT, Hon Thomas Anthony; s of Baron Hewlett, CBE (Life Peer, d 1979), and Millicent, *née* Taylor (d 1991); *b* 31 March 1952; *Educ* Oundle, Magdalene Coll Cambridge (MA); *m* 2 Oct 1980, Jane Elizabeth, da of Brian A Dawson, of Aldeburgh, Suffolk; 2 da (Emily b 14 Feb 1983, Georgina b 24 July 1984), 2 s (Harry, Charles (twins) b 30 Dec 1986); *Career* dir: Anchor Chemical Gp plc 1976–88, V Berg & Sons Ltd 1986–91; vice-pres Morgan Guaranty Tst 1974–84; owner Portland Gallery 1985–; Freeman City of London, Liveryman Worshipful Co of Tin Plate Workers; *Books* Cadell - A Scottish Colourist (1988); *Recreations* golf, tennis; *Clubs* Garrick, Aldeburgh Golf, Royal St Georges Golf; *Style*— The Hon Thomas Hewlett; ✉ Kyson House, Woodbridge, Suffolk IP12 4DN (tel 0139438 3441); Portland Gallery, 8 Bennet Street, London SW1A 1RP

HEWSON, Paul; *see:* Bono

HEY, Prof John Denis; s of George Brian Hey (d 1991), of Adlington, Cheshire, and Elizabeth Hamilton, *née* Burns; *b* 26 September 1944; *Educ* Manchester Grammar, Univ of Cambridge (BA), Univ of Edinburgh (MSc); *m* 18 Oct 1968 (m dis 1998), Marlene Robertson, da of Thomas Bissett (d 1958), of Perth; 2 da (Clare b 1979, Rebecca b 1984), 1 s (Thomas b 1981); *Career* econometrician Hoare & Co Stockbrokers 1968–69; lectr in econs: Univ of Durham 1969–73, Univ of St Andrews 1974–75; Univ of York: lectr in social and econ statistics 1975–81, sr lectr 1981–84, prof of econs and statistics 1984–98 (part-time 1998), co-dir Centre for Experimental Econs 1986–; professore ordinario Universita di Bari Italy 1998–2006, professore ordinario LUISS Rome Italy 2006–; ed Economic Journal 1986–96, author of articles for numerous jls; memb: RES, AEA; *Books* Statistics in Economics (1974), Uncertainty in Microeconomics (1979), Britain in Context (1979), Economics in Disequilibrium (1981), Data in Doubt (1984), A Century of Economics (ed, 1990), Experiments in Economics (1991), Recent Developments in Experimental Economics (ed, 1993), The Economics of Risk and Uncertainty (ed, 1996), Intermediate Microeconomics (2003), Microeconomia (2007); *Recreations* cycling, walking, eating; *Style*— Prof John Hey; ✉ Department of Economics, University of York, York YO1 5DD (tel 01904 433786, fax 01904 433759, e-mail jdh1@york.ac.uk)

HEYER, Elizabeth Anne; da of Aubrey Thomas Heyer, of Reigate, Surrey, and Anne, *née* Arnott; *b* 3 June 1956; *Educ* Bishop Simpson Girls' Sch, Poly of Central London (BA), Inst of Health Serv Mangrs (Dip), Cranfield Univ (MBA); *ptnr* Martin Stewart Clyne Hunter; *Career* clerical offr Guy's Hosp London 1974–75, mgmnt trainee SW Thames RHA 1975–78, asst hosp admin Queen Mary's Hosp Sidcup 1978–81, asst hosp sec The London Hosp Whitechapel 1981–84, planning admin The Middx and UC Hosps London 1984–86, unit gen mangr of mental health and mental handicap servs Harrow Health Authy 1986–88, unit gen mangr then chief exec Harrow Community Health Servs NHS Tst 1988–94, chief exec Harrow and Hillingdon Healthcare NHS Tst 1994–97, chief exec Chase Farm Hosps NHS Tst 1997–; MHSM (prizewinner 1976), memb Stategic Planning Soc, Cranfield Mgmnt Assoc; *Recreations* Austin Healey cars, swimming, foreign travel; *Style*— Ms Elizabeth Heyer; ✉ Chase Farm Hospitals NHS Trust, The Ridgeway, Enfield, Middlesex EN2 8JL (tel 020 8366 9101)

HEYES, David; MP; *b* 2 April 1946, Manchester; *Educ* Blackley Tech HS, Open Univ; *Career* dep dist mangr Manchester CAB; cncllr (Lab) Oldham MBC 1992– (sec Lab Gp 1994–2000, chair Personnel Ctee 1994–2000), MP (Lab) Ashton-under-Lyne 2001–; vice-chair Ashton-under-Lyne Lab Pty; memb Unison; *Style*— David Heyes, Esq, MP; ✉ House of Commons, London SW1A 0AA

HEYGATE, Sir Richard John Gage; 6 Bt (UK 1831), of Southend, Essex; s of Sir John Edward Nourse Heygate, 4 Bt (d 1976), suc bro, Sir George Lloyd Heygate, 5 Bt (d 1991); *b* 30 January 1940; *Educ* Repton, Balliol Coll Oxford; *m* 1, 1968 (m dis 1972), Carol Rosemary, da of late Cdr Richard Michell, RN, of Amberley, W Sussex; m 2, 1974 (m dis 1988), Jong-Ja Hyun, da of In Suk, of Seoul, South Korea; 1 da (Eun-Hee Isobella Gage b 1977); m 3, 1988, Susan Fiona, da of late Robert Buckley, of Peasmarsh, E Sussex; 2 s (Frederick Carysfort Gage b 1988, Robert George Liam b 1991); *Heir* s, Frederick Heygate; *Career* IBM (United Kingdom) Ltd 1967–70, McKinsey & Co Inc 1970–77; dir: Olaf Foods Ltd 1977–85, Index Group 1985–87; princ McKinsey & Co Inc 1997–98, ceo Sophron Partners 1998–2005; chm: Mouse Smart Software 2004–, Birgate Partnership 2006–, Welford Technol Ptnrs 2006–; dir Isis Technology 1999–2001; *Style*— Sir Richard Heygate, Bt

HEYHOE FLINT, Rachael; MBE (1971), DL (W Midlands 1997); da of Geoffrey Heyhoe (d 1972), of Penn, Wolverhampton, and Roma Kathleen, *née* Crocker (d 1978); *b* 11 June 1939; *Educ* Wolverhampton Girls' HS, Dartford Coll of PE (DipPhysEd); *m* 1 Nov 1971, Derrick Flint, s of Benjamin Flint, of Underwood, Notts; 1 s (Benjamin b 8 June 1974); *Career* Women's Cricket Int England 1960–83, Capt 1966–77, scored 179 v Aust (Oval) 1976 (world record score for England, world's fifth highest score by woman in tests); Women's Hockey Int England 1964; journalist; PR conslt: La Manga Club Spain, Wolverhampton Wanderers FC; vice-pres Cricketers Club of London; PR dir Wolverhampton Wanderers FC, memb Bd Family Investments Ltd; hon life memb MCC (first lady appointed) 1999– (memb Mktg Ctee 2003–, memb Main Ctee 2004); pres Lady Taverners 2001–; Best After Dinner Speaker Guild of Professional Toastmasters 1972; hon fell Univ of Wolverhampton 2002, Hon DUniv Bradford 2002, Hon DSc Univ of Greenwich 2003; *Books* Fair Play, History of Women's Cricket (1976), Heyhoe (autobiography, 1978); *Recreations* golf; *Clubs* South Staffs Golf (Wolverhampton), La Manga Club Resort (Spain), Patshull Park Golf and Country (Wolverhampton); *Style*— Mrs Rachael Heyhoe Flint, MBE, DL; ✉ Danescroft, Wergs Road, Tettenhall, Wolverhampton, West Midlands WV6 9BN (fax 01902 756111)

HEYLIN, Angela Christine Mary (Mrs Maurice Minzly); OBE (1997); da of Bernard Heylin (d 1985), and Ruth Victoria, *née* D'Arcy (d 1997); *b* 17 September 1943; *Educ* Apsley GS, Watford Coll; *m* 13 March 1971, Maurice Minzly, s of Solomon Minzly (d 1974); 1 s (James b 1982); *Career* chief exec Charles Barker Lyons 1984 (formerly dir F J Lyons, dir 1976, jt md 1980), chm and chief exec Charles Barker Gp 1988 (dir 1984), chm Charles Barker BSMG (formerly Charles Barker plc) 1996–98 (chief exec 1992–96), UK pres Charles Barker BSMG Worldwide 1999–2001; non-exec dir: Mothercare plc 1997–2004, Provident Financial plc 1998–2003, Austin Reed plc 2001–06; tstee Historic Royal Palaces 1998–2007; chm The House of St Barnabas 2001–04, chm PRCA 1990–92; memb Citizen's Charter Advsy Panel 1993–97; FIPR 1987; *Recreations* theatre, gardening; *Style*— Miss Angela Heylin, OBE; ✉ 46 St Augustine's Road, London NW1 9RN (tel 020 7485 4815, mobile 07767 491508, e-mail angela@heylin.com)

HEYMAN, Norma Frances; *b* Liverpool; *Career* film and TV prodr; former actress; memb Cncl BAFTA, fndr memb Bd Women in Film and TV, memb American Acad, memb Advsy Ctee Br Ind Film Awards; Women in Film Business Award 1992, Special Jury Prize British Ind Film Awards 2004, 25th Anniversary Award London Critics' Circle Film Awards 2005, Women in Film and Television Lifetime Achievement Award 2006; *Films* credits incl: The Honorary Consul (first woman in Br to produce a solo independent prodn) 1983, Burning Secret 1987, Buster (Oscar nomination) 1988, Dangerous Liaisons 1989 (3 Oscars, 7 Academy Award nominations, 10 BAFTA's, César Best Foreign Film), Clothes in the Wardrobe (for BBC, theatrical release in the USA as The Summer House (film won Writers' Guild Award, BAFTA nomination)) 1992, Sister My Sister 1993–94, The Secret Agent 1995–96, Gangster No 1 2000, Kiss Kiss (Bang Bang) 2000, Mrs Henderson Presents (winner: Ensemble Award Nat Bd of Review, London Film Critics' Circle Award; nominated for: 2 Oscars, 3 Golden Globes, 4 BAFTAs) 2006; *Style*— Mrs Norma Heyman; ✉ c/o NFH Ltd & Heyman-Hoskins, 37 Ovington Square, London SW3 1LJ (tel 020 7584 3355, fax 020 7589 1863)

HEYS, Prof Steven Darryll; s of Keith Heys, and Alice, *née* McNamee; *b* 5 July 1956; *Educ* St Mary's Coll Blackburn, Univ of Aberdeen (BMedBiol, MB ChB, MD, PhD); *m*; 3 c; *Career* Capt RAMC (V) 252 Highland Field Ambulance 51 Highland Bde 1985–89; SHO Aberdeen Royal Infirmary 1982–84 (house offr 1981–92), memb Health Bd Aberdeen 1984–87, registrar (neurosurgery, orthopaedics, plastic surgery and gen and vascular surgery) Aberdeen Royal Infirmary 1984–86, registrar (gen surgery (gastroenterology)) Woodend Hosp Aberdeen 1985–86, registrar (gen, paediatric and urology) Dr Grays Dist Gen Hosp Elgin 1986–87, Wellcome research trg fell and hon research assoc Rowett Research Inst and Dept of Surgery Univ of Aberdeen 1987–89, hon sr registrar Grampian Health Bd 1989–92; locum conslt surgn: Dr Grays Hosp Elgin 1988, 1989 and 1990, Balfour Hosp Orkney 1990, 1992, 1993 and 1994; hon conslt surgn Aberdeen Royal Hosps NHS Tst 1992–; Univ of Aberdeen: tutor in surgery 1984–87, lectr 1989–92, sr lectr 1992–96, dir Surgical Nutrition and Metabolism Unit Dept of Surgery 1995–, reader 1996–99, prof of surgical oncology 1999–, specialist assessor readership appointments, memb Strategic Planning Gp for Med Sch 1991, memb Med Sch Curriculum Steering Gp 1995–, memb Dean's Advsy Research Ctee Faculty of Med 1996–, cancer research program ldr 2004–; clinical tutor in minimal access therapy (gen surgery) Minimal Access Therapy Trg Unit for Scotland Scottish Royal Colls 1994–97; hon professorial research fell Rowett Research Inst 1992–; external examiner: Queen's Univ Belfast, RCS, Univ of Southampton, Univ of Dundee, Univ of Belfast; examiner in surgery for fellowship RCPSGlas, external assessor for Francis Mitchell Caird Prize in Surgery RCS(Ed), assessor Scottish Mortality Study; specialist assessor for professorial appointments Queen's Univ Belfast; reviewer: NHS R&D prof, Health Technol Bd for Scotland; chm: Aberdeen Breast Res Gp 1998–, Symptomatic Breast Service Grampian Univ Hosps NHS Tst 2000–03; vice-chm NE of Scotland Clinical and Audit Focus Gp Breast Cancer; Br Assoc of Surgical Oncology memb Surgical Advsy Bd RCS(Ed) 2001–, Br Assoc of Surgical Oncology Scottish Rep UK Ctee for Breast Surgery 2001–; GMC inspr new med sch UEA 2000–; memb Editorial Bd World Jl of Surgical Oncology; assessor and reviewer for pubns incl: Clinical Immunotherapeutics, Br Jl of Surgery, The Cancer Jl, Br Jl of Nutrition, Clinical Science, Nutrition and Cancer, Jl of the Royal Coll of Surgns of Edinburgh, BMA Annual Book Competition, Euro Jl of Applied Physiology and Occupational Med, Br Jl of Cancer, Surgical Oncology; memb: Surgical Res Soc, Br Assoc of Surgical Oncology, Nutrition Soc, BMA; FRCSGlas 1985, FRCS (ad eundem) 1998, FRCSEd (without examination) 1999, fell HE Acad 2007; *Awards* as student: Alexander Smith Cardno Prize 1976, George Thomson Bursary 1976, Durno Prize 1977, MRC Trg Award 1977–78, Scot Prize 1979, Russel Gold Medal 1979, Ogston Prize 1979, Munday and Venn Prize 1980, Dyce Davison Medal 1981, McQuibban Prize 1981 (dux in surgery), McQuibban Prize 1981 (dux in med), Smith Davidson Prize 1981, Lyon Prize 1981, David Tomory Prize 1981, Murray Medal and Scholarship 1981; travelling fellowships: Chest, Heart and Stroke Assoc 1980 (at Northwestern Univ Chicago), Wellcome Travelling fell 1988 (at Huddinge Univ Hosp Karolinska Inst Stockholm), Br Jl of Surgery Soc 1993 (at oncological centres of excellence in Europe); *Publications* author of over 180 scientific papers, 450 presentations to learned societies and 23 book chapters; *Recreations* flying, karate, Hispanic studies, hill walking; *Style*— Prof Steven Heys; ✉ University of Aberdeen, Medical School Buildings, Foresterhill, Aberdeen AB9 2ZD (tel 01224 552105, e-mail s.d.heys@abdn.ac.uk)

HEYWOOD, John Kenneth; s of Samuel George Heywood (d 1987), of Devon, and Hilda Kathleen, *née* Lamey (d 1985); *b* 29 January 1947; *Educ* Shebbear Coll, UCL (LLB), INSEAD Fontainebleau (Advanced Mgmnt Course); *m* 1976, Susan Ann Heywood; 2 s (James Samuel b 15 Nov 1981, William John b 22 Oct 1984), 1 da (Sophie Elizabeth b 4 May 1990); *Career* PricewaterhouseCoopers (formerly Price Waterhouse before merger 1998): joined 1968, ptnr 1980–2006, dir London office and memb UK Exec 1991–95, chm E European firm 1993–2006, memb Euro Mgmnt Bd 1993–98, dir PricewaterhouseCoopers China 1996–98; non-exec dir Home Office 2007– (chair Audit Ctee); tstee UCL Friends Tst, govr and memb Ct Herts Univ; FCA; *Recreations* golf, tennis, opera, history; *Style*— John Heywood, Esq

HEYWOOD, Matthew David; s of David Main Heywood (d 1999), and Patricia Ann, *née* Robinson; *b* 26 December 1970, Derby; *Educ* Dunfermline HS, Duncan of Jordanstone Coll of Art Univ of Dundee (BSc, BArch); *m* 10 Aug 2002, Sarah Elizabeth, *née* Casemore; *Career* architect; T P Bennett Partnership 1994–96, J R Wilks & G R Vaughen-Ellis Architects 1991–92; assoc dir Future Systems 2000–03 (joined 1996), dir Matthew Heywood Architecture 2003–; projects incl: NatWest Media Centre Lord's Cricket Ground 1996–99, Selfridges Birmingham 1999–2003; exhbns: Future Systems (ICA London) 1998, Venice Biennale 2002; memb St Mark's Church Battersea; RIBA 1995, memb ARB 1995; *Style*— Matthew Heywood, Esq; ✉ Matthew Heywood Architecture, 1 Munro Terrace, London SW10 0DL (tel 020 7352 7583, e-mail email@matthewheywood.com)

HEYWOOD, Sir Peter; 6 Bt (UK 1838), of Claremont, Lancashire; s of Sir Oliver Kerr Heywood, 5 Bt (d 1992), and Denise, *née* Godefroi; *b* 10 December 1947; *Educ* Bryanston, Keble Coll Oxford (MA); *m* 1970, Jacqueline Anne, da of Sir Robert Frederick Hunt, CBE (d 2004); 2 da (Vanessa Jane (Mrs Paul Fewell) b 1975, Annabel Sarah (Mrs Nicholas Gibson) b 1976); *Heir* bro, Michael Heywood; *Career* company director; *Style*— Sir Peter Heywood, Bt; ✉ 64 Newbridge Road, Weston, Bath BA1 3LA

HEYWOOD, Victoria Mary Taylor (Vikki); da of Kenneth Heywood Taylor, *qv*, and Gillian Dorothea, *née* Black; sis of Matthew Taylor, MP, *qv*; *b* 25 June 1956, London; *Educ* Truro HS, Fortismere Sch London, Central Sch of Speech and Drama (Dip); *m* 1, 1988, Christopher Wright; 1 s (Thomas b 11 Feb 1992); m 2, 2004, Clive Jones, CBE, *qv*; *Career* stage mangr 1977–84, gen mangr London Bubble Theatre Co 1986–89, exec dir Contact Theatre Manchester 1989–93, gen mangr London Int Festival 1994, exec dir Royal Court Theatre 1994–2001, exec dir RSC 2003– (govr 2006–); vice-chm: Lyric Theatre Hammersmith 1999–2004, Young Vic Theatre 2002–06; tstee Shakespeare Birthplace Tst 2004–; FRSA 2005; *Recreations* sleeping, eating, reading, walking; *Style*— Mrs Vikki Heywood; ✉ Royal Shakespeare Company, Royal Shakespeare Theatre, Waterside, Stratford-upon-Avon, Warwickshire CV37 6BB (tel 01789 403444, fax 01789 262341, e-mail info@rsc.org.uk)

HEYWORTH, John; s of Lt-Col Reginald Francis Heyworth (ka 1941), and Hon Moyra, *née* Marjoribanks, da of 3 Baron Tweedmouth; *b* 21 August 1925; *Educ* Eton; *m* 10 June 1950, Susan Elizabeth, da of Sir John Henry Burder, ED, of Burford, Oxford; 1 s (Reginald b 1961), 3 da (Caroline b 1952, Jane b 1953, Joanna b 1957); *Career* Royal Dragoons NW Europe 1943–47; farmer and owner of The Cotswold Wild Life Park; High Sheriff Oxon 1962; *Style*— John Heyworth, Esq; ✉ Bradwell Grove, Burford, Oxfordshire OX18 4JW (tel 01993 823154, fax 01993 824050)

H

HIBBERD, Dr Alan Ronald; s of George Peter Hibberd (d 1946), of Bendigo, Victoria, Aust, and Flora Gertrude, *née* Dainty (d 1973); *b* 25 October 1931; *Educ* High Sch Bendigo (Alexander Rushall scholarship), Ridley Coll Melbourne, Victorian Coll of Pharmacy Melbourne (PhC), Chelsea Coll London (DCC, PhD); *m* 1, 1954, Doreen Imilda, da of James Collier; 2 s (David b 1954, Andrew b 1957), 2 da (Wendy b 1959, Christine b 1962); m 2, 1974, Lois, da of Howard Kenneth Stratton; *Career* specialist in clinical ecology/clinical toxicology; community pharmacy practice Melbourne 1953–73; dir: ARH Pharmaceuticals 1959–74, Pressels Laboratories 1959–74; pt/t demonstrator in practical pharmaceutics Victorian Coll of Pharmacy 1961–64; Victorian Branch Aust Dental Assoc 1966–74: lectr to postgrads in pharmacology and therapeutics, conslt in dental therapeutics and prescribing; i/c of Drug Info Dept and Ward Pharmacy Services Hackney Hosp London 1975, res fell Pharmacy Dept Chelsea Coll London 1976–79, lectr Sch of Pharmacy Univ of London 1980–81, tutor in clinical pharmacy Northwick Park Hosp Harrow 1980–81, first course organiser and supervisor MSc course in clinical pharmacy Univ of London (first clinical pharmacy degree course in SE England) 1980–81, dir Hibbro Research Hereford 1981–84, private practice in clinical ecology and toxicology London 1985–, conslt in clinical pharmacology and toxicology Biocare Ltd 1989–, conslt in clinical biochem/pharmacology to Soc for Promotion of Nutritional Therapy (UK) 1992–2001, scientific advsr to Register of Nutritional Therapists (UK) 1993–; author of numerous articles and scientific papers on drug metabolism and relating to specialist field and contrib to many learned pubns; vice-pres The Int Acad of Oral Med and Toxicology (UK) 1994–98; memb: Pharmaceutical Soc of Victoria 1953 (fell (by examination) 1961), Royal Soc of Victoria 1968–74, Br Dental Soc for Clinical Nutrition 1985–98, Nutrition Assoc 1987, Environmental Dental Association USA 1991–98, British Soc for Ecological Medicine (BSEM, formerly British Soc for Allergy, Environmental and Nutritional Medicine) 1993, Br Assoc for Nutritional Therapy 2001; FRSH 1971, MRPharmS 1974–2005, fell Pharmaceutical Soc of Aust 1983 (life fell 1991), FRSM 2003; *Recreations* golf, flying light aircraft, bridge, travelling, languages, music; *Clubs* Ross-on-Wye Golf, Herefordshire Flying, Greenacres Golf (Melbourne); *Style*— Dr Alan Hibberd; ✉ Bayswater Clinic, 25B Clanricarde Gardens, London W2 4JL (tel and fax 020 7229 9078)

HIBBERD, Dr (John William) Dominic; s of Charles John Leslie Hibberd, CVO (d 1993), and Winifred Alice Nattriss (d 1979); *b* 3 November 1941, Guildford; *Educ* Rugby, King's Coll Cambridge (exhibitioner, MA), Univ of Exeter (PhD); *Career* author; former teacher at univs in GB, USA and China; hon vice-pres Wilfred Owen Assoc, hon fell War Poets Assoc; FRSL 2002; *Publications* as author: Owen the Poet (1986), Wilfred Owen: The Last Year (1992), Harold Monro: Poet of the New Age (2001), Wilfred Owen: A New Biography (2002); as ed: War Poems and Others, Wilfred Owen (1973), Poetry of the Great War: An Anthology (1986), The Diary of a Dead Officer, Arthur Graeme West (1991), Strange Meetings: Poems by Harold Monro (2003); author of numerous articles and reviews; *Recreations* travel; *Style*— Dr Dominic Hibberd

HIBBERT, Christopher; MC (1945); s of Canon H V Hibbert (d 1980); *b* 5 March 1924; *Educ* Radley, Oriel Coll Oxford (MA); *m* 1948, Susan, da of Rayner Piggford (d 1978); 2 s (James, Tom), 1 da (Kate); *Career* Capt London Irish Rifles Italy 1944–45; ptnr firm of land agents and auctioneers 1948–59; author 1959–; Heinemann Award for Lit 1962, McColvin Medal 1989; Hon DLitt Univ of Leicester; FRSL, FRGS; *Books* incl: The Destruction of Lord Raglan (1961), Corunna (1961), Benito Mussolini (1962), The Battle of Arnhem (1962), The Court at Windsor (1964), The Roots of Evil (1964), Agincourt (1965), Garibaldi and his Enemies (1966), The Making of Charles Dickens (1967), London: Biography of a City (1969), The Dragon Wakes: China and the West (1970), The Personal History of Samuel Johnson (1971), George IV (1972, vol 2 1973), The Rise and Fall of the House of Medici (1974), Edward VII (1976), The Great Mutiny: India 1857 (1978), The French Revolution (1980), The London Encyclopaedia (ed, 1983), Rome: Biography of a City (1985), The English: A Social History (1986), The Grand Tour (1987), Venice: The Biography of a City (1988), The Encyclopaedia of Oxford (ed, 1988), The Virgin Queen: The Personal History of Elizabeth I (1990), Redcoats and Rebels: The War for America, 1770–1781 (1990), The Story of England (1992), Cavaliers and Roundheads: The Civil War in England 1642–49 (1993), Florence: The Biography of A City (1993), Nelson: A Personal History (1994), Soldier of the Seventy-first: The Journal of a Soldier in the Peninsular War (ed, 1996), No Ordinary Place: Radley College and the Public School System (1997), Wellington: A Personal History (1997), George III: A Personal History (1998), Queen Victoria: A Personal History (2000), The Marlboroughs: John and Sarah Churchill, 1650–1744 (2001), Napoleon: His Wives and Women (2002), Disraeli: A Personal History (2005); *Recreations* cooking, crosswords, gardening, travel; *Clubs* Army and Navy, Garrick; *Style*— Christopher Hibbert, Esq, MC; ✉ 6 Albion Place, West Street, Henley-on-Thames, Oxfordshire RG9 2DT

HIBBERT, William John; s of Sir Reginald Hibbert, GCMG (d 2002), of Machynlleth, Powys, and Ann Alun, *née* Pugh; *b* 23 February 1957; *Educ* Charterhouse, Worcester Coll Oxford (MA); *m* 1, (Caroline) Maria, da of Sir John Lucas-Tooth, 2 Bt, *qv*; m 2, Julia Mair Wheldon, da of Anthony Smith, QC; 3 da (Cosima Mary b 1984, Clover Frances b 1988, Saffron Lucy b 2005); *Career* called to the Bar Inner Temple 1979; *Style*— William Hibbert, Esq; ✉ Gough Square Chambers, 6/7 Gough Square, London EC4A 3DE (tel 020 7353 0924, fax 020 7353 2221, e-mail william.hibbert@goughsq.co.uk)

HIBBIN, Sally; da of Eric Hibbin (d 2001), and Nina, *née* Masel (d 2004); *b* 3 July 1953; *Educ* Tottenham Sch, Keele Univ (BA), Open Univ (MA); *Career* journalist and producer; memb: BAFTA, WFTV; *Films* as documentary film-maker for Channel 4 incl: Live A Life 1982, The Road to Gdansk 1985 and Great Britain United 1991; as prodr credits incl: A Very British Coup 1988, Riff-Raff 1991 (European Film of the Year and Cannes Critics' Award), Raining Stones 1992 (Cannes Jury Prize and Evening Standard Award for Best Film), Ladybird Ladybird 1993, i.d. 1994, Carla's Song 1995, Stand and Deliver 1998, Hold Back the Night 1999, Dockers; as exec prodr credits incl: Bad Behaviour 1992 (Evening Standard Award - Peter Sellers Best Comedy), London South-West (short) 1992, Tomorrow Calling (short) 1993, Land and Freedom 1994, The Englishman Who Went Up A Hill But Came Down A Mountain 1994, The Governess, Liam 2000, The Intended, Blind Flight 2003, Yasmin 2004, Almost Adult 2006; *Publications* The Making of Licence to Kill, The Making of Back to the Future; *Recreations* walking, Spurs FC, cooking, bridge; *Clubs* The Union; *Style*— Ms Sally Hibbin; ✉ Parallax Pictures Ltd, Victoria Chambers, St Runwald Street, Colchester CO1 1HF

HIBBITT, Tari; da of Suwondo Budiardjo (d 1996), of London, and Carmel, *née* Brickman; *b* 18 June 1951; *m* 1, 1971 (m dis 1996), Roger Hibbitt, s of John A Hibbitt; 1 da (Claire b 28 June 1976), 1 s (Laurence b 9 June 1978); m 2, 2002, Dr Brian Andrew Lang, *qv*, s of Andrew Ballantyne Lang; *Career* fndr dir Clasma Software Ltd 1980–86, jt md UK The Rowland Co 1988–95, chief exec UK ops Edelman Public Relations Worldwide 1998–2002 (dep md UK and md European Business and Technol 1995–98), founding ptnr ReputationInc 2002–; MIPR 1989, MInstD 1990; *Recreations* theatre, cinema, opera; *Style*— Ms Tari Hibbitt; ✉ ReputationInc, 8 Grafton Street, London W1S 4EL

HICHENS, Antony Peverell; RD (1969); s of Lt Cdr Robert Peverell Hichens, DSO and bar, DSC and two bars, RNVR, and Catherine Gilbert Enys; *b* 10 September 1936; *Educ* Stowe, Magdalen Coll Oxford, Univ of Pennsylvania; *m* 1963, Sczerina Neomi, da of Dr F T J Hobday; 1 da (Tamsin); *Career* Nat Serv Midshipman RNVR 1954–56, ret as Lt Cdr RNR 1969; called to the Bar Inner Temple, dep md Redland Ltd 1979 (fin dir 1972), md fin Consolidated Gold Fields plc 1981–89; chm: Caradon plc 1987–89, Y J Lovell (Holdings) plc 1990–93, Caradon plc 1990–98, LASMO plc 2000–01 (dep chm 1995–2000), DS Smith plc 1999–2006, WaterRower (UK) Ltd; dir: Greenfriar Investment Co plc 1985–98, Candover Investments plc 1989– (dep chm 1991–2004), South Western Electricity plc 1990–95, Courtaulds Textiles plc (dep chm) 1990–99, British Coal Corporation 1992–96, Fleming Income & Capital Investment Trust 1992–, Limit plc (formerly London Insurance Market Investment Trust) 1993–2000, Global Stone Corp 1994–98; memb: Takeover Panel 2002–, Oxford Ct of Benefactors; Waynflete fell Magdalen Coll Oxford 1996; *Recreations* travel, shooting, marine paintings, wine; *Clubs* Brooks's, Naval; *Style*— Antony Hichens, Esq; ✉ Slape Manor, Netherbury, Bridport, Dorset DT6 5LH

HICKEY, Christopher John (Chris); s of William Hickey (d 1971), and Mary, *née* Watkins (d 1995); *b* 8 November 1951; *Educ* Monmouth, Univ of Sheffield (BA), Univ of Leeds (PGCE), RSA (Dip TEFL), UCL (MPhil), London Business Sch (Sr Exec Prog); *m* Dec 1984, Pauline; 1 da (Caroline b 1986), 1 s (Michael b 1988); *Career* British Cncl: first sec (educn) Ivory Coast 1986–90, English language offr Barcelona 1990–93, head Educn Enterprises Spain 1993–95, dir Educn Enterprises 1999–2000 (dep dir 1996–99), dir Greece 2000–03, dir Spain 2003–; chair British Nat Ctee for Cultural Olympiad 2001–04, memb Exec Ctee Fundacion Hispano-Britanica Madrid 2003–; *Books* The Influence of Malraux on Camus (1986); *Recreations* literature, language, the arts, watching football, restaurants; *Style*— Chris Hickey, Esq; ✉ British Council, 31 Martinez Campos, 28010 Madrid, Spain (tel 00 34 91 337 3590, e-mail chris.hickey@britishcouncil.es)

HICKEY, (James) Kevin; MBE (1987); s of James Francis Hickey (d 1972), of Blackpool, and Mary Veronica, *née* Queenan; *b* 25 July 1941; *Educ* St Joseph's Coll Blackpool, De La Salle Coll Middleton, St Mary's Coll Twickenham; *m* Kyra Marjorie, da of George C Collen; 2 s (Sean Francis b 11 May 1965, Adrian Kevin b 12 April 1966), 1 da (Katherine Kyra b 24 Nov 1969); *Career* sports coach and administrator; teacher 1962–69, nat coach ABA 1969–89 (dir of coaching 1973–89), tech dir Br Olympic Assoc 1989–2000, high performance conslt 2001–, conslt Irish Sports Cncl 2001–; dep chef de mission (technical) to GB Olympic teams: Barcelona 1992, Albertville 1992, Lillehammer 1994, Nagano 1996, Atlanta 1996, Sydney 2000; vice-chm Euro Coaches Fedn 1982–89, chm Br Assoc of Nat Coaches 1986–89; conslt IOC; memb: Grants Ctee Sports Aid Fndn, Cncl Br Inst of Sports Coaches 1989–92, World Safety Cmmn 1986–89, World Class Advsrs Panel Sport England 2000–, Strength and Conditioning Steering Gp EIS 2002; lectured worldwide, contrib to various coaching gps incl Coaching Review Panel 1989–90 and 1998–99; conceived and implemented: Schs' ABA Standards Scheme, Golden Gloves Award; sporting achievements: co youth player rugby, represented London Colls at rugby, British schools boxing champion 1955–57; coaching achievements: coached GB Boxing Team Olympic Games 1972, 1976, 1980, 1984 and 1988 (total 7 medals), coached England Boxing Team Cwlth Games 1970, 1974, 1978, 1982 and 1986 (total 33 medals, every English boxer won medals 1984 and 1988); fell Br Inst of Sports Coaches 1989, Sports Writers' J L Manning Award 1987, UK Coach of the Year Br Assoc of Nat Coaches 1989, Sportscoach UK Coaching Hall of Fame 1998, BBC Team of the Year (GB Olympic Team Sydney) 2000; *Books* Know the Game, ABA Coaching Manual; *Recreations* keep fit activities including running and weight training, outdoor pursuits, fell walking, golf; *Style*— Kevin Hickey, Esq, MBE; ✉ 180 West Park Drive, Blackpool, Lancashire FY3 9LW (tel 01253 64900)

HICKEY, Dr Stephen Harald Frederick; s of Rev Dr James Peter Hickinbotham (d 1990), and Ingeborg Alice Lydia, *née* Manger; *b* 10 July 1949; *Educ* St Lawrence Coll, Corpus Christi Coll Oxford (BA), St Antony's Coll Oxford (DPhil); *m* 1976, Janet Elizabeth, *née* Hunter; 3 s (James b 1979, Thomas b 1982, Edward b 1985); *Career* DHSS: admin trainee and higher exec offr (admin) 1974–79, asst private sec to Sec of State 1978–79 and 1984–85, princ 1979–85, asst sec 1985–89, seconded to Rank Xerox (UK) Ltd 1989–90, asst sec Benefits Agency 1990–92; Fin Div DSS 1992–94; under sec and chief exec Civil Serv Coll Cabinet Office 1994–98; princ fin offr DSS 1998–2000, DG corp servs DSS/DWP 2000–02, DG Dept for Tport 2003–; *Books* Workers in Imperial Germany: The Miners of the Ruhr (1985); *Recreations* music, walking, tennis; *Style*— Dr Stephen Hickey; ✉ Department for Transport, Zone 1/33 Great Minster House, 76 Marsham Street, London SW1P 4DR (e-mail stephen.hickey@dft.gsi.gov.uk)

HICKIE, Denis; *b* 13 February 1976; *Educ* St. Mary's Coll Rathmines, UC Dublin; *Career* rugby union player (back); clubs: St Mary's Coll, Leinster (provincial team) 1996– (over 80 appearances); Ireland: 56 caps, debut v Wales 1997, memb squad World Cup 2003; memb British and Irish Lions touring squad NZ 2005; *Style*— Mr Denis Hickie; ✉ c/o Leinster Rugby, 55 Main Street, Donnybrook, Dublin 4, Ireland

HICKINBOTTOM, His Hon Judge Gary Robert; s of Samuel Geoffrey Hickinbottom, and Jean Irene, *née* Greaney; *Educ* Queen Mary's GS Walsall, UC Oxford (MA); *m* Caroline Hamilton; *Career* lectr: PCL 1980–2, UC Oxford 1987–89; admitted solicitor 1981, ptnr CMS Cameron McKenna (formerly McKenna & Co) 1986–2000, admitted solicitor-advocate (all courts) 1997, asst recorder 1994–98, recorder 1998–2000, circuit judge (Wales & Chester Circuit) 2000– dep High Court judge 2001–, sr circuit judge 2003–, chief social security and child support cmmr 2003–, chief pensions appeal cmmr 2005–, judge Technol and Construction Court 2005–, designated civil judge for S Wales, Dyfed, Powys and Gwent 2005–06, designated civil judge for Wales 2007–, judge Admin Court 2007–, judge Mercantile Court 2007–; memb: Gen Bar Cncl and Law Soc working pty on the civil courts 1992–93, Law Soc working pty on group actions 1994–2000, Central London County Court Mediators Panel 1996–98, Acad of Experts' Disciplinary Ctee 1996–2000, Judicial Technol Bd 2004–05; parking adjudicator Parking Appeals Service (London) and Nat Parking Adjudication Serv 1994–2000, asst cmmr Boundary Cmmn for England 2000; author of various articles and contributions to books on law and legal procedure; registered mediator; Fell Soc of Advanced Legal Studies; FCIArb (DipCIArb); *Recreations* choral singing, opera and ballet, sport; *Clubs* London Welsh; *Style*— His Hon Judge Hickinbottom; ✉ Cardiff Civil Justice Centre, 2 Park Street, Cardiff CF10 1ET (tel 029 2037 6400)

HICKISH, Dr Tamas Frederick Gordon; s of Gordon Walter Hickish, and Aileen, *née* Key; *Educ* Brockenhurst Coll, KCL, The Queen's Coll Oxford (MA), Westminster Med Sch (MB BS), Univ of London (MD); *Career* conslt med oncologist Poole and Royal Bournemouth Hosps 1995–; author and co-author of publications on oncology; tstee Youth Cancer Tst; FRCP (2000), MRCP (1988); *Recreations* marathon running; *Style*— Dr Tamas Hickish

HICKMAN, Sir (Richard) Glenn; 4 Bt (UK 1903), of Wightwick, Tettenhall, Staffordshire; s of Sir (Alfred) Howard Whitby Hickman, 3 Bt (d 1979), and late Margaret Doris, *née* Kempson (formerly Thatcher); *b* 12 April 1949; *Educ* Eton; *m* 1981, Heather Mary Elizabeth, er da of Dr James Moffett (d 1982), of Swindon, and Dr Gwendoline Moffett (d 1975); 2 s (Charles Patrick Alfred b 1983, Edward William George b 1990), 1 da (Elizabeth Margaret Ruth b 1985); *Heir* s, Charles Hickman; *Clubs* Turf; *Style*— Sir Glenn Hickman, Bt; ✉ Manor Farm House, Liddington, Wiltshire SN4 0HD

HICKMAN, James; *b* 2 February 1976; *Educ* William Hulmes GS, Univ of Manchester; *Career* swimmer; memb: Stockport Metro Swimming Club, City of Manchester Aquatics Club, City of Leeds Swimming Club; 100m butterfly: finalist Olympic Games 1996, finalist World Championships 1997, European record holder 1997 and 1998, world record holder 1998, third World Short-Course Championships 1999, fourth Cwlth Games 2002, second World Short-Course Championships 2004; 200m butterfly: Br record holder 1993, Gold medal European Jr Championships 1993, Bronze medal Cwlth Games 1994, finalist Olympic Games Atlanta 1996, Gold medal World Short-Course Championships 1997,

1999, 2000, 2002 and 2004, finalist World Championships 1998, Gold medal Cwlth Games (championship record) 1998, world record holder 1998, Bronze medal Cwlth Games 2002; 4x100m medley: Gold medal European Junior Championships 1993, Bronze medal Cwlth Games 1994, Bronze medal World Short-Course Championships 1997, Silver medal Cwlth Games 1998, Bronze medal World Championships 1999, Silver medal Cwlth Games 2002; 200m individual medley: Silver medal Cwlth Games 1998, Gold medal European Short-Course Championships 1998, Silver medal World Short-Course Championships 1999; Silver medal 400m individual medley Cwlth Games 1998, Br record holder 200m Backstroke 1998 (Br junior record holder 1991), Cwlth record holder 100m and 200m individual medley 1998; ret 2004; dir Made in Manchester Prodns (PR for the 2008 World Swimming Championships Manchester 2006–, also prodns for ITV and BBC Radio 2, 4 and World Serv) Young Mancunian of the Year 1994 and 1996, Mancunian of the Year 1998; *Style*— James Hickman, Esq; ✉ Made in Manchester, Suite 444, Great Northern House, 275 Deansgate, Manchester M3 4EL (tel 01509 618700, website www.jameshickman.com)

HICKMAN, District Judge Neil Edward; s of late Tony (Albert Frederick William) Hickman, and Nellie Elizabeth Hickman; *b* 13 May 1951; *Educ* after leaving King Edward's Sch Birmingham, Worcester Coll Oxford (MA); *m* 1973, Susan Mary, da of late William Charles Tucker, and Mary Elayne Tucker; 1 da (Jo), 1 s (Ben); *Career* admitted slr 1976, appointed dep registrar/district judge 1986, sr ptnr Batcheldors 1997–98, district judge (SE (Provincial) Circuit) 2000–; pres Bedfordshire Law Soc 1994–95; chm Bedford Divnl Liberal Assoc 1978–79, hon slr Bedfordshire Housing Aid Centre 1985–2000, fndr memb Bedfordshire Pilgrims Housing Assoc Steering Ctee 1989; author of various articles in legal periodicals; contrib: Practical Civil Courts Precedents, Family Court Practice; jt gen ed Civil Court Service; *Recreations* chess, singing, bellringing, family and ecclesiastical history; *Style*— District Judge Hickman; ✉ Milton Keynes County Court, 351 Silbury Boulevard, Central Milton Keynes MK9 2DT (tel 01908 302800)

HICKOX, Richard Sidney; CBE (2002); s of Sidney Edwin Hickox (d 1988), and Jean MacGregor, *née* Millar; *b* 5 March 1948; *Educ* Royal GS High Wycombe, Royal Acad of Music (LRAM), Queens' Coll Cambridge (organ scholar, MA, ChM); *m* 1, 1970 (m dis), Julia Margaret, *née* Smith; m 2, 1976 (m dis), Frances Ina, *née* Sheldon-Williams; 1 s (Thomas Richard Campbell b 1981); m 3, 1995, Pamela, *née* Helen Stephen; 1 s (Adam b 1996); *Career* organist and master of music St Margaret's Westminster 1972–82, Promenade debut 1973; artistic dir: Woburn Festival 1967–89 (now pres), St Endellion Festival 1974–, London Symphony Chorus 1976–, ChCh Spitalfields Festival 1978–, Truro Festival 1981–, Northern Sinfonia 1982–90 (conductor emeritus 1996–), Chester Summer Music Festival 1989–; conductor and musical dir: City of London Sinfonia (fndr 1971), Richard Hickox Singers; co-fndr (with Simon Standage) Collegium Musicum '90 1990; princ guest conductor Bournemouth Symphony Orch 1992–95, assoc conductor LSO 1985–; regular conductor: RPO, Bournemouth Symphony Orch and Sinfonietta, Royal Liverpool Philharmonic Orch, BBC Symphony and Welsh orchs; conductor for many int orchestras; conducted anniversary performance of Mendelssohn's Elijah (BBC Proms) 1996; FRCO (cncl memb), ARAM; *Opera* performances incl: Walton's Troilus and Cressida (Opera North) 1995, Rusalka (Rome Opera) 1995, Gluck's Armide (Spitalfields Festival), A Midsummer Night's Dream (Opera London), Handel's Julius Caesar (Komische Oper Berlin and Australian Opera Sydney), Seraglio (Scottish Chamber Orch at Istanbul Festival), Cunning Little Vixen (ENO) 1996, Fidelio (Australian Opera Sydney), Ariadne auf Naxos (Australian Opera) 1997, Vaughan Williams' Pilgrim's Progress (Royal Opera House) 1997, Vaughan Williams' Riders to the Sea and Purcell's Dido and Aeneas (Royal Opera House), Lohengrin (Spoleto Festival Italy); *Recordings* over 150 recordings incl: Britten War Requiem, Delius Sea Drift (with Bournemouth Symphony Orch), works by Bach, Handel and Telemann (with Collegium Musicum '90), Troilus and Cressida (Opera North), Walton The Bear, Vaughan Williams Riders to the Sea, Holst The Wandering Scholar (with Northern Sinfonia), complete Haydn masses (with Collegium Musicum '90), Peter Grimes (with City of London Sinfonia and London Symphony Chorus); *Television* incl: South Bank Show (Ken Russell film with Bournemouth Symphony), Dido and Aeneas with Collegium Musicum '90 and Maria Ewing (BBC); *Awards* Gramophone Award for best choral recording (Britten's War Requiem) 1992, Gramophone Award for best choral recording (Delius' Sea Drift) 1994, Nat Fedn of Music Socs' first Sir Charles Groves Prize for Services to Br Music, Royal Philharmonic Soc Music Award 1995 (for Opera North's Troilus and Cressida and first ever complete cycle of Vaughan Williams' symphonies with Bournemouth Symphony Orch), Gramophone Opera Award 1995 (for Walton's Troilus and Cressida), Deutsche Schallplattenpreis, Diapason d'Or; *Recreations* watching football and tennis, surfing, politics; *Style*— Richard Hickox, Esq, CBE; ✉ c/o Intermusica Artists' Management, 16 Duncan Terrace, London N1 8BZ (tel 020 7278 5455, fax 020 7278 8434)

HICKS, Air Cdre Alan George; CBE (1990); s of late William John Hicks, TD, of Verwood, Dorset, and late Ellen Rose, *née* Packer; *b* 18 February 1936; *Educ* Fosters Sch Sherborne, St Catharine's Coll Cambridge (MA); *m* 30 Oct 1961, Jessie Elizabeth, da of James Hutchison, of Perth, Scotland; 1 s (Jeremy b 8 Aug 1962), 3 da (Cressida b 22 Aug 1963, Gemma b 10 June 1965, Clare b 27 March 1967); *Career* cmmnd RAF 1957, 42 Sqdn 1962–65, 204 Sqdn 1965–67, Avionics Spec RAF Coll Manby 1969–71, Flt Cdr 203 Sqdn Malta 1973–76, OC 42 Sqdn 1976–78, Directing Staff RAF Staff Coll 1978–80, Central Tactics and Trials Orgn 1981, Station Cdr RAF Turnhouse 1982–84, MOD Concepts Staff 1985–87, MOD Dir of Def Commitments 1987–90, head Gulf War Report Team 1990–91 (ret 1991); sec gen UK Industrial Space Ctee 1993–2006 (conslt to chm 2006–); chm United Servs Catholic Assoc 1984–90; CEng, MRAeS, MIERE 1971; *Recreations* Italian studies, art; *Clubs* RAF, Army and Navy; *Style*— Air Commodore Alan Hicks, CBE; ✉ c/o National Westminster Bank, 50 Cheap Street, Sherborne, Dorset

HICKS, Dr Colin Peter; CB (2007); s of George Stephen Frederick Hicks (d 1976), and Irene Maud, *née* Hargrave; *b* 1 May 1946; *Educ* Rutlish Sch Merton, Univ of Bristol (BSc, PhD); *m* Elizabeth Joan, da of Rev Sidney Eric Escourt Payne, of Birmingham; 2 da (Rachel Heather b 1970, Joanna Katharine b 1972); *Career* lectr in chemistry Univ of the West Indies 1970–73, ICI research fell Univ of Exeter 1973–75, researcher Nat Physical Laboratory 1975–80, various research positions DTI 1980–83, tech advsr Barclays Bank 1983–84, dep dir Laboratory of the Govt Chemist 1984–87, sec Industrial Devpt Advsy Bd 1988–90, under sec i/c res and technol policy DTI 1990–94, under sec i/c environment and energy technologies DTI 1994–96, dir Environment Directorate DTI 1996–99, dir of space DTI and DG British National Space Centre 1999–2006; sec Teddington Baptist Church 1979–1990, memb London Baptist Assoc Cncl 1986–2001, memb London Baptist Assoc Bd 2002–, FRSC 1985; *Recreations* computing; *Style*— Dr Colin Hicks, CB

HICKS, James Frederick (Jim); s of Fred Hicks, of Beccles, Suffolk, and Doreen, *née* Tulip; *b* 8 July 1960, Sunderland; *Educ* Damelin Coll Johannesburg; *m* 21 Nov 2003, Lisa, da of Carlo Capaldi; 2 da from previous m (Lucy Joanna b 2 July 1990, Anna Olivia b 21 Sept 1995); *Career* prog dir 96.3 Aire FM and Magic 828 1995–97, prog dir Galaxy 102 Manchester 1997–99, launch md Galaxy 105–106 (NE England) 1999, gp prog dir Chrysalis Radio 1999–; a dir Radio Acad 2003–, chair Annual Music Conf Steering Ctee Radio Acad 2004; master practitioner Neuro-Linguistic Programming (NLP); *Clubs* Teatro; *Style*— Jim Hicks, Esq; ✉ c/o Chrysalis Radio, Bramley Road, London W10 6SP (tel 020 7465 6218)

HICKS, Michael Frank; s of Frank Henry Hicks (d 1985), and Annie Elizabeth Lydia, *née* Beeson (d 1988); *b* 11 March 1935; *Educ* Fairlop Secdy HS Hainault, Dane Secdy Modern Ilford; *m* 1, 19 Sept 1959 (m dis), Veronica Constance, da of Frederick Edwin Martin; 2 da (Corinne Veronica b 14 May 1962, Anne Christine b 15 April 1964); m 2, 19 Oct 2002, Sally Diana Critchley, da of Ken Green; *Career* Nat Serv RAF 1953–55, serv 66 Sqdn Aden; stockbroker: HE Goodison 1948–56, Blount 1956–59; ptnr Simon and Coates 1959–80, equity ptnr Statham Duff Stoop 1980–86; dir: Prudential Bache Capital Funding 1986–89, Société Générale Strauss Turnbull Securities Ltd 1989–98, KAS Associate NV 1998–99; md Hicks Int Ltd Trade and Finance (Introductions), non-exec dir Netwindfall Ltd 2000–01, conslt ITG Europe 1999–2001, chm Alexander David Securities Ltd 2007–; cncllr St Osyth Parish Cncl until 2007; MSI, MInstD; *Recreations* tennis, walking, spreadbetting; *Style*— Michael F Hicks, MSI; ✉ The Poplars, The Green, Great Bentley, Colchester, Essex CO7 8PJ (tel 01206 250789, e-mail hicks427@btinternet.com); Alexander David Securities Limited, 10 Finsbury Circus, London EC2A 1AD (tel 020 7556 1072)

HICKS, Nicola Katherine; MBE (1995); da of Philip Lionel Shalto Hicks, of Radcot House Bampton Oxfordshire, and Jill Tweed; *b* 3 May 1960; *Educ* Frensham Heights Sch, Chelsea Sch of Art (BA), RCA (MA); *m* 1 (m dis); m 2, 28 Feb 1992, Daniel Flowers; 1 s (William Gabriel Sholto b 31 March 1992), 1 da (Edith Lilly b 13 September 1994); *Career* artist; RWA, FRBS; *Solo Exhibitions* incl: Angela Flowers Gallery London 1985 and 1986, Angela Flowers Co Cork 1986, Beaux Arts Gallery Bath 1987, Flowers East London 1988, 1989, 1992, 1994, 1995, 1996 and 1998, Tegnerforbundet Oslo 1991, Fire and Brimstone (Flowers East and Watermans Art Centre Brentford) 1991, Peter Scott Gallery Lancaster Univ 1993, Castlefield Gallery Manchester 1993, Djanogly Art Gallery Univ of Nottingham 1995, Furtive Imagination at Whitworth Art Gallery Manchester and Yorkshire Sculpture Park 1996, Riverside Studios London 1997, Galerie de Bellefeuille Quebec 1997, Outrageous Fortune (Flowers East London) 1998, Flowers West Santa Monica CA 1999, Galerie Rachlin Lemarié Beaubourg Paris 1999, Outrageous Fortune (Ferens Art Gallery Hull) 1999; *Group Exhibitions* incl: Christie's Inaugural Graduate Exhibition London 1982, Mixed Christmas Show (New Grafton Gallery) 1982, Current Issues (RCA London) 1982, Portland Clifftops Sculpture Park 1983, Sculptural Drawings (Ruskin Coll Oxford) 1983, Int Garden Festival Liverpool: Sculpture Garden 1984, Hayward Annual (Hayward Gallery London) 1985, Basel Art Fair 1985 and 1986, '85 Show (Serpentine Gallery London) 1985, Opening Exhibition (Damon Brandt Gallery NY) 1985, Sixteen (Angela Flowers Gallery London) 1986, The Living Art Pavillion (The Ideal Home Exhibition London) 1986, Beaux Arts Summer Exhibition Bath 1986, Antithesis (Angela Flowers Gallery) 1986, Chicago Art Fair 1987 and 1988, The Scottish Gallery Edinburgh 1987, Art In The City (Lloyds Building London) 1987, Rocket 6–1 (installed at the Economist Building Piccadilly London) 1988, Hakone Open Air Museum 1988, Veksolund Udstilling For Sculptor Copenhagen 1988, Out of Clay (Manchester) 1988, Daley Hicks Jeffries Jones Kirby Lewis (Flowers East London) 1989, Los Angeles Art Fair 1990, Sculptors Drawings (Cleveland Bridge Gallery Bath) 1990, The Drawings Show (Thumb Gallery) 1990, Bryan Kneale's Choice (Dover Street Arts Club) 1990, The Discerning Eye (Mall Galleries) 1990, Inaugural Exhibition (Lannon Cole Gallery Chicago) 1991, Millfield British 20th Century Sculpture Exhibition 1992, RA Summer Exhibition 1993, New Grafton Gallery 1993, Beaux Arts Gallery Bath 1993, first RWA Open Sculpture Exhibition 1993 (Morris Singer Award), Norrkopings Museum Sweden 1993, Dialogue with the Other (Kunsthallen Brandts Odense Denmark and Norrkopings Museum Sweden) 1994, Flowers East 1993–94, Flowers (Koplin Gallery LA) 1995, The Hare (The City Gallery Leicester) 1996, Foundations of Fame (London Inst) 1997, The Body Politic (Wolverhampton Art Gallery) 1997, Galerie Rachlin Lemarié Beauborg Paris 1998, British Figurative Art Part 2: Sculpture (Flowers East London) 1998, The Shape of the Century - 100 Years of Sculpture in Britain (Salisbury Cathedral) 1999; work in various collections incl: Arthur Andersen, Contemporary Arts Soc, Chase Manhattan Bank, Castle Museum Norwich, Coopers & Lybrand, Govt Art Collection, Huddersfield Art Gallery, Hakone Open Air Museum, Ipswich Cncl; cmmn for monument in Battersea Park; artist in residence Brentwood HS; *Recreations* poker, backgammon, dice, dog and horse racing, travelling, searching for horned rhino on elephantback and white water surfing, gardening and gaming; *Clubs* Chelsea Arts; *Style*— Nicola Hicks, MBE; ✉ c/o Flowers East, 82 Kingsland Road, London E2 8DP (tel 020 8985 3333, fax 020 8985 0067, e-mail gallery@flowerseast.co.uk, website www.flowerseast.co.uk)

HICKS, Philip; s of Brig Philip Hugh Whitby Hicks, CBE, DSO, MC (d 1967), and Patty, *née* Fanshawe (d 1985); *b* 11 October 1928; *Educ* Winchester, RMA Sandhurst, Royal Acad Schs (Dip RAS); *m* 22 July 1952, Jill, da of Maj Jack Tweed (d 1979); 1 da (Nicola b 1960), 1 s (David b 1971); *Career* Irish Gds 1946–47, 2 Lt Royal Warwicks Regt 1948–49; artist (represented by David Messum Fine Art Cork St); pt/t teacher various art schs 1960–85, concentrated full time on painting 1986–; solo exhibitions incl: Camden Arts Centre 1971, Richard Demarco Gallery Edinburgh 1971, Robert Self Gallery London 1971, Imperial War Museum 1975, Galerie VFCU Antwerp 1977–79, Battersea Arts Centre 1977, Gallery 22 Dublin 1980, New Art Centre (London) 1980–82, Galleri Engstrom Stockholm 1985, Gallery 10 London 1986–91, Bohun Gall Henley 1986–90, Heffer Gallery Cambridge 1992, Courcoux and Courcoux Fine Art Salisbury 1992, David Messum Fine Art London 1996, 1997, 1998, 2000 and 2001; mixed exhibitions incl: Tate Gallery London 1976, Mall Galleries London 1980, Israel Israel Museum Jerusalem 1980–81, Serpentine Gallery London 1982, Angela Flowers Gallery 1985, Art '89 London 1989; works in public collections incl: Tate Gallery, Contemporary Art Soc, V&A, Imperial War Museum; Br Cncl award 1977; also performed professionally as a jazz pianist; past chm and vice-pres Artists Gen Benevolent Inst; *Recreations* music; *Clubs* Chelsea Arts, Royal Over-Seas League; *Style*— Philip Hicks, Esq; ✉ Radcot House, Buckland Road, Bampton, Oxfordshire OX18 2AA (tel 01993 850347, fax 01993 851733); c/o Messum's, 8 Cork Street, London W1X 1PB

HICKS, Sir Robert Adrian; kt (1996); s of W H Hicks of Horrabridge, Devon; *b* 18 January 1938; *Educ* Queen Elizabeth GS, UCL, Univ of Exeter; *m* 1, 1962 (m dis 1987), Maria, da of Robert Gwyther of Plympton, Devon; 2 da; m 2, 1991, Mrs Glenys Foote; *Career* nat vice-chm Young Cons 1964–66, tech coll lectr 1964–70, Parly candidate (Cons) Aberavon 1966; MP (Cons): Bodmin 1970–74 and 1974–83, Cornwall SE 1983–97; chm Horticultural Ctee 1971–73, asst govt whip 1973–74, memb Select Ctee on European Secdy Legislation 1973–97; vice-chm: Cons Pty Agric Ctee 1971–73 and 1974–81, Cons Pty European Affrs Ctee 1979–81; chm: Westcountry Cons Membs Ctee 1977–78 (sec 1970–73), UK Branch Parly Assoc for Euro-Arab Co-operation 1983–97, Cons Pty Agric Ctee 1988–90; vice-chm Cons Pty Middle East Cncl 1992–96 (treas 1979–92), memb Speaker's Panel of Chairmen 1992–97; Parly advsr: Br Hotels Restaurants and Caterers Assoc 1974–96, Milk Mktg Bd 1985–97; pres Plymouth Albion RFC 1991–96; chm: Westcountry Enterprises Ltd 1997–2002, Silvanus Tst 1997–, Midas Consortium Ltd 2003–, Resound Health (Plymouth) Ltd 2004–; tstee Peninsula Med Sch 1997–2002, chm of govr Plymouth Coll 2004– (govr 1997–); *Recreations* cricket, golf, walking, gardening; *Clubs* MCC, Farmers'; *Style*— Sir Robert Hicks; ✉ Burndoo, Luckett, Callington, Cornwall

HICKS, Sophie; da of late Richard Hicks, and Joan Hicks; *b* 18 September 1960; *Educ* AA Sch of Architecture (AADipl), RIBA; *m* 1988, Roderick Campbell; 1 s (Arthur b 1988), 2 da (Edie b 1990, Olympia b 1995); *Career* fashion ed British Vogue and Tatler magazines 1977–86, acted in the film L'Intervista (dir Federico Fellini) 1986, stylist with Azzedine Alaïa 1986–88, student AA 1987–93, in private practice SH Ltd Architects 1990–; projects: various private house designs 1991–98, architect for Paul Smith's Westbourne House shops 1997–98 and International Shops 1997–2001, architect for Royal Acad exhbns Sensation, Young British Artists from the Saatchi Collection 1997 and Picasso:

H

Painter and Sculptor in Clay 1998, concept for Chloe Stores Worldwide 2001–04 (architect of flagship stores in London, Paris, Tokyo and Hong Kong, plus 100 other stores worldwide); memb Cncl AA 1993–99 (vice-pres 1997–99); *Recreations* travelling; *Style*— Ms Sophie Hicks; ✉ SH Architects Limited, 17 Powis Mews, London W11 1JN (tel 020 7792 2631, fax 020 7727 3328, e-mail sophie@sophiehicks.com, website www.sophiehicks.com)

HICKS, William David Anthony; QC (1995); s of Maj-Gen (William) Michael Ellis Hicks, of Wilts, and Jean Hillary, *née* Duncan; *b* 11 June 1951; *Educ* Eton, Magdalene Coll Cambridge (MA); *m* 1982, Jennifer Caroline, da of Dr Louis Ross; 2 da (Julia Rebecca b 6 June 1986, Olivia Clare b 4 May 1988), 1 s (George David Alexander b 1 March 1990); *Career* called to the Bar Inner Temple 1975; *Recreations* real tennis, fishing, skiing, walking; *Clubs* Flyfishers', MCC; *Style*— William Hicks, Esq, QC; ✉ Landmark Chambers, 180 Fleet Street, London EC4A 2HG (tel 020 7430 1221, fax 020 7421 1399, e-mail clerks@landmarkchambers.co.uk)

HICKSON, Peter Charles Fletcher; s of Geoffrey Fletcher Hickson (d 1978), of Cambridge, and Jane Margaret Amy, *née* Cazenove (d 1993); *b* 30 May 1945; *Educ* Uppingham, Fitzwilliam Coll Cambridge (MA); *m* Rosemary, da of Hugh and Margaret Dawson, of Newport, Gwent; 1 da (Sally b 1978), 3 s (Richard b 1979, David b 1981, James b 1983); *Career* articled clerk Chalmers Impey 1967–71, chief accountant Doulton Glass Industries 1971–78, fin dir Wimpey Asphalt 1978–80, fin dir Tarmac Building Products 1980–85, dep chief exec United Scientific Holdings 1986–89, fin dir MAI plc 1991–96, fin dir PowerGen plc 1996–2002, chm Anglian Water Gp Ltd (formerly AWG plc) 2003–; non-exec dir: Meridian Broadcasting Ltd 1991–95, Intrum Justitia NV 1993–97, Anglia Television 1993–95, RAC plc 1994–2002, Telent plc (formerly Marconi Corp) 2004–, Scottish Power 2006–07, London & Continental Railways Ltd 2007–; govr St John's Sch Leatherhead 2003– (chm 2006–); FCA 1970; *Recreations* cricket, bridge, golf, music; *Clubs* Oxford and Cambridge, City of London, MCC, Royal Wimbledon Golf, Wimbledon Park Golf, Real Club de Golf Las Brisas, Isle of Harris Golf; *Style*— Peter Hickson, Esq; ✉ Anglian Water Group Limited, 111 Park Street, London W1Y 4JL (tel 020 7441 7400, fax 020 7441 7405, e-mail pcfhickson@awg.com)

HIDDLESTON, Prof James Andrew; s of J A Hiddleston, and Helen, *née* Hall; *b* 20 October 1935; *Educ* George Watson's Coll Edinburgh, Univ of Edinburgh (MA, PhD); *m* 1971, Janet Taylor (d 2000); 2 da (Anna b 1972, Jane b 1974); *Career* lectr in French Univ of Leeds 1960–66, fell Exeter Coll Oxford 1966–2003, prof of French Univ of Oxford 1996–2003; DLitt Univ of Oxford 2006; Officier de l'Ordre des Arts et des Lettres (France) 2002; *Books* L'Univers de Jules Supervielle (1965), Malraux: "La Condition humaine" (1973), Poems: Jules Laforgue (ed, 1975), Essai sur Laforgue et les derniers vers, suivi de Laforgue et Baudelaire (1980), Baudelaire and "Le Spleen de Paris" (1987), Laforgue aujourd'hui (ed, 1988), Baudelaire and the Art of Memory (1999), Victor Hugo: Romancier de l'abîme (ed, 2002); *Recreations* golf, hill walking; *Style*— Prof James Hiddleston; ✉ Exeter College, Oxford OX1 3DP (tel 01865 279600)

HIDE, Prof Raymond; CBE (1990); s of Stephen Hide (d 1940), and Rose Edna, *née* Cartlidge (later Mrs Thomas Leonard, d 1995); *b* 17 May 1929; *Educ* Percy Jackson GS, Univ of Manchester (BSc), Univ of Cambridge (PhD, ScD); *m* 1958, (Phyllis) Ann, da of Gerald James William Licence (d 1949), and Margaret, *née* Davis; 1 s (Stephen), 2 da (Julia, Kathryn); *Career* research assoc in astrophysics Univ of Chicago 1953–54, sr res fell Gen Physics Div AERE Harwell 1954–57, lectr in physics Univ of Durham 1957–61, prof of geophysics and physics MIT 1961–67, head Geophysical Fluid Dynamics Laboratory UK Meteorological Office 1967–90, dir Robert Hooke Inst and visiting prof of physics Univ of Oxford 1990–92, research prof Dept of Physics and Earth Scis Univ of Oxford 1992–94 (emeritus prof 1994–), sr research investigator Dept of Mathematics Imperial Coll London 2000–; visiting prof: Dept of Meteorology Univ of Reading 1970–90, Dept of Mathematics UCL 1970–82, Depts of Earth Scis and Maths Univ of Leeds; Adrian fell Univ of Leicester 1980–83, Gresham prof of astronomy Gresham Coll City of London 1985–90, hon sr res fell Inst of Oceanographic Scis Deacon Lab 1990–, hon scientist Rutherford Appleton Lab 1992–; author of numerous scientific papers in learned jls; pres: RMS 1975–76 (hon fell 1989), Euro Geophysical Soc 1982–84 (hon fell 1988), RAS 1983–85; Charles Chree Medal and Prize Inst of Physics 1974, Holweck Medal and Prize Société Française de Physique and Inst of Physics 1982, Gold Medal RAS 1989, William Bowie Medal American Geophysical Union 1997, Hughes Medal Royal Soc 1998, Richardson Medal European Geophysical Soc 1999, Symons Gold Medal Royal Meteorological Soc 2003; Hon DSc: Univ of Leicester 1985, UMIST 1994, Paris 1995; hon fell: Jesus Coll Oxford 1997 (fell 1983–97), Gonville & Caius Coll Cambridge 2001; memb: Academia Europaea 1988, Pontifical Acad of Scis 1996; FAAAS 1964, FRS 1971; *Style*— Prof Raymond Hide, CBE, FRS; ✉ Department of Mathematics, Imperial College London, London SW7 2BZ (e-mail arhide@ntlworld.com)

HIDER, (Kenneth) Mark; s of Maj Kenneth George Hider, RA, of Hampstead, London, and Marian, *née* Richards; *b* 18 September 1953; *Educ* Sir William Borlase's Sch Marlow, Trinity Coll Oxford (MA); *m* 20 June 1981, Nicola Louise, da of John Haigh; 3 s (Tom, Ben, George); *Career* former media res controller Scottish Television, subsequently analyst rising to a sr planner Masius advtg; Ogilvy & Mather advtg: initially sr planner, estab Strategic Analysis Unit, planning dir 1988–91, business devpt dir 1991–92, worldwide dir of strategy 1992–; memb: Mktg Soc, Market Res Soc; MIPA; *Recreations* cricket, soccer, theatre, walking the dog, supporting Manchester United FC, travel; *Style*— Mark Hider, Esq

HIGGINBOTTOM, Dr Edward; s of Walter Higginbottom (d 1973), and Phyllis Higginbottom (d 1994); *b* 16 November 1946; *Educ* Leamington Coll for Boys, CCC Cambridge (John Stewart of Rannoch scholarship in sacred music, organ scholar, BA, MusB, PhD), FRCO (Harding and Read Prizes); *m* Caroline Marie Florence, *née* Barrowcliff; 4 da, 3 s; *Career* res fell Corpus Christi Coll Cambridge 1973–76, fell, organist and tutor in music New Coll Oxford 1976–; advsr to French Miny of Culture on choir schs; memb various local and nat ctees; recorded over 80 CDs as dir or supervisor New College Choir; author various articles in New Grove Dictionary of Music and jls; ed music by Couperin and Telemann; folksong arrangements published by OUP; Commandeur de l'Ordre des Arts et des Lettres (France) 2004 (Officier 1989); hon fell: Guild of Church Musicians, Royal Sch of Church Music; *Recreations* playing the piano, walking, eating oysters; *Style*— Dr Edward Higginbottom; ✉ New College, Oxford OX1 3BN (tel 01865 279519, fax 01865 279590, e-mail edward.higginbottom@new.ox.ac.uk)

HIGGINS, Dr Andrew James; s of Edward James Higgins (d 1966), and Gabrielle Joy, da of Sir John Kelland; *b* 7 December 1948; *Educ* St Michael's Coll Leeds, RVC, Univ of London (BVetMed, PhD), Centre for Tropical Veterinary Med Univ of Edinburgh (MSc); *m* 19 Dec 1981, Nicola Lynn, da of Peter Rex Eliot (d 1980); 1 s (Benjamin b 1982), 3 da (Amelia b 1984, Joanna b 1986, Venetia b 1993); *Career* cmmnd RAVC 1973, Capt, served Dhofar War 1974; veterinary offr HM The Sultan of Oman 1975–76, veterinary advsr The Wellcome Fndn 1977–82, conslt FAO 1981–86, scientific dir and chief exec Animal Health Tst 1988–99, chm Strata Technol Ltd, managing conslt Compton Int Ltd; hon vet advsr to Jockey Club 1988–99, hon scientific advsr Fédération Equestre Internationale 1991– (memb Veterinary Ctee, chm Medication Advsy Gp and Welfare Sub-Ctee); memb: Welfare and Ethics Ctees Zoological Soc of London 1987–, Govt Advsy Ctee on Quarantine 1997–98, Lord Chancellor's Advsy Sub-Ctee for W Suffolk; ed The Veterinary Jl 1991– (dep ed 1990–91); tstee: Dogs Tst, Animals in War Meml Fund; Univ of London Laurel 1971, Equine Veterinary Jl Open Award 1986, Central Veterinary Soc Centenary Prize 1986, Br Veterinary Jl George Fleming Prize 1987, Ciba-Geigy Prize for Research in Animal Health 1985, Pres's Medal Veterinary Mktg Assoc 1997; Liveryman Worshipful Co of Farriers; FIBiol, scientific fell Zoological Soc of London; *Books* An Anatomy of Veterinary Europe (contrib, 1972), The Camel in Health and Disease (ed and contrib, 1986), The Equine Manual (ed, 1995, 2 edn 2005); papers in scientific and general pubns and communications to learned societies; *Recreations* skiing, riding, opera, camels; *Clubs* Buck's, RSM; *Style*— Dr Andrew Higgins; ✉ PO Box 274, Bury St Edmunds, Suffolk IP29 5LW (fax 01284 725463)

HIGGINS, Benny; *Educ* Univ of Glasgow (Football blue); *Career* Standard Life: joined 1983 (qualified actuary 1986), various sr appts, appointed gen mangr (sales) 1996; Royal Bank of Scotland: joined 1997, chief operating offr Tesco Personal Finance 1997–98 (memb Bd), appointed md Retail Banking 1998, chief exec Retail Banking 1999–2006, chm Royal Scottish & Nat West Life, chm RBSG Independent Financial Services; head of retail businesses HBOS plc 2006–; memb Bd Citizens in the USA; *Recreations* reading, art, music, sport - particularly football (former capt Celtic Youth Team); *Style*— Benny Higgins, Esq

HIGGINS, Prof Christopher Francis; s of Prof Philip John Higgins, of Durham, and Betty Ann, *née* Edmonds; *b* 24 June 1955; *Educ* Raynes Park Grammar/Comp Sch, Univ of Durham (scholar, BSc, PhD, W E Foster prize), Royal Coll of Music (exhibitioner, Hugh Bean prize), Univ of Oxford (MA); *m* 1, 1978 (m dis), Elizabeth Mary Joy; 2 da (Alison Elizabeth b 1982, Julia Katherine b 1984); m 2, 1994 (m dis), Suzanne, *née* Wilson; 3 da (Katherine Ann b 1989, Jennifer Dorothy b 1992, Emily Frances b 1995); *Career* SERC/NATO fell Univ of Calif Berkeley 1979–81, prof of molecular genetics Univ of Dundee 1988–89 (lectr 1981–87, reader 1987–88); Univ of Oxford: princ scientist Imperial Cancer Res Fund 1989–93, dep dir Inst of Molecular Med; prof and head Nuffield Dept of Clinical Biochemistry 1993–97; fell: Keble Coll Oxford 1989–93, Hertford Coll Oxford 1993–97; dir MRC Clinical Sciences Centre Imperial Coll London 1998–, prof and head of Div of Clinical Sciences; res fell Lister Inst 1983–89, Howard Hughes int res scholar 1993–98; chair Spongiform Encephalopathy Advsy Ctee (SEAC) 2004–; memb: Cncl BBSRC 1997–2000, Cncl Acad Med Sci 2001–03, Human Genetics Cmmn 2006–, Exec Ctee Assoc of Medical Research Charities; tstee: 2Higher Ground 2001–04, Future Harvest UK 2001–05, Kennedy Inst for Rheumatology 2004–; Fleming award Soc for General Microbiology 1987, CIBA medal and prize Biochemical Soc 1994; fell European Molecular Biology Orgn 1989; FRSE 1990, FMedSci 1998, FRSA 2006; *Recreations* daughters, science, violin playing, opera, classical music; *Style*— Prof Christopher Higgins, FRSE, FMedSci

HIGGINS, Clare Frances Elizabeth; da of James Stephen Higgins, and Paula Cecilia, *née* Murphy; *Educ* St Philomena's Convent Sch, Ecclesbourne Sch, LAMDA; *Career* actress; *Theatre* Royal Exchange: Isabella in Measure for Measure, Alexis in Rollo, Judith in Blood Black and Gold, The Deep Man; Greenwich: Kay in Time and the Conways, Julie in The Rivals, Stella in A Street Car Named Desire; RSC: Titania in A Midsummers Night's Dream 1989–90, Gertrude in Hamlet 1989–90, Cleopatra in Antony and Cleopatra 1992–93; RNT: Lili Brik in The Futurists 1986, Katherine in The Secret Rapture 1988, Queen Elizabeth in Richard III 1990–91, Regan in King Lear 1990–91, Amelia in Napoli Milionaria 1991, Lyndsey Fontaine in The Absence of War 1993–94, Princess Kosmanopolis in Sweet Bird of Youth 1995 (Best Actress: Olivier Award, Critics' Circle Award and Time Out Reader's Award 1995), Martha Dobie in The Children's Hour 1995 (Critics' Circle Best Actress Award 1995), Stella in The Walls 2001, Ursula in Vincent in Brixton (also at Wyndam's Theatre, Golden Theatre, Broadway, The Playhouse Theatre) 2002 (Best Actress Olivier Award, Critics' Circle Award, Evening Standard Award, Tony Nomination); other credits incl: A View from the Bridge (Harrogate), The White Devil (Oxford Playhouse), Beethoven's Tenth (Vaudeville), Jenkin's Ear (Royal Court), The Ride Down Mt Morgan (Wyndhams, world premiere), A Letter of Resignation (Comedy Theatre) 1998, Arkadina in The Seagull, Liz in Private Lives (West Yorkshire Playhouse) 1998–99, Hesione Hushabye in Heartbreak House (Chichester) 2000, Martha in Who's Afraid of Virginia Woolf (Bristol Old Vic) 2002, Hecuba (Donmar Warehouse) 2004 (Best Actress Olivier Award), Death of a Salesman (Lyric Theatre) 2005, Night of the Iguana (Lyric) 2006, Phaedra (Donmar Warehouse) 2006; *Television* incl: Pride and Prejudice, Unity, Byron, The Concubine, Mitch, The Citadel, Cover Her Face, Foreign Body, Beautiful Lies, After the War, Downtown Lagos, Boon, Inspector Alleyn, Circle of Deceit, Men of the Month, Absence of War, Kavanagh QC, Silent Witness; *Film* incl: 1919, Hellraiser, Hellbound, The Fruit Machine, Bad Behaviour, Small Faces, The House of Mirth, Caught in the Act, The Libertine, The Golden Compass; *Recreations* yoga, being in the country, reading, theatre-going, seeing friends, cats; *Style*— Miss Clare Higgins; ✉ c/o Conway van Gelder Ltd, 18–21 Jermyn Street, London SW1Y 6HP (tel 020 7287 0077, fax 020 7287 1940)

HIGGINS, David Charles; s of Prof Peter Higgins, and Jean Margaret Lindsey, *née* Currie; *b* 23 June 1958, Birmingham; *Educ* St Bedes Sch Bishton, Ampleforth, Oxford Brookes Univ (BSc); *Career* grad trainee VNU Business Pubns 1982–85, account exec Lloyd Chapham Assoc 1985–87, fndr and ceo Harvey Nash plc 1987– (Best Small Business Deloitte 1996); RSA 2006; *Recreations* cricket, rugby, golf, travel; *Clubs* RAC; *Style*— David Higgins, Esq; ✉ Harvey Nash Group, 13 Bruton Street, London W1H 7AH

HIGGINS, Prof James; s of Peter Higgins (d 1998), and Annie, *née* McShane (d 2002); *b* 28 May 1939; *Educ* Our Lady's HS Motherwell, Univ of Glasgow (MA), Univ of Lyons (Licence-ès-lettres), Univ of Liverpool (PhD); *m* 1962, Kirstine Anne, da of John Atwell; 2 s (Anthony James b 1964 d 2001, Graham b 1967); *Career* Univ of Liverpool: asst lectr in Latin American Studies 1964–67, lectr 1967–73, sr lectr 1973–83, reader 1983–88, prof of Latin American literature 1988–2004, emeritus prof 2004–; visiting prof: Univ of Pittsburgh PA 1968, Univ of Waterloo Ontario 1974, Univ of WI Trinidad 1979, Univ of Wisconsin-Madison 1990; hon prof: Universidad Nacional Mayor de San Marcos Lima 1984, Univ of Stirling 2006; corresponding fell Peruvian Acad 2002; FBA 1999; Comendador de la Orden al Mérito (Peru) 1988; *Books* César Vallejo: An Anthology of His Poetry (1970), Visión del hombre y de la vida en las últimas obras poéticas de César Vallejo (1970), The Poet in Peru (1982), A History of Peruvian Literature (1987), César Vallejo: A Selection of His Poetry (1987), César Vallejo en su poesía (1990), Cambio social y constantes humanas. La narrativa corta de J R Ribeyro (1991), Hitos de la poesía peruana (1993), Myths of the Emergent. Social Mobility in Contemporary Peruvian Fiction (1994), The Literary Representation of Peru (2002), Lima: A Cultural and Literary History (2005), Historia de la Literatura Peruana (2006); *Recreations* reading, walking, gardening, whisky, Celtic FC; *Style*— Prof James Higgins; ✉ 6 Carlton House, 15 Snowden Place, Stirling FK8 2NR (tel 01786 470641, e-mail james@jameshiggins.wanadoo.co.uk)

HIGGINS, John; s of John and Josephine Higgins; *b* 18 May 1975; *Educ* St Aiden's HS Wishaw; *Career* professional snooker player 1992–; tournament winner: Australian Open 1994, Grand Prix 1994, 1999 and 2005, British Open 1995 and 1998, German Open 1995 and 1997, International Open 1995 and 1996, Castrol/Honda World Team Cup 1996, European Open 1997, Liverpool Victoria Charity Challenge 1997 and 1999, Embassy World Championship 1998 and 2007, Liverpool Victoria UK Championship 1999 and 2000, Benson & Hedges Masters 1999 (runner-up 1995 and 2005), Regal China International 1999, Riley Premier Snooker League 1999, Benson & Hedges Irish Masters 2000, Regal Welsh 2000, Nations Cup 2001, Champions Cup 2001, Scottish Regal Masters 2001, British Open Championship 2001 and 2004, Irish Masters 2002, Saga Masters 2006;

memb Br Inst for Brain Injured Children; *Recreations* golf, football; *Clubs* Wishaw Golf, Southerness Golf; *Style—* John Higgins, Esq (The Wizard of Wishaw)

HIGGINS, Prof Dame Julia Stretton; DBE (2001, CBE); da of George Stretton Downes, and Sheilah, *née* Gavigan; *Educ* Somerville Coll Oxford (BA), Univ of Oxford (DPhil), Univ of London; *Career* SRC research student Physical Chem Lab Oxford 1964–66, physics teacher Mexborough GS 1966–68, SRC research fell Dept of Chem Univ of Manchester 1968–72, research fell Centre de Recherche Macromoleculaire CNRS Strasbourg 1972–73, physicist Institut Laue-Langevin Grenoble 1973–76; Imperial Coll London: lectr 1976–85, reader in polymer sci 1985–89, postgraduate tutor 1989–94, prof of polymer sci Dept of Chem Engrg 1989–, princ Faculty of Engrg 2006–, coll tutor 1990–93, pt/t dean City and Guilds Coll 1993–97; chm Neutron Scattering Gp of Inst of Physics and RSC 1980–84; RSC: memb Faraday Cncl 1984–87 and 1996–98, chm Research Fund Ctee 1991–96, memb Faraday Ed Bd 1994–97, chm Sci Advsy Bd 1998–; memb SERC: Neutron Beam Res Ctee 1979–83 and 1988–91, Sci Planning Gp for Spallation Neutron Source 1977–85, Chem Sub-Ctee ILL Grenoble 1978–81, Polymers and Composites Ctee 1989–94, Materials Cmmn 1991–94; chm EPSRC 2003– (memb Cncl 1994–2000); memb: Instrument Sub-Ctee ILL Grenoble 1986–89, Sci Advsy Cncl of Br Cncl 1993–98, Materials Sector Panel Technol Foresight Prog 1994–98, Cncl for the Central Laboratories of the Research Cncls 1995–2000, Editorial Advsy Bd Jl of Polymer Sci, Cncl for Sci and Technol 1998–, Research Ctee HEFCE 1998–2002; foreign memb Ed Advsy Bd of Macromolecules ACS Jl 1984–87, tstee Daphne Jackson Meml Fellowships 1994– hon fell Somerville Coll Oxford; Hon DSc: Univ of Nottingham 1999, Univ of Oxford 2003, Univ of Sheffield 2003; Hon DEng Heriot-Watt Univ 2000; MACS, CChem, FRSC, FCGI, FIM (memb Cncl 1996–99), FInstP (memb Polymer Physics Ctee 1987–93), FIChemE, CEng, FREng, FRS (memb Cncl 1998 and 1999, foreign sec 2001–); *Publications* over 200 articles in jls; *Recreations* opera, theatre, travel; *Style—* Prof Dame Julia Higgins, DBE, FRS, FREng; ✉ Department of Chemical Engineering, Imperial College, London SW7 2BY

HIGGINS, Mark; s of Andrew Higgins (d 1991), and Kathleen, *née* Monaghan; *b* 31 January 1970, Glasgow; *Educ* Univ of Glasgow (LLB, DipLP); *m* 5 Sept 1997, Rachel, *née* Macleod; 2 da (Leah b 19 July 2001, Amy b 20 May 2003); *Career* admitted slr 1993; ptnr Irwin Mitchell Slrs 1999–; chm E Dunbartonshire Constituency Cons Assoc; memb Law Soc of Scotland 1993; *Publications* Scottish Repossessions (2002); *Recreations* reading, astronomy, football; *Style—* Mark Higgins, Esq; ✉ 5 Drymen Wynd, Bearsden, Glasgow G61 2UB (tel 0141 942 2866); Irwin Mitchell Solicitors, Stewart House, 123 Elderslie Street, Glasgow G3 7AR (tel 0870 150 0100, e-mail mark.higgins@irwinmitchell.com)

HIGGINS, Prof Peter Matthew; OBE (1986); s of Peter Joseph Higgins (d 1952), of Stamford Hill, London, and Margaret, *née* De Lacey (d 1981); *b* 18 June 1923; *Educ* St Ignatius Coll London, UCL, UCH (MB BS); *m* 27 Sept 1952, Jean Margaret Lindsay, da of Capt Dr John Currie, DSO (d 1932), of Darlington, Co Durham; 3 s (Nicholas b 1954, Anthony b 1956, David b 1958), 1 da (Jane b 1959); *Career* Capt RAMC 1948–49; asst med registrar UCH (house physician med unit 1947 and 1950, res med offr 1951–52); princ in gen practice: Rugeley Staffs 1954–65, Castle Vale Birmingham 1966–67, Thamesmead London 1968–88; regnl advsr in gen practice SE Thames 1970–88, prof in gen practice Guy's Hosp Med Sch 1974–88 (sr lectr 1968–73); vice-chm SE Thames RHA 1976–92 (memb 1974–92); chm: Thamesmead Family Serv Unit 1983–91, Kent Family Health Servs Authy 1990–92, Inquiry into A&E Dept King's Coll Hosp 1992, Nurse Practitioner Project Steering Ctee 1992–94, Review (into emergency admission arrangements) Ealing Hosp 1994; pres Section of Gen Practice RSM 1969; memb: Jt Ctee on Hosp Treatment of Acute Poisoning 1966–68 (sec 1968), Standing Med Advsy Ctee DHSS 1970–74, Attendance Allowance Bd 1971–74, Nat Cncl of Family Serv Units 1983–95 (memb Nat Exec 1991–95), London Health Partnership 1994–96; formerly tstee: Thamesmead Community Assoc, Tst Thamesmead; formerly vice-chm of govrs Linacre Centre for Study of Med Ethics; memb: Court Univ of Kent 1979–88, Assembly Univ of Greenwich 1998–; Hon DSc Univ of Greenwich 1998; FRSM 1950, FRCP, FRCGP; *Recreations* reading, music; *Style—* Prof Peter Higgins, OBE; ✉ Wallings, Heathfield Lane, Chislehurst, Kent BR7 6AH (tel 020 8467 2756)

HIGGINS, Rodney Michael; s of Ronald George Platten Higgins (d 1952), and Mina Emily, *née* Botterill (d 1993); *b* 24 October 1927; *Educ* Hurstpierpoint Coll, Univ of Durham (BSc); *m* (Lilian) Joyce, da of late Thomas Bookless (d 1956); 1 s (Michael), 3 da (Lesley, Frances, Nicola); *Career* RE 1946–50; engr; designer and estimator British Reinforced Concrete 1952–54, designer Clarke Nichols & Marcel Bristol 1954–55, Kellogg International Corporation 1955–56, in private practice London 1958–64; princ: Cooper Higgins & Ptnrs Newcastle 1964–76, RM Higgins Assoc 1976–91, Higgins RTJ 1992–95, Higgins-WSP 1995–96, RM Higgins Assoc 1997–99, Crawford Higgins Assoc 2000–; FIStructE 1966, MConsE 1966; *Recreations* industrial archaeology, folklore traditions of wild flowers, genealogy, local history; *Style—* Rodney Higgins, Esq; ✉ Munro, 49 Leazes Park, Hexham, Northumberland NE46 3AX (tel 01434 602941, fax 01434 608519)

HIGGINS, HE Judge; Dame Rosalyn; DBE (1995), QC (1986); da of Lewis Cohen, and Fay, *née* Inberg; *b* 2 June 1937; *Educ* Burlington GS London, Girton Coll Cambridge (minor and major scholar, Campell scholar, Bryce-Tebbs scholar, BA, MA, LLB, Montefiore award), Yale Univ (JSD); *m* 1961, Baron Higgins, KBE, PC, DL (Life Peer), *qv*; 1 s, 1 da; *Career* UK intern Office of Legal Affairs UN 1958, Cwlth Fund fell 1959, visiting fell Brookings Inst Washington DC 1960, jr fell in int studies LSE 1961–63, staff specialist in int law RIIA 1963–74, visiting lectr in law Yale Law Sch 1966 and 1975, visiting fell LSE 1974–78; visiting prof of law: Stanford Law Sch 1975, Yale Law Sch 1977; prof of int law: Univ of Kent Canterbury 1978–81, Univ of London 1981–95; judge Int Court of Justice 1995–; bencher Inner Temple 1989; memb: UN Ctee on Human Rights 1984–95, Gen Course in Public Int Law Hague Acad of Int Law 1991; vice-pres and chm Advsy Cncl British Inst of Int and Comparative Law; guest lectr at numerous univs in Europe and America, memb Bd of Eds American Jl of Int Law 1975–85; Hon Doctorate: Univ of Paris 1980, Univ of Dundee 1992, Univ of Durham 1995, Univ of London 1995, Univ of Greenwich 1996, City Univ London 1996, Univ of Essex 1996, Univ of Cambridge 1996, Univ of Kent 1996, Univ of Sussex 1996, Univ of Birmingham 1997, Univ of Leicester 1997, Univ of Glasgow 1997, Univ of Nottingham 1999, Univ of Bath 2001, Univ of Paris II 2001, Univ of Oxford 2002, Univ of Reading 2003; Yale Univ Medal of Merit 1997; Manley Hudson Medal ASIL 1998; memb Int Law Assoc; hon vice-pres American Soc of Int Law hon life memb American Soc of Int Law, hon memb American Acad of Arts and Sciences; memb Int Law Assoc, memb Institut de Droit International 1991 (assoc 1987); Ordre des Palmes Académiques; *Books* The Development of International Law Through the Political Organs of the United Nations (1963), Conflict of Interests: International Law in a Divided World (1965), The Administration of the United Kingdom Foreign Policy Through the United Nations (1966), UN Peacekeeping: Documents and Commentary (Vol I ME 1969, Vol II Asia 1970, Vol III Africa 1980, Vol IV Europe 1981), Law in Movement-Essays in Memory of John McMahon (jt ed with James Fawcett, 1974), The Taking of Property by the State (1983), International Law and the Avoidance, Containment and Resolution of Disputes (General Course on Public International Law), Vol 230 Recueil des cours (Martinus Nijhoff, 1991), Problems and Process: International Law and How We Use It (1994); author of numerous articles for law jls and jls of int relations; *Recreations* golf, cooking, eating; *Style—* HE Judge Rosalyn Higgins, DBE, QC; ✉ International Court of Justice, Peace Palace, The Hague 2517 KJ, Netherlands

HIGGINS, Baron (Life Peer UK 1997), of Worthing in the County of West Sussex; Rt Hon Sir Terence Langley Higgins; PC (1979), KBE (1993), DL (W Sussex 1988); s of Reginald Higgins, and Rose Higgins; *b* 18 January 1928; *Educ* Alleyn's Sch Dulwich, Gonville & Caius Coll Cambridge (MA, pres Cambridge Union); *m* 1961, HE Judge Rosalyn Higgins, DBE, QC, *qv*, *née* Cohen; 1 s, 1 da; *Career* NZ Shipping Co 1948–55, lectr in econ principles Yale Univ 1958–59, economist Unilever 1959–64; MP (Cons) Worthing 1964–97; min of state Treasy 1970–72, fin sec to Treasy 1972–74; oppn spokesman: on Treasy and Econ Affrs 1966–70 and 1974, on Trade 1974–76, on social security and Treasy House of Lords 1997–2001, on work and pensions House of Lords 2001–05; chm: Cons Parly Sports Ctee 1979–81, Cons Parly Tport Ctee 1979–90, House of Commons Liaison Ctee 1983–97, Treasy and Civil Serv Select Ctee 1983–91 (memb 1980–91); memb Ctee on the Speakership of the House of Lords 2005; chm Public Accounts Commission 1996–97 (memb 1983–97), chm Cncl Inst of Advanced Motorists 1997; govr: Dulwich Coll 1978–95, Alleyn's Sch 1995–2000; memb Cncl: NIESR 1989–, Policy Studies Inst 1988–95; tstee Indust and Parly Tst 1987–91; dir: Warne Wright Group 1976–84, Lex Service Group 1980–92 (chm Lex Service Pension Tstees 1992–2002), First Choice Holidays plc (formerly Owners Abroad Group plc) 1991–97; arbitrator Claims Resolution Tbnl for Dormant Accounts in Switzerland 1998–2002; memb Br Olympic Athletics Team 1948 and 1952; *Clubs* Reform, Hawks' (Cambridge), Royal Blackheath Golf, Koninklijke Haagrche Golf; *Style—* The Rt Hon the Lord Higgins, KBE, PC, DL; ✉ House of Lords, London SW1A 0PW

HIGGINSON, Lucy Amanda; da of Keith Higginson, of Hale Barns, Cheshire, and Judith Rosemary Britain, *née* Godber; *b* 13 March 1970, Gothenburg, Sweden; *Educ* Manchester HS for Girls, Coll of St Hild and St Bede Durham (BA); *m* 27 March 1999, Dr Alexis Warnes; 1 da (Madeleine Charlotte b 4 Sept 2005); *Career* journalist; sub ed rising to dep ed The Field, ed Horse & Hound 2002– (first female ed); *Recreations* riding, hunting, dog walking, rowing; *Clubs* Farmers'; *Style—* Ms Lucy Higginson; ✉ Horse & Hound, IPC Media Ltd, Blue Fin Building, 110 Southwark Street, London SE1 0SU (tel 020 3148 4550, e-mail lucy_higginson@ipcmedia.com)

HIGGS, Brian James; QC (1974); s of James Percival Higgs (d 1984), and Kathleen Anne, *née* Sullivan (d 1993); *b* 24 February 1930; *Educ* Wrekin Coll, Univ of London; *m* 1, 1953 (m dis), Jean Cameron Dumerton; 2 s (Jeremy b 1953, Jonathan b 1963), 3 da (Antonia b 1955, Nicola b 1962, Juliet b 1969); m 2, Vivienne Mary, da of Vivian Oliver Johnson, of Essex; 1 s (Julian b 1982); *Career* cmmnd RA, served 1948–50; called to the Bar Gray's Inn 1955 (bencher 1986), recorder of the Crown Court 1974–98, head of chambers, memb (ad eundem) Hon Soc of Inner Temple; contested (Cons) Romford 1966; *Recreations* gardening, golf, wine, chess, bridge; *Style—* Brian Higgs, Esq, QC; ✉ 5 King's Bench Walk, Temple, London EC4 (tel 020 7353 5638)

HIGGS, Sir Derek Alan; kt (2004); s of Alan Edward Higgs (d 1979), and Freda Gwendoline, *née* Hope (d 1984); *b* 3 April 1944; *Educ* Solihull Sch, Univ of Bristol (BA, LLD); *m* 1970, Julia Mary, da of Robert T Arguile, of Leics; 2 s (Oliver b 1975, Rowley b 1980), 1 da (Josephine b 1976); *Career* S G Warburg & Co Ltd 1972–96 (chm 1994–96), bd dir Prudential plc 1996–2000, sr advsr in UK UBS Investment Bank 2001–05; chm: Business in the Environment 1999–2004, Partnerships UK plc 2000–07, IPD Index Consultative Gp 2001–, Bramdean Gp LLP 2005–, Alliance & Leicester plc 2005–; dep chm: Fund Managers Assoc 1998–2000, Business in the Community 1999–2006, British Land Co plc 2001–06; dir: Coventry City FC Holdings Ltd 1996–, Jones Lang LaSalle Inc 1999–, London Regional Transport 1999–2003, Egg plc 2000–05, Allied Irish Banks plc 2000–05, Arena Coventry Ltd 2003–; tstee: The Alan Edward Higgs Charity 1979–, Textile Conservation Centre Fndn 1979–, Architecture Fndn 1998–2002; memb: City Arts Tst 1995–2001, Financial Reporting Cncl 1996–2005, Advsy Ctee Enviromental Change Inst 2000–04, FTSE4Good Advsy Ctee 2001–03; pro-chllr Univ of Bristol 2002–; CCMI, FCA, FRSA; *Publications* The Role and Effectiveness of Non-Executive Directors (2003); *Style—* Sir Derek Higgs; ✉ 2C Melbury Road, London W14 8LP; Alliance & Leicester plc, 17 Ulster Terrace, London NW1 4PJ (tel 020 7908 3006)

HIGGS, Prof Roger Hubert; MBE (1987); s of Rt Rev Hubert Lawrence Higgs, Bishop of Hull (d 1992), and Elizabeth Higgs, of Chediston, Suffolk; *b* 10 December 1943; *Educ* Marlborough (fndn scholar), Christ's Coll Cambridge (Classics and Tancred scholar, MA, MB BChir, pres JCR, Coll 1st VIII Boat), Westminster Med Sch (Hart prize); *m* 9 Jan 1971, Susan, da of Prof Tom Hewer, and Anne Hewer, of Henbury, Bristol; 1 s (Ben b 18 Dec 1971), 1 da (Jessie b 2 July 1975); *Career* VSO Starehe Boys' Centre Nairobi Kenya 1961–62; house offr posts: Westminster Hosp 1969–70, W Middx Hosp 1970, Whittington Hosp 1970–71; resident med offr Whittington Hosp 1971–72, med registrar St George's Hosp 1972–74, gen practice trainee Dr McEwan and Partners 1974–75, currently princ in gen practice partnership Drs Higgs, Haigh, Herzmark, Nixon, Maycock and Osonuga Walworth London 1975–2004 (founded as solo practice 1975); ldr Lambeth Community Care Centre Devpt Gp 1979–85; King's Coll Sch of Med (now GKT): lectr in gen practice 1978–81, sr lectr and head of dept 1981–89, chair Dept of Gen Practice and Primary Care 1989–2004, dep head Division of Primary Care and Public Health 1998–2004; emeritus prof of gen practice and primary care KCL 2004–; fndr Jl of Med Ethics, chair Editorial Bd and consltg ed Case Conference 2001– (ed 1974–96); memb CND; memb Worshipful Soc of Apothecaries 1978; FRCGP 1986, FRCP 1993; *Books* In That Case (with Alastair Campbell, 1982), A Case Study in Developing Primary Care: The Camberwell Report (1991), Mental Health and Primary Care: A Changing Agenda (1993), New Dictionary of Medical Ethics (1997); also author of papers on medical ethics, devpt and psychosocial issues in primary healthcare; *Recreations* playing oboe, planting trees, listening to classical music and jazz; *Style—* Prof Roger Higgs, MBE; ✉ Department of General Practice and Primary Care, Guy's, King's and St Thomas' Medical School, King's College London, 5 Lambeth Walk, London SE11 6SP (e-mail roger.higgs@kcl.ac.uk)

HIGHAM, John Arthur; QC (1992); s of Frank Greenhouse Higham (d 1988), and Muriel, *née* King; *b* 11 August 1952; *Educ* Shrewsbury, Churchill Coll Cambridge (scholar, MA, LLM); *m* 1, 1982, Francesca Mary Antonietta, *née* Ronan (d 1988); 2 da (Miranda Elizabeth Francesca b 9 April 1983, Charlotte Daisy Emilia b 14 August 1984), 1 s ((John) Christian Alexander b 3 March 1987); m 2, 1988, Catherine Ennis, *qv*; 2 s (Patrick Rupert James b 14 Sept 1989, Edmund George Christopher b 24 March 1992), 1 da (Cecily Mary Catherine b 17 Jan 1994); *Career* called to the Bar Lincoln's Inn 1976 and Gray's Inn (ad eundem) 1989, asst recorder 1998–2000, recorder 2000–; admitted slr and authorised slr advocate 1999, ptnr Stephenson Harwood 2000–04, ptnr White & Case 2004–; *Books* Loose on Liquidators (jt ed, 1981), A Practitioner's Guide to Corporate Insolvency and Corporate Rescues (contrib, 1991), Corporate Administrations and Rescue Procedures (jt ed, 2004); *Recreations* opera, gardening, cricket; *Clubs* Lancashire CCC; *Style—* John Higham, Esq, QC; ✉ White & Case, 5 Old Broad Street, London EC2 (tel 020 7532 1000, fax 020 7532 1001, e-mail jhigham@whitecase.com)

HIGHAM, Nicholas Geoffrey (Nick); s of Geoffrey Arthur Higham, of Abingdon, Berks, Audrey Mary, *née* Hill; *b* 1 June 1954; *Educ* Bradfield, St Catharine's Coll Cambridge (BA); *m* 1981, Deborah Joan, da of Brig J G Starling, CBE, MC; 1 s (William b 12 May 1987), 1 da (Catherine b 10 July 1989); *Career* freelance journalist 1978–88, media corr BBC News and Current Affrs 1988– (arts and media corr 1993–2003), analyst and corr BBC News 24 2003–; presenter of progs on BBC2, BBC Radio 4, BBC Radio Five Live, BBC World Service; *Style—* Nick Higham, Esq; ✉ BBC News and Current Affairs, Television Centre, Wood Lane, London W12 7RJ (tel 020 8743 8000, e-mail nick.higham@bbc.co.uk)

HIGHFIELD, Ashley; s of Roy Highfield, and Sheila, *née* Whitmore; *b* 3 May 1965; *Educ* City Univ Business Sch London; *m* 2005, Charlotte Payter; *Career* media and IT conslt Coopers & Lybrand 1988–94 (participated in launch of Vodacom in South Africa), head of IT and new media NBC 1995–96, dir Flextech Interactive 1996–2000, dir New Media and Technol Div BBC 2000–; *Clubs* Soho House; *Style*— Ashley Highfield, Esq; ✉ BBC, 5th Floor, Broadcast Centre, BBC Media Village, 201 Wood Lane, London W12 7TP (tel 020 8008 5050, fax 020 8008 5090, e-mail ashley.highfield@bbc.co.uk)

HIGHFIELD, Dr Roger; s of Ronald Albert Highfield, of Enfield, Middx, and Dorothea Helena, *née* Depta; *b* 11 July 1958; *Educ* Christ's Hosp, Pembroke Coll Oxford (Domus scholar, MA, DPhil), Queen Elizabeth House Oxford (Leverhulme fell), Balliol Coll Oxford (sabbatical fell); *m* Julia Brookes; 1 da (Holly Elizabeth), 1 s (Rory James Charles); *Career* news/clinical reporter Pulse 1983–84 (dep features ed), news ed Nuclear Engineering International 1984–86; The Daily Telegraph: technol corr 1986, technol ed 1987, science ed 1988–; memb: Bioscience Futures Forum, Health Protection and Soc Advsy Gp, Communications and Public Enjoyment Ctee, Royal Acad of Engineering; former organiser of Live Lab nat experiments; organiser: Science Writer Awards, Visions of Science Awards; advsr Cheltenham Sci Festival; *Awards* Medical Journalist Assoc Award 1987 and 1999 (runner-up 2001), Assoc of Br Sci Writers Awards 1988, 1995, 1997 and 1998, Br Press Awards Specialist Corr of the Year 1989 (commended 1991 and 2001), cited by Save British Science as Campaigning Journalist of the Year, Cwlth Media Award 1994, Chemical Industries Assoc Award 1997; *Books* The Arrow of Time (1990), The Private Lives of Albert Einstein (1993), Frontiers of Complexity (1995), Can Reindeer Fly? (1998), The Science of Harry Potter: How Magic Really Works (2002), After Dolly (2006); *Recreations* care of small children; *Style*— Dr Roger Highfield; ✉ Daily Telegraph, 111 Buckingham Palace Road, London SW1W 0DT (tel 020 7731 2000, fax 020 7731 2876, e-mail science@telegraph.co.uk, website www.rogerhighfield.com)

HIGHTON, David Peter; s of Allan Peter Highton, of Sittingbourne, Kent, and May Highton; *b* 22 May 1954; *Educ* Borden GS, Univ of Bristol (BSc); *m* Wendy Ann; 1 da (Emily Katherine Highton b 7 May 1990); *Career* Turquands Barton Mayhew (now Ernst & Young): articled clerk 1975–78, qualified CA 1978, audit sr 1978–79, audit supr 1979; fin accountant Tunnel Avebe Starches Ltd 1979–81, London controller R P Martin plc 1981–83, fin planning and analysis mangr Watney Mann & Truman Ltd 1986–87 (fin controller (central staffs and Cos) 1983–86), regnl fin dir SE Region Prudential Property Services 1987–89, md Property Mail (pt of Prudential Group until 1990) 1989–90, chief exec Ealing HA 1991–92 (dir of fin and purchasing 1990–92), dir of fin and business devpt Riverside Hosps 1992–94, tst project mangr Chelsea and Westminster Hosp 1993–94; chief exec: Chelsea and Westminster Healthcare NHS Tst 1994–2000, St Mary's Hosp NHS Tst 1998–99 (on secondment), Oxford Radcliffe Hospitals NHS Trust 2000–03; chm Healthwork UK 2001–05, chm Skills for Health 2002–03, md Clinicenta Ltd (formerly Patient Choice Ptnrs) 2003–; pres Sittingbourne RUFC 1999– (chm 1991–94 and 1997–99, treas 1976–90), vice-pres Imperial Medical RFC 1999–, fin sec Gore Court Cricket Club 1994–97; FCA 1989; *Recreations* rugby, cricket; *Style*— David Highton, Esq; ✉ White Cottage, New Yatt, Witney, Oxfordshire OX29 6TF (tel 01993 868432, fax 01993 869043, e-mail david.highton@clinicenta.com)

HIGLETT, Simon Ian; s of John Higlett, of Allesley, Coventry, and Patricia Anne, *née* Such; *b* 30 May 1959; *Educ* Wimbledon Sch of Art (BA), Slade Sch of Fine Art (Higher Dip Fine Art, Leslie Hurry Prize for Theatre Design); *m* 21 Aug 1988, Isobel, da of Alan Arnett, of Tuffley, Gloucester; 2 da (Charlotte Hope b 27 Sept 1994, Emily Georgina b 9 June 1997); *Career* theatre designer; asst to Tim Goodchild 1982–84, head of design New Shakespeare Co 1986–89; bd dir: Arundel Festival, Soc of Br Theatre Designers; artistic assoc (design) Chichester Festival Theatre; *Productions* West End: The Prisoner of Second Avenue (with Richard Dreyfuss and Marsha Mason), A Song at Twilight, Antony and Cleopatra, The Taming of the Shrew (all with Vanessa Redgrave), Blithe Spirit, Man and Boy, The Dresser, The Witches; Comedy Theatre: Talking Heads (with Maggie Smith), Kean (dir Sam Mendes, with Derek Jacobi), Medea (with Eileen Atkins); RSC: Singer (dir Terry Hands, with Antony Sher), The Chiltern Hundreds, A Russian In The Woods, A Long Days Journey Into Night (with Jessica Lange), Thomas More; Chichester: Our Betters (with Kathleen Turner), Beethoven's Tenth (with Peter Ustinov), Mansfield Park, The Miser, A Doll's House, Three Sisters, Scenes from a Marriage; Houston Grand Opera: Resurrection, The Barber of Seville, The Rake's Progress, Don Giovanni, La Traviata, La Cenerentola, The Marriage of Figaro, The Magic Flute; regional tours: The Lion in Winter (with David McCallum), Peer Gynt, The Ride Down Mount Morgan; other credits incl: The Magistrate (Savoy), Lady Windermere's Fan (Haymarketn), In a Little World of Our Own (Donmar), The Force of Change (Royal Court), The Country Wife (Shakespeare Theater Washington DC), Three Sisters: Elizabeth Rex: Accidental Death of an Anarchist (Donmar Warehouse, TMA Designer of the Year Award 2002), Whistling Psyche (Almeida), Of Mice and Men (Savoy), Hay Fever (Haymarket) 2006, Albert Herring (Darmsdadt) 2006, Barber of Seville (Scottish Opera) 2007; *Recreations* reading, drawing, theatre; *Style*— Simon Higlett, Esq; ✉ Oak Tree House, 16 Torton Hill Road, Arundel, West Sussex BN18 9HE (tel 01903 882586)

HIGSON, Charlie; *b* 1958; *Career* writer and comedian; lead vocalist The Higsons 1980–86; *Television* as writer, prodr and actor incl: The Fast Show 1994, Ted & Ralph 1998, Swiss Tony 2003; as writer, prodr and dir: Randall & Hopkirk (Deceased) 2000; *Publications* as Charles Higson: King of the Ants (1992), Happy Now (1993), Full Whack (1995), Getting Rid Of Mister Kitchen (1996); as Charlie Higson: SilverFin: A James Bond Adventure (2005), Blood Fever (2006), Hurricane Gold (2007); *Style*— Charlie Higson; ✉ c/o Curtis Brown Agency, 5th Floor, Haymarket House, 28–29 Haymarket, London SW1Y 4SP (tel 020 7393 4400, fax 020 7393 4401)

HILDITCH, David; MLA; s of David Hilditch, and Agnes, *née* Smith (d 2003); *b* 23 July 1963, Larne, Co Antrim; *Educ* Carrickfergus GS, E Antrim Inst of Further and Higher Educn; *m* 23 July 1987, Wilma; 2 s (Stuart b 1 Aug 1981, Michael b 13 Oct 1989); *Career* worked in building and construction industry 1980–87, with Royal Mail 1987–2004, MLA (DUP) E Antrim 1998– (vice-chair Dept of Social Devpt); memb NI Assembly 1999–; memb Carrickfergus BC 1991– (memb numerous ctees), mayor Carrickfergus 1997–98 and 2005–06 (dep mayor 1995–96); memb: Carrickfergus Dist Policing Partnership, NE Gp Building Control, Ulster Tourist Devpt Assoc, Antrim Coast and Glens Tourist Orgn; RUC Bravery Award 1997; *Style*— David Hilditch, Esq, MLA; ✉ Constituency Office, 31 Lancasterian Street, Carrickfergus, Co Antrim BT38 7AB (tel 028 9332 9980, fax 028 9332 9979, e-mail david.hilditch@btconnect.com); Northern Ireland Assembly, Parliament Buildings, Stormont Estate, Belfast BT4 3XX

HILDYARD, Robert Henry Thoroton; QC (1994); s of Sir David Henry Thoroton Hildyard, KCMG, DFC (d 1997), of London, and Millicent, *née* Baron (d 1998); *b* 10 October 1952; *Educ* Eton, ChCh Oxford (MA); *m* 9 Aug 1980, Isabella Jane, da of James Rennie (d 1964); 3 da (Catherine b 31 Oct 1983, Camilla b 15 May 1985 d 1987, Alexandra b 15 Sept 1988); *Career* called to the Bar: Inner Temple 1977, Lincoln's Inn (ad eundem) 1994 (bencher 2005); jr counsel to the Crown (Chancery) 1992–94, dep judge of the High Court 2001–, attorney-gen to Duchy of Lancaster 2006–; memb Fin Reporting Review Panel 2002–; *Books* contrib to: Butterworths Forms and Precedents: Company Law, Tolleys Company Law; *Recreations* tennis, shooting; *Clubs* Hurlingham; *Style*— Robert Hildyard, Esq, QC; ✉ 4 Stone Buildings, Lincoln's Inn, London WC2A 3XT (tel 020 7242 5524, fax 020 7831 7907)

HILHORST, Rosemary; OBE (2003); da of Raymond Bowditch (d 2002), of Portesham, Dorset, and June, *née* Ebdon; *b* 10 April 1954; *Educ* Woodroffe Sch Lyme Regis, UCL (BSc), Chelsea Coll (PGCE); *m* 10 April 1981, Francis Hilhorst, s of Henk Hilhorst (d 1991); 1 da (Malaika b 5 April 1982), 1 s (Sean b 6 Jan 1985); *Career* physics/integrated science teacher: Portslade Community Coll 1976–80, Int Sch of Tanganyika Dar es Salaam 1980–82, American Cultural Assoc Turin 1982–83, Portesham CE Primary Sch (pt/t) 1983–84; British Council: science advsr 1985–86, asst rep Khartoum 1986–88, head Exchanges Unit Khartoum 1988–89, head Project Devpt Dept (asst dir 1989–90), dir Bratislava 1991–93, dir Slovakia 1993–95, UK 1995–97, dir Tanzania 1997–2000, UK 2000–03, dir Portugal 2003–; memb Governing Body Br Assoc for Central and Eastern Europe 2000–02; *Recreations* family, literature, walking, running and cycling; *Style*— Mrs Rosemary Hilhorst, OBE; ✉ c/o British Council, Rua Luis Fernandes I, 1249–062, Lisbon, Portugal (tel 00 351 213 214 542)

HILL, Alfred Edward; MBE (2006); s of Mervyn Ewart Phillips Hill, of Gozo, and Betty Deborah Jane Matilda, *née* Bennett; *b* 29 August 1945; *Educ* Clifton, IMEDE (MBA); *m* 14 July 1973, Rosemary Scarth, da of John William Chandos Lloyd-Kirk; 2 c (Charlotte Rosina b 13 Aug 1975, Rupert Alfred b 23 Dec 1977); *Career* articled clerk: Monahans Swindon 1964–66, Grace Ryland (formerly CJ Ryland & Co) 1966–69; qualified CA 1969, seconded to Spafax SA 1972; ptnr: Thomson McLintock 1974–87, KPMG 1987–95 (conslt 1995–96); underwriting memb Lloyd's 1979–93; fndr chm Freeways Tst for the disabled 1976–2004, govr Clifton Coll 1989–; FCA 1979 (ACA 1969); *Clubs* Clifton, Bristol Savages; *Style*— Alfred Hill, Esq, MBE, FCA; ✉ Campfield, Church Road, Abbots Leigh, Bristol BS8 3QU (tel 01275 372104, fax 01275 374937, e-mail aers.hill@fish.co.uk)

HILL, Prof (Hugh) Allen Oliver; s of Hugh Rankin Stewart Hill (d 1974), and Elizabeth, *née* Burns; *b* 23 May 1937; *Educ* Royal Belfast Academical Inst, Queen's Univ Belfast (BSc, DPh, Hon DSc), Univ of Oxford (MA, DSc); *m* 29 June 1967, Dr Boglarka Anna, da of Pal Pinter (d 1945); 2 s (Alister Pal Stewart b 1969, Roderick Ferenc Allen b 1972), 1 da (Natalie Elizabeth Margit b 1974); *Career* Univ of Oxford: DSIR res fell Inorganic Chemistry Lab 1962–64, Wadham Coll 1962–64, Turner and Newall res fell 1964–65, Weir jr res fell UC 1964, fell and tutor in chemistry The Queen's Coll 1965–2004 (now emeritus), departmental demonstrator in inorganic chemistry 1965–67, lectr in inorganic chemistry 1967–90, sr proctor 1976–77, reader in bioinorganic chemistry 1990–92, prof of bioinorganic chemistry 1992–2004 (now emeritus); strategic technologies dir Oxford Biosciences Ltd; visiting lectr Dept of Biological Chemistry Harvard Univ 1970–71, visiting prof Harvard Univ 1996–2002, assoc Dept of Med Peter Bent Brigham Hosp Boston 1970–71, Cwlth visiting fell Univ of Sydney Aust 1973, inorganic lectr W Coast USA 1981, visiting prof Univ of Calif 1982; hon fell Wadham Coll Oxford 2002; FRSC 1978 (Interdisciplinary award 1987, Chemistry and Electrochemistry of Transition Metals medal 1990, Robinson award 1994), Breyer medal Royal Aust Chemical Inst; FRS 1990 (Mullard medal 1993); *Publications* Physical Methods in Advanced Inorganic Chemistry (Interscience London, ed with P Day, 1968), Inorganic Biochemistry Vol 1 2 & 3 (specialist periodical report RSC London, 1979), Chemical and Biochemical Aspects of Superoxide Dismutases (Elsevier/North-Holland NY, ed with J V Bannister, 1980); *Recreations* opera, theatre, film, gardening; *Style*— Prof Allen Hill, FRS; ✉ The Queen's College, Oxford OX1 4AW (tel 01865 279120); Inorganic Chemistry Laboratory, South Parks Road, Oxford OX1 3QR (tel and fax 01865 275900, e-mail allen.hill@chem.ox.ac.uk)

HILL, Prof (Norman) Berkeley; s of Ewart Edward Wesley Hill (d 1984), and Doris May, *née* Nelson; *b* 6 May 1944; *Educ* Univ of Nottingham (BSc), Univ of Reading (PhD); *m* 1970, Hilarie Angela, *née* Scott; 2 da (Deborah b 1966, Emily b 1974), 1 s (Timothy b 1972); *Career* lectr, sr lectr and reader in agricultural economics Wye Coll Univ of London 1970–99, prof of policy analysis Dept of Agricultural Sciences Imperial Coll London (formerly Wye Coll) 1999–2005 (emeritus prof 2005–); conslt/advsr: Eurostat, European Cmmn, NAO, Defra, OECD, UNECE; memb Agricultural Economics Soc 1967; *Books* incl: Size and Efficiency in Farming (with D K Britton, 1975), An Introduction to Economics for Students of Agriculture (1980, 3 edn 2006), Farm Tenure and Performance (with Ruth Gasson, 1984), Economics for Agriculture: Food, Farming and the Rural Economy (with Derek Ray, 1987), Farm Incomes, Wealth and Agricultural Policy (1989, 3 edn 2000), Policy Reform and Adjustment in the Agricultural Sectors of Developed Countries (with David Blandford, 2006); *Recreations* choral conductor and organist; *Style*— Prof Berkeley Hill; ✉ 1 Brockhill Road, Hythe, Kent CT21 4AB (tel 01303 265312, fax 01303 237381); Imperial College London, Wye Campus, Ashford, Kent TN25 5AH (e-mail b.hill@imperial.ac.uk)

HILL, Bernard; *b* 17 December 1944; *Career* actor; *Theatre* incl: John Lennon in John, Paul, George, Ringo... and Bert (West End), Toby Belch in Twelfth Night, title role in Macbeth (Leicester Haymarket), Lopakhin in The Cherry Orchard (Aldwych), Eddie in A View From the Bridge (Bristol Old Vic and Strand Theatre); *Television* for BBC: Boys from the Blackstuff, John Lennon - A Journey in the Life, The Burston Rebellion, New World, Permanent Red, The Lawlord, Olly's Prison - Edward Bond Trilogy Once Upon a Time in the North; for Channel 4: Squaring the Circle, Lipstick on your Collar, Without Walls - The Art of Tripping; other credits incl: The Mill on the Floss, Great Expectations; *Film* incl: The Bounty, Gandhi, The Chain, Restless Natives, No Surrender, Bellman and True (and TV series), Drowning By Numbers, Shirley Valentine, Mountains of the Moon, Skallagrigg (also TV release), The Wind in the Willows, The Ghost and the Darkness, Titanic, Short Stories, True Crime, A Midsummer Night's Dream, The Loss of Sexual Innocence, Blessed Art Thou, The Criminal, The Lord of the Rings - The Two Towers, The Lord of the Rings - The Return of the King, The Scorpion King, The Boys from County Clare, Gothika; *Recreations* skiing, squash, tennis, swimming, fishing, Apple Macintosh; *Style*— Bernard Hill, Esq; ✉ c/o ARG Talent, 4 Great Portland Street, London W1W 8PA

HILL, Sir Brian John; s of Gerald A Hill, OBE (d 1974); *b* 19 December 1932; *Educ* Stowe, Univ of Cambridge (MA); *m* 1959, Janet Joyce, da of Alfred S Newman, OBE; 3 c; *Career* Nat Serv Army; gp md Higgs and Hill Ltd 1972–83, exec chm Higgs and Hill plc 1989–92 (chm and chief exec 1983–89); chm: Goldsborough Holdings 1993–97, The Children's Tst Tadworth 1998–; dir: Building Centre 1981–85, Lazard Property Unit Trust 1982–98, Sackville Property Unit Tst 1998–, Lancs and Yorks Property Management Ltd 1985–93, Etonbrook Property plc 1985–93, Property Services Agency 1986–88, Southern Regnl Bd National Westminster Bank 1990–92, London Docklands Development Corp 1994–98; memb Advsy Bd Property Services Agency 1981–86; pres: Bldg Employers' Confedn 1992–95 (pres London Region 1981–82, chm Nat Contractors Gp 1983–84), Chartered Inst of Building 1987–88, Health Projects Abroad 1992–99; chm Vauxhall Coll of Bldg and Further Educn 1976–86; dir Gt Ormond Street Hosp for Children NHS Tst 1984– (chm 1992–97, special tstee 1997–2000), chm Children's Tst 1998–; govr: Aberdour Sch Tadworth 1987–, Pangbourne Coll 2000–04; external examiner Univ of Reading 1993–97; tstee Falklands Islands Meml Chapel 1997–; Hon DSc, Hon LLB; memb Ct of Assts Worshipful Co of Chartered Surveyors (Master 1994–95); FRICS, FCIOB, Hon FIStructE, Hon FCGI; *Recreations* travelling, tennis, gardening, amateur dramatics; *Clubs* RAC; *Style*— Sir Brian Hill; ✉ Corner Oak, 5 Glen Close, Kingswood, Surrey KT20 6NT (tel 01737 832424)

HILL, (Robert) Charles; QC (1974 NI); s of Benjamin Morrison Hill (d 1968), of Belfast, and Mary, *née* Roche (d 1980); *b* 22 March 1936; *Educ* St Paul's Sch Belfast, St Malachy's Coll Belfast, Queen's Univ Belfast (LLB), Trinity Coll Dublin (MA); *m* 1961, Kathleen, *née* Allen, da of Robert Wilson Allen; 1 da (Kathryn Elizabeth b 18 Nov 1962), 3 s

(Robert Charles Michael b 30 Dec 1963, Niall Benjamin Morrison b 19 March 1969, Alan Lawther Roche b 13 March 1974); *Career* called to the Bar: NI 1959 (bencher 1988), Gray's Inn 1971, King's Inn Dublin 1986; sr counsel Ireland 1987; referee under Finance Act 1976; chm: Statutory Ctee of Pharmaceutical Soc of NI 1977–92, Poisons Bd of NI 1982–92, Standing Advsy Cmmn on Human Rights in NI 1992–95 (memb 1990–95); *Recreations* farming, forestry; *Style*— Charles Hill, Esq, QC

HILL, Dr Christina Bernadette Thérèse; DL (Berks 2005); da of Howard E Hill (d 1971), and Elsie, *née* Punnett-Beale (later Mrs Robert L Hall, d 2003); *Educ* Univ of Wales (BA), Univ of Birmingham (MA, PhD); *partner* (David) Clive Harries Williams, OBE; 1 step da (Rebecca b 1975), 1 step s (Robert b 1977); *Career* Tidy Britain Gp: field offr 1977, dir Midlands 1977–81, dir Devpt and Trg 1981–88, head of research and legislation 1988; dir of public affrs Aviation Environment Fedn & Tst 1988–89, nat dir Sch & Gp Travel Assoc (SAGTA) 1988–94; environmental and educnl conslt 1988–; UK Environmental Law Assoc (UKELA): hon dir of conferences and hon annual conference organiser 1989–93, memb Cncl of Mgmnt 1989–95, memb Noise Working Pty 1989–96, co sec 1995–96, gen sec 1996–2006, life memb 2006; co sec TecKnow Ltd 1995–98; lay interviewer Ind Tribunal Service 1999, census enumerator 2001; vice-chm Berks Environment Tst 1990–92 (memb Exec Ctee 1989–92); Berks Healthcare Tst: non-exec dir 2001–, co-convenor 2002–04, chair Clinical Effectiveness Ctee 2002–04, chair Improving Working Lives Steering Gp 2004–; memb Lord Chllr's Advsy Ctee on JPs and Appointments Panel (Berks) 1998– (chm Appointments Panel 2001–, memb W Berks Advsy Sub-Ctee 2001–), chm Berks Gen Cmmrs of Income Tax 2004– (gen cmmr 1998–, divnl vice-chm 2001–03), presenter and facilitator Nat Training Prog for Gen Cmmrs 2004–, memb Berks Advsy Ctee for Gen Cmmrs of Income Tax 2006–; YWCA: chair Steering Gp for Major Appeal Ctee 1993, acting chair Appeal Ctee 1994, chair Open The Door Appeal Ctee 1994–95, chair Special Events Ctee 1996, memb YWCA Incorporated Co 1996–, YWCA Bd of Govrs and Audit Ctee 1996–99; advsr Bd of Tstees Prisoners Abroad 1990–95 (vice-chair Fundraising Ctee 1988, memb Fundraising Working Gp 1990–93), memb Exec Ctee SPISE (Sane Planning in the SE) 1989– (memb Working Gp 1989–91, memb Policy Gp 1991–93), vice-patron Abbeyfield House Reading 2000– (vice-patron Appeal 1998–2000); CPRE Berks: memb Exec Ctee 2002–, vice-chm 2003–06, chm 2006–; author various pubns for Tidy Britain Gp and SAGTA, ed SAGTA News 1989–92; affiliate memb Inst of Wastes Mgmnt 1994– (assoc memb 1981–94), assoc memb Chartered Inst of Environmental Health 1988; FIPD 1985–96, FRGS 1989, FRSA 1989; *Recreations* reading, theatre, music, walking, skiing, gardening, keeping ducks; *Style*— Dr Christina Hill, DL; ✉ Honeycroft House, Pangbourne Road, Upper Basildon, Berkshire RG8 8LP (tel and fax 01491 671631)

HILL, Rt Rev Christopher John; *see:* Guildford, Bishop of

HILL, Damon Graham Devereux; OBE (1997); s of (Norman) Graham Hill, OBE (d 1975, twice Formula 1 world champion 1962 and 1968), and Bette Hill; *b* 17 September 1960; *Educ* Haberdashers' Aske's; *m* 21 Oct 1988, Georgie; 2 s, 2 da; *Career* Formula 1 racing driver; Williams test driver 1991 and 1992, first Grand Prix (Silverstone) 1992 (driving for Brabham team); driver with: Canon Williams team 1993, Rothmans Williams Renault team 1994, 1995 and 1996, Danka Arrows Yamaha team 1997, Benson and Hedges Jordan team 1998–99, ret; winner: Hungarian Grand Prix 1993 and 1995, Belgian Grand Prix 1993, 1994 and 1998, Italian Grand Prix 1993 and 1994, Spanish Grand Prix 1994, British Grand Prix 1994, Portuguese Grand Prix 1994, Japanese Grand Prix 1994 and 1996, Argentinian Grand Prix 1995 and 1996, San Marino Grand Prix 1995 and 1996, Australian Grand Prix 1995 and 1996, Brazilian Grand Prix 1996, Canadian Grand Prix 1996, French Grand Prix 1996, German Grand Prix 1996; Formula 1 World Drivers' Championship: third place 1993, second place 1994 and 1995, world champion 1996; 84 Grand Prix starts, 21 wins, 20 pole positions, 19 fastest laps, 41 podium finishes; pres British Racing Drivers' Club 2006–; chm: Damon Hill BMW, P1 International Ltd; *Awards* Sportsman of the Year Daily Express 1993, Newsround's Sportsman of the Year 1994, RAC Trophy 1994, Gold Star Award for Courage Daily Star 1994, International Racing Driver of the Year Autosport Awards 1994 and 1996, British Competition Driver of the Year Autosport Awards 1995 and 1996, Driver of the Year Guild of Motoring Writers 1994, BBC Sports Personality of the Year 1994 and 1996, sixteen awards (incl Gold Stars 1993, 1994, 1995 and 1996) British Racing Drivers' Club 1993, 1994, 1995 and 1996, Abbey National RADAR People of the Year Award 1996, Autosprint Golden Helmet Award 1996, l'Automobile Magazine Trophy 1996, Daily Mirror Sports Personality of the Year 1996, Barclaycard Daily Telegraph Champion of British Sport 1996, Bluebird Trophy for British Achievement 1996, Blue Peter Gold Badge 1996, Sunshine Award The Sun 1997; *Books* Damon Hill Grand Prix Year (1994), Damon Hill My Championship Year (1996); *Video* Damon Hill The Fight for Victory (1996); *Recreations* golf, music, motorcycles, skiing, playing the guitar, training; *Style*— Damon Hill, Esq, OBE

HILL, David Neil; *b* 13 May 1957; *Educ* Chetham's Sch Manchester, St John's Coll Cambridge (organ scholar); *Career* asst to Dr George Guest St John's Coll Cambridge, studied under Gillian Weir and Peter Hurford; sub-organist Durham Cathedral, master of music Westminster Cathedral 1982–87, dir of music Winchester Cathedral 1987–2002; artistic dir Philharmonia Chorus 1992–98, dir Waynflete Singers 1987–2002, music dir Bach Choir 1998–, organist and dir of music St John's Coll Cambridge 2003–07, chief conductor BBC Singers 2007–; princ conductor: Southern Sinfonia 2003, Leeds Philharmonic 2004; dir numerous choral workshops and summer schs UK, USA, Australasia; FRCO 1974; Hon DMus Univ of Southampton 2002; *Performances* organ recitals: NY, Chester Cathedral, Colston Hall Bristol, Lincoln Cathedral, Truro Cathedral, Bridgewater Hall Manchester, Royal Festival Hall, St Alban's; *Recordings* incl: William Byrd and John Blow Anthems (works by Stanford), Rachmaninov Vespers (with Philharmonia Chorus), Fauré's Requiem, Elgar's The Dream of Gerontius (with Bournemouth Symphony Orch), works by Mendelssohn, Bairstow and Jongen (with Choir of St John's Coll), works by Howells (with Bach Choir), works by Finzi (with Bournemouth Symphony Orch and Chorus); as conductor of: Bournemouth Symphony Orch, Brandenburg Consort, City of London Sinfonia, Parley of Instruments, Philharmonia Orch, English Chamber Orch, Liverpool Philharmonic Orch, BBC Philharmonic Orch, London Philharmonic Orch, Florilegium, Britten Sinfonia, Ulster Orch, Orch of the Age of Enlightenment, Westminster Cathedral Choir, Winchester Cathedral Choir, The Bach Choir, Waynflete Singers, Choir of St John's Coll; *Books* Giving Voice (jtly); *Clubs* Athenaeum; *Style*— David Hill, Esq; ✉ c/o Caroline Phillips Management, The Old Brushworks, 56 Pickwick Road, Corsham, Wiltshire SN13 9BX

HILL, Dominic; *b* 22 April 1969, Wimbledon; *Educ* Douai Sch, Lincoln Coll Oxford (BA); *Career* dir The Room Orange Tree Studio Theatre 1993–94, asst dir Perth Theatre 1994–96, asst dir RSC 1997, assoc dir Orange Tree Theatre 1998–99, currently artistic dir Dundee Rep Theatre (previously assoc dir, best dir Scottish Critics Awards for Scenes from an Execution 2004, nomination best dir TMA/Barclays Theatre Awards for The Winter's Tale 2001); prodns as freelance dir at Mercury Theatre Colchester, Salisbury Playhouse, Greenwich Theatre, Derby Playhouse, Northcott Theatre Exeter, Cotteloe Theatre RNT, Nuffield Theatre Southampton, Bath Theatre Royal, Bush Theatre, Open Air Theatre Regent's Park; *Style*— Dominic Hill, Esq; ✉ Dundee Rep Theatre, Tay Square, Dundee DD1 1PB (tel 01382 227684, e-mail dhill@dundeereptheatre.co.uk)

HILL, Prof (Anthony) Edward (Ed); s of Anthony Sidney Hill, and Philomena Ward; *b* 30 December 1959, Coventry; *Educ* Bishop Wulstan RC HS Rugby, Univ of Sheffield (BSc), UCNW Bangor (MSc, PhD); *m* 1989, Jacqueline Patricia, *née* Caukwell; 2 s (Oliver b 1991, Patrick b 1993); *Career* lectr then sr lectr in oceanography UCNW Bangor (latterly Univ of Wales Bangor) 1986–99, dir Proudman Oceanographic Lab NERC 1999–2005, hon visting prof Univ of Liverpool 1999–2004, dir Nat Oceanography Centre Southampton 2005–; memb Exec Bd NERC 2001–, chm Bd Nat Centre for Ocean Forecasting 2005–07; author of numerous pubns on shelf sea oceanography in learned jls; memb Challenger Soc for Marine Sci; FIMarEst, chartered marine scientist 2006; *Recreations* oil painting, visiting historic monuments, walking; *Style*— Prof Ed Hill; ✉ National Oceanography Centre, University of Southampton, Waterfront Campus, European Way, Southampton SO14 3ZH (tel 023 8059 6666, e-mail ehill@noc.soton.ac.uk)

HILL, Prof Geoffrey William; *b* 18 June 1932, Bromsgrove, Worcs; *Educ* Co HS Bromsgrove, Keble Coll Oxford (MA); *Career* poet; prof of English lit Univ of Leeds 1976–80, univ lectr in English Univ of Cambridge and fell Emmanuel Coll Cambridge 1981–88; Boston Univ: prof of lit and religion 1988–2006, co-dir Editorial Inst 1998–2004, univ prof emeritus and prof emeritus of lit and religion; Churchill fell Univ of Bristol 1980, hon fell Keble Coll Oxford 1981–, hon fell Emmanuel Coll Cambridge 1990–, assoc fell Centre for Research in Philosophy and Lit Univ of Warwick 2004–; Joseph Bard meml lectr RSL 1979, Judith Wilson lectr Univ of Cambridge 1980, F W Bateson meml lectr Univ of Oxford 1984, Clark lectr Trinity Coll Cambridge 1986, T S Eliot centenary lectr Univ of Leeds 1988, Warton lectr Br Acad 1998, Morris Gray lectr Harvard Univ 1998, Tanner lectr BNC Oxford 2000, Ward-Phillips lectr Univ of Notre Dame 2000, President's lectr Univ of Montana 2000, TS Eliot meml lectr St Louis 2001, Sidney Keyes lectr Queen's Coll Oxford 2003, Charles Rosenthal lectr Brown Univ 2004, Empson lectr Cambridge Univ 2005, Goldsmith lectr Univ of Leeds 2006; MA by incorporation Univ of Cambridge 1984; DLitt (hc) Univ of Leeds 1988; FRSL 1972, FAAAS 1996; *Awards* Gregory Award for Poetry 1961, Hawthornden Prize 1969, Geoffrey Faber Meml Prize 1970, Whitbread Award 1971, Heinemann Award 1971 and 1999, Alice Hunt Bartlett Award 1971, Duff Cooper Meml Prize 1979, Loines Award American Acad and Inst of Arts and Letters 1983, Ingram Merrill Fndn Award in Lit 1985, Kahn Award 1998, Cholmondeley Award Soc of Authors 1999, T S Eliot Prize Ingersoll Fndn 2000; *Publications* Henrik Ibsen's Brand: A Version for the Stage (1978, 3 edn 1996), The Lords of Limit: Essays on Literature and Ideas (1984), The Enemy's Country: Words, Contexture and other Circumstances of Language (1994), Style and Faith (2003); *Poetry* For the Unfallen (1959), King Log (1968), Mercian Hymns (1971), Somewhere is Such a Kingdom: Poems 1952–1971 (1975), Tenebrae (1978), The Mystery of the Charity of Charles Péguy (1983), Collected Poems (1985), New and Collected Poems 1952–1992 (1994), Canaan (1996), The Triumph of Love (1998), Speech! Speech! (2000), The Orchards of Syon (2002), Scenes from Comus (2005), Without Title (2006), Selected Poems (2006), A Treatise of Civil Power (2007); *Style*— Prof Geoffrey Hill

HILL, Harry Douglas; s of Jack Hill, of S Yorks, and Katheline Francis, *née* Curran; *b* 4 April 1948; *Educ* Holgate GS Barnsley; *m* 1 (m dis 1979), Glenis Margaret, *née* Brown; 2 s (Jonathan b 1973, Matthew b 1975); *m* 2, 23 Nov 1985, Mandy Elizabeth, da of Frederick Aldred, of Downham Market, Norfolk; 3 s (William b 1986, Joshua b 1987, Rupert b 1992); *Career* surveyor; articles A E Wilby & Son Barnsley 1964–67, various surveying appts 1967–74; ptnr: David Bedford Norfolk 1974–82, Hill Nash Pointen 1982–84, James Abbott Partnership 1984–86; dir Mann & Co 1986–87; Countrywide Assured Gp plc: dir 1987–88, md 1988–2006, chm 2007–; *Style*— Harry Hill, Esq; ✉ Countrywide Assured Group plc, Countrywide House, Perry Way, Witham, Essex CM8 3SX (tel 01376 533700, fax 01376 520465)

HILL, (Michael) Hedley; s of late Kenneth Wilson Hill, and Dorothy, *née* Etchells (d 1984); *b* 3 February 1945; *Educ* Rydal Sch Colwyn Bay, St John's Coll Cambridge; *Career* admitted slr 1969; NP; ptnr Weightmans Liverpool 1971–95 (conslt 1995–97); gen cmmr for Income Tax 1996–; pres Liverpool Law Soc 1992–93 (vice-pres 1991–92), former chm Liverpool Young Slrs Gp; dir: Slrs' Benevolent Assoc 1999–2006, Liver Housing Assoc (chm 2001); memb Bd Arena Housing Gp 2006–; former pres Old Rydalian Club; dep chm Arena Housing Assoc 2001–05; memb: Law Soc, Liverpool Law Soc; *Recreations* canal boating, oenology; *Clubs* Union Soc Cambridge; *Style*— Hedley Hill, Esq; ✉ Fulwood Park Lodge, Liverpool L17 5AA (tel 0151 727 3411, e-mail michael@hedleyhill.com)

HILL, Sir James Frederick; 4 Bt (UK 1916), of Bradford; OBE (2000), DL (W Yorks 1994); s of Sir James Hill, 3 Bt (d 1976), and Marjory, *née* Croft; *b* 5 December 1943; *Educ* Wrekin Coll, Univ of Bradford; *m* 1966, Sandra Elizabeth, da of late J C Ingram, of Ilkley, W Yorks; 3 da (Juliet Clare (Mrs Kaberry-Hill) b 1969, Georgina Margaret b 1971, Josephine Valerie b 1976), 1 s (James Laurence Ingram b 1973); *Heir* s, James Hill; *Career* chm Sir James Hill (Wool) Ltd; Hon DUniv 1997; *Recreations* walking, sailing, golf; *Clubs* RAC, Bradford, Ilkley, St Enodoc; *Style*— Sir James F Hill, Bt, OBE, DL; ✉ Roseville, Moor Lane, Menston, Ilkley, West Yorkshire LS29 6AP (tel 01943 874624)

HILL, Jeremy Adrian; s of Lt-Col Cecil Vivian Hill (d 1978); *b* 16 January 1940; *Educ* Eton, ChCh Oxford; *m* 1965, Virginia Ann, da of Maj Gordon Darwin Wilmot; 3 s; *Career* chm: Schroder Japan Growth Fund plc, Colne Stour Countryside Assoc; Liveryman Worshipful Co of Goldsmiths; *Recreations* tennis, shooting, tree planting; *Style*— Jeremy Hill, Esq; ✉ Peyton Hall, Bures, Suffolk; Schroder Investment Management Ltd, 31 Gresham Street, London EC2V 7QA (tel 020 7658 6000)

HILL, Prof (William) John; s of Rowan Jardine Hill, and Dorothy Isobel Hill; *b* 15 February 1954; *Educ* The Acad Annan, Univ of Glasgow (MA), Univ of York (PhD); *Career* Univ of Ulster: lectr 1978–88, sr lectr 1988–98, prof of media studies 1998–2004; prof of media Royal Holloway Univ of London 2004–; visiting prof of film Hochschule für Fernsehen und Film Munich 1994–95, visiting prof of media studies Aichi Shukutoku Univ Nagoya 1997–98, sr res fell AHRB Centre for Br Film and Television Studies 2001–02; dir UK Film Cncl 1999–2004 (chair Working Pty on Specialised Exhbn and Distribution 2001–02), chair NI Film Cncl 1994–97, govr BFI 1994–97; chair Working Gp on the Film Industry in Europe European Inst for the Media 1998–2004, memb Communications, Cultural and Media Studies Panel HEFCE Res Assessment Exercise 1996; founding chair Foyle Film Festival 1987; FRSA; *Books* Sex, Class and Realism: British Cinema 1956–63 (1986), Cinema and Ireland (jtly, 1987), Border Crossing: Film in Ireland, Britain and Europe (co-ed, 1994), Big Picture, Small Screen: The Relations Between Film and Television (co-ed, 1996), The Oxford Guide to Film Studies (co-ed, 1998), British Cinema in the 1980s (1999), Film Studies (co-ed, 2000), American Cinema and Hollywood (co-ed, 2000), World Cinema (co-ed, 2000), National Cinema and Beyond (co-ed, 2004), Film History and National Cinema (co-ed, 2005), Cinema and Northern Ireland (2006), National Cinemas and World Cinema (2006); *Style*— Prof John Hill; ✉ Department of Media Arts, Royal Holloway, University of London, Egham, Surrey TW20 0EX (tel 01784 414684, e-mail john.hill@rhul.ac.uk)

HILL, Jonathan Hopkin; CBE (1995); s of Rowland Louis Hill, and Paddy Marguerite, *née* Henwood; *b* 24 July 1960; *Educ* Highgate Sch, Trinity Coll Cambridge (MA); *m* 3 Sept 1988, Alexandra Jane, da of John Nettelfield, MC; 2 da (Georgia Elizabeth b 9 Oct 1991, Harriet Victoria b 10 Jan 1993), 1 s (Archie William Augustus b 1 June 1995); *Career* RIT & Northern 1983, Hamish Hamilton 1984–85, Cons Research Dept 1985–86, special advsr to Rt Hon Kenneth Clarke at Dept of Employment, DTI and Dept of Health 1986–89, Lowe Bell Communications 1989–91, No 10 Policy Unit 1991–92, political sec to PM 1992–94, sr conslt Bell Pottinger Communications (formerly Lowe Bell Communications) 1994–98, dir Quiller Consultants 1998–; memb: Cncl Nat Literacy Tst,

Advsy Bd Reform; govr: Highgate Sch, Hanford Sch; *Books* Too Close to Call (with Sarah Hogg, 1995); *Style*— Jonathan Hill, Esq, CBE; ✉ Quiller Consultants, 11–12 Buckingham Gate, London SW1E 6LB

HILL, Judith Lynne; LVO (1995); da of Dr Michael James Raymond (d 1996), and Joan, *née* Chivers; *b* 8 October 1949; *Educ* Brighton and Hove HS, Univ of Cambridge (MA); *m* 1, 9 Oct 1976 (m dis 1986), Brent Arthur Hill; 1 da (Olivia b 1981); m 2, 6 March 1987, Edward Richard Regenye, s of Edward Joseph Regenye (d 1987), of New Jersey, USA; *Career* admitted slr 1975, ptnr Farrer and Co 1986; former chm: Ctee 20 Int Bar Assoc, Charity Law Assoc; memb Law Soc; *Recreations* travel, gardening; *Clubs* Reform; *Style*— Mrs Judith Hill, LVO; ✉ Messrs Farrer & Co, 66 Lincoln's Inn Fields, London WC2A 3LH (tel 020 7242 2022, fax 020 7831 9748, e-mail jlh@farrer.co.uk)

HILL, Rt Hon (Trevor) Keith; PC (2003), MP; s of late George Ernest Hill, and late Ena Ida, *née* Dakin; *b* 28 July 1943; *Educ* City of Leicester Boys' GS, CCC Oxford (MA), UC Wales Aberystwyth (DipEd); *m* 19 May 1972, Lesley Ann Sheppard, da of late Heinz Doktor; *Career* tutorial asst in politics Univ of Leicester 1966–68, Belgian Govt scholar Brussels 1968–69, lectr in politics Univ of Strathclyde 1970–73 (res asst 1969–70), res offr Lab Pty International Dept 1974–76, political offr RMT (formerly NUR) 1976–92; MP (Lab) Streatham 1992–; asst Govt whip 1998–99, Parly under-sec of state DETR 1999–2001, Treas of HM Household (dep Govt chief whip House of Commons) 2001–03, min for housing and planning ODPM 2003–05, PPS to the PM 2005–; *Books* European Political Parties (contrib, 1969), Electoral Behaviour (contrib, 1974); *Recreations* films, books, music, walks; *Style*— The Rt Hon Keith Hill, MP; ✉ 110 Wavertree Road, London SW2 3SN (tel 020 8674 0434); House of Commons, London SW1A 0AA (tel 020 7219 6980)

HILL, Kenneth Leslie (Ken); s of William Leslie Hill (d 1965), of Great Barr, Birmingham, and Doris Agnes, *née* Clarke (d 1975); *b* 13 May 1941; *Educ* West Bromwich Tech HS, West Bromwich Tech Coll, Wolverhampton Poly, Alban & Lamb Coll, Harvard Business Sch; *m* 2 Sept 1964, Wendy, da of George Somerville; 2 da (Suzanne Marie b 8 Aug 1965, Lisa Joanne b 28 Nov 1971), 2 s (Christopher David, Richard Anthony (twins) b 28 July 1966); *Career* accountant West Bromwich CBC 1957–62, sr accountant Walsall CBC 1962–67, chief accountant Harlow Development Corp 1967–69, chief fin offr Essex River Authy 1969–72, chief fin offr Glamorgan River Authy 1972–73, dir of fin Severn Trent Water 1973–89, gp dir of fin Pennon Group plc (formerly South West Water plc) 1989–2002; chm: Eden Project Ltd 1999–, Vocalis plc 2000–04, Clear Communications Ltd; chm Westcountry Rivers Tst; CIPFA 1963; *Recreations* golf, cricket, squash, tennis; *Clubs* Harvard Business, Isle of Purbeck Golf; *Style*— Ken Hill, Esq; ✉ Eden Project Ltd, Bodelva, Cornwall PL24 2SG (tel 01726 811918, fax 01726 811959)

HILL, Rt Rev Michael Arthur; *see:* Bristol, Bishop of

HILL, Prof Peter David; s of Derryck Albert Hill (d 1988), and Phyllis Mary, *née* Carn; *b* 16 March 1945; *Educ* Leighton Park Sch Reading, Univ of Cambridge and St Bartholomew's Hosp London (MA, MB BChir); *m* 10 June 1972, Christine Margaret, da of Stanley William Seed (d 1996), of Seaton, Devon; 2 s (Gulliver b 1974, Luke b 1976), 1 da (Jessica b 1981); *Career* registrar then sr registrar Maudsley Hosp 1972–79, hon conslt St Thomas' Hosp 1981–89, conslt Tadworth Court Children's Hosp 1987–, sr lectr then prof of child mental health, head of section and conslt in child and adolescent psychiatry St George's Hosp and Med Sch Univ of London 1992–98, conslt, departmental head and prof Great Ormond St Hosp for Children 1998–2003 (hon conslt 2003–), emeritus prof Univ of London 1998–, visiting prof St George's Hosp 1999–; conslt advsr Huntercombe Manor Hosp 1998–, conslt advsr British Army, med advsr Tourette Syndrome (UK) Assoc, advsr Select Ctee on Health 1995–97, specialist advsr Health Advisory Serv 1999–2003; currently ind medical practictioner; pres Union Européene des Médecins Spécialistes (Child and Adolescent Psychiatry) (UEMS-CAPP) 2002–06; chm Child and Adolescent Specialist Section RCPsych 1993–97; memb Professional Bd Addiss; FRCPsych 1987 (MRCPsych 1975), FRCP 1994 (MRCP 1972), FRCPCH 1997 (MCPCH 1996); *Books* Essentials of Postgraduate Psychiatry (jtly, 1979, 1986 and 1997), A Manual of Practical Psychiatry (jtly, 1986), Adolescent Psychiatry (1989), The Child Surveillance Handbook (jtly, 1990 and 1994), The Child with a Disability (jtly, 1996), Child Mental Health in Primary Care (jtly, 2001), A Perfect Start (jtly, 2007); *Recreations* jazz trumpet, house restoration; *Style*— Prof Peter Hill; ✉ Strand End, 78 Grove Park Road, London W4 3QA; 17 Wimpole Street, London W1G 8GB (tel 020 7323 1535, fax 020 7323 9126)

HILL, 9 Viscount (UK 1842) Peter David Raymond Charles Clegg-Hill; 11 Bt (GB 1727); also Baron Hill of Almarez and of Hardwick (UK 1814); the full title of the Viscountcy is Viscount Hill of Hawkstone and of Hardwick; s of Maj Hon Frederic Raymond Clegg-Hill (ka 1945), 2 s of 6 Viscount Hill, and Hon Mrs Frederic Clegg-Hill; suc cous, 8 Viscount Hill (d 2003); *b* 17 October 1945, (posthumously); *Educ* Tabley House Sch; *m* 1973 (m dis 2000, remarried 2002), Sharon Ruth Deane (changed name by deed poll to Savanna Summer Dawson), of NZ; 5 da (Hon Catherine b 1974, Hon Jennifer b 1976, Hon Susan b 1980, Hon Rachel b 1984, Hon Melissa b 1986), 2 s (Hon Paul Andrew Raymond b 1979 d 2003, Hon Michael Charles David b 1988); *Heir* s, Hon Michael Hill; *Career* farmer; *Style*— The Rt Hon the Viscount Hill

HILL, Reginald Charles; s of Reginald Hill (d 1961), and Isabel, *née* Dickson; *b* 3 April 1936; *Educ* Carlisle GS, St Catherine's Coll Oxford (BA); *m* 1960, Patricia, da of Leslie Ruell; *Career* worked for Br Cncl Edinburgh 1960–61; English teacher: Royal Liberty Sch Romford 1962–64, Fryerns Sch Basildon 1964–67; English lectr Doncaster Coll of Educn 1967–81; author; Crimewriters' Assoc Gold Dagger Award 1990, Diamond Dagger Award 1995; memb: Crime Writers' Assoc 1971, The Detection Club 1978, Soc of Authors 1984; FRSL; *Books* A Killing Kindness (1980), Who Guards A Prince (1982), Traitor's Blood (1983), Deadheads (1983), Exit Lines (1984), No Man's Land (1985), Child's Play (1987), The Collaborators (1987), Under World (1988), Bones and Silence (1990), Recalled to Life (1992), Blood Sympathy (1993), Pictures of Perfection (1994), The Wood Beyond (1996), Killing the Lawyers (1997), On Beulah Height (1998), Singing the Sadness (1999), Arms and the Women (2000), Dialogues of the Dead (2001), Death's Jest-Book (2002), Good Morning, Midnight (2004), The Stranger House (2005), The Death of Dalziel (2007); novels under the pseudonym of Patrick Ruell incl: The Long Kill (1986), Death of a Dormouse (1987), Dream of Darkness (1989), The Only Game (1991); novels under the pseudonym of Dick Morland: Heart Clock (1973), Albion! Albion! (1974); novels under the pseudonym of Charles Underhill: Captain Fantom (1978); short story collections: Pascoe's Ghost (1979), There are No Ghosts in the Soviet Union (1987); *Plays* An Affair of Honour (BBC, 1972), Ordinary Levels (Radio 4, 1982); *Recreations* fell walking, listening to classical music, watching rugby, Siamese cats; *Style*— Reginald Hill, Esq; ✉ c/o Caradoc King, A P Watt Ltd, Literary Agents, 20 John Street, London WC1N 2DR (tel 020 7405 6774, fax 020 7831 2154)

HILL, Richard Anthony; MBE (2004); *b* 23 May 1973, Dormansland, Surrey; *Educ* Stratford-sub-Castle Sch Salisbury, Bishop Wordsworth Sch Salisbury, Brunel Univ; *Career* rugby union player (flanker); currently with Saracens RUFC; England: 71 caps, debut v Scotland 1997, winners Six Nations Championship 2000, 2001 and 2003 (Grand Slam 2003), ranked no 1 team in world 2003, winners World Cup Aust 2003, capt v NZ Barbarians 2003; memb Br & I Lions touring squad South Africa 1997, Aust 2001 and NZ 2005; *Style*— Mr Richard Hill, MBE

HILL, District Judge Robert Nicholas; s of Edward Hill, and Sylvia Grace, *née* Kingham; *b* 19 October 1947; *Educ* Salford GS, Manchester Coll of Commerce, Coll of Law Lancaster Gate; *m* 30 Sept 1967, Ann Elizabeth, da of Bernard Frost, and Lily Frost; 1 s (Giles Robert b 20 Aug 1976), 1 da (Shona Ann b 1 Jan 1980); *Career* jr clerk Messrs Hall Brydon & Co Slrs Manchester 1964–67, articled to Michael Bowman Bowman's Slrs Minehead 1968–73, admitted slr 1974 (John Mackrell Prize); Coll of Law Chester: lectr 1974–78, sr lectr 1978–83, princ lectr 1983–88, memb Bd of Mgmnt 1988–92; princ Coll of Law York 1988–92, dist judge 1992–, asst recorder 1996–2000, recorder 2000–; visiting prof of law Leeds Metropolitan Univ 1998–; memb: Law Soc 1974–, Assoc of Dist Judges 1992–; fell Inst of Legal Execs 1972 (associate 1967); TA: joined 1978, trg RMA Sandhurst 1980, cmmd 33 Signal Regt, RARO York 1988–2002; *Books* Civil Litigation (with John O'Hare, 1980, 10 edn 2001), How To Survive Your Articles (1987), Supreme Court Practice (The White Book) (ed 1997–2000, sr ed 2000–), A Practical Guide to Civil Litigation (with Helen Wood and Suzanne Fine, 2003, 2 edn 2006); author of numerous articles; *Style*— District Judge Robert Hill; ✉ Scarborough County Court, Pavilion House, Valley Bridge Road, Scarborough, North Yorkshire YO11 2JS (tel 01723 366361)

HILL, Robin Arthur; s of Paul Colin Hill, and Ellen, *née* Barclay-Moore (d 1993); *b* 2 January 1956; *Educ* Victoria Univ of Manchester (BA (Arch), BArch); *m* 1985, Dawn Rebecca Teago; 1 da (Tamsin b 1992), 1 s (Tobias b 1998); *Career* architect in private practice 1988–; expert witness 1992–; memb Nat Cncl RIBA 1997–2003; MAE, corp memb RIBA 1985; *Style*— Robin Hill, Esq; ✉ Robin Hill Chartered Architects, 93 Ashley Road, Altrincham, Cheshire WA14 2LX (tel 0161 928 7143, fax 0161 928 7144, e-mail robinhill@riba.demon.co.uk)

HILL, Selima; da of James Wood, and Elisabeth, *née* Robertson (d 1991); *b* 13 October 1945; *Educ* New Hall Cambridge; *m* 1968, Roderic Hill; 1 da (Maisie b 1970), 2 s (Moby 1972, Albert 1977); *Career* author; writer in residence: Royal Festival Hall 1992, Science Museum London 1996; writing fell UEA 1991, tutor Exeter and Devon Arts Centre 1990–96, tutor South Bank Centre 2001, Royal Literary Fund fell 2003; exhibitor Imperial War Museum 1996; judge T S Eliot Prize 1999; memb Assoc Faculty Schumacher Coll 19920, cultural exchange visit to Mongolia 1993 and 1994; winner: Cholmondeley Award for Lit 1989, Arvon Observer Int Poetry Competiton 1989, Arts Cncl writers bursary 1993; shortlisted: T S Eliot Prize, Forward Prize and Whitbread Poetry Award 1997; *Books* Saying Hello at the Station (1984), My Darling Camel (1987), The Accumulation of Small Acts of Kindness (1988), Point of Entry (multimedia work Imperial War Museum, 1990), A Little Book of Meat (1993), Trembling Hearts in the Bodies of Dogs (1994), Violet (1996), Bunny (2001, winner Whitbread Poetry Book of the Year 2001), Portrait of My Lover as a Horse (2002); *Recreations* swimming, learning Mongolian; *Style*— Ms Selima Hill; ✉ c/o Bloodaxe Books, PO Box 1SN, Newcastle upon Tyne NE99 1SN (tel 01830 520590, fax 01830 520596)

HILL, Shaun Donovan; s of George Herbert Hill (d 1969), and Molly, *née* Cunningham, of London; *b* 11 April 1947; *Educ* The London Oratory, St Marylebone GS; *m* 11 June 1966, Anja Irmeli, da of Martti Toivonen, of Lahti, Finland; 1 s ((Kim) Dominic b 18 Jan 1967), 2 da (Maija b 9 April 1972, Minna b 10 June 1975); *Career* cook: Carrier's Restaurant London 1968–71, The Gay Hussar London 1972–74, Intercontinental Hotel London 1975–76; head chef: Capital Hotel Knightsbridge 1976–77, Blakes Chelsea 1978–80, Lygon Arms Broadway 1981–82; chef and patron Hill's Stratford-upon-Avon 1983–85, chef and md Gidleigh Park Chagford 1985–94, chef and proprietor Merchant House Ludlow 1995– (8 out of 10 Good Food Guide 1999 and 2000); memb Académie Culinaire de France 1982, elected master chef by Master Chef's Inst 1983, Egon Ronay Guide Chef of the Year 1992, Catey Chef Award 1993; research fell Dept of Classics Univ of Exeter; *Books* Shaun Hill's Gidleigh Park Cookery Book, Quick and Easy Vegetables, Masterclass, Cooking at the Merchant House (2000), How To Cook Better (2004), The Cook's Book (jtly, 2005), Food in Ancient World (jtly, 2006); *Recreations* eating and drinking (not necessarily in that order); *Style*— Shaun Hill, Esq; ✉ 24 Droitwich Road, Worcester WR3 7LH

HILL, Stanley Arthur; s of John Henry Hill (d 1976), and Edith Muriel, *née* Mathews (d 1985); *b* 22 May 1935; *Educ* Townsend C of E Sch St Albans; *m* 9 July 1960, Elizabeth Scott (Betty), da of late James McKay; 2 da (Elizabeth Scott b 19 Feb 1962, Catherine McKay b 11 Nov 1963); *Career* Nat Serv RMP 1953–55, served ME; gp md Coopers Holdings Ltd until 1994; Queen's Award for Export 1982 and 1986; pres Br Scrap Fedn 1993–94; Br vice-pres Bureau Int de la Recuperation (BIR) 1989–94; memb Ctee: 1986 Industry Year, Lechlade Soc; FInstD 1968; *Recreations* cricket, golf; *Clubs* Burford Golf (pres 1996–), Parkstone Golf; *Style*— Stanley Hill, Esq; ✉ The Butts, Bryworth Lane, Lechlade, Gloucestershire GL7 3DY (tel 01367 252598, fax 01367 253232); Forsyte Shades, Canford Cliff, Poole, Dorset (tel 01202 701449)

HILL, Stephen Guy; s of Michael Lawrence Hill, and Joan Florence, *née* Luce; *b* 19 July 1960; *Educ* King Edward VII Sch Lytham, St John's Coll Cambridge (MA), Harvard Grad Sch of Business (Prog for Mgmnt Devpt); *Career* conslt Boston Consulting Gp 1982–85, exec asst to ceo Guinness plc 1985–87, dir of strategy Pearson plc 1987–92, md Watford Observer Newspapers Ltd 1992–93, md Oxford and County Newspapers Ltd 1993–95; chief exec: Westminster Press Ltd 1995–96, The Financial Times Newspaper Ltd 1996–98, The Financial Times Group Ltd 1998–2002, The Sporting Exchange Ltd 2003–05; chm Interactive Data Corp 2000–02, fndr and chm The Harbour Gp 2002–; dir: MarketWatch.com 2000–02, RAW Communications 2000–02, Royal & SunAlliance plc 2000–04, Psion plc 2003–, Channel 4 2006–; memb Mgmnt Bd Pearson plc 1998–2002; memb Devpt Cncl Whitechapel Art Gallery 2000–03; *Recreations* triathlon, gardening, travel; *Style*— Stephen Hill, Esq

HILL, Susan Elizabeth (Mrs Stanley Wells); da of R H Hill, and Doris, *née* Bailey; *b* 5 February 1942, Scarborough; *Educ* Scarborough Convent, Barr's Hill Sch Coventry, KCL (BA); *m* Prof Stanley Wells, *qv*; 3 da (Jessica b 1977, Imogen b 1984 d 1984, Clemency b 1985); *Career* novelist, playwright, book reviewer; *Novels* The Enclosure (1961), Do Me A Favour (1963), Gentleman and Ladies (1968), A Change for the Better (1969), I'm the King of the Castle (1970), Strange Meeting (1971), The Bird of Night (1972), In the Springtime of the Year (1974), The Woman in Black (1983), Air and Angels (1991), The Mist in the Mirror (1992), Mrs de Winter (1993), The Service of Clouds (1997), The Various Haunts of Men (2004), The Pure in Heart (2005), The Risk of Darkness (2006), The Man in the Picture (2007); *Non-Fiction* The Magic Apple Tree (autobiography, 1982), People (ed, 1983), Through the Kitchen Window (1984), Through the Garden Gate (1986), The Lighting of the Lamps (1987), Shakespeare Country (1987), The Spirit of the Cotswolds (1988), Family (autobiography, 1989), Reflections from a Garden (1995); *Children's Books* One Night at a Time (1984), Mother's (1985), Can it be True? (1987), Susie's Shoes (1989), I've Forgotten Edward (1990), I Won't Go There Again (1990), Pirate Poll (1991), The Glass Angels (1991), Beware, Beware (1993), King of King's (1994), The Christmas Collection: An Anthology (1995); *Short Stories* The Albatross (1970), A Bit of Singing and Dancing (1973), The Penguin Book of Modern Women's Short Stories (ed, 1991), The Penguin Book of Contemporary Women's Short Stories (ed, 1995), The Second Penguin Book of Women's Short Stories (ed, 1997), Listening to the Orchestra (1997), The Boy Who Taught the Beekeper to Read (2003); *Style*— Miss Susan Hill; ✉ website www.susan-hill.com

HILL, Prof William George; OBE (2004); s of William Hill (d 1984), of Hemel Hempstead, Herts, and Margaret Paterson, *née* Hamilton (d 1987); *b* 7 August 1940; *Educ* St Albans Sch, Wye Coll London (BSc), Univ of Calif Davis (MS), Iowa State Univ, Univ of Edinburgh (PhD, DSc); *m* 1 July 1971, (Christine) Rosemary, da of John Walter Austin (d 2002), of Kingskerswell, Devon; 2 da (Louise b 1973, Rachel b 1974), 1 s (Alastair b 1977); *Career* Univ of Edinburgh: lectr 1965–74, reader 1974–83, prof of animal genetics 1983–2002 (emeritus prof 2003–), head Inst of Cell, Animal and Population Biology

1990–93, head Div of Biological Sciences 1993–98, dean and provost Faculty of Sci and Engrg 1999–2002; visiting prof and visiting research assoc: Univ of Minnesota 1966, Iowa State Univ 1967–78, N Carolina State Univ 1979, 1985 and 1988–2005; ed: Animal Production 1971–78, Livestock Production Science 1994–95, Genetical Research 1996–; ed-in-chief Proceedings of the Royal Soc B 2005–; memb: Sci Study Gp Meat and Livestock Cmmn 1969–72, AFRC Animals Res Grant Bd 1986–92, Dir's Advsy Gp AFRC Animal Breeding Res Orgn 1983–87, AFRC Inst of Animal Physiology and Genetics Res 1987–93, Bd of Govrs Roslin Inst 1994–2002 (dep chair 1998–2002), Cncl Royal Soc 1993–94, RAE Biological Scis Panel 1995–96 and 1999–2001 (chair 1999–2001); chair Nat Conservation Ctee Animal Genetic Research 2001–02; pres: Br Soc of Animal Sci 1999–2000 (vice-pres 1997–99), Cwlth Scholarships Cmmn 1998–2004 (dep chair 2002–04); vice-pres Genetics Soc 2004–; Hon DSc N Carolina State Univ 2003, Dr (hc) Univ of Edinburgh 2005; FRSE 1979, FRS 1985; *Books* Benchmark Papers on Quantitative Genetics (1984), Evolution and Animal Breeding (1989); *Recreations* farming, bridge; *Clubs* Farmers'; *Style—* Prof William Hill, OBE, FRS, FRSE; ✉ 4 Gordon Terrace, Edinburgh EH16 5QH (tel 0131 667 3680); Institute of Evolutionary Biology, School of Biological Sciences, University of Edinburgh, West Mains Road, Edinburgh EH9 3JT (tel 0131 650 5705, fax 0131 650 6564, e-mail w.g.hill@ed.ac.uk)

HILL ABRAHAMS, Rosalind Margaret; da of Brian Percival Hill (d 1992), and Joan Barbara Warren, *née* Rollinson (d 2004); *b* 18 April 1955; *Educ* St Margaret's Convent Sussex, Univ of Exeter (BA); *m* 7 June 1997, David Jacques Abrahams; *Career* Ernst & Young 1977, J Henry Schroder Wagg & Co Ltd 1986, dir corporate fin P&P plc 1988–92; dir: Capita Corporate Finance Ltd 1992–93, Beaumont Cornish Ltd 2000–, Consilium Capital Ltd 2006; independent corp advsr Warren Hill & Co 1992–; memb: The Pilgrims, Int Fundraising Ctee of Br Red Cross; Liveryman Worshipful Co of Glaziers and Painters of Glass; MInstD, ACA 1981, FRSA 2001; *Recreations* travel, entertaining, the arts; *Style—* Mrs Rosalind Hill Abrahams; ✉ Warren Hill & Co, 93 Cheyne Walk, London SW10 0DQ (tel 020 7352 8617)

HILL-ARCHER, Clive; s of late Malcolm Hill-Archer, and Agnes Keech, *née* Harrison, of Headley, Hants; *b* 23 March 1946; *Educ* Duke of York Sch Nairobi, Dulwich Coll, SW London Tech Coll (HND Business Studies), DipM (CIM), Univ of Strathclyde (MSc); *m* 2 April 1966, Valerie Frances, *née* Balchin; 2 da (Maxine Louise b 6 Feb 1969, Naomi Angelina b 29 Aug 1970); *Career* account mangr/dir with several advtg agencies incl Garland Compton, Dorland Grey (Paris) and Allen Brady & Marsh 1967–80, Univ of Strathclyde 1980–82, new technol mangr Thames Television Ltd 1982–84, mktg dir Thorn EMI Cable Television Ltd 1984–86, mktg devpt dir Tupperware UK and Ireland 1986–87, mangr mktg consultancy Pannell Kerr Forster Associates 1987–92, non-exec dir International Weather Productions 1990–93, owner/managing conslt Niche Marketing & Communications 1992–97, head of mktg Hempsons 1997–; interim exec mktg mangr The Wine Soc 1996; memb Nat Cncl CIM 1990–97 (Pres's Award 1993); visiting lectr in mktg London Guildhall Univ 1988–95; external examiner: Univ of E London 1995–98, South Bank Univ 1999–2002; memb: Wine Soc, BASC; memb: PCC St Bride's 2005, Guild of St Bride's 2006; Freeman City of London 1991, Liveryman Worshipful Co of Marketors 1991; Assoc of MBAs 1986, memb Professional Services Mktg Gp 1997; FCIM 1990 (MCIM 1969), MIMC 1997, certified mgmnt conslt 1997, chartered marketer 1998; *Recreations* rambling, driving (follower of motor sport), shooting, wine, the Arts (ballet, music, theatre and art); *Style—* Clive Hill-Archer, Esq; ✉ 127 Turney Road, Dulwich Village, London SE21 7JB (tel 020 7274 5235, fax 020 7274 4482, e-mail chillarcher@aol.com); Office (tel 020 7839 0278 ext 742, e-mail c.hill-archer@hempsons.co.uk)

HILL-NORTON, Vice Adm the Hon Sir Nicholas John; KCB (1991); s of Adm of the Fleet Baron Hill-Norton, GCB (Life Peer, d 2004); *b* 1939; *Educ* Marlborough, BRNC Dartmouth; *m* 1966, Ann Jennifer, da of Vice Adm Dennis Mason, CB, CVO (d 1996); 2 s (Simon b 1967, Tom b 1975), 1 da (Claudia b 1969); *Career* RN: Capt HMS Invincible 1983–84, Flag Offr Gibraltar 1987–90, Flag Offr Flotilla Three and Cdr Anti-Submarine Warfare Striking Force Atlantic 1990, Flag Offr Surface Flotilla 1992, DCDS 1992; HQ dir and defence advsr Marconi Electronic Systems Ltd 1995–2000; dir: Matra Marconi Space 1996–2000, Lear Astronics USA 1996–99, Marconi North America (USA) 1996–2000; vice-pres RUSI 1999–2003; chm: British Greyhound Racing Bd 2000–02, King George's Fund for Sailors 2003–2007; memb UK Advsy Bd Tenix Pty Ltd (Aust) 2003–07; *Recreations* travel, good food, fishing, shooting, golf, tennis, cooking, extended family; *Clubs* Farmers', Royal Navy of 1765 and 1785; *Style—* Vice Admiral the Hon Sir Nicholas Hill-Norton, KCB; ✉ King George's Fund for Sailors, 8 Hatherley Street, London SW1P 2YY (tel 020 7932 0000); e-mail nick.hill-norton@tenix.com

HILL SMITH, Marilyn; da of George Francis Smith, and Irene Charlotte, *née* Clarke; *b* 9 February 1952; *Educ* Nonsuch HS For Girls Ewell Surrey, Guildhall Sch of Music & Drama; *Career* opera singer; soprano soloist: Viennese Gala Performances Southbank and touring 1975–80, Gilbert & Sullivan For All touring England Australasia (1974) USA/Canada (1975–76) 1969–75; debut: BBC Radio 1975, princ soprano ENO 1978 (memb co 1978–84), Royal Opera House 1981, New Sadler's Wells Opera 1981, Canadian Opera 1984, Welsh Nat Opera 1987, Scottish Opera 1988, New D'Oyly Carte Opera 1990, Singapore Opera 1992 and 1993; festivals incl: Aldeburgh, Henley, Versailles, Nurenburg, Cologne, Athens, Granada, Bologna, Siena, Rome, Zimbabwe, Hong Kong; TV incl: Top C's and Tiaras (C4) 1983, Queen Mother's 90 Birthday Celebration 1990; recordings incl: Dixit Dominus (CBS Masterworks) 1977, The Songwriters (BBC) 1978, Christopher Columbus (Opera Rara) 1978, La Princesse de Navarre (Erato) 1980, Dinorah (Opera Rara) 1980, Robinson Crusoe (Opera Rara) 1981, Count of Luxembourg and Countess Maritza (New Sadler's Wells Opera) 1983, Vienna Premiere Vol I (Chandos, Music Retailers Assoc award 1984) 1983, Friday Night is Music Night (BBC Records) 1985, Treasures of Operetta Vol I (Chandos Retailers Assoc award 1985) 1985, Vienna Premiere Vol II (Chandos) 1987, Ruddigore (New Sadler's Wells) 1987, Candide (Bernstein, Scottish Opera) 1988, Treasures of Operetta Vol III (Chandos) 1989, Pirates of Penzance (New D'Oyly Carte, Music Retailers Assoc) 1990, Student Prince (TER) 1990, Marilyn Hill Smith sings Kálmán and Lehár (Chandos) 1991, Is It Really Me? (TER) 1991, Edwardian Echoes (Chandos) 1992, Novello Centenary (Chandos) 1992, Celebrating the Musicals (BBC) 1998, Friday Night is Music Night (BBC) 1998, The Rose of Persia (BBC) 1999; patron: Epsom Light Opera 1998, Central Festival Opera 1999, Ivor Novello Appreciation Bureau 2001, Bromley OEcumenical Singers 2005, Sinfonia Britannia 2006; teacher and adjudicator Fedn of Music Festivals; *Recreations* cooking, reading, sleeping; *Style—* Ms Marilyn Hill Smith; ✉ c/o Music International, 13 Ardilaun Road, Highbury, London N5 2QR (tel 020 7359 5183, fax 020 7226 9792)

HILL-WOOD, Peter Denis; s of Denis John Charles Hill Hill-Wood, MC (d 1982), of Hartley Wintney, Hants, and Mary Cecilia, *née* Martin Smith (d 1997); *b* 25 February 1936; *Educ* Eton; *m* 1971, Sarah, *née* Andrews; 1 da (Sarah Frances b 5 July 1972), 2 s (Julian Peter b 16 Jan 1974, Charles Denis b 21 April 1976); *Career* with David A Bevan Simpson & Co (later de Zoete & Bevan) stockbrokers 1956–60; Hambros Bank Ltd: joined 1960, exec dir i/c fund mgmnt 1968, vice-chm 1987, non-exec dir 1994–96, ret; chm: Arsenal Football Club plc, Top Technology Ltd; dir Peter Hambro Mining plc 2003–, non-exec dir Delphi Group plc 1996–98; *Recreations* association football, golf, country pursuits; *Clubs* White's, Pratt's; *Style—* Peter Hill-Wood, Esq

HILLARY, Sir Edmund Percival; KG (1995), KBE (1953); s of Percival Augustus Hillary, of Remuera, Auckland, NZ; *b* 20 July 1919; *Educ* Auckland GS, Auckland UC; *m* 1, 1953, Louise Mary Rose (d 1975); 1 s (Peter), 2 da (Sarah, Belinda (d 1975)); m 2, 21 Dec 1989, June Mulgrew, wid of Peter Mulgrew; *Career* mountaineer, explorer, author, lectr; served navigator RNZAF Pacific Theatre WWII; first person to reach summit of Mt Everest (with Sherpa Tensing) Br Mount Everest Expdn 1953; leader: NZ section Br Trans Antarctic Expdn 1957–58 (supervised building of Scott Base in McMurdo Sound), various Himalayan expdns 1960–66, Antarctic Expdn 1967 (first ascent of Mt Herschel); other expdns incl: river journey E Nepal 1968, river journey up the Ganges from ocean to source in Himalayas 1977, American expdn to China and Tibet 1981, twin engined ski plane landing at North Pole (with Neil Armstrong) 1985; NZ High Cmmr to India, Nepal and Bangladesh 1985–89, formerly pres NZ Voluntary Service Abroad, int dir WWF, dir Field Educn Enterprises of Australasia Pty Ltd, advsr on camping activities to Sears Roebuck and Co Chicago and Toronto, appointed UNICEF special rep for children of the Himalayas 1991–; involved with extensive fund raising and aid activities in Himalayas 1960– (incl construction of schs, hosps, bridges, airfields, pipelines, etc), honoured by UN Environmental Prog for conservation work; Founders medal RGS, Hubbard medal Nat Geographical Soc, Polar medal, Cdr Mérite et Sportif, Star of Nepal (1st Class), ONZ; *Books* incl: High Adventure (1956), East of Everest (with George Lowe, 1956), No Latitude for Error (1961), High in the Thin Cold Air (with Desmond Doig, 1963), Schoolhouse in the Clouds (1965), Nothing Venture Nothing Win (autobiography, 1975), From the Ocean to the Sky (1979), Two Generations (with Peter Hillary, 1983); *Recreations* skiing, camping, mountaineering; *Clubs* Explorers (NY, hon pres), New Zealand Alpine (hon memb); *Style—* Sir Edmund Hillary, KG, KBE; ✉ 278A Remuera Road, Auckland, New Zealand

HILLER, Susan; *b* 1942; *Educ* Smith Coll US (AB), Tulane Univ (MA); *Career* artist; lectr Maidstone Coll of Art and tutor St Martin's Sch of Art 1975–80, postgrad tutor Slade Sch of Fine Art 1980–91, assoc prof of art Dept of Fine and Applied Arts Univ of Ulster 1991–, Baltic chair in contemporary art Univ of Newcastle upon Tyne 2000–; distinguished visiting prof Dept of Art Calif State Univ Long Beach 1988, visiting prof of new genres UCLA 1991, visiting Art Cncl chair Dept of Fine Art UCLA 1992; external examiner CNAA (various BA and MA Fine Art courses); curator Dream Machines Arts Cncl touring exhbn 2000–01, selector Bienale of Sydney 2002; memb Visual Arts Panel Greater London Arts Assoc 1976–81; memb Visual Arts Panel Arts Cncl of England 1997–99; artist in residence Univ of Sussex 1975, Visual Artist's Award GB (Gulbenkian Fndn) 1976 and 1977, Nat Endowment for the Arts fell (USA) 1982, Guggenheim fell (USA) 1998; work in public collections incl: Arts Cncl of GB, Tate Gallery, V&A, Contemporary Arts Soc; *Works* incl: Belshazzar's Feast (video installation), Monument (photography and audio), From the Freud Museum 1991–97 (mixed media installation), An Entertainment (video installation), Wild Talents (video installation), Psi Girls (video installation), Witness (audio sculpture); *Exhibitions* solo incl: Gallery House 1973, Hester van Royen 1976 and 1978, Serpentine Gallery 1976, MOMA Oxford 1978, Gimpel Fils London (various 1980–95), A Space Toronto 1981, Akumulatory Warsaw 1982, Roslyn Oxley Gallery Sydney 1982, Interim Art 1984, ICA 1986, Pat Hearn NY 1988–90, Kettle's Yard Cambridge 1989, Mappin Gallery Sheffield 1990, Matt's Gallery London 1991, Pat Hearn Gallery NY 1991, Nicole Klagsbrun NY 1991, Third Eye Centre Glasgow 1991, Tate Gallery Liverpool 1996, Art Angel cmmn 2000, Testa Konsthalle Stockholm 2000, Gagosin Gallery NY 2001, Tate Modern monograph room 2000–01, Gagosian Gallery NY 2001, Fondacion Mendoza Caracas Venezuela 2001, Museet for Samtidskunst Roskilde Denmark 2002, Galerie Volker Diehl Berlin 2003, Baltic Centre for Contemporary Art Newcastle England 2004, Museu Seralves Porto Portugal 2004, Kunsthalle Basle Switzerland 2004; group incl: From Britain 75 (Taidehall Helsinki) 1975, Hayward Annual 1978, The British Art Show (Arts Cncl of GB) 1984, Kunst mit Eigen-Sinn (Museum Moderner Kunst Vienna) 1985, Staging the Self (Nat Portrait Gallery) 1986, Towards a Bigger Picture (V&A) 1987, 100 Years of Art in Britain (Leeds City Museum) 1988, Lifelines (Br Cncl, BASF, Tate, Ludwigshafen and Liverpool) 1989–90, Great British Art (Maclellon Galleries Glasgow) 1990, Ten Artists (Ceibu Caison Tokyo) 1990, Now for the Future (Hayward Gallery London) 1990, At One/At War with Nature (Pratt Inst Galleries NY) 1991, In Vitro (Joan Miro Fndn Barcelona), Rites of Passage (Tate Gallery London) 1995, Sydney Biennale 1996, Inside the Visual (ICA Boston) 1996, Material culture: the object in British art of the 1980s and 90s (Hayward Gallery London) 1997, Now/Here (Louisiana Museum, Humlebaek Denmark) 1997, The Object of Performance (Museum of Contemporary Art LA) 1998, The Muse in the Museum (MOMA NY) 1998, Amateur/Eksdal (Gothenburg Museum) 2000, Intelligence (Tate Britain) 2000, The British Art Show 2000–01, Memory (Br Museum) 2003, Dream Extensions (SMAK Ghent) 2004; *Books* Dreams - Visions of the Night (co-author), The Myth of Primitivism (ed), After the Freud Museum (1996), Thinking About Art: Conversations with Susan Hiller (1997); various artists books and monographs; *Style—* Ms Susan Hiller

HILLIARD, Spenser Rodney; s of Alfred Hilliard (d 1982), of London, and Kathleen Claribelle Hilliard (d 2006); *b* 14 March 1952; *Educ* City of London Sch, QMC, Univ of London (LLB); *m* 1 May 1993, Rachel Frances, *née* Hindle; 4 c (Daisy Isobel b 2 April 1994, Chloë Valentine b 14 Feb 1996 d 1998, Cora Columbine b 31 March 1999, Digby Easter b 15 April 2001); *Career* called to the Bar Middle Temple 1975, practising barr; memb Hon Soc of Middle Temple; *Recreations* wine; *Style—* Spenser Hilliard, Esq; ✉ Lamb Building, Temple, London EC4Y 7AS (tel 020 7797 7788, fax 020 7353 0535)

HILLIER, Bevis; s of late Jack Ronald Hillier, and late Mary Louise, *née* Palmer; *b* 28 March 1940, Redhill, Surrey; *Educ* Reigate GS, Magdalen Coll Oxford (Demy, Gladstone prizeman); *Career* editorial staff The Times 1963–68, ed British Museum Society Bulletin 1968–70, antiques corr The Times 1970–84, guest curator Minneapolis Inst of Arts 1971, ed The Connoisseur 1973–76, dep literary ed The Times 1980–82, features ed Sunday Telegraph magazine 1983–84 (exec ed 1982–83), columnist and assoc ed Los Angeles Times 1984–88, ed Sotheby's Preview 1990–93; freelance work incl: TV critic New Statesman (as Garry Reffell), restaurant critic Vogue (Corning Glass Award 1980), antiques columnist Punch, Country Living and Harpers & Queen; frequent broadcaster on radio and TV; presenter: Collecting on a Shoestring (TV series), and Trash or Treasure? (TV series); co-fndr and first chm The Thirties Soc (now The Twentieth-Century Soc) 1979, vice-pres Betjeman Soc 1988–; FRSA 1967, FRSL 1997; Commedatore Order of Merit Republic of Italy 1976; *Publications* Master Potters of the Industrial Revolution: The Turners of Lane End (1965), Pottery and Porcelain 1700–1914 (1968), Art Deco of the 1920s and 30s (1968), Posters (1969), Cartoons and Caricatures (1970), The World of Art Deco (1971), 100 Years of Posters (1972), Travel Posters (1973), Victorian Studio Photographs (1974), Façade (jtly, 1974), Austerity/Binge: Decorative Arts of the 1940s and 1950s (1975), Punorama (1975), Dead Funny (1975), A Tonic to the Nation: The Festival of Britain, 1951 (jt ed, 1976), The New Antiques (1977), Fougasse (1978), Ealing Film Posters (1981), Bevis Hillier's Pocket Guide to Antiques (1981), John Betjeman, Uncollected Poems (ed, 1982), The Style of the Century 1900–1980 (1983), John Betjeman: A Life in Pictures (1984), Mickey Mouse Memorabilia (1986), Young Betjeman (1988), Early English Porcelain (1992), Art Deco Style (jtly, 1997), John Betjeman: New Fame, New Love (2002), Betjeman: The Bonus of Laughter (2004); author of numerous articles in newspapers and learned jls; *Recreations* piano, collecting; *Clubs* Garrick; *Style—* Bevis Hillier, Esq

HILLIER, John Michael; s of Clifford Henry Hillier (d 1952), and Alice Jane, *née* Lane (d 1999); *b* 8 October 1941; *Educ* Royal Masonic Sch Bushey, Wycliffe Coll, Univ of Sheffield

H

(BA); *m* 1994, Lesley Patricia, *née* Forrest; 2 s from previous m; *Career* HM inspr of taxes Inland Revenue 1963–64, educn officer and prodn mangr Pilkington Bros 1964–67, gp trg advsr Warrington Gp Trg Assoc 1967–68, sr conslt Industrial Trg Serv 1968–73, successively trg mangr, salary systems mangr, employee rels mangr then personnel mangr W D and H O Wills 1973–86, chief exec Tobacco Industry Trg Orgn 1986–90; NCVQ: dir accreditation 1990–91, chief exec 1991–97; chm: Nat Cncl Industry Trg Orgns 1988–90, Int Training Serv Ltd 1999–; dir: Glass Training Ltd 1997–, EMTA Awards Ltd 1997–; tstee London C of C Commercial Educn Tst 2002–; CIMgt; *Recreations* music, drama, tennis; *Style*— John Hillier, Esq; ✉ 3 Dwry Carneddau, Glan Conwy, Conwy LL28 5SW (tel 01492 573906, e-mail jhil331307@aol.com)

HILLIER, Meg; MP; *Educ* St Hilda's Coll Oxford, City Univ; *Career* freelance journalist 1998–2000; mayor of Islington 1998–99; memb London Assembly 2000–04, former chair Culture, Sport and Tourism Ctee; MP (Lab/Co-op) Hackney S and Shoreditch 2005–; tstee War Memorials Tst; memb: TGWU, Fabian Soc; *Style*— Ms Meg Hillier, MP; ✉ House of Commons, London SW1A 0AA

HILLIER, Prof Sheila Mary Bernadette; da of John Francis Kelleher, of Penwortham, Lancs, and Bridget Cecilia, *née* O'Riordan; *b* 5 October 1944; *Educ* Convent of the Holy Child Jesus Preston, LSE (BSc), Bedford Coll London (MSc(Econ)), Univ of London (PhD), Renmin Daxue (People's Univ) Beijing (Dip Chinese), London Hospital Medical Coll (certified bereavement cnsllr); *m* William Robert George Hillier, s of late Reginald Hillier; 1 da (Martha Tamar Riordan b 6 Sept 1975); *Career* research asst Dept of Social Admin LSE 1965–66, researcher Dept of Social Med Guy's Med Sch 1966–68, research asst Statistical Research Unit DHSS 1968–70; Bedford Coll London: research offr Social Research Unit 1971–73, lectr in med sociology 1973–74; St Bartholomew's and the Royal London Sch of Med and Dentistry: lectr in med sociology 1974–86, sr lectr 1986–94, head Dept of Human Science and Med Ethics 1990–, prof 1994–, head Div of Community Sciences 1998–2001; memb: Br Sociological Assoc 1984, RSM 1987, RHS 1991; *Books* Health-Care and Traditional Medicine in China 1800–1982 (with J A Jewell, 1983), Researching Cultural Differences in Health (with D Kelleher, 1995); *Recreations* early music, cookery, gardening; *Style*— Prof Sheila Hillier; ✉ 409 Mountjoy House, Barbican, London EC2Y 8BP; Unit of Human Science and Medical Ethics, St Bartholomew's and The Royal London Hospital School of Medicine and Dentistry, Turner Street, London E1 2AD (tel 020 7882 7083)

HILLIER, William Edward; s of William Edward Hillier (d 1976), and Ivy, *née* Elliott; *b* 11 April 1936; *Educ* Acton Co GS, Luton Tech Coll (HNC, DMS), Open Univ (BA); *m* 12 April 1958, Barbara Mary, da of William Victor Thorpe (d 1980); 1 da (Joy Marie b 1961), 1 s (William Edward b 1963); *Career* Nat Serv 1955–57; missile electronic systems De Havilland Propellors Ltd 1957, semiconductor mfrg Texas Instruments Ltd 1960, tech dir Racal-Redac Ltd 1974 (involved with computer aided engrg systems 1970), computer integrated mfrg Racal Group Services 1984; EPSRC: dir Application of Computers and Manufacturing-Engineering Directorate 1985–94, dir IT 1991–94, head of mktg and industrial policy 1994–96; visiting industrial fell Engrg Dept Univ of Cambridge 1996–; IEE: chm Computing and Control Bd 1993–94, memb Cncl 1992–94, memb membership Ctee 1995–2000, memb Mfrg Bd 1996–99, memb Informatics Bd 1997–99; dir Heritage Railway Assoc 2000–; CEng, FIEE, FIMgt; *Recreations* railway preservation (dir and company sec Gloucestershire & Warwickshire Steam Railway plc); *Style*— William Hillier, Esq; ✉ 19 Simon de Montfort Drive, Evesham, Worcestershire WR11 4NR (tel 01386 443449, e-mail billhillier@iee.org.uk)

HILLMAN, David; s of Leslie Hillman (d 1969), and Margery Joan, *née* Nash (d 1988); *b* 12 February 1943; *Educ* Aristotle Central Sch, London Sch of Printing (Graphic Art NDD); *m* 1, 27 Oct 1963 (m dis 1983), Eileen Margaret, *née* Griffin; 1 da (Jane b 1965), 1 s (Stephen b 1968); m 2, 2 July 1983, Jennie Diana, da of Max David Keith Burns, of Burley, Hants; 2 s (James Daniel b 3 July 1992, Thomas David b 3 July 1995); *Career* asst Sunday Times Magazine 1962–65; art ed: London Life 1965–66, Sunday Times 1966–68; ed Design for Living Section Sunday Times Magazine 1968–75, art dir and dep ed Nova Magazine 1968–75, freelance practice London 1975–76; art dir: Wolff Olins Ltd 1976–77, Le Matin de Paris 1977–78; ptnr Pentagram Design 1978–2007; estab Studio David Hillman 2007; sr fell RCA 2004; D&AD: Gold Award for Design 1973, Silver Award 1972–73, 1975, 1983, 1984, 1989, 1994 and 2001; NY Art Dirs Int Silver Award 1992, Critics Award Critique Magazine USA 2000; memb AGI (int pres 2003–04), FCSD, RDI 1997, FRSA 1998; *Books* Ideas on Design (co-ed, 1986), Puzzlegrams (1989), Pentagames (1990), Phantasmagrams (1992), Pentagram, The Compendium (co-ed 1993), Nova 1965–75 (co-author, 1993), Puzzlegrams Too! (1994), Century Makers (co-author, 1999), Pentagram Book 5 (co-author, 1999), Terence Donovan. The Photographs (co-author, 2000); *Style*— David Hillman, Esq; ✉ The Barns, Wortley, Wotton-under-Edge, Gloucestershire GL12 7QP (tel 01453 844266); Studio David Hillman Limited, Unit 100, Barlby Road, London W10 6BL (tel 020 8960 1717, e-mail hillman@studiodavidhillman.com)

HILLMAN, Prof John Richard; s of Robert Hillman (d 1990), of Farnborough, Kent, and Emily Irene, *née* Barrett; *b* 21 July 1944; *Educ* Chislehurst and Sidcup GS, UC Wales (BSc, PhD); *m* 23 Sept 1967, Sandra Kathleen, da of George Palmer (d 1997), of Luton, Beds; 2 s (Robert George b 1968, Edmund John b 1969); *Career* lectr in physiology and environmental studies Univ of Nottingham 1969–71 (asst lectr 1968–69); Univ of Glasgow: lectr in botany 1971–77, sr lectr 1977–80, reader 1980–82, prof and head of dept 1982–86; dir Scottish Crop Research Inst 1986–2005, dep chm and fndr Mylnefield Research Services Ltd 1989–2005; visiting prof: Univ of Dundee 1986–, Univ of Strathclyde 1986–97, Univ of Edinburgh 1988–, Univ of Glasgow 1991–; author of papers in scientific jls and books on plant physiology, agriculture and horticulture, plant biochemistry and biotechnology; chm and memb numerous ctees and panels; Bawden lectr 1993; chm Technology Foresight Panel: on Agric, Natural Resources and Environment 1994–95, on Agric, Horticulture and Forestry 1995–97; pres Agric and Food Section BAAS 2001–02; memb: Bd BioIndustry Assoc 1998–2004 (chair Industrial Applications Ctee), Ct Univ of Abertay Dundee 1998–2005; dir: The Mylnefield Tst 2000–05, Mylnefield Holdings Ltd 2000–05; tstee Jl of Horticultural Science and Biotechnology 2003–, tstee Scottish Soc of Crop Research 2006–, vice-pres Scotia Agricultural Soc 2006–; Br Potato Industry Award 1999, World Potato Industry Award 2000, Scottish Horticultural Medal 2003; Hon DSc: Univ of Strathclyde 1994, Univ of Abertay Dundee 1996; FIBiol, CBiol 1985, FLS 1982, FRSE 1985, MInstD 1995, FRSA 1997, FIHort 1998, FCMI (FIMgt 1987); *Books* ed: Isolation of Plant Growth Substances (1978), Biosynthesis and Metabolism of Plant Hormones (with A Crozier, 1984), Biochemistry of Plant Cell Walls (with C T Brett, 1985), Opportunities and Problems in Plant Biotechnology (with W Powell, 1992); *Recreations* landscaping, building renovations, horology, reading, Arab affairs; *Clubs* Farmers'; *Style*— Prof John Hillman, FRSE; ✉ Scottish Crop Research Institute, Invergowrie, Dundee DD2 5DA (tel 01382 562731, fax 01382 561412, e-mail j.hillman@tiscali.co.uk)

HILLS, Barrington William (Barry); s of William George (d 1967), of Upton upon Severn, Worcs, and Phyllis, *née* Biddle; *b* 2 April 1937; *Educ* Ribston Hall Gloucester, St Mary's Convent Newmarket, Mr Whittaker's Worcester; *m* 1, 21 Nov 1959 (m dis 1977), Maureen, da of late Patrick Newson; 3 s (John b 1960, Michael b 1963, Richard b 1963); m 2, 1 Sept 1977, Penelope Elizabeth May, da of John Richard Woodhouse; 2 s (Charles b 1978, George b 1983); *Career* Nat Serv King's Troop RHA, racehorse trainer 1969–; won: Prix de L'Arc de Triomphe, Budweiser Irish Derby, Irish 1000 Guineas (twice), Irish Oaks (twice), Prix Royal-Oak, 2000 Guineas Newmarket (twice), 1000 Guineas Newmarket, St Leger, Prix de l'Abbaye; second place Epsom Derby three times; *Recreations* hunting, shooting, golf; *Clubs* Turf; *Style*— Barry W Hills, Esq; ✉ B W Hills Southbank Ltd, Wetherdown House, Lambourn, Hungerford, Berkshire RG17 8UB (tel 01488 71548, e-mail info@barryhills.com, website www.barryhills.com)

HILLS, Prof John Robert; CBE; s of Derrick Walter Hills (d 1979), and Valerie Jean, *née* Gribble; *b* 29 July 1954, Luton, Beds; *Educ* Univ of Cambridge (BA), Univ of Birmingham (MSocSc); *m* 1989, Prof Anne Power; *Career* Dept of the Environment 1979–80, House of Commons Treasy Ctee 1980–82, Inst for Fiscal Studies 1982–84, Cmmn of Inquiry into Taxation in Zimbabwe 1984–86, Welfare State Prog LSE 1986–97, dir Centre for Analysis of Social Exclusion and prof of social policy LSE 1997–; memb Pensions Cmmn 2003–06; FBA 2002; *Publications* New Inequalities (ed, 1996), The State of Welfare (co-ed, 1998), Understanding Social Exclusion (co-ed, 2002), Inequality and the State (2004), A more equal society? New Labour, poverty, inequality and exclusion (co-ed, 2005); *Recreations* fell walking; *Style*— Prof John Hills, CBE; ✉ Centre for Analysis of Social Exclusion, London School of Economics and Political Science, Houghton Street, London WC2A 3AE (tel 020 7955 6562, fax 020 7955 6951, e-mail j.hills@lse.ac.uk)

HILLS, Prof Paul; *Educ* Univ of Cambridge, Courtauld Inst of Art London (MA, PhD); *Career* lectr Univ of Warwick 1976–98, Andrew Mellon visting prof Courtauld Inst of Art London 2003, prof Courtauld Inst of Art London 2004–; sometime visiting prof: Inst of Fine Arts NY, Villa I Tatti, Harvard Center for Renaissance Studies, RCA; *Books* incl: David Jones (1981), The Light of Early Italian Painting (1987), David Jones: Artist and Poet (ed, 1997), Venetian Colour: Marble, Mosaic, Painting and Glass, 1250–1550 (1999); *Style*— Prof Paul Hills; ✉ Courtauld Institute of Art, Somerset House, Strand, London WC2R 0RN

HILLS, Prof William; MBE (2002); s of Robert Hills, of Wallsend, and Mary, *née* Bulman; *b* 12 January 1941; *Educ* Western Secdy Modern Wallsend, Sunderland Poly (BSc, MPhil); *m* March 1965, Joyce Louise, da of Alfred Miller; 1 s (Paul William b 9 August 1967), 1 da (Helen Louise b 25 June 1970); *Career* graduate apprentice designer then asst naval architect Swan Hunter Shipyard Wallsend 1956–68, lectr and princ lectr in naval architecture Sunderland Poly 1962–82 (sr lectr 1982–88), dir Engrg Design Centre Univ of Newcastle 1988–98, prof of engrg design Univ of Newcastle 1996–98 (emeritus 1998–); Prince Philip Designer Prize 1999; FRINA 1982, CEng 1982, FIED 1997, FRSA 1997; *Publications* author of over 150 papers in engrg jls and professional transactions; *Recreations* ornithology, walking; *Style*— Prof William Hills, MBE; ✉ Engineering Design Centre, Armstrong Building, University of Newcastle upon Tyne, Newcastle upon Tyne NE1 7RU (tel 0191 222 8701)

HILTON, Anthony Victor; s of Dr Raymond W Hilton (d 1975), and Miriam Eileen Norah, *née* Kydd (d 2003); *b* 26 August 1946; *Educ* Woodhouse Grove Sch Bradford, Aberdeen Univ (MA); *m* 1 (m dis); 1 s (Steven b 1969); m 2, Cyndy Miles; 2 s (Michael b 1985, Peter b 1987), 1 da (Emily b 1991); *Career* city ed The Times 1982–83; Evening Standard: city ed 1984–89 and 1996–2002, md 1989–95, fin ed 2002–; dir Associated Newspapers plc 1989–95, chm Newsdesk Communications Ltd 2003–; Wincott Journalist of the Year 2003, London Press Club Business Journalist of the Year 2005, World Leadership Forum Decade of Excellence Award 2007; memb Stock Exchange Ctee on Private Share Ownership (Weinberg Ctee) 1995–96; dir: London Forum 1993–96, London First 1993–96, St John's Ambulance Nat Fundraising Appeal 1993–95; vice-pres Children's Film Unit 1993–95; *Books* Employee Reports (1978), City within a State (1987); *Recreations* after dinner speaking; *Clubs* Lansdowne, Reform; *Style*— Anthony Hilton, Esq; ✉ Evening Standard, Northcliffe House, Derry Street, London W8 5EE (tel 020 7938 6000)

HILTON, Colin John; s of Herbert Jackson Mason Hilton, of Boston, Lincs, and Marjorie, *née* Wray (d 1975); *b* 17 August 1945; *Educ* Boston GS, Univ of Newcastle Med Sch (MB BS); *m* 15 Feb 1969, Helen, da of Flt Lt Joseph William Atkinson, DFC, of Newcastle upon Tyne; 1 da (Nicola b 27 Sept 1972); *Career* locum registrar in thoracic and gen surgery Queen Elizabeth Hosp Birmingham and Wolverhampton Royal Infirmary 1973, locum sr registrar in cardiothoracic surgery Harefield Hosp 1975–76 (registrar 1973–75), registrar in cardiac surgery Nat Heart Hosp 1976, sr registrar in cardiothoracic surgery Papworth Hosp Cambridge 1976–77, res fell Brown Univ Providence Rhode Is 1978, sr registrar St Bartholomew's Hosp 1979, conslt cardiothoracic surgn Freeman Hosp Newcastle 1979–; postgrad dean Soc of Cardiothoracic Surgns 1991–95; RCS: chm Specialist Advsy Ctee in Cardiothoracic Surgery 1995–99, memb Cncl 2002–; pres Soc of Cardiothoracic Surgeons 2002–; memb Senate of Surgery 2002–; memb Ctee Soc of Cardiothoracic Surgns of GB and NI; FRCS 1973, fell Euro Bd of Thoracic and Cardiovascular Surgeons 2000; *Recreations* golf, skiing; *Clubs* Northumberland Golf; *Style*— Colin Hilton, Esq; ✉ Rodborough, 8 Westfield Grove, Gosforth, Newcastle upon Tyne NE3 4YA (tel 0191 284 7394); Regional Cardiothoracic Centre, Freeman Hospital, Freeman Road, High Heaton, Newcastle upon Tyne NE7 7DN (tel 0191 284 3111 ext 26587, fax 0191 213 1968, e-mail c.j.hilton@ncl.ac.uk)

HILTON, Isabel N; da of Dr Raymond W Hilton (d 1975), and Miriam Evelyn, *née* Kydd (d 2003); *b* 25 November 1947; *Educ* Bradford Girls' GS, Walnut Hills HS Ohio, Univ of Edinburgh (MA), Peking Languages Inst, Univ of Fudan Shanghai (scholar); *m* 1 (m dis 1975), John Armstrong Black; m 2, Charles Neal Ascherson; 1 s, 1 da; *Career* journalist; teaching asst Chinese Dept Univ of Edinburgh 1972–73, Scottish TV 1976–77, Sunday Times 1977–86 (special corr China, feature writer, news reporter, Latin America ed, asst foreign ed); The Independent: Latin America ed 1986, European Affrs ed 1989, chief feature writer 1991–95; presenter The World Tonight (BBC radio) 1995–99, presenter Night Waves (BBC Radio 3) 1999–; corr (BBC2); columnist The Guardian, staff writer The New Yorker, ed chinadialogue.net; reg contrib: New Statesman, Time Magazine, El Pais, New York Times; memb: Chatham House (RIIA) 1977, Br Assoc of China Studies 1978; Hon DLitt (hc) Univ of Bradford 2003; IISS 1989, FRSA 2007; *Books* The Falklands War (jtly, 1982), The Fourth Reich (jtly, 1984), Betrayed (contrib, 1988), The General (1990), The Search for the Panchen Lama (1999), The Thinking Man's Guide to the World Cup (contrib, 2006); *Recreations* family, gardening; *Style*— Ms Isabel Hilton; ✉ c/o Gillon Aitken Associates Ltd, 18–21 Cavaye Place, London SW10 9PT (e-mail isabelhilton@mac.com)

HILTON, Jane Elizabeth Anne; s of Derek George Ernest Hilton, and Anne Kathleen, *née* Stacy; *b* 3 November 1962; *Educ* Beaconsfield HS, Lancaster Univ (BA); *Career* professional photographer and film maker (specializes in people, quirky situations and the USA); clients incl: Nescafe, BT, Next, Sunday Times Magazine, Telegraph Magazine, BBC; work incl The Brothel (10–part documentary series for BBC); *Style*— Jane Hilton; ✉ mobile 07785 795158, e-mail jane@janehilton.com

HILTON, (Alan) John Howard; QC (1990); s of Alan Howard Hilton, (d 1986), of Bowdon, and Barbara Mary Campbell, *née* Chambers, (d 1958); *b* 21 August 1942; *Educ* Haileybury, Univ of Manchester (LLB); *m* 21 Dec 1978, Nicola Mary, da of Percy Harold Bayley (d 1977), of Brighton; 1 s (Felix b 24 Dec 1983); *Career* called to the Bar Middle Temple 1964; in practice 1964–, recorder 1985–; *Books* Fish Cookery (1981), Opera Today (1985); *Recreations* opera, conjuring, 19th century females in oils, cooking; *Clubs* Garrick, Les Six; *Style*— John Hilton, Esq, QC; ✉ Queen Elizabeth Building, Temple EC4Y 9BS (tel 020 7583 5766, fax 020 7353 0339, e-mail john.hilton@holliswhiteman.co.uk)

HILTON, Prof Julian; s of R K Hilton; *b* 11 September 1952; *Educ* Canford Sch, BNC Oxford, Univs of Grenoble, Munich and Salamanca (MA, D Phil); *m* 1, 10 July 1976, Hanne, da of H J Boenisch; 1 da (Ruth b 18 Feb 1978); m 2, 29 Aug 1996, Malika, da of B Moussaid;

1 da (Nermeen b 11 Nov 1996), 1 s (Kenz b 24 May 2002); *Career* res fell Alexander van Humboldt Stiftung 1976, fell Stiftung Maximilianeum Munich 1977, prof of drama and communications UEA 1988–91 (lectr 1977, sr lectr 1987, dir Audio-visual Centre 1987–91); fndr and ptnr Technol Arts Info 1985–98, project mangr AIM prog EC 1989–91, dir AVC Multimedia Ltd 1991–93, md Telos Consulting Ltd 1993–95, pres Telos Gp 1995–98, chm Aleff Gp Ltd 1999–; jt project mangr COMETT proj EC 1991–94, dir Value Project EC DGXIII; conslt: IAEA Vienna 1991–, WHO 1995–, FAO Rome 1997–; memb Bd Global Assoc of Clinical Res Professionals Washington DC 1998–2000; dir Advanced Veterinary Information System (AVIS) project FAO 1992–, princ investigator Milo Project Florida Inst of Phosphate Res 1999–, princ investigator Beneficial Uses of Phosphogypsum 2006–; chm Artificial Intelligence and Interactive Systems Gp; memb Bd Theatre Royal Norwich, vice-chm Norfolk Arts Forum; fell Swedish Center for Working Life; visiting prof Tech Univ Vienna; dean Inst ACRP 2000–02; *Books* Georg Buchner (1982), Performance (1987), New Directions in Theatre (1992); plays incl: The Enchanted Bird's Nest (1985), Broken Ground (1986), The Marriage of Panurge (1986), Courage (1989); *Recreations* opera, walking, shopping; *Style—* Prof Julian Hilton; ✉ Aleff Group, 53/54 Skylines, Limeharbour, London E14 9TS (tel 020 7515 9009, fax 020 7515 5465, e-mail jhilton@aleffgroup.com)

HILTON, Mark William; s of Peter Entwistle Hilton, of Ripley, N Yorks, and Monica, *née* Smith; *b* 15 July 1958, Bradford; *Educ* Wrekin Coll, Univ of Leeds (LLB); *m* 25 April 1987, Catharine, da of George Canavan, of Ripon; 1 da (Camilla b 21 July 1991), 1 s (Thomas b 26 March 1994); *Career* admitted slr 1982; Last Suddards Bradford 1980–82, Barlow Lyde & Gilbert London 1982–85, ptnr Last Suddards Leeds 1986–88 (joined 1982, rejoined 1985), ptnr and head of construction and engrg Hammond Suddards Leeds 1988–2000, Hammond Suddards Edge 2001–03, Hammonds 2003–05, ptnr Addleshaw Goddard 2005–; memb Law Soc 1979–; FCIArb 1995, CEDR accredited mediator 2000; *Recreations* skiing, scuba diving, tennis; *Clubs* RAC; *Style—* Mark Hilton, Esq; ✉ Addleshaw Goddard, Sovereign House, PO Box 8, Sovereign Street, Leeds LS1 1HQ (tel 0113 209 2476, fax 0113 209 2060, e-mail mark.hilton@addleshawgoddard.com)

HILTON, Nicholas David; s of John David Hilton, and Dorothy Gwendoline, *née* Eastham; *b* 27 June 1952; *Educ* Marlborough; *m* 14 July 1984, Vanessa Jane, da of late Brig W John Reed; 2 da (Lucy Vanessa b 1989, Emma Rachel b 1992); *Career* CA 1974; ptnr Moore Stephens 1979–; FCA 1979, MCIM 1996; *Recreations* golf, skiing, mah-jong, entertaining; *Style—* Nicholas Hilton, Esq; ✉ Moore Stephens, St Paul's House, Warwick Lane, London EC4M 7BP (tel 020 7334 9191, fax 020 7248 3408, e-mail nick.hilton@moorestephens.com)

HILTON-BARBER, Miles Anthony; s of Lt-Col Maurice Clinton Hilton-Barber, OBE, DFC, and Moira Yvonne Hilton-Barber; *m* 1976, Stephanie Evans; 2 da (Deborah, Abigail), 1 s (David); *Career* adventurer, marathon runner and author; achievements incl: London Marathon 1998, Marathon des Sables (250km ultra-marathon in Sahara Desert) 1999, climbed 17,500 feet in Himalayas 2000, reached summit of Kilimanjaro 2000, Highest and Deepest Project Mont Blanc 2000, first blind person to manhaul a sledge 400km across Antarctica 2000 (frostbite prevented contintuation of bid to be first blind person to reach S Pole), 11-day 200km ultra-marathon across parts of ancient Silk Road in China 2001, climbed Ben Nevis 2001, abseiled down several tower blocks for charity 2001, Siberian Ice Marathon 2002, memb 5-man team which set new world record for non-stop unsupported 200km crossing of Qatar Desert 2002, Around the World in 80 Ways Project 2002 (part of team of 3 people with disabilities circumnavigating the globe using at least 80 of the most challenging forms of transport), first blind person to fly English Channel in a microlight 2003, set new world high-altitude record (20,300ft) in tandem microlight 2004, did wing-walk on Boeing Steerman 2004, first blind person to do solo kamakazi skeleton run down 5G Olympic bobsleigh track Lillehammer 2005, participated in Bad Water Ultra-Marathon across Death Valley 2005, cage-diving with great white sharks 2006, first blind person to abseil 350 feet down Table Mountain 2006, competed in 3 day int canoe race Atlantic to Pacific via Panama Canal 2006, co-piloted 3 engined 1932 Dornier float plane Austrian air display 2006; also competed in tandem cycling marathons, hot-air ballooning, para-sailing, and made 40 sky-diving jumps; qualified scuba diver, Grade 5 Zambesi white water rafting, Scottish Grade 3 technical ice climbing; subject of TV documentaries: Against All Odds (Carlton, three int film festival Gold Awards), Blind Faith (Carlton, int film festival Gold Award), National Geographic Channel Antarctica documentary; int motivational speaker and writer; hon master Univ of Derby 2003; *Style—* Miles Hilton-Barber, Esq; ✉ 10 Ferrers Crescent, Duffield, Belper, Derbyshire DE56 4DH (tel 01332 843590, mobile 07973 360470, e-mail miles@mhb.demon.co.uk)

HINCH, (Edward) John; s of Joseph Edward Hinch, of Waterbeach, Cambridge, and Mary Grace, *née* Chandler; *b* 4 March 1947; *Educ* Edmonton County GS, Trinity Coll Cambridge (BA, PhD); *m* 28 June 1969, Christine Bridges; 1 da (Clare b 9 Dec 1975), 1 s (Robert b 22 Aug 1977); *Career* Univ of Cambridge: asst lectr in mathematics 1972–75, lectr in mathematics 1975–94, reader in fluid mechanics 1994–98, prof in fluid mechanics 1998–; fell Trinity Coll Cambridge 1971–; FRS 1997; Chevalier de l'Ordre Nationale du Mérite (France) 1997; *Books* Perturbation Methods (1991); *Style—* Prof John Hinch, FRS; ✉ Trinity College, Cambridge CB2 1TQ (tel 01223 338427, fax 01223 337918, e-mail e.j.hinch@damtp.cam.ac.uk)

HINCHCLIFFE, Christian; *b* 7 March 1973, London; *Educ* Eton, Univ of Bristol; *Career* started career in advtg at Ogilvy Gp 1996; Euro RSCG: joined as account mangr 1998, rising to account dir, new business dir and bd memb 2002–04; mktg dir McCann Erickson 2004–; Top 10 New Business Director Campaign Magazines 2002; memb: Cncl IPA, Mktg Soc; *Recreations* golf, tennis; *Clubs* The Berkshire, Queen's, RAC, Soho House; *Style—* Christian Hinchcliffe, Esq; ✉ McCann Erickson Advertising Limited, 7–11 Herbrand Street, London WC1N 1EX (tel 020 7961 2267)

HINCHCLIFFE, Prof Ronald; s of Charles Hinchcliffe, and Fenella, *née* Pearce; *b* 20 February 1926; *Educ* Bolton Sch, Univ of Manchester, Harvard Univ, Univ of London; *m* 4 July 1953 (m dis 1980), Doreen, *née* Lord; *Career* Sqdn Ldr and RAF med servs offr i/c RAF Acoustics Laboratory 1951–55; res fell Psycho-Acoustic Laboratory Harvard Univ 1955–56, scientific staff MRC 1956–60, assoc prof of otolaryngology Univ of Iowa 1960–63, hon conslt neuro-otologist Royal Nat ENT Hosp London 1967–91, prof of audiological med Univ of London 1977–91, conslt to Hearing and Balance Centre Portland Hosp London 1991–2001; vice-chm Hearing Conservation Cncl 1999–; past pres Int Soc of Audiology; memb: Collegium Otorhinolaryngologicum Amicitiae Sacrum 1969–, Bárány Soc 1972–; *Books* Scientific Foundations of Otolaryngology (jt ed, 1976), Hearing and Balance in the Elderly (ed, 1983), Noise and Hearing Vol 1 (jt author, 2001); *Recreations* travel; *Clubs* Athenaeum; *Style—* Prof Ronald Hinchcliffe; ✉ University College London, 330 Gray's Inn Road, London WC1X 8EE (tel 020 7580 4400, fax 01462 454394, e-mail rondlanor@aol.com)

HIND, Andrew; *b* 29 September 1955, Portsmouth, Hants; *Educ* Portsmouth GS, Univ of Southampton (BSc); *m* 1985, Christina; 3 s; *Career* Ernst & Young 1976–80, Pannell Kerr Forster Kenya 1980–83, divnl financial controller Balfour Beatty Ltd 1983–86; ActionAid: dir of fin 1986–89, dep chief exec 1989–91; dir of fin and corporate servs Barnardo's 1992–95; BBC World Serv: dir of finance and business devpt 1995–2002, chief operating offr 2002–04; chief exec Charity Cmmn for England and Wales 2004–; *Publications* Charity Managers and Charity Trustees: Meeting the challenges of the 1990s (jt ed, 1993), The Charity Finance Handbook (ed, 1994), The Governance and Management of Charities (1995); *Recreations* running, golf, travel, collecting old books on Africa; *Style—* Andrew Hind, Esq; ✉ 11 Byng Road, High Barnet, Hertfordshire EN5 4NW; Charity Commission for England and Wales, Harmsworth House, 13–15 Bouverie Street, London EC4Y 8DP (tel 020 7674 2473, fax 020 7674 2309, e-mail andrew.hind@charitycommission.gsi.gov.uk)

HIND, Dr Charles Robert Keith; s of Col (Robert) Keith Hind, of Derby, and Dorothy, *née* Kinsey; *b* 7 June 1953; *Educ* King's Coll Taunton, Univ of London Med Sch (BSc, MB BS, MD); *m* 21 July 1985, Fiona, da of Maj Alexander Hugh Fraser, of Cradley, Worcs; 2 s (James b 1986, Alexander b 1992), 1 da (Eleanor b 1989); *Career* conslt physician gen and respiratory med: The Cardiothoracic Centre Liverpool 1987– (med dir 2000–04), Royal Liverpool Hosp 1987–2001; censor and dir of publications RCP 1997–2000, ed Postgraduate Medical Jl 1994–98; pres Int Soc of Internal Med 2002–04; FRCP, FRCPE, FACP; *Books* X-Ray Interpretation for the MRCP (1983), Short Cases for the MRCP (1984), Amyloidosis and Amyloid P Component (1986), Communication Skills in Medicine (1997); *Style—* Dr Charles Hind; ✉ 47 Rodney Street, Liverpool L1 9EW (tel and fax 0151 327 5107); The Cardiothoracic Centre, Liverpool L14 3PE (tel 0151 293 2395, fax 0151 220 8573)

HIND, Rt Rev John William; *see:* Chichester, Bishop of

HIND, Kenneth Harvard; CBE (1995); *b* 15 September 1949; *Educ* Woodhouse Grove Sch Bradford, Univ of Leeds; *m* Patricia Anne, *née* Millar; 1 s, 1 da; *Career* called to the Bar Gray's Inn 1973, practising barr Leeds until 1983, in practice Temple 1992–; MP (Cons) Lancs W 1983–92; PPS to: Lord Trefgarne MOD 1986–87, John Cope as Min of State DOE 1987–90, Rt Hon Peter Brooke as Sec of State for NI 1990–92; chm Assoc of Conservative Parliamentary Candidates; *Recreations* sailing, skiing; *Clubs* Carlton, Saracens RUFC; *Style—* Kenneth Hind, Esq, CBE; ✉ 3 Temple Gardens, Temple, London EC4Y 9AU (tel 020 7583 1155)

HINDE, David Richard; s of Walter Stanley Hinde (d 1952), and Marjorie Jewell Grieg, *née* Butcher (d 1970); *b* 16 August 1938; *Educ* Marlborough, Univ of Cambridge; *m* 1963, Rosemary Jill, da of Malcolm Hartree Young (d 1965); 3 da (Sasha Karen b 1966, Rachel Olivia b 1968, Anna-Louise b 1972); *Career* asst slr Slaughter and May 1961–69; exec dir: Wallace Bros Group 1969–77, Wardley Ltd 1977–81, Samuel Montagu and Co Ltd 1981–95, Dah Sing Financial Hong Kong 1995–2004; chm: Invesco Asia Tst plc 2005–, Macau Property Opportunities Fund Ltd 2006–; Liveryman Emeritus Worshipful Co of Woolmen; *Recreations* skiing, tennis, golf, gardening, travel; *Clubs* MCC, City of London, Hong Kong; *Style—* David Hinde, Esq; ✉ The Martins, High Street, Chipping Campden, Gloucestershire GL55 6AG (tel and fax 01386 841328, e-mail david.hinde@yahoo.com)

HINDE, Keith Stevens Gleave; OBE (1998), TD (1969); s of Wing Cdr Sydney Arthur Hinde, OBE, DL (d 1977), of West Mersea, Essex, and Guinevere Waneeta Ashore, *née* Gleave (d 1974); *b* 4 October 1934; *Educ* Colchester Royal GS, CCC Cambridge (MA); *m* 8 May 1965, Gillian Myfanwy, da of William Godfrey Morgan (d 1955), of Coventry, Warks; 1 s (Edward Morgan Stevens b 1976); *Career* 2 Lt RA 1953–55, Battery Capt Suffolk & Norfolk Yeo 1955–67, Maj Suffolk/Cambs Regt (S and NY) 1967–69; admitted slr 1961; conslt (former ptnr) Pothecary & Barratt 1994–2006; chm Stretham Engine Tst, chm Willingham (West Fen) Tst, tstee Suffolk & Norfolk Yeo Tst; Master Worshipful Co of Slrs 1988–89 (Liveryman 1966, Clerk 1969–76), Liveryman Worshipful Co of Cutlers 2001 (Clerk 1975–2001); *Books* Steam in the Fens (1974, 5 edn 2001), History of The City of London Solicitors Company (1994), London-made Knives and their Marks (jtly, 2005), Fenland Pumping Engines (2006); *Recreations* history (local and general), country pursuits; *Clubs* Oxford and Cambridge; *Style—* Keith Hinde, Esq, OBE; ✉ Denny House, Waterbeach, Cambridgeshire CB25 9JU (tel 01223 860895)

HINDE, Stephen Victor Cecil; s of Eric Stanley Hinde (d 1972), and Joyce, *née* Ball (d 1994); *b* 31 August 1948; *Educ* Plymouth Coll; *m* 1 July 1978, Mary Elizabeth Margaret, da of Basil Wilfred Mulligan; 2 da (Clare Venetia b 26 June 1980, Laura Mary b 7 March 1982); *Career* articled clerk Grace Darbyshire & Todd (now KPMG) 1966–71, audit sr Arthur Young McClelland Moores (now Ernst & Young) 1972, computer audit mangr Rediffusion Group 1972–78, audit servs mangr Brooke Bond Foods 1978–88, sr gp mangr computers Unilever plc 1988–90, gp mangr Courage Internal Audit Fosters Brewing Group 1990–95, gp info protection mangr BUPA 1995–; Faculty of Info Technol ICAEW: memb 1988–, chm Communications Ctee 1991–94, chm Professional Educn and Qualifications Ctee 1994–, chm Data Protection Panel 1995–2000, lead examiner Advanced Case Study (ACA) 2002–06; Inst of Internal Auditors UK & Ireland: memb 1976–, jt fndr of qualification in computer auditing and chm QiCA Ctee 1981–88, jt fndr and chm Int Conf on Computer Audit Control and Security (COMPACS) 1981–91, chm Educn Co-ordinating Ctee 1983–85 (memb 1981–86), memb Cncl 1982–88, memb Res Co-ordinating Ctee 1983–85, chm EDP Res Ctee 1982–85 (memb 1980–2000), chm EDP Educn Ctee 1982–84 (memb 1981–86), memb Editorial Bd 1982–88, dir 1984–88, pres 1986–87, chm Disciplinary Ctee 1988–96, chm Data Protection Panel 1995–2000, computer audit examiner; chm Confidentiality Working Gp Independent Healthcare Advsy Serv 2000–, chm pmi Data Protection Working Pty 2000–; memb Advanced Technol Ctee Inst of Internal Auditors Inc USA 1983–87, UK rep of Admin Cncl Euro Confedn of Inst of Internal Auditors 1986–88; memb Assurance Advsy Cncl Director's Information Assurance Network 2003–06; fndr ed Computer Audit Update Jl 1987–98, computer auditor ed Computers & Security Jl 1998–2005, fndr ed Information Systems Auditor 1998–2003; memb: Data Protection Panel ABI 1995– (chm 2004–), Advisor Skills Initiative Advsy Cncl DTI 1998–2000, Cncl of Europe Insurance Working Pty ABI 2000–01; NHS Scotland: Data Protection Forum 2003–, Information Governance Network Steering Gp 2007–; jt fndr UK Cncl of Caldicott Guardians 2003– (chm 2006–); chm Int Food & Wine Soc - Young Membs 1981–85 (hon treas 1979–82); govr St James's C of E First and Middle Sch Weybridge 1992–93; capt 4 XV Old Redcliffians RFC (Bristol); FCA 1971, MIIA 1981, FIIA 1986; *Books* Control & Audit of Mini Computer Systems (contrib, 1981), Use of Generalized Audit Software (contrib, 1983), Comparison of Access Control Software (ed, 1983), Internal Auditing (co-author, 1990, 3 edn 1999), Manual of Internal Audit Practice (1990), Information Security Guide (1990), Computer Auditing (co-author, 1991), Computer Audit and Control Handbook (contrib, 1995); *Recreations* Church activities, wine and food, history, literature; *Style—* Stephen Hinde, Esq; ✉ BUPA House, 15–19 Bloomsbury Way, London WC1A 2BA (tel 020 7656 2311, e-mail hindes@bupa.com)

HINDE, Thomas; *see:* Chitty, Sir Thomas

HINDLE, Charlotte; da of Tom Hindle, and Pauline, *née* Howton; *Educ* Univ of Leicester (BA); *Career* export sales and mktg mangr Lonely Planet Aust HQ 1988–91, general mangr Lonely Planet London 1991–2002; *Recreations* travel, photography, art history; *Style—* Ms Charlotte Hindle

HINDLEY, Her Hon Judge Estella Jacqueline; QC (1992); da of Arthur John Hindley, of Sutton Coldfield, and Olive Maud, *née* Stanley; *b* 11 October 1948; *Educ* Sutton Coldfield Girls GS, Univ of Hull (LLB); *m* 1, Timothy Raggatt, QC; 1 s (Andrew Timothy Hindley b 14 May 1977); m 2, John Gilbert Harvey; *Career* called to the Bar Gray's Inn 1971; recorder of the Crown Court 1989–97, circuit judge (Midland & Oxford Circuit) 1997–; memb Parole Bd; chm and non-exec dir Birmingham Children's Hosp NHS Tst 1993–2003; pres Birmingham Medico-Legal Soc 1999–2001, sec UK Assoc of Women Judges 2006–; *Recreations* book collecting, painting, music; *Style—* Her Hon Judge E Hindley, QC; ✉ Birmingham Civil Justice Combined Court Centre, 33 Bull Street, Birmingham B4 6DS (tel 0121 681 3000)

HINDLIP, 6 Baron (UK 1886); Sir Charles Henry Allsopp; 6 Bt (UK 1880); s of 5 Baron Hindlip, JP, DL (d 1993), and Cecily Valentine Jane, *née* Borwick (d 2000); *b* 5 August 1940; *Educ* Eton; *m* 18 April 1968, Fiona Victoria Jean Atherley, da of late Hon William Johnston McGowan, 2 s of 1 Baron McGowan; 3 da (Hon Kirstie Mary b 1971, Hon Sophia Atherley b 1980, Hon Natasha Fiona b 1986), 1 s (Hon Henry William b 1973); *Heir* s, Hon Henry Allsopp; *Career* Coldstream Gds 1959–62, Lt; Christie's: joined 1962, gen mangr NY 1965–70; Christie Manson & Wood: dir 1970–96, dep chm 1985–86, chm 1986–96; CIL plc: dir 1986–, chm 1996–2003; *Recreations* painting; *Clubs* White's, Pratt's, Corviglia Ski; *Style*— The Rt Hon the Lord Hindlip; ✉ Lydden House, King's Stag, Dorset DT10 2AU

HINDMARCH, Anya (Mrs James Seymour); da of Michael Hindmarch, and Susan Hindmarch; *b* 7 May 1969; *m* 1996, James Seymour; 4 s (Hugo, Bertie, Felix, Otto), 1 da (Octavia); *Career* fashion designer; Anya Hindmarch (own label specialising in bags): first store opened London 1993, subsequent stores in NY, LA, Tokyo and Hong Kong, concessions worldwide, launched Blue Label 1999, launched Be a Bag (charity promotion) 2001, launched shoe range 2002; conslt Br Airways (designer First Class amenity kit); Best British Accessories Designer Br Fashion Cncl 2001; *Style*— Ms Anya Hindmarch; ✉ The Stable Block, Plough Brewery, 516 Wandsworth Road, London SW8 3JX (tel 020 7501 0177, fax 020 7501 0170, website www.anyahindmarch.com)

HINE, Dame Deirdre Joan; DBE (1997); da of David Alban Curran (d 1987), and Noreen Mary, *née* Cliffe; *b* 16 September 1937; *Educ* Charlton Park Sch Cheltenham, WNSM (DPH, MB BCh); *m* 12 Sept 1963, Raymond Hine; 2 s (Jonathan David b 2 Feb 1966, Andrew James b 17 Sept 1967); *Career* house physician and surgn Cardiff Royal Infirmary 1961–62, MO Glamorgan CC 1964–74 (asst MO 1962–64), specialist in community med S Glamorgan HA 1974–82, sr lectr in geriatric med Univ of Wales Coll of Med 1982–84, dep chief MO Welsh Office 1984–87, dir Breast Cancer Screening Serv Breast Test Wales 1987–90, chief MO Welsh Office 1990–97; pres: RSM 2000–02, BMA 2005–06; vice-pres Marie Curie Cancer Care; chm: No Smoking Day Bd 1999–2001, Cmmn for Health Improvement 1999–2004, BUPA Fndn 2004–, Press Bd RSM 2004–; ind memb House of Lords Appointments Cmmn 2000–05, non-exec dir Glas Cymru 2001–; Hon FRCS, Hon FRCA, Hon FRCGP, FRCP, FFPHM; *Recreations* reading, walking, canal cruising, classical music; *Style*— Dame Deirdre Hine, DBE; ✉ The Red House, Mill Road, Lisvane, Cardiff (tel 029 2076 6729, e-mail deirdrehine@aol.com)

HINE, John; s of late Leonard John Hine, and Elizabeth Jane, *née* Jenkins; *b* 21 January 1946; *Educ* Taunton Sch, Univ of Bristol (LLB); *m* 14 Dec 1974, Margaret Alice Stuart, *née* Morton; 3 c (Louise b 10 Jan 1977, Alice b 29 Sept 1978, William b 30 June 1981); *Career* articled clerk Dodson & Pulman Taunton 1968–70; asst slr: Wragge & Co Birmingham 1970–73, Lovell White & King 1974–80; ptnr Slaughter and May 1983–2000 (joined 1980); commercial mediator 2000–, CEDR registered mediator 1997; memb Mgmnt Ctee Royal Courts of Justice Citizens Advice Bureau; govr Taunton Sch, tstee Garden Opera; Freeman Worshipful Co of Slrs 1974; memb Law Soc; FIArb 1994; *Recreations* theatre, opera, architecture, railway history, occasional cycling; *Style*— John Hine, Esq; ✉ 50 Blackheath Park, London SE3 9SJ (tel 020 8852 7430, fax 020 8297 2489, e-mail john.hine@50bhp.co.uk)

HINES, (Melvin) Barry; s of Richard Lawrence Hines (d 1963), and Annie Westerman; *b* 30 June 1939; *Educ* Ecclesfield GS, Loughborough Coll of Educn (Teaching Cert); *m* (m dis), Margaret; 1 da (Sally b 1967), 1 s (Thomas b 1969); *Career* writer; teacher in various schs: London 1960–62, S Yorks 1963–72; hon fell Sheffield City Poly 1985; FRSL 1977; *Films* Kes 1970, Looks and Smiles 1981; *TV* Billy's Last Stand 1970, Speech Day 1973, Two Men From Derby 1976, The Price of Coal (two films, 1977), The Gamekeeper 1979, A Question of Leadership 1981, Threads 1984, Shooting Stars 1990, Born Kicking 1992; *Books* The Blinder (1966), A Kestrel for a Knave (1968), First Signs (1972), The Gamekeeper (1975), The Price of Coal (1979), Looks and Smiles (1981), Unfinished Business (1983), The Heart of It (1994), Elvis over England (1998); *Style*— Barry Hines, Esq, FRSL; ✉ c/o The Agency, 24 Pottery Lane, Holland Park, London W11 4LZ (tel 020 7229 9216)

HINES, Prof Peter; *b* 8 August 1962; *Educ* Univ of Cambridge (MA, William Vaughan Lewis Prize), Cardiff Business Sch (MBA, Alexander Duckhams Meml Trophy, PhD, Euro Fedn of Quality Mgmnt Bronze Plate); *m*; 2 c; *Career* purchasing mangr Madison Cycles 1985–88, supply chain manager Spong Housewares 1988–91, freelance conslt 1991–92; Cardiff Business Sch Wales: co-ordinator Materials Mgmnt Unit 1992–94, dir Lean Enterprise Res Centre 2000– (dep dir 1994–97, co-dir 1997–2000), prof of supply chain mgmnt 1997–; conslt ed Casebook, ed Lean Logistics, ed Int Jl of Logistics: Res & Applications 1998–; chm SA Partners 2000–; memb Ed Advsy Bd: Euro Jl of Purchasing & Supply Mgmnt, Int Jl of Logistics Mgmnt, Supply Chain Forum; chm of nat and int conferences on mgmnt and logistics; fndr ctee chm Logistics Res Network 1996–2001; Euro Best Practice Benchmarking Award 1998; *Books* Creating World Class Suppliers: Unlocking Mutual Competitive Advantage (1994), Selected Readings in Purchasing & Supply (ed with David Jessop, 1994), Selected Readings in Supply Chain Management (ed with David Jessop, 1996), The Lean Enterprise: Designing and Managing Strategic Processes for Customer Winning Performance (with Dan Dimancescu and Nick Rich, 1997), Advanced Supply Management: The Best Practice Debate (ed with Andrew Cox, 1997), Value Stream Management: Strategy and Excellence in the Supply Chain (with Richard Lamming, Dan Jones, Paul Cousins and Nick Rich, 2000); also author of numerous res papers; *Style*— Professor Peter Hines; ✉ Lean Enterprise Research Centre, Cardiff Business School, Aberconway Building, Colum Drive, Cardiff CF10 3EU (tel 029 20 876005, fax 029 20 874556, e-mail hinespa@cardiff.ac.uk)

HINGLEY, Gerald Bryan Grosvenor; s of late Martin Ward Hingley, of South Broughton, Cleveland, and late Mary Hingley; *b* 2 July 1943; *Educ* Shrewsbury, Univ of Nottingham (BA); *m* 28 July 1978, Veronica Mary, da of John Hird (d 1972), of York; 1 da (Helen b 1979), 2 s (John b 1981, David b 1986); *Career* admitted slr 1970; ptnr Wragge & Co 1974–2004; tstee: Rowlands Tst, W Midlands Chest Fund; memb Assoc of Pension Lawyers; *Recreations* sailing; *Clubs* English Speaking Union, RYA; *Style*— Gerald Hingley, Esq

HINKES, Alan Charles; OBE (2006); *b* 26 April 1954; *Children* 1 da (Fiona); *Career* mountaineer; first Briton and thirteenth person to climb the world's highest mountains, the fourteen peaks over 8000m: Shisha Pangma 1987, Manaslu 1989, Cho Oyu 1990, Broad Peak 1991, K2 1995, Everest 1996, Gasherbrum I 1996, Gasherbrum II 1996, Lhotse 1997, Nanga Parbat 1998, Makalu 1999, Annapurna 2002, Dhaulagiri 2004, Kangchenjunga 2005; int mountain guide Int Fedn of Mountain Guides Assocs (UIAGM), inspirational/motivational speaker, columnist Trail magazine, produced 11 documentaries for ITV; currently works with Br Mountaineering Cncl; environmental and organic supporter, charity work with Water Aid (Pres's Award for outstanding vol contribution to Water Aid), Cystic Fibrosis Tst, Duke of Edinburgh's Award Scheme and Outward Bound; Hon Dr Univ of York; hon citizen Northallerton N Yorks, hon fell Univ of Sunderland, Yorkshireman of the Year 2005–06; *Style*— Alan Hinkes, OBE; ✉ c/o Brandscape, Mouldings Green, Kenilworth Road, Meriden CV7 7LJ

HINKS, Frank Peter; QC (2000); s of Henry John Hinks, and Patricia May, *née* Adams; *b* 8 July 1950; *Educ* Bromley GS, St Catherine's Coll Oxford (MA, BCL); *m* 31 July 1982, Susan Mary, da of Col John Arthur Haire; 3 s (Julius b 1984, Alexander b 1985, Benjamin b 1987); *Career* called to the Bar Lincoln's Inn 1973, Chancery Bar 1974–; writer, illustrator and publisher of children's stories 1992–, exhbns incl The Chapel Gallery Hall Place Bexley 2002; churchwarden Shoreham PC 1995–2005; Liveryman Worshipful Co of Innholders 1991; *Books* The Land of Lost Hair and The Vicar's Chickens (2003, originally published as part of Shoreham Festival of Music 1992), The Crystal Key (2003), Creatures of the Forest (2003), Ramion (2003), The Dim Daft Dwarves (2004), The Bands of Evil (2004), The Magic Magpie (2004), The Cruel Count (2004), Realm of Ramion (2004), The Seven Stones of Lliana (2005), The Black Marchesa (2005), Gary the Frog Prince (2005), The Embodiment of Evil (2005), Swords of Ramion (2005); *Recreations* gardening, collecting jugs; *Clubs* Knole; *Style*— Frank Hinks, Esq, QC; ✉ Serle Court, 6 New Square, Lincoln's Inn, London WC2A 3QS (tel 020 7242 6105, fax 020 7405 4004)

HINNELLS, Prof John Russell; s of William Hinnells (d 1978), and Lilian, *née* Jackson; *b* 27 August 1941; *Educ* Derby Coll of Art, KCL (BD, AKC), SOAS Univ of London; *m* 24 June 1965, Marianne Grace, da of William Bushell (d 1973); 2 s (Mark b 11 June 1966, Duncan b 9 Oct 1968); *Career* lectr Univ of Newcastle 1967–70; Univ of Manchester: joined 1970, prof 1985–93, dean Faculty of Theology 1987–88; prof of comparative religion SOAS Univ of London 1993–98; res prof of comparative religion Derby Univ 1999–2002, prof of comparative religion Liverpool Hope Univ 2002–; visiting appts: sr lectr Open Univ 1975–77, govt res fellowship lectr Bombay 1975, Shann lectr Univ of Hong Kong 1986, Ratanbai Katrak lectr Univ of Oxford 1986; visiting prof: Univ of London 1998–, Univ of Stirling 1998–; author of numerous articles on religious and theological topics published in books and jls; series ed: Library of Religious Beliefs and Practices, Sources for the Study of Religion, Religion and the Arts, Sherman Studies on Judaism in Modern Times; advsr on religion: Penguin Books (Penguin Classics on Religion), Routledge; sec gen Soc for Mithraic Studies, fndr and first sec Shap Working Pty on world Religions in Educn 1968–75; memb: Governing Cncl Br Inst of Persian Studies 1982–86, Cncl of the Br Acad Soc of South Asian Studies 1996–; convenor Int Congress of Mithraic Studies Manchester (first) 1971, Tehran (second) 1975, Rome (Fourth) 1990, chm UNESCO Int Symposium on the Conception of Human Rights in World Religions Inter-Univ Centre Dubrovnik 1985, chief speaker American Acad of Religious Conference LA USA 1985; pres Assoc of Univ Depts of Theology and Religious Studies 1997–2000; life memb Clare Hall Cambridge 1998, sr memb Robinson Coll Cambridge 1999; FSA, FRAS; *Books* incl: Comparative Religion in Education (1970), Hinduism (ed, 1972), Persian Mythology (1974), Mithraic Studies (2 vols, ed, 1975), Spanning East and West (1978), Zoroastrianism and Parsis (1981), Penguin Dictionary of Religions (ed, 1984), Handbook of Living Religions (ed, 1985), Who's Who of World Religions (1991), Studies in Mithraism (1993), New Dictionary of Religions (ed, 1995), Zoroastrians in Britain (1996), Religion, Health and Suffering (jt ed, 1999), The South Asian Religious Diaspora in Britain, Canada and the United States (jt ed, 2000), Zorastrian and Parsi Studies: Selected Works of John R Hinnells (2000), The Zoroastrian Diaspora (2005), Sufism in the West (jt ed, 2006), The Routledge Companion to the Study of Religion (ed, 2006), Religion and Violence in South Asia: Theory and practice (jt ed, 2007), Handbook of Ancient Religion (ed, 2007), Religious Reconstruction in the South Asia Diasporas (ed, 2007); *Recreations* drawing, painting, photography; *Style*— Prof John Hinnells, FSA; ✉ e-mail jhinnells@btinternet.com

HINTON, Kevin Leslie; s of Ernest Leslie Hinton, of Oxford, and Diana, *née* Churchill; *b* 27 November 1955; *Educ* Oxford Sch, Newcastle upon Tyne Poly (BA); *m* 7 May 1988, Carolyn, da of Robert Ian Tricker; 2 da (Lauren Kay b 12 Nov 1990, Fern Elise b 24 July 1998), 1 s (Jack Samuel b 16 May 1993); *Career* design asst Hancock Museum Newcastle upon Tyne 1977–78, graphic designer VAP Kidlington 1978–80, sr designer The Medicine Group Abingdon 1980–89, fndr ptnr The Hinton Chaundy Design Partnership 1989–98 (ind conslt 1998–2000), fndr dir The Blake Project Ltd 2000–; MCSD 1988 (chm S of England Region 1994–97 and 1999, memb Cncl 2001–03); *Recreations* reading, drawing, enjoying my family; *Style*— Kevin Hinton, Esq; ✉ Mill Lane House, Cassington, Oxfordshire OX29 4DL

HINTON, Leslie Frank; s of late Frank Arthur Hinton, and Lilian Amy, *née* Bruce; *b* 19 February 1944, Bootle; *Educ* Br Army Schs in Germany, Libya, Egypt, Ethiopia and Singapore; *m* 1968, Mary Christine Weadick; 4 s, 1 da; *Career* reporter Adelaide News Aust 1960–65, desk ed Br United Press London 1965–66, reporter The Sun 1966–69, writer ed Adelaide News 1969–70, reporter The Sun 1971–76, US corr News International NYC 1976–78; The Star NYC: news ed 1978–80, managing ed 1980–82; assoc ed Boston Herald 1982–85; Murdoch Magazines: ed-in-chief Star magazine 1985–87, exec vice-pres 1987–90, pres 1990–91; pres and ceo News America Publishing Inc NYC 1991–93, chm and ceo Fox TV Stations Inc and Fox News Inc LA 1993–95, exec chm News International plc 1995–, dir British Sky Broadcasting plc 1999–2003; non-exec dir Johnston Press plc 2005–; memb Bd of Dirs Press Assoc 1996–, chm Code of Practice Ctee PCC 1998–, memb Cncl CPU 1999–; memb Bd of Tstees American Sch in London 1999–; *Style*— Les Hinton, Esq; ✉ News International, 1 Virginia Street, London E98 1EX (tel 020 7782 6000, fax 020 7488 3245)

HINTON, Wendy Pamela; da of Norman George Hinton (d 1991), and Jean Clarise, *née* Swain (d 1999); *b* 14 July 1962; *Educ* Benedictine Convent Sch Dumfries, Emerson Park Sch Hornchurch, Havering Tech Coll Hornchurch, London C of C and Industry; *m* 18 Sept 1987, Paul Doherty, s of Llewellyn Patrick John Doherty; 1 da (Jasmine Anne b 4 July 1991), 1 s (Jordan Llewellyn George b 13 Nov 1996); *Career* Woman's Journal magazine 1981–86, Signature magazine 1986–87, picture ed ES Magazine 1987–2001, picture dir InStyle UK magazine 2001–; judge: Assoc of Photographers Twelfth Awards 1995, London Photographic Awards 1998 and 2003, Assoc of Photographers' Assistants Awards 2001; Newspaper Supplement of the Year Br Picture Eds Award (for ES) 2000, highly commended Picture Ed of the Year IPC Media Editorial Awards 2004; *Recreations* photography exhibitions, being a mother; *Style*— Mrs Wendy Hinton; ✉ InStyle UK, Blue Fin Building, 110 Southwark Street, London SE1 0SU (tel 020 3148 7385, fax 020 3148 8166, e-mail wendy_hinton@instyleuk.com)

HINTON COOK, Gavin; s of Ronald Edward William Cook, and Gwendolin Bessie Hinton; *b* 9 April 1947; *Educ* Kingsbury GS, Architectural Assoc Sch of Architecture (AA Dipl); *m* 11 Sept 1971, Janine Dewar, da of Wing Cdr William Charles Ramsay (d 1979); *Career* chartered architect: WF Johnson and Assoc, Melvin and Lansley, London Borough of Lambeth, Philip Mercer RIBA; project architect Milton Keynes Devpt Corp 1976–79 (chief architect 1979–85, completed 2400 houses and co-ordinated Energy World at MK); md Orchard Design 1985– (39 current design projects, complete site development, engrg and total integration managed); lectr architectural studies Univ of Birmingham; awards: Arch Design Magazines, Best of Br Architecture Design Award Commendation, RIBA S Regn Energy Award; ARIBA; *Recreations* sailing, squash, cycling; *Style*— Gavin Hinton Cook, Esq

HIRSCH, Prof Steven Richard; *b* 12 March 1937; *Educ* Amherst Coll MA (BA), Johns Hopkins Univ (MD); *m* Teresa; 1 s (Phineas), 3 da (Georgina, Colette, Eleanor); *Career* attached res worker MRC social psychiatry Maudsley Hosp 1971–73 (sr registrar and lectr 1967–71), sr lectr and hon conslt Westminster and Queen Mary's Hosp 1973–75, prof and head Dept of Psychiatry Imperial Coll Sch of Med at Charing Cross Hosp until 2002 (Charing Cross and Westminster Med Sch until merger 1997) and hon conslt Charing Cross Hosp 1975–2005; in private practice (psychiatry) Priory Hosp Roehampton; dir of teaching governance W London Mental Health Tst 2002–05; former pres Psychiatry Section RSM; former chm: Assoc of Professors of Psychiatry, Assoc of Univ Teachers of Psychiatry, Psychopharmacology Sub-Ctee RCPsych; former dep chm Mental Health Cmmn BMA; convenor of Psychiatry Subject Panel Faculty of Med Univ of

London; memb: BMA, RCPsych, Soc of Apothecaries; FRCPsych 1979, FRCP 1983; *Books* Themes and Variations in European Psychiatry: An anthology (ed with M Shepherd, 1974), Abnormalities in Parents of Schizophrenics: Review of the Literature and an Investigation of Communication Defects and Deviances (with J Leff, 1975), The Suicide Syndrome (ed with R Farmer, 1980), Social Behaviour Assessment Schedule. Training Manual and Rating Guide (with S Platt and A Weyman, 1983), The Psychopharmacology and Treatment of Schizophrenia (ed with P B Bradley, 1986), Consent and the Incompetent Patient: Ethics, Law and Medicines (ed with J Harris, 1988), Learning Psychiatry through MCQ: a comprehensive text (with T E Sensky, C Thompson et al, 1988), Schizophrenia (ed with D Weinberger, 1995, 2 edn 2003); author of reports incl: Psychiatric Beds and Resources: Factors Influencing Bed Use and Service Planning RCPsych 1988, Services for Patients with Chronic Disabilities Resulting from Mental Illness RCPsych 1993; author of 300 abstracts, chapters and published scientific papers; *Recreations* skiing, ju jitsu; *Style*— Prof Steven Hirsch; ✉ Division of Neuroscience and Psychological Medicine, Imperial College Faculty of Medicine at Charing Cross Hospital, St Dunstan's Road, London W6 8RP (tel 020 8846 7342, e-mail s.hirsch@ic.ac.uk)

HIRST, Chris; s of R C C Hirst, and P Hirst, *née* Snell; *b* 4 April 1971, Cannock, W Midlands; *Educ* Haydon Bridge Co HS, BNC Oxford (MEng); *m* 27 May 2000, Ann, *née* Jenkins; 2 s (Dylan b 28 March 2003, Sam b 18 Dec 2004); *Career* Bartle Bogle Hegarty 1995–99, client servs dir Fallon London 1999–2003, md Grey London 2003–; FRSA; *Recreations* lots of tennis, a little golf, running, reading, writing, the kids; *Clubs* Groucho; *Style*— Chris Hirst, Esq; ✉ Grey London, 77 Hatton Garden, London EC1N 8JS (tel 020 3037 3030, e-mail chris.hirst@greyeu.com)

HIRST, Christopher Halliwell; s of John Kenneth Hirst, of Hutton Buscel, N Yorks, and Marian Harrison, *née* Smith; *b* 27 May 1947; *Educ* Merchant Taylors', Trinity Hall Cambridge (MA); *m* 1, 12 Aug 1972 (m dis 1985), (Moira) Cecilia, da of Arthur Tienken, of Minneapolis, USA; 1 s (William b 1974), 1 da (Elizabeth b 1976); m 2, 28 March 1987, Sara Louise, da of Arthur James Petherick, of Bodmin, Cornwall; 3 da (Victoria b 1988, Catherine b 1989, Emily b 1991); *Career* trainee exec Bank of London & S America Chile 1969–71; asst master Radley Coll 1972–85 (housemaster 1978–85), headmaster Kelly Coll Tavistock 1985–95, headmaster Sedbergh Sch 1995–; HMC: chm Sports Sub-Ctee 1995–2001, memb HMC Ctee 1998–2002, chm NE Div 2002; govr Newcastle Sch for Boys; *Recreations* antiquarian, literary, sporting, memb Ctee Cumberland CCC; *Clubs* East India, Lansdowne, Free Foresters, Jesters, MCC, Lord's Taverners; *Style*— Christopher Hirst, Esq; ✉ Birksholme, Sedbergh, Cumbria LA10 5HQ (tel 01539 620491); Sedbergh School, Sedbergh, Cumbria LA10 5HG (tel 01539 620535, fax 01539 621301, e-mail hm@sedbergh.sch.uk, website www.sedbergh.cumbria.sch.uk)

HIRST, Damien; *b* 1965, Bristol; *Educ* Goldsmiths Coll London; *Career* artist; guest ed The Big Issue 1997; co fndr and owner Pharmacy 1998–2003, prop The White Hart Bar Ifracombe Devon 2004–; Prix Eliette von Karajan 1995, Turner Prize 1995; *Solo Exhibitions* incl: In & Out of Love (Woodstock Street London) 1991, When Logics Die (Emmanuel Perrotin Paris) 1991, Internal Affairs (ICA London) 1991, Where's God Now? (Jay & Donatella Chiat NY) 1992, Marianne, Hildegard (Unfair/ Jay Jopling Cologne) 1992, Pharmacy (Cohen Gall NY) 1992, Visual Candy (Regen Projects LA) 1993, Damien Hirst (Galerie Jablonka Cologne) 1993, Making Beautiful Drawings (Bruno Brunnet Fine Arts Berlin) 1994, Currents 23 (Milwaukee Art Museum) 1994, A Bad Environment for White Monochrome Paintings (Mattress Factory Pittsburgh) 1994, A Good Environment for Coloured Monochrome Paintings (DAAD Gall Berlin) 1994, Pharmacy (Dallas Museum) 1994, Pharmacy (Kukje Gall Seoul) 1995, Still (White Cube/Jay Jopling London) 1995, Prix Eliette von Karajan '95 (Max Gandolph-Bibliothek Salzburg) No Sense of Absolute Corruption (Gagosian Gall NY) 1996, The Beautiful Afterlife (Bruno Bischofberger Zürich) 1997, Damien Hirst (Astrup Fearnley Museum Oslo) 1997, Damien Hirst (Southampton City Art Gall) 1998, Pharmacy (Tate Gall London) 1999, Damien Hirst (Sadler's Wells London) 2000, Theories, Models, Methods, Approaches, Assumptions, Results and Findings (Gagosian Gall NY) 2000, Damien Hirst's art education (The Reliance Leeds) 2002, Damien Hirst in a Spin; The Action of the World on Things (Galerie Aurel Scheibler) 2003, Damien Hirst (The Saatchi Gall London) 2003, From the Cradle to the Grave: Selected Drawings (25th Int Biennale of Graphic Arts Ljubljana and The Marble Palace St Petersburg) 2003, Romance in the Age of Uncertainty (White Cube London) 2003, The Agony and The Ecstasy: Selected works 1989–2004 (Archaeological Museum Naples) 2004, A Selection of Works by Damien Hirst from Various Collections (MFA Boston) 2005, Damien Hirst - Works on Paper (Andipa Gall London) 2005, Damien Hirst. In a Spin (Gascoigne Gall Harrogate) 2005, The Elusive Truth! (Gagosian Gall NY) 2005, Damien Hirst (Static Gall Liverpool 2005), Damien Hirst (Astrup Fearnley Museet fur Moderne Kunst Oslo) 2005, In the darkest hour there may be light: works from Damien Hirst's murderme collection (Serpentine Gall London) 2006; *Group Exhibitions* incl: Freeze (Surrey Docks London) 1988, New Contemporaries (ICA London) 1989, Third Eye Centre Glasgow 1989, Modern Medicine (Building One London) 1990, Broken English (Serpentine Gall London) 1991, Young British Artists (Saatchi Collection London) 1992, British Art (Barbara Gladstone Gall NY) 1992, Turner Prize Exhbn (Tate Gall London) 1992, The 21st Century (Kunsthalle Basel) 1993, Aperto: Venice Biennial (Aperto Section Venice) 1993, Some Went Mad, Some Ran Away (Serpentine Gall London and tour) 1994, Virtual Reality (Nat Gall of Aust Canberra) 1994, Art Unlimited (Centre for Contemporary Art Glasgow and tour) 1994, Drawing the Line (Southampton City Art Gall, Manchester City Art Gall, Ferens Art Gall Hull, Whitechapel Art Gall London) 1995, Turner Prize Exhbn (Tate Gall London) 1995, British Art Show 4 (touring exhbn) 1995, Spellbound (Art and Film exhbn, Hayward Gall London) 1996, A Small Shifting Sphere of Serious Culture (ICA London) 1996, Dimensions Variable (British Cncl touring exhbn) 1997, Sensation (Royal Acad of Arts London) 1997, Picture Britannica: Art from Britain (Museum of Contemporary Art Sydney, Art Gall of S Aust Adelaide, Te Papa Wellington) 1997, Wall Projects (Museum of Contemporary Art Chicago) 1998, London Calling (British Sch of Rome/Galleria Nazionale d'Art Moderne Guarene) 1998, Damien Hirst, Jeff Koons, Charles Ray (11 Duke Street London) 1998, Modern British Art (Tate Gall Liverpool) 1998, On the Sublime (Rooseum Center for Contemporary Art Malmö) 1999, Examining Pictures (Whitechapel Art Gall London, Museum of Contemporary Art Chicago) 1999, Fourth Wall (South Bank London) 1999, The History of the Turner Prize (ArtSway Sway) 1999, Sincerely Yours: British Art from the 90's (Astrup Fearnley MOMA Oslo) 2000, Art in Sacred Spaces (St Stephen's Church London) 2000, Out There (White Cube 2 London) 2000, Ant Noises (Saatchi Gall London) 2000, Video Vibe: Art, Music and Video in the UK (British Sch of Rome) 2000, The History of the Turner Prize 1983–1999 and People's Show 2: Pictures selected by the public (Victoria Art Gall Bath) 2000, Peter Blake: About Collage (Tate Gall Liverpool) 2000, Century City (Tate Modern London) 2001, Breaking the Mould: 20th Century British Sculpture from Tate (Norwich Castle Museum and Art Gall) 2001, Public Offerings (Museum of Contemporary Arts LA) 2001, Warhol/Koons/Hirst: Cult and Culture Selections from the Vicki and Kent Logan Collection (Aspen Art Museum Colorado) 2001, Beautiful Productions. Art to play, art to wear, art to own (Whitechapel Art Gall London) 2001, Art > Music, Rock Pop Techno (MOMA Sydney) 2001, Artist's London: Holbein to Hirst (Museum of London) 2001,The Rowan Collection. Contemporary British & Irish Art (Irish MOMA Dublin) 2002, Le Part de l'Autre (Carre d'Art Musée d'aer Contemporaine Nimes) 2002, In Good Form: Recent Sculpture from the Arts Cncl Collection (Yorkshire Sculpture Park Wakefield) 2003, Dreams and conflicts: the Dictatorship of the Viewer (50th Venice Biennale) 2003, In-A-Gadda-Da-Vida (Tate Britain London) 2004, Singular Forms (Sometimes Repeated) (Solomon R Guggenheim Museum NY) 2004, The Stations of the Cross (Gagosian Gall London) 2004, Summer Exhibition (Royal Acad of Arts London) 2004, Den Haag Sculpture Project 2004, Imageless Icons: Abstract Thoughts (Gagosian Gall London) 2005, Logical Conclusions (Pacewildenstein NY) 2005, An International Legacy: Selections from Carnegie Museum of Art (Columbus Museum of Art) 2005, Figure It Out (Hudson Valley Center for Contemporary Art NY) 2005; *Works in Collections* incl: Saatchi Gall London, Tate Gall London, Br Cncl, Arts Cncl, Contemporary Art Museum Kanazawa, Denver Art Museum, Deste Fndn for Contemporary Art Athens, Deutsche Bank London, Fondazione Prada Milan, Hirshhorn Museum Washington, MOMA NY, Samsung Museum Seoul, San Diego Museum of Contemporary Art, San Francisco MOMA, Scottish Nat Gall of Modern Art Edinburgh, Stedelijk Museum Amsterdam, Weltkunst Fndn Dublin, Yale Center for British Art New Haven; *Film* dir Breath (Beckett on Film Channel 4 and RTÉ) 2001; *Books* I Want to Spend the Rest of My Life Everywhere, with Everyone, One to One, Always, Forever, Now (1997), On the Way to Work (with Gordon Burn, 2001); *Style*— Damien Hirst, Esq; ✉ White Cube, 48 Hoxton Square, London N1 6PB (tel 020 7930 5373, fax 020 7749 7480)

HIRST, Rt Hon Sir David Cozens-Hardy; kt (1982), PC (1992); er s of Thomas William Hirst (d 1965), of Aylsham, Norfolk, and Margaret Joy, *née* Cozens-Hardy (niece of 1 Baron Cozens-Hardy) (d 1984); *b* 31 July 1925; *Educ* Eton, Trinity Coll Cambridge; *m* 1951, Pamela Elizabeth Molesworth, da of Col Temple Percy Molesworth Bevan, MC, of London (s of Hon Charlotte Molesworth, 2 da of 8 Viscount Molesworth); 3 s (one of whom Jonathan William Hirst, QC, *qv*), 2 da (one of whom Rachel Joy Hirst, *qv*); *Career* served WWII, RA and Intelligence Corps, Capt 1946; called to the Bar Inner Temple 1951, reader 1994, treas 1995, QC 1965, judge of the High Court of Justice (Queen's Bench Div) 1982–92, Lord Justice of Appeal 1992–99, treas Inner Temple 1995; memb: Lord Chllr's Law Reform Ctee 1966–80, Cncl on Tbnls 1966–80, Ctee to Review Defamation Act, Supreme Ct Rule Ctee 1984; chm of the Bar 1978–79 (vice-chm 1977–78); chm Spoliation Advsy Panel 2000–; chm Stewards RAC 2001–; *Recreations* theatre and opera, growing vegetables; *Clubs* Boodle's, MCC; *Style*— Sir David Hirst; ✉ Royal Courts of Justice, Strand, London WC2A 2LL

HIRST, (Nathania) Gemma Louise; da of Peter John Hirst, of Surrey, and Anne Jennifer, *née* Steele; *b* 1 September 1970, Cuckfield, Sussex; *Educ* Croham Hurst Sch Croydon (scholar, head girl), Newnham Coll Cambridge (MA); *Career* foreign rights asst Kingfisher Larousse plc 1993–94, asst agent Deborah Owen Ltd 1994–97, media agent David Higham Assocs Ltd 1997–; affiliate memb of Writers' Guild; memb Bafta Children's Jury 2005; *Recreations* film, books, theatre, travel, gourmet cuisine; *Style*— Miss Gemma Hirst; ✉ David Higham Associates Limited, 5–8 Lower John Street, Golden Square, London W1F 9HA (tel 020 7434 5900, fax 020 7437 1072, e-mail gemmahirst@davidhigham.co.uk)

HIRST, Jonathan William; QC (1990); s of Sir David Hirst, *qv*, and Pamela Elizabeth Molesworth, *née* Bevan; *b* 2 July 1953; *Educ* Eton, Trinity Coll Cambridge (MA); *m* 20 July 1974, Fiona Christine Mary, da of Dr Peter Anthony Tyser; 2 s (Thomas James b and d 1991, Charles John b 1993); *Career* called to the Bar Inner Temple 1975 (bencher 1994); in practice at commercial bar SE Circuit, recorder 1997– (asst recorder 1993–97), dep High Court judge 2002–, jt head Brick Court Chambers 2005–; memb Gen Cncl of Bar 1986–2000 (vice-chm 1999, chm 2000); chm: Law Reform Ctee 1992–94, Professional Standards Ctee 1996–98; govr Taverham Hall Sch Norfolk 1990–95, govr Goodenough Coll London 2001– (memb Bd 2006–); *Recreations* shooting, gardening, music; *Clubs* Boodle's, Norfolk, Hurlingham; *Style*— Jonathan Hirst, Esq, QC; ✉ Brick Court Chambers, 7–8 Essex Street, London WC2R 3LD (tel 020 7379 3550, fax 020 7379 3558, e-mail jonathan.hirst@brickcourt.co.uk)

HIRST, Dr Linda Margaret; da of Harold Bruce Hirst, of Huddersfield (d 1987), and Margaret, *née* Binns (d 1993); *b* 19 November 1947, Huddersfield; *Educ* Greenhead HS Huddersfield, Guildhall Sch of Music and Drama (AGSM); *m* 1, 1978 (m dis 1990), Terry Edwards; 1 s (Timothy b 30 June 1979), 1 da (Helen b 24 Sept 1982); m 2, 1991, Gillean Craig; *Career* singer; Swingle Singers 1974–78, co-fndr Electric Phoenix, head Vocal Faculty Trinity Coll of Music 1995–; numerous masterclasses nationally and internationally; recordings include: Ligeti's Aventures and Nouvelles Aventures, Muldowney's Lonely Hearts and Duration of Exile (BBC Radio 3), Weir's Consolations of Scholarship (BBC2); tstee Hinrichsen Fndn, fell Dartington Coll of Arts; Hon DLitt Univ of Huddersfield 2001; *Publications* Alternative Voices (in Cambridge Companion to Singing); *Recreations* languages, cooking, swimming, reading; *Style*— Dr Linda Hirst; ✉ St Mary Abbots Vicarage, Vicarage Gate, London W8 4HN (tel 020 7937 9490); Trinity College of Music, King Charles Court, Old Royal Naval College, Greenwich, London SE10 9JA (e-mail lhirst@tcm.ac.uk)

HIRST, Sir Michael William; kt (1992); s of John Melville Hirst (d 1969), and Christina Binning, *née* Torrance (d 2002); *b* 2 January 1946; *Educ* Glasgow Acad, Univ of Glasgow (LLB), Univ of Iceland (exchange student); *m* 1, 21 Sept 1972, Naomi Ferguson, da of Robert Morgan Wilson (d 1977); 2 da (Sarah b 1974, Kate b 1979), 1 s (John b 1976); *Career* qualified CA 1970, ptnr Peat Marwick Mitchell & Co 1977–83, conslt KPMG Peat Marwick 1983–92, Michael Hirst Assocs 1987–; MP (Cons) Strathkelvin and Bearsden 1983–87, PPS Dept of Energy 1985–87; company director; pres Scottish Cons and Unionist Assoc 1989–92, chm Scottish Cons and Unionist Pty 1993–97 (vice-chm 1987–89); Diabetes UK: tstee 1988–2006, hon sec 1993–98, vice-chm 1998–2001, chm 2001–06; vice-pres Int Diabetes Fedn 2006–; chm The Park Sch Educn Tst 1986–; dir: Erskine Hosp Ltd 1979–, Weavers Soc of Anderston 1981–, Childrens Hospice Assoc Scotland 1993–2005; memb Ct Glasgow Caledonian Univ (chm Audit Ctee 1992–98), memb Cncl Imperial Soc of Knights Bachelor 2002– (chm Scottish Div); elder: Kelvinside Hillhead Parish Church 1975–98, Kippen Parish Church 1999–; chm Friends of Kippen Kirk Tst 2004–; Hon DLitt Glasgow Caledonian Univ 2004; FRSA 1993, MCIPR 2003; *Recreations* golf, hill walking, theatre, skiing; *Clubs* Carlton, Western (Glasgow); *Style*— Sir Michael Hirst; ✉ Glentirran, Kippen, Stirlingshire FK8 3JA (tel 01786 870283, fax 01786 870679, e-mail smh@glentirran.co.uk)

HIRST, Neil Alexander Carr; s of Theodore James Hirst, and Valerie Adamson Hirst; *b* 16 May 1946; *Educ* Canford Sch, Lincoln Coll Oxford (BA), Cornell Univ (Telluride scholar, MBA); *m* 1984, Caroline Rokeby, da of Peter Blumfeld Collins; 2 da (Emily Clare Collins b 10 Dec 1987, Alice Lydia Collins b 25 March 1993); *Career* jr reporter Eastbourne Gazette 1964–65; civil service: asst princ Fin and Econ Appraisal then Coal Div 1970–73, asst private sec to Min for Indust then two Mins for Energy and Sec of State for Trade 1973–75, princ Dept of Energy 1975–78, Atomic Energy Div Dept of Energy 1978–81, seconded to Goldman Sachs NY 1981, public flotation of Britoil 1982, asst sec Br Nuclear Fuels plc 1983–85, energy cnsllr FCO Washington DC 1985–88, DTI (projects incl legislation for privatisation of coal indust) 1992–95, dir Nuclear Industries 1995–98, dep DG Energy 1998–2002, head of Energy Markets Unit DTI 2002–04; dir energy technol and R&D International Energy Agency 2005–; *Recreations* gardening, music, theatre, walking, squash; *Clubs* Oxford and Cambridge; *Style*— Neil Hirst, Esq

HIRST, Prof Paul Heywood; s of Herbert Hirst (d 1971), of Huddersfield, W Yorks, and Winifred, *née* Michelbacher; *b* 10 November 1927; *Educ* Huddersfield Coll, Trinity Coll Cambridge (MA), Univ of London (Dip), ChCh Oxford (MA); *Career* lectr and tutor Dept of Educn Univ of Oxford 1955–59, lectr in philosophy of educn Inst of Educn Univ of Oxford 1959–65; prof of educn: KCL 1965–71, Univ of Cambridge 1971–88 (emeritus prof

1988–); fell Wolfson Coll Cambridge 1971–; visiting prof Univs of: Br Columbia, Malawi, Otago, Melbourne, Puerto Rico, Sydney, Alberta, London; CNAA: vice-chm Ctee for Educn 1975–81, chm Res Ctee 1988–92; vice-pres Philosophy of Educn Soc of GB 1979–; chm Univ Cncl for the Educn of Teachers 1985–88; memb: Cncl Royal Inst of Philosophy 1972–89, Educn Sub Ctee UGC 1974–80, Ctee for Enquiry into the Educn of Children from Ethnic Minorities (Lord Swann Ctee) 1981–85; Hon DEd CNAA 1992, Hon DPhil Cheltenham and Gloucester Coll of HE 2000, Hon DLitt Univ of Huddersfield 2002; elected memb Royal Norwegian Soc of Scis and Letters 1995; *Books* Knowledge and the Curriculum (1974), Moral Education in a Secular Society (1974), Education and its Foundation Disciplines (jtly, 1983), Initial Teacher Training and the Role of the School (jtly, 1988), Philosophy of Education: Major Themes in the Analytic Tradition (jtly, 1998); *Recreations* music (especially opera); *Clubs* Athenaeum; *Style—* Prof Paul H Hirst; ✉ Flat 3, 6 Royal Crescent, Brighton BN2 1AL (tel 01273 684118)

HIRST, Rachel Joy; da of Sir David Hirst, *qv*, and Pamela Elizabeth Molesworth, *née* Bevan; *b* 14 November 1960; *Educ* Cranborne Chase Sch; *m* 1998, Leslie Johnston; *Career* PR exec; with Good Relations 1982–85; dir: Valin Pollen 1990 (joined 1985), Gavin Anderson & Co 1991–94, Shandwick Consultants 1994–97; fndr ptnr The Hogarth Partnership 1997; dir and memb Cncl Benenden Sch 1993–; *Style—* Ms Rachel Hirst; ✉ The Hogarth Partnership, No 1 London Bridge, London SE1 9BG (tel 020 7357 9477)

HISCOCK, David Miles; s of Jeffrey Hiscock, of Coombe Bissett, Wilts and Rosalind Mary, *née* Marshall; *b* 20 September 1956; *Educ* Bishop Wordsworths GS, Salisbury Art Sch, St Martin's Sch of Art (BA), RCA (MA); *m* Anna Maria Russell; 1 s (Hunter Mannix Russell-Hiscock b 24 March 2000); *Career* freelance photographer and artist; editorial, advertising cmmns and commercials dir 1985–; Pentax bursaries 1983–85, Vogue Award for photography 1985, Madame Tussaud's Award for figurative work 1985, official VISA Olympic artist 1992; FRCA 1996; *Solo Exhibitions* incl: RPS Bath 1987, Pomeroy Purdey Gallery London 1988, 1990 and 1992, Parco Gallery Tokyo 1990, Norwich Arts Centre Norwich 1990, The Chateau d'Eau Gallery Toulouse 1991, Olympic Works (Zelda Cheatle Gallery London) 1992, Zelda Cheatle Gallery London 1993 and 1995, Transmutations (Purdy Hicks Gallery London) 1994, Strokes (Purdy Hicks Gallery and Focal Point Gallery Southend on Sea) 1997; *Selected Group Exhibitions* 1990: Identities (Philadephia Art Alliance USA), Rencontres Photographiques (Carcassonne France), Face On (Zelda Cheatle Gallery London), David Hiscock and Calum Colvin (Seagate Gallery), Dundee and Theatre Clwyd (Mold), Works by 54 Master Printers (John Jones Gallery London) 1992, The Figure Laid Bare (Pomeroy Purdy Gallery London) 1992, Print Center Editions (Pomeroy Purdy Gallery London) 1992, Fictions of the Self (Weatherspoon Art Gallery USA and tour) 1993, Time Machine (British Museum London) 1994, Little Boxes (Photofusion Gallery London and Cambridge Dark Room) 1997, Wait and See What's for Dinner (Towner Art Gallery Eastbourne) 1997, History the Mag Collection (Ferens Art Gallery Hull and Fruit Market Gallery Edinburgh), In To The Light (RPS Bath) 1999, Revelation (Purdy Hicks Gallery London) 1999, Revelation (Tullie House City Museum Carlisle) 2000, Visual Arts Scotland Annual Exhbn Edinburgh 2000, Bittersweet (Danielle Arnaud Gallery London) 2001; *Work in Collections* incl: Madame Tussauds's London, Nat Portrait Gallery, Haggerty Museum USA, Chateau D'Eau, Toulouse, Leeds City Art Gallery, Deutsche Bank, Mag Collection Ferens Art Gallery Hull, P&O Oriana Collection, RPS Bath, Tullie House City Museum Carlisle; *Books* David Hiscock - Work from 1982–90 (SKOOB Books, 1992), David Hiscock (Zelda Cheatle Press, 1994); *Style—* David Hiscock, Esq; ✉ Robert Montgomery and Partners, 3 Junction Mews, London W2 1PN (tel 020 7439 1877)

HISCOCK, (Nicholas) Toby; s of David Hiscock, of Bourton-on-the-Water, Glos, and Anne Kathleen Audrey Mary Elizabeth, *née* Clark; *b* 8 January 1960, Chelmsford, Essex; *Educ* Sexey's GS Blackford, Wells Cathedral Sch, Hertford Coll Oxford (MA); *m* 21 Aug 1982, Gail Shirley, *née* Audley-Miller; 1 da (Camilla Anne Ismay b 29 May 1990, Charles Cosmo Hugh b 11 March 1993); *Career* Binder Hamlyn Chartered Accountants 1981–88, sr audit mangr Midland Bank plc 1988–92; Henderson Group plc: joined 1992, dir of finance 1996, chief financial officer 2003–; FCA 1996 (ACA 1986); *Recreations* the arts, cycling, travel; *Style—* Toby Hiscock, Esq; ✉ Henderson Group plc, 4 Broadgate, London EC2M 2DA (tel 020 7818 4723, e-mail toby.hiscock@henderson.com)

HISCOX, Robert Ralph Scrymgeour; s of Ralph Hiscox, CBE (d 1970), and Louisa Jeanie, *née* Boal; *b* 4 January 1943; *Educ* Rugby, CCC Cambridge (MA); *m* 1, 1966 (m dis 1978), Lucy (d 1996), da of Charles Henry Mills; 2 s (Renshaw b 5 June 1968, Frederick b 5 June 1972); m 2, 1985, Lady Julia Elizabeth, da of 6 Earl of Clanwilliam (d 1989); 3 s (Milo Edmund b 4 Jan 1987, Henry Charles b 23 Sept 1989, Sidney John b 24 Jan 1993); *Career* chm Hiscox Ltd and other cos in the Hiscox Group; chm: Lloyd's Corporate Capital Assoc 1998–99, Lloyd's Market Assoc 1999–2000; dep chm Lloyd's of London 1993–95, memb Lloyd's 1967–98; dir Grainger Tst plc 2002–; treas: Friends of the Tate Gallery 1990–93, Museums and Galleries Cmmn 1996–2000; tstee and treas Campaign for Museums 1998–2004; tstee: Wilts Bobby Van Tst 1998– (chm 2002–), 24 Hour Museum 2000–01, Public Catalogue Fndn 2004–; govr St Francis Sch Pewsey 1994–97; ACII; *Recreations* family life, country life, fine art; *Style—* Robert Hiscox, Esq; ✉ Rainscombe Park, Oare, Marlborough, Wiltshire SN8 4HZ (tel 01672 563491, fax 01672 564120); Hiscox Ltd, 1 Great St Helen's, London EC3A 6HX (tel 020 7488 6011, fax 020 7488 6598, e-mail robert.hiscox@hiscox.com)

HISKEY, Rex Arthur; s of Harry Charles Hiskey, and Gwynneth, *née* Bush (d 1999); *b* 9 March 1947; *Educ* Chelmsford Tech HS, Univ of Birmingham (LLB); *m* 2 Oct 1971, Christine Elizabeth, da of Maurice Henry Cobbold (d 1997); 1 s (Thomas b 1981), 2 da (Florence b 1986, Clara b 1990); *Career* slr; in private practice holding various local appts, ptnr Hayes & Storr; *Recreations* reading, sailing; *Style—* Rex Hiskey, Esq; ✉ tel 01328 710210, fax 01328 711261

HISLOP, Ian David; s of late David Atholl Hislop, and Helen Hislop; *b* 13 July 1960; *Educ* Ardingly, Magdalen Coll Oxford (BA); *m* 16 April 1988, Victoria, *née* Hamson; 1 da (Emily Helen b 3 Oct 1990), 1 s (William David b 26 June 1993); *Career* ed Private Eye 1986–; scriptwriter Spitting Image 1984–89, columnist The Listener 1985–89, TV critic The Spectator 1994–96, columnist Sunday Telegraph 1996–2003; regular book reviewer and contrib to various newspapers and magazines; writer and broadcaster for radio and TV; team capt Have I Got News For You (BBC 2) 1991–; presenter: Canterbury Tales (Channel 4) 1996, School Rules (Channel 4) 1997, Pennies from Bevan (Channel 4) 1998, Great Railway Journeys East to West 1999, A Revolution in 5 Acts (BBC Radio 4) 2001, The Real Patron Saints (BBC Radio 4) 2002, A Brief History of Tax (BBC Radio 4) 2003, The Choir Invisible (BBC Radio 4) 2003, There'll be Blue Birds over the White Cliffs of Dover (BBC Radio 4) 2004, Are we being offensive enough? (BBC Radio 4) 2004, Who do you think you are? (BBC 2) 2004, Not Forgotten (Channel 4) 2005, Not Forgotten: Shot at Dawn (Channel 4) 2007, Scouting for Boys (BBC 4) 2007; TV plays (all co-written with Nick Newman): The Stone Age (BBC 2) 1990, Briefcase Encounter (ITV) 1991, He Died a Death (BBC 2) 1991, The Case of the Missing (BBC 2) 1991, Mangez Merveillac (BBC 2) 1993, Dead on Time (BBC 2) 1995, Gobble (BBC 2) 1996, My Dad's The Prime Minister (BBC 1) 2003 and 2004; *Publications* incl various Private Eye compilations; *Style—* Ian Hislop, Esq; ✉ Private Eye, 6 Carlisle Street, London W1V 5RG (tel 020 7437 4017, fax 020 7437 0705)

HITCHCOCK, Teresa Caroline; *b* 22 January 1960; *Educ* Ripley Tech Sch, Trent Poly (Dip), Nottingham Trent Univ (LLB, Dip); *m* 15 Aug 1981, Michael Hitchcock; *Career* admitted slr 1993; Erewash BC: dist environmental health offr 1981–84, sr grade environmental health offr 1984–86; princ grade environmental health offr NW Leics DC 1986–90, ptnr DLA Piper Slrs 1996–; memb Bd Sheffield First for Environment, hon legal advsr S Yorks Green Business Club; memb: Chartered Inst of Environmental Health, Law Soc, UK Environmental Law Assoc; *Publications* A Guide to the Food Safety Act 1990 (1989–90), Department of Environment Liability from Methane Generation (jt paper, 1994), DTI Sequestration of CO2: Onshore Actvities (2002); *Recreations* equestrian pursuits, netball, walking; *Style—* Mrs Teresa Hitchcock; ✉ DLA Piper UK LLP, 1 St Paul's Place, Sheffield S1 2JX (tel 0114 283 3302, fax 0114 276 6720, e-mail teresa.hitchcock@dlapiper.com)

HITCHCOX, John; s of Brian Hitchcox, OBE, and Jean Hitchcox; *b* Sussex; *Educ* Michael Hall Sch; *Career* property developer; co-fndr (with Harry Handlesman) Manhattan Loft Corp 1992–99, co-creator (with Philippe Starck) and dir YOO 1999–; memb The Prince's Youth Business Tst, supporter Amnesty Int; *Recreations* playing music, sailing, yoga, tennis, spending time with his children; *Style—* John Hitchcox, Esq; ✉ YOO, 2 Bentinck Street, London W1U 2FA (tel 020 7009 0100, website www.yoo.com)

HITCHENS, Peter Jonathan; s of Eric Hitchens (d 1987), and Yvonne, *née* Hickman (d 1974); *b* 28 October 1951; *Educ* The Leys Sch Cambridge, Oxford Coll of FE, Univ of York (BA); *m* 1983, Eve, da of David and Tamara Ross; 1 da, 2 s; *Career* journalist; with: Socialist Worker 1972, Swindon Evening Advertiser 1973–76, Coventry Evening Telegraph 1976; Daily Express: joined 1977, sometime industrial reporter, educn reporter, labour corr, dep political ed, diplomatic corr, Moscow corr 1990–92, Washington corr 1993–95, asst ed 1995–2001, columnist 1997–2001; Mail on Sunday 2001–; *Books* The Abolition of Britain (1999), The Rape of the Constitution (contrib, 2000), Monday Morning Blues (2000), A Brief History of Crime (2003), The Abolition of Liberty (2004); *Recreations* long train journeys, second-hand bookshops; *Style—* Peter Hitchens; ✉ Mail on Sunday, 2 Derry Street, London W8 5TS (tel 020 7938 7073, e-mail peter.hitchens@mailonsunday.co.uk)

HITCHIN, Prof Nigel James; s of Eric Wilfred Hitchin (d 1987), and Bessie, *née* Blood (d 1993); *b* 2 August 1946; *Educ* Jesus Coll Oxford (jr mathematical prize, BA), Wolfson Coll Oxford (DPhil); *m* 17 Aug 1973, Nedda Vejarano Bernal, da of Luis Vejarano; 1 da (Gloria Louise b 1977), 1 s (Julian James b 1981); *Career* research asst Inst for Advanced Study Princeton 1971–73, instructor Courant Inst NYU 1973–74; Univ of Oxford: successively research asst, jr research fell, research fell Wolfson Coll 1974–79, fell and tutor in mathematics St Catherine's Coll 1979–90; prof of mathematics Univ of Warwick 1990–94, Rouse Ball prof of mathematics Univ of Cambridge and professorial fell Gonville & Caius Coll Cambridge 1994–97, Savilian prof of geometry Univ of Oxford and professorial fell New Coll Oxford 1997–; visiting appts: Institut des Hautes Etudes Scientifiques 1975, 1979, 1987, 1990, 1994, 1997, École Normale Superieure Paris 1979, Univ of Bonn 1979, Inst for Advanced Study Princeton 1982, SUNY 1983–84, École Polytechnique 1988; pres London Mathematical Soc 1995–96 (memb Cncl 1992–96); memb: SERC Mathematics Panel 1991–94, Cncl Royal Soc 2002–04; memb Academia Europaea; jr Whitehead Prize London Mathematical Soc 1981, sr Berwick Prize London Mathematical Soc 1990, Royal Soc Sylvester Medal 2000, Polya Prize London Mathematical Soc 2002; hon fell Jesus Coll Oxford 1998; Hon DSc Univ of Bath 2003; FRS 1991; *Publications* author of over 70 learned articles in scientific jls; *Style—* Prof Nigel Hitchin, FRS; ✉ Mathematical Institute, 24–29 St Giles, Oxford OX1 3LB (tel 01865 273515, fax 01865 273588, e-mail hitchin@maths.ox.ac.uk)

HITCHING, His Hon Alan Norman; s of Norman Henry Samuel Hitching (d 1987), and Grace Ellen, *née* Bellchamber (d 1992); *b* 5 January 1941; *Educ* Forest Sch, ChCh Oxford (MA, BCL); *m* 1, 1967, Hilda Muriel (d 2000), da of Arthur William King (d 1984); 1 da (Isabel b 1969), 2 s (Malcolm b 1972, Robert b 1977); m 2, 13 Sept 2003, Susan Mary, née Banfield, wid of Michael Henry Cotton; *Career* called to the Bar Middle Temple 1964, recorder 1985–87, circuit judge (SE Circuit) 1987–2006, resident judge Blackfriars Crown Court 1998–2006; *Style—* His Hon Alan Hitching; ✉ Blackfriars Crown Court, Pocock Street, London SE1 0BJ

HITCHINSON, David Anthony; s of Rev Prebendary William Henry Hitchinson (d 2003), of Middx, and Joan Lucretia, *née* Blakeley (d 2006); *b* 8 July 1948; *Educ* Merchant Taylors', Rose Bruford Coll of Speech and Drama (RBC Dip), Univ of Kent (BA); *m* Jean, *née* Braithwaite; 1 step da (Sarah Turner); *Career* BBC: radio drama 1972–80, Radio 4 newsreader 1980–85, sr prodr drama World Serv 1985–96 (Sony Best Prodn Award 1993 and 1995, NY Best Drama Award 1996 and 1997), ed Westway 1997–2004 (Race in the Media Award Cmmn for Racial Equality 2001), exec-prodr World Service Drama 2004–06, audio and radio drama conslt 2006–; *Recreations* music, swimming, theatre; *Clubs* BBC; *Style—* David Hitchinson, Esq; ✉ 10 Abbey Close, Pyrford, Surrey GU22 8RY (e-mail hitchinson695@btinternet.com)

HITCHMAN, Frank Hendrick; s of Sir (Edwin) Alan Hitchman, KCB (d 1980), of London, and Katharine Mumford, *née* Hendrick (d 1996); *b* 21 July 1941; *Educ* Westminster, Univ of St Andrews (BSc); *Career* Coopers & Lybrand 1964–69, Samuel Montagu & Co Ltd 1970–73, Sedgwick Group plc 1973–89 (sec 1980–85), dir E W Payne Co Ltd 1985–89; Greig Fester Group Ltd: gp sec 1989–97, dep gp fin dir 1989–91, gp fin dir 1992–97; various charitable appts in London and Scotland; Hon MA Univ of Stirling 2006; FCA 1978; *Recreations* opera, travel, collecting; *Style—* Frank Hitchman, Esq; ✉ 34 Moray Place, Edinburgh EH3 6BX (tel and fax 0131 225 4130)

HITCHMAN, Prof Michael L; s of Leslie S Hitchman (d 1993), and Grace H Hitchman, *née* Callaghan (d 1991); *b* 17 August 1941; *Educ* Stratton GS Biggleswade, QMC London (BSc), King's Coll London (PGCE), UC Oxford (DPhil); *Family* 2 da (Natasha M b 8 July 1971, Fiona E b 17 May 1977), 1 s (Timothy S b 8 Feb 1973); *Career* asst lectr in chemistry Leicester Regnl Coll of Technol 1963–65, jr res fell Wolfson Coll Oxford 1968–70, ICI postdoctoral res fell Physical Chemistry Laboratory Oxford 1968–70, chief scientist Orbisphere Corporation Geneva 1970–73, staff scientist Laboratories RCA Ltd Zurich 1973–79, lectr then sr lectr Univ of Salford 1979–84; Univ of Strathclyde: Young prof of chemical technol 1984–2004, chm Dept of Pure and Applied Chemistry 1986–89, vice-dean Faculty of Sci 1989–92; hon prof Taiyuan Univ of Technol China 1994–; treas Electrochemistry Gp RSC 1984–90, chm Electroanalytical Gp RSC 1985–88; memb Advsy Bd EUROCVD 1985– (chm 1989–92); memb SERC ctees on: chemistry 1987–90, semiconductors 1988–90, non-metallic materials 1986–88; dir: Thin Film Innovations (TFI) Ltd, Jinju Consultancies Ltd; co-chm W Scotland Sci Park Advsy Ctee 1988–92; memb: Electrochemical Soc, Int Soc of Electrochemistry, Br Assoc of Crystal Growth, Materials Research Soc; British Vacuum Cncl medal and prize 1992; CSci, CChem, FRSC, FRSA, FRSE; *Publications* Ring Disk Electrodes (jtly, 1971), Measurement of Dissolved Oxygen (1978), Proceedings of the Eighth European Conference on Chemical Vapour Deposition (ed, 1991), Chemical Vapour Deposition (ed, 1992), Advanced Materials Chemical Vapour Deposition (ed, 1995–), Proceedings of the Fifteenth International Symposium on Chemical Vapour Deposition (jtly ed, 2000), Proceedings of EUROCVD 15 (jtly ed 2005); *Recreations* humour, cooking, eating, walking, losing weight; *Style—* Prof Michael L Hitchman; ✉ Thin Film Innovations Ltd, Block 7 Kelvin Campus, West of Scotland Science Park, Glasgow G20 0TH (tel 0141 5793028)

HITCHON, (George) Michael; s of Alfred Clifford Hitchon (d 1987), and Beatrice Helen, *née* Daniels (d 1982); *b* 26 November 1944; *Educ* King Edward's Five Ways Sch, Newent Sch, Univ of Nottingham (MSc); *Career* horticulturist at Scot Agric Coll 1969–2006; treas Ayr Arts Guild 1982–, dir Ayr Arts Festival 1983– (co sec 1991–), pres Kyle and Carrick Civic Soc 1981–, sec Int Soc of Horticultural Science's First Int Conf on Educn and Trg in Horticulture at Scottish Agric Coll 1992, memb Gardens Ctee Nat Tst for Scotland 2001–06, treas Scottish branch Inst of Horticulture 2003–, memb Bicentenary Ctee Royal Caledonian Horticultural Soc 2006–; memb: Ayr Guildry Dean's Cncl 2003–06, S Ayrshire Sustainability Forum 2005–, Cncl Strathclyde Building Preservation Tst 2005–; treas Fort, Seafield and Wallacetown CC 1992–; Worshipful Co of Fruiterers Prize and Medal 1967, S Ayrshire Cncl Queen's Jubilee Medal 2002, Royal Caledonian Horticultural Soc Dr Andrew Duncan Medal 2005; Churchill fell 1973; MIHort (chm Scottish Branch 1996–98); *Books* Growing in Perlite (1991), Education and Training for Horticulture (1993); *Recreations* music, conservation, architectural history, curling; *Clubs* Auchincruive Curling, Ayr Curling; *Style*— G Michael Hitchon, Esq; ✉ 1 Barns Terrace, Ayr KA7 2DB (tel and fax 01292 619800, e-mail m.hitchon@tiscali.co.uk)

HITMAN, Prof Graham Alec; s of Maxwell Hitman (d 1987), and Annette Hitman (d 1968); *b* 19 January 1953; *Educ* Bromley GS, UCH Med Sch (MB BS), Univ of London (MD); *m* Avril Froma, da of Ivor Sevitt, of Chislehurst; 1 da (Nadia b 1978), 1 s (Oliver b 1980); *Career* formerly: SHO and registrar King's Coll Hosp London, RD Lawrence res fell Bart's; Bart's and London Queen Mary Sch of Med and Dentistry: successively lectr Med Unit, asst dir, then reader, currently prof of molecular med, hon conslt, head of dept of diabetes and metabolic med; memb: Br Diabetic Assoc, American Soc of Human Genetics; FRCP; *Recreations* windsurfing, tennis, running; *Style*— Prof Graham Hitman; ✉ 2 Yester Road, Chislehurst, Kent BR6 5LT (tel 020 8467 3331); Department of Diabetes and Metabolic Medicine, 7th Floor, John Harrison House, Royal London Hospital, Whitechapel, London E1 1BB (tel 020 7377 7111, fax 020 7377 7636, e-mail g.a.hitman@qmul.ac.uk)

HIVES, 3 Baron (UK 1950); Matthew Peter Hives; s of Hon Peter Anthony Hives (d 1974), and Dinah, *née* Wilson-North; suc unc, 2 Baron Hives, CBE, 1997; *b* 25 May 1971; *Educ* Haileybury Coll, Univ of Newcastle (BEng), Univ of Aberdeen (MSc); *Heir* unc, Hon Michael Hives; *Career* MIMechE; *Recreations* fly fishing; *Clubs* Farmers'; *Style*— The Rt Hon the Lord Hives; ✉ Le Tapon Cottage, La Rue Du Tapon, St Savior, Jersey JG2 7UL

HIX, Mark Ernest; s of Ernest Hix, and Gillian, *née* Ward; *b* 10 December 1962, Dorset; *Educ* Colfox Sch Bridport, South Dorset Tech Coll Weymouth; *m* 1, (m dis) Suzie; 2 da (Lydia, Ellie (twins) b 2 Nov 1994); partner Clare Lattin; *Career* chef; Grosvenor House Park Lane 1981, Park Lane W1 1983, Dorchester Hotel Grill Room 1983, Park Lane W1 1984; Mr Pontac's Candlewick Restaurant: sous chef 1985, head chef 1985, exec chef 1986; head chef Le Caprice 1990, exec chef Le Caprice and The Ivy 1993, chef dir Caprice Holdings Ltd 2000–; memb: Mutton Renaissance, Leuka, Acad of Culinary Arts, Serpentine Gallery, Guild of Food Writers; Glenfiddich Award Newspaper Cookery Writer of the Year 2003, Guild of Food Writers Best Cookery Writer 2005; *Publications* The Ivy: The restaurant and its recipes (1997), Le Caprice (1999), Eat Up (2000), British (2003), Fish Etc (2004), The Simple Art of Marrying Food and Wine (2005); *Recreations* fishing, foraging; *Style*— Mark Hix, Esq; ✉ Caprice Holdings Ltd, 3–5 Rathbone Place, London W1T 1HJ (tel 020 7307 5763, fax 020 7307 5787, e-mail mhix@caprice-holdings.co.uk)

HO-YEN, Dr Darrel Orlando; s of Basil Orlando Ho-Yen, and Cicely Ho-Yen; *b* 1 May 1948; *Educ* Univ of Dundee (BMSc, MB ChB, MD, DSc); *Children* 2 s (Gregory Orlando b 9 Aug 1977, Colan Maxwell b 2 Oct 1979); *Career* dir S Toxoplasma Reference Laboratory 1987–, head Microbiology Raigmore Hosp Inverness 1995– (conslt microbiologist 1987–), hon clinical sr lectr Univ of Aberdeen 1987–, dir nat Lyme Disease testing; memb: Br Soc for Study of Infection, Assoc of Clinical Pathologists, Soc of Authors; FRCPath (MRCPath 1986), FRCPEd; *Books* Better Recovery From Viral Illnesses (2 edn, 1987, 3 edn 1993, 4 edn 1999), Diseases of Infection (jtly, 1987, 2 edn 1993), Unwind! Understand and Control Life, Be Better!! (1991), Human Toxoplasmosis (jtly, 1992), Climbing Out (1995), Ticks (1998, 2 edn 2006), A Scientist's Quest for God (2003); *Style*— Dr Darrel Ho-Yen; ✉ Microbiology Department, Raigmore Hospital, Inverness (tel 01463 704207)

HOARE, Prof Sir Charles Antony Richard; kt (2000); s of late Henry Samuel Malortie Hoare, and Marjorie Francis, *née* Villiers; *b* 11 January 1934; *Educ* King's Sch Canterbury, Merton Coll Oxford (MA), Moscow State Univ; *m* 13 Jan 1962, Jill, da of late John Pym, of Brasted Chart, Kent; 2 s (Thomas b 1964, Matthew b 1967 d 1981), 1 da (Joanna b 1965); *Career* Nat Serv RN 1956–58, Lt RNR 1958; Elliot Bros Ltd 1960–68: programmer, chief engr, tech mangr, chief scientist; prof of computer sci Queen's Univ Belfast 1968–77, prof of computation Univ of Oxford 1977–93, James Martin prof of computing Univ of Oxford 1993–99 (fell Wolfson Coll 1977–), princ researcher Microsoft 1999–; Turing award 1980, Faraday medal 1985, Kyoto prize 2000; Hon DSc: Univ of Southern Calif 1979, Univ of Warwick 1985, Univ of Pennsylvania 1986, Queen's Univ Belfast 1987, Univ of York 1989; Hon DUniv: Essex 1991, Bath 1993, Oxford Brookes 2000, Queen Mary Coll 2005; hon fell: Kellogg Coll Oxford 1998, Darwin Coll Cambridge 2001, Merton Coll Oxford 2004; Soc Stran Accad dei Lincei 1988, corresponding memb Bayerische Akad der Wissenschaften 1997, foreign assoc US Nat Acad 2006, Einstein prof Chinese Academy of Science 2006 Distinguished FBCS 1978, FRS 1982, FREng 2005; *Books* Structured Programming (1972), Communicating Sequential Processes (1985), Essays in Computing Science (1988), Unifying Theories of Programming (1998); *Recreations* reading, walking, music, travel; *Style*— Prof Sir Tony Hoare, FRS; ✉ Microsoft Research Ltd, 7 JJ Thomson Avenue, Cambridge CB3 0FB (tel 01223 479800, fax 01233 479999, e-mail thoare@microsoft.com)

HOARE, Christopher Henry St John (Toby); s of J Michael Hoare, and Ann St John, *née* Kingham; *b* 2 February 1960; *Educ* Harrow; *m* 2 Aug 1986, Hon Sarah Jane, da of Baron Dixon-Smith (Life Peer), *qv*; 2 s (Oscar b 16 July 1988, Giles b 22 June 1990); 1 da (Camilla b 18 Nov 1994); *Career* mgmnt trainee Distillers Co Ltd 1979–80, Express Newspapers 1980–84, Centaur Communications 1984–85, Dorland Advertising Ltd 1985–87; Young & Rubicam Ltd: joined 1987, dir 1989, business devpt dir 1991–94, md 1994–96, chief exec 1996–99; gp chief exec Bates UK Gp 1999–2002, chm Bates Gp Europe 2002–; global client leader (ceo HSBC team) WPP plc 2004–, head of UK ops JWT 2005–; govr Harrow Sch 2001; Freeman City of London 1987, Liveryman Worshipful Co of Distillers 1982; *Recreations* shooting, golf, music, wine; *Clubs* Garrick, Royal Worlington Golf; *Style*— Toby Hoare, Esq; ✉ 17 Stanley Crescent, London W11 2NA (e-mail thoare@wpp.com)

HOARE, Sir David John; 9 Bt (GB 1786), of Barn Elms, Surrey; s of Sir Peter William Hoare, 7 Bt (d 1973); suc bro, Sir Peter Richard David Hoare, 8 Bt (d 2004); *b* 8 October 1935; *Educ* Eton; *m* 1, 1965, Mary Vanessa, yr da of Peter Cardew, of Westhanger, Cleeve, Bristol; 1 s (Simon Merrik b 1967); m 2, 1984, Virginia Victoria Labes, da of Michael Menzies, of Long Island, NY; *Heir* s, Simon Hoare; *Career* banker; chm C Hoare & Co 2001–06 (managing ptnr 1964–); *Recreations* fishing, shooting, golf, skiing; *Clubs* White's, Royal St George's Golf, Swinley; *Style*— Sir David Hoare, Bt; ✉ Luscombe Castle, Dawlish, Devon; C Hoare & Co, 37 Fleet Street, London EC4P 4DQ (tel 020 7353 4522)

HOARE, Henry Cadogan; s of Henry Peregrine Rennie Hoare (d 1981), and Lady Beatrix Lilian Ethel Cadogan (d 1999); *b* 23 November 1931; *Educ* Eton, Trinity Coll Cambridge (MA); *m* 1, 30 May 1959 (m dis 1970), Pamela Saxon, da of late Col G F Bunbury, OBE; 2 s (Timothy b 1960, Nicholas b 1964), 1 da (Arabella b 1968); m 2, 16 June 1977, Caromy Maxwell Macdonald, da of Robert Jenkins, CBE, JP; *Career* banker; sr ptnr C Hoare & Co 2001– (managing ptnr 1959–, chm 1988–2001); *Style*— Henry Hoare, Esq; ✉ C Hoare & Co, 37 Fleet Street, London EC4P 4DQ (tel 020 7353 4522, fax 020 7353 4521)

HOARE, Jonathan Michael Douro; s of Capt Michael Douro Hoare, of Downsland Court, Ditchling, E Sussex, and Valerie Ann, *née* James; *b* 21 October 1953; *Educ* Eton, Oriel Coll Oxford (MA); *m* 7 Aug 1982, Clare Elizabeth, da of Peter Parsons, of The Grove, Stocklinch, Somerset; 2 s (Timothy Jonathan b 4 Oct 1986, Sebastian Michael b 18 Dec 1989), 1 da (Natasha Ruth b 1 June 1984); *Career* advertising mangr The Economist 1977–83, business devpt mangr Valin Pollen 1983–85, chief exec BMP Business 1985–91, chief exec Hoare Wilkins Advertising Ltd 1991–94; TBWA: md (following merger) 1994–96, chm 1996–97; chm TBWA Simons Palmer (following merger with Simons Palmer Clemmow Johnson) 1997–98, md Griffin Bacal 1998, currently with Burkitt DDB; Freeman City of London, Liveryman Worshipful Co of Marketors; memb: IAA, IPA, Inst of Mktg, Mktg Soc; *Books* Racial Tension in the Twelfth Century in the Holylands (1975), The Third Crusade (1974); *Recreations* tennis, cricket, real tennis, golf, shooting; *Clubs* RAC, Queen's, Hurlingham, White's, MCC, Wentworth Golf, Piltdown Golf; *Style*— Jonathan Hoare, Esq

HOARE, Prof Michael; s of Ernest Charles Hoare (d 1992), and Pat, *née* Morgan; *b* 28 February 1950; *Educ* Penarth County GS, UCL (BSc, MSc, PhD); *m* 16 April 1983, Deborah, da of Derek Heywood-Waddington (d 1996); 2 s (Benjamin David b 11 June 1986, Simon Gareth b 18 May 1988), 1 da (Megan Kathleen Mary b 7 March 1991); *Career* scientist/mangr Unilever Research Lab Colworth House Beds 1971–74, biochemical engr UCL/UKAEA Harwell 1974–78; UCL: lectr 1978, reader 1984, prof of biochemical engrg 1991–, head of Dept of Biochemical Engrg 1998–, dir Advanced Centre for Biochemical Engrg; memb Editorial Bd: Trends in Biotechnology, Pharmaceutical Technology International, Jl of Biotechnology; Donald Medal for Contributions to Biochemical Engineering; FIChemE, FREng 1997; *Recreations* Wales, chamber music; *Style*— Prof Michael Hoare, FREng; ✉ Department of Biochemical Engineering, University College London, Torrington Place, London WC1E 7JE

HOARE, Richard John; s of Wing Cdr Charles Frederick Hoare, of Farnham, Surrey, and Joyce Mary, *née* Stamp; *b* 5 October 1952; *Educ* Mill Hill Sch; *m* 1993, Jennifer Grace Agnes, da of William Thomas Patrick Donohue, of Marlborough, Wilts; 1 da (Héloïse Trafalgar Agnès Archer b 30 Nov 1996), 1 s (Lancelot Theodore Richard Falconer b 25 Aug 1998); *Career* ptnr: Barlow Lyde and Gilbert 1983–93 (joined 1973), Wilkinson Maughan 1993–95; slr to Hinduja Group 1995–, gen counsel Gulf Oil Int Ltd 1995–; Freeman City of London 1984; memb Law Soc 1978; *Publications* Personal Injury Precedents and Pleadings; *Recreations* gardening, sport, fine arts; *Style*— Richard Hoare, Esq; ✉ 18 Woodseer Street, London E1 5HD (tel 020 7375 2856); Chateau de Villeneuve Les Montreal, Villeneuve Les Montreal, 11290, Aude, France; Richard Hoare, 3rd Floor, 16 Charles II Street, London SW1Y 4QU (tel 020 7321 5530, fax 020 7839 2399, e-mail richard@gulfoilltd.com)

HOARE, Richard Quintin; OBE (2007), DL (Hants 1997); s of Quintin Vincent Hoare, OBE, and Lucy Florence, *née* Selwyn; *b* 30 January 1943; *Educ* Eton; *m* 19 Oct 1970, Hon Frances Evelyn Hogg, da of Baron Hailsham of St Marylebone, KG, CH, PC (d 2001); 2 s (Alexander b 1973, Charles b 1976), 1 da (Elizabeth b 1978); *Career* HAC 1963–68, Home Serv Force HAC Detachment 1985–88; managing ptnr C Hoare & Co Bankers 1969– (also dep chm); chm: Bulldog Holdings Ltd 1986– (dir 1964), The Bulldog Trust 1983–; dir Placehill Ltd 1992–; govr Westminster Med Sch 1972–76, memb Cncl Univ of Buckingham 1999–2001; treas Old Etonian Assoc 1984–95, hon tstee African Med Research Fndn (memb Cncl 1977–84), pres Interbank Athletics Assoc 1980, chm Meridian Tst 2004–06; *Recreations* travel, walking, stalking, reading, collecting antiques; *Clubs* Boodle's, HAC; *Style*— Richard Hoare, Esq, OBE; ✉ Tangier House, Wootton St Lawrence, Basingstoke, Hampshire RG23 8PH (tel 01256 780240); The Bulldog Trust, 2 Temple Place, London WC2R 3BD (tel 020 7240 6044); C Hoare & Co, 37 Fleet Street, London EC4P 4DQ (tel 020 7353 4522, fax 020 7353 4521)

HOARE, Rt Rev Dr Rupert William Noel; s of Julian Hoare, and Edith, *née* Temple; *b* 3 March 1940; *Educ* Dragon Sch, Rugby, Trinity Coll Oxford (MA), Kirchliche Hochschule Berlin, Fitwilliam House and Westcott House Cambridge (MA), Univ of Birmingham (PhD); *m* Jan 1965, Gesine Pflüger; 3 s (Christopher, Martin, Nicholas), 1 da (Rebecca); *Career* curate St Mary's Oldham 1964–67, ordained priest 1965, lectr Queen's Coll Birmingham 1968–72, canon theologian Coventry Cathedral 1970–75, rector Parish of the Resurrection Beswick E Manchester 1972–78, canon residentiary Birmingham Cathedral 1978–81, princ Westcott House Cambridge 1981–93, bishop of Dudley 1993–99, dean of Liverpool 2000–; *Recreations* walking, gardening (sometimes); *Style*— The Rt Rev Dean of Liverpool; ✉ Liverpool Cathedral, Liverpool L1 7AZ (tel 0151 702 7220, fax 0151 702 7292)

HOARE, SaraJane; da of Jeff Hoare, of Strand on the Green, London, and late Elizabeth Jane Hoare; *b* 27 June 1955; *Educ* Univ of Warwick (BA); *Career* fashion dir Observer newspaper 1985–87, sr fashion ed Vogue 1987–, fashion dir British Vogue 1989–92, ed-at-large Harpers Bazaar NYC 1992–2001, fashion ed Vanity Fair NYC 2001–; *Books* Talking Fashion (2001); *Style*— Miss SaraJane Hoare

HOARE, Sir Timothy Edward Charles; 8 Bt (I 1784), of Annabella, Co Cork, OBE (1996); s of Maj Sir Edward O'Bryen Hoare, 7 Bt (d 1969), and Nina Mary, *née* Hope-Wallace (d 1995); *b* 11 November 1934; *Educ* Radley, Worcester Coll Oxford (MA), Birkbeck Coll London (MA); *m* 1969, Felicity Anne, da of late Peter Boddington, JP, of Stratford-upon-Avon; 1 s (Charles James b 1971), 2 da (Louisa Hope, Kate Annabella (twins) b 1972); *Heir* s, Charles Hoare; *Career* dir: Career Plan Ltd 1971–2005, New Metals and Chemicals Ltd; memb: Church Assembly 1960–70, C of E Gen Synod 1970–2000, Crown Appointments Cmmn 1987–92; delegate: WCC Conference 1991, Chadwick Cmmn on Church and State; dir World Vision of Britain 1984–95; fell Linnean Soc, FZS; *Recreations* the creative works of God in nature and of man in art; *Clubs* MCC, National; *Style*— Sir Timothy Hoare, Bt, OBE; ✉ 10 Belitha Villas, London N1 1PD (tel 020 7607 7359)

HOBAN, Mark; MP; s of Tom Hoban, of Durham, and Maureen, *née* Orchard; *b* 31 March 1964; *Educ* LSE (BSc); *m* 6 Aug 1994, Fiona Jane, da of Peter and Sally Barrett; *Career* chartered accountant with PricewaterhouseCoopers and predecessor firms 1985–2001 (mangr 1990–92, sr mangr 1992–2001); MP (Cons) Fareham 2001–, oppn whip 2002–03, shadow min for educn 2003–05, shadow financial sec to the Treasy 2005–; House of Commons: Select Ctee on Sci and Technol 2001–03, All Pty Local Hosp Gp, All Pty Small Business Gp; hon vice-pres Soc of Maritime Industries 2003–; Freeman City of London 2003, Liveryman Worshipful Co of Fruiterers 2003–; ACA 1988; *Recreations* cooking, reading, travel, entertaining; *Style*— Mark Hoban, Esq, MP; ✉ House of Commons, London SW1A 0AA (tel 020 7219 8228, e-mail mail@markhoban.com)

HOBAN, Russell Conwell; s of Abram Hoban, and Jenny, *née* Dimmerman; *b* 4 February 1925; *Educ* Lansdale HS Pennsylvania, Philadelphia Museum Sch of Industrial Art; *m* 1, 1944 (m dis 1975), Lillian Aberman; 1 s, 3 da; m 2, 1975, Gundula Ahl; 3 s; *Career* Army, served 339 Infantry 85 Div 5 Army Italian Campaign (Bronze Star Medal); various jobs 1946–56 incl TV art dir Batten Barton Durstine & Osborn; freelance illustrator 1956–65; assignments incl: Sports Illustrated, Fortune, Time; copywriter Doyle Dane Bernbach NY 1965–67; full-time author 1967–; FRSL 1988; *Books* novels: The Mouse and His Child (1967, made into film 1977, The Lion of Boaz-Jachin and Jachin-Boaz (1973), Kleinzeit (1974), Turtle Diary (1975, made into film 1984), Riddley Walker (1980, John W Campbell Meml award 1982, Aust Sci Fiction Achievement award 1983, expanded edition 1998), Pilgermann (1983), The Medusa Frequency (1987), Fremder (1996), The Trokeville Way (1996), Mr Rinyo - Clacton's Offer (1998), Hoban Omnibus (1999), Angelica's Grotto (1999), Amaryllis Night and Day (2001), The Bat Tattoo (2002), Her Name Was Lola (2003), Come Dancing With Me (2005); The Moment Under the Moment (stories, essays and a libretto, 1992), The Second Mrs Kong (opera, music by Sir Harrison Birtwistle,

H

Glyndebourne 1994), The Last of the Wallendas (poetry collection, 1997); 64 children's picture books incl: Charlie the Tramp (1966, Boys' Club Junior Book Award 1968), Emmet Otter's Jug-Band Christmas (1971, Lewis Carroll Looking-Glass Shelf award and Christopher award 1972), How Tom Beat Captain Najork and His Hired Sportsmen (1974, Whitbread award 1974); also author of essays and fragments, short stories, verse for children, and theatre pieces; *Style*— Russell Hoban, Esq, FRSL; ✉ c/o David Higham Associates, 5–8 Lower John Street, Golden Square, London W1R 4HA (tel 020 7437 7888, fax 020 7437 1072)

HOBART, Sir John Vere; 4 Bt (UK 1914), of Langdown, Co Southampton; s of Sir Robert Hampden Hobart, 3 Bt (d 1988), and his 1 w Sylvia, *née* Argo (d 1965); gggs of 3 Earl of Buckinghamshire and hp to kinsman 10 Earl, *qv*; *b* 9 April 1945; *m* 1980, Kate, o da of late George Henry Iddles, of Cowes, Isle of Wight; 2 s (George Hampden b 1982, James Henry Miles b 1986); *Heir* s, George Hobart; *Style*— Sir John Hobart, Bt; ✉ Dottens Farm, Woodvale Road, Gurnard, Isle of Wight PO31 8EA

HOBBS, Prof Kenneth Edward Frederick (Ken); s of Thomas Edward Ernest Hobbs (d 1951), of Suffolk, and Gladys May, *née* Neave (d 1986); *b* 28 December 1936; *Educ* W Suffolk Co GS Bury St Edmunds, Guy's Hosp Med Sch Univ of London (MB BS), Univ of Bristol (ChM); *Career* surgical res fell Harvard Univ 1968–69, sr lectr in surgery Univ of Bristol 1970–73 (lectr 1966–70), prof of surgery Royal Free Hosp Sch of Med 1973–98 (now Royal Free and Univ Coll Sch of Med), hon conslt surgn Royal Free Hosp Hampstead (now Royal Free Hampstead NHS Tst) 1973–98, dean Faculty of Med Univ of London 1994–98, (elected memb of Senate 1985–98, memb Cncl 1985–98), emeritus prof of surgery Royal Free and Univ Coll Sch of Med 1998–; memb MRC Ctee Systems Bd 1982–86, chm MRC Grants Ctee A 1984–86; memb: UGC Med Sub Ctee (now Univ Funding Cncl) 1986–89, UFC Med Ctee 1991–93, GMC 1996–2001 (dep chm Professional Conduct Ctee 1999–2001); chm Mason Medical Fndn 1993–98, pres Stanley Thomas Johnson Fndn 1996–2004 (memb 1976–96); professional memb GMC Fitness to Practice Ctees 2002–06; Int Master Surgeon Int Coll of Surgeons 1994; hon fell The Sri Lanka Coll of Surgeons 1995; hon fell Chinese Univ Hong Kong 2002; memb RSM; FRCS 1964; *Books* contrib: Surgical Techniques Illustrated (1985), Operative Surgery and Management (1987), Surgery of the Liver and Biliary Tract (1988), Oxford Textbook of Hepatology (1991), Liver and Biliary Disease (1992), General Surgical Operations (1994), Oxford Textbook of Hepatology (1998); *Recreations* gourmet dining, the countryside; *Style*— Prof Ken Hobbs; ✉ The Rookery, New Buckenham, Norfolk NR16 2AE (tel 01953 860558, e-mail profkenhobbs@aol.com)

HOBBS, Peter Thomas Goddard; s of Reginald Stanley Hobbs, BEM (d 1970), of Gloucester, and Phyllis Gwendoline, *née* Goddard; *b* 19 March 1938; *Educ* Crypt Sch Gloucester, Exeter Coll Oxford (MA); *m* Victoria Christabel, da of Rev Alan Matheson (d 1988), of Clifton Campville, Staffs; 1 da (Katharine b 1971); *Career* Nat Serv 2 Lt RASC 1957–59, Capt RCT TA 1959–68; ICI Ltd 1962–79 (rising to jt personnel mangr Mond Div), gp personnel dir Wellcome Fndn and Wellcome plc 1979–92; HM Inspector of Constabulary 1993–98; dir Forensic Science Service 1996–2006; Chemical Industries Assoc: dep chm Pharmaceuticals and Fine Chemicals Jt Industrial Cncl 1979–89, chm Trg Ctee 1985–89, chm Employment Affr Bd 1989–91, memb Cncl 1989–92, chm Chemical Industry Educn Centre Univ of York 1992–94; dir Employment Conditions Abroad Ltd 1984–91 and 1993, vice-pres Int Inst of Personnel Mgmnt 1987–89 and 1990–91, dir and dep chm Roffey Park Inst 1989–93, dir London Business Sch Centre for Enterprise 1989–92; CBI: memb Task Force on Vocational Educn and Trg 1989–90, memb Educn and Trg Policy Ctee 1990–94; Business in the Community: memb Target Team for Industry/Educn Partnerships 1988–90, memb Target Team for Priority Hiring 1988–91; chm Learning from Experience Tst 1992–93 and 1998– (tstee 1988–); memb Advsy Cncl Mgmnt Centre Europe Brussels 1989–97, fndr chm Employers' Forum for Disability 1987–93; memb: Employment Ctee IOD 1989–98, Nat Advsy Cncl on Employment of People with Disabilities 1991–93, Cncl Contemporary Applied Arts 1990–92, Industry Advsy Gp Nat Curriculum Cncl 1990–92, Personnel Standards Lead Body 1992–94, Cncl BTEC (now EDEXCEL Fndn) 1994–98; Dr (hc) Int Mgmnt Centre 2000; CCIPD, FInstD, FRSA; *Recreations* history, topography, moving earth; *Clubs* Oxford and Cambridge; *Style*— Peter Hobbs, Esq; ✉ 105 Blenheim Crescent, London W11 2EQ (tel 020 7727 3054, fax 020 7221 9542)

HOBBS, Philip John; s of Anthony Lewis Hobbs, and Barbara, *née* Thomas; *b* 26 July 1955; *Educ* King's Coll Taunton, Univ of Reading (BSc); *m* 12 June 1982, Sarah Louise, da of Albert Edwin Hill; 3 da (Caroline Elizabeth, Katherine Louise, Diana Margaret); *Career* professional jockey for 10 years (160 winners); racehorse trainer 1985–: currently trg 100 horses, over 1,000 winners incl Mackenson Gold Cup, Queen Mother Champion Chase, Hennesy Gold Cup, County Hurdle, Racing Post Chase (twice), Champion Hurdle and Scottish Champion Hurdle; *Recreations* shooting, skiing; *Clubs* Sportsman; *Style*— Philip Hobbs; ✉ Sandhill, Bilbrook, Minehead, Somerset (tel 01984 640366, fax 01984 641124, website and e-mail www.pjhobbs.co.uk)

HOBDAY, Peter; *b* 16 February 1937; *Educ* St Chad's Coll Wolverhampton, Univ of Leicester; *Career* journalist, broadcaster; Wolverhampton Express and Star & Chronicle 1960–61; formerly with BBC World Service, progs incl The Financial World Tonight (Radio 4), The Money Programme (BBC2) 1979–81, Newsnight (BBC2) 1980–82, Today (Radio 4) 1981–96; other work for TV incl: The Business Programme (Channel 4), Pebble Mill Midlands at Westminster, European Business Weekly (satellite TV); *Books* Saudi Arabia Today (1979), In the Valley of the Fireflies; *Style*— Peter Hobday, Esq; ✉ home fax 020 7371 1002

HOBHOUSE, Sir Charles John Spinney; 7 Bt (UK 1812), of Broughton-Gifford, Bradford-on-Avon, and of Monkton Farleigh, Wiltshire; o s of Sir Charles Chisholm Hobhouse, 6 Bt, TD (d 1991), and his 2 w Elspeth Jean, *née* Spinney; *b* 27 October 1962; *Educ* Eton; *m* 5 June 1993 (m dis), Katrina, da of Maj-Gen Sir Denzil Macarthur-Onslow, CBE, DSO, ED (d 1984); *Heir* unc, John Hobhouse, AFC; *Recreations* sport, travel; *Style*— Sir Charles Hobhouse, Bt; ✉ The Manor, Monkton Farleigh, Bradford-on-Avon, Wiltshire (tel 01225 858558)

HOBHOUSE, Penelope (Mrs Malins); da of Capt James Jackson Lenox-Conyngham Chichester-Clark, DSO, RN (d 1933), and Marion Caroline Dehra, *née* Chichester (d 1976); sis of Sir Robin Chichester-Clark, *qv*; *b* 20 November 1929; *Educ* North Foreland Lodge, Girton Coll Cambridge (BA); *m* 1, 17 May 1952 (m dis 1983), Paul Rodbard Hobhouse (d 1994), s of Sir Arthur Hobhouse (d 1965), of Castle Cary, Somerset; 1 da (Georgina Dehra Catherine b 9 March 1953), 2 s (Niall Alexander b 29 Aug 1954, David Paul b 9 Sept 1957); m 2, 1983, Prof John Melville Malins (d 1992); *Career* writer and garden designer; Hon DLitt: Univ of Birmingham, Writtle Coll Univ of Essex; *Books* incl: The Country Gardener (1976), The Smaller Garden (1981), Gertrude Jekyll on Gardening (1983), Colour in Your Garden (1985), The National Trust: A Book of Gardening (1986), Private Gardens of England (1986), Garden Style (1988), Borders (1989), The Gardens of Europe (1990), Flower Gardens (1991), Plants in Garden History (1992), Penelope Hobhouse on Gardening (1994), Penelope Hobhouse's Garden Designs (1997), Penelope Hobhouse's Natural Planting (1997), Gardens of Italy (1998), The Story of Gardening (2002), The Gardens of Persia (2003); *Style*— Ms Penelope Hobhouse; ✉ The Coach House, Bettiscombe, Bridport, Dorset DT6 5NT (tel 01308 868560, fax 01308 867560, e-mail p.malins560@btinternet.com)

HOBLEY, Mary Elizabeth Agnes; da of George Frederick Hobley (d 1992), Maria Wilhelmina, *née* Meiresonne, of Dorchester, Dorset; *b* 9 December 1961; *Educ* Sacred Heart HS for Girls, UCNW Bangor (BSc), Australian Nat Univ Canberra (PhD); *m* 18 July 1987, (Michael) Mark Agnew; 1 s (Alexander Michael Hobley Agnew b 28 June 2000); *Career* rural devpt forestry res fell ODI 1987–95, ptnr in local governance, nat resource mgmnt and planning consultancy 1995–; worldwide consultancies for IUCN, DFID, World Bank and ODI; extensive res in India, Nepal and Australia; devpt of teaching modules for masters, diplomas and short courses for foresters, agric lectures and rural devpt professionals; Westoby mem lectr ANU 2007; memb numerous forestry ctees, review panels and gps on forestry issues; Cwlth Scholarship 1984, Amy Rustomjee Scholarship 1985; memb: Cwlth Forestry Assoc, RFS; *Publications* Participatory Forestry: The Process of Change in India and Nepal (1996); also numerous learned papers, courses, reports and chapters on forestry, poverty and organisational change; *Recreations* walking, swimming, antiquarian book collecting; *Style*— Dr Mary Hobley; ✉ Mary Hobley & Associates, Glebe House, Thorncombe, Chard, Somerset TA20 4NE (tel 01460 30385, e-mail mary@maryhobley.co.uk)

HOBLEY, Tina; *b* 20 May 1971; *Educ* Webber Douglas Sch of Drama London; *m* 16 Dec 2006, Oliver Wheeler, *qv*; 1 da (Isabella b 9 April 1999); *Career* actress; *Theatre* View from a Bridge (Colchester), Only When I Laugh (Bath, World Tour), The Taming of the Shrew (Chichester); *Television* Coronation Street (Granada) 1996–98, Harbour Lights (BBC) 1998–99, Holby City (BBC) 2000–; *Style*— Ms Tina Hobley; ✉ c/o Paul Lyon-Maris, ICM, Oxford House, 76 Oxford Street, London W1N 0AX (tel 020 7636 6565)

HOBMAN, Anthony (Tony); s of late David Burton Hobman, CBE, and Erica Agatha, *née* Irwin; *b* 5 July 1955; *Educ* De La Salle Coll, Cardinal Newman Sch Hove, N Staffs Poly (BA); *m* 1, 1978 (m dis 1994), Catherine Fenton; 1 s, 2 da; m 2, 2001, Victoria Richards *née* Maynard; 1 da, 2 step s; *Career* Barclays Bank plc: joined as grad mgmnt trainee 1976–81, various roles in mktg, project, change and serv mgmnt 1982–95; ProShare Ltd: head of investor servs 1996–99, ceo 1999–2000; ceo: Money Channel plc 2000–01, Occupational Pensions Regulatory Authy 2002–05, Pensions Regulator 2005–; memb: Consultative Ctee Co Law Review DTI 1999–2000, Advsy Gp Employer Task Force on Pensions DWP 2003–04; tstee David Hobman Charitable Tst 1987–96; *Clubs* Reform; *Style*— Tony Hobman, Esq; ✉ The Pensions Regulator, Napier House, Trafalgar Place, Brighton BN1 4DW (tel 01273 627612, fax 01273 627630)

HOBSON, Anthony John; *b* 1947; *Career* gp fin dir Legal & General Group plc 1987–2001; non-exec chm: Northern Foods plc 2005– (non-exec dep chm 2002–05), Sage Gp plc 2007– (non-exec dir 2004–); non-exec dir: Thames Water plc 1994–2000, HBOS plc (formerly Halifax) 2001–, Glas Cymru Cyfyngedig 2001–, Jardine Lloyd Thompson Gp 2002–; *Style*— Antony Hobson, Esq

HOBSON, David Llewelyn (Daf); s of Alan Hobson, and Mary Ellen, *née* Roberts; *Educ* Caernarfon GS, Jacob Kramer Coll of Art and Design Leeds, Leeds Coll of Art and Design (DipAD); *Career* cinematographer; asst cameraman World in Action Granada 1974–75, dir film and TV 1974–81, estab Woodthrush Ltd 1981, dir of photography S4C 1981–92, dir of photography and facilities supply BBC, ITV and Channel 4 features 1992–; inventor Wonkycam; memb BSC 1998–; annual govr RNLI; *Television* Family (BBC 1) 1993 (Best Photography and Lighting BAFTA Awards 1994), Bramwell (ITV) 1994 (Best Photography and Lighting RTS Awards 1995), Y Wisg Sidan (S4C) 1995 (nomination BAFTA Cymru Awards 1996), The Tenant of Wildfell Hall (BBC 1) 1996 (Best Camera RTS Awards 1997, nomination Best Photography and Lighting BAFTA Awards 1997), The Lakes (BBC 1) 1997 (nomination Best Photography and Lighting BAFTA Awards 1998), Births Marriages and Deaths (BBC 2) 1998, Spoonface Steinberg (BBC 2) 1998, Eureka Street (BBC 2) 1999 (Best Photography and Lighting Irish Film and TV Acad 1999), Sword of Honour (Channel 4) 2000, Swallow (Channel 4) 2001, Othello (ITV) 2001 (winner Best Photography and Lighting BAFTA Awards 2002, Best Photography and Lighting RTS Awards 2002); *Film* Welcome to Sarajevo 1996, Tatoo (short film) 2002 (Kodak Swan Award, nomination BAFTA Awards 2002); *Recreations* my family, sailing, building our house; *Clubs* NW Venturers Yacht; *Style*— Daf Hobson, Esq; ✉ e-mail daf@dafhobson.com

HOCHGREB, Prof Simone; *Educ* Princeton Univ (PhD); *Career* assoc prof MIT 1999, princ investigator Combustion Research Facility Sandia Nat Labs 2000, managing engr Exponent Failure Analysis Assocs 2002, prof of experimental combustion Univ of Cambridge 2002–; *Style*— Prof Simone Hochgreb; ✉ Department of Engineering, Trumpington Street, Cambridge CB2 1PZ

HOCHHAUSER, Andrew Romain; QC (1997); s of Jerome Romain Hochhauser, MD, FRCSE (d 1978), and Ruth, *née* Binks (d 2002); *b* 16 March 1955; *Educ* Highgate Sch, Univ of Bristol (LLB), LSE (LLM); *Career* called to the Bar Middle Temple 1977 (Harmsworth scholar, bencher 2000); recorder 2004–; hon counsel to Westminster Abbey 2004; pt/t memb Law Sch LSE 1979–86; chm Dance Umbrella 2007–; FCIArb 1995; *Recreations* collecting paintings, swimming with sharks; *Clubs* Reform; *Style*— Andrew Hochhauser, QC; ✉ Essex Court Chambers, 24 Lincoln's Inn Fields, London WC2A 3ED (tel 020 7813 8000, fax 020 7813 8080)

HOCKING, Mary; da of Charles Hocking (d 1965), and Eunice, *née* Hewett (d 1962); *b* Acton, London; *Educ* Haberdashers' Aske's Sch for Girls; *Career* writer; memb: Soc of Authors, PEN; FRSL; *Books* incl: Good Daughters, Indifferent Heroes, Welcome Strangers, Letters from Constance, He Who Plays The King, A Particular Place, The Meeting Place; *Recreations* theatre; *Style*— Miss Mary Hocking; ✉ c/o A M Heath & Co, 6 Warwick Court, London WC1R 5DJ

HOCKMAN, Stephen Alexander; QC (1990); s of late Dr Nathaniel Hockman, of London, and Trude, *née* Schlossman; *b* 4 January 1947; *Educ* Eltham Coll, Jesus Coll Cambridge; *m* August 1998, Elizabeth St Hill Davies; *Career* called to the Bar Middle Temple 1970; recorder of the Crown Court 1987, dep judge of the High Court 1998–, ldr SE Circuit 2001–03, head of chambers 6 Pump Court; chair Bar Cncl 2006 (vice-chair 2005); *Clubs* Garrick, RAC; *Style*— Stephen Hockman, Esq, QC; ✉ 6 Pump Court, Temple, London EC4Y 7AR (tel 020 7797 8400, fax 020 7797 8401, e-mail stephenhockmanqc@6pumpcourt.co.uk)

HOCKNEY, David; CH (1997); s of Kenneth and Laura Hockney; *b* 9 July 1937, Bradford, Yorks; *Educ* Bradford GS, Bradford Coll of Art, RCA, Univ of Aberdeen; *Career* artist; Hon Dr RCA; RA 1991 (ARA 1985); *Solo Exhibitions* incl: Kasmin Gallery London 1963–89, Museum of Modern Art NY 1964 and 1968, Stedelijk Museum Amsterdam 1966, Whitechapel Gallery London 1970, Andre Emmerich Gallery NY 1972–96, Musée des ArtsDecoratifs Paris 1974, Museo Tamayo Mexico City 1984, LA Louver CA 1986, 1989, 1995, 1998 and 2005, Nishimura Gallery Tokyo 1986, 1989, 1990 and 1994, Met Museum of Art 1988, LA County Museum of Art 1988, 1996 and 2006, Tate Gallery London 1988, 1992 and 2007, Royal Acad of Arts London 1995 and 1999, Hamburger Kunsthalle 1995, Nat Museum of American Art WA 1997 and 1998, Museum Ludwig Cologne 1997, MFA Boston 1998 and 2006, Centre Georges Pompidou Paris 1999, Musée Picasso Paris 1999, Museum of Contemporary Art LA 2001, Kunst-Und Ausstellung Halle Bonn 2001, La Museum of Modern Art Copenhagen 2001, Annely Juda Fine Art London 1997, 1999, 2003 and 2006, Richard Gray Gallery Chicago and NY 1992, 1999, 2002 and 2004, Nat Portrait Galley London 2003 and 2006, Whitney Biennial NY 2004; designer Rake's Progress (Glyndebourne UK) 1975; set designer for: Magic Flute (Glyndebourne) 1978, Parade Triple Bill, Stravinsky Triple Bill (Met Opera House) 1980–81, Tristan und Isolde (LA Music Opera) 1987, Turnadot (Lyric Opera Chicago and San Francisco Opera) 1992–, Die Frau Ohne Schatten (Covent Garden London) 1992; *Awards* Guinness Award first prize for etching 1961, Gold Medal Royal Coll of Art 1962,

Graphic Prize Paris Biennale 1963, first prize 8th Int Exhibition Drawings Lugano Italy 1964, first prize John Moores Exhibition Liverpool 1967, German Award for Excellence 1983, Praemium Inperiale Japan Art Assoc 1989, fifth annual Govt CA Visual Arts Award 1994, Charles Wollaston Award Royal Acad of Arts 1999; *Books* Six Fairy Tales of the Brothers Grimm (illustrator, 1969), David Hockney by David Hockney (1976), The Blue Guitar (illustrator, 1977), David Hockney: Travels with Pen, Pencil and Ink (1978), Paper Pools (1980), David Hockney Photographs (1982), Cameraworks (1983, Kodak Photography Book Award 1984), David Hockney: A Retrospective (1988), Hockney Paints the Stage (1983), Hockney's Alphabet (illustrator, 1991), That's the Way I See It (1993), David Hockney's Dog Days (1998), Hockney on Art (1999), Secret Knowledge: Rediscovering the Lost Techniques of the Old Masters (2001), Hockney's Portaits and People (2003), Hockney's Pictures (2004), David Hockney: Portraits; *Style*— David Hockney, CH, RA; ✉ 7508 Santa Monica Boulevard, Los Angeles, CA 90046–6407, USA

HOCKNEY, Michael Brett; s of Stanley Waller Hockney, of Lytham, Lancs, and Jean, *née* Duston; *b* 29 July 1949; *Educ* Beechenhurst, King Edward Sch Lytham, Univ of Manchester, LSE; *m* 30 July 1983, Dr Elizabeth Anne Hockney, da of Bruce Cryer, of Richmond, Surrey; *Career* account planner J Walter Thompson 1972–75, assoc dir Boase Massimi Pollitt Partnership 1975–80, bd dir and memb Exec Ctee BMP plc 1980–87, gp chm and md BDDH Gp plc 1987–93, gp mktg dir and memb Mgmnt Bd Christie's International 1993–95, advsr to MOD 1995–99, exec dir ICAEW 1999–2001, chief exec D&AD 2003–07; non-exec dir: Adjutant Gen's Mgmnt Bd 1996–99, BCMG Ltd 1996–2005; memb Cncl: Inst of Practitioners in Advtg 1981–93, Advtg Assoc 1989–93; chm UK Advtg Effectiveness Awards 1984–94; vice-chm Berkeley Square Ball Charitable Trust 1986–90, dep chm Cncl Royal Sch of Church Music 2000–04 (memb Cncl and tstee 1986–2004); tstee and memb Bd: English Chamber Orchestra 1994–, Army Benevolent Fund 1998– (chm Devpt Ctee 2000–), Christian Aid 1995–2001; co-opted memb Gtr London RFCA 1999–; memb Min for Veterans' Affrs Working Party 2000–03, Nikaean 2004–, memb Bd of Govrs Univ of Berlin Sch of Creative Leadership 2006–; govr Army Fndn Coll 1999–2003; organist and choir master All Saints Church London 1976–98; Liveryman Worshipful Co of Musicians 2005; FRSA, FCIM, FCMI, FIPA, FRSCM 2004; *Recreations* the organ, baroque opera, early music, 18th century Worcester porcelain, French wine, English furniture, architecture, biography; *Clubs* Athenaeum; *Style*— Michael B Hockney, Esq; ✉ c/o The Athenaeum, Pall Mall, London SW1

HODDER, Elizabeth; da of late Jack Scruton, and late Beryl, *née* Haines; *b* 5 September 1942; *Educ* High Wycombe HS, Univ of London (BSc); *m* 1, Barry Quirke; 2 da (Anna, Louise); *m* 2, Dick Hodder (d 2006); 3 step s (Ian, Greg, Rupert), 2 step da (Jean, Tamsin); *Career* area offr Nat Assoc of Citizens Advice Bureaux 1978–91, cmmr Meat and Livestock Cmmn (also chm Consumer Ctee) 1992–98, cmmr Equal Opportunities Cmmn 2000–02 (dep chair 1996–2000), chm Lifespan Healthcare NHS Tst 2000–02; memb: Nat Consumer Cncl 1981–87, Cncl Bldg Socs Ombudsman 1987–2001, Review Ctee Code of Banking Practice 1992–2000; fndr and hon pres Stepfamily (nat stepfamily assoc) 1983–; chm: Cambridge Civic Soc 1976–80, Cambridge Relate 1986–89; dining fell Lucy Cavendish Coll Cambridge 1987; FRSA 1997; *Recreations* painting, hill walking, gardening, Italy, cooking; *Style*— Mrs Elizabeth Hodder; ✉ 4 Ascham Road, Cambridge CB4 2BD (tel 01233 301086, e-mail e.hod@btinternet.com)

HODDER, Prof Ian Richard; s of Bramwell William (Dick) Hodder, and Noreen Victoria Hodder; *b* 23 November 1948; *Educ* Magdalen Coll Sch Oxford, Inst of Archaeology Univ of London (BA), Univ of Cambridge (PhD); *m* 1, (m dis), Françoise Hivernel; 2 s (Christophe b 1976, Gregoire b 1979); *m* 2, Christine Hastorf; 2 s (Kyle, Nicholas (twins) b 1991); *Career* lectr Dept of Archaeology Univ of Leeds 1974–77; Univ of Cambridge: asst lectr Dept of Archaeology 1977–81, lectr Dept of Archaeology 1981–90, reader in prehistory 1990–96, prof of archaeology 1996–2000, fell McDonald Inst 2001–; fell Darwin Coll Cambridge 1990–2000; Stanford Univ: co-dir Archaeology Center 1999–2002, prof Dept of Cultural and Social Anthropology 1999–, Dunlevie Family prof Sch of Humanities and Sciences 2002–; adjunct asst prof of anthropology SUNY 1984–89, adjunct prof and visiting prof Dept of Anthropology Univ of Minnesota 1986–; visiting prof: Van Giffen Inst for Pre- and Proto-history Amsterdam 1980, Univ of Paris I Sorbonne 1985; fell Center for Advanced Study in the Behavioural Scis Stanford CA 1987; dir gen Cambridge Archaeological Unit 1990–2000; memb Ed Bd: New Directions in Archaeology 1978–89, Anthropology Today, Archeologia e Calcolatori, Cambridge Archaeological Jl, Jl of European Archaeology; memb Advsy Bd: Rural History: Economy, Society, Culture, Jl of Material Culture; Gordon Childe prize Inst of Archaeology; memb Founding Ctee Euro Assoc of Archaeologists 1991–95; memb Prehistoric Soc, Associate Inst of Field Archaeologists (memb Cncl 1986–89); FRAI (memb Cncl 1985–88), FSA, FBA 1996; *Publications* authored volumes: Spatial analysis in archaeology (with C Orton, 1976), Symbols in action. Ethnoarchaeological studies of material culture (1982), The Present Past. An Introduction to anthropology for archaeologists (1982), Reading the Past. Current approaches to interpretation in archaeology (1986, revised edn, 1991), The domestication of Europe: structure and contingency in Neolithic societies (1990), Theory and practice in archaeology (1992), The archaeological process (1999), Archaeology beyond dialogue (2003); edited volumes incl: The Archaeology of contextual meanings (1987), Archaeology as long term history (1987), The meanings of things: material culture and symbolic expression (1989), Archaeological Theory in Europe. The last three decades (1991), Interpreting Archaeology (with M Shanks, 1994), Archaeology in Theory. A Reader (with R Preucel, 1996); also author of numerous articles and reviews in learned jls; *Recreations* playing piano and violin, sports especially tennis, sailing and golf; *Style*— Prof Ian Hodder, FBA, FSA; ✉ Department of Anthropology, Stanford University, Stanford, CA 94305, USA (tel 00 1 650 723 1197, e-mail ihodder@stanford.edu)

HODDER-WILLIAMS, Richard; s of Paul Hodder-Williams, and Felicity, *née* Blagden (d 1985); *b* 18 March 1943; *Educ* Rugby (mathematics scholar), CCC Oxford (MA, Coll prize), UC of Rhodesia and Nyasaland (Miny of Overseas Devpt scholar); *m* 1972, Rhiain Rhys, *née* Morgan; 2 s (Matthew b 1 June 1975, John-Paul b 27 Jan 1979); *Career* Univ of Bristol: lectr in politics 1967–81, reader 1981–91, prof of politics 1991–, dean Faculty of Social Sciences 1996–99, pro-vice-chllr 1999–2004; visiting lectr: Univ of South Africa 1976, Univ of Cape Town 1980 and 1981, Univ of Nairobi 1981, Chllr Coll Univ of Malawi 1981; visiting prof of political science Univ of Calif Berkeley 1984–85, visiting fell ANU 1988, dep to Mellon chair of American politics Univ of Oxford 1990, visiting scholar Inst of Governmental Studies Univ of Calif Berkeley 1996; co-ed Jl of Southern African Studies 1973–76; memb Editorial Bd: Jl of American Studies 1985–88, African Affrs 1987– (jt ed 1977–87), Politikon 1991–99; memb: Exec Ctee VSO 1979–82, Royal African Soc (memb Cncl 1978–98, vice-pres 1998–), African Studies Assoc of the UK (pres 1994–96, treas 1999–), Political Studies Assoc, American Political Studies Assoc; govr: Sherborne Sch 1979– (vice-chm 2001–), Cheltenham Coll 1991–98, Fairfield Sch 1981–99 (chm 1985–99), Badminton Sch 1994– (chm 1998–); tstee African Educnl Tst 2004–; FRSA; *Books* Public Opinion Polls and British Politics (1971), The Politics of the US Supreme Court (1983), An Introduction to the Politics of Tropical Africa (1984), White Farmers in Rhodesia (1984), USA and UK: a comparative study (ed with James Ceaser, 1986), From Churchill to Major: the British Prime Ministership (ed with Donald Shell, 1995), Directory of Africanists in Britain (ed, 3 edns), Judges and Politics in the Contemporary Age (1997); *Recreations* cricket, golf, listening to classical music, playing the piano; *Clubs* Vincent's (Oxford), Royal Cwlth Soc, Château des Vigiers GC, Eymetois de Cricket (vice-pres

2001–04, treas 2004–), Clifton; *Style*— Prof Richard Hodder-Williams; ✉ e-mail hodderw@wanadoo.fr

HODDINOTT, Prof Alun; CBE (1983); s of Thomas Ivor Hoddinott, MM (d 1974), and Gertrude Jones (d 1964); *b* 11 August 1929; *Educ* Gowerton GS, UC Cardiff (Glamorgan music scholar, BMus, DMus, Walford Davies prize, Arnold Bax medal); *m* (Beti) Rhiannon, da of Rev Llewellyn C Huws (d 1982); 1 s (Huw Ceri); *Career* lectr: Welsh Coll of Music and Drama 1951–59, UC Cardiff 1959–66; reader Univ of Wales 1966–67, prof and head Dept of Music UC Cardiff 1967–87 (now prof emeritus), fndr and artistic dir Cardiff Festival of Music 1967–90 (currently pres), fndr and chm Oriana Records 1983–91, govr St John's Coll Cardiff, patron Live Music Now; Hopkins medal St David's Soc of NY 1981, Glyndwr medal 1997; Hon DMus Univ of Sheffield 1993, Hon DUniv Wales; Hon RAM, Millenium Centre Hons; fell: RNCM, UCW, Welsh Coll of Music and Drama, Swansea Inst; *Works* incl: String Trio (Cardiff) 1949, Concerto for harp and orchestra (Cheltenham Festival) 1957, Concerto for piano, wind and percussion (London) 1960, Carol for SSA (Cardiff) 1961, Sinfonia for string orchestra (Bromsgrove Festival) 1964, Fioriture for orchestra (Aberdeen) 1968, Suite for orchestra (Southampton) 1970, The Sun The Great Luminary music for orchestra (Swansea Festival) 1970, Sonata for horn and piano (St Donats) 1971, The Silver Swimmer (Manchip White) for mixed voices and piano duet (Austin TX) 1973, Sinfonia fidei for soprano, tenor, chorus and orchestra (Llandaff Festival) 1977, Scena for String Quartet (Portsmouth) 1979, Six Welsh Folk Songs (Cardiff Festival) 1982, Ingravescentum Aetatem (Manhattan KS) 1983, Piano Sonata No 7 (London) 1984, Passacaglia and Fugue (St Davids) 1985, Concerto for Clarinet and Orchestra (Manchester) 1987, Piano Sonata No 9 (Cheltenham Festival) 1989, Star Children for orchestra (London Proms) 1989, Noctis Equi for cello and orchestra (Rostropovitch London) 1989, Emynau Pantycelyn (Rhymni) 1990, Sonata for flute and piano (Harrogate Festival) 1991, Advent Carols (St John's Coll Cambridge) 1991, Sonata No 5 for violin and piano (NY) 1992, A May Song (Wales Garden Festival) 1992, Symphony for brass and percussion (Cardiff Festival) 1992, Chorales, Variants and Fanfares for organ and brass quintet (Swansea Festival) 1992, Gloria for chorus and organ (Tenby Festival) 1992, A Vision of Eternity symphony for soprano and orch (Gwyneth Jones) 1993, Three Motets for chorus and organ (Atlanta GA) 1993, Wind Quintet (Gower Festival) 1993, Piano Sonata II (Griccieth Festival) 1993, Piano Sonata 12 (London) 1994, Missa Sancti David (Fishguard Festival) 1994, Six Bagatelles for Quartet (Lower Machen Festival) 1994, Three Hymns for Mixed Chorus and Organ (N Wales Festival) 1994, Shakespeare Songs for Mixed Voices (Swansea Festival) 1994, Five Poems of G A Becquer for baritone and piano (Manchester) 1994, One Must Always Have Love songs for high voice and piano (Atlanta GA) 1994, Concerto for violin and orchestra (BBC) 1995, Concerto for trumpet and orchestra (Hallé) 1995, Sonata for Oboe and Harp (Cardiff) 1995, Magnificat and Nunc Dimittis (St David's Festival) 1996, String Quartet No 4 (Mach Ynlleth Festival) 1996, Piano Trio No 3 (Fishguard Festival) 1996, Sonata No 2 for clarinet and piano (Cardiff) 1997, Sonata No 6 for violin and piano (Machen Festival) 1997, Tempi Sonata for harp (N Wales Festival) 1997, The Poetry of Earth songs for baritone and harp (London) 1997, Island of Dragons variants for cello (Rhymni) 1998, Dragonfire concertanti for timpani, percussion and orchestra (BBC) 1998, Grongar Hill for baritone, string quartet and piano (Beaumaris Festival) 1998, Lizard variants for recorder (Tenby Festival) 1998, Camargue Mass (S4C) 1998, Celebration Dances for orchestra (Cardiff) 1999, Bagatelles for wind quintet (Fishguard Festival) 1999, Tower: Opera in Three Acts (Swansea) 1999, Symphony No 10 (N Wales Festival) 1999, La Serenissima songs for baritone and piano (London) 2000, Doubles Quintet for oboe, piano and string trio (London) 2000, Concerto for Percussion and Brass (Fishguard Festival) 2000, Piano Sonata 13 (N Wales Festival) 2001, String Quartet No 5 (Aberystwyth) 2001, Bagatelles for 11 instruments (London) 2001, Three Welsh Folk Songs on cello and piano (London) 2002, Lizard: concerto for orchestra (BBC) 2002, Sonata for euphonium and piano (London) 2003, Promontory of Dreams: cycle for baritone, horn and strings (Fishlock, Wrexham) 2004, Badger in the Bag (Cardiff) 2004, BBC Concerto for trombone and orchestra 2004, Bagatelles for Four Trombones (New York) 2004, Concerto Grosso for Brass (Fishguard Festival) 2004, Sonata for Piano Duet (Bangor) 2004, Celebration Fanfare (Royal Wedding, Windsor) 2005, La Serenissima: Images of Venice for soprano, baritone and orchestra 2005, Towy Landscape songs for soprano, baritone and piano duet 2006, Blake Songs for baritone and violin; *Style*— Prof Alun Hoddinott, CBE

HODGART, Alan William; s of late William George Hodgart, of Australia, and late Hilda Murial Herschel, *née* Hester; *b* 19 July 1940; *Educ* Univ of Melbourne (MA), Univ of Cambridge; *Career* mgmnt conslt Cortis Powell Ltd (UK) 1967–76; Deloitte Haskins and Sells: md DHS Consultants Ltd 1976–83, dep managing ptnr Deloitte Haskins & Sells Australia 1983–84, dir int strategy NY 1984–88; md Spicers Consultants Group Ltd (UK) 1988–90, chm Hodgart Consulting Ltd 1990–99, chm Carey Howells, Jeans & Spiro Ltd 1993–99, dir European ops Hildebrandt Int 1999; *Books* The Economics of European Imperialism (1978); *Recreations* literature, 19th century music and opera, walking; *Clubs* Athenaeum, Princeton Univ; *Style*— Alan Hodgart, Esq

HODGE, His Hon Judge David Ralph; QC (1997); s of Ralph Noel Hodge, CBE, and Jean Margaret Hodge; *b* 13 July 1956; *Educ* St Margaret's Sch Liverpool, UC Oxford (scholar, BA, BCL); *m* 2003, Jane, yst da of Tom and Mabel Woosey; *Career* called to the Bar Inner Temple 1979, admitted to Lincoln's Inn 1980 (bencher 2000); practising barr and memb of chambers: 9 Old Square 1980–2004, Maitland Chambers 2004–05; recorder 2000–05 (asst recorder 1998–2000), dep judge of the High Court 2004–05, specialist chancery circuit judge (Northern Circuit) 2005–, pt/t judge of the Court of Protection 2007–; chm Lincoln's Inn Bar Representation Ctee 1997–98; *Publications* contrib chapter on Chancery matters to The Law and Practice of Compromise (6 edn, 2005); *Recreations* theatre, wine and wife; *Clubs* Garrick; *Style*— His Hon Judge Hodge, QC; ✉ c/o Manchester Civil Justice Centre, 1 Bridge Street West, Manchester M60 9DJ

HODGE, Prof Ian David; s of Robert Hodge (d 1982), and Georgina, *née* Padfield; *b* 1952, Chelmsford, Essex; *Educ* Univ of Reading (BSc), Wye Coll London (PhD); *m* 1979, Bridget, *née* Palmer; 3 da (Rebecca b 1982, Susannah b 1987, Louisa b 1990), 1 s (David b 1984); *Career* research assoc and lectr Univ of Newcastle upon Tyne 1976–78, lectr in agric economics Univ of Queensland 1979–83; Dept of Land Economy Univ of Cambridge: Gilbey lectr 1983–2000, univ sr lectr 2000–01, reader in rural economy 2001–05, head of dept 2002–, prof of rural economy 2005–; fell Hughes Hall Cambridge 2004–; govr: Macaulay Land Use Research Inst 1998–2003, Cambridge Int Land Inst 2003–; pres Agricultural Economics Soc 2007–08; memb: Socio Economic Advsy Gp English Nature 1994–, Broads Research Advsy Panel 1999–2003, MAFF/DEFRA Academic Economist Panel 1999–, MAFF Task Force for the Hills 2000–01; tech assessor Salmon and Freshwater Fisheries Legislation Review Gp 1999; memb Cncl of Chiefs Essodo community Enugu state Nigeria; FRICS 2004–; *Publications* Rural Employment: Trends, Options, Choices (with Martin Whitby, 1981), Environmental Economics: Individual Incentives and Public Choice (1995), Countryside in Trust: Land Management by Conservation, Recreation and Amenity Organisations (with Janet Dwyer, 1996); also author of articles in academic jls and other professional pubns; *Recreations* gardening, walking; *Style*— Prof Ian Hodge; ✉ Department of Land Economy, University of Cambridge, 19 Silver Street, Cambridge CB3 9EP (tel 01223 337134, fax 01223 337132, e-mail idh3@cam.ac.uk)

H

HODGE, Sir James William; KCVO (1996), CMG (1996); s of William Hodge (d 1994), of Edinburgh, and Catherine, *née* Carden (d 1977); *b* 24 December 1943; *Educ* Holy Cross Acad Edinburgh, Univ of Edinburgh (MA); *m* 20 June 1970, Frances Margaret, da of Michael Coyne (d 1995), of Liverpool; 3 da (Catherine b 1973, Fiona b 1975, Claire b 1979); *Career* Cwlth Office 1966, third sec Tokyo 1967–69, second sec Tokyo 1970–72, FCO 1972–75, first sec Lagos 1975–78, FCO 1978–81, first sec Tokyo 1981–82, cnsllr (commercial) Tokyo 1982–86, cnsllr and head of Chancery Copenhagen 1986–90, cnsllr FCO 1990–93, RCDS 1994, min Peking 1995–96, ambass to Thailand 1996–2000 (concurrently non-resident ambass to Laos), consul-gen Hong Kong 2000–03 (concurrently non-resident consul-gen Macao); chm Soc of Pension Cnslts 2007–; Hon DLitt Univ of Ulster 2003, Hon LLD Univ of Liverpool 2004; MCIL 1990; Knight Grand Cross Order of the White Elephant (Thailand) 1996; *Recreations* books, music; *Clubs* MCC, Oriental, Royal Over-Seas League, Hong Kong, Foreign Correspondents' (Hong Kong), China (Hong Kong), Macao Jockey; *Style*— Sir James Hodge, KCVO, CMG

HODGE, Rt Hon Margaret Eve; MBE (1978), PC (2003), MP; da of Hans and Lisbeth Oppenheimer; *b* 8 September 1944; *Educ* Bromley HS, Oxford HS, LSE (BSc(Econ)); *m* 1, 1968 (m dis 1978), Andrew Watson; 1 s (Nick), 1 da (Lizzi); m 2, 1978, Henry Hodge; 2 da (Anna, Amy); *Career* teacher and int market research 1966–73; London Borough of Islington: cncllr 1973–94, chm Housing Ctee 1975–79, dep ldr 1981, ldr 1982–92; sr conslt Price Waterhouse 1992–94, MP (Lab) Barking 1994–; chm: Lab Pty's inquiry team on early years educn 1994–97, London Gp of Lab MPs, Educn and Employment Select Ctee 1997–98; Parly under sec Dept for Educn and Employment 1998–2001, min of state for lifelong learning and HE DfES 2001–03, min of state for children, young people and families DfES 2003–05, min of state for work DWP 2005–06, min of state DTI 2006–; fndr and chm Assoc of London Authorities 1984–92, vice-chm AMA 1991–92, chm Circle 33 Housing Assoc 1993–96; dir CILNTEC 1990–92, non-exec dir London First 1992–94, former memb Cncl Univ of London; govr LSE 1990–2001; chm Fabian Soc 1997–98 (memb Exec Ctee 1990–99); visiting fell Inst of Public Policy Research 1992–, hon fell Univ of North London, Hon DCL City Univ; *Publications* Quality, Equality and Democracy: Improving Public Services (1991), Beyond the Town Hall - Reinventing Local Democracy (1994), More than the Flower Show: elected mayors and democracy (1997); contrib chapters to: Reinventing the Left (ed David Miliband), Making Gender Work (ed Jenny Shaw); *Recreations* family, cooking, cycling, theatre and opera; *Style*— The Rt Hon Margaret Hodge, MBE, MP; ✉ House of Commons, London SW1A 0AA (tel 020 7219 6666, fax 020 7219 3640)

HODGE, Patricia Ann; da of Eric Hodge (d 1988), and Marion, *née* Phillips; *b* 29 September 1946; *Educ* Grimsby Wintringham Girls' GS, St Helen's Sch for Girls Northwood, Maria Grey Teachers' Training Coll Isleworth, LAMDA (Eveline Evans Award for Best Actress on graduating); *m* 31 July 1976, Peter Douglas Owen; 2 s (Alexander Richard Charles b 18 Feb 1989, Edward Frederick James b 27 Dec 1991); *Career* actress; *Theatre* incl: All My Sons, Say Who You Are, The Birthday Party, The Anniversary (dir Peter Farago, Gateway Theatre Chester) 1971, Two Gentlemen of Verona (musical, dir Mel Shapiro, Phoenix) 1993, Hair (dir Rufus Collins, Queen's) 1974, The Beggar's Opera (dir Max Stafford-Clarke, Nottingham Playhouse) 1975, Pal Joey, Look Back In Anger (dir Phillip Hedley, Oxford Playhouse) 1976, Then and Now (Hampstead) 1979, The Mitford Girls (Chichester Festival Theatre) 1981, Noel and Gertie (Comedy Theatre) 1989/90, Separate Tables 1993, A Talent to Amuse 1993, The Prime of Miss Jean Brodie (Strand) 1994, A Little Night Music (RNT) 1995, Heartbreak House (Almeida) 1997, Money (RNT0 1999, Summerfolk (RNT) 1999, Noises Off (RNT) 2000, His Dark Materials (NT, 2004); *Television* for BBC incl: Valentine (series) 1973, The Girls of Slender of Means 1975, Jackanory Playhouse 1977, Act of Rape 1977, Crimewriters 1978, Hotel du Lac 1985, The Life and Loves of a She Devil 1986, The Legacy of Reginald Perrin 1996, The Moonstone 1996; for Thames incl: The Naked Civil Servant 1975, Rumpole of the Bailey (various) 1978–90, Edward and Mrs Simpson 1978, Rumpole's Return 1980, Jemima Shore Investigates 1982, Rumpole and the Female Species 1983; other credits incl: The Professionals (Mark 1 Prodns) 1979, Holding the Fort (LWT, 3 series) 1979–82, Robin of Sherwood (HTV) 1985, Time for Murder (Granada) 1985, Inspector Morse (Central) 1988, The Shell Seekers (ABC/Central) 1989, The Secret Life of Ian Fleming (Turner Entertainment) 1989, Rich Tea and Sympathy (Yorkshire) 1991, The Cloning of Joanna May (Granada) 1991, The Falklands Play 2002, Sweet Medicine 2003; *Films incl* The Disappearance (dir Stuart Cooper) 1977, The Elephant Man 1979, Betrayal (dir David Jones) 1982, Sunset (dir Blake Edwards) 1987, Just Ask for Diamond (dir Stephen Bayly) 1988, The Leading Man 1996, Jilting Joe 1997, Before You Go 2002; *Awards* Olivier Award Best Supporting Actress (for Money) 1999; nominations for: 2 Olivier Awards, 1 Br Acad Award, 1 Ace Award (USA); Hon DLitt Univ of Hull, Hon DLitt Brunel Univ, Hon DLitt Univ of Leicester; *Style*— Miss Patricia Hodge; ✉ c/o ICM Ltd, Oxford House, 76 Oxford Street, London W1D 1BS (tel 020 7636 6565, fax 020 7323 0101)

HODGE, Ralph Noel; CBE (2001); s of Ralph Hodge, of Ardbrecknish, Argyll, and Helena Florence, *née* Mason; *b* 1 November 1934; *Educ* Culford Sch, Univ of Liverpool (BEng); *m* 11 Sept 1954, Jean Margaret, *née* Rowlands; 2 s (David Ralph b 13 July 1956, Ian William b 5 May 1962), 2 da (Jackie Ann b 28 April 1959, Andrea Jane b 29 June 1966); *Career* cadet pilot RAFVR; ICI 1956–92: joined as graduate trainee 1956, division dir 1976, division dep chm 1978, gen mangr personnel 1981, chm Petrochemicals and Plastics Div 1985, ceo ICI Chemicals and Polymers 1990–92 (dep ceo 1987–90); dir: Halifax Building Society (now Halifax plc) 1992–98, Coal Investments plc 1993–96, BTP plc 1995–2000 (dep chm 1997–2000), Organisation Resources Counsellors Inc; chm: Enron Europe Ltd 1992–98, Tech Board Ltd 1993–99, WRc plc 1994–2004, Addis Ltd 1997–2000, Wessex Water Services Ltd 1998–2000, Azurix Europe Ltd 1998–2000, BCT Ltd 1999–, Serco plc 2000–; Melchett Medal for services to UK energy industries 1991; memb British Standards Bd 1992–97; memb Cncl Nat Forum of Mgmnt Educn and Devpt; FIPM; *Recreations* farming; *Style*— Ralph Hodge, Esq, CBE; ✉ Ralph Hodge Associates (tel 01323 502392, e-mail ralph.hodge@bctltd.co.uk)

HODGE, Stephen Murley Garfield; s of Raymond G Hodge (d 1960), and Ruth Egar (d 1997); *b* 11 March 1942, Peterborough; *Educ* Univ of Oxford; *m* 5 Aug 1967, Leila; 1 s (Thomas b 7 Aug 1975); *Career* admitted slr 1966; early career in various financial roles UK, Venezuela, Argentina, the Netherlands and Australia, treas then finance dir Shell Australia 1979–86, dep gp treas then gp treas Shell Int Petroleum Co, dir of finance Royal Dutch/Shell Gp of Cos until 2001, currently chm Shell Pensions Tst, non-exec dep chm O2 plc 2005–06 (non-exec dir 2001–06), dep chm Franchise Bd Lloyd's of London; memb Editorial Advsy Cncl CFO Europe magazine; memb Bd of Advsrs City Univ Business Sch; MCT; *Style*— Stephen Hodge, Esq; ✉ Shell Pensions Trust, Shell Centre, London SE1 7NA

HODGES, Dr Christopher John Stratford; s of John Henderson Hodges, and Norah, *née* Stratford; *b* 19 March 1954; *Educ* King Edward's Sch Birmingham, RMA Sandhurst, New Coll Oxford (MA), KCL (PhD); *m* Fiona Mary, *née* Ewart; 3 da; *Career* admitted slr 1979; slr Slaughter and May 1979–85 (articled clerk 1977–79), slr Clifford Chance 1986–89, ptnr McKenna & Co (now CMS Cameron McKenna) 1990–2005; visiting lectr Univ of Surrey 1994–97, visiting research fell Centre for Socio-Legal Studies Univ of Oxford 2003–04 (assoc fell and head of res prog on civil justice systems 2005–); memb Editorial Bd: Consumer Law Jl 1993–98, Int Business Law 2001–03; memb Editorial Advsy Bd The Regulatory Affrs Jl (Devices) 1993–; contrib: Law Quarterly Review, Common Market Law Review, European Business Law Review, Int Business Lawyer, Jl of Personal Injury Litigation; chair Legal Issues Ctee European Confedn of Med Devices Assocs (EUCOMED)/European Diagnostic Mfrs Assoc (EDMA) 2000–, vice-chair Cncl Assoc of Br Health-Care Industries (memb 1992–, chair Legal Ctee 1995–, chair Tech Policy Gp 2005–, co-chair Health Industries Task Force Working Gp on Regulation 2002–07), chair Pharmaceutical Services Negotiating Ctee 2007–; memb: Consumer Affrs Panel CBI 1992– (chair Working Ptys: Product Liability 1998–, Representative Claims 2000–), Academic Advsy Panel on Consumer Law DTI 2001–, Med Res Ethics Ctee Harrow HA 1990–97 (vice-chair 1992–97); tstee and dir The Sixteen 1989–2007, chair Bampton Classical Opera 2005–; memb Equity 1980–, memb RHS 1998–; Freeman: City of London 1982, City of London Slrs Co 1982; Yeoman Worshipful Soc of Apothecaries 2005; hon res assoc New Coll Oxford 2001–04; memb: Int Bar Assoc 1993–2003 (chair Ctee on Product Liability, Advtg, Unfair Competition and Consumer Affrs 2001–03), Int Assoc of Def Counsel, Def Res Inst, Soc of Legal Scolars 2005–; fell Inst of Continuous Professional Devpt 1998, fell Soc of Advanced Legal Studies 2000; *Publications* Product Liability: European Laws and Practice (1993), Product Safety (jtly, 1995), Multi-Party Actions (2001), European Regulation of Consumer Product Safety (2005); also author of various book chapters and numerous articles; *Recreations* singing and conducting classical music, horticulture; *Style*— Dr Christopher Hodges; ✉ Centre for Socio-Legal Studies, Manor Road, Oxford OX1 3UQ (tel 01869 284245, e-mail christopher.hodges@csls.ox.ac.uk)

HODGES, Mike; s of Graham Hodges (d 1987), and Norah, *née* Cottrell (d 1994); *b* 29 July 1932; *Educ* Prior Park Coll Bath, ACA; *m* 1964 (m dis 1982), Jean Alexandrov (d 1990); 2 s (Ben b 22 Dec 1964, Jake b 23 July 1966); *Career* writer, film producer and director; memb: Amnesty, Intermediate Technology, VES; Hon DLitt UWE 2005; *Television* World in Action (prodr/dir) 1963–65, Tempo (exec prodr and dir, ABC arts prog) 1965–68, Rumour (writer, dir and prodr) 1967, Suspect (writer, dir and prodr) 1968, Murder By Numbers (dir, documentary) 2001; *Radio* writer and dir: Shooting Stars and Other Heavenly Pursuits (BBC Radio 3) 2003, King Trash (BBC Radio 4) 2005; *Theatre* Soft Shoe Shuffle (writer, Hammersmith Lyric) 1985, Shooting Stars and Other Heavenly Pursuits (writer anddir, Old Red Lion) 2001; *Films* as writer and dir incl: Get Carter 1970, Pulp 1972, Missing Pieces 1982, Black Rainbow 1991; as writer, dir and prodr incl: The Terminal Man 1974; as dir incl: Flash Gordon 1979, Squaring the Circle 1984, Morons from Outer Space 1986, Florida Straits 1987, A Prayer for the Dying 1988, Dandelion Dead 1993, The Healer 1994, Croupier 1996, I'll Sleep When I'm Dead 2002; *Recreations* drawing, painting, playing clarinet, walking, gardening; *Style*— Mike Hodges, Esq; ✉ c/o Stephen Durbridge, The Agency, 24 Pottery Lane, London W11 4LZ (tel 020 7727 1346, fax 020 7727 9037)

HODGES, Peter Lewis (Lew); *b* 29 February 1956; *Educ* Peter Symonds GS Winchester, UCL (BA), London Business Sch (MBA); *Career* asst fin dir Arts Council 1985–87, head of fin and personnel CNAA 1987–89, dir of fin and resources Arts Council 1989–96, fin dir Sports Council 1996–97, head of fin RNT 1997–2000, dir of fin London Arts 2000–01, dir of fin Arts & Business 2001–05, dir of fin and resources Leadership Fndn 2006–; dir: English Touring Theatre, Artsadmin, Space, Lamda; memb Inner London Probation Ctee 1996–2001; FCA; *Clubs* South Bank Squash; *Style*— Lew Hodges, Esq; ✉ Leadership Foundation, 88 Kingsway, London WC2B 6AA

HODGES, Prof Richard Andrew; OBE (1995); s of Roy Clarence Hodges, of Box, Wilts, and Joan Mary, *née* Hartnell; *b* 29 September 1952; *Educ* City of Bath Boys' Sch, Univ of Southampton (BA, PhD); *m* (m dis 1998), Deborah, da of F C P Peters; 1 s (William b 15 March 1984), 1 da (Charlotte b 25 Oct 1986); *Career* archaeologist; Univ of Sheffield: lectr 1976–86, sr lectr 1986–88, prof 1993–95; prof UEA 1995–; visiting prof: SUNY-Binghamton 1983, Univ of Siena 1984–87, Univ of Copenhagen 1987–88; dir Br Sch at Rome 1988–95, dir Prince of Wales' Inst of Architecture 1996–98; princ advsr Min of Culture Albania 1999, princ advsr Packard Humanities Inst Albania 2000–07; maj archaeological excavations: Roystone Grange Derbyshire 1978–88, San Vincenzo al Volturno 1980–98, Montarrenti Siena 1982–87, Butrint Albania 1994–; memb Packard Humanities Bd 2003–; FSA 1984; *Books* The Hamwih Pottery (1981), Dark Age Economics (1982), Mohammed, Charlemagne and Origins of Europe (1983), Primitive and Peasant Markets (1988), The Anglo-Saxon Achievement (1989), Wall-to-Wall History (1991), San Vincenzo al Volturno I (1993), San Vincenzo al Volturno 2 (1995), Light in the Dark Ages (1997), Tours and Trade in the Age of Charlemagne (2000), Visions of Rome: Thomas Ashby, Archaeologist (2000), Villa to Village (with R Francovich, 2003), Byzantine Butrint (ed, 2004), Goodbye to the Vikings (2006), Eternal Butrint (2006); *Recreations* hill walking, listening to classical music, tennis; *Style*— Prof Richard Hodges, OBE, FSA; ✉ 64A The Close, Norwich NR1 4DW (tel 01603 615932)

HODGES, Stephen Richard; *b* 23 May 1954; *Educ* Latymer Upper Sch, Trinity Hall Cambridge (MA); *m* 1980, Felice; 1 s, 1 da; *Career* barr-at-law 1976; Close Brothers Ltd: joined 1985, md 1990–2002, chm 2002–; md Close Brothers Group plc 2002– (dir 1995–2002); *Recreations* fishing, walking, bridge, rare books; *Clubs* Flyfishers'; *Style*— Stephen Hodges, Esq; ✉ Close Brothers Ltd, 10 Crown Place, London EC2A 4FT (tel 020 7655 3100, fax 020 7247 1203)

HODGKIN, Sir (Gordon) Howard Eliot; kt (1992), CH (2003), CBE (1977); s of Eliot Hodgkin, and Hon Katherine Mary Hodgkin, *née* Hewart; *b* 6 August 1932, London; *Educ* Camberwell Sch of Art London, Bath Acad of Art Corsham; *m* 16 April 1955, Julia Hazel Ann, da of Albert Ernest Lane; 2 s (Louis b 23 Oct 1957, Sam b 20 Feb 1960); *Career* artist (represented by Gagosian Gallery and Galleria Lawrence Rubin Milan); teacher: Charterhouse 1954–56, Bath Acad of Art Corsham 1956–66, Chelsea Sch of Art 1966–72; visiting lectr Slade and Chelsea Schs of Art London 1976–77, artist in residence BNC Oxford 1976–77; tstee: Tate Gallery London 1970–76, Nat Gallery London 1978–85; memb Exec Ctee Nat Art Collections Fund 1988–; second prize John Moore's Liverpool Exhibition 1976 and 1980, Turner Prize Tate Gallery London 1985, Shakespeare Prize 1997; hon fell BNC Oxford 1988; Hon DLitt Univ of London 1985, Hon DLitt Univ of Oxford 2000 *Collections* incl: Arts Cncl of GB, Br Cncl London, Govt Picture Collection London, Contemporary Art Soc London, Tate Gallery London, V&A London, The Br Museum London, MOMA Edinburgh, MOMA NY, Met Museum of Art NY, Museum of Art Carnegie Inst, Nat Gallery of Washington, Fogg Art Museum Cambridge Mass, Louisiana Museum Denmark, Modern Art Museum Fort Worth, Oldham Art Gallery, São Paulo Museum Brazil, St Louis Art Museum, Walker Art Center Minneapolis, S Aust Art Gallery Adelaide; *One Man Exhibitions* incl: Arthur Tooth and Sons London 1962, 1964 and 1967, Kasmin Gallery London 1969 and 1971, Arnolfini Gallery Bristol 1970, Galerie Muller Cologne 1971, Kornblee Gallery New York 1973, Serpentine Gallery London 1976, Waddington/Kasmin Galleries London 1976, MOMA Oxford 1976 and 1977, Andre Emmerich New York and Zurich 1977, Br Cncl exhbn touring India 1978 (graphics), Bernard Jacobson NY 1980 and 1981, LA 1981 and London 1982 (graphics), M Knoedler & Co New York 1981, 1982, 1984, 1986, 1988, 1990 and 1993–94, Waddington Galleries London 1980, 1988 and 1991 (graphics), Macquarie Galleries Sydney 1981, Tate Gallery London 1982, Br Pavilion Venice Biennale 1984, Phillips Collection Washington DC 1984, Yale Center for Br Art 1985, Kestner-Gesellschaft Hanover 1985, Whitechapel Art Gallery London 1985, Tate Gallery London 1985 (graphics), Michael Werner Gallery Cologne 1990, Anthony d'Offay Gallery London 1993 and 1999–2000, retrospective exhbn Metropolitan Museum of Art NY to Modern Art Museum Fort Worth then Der Kunstverein Düsseldorf and Hayward Gallery 1995–97, Galerie Lawrence Rubin Zurich 1997, Gagosian Gallery New York 1998 and 2003, Haas and Fuchs Galerie Berlin 1998,

Galleria Lawrence Rubin Milan 2001, Dulwich Picture Gallery London 2001, Scottish Nat Gallery of Modern Art Edinburgh 2002, Gagosian Gallery LA 2004, Irish Museum of Modern Art Dublin (major retrospective touring to Tate Britain London and Reina Sofia Madrid) 2006; *Style*— Sir Howard Hodgkin, CH, CBE; ✉ c/o Gagosian Gallery, 6–24 Britannia Street, London, WC1X 9JD (tel 020 7841 9960)

HODGKINSON, (James) Andrew; s of Peter George Hodgkinson (d 1986), of Lincoln, and Gwyneth Anne, *née* Evans (d 1984); *b* 22 January 1952; *Educ* City Sch Lincoln, Brighton Poly (BA); *m* 6 Sept 1996, Mariann Halkjaer; *Career* dir John Michael Design Consultants 1975–80, fndr and md Simons Design 1980–94, Main Bd dir and shareholder of The Simons Gp, fndr and md Hodgkinson & Co 1994; MInstD, MCSD 1989; *Recreations* design, art, polo and numerous sports, ethnography, natural history; *Clubs* Guards Polo; *Style*— Andrew Hodgkinson, Esq; ✉ Hodgkinson & Co, 29 Alexander Street, London W2 5NU

HODGKINSON, Catherine; da of Richard Hodgkinson (d 1992), and (Joyce) Marten, *née* Green (d 1990); *b* 19 December 1946; *Educ* New Hall Chelmsford, Institut d'Art et d'Archeologie Paris (LèsL); *m* 19 Dec 1975 (m dis 1985), John Louis Rishad Zinkin, s of Maurice Zinkin, OBE, of London; 1 da (Kate b 1977); *Career* art dealer; md Lumley Cazalet Ltd 1973–2002, private dealer 2002–; *Recreations* theatre, art, travel; *Style*— Miss Catherine Hodgkinson; ✉ PO Box 33729, London SW3 3ZQ (tel 020 7376 7062, fax 020 7376 5941, e-mail catherine@hodgkinsonart.com)

HODGKINSON, Sir Michael S (Mike); kt (2003); *Educ* Univ of Nottingham; *Career* formerly: md Land Rover Ltd, md UK Ops Express Dairy Gp, chief exec European Foods Div Grand Metropolitan plc; chief exec BAA plc 1999–2003 (gp airports dir 1992–99); non-exec chm: Post Office Ltd 2003–, First Choice Holidays plc 2004–; non-exec dir: FKI plc 2000–, Royal Mail plc 2003–; memb Ct of Directors Bank of Ireland 2004–; chm Airports Advsy Cncl; memb Bd: Cmmn for Integrated Transport, Transport for London, Dublin Airport Authority; *Style*— Sir Mike Hodgkinson; ✉ Post Office Ltd, 80 Old Street, London EC1V 9NN (tel 020 7320 7430)

HODGKINSON, Paul Richard; CBE (2001); s of Peter George Hodgkinson, DL (d 1986), of St Georges House, Lincoln, and Gwyneth Anne, *née* Evans (d 1984); *b* 9 March 1956; *Educ* Lincoln GS, Oxford Poly (BA, DipArch); *m* 13 Oct 1984, Catherine Ann, da of George Giangrande, of New Vernon, NJ, USA; 2 s (Christopher Peter, Alexander George); *Career* Shepherd Epstein & Hunter 1975–76, Capital and Counties plc 1979–81, Simons Design Conslts 1981–86, chm and chief exec Simons Group Ltd 1986–; chm E Midlands Regional Ctee CBI 1997–98, chm Lincolnshire Training and Enterprise Cncl 1989–94; RIBA 1980, ARCUK, MInstD, RSA 1986; *Recreations* tennis, reading, golf, food; *Style*— Paul Hodgkinson, Esq, CBE; ✉ Simons Group Ltd, 991 Doddington Road, Lincoln LN6 3AA (tel 0808 202 3991, fax 0845 072 1800, e-mail paul.hodgkinson@simonsgroup.com)

HODGKINSON, (Claude) Peter; s of Claude Harold Hodgkinson, of Stoke-on-Trent, and Gweneth Mary, *née* Cupit; *b* 26 June 1943; *Educ* Ratcliffe Coll Leicester, Univ of Manchester (BA); *m* 27 Nov 1974, Julie Margaret Wesley Thompson, of Birmingham; 1 s (Oliver b 1976), 1 da (Sophie b 1982); *Career* dir: Hanley Economic Building Society 1972–2001, A G (Plaster) Ltd 1978–2003; memb The Ancient Corporation of Hanley; FCA 1968; *Recreations* gentleman farmer of rare breed sheep (Balwens) and cattle (Dexters), golf, good food and fine wines, holidays; *Clubs* Trentham Golf, British Pottery Mfrs Fedn, Builders and Allied Trades Golf (pres); *Style*— Peter Hodgkinson, Esq; ✉ Holly Cottage, Maer, Newcastle, Staffordshire ST5 5EF (tel 01782 680255)

HODGSON, Carole; *b* 1940, London; *Educ* Wimbledon Sch of Art, Slade Sch of Fine Art; *Career* artist; visiting prof of sculpture and painting Univ of Wisconsin 1968 and 1980, pt/t lectr Univ of Reading 1964–71, lectr in art Univ of London Inst of Educn 1975–79, visiting lectr Norwich Sch of Art 1979–87, visiting tutor RCA Painting Sch 1981–86; currently prof of sculpture Kingston Univ; appears in Br Sculptors of the Twentieth Century; fell RBS 1997; *Solo Exhibitions* Angela Flowers Gallery London 1973, 1977, 1979, 1984, 1989, 1994, 2005 and Flowers East London 1992, 1997, 2000 and 2005, UCW 1973, Royal Shakespeare Theatre Stratford 1975, Welsh Arts Cncl 1976, The Fine Arts Galleries Univ of Wisconsin 1980, The Wustum Museum Racine 1981, Lawrence Univ Appleton 1981, The Bedford Way Gallery Univ of London 1981, Llanelli Festival 1984, Christie's Fine Arts Courses London 1986, Whitefriars Museum Coventry 1991, New Ashgate Gallery Farnham 1991, Centro Cultural Recoleta Buenos Aires 1995, GEC Mgmnt Coll Rugby 1995, Sudbury bronzes in garden Gainsborough's house 1996, Patrick & Beatrice Haggerty Museum of Art Milwaukee 1999, Flowers West Santa Monica 1999, Flowers East Graphics Monoprints 2001, Monoprints (Wingfield Arts Suffolk) 2002; *Group Exhibitions* incl: Br Art Show (Arts Cncl of GB touring Sheffield, Newcastle and Bristol) 1979, Probity of Art (Welsh Arts Cncl touring Wales, England, Spain and Turkey) 1980–82, RCA Painting Staff Exhibition 1981, City Gallery Arts Tst Milton Keynes 1984, Int Contemporary Art Fair London 1986, The Artist Day Book (Smiths Gallery London) 1987, Chicago Art Fair 1989, Bath Contemporary Print Fair 1990, Royal Acad Summer Exhibition 1990, Print of the Month (Flowers East London) 1990, Royal Acad Print Fair 1991, Islington Business Centre Art Fair 1991, Chelsea Harbour Sculpture 1993, Downeen Decade (Angela Flowers Ireland) 1994, Instituto Chileno-Britancio de Cultura Santiago1995, Grafica International Museo de Arte Contemporánea Santiago 1995, The Gallery Garden Broughton Stockbridge 1996, New Ashgate Gallery Farnham 1997 and 1998, Grand Valley State Univ 1999, Landscape (Angela Flowers) 1999, Gallery Artist Flowers Central 2000 and 2001, Palazzo Vendramin dei Carnini Venice 2000, Royal British Soc of Sculptors 2001, Oxford Brookes Univ 2001, FIDEM Paris 2002, Flowers East 2002, Flowers Central 2002, Pitshanger Manor 2003, Drawing as Process 2003, Martini Arte Internazionale Manufactured in the UK Turin 2003; *Commissions* incl: bronze sculpture for British Aerospace Kingston upon Thames 1986–87, medal for Br Medal Soc (commemorating' Bogman' exhibition Br Museum) 1987, bronze 'River Celebration' cmmnd by Royal Borough of Kingston upon Thames 1988–90, still life bronze cmmnd by Knee Surgery Unit Wellington Hosp 1996, wall sculpture cmmnd by Wingfield Arts Suffolk 2002; *Work in Collections* Arts Cncl of GB, Dept of the Environment, Br Cncl, Contemporary Arts Soc, Univ of London, Unilever House, Welsh Contemporary Arts Soc, Pontevedra Museum, Bello Piñeiro Museum Ferrol, La Escuelo Nacional de Bellas Artes Buenos Aires, Universidad Católica Santiago, Manpower, private collections in Europe, USA, Mexico and Aust; *Awards* Univ of Reading res grant to travel Mexico 1968, Arts Cncl of GB Award 1973, Br Cncl Award 1978 and 1980, The Elephant Tst Award 1979 and 1986, Grocers' Co bursary Br Sch at Rome 1982, Kingston Univ res grant to travel to China 1993 and to Chile and Argentina 1995, Br Cncl USA Exhibitions 1998, Kingston Univ res grant 1999, Humanity Medal (Honorarium Prize) RBS/Worshipful Co of Goldsmiths 1993, Purchase Prize X Premio de Grabado Maximo Ramos Ferrol Spain; *Publications* contrib TES: Women Artist (1978), Sculpture a Missing Dimension in School Art (1980), From the Sea to the Wall (1995), Monograph (1999), From City to Lake (2005); *Style*— Ms Carole Hodgson; ✉ c/o Flowers East, 82 Kingsland Road, London E2 8DP (website www.flowerseast.co.uk)

HODGSON, Charles Christopher (Charlie); s of Christopher Hodgson, and Christine Hodgson; *Educ* Bradford GS, Univ of Durham; *m* Daisy, *née* Hartley; *Career* rugby union player; Sale Sharks 2000– (winners European Challenge Cup 2005, winners Guinness Premiership 2006); England: 29 caps, full debut v Romania 2001 (highest English individual point scorer with 44 points), also represented Under 18s and Under 21s (incl World Championships Australia 2001); memb squad Br & I Lions tour to NZ 2005; patron Yorkshire Air Ambulance Charity; *Recreations* listening to music, tennis, golf; *Clubs* West End Golf Halifax; *Style*— Charlie Hodgson, Esq; ✉ c/o Sale Sharks Rugby Union Club, Edgeley Park, Stockport, Cheshire SK3 9DD (tel 0161 283 1861)

HODGSON, Godfrey Michael Talbot; s of Arthur Benjamin Hodgson (d 1962), of York, and Jessica, *née* Hill (d 1947); *Educ* Winchester (open scholar, Goddard leaving scholarship, cricket first XI), Magdalen Coll Oxford (Demy open scholar, MA), Univ of Pennsylvania (MA); *m* 1, 1958 (m dis 1970), Alice Anne Simone, da of Jacques Vidal, Légion d'Honneur, MM; 2 s (Pierre Thomas Godfrey b 1959, Francis James Samuel b 1960); m 2, 1970, Hilary Mary, da of Brian F C Lamb; 2 da (Jessica b 1971, Laura b 1974); *Career* reporter TES 1956, reporter The Times 1958; The Observer: wrote Mammon column 1960, Washington corr 1962–65; reporter This Week (ITV) 1965–67; ed Insight Sunday Times 1967–71, foreign features ed 1971; freelance 1972–90, presenter The London Programme (LWT) 1976–81, presenter of progs incl The Great Depression (ITV) 1981 and Reagan on Reagan (Channel 4) 1988; foreign ed The Independent and The Independent on Sunday 1990–92, dir Reuter Fndn Prog Univ of Oxford 1992–2001; fell Green Coll Oxford 1993–2001, assoc fell Rothermere American Inst Univ of Oxford; contrib articles and reviews to numerous pubns incl: Sunday Times, The Economist, New Statesman, NY Times, FT, Washington Post, The Independent, and various academic jls; Sarah Tryphena Phillips lectr Br Acad 1999; memb Soc of American Historians; *Books* incl: Carpetbaggers et Ku-Klux Klan (in French, 1965), An American Melodrama (with L Chester and B Page, 1969), Do You Sincerely Want to Be Rich? (with B Page and C Raw, 1970), In Our Time (1976), All Things to All Men (1980), Lloyd's of London (1986), The Colonel (1990), A New Grand Tour (1995), People's Century (1995), The World Turned Right Side Up (1996), The Gentleman from New York (2000), More Equal Than Others (2004), Woodrow Wilson's Right Hand: The Life of Colonel Edward M House (2006), A Great and Godly Adventure (2006); *Recreations* travelling, reading, listening to classical music, watching cricket; *Clubs* Beefsteak; *Style*— Godfrey Hodgson, Esq; ✉ 55 High Street, Finstock, Oxfordshire OX7 3DA (tel 01993 868867, e-mail godfrey.hodgson@dial.pipex.com)

HODGSON, Prof Humphrey Julian Francis; s of Harold Robinson Hodgson (d 1985), and Celia Frances Hodgson; *b* 5 May 1945; *Educ* Westminster (Queen's scholar), ChCh Oxford (scholar, MA, BSc, Martin Wronker Prize), St Thomas' Hosp Med Sch London (BM BCh, DM, Charles Box Prize in Med); *m* Shirley Victoria, da of Prof Lionel Penrose; 1 s (Julian b 1973), 1 da (Anna b 1974); *Career* research fell Massachusetts Gen Hosp Boston 1976–77, conslt physician Hammersmith Hosp 1978–99; Imperial Coll Sch of Med Hammersmith Hosp (Royal Postgraduate Med Sch until merger 1997): vice-dean 1989–97, prof of gastroenterology 1990–95, prof of med 1995–99; prof of med (Sheila Sherlock Chair) Royal Free and Univ Coll School of Med 1999–; vice-dean Royal Free and Univ Coll Medical Sch 2001–; non-exec dir Royal Free Hampstead NHS Tst 2002–; Radcliffe travelling fell UC Oxford 1976, Humphrey Davy Rolleston lectr RCP London 1991, Fitzgerald Peel lectr Scot Soc of Physicians 1993, Croonian lectr RCP London 2002; academic registrar RCP London 1993–97; author of books and original articles on gastrointestinal and liver disease; pres Br Assoc of Study of the Liver 2003–; chm: Liver Group Charity 1993–, Scientific Co-ordinating Ctee Arthritis Res Campaign 1996–2003; FMedSci; FRCP 1982 (MRCP 1972); *Recreations* walking, reading; *Style*— Prof Humphrey Hodgson; ✉ 40 Onslow Gardens, London N10 3JU (tel 020 8883 8297); Royal Free and University College School of Medicine, Rowland Hill Street, London NW3 2PF (tel 020 7433 2851, fax 020 7433 2852, e-mail h.hodgson@medsch.ucl.ac.uk)

HODGSON, Jonathan James; s of John Hodgson, of Sutton Coldfield, and Barbara, *née* Middlemiss; *b* 6 May 1960; *Educ* Park Hall Comp, Solihull Coll of Technol, Liverpool Poly (BA), RCA (MA); *Career* animation director, musician and soundtrack composer; co fndr Unicorn Productions 1985; freelance dir: Barry Joll Associates 1985–88, Practical Pictures 1985–88, Felix Films 1988–90, Bermuda Shorts 1991–93, Mojo Working 1993–4, Speedy Films 1995; co-fndr (with Jonathan Bairstow) Sherbet Ltd 1996; commercials, title sequences and short films for clients incl: UN, Brooke Bond, McVities, MTV, BBC, Channel Four, Lambie-Nairn, English-Markell-Pockett, Thames TV, SAAB USA, Prince Matchabelli, Initial TV, Bank of Switzerland, Bell Atlantic, Unilever; films credits incl: An Unseen Flight 1980, Dogs (first prize Stuttgart Trickfilmtage) 1981, Experiments In Movement and Line 1981, Night Club (6 int awards) 1983, Menagerie 1984, Train of Thought 1985, The Doomsday Clock (cmmnd by UN) 1987, Feeling My Way 1997 (5 int awards), The Man with the Beautiful Eyes 1999 (BAFTA award for Best Short Animation 2000 and 10 int awards), Camouflage 2001; art work published in European Illustration 1981–; *Recreations* digging; *Style*— Jonathan Hodgson, Esq; ✉ Sherbet Ltd, 112–114 Great Portland Street, London W1N 5PE (tel 020 7636 6435, fax 020 7436 3221, e-mail jh@sherbet.co.uk)

HODGSON, Mark Thomas; s of Thomas Hodgson (d 1975), and Joyce, *née* Page; *b* 2 December 1957, Bishop Auckland, Co Durham; *Educ* Barnard Castle Sch, Emmanuel Coll Cambridge (MA); *m* 5 June 1982, Janet, *née* Annas; 2 s (James b 30 July 1987, Edward b 13 Jan 1991), 1 da (Louise b 10 March 1993); *Career* slr; Woodham Smith 1981–84, ptnr Simmons & Simmons 1994–99 (joined 1984), ptnr and head Life Sciences Gp Taylor Wessing 1999–; chm Intellectual Property Lawyers Assoc; memb: Intellectual Property Court Users Ctee, Int Assoc for the Protection of Intellectual Property (AIPPI), Intellectual Property Owners Assoc (IPO), City of London Slrs' Co; *Recreations* sport, travel, gardening; *Style*— Mark Hodgson, Esq; ✉ Taylor Wessing, 50 Victoria Embankment, Blackfriars, London EC4Y 0DX (tel 020 7300 7000, fax 020 7300 7100, e-mail m.hodgson@taylorwessing.com)

HODGSON, Dame Patricia Anne; DBE (2004, CBE 1995); da of Harold Hodgson, of Brentwood, Essex, and Lilian Mary, *née* Smith; *b* 19 January 1947; *Educ* Brentwood Co HS, Newnham Coll Cambridge (MA); *m* 23 July 1979, George Edward Donaldson, s of Edward George Donaldson, of Donington-le-Heath, Leics; 1 s; *Career* Cons Research Dept 1968–70, prodr BBC Open Univ (specialising in history and philosophy) 1970–82 (TV series incl: English Urban History 1978, Conflict in Modern Europe 1980, Rome in the Age of Augustus 1981), broadcaster and freelance journalist in UK and USA, ed Crossbow 1976–80; BBC: dep sec 1982–83, the sec 1985–87, head Policy and Planning Unit 1987–92, dir Policy and Planning 1993–99, dir Public Policy 2000; chief exec ITC 2000–03; chm Bow Group 1975–76; dir BARB 1987–98; chair HE Regulatory Review Gp 2004–; memb: Monopolies & Mergers Cmmn 1993–99, London Arts Bd 1991–96, Statistics Cmmn 2000–06, Cncl Competition Cmmn 2003–, Ctee on Standards in Public Life 2004–, Bd HEFCE 2005–, BBC Tst 2006–; govr Wellcome Tst 2004–; non-exec dir GCap Media Gp plc 2004–06; Parly candidate (Cons) Islington 1974; princ Newnham Coll Cambridge 2006– (assoc fell 1994–96, visiting bye-fell 2004); *Recreations* quietness; *Clubs* Oxford and Cambridge; *Style*— Dame Patricia Hodgson, DBE

HODGSON, Peter Barrie; s of Clive Ward (d 1980), and Gladys Stewart, *née* Ross (d 1983); *b* 12 March 1942; *Educ* Clayesmore Sch, St Peter's Coll Oxford (BA); *m* 10 Feb 1973, Audrone Ona, da of Jonas Grudzinskas (d 1992), formerly of Kretinga, Lithuania; 1 s (Lindsay Matthew Oliver b 3 Aug 1977); *Career* dir: Opinion Research Centre 1973–75, Professional Studies Ltd 1975–77; md: Professional Studies Ireland 1977, Action Research Ltd 1977–78; chm and md Travel and Tourism Research Ltd 1978–; dir: City Research Associates Ltd 1981–89, Quay Management (Waterside) Ltd 1999–; chm: Assoc of Br Market Research Cos 1987–89, Assoc of Euro Market Research Insts 1991–94; memb Editorial Bd Jl of Consumer Research 2000–; memb: Cncl Market Research Soc 1978–81, Tourism Soc 1981–84, Market Research Soc, Euro Soc for Opinion & Marketing Res; fndr memb Social Research Assoc; dep chm and memb Cncl Br Market Research Assoc

1998–2004; fell Tourism Soc 1980, FInstTT 1989; *Publications* author of articles in: Espaces (Paris), Imprints (Canada), Marketing, Jl of the Market Res Soc, Jl of the Professional Market Res Soc of Canada, Research Magazine, Research Plus, Jl of Travel Research (US), Survey, Tourism Management; *Recreations* opera, wine, travel; *Style*— Peter Hodgson, Esq; ✉ Travel and Tourism Research Ltd, 4 Cochrane House, Admirals Way, London E14 9UD (tel 020 7538 5300, fax 020 7538 3299, e-mail pb.hodgson@virgin.net)

HODGSON, Peter Gerald Pearson; s of Thomas William Hodgson, of Elloughton, N Humberside, and Edna, *née* Pearson; *b* 13 July 1934; *Educ* Reade Sch, Univ of Hull (BSc), Imperial Coll London (DIC); *m* 30 Sept 1956, Noreen, da of Albert James Warnes, of Byfleet, Surrey; 2 s (Michael Charles Peter b 1966, John Paul Richard b 1967); *Career* chm: Petrocon Group plc 1963–89 (chief exec 1963–88), Richards Group plc 1987–93, Loma Group plc 1990–95, HAT Property Services Ltd 1994–98, Service Team Ltd 1995–2001; MIChemE 1965, FInstPet (1968); *Recreations* golf, horse racing (owner), watching cricket; *Clubs* MCC, RAC; *Style*— Peter Hodgson, Esq; ✉ Arlington, Ashtead Park, Ashtead, Surrey KT21 1EG (tel 01372 277579, fax 01372 277509)

HODGSON, Peter John Dixon; CBE (1992, OBE 1979), DL (Cornwall 2006); s of John Dixon Hodgson (d 1998), of Manaton, Launceston, Cornwall, and Dorothy Blanche, *née* Saunders (d 1991); *b* 21 March 1947; *Educ* Charterhouse; *m* 18 July 1970, Cecilia Anne, da of Brig Arnold de Lerisson Cazenove, CBE, DSO, MVO (d 1969); 2 s (James b 1973, Timothy b 1975), 1 da (Charlotte b 1977); *Career* chartered accountant, sr ptnr Hodgsons; chm: Fin Ctee Red Cross Cornwall 1988–95, Western Area Nat Union of Cons and Unionist Assocs 1991–94, SRC Nat Union of Cons and Unionists Assocs 1995–98; chm of govrs: UC Falmouth (formerly Falmouth Coll of Arts) 1999–2007 (govr 1997–2007), Mount House Sch 2000–06 (govr 1993–2006); High Sheriff Cornwall 2005–06; FCA 1970; *Recreations* gardening, fishing; *Style*— Peter Hodgson, Esq, CBE, DL; ✉ Manaton, Launceston, Cornwall PL15 9JE (tel 01566 772880); Hodgsons, 12 Southgate Street, Launceston, Cornwall PL15 9DP (tel 01566 772177)

HODGSON, Sharon; MP; *b* 1 April 1966; *Educ* Heathfield Sr HS, Newcastle Coll; *Career* Lab link co-ordinator Unison; MP (Lab) Gateshead E and Washington W 2005–; memb: GMB, Fabian Soc, Christian Socialist Movement; *Style*— Mrs Sharon Hodgson, MP; ✉ House of Commons, London SW1A 0AA

HODGSON, Prof Shirley Victoria; da of Lionel Sharples Penrose, and Margaret, *née* Leathes; *b* 22 February 1945; *Educ* Hendon Co GS, UCL (BSc), Somerville Coll Oxford (BM BCh), Univ of Oxford (DM, DCH); *Career* house surgn Churchill Hosp Oxford 1969–70, house physician Cowley Rd Hosp Oxford 1970, house surgn (obstetrics and gynaecology) N Middx Hosp London 1970–71, registrar (paediatrics and med) Saadi and Pahlavi Hosps Shiraz Iran 1971–72, SHO (paediatrics) St Stephen's Hosp Chelsea 1972–73, registrar (paediatrics) Whittington Hosp London 1973–74, paediatric offr Islington Local HA 1974–75, trainee GP 1975–76, fell in paediatrics Psychosomatic Unit Children's Hosp Boston Mass 1976–77, asst GP Canonbury 1977–79, locum registrar S Thames (E) Regnl Genetics Centre Guy's 1979–80, registrar (paediatrics) Chase Farm Hosp Enfield 1980–83, sr registrar (clinical genetics) S Thames (E) Regnl Genetics Centre Guy's 1983–88, conslt clinical geneticist E Anglian Regnl Genetics Centre Addenbrooke's Hosp Cambridge 1988–90, dir Family Cancer Clinic St Mark's Hosp Northwick Park 1990–96, hon conslt clinical geneticist S Thames (E) Regnl Genetics Centre Guy's and St Thomas' NHS Tst Guy's 1990–2003, sr lectr in clinical genetics St Mark's Hosp and Bart's 1990–96, sr lectr in clinical genetics Div of Med and Molecular Genetics UMDS 1990–98, reader in clinical genetics GKT 1998–2003, prof of cancer genetics Dept of Clinical Developmental Sciences St George's Hospital London 2003–; delivered lectures internationally, memb of organising ctees for symposia incl Euro Biomed conf Heidelberg 1999; memb: InSIGHT (International Society for Gastrointestinal Hereditary Tumours) 1990, Steering Ctee Thames Cancer Registry 1999–, Public and Professional Policy Ctee Soc for Human Genetics 2001–, Exec Ctee UK Forum of Genetics and Insurance, Steering Ctee Cancer Genetics Gp (also memb Bd), Bd Genetics Interest Gp (also advsr), Ctee on Medical Aspects of Radiation in the Environment (COMARE); participant Euro Biomed II collaboration on breast cancer genetics services; genetics advsr to Cancer BACUP; memb Editorial Bd: Clinical Medicine RCP, Kluwer Academic Publishers; awarded Wellington Travelling scholarship; D(Obst)RCOG 1970; FRCP 1993 (MRCP 1982); *Publications* A Practical Guide to Human Cancer Genetics (jt ed, 1993, 2 edn 1999), Inherited Susceptibility to Cancer: Clinical, Predictive and Ethical Perspectives (jt ed, 1998), Familial Breast and Ovarian Cancer (jt ed, 2002); numerous book chapters and jl papers; *Recreations* cycling, walking, painting, classical music; *Style*— Prof Shirley Hodgson; ✉ Department of Clinical Development Sciences, Medical Genetics, St George's Hospital Medical School, Jenner Wing, Cranmer Terrace, London SE17 0RE (tel 020 8725 5279, fax 020 8266 6410, e-mail shodgson@sgul.ac.uk)

HODGSON OF ASTLEY ABBOTTS, Baron (Life Peer UK 2000), of Nash in the County of Shropshire; Robin Granville; CBE (1992); s of late Henry Edward Hodgson, of Astley Abbotts, Salop, and Natalie Beatrice, *née* Davidson; *b* 25 April 1942; *Educ* Shrewsbury, Univ of Oxford (BA), Wharton Sch Univ of Pennsylvania (MBA); *m* 8 May 1982, Fiona Ferelith, da of Keith Storr Allom; 4 s (Barnaby Peter Granville b 1986, James Maxwell Gower (twin) b and d 1986, Toby Henry Storr b 1988, Hugo Edward Valentine b 1992), 1 da (Poppy Ferelith Alice b 1990); *Career* Lt 4 Bn Kings Shrops LI TA 1960–64; chm: Granville Baird Gp (investment bankers) 1972–2003 (also former gp chief exec), Nasdim 1979–85, Rostrum Gp 2000–, Nova Capital Gp 2002–; non-exec chm: Spotlaunch plc, Walter Alexander plc 1990–92; dir: Dominic Hunter plc 1992–2002, Community Hospital plc 1995–2001, Staffordshire Building Society 1995–; non-exec dir Marston's plc (formerly Wolverhampton and Dudley Breweries plc) 2002–; memb West Midland Industrial Devpt Bd 1988–96; dir: Securities and Investment Bd 1985–89, Securities and Futures Authy 1991–2002; MP (Cons) Walsall N 1976–79, chm Cons Party W Midlands Area 1991–94 (treas 1985–91); Nat Union of Cons Assocs: memb Exec Ctee 1988–98, vice-pres 1995–96, chm 1996–98; dep chm Cons Pty 1998–2000, chm Nat Cons Convention 1998–2000; tstee Shrewsbury Sch Fndn; Liveryman Worshipful Co of Goldsmiths; tstee and hon fell St Peter's Coll Oxford; *Style*— The Rt Hon the Lord Hodgson of Astley Abbotts, CBE; ✉ Nash Court, Nash, Ludlow, Shropshire SY8 3DF (tel and fax 01584 811677); 15 Scarsdale Villas, London W8 (tel and fax 020 7937 2964); Nova Capital Management Ltd, 11 Strand, London WC2N 5HR

HODKINSON, James Clifford (Jim); s of John Eric Thomas Hodkinson (d 1985), of Ferndown, Dorset, and Edith Lilian, *née* Lord; *b* 21 April 1944; *Educ* Salesian Coll Farnborough; *m* 8 Feb 1969, Janet Patricia, da of George William Lee (d 1941); 1 da (Justine b 30 April 1970); *Career* trainee mangr F W Woolworth 1962–71; B & Q plc: mangr Bournemouth Store 1971–74, sales mangr in South 1974–79, ops dir 1979–84, ops and personnel dir 1984–86, chief exec 1986–92, int devpt dir 1992–94, chm and chief exec 1994–1998; chm (DIY) Kingfisher plc 1994–1998; chief exec New Look plc 1998–2000; non-exec chm: Furniture Village plc 2002–, Ideal Shopping Direct 2004–07, Wyevale Garden Centres 2005–; non-exec dir: Hamleys plc 1994–2003, Provident Financial plc 1998–2000, B&Q Int Ltd 2002–03, Polymer Logistics Hldgs Ltd 2002–, Big Ideas Mgmnt Ltd 2002–, Edinburgh Woollen Mill plc 2004–; FInstD, CIMgt; *Recreations* golf, shooting; *Style*— Jim Hodkinson, Esq

HODSON, Beverley; OBE (2003); da of Clifford Vernon Hodson (d 1984), of London, and Frances Jeanne Hodson, *née* Cox (d 1971), of London; *Educ* Univ of Cambridge (BA, Women's Lawn Tennis capt and blue); *m* Peter John Cottingham; 1 s (Thomas Hodson Cottingham b 14 April 1988); *Career* business gen mangr Boots The Chemist 1989–95 (various positions 1978–89); md: Childrens World 1995–96, Dolcis Cable 1996–97, WH Smith 1997–2004; non-exec dir: Trent FM GWR Radio 1990–97, M&G (Fin Services/Unit Tst) 1998–99, Legal & General 2000–07, First Milk 2005–, Robert Wiseman Dairies 2005–, Vedior NV 2006–; hon sec AT Med Research Tst; memb Regnl Devpt Agency Yorks and N Humberside 1990–97; memb Nat Coll of Sch Leadership 1999–2005; memb: RSA, Women's Advtg Club of London (WACL); *Recreations* tennis, skiing, walking, swimming, reading, theatre, music, cinema, gardening, cookery; *Style*— Beverley Hodson, OBE

HODSON, Clive; CBE (1992); s of Stanley Louis Hodson (d 1993), and Elsie May, *née* Stratford (d 2003); *b* 9 March 1942; *Educ* Erith GS; *m* 18 Sept 1976, Fiona Mary, *née* Pybus; 1 s (James Andrew b 12 Feb 1983), 1 da (Kate Alexis b 19 Jan 1985); *Career* Fin Dept London Transport 1960–69, asst co sec and accountant London Country Bus Services Ltd 1970–74, mgmnt accountant London Transport 1974–78, fin dir London Buses 1978–89, md London Buses Ltd 1989–95, project dir (bus privatisation) London Transport 1993–95, md London Transport Buses 1994–2000, project dir Croydon Tramlink 1995–2000, chm Victoria Coach Station Ltd 1995–2000; memb Bd London Transport 1995–2000; chm: London River Services Ltd 1998–2000, LRT Pension Fund Tstee Co Ltd 1998–2003, London Buses Ltd 2000; md London Bus Services Ltd 2000; non-exec dir Capital Value Brokers Ltd 2000–04; Freeman City of London 1995, Liveryman Worshipful Co of Carmen 1995; CTA 1968; FCCA 1967, FCILT 1969; *Recreations* travel, walking, reading; *Style*— Clive Hodson, Esq, CBE; ✉ tel 01737 210910

HODSON, Daniel Houghton; s of Henry Vincent Hodson, of London, and Margaret Elizabeth, *née* Honey; *b* 11 March 1944; *Educ* Eton, Merton Coll Oxford (MA); *m* 22 Feb 1979, Diana Mary, da of Christopher Breen Ryde, of Middleton-on-Sea, W Sussex; 2 da (Susannah Fleur b 1980, Emma Katharine b 1982); *Career* Chase Manhattan Bank NA 1965–73, dir Edward Bates & Sons Ltd 1974–76 (joined 1973), gp fin dir Unigate plc 1981–87 (gp treas 1976–81), pres Unigate Inc 1986–87, chm Davidson Pearce Group plc 1988 (chief exec 1987–88), dep chief exec and gp fin dir Nationwide Building Society 1989–92, chief exec LIFFE 1993–98; chm: Medialink International 1999–2003, Design and Artists Copyright Soc 2000–05, Insulation and Machining Services Ltd 2001–07, The Lokahi Fndn 2005–; Gresham Coll prof of commerce (Mercer's Sch Meml) 1999–2002 (memb Cncl 2006–); non-exec dir: The Post Office 1984–95, Girobank plc 1986–89, Ransomes plc 1993–98, Independent Insurance Group plc 1995–2001, The London Clearing House 1996–98, Rolfe and Nolan plc 1999–2003, Norland Managed Services Ltd 1999–2006, Berry Palmer and Lyle Holdings 2000–, SVM Global Fund plc 2004–; chm Euro Ctee of Options and Futures Exchanges (ECOFEX) 1996–98; pres Assoc of Corporate Treasurers 1992–93 (chm 1984–86); govr: The Yehudi Menuhin Sch 1984–2005, Univ of Winchester 2000– (chm 2001–06), Peter Symonds' Coll Winchester 1999–2002; chm Fulham Carnival 1979–81; memb Worshipful Co of Mercers 1965 (Upper Warden 2007); Hon FCT 1994 (FCT 1979); *Books* Businessman's Guide to the Foreign Exchange Market (jtly), Corporate Finance and Treasury Management (founding ed 1984–); *Recreations* music, travel, skiing, gardening; *Clubs* Brooks's; *Style*— Daniel Hodson, Esq; ✉ 21 Maltravers Street, Arundel, West Sussex BN18 9AP (tel 01903 883234, fax 01903 883739, e-mail d.h.hodson@btinternet.com)

HODSON, His Hon Judge (Thomas) David Tattersall; s of Thomas Norman Hodson (d 1987), and Elsie Nuttall Hodson (d 1987); *b* 24 September 1942; *Educ* Sedbergh, Univ of Manchester (LLB); *m* 9 Aug 1969, Patricia Ann, da of Robert Arthur Vint (d 1967); 2 s (Nicholas b 1970, Benjamin b 1979), 1 da (Philippa b 1972); *Career* leader writer The Yorkshire Post 1964–65; called to the Bar Inner Temple 1966 (bencher 2001); in practice Northern Circuit 1966–87 (jr 1968), recorder Crown Court 1983–87, circuit judge (Northern Circuit) 1987–97, sr circuit judge, resident judge Newcastle Crown Court and hon recorder Newcastle upon Tyne 1997–; dep chllr Dio of Newcastle 2003–; memb Parole Bd 1996–97; pres S Lancs Branch Magistrates' Assoc 1994–97, chm Northumbria Area Criminal Justice Strategy Ctee 2000–03; memb Ct Univ of Newcastle upon Tyne 2000–; Hon LLD Univ of Sunderland 2002; *Books* One Week in August: The Kaiser at Lowther Castle 1895 (1995); *Recreations* music, fell walking, family history; *Style*— His Hon Judge Hodson; ✉ c/o The Law Courts, The Quayside, Newcastle upon Tyne NE1 3LA (tel 0191 201 2000)

HODSON, Denys Fraser; CBE (1982); s of Rev Harold Victor Hodson, MC (d 1977), of Glos, and Marguerite Edmée (Madge), *née* Ritchie (d 1996); *b* 23 May 1928; *Educ* Marlborough, Trinity Coll Oxford (MA); *m* 1954, Julie Compton, da of Harold Goodwin (d 1984), of Warks; 1 da (Lucy b 1963), 1 s (Nicholas b 1965); *Career* dir arts and recreation Thamesdown BC 1970–92; dir Arts Research Ltd 1994– (chm 1999–2006); chm: Southern Arts Assoc 1975–81 and 1985–87, Cncl Regnl Arts Assoc 1976–81; dir Oxford Playhouse Co 1974–86, govr Br Film Inst 1976–87 (dep chm 1985–87), memb Arts Cncl GB 1987–94 (vice-chm 1989–94), dir Brewery Arts 1991– (chm 1994–98), vice-pres Voluntary Arts Network (VAN) 1998– (vice-chm 1991–94, chm 1994–98), chm Public Arts Cmmns Agency 1993–2000; chm: Friends of Fairford Church 1995–, Friends of Lydiard Park 2005–; *Recreations* arts, fishing, bird watching; *Style*— Denys Hodson, Esq, CBE; ✉ Manor Farm House, Fairford, Gloucestershire GL7 4AR (tel and fax 01285 712462, e-mail denys.hodson@btinternet.com)

HODSON, Prof Howard Peter; s of Edward Hodson, and late Kathleen Janette Hodson; *b* 18 February 1957; *Educ* Churchill Coll Cambridge (MA, PhD); *m* 1978, Dr Jane Hodson; *Career* engr Perkins Engine Co Ltd 1978–79; Dept of Engrg Univ of Cambridge: res asst Whittle Lab 1982–85, sr asst in res 1985–89, lectr 1989–98, reader in thermofluid engrg 1998–2000, prof of aerothermal technol 2000–; Girton Coll Cambridge: res fell 1984–85, dir of studies 1985–2000, lectr 1985–, professorial fell 2000– (official fell 1985–2000); dir and sec CTC Ltd 1983–2005; CEng 1999, FRAeS 1999, FASME 2002, FREng 2005; *Publications* author of papers published in transactions of: ASME, American Inst of Aeronautics and Astronautics, IMechE; *Recreations* gardening, vehicle restoration; *Style*— Prof Howard Hodson; ✉ Whittle Laboratory, Department of Engineering, University of Cambridge, Madingley Road, Cambridge CB3 0DY (tel 01223 337588, fax 01223 337596, e-mail hph@eng.cam.ac.uk)

HODSON, John; s of late Arthur Hodson, of Stoke-on-Trent, and Olga, *née* Vernon; *b* 19 May 1946; *Educ* Hanley HS Stoke-on-Trent, Worcester Coll Oxford (BA); *m* 1970, Christina, *née* McLeod; 2 da (Sarah b 3 Jan 1972, Lucinda b 7 Oct 1978), 1 s (Jonathan b 13 Feb 1973); *Career* graduate trainee Fin Div Bowater Paper Corp 1967–68, Burroughs Machines 1968–70; Singer & Friedlander: joined 1970, asst dir 1974, dir 1983, head of investments 1985–90, memb Bd Singer & Friedlander Gp 1987–2004, chief exec Singer & Friedlander Hldgs 1990–2004 (dir 1986–2004), chief exec Singer & Friedlander Gp plc 1993–2004, chm Singer & Friedlander Gp plc 2000–03; non-exec dir: SVB Holdings plc (formerly Syndicate Capital Tst) 1994–2000, Associated Nursing Services plc 1994–2002, Miller Fisher Gp plc (formerly Fishers International Gp plc) 1993–2004, Intrinsic Value plc 1999–2004, Domino's Pizza UK and Ireland plc 2005–; other current directorships: Boddington Hill Management Ltd, Prestbury Residual Ltd, Fulham Park Gardens Ltd; other past directorships incl: Carnegie Holding AB (Sweden), Ancomass Ltd, Collins Stewart Ltd, Coventbrook Ltd, Ecom Group Ltd, Gilbert Estates Ltd, Haxted Investment Mgmnt Ltd, Hillgrove Devpts Ltd, Sinjul Investments Ltd, Syndicate Capital Underwriting Ltd; *Recreations* tennis, family; *Style*— John Hodson, Esq

HODSON, Sir Michael Robin Adderley; 6 Bt (I 1787), of Holybrooke House, Wicklow; s of Maj Sir Edmond Adair Hodson, 5 Bt, DSO (d 1972); *b* 5 March 1932; *Educ* Eton; *m* 1, 1963 (m dis 1978), Katrin Alexa, da of late Erwin Bernstiel, of St Andrew's Major, Dinas Powis; 3 da (Tania Elizabeth (Mrs Guy Deacon) b 1965, Alexa Adderley (m Christopher M Chambers, *qv*) b 1966, Jane Katrina b 1970); m 2, 1978, Catherine, da of John Henry Seymour, of London; *Heir* bro, Patrick Hodson; *Career* Capt (ret) Scots Gds; *Style*— Sir Michael Hodson, Bt; ✉ Nantyderry House, Nantyderry, Abergavenny NP7 9DW

HODSON, Phillip I; *Educ* Univ of Oxford; *Partner* Anne Hooper; 1 s (Alexander), 2 step s (Barnaby, Joel); *Career* psychotherapist, broadcaster, lecturer and writer; ed Forum (int jl of human rels) 1972–79; problem page columnist: Psychology Today, SHE Magazine (columnist of the year 1984), Woman's World, Family Circle, TV Quick, Today newspaper, Daily Star, OK Weekly, Woman's Journal; contributing ed Cosmopolitan Magazine 1994–96, regular contrib The Times 2003–; host LBC Radio problem phone-in 1976–91, agony columnist News of the World 1992–94, counsellor BBC Radio 2 1995–99, counsellor Talk Radio 1996–98; numerous appearances on TV incl own shows for TVS, LWT, and as presenter of BBC1's Daytime UK and Going Live!, prodr-presenter of award winning films on counselling skills; author of numerous books on related subjects and also on opera; past chm and tstee Impotence Assoc; fell and head of media relations British Assoc for Counselling and Psychotherapy; past pres Tetbury CC; *Books* Wagner (1984), Cosmopolitan Guide to Love, Sex and Relationships (1997), How to Make Great Love to a Man/Woman (2000), How 'Perfect' is your Partner? (2004); *Recreations* playing cricket, piano, opera; *Clubs* Groucho; *Style*— Phillip Hodson, Esq; ✉ website www.philliphodson.co.uk

HOERNER, John Lee; s of Robert Lee Hoerner (d 1990), and Lulu Alice, *née* Stone, of St Louis, MO; *b* 23 September 1939; *Educ* Univ of Nebraska (BS, BA); *m* 1, 9 Aug 1959 (m dis 1971), Susan Kay, da of Fred W Morgan, of Lincoln, NE; 1 s (John Scott b 30 May 1960), 1 da (Joanne Lynne b 21 Sept 1962); m 2, 16 Feb 1973, Anna Lea, da of Leonard O Thomas, of Kansas City, MO; *Career* Hovland-Swanson Lincoln NE 1959–68, Woolf Brothers Kansas City MO 1968–72, Hahnes NJ 1972–73, pres and ceo First 21st Century Corp McLean VA, Hahnes NJ 1974–81; Associated Dry Goods Corp/May Co: chm and chief exec H & S Pogue Co Cincinnati OH 1981–82, chm and chief exec L S Ayres & Co Indianapolis IN 1982–87; The Burton Gp plc: chm Debenhams 1987–92, chm Harvey Nichols 1988–91, gp chief exec 1992–98; chief exec Arcadia Gp plc (following demerger) 1998–2000; Tesco plc: chief exec clothing 2001–05, ceo Central Europe Clothing 2005–; non-exec dir BAA plc 1998–2004; chm British Fashion Cncl 1997–2000; chm The Dogs' Home Battersea 2002–06 (vice-chm 1995–2002); *Books* Ayres Adages (1983), The Director's Handbook (1991); *Recreations* dogs, riding, flying; *Clubs* The Air Squadron, Groucho; *Style*— John Hoerner, Esq; ✉ Cornwell Glebe, Chipping Norton, Oxfordshire OX7 6TX (tel 01608 658549, fax 01608 658818, e-mail john.hoerner@zoom.co.uk); Tesco Stores Limited, Progress House, The Boulevard, Shire Park, Welwyn Garden City, Hertfordshire AL7 1GB (tel 01707 359407, fax 01707 297603, e-mail john.hoerner@uk.tesco.com)

HOEY, Catharine Letitia (Kate); MP; da of Thomas Hoey, and Letitia Hoey; *b* 21 June 1946; *Educ* Belfast Royal Acad, Ulster Coll of Physical Educn, City of London Coll (BSc); *Career* lectr Southwark Coll 1972–76, sr lectr Kingsway Coll 1976–85, educnl advsr to London Football Clubs 1985–89; memb Hackney Borough Cncl 1978–82, Parly candidate (Lab) Dulwich 1987, MP (Lab) Vauxhall June 1989–, shadow min for Citizens Rights and Equality 1992–93; memb: Select Ctee on Broadcasting, Political Ctee South East CWS 1984–, Select Ctee on Social Security 1994–97; PPS to Rt Hon Frank Field, MP as min of state for Welfare Reform DSS 1997–98, Parly under sec Home Office 1998–99, Parly under-sec of state Dept of Culture, Media and Sport (sport) 1999–2001; author of various articles on sport; *Recreations* watching soccer, keeping fit; *Style*— Kate Hoey, MP; ✉ House of Commons, London SW1A 0AA

HOFFBRAND, Prof (Allan) Victor; s of Philip Hoffbrand (d 1959), and Minnie, *née* Freedman; *b* 14 October 1935; *Educ* Bradford GS, The Queen's Coll Oxford (MA, DM), London Hosp Med Sch (BM BCh); *m* 3 Nov 1963, (Irene) Jill, da of Michael Mellows, of Wembley Park, Middx; 1 da (Caroline b 21 March 1966), 2 s (Philip b 11 May 1967, David b 12 July 1970); *Career* jr hosp doctor London Hosp 1960–62, lectr in haematology Bart's 1966–67, MRC res scholar Tufts Univ Boston 1967–68, lectr and sr lectr in haematology Royal Postgrad Med Sch 1968–74 (registrar and res fell 1962–66), prof of haematology Royal Free Sch of Med 1974–96; hon conslt Royal Free Hosp 1974–; DSc 1987; Hon FRCPEd 1986, FRCP 1976, FRCPath 1980, FMedSci 2000; *Books* Essential Haematology (jtly 1980, 5 edn 2006), Clinics in Haematology (ed Vol 5.3 1976, Vol 15.3 1986, Vol 15.1 2002), Clinical Haematology Illustrated (jtly, 1988), Recent Advances in Haematology (ed, 8 edn 1996), Atlas of Clinical Haematology (jtly, 1988, 3 edn 2000), Postgraduate Haematology (jt ed, 5 edn 2005), Haematology at a Glance (jtly, 2000, 2 edn 2005); also author of numerous scientific papers; *Recreations* gardening, bridge, antiques, music; *Style*— Prof Victor Hoffbrand; ✉ 12 Wedderburn Road, London NW3 5QG (tel 020 7435 9413); Department of Haematology, Royal Free Hospital, London NW3 2QG (tel 020 7435 1547, fax 020 7431 4537)

HOFFMAN, Anthony Edward; s of late Geoffrey and late Jean Hoffman; *b* 21 February 1937; *Educ* City of London Sch; *Career* admitted slr 1960; slr advocate (Higher Courts Civil); sole practitioner 1960–62, former sr ptnr and head of litigation Hamlin Slowe, conslt slr Edwin Coe Slrs; currently dep costs judge, dep Chancery master and dep Queen's Bench master Supreme Court, dep dist judge Princ Registry Family Div, dep dist judge County Court; chm Friends of St Pancras Housing 1995–2001, vice-chm St Pancras Properties Ltd 1995–2001, vice-chm Shadow Bd Merlin Housing Soc 2005–; *Books* Civil Costs Cases: Taxation Handbook (1997, 3 edn 2003); *Recreations* game shooting, hill walking, theatre, arts, architecture; *Clubs* Circolo Unione Venezia, Garrick; *Style*— Anthony E Hoffman, Esq

HOFFMAN, Gary Andrew; s of Dennis Hoffman, of Coventry, Warks, and Joyce, *née* Watkins; *Educ* Bablake Sch Coventry, Queens' Coll Cambridge (BA), Henley Mgmnt Coll; *m* 2003, Nicola; 1 s (Nathan b 22 March 2003); *Career* Barclays Bank plc: joined 1982, chief exec UK retail banking 1998, md mktg and distribution 1999–2001, chief exec Barclaycard 2001–06, gp vice-chm 2006–; non-exec dir Trinity Mirror plc 2005–; *Recreations* Coventry City FC, golf; *Clubs* Coventry Sch Former Pupils Assoc; *Style*— Gary Hoffman, Esq; ✉ Barclays Bank plc, 54 Lombard Street, London EC3P 2AH

HOFFMAN, George Henry; s of George Hoffman (d 1993), and Anna Cecilia, *née* Hojnowski (d 2004); *b* 30 October 1939; *Educ* Cornell Univ (BA), Columbia Univ (MA); *m* 1961 (m dis 1998); 2 da (Erika b 1962, Bridgit b 1965), 1 s (Philip b 1968); *Career* banker 1962–88, chm and chief exec GHH Mgmnt Conslts 1988–; memb Ad Hoc Cncl Euro Govt Business Relations Cncl 1979–; former dir American C of C UK; *Recreations* tennis, scuba diving, reading; *Clubs* Gravetye; *Style*— George Hoffman; ✉ c/o GHH Management Consultants, PO Box 71, Guildford, Surrey GU3 3XY (tel 01483 306820, e-mail ghhoffman@gmail.com, website www.georgehhoffman.com)

HOFFMAN, Mark; s of Dr Mark Hoffman (d 1975), of USA; *b* 14 December 1938; *Educ* Harvard Univ (AB), Trinity Coll Cambridge (MA), Harvard Business Sch (MBA); *m* 1968, Mary Jo, da of John C Pyles, of Washington DC, USA; 3 s (Nicholas b 1969, John b 1972, James b 1978); *Career* E African Common Services Orgn/MIT (Africa/USA) 1964–66, World Banks International Finance Corp (Washington) 1966–68, Olympic Investment Gp (Paris) 1968–69; dir: Hambros Bank (UK) 1970–74, Millipore Corp (USA) 1975–, George Weston Ltd (Canada) 1975– (fin dir 1975–80, pres Weston Resources 1980–82), Guinness Peat Group plc (UK) 1982–84 (gp md 1982–83), LAC Minerals (Canada) 1984–86, Guinness Flight Global Asset Management Ltd (UK) 1989–97, Advent International Inc (Boston) 1989–; chm: International Financial Markets Trading Ltd (UK) 1984–93, Cambridge Research Group Ltd 1990–, Guinness Flight Venture Capital Trust plc 1997–, Hermes Focus Asset Management Ltd 1998–2001 (dir 2002–); int dir Harvard Alumni Assoc 1989–92, vice-pres United World Colls Int and Exec Bds 1999– (chm 1993–99); chm Oxford and Cambridge Rowing Fndn 1990–94; *Clubs* Boodle's, Leander (chm 1989–93), Oxford and Cambridge, Hawks' (Cambridge), Guards Polo, Toronto, Harvard (UK pres 1988–93); *Style*— Mark Hoffman, Esq; ✉ 21 Campden Hill Square, London W8 7JY; Cambridge Research Group Ltd, Salisbury House, Station Road, Cambridge CB1 2LA

HOFFMAN, Maxine; da of Philip Porter (d 2002), and Beatrice, *née* Sims; *b* 5 January 1951, London; *m* 9 Jan 1972, Anthony Hoffman; 1 s (Nick b 17 Sept 1976), 1 da (Zoë b 18 Dec 1979); *Career* with Citizens Advice Bureau 1983–87, with J M Associates 1992–94, agent London Management 1994–2002, agent Curtis Brown Gp 2002–; *Recreations* theatre, cinema, reading; *Style*— Mrs Maxine Hoffman; ✉ Curtis Brown Group Ltd, Haymarket House, 28–29 Haymarket, London SW1Y 4SP (tel 020 7393 4470, fax 020 7393 4401, e-mail hoffman@curtisbrown.co.uk)

HOFFMAN, Tom; s of Dirk Hoffman (d 1986), of Cambridge, and Marie-Luise, *née* Leyser (d 1999); *b* 9 August 1945; *Educ* The Leys Sch Cambridge, Univ of Exeter (LLB); *m* June 1971, Verena; 1 s (Alexander b 1975); *Career* chartered accountant Spicer & Pegler 1963–70, Arthur Andersen 1970–71, Williams & Glyn's Bank 1971–76, Hill Samuel & Co 1976–78, dir of capital markets Lloyds Bank International 1978–84, dep md Fuji International Finance 1984–89, head of corporate banking in UK Algemene Bank Nederland NV 1989–91, UK gen mangr Banco Espirito Santo 1991–2003, dir Espirito Santo plc 1999–2005; dir Tower Bridge Square Management 1991–; UK advsr: Bd Banco Int do Funchal, Bd Banif Investment Bank 2004–; memb Advsy Bd London Festival Orch 1996– (chm 2004–), memb Advsy Bd The Sixteen Choir and Orch 2000– (chm 2004–), tstee Maryport Heritage Tst Cumbria 1990–97; tstee City Arts Tst/City of London Festival 2003–, tstee and hon treas Portuguese Arts Tst 1993–2001; memb Ct of Assts Corp of the Sons of the Clergy 1996–, memb Mgmnt Ctee of Friends of the Clergy Corp 2005–; memb Ct City Univ 2001–06; Univ of Exeter: memb Audit Ctee 1999–2005 (chm 2003–05), memb Cncl 2003–06; govr: City of London Sch for Girls 2002– (chm 2003–06), Guildhall Sch of Music and Drama 2003– (dep chm 2007–), Christ's Hospital 2004– (memb Cncl 2004–, chm Finance Ctee 2006–), Birkbeck Coll Univ of London 2004– (memb Finance and Investment Ctees 2005–), King's Coll Hospital 2004– (memb Research and Devpt Ctee 2005–); memb Cncl UK-Portuguese C of C 1993–2003 (chm 1998–2001); memb Corp of London: Ct of Common Cncl 2002–, Community Servs Ctee 2002–04, Markets Ctee 2002–04, Planning and Transportation Ctee 2002–, City Lands and Bridge House Estates Ctee 2004–06, Port Health and Environmental Servs Ctee 2004–, Livery Ctee 2005–, Gresham Ctee 2005–, Finance Ctee 2006–, Libraries, Archives and Guildhall Art Gallery Ctee 2005–; hon treas: Ward of Cordwainer Club London 1985– (chm 1993–94), Vintry and Dowgate Wards Club (chm 2001–02); memb Ct Hon Irish Soc 2004–; memb Guildhall Historical Assoc; Worshipful Co of Tylers and Bricklayers 1979– (Master 2006–07); memb Royal Soc for Asian Affrs 1989–; fell Royal Cwlth Soc 1964, FCA 1971, FRSA 1990; *Publications* various articles in banking, finance and accountancy journals, and on history of guilds; *Recreations* gardening, music, guild history, collecting books on rowing; *Clubs* Leander, City Livery, Royal Cwlth; *Style*— Tom Hoffman; ✉ Old Curteis, Biddenden, Kent TN27 8JN; 72 Gainsford Street, Tower Bridge Square, London SE1 2NB

HOFFMANN, Baron (Life Peer UK 1995), of Chedworth in the County of Gloucestershire; Sir Leonard Hoffmann; kt (1985), PC (1992); s of B W Hoffmann, of South Africa; *b* 8 May 1934; *Educ* South African Coll Sch Cape Town, Univ of Cape Town (BA), The Queen's Coll Oxford (Vinerian Law scholar, MA, BCL); *m* 1957, Gillian Lorna, *née* Sterner; 2 da; *Career* advocate Supreme Court of South Africa 1958–60, called to the Bar Gray's Inn 1964 (bencher 1984), QC 1977, judge Courts of Appeal Jersey and Guernsey 1980–85, judge of the High Court of Justice (Chancery Div) 1988–92, a Lord Justice of Appeal 1992–95, a Lord of Appeal in Ordinary 1995–; Hon DCL City Univ 1992, hon fell The Queen's Coll Oxford 1992; *Style*— The Rt Hon Lord Hoffmann, PC; ✉ House of Lords, London SW1A 0PW

HOFMEYR, Stephen Murray; QC (2000); s of late Jan Murray Hofmeyr, of Cape Town, and Stella Mary, *née* Mills; *b* 10 February 1956; *Educ* Diocesan Coll Rondebosch, Univ of Cape Town (BCom, LLB), UC Oxford (MA); *m* 28 June 1980, Audrey Frances, da of late James Murray Cannan, of Cape Town; 3 c (Timothy, Paul, Rebecca (triplets) b 6 July 1986); *Career* called to the Bar Gray's Inn 1982, recorder 2005; *Recreations* photography, bird watching; *Clubs* Vincent's (Oxford); *Style*— Stephen Hofmeyr, Esq, QC; ✉ Acre Holt, One Tree Hill Road, Guildford GU4 8PJ; 7 King's Bench Walk, Temple, London EC4Y 7DS (tel 020 910 8300, fax 020 910 8400, e-mail shofmeyr@7kbw.co.uk)

HOGAN, Desmond; s of William Hogan (d 1979), of Ballinasloe, and Christina, *née* Connolly (d 1999); *b* 10 December 1950; *Educ* Garbally Coll Ballinasloe, UC Dublin (BA, MA); *Career* author; hon chair Dept of English Univ of Alabama 1989; *Awards* Hennessy Award 1971, Rooney Prize 1977, John Llewelyn Rhys Meml Prize 1981, Irish Post Award 1985, DAAD Award Deutsch Acad 1991; *Work incl* Jimmy (radio play) 1978, The Mourning Thief (TV play) 1984, Through Other Eyes (TV documentary) 1987; *Publications* incl: The Ikon Maker (1976), The Diamonds at the Bottom of the Sea (stories, 1979), The Leaves on Grey (1980), Children of Lir (stories, 1981), Stories (1982), A Curious Street (1984), A New Shirt (1986), Lebanon Lodge (stories, 1988), A Link with the River (collected stories, 1989), The Edge of the City (a scrap-book 1976–91, 1993), A Farewell to Prague (1995), Lark's Eggs (new and selected stories, 2005); *Style*— Desmond Hogan, Esq

HOGAN, Prof Eileen Mary; da of Thomas Matthew Hogan (d 1996), and Marjorie Coyle (d 1982); *b* 1 March 1946; *Educ* Streatham Hill and Clapham HS, Camberwell Sch of Arts and Crafts, Royal Acad Schs, Br Sch of Archaeology Athens, RCA (BA, MA); *m* (m dis) Kenneth Ersser; *Career* artist; princ lectr and dir Camberwell Press 1985, dean Sch of Applied and Graphic Arts 1989–98; represented by The Fine Art Soc 1979; numerous work in public collections; *Solo Exhibitions* incl: Br Cncl Athens 1971 and 1983, New Grafton Gallery 1972, RCA 1974 and 1977, The Fine Art Soc London 1980, 1982, 1984, 1985, 1986, 1988, 1992, 1997, 2000 and 2006, The Imperial War Museum 1984, Bankside Gallery 1999; *Commissions* incl: Women at Work in the Royal Navy (for Artistic Records Ctee of Imperial War Museum) 1983–84, The Queen presenting Colours to the Portsmouth Fleet (for HMS Nelson) 1986, stamps for Royal Mail 1989, 1990, 1993 and 2001; *Publications* A Selection of Poems by C P Cavafy (1985), On Common Ground (1987), Anaskaphes (1989), All Over the Place (1993), Under the Influence (1997), A Day Out For Mehmet Erbil by Louis de Bernieres (1999), A Green Place (1999), Early Japanese Stories by Kazuo Ishiguro (2000), Murder in Triplicate by PD James (2001), Three Easy Pieces by Peter Carey; *Clubs* Chelsea Arts, Double Crown; *Style*— Prof Eileen Hogan; ✉ 13 Wythburn Place, London W1H 7BU

HOGAN, James; s of Reg Hogan, of Mornington, Victoria, Aust, and Lorna, *née* Thomson (d 1988); *b* 28 November 1956, Melbourne, Aust; *Educ* Ivanhoe GS Victoria Aust; *m* 28 Nov 1981, Heather, *née* Debney; 2 s (Mark b 24 March 1985, Andrew b 27 Nov 1987), 1 da (Nicole b 21 April 1990); *Career* formerly: vice-pres mktg/sales Europe Hertz Corp, worldwide sales dir Forte Hotels Ltd, chief operating offr bmi British Midland; pres and

H

chief exec Gulf Air 2002–; non-exec dir Gallaher Ltd, vice-chm Bahrain Hotels Corp; fell Aust Mktg Inst; *Clubs* Melbourne CC, Sydney CC; *Style*— James Hogan, Esq; ✉ Gulf Air, PO Box 138, Kingdom of Bahrain (tel 00973 17 338888, fax 00973 17 335568)

HOGAN, James V J; s of Thomas Joseph Hogan, and Bridget, née Lemon; *b* 12 September 1951; *Educ* Lancaster Univ (BA), St Edmund Hall Oxford (MLitt); *m* Jane Eveline, née Kinnock; 1 da (Cassandra Jane Eveline b 1983), 1 s (Alexander James William b 1987); *Career* BBC TV News and Current Affrs 1978–91: asst prodr/researcher Nationwide, Westminster, and Tonight 1978–80, prodr Newsweek, The Pursuit of Power, and 20th Century Remembered 1980–84, sr prodr Panorama and Newsnight 1984–88, ed This Week Next Week 1987–88, ed BBC News Event Unit (exec prodr of Gen Election progs, Party Political Confs and major current affrs documentaries on domestic and foreign topics) 1988–90, ed BBC Question Time 1990–91, md subsid of Zenith Prodns 1992–94, dir subsid of SelecTV plc 1994–96, ptnr Brunswick Group Ltd 1996–; memb Cncl Britain in Europe; Robert McKenzie fell LSE 1993–94, memb Advsy Bd Oxford Business Sch; MInstD, MIPR; memb: RTS, BAFTA, Media Soc Cncl, Br in Europe; fell LSE; *Publications* BBC Review of the Year (ed, 1990 and 1991), From Demigods to Democrats? the Television Revolution 1976–96 (1997), LSE working papers; *Recreations* writing, classical music, opera, food, fine wine, post-war English abstract art, horse racing, sport; *Clubs* Savile, Mosimann's; *Style*— James Hogan, Esq; ✉ Brunswick Group Ltd, 16 Lincoln's Inn Fields, London WC2A 3ED (tel 020 7404 5959, fax 020 7831 2823)

HOGAN, John Anthony; s of John and Margaret Hogan; *b* 14 April 1953; *Educ* KCL (BA); *m* 1977, Jane, da of Frederick J Ford; 2 da (Jennifer b 23 March 1980, Katherine b 7 June 1982), 1 s (James b 19 Feb 1985); *Career* exploration geologist Elf UK, BNOC and Shell 1974–81, regnl explorationist LASMO plc 1981–84, sr vice-pres LASMO Energy Corp USA 1984–89, md LASMO North Sea plc 1989–93, chief operating offr LASMO plc 1993–2001, chm Acteon Gp 2001–, dir Caledonia Oil and Gas 2003–, chief exec Argos Resources 2005–, dir Noreco AS 2005–; *Recreations* walking, reading, clay pigeon shooting, rugby; *Style*— John Hogan, Esq

HOGAN, William Patrick (Bill); s of William Daniel Hogan (d 1983), of Laindon, Essex, and Lilian, *née* Morley (d 2003); *b* 7 September 1943; *Educ* Christ's Hosp; *m* 20 March 1971, Audrey Margaret, da of Arthur Willber; 2 c (Neil b 28 May 1975, Natalie b 15 Dec 1982); *Career* qualified chartered accountant 1966, ptnr Baker Tilly CAs; int tax specialist; writer and lectr; FCA 1976 (ACA 1966); *Recreations* travel, biographies, theatre, golf; *Clubs* Christ's Hosp, Stock Brook Manor; *Style*— Bill Hogan, Esq; ✉ Baker Tilly, 2 Bloomsbury Street, London WC1B 3ST (tel 020 7413 5100, fax 020 7413 5101)

HOGAN-HOWE, Bernard; QPM (2004); Bernard Howe (d 2000), and Cecilia Teresa, *née* Hogan; *b* 25 October 1957; *Educ* Sheffield Poly (HNC), Merton Coll Oxford (MA), Fitzwilliam Coll Cambridge (Dip), Univ of Sheffield (MBA); *m* Marion White; *Career* Supt S Yorks Police 1994–97, Asst Chief Constable Mersyside Police 1997–2001, Asst Cmmr Met Police 2001–04, Chief Constable Merseyside Police 2004–; *Recreations* horse riding, opera, Sheffield Wednesday FC, playing football; *Style*— Bernard Hogan-Howe, Esq, QPM; ✉ Merseyside Police Headquarters, PO Box 59, Liverpool L69 1JD (tel 0151 777 8000, fax 0151 777 8020, e-mail chief@merseyside.police.uk)

HOGARTH, Adrian John; s of Prof Cyril Alfred Hogarth (d 2006), of Gerrards Cross, Bucks, and Audrey, *née* Jones; *b* 7 July 1960; *Educ* St Paul's, Magdalene Coll Cambridge (MA, LLM), Inns of Court Sch of Law; *m* 20 July 1996, Archana, da of K P Singh; *Career* called to the Bar Inner Temple 1983; joined Office of the Parly Counsel 1985, on secondment to Law Cmmn 1992–94, currently Parly counsel; memb Hon Soc of the Inner Temple; FRSA; *Recreations* travel, cricket, tennis; *Style*— Adrian Hogarth, Esq; ✉ Office of the Parliamentary Counsel, 36 Whitehall, London SW1A 2AY (tel 020 7210 6619)

HOGARTH, Peter Laurence; s of Michael Hogarth, of Swindon, and Joyce, *née* Ponder; *b* 10 July 1949; *Educ* Haileybury; *m* 15 July 1972, Margaret Rosemary, da of Alexander Sidney Alison; 1 s (Ian b 30 Jan 1982), 2 da (Rosemary b 6 June 1983, Juliet b 25 April 1988); *Career* CA 1972; KPMG 1967–88, Société Générale Strauss Turnbull Securities 1988–90, exec dir London Stock Exchange 1991–92, fndr and dir The Change Partnership Ltd 1994–2001, Whitehead Mann Change Partnership 2001–05, chm Praesta Partners LLP, dir JCA Gp 2006–; memb Cncl Toynbee Hall 1995–2000; govr James Allen Girls' Sch 1996–2006; Master Worshipful Co Joiners and Ceilers 1995–96; MSI 1992, FRSA 1992; *Recreations* golf, bridge, chess, cooking; *Clubs* MCC, Reform; *Style*— Peter Hogarth, Esq; ✉ 6 Frank Dixon Way, Dulwich, London SE21 7BB (tel 020 8693 8881, e-mail peterhogarth@jcagroup.net)

HOGBEN, Dr Neil; s of Eric O'Neill Hogben (d 1984), and Alma, *née* Ault (d 1986); *b* 23 March 1923; *Educ* St Paul's, Univ of Durham (1851 exhbn postgrad res scholarship in naval architecture, BSc, PhD); *m* 1958, Edith Cornelia, da of Wilhelm Leister (d 1971); 2 da (Anita Ruth b 1959, Kim Frances b 1960), 1 s (Giles Dominic b 1971); *Career* history scholarship Magdalene Coll Cambridge (declined due to War Serv) 1941; served WWII: gunner RA 1942–47, 72 Anti Tank Regt N Africa, Italy and Austria; mgmnt trainee J L Thompson Shipbuilders 1947–51, tech asst Rotol Propeller Co 1951–52; National Physical Laboratory (Ship Div merged to National Maritime Inst 1976 became NMI Ltd 1982): princ scientific offr 1956, sr princ scientific offr (individual merit) 1967, dep chief scientific offr (individual merit) 1979, sr res advsr to NMI Ltd 1983–85; pt/t conslt BMT (British Maritime Technology) Fluid Mechanics Ltd 1985–; chm: Environmental Conditions Ctee Int Ship Structures Congress 1964–70 and 1973–79, Working Gp on Surface Waves for Engrg Ctee on Oceanic Resources 1972–76; RINA: Silver Medal (Experience in Computing Wave Loads on Large Bodies) 1974, Bronze Medal (Wave Climate Synthesis Worldwide) 1984, Bronze Medal (Increases in Wave Heights over the N Atlantic) 1996; ICE George Stephenson Medal (Estimation of Fluid Loading on Offshore Structures) 1977, MOD Award for Oceanography 1989 (from Soc for Underwater Technol); assoc memb NE Coast Instn of Engrs and Shipbuilders 1956; FRINA 1967, FREng 1988; *Books* Ocean Wave Statistics (jtly, 1967), Global Wave Statistics (jtly, 1986); contrib to: Advances in Hydroscience Vol 4 (1967), The Sea Vol 9 pt A (1990), Encyclopaedia of Fluid Mechanics Vol 10 (1990); *Recreations* music (piano playing of a sort); *Style*— Dr Neil Hogben, FREng; ✉ 60 Foley Road, Claygate, Surrey KT10 0ND (tel 01372 462966); BMT (British Maritime Technology) Fluid Mechanics Ltd, Orlando House, 1 Waldegrave Road, Teddington, Middlesex TW11 8LZ

HOGG, Sir Christopher; kt (1985); *b* 2 August 1936; *Educ* Marlborough, Trinity Coll Oxford (MA), Harvard Univ (MBA); *m* (m dis); 2 da; *Career* Nat Serv 1955–57; IMEDE Business Sch Lausanne 1962, Philip Hill Higginson Erlangers Ltd (now Hill Samuel & Co Ltd) 1963–66, Industrial Reorganisation Corporation 1966–68; Courtaulds plc: joined 1968, dir 1973–, dep chm 1978, chief exec and chm designate 1979, chm and chief exec 1980–91, non-exec chm until July 1996; non-exec chm: Reuters Gp plc 1985–2004 (non-exec dir 1984), Courtaulds Textiles plc 1990–95, Allied Domecq plc 1996–2002 (dep chm 1995–96), GlaxoSmithKline plc 2002–04 (memb Bd: Smithkline Beecham 1993–2000, GlaxoSmithKline 2000–04); memb International Cncl J P Morgan 1988–2003; non-exec dir Bank of England 1992–96, chm Financial Reporting Cncl 2006–; memb: Bd of Tstees Ford Fndn 1987–99, Dept of Industry's Industrial Advsy Bd 1976–80; chm Royal National Theatre 1995–; Centenary medal Soc Chem Indust 1989, Alumni Achievement award Harvard Business Sch 1989, Gold medal BIM 1986; Hon DSc Cranfield Inst of Technol 1986, Hon DSc Aston Univ 1988; hon fell Trinity Coll Oxford 1982; Hon FCSD, Hon FCGI; *Recreations* theatre, reading, skiing, walking; *Style*— Sir Christopher Hogg

HOGG, Douglas; *see:* Hailsham, 3 Viscount

HOGG, James Dalby; s of Sir James Cecil Hogg, KCVO (d 1973), of London, and Lady Hogg (d 2003); *b* 9 July 1937; *Educ* Eton; *m* 19 Aug 1964, Joan, da of Richard Blackledge; 2 s (James b 1965, Samuel b 1966); *Career* reporter: Bolton Evening News 1960–64, Morning Telegraph Sheffield 1964–65, BBC Manchester 1965–66, BBC Leeds 1967–69, 24 Hours BBC London 1970–72, Nationwide 1972–83, Newsnight 1983–88; writer and presenter of numerous documentaries; *Books* Lord Emsworth's Annotated Whiffle (1991), The Queen Mother Remembered (2002); *Recreations* keeping animals, reading, jazz, trying to play the piano; *Clubs* Drones (NY); *Style*— James Hogg, Esq; ✉ Noon's Folly Cottage, Melbourn, Cambridgeshire SG8 7NG (tel 01763 241844, e-mail jmshogg@aol.com); BBC TV, Television Centre, London W12 7RJ (tel 020 8743 8000)

HOGG, Hon Mrs Justice; Dame Mary Claire; DBE (1995); eld da of Baron Hailsham of St Marylebone, KG, CH, PC (d 2001), and Mary Evelyn, *née* Martin (d 1978); *b* 15 January 1947; *Educ* St Paul's Girls' Sch; *m* 11 Sept 1987, Eric Koops, *qv*, s of late Lendeert Koops; 1 da (Katharine Mary b 17 March 1989), 1 s (William Quintin Eric b 21 Dec 1991); *Career* called to the Bar: Lincoln's Inn 1968 (bencher 1995), NI 1993; QC 1989, recorder of the Crown Court 1990–95 (asst recorder 1986–90), judge of the High Court of Justice (Family Div) 1995–; govr Univ of Westminster 1992– (govr Poly of Central London 1982–92), tstee The Harrison Homes 1983–; memb Cncl Church of England's Children's Soc 1990–95; Hon LLD Univ of Westminster 1995; Freeman City of London 1981; FRSA; *Style*— The Hon Mrs Justice Hogg, DBE; ✉ c/o Royal Courts of Justice, Strand, London WC2A 2LL

HOGG, Baroness (Life Peer UK 1995), of Kettlethorpe in the County of Lincolnshire; Sarah Elizabeth Mary Hogg; yr da of Baron Boyd-Carpenter, PC, DL (Life Peer) (d 1998); *b* 14 May 1946, 1946; *Educ* St Mary's Convent Ascot, Lady Margaret Hall Oxford; *m* 6 June 1968, Rt Hon Douglas Hogg, QC, MP, 3 Viscount Hailsham, *qv*; 1 s, 1 da; *Career* Economist Newspaper 1968–81; economics ed: Sunday Times 1981–82, The Times 1983–86; presenter and economics ed Channel 4 News 1982–83, dir London Broadcasting Co 1985–90, govr Centre for Economic Policy Research 1985–90, asst ed, business and fin ed The Independent 1986–89, dir National Theatre 1987–90, economics ed The Daily Telegraph and The Sunday Telegraph 1989–90, head of Policy Unit No 10 Downing St with rank of second permanent sec 1990–95; govr of the BBC 2000–04; chm: London Economics 1997–99, Foreign and Colonial Small Companies 1997–2002 (dir 1995–2002), Frontier Economics 1999–, 3i Group 2002–; non-exec dir: GKN plc 1996–2006 (dep chm and sr ind dir 2003–06), National Provident Institution 1996–99, P&O 1999–2000, P&O Princess 2000–03, Carnival Corp and Carnival plc 2003–, BG Gp 2005–; memb: Cncl Hansard Soc 1995–98, House of Lords Select Ctee on Sci and Technol 1996–99, Inst of Fiscal Studies 1996–2005, Select Ctee on Monetary Policy 2000–03, Financial Reporting Cncl 2005–, Cncl London Business Sch 2005–; Martin Curie Portfolio Tst 1999–2002; Wincott Fndn Fin Journalist of the Year 1985; fell Eton Coll 1996–, hon fell LMH Oxford; Hon MA Open Univ 1987, Hon DLitt Loughborough Univ 1992, Hon DL Univ of Lincoln 2001, Hon DSc City Univ 2002; *Books* Too Close to Call (with Jonathan Hill, 1995); *Style*— The Baroness Hogg; ✉ House of Lords, London SW1A 0PW

HOGG OF CUMBERNAULD, Baron (Life Peer UK 1997), of Cumbernauld in North Lanarkshire; Norman Hogg; *b* 12 March 1938; *Educ* Ruthrieston Secdy Sch; *m* 1964, Elizabeth McCall Christie; *Career* dist offr Nat and Local Govt Offrs Assoc 1967–79, memb Tport Users' Consultative Ctee for Scotland 1977–79; non-exec dir Kelvin Central Buses Ltd 1990–96; MP (Lab): E Dunbartonshire 1979–83, Cumbernauld and Kilsyth 1983–97; memb Select Ctee: Scottish Affrs 1979–82, Public Accounts 1991–92; Scottish Lab whip 1982–83, Lab dep chief whip 1983–87; oppn front bench spokesman for Scottish Affrs 1987–88, memb Chairman's Panel 1989–97; memb Delegated Powers and Regulatory Reform Ctee 1999–2002; dep speaker House of Lords 2002–04; patron The Scottish Centre for Children with Motor Impairments 1997–; hon pres YMCA Scotland 1998–2005; hon vice-pres Cncl of Christians and Jews 1998–; Lord High Cmmr to the 1998 and 1999 Gen Assembly of the Church of Scotland; chm Bus Appeals Body 2000–; LLD Univ of Aberdeen 1999; FSA Scot 2002; *Style*— The Rt Hon Lord Hogg of Cumbernauld; ✉ House of Lords, London SW1A 0PW (tel 020 7219 4214, e-mail hoggnorman@aol.com)

HOGGARD, Matthew James; MBE (2006); *b* 31 December 1976, Leeds; *Educ* Pudsey Grangefield Sch Leeds; *m* Sarah; *Career* cricketer (bowler); Yorkshire CCC 1996– (more than 100 first class appearances); England: 64 test caps, 26 one day appearances, test debut v West Indies Lord's 2000, one day debut v Zimbabwe 2001, best bowling 7–61 v SA Johannesburg 2005 (12–205 in the match), memb Ashes-winning team 2005; ranked 4th best Test match bowler in the world 2006; NBC Denis Compton Award 1998, Wisden Cricketer of the Year 2006; *Style*— Mr Matthew Hoggard, MBE; ✉ c/o Jim Souter, 4 Sports, 1 Furzeground Way, Stockley Park UB11 1BD (tel 07769906295)

HOGGART, (Herbert) Richard; s of Tom Longfellow Hoggart, and Adeline Hoggart; *b* 24 September 1918; *Educ* schs in Leeds, Univ of Leeds (MA, LittD); *m* 1942, Mary Holt France; 2 s (one of whom, Simon Hoggart, *qv*), 1 da; *Career* served WWII RA; staff tutor and sr staff tutor UC Hull 1946–59, sr lectr in English Univ of Leicester 1959–62, prof of English Univ of Birmingham 1962–73 (dir Centre for Contemporary Cultural Studies 1964–73), asst DG UNESCO 1970–75, visiting fell Inst of Devpt Studies Univ of Sussex 1975, warden Goldsmiths Coll London 1976–84; visiting prof Rochester Univ (NY) 1956–57; hon prof UEA 1984–, Reith lectr 1971; memb: British Cncl Br Books Overseas Ctee 1959–64, BBC Gen Advsy Cncl 1959–60 and 1964–, Pilkington Ctee on Broadcasting 1960–62, Culture Advsr Ctee of UK Nat Cmmn for UNESCO, Arts Cncl 1976–81 (chm Drama Panel 1977–80, vice-chm 1980–81), Editorial Bd New Univs Quarterly, Cncl Soc of Authors 1991–; chm: Advsy Cncl for Adult and Continuing Educn 1977–83, Euro Museum of the Year Award Ctee 1977–95, Statesman and Nation Publishing Co 1978–81 (publishers New Statesman), Nat Broadcasting Res Unit 1981–91, The Book Trust 1995–; govr Royal Shakespeare Theatre until 1988; pres Br Assoc Former UN Civil Servants 1979–86; Liveryman Worshipful Co of Goldsmiths; Hon Dès Lettres Univ of Bordeaux 1975, Hon DUniv Surrey 1981, Hon LLD Cncl for Nat Academic Awards 1982, Hon LLD York Univ Toronto, Hon DLitt: Open Univ 1973, Univ of Leicester, Univ of Hull, Leeds Metropolitan Univ 1995, Keele Univ 1995, Univ of Westminster 1997, Univ of Sheffield 1999, London Met Univ 2003; Hon DUniv UEA 1986, Hon Dès Lettres Paris 1987, Hon DEd Univ of East London 1998, Hon DLit Univ of London 2000; hon fell Sheffield Poly 1983, hon fell Goldsmiths Coll 1985; FRSL 2003; *Books* The Uses of Literacy (1957), various works on W H Auden, Speaking to Each Other (1970), Only Connect (1972), An Idea and Its Servants (1978), An English Temper (1982), An Idea of Europe (with Douglas Johnson, 1987), A Local Habitation (1988), A Sort of Clowning (1990), An Imagined Life (1992), Townscape with Figures (1994), The Way We Live Now (1995), First and Last Things (1999), Between Two Worlds (2001), Everyday Language and Everyday Life (2003), Mass Media in a Mass Society: Myth and Reality (2004), Promises to Keep (2005); *Style*— Richard Hoggart, Esq

HOGGART, Simon David; s of (Herbert) Richard Hoggart, *qv*, of Norwich, Norfolk, and Mary Holt, *née* France; *b* 26 May 1946; *Educ* Hymers Coll Hull, Wyggeston GS Leicester, King's Coll Cambridge (MA); *m* 9 July 1983, Alyson Clare, da of Cdr Donald Louis Corner, RN, of Rusper, W Sussex; 1 da (Amy b 1986), 1 s (Richard b 1988); *Career* political corr: The Guardian 1973–81 (reporter 1968–71, NI corr 1971–73), Punch 1979–85; The Observer: reporter 1981–85, US corr 1985–89, columnist 1989–93, political ed 1992–93; Parly corr The Guardian 1993–, chm The News Quiz (BBC Radio 4) 1996–2006, TV critic The Spectator 1996–, wine corr The Spectator 2001–; *Books* incl: The Pact (with

Alistair Michie, 1978), Michael Foot: A Portrait (with David Leigh, 1981), On The House (1981), Back On The House (1982), House of Ill Fame (1985), House of Cards (ed, 1988), America - A User's Guide (1990), House of Correction (1994), Bizarre Beliefs (with Mike Hutchinson, 1995), Live Briefs (with Steve Bell, 1996), Playing to the Gallery (2002), Punch Lines (2003), The Cat That Could Open the Fridge (2004), The Hamster that Loved Puccini (2005), Don't Tell Mum: Hair-Raising Messages Home from Gap-Year Travellers (jtly, 2006), The Hand of History (2007); *Recreations* reading, writing, travel; *Style—* Simon Hoggart, Esq; ✉ The Guardian, 119 Farringdon Road, London EC1R 3ER (tel 020 7278 2332, e-mail simon.hoggart@guardian.co.uk)

HOGGETT, Brenda Marjorie; *see:* Hale of Richmond, Baroness

HOGGETT, Dr (Anthony) John Christopher; QC (1986); s of Christopher Hoggett (d 1989), and Annie Marie, *née* Barker (d 1991); *b* 20 August 1940; *Educ* Leeds GS, Hymers Coll Hull, Clare Coll Cambridge (scholar, MA, LLB), Univ of Manchester (PhD); *m* 1968 (m dis 1992), Brenda Marjorie (Baroness Hale of Richmond, DBE, PC (Life Peer)), *qv*, da of Cecil Frederick Hale (d 1958); 1 da (Julia Anne b 1973); *Career* lectr in law Univ of Manchester 1963–69, res fell Univ of Michigan 1965–66; called to the Bar 1969; head of chambers 1985–96, recorder of the Crown Court 1988–; formerly dir European Youth Parliament Ltd; memb Advsy Cncl Rural Buildings Preservation Tst (tstee 2000–02); former memb: DOE's Final Selection Bd for Planning Insprs, Editorial Bd Environmental Law Reports; *Recreations* swimming; *Style—* Dr John Hoggett, QC

HOGWOOD, Christopher Jarvis Haley; CBE (1989); s of Haley Evelyn Hogwood (d 1982), of Saffron Walden, Essex, and Marion Constance, *née* Higgott; *b* 10 September 1941; *Educ* Nottingham HS, Skinners' Sch Tunbridge Wells, Univ of Cambridge (MA), Charles Univ Prague; *Career* harpsichordist, conductor, musicologist; fndr memb Early Music Consort of London 1965–76, fndr dir The Acad of Ancient Music 1973–2006 (emeritus dir 2006–), memb Music Faculty Univ of Cambridge 1975–; Handel & Haydn Soc Boston USA: artistic dir 1986–2001, conductor laureate 2001–; princ guest conductor Saint Paul Chamber Orch Minnesota USA 1992–98 (dir of music 1987–92), int prof of early music performance Royal Acad of Music London 1992–, visiting prof Dept of Music KCL 1992–96, NSO artistic dir Summer Mozart Festival 1993–2001, assoc dir Beethoven Academie Antwerp 1998–2002; princ guest conductor: Kammerorchester Basel 2000–06, Orquesta Ciudad de Granada 2001–04, Orchestra Sinfonica di Milano Giuseppe Verdi 2003–06; hon prof of music: Keele Univ 1986–90, Univ of Cambridge 2002–; various pubns in jls; fell Handel & Haydn Soc (named in his honour 'The Christopher Hogwood Historically Informed Performance Fellowship'); Freeman Worshipful Co of Musicians 1989 (Willson Cobbett Medal 1986); Hon DMus Keele Univ 1991; hon fell: Jesus Coll Cambridge 1989, Pembroke Coll Cambridge 1992; hon dr Zurich Univ 2007; Hon RAM; FRSA 1982; *Awards* Finalist Giovanni Comisso Prize for Biographies, Award for Artistic Excellence Univ oc California 1996, Scotland on Sunday Music Prize Edinburgh Int festival 1996, Incorporated Soc of Musicians Distinguished Musician Award 1997, Bohuslav Martinu Fndn Prague Martinu Medal 1999; *Books* Music at Court (1977), The Trio Sonata (1979), Haydn's Visits to England (1980), Music in Eighteenth-Century England (jtly, 1983), Handel (1984, revised edn 2007), New Grove Dictionary of Music and Musicians (contrib), The Life of Mozart by Edward Holmes (ed, 1991), The Keyboard in Baroque Europe (ed, 2003); *Style—* Christopher Hogwood, Esq, CBE; ✉ 10 Brookside, Cambridge CB2 1JE (tel 01223 363975, fax 01223 327377, website www.hogwood.org)

HOGWOOD, Paul Arthur; s of Robert Thomas Hogwood, of Forest Hill, and Hilda Jesse, *née* Marshall; *b* 18 July 1949; *Educ* Haberdashers' Aske's, Univ of Hull (BSc); *m* 30 Oct 1971, Sylvia Ann, da of Gordon McCulloch (d 1971); 2 s (James b 1978, Christopher b 1980); *Career* CA; audit mangr Coopers & Lybrand 1970–78, project fin asst dir Morgan Grenfell & Co Ltd 1983–86 (chief internal auditor 1978–83); co sec: Morgan Grenfell Securities Holdings Ltd 1986–88, Anglo & Overseas Trust plc 1989–, The Overseas Investment Trust plc 1989–99, Deutsche Equity Income Trust plc 1991–; dir DWS Investment Funds Ltd 1993–; co sec: Deutsche Latin American Companies Trust plc 1994–2005, Deutsche Asset Management Gp Ltd 1996–; FCA 1974; *Recreations* travel, theatre; *Style—* Paul Hogwood, Esq; ✉ 15 Ambleside, Epping, Essex CM16 4PT (tel 01992 570264); Deutsche Asset Management Group Ltd, One Appold Street, London EC2A 2UU (tel 020 7545 0036, fax 020 7547 1042, telex 920286 MGAM G)

HOLBEN, Terence Henry Seymour; s of Henry George Seymour Holben (d 1991), and Ivy Blanche, *née* Blomfield; *b* 4 March 1937; *Educ* Mark House Sch, SW Essex Tech Coll, London Coll of Printing; *m* 7 Oct 1961, June Elizabeth, da of Alan John Elliot, of Uckfield, E Sussex; 2 s (Matthew Seymour b 1966, Simon Lee b 1969); *Career* Royal Navy 1955–57; advtg art dir: J Walter Thompson 1958–60, McCann Erickson 1960–66, Graham and Gillies 1967–77; Ogilvy & Mather: art dir 1977–91, dir 1983–91, European creative dir 1991–2007, ret; *Recreations* graphic arts, wife, two sons and four grandchildren; *Style—* Terence H S Holben, Esq; ✉ Oakwood, 19 London Road, Stanford Rivers, Ongar, Essex CM5 9PH

HOLBOROW, Jonathan; s of Eric John Holborow, of Henley-on-Thames, Oxon, and Cicely Mary, *née* Foister; *b* 12 October 1943; *Educ* Charterhouse; *m* 1, 12 June 1965, Susan, *née* Ridings (d 1993); 1 da (Rachel Katherine b 16 Sept 1971), 1 s (Matthew Daniel b 12 May 1974); m 2, 21 Oct 1994, Mrs Vivien Claire Ferguson; *Career* jr reporter Maidenhead Advertiser 1961–65; reporter: Lincolnshire Echo 1965–66, Lincoln Chronicle 1966–67, Daily Mail Manchester 1967–69; Scottish news ed Daily Mail Glasgow 1969–70; Daily Mail Manchester: northern picture ed 1970–72, northern news ed 1972–74; Daily Mail London: dep news ed 1974–75, news ed 1975–80; ed Cambrian News 1980–82, asst ed then assoc ed The Mail on Sunday 1982–86; dep ed Today 1986–87, dep ed Daily Mail 1988–92 (asst ed then assoc ed 1987–88), ed The Mail on Sunday 1992–98, dir Associated Newspapers Ltd 1992–98; currently media conslt and broadcaster; delegate to European Inst for the Media 2001; chm Folkestone & Hythe Cons Assoc 2003–; *Recreations* golf, reading, theatre, Saxon and Norman churches in SE England; *Style—* Jonathan Holborow, Esq; ✉ e-mail jholborow@btopenworld.com

HOLBOROW, Lady Mary Christina; *née* Stopford; JP (1970); da (by 1 m) of 8 Earl of Courtown, OBE, DL, TD (d 1976); *b* 19 September 1936; *m* 8 Aug 1959, Geoffrey Jermyn Holborow, OBE; 1 s, 1 da; *Career* memb Regnl Bd Trustee Savings Bank 1981–89, dir South West Water plc 1989–95; dir Devon and Cornwall TEC 1990–96, vice-chm Cornwall & Isles of Scilly HA 1990–2000; chm: Cornwall Ctee Rural Devpt Cmmn 1987–99, Cornwall Macmillan Serv 1982–2002; cmmr St John Ambulance Cornwall 1982–87; patron and pres of numerous voluntary orgns; HM Lord-Lt Cornwall 1994–; Hon LLD Univ of Exeter; DStJ 1987; *Style—* The Lady Mary Holborow; ✉ Ladock House, Ladock, Truro, Cornwall (tel 01726 882274)

HOLBROOK, David Kenneth; s of Kenneth Redvers Holbrook (d 1968), of Norwich, Norfolk, and Elsie Eleanor Holbrook (d 1956); *b* 9 January 1923; *Educ* City of Norwich Sch, Downing Coll Cambridge (MA); *m* 23 April 1949, Frances Margaret (Margot), da of Charles Davies-Jones (d 1938), of Bedwas, Wales; 2 da (Susan (Suki) b 1950, Kate b 1953), 2 s (Jonathan b 1956, Thomas b 1966); *Career* Lt E Riding Yeomanry RAC 1942–45, serv Normandy Invasion and NW Europe; asst ed Bureau of Current Affrs 1947–52, tutor Bassingbourn Village Coll Cambridge 1954–61, fell King's Coll Cambridge 1961–65, sr Leverhulme res fell 1965, writer in residence Dartington Hall 1971–73; Downing Coll Cambridge: asst dir 1973–75, fell and dir of Eng studies 1981–88, emeritus fell 1988; Hooker visiting prof MacMaster Univ Hamilton Ontario 1984, sr Leverhulme res fell 1988–90; Arts Cncl Writers' Grant 1968, 1976 and 1980; memb Editorial Bd Universities Quarterly 1978–86; founding fell Eng Assoc; *Books* Imaginings (1961), English for Maturity (1961), English for the Rejected (1964), The Quest for Love (1965), Flesh Wounds (1966), The Exploring Word (1967), Object Relations (1969), Human Hope and the Death Instinct (1971), The Pseudo-Revolution (1972), Gustav Mahler and the Courage to be (1974), A Play of Passion (1977), Selected Poems (1980), English for Meaning (1980), Nothing Larger than Life (1987), The Novel and Authenticity (1987), Worlds Apart (1988), Images of Woman in Literature (1990), A Little Athens (1990), Jennifer (1990), The Skeleton in the Wardrobe: the Fantasies of C S Lewis (1991), Edith Wharton and the Unsatisfactory Man (1991), The Gold in Father's Heart (1992), Where D H Lawrence Was Wrong About Woman (1992), Charles Dickens and the Image of Woman (1993), Even if They Fail (1994), Creativity and Popular Culture (1994), Tolstoy, Women and Death (1997), Wuthering Heights: A Drama of Being (1997), Getting it Wrong with Uncle Tom (1998), Bringing Everything Home (poems, 1999), George MacDonald and the Phantom Woman (2000), Lewis Carroll: Nonsense Against Sorrow (2001), Going Off the Rails (2003), English in a University Education (2006); *Recreations* oil painting, foreign travel, cooking; *Style—* David Holbrook, Esq; ✉ 1 Tennis Court Terrace, Cambridge CB2 1QX (tel 01223 328341); Downing College, Cambridge (tel 01223 331108)

HOLCROFT, Sir Peter George Culcheth; 3 Bt (UK 1921), of Eaton Mascott, Berrington, Shropshire, JP (Shropshire 1976); s of Sir Reginald Culcheth Holcroft, 2 Bt, TD (d 1978), and his 1 w, Mary Frances, *née* Swire (d 1963); *b* 29 April 1931; *Educ* Eton; *m* 21 July 1956 (m dis 1987), Rosemary Rachel, yr da of late Capt George Nevill Deas, 8 Hussars; 3 s (Charles Anthony Culcheth b 1959, Thomas Marcus Culcheth b 1967, Alexander James Culcheth b 1969), 1 da (Tania Melanie b 1961); *Heir* s, Charles Holcroft; *Career* High Sheriff Shropshire 1969–70; *Style—* Sir Peter Holcroft, Bt; ✉ Appartado de Correos 223, 07210 Algaida, Mallorca, Spain

HOLDEN, Anthony Ivan; s of John Holden (d 1985), of Southport, Lancs, and Margaret Lois, *née* Sharpe (d 1985); *b* 22 May 1947; *Educ* Oundle, Merton Coll Oxford (MA); *m* 1, 1 May 1971 (m dis 1988), Amanda Juliet, da of Sir Brian Warren; 3 s (Sam b 1975, Joe b 1977, Ben b 1979); m 2, 21 July 1990, Cynthia Blake, da of Mrs Rosemary Blake; *Career* trainee reporter Evening Echo Hemel Hempstead 1970–73; The Sunday Times: home and foreign corr 1973–77, Atticus column 1977–79; Washington and chief US corr The Observer 1979–81, Transatlantic Cables columnist Punch 1979–81, features ed and asst ed The Times 1981–82, exec ed Sunday Today 1985–86, classical music critic The Observer 2002–; fell Center for Scholars and Writers NY Public Library 1999–2000; Br Press Awards: Young Journalist of the Year 1972, Reporter of the Year 1976, Columnist of the Year 1977; freelance journalist and author: Holden At Large column Sunday Express magazine 1982–85, presenter In the Air BBC Radio 4 1982–83; TV documentaries: The Men who Would be King 1982, Charles at Forty 1988, Anthony Holden on Poker 1992, Who Killed Tchaikovsky? 1993; opera translations (with Amanda Holden): Don Giovanni ENO 1985, La Boheme Opera North 1986, The Barber of Seville ENO 1987; memb Bd of Govrs South Bank Centre 2002–; *Books* Aeschylus' Agamemnon (translated and ed, 1969), The Greek Anthology (contrib, 1973), Greek Pastoral Poetry (translated and ed, 1974), The St Albans Poisoner (1974), Charles, Prince of Wales (1979), Their Royal Highnesses (1981), Anthony Holden's Royal Quiz - The Penguin Masterquiz (1983), Of Presidents, Prime Ministers and Princes (1984), The Queen Mother (1985, revised edns 1990 and 1993), Don Giovanni (1987), Olivier, A Biography (1988), Charles, A Biography (1989), Big Deal: A Year as a Professional Poker Player (1990), The Last Paragraph: The Journalism of David Blundy (ed, 1990), The Oscars: A Secret History of Hollywood's Academy Awards (1993), The Tarnished Crown: Crisis in the House of Windsor (1993), Power and the Throne (contrib, 1994), Tchaikovsky (1995), Diana: A Life and a Legacy (1997), Charles (1998), William Shakespeare (1999), The Mind Has Mountains (co-ed with Sir Frank Kermode, *qv*, 1999), There are Kermodians (co-ed with Ursula Owen, 1999), The Drama of Love, Life and Death in Shakespeare (2000), William Shakespeare: An Illustrated Biography (2002), The Wit in the Dungeon: A Life of Leigh Hunt (2005); *Recreations* poker, Arsenal FC, Lancashire CCC; *Clubs* Victoria Casino, MCC; *Style—* Anthony Holden, Esq; ✉ c/o Rogers Coleridge & White Ltd, Literary Agents, 20 Powis Mews, London W11 1JN (tel 020 7221 3717, fax 020 7229 9084)

HOLDEN, His Hon Derek; s of Frederic Holden, of Sussex, and Audrey Lilian Holden (d 1985); *b* 7 July 1935; *Educ* Cromwell House, Staines GS; *m* 1961, Dorien Elizabeth, da of Henry Douglas Bell, of Sunningdale; 2 s (Derek Grant b 1968, Derek Clark b 1970); *Career* Lt East Surrey Regt 1953–56, ptnr Derek Holden and Co (slrs) 1966–82, recorder 1980–84, circuit judge (SE Circuit) 1984–2000, ret; slr Supreme Ct (with rights of audience in all cts) 2001–; pres 1990–92: Social Security Appeal Tbnls, Med Appeal Tbnls, Vaccine Damage Tbnls, Disability Appeal Tbnls; chm Asylum and Immigration Tbnl (formerly Immigration Appeal Tbnl) 2001–, legal memb Criminal Injuries Compensation Panel 2000–; chm: Appeals Body Office for the Supervision of Standards of Telephone Info 2001–, Appeals Panel Ind Mobile Classification Body 2006–; chm Tbnls Ctee Judicial Studies Bd 1990–92; memb Law Soc 1966–; *Recreations* sailing, rowing, photography, music; *Clubs* Leander, Royal Solent Yacht, Remenham, Staines Boat, Burway Rowing, Eton Excelsior Rowing, Western (Glasgow), Sonata Assoc; *Style—* His Hon Derek Holden; ✉ e-mail derekholden1@googlemail.com

HOLDEN, Harold Benjamin; s of Reginald Holden (d 1979), and Frances Hilda, *née* Haslett (d 1983); Haslett family built and manned the first lifeboats on the Sussex coast (circa 1880–1910); *b* 2 June 1930; *Educ* Highgate Sch, Charing Cross Hosp Med Sch London (MB BS); *m* 1, Nov 1963, Ann, da of Archibald Sinclair, of Cardiff; 2 s (Andrew b 1964, Michael b 1970), 1 da (Sarah b 1966); m 2, March 1978, Lydia, da of Dr Ronald James, of Toronto, Canada; 2 s (Benjamin b 1978, Robin b 1979); *Career* surgn; formerly: postgraduate dean Charing Cross Hosp Med Sch, dir ENT Unit Charing Cross and Westminster Hosp Med Sch London (currently hon conslt and sr lectr); emeritus conslt Cromwell Hosp London; fell Harvard Univ; FRCS; *Recreations* yachting, flying, golf; *Clubs* Royal Southampton YC, British Med Pilots Assoc, St Georges Hill GC; *Style—* Harold B Holden, Esq; ✉ ENT Unit, Cromwell Hospital, London SW5 0TU (tel 020 7460 2000, fax 020 7244 9975)

HOLDEN, Sir John David; 4 Bt (UK 1919), of The Firs, Leigh, Co Lancaster; s of David George Holden (d 1971, eldest s of Sir George Holden, 3 Bt), and Nancy, *née* Marwood; suc gf 1976; *b* 16 December 1967; *m* 29 Aug 1987, Suzanne, *née* Cummings; 3 da; *Heir* unc, Brian Holden; *Style—* Sir John Holden, Bt

HOLDEN, Lawrence; DL (1992); s of Trevor Holden, of Liverpool (d 1983), and Alice Mary Christine, *née* Roper (d 1991); *b* 19 September 1940, Liverpool; *Educ* Liverpool Coll, Univ of Liverpool (LLB), Coll of Law; *m* 17 Sep 1966, Rosemary Anne, *née* Sutton; 2 s (Rupert b 2 Nov 1967, Timothy b 1 Oct 1969), 1 da (Alison Rebecca b 14 Dec 1971); *Career* admitted slr 1965; ptnr Duncan Oakshott & Co 1966; Brabner Holden Banks Wilson (following merger): managing ptnr 1989, sr ptnr 1994; conslt Brabners Chaffe Street LLP 2001–; pres Liverpool Law Soc 1990–91; memb: Cncl Soc for Computers and Law 1982–87, Law Office Mgmnt and Technology Ctee Law Soc 1983–88, National Inquiry into Governance of Housing Assocs 1994–95, Liverpool City Cncl Advsy Panel on Urban Design and Conservation 1999–; Univ of Liverpool: memb Cncl 1982–2004, pres 1993–99, pro-chllr 1999–2004; vice-pres Liverpool Cncl of Charity and Voluntary Service 1992– (treas 1983–92); Hon LLD Univ of Liverpool 2005; memb Law Soc 1965; *Recreations* mountain walking, painting, sculpture; *Clubs* Athenaeum (Liverpool); *Style—* Lawrence Holden, Esq; ✉ Hollybank, 12 Pine Walks, Birkenhead, Merseyside CH42 8LQ (tel 0151 608 2884, e-mail lawrence.holden@btinternet.com)

H

HOLDEN, Dr Michael Preston; s of Capt Malcolm Holden (d 1971), and Mary Agnes, *née* Preston (d 1985); *b* 10 May 1939; *Educ* Friends Sch Lancaster, Univ of Leeds (MB ChB); *m* 1 April 1963, Susan Margaret, da of Raymond Ashton, of Wilsden; 1 s (David Mark b 1970), 1 da (Helen Jane b 1967); *Career* lectr in anatomy Univ of Glasgow 1964, first asst cardiovascular surgery Auckland NZ 1973, sr registrar cardiothoracic surgery Leeds 1966, sr conslt cardiothoracic surgn Univ of Newcastle 1974–; sr examiner RCS; FRCS 1967, DObst RCOG 1966, FACN 1982; *Books* Towards Safer Cardiac Surgery (1980), Cardiothoracic Surgery (1981); *Recreations* gardening, horse riding, wood turning, dogs; *Style*— Dr Michael Holden

HOLDEN, Patrick Brian; s of Reginald John Holden, of Hants, and Winifred Isabel Holden; *b* 16 June 1937; *Educ* All Hallows Sch, St Catharine's Coll Cambridge (MA); *m* 1972, Dr Jennifer Ruth (m dis 2001), da of Francis Meddings (d 1985); *Career* served Royal Hampshire Regt 1955–57, seconded 1 Ghana Regt RWAFF; Fine Fare Group 1960–69 (legal and property dir 1965–69), Pye Telecom 1969–74 (int dir 1971–74), sec New Towns Assoc 1974–75, dir and sec Oriel Foods Group 1975–81; chm: Steak Away Foods Ltd 1982–, Ainsfield plc 1991–; non-exec Mortimer Growth II plc 1996–; FCIS; *Publications* Map of Tewin and its Rights of Way (1991), A-Z of Dog Training & Behaviour (1999, Chinese version 2001), The Old School House, A Dickensian School (1999), Agility: A Step by Step Guide (2001); *Recreations* walking, bridge, cartoons, travel, dog training; *Clubs* Naval and Military; *Style*— Patrick Holden, Esq; ✉ The Old School House, Lower Green, Tewin, Welwyn, Hertfordshire AL6 0LD (tel 01438 717573)

HOLDEN, Robert David; s of Major Hubert Robert Holden, MC (d 1987), of Sibdon Castle, Craven Arms, Salop, and Lady Elizabeth, *née* Herbert (d 1999); *b* 14 January 1956; *Educ* Eton; *m* 18 June 1988, Susan Emily Frances, da of Sir Joshua Rowley, 7 Bt (d 1997); 2 c (Hubert Joshua Robert, Lucia Hermione Sophia (twins) b 10 March 1997); *Career* chm Robert Holden Ltd 1978–, dir Fine ART Travel Ltd 1985–; patron of the living of Sibdon; *Clubs* Army and Navy; *Style*— Robert Holden, Esq; ✉ Sibdon Castle, Craven Arms, Shropshire SY7 9AQ; 94, Frithville Gardens, London W12 7JW; Robert Holden Limited, 13 Old Burlington Street, London W1S 3PJ (tel 020 7437 6010, fax 020 7437 1733, e-mail robertholden@robertholden.com)

HOLDEN, Sue; *b* 13 May 1966, Morden; *Educ* Univ of Cambridge (MA); *Career* early career with Shell Int and Shell UK; various operational roles rising to business admin dir National Tst 1996–2005, chief exec Woodland Tst 2005–; *Style*— Ms Sue Holden; ✉ The Woodland Trust, Autumn Park, Dysart Road, Grantham, Lincolnshire, NG31 6LL (tel 01476 581111, fax 01476 590808)

HOLDEN, Wendy; da of Anthony Holden, and Elaine, *née* Murgatroyd; *Educ* Whitcliffe Mount Sch Cleckheaton, Girton Coll Cambridge (MA); *m* Jonathan McLeod; 1 s (Andrew Arthur b 2002), 1 da (Isabella b 2004); *Career* writer and journalist; dep ed Style section Sunday Times 1996–97, dep ed Tatler 1997–98, sr ed You magazine Mail on Sunday 1998–2000; *Books* Simply Divine (1999), Bad Heir Day (2000), Pastures Nouveaux (2001), Fame Fatale (2002), Azur Like It (2003), The Wives of Bath (2005), The School for Husbands (2006); *Style*— Miss Wendy Holden; ✉ c/o Jonathan Lloyd, Curtis Brown, 4th Floor, Haymarket House, 28–29 Haymarket, London SW1Y 4SP (tel 020 7393 4400, e-mail jonathan@curtisbrown.co.uk)

HOLDEN-BROWN, Heather; da of Sir Derrick Holden-Brown, and Patricia, *née* Mackenzie (d 2001); *b* 13 August 1951; *Educ* Hampden House, Tudor Hall, QMC London (BA); *Career* The Economist 1975–81, Waterstone's Firethorn Press 1985–86, Harrap 1986–87, BBC Books 1988–97, non-fiction publisher and dir Headline Book Publishing Ltd 1997–2003, dir hhb agency ltd 2005–; govr Tudor Hall Sch, tstee Sparrow Schs Fndn; *Recreations* reading, exploring London and the Thames, visiting historic houses and churches, theatre, cooking for friends; *Style*— Ms Heather Holden-Brown; ✉ hhb agency ltd, 6 Warwick Court, London WC1R 5DJ (tel 020 7405 5525, e-mail heather@hhbagency.com)

HOLDER, Prof Derek Alfred; s of Jesse Alfred Holder, of Isleworth, Middx, and Vera Helen, *née* Haynes; *b* 7 September 1951; *Educ* Isleworth GS, Univ of Manchester (BSc); *Career* mgmnt trainee BOAC 1970–71, mktg grad Ford Motor Company 1974–75, sales mangr then marketing mangr McGraw-Hill Book Company 1975–79, mktg mangr Readers Digest Assoc 1979–80, sr lectr then princ lectr Kingston Poly Business Sch 1980–87, fndr md Inst of Direct Mktg (IDM) 1987–; visiting prof Kingston Univ 1997–; creator IDM Dip in Direct Mktg 1981; govr CAM Fndn; memb: DMA 1981, Direct Mktg Assoc (USA) 1983; FInstD 1985; *Recreations* squash, running, snooker, world travel; *Style*— Prof Derek Holder; ✉ The Institute of Direct Marketing, 1 Park Road, Teddington, Middlesex TW11 0AR (tel 020 8977 5705, fax 020 8943 2535)

HOLDER, Sir (John) Henry; 4 Bt (UK 1898), of Pitmaston, Moseley, Worcs; s of Sir John Eric Duncan Holder, 3 Bt (d 1986), and his 1 w, Evelyn Josephine, *née* Blain; *b* 12 March 1928; *Educ* Eton, Univ of Birmingham (Dip Malting and Brewing); *m* 1, 10 Sept 1960, Catharine Harrison (d 1994), da of Leonard Baker (d 1973); 2 s (Nigel John Charles, Hugo Richard (twins) b 1962), 1 da (Bridget Georgina b 1964); m 2, 14 Sept 1996, Josephine Mary Rivett, da of Alfred Elliott (d 1937); *Heir* s, Nigel Holder; *Career* prodn dir and head brewer Elgood and Son Ltd (Wisbech) 1975–93, ret 1993; chm E Anglian Section Incorporated Brewers' Guild 1981–83; dip memb Inst of Brewing; *Recreations* sailing; *Clubs* Brancaster Staithe Sailing; *Style*— Sir Henry Holder, Bt; ✉ Westering, Holt Road, Cley next the Sea, Holt, Norfolk NR25 7UA

HOLDER, John Wakefield; s of Charles Holder (d 1968), of Barbados, and Carnetta, *née* Blackman (d 1984); *b* 19 March 1945; *Educ* Combermere HS Barbados, Rochdale Coll; *m* Glenda Ann; 2 s (Christopher Paul b 1968, Nigel Anthony John b 1970); *Career* cricket umpire 1983–; playing career: Combermere HS 1957–63, Central CC Barbados 1964, Caribbean CC London 1965, BBC Motspur Park 1965–66, Hampshire CCC 1966–72; professional: Rawtenstall 1974, Norden 1975, Slaithwaite 1976, Royton 1977–78 and 1980–82, Austerlands 1979; test match umpire: debut England v Sri Lanka (Lord's) 1988, England v Australia (Edgbaston) 1989, England v Australia (Headingley) 1989, Pakistan v India series (Karachi, Faisalabad, Lahore, Sialkot) 1989, England v New Zealand (Edgbaston) 1990, England v India (Old Trafford) 1990, England v West Indies (Oval) 1991, England v Australia (Lord's) 2001; Texaco Trophy One Day Int umpire: England v Sri Lanka (Oval) 1988, England v Australia (Old Trafford) 1989, England v India (Headingley) 1990; One Day Int: England v Pakistan 1996, England v Zimbabwe (Old Trafford) 2000, Zimbabwe v West Indies (Riverside), England v Australia (Old Trafford) 2001, England v Pakistan (Headingley) 2001; umpire India Nehru Cup (Delhi, Bombay, Calcutta, Madras, Jullundur) 1989, umpire CBFS Pepsi Champions Trophy 1993; first English umpire (with John Hampshire) to officiate in a test match series abroad Pakistan 1989; *Recreations* keep fit, supporting Manchester United FC; *Style*— John Holder, Esq; ✉ 1 Heald Close, Shawclough, Rochdale OL12 7HJ (tel 01706 665928); England and Wales Cricket Board, Lord's Cricket Ground, London NW8 8QZ (tel 020 7432 1200)

HOLDER, Kevin John; s of K Holder, of Bracknell, Berks, and L Holder, *née* Warboys; *b* 6 November 1958; *Educ* Windsor GS, RMA Sandhurst; *m* (m dis); 1 da (Katherine Anne b 22 Dec 1988), 2 s (Michael Anthony, James Simon (twins) b 18 Nov 1992); *Career* cmmnd RAPC 1981, left Army as Maj 1994; dir of corp affrs Lincs HA 1994, dir of ops Community Healthcare Serv (CHS) Southern Derbys 1998, chief exec NE Derbys PCT 2001–; assoc ICSA 1993; *Recreations* golf, skiing, photography, travel; *Style*— Kevin Holder, Esq; ✉ North Eastern Derbyshire Primary Care Trust, St Mary's Court, St Mary's Gate, Chesterfield, Derbyshire S41 7TD (tel 01246 544610, fax 01246 544689, e-mail kevin.holder@nederbypct.nhs.uk)

HOLDER, Nicholas Paul; TD (1982); s of late Air Marshal Sir Paul Holder, KBE, CB, DSO, DFC, of Hindhead, Surrey, and Mary Elizabeth, *née* Kidd; *b* 10 November 1942; *Educ* Sherborne; *Career* Royal Scots Greys (2 Dragoons) 1963–71, Royal Scots Dragoon Gds Reserve of Offrs 1971–82; cmmnd Inns of Court and City Yeo Home Service Force 1987–91; assoc dir Kleinwort Benson Ltd 1984–87, dir Fuji International Finance (merchant banking subsid of Fuji Bank Tokyo) 1987–94, dir Silverdale Investment Management Ltd 1994–, md Party-Time.co.uk Ltd 2000–; memb: Br Jostedhals Glacier Expedition 1967, Br White Nile Hovercraft Expedition 1969; treas Br Ski Mountaineering Assoc; Freeman City of London 1999, Liveryman Worshipful Co of Fanmakers 1999; *Recreations* mountaineering, skiing, gardening, tennis; *Clubs* Boodle's, Alpine, Lloyd's; *Style*— Nicholas Holder, Esq, TD; ✉ Winkford House, Witley, Godalming, Surrey GU8 5PR; Silverdale Investment Management Limited, 137 Station Road, Hampton, Middlesex TW12 2AL

HOLDERNESS, Sir Martin William; 4 Bt (UK 1920), of Tadworth, Surrey; s of Sir Richard William Holderness, 3 Bt (d 1998), and Pamela, *née* Chapman; *b* 24 May 1957; *m* 2 Oct 1984, Elizabeth D, da of Dr W Thornton; 1 s (Matthew William Thornton b 23 May 1990), 1 da (Tessa Elizabeth Mary b 8 Sept 1992); *Heir* s, Matthew Holderness; *Style*— Sir Martin Holderness, Bt

HOLDGATE, Sir Martin Wyatt; kt (1994), CB (1978); s of Francis Wyatt Holdgate, JP (d 1981), of Lancs, and Lois Marjorie, *née* Bebbington (d 1990); *b* 14 January 1931; *Educ* Arnold Sch Blackpool, Queens' Coll Cambridge (BA, MA, PhD); *m* 2 April 1963, Elizabeth Mary, *née* Dickason; 1 s (Nicholas Michael David b 1965); 1 step s (Martin Robert Arnold Weil b 1956); *Career* research fell Queens' Coll Cambridge 1953–56, sr scientist and jt ldr Gough Island Sci Survey 1955–56; lectr in zoology: Univ of Manchester 1956–57, Univ of Durham 1957–60; ldr Royal Soc expdn to Southern Chile 1958–59, asst dir of research Scott Polar Research Inst Cambridge 1960–63, sr biologist Br Antarctic Survey 1963–66, dep dir The Nature Conservancy 1966–70, dir Central Unit on Environmental Pollution DOE 1970–74, Inst of Terrestrial Ecology NERC 1974–76, DG of research (and dep sec) DOE and Dept of Tport 1976–83, dep sec (environment protection) and chief environment scientist DOE 1983–88, chief sci advsr Dept of Tport 1983–88, DG IUCN (The World Conservation Union) 1988–94, chm UK Energy Advsy Panel 1993–96, pres Zoological Soc of London 1994–2004; chm Int Inst for Environment and Devpt 1994–99, jt chm Intergovernmental Panel on Forests 1995–97; chm of govrs Arnold Sch 1997–2004; pres Freshwater Biological Assoc 2002–; UNEP 500 Award 1988, UNEP Silver Medal 1983, Bruce Medal RSE 1964, Patron's Medal RGS 1992, Livingstone Medal RSGS 1993; Hon DSc: Univ of Durham 1991, Univ of Sussex 1993, Lancaster Univ 1995, Queen Mary Univ of London 2006; hon memb IUCN 2000; hon fell Royal Holloway Univ of London 1997; hon fell Zoological Soc of London 2005; CBiol, FIBiol; Cdr Order of the Golden Ark (Netherlands) 1991; *Books* Mountains in the Sea (1958), Antarctic Ecology (ed, 1970), A Perspective of Environmental Pollution (1979), The World Environment 1972–82 (jt ed, 1982), From Care to Action (1996), The Green Web: A Union for World Conservation (1999), Penguins and Mandarins: Memories of Natural and Un-Natural History (2003), The Story of Appleby in Westmorland (2006); numerous papers in biological and environmental jls and works on Antarctic; *Recreations* hill walking, local history, natural history; *Clubs* Athenaeum; *Style*— Sir Martin Holdgate, CB; ✉ Fell Beck, Hartley, Kirkby Stephen, Cumbria CA17 4JH (tel 01768 372316, e-mail martin@holdgate.org)

HOLDSWORTH, Brian John; s of Reginald Hugh Holdsworth (d 1996), of Long Eaton, Derbys, and Dorothy, *née* Ellis; *b* 27 January 1950; *Educ* Southwell Minster GS, Guy's Hosp Med Sch (BSc, MB BS); *m* 21 Sept 1974, Ursula Jean, da of Victor Robert Lees (d 1974), of Roehampton, London; 3 s (Matthew b 1978, Thomas b 1982, Christopher b 1989); *Career* house jobs Guy's Gp of Hosps 1973–76, registrar in surgery Royal Infirmary Sheffield 1976–78, sr orthopaedic registrar Nottingham Hosps 1981–86 (orthopaedic registrar 1978–81); conslt orthopaedic surgn: Harlow Wood Orthopaedic Hosp nr Mansfield 1986–95, Univ Hosp Nottingham 1986–; FRCS 1978, FBOA 1987; *Publications* Frontiers of Fracture Management (contrib, 1989), Principles of Fracture Management (contrib, 2000), Oxford Book of Trauma (contrib, 2002); author various papers on traumatic conditions of the elbow joint; *Recreations* photography, picture framing, growing cacti; *Style*— Brian Holdsworth, Esq; ✉ 32 Victoria Crescent, Sherwood, Nottingham NG5 4DA (tel and fax 0115 960 4142)

HOLDSWORTH HUNT, Christopher; s of Peter Holdsworth Hunt (d 1996), of London, and Monica, *née* Neville (d 1971); *b* 2 August 1942; *Educ* Eton, Univ of Tours; *m* 1, 24 Feb 1969 (m dis), Charlotte Folin; m 2, 24 June 1976, Joanne Lesley Starr Minoprio, *née* Reynolds; 2 s (Rupert Daniel b 10 Sept 1976, Piers Richard b 4 July 1980); *Career* cmmnd Coldstream Gds 1961–64; joined Murton & Adams Stockjobbers 1964 (firm acquired by Pinchin Denny 1969), memb Mgmnt Ctee Pinchin Denny 1985 (ptnr 1971, firm acquired by Morgan Grenfell 1986), dir Morgan Grenfell Securities 1987, fndr Peel Hunt & Company Ltd 1989–2004, chm Melchior Japan Investment Tst 2006–; Freeman City of London 1970, memb Ct of Assts Worshipful Co of Grocers 1988 (Master 1994–95); *Recreations* opera, ballet, theatre, golf, tennis, walking; *Clubs* White's, City of London, Sunningdale Golf, Swinley Forest Golf; *Style*— Christopher Holdsworth Hunt, Esq

HOLE, Max; s of Anthony Frederick Hole (d 1975), of London, and Barbara Mary Hole; *b* 26 May 1951; *Educ* Haileybury, Univ of Kent at Canterbury; *m* 1 (m dis), Cynthia; 2 s (Jamie b 23 June 1979, Mark b 24 Jan 1984); m 2, Jan Ravens, *qv* (actress); 1 s (Louis b 20 May 1998); *Career* fndr (with Geoff Jukes): Gemini Artists 1972 (clients incl Camel, Mungo Jerry, Arthur Brown), Criminal Records 1976 (signings incl Bram Tchaikovsky, Robin Williamson, Susan Fassbender); mangr: Chris Hughes, Ross Cullum; WEA: A&R mangr 1982–83, dir of A&R 1983–87, md UK div 1987–90; md East West Records (following splitting of WEA into 2 cos) 1990–98, currently pres Asia Pacific and exec vice-pres Universal Music Gp Int (formerly sr vice-pres of mktg and A&R); *Recreations* walking and boating at my house in Cornwall, watching cricket; *Clubs* MCC, Groucho; *Style*— Max Hole, Esq; ✉ Universal Music International, 364–366 Kensington High Street, London W14 8NS (tel 020 7471 5603, fax 020 7471 5605)

HOLES, Prof Clive Douglas; s of Douglas John Holes, and Kathryn Mary, *née* Grafton; *b* 29 September 1948; *Educ* Trinity Hall Cambridge (MA), Univ of Birmingham (MA), Wolfson Coll Cambridge (PhD); *m* 8 March 1980 (m dis 2003), Gillian Diane, da of late James Herbert Pountain; 2 s (Timothy Peter b 23 March 1984, Michael James b 21 March 1988); m 2, 7 Aug 2004, Deidre Margaret, da of Charles William Allen; *Career* British Cncl offr Bahrain, Kuwait, Algeria, Iraq and Thailand 1971–83, lectr then sr lectr in applied linguistics Univ of Salford 1983–85, dir Language Centre Sultan Qaboos Univ Oman 1985–87; Univ of Cambridge: lectr in Islamic Studies 1987–96, reader in Arabic 1996, fell Trinity Hall 1989–96; Khalid Bin Abdallah Al-Saud prof for the study of the contemporary Arab world Univ of Oxford 1997–, fell Magdalen Coll; memb: Philological Soc 1985, Br Soc for Middle Eastern Studies 1985; FBA 2002; *Books* Colloquial Arabic of the Gulf & Saudi Arabia (1984), Language Variation and Change in a Modernising Arab State (1987), Gulf Arabic (1990), Modern Arabic (1995), Dialect, Culture and Society in Eastern Arabia (Vol I 2001, Vol II 2005); also author of numerous professorial jl articles on the Arabic language; *Recreations* keeping fit, watching soccer and rugby, visiting the Arab world, cooking; *Style*— Prof Clive Holes; ✉ Magdalen College, Oxford OX1 4AU; Oriental Institute, Pusey Lane, Oxford OX1 2LE (e-mail clive.holes@orinst.ox.ac.uk)

HOLGATE, David John; QC (1997); s of John Charles Holgate, of Loughton, Essex, and Catherine Philbin, *née* Rooney; *b* 3 August 1956; *Educ* Davenant Fndn GS, Exeter Coll Oxford (BA); *Career* called to the Bar Middle Temple 1978 (bencher 2004); recorder of the Crown Court 2001–; memb Supplementary Panel of Jr Counsel to the Crown (Common Law) 1986–97, Standing Jr Counsel to the Inland Revenue in Rating and Valuation Matters 1990–97; admitted Hong Kong Bar 2000; *Recreations* music (particularly opera), travel, reading; *Clubs* Travellers; *Style*— David Holgate, QC; ✉ 4 Breams Buildings, London EC4A 1AQ (tel 020 7430 1221, fax 020 7421 6060, e-mail clerks@landmarkchambers.co.uk)

HOLGATE, Peter Alan; s of Harold Holgate, of Leeds, and Ivy, *née* Instrell; *b* 8 February 1953; *Educ* West Leeds Boys HS, Univ of Bradford (MSc); *m* 1980, Dr Nelda Elizabeth Frater; 1 s (Andrew b 25 Nov 1985); *Career* articled clerk John Gordon Walton & Co CAs Leeds 1970–74, audit sr and asst mangr Coopers & Lybrand London and Nairobi 1975–78, fin controller Mitchell Cotts Kenya Ltd 1978–79, business planning mangr Hertz Europe Ltd London 1979–81; under sec then sec Accounting Standards Ctee 1981–86; sr tech mangr Deloitte Haskins & Sells 1986–90, sr accounting tech ptnr PricewaterhouseCoopers (formerly Coopers & Lybrand before merger) 1990–; author of numerous articles in professional jls, frequent speaker at accounting confs; chm Centre for Business Performance ICAEW 2006–; memb: Fin Reporting Ctee ICAEW 1990–98, Main Ctee and Tech Ctee LSCA 1990–93 (chm Tech Ctee 1991–93), Accounting Standards Bd's Urgent Issues Task Force 1994–, Int Accounting Ctee CCAB 1996–2000; FCA; *Books* A Guide to Accounting Standards - Accounting For Goodwill (1985, updated 1990), A Guide To Accounting Standards - SSAP 23 Accounting For Acquisitions and Mergers (1986), A Guide to Accounting Standards - SSAP 12 revised Accounting for Depreciation (1987), Goodwill, Acquisitions & Mergers (1990), Operating and Financial Review (1994), The Coopers & Lybrand Manual of Accounting (princ author, 1995, 1996, 1997 and 1998), The PricewaterhouseCoopers Manual of Accounting- UK GAAP (princ author, annually 1999–2007), The PricewaterhouseCoopers Manual of Accounting - IFRS for the UK (princ author, annually 2005–07), Accounting Principles for Lawyers (2006); *Recreations* music, visiting second hand bookshops, reading; *Style*— Peter Holgate, Esq; ✉ PricewaterhouseCoopers, 1 Embankment Place, London WC2N 6NN (tel 020 7583 5000, e-mail peter.a.holgate@uk.pwc.com)

HOLGATE, Peter Roy; s of Leonard George Holgate (d 1984), of Sussex, and Phyllis Evelyn, *née* Haynes (d 1995); *b* 24 March 1942; *Educ* Eltham Coll London; *m* 28 June 1969, Carol Priscilla, da of Edward Charles Thewlis; 1 da (Charlotte Amanda b 20 Sept 1972), 1 s (Matthew James b 20 Sept 1974); *Career* chartered accountant; sr ptnr Callingham Crane until 1991, ptnr Kingston Smith LLP (following merger with Callingham Crane) 1991–; memb Cncl ICAEW 1993–; Freeman City of London; Liveryman: Worshipful Co of Needlemakers, Worshipful Co of Coopers; FCA (ACA 1965), MSI 1994; *Recreations* cricket, gardening, forestry; *Style*— Peter Holgate, Esq; ✉ Kingston Smith LLP, Chartered Accountants, Devonshire House, 60 Goswell Road, London EC1M 7AD (tel 020 7566 4000, fax 020 7566 4010, mobile 077 6822 2964, e-mail pholgate@kingstonsmith.co.uk)

HOLL-ALLEN, Dr Robert Thomas James; s of Robert Thomas James Allen (d 1988), and Florence Janet Rachel (d 1972); *b* 3 December 1934; *Educ* Warwick Sch, Univ of London, Harvard Med Sch (BSc, MD, MS, DLO); *m* 1, 2 June 1962 (m dis 1972), Barbara Mary, da of Leslie Thomas Holl (d 1971); 1 s (Jonathan Guy b 7 April 1966); m 2, 2 March 1974 (m dis 1989), Diana Elisabeth Tootill; 1 s (Robert (Robin) Gerald b 10 Jan 1975), 1 da (Amanda Jane b 23 Nov 1976); m 3, 2 Sept 1992, Julia Anne Gollance, *née* Rush; *Career* house physician UCH 1959, registrar Radcliffe Infirmary Oxford 1963–65, sr surgical registrar W Midland RHA 1966–72, conslt surgn Birmingham Heartlands and Solihull Hosp 1972–96, hon sr clinical lectr Univ of Birmingham; research fell Harvard Med Sch 1968–69; visiting overseas professorships; FRCS 1963, FRSM 1964, FACS 1974, fell Int Coll of Surgeons 1974, memb NY Acad of Scis; *Recreations* golf, travel, good food; *Clubs* Squire, Tennessee; *Style*— Dr Robert Holl-Allen; ✉ 1 Avenbury Drive, Solihull, West Midlands B91 2QZ (tel 0121 704 4488, fax 0121 704 0809, e-mail hollallen@aol.com)

HOLLAND, Sir (John) Anthony; kt (2003); s of late Maj John Holland, of Yelverton, Devon, and Dorothy Rita, *née* George; *b* 9 November 1938; *Educ* Ratcliffe Coll, Univ of Nottingham (LLB), Univ of the West of England (MPhil); *m* 1 June 1963, Kathleen Margaret (Kay), da of John Smellie Anderson (d 1978); 3 s (Andrew John, Christopher Iain, Nicholas Alexander); *Career* admitted slr 1962, sr ptnr Foot & Bowden Plymouth 1980–97, princ ombudsman PIA 1997–2000; chm: Regnl Advsy Cncl BBC SW 1984–87, Social Security Appeals Tbnl 1991–97, Plymouth C of C and Industry 1994–96, Exec Bd Justice 1997–2000 (memb Cncl 1991–2003), Jt Insolvency Monitoring Unit 2000–04, NI Parades Cmmn 2000–05, Standards Bd for England 2001–08, Access Dispute Ctee 2002–, NI Legal Servs Cmmn 2004–07; chm (jtly) Securities and Futures Authy 1993–2001; dep chm Regulatory Decisions Ctee FSA 2002–04, complaints cmmr to FSA 2004–; govr Coll of Law 1991–97; memb: Cncl Howard League for Penal Reform, Marre Ctee, Criminal Injuries Compensation Appeals Panel 2000–05; pres: Plymouth Law Soc 1986, Cornwall Law Soc 1988; hon memb Soc of Legal Slrs 1992; memb Law Soc 1962 (elected to Cncl 1976, vice-pres 1989, pres 1990); *Books* Principles of Registered Land Conveyancing (1968), Landlord and Tenant (1970), Mines and Quarries Section Butterworths Encyclopedia of Forms and Precedents (jt consulting ed, 1989–2005), Cordery on Solicitors (gen ed, 9 edn); *Recreations* opera, travel, sailing; *Clubs* Royal Western Yacht of England, Athenaeum; *Style*— Sir Anthony Holland; ✉ 262 Lauderdale Tower, Barbican, London EC2Y 8BY (tel 020 7638 5044)

HOLLAND, Barry K; s of Frank Hope Holland, of Wallasey, Merseyside, and Mary, *née* Kay; *b* 6 February 1947; *Educ* Wallasy GS, Univ of Nottingham (LLB); *m* 1 Dec 1973, Lois Bradley, da of Dr T H H Green, of Wallasey, Merseyside; 2 s (James b 7 Aug 1974, Benjamin b 13 Nov 1975), 2 da (Samantha b 15 Aug 1969, Nathalie b 25 Feb 1972); *Career* admitted slr 1970, NP 1980; ptnr Percy Hughes & Roberts 1972–85, sole princ Hollands 1985–86, ptnr Davies Wallis 1986–91, ptnr Elliotts & Co 1991–2006, sole princ 2006–; fndr chm The Caldy Soc 1985–2006, chm Food Law Gp 1996–; memb Law Soc 1970; *Style*— Barry K Holland, Esq; ✉ Butts Mead, East Farm Mews, Caldy, Wirral CH48 1QB (tel 0151 625 7413, fax 0151 625 3131); 47 Hamilton Square, Wirral CH41 5BD (tel 0151 666 2181, fax 0151 647 1025, e-mail barry@barryholland.com)

HOLLAND, Hon Mr Justice; Sir Christopher John Holland; kt (1992); s of Frank Holland (d 1979), of Leeds, and Winifred Mary, *née* Pigott (d 1984); *b* 1 June 1937; *Educ* Leeds GS, Emmanuel Coll Cambridge (MA, LLB); *m* 11 Feb 1967, Jill Iona; 1 s (Charles Christopher b 20 May 1969), 1 da (Victoria Joanna b 1 June 1971); *Career* Nat Serv 3 Royal Tank Regt 1956–58; called to the Bar Inner Temple 1963 (bencher 1985); practised NE Circuit, QC 1978, recorder NE Circuit 1992, judge of the High Court of Justice (Queen's Bench Div) 1992–, presiding judge NE Circuit 1993–97; judge Employment Appeal Tbnl 1994–; memb Criminal Injuries Compensation Bd 1992; vice-chm Ctee of Inquiry into the Outbreak of Legionnaires' Disease at Stafford 1985; chm Lower Washburn Parish Cncl 1976–91; *Style*— The Hon Mr Justice Holland; ✉ Royal Courts of Justice, London WC2A 2LL

HOLLAND, Darryll; s of Lenord Holland, and Anne, *née* Tynan; *b* 14 June 1972, Manchester; *m* 16 Sept 2001, Jacqueline Elizabeth, *née* Merchant; *Career* jockey (flat racing); ridden in UK, Europe, Asia and N America; Group 1 wins incl: Yorkshire Oaks, Singapore Derby, July Cup, St James Palace Stakes, Juddmonte Int, Queen Elizabeth II Stakes, Dewhurst Stakes, Gran Criterium, Italian Oaks, Coronation Cup, Coral Eclipse (twice), Pretty Polly, Fillies Mile; other wins incl: Goodwood Cup, Doncaster Cup, Italian 2000 Guineas, German 2000 Guineas; *Recreations* golf, football, tennis, skiing; *Clubs* Links Golf (Newmarket); *Style*— Darryl Holland, Esq; ✉ c/o Peter Merchant, Baden Lodge, 184 High Street, Cheveley, Newmarket CB8 9DG (tel and fax 01638 731050, e-mail petermerchant@lineone.net)

HOLLAND, Julian Miles (Jools); OBE (2003); s of Derek Holland, of London, and June Rose, *née* Lane; *b* 24 January 1958; *Educ* Park Walk Sch, Invicta Sherington Sch, Shooters' Hill Sch; *Partner* (until 1986), Mary Leahy; 2 c (George Soloman b 14 April 1984, Rosie Areatha Mae b 1 Oct 1985); m, Aug 2005, Christabel Durham; 1 da (Mabel Ray Brittania b 22 Nov 1990); *Career* pianist 1975–78; keyboard player Squeeze 1978–80 (hits incl Take Me I'm Yours, Cool for Cats, Up The Junction, Hourglass, Annie Get Your Gun, Pulling Mussels from a Shell, Tempted, Slap and Tickle), regularly tours UK, concerts at Royal Albert Hall; solo albums: A World of His Own 1990, Full Compliment 1991, A-Z Of Piano 1993, Live Performance 1995, Solo Piano 1995, Sex, Jazz & Rock and Roll 1996, Lift The Lid 1997, Best of 1998, As The Sun Sets Over London 1999, Hop the Wag 2000, Small World Big Band 2001, Small World Big Band Vol II - More Friends 2002, Small World Big Band Friends III 2003; band leader Rythm & Blues Orchestra 1993–; extensive touring and guest performances with numerous artists incl: BB King (duet Deuces Wild CD), Elvis Costello, Sting, Al Green, Dr John, The The, Fine Young Cannibals, George Harrison; TV Presenter: The Tube (Channel 4) 1981–86, Juke Box Jury (BBC2) 1989, Sunday Night (with David Sanborn, NBC) 1990, The Happening (BSB) 1990, Later With Jools Holland (series, BBC2) 1993–; presenter The Jools Holland Show (Radio 2); writer: The Groovy Fellers (Channel 4) 1988, wrote and produced films: Walking To New Orleans 1985, Mr Roadrunner (Channel 4) 1991, Spiceworld The Movie (cameo) 1997, Beat Route 1998, Jools Meets The Saint 1999; wrote film score for feature film Milk 1999; *Recreations* sketching, architecture; *Style*— Jools Holland, Esq, OBE; ✉ One-Fifteen, 1 Prince of Orange Lane, Greenwich, London SE10 8JQ (tel 020 8293 0999, fax 020 8293 9525)

HOLLAND, Katharine Jane; da of Wilfred Holland, and Margaret Holland; *Educ* Lady Manners Sch, Hertford Coll Oxford (BA, BCL); *Career* called to the Bar 1989; memb: Hon Soc of Middle Temple, Hon Soc of Lincoln's Inn, Chancery Bar Assoc, Professional Negligence Assoc; *Style*— Ms Katharine Holland; ✉ Landmark Chambers, 4 Bream's Buildings, London EC4A 1AQ

HOLLAND, Prof Peter William Harold; s of Franklin Holland, and Christine, *née* Bartrop; *b* 17 August 1963, Hyde; *Educ* Marple Hall Sch, The Queen's Coll Oxford (MA), Nat Inst for Med Research and Univ of London (PhD), Univ of Reading (DSc); *m* 1996, Amanda Susan, *née* Horsfall; 2 s; *Career* demonstrator in zoology Univ of Oxford 1987–91, Browne research fell The Queen's Coll Oxford 1988–91, Royal Soc univ research fell Univ of Oxford 1991–94, prof of zoology Univ of Reading 1994–2002, Linacre prof of zoology and assoc head Dept of Zoology Univ of Oxford 2002–, fell Merton Coll Oxford 2002–; editor of two books and author of numerous research papers in scientific jls; Scientific Medal Zoological Soc of London 1996, De Snoo Medal 1999, Genetics Soc Medal 2004, Blaise Pascal Medal 2005; FLS 2002, FRS 2003; *Style*— Prof Peter Holland; ✉ Department of Zoology, University of Oxford, South Parks Road, Oxford OX1 3PS (tel 01865 271185, fax 01865 271184)

HOLLAND, Prof Walter Werner; CBE (1992); s of Henry H Holland (d 1959), of London, and Hertha, *née* Zentner; *b* 5 March 1929; *Educ* Rugby, Univ of London, St Thomas' Hospital Med Sch (BSc, MB BS, MD); *m* 29 Oct 1964, Fiona, da of Douglas C Love (d 1976), of Bristol; 3 s (Peter b 1965, Richard b 1967, Michael b 1970); *Career* Flying Offr and Flt Lt RAF 1956–58; res fell: MRC 1959–61, Johns Hopkins Univ 1961–62; prof (former sr lectr and reader) St Thomas' Hosp 1962–94 (casualty offr 1955–56), visiting professor LSE Health London Sch of Economics 1995–, chm Euro Health Policy Network 1996–; author of over 315 articles and books; inaugural lectr Johns Hopkins Univ 1977 (elected lifetime memb Soc of Scholars 1970), Fogarty Scholar-in-Residence NIH Bethesda USA 1984–85, Theodore Badger visiting prof Harvard Univ 1984, first Sawyer Scholar in Res Case Western Reserve Med Sch Cleveland USA 1985, Europe et Médecine Prize Institut des Sciences de la Santé 1994, Queen Elizabeth The Queen Mother lectr Faculty of Public Health Med RCP 1995, Harben lectr Royal Inst of Public Health 1995, Cruickshank lectr Int Epidemiological Assoc 1996, Rock Carling lectr Nuffield Provincial Hosps Tst 1996/97; pres Int Epidemiological Assoc 1987–90, pres Faculty of Public Health Med 1989–92, vice-chm W Lambeth HA 1983–86, hon memb American Epidemiological Soc 1985; hon fell Italian Soc of Hygiene, Preventative Medicine and Public Health 2005; Hon DUniv Bordeaux Univ 1981, Hon DUniv Free Univ of Berlin 1990; memb: RSM, Soc for Social Med, Royal Statistical Soc, Int Epidemiological Assoc; FFPHM, FRCPE, FRCPath, FRCP, FRCGP, FFPHMI; *Clubs* Athenaeum; *Style*— Prof Walter Holland, CBE; ✉ South End Cottage, Orleans Road, Twickenham, Middlesex TW1 3BL

HOLLAND, Wright Henry (Harry); s of Joseph Holland (d 1942), of Glasgow, and Joan Rose, *née* Goddard; *b* 11 April 1941; *Educ* Rutlish Sch Merton, St Martin's Sch of Art (DipAD); *m* Maureen, da of Lucien Coulson; 2 da (Samantha Joan b 18 June 1964, Emma Corinna b 6 May 1967); *Career* artist; lectr 1969–78 (Coventry, Hull, Stourbridge, Cardiff); *Solo Exhibitions* Roundhouse Gallery 1979, Oriel Gallery Cardiff 1979, Welsh Arts Cncl Touring Exhibition 1980, Mineta Move Gallery Brussels 1981, Robin Garton Gallery London 1982 and 1983, Arnold Katzen Gallery NY 1982, FIAC Paris (Mineta Move) 1983 and 1984, Ian Birksted Gallery 1984, Artiste Gallery Bath 1985, Edinburgh Demarcations (Garton & Cooke) 1985, Chicago Art Fair (Ian Birksted Gallery) 1986, New Drawings (Birksted Gallery) 1986, Andrew Knight Gallery Cardiff 1987, Bohun Gallery Henley 1987 and 1989, Thumb Gallery 1988 and 1990, Garton & Co 1988, Forum Art Fair Hamburg (Thumb Gallery) 1989, Beaux Arts Bath 1993, Jill George Gallery London 1994, 1996 and 1998, Martin Tinney Gallery Cardiff 1994 and 1997, Oriel Gallery Cardiff 1995, Ferens Gallery Hull 1995, Rooryk Gallery Knokke 1997, Mineta Move Gallery Brussels 1999, Il Pollitico Gallery Rome 2002, Mineta Move Gallery Brussels 2001, Martin Tinney Gallery Cardiff 2001; *Group Exhibitions* incl: Aspects of Realism 1976–78, From Wales 1977, Fruitmarket Gallery Edinburgh 1977, Nat Eisteddfod of Wales (prizewinner) 1978, Grandes et Jeunes d'Aujourd'hui (Grand Palais Paris) 1979, Probity of Art (Welsh Arts Cncl touring exhibition) 1980, Br Art Show (Arts Cncl of GB) 1980, Art of the Eighties (Walker Art Gallery) 1981, Euro Print Biennale Heidelberg 1983, The Male Nude (Ebury Gallery) 1983, Bradford Print Biennale 1984, second Int Contemporary Art Fair 1985, Int Contemporary Art Fair LA (Thumb Gallery) 1986, 1987 and 1988, Bruton Gallery 1987, Self Portrait - A Modern View (touring) 1987, The Drawing Show (Thumb Gallery) 1988, Ways of Telling (Mostyn Gallery Wales) 1989, Fourth Int Contemporary Art Fair LA (Thumb Gallery) 1989, Disclosures (Wales & Barcelona) 1997, Art of the Ideal (Gallery of Modern Art Verona) 2002, Between Earth and Heaven (Gallery of Modern Art Ostend) 2001; *Collections* Contemporary Art Soc, Tate Gallery, Newport Museum and Art Gallery, Glynn Yivian Art Gallery and Museum Swansea, Nat Museum of Wales Cardiff, Welsh Arts Cncl, Contemporary Arts Soc for Wales, Metropolitan Museum of Art NYc, Heineken Collection Amsterdam, Euro Parl Collection, Belgian Nat Collection, British Museum, Fitzwilliam Museum, Scottish Equitable, Gartmore Investment Mgmnt Ltd; memb Royal Cambrian Acad; *Clubs* Chelsea Arts; *Style*— Harry Holland, Esq; ✉ Harry Holland, 19 Plasturton Gardens, Pontcanna, Cardiff CF11 9HG (tel 029 2048 0414)

HOLLAND-MARTIN, Robert George (Robin); s of Cyril Holland-Martin (d 1983), and Rosa, *née* Chadwyck-Healey (d 1997); *b* 6 July 1939; *Educ* Eton; *m* 1976, Dominique, da of Maurice Fromaget; 2 da; *Career* Cazenove & Co 1960–74 (ptnr 1968–74), fin dir Paterson Products Ltd 1976–86, conslt Newmarket Venture Capital plc 1982–94, dir Henderson

H

plc 1983–98; non-exec dir: Dorling Kindersley Holdings plc 1992–2000, The Fine Art Soc plc 1995–, Service Point Solutions SA (formerly Grupo Picking Pack SA) 1998–2006, Grapes Direct Ltd 2000–06; conslt Investindustrial Group of Companies 1997–; memb: Met Hosp-Sunday Fund 1964–2002 (chm 1977–2002), Homoeopathic Tst 1970–90 (vice-chm 1975–90), Advsy Cncl V&A 1972–83, Assocs of V&A Ctee 1976–85 (chm 1981–85), Visiting Ctee RCA 1982–93 (chm 1984–93); tstee V&A 1983–85 (dep chm); hon dep treas Cons and Unionist Pty 1979–82; pres Blackie Fndn Tst 1998– (tstee 1971–96, chm 1987–96), tstee King's Med Res Tst 2000–, tstee City & Guilds of London Art Sch 2001– (chm 2002–); memb Ct of Assts Worshipful Co of Fishmongers 1999–; *Clubs* White's, RAC; *Style—* Robin Holland-Martin, Esq; ✉ 18 Tite Street, London SW3 4HZ (tel 020 7352 7871)

HOLLANDER, Charles Simon; QC (1999); s of Paul Hollander, of London, and Eileen, *née* Flanagan; *b* 1 December 1955; *Educ* UCS Hampstead (nat schoolboy bridge champion, rep Univ of Cambridge, Cambs and Hunts), King's Coll Cambridge (Douton entrance scholar, sr scholar, MA); *m* 1986, Heather, da of Trevor Pilley; 2 da (Jennifer b 19 April 1990, Hilary b 15 Jan 2000), 2 s (Andrew b 11 May 1993, Ian b 1 Nov 1997); *Career* called to the Bar Gray's Inn 1978, in private practice specialising in commercial litigation 1978–, recorder 2000; *Books* Documentary Evidence (1 edn 1985, 7 edn 2000), Conflicts of Evidence and Chinese Walls (2000), Phipson on Evidence (contrib and ed, 15 edn 1999); *Recreations* tennis, food, wine; *Style—* Charles Hollander, Esq, QC; ✉ Brick Court Chambers, 7/8 Essex Street, London WC2R 3LD (tel 020 7379 3550, fax 020 7379 3558, e-mail hollander@brickcourt.co.uk)

HOLLENDEN, 4 Baron (UK 1912); Ian Hampden Hope-Morley; s of 3 Baron Hollenden (d 1999); *b* 23 October 1946; *Educ* Eton; *m* 1, 1972 (m dis 1995), Beatrice Saulnier, da of Baron Pierre d'Anchald, of Paris; 1 da (Hon Juliette b 1974), 1 s (Hon Edward b 1981); m 2, 10 Oct 1988, Caroline N, o da of Kim Ash, of Johannesburg; 2 s (Hon Alastair Kim b 1990, Hon Henry Gordon (Harry) b 1993); *Heir* s, Hon Edward Hope-Morley; *Career* estate mangr The Hampden Estate; formerly ship broker and wine importer; Liveryman Worshipful Co of Fishmongers; *Clubs* Brooks's; *Style—* Lord Hollenden; ✉ c/o The Estate Office, Great Hampden, Great Missenden, Buckinghamshire HP16 6RE

HOLLICK, Baron (Life Peer UK 1991), of Notting Hill in the Royal Borough of Kensington and Chelsea; Clive Richard Hollick; *Educ* Taunton's Sch, Univ of Nottingham; *m*; 3 da; *Career* dir various United Business Media plc subsids, chief exec United Business Media plc until 2005, ptnr Kohlberg Kravis Roberts 2005–; dir: Hambros Bank 1973–96, Diageo plc, TRW Inc 2000–02, Honeywell Inc; special advsr to Pres Bd of Trade 1997–98; chm South Bank Bd 2002–; fndr tstee IPPR; *Style—* The Rt Hon Lord Hollick

HOLLIDAY, (Peter) David; OBE (1997); s of Leslie John Holliday, of Berkhamsted, and Kathleen Joan Marjorie, *née* Stacey; *b* 20 July 1947; *Educ* Brixton Sch of Bldg, London Business Sch; *m* 1972, Diana Patricia, da of Philip Shirley Christian Aldred, of Surrey; 2 da (Rebecca Louise b 1976, Amanda Alice b 1982), 1 s (Michael Stuart b 1978); *Career* chm: Laing Homes 1983–88, Super-Homes 1983–88, John Laing Homes Inc (California) 1985–88; chm and chief exec Ward Holdings plc 1998–2004, chief exec Admiral Homes Ltd 1988–97; chm: Tamsdown plc 1999–, Riverbank Associates 2000–, Bison Gp 2004–, RD Ltd 2004–; dir John Laing plc 1984–88; non-exec dir: Ben Bailey plc 1997–2000, Bowey Gp plc 1999–2006; pres House Builders' Fedn 1991–92 (vice-pres 1988–91), dir National House Building Cncl 1994–2000; Freeman: City of London 1987, Worshipful Co of Plaisterers (Master 2004); MCIOB, FInstD; *Recreations* sailing, golf; *Clubs* Royal Southern Yacht, City Livery Yacht, Berkhamsted Golf, Ashridge Golf; *Style—* David Holliday, Esq, OBE; ✉ Dundry, Water End Road, Potten End, Berkhamsted, Hertfordshire HP4 2SG (tel 01442 865556, e-mail dhol5556@aol.com)

HOLLIDAY, Prof Sir Frederick George Thomas; kt (1990), CBE (1975); s of Alfred Charles Holliday (d 1996), and Margaret, *née* Reynolds (d 1996); *b* 22 September 1935; *Educ* Bromsgrove Co HS, Univ of Sheffield (BSc, DSc), Univ of Durham (DCL); *m* 1957, Philippa Mary, da of Charles Davidson (d 1985); 1 da (Helen Kirstin b 1961), 1 s (Richard John b 1964); *Career* Devpt Cmmn fisheries res student Aberdeen 1956–58, sci offr Marine Lab Aberdeen 1958–61, acting princ and vice-chllr Univ of Stirling 1973–75 (prof and head Dept of Biology 1967–75, dep princ 1972–73), prof of zoology Univ of Aberdeen 1975–79 (lectr in zoology 1961–66), vice-chllr and warden Univ of Durham 1980–90; chm: Lloyds Bank Northern Regnl Bd 1986–89 (dir 1985–90, dep chm 1989–90), BR Eastern Region Bd 1986–90 (non-exec dir 1983–90), Northumbrian Water Group plc 1993–2006 (non-exec dir 1991–2006), Northern Venture Tst plc 1996–, Go-Ahead Group plc 1998–2002 (non-exec dir 1997–2002), Brewin Dolphin Holdings plc (formerly Wise Speke plc) 2003–05 (non-exec dir 1997–2005, memb Bd 1998–2003); non-exec dir: Shell UK Ltd 1980–99, BR Main Bd 1990–93, Bd Union Railways 1993–97; dir Northern Investors Ltd 1984–89; chm Nature Conservancy Cncl 1977–80 (memb 1975–80), vice-pres Scottish Wildlife Tst 1980–, chm Ind Review of Disposal of Radioactive Waste at Sea 1984, chm Jt Nature Conservation Ctee 1990–91, pres Freshwater Biological Assoc 1995–99, pres Br Tst for Ornithology 1997–2002; memb: Leverhulme Tst Res Awards Advsy Ctee 1978–95 (chm 1987–95), Environment Ctee CBI 1994–2006, Bd Suez Lyonnaise des Eaux 1996–2001, Lyonnaise Europe 1996; tstee: The Scottish Civic Tst 1984–87, The Nat Heritage Meml Fund 1980–91, Water Aid Cncl 1995–97; DL Co Durham 1985–90; FRSE 1971; *Recreations* ornithology, hill walking, vegetable gardening; *Clubs* Cwlth Tst, Fettercairn Farmers'; *Style—* Prof Sir Frederick Holliday, CBE, FRSE; ✉ Northern Venture Trust, Northumberland House, Princess Square, Newcastle upon Tyne NE1 8ER (tel 0191 244 6000)

HOLLIDAY, Raymond (Ray); OBE (1999); s of Ronald Holliday (d 1992), and Mary Louisa, *née* Cowen; *b* 30 May 1949; *Educ* Boteler GS Warrington, Univ of Newcastle upon Tyne (BA, PGCE, MEd), Newcastle upon Tyne Poly (TEFL Dip (RSA)); *m* 1, 1975 (m dis 2003), Régine, da of Gérard Leclerc; 4 da (Kristelle b 6 May 1981, Chloé b 13 April 1985, Loriane b 19 April 1987, Géraldine b 8 Aug 1992), 1 s (Marc Alexandre b 20 Feb 1988); m 2, 2004, Cécile, da of Roland Bonnin; 1 da (Océne Cécilia b 9 Feb 2004); *Career* teacher of French and English Seaton Sluice Middle Sch Northumberland 1975–80, dep head Blyth Wensleydale Middle Sch Northumberland 1982–87(year ldr 1980–82); British Council School of Madrid: dep head 1987–93, actg head 1993–94, head 1994–2001; head French American Int Sch of Boston 2001–; *Recreations* reading, music, cycling, a wide variety of sports with no great level in any; *Style—* Ray Holliday, Esq, OBE; ✉ French American International School of Boston, 43 Matignon Road, Cambridge, MA 02140, USA (tel 00 1 617 499 1455, fax 00 1 617 499 1454, e-mail rholliday@ecolebilingue.org)

HOLLINGHURST, Alan James; s of James Kenneth Hollinghurst (d 1991), and Elizabeth Lilian, *née* Keevil; *b* 26 May 1954; *Educ* Canford Sch Dorset, Magdalen Coll Oxford (BA, MLitt); *Career* dep ed Times Literary Supplement 1985–90 (on staff 1982–95); FRSL; *Books* The Swimming-Pool Library (1988, Somerset Maugham Award, American Acad of Arts and Letters E M Forster Award), The Folding Star (1994, James Tait Black Memorial Prize, shortlisted Booker Prize), The Spell (1998), The Line of Beauty (2004, Man Booker Prize); *Recreations* listening to music, looking at buildings; *Style—* Alan Hollinghurst, Esq, FRSL; ✉ Antony Harwood Ltd, 103 Walton Street, Oxford OX2 6EB (tel 01865 559615, fax 01865 310660, e-mail mail@antonyharwood.com)

HOLLINGSWORTH, Michael Charles (Mike); s of Albert George Hollingsworth, of Petersfield, Hants, and Gwendolen Marjorie Hollingsworth; *b* 22 February 1946; *Educ* Reading Sch, Carlisle Sch, Ruskin Coll Oxford (MA); *m* 1, 10 Aug 1968 (m dis 1988), Patricia Margaret Jefferson Winn; 1 da (Rebecca b 7 Oct 1974); m 2, 1 Jan 1989 (m dis 1999), Anne Margaret Diamond; 5 s (Oliver b 12 July 1987, Jamie b 21 Dec 1988, Sebastian b and d 1991, Jacob b 21 May 1993, Conor b 17 March 1995); *Career* prodr radio and TV BBC 1967–75; ed news and current affairs: Southern TV Ltd 1975–79, ATV Network Ltd/Central TV 1979–82; sr prodr current affairs BBC 1982–84, dir of progs TV-am Ltd 1984–85, md Music Box Ltd 1985–88, chief exec Venture Television and md Venture Artistes 1988–, fndr Daytime TV 1990, ed Good Morning with Anne and Nick (BBC1) until 1994, conslt on daytime programming to Sky TV until 1994, md Liberty Broadcasting 1996–97; presenters' agent 1994–; dir: Venture Television Ltd, Good Morning Britain Ltd; former dir TV-am Ltd and TV-am News Ltd (resigned 1986); currently head of celebritiy liaison Cancer Research UK; FRSA; *Recreations* polo, house renovation; *Style—* Mike Hollingsworth; ✉ Macready House, 75 Crawford Street, London W1H 5LP (tel 07836 637086, e-mail venturemike@btinternet.com)

HOLLINGTON, Geoffrey Arnold (Geoff); s of Henry Cecil Hollington (d 1983), of West Wickham, Kent, and Eileen Caroline, *née* Fletcher; *b* 5 February 1949; *Educ* Beckenham GS, Central Sch of Art and Design London (BA), RCA London (MA); *m* 1, 1971 (m dis 1984) Judith Ann, da of Dennis Frederick Leonard Fox; 1 s (Simon James b 7 Feb 1979); m 2, 1984, Elizabeth Ann Beecham, da of Clement Joseph Lawton; 3 da (Gemma Beecham (adopted 1987) b 27 Oct 1977, Emily b and d 29 Feb 1985, Sophy Imogen b 18 July 1989), 1 s (James Henry b 23 Sept 1986); *Career* industrial designer; Milton Keynes Devpt Corp 1976–78, ptnr Glickman & Hollington 1978–80, princ Hollington Associates 1980–; clients incl: Herman Miller Inc USA, Parker Pen, Ericsson; memb: Industrial Design Soc of America 1991; FRSA 1988, FCSD 1994; *Publications* Hollington: Industrial Design (1990); *Recreations* family, theatre, music, opera, reading, writing; *Style—* Geoff Hollington, Esq

HOLLINGWORTH, Corinne Ann; da of George Hollingworth, and Dorothy, *née* Grice; *b* 25 May 1952; *Educ* Sherwood Hall GS, Drama Dept Univ of Bristol (BA), Webber Douglas Acad of Dramatic Art; *m* 1983, Robert Gabriel; 1 s (Jonathan William Hamilton b 1985); *Career* BBC TV: prodr Eastenders 1988–91, prodr Eldorado 1992–93, prodr Casualty 1993–95, exec prodr Eastenders 1994–96; controller of drama Channel 5 1996–2003, head of continuing series ITV 2004–; memb: BAFTA 1996, RTS 1996; *Style—* Ms Corinne Hollingworth

HOLLINS, Peter; *Educ* East Barnet GS, Hertford Coll Oxford (BA); *Career* ICI 1973–1992, chief operating offr European Vinyls Corp 1992–98, ceo British Energy 1998–2001, various roles as chm and non-exec dir 2001–03, chief exec British Heart Fndn 2003–; *Recreations* music (especially opera), European history; *Style—* Peter Hollins, Esq; ✉ British Heart Foundation, 14 Fitzhardinge Street, London W1H 6DH (tel 020 7935 0185, fax 020 7486 5820)

HOLLINS, Prof Sheila Clare; da of Capt Adrian M Kelly (d 1995), of Bristol, and Monica Dallas, *née* Edwards (d 2005); *b* 22 June 1946; *Educ* Notre Dame HS Sheffield, St Thomas' Hosp Med Sch London (MB BS); *m* 7 June 1969, Martin Prior Hollins, s of Harry Pryor Hollins (d 1985), of Cheadle Hulme; 3 da (Kathryn b 1971, Emily b 1976, Abigail b 1978), 1 s (Nigel b 1973); *Career* sr registrar in child psychiatry Earls Court Child Guidance Unit and Westminster Children's Hosp 1979–81; St George's Hosp Med Sch London: sr lectr in the psychiatry of learning disability St George's Hosp Med Sch (prof 1990–), head Dept of Psychiatry of Disability 1986–2002, head Div of Mental Health 2002–05; hon conslt Wandsworth Community Health Tst and Richmond Twickenham and Roehampton Healthcare Tst 1981–99, hon conslt SW London Mental Health Tst 1999–; Dept of Health: seconded to Policy Div as pt/t sr policy advsr on learning disability 1993–94 and 2001–03; memb: Minister's Advsy Gp on Learning Disability 1999–2001, Nat Learning Disability Taskforce 2001–, Independent Inquiry into Access to Healthcare for People with Learning Disabilities 2007; chair NHS Working Party on Breast and Cervical Screening in Learning Disability 1999–2000, chair External Advsy Gp Nat Confidential Inquiry into Suicides and Homicides 2007–; RCPsych: chair Exec Ctee Psychiatry of Learning Disability Faculty 1994–98, memb Ct of Electors 1999–, vice-pres 2003–, pres 2005–; vice-pres Inst of Psychiatry and Disability 2001–; memb lay community St Benedict; Winston Churchill fell 1993; memb APP, FRCPsych 1988 (MRCPsych 1978), FRCPCH, FRCP, FRSM; *Books* Mental Handicap: A Multi Disciplinary Approach (ed with M Craft, J Bicknell, 1985), Going Somewhere - Pastoral Care for People with Mental Handicap (with M Grimer, 1988), Understanding Depression in People with Learning Disabilities (with J Curran, 1996), Understanding Grief (with L Sireling, 1999); ed and co-author of 31 titles in Books Beyond Words series incl: When Dad Died and When Mum Died (2 books with L Sireling, 1990), Jenny Speaks Out (with V Sinason, 1992), Bob Tells All (with V Sinason, 1992), Hug Me, Touch Me (Best Author Read Easy Awards Book Tst and Joseph Rowntree Fndn 1994), Getting on With Epilepsy (with J Bernal, 1999), Looking After My Breasts (2000), George Gets Smart (with M Flynn and P Russell, 2001), Mugged (with V Sinason, 2002), You and Your Child: Making Sense of Learning Disability (with M Hollins, 2005); author of numerous peer reviewed papers and chapters on mental health and learning disability; *Recreations* family, walking, music; *Style—* Prof Sheila Hollins; ✉ Division of Mental Health, St Georges, University of London, Cranmer Terrace, London SW17 0RE (tel 020 8725 5501, fax 020 8672 1070, e-mail s.hollins@sgul.ac.uk)

HOLLIOAKE, Adam; *b* 5 September 1971; *Career* professional cricketer; debut Surrey CCC 1992 (currently capt, highest score 138 v Leics); memb England U19 team to NZ 1992; England: debut v Australia 1997, capt team for Sharjah Cup (winners) 1997, memb team touring West Indies 1998, one-day capt 1998, memb squad Emirates Trophy 1998, capt Wills International Cup squad Bangladesh 1998, 4 test matches, 35 one-day ints; *Style—* Adam Hollioake, Esq; ✉ c/o Surrey CCC, Kennington Oval, London SE11 5SS (tel 020 7582 6660)

HOLLIS, Arthur Norman; OBE (1985), DFC (1943); s of Egerton Clark Hollis (d 1967), of Eastbourne, E Sussex, and Vera Lina, *née* Leigh (d 1944); *b* 11 August 1922; *Educ* Dulwich Coll; *m* 2 Dec 1944, Elizabeth, da of Reginald Chase Edmunds (d 1986), of Westwell, Kent; 2 da (Jennifer b 1945, Sylvia b 1949), 1 s (Richard b 1953); *Career* RAFVR 1941–46, Sqdn Ldr 1945–46; memb HAC 1978; chartered accountant; ptnr: Limebeer & Co 1953–75, Russell Limebeer 1975–88; sr ptnr based in City of London specialising in countries of W Europe; dir various cos; memb Mgmnt Ctee Yehudi Menuhin Sch 1964–88 (vice-pres 1989), govr Live Music Now 1977–90, offr of various Cons Assocs; chm: Ashford Constituency 1980–83 (vice-pres 1991), Kent East Euro Constituency 1985–88 (pres 1991–96); chm Westwell PC 1976–79; Master Worshipful Co of Woolmen 1982–83; FCA 1958, FRSA 1983; *Recreations* travel, shooting, country pursuits; *Clubs* Travellers, City of London, United and Cecil; *Style—* Arthur Hollis, Esq, OBE, DFC; ✉ Court Lodge, Westwell, Ashford, Kent TN25 4JX (tel 01233 712555)

HOLLIS, Rt Rev Crispian; *see:* Portsmouth, Bishop of (RC)

HOLLIS, His Hon Judge Keith; s of Eric Hollis (d 2005), and Joan, *née* Gore; *b* 9 June 1951, London; *Educ* Whitgift Sch Croydon; *m* 28 April 1979, Mariana, *née* Roberts; 1 s (George b 11 Oct 1981), 1 da (Isabel b 27 Sept 1983); *Career* slr 1974, district judge 1991, circuit judge 2000–; dir of studies Cwlth Magistrates and Judges Assoc 1998–; *Recreations* music; *Clubs* ESU; *Style—* His Hon Judge Hollis

HOLLIS, Prof Malcolm Richard Arthur; s of Arthur Edwin Hollis (d 1970), of Southport, Merseyside, and Esmé Muriel, *née* Pettit (d 2002); *b* 17 March 1944; *Educ* King George V GS Southport, Univ of South Wales and Monmouth, Univ of London (BSc); *m* 11 Sept 1965, Andrea Joan, da of Sqdn Ldr John Edward Fuller (d 1989), of West Chiltington, W Sussex; 2 s (Richard b 1969, Gavin b 1976), 1 da (Tricia b 1970); *Career* chartered building surveyor; ptnr Best Gapp & Ptnrs 1969, princ Malcolm Hollis Associates

1972–80, ptnr Baxter Payne & Lepper (incl Malcolm Hollis Associates) 1980–91 (dep chm 1986–88), sr ptnr Malcolm Hollis & Partners 1991–95; chm Acutec UK 1995–; Surveyor to the Fabric Worshipful Co of Skinners 1982–, mangr professional servs Nationwide Anglia Estate Agents 1987–91, memb Cncl RICS Bldg Surveyors 1988–92 and 1998–2001; over 100 appearances on TV and radio 1984–; prof Univ of Reading 1989–, visiting prof Univ of Malaya Malaysia 2006–, visiting prof Politecnic of Bari Italy 2007–; ed Jl of Building Appraisal 2002–; cncllr London Borough of Lambeth 1977–81; govr Woodmansterne Sch 1978–81 (chm 1979–81); tstee Upkeep (incl The Upkeep Building Museum); Freeman City of London 1983, Freeman Worshipful Co of Chartered Surveyors 1982; FSVA 1969, FBEng 1969, FRICS 1970, MCIArb 1974, MAE 1997; *Books* Surveying Buildings (1983, 5 edn 2003), Householders Action Guide (1984), Model Survey Reports (1985, 2 edn 1989), Surveying for Dilapidations (1988), Cavity Wall Tie Failure (1990), Dilapidations (1992, 2 edn 1996), Introduction to Dilapidations (1999, 2 edn 2003), Surveyors Fact Book (2001, revised edn 2007), Surveying Buildings Pocket Book (2002, 2 edn 2006); *Recreations* writing, photography, skiing, thinking; *Clubs* Charthills GC, Dartmouth Golf; *Style*— Prof Malcolm Hollis; ✉ 6 Rydal Road, London SW16 1QN (tel 020 8769 9927, fax 020 8769 2670, e-mail mh@malcolmhollis.org)

HOLLIS OF HEIGHAM, Baroness (Life Peer UK 1990), of Heigham in the City of Norwich; Patricia Lesley Hollis; PC (1999), DL (Norfolk 1994); da of H L G Wells, of Norwich, and (Queenie) Rosalyn, *née* Clayforth; *b* 24 May 1941; *Educ* Plympton GS, Univ of Cambridge (MA), Univ of Calif Berkeley, Columbia Univ NY, Nuffield Coll Oxford (MA, DPhil); *m* 18 Sept 1965, Prof (James) Martin Hollis (d 1998), s of (Hugh) Mark Noel Hollis, of Oxted, Surrey; 2 s (Hon Simon b 1969, Hon Matthew b 1971); *Career* Harkness fell 1962–64, Nuffield scholar 1964–67, reader (formerly sr lectr and lectr) modern history UEA 1967–, dean Sch of English and American Studies UEA 1988–90; Parly under sec of state DSS 1997–2001, min for Children and the Family Dept of Work and Pensions 2001–; councillor Norwich City 1968–91 (ldr 1983–88); memb: E Anglia Economic Planning Cncl 1975–79, Regnl Health Authy 1979–83, BBC Regnl Advsy Ctee 1979–83, Norfolk CC 1981–85; dir Radio Broadland 1983–95; Parly candidate Great Yarmouth 1974 and 1979; nat cmmr English Heritage 1988–91, memb Press Cncl 1989–91; hon fell Girton Coll Cambridge 2000; FRHistS; *Books* The Pauper Press (1970), Class and Class Conflict 1815–50 (1973), Women in Public 1850–1900 (1979), Pressure from Without (1974), Ladies Elect: Women in English Local Govt 1865–1914 (1987), Jennie Lee, A Life (1997); *Recreations* singing, boating on the broads, domesticity; *Style*— The Rt Hon Baroness Hollis of Heigham, PC, DL; ✉ House of Lords, London SW1A 0PW (tel 020 7219 3000)

HOLLOBONE, Philip; MP; *b* 7 November 1964; *Educ* Lady Margaret Hall Oxford; *Career* industry research analyst 1987–2004; cncllr (Cons): Bromley BC 1990–94, Kettering BC 2003–; Parly candidate (Cons) Kettering 2001, MP (Cons) Kettering 2005–; *Style*— Philip Hollobone, Esq, MP; ✉ House of Commons, London SW1A 0AA (tel 020 7219 8373, fax 020 7219 8802, e-mail hollobonep@parliament.uk)

HOLLOWAY, Adam; MP; *Educ* Univ of Cambridge (MA), Imperial Coll London (MBA); *Career* former offr Grenadier Guards; TV journalist and undercover reporter, Bosnia reporter ITN; worked on programs incl: Newsnight, World in Action, News At Ten, No Fixed Abode; MP (Cons) Gravesham 2005–, memb House of Commons Defence Select Ctee; former memb Bd Christian Aid; *Style*— Adam Holloway, Esq, MP; ✉ House of Commons, London SW1A 0AA (tel 020 7219 8402, e-mail adamholloway@ntlworld.com, website www.adamholloway.co.uk)

HOLLOWAY, His Hon Judge (Frederick Reginald) Bryn; s of William Herbert Holloway, of Alberbury, Shrewsbury, and Audrey Eileen, *née* Hull-Brown; *b* 8 January 1947; *Educ* Wrekin Coll, Holborn Coll of Law London; *m* 6 Aug 1974, Barbara, da of William Archie Bradley; 2 s (Christopher Reginald Bradley b 11 Sept 1978, William Benjamin b 30 Oct 1979); *Career* called to the Bar Lincoln's Inn 1971; pupillage with His Hon Judge Henry Lachs 1972, recorder 1989–92 (asst recorder 1984–89), circuit judge (Northern Circuit) 1992–; *Recreations* gardening, Shrewsbury Town FC, cricket, rugby; *Style*— His Hon Judge Holloway; ✉ Queen Elizabeth II Law Courts, Derby Square, Liverpool (tel 0151 473 7373)

HOLLOWAY, James; s of Roland David Holloway (d 1987), and Nancy Briant Evans (d 1981); *b* 24 November 1948; *Educ* Marlborough, Courtauld Inst of Art; *Career* research asst National Gallery of Scotland 1972–80, asst keeper National Museum of Wales 1980–83, dir Scottish National Portrait Gallery 1997– (dep keeper 1983–97); pres The Scottish Soc; memb Ctee: Scottish Indian Arts Forum, Scottish Sculpture Trust; curatorial ctee memb National Trust for Scotland; FSA Scot 1984; *Publications* The Discovery of Scotland (1978), James Tassie (1986), Jacob More (1987), William Aikman (1988), Patrons of Painters Art: in Scotland 1650–1760 (1989), The Norie Family (1994); *Recreations* motorbikes, India; *Clubs* Puffins, New; *Style*— James Holloway, Esq; ✉ Scottish National Portrait Gallery, 1 Queen Street, Edinburgh EH2 1JD (tel 0131 624 6401, fax 0131 558 3691, e-mail jholloway@nationalgalleries.org)

HOLLOWAY, Prof John Henry; OBE (2000); s of William Henry Holloway (d 1983), of Coalville, and Ivy May, *née* Sarson (d 1997); *b* 20 December 1938; *Educ* Ashby-de-la-Zouch Boys' GS, Univ of Birmingham (BSc, PhD, DSc); *m* 14 April 1962, Jennifer, da of Albert Burne (d 1993); 2 da (Sarah b 1964, Amanda b 1965), 1 s (Mark b 1969); *Career* Univ of Aberdeen: asst lectr 1963–64, lectr 1964–70; Univ of Leicester: lectr 1971–78, sr lectr 1978–87, prof and head of chemistry 1987–96, dean of science 1997–99, pro-vice-chllr 1999–2001, sr pro-vice-chllr 2001–03, prof emeritus 2004; Royal Soc of Chemistry: memb Disciplinary Ctee, memb Industrial Inorganics Sector Ctee, memb Ctee for Health and Safety at RSC Events; BAAS: memb Cncl, memb Audit Ctee; author of over 300 papers on fluorine chemistry; past chm HE Chemistry Conf; chm of dirs EMMAN (E Midlands Met Area Network) Ltd; CChem, FRSC; *Books* Noble Gas Chemistry (1968); *Recreations* painting, drawing, sailing, classic car restoration; *Style*— Prof John Holloway, OBE; ✉ 5 Hall Gardens, High Street East, Uppingham, Rutland LE15 9HG (tel 01572 820276); Pro-Vice-Chancellors' Office, University of Leicester, Leicester LE1 7RH (tel 0116 252 2326, fax 0116 255 8691, e-mail jhh2@le.ac.uk)

HOLLOWAY, Julian Pendrill Warner; s of Adrian George Warner Holloway, JP, of Minchinhampton, Glos, and Helen Pendrill, *née* Charles; *b* 6 May 1954; *Educ* Winchester, Univ of Durham (BA); *m* 4 Oct 1980 (m dis 1998), Emma Jane Caroline, da of Col Peter Charles Ormrod, MC, JP, DL, of Pen-y-Lan Ruabon, Clwyd; 1 da (Lavinia b 28 April 1984), 3 s (James b 29 June 1986, Thomas b 14 March 1988, Alexander b 29 Aug 1991); m 2, 1999, Sarah Louise Balfe, da of Jeremy Bennett, Esq, OBE, of Sherborne, Dorset; *Career* articled clerk Denton Hall & Burgin 1979–81, admitted slr to the Supreme Ct 1981, asst slr Brecher & Co 1981–83, ptnr McKenna & Co 1988–92 (asst slr 1984–88), ptnr Greenwoods 1993–2000, ptnr Berwin Leighton Paisner 2001–; dir Centre for Dispute Resolution, case-notes ed Construction Law Jl; memb Law Soc; *Recreations* tennis, skiing, shooting; *Clubs* Hurlingham; *Style*— Julian Holloway, Esq; ✉ 64 Alderbrook Road, London SW12 8AB (tel 020 8675 0308); Berwin Leighton Paisner, Adelaide House, London EC4R 9HA (tel 020 7760 1000, fax 020 7760 1111)

HOLLOWAY, Laurence (Laurie); s of Marcus Holloway (d 1978), of Oldham, Lancs, and Annie, *née* Gillespie (d 1992); *b* 31 March 1938; *Educ* Oldham GS; *m* 1, 31 March 1956, Julia Planck, da of Rufus Macdonald (d 1975), of Rothesay, Isle of Bute; 1 da (Karon Julie b 9 Jan 1957); m 2, 16 June 1965, Marian Montgomery (d 2002), singer, da of Forrest Marion Runnels (d 1966), of Atlanta, Georgia; 1 da (Abigail Ann Montgomery Hellens b 31 Jan 1967); *Career* pianist, composer, arranger; studio musician 1959–69; compositions incl: A Dream of Alice (BBC TV), pop preludes, About Time (C5 Records); musical dir: Engelbert Humperdinck 1969–74, Dame Edna Everage 1980– (currently md), Elaine Paige 1992–, Piaf (musical) 1992, Bob Monkhouse, Lily Savage TV Special, Bob Downe TV Special, Bob Holness radio series, Parkinson TV series 1998–, Strictly Come Dancing (BBC TV) 2004–05; pianist for: Judy Garland and Liza Minnelli London Palladium 1964, Dame Kiri Te Kanawa on Popular Recordings (special guest at concert); composer TV signature tunes incl Blind Date, occasional guest conductor London Symphony Orch; tstee Montgomery-Holloway Music Tst; subject of This is your Life 2000; *Recreations* golf, music, shooting, fishing; *Clubs* Temple Golf; *Style*— Laurie Holloway, Esq; ✉ Elgin, Fishery Road, Bray-on-Thames, Berkshire SL6 1UP (tel 01628 637715, fax 01628 776232, e-mail laurence.holloway@btinternet.com)

HOLLOWAY, Neil; *Educ* Univ of Bath (BSc), Univ of Cambridge (MPhil); *Career* md Migent UK until 1990; Microsoft Corporation: joined 1990, md Microsoft Ltd 1998–2000, vice-pres for sales, mktg and servs EMEA 2000–05, pres EMEA 2005, corporate vice-pres 2003–; *Recreations* football, swimming, golf, family; *Style*— Neil Holloway, Esq; ✉ Microsoft Ltd, Microsoft Campus, Thames Valley Park, Reading RG6 1WG

HOLLOWAY, Prof Robin Greville; s of Robert Charles Holloway (d 1986), and Pamela Mary, *née* Jacob (d 1996); *b* 19 October 1943; *Educ* St Paul's Cathedral Choir Sch, KCS Wimbledon, King's Coll Cambridge, New Coll Oxford; *Career* composer; Univ of Cambridge: lectr in music 1975–, prof of musical composition 2001–; compositions incl: Scenes from Schumann (Cheltenham) 1970, Domination of Black (London) 1974, Second Concerto for Orchestra (Glasgow) 1979, Seascape and Harvest (Birmingham) 1986, Clarissa (ENO) 1990, The Spacious Firmament (Birmingham) 1992, Violin Concerto (Manchester) 1992, Frost at Midnight (Bournemouth) 1994, Third Concerto for Orchestra (London) 1996, Clarinet Concerto (Canterbury) 1997, Scenes from Antwerp (Antwerp) 1998, Clarissa - Sequence (San Francisco) 1998, Double Bass Concerto 1999, Symphony (London) 2000, Fourth Concerto for Orchestra 2001–06, Missa Caiensis 2002, String Quartet No 1 2003, String Quartet No 2 2004; *Books* Debussy and Wagner (1978), On Music: Essays and Diversions (2003); *Style*— Prof Robin Holloway; ✉ Gonville & Caius College, Cambridge CB2 1TA (tel and fax 01223 335424); 531 Caledonian Road, London N7 9RH (tel 020 7607 2550)

HOLM, Sir Ian; kt (1998), CBE (1990); *b* 12 September 1931; *Educ* RADA; *m* 2003, Sophie de Stempel, *qv*; *Career* actor; *Theatre* debut in Othello (Shakespeare Memorial Theatre) 1954, Worthing Rep 1956, at Stratford 1957–60: roles incl Verges, Puck, The Fool in King Lear, Lorenzio and Gremio; with RSC (Aldwych) until 1967: Ondine, The Devils, Becket, The Taming of the Shrew, The Cherry Orchard; other RSC prodns until 1967: Troilus and Cressida (Stratford), The Tempest, Edward IV, Richard III, Henry IV and Henry V (Evening Standard for Best Actor) 1964, Edward IV 1964, Richard III 1964, The Homecoming (Aldwych) 1965 and (Music Box NY) 1967 (Tony Award for Best Supporting Actor in a Drama), Henry IV (I and II) 1966, Henry V 1966, Twelfth Night 1966, Romeo and Juliet 1967; other prodns incl: The Friends (Roundhouse) 1970, A Bequest to the Nation (Haymarket) 1970, Caravaggio Buddy (Traverse Theatre, Edinburgh) 1972, Hatch in the Sea (Royal Court), Other People (Hampstead) 1974, The Iceman Cometh (Aldwych) 1976, The Devil's Disciple (Aldwych) 1976, Uncle Vanya (Hampstead) 1979, The Room (Pinter benefit, Haymarket) 1989, Moonlight (Almeida) 1993 (Evening Standard Award for Best Actor), Moonlight and Landscape (Pinter Festival Gate Theatre Dublin) 1994, Landscape (RNT) 1994, King Lear (RNT) 1997 (Evening Standard Award for Best Actor, Olivier Award for Best Actor), The Homecoming (Comedy Theatre) 2001; *Television* for BBC: Flayed, The Lost Boys, The Misanthrope, Lloyd George, We The Accused, The Bell, After The Party, The Browning Version, Mr and Mrs Edgehill, Uncle Vanya, The Last Romantics, The Borrowers, Landscape, King Lear; for Granada: Night School, Strike, Game Set and Match, Mirage; other credits incl: Napoleon in Love, Jesus of Nazareth, The Road From Mandalay, SOS Titanic, All Quiet on the Western Front, Inside The Third Reich, Death Can Add (Anglia TV), The Endless Game (HTV), Taylor of Gloucester (Thames), Alice Through The Looking Glass (Channel 4); *Film* A Midsummer Night's Dream, The Fixer, The Bofors Gun (BAFTA for Best Supporting Actor), The Homecoming, Juggernaut, Shout at the Devil, The Man in the Iron Mask, March or Die, Thief of Baghdad, Alien, Chariots of Fire (BAFTA for Best Supporting Actor, Cannes Film Festival Best Supporting Actor, Oscar nomination), The Time Bandits, The Return of the Soldier, Dead as they Come, Greystoke, Brazil, Laughterhouse, Dance with a Stranger, Wetherby, Dreamchild, Another Woman, Henry V, Michaelangelo, Hamlet, Kafka, The Naked Lunch, Blue Ice, The Hour of the Pig, Frankenstein, Dr Willis in The Madness of King George 1994 (BAFTA nomination), Loch Ness 1995, Big Night 1995, Nighty Falls on Manhattan 1995, The Fifth Element 1996, A Life Less Ordinary 1996, The Sweet Hereafter 1996, Simon Magus 1998, Existenz 1998, The Match 1998, Beautiful Joe 1999, Bless the Child 1999, Joe Gould's Secret 1999, Esther Kahn 1999, Lord of the Rings: The Fellowship of the Ring 2001, From Hell 2002, Lord of the Rings: the Return of the King 2003, Garden State 2004, The Day After Tomorrow 2004, The Treatment 2005, Lord of War 2005, Chromophobia 2005, Beyond Friendship 2005; *Style*— Sir Ian Holm, CBE

HOLM, Dr Jessica Lynn; da of Sir Ian Holm, CBE, *qv*, and Lynn Mary, *née* Shaw; *b* 29 March 1960; *Educ* Putney HS for Girls, Royal Holloway Coll London (BSc, PhD); *m* 27 Feb 1988, Gavin Bernard Chappell, s of Lt-Col Robin Chappell, OBE; 2 c (Tierney Brook b 15 Oct 1997, Karris Layne b 27 Sept 2000); *Career* zoologist and broadcaster BBC Natural History Unit and others; BBC Natural History Unit films: The Case of the Vanishing Squirrel 1987, Daylight Robbery 1988, Badger Watch 1990, Daylight Robbery II 1991, Nightshift 1993; presenter: Natural History Progamme (BBC Radio 4) 1988–93, Wild about the West (TSW) 1988, Up Country (Tyne Tees TV) 1990, 1991, 1992 and 1993, Crufts (BBC TV) 1991–2007, Wild West Country (WCTV) 1994, 1995 and 1996, Cross Country (HTV) 1999, Changing Places (BBC Radio 4) 2001–02; commentator The Underdog Show (BBC 2) 2007; regular columnist and cartoonist Dog World newspaper; painter; Slipper Thief (first limited edn print, Greenwich Workshop) 1996, I Spy Summer (second limited edn print, Greenwich Workshop) 1997, Five Persians (third limited edn print) 1998, The Sentry (fourth limited edn print) 1998, solo exhibition The Kennel Club 1997; *Publications* Squirrels (1987), The Red Squirrel (1989); contrib various articles to wildlife and conservation magazines; *Recreations* my children, my dogs, my vegetable garden; *Style*— Dr Jessica Holm; ✉ c/o Rachel Daniels, Berlin Associates, 14 Floral Street, London WC2E 9DH (tel 020 7836 1112); Greenwich Workshop, One Greenwich Place, PO Box 875, Shelton, Connecticut 06484–4675, USA (tel 00 1 203 925 0131, e-mail jessica.holm@btinternet.com)

HOLMAN, Barry William; s of Ronald Cecil Holman, of Loughton, Essex, and Irene Winifred Holman; *b* 7 July 1949; *Educ* Coopers' Co GS; *m* 17 Aug 1974, Christine, da of Norman Thomas Richards; *Career* chartered accountant: B W Holman & Co (own practice), Newman Harris & Co, Silver Altman & Co, Lewis Bloom, Macnair Mason; FCA; *Recreations* golf, horse riding, clay pigeon shooting, music, chess; *Clubs* Abridge Golf and Country, Beldlam Golf Soc (past capt); *Style*— Barry W Holman, Esq; ✉ Brook House, Ongar Road, Abridge, Essex RM4 1UH (tel 01992 813079); B W Holman & Co, First Floor Suite, Enterprise House, 10 Church Hill, Loughton, Essex IG10 1LA (tel 020 8508 9228, fax 020 8502 4772)

HOLMAN, Hon Mr Justice; Sir (Edward) James Holman; kt (1995); s of Edward Theodore Holman (d 2001), and Mary Megan, *née* Morris, MBE (d 2006), formerly of Ringwood, Hants and Manaccan, Cornwall; *b* 21 August 1947; *Educ* Dauntsey's Sch West Lavington, Exeter Coll Oxford (MA); *m* 14 July 1979, Fiona Elisabeth, da of late Dr Ronald Cathcart

H

Roxburgh, of Wiggenhall St Mary, Norfolk; 1 da (Charlotte b 1984), 2 s (Edward b 1988, Henry b 1991); *Career* called to the Bar Middle Temple 1971 (bencher 1995); memb Western Circuit, QC 1991, recorder of the Crown Court 1993–95, judge of the High Court of Justice (Family Div) 1995–, Family Div liaison judge for Western Circuit 1995–2002; standing counsel to the Treasury (Queen's Proctor) 1980–91, legal assessor UK Central Cncl for Nursing Midwifery and Health Visiting 1983–95; Family Law Bar Assoc: sec 1988–92, chm 1992–95; ex officio memb Gen Cncl of the Bar 1992–95; memb: Family Proceedings Rules Ctee 1991–95, Supreme Court Procedure Ctee 1992–95; memb: Cncl RYA 1980–83, 1984–87 and 1988–91, Ctee Royal Ocean Racing Club 1984–87; *Recreations* sailing, skiing, music; *Clubs* Royal Yacht Sqdn, Royal Ocean Racing; *Style—* The Hon Mr Justice Holman; ✉ Royal Courts of Justice, Strand, London WC2A 2LL

HOLMAN, His Hon Judge Richard Christopher; s of Frank Harold Holman (d 1984), and Joan, *née* Attrill (d 1988); *b* 16 June 1946; *Educ* Eton, Gonville & Caius Coll Cambridge (MA); *m* 9 Aug 1969, Susan Holman, MBE, DL (d 2007), da of George Amos Whittaker, of Wilmslow, Cheshire; 2 s (Nicholas b 12 Jan 1973, Simon b 26 May 1977); *Career* admitted slr 1971, dep dist registrar of High Court and dep registrar County Court 1982–88, asst recorder 1988–92, recorder Northern Circuit 1992–94, circuit judge (Northern Circuit) 1994–, designated civil judge, Manchester (central) 1998–, sr circuit judge 2002–; memb Civil Procedure Rule Ctee 1997–2002; managing ptnr Davies Wallis Foyster 1988–89 (ptnr 1973); memb: Cncl Manchester Law Soc until 1990, Area Ctee NW Legal Aid until 1994; chm Pownall Hall Sch 1993–98 (govr 1990–98); *Recreations* golf, gardening, theatre, wine; *Clubs* Wilmslow Golf (capt 1998–99); *Style—* His Hon Judge Holman; ✉ Manchester Civil Justice Centre, 1 Bridge Street West, Manchester M3 3FX

HOLME OF CHELTENHAM, Baron (Life Peer UK 1990), of Cheltenham in the County of Gloucestershire; Richard Gordon Holme; CBE (1983), PC (2000); s of J R Holme (d 1940), and E M Holme, *née* Eggleton; *b* 27 May 1936; *Educ* St John's Coll Oxford (MA); *m* 1958, Kay Mary, da of Vincent Powell; 2 da (Hon Nicola Ann b 1959, Hon Penelope Jane b 1962), 2 s (Hon Richard Vincent, Hon John Gordon (twins) b 1966); *Career* chm: Constitutional Reform Centre 1984–94, Threadneedle Publishing Gp 1988–, Prima Europe Ltd 1991–95; dep chm ITC 1999–, dir Rio Tinto plc (formerly RTZ Corp plc) 1995–98; sec Parly Democracy Tst 1979–95, pres Lib Pty 1981, Lib Dem Parly spokesman on N Ireland 1990–2000; chm: English Coll in Prague 1991–, Cncl Cheltenham Ladies' Coll 1998–2000, Advsy Bd Br American Project 1999–, Broadcasting Standards Cmmn 1999–2000, Hansard Soc for Parly Govt 2001–; advsy dir NTL 2001–; chllr Univ of Greenwich 1998–; *Recreations* reading, walking, opera; *Clubs* Reform, Brooks's; *Style—* The Rt Hon Lord Holme of Cheltenham, CBE, PC; ✉ House of Lords, London SW1A 0PW

HOLMES, Alan Wilson Jackson; s of Luke Jackson Holmes (d 1979); *b* 13 September 1945; *Educ* Portora Royal Sch Enniskillen, Univ of Cambridge; *m* 1970, Frances-Maria, *née* Kadwell; 3 s, 1 da; *Career* dir Courage (Central) Ltd 1973–81, chm Courage (Scotland) Ltd 1979–81, dir Courage Ltd 1982–96, dir Scottish Courage Ltd 1996–2000, dir (int beer) Scottish & Newcastle plc 2000– (dir Central and Eastern Europe 2002–); memb Ct of Assts Worshipful Co of Brewers; *Recreations* golf, modern jazz, theatre; *Clubs* Royal & Ancient, Loch Lomond Golf, Huntercombe Golf; *Style—* Alan Holmes, Esq; ✉ 26a Royal Terrace, Edinburgh EH7 5AH (tel 0131 557 9788); Scottish & Newcastle plc, 33 Ellersly Road, Edinburgh EH12 6HX (tel 0131 528 2000, fax 0131 528 2305)

HOLMES, Prof Andrew Bruce; AM (2004); s of late Bruce Morell Holmes, and Frances Henty Graham Holmes; *b* 5 September 1943; *Educ* Scotch Coll Melbourne, Ormond Coll Univ of Melbourne (BSc, MSc), UCL (PhD), Univ of Cambridge (ScD); *m* 1971, Jennifer Lesley, *née* Hodson; 3 s; *Career* Royal Soc European postdoctoral fell ETH-Zürich 1971–72; Univ of Cambridge: demonstrator 1972–77, lectr 1977–99, dir Melville Lab for Polymer Synthesis 1994–2004, reader in organic and polymer chemistry 1995–98, prof of organic and polymer chemistry 1998–2004; prof of chemistry Imperial Coll London 2004–, ARC fedn fell and prof of chemistry Univ of Melbourne/CSIRO Molecular and Health Technologies; fell Clare Coll Cambridge 1973–; visiting fell La Trobe Univ 1977, visiting prof Univ of Calif Berkeley 1984, visiting prof Univ of Calif Irvine 1991; Royal Soc Leverhulme sr research fell 1993–94, Wilsmore fell Univ of Melbourne 2002–03; W G Dauben lectr Univ of Calif Berkeley 1999–2000, Aggarwal lectr Cornell Univ 2002, W Heinlen Hall lectr Bowling Green State Univ 2006; princ ed Jl of Materials Research 1994–99, chm Editorial Bd Chemical Communications 2000–03; memb: Bd of Editors Organic Syntheses Inc 1996–2001, Int Advsy Bd Jl of Materials Chemistry 1996–2006, Int Advsy Bd Macromolecular Chemistry and Physics 1999–2006; memb Editorial Bd: New Jl of Chemistry 2000–03, Chemical Communications 2004–, Chemistry World 2004–, Australian Jl of Chemistry 2004–, Bulletin of the Chemical Society of Japan 2004–, Angewandte Chemie 2006–; assoc ed Organic Letters 2006–; author of numerous articles in learned jls; Alfred Bader Award 1994, Materials Chemistry Award 1995, EU Descartes Prize 2003, Tilden lectr RSC 2003–04, Macro Gp Medal RSC 2004, Merck-Pfister lectr MIT 2005; dir Cambridge Quantum Fund 1995–2004, memb CUP Syndicate 2000–04; FRS 2000, FAA 2006, FTSE 2006; *Recreations* music appreciation, walking, skiing; *Style—* Prof Andrew Holmes, AM, FRS; ✉ Department of Chemistry, Imperial College, South Kensington, London SW7 2AY; Bio21 Institute, University of Melbourne, Victoria 3010, Australia (tel 00 61 3 8344 2344, fax 00 61 3 8344 2384, e-mail aholmes@unimelb.edu.au); CSIRO Molecular and Health Technologies, Bag 10, Clayton, Victoria 3169, Australia

HOLMES, Christopher; MBE (1993); *b* 15 October 1971, Peterborough; *Educ* Harry Cheshire Comp Sch Kidderminster, King's Coll Cambridge (MA), BPP Law Sch (Dip); *Career* swimmer, memb GB swimming team 1985–2001 (capt for 5 years), competed in 4 Paralympic Games (9 Paralympic Gold Medals), 2 World Championships and 7 European Championships, held 7 world records, 10 European records and 12 GB records; freelance journalist 1994–2000, project conslt Royal Mail Olympic Sponsorship Team 1995–97, slr specialising in employment and pensions law Ashurst London 2002–; cmmr Disability Rights Cmmn 2002–; memb: Implementation Bd UK Sports Inst 1999–2000, Panel UK Sport Awards 2001–04, Bd UK Sport 2005–; ambass London 2012 Olympic bid 2003–05; sporting patron Youth Sport Tst 1994–, patron Br Paralympic Assoc 2005–; vol Action for Blind People 1995–97; Sports Personality of the Year 1992, Bass Midlander of the Year 1992, SAF Paul Zetter Award 1996, Sports Personality of the Year Variety Club of GB 1997; *Style—* Christopher Holmes, Esq, MBE; ✉ Ashurst, Broadwalk House, 5 Appold Street, London EC2A 2HA

HOLMES, David Frederick Cecil; s of Norman Holmes (d 1995), and Kathleen Alice, *née* Bennett (d 1983); *b* 10 September 1933; *Educ* Little Ealing Sr Boys' Sch, Ealing Coll of Art, Shrewsbury Coll of Art, Central Sch of Art (pt/t); *m* 16 April 1960, Marie Lily Theresa, da of James Frederick Wilkinson; 2 s (Toby John b 20 Oct 1962, Rupert James b 20 May 1964), 1 da (Polly Victoria b 18 Nov 1967); *Career* joined Colman Prentis & Varley as junior 1950–52; Nat Serv RAOC 1952–54; jr creative Colman Prentis & Varley 1954–55, jr art dir W S Crawford Advertising 1955–58, art dir Mather & Crowther 1958–63, gp head of art Colman Prentis & Varley 1963–65, sr art dir (later ptnr and head of art) Kingsley Manton & Palmer Partnership 1965–71, dir and art dir The Television Department Ltd 1971–75, prop David Holmes & Partners (creative consultants) 1975–77, jt fndr dir and creative dir Holmes Knight Keeley Ltd (later Holmes Knight Ritchie WRG Ltd) 1977–92, exec creative dir TBWA/Holmes Knight Ritchie Ltd 1990–92, freelance artist, art dir and film maker 1992–, jt fndr dir Messrs Holmes & Watson Ltd 1994–; winner: numerous D&AD awards 1966–, Campaign Poster award for The Macallan 1986, Clio award for the Macallan poster 1988, D&AD Silver medal for Singapore Brochure design 1988 (also Gold award Aust Art Dirs' and Writers' Club 1988), shortlist certificate for The Long Sleep (The Macallan Malt Whisky cinema commercial) 1990 (also winner The One Show merit award 1990, Clio award 1990 and Oscar Br Animation awards 1990), 4 Gold awards Scotmedia Advertising Awards 1991; memb: D & AD 1968– (memb Ctee 1971–72), The Advertising Creative Circle 1967– (memb Cncl and sec 1979–81); *Publications* created books for Pan Books: My First Watch (Timex), My First Torch (Duracell), My First Toothbrush (Wisdom), My First Fountain Pen (Platignum), My First Crayons (Platignum); *Recreations* painting, playing the bagpipes, theatre; *Style—* David Holmes, Esq; ✉ Studio, 5 Calvert Street, Primrose Hill, London NW1 8NE (tel 020 7586 0363)

HOLMES, Dr Geoffrey Kenneth Towndrow; s of Kenneth Geoffrey Holmes (d 1974), and Majorie, *née* Towndrow; *b* 15 February 1942; *Educ* Tupton Hall GS, Univ of Birmingham (BSc, MB ChB, MD), DRCOG, PhD; *m* 4 May 1970, Rosemary, da of Stanley Alfred Guy, MBE (d 1997); 2 da (Rachel b 1971, Emma b 1976), 1 s (Simon b 1973); *Career* res fell Birmingham Gen Hosp and Dept of Experimental Pathology Univ of Birmingham 1971–74, sr med registrar United Birmingham Hosps 1974–78, conslt physician and gastroenterologist Derbyshire Royal Infirmary 1978–, clinical teacher Univ of Nottingham 1980–; examiner RCP 1990; author various research papers on gastrointestinal disorders particularly coeliac disease; memb Br Soc of Gastroenterology 1973, med advsr Derby and Dist Coeliac Soc 1980–, memb Medical Advsy Cncl Coeliac UK; pres: Derby and Burton Ileostomy Assoc 1986, Midland Gastroenterological Soc 2002–03; memb BMA 1966; FRCP (MRCP); *Books* Coeliac Disease Inflammatory Bowel Disease and Food Intolerance in Clinical Reactions to Food (1983), Coeliac Disease (1984), Coeliac Disease in Bockus Gastroenterology (1985), Coeliac Disease (2000); *Recreations* gardening, reading, theology; *Style—* Dr Geoffrey Holmes; ✉ Derbyshire Royal Infirmary, London Road, Derby (tel 01332 347141)

HOLMES, James Christopher (Jim); s of Herbert Frederick Holmes (d 1978), and Dorothy Gladys, *née* Thomas (d 2001); *b* 21 November 1948; *Educ* Tottenham Co GS, Univ of Sheffield (BA), London Opera Centre (repetiteurs dip); *Children* 2 s (Edward b 1983, Robert b 1985); *Career* conductor; ENO: chorus master 1973–78, princ coach 1978–96, resident conductor 1985–96; head of music/asst music dir Opera North 1996–; princ coach Glyndebourne Festival 1986–94; memb Editorial Advsy Bd Kurt Weill Edn 1994–; memb Br Voice Assoc; *Repertoire* incl: Orpheus in the Underworld, The Magic Flute, Mikado, Princess Ida, Die Fledermaus, Hänsel and Gretel, Peter Grimes, Turn of the Screw, Falstaff, Oedipus Rex, Pacific Overtures, La Belle Vivette, Fidelio, Mahagonny, Katya Kabanova, The Cunning Little Vixen, Paradise Moscow, Pelleas and Melisande, Marriage of Figaro, Gloriana, Sweeney Todd, One Touch of Venus, Seven Deadly Sins, Arms and the Cow, Tannhäuser, Cosi Fan Tutte, Don Giovanni, Peter Grimes, Albert Herring; other prodns incl: assoc music dir Carousel RNT 1993, I'm A Stranger Here Myself - Kurt Weill in America (BBC TV/Hessischer Rundfunk), Street Scene (Theater des Westens Berlin, Theater im Pfalzbau Ludwigshafen) 1994–95, debut Montreal Symphony Orch 1995, City of Birmingham Symphony Orch 2002, Norwegian Radio Orch 2002, Almeida Festival 2003, Hallé Orchestra 2005, BBC Nat Orchestra of Wales 2006, RLPO 2007; *Recordings* Pacific Overtures (Grammy Award nomination 1989), Soprano in Red (with Lesley Garrett, Gramophone Award) 1996, Porgy and Bess (musical asst to Sir Simon Rattle), Something Wonderful / If Ever I Would Leave You (with Bryn Terfel, arranger/musical asst); *Recreations* reading, crosswords, cinema, physical fitness, soccer (lifelong Spurs fan); *Style—* Jim Holmes, Esq; ✉ c/o Opera North, Grand Theatre, New Briggate, Leeds LS1 6NU (tel 0113 223 3512, fax 0113 244 0418, e-mail jim.holmes@operanorth.co.uk)

HOLMES, Dr Jeremy Alan; s of Robin Holmes (d 1985), of Oare, Wilts, and Marjorie, *née* Brown (d 1988); *b* 21 February 1943; *Educ* Westminster, King's Coll Cambridge (MA, MB BCh), UCH London; *m* 1, 1964 (m dis 1975), Margaret Simpson; m 2, 1978, Rosamund, da of Erroll Bruce; *Children* 3 s (Jacob b 1967, Matthew b 1969, Joshua b 1983), 1 da (Lydia b 1971); *Career* house physician London 1968–71, lectr in med Tanzania 1971–73, registrar then sr registrar in psychiatry Maudsley Hosp London 1973–77, conslt psychiatrist and hon sr lectr UCH London 1977–86, conslt psychiatrist N Devon, conslt psychotherapist and sr clinical lectr Univ of Bristol 1986–2003; visiting prof: UCL 2002–, Univ of Exeter; chair SW Assoc for Psychoanalytic Psychotherapy 2005–, former chair Psychotherapy Faculty RCPsych; Wellcome sr research fell 1992; MRCP, FRCPsych 1986; *Books* Textbook of Psychotherapy in Psychiatric Practice (ed, 1971), The Values of Psychotherapy (jtly, 1989), Between Art and Science - Essays in Psychiatry and Psychotherapy (1992), John Bowlby and Attachment Theory (1993), The Good Mood Guide (jtly, 1993), Introduction to Psychoanalysis (jtly, 1995), Attachment, Intimacy, Autonomy (1996), Healing Stories (jtly, 1998), The Search for the Secure Base (2001), Oxford Textbook of Psychotherapy (ed, 2005); *Recreations* family, literature and the Arts; *Style—* Dr Jeremy Holmes; ✉ North Devon District Hospital, Barnstaple, Devon EX31 4JB (e-mail j.a.holmes@btinternet.co.uk)

HOLMES, HE Sir John Eaton; GCVO (2004, CVO 1998), KBE (1999), CMG (1997); s of Leslie Howard Holmes, of Preston, Lancs, and Joyce Mary, *née* Stone; *b* 29 April 1951; *Educ* Preston GS, Balliol Coll Oxford (MA); *m* 1976, Penelope, da of Lt Col Rev E I Morris; 3 da (Sarah Victoria b 21 Jan 1981, Lucy Alexandra Mary b 22 Sept 1982, Emilie Catherine b 27 Nov 1985); *Career* FCO: joined 1973, third then second sec Moscow 1976–78, Near East and North Africa Dept 1978–82, private sec to Foreign Sec 1982–84, first sec Paris 1984–87, dep head Soviet Dept 1987–89, seconded to Thomas de la Rue plc 1989–91, cnsllr (econ and commercial) New Delhi 1991–95, head EU Dept (external) FCO 1995, princ private sec (overseas affairs) 10 Downing St 1997–99 (private sec 1996–97), ambass to Portugal 1999–2001, ambass to France 2001–07; under sec-gen for humanitarian affrs and emergency relief co-ordinator UN 2007–; *Recreations* golf, tennis, music; *Style—* HE Sir John Holmes, GCVO, KBE, CMG

HOLMES, Jon; *Educ* Christ Church Coll Canterbury; *Career* writer, comedian and presenter; host Mojo Awards 2005; *Television* Stop The World (BBC Choice) 1998, Footage and Mouth (Play UK) 1998, Wish We Were There (BBC Choice) 1999, The Way It Is (TV pilot, BBC1) 2000, The 11 O'Clock Show (Channel 4) 2000, I Love... (BBC2) 2000, Dead Ringers (BBC2) 2000–, The State We're In (BBC3) 2002–03, Gash (Channel 4) 2003; writer, script ed and actor The Impressionable Jon Culshaw (BBC) 2004; writer: V Graham Norton (prog conslt, Channel 4), Spitting Image (ITV), Patrick Keilty Almost Live (BBC1), Jim Tavare In Cabaret (five), Have I Got News For You (BBC1), Harry Hill (Channel 4), Comedy Nation (BBC2), Br Acad Film Awards 2005, Br Acad Television Craft Awards 2005; voice artist: Crash Test Danny (Discovery Kids), 7 Days (BBC 3); *Radio* comedy for Radio 4: Grievous Bodily Radio 1997, The Way It Is 1998–2002, The Now Show 1998–, Dead Ringers 2000– (Best Radio Prog Broadcasting Press Guild Awards 2001, Gold Comedy Award Sony Radio Awards 2001), Concrete Cow 2002, The 99p Challenge, The Armando Iannucci Show 2004, Armando Iannucci's Charm Offensive (presenter) 2005; writer for Radio 4: Yes Sir, I Can Boogie, The Very World of Milton Jones (Bronze Comedy Award Sony Radio Awards 2000), Harry Hill's Fruit Corner, Big Town All Stars, This is Your Life (also script ed); music radio: Jon & Andy on 106 CTFM 1997–98 (Presentation Newcomer of the Year KPMG Awards 1999), Jon & Andy on Power FM 1999–2000 (Gold Entertainment Award Sony Radio Awards 2000), TFI Galaxy Celebrity Pantomime (Galaxy Network) 1999, Jon Holmes on Xfm 2000, Jon Holmes on Virgin Radio 2001–02, Jon Holmes on LBC 97.3 2003–, presenter BBC6 Music 2003–, The Day the Music Died (Radio 2) 2003–, Jon Holmes on Radio One 2005, Jon Holmes on BBC6 (6Music) 2006–, Listen Against (Radio 4) 2007; *Awards* incl: 1 Silver Award Sony Radio Awards, 3 Bronze Awards Sony Radio Awards; *Books* Status Quo and the Kangaroo (2007); *Style*— Jon Holmes, Esq; ✉ c/o The Richard Stone Partnership, 2 Henrietta Street, London WC2E 8PS (tel 020 7497 0849, fax 020 7497 0869)

HOLMES, Katherine; da of Idwal Humphrey, of Woodbridge, Suffolk, and Agnes, *née* Richard; *b* 10 May 1952, Porchester, Hants; *Educ* Coll of Law London; *m* 20 July 1985, Christopher Holmes; *Career* called to the Bar 1973; barr in private practice 1973–76, head of commercial law CBI 1976–81, lawyer Distillers Co Ltd 1981–87, head of competition law Guinness plc 1987–89, ptnr Richards Butler (latterly Reed Smith Richards Butler) 1991– (lawyer 1989–91); memb: Senate Inns of Court and Bar 1979–83, Senate/Bar Cncl 1985–86 and 1987 (memb various sub-ctees 1979–90); Bar Assoc for Finance and Industry: chm 1986–87, sr vice-chm 1987–88, vice-pres 1988–90; vice-chm ICC Cmmn on Competition 1989–93, chm Jt Working Party of the Bars and Law Socs of the UK of Competition Law 1998–2005; tstee Guinness Gp Pension Fund 1988–89; dir Scotch Whisky Assoc 1987–89; memb Law Soc 1990; *Publications* Fiscal Frontiers (1993), Guide to Competition Act 1988 (1988), Guide to Competition Law in the UK (2002); *Recreations* sailing, skiing, entertaining; *Style*— Mrs Katherine Holmes; ✉ Reed Smith Richards Butler, Beaufort House, 15 St Botolph Street, London EC3A 7EE (tel 020 7247 6555, fax 020 7539 5208, e-mail kholmes@reedsmith.com)

HOLMES, Dame Kelly; DBE (2005, MBE 1998); da of Pamela, *née* Norman; *b* 19 April 1970; *Educ* Hugh Christie Comp Sch; *Career* athlete; memb Ealing Southall and Middx Athletics Club; English Schs winner 1,500m 1983 and 1987, Gold medal 800m Mini Youth Olympics 1987, Gold medal 1,500m GB Int Germany and Ipswich 1987, semi-finalist World Championships 1993, Silver medal 1,500m European Championships 1994, Gold medal 1,500m Cwlth Games Victoria 1994, Silver medal 1,500m and Bronze medal 800m World Championships 1995, Silver medal 1,500m Cwlth Games Kuala Lumpur 1998, Bronze medal 800m Olympic Games Sydney 2000, Silver medal 800m Goodwill Games 2001, Gold medal 1,500m Cwlth Games Manchester 2002, Bronze medal 800m European Championships 2002, Silver medal 1,500m World Indoor Championships 2003, Silver medal 800m World Championships 2003, Gold medal 800m and Gold medal 1,500m Olympic Games Athens 2004; English and Br record holder 800m, Br and Cwlth record holder 1000m and 1,500m, Br record holder 800m and 1500m indoors; ranked no 1 in world for 1,500m 1997 and 2004, ranked no 3 in the world for 800m 2001; Army judo champion, Army volleyball player; Army Athlete of the Year 1989–97, Combined Servs Sports Woman of the Year 1993 and 1994, Middx County Sports Woman of the Year 1994 and 1995, Athlete of the Year Sports Writers' Assoc 1995, nominated Mover & Shakers Award Company magazine 1995, Br Athletics Female Athlete of the Year 1995, 3rd place Carlton TV Sports Personality of the Year 1997, BBC Sports Personality of the Year 2004, European Athlete of the Year 2004, IAAF Female Performance of the Year 2004, Int Athlete of the Year 2004, Sports Writers Assoc Sports Woman of the Year 2004, Br Athletic Writers Assoc Female Athlete of the Year 2004, Laureus World Sportswoman of the Year 2005; non-sporting career: nursing asst 1986–87, Sgt (HGV driver then army physical trg instr) HM Forces 1988–97, md Double Gold Enterprises Ltd 1997–; fndr and dir On Camp with Kelly 2004–, fndr Believe to Achieve with Kelly, nat sch sport champion, motivational speaker; Hon Dr in Sports Science Leeds Met Univ 2005, Hon DCL Univ of Kent 2005; *Style*— Dame Kelly Holmes, DBE; ✉ tel 01732 838800, e-mail info@doublegold.co.uk, website www.doublegold.co.uk

HOLMES, Dr (Janet) Martha Lee; da of Sir Peter Holmes (d 2002), and Judith Holmes (d 2003); *Educ* Bryanston, Univ of Bristol (BSc), Univ of York (DPhil); *Career* broadcaster and prodr with BBC Natural History Unit; presenter: Reefwatch 1988, Sea Trek 1991, The Blue Planet Deep Trouble 2001; asst prodr Life in the Freezer 1993; prodr: Wildlife Special Polar Bear 1997, The Blue Planet 2001; series prodr: The Nile 2004, Man Hunters 2005; RGS Cherry Kearton Medal and Award 1999; *Publications* Sea Trek (1991), Wildlife Specials (1997), The Blue (1999), The Blue Planet (2001), Nile (2004); *Style*— Dr Martha Holmes; ✉ BBC-NHU, Whiteladies Road, Bristol BS8 2LR (tel 0117 974 7677, e-mail martha.holmes@bbc.co.uk)

HOLMES, Paul; MP; *Career* MP (Lib Dem) Chesterfield 2001–; Lib Dem spokesperson for disability issues 2001–02, Lib Dem spokesperson for disability issues and work and pensions 2002–05, chair Lib Dem Parly Pty 2005–, memb Select Ctee on Educn and Skills 2001–05; cncllr Chesterfield BC 1987–95 and 1999–2003; vice-pres Local Govt Assoc 2001–; *Style*— Paul Holmes, Esq, MP; ✉ House of Commons, London SW1A 0AA

HOLMES, Peter Sloan; s of George Horner Gaffikin Holmes (d 1971), of Newcastle, Co Down, and Anne Sloan, *née* Reid (d 1987); *b* 8 December 1942; *Educ* Rossall Sch, Magdalen Coll Oxford (BA); *m* 14 April 1966, Patricia, da of Frederick Alexander McMahon (d 1984), of Belfast; 2 s ((Christopher) Paul b 25 Jan 1967, Patrick Michael b 4 June 1969); *Career* Lt RNR 1965–68; teacher Eastbourne Coll 1965–68, head of English Grosvenor HS Belfast 1968–71, lectr and sr lectr Stranmillis Coll of Educn Belfast 1971–75; Dept of Educn: joined 1975, sr inspector 1980–82, staff inspector 1982–83, asst sec 1983–87, under sec 1987–96, dep sec 1996–2000; chief exec: Sheridan Gp, Sheridan Millennium Ltd; chm Arts and Business NI until 2006; *Recreations* singing, sailing, gliding; *Style*— Peter Holmes, Esq; ✉ 303 Comber Road, Lisburn BT27 6TA (tel 028 9263 9495), e-mail peter.holmes@sheridangroup.com)

HOLMES, Prof (Edward) Richard; CBE, TD, JP (NE Hampshire); s of Edward William Holmes (d 1965), and Helen, *née* Jacques (d 1990); *b* 29 March 1946; *Educ* Forest Sch, Emmanuel Coll Cambridge (scholar, MA), Northern Illinois Univ (travelling fell), Univ of Reading (PhD); *m* 1975, Katharine Elizabeth, da of William Richard Dawson Saxton (sr princ surveyor Lloyd's Register of Shipping); 2 da (Jessica Helen b 1980, Sara Corinna b 1983); *Career* military historian, author and broadcaster; RMA Sandhurst 1969–85 (lectr in war studies, sr lectr, dep head of dept), Lt-Col cmdg 2 Bn The Wessex Regt (Vol) 1985–88, co-dir Cranfield Security Studies Inst 1990–; conslt historian Army Staff Coll 1988–97, prof of military and security studies Cranfield Univ 1995–; TA: enlisted 1964, cmmnd 1965, dir Reserve Forces and Cadets 1998–2001; Col Princess of Wales's Royal Regt 2000–07; pres: Br Cmmn for Mil History, The Battlefields Tst, Corps of Drums Soc; vice-pres The Sealed Knot, hon pres Napoleonic Assoc, patron Guild of Battlefield Guides, tstee Royal Armouries; Hon DLitt Univ of Leicester 2006, Hon DLitt Univ of Kent 2007; MRUSI; Cdr (First Class) Order of the Dannebrog (Denmark); *Television* credits (writer/presenter) incl: Comrades in Arms 1980, Soldiers 1985, The War Within 1990, Tales from the Map Room: Burma 1995, War Walks 1996, War Walks 2 1997, The Western Front 1999, Battlefields 2001, Wellington - The Iron Duke 2002, Rebels and Redcoats 2003, In the Footsteps of Churchill 2005; *Books* incl: The English Civil War (with Brig Peter Young, 1974), The Little Field-Marshal - Sir John French (1981), The Road to Sedan (1984), Firing Line (1985, US title Acts of War), Soldiers (jtly, 1985), Nuclear Warriors (1991), Fatal Avenue (1992), Riding the Retreat: Mons to the Marne 1914 Revisited (1995), War Walks (1996), War Walks 2 (1997), The Western Front (1999), The Imperial War Museum Second World War in Photographs (2000), The Oxford Companion to Military History (gen ed, 2001), Battlefields (2001), Redcoat (2001), The Imperial War Museum First World War in Photographs (2001), Wellington - The Iron Duke (2002), Tommy (2004), The D-Day Experience (2004), In the Footsteps of Churchill (2005), Sahib (2005), Dusty Warriors (2006), The Age of Napoleon (2006); *Recreations* travelling, riding; *Clubs* Naval and Military; *Style*— Prof Richard Holmes, CBE, TD; ✉ Cranfield Security Studies Institute, Defence College of Management and Technology, Shrivenham, Swindon, Wiltshire SN6 8LA (tel 01793 785474, fax 01793 785459, e-mail s.b.muir@cranfield.ac.uk)

HOLMES, Dr William Francis (Bill); s of William Francis Holmes (d 1970), and Margaret Mary, *née* Carty; *b* 7 May 1954; *Educ* St Mary's Coll Crosby, Univ of Nottingham; *m* Dr Sheelagh Littlewood; *Career* GP 1980–; ptnr Health at Work 1987–; special lectr Dept of Respiratory Med Univ of Nottingham 1992–2000; memb GMC 1994–99; dir Nestor Healthcare Gp plc 2001–06; FRCP, FRCGP; *Recreations* golf; *Clubs* Athenaeum, Royal and Ancient Golf; *Style*— Dr Bill Holmes; ✉ Health at Work, Church House, Beckhampton Road, Nottingham NG5 5NG (0115 920 9901, e-mail holmes@mail.com)

HOLMPATRICK, 4 Baron (UK 1897), of HolmPatrick, Co Dublin; Hans James David Hamilton; eldest s of 3 Baron HolmPatrick (d 1991), and Anne Loys Roche, *née* Brass (d 1998); *b* 15 March 1955; *Educ* Harrow; *m* 19 July 1984, Mrs Gill Francesca Anne du Feu, eldest da of Kenneth James Harding (d 1990), of Binisafua, Minorca; 1 s (Hon James Hans Stephen b 6 Oct 1982), 1 step s (Dominic Mark du Feu b 15 Jan 1975); *Heir* bro, Hon Ion Hamilton; *Style*— The Rt Hon Lord HolmPatrick

HOLROYD, (William) Andrew Myers; OBE (2003); s of William Holroyd (d 1992), of Bradford, and Joan, *née* Myers (d 1993); *b* 13 April 1948; *Educ* Bradford GS, Univ of Nottingham (BA); *m* 26 July 1975, Caroline Irene, da of Jack Skerry, of Southport; 2 da (Emma b 1 Feb 1977, Clare b 5 Dec 1979); *Career* VSO Indonesia 1970–72, articled clerk Alsop Wilkinson 1972–74, managing ptnr Jackson & Canter Liverpool (ptnr 1977–); Law Soc: memb 1974–, memb Cncl 1996–, dep vice-pres 2005–06, vice-pres 2006–07, pres 2007–08; Liverpool Law Soc: memb Ctee 1983–95, vice-pres 1993, pres 1994; memb Ctee: Princes Park Methodist Centre Toxteth; Methodist local preacher; *Recreations* music, walking; *Clubs* RAC; *Style*— Andrew Holroyd, Esq, OBE; ✉ Jackson & Canter, 88 Church Street, Liverpool L1 3HD (tel 0151 282 1961, fax 0151 282 1963, e-mail aholroyd@jacksoncanter.co.uk)

HOLROYD, Air Marshal Sir Frank Martyn; KBE (1989), CB (1985); s of George Lumb Holroyd (d 1987), and Winifred Hetty; *b* 30 August 1935; *Educ* Southend-on-Sea GS, Cranfield Univ (MSc); *m* 1 Feb 1958, Veronica Christine (d 2001), da of Arthur George Booth (d 1984); 2 s (Martyn Paul b 26 Jan 1959, Myles Justin b 9 Nov 1966), 1 da (Bryony Jane b 4 June 1961); *Career* joined RAF 1956, appt Fighter Stations RAF Leconfield and RAF Leeming, No 14 Grad Course RAF Tech Coll 1959, Blind Landing Experimental Unit RAE Bedford 1960–63, HQ Fighter Cmd 1965–67, OC Electrical Engrg Sqdn RAF Changi Singapore 1967–69, Wing Cdr Staff Coll RAF Bracknell 1970, MOD 1970–72, OC Engrg Wing RAF Brize Norton 1972, Gp Capt 1974, Station Cdr No 1 Radio Sch RAF Locking 1974–76, sr engrg offr HQ 38 Gp 1976, Air Cdre dir Aircraft Engrg MOD 1977, RCDS 1981, dir Weapons and Support Engrg 1982, Air Vice Marshal dir gen Strategic Electronic Engrg MOD (PE) 1982, air offr engrg HQ Strike Cmd 1986, Air Marshal chief engr RAF 1988–91, chief Logistics Support RAF 1989–91; chm: AVR Communications Ltd 1991–95, Composite Technology Ltd 1992–2004, Electronica (UK) Ltd 1992–95, Military Aircraft Spares Ltd 2004–06 (dep chm 1999–2004), Troy Court Mgmnt Ltd 2004–07, Military Asset Services Ltd 2007–; dir: Admiral plc 1992–2000, REW Communications Services plc 1995–96, Ultra Electronics plc 1995–2003, Airinmar Ltd 1996–2001; memb: BBC Engrg Advsy Bd 1984–90, Advsy Cncl RMCS 1988–91, Cncl Cranfield Univ 1988–2005 (memb Ct 1988–, dep chm Cncl 1997–2005), Cncl (now Senate) Engrg Cncl 1990–2000 (chm Fin & Audit Ctee), BIM Bd of Companions 1991–99 (chm 1998–99), Tribology Tst Ctee 1997–; pres RAeS 1992–93, life vice-pres Chelmsford RAFA 1992; MacRobert Award tstee Royal Acad of Engrg 1994–98, chm tstees Eng Cncl Pension Fund 2000–; memb Ct Cranfield Univ 1997–; Hon DSc Cranfield Univ 2006; CEng, FREng 1992, FRAeS, FIEE, CIMgt; *Recreations* shooting, gardening, maintaining 14th century house, travel; *Clubs* RAF; *Style*— Air Marshal Sir Frank Holroyd, KBE, CB, FREng; ✉ c/o RAF Club, 128 Piccadilly, London W1V 0PY

H

HOLROYD, Sir Michael de Courcy Fraser; kt (2007), CBE (1989); s of Basil de Courcy Fraser Holroyd, of Surrey, and Ulla, *née* Hall; *b* 27 August 1935; *Educ* Eton; *m* 1982, Margaret Drabble, *qv*, da of John Frederick Drabble, QC (d 1983), of Suffolk; *Career* biographer; chm: Soc of Authors 1973–74, Nat Book League 1976–78; pres English PEN 1985–8, Royal Soc of Literature 2003– (chm 1997–2001); chm: Arts Cncl Literature Panel 1992–95, Public Lending Right Ctee 1997–2000; memb Arts Cncl of GB 1992–95; David Cohen Prize for Literature 2005; Hon DLitt: Univ of Ulster 1992, Univ of Sheffield 1993, Univ of Warwick 1993, UEA 1994, LSE 1998; CLit (FRSL 1968), FRHistS; *Books* Lytton Strachey (1967–68 and 1994), Augustus John (1974–75 and 1996), Bernard Shaw (1988–92 and 1997), Basil Street Blues (1999), Works on Paper (2002), Mosaic: Portraits in Fragments (2004); *Recreations* listening to music and stories, watching people dance; *Style*— Sir Michael Holroyd, CBE, CLit; ✉ 85 St Mark's Road, London W10 6JS (tel 020 8960 4891, fax 020 8968 6295)

HOLROYD, Richard Norton; s of Maj C I P Holroyd (d 1976), and Lady Sheila Holroyd, *née* Cairns (d 2001, da of 4 Earl Cairns); *b* 25 December 1946, Bath; *Educ* Marlborough, Selwyn Coll Cambridge, Indiana Univ Grad Sch of Business; *m* 12 Nov 1977, Karine Phèlip; 3 s (Wilfrid Andrew b 15 Nov 1980, Alistair Hugo b 15 April 1985, Alexander Ivor b 17 May 1987), 1 da (Annabel Juliette b 19 July 1983); *Career* European dir Reckitt & Colman 1988–91, ceo Colman's of Norwich 1991–95, sr mangr Shell Int 1995–2001, non-exec dir Cantrell & Cochrane plc 2001–; memb Competition Cmmn; non-exec dir ABRO (MOD trading fund); *Recreations* opera, history, skiing; *Style*— Richard Holroyd, Esq; ✉ Flat 8, 37 De Vere Gardens, London W8 5AW (tel 020 7938 2522, fax 020 7376 1105, e-mail rnholroyd@aol.com)

HOLROYDE, Timothy Victor (Tim); QC (1996); s of Frank Holroyde, and Doreen, *née* Bell; *b* 18 August 1955; *Educ* Bristol GS, Wadham Coll Oxford (BA); *m* 1980, Miranda Elisabeth, da of Alex Stone; 2 da (Caroline Louise b 26 Dec 1986, Imogen Sarah b 15 Sept 1989); *Career* called to the Bar Middle Temple 1977 (bencher), in practice Northern Circuit, currently recorder; *Recreations* tennis; *Style*— Tim Holroyde, Esq, QC; ✉ Exchange Chambers, Pearl Assurance House, Derby Square, Liverpool L2 9XX (tel 0151 236 7747, fax 0151 236 3433, e-mail holroydeqc@exchangechambers.co.uk)

HOLT, HE Denise Mary; CMG (2002); da of William Dennis Mills (d 1971), and Mary Joanna, *née* Shea; *b* 1 October 1949; *Educ* New Hall Sch Chelmsford, Univ of Bristol (BA); *m* John David Fletcher Holt; 1 s (Patrick David Mills Holt b 1987); *Career* diplomat; joined FCO 1970, res analyst for Iberia 1970–83, first sec (political) Dublin 1984–87, head of section FCO 1988–90, first sec (political) Brasilia 1991–93, dep head Eastern Dept FCO 1993–94, asst dir (personnel) FCO 1996–98, dep head of mission Dublin 1998–99, dir (personnel) FCO 1999–2001, ambass to Mexico 2002–05, dir (migration) FCO 2005–07, ambass to Spain 2007– (concurrently non-resident ambass to Andorra); *Recreations* reading, cooking, sewing; *Style*— HE Mrs Denise Holt, CMG; ✉ c/o Foreign & Commonwealth Office (Madrid), King Charles Street, London SW1A 2AH (e-mail denise.holt@fco.gov.uk)

HOLT, (Roma) Hazel Kathryn; da of Charles Douglas Young (d 1986), of Clearwell, Glos, and Roma, *née* Simpson; *b* 3 September 1928; *Educ* King Edward VI HS Birmingham, Newnham Coll Cambridge (BA); *m* Geoffrey Louis Holt; 1 s (Thomas Charles Louis Holt, *qv* b 13 Sept 1961); *Career* editorial asst International African Institute 1950–79, feature writer and reviewer Stage and Television Today 1979–82; *Books* edited for posthumous publication the novels of Barbara Pym (literary executor); A Very Private Eye (with Hilary Pym, 1984), Gone Away (1989), A Lot to Ask: A Life of Barbara Pym (1990), The Cruellest Month (1991), The Shortest Journey (1992), Uncertain Death (1993), Murder on Campus (1994), Superfluous Death (1995), Death of a Dean (1996), The Only Good

Lawyer... (1997), Dead and Buried (1998), Fatal Legacy (1999), Lilies That Fester (2000), Delay of Execution (2001), Leonora (2002), Death in Practice (2003), The Silent Killer (2004), Death in Practice (2005), A Death in the Family (2006); *Recreations* reading, writing and watching cats; *Clubs* Univ Women's; *Style—* Mrs Hazel Holt; ✉ Tivington Knowle, Minehead, Somerset TA24 8SX (tel 01643 704707, e-mail hazelholt9@aol.com)

HOLT, Jeremy Martin; s of Graham John Holt, of Brampton, Cambs, and Doreen Marie, *née* Boud; *b* 1 June 1956, London; *Educ* Sexey's Sch Bruton, Exeter Coll Oxford (MA); *m* Antonia; 2 da (Georgina b 23 Dec 1988, Katharine b 10 July 1991); *Career* admitted slr 1980; articled clerk Macfarlanes 1978–80, slr Herbert Oppenheimer Nathan & Vandyk 1980–83, slr Compton Carr 1983–84, ptnr Peake & Co 1986–89 (slr 1984–86), ptnr Charles Russell 1989–95, co-fndr and ptnr Clark Holt Commercial Slrs 1995–; *Publications* A Manager's Guide to IT Law (2004); author of numerous magazine articles on law and IT; *Recreations* military history, long-distance running; *Clubs* Hon Artillery Co (veteran memb); *Style—* Jeremy Holt, Esq; ✉ 14 Belmont Crescent, Swindon, Wiltshire SN1 4EY; Clark Holt Commercial Solicitors, Hardwick House, Prospect Place, Swindon, Wiltshire SN1 3LJ (tel 01793 617444, fax 01793 617436, e-mail jeremyh@clarkholt.com)

HOLT, John Antony; *b* 31 March 1938; *Educ* Imperial Coll London (BSc(Eng), ACGI, Dip Imperial Coll, MSc), Henley Mgmnt Centre; *m*; 2 c; *Career* sr industrial fell Univ of Leeds 1969–71, chief systems engr (space) and head of New Space Technol Electronic and Space Systems Guided Weapons Div British Aircraft Corporation 1971–76 (joined 1960), gen mgmnt course Henley Mgmnt Centre 1976; British Aerospace: head of Guided Weapons New Projects British Aerospace Dynamics Gp (Bristol) 1976–80, engrg dir 1980–82, tech dir British Aerospace Dynamics Gp 1982–85, md British Aerospace Space and Communications Ltd 1985–92; fndr dir McLaurin-Holt Associates Ltd 1993–2002; chm Surrey Satellite Technology Ltd 2005–06 (non-exec dir 1994–2005); non-exec dir: Orion Network Systems Inc 1989–92, Arthur C Clarke Fndn USA 2003–; visiting prof RMCS 1985; chm: Euro MESH consortium for collaboration on space projects 1987–92, UK Electronic Industry Component Policy Cncl 1987–91, UK Industrial Space Ctee 1988–90, UK Electronic Components Policy Cncl 1993–, ESYS Ltd 1997–2001 and 2003– (non-exec dir 1995–97 and 2001–03); memb Advsy Bd: Inst of Engrg Survey and Space Geodesy Univ of Nottingham 1990–94, Centre for Space Engrg Research Univ of Surrey 1991–97; memb Ct Cranfield Univ, memb Ct Univ of Surrey; Hon DSc Capitol Coll Maryland 1992; MInstD, FRAeS, FREng 1985; *Style—* John Holt, Esq, FREng; ✉ tel 01462 436626, fax 01462 452885, e-mail holtja@compuserve.com

HOLT, His Hon Judge John Frederick; s of Edward Basil Holt (d 1984), and Monica, *née* Taylor; *b* 7 October 1947; *Educ* Ampleforth, Univ of Bristol (LLB); *m* 26 Sept 1970, Stephanie Ann, da of Peter Watson, of Belaugh, Norfolk; 3 s (Samuel John b 16 June 1973, Benjamin Alexander b 2 Sept 1974, Edward Daniel b 11 Oct 1980); *Career* called to the Bar Lincoln's Inn 1970 (former head of East Anglian Chambers), asst recorder 1988–92, recorder of the Crown Court 1992–98, circuit judge (SE Circuit) 1998–; memb Co Court Rules Ctee 1981–85; *Recreations* cricket, restoring vintage motor cars; *Clubs* Twinstead Cricket, Strangers (Norwich); *Style—* His Hon Judge Holt; ✉ Ipswich Crown Court, Civic Drive, Ipswich, Suffolk IP1 2DX (tel 01473 213841)

HOLT, Nicholas John; s of Eric Holt and Eileen Patricia, *née* Macritchee; *b* 2 April 1958; *Educ* Manchester Grammar, Fitzwilliam Coll Cambridge (BA, MA); *m* 14 April 1984, Georgina Mary, da of Dr William Mann; 2 s (William James Edward b 1987, Frederick Nicholas Jack b 1993), 1 da (Alexandra Olivia b 1989); *Career* articled clerk then asst slr Coward Chance 1980–84, asst slr then mangr Corp Legal Dept Jardine Matheson & Co Hong Kong 1984–87, legal and compliance dir Smith New Court plc 1989–92 (gp legal advsr 1987–89), chief exec Smith New Court Far East Ltd 1992–94, dir Merrill Lynch International Ltd 1994–95, ptnr Weil Gotshal & Manges 1995–2000, managing ptnr McGrigors London (formerly KLegal) 2000–04, ptnr Global Legal Search 2004–; memb Law Soc; *Recreations* football, squash, cricket; *Clubs* Reform; *Style—* Nicholas Holt, Esq

HOLT, Thelma Mary Bernadette; CBE (1994); da of David Holt (d 1941), and Ellan, *née* Finnagh Doyle (d 1969); *b* 4 January 1933; *Educ* St Anne's Coll for Girls, RADA; *m* 1, 31 March 1957 (m dis), Patrick Graucob; m 2, 6 Oct 1968 (m dis), David Pressman; *Career* producer; actress 1955–68; jt art dir Open Space Theatre 1968–77, art dir Round House Theatre 1977–83, exec prodr Theatre of Comedy 1983–85, head of touring and commercial exploitation Nat Theatre 1985–88, exec prodr Peter Hall Co 1988; prodr Int Theatre, Nat Theatre 1989–, assoc prodr RSC 2004–; Cameron Mackintosh prof of contemporary theatre Univ of Oxford 1998; emeritus fell St Catherine's Coll Oxford 2003; dir: Thelma Holt Ltd, Theatre Investment Fund Ltd, Almeida Theatre 2001–; chm Yvonne Arnaud Theatre 2002–05; vice-pres Citizens' Theatre Glasgow; Observer Award for Special Achievement in Theatre 1987; memb Cncl: RADA, Arts Cncl of England 1993–98 (chm Drama Advisory Panel); Special Award for Inidivdual Achievement TMA Awards 2006; patron Oxford Univ Dramatic Soc; Hon DUniv Middx 1994, Hon DLitt UEA 2003; companion Liverpool Inst for Performing Arts 2002, distinguished friend Univ of Oxford 2006; Order of the Rising Sun (Japan) 2004; *Style—* Miss Thelma Holt, CBE; ✉ Thelma Holt Ltd, Noel Coward Theatre, 85 St Martin's Lane, London WC2N 4AU (tel 020 7812 7455, fax 020 7812 7550, e-mail thelma@dircon.co.uk)

HOLT, Thomas Charles Louis; s of Geoffrey Louis Holt, and (Roma) Hazel Kathryn Holt, *qv*, *née* Young; *b* 13 September 1961; *Educ* Westminster, Wadham Coll Oxford, Coll of Law Chancery Lane; *m* 6 Aug 1988, Kim Nicola, da of John Clifford Foster; 1 da (Natalie Alicia Alexandria b 12 March 1992); *Career* author; *Publications* incl: Poems by Tom Holt 1973, Lucia in Wartime (1985, US 1986), Lucia Triumphant (1986, US 1986), Expecting Someone Taller (1987, US 1988), Who's Afraid of Beowulf? (1988, US 1989), Goatsong (1989, US 1990), I Margaret (with Steve Nallon, 1989), The Walled Orchard 1990, Flying Dutch (1991, US 1992), Ye Gods! (1992), Overtime (1993), Here Comes The Sun (1993), Grailblazers (1994), Faust Among Equals (1994), Odds and Gods (1995), Djinn Rummy (1995), My Hero (1996), Paint Your Dragon (1996), Open Sesame (1997), Wish You Were Here (1998), Valhalla (1998), Only Human (1998), Snow White & The Seven Samurai (1999), Nothing But Blue Skies (2000), Falling Sideways (2001), Little People (2002), The Portable Door (2003), A Song For Nero (2003); *Recreations* engineering; *Style—* Thomas Holt, Esq; ✉ c/o James Hale, 47 Peckham Rye, London SE15 3NX (tel and fax 020 7732 6338)

HOLT, Prof (David) Tim; CB (2000); s of Ernest Frederick Holt (d 1989), and Catherine Rose, *née* Finn (d 2001); *b* 29 October 1943; *Educ* Coopers' Company's Sch, Univ of Exeter (BSc, PhD); *m* 1966, Jill, *née* Blake; 1 s (Dickon Stuart b 6 Nov 1969), 1 da (Sarah Helen Rachel b 9 Sept 1972); *Career* research fell Univ of Exeter 1969–70, survey statistician Statistics Canada 1970–73; Univ of Southampton: lectr in social statistics 1973–80, Leverhulme prof of social statistics 1980–, dean Faculty of Social Science 1981–83, dep vice-chllr 1990–95, prof of social statistics 2000–; dir Office for National Statistics, Registrar General for England and Wales and head Govt Statistical Service 1996–2000; scientific advsr to Chief Scientist DHSS 1983–88; conslt: Statistics Canada 1974–75, Statistics NZ 1981, OPCS 1983, 1987 and 1991, ESRC 1990, Australian Bureau of Statistics 1990, EU 2001–02, UN 2001–02, IMF 2002; ed Jl of RSS A (Statistics and Society) 1991–94; assoc ed: Jl of RSS B 1983–88, Survey Methodology 1988–; pres Royal Statistical Soc 2005–07 (vice-pres 2002–03); vice-pres: Int Assoc of Survey Statisticians 1989–91 (memb 1973–, scientific sec 1985–87), UN Statistical Cmmn 1997–99; elected memb Int Statistical Inst 1985– (vice-pres 1999–2001), pres ILO Int Conf Lab Statisticians 1998; tstee Newitt Tst; Hon DSocSc Univ of Southampton 2000; FRSS 1973, fell American Statistical Assoc 1990, FRSA 1995, AcSS 2000; *Books* Analysis of Complex Surveys (with C J Skinner and T M F Smith, 1989); also author of articles in academic jls; *Recreations* orienteering, theatre, walking, food; *Style—* Prof Tim Holt; ✉ Department of Social Statistics, University of Southampton, Southampton SO17 1BF (e-mail tholt@socsci.soton.ac.uk)

HOLTHAM, Gerald Hubert; s of Denis Arthur Holtham (d 1995), of Quinton, Birmingham, and Dilys Maud, *née* Bull (d 1999); *b* 28 June 1944, Aberdare, Glamorgan; *Educ* King Edward's Sch Birmingham, Jesus Coll Oxford (BA), Nuffield Coll Oxford (MPhil); *m* 1, 1969 (m dis), Patricia Mary, *née* Blythin; 1 da (Clare Miriam b 1971); m 2, 1979, Edith, *née* Hodgkinson; 1 da (Sophie Maud b 1976), 1 s (Rhodri Huw b 1982); *Career* journalist 1962–66 and 1969–70, at Oxford 1967–69 and 1971–73, res offr Overseas Devpt Inst London 1973–75, head Gen Econs Div Econs Dept Orgn for Econ Co-operation and Devpt (OECD) Paris 1982–85 (economist 1975–81), visiting fell Brookings Instn Washington DC 1985–87, chief int economist Credit Suisse First Boston London 1987–88, chief international economist Shearson Lehman Hutton London 1988–91, fell and tutor in econs Magdalen Coll Oxford 1991–92, chief economist Europe Lehman Brothers London 1992–94, dir IPPR 1994–98, head of global strategy Norwich Union Investment Mgmnt 1998–2000, chief investment offr Morley Fund Mgmnt 2000–04, managing ptnr Cadwyn Capital LLP; visiting prof Univ of Strathclyde 1990–93, affiliated prof London Business Sch 1993–99, visiting prof Cardiff Univ Business Sch 2004–; *Books* Aid and Inequality in Kenya (with A Hazlewood, 1976), Deficits and the Dollar (with R Bryant and P Hooper, 1988), Empirical Macroeconomics for Interdependent Economies (jtly, 1988); also author of numerous articles in learned jls; *Recreations* gardening, windsurfing, listening to jazz; *Style—* Gerald Holtham, Esq; ✉ 13 Lansdowne Gardens, London SW8 2EQ (tel 020 7622 8673, e-mail gerald@holtham.fsnet.co.uk)

HOLWELL, Peter; s of Frank Holwell (decd), and Helen, *née* Howe (decd); *b* 28 March 1936; *Educ* Palmers Endowed Sch Grays, Hendon GS, LSE (BSc(Econ)); *m* 1959, Jean Patricia Ashman; 1 da (Felicity b 18 May 1964), 1 s (William b 22 June 1967); *Career* mgmnt conslt Arthur Andersen & Co 1961–64 (articled clerk 1958–61); Univ of London: head of computing Sch Exams Bd 1964–67, head of Univ Computing and O & M Unit 1966–67, sec for accounting and admin computing 1977–82, clerk of the Ct 1982–85, princ 1985–97; conslt: Prince of Wales's Inst of Architecture 1997–99, Chatham Historic Dockyard Tst 1999–2001; memb CVCP 1985–94; dir: Sch Exams Cncl 1988–94, Univ of London Examinations and Assessment Cncl 1991–97; memb Advsy Bd Samuel Courtauld Inst 1985–97; non-exec dir: NE Thames Regnl HA 1989–94, Edexcel Fndn 1996–97; chm: City and E London FHSA 1994–96, St Mark's Research Fndn and Educn Tst 1995–2000; vice-chm: Governing Body Wye Coll London 1996–2000, Cncl Sch of Pharmacy 1996–2001; tstee Chartered Accountants' Employees Superannuation Scheme 1998–2004; tstee Leeds Castle Fndn 2001–03; FCA 1972; *Recreations* walking, music, horology; *Clubs* Athenaeum, RSM; *Style—* Peter Holwell, Esq; ✉ Hookers Green, Bishopsbourne, Canterbury, Kent CT4 5JB (tel 01227 830135, e-mail holwells@waitrose.com)

HOM, Ken; s of Thomas Hom (d 1950), and Ying Fong Hom; *b* 3 May 1949; *Educ* Univ of Calif; *Career* chef and food writer; Oriental Restaurant Gp: conslt 1993–99, gp chef conslt 1999–; prop Yellow River Café 1999–2001, following takeover by Noble House Leisure dir and chief conslt 2001– (currently 7 Yellow River Cafés in UK); Ken Hom brands incl: Ken Hom Wok and Accessories, Ken Hom Ready-Cooked Meals, Ken Hom Sauces; contrib: NY Times, The Financial Times; supporter of various charities incl: Barnardo's, NSPCC; *Television* credits incl: Ken Hom's Chinese Cookery (BBC series), Ken Hom's Hot Wok (BBC series), Ken Hom Travels with a Hot Wok (BBC series); *Books* Ken Hom's Encyclopaedia of Chinese Cookery Techniques (1984), Ken Hom's Chinese Cookery (1984), Ken Hom's East Meets West Cuisine (1987), Ken Hom's Vegetable & Pasta Book (1987), Ken Hom's Quick & Easy Chinese Cookery (1989), The Taste of China (1990), Fragrant Harbour Taste (1991), Cooking of China (1993), Ken Hom's Illustrated Chinese Cookery (1993), Ken Hom's Chinese Kitchen (1994), Chinese Recipes (1994), Ken Hom's Vegetarian Cookery (1995), Ken Hom Cooks Chinese (1996), Ken Hom's Hot Wok (1996), Ken Hom Travels with a Hot Wok (1998), Easy Family Dishes: A Memoir with Recipes (1998, Andre Simon Meml Book of the Year), Ken Hom Cooks Thai (1999), Ken Hom's Foolproof Chinese Cookery (2000), Ken Hom's Quick Wok (2001), Ken Hom's Foolproof Thai Cookery (2002), Ken Hom's Foolproof Asian Cookery (2003), 100 Top Stir Fries (2004); *Recreations* wines (claret), swimming, cycling; *Style—* Ken Hom, Esq

HOMA, Peter Michael; CBE (2000); *b* 1957; *Educ* Ernest Bevin Sch Tooting, Univ of Sussex (BA), Univ of Hull (MBA), IHSM (DipHSM), Brunel Univ (DBA); *m* 1; 1 s (b 1988), 1 da (b 1990); m 2, 16 July 2006, Deborah Hallas; *Career* health serv mangr; self-employed 1979–81, nat admin trainee SW Thames RHA 1981–82, operational servs administrator St George's Hosp London 1982–84, dep unit administrator Bristol Children's and Maternity Hosps 1984–86, dep unit gen mangr Acute Servs Unit Bromsgrove and Redditch HA 1986–89; The Leicester Royal Infirmary: assoc gen mangr 1989–90, unit gen mangr 1990–93, chief exec The Leicester Royal Infirmary NHS Tst 1993–98; head of National Patients' Access Team NHS Exec 1998–99, chief exec Cmmn for Health Improvement 1999–2003, chief exec St George's Healthcare NHS Tst 2003–06, chief exec Nottingham Univ Hosps NHS Tst 2006–; visiting prof Postgrad Med Sch Univ of Surrey 2006; IHSM: vice-chm 1996–97, chm 1997–98, pres 1998–99; pres Infirmary Drama and Operative and Literary Soc (IDOLS) 1990–98; companion Inst of Health Mgmnt 2003; *Recreations* rock climbing, running, cycling, picture framing, car mechanics, photography, writing, reading; *Clubs* Royal Over-Seas League; *Style—* Dr Peter Homa, CBE; ✉ Nottingham University Hospitals NHS Trust, C Floor, South Block, Derby Road, Nottingham NG7 2UH (tel 0115 942 2152)

HOMAN, Lawrence Hugh Adair; s of Lawrence William Nicholson Homan (d 1981), of Harpenden, Herts, and Mary Graves, *née* Adair (d 2003); *b* 26 June 1945; *Educ* Sherborne, Worcester Coll Oxford (MA); *Children* 1 s (Alexander b 1973), 1 da (Olivia b 1976); *Career* admitted slr 1970; asst slr Allen & Overy 1968–73, ptnr Berwin Leighton Paisner 1975–99, conslt 1999–; memb Law Soc; *Recreations* sailing, fishing; *Style—* Hugh Homan; ✉ The Malthouse, Teffont, Salisbury, Wiltshire SP3 5QY (tel 01722 717960, fax 01722 717961, e-mail hh@hugh-homan.com)

HOMAN, (John) Richard Seymour; CBE (1985); s of Capt Charles Edward Homan (d 1936), of London and Hants, and Mary Muriel, *née* Hewetson (d 1979); *b* 7 January 1925; *Educ* Radley, ChCh Oxford (MA); *m* 7 April 1961, Hon Mrs (Mary Graham) Homan (d 1999), da of 2 Baron Wrenbury (d 1940), of E Sussex and London; 1 s (Robert b 1964), 2 da (Frances (Mrs Gerald Homan Jue) b 1967, Rosalind b 1969); *Career* RNVR 1943, Sub Lt RNVR 1944–46; Second Sea Lord's Dept Admiralty London 1944, HMS Tracker 1944–45, Underwater Weapons Div 1945–46; corp internal mgmnt conslt Head Office ICI 1950–57, corp planner and export sales mangr ICI Metals/IMI 1957–64, head Computing and Mgmnt Servs Agric Div ICI 1964–68; NEDO: Br head Industrial Div 1968–72, head Assessment Div 1972–74, asst industrial dir 1974–77, actg industrial dir 1977–79, dep industrial dir 1979–83, industrial dir 1984–85, chm Speciality Chemicals Sector Gp 1986–90; author of various NEDO reports on Industrial Policies and Issues 1977–85, conslt CEGB and successor companies 1986–96, memb Advsy Ctee on Hazardous Substances 1991–94; chm: Govrs Uplands Community Coll Wadhurst 1989–94 and 1996–97, E Sussex Strategic Forum 1995–99; dep chm Salters Inst of Industrial Chemistry 2003– (chm 1995–2003); Hon DUniv York 2005; memb Ct of Assts Worshipful Co of Salters (Master 1994–95), Freeman City of London (Liveryman 1957); *Recreations* walking, music, reading; *Style—* Richard Homan, Esq, CBE; ✉ 30 High Street, Ticehurst, Wadhurst, East Sussex TN5 7AS (tel and fax 01580 200651)

HOMAN, Prof Roger Edward; s of Edward Alfred Homan (d 1997), and Olive Florence, *née* Dent (d 1988); *b* 25 June 1944; *Educ* Varndean GS Brighton, Univ of Sussex (BA), Lancaster Univ (PhD), LSE (MSc); *Career* Brighton Coll of Educn: lectr in religious studies 1971–73, lectr in educn 1973–76; University of Brighton (formerly Brighton Poly): lectr in religious educn 1976–85, princ lectr in religious studies 1985–, prof of religious studies 1998–; memb: Prayer Book Soc (current vice-pres), Victorian Soc; fell Victoria Coll of Music 1994; *Recreations* sweet peas and auriculas, church music, chapel hunting, poetry, aesthetics; *Style*— Prof Roger Homan; ✉ University of Brighton, Falmer, East Sussex BN1 9PH (tel 01273 643405)

HOME, Anna Margaret; OBE (1993); da of James Douglas Home (d 1989), and Janet Mary, *née* Wheeler (d 1974); *b* 13 January 1938; *Educ* Convent of Our Lady St Leonards-on-Sea, St Anne's Coll Oxford (MA); *Career* joined: BBC Radio 1961, BBC TV 1964; researcher, dir and prodr Children's Programmes 1964–70, exec prodr Children's Drama 1970–81; controller of programmes (later dep dir programmes) TVS 1981–86, head of Children's Programmes BBC TV 1986–97, chief exec Children's Film and Television Fndn (CFTF) 1998–; chair: Second World Summit on Television for Children 1998, Cinemagic 1999–2005, Eurokidnet 2002–06, Kidnet 2006–; memb Bd Unicorn Children's Theatre 2004–, chair Showcomotion Children's Media Conf 2004–, tstee Prince of Wales Arts and Kids Fndn 2006–; Women in Film and Television Lifetime Achievement Award 1996, BAFTA Special Award for Lifetime Achievement 1997; FRTS, FRSA; *Recreations* reading, theatre, gardening; *Style*— Miss Anna Home, OBE; ✉ 3 Liberia Road, London N5 1JP

HOME, 15 Earl of (S 1605); David Alexander Cospatrick Douglas-Home; CVO (1997), CBE (1991); also Lord Dunglass (S 1605), Lord Home (S 1473), and Baron Douglas (UK 1875); only s of Baron Home of the Hirsel, KT, PC, who disclaimed the Earldom of Home for life 1963 (d 1995), and Elizabeth Hester, *née* Alington (d 1990); *b* 20 November 1943; *Educ* Eton, ChCh Oxford; *m* 1972, Jane Margaret, yr da of Col John Williams-Wynne, CBE, DSO, JP (d 1998); 2 da (Lady Iona Katherine b 1980, Lady Mary Elizabeth b 1982), 1 s (Michael David Alexander, Lord Dunglass b 1987); *Heir* s, Lord Dunglass; *Career* dir Morgan Grenfell & Co Ltd 1974–99, chm Deutsche Export Services Ltd 1984–99, chm Deutsche (Scotland) Ltd 1986–99 (dir 1978–99), chm Morgan Grenfell International Ltd 1987–98, dir Deutsche Morgan Grenfell Hong Kong Ltd 1989–99, dir Deutsche Morgan Grenfell Asia Pacific Holdings Pte Ltd 1989–99, pres cmmr PT Deutsche Morgan Grenfell Indonesia 1993–99, dir Deutsche Morgan Grenfell Group plc 1996–99 (chm 1999); chm: Tandem Group plc (formerly EFG plc) 1991–96 (dir 1981–96), Cegelec Controls Ltd 1991–94, Coutts & Co 1999–, MAN Ltd 2000–, Coutts (Switzerland) Ltd 2000–04, Bank von Ernst 2003–04, Coutts Bank von Ernst 2004–; dir: Douglas and Angus Estates 1966–, Agricultural Mortgage Corporation 1979–93, Credit for Exports plc 1984–94, K & N Kenanga Holdings Bhd (formerly K & N Kenanga Sdn Bhd until 1996) 1993–99, Kenanga Deutsche Futures Sdn Bhd 1995–99; tstee Grosvenor Estate 1993–, non-exec dir Grosvenor Estate Holdings 1993–2000, chm Grosvenor Gp Ltd 2007– (non-exec dir 2005–); govr The Ditchley Fndn 1976– (memb Cncl of Mgmnt 1976–2003); chm Ctee for ME Trade 1986–92, memb Export Guarantee Advsy Cncl ECGD 1988–93, govr Cwlth Inst 1988–98; memb: Offshore Industry Export Advsy Gp 1989–93, Cncl RASE 1990–, Bd Dubai FSA 2005–; pres Old Etonian Assoc 2002–03; sits as Cons House of Lords, oppn front bench spokesman on trade and industry 1997–98; *Recreations* outdoor sports; *Clubs* Turf; *Style*— The Rt Hon the Earl of Home, CVO, CBE; ✉ 99 Dovehouse Street, London SW3 6JZ (tel 020 7352 9060); The Hirsel, Coldstream, Berwickshire TD12 4LP (tel 01890 882345); Castlemains, Douglas, Lanarkshire ML11 0RX (tel 01555 851241); Coutts & Co, 440 Strand, London WC2R 0QS (tel 020 7753 1000, fax 020 7753 1066)

HOME, Prof Philip David; s of Philip Henry Home, and Kathleen Margaret, *née* Young; *b* 11 January 1948; *Educ* Birkenhead Sch, Univ of Oxford (MA, DM, DPhil), Guy's Hosp (BM BCh); *m* 28 Aug 1971, Elizabeth Mary, da of Sidney Thomas Broad; 1 s (Jonathan Paul b 1979), 1 da (Deborah Mary b 1976); *Career* Wellcome Tst sr res fell in clinical sci 1982–86, prof Univ of Newcastle upon Tyne 1993– (reader 1986–93); conslt physician Freeman Hosp Newcastle 1986–; ed Diabetic Medicine 1987–91, ed Diabetes Voice 2002–04; author of over 350 articles on aspects of diabetes med; vice-pres Int Diabetes Fedn 1997–2003; FRCP 1989; *Recreations* gardening, travel, work; *Style*— Prof Philip Home; ✉ SCMS-Diabetes, Framlington Place, Newcastle upon Tyne NE2 4HH (tel 0191 222 7019, fax 0191 222 0723, e-mail philip.home@ncl.ac.uk)

HOME, Sir William Dundas; 14 Bt (NS 1671), of Blackadder, Co Berwick; o s of John Home (d 1988, er s of Sir David George Home, 13 Bt), and Nancy Helen, *née* Elliott (now Lady Gorton); suc gf 1992; *b* 19 February 1968; *Educ* Cranbrook Sch Sydney; *m* 30 Sept 1995, Dominique Meryl, da of Sydney Fischer, OBE; 1 s (Thomas John b 29 Nov 1996), 1 da (Petra Sydney b 23 June 1998); *Heir* s, Thomas Home; *Career* horticulturalist and arboriculturalist; memb: Int Soc of Arboriculture, Aust Inst of Horticulture, Nat Arborist Assoc; *Recreations* tennis, golf, fly fishing; *Clubs* Royal Sydney Golf; *Style*— Sir William Home, Bt

HOME ROBERTSON, John David; s of Lt-Col John Wallace Robertson, TD, JP, DL (d 1979), and Helen Margaret (d 1987), eld da of Lt-Col David Milne-Home (assumed additional name of Home by Scottish licence 1933); *b* 5 December 1948; *Educ* Ampleforth, West of Scotland Agric Coll; *m* 1977, Catherine Jean, da of Alex Brewster, of Glamis, Angus; 2 s (Alexander b 1979, Patrick b 1981); *Career* farmer; memb: Berwickshire Dist Cncl 1974–78, Borders Health Bd 1975–78; MP (Lab): Berwick and East Lothian Oct 1978–83, E Lothian 1983–2001; MSP E Lothian 1999–2007; House of Commons: memb Select Ctee Scottish Affrs 1979–83, chm Scottish Gp of Lab MPs 1983, Scottish Labour whip 1983–84; oppn spokesman: on agriculture 1984–87, Scottish affrs 1987–88, agriculture 1988–90; memb Select Ctee on Defence 1990–97, PPS to Rt Hon Dr Jack Cunningham, MP as Min of Agric 1997–99; memb Br-Irish Parly Body 1994–99, dep min Rural Affairs 1999–2000; Scot Parl: convener Holyrood Progress Gp 2000–07, dep convenor European Ctee 2000–03; *Clubs* Prestonpans Labour, East Lothian Labour, Haddington Labour; *Style*— John Home Robertson, Esq, MSP

HOMER, Andy; s of Charles Henry Homer (d 1982), and Kathleen Homer, *née* Welch (d 2004); *b* 2 March 1953; *Educ* St Chad's Coll Wolverhampton, Becket GS Nottingham, Wharton Sch Univ of Philadelphia; *m* 1971, Maria; 2 s (Oliver Charles b 1980, Alexander Charles b 1983); *Career* Commercial Union plc: dep corp fin and planning mangr 1992–93, dir of fin UK 1994–96, gen mangr UK General Insurance 1996–98; chief exec Axa Insurance plc 1998–, exec dir AXA UK plc 1999–2001; chief exec Folgate Partnership 2001–05, chief exec Towergate Partnership 2005–; chm Motor Insurers Bureau UK 1998–2001, pres CII 2003 (vice-pres 1999–2003); Freeman City of London Co of Firefighters 1997; FCII 1976; *Recreations* aerobics, raquet ball, jogging; *Clubs* Worcestershire CC, West Bromwich Albion FC; *Style*— Andy Homer, Esq

HON, Prof (Kwok Keung) Bernard; s of Chung Ki Hon, and Yuet Seen, *née* Shaw; *b* 16 January 1950; *Educ* Hong Kong Tech Coll, Univ of Birmingham (MSc, PhD); *m* 18 Dec 1976, Yuk Ching Metis, da of late Yat Chow Hui; 2 s (Chen Yue (Daniel) b 1979, Wai Yue (Adrian) b 1982); *Career* lectr: Univ of Bath 1979–81, Univ of Birmingham 1981–87, prof of mfrg systems Univ of Dundee 1987–90; Univ of Liverpool: prof of mfrg systems 1990–, head Dept of Industrial Studies 1990–97, dep dean of engrg 1997–2000; dir: Merseyside Innovation Centre 1992–96, Rapid Prototyping Centre 1994–, Product Innovation and Development Centre 1995–2003, Merseyside TCS Centre 1995–2003; memb Technology Foresight Manufacturing Production and Business Processes Panel 1994–98; academic advsr: Hong Kong Poly Univ 1996–2001, Hong Kong Univ of Science and Technology 2001–03; visiting lectr Univ of Hong Kong 2004; founding chm Int Conference on Design and Manufacture for Sustainable Devpt; Outstanding PolyU Alumni Award Hong Kong Poly Univ 2007; fell CIRP (Int Acad for Production Engrg) 2001; FIEE 1990; *Recreations* badminton, music; *Style*— Prof Bernard Hon; ✉ Department of Engineering, University of Liverpool, PO Box 147, Liverpool L69 7BZ (tel 0151 794 4680, fax 0151 794 9364, e-mail hon@liv.ac.uk)

HONAN, Corinna Jeannette; da of Prof Park Honan, of Burley, Leeds, and Jeannette, *née* Colin; *b* 7 May 1953, St Germain-en-Laye, France; *Educ* Classical HS RI USA, King Edward VI HS for Girls Birmingham, St Hugh's Coll Oxford (BA), NCTJ; *m* 21 July 1984, Nicholas Inge, s of Edward Inge; 2 da (Anabel India Kitty b 20 June 1985, Sophie Georgia Rachelle b 12 April 1989); *Career* news reporter Newcastle Journal 1975–78, staff feature writer Woman magazine 1978–81; Daily Mail: news reporter 1981–83, TV and foreign correspondent 1984–87, showbusiness ed 1987–91, feature writer and personality interviewer 1991–95; Daily Telegraph: features ed 1995–97, asst ed (features) 1997–2005, asst ed 2005–07, no 2 on Saturday edn 2003–05; conslt ed (features) Daily Mail 2007–; *Recreations* nineteenth-century novels, antiques, walking; *Style*— Ms Corinna Honan; ✉ Daily Mail, Northcliffe House, 2 Derry Street, Kensington, London W8 (tel 020 7538 6133, e-mail corinna.honan@dailymail.co.uk)

HONAN, Prof Park; s of Dr William Francis Honan, FACS, Lt Col US Med Corps, and Annette Neudecker Honan; *b* 17 September 1928, Utica, NY; *Educ* Bronxville HS, Deep Springs Jr Coll, Univ of Chicago (MA), Univ of London (PhD); *m* 22 Dec 1952, Jeannette, *née* Colin; 2 da (Corinna b 1953, Natasha b 1958), 1 s (Matthew (twin) b 1958); *Career* successively lectr, sr lectr and reader in English Univ of Birmingham 1968–83, prof of English and American literature Univ of Leeds 1984–93; Guggenheim fell 1962 and 1973, Andrew Mellon research fell 1990; patron London branch Jane Austen Soc, hon vice-pres Marlowe Soc; hon degree Brown Univ RI; FRSL 1998; *Books* Browning's Characters (1961), The Book, the Ring and the Poet (with W Irvine, 1975), Matthew Arnold: A Life (1983), Jane Austen: Her Life (1987), Authors' Lives (1990), Shakespeare: A Life (1998), Christopher Marlowe: Poet and Spy (2005); *Recreations* walking, inspecting nature, museum-going, travel, letter writing; *Style*— Prof Park Honan; ✉ 11 Vinery Road, Burley, Leeds LS4 2LB (e-mail park.honan@tiscali.co.uk)

HONDERICH, Prof Edgar Dawn Ross (Ted); s of John William Honderich (d 1956), and Rae Laura, *née* Armstrong (d 1952); *b* 30 January 1933; *Educ* Univ of Toronto (BA), UCL (PhD); *m* 1, 22 Aug 1964 (m dis 1976), Pauline da of Paul Goodwin (d 1976), of Dunlavin; 1 da (Kiaran Aeveen b 1960), 1 s (John Ruan b 1962); m 2, 8 Dec 1989, Jane, da of Maj Robert O'Grady, MC, of Midford Place, Bath; m 3, 4 July 2003, Ingrid Coggin Purkiss, da of Maurice Coggin, of Cambridge; *Career* lectr in philosophy Univ of Sussex 1962–64; UCL: lectr 1964–72, reader 1972–83, prof 1983–88, Grote prof of philosophy of mind and logic 1988–; visiting prof: Yale Univ 1970, City Univ of NY 1971, Univ of Bath 2005–; chm Royal Inst of Philosophy 2006– ed: International Library of Philosophy And Scientific Method 1965–, The Arguments of the Philosophers 1970–, The Problems of Philosophy 1983–; advsy ed Penguin Philosophy 1965–; memb: Mind Assoc, Aristotelian Soc; memb Lab Pty; *Books* Punishment: The Supposed Justifications (1969), Essays on Freedom of Action (ed, 1973), Social Ends and Political Means (ed, 1976), Philosophy As It Is (ed with M Burnyeat, 1979), Violence for Equality: Inquiries in Political Philosophy (1980), Philosophy Through its Past (ed, 1984), Morality and Objectivity (ed, 1985), A Theory of Determinism: The Mind, Neuroscience and Life-Hopes (1988), Conservatism (1990, revised edn 2004), How Free are You? The Determinism Problem (1993, 2 edn 2002), The Oxford Companion to Philosophy (ed, 1995, new edn 2005), Philosopher: a Kind of Life (2000), After the Terror (2002), On Political Means and Social Ends (2003), Terrorism for Humanity: Inquiries in Political Philosophy (2003), On Consciousness (2004), On Political Means and Social Ends (2004), On Determinism and Freedom (2005), Punishment: The Supposed Justifications Reconsidered (2005), Humanity, Terrorism, Terrorist War: Palestine, 9/11, Iraq, 7/7... (2006), Radical Externalism: Honderich's Theory of Consciousness Discussed (contrib, 2006); *Recreations* wine, music, old house; *Clubs* Garrick; *Style*— Prof Ted Honderich; ✉ Fountain House, Gould's Grove, Frome, Somerset BA11 3DW (tel 01373 466854, e-mail t.honderich@ucl.ac.uk)

HONE, His Hon Judge Richard Michael; QC (1997); s of late Maj-Gen Sir (Herbert) Ralph Hone, KCMG, KBE, GCStJ, MC, TD, QC, and Sybil Mary, *née* Collins; *b* 15 February 1947; *Educ* St Paul's (scholar), UC Oxford (MA); *m* 1, Sarah Nicholl-Carne; 2 s (Nathaniel b 1987, Rufus b 1989); m 2, Diana Pavel; 2 s (Adam b 1995, Charles b 1997); *Career* called to the Bar Middle Temple 1970 (bencher 1994); recorder of the Crown Court 1987–2004, circuit judge (SE Circuit) 2004–, sr circuit judge Central Criminal Court 2005–; Cocks' referee 1988–94; chm Jt Regulations Ctee 1995–2000; memb Professional Conduct Ctee of the Bar 1993–97, legal memb MHRT 2000–; KStJ 2000 (CStJ 1993, OStJ 1972); *Recreations* wine, reading, travel; *Clubs* Boodle's, Pratt's; *Style*— His Hon Judge Hone, QC; ✉ Central Criminal Court, Old Bailey, London EC4M 7EH (tel 020 7248 3277)

HONER, Julian Anthony; s of John David Honer, of Cambridge, and Shirley, *née* Gerrish; *b* 19 February 1961; *Educ* Lewes Priory Sch, Univ of Stirling (BA), Univ of Birmingham, Barber Inst of Fine Arts (MPhil); *m* 1997, Alison, *née* Starling; 1 da (Charlotte Miranda b 22 March 2005); *Career* researcher and cataloguer Dept of Modern Br Pictures Bonhams Fine Art Auctioneers 1986–88, fine art insurance underwriter Eagle Star (Star Assurance Soc Ltd) 1988–89, account exec Frizzell Fine Art Insurance 1989–90; ed: The Art Directory 1990–93, The Dictionary of Art 1992–95; Macmillan: managing ed 1995–97, sr commissioning ed 1997–98; Merrell Publishers London: ed 1998–99, editorial dir 1999–; author of a number of articles; *Recreations* travel, art, architecture, photography, music; *Style*— Julian Honer, Esq; ✉ Merrell Publishers Ltd, 81 Southwark Street, London SE1 0HX (tel 020 7928 8880, fax 020 7928 1199, e-mail jh@merrellpublishers.com)

HONEYBALL, Mary Hilda Rosamund; MEP (Lab) London; da of Stanley James Honeyball, of Yate, Bristol, and late Betty Gath, *née* Tandy; *b* 12 November 1952; *Educ* Pate's GS for Girls Cheltenham, Somerville Coll Oxford (MA); *Career* administrative offr GLC 1975–77, negotiations offr Soc of Civil and Public Servants 1977–83, political organiser Royal Arsenal Co-operative Soc 1983–85, gen sec Newham Voluntary Agencies Cncl 1986–90, service mangr Spastics Soc 1990–91, chief exec Gingerbread (lone parents' support orgn) 1992–94, gen sec Assoc of Chief Offrs of Probation 1994–98, MEP (Lab) London 2000–; cncllr Barnet BC 1978–86; chair Women's Ctee Gtr London Lab Pty 1983–85, memb Nat Alliance of Women's Orgns 1992–94; chair Docklands Forum 1987–90; govr: Grahame Park Sch London 1978–84, Deptford Green Sch London 1986–95, Sir Francis Drake Primary Sch London 1986–95; *Recreations* art, literature, food and wine; *Clubs* Reform; *Style*— Ms Mary Honeyball, MEP; ✉ 4G Shirland Mews, London W9 3DY (tel 020 8964 9815, fax 020 8960 0150, e-mail mary@maryhoneyball.net)

HONEYBORNE, Dr Christopher Henry Bruce; s of Henry Thomas Honeyborne (d 1998), and Lily Margaret, *née* Fox (d 1991); *b* 5 December 1940; *Educ* Cambs HS for Boys, St Catharine's Coll Cambridge (MA, DipAgSci), Univ of Reading (PhD); *m* 12 Oct 1968, (Anne) Veronica, da of Stephen Sullivan (d 2003), of Guernsey; 1 s (James b 1970), 2 da (Clare b 1975, Katharine b 1986); *Career* res demonstrator Univ of Reading 1964–68, res scientist ARC Univ of Bristol 1968–70, mangr Cuprinol Ltd 1971–72, sr mangr Lazard Bros & Co Ltd 1972–77 (seconded to Dalgety Ltd 1976–77), Banque Paribas 1977–89 (dep gen mangr London Branch 1977–86, chief exec Quilter Goodison Co Ltd 1986–88); chief exec Bank of N T Butterfield & Son Ltd London Branch and Seymour Pierce Butterfield Ltd 1993–94; chm: Finotel plc 1989–98 (dir 1983), Cameron Richard and Smith (Holdings) Ltd 1989–, Gremlin Group plc 1997–99, Aerosol Products Ltd 1999–2004,

H

Aspect Internet Hldgs Ltd 2003–04, Dyson Gp plc 2006, ZOO Digital Group plc (formerly KAZOO3D plc) 2006– (dir 2000–); dir: Cartier Ltd 1979–97, Secure Retirement plc 1991–93, Yorkshire Water plc 1993–98, Kunick plc 1995–2002, BWDAimVCT plc (now Rensburg Aim VCT plc) 1999–2005, Coolbeans Productions Ltd 1999–2001, ukphonebook.com ltd (now Simunix Ltd) 1999–2005, Bede plc 2000, Birse Group plc 2000–06, Bannatyne Fitness Ltd 2001–03, LBIconAB(publ) 2005–06, Matica plc 2007; MIBiol, MSI; *Recreations* gardening, shooting, viewing art; *Clubs* City of London, The Arts, United & Cecil; *Style*— Dr Christopher Honeyborne; ✉ Scawton Croft, Rievaulx, York YO62 5LE (tel 01439 770392); office (tel and fax 01439 771900, mobile 07710 904550, e-mail chbhoneyborne@aol.com)

HONEYBOURNE, Dr David; *b* 26 March 1951; *Educ* Redditch HS, Univ of Bristol Med Sch (MB ChB, MD), Univ of Wales (MSc); *m* 30 Aug 1980, Jane Elizabeth, da of Dr David John Rudman, of Whitton, London; 2 da (Laura Ann b 1982, Clare Louise b 1985); *Career* house physician Bristol Gen Hosp 1974; SHO: Southmead Hosp Bristol 1975–76 (house surgn 1975), Brook Hosp London 1976–77; registrar in med KCH London 1977–78, res fell KCH Med Sch London 1978–80, sr registrar in med Manchester 1980–85; conslt physician specialising in chest diseases: City Hosp Birmingham 1985–98, Birmingham Heartlands Hosp 1998–; sr clinical lectr in med Univ of Birmingham, hon clinical reader Univ of Warwick; author of books and pubns on chest diseases; memb: Br Thoracic Soc, Euro Respiratory Soc, American Thoracic Soc; FRCP 1993 (MRCP 1977); *Recreations* golf, photography; *Style*— Dr David Honeybourne; ✉ Priory Hospital, Priory Road, Edgbaston, Birmingham B5 7UG (tel 0121 446 1671); Department of Respiratory Medicine, Birmingham Heartland, Birmingham B9 5SS (tel 0121 424 3731, fax 0121 424 1661, e-mail davidhoneybourne@aol.com)

HONEYMAN BROWN, Christopher; s of Edward Honeyman Brown (d 1981), of St Mawes, and Nancy Elisabeth Ellen Odgers, *née* Hall (d 1991); *b* 2 June 1948; *Educ* Stowe; *m* 7 Sept 1973, Rosamund, da of late Peter Bluett Winch; 1 da (Emma b 15 Sept 1976), 1 s (Thomas b 2 Nov 1978); *Career* ptnr: Croydon & Co (chartered accountants) 1977–85, Binder Hamlyn (chartered accountants) 1986–96; chief exec Alsop Wilkinson (slrs) 1996, dir of ops Dibb Lupton Alsop (slrs) 1996–98; ptnr Horwath Clark Whitehill (chartered accountants) 1998–2001, chief exec asb law (slrs) 2001–06; chm of govrs Stowe Sch; Liveryman Worshipful Co of Fletchers; FCA 1979 (ACA 1973), FRSA; *Recreations* music, cars; *Style*— Christopher Honeyman Brown, Esq; ✉ 31 Old Glebe, Fernhurst, Haslemere, Surrey GU27 3HT (tel 01428 645911, e-mail christopher@honeymanbrown.freeserve.co.uk)

HONYWOOD, Sir Filmer Courtenay William; 11 Bt (E 1660), of Evington, Kent; s of Col Sir William Wynne Honywood, 10 Bt, MC (d 1982), and Maud, yr da of William Hodgson-Wilson, of Hexgrave Park, Southwell, Notts; *b* 20 May 1930; *Educ* Downside, RMA Sandhurst, RAC Cirencester (MRAC Dip); *m* 1956, Elizabeth Margaret Mary Cynthia (d 1996), 2 da of late Sir Alastair George Lionel Joseph Miller, 6 Bt; 2 s (Rupert Anthony b 1957, Simon Joseph b 1958), 2 da (Mary Caroline (Mrs C Bear) b 1961, Judith Mary Frances (Mrs Paul Baker) b 1964); *Heir* s, Rupert Honywood; *Career* 3 Carabiniers (Prince of Wales's Dragoon Gds) 1950–51; farmed 1954–64 (Suffolk Co Dairy Herd Production awards 1955 and 1956); Agricultural Land Serv MAFF Maidstone 1964, asst land cmmr 1966, surveyor Cockermouth Cumbria 1973–74; sr lands offr SE Region CEGB 1974–78, Regnl Surveyor and Valuer 1978–88, conslt on agric restoration and compensation to UK Nirex Ltd 1989–90, pt/t sr valuer Inland Revenue Folkestone 1989–90; land agency conslt Nuclear Electric plc 1993–94; examiner in agriculture: Incorporated Soc of Estates & Wayleaves Offrs 1988–95, Soc of Surveying Technicians 1996–97; FRICS; *Style*— Sir Filmer Honywood, Bt; ✉ Greenway Forstal Farmhouse, Hollingbourne, Maidstone, Kent ME17 1QA (tel 01622 880418)

HOOD, Dr Alison Sinclair; da of Alexander B Hood (d 1986), and Agnes Prise, *née* Edgar (d 1989); *b* 21 January 1952; *Educ* Univ of Glasgow (PhD); *Career* princ Lipton Orthoptic Inst Sch of Orthoptics Glasgow and head Lipton Orthoptic Inst Glasgow 1979–84, head Sch of Orthoptics The Queen's Coll Glasgow 1984–90, sr lectr in orthoptics Dept of Vision Sciences Glasgow Caledonian Univ 1990–92, md Eye Scan (UK) Ltd 1993–; Scottish memb Orthoptists' Bd Cncl for Professions Supplementary to Med (CPSM) 1979–93; memb Br Orthoptic Soc 1973–; *Recreations* art, golf; *Style*— Dr Alison Hood; ✉ Eye Scan (UK), 30 Lanton Road, Lanton Park, Newlands, Glasgow G43 2SR (tel 0141 637 7503, mobile 07860 735911, e-mail alison.eyescan@talk21.com)

HOOD, Andrew; s of Dr Christopher Allen Hood, and Alison Julia Annabelle, *née* Clair; *b* 5 April 1966; *Educ* Lord Williams's Comp Sch, New Coll Oxford (BA), Birkbeck Coll London (MSc); *m* 17 June 2001, Katherine, *née* Rainwood; *Career* tutor 1989–94, researcher for Rt Hon Tony Benn, *qv*, 1990–92, co-author (with Tony Benn) of Common Sense, a new constitution for Britain 1991–92, ptnr Ashdown Hood (film prodn co) 1993–94; special advsr to: Rt Hon Robin Cook MP 1997–2000 (policy advsr 1994–97), Rt Hon Geoffrey Hoon MP, *qv*, 2000–; fndr and chm Foreign Policy Centre 1997–, fndr and memb Bd Policy Network 2000– (exec dir 2000–01); *Style*— Andrew Hood, Esq

HOOD, Prof Christopher Cropper; s of David White Hood (d 2003), and Margaret, *née* Cropper (d 1985); *b* 5 March 1947; *Educ* Univ of York (BA, DLitt), Univ of Glasgow (BLitt); *m* 1979, Gillian Thackwray White; 2 da; *Career* jr research fell Carnegie Corporation Project 1970–72, lectr Dept of Politics Univ of Glasgow 1972–77, research fell SSRC Machinery of Govt Project Univ of York 1977–79, lectr Dept of Politics Univ of Glasgow 1979–86, sr teaching fell Faculty of Law Nat Univ of Singapore 1984–85, prof of govt and public admin Univ of Sydney 1986–89, prof of public admin and public policy LSE 1989–2000, Gladstone prof of government and fell All Souls Coll Oxford 2001–; chair Section S5 (Politics and Int Relations) Br Acad 2002–05; FBA 1996, AcSS 2001; *Books* The Limits of Administration (1976), Bureaumetrics (with Prof A Dunsire, 1981), Big Government in Hard Times (ed with Prof M Wright, 1981), The Tools of Government (1983), Administrative Analysis: An Introduction to Rules, Enforcement and Organization (1986), Delivering Public Services: Sharing Western European Experience (1988), Cutback Management in Public Bureaucracies (with Prof A Dunsire, 1989), Administrative Argument (with Prof M W Jackson, 1991), Rewards at the Top (ed with Prof Guy Peters, 1994), Explaining Economic Policy Reversals (1994), The Art of the State (1998), Regulation inside Government (with Colin Scott and others, 1999), The Government of Risk: Understanding Risk Regulation Regimes (with Henry Rothstein and Robert Baldwin, 2001), Reward for High Public Office: Asian and Pacific Rim States (ed with Prof Guy Peters, 2003), Controlling Modern Government (jt ed, 2004), The Politics of Public Service Bargains (with Martin Lodge, 2006), The Tools of Government in the Digital Age (with Helen Margetts, 2007), Transparency: The Key to Better Governance (jt ed, 2006); also author of numerous book chapters and articles in learned jls; *Style*— Prof Christopher Hood, FBA; ✉ All Souls College, Oxford OX1 4AL

HOOD, (Hilary) David Richard; s of Maj Hilary Ollyett Dupuis Hood, RA (d 1982), and Mrs Patrick Reid, *née* Sampson; *b* 6 February 1955; *Educ* Radley, Millfield, KCL (LLB); *Career* called to the Bar Inner Temple 1980; *Style*— David Hood, Esq; ✉ 90 Overstrand Mansions, Prince of Wales Drive, London SW11 4EU (tel 020 7622 7415, fax 020 7622 6929)

HOOD, 8 Viscount (GB 1796); Sir Henry Lyttelton Alexander; 8 Bt (GB 1778); also Baron Hood (I 1782 and GB 1795); s of 7 Viscount Hood (d 1999); Lord Hood is seventh in descent from 1 Viscount, the naval hero who captured Corsica 1793; *b* 16 March 1958; *m* 5 Oct 1991, Flora, yr da of Cdr Michael Bernard Casement, OBE, RN, of Dene Cottage, West Harting, Petersfield, Hants; 3 s (Archibald Lyttelton Samuel b 16 May 1993, Atticus Michael Alexander b 20 Oct 1995, Willoughby Henry Caspar b 11 Nov 1998); 2 da (Edith Clementine Matilda (twin) b 11 Nov 1998, Darcy Ellen Fynvola b 8 July 2002); *Career* slr; *Style*— The Rt Hon Viscount Hood; ✉ 29 Lansdowne Road, London W11 2LQ

HOOD, James (Jim); MP; *m* Marion; 1 s, 1da; *Career* cncllr Newark and Sherwood DC 1979–87; MP (Lab): Clydesdale 1987–2005, Lanark and Hamilton E 2005–; House of Commons: fndr chm All-Pty Gp on ME 1987–92, memb Defence Select Ctee 1997–2001, memb Liaison Ctee 1992–2006, chm European Scrutiny Select Ctee 1998–2006, memb Speaker's Panel of Chm 1997–; memb NATO UK Parly Assembly 2005–; ldr Nottingham striking miners 1984–85; fell Industry and Parl Tst, memb Armed Forces Parly Scheme; *Style*— Jim Hood, Esq, MP; ✉ House of Commons, London SW1A 0AA (tel 020 7219 4585, fax 020 7219 5872, e-mail hoodj@parliament.uk, website www.jimhoodmp.co.uk); Constituency Office: Council Offices, South Vennel, Lanark ML11 7JT (tel 01555 673177, fax 01555 673188)

HOOD, (William) Nicholas (Nick); CBE; s of Sir Tom Hood, KBE, CB, TD, and Joan, *née* Hellyar; *b* 3 December 1935; *Educ* Clifton; *m* 1, 1963 (m dis 1990), Angela, *née* Robinson; 1 s, 1 da; m 2, 1994 (m dis 2003), Ann E H Reynolds; m 3, 2006, Patricia Lang; *Career* served DCLI 1955–57; NEM General Insurance Association Ltd and Credit Insurance Association Ltd 1958–64, G B Britton UK Ltd 1964–70 (rising to sales and mktg dir); UBM Group plc: various positions rising to dir Central Region 1970–84, md UBM Overseas Ltd 1972–82; dir HAT Group Ltd 1984–86; chm: Wessex Water Authy 1987–89, Winterthur Life plc 1988–2007, Wessex Water plc 1989–98, Wessex Water Ltd 1998–99, MHIT plc 1998–2003, Clifton College Services Ltd 1998–, Frogmat International Ltd 2001–, Winterthur Life (UK) Ltd 2002–07, Wessex Water Services Ltd, Wessex Water Commercial Ltd, Wessex Waste Management Ltd; vice-chm Azurix Ltd 1998–99; dir QHIT plc 1998–2004; non-exec dir: Bremhill Industries plc 1987–93, Commercial Union Environmental Trust plc 1992–98, APV plc 1994–97, Brewin Dolphin Holdings plc 2000– (dep chm); cncl memb Water Trg Cncl 1987–99, Fndn for Water Research 1989–99, chm WaterAid 1990–95 (memb Cncl 1989–96), pres International Water Services Assoc 1997–99 (vice-pres 1993–97), life vice-pres Int Water Assoc 2002, memb Cncl Water Servs Assoc (vice-chm 1994, chm 1995), tstee West Country Rivers Tst 2000–; memb Advsy Cncl for Business and the Environment 1990–93; dep chm Business in the Community 1993–2007; chm @Bristol 1994–2002 (life vice-pres 2002); dir: The Harbourside Centre 1995–2001, The Harbourside Foundation 1996–2001, West of England Philharmonic Orch 2003–; chm of tstees Bristol Cancer Help Centre 2000–; memb Duchy of Cornwall Cncl 1992–; Liveryman Worshipful Co of Plumbers; Hon MBA UWE 2000; *Recreations* music, fishing, cricket, painting; *Clubs* Army and Navy, MCC, Boodle's; *Style*— Nick Hood, Esq, CBE; ✉ One Queen's Parade, Bath BA1 2NJ (tel 01225 334423)

HOOD, Prof Roger Grahame; CBE (1995); s of Ronald Hugo Frederick Hood (d 1996), of Aldridge, W Midlands, and Phyllis Eileen, *née* Murphy (d 1991); *b* 12 June 1936; *Educ* King Edward's Sch Five Ways Birmingham, LSE (BSc), Downing Coll Cambridge (PhD), Univ of Oxford (DCL); *m* 1, 15 June 1963 (m dis 1985), Barbara, da of Donald Waldo Smith (d 1979), of Washington, IL; 1 da (Catharine b 1964); m 2, 5 Oct 1985, Nancy Colquitt, da of Maj John Heyward Lynah (d 1984), of Charleston, SC; 2 step da (Clare b 1964, Zoe b 1969); *Career* research offr LSE 1961–63, lectr in social admin Univ of Durham 1963–67, asst dir of research Inst of Criminology Univ of Cambridge 1967–73, fell Clare Hall Cambridge 1969–73; Univ of Oxford: reader in criminology 1973–96, dir Centre for Criminological Res 1973–2003, prof of criminology 1996–2003; fell All Souls Coll Oxford 1973–2003 (sub-warden 1994–96, emeritus fell 2003–); distinguished visiting prof Univ of Hong Kong 2003–04, visiting prof Univ of Virginia Law Sch 2005–07; Sellin-Glueck Award for Int Contribs to Criminology 1986; memb: Parole Bd 1973, SSRC Ctee on Social Science and Law 1975–79, Judicial Studies Bd 1979–85, Dept Ctee to Review the Parole System 1987–88; expert conslt UN Ctee on Crime Prevention and Control 1988–95, 1999–2001 and 2004–05, memb Foreign Sec's Death Penalty Panel 1998–, pres Br Soc of Criminology 1986–89; hon QC 2000; FBA 1992; *Books* Sentencing in Magistrates Courts (1962), Borstal Re-Assessed (1965), Key Issues in Criminology (jtly, 1970), Sentencing the Motoring Offender (1972), Crime, Criminology and Public Policy - Essays in Honour of Sir Leon Radzinowicz (ed, 1974), A History of English Criminal Law - Vol 5, The Emergence of Penal Policy (jtly, 1986), The Death Penalty - A Worldwide Perspective (1989, 3 edn 2002), Race and Sentencing (1992), The Parole System at Work (jtly, 2000), Differences or Discrimination? Minority ethnic young people in the youth justice system (jtly, 2004), A Fair Hearing? Ethnic Minorities in the Criminal Courts (jtly, 2005); *Recreations* travel, cooking; *Style*— Prof Roger Hood, CBE, QC, DCL, FBA; ✉ 36 The Stream Edge, Fisher Row, Oxford OX1 1HT (tel and fax 01865 243140); All Souls College, Oxford OX1 4AL (tel 01865 279379, fax 01865 274445, e-mail roger.hood@all-souls.ox.ac.uk)

HOOD, Stephen John; s of Leslie Gilbert Hood, of Australia, and Margaret, *née* Vinnicombe; *b* 12 February 1947; *Educ* Brisbane Boys Coll, Univ of Queensland, Univ of London (LLM); *Children* 5 s (Ludovic b 1973, William b 1974, Roderick b 1978, Frederick b 1980, Anthony b 2004), 1 da (Victoria b 1985); *Career* ptnr Clifford Chance 1978–; chm: Royal Cwlth Soc in Hong Kong 1983–86, Exec Ctee Sir Robert Menzies Meml Tst 1988–98, Latin American Advsy Gp British Invisibles 1999–; Freeman City of London, Liveryman City of London Solicitors' Co; *Books* Equity Joint Ventures in The People's Republic of China, Technology Transfer in The People's Republic of China; *Recreations* viticulture, fly fishing, skiing, contemporary art; *Clubs* Garrick, Oriental, Union (NY), Anglers (NY); *Style*— Stephen Hood, Esq; ✉ Clifford Chance, 10 Upper Bank Street, Canary Wharf, London E14 5JJ (tel 020 7600 1000, fax 020 7600 5555)

HOODLESS, Dame Elisabeth Ann Marion Frost; DBE (2004, CBE 1992); da of late Maj Raymond Evelyn Plummer, TD, of Sevenoaks, Kent, and late Maureen Grace, *née* Frost; *b* 11 February 1941; *Educ* Redland HS Bristol, Univ of Durham (BA), LSE (Dip); *m* 28 Aug 1965, Donald Bentley Hoodless, s of Ernest William Hoodless, of Ticehurst, E Sussex; 2 s (Christopher, Mark); *Career* Community Service Volunteers: asst dir 1963, dep dir 1975, exec dir 1986; cncllr London Borough of Islington 1964–68, JP Inner London 1969; chm Juvenile Court 1985–; memb Inst of Med Social Work 1963, Churchill fellowship 1966, Sec of State's nominee to Personal Social Services Cncl 1973–80, Cwlth Youth fellowship to Jamaica 1974, pres Volonteurope 1988–; dep chm Speaker's Cmmn on Citizenship 1987–90; memb: Home Sec's Ctee on Volunteering 1994–96, Dept of Health Task Force on Volunteering 1994–96, DfEE Advsy Bd on Citizenship 1997–98; dir The Experience Corps 2001–03; memb: Community Advsy Bd IBM 1988–91, Bd Innovation in Civic Participation 2001–, Nat Assoc of Hosp and Community Friends 2002–; chm of govrs Barnsbury Sch 1971–89; govr: Reeves Fndn 1981–2003, Elizabeth Garrett Anderson Sch 1985–98, Sevenoaks Sch 1991–97; Freedom City of London 1992; Hon Dr Sheffield Hallam Univ 2004; *Recreations* ballet, grand-daughters, travel; *Style*— Dame Elisabeth Hoodless, DBE; ✉ Flat 10, 26 The Eclipse, Laycock Street, London N1 1AH (tel and fax 020 7359 0231); Weald Ridge, Ticehurst, East Sussex TN5 7HT (tel 01580 200256); Community Service Volunteers, 237 Pentonville Road, London N1 9NJ (tel 020 7278 6601, fax 020 7837 9621, e-mail ehoodless@csv.org.uk)

HOOK, Prof Andrew; s of Wilfred Thomas Hook (d 1964), and Jessie, *née* Dunnett (d 1984); *b* 21 December 1932; *Educ* Wick HS, Daniel Stewart's Coll Edinburgh, Univ of Edinburgh (MA), Princeton Univ (PhD); *m* 18 July 1966, Judith Ann (d 1984), da of George Hibberd, of Comberton, Cambridge; 1 da (Sarah b 1964 d 1995), 2 s (Caspar b 1968 d 2006, Nathaniel b 1975); *Career* Nat Serv NCO Intelligence Corps 1954–56; lectr in American lit Univ of Edinburgh 1961–70, sr lectr in English Univ of Aberdeen 1970–79, Bradley prof of English lit Univ of Glasgow 1979–98; visiting prof: English Dept Princeton Univ 1999–2000, Dartmouth Coll 2003, 2006 and 2007, Univ of St Thomas Minnesota 2005; Gillespie visiting prof Coll of Wooster Ohio 2001–02; CNAA: chm Ctee on Humanities, memb Ctee on Academic Affrs 1986–92; chm: English Panel Scottish Univ Cncl on Entrance, English Panel (Scotland) UCAS 1994–98; memb: Scottish Exam Bd 1986–92, English Panel Scottish Qualifications Authy 1997–99; pres Eighteenth Century Scottish Studies Soc 1990–92; FRSE 2000, FBA 2002; *Books* ed: Scott's Waverley (1972), Charlotte Brontë's Shirley (with Judith Hook, 1974), John Dos Passos Twentieth Century Views (1974); Scotland and America - A Study of Cultural Relations 1750–1835 (1975), American Literature in Context 1865–1900 (1983), History of Scottish Literature Vol II 1660–1800 (1987), Scott Fitzgerald (1992), The Glasgow Enlightenment (with Richard Sher, 1995), From Goosecreek to Gandercleugh: Studies in Scottish-American Literary and Cultural History (1999), Scott's The Fair Maid of Perth (with Donald Mackenzie, 1999), F Scott Fitzgerald: A Literary Life (2002); *Recreations* theatre, opera, reading; *Style—* Prof Andrew Hook, FBA, FRSE; ✉ 5 Rosslyn Terrace, Glasgow G12 9NB (tel 0141 334 0113, e-mail nassau@palio2.vianw.co.uk)

HOOK, Brian Laurence; s of Laurence Hook (d 2002), and Joan Brookes, *née* Read; *b* 31 December 1934; *Educ* Christ's Hosp, Oxford Sch of Architecture (DipArch), Oxford Brookes Univ (MSc); *m* 26 March 1960, (Thelma) Jill, da of Morton Griffiths Mathias (d 1974), of Deddington, Oxford; 3 da (Caroline Sanderson, Dr Sarah Hall, Philippa Rothwell); *Career* Nat Serv 2 Lt RE served Malta and N Africa 1958–60, Lt RE (TA) 1961–64; architect; assoc Peter Bosanquet & Partners Oxford 1966–70, princ in own practice Brian Hook & Partners Wantage and Oxford 1970–; cncllr Berks CC 1971–74; Oxfordshire CC: cncllr 1973–81 and 1989–2005, chm Environmental Ctee 1979–81, chm 1998–99; chm: Wantage Constituency Cons Assoc 1987–91, Wilts Cons European Constituency Cncl 1991–93, Soldiers of Oxfordshire Tst 2000–; chm of govrs Sch of St Helen and St Katharine Abingdon 1985–90; memb Ct Oxford Brookes Univ 1999–; ARIBA 1959, FRSA 1995; *Recreations* sailing, travel, water colour painting; *Clubs* Frewen (Oxford); *Style—* Brian Hook, Esq; ✉ Green Farm, 1 The Green, Charney Bassett, Wantage, Oxfordshire OX12 0EU (tel 01235 868477, e-mail brian.l.hook@btinternet.com)

HOOK, Neil; MVO (1983); s of George Edward (d 1999), and Winifred Lucy, *née* Werrell, of Brighton; *b* 24 April 1945; *Educ* Varndean GS Brighton, Univ of Sheffield (Japanese Studies, Dip Mgmnt Studies); *m* 1973, Pauline Ann, *née* Hamilton, da of Leonard and Grace Hamilton; 1 da (Sonya Felicity b 4 April 1975), 1 s (Richard Alexander b 11 July 1977); *Career* HM Dip Service: FCO 1968–70, Moscow 1970–71, FCO 1971–74, Tokyo 1975–79, Dhaka 1980–83, SA Dept FCO 1984, S Asia Dept FCO 1985–86, Tokyo 1987–92, N America Dept FCO 1993–95, ambass to Turkmenistan 1995–98, high cmmr Swaziland 1999–2001, consul-gen Osaka 2001–05, UK cmmr-gen Expo 2005; *Recreations* bridge, Hash House Harriers, photography; *Style—* Mr Neil Hook, MVO

HOOKE, Robert Lowe, Jr; s of Robert Lowe Hooke, of Greenport, NY, and Sag Harbor, NY, and Elizabeth, *née* Salter; *b* 12 September 1942; *Educ* Millburn HS, Bowdoin Coll ME (BA), Columbia Univ NYC (MBA), NY Sch of Visual Arts; *Career* investment advsr and sculptor; Lt USN 1966–70, Vietnam Patrol Boat Cmd, Bronze Star and Navy Commendation Medal; account exec Merrill Lynch 1970–73, md London Donaldson Lufkin & Jenrette Inc 1979–86 (account exec NYC and md London 1979–86), dir Euro-equities Paribas Capital Markets London 1986–90; md: Art Scene Ltd 1986–93, Research Vision Ltd 1993–; exhbns of sculpture 1982–2006: London, NY, Paris, Geneva, Basel, Zürich, Baden Baden, Amsterdam, Sydney, Johannesburg, Cape Town; sculpture in public collections: Compton Gardens Poole, Bowdoin Coll, Oppenheimer Collection Durban; memb RSBS; *Sporting Achievements* Atlantic yacht crossings (single-handed) 1986 and 1990 and (two-handed) 1995, BOC Single-Handed Around the World Race 1990–91, Transatlantic Route de Café 1997, Dusi Canoe Marathon South Africa 2000 and 2001, Fish River Canoe Marathon South Africa 2000, CMH heli-skiing (2 million vertical feet); *Recreations* sky diving, polo, tennis; *Clubs* Ascot Park Polo, Annabel's, Clermont; *Style—* Robert Hooke, Jr; ✉ 14 Royal Crescent, London W11 4SL (tel 020 7603 1370); Northampton Shores, Sag Harbor, NY 11963, USA; ERF16, Hilltop Road, Scarborough, Cape Town, South Africa; Research Vision Ltd, 76 Brook Street, London W1K 5EE (tel 020 7495 6009, fax 020 7495 6011, e-mail bhooke@researchvision.com)

HOOKER, David Symonds; s of Cdr John Joseph Symonds Hooker, RN, and Pamela Bowring, *née* Toms; *b* 9 October 1942; *Educ* Radley, Magdalene Coll Cambridge (MA), Royal Sch of Mines (MSc); *m* 16 Jan 1965, (Catharine) Sandra, da of Maurice Hilary Thornely Hodgson (d 1986); 1 da (Samantha b 1966), 2 s (Benjamin b 1969, Joshua b 1979); *Career* Pennzoil Co 1965–73, Edward Bates & Sons Ltd 1973–75; md: Candecca Resources plc 1978–82, Plascom Ltd 1982–85, Hurricane International Ltd 1985–87, Aberdeen Petroleum plc 1987–93: chm: Bakyrchic Gold plc 1993–96, Goshawk Insurance Holdings plc 1996–2003, Ocean Hover Ltd 2003–; *Style—* David Hooker, Esq; ✉ 12 Lindsay Square, London SW1V 3SB; Ardura, Isle of Mull

HOOKER, Prof Morna Dorothy; da of Percy Francis Hooker (d 1975), of High Salvington, W Sussex, and Lily, *née* Riley (d 1988); *b* 19 May 1931; *Educ* Univ of Bristol (BA, MA), Univ of Manchester (PhD), Univ of Cambridge (DD); *m* 30 March 1978, Rev Dr (Walter) David Stacey (d 1993), s of Walter Stacey (d 1957); *Career* res fell Univ of Durham 1959–61, lectr in New Testament King's Coll London 1961–70; Univ of Oxford: lectr in theology 1970–76, fell Linacre Coll 1970–76, lectr in theology Keble Coll 1972–76; Lady Margaret's prof of divinity Univ of Cambridge 1976–98 (now emeritus); visiting prof: McGill Univ Montreal 1968, Duke Univ N Carolina 1987 and 1989; visiting fell Clare Hall Cambridge 1974; jt ed Jl of Theological Studies 1985–2005; fell: Robinson Coll Cambridge 1977–, King's Coll 1979–; hon fell: Linacre Coll Oxford 1980–, Westminster Coll Oxford 1996–; pres Studiorum Novi Testamenti Societas 1988–89 (memb 1959–); Burkitt Medal for Biblical Studies 2004; Hon DLitt Univ of Bristol 1994, Hon DD Univ of Edinburgh 1997; *Books* Jesus and The Servant (1959), The Son of Man in Mark (1967), What about The New Testament? (ed, 1975), Pauline Pieces (1979), Studying The New Testament (1979), Paul and Paulinism (ed, 1982), The Message of Mark (1983), Continuity and Discontinuity (1986), From Adam to Christ (1990), A Commentary on the Gospel According to St Mark (1991), Not Ashamed of the Gospel (1994), The Signs of a Prophet (1997), Beginnings: Keys that Open the Gospels (1997), Paul: A Short Introduction (2003), Endings: Invitations to Discipleship (2003), Not in Word Alone (ed, 2003); *Recreations* molinology, music, walking; *Style—* Prof Morna Hooker; ✉ Robinson College, Cambridge CB3 9AN (tel 01223 339100, fax 01223 351794, e-mail mdh1000@cam.ac.uk)

HOOLE, John George Aldick; s of John Aldick Hoole (d 1992), and Pamela Betty, *née* Coleman (d 2003); *b* 3 February 1951; *Educ* Canford Sch, Lawrenceville Sch NJ, Southampton Coll of Technol, UEA (BA); *m* 1975, Lindsey Gladstone, *née* Rushworth; 1 da (Poppy Imogen b 9 Nov 1983), 1 s (Theodore Edmund Inigo b 23 June 1990); *Career* asst keeper of art Southampton Art Gallery 1974–78, asst dir MOMA Oxford 1978–82, dir Barbican Art Gallery 1982–2001, Arts and Culture worker Oxford Brookes Univ 2003–; *Exhibitions curated* James Dickson Innes (Southampton Art Gallery) 1977, John Piper (MOMA) 1980, The Young Ones (Saïd Business Sch Univ of Oxford) 2005; Barbican Art Gallery: Matthew Smith 1983, Patrick Heron 1985, The Edwardian Era 1987, Stanley Spencer 1991, The Cutting Edge 1992, Alphonse Mucha 1993; *Recreations* collecting books and art; *Style—* John Hoole, Esq; ✉ e-mail jhoole@appleinter.net

HOOLEY, Peter; *b* 13 June 1946; *Educ* Rishworth Sch, Univ of Bradford (MSc); *m* 1978, Marianne Patricia; 1 s (James), 1 da (Rebecca); *Career* assoc fin dir Matthew Hall plc 1977–85, gp fin controller BICC plc 1985–91, gp fin dir Smith & Nephew plc 1991–2006, chm BSN Medical 2006–; non-exec dir Cobham plc 2002–; FCA; *Recreations* shooting, horse racing, rugby, theatre, holidays; *Style—* Peter Hooley, Esq

HOON, Rt Hon Geoffrey William; PC (1999), MP; s of Ernest Hoon, and June, *née* Collett; *b* 6 December 1953; *Educ* Nottingham HS, Jesus Coll Cambridge (MA); *m* 4 April 1981, Elaine Ann Dumelow; 1 s (Christopher b 15 May 1985), 2 da (Julia b 4 Nov 1987, Nathalie b 21 May 1990); *Career* lectr Univ of Leeds 1976–82, visiting prof of law Univ of Louisville 1979–80, barr 1982–84; MEP (Lab) Derbyshire 1984–94, MP (Lab) Ashfield 1992–; Treasy whip 1994–95, shadow min for industry 1995–97; Parly sec Lord Chllr's Dept 1997–98 (min of state 1998–99), min of state FO 1999, sec of state for defence 1999–2005, ldr of the House of Commons 2005–06, min of state for Europe FCO 2006–07, Govt chief whip and Parly sec to the Treasy 2007–; vice-chm Bd of Govrs Westminster Fndn for Democracy 1995–97; *Recreations* sport, cinema, music; *Style—* The Rt Hon Geoffrey Hoon, MP; ✉ House of Commons, London SW1A 0AA (tel 020 7219 2701, fax 020 7219 2428); c/o 8 Station Street, Kirkby-in-Ashfield, Nottinghamshire NG17 7AR (tel 01623 720399, fax 01623 720398)

HOOPER, Rt Hon Lord Justice; Rt Hon Sir Anthony; kt (1995), PC (2004); *Educ* Univ of Cambridge (MA, LLB); *Career* called to the Bar Inner Temple 1965, QC 1987, recorder of the Crown Court until 1995, judge of the High Court of Justice (Queen's Bench Div) 1995–2004, presiding judge NE Circuit 1997–2000, judge of the Court of Appeal 2004–; bencher Inner Temple 1993; chm Inns of Court Sch of Law 1996–99; former prof of law Osgoode Hall Law Sch Toronto; memb Bar Br Columbia; *Style—* The Rt Hon Lord Justice Hooper; ✉ Royal Courts of Justice, Strand, London WC2A 2LL (tel 020 7947 7177)

HOOPER, Baroness (Life Peer UK 1985), of Liverpool and St James's in the City of Westminster; Gloria Hooper; CMG (2002); da of Frederick Hooper (d 1977), of Shawford, Hants, and Frances, *née* Maloney (d 1984); *b* 25 May 1939; *Educ* Univ of Southampton (BA); *Career* slr 1973, ptnr Taylor & Humbert 1974–85; MEP (Cons) Liverpool 1979–84; baroness-in-waiting and govt whip House of Lords 1985–87; Parly under sec of state: Dept for Educn and Science 1987–88, Dept of Energy 1988–89, Dept of Health 1989–92; dep speaker House of Lords 1993–, memb Parly Delgn to Cncl of Europe and WEU 1992–97 and 2002–; SmithKline Beecham plc 1994–2001, Winterthur Life UK Ltd 1999–2002, Deutsche Latin American Companies Trust plc 1996–2004, The Tablet Publishing Company Ltd 1992–2003; govr Centre for Global Energy Studies; vice-pres Hispanic and Luso Brazilian Cncl (Canning House), tstee Industry and Parl Tst, tstee St George's House Windsor Caslte 2006–; *Style—* The Rt Hon Baroness Hooper, CMG; ✉ House of Lords, London SW1A 0PW

HOOPER, (Arthur) John; s of Arthur Leonard Hooper (d 2000), and Gladys Ivy, *née* Bullock (d 1989); *b* 4 December 1938, Kenton, Middx; *Educ* Worthing HS for Boys (head boy), Univ of London (LLB); *m* 22 Oct 1966, Celia, *née* Willard; 2 da (Gillian (Mrs Winnifrith) b 14 Oct 1970, Christine b 17 Jan 1974), 1 s (Richard John b 27 May 1980); *Career* admitted slr 1962, higher courts advocate 1994; ptnr: Selwood Leathes Hooper Slrs 1963–97, Wynne Baxter (following merger) 1997–2005 (sr ptnr 2000–05); dep dist judge High Court and County Court (SE Circuit) 1989–; dep coroner City of Brighton and Hove 2004–; pres Sussex Law Soc 1988–89; memb: South Eastern Legal Aid Area Ctee Funding Review Ctee 1988–2005, Law Soc 1962, Coroners' Soc of England and Wales 2004; non-exec dir Worthing Priority Care NHS Tst 1992–2002 (actg chair 2000–02); dir and tstee: Isaac Newton Arts Tst 2002–, Sussex Autistic Community Tst 2007–; ind memb Standards Ctee West Sussex CC 2003–; *Recreations* walking, cycling, visiting historic properties and gardens, gardening, going to the theatre, caravanning whenever possible, especially in France; *Style—* John Hooper, Esq; ✉ The Coroner's Office, Woodvale, Lewes Road, Brighton, East Sussex BN2 3QB (tel 01273 292046)

HOOPER, John Charles; CBE (1997); *b* 18 November 1940; *Educ* Wallington Co GS, Univ of Leeds (BA); *m* three times; 2 c, 4 step c; *Career* Procter & Gamble Ltd 1962–68 (copy supervisor, sr brand mangr), Glendinning Companies Inc 1968–72 (mktg conslt, head of manufacturer promotions, retail promotion conslt Westport CT, head of promotions Frankfurt Germany, md Danbury Mint), fin dir Scott International Marketing 1972–73, md Clarke Hooper plc 1974–91, managing ptnr Scorpion promotional mktg consultancy 1991–94, DG Incorporated Soc of British Advertisers (ISBA) 1995–2000; chm: Euro Advtg Tripartite 1999–2001, Radio Advertising Bureau 2001–04, Zed Media 2001–05, Mentor Media & Investment 2001–04, Ninah Consulting 2002–05; vice-pres Sales Promotion Conslts Assoc, past chm Ctee of Advtg Practice; vice-chm Lord's Taverners 2007– (tstee 2003–); Freeman City of London 2000; fell Mktg Soc (past chm), fell CAM Fndn, FISP; *Clubs* Lord's Taverners; *Style—* John Hooper, CBE; ✉ Cedar House, 7 Hethersett Close, Reigate, Surrey RH2 0HQ (tel 01737 241771, e-mail jchooper@btinternet.com)

HOOPER, Dr John David; s of Wilfred John Hooper (d 1976), and Vera, *née* Bradbury (d 2005); *b* 22 March 1947; *Educ* Univ of Bath (BSc), Univ of Salford (MSc), Columbia Pacific Univ Calif (PhD); *m* Veronica Jane; 1 s (Robert b 1972), 1 da (Suzanne b 1983); *Career* apprentice engr UK Atomic Energy 1964–69, project engr United Glass Ltd 1969–74, sr project engr Cadbury Schweppes Ltd 1974–78, sales mangr, gp energy mangr, dep gp chief engr Glaxo Pharmaceuticals plc 1978–85; chief exec Chartered Inst of Building 1985–87, dir of Pan-European Ops Carlson Mktg Gp Inc 1987–90, business strategy mangr Scottish Hydro-Electric plc 1990–94, chief exec Br Sports and Allied Industries Fedn 1994–97, chief exec RoSPA 1997–2004, chief exec Inst of Clinical Research 2004–; chartered dir 2000, memb IOD Examinations Bd, chartered dir interviewer; patron: Lifeskills, Learning for Living; advsr to Business in the Arts; ambass to Highlands and Islands of Scotland; tstee RIPH; CEng 1980, FCMI 1985, FInstD 1986, FRSA 2000, FRIPH 2002; *Publications* Heat Energy Recovery in the Pharmaceutical Industry (1982), Energy Management and Marketing in the UK Pharmaceutical Industry (1985); *Recreations* flying light aircraft, DIY; *Style—* Dr John Hooper; ✉ 45 Hunsbury Close, Northampton NN4 9UE

HOOPER, John Edward; s of William John Henry Hooper (d 1996), and Noëlle Patricia Thérèse, *née* Lang (d 1979); *b* 17 July 1950; *Educ* St Benedict's Abbey London, St Catharine's Coll Cambridge (BA); *m* 19 July 1980, Hon Lucinda Mary Evans, da of 2 Baron Mountevans (d 1974); *Career* reporter BBC Current Affrs 1971–73, dip corr Independent Radio News 1973–74, Cyprus corr BBC, Guardian and Economist 1974–76; Guardian: corr Spain and Portugal 1976–79, London staff 1979–88; presenter Twenty Four Hours BBC World Service 1984–88; corr (Guardian and Observer): Madrid 1988–94, Rome 1994–99, Berlin 1999–2003; Rome corr Economist and Guardian 2003–; winner Allen Lane award best first work of history or lit 1987; memb Soc of Authors; *Books* The Spaniards: a portrait of the new Spain (1986 and 1987), The New Spaniards (1995); *Recreations* reading, contemporary art, motor boating; *Style—* John Hooper, Esq; ✉ c/o The Guardian, 119 Farringdon Road, London EC1R 3ER (tel 020 7278 2332)

HOOPER, Rt Rev Michael Wrenford; *see:* Ludlow, Bishop of

HOOSON, Baron (Life Peer UK 1979), of Montgomery in the County of Powys; (Hugh) Emlyn Hooson; QC (1960); s of Hugh Hooson, of Denbigh; *b* 26 March 1925; *Educ* Denbigh GS, Henry Ford Inst of Agriculture Boreham Hall, UCW Aberystwyth; *m* 1950, Shirley Margaret Wynne, da of Sir George Hamer, CBE, of Powys; *Career* served RN 1943–45; sits as Lib Dem peer in House of Lords; called to the Bar Gray's Inn 1949 (bencher 1968, vice-treas 1985, treas 1986), dep chm Merioneth QS 1960–67 (chm 1967–71), dep chm Flintshire QS 1960–71, recorder Merthyr Tydfil 1971 and Swansea 1971, recorder Crown Court 1972–93, ldr Wales & Chester circuit 1971–74; MP (Lib) Montgomeryshire 1962–79, ldr Welsh Lib Pty 1966–79, vice-chm Political Ctee Atlantic Assembly 1976–79; non-exec chm: Severn River Crossing plc 1991–2000, Laura Ashley Holdings Ltd 1995–96

H

(non-exec dir 1985–96); vice-pres Peace Through NATO 1985–; pres Llangollen Int Eisteddfod 1987–93; memb Governing Body Inst of Grass and Environmental Research 1989–93; hon professorial fell Univ Coll of Wales 1971–; Hon LLD Univ of Wales 2003; *Style*— The Lord Hooson, QC; ✉ House of Lords, London SW1A 0PW (tel 020 7219 5226)

HOPE, Christopher David Tully; s of Dudley Mitford Hope, and Kathleen Mary, *née* McKenna; *b* 26 February 1944; *Educ* Christian Brothers Coll Pretoria, Univ of the Witwatersrand (BA, MA), Univ of Natal (BA); *m* 18 Feb 1967, Eleanor Marilyn Margaret, da of Hans Richard Klein (d 1977); 2 s (Jasper Antony b 1969, Daniel Clement b 1973); *Career* author and poet; FRSL 1990; *Publications* A Separate Development (1981), The King, the Cat and the Fiddle (with Yehudi Menuhin, 1983), Kruger's Alp (1984), The Dragon Wore Pink (1985), The Hottentot Room (1986), Black Swan (1987), White Boy Running (1988), My Chocolate Redeemer (1989), Learning to Fly and Other Tales (1990; originally published as Private Parts, 1982), Moscow! Moscow! (1990), Serenity House (1992, shortlisted Booker Prize 1992), The Love Songs of Nathan J Swirsky (1993), Darkest England (1996), Me, The Moon and Elvis Presley (1997), Signs of the Heart: Love and Death in Languedoc (1999), Heaven Forbid (2002), Brothers Under The Skin (Travels in Tyranny) (2003); *Poetry* Cape Drives (1974), In the Country of the Black Pig (1981), Englishmen (1985); *Awards* Cholmondeley Award 1972, David Higham Award 1981, Whitbread Prize for Fiction (for Kruger's Alp) 1985, CNA Literary Award (South Africa) 1989, Travelex Travel Writer Award 1997; *Recreations* getting lost; *Style*— Christopher Hope, Esq, FRSL; ✉ c/o Rogers, Coleridge & White, 20 Powis Mews, London W11 1JN (tel 020 7221 3717, fax 020 7229 9084)

HOPE, His Hon Judge (Antony) Derwin; *b* 22 August 1944; *Educ* King's Coll Taunton, Leighton Park Sch Reading, Coll of Estate Mgmnt London (BSc), Coll of Law; *m* 5 May 1979, Heidi; 1 s (Matthew b 3 June 1983), 1 da (Zoe b 18 Oct 1985); *Career* called to the Bar 1970; in practice 3 Paper Buildings, London, Winchester, Oxford and Bournemouth 1970–2002, circuit judge (Northern Circuit) 2002–04, circuit judge (Western Circuit) 2004–, resident judge Southampton Combined Court; UK rep Int Assoc of Judges; *Recreations* walking, cricket, travelling, historical studies; *Style*— His Hon Judge Hope

HOPE, Emma Mary Constance; da of Capt John David Hope, RN, and Margaret Daphne, *née* Boutwood; *Educ* Reigate Co Sch for Girls, Sevenoaks Sch, Cordwainers Coll (SIAD Dip); *Career* shoe designer; fndr own business, opened 3 shops in London (Notting Hill, Sloane Square and Islington); has designed for: Laura Ashley, Betty Jackson, Jean Muir, Nicole Farhi, Anna Sui, Paul Smith; speaker Oxford Union against 'High Fashion: Does this house think we pay too high a price?' 2004; FRSA 1993; *Awards* 5 Design Cncl Awards for Footwear 1987–88, Martini Style Award 1988, Harpers and Queens Award for Excellence 1988, DTI/Clothes Show Award for Best Accessories 1996; *Recreations* surfing, hunting, golf, shopping; *Style*— Miss Emma Hope; ✉ Emma Hope's Shoes, 14–16 St Marks Road, London W11 1RQ (tel 020 7792 7800, fax 020 7792 5351, e-mail mail@emmahope.co.uk)

HOPE, Sir John Carl Alexander; 18 Bt (NS 1628), of Craighall, Co Fife; s of Gp Capt Sir Archibald Philip Hope, OBE, DFC, AE (d 1987), and Ruth (d 1986), da of Carl R Davis; *b* 10 June 1939; *Educ* Eton; *m* 1968, Merle Pringle, da of late Robert Douglas, of Holbrook, Suffolk; 1 s (Alexander Archibald Douglas b 1969), 1 da (Natasha Anne (Mrs Jon Reid) b 1971); *Heir* s, Alexander Hope; *Style*— Sir John Hope, Bt; ✉ 29 Nicholas Court, Corney Reach Way, London W4 2TS (tel 020 8742 2986)

HOPE, Philip Ian (Phil); MP; *b* 19 April 1955; *Educ* Wandsworth Comp Sch, St Luke's Coll Univ of Exeter (BEd); *m* 25 July 1980, Allison; 1 s (Nicholas), 1 da (Anna); *Career* successively: teacher Kettering Sch for Boys, youth policy advsr Nat Cncl for Voluntary Orgns, head Young Volunteer Resources Unit National Youth Bureau, memb Framework (ind mgmnt and community work consltS) 1985–97; MP (Lab) Corby 1997–; PPS to Rt Hon John Prescott, MP 2001–03, Parly under sec of state ODPM 2003–05, Parly under sec of state for skills DfES 2005–07, min for the third sector 2007–; memb Public Accounts Ctee 1997–99, chm All-Pty Parly Gp for Charities and the Voluntary Sector 1997–2001, vice-chm PLP Soc Servs Departmental Ctee 1997–2001; memb: Lab Pty Leadership Campaign Team 1997–2001, Cwlth Parly Assoc 1997–, All Pty Parly Gps on Parenting, Children, Youth Race Equality and Youth Affairs 1997–, Nat Advsy Gp on Personal, Social and Health Educn DfEE 1998–, Devpt Awareness Working Gp DfID 1998–2000; cncllr (Lab): Kettering BC 1983–87, Northamptonshire CC 1993–97; dir Framework in Print (publishing co-op); memb: Midland Co-op Soc, Wine Soc Co-op; *Publications* author of numerous youth policy documents, curriculum materials and mgmnt texts incl: Making the Best Use of Consultants (1993), Education for Parenthood (1994), Performance Appraisal (1995), Analysis and Action on Youth Health (1995); *Recreations* tennis, juggling, computing, gardening; *Style*— Phil Hope, Esq, MP; ✉ House of Commons, London SW1A 0AA (tel 020 7219 4075, fax 020 7219 2964, e-mail hopep@parliament.uk); constituency office: 2nd Floor, Chisholm House, Queen's Square, Corby, Northamptonshire NN17 1PD (tel 01536 443325, fax 01536 269462)

HOPE, Prof Ronald Anthony (Tony); s of Ronald Sidney Hope, and Marion Nuttall, *née* Whittaker; *Educ* Dulwich Coll, New Coll Oxford (Bosanquet open scholarship, MA), Univ of London (PhD), Univ of Oxford (BM BCh); *Career* SHO and registrar trg in psychiatry Oxford 1981–85, Wellcome Tst trg fell 1985–87, clincal lectr in psychiatry 1987–90; Univ of Oxford: fell St Cross Coll 1990–, lectr in practice skills 1995–2000, prof of med ethics 2000–; ldr Oxford Practice Skills Project 1990–95; Research Prize and Medal RCPsych 1989; memb Inst of Med Ethics (memb Governing Body 1998–); FRCPsych 1997 (MRCPsych 1985); *Publications* Oxford Handbook of Clinical Medicine (1985, 4 edn 1998), Manage Your Mind (1995); numerous articles and papers in med ethics and Alzheimer's Disease; *Recreations* family, literature, wine and food; *Style*— Prof Tony Hope; ✉ Ethox Centre, Institute of Health Sciences, Old Road, Oxford OX3 7LF (tel 01865 226936, fax 01865 226938, e-mail admin@ethox.ox.ac.uk)

HOPE, Simon Richard; s of Richard Hope, and Carole, *née* Byrom; *b* 1 July 1964, Congleton, Cheshire; *Educ* King Edward VI GS Macclesfield, RAC Cirencester, Univ of Reading (MBA); *m* 1994, Margaret, *née* Carnell; 4 da (Camilla, Laura, Eleanor, Georgina); *Career* Savills plc: RICS qualification 1986–88, West End office 1989–, dir 1992–, memb Bd 1999–; chm Dinton and Ford Cons Assoc, memb Bd Charities Property Fund; MRICS; *Recreations* golf, racing, tennis, hunting, shooting; *Clubs* Oxfordshire Golf, Turf, Lansdowne, Vale of Aylesbury Hunt; *Style*— Simon Hope, Esq; ✉ Aston Mullins Farm, Chapel Road, Ford, Aylesbury, Buckinghamshire HP17 8XG (tel 01296 748400, fax 01296 748110, e-mail s.r.hope@btinternet.com); Savills plc, 20 Grosvenor Hill, Berkeley Square, London W1K 3HQ (tel 020 7409 8725, e-mail shope@savills.com)

HOPE, (David) Terence; s of George Charles Oswald Hope (d 1988), and Lucy, *née* Bollom (d 1970); *b* 2 April 1946; *Educ* Rutherford GS Newcastle upon Tyne, Univ of Liverpool (MB ChB, ChM); *Children* 1 s ((Charles) Benjamin b 1976), 2 da (Lucy Alexandra b 1979, Victoria Mary b 1983); m, August 2003, Alexandra Frances, *née* Crabbie; *Career* served in RNR; conslt neurosurgeon: Aberdeen 1982, Univ Hosp of Nottingham 1985–; prof of neurosurgery Bir Hosp Kathmandu Nepal; author of chapters in books on vascular neurosurgery; examiner: RCS, Intercollegiate Bd of Examiners in Neurosurgery; sec Intercollegiate Bd of Neurosurgery 1999; memb: Soc of British Neurological Surgeons, Ct of Examiners RCS; FRCS 1985; *Recreations* fishing, shooting, gardening; *Clubs* Athenaeum; *Style*— Terence Hope, Esq; ✉ The Nunnery, Hemington, Derby DE74 2SQ (tel 01332 811724, fax 01332 811724, e-mail terencehope@btinternet.com); Department of Neurosurgery, University Hospital, Queen's Medical Centre, Nottingham NG7 2UH (tel 0115 970 9102)

HOPE-DUNBAR, Sir David; 8 Bt (NS 1664), of Baldoon; o s of Maj Sir Basil Douglas Hope-Dunbar, 7 Bt (d 1961), and Edith Maude Maclaren, *née* Cross; *b* 13 July 1941; *Educ* Eton, RAC Cirencester; *m* 1971, Kathleen Ruth, yr da of late J Timothy Kenrick; 2 da (Philippa b 1973, Juliet Antonia b 1976), 1 s (Charles b 1975); *Heir* s, Charles Hope-Dunbar; *Career* founded Dunbar & Co (now Allied Dunbar) 1962, chartered surveyor; ARICS; *Recreations* fishing, tennis, shooting; *Style*— Sir David Hope-Dunbar, Bt; ✉ Banks House, Kirkcudbright DG6 4XF (tel 01557 330424)

HOPE-FALKNER, Patrick Miles; s of Robert E Hope-Falkner (d 1991), and Diana, *née* Hazlerigg (d 1977); *b* 1 December 1949; *Educ* Wellington; *m* 1972 (m dis 1994), Wendy Margaret, *née* Mallinson; 2 s (Timothy Douglas b 1980, James Edward b 1982); *Career* articles 1968–73, admitted slr 1973, Freshfields 1973–84, Lazard Brothers & Co Ltd 1985–90; dir: Lazard Investors Ltd 1985–90, Lazard Brothers & Co (Jersey) Ltd 1985–89; ptnr Crossman Block 1991–94; sr dir: American Express Bank 1995–2005, Merril Lynch Int Bank Ltd 2006–; memb Law Soc; *Clubs* Brooks's, Cowdray Polo; *Style*— Patrick Hope-Falkner, Esq; ✉ Merrill Lynch International Bank, 2 King Edward Street, London EC1A 1HQ (tel 020 7996 8084)

HOPE OF CRAIGHEAD, Baron (Life Peer UK 1995), of Bamff in the District of Perth and Kinross; (James Arthur) David Hope; PC (1989); s of Arthur Henry Cecil Hope OBE, TD, WS (d 1986), of Edinburgh, and Muriel Ann Neilson, *née* Collie; *b* 27 June 1938; *Educ* Edinburgh Acad, Rugby, St John's Coll Cambridge (MA), Univ of Edinburgh (LLB); *m* 11 April 1966, (Katharine) Mary, da of William Mark Kerr, WS (d 1985), of Edinburgh; 2 s (Hon William Thomas Arthur, Hon James David Louis (twins) b 1969), 1 da (Hon Lucy Charlotte Mary b 1971); *Career* Nat Serv cmmnd Seaforth Highlanders 1957, Lt 1959; admitted Faculty of Advocates 1965, standing jr counsel in Scotland to Bd of Inland Revenue 1974–78, QC (Scot 1978), advocate depute 1978–82, chm Med Appeal Tbnls 1985–86, legal chm Pensions Appeal Tbnl 1985–86; memb Scottish Ctee on Law of Arbitration 1986–89; elected dean of Faculty of Advocates 1986; senator of the Coll of Justice, a Lord of Session with the title of Lord Hope, Lord Justice General of Scotland and Lord President of the Court of Session 1989–96; a Lord of Appeal in Ordinary 1996–; chm Sub-Ctee E House of Commons Select Ctee on EU 1998–2001; chllr Univ of Strathclyde 1998–; pres: The Stair Soc, Int Criminal Lawyers Assoc, Cwlth Magistrates' and Judges' Assoc 2003–06; hon prof of law Univ of Aberdeen; hon fell: St John's Coll Cambridge 1995, Univ of Strathclyde 2000, American Coll of Trial Lawyers 2000; hon memb: Canadian Bar Assoc 1987, Soc of Public Teachers of Law 1991; hon bencher: Gray's Inn 1989, Inn of Court of N Ireland 1995; Hon LLD: Univ of Aberdeen 1991, Univ of Strathclyde 1993, Univ of Edinburgh 1995; fell Univ of Strathclyde 2000; FRSE 2003; *Books* Gloag and Henderson's Introduction to the Law of Scotland (jt ed 7 edn 1968, asst ed 8 edn 1980 and 9 edn 1987, contrib ed 11 edn 2001), Armour on Valuation for Rating (jt ed 4 edn 1971, 5 edn 1985), Court of Session Practice (contrib); *Recreations* walking, music, ornithology; *Clubs* New (Edinburgh); *Style*— The Rt Hon Lord Hope of Craighead, PC, FRSE; ✉ 34 India Street, Edinburgh EH3 6HB (0131 225 8245); Law Lords Corridor, House of Lords, London SW1A 0PW (tel 020 7219 3202, fax 020 7219 6156, e-mail hopejad@parliament.uk)

HOPE OF THORNES, Baron (Life Peer UK 2005), of Thornes in the County of West Yorkshire; Rt Rev Dr David Michael Hope; KCVO (1995), PC (1991); s of Jack Hope, by his w Florence; *b* 14 April 1940; *Educ* Queen Elizabeth GS Wakefield, Univ of Nottingham (BA), Linacre Coll Oxford (DPhil), St Stephen's House Oxford; *Career* asst curate St John Tuebrook Liverpool 1965–70, chaplain Bucharest 1967–68, vicar St Andrew Warrington 1970–74, princ St Stephen's House Oxford 1974–82; vicar All Saints' Margaret St London 1982–85, bishop of Wakefield 1985–91, bishop of London 1991–95, archbishop of York 1995–2005, parish priest Ilkley W Yorks 2005–; dean of HM's Chapels Royal 1991–95; memb House of Lords 1990–2005; Hon DD: Univ of Nottingham 1999, Univ of Hull 2005; hon fell Linacre Coll Oxford 1993; *Recreations* theatre, walking, travel; *Style*— The Rt Rev and Rt Hon the Lord Hope of Thornes, KCVO, PC

HOPE-STONE, Dr Harold Francis; s of Sidney Hope-Stone (d 1933), of Liverpool, and Doris, *née* Cohen (d 1943); *b* 20 August 1926; *Educ* The Liverpool Inst GS for Boys, Strathcona Acad Montreal, The London Hosp Med Coll (MB BS, LRCP, MRCS); *m* 20 Aug 1954, Shelagh, da of Harold William Gallimore; 2 s (Rodney Alan b 5 July 1957, Hugh William b 10 Dec 1960), 1 da (Laura Doris b 16 Feb 1963); *Career* Capt RAMC RMO 13/18 Royal Hussars and King's African Rifles 1952–54; house surgn Poplar Hosp 1951; The London Hosp: house physician 1952, registrar Whitechapel Clinic 1955, registrar Radio Therapy Dept 1956–59, sr registrar Radio Therapy Dept 1959–63, conslt radiotherapist and oncologist 1963–, conslt in admin charge Dept of Radiotherapy and Oncology 1975–91; hon conslt radiotherapist and oncologist: Whipps Cross Hosp 1965–91, Harold Wood Hosp Romford 1968–, The Royal London Hosp 1991–, Cromwell Hosp 1991–, London Independent Hosp 1991–; lectr in radiotherapy and oncology Univ of London 1968–, advsr in radiation protection QMC 1973–; chm: Medical Advsy Ctee The London Ind Hosp 1985–89, Regnl Advsy Ctee on Radiotherapy and Oncology NE Thames RHA 1970–79, Working Party Radiotherapy Servs NE Thames Region 1977–79; memb London Univ Bd Studies in Medicine 1970–, examiner RCR 1978–81, vice-pres Section of Radiology RSM 1979–82 and 1986–88 (hon sec 1985–86), examiner for MD in radiotherapy Colombo Sri Lanka 1986–, examiner Royal Coll of Radiologists 1978–81; The London Hosp: memb Academic Bd 1971–74 and 1990–91, chm Ctee Sch of Radiology and Radiotherapy 1976–80, chm Medical Records Sub Ctee Medical Cncl 1972–77, chm Div of Surgery 1980–84, chm Private Practice Sub Ctee of Medical Cncl 1977–85, Medical Cncl rep Final Medical Ctee 1978–80, memb Exec Ctee Scanner Appeal 1984–85, chm Medical Cncl 1988–91 (vice-chm 1985–89); med audit advsr London Ind Hosp 1994–; memb: BIR, Section of Radiology RSM, Section of Oncology RSM, Euro Soc of Therapeutic Radiology and Oncology, Br Oncological Soc; DMRT 1957, FRCR 1959; *Books* Tumours of the Testicle (jtly, 1970), Malignant Diseases in Children (contrib, 1975), Radiotherapy in Modern Clinical Practice (ed, 1976), Bladder Cancer (contrib, 1981), Urology I: Bladder Cancer (contrib, 1984), Radiotherapy in Clinical Practice (ed, 1986), Urological and Genital Cancer (co-ed, 1989), A History of Radiotherapy of The London Hospital 1896–1996 (1999), No Stone Unturned: An Autobiography (2001); *Recreations* gardening, tennis, skiing, sailing, opera, ballet, theatre, travelling; *Style*— Dr Harold F Hope-Stone; ✉ tel 01763 838461

HOPES, Rt Rev Alan Stephen; s of William Hopes, and Beatrice, *née* Tate; *b* 17 March 1944, Oxford; *Educ* Oxford HS, Enfield GS, KCL (BD, AKC), St Boniface Coll Warminster; *Career* asst priest Our Lady of Victories Kensington 1995–97, parish priest Our Most Holy Redeemer and St Thomas More Chelsea 1997–2001, vicar gen Dio of Westminster 2001, ordained bishop (titular see Cuncacestre) 2003, auxiliary bishop (RC) of Westminster 2003–; *Style*— The Rt Rev Alan Hopes; ✉ Archbishop's House, Ambrosden Avenue, London SW1P 1QJ (tel 020 7798 9033, fax 020 7798 9077, e-mail alanhopes@rcdow.org.uk)

HOPEWELL, Martin; s of late Tom Clifford Hopewell, and Joan, *née* Walker; *b* 27 May 1951; *Educ* Nottingham HS for Boys, Univ of Reading (BA); *m* (m dis); 1 da (Kate Laura b 1981), 1 s (Tom Martin b 1984); partner Patsy Politoff; *Career* music agent and conf organiser; agent Noel Gay Orgn 1972, agent Chrysalis Gp (successively Chrysalis Agency, Cowbell Agency and World Service Agency); former clients incl: The Jam, The Cure, The Eurythmics, The Pretenders, Fine Young Cannibals, Bronski Beat, The Style

Council, The Sex Pistols, Marc Almond; chm: Primary Talent International Ltd, International Live Music Conference Ltd; memb Cncl Agents Assoc of GB; inducted Br Music Roll of Honour 1999; *Recreations* clay target shooting, astronomy, gliding; *Style*— Martin Hopewell, Esq; ✉ Primary Talent International/International Live Music Conference, Fifth Floor, 2–12 Pentonville Road, London N1 9PL (tel 020 7833 8998, fax 020 7833 5992, e-mail martin@rimary.uk.com)

HOPKIN, Prof Deian Rhys; s of Islwyn Hopkin (d 1951), of Llanelli, and Charlotte, *née* Rees (d 1969); *b* 1 March 1944; *Educ* Llandovery Coll, Univ of Wales Aberystwyth (BA, PhD); *m* 1, 11 June 1966 (m dis 1989), Orian, da of Edryd Jones; 2 da (Elinor Mair b 1970, Gwenno Eleri b 1974), 2 s (Kieran, Liam (twins) b 1981); m 2, 13 Sept 1989, Lynne, da of Richard Hurley; *Career* tutor QMC London 1966–67, lectr in modern history Univ of Wales Aberystwyth 1967–84, staff tutor in arts (secondment) Open Univ 1974–76, sr lectr Dept of History Univ of Wales Aberystwyth 1984–91 (head of dept 1990–91), dean of human sciences City of London Poly (later London Guildhall Univ) 1992–96, vice-provost London Guildhall Univ 1996–2001, vice-chllr and chief exec London South Bank Univ 2001–; chm and tstee UNIAID, chair Univs UK Skills Task Force; vice-chm: Cncl for Assisting Refugee Academics 2003–, London Higher 2004–; jt chair HE Engagement Bd DfES 2006–; memb: Exec Ctee UK Arts and Humanities Data Serv 1997–2002, Exec Ctee Coalition of Modern Universities (CMU) 2003–; memb Cncl UCL Hosp Fndn NHS Tst 2004–05; chm Cityside Regeneration Ltd 1996–2002; memb: London European Progs Ctee 2000–04, Bd Central London Partnership 2001–, Bd One London Ltd 2002–06, Bd South Bank Employers' Gp 2004–06, Bd Skills for Health UK 2004–, Bd Fndn Degree Forward 2007–, London Skills and Employment Bd 2007–; govr: Hackney Community Coll Corp 1999–2001, Lambeth Coll Corp 2001–05; govr and tstee Bishopsgate Fndn and Inst 1997–2003, tstee Aldgate, All Hallows and Barking Exhbn Tst (Sir John Cass's Fndn) 2003–06, dir Elephant and Castle Tst 2006–, memb Bd Southwark Alliance 2006–; memb Gen Advsy Cncl BBC 1988–96; Nat Library of Wales: govr and memb Cncl 1975–90, memb Advsy Bd The Welsh Political Archive 1984–; Freeman City of London 1999, Freeman Worshipful Co of Information Technologists 1999, Liveryman Guild of Educators 2004; hon fell Univ of Wales Aberystwyth 2003; FRHistS 1978, FRSA 1996; *Publications* incl: History and Computing (jt ed, 1987), Class, Community and the Labour Movement: Wales and Canada, 1880–1930 (jt ed, 1989), The Labour Party in Wales, 1900–2000 (jt ed, 2000), The Role of Universities in the Modern Economy (2002); also author of numerous book chapters and articles, reviews and features in jls incl: Int Review of Social History, Jl of Contemporary History, English Historical Review, Welsh History Review, Anglo-Welsh Review, History, Times Higher Educn Supplement, Educn Guardian, Taliesin; *Recreations* music (especially jazz), writing, broadcasting; *Clubs* Athenaeum; *Style*— Prof Deian Hopkin; ✉ London South Bank University, 103 Borough Road, London SE1 0AA (tel 020 7815 6001, fax 020 7815 6099, e-mail deian.hopkin@lsbu.ac.uk)

HOPKIN, Prof Julian; s of Meurglyn Hopkin, and Mair, *née* Watkins; *Educ* Maesydderwen Sch Ystradgynlais, WNSM Univ of Wales (MB BCh, MD), Univ of Edinburgh (MSc); *Career* clinical scientist MRC 1978–79, conslt physician Oxford 1984–99, sr clinical lectr Univ of Oxford 1984–99, fell BNC Oxford 1992–99; Univ of Wales Swansea: prof of med 1999–, head Sch of Med 2004–; visiting prof: Osaka 1994, Rome 2001, Kyoto 2002; exec ed Quarterly Jl of Med 1992–2000; Daiwa-Adrian Prize in Med 2001; FRCP 1988, FRCPEd 1999, FMedSci 2005; *Publications* Pneumocystis Carinii (monograph, 1991); author of over 150 medical and scientific papers and articles; *Recreations* the outdoors; *Style*— Prof Julian Hopkin; ✉ University of Wales Swansea, The School of Medicine, Swansea SA2 8PP (tel 01792 295149, fax 01792 513054, e-mail j.m.hopkin@swan.ac.uk)

HOPKINS, Sir (Philip) Anthony; kt (1993), CBE (1987); s of Richard Arthur Hopkins (d 1981), and Muriel Annie Yeates; *b* 31 December 1937; *Educ* Cowbridge GS, Welsh Coll of Music and Drama, RADA; *m* 1, 1968 (m dis), Petronella; 1 da (Abigail b 1968); m 2, 1973 (m dis), Jennifer Ann, da of Ronald Arthur Lynton; m 3, 2003, Stella Arroyave; *Career* actor and director; first joined Nat Theatre 1965, Broadway debut Equus 1974 (NY Drama Desk Award for Best Actor, Outer Critics' Circle Award, American Authors and Celebrities Forum Award, LA Drama Critics' Award); lived and worked in USA 1975–84, returned to England 1984, took US citizenship 2000; Hon DLitt Univ of Wales 1988, hon fell St David's Coll Lampeter Wales; Commandeur de l'Ordre des Arts et des Lettres (France) 1996; *Theatre* incl: Julius Caesar (debut) 1964, A Flea in Her Ear (NT) 1966, The Three Sisters, Dance of Death (NT) 1967, As You Like It 1967, The Architect and The Emperor of Assyria, A Woman Killed with Kindness, Coriolanus (NT) 1971, The Taming of the Shrew (Chichester) 1972, Macbeth (NT) 1972, Equus (Plymouth Theatre NY) 1974–75 and (Huntington Hartford Theatre LA) 1977, The Tempest (The Mark Taper Forum Theatre LA) 1979, Old Times (Roundabout Theatre NY) 1983, The Lonely Road (Old Vic) 1985, Pravda (NT) 1985 (Variety Club Stage Actor Award, Br Theatre Assoc Best Actor Award, The Observer Award for Outstanding Achievement (Olivier Awards)), King Lear 1986, Antony and Cleopatra 1987, M Butterfly (Shaftesbury) 1989, August (also dir) 1994; *Television* incl: A Heritage and Its History (ATV) 1968, A Company of Five (ATV) 1968, The Three Sisters (BBC) 1969, The Peasants Revolt (ITV) 1969, Dickens (BBC) 1970, Danton (BBC) 1970, The Poet Game (BBC) 1970, Uncle Vanya (BBC), Hearts and Flowers (BBC), Decision to Burn (Yorkshire) 1970, War and Peace (BBC) 1971 & 1972 (BAFTA Best Television Actor Award), Cuculus Canorus (BBC) 1972, Lloyd George (BBC) 1972, QB VII (ABC) 1973, Find Me (BBC) 1973, A Childhood Friend (BBC) 1974, Possessions (Granada) 1974, All Creatures Great and Small (NBC) 1974, The Arcata Promise (Yorkshire) 1974, Dark Victory (NBC) 1975, The Lindbergh Kidnapping Case (NBC) 1975 (Emmy Award for Best Actor), Victory at Entebbe (ABC) 1976, Kean (BBC) 1978, The Voyage of the Mayflower (CBS) 1979, The Bunker (CBS) 1980 (Emmy Award for Best Actor), Peter and Paul (CBS) 1980, Othello (BBC) 1981, Little Eyolf (BBC) 1981, The Hunchback of Notre Dame (CBS) 1981, A Married Man (LWT/ Channel 4) 1982, Strangers and Brothers (BBC) 1983, The Arch of Triumph (CBS) 1984, Mussolini and I (RAI Italy) 1984 (Ace Award), Hollywood Wives (ABC) 1984, Guilty Conscience (CBS) 1984, Blunt (BBC) 1985, Across the Lake (BBC) 1988, Heartland (BBC) 1988, The Tenth Man (CBS) 1988, Magwitch in Great Expectations (Disney Primetime TV USA) 1988, To Be The Best (USA mini series) 1990, Big Cats (wildlife documentary) 1993; *Films* The Lion in Winter (debut) 1967, The Looking Glass War 1968, Hamlet 1969, When Eight Bells Toll 1969, Young Winston 1971, A Doll's House 1972, The Girl from Petrovka 1973, Juggernaut 1974, A Bridge Too Far 1976, Audrey Rose 1976, International Velvet 1977, Magic 1978, The Elephant Man 1979, A Change of Seasons 1980, The Bounty 1983 (Variety Club Film Actor of 1983 Award), The Good Father 1985, 84 Charing Cross Road 1986 (Moscow Film Festival Best Actor Award), The Dawning 1987, A Chorus of Disapproval 1988, The Desperate Hours 1989, The Silence of the Lambs 1990 (Academy Award for Best Actor, BAFTA Award for Best Film Actor, NY Film Critics' Circle Award for Best Actor, Chicago Film Critics' Award for Best Actor, Boston Film Critic's Award for Best Actor), Spotswood 1990, One Man's War 1990, Howard's End 1991, Freejack 1992, Chaplin 1992, Bram Stoker's Dracula 1992, The Trial 1993, Remains of the Day 1993 (BAFTA Award for Best Film Actor, Guild of Regnl Film Writers Award for Best Actor, LA Film Critics' Assoc Award for Best Actor, Variety Club Film Actor of 1993 Award, Japan Critics' Awards Best Actor in a Foreign Film), Shadowlands 1993 (US Nat Bd of Review Best Actor Award, LA Film Critic's Assoc Best Actor Award, Mexican Int Film Festival Best Actor Award), Legends of the Fall 1994, The Road to Welville 1994, August (also dir) 1994, Nixon 1995, Surviving Picasso 1995, The Edge 1996, Amistad 1997 (Oscar nomination for Best Supporting Actor), The Mask of Zorro 1997, Meet Joe Black 1997, Instinct 1998, Titus 1999, The Grinch (voice) 2000, Mission: Impossible II 2000, Hannibal 2001, Hearts in Atlantis 2001, The Devil and Daniel Webster 2001, Bad Company 2002, Red Dragon 2002, The Human Stain 2003; *Awards* Award for Career Excellence (Montreal Film Festival) 1991, Evening Standard Film Awards' Special Award for UK Body of Work 1994, The US Film Advisory Bd Special Career Achievement Award for US Body of Work 1994, US BAFTA The Britannia Award for Outstanding Contribution to the Int Film and TV Industry 1995, Spencer Tracy Award for Excellence on Stage and Screen 1996, Donostia Award 1998; *Recreations* piano, reading; *Style*— Sir Anthony Hopkins, CBE

HOPKINS, Anthony Strother; CBE (1996); *b* 1940; *Educ* Queen's Univ Belfast (BSc(Econ)); *Career* sr mangr Audit Dept Thomson McLintock & Co (now KPMG), CA Industrial Development Organisation Dept of Commerce 1971–76; chief exec: Northern Ireland Development Agency 1979–82 (joined 1976, subsequently head of corp fin, dep chief exec), Industrial Development Bd for NI 1988–92 (joined as dep chief exec Inward Investment 1982, dep chief exec Home Industry 1984); managing ptnr NI Touche Ross (now Deloitte & Touche) 1992–; chm: Milk Marketing Bd for NI 1995–, Laganside Corp 1996– (dep chm 1995–96); dep chm Probation Bd for NI 1997–98; visiting prof Univ of Ulster (memb Advsy Bd Ulster Business Sch); memb NI Tourist Bd 1992–98; FCA, CIMgt (chm NI region 1992–97); *Style*— Anthony Hopkins, Esq, CBE; ✉ Deloitte & Touche, 19 Bedford Street, Belfast BT2 7EJ (tel 028 9032 2861)

HOPKINS, Prof Colin Russell; s of Bleddyn Hopkins (d 1939), and Vivienne, *née* Jenkins; *b* 4 June 1939; *Educ* Pontypridd Boys GS, Univ of Wales (BSc, PhD); *m* Aug 1964, Hilary, da of Fredrick Floyd (d 1973); 1 s (Laurence b 1973), 1 da (Sally b 1970); *Career* prof of molecular cell biology Imperial Coll London, dir MRC Inst for Molecular Cell Biology, Rank prof of physiological biochemistry Imperial Coll London, prof of med cell biology Univ of Liverpool Med Sch; Fulbright fell Rockefeller Univ NY; *Recreations* music; *Style*— Prof Colin Hopkins; ✉ Department of Biological Sciences, Imperial College, London SW7 2AZ

HOPKINS, Brig Graham Owen; s of Ivor Hopkins (d 1978), and Sarah Elizabeth, *née* Owen (d 1999); *b* 16 December 1943; *Educ* Llanelli GS, Newton le Willows GS, Bart's Med Coll (MB BS); *m* 1, 1970, Rita Janis, *née* Howlett; 2 s (Simon Owen b 1973, Peter Edward b 1981); m 2, 2003, Vanessa Maria, *née* Cartmell; 1 step da (Eleanor Jayne b 1992); *Career* cmmnd 1966; MO 23 Parachute Field Ambulance 1970, MO 16 Parachute Bde 1970–71, MO 3 Bn Parachute Regt 1971, trainee specialist Jt Servs Med Rehabilitation Unit (JSMRU) Chessington 1974, SHO and registrar Cambridge Mil Hosp 1977, sr specialist in rheumatology and rehabilitation JSMRU, conslt in rheumatology and rehabilitation Queen Elizabeth Mil Hosp 1982, conslt rheumatology and rehabilitation Cambridge Mil Hosp Aldershot 1985, QHP 1999–2005, conslt dir of defence rehabilitation and Cdr Defence Services Med Rehabilitation Centre Headley Ct 2002–05; hosp appointments: house surgn (orthopaedics) Bart's 1969, house physician (gen med) Brook Hosp 1970, SHO (gen surgery) 1970, clinical asst sr registrar post Middx Hosp 1980, hon conslt St Thomas' Hosp London; RCM rep and memb Investigation Ctee Ctee for Professions Supplementary to Med (CPSM) 1994–97, examiner Intercollegiate Academic Bd for Sport and Exercise Med 2000–; memb: Br Soc for Rheumatology 1980–, Br Rehabilitation Soc 1980–, Br Assoc of Sport and Exercise Science 1982–; ed Jl of the RAMC 1992–99; fndr chm Army Martial Arts 1995–99 (pres 1999–), chm Combined Servs Martial Arts, 4th Dan Black Belt Wado Ryu Karate, English Karate Governing Body Reg Coach; LTA Intermediate Tennis Coach, memb Professional Tennis Coaches Assoc 1982–95; FRCPEd 1991, fell Inst of Sports Med 1993, FRCP 1997 (MRCP 1978), FFSEM(I) 2003, FFSEM (UK) 2006; OStJ 2006; *Publications* articles: Snake Bite in Cyprus (1974), A Co-location System for the Management of Brain Damaged Patients (jtly, 1981), Muscle Changes in Ankylosing Spondylitis (jtly, 1983), Multiple Joint Tuberculosis Presenting as HLA B27 Disease (1983), Food Antibodies in Palindromic Rheumatism (jtly), Lone Axillary Nerve Injury due to Non Dislocating Injury of the Shoulder (jtly), Double Blind Cross Over Trial of Infra Red Laser in the Treatment of Tennis Elbow (1985), Osteoarticular Tuberculosis - A Review (1986), Stress Fractures in Parachute Regiment Recruits (jtly, 1988); *Recreations* walking, karate, music, sketching; *Style*— Brig Graham Hopkins; ✉ DSMRC, Headley Court, Epsom, Surrey KT18 6JN (tel 01372 381000, fax 01372 363849, e-mail grahhopk@dsca.mod.uk)

HOPKINS, Joel; s of Sir Michael John Hopkins, and Patricia Ann, *née* Wainwright; *b* 6 September 1970; *Educ* Highgate Sch, Christ Church Coll Canterbury (BA), NYU (MA); *Career* filmmaker; *Films* The South Bank - A Day in the Life (documentary) 1994, Just William (documentary) 1995, Growth (short) 1996, Jorge (short) 1998, The Independent 1999, Jump Tomorrow 2001; *Awards* for Growth: Craft award for Outstanding Acting, Craft award for Outstanding Directing; for Jorge: Best Dramatic Film BBC British Short Film Festival, Wasserman Award, Best Short Minneaolis Film Festival, Best Short USA Film Festival, Official Selection Sundance Film Festival; for Jump Tomorrow: BAFTA Carl Foreman Award Most Promising Newcomer to Br Film, Audience Award Deauville American Film Festival, Richard Vague Production Grant, one of Festival Dir's Best of Festival Edinburgh Film Festival, official selection Sundance Film Festival, finalist Perrier Award, nominated five BIFA Awards (Best Br Ind Film, Best Screenplay, Douglas Hicock Award Best Feature Debut, Best Music, Most Promising Newcomer); *Style*— Joel Hopkins, Esq; ✉ c/o Natasha Galloway, PFD, Drury House, 34–43 Russell Street, London WC2B 5HA (tel 020 7344 1048)

HOPKINS, Dr Justine Tracy; da of John Richard Hopkins, of Los Angeles, and Prudence Anne, *née* Balchin; *b* 1 October 1960; *Educ* Univ of Bristol (Eric Pendry prize, Tucker-Cruze prize, Thomas David Taylor prize, BA), Courtauld Inst (Br Acad state studentship, MA), Birkbeck Coll London (Br Acad state studentship, PhD); *Career* exhbn offr for Michael Ayrton and the Maze exhbn Victoria Art Gallery Bath 1983, gallery invigilator and exhbns guide Arnolfini Gallery Bristol 1984, asst restorer W of England Restoration Studios Bristol 1984, excavations illustrator (ceramics) Cuello Archaeological Project Belize 1987 and 1990–93; pt/t lectr: Sch of Humanities Leicester Poly 1988–89 and 1991, Birkbeck Coll London 1993–94, History of Arts Dept Univ of the West of England 1994–, Dept of Continuing Educn Univ of Bristol 1995–; former visiting lectr: Sotheby's Fine Arts Educn Dept 1989, Birkbeck Coll London 1989 and 1990, City of London Poly 1990; currently visiting lectr: Tate Gallery, V&A, Barbican Art Gallery, Friends of Covent Garden, Christies Education Dept, National Gallery, National Portrait Gallery, NADFAS; Harold Hyam Wingate scholar 1993/94; *Publications* A Way Through the Maze - Michael Ayrton's Labyrinths (exhbn catalogue, 1983), Michael Ayrton (1921–75) - Paintings, Drawings, Sculpture and Graphics (1990), Wright of Derby (slide pack with commentary, 1990), Samuel Palmer: Visionary Printmaker (exhbn review, Apollo Magazine, 1991), Ben Nicholson (exhbn guide, 1993), Michael Ayrton: a biography (1994), Drawing on these Shores (exhbn review, 1994), Good Company: Diaries of Frances Partridge (book review, Charleston Magazine, 1995), The Enemy as Mentor: Michael Ayrton and Wyndham Lewis (Wyndham Lewis Annual, 1995), John Singer Sargent (Charleston Magazine, 1998), On Reflection (RA Magazine, 1998), LIX pittura in Europa: La pittura Inglese (1998), Holland Park Artists (Charleston Magazine, 2000); Fields of Influence: Conjunctions of Artists & Scientists 1815–1860 (2001); various articles in Macmillan's Dictionary of Art 1996 and Dictionary of Western Art 1999; pottery illustrations in various archaeological jls incl Antiquity and National Geographic;

H

Recreations travel, theatre and the performing arts, art conservation and restoration, photography, walking, reading; *Style*— Dr Justine Hopkins

HOPKINS, Kelvin Peter; MP; s of Prof Harold Horace Hopkins, FRS (d 1994), and Joan Avery Frost; *b* 22 August 1941; *Educ* Queen Elizabeth's GS Barnet, Univ of Nottingham (BA); *m* 1965, Patricia, da of Alfred Thomas Langley; 1 s (Daniel Robert b 29 Sept 1969), 1 da (Rachel Louise b 30 March 1972); *Career* with Econ Dept TUC 1969–70 and 1973–77, lectr St Alban's Coll of FE 1971–73, policy and research offr Nalgo/Unison 1977–94, MP (Lab) Luton N 1997–; chm of govrs Luton Coll of HE (now Luton Univ) 1985–89; hon fell Univ of Luton 1993; *Recreations* music, theatre, photography, sailing on the Norfolk Broads; *Clubs* Luton Socialist, Lansdowne (Luton); *Style*— Kelvin Hopkins, Esq, MP; ✉ House of Commons, London SW1A 0AA (tel 020 7219 6670)

HOPKINS, Sir Michael John; kt (1995), CBE (1989); s of late Gerald Hopkins, and Barbara Hopkins; *b* 7 May 1935; *Educ* Sherborne, Architectural Assoc (AADipl); *m* 1962, Patricia Ann, *née* Wainwright; 1 s, 2 da; *Career* architect: worked in offices of Sir Basil Spence, Leonard Manasseh and Tom Hancock; partnership with: Norman Foster 1969–75, Patricia Hopkins 1976–; fndr ptnr Michael Hopkins and Partners 1976–; projects incl: own house and studio Hampstead 1976 (RIBA Award, Civic Tst Award), Greene King brewery bldg 1979 (RIBA Award, FT Award), Patera Bldg System 1984, research centre for Schlumberger Cambridge 1984 (FT Award, RIBA Award, Civic Tst Award), infants sch Hants 1986 (RIBA Award, Civic Tst Award), Bicentenary Stand Lord's Cricket Ground 1987 (RIBA Award, Civic Tst Award), R&D centre Solid State Logic 1988 (RIBA Award, Civic Tst Award), London Office and country workshop for David Mellor 1989 and 1991 (FT Award, two RIBA Awards, Civic Tst Award), redevelopment of Bracken House St Paul's for Ohbayashi Corp 1992 (RIBA Award, FT Award, Civic Tst Award), offices at New Square Bedfont Lakes 1992 (FT Award), Glyndebourne Opera House 1994 (RIBA Award, Royal Fine Art Cmmn Award, Civic Tst Award, FT Award), Inland Revenue Centre Nottingham 1995 (Civic Tst Award), Queen's Bldg Emmanuel Coll Cambridge 1995 (RIBA Award, Royal Fine Art Cmmn Award), Jewish Care residential home for the elderly 1996, Saga Gp HQ 1999, Jubilee Campus Univ of Nottingham 1999 (Br Construction Industry Award, RIBA Award), Dynamic Earth Edinburgh 1999 (Civic Tst Award, RIBA Award), Westminster Underground Station 1999 (Br Construction Industry Award, Royal Fine Art Cmmn Award), Portcullis House Westminster 2000 (Civic Tst Award, RIBA Award, Concrete Award), Wildscreen Bristol 2000 (Civic Tst Award, DTLR Urban Design Award), Pilkington Labs Sherborne Sch 2000, housing at Charterhouse 2000, Goodwood Racecourse 2001, (Ind Fabric Assoc Award) 2001, Manchester Art Gall 2002, The Forum Norwich 2002, Haberdashers' Hall London 2002, Nat Coll of Sch Leadership Univ of Nottingham 2002; pres Architectural Assoc 1997–99 (vice-pres 1987–93); cmmr Royal Fine Art Cmmn; memb: Architecture Advsy Panel Arts Cncl, Cncl Architecture Assoc, Cncl RIBA, London Advsy Ctee English Heritage; hon memb Bund Architekten 1996; tstee: British Museum 1993–, Thomas Cubitt Tst; Royal Gold Medal for Architecture 1994, Prince Philip Prize for Designer of the Year 1994; Dr (hc) RCA 1994, Hon DLitt Univ of Nottingham 1995, Hon DTech London Guildhall Univ 1996; RIBA 1966, RWEA 1989, RA 1992, Hon FAIA 1996, Hon FRIAS 1996; *Recreations* Blackheath, sailing, Catureglio; *Style*— Sir Michael Hopkins, CBE, RA; ✉ 49A Downshire Hill, London NW3 1NX (tel 020 7435 1109); Hopkins Architects, 27 Broadley Terrace, London NW1 6LG (tel 020 7724 1751)

HOPKINS, Rowland Rhys; s of David Verdun Hopkins, of Ammanford, Carmarthenshire, and Phyllis, *née* Dyson; *b* 19 December 1948; *Educ* Lawrence Sheriff Sch Rugby, UCL (LLB); *m* 12 Dec 1987, Elizabeth Ann, da of Ronald Williams (d 1980), of Church Stretton, Salop; 1 da (Sarah Elizabeth b 24 Oct 1989); *Career* called to the Bar Inner Temple 1970; barr 1984–; pt/t immigration adjudicator 2001–05, pt/t immigration judge 2005–; memb Gen Synod C of E 1985–90, chm House of Laity of Birmingham Diocesan Synod C of E 1988–94; *Recreations* skiing, fell walking; *Style*— Rowland Hopkins, Esq; ✉ Rowchester Chambers, 4 Rowchester Court, Whittall Street, Birmingham B4 6DH (tel 0121 233 2327)

HOPKINS, Russell; OBE (1989); s of Charles Albert Hopkins (d 1948), of Sunderland, Co Durham, and Frances Doris, *née* Baldwin (d 1980); *b* 30 April 1932; *Educ* Barnard Castle Sch, Univ of Durham (BDS), Univ of London; *m* 25 April 1970, Jill Margaret, da of Dudley Frederick Pexton (d 1961); 2 s (Richard Jonathon b 6 May 1971, Robert Geoffrey Russell b 24 April 1979), 1 da (Claire Louise b 31 May 1972); *Career* gen dental practice Salisbury Rhodesia 1957–58 (Cambridge 1956–57), SHO (oral surgery) Nottingham Gen Hosp 1959, registrar (oral surgery) St Peter's Hosp Chertsey 1959–61, house surgn (surgery) Bolingbroke Hosp Wandsworth 1964, house physician (med) Mayday Hosp 1964, surgn Union Castleline 1965, sr registrar (oral surgery) Royal Victoria Infirmary Newcastle upon Tyne 1965–68, gen mangr Univ Hosp of Wales 1985–91 (conslt in oral maxillo and facial surgery 1968–95), dir Med Audit S Glamorgan HA 1991–95; chm Hosp Dental Staff Ctee 1976–78, Hosp Med Staff Ctee and Med Bd 1980–82, chm Welsh Conslts and Specialists Ctee 1990–94, memb Joint Conslts Ctee 1980–93, Central Ctee Hosp Med Services 1975–90; chm: Glan-Y-Môr NHS Tst 1995–99, Bro' Morgannwg NHS Tst 1999–2005 (lead chair 2002–04); BMA: chm Gen Mangrs Gp 1987–90, chm Welsh Cncl 1990–94, memb Cncl 1990–95; memb Joint Conslts Ctee 1980–93, Central Ctee Hosp Med Services 1975–90; pres BAOMS 1992–93 (hon treas 1978–80); external examiner Univ of Hong Kong 1991–93; Llandudno Vase BAOMFS 1980, Down Surgical Prize 1993; memb EAOMS, fell BMA 1998; FDSRCS 1961, MRCS 1964, LRCP 1964; *Books* Mandibular Fractures in Maxillo Facial Injuries (1985), Atlas of Oral Preprosthetic Surgery (1986), Preprosthetic Surgery in Surgery of Mouth & Jaws (1986), Bone Dysplasias in Clinical Dentistry (1986), Farbatlas Der Präprothelischen Chirurgie (1990); *Recreations* golf, photography, work; *Clubs* Cardiff and County; *Style*— Russell Hopkins, Esq, OBE; ✉ 179 Cyncoed Road, Cyncoed, Cardiff, South Glamorgan CF23 6AH (tel 029 2075 2319)

HOPKINSON, Prof Brian Ridley; s of Rev E A E Hopkinson (d 1982), of Cheltenham, Glos, and May Olive, *née* Redding (d 1986); *b* 26 February 1938; *Educ* Univ of Birmingham (MB ChB, ChM); *m* 14 April 1962, Margaret Ruth, da of Percival Bull (d 1945), of Burton upon Trent, Staffs; 3 s (Nicholas b 1967, Adrian b 1968, Jonathan b 1969), 1 da (Susannah b 1971); *Career* RSO West Bromwich Hosp 1964 (house surgn 1961), lectr in surgery Queen Elizabeth Hosp Birmingham 1968–73, conslt surgn Nottingham Gen Hosp 1973–, prof of vascular surgery Univ of Nottingham 1996–2003; Hunterian prof RCS 1970; chm Annual Representatives Meeting BMA 1998–2001 (dep chm 1995–98); former memb: Exec Ctee Vascular Surgical Soc of GB and Ireland, Cncl BMA; licensed lay reader C of E 1961–; FRCS 1964; *Recreations* steam boating and motor caravanning at home and abroad; *Clubs* BMA; *Style*— Prof Brian Hopkinson; ✉ Lincolnsfield, 18 Victoria Crescent, Private Road, Sherwood, Nottingham NG5 4DA (tel 0115 960 4167); Consulting Rooms: 34 Regent Street, Nottingham NG1 5BT (tel 0115 947 2860)

HOPKINSON, David Adrian; s of Jonathan Adrian Hopkinson (d 1997), and Hilda Florence, *née* Greening (d 1996); *b* 21 December 1956; *Educ* Queen Elizabeth Sch Wimborne, Poole Coll, Univ of Kent (BA), Int House London (RSA Dip); *m* 2 Sept 1989, Umi Djulianti; *Career* teacher of English English Educn Centre Jakarta Indonesia 1985–87; Br Cncl: teacher of English Seoul South Korea 1990–92, teacher of English Sana'a Yemen 1993–94, satellite mangr Subang Jaya Selangon Malaysia 1994–98, branch mangr Kandy Sri Lanka 1998–2001, dir Chiang Mai Thailand 2001–04, country examinations mangr Philippines 2004–; hon Br consul Chiang Mai Thailand 2002–04; *Recreations* reading (especially non-fiction), travel, photography; *Clubs* Chiang Mai Gymkhana; *Style*—David Hopkinson, Esq; ✉ British Council, 10F Taipan Place, Emerald Avenue, Ortigas Centre, Pasig City 1620, Philippines (tel 00 63 2 9141011, fax 00 63 2 9141020, e-mail david.hopkinson@britishcouncil.org.ph)

HOPKINSON, Jeremy Stephen Frederick; s of John Gordon Hopkinson, of Kensworth, Dunstable, and Edith, *née* Lord; *b* 28 August 1943; *Educ* Berkhamsted Sch; *m* 14 Sept 1968, Helle, da of Alfred Holter, of Brevik, Norway; 1 s (Peter John b 18 Nov 1969), 2 da (Cecilia Ann b 22 Feb 1972, Theresa Janet b 19 July 1974); *Career* articled clerk Robert H Marsh & Co CA 1961–68, qualified 1966, Hillier Hills Frary & Co 1968–70; ptnr Marsh Wood Drew & Co 1972–78 (joined 1970), ptnr Dearden Farrow 1978–88 (chm Tax Ctee 1983–86), joined Binder Hamlyn 1988, ptnr (following merger) Arthur Andersen from Oct 1994 (ret); princ Jeremy Hopkinson & Co 1999–; tstee Milton Keynes City Centre Counselling, tstee Assoc of Church Accountants and Treasurers London (chm 1999–2004), conslt numerous charities; reader C of E 2003–, memb local church and treas Mursley Deanery Synod; FCA 1976 (ACA 1966); Freemason (Gadebourne Lodge, King Henry VIII Chapter and Berkhamsted Rose Croix); *Recreations* golf, choir singing, marquetry; *Clubs* Woburn Golf & Country; *Style*— Jeremy Hopkinson, Esq; ✉ Lynghouse, 12 Heath Road, Great Brickhill, Milton Keynes, Buckinghamshire MK17 9AL (tel 01525 261674, fax 0709 200 8274)

HOPKINSON, Martin James; *b* 6 August 1946; *Career* Walker Art Gallery Liverpool: asst keeper Br art 1973–74, asst keeper foreign art 1974–77; curator of prints and non-Scottish art Hunterian Art Gallery Univ of Glasgow 1977–97, currently hon fell Hunterian Nat Gallery Univ of Glasgow; assoc ed (books) Br Art Jl; *Publications* Foreign Schools catalogue 2 vols (with Edward Morris for Walker Art Gallery, 1977), Alexander Mann 1853–1908 - sketches and correspondence with his wife and family (Fine Art Soc, 1985), No Day Without a Line (Ashmolean Museum, 1999); *Exhibition Catalogues* The Macfie Collection (1980), Whistler in Europe (and James McNeill Whistler at the Hunterian Art Gallery - An Illustrated Guide, 1990), James McNeill Whistler (with Denys Sutton, Isetan Museum of Art Tokyo, 1987), Printmaking in Paris 1900–1940 (1991), The Italian Renaissance Print (Hunterian Art Gallery, 1994), Colour and Line: Five Centuries of Colour Woodcuts (Hunterian Art Gallery, 1994), Picasso and his Contemporaries: Printmaking in Paris 1905–1975 (with Stephen Coppel and Jane Lee, British Museum, 1997), A Ramble on Copper. Two Centuries of Scottish Etchings 1750–1950 (with B K Smith, Fleming Collection, 2003), Italian Prints 1875–1975 (British Museum, 2007); *Style*— Martin Hopkinson, Esq; ✉ 44 Victoria Road, Deal, Kent CT14 7BQ

HOPKINSON, Simon Charles; s of Frederick Bruce Hopkinson, of Pembrokeshire, and Anne Dorothie Mary, *née* Whitworth; *b* 5 June 1954; *Educ* St John's Coll Cambridge (chorister), Trent Coll; *Career* Normandie Hotel Birtle 1970–71, Hat & Feather Knutsford 1971–72, St Non's Hotel St Davids 1972–74, Druidstone Hotel Little Haven 1974–75; chef and proprietor: Shed Restaurant Dinas 1975–77, Hoppy's Restaurant 1977–78; inspr Egon Ronay 1978–80; chef: private house 1980–83, Hilaire London 1983–87; founding chef and co-prop Bibendum 1987–95; former cookery writer The Independent (winner Glenfiddich Award for Cookery writing (three times)); *Books* Roast Chicken and Other Stories (1994, Andre Simon Award 1995, Glenfiddich Award 1995, Most Useful Cookery Book Ever Waitrose Food Illustrated 2005), The Prawn Cocktail Years (1997), Gammon and Spinach and Other Recipes (1998), Roast Chicken and Other Stories: Second Helpings (2001); *Recreations* dining; *Clubs* The Groucho, Colony Room; *Style*— Simon Hopkinson, Esq

HOPKINSON, (George) William; s of William Hartley Hopkinson (d 1971), and Mary, *née* Ashmore; *b* 13 September 1943; *Educ* Tupton Hall GS, Pembroke Coll Cambridge (MA); *m* (m dis 1997), Mary Agnes, *née* Coverdale; 1 s (William St John b 9 Nov 1974); *Career* Inland Revenue: joined 1965, Civil Serv Dept 1973–76, private sec to Min of State 1976–77, asst sec 1978–81; HM Treasy 1981–86; MOD: head Defence Arms Control Unit 1988–92, head Defence Lands Serv 1992–93, asst under sec of state (Policy) 1993–97; dep dir and dir of studies RIIA 1999–2000 (head of int security prog 1997–99, assoc fell); visiting fell Univ of Cambridge 1991, sr visiting fell WEU Inst Paris 2001; contrib to pubns on security policy, writer and speaker on int relations; assoc fell RUSI; *Publications* The Making of British Defence Policy (2000), Enlargement: A New NATO (2001), Sizing and Shaping European Armed Forces (2004), The Atlantic Crises: Britain, Europe and Parting from the United States (2005); *Recreations* walking, reading; *Clubs* Oxford and Cambridge; *Style*— William Hopkinson, Esq; ✉ Woodlands, Rimpton, Somerset BA22 8AJ (tel 01935 851069, e-mail g.w.hopkinson@btinternet.com)

HOPKIRK, (Margaret) Joyce; da of late Walter Nicholson, of Newcastle, and late Veronica, *née* Keelan; *Educ* Middle St Secdy Sch Newcastle; *m* 1, 1964, Peter Hopkirk; 1 da (Victoria b 11 April 1966); m 2, 9 Aug 1974, William James (Bill) Lear, s of Maj Cyril James Lear (d 1988), of Newick, E Sussex; 1 s (Nicholas b 22 Nov 1975); *Career* women's ed (launch) Sun Newspaper 1969, ed (launch) Br Cosmopolitan 1970, asst ed Daily Mirror 1972–78, women's ed Sunday Times 1986, ed dir (launch) Br Elle 1987, ed She magazine 1987–89, ed Chic magazine 1993–94 (fndr ed), conslt ed TV Plus 1991–, conslt to ed Sunday Express 1992–; co-chm PPA Awards; media memb Competition Cmmn 2001–06; FRSA; *Books* Splash (co-author, 1995), Best of Enemies (1996), Double Trouble (1997), Unfinished Business (1998), Relative Strangers (1999), The Affair (2000); *Style*— Mrs Joyce Hopkirk

HOPMEIER, George Alan Richard; JP (Inner London); s of Dr Lucian Hopmeier (d 1981), and Yolanda Hopmeier; *b* 23 September 1948; *Educ* Dulwich Coll, UCL (BA); *Chidren* 1 da (Charlotte b 29 March 1981); *Career* chief exec: First Trade Ltd 2003–, Brand Collection Ltd, Exclusive World Resorts Ltd; *Recreations* boating, reading, flying; *Clubs* RAC, Citrus (USA); *Style*— George Hopmeier, Esq; ✉ Unit 1, Kingfisher House, Juniper Drive, London SW18 1TX (tel 020 7350 2020, fax 020 7350 2545, e-mail hopmeier@msn.com)

HOPPÉ, Benjamin Finley; OBE (2004); s of Benjamin Finley Hoppé, and Gwendoline May, *née* Evans; *b* 7 May 1933, Swansea; *Educ* Swansea GS; *m* 10 June 1957, Valerie, *née* Rowe; 2 s (Andrew Finley b 7 Oct 1958, Ian David b 18 Dec 1963), 1 da (Angela Gillian b 31 Jan 1960); *Career* apprentice structural draughtsman Dawnays Ltd 1950–54, cmmnd Nat Serv Royal Engrs Sch of Mil Engrg Chatham 1955–57, site engr Braithwaite Engrs Ltd 1957–59, site agent Metal Construction Ltd 1959–61, area agent Rees and Kirby Ltd 1961–68, fndr Rowecord Engrg Ltd 1968, currently chm Rowecord Holdings Ltd; pres Br Constructional Steelwork Assoc 1996–98, chm Newport Successful City Status Bid 2003, chm Newport Gwent Enterprises Agency 1993–2005; hon fell Univ of Wales Newport 2002; Wales Business Achiever of the Year 2003; *Clubs* Newport Fugitives CC (pres), Newport Golf; *Style*— Benjamin Hoppé, Esq, OBE; ✉ Newholme, Glasllwch Lane, Newport, Gwent NP20 3PT (tel 01633 258527, fax 01633 267253); Rowecord Holdings Ltd, Neptune Works, Uskway, Newport NP20 2SS (tel 01633 250511, fax 01633 253219, e-mail benhoppe@rowecord.com)

HOPPEN, Prof (Karl) Theodore; s of Paul Ernst Hoppen (ka 1941), of Mönchengladbach, Germany, and Edith Margaretha, *née* van Brussel (d 2005); *b* 27 November 1941; *Educ* Glenstal Abbey Sch Co Limerick, UC Dublin (BA, MA), Trinity Coll Cambridge (PhD); *m* 1, 8 Aug 1970, Alison Mary (d 2002), da of Dr Samuel Buchan; 2 da (Martha Alice b 3 Jan 1974, Katherine Edith b 3 Nov 1975), 1 s (Theodore Samuel b 3 May 1979); m 2, 1 June 2007, Anne Drakeford, *née* Oldfield; *Career* Univ of Hull: asst lectr 1966–68, lectr 1968–74, sr lectr 1974–86, reader 1986–96, prof 1996–2003, ret; Benjamin Duke visiting fell Nat Humanities Center N Carolina 1985–86, visiting fell Sidney Sussex Coll Cambridge 1988; Br Acad res reader in the humanities 1994–96; FRHistS 1978, FBA 2001; *Books* The Common Scientist in the Seventeenth Century (1970), The Papers of the Dublin Philosophical Society 1683–1708 (ed, 1982, 2 edn 2007), Elections, Politics and

Society in Ireland 1832–1885 (1984), Ireland since 1800: Conflict and Conformity (1989, 2 edn 1999), The Mid-Victorian Generation 1846–1886 (1998); author of numerous articles in learned jls; *Recreations* idleness, bel canto operas; *Clubs* Oxford and Cambridge; *Style*— Prof Theodore Hoppen; ✉ 1 Greyfriars Crescent, Beverley, East Yorkshire HU17 8LR (tel 01482 861343, e-mail k.t.hoppen@hull.ac.uk)

HOPPER, Prof Andrew (Andy); CBE (2007); *Educ* Univ of Wales Swansea (BSc), Univ of Cambridge (PhD); *Career* fndr Olivetti Research 1986, md AT&T Laboratories Cambridge until 2002, currently prof of computer technol and head Computer Laboratory Univ of Cambridge, fell CCC Cambridge; co-fndr 13 ICT cos incl Acorn Computer and Virata; chm: RealVNC, Ubisense, Adventiq; dir Solarflare (formerly Level5 Networks); Royal Soc Clifford Paterson Lecture 1999, Royal Acad of Engrg Silver Medal 2002, Assoc of Computing Machinery SIGMOBILE Outstanding Contribution Award 2004, IEE Mountbatten Medal 2004; hon fell Swansea Univ 2005; tstee IEE, FREng, FRS 2006; *Style*— Prof Andy Hopper, CBE; ✉ University of Cambridge Computer Laboratory, William Gates Building, 15 J J Thomson Avenue, Cambridge CB3 0FD

HOPPER, William Joseph; s of late Isaac Vance Hopper, and late Jennie Josephine Black; *b* 9 August 1929; *Educ* Queen's Park Secdy Sch, Univ of Glasgow (MA); *m* 1 (m dis); 1 da (Catherine b 1972); m 2, 1987 (m dis), Marjorie; *Career* Pilot Offr RAF 1952–55; fin analyst W R Grace and Co New York 1956–59, London office mangr H Hentz and Co (memb NYSE) 1960–66, gen mangr S G Warburg and Co Ltd 1966–69; dir: Hill Samuel and Co Ltd 1969–74, Morgan Grenfell and Co Ltd 1975–79 (advsr 1979–86), Wharf Resources Ltd (Calgary) 1984–87, Manchester Ship Canal Co 1985–87; exec chm Shire Trust Ltd 1986–91, chm Robust Mouldings Ltd 1986–90, exec chm W J Hopper & Co Ltd (investment bankers)1996–; fndr chm (now memb Exec Ctee) Inst for Fiscal Studies 1969–, treas Action Resource Centre 1985–94, tstee Nat Hosp for Nervous Diseases Devpt Fndn 1986–90, tstee Hampstead Wells and Campden Tst 1989–99; memb Ct of Mgmnt Rosslyn Hill Unitarian Chapel 1995–2000 (chm 1995–98) and 2004–, memb London Dist and South Eastern Provincial Assembly of Unitarian and Free Christian Churches 2000–04; MEP (Cons) Greater Manchester W 1979–84; *Recreations* listening to music, gardening; *Clubs* Garrick, RAF; *Style*— W J Hopper; ✉ 9A Flask Walk, London NW3 1HJ (tel 020 7435 6414, fax 020 7431 5568, e-mail will@wjhopper.com)

HOPPS, Stuart Gary; s of Alec Hopps (d 1973), of London, and Lucie, *née* Dombek; *b* 2 December 1942; *Educ* Stratford GS, KCL (BA), MFA Sarah Lawrence Coll; *Career* choreographer; Dance Dept Dartington Coll of Art 1970–71, assoc dir Scottish Ballet 1971–76, fndr dir SB's movable Workshop, fndr chm Dance Panel Gr London Arts, chm Br Assoc of Choreographers, memb Dance Panel Arts Cncl of GB 1976–80, dir MA Studies Laban Centre 1986–89, memb Accreditation Ctee Cncl for Dance Educn & Training; fndr chm Br Assoc of Choreographers; *Theatre* incl: Elizabeth (Ginza Saison Theatre Tokyo), Medea (Barcelona Cultural Olympics), A Midsummer Night's Dream, Salome, Candide (Edinburgh Festival), The Oresteia, Animal Farm (NT), Henry VIII, As You Like It and Beauty and the Beast (RSC), Oliver (Nat Youth Music Theatre), Chips With Everything (NT), Galileo (NT); theatre in West End: Pal Joey, Girl Friends, The Rocky Horror Show, Carmen Jones, The Betrayal of Laura Blake; *Opera* incl: The Cunning Little Vixen, The Silver Tassie and Christmas Eve (ENO), Orfeo ed Euridice (Glyndebourne), Carmen, Idomeneo, Onegin and The Merry Widow (WNO), HMS Pinafore and The Merry Widow (Sadler's Wells), The Cunning Little Vixen and Carmen (Royal Opera), Macbeth (Metropolitan Opera), Peter Grimes (Kent Opera); *Television* The Passion (BBC 2); *Films* incl: Sense and Sensibility, Twelfth Night, Kenneth Branagh's Much Ado About Nothing, Hamlet and Love's Labour's Lost, A Knight's Tale, The Magic Flute; *Style*— Stuart Hopps, Esq; ✉ c/o Simpson Fox Associates, 52 Shaftesbury Avenue, London W1D 6LP (tel 020 7434 9167, fax 020 7494 2887, e-mail cary@simpson-fox.demon.co.uk)

HOPSON, Christopher Ian (Chris); s of David Joseph Hopson (d 2001), of Newbury, Berks, and Susan, *née* Buckingham; *b* 9 April 1963; *Educ* Marlborough, St Andrews Sch Middletown Delaware USA (ESU Scholarship), Univ of Sussex (BA), Cranfield Sch of Mgmnt (MBA); *m* May 1994, Charlotte, da of Keith Gascoigne; 2 s (Matthew James b 4 July 1998, Nicholas Henry b 1 Sept 2000); *Career* SDP 1985–90: sometime constituency agent, Pty researcher (Rosie Barnes), dir elections and campaigns and chief exec; communications conslt Corporate Communications Strategy 1990–91, political adviser to David Mellor (then Sec of State for National Heritage) 1992, corporate affrs dir Granada Media Group 1993–2000, md Result educn serv 1999–2002, conslt DfES 2002–04; HMRC: communications and mktg dir 2005–07, memb Bd 2006–, change and capability dir 2007–; chm Foyer Fedn 2004– (memb Bd 2001–); memb Cncl RTS 1995–98; *Recreations* walking, travel, reading, theatre, good food and wine (not necessarily in that order); *Style*— Chris Hopson, Esq; ✉ 5 Estelle Road, London NW3 2JX (e-mail chris.hopson@dial.pipex.com)

HOPWOOD, Prof Anthony George; s of George Hopwood (d 1986), of Stoke-on-Trent, and Violet, *née* Simpson (d 1986); *b* 18 May 1944; *Educ* Hanley HS, LSE (BSc), Univ of Chicago (MBA, PhD); *m* 31 Aug 1967, Caryl, da of John H Davies (d 1981), of Ton Pentre, Mid Glamorgan; 2 s (Mark b 1971, Justin b 1974); *Career* lectr in mgmnt accounting Manchester Business Sch 1970–73, sr staff Admin Staff Coll Henley-on-Thames 1973–75, professorial fell Oxford Centre for Mgmnt Studies 1976–78, ICA prof of accounting and fin reporting London Business Sch 1978–85, Ernst and Young prof of int accounting and fin mgmnt LSE 1985–95; Univ of Oxford: fell Templeton Coll 1995–97, prof of mgmnt studies 1995–97, American Standard Companies prof of ops mgmnt 1997–, student ChCh 1997–, dean Saïd Business Sch 1999–2006 (dep dir 1995–98); visiting prof of mgmnt European Inst for Advanced Studies Mgmnt Brussels 1972–2003 (pres of Bd 1995–2003), visiting distinguished prof of accounting Pennsylvania State Univ 1983–88; chm Prince's Fndn for the Built Environment 2006–; pres Euro Accounting Assoc 1977–79 and 1987–88, distinguished int lectr American Accounting Assoc 1981 (presidential scholar 2006), John V Ratcliffe Meml lectr Univ of NSW 1988; accounting advsr to: Euro Cmmn 1989–90, OECD 1990–91; memb: Mgmnt and Industrial Rels Ctee SSRC 1975–79; foreign memb Swedish Royal Soc of Sciences 2003; Lifetime Achievement Award American Accounting Assoc 2002, Academic Leadership Award European Accounting Assoc 2005; Hon DEcon Turku Sch of Econs 1989, Hon DEcon Univ of Gothenburg 1992, Hon DSc Univ of Lincolnshire and Humberside 1999, Hon Dr Merc Copenhagen Business Sch 2000, Hon Dr Univ of Siena; *Books* An Accounting System and Managerial Behaviour (1973), Accounting and Human Behaviour (1974), Essays in British Accounting Research (with M Bromwich, 1981), Auditing Research (with M Bromwich and J Shaw, 1982), Accounting Standard Setting - An International Perspective (with M Bromwich, 1983), European Contributions to Accounting Research (with H Schreuder, 1984), Issues in Public Sector Accounting (with C Tomkins, 1984), Research and Current Issues in Management Accounting (with M Bromwich, 1986), Accounting from the Outside (1989), International Pressures for Accounting Change (1989), Understanding Accounting in a Changing Environment (with M Page and S Turley, 1990), Accounting and the Law (with M Bromwich, 1992), Accounting as Social and Institutional Practice (with P Miller, 1994), The Economics and Politics of Accounting (with C Lenz and D Pfaff, 2004), Handbook of Management Accounting Research vols 1 and 2 (with C Chapman and M Shields, 2006); *Style*— Prof Anthony Hopwood; ✉ Saïd Business School, University of Oxford, Park End Street, Oxford OX1 1HP (tel 01865 288800, fax 01865 288810)

HOPWOOD, Prof Sir David Alan; kt (1994); s of Herbert Hopwood (d 1963), of Lymm, Cheshire, and Dora, *née* Grant (d 1972); *b* 19 August 1933; *Educ* Purbrook Park Co HS, Lymm GS, Univ of Cambridge (MA, PhD), Univ of Glasgow (DSc); *m* 15 Sept 1962, Joyce Lilian, da of Isaac Bloom (d 1964), of Hove, E Sussex; 2 s (Nicholas Duncan b 1964, John Andrew b 1965), 1 da (Rebecca Jane b 1967); *Career* John Stothert bye-fell Magdalene Coll Cambridge 1956–58, univ demonstrator and asst lectr in botany Univ of Cambridge 1957–61, res fell St John's Coll Cambridge 1958–61, lectr in genetics Univ of Glasgow 1961–68, John Innes prof of genetics UEA 1968–98 (emeritus prof 1998–); formerly head Genetics Dept John Innes Centre (emeritus fell 1998–); hon prof: Chinese Acad Med Sciences 1987, Chinese Acad of Sciences (Insts of Microbiology and Plant Physiology) 1987, Huazhong Agric Univ Wuhan China 1989, Guangxi Univ Nanning China 2004, Jaio Tong Univ Shanghai China 2004; hon fell: UMIST 1990, Magdalene Coll Cambridge 1992; memb: Genetical Soc of GB 1957 (pres 1984–87), Euro Molecular Biology Orgn 1984, Academia Europaea 1988; hon memb: Spanish Microbiological Soc 1985, Hungarian Acad of Sciences 1990, Soc Gen Microbiology (pres 2000–03); foreign fell Indian Nat Sci Acad 1987; Hon DSc: ETH Zürich 1989, UEA 1998; Hon FIBiol 2001, FRS 1979; *Publications* author of over 270 articles in scientific jls and books; *Recreations* cooking, gardening; *Style*— Prof Sir David Hopwood, FRS; ✉ John Innes Centre, Norwich Research Park, Colney, Norwich NR4 7UH (tel 01603 450000, fax 01603 450778, e-mail david.hopwood@bbsrc.ac.uk); 244 Unthank Road, Norwich NR2 2AH (tel 01603 453488)

HORAM, John Rhodes; MP; s of Sydney Horam, of Preston, Lancs, and Catherine Horam; *b* 7 March 1939; *Educ* Silcoates Sch Wakefield, St Catharine's Coll Cambridge; *m* 1, 1977, Iris Crawley; m 2, 1987, Judith Margaret Jackson; *Career* former fin journalist: Financial Times, The Economist; MP (Lab 1970–81, SDP 1981–83) Gateshead West 1970–83, joined Cons Pty Feb 1987, MP (Cons) Orpington 1992–; Parly under sec for Tport 1976–79, memb Public Accounts Ctee 1992–95, Parly sec Office of Public Service 1995, Parly under sec Dept of Health 1995–97; chm Environmental Audit Ctee 1997–2003, memb Exec 1922 Ctee of Cons MPs 2004–, memb Foreign Affrs Ctee 2005–; CRU International Ltd: md 1968–70 and 1983–92, dep chm 1992–95, non-exec dir 1997–; *Style*— John Horam, Esq, MP; ✉ House of Commons, London SW1A 0AA

HORAN, Francis Thomas (Frank); s of Leo Patrick Horan (d 1979), and Rose, *née* Finch (d 1983); *b* 24 July 1933; *Educ* Torquay GS, St Mary's Hosp Med Sch, RCS, McGill Univ Montreal (MSc); *m* 17 Feb 1962, Cynthia Anne, da of Percy John Reginald Bambury (d 1988), of Bournemouth, Dorset; 2 s (Thomas Charles b 1965, John Patrick b 1968), 1 da (Julia Anne b 1968); *Career* former med dir and consult orthopaedic surgn Princess Royal Hosp Haywards Heath; former hon orthopaedic surgn: Lord's Cricket Ground, Middlesex CCC; former hon med advsr: English Basketball Assoc, Br and Irish Basketball Fedn, ECB (formerly TCCB); formerly ed now emeritus ed Jl of Bone and Joint Surgery, former chm Editorial Bd and English language ed Int Orthopaedics, former ed Br Orthopaedic News; former pres Br Orthopaedic Sports Trauma Assoc (BOSTA); memb Medical Cmmn FIBA; memb Ctee Sussex CCC 1990–97; Robert Jones Gold Medal BOA; membre d'honneur Societé International de Chirugie Orthopedie et Traumatologie (former memb Int Ctee), hon memb Hellenic Orthopaedic and Trauma Soc; LRCP, Hon FBOA (memb Cncl 1987–89 and 1991–2000), FRCS 1966 (MRCS 1959); *Books* Orthopaedic Problems in Inherited Skeletal Disorders (1982), The Mary's Men: A History of St Mary's Hospital RFC (2003), Harris's Orthopaedics (contrib), Medicine Sport and the Law (contrib), Modern Trauma Management (contrib); *Recreations* sport, travel, food; *Clubs* Athenaeum, MCC (hon life memb), Middlesex CCC, Sussex CCC; *Style*— Frank Horan, Esq; ✉ Providence, Plumpton, East Sussex BN7 3AJ (tel 01273 890316, fax 01273 890482); Consulting Rooms, 40 Wilbury Road, Hove, East Sussex BN3 3JP (tel 01273 206206); 71 Park Street, London W1K 7HW (tel 020 7629 3763)

HORE, Dr Brian David; s of late William Harold Banks Hore, and Gladys Hilda, *née* Preedy; *b* 21 September 1937; *Educ* Lower Sch of John Lyon Harrow, Bart's Med Coll London, Maudsley Hosp London (BSc, MB BS, MPhil); *m* 1, Eva Elliot (d 1998), da of George Elliot Shepherd (d 1955); 2 s (Ian b 19 March 1968, Andrew b 29 Jan 1971); m 2, Janette Elisabeth da of Richard Kendall (d 1970); *Career* house offr Bart's London 1963–65, registrar in psychiatry Maudsley Hosp 1967–70, sr registrar in psychological med Hammersmith Hosp 1970–71; conslt psychiatrist: Withington Hosp Manchester 1972–98, Univ Hosp of S Manchester 1972–; hon lectr in psychiatry Univ of Manchester 1972– (lectr and hon conslt 1971–72), hon conslt psychiatrist Univ Hosp of S Manchester, staff conslt psychiatrist Altrincham Priory Hosp; hon vice-pres Bd of Dirs ICAA Lausanne, memb Exec Ctee and Jt Ctee Med Cncl on Alcoholism, temp advsr WHO regnl Euro office; memb BMA 1963, FRCPsych 1981, FRCP 1983; *Books* Alcohol Dependence (1976), Alcohol Problems in Employment (jt ed and contrib, 1981), Alcohol and Health (jtly, 1986), Alcohol Our Favourite Drug (jtly, 1986); *Recreations* theatre, cinema, soccer (Manchester City FC); *Style*— Dr Brian Hore; ✉ 17 St John Street, Manchester M3 4DR (tel 0161 834 5775)

HORLICK, Sir James Cunliffe William; 6 Bt (UK 1914), of Cowley Manor, Co Gloucester; s of Sir John James Macdonald Horlick, 5 Bt (d 1995), and June, *née* Cory-Wright; *b* 19 November 1956; *Educ* Eton; *m* 1, 1985 (m dis 1997), Fiona Rosalie, eldest da of Andrew Mclaren, of Alcester, Warks; 3 s (Alexander b 1987, Jack b 1989, Hugo b 1991); m 2, 1999, Georgina Hudson, da of Roy Ticey, of London; *Heir* s, Alexander Horlick; *Career* 2 Lt Coldstream Guards; co dir; *Style*— Sir James Horlick, Bt

HORLICK, Nicola Karina Christina; da of Michael Robert Dudley Gayford (d 1997), of Chichester, W Sussex, and Suzanna Christina Victoria, *née* Czyzewska; *b* 28 December 1960; *Educ* Cheltenham Ladies' Coll, Birkenhead HS GPDST, Phillips Exeter Acad (USA), Balliol Coll Oxford (BA); *m* 1, 23 June 1984 (m dis 2005), Timothy Piers Horlick, s of Vice-Adm Sir Ted Horlick, KBE, FREng; 4 da (Georgina b 19 Oct 1986 d 27 Nov 1998, Alice b 17 Nov 1988, Serena b 2 Nov 1990, Antonia b 10 June 1996), 2 s (Rupert b 1 Dec 1993, Benjamin b 18 Sept 1999); m 2, 8 Sept 2006, Martin Francis Damian Baker; *Career* Mercury Asset Management 1983–91, md Morgan Grenfell Investment Management (UK Institutional Business) Morgan Grenfell Asset Management 1991–97 (resigned), with SG Asset Management 1997–2003, fndr and chief exec Bramdean Gp LLP 2004–; *Recreations* music, theatre, skiing; *Style*— Mrs Nicola Horlick; ✉ Bramdean Group LLP, 100 Brompton Road, London SW3 1ER

HORLOCK, Timothy John; QC (1997); s of John Harold Horlock, and Sheila, *née* Stuteley; *b* 4 January 1958; *Educ* Manchester Grammar, St John's Coll Cambridge (BA); *m* (m dis); 3 s (Matthew b 1985, Alex b 1987, Guy b 1991); *Career* called to the Bar Middle Temple 1981, in practice Northern Circuit, asst recorder 1997–; *Recreations* football, tennis, cricket; *Style*— Tim Horlock, QC; ✉ 9 St John Street, Manchester M3 4DN (tel 0161 955 9000, fax 0161 955 9001)

HORLOCK, (Henry) Wimburn Sudell; s of Rev Dr Henry Darrell Sudell Horlock, DD (d 1953), and Mary Haliburton, *née* Laurie (d 1953); *b* 19 July 1915; *Educ* Pembroke Coll Oxford (MA); *m* 21 July 1960, Jeannetta Robin, da of Frederick Wilfred Tanner, JP (d 1958), of Farnham Royal, Bucks; *Career* serv WWII Army 1939–42; civil serv 1942–60; fndr and dir Stepping Stone Sch 1962–87; memb Ct of Common Cncl City of London 1969–2001, Sheriff City of London 1972–73, dep Ward of Farrington Within (North Side) 1978–98; chm: City of London Sheriffs' Soc 1985–2002, West Ham Park Ctee 1979–82, Police Ctee 1987–90; memb: City Livery Club 1969– (pres 1981–82), Farringdon Ward Club 1970– (pres 1978–79), United Wards Club 1972– (pres 1980–81), Guild of Freemen 1972– (Master 1986–87), Royal Soc of St George (City of London Branch) 1972– (chm 1989–90); Freeman City of London 1937; Liveryman Worshipful Co of: Saddlers 1937

H

(Master 1976–77), Parish Clerks 1966 (Master 1981–82), Plaisterers 1975, Fletchers 1977, Gardeners 1980; hon memb Soc of Young Freeman 1994; Cdr Order of Merit FRG 1972, Cdr Nat Order of Aztec Eagle of Mexico 1973, Cdr Du Wissam Alouite of Morocco 1987; *Recreations* country pursuits, freemasonry; *Clubs* Athenaeum, Guildhall; *Style*— Wimburn Horlock, Esq; ✉ Copse Hill House, Lower Slaughter, Gloucestershire GL54 2HZ (tel 01451 820276)

HORN, Bernard P; *Educ* Catholic Coll Preston, John Dalton Faculty of Technol Manchester (DMS), Harvard Business Sch (Exec Prog); *m*; *Career* National Westminster Bank plc: joined 1965, in retail banking in N of England 1965–70, joined International Div 1972, dir of corp and institutional fin 1988–89, gen mangr Gp Chief Exec's Office 1989–90, gen mangr i/c gp strategy and communications 1990–91, chief exec NatWest Gp Int Businesses 1991–96, gp main bd dir 1995–2000, exec dir Gp Ops 1996–2000; chm: Rock Consulting 2001–07, Netik Holdings Ltd 2002–, Eontec Ltd (Dublin) 2003–04, E-Box 2004–, Econiq (Ireland) 2007; advsr Tuberous Sclerosis Assoc 2005–06, chm Magic Bus (UK) 2007; Freeman City of London 2002, memb Worshipful Co of Information Technologists; FCIB, FRSA; *Recreations* keeping fit, theatre, ballet, opera, playing the piano; *Style*— Bernard P Horn, Esq; ✉ E-Box, The Dome Building, 4 The Square, Richmond, Surrey TW9 1DT (e-mail bph@bernardhorn.com)

HORN, Prof Sir Gabriel; kt (2002); s of Abraham Horn (d 1946), of Birmingham, and Anne, *née* Grill (d 1976); *b* 9 December 1927; *Educ* Univ of Birmingham (BSc, MB ChB, MD), Univ of Cambridge (MA, ScD); *m* 1, 29 Nov 1952 (m dis 1979), Hon Ann Loveday Dean, da of Baron Soper (Life Peer) and Marie Soper, *née* Dean; 2 da (Amanda b 1953, Melissa b 1962), 2 s (Nigel b 1954, Andrew b 1960); m 2, 30 Aug 1980, Priscilla, da of Edwin Victor Barrett (d 1976), of Cape Town, and Sarah Eliza, *née* McMaster (d 1989); *Career* Educn Branch RAF 1947–49; house appts Birmingham Children's and Birmingham and Midland Eye Hosps 1955–56; Univ of Cambridge: demonstrator and lectr in anatomy 1956–72, reader in neurobiology 1972–74, prof of zoology 1978–95, head Dept of Zoology 1979–94, fell King's Coll 1962–74, 1978–98 and 1999–, master Sidney Sussex Coll 1992–99 (fell 1999–), dep vice-chllr 1994–98; sr res fell in neurophysiology Montreal Inst McGill Univ 1957–58, Kenneth Craik Award in Physiological Psychology 1962, visiting prof Univ of Calif Berkeley 1963, visiting res pres Ohio State Univ 1965, visiting prof of zoology Makerere UC Uganda 1966, dir Cambridge Consultants Ltd 1966–69, Leverhulme res fell Laboratoire de Neurophysiologie Cellulaire France 1970–71, prof of anatomy and head of dept Univ of Bristol 1974–77, sr conslt PA technology Melbourne 1976–86, distinguished visiting prof Univ of Alberta 1988, visiting Miller prof Univ of Calif Berkeley 1989, visiting prof Chinese Univ of Hong Kong 1995; Charnock Bradley lectr Univ of Edinburgh 1988, Crisp lectr Univ of Leeds 1990; chm: BBSRC Working Pty on Biology of Spongiform Encephalopathies 1991–94, Animal Sciences and Psychology Research Ctee BBSRC 1994–96 (memb Science and Engrg Bd 1994–96), Core Ctee Univ of Cambridge Govt Policy Programme 1998–, Review Ctee on the Origin of Bovine Spongiform Encephalopathy 2001, Working Pty on Brain Sciences, Addiction and Drugs Acad of Medical Sciences 2005–; memb: Biological Sciences Advsy Panel and Ctee Scientific Res Cncl 1970–75, Res Ctee Mental Health Fndn 1973–78, Advsy Bd Inst of Animal Physiology Babraham Cambridge 1980–85, Cncl AFRC 1991–94; memb and sometime chm Scientific Advsy Bd Parke-Davis Cambridge 1988–99; Leverhulme emeritus fell 2002–04; dir Co of Biologists 1980–93; Royal Medal of The Royal Soc 2001; hon memb: Euro Brain and Behaviour Soc, Anatomical Soc; foreign memb Georgian Acad of Sciences; pubns in various scientific journals; Hon DSc: Univ of Birmingham 1999, Univ of Bristol 2003, Inst of Physiology Georgian Acad of Sciences; FRS 1986, Hon FRCP 2007; *Books* Memory, Imprinting and the Brain (1985), Short-term Changes in Neural Activity and Behaviour (jt ed, 1970), Behavioural and Neural Aspects of Learning and Memory (jt ed, 1991); *Recreations* cycling, walking, listening to music, wine and conversation; *Style*— Prof Sir Gabriel Horn, FRS, FRCP; ✉ Sub Department of Animal Behaviour, Madingley, Cambridge CB3 8AA (tel 01223 741813, fax 01223 330869, e-mail gh105@cam.ac.uk)

HORN, Trevor; s of Robert Horn, of Durham, and Elizabeth, *née* Lambton; *b* 15 July 1949; *Educ* Johnson GS; *m* 1980, Jill, da of David Sinclair; 1 s (Aaron b 15 Dec 1983), 3 da (Alexandra b 24 April 1982, Rebecca b 25 March 1990, Gabriella b 17 April 1995); *Career* record prodr; formerly vocalist of pop bands Buggles and Yes, fndr memb and innovator The Art of Noise, fndr ZTT records, dir SPZ Group, estab Perfect Songs; past prodn credits incl: Buggles' The Age of Plastic (1980, gold disc), ABC's Lexicon of Love (1982, platinum), Malcolm McClaren's Duck Rock (1983, gold), Yes' 90125 (multi platinum), Frankie Goes To Hollywood's Welcome To The Pleasure Dome (multi platinum), Simple Minds' Street Fighting Years (platinum), Seal (multi platinum), Mike Oldfield's Tubular Bells II, Pet Shop Boys' Fundamental; prodr of many other artists incl: Grace Jones, Spandau Ballet, Foreigner, Godley and Creme, Paul McCartney, Rod Stewart, Pet Shop Boys, Propaganda, Dollar, Tina Turner, Tom Jones, Tatu; writer Pass the Flame (Official Olympics 2004 song); songwriter for film and TV incl: Toys, Coyote Ugly, Mona Lisa Smile, The Glam Metal Detectives; Prince's Tst charity concert at Wembley Arena celebrating 25 years as record prodr 2004; memb band The Producers; BPI Br Prodr of the Year 1983, 1985 and 1991 (nominated 1983, 1984, 1985, 1986, 1987, 1988 and 1994), Radio 1 Award for contribution to pop music 1984; Ivor Novello Awards: best recorded record for Owner of a Lonely Heart 1983, best contemporary song for Relax 1984, most performed work for Two Tribes 1984; 49 Grammy Award nominations incl: winner Best Instrumental (Cinema 90125), nomination Best Prodr 1994, Best Record (for Kiss From a Rose by Seal) 1996, Best Dance Song (I'm with Stupid by the Pet Shop Boys); Brit Award Best Br Prodr 1982, 1983 and 1992, BMI Award for Owner of A Lonely Heart 1984, Q Magazine Best Prodr Award 1991, Music Week Best Prodr Award 1991, Music Week Prodr of the Year Award 2004; *Style*— Trevor Horn, Esq; ✉ Sarm Productions, 42–46 St Luke's Mews, London W11 1DG (tel 020 7221 5101, fax 020 7221 3374)

HORN-SMITH, Sir Julian; kt (2004); *Career* Rediffusion 1972–78, Philips 1978–82, Mars GB 1982–84; Vodafone Gp plc: joined 1984, memb Bd 1996–2006, chief exec Vodafone AirTouch International Limited and exec dir Vodafone AirTouch plc 1999–2001, gp chief operating offr 2001–05, dep chief exec 2005–06, chm Supervisory Bd Vodafone Deutschland GmbH; chm Sage Gp plc 2006–07; non-exec dir: Smiths Gp plc 2000–06, Lloyds TSB Gp 2005–; *Style*— Sir Julian Horn-Smith

HORNBY, Sir Derek Peter; kt (1990); s of F N Hornby (d 1942), of Bournemouth, Dorset, and Violet May, *née* Pardy; *b* 10 October 1930; *Educ* Canford Sch; *m* 1, 1953 (m dis), Margaret Withers; 1 s (Nicholas Peter John b 1957), 1 da (Gillian Margaret (m Robert Harris, *qv*) b 1959); m 2, 1971, Sonia Margaret, da of Sidney Beesley (d 1985), of Birmingham; 1 s (Jonathan Peter Hornby, *qv*, b 1967), 1 da (Victoria Jane b 1968); *Career* Mars Ltd 1960–64, Texas Instruments 1964–73, dir international operations Xerox Corp USA 1973–80, md Rank Xerox Services Ltd 1980–84, chm Rank Xerox UK Ltd 1984–90; memb Br Overseas Trade Bd 1987– (chm 1990–95), pres European Cncl of Management 1992–94; chm: Video Arts Ltd 1993–96, London and Continental Railways 1994–98, Morgan Sindall plc 1995–2000, IRG plc; dir: Dixons Group plc 1990–97, Sedgewick Group 1993–99, AMP Asset Management 1994–98, Morgan Sindall plc 2000–02, Pillar Properties plc; chm Phillipines British Business Cncl; Liveryman Worshipful Co of Loriners; Hon DSc Aston Univ; CIMgt, FRSA, FInstD; *Recreations* cricket, real tennis, theatre; *Clubs* Garrick, MCC, Leamington Real Tennis; *Style*— Sir Derek Hornby; ✉ Badgers Farm, Idlicote, Shipston-on-Stour, Warwickshire CV36 5DT (tel 01608 661890)

HORNBY, John Fleet; s of John Fleet Hornby, of Cumbria (d 1997), and Marion, *née* Charnley (d 1981); *b* 23 December 1945; *Educ* Dowdales Co Sch Cumbria; *m* 1976, Elizabeth, da of John Chorley, of Cumbria (d 1988); 1 s (Paul b 1978); *Career* chartered accountant; audit mangr R F Miller & Co 1968–69 (articled clerk 1963–68); James Fisher & Sons plc (shipowners and port operators): accountant special duties 1969, asst co sec 1969–70, PA to md 1970–71, group accountant 1971–78, divnl dir of fin 1978–81, fin dir 1981–86, commercial dir 1986–88, md 1988–89, chm and md 1989–93; princ J F Hornby & Co Chartered Accountants 1994–, business conslt 1994–, assoc conslt Armstrong Watson & Co Chartered Accountants 1994–99; former dir/chm numerous other companies; dir Chamber of Shipping 1991–94, memb Gen Ctee Lloyd's Register of Shipping 1992–94; chm: Cumbria Christian Crusade Tst 1990–2000, Mgmnt Ctee The Sea Cadet Corps Barrow-in-Furness Unit 23 TS Sovereign; pres Barrow Chrysanthemum Soc, dep chm Governing Body Dowdales Sch 1995–2000; hon consul of Norway at Barrow-in-Furness; Freeman City of London, Liveryman Worshipful Co of Shipwrights; FCA 1968, FInstD, FRSA; Knight First Class Royal Norwegian Order of Merit; *Recreations* fell walking, fitness, travelling, reading; *Style*— John Hornby, Esq; ✉ Hillside, Guards Road, Lindal, Ulverston, Cumbria LA12 0TN (tel 01229 465614, fax 01229 588061, e-mail jfh@jfhornby.com)

HORNBY, John Hugh; s of Richard Phipps Hornby, of Bowerchalke, Wilts, and Stella, *née* Hichens; *b* 23 January 1954; *Educ* Winchester, Univ of Exeter (BSc); *m* 18 June 1983, Anne Elizabeth Meredydd, da of George Hugh Kenefick Rae (d 1989); 3 s (David Hugh b 1988, Edward John b 1990, Julian Patrick b 1992); *Career* admitted slr 1980, Macfarlanes: joined 1977, ptnr 1987–, currently specialising in property (housing, leisure and agric); *Recreations* ball game sports, vocal classical music; *Clubs* Hurlingham; *Style*— John Hornby, Esq; ✉ Macfarlanes, 10 Norwich Street, London EC4A 1BD (tel 020 7831 9222, fax 020 7831 9607, e-mail john.hornby@macfarlanes.com)

HORNBY, Jonathan Peter; s of Sir Derek Hornby, *qv*, and Sonia Margaret, *née* Beesley; *b* 29 March 1967; *Educ* Marlborough, Univ of Edinburgh (MA); *m* 1; 2 s (Benedict b 1994, Joseph b 1997), 1 da (Arabella b 1995); m 2, Clare, née Griffiths; 2 da (Madeleine b 2004, Grace b 2005); *Career* account dir Ogilvy & Mather Advertising 1993–94 (joined as graduate trainee 1990), client servs dir Collett Dickenson Pearce & Partners 1996–98 (bd account dir 1995–96), jt md TBWA GGT Simons Palmer 1998–2001; fndr Clemmow Hornby Inge 2001; assoc memb D&AD; *Recreations* real tennis (Br Open Handicap champion 1986), lawn tennis, Arsenal FC season ticket holder; *Clubs* Thirty, Marketing Group of GB, Century, Soho House, Home House; *Style*— Johnny Hornby, Esq; ✉ Clemmow Hornby Inge, 7 Rathbone Street, London W1T 1LY (tel 020 7462 8514, e-mail johnny.hornby@chiadvertising.com)

HORNBY, His Hon Judge Keith Anthony Delgado; s of James Lawrence Hornby (d 1993), of Heathfield, E Sussex, and Naomi Ruth, *née* Delgado (d 2003); *b* 18 February 1947; *Educ* Oratory Sch, Trinity Coll Dublin (BA); *m* 14 Feb 1970, Judith Constance, da of Patrick Yelverton Fairbairn; 1 da (Katya Eugenie b 13 Dec 1973), 2 s (Jamie Alexander Fairbairn b 11 Oct 1976, Nicholas Thomas Fairbairn b 11 May 1980); *Career* lectr in commercial law 1969–70; called to the Bar Gray's Inn 1970; recorder of the Crown Court 1992–95 (asst recorder 1988–92), circuit judge (SE Circuit) 1995–; *Recreations* art, theatre, music, golf, tennis, squash; *Clubs* Hurlingham; *Style*— His Hon Judge Keith Hornby; ✉ Bow County Court, 96 Romford Road, Stratford, London E15 4EG (tel 020 8536 5200)

HORNBY, Nicholas Peter John (Nick); s of Sir Derek Hornby, *qv*, and Margaret Withers; *b* 17 April 1957, Maidenhead, Berks; *Educ* Maidenhead GS, Univ of Cambridge; *m* 1, 1993 (m dis), Virginia Bovell; 1 s (Danny b 1993); m 2, 2006, Amanda Posey; 2 s (Lowell b 2002, Jesse b 2004); *Career* author and freelance journalist; former teacher; E M Forster Award American Acad of Arts and Letters 1999, W H Smith Award for Fiction 2002, Writers' Writer Award Orange Word Int Writers Festival 2003; co-fndr TreeHouse (nat educnl charity for children with autism); FRSL; *Books* novels: High Fidelity (1995, film adaptation 2000), About a Boy (1998, film adaptation 2002), How to be Good (2001), A Long Way Down (2005, shortlisted Whitbread Novel of the Year 2005), Slam (2007); non-fiction: Fever Pitch (1992, film adaptations 1997 and 2005), 31 Songs (2003), The Complete Polysyllabic Spree (2006); anthologies: My Favourite Year (ed, 1993), Speaking with the Angel (ed, 2000); *Recreations* Arsenal FC; *Style*— Nick Hornby, Esq; ✉ c/o Caroline Dawnay, Peters Fraser & Dunlop, Drury House, 34–43 Russell Street, London WC2B 5HA (tel 020 7344 1000, fax 020 7836 9539, e-mail postmaster@pfd.co.uk)

HORNBY, Sir Simon Michael; kt (1988); er s of Michael Charles St John Hornby (d 1987), of Pusey House, Faringdon, and Nicolette Joan, *née* Ward (d 1988); *b* 29 December 1934; *Educ* Eton, New Coll Oxford; *m* 15 June 1968, (Ann) Sheran, da of Peter Victor Ferdinand Cazalet, of Kent; *Career* 2 Lt Grenadier Gds 1953–55; W H Smith Group plc: joined 1958, merchandise dir 1968, retail dir 1974, retail md 1977, gp chief exec 1978, chm 1982–94; non-exec chm Lloyds Abbey Life plc 1992–97 (dir 1991–97); non-exec dir: Pearson plc 1978–97, Lloyds Bank plc (now Lloyds TSB Group plc) 1988–99; tstee Br Museum 1975–85, chm Nat Book League 1978–80; memb Cncl: Nat Tst 1978–2001 (memb Exec Ctee 1966–93), RSA 1985–90, Royal Horticultural Soc 1992–2001; chm: Design Cncl 1986–92, Assoc of Business Sponsorship of the Arts 1988–98; pres: Newsvendors' Benevolent Inst 1989–94, The Book Tst 1990–96, RHS 1994–2001, Chelsea Soc 1995–2001, Nat Literacy Tst 2001– (chm 1993–2001); Hon DUniv: Stirling 1993, Reading 1996; Hon DLitt Univ of Hull 1994; FIMgt, FRSA; *Recreations* gardening, music; *Style*— Sir Simon Hornby; ✉ The Ham, Wantage, Oxfordshire OX12 9JA

HORNBY PRIESTNALL, Cdr (Thomas) Keith; VRD (1963 and Clasp 1975); s of Rev Thomas Hornby Priestnall (d 1956), and Norah Hayward (d 1961); *b* 22 June 1925; *Educ* Burton Sch, Univ of Nottingham; *m* 2 Sept 1982, Gillian Christine, da of Police Supt William Edward Thomas Hinckley (d 1977), of Staffs; 1 da (Daniella b 1959); *Career* served WWII Midget Subs (X Craft); chm and md Salesprint and Display Ltd and Salesprint Temple Group Ltd 1963–83, chm Peel House Publicity 1983–; vice-pres E Midland Areas C of C; dir BDI Events and Promotions Ltd; tstee and former nat chm Brewing, Food and Beverage Assoc, chm Burton upon Trent & Uttoxeter SSAFA - Forces Help, pres Trg Ship Modwena Sea Cadet Corps, vice-pres Burton Cons Assoc; memb: Inst of Brewing, Equity; *Recreations* riding, bird watching, sailing; *Clubs* Naval and Military, Army and Navy, The Burton; *Style*— Cdr Keith Hornby Priestnall, VRD*; ✉ Middleton Farm Cottage, Collycroft, Clifton, Asbourne, Derbyshire DE6 2GN (tel 01335 343454, fax 01335 346319, e-mail bdi4keith@aol.com)

HORNE, Sir Alistair Allan; kt (2003), CBE (1992); s of late Sir (James) Allan Horne, and Auriol Camilla, *née* Hay; *b* 9 November 1925; *Educ* Jesus Coll Cambridge (MA, LittD 1993), Le Rosey Switzerland, Millbrook USA; *m* 1, 1953 (m dis 1982), Renira Margaret, da of Adm Sir Geoffrey Hawkins, KBE, CB, MVO, DSC; 3 da; m 2, 1987, Sheelin Ryan Eccles; *Career* served RAF 1943–44, Coldstream Gds 1944–47, Capt attached to Intelligence Serv (ME); foreign corr Daily Telegraph 1952–55; founded Alistair Horne Research Fellowship in Modern History St Antony's Coll Oxford 1969 (supernumerary fell 1978–88, hon fell 1988–), fell Woodrow Wilson Centre Washington DC 1980–81, hon fell Jesus Coll Cambridge 1996–, distinguished visiting scholar Library of Congress USA 2005; lectr, journalist and contrib to a number of books and various periodicals; memb: Mgmnt Ctee Royal Literary Fund 1969–90, Franco-Br Cncl 1979–94, Ctee of Mgmnt Soc of Authors 1979–81; tstee Imperial War Museum 1975–82; Chevalier Légion d'Honneur 1993; FRSL; *Publications* Back into Power (1955), The Land is Bright (1958), Canada and the Canadians (1961), The Price of Glory: Verdun 1916 (1962, Hawthornden Prize 1963), The Fall of Paris: The Siege and the Commune 1870–71 (1965), To Lose a Battle: France

1940 (1969), Death of a Generation (1970), The Terrible Year: The Paris Commune (1971), Small Earthquake in Chile (1972), A Savage War of Peace: Algeria 1954–62 (1972, Yorkshire Post Book of the Year Prize 1978, Wolfson Literary Award 1978), Napoleon Master of Europe 1805–07 (1979), The French Army and Politics 1870–1970 (1984, Enid Macleod Prize), Macmillan 1894–1956, Vol I (1988), Macmillan 1957–86, Vol II (1989), A Bundle from Britain (1993), The Lonely Leader: Monty 1944–45 (1994), How far from Austerlitz? Napoleon 1805–1815 (1996), Telling Lives: From W B Yeats to Bruce Chapman (ed, 2000), Seven Ages of Paris (2002), Age of Napoleon (2004), Friend or Foe (2004); *Recreations* thinking about skiing, talking to dogs, gardening; *Clubs* Garrick, Beefsteak; *Style—* Sir Alistair Horne, CBE, LittD; ✉ The Old Vicarage, Turville, Henley-on-Thames, Oxfordshire RG9 6QU

HORNE, Christopher Malcolm; CVO (1996); s of Gerald Fitzlait Horne (d 1970), and Dora, *née* Hartley; *b* 14 June 1941; *Educ* King Edward VI Chelmsford; *m* 12 Sept 1964, Christine Ann, da of Reginald Arthur Fradley (d 1985); 2 s (Darren James b 7 Feb 1968, Alec Gerald b 20 Jan 1970); *Career* Coutts & Co 1958–97: head of personnel 1980–88, assoc dir 1980–89, sec of Bank 1988–, sr assoc dir 1989–97, co sec Coutts & Co Group 1991–97; memb Vines Rochester United Reformed Church, chm of tstees Vines Centre Tst 1998–2001; *Recreations* golf, gardening, interest in most sports; *Clubs* Rochester & Cobham Park Golf, Castle (Rochester); *Style—* Christopher Horne, Esq, CVO; ✉ Silver Birches, 151 Maidstone Road, Chatham, Kent ME4 6JE (tel 01634 847594, fax 01634 306291, e-mail chrishorne@blueyonder.co.uk)

HORNE, Geoffrey Norman; s of Albert Edward Horne (d 1982), of Berks, and Doris Irene, *née* Blackman; *b* 7 February 1941; *Educ* Slough GS, Open Univ (BA); *m* 1, 1967 (m dis 1977), Barbara Ann Mary; 1 s (Rupert b 1971); m 2, 1980, Davina Dorothy, da of David Lockwood London, of Dyfed; 2 s (Edward b 1984, Richard b 1986); *Career* advertising exec; sr writer: CDP 1973–74, Davidson Pearce Berry and Spottiswoode 1974–77, Saatchi and Saatchi 1985–88; bd dir: KMP Partnership 1978–84 (creative dir 1977–84), Grandfield Rork Collins 1984–85 (creative gp head 1984–85), Saatchi and Saatchi 1985–88, Freeland 1988–; over 70 advtg awards incl: Br Advertising Press awards, D & AD Assoc awards, NY One Show, Br Advertising TV awards, The Creative Circle; MIPA, MCAM; *Recreations* cooking, reading, travel; *Clubs* Phyllis Court; *Style—* Geoffrey Horne, Esq; ✉ Pine Ridge, 46 Altwood Road, Maidenhead, Berkshire

HORNE, Sir (Alan) Gray Antony; 3 Bt (UK 1929), of Shackleford, Surrey; s of Antony Edgar Alan Horne (d 1954; only s of 2 Bt, Sir Alan Edgar Horne, MC, who died 1984), and Valentine Antonia (d 1981), da of Valentine Dudensing, of Thenon, Dordogne, France and 55 East 57th St, New York City; *b* 11 July 1948; *m* 1980, Cecile Rose, da of Jacques Desplanche, of 5 rue de Cheverny, Romorantin, France; *Heir* none; *Style—* Sir Gray Horne, Bt

HORNE, Dr Nigel William; s of Eric Charles Henry Horne (d 1963), and late Edith Margaret, *née* Boyd; *b* 13 September 1940; *Educ* Lower Sch of John Lyon Harrow, Univ of Bristol (BSc), Univ of Cambridge (PhD); *m* 30 Oct 1965, Jennifer Ann, da of William Henry Holton (d 1988); 2 da (Catherine b 1967, Joanna b 1973), 1 s (Peter b 1970); *Career* dir and gen mangr GEC Telecommunications Ltd 1976–81, md GEC Information Systems Ltd 1981–83, dir Tech and Corp Devpt STC plc 1983–89, IT ptnr KPMG Peat Marwick 1989–92 (special advsr 1992–98); non-exec chm: Alcatel UK Ltd 1992–2001, STC Submarine Systems 1994–96, IMS Maxims plc 2000, Aspex Semiconductor 2002–; dir: Abingworth plc 1985–90, Abingworth Management Ltd 1993–97, FI Group plc 1993–98, Wireless Systems International Ltd 1995–2001, Onyvax Ltd 1997–2002, Foresight VCT plc 1997–, Parc Technologies Ltd 1999–2000, Sarantel Ltd 2000–02, Jersey Telecom Gp 2002–, Alan Dick Ltd 2006–; interim dir of engrg Nat Air Traffic Servs 2005–06; memb Esprit Advsy Bd EC 1986–93, chm IT Advsy Bd DTI 1988–91, memb ACOST Cabinet Office 1990–93, memb Strategy Advsy Gp DGIII EC 1994–98 (chm Software and Multimedia Advsy Gp); visiting prof Univ of Bristol 1990–98; Hon DEng Univ of Bristol 1993; Hon DSc: Univ of Hull 1993, City Univ London 1994; Freeman City of London, memb Worshipful Co of Info Technologists; FIIM 1979, FREng 1982, FRSA 1983, FIEE 1984, CIMgt 1992; Caballeros del Monasteria de Yuste (Spain) 1993; *Recreations* piano, music, gardening; *Clubs* Athenaeum; *Style—* Dr Nigel Horne, FREng

HORNE, Prof (Charles Hugh) Wilson; MBE; s of Charles Hugh Wilson Horne (d 1977), and Jean, *née* Wells; *b* 13 September 1938; *Educ* Ardrossan Acad, Univ of Glasgow (MB ChB, MD), Univ of Aberdeen (DSc); *m* 5 Sept 1964, Agnes Irvine, da of Joseph Scott (d 1977); 1 da (Glenda May b 16 Nov 1966), 1 s ((Charles Hugh) Wilson b 25 Oct 1969); *Career* lectr in pathology Univ of Glasgow 1966–73; Univ of Aberdeen: sr lectr in pathology 1973–80, prof of immunopathology 1980–84; Univ of Newcastle upon Tyne: prof of pathology 1984–97, head Sch of Pathological Sciences 1988–95; chm Novocastra Labs Newcastle upon Tyne 1989–2005, conslt Vision Biosystems 2005–06; author of numerous pubns on immunology and pathology; FRCPath, FRCPEd; *Recreations* philately, rugby union; *Style—* Prof Wilson Horne, MBE; ✉ 12 Adderstone Crescent, Jesmond, Newcastle upon Tyne NE2 2HH (tel 0191 281 3695, e-mail chorne@aol.com)

HORNE-ROBERTS, Jennifer; da of Frederick William Horne (d 1969), and Daisy Jessie Elizabeth, *née* Norman; *b* 15 February 1949; *Educ* State Schs NW London, Univ of Perugia (Dip Italian), Univ of London (BA); *m* 29 April 1987, Keith Michael Peter Roberts, s of Gerald Roberts (d 1962); 1 s (Harry Alexander b 29 June 1989), 1 da (Francesca Elizabeth b 24 July 1990); *Career* called to the Bar Middle Temple 1976, ad eundem memb Inner Temple; dir of family co; contrib pubns on: political issues, family law, employment law, human rights, literature; Parly candidate: (Lab) Fareham 1974, (Alliance) Medway 1987, (Lib Dem) Holborn and St Pancras 1992; cncllr (Lab) Camden 1971–74; founder and first chair Assoc of Women Barristers; memb: Bar Assocs, Family Law Bar Assoc, Bar European Gp, Soc of Labour Lawyers (chair Family Law Ctee, memb Exec Ctee), Human Rights Lawyers Assoc (memb Exec Ctee), Personal Injury Bar Assoc; former memb Young Bar Ctee; fndr Alliance for Govt of National Unity 1994; memb: Tate Gallery, Royal Acad of Arts, Highgate Literary and Scientific Inst; former govr Parliament Hill Secdy Sch London; *Books* Trade Unionists and the Law (1984), Justice for Children (1992), New Frontiers in Family Law (1998), Labour's True Way Forward (2000), Labour's Agenda (2002), Selected Poems (2002), In Harm's Way: The MMRIO Story (co-author, 2006), Access to Justice (co-author, 2006); *Recreations* art, writing, visual and literary arts, politics, travel; *Clubs* Highgate Golf, Arts; *Style—* Mrs Jennifer Horne-Roberts; ✉ Goldsmith Chambers, Temple, London EC4Y 7BL (tel 020 7272 2245, e-mail e-mail keith@horne-roberts.co.uk, website www.horne-roberts.co.uk)

HORNER, John Patrick Francis; s of Arthur William Horner, CMG, TD (d 1999), and Patsy Denise, *née* Campbell (d 1993); *b* 20 September 1946; *Educ* St Mary's Sch Nairobi, Stafford House Tutorial Coll London; *m* 1, 1964 (m dis 1973), Diana Pring; 1 s (Jeremy b 20 Sept 1964), 2 da (Geraldine b 4 Oct 1968, Annelise b 16 Aug 1980); m 2, 1974 (m dis 1982), Nicola Bates; 2 da (Sophie b 4 June 1985, Clio b 17 June 1988); m 3, 1999, Penelope, da of late Christopher Gray; *Career* in advtg: Dorland 1965–68, Leo Burnett 1968–73, Kirkwood Co 1973–83 (md 1981–83); fndr Horner, Collis and Kirvan 1983 (subsequently sold to Eurocom Gp), joined Conzept Strategic Systems 1993, headhunted by J Walter Thompson to set up Blue Logic (strategic brand and new product devpt consultancy) 1997; clients incl: Kellogg's, Boots, The Post Office, Sainsbury's, Homebase, CPC; chief exec Models 1 1999– (led mgmnt buyout), dir of mktg Dr Foster Ltd, non-exec chm Shownet, non-exec dir Snowteam; small business mentor Prince's Tst, tstee Jaipur Heritage; memb Cncl Assoc of Model Agencies 1999; FIPA 1992; *Recreations* classical music, travel, cooking, reading, business; *Style—* John Horner, Esq; ✉ Models 1 Ltd, 12 Macklin Street, London WC2B 5SZ (e-mail jh@johnhorner.com)

HORNER, Prof (Robert) Malcolm Wigglesworth; s of James William Horner (d 1986), and Emma Mary, *née* Wigglesworth (d 1977); *b* 27 July 1942; *Educ* Bolton Sch, UCL (BSc, PhD); *m* 21 March 1970, Beverley Anne, *née* Wesley, da of Ewart Alexander (d 1986); 1 da (Victoria b 10 Sept 1977), 1 s (Jonathan b 3 Oct 1980); *Career* Taylor Woodrow Construction Ltd: civil engr 1966–72, engrg rep W Germany 1972–74, site agent 1974–77; Univ of Dundee: lectr Dept of Civil Engrg 1977–83, sr lectr 1983–86, head of dept 1985–91, prof of engrg mgmnt 1986–2006 (emeritus prof of engrg mgmnt 2006–), chair Sch of Engrg and Physical Sciences 1997–99, dir of enterprise mgmnt 2000–05, dep princ 2002–06; dir Atlantic Power and Gas Ltd 1993–99, dir Objective 3 Partnership 2000–03 (dep chair 2002–03); chm Winton Caledonian Ltd 1995–97, md International Maintenance Management 1996–97; dir Scottish Enterprise Tayside 2003– (chair 2005–), fndr chm Tayside branch Opening Windows on Engrg 1980–85, chm ICE Scotland Mgmnt Bd 2007–; memb: ICE Working Pty on Strategy Construction Mgmnt Res 1987–89, Technol Foresight Construction Sector Panel 1994–98, Science and Engrg Advsy Ctee Br Cncl 1992–2005, Editorial Bd Construction Mgmnt and Economics 1991–94, Bd and Mgmnt Exec Scottish Inst for Enterprise 2000–05 (chair Mgmnt Exec 2003–05); govr Duncan of Jordanstone Coll of Art 1990–92; chm: Educn Ctee Engrg Cncl Regnl Orgn Mgmnt Ctee (E Scotland) 1988–91, Scottish Int Resource Project Steering Gp 1993–95, Friends of St Paul's Cathedral 1993–95; dir: Dundee Repertory Theatre Ltd 1991–2006, CAB Dundee 2003–05; memb Cncl Nat Conf of Univ Profs 1989–93; CEng, FRSE, FICE, MCMI; *Recreations* gardening, amateur dramatics; *Clubs* Rotary; *Style—* Prof Malcolm Horner; ✉ Westfield Cottage, 11 Westfield Place, Dundee DD1 4JU (tel 01382 225933, fax 01382 229721); Division of Civil Engineering, The University, Dundee DD1 4HN (tel 01382 344350, fax 01382 344816, telex 76293, e-mail r.m.w.horner@dundee.ac.uk)

HORNSBY, Guy Philip; s of Norman Dalton Hornsby (d 1970), and Yvonne Betty Hornsby (d 1997), of Twickenham, Middx; *b* 24 March 1958; *Educ* Emanuel Sch; *Partner* (civil partnership, 8 July 2006), Michael Clement Charles Gray, s of Robert Arnold Gray (d 2005), and Dolores Ameé Alexandra Gray; *Career* computer programmer and company liaison supervisor Head Office Honda (UK) Ltd 1978–79; BBC Radio London: joined 1979 as reporter and prodn asst on daily arts prog, variously asst prodr Robbie Vincent Prog, prodr Tony Blackburn Show, presenter/prodr London Weekend and London This Week, exec prodr Radio London Unemployment Festival of Music, prodr BBC Children in Need prog, prodr daily afternoon music prog; outside broadcast presenter Saturday Superstore BBC TV 1984, prodr Popular Music Unit BBC World Service 1984–85, continuity announcer TVS Southampton 1986–90; Southern Radio plc (formerly Ocean Sound plc): presenter breakfast show then prodr and presenter afternoon prog 1986–90, prog mangr Ocean Sound and South Coast Radio 1990–92, gp prog controller Southern Radio plc 1992–94; md Kiss 102 Manchester 1994–96, gp chief exec Kiss 102 Manchester and Kiss 105 Yorkshire 1996–97; dir: IT Computer Systems Ltd 1999–, Out UK 2000–, Out Europe 2000–; exec dir Riverside Studios Hammersmith 2006–; chief exec Assembly Media Gp 2006–; International Radio Award for Sweet Soul Music series BBC World Service 1985 (prodr and writer); memb: BFI, Stonewall; *Recreations* music, cinema, computers, swimming; *Style—* Guy Hornsby; ✉ Roosveltlaan 95/1, 1079AG, Amsterdam, The Netherlands (tel 00 31 20 6464 281); 1928 Willow Wood Drive, Kissimmee, Florida 34746, USA (tel 00 1 407 933 1928, fax 00 1 407 933 1924, e-mail guyhornsby@consultant.com, website www.guyhornsby.com)

HORNSBY, Timothy Richard; s of Harker William Hornsby (d 1973), and Agnes Nora Phillips (d 1992); *b* 22 September 1940; *Educ* Bradfield Coll, ChCh Oxford (MA); *m* 1971, Charmian Rosemary, da of Frederick Cleland Newton (d 2001), of Weybridge, Surrey; 1 da (Gabrielle b 1975), 1 s (Adrian b 1977); *Career* Harkness fell 1961–63, res lectr ChCh Oxford 1964–65, HM Treasy 1971–73, dir ancient monuments historic bldgs and rural affrs DOE 1983–88, DG Nature Conservancy Cncl 1988–91; chief exec: Royal Borough of Kingston upon Thames 1991–95, National Lottery Charities Board 1995–2001; cmmr National Lottery Cmmn 2001–; chair: Public Fundraising Regulatory Assoc 2002–, Harkness Fellows Assoc 2002–, Horniman Museum 2004–; memb Bd Consumer Cncl for Water; tstee Charles Darwin Tst, govr Legacy Tst, tstee Int Inst for Environment and Devpt, tstee Royal Botanic Gardens Kew 2007–; *Recreations* conservation, skiing; *Clubs* Athenaeum; *Style—* Timothy Hornsby, Esq; ✉ The National Lottery Commission, 101 Wigmore Street, London W1U 1QU (tel 020 7016 3434, mobile 07785 376172, e-mail thornsby@timothyhornsby.freeserve.co.uk)

HORNYOLD-STRICKLAND, 8 Count Della Catena (Malta 1745); Henry Charles; s of Lt Cdr Thomas Henry Hornyold-Strickland, DSC, RN, 7 Count della Catena (d 1983), of Sizergh Castle, Kendal, Cumbria, and Angela Mary, *née* Engleheart; *b* 15 December 1951; *Educ* Ampleforth, Exeter Coll Oxford (BA), INSEAD Fontainebleau (MBA); *m* 1979, Claudine Thérèse, da of Clovis Poumirau, of Hossegor, France; 2 s (Hugo b 1979, Thomas b 1985); *Career* engr Rolls Royce Ltd 1970–76, mgmnt conslt Arthur D Little Ltd 1977–84, ind mgmnt conslt 1984–; dir: Allied Newspapers Ltd (Malta) 1988–, Progress Press (Malta) 1988–, Allied Insurance Agency (Malta) 1991–2002, Logical Processes Ltd 1997–98, Oxford Creativity Ltd 2000–06, Media Maker Ltd (Malta) 2004–; Knight of Honour and Devotion SMOM 1977; *Clubs* IOD; *Style—* Henry Hornyold-Strickland, Esq (Count della Catena); ✉ Sizergh Castle, Kendal, Cumbria LA8 8AE (fax 015395 61481, mobile 07775 894650, e-mail hstrickland@luna.co.uk)

HOROVITZ, Joseph; s of Dr Bela Horovitz (d 1955), and Lotte Horovitz (d 2003); *b* 26 May 1926; *Educ* City of Oxford HS, New Coll Oxford (MA, BMus); *m* 16 Aug 1956, Anna Naomi, da of Frederic Moses Landau, of London; 2 da; *Career* WWII Army Educn Corps 1943–44; music dir Bristol Old Vic 1949–51, conductor Ballets Russes 1952, music staff Glyndebourne Opera 1956, prof of composition RCM 1961–, dir Performing Rights Soc 1969–96, pres Conseil International des Auteurs de Musique 1981–89; compositions incl: 16 ballets incl Alice in Wonderland, Ninotchka (opera), two one act operas, five string quartets, eleven concertos, works for orchestra, brass band, wind band and choirs incl Capt Noah and his Floating Zoo; Son et Lumière incl: St Paul's Cathedral, Canterbury Cathedral, Royal Pavilion Brighton, Chartwell; numerous TV scores incl: Search for the Nile, Lillie, The Tempest, Twelfth Night, Agatha Christie Series, Dorothy L Sayers Series, Rumpole of the Bailey; memb: Royal Soc of Musicians 1968, Cncl Composers Guild of GB 1970–99; winner: Cwlth Medal for Composition 1959, Ivor Novello Award 1976 and 1979, Nino Rota Prize Italy 2002; FRCM 1981; Gold Order of Merit of Vienna 1996; *Recreations* books; *Style—* Joseph Horovitz, Esq; ✉ The Royal College of Music, Prince Consort Road, London SW7

HOROWITZ, Anthony; *b* 1956, Stanmore, Middx; *Educ* Rugby, Univ of York (BA); *m* Jill Green, *qv*; 2 s (Nicholas b 1989, Cassian b 1991); *Career* novelist, children's author and scriptwriter; early career as advtg copywriter with McCann Erickson; *Theatre* Theatre Mindgame; *Television* Foyle's War (ITV), Midsomer Murders (ITV), Murder in Mind (BBC), Agatha Christie's Poirot (ITV), Murder Most Horrid (BBC), Crime Traveller (BBC), Anna Lee (ITV), The Last Englishman (BBC), Robin of Sherwood (ITV); *Film* The Gathering, Just Ask For Diamond, Stormbreaker; *Awards* Red House Children's Book Award 2003 (for Skeleton Key), Lew Grade Audience Award 2003 (for Foyle's War); *Books* The Alex Rider series, Raven's Gate, The Killing Joke, Granny, The Switch, Groosham Grange, Return to Groosham Grange, Horowitz Horror, More Horowitz Horror, Myths and Legends, The Sinister Secret of Frederick K Bower, Misha, The Magician and the Mysterious Amulet, The Devil's Doorbell, The Night of The Scorpion, The Silver

H

Citadel, The Day of the Dragon, Evil Star; *Recreations* scuba diving, cinema; *Style*— Anthony Horowitz, Esq; ✉ c/o Walker Books, 87 Vauxhall Walk, London SE11 5HJ (tel 020 7793 0909)

HORRIDGE, Chris P; s of Colin Horridge, of Lincoln, and Carol Ann, *née* Blain; *b* 2 June 1970, RAF Nocton Hall, Lincs; *Educ* Castle Hills Sch Gainsborough, Gainsborough Coll of FE, Tidworth Coll; *Career* RAF 1988–97, sr chef de partie Le Petit Blanc restaurant Oxford 1997–98, demi chef de partie to sr sous chef Le Manoir aux Quat'Saisons Great Milton 1998–2003, Gordon Ramsay Holdings (Petrus, Gordon Ramsay at Royal Hospital Road, Marcus Wareing at The Savoy) 2003, private chef to Canadian entrepreneur 2003–05, head chef The Bath Priory 2005– (1 Michelin Star); Caterer and Hotel Keeper Acorn Award 2000; *Recreations* botany, country pursuits, gastronomy, classic cars; *Clubs* Wine Soc, Salisbury and Dist Angling; *Style*— Chris Horridge, Esq; ✉ The Bath Priory, Weston Road, Bath BA1 2XT (tel 01225 478394, e-mail chris.horridge@thebathpriory.co.uk)

HORROCKS, (Barbara) Jane; da of John Horrocks, of Rossendale, Lancs, and Barbara, *née* Ashworth; *b* 18 January 1964; *Educ* Fearns Co Secdy Sch, Oldham Coll of Technol, RADA (Bronze medal); *Career* actress; *Theatre* RSC (joined 1985) incl: Hetty in The Dillon, Flo in Mary After the Queen, Phoebe in As You Like It; other roles incl: Fanny in Ask For The Moon (Hampstead) 1986, various parts in Road (Royal Court) 1987, Beatrice in A Colliers Friday Night (Greenwich) 1987, Sherry in Valued Friends (Hampstead) 1989, Teddy in The Debutante Ball (Hampstead) 1989, Sylvie in Our Own Kind (Bush) 1991, Little Voice in The Rise and Fall of Little Voice (RNT and Aldwych) 1992, Sally Bowles in Cabaret (Donmar) 1994, Lady Macbeth in Macbeth (Greenwich) 1995, Mrs Trevel in Sweet Panic (Duke of York's) 2003–04; *Television* BBC incl: Road 1987, Heartland 1988, Nona 1990, Alive and Kicking 1991, Came Out, It Rained, Went Back In Again 1991, Roots 1991, Absolutely Fabulous (5 series) 1992–94 and 2001–03, Bad Girl 1992, Suffer the Little Children 1994, Nightlife (BBC Scotland) 1995, Henry IV (parts I and II) 1995, Mirrorball 2000, Linda Green 2002; Channel 4 incl: Storyteller 1988, Self Catering (TV film) 1993, Never Mind the Horrocks 1996; other credits incl: Cabaret (Carlton) 1994, Some Kind of Life (Granada) 1995, Tales from the Crypt (HBO) 1996, Hunting Venus 1998, The Flint Street Nativity (ITV) 1998, Jericho (ITV) 2005, The Street (BBC) 2005, The Amazing Mrs Pritchard (BBC) 2006; *Film* incl: The Dressmaker 1987, The Wolves of Willoughby Chase 1988, Witches 1988, Getting It Right 1988, Memphis Belle 1989, Life Is Sweet 1990, Deadly Advice 1993, Second Best 1993, Bring Me the Head of Mavis Davis 1996, Little Voice 1997, Born Romantic 2000, Chicken Run 2000, Feathers (short) 2002, Corpse Bride 2006; *Awards* LA Film Critics' Award and American Nat Soc of Film Critics' Award for Best Supporting Actress 1991 (for Life Is Sweet); Royal Television Soc Award for Best Actress and Banff Television Festival Special Jury Award (for Suffer the Little Children); *Recordings* The Further Adventures of Little Voice (2000); *Style*— Ms Jane Horrocks; ✉ c/o ICM, Oxford House, 76 Oxford Street, London W1D 1BS (tel 020 7636 6565)

HORROCKS, Peter Leslie; s of (Arthur Edward) Leslie Horrocks (d 2005), of Beaconsfield, Bucks, and Phillis Margaret Chiene, *née* Bartholomew; *b* 31 January 1955; *Educ* Winchester, Trinity Hall Cambridge (MA); *m* 15 Sept 1995, Catherine Alicia Brinsley, er da of Dr (Moryd) Brinsley Sheridan; 1 s (Edward Leslie Sheridan b 26 March 1997); *Career* called to the Bar Middle Temple 1977 and Lincoln's Inn 1987, in private practice 1978–; memb Cncl Royal Stuart Soc 1987–, pres Covent Garden Minuet Co 2004–, chm Sherlock Holmes Soc of London 1999–2003; Freeman City of London 1982; FRAS 1984; *Recreations* travel, real tennis, cricket, Sherlock Holmes, opera, collecting books, dancing the minuet; *Clubs* MCC, Travellers, Royal Tennis Court, City Pickwick; *Style*— Peter Horrocks, Esq; ✉ 1 Garden Court, Temple, London EC4Y 9BJ (tel 020 7797 7900, fax 020 7797 7929)

HORROX, Alan; s of Stanley Horrox, and Gudrun Jonsdottir; *b* 3 January 1947; *Educ* St John's Sch Leatherhead, Christ's Coll Cambridge; *m* Viveka Britt Inger, da of Torsten Nyberg, of Föllinge, Sweden; 2 da (Anna Helga b 1981, Katarina b 1983); *Career* prodr-dir of children's progs BBC, educn progs, dramas and documentaries Thames TV (controller Children's and Educn Dept 1986–92), md Tetra Films 1992–, prof of film and media Univ of Hertfordshire 2006–; *Television* incl: Our People, Small World, Accidental Death of an Anarchist, A Foreign Body, Voices in the Dark, The Belle of Amherst, Rose, The Gemini Factor, Catherine, Ingmar Bergman-The Magic Lantern, The Thief, Young Charlie Chaplin, The Green Eyed Monster, Brief Lives, Rosie The Great, Somewhere to Run, Handle with Care, Spatz, Lorna Doone, Forget About Me, Long Way Home, The Strangers, Sea Dragon, A Small Dance, Time Riders, Pirate Prince, Romeo and Juliet, Tomorrow People, The Merchant of Venice, Delta Wave, Treasure Seekers, Canterville Ghost, The Gift, Bill's New Frock, Magic with Everything, What Katy Did; *Film* London Film Festival Screenings: Forget About Me 1990, A Small Dance 1991, Under The Sun 1992, Faith 1996; *Awards* Int Emmy 1987, Special Jury Award at the San Francisco Film Festival 1988, Valladolid Int Film Festival Award 1988, Special Prize for Fiction Prix Europa 1988, 1989 and 1991, Prime Time Emmy Nomination 1989, BAFTA Nominations 1989, 1990, 1991, 1995, 1996, 1997 and 1998 Chicago Int Film Festival Special Live Action Award 1990, RTS Enid Love Award Nomination 1990 and 1991, Writers' Guild Award B&B 1992 (nomination 1995), Japan Prize 1996, runner up BFI Children's Award 1995, Special FX Monitor Award 1996, RTS Award 1996, 1997 and 1998, Houston Gold Award 1997 and 1998, Best TV Movie Monte Carlo 1999; *Style*— Alan Horrox; ✉ Tetra Films Ltd, 24 Stormont Road, London N6 4NP (tel 020 8374 4553, e-mail horrox@blueyonder.co.uk)

HORSBRUGH, Oliver Bethune; s of Archibald Walter Bethune Horsbrugh (d 1973), of London, and Sheila May, *née* Beckett-Overy; *b* 13 November 1937; *Educ* St Pauls; *m* 6 Oct 1962, Josephine Elsa, *née* Hall; 1 s (Edward b 8 Feb 1966 d 10 Dec 2005), 1 da (Rebecca b 1 Feb 1969); *Career* Nat Serv RN 1956–58, GSM 1957; TV 1958–: BBC TV staff dir 30 minute theatres Newcomers and Boy Meets Girl 1968–71; freelance TV dir 1971– incl: Z Cars, The Brothers, Crown Court, Coronation Street, Emmerdale (winner Best Soap BAFTA Awards 2000), A Kind of Loving, Cribb, Fallen Hero, Bergerac, Juliet Bravo, The Gibraltar Inquest, Birmingham 6 Appeal; dir: various corp videos, trg films, ITN bulletins; memb Dir's Guild of GB, BAFTA; *Recreations* sport, photography, enjoying food and wine, visiting the cinema and theatre, history of cinema buildings; *Clubs* MCC, BAFTA; *Style*— Oliver Horsbrugh, Esq; ✉ 23 Bishops Mansions, Bishops Park Road, Fulham, London SW6 6DZ (tel 020 7731 8325)

HORSBRUGH-PORTER, Sir John Simon; 4 Bt (UK 1902), of Merrion Sq, City and Co of Dublin; s of Col Sir Andrew Marshall Horsbrugh-Porter, 3 Bt, DSO and Bar (d 1986), and (Annette) Mary, *née* Browne-Clayton (d 1992); *b* 18 December 1938; *Educ* Winchester, Trinity Coll Cambridge; *m* 18 July 1964, Lavinia Rose, 2 da of Ralph Meredyth Turton, of Kildale Hall, Whitby; 2 da (Anna (Mrs Nicholas McNulty) b 1965, Zoë (Mrs Nicholas Curtis) b 1967), 1 s ((Andrew) Alexander Marshall b 1971); *Heir* s, Alexander Horsbrugh-Porter; *Career* Nat Serv 2 Lt 12 Lancers (Germany and Cyprus) 1957–59; schoolmaster; *Recreations* music, literature; *Style*— Sir John Horsbrugh-Porter, Bt; ✉ Bowers Croft, Coleshill, Amersham, Buckinghamshire HP7 0LS (tel 01494 724596, e-mail horsb.bower@virgin.net)

HORSBURGH, (Monica) Jill; da of Edward Michael Horsburgh, and Jean Isabella, *née* McKie; *Educ* Ipswich HS GDST, St Hilda's Coll Oxford, Univ of Leicester (CertEd); *Career* history teacher Downe House 1974–78; Benenden: head of history 1978–88, housemistress 1982–93, dep head and dir of residence 1988–96; headmistress Godolphin 1996–; inspector ISI 2001; memb: GSA 1996, SHA 1996; *Recreations* equestrianism; hill walking, the countryside, travel, literature, music, dogs; *Style*— Ms Jill Horsburgh; ✉ The Wilderness, Shady Bower, Salisbury, Wiltshire SP1 2RE (tel 01722 430518); The Godolphin School, Milford Hill, Salisbury, Wiltshire SP1 2RA (tel 01722 430500, fax 01722 430521, e-mail horsburghjill@godolphin.wilts.sch.uk)

HORSEY, John Sebastian Norman James; s of Rev Frank Bokenham Horsey (d 1970), of Broadwindsor, Dorset, and Maria Luisa de Montezuma (d 1973); *b* 26 November 1938; *Educ* St John's Sch Leatherhead, City Univ London (Dip Horology and Instrument Technol); *m* 1 (m dis); 3 s (Jonathan Charles b 25 Dec 1964, Guy Anthony b 29 July 1966, Mark Edward b 14 Sept 1968), 1 da (Charlotte Rosemary Louise b 23 June 1973), 1 step s (Thomas Duncan Stewart b 20 Feb 1972); *m* 2, 28 Oct 1978 (Eveline) Theresa Paton, slr and dep dist judge, da of Dr Edward Harry Stewart Weston (d 1968), of Charter Alley, Hampshire; 1 s (Oliver George Sebastian b 10 Dec 1979), 1 da (Natasha Annabel Clare b 13 April 1985); *Career* admitted slr 1966; sr ptnr Horsey Lightly Fynn Slrs; vice-chm: W Berkshire Mencap, Parochial Church Cncl St Katharine's Savernake Forest; chm Savernake Team Cncl, tstee Berkshire Community Fndn; memb Law Soc 1966; *Recreations* music, riding, tennis, motorcycling, shooting, golf; *Style*— John Horsey, Esq; ✉ Durley House, Durley, Marlborough, Wiltshire SN8 3AZ (tel 01672 810217); Horsey Lightly Fynn, 20 West Mills, Newbury, Berkshire (tel 01635 580858, fax 01635 582813)

HORSFALL TURNER, Jonathan; s of Harold Horsfall Turner, CBE (d 1981), and Eileen Mary, *née* Jenkins (d 1999); *b* 27 November 1945; *Educ* The King's Sch Canterbury, Gonville & Caius Coll Cambridge (MA); *m* 25 Aug 1973, Yvonne Roberts, da of Angus Munro Thomson (d 1971); 1 da (Olivia Jane b 1980); *Career* admitted slr 1970; Allen & Overy: ptnr 1973–2001, conslt 2001–05; carried out res on Eng Medieval Graffiti of Canterbury Cathedral 1963–67 (manuscripts in cathedral library and results published by Canterbury Cathedral Chronicles); Freeman Worshipful Co of Slrs 1973; memb Law Soc 1970; *Recreations* architecture, antiques, opera, canals; *Clubs* Garrick; *Style*— Jonathan Horsfall Turner, Esq

HORSHAM, Bishop of 1993–; Rt Rev Lindsay Goodall Urwin; s of William Edward Urwin, and Beryl Jesse, *née* Towler; *b* 13 March 1956, Melbourne, Australia; *Educ* Camberwell C of E Boys' GS Canterbury Victoria Aust, Trinity Coll Melbourne, Ripon Coll Cuddesdon Oxford (CertTheol (Oxon)), Heythorp Coll London (MA); *Career* clerk Dept of Social Servs Australian Govt 1973 and 1975–76, on staff Double M Club community and social centre St Mary Magdalen Munster Square London 1976–77; ordained 1980; asst curate St Peter Walworth Southwark Dio 1980–83, vicar St Faith Red Post Hill Southwark Dio 1983–88, diocesan missioner Chichester Dio 1988–93; guardian Shrine of Our Lady of Walsingham 2006–; memb: Southwark Diocesan Synod 1982 and 1986–88, Archdeaconry Pastoral Ctee 1986–88; chm Southwark Diocesan Church Union 1985–88, diocesan dir Cursillo spiritual renewal movement Southwark Dio 1985–88; nat chm Church Union 1995–99; memb: At Home Ctee Gen Synod Bd of Mission, Renewal and Evangelism 1992–95, Diocesan Ctee for Social Responsibility Chichester Dio 1991–94; tstee Cuthbert Bardsley Evangelism Award; provost Southern Region Woodland Corp of Schs 2006–; memb Archbishop's Coll of Evangelists 2000–; OGS 1991 (UK Provincial 1996–2005); *Publications* study courses: Before We Go (audio, 1989), Prayer Together for the New Evangelisation (1991), Food for the Journey (1993), Credo (1997), A Youthful Spirit (co-ed, 1998); *Style*— The Rt Rev the Bishop of Horsham, OGS; ✉ Bishop's House, 21 Guildford Road, Horsham, West Sussex RH12 1LU (tel 01403 211139, fax 01403 217349, e-mail bishhorsham@clara.net)

HORSLER, Valerie Anne (Val); da of Terence Patrick Sheen, and Gwenllian Margaret, *née* Jones; *Educ* Ursuline Convent Wimbledon, Girton Coll Cambridge (open exhbn, Netball half blue); *Family* 2 da (Emily Katharine Allison b 1981, Polly Elizabeth Allison b 1985); *Career* managing ed Cncl for Br Archaeology 1977–86; English Heritage: memb pubns team 1986–94, head of publishing 1994–2004; *Books* England's Heritage (contrib, 2001), Royal Heritage: Kings and Queens at English Heritage Sites (2002), Living The Past (2003), This Spectred Isle (co-written with Susan Kelleher, photographed by Sir Simon Marsden, Bt, *qv*, 2005), All for Love: Seven Centuries of Illicit Liaison (2006), Jack the Ripper (2007); *Recreations* travel, history, cookery, The Times crossword; *Style*— Ms Val Horsler; ✉ 4C Prince of Wales Terrace, Deal, Kent CT14 7BS (tel 01304 360505, e-mail val.horsler@virgin.net)

HORSLEY, Adrian Mark; JP; s of (Ian) Mark Horsley (d 1999) and Patricia Horsley, JP, *née* Farrell (d 1994); *b* 12 April 1949; *Educ* Ampleforth, Leicester Sch of Architecture (DipArch); *m* 28 Sept 1974, Louise Jane, da of Peter Bentham Oughtred, JP (d 1999); 2 s (Adam b 1979, Luke b 1982); *Career* architect; Gelder & Kitchen: joined 1974, ptnr 1978–2004, managing ptnr 1994–2004, conslt 2004–; former pres N Humberside Soc of Architects, former chm Yorks Region RIBA; memb: Magistrates' Assoc of E Yorks, Hull Civic Soc, Georgian Soc of E Yorks; tstee: Hull and E Riding Charitable Tst, Lees Rest Homes; Govr Co of Merchant Adventurers of the City of York 2004 (joined 1978); RIBA 1976, ACIArb 1980, memb Assoc of Project Mangrs 1994; *Recreations* shooting, tennis, croquet, gardening; *Style*— Adrian Horsley, Esq; ✉ Gelder & Kitchen, Architects, Maister House, High Street, Hull HU1 1NL (tel 01482 324114, fax 01482 227003, mobile 07710 919873, e-mail adrianhorsley@gelderandkitchen.co.uk)

HORSLEY, Very Rev Dr Alan Avery; s of Reginald James Horsley, of Staffs, and Edith Irene, *née* Allen; *b* 13 May 1936; *Educ* Worcester Royal GS, Northampton GS, St Chad's Coll Durham (BA), The Queen's Coll at Birmingham Univ of Birmingham, Pacific Western Univ (MA, PhD); *Career* curate: Daventry 1960–63, St Giles Reading 1963–64, St Paul Wokingham 1964–66; vicar St Andrew Yeadon 1966–71, rector Heyford with Stowe-Nine-Churches 1971–78, rural dean Daventry 1976–78, vicar Oakham with Hambleton and Egleton 1978–86 (with Braunston and Brooke from 1980–), non-residentiary canon Peterborough 1979–86, canon emeritus 1986–, vicar Lanteglos-by-Fowey 1986–88, provost of St Andrew's Cathedral Inverness 1988–91; priest i/c: St Mary-in-the Fields Culloden 1988–91, St Paul Strathnairn 1988–91; vicar Mill End and Heronsgate with W Hyde 1991–2001, acting rural dean Rickmansworth 1998–2000, rural dean Rickmansworth 2000–01, ret; *Publications* A Lent Course (with Mary Horsley, 1967, 3 edn 1997), Lent with St Luke (1978), Action at Lanteglos and Poluran (1987), The Parish Church at Mill End, Rickmansworth, Hertfordshire (Part I 1999, Part II 2000); contrib Rutland Record Soc Jl; *Recreations* music (piano and organ), cultivation of flowers, research; *Style*— The Very Rev Dr Alan Avery Horsley; ✉ Boswartha, High Burrow, Porthleven, Helston, Cornwall TR13 9EU (tel 01326 562404)

HORSLEY, William Frederick Moreton; *b* 28 January 1949, Macau; *Educ* St Edward's Sch Oxford, Pembroke Coll Oxford (exhibitioner, MA); *m* 1979, Noriko, *née* Makuuchi; *Career* prodr BBC Far Eastern Serv External Servs 1971–74, BBC secondee to Radio Japan (Japan Broadcasting Co Tokyo 1974–76, prodr Special Current Affairs unit BBC and The World Tonight 1977–80, prodr and news presenter Newsnight BBC TV 1981, reporter The World Tonight and BBC Radio News 1981–83, Tokyo corr and bureau chief BBC Tokyo 1983–90, corr for radio and TV BBC Bonn 1991–97, BBC European Affairs corr 1997–2007; chm Foreign Press 1984–88; chm Br branch AEJ 2002–, media freedom rep of Int AEJ 2007–; Assoc of Euro Journalists Euro Journalism Prize 2000; *Books* Newspapers and Democracy (contrib, 1980), Nippon - New Superpower (with Roger Buckley, 1990); author of numerous articles on Japan, Germany and int affairs in The Listener, The World Today, International Herald Tribune and other jls; *Style*— William Horsley, Esq; ✉ Flat 1, 30 Bina Gardens, London SW5 0LA (tel 07711 912499, e-mail wh@williamhorsley.com)

HORSMAN, Prof Michael John; s of late Graham Joseph Vivian Horsman, of Dollar, Scotland, and Ruth, *née* Guest; *b* 3 March 1949; *Educ* Dollar Acad, Univ of Glasgow (MA), Balliol Coll Oxford (Snell exhibitioner, Brackenbury scholar); *m* 1977, Anne Margaret, da of late John Marley; 3 s (Graham John b 10 Dec 1979, Ian Michael b 17 Feb 1982, William David b 27 April 1986); *Career* Dept of Employment: joined 1974, sec to Chm of Manpower Services Cmmn 1978–79, area mangr 1982–84, dir Professional and Exec Recruitment 1984–85, head of MSC Fin Policy and resource controller 1985–87, head of Employment Serv Ops Branch 1987–89, regnl dir Employment Serv London and SE 1989–92, dir Office of Manpower Economics 1992–2003; ind memb House of Commns Sr Pay Panel 2003–, inquiry dir Competition Cmmn 2005–; special prof Nottingham Univ Business Sch 2003–; *Recreations* reading, historical research, cycling; *Clubs* Cyclist Touring; *Style*— Prof Michael Horsman; ✉ 19 Harwood Close, Tewin, Hertfordshire AL6 0LF (tel 01438 840566, e-mail professormhorsman@hotmail.com)

HORSMAN, Peter James; s of Markham Henry Horsman, of Pinner, Middx, and Barbara, *née* Blow; *b* 11 January 1956; *Educ* Harrow Co Sch; *m* 5 April 1980, Ruth Margaret, da of Rev Kenneth Thomas Jarvis; 1 s (James Edward b 2 Feb 1985), 1 da (Julia Katherine b 22 Feb 1988); *Career* articled clerk Allfields (now Stoy Hayward) 1976–80, lectr Financial Training Co 1980–85, ptnr Armitage & Norton CAs 1987 (joined 1985); Saffery Champness: ptnr 1987–, nat tax ptnr 1990–; memb: Chartered Inst of Taxation 1985 (memb Cncl 1995–), Assoc of Taxation Technicians 1994 (memb Cncl 1994–); FCA 1990 (ACA 1980); *Recreations* country pursuits, motor racing; *Style*— Peter Horsman, Esq; ✉ Hockley Threshing Barn, Latimer, Buckinghamshire HP5 1XA; Saffery Champness, Lion House, Red Lion Street, London WC1R 4GB (tel 020 7841 4000, fax 020 7841 4100)

HORT, Sir Andrew Edwin Fenton; 9 Bt (GB 1767), of Castle Strange, Middlesex; s of Sir James Fenton Hort, 8 Bt (d 1995), and Joan Mary, *née* Peat; *b* 15 November 1954; *m* 15 Nov 1986, Mary, da of Jack Whibley, of Spalding, Lincs; 1 da (Jennifer Briony b 1987), 1 s (James John Fenton b 1989); *Heir* s, James Hort; *Style*— Sir Andrew Hort, Bt

HORTON, Gavin Tobias Alexander Winterbottom (Toby); s of late Alistair Winterbottom (bro of late Lord Winterbottom), and Maria Kersti; *b* 18 February 1947; *Educ* Westminster, ChCh Oxford (MA); *m* 1977, Hon Fiona Catherine Peake, da of 2 Viscount Ingleby; 2 da (Alice Emily Rose (Mrs Robert Procopé) b 1978, Violet Constance Lily b 1980), 2 s (George William Arthur b 1983, Thomas Henry Ralph b 1985); *Career* md Sound Broadcasting (Teesside) 1979–83, dir and head Corp Fin Dept Minster Trust Ltd 1984–90; md Heritage Media Ltd 1993–, chm Classic Rock (UK) Ltd 2000–, chm 59–75 (odd) Onslow Square Freehold Ltd 2004–; Parly candidate (Cons) Sedgefield 1983, Parly agent (Cons) Bethnal Green and Stepney 1987, Euro Parly candidate (Cons) Yorkshire SW 1989, Parly candidate (Cons) Rother Valley 1992, chm Richmond Cons Assoc 1996–99, memb UKIP 2006–; *Books* Going to Market: New Policy for the Farming Industry (1985), Programme for Reform: a New Agenda for Broadcasting (1987); *Recreations* radio, country pursuits; *Clubs* Royal Over-Seas League; *Style*— Toby Horton, Esq; ✉ Whorlton Cottage, Swainby, Northallerton, North Yorkshire DL6 3ER (tel 01642 700213, fax 01642 701615); Flat 1, 61 Onslow Square, London SW7 3LS (tel 020 7589 0609)

HORTON, Geoffrey; s of Leonard Horton (d 1987), and Joan, *née* Bissell (d 1997); *b* 23 July 1951; *Educ* Bristol GS, Exeter Coll Oxford (MA), UCL (MSc); *m* 1991, Dianne Alexandra (Alex), da of Dr Eric Craker; 2 da (Camilla b 1993, Beatrice b 1996); *Career* econ asst HM Treasy 1974–76, lectr in econ UC Swansea 1976–78, econ advsr HM Treasy 1978–85, chief economist DRI (Europe) Ltd 1985–88, sr econ advsr Dept of Energy 1988–90, pt/t sr conslt Nat Econ Research Assocs 1990–92, pt/t dir of regulation and business affairs Office of Electricity Regulation (GB) 1990–95, pt/t DG (electricity supply) Office of Electricity Regulation (NI) 1992–95, dir of consumer affairs OFT 1995–98, dir Horton 4 Consulting 1998–; *Publications* working papers: Modelling the World Economy (1984), The Economic Effects of Lower Oil Prices (with Stephen Powell, 1984); Links between Environmental and International Trade Policies: A Study on the Implications of Greenhouse Gas Emissions Control Policies for Trade (with James Rollo and Alistair Ulph, 1992), British Electricity Privatisation: The Customer's Standpoint (proceedings of BIEE conf, 1995); contrib various reports for EC, articles in economic jls and seminar papers; *Recreations* sailing, reading, cooking; *Style*— Geoffrey Horton; ✉ 43 Grove Park, London SE5 8LG (tel 020 7733 6587, fax 020 7771 9239, e-mail geoff@horton4co.uk)

HORTON, Matthew Bethell; QC; s of Albert Leslie Horton, of Tunbridge Wells, Kent, and Gladys Rose Ellen, *née* Harding; *b* 23 September 1946; *Educ* Sevenoaks, Trinity Hall Cambridge (MA, LLM); *m* 1, 22 May 1972 (m dis 1983), Liliane, da of Henri Boleslawski, of Nice, France; 1 s (Jerome b 1971), 1 da (Vanessa b 1973); m 2, 10 Oct 1999, Jane Louise Pendower, da of John Pendower FRCS, of Purley, Surrey; 1 da (Ursula b 1998), 1 s (James b 2001); *Career* called to the Bar Middle Temple 1969; in private practice specialising in: commercial property law, planning, environmental and local govt law, admin law, Parly law; *Recreations* tennis, skiing, windsurfing; *Style*— Matthew Horton, Esq, QC; ✉ 39 Essex Street, London WC2R 3AT (tel 020 7832 1111, fax 020 7832 3978, e-mail clerks@39essex.com, DX 298 London/Chancery Lane)

HORTON, Prof Michael Anthony; s of Dr (John Anthony) Guy Horton, of Newcastle upon Tyne, and Margaret Louisa, *née* Jenkins; *b* 6 May 1948; *Educ* Oundle, Bart's Med Coll Univ of London (BSc, MB BS); *m* 10 Aug 1968, Susan Geraldine Horton, JP, da of Capt Gerald Taylor, MBE (d 1973); 1 da (Rachel b 1971), 1 s (Benjamin b 1977); *Career* MRC fell UCL 1976–79; Bart's: sr lectr and conslt haematologist 1979–94, Wellcome Tst clinical res fell 1979–84, princ scientist Imperial Cancer Res Fund 1984–94; head Bone and Mineral Centre Dept of Medicine and prof in medicine UCL Med Sch 1995–; nanotechnologist, dir of life sciences London Centre for Nanotechnology 2003–; visiting scientist MRC Lab of Molecular Biology Cambridge 1991, visiting prof Meikai Univ Japan 1992; memb American Soc for Bone and Mineral Research; past pres Bone and Tooth Soc; author of various publications on haematology, immunology, bone biology and diseases, and nanomedicine; memb Lib Dems; FRCP, FRCPath; *Recreations* gardening, archaeology, family history; *Style*— Prof Michael Horton; ✉ The Priory, Quendon, Essex CB11 3XJ (tel 01799 543255); Department of Medicine, UCL Medical School, The Rayne Institute, University Street, London WC1E 6JJ (tel 020 7679 6169, fax 020 7679 6219, e-mail m.horton@ucl.ac.uk)

HORTON, (John) Philip (Phil); s of Frank Horton (d 1982), and Elsie, *née* Gill; *b* 19 January 1956; *Educ* Bournemouth Boys' Sch, Univ of Southampton (BA); *m* 1997; *Career* various positions in sales and mktg Ford of Britain 1977–85, Mktg Dept Ford of Europe 1985–90, dir of communications (i/c advtg, promotions and PR activities) Renault UK 1990–97, mktg dir BMW (GB) 1997–; *Recreations* motorcycling, skiing, tennis; *Style*— Phil Horton; ✉ BMW (GB) Ltd, Ellesfield Avenue, Bracknell, Berkshire RG12 8TA (tel 01344 426565)

HORTON, Sir Robert Baynes; kt (1997); s of W H Horton (d 1969), of Pangbourne; *b* 18 August 1939; *Educ* King's Sch Canterbury, Univ of St Andrews (BSc), MIT (SM); *m* 1962, Sally Doreen, da of Edward Wells (d 1971), of Beverley, E Yorks; 1 s, 1 da; *Career* joined BP Co Ltd 1957, gen mangr BP Tanker Co 1975–76 and corp planning BP 1976–79, md and chief exec BP Chemicals International 1980–83, chm and ceo Standard Oil (Ohio) 1986–88; British Petroleum plc: jt md 1983–86 and 1988–92, dep chm 1989–90, chm and chief exec 1990–92; vice-chm British Railways Bd 1992–94, chm Railtrack plc 1993–99; chm: Chubb plc 2002–03, Betfair 2004–06; non-exec dir: ICL plc 1982–84, Pilkington Bros plc 1985–86, Emerson Electric Co 1987–, Partner Re 1993–2002, Premier Farnell plc 1995–2004; pres: Chemical Industriess Assoc 1982–84, BESO 1993–97; vice-chm ABSA 1992–97; memb: SERC 1985–86, Bd of MIT 1987–97 (chm Sloan Visiting Ctee 1991–97), UFC 1989–92; tstee: Case Western Reserve Univ 1987–92, Cleveland Orch 1987–93; chm Bodleian Libraries Devpt Bd 2000–06; chllr Univ of Kent at Canterbury 1990–95; govr emeritus King's Sch Canterbury 2005– (govr 1983–2005); pres Railway Benevolent Fund 1999–2005; Hon LLD: Univ of Dundee 1988, Univ of Aberdeen 1992; Hon DSc: Cranfield Univ 1992, Kingston Univ 1993; Hon DCL Univ of Kent 1990, Hon DBA Univ of N London 1991, Hon DUniv Open Univ 1993; Hon FCGI, FIChemE, CIMgt, FCIT; *Recreations* music, country pursuits, rare books; *Clubs* Leander, Athenaeum, Huntercombe; *Style*— Sir Robert Horton; ✉ Stoke Abbas, South Stoke, Oxfordshire RG8 0JT (tel 01491 873996)

HORWICH, Prof Alan; s of late William Horwich, and late Audrey Miriam Lindley, *née* Rigby; *b* 1 June 1948; *Educ* William Hulme's GS, UCL, UCH Med Sch (MB BS, PhD); *m* 1981, Pauline Amanda, da of A R Barnes; 2 s (Oscar Samuel b 18 May 1985, Barnaby James b 24 March 1987), 1 da (Florence Harriet b 27 April 1989); *Career* house physician/surgn UCH 1972–73, house physician Royal N Hosp London 1973, SHO Hammersmith Hosp 1974, fell in oncology Harvard Med Sch Boston 1974–75, res fell ICRF 1975–78, registrar The Royal Marsden Hosp 1979–81, lectr Inst of Cancer Res 1981–83, MRC sr grade scientist MRC Radiobiology Unit 1983–84; Inst of Cancer Res and Royal Marsden Hosp: sr lectr 1984–86, prof of radiotherapy 1986– (head of section), dean 1993–97 and 2005–, dir of clinical res 1994–2005; Warden RCR 1998–2002; memb RSM; FRCR (MRCR), FRCP (MRCP); *Books* Testicular Cancer (1991, 2 edn, 1996), Combined Radiotherapy and Chemotherapy in Clinical Oncology (1992), Oncology: A Multidisciplinary Textbook (1995); *Style*— Prof Alan Horwich; ✉ The Royal Marsden Hospital, Downs Road, Sutton, Surrey SM2 5PT (tel 020 8661 3274, fax 020 8643 8809, e-mail alan.horwich@icr.ac.uk)

HORWOOD, Martin; MP; *b* 12 October 1962, Cheltenham, Glos; *Educ* Cheltenham Coll, The Queen's Coll Oxford (BA); *m* 1995, Dr Shona Arora; 2 c; *Career* joined Cheltenham Young Liberals 1979; account exec Ted Bates Advtg 1985–86, dir of devpt Br Humanist Assoc 1986–88, creative co-ordinator Help the Aged 1988–90, donor mktg mangr then dir of mktg and fundraising (India) Oxfam 1990–96, dir of fundraising Alzheimer's Soc 1996–2001, sr conslt then head of consultancy Consultancy Target Direct 2001–05; MP (Lib Dem) Cheltenham 2005– (Parly candidate (Lib Dem): Oxford E 1992, Cities of London and Westminster 2001); Lib Dem spokesperson for: home affrs 2005–06, environment 2006–; memb Select Ctee on ODPM 2005–, sec All Pty Corp Responsibility Gp 2005–; cncllr Vale of White Horse DC 1991–95 (dep ldr Lib Dem Gp 1993–95) memb: Ashridge Mgmnt Coll Assoc, World Devpt Movement 1988–, Alzheimer's Soc 1996–, Amnesty Int 1999–, TGWU, Amicus; memb Inst of Fundraising 1996; *Style*— Martin Horwood, Esq, MP; ✉ House of Commons, London SW1A 0AA (e-mail martin@martinhorwood.net, website www.martinhorwood.net); Constituency Office, 16 Hewlett Road, Cheltenham, Gloucestershire GL52 6AA

HORWOOD, Air Cdre Raymond James; CBE (2001, OBE 1991); *b* 1949; *Educ* Abbs Cross Sch Hornchurch, trg RAF Gaydon/Stradishall, RAF Staff Coll Bracknell, Canadian Nat Defence Coll; *m* 1972, Gwyneth Mary Bridge; 3 c (Andrew, Emma, Anna); *Career* Navigator 6 Sqdn (Phantom) RAF Coningsby 1970–73, 17 and 31 Sqdn (Phantom) RAF Brüggen Germany 1973–76, instr Navigation Sch RAF Finningley 1976–79, 16 Strike/Attack Sqdn (Buccaneer) RAF Laarbruch Germany 1979–84, mgmnt Offensive Weapons MOD 1984–85, HQ STC 1985–87, OC Ops Wing RAF Marham 1987–90, Wing Cdr Strike/Attack Gp Upavon 1990–92, Head of Ops Muharraq Bahrain (Gulf War), Air Warfare Centre 1993–96, Cdr Br Forces Riyadh Saudi Arabia 1994, Detachment Cdr Jaguar/Harrier Ops Gioia Del Colle S Italy 1997, Air Cdr and Jt Force Cdr UK tri-service evacuation of Br Nationals Albania, Station Cdr RAF Waddington 1998, Cmdt Air Warfare Centre/Defence EW Centre 1998–2000, Dep Force Cdr/COS NATO Airborne Early Warning and Control Force 2000–04; chief exec Nat Fedn of Roofing Contractors 2004–; Liveryman Worshipful Co of Tylers and Bricklayers; QCVSA 1973; FRAeS 1998; Order of Bahrain 1991; *Recreations* golf, ice skating; *Style*— Air Commodore Raymond Horwood, CBE, FRAeS; ✉ 31–41 Worship Street, London SE2A 2DX

HORWOOD-SMART, Rosamund; QC (1996); da of John Horwood-Smart (d 1997), of Cheveley, Cambs, and Sylvia, *née* Nutt; *b* 21 September 1951; *Educ* Felixstowe Coll, Cambridgeshire HS for Girls, Inns of Court Sch of Law; *m* 1, 16 July 1983 (m dis 1994), Richard Clive Blackford; 1 s (Frederick John b 3 Sept 1986), 1 da (Eleanor Kate b 30 Aug 1989); m 2, 22 Feb 1996, Richard Oliver Bernays, *qv*; *Career* called to the Bar Inner Temple 1974 (master of the bench 1998), recorder 1995–; memb: S Eastern Circuit, Criminal Bar Assoc; vice-pres Int Students House; *Recreations* music, gardening, theatre; *Style*— Miss Rosamund Horwood-Smart, QC; ✉ 18 Red Lion Court, London EC4A 3EB (tel 020 7520 6000, fax 020 7520 6248)

HOSEASON, James William Nicholson; OBE (1990); s of William Ballantyne Hoseason (d 1950), of Lowestoft, and Jessie Mary Hoseason (d 1972); *b* 6 November 1928; *Educ* Lowestoft GS; *m* 20 March 1965, Lesley Jean, da of Leslie Charles Edmonds (d 1964), of Chedgrave, nr Norwich; 1 s (James Charles William b 6 Feb 1967); *Career* articled pupil then chartered civil engr and chartered structural engr Sir Owen Williams & Partners 1945–50; Hoseasons Holidays Ltd: trainee 1950, md 1952–64, chm and jt md 1964–90, chm 1990–98; memb Inland Waterways Amenity Advsy Cncl 1972–80, govt appointed memb Anglian Water 1973–76, river cmmr Norfolk Broads 1982–88, past chm Br Hire Cruiser Fedn; Bd memb English Tourist Bd 1989–93, memb Broads Authy (memb Navigation Ctee); FTS 1973, FIMgt 1974, FCIM 1976; *Books* The Thousand Day Battle (1979, 3 edn 1990); *Recreations* sailing, writing, flying light aircraft, gardening; *Clubs* RAC, Royal Norfolk & Suffolk Yacht; *Style*— James Hoseason, Esq, OBE

HOSFORD, David Jeremy; s of Desmond James Hosford, of Belfast, and Heather, *née* Wallace; *b* 21 March 1969, Londonderry; *Educ* Royal Belfast Academical Instn, Univ of Warwick (LLB), Coll of Law Chester; *m* 8 Sept 2001, Sarah Elizabeth, *née* Hallam; 2 da (Elizabeth Laura b 17 Oct 2002, Chloe Imogen b 1 Aug 2004); *Career* slr; Burges Salmon 1993–2001, Pitmans 2001–; memb: Assoc of Pension Lawyers, Int Tstee Gp; assoc Pensions Mgmnt Inst; *Recreations* windsurfing, walking; *Style*— David Hosford, Esq; ✉ Pitmans, 47 Castle Street, Reading RG1 7SR (tel 0118 957 0393, fax 0118 957 0372, e-mail dhosford@pitmans.com)

HOSFORD-TANNER, (Joseph) Michael; s of late Dr Hubert Hosford-Tanner, of London, and Betty, *née* Bryce; *b* 8 August 1951; *Educ* Midleton Coll, Trinity Coll Dublin (BA, LLB); *Career* called to the Bar Inner Temple 1974; legal assessor: Farriers Registration Cncl 1985–, CIMA 2001–, Gen Chiropractic Cncl 2001–, Nursing and Midwifery Cncl Panel 2003–; *Recreations* horses, cricket, motorcycles; *Clubs* Chelsea Arts, Kildare Street and Univ; *Style*— Michael Hosford-Tanner, Esq; ✉ Queen Elizabeth Building, Temple, London EC4Y 9BS (tel 020 7797 7837, fax 020 7353 5422)

HOSIE, Stewart; MP; *b* 1963, Dundee; *Educ* Carnoustie HS, Bell Street Tech Coll; *Career* former IT conslt Scottish Telecom; SNP: nat sec 1999–2003, orgn convener 2003–05; MP (SNP) Dundee E 2005– (Parly candidate (SNP) Dundee E 2001); *Style*— Stewart Hosie, Esq, MP; ✉ House of Commons, London SW1A 0AA

HOSKING, Prof Geoffrey Alan; s of late Stuart William Steggall Hosking, and late Jean Ross *née* Smillie; *b* 28 April 1942; *Educ* Maidstone GS, King's Coll Cambridge (BA), Moscow State Univ, St Antony's Coll Oxford, Univ of Cambridge (MA, PhD); *m* 19 Dec 1970, Anne Lloyd Hirst; 2 da (Katya b 1974, Janet b 1978); *Career* Univ of Essex: lectr Dept of Govt 1966–71, lectr Dept of History 1972–76, reader Dept of History 1976–80 and 1981–84; SSEES Univ of London: prof of Russian history 1984–99 and 2004–, dep dir 1996–98; visiting prof: Dept of Political Science Univ of Wisconsin 1971–72,

Slavisches Inst Univ of Cologne 1980–81; Leverhulme personal research prof SSEES UCL 1999–2004, memb Inst of Advanced Study Princeton 2006–07; Reith lectr BBC 1988, memb jury Booker Prize for Russian Fiction 1993; memb: Cncl of Writers and Scholars Int 1985–, Cncl Moscow Sch of Political Studies 1992–, Overseas Policy Ctee Br Acad 1994–2000, Br Univs Assoc for Soviet and E Euro Studies, Royal Inst for Int Affrs, Exec Ctee Britain-Russia Centre 1992–2000, Acad Cncl Museum of Contemporary History Moscow, Inst for Advanced Study Princeton Univ 2006–07; memb Editorial Bd: Nations and Nationalism, Nationalities Papers, Ab Imperio, Otechestvennaia Istoriia; Hon Doctorate Russian Acad of Scis 2000; FBA 1993, FRHistS 1995; *Books* The Russian Constitutional Experiment: Government & Duma 1907–14 (1973), Beyond Socialist Realism: Soviet Fiction since Ivan Denisovich (1980), A History of The Soviet Union (1985, 3 edn 1992, Los Angeles Times History Book Prize 1986), The Awakening of The Soviet Union (1990, 2 edn 1991), The Road to Post-Communism: independent political movements in the Soviet Union 1985–91 (with J Aves and P Duncan, 1992), Russia: People and Empire 1552–1917 (1997), Myths & Nationhood (ed with G Schöpflin, 1998), Russian Nationalism Past and Present (ed with R Service, 1998), Reinterpreting Russia (ed with R Service, 1999), Russia and the Russians: A History (2001, American Independent Publishers' History Book Prize 2002), Rulers and Victims: The Russians in the Soviet Union (2006); *Recreations* walking, music, chess; *Style*— Prof Geoffrey Hosking, FBA; ✉ School of Slavonic & East European Studies, University College London, Gower Street, London WC1E 6BT (tel 020 7679 8815, fax 020 7679 8777, e-mail g.hosking@ssees.ucl.ac.uk)

HOSKING, Patrick Anthony James; s of Roger Michael Hosking, and Mollie June, *née* Allen; *b* 8 February 1960; *Educ* Rugby, Pembroke Coll Cambridge; *m* Amanda Clare, *née* Lindsay; *Career* asst ed Inst for Int Research 1981–83, newsletter ed Stonehart Publications 1983–86, business reporter then banking corr The Independent 1986–90; business corr: The Age Melbourne 1990–91, The Independent 1991–93; The Independent on Sunday: sr business writer 1993–94, dep City ed then City ed 1994–96; dep business ed The Age Australia 1996–97, City Office Evening Standard 1997–2000, City head Express Newspapers and City ed Daily Express 2000–01, columnist Investors Chronicle 2002–04, columnist New Statesman 2002–05, dep City ed Evening Standard 2002–04 (freelance contrib 2001–02), investment ed then banking and finance ed The Times 2004–; tstee News Int Pension Plan 2006–; *Style*— Patrick Hosking, Esq; ✉ tel 020 7782 5040, e-mail patrick.hosking@thetimes.co.uk

HOSKINS, Arthur Henry James; CBE; s of Alfred George Hoskins; *b* 14 January 1923; *m* 1949, Margaret Lilian Rose, da of Albert Davis (d 1959); 1 c; *Career* certified accountant, chartered sec; md and dep chm Matthew Hall plc 1939–86; *Recreations* reading, walking; *Style*— Arthur Hoskins, Esq, CBE; ✉ 2 Acorn Close, Chislehurst, Kent BR7 6LD (tel 020 8467 0755)

HOSKINS, Prof Sir Brian John; kt (2007), CBE (1998); s of George Frederick Hoskins (d 1979), and Kathleen Matilda Louise, *née* Rattue; *b* 17 May 1945; *Educ* Bristol GS, Trinity Hall Cambridge (MA, PhD); *m* 25 May 1968, Jacqueline, *née* Holmes; 2 da (Brooke b 22 Sept 1972, Bryony b 7 Oct 1974); *Career* prof of meteorology Univ of Reading 1981– (reader in atmospheric modelling 1976–81, head of dept 1990–96); Rothschild visiting prof Isaac Newton Math Inst Cambridge 1996, Royal Soc research prof 2001–; special advsr to Sec of State for Tport 1989–90; memb Cncl NERC 1988–94, pres Int Assoc for Meteorology and Atmospheric Physics 1991–95; Starr Meml lectr MIT 1989, Br Geological Survey distinguished lectr 1992, Haurwitz lectr American Meteorological Soc 1995, Welsh lectr Univ of Toronto 2006; Royal Meteorological Soc: L F Richardson prize 1972, Buchan prize 1976, Symons Meml lecture 1982, pres 1998–2000; memb Royal Commission for Environmental Pollution 1998–2005; vice-chm Jt Scientific Ctee Work Climate Res Programme; Royal Soc: chm Global Environmental Res Ctee, memb Cncl 1999–2001; Charles Chree Silver medal Inst of Physics 1987, Carl-Gustaf Rossby Res medal American Meteorological Soc 1988, Geophysical Soc Bjerknes prize 1997, Symons medal RMS 2007; hon prof Chinese Acad of Sciences 1998; foreign assoc US Nat Acad of Sciences 2002, foreign memb Chinese Acad of Sciences 2002; FRMetS 1970, FRS 1988, fell Academia Europaea 1990, Hon FRMetS 2001; *Books* Large-Scale Dynamical Processes in the Atmosphere (1982), author of 130 papers in learned jls; *Recreations* singing, gardening; *Style*— Prof Sir Brian Hoskins, CBE, FRS; ✉ Department of Meteorology, University of Reading, Whiteknights, Reading RG6 6BB (tel 0118 378 8953, fax 0118 378 8905, e-mail b.j.hoskins@reading.ac.uk)

HOSKINS, Robert (Bob); s of Robert Hoskins, and Elsie Lilian Hopkins; *b* 26 October 1942; *Educ* Stroud Green Sch; *m* 1, Jane Livesey; 1 s (Alexander b 8 Aug 1968), 1 da (Sarah b 30 Dec 1972); m 2, Linda Banwell; 1 da (Rosa Louise b 27 May 1983), 1 s (Jack Anthony b 5 March 1985); *Career* actor; previously held numerous jobs incl accountant; theatre debut Unity Theatre London, early experience on tour with Ken Campbell's Road Show; *Theatre* Victoria Theatre Stoke-on-Trent 1968: Romeo and Juliet, Toad of Toad Hall, Christopher Pee in Heartbreak House; Century Theatre 1969: Marker in A View From the Bridge, Pinchwife in The Country Wife, Hiring in The Anniversary, Menelaus in The Trojan Women; Lenny in the Homecoming 1969 and Richard in Richard III 1970 (Hull Arts Theatre), Azdac in The Caucasian Chalk Circle and Lear (Royal Court) 1970–71, Bernie the Volt in Veterans (Royal Court) 1972, Sextus Pompeius in Antony and Cleopatra (Globe) 1973, Lear in Lear (Dartington Hall) 1973, Mr Doolittle in Pygmalion (Albery) 1974, Common Man in A Man For All Seasons (Sixty Nine Theatre Co) 1974, Geography of a Horse Dreamer (Royal Court) 1974, Touchstone in As You Like It (Oxford Playhouse) 1975, Biu Cracker in Happy End (Lyric) 1975–76; RSC 1976 incl: Rocky in The Iceman Cometh, Seargeant in The Devil's Disciple; other roles incl: The Bystander (also writer, Soho Poly Theatre) 1977, The World Turned Upside Down and Has Washington Legs? 1978, Lee in True West 1981, Nathan Detroit in Guys and Dolls 1982, Bosola in The Duchess of Malfi 1983, Professor Mashkan in Old Wicked Songs (Gielgud Theatre) 1996; *Television* 1971–1984 incl: Joe Gramaldi in Omnibus - It Must Be Something in the Water, Knocker in Villains, Woodbine in Her Majesty's Pleasure, All Who Sail Around Her. On the Road, Crown Court, New Scotland Yard, Sexton in If there Weren't Any Blacks..., Doobs in Thick as Thieves, Schmoedius, Shoulder to Shoulder, Thriller - To Kill Two Birds, Omnibus on Brecht, Three Piece Suite, In The Looking Glass, Napoleon in Peninsular, Arthur Parker in Pennies From Heaven, Chorus in Mycenae and Men, Sheppey in Sheppey, Arnie Cole in Flickers, Iago in Othello, Eddie Reed in You Don't Have to Walk to Fly, The Beggars Opera; most recently incl: The Changeling (BBC) 1993, World War II: And then there were Giants (NBC) 1994, David Copperfield, The Lost World 2001, The Good People; *Films* incl: Foster in The National Health 1973, Royal Flash 1974, Big Mac in Inserts 1975, Colour Sergeant Major Williams in Zulu Dawn 1979, Harold Shand in The Long Good Friday 1980, Rock and Roll Manager in The Wall 1982, Colonel Perez in The Honorary Consul (titled Beyond The Limit in USA) 1983, Owney Madden in The Cotton Club 1984, Spoor in Brazil 1985, Stanley in Sweet Liberty 1986, George in The Woman Who Married Clark Gable 1986, George in Mona Lisa 1986, The Priest in A Prayer For The Dying 1987, Madden in The Lonely Passion of Judith Hearne 1987, Eddie Valiant in Who Framed Roger Rabbit? 1988, Darky in The Raggedy Rawney (also writer, dir) 1988, Lou Landsky in Mermaids 1989, Jack Moony in Heart Condition 1990, Shattered 1990, The Favour The Watch and The Very Big Fish 1990, The Projectionist 1990, Hook 1991, Passed Away 1992, Mario in Mario Bros 1993, Super Mario Brothers 1993, Balto (animation) 1995, Rainbow (also dir) 1995, Nixon 1995, Michael 1996, Spiceworld The Movie (cameo role) 1997, The Secret Agent, Cousin Bette 1997, Twenty-Four Seven 1997, Inch over the Horizon 1997, Felcia's Journey, A Room for Romeo Brass, Sleeping Dictionary, Where Eskimos Live, Enemy at the Gates 2001, Last Orders 2001, Den of Lions, Maid in Manhattan, Danny the Dog, Vanity Fair, Stay, Beyond the Sea, Son of the Mask, Mrs Henderson Presents 2005; *Awards* for Pennies From Heaven BAFTA nomination; for The Long Good Friday incl: Evening Standard Award for Best Actor, nominated for Best Actor Award British Acad of Film & Television Arts; for Mona Lisa incl: Oscar nomination for Best Actor, winner New York Critics and Golden Globe Awards, Best Actor Award Cannes Film Festival; Variety Club of GB Best Actor Award 1997; *Style*— Bob Hoskins, Esq; ✉ c/o ICM, Oxford House, 76 Oxford Street, London W1D 1BS

HOSKYNS, Sir Benedict Leigh; 16 Bt (E 1676), of Harewood, Herefordshire; 3 s of Rev Sir Edwyn Clement Hoskyns, 13 Bt, MC, DD (d 1937), and Mary Trym, *née* Budden (d 1994); suc bro, Sir John Chevallier Hoskyns, 15 Bt, 1956; *b* 27 May 1928; *Educ* Haileybury, Corpus Christi Coll Cambridge (MB BChir), London Hosp; *m* 19 Sept 1953, Ann, da of Harry Wilkinson, of London; 2 da (Janet Mary b 1954, Sarah Leigh (Mrs Julian P C Raphael) b 1959), 2 s (Edwyn Wren b 1956, John Chandos b 1961); *Heir* s, Dr Edwyn Hoskyns; *Career* Capt RAMC (ret); in general med practice 1958–93, ret; DObstRCOG 1958; *Style*— Sir Benedict Hoskyns, Bt; ✉ Russell House, Wherry Corner, High Street, Manningtree, Essex CO11 1AP (tel 01206 396432, e-mail ann@russell-house.co.uk)

HOSSAIN, Ajmalul; QC (1998); s of Asrarul Hossain, Barrister and Sr Advocate Supreme Ct of Bangladesh (d 2002), and Rabia *née* Ahmed (d 1992); *b* 18 October 1950, Dhaka, Bangladesh; *Educ* King's Coll London (LLB, LLM); *m* Nasreen, da of Prof M U Ahmed (decd); 2 c (Syed Ahrarul b 8 June 1979, Syed Afsar b 14 Nov 1981); *Career* called to the Bar Lincoln's Inn 1976 (Buchanan Prize); Supreme Ct of Bangladesh: High Ct Div 1977, Appellate Div 1986, Senior Advocate 1998; FCIArb 1994, pt/t chm Employment Tbnls 1995–2005; memb: SE Circuit, Chancery Bar Assoc, Supreme Ct Bar Assoc Bangladesh, Int C of C Int Ct of Arbitration 2006–; memb Int Cricket Cncl Code of Conduct Cmmn 2006–; fell Soc of Advanced Legal Studies; *Recreations* travel, bridge; *Style*— Ajmalul Hossain, Esq, QC; ✉ Selborne Chambers, 10 Essex Street, London WC2R 3AA (tel 020 7420 9500, fax 020 7420 9555, e-mail ajmalul.hossain@selbornechambers.co.uk)

HOSTOMBE, Roger Eric; s of late Eric Rudolf Hostombe, of Sheffield, and late Irene, *née* Baxter; *b* 22 December 1942; *Educ* Sedbergh; *m* 20 Sept 1975, Susan Mary, da of late Frank Ian Cobb, of Sheffield; 5 da (Clare b 1976, Natalie b 1979, Annabel b 1982, Lucinda b 1982, Sophie b 1989); *Career* CA 1968, exec chm Hostombe Group Ltd 1975–; underwriter Lloyd's 1975–; regnl cncllr CBI Yorkshire and Humberside branch 1981–87; *Recreations* tennis, skiing, gardening; *Style*— Roger E Hostombe, Esq; ✉ Stylewood Hall, Sheffield S10 4PA (tel and fax 0114 230 2148); Hostombe Group Ltd, Minalloy House, Regent Street, Sheffield S1 3NJ (tel 0114 272 4324, fax 0114 272 9550, e-mail roger.hostombe@hostombe.co.uk)

HOTHAM, Anthony; TD (1969); s of Edward Hotham (d 1985), and Freda Elizabeth, *née* Smith (d 1988); *b* 30 May 1933; *Educ* Warwick Sch; *m* 6 Nov 1954, Patricia Margaret, da of George Henry Day (d 1956); 2 s (Charles Anthony b 7 Sept 1959, Timothy Edward b 9 Oct 1961); *Career* Nat Serv 1952, cmmnd RASC 1953, TA 1954, Capt 1957, Maj 7 Bn Worcs Regt TA 1967, ret 1969; md Starr Roadways Ltd 1968–72; called to the Bar Middle Temple 1971, in practice 1973–91; pt/t pres Mental Health Review Tbnl 1987–2006; chm Starr Roadways Ltd 1985–2001; cncllr Wychavon DC 1991–2003 (chm 2001–02); memb CIT (until 1982); *Recreations* golf; *Style*— Anthony Hotham, Esq, TD; ✉ 5 Fountain Court, Steelhouse Lane, Birmingham B4 6DR (tel 0121 606 0500, fax 0121 606 1501)

HOTHAM, 8 Baron (I 1797); Sir Henry Durand Hotham; 18 Bt (E 1622), DL (Humberside 1981); 3 s of 7 Baron Hotham, CBE (d 1967), and Lady (Letitia Sibell) Winifred Cecil (d 1992), da of 5 Marquess of Exeter, KG, CMG, TD; *b* 3 May 1940; *Educ* Eton; *m* 1972, Alexandra Mary, 2 da of Maj Andrew Charles Stirling Home Drummond Moray; 2 s (Hon William Beaumont b 1972, Hon George Andrew b 1974), 1 da (Hon Elizabeth Henrietta Alexandra b 1976); *Heir* s, Hon William Hotham; *Career* former Lt Grenadier Gds; patron of 1 living; ADC to Govr of Tasmania 1963–66; *Style*— The Rt Hon Lord Hotham, DL; ✉ The Dower House, Mere Lane, South Dalton, Beverley, East Yorkshire HU17 7PL

HOTHFIELD, 6 Baron (UK 1881), of Hothfield, Co Kent; Sir Anthony Charles Sackville Tufton; 7 Bt (UK 1851), DL (Cumbria); s of 5 Baron Hothfield, TD, DL (d 1991), and Evelyn Margarette, *née* Mordaunt (d 1989); *b* 21 October 1939; *Educ* Eton, Magdalene Coll Cambridge (MA); *m* 1975, Lucinda Marjorie, da of Capt Timothy John Gurney, and formerly w of Capt Graham Morison Vere Nicoll; 1 da (Hon Emma b 1976), 1 s (Dr the Hon William Sackville b 1977); *Heir* s, Dr the Hon William Tufton; *Career* civil engrg; CEng, MICE; *Recreations* real tennis (amateur champion 1964, doubles 1962, 1963 and 1964), lawn tennis, bridge, shooting; *Style*— The Rt Hon Lord Hothfield, DL; ✉ Drybeck Hall, Appleby-in-Westmorland, Cumbria CA16 6TF

HOTUNG, Eric Edward; CBE (2001); s of Edward Sai Kim Hotung (d 1957), and Mordia Alice, *née* O'Shea (d 1992); gs of Sir Robert Hotung; *b* 8 June 1926; dual Anglo-Chinese nationality; *Educ* St Francis Xavier Coll Shanghai, Georgetown Univ Washington DC (BSS), NY Inst of Finance NYC; *m* 17 Jan 1959, Patricia Anne, da of Michael Shea (d 1938); 6 s (Michael Alexander b 1959, Michael Eric b 8 Jan 1960, Robert Eric 1961, Eric Shea-kim b 1963, Sean Eric b 1965, Anthony Eric b 1966), 4 da (Barbara b 1960, Mara Tegwen b 1967, Gabrielle Marie b 1971, Sheridan Patricia b 1972); *Career* security analyst Henry Hentz & Co NY 1951, admin asst to dir Pacific Area Foreign Distributors Div General Motors 1953–58, dir Hong Kong & Kowloon Entertainment Co 1958, chm Hotung Int Ltd 1960, fndr chm Hong Kong Devpt Ltd and Cosmopolitan Properties & Securities Ltd 1970–, chm Hotung Int Devpt; memb Hong Kong Stock Exchange and Hong Kong Gold and Silver Exchange 1958; special advsr on Chinese affrs Centre for Strategic and Int Studies Washington DC 1975, dir US Nat Ctee on US-China Relations 1986, US Senate-China Trade Caucus 'In the decade ahead' 1987, econ and fin advsr to Tianjin Govt of China 1990, fin advsr Municipal Govt of Xuzhou 1999, advsr to Wai Hai Operation Res Museum 1999, special econ and fin advsr to the Nat Cncl of Timorese Resistance East Timor 1999, memb Advsy Cncl Bd of Fundacao Luso-Americana Lisboa 2000; fndr Hotung Inst; fndr/sponsor numerous philanthropical, charitable and other projects incl: Convent of Santa Rosa de Lima Macáu 1962, Low Cost Home Ownership and Financing Schemes Hong Kong 1964–93, Eric Hotung Tst Fund for Secdy Educn 1965, initial funding for restoration of Castle Mailberg and Church of St John the Baptist 1974, radio stations for marginados (underprivileged youth) Costa Rica 1975, Georgetown Univ Trauma Team for Vietnamese refugees in Cambodia and other projects 1978, Intercultural Centre Georgetown Univ (jt sponsor with US Govt) 1980, Brathay Expdn and Operation Drake 1980, visit of Cardinal Sin of the Philippines to China 1984, US-China Trade Confs at US Senate (advocating unconditional renewal of China's Most Favoured Nation trading status) 1987, SES Expdn to Mt Xixibangma Tibet 1987, co-sponsor (with US-China Business Cncl) conf on Reassessing US-China Ties: Economic Policy and the Role of Business at US State Dept 1990, co-host (with US Nat Ctee on US-China Relations) to Chinese Mayors' Delgn at US Senate and State Dept 1990, founding benefactor East Timor Good Samaritan Fndn 2000, funding and construction of accomodation for East Timorese students 2002, estab Eric Hotung Research Fellowship to promote research and enhance the research profile of the Sch of Law Univ of Canterbury NZ 2005; co-host (with China Inst for Int Stategic Studies) an Int Symposium on: 'Asia-Pacific Security Situation' 2002, 'Sino-US-European Relations in the

New Century: Opportunities and Challenges' 2003, 'Int Counter-Terrorism Situation and Cooperation' 2004, 'Non-traditional Security: Challenges and Responses' 2005; tstee Marine Mil Acad Harlingen TX 1978; vice-pres: Operation Drake 1979, Operation Raleigh 1984; dir Soong Ching Ling Fndn for Children 1987, patron Hotung Tech Sch for Girls 1988; hon memb 22nd Special Service Regt 1985, chm Non-Combatants Pacific War 1937–45 Assoc Inc 1994, chm China AIDS Fund Inc 2003; patron: Royal British Legion, Hong Kong Ex-Serviceman's Assoc, WWII Veterans Assoc 1998; tstee: Spirit of Normandy Int Appeal 1994, Spirit of Normandy Tst 2000, Soc for Aid and Rehabilitation of Drug Abusers Hong Kong 2000, Bd of China Inst in America 2001; sponsor: Hotung Pavilion, Shanghai Museum 1996, hosp ship East Timor 1999; donation of plaques to the Wai Hai Cemetery 1999, donation to Chinese Scholar's Garden Staten Island NY 1999 (fndr memb Scholar's Soc of NY Chinese Scholar's Garden 1999), donation incl the former RAN vessel HMAS Moresby (renamed as 'MV Patricia Anne Hotung') to East Timor 1999, donation to Eye Hosp China Acad of Traditional Chinese Med Beijing 2000, donation to Georgetown Univ Law Center (building named Eric Hotung Int Law Center) 2000; memb Bd of Dirs Community Chest Hong Kong 2000; established free clinic in Dili East Timor 2000; ambass at large of the Democratic Republic of East Timor 2002–; hon pres China Soc for People's Friendship Studies 2005; Scientific Exploration Soc: hon memb 1980, hon vice-pres 2005; memb Frank Hogan Soc Georgetown Univ 2004; life memb: Hong Kong Arts Centre 1984, RPO 1984; companion St George's Chapel Windsor 2006 (friend 1984); Charter Award from Bd of Dirs Georgetown Univ 1985, charter memb 1789 Soc Georgetown Univ 1997, John Carroll Award Georgetown Univ 1997; sr assoc memb St Antony's Coll Oxford 1999, fndn fell St Antony's Coll Oxford 1999, memb Chllr's Ct of Benefactors Univ of Oxford 2000; The Path to Peace Fndn Servitor Pacis Award 2003 (Vatican Award) 2003; Freeman City of San Francisco 1972, Hon Citizen Pyongyang City N Korea 2002; Hon Dr Georgetown Univ 1984; fell Hong Kong IOD 2000; Knight of Malta Grand Cross with Star Pro Merito Meletensi 1974, Cruz de Caballero de la Orde de Isabel la Católica 1973, Das Kommitur Cruz Mit Stern Leichtenstein 1974, Knight of St Sylvester 1984, Grand Cross of the Order of NS DA Conceicao de Vila Vicosa Portugal 1985, CStJ 1995 (OStJ 1966), Marquez de Baucau de Timor 1997, Cert of Friendship Order N Korea 2002, Medalha de Ouro da Resistenca das Falintil 2002; *Recreations* game fishing, calligraphy; *Clubs* Carlton, Metropolitan (Washington DC), Chinese (Hong Kong), China (Beijing), American (Hong Kong), Foreign Correspondents' (Hong Kong), Hong Kong Country, Jockey, Hong Kong Golf; *Style*— Eric Hotung, Esq, CBE; ✉ Hotung International Development Ltd, 7/F The Chinese Club Building, 21–22 Connaught Road C, Hong Kong (tel 00 852 2526 2272, fax 00 852 2526 2812, e-mail erichotung_therealmccoy@hotung.org)

HOUGH, Robert Eric; DL (Gtr Manchester 1997); s of Gordon Hough, and Joyce, *née* Davies; *b* 18 July 1945; *Educ* William Hulme's GS Manchester, Univ of Bristol (LLB); *m* 14 June 1975, Pauline Elizabeth, da of Austin David Gilbert Arch, and Amy Jean, *née* Watt; 2 s (Mark Ian b 11 Oct 1979, Christopher James b 21 Feb 1985); *Career* admitted slr 1970, NP; ptnr Slater Heelis (slrs) Manchester 1974–89; exec chm The Manchester Ship Canal Co 1989–2002 (chm 1987–2002); Peel Holdings plc: dir 1986–, exec dep chm 1989–2002, non-exec dep chm 2002–; chm Liverpool Airport plc 1997–, non-exec chm: New East Manchester Ltd 2002–, Cheshire Building Soc 2006– (non exec dir 2002–); non-exec dir: Alfred McAlpine plc 2003–, Styles & Wood Gp plc 2006–, Provident Financial plc 2007–; memb Exec Bd NW Regnl Assembly 2006–, past pres Manchester C of C, former vice-pres and former chm Manchester Cwlth Games 2002, former chm NW Business Leadership Team; govr Univ of Manchester 2005–; High Sheriff Gtr Manchester 2004; Hon DBA Manchester Metropolitan Univ 1996, Hon DLitt Univ of Salford 1996; memb Law Soc; *Recreations* golf, gardening, sport; *Clubs* Hale Golf; *Style*— Robert Hough, Esq, DL; ✉ Peel Holdings (Management) Limited, Peel Dome, The Trafford Centre, Manchester M17 8PL (tel 0161 629 8200, fax 0161 629 8333, e-mail rhough@peel.co.uk)

HOUGH, Stephen; *b* 1961, Cheshire; *Educ* RNCM, Juilliard Sch NY; *Career* concert pianist; performed with orchs incl: Philharmonia, Royal Philharmonic, LSO, London Philharmonic, BBC Symphony, Eng Chamber, City of Birmingham Symphony, NY Philharmonic, Cleveland, Chicago Symphony, Detroit Symphony, Hong Kong Philharmonic, Toronto Symphony, Monte Carlo Philharmonic, Philadelphia, LA Philharmonic, Lausanne Chamber, Orch of St Cecilia Rome, Deutsche Symphonie Orch Berlin, Orchestre National de France; worked with conductors incl: Claudio Abbado, Klaus Tennstedt, Mstislav Rostropovich, James Levine, Simon Rattle, Charles Dutoit, Esa-Pekka Salonen, Christoph von Dohnányi, Yuri Temirkanov, Jeffrey Tate; performed at festivals incl: Ravinia, Blossom, Spoleto, NY Mostly Mozart, Sorrento, Tivoli, Bath, Cheltenham, La Grange de Meslay, BBC Promenade Concerts, Edinburgh, Salzburg, Aldeburgh. Sapporo; Terence Judd award 1982, first prize Naumburg Int Piano Competition 1983, awarded MacArthur Fellowship 2001; memb RAM 2003; FRNCM 1996; *Recordings* incl: Hummel piano concertos (with the Eng Chamber Orch, Gramophone magazine best concerto record 1987), The Piano Album (collection of favourite encores), Brahms piano concerto no 1 and no 2 (with the BBC Symphony Orch and Andrew Davis, various works by Britten, Schumann and Liszt (awarded Deutsche Schallplattenpreis), Scharwenka and Sauer piano concertos (Gramophone Record of the Year 1996), York Bowen piano music (awarded Diapason d'Or), Franck piano music (awarded Deutsche Schallplattenpreis), Mompou piano music (Gramaphone magazine Best Instrumental Record 1998), Mendelssohn complete works for piano and orch, Liebermann piano concertos, New York Variations recital (Grammy nomination), Schubert piano sonatas, new piano album, complete works for piano and orch by Saint-Saens (Grammy nomination, Gramophone Record of the Year 2002), English Piano Album, Lizst sonata (Grammy nomination), Brahms F minor sonata, Rachmaninoff and Franck cello sonatas (with Steven Isserlis), Hummel piano sonatas, Chopin Ballades and Scherzos; *Publications* incl five volumes of solo pieces and transcriptions; *Style*— Stephen Hough, Esq; ✉ c/o Harrison/Parrott, 12 Penzance Place, London W11 4PA (tel 020 7229 9166, fax 020 7221 5042, website www.stephenhough.com)

HOUGHAM, John William; CBE (1996); s of William George Hougham (d 2001), of Ash, Kent, and Emily Jane, *née* Smith (d 2006); *b* 18 January 1937; *Educ* Sir Roger Manwood's Sch Sandwich, Univ of Leeds (BA); *m* 26 Aug 1961, Peggy Edith (d 2006), da of Ernest Grove (d 1972), of Halesowen, Worcs; 1 da (Elizabeth b 1965), 1 s (Simon b 1967); *Career* Royal Regt of Artillery 1955–57 (2 Lt 1956), TA 1957–60 (Lt 1959); dir industrial rels Ford España SA Valencia Spain 1976–80, dir industrial relations mfrg Ford of Europe Inc 1982–86, exec dir for personnel Ford Motor Co Ltd 1986–93, chm Advisory, Conciliation and Arbitration Serv (ACAS) 1993–2000; visiting fell City Univ 1991–, visiting prof Univ of E London 1991–; pres Manpower Soc 1997–2001; vice-pres Involvement and Participation Assoc 1994–2001 (hon vice-pres 2001–); chm: Employment Occupational Standards Cncl 1994–97, Employment National Training Organization 1997–2003, ENTO 2003–; dep chm and cmmr Disability Rights Cmmn 2000–07; memb: Cncl CRAC 1986–2000, CBI Employment Policy Ctee 1987–93, Engrg Industry Trg Bd 1987–91, IPM Ctee on Equal Opportunities 1987–92, Bd Personnel Management Services Ltd 1989–93, Cncl Engineering Training Authority Ltd 1990–93, Trg and Employment Agency Bd NI 1990–93, Editorial Advsy Bd Human Resource Mgmnt Jl 1991–2000, Editorial Advsy Bd Personnel Mgmnt Magazine 1993–2003, Review Body on Doctors' and Dentists' Remuneration 1992–93, Advsy Bd Civil Serv Occupational Health Serv 1992–97, Employment Appeal Tbnl 1992–93 and 2000–07, Cncl of Reference Ridley Hall Fndn Cambridge 1993–, Advsy Bd Business Sch Univ of Leeds 1996–2005; tstee The Ellenor Fndn 2005–; reader Diocese of Rochester 1998; sch govr: St George's Church of England Secdy Sch Gravesend 1989–, Gravesend GS 1989–2003; Freeman City of London 1997; Hon LLD Univ of Leeds 1997, Hon DBA De Montfort Univ 1997; CIPM 1991, CIMgt 1986; FRSA 1999; *Recreations* vintage cars, collecting books on Kent; *Clubs* Harlequin FC; *Style*— John Hougham, Esq, CBE; ✉ 12 Old Road East, Gravesend, Kent DA12 1NQ

HOUGHTON, Frances; *b* 19 September 1980; *Educ* King's Sch Canterbury, King's Coll London (BA, Jelf Medal, Sir Douglas Logan Award); *Career* amateur rower; achievements incl: Bronze medal double sculls World Jr Championships 1998, Gold medal double sculls World Under 23 Championships 1999, Silver medal double sculls and Silver medal quadruple sculls Cwlth Regatta 1999, ninth place double sculls Olympic Games Sydney 2000, winner double sculls World Cup 2002, winner quadruple sculls World Cup 2004 and 2005, Silver medal quadruple sculls Olympic Games Athens 2004, Gold medal quadruple sculls World Championships 2005 and 2006; jr champion World Indoor Rowing Championships 1999; ITV Sporting Midlander of the Year 2004; hon life memb Univ of London Union 2005; *Style*— Miss Frances Houghton

HOUGHTON, Sir John Theodore; kt (1991), CBE (1983); s of Sidney Maurice Houghton (d 1987), of Abingdon, Oxon, and Miriam, *née* Yarwood (d 1974); *b* 30 December 1931; *Educ* Rhyl GS, Jesus Coll Oxford (MA, DPhil); *m* 1, 1962, Margaret Edith (d 1986), da of Neville Broughton, of Colne, Lancs; 1 da (Janet b 1964), 1 s (Peter b 1966); m 2, 1988, Sheila, da of Sydney Thompson, of Bradford, W Yorks; *Career* res fell Royal Aircraft Estab, lectr in atmospheric physics Univ of Oxford 1958 (reader 1962, prof 1976), official fell and tutor in physics Jesus Coll Oxford 1960–73 (prof fell 1973, hon fell 1983), visiting prof UCLA 1969; dir Appleton Sci and Engrg Res Cncl 1979–83, DG (later chief exec) Meteorological Office 1983–91, hon scientist Rutherford Appleton Lab 1991–; developed: Selective Chopper Radiometer (for the Nimbus 4 and 5 satellites), Pressure Modulator Radiometer (flown on Nimbus 6) 1975, Stratospheric and Mesopheric Sounder (flown on Nimbus 7) 1978; chm: Jt Scientific Ctee for World Climate Res Programmes 1981–84, Scientific Assessment Intergovernmental Panel on Climate Change 1988–2002, Jt Scientific and Technical Ctee Global Climate Observing System 1992–95, Royal Cmmn on Environmental Pollution 1992–98; vice-pres World Meteorological Orgn 1987–91; pres John Ray Initiative 2006– (chm 1997–2006); tstee Shell Fndn 2000–; Darton Prize (RMS) 1954, Buchan Prize (RMS) 1966, Charles Chree Medal Inst of Physics 1979, Glazebrook Medal Inst of Physics 1989, Rank Prize for opto electronics 1989 (jtly), Symons Gold Medal Royal Meteorological Soc 1991, Bakerian lectr Royal Soc 1991, Global 500 Award UN Environment Prog 1994, Gold Medal Royal Astronomical Society 1995, Int Meterological Orgn Prize 1998, Japan Prize 2006; Hon DUniv Stirling 1992; Hon DSc: Univ of Wales 1991, UEA 1993, Univ of Leeds 1995, Heriot-Watt Univ 1997, Univ of Greenwich 1997, Univ of Glamorgan 1998, Univ of Reading 1999, Univ of Birmingham 2000, Univ of Glos 2001, Univ of Hull 2002, Univ of Oxford 2006; hon memb American Meteorological Soc; fell Optical Soc of America; FRS, FInstP, FRMetS (pres 1976–78, hon memb), Hon FRIBA 2001; *Books* Infra Red Physics (with S D Smith, 1966), The Physics of Atmospheres (1977, ed 1986, 3 edn 2002), Remote Sensing of Atmospheres (with F W Taylor and C D Rodgers, 1984), The Global Climate (ed, 1984), Does God Play Dice? (1988), Global Warming: The Complete Briefing (1994, 3 edn 2004), The Search for God: can science help? (1995); *Style*— Sir John Houghton, CBE, FRS

HOULDER, Bruce Fiddes; QC (1994); s of Dr Charles Alexander Houlder (d 1993), and Jessie, *née* Fiddes; *b* 27 September 1947; *Educ* Felsted; *m* 1974, Stella Catherine, da of Dr Michael Mattinson, and Barbara, *née* Wilkins; 2 da (Diana Elizabeth b 3 March 1981, Francesca Maria b 20 Aug 1983); *Career* called to the Bar Gray's Inn 1969 (bencher 2001); recorder 1991–; memb General Cncl of the Bar 1995–2000 and 2003–05, vice-chm Professional Standards Ctee 1995–2000, chm Public Affairs Ctee Bar Cncl 1998–2000 and 2004–05 (vice-chm 1996–98), vice-chm IT Panel Bar Cncl 2004–, chm Bar Quality Advsy Panel 2007–, Bar Cncl memb responsible for criminal justice modernisation prog; chm Criminal Bar Assoc of England and Wales 2001–02 (vice-chm 2000–01), memb Criminal Ctee Judicial Studies Bd 2001–04; dir Bar Services Co Ltd 2003–; vice-chm Millennium Bar Conference 2000; fell Soc for Advanced Legal Studies; *Recreations* painting, walking, theatre; *Style*— Bruce Houlder, Esq, QC; ✉ 6 King's Bench Walk, Temple, London EC4Y 7DR (tel 020 7583 0410, fax 020 7353 8791, e-mail bhqc@aol.com)

HOULDSWORTH, Philippa Caroline (Pippy); da of Maj Ian George Henry Houldsworth, TD, JP (d 1963), of Dallas, Moray, and Clodagh Houldsworth, JP, *née* Murray; *b* 17 August 1957; *m* 18 Aug 1995 (m dis 2004), Matthew Julius Radford; 2 s (Frederick b 1994, Cosmo b 1996); *Career* head buyer Children's Book Centre 1978–80, ed Children's Book News 1981–82, New Art Centre 1986–87, proprietor Houldsworth Gallery 1987–; patron of new art Tate Gallery 1992–2001, memb Exec Ctee Soc of London Art Dealers 2000–02; *Recreations* reading, visiting galleries, photography; *Style*— Pippy Houldsworth; ✉ Houldsworth Gallery, 50 Pall Mall Deposit, 124–128 Barlby Road, London W10 6BL

HOULDSWORTH, Sir Richard Thomas Reginald; 5 Bt (UK 1887), of Reddish, Manchester, Co Lancaster, and Coodham, Symington, Ayrshire; s of Sir Reginald Douglas Henry Houldsworth, 4 Bt, OBE, TD (d 1989), and Margaret May, *née* Laurie (d 1995); *b* 2 August 1947; *Educ* Bredon Sch Tewkesbury; *m* 1, 1970 (m dis 1979), Jane, o da of Alistair Orr, of Sydehead, Beith, Ayrshire; 2 s (Simon Richard Henry b 1971, Nicolas Peter George b 1975); m 2, 2 May 1992, Ann Catherine, da of late Capt Jean Jacques Tremayne, and Mrs Stella Mary Tremayne; 1 s (Matthew James b 12 Nov 1992); *Heir* s, Simon Houldsworth; *Style*— Sir Richard Houldsworth, Bt; ✉ Kirkbride, Glenburn, Crosshill, Maybole, Ayrshire

HOULIHAN, Michael Patrick; s of Michael Houlihan, and Kathleen, *née* Small (d 2007); *b* 27 September 1948; *Educ* St Francis Xavier's Coll Liverpool, Univ of Bristol (BA); *m* 1969, Jane, *née* Hibbert; 1 s (Sean b 11 May 1970), 1 da (Sarah b 7 Sept 1974); *Career* Imperial War Museum: research asst 1971–75, dep keeper Dept of Exhibits 1975–76, keeper Dept of Permanent Exhbns 1976–84; dir Horniman Museum and Gardens 1994–98 (dep dir 1984–94), chief exec Nat Museums and Galleries of NI 1998–2003, dir Amgueddfa Cymru-Nat Museum Wales 2003–; chm MDA (Museum Documentation Association) 2003–; memb: Br Cmmn for Military History 1982–, NI Ctee Br Cncl 1998, Bd NI Museum Cncl 1998; visiting prof Univ of Ulster 1999; tstee: Nat Self-Portrait Collection of Ireland 1998–2003, Nat Coal Mining Museum 2004–; memb Cncl Goldsmiths Coll London 1997–98; *Publications* Trench Warfare 1914–18 (1974), No Man's Land (jtly, 1984); *Recreations* military history, cycling, Romanesque architecture, battlefields; *Style*— Michael Houlihan, Esq; ✉ Amgueddfa Cymru - National Museum Wales, Cathays Park, Cardiff CF10 3NP

HOULSBY, Prof Guy Tinmouth; s of Thomas Tinmouth Houlsby (d 1998), of South Shields, and Vivienne May, *née* Ford; *b* 28 March 1954; *Educ* Trinity Coll Glenalmond (War Meml scholar), St John's Coll Cambridge (Whytehead open scholar, MA, PhD, Rex Moir prize, Roscoe prize, Archibald Denny prize); *m* 28 March 1985, Jenny Lucy Damaris, da of Dr Ronald M Nedderman; 2 s (Neil Matthew Tinmouth b 16 Oct 1987, Ian Thomas Tinmouth b 13 Oct 1990); *Career* civil engr: Binnie & Partners 1975–76, Babtie Shaw & Morton 1976–77; Univ of Oxford: jr res fell Balliol Coll 1980–83, lectr in engrg and fell Keble Coll 1983–91, prof of civil engrg and fell Brasenose Coll 1991–; Br Geotechnical Soc prize 1985, Geotechnical Res medal ICE 1989, Telford Prize ICE 2001; DSc Univ of Oxford 2003; CEng 1983, FICE 1997 (MICE 1983), FREng 1999; *Books* Basic Soil Mechanics (with G W E Milligan, 1984), Predictive Soil Mechanics - Proceedings of the Wroth Memorial Symposium (ed), Principles of Hyperplasticity (with A M Puzrin, 2006);

H

Recreations ornithology, woodwork, Northumbrian small pipes, rowing; *Style*— Prof Guy Houlsby; ✉ 25 Purcell Road, Marston, Oxford OX3 0HB (tel 01865 722128); Department of Engineering Science, Parks Road, Oxford OX1 3PJ (tel 01865 273138, fax 01865 283301, e-mail guy.houlsby@eng.ox.ac.uk)

HOULT, David; s of Percy Frederick Hoult, of Exmouth, Devon, and Flora, *née* Macdonald; *b* 18 April 1948; *Educ* Univ of Manchester (MusB), Royal Manchester Coll of Music (GRSM, ARMCM), Lancaster Univ (MPhil); *m* 21 Aug 1971, Mary Agnes, da of Richard Percy Fentiman; 1 da (Alice Agnes b 6 April 1982), 2 s (Thomas William b 7 Oct 1985, George Frederick b 6 Feb 1990); *Career* dir of music Cheadle Hulme Sch 1974–79, head of music UC Salford 1988–93 (sr lectr 1984–87), princ Leeds Coll of Music 1993–; also: horn player, singer, teacher, broadcaster, conductor and adjudicator; ISM 1993; *Recreations* brewing, walking; *Style*— David Hoult, Esq; ✉ Leeds College of Music, 3 Quarry Hill, Leeds LS2 7PD (tel 0113 222 3456, fax 0113 222 3455, e-mail d.hoult@lcm.ac.uk)

HOUSE, Prof John Peter Humphry; s of (Arthur) Humphry House (d 1955), and Madeline Edith, *née* Church (d 1978); *b* 19 April 1945; *Educ* Westminster, New Coll Oxford (BA), Courtauld Inst of Art London (MA), Univ of London (PhD); *m* 31 Aug 1968, Jill Elaine, da of Ernest Sackville Turner, OBE, of Kew, Surrey; 2 s (Adam b 1973, Joseph b 1975); *Career* lectr: UEA 1969–76, UCL 1976–80, Courtauld Inst of Art London 1980–87; Slade prof of fine art Univ of Oxford 1986–87; Courtauld Inst of Art London: reader 1987–95, prof 1995–, dep dir 1996–99; awarded Br Acad Res Readership 1988–90; organiser Impressionism exhibition Royal Acad of Arts 1974, co-organiser Post-Impressionism exhbn (Royal Acad of Arts) 1979–80, co-organiser Renoir exhbn (Arts Cncl of GB) 1985, curator Landscapes of France: Impressionism and its Rivals (Hayward Gallery) 1995, curator Impressionists by the Sea exhbn (Royal Acad of Arts) 2007; *Books* Monet (1976, enlarged edn 1981), Monet: Nature into Art (1986), Impressionist and Post-Impressionist Masterpieces: The Courtauld Collection (co-author, 1987), Impressionism for England: Samuel Courtauld as Patron and Collector (co-author, 1994), Renoir: La Promenade (1997), Impressionism: Paint and Politics (2004); *Recreations* second-hand bookshops; *Style*— Prof John House; ✉ Courtauld Institute of Art, University of London, Somerset House, The Strand, London WC2R ORN (tel 020 7848 2519, fax 020 7848 2410, e-mail john.house@courtauld.ac.uk)

HOUSE, Keren Ruth (Mrs John Hookway); da of Alan Sidney House, of Purley, Surrey, and Maureen Elizabeth Evelyn, *née* Atkinson; *b* 1 June 1951; *Educ* Purley Co GS for Girls, London Coll of Printing (BA), RCA (MA); *m* 9 Feb 1980, John Hookway, s of Leslie Hookway; 3 da (Jessica Rose b 27 Aug 1984, Eleanor Kate b 22 Oct 1987, Meredith Anne b 17 June 1992); *Career* lectr in graphic design Pennsylvania State Univ 1976–78; graphic designer: Bloomfield/Travis London 1978–79, Pentagram London 1979–81; pt/t lectr in graphic design Harrow Sch of Art 1981–82, fndr ptnr (with David Stuart) The Partnership 1981–83, fndr ptnr and dir The Partners 1983–87, art dir Glenn Travis Associates 1988–90; creative dir: Design Bridge 1990–98, Siebert Head 1998–2003, Aricot Vert 2003–; external assessor on BA and MA courses in graphic design; work accepted: D&AD Annual and exhbn 1979, 1981, 1983, 1985, 1987 and 1989, Communication Arts Annual (USA) 1982, 1986 and 1989, Design Effectiveness Awards 1995, 1997, 2001 and 2005, Brand Design Awards 2002; memb D&AD 1978 (memb Exec Ctee 2000–03); FRSA 1999; *Recreations* everything I can't do at work; *Style*— Ms Keren House

HOUSHIARY, Shirazeh; *b* 10 January 1955, Iran; *Educ* Chelsea Sch of Art London; *Career* artist/sculptor; work subject of numerous exhibition catalogues, articles and reviews; jr fell Cardiff Coll of Art 1979–80; prof London Inst 1997–; *Solo Exhibitions:* Chapter Arts Centre 1980, Kettle's Yard Gallery Cambridge 1982, Centro d'Arte Contemporanea Siracusa Italy 1983, Galleria Massimo Minini Milan 1983, Galerie Grita Insam Vienna 1983, Lisson Gallery London 1984, Galerie Paul Andriesse Amsterdam 1986, Breath (Lisson Gallery London) 1987, Centre d'Art Contemporain Musée Rath Geneva (travelling to MOMA Oxford) 1988–89, Valentina Moncada Rome 1992, Lisson Gallery London 1992, Camden Arts Centre London (travelling to Douglas Hyde Gallery Dublin), Fine Arts Centre Univ of Massachusetts (travelling to Art Gallery of York Univ Canada) 1993–94, The Sense of Unity (Lisson Gallery London) 1994, Isthmus (Le Magasin Centre National d'Art Contemporain Grenoble, travelling to Munich, Maastricht and Vienna) 1995–96, Islamic Gallery British Museum 1997; *Group Exhibitions* incl: London/New York 1982 (Lisson Gallery London) 1982, The Sculpture Show (Arts Cncl of GB, Hayward Gallery and Serpentine Gallery London) 1983, New Art (Tate Gallery London) 1983, British Art Show - Old Allegiances and New Directions 1979–84 (Arts Cncl of GB, travelling to Birmingham Museum and Art Gallery, Ikon Gallery Birmingham, Royal Scottish Acad Edinburgh, Mappin Art Gallery Sheffield and Southampton Art Gallery) 1984, Galerie Montenay-Delsol Paris 1985, The British Show (Art Gallery of NSW Sydney and Br Cncl, travelling to Art Gallery of Western Aust Perth, Art Gallery of NSW Sydney, Queensland Art Gallery Brisbane, The Exhibition Hall Melbourne and Nat Art Gallery Wellington NZ) 1985, Jack Shainman Gallery NY 1987, Walk out to Winter (Bess Cutler Gallery NY) 1988, Magiciens de la Terre (Centre Georges Pompidou Paris) 1989, Terskel II/Threshold II (Museet for samtidskunst Oslo Norway) 1990, Studies on Paper - Contemporary British Sculptors (Connaught Brown London) 1990, Now for the Future (Arts Cncl of GB, Hayward Gallery London) 1990, Dujourie, Fortuyn/O'Brien, Kapoor, Houshiary (Rijksmuseum Kröller-Müller Otterlo Holland) 1990, Rhizome (Haags Gemeentemuseum Netherlands) 1991, Misure e Misurazioni (Naples) 1992, Bruges La Morte Gallery Belgium 1992, II Tyne Int Newcastle 1993, Venic Biennale 1993, Travellers Treasures (Mechitarist Monastery Venice) 1993, Int Biennale of Obidos Portugal 1993, Sculptors' Drawings The Body of Drawing (Univ of Warwick Coventry and The Mead Gallery) 1993, Sculptors' Drawings presented by the Weltkunst Fndn (Tate Gallery London) 1994, Turner Prize Shortlist Artists' Exhibition (Tate Gallery London) 1994, Sculpture at Goodwood (The Hat Hill Sculpture Fndn Goodwood) 1994 and 1997, Contemporary British Art in Print (Scottish Nat Gallery of Modern Art Edinburgh touring to Yale Center for British Art New Haven) 1995, Dialogues of Peace (Palais de Nations Geneva) 1995, A Changing World - 50 Years of Sculpture from the British Council Collection (Castle Riding Hall Prague) 1995, Negotiating Rapture (Museum of Contemporary Art Chicago) 1996, 23rd Bienal Internacioal de Sao Paolo 1996, Meditation (Madras Ibn Youssef Marakesh) 1997, Follow Me - Britische Kunst an der Unterelbe (Schloss Agathenburg) 1997; *Style*— Ms Shirazeh Houshiary; ✉ Lisson Gallery London Ltd, 67 Lisson Street, London NW1 5DA (tel 020 7724 2739, fax 020 7724 7124)

HOUSLAY, Prof Miles Douglas; s of (Edwin) Douglas Houslay, of Wolverhampton, and Georgina Marie (Molly), *née* Jeffs; *b* 25 June 1950; *Educ* The Grammar Sch Brewood, UC Cardiff (BSc), King's Coll Cambridge (PhD); *m* 29 July 1972, Rhian Mair, da of Charles Henry Gee, of Aberystwyth, Wales; 1 da (Emma b 14 Feb 1978), 2 s (Thomas b 29 March 1981, Daniel b 21 Feb 1988); *Career* res fell Queens' Coll Cambridge 1975–76 (ICI postdoctoral res fell Dept of Biochemistry 1974–76), reader in biochemistry UMIST 1982–84 (lectr 1976–82), Gardiner prof of biochemistry Univ of Glasgow 1984–; memb: Res Ctee British Diabetic Assoc 1986–91, MRC Cell Biology & Disorders Bd 1990–94 (memb Grant Ctee A 1989–93 (chm 1990–93)), Clinical Biomedical Res Ctee Scottish Office Home & Health Dept 1991–93, AFRC Cell Signalling Initiative Grant Ctee 1992–97, HEFC Res Assessment Panel (Basic Medical and Dental Sciences) 1992 and 1996, Cell and Biochemistry Grant Panel Wellcome Trust 1996–2002, Advsy Bd for External Appts Univ of London 1990–97, Ctee of the Biochemical Soc of GB 1983–86; external assessor Univ of Malaysia 1991–97; ed-in-chief Cellular Signalling 1987–; Br Heart Fndn: tstee 1997–99, chm Projects Grant Ctee 1997–99, memb Chairs and Programme Grants Ctee 1997–99; memb Editorial Bd: Biochemical Jl 1981–88 (dep chm 1985–88), Biochem Biophys Acta 1982–93, Biochemical Pharmacology 1988–90, Progress in Growth Factor Res 1988–93; hon sr res fell: California Metabolic Res Fndn 1982–94, Hannah Res Inst 1988–2004, Celgene Corp 2000– (memb Scientific Advsy Bd 2002–05); memb Scientific Advsy Bd Fission Pharmaceuticals 2007–; Selby fell Australian Acad of Sci 1984; Colworth Medal Biochemical Soc GB 1985, Most Cited Scientist in Scotland 1992 (period 1986–91); FRSE 1986, founding fell Acad Med Sci, FIBiol, CBiol, FRSA; *Books* Dynamics of Biological Membranes (with K K Stanley, 1983); author of over 490 res pubns; *Recreations* reading, hill walking, travel, driving, cooking; *Style*— Prof Miles Houslay, FRSE; ✉ Molecular Pharmacology Group, Division of Biochemistry & Molecular Biology, IBLS, Wolfson Building, University of Glasgow, Glasgow G12 8QQ (tel 0141 330 4624, fax 0141 330 4365, e-mail m.houslay@bio.gla.ac.uk)

HOUSLEY, Dr Edward; s of Albert Edward Housley (d 1980), and Minnie, *née* Davis (d 1934); *b* 10 January 1934; *Educ* Mundella GS, Univ of Birmingham (MB ChB); *m* 1, 8 July 1956 (m dis 1997), Alma Mary, da of Harold Ferris (d 1968); 1 da (Lucy Elizabeth b 1962); *m* 2, 10 Oct 1997 Penelope Mary, da of Francis Hugh Thomas (d 1987); *Career* short serv cmmn RAMC 1960–63; conslt physician Royal Infirmary Edinburgh 1970–2000, hon sr lectr in med Univ of Edinburgh 1970–2000; med specialist Armed Forces Scotland 1975–2007, hon conslt in med to the Army in Scotland 1998–2007; dir Murrayfield plc 1982–92; chm MRCP (UK) Part I Examining Bd 1990–95; FRCPEd 1975, FRCP 1979, FRSM 1986; *Recreations* skiing, crossword puzzles, travel; *Style*— Dr Edward Housley; ✉ 6 Kew Terrace, Edinburgh EH12 5JE (tel 0131 337 5114, fax 0131 313 2757, e-mail edhousley@btinternet.com)

HOUSTON, Maj-Gen David; CVO (2005), CBE (1975, OBE 1972), JP (1991); s of late David Houston, and Christina Charleson, *née* Dunnett; *b* 24 February 1929; *Educ* Latymer Upper Sch; *m* 1959, Jancis Veronica Burn; 2 s; *Career* cmmnd Royal Irish Fus 1949; cmd 1 Loyals then 1 QLR 1969–71, 8 Inf Bde 1974–75, Br Mil Attaché Washington 1977–79, BGS HQ UKLF 1979–80; pres Regular Cmmns Bd 1980–83, Col Queen's Lancs Regt 1983–92; Hon Col Manchester and Salford Univ OTC 1985–90; Lord-Lt Highland Region (Dist of Sutherland) 1991–96 (DL 1990), Lord-Lt Area of Sutherland 1996–2004; *Style*— Maj-Gen David Houston, CVO, CBE; ✉ c/o Bank of Scotland, Dornoch, Sutherland IV25 3ST

HOUSTON, John; OBE (1990); s of Alexander Anderson Houston (d 1947), of Fife, and Alison Crichton, *née* McKelvie (d 2002); *b* 1 April 1930; *Educ* Buckhaven HS, Edinburgh Coll of Art (Dip Drawing and Painting, Postgrad Dip, Andrew Grant travelling scholarship), Moray House Teachers Trg Coll (Teachers Trg Cert); *m* 1956, Elizabeth Violet Blackadder, DBE, RA, RSA, *qv*, da of Thomas Blackadder; *Career* artist; dep head Sch of Drawing and Painting Edinburgh Coll of Art 1982–89 (teacher 1955–89); memb: SSA, RGI, RSW; RSA 1972; *Works* incl: Dusk (Scot Arts Cncl) 1971, Bathers (Carlsberg Breweries Copenhagen) 1966, Wisconsin Landscape 1969, Dune Sounds 1971, Lake Owen Wisconsin 1970–71, Summer In Fife (private collection Sweden) 1968, Low Tide, North Berwick 1982, Winter Walk 1985, Beach Party 1986–90, A Day By The Sea, Summer 1990; exhibits regularly with: Scot Gallery Edinburgh, Browse Darby London, Royal Scot Acad, Royal Acad, RGI; Guthrie Award (Royal Scot Acad, 1964), Cargill Prize (RGI, 1965 and 1988), Sir William Gillies Prize (RSW, 1990); Hon LLD Heriot Watt Univ 2004; *Recreations* golf; *Clubs* Gullane Golf, Lansdowne; *Style*— John Houston, Esq, OBE; ✉ 57 Fountainhall Road, Edinburgh EH9 2LH (tel 0131 667 3687)

HOUSTON, John McLellan; *b* 18 July 1944; *Career* dir Coats Patons plc/Coats Viyella plc 1985–88, dir Kwik-Fit Holdings plc 1988–2002, non-exec dir Br Polythene Industries plc 1999–; *Style*— John Houston, Esq; ✉ 3 Douglas Avenue, Langbank, Port Glasgow PA14 6PE (tel 01475 540683, mobile 07881 781755)

HOUSTON, Robert Ian; s of Ivan Thomas Houston (d 1985), of Gloucester, and Joy, *née* Meehan (d 1987); *b* 18 October 1950; *Educ* Sebright Sch, Nottingham Trent Univ (BSc); *m* Gillian Duret, da of Frederick John Floyd; 2 s (Ian David b 8 July 1979, Andrew Robert b 6 May 1983), 1 da (Claire Alexandra b 10 March 1981); *Career* chartered surveyor; Richard Ellis 1972–80, chief exec Rowe & Pitman Property Services 1980–84, chm ING Real Estate Investment Management Ltd (formerly Baring, Houston & Saunders) 1984–; chm Boost Charitable Tst; Liveryman Worshipful Co of Chartered Surveyors; FRICS; *Recreations* cricket; *Style*— Robert Houston, Esq; ✉ Winkford Lodge, Church Lane, Witley, Godalming, Surrey GU8 5PR (tel 01428 683016); ING Real Estate Investment Management Ltd, 6th Floor, 60 London Wall, London EC2M 5TQ (tel 020 7767 5559, fax 020 7767 7772)

HOUSTOUN-BOSWALL, Sir (Thomas) Alford; 8 Bt (UK 1836); s of Sir Thomas Houstoun-Boswall, 7 Bt (d 1982), by his 1 w (*see* Houstoun-Boswall, Margaret, Lady); *b* 23 May 1947; *m* 1971 (m dis 1996), Eliana Michele, da of Dr John Pearse, of New York; 1 s (Alexander Alford b 1972), 1 da (Julia Glencora b 1979); *Heir* s, Alexander Houstoun-Boswall; *Style*— Sir Alford Houstoun-Boswall, Bt; ✉ 18 Rue Basse, Biot 06410, France (tel 00 33 93 65 72 44); 11 East 73rd Street, New York City, NY 10021, USA (tel 212 517 8057); c/o The Harrodian School, Lonsdale Road, London SW13 9QN (tel 020 8748 6117)

HOW, Peter Cecil; s of Cecil P How (d 1995, aged 100), of Rugeley, Staffs, and Dora, *née* Marshall (d 1960); *b* 27 June 1931; *Educ* Oundle, Open Univ (BA); *m* 21 Sept 1951, Jane, da of Thomas Erickson (d 1936); 2 s (Neil b 1952, Adam b 1954); *Career* dir Froggatt & Prior Ltd 1955–63; chm: How Group Ltd and assoc cos 1974–86 (dir 1963), H & V Welfare Ltd 1974–90, How Group plc 1986–97, Hansgross Estates plc 1986–97; non-exec dir Hazard Chase Ltd 2000–; pres Genie Climatique International 1986–88 (hon pres 1994–); memb W Midlands Regnl Cncl CBI 1979–85; pres Heating and Ventilating Contractors' Assoc 1975–76; memb Chm's Circle Symphony Hall Birmingham 2002–; Liveryman Worshipful Co of Fan Makers 1975; *Recreations* travel, theatre, opera, music, books, gardening, memb Magic Circle; *Clubs* East India, City Livery; *Style*— Peter How, Esq; ✉ 11 The Regents, Norfolk Road, Edgbaston, Birmingham B15 3PP (tel 0121 454 4777, fax 0121 246 1572); 7047 Vilamoura Place, Lakewood Ranch, FL 34202, USA (tel 00 1 941 907 0239, fax 00 1 941 907 0392)

HOW, Ronald Mervyn; s of Mervyn Darvell How (d 1973), of Bucks, and Kathleen Dorothy, *née* Honour (d 1990); *b* 24 December 1927; *m* 30 June 1951, Brenda (d 1989), da of Harold Brown (d 1976), of Herts; 1 s (David b 1953), 1 da (Margaret b 1956); *Career* RAF AC1 1946–47; farmer; dir: Br Turkey Fedn 1978–99 (fndr memb, treas 1984–88), Br Poultry Meat Fedn 1978–99; Central Region turkey delg NFU HQ Poultry Ctee 1992–98; memb Rotary Club 1973– (pres Chesham branch 1981, treas Chesham branch 1983–92); memb Ctee Hawridge Commons Preservation Soc 1970–99, pres (former chm) Amersham Hosp League of Friends (memb Ctee 1979–), memb Chesham Town Cncl Environmental Sub-Gp Ctee 2000–, treas Friends of St Mary's Church 1994–2000, working with LabAid 2001–; Goodchild Trophy for Service to Turkey Industry 1987; *Recreations* tennis, computer programming, photography; *Clubs* Chesham Rotary, Amersham Photographic Soc; *Style*— Ronald How, Esq; ✉ Mayfield, North Road, Chesham Bois, Amersham HP6 5NA (tel 01494 723577, e-mail rturkey1@btinternet.com)

HOW, Timothy; s of Mervyn How and Margaret How, of Norwich; *b* 29 December 1950; *Educ* Churchill Coll Cambridge (MA), London Business Sch (MSc); *m* Elizabeth; 4 da (Jennifer, Rachel, Caroline, Susan); *Career* gen mangr Polaroid (UK) Ltd 1979–83; Bejam Freezer Food Centres Ltd: mktg dir 1983–85, trading dir 1985–87, managing dir 1987–89; chief exec Majestic Wine plc 1989–; non-exec chm Framlington AIM VCT plc, non-exec dep chm Austin Reed Gp plc; *Recreations* dinghy racing; *Clubs* Oxford and Cambridge Sailing Soc, Brancaster Staithe Sailing; *Style*— Timothy How, Esq; ✉ 47 Battlefield Road, St Albans AL1 4DB (tel 01727 857884); Majestic Wine Warehouses Ltd, Majestic House, Otterspool Way, Watford WD25 8WW (tel 01923 298200, fax 01923 819105)

HOWARD, *see also:* Fitzalan Howard

HOWARD, Anthony John; s of Peter Dunsmore Howard (d 1965, former Capt England Rugby Team), of Sudbury, Suffolk, and Doris Emily, *née* Metaxas (former winner Wimbledon Ladies Doubles); *b* 31 December 1937; *Educ* Eton, Trinity Coll Oxford; *m* 12 Oct 1963, Elisabeth Ann, da of Capt Roddie Casement, OBE, RN (d 1987); 1 s (Tom), 2 da (Katie, Emma); *Career* film researcher, producer, dir and writer for TV; 2500 films and progs for TV incl: Greece - The Hidden War, A Passage to Britain, A Full Life, Dick Barton - Special Agent, Country Ways (24 series), Every Night Something Awful, The Missa Luba, The Cathedrals of Britain, Country Faces, Great House Cookery, Pub People, Land Girls, Michael Barry's Undiscovered Cooks, Reflections on Science, Tool Box, Coastal Ways (10 series), Famous Foods of the South (2 series); fndr chief exec Countrywide Films Ltd 1989–2005 (taken over by da Katie Judd); currently freelance writer, prodr and dir; *Books* thirteen books published on the English countryside; *Recreations* walking, talking, shepherding, reading, wood clearing; *Style*— Anthony Howard, Esq; ✉ Drove Cottage, Newbridge, Cadnam, Southampton, Hampshire SO40 2NW (tel 023 8081 3233); Countrywide Films Ltd, Production Office, Tatchbury House, Loperwood, Calmore, Southampton, Hampshire SO40 2RN (tel 023 8066 9006)

HOWARD, Dr Anthony John (Tony); MBE (2007); *b* 14 April 1949; *Educ* Surbiton GS for Boys, King's Coll London (AKC, MB BS, MSc), St George's Hosp Med Sch London (Brackenbury prize in surgery); *m*; 2 c; *Career* St George's Hosp London: house physician 1972–73, house surgn 1973, SHO in pathology 1972–74, registrar in med microbiology 1974–76; sr lectr in med microbiology London Hosp Med Coll 1979–81 (lectr 1976–79), conslt in med microbiology Gwynedd Dist Hosp Bangor 1981–93, dir Bangor Public Health Lab 1993–95, chm R&D Ctee and asst med dir Gwynedd Hosps NHS Tst 1994–95, dir Public Health Lab Serv Wales 2000– (gp dir 1995–2000), dir Cardiff Public Health Lab 1998–; memb: Welsh Microbiology Standing Specialist Advsy Ctee 1981– (chm 1989–94), Dept of Health Infection Working Gp 1992–94; Assoc of Med Microbiologists: Welsh rep Clinical Servs Sub-Ctee 1985–93, memb Educn Sub-Ctee 1986–89; Welsh Microbiology Assoc: sec 1984–87, vice-pres 1987–90, pres 1990–93; memb Cncl: Hosp Infection Soc 1985–90 (gen sec 1986–89), Br Soc for the Study of Infection 1989–91 (memb Ctee English Branch 1987–90), Br Soc for Antimicrobial Chemotherapy 1992–94, RCPath 1994–96 (Welsh regional rep 1992–94); Gillson scholar in pathology Soc of Apothecaries London 1979, Br Cncl travelling fell Turkey 1993; memb: American Soc for Microbiology, Med Scis Historical Soc, Y Gymdeithas Feddygol; contrib various book chapters and author of numerous papers in scientific jls; asst ed Jl of Hosp Infection 1987–93, section ed Current Opinions in Infectious Diseases 1991; FRCPath 1990 (MRCPath 1978); *Recreations* book collecting, history, cricket, music, food and wine; *Style*— Dr Tony Howard, MBE; ✉ Public Health Laboratory Service, University Hospital of Wales, Heath Park, Cardiff CF4 4XW (tel 029 2074 4515)

HOWARD, Anthony Michell; CBE (1997); s of late Canon Guy Howard, and Janet Rymer Howard; *b* 12 February 1934; *Educ* Westminster, ChCh Oxford; *m* 1965, Carol Anne Gaynor; *Career* political journalist; called to the Bar Inner Temple 1956; Nat Serv 2 Lt Royal Fus 1956–58; political corr Reynolds News 1958–59, Editorial Staff Manchester Guardian 1959–61 (Harkness fell USA 1960), political corr New Statesman 1961–64, Whitehall corr Sunday Times 1965, Washington corr Observer 1966–69 (political columnist 1971–72), ed The New Statesman 1972–78 (asst ed 1970–72), ed The Listener 1979–81, dep ed The Observer 1981–88, reporter BBC TV 1989–92, Obituaries ed The Times 1993–99; presenter: Face the Press (Channel 4) 1982–85, The Editors (Sky) 1989–90; Gerald Barry What the Papers Say Award 1998; Hon LLD Univ of Nottingham 2001, Hon DLitt Univ of Leicester 2003, hon student ChCh Oxford 2003; *Books* The Baldwin Age (contrib, 1960), Age of Austerity (contrib, 1963), The Making of the Prime Minister (with Richard West, 1965), The Crossman Diaries (ed, 1979), RAB: The Life of R A Butler (1987), Crossman: The Pursuit of Power (1990), Secrets of the Press (contrib, 1999), Basil Hume: The Monk Cardinal (2005); *Clubs* Garrick, Beefsteak; *Style*— Anthony Howard, Esq, CBE; ✉ 11 Campden House Court, London W8 4HU (tel 020 7937 7313); Dinham Lodge, Ludlow, Shropshire SY8 1EH (tel 01584 878457)

HOWARD, Charles Anthony Frederick; QC (1999); s of John Howard (d 1970), of London, and Mrs Naida Royal, formerly Howard, *née* Guest (d 1997); *b* 7 March 1951; *Educ* Sherborne, St John's Coll Cambridge (open history scholarship, McMahon studentship); *m* 1, (m dis), Geraldine Howard; 1 s (Alexander b 27 April 1981), 1 da (Francesca b 22 Dec 1982); m 2, Rosie Boycott, *qv*, da of Maj Charles Boycott; 1 step da (Daisy Leitch b 9 Aug 1983); *Career* called to the Bar 1975; barrister in private practice 1975–; memb Family Law Bar Assoc; *Recreations* cricket, tennis, films, gardening, breeding pigs and walking; *Clubs* Groucho, Somerset CCC; *Style*— Charles Howard, Esq, QC; ✉ 1 King's Bench Walk, Temple, London EC4Y 7DB (tel 020 7936 1500, fax 020 7936 1590)

HOWARD, Sir David Howarth Seymour; 3 Bt (UK 1955), of Great Rissington, Co Gloucester; s of Sir (Hamilton) Edward de Coucey Howard, 2 Bt, GBE (d 2001); *b* 29 December 1945; *Educ* Radley, Worcester Coll Oxford (MA); *m* 15 June 1968, Valerie Picton, o da of late Derek Weatherly Crosse, of Broadstairs, Kent; 2 da (Caroline Picton Seymour b 1970, Victoria Picton Seymour b 1975), 2 s (Robert Picton Seymour b 1971, James Picton Seymour b 1979); *Heir* s, Robert Howard; *Career* chm Charles Stanley & Co Ltd (Stockbrokers) 1999– (md 1971–); dir: Assoc of Private Client Investment Mangrs and Stockbrokers (APCIMS) 2001–, Securities Inst 2002– (chm Examination Bd 2003–); pres City of London Branch Chartered Mgmnt Inst 2002–; pro-chllr and chm of Cncl City Univ 2003–; Alderman City of London 1986–, Common Councilman City of London 1972–86, Sheriff City of London 1997–98, Lord Mayor of London 2000–01; councillor London Borough of Sutton 1974–78; chm London Gardens Soc 1996–; Master Worshipful Co of Gardeners 1990–91; Hon FSI; KStJ 2000, Grand Cordon (First Class) of the Order of Independence (Jordan) 2001; *Style*— Sir David Howard, Bt; ✉ 25 Luke Street, London EC2A 4AR

HOWARD, Prof David Martin; s of Jack Bruere Howard, of Rochester, Kent, and Philis Joan, *née* Probert; *b* 13 April 1956; *Educ* King's Sch Rochester, UCL (BSc(Eng), Clinton prize, PhD); *m* 3 October 1981, Clare, da of Robert Hilton Wake; 1 s (Joseph Leo b 11 March 1993), 1 da (Antonia Elizabeth b 11 June 1996); *Career* trainee offr RN BRNC Dartmouth 1974–78; lectr in experimental phonetics UCL 1979–90; Univ of York: lectr in music technol 1990–93, sr lectr 1993–96, prof 1996–, head Dept of Electronics 1996–2000; fndr ed Voice 1992–95; ed-in-chief Logopedics Phoniatrics Vocology 2002–; chm Engrg Professors' Cncl 1999–2001, vice-pres and tstee Instn of Engrg and Technol 2004–; memb Editorial Bd: Forensic Linguistics Int Jl of Speech Language and the Law 1999–, Organised Sound 2001–; memb: Br Assoc of Academic Phoneticians 1988–, Br Voice Assoc 1990–, Int Assoc of Forensic Phoneticians 1991–; choral dir The Beningbrough Singers, dep tenor songman York Minster 2004–; Ferens Inst of Otolaryngology Prize 1989, Design Cncl/BAe Engrg Design Award 1992, Ken Brodie Award 1993, Thorn EMI Prize 1994; memb and dir Audio Engrg Soc; CEng 1995, FIEE 1997; *Recreations* organist, keyboard playing, choral direction, choir singing, sailing, skiing, walking; *Style*— Prof David Howard; ✉ Department of Electronics, University of York, Heslington, York YO10 5DD (tel 01904 432405, fax 01904 432335, e-mail dmh@ohm.york.ac.uk)

HOWARD, Prof Deborah Janet; da of Thomas Were Howard (d 1997), and Isobel, *née* Brewer (d 1990); *b* 26 February 1946; *Educ* Loughton HS for Girls, Newnham Coll Cambridge (MA), Courtauld Inst of Art (MA, PhD); *m* 26 Sept 1975, Prof Malcolm Sim Longair, s of James Longair; 1 s (Mark Howard b 13 Sept 1976), 1 da (Sarah Charlotte b 7 March 1979); *Career* Leverhulme fell in history of art Clare Hall Cambridge 1972–73, lectr in history of art UCL 1973–76, visiting lectr Yale Univ 1977 and 1980, pt/t lectr, sr lectr then reader Dept of Architecture Univ of Edinburgh 1982–91, pt/t lectr Courtauld Inst of Art 1991–92; Univ of Cambridge: librarian to Faculty of Architecture and History of Art 1992–96, fell St John's Coll 1992–, reader in architectural history 1996–2001, prof of architectural history 2001–, head Dept of History of Art 2002–05 and 2007–08; Kennedy prof of Renaissance studies Smith Coll Massachusetts 2006, visiting prof Harvard Univ Center for Italian Renaissance Studies Florence 2007; cmmr: Royal Fine Art Cmmn for Scotland 1985–95, Royal Cmmn on Ancient and Historic Monuments of Scotland 1989–99, chm Soc of Architectural Historians of GB 1997–2000; FSA 1984, FSA Scot 1991, Hon FRIAS 1996, FRSE 2004; *Books* Jacopo Sansovino: Architecture & Patronage in Renaissance Venice (1975, 2 edn 1987), The Architectural History of Venice (1980, revised edn 2002), William Adam (Architectural Heritage I, ed 1990), Scottish Architects Abroad (Architectural Heritage II, ed 1991, Glenfiddich Award), Scottish Architecture from the Reformation to the Restoration (1995), La Scuola Grande della Misericordia di Venezia (co-author, 1999), Venice and the East: The Impact of the Islamic World on Venetian Architecture 1100–1500 (2000), Architettura e musica nella Venezia del Rinascimento (co-ed, 2006); *Recreations* music (especially opera and chamber music), hill-walking, gardening, photography; *Style*— Prof Deborah Howard, FSA, FRSE; ✉ Faculty of Architecture and History of Art, University of Cambridge, 1 Scroope Terrace, Cambridge CB2 1PX (tel 01223 332975, fax 01223 332960); St John's College, Cambridge CB2 1TP (tel 01223 339360, fax 01223 740399, e-mail djh1000@cam.ac.uk)

HOWARD, Elizabeth Jane; CBE (2000); da of David Liddon Howard (d 1962), and Katharine Margaret Somervell (d 1975); *b* 26 March 1923; *m* 1, (m dis), Peter Markham Scott (later Sir Peter Scott, CH, CBE, DSC, FRS, d 1989), s of Capt Robert Falcon Scott; 1 da (Nicola); m 2, James Douglas-Henry; m 3, (m dis), Sir Kingsley William Amis, CBE (d 1995); *Career* novelist, playwright of 14 TV plays; FRSL; *Books* The Beautiful Visit (1950), The Long View (1956), The Sea Change (1959), After Julius (1965), Something in Disguise (1969), Odd Girl Out (1972), Mr Wrong (short stories, 1975), Lovers' Companion (ed, 1978), Getting It Right (1982), The Light Years (1990), Green Shades (1991), Marking Time (1991), Confusion (1993), Casting Off (1995), Marriage (anthology, 1997), The Lover's Companion (anthology, 1998), Falling (1999), Slipstream (autobiography, 2002); *Recreations* gardening, cooking, reading, music; *Style*— Miss Elizabeth Jane Howard, CBE, FRSL; ✉ c/o Jonathan Clowes, 10 Iron Bridge House, Bridge Approach, London NW1 8BD (tel 020 7722 7674)

H

HOWARD, Francis John Adrian; s of Ewen Storrs Howard (d 1979), of Cape Town, South Africa, and Cynthia Beatrice, *née* Wallace (d 2000); *b* 11 July 1935; *Educ* Michaelhouse Sch South Africa, Univ of Natal (BCom); *m* 30 Sept 1961, Lynette, da of John Ashford Mader (d 1988), of South Africa; 2 s (Gregory Andrew b 1964 d 1996, Philip Ewen b 1966); *Career* dir: The Diamond Trading Co 1973–75, Beralt Tin and Wolfram Ltd 1977–86, Cape Industries plc 1977–86, Charter Consolidated plc 1978–87, Anderson Strathclyde Ltd 1980–87, Howard Perry Assocs Ltd 1987–98, Nestor Healthcare Group plc 1987–99, Hawtal Whiting Holdings plc 1988–95, Consolidated Communications Management Ltd (non-exec chm) 1989–2001, I Hennig and Co Ltd 1990–, International Training Equipment Conference Ltd (chm) 1991–96; chm JUS Ltd 2000–01; dir African Medical and Research Fndn UK 1990–2005 (chm 1990–99), dir African Medical and Research Fndn Kenya 1990–2003, tstee AMREF Tst Fund 1995–2005; tstee Action in the Community Environment 2005–; *Recreations* gardening, painting, wine-making, shooting, fishing; *Clubs* Boodle's, Rand (Johannesburg); *Style*— Francis Howard, Esq; ✉ 6 Varsity Row, London SW14 7SA (tel 020 8876 2905, e-mail fhoward@dialstart.net)

HOWARD, Prof Ian; s of Harold Geoffrey Howard, of Aberdeen, and Violet, *née* Kelly; *b* 7 November 1952; *Educ* Aberdeen GS, Univ of Edinburgh, Edinburgh Coll of Art; *m* 1977, Ruth, da of Henry D'Arcy; 2 da (Francesca b 21 April 1982, Annabelle b 25 Jan 1986); *Career* artist; travelling scholarship Italy 1976, lectr in painting Grays Sch of Art Aberdeen 1977–86, head of painting Duncan of Jordanstone Coll of Art and Design Dundee 1986–95, prof of fine art Univ of Dundee 1995–2001, dean of faculty Duncan of Jordanstone Coll of Art Univ of Dundee 1999–2001, princ Edinburgh Coll of Art 2001–; William Gillies Bequest Scholarship 1990 (travelled in India and Thailand); over 80 exhibitions incl: Different Realists (Talbot-Rice Art Centre Edinburgh) 1973, Edinburgh Int Film Festival 1976, Recent Acquisitions Scot Arts Cncl Gallery 1979 and 1981, Grease & Water (Scot Arts Cncl touring) 1982, Dunbar & Howard (Glasgow Arts Centre) 1984, Contemporary Scottish Printmakers (Mercury Gallery London) 1984, Sculptors' Drawings (Arts Cncl touring) 1984–85, New Drawings (Compass Gallery Glasgow) 1985, The Human Touch (Fischer Fine Art London) 1986, Br Cncl British/Malaysian Exhibition Kuala Lumpur 1986, Br Cncl touring exhibition (Bangkok, Singapore, Hong Kong) 1987, Scottish Contemporary Art (Clare Hall Cambridge) 1987, Scottish Art in Yugoslavia 1988, Fine Art Soc (Edinburgh and Glasgow) 1990, Print Works Chicago 1996, Dubrovnik Festival 1997, Iwate Festival Japan 1998, John David Mooney Fndn Chicago 2000; work in collections incl: Edinburgh Coll of Art, Scot Arts Cncl, Contemporary Arts Soc, Hunterian Gallery Glasgow, Unilever plc, Arts Cncl of England, ICI plc, Clare Coll Cambridge, City Arts Centre Edinburgh, Aberdeen Hosps Art Project, Fleming's Bank Collection; awards incl: Guthrie award Royal Scot Acad 1978, Scot Arts Cncl award 1979, Scot Arts Cncl major bursary 1984–85, first prize Scot Open Drawing competition 1985, Shell Premier award 1985, prizewinner Tolly-Cobbold Eastern Arts Nat competition 1985, Chicago prize 2000; Royal Scot Acad: associate 1984–, academician 1998–; dir: ALBA magazine 1989–, Dundee Contemporary Arts (DCA) 1998–; memb Scot Arts Cncl Awards Panel and Purchasing Ctee 1990–96, memb Faculty of Fine Art Br Sch at Rome 1995–2001; FRSA; *Style*— Prof Ian Howard; ✉ Edinburgh College of Art, 74 Lauriston Place, Edinburgh EH3 9DF (tel 0131 221 6060, fax 0131 221 6058, e-mail i.howard@eca.ac.uk)

HOWARD, John; s of Henry Vivian Howard, and Florence Elizabeth, *née* Pulley; *b* 11 February 1951; *Educ* Strode's Sch Egham; *m* Angela Margaret; 2 da (Sasha Sophie, Tamzin Alice); *Career* admitted slr 1979; presenter: You and Yours (Radio 4) 1980–95, Nature (BBC TV) 1988–89, The Leading Edge (Radio 5), An Unfortunate Turn of Events (Radio 4) 1995, BBC World TV 1996–99; dir Sharp End Productions; dir Mortgage Code Compliance Bd 2000–05, memb Fin Servs Consumer Panel 2000 (chm 2005); Soc of Authors/Pye Radio Award Best Light Entertainment Programme Radio 1979, RICS Radio Award Best Investigative Programme Radio 1983, Argus Consumer Journalist Award Radio 1985, Sony Award for Best Social Affairs Programme Radio 1989; *Style*— John Howard, Esq; ✉ 28 Royal Crescent, Holland Park, London W11 4SN; office: (tel 01488 657485)

HOWARD, Prof (James) Ken; s of Frank Howard (d 1974), of Mousehole, Cornwall, and Elizabeth Crawford, *née* Meikle (d 1987); *b* 26 December 1932; *Educ* Kilburn GS, Hornsey Coll of Art, RCA (ARCA); *m* 1, 1961 (m dis 1974), Margaret Ann, da of Philip Popham, of Ickenham, Middx; m 2, 1991, Christa Gaa, *née* Koehler, ARWS (d 1992), formerly wife of Hartmut Gaa; 2 step da; m 3, 2000, Dora Bertolutti, formerly wife of Bruno Di Giorgio; *Career* Nat Serv RM 1953–55; artist; Br Cncl scholarship Florence 1958–59, taught at various London art schs 1959–73, official artist Imperial War Museum NI 1973 and 1978;

painted for Br Army: NI, Germany, Cyprus, Hong Kong, Brunei, Nepal, Belize, Norway, Lebanon; Hon RBA 1988, Hon ROI 1988; past pres New English Art Club (PPNEAC); NEAC 1962 (pres 1998), RWA 1981, RWS 1983, RBSA 1991, RA 1992 (ARA 1983); *Solo Exhibitions* Plymouth Art Centre 1955, John Whibley Gallery 1966–68, New Grafton Gallery 1971–2000, Hong Kong 1979, Jersey 1980, Nicosia 1982, Delhi 1983, Oscar J Peter Johnson 1986–92, Duncalfe Gallery Harrogate 1987–, Sinfield Gallery 1991, 1993 and 1995, Hollis Taggart Inc Washington DC 1993, Everard Reed Gallery Johannesburg 1998 and Cape Town 2001, Richard Green Gallery 2002, 2003, 2004, 2005 and 2006; *Work in Collections* Plymouth Art Gallery, Imperial War Museum, Guildhall Art Gallery, Ulster Museum, Nat Army Museum, Southend Art Gallery, HNC Art Gallery, Sheffield Art Gallery, Bankside Gallery; *Portraits* incl: Gerald Durrell, Gen Sir Martin Farndale; *Commissions* Drapers' Co, Haberdashers' Co, States of Jersey, HQ Br Army of the Rhine, HM Forces in Cyprus, The Stock Exchange, Lloyd's of London, Royal Hosp Chelsea, Banque Paribas, *Video* Inspired by Light 1996, Vision of Venice in Watercolour 1998, Vision of Venice in Oils 2000; *Books* The War Artists (1986), Art Class (1989), Venice - The Artist's Vision (1990), Visions of Venice (1990), The Paintings of Ken Howard (1992), Ken Howard - a Personal View (1998); *Style*— Prof Ken Howard, Esq, RA; ✉ 8 South Bolton Gardens, London SW5 0DH (tel 020 7373 2912, fax 020 7244 6246); St Clements Studio, Paul Lane, Mousehole, Cornwall TR19 6TR (tel 01736 731596); Cannaregio 6262, Venice, Italy (tel 0039 041 5202277)

HOWARD, Dr Laurence; s of Henry Lovering Howard (d 1990), of Surrey, and Beryl Cicely Howard; *b* 29 March 1943, Woking, Surrey; *Educ* Strode's Sch Egham, Univ of Nottingham (BSc), Univ of Leicester (PhD); *m* 1966, Christine Mary, da of William Kinver; 1 da (Anna b 16 July 1972), 1 s (Stephen b 29 May 1974); *Career* Wolfson research fell Univ of Leeds 1970–73, lectr in physiology Univ of Leicester 1974–90, sub dean Leicester Med Sch 1990–2003; author of various articles in physiological jls; memb Physiological Soc 1980; HM Lord-Lt Rutland 2003–; chm: Rutland Bench 1991–97, Central Cncl of Magistrates' Courts Ctees 2002–03; memb Bd Unified Courts Admin Prog 2003–04; pres: Leicester and Rutland Magistrates' Assoc, Leicester and Rutland Headway; fell UC Northampton; *Recreations* horses and music; *Style*— Dr Laurence Howard; ✉ Daventry House, Main Street, Whissendine, Rutland LE15 7ET (tel 01664 474662); Leicester Medical School, Leicester LE1 9HN (tel 0116 252 2967, fax 0116 252 3013, e-mail lh31@le.ac.uk)

HOWARD, Margaret; da of John Bernard Howard (d 1969), and Ellen Corwena, *née* Roberts; *b* 29 March 1938; *Educ* St Mary's Convent Rhyl, St Teresa's Convent Sunbury-on-Thames, Guildhall Sch of Music and Drama (LGSM), Univ of Indiana; *Career* BBC announcer 1966–69, reporter World This Weekend 1971–74, presenter Pick of the Week 1974–91, radio columnist Sunday Express 1991–92; Classic FM: presenter Classic Reports 1992–94, ed and presenter Howard's Week 1994–97, presenter Masterclass 1994–98, presenter Hot Ticket Hour, Vienna City of Dreams and Classic Discoveries 1997–99; radio critic The Tablet 1991–2001, columnist The Universe 1973–79, classical CD reviewer Chic Magazine 1995–98; presenter: Viva Verdi GB Concert Tour with Opera Nazionale Italiana 2001, Haydn's Seven Last Words From The Cross with the Medici Quartet Geneva and London 2001 and 2002, Coverwood Farm Concert 2002; conslt and recording artist Classical Communications Ltd 2003–, interviewer Appreciating Great Music CD series for Haysbridge (UK) Ltd 2003–; female UK Personality of the Year Sony Awards 1984, Sony Radio Awards Roll of Honour 1988, Voice of the Listener Award for Excellence 1991, Radio Personality of the Year Television and Radio Industries Club Awards 1996; memb: LRAM, LGSM; *Books* Margaret Howard's Pick of the Week (1984), Court Jesting (1986); *Recreations* riding, swimming, dog walking, wine tasting; *Clubs* South London Swimming (Tooting Bec Lido); *Style*— Miss Margaret Howard; ✉ 215 Cavendish Road, London SW12 0BP (tel 020 8673 7336, e-mail margaret.howard@virgin.net)

HOWARD, Dr Mary Elizabeth; da of William Joseph Howard (d 1974), and Mary, *née* Breaden (d 1979); *b* 17 April 1953; *Educ* Notre Dame HS Glasgow, Univ of Glasgow (MB ChB); *m* 14 July 1976, John Hilary Higgins, s of John Joseph Higgins, MBE (d 1972); 1 da (Louise Mary Anne b 1985); *Career* sr registrar in histopathology Gtr Glasgow Health Bd 1980–83 (house surgn and house physician 1976–77, registrar 1977–80), conslt histopathologist Wishaw General Hosp (now part of Lanarkshire Acute Hospitals Tst) 1983–; memb: BMA, Assoc of Clinical Pathologists, Mensa; FRCPath 1994 (MRCPath 1982); *Recreations* music, arts and crafts, reading; *Style*— Dr Mary Howard; ✉ Department of Histopathology, Wishaw General Hospital, 50 Netherton Street, Carluke, Lanarkshire ML2 0DP (tel 01698 366325, fax 01698 366333, e-mail mary.howard@laht.scot.nhs.uk)

HOWARD, Rt Hon Michael; PC (1990), QC (1982), MP; s of late Bernard Howard, and Hilda Howard; *b* 7 July 1941; *Educ* Llanelli GS, Peterhouse Cambridge; *m* 1975, Sandra Clare, da of Wing Cdr Saville Paul; 1 s, 1 da, 1 step s (Sholto Douglas-Home, *qv*); *Career* pres Cambridge Union 1962, called to the Bar Inner Temple 1964, chm Bow Group 1970; Parly candidate (Cons) Liverpool Edge Hill 1966 and 1970, MP (Cons) Folkestone and Hythe 1983–; memb: Cons Gp for Europe, Euro Movement Exec Ctee 1970–73; PPS to Slr-Gen 1984–85, Parly under sec of state for Consumer and Corporate Affrs 1985–87, min for Local Govt 1987–88, min for Water and Planning 1988–90, sec of state for Employment 1990–92, sec of state for the Environment 1992–93, home sec 1993–97; shadow foreign sec 1997–99, shadow Chllr of the Exchequer 2001–03, ldr Cons Pty and HM Oppn 2003–05 (Cons Pty leadership challenger 1997); memb Cons Pty Policy Bd 2001–03; chm: Coningsby Club 1972–73, Atlantic Partnership 2000–03; Parliamentarian of the Year Spectator Awards 2003; *Recreations* watching sport, reading; *Clubs* Carlton, Pratt's; *Style*— The Rt Hon Michael Howard, QC, MP; ✉ House of Commons, London SW1 (tel 020 7219 5493, fax 020 7219 5322)

HOWARD, Sir Michael Eliot; OM (2005), CH (2002), kt (1986), CBE (1977), MC (1943); s of Geoffrey Eliot Howard (d 1956), of Ashmore, Dorset, and Edith Julia Emma Edinger (d 1977); *b* 29 November 1922; *Educ* Wellington, ChCh Oxford (MA, DLitt); *Career* served Italian Theatre with 2 & 3 Bns Coldstream Gds (Capt) 1943–45; prof of war studies KCL 1963–68, Chichele prof of history of war Univ of Oxford 1977–80, regius prof of modern history Univ of Oxford 1980–89, prof of history Yale Univ 1989–93, pres Int Inst of Strategic Studies; DLitt, FRHistS, FBA 1970; *Books* The Franco-Prussian War (1961), Grand Strategy, Vol IV in UK Official History of World War II (1972), The Continental Commitment (1972), War in European History (1976), The Causes of Wars (1983), Strategic Deception in World War II (1990), The Lessons of History (1991), The Oxford History of the 20th Century (jtly, 1998), The Invention of Peace (2000), The First World War (2002); *Recreations* music; *Clubs* Athenaeum, Garrick, Pratt's; *Style*— Sir Michael Howard, OM, CH, CBE, MC, FBA; ✉ The Old Farm, Eastbury, Hungerford, Berkshire RG17 7JN

HOWARD, Michael Newman; QC; s of late Henry Ian Howard, and Tilly Celia, *née* Newman; *b* 10 June 1947; *Educ* Clifton, Magdalen Coll Oxford (MA, BCL); *Career* lectr in law LSE 1970–74; called to the Bar Gray's Inn 1971 (bencher 1995); in practice at the Bar 1972–, recorder of the Crown Court 1993– (asst recorder 1989–93); ldr Admiralty Bar 2000–; visiting prof of law Univ of Essex 1987–92, visiting prof of maritime law UCL 1996–99; panel memb Lloyds Salvage Arbitrators 1988–; *Books* Phipson on Evidence (jt ed, 12 edn 1976, 13 edn 1982, 14 edn 1990, 15 edn 2000), Force Majeure and Frustration of Contract (contrib, 1991, 2 edn 1994), Halsbury's Laws of England (4 edn, contrib Damages), Consensus ad idem: Essays on Contract in Honour of Guenter Treitel (contrib, 1996); *Recreations* books, music, sport; *Clubs* Oxford and Cambridge, RAC, Garrick; *Style*— M N Howard, Esq, QC; ✉ Quadrant Chambers, Quadrant House, 10 Fleet Street, London EC4Y 1AU (tel 020 7583 4444, fax 020 7583 4455, e-mail michael.howard@quadrantchambers.com)

HOWARD, Dr Norman; s of Philip Howard (d 1987), and Deborah Howard (d 1952); *b* 25 November 1926; *Educ* Haberdashers' Aske's, Wadham Coll Oxford (MA, DM), UCH London; *m* 26 June 1955, Anita, da of H Selby; 2 s (Anthony b 1956, David b 1959); *Career* registrar and sr registrar Royal Marsden Hosp 1956–63; conslt radiotherapy and oncology: Charing Cross Hosp 1963–91 (dir 1980–91), Wembley Hosp 1965–91 (hon conslt 1991–), Royal Marsden Hosp 1970–; conslt in clinical oncology Cromwell Hosp 1982–2001; chm: Royal Coll of Radiologists Res Appeal 1993–2003, Gunnar Nilsson Cancer Res Tst Fund, Med Staff Ctee Charing Cross Hosp 1974–79; memb Final Fellowship Bd RCR 1981–91 (chm 1986–91); memb Cncl Medical Insurance Agency Ltd; DMRT 1956, FFR 1958, FRCR 1975; memb: BMA, RSM; Commendatore Order of Merit Republic of Italy 1976; *Books* Mediastinal Obstruction in Lung Cancer (1967); author of numerous chapters and papers on cancer; *Recreations* reading, theatre; *Style*— Dr Norman Howard; ✉ 5A Clarendon Road, London W11 4JA (tel 020 7229 6704, mobile 07831 875082); Old Malthouse Cottage, Shurlock Row, Reading RG10 0PL (tel 0118 934 3368)

HOWARD, Philip Ewen; s of Francis John Adrian Howard, of London, and Lynnette, *née* Maider; *b* 5 June 1966; *Educ* Bradfield Coll, Univ of Kent at Canterbury (BSc); *m* 15 Dec 1990, Jennifer Elizabeth, da of Robert Collier; 1 da (Amelia Mae b 7 July 1995), 1 s (Alexander Gregory Robert b 1 Feb 1999); *Career* trg/apprenticeship: with Roux Restaurants Ltd 1988–89, under Marco Pierre White Harvey's Restaurant 1989–90, under Simon Hopkinson Bibendum 1990–91; head chef/jt owner The Square 1991– (8 out of 10 Good Food Guide 1999–2006, second Michelin star 1998– (first 1994)), jt owner The Ledbury 2005–; *Style*— Philip Howard, Esq; ✉ 84 Madrid Road, Barnes, London SW13 9PG; The Square, 6–10 Bruton Street, Mayfair, London W1J 6PU (tel 020 7495 7100, fax 020 7495 7150, e-mail phil@squarerestaurant.com, website www.squarerestaurant.com)

HOWARD, Philip Nicholas Charles; s of Peter Dunsmore Howard (d 1965), and Doris Emily Metaxa; *b* 2 November 1933; *Educ* Eton, Trinity Coll Oxford (MA); *m* 1959, Myrtle Janet Mary, da of Sir Reginald Houldsworth, 5 Bt, *qv*; 2 s, 1 da; *Career* Nat Serv Lt Black Watch; newspaper reporter, columnist and author; Glasgow Herald 1959–64, columnist, ldr writer and composer of Word Watching and Modern Manners The Times 1990– (joined 1964, literary ed 1978–90), London ed Verbatim 1977–; pres Classical Assoc 2001–, fndr patron Friends of the Classics; Liveryman Worshipful Co of Wheelwrights; FRSL; *Books* The Black Watch (1968), The Royal Palaces (1970), London's River (1975), New Words for Old (1977), The British Monarchy (1977), Weasel Words (1978), Words Fail Me (1980), A Word in Your Ear (1983), The State of the Language (1984), We Thundered Out, 200 Years of The Times 1785–1985 (1985), Winged Words (1988), Word-Watching (1988), A Word in Time (1990), The Times Bedside Book (ed, 1990 and 1992); *Recreations* reading, walking, talking; *Style*— Philip Howard, Esq; ✉ Flat 1, 47 Ladbroke Grove, London W11 3AR (tel 020 7727 1077, fax 020 7221 7626, e-mail philip.howard@the-times.co.uk)

HOWARD, Ronald John Frederick; s of Frederick Perceval Howard (d 1947), and Lydia Mary Howard (d 1976); *b* 1 September 1921; *Educ* Whitgift Middle Sch; *m* 1, 1944, (Sylvia) Betty (d 1974); m 2, 1976 (m dis 1991), (Ann) Veronica, da of Ward Turner Nicholson (d 1967); *Career* Metal Industries Ltd 1947–67 (dir 1959–67), dep gen mangr AEI/GEC Controls Gp 1967–68; chief exec dir: Plantation Holdings Ltd 1969–78, Phicom plc 1978–81 (chm 1981–84); non-exec dir: Fothergill and Harvey plc 1973–87, Graseby plc (formerly Cambridge Electronic Industries plc) 1980–92; dir: Cynanamid-Fothergill Ltd 1981–87, Infrared Assocs Inc 1985–88; fndr bd dir and dep chm Chiltern Radio plc 1980–95; chm: The Rank Phicom Video Gp Ltd 1981–84, Technology Mgmnt Services Ltd 1981–, Baird UK Holdings Ltd 1982–89, Silver Chalice Productions Intl Ltd (Bermuda) and Silver Chalice Productions Ltd 1983–86, Reflex Holdings Ltd 1986–88, Commtel Consumer Electronics plc 1987–88, Synoptics Ltd 1988–, Universal Machine Intelligence Gp Ltd 1989–90, SyFA Data Systems plc 1990–93, Solix Systems Ltd 1993–94, The Univ of Manchester Venture Fund Mgmnt Ltd 1999–2007, Eights Mgmnt Co Ltd 1999–2007; dir: Kratos Gp plc (formerly Spectros Int plc) 1984– (vice-chm 1984–91), Myriad Solutions Ltd 1995–, UMIST Ventures Ltd 1997–2004, Synoptics Inc 2000–2003, Gallery of Galleries Ltd 2006–; CCMI, FCIM; *Recreations* sailing, photography; *Clubs* City of London, Savile, Royal Thames Yacht; *Style*— Ronald Howard, Esq, CCMI, FCIM; ✉ 5 Ordnance Mews, St John's Wood, London NW8 6PF (tel 020 7586 8693, mobile 07721 959779, e-mail rjfhoward@dial.pipex.com); Technology Management Services Ltd, PO Box 1775, London NW8 6PQ (tel 020 7722 2521, fax 020 7586 6307, e-mail tms@dial.pipex.com)

HOWARD, Hon Simon Bartholomew Geoffrey; 3 s of Baron Howard of Henderskelfe (Life Peer; d 1984); *b* 26 January 1956; *Educ* Eton, RAC Cirencester, Study Centre for Fine and Decorative Arts; *m* 1, 1983 (m dis 2000), Annette Marie, Countess Compton, er da of Charles Antony Russell Smallwood, and formerly 2 w (m dis 1977), of Earl Compton (now 7 Marquess of Northampton); m 2, 2001, Rebecca Verassana, da of Jonathan and Angela Sieff; 2 c (Merlin, Octavia (twins) b 2002); *Career* chm of estate co 1984–; landowner (10,000 acres); chm Yorkshire Regnl HHA 1986–97; non-exec dir Sotheby's 1998–; High Sheriff North Yorks 1995–96; *Recreations* photography, wine, country sports; *Style*— The Hon Simon Howard; ✉ Castle Howard, York YO60 7DA (tel 01653 648444)

HOWARD, Timothy Charles Maxwell (Tim); s of Edward Maxwell Howard (d 1970), and Eleanor Monica Newsum; *b* 29 July 1947; *Educ* Uppingham, Univ of Dundee (LLB), Coll of Law; *m* 1, 1970 (m dis 1993), Elizabeth Marion; 3 s (Andrew Oliver Maxwell b 30 April 1976, Edward William b 25 May 1978, Thomas Timothy b 26 May 1982); m 2, 1994, Gillian Lesley; *Career* Norton Rose: joined 1970, asst slr 1973–78, ptnr 1978–2003, recruitment ptnr 1988–90, memb Mgmnt Ctee 1988–91, sr conslt Norton Rose Consultants OE Greece 1995–2000, managing ptnr Norton Rose Paris 2001–03; princ Law Office Howard Greece 2000–01; memb Editorial Bd: European Transport Law, Charterparty International, Maritime Focus, Jl of Maritime Law and Commerce; jt pres Br Hellenic C of C 1998–2001; Liveryman City of London Slrs Co 1978; memb: Law Soc 1970, Baltic Exchange London, Maritime Arbitrators Assoc 1978; *Recreations* theatre, golf, DIY, travel; *Style*— Tim Howard, Esq

HOWARD DE WALDEN, Baroness (E 1597); (Mary) Hazel Caridwen Czernin; eldest da of 9 Baron Howard de Walden and 5 Baron Seaford (d 1999) and Lady Howard de Walden, *née* Countess Irene Harrach (d 1975); suc on termination of abeyance 2004; *b* 12 August 1935; *m* 1957, Count Joseph Czernin; 5 da (Hon Charlotte Mary Sidonia b 1958, Hon Henrietta Mary Rosario b 1960, Hon Alexandra Mary Romana b 1961, Hon Philippa Mary Loretta b 1963, Hon Isabelle Mary Benedicta b 1967), 1 s (Hon Peter John Joseph b 1966); *Heir* s, Hon Peter Czernin; *Style*— The Rt Hon the Lady Howard de Walden; ✉ White Oak House, Highclere, Newbury, Berkshire RG20 9RJ

HOWARD-LAWSON, Sir John Philip; 6 Bt (UK 1841), of Brough Hall, Yorks; s of Sir William Howard Lawson, 5 Bt (d 1990); assumed by Royal Licence surname and arms of Howard 1962; *b* 6 June 1934; *m* 1960, Jean Veronica (d 2001), da of late Col John Evelyn Marsh, DSO, OBE; 2 s (Philip William b 1961, Thomas John b 1963), 1 da (Julia Frances b 1964); *Heir* s, Philip Howard; *Style*— Sir John Howard-Lawson, Bt; ✉ Hunter Hall, Great Salkeld, Penrith, Cumbria CA11 9NA

HOWARD OF PENRITH, 3 Baron (UK 1930) Philip Esme; s of 2 Baron Howard of Penrith (d 1999); *b* 1 May 1945; *Educ* Ampleforth, ChCh Oxford; *m* 1969, Sarah, da of late Barclay Walker; 2 da (Hon Natasha Mary b 1970, Hon Laura Isabella b 1976), 2 s (Hon Thomas Philip b 1974, Hon Michael Barclay b 1984); *Style—* The Rt Hon the Lord Howard of Penrith; ✉ 45 Erpingham Road, London SW15

HOWARD OF RISING, Baron (Life Peer UK 2004), of Castle Rising in the County of Norfolk; Greville Patrick Charles Howard; s of Col Henry Redvers Greville Howard (d 1978), and Patience Nichol (d 1987); *b* 22 April 1941; *Educ* Eton; *m* 1, 1968 (m dis 1972), Zoe Rosaleen, da of Douglas Walker; m 2, 1978, Mary Rose (d 1980), da of Sir (Edward) John Chichester, 11 Bt; m 3, 1981, Mary Cortlandt, da of Robert Veitch Culverwell; 2 s (Hon Thomas Henry Greville b 1983, Hon Charles Edward John b 1986), 1 da (Hon Annabel Rosemary Diana b 1984); *Career* landowner; Liveryman Worshipful Co of Mercers; *Recreations* reading; *Style—* The Rt Hon the Lord Howard of Rising; ✉ Castle Rising, Kings Lynn, Norfolk PE31 6AF

HOWARTH, David; MP; *Educ* Queen Mary's GS, Univ of Cambridge (MA), Yale Univ (LLM, MA, MPhil); *Career* reader in law and economics Univ of Cambridge 2005– (lectr 1988–2005); Cambridge CC: cncllr 1987–2004, ldr Lib Dems 1990–2003, ldr oppn 1992–2000, ldr 2000–03; Parly candidate (Lib Dem): Cambridge 1992 and 2001, Peterborough 1997; MP (Lib Dem) Cambridge 2005–; memb: Lib Dem Federal Policy Ctee 1989–2000, European Lib Dem Cncl; former chair Lib Dem Economic Policy Working Gp; writer of numerous jl articles and book chapters; Butterworth Prize Best New Legal Textbook 1995; *Style—* David Howarth, Esq, MP; ✉ House of Commons, London SW1A 0AA

HOWARTH, Elgar; s of Oliver Howarth (d 1976), and Emma, *née* Wall (d 1979); *b* 4 November 1935; *Educ* Eccles GS Manchester, Univ of Manchester (BMus), Royal Manchester Coll of Music; *m* 22 May 1958, Mary Bridget, da of John Francis Neary (d 1953); 2 da (Theresa b 1960, Maria b 1963), 1 s (Patrick b 1962); *Career* trumpeter and conductor; trumpeter: Royal Opera House Orch 1958–63, Royal Philharmonic Orch 1963–70, London Sinfonietta and Nash Ensemble 1968–74, Philip Jones Brass Ensemble 1965–75; freelance conductor 1969–, princ guest conductor Opera North 1985–90; musical advsr: Grimethorpe Colliery Band 1972–97, English Northern Philharmonia 1997–98; various compositions and arrangements published by Novello, Chester and Rosehill; Olivier Award for outstanding achievement in opera; Hon DUniv: Central England Birmingham Conservatoire of Music 1993, York 1999, Salford 2003; Hon DMus Keele Univ 1995, hon fell UC Salford 1992; fell Royal Manchester Coll of Music, Hon ARAM 1990, FRNCM 1994, FWCMD 1997, FRCM 2000; *Books* What a Performance (jtly with son Patrick Howarth); *Recreations* cycling; *Style—* Elgar Howarth, Esq; ✉ c/o Allied Artists, 42 Montpelier Square, London SW7 1JZ (tel 020 7589 6243, fax 020 7581 5269)

HOWARTH, George; PC (2005), MP; Rt Hon; *Career* MP (Lab): Knowsley N 1986–97, Knowsley N and Sefton E 1997–; Parly under-sec of state: Home Office 1997–99, NI 1999–2001; memb Intelligence and Security Ctee 2005–; *Style—* The Rt Hon George Howarth, MP; ✉ House of Commons, London SW1A 0AA (tel 020 7219 3000)

HOWARTH, (James) Gerald Douglas; MP; s of late James Howarth, of Hurley, Berks, and Mary Howarth; *b* 12 September 1947; *Educ* Bloxham Sch, Univ of Southampton; *m* 1973, Elizabeth; 1 da, 2 s; *Career* gen sec Soc for Individual Freedom 1969–71, Bank of America International 1971–76, European Arab Bank 1976–81, Standard Chartered Bank plc 1981–83 (loan syndication mangr); MP (Cons): Cannock and Burntwood 1983–92, Aldershot 1997–; PPS to: Michael Spicer at the Dept of Energy 1987–90, Sir George Young at the DOE 1990–91, Rt Hon Margaret Thatcher 1991–92; shadow def min 2002–; memb Home Affairs Select Ctee 1997–2001, memb Defence Select Ctee 2001–03; chm Parly Aerospace Gp 1998–99 (vice-chm 1997–98, 1999–), vice-chm Cons Parly Environment, Tport and the Regions Ctee 1997–99, vice-chm Cons Home Affairs Ctee 1999–2002, chm Lords and Commons Family and Child Protection Gp, hon sec Cons Parly Aviation Ctee 1983–87, memb Exec 1922 Ctee 1999–2002; jt md Taskforce Communications Ltd 1993–95; pres Air Display Assoc Europe, memb Cncl Air League 2004–; chm 92 Gp 2001–; cncllr London Borough of Hounslow 1982–83; Freeman GAPAN 2004; fell Industry and Parly Tst; *Publications* No Turning Back (1985) and other publications of the No Turning Back Group; *Recreations* flying (Britannia Airways Parly Pilot of the Year 1988), photography, walking, DIY; *Style—* Gerald Howarth, Esq, MP; ✉ House of Commons, London SW1A 0AA (tel 020 7219 5650, fax 020 7219 1198, website www.geraldhowarth.com)

HOWARTH, His Hon Nigel John Graham; s of Vernon Howarth (d 1960), of Sale, Cheshire, and Irene, *née* Lomas (d 1962); *b* 12 December 1936; *Educ* Manchester Grammar, Univ of Manchester (LLB, LLM); *m* 9 June 1962, Janice Mary, da of Francis Harry Hooper; 1 da (Rosamond Irene b 19 June 1963), 2 s (Charles Vernon b 12 Oct 1965, Laurence Francis b 19 Jan 1973); *Career* called to the Bar Gray's Inn 1960 (Macaskie scholar 1960, Atkin scholar 1962), in practice Chancery Bar Manchester 1961–92, recorder of the Crown Court 1989–92 (asst recorder 1983–89), circuit judge (Northern Circuit) 1992–2006; chm Northern Chancery Bar Assoc 1990–92, former pres Inc Law Library Soc Manchester, actg deemster Isle of Man 1985 and 1989, vice-pres Disabled Living; *Recreations* music, theatre, fell walking, keen supporter Altrincham FC; *Style—* His Hon Nigel Howarth; ✉ c/o Circuit Administrator, Northern Circuit Office, 15 Quay Street, Manchester M60 9FD

HOWARTH OF BRECKLAND, Baroness (Life Peer UK 2001), of Parson Cross in the County of South Yorkshire; Valerie Georgina Howarth; OBE (1999); *b* 5 September 1940; *Educ* Abbeydale Girls' GS, Univ of Leicester (Sheila McKay Meml Prize); *Career* mgmnt trainee Walsh's Ltd 1959–60, family caseworker Family Welfare Assoc 1963–68; London Borough of Lambeth: sr child care worker and trg offr 1968–70, area co-ordinator 1970–72, chief co-ordinator of social work 1972–76, asst dir of personal services 1976–82; dir of social services London Borough of Brent 1982–86, chief exec ChildLine 1987–2001; chair: Lambeth and Brent Area Review Ctee, London Directors' Child Care Gp; advsr to: London Boroughs' Regnl Planning Ctee, Women's Refuges; conslt to: John Grooms Assoc for Disabled People 1987 (tstee 1988–), Thomas Coram Fndn 1987, Ind Ctee for the Supervision of Telephone Information Systems (ICSTIS) 1988–2001; tstee: National Cncl for Voluntary Child Care Orgns 1990–95 (vice-chair), Lucy Faithfull Fndn 1992– (vice-chm), National Children's Bureau 1993–94; UK rep Euro Forum for Child Welfare 1994–97; fndr memb: Telephone Helplines Assoc 1995–96 (first chair), King's Cross Homelessness Project (first chair), London Homelessness Forum, NCH Commn considering Children as Abusers 1991–92, NSPCC Professional Advsy Panel 1993–95, Working Gp on Children and the Law (resulting in Child Witness Pack 1991–94 and trg video for judges 1997), Home Office Steering Gp on Child Witnesses; bd memb Food Standards Agency 2000–07; tstee Sieff Fndn 1992–; memb Br Assoc of Social Workers (BASW), Nat Care Stadards Cmmn 2001–05, patron Little Hearts Matter 2002–, children's helpline asst 2003–07, memb Select Ctee House of Lords 2005–; hon degree Open Univ 2007; assoc memb Assoc of Directors of Social Services; *Style—* The Rt Hon the Baroness Howarth of Breckland, OBE; ✉ House of Lords, London SW1A 0PW

HOWARTH OF NEWPORT, Baron (Life Peer UK 2005), of Newport in the County of Gwent; Alan Thomas Howarth; CBE (1982), PC (2000); *b* 11 June 1944; *Educ* Rugby, King's Coll Cambridge; *m* 1967 (m dis 1996), Gillian Martha, da of Arthur Chance, of Dublin; 2 s, 2 da; *Career* former head Chm's Office CCO (private sec to Rt Hon William Whitelaw and Rt Hon Lord Thorneycroft as Pty Chm), dir Cons Res Dept 1979–81, vice-chm Cons Pty Orgn 1980–81; MP: Stratford-upon-Avon 1983–97 (resigned Cons Pty 1995, memb Lab Pty 1995–), (Lab) Newport E 1997–2005; PPS to Dr Rhodes Boyson 1985–87, asst Govt whip 1987, a Lord Cmmr of HM Treasy (Govt whip) 1988, min for Schools 1989–92, min for HE and Sci 1990–92, Employment min and min for Disabled People 1997–98, min for the Arts 1998–2001, memb Intelligence and Security Ctee 2001–; memb: Nat Heritage Select Ctee 1992–93, Social Security Select Ctee 1996–97; *Books* Changing Charity (jtly, 1984), Monty At Close Quarters (1985), Save Our Schools (1987), Arts: The Next Move Forward (1987), Cities of Pride (jtly, 1994); *Recreations* books, arts, hill walking; *Style—* The Rt Hon the Lord Howarth of Newport, CBE, PC

HOWAT, John Michael Taylor; s of Henry Taylor Howat, CBE, of Bramhall, Cheshire, and Rosaline, *née* Green; *b* 18 April 1945; *Educ* Manchester Warehousemen and Clerks Orphan Sch Cheadle Hulme, Victoria Univ of Manchester (MB ChB, MD); *m* 16 July 1988, Dr Trudie Elizabeth Roberts, da of John Roberts, of Millbrook, Stalybridge; 2 da (Fiona Katherine b 17 Oct 1989, Alexandra Helen b 19 June 1992); *Career* conslt surgn N Manchester gp of hosps 1982–; FRCS 1973; *Recreations* industrial archaeology, photography, clock restoration; *Style—* John Howat, Esq; ✉ Department of Surgery, North Manchester General Hospital, Delauneys Road, Manchester M8 6RB (tel 0161 795 4567 ext 2608)

HOWDEN, Alan Percival; s of C P Howden (d 1986), of Scarborough, N Yorks, and Marian, *née* Grindell (d 1980); *b* 28 August 1936; *Educ* Sale GS, UMIST (BSc Tech); *m* Judith, da of Edward L South; 1 da (Charlotte b 1981); *Career* BBC TV: exec Purchased Progs 1964–77, head of Purchased Progs 1977–83, gen mangr Prog Acquisition 1983–91, Bd memb BBC Enterprises 1989–94, head of Prog Acquisition 1991–97, controller Prog Acquisition 1997–99, conslt Prog Acquisition 1999–2000; dir Picturedrome Ltd 2000–; Br Fedn of Film Socs: vice-chm 1965–80, chm 1980–82, vice-pres 1982–; govr BFI 1994–2000; chm BFI Film Educn Working Gp 1998; memb: BAFTA 1990, Br Kinematograph Sound and Television Soc (BKSTS) 1995, RTS 1995; *Recreations* theatre, early music, English countryside; *Clubs* Soho House; *Style—* Alan Howden, Esq; ✉ 31 Thornton Road, London SW19 4NG (tel 020 8944 1921, e-mail alanhowden@beeb.net)

HOWE, Prof Christopher Barry; MBE (1997); s of Charles Roderick Howe, and Patricia, *née* Creeden; *b* 3 November 1937; *Educ* William Ellis Sch Highgate, St Catharine's Coll Cambridge (MA), Univ of London (PhD); *m* 2 Dec 1967, Patricia Anne, da of L G Giles; 1 da (Emma Claire (Mrs Dominic Soares) b 1968), 1 s (Roderick Giles b 1972); *Career* Econ Directorate Fedn Br Industries 1961–63; SOAS Univ of London: res fell and lectr 1963–72, reader in the economics of Asia 1972–79, prof 1979–, prof of Chinese business mgmnt 2001 (prof emeritus 2003); head Contemporary China Inst 1972–78; memb: Hong Kong Univ and Poly Grants Ctee 1974–93, UGC 1979–84, Hong Kong RGC 1991–; fell 48 Gp Club; FBA 2001; *Books* Employment and Economic Growth in Urban China (1971), Wage Patterns and Wage Policies in Modern China (1973), China's Economy: A Basic Guide (1978), Shanghai (1980), Foundations of the Chinese Planned Economy (1989), The Origins of Japanese Trade Supremacy (1995), China and Japan (1996), Chinese Technology Transfer in the 1990s (1997), China's Economic Reform (2003); *Recreations* walking, swimming, cycling, antiquarian books, France, music, photography; *Style—* Prof Christopher Howe, MBE; ✉ School of Oriental and African Studies, Thornaugh Street, Russell Square, London WC1A 0XG (tel 020 7637 2388)

HOWE, Prof Daniel Walker; s of Maurice Langdon Howe (d 1945), and Lucie, *née* Walker; *b* 10 January 1937; *Educ* East HS Denver, Harvard Univ (Phi Beta Kappa), Magdalen Coll Oxford (MA), Univ of Calif Berkeley (PhD); *m* 3 Sept 1961, Sandra Fay, da of Gaylord David Shumway; 1 da (Rebecca b 1964), 2 s (Christopher Shumway b 1967, Stephen Walker b 1971); *Career* Lt US Army 1959–60; Yale Univ: instr 1966–68, asst prof 1968–72, assoc prof 1972–73; UCLA: assoc prof 1973–77, prof 1977–92, chm Dept of History 1983–87; Harmsworth prof of American history and fell The Queen's Coll Oxford 1989–90, Rhodes prof of American history and fell St Catherine's Coll Oxford 1992–2002; fell: Charles Warren Center for Studies in American History Harvard Univ 1970–71, Nat Endowment for the Humanities 1975–76, John Simon Guggenheim Meml Fndn 1984–85; res fell Henry E Huntington Library San Marino 1991–92, 1994 and 2002–03, Cardozo lectr Yale Univ 2001; pres Soc for Historians of the Early American Repub 2000–01; memb: American Historical Assoc, Inst of Early American History and Culture, Br Assoc for American Studies, Soc of American Historians; FRHS; *Publications* The Unitarian Conscience (1970, 2 edn 1988), Victorian America (1976), The Political Culture of the American Whigs (1980), Making the American Self (1997), What Hath God Wrought: The Transformation of America 1815–1848 (2007); *Recreations* music; *Clubs* Oxford and Cambridge; *Style—* Prof Daniel Howe; ✉ St Catherine's Coll, Oxford OX1 3UJ; 3814 Cody Road, Sherman Oaks, California, 91403 USA (e-mail howe@history.ucla.edu)

HOWE, Elizabeth; da of Allen Howe (d 1998), and Katherine, *née* Davies; *b* 22 March 1956; *Educ* Howell's Sch Llandaff, Univ of Exeter (LLB); *m* 11 Oct 1986, Patrick; 1 da (Emily b 2 April 1991), 1 s (David b 2 July 1994); *Career* chief crown prosecutor Kent 1999–; chair Kent Criminal Justice Bd 2003–; memb: Kent Law Soc, London Criminal Courts Assoc, Law Soc, Int Assoc of Prosecutors; *Recreations* riding, tennis, swimming, theatre; *Style—* Miss Elizabeth Howe; ✉ Crown Prosecution Service, Priory Gate, 29 Union Street, Maidstone, Kent ME14 1PT (tel 01622 356300, fax 01622 356340, e-mail elizabeth.howe@cps.gsi.gov.uk)

HOWE, 7 Earl (UK 1821); Frederick Richard Penn Curzon; also Baron Howe of Langar (GB 1788), Baron Curzon of Penn (GB 1794) and Viscount Curzon of Penn (UK 1802); s of Cdr (Chambré) George William Penn Curzon, RN (d 1976), and Enid Jane Victoria (d 1997), da of late Malcolm Mackenzie Fergusson; suc cous, 6 Earl Howe, CBE (d 1984); *b* 29 January 1951; *Educ* Rugby, ChCh Oxford (MA); *m* 1983, Elizabeth Helen (DL Bucks 1995), elder da of late Capt Burleigh Edward St Lawrence Stuart, of Ickford, Bucks; 3 da (Lady Anna Elizabeth b 19 Jan 1987, Lady Flora Grace b 12 June 1989, Lady Lucinda Rose b 12 Oct 1991), 1 s (Thomas, Viscount Curzon b 22 Oct 1994); *Heir* s, Viscount Curzon; *Career* banker and farmer; dir: Adam & Co plc 1987–90, Provident Life Assoc Ltd 1988–91, Andry Montgomery Ltd 2000–; Lord-in-Waiting to HM The Queen (Govt Whip) 1991–92; Govt spokesman: on Employment and Transport 1991, on Environment and Def 1992; Parly sec: MAFF 1992–95, MOD 1995–97; oppn spokesman on health House of Lords 1997–; chm LAPADA 1999–; pres: Nat Soc for Epilepsy, RNLI (Chilterns Branch), South Bucks Assoc for The Disabled; memb: Cncl RNLI, RAFT; govr: King William IV Naval Fndn, Milton's Cottage Tst; patron: DEMAND, The Chiltern Soc; ACIB 1976; *Recreations* musical composition; *Style—* The Rt Hon the Earl Howe; ✉ House of Lords, London SW1A 0PW (tel 020 7219 5353, e-mail howef@parliament.uk)

HOWE, Prof Geoffrey Leslie; TD 1962 (and Bars 1969, 1974); s of Leo Leslie John Howe (d 1934), of Maidenhead, Berks, and Ada Blanche, *née* Partridge (d 1973); *b* 22 April 1924; *Educ* Royal Dental Hosp, Middx Hosps; *m* 1, 8 April 1948, Heather Patricia Joan, *née* Hambly (d 1997); 1 s (Timothy John b 1958 d 1997); m 2, 1 Dec 2003, Mrs Margaret Samuel, *née* Hall; *Career* dental offr RADC 1946–49, Col RADC (V) 1972–75, Col RARO 1973–89 (Hon Col Cmdt RADC 1975–90); prof of oral surgery Univs of Durham and Newcastle upon Tyne 1959–67, dean Royal Dental Hosp London Sch of Dental Surgery 1973–78 (prof of oral surgery 1967–78), prof Univ of Hong Kong 1978–84 (fndr dean of dentistry 1978–83), dean Faculty of Dentistry Jordan Univ of Sci and Technol 1988–90 and 1993–96 (prof of oral surgery 1986–90, prof of oral surgery and med 1993–96); memb Cncl RCS 1977–78, vice-pres BDA 1979– (vice-chm 1971–73, chm Cncl 1973–78); Int Freeman New Orleans USA, Freeman Louisville USA; Liveryman Worshipful Soc of Apothecaries; hon fell: Philippine Coll of Oral and Maxillo-Facial Surgns 1979, Acad of Dentistry Int (USA) 1982; fell Int Coll of Dentists, hon memb American Dental Assoc;

H

LRCP, MRCS 1954, FDSRCS 1955 (LDSRCS 1946), MDS 1961, FFDRCSI 1964; OStJ; *Books* Extraction of Teeth (2 edn, 1980), Local Anaesthesia in Dentistry (with F I H Whitehead, 3 edn, 1990), Minor Oral Surgery (3 edn, 1989), Reflections of a Fortunate Fellow (2002); *Recreations* sailing, reading, music, club life; *Clubs* Gents, Hong Kong, Royal Hong Kong Yacht, Savage; *Style*— Prof Geoffrey Howe, TD; ✉ 70 Croham Manor Road, South Croydon, Surrey CR2 7BF (tel 020 8686 0941); Villa 2–1, Marina de Casares, Km 146 Ctrà Cadiz/Malaga CN 340; Casares 29691, Andalucia, Spain

HOWE, Geoffrey Michael Thomas; s of Michael Edward Howe, and Susan Dorothy, *née* Allan; *b* 3 September 1949; *Educ* Manchester Grammar, St John's Coll Cambridge (MA); *Career* admitted slr 1973; ptnr Co Dept Clifford-Turner 1980 (joined 1975), managing ptnr Clifford Chance 1989–97; general counsel and dir Robert Fleming Holdings Ltd 1998–2000, chm Railtrack Gp plc 2002, chm Jardine Lloyd Thompson plc 2006– (non-exec dir 2002–); non-exec dir: JPMorgan Fleming Overseas Investment Tst 1999–, Gateway Electronic Components Ltd 2000–, Investec plc 2003–, Nationwide Building Soc 2005–; Freeman Worshipful Co of Slrs; memb Law Soc 1973; *Recreations* wine, antiques, opera; *Style*— Geoffrey Howe, Esq

HOWE, Ven George Alexander; s of Eugene Howe, of Parkgate, Cheshire, Olivia Lydia Caroline, *née* Denroche; *b* 22 January 1952; *Educ* Liverpool Inst HS, St John's Coll Durham (BA), Westcott House Cambridge; *m* 3 Oct 1980, Jane, da of Allen Corbould (decd); 1 da (Katharine Rachel b 19 May 1982), 1 s (Simon Andrew 22 Feb 1984); *Career* curate St Cuthbert Peterlee 1975–79, curate St Mary Norton Stockton-on-Tees 1979–81, vicar Hart with Elwick Hall 1981–85, rector St Edmund Sedgefield 1985–91, rural dean of Sedgefield 1988–91, vicar Holy Trinity Kendal 1991–2000, rural dean of Kendal 1994–99, hon canon of Carlisle Cathedral 1994–, archdeacon of Westmorland and Furness 2000–; chm Church and Community Fund 2007–; *Style*— The Ven the Archdeacon of Westmorland and Furness; ✉ The Vicarage, Windermere Road, Lindale, Grange-over-Sands, Cumbria LA11 6LB (tel 01539 534717, fax 01539 535090, e-mail archdeacon.south@carlislediocese.org.uk)

HOWE, Graham Edward; *Career* formerly with: Hutchison Telecom, First Pacific Company, Touche Ross Mgmnt Conslts; co-fndr Orange 1992, chief financial offr Orange 1996, dep ceo Orange plc 1996–2003; currently chm Promethean; non-exec dir Cable and Wireless plc 2003–06; *Style*— Graham Howe, Esq

HOWE, John Francis; CB (1996), OBE (1974); s of late Frank Howe, OBE, of Devon, and Marjorie Alice, *née* Hubball; *b* 29 January 1944; *Educ* Shrewsbury, Balliol Coll Oxford (MA); *m* 1981, Angela Ephrosini, da of Charalambos Nicolaides (d 1973), of Alicante and London; 1 da (Alexandra b 1983), 1 step da (Caroline b 1973); *Career* Civil Serv: princ MOD 1972 (asst princ 1967), civil advsr GOC NI 1972–73, private sec to Perm Under Sec 1975–78, asst sec MOD 1979, seconded FCO, cnsllr UK Delgn to NATO 1981–84, head Def Arms Control Unit 1985–86, private sec to Sec of State for Def 1986–87, asst under sec of state (personnel and logistics) 1988–91, dep under sec of state (civilian mgmnt) 1992–96, dep chief of defence procurement (support) 1996–2000, seconded as exec dir to Thales plc (formerly Thomson-CSF Racal plc) 2000–02; vice-chm Thales UK 2002–; chm Citylink Telecommunications 2004–; *Books* International Security and Arms Control (contrib); *Recreations* travel, gardening, pictures; *Clubs* Athenaeum; *Style*— John Howe, Esq, CB, OBE; ✉ Thales UK, 2 Dashwood Lang Road, Addlestone, Weybridge, Surrey KT15 2NX (tel 01932 824809)

HOWE, Leslie Clive; s of Alexander Leslie Howe, of Cheshunt, Herts, and Patricia Ann, *née* Lord; *b* 21 April 1955; *Educ* Cheshunt GS, Royal Dental Hosp Univ of London (BDS); *Career* house surgn Royal Dental Hosp 1979, sr house surgn London Hosp 1979–80; lectr in conservative dentistry: Royal Dental Hosp 1980–85, Guy's Dental Sch 1985–; conslt in restorative dentistry Guy's Hospital 1993–; Lunt prize, Sounders scholar, Baron Cornelius ver Heyden de Lancey award; memb: Br Soc for Restorative Dentistry, Br Soc for Dental Res; Accreditation in Restorative Dentistry 1989; FDSRCS 1983; *Books* Inlays, Crowns and Bridges (1993), Implants in Clinical Dentistry (2000); *Style*— Leslie Howe, Esq; ✉ Conservation Department, Guy's Hospital Dental School, London Bridge, London SE1 9RT (tel 020 7955 4533); 21 Wimpole Street, London W1G 8GG (tel 020 7636 3101, fax 020 7735 8810, e-mail lesliechowe@hotmail.com)

HOWE, Martin Russell Thomson; QC (1996); s of Colin Thomson Howe, FRCS (d 1988), of Kenley, Surrey, and Dr Angela Mary, *née* Brock (d 1977), da of Baron Brock (Life Peer; d 1979); *b* 26 June 1955; *Educ* Trinity Hall Cambridge (MA); *m* 30 Dec 1989, Lynda, *née* Barnett; 1 s (Philip Anthony b 19 Oct 1990), 3 da (Julia Angela b 13 Nov 1992, Jennifer Rosalind b 19 Feb 1996, Elizabeth Florence b 6 Nov 1999); *Career* called to the Bar Middle Temple 1978; specialising in EC law and intellectual property; jt ed Halsbury's Laws of England section on Trade Marks, Trade Names and Designs; Parly candidate (Cons) Neath 1987, memb Hammersmith and Fulham Borough Cncl 1982–86 (chm Planning Ctee), memb Cons Pty Cmmn on a Bill of Rights for the UK; *Publications* Russell-Clarke and Howe on the Legal Protection of Industrial Designs (6 edn, 1998, 7 edn 2005), A Legal Assessment of the European Constitution Today (2005); author of other pubns on EC constitutional law; *Recreations* sailing; *Style*— Martin Howe, Esq, QC; ✉ 8 New Square, Lincoln's Inn, London WC2A 3QP (tel 020 7405 4321)

HOWE OF ABERAVON, Baron (Life Peer UK 1992), of Tandridge in the County of Surrey; Sir (Richard Edward) Geoffrey Howe; kt (1970), CH (1996) PC (1972), QC (1965); er s of late B Edward Howe, of Port Talbot, Glamorgan, and Mrs E F Howe, JP, *née* Thomson; *b* 20 December 1926; *Educ* Winchester, Trinity Hall Cambridge; *m* 1953, Elspeth Rosamund (Baroness Howe of Idlicote, CBE, JP, *qv*), da of late Philip Morton Shand; 2 da (Hon Caroline (Hon Mrs Ralph) b 1955, Hon Amanda (Hon Mrs Glanvill) b 1959), 1 s (Hon Alexander Edward Thomson (twin) b 1959); *Career* called to the Bar 1952; memb Gen Cncl of the Bar 1957–61, memb Cncl of Justice 1963–70, dep chm Glamorgan QS 1966–70, Parly candidate (Cons) Aberavon 1955 and 1959; chm Bow Gp 1955, ed Crossbow 1960–62 (md 1957–60); MP (Cons): Bebington 1964–66, Reigate 1970–74, Surrey E 1974–92; oppn front bench spokesman on labour and social servs 1965–66, SG 1970–72, min for trade and consumer affrs 1972–74; oppn front bench spokesman: on social servs 1974–75, on Treasy and econ affrs 1975–79; Chllr of the Exchequer and Lord Cmmr of the Treasy 1979–83, chm IMF Policy-Making Interim Ctee 1982–83, ldr team of Policy Gps preparing Cons Gen Election Manifesto 1982–83, sec of state for foreign and Cwlth affrs 1983–July 1989, Leader of the Commons and Lord Pres of the Cncl July 1989–Nov 1990, dep PM July 1989–Nov 1990; non-exec dir: Glaxo Wellcome plc (formerly Glaxo Hldgs plc) 1991–96, BICC plc 1991–97; chm Framlington Russian Investment Fund 1994–2003, special advsr on Euro and international affrs Jones Day Reavis and Pogue 1991–2000; memb: J P Morgan Int Advsy Cncl 1992–2001, Bertelsmann Fndn Int Advsy Cncl 1992–96, Carlyle Gp Advsy Bd 1996–2001, Fuji Bank Euro Advsy Cncl 1996–2003; chm Thomson Fndn 2004–07 (tstee 1994–2007); jt pres Wealth of Nations Fndn 1991–; pres: Which? (formerly Assoc of Consumer Res) 1992–, GB-China Centre 1992–, Academy of Experts 1996–2005; chm Steering Ctee Tax Law Rewrite 1996–2005; vice-pres RUSI 1992–; memb: Int Advsy Cncl Inst of Int Studies Stanford Univ 1990–2004, Steering Ctee Project Liberty 1991–93, Advsy Cncl Presidium of the Supreme Rada of Ukraine 1991–98; patron Enterprise Europe 1990–2004, patron UK Metric Assoc 1999–; visiting fell John F Kennedy Sch of Government Harvard Univ 1991–92, visitor to Sch of Oriental and African Studies of Univ of London 1991–2001, Herman Phleger visiting prof Stanford Law Sch 1992–93; Paul Harris fell Rotary Int 1995; Joseph Bech prize FVS Stiftung of Hamburg 1993; hon fell: Trinity Hall 1992–, UCW Swansea 1996, Univ of Cardiff 1999, American Bar Fndn 2001, Inst of Taxation 2001, SOAS Univ of London 2003; Hon LLD Wales 1988, Hon LLD LSE 2004, Hon LLD Univ of Glamorgan 2004, Hon DCL City of London; Hon Freeman Port Talbot 1992, Hon Freeman Co of Tax Advsrs 2004; Grand Cross Order of Merit: Portugal 1987, Germany 1992; Order of Ukraine for Public Service 2001; *Publications* Conflict of Loyalty (autobiography, 1994); *Style*— The Rt Hon the Lord Howe of Aberavon, CH, PC, QC; ✉ House of Lords, London SW1A 0PW

HOWE OF IDLICOTE, Baroness (Life Peer UK 2001), of Shipston on Stour in the County of Warwickshire; Elspeth Rosamund Morton Howe; CBE (1999), JP (Inner London 1964); da of late Philip Morton Shand and Sybil Mary, *née* Sissons; *b* 8 February 1932; *Educ* Bath HS, Wycombe Abbey, LSE (BSc); *m* Aug 1953, Baron Howe of Aberavon (Life Peer), *qv*; 2 da (Hon Caroline b 1955, Hon Amanda b 1959), 1 s (Hon Alexander (twin) b 1959); *Career* sec to princ of AA Sch of Architecture 1952–55, dep chm Equal Opportunities Cmmn Manchester (chm Legal Ctee) 1975–79; chm Inner London Juvenile Cts: Southwark 1970–80, Greenwich 1980–83, Lambeth 1983–86, Wandsworth 1987–90; non-exec dir: Kingfisher (Holdings) plc (formerly Woolworth Holdings plc) 1986–2000, United Biscuits (Holdings) Ltd 1988–94, Legal and General Group plc 1989–97; chm BOC Foundation 1990–2003; pres: Peckham Settlement 1976–, Fedn of Recruitment and Employment Servs 1980–94, UNICEF UK 1993–2002; chm: Business in the Community Opportunity 2000 Initiative 1991–98, NACRO Working Pty on Fine Enforcement 1980–81, NACRO Drugs Advsy Gp 1988–93, Local Govt Mgmnt Bd Inquiry and Report 'The Quality of Care' 1991–92, The Archbishops' Cmmn on Cathedrals 1992–94, Broadcasting Standards Cmmn 1993–99; vice-pres Pre-School Playgroups Assoc 1978–83; vice-chm Cncl Open Univ 2001–03 (memb Cncl 1996–2003); memb: Lord Chllr's Advsy Ctee on Legal Aid 1971–75, Parole Bd For England and Wales 1972–75, Advsy Cncl Inst of Business Ethics 1990– (vice-pres 2002–), The Justice Ctee on the English Judiciary 1992; tstee The Westminster Fndn for Democracy 1992–96; govr LSE 1985–2007; memb Cncl St George's House Windsor 1989–93; contrib articles to: The Times, FT, The Guardian, New Society; Hon LLD Univ of London 1990, Hon DUniv Open Univ 1993; Hon DLitt: Univ of Bradford 1993, Univ of Aberdeen 1994, Univ of Liverpool 1994, Univ of Sunderland 1995, South Bank Univ 1995; hon fell LSE 2001; *Style*— The Baroness Howe of Idlicote, CBE; ✉ House of Lords, London SW1A 0PW (tel 020 7219 6581, fax 020 7219 5979, e-mail howee@parliament.uk)

HOWELL, Geoffrey Colston; s of Leonard Colston Howell (d 1968), and Leah Emily, *née* Probert (d 1971); *b* 17 July 1932; *Educ* Latymer Upper Sch, St John's Coll Cambridge (MA, MSc); *m* 1, 23 April 1957 (m dis 1992), Elizabeth Mary, *née* Dutton; 2 da (Jacqueline Mary b 18 July 1958, Philippa Joan b 16 Feb 1965), 2 s (Martin Colston b 29 May 1960, Antony Gerald b 17 June 1961); m 2, 16 May 1992, Margaret Anne, *née* Worger; *Career* RAE Farnborough: scientific offr 1955–60, sr scientific offr 1960–64, princ scientific offr 1964–71, supt Controls and Displays Div 1971–72; chief supt RAE Bedford 1977–80 (head Blind Landing Experimental Unit 1972–77), head Flight Systems Dept RAE Farnborough 1980–82, dir of aircraft equipment and systems (MOD) PE 1982–84, chief scientist CAA 1988–92 (dir of research 1984–88), self-employed aviation conslt 1992–; pres RAeS 1990–91; FRAeS 1974, FRSA 1988, FREng 1992; *Recreations* music, reading; *Style*— Geoffrey Howell, Esq, FREng; ✉ Thenon, Razac de Saussignac, Dordogne 24240, France (tel 00 33 5 53 27 99 74, e-mail geoffrey.howell@wanadoo.fr)

HOWELL, Gwynne Richard; CBE (1998); s of Gilbert Lewis Howell (d 1991), and Ellaline, *née* Richards (d 1986); *b* 13 June 1938; *Educ* Pontardawe GS, Univ Coll Swansea (BSc), Univ of Manchester (DipTP); *m* 26 Oct 1968, Mary Edwina, da of Edward Morris (d 1988); 2 s (Richard b 23 May 1970, Peter b 31 May 1972); *Career* bass; sr planning offr Corporation of Manchester 1965–68; commenced professional music career 1968; with Sadler's Wells Opera (now ENO) 1968–72, Royal Opera 1972; given concerts with numerous leading conductors incl: Claudio Abbado, Daniel Barenboim, Pierre Boulez, Leonard Bernstein, Sir Colin Davis, Sir Bernard Haitink, James Levine, Zubin Mehta, Riccardo Muti, Tadaaki Ozawa and Sir Georg Solti; *Performances* notable operatic roles incl: First Nazarene in Salome (Covent Garden debut) 1969, Arkell in Pelleas and Melisande (Glyndebourne and Covent Garden 1969 and 1982), Otello (Met Opera NY debut) 1985, Hans Sachs in Die Meistersinger (ENO), Bluebeard in Bluebeard's Castle (ENO) 1991, Phillip II in Don Carlos (ENO) 1992, Boris Godunov (San Francisco Opera) 1992, Iolanta (Opera North) 1993, Fidelio (ENO) 1996, King Marke in Tristan und Isolde (ENO) 1996, King in Ariodante (ENO) 1996, The Croucher Silver Tassie (ENO premier) 2000, Thomas Adé's The Tempest (world premier Covent Garden) 2004; concert performances incl: St Matthew Passion (US debut, with Chicago Symphony Orch) 1974, Oedipus Rex (with Chicago Symphony Orch under Solti and with NY Philharmonic), numerous others at festivals incl Salzburg and Edinburgh; *Recordings* incl: Mahler's 8th Symphony (with Boston Symphony Orch under Ozawa), Un Ballo in Maschera, Luisa Miller and Rossini's Stabat Mater (all under Muti), Handel's Messiah (under Solti), Beethoven's 9th Symphony (under Kurt Masur); fell Welsh Coll of Music and Drama 1994; *Recreations* tennis, golf, gardening, good wine, walking; *Style*— Gwynne Howell, Esq, CBE; ✉ 197 Fox Lane, London N13 4BB

HOWELL, Dr John Frederick; s of Frederick Howell (d 1996), and Glenys Griffiths (d 1990); *b* 16 July 1941; *Educ* Welwyn Garden City GS, UC Swansea (BA), Univ of Manchester (MA), Univ of Reading (PhD); *m* 1993, Paula Wade; 2 s, 1 step s; *Career* lectr Univ of Khartoum 1966–73, sr lectr Univ of Zambia 1973–77, dir ODI 1987–97 (res fell 1977–87), advsr to Min for Agric and Land Affairs Govt of South Africa 1997–2001, sr res fell ODI 2001–; visiting prof Wye Coll London 1988–96; pres UK Chapter Soc for Int Devpt, advsr All-Pty Parly Gp on Overseas Devpt; *Style*— Dr John Howell; ✉ Overseas Development Institute, 258 Indus Street, Waterkloof Ridge, Pretoria 0181, South Africa (e-mail jhowell@mweb.co.za)

HOWELL, Lee Thomas; s of Howard Ungoed Howell, and Linda Annette, *née* Wilson; *b* 13 September 1969, Aldershot, Hants; *Educ* Univ of Reading (MBA), South Bank Univ (BEng); *m* 20 July 2002, Fiona Catherine, *née* Holland; 1 da (Jemima Jane), 1 s (Barnaby Thomas); *Career* firefighter 1988–91, jr offr 1991–94, station offr 1994–98, asst divnl offr 1998–2000, divnl offr 2000–02, sr divnl offr 2002–03, HM inspr of fire servs 2003, asst chief fire offr 2003–04, chief fire offr 2004– (also dir of public protection Suffolk CC); regnl lead offr Regnl Mgmnt Bd Fire Service Procurement 2004–, nat lead offr Children and Young People Chief Fire Offrs Assoc 2005–, ind memb Nat Sounding Bd Chief Fire Offrs Assoc 2007–; former chm: Regnl Fire & Rescue Serv Procurement Bd, Suffolk Resilience Forum; Millennium scholar Cwlth and Overseas Fire Serv Assoc 2000; memb Chief Fire Offrs Assoc 2004 (nat lead offr on children and young people issues), MInstD 2006; FIFireE 2000; *Recreations* golf, skiing, reading; *Style*— Lee Howell, Esq; ✉ Suffolk County Council, Endeavour House, Russell Road, Ipswich IP1 2BX

HOWELL, Lisbeth Edna (Lis); da of Frederick Baynes, and Jessica Edna Baynes; *b* 23 March 1951; *Educ* Liverpool Inst HS for Girls, Univ of Bristol (BA); *Partner* Ian Prowiewicz; 1 da (Alexandra b 19 Sept 1984); *Career* reporter BBC local radio 1973–77; reporter/presenter: Border TV 1977–79, Granada TV 1978–80, Tyne Tees TV 1981–84; Border TV: head of news 1986–88, dep dir of progs 1988–89; managing ed Sky News 1990–91, dir of progs GMTV 1991–93, conslt United Artists Programming 1993, dir of progs UK Living satellite and cable channel 1993–97, vice-pres Flextech Programming 1997–; *Books* After the Break (novel, 1995), The Director's Cut (novel, 1996), A Job to Die For (novel, 1997); *Style*— Ms Lis Howell

HOWELL, Margaret; CBE (2007); *b* 5 September 1946; *Educ* Goldsmiths Coll London; *Children* 2 c; *Career* first of new Br fashion designers to modernise the classics of Br clothing using traditional fabrics; postgrad experience mfrg accessories 1969, expanded to produce clothing collections (wholesaled internationally) from own studio 1970–, shops on Wigmore St and Fulham London and in Richmond Surrey, concessions in Selfridges and Bon Marché Paris, jt venture with Anglobal Tokyo 1990, currently produces mens and womenswear with 50 retail outlets worldwide incl UK, Japan, France; outfits donated to Costume Museum Bath and Costume Dept V&A; engaged in promoting post-war Br modern design and architecture; *Recreations* walking, art exhibitions, films and photography; *Style*— Ms Margaret Howell; ✉ Margaret Howell Ltd, 6 Welbeck Way, London W1G 9RZ

HOWELL, Michael John; s of Jack Howell, and Emmie Mary Elizabeth Howell; *b* 9 June 1939; *Educ* Strodes, KCL (LLB), Chicago Univ (JD), Univ of Cape Town; *m* 14 May 1966, Caroline Sarah Eifiona, da of Charles Herbert Gray; 2 da (Juliet b 1967, Lucy b 1973); *Career* admitted slr 1966; ptnr Clifford Chance (formerly Clifford-Turner) 1969–98 (joined 1964); Worshipful Co of Coopers (Under Warden 1988–89, Upper Warden 1989–90, Master 1999–2000); *Style*— Michael Howell, Esq; ✉ Woodhouse Farm, Montacute, Somerset TA15 6XL (tel 01935 829007)

HOWELL, Michael William Davis; s of Air Vice Marshal Evelyn Michael Thomas Howell, CBE, and Helen Joan, *née* Hayes (d 1976); *b* 11 June 1947; *Educ* Charterhouse, Trinity Coll Cambridge, INSEAD and Harvard Business Sch (MBA); *m* 1975, Susan Wanda, da of Andrew Adie (d 1986); 2 s (William b 1982, Andrew b 1988), 1 da (Anna b 1990); *Career* BL Truck & Bus Div 1969–74, vice-pres Cummins Engine Co Inc 1976–88; gen mangr Gen Electric Co (US) Inc 1988–91; dir: Arlington Capital Partners Ltd 1991–, Fenner plc 1993–96; commercial dir Railtrack Group plc 1996–97, exec chm FPT Group Ltd 1998–2002, chief exec Transport Initiatives Edinburgh Ltd 2002–06, chm City and Guilds Inst 2006– (treas 2001–06); dir: Westinghouse Airbrake Technology Corp 2003–, Hutchison China Meditech Ltd 2006–; memb Ct of Assts Worshipful Co of Clothworkers, memb Edinburgh Merchant Co; *Recreations* aviation, walking; *Clubs* Oxford and Cambridge; *Style*— Michael Howell, Esq; ✉ Shawhill, Dundrennan DG6 4QS (tel 0131 552 2644, e-mail mwdhowell@aol.com)

HOWELL, Patrick Leonard; QC (1990); *Educ* Univ of Oxford (MA), Univ of London (LLM); *Career* called to the Bar: Inner Temple 1966, Lincoln's Inn; social security cmmr 1994–; *Style*— Patrick Howell, Esq, QC; ✉ Social Security and Child Support Commissioners, 3rd Floor, Procession House, 55 Ludgate Hill, London EC4M 7JW

HOWELL, Peter Adrian; s of Lt Col Harry Alfred Adrian Howell, MBE (d 1985), of Chester, and Madge Maud Mary, *née* Thompson (d 1992); *b* 29 July 1941; *Educ* Downside, Balliol Coll Oxford (MA, MPhil); *Career* Univ of London: asst lectr then lectr Dept of Latin Bedford Coll 1964–85, sr lectr Dept of Classics Royal Holloway and Bedford New Coll 1994–99 (lectr 1985–94), hon res fell 1999–; memb: Westminster Cathedral Art Ctee 1974–91, Dept of Art and Architecture Liturgy Cmmn Roman Catholic Bishops' Conf for Eng and Wales 1977–84, Churches Ctee English Heritage 1984–88, Westminster Cathedral Art and Architecture Ctee 1993–, Archdiocese of Westminster Historic Churches Ctee 1995–99, RC Historic Churches Ctee for Wales and Herefordshire 1995–; chm Victorian Soc 1987–93 (memb Ctee 1968–2005), dep chm Jt Ctee Nat Amenity Socs 1991–93; *Books* Victorian Churches (1968), Companion Guide to North Wales (with Elisabeth Beazley, 1975), Companion Guide to South Wales (with Elisabeth Beazley, 1977), A Commentary on Book I of the Epigrams of Martial (1980), The Faber Guide to Victorian Churches (ed with Ian Sutton, 1989), Martial: The Epigrams, Book V (1996); *Style*— Peter Howell, Esq; ✉ 127 Banbury Road, Oxford OX2 6JX (tel 01865 515050)

HOWELL, Robert Stuart (Rob); s of Stuart Henry Howell, and Doreen Marjorie Howell; *Educ* Birmingham Poly (BA); *m* Gail; 2 s (Oscar, Dexter); *Career* theatre designer; res design asst RSC 1990–92, freelance set and costume designer 1992–; *Theatre* credits incl: Relative Values (Chichester Festival Theatre and UK tour) 1993, Eurovision (Sydmonton Festival and Vaudeville Theatre) 1993, Oliver (Crucible Theatre Sheffield) 1993, Private Lives (Dalateatern Sweden) 1994, Julius Caesar (Royal Exchange Theatre) 1994, The Shakespeare Revue (RSC) 1994, True West (Donmar Warehouse) 1994, Simpatico (Royal Court Theatre) 1995, The Painter of Dishonour (RSC) 1995, The Glass Menagerie (Donmar Warehouse) 1995 (nominated for Olivier Award Best Set Designer 1996), Tartuffe (Almeida Theatre) 1996, The Loves of Cass Maguire (Druid Theatre Co) 1996, Habeas Corpus (Donmar Warehouse) 1996, Peter Pan (W Yorks Playhouse) 1996, Little Eyolf (RSC) 1996, Tom and Clem (Aldwych Theatre) 1997, Chips with Everything (RNT) 1997 (nominated for Olivier Award for Best Set Designer 1997), Entertaining Mr Sloane (Theatre Clwyd) 1997, The Government Inspector (Almeida Theatre) 1997, Eddie Izzard - Glorious (tour) 1997, How I Learned to Drive (Donmar Warehouse) 1998, Richard III (RSC) 1998 (Olivier Award Best Set Designer 2000), Real Classy Affair (Royal Court Theatre) 1998, Vassa (Almeida Theatre) 1999 (Olivier Award Best Set Designer 2000), Troilus and Cressida (RNT) 1999 (Olivier Award Best Set Designer 2000, nominated for Olivier Award for Best Costume Design 2000), Money (RNT) 1999 (nominated for Olivier Award for Best Costume Design 2000), Family Reunion (RSC) 1999, Betrayal (Theatre d'Atelier Paris) 1999, Battle Royal (RNT) 1999, Eddie Izzard - UK Tour 1999–2000, Hard Fruit (Royal Court Theatre) 2000, Turn of the Screw (WNO) 2000, Conversations after a Burial (Almeida Theatre) 2000, The Caretaker (Comedy Theatre) 2000 (nominated for Olivier Award for Best Set Designer 2001), Lulu (Almeida Theatre and Kennedy Center Washington) 2001, Howard Katz (RNT) 2001, Sunset Boulevard (UK tour) 2001, Faith Healer (Almeida Theatre) 2001, The Graduate (Gielgud Theatre and Broadway) 2002, Proof (Donmar Warehouse) 2002, Our House (Cambridge Theatre) 2002, Sophie's Choice (Royal Opera House) 2002, Simply Heavenly (Young Vic Theatre) 2003, Tell Me on a Sunday (Gielgud Theatre) 2003, The Lady fron the Sea (Almeida Theatre) 2003, Endgame (Albery Theatre) 2004, Buried Child (RNT) 2004, Hedda Gabler (Almeida) 2005 (Best Set Design Olivier Awards 2006 (nominated Best Costume Design)), Lord of the Rings (Toronto) 2006 (Best Costume Design Dora Mavor Award 2006 (nominated Best Set Design)), Bash (The Trafalgar Studios) 2007, Boeing Boeing (The Comedy Theatre) 2007, The Reporter (Nat Theatre) 2007, Lord of the Rings (Theatre Royal) 2007; *Style*— Rob Howell, Esq; ✉ c/o Judy Daish Associates, 2 St Charles Place, London W10 6EG (tel 020 8964 8811, fax 020 8964 8966)

HOWELL, Rupert Cortlandt Spencer; s of Lt-Col F R Howell, of Seaview, IOW, and Sheila Dorothy Lorne McCallum; *b* 6 February 1957; *Educ* Wellington, Univ of Warwick (BSc); *m* 4 Sept 1987, Claire Jane, da of Dr Nigel Ashworth; 1 da (Amy Jane b 8 Aug 1991), 1 s (Dominic James Spencer b 4 Feb 1995); *Career* account exec Mathers Advertising (now Ogilvy and Mather Partners) 1979–80, account supervisor Grey Advertising 1982–83 (account mangr 1981); Young and Rubicam: account dir 1983–84, dir 1984–87, jt head of Account Mgmnt 1987; fndr ptnr HHCL and Partners (formerly Howell Henry Chaldecott Lury) 1987–97 (UK Agency of the Decade Campaign magazine), jt ceo Chime Communications plc 1998–2002, pres EMEA and chm UK and I McCann Erickson 2003–07; pres IPA 2000–01; memb Govt Communications Review Gp; memb Advsy Bd Warwick Business Sch; FIPA 1995 (MIPA 1989); *Recreations* cricket, golf, tennis (playing and spectating), rugby and soccer (spectating only!); *Clubs* MCC, London Rugby, Sandown & Shanklin Golf, Seaview Yacht; *Style*— Rupert Howell, Esq; ✉ tel 020 7961 2301, mobile 07770 381300

HOWELL, Prof Simon Laurence; s of Laurence James Howell, of Eastbourne, E Sussex, and Rosemary, *née* Wheelwright (d 1984); *b* 29 June 1943; *Educ* St John's Sch Leatherhead, Chelsea Coll London (BSc), KCL (PhD), Univ of London (DSc); *m* 1969, Linda Margaret, *née* Chapman; 1 da (Tessa Louise); *Career* research fell Univ of Sussex 1968–78, lectr Charing Cross Hosp Med Sch 1978–80; KCL: reader then prof of endocrine physiology 1980–, head Div of Biomedical Scis 1988–98, head Sch of Biomedical Scis 1998–2003, research dean Sch of Biomedical Scis 2003–06, dir research devpt (health) 2007–; chair Diabetes UK 2006– (vice-chair 2002–06); memb Cncl: Br Diabetic Assoc 1985–91 (chm Research Ctee 1987–90), Assoc of Medical Research Charities 1989–92, European Assoc for the Study of Diabetes 1992–95, KCL 1992–96; R D Lawrence Lecture Br Diabetic Assoc 1976, Minkowski Prize European Assoc for the Study of Diabetes 1983; *Books* Biochemistry of the Polypeptide Hormones (with M Wallis and K W Taylor, 1985), Diabetes and its Management (with P Watkins and P Drury, 1996 and 2003), Biology of the Pancreatic Beta Cell (1999); *Recreations* gardening, opera; *Style*— Prof Simon Howell; ✉ School of Biomedical Sciences, King's College London, Hodgkin Building, Guys Campus, London SE1 9UL (tel 020 7848 6390, fax 020 7848 6394, e-mail simon.howell@kcl.ac.uk)

HOWELL OF GUILDFORD, Baron (Life Peer UK 1997), of Penton Mewsey in the County of Hampshire; David Arthur Russell Howell; PC (1979); s of Col Arthur Howard Eckford Howell, DSO, TD, DL (d 1980), and Beryl Stuart, *née* Bowater; *b* 18 January 1936; *Educ* Eton, King's Coll Cambridge (MA); *m* 1967, (Cary) Davina, da of Maj David Wallace (ka 1944); 2 da (Hon Frances Victoria (Mrs George Osborne) b 1969, Hon Kate Davina b 1970), 1 s (Hon Toby David b 1975); *Career* serv Coldstream Gds 1954–56, 2 Lt; worked in Econ Section Treasy 1959–60, ldr writer Daily Telegraph 1960–64, chm Bow Gp 1961–62, ed Crossbow 1962–64, Parly candidate (Cons) Dudley 1964, dir Cons Political Centre 1964–66, MP (Cons) Guildford 1966–97, lord cmmr Treasy 1970–71, Parly sec CSD 1970–72; Parly under sec: Employment 1971–72, NI March-Nov 1972; min of state: NI 1972–74, Energy 1974; oppn spokesman on: Treasy and financial affrs 1974–77, home affrs 1977–79, sec of state for: Energy 1979–81, Transport 1981–83; chm: House of Commons Foreign Affrs Ctee 1987–97, House of Lords European Sub-Ctee on Common Foreign and Security Policy 1999–2000; House of Lords: oppn spokesman on foreign and Cwlth affrs 2001–, dep ldr of the Oppn 2005–; chm UK Japan 21st Century Gp 1989–2001; non-exec dir: Queens Moat Hotels plc 1989–93, Trafalgar House plc 1990–96, Monks Investment Trust 1993–2004, Jardine Insurance Brokers 1994–97, John Laing plc 2000–03; advsr: Wood Mackenzie 1976–79, Merck, Sharp and Dohme 1976–79; conslt: Savory Milln plc 1983–86, Coopers and Lybrand 1984–89; memb Int Advsy Bd Swiss Bank Corporation 1987–96, advsy dir Warburg Dillon Read 1997–2000, sr advsr Japan Central Railway Co 2001–, European adsvsr Mitsubishi Electric BV 2003–, memb Financial Advsy Bd Kuwait Investment Authority 2003–; pres Br Inst of Energy Economists 2003–, co-chm Windsor Energy Gp, memb Governing Bd Centre for Global Energy Studies 2006–; columnist Japan Times 1983–; govr Sadlers Wells Fndn 1998–2000, tstee Shakespeare's Globe Theatre 2000–; visiting fell: Policy Studies Inst 1983–85, Nuffield Coll Oxford 1983–2001; Liveryman Worshipful Co of Clothworkers; *Publications* A New Style of Government (1970), Time to Move On (1976), Freedom and Capital (1981), Blind Victory (1986), The Edge of Now (2000), Out of the Energy Labyrinth (2007); *Recreations* tennis, writing, DIY; *Clubs* Beefsteak; *Style*— The Rt Hon Lord Howell of Guildford, PC; ✉ House of Lords, London SW1A 0PW (e-mail howelld@parliament.uk, website www.lordhowell.com)

HOWELL-RICHARDSON, Phillip Lort; s of Graham Howell-Richardson (d 1980), and Jean, *née* McDonald; *b* 21 June 1950, Cardiff; *Educ* Univ of Kent at Canterbury (BA), Coll of Law Guildford; *m* 20 May 1978, Sally Anne, *née* Chamberlin; 1 s (James b 14 May 1980), 2 da (Victoria b 13 March 1982, Charlotte b 5 Oct 1983); *Career* admitted slr 1975; asst slr Osborne Clarke Bristol 1976–81; Morgan Cole: ptnr London Thames Valley and Wales 1982–2005, head of commercial litigation 1985–98, memb Bd 1998–2000; mediator and conslt in alternative dispute resolution S J Berwin 2005–; fndr memb Panel of Ind Mediators 1995, co-chm ADR Gp 1995–; memb: Panel of Ct of Appeal Mediators, In Place of Strife, Construction Conciliation Gp, Panel of Mediators Fedn Against Software Theft, Technol & Construction Slrs Assoc, CMAP Paris, Exec Advsy Bd CPR NY; conslt ed Inst of Advanced Legal Studies; vice-chm of govrs Clifton Coll Bristol; memb Law Soc 1975, accredited mediator ADR Gp 1990, MCIArb 1998, fell Inst of Professional Devpt 1999, fell Int Acad of Mediators; *Publications* Mediators on Mediations (contrib, 2005), many articles in periodicals; *Recreations* sailing, mountain biking, modern art; *Clubs* Royal Dart Yacht; *Style*— Phillip Howell-Richardson, Esq; ✉ Flat 7, 198 St John Street, London EC1V 4JY (tel 07720 700228); S J Berwin LLP, 10 Queen Street Place, London EC4R 1BE (tel 020 7111 2566, fax 020 7111 2000, e-mail phillip.howell-richardson@sjberwin.com)

HOWELLS, Anne Elizabeth; da of Trevor William Howells, and Mona, *née* Hewart; *b* 12 January 1941; *Educ* Sale GS for Girls, Royal Northern (then Manchester) Coll of Music (ARMCM, Curtis Gold Medal, Ricordi Opera Prize); *Career* opera singer; mezzo soprano; performances incl: lead role in L'Ormindo, Rosina in The Barber of Seville, Cherubino in The Marriage of Figaro, Zerlina in Don Giovanni, Dorabella and Despina in Cosi Fan Tutte, Octavian in Der Rosenkavalier, Giulietta in The Tales of Hoffmann, Orsini in Lucrezia Borgia, Annius in La Clemenza di Tito, Ascanius in Benvenuto Cellini, Mélisande in Pelléas et Mélisande, Ophelia in Hamlet, Lena in Victory, Cathleen Sweeney in Rising of the Moon, Lady Hautdesert in Gawain and the Green Knight, Helen in King Priam; as freelance sang with all major Euro and British Cos incl Judit in Bluebeard's Castle (Rotterdam Philharmonic); visitor: La Scala Milan, The Metropolitan NY, Salzburg Festival, Opera Houses of LA, San Francisco, Chicago, Geneva and Paris; prof RAM 1997–; hon fell RMCM; *Recreations* reading, theatre; *Style*— Miss Anne Howells

HOWELLS, Prof Christina; da of John Mitchell, of Frimley, Surrey, and Elizabeth, *née* Johnson; *b* 13 April 1950; *Educ* Merrow Grange Covent Sch Guildford, KCL (BA, PhD); *m* 21 July 1973, Bernard Howells; 1 da (Marie-Elise b 1 Feb 1984), 1 s (Dominic b 2 March 1986); *Career* temporary posts Philippa Fawcett Coll, Stockwell Coll and KCL 1975–79; fell in French Wadham Coll Oxford 1979–; Univ of Oxford: CUF lectr 1979, reader 1996, prof of French 1999–; delivered numerous lectures and papers and chaired sessions at colloquia and confs in GB, Europe and USA; fndr memb and Br rep Groupe d'Etudes Sartriennes (also co-ed jl), assoc memb Conseil National des Programmes (CNP) 2001–; memb: Int Assoc of Philosophy and Literature (IAPL), Forum for European Philosophy; co-ed Sartre Studies International 1995–; Officier dans l'Ordre des Palmes Académiques (France); *Publications* Sartre's Theory of Literature (1979), Sartre: The Necessity of Freedom (1988), Sartre: A Companion (ed and contrib, 1992), Sartre (ed and contrib, 1995), Derrida: Deconstruction from Phenomenology to Ethics (1998), French Women Philosophers: Subjectivity, Identity, Alterity (2004); also author of numerous essays, chapters and reviews; *Recreations* theatre, opera, cinema, reading, travel, friends; *Style*— Prof Christina Howells; ✉ Wadham College, Oxford OX1 3PN (tel 01865 277985, e-mail christina.howells@wadh.ox.ac.uk)

HOWELLS, David John; s of Ivor Mervyn Howells, of Shrewsbury, and Veronica Carey, *née* Jones; *b* 14 March 1953; *Educ* London Hosp Med Coll (BDS), Univ Hosp of Wales (MScD); *Family* 2 da (Lowri b 1989, Ffion b 1991); *Career* postgrad training in orthodontics Welsh Nat Sch of Med, registrar Queen Alexandra Hosp Portsmouth 1982–84, sr registrar Birmingham Dental Hosp 1984–87, conslt orthodontist to Morriston Hosp Swansea and Prince Phillip Hosp Llanelli 1987–, clinical dir Morriston Hosp 1990–95, chm W Glam Dist Dental Ctee 1991–96, chm Iechyd Morgannwg Dist Dental Ctee 1996–2002; also in private orthodontic practice in Llanelli and Carmarthen; author of several academic papers in specialist jls; LDS, DOrth, MOrth, FDSRCS (Eng); *Recreations* scuba diving, hiking, photography, nature conservation; *Style*— Dr David

H

Howells; ✉ Consulting Rooms, Pencastell, 1 Murray Street, Llanelli (tel 01554 777799, fax 01554 776699, e-mail dr.howells@orthodontics.demon.co.uk)

HOWELLS, Dr Kim Scott; MP; s of late Glanville James Howells, of Aberdare, Mid Glamorgan, and Glenys Joan, *née* Edwards; *b* 27 November 1946; *Educ* Mountain Ash GS, Hornsey Coll of Art, Cambridge Coll of Advanced Technol (BA), Univ of Warwick (PhD); *m* 22 Oct 1983, Eirlys, da of William Elfed Davies, of Neath, W Glamorgan; 1 da (Seren Rachel Morgans b 23 Dec 1976), 2 s (Cai James b 26 April 1984, Scott Aled b 20 Feb 1988); *Career* steel worker 1969–70, coal miner 1970–71, lectr 1975–79; res offr: Univ of Wales 1979–82, NUM S Wales 1982–89 (also ed); TV presenter and writer 1986–89; MP (Lab) Pontypridd 1989–; oppn front bench spokesman on: Overseas Co-operation and Devpt 1993, Foreign Affrs 1994, Home Affrs 1994–95, Trade and Industry 1995–97; Parly under sec of state: DfEE 1997–98, DTI 1998–2001, DCMS (min for Tourism, Film and Broadcasting) 2001–03; min of state Dept for Tport 2003–04, min of state DfES 2004–05, min for the Middle East FCO 2005–; House of Commons: memb Select Ctee on Welsh Affrs, memb Select Ctee on the Environment, memb Public Accounts Ctee; memb Br Mountaineering Cncl; *Publications* various essays in collections dealing mainly with mining history, trade unionism, literature and the environment; *Recreations* mountaineering, jazz, cinema, painting; *Clubs* Llantwit Fadre CC, Pontypridd CC, Hopkinstown CC, Pontypridd RFC; *Style—* Dr Kim Howells, MP; ✉ 16 Tyfica Road, Pontypridd CF37 2DA (tel 01443 402551, fax 01443 485628); House of Commons, London SW1A 0AA (tel 020 7219 3000)

HOWELLS, Michael Sandbrook; s of Benjamin George Howells (d 1971), of Pembroke Dock, and Blodwen, *née* Francis (d 1978); *b* 29 May 1939; *Educ* Dean Close Sch Cheltenham, UCL; *m* 18 June 1966, Pamela Vivian, da of Gordon Harry Francis, of Clandon, Surrey; 2 s (Luke b 1970, Toby b 1972); *Career* admitted slr 1966; sr ptnr Price and Kelway Slrs 1980–95 (ptnr 1971), princ Michael S Howells Slrs 1995–2003; HM coroner Pembrokeshire 1980; conducted inquests into: Richard and Helen Thomas (double murder), 1985, explosion on tanker Pointsman 1985, Peter and Gwenda Dixon (double murder) 1989, loss of fishing vessel Inspire 1990, ferry Norrona fire 1991, the Tregwynt Hoard (last Treasure Trove inquest in Wales) 1997; memb: Cncl Law Soc 1983–99 (dep treas 1992–95, treas 1995–96), Supreme Court Rules Ctee 1985–88, Cncl of Coroners' Soc of England and Wales 1986– (vice-pres 1997–98, pres 1998–99, conf sec 2002–), Lord Chancellor's Standing Ctee for the Welsh Language 2003–; High Ct costs assessor 1988–2003; pres Pembrokeshire C of C 1995–96, pres Milford Haven Rotary Club 1997–98; *Recreations* theatre, messing about in boats; *Clubs* RAC, Waterloo, Milford Haven, Neyland Yacht; *Style—* Michael Howells, Esq; ✉ Glenowen, Mastlebridge, Milford Haven, Pembrokeshire SA73 1QS (tel 01646 600208, e-mail mike_howells8@btinternet.com); Town Hall, Hamilton Terrace, Milford Haven, Pembrokeshire SA73 3JW (tel 01646 698129, fax 016462 690607)

HOWELLS OF ST DAVIDS, Baroness (Life Peer UK 1999), of Charlton in the London Borough of Greenwich; Rosalind Patricia-Anne Howells, *née* George; OBE (1994); *b* 10 January 1931; *Educ* St Joseph's Convent Grenada, SW London Coll; *Career* black community ldr and campaigner for racial equality; former equal opportunities dir and chair Greenwich Racial Equalities Cncl, former dep high cmmr for Grenada; first black: public library employee, vice-chair London Voluntary Services Cncl, tstee City Parochial Fndn, female memb Ct of Govrs Univ of Greenwich, female memb GLC Trg Bd; memb Constitution Ctee House of Lords, memb Parly Cwlth Ctee; former chair: Charlton Consortium, Carnival Liaison Ctee, Gtr London Action on Race Equality; former memb: Advsy Ctee to the Home Sec, Lay Visitors Panel, Commonwealth Countries League, Greenwich Police/Community Consultative Gp, Greenwich Waterfront Devpt Bd; currently: dir Smithville Associates, pres Grenada Convent Past Pupils Assoc, chair Talawa Theatre, chair Jalawa Westminster Theatre, memb Woman of the Year Ctee, tstee West Indian Standing Conf, tstee Museum of Ethnic Arts, patron Grenada Arts Cncl, patron Mediation Service; Hon Degree Univ of Greenwich; *Style—* The Rt Hon the Baroness Howells of St Davids, OBE; ✉ House of Lords, London SW1A 0PW (tel 020 7219 8655)

HOWES, Sir Christopher Kingston; KCVO (1999, CVO 1997), CB (1993); s of Leonard Arthur Howes, OBE (d 1999), of Norfolk, and Marion Amy, *née* Bussey (d 1999); *b* 30 January 1942; *Educ* Gresham's, Univ of London, Coll of Estate Mgmnt (BSc), Univ of Reading (MPhil); *m* 1967, Clare, da of Gordon Edward Cunliffe (d 1987), of Sussex; 2 da (Catherine b 1973, Rosalind b 1975 (decd)), 2 s (Robert b 1976, Michael b 1977 (decd)); *Career* GLC Planning and Valuation Depts 1965–67; ptnr (later sr ptnr) Chartered Surveyors & Planning Conslts 1967–79, dep dir Land Economy Directorate DOE 1979–80 (dir Land Economy 1981–84), dir Land and Property 1985–89, second Crown Estate cmmr and chief exec Crown Estate 1989–2001; non-exec dir: Norwich & Peterborough Building Society 1998–2005, Howard de Walden Estates Ltd 2002–, Compco Hldgs 2004–; memb Advsy Bd Barclays Private Bank Ltd 2001–, non-exec chm Property Finance Team Barclays Bank 2005–; memb Advsy Bd Three Delta LLP; visiting lectr Univs of London, E Anglia (sr visiting fell 1973), Cambridge, Reading and Aberdeen 1966–, UCLA and Univ of Calif South LA 1983, Harvard 1985, North Carolina Chapel Hill 1985; visiting prof UCL 1985–; memb Norwich Cncl 1970–74, magistrate for Norfolk 1973–79, memb Ct of Advsrs St Paul's Cathedral 1980–99, steward and hon surveyor to Dean and Chapter Norwich Cathedral 1972–79; RICS: memb Policy Review Ctee 1979–81, memb Planning & Devpt Divnl Cncl 1984–92; memb Cncl Duchy of Lancaster 1993–2005, memb Sec of State for the Environment's Thames Advsy Gp 1995–98; hon memb Cambridge Univ Land Soc 1989; jt chm World Land Policy Congress 1986; memb: OECD Urban Policy Gp 1985–87 HRH Prince of Wales's Cncl 1990–, Cncl Br Property Fedn 1992–2001, Ct UEA 1992–; tstee: HRH Prince of Wales's Inst of Architecture 1991–99, Br Architectural Library Tst 1997–; first hon fell Local Authy Valuers' Assoc 1990, Hon DLitt UEA 2000; Hon FRIBA 1995; *Books* Value Maps: Aspects of Land and Property Values (1980), Economic Regeneration (1988), Urban Revitalization (1988); contributor to many books and articles in learned journals; *Recreations* watching sport, music, painting, sailing; *Clubs* Athenaeum, Garrick, Norfolk (Norwich), Aldeburgh Yacht; *Style—* Sir Christopher Howes, KCVO, CB; ✉ 8 Millennium House, 132 Grosvenor Road, London SW1V 3JY (tel 020 7828 9920)

HOWES, Colin; s of Russell Howes, of Norwich, and Toby, *née* Jones; *b* 3 March 1956, Norfolk; *Educ* Ipswich Sch, Oriel College Oxford (MA), Coll of Law Chester; *m* 29 Aug 1983, Deborah, *née* Sherry; 1 s (Alexander b 9 Sept 1987), 2 da (Rosalind b 19 June 1990, Juliet b 13 July 1995); *Career* slr; Harbottle & Lewis: joined 1979, slr 1981–84, ptnr 1984–, managing ptnr 1992–2000; non-exec dir Pola Jones Assoc Ltd; sec Virgin Fndn/Virgin Unite; tstee: Comic Relief, Timebank; memb Law Soc 1981; *Recreations* music, theatre, golf; *Clubs* Hampstead Golf; *Style—* Colin Howes, Esq; ✉ Harbottle & Lewis LLP, Hanover House, 14 Hanover Square, London W1S 1HP (tel 020 7667 5000, fax 020 7667 5100)

HOWES, Jacqueline Frances (Jaki); da of Frank Bernard Allen (d 1974), of Hardingstone, Northants, and Hilda Evelyn, *née* Bull (d 1998); *b* 5 April 1943; *Educ* Northampton HS, Univ of Manchester (BA); *m* (m dis 1982), (Anthony) Mark Howes, s of Anthony Cecil George Howes (d 1974); 1 da (Josephine); *Career* Guardian and Manchester Evening News Manchester 1969–71, Leach Rhodes and Walker 1971–72, sr lectr Sch of Architecture Huddersfield Poly 1972–89, conslt to Geoffrey Alsop Practice Manchester 1983–85, princ lectr in architecture Leeds Metropolitan Univ (formerly Leeds Poly) 1990–; dir Constructing Excellence in Yorkshire and Humber 2003–04; Freeman City of London 1993; memb Ct of Assts Worshipful Co of Chartered Architects (Liveryman 1994); ARCUK 1970, RIBA 1976; *Books* The Technology of Suspended Cable Net Structures (with Chaplin and Calderbank, 1984), Computers Count (1989), Computers in Architectural Practice (with Christopher Woodward, 1997); *Recreations* sailing, music, cartoons; *Style—* Mrs Jaki Howes; ✉ School of Architecture, Landscape and Design, Hepworth Point, Claypit Lane, Leeds LS2 8BQ (tel 0113 218 1714)

HOWES, Prof Michael John; s of Lt Cdr Ernest Stanley George Howes (d 1984), of Lowestoft, Suffolk, and Louisa Anne, *née* Hart (d 1976); *b* 19 January 1941; *Educ* Lowestoft GS, Univ of Leeds (BSc, PhD); *m* 8 Oct 1960, Dianne Lucie, da of Rex Crutchfield, of Stevenage, Herts; 1 da (Emma); *Career* scientific offr MAFF 1957–62; Univ of Leeds: lectr 1967–78, sr lectr 1978–80, head of dept and prof of electronic engrg 1984–95; visiting prof Cornell Univ USA 1980–81, tech dir MM Microwave Yorks 1981–84; author of numerous engrg and scientific pubns; MInstP, FIEE, FIEEE, FRSA; *Books* incl: Solid State Electronics (with D V Morgan, 1973), Microwave Devices (ed with D V Morgan, 1976), Optical Fibre Communications (ed with D V Morgan, 1980), Reliability and Degradation (ed with D V Morgan, 1982), Worked Examples in Microwave Subsystem Design (jtly, 1984), Reliability and Degradation (ed with D V Morgan, 1985); *Recreations* golf; *Clubs* Moortown Golf; *Style—* Prof Michael Howes; ✉ 32 West Park Drive, Leeds LS16 5BL (tel 0113 275 2156); Department of Electronic and Electrical Engineering, The University, Leeds LS2 9JT (tel 0113 233 2014, fax 0113 233 2032, e-mail m.j.howes@leeds.ac.uk)

HOWGEGO, Charles; s of David Howgego, of Wild Hill, Herts, and Sybil, *née* Jones; *b* 8 January 1971, Welwyn Garden City, Herts; *Educ* St Albans Sch, Sheffield Hallam Univ; *Partner* Carolyn Fearn; 2 s (Evan, Jonah), 1 da (Yasmin); *Career* ed The Big Issue; memb CAMRA; *Style—* Charles Howgego, Esq

HOWGRAVE-GRAHAM, Christopher Michael; s of Hamilton Stuart Howgrave-Graham, of Salisbury, Wilts, and Joyce Mary, *née* Rowlatt (d 2000); *b* 18 February 1949; *Educ* Ardingly, UEA (BA), Institut d'Etudes Politiques; *m* 5 Aug 1972, Rossana, da of Giliande Mastroddi; 2 s (Jonathan b 7 Dec 1977, Matthew b 28 March 1981); *Career* NHS trainee (Winchester, Portsmouth, Kings Fund Coll London) 1971–73; planner: East Birmingham HMC 1973–74, South Birmingham HA 1974–75; house governor St Stephen's Hosp 1975–80 (latterly sector admin Chelsea & Kensington), dep dist admin and acute servs mangr Redbridge HA 1980–85, gen mangr Community & Mental Health Servs Barking Havering and Brentwood HA 1986–88, dir of acute servs Bloomsbury and Islington HA 1989–90, mangr Middlesex Hosp, UCH and associated hosps, Whittington Hosp and Royal Northern Hosps 1990–92, London review co-ordinator NE Thames RHA 1992–; chief exec Coventry HA 1993–2002, assoc Modernisation Agency 2002–; sec Special Tstees of Middx Hosp 1990–92; memb Cncl Univ of Warwick 2000–; MIHSM 1976; *Books* The Hospital in Little Chelsea (with Dr L Martin, 1978); *Recreations* keeping fit, gardening, seeing the family; *Style—* Christopher Howgrave-Graham, Esq; ✉ Department of Health, 133–135 Waterloo Road, London SE1 8UG (tel 020 7972 4174, e-mail chris.howgrave-graham@doh.gsi.gov.uk)

HOWICK OF GLENDALE, 2 Baron (UK 1960); Charles Evelyn Baring; s of 1 Baron Howick of Glendale, KG, GCMG, KCVO (d 1973; formerly Hon Sir Evelyn Baring, sometime govr Kenya and yst s of 1 Earl of Cromer), and Lady Mary Grey (d 2002), da of 5 Earl Grey; *b* 30 December 1937; *Educ* Eton, New Coll Oxford; *m* 1964, Clare, yr da of Col Cyril Darby, MC, of Kemerton Court, Tewkesbury; 3 da (Hon Rachel Monica (Hon Mrs Lane Fox) b 1967, Hon Jessica Mary Clare (Hon Mrs Laithwaite) b 1969, Hon Alice Olivia (Hon Mrs Ward-Thomas) b 1971), 1 s (Hon David Evelyn Charles b 1975); *Heir* s, Dr the Hon David Baring; *Career* md Baring Bros & Co 1969–82, dir London Life Assoc 1972–82, dir Northern Rock plc 1988–2001; memb: Exec Ctee Nat Art Collections Fund 1973–88, Cncl The Baring Fndn 1982–99; tstee: Chelsea Physic Garden 1994–, The Northern Rock Fndn 1997–, Royal Botanic Garden Edinburgh 2001–; memb Advsy Cncl Westonbirt Arboretum 1999–; *Style—* The Lord Howick of Glendale; ✉ Howick, Alnwick, Northumberland NE66 3LB (tel 01665 577624)

HOWIE, Prof Archibald; CBE (1998); s of Robert Howie (d 1992), of Grange, Kirkcaldy, Fife, and Margaret Marshall, *née* McDonald (d 1971); *b* 8 March 1934; *Educ* Kirkcaldy HS, Univ of Edinburgh (BSc), Caltech (MS), Univ of Cambridge (PhD); *m* 15 Aug 1964, Melva Jean, da of Ernest Scott (d 1959), of Tynemouth, Northumberland; 1 s (David Robert b 9 Oct 1965, d 1986), 1 da (Helena Margaret b 14 July 1971); *Career* Univ of Cambridge: ICI fell 1960–61, demonstrator in physics 1962–65, lectr 1965–78, reader 1978–86, prof 1986–2001, head Dept of Physics 1989–97; Churchill Coll Cambridge: fell 1960–, res fell 1960–61, teaching fell in physics 1962–86; visiting prof of physics: Aarhus 1974, Bologna 1984; NPL Management Ltd 1995–2001; pres: Royal Microscopical Soc 1984–86, Int Fedn of Societies for Electron Micoscopy 1999–2002; Hughes Medal Royal Soc (with Dr M J Whelan) 1988, Royal Medal Royal Soc 1999; Hon Dr of Physics: Bologna 1989, Thessaloniki 1995; FRS 1978, FInstP 1978, Hon FRMS 1978, Hon FRSE 1995; *Books* Electron Microscopy of Thin Crystals (jtly 1965, revised 1977), Electron Optical Imaging of Surfaces (jtly); *Recreations* winemaking; *Style—* Prof Archibald Howie, CBE, FRS; ✉ 194 Huntingdon Road, Cambridge CB3 0LB (tel 01223 570977); Cavendish Laboratory, Madingley Road, Cambridge CB3 0HE (tel 01223 337335, fax 01223 363263, e-mail ah30@cam.ac.uk)

HOWIE, Prof John Mackintosh; CBE (1993); s of Rev David Yuille Howie (d 1995), of Aberdeen, and Janet Macdonald, *née* Mackintosh (d 1989); *b* 23 May 1936; *Educ* Robert Gordon's Coll Aberdeen, Univ of Aberdeen (MA, DSc), Balliol Coll Oxford (DPhil); *m* 5 Aug 1960, Dorothy Joyce Mitchell, da of Alfred James Miller, OBE (d 1980), of Aberdeen; 2 da (Anne b 1961, Katharine b 1963 d 1998); *Career* asst in maths Univ of Aberdeen 1958–59, asst then lectr in maths Univ of Glasgow 1961–67, sr lectr in maths Univ of Stirling 1967–70, regius prof of maths Univ of St Andrews 1970–97 (dean Faculty of Sci 1976–79); visiting appts: Tulane Univ 1964–65, Univ of Western Aust 1968, SUNY Buffalo 1969 and 1970, Monash Univ 1979, Northern Illinois Univ 1988, Univ of Lisbon 1996; chm: Scot Central Ctee on Mathematics 1975–81, Dundee Coll of Educn 1983–87, Ctee to Review Fifth and Sixth Years (The Howie Ctee) 1990–92; memb Ctee to Review Examinations (The Dunning Ctee) 1975–77, vice-pres London Mathematical Soc 1984–86 and 1990–92; Hon DUniv Open Univ 2000; FRSE 1971; *Books* An Introduction to Semigroup Theory (1976), Automata and Languages (1991), Fundamentals of Semigroup Theory (1995), Real Analysis (2001), Complex Analysis (2003), Fields and Galois Theory (2006); author of articles for various mathematical jls; *Recreations* music, gardening; *Style—* Prof John M Howie, CBE, FRSE; ✉ Longacre, 19 Strathkinness High Road, St Andrews, Fife KY16 9UA (tel 01334 474103); Mathematical Institute, University of St Andrews, North Haugh, St Andrews, Fife KY16 9SS (tel 01334 463746, fax 01334 463748, e-mail jmh@st-andrews.ac.uk)

HOWIE OF TROON, Baron (Life Peer UK 1978), of Troon in Kyle and Carrick; William Howie; s of Peter Howie; *b* 2 March 1924; *Educ* Marr Coll Troon, Royal Tech Coll Glasgow; *m* 1951, Mairi (d 2005), da of John Sanderson; 2 da, 2 s; *Career* civil engr, journalist and publisher; MP (Lab) Luton 1963–70, asst whip 1964–66, lord cmmr Treasy 1966–67, comptroller HM Household 1967–68, vice-chm PLP 1968–70, dir of internal rels Thos Telford Ltd 1976–95; pro-chllr City Univ 1984–91 (memb Cncl 1968–91); MSocIS (France), FICE; *Style—* The Rt Hon Lord Howie of Troon; ✉ 34 Temple Fortune Lane, London NW11 7UL (tel 020 8455 0492)

HOWITT, Richard; MEP (Lab) East England; *Educ* Lady Margaret Hall Oxford (BA), Univ of Hertfordshire (Dip Mgmnt Studies); *Career* co-ordinator Harlow Cncl for Voluntary

Service 1982–86, specialist in community care for the disabled Waltham Forest Social Services 1986–94; chm South-East Economic Devpt Strategy (SEEDS) 1986–94, memb Bd Centre for Local Economic Strategies (CLES) 1988–91, UK rep Helios Prog 1988–91; Harlow DC: cncllr 1984–94, chm Planning and Economic Devpt Ctee 1985–91, leader 1991–94; MEP (Lab): Essex South 1994–99, E England 1999–; pres All-Pty Disability Gp of MEPs; vice-pres Regional Affrs Ctee; memb: Devpt Ctee, Delgn with S America; sec Lab Gp of MEPs in South East; *Recreations* photography, travel, opera and cricket; *Style*— Richard Howitt, MEP; ✉ Labour European Office, Unit 3, Frohock House, 222 Mill Road, Cambridge CB1 3NF (tel 01223 240202, fax 01223 241900, e-mail richard.howitt@geo2.poplet.org.uk, website www.richardhowittmep.com)

HOWKINS, Ben Walter; s of Col Walter Ashby (Tim) Howkins (d 1977), and Lesley, *née* Stops (d 2003), of Olney, Bucks; *b* 19 August 1942; *Educ* Rugby, Amherst Coll Massachusetts; *m* 6 Nov 1976, Clarissa Jane, da of Thomas John Fairbank, of Cambridge; 1 s (James b 1980), 1 da (Lucy b 1981); *Career* Vintners scholar 1963, Lt Northants Yeo TA 1964–69; brand mangr IDV UK 1968–70, int sales and mktg dir Croft & Co 1970–80, md Morgan Furze 1980–89, dir Taylor Fladgate & Yeatman 1989–90, chm Wine Promotion Bd 1990–93, wine conslt Waddesdon Manor 1991–, md Royal Tokay Wine Co 1993–; memb Cncl Wine Guild of UK 1995–2003, tstee Wine and Spirit Educn Tst 2000–04; Freeman City of London 1986, Liveryman Worshipful Co of Vintners 1986; *Books* Rich, Rare and Red - A Guide to Port (1982, paperback edn 1987, 3 edn 2003), Tokaji - A Classic Lost and Found (1999); *Recreations* skiing, tennis, shooting; *Clubs* Brooks's; *Style*— Ben Howkins, Esq; ✉ Staverton Manor, Staverton, Northamptonshire NN11 6JD (tel 01327 703600); 202 Fulham Road, London SW10 9PJ (tel 020 7495 3010, fax 020 7823 3510, e-mail benhowkins@royal-tokaji.com)

HOWKINS, John Anthony; s of Col Ashby (Tim) Howkins (d 1977), and Lesley, *née* Stops; *b* 3 August 1945; *Educ* Rugby, Keele Univ (BA), AA Sch of Architecture (AADipl); *m* 1, 1971, Jill, da of Ian Liddington; m 2, 1977, Annabel, da of John Whittet; *Career* mktg mangr Lever Bros 1968–70, TV ed Time Out 1971–74, fndr TV4 Gp 1971, dir Whittet Books 1976–84, chm Pool Video Graz Austria 1976, ed Vision 1977–79, chm London Film Sch 1979–84, TV columnist Illustrated London News 1981–83, exec ed Nat Electronics Review 1981–90, exec dir Int Inst of Communications 1984–89, conslt and dir ETR & Co 1989–, assoc Coopers & Lybrand Deloitte 1990–91, chm Createc 1996–2001, dir Equator Gp plc 1999–2006, chm Tornado Productions Ltd 2000–04; dir: Handmade plc 2006, Hotbed Media Ltd 2006; memb: Interim Action Ctee on the Film Industry DTI 1980–85, Exec Ctee Broadcasting Research Unit 1981–90; European advsr HBO Time Warner 1981–96, specialist advsr Select Ctee on European Communities House of Lords 1985, advsr Polish Radio and TV 1989–95, advsr Min for Film Poland 1991–93; vice-chm Assoc of Ind Prodrs 1984–85, dep chm Br Screen Advsy Cncl 1991– (memb 1985–); project dir World Learning Network 1996–2002, dir Adelphi Charter on Creativity, Innovation and Intellectual Property 2005–07; co-ordinator European Audiovisual Conf 1998; visiting prof: Lincoln Univ 2004–, Shanghai Theatre Acad China 2006–; *Books* Understanding Television (1977), Mass Communications in China (1982), New Technologies, New Policies (1982), Satellites International (1987), Four Global Senarios on Information and Communication (1997), The Creative Economy (2001), Code (2002); *Style*— John Howkins, Esq; ✉ E6 Albany, Piccadilly, London W1J 0AR (tel 020 7434 1400, e-mail john@johnhowkins.com)

HOWKINS, John David; s of Gordon Arthur Howkins, and Olga Annie, *née* King; *b* 4 February 1955; *Educ* Windsor GS, Univ of Exeter (BSc); *m* 14 April 1984, Susan, da of Richard Andreas Oakley; 2 da (Lily May b 23 May 1988, Scarlett Hannah b 20 Feb 1991); *Career* media trainee rising to dep media dir D'Arcy McManus Masius advtg agency 1976–82, assoc dir of planning DMB&B 1982–84, planning dir Lowe Howard-Spink 1984–88, ptnr Elgie Stewart Smith 1988–90, md Planning Consultancy 1990–91, md DDM Advertising 1991–93, strategic planning dir McCann-Erickson 1993–97, planning ptnr Rainey Kelly Campbell Roalfe/Y&R Ltd 1997–2005, consumer planning dir HTW Ltd 2005–07, fndr The Nub Consultancy 2007–; memb Market Res Soc 1982; *Recreations* media journalism, campanology; *Clubs* Royal Scottish Automobile; *Style*— John Howkins, Esq; ✉ Hermongers Barn, Rudgwick, West Sussex RH12 3AL (tel 01403 822476); The Nub Consultancy (tel 07801 019778)

HOWLAND JACKSON, Anthony Geoffrey Clive; s of Arthur Geoffrey Howland Jackson, MBE (d 1996), and Pamela Foote, *née* Wauton; *b* 25 May 1941; *Educ* Sherborne; *m* 15 June 1963, Susan Ellen, da of Geoffrey Hickson (d 1984); 1 s (James Geoffrey b 10 Feb 1965), 2 da (Anna Kate b 10 July 1968, Louisa Jane b 13 May 1971); *Career* md: Clarkson Puckle 1979–87, Bain Clarksons 1987; exec dir Gill & Duffus plc 1983–87; chm and chief exec Hogg Group plc 1987–94, chm Bain Hogg plc 1994–96, dir Aon Holdings 1999–2000, dir Hiscox plc 1997–; memb Lloyd's Regulatory Bd 1993–2002, chm Lloyd's Insurance Brokers' Ctee (LIBC) 1996, 1998 and 1999; chm General Insurance Standards Cncl 1999–; Freeman City of London, Liveryman Worshipful Co of Insurers; *Recreations* shooting, cricket, racing; *Clubs* Turf, City of London; *Style*— A G C Howland Jackson, Esq; ✉ Little Loveney Hall, Wakes Colne, Colchester, Essex CO6 2BH (tel 01787 222282); General Insurance Standards Council, 110 Cannon Street, London EC4N 6EU (tel 020 7648 7800)

HOWLETT, Elizabeth; JP (Wimbledon 1985), AM; da of Walter James Robson, and Lizzie Mason, *née* Houston; *b* 17 January 1938; *Educ* Royal Scottish Acad of Music (DRSAM); *m* 1962 (m dis 1987), Neil Baillie Howlett; 2 da (Alexandra b 24 March 1971, Olivia b 8 Sept 1974); *Career* leading soprano: Lyric Sadlers Wells Opera Co (Lyric) 1961–65, Royal Opera Covent Garden 1965–1972, Staatsoper 1970–74; guest engagements 1974–: Milan, Naples, Florence, Toulouse, Bordeaux, Aix-en-Provence, Strasbourg, Mulhouse, Colmar, Paris, Ghent, Antwerp, Amsterdam, Hamburg, Geneva, South Africa, Japan, Korea, Canada, USA, Scottish Opera, Welsh National Opera, Opera North, ENO; prof of singing Royal Coll of Music 1989–, adjudicator Festivals Musicales Buenos Aires 1995–2004, nat and int examiner 1997–; memb Wandsworth BC 1986– (chief whip 1999–2000), mayor of Wandsworth 1998–99, memb London Assembly GLA (Cons) Merton & Wandsworth 2000–; non-exec dir and chm The Nat Hosp Neurology and Neurosurgery 1990–96; chm: Social Service Ctee 1989–92, Educn Ctee 1992–98; memb Inner London Probation Bd 1995–2001, tstee Fndn for Young Musicians 1996–, hon vice-patron Ystradgynlasi Male Voice Choir 1985–, fndr and tstee Margaret Dick Award; awarded Eschandon of Roi Rene Aix-en-Provence 1970; Freeman City of London; *Recreations* walking, theatre, music; *Style*— Ms Elizabeth Howlett, AM; ✉ London Assembly, City Hall, The Queen's Walk, London SE1 2AA

HOWLETT, Gen Sir Geoffrey Hugh Whitby; KBE (1984, OBE 1972), MC (1952); s of Brig Bernard Howlett, DSO (ka 1943), and Joan, *née* Whitby; *b* 5 February 1930; *Educ* Wellington, RMA Sandhurst; *m* 1955, Elizabeth Anne, da of Sqdn Ldr Leonard Aspinal, of Speldhurst, Kent; 1 s (Nigel b 1957), 2 da (Diana b 1958, Alexandra b 1963); *Career* cmmnd Queen's Own Royal W Kent Regt 1950, transferred Parachute Regt 1959, cmd 2 Para 1971–73, RCDS 1973–75, cmd 16 Para Bde 1975–77, dir Army Recruiting 1977–79, GOC 1 Armoured Div (Lower Saxony, W Germany) 1979–82, Cmdt RMA Sandhurst 1982–83, GOC SE Dist 1983–85; C-in-C Allied Forces Northern Europe (Oslo) 1986–89; Col Cmdt: Army Catering Corps 1981–89, Parachute Regt 1983–90; chm: Services Sound and Vision Corp 1990–99 (vice-pres 1999–), Leonard Cheshire Fndn 1990–95 (tstee 1988–95, vice-pres 1997–); pres: Stragglers of Asia Cricket Club 1989–94, CCF 1989–2000, Dorset Army Benevolent Fund 1993–2000; Regular Forces Employment Assoc: chm 1990–93, pres 1993–96; cmmr Royal Hosp Chelsea 1989–95, chm Cncl Milton Abbey Sch 1994–2000 (visitor 2001–05); Liveryman Worshipful Co of Cooks 1991; *Recreations* cricket, shooting, racing; *Clubs* MCC; *Style*— Gen Sir Geoffrey Howlett, KBE, MC; ✉ Flat 58, Hascombe Court, Somerleigh Road, Dorchester DT1 1AG (tel 01305 269222)

HOWLETT, Liam; *b* 21 August 1971, Braintree, Essex; *Career* musician and prodr The Prodigy; *Albums* Experience 1992, Music for the Jilted Generation 1994 (UK no 1, nominated Mercury Music Prize), The Fat of the Land 1997 (UK no 1, US no 1), Prodigy presents The Dirtchambers Sessions, Vol 1 (solo mix album) 1999, Always Outnumbered, Never Outgunned 2004, Their Law: The Singles 1990–2005 2005; *Singles* What Evil Lurks 1991, Charly 1991 (UK no 3), Everybody in the Place 1991, Fire/Jericho 1992, Out of Space 1992, One Love 1993, Wind it Up (Rewound) 1993, No Good (Start the Dance) 1994, Voodoo People 1994, Poison 1995, Firestarter 1996 (UK no 1), Breathe 1996 (UK no 1), Poison 1997, Smack My Bitch Up 1997, Baby's Got a Temper 2002, Girls 2004, Hot Ride 2004, Spitfire 2005; *Style*— Liam Howlett, Esq; ✉ website www.theprodigy.com

HOWLETT, Neil Baillie; s of Terence Howlett (d 1975), of Storrington, W Sussex, and Margaret Marshall, *née* Baillie (d 1983); *b* 24 July 1934; *Educ* Trent Coll, King's Coll Cambridge (MA), Hochschule Für Musik Darstellende Kunst Stuttgart; *m* 1, 1962 (m dis 1988); 2 da (Alexandra b 1971, Olivia b 1974); m 2, 1988, Carolyn Margaret, *née* Hawthorn; *Career* opera singer; Eng Opera Gp (Aldeburgh Festival, Soviet Union Tour) 1964; Glyndebourne tour: L'Ormindo 1967, Idem 1968, Macbeth; Aix-en-Provence Festival: Don Giovanni 1970, Falstaff 1971; ENO 1972–89; guest appearances in: Cologne, Frankfurt, Hamburg, Royal Opera House Covent Garden, Athens Festival, Buenos Aires, Vichy Festival, Trieste, Netherlands Opera, Trondheim, Catania, ENO; concerts with: LPO, LSO, CBSO, SNO, Oslo Philharmonic, Orquesta Nacional Madrid, Orquesta de Cataluna Barcelona, Radio Orch Katowice and Warsaw, Slovenian Philharmonic, Maggio Musicale Firenze; recording Otello (with ENO 1984 and 1990); prof Guildhall Sch of Music 1974–92, dir of repertoire studies Royal Northen Coll of Music 1996– (head of Sch of Vocal Studies 1992–96); Kathleen Ferrier Meml Scholarship 1957; *Recreations* sport, history, philosophy, piano, gardening, theatre, reading; *Style*— Neil Howlett, Esq; ✉ Royal Northern College of Music, 124 Oxford Road, Manchester M13 9RD (tel 0161 273 6283, fax 0161 273 7611); c/o Ingpen & Williams Ltd, 7 St George's Court, 131 Putney Bridge Road, London SW15 2PA (tel 020 8874 3222, fax 020 8877 3113)

HOWLETT, Stephen William; s of Ivan William Howlett (d 1955), and Marjorie Elsie Howlett (d 1997); *b* 18 November 1951, Sudbury, Suffolk; *Educ* King Edward VI Sch Bury St Edmunds, Thames Poly (BA); *m* 1989, Jane Elizabeth, *née* Everton; 2 s (William b 1 Aug 1989, George b 16 April 1994), 1 da (Emma b 1 July 1996); *Career* admin offr Housing Corporation 1975–76, housing offr Warden Housing Assoc 1976–78, London regnl offr Nat Fedn of Housing Assocs 1978–82, dir Croydon Churches Housing Assoc 1982–88, dir Notting Hill Housing Tst 1988–92, chief exec Swale Housing Assoc 1992–99, chief exec Amicus Gp Ltd 1999–2004, chief exec Peabody Tst 2004–; memb Bd Asset Skills 2004–; former memb Bd: Nat Housing Fedn, New Islington and Hackney Housing Assoc, USIMA Housing Assoc; memb Bd Canterbury Coll 1995–2004 (vice-chair 1999–2004); *Recreations* my children's sporting and musical activities, cinema, opera, sport; *Clubs* MCC, Blackheath FC; *Style*— Stephen Howlett, Esq; ✉ Peabody Trust, 45 Westminster Bridge Road, London SE1 7JB (tel 020 7021 4230, fax 020 7021 4070, e-mail stephenh@peabody.org.uk)

HOWLETT, Dr Trevor Anthony; s of Ivan William Howlett, of Cambridge, and Daphne May, *née* Long; *b* 20 July 1952; *Educ* Perse Sch Cambridge, Gonville & Caius Coll Cambridge (MA, MB BChir, MD), KCH Med Sch London; *Career* house physician KCH 1977–78, SHO Central Middx Hosp London 1978–79, med registrar Frimley Park Hosp Surrey 1980–81, lectr in endocrinology Dept of Endocrinology Bart's 1985–88 (MRC trg fell 1981–85), conslt physician and endocrinologist Leicester Royal Infirmary 1988–, dir of R&D Leicester Royal Infirmary NHS Tst 1996–2001, lead Leics, Northants and Rutland Deanery Shadow Specialty Sch of Medicine 2006–; sec Endocrine Section RSM 1992–96, UK rep Euro Bd Endocrinology 1994–, regnl advsr RCP 2002–06; chair Specialist Working Gp in Endocrinology to the Clinical Terms Project (NHS Mgmnt Exec Info Mgmnt Gp); numerous scientific articles on clinical endocrinology and endogenous opioid peptides; memb Soc for Endocrinology; FRCP; *Recreations* gardening, skiing; *Style*— Dr Trevor Howlett; ✉ Leicester Royal Infirmary, Leicester LE1 5WW (tel 0116 254 1414)

HOWORTH, Prof Jolyon Michael; s of Joseph Alfred Howorth (d 1966), and Constance, *née* Styles; *b* 4 May 1945; *Educ* Rossall and Henry Box Schs, Univ of Manchester (BA), Univ of Reading (PhD), Univs of Lausanne and Geneva; *m* 1, 27 Aug 1966 (m dis 1982), Pauline, *née* Macqueen; 1 da (Stephanie Jeanne b 1974); m, 6 Oct 2001, Prof Vivien, *née* Schmidt; 1 da (Emily Kirstine b 1988) and 1 s (Alexander Boris b 1989) by previous m; *Career* lectr: Univ of Paris III (Sorbonne Nouvelle) 1969–76, sr lectr Aston Univ 1979–85 (lectr 1976–79); Univ of Bath: prof of French civilisation 1985–2004, Jean Monnet prof of European politics 1992–; visiting prof Univ of Wisconsin Madison 1974–75, visiting scholar Harvard Univ 1981–82, 1983–84, 1985 and 2002–03, visiting fell Institut Français des Relations Internationales (IFRI) Paris 1999–2000 (res assoc 2000–), sr res fell Inst for Security Studies WEU Paris 2000, Marshall Monnet distinguished scholar in residence Univ of Washington Seattle 2001; visiting prof: NYU 2002, Columbia Univ 2002, Yale 2003–; dir: EU/US Transatlantic Studies Prog, Language Conslts for Industry Bath 1986–91; conslt: Univs Funding Cncl, FCO, RIIA, EU, US State Dept, Govt of Canada, Boeing, Thales, BAES, UEFA; European def analyst Oxford Analytica; memb: Centre National Jean Jaurès, Mgmnt Bd Centre for Def Studies 1996–2002, Advsy Bd Centre for the Study of Security and Diplomacy 1999–, Scientific Advsy Ctee European Inst for Public Admin Maastricht 2002–, Conseil Scientifique Centre National Jean Jaures; fndr memb Assoc for Study of Modern and Contemporary France, pres Br Assoc for the Study of European Languages and Socs 1993–96; memb: RIIA, IISS, Soc for French Hist Studies, Institut Français d'Histoire Sociale; Chev dans l'Ordre des Palmes Académiques; *Books* Elites in France: Origins, Reproduction and Power (with P Cerny, 1981), Edouard Vaillant et La Création de l'Unité Socialiste en France (1982), France: The Politics of Peace (1984), Defence and Dissent in Contemporary France (with P Chilton, 1984), Contemporary France: A Review of Interdisciplinary Studies (with George Ross, vol 1 1987, vol 2 1988, vol 3 1989), Europeans on Europe: Transnational Visions of a New Continent (with M Maclean, 1992), The European Union and National Defence Policy (with A Menon, 1997), Language, Politics and Society (co-ed, 2000), European Integration and Defence: The Ultimate Challenge (2000), Defending Europe: NATO and the Quest for European Autonomy (2003), Security and Defence Policy in the European Union (2007); *Recreations* travel, skiing, numismatics, ballet, opera; *Style*— Prof Jolyon Howorth; ✉ 126 Amory Street, Brookline, Ma 02446, USA (e-mail jolyon.howorth@yale.edu)

HOWSE, Dr Michael Gilbert James William; OBE (2000); *b* 20 June 1942; *Educ* Witney GS, Univ of Reading (BSc, PhD); *m* Valerie; *Career* Rolls Royce plc: res engr 1968, asst chief engr 1981–83, chief devpt engr 1983–84, chief engr RB211 In-service Engines 1984–87, chief engr RB211 Devpts 1987–89, head of advanced engrg Aerospace Gp 1989–91, dir of engrg Military Engine Gp 1991–95, dir of engrg Rolls Royce Commercial Aero Engines Ltd (now Airlines, Rolls Royce plc) 1995–2000, dir of engrg & technol Civil Aerospace 2000–01, dep dir Engrg & Technol 2001, dir Engrg & Technol 2001–, exec dir 2001–; memb: Tech Bd SBAC 1991–99 (chm 1996–98), Technology Strategy Bd DTI 2004–; visiting prof Sch of Mech Engrg Cranfield Univ 1996–; Sir Roy Fedden Lecture RAeS 1998; FRAeS 1998, CEng 1998, FREng 2000; *Style*— Dr Michael Howse, OBE, FREng;

✉ Rolls-Royce plc, PO Box 31, Derby DE24 8BJ (tel 01332 248216, e-mail mike.howse@rolls-royce.com)

HOWSON, Prof John Orrell; JP (1990); s of Harold Howson (d 1998), and Joan, *née* Boxall (d 1991); *b* 16 May 1947, London; *Educ* Tottenham Co Sch, LSE (Westminster Bank exhibitioner, BSc), Worcester Coll Oxford (MSc); *Career* dep head Sch of Educn Oxford Brookes Univ 1987–96, chief professional advsr Teacher Training Agency 1996–97, dir Education Data Surveys Ltd 1997–; author: Senior Staff in Schools Workforce Surveys (23 edns) 1984–2007, various reports on teacher supply for govt bodies, professional assocs and other groups; memb Nat Cncl and tstee Magistrates' Assoc; FRSA 1986; *Recreations* reading, walking, railways; *Clubs* National Liberal; *Style—* Prof John Howson; ✉ Education Data Surveys Limited, 27 Park End Street, Oxford OX1 1HU (tel 01865 242468, e-mail educationdatasurveys@gmail.com)

HOWSON, Peter John; s of Tom William Howson, of Prestwick, Scotland, and Janet Rosemary, *née* Smith; *b* 27 March 1958; *Educ* Prestwick Acad, Glasgow Sch of Art (BA); *m* 1, 1983 (m dis 1984), Francis, *née* Nevay; m 2, 1989, Terry Jane, da of James Peter Cullen; 1 da (Lucie Elizabeth b 19 May 1986); *Career* artist; RHF 1977, warehouseman Tesco Stores Ltd 1978, bouncer Caledonian Hotel 1978, shelf filler Safeway plc 1983, labourer 1983; official Br war artist Bosnia 1993, The London Times war artist in Kosovo 1999; painter; Hon Doctorate Strathclyde Univ 1996; *Exhibitions* incl: Flowers East London 1993, 1994, 1996, 1997, 1999 and 2003, McLellan Galleries Glasgow 1993, Imperial War Museum (series of paintings of Bosnia) 1994, The Drawing and Art Assoc of Norway Oslo 1996, Galleri Christian Dam Copenhagen 1997, Flowers West LA 2001, Maclaurin Gallery Ayr 2002; *Public Collections*: BBC, Br Cncl, Br Museum, Cartwright Hall Bradford, Christie's Corporate Collection, Contemporary Art Soc, Fitzwilliam Museum Cambridge, Glasgow Art Gallery and Museum, Glasgow Royal Concert Hall, Gulbenkian Collection Lisbon, Hunterian Museum Glasgow, Imperial War Museum London, Library of Congress Washington DC, Metropolitan Museum of Art NY, MOD London, MOMA NY, National Gallery of Norway Oslo, NY Library, Arts Cncl of GB, Scot Arts Cncl, Scot National Gallery of Modern Art Edinburgh, STV, Tate Gallery London, V&A, Aberdeen Art Gallery, City Art Centre Edinburgh, Dundee Art Gallery, Paul Mellon Centre, Yale Univ, Scottish Television, Flemings Bank; *Awards* Scottish Drawing Prize 1985, Edwin Morgan Prize 1987, First Prize European Painters Sofia Bulgaria 1989, Henry Moore Prize Bradford International Print Biennia, Lord Provost's Medal Glasgow 1995, Lord Provost's Prize Glasgow 1998; *Recreations* walking, reading; *Clubs* Caledonian, Glasgow Art; *Style—* Peter Howson, Esq; ✉ c/o Matthew Flowers, Flowers East, 82 Kingsland Road, London E2 8DP (tel 020 8985 3333)

HOY, David Forrest; s of Peter Harold Hoy, of Epsom, Surrey, and Helena Muriel, *née* Blackshaw; *b* 7 April 1946; *Educ* Leeds GS, Merchant Taylors'; *m* 11 Sept 1971, Angela, da of John Piddock; 1 da (Susanne Mary b 4 April 1976); *Career* asst internal auditor Dunlop Co Ltd 1964–67, accountant Redwood Press Ltd 1967–68, gen mangr Guinness Superlatives Ltd 1974–76 (co accountant 1968–74), md Guinness Publishing Ltd 1976–88, project dir Guinness Enterprises Ltd 1989–90; vice-pres: Gleneagles Group Inc, Champneys Group Inc 1991–92; commercial dir Guinness Nigeria plc 1992–95, fin dir Guinness Brewing Worldwide Ltd (Africa) 1995–96, strategic and devpt dir Park Royal Partnership 1996–97, dir Strategic Devpt Guinness Ltd 1997–2000, facilities and devpt dir Guiness UDV 2000–01, property devpt dir Diageo plc 2001–06; FCCA, FRSA; *Recreations* skiing, tennis, powerboating, sailing, photography, philately; *Style—* David Hoy, Esq; ✉ 9 Heidegger Crescent, Barnes, London SW13 8HA

HOYER MILLAR, Gurth Christian; s of Edward George Hoyer Millar, and Phyllis Edith Amy Wace (d 1956); *b* 13 December 1929; *Educ* Harrow (head of sch), Univ of Oxford (LLB, Boxing and Rugby blue), Michigan Univ (Master of Laws); *m* 17 March 1956, Jane Taylor, da of Harold John Aldington; 2 s (Christian b 1959, Luke b 1962), 1 da (Eliza b 1965); *Career* cmmnd Malaya 1949–50, cmmnd Reserve Bn SAS 1950–58; called to the Bar Middle Temple; exec dir J Sainsbury plc 1967–91; chm: J Sainsbury (Properties) Ltd until 1991, Homebase Ltd 1979–91, Bonham's Fine Art Auctioneers 1988–96, T J Hughes 1991–96, Checkmate plc 1999–; non-exec dir: Hudson's Bay Co of Canada 1976–2000, P&O Steam Navigation Co 1980–89, London & Edinburgh Trust plc 1988–91; dir Br Property Fedn until 1989; tstee Oxfam 1976–88, tstee Howard de Walden Estate 1990–, dep chm Northern Ballet Theatre; played rugby Oxford and Scotland 1952; *Clubs* Garrick, MCC (playing memb), Special Forces, Pitt; *Style—* Gurth Hoyer Millar, Esq; ✉ 15 Selwood Place, London SW7 3QL

HOYLAND, Prof Daniel Victor (Vic); s of Frank Hoyland (d 2000), of Yorks, and Nanette, *née* Tingle; *b* 11 December 1945; *Educ* Univ of Hull (BA), Univ of York (PhD); *Career* composer; commnd by UK ensembles incl: Lontano, Birmingham Contemporary Music Gp, BBC Symphony Orch, Arditti Quartet, Vocem, Lindsay Quartet; cmmnd by UK festivals incl: Aldeburgh, Almeida, Bath, Cheltenham, Huddersfield, South Bank, York; visiting composer in residence Univ of Calif San Diego, Hayward fell Barber Inst of Fine Art Univ of Birmingham 1980–83, visiting lectr Univ of York, currently prof in composition Univ of Birmingham (sometime lectr); dir Northern Music Theatre (NMT); involved with SPNM and Royal Philharmonic Soc; *Compositions* incl: Em 1970, Es 1971, Jeux thème 1973, Ariel 1974–75, Esem 1975, Seranade 1979, Xingu 1979, Andacht zum Kleinen 1980, Reel 1980, Michelagniolo 1981, Quartet movement 1982, Fox 1983, Head and 2 Tails 1983–84, Quintet of Brass 1984, Seneca - Medea 1985, String Quartet 1985, In Transit 1987, Work-out 1987, Hoquetus David 1987, Crazy Rosa - La Madre 1988, Work-out 1988, Of Phantasy, of Dreams and Ceremonies 1989, Trio 1989, Quintet 1990, The Other Side of Air 1991–92, November 2nd P.P.P. 1992, Chamber Concerto 1993, String Quartet No 3 (Bagatelles) 1995, Vixen (A-vixen-A) 1996, Shadow-Show 2002, Qibti 2003, The Attraction of Opposites 2003, Sicilian Vespas 2006, Phoenix 2007; *Recordings* incl: The Other Side of the Air (piano solo) 1994, In Transit and Vixen (conducted by Martyn Brabbins, *qv*) 2002; *Recreations* travel, archaeology, mediterranean food and wine; *Style—* Prof Vic Hoyland; ✉ c/o W M Colleran, Colleran Associates, Yew House, Hascombe Road, Munstead, Godalming, Surrey GU8 4AA (tel 01483 416653, fax 01483 418409)

HOYLAND, Prof John; *b* 12 October 1934; *Educ* Sheffield Coll of Art, Royal Acad Schs London; *m* 1958 (m dis 1968), Airi; 1 s (Jeremy b 1958); *Career* artist and sculptor; taught at Hornsey, Oxford, Croydon, Luton and Chelsea Schs of Art 1960s, taught at St Martin's Sch of Art 1970s and Slade Sch of Fine Art 1970s until resigned 1989; set designs for Zansa Sadler's Wells, prof of painting Royal Acad Schs London 2000–; designer: The Don Restaurant London 2001, mural mosaic for Metro Rome 2001; memb Rome Scholarship Ctee (printmaking) 1975; foreign painter academician Accademia Nationale di San Luca 2000; Hon Dr Sheffield Hallam Univ 2002; RA 1991 (ARA 1983); *Solo Exhibitions* incl: Marlborough New London Gallery London 1964, Whitechapel Art Gallery London 1967, Waddington Galleries London 1970, Andre Emmerich Gallery NY 1972, Paintings 1966–68 (Waddington Galleries London) 1976, Galeria Modulo Lisbon 1976–77, Serpentine Gallery London touring to Birmingham City Art Gallery and Mappin Art Gallery Sheffield (retrospective) 1979–80, Univ Gallery Univ of Melbourne touring to Art Gallery of S Aust Adelaide and Macquarie Galleries Sydney 1980, Gump's Gallery San Francisco 1981, Castlefield Gallery Manchester 1984, Erika Meyerovich Gallery San Francisco 1988, Waddington Galleries London 1990, Eva Cohen Gallery Chicago 1991, Galerie Josine Bokhoven Amsterdam 1992, Graham Modern Gallery NYC 1992, CCA Gallery London (ceramic sculptures) 1994, Bali Paintings (Theo Waddington Gallery London) 1994, Royal Acad of Arts London (retrospective) 1999, Galerie Fine London 1999, Univ of Leatherbridge Alberta (retrospective) 2000, Galerie Josine Bokhoven Amsterdam 2000, Galerie Christian Dam Oslo 2001, Graves Art Gallery Sheffield (retrospective) 2001, Nevill Keating Pictures Ltd London 2001, Beaux Art Gallery London 2001, Galerie Aalders La Garde Freinet 2002; *Two-Man Exhibitions* incl: Biennial de São Paulo 1969, Waddington Graphics London 1979, Van Straaten Gallery Chicago 1980, Hokin Gallery Miami 1981; *Group Exhibitions* incl: Summer Exhbn (Royal Acad of Arts London)1956, 1957, 1958, 1993, 1998 and 2001, 7th Tokyo Biennial 1963, 4th Biennial Exhbn of Young Artists (Musée d'Art Moderne de la Ville de Paris) 1965, Documenta IV Kassel 1968, Affinities in Paint (Crane Gallery London) 1991, Peter Stuyvesant Fndn Kunst Werkt Artworks (touring Holland, Spain and France) 1992, Painting of the Sixties (Arts Cncl Collection Royal Festival Hall and tour) 1992, Redfern Gallery 1992, Galerie zur alten Deutschen Schule Thun 1992, New Realities: Art From Post-War Europe 1945–1968 (Tate Liverpool) 1993, RA Collection (Sackler Galleries Royal Acad of Arts London) 1993, The Sixties Art Scene in London (Barbican London) 1993, Abstract Paintings and Prints (Advanced Graphics London) 2001, Master Class (Stephen Lacey Gallery London) 2001, Master Class (Alan Gaillard Paris) 2001, This Was Tomorrow: Art and the 60s (Tate Britian London) 2004; *Awards* prizewinner: John Moores Liverpool Exhbn 1965, Open Paintings Exhbn Belfast 1966; first prize: Edinburgh Open 100 Exhbn (with Robyn Denny) 1969, Chichester Nat Art Exhbn 1975, John Moores Liverpool Exhbn 1982, Korn Ferry Int Award Exhbn (with William Scott) 1986, Athena Art Awards Exhibition 1987, Charles Wollaston Award for most distinguished work Summer Exhbn Royal Acad of Arts 1998; *Style—* Prof John Hoyland, RA; ✉ c/o Royal Academy of Arts, Piccadilly, London W1V 0DS

HOYLE, Baron (Life Peer 1997), of Warrington in the County of Cheshire; (Eric) Douglas Harvey Hoyle; JP (1958); s of late William Hoyle, of Adlington, Lancs, and Leah Ellen Hoyle; *b* 17 February 1930; *Educ* Adlington Sch, Horwich and Bolton Tech Colls; *m* 1953, Pauline (d 1991), da of William Spencer, of Blackrod, Lancs; 1 s (Lindsay Hoyle, MP, *qv*); *Career* sales engr; Parly candidate (Lab) Clitheroe 1964; MP (Lab): Nelson and Colne 1974–79 (contested same 1970 and 1974), Warrington (by-election) July 1981–83, Warrington N 1983–97; chm PLP 1992–97, memb shadow cabinet 1992–97; a Lord in Waiting (Govt whip) 1997–99; memb Manchester Regnl Hosp Bd 1968–74, pres ASTMS 1985–88 (memb 1958, vice-pres 1981–85), pres MSF 1990–91 (jt pres 1988–90), memb Lab Pty NEC 1978–82 and 1983–85 (chm Home Policy Ctee 1983), chm PLP Trade and Industry Ctee 1987–92; memb: House of Commons Trade and Industry Select Ctee 1985–92, House of Lords Select Ctee on Procedure 2003–; non-exec dir Debt Free Direct Gp 2004–; chm Warrington Wolves RLFC 1999–; *Style—* The Rt Hon Lord Hoyle; ✉ House of Lords, London SW1A 0PW

HOYLE, Jonathan Wilson; CBE (2005); s of Walter Hoyle (d 2002), and Barbara, *née* Wilson; *b* 5 December 1960; *Educ* Baines GS, Univ of Hull (BA), Cranfield Univ (MBA); *m* 27 Oct 1991, Amanda, *née* Catlow; *Career* civil servant 1982–, currently project dir main building redevelopment MOD; non-exec dir Luminus Group (housing agency); *Recreations* golf; *Clubs* Abbotsley Golf; *Style—* Jonathan Hoyle, Esq, CBE; ✉ 8th Floor, Main Building, Whitehall, London SW1A 2HB (tel 020 7218 7599, e-mail dmbr@defence.co.uk)

HOYLE, Lindsay; MP; *Career* Chorley BC: cncllr 1980–98, dep ldr 1994–97; mayor of Chorley 1997–98; MP (Lab) Chorley 1997–; memb Catering Ctee 1997–; memb Trade and Industry Select Ctee 1998–; vice-chair All-Pty Rugby League Gp, treas All-Pty Parly Cricket Gp, chair All-Pty Gibraltar Gp 2000; *Style—* Lindsay Hoyle, Esq, MP; ✉ House of Commons, London SW1A 0AA (tel 020 7219 3515, fax 020 7219 3831)

HOYLE, Susan (Sue); da of Roland Hoyle, and Joan, *née* Dickson; *b* 7 April 1953; *Educ* Nottingham HS for Girls, Univ of Bristol; *Career* educn offr Eng Nat Ballet (formerly London Festival Ballet) 1980–83, admin Extemporary Dance Theatre 1983–86, dance dir Arts Cncl 1989–94 (dance and mime offr 1986–89), dep sec-gen Arts Cncl 1994–97, head of arts Br Cncl France 1997–98, lead advsr (dance) Arts Cncl 2003–, memb Franco-Br Cncl 2000–06; exec dir The Place 1998–2003, dep dir Clore Cultural Leadership Programme 2003–, chair CreateKX 2003–06, chair DV8 Physical Theatre 2004–; *Style—* Ms Sue Hoyle; ✉ Clore Leadership Programme, Somerset House, Strand, London WC2R 1LA

HOYLES, Prof Celia Mary; OBE (2004); da of Harold Gainsford French, of Loughton, Essex, and Elsie Florence, *née* Last; *b* 18 May 1946; *Educ* Univ of Manchester (BSc), Univ of London (MEd, PhD); *m* (m dis); *Career* mathematics teacher in secdy schs 1967–72, sr lectr then princ lectr Poly of N London 1972–84, prof of mathematics educn Univ of London 1984–; presenter: Fun and Games YTV 1987–, several TV shows on gender and computing; chair Jt Mathematical Cncl of the UK 1999–2003; *Books* Logo Mathematics in the Classroom (with R Sutherland, 1989), Learning Mathematics and Logo (with R Noss, 1992), Windows on Mathematical Meanings: Learning Cultures and Computers (with R Noss, 1996); *Recreations* tennis, swimming; *Style—* Prof Celia Hoyles, OBE; ✉ Institute of Education, University of London, 20 Bedford Way, London WC1H 0AL (tel 020 7612 6659, e-mail c.hoyles@ioe.ac.uk)

HRUSKA, Dr Jan; s of Prof Ivan Hruska (d 1998), and Bozena Bozicek-Ferrari (d 1983); *b* 22 April 1957, Zagreb, Croatia; *Educ* Downing Coll Cambridge (BA), Magdalen Coll Oxford (DPhil); *m* 2000, Regula Voellm; *Career* co-fndr and jt ceo (with Peter Lammer, *qv*) Sophos plc 1985–2005 (non-exec dir 2006–), md LogicIQ Ltd 2006–; *Publications* Computer Viruses and Anti-Virus Warfare (1990, 2 edn 1992); *Recreations* sub-aqua diving, running, flying, piano; *Style—* Dr Jan Hruska; ✉ Sophos plc, The Pentagon, Abingdon Science Park, Abingdon, Oxfordshire OX14 3YP (tel 01235 559933, fax 01235 559935, e-mail jh@sophos.com)

HUBAND, Neil; *b* 22 April 1948; *Career* journalist 1967–82 (initially with regnl newspapers, latterly as Parly corr for BBC TV and Radio), account dir Shearwater Communications 1982–83, dir O&M PR Ltd and dep ceo O&M Corporate Financial Ltd 1983–87; dir: Gresham Financial 1988–, Shandwick Network 1988–, Shandwick Consultants Ltd 1988–; MIPR; *Style—* Neil Huband, Esq

HUBBARD, (Richard) David Cairns; OBE (1995); s of John Cairns Hubbard (d 1997), and Gertrude Emilie, *née* Faure (d 1967); *b* 14 May 1936; *Educ* Tonbridge, Harvard Business Sch; *m* 7 Feb 1964, Hannah Neale, da of Arthur Gilbert Dennison (d 1987); 3 da (Katy-Jane b 1966, Juliet b 1970, Nicola b 1973); *Career* Nat Serv RA 1955–57; Peat Marwick Mitchell & Co London 1957–64, sec and gp fin dir Cape Asbestos plc 1965–73, dir of fin and admin Bache & Co London 1974–76; chm Exco plc 1996–98; chm Powell Duffryn plc 1986–96 (gp fin dir 1976), chm London & Manchester Gp plc 1993–98; non-exec dir: Blue Circle Industries plc 1986–96, Southern Advsy Bd National Westminster Bank plc 1988–91, The City of London Investment Tst plc 1989–2002, Shandwick plc 1991–97, Slough Estates plc 1994–2001, Medical Defence Union Ltd 1998–2000; memb Bd of Crown Agents 1986–89; chm Cncl Cancer Res Campaign 1995–98, pres The Berkshire Golf Club 1999–2004 (treas 1980–93), capt The Elders GS; Freeman City of London, Liveryman Worshipful Co of Skinners; FCA; *Recreations* golf, skiing, family; *Style—* David Hubbard, Esq, OBE; ✉ Meadowcroft, Windlesham, Surrey GU20 6BJ (tel 01276 472198)

HUBBARD, Deirdre; da of Richard L Hubbard (d 1993), and Betty (d 1967); *b* 28 October 1935; *Educ* Dalton Sch NYC, Radcliffe Coll Harvard (BA), Chelsea Art Sch; *m* 1957, Dr John Wilson; 3 s (Michael b 1958, James b 1959, Adam b 1963); 1 da (Nicola b 1961); *Career* sculptor; trained in studio of Elisabeth Frink 1963–65; work in public and corporate collections: Royal Free Hosp, Univ of London, Usher Gall, Towner Gall

Eastbourne, Bryn Mawr Coll Pennsylvania, Robert Fleming Holdings plc, Molins plc Milton Keynes, Sumitomo Corporation Tokyo, Univ of Leicester; Hon DLitt Univ of Leicester 2007; memb Free Painters and Sculptors 1966, FRBS 1999 (memb 1981, fell 1999); *Exhibitions* Royal Acad, RGI, Nat Museum of Wales, Bristol Cathedral, Lincoln Cathedral, St Paul's Cathedral, House of Commons, Gardner Centre Univ of Sussex, Bedford Way Gall Univ of London, Usher Gall Lincoln, Towner Gall Eastbourne, Penwith Galleries St Ives, Scone Palace Perth, Barbican Centre, Camden Arts Centre London, Sandford Gall London, Anderson-Woods Fine Arts London, McHardy Sculpture Co London, Thompsons Gallery London, Jonathan Clark Fine Art London; *Awards* Art and Work award to Robert Fleming Holdings 1987; *Recreations* music, literature; *Clubs* Harvard Club of GB; *Style*— Ms Deirdre Hubbard; ✉ 101 Woodsford Square, London W14 8DT (tel and fax 020 7603 6118); 3 Fleming Close Studios, Winterton Place, London SW10

HUBBARD, Michael Joseph; QC (1985); s of Joseph Thomas Hubbard, of Sussex, and Gwendoline Phyllis, *née* Bird (d 1957); *b* 16 June 1942; *Educ* Lancing; *m* 1967, Ruth Ann, *née* Logan; 5 s (Mark b 1968, Duncan b 1970, Lucian b 1972, Angus b 1974, Quinten b 1976); *Career* slr 1966–72, called to the Bar Gray's Inn 1972, initially in practice Western Circuit; prosecuting counsel to Inland Revenue Western Circuit 1983–85; recorder of the Crown Ct 1984–; *Recreations* sailing - yacht 'Wild Confusion'; *Style*— Michael Hubbard, QC; ✉ 1 Paper Buildings, Temple, London EC4Y 7EP (tel 020 7353 3728, fax 020 7353 2911)

HUBER, Peter John; s of James Huber (d 1989), and Doris, *née* Fickling (d 1960); *b* 1 April 1940; *Educ* St Benedict's London, Columbia Univ NY USA; *m* Evelyn, da of William Hayhow (d 2003); 2 da (Belinda b 13 Sept 1971, Gillian b 21 Jan 1974); *Career* advtg exec; J Walter Thompson: joined 1960, NY 1961–62, Amsterdam 1962–63, assoc dir London 1963–73, account dir 1973–79, Bd dir 1979, currently conslt; MIPA 1985; *Clubs* MCC, Surrey CCC, Ealing Squash (chm 1976–), Veterans Squash Club of GB; *Style*— Peter Huber, Esq

HUCK, Prof Steffen; s of Jochen Huck, of Mainhausen, Germany, and Waltrand Huck; *b* 2 October 1968, Seligenstadt, Germany; *Educ* Goethe Univ Frankfurt, Humboldt Univ Berlin; *Partner* Heike Harmgart; *Career* sr lectr Royal Holloway Univ of London 2000–01; UCL: exec memb Centre for Economic Learning and Social Evolution 2001–, reader in economics 2002–03, prof of economics 2003–; memb Sozialdemokratische Partei Deutschland (SPD), memb Royal Opera House Tst; Philip Leverhulme Prize 2004; *Publications* contrib to numerous jls incl: American Economic Review, American Political Science Review, Jl of Theoretical Biology; ed first German edn of Wilfred Owen's war poems (published 1993); *Recreations* jogging and champagne; *Style*— Prof Steffen Huck; ✉ University College London, Department of Economics, Gower Street, London WC1E 6BT (tel 020 7679 5895, e-mail s.huck@ucl.ac.uk)

HUCKNALL, Mick; *b* 8 June 1960; *Career* singer and songwriter; formerly with own punk band Frantic Elevators, fndr/lead singer Simply Red 1984–; tours incl: support on James Brown's UK tour 1984, world tours 1989–90, 1992–93, 1995–96 and 1999–2000; albums: Picture Book (1985), Men and Women (1987), A New Flame (1989), Stars (1991, nominated Mercury Music Award 1992), Life (1995), Greatest Hits (1996), Blue (1998), Love and the Russian Winter (1999), It's Only Love (2000), Home (2003); singles incl: Money's Too Tight To Mention, Holding Back the Years (reached number 1 USA 1985), The Right Thing, A New Flame, Something Got Me Started, Stars, Fairground, Angel, Night Nurse, Say You Love Me, Ain't That A Lot of Love, Sunrise, Fake, You Make Me Feel Brand New, Home; Best Group BRIT Awards (BPI) 1992 (jtly) and 1993, Ivor Novello Award for Outstanding Song Collection 2002; *Style*— Mick Hucknall, Esq; ✉ c/o Silentway Management Ltd, 1 Chilworth Mews, Paddington, London W2 3RG (website www.silentway.co.uk)

HUDD, Dr Nicholas Payne (Nick); s of Harold Payne Hudd (d 1977), of Essex, and Marguerita Eva, *née* Clarke; *b* 11 October 1945; *Educ* Palmer's Sch, Sidney Sussex Coll Cambridge (MA, MB BChir, first boat colours), Westminster Hosp; *m* 11 Oct 1969, Gwendeleen Mary, da of John Johnstone, of Glasgow; 2 s (Alastair Payne b 28 Dec 1973, Robert Nicholas Harold b 23 June 1984), 1 da (Anne Marguerita Jane b 10 Dec 1976); *Career* house surgn Westminster Children's Hosp 1970, house physician Princess Alexandra Hosp Harlow 1971, SHO Orsett Hosp 1972, med registrar St Andrew's Hosp Billericay and Basildon Hosp 1972–74, haematology registrar Orsett Hosp 1974–76; sr med registrar: Withington Hosp and Manchester Royal Infirmary 1976–78, Benenden Hosp 1978–79; conslt physician Benenden Hosp 1980–2004; memb: BMA, Br Diabetic Assoc, Euro Assoc for Study of Diabetes, Historical Assoc, Royal Nat Rose Soc; chm Romney Marsh Historic Churches Tst 1988–96 (vice-chm 1982–88), pres The Rising Mercury Soc (Benenden Ex-Patients) 1993–2004; FRCP 1995; *Recreations* golf, music (singing and conducting), rose-growing, cricket, history, talking; *Clubs* Tenterden Golf, Kent CCC, RSM; *Style*— Dr N P Hudd; ✉ 13 Elmfield, Tenterden, Kent TN30 6RE (tel 01580 763704, e-mail nphudd@nphudd.com, website www.nphudd.com)

HUDD, Roy; OBE (2004); s of Harold Hudd, of London, and Evelyn, *née* Barham; *b* 16 May 1936; *Educ* Croydon Secdy Tech Sch; *m* 25 Sept 1988, Deborah Ruth, da of Gordon Flitcroft (d 1986), of Lytham, Lancs; *Career* comedian, playwright, author and actor; commercial artist 1952–55, Nat Serv RAF 1955–57, entered show business 1958; pres: Br Music Hall Soc, Max Miller Appreciation Soc; Centenary King Rat of The Grand Order of Water Rats 1989 and 2000; monthly column Yours magazine; *Theatre* incl: seasons at Richmond Theatre and The Young Vic, the clown in The Birth of Merlin (Theatr Clwyd), Fagin in Oliver!, Stanley Gardner in Run For Your Wife (Whitehall and Criterion), The Fantasticks (Open Air Theatre) 1990, Babes in the Wood (Ashcroft Theatre Croydon 1990, Theatre Royal Plymouth 1991, New Theatre Cardiff 1992, Pavilion Theatre Bournemouth 1993, Sadler's Wells 1994), Midsummer Night's Dream (Open Air Theatre) 1991, George Pigden in Two into One 1993, A Funny Thing Happened on the Way to the Forum (Open Air Theatre) 1999, Hard Times (Theatre Royal Haymarket) 2000, Theft (nat tour) 2001, The Solid Gold Cadillac (Garrick Theatre) 2005, Roy Hudd's Exeedingly Entertaining Evening (nat tour); writer of stage prodns: The Victorian Christmas, Roy Hudd's very own Music Hall, Just a Verse and Chorus, Beautiful Dreamer, While London Sleeps, Underneath the Arches (winner Best Actor in a Musical from Soc of West End Theatre), numerous pantomimes; *Radio* incl: Workers' Playtime, The News Huddlines, Like They've Never Been Gone, Tickling Tunes, disc jockey Radio 2; *Television* incl: Not So Much a Programme More a Way of Life, The Maladjusted Busker (winner Montreaux Press Prize), Hudd, The Illustrated Weekly Hudd, Comedy Tonight, The 607080 Show, Movie Memories, Halls of Fame, The Puppet Man, Hometown, regular panelist on What's My Line?, Lipstick on Your Collar, Common as Muck, Karaoke, Common as Muck 2, The Quest, Coronation Street, The Quest Two, The Quest Three, All About George, Hollyoaks in the City; *Awards* incl: Sony Gold Award 1990 for outstanding contrib to radio, LWT Lifetime Achievement for Radio Comedy Award 1990, Variety Club BBC Radio Personality 1979 and 1993, Columnist of the Year EMAP 1994, Roy Castle Award for Outstanding Services to Variety 2003; *Books* Music Hall (1970), Roy Hudd's Book of Music Hall, Variety and Showbiz Anecdotes (1993), Roy Hudd's Cavalcade of Variety Acts (1997); *Recreations* walking, singing, napping; *Clubs* Garrick; *Style*— Roy Hudd, Esq, OBE; ✉ PO Box 604, Ipswich IP6 9WZ

HUDSON, Prof Anthony Hugh; s of Dr Thomas Albert Gibbs Hudson (d 1959), and Bridget, *née* Quinn (d 1979); *b* 21 January 1928; *Educ* St Joseph's Coll Blackpool, Pembroke Coll Cambridge (MA, LLB), Univ of Manchester (PhD); *m* 10 Jan 1962, Joan Bernadette, da of Anthony O'Malley (d 1953); 1 s (Michael Hugh b 1963), 3 da (Mary Bridget b 1962, Margaret Mary Theresa b 1964, Catherine Agnes b 1965); *Career* called to the Bar Lincoln's Inn 1954, lectr Univ of Hull 1954–57 (asst lectr 1951–54), lectr in common Law Univ of Birmingham 1957–62, lectr Univ of Manchester 1962–64; Univ of Liverpool: sr lectr 1964–71, prof of law 1971–77, dean Faculty of Law 1971–78 and 1984–91, prof of common law 1977–92, prof emeritus and sr fell 1992–; *Books* jtly: Hood Phillips First Book of English Law (1977 and 1988), Pennington, Hudson & Mann Commercial Banking Law (1978), Stevens and Borrie Mercantile Law (1978); *Recreations* history, gardening, walking; *Style*— Prof Anthony Hudson; ✉ University of Liverpool, Faculty of Law, PO Box 147, Liverpool L69 3BX (tel 0151 794 2000, fax 0151 794 2829, telex 627095 UNILPL G)

HUDSON, Christopher John; s of John Augustus Hudson, of Benenden, Kent, and Margaret Gwendolen, *née* Hunt; *b* 29 September 1946; *Educ* The King's Sch Canterbury, Jesus Coll Cambridge (MA); *m* 10 March 1978, (Margaret) Kirsty, da of Alexander Drummond McLeod, of Ticehurst, E Sussex; 1 s (Rowland Alexander b 1983); *Career* ed Faber & Faber 1968–70, literary ed The Spectator 1971–73, Harkness fell 1975–77, columnist Evening Standard 1985–91 (leader writer 1978–81, literary ed 1982–85), leader page ed Daily Telegraph 1991–94; memb: Soc of Authors, PEN; *Books* Overlord (filmed 1975), The Final Act (1979), Insider Out (1981), The Killing Fields (1984), Colombo Heat (1986), Playing in the Sand (1989), Spring Street Summer - A Journey of Rediscovery (1992); *Clubs* Beefsteak; *Style*— Christopher Hudson, Esq; ✉ Domons, Higham Lane, Northiam, East Sussex TN31 6JT

HUDSON, David Charles; *b* 10 April 1950; *Educ* King's Sch Pontefract, The Queen's Coll Oxford (MA); *m*; 3 c; *Career* asst brand mangr rising to brand mangr (petfoods) Spillers Foods 1971–74, gen mktg mangr (milks, healthcare, petfoods) Nestlé UK 1985–88 (successively brand mangr, brand gp mangr, mktg mangr 1977–85), gen mktg mangr (retail products) Nestlé Japan 1988–92, dir of mktg Nestlé Food Div 1992–95, dir of communication and corporate affrs Nestlé UK 1995–2005; memb Ct Whitgift Fndn; *Style*— David Hudson, Esq; ✉ e-mail dchudson@blueyonder.co.uk

H

HUDSON, David Norman; s of Sir Edmund Peder Hudson (d 1978), of Edinburgh, and Bodil Catharina, *née* Boschen (d 1997); *b* 29 May 1945; *Educ* Marlborough, Balliol Coll Oxford; *m* 1, 1967 (m dis 1993), Rosemary McMahon, *née* Turner; 1 s (Stephen b 1969), 2 da (Isobel b 1971, Sarah b 1976); m 2, 1993, Carole Annis, *née* Williams; 1 s (Christopher b 1995); *Career* merchant banker, dir Samuel Montagu & Co Ltd 1974–81, asst gen mangr Arlabank 1981–84, ptnr and head of corporate fin James Capel & Co 1984–87, dep chm and chief exec Henry Ansbacher & Co Ltd 1987–89, dir and shareholder Campbell Lutyens Hudson & Co Ltd 1989–93; chm David Hudson & Co 1992–; dir: MacArthur & Co 1993–97, Winterbotham Tst Co 1994–; *Recreations* natural history, bridge, opera, equestrianism; *Style*— David Hudson, Esq; ✉ David Hudson & Co Ltd, The Highlands, Hatches Lane, Great Missenden, Buckinghamshire HP16 0JP (tel 01494 564300, fax 01494 562854)

HUDSON, David Pelham; s of William Henry Hudson (d 1989), of Bradford, W Yorks, and Alma Myrtle, *née* Fynes (d 1952); *b* 19 August 1936; *Educ* Univ of Liverpool (LLB); *m* 3 May 1957, June Millicent; 2 s (Steven John b 3 Oct 1957, Nigel James b 19 May 1960), 2 da (Sally Jane Nightingale b 10 April 1959, Clare Elizabeth b 17 Aug 1968); *Career* admitted slr 1962; City of Bradford: articled clerk 1958–61, asst slr 1962–64, sr asst slr 1964–67; dep town clerk City of Exeter 1967–73, town clerk and chief exec Torbay Cncl 1973–96; currently: chm S Devon Healthcare NHS Tst; formerly: sec Devon Branch and advsr Assoc of Dist Cncls, advsr Br Resorts Assoc, memb Advsy Ctee on the Oil Pollution of Sea; pres Torquay St John Ambulance; *Recreations* cricket, football, rugby, walking; *Style*— David Hudson, Esq; ✉ Saltaire Cottage, Headland Road, Torquay, Devon TQ2 6RD (tel and fax 01803 297298, e-mail hudsonpelham@blueyonder.co.uk); South Devon Healthcare NHS Trust, Hengrave House, Torbay Hospital, Lawes Bridge, Torquay TQ2 7AA (tel 01803 654310, fax 01803 616334)

HUDSON, Gaye; da of Rt Hon Sir Peter Emery, and Elizabeth, *née* Nicholson; *b* 14 February 1957; *Educ* Westonbirt Sch, Eastbourne Coll, Coll of Distributive Trade; *m* 2 Oct 1982, Jonathan Michael Hudson; 1 da (Holly Elizabeth b 13 Feb 1988), 1 s (Charles Peter Meadows b 22 Dec 1989); *Career* formerly with Young and Rubicam advtg agency; dir Burson-Marsteller, main bd dir and head of mktg Hill and Knowlton int PR consultancy, currently vice-pres corporate communications Oracle Corporation; *Recreations* total love of skiing; *Style*— Mrs Gaye Hudson; ✉ The Tree House, Station Road, Wargrave, Berkshire RG10 8EU

HUDSON, Gillian Grace (Gill); da of Brian Hudson (d 1985), of East Grinstead, W Sussex, and Grace Iris, *née* Hill; *b* 23 March 1955; *Educ* Univ of Sussex (BA); *Children* 1 da (Alexia b 15 Jan 1994); *Career* press offr Eng Tourist Bd 1978–81, ed Home and Country Magazine 1981–83, dep ed then ed Fitness Magazine 1984–85, ed Cook's Weekly 1986, dep ed then ed Company Magazine 1987–92, ed New Woman 1992–95; editorial dir: Maxim 1995–99, Stuff 1996–99, Eve 1999–2002; editorial dir (new devpts) BBC Magazines 2002, ed Radio Times 2002–; BSME: memb 1981, memb Ctee 1993–96, chm 1993, memb Periodicals Trg Ctee 2001–; PPA Campaign of the Year Award 1991 and 1993, BSME Men's Magazine Ed of the Year 1997, BSME Entertainment Magazine Ed of the Year 2003, BBC Magazines Ed of the Year 2005, PPA Ed of the Year 2006; *Clubs* Groucho; *Style*— Ms Gill Hudson

HUDSON, Hugh; s of Michael Donaldson-Hudson (d 1965), and Jacynth Mary, *née* Ellerton (later Lady Lawrence, d 1987); *b* 25 August 1936; *Educ* Eton; *m* 25 Aug 1977, Susan Caroline, *née* Michie; 1 s (Thomas John b 8 May 1978); *Career* director and film maker; memb: Exec Ctee Cinema 100, 2nd Decade Cncl of AFI, BAFTA, Acad of Motion Picture, Arts and Sci (USA); Liveryman Worshipful Co of Haberdashers; *Films* incl: Chariots of Fire 1980 (5 BAFTA Awards, 4 Oscars, Golden Globe Award for Best Foreign Film, Best Picture UK & USA 1982), Greystoke - Legend of Tarzan 1983 (6 BAFTA & 5 Oscar nominations, BFI Technical Achievement Award), Revolution 1985 (BFI Anthony Asquith Award for Music), Lost Angels 1989, Lumière and Company (multi-directional participation in film to celebrate cinema's centenary) 1992, A Life So Far 1997, I Dreamed of Africa 1998; *Documentary* incl: A is for Apple (BAFTA nomination for Best Short Film 1963, Screenwriters' Guild Award), Tortoise & Hare (BAFTA nomination, Venice Festival Documentary Award), Fangio; *Political Films* Labour Party Election Broadcasts 1987–92 (incl Kinnock the Movie); *Advertising* over 600 commercials produced 1968–92 for clients incl: Levis, Coty, Benson & Hedges, Fiat Strada, Courage (Gercha), British Airways (Island and Face); *Awards* incl: 3 times D&AD Gold & Best Dir Awards, 5 Gold and 6 Silver Cannes Awards 1975–85, Cannes Grand Prix, Venice Grand Prix; *Style*— Hugh Hudson, Esq; ✉ Hudson Film Ltd, 24 St Leonards Terrace, London SW3 4QG (tel 020 7730 0002, fax 020 7730 8033, e-mail hudsonfilm@dsl.pipex.com)

HUDSON, Ian; s of Allen Hudson, and Ivy, *née* Angell; *Educ* Queen Elizabeth GS Gainsborough, Univ of Derby, Henley Mgmnt Coll; *m* Nicola; 2 s (Elliot, Tom), 1 da (Georgia); *Career* Marshall Cavendish Ltd: fin controller 1988–90, Euro ops mangr 1990–92; The Random House Gp: dep gp fin dir 1992–96, md Random House Children's Books 1996–97, gp commercial dir 1997–98, gp md 1998–2005, dep gp ceo 2005–; chm Trade Publishers' Cncl, vice-pres Publishers' Assoc; memb: Information Age Partnership, Young Presidents Org; FCMA 1987 (memb 1985); *Recreations* family life, reading, tennis, golf, skiing, music, travelling; *Clubs* High Road House, Hogarth; *Style*— Ian Hudson, Esq; ✉ The Random House Group Ltd, Random House, 20 Vauxhall Bridge Road,

London SW1V 2SA (tel 020 7840 8876, fax 020 7233 6115, e-mail ihudson@randomhouse.co.uk)

HUDSON, John; s of Don Hudson, of Barnsley, S Yorks, and Joyce, *née* Winterbottom (d 1995); *b* 16 February 1961; *Educ* Worsborough HS Barnsley, Gravnille Art Coll Sheffield, GSM; *m* Claire Elizabeth Olwen, da of Richard John Foulkes Taylor; *Career* tenor; memb chorus Welsh Nat Opera 1992–93, co princ ENO 1993–; performances incl: Paris, Auckland, Ireland, Canada, Barbican, Kenwood, Birmingham Symphony Orch, Royal Albert Hall; appeared with Lesley Garratt Viva La Diva (BBC 2) 1996; subject of various articles in magazines and newspapers; *Recreations* tennis, painting, cooking, playing cricket; *Clubs* Savage, London Sketch; *Style*— John Hudson, Esq

HUDSON, John Lewis; OBE (2003); s of Wilfred Hudson, and Edith Hudson; *Educ* Aston Univ (MSc), Birmingham Poly; *m* 22 Sept 1973, Eileen Cornelia; 1 s (Mark Standring b 7 Feb 1975), 1 da (Vicki Samantha b 24 Sept 1977); *Career* BSA Motorcycles Ltd 1960–71, Chrysler (UK) Ltd 1971–72, md Morphy Richards Ltd 1972–78; Delta Group plc: md Sperryn & Co Ltd 1978–82, divnl dir and gen mangr Gas Controls and Engrg Div Delta Group 1982–84, divnl md Fluid Controls Div 1984–86, gp chief exec Wagon Industrial Holdings 1986–97; chm and chief exec Calder Industrial Materials Ltd 1998–2006; chm: Birmingham International Airport 1997–, Metal Castings Ltd 1998–2006, Whittan Group Ltd 2002–06; non-exec dir: Senior Engineering Group plc 1991–2001, Temple Bar Investment Trust plc 1991–2005; pres Birmingham C of C 1999–2000, chm W Midlands Industrial Devpt Bd 1999–2001; memb Cncl Aston Univ 1992–97; CEng, FIET, FIMechE; *Recreations* walking, chess; *Style*— John Hudson, Esq, OBE; ✉ Birmingham Airport, Birmingham B26 3QJ (tel 0121 767 7100, fax 0121 767 7310)

HUDSON, Lucian; *b* 5 July 1960; *Educ* Lycee Francais de Londres, St Catherine's Coll Oxford (scholar, MA); *m* 1982, Margaret Prythergch; *Career* trainee journalist Central TV 1983–84, asst prodr Newsnight BBC 1984–85, sr researcher TVS 1985–88, prodr then sr prodr BBC Nine O'Clock News and Weekends 1988–93, output ed BBC Breakfast News 1993–94, chief asst to controller Radio 5 Live 1994, ed party confs BBC TV News 1994, ed Newsdesk, News Hour, Live Events and Breaking News BBC World 1994–97, head of programming (int channels) BBC Worldwide 1997–99, editorial dir Armstrong International, Skillcapital and Justpeople.com 2000, dir of e-communications Cabinet Office 2000–01; dir of communications: DEFRA (also chief knowledge offr) 2001–04, Dept for Constitutional Affrs 2004–06, FCO 2006–; chm Cncl Tavistock Inst of Human Relations 2003–07; chm Rory Peck Tst 1998–2000; *Recreations* travel, reading, music, swimming, watching rugby; *Style*— Lucian Hudson, Esq; ✉ Foreign and Commonwealth Office, King Charles Street, London SW1A 2AH

HUDSON, Manley O (Jr); s of Judge Manley O Hudson (d 1960), of Cambridge, Mass, and Janet A Hudson, *née* Aldrich (d 2003); *b* 25 June 1932; *Educ* Middx Sch Concord MA, Harvard Univ (AB), Harvard Law Sch (LLB); *m* 1 July 1971, Olivia (d 2000), da of Count Olivier d'Ormesson, of Ormesson-sur-Marne, France; 1 s (Nicholas b 1989), 1 da (Antonia b 1992); *Career* sec to Justice Reed Supreme Ct of the US 1956–57, ptnr Cleary Gottlieb Steen & Hamilton 1968–2001 (assoc 1958–68); memb Cncl on Foreign Relations; *Clubs* Century Assoc (NY), Knickerbocker (NY), White's; *Style*— Manley O Hudson, Jr; ✉ Cleary, Gottlieb, Steen & Hamilton, Level 5, City Place House, 55 Basinghall Street, London EC2V 5EH (tel 020 7614 2200, fax 020 7600 1698)

HUDSON, (Anthony) Maxwell; s of Peter John Hudson, CB, of Haslemere, Surrey, and Joan Howard Hudson (d 1998), *née* Fitzgerald; *b* 12 April 1955; *Educ* St Paul's, New Coll Oxford (MA); *m* 14 Sept 1991, Cordelia Jennifer, da of Nigel Roberts, of Haslemere; 1 s (James Nicholas Maxwell b 10 Sept 1994), 1 da (Katharine Jennifer Sophie b 27 March 1997); *Career* admitted slr 1980; ptnr: Frere Cholmeley 1987–95, Payne Hicks Beach 1995–; *Recreations* wine, military history, architecture; *Clubs* Oxford and Cambridge; *Style*— Maxwell Hudson, Esq; ✉ Payne Hicks Beach, 10 New Square, Lincoln's Inn, London WC2A 3QG (tel 020 7465 4300, fax 020 7465 4400, e-mail mhudson@phb.co.uk)

HUDSON, Nigel Gary; s of Ronald and June Hudson; *Educ* Repton, Univ of Nottingham (MBA); *Career* Sage Group plc: mktg mangr 1993–94, product mangr 1994–97, business devpt mangr 1997–98, mktg mangr (Germany) 1998–2000, mktg dir 2001, md New Business Div 2001–; *Recreations* sports, my children; *Style*— Nigel Hudson, Esq; ✉ Sage Group plc, Sage House, Benton Park Road, Newcastle upon Tyne NE7 7LZ (tel 0191 255 3000, e-mail nigel.hudson@sage.com)

HUDSON, Prof Ray; s of Jack Hudson (d 1977), and Jean, *née* Macfarlane (d 1982); *b* 7 March 1948, Alnwick, Northumberland; *Educ* Alnwick Dukes GS, Univ of Bristol (BA, PhD, DSc); *m* 2 Aug 1975, Geraldine, *née* Holder Jones; 1 s (Matthew b 23 March 1979), 1 da (Anna b 28 May 1981); *Career* Univ of Durham: lectr 1972, sr lectr 1984, reader 1987, prof of geography 1990–, dir Wolfson Research Inst 2003–; various visiting appts incl prof Copenhagen Business Sch 1984; Edward Heath award RGS 1988, Victoria medal RGS 2005; Hon DSc Roskilde Univ 1987; FRGS 1989, AcSS 2002, FBA 2006; *Books* Wrecking a Region (1989), Producing Places (2001), Placing the Social Economy (2002), Geographies of Economies (2005); *Recreations* travel, walking, sport, reading; *Style*— Prof Ray Hudson; ✉ University of Durham, Wolfson Research Institute, Queen's Campus, Thornaby, Stockton-on-Tees TS17 6BH (tel 0191 334 0070, fax 0191 334 0075, e-mail ray.hudson@durham.ac.uk)

HUDSON, Prof Richard Anthony; s of Prof John Pilkington Hudson, and Mary Greta, *née* Heath (d 1989); *b* 18 September 1939; *Educ* Loughborough GS, CCC Cambridge (open major scholar, BA), SOAS London (PhD); *m*; 2 c; *Career* UCL: research asst to Prof M Halliday 1964–70, lectr in linguistics 1970–80, reader 1980–89, prof of linguistics 1989–, vice-dean Faculty of Arts 1993–96; pres Linguistics Assoc of GB 1997–2000; formerly fndr memb Ctee for Linguistics in Educn (CLIE); conslt on grammar DFES 2000–; regular contrib on grammar TES; conslt ed Cognitive Linguistics; FBA 1993; *Books* Arguments for a Non-transformational Grammar (1976), Sociolinguistics (1980, new edn 1996), Word Grammar (1984), English Word Grammar (1990), Teaching Grammar: A Guide for the National Curriculum (1992), Word Meaning (1995), English Grammar (1998); Linguistic Theory Guides (initiator and ed), Routledge Language Workbooks (initiator and ed, 1994–); also author of numerous articles in learned jls; *Style*— Prof Richard Hudson, FBA; ✉ Phonetics and Linguistics Department, University College London, Gower Street, London WC1E 6BT (e-mail dick@ling.ucl.ac.uk)

HUDSON, Richard Bayliss; *b* 9 June 1954; *Educ* Peterhouse Sch Zimbabwe, Wimbledon Sch of Art (BA); *Career* set and costume designer for theatre and opera 1980–; FRSA, RDI; *Theatre* RSC: The Master Builder, A Clockwork Orange, Travesties, The Cherry Orchard, Women Beware Women, Coriolanus; RNT: The Misanthrope, Volpone, Blue Remembered Hills, The Ends of the Earth; Old Vic: Andromache, One Way Pendulum, Too Clever by Half, Bussy d'Ambois, The Tempest, Candide; Young Vic: 'Tis Pity She's a Whore, The Skin of our Teeth, Doctor Faustus; other credits inc: The Emperor (Royal Court), Desire (Almeida), Hippolytos (Almeida), La Bete (NY and London), The Lion King (NY, Tokyo, Osaka, London, Toronto, Los Angeles and Hamburg); *Opera* Glyndebourne Festival Opera: The Queen of Spades, Eugene Onegin, Ermione, Manon Lescaut, Le Nozze di Figaro, Don Giovanni, Cosi Fan Tutte; ENO: Figaro's Wedding, The Force of Destiny, The Ring of the Nibelung; Scottish Opera: La Vie Parisienne, Candide, The Vanishing Bridegroom, Maria Stuarda; Vienna State Opera: Ernani, Guillaume Tell, Les Contes d'Hoffmann; other credits incl: Die Meistersinger von Nurnberg (Royal Opera), Samson et Dalila (Met Opera NY), The Rake's Progress (Chicago Lyric Opera and Saito Kinen Festival Japan) I Puritani (Gran Teatro la Fenice Venice), L'Inganno Felice (Rossini Opera Festival Pesaro), Lucia di Lammermoor (Zurich and Bayerisches Staatsoper Munich), A Night at the Chinese Opera (Kent Opera), Count Ory (Kent Opera), The Queen of Spades (Chicago), Idomeneo (Florence), Tamerlano (Florence), Of Mice and Men (Bregenz, Houston and Washington), Khovanshchina (Paris Opera), Benvenuto Cellini (Zurich), Les vêpres siciliennes (Paris), The Makropulos Case (Copenhagen), Fall of the House of Usher (Bregenz); Olivier Award 1989, Tony Award for The Lion King on Broadway 1998, Critics Choice Award NY 1998 and London 2000, Gold Medal for Set Design Prague Quadreniale 2003; Br scenography cmmr to Organisation International des Scenographes, Techniciens, et Architects de Théatre (OISTAT) 1997; Hon Dr Surrey Univ 2005; RDI 1999; *Style*— Richard Hudson, Esq; ✉ c/o Judy Daish Associates, 2 St Charles Place, London W10 6EG (tel 020 8964 8811)

HUDSON, Robert L F; s of Lionel Derek Hudson (d 1985), of Kidderminster, and Moreen, *née* Glarvey; *b* 18 February 1952; *Educ* King Charles I GS, Univ of Nottingham (BSc); *m* 1974, Katrina Susan, da of Charles Peter Poulsen; 1 da (Coralie Kate b 12 May 1978), 1 s (Alexander Robert b 23 Sept 1980); *Career* Arthur Andersen & Co: articled clerk 1973–76, audit sr 1976–80, audit mangr 1980–84; PKF (formerly Pannell Kerr Forster): audit mangr 1984–87, ptnr 1987–; dir of Audit and Accountancy 1990 and 1991; memb: Nat Audit and Accounting Standards Ctee 1989–95, Nat Audit and Accounting Tech Bd 1994–97; Midlands region internal quality control review ptnr 2005–; pres The Three Counties C of C and Indust 1994–96, pres Herefordshire and Worcester C of C Training and Enterprise 1997–2002, chm Worcester Business Breakfast Club 1997–99, chm Advantage West Midlands Business and Professional Servs Cluster Opportunities Gp 2006– (memb 2003–06); vice-chm: Worcester Gp of CAs 1994–2000, West Midlands Regional Gp of C of C 1998–2000; Scout Assoc: Medal of Merit and bar, asst Co Cmmn for activities (Hereford and Worcester) 1992–2002; Herefordshire and Worcestershire County Scout Network Cmmr 2002–03; FCA 1976; *Recreations* caravanning, hill walking, off-road driving; *Style*— Robert Hudson, Esq; ✉ PKF (UK) LLP, New Guild House, 45 Great Charles Street, Queensway, Birmingham B3 2LX (tel 0121 212 2222, fax 0121 212 2300, mobile 07778 412390, e-mail robert.hudson@uk.pkf.com)

HUDSON, Prof Robin Lyth; s of Frederick Lyth Hudson (d 2001), and Enid, *née* Wright (d 1982); *b* 4 May 1940; *Educ* King Edward VI GS Stourbridge, Stockport GS, Univ of Oxford (BA, DPhil); *m* 22 July 1962, Geraldine Olga Margaret, da of Percival George Beak, MBE (d 1995), of Dorchester on Thames, Oxon; 3 s (Daniel b 1965, Hugh b 1966, Michael b 1975), 1 da (Lucy b 1968); *Career* Dept of Mathematics Univ of Nottingham: asst lectr 1964–66, lectr 1966–76, reader 1976–85, prof 1985–87, head of Mathematics 1987–90, prof emeritus; sr research fell Mathematical Inst Slovak Acad of Sciences 1997–2000, pt/t research fell Nottingham Trent Univ 1998–2005; visiting prof: Univ of Heidelberg 1978, Univ of Denver 1980, Univ of Texas 1983, Univ of Colorado 1996, Indian Statistical Inst 1987 and 1996, Univ of Grenoble 1999, Univ of Łódź 2002, Loughborough Univ 2005– (pt/t); memb: London Mathematical Soc, American Mathematical Soc; memb: Amnesty International, CND, Republic, UK Shostakovich Soc; *Recreations* music, literature; *Style*— Prof Robin Hudson; ✉ School of Mathematics, Loughborough University, Leicestershire LE11 3TU (tel 01509 222861, fax 01509 223969, e-mail r.hudson@lboro.ac.uk)

HUDSON-WILKIN, Rev Rose Josephine; da of Joseph Hudson (d 1994), of Jamaica, and Eunice, *née* Desporte; *b* 19 January 1961; *Educ* Montego Bay HS, Queen's Theol Coll, Univ of Birmingham (BPhil); *m* 23 April 1983, Kenneth Wilkin, s of Matthew Wilkin; 2 da (Amanda b 1986, Hannah b 1988), 1 s (Jamie b 1990); *Career* Christian educn offr Dioc of Jamaica 1982–85, asst curate St Matthew's Wolverhampton 1991–95, diocesan offr Lichfield and assoc priest Church of the Good Shepherd West Bromwich 1995–98, vicar Holy Trinity Dalston and All Saints Haggerston 1998–; Broadcasting Standards cmmr 1998–2003; chair: Nat Ctee for Minority Ethnic Anglicans, Worldwide Ctee SPCK until 2004; *Recreations* cooking, reading, entertaining, tennis; *Style*— The Rev Rose Hudson-Wilkin; ✉ The Vicarage, Livermere Road, London E8 4EZ (tel and fax 020 7254 5062, e-mail revdrose@aol.com)

HUDSPETH, Neil; *Educ* UCLA (BA); *Career* md Lloyd Northover; dir: Design Business Assoc, Bd Int Design in Business Assoc; memb Writers' Guild of America; *Style*— Neil Hudspeth, Esq; ✉ Lloyd Northover, 2 Goodge Street, London W1T 2QA (tel 020 7420 4850)

HUE WILLIAMS, Charles James; s of Charles Anthony Hue Williams (d 1969), and Joan, *née* Winfindale (d 1991); *b* 28 September 1942; *Educ* Harrow; *m* 14 March 1964, Joey Oriel Marie-Lou, da of Charles George Clover, of South Stoke; 1 da (Sarah b 27 June 1966), 1 s (Mark b 29 Oct 1968); *Career* ptnr Wedd Durlacher Mordaunt & Co 1970–85; dir: Kleinwort Benson Ltd 1986–90, Kleinwort Benson Securities 1986–90 (md 1989–90), Kleinwort Benson Holdings plc 1989–90, Henderson Crosthwaite Institutional Brokers Ltd 1992–99, Investec Securities (formerly Investec Henderson Crosthwaite Securities) 1999–2002, Lambert Energy Advisory Ltd 2002–; *Recreations* rackets, lawn tennis, real tennis, golf; *Clubs* Tennis and Rackets Assoc, Queen's, Turf, Swinley, Prestwick, Royal St George's Sandwich, Royal & Ancient, Berkshire, MCC; *Style*— Charles Hue Williams, Esq; ✉ Headley Meadows, The Hanger, Headley, Hampshire GU35 8SQ (tel 01428 713970); Lambert Energy Advisory Ltd, 17 Hill Street, London W1J 5LT (tel 020 7491 4473)

HUEY EVANS, Gay; da of C Calvin Huey (d 1989), and Frances, *née* Wismar; *b* 17 July 1954, USA; *Educ* Bucknell Univ Lewisburg PA (BA); *partner* Angus Broadbent; 1 da (Alexandra Evans b 12 Nov 1986); *Career* with Bankers Tst Co 1984–98 (sr md of risk mgmnt servs); FSA: dir of markets and exchanges 1998–2003, dir of markets 2003–05, capital markets sector ldr 2004–05; pres Tribeca Global Mgmnt (Europe) Ltd 2005–; memb Bd Krupaco Finance (UK) Ltd; chair: Int Swaps and Derivatives Assoc (ISDA) 1994–98, Jt Forum 2003–05; memb EC Experts Gp on Alternative Investments 2006; govr Benjamin Franklin House, co-opted tstee Tate Audit Ctee, tstee Wigmore Hall, tstee Cambridge Endowment Research Facility; *Recreations* tennis, reading, walking, piano playing; *Style*— Ms Gay Huey Evans; ✉ 41 Berkeley Square, London W1J 5AN (tel 020 7508 8622)

HUGGETT, Monica Elizabeth; da of Victor Lewis Huggett (d 1983), of Epsom, and Monica Germaine, *née* May; *b* 16 May 1953; *Educ* Green Sch for Girls, Isleworth, RAM London; *Career* violinist; ldr Amsterdam Baroque Orchestra 1979–87, ldr/dir The Hanover Bond 1983–86 (recordings incl Beethoven Symphonies), dir Sonnerie (baroque ensemble), first violin of Hausmusik (romantic chamber ensemble), artistic dir Portland Baroque Orchestra USA 1995, teacher of baroque and classical violin RAM London; recordings incl: J S Bach solo sonatas and partitas, Bach sonatas with Ton Koopman, Vivaldi concertos with The Academy of Ancient Music, Mozart concertos, Beethoven concerto and Mendelssohn concerto with the Orchestra of the Age of Enlightenment; memb Musicians' Union; fell RAM London 1994; *Recreations* gardening, cycling, narrow-boating; *Style*— Ms Monica Huggett

HUGGINS, Rodney Philip; s of Maj Rowland Huggins (d 1961), of Reading, Berks, and Barbara Joan Trowbridge, *née* Hayter; *b* 26 November 1935; *Educ* Reading Sch, Lycée Lakanal Sceaux Paris; *m* 30 March 1959, José Rhoda, da of Charles Hatch; 1 s (Jeremy b 1963); *Career* slr 1958; Kenya advocate 1960, fndr and sr ptnr RP Huggins & Co Slrs Reading 1961–85; chm: Nat Insurance Local Tbnl 1975–84, Industrial Tbnls 1981–84, Vaccine Damage Tbnl 1984–, VAT Tbnls 1988–; regnl chm Social Security Appeals Tbnls 1984–92; nat chm Ind Tbnl Serv 1992–97; gen tax cmmr 1983–; legal memb Criminal Injuries Compensation Panel 2001–; pres Nat Assoc of Round Tables of GB and I 1975–76, govr Dist 1090 Rotary Int 1987–88, pres Rotary Int in GB and Ireland

1997–98 (vice-pres 1996–97); hon slr Nat Assoc Ex Tablers Clubs 1984–2004; Freeman City of London 1981, Liveryman Worshipful Co of Arbitrators 1981; FCIArb, FRSA; *Books* Guide to Procedure in Social Security Appeal Tribunals (1985), Guide to Procedure in Medical Appeal Tribunals; *Recreations* golf, singing, swimming, bridge; *Clubs* MCC, Leander, Royal Over-Seas League, RAC, Sonning Golf; *Style*— Rodney Huggins, Esq; ✉ The Quarries, 10 West Drive, Sonning-on-Thames, Berkshire RG4 6GD (tel 0118 969 3096, e-mail rod2h@aol.com); 22 Cerro Grande, Albufeira 8200, Algarve, Portugal

HUGH SMITH, Sir Andrew Colin; kt (1992); s of Lt-Cdr Colin Hugh Smith, RN (d 1975); *b* 6 September 1931; *Educ* Ampleforth, Trinity Coll Cambridge; *m* 1964, Venetia, da of Lt-Col Peter Flower (d 1993); 2 s; *Career* called to the Bar Inner Temple 1956; sr ptnr Capel-Cure Myers 1979–85, chm London Stock Exchange 1988–94; chm: Holland & Holland plc 1987–95, Penna plc 1995–2001; *Recreations* reading, shooting, fishing, gardening; *Clubs* Brooks's, Pratt's; *Style*— Sir Andrew Hugh Smith; ✉ c/o National Westminster Bank plc, 1 Princes Street, London EC2R 8PA

HUGHES, Prof Alan; s of Benjamin Redshaw Hughes (d 1957), and Lilias, *née* Eyre; *b* 1 August 1946, Sunderland; *Educ* King's Coll Cambridge (BA); *m* 17 Aug 1968, Jean, *née* Braddock; 1 da (Rachel Sarah b 29 June 1979), 2 s (John Redshaw, Robert Benjamin (twins) b 17 Dec 1981); *Career* sr economic asst NEDO 1971–73, fell Sidney Sussex Coll Cambridge 1973–; Univ of Cambridge: univ asst lectr then lectr in economics 1973–94, chm Faculty Bd of Economics and Politics 1983–88, dir ESRC Small Business Research Centre Dept of Applied Economics 1989–93, dir Centre for Business Research 1994–, Margaret Thatcher prof of enterprise studies Judge Business Sch 1999–, dir of research Judge Business Sch 2001–04, dir Nat Competitiveness Network Prog Cambridge-MIT Inst 2002–03; visiting prof: Coll of Business Florida State Univ 1983, Univ of Social Sciences Toulouse 1993–95 and 1998, Doshisha Univ Kyoto 2005, Univ of Queensland Business Sch Brisbane 2006; memb: Cmmn on Public Policy and Br Business 1995–96, Advsy Bd Centre for Research on Innovation and Competition 1997–, Expert Panel on Educn, Learning and Lifelong Skills DfES 2000–05, Cncl for Science and Technol 2004–; sometime advsr to UK and Dutch Govts on business support policies and and German Govt on science educn; *Books* incl: Finance and the Small Firm (jtly, 1994), The Changing State of British Enterprise: Growth Innovation and Competitive Advantage in SMEs 1986–95 (jt ed, 1996), Enterprise and Community: New Directions in Corporate Governance (jt ed, 1997), Enterprise Challenged: Policy and Performance in the British SME Sector 1999–2002 (jt ed, 2003), UK Plc: Just How Innovative Are We? (jtly, 2006), British Enterprise: Thriving or surviving? SME growth, innovation and public policy 2001–2004 (jt ed, 2007); author of 200 other pubns; *Recreations* photography, walking, golf, gardening, watching football and rugby; *Style*— Prof Alan Hughes; ✉ Centre for Business Research, Judge Business School, University of Cambridge, Trumpington Street, Cambridge CB2 1AG (tel 01223 765335, fax 01223 765338, e-mail a.hughes@cbr.cam.ac.uk)

HUGHES, Alan Renatus Frederick; s of Wilfred Alan Hughes (d 1985), and Lily Hughes; *b* 1951, Blackpool; *Educ* Arnold Sch Blackpool, Henley Mgmnt Coll (MBA); *Partner* Dr Sandy Hewitt; 1 da (Anna b 1 Oct 1980), 1 s (Thomas b 22 Nov 1984); *Career* area dir Midland Bank plc Cambridge 1987–89, md Griffin Credit Services Ltd 1989–97, gen mangr mktg HSBC Bank plc 1997–1999, chief exec first direct 1999–2004, chm first direct Investments (UK) Ltd 2001–04; chm Ind Assurance Panel Govt Identity Card Scheme 2005–; dir Forward Tst Gp Ltd 1997–2000; memb Bd of the Banking Ombudsman 1997–99; memb DTI E-Strategy Gp 2003–04; vice-chm Factors Chain Int Amsterdam 1994–97, chm UK Factors and Discounters Assoc 1995–97; memb Advsy Bd Univ of Leeds Business Sch 2001–; FRSA, FCIB; *Recreations* family, reading, hill walking, old cars; *Clubs* Sloane; *Style*— Alan Hughes, Esq; ✉ e-mail alan@renatus.net

HUGHES, Aneurin Rhys; s of William Hughes, of Swansea, and Hilda Hughes; *b* 11 February 1937; *Educ* Swansea GS, Oregon City HS USA, UCW Aberystwyth (BA); *m* 2001, Lisbeth Lindback; 2 s; *Career* pres NUS 1962–64, research on HE in South America; HM Dip Serv: FO London 1966–68, first sec Political Advsr's Office (later Br High Cmmn) Singapore 1968–70, first sec Br Embassy Rome 1971–73; Secretariat General of the Euro Community: head Div for Internal Coordination 1973–76, advsr to Spokesman and DG for Info 1977–80, chef de cabinet of Ivor Richard (memb Euro Cmmn) 1981–85, chm Selection Bd for Candidates from Spain and Portugal 1985–87, organiser Conf on Culture Econ New Technol (Florence) 1986–87; ambass and head of Delgn of the Euro Cmmn: to Oslo Norway 1987–95, to Aust and NZ 1995–2002; *Recreations* golf, music, hashing; *Style*— Aneurin Hughes, Esq; ✉ e-mail aneurin_hughes@hotmail.com

HUGHES, Rt Hon Lord Justice; Sir Anthony Philip Gilson Hughes; kt (1997), PC (2006); s of late Patrick and Patricia Hughes; *b* 11 August 1948; *Educ* Tettenhall Coll, Univ of Durham (BA); *m* 1972, Susan Elizabeth March; 1 s, 1 da; *Career* lectr in law Univ of Durham and QMC 1969–71; called to the Bar Inner Temple 1970, recorder of the Crown Court until 1997, head of chambers until 1997, QC 1990; judge of the High Court of Justice: (Family Div) 1997–2003, (Queen's Bench Div) 2004–06; Lord Justice of Appeal 2006–; presiding judge Midland circuit 2000–04; *Style*— The Rt Hon Lord Justice Hughes; ✉ Royal Courts of Justice, Strand, London WC2A 2LL

HUGHES, Anthony (Tony); s of Richard Hughes (d 1944), and Lucy Cotton, *née* Sproule (d 1989); *b* 24 September 1944; *Educ* Blackfriars Sch, UCL, Univ of Edinburgh (MA); *m* 1975, Marie-Estelle, da of Jean Dufournier; 1 da (Chantal Madeleine Lucy b 26 Sept 1980), 2 s (Timothy Anthony Jean b 16 March 1983, Christopher François Wilfrid b 27 Aug 1986); *Career* film ed BBC 1970–74; called to the Bar Inner Temple 1975 (scholar 1973), barr 1975–77; tax mangr Peat Marwick Mitchell 1978–82; PricewaterhouseCoopers (formerly Deloitte Haskins & Sells then Coopers & Lybrand): tax mangr 1982–86, ptnr 1986–; memb Dell Ctee 1982; contrib to Financial Times and professional jls; ATII 1979; *Books* International Tax Planning for UK Companies (1984, 1990 and 1994); *Recreations* music, theatre, bridge, tennis; *Clubs* Wimbledon Lakeside; *Style*— Tony Hughes, Esq; ✉ PricewaterhouseCoopers, 1 Embankment Place, London WC2N 6NN (e-mail hughesapc@hotmail.com)

HUGHES, Dr Antony Elwyn; s of Ifor Elwyn Hughes, and Anna Betty, *née* Ambler; *b* 9 September 1941; *Educ* Newport HS Gwent, Jesus Coll Oxford (Scott Prize in Physics); *m* 1963, Margaret Mary, da of Arthur James Lewis (d 1978); 2 s (1 d 1997), 2 da; *Career* Harkness fell Cornell Univ USA 1967–69; UKAEA: scientific offr 1963–67, sr scientific offr 1969–72, princ scientific offr 1972–75, individual merit appt 1975–81, sr personal appt 1981–83, ldr Defects in Solids Gp 1973–78, ldr Solid State Scis Gp 1978–83, head Materials Physics Div 1983–86, dir Underlying Research and Non-Nuclear Energy Research 1986–87, chief scientist and dir Nuclear Research 1987–88; dir Laboratories SERC 1988–91, dir Progs and dep chm SERC 1991–94, dir of engrg and science and dep chief exec EPSRC 1994–96; conslt 1996–; memb NI HE Cncl 1993–2001, memb Cncl CRAC 1994–2007, memb Cncl Royal Instn GB 1995–98; chm Winterbrook Youth Club Harwell 1980–93, govr Didcot Girls' Sch 1981–88; FInstP 1972, CPhys; *Books* Real Solids and Radiation (1975), Defects and Their Structure in Non-Metallic Solids (ed 1976); *Recreations* walking, watching rugby and cricket, music, playing the trumpet, gardening; *Style*— Dr Antony E Hughes; ✉ Kingswood, King's Lane, Harwell, Didcot, Oxfordshire OX11 0EJ (tel 01235 835301, fax 01235 832667)

HUGHES, Rt Hon Beverley June (Bev); PC (2004), MP; da of Norman Hughes (d 1987), and Doris, *née* Gillard; *b* 30 March 1950; *Educ* Ellesmere Port Girls' GS, Univ of Manchester (BSc), Univ of Liverpool (DSA), Univ of Manchester (MSc); *m* 1973, Thomas Kevin McDonald; 2 da (Anna 1979, Sarah b 1980), 1 s (Michael b 1984); *Career* probation offr Merseyside 1971–76; Univ of Manchester: research assoc 1976–81, lectr 1981–94, sr lectr and head Dept of Social Policy and Social Work 1994–97; MP (Lab) Stretford and Urmston 1997–; Parly under sec of state DETR 1999–2001, Parly under sec of state Home Office 2001–02, min of state Home Office 2002–04, min of state DfES 2006–07, min of state for Children and Youth Justice 2007–; ldr Trafford MBC 1995–97 (cncllr 1986–97); non-exec dir: Trafford Park Devpt Corporation 1992–97, Manchester Airport plc 1995–97, G-Mex Ltd, Modesole Ltd; chm Age Concern Trafford; *Books* Older People and Community Care (1995); also author of numerous academic journal and conference papers; *Recreations* jazz, walking, reading, gardening; *Style*— The Rt Hon Bev Hughes, MP; ✉ House of Commons, London SW1A 0AA (tel 020 7219 3000); constituency office (tel 0161 749 9120)

HUGHES, Charles Edward; s of Frank Hughes (d 1967), and Irene, *née* Holt (d 1970); *b* 15 September 1946, Manchester; *Educ* Stockport GS, Univ of Manchester (BSc); *m* 5 May 1973, Beverley Dawn, da of Maurice Kennerley Humphreys, of Grimsby; 1 s (Daniel Charles b 14 March 1977), 1 da (Samantha Louise b 29 Jan 1979); *Career* ICL 1967–99 (dir 1985), seconded as project dir DTI 1995–97, fndr and ceo eManagement Ltd 1999–; chm: European Computer Res Centre GmbH 1988–91, Sherwood-CFM Ltd 1996–97; non-exec dir: PERQ Systems Corp 1984–85, ICL Australia pty 1989–90, Screen plc 2000–; exec offr and memb Cncl Parly IT Ctee; pres BCS 2005–06 (vice-pres 2001–04, dep pres 2004–05), memb Cncl Inst for the Mgmnt of Information Systems 2000–03, memb Spectrum Mgmnt Advsy Bd 2001–03; chm and cncllr Smallwood Parish Cncl 1987–93; Freeman City of London, Liveryman and memb Ct of Assts Worshipful Co of Information Technologists; MCMI 1974, MCIPS 1991, fell Inst for the Mgmnt of Information Systems (FIMIS), FBCS, CEng, CITP; *Recreations* sport, travel, gardening, philately; *Clubs* Real Time (past chm), Goring and Streatley Tennis; *Style*— Charles Hughes, Esq; ✉ eManagement Ltd, The Ridge, Lower Basildon, Berkshire RG8 9NX

HUGHES, Christopher Carl; s of Norman Alfred Hughes (d 1983), of Sheffield, and Betty, *née* Roebuck; *b* 19 August 1950; *Educ* Harrow Weald Co GS, Univ of Sheffield (BSc); *m* 26 Aug 1972 (m dis 1996), Julia Clare, da of Dr Maxwell Chapman Pennington, of Caerphilly; 1 s (Daniel Andrew b 13 Feb 1983); *Career* BBC: studio mangr World Serv 1971–73, prodr Radio Sheffield 1975–79 (station asst 1973–75), prodr Special Current Affrs Unit Radio 4 1979–80; Radio Trent Ltd: prog controller 1980–89, md 1989–; memb Radio Acad; *Recreations* birdwatching, gardening, vegetarian cookery; *Style*— Christopher Hughes, Esq; ✉ Radio Trent Ltd, 29–31 Castlegate, Nottingham NG1 7AP (tel 0115 912 9301, fax 020 7912 9302, e-mail chris.hughes@musicradio.com)

H

HUGHES, Christopher Wyndham; s of Dr John Philip Wyndham Hughes (d 1981), and Christine, *née* Jolley (d 1947); *b* 22 November 1941; *Educ* Manchester Grammar, King Edward's Sch Birmingham, UCL (LLB); *m* 31 Dec 1966, Gail, da of Percival Eric Ward (d 1957); 3 s (Christian Wyndham, Marcus Wyndham (twins) b 29 Feb 1968, Dominic Wyndham b 20 June 1974); *Career* admitted slr 1966; Wragge & Co Birmingham: articled clerk and slr until 1970, ptnr 1970–2005, managing ptnr 1994–95, head of int 2005–; NP; memb Bd Severn Trent Water Authy 1982–84, non-exec chm Newman Tonks Group plc 1995–97; non-exec dir Pension Protection Fund 2004–; memb and later chm Solihull Ctee of Cancer Research Campaign 1972–85; govr The Schs of King Edward VI Birmingham 1984–; memb: Law Soc 1966, Birmingham Law Soc 1966 (memb Cncl 1977–91, jt hon sec 1977–84, vice-pres 1988–89, pres 1989–90), The Notaries Soc 1979; *Recreations* travel, theatre, sport, languages, old buildings; *Clubs* Warwickshire CCC; *Style*— Christopher Hughes, Esq; ✉ Cuttle Pool Farm, Cuttle Pool Lane, Knowle, Solihull, West Midlands B93 0AP (tel 01564 772611); Wragge & Co LLP, 55 Colmore Row, Birmingham B3 2AS (tel 0121 233 1000, fax 0121 214 1099, e-mail christopher_hughes@wragge.com)

HUGHES, Prof Colin; s of Joseph Hughes (d 2000), and May, *née* Roberts; *b* 14 March 1953, St Asaph; *Educ* Univ of Kent (PhD), Univ of Cambridge (ScD); *Career* research fell: Sandoz Research Inst Vienna 1977–80, Univ of Wurzburg 1980–84, SmithKline Research Philadelphia 1984–85; Univ of Cambridge: lectr 1985–96, reader 1996–2001, prof of microbiology 2001–; fell Trinity Coll Cambridge 1997–; author of ca 130 publications in molecular microbiology in learned jls; *Style*— Prof Colin Hughes; ✉ Trinity College, Cambridge CB2 1TQ (tel 01223 338538)

HUGHES, David Campbell; yr s of Trevor George Hughes (d 1988), of Herefordshire, and Flora Jean, *née* Britton; *b* 13 December 1953; *Educ* Millfield, KCL (LLB, pres Union 1975–76); *m* 1992, Claire Margaret, da of Ian Mitchell Bennet (d 1990), and Doreen Margaret, *née* Wilson, of Cheshire; 2 da, 1 s; *Career* admitted slr 1979, admitted slr Hong Kong 1992; ptnr Allen & Overy 1985–2003; md DC Hughes Ltd 2003–; Parly candidate (Cons) Bow and Poplar 1987; memb Law Soc, MInstD; *Recreations* golf; *Clubs* Oriental, Falmouth Golf; *Style*— David C Hughes, Esq; ✉ DC Hughes Limited, Kingham, Oxfordshire OX7 6YD (tel 01608 659505, fax 01608 659745)

HUGHES, David Clewin; s of Harry Alfred Hughes, and Margaret Eileen Hughes; *b* 14 October 1953; *Educ* Whitgift Sch, Univ of Oxford (MA); *m* 16 July 1977, Rosanne Margaret, da of Ian Brunton Graham; 3 da (Katherine Rosanne b 26 March 1982, Victoria Louise b 25 June 1985, Emily Charlotte b 13 May 1988); *Career* ptnr Arthur Andersen 1987 (joined 1976); FCA; *Recreations* sport, theatre, travel, gardening, wine; *Clubs* RAC, Old Whitgiftians; *Style*— David C Hughes, Esq

HUGHES, Prof David John; *b* 5 May 1947, London; *Educ* Royal GS High Wycombe, Aston Univ (MSc); *m* 7 Nov 1970, Dawn Anne, *née* Newman; 2 da (Rachel Sarah b 8 Oct 1972, Elizabeth Jane b 30 July 1975); *Career* Ford Motor Co Ltd 1970–91 (latterly head of electrical/electronic systems Ford of Europe), dir advanced vehicle systems Lucas plc (then Lucas Varity plc) 1991–97, exec vice-pres technol mgmnt GEC-Marconi plc 1997–2001, special projects dir avionics BAE Systems plc 2002, DG Innovation Gp and chief scientific advsr DTI 2002–06, md The Business Innovation Gp LLP 2006–; visiting prof of engrg mgmnt City Univ 2006–; author of numerous articles for various jls and conferences; memb: Technol and Innovation Ctee CBI 1999–2003, EPSRC 2003–06, Innovation and Engagement Bd Cardiff Univ 2005–; MInstD; CEng 1975, FIMechE 1996, MIEEE 2000, FREng 2000, CDir 2005; *Recreations* walking, 20th century British art, antique metalware, African tribal art; *Style*— Prof David Hughes, FREng; ✉ School of Engineering and Mathematical Sciences, City University, Northampton Square, London EC1V 0HB (tel 07801 712139, e-mail david.hughes@thebigpartnership.com)

HUGHES, David John; s of John David Hughes (d 1994), of Wendover, Bucks, and Mary Deirdre, *née* Lowen; *Educ* St Paul's, Univ of Southampton (BA, pres Students' Union 1975–76); *m* 21 Oct 1995 (m dis 2003), Jane Wynsome Katherine, *née* Anstiss; 2 da (Alice b 1 Aug 1996, Lucy b 22 Sept 2000), 1 s (Harry b 5 July 1999); *Career* mktg exec Express Newspapers 1979–82, Parly and external affrs offr Fedn of Civil Engrg Contractors 1982–85, exec sec Cncl for Environmental Conservation 1985–88, sr conslt then bd dir Shandwick Public Affairs 1988–93, dir of govt rels and public affrs The Communication Gp plc 1993–95, jt md The Rowland Co and Rowland Sallingbury Casey 1995–97, fndr Cothelstone Consulting Ltd 1996–, dir Precise Communications Gp 1998–2001, dir Burlington Entertainment Ltd 1999–, md Palliser Public Counsel Ltd 2002–; conslt ESL & Network SA (Paris) 1998–; nat chm Lib Students 1976–77; Parly candidate: (Lib) Southampton Test 1979, (Lib-SDP Alliance) Westbury 1983 and 1987; nat chm Parly Candidates Assoc 1984–87, vice-chm Lib Pty 1985–88; memb: Hansard Soc for Parly Govt 1991, Int Assoc of Political Conslts 1995, Political Studies Assoc 2001; MInstD 1996; *Books* Liberals and Social Democrats: the Case for an Alliance (1981), Guide to Westminster and Whitehall (1994), Marketing in the Voluntary Sector (2001); various articles in New Statesman, PR Week and other pubns; *Recreations* historical and political biography, theatre and cinema; *Clubs* National Liberal; *Style*— David Hughes, Esq; ✉ Suite 130, 34 Buckingham Palace Road, London SW1W 0RH (tel 020 7834 0019, e-mail davidhughes@polvoice.org.uk)

HUGHES, David John; s of Glynn Hughes (d 1985), and Gwyneth Mary, *née* Jenkins; *b* 19 March 1955; *Educ* Wolverhampton GS, Jesus Coll Oxford (MA); *m* 4 Sept 1987, Linda Anne, da of Thomas Hunt (d 1991), of Wolverhampton; 1 s (Richard b 1987), 1 da (Lisa b 1990); *Career* asst slr: Nabarro Nathanson 1980–82, Slaughter and May 1982–85; ptnr Pinsent Curtis Biddle (formerly Pinsent & Co) 1987– (asst slr 1985–87); memb: Law Soc, IOD; *Recreations* music, theatre; *Style*— David Hughes, Esq; ✉ Pinsent Curtis Biddle, 3 Colmore Circus, Birmingham B4 6BH (tel 0121 200 1050, fax 0121 626 1040, e-mail david.hughes@pinsents.com)

HUGHES, Dr David Treharne Dillon; s of Maj-Gen W D Hughes, CB, CBE (d 1999), of Farnham, Surrey, and Kathleen Linda Elizabeth, *née* Thomas (d 1976); *b* 31 October 1931; *Educ* Cheltenham Coll, Trinity Coll Oxford (BSc, MA), London Hosp Med Coll (BM BCh); *m* 14 Nov 1959, Gloria Anna; 2 da (Carly Anna b 22 Sept 1960, Mandy Lou b 19 Oct 1962), 1 s (David Edward Treharne b 29 March 1974); *Career* Capt RAMC 1959–61 (jr med specialist BMH Hong Kong); jr research fell MRC Univ of Oxford 1953–54, research fell Univ of Calif 1963–64, conslt physician Royal London Hosp 1970–96 (jr appts 1957–68), head Dept of Clinical Investigation Wellcome Research Laboratories 1978–93; tstee Hunterian Soc (former pres); memb Int Soc of Internal Med (former pres), memb GMC 1993–96; chm Bd of Govrs Moving Theatre Tst 1994–2000; Freeman City of London, past Master Worshipful Soc of Apothecaries (memb Court of Assts 1981); memb RSM, FRCP; *Books* Tropical Health Science (1967), Human Biology and Hygiene (1969), Lung Function for the Clinician (1981); *Recreations* cricket, horseracing, theatre, film; *Clubs* Savage, Garrick, Leander (Henley); *Style*— Dr David Hughes; ✉ 94 Overbury Avenue, Beckenham, Kent BR3 6PY (tel 020 8650 3983)

HUGHES, Diane Bridget; da of Dr Brynfor Dennis Hughes (decd), and Patricia O'Brien Hughes, *née* Shenton; *b* 28 October 1957; *Educ* Univ of New Hampshire (BA), Univ of Manchester (LLB, R G Lawson Prize), Manchester Metropolitan Univ (PGCE); *Family* 1 s (Alexander James David Waterhouse Wood b 5 Dec 1985); m, 28 April 2005, Raymond Scobie; *Career* legal research asst Law Cmmn 1984–85; lectr in law: Univ of Buckingham 1985–87, Univ of Leeds 1987–90 (seconded to NCUK Malaysia 1988–89); conslt dir of trg Davies Wallis Foyster (Slrs) 1990–98, sr lectr in law and admissions tutor Manchester Metropolitan Univ 1991–2001 (academic dir Centre for Continuing Professional Devpt 1994–96), memb Police Complaints Authy 2001–03, princ lectr Sch of Law Manchester Metropolitan Univ 2003–06, ret; patron Sailfin Swimming Club for the Disabled; exhibited Pastel Exhbn Mall Gallery 2003; former JP (Manchester City); *Recreations* meditation, P G Wodehouse, Sale Rugby Club; *Style*— Ms Diane Hughes

HUGHES, Frances Mary Theresa; da of Noel Hughes, and Joanna, *née* Cartledge; *b* 15 June 1954, Richmond, Surrey; *Educ* Ursuline Convent Wimbledon, St Anne's Coll Oxford (MA); *m* 5 August 2003, Jonathan Buckeridge, s of Paul Buckeridge; 1 da (Florence b 28 Nov 1987), 2 s (Sydney b 18 Feb 1989, Nathaniel b 3 Feb 1993); *Career* admitted slr 1981; Theodore Goddard: articled clerk 1979–81, slr 1981–83; ptnr and head Family Dept Bates Wells & Braithwaite 1983–2001, fndr and sr ptnr Hughes Fowler Carruthers 2001–; vice-pres Int Acad of Matrimonial Lawyers (European Chapter); memb: Law Soc, Slr's Family Law Assoc, Poetry Soc; fell and govr-at-large Int Acad of Matrimonial Lawyers; FRSA; *Recreations* opera, gardening, playing the viola; *Style*— Ms Frances Hughes; ✉ Hughes Fowler Carruthers, Academy Court, 94 Chancery Lane, London WC2A 1DT (tel 020 7421 8383, fax 020 7421 8384, e-mail f.hughes@hfclaw.com)

HUGHES, Gary William; s of William Muir Hughes, of Paisley, and Frances, *née* Carruthers; *b* 23 April 1962; *Educ* Castlehead HS Paisley, Univ of Strathclyde (BA); *m* July 1990, Margaret Frances, da of Frank Swallow; 2 s (Gavin Andrew b June 1996, Scott William b Nov 1999); *Career* accountant Ernst & Whinney 1985–89 (articled clerk 1985–87); Guinness plc/United Distillers: gp accountant 1989–90, controller mergers and acquisitions Guinness plc 1990–92, vice-pres fin United Distillers N America 1992–94; dir of financial control Forte plc 1994–96, commercial dir Forte Hotels Div Granada plc Feb-May 1996, finance dir Scottish Media Group plc (formerly Scottish Television plc) 1996–2000, finance dir Emap plc 2000–04, chm Emap Performance 2004–05, chief exec CMP Information 2006–; FCA 1997 (ACA 1987); *Recreations* golf, tennis, cooking, running, reading, football; *Style*— Gary Hughes, Esq

HUGHES, Geoffrey; s of Ceredig (Ceri) Hughes (d 1985), and Megan, *née* Jones (d 2000); *b* 4 August 1950, Usk, Monmouthshire; *Educ* Monmouth, Cardiff Coll of Educn (CertEd), Open Univ (BA, MBA), Univ of Wales (MEd); *m* 18 Aug 1973, Susan Janet, *née* Carthey; 1 s (Rhys John b 1 April 1976), 1 da (Bethan Jane b 3 Feb 1978); *Career* PE teacher 1972–81; joined HM Prison Serv as asst govr 1981, asst govr HM Young Offenders Instn Onley, HMP Wandsworth and HM Young Offenders Instn Feltham, dep govr HMP Brixton 1991–94, govr HMP Drake Hall 1994–98, team ldr HM Inspectorate of Prisons 1998–2002, govr HMP Belmarsh 2002–05, head of security gp HM Prison Serv 2005–; memb Cncl Royal London Soc; Winston Churchill travelling fell 1999; *Recreations* rugby union football, skiing, travel; *Clubs* Usk RFC, Newport (Salop) RFC, Blackheath RFC; *Style*— Geoffrey Hughes, Esq; ✉ Geneva Cottage, Llansoy, Usk, Monmouthshire NP15 1DE

HUGHES, Rev Dr Gerard J; *b* 6 June 1934; *Educ* St Aloysius Coll Glasgow, Inst of Educn Univ of London (DipEd), Campion Hall Oxford, Univ of Michigan (PhD); *Career* Soc of Jesus: entered 1951, ordained priest 1967, vice-provincial with responsibility for the trg of Jesuits in the British Province 1982–88; Heythrop Coll London: lectr in philosophy 1970–98, head Dept of Philosophy 1974–95, vice-princ 1983–98; master Campion Hall Oxford 1998–; memb Academic Cncl and Senate Univ of London 1986–94; Austin Fagothey/Bannan visiting prof Univ of Santa Clara Calif 1988, 1992 and 1996; author of numerous articles for learned jls incl The Heythrop Jl, Religious Studies and Philosophical Quarterly; *Books* Authority in Morals: An Essay in Christian Ethics (1978), Moral Decisions (1980), The Philosophical Assessment of Theology: Essays in Honour of Frederick C Copleston (ed and contrib, 1987), The Nature of God (1995), Aristotle on Ethics (2000), Is God to Blame? (2007); *Style*— The Rev Dr Gerard J Hughes, SJ; ✉ Campion Hall, Oxford OX1 1QS

HUGHES, (George) Graham McKenny; s of George Hughes (d 1982), of London, and Peggy, *née* Graham (d 1965); *b* 17 April 1926; *Educ* Eton, Trinity Coll Cambridge (exhibitioner); *m* 1951, Serena, da of Sir Stanley Robinson (d 1976); 3 da (Emma b 1953, Clare b 1956, Harriot b 1959), 1 s (Benjamin b 1960); *Career* exhibition sec then art dir Goldsmiths' Hall (Worshipful Co of Goldsmiths) 1951–80, head of design Royal Mint 1973–77; owner and ed Arts Review magazine 1980–92; currently head Starcity Ltd (Publishers); hon chm Crafts Centre of GB 1966–75; organiser of exhibitions of modern silver, jewellery and crafts throughout the world incl: Br Fair NY 1960 (consequently estab perm showrooms for artists' products in NY and Tokyo), Int Exhibition of 20th Century Artists' Jewellery (Goldsmiths' Hall) 1961; RSA Gold Medal 1966; hon memb: Soc of Antiquaries, Royal Soc of Arts, RCA (hon sr fell 1998), Sheffield Hallam Univ, Düsseldorf Goldsmiths' Guild, German Goldsmiths' Soc, Art Workers' Guild; Liveryman Worshipful Co of Goldsmiths; Hon FSA; *Publications* The Sculpture of David Wynne (1974), Rural Barns of Britain (1985), Sven Boltenstern Jeweller of Vienna (biog, 1993), Marit Guinness Aschan Enamellist of our Time (biog, 1995)), Renaissance Cassoni - Masterpieces of early Italian art; painted marriage chests 1400–1550 (1997), Gerald Benney - Goldsmith, the Story of 50 Years at the Bench (1998), Treasures at Salters' Hall - silver and manuscripts (2000), Andrew Grima - international jewellery pioneer since 1947 (biog, 2002), Grima, a Jeweller's World: A Study of Golden Grima the Master Jeweller by Appointment Jeweller to HM Queen Elizabeth II 1970–86 (2003); also author of numerous books, articles and catalogues on silver, jewellery and crafts; *Recreations* playing clarinet; *Style*— Graham Hughes, Esq, FSA; ✉ Burnt House Cottage, Dukes Green, Alfriston, Polegate, East Sussex BN26 5TS (tel 01323 870 231); 69 Faroe Road, London W14 0EL (tel 020 7603 6563)

HUGHES, Prof Graham Robert Vivian; s of Robert Arthur Hughes, and Emily Elizabeth Hughes (d 1989); *b* 26 November 1940; *Educ* Cardiff HS For Boys, London Hosp Med Coll (MD); *m* 2 March 1966, Monica Ann; 1 da (Sarah Imogen b 19 Oct 1967), 1 s (Richard John Vivian b 7 July 1971); *Career* rheumatologist; trained London Hosp; successively: res fell Columbia Presbyterian Hosp, reader in med and head of Dept of Rheumatology Royal Postgrad Med Sch London; currently head London Lupus Centre London Bridge Hosp and emeritus conslt physician St Thomas' Hosp London (formerly head Lupus Arthritis Research Unit); conslt rheumatologist RAF, 900 pubns on arthritis res; Ciba Geigy ILAR int res prize for rheumatology res 1993; ed LUPUS, life pres LUPUS UK, tstee St Thomas' Lupus Tst, patron Hughes' Syndrome Fndn; master American Coll of Rheumatology 2006; hon memb: Aust Rheumatology Soc, Scandinavian Rheumatology Soc, Hong Kong Rheumatology Soc, Portugese Rheumatology Soc, Turkish Rheumatology Soc, memb: American Lupus Hall of Fame, Assoc of Physicians of GB & I; AESKU Lifetime Achievement Award Int Soc for Immunology 2006; Dr (hc): Université de la Méditerranée 2001, Barcelona Univ 2004; FRCP; *Books* Connective Tissue Diseases (1971, 4 edn, 1994), Modern Topics in Rheumatology (1978), Systemic Lupus Erythematosus (1982), Lecture Notes in Rheumatology (1987), Problems in The Rheumatic Diseases (1988), SLE: A Guide for Patients (1988), Phospholipid Binding Antibodies (1991), Understanding Lupus (1996), Hughes' Syndrome: a patient's guide to the Antiphospholipid Syndrome (1997); *Recreations* tennis, piano; *Style*— Prof Graham Hughes; ✉ London Lupus Centre, London Bridge Hospital, London SE1 2PR (tel 020 7234 2155, website www.thelondonlupuscentre.com); c/o Lupus Research Unit, Rayne Institute, St Thomas' Hospital, London SE1 (tel 020 71883570, fax 020 7633 9422, e-mail graham.hughes@kcl.ac.uk)

HUGHES, Gwen; *Educ* St Hilda's Coll Oxford; *m* 31 March 1995, Ian Brunskill; 1 da (Amy Catrin b 19 June 1997), 1 s (Thomas Frederick Huw b 18 Feb 2000); *Career* editor Opera BBC Radio 3 1995–97, editor Live Music BBC Radio Classical Music 1997–99, head of music policy BBC Radio 3 1999–2000, head of BBC Classical Music Online 2000–01, head of classical music Arts Cncl of England 2001–; *Style*— Ms Gwen Hughes

HUGHES, Howard; s of Charles William Hughes (d 1969), of West Kirby, Cheshire, and Ethel May, *née* Howard (d 1994); *b* 4 March 1938; *Educ* Rydal Sch; *m* 1, 20 June 1964, Joy Margaret (d 1984), da of Charles Francis Pilmore-Bedford (d 1966), of Keston, Kent; 2 s (Quentin b 1969, Edward b 1971), 1 da (Charlotte b 1974); m 2, 2 April 1988, Christine Margaret, da of Walter George Miles (d 1998); 1 s (Andrew b 1982); *Career* chartered accountant; articled clerk Bryce Hanmer & Co Liverpool 1955–60; PricewaterhouseCoopers (formerly Price Waterhouse before merger): joined 1960, ptnr 1970–98, memb Policy Ctee 1979–98, dir London office 1982–85, managing ptnr UK 1985–88, memb World Bd 1988–98, managing ptnr Europe 1988–91, dep chm Europe 1991–92, world managing ptnr 1992–98; tstee Royal London Soc for the Blind (chm 2000–05); memb Cncl Br Heart Fndn 2000– (chm of tstees 2007–); chm of govrs Dorton House Sch 1998–2001, chm United Westminster Schools 2002–; govr: Westminster City Sch, Emannuel Sch, Sutton Valance Sch; Liveryman Worshipful Co of Chartered Accountants; FCA 1960; *Recreations* golf, music; *Clubs* Carlton, MCC, Wildernesse Golf; *Style*— Howard Hughes, Esq; ✉ Witham, Woodland Rise, Seal, Sevenoaks, Kent TN15 0HZ (tel 01732 761161, fax 01732 763553)

HUGHES, Prof Ieuan Arwel; s of Arwel Hughes, OBE (d 1988), of Cardiff, and Enid Phillips, *née* Thomas (d 1995); bro of Owain Arwel Hughes, OBE,, *qv*; *b* 9 November 1944; *Educ* Univ of Wales Coll of Med (MB BCh, MD), Univ of Cambridge (MA); *m* 26 July 1969, Margaret Maureen (Mac), da of William Edgar Davies; 2 s (Gareth Arwel, Wiliam Arwel), 1 da (Mari Jones, *née* Arwel); *Career* reader in child health Univ of Wales Coll of Med 1985–89 (sr lectr 1979–85), prof of paediatrics Univ of Cambridge 1989–; fell Clare Hall Cambridge; chm Ctee on Toxicity of Chemicals in Food, Consumer Products and the Environment 2002; pres: Endocrine Section RSM, Euro Soc of Paediatric Endocrinology 1993 (sec 1987–92, Andrea Pradar Prize 2006), Assoc of Clinical Professors of Paediatrics 1995–99; fndr fell Acad of Med Scis 1998; FRCP(C) 1975, FRCP 1984, FRCPCH 1997; *Publications* Handbook of Endocrine Tests In Children (1989), Doctor to the Genome (ed, 1999) also author of papers on genetic endocrine disorders; *Recreations* music (memb Ralph Vaughan Williams Soc), travel, squash, cycling, hill walking; *Style*— Prof Ieuan Hughes; ✉ University of Cambridge, Department of Paediatrics, Addenbrooke's Hospital, Hills Road, Cambridge CB2 2QQ (tel 01223 336885, fax 01223 336996, e-mail iah1000@cam.ac.uk)

HUGHES, Jeremy Michael; s of Martyn Lawrence Hughes, of Calgary, Canada, and Mary Dorothea, *née* Kempe; *b* 15 August 1957, Oakham, Rutland; *Educ* Harrow, St Edmund Hall Oxford (MA); *m* 2 Sept 1989, Caroline Anne; 2 s (Edward Fauchon b 31 Jan 1991, Alistair John b 13 March 1993); *Career* md LMS PR 1983–89, assoc dir policy and info NCH Action for Children 1989–92, mktg and communications dir Muscular Dystrophy Gp 1992–93, dir of public affrs Leonard Cheshire 1994–99, dir of mktg and income generation Br Red Cross 1999–2003, head external rels and communications Int Fedn of Red Cross and Red Crescent Socs 2003–05, chief exec Breakthrough Breast Cancer 2005–; tstee Sight Savers Int; *Style*— Jeremy Hughes, Esq; ✉ Breakthrough Breast Cancer, Weston House, 3rd Floor, 246 High Holborn, London WC1V 7EX (tel 020 7025 2400, fax 020 7025 2401)

HUGHES, Prof John; s of Joseph Henry Hughes (d 1956), and Edith Annie Hughes; *b* 6 January 1942; *Educ* Mitcham Co GS, Chelsea Coll London (BSc), King's Coll London (PhD), Univ of Cambridge (MA); *m* 1, (m dis 1981), Madeleine Carol; 1 da (Katherine b 1967); m 2, 1997, Ann Rosemary Elizabeth Mutti; 4 c by previous partner (Georgina Anne b 1984, Joseph Francis b 1986, John Stephen b 1988, Tomas James b 1990); *Career* sr lectr and dep dir Unit for Res on Addictive Drugs Univ of Aberdeen 1973–77 (lectr in pharmacology 1969–73), prof in pharmacological biochemistry Imperial Coll London 1979–83 (reader in biochemistry 1977–79), dir Parke-Davis Res Centre Cambridge 1983–, fell Wolfson Coll Cambridge 1983–, vice-pres of res Parke-Davis (Warner-Lambert Corp) 1988–; hon prof of: neuropharmacology Univ of Cambridge 1989–, pharmacology Univ of Aberdeen 1998–; jt chief ed Neuropeptides 1980–; chm Persistent Viral Disease Res Fndn; memb Substance Abuse Ctee Mental Health Fndn; sch govr Local Educn Authy Swaffham Prior Community Sch; Hon Dr of Med Univ of Liège 1978; memb of honour Romanian Acad of Sciences, memb Biochemical Soc, MPS, FRS 1993; *Books* Centrally Acting Peptides (1978), Opioid Peptides (1983), Opioids Past Present and Future (1984), The Neuropeptide Cholecystokinin (1989); *Recreations* gardening, dogs; *Style*— Prof John Hughes, FRS

HUGHES, HE Dr (Edgar) John; *b* 1947, Pengam; *Educ* LSE, Lehigh Univ Bethlehem PA, Pembroke Coll Cambridge; *m* Lynne; 2 s; *Career* diplomat; entered HM Dip Serv 1973, posted Washington DC 1976–77, Research Dept FCO then on loan to Cabinet Office 1977–79, first sec (conf offr) Madrid 1981–82, first sec (political) Santiago 1983–95, first sec (info) Washington DC 1985–88, dep head rising to head Aviation and Maritime Dept FCO 1989–92, dep head of mission Oslo 1993–97, change mangr FCO 1997–99, seconded to BAE Systems 1999, ambass to Venezuela 2000–03, vice-pres int relations (on secondment) Shell 2003–04, ambass to Argentina 2004–; *Style*— HE Dr John Hughes; ✉ c/o Foreign & Commonwealth Office (Buenos Aires), King Charles Street, London SW1A 2AH

HUGHES, Her Hon Judge Judith Caroline Anne; QC (1994); 3 da of William Frank Hughes, and Eva-Ruth, *née* Meier; *b* 13 October 1950; *Educ* Woodhouse GS Finchley, Univ of Leeds (LLB); *m* 1, 27 Aug 1977 (m dis 1998), Mark G Warwick; 2 da (Sarah b 1981, Lucy b 1985); m 2, 31 March 2004, His Hon Inigo Bing; *Career* called to the Bar Inner Temple 1974 (bencher 1994); recorder of the Crown Court 1995 (asst recorder 1991–95), dep judge of the High Court of Justice 1997, circuit judge (SE Circuit) 2001–; vice-chair Legal Service Ctee Bar Cncl 1999; memb: SE Circuit 1974–2001, Family Bar Assoc 1983–2001; tstee: Gilbert Place Centre 1995–98, The Children's Soc 1996–2003, HASTE 1998– (chair 2000–); memb Ctee Bottoms Up 2001–03; memb PTA S Hampstead HS 1997–98; *Publications* Butterworth's Guide to Family Law (jt author, 1996); *Recreations* reading, theatre, philately, gardening, handicrafts; *Style*— Her Hon Judge Judith Hughes, QC; ✉ Snaresbrook Crown Court, 75 Hollybush Hill, Wanstead, London E11 1QW

HUGHES, Katherine; da of William Frank Hughes, and Eva Ruth Hughes; *b* 24 July 1949; *Educ* Woodhouse GS Finchley, UEA (BA), Univ of Wales (MSc); *Career* res assoc Univ of Wales 1973–75, asst planning offr Mid Glamorgan CC 1975–77, dir Welsh Consumer Cncl 1978–94 (res offr 1977–78); acting head Wales office Nat Fedn of Women's Institutes 1994–95; chair Planning Aid Wales 2004– (dir 1995–2001); memb: Welsh Ctee Butler Tst 1996–2003, Bd Tai Cymru/Housing for Wales 1997–98, Ct and Cncl Nat Library of Wales 1997–2003; tstee: Rhondda Housing Assoc 1999–, Encams Cymru 2000–; ed Int Jl of Consumer Studies (formerly Jl of Consumer Studies and Home Economics) 1998–; chair Keep Wales Tidy 2005–; MRTPI, FRSA; *Style*— Miss Katherine Hughes; ✉ Katherine Hughes Associates, 26 Bryngwyn, Caerphilly CF83 1ET (tel 029 2088 6569, fax 029 2086 0848, e-mail katherine.hughes@btconnect.com, website www.katherinehughes.org)

HUGHES, Lee Terence; CBE (2004); s of Thomas John Hughes (d 1989), and Joyce Ellen, *née* Lee (d 1984); *b* 16 January 1951; *Educ* Surbiton Co GS, Middx Poly (BA), Univ of Birmingham (Postgrad Cert Public Sector Mgmnt); *Career* civil servant; sec Police Nat Computer Bd 1986–89, sec Advsy Bd on Restricted Patients 1990–93, memb joint Dept of Health and Home Office review of services for mentally disordered offenders 1991–93, memb Cncl of Europe Ctee on Corruption (chm criminal law working gp) 1995–97, head of bill team Protection from Harrassment Act 1997; head Freedom of Information Unit (Constitutional and Community Policy Directorate) Home Office 1998–2001, head Freedom of Information and Data Protection Div Lord Chllr's Dept 2001–03, head Administrative Justice Div Lord Chancellor's Dept (now Dept for Constitutional Affrs) 2003, sec Hutton Inquiry 2003–04, dir (courts appts) Judicial Appts Cmmn 2004–; memb Advsy Gp on Openness in the Public Sector 1999, memb Lord Chllr's Advsy Gp on the Implementation of Freedom of Information Act 2002–03; *Style*— Lee Hughes, Esq, CBE; ✉ Judicial Appointments Commission, Steel House, 11 Tothill Street, London SW1H 9LH (tel 020 7210 1484, fax 020 7210 0300)

HUGHES, Lewis Harry (Lew); CB (1996); s of Reginald Hughes (d 1975), and Gladys Hughes; *b* 6 March 1945; *Educ* Devonport HS, City of London Coll; *m* July 1975, Irene, *née* Nash; 1 s (Robert David b 27 May 1977); *Career* Nat Audit Office: asst auditor then sr auditor 1963–79, audit mangr then dep dir 1979–88, dir 1988–89, asst auditor gen 1990–2000, dep auditor gen for Wales 2000–05; memb UK Auditing Practices Bd; memb CIPFA; *Recreations* golf, music, family life; *Clubs* Redbourn Golf, The Friars; *Style*— Lew Hughes, Esq, CB; ✉ 1 Wood End Road, Harpenden, Hertfordshire AL5 3EB (tel 01582 764992, fax 01582 469396)

HUGHES, Prof Martin; *b* 15 May 1949; *Educ* Manchester Grammar, UC Oxford (BA), Univ of Edinburgh (PhD); *Career* research offr Thomas Coram Research Unit Inst of Education Univ of London 1974–78, research fell Univ of Edinburgh 1978–84; Univ of Exeter: lectr in educn 1984–91, reader in educn 1991–94, prof of educn 1994–99; prof of educn Univ of Bristol 1999– (head Grad Sch of Educn 2000–03); memb ESRC Research Grants Bd 1996–2000 (vice-chair 1999–2000); panel conslt Nat Science Fndn Washington USA 2000; assoc ed: Br Jl of Developmental Psychology 1988–93, European Jl of the Psychology of Educn 1996–; author of numerous book chapters, conf proceedings, papers and reports, regular referee of papers for academic jls and of research proposals for ESRC, Leverhulme Tst and Nuffield Fndn; memb: BERA, European Assoc for Research on Learning and Instruction (EARLI), American Educnl Research Assoc (AERA); MBPsS; *Books* Nurseries Now (jtly, 1980), Young Children Learning (jtly, 1984, 2 edn 2002), Children and Number (1986, Standing Conf on Educn Book Prize), Cognition and Computers: Studies in Learning (jtly, 1986), Involving Parents in the Primary Curriculum (ed, 1986), Understanding Children: Essays in Honour of Margaret Donaldson (jt ed, 1990), Parents and their Children's Schools (jtly, 1994), Perceptions of Teaching and Learning (ed, 1994), Progression in Learning (ed, 1995), Teaching and Learning in Changing Times (ed, 1996), Numeracy and Beyond: Applying Mathematics in the Primary School (jtly, 2000); for children: Harlem Globetrotters (1984), Winston and the Robot Report (1986); *Style*— Prof Martin Hughes; ✉ Graduate School of Education, University of Bristol, 35 Berkeley Square, Bristol BS8 1JA (tel 0117 928 7007, fax 0117 925 5412, e-mail martin.hughes@bristol.ac.uk)

HUGHES, Melvyn; s of Evan Llewellyn Hughes, of Newcastle upon Tyne, and Irene Kathleen, *née* Spires; *b* 18 November 1950; *Educ* Royal GS Newcastle upon Tyne, St Catherine's Coll Oxford (MA); *m* 6 July 1974, Diane, da of Percival Moffett (d 1987); 1 da (Alexandra b 28 Oct 1980), 2 s (Richard b 2 Nov 1983, David b 9 March 1990); *Career* Slaughter and May: articled clerk 1974–76, asst slr 1976–83, ptnr 1983–, exec ptnr 1989–; memb: City of London Slrs' Co, Law Soc; Freeman City of London; *Recreations* reading, cars, sport; *Clubs* RAC; *Style*— Melvyn Hughes, Esq; ✉ Slaughter and May, 1 Bunhill Row, London EC1Y 8YY (tel 020 7600 1200, fax 020 7600 0289/1455)

HUGHES, His Hon Judge (Thomas) Merfyn; QC (1994); s of John Medwyn Hughes (d 2001), of Beaumaris, Anglesey, and Jane Blodwen, *née* Roberts; *b* 8 April 1949; *Educ* Rydal Sch Colwyn Bay, Univ of Liverpool (LLB); *m* 16 April 1977, Patricia Joan Hughes, DL (High Sheriff Gwynedd 2002–03), da of John Edmund Talbot (d 1982), of Brentwood, Essex; 1 da (Caitlin Mary b 19 Feb 1980), 2 s (Thomas Jenkin Edmund b 14 Sept 1982, Joshua Edward Talbot b 7 Dec 1987); *Career* called to the Bar Inner Temple 1971; in practice Wales & Chester Circuit, recorder 1991–2001 (asst recorder 1987–91), circuit judge (Wales & Chester Circuit) 2001–; pres Restricted Patients Panel of Mental Health Review Tbnl 1999–, chm Sports Dispute Resolution Panel 2000–01; memb: Parole Bd for England and Wales 2004–, N Wales Courts Bd 2005–, N Wales Probation Bd 2005–; former Lab Pty candidate Caernarfon; *Recreations* sailing, rugby; *Clubs* Royal Anglesey Yacht, Bangor RFC; *Style*— His Hon Judge Merfyn Hughes, QC; ✉ c/o The Crown Court, Shirehall, Mold, Flintshire CH7 1AE

HUGHES, Michael; CBE (1998); s of Leonard Hughes (d 1998), of Clwyd, and Gwyneth Mair, *née* Edwards (d 1997); *b* 26 February 1951; *Educ* Rhyl GS, Univ of Manchester (BA), LSE (MSc); *m* 11 Feb 1978, Jane Ann, da of Percival Frederick Gosham (d 1977), of Ipswich, Suffolk; 2 da (Sophie b 1979, Harriet b 1981); *Career* economist BP Pension Fund 1973–75, chief economist and ptnr de Zoete and Bevan 1976–86, dir Barclays de Zoete Wedd Securities Ltd; BZW: Capital Markets 1986, exec dir Gilts Ltd 1986–89, md Economics and Strategy 1989–97, chm BZW Pensions Ltd 1996; gp economic advsr Barclays Capital 1997–98; chief investment offr Baring Asset Management 2000– (dir and memb strategic policy gp 1998–2000); memb: ESRC 1995–98, Cncl Univ of Essex 1997–2006; chm Fin Panel Foresight Prog DTI 1994–97; AMSIA 1977, FSI, FRSA 2005; *Recreations* horses, gardens; *Clubs* National Liberal, City of London; *Style*— Michael Hughes, Esq, CBE; ✉ Baring Asset Management, 155 Bishopsgate, London EC2M 3XY (tel 020 7628 6000)

HUGHES, Prof (John) Michael Barton; s of Dr Stanley Barton Hughes (d 1963), of Helen's Bay, Co Down, and Dorothy Jane Augusta, *née* Tornblad (d 1990); *Educ* Lancing, Trinity Coll Oxford (BM BCh, MA, DM); *m* 22 Feb 1963, Shirley Ann, da of Hedley Frank Stenning (d 1977); 2 da (Penelope Barton b 1971, Caroline Barton b 1975); *Career* house physician med unit London Hosp 1963–64, house physician and res fell Hammersmith Hosp 1965–68, MRC travelling fell Harvard Sch of Public Health 1968; conslt physician Hammersmith Hosp 1974–97 (Cournand lectr 1975, Fleischner lectr 1989–, E S Garnett lectr 2000, Ludwig Engel lectr 2004); Imperial Coll Sch of Med at Hammersmith Hosp (Royal Postgrad Med Sch until merger 1997): lectr, sr lectr then reader 1969–93, prof of thoracic med 1993–97, emeritus prof 1997; author of chapters on lung gas exchange, pulmonary circulation, radioisotopes and lung function, over 150 sci articles on pulmonary physiology, pharmacology and lung disease; memb: Med Res Soc, Assoc Physicians, Physiological Soc, American Physiological Soc, British Thoracic Soc, Euro Resp Soc; FRCP 1979; *Books* Pulmonary Function Tests (with N B Pride, 1999), Pulmonary Circulation (with N W Morrell, 2001); *Recreations* golf, ornithology, round tower churches; *Clubs* Royal West Norfolk Golf, Hunstanton Golf; *Style*— Prof Michael Hughes; ✉ Respiratory Medicine, NHLI, Imperial College, Hammersmith Hospital, London W12 0HS (tel 020 8383 3269, e-mail mike.hughes@imperial.ac.uk)

HUGHES, Michael James Hamilton; s of George Hamilton Hughes, of S Queensferry, Scotland, and Beatrice, *née* Bartlett; *b* 1 October 1948; *Educ* George Watson's Coll, Univ of Edinburgh (BCom); *m* 1974, Tytti, *née* Marttila; 4 s (Andrew Hamilton b 1979, Simon Tapio b 1981, Eric Michael b 1986, Alexander Peter b 1989); *Career* KPMG: joined 1970, CA 1973, mangr 1975, ptnr 1977–, memb Bd 1991, head of audit until 2005, chm Global Audit Steering Gp 2005–; *Recreations* sailing, travel; *Style*— Michael Hughes, Esq

HUGHES, Nerys (Mrs Turley); da of Roger Edward Kerfoot Hughes (d 1974), of Rhyl, N Wales, and Annie Myfanwy, *née* Roberts; *b* 8 November 1941; *Educ* Howells Sch Denbigh, Rose Bruford Coll; *m* 13 May 1972, (James) Patrick Turley, s of James Turley (d 1983), of Wednesbury, Staffs; 1 s (Ben b 1974), 1 da (Mari-Claire b 1978); *Career* actress; vice-pres Nat Children's Home, hon fell Univ of Wales; *Theatre* work incl: BBC Rep Co, RSC, English Stage Co Royal Court Theatre, RNT (Under Milk Wood 1995); *Television* series incl: Diary of a Young Man, The Liver Birds (revival 1996), The District Nurse, How Green was my Valley, Alphabet Zoo (children's TV), Bazaar (BBC) 1990, With A Little Help (BBC Wales) 1995, Capital Woman 1997, Molly 1997, Queen's Nose (BBC)1998, Liverpool Mums (Channel Five) 1998 and 1999, Labour of Love (BBC Wales) 1999, Labour of Love (BBC Wales) 2000, Fun in the Funeral Parlour (BBC) 2002, The Secret (BBC) 2002, Promenade Rock 2003, Hospital (BBC Cardiff) 2004 and 2005; *Film* Second Best 1993, Handmade Moon (for TV) 1993, Swing 1999, Hospital (BBC Wales) 2003, Autumn Girls (BBC Wales) 2004, CBeebies (BBC) 2004; *Awards* incl: Pye Female Comedy Star Award 1974, Variety Club TV Actress of the Year 1984; *Recreations* gardening, reading; *Style*— Miss Nerys Hughes; ✉ c/o Barry Burnett Organisation Ltd, 3 Clifford Street, London W1S 2LF (tel 020 7437 8008, fax 020 7257 3239)

HUGHES, Nicholas Maxwell Lloyd; s of late Glyn Hughes, of Brighton, E Sussex, and late (Muriel) Joyce, *née* Hardaker; *b* 10 October 1955; *Educ* Univ of Sheffield (BA); *m* 8 June 1985, (Margaret) Ruth, da of Prof David Cornelius Morley, CBE, of Harpenden, Herts; 2 da (Olivia Emily b 3 July 1990, Eleanor Joyce b 27 July 1993), 1 s (Russell David Glyn b 12 Jan 1997); *Career* admitted slr 1981; ptnr Barlow Lyde & Gilbert 1984–; dir AIRMIC 1992–; consulting ed Transport Law and Policy Jl 1993–, author of articles on aviation and environmental law; Freeman City of London, Liveryman City of London Slrs' Co; memb Law Soc, MRAeS; *Publications* Contracts for the Carriage of Goods by Land, Sea and Air (gen ed, 1993); *Recreations* wine, antique furniture, golf, opera; *Clubs* City of London; *Style*— Nicholas Hughes; ✉ Beaufort House, 15 St Botolph Street, London EC3A 7NJ (tel 020 7643 8459, fax 020 7071 9501, e-mail nhughes@blg.co.uk)

HUGHES, Nigel; *Career* head Southbank Int Sch London 2001–; *Style*— Nigel Hughes, Esq; ✉ Southbank International School, 36–38 Kensington Park Road, London W11 3BU

HUGHES, Owain Arwel; OBE (2004); s of Arwel Hughes, OBE (d 1988), of Cardiff, and Enid Phillips, *née* Thomas (d 1995); bro of Prof Ieuan Hughes, *qv*; *b* 21 March 1942; *Educ* Howardian HS Cardiff, Univ Coll Cardiff, RCM London; *m* 23 July 1966, Jean Bowen, da of William Emlyn Lewis; 1 da (Lisa Margaret b 25 Dec 1970), 1 s (Geraint John b 15 Feb 1974); *Career* conductor; since 1970 has conducted all the UK symphony orchs and their respective choirs, in particular The Hallé, London Philharmonic and The Royal Philharmonic; assoc conductor: BBC Welsh Symphony Orch 1980–86, Philharmonia Orch London 1985–90; musical dir Huddersfield Choral Soc 1980–86, fndr, artistic dir and conductor the Annual Welsh Proms 1986–, creator and musical dir The World Choir (10,000 male voices) 1992; princ conductor Aalborg Symphony Orch Denmark 1995–, princ assoc conductor Royal Philharmonic Orch 2003–, musical dir Nat Youth Orch of Wales 2003–; performances in Norway, Sweden, Finland, Iceland, Luxembourg, France, Germany, Portugal, Hong Kong, Japan and NZ; many TV appearances in concert or special projects incl Mahler Symphony No 8, Requiem series, Holy Week series, Much Loved Music series, 40 anniversary concert of Granada TV (with Hallé and Royal Liverpool Philharmonic Orchs); memb Inst of Advanced Motorists, vice-pres Nat Children's Home; hon bard Royal Nat Eisteddfod of Wales; fell UC Cardiff, fell Univ of Glamorgan Hon DMus: CNAA London, Univ of Wales; *Recordings* incl: Music of Delius (Philharmonia Orch), London Symphony by Vaughan Williams (Philharmonia Orch), Music of Paul Patterson (London Philharmonic), Much Loved Music Vols I and II (Hallé Orch), Carols Album and Hymns Album (Huddersfield Choral Soc), St David by Arwel Hughes (BBC Welsh Orch and Choir), African Sanctus by David Fanshawe (Ambrosian Chorus and Instrumentalists), complete cycle of Holmboe twelve symphonies (with Aarhus Symphony Orch), Handel Messiah (with RPO and Royal Choral Soc), Verdi Requiem (with RPO, Royal Choral Soc and Brighton Festival Chorus), Sullivan Irish Symphony (with BBC Concert Orch), Holmboe Symphony No 13 & Koepell Oratorio Moses da Capo (with Danish Radio Symhony Orch), Ludolf Nielsen Oratorio Tower of Babel (with Danish Radio Symhony Orch), Sibelius Symphony No 1 (with BBC Concert Orch), Rachmaninov Piano Concerto's 1, 2, 3 and 4 and Paganini Variations (with Malmo Symphony Orch), Holmboe Orchestral Tone Poems, Brass and Woodwind Concertos, and Chamber Symphonies (with Aalborg Symphony Orch), Borresen Symphony No 1 (Aalborg Symphony Orch), Borresen Violin Concerto (Aalborg Symphony Orch), Borresen Symphonies 2 and 3 (Aalborg Symphony Orch), Horniman Theatre Music (Aalborg Symphony Orch), Norby Orchestral Music (Aalborg Symphony Orch), Rachmaninov Symphonies 1, 2 and 3 (Youth Symphony and Royal Scottish Nat Orch), Tchaikovsky Piano Concertos 1, 2 and 3 (Aalborg Symphony Orch), Choral Classics (Royal Philarmonic Orch), Opera Classics (Royal Philarmonic Orch); *Awards* Gold medal Welsh Tourist Bd, Communicator of the Year, 2 Gold Discs BPI; *Recreations* rugby, cricket, golf, motoring, travel; *Clubs* Rugby Club of London, London Welsh Assoc, London Welsh Rugby; *Style*— Owain Arwel Hughes, Esq, OBE; ✉ 7 Chartwell Place, Middle Road, Harrow-on-the-Hill, Middlesex HA2 0HE; Hazard Chase, Norman House, Cambridge Place, Cambridge CB2 1NS

HUGHES, Paul; s of James Henry Hughes (d 1986), of Dublin, and Mary, *née* O'Hanlon; family in wool business handed down some 200 years; *b* 22 June 1956, Dublin; *m* 24 June

1983, Liliane Niederer; 1 s (Kean b 11 Sept 1990); *Career* studied knitwear design Antwerp 1973–76, fndr and knitwear designer Cachaca (later Liberated Lady) shop King's Road 1976–79, travel through Latin America and Africa (studying and collecting ethnic textiles) 1979, subsequently studied textile collections at Met Museum of Art NY, Br Museum, Washington Textile Museum and V&A whilst serving an internship handling conservation co-ordination and customer serv at Artweave Textile Gallery NY, opened own textile gallery NY 1980, relocated to San Francisco 1981, fndr/proprietor Paul Hughes Gallery London 1983–; exhbns co-ordinated and curated in London 1983–91: Pre-Columbian Andean Textile Art & 2,000 Years of Andean Textile Art (both Wilson Hale Gallery London), European Textiles 15th-20th Century (Centre for Embroidery, Fashion and Textile Studies London), Kuba Raffia Textiles from Zaïre, 17th Century English Embroideries, Textiles of Africa & Pre-Columbian and Coptic Textiles (all Paul Hughes Gallery London); int and travelling exhbns co-ordinated and curated 1989–96: Pre-Columbian Textile Art (Grasse Austria, 1989, Milan Italy 1991), Tiger Rugs of Tibet (Milan) 1992, African Majesty (Antwerp Belgium) 1992, Rediscovery of Pre-Columbian Textiles (Antwerp) 1993, Time Warps (Sammlung, Hauser & Wirth Zurich, Gallerie Asbek Copenhagen, Le Monde d'Art Paris, Paul Kasmin Gallery NY) 1995, Andean Textile Art (Kasmin Gallery NY, also Japan) 1996; author of exhibition catalogues and contribs to magazines; *Style*— Paul Hughes, Esq; ✉ The Gallery, 3A Pembridge Square, London W2 4EW (tel 020 7243 8598, fax 020 7221 8785)

HUGHES, Peter Thomas; QC (1993); s of Peter Hughes, JP (d 1991), and Jane Blakemore, *née* Woodward (d 2002); *b* 16 June 1949; *Educ* Bolton Sch, Univ of Bristol; *m* 20 July 1974, Christine Stuart, da of Rex Taylor, of West Kirby, Wirral; 1 da (Rosemary b 27 May 1982), 1 s (Richard b 12 July 1985); *Career* called to the Bar Gray's Inn 1971 (bencher 2001); in practice Wales & Chester Circuit, asst recorder Wales & Chester Circuit 1988–92, recorder 1992–, dep judge of the High Court 2001–; chm: Med Appeal Tbnl 1988–93, Registered Homes Tbnl 1993–2002 (lead chm 2000–2002), Mental Health Review Tbnl 1999–; memb Gen Cncl of the Bar 1993–98; circuit jr 1991, circuit treas 1999–2000; chm: City of Chester Cons Assoc 1983–86, Euro Constituency Cncl 1984–87; Freeman Worshipful Co of Clockmakers 2005; *Recreations* fell walking, book collecting, taming an unruly garden; *Clubs* Army and Navy, Lancashire County Cricket; *Style*— Peter Hughes, Esq, QC; ✉ 22 Nicholas Street, Chester CH1 2AH (tel 01244 323886, fax 01244 347732); Tanfield Chambers, 2–5 Warwick Court, London WC1R 5DJ (tel 020 7421 5300, fax 020 7421 5333)

HUGHES, Peter Travers; OBE (1993); *b* 24 December 1946; *Educ* Wishaw HS Lanarkshire, Tech Coll Coatbridge (HNC Metallurgy), Univ of Strathclyde (DMS), Univ of Dundee (MBA); *m* 1; 2 s (Alan, William); m 2, (m dis); 1 s (Alexander); *Career* trainee metallurgist Clyde Alloy (latterly British Steel), foundry metallurgist rising to foundry mangr North British Steel Gp 1968–76, gen mangr Lake & Elliot Essex 1976–80 (also dir 1977–80), md National Steel Foundry (1914) Ltd (subsid of Lake & Elliot) 1980–83, initiated MBO forming Glencast Ltd 1983 (co sold to NACO Inc Illinois USA 1994), chm and md Glencast Ltd 1983–98 (winners Queen's Award for Technological Achievement 1990), chief exec Scottish Engineering 1998– (pres 1993); chm: Steel Castings Research and Trade Assoc 1988–92 (chm Research Ctee 1985–88), DTI Steering Ctee on UK Devpt of Solidification Simulation Prog for Castings 1988–89; guest lectr at various confs UK and abroad; UK pres Inst of Br Foundrymen 1994–95 (pres Scottish Branch 1984–85), former chm Scottish Steel Founders' Assoc; former govr and memb Ct Univ of Abertay (formerly Dundee Inst of Technol), memb Ct Univ of Strathclyde; chm Bd New Park Preparatory Sch 1998–2001; elder Church of Scotland 1976; Hon Dr: Univ of Paisley 2001, Univ of Strathclyde 2006, Napier Univ 2006; fell Univ of Abertay 2001 FIMgt 1986, FIBF 1988, FIM 1993, CEng 1994, FREng 1995; *Recreations* soccer, golf, tennis, curling, music, church, after dinner speaking; *Clubs* Thorn Park Tennis, Bearsden; *Style*— Dr Peter T Hughes, OBE, FREng, FIMMM; ✉ Scottish Engineering, 105 West Street, Glasgow G2 1QL (tel 0141 221 3181, fax 0141 204 1202, e-mail peterhughes@scottishengineering.org.uk)

HUGHES, Philip Arthur Booley; CBE (1982); s of Leslie Booley Hughes, and Elizabeth Alice, *née* Whyte; *b* 30 January 1936; *Educ* Bedford Sch, Univ of Cambridge (BA); *m* 21 Aug 1964, Psiche Maria Anna Claudia, da of Bertino Bertini (d 1971); 2 da (Francesca b 1966, Simona b 1968), 2 step da (Pauline b 1952, Carole b 1954); *Career* engr Shell International Petroleum Co 1957–61, computer conslt Scicon (formerly CEIR) 1961–69, dir Logica plc 1990–95 (co-fndr, chm and md 1969–72, chm 1972–90); artist; official visiting artist Br Antartica Survey to Antartica 2001–02; chm Bd of Tstees National Gallery London 1996–2000 (tstee 2000–02); dir Thames & Hudson Ltd; *Solo Exhibitions* Parkway Focus Gallery London 1976, Angela Flowers Gallery London 1977, Gallery Cance Manguin Vaucluse 1979, 1985 and 2000, Francis Kyle Gallery London 1979, 1982, 1984, 1987, 1989, 1992, 1994, 1997, 2000, 2003 and 2007, Inverness Museum 1990, Lesley Craze Gallery London 1992, Galerie Le Tour des Cardinaux Vaucluse France 1993, L'Ambassade de l'Australie Paris 1995, Museo Marco Monterrey Mexico 1997, Museo Tameyo Mexico 1998, Drill Hall Gallery Canberra 1998 and 2002–, Volvo Gallery Sydney 1999, George Adams Gallery Melbourne 1999, Tate Gallery St Ives 2000, Victoria and Albert Museum 2001, Musée Chatillonais Chatillon-sur-Seine France 2002, Star Gallery Lewes 2004, Chateau La Nerthe Vaucluse 2004, Watermill Gallery Aberfeldy 2005, Rex Irwin Gallery Sydney 2005, Maison de la Truffe et du Vin Ménerbes France 2007, Gallerie Pascal Lainé Méerbes France 2007; *Group Exhibitions* incl: Monks Gallery Sussex (with Beryl Bainbridge) 1972, Contemporary Br Painting (Madrid) 1983, Contemporary Painters (Ridgeway Gallery Swindon) 1986, Sherman Gallery Sydney (with Philip Wolfhagen) 2002, Churchill Coll Cambridge (with Keith Grant) 2003; *Style*— Philip Hughes, Esq, CBE

HUGHES, Richard; s of Lt Walter Cyril Hughes, RA (d 1947), of Cardiff, and Emily, *née* Palfrey (d 1941); *b* 15 April 1938; *Educ* Cardiff HS, Eaton Hall Offr Cadet Sch, Mons Offr Cadet Sch, Queens' Coll Cambridge (MA, LLM), Coll of Law Guildford; *m* 11 June 1963, Marie Elizabeth, da of William Rieb (d 1972), of Somerset West, South Africa; 1 s (David b 31 March 1964); *Career* cmmnd 2 Lt The Welch Regt 1958, serving Cyprus (GSM) and Libya 1958–59; legal advsr: Royal Insurance Group 1963–65, South African Mutual Life Assurance Soc 1965–66; slr of the Supreme Court 1969, sr ptnr Sprake and Hughes 1982–91 (ptnr in private practice 1969–91); literary critic and reviewer The Cape Times 1964–66; memb Law Soc; *Recreations* travel, walking, reading, music; *Style*— Richard Hughes, Esq; ✉ Apple Acre, Low Road, Norton Subcourse, Norwich, Norfolk NR14 6SA (tel 01508 548316); 70 Queenswood Gardens, Blake Hall Road, Wanstead, London E11 3SF

HUGHES, Prof Richard Anthony Cranmer; s of late Dr Anthony Chester Cranmer Hughes, of Chester, and Lilian Mildred, *née* Chrisp; *b* 11 November 1942; *Educ* Marlborough, Clare Coll Cambridge, Guy's Hosp Med Sch London; *m* 17 Feb 1968, Coral Stephanie, da of James Albert Whittaker (d 1983); 2 da (Polly b 1970, Romany b 1971), 1 s (Henry b 1975); *Career* conslt neurologist Guy's Hosp 1975, prof of neurology UMDS 1987, head Dept of Clinical Neurosciences Guy's, King's and St Thomas' Sch of Med 1998; chm: Neurology Ctee RCP 1989–97, Med and Dental Advsy Ctee Guy's and St Thomas' Hosps Tst 1998, Sci Ctee Euro Fedn of Neurological Socs 1998, Sci Ctee World Congress of Neurology 2001 1998; ed Jl of Neurology, Neurosurgery and Psychiatry 1979–96; govr Highgate Sch 1990–95; FRCP 1980; *Books* Immunology of The Nervous System (1983), Guillain-Barré Syndrome (1990), Neurological Emergencies (2003); *Recreations* tennis, sailing, botany, theatre; *Clubs* RSM, Athenaeum; *Style*— Prof Richard Hughes; ✉ c/o Department of Clinical Neurosciences, King's College London, Guy's Hospital, London SE1 1UL

HUGHES, Robert Charles; s of Clifford Gibson Hughes, of Walton-On-The-Hill, Surrey, and Elizabeth Joan, *née* Goodwin; *b* 20 January 1949; *Educ* Westminster, Emmanuel Coll Cambridge (MA); *m* 1, 1973 Cindy *née* Kirby-Turner (m dis 1998); 3 da (Zoe b 1975, Emma b 1976, Sophie b 1980); m 2, 2000, Annie *née* Bennett; *Career* Ernst & Young (formerly Barton Mayhew & Co): joined 1970, ptnr London 1978–81, ptnr Dubai UAE 1981–86, London 1986–; FCA; *Recreations* golf, puzzles; *Clubs* RAC, Sutton Tennis and Squash, Cuddington Golf; *Style*— Robert Hughes, Esq; ✉ Crazes, Heather Close, Kingswood, Surrey KT20 6NY (tel 01737 832 256); Ernst & Young, Becket House, 1 Lambeth Palace Road, London SE1 7EU (tel 020 7951 2000, fax 020 7951 1345, e-mail rhughes1@cc.ernsty.co.uk)

HUGHES, Rodger Grant; s of Eric Hughes, of Rhyl, Clwyd, and Doreen, *née* Barnes; *b* 24 August 1948; *Educ* Rhyl GS, Queens' Coll Cambridge (MA); *m* 9 June 1973, Joan Clare, da of James Barker; 2 s (Marcus b 9 July 1979, Oliver b 2 Feb 1983); *Career* PricewaterhouseCoopers (formerly Price Waterhouse before merger): joined 1970, ptnr 1982–, ptnr i/c Ind Business Gp 1988–91, ptnr i/c NW Region 1991–95, memb Supervisory Ctee 1991–95, UK dir Audit and Business Advisory Services (ABS) 1995–97, ABS dir UK, Scandinavia and Netherlands 1997–98, UK head ABAS, memb Euro and ME ABAS Exec and Global ABAS Mgmnt Team 1998–2002, UK managing ptnr 2002–; FCA 1973; *Style*— Rodger Hughes, Esq; ✉ PricewaterhouseCoopers, 1 Embankment Place, London WC2N 6RH (tel 020 7213 5619, fax 020 7213 4433)

HUGHES, Dr Roger Llewellyn; s of Flt-Lt Clifford John Silke Hughes (d 1963), and Jean Christine Roger, *née* Stewart (d 1999); *b* 2 June 1947; *Educ* The HS of Glasgow, Univ of Glasgow (MB ChB, MD); *m* 14 Oct 1971, Pamela Jane, da of Dr Finlay Finlayson (d 1983); 4 da (Vivienne b 1972, Caroline b 1974, Zoe b 1979, Jennifer b 1981); *Career* sr registrar Glasgow Royal Infirmary 1975 (sr house offr 1971–72, registrar of anaesthesia 1972–75), conslt in anaesthesia Stobhill Hosp Glasgow 1980–, currently hon clinical sr lectr Univ of Glasgow (lectr in anaesthesia 1975–80); author of papers on liver blood flow and baroreceptor reflex; chm of jr gp Assoc of Anaesthetists of GB and I 1977–79; memb: BMA, Intensive Care Soc; FRCP, FRCA; *Recreations* gardening, walking; *Style*— Dr Roger Hughes; ✉ 7 Ballaig Avenue, Bearsden, Glasgow G61 4HA (tel and fax 0141 942 5626, e-mail llewellynroger@ntlworld.com); Stobhill Hospital, Glasgow G21 (tel 0141 201 3005); Glasgow Nuffield Hospital, Glasgow G12

HUGHES, Sean; *Career* comedian, writer and actor; stand up comic London clubs 1987; performances incl: Edinburgh Fringe, A One Night Stand with Sean Hughes (Int tour, Perrier Award 1990), Patrick's Day (Edinburgh Critics' Award 1991), nat UK and Eire tour 1994, Melbourne Comedy Festival 1994, live tour Aust 1995, Thirtysomehow (nat tour, also TV) 1995, The Montreal Comedy Festival 1997, Edinburgh 1997, Alibis for Life (nat tour, Aust, NZ) 1997, The World Comedy Tour - Melbourne 2001; *Theatre* with Owen O'Neill: Dehydrated, Travellin' Light; Art (Wyndhams Theatre) 2000; *Radio* own show GLR 1997, own show London Live 2000, The Sunday Lie-in (BBC), 6 Music (BBC); *Television* incl: Sean's Show (Channel Four), Sean's Shorts (BBC), Aaaah Sean (Channel Four), The Signal Box (Parallel Films) 1995, Never Mind The Buzzcocks (team captain, 10 series and various specials, BBC) 1996–2002, The Greatest Store in the World (BBC) 1999, Inside Tracks (BBC Choice) 2000, Gormenghast (BBC/WGBH) 2000, Turn The World Down (Channel 4) 2001, Celebrity Blind Man's Bluff (Channel 4) 2001, The Last Detective (ITV) 2002, The Last Detective (second series, ITV) 2004; *Films* incl: The Commitments (debut) 1991, Snakes and Ladders (Livia Films) 1995, The Butcher Boy (Warner Bros) 1997, Fast Food (Twin Pictures) 1998, Puckoon (Insight Pictures) 2001; *Video* Sean Hughes Live and Seriously Funny; winner for Outstanding Production of New Work Fringe First award Edinburgh Festival 1999; *Books* Sean's Book (1993), The Grey Area (1995), The Detainees (1997), It's What He Would Have Wanted (1999); *Style*— Sean Hughes, Esq; ✉ c/o PBJ Management Ltd, 7 Soho Street, London W1D 3DQ (tel 020 7287 1112, fax 020 7287 1191, e-mail general@pbjmgt.co.uk, website www.pbjmgt.co.uk)

HUGHES, Prof Sean Patrick Francis; s of Dr Patrick Hughes (d 1995), and Kathleen Ethel, *née* Bigg (d 2001); *b* 2 December 1941; *Educ* Downside, St Mary's Hosp Med Sch Univ of London (MB BS, MS); *m* 22 Jan 1972, Dr Felicity Mary Anderson; 2 da (Sarah Jane (Mrs Kristen Glynn) b 28 Nov 1972, Emily Anne (Mrs Andrew Hills) b 25 July 1974), 1 s (John Patrick b 3 Feb 1977); *Career* successively: MO Save the Children Fund Nigeria, sr registrar in orthopaedics The Middx Hosp and Royal Nat Orthopaedic Hosp London, res fell Mayo Clinic USA, sr lectr/hon conslt orthopaedic surgn Royal Postgrad Med Sch Hammersmith Hosp London, prof and head Dept of Orthopaedic Surgery Univ of Edinburgh, hon conslt orthopaedic surgn Royal Infirmary Edinburgh and Princess Margaret Rose Orthopaedic Hosp Edinburgh, prof and head of orthopaedic surgery Royal Postgrad Med Sch Univ of London, prof of orthopaedic surgery Imperial Coll London (following merger with Royal Postgrad Med Sch), dir Inst of Musculoskeletal Surgery Ravenscourt Park Hospital Hammersmith Hosps NHS Tst; currently: emeritus prof of musculoskeletal surgery Imperial Coll London, hon conslt orthopaedic surgn Hammersmith Hosps, hon conslt Nat Hosp for Neurology and Neurosurgery Queen's Square, hon civilian orthopaedic conslt to RN; non-exec dir W Middx Univ Hosp 2001–05; pres Br Orthopaedic Res Soc 1996–98; vice-pres RCSEd 1995–97; memb Int Soc for Study of the Lumbar Spine; FRCS, FRCSI, FRCSEd Orth, FRSA; *Books* Short Textbook of Orthopaedics and Traumatology (5 edn), Orthopaedics: The Principles and Practice of Musculoskeletal Surgery (1987); *Recreations* walking, skiing, music, golf; *Clubs* Athenaeum, Naval; *Style*— Prof Sean Hughes; ✉ The Old Dairy, Maugersbury, Cheltenham, Gloucestershire GL54 1HR (e-mail s.hughes@imperial.ac.uk)

HUGHES, (Winifred) Shirley; OBE (1999); da of Thomas James Hughes (d 1933), of Liverpool, and Kathleen, *née* Dowling (d 1971); *b* 16 July 1927, West Kirby, Wirral; *Educ* West Kirby HS for Girls, Liverpool Sch of Art, Ruskin Sch of Fine Art Oxford; *m* 26 April 1952, John S P Vulliamy, s of C E Vulliamy; 2 s (Edward b 1954, Thomas b 1956), 1 da (Clara b 1962); *Career* author and freelance illustrator; total sales over 11.5 million by 2006; exhbns of artwork at Ashmolean Museum Oxford 2002 and Walker Art Gallery Liverpool 2003; Eleanor Farjeon Award for Services to Children's Literature 1984, UK nominee Hans Anderson Award 1997; Hon DLitt: UEA 2004, Univ of Liverpool 2004; hon fell Liverpool John Moores Univ 2004; hon fell CILIP 1997, FRSL 2000; *Books* for the very young: Lucy and Tom's Day Out, Lucy and Tom Go to School, Lucy and Tom's Christmas, Lucy and Tom at the Seaside, Lucy and Tom's ABC, Lucy and Tom's 123, Out and About, Giving, Bouncing, Chatting, Hiding, Noisy, Colours, Bathwater's Hot, All Shapes and Sizes, Two Shoes New Shoes, When We Went to the Park, Olly and Me, Alfie's Alphabet, Alfie's Numbers, Rhymes for Annie Rose, Annie Rose is My Little Sister; story picture books: Dogger (Kate Greenaway Medal 1977), Moving Molly, The Trouble with Jack, Stories by Firelight, Enchantment in the Garden, The Lion and the Unicorn, Alfie Wins a Prize, Alfie Gets In First, Alfie Gives a Hand, An Evening at Alfie's, Alfie's Feet, Alfie and the Birthday Surprise, Alfie Weather, Alfie and the Big Boys, The Big Alfie and Annie Rose Story Book, The Big Alfie Out of Doors Story Book, Alfie's World, Helpers (The Other Award 1976), Sally's Secret, Up and Up, Abel's Moon, Ella's Big Chance (Kate Greenaway Medal 2004), The Shirley Hughes Collection; to read alone: Chips and Jessie, Another Helping of Chips, Here Comes Charlie Moon, Charlie Moon and the Big Bonanza Bust Up, Angel Mae, The Big Concrete Lorry, Wheels, The Snow Lady, It's Too Frightening for Me; A Life Drawing (illustrated memoir), A Brush with the Past 1900–1950 (memoir); *Recreations* looking at paintings, sewing, wandering about with a sketchbook; *Style*— Ms Shirley Hughes, OBE; ✉ c/o Random House Children's Books, 61–63 Uxbridge Road, Ealing, London W5 5SA (tel 020 8231 6800, fax 020 8231 6737)

HUGHES, Simon Henry Ward; MP; s of James Henry Annesley Hughes (d 1976), and Sylvia, *née* Ward; *b* 17 May 1951; *Educ* Christ Coll Brecon, Selwyn Coll Cambridge (MA), Inns of Court Sch of Law, Coll of Europe Bruges (Cert Higher Euro Studies); *Career* called to the Bar Inner Temple 1974, trainee EEC Brussels 1975–76, trainee and memb Secretariat, Directorate and Cmmn on Human Rights Cncl of Europe Strasbourg 1976–77, in practice as barr 1978–; MP (Lib 1983–88, Lib Dem 1988–): Southwark and Bermondsey 1983–97, Southwark N and Bermondsey 1997–; Parly spokesman: (Lib) on Environment 1983–87 and 1987–88, (Alliance) on Health 1987, (Lib Dem) on Environment 1988, on Educn, Sci and Trg 1988–90, on Environment, Natural Resources and Food 1990–94, on Community & Urban Affrs and Young People and on the C of E 1994–95, on Health & Social Welfare 1995–97, Health 1997–99; Lib Dem dep whip 1989–97, Lib Dem shadow home sec 1999–; memb Ecclesiastical Ctee 1987–; pres: Southwark C of C, Redriff Club, Ethnic Minority Lib Dems; vice-pres Br Assoc of Communicators in Business; jt Parly chair Cncl for Educn in the Cwlth; chair of govrs St James C of E Sch Bermondsey; tstee: Salmon Youth Centre Bermondsey, Rose Theatre Tst; hon fell South Bank Univ; *Publications* jtly: Human Rights in Western Europe - The Next Thirty Years (1981), The Prosecutorial Process in England and Wales (1981), Across the Divide - Liberal Values for Defence and Disarmament (1986), Pathways to Power (1992), Asylum - Opportunity not Crisis (2002); *Recreations* music, theatre, sport (Millwall and Hereford FC, Glamorgan CCC and Wales RFU), the open air; *Style*— Simon Hughes, Esq, MP; ✉ House of Commons, London SW1A 0AA (tel 020 7219 6256, e-mail simon@simonhughesmp.org.uk)

HUGHES, Simon Peter; s of Peter Clowe Hughes, and Erica Christine, *née* Brace; *b* 20 December 1959; *Educ* Latymer Upper Sch, Coll of St Hild & St Bede Durham; *m* 1, 1990 (m dis); m 2, 10 June 1994, Tanya Rimmer; *Career* former professional cricketer; Middlesex CCC: debut 1980, awarded county cap 1981, benefit 1991; Durham CCC 1992–93; rep: England Young Cricketers 1979, England A team v Sri Lanka 1981, Northern Transvaal SA 1982–83 (25 appearances); honours with Middlesex CCC: County Championship winners 1980, 1982, 1985 and 1990, NatWest Trophy 1980, 1984 and 1988, Benson & Hedges Cup 1983 and 1986, Refuge League Cup 1990; columnist: From the Inside (Cricketer International) 1982–88, Cricketers' Diary (The Independent) 1987–94, The Daily Telegraph 1994–; TV commentator and reporter: formerly BBC, currently Channel 4; *Books* From Minor to Major (1992), A Lot of Hard Yakka (1997, winner William Hill Sports Book of the Year Award); *Recreations* Asian food, piano and Hammond organ, acid jazz, people, modern art; *Style*— Simon Hughes, Esq

HUGHES, Stephen Skipsey; MEP; *b* 19 August 1952; *Educ* St Bede's Sch Lanchester, Newcastle Poly; *m* (m dis), Cynthia, 2 s, 3 da (2 of whom twins); *Career* local govt offr; memb GMB; MEP: (Lab) Durham 1984–99, NE England 1999–; dep ldr European Parly Lab Pty 1991–93, former health and safety spokesperson for Socialist Gp of European Parl, chair Social Affairs and Employment Ctee 1994–99 (currently Socialist Gp co-ordinator); memb Advsy Ctee Roebens Inst 1994–; *Style*— S S Hughes, Esq, MEP; ✉ Room 4/38, County Hall, Durham DH1 5UR (tel 0191 384 9371, fax 0191 384 6100)

HUGHES, William Young; CBE (1987); s of Hugh Prentice Hughes, and Mary Henderson Hughes; *b* 12 April 1940; *Educ* Firth Park GS Sheffield, Univ of Glasgow (BSc), Univ of Strathclyde; *m* 1964, Anne MacDonald Richardson; 2 s, 1 da; *Career* lectr in Dept of Pharmacy Heriot-Watt Univ 1964–66, ptnr R Gordon Drummond Retail Chemists 1966–70, md MSJ Securities Ltd 1970–76, chm and chief exec Grampian Holdings plc 1976–98; chm: Aberforth Smaller Companies Trust plc 1990–2005, Scottish Churches Industrial Mission Tst 2000–, The Princes Scottish Youth Business Tst 2000, The Princes Tst Scot 2003–; tstee The Princes Tst UK 2003–; dir Royal Scottish Nat Hosp and Community NHS Tst 1992–95, Central Scotland NHS Tst 1995–98; dep chm Scottish Conservative Party 1989–92 (treas 1993–96), chm Euro Summer Special Olympic Games 1990, chm CBI Scotland 1987–89; memb Davidson's Mains Church Edinburgh; *Recreations* golf; *Style*— William Hughes, Esq, CBE; ✉ Flat 7, 1 Succoth Avenue, Edinburgh EH12 6BE

HUGHES-D'AETH, (Wyndham) Jonathan; TD (1999); s of (Wyndham) Peter Hughes-D'Aeth, TD (d 2004), and (Gertrude Marion) Joy, *née* Hird; *Educ* Haileybury (head of sch), Univ of Liverpool (BA), Queens' Coll Cambridge (PGCE); *Career* asst master Rugby Sch 1979, asst master (on exchange) Melbourne GS Aust 1987, housemaster Rugby Sch 1990, headmaster Milton Abbey Sch 1995; memb: Ctee Bloxham Project 1994, SHMIS 1995 (memb Exec Ctee 2001), Ctee Boarding Schools Assoc 2001 (chm 2004–05), inf offr TA 5 Bn Royal Regt of Fusiliers 1978–91; *Recreations* family, field sports, military history; *Clubs* East India, Public Schools; *Style*— Jonathan Hughes-D'Aeth, Esq, TD; ✉ Milton Abbey School, Blandford, Dorset DT11 0BZ (tel 01258 880484)

HUGHES HALLETT, Prof Andrew Jonathan; s of Vice Adm Sir Charles Hughes Hallett, KCB, CBE (d 1985), of Salisbury, Wilts, and Joyce Plumer, *née* Cobbold (d 1996); *b* 1 November 1947; *Educ* Radley, Univ of Warwick (BA), LSE (MSc), Nuffield Coll Oxford (DPhil); *m* 22 July 1982, Claudia Ilse Luise, da of Karl Becker (d 1988), of Kassel, W Germany; 2 s (David b 1983, James b 1986), 1 da (Nicola b 1990); *Career* lectr in economics Univ of Bristol 1973–77, assoc prof of economics Erasmus Univ Rotterdam 1977–85, David Dale prof of economics Univ of Newcastle upon Tyne 1985–89, Jean Monnet prof of economics Univ of Strathclyde 1989–2001, prof of economics Vanderbilt Univ 2001–06, prof of economics and public policy George Mason Univ 2006–; visiting prof: Princeton Univ, Univs of Rome, Berlin, Frankfurt and St Andrews; author of papers on: theory of economic policy, int economic policy, (european) economic integration, commodity markets and economic devpt, game theory, numerical analysis; reg broadcasts on economic affairs; conslt to: IMF, UN, World Bank, EEC Cmmn, OECD, UNESCO, various govts; memb: Royal Econ Soc 1975, Euro Econ Assoc 1985, Scot Econ Assoc 1998, American Econ Assoc 1998, American Mathematical Soc 2000; fell Centre for Econ Policy Res; FRSE (convenor Econ Ctee); *Books* Quantitative Economic Policies and Interactive Planning (1983), Stabilising Speculative Commodity Markets (1987), Optimal Control, Expectations and Uncertainty (1989), Fiscal Aspects of European Monetary Integration (1999); *Recreations* hill walking, beer, blues, history; *Style*— Prof Andrew Hughes Hallett

HUGHES-HALLETT, James Wyndham John; s of Michael Hughes-Hallett, and Penelope, *née* Fairbairn; bro of Lucy Hughes-Hallett and Tom Hughes-Hallett, *qqv*; *b* 10 September 1949; *Educ* Eton, Merton Coll Oxford; *m* 1991, Lizabeth Louise Hall; 2 da; *Career* articled clerk Dixon Wilson Tubbs & Gillett 1970–73, with Swire Gp 1976–; chm: Cathay Pacific Ltd 1999–2005, Swire Pacific Ltd 1999–2005, John Swire & Sons (Hong Kong) Ltd 1999–2005, John Swire & Sons Ltd 2005–; dir HSBC Holdings Ltd 2005–; tstee: Dulwich Picture Gallery 2005–, Esme Fairbairn Fndn 2005–; govr SOAS 2005–; FCA 1973; Silver Bauhinia Star (Hong Kong) 2004; *Style*— James Hughes-Hallett, Esq; ✉ John Swire & Sons Ltd, Swire House, 59 Buckingham Gate, London SW1E 6AJ

HUGHES-HALLETT, Lucy Angela; da of Michael Hughes-Hallett, of Glos, and Penelope, *née* Fairbairn; sis of James Hughes-Hallett and Tom Hughes-Hallett, *qqv*; *b* 7 December 1951; *Educ* St Mary's Calne, Bedford Coll London (BA); *m* 1985, Dan J Franklin, s of Michael Franklin, of Much Hadham, Herts; 2 da (Lettice, Mary (twins) 1 March 1990); *Career* writer and critic 1973–; *Books* Cleopatra: Histories, Dreams and Distortions (1990), Heroes (2004); *Awards* Catherine Pakenham Award 1980, Emily Toth Award 1990, Fawcett Book Prize 1992; *Style*— Lucy Hughes-Hallett; ✉ c/o Lutyens & Rubinstein, 231 Westbourne Park Road, London W11 1EB (tel 020 7792 4855)

HUGHES-HALLETT, Thomas; s of Michael Hughes-Hallett, and Penelope, *née* Fairbairn; bro of James Hughes-Hallett and Lucy Hughes-Hallett, *qqv*; *b* 28 August 1954; *Educ* Eton, Univ of Oxford (MA), Coll of Law; *m* Juliet, da of Col Anthony Rugge-Price, and Joy Rugge-Price; 2 s, 1 da; *Career* Robert Fleming & Co Ltd: chm Robert Fleming Securities 1993–99, chm Fleming Private Asset Mgmnt, memb Bd Fleming Asset Mgmnt and chm Flemings Private Bank 1999–2000; chief exec Marie Curie Cancer Care 2000–; chm Michael Palin Centre for Stammering Children, special tstee Great Ormond St Hospital Children's Charity 2004–; *Recreations* music, tennis, cooking, walking; *Style*— Thomas Hughes-Hallett, Esq; ✉ Marie Curie Cancer Care, 89 Albert Embankment, London SE1 7TP (tel 020 7599 7130, fax 020 7599 7131)

HUGHES OF WOODSIDE, Baron (Life Peer UK 1997), of Woodside in the City of Aberdeen; Robert Hughes; *b* 3 January 1932; *Educ* Robert Gordon's Coll Aberdeen, Benoni HS Transvaal, Pietermaritzburg Tech Coll; *m* 1957, Ina, *née* Miller; 2 s, 3 da; *Career* formerly engrg apprentice in SA, chief draughtsman C F Wilson & Co 1932 Ltd (Aberdeen until 1970); Parly candidate N Angus and Mearns 1959, memb Aberdeen Town Cncl 1962–70 (convenor of Health and Welfare Ctee 1963–68 and Social Work Ctee 1969–70), MP (Lab) Aberdeen N 1970–97; memb: Standing Ctee on Immigration Bill 1971, Scot Affairs Select Ctee 1971 and 1992–97; Parly under sec of state Scot Office 1974–75, jr oppn spokesman 1981–83; princ oppn spokesman: agriculture 1983–84, transport 1985–88; memb PLP Shadow Cabinet 1985–88; chm Aberdeen City Lab Party 1961–69, chm Anti-Apartheid Movement 1976–94 (vice-chm 1975–76), chm Action for Southern Africa (successor to AAM) 1994–99 (hon pres 1999–), chm Aberdeen CND (founder memb); memb: AEU 1952–, GMC 1976–79, Scot Poverty Action Gp; hon pres Mozambique Angola Ctee 2002–; tstee Canon Collins Educnl Tst for Southern Africa 1997–; *Recreations* fishing, golf; *Style*— The Rt Hon Lord Hughes of Woodside; ✉ House of Lords, London SW1A 0PW

HUGHES-ONSLOW, James Andrew; s of Andrew Hughes-Onslow (d 1979), and Betty Lee (now Mrs David Crichton), half-sister of Lord Rossmore; gs of Capt Oliver Hughes-Onslow (d 1972), of Ayrshire; *b* 27 August 1945; *Educ* Castle Park Dublin, Eton; *m* 1982, Christina Louise, da of Peter Henry Hay, bro of Sir David Hay, of Aust; 1 s (Andrew b 1985), 3 da (Flora b 1988, Marina b 1990, Harriet b 1993); *Career* sub ed and feature writer The Field 1968–70; reporter: Sunday Telegraph 1970–71, Daily Express 1971–73; columnist: The Spectator 1974–75, What's On in London 1976–82; columnist and feature writer: Evening Standard 1983–96, The Express (Beachcomber Column) 1996–; articles and reviews in: Punch, The Times, The Field, Books and Bookmen, Business Traveller, The Spectator, Tatler, Country Times, Southside, The Illustrated London News, Country Living, The Melbourne Age, Sydney Morning Herald; *Clubs* Boodle's; *Style*— James Hughes-Onslow, Esq; ✉ 42 Knatchbull Road, Camberwell, London SE5 9QY (tel 020 7274 9347); The Express, 245 Blackfriars Road, London SE1 9UX (tel 020 7928 8000)

HUGHES-PARRY, Thomas Antony; s of Maj Thomas Garrard Hughes-Parry (d 1987), of Llangollen, Denbighshire, and Rachael Constance Luz, *née* Boger (d 2000); *b* 9 February 1949; *Educ* Canford Sch, Univ of Exeter (BSc); *m* 1 May 1976, Rosemary Constance, da of Robert James Foster; 2 s (Thomas David b 9 Sept 1981, Philip John b 19 Sept 1983); *Career* articled clerk Harmood Banner 1969–73, chartered accountant Investigation Dept Deloitte Haskins & Sells 1974–78, ptnr Beer Aplin 1979–2004, ptnr Thomas Westcott 2004–06 (conslt 2006–); memb SW Soc Chartered Accountants: Tech Advsy Ctee 1979–91 (del to London Ctee 1988–91), GP Panel 1991– (del to London Ctee); chm ICAEW Charity and Voluntary Sector Gp 1999–2004; Exeter District Soc of Chartered Accountants: careers advsr 1980–84, vice-chm 1989–90, chm 1990–91; vice-treas Exeter Cncl for Voluntary Service 1980–88, various offices Dawlish Round Table 1980–89, bursar and sec to the govrs Maynard Sch 1981–, sec to the govrs Royal West of England Residential Sch for the Deaf 1986–, adult educn lectr 1986–, chm Exeter Voluntary Trading Enterprizes 1988–2004, chm Devon & Exeter Deaf Soc 2005–; FCA, ACIArb; *Recreations* swimming, walking, gardening, yoga, boating, classical music, reading; *Style*— Tom Hughes-Parry, Esq; ✉ 8 Cavendish Close, Dawlish EX7 9ED (tel 01626 863653, e-mail rosemaryhparry@f2s.com)

HUGHESDON, Charles Frederick; AFC (1943); *b* 10 December 1909; *Educ* Raine's GS; *m* 1, 1937, Florence Elizabeth (the actress Florence Desmond d 1993), *née* Dawson, wid of Capt Tom Campbell Black; 1 s (Michael); m 2, 1993, Carol Elizabeth, wid of Baron Havers, PC, QC (Life Peer, d 1992), and da of Stuart Lay, of London; *Career* cmmnd RAFO 1934, ret 1946; chm: Stewart Smith Group of Companies, Stewart Wrightson Group of Companies (until ret 1976), Tradewinds Helicopters Ltd, Charles Street Co; formerly: chm and dir Tradewinds Airways Ltd, dir Aeronautical Trust Ltd; memb: Guild of Air Pilots and Air Navigators, Gunmakers' Guild; Upper Freeman City of London; FRAeS (hon treas 1969–85); Knight of the Order of the Cedar (Lebanese Republic) 1972; *Recreations* shooting, water skiing, yachting; *Clubs* RAF, Royal Thames Yacht, Garrick, Mark's; *Style*— Charles Hughesdon, Esq, AFC, FRAeS; ✉ 5 Grosvenor Square, London W1X 9LA (tel 01493 1494, fax 01488 638808); Leckhampstead House, Leckhampstead, Newbury, Berkshire RG20 8QH (tel 01488 638229)

HUGHESDON, John Stephen; s of Eric Hughesdon (d 1994), and Olive Mona, *née* Quirk (d 1980); *b* 9 January 1944; *Educ* Eltham Coll; *m* Mavis June, da of Charles Henry George Eburne, OBE; 1 da (Fiona Louise b 22 Nov 1975), 1 s (Simon Charles b 18 Aug 1978); *Career* Peat Marwick Mitchell 1962–73, ptnr Mazars (formerly Neville Russell) 1977–2004 (mangr 1973–76), conslt 2004–; hon treas: Girls' Bde Nat Cncl Eng & W 1979–91, TEAR Fund 1992–96; govr Bishopsgate Fndn 1993–97, almoner Christ's Hosp Fndn 1993–, tstee: Br and Foreign Bible Soc 1997–, Southwark Welcare, City of London Endowment Tst for St Paul's 2004–, UCLH Charitable Fndn 2004–06; pres Boys' Brigade London Dist 2005–; Liveryman Worshipful Co of Coopers (Master 2006–07), Liveryman Worshipful Co of Chartered Accountants, Freeman City of London, Freeman Worshipful Co of Parish Clerks, Freeman Co of Waterman and Lightermen of the River Thames; Sheriff City of London 2004–05; memb: Guild of Freemen of City of London, Royal Soc of St George, Ct of Common Cncl City of London 1991–97; Alderman Billingsgate Ward 1997–; FCA 1977 (ACA 1967), FRSA 1990; *Recreations* church, golf; *Clubs* City Livery, National, Billingsgate Ward, Bishopsgate Ward, Broad Street Ward; *Style*— John Hughesdon, Esq; ✉ 44 Speen Lane, Speen, Newbury, Berkshire RG14 1RN (e-mail john.hughesdon@cityoflondon.gov.uk)

HUGILL, John; QC (1976); s of John Alfred Hugill (d 1950), and Alice, *née* Clarke (d 1982); *b* 11 August 1930; *Educ* Sydney C of E GS Aust, Fettes, Trinity Hall Cambridge (MA); *m* 1956, Patricia Elizabeth, da of Stanley Welton (d 1966), of Cheshire; 2 da (Gail b 1962, Rebecca b 1968); *Career* RA 1949–50 2 Lt, Capt RA (T); called to the Bar Middle Temple 1954 (bencher 1984–), asst recorder Bolton 1971, recorder 1972–96, dep High Ct judge 1985–96; memb: Senate of the Inns of Ct and the Bar 1984–86, Gen Cncl of the Bar 1987–89, Criminal Injuries Compensation Bd 1998–2000, Criminal Injuries Panel 2000–02; chm: Darryn Clarke Inquiry 1979, Stanley Royd Inquiry 1985; hon legal advsr Clay Pigeon Shooting Assoc (CPSA); *Clubs* Army and Navy; *Style*— John Hugill, Esq, QC; ✉ 45 Hardman Street, Manchester M3 3HA (tel 0161 832 3791, fax 0161 835 3054)

HUHNE, Christopher Murray Paul (Chris); MP; s of Peter Ivor Paul Huhne, and Margaret Ann Gladstone, *née* Murray; *b* 2 July 1954; *Educ* Westminster, Sorbonne, Magdalen Coll Oxford (BA); *m* 19 May 1984, Vicky Pryce, *qv*; 2 s, 1 da, 2 step da; *Career* journalist

H

1975–94; md of sovereign ratings and economics dir IBCA Ltd 1994–97, gp md Fitch IBCA Ltd 1997–99; memb Cncl Royal Econ Soc 1993–98; Financial Journalist of the Year (Wincott award) 1990; Lib Dem Pty: Parly candidate (SDP Lib Alliance) 1983 and 1987, chm Press and Broadcasting Policy Panel 1994–95, economic advsr Gen Election 1997, memb Economic Policy Cmmn 1997–98, chair Expert Cmmn on Britain's Adoption of the Euro Law, chair (joint with Lord Wallace) Global Security and Sustainability Policy Panel 1999–2000, MEP (Lib Dem) SE England 1999–2005, economic spokesman of Gp of Euro Lib Dems and Reformist Parties in Euro Parl, memb Economic and Monetary Affairs Ctee Euro Parl, rapporteur first report on the Euro Central Bank 1999, substitute memb Budget Ctee, memb Cncl Britain in Europe 2000–05, chair Public Servs Policy Panel 2001–02, rapporteur prospectus directive 2001–03; MP (Lib Dem) Easleigh 2005–; shadow sec for environment, food and rural affrs 2006–; pres Oxfordshire Branch Euro Movement 2000–, memb Cncl Consumers' Assoc 2002–04; *Books* Debt and Danger - The World Financial Crisis (with Lord Lever, 1985), Real World Economics (1990), The Ecu Report (with Michael Emerson, 1991), Both Sides of the Coin (with James Forder, 1999, 2 edn 2001); *Recreations* family, cinema; *Clubs* Hurlingham, Nat Liberal; *Style*— Chris Huhne, MP; ✉ House of Commons, London SW1A 0AA (tel 020 7219 4997, e-mail chris@chrishuhne.org.uk)

HUISMANS, Sipko; s of Jouko Huismans, and Roeloffina Huismans; *b* 28 December 1940; *Educ* Univ of Stellenbosch (BA); *m* 1969, Janet, *née* Durston; 2 s (Jake, Nicholas), 1 da (Emma); *Career* Usutu Pulp Co Swaziland 1961–68; Courtaulds plc: sales mangr 1968, gen mangr Springwood Cellulose Co Ltd 1968, md Courtaulds Central Trading (formerly Lustre Fibres Ltd) 1973, md Fibres Bd 1982, main bd dir 1984–96, non-exec dir BCL 1985–86, ldr Chem and Industry Task Force 1986–88, chm International Paint 1986–96, chm Chemical and Industrial Executive 1988–90, gp md 1990, chief exec 1991–96; non-exec dir: Vickers plc 1994–99, Imperial Tobacco plc 1996–; ceo Volharding (UK) Ltd; *Recreations* motor racing, sailing; *Style*— Sipko Huismans, Esq

HULBERT, (Evelyn) Gervase Carson; OBE (1993); s of Lt Col John Harvey Hulbert (d 1981), and Elisabeth, *née* Lovett (d 1985); *b* 1 April 1942; *Educ* Winchester, Univ of Paris; *m* 23 March 1968, Susannah Mary, da of Lt Cdr Ralph Henry Hood Laurence Oliphant, RN (ret) (d 1995); 2 s (George Gervase b 24 Nov 1970, William Laurence b 12 June 1972); *Career* Moore Stephens: articled clerk 1962–67, Moore Stephens & Butterfield Bermuda 1968–69, ptnr 1970, chm Moore Stephens International 1989–; co-chm Polish British Accountancy Assoc 1990–94; FCA; *Recreations* collecting antiques, pictures, classic cars; *Style*— Gervase Hulbert, Esq, OBE; ✉ Moore Stephens, St Paul's House, Warwick Lane, London EC4P 4BN (tel 020 7334 9191, fax 020 7651 1637)

HULL, Prof Derek; s of William Hull (d 1974), of Blackpool, Lancs, and Nellie, *née* Hayes (d 1958); *b* 8 August 1931; *Educ* Baines GS Poulton-Le-Fylde, Univ of Wales (BSc, PhD, DSc); *m* 5 Aug 1953, Pauline, da of Norman Scott (d 1950), of Halifax, W Yorks; 1 s (Andrew b 1956), 4 da (Sian b 1958, Karen b 1961, Beverley b 1965, Alison b 1967); *Career* section ldr AERE Harwell 1956–60; Univ of Liverpool: lectr 1960–62, sr lectr 1962–64, prof 1964–84, dean of engrg 1971–74, pro-vice-chllr 1983–84; Goldsmiths prof Univ of Cambridge 1984–91 (emeritus prof 1991–), sr fell Univ of Liverpool 1991–; Hon DTech Tampere Univ Finland 1987; Liveryman Worshipful Co of Goldsmiths; FIM 1966, FPRI 1978, FREng 1986, FRS 1989; *Books* Introduction to Dislocations, An Introduction to Composite Materials, Fractography: Observing Measuring and Interpreting Fracture Surface Topography, Celtic and Anglo-Saxon Art: Geometric Aspects; *Recreations* golf, fell walking, music, early Medieval art; *Clubs* Heswall Golf; *Style*— Prof Derek Hull, FRS, FREng; ✉ Department of Engineering, University of Liverpool, Liverpool L69 3BX (tel 0151 794 4669, fax 0151 794 4675, e-mail derekh@liv.ac.uk)

HULL, Janet Elizabeth; da of Thomas Edward Lacy (d 1989), of Southport, and Marjorie, *née* Forster (d 2003); *b* 20 March 1955; *Educ* Southport HS for Girls, St Anne's Coll Oxford (MA), Napier Coll Edinburgh (DEML), Inst of Direct Mktg (DipIDM); *Children* 1 s (Archibald Campbell b 19 Dec 1991), 1 da (Florence Campbell b 2 March 1998); *Career* Ted Bates 1979–80, Abbott Mead Vickers 1980–85, Young & Rubicam 1985–9, Burson-Marsteller 1992–93, IPA 1993–99, Lewis Moberly 2000–02, IPA 2003–; memb: The Marketing Soc, Women's Advtg Club of London (WACL), RHS; memb Worshipful Co of Marketors; *Recreations* piano, art, travel; *Style*— Ms Janet Hull; ✉ 4 Edith Grove, London SW10 0NW

HULL, Bishop of 1998–; Rt Rev Richard Michael Cokayne Frith; s of Canon Roger Cokayne Frith (d 1989), and Joan Agnes, *née* Pearson; *b* 8 April 1949; *Educ* Marlborough, Fitzwilliam Coll Cambridge (MA), St John's Coll Nottingham; *m* 1, 1975 (m dis 2000), Jill, da of Norman Richardson; 2 s (James b 1977, Timothy b 1982), 2 da (Rachel b 1979, Elizabeth b 1985); m 2, 2006, Kay Gledhill.; *Career* ordained: deacon 1974, priest 1975; curate Mortlake with E Sheen (Dio of Southwark) 1974–78, team vicar Thamesmead (Dio of Southwark) 1978–83, team rector Keynsham (Dio of Bath and Wells) 1983–92, archdeacon of Taunton 1992–98; *Recreations* cricket, theatre; *Clubs* MCC; *Style*— The Rt Rev the Bishop of Hull

HULL, Robert David (Rob); s of David Archibald Hull, of Normandy, Surrey, and Rosalie Joy, *née* Cave; *b* 17 December 1950; *Educ* Royal GS Guildford, Jesus Coll Cambridge (MA, PhD); *m* 23 June 1973, Sarah Ann (Sally), *née* Cockett; 1 s (George Thomas Bernard b 1 Sept 1983), 1 da (Sarah Lucy Felicity b 11 Oct 1986); *Career* Civil Service Dept 1974–81, DES 1982–94, sec HEFCE 1994–98, dir for qualifications and young people DfES 1998–2004, freelance conslt 2005–; chair E London Advanced Technol Trg 2005–; govr Holloway Sch; chair On Golden Lane 2007–; *Recreations* chess, writing, photography; *Clubs* Cavendish Chess, Surrey CCC; *Style*— Rob Hull; ✉ 27 Myddelton Square, London EC1R 1YE (e-mail rob.hull@dsl.pipex.com)

HULME, Geoffrey Gordon; CB (1984); s of Alfred Hulme, and Jessie Hulme; *b* 8 March 1931; *Educ* King's Sch Macclesfield, CCC Oxford (MA); *m* 1951, Shirley Leigh (d 2003), da of Herbert and Doris Cumberlidge; 1 s (Andrew), 1 da (Alison); *Career* DHSS: joined min 1953, under sec 1974, dep sec and princ fin offr 1981–86; dir Public Expenditure Policy Unit 1986–91; conslt 1991–; memb Editorial Bd Office of Health Economics 1990–; chm Knowledge Aid for Sierre Leone 2001–, tstee Disabled Living Fndn 2001– (chm 2001–06); *Recreations* most of the usual things, collecting edible fungi; *Clubs* RAC; *Style*— Geoffrey Hulme, Esq, CB; ✉ Stone Farm, Little Cornard, Sudbury, Suffolk (tel 01787 312728, e-mail g.hulme@tesco.net)

HULME, Cdr Laon Stuart Grant; OBE (1999); s of Capt James Edmund Hulme, and Dorothea Valentia, *née* Valless (d 2000); *b* 2 November 1944; *Educ* Hardye's Dorchester, BRNC Dartmouth; *m* 1968, Karen Mary, *née* Welch; 2 da (Sara-Louise b 9 May 1970, Anna-Marie b 21 July 1972); *Career* RN 1963–98; qualified aircraft control/air direction; memb trg staff: RNAS Yeovilton (fighter control), FOST (operational sea trg), SMOPS (i/c ops trg); specialised in NATO Command systems/data links; cmd: HMS Hubberston (minehunter), HMS Galatea (frigate); exec offr HMS Brilliant (Falklands War, mentioned in dispatches); seagoing flag staff Ops Offr, head Warfare Branch Implementation Team; ed Broadsheet (RN annual magazine, BACB awards) MOD, ret as Cdr 1998; sec/chief exec Insurance Inst of London 1998–, ed New London Jl (Insurance Inst of London magazine) 2000–; vice-pres Insurance Orch 2000–, vice-pres Insurance Charities 2001; memb: Insurance Golfing Soc of London, Worshipful Insurers Golf Soc; Freeman City of London 1999, memb Worshipful Co of Insurers 1999; MInstD 1996 (memb Business Panel); *Recreations* golf, being with family and friends; *Clubs* Royal Navy of 1765 and 1795, City Livery, Anchorites, Rowlands Castle Golf, Lime Street and Bassishaw Ward; *Style*— Cdr Laon Hulme, OBE; ✉ Insurance Institute of London, 20 Aldermanbury, London EC2V 7HY (tel 020 7600 1343, fax 020 7600 6857, e-mail laon.hulme@cii.co.uk)

HULME, Prof Mike; s of Ralph Hulme (d 1989), and Shelagh Mary, *née* Close; *b* 1960, London; *Educ* Madras Coll St Andrews, Univ of Durham (BSc), Univ of Swansea (PhD); *m* 1987, Gillian Margaret, *née* Walker; 1 da (Emma Jane b 1992); *Career* lectr in physical geography Univ of Salford 1984–88; Sch of Environmental Sciences UEA: sr research assoc Climatic Research Unit (CRU) 1988–98, reader CRU 1998–2000, founding dir Tyndall Centre for Climate Change Research 2000–07, prof of environmental science 2002–; conslt: World Bank, UNDP, UNEP, ODA, Inst of Terrestrial Ecology, BP-Amoco, W S Atkins, Mott McDonald Ltd, Club du Sahel; ed: Climate Research 1997–2000, Global Environmental Change 2003–; memb Editing Ctee Int Jl of Climatology 1994–99, editorial advsr Progress in Physical Geography 1999–2002, memb Editorial Bd Climate Policy; contrib The Guardian 1988–2001 (monthly climate summaries); Hugh Robert Mill Prize Royal Meteorological Soc 1995; memb Royal Meteorological Soc 1982; *Books* incl: An Annotated Bibliography of the Climate of Sudan (1987), Climate Change, Desertification and Desiccation, with Particular Emphasis on the African Sahel (with Mick Kelly, 1993), The Impact of Climate Changes on Africa (1995), Climate of the British Isles: Present, Past and Future (ed with Elaine Barrow, 1997), Climate Change Scenarios for the UK (ed, 1998, 2 edn 2002); *Recreations* cricket, genealogy, modern history; *Style*— Prof Mike Hulme; ✉ School of Environmental Sciences, University of East Anglia, Norwich NR4 7TJ

HULME, Bishop of 1998–; Rt Rev Stephen Richard Lowe; *b* 3 March 1944; *Educ* Leeds GS, Reading Sch, Birmingham Poly (BSc Univ of London), Ripon Hall Oxford; *m* Pauline Amy, *née* Richards; 1 s (Michael b 12 April 1969), 1 da (Janet b 7 Dec 1972); *Career* curate St Michael's Anglican Methodist Church Birmingham 1968–72, min in charge Woodgate Valley Conventional dist 1972–75, team rector East Ham 1975–88, hon canon Chelmsford Cathedral 1985–88, urban offr Chelmsford Diocese 1986–88, archdeacon of Sheffield 1988–98; Bishop for Urban Life and Faith 2006–; travelling fellowship Winston Churchill Meml Trust 1980, Paul Cadbury fell 1996; memb: BBC N Regnl Advsy Cncl 1993–95, Archbishop's Cmmn on the Organisation of the C of E 1994–96, Gen Synod, House of Bishops 2001–, Bishops' Urban Panel 2001–, Urban Life and Faith Cmmn 2003–; Bishop's liaison offr with HM Prison Serv Chaplaincy Dept 1993–98, chair Sheffield Somalian Refugees Tst 1993–95; responsible for drawing up and implementation of Church Major Incident Plan following Hillsborough disaster; chm: Diocesan Social Responsibility and Faith in City Ctees 1988–99, Urban Bishops Panel 2006–; memb: Duke of Edinburgh's Study Conf 1989, Bishoprics and Cathedrals Ctee 1999–, Governing Body Westcott House Cambridge 1999–, Governing Body Northern Ordination Course 1999–, House of Bishops 2001–; tstee Church Urban Fund 1991–97 (chm Grants Ctee 1994–97), church cmmr 1992–98 and 2001– (memb Houses Ctee 1993–95, memb Bd of Govrs 1994–98 and 2001–, dep chair Bishoprics Ctee 2001– (memb 1996–98)); chair William Temple Fndn 2006–; *Books* The Churches' Role in the Care of the Elderly (1969); *Recreations* watching football, travel, theatre, cinema, photography; *Clubs* Commonwealth Soc; *Style*— The Rt Rev the Bishop of Hulme; ✉ 14 Moorgate Avenue, Withington, Manchester M20 1HE (tel 0161 445 5922, fax 0161 448 9687, e-mail lowehulme@btinternet.com)

HULSE, Sir Edward Jeremy Westrow; 10 Bt (GB 1739), of Lincoln's Inn Fields; DL (Hants 1989); s of Sir (Hamilton) Westrow Hulse, 9 Bt (d 1996), and his 1 w, Philippa Mabel, *née* Taylor; *b* 22 November 1932; *Educ* Eton; *m* 1957, Verity Ann, da of William Pilkington, of Bournemouth, Dorset; 1 s ((Edward) Michael Westrow b 1959), 1 da (Camilla Ann (Mrs Luca M Corona) b 1962); *Heir* s, Michael Hulse; *Career* late Capt Scots Gds; High Sheriff Hants 1978; *Style*— Sir Edward Hulse, Bt, DL; ✉ Breamore House, Fordingbridge, Hampshire SP6 2DF (tel 01725 512233, fax 01725 512858, e-mail breamore@internet.com)

HUM, Sir Christopher Owen; KCMG (2003, CMG 1996); s of Norman Charles Hum (d 1950), and Muriel Kathleen, *née* Hines (d 2001); *b* 27 January 1946; *Educ* Berkhamsted Sch, Pembroke Coll Cambridge (MA), Univ of Hong Kong; *m* 31 Oct 1970, Julia Mary, da of Hon Sir Hugh Park (d 2001), of London and Cornwall; 1 da (Olivia b 1974), 1 s (Jonathan b 1976); *Career* FCO: joined 1967, Hong Kong 1968–70, Peking 1971–73, office of UK Perm Rep to the EEC Brussels 1973–75, FCO 1975–79, Peking 1979–81, Paris 1981–83, head Hong Kong Dept 1986–89 (asst head 1983, cnsllr 1985), dep head Falkland Islands Dept 1985–86, cnsllr and head of Chancery UK Mission to the UN NYC 1989–92, asst under sec of state (Northern Asia) 1992–94, asst under sec of state (Northern Asia and Pacific) 1994–95, ambass Poland 1996–98, dep under-sec and chief clerk 1998–2001, ambass to China 2002–05; master Gonville and Caius Coll Cambridge 2006–; non-exec dir The Laird Gp plc 2006–; memb GB China Centre 2006–; govr SOAS Univ of London 1998–2001; hon fell Pembroke Coll Cambridge 2004; hon LLD Univ of Nottingham 2006, Hon PhD London Met Univ 2006; *Recreations* music (piano, viola), walking; *Clubs* Athenaeum; *Style*— Sir Christopher Hum, KCMG; ✉ Gonville & Caius College, Trinity Street, Cambridge CB2 1TA

HUMAN, (Henry) Robin John; s of Roger Henry Charles Human (d 1942), and Rosalind Mary, *née* Gepp (d 1991); *b* 5 October 1937; *Educ* Repton, Clare Coll Cambridge (BA); *m* 4 Nov 1961, Alison Phyllida, da of Dr Oliver Frederick Thompson; 1 s (Charles Robin Graham b 21 June 1963), 1 da (Joanna Alison b 7 April 1965); *Career* admitted slr 1965; Linklaters & Paines 1962–95: ptnr 1969–95, conslt 1995–98; memb City of London Solicitors Co; Bd of Crown Agents 1986–92; govr Brentwood Sch 1997–2006, tstee Firstsite Art Gallery Colchester 1997–2004; *Recreations* golf, shooting, painting; *Clubs* MCC, Hawks' (Cambridge); *Style*— Robin Human, Esq; ✉ Perrymans, Boxted, Colchester, Essex CO4 5SL (tel 01206 272297, fax 01206 271344)

HUMBLE, James Kenneth; OBE (1996); s of Joseph Humble (d 1993), and Alice, *née* Rhodes (d 1992); *b* 8 May 1936; *m* 1962, Freda, da of George Frederick Holden, OBE (d 1964); 3 da (Josephine Clare b 1964, Rebecca Jane b 1965, Sarah Louise b 1966); *Career* Nat Serv RN 1954–56; Weights and Measures Oldham 1956–62, asst supt metrology Nigeria 1962–66, chief dep trading standards offr Croydon 1966–73, asst dir of consumer affrs Office of Fair Trading 1973–78, dir of Metrication Bd 1978–80, chief exec Local Authorities Co-ordinating Body on Food and Trading Standards (LACOTS) 1980–98; dir Nat Metrological Co-ordinating Unit 1980–88; vice-pres Inst of Trading Standards 1998–, dir National Consumer Cncl 1998–2002, non-exec dir Wine Standards Bd 1999–2003, memb Exec Ctee Consumer Congress 1995–99; memb: Methven Ctee 1976, Eden Ctee 1987, Forum of Euro Food Law Enforcement Practitioners (FLEP) 1990–98, Western Euro Legal Metrologists Cooperative (WELMEC) 1989–98, Euro Product Safety Enforcement Gp (PROSAFE) 1991–98, Cars Ctee 1984–96; chm (various) Euro Ctee of Experts 1976–82; tstee Golden Leaves 2002–, memb Bd Dignity in Dying 2007–; orator TSi Coll of Fells 1999–; sport: capt Oldham RU 1957–59, professional rugby league Leigh RFC 1959–65; chm Addiscombe and Shirley Round Table 1980–81; *Recreations* golf, bridge, opera; *Style*— James K Humble, Esq, OBE; ✉ 153 Upper Selsdon Road, Croydon, Surrey (tel 020 8657 6170)

HUMBLE, Jovanka (Joan); JP, MP; *b* 3 March 1951; *Career* civil servant 1972–77, cncllr (Lab) Lancashire CC 1985–97, MP (Lab) Blackpool N and Fleetwood 1997–; memb: Lab Pty, Co-op Pty, Christian Socialist Movement, TGWU; *Style*— Mrs Joan Humble, JP, MP; ✉ House of Commons, London SW1A 0AA

HUME, Gary; *b* 1962, Kent; *Educ* Goldsmiths Coll London; *Career* artist; *Selected Solo Exhibitions* Recent Works (Karsten Schubert Ltd London) 1991, The Dolphin (Karsten

Schubert Ltd London) 1991, Tarpaulins (Galerie Tanja Grunert Cologne) 1991, Recent Paintings (Daniel Weinberg Gallery Santa Monica CA) 1992, Gary Hume (Galerie Tanja Grunert Cologne) 1993, Gary Hume (Matthew Marks Inc New York) 1994, My Aunt and I Agree (Habitat London) 1995, Gary Hume (ICA London and Spacex Gallery Exeter) 1995, Gary Hume (Jay Jopling/White Cube London) 1995, Gary Hume (Galerie Gebauer and Thumm Berlin) 1996, Turner Prize 96 (Tate Gallery London) 1996, São Paulo Biennale (São Paulo Brazil) 1996, Gary Hume (Bonnefantenmuseum Maastricht) 1996, New Work (Dean Edinburgh) 1999, New Work (Whitechapel Art Gallery London) 1999, Gay Hume (UMA Casa de Mundo Lisbon) 2000, Fondació "La Caixa" Barcelona 2000, Matthew Marks Gallery NY 2001, White Cube London 2002, Irish MOMA Dublin 2003, Galleria Massimo De Carlo Milan 2003, The Bird Has A Yellow Beak (Kunsthaus Bregenz) 2004, Carnival (Kestnergesellschaft Hannover) 2004, Carnival (Matthew Marks Gallery NY) 2005, Cave Paintings (White Cube) 2006; *Selected Group Exhibitions* Freeze Part II (Surrey Docks London) 1988, A Painting Show (Karsten Schubert Ltd London) 1990, The British Art Show (McLellan Galleries Glasgow, Leeds City Art Gallery and Hayward Gallery London) 1990, Artists Sketchbooks (Matthew Marks Inc New York) 1991, Broken English (Serpentine Gallery London) 1991, Confrontations (Rena Sofia Madrid) 1991, Act-Up Benefit (Paula Cooper Gallery New York) 1991, 5th Anniversary Show (Karsten Schubert Ltd London) 1992, Etats Spécifiques (Musée des Beaux-Arts Le Havre) 1992, New Voices: New Works (British Council Collection Centre de Conférence Brussels) 1992, Instructions Received By (Gio Marconi Gallery Milan) 1992, New Voices (Musée National d'Histoire Luxembourg) 1993, Wonderful Life (Lisson Gallery London) 1993, Close Up (Time Square New York) 1993, Portraits (Karsten Schubert London) 1993, Beauty is Fluid (PPQ London) 1993, Unbound (Hayward Gallery London) 1993, Wild Walls (Stedelijk Museum Amsterdam) 1995, Hardcore Part II (Factual Nonsense London) 1995, British Art Show 4 (Manchester, Edinburgh, Cardiff) 1995, Brilliant! (Walker Art Center Minneapolis) 1995, From Here (Waddington Galleries and Karsten Schubert Gallery London) 1995, Minky Manky (South London Gallery London and Arnolfini Bristol) 1995, Venice Biennial 1995, A Small Shifting Sphere of Serious Culture (ICA London) 1996, Other Menus Flowers (Aurel Scheibler Cologne) 1996, Young British Artists (Saatchi Collection London) 1997, Truce: Echoes of Art in an Age of Endless Conclusions (Site Santa Fe New Mexico) 1997, Sensation (Royal Acad London and Hamburgher Bahnof Berlin) 1998–99, Summer Exhibition (Royal Acad London) 1998, London Calling (British Sch at Rome) 1998, Distinctive Elements (Mat Museum of Contemporary Art Korea) 1998, Graphic! British Prints Now (Yale Center for British Art New Haven) 1999, Now it's my Turn to Scream (Haines Gall San Francisco) 1999, British Pavilion Venice Biennial (Venice) 1999, Liverpool Biennial of Contemporary Art Liverpool 1999, Ant Noises (Saitchi Gallery London) 2000, Out There (White Cube 2 London) 2000, Painting the Century: 101 Portrait Masterpieces 1900–2000 (Nat Portrait Gallery London) 2000, Seven Print Projects from the The Paragon Press (Gimpel Fils London) 2000, Century City (Tate Modern London) 2001, Heads and Hands (Decatur House Museum Washington) 2001, Remix: Contemporary Art and Pop (Tate Liverpool) 2002, Summer Exhibition (Royal Acad of Arts London) 2002, Independence (South London Gallery) 2003, Art of the Garden (Tate Britain London, Ulster Museum Belfast and Manchester Art Gallery) 2004, The Flower as Image (Louisiana Museum Denmark) 2004, Supernova (Galeria Sztuki Współczesnej Bunkier Sztuki Krakow) 2005, Summer Exhibition (Royal Acad of Arts) 2005; *Awards* Turner Prize nominee 1996, winner Jerwood Painting Prize 1997; *Style—* Gary Hume, Esq

HUME, James Douglas Howden; CBE (1983); s of James Howden Hume (d 1981), and Kathleen Douglas, *née* Macfarlane (d 1973); *b* 4 May 1928; *Educ* Loretto, Royal Tech Coll, Univ of Glasgow (BSc), Univ of Strathclyde (LLD); *m* 1950, June Katharine (d 2004), da of Sir Frank Spencer Spriggs, KBE (d 1969); 1 s (Duncan), 2 da (Evelyn (d 1989), Clare); *Career* chm: Howden Group 1987 (dir 1957, md 1963, dep chm and md 1973), Drimard 1988–98; non-exec dir Magnum Power plc 1992–98 (chm 1993–96); FIMechE; *Recreations* sailing; *Clubs* Royal Northern and Clyde Yacht; *Style—* J D H Hume, CBE; ✉ Drimard, 22 East Lennox Drive, Helensburgh, Dunbartonshire G84 9JD (tel 01436 75132)

HUME, Dr Robert; *b* 6 January 1928; *Educ* Ayr Acad, Bellahouston Acad, Univ of Glasgow (MB ChB, MD, DSc); *m* 1 June 1959, Kathleen Ann Ogilvie; 2 s (Robert, David), 1 da (Morag); *Career* Nat Serv Intelligence Corps, cmmnd Gordon Highlanders India and Germany 1946–48; Univ of Glasgow: Hutcheson res scholar 1955–56, Hall fellowship 1956–59, hon clinical lectr 1965, hon sub dean Faculty of Med 1988; conslt physician Southern Gen Hosp Glasgow 1965–93, ret 1993; memb Bd Health Care International 1995–; author of numerous pubns on haematological and vascular disorders; memb BMA 1954, memb Scot Soc for Experimental Med 1955–, memb Br Soc for Haematology 1960, memb Res Support Gp Gtr Glasgow Health Bd 1978–90, memb Intercollegiate Standing Ctee on Nuclear Med UK 1980–83, memb Scot Cncl BMA 1980–83, chm Sub-Ctee in Med Gtr Glasgow Health Bd 1985–90, memb Bd of Dirs HCI (Scotland) Clydebank 1995–2003; RCPS: hon registrar for examinations 1971–83, visitor and pres elect 1988, pres 1990–92; chm: Conf of Scot Royal Colls and Faculties 1991–92, Jt Ctee on Higher Med Trg of Royal Colls of UK 1990–93; memb Scot Soc of Physicians 1965, FRCPS 1968, FRCPE 1969, hon memb Assoc of Physicians of GB and Ireland 1971, Hon FACP 1991, Hon RACP 1991, memb Acad of Med of Malaysia 1991, Hon FCM (SA), Hon FRCPS (Canada), FRCPath, FRCSEd 1992, FRCPI 1993; *Recreations* hill walking, reading, opera, TV; *Clubs* Royal Scottish Automobile, Glasgow Antiques and Fine Arts Soc, Royal Philospophical Soc of Glasgow, Nat Tst for Scotland, Buchanan Castle Golf; *Style—* Dr Robert Hume; ✉ 6 Rubislaw Drive, Bearsden, Glasgow G61 1PR (tel 0141 586 5249)

HUMFREY, HE Charles Thomas William; CMG (1999); s of Brian Humfrey (d 1977), of St James, Barbados, and Marjorie Humfrey (d 2006); *b* 1 December 1947; *Educ* The Lodge Sch Barbados, St Edmund Hall Oxford (BA); *m* 1971, Enid, *née* Thomas; 2 s (James b 2 May 1975, Nicholas b 15 May 1983), 1 da (Susannah b 7 July 1977); *Career* HM Dip Serv: joined FCO 1969, Br Embassy Tokyo 1971–76, SE Asian Dept FCO 1976–79, private sec to Min of State FCO 1979–81, UK Mission NY 1981–85, Southern African Dept FCO 1985–87, cnsllr Ankara 1988–90, cnsllr (economic) Tokyo 1990–94, head African Dept (Southern) FCO 1994–95, min Tokyo 1995–99, ambass to Repub of Korea 2000–03, ambass to Repub of Indonesia 2004–; *Style—* HE Mr Charles Humfrey, CMG; ✉ c/o Foreign & Commonwealth Office (Jakarta), King Charles Street, London SW1A 2AH

HUMM, Roger Frederick; s of Leonard Edward Humm, MBE (d 1964), and Gladys, *née* Prevotat (d 1986); *b* 7 March 1937; *Educ* Hampton Sch, Univ of Sheffield (BA); *m* 1966 (m dis), Marion Frances, *née* Czechman; *Career* md Ford Motor Co Ltd 1986–90 (dir 1980–90); dir: Ford Motor Credit Co Ltd 1980–90, Imperial Hospitals Ltd 1991–2001; vice-chm and chief exec Alexanders Holdings plc 1992–2000 (non-exec dir 2000–02), dir Andrew Macdonald (London) Ltd 2002–, Mount Securities Ltd 2005, St James and Country Estates Ltd 2005; Freeman City of London 1986, Liveryman Worshipful Co of Carmen; FIMI, FInstD, FRSA; *Recreations* golf, scuba diving, writing; *Clubs* RAC, Variety Club of GB, Lord's Taverners; *Style—* Roger F Humm, Esq; ✉ c/o The Clock House, Kelvedon, Essex CO5 9DG

HUMPHERY-SMITH, Cecil Raymond Julian; OBE (2004); s of Frederick Humphery-Smith, MBE (d 1979), and Violet Agnes, *née* Boxall (d 1990); *b* 29 October 1928; *Educ* St John's Hurstpierpoint, Univ of London Sch of Hygiene and Tropical Med, Parma, Univ of Kent; *m* 1951, Alice Elizabeth Gwendoline, da of late Charles Thomas Cogle; 1 s, 5 da; *Career* mangr Consumer Servs Dept H J Heinz Co 1955–60, conslt De Rica Spa 1961–74, md Achievements Ltd 1961–81 (chm 1981–91); fndr, princ and tstee Inst of Heraldic and Genealogical Studies 1961– (chm of Ct 1961–77 and 1990–97); dir Tabard Press 1959–94; ed Family History 1962–; co-fndr Fedn Family History Societies 1974; exec prodr Prospero Films 2003–; lectr in extra mural studies Univs of: London 1951–96, Kent 1951–96, Oxford 1960–65; visiting prof Univs of: Minho 1970–72, Bologna 1996; memb Governing Cncl Rutherford Coll 1992–2001; sec gen: XIII Int Congress of Genealogy and Heraldry 1976, VIII Colloquium Internationale d'Héraldique 1993, Bureau Permanent des Congrès Internationaux des Sciences Généalogique et Héraldiques 1976–; memb Cncl Heraldry Soc 1953– (vice-pres 1993–); pres Int Fedn Schs of Family History Studies 2001; vice-pres: Cambridge Univ Heraldic and Genealogical Soc 1954–, Assoc of Genealogists and Record Agents 1994–; UNESCO, ISSC, corr Int Archives Cncl; Arvid Bergman lauriat 1961, d'Altenstein Prize 1961, academician l'Académie Internationale d'Héraldique 1976 (memb Cncl 1986–), Julian Bickersteth Meml Medal 1986, Prix Delenda 1995, Gustaf von Numers Prize 1996; Freeman City of London 1967, Liveryman Worshipful Cos of Broderers and Scriveners (hon historian); fell Heraldry Soc, FSA; Knight of Obedience SMOM, co-fndr OMV; *Publications* books incl: The Colour of Heraldry (jtly), General Armory Two, Heraldry in Canterbury Cathedral, Chronicles of Thomas Chough, Anglo-Norman Armory (2 vols), An Atlas and Index of Parish Registers, Introducing Family History (1957), Sonnets of Life, Hugh Revel, Master of the Hospital, 1258–1277; author of several film scripts, books, numerous articles and lectures on subjects auxiliary to history, heraldry and family history; *Recreations* designing coats of arms, writing sonnets, walking, enjoying the company of grandchildren and great-grandchildren; *Clubs* Athenaeum; *Style—* Cecil Humphery-Smith, Esq, OBE, FSA; ✉ Saint Michael's, Allan Road, Seasalter, Kent CT5 4AH (tel 01227 275791, fax 01227 765617, e-mail principal@ihgs.ac.uk)

HUMPHREY, Anthony Robert; s of Idwal Robert Humphrey, of Suffolk, and Mary Agnes, *née* Richards; *b* 12 January 1951; *Educ* Douai Sch, Univ of Durham (BA); *m* Sarah Jane, *née* Martin; 3 s; *Career* ptnr (specialising in fin and corp law) Allen & Overy 1981– (joined 1973); memb: Law Soc, Int Bar Assoc; *Recreations* point-to-point riding, hunting, tennis, skiing; *Clubs* RAC; *Style—* Anthony Humphrey, Esq; ✉ Allen & Overy, One New Change, London EC4M 9QQ (tel 020 7330 3000, fax 020 7330 9999, e-mail anthony.humphrey@allenovery.com)

HUMPHREY, (Ann Margaret) Emma; da of Rev Roger Douglas St John Smith (d 2002), of Prestatyn, Clwyd, and Frances Mary, *née* Calderbank; *b* 21 June 1948; *Educ* St Elphin's C of E Public Sch for Girls, Derby and Dist Coll of Technol, Univ of London (BSc (external)); *Career* postgrad research and staff appt Royal Instn of GB 1969–72, exhbn work Nat Museum of Wales Cardiff 1972, PR offr Science Museum London (incl regnl outstations) 1973–83, museum mangr Helmshore Textile Museums 1983–85, press sec Westminster Abbey 1986–98, mangr Derby Cards for Good Causes 2003–05, press offr Derby Cathedral 2005; conslt to TV progs: Westminster Abbey: a video history and guide (BBC Enterprises) 1988, Songs of Praise with Bells and Bellringers (BBC) 1992; co-prodr The Abbey - with Alan Bennett (BBC) 1995; memb Cncl Friends of Nat Railway Museum 1977–80, asst sec Friends of Derby Cathedral 2003–06; memb LTB Guides Cncl 1995–98; hon memb: Central Cncl of Church Bellringers 1991–97, Guild of Registered Tourist Guides; Freedom City of London 1991; FIPR 1999 (MIPR 1977); *Recreations* interior design and decoration, campanology, cooking and entertaining; *Style—* Mrs Emma Humphrey; ✉ 3 Market Square, Tideswell, Buxton, Derbyshire SK17 8LQ (tel 01298 871976)

HUMPHREY, Dr Peter Ronald David; *b* 19 March 1946; *Educ* Merchant Taylors', St John's Coll Oxford (scholar, MA), Univ of Oxford Med Sch (BM BCh, DM); *m*; 2 c; *Career* house physician Radcliffe Infirmary Oxford 1973, house surgn Royal S Hants Hosp Southampton 1973–74, SHO rotation Knowle Hosp, Southampton Gen Hosp, Wessex Neurological Centre and Royal S Hants Hosp Southampton 1974–75, med registrar Southampton Gen Hosp 1975–76, registrar in neurology Wessex Neurological Centre 1977–78; Nat Hosps for Nervous Diseases London: SHO (neurology) 1976–77, cerebral blood flow res registrar 1978–80, locum registrar in neurophysiology 1980, sr registrar 1980–83; sr registrar Bart's 1980–83, hon reader in neurology Univ of Liverpool 1983–, conslt neurologist Walton Centre for Neurology and Neurosurgery (WCNN) Liverpool 1983– (neurology dir 1994–99, res and educn dir WCNN Tst Bd 1999–2005, med dir WCNN Tst Bd 2005–06); pres N of Eng Neurological Assoc 2006 (memb Cncl 1988–91), pres-elect Br Assoc of Stroke Physicians 2006–, memb Cncl Assoc of Br Neurologists 1994– (sec 1995–2001, memb Servs Ctee 1986–93 (sec 1989–94)); membs rep Neurology Standing Ctee RCP 1980–83; memb: RCP Ctee on Neurology 1989–, R&D Ctee Stroke Assoc 1995–99, Stroke Task Force, Stroke Project Gp, Organizing Ctee and Scietific Panel World Congress of Neurology Meeting London 2001; neurological rep S Sefton Ethical Med Ctee 1987–93; participant in numerous clinical trials incl European Carotid Artery Surgery Trial 1983–96; memb Editorial Bd Jl of Neurology, Neurosurgery and Psychiatry 1995–98; hon reader Univ of Liverpool; FRCP 1989; *Publications* numerous pubns on strokes in learned jls; *Recreations* sailing, golf, survival in the NHS!; *Style—* Dr Peter Humphrey; ✉ Walton Centre for Neurology and Neurosurgery, Lower Lane, Liverpool L9 7LJ (tel 0151 529 5717, fax 0151 529 5512)

HUMPHREY, Raymond John; s of Thomas Geoffrey Humphrey, and Mary Irene, *née* Warwick; *b* 4 October 1951; *Educ* St Joseph's GS Blackpool, Blackpool Sch of Technol & Art; *m* 1, 16 Aug 1975 (m dis); 1 s (Liam Jason b 4 Nov 1976); m 2, 26 May 1990, Lynne Roberta, da of Robert Fraser Andrews; 1 da (Charlotte Elizabeth b 30 Oct 1992); *Career* professional photographer; formerly: industrial photographer Winter & Kidson Preston, retinal photographer RPMS, commercial and advertising photographer Gordon Hammonds Photography Co Southampton, dir of own co Picture IT Eastleigh 1982–; FBIPP; *Awards* Kitchenham Trophy (Industrial) 1979–80, Wessex Colour Plaque (Industrial and Commercial) 1980–81, 1982–83 and 1984–86, Master Photographers Industrial Award 1981–82, Master Photographers Pictorial Photography Gold Certificate, 3M Award for Best Use of Colour in Industrial and Commercial Photography 1981, Inst of Incorporated Photographers Industrial and Commercial Photographer of the Year 1981–82, World Cncl of Professional Photographers Gold Certificate 1988, winner Regnl BIPP Competitions 1993 and 1994, Gold and Silver Certs BIPP Nat Awards 1996, Gold Cert BIPP Nat Awards 1997; *Recreations* motorcycling, jogging; *Style—* Raymond Humphrey, Esq; ✉ Picture IT, Foxhills, 36 Ruskin Road, Eastleigh, Hampshire SO50 4JS (tel 023 8064 1237, e-mail ray@pictureit-uk.com, website www.picture-it.com)

HUMPHREY OF DINNET, (James Malcolm) Marcus; CBE (1993), DL (Aberdeenshire 1989); s of Lt Col James McGivern Humphrey, MC (d 1979), and Violet Joan (d 1999), da of Col Sir Malcolm Barclay-Harvey of Dinnet, Govr of S Aust 1939–44 and for many years MP for Kincardine and W Aberdeenshire; *b* 1 May 1938; *Educ* Eton, ChCh Oxford (MA); *m* 15 Oct 1963, Sabrina Margaret, da of Lt Cdr Thomas Edward Pooley, RN (ret); 2 s (Edward b 1965, Simon b 1978), 2 da (Tania b 1966, Natasha b 1972); *Career* chartered surveyor; landowner; chm N of Scotland Bd Eagle Star Group 1971–91; memb: NFU of Scotland HQ Cncl 1968–73, Grampian Regnl Cncl 1974–94 (chm of fin 1974–78); non-exec dir Grampian Healthcare NHS Tst 1993–99; alternate memb UK Delegation Euro Ctee of the Regions 1994–2002; Parly candidate (Cons): N Aberdeen 1966, Kincardine and Deeside By-election 1991; chm of fin Aberdeen CC 1973–75, memb Aberdeenshire Cncl 1995– (ldr Cons Gp 1999–, dep provost 2007–); memb Bd Cairngorms Nat Park Authy 2004–; Grand Master Mason of Scotland 1983–88, memb Queen's Body Guard for Scotland (Royal Co of Archers) 1969–; FRICS; OStJ 1970; *Recreations* fishing, shooting, photography, philately; *Clubs* Royal Northern and Univ (Aberdeen); *Style—* Marcus Humphrey of Dinnet, CBE, DL; ✉ Estate Office, Dinnet, Aboyne AB34 5LL (tel 01339 885341, fax 01339 885319)

HUMPHREYS, Prof Colin John; CBE (2003); s of Arthur William Humphreys (d 1994), of Syston, Leics, and Olive Annie Harton (d 1965); *b* 24 May 1941; *Educ* Luton GS, Imperial Coll London (BSc), Churchill Coll Cambridge (PhD), Jesus Coll Oxford (MA); *m* 30 July 1966, Sarah Jane, da of Henry Matthews, of Cottingham, N Humberside; 2 da (Katherine Jane b 1968, Elizabeth Mary Louise b 1971); *Career* Univ of Oxford: sr research offr 1971–80, sr research fell Jesus Coll 1974–85, lectr in metallurgy and science of materials 1980–85; Henry Bell Wortley prof of materials engrg and head Dept of Materials Science and Engrg Univ of Liverpool 1985–89; Univ of Cambridge: prof of materials science 1990–92, professorial fell Selwyn Coll 1990–, head Dept of Materials Science and Metallurgy 1991–95, Goldsmiths' prof of materials science 1992–; prof of experimental physics Royal Instn of GB 1999–; visiting prof: Arizona State Univ 1979, Univ of Illinois 1982–86; dir Rolls Royce Univ Technol Centre 1994–; hon pres Canadian Coll for Chinese Studies 1996–; chm: Cmmn on Electron Diffraction Int Union of Crystallography 1984–87 (memb Cmmn on Int Tables), Materials Science and Engrg Cmmn SERC 1988–92; pres Inst of Materials, Minerals and Mining 2002–03 (memb Cncl 2002–, chm Managing Bd 2004–05); sr vice-pres Inst of Materials 2000– (memb Cncl 2000–), vice-pres Inst of Metals 1993–96 (memb Cncl 1992–96); memb Cncl: SERC 1988–92, Inst of Metals 1989–92; vice-chm Technol Foresight Ctee on Materials DTI 1994–99, memb Nat Advsy Ctee on Electronic Materials and Devices 1999–; chm Int Advisory Bd Nat Inst for Materials Science Tsukuba Japan 2003–, memb Int Advsy Panel Etisalat Univ UAE 2003–, chm Int Review Panel Dept of Materials The Technion Israel 2004; Inst of Physics fell in the public understanding of physics 1997–99; pres Physics Section BAAS 1998–99; RSA Medal 1963, Reginald Mitchell Medal 1989, Rosenhain Medal and Prize 1989, Templeton Award 1994, Elegant Work Prize Inst of Materials 1996, Kelvin Medal and Prize Inst of Physics 1999, Euro Materials Gold Medal Fedn of Euro Materials Socs 2001, Robert Franklin Mehl Gold Medal Minerals Metals and Materials Soc USA 2003; D K C MacDonald meml lectr Canada 1993, Hume-Rothery meml lectr Oxford 1997, Gladstone lectr London 1999, Hatfield meml lectr Sheffield 2000, Sterling lectr Singapore and Malaysia 2001, John Matthews meml lectr Durban South Africa 2002, Robert Warner lectr London 2002; memb: Ct Univ of Bradford 1990–94, Ct Cranfield Univ 1997–, John Templeton Fndn 1994–, BBC Panel on Engrg and Technol progs 1995–96; tstee Link House 1994–; Freeman City of London 1994, Liveryman Worshipful Co of Goldsmiths 1997, Liveryman Worshipful Co of Armourers and Brasiers 2001 (Freeman 1998, memb Ct of Assts 2004); Hon DSc Univ of Leicester 2001; CEng 1980, FIM 1985, FInstP 1985, memb Academia Europaea 1991, FREng 1996, Selby fell Australian Acad of Science 1997; *Books* High Voltage Electron Microscopy (ed, 1974), Electron Diffraction 1927–77 (ed, 1978), Creation and Evolution (1985, translated into Chinese 1988), Understanding Materials (ed, 2002), The Miracles of Exodus (2003); *Recreations* chronology of biblical events, contemplating gardening; *Style—* Prof Colin Humphreys, CBE, FREng; ✉ 8 Diamond Close, Cambridge CB2 2AU; Department of Materials Science and Metallurgy, University of Cambridge, Pembroke Street, Cambridge CB2 3QZ (tel 01223 334457, fax 01223 334437, e-mail colin.humphreys@msm.cam.ac.uk)

HUMPHREYS, David George; MBE (2004); s of William George Humphreys, and Ann Deirdre, *née* Houston; *Educ* Ballymena Acad, Queen's Univ Belfast (LLB), St Cross Coll Oxford (Rugby blue), Inst of Professional Legal Studies Belfast; *m* June 1998, Jayne, *née* McAllister; 1 da (Katie Jayne b 11 July 2000), 1 s (James David b 4 Nov 2001); *Career* professional rugby player; former clubs: Queen's Univ Belfast 1990–94 (capt 1994), Oxford Univ 1995, London Irish 1995–98; with Dungannon RFC 1998–, winner All Ireland League Winners Medal 2001; Ulster: debut 1992, capt 1998–2000, winners Euro Cup 1999, 86 caps, leading points scorer; Ireland: debut v France 1996, capt v Italy 2002, 56 caps, leading points scorer in Irish history, memb squad World Cup Aust 2003; capt Ireland Schs 1990 (winners Triple Crown); Irish Rugby Writers Player of the Year 1996 and 1999, Texaco Sports Star Award 1999, Queen's Univ Belfast Grad of the Year 1999; slr, memb Law Soc of NI; Hon DUniv Ulster 2003; *Recreations* golf (handicap 8 at Royal Portrush Golf Club), family; *Style—* David Humphreys, Esq, MBE; ✉ IRFU (Ulster Branch), Ravenhill Grounds, 85 Ravenhill Park, Belfast BT6 0DG (tel 028 9064 9141)

HUMPHREYS, Emyr Owen; s of William Humphreys, of Prestatyn, Flints, and Sarah Rosina Humphreys; *b* 15 April 1919; *Educ* UC Aberystwyth, UC Bangor; *m* 1946, Elinor Myfanwy, da of Rev Griffith Jones, of Bontnewydd, Carns; 3 s, 1 da; *Career* author; Somerset Maugham Award 1953, Hawthornden Prize 1959, Welsh Arts Cncl Prize 1972, Soc of Authors Travelling Award 1979, Welsh Arts Cncl Non Fiction Prize 1984, Book of the Year Welsh Arts Cncl 1992 and 1999; Gregynog Arts fell 1974–75; hon prof of English UCNW Bangor; hon fell: Univ of Wales Aberystwyth, UC Swansea; Hon DLitt Univ of Wales; FRSL; *Books* The Little Kingdom (1946), The Voice of a Stranger (1949), A Change of Heart (1951), Hear and Forgive (1952), A Man's Estate (1955), The Italian Wife (1957), Y Tri Llais (1958), A Toy Epic (1958), The Gift (1963), Outside the House of Baal (1965), Natives (1968), Ancestor Worship (1970), National Winner (1971), Flesh and Blood (1974), Landscapes (1976), The Best of Friends (1978), Penguin Modern Poets number 27 (1978), The Kingdom of Brân (1979), The Anchor Tree (1980), Pwyll a Riannon (1980), Miscellany Two (1981), The Taliesin Tradition (1983), Jones (1984), Salt of the Earth (1985), An Absolute Hero (1986), Darn o Dir (1986), Open Secrets (1988), The Triple Net (1988), Bonds of Attachment (1991), Outside Time (1991), Unconditional Surrender (1996), The Gift of a Daughter (1998), Collected Poems (1999), Dal Pen Rheswm (1999), Ghosts and Strangers (2001), Conversations and Reflections (2002), Old People are a Problem (2003), The Shop (2005); *Recreations* rural pursuits; *Style—* Emyr Humphreys, Esq, FRSL; ✉ Llinon, Penyberth, Llanfairpwll, Ynys Môn, Gwynedd LL61 5YT (tel 01248 714540)

HUMPHREYS, Nigel Craven; s of Gordon Stephen Humphreys (d 1985), of Godalming, Surrey, and Joan Olive, *née* Mudditt; *b* 15 March 1938; *Educ* Sherborne, New Coll Oxford (MA); *m* 29 Sept 1962, Jennifer Nan, da of Maj Adrian Hugh Lovegrove, TD (d 1993), of Over Stratton, Somerset; 2 da (Julia Jane Craven (Mrs Michael Parker) b 1964, Annabella Claire Gough (Mrs Andrew Wass) b 1966); *Career* RB 1956–58, cmmnd 1957, seconded to 3 Bn King's African Rifles Kenya; Courtaulds Ltd 1961–65, Andrews & Partners 1965–68, Chaucer Estates Ltd 1968–71, md Mitropa Group Brussels 1971–77; Tyzack & Partners Ltd: conslt 1977, ptnr 1978–84, managing ptnr 1984–95, ptnr Accord Group Tyzack Ltd (after name change) 1995–96; chm: Accord Group Ltd 1995–2000, North and Mid Hants HA 2001–02, Hants and IOW Youth Clubs 2003–; non-exec dir: Hants Ambulance NHS Tst 1996–2000, Sector Public Relations Ltd 1998–2000; memb: Vol Serv Housing Soc 1966–68, Cherwell Housing Tst 1968–71; tstee Chawton House Library 1998–2007; chm of govrs The Old Ride Sch 1989–91; Freeman City of London 1984, Liveryman Worshipful Co of Glovers 1984 (memb Ct of Assts 1990–94); *Recreations* opera, country sports, uninhabited places; *Clubs* Royal Green Jackets; *Style—* Nigel Humphreys, Esq; ✉ Little Westcombe House, Westcombe, Somerset BA4 6ES

HUMPHREYS, Stephen Alan; *b* 12 March 1959; *Educ* Open Univ (BA); *m* 3 Sept 1994, Elizabeth, *née* Goode; *Career* Miny of Justice (formerly Lord Chllr's Dept then Dept for Constitutional Affrs): joined 1978, head Remuneration and Costs Branch Legal Aid Div 1993–99, dep sec of cmmns 1999–2002, sec to Corp Bd 2002–03, chief exec Law Cmmn 2004–; *Recreations* numismatics, photography, theatre, eating out and music; *Clubs* Athenaeum, Middlesex CCC; *Style—* Stephen Humphreys, Esq; ✉ Law Commission, Conquest House, 37–38 John Street, Theobalds Road, London WC1N 2BQ (tel 020 7453 1250, e-mail steve.humphreys@lawcommission.gov.uk)

HUMPHRIES, (John) Barry; AO (1982), CBE (2007); *b* 17 February 1934; *Career* actor and writer; stage characters incl: Dame Edna Everage, Sir Les Patterson, Sandy Stone; Hon DUniv Griffith Aust 1994; *Theatre* incl: Estragon in Waiting for Godot (Melbourne), Fagin in Oliver (Piccadilly and Palladium), Maggie May (Adelphi), Bed-Sitting Room (Comedy Theatre), Long John Silver in Treasure Island (Mermaid), Just A Show (one man show, Australia and Fortune Theatre), Housewife Superstar (Apollo and Globe), A Night with Dame Edna (Piccadilly), An Evening's Intercourse (Drury Lane), Song for Australia (Albert Hall), Back with A Vengeance (Strand, Royal and tour), Edna, The Spectacle (Haymarket), Edna, The Royal Tour (San Francisco) Remember You're Out (Australia/New York), Royal Tour (Broadway and N America tour), numerous one man shows in Aust; *Television* incl: The Bunyip (Channel 7), The Barry Humphries Scandals (BBC), The Dame Edna Experience (LWT), Audience With Dame Edna (LWT), A Profile of Barry Humphries (LWT), Single Voices (BBC), Selling Hitler (Euston Films), Dame Edna's Hollywood (NBC), Dame Edna's Neighbourhood Watch (series of 12, LWT), Dame Edna's Work Experience (BBC), Flashbacks with Barry Humphries, The Talk Show Story, Heroes of Comedy (Thames Television), Biography (ABC News Productions); *Film* incl: Bedazzled, Bliss of Mrs Blossom, The Adventures of Barry McKenzie, Barry McKenzie Holds His Own, Sir Les Saves the World, The Getting of Wisdom; *Awards* SWET Award Best Comedy of the Year (for A Night with Dame Edna) 1979, BAFTA Award nomination Best Arts Programme (for A Profile of Barry Humphries), TV Personality of the Year 1990, Golden Rose of Montreux Award (for A Night with Dame Edna) 1991, JR Ackerley Prize 1994 (for More Please), Bay Area Theatre Critics Outstanding Achievement Award 1998, Tony Award 2000 (nomination 2005), Drama Desk Award 2000, Outer Critics Circle Award 2000, League of American Theatres Award 2001; *Books* incl: Bizarre, The Wonderful World of Barry McKenzie (1970), Dame Edna's Coffee Table Book (1976), Les Patterson's Australia (1979), The Traveller's Tool (1985), My Gorgeous Life: The Autobiography of Dame Edna Everage (1989), More Please (autobiography, 1992), Women in the Background (debut novel, 1995), My Life As Me: A Memoir (2002); *Style—* Barry Humphries, Esq, AO, CBE

HUMPHRIES, Chris; CBE (1998); *b* 31 August 1948; *Educ* Univ of NSW (BA); *m* Hazel Maxwell, *née* Cross; 1 s (Jesse b 28 Jan 1977), 2 da (Samantha b 11 Feb 1987, Katie b 10 April 1989); *Career* media resources offr ILEA 1975–79, prodr Promedia 1979–82; Cncl for Educnl Technol (CET): IT prog mangr 1982–84, asst dir 1984–87; prodn mangr ICL Interactive Learning Services 1987–88, educn business unit mangr Acorn Computers Ltd 1988–91, chief exec Herts TEC 1991–94, dir then chief exec TEC Nat Cncl 1994–98, DG Br Chambers of Commerce 1998–2001, DG City & Guilds of London Inst 2001–; chm: Nat Skills Task Force 1998–2000, UK Skills 2000–; memb: Nat Learning and Skills Cncl 2000–02, Nat Adult Learning Ctee 2000–, Cncl for Excellence in Leadership and Mgmnt 2001–02, Educn Advsy Gp BBC 2002–, Skills Strategy Steering Gp 2002–; memb: Bd NHSU Tst 2003–05, Cncl Gresham Coll 2003–; *Style—* Chris Humphries, Esq, CBE

HUMPHRIES, Prof (Katherine) Jane; *b* 1948; *Educ* Univ of Cambridge (BA), Cornell Univ (MA, PhD); *Career* prof of economic history Univ of Oxford, fell All Souls Coll Oxford; *Publications* Gender and Economics (ed, 1995), The Economics of Equal Opportunities (ed with Jill Rubery, 1995); also other edited collections and many articles in social science history jls; *Style—* Prof Jane Humphries; ✉ All Souls College, Oxford OX1 4AL; Faculty of Modern History, Broad Street, Oxford OX1 3BD

HUMPHRISS, Dr David Bryan; s of Bryan Eric Humphriss, and Jean Beverley Humphriss; *b* 30 March 1962, Liverpool; *Educ* Liverpool Coll (scholar), Univ of Liverpool (BSc, MB ChB); *Career* house offr Royal Liverpool Hosp 1985–86, SHO Fazakerley and Walton Hosps 1986–88, med registrar Merseyside rotation 1988–90, med registrar Freeman Hosp Newcastle upon Tyne 1990–91, res registrar Univ of Newcastle upon Tyne 1991–94, sr registrar Newcastle upon Tyne 1994–96, conslt physician specialising in gen med, diabetes and endocrinology Scarborough Hosp 1996–, hon sr lectr Hull York Med Sch 2005–; immediate care practitioner and motorsport dr 1990–, instructor in major incident mgmnt 2000–; author of numerous papers and abstracts; memb: Diabetes UK 1990–, UK Prospective Diabetes Study Gp 1996–2002, Br Assoc for Immediate Care (BASICS); chm Hosp Arts for NE Yorks 1999–; MRCP 1988, FRCPEd 2006; *Recreations* gardening, reading, cycling, juggling, trying to keep up with the children and the dog; *Style—* Dr David Humphriss; ✉ Scarborough Hospital, Woodlands Drive, Scarborough, North Yorkshire YO12 6QL (tel 01723 368111)

HUMPHRYS, John Desmond; s of Edward George Humphrys, and Winifred May Humphrys (d 1988); *b* 17 August 1943, Cardiff; *Educ* Cardiff HS; *m* 5 Sept 1964 (m dis), Edna Wilding (d 1997); 1 s (Christopher b 30 April 1967), 1 da (Catherine b 21 July 1969); 1 s (with Valerie Sanderson, Owen b 2000); *Career* BBC TV: joined as reporter Liverpool 1966, northern industrial corr 1967, foreign corr USA and SA 1970–80, dip corr 1980–81, presenter 9 O'Clock News 1981–86; presenter: Today Programme (BBC Radio 4) 1987–, On the Record (BBC TV) 1993–2002, BBC TV News, Mastermind; Journalist of the Year House Magazine/Channel 4 2000, Gold Sony Radio Award 2003; *Books* Devil's Advocate (1998), The Great Food Gamble (2001), Lost for Words (2004), Beyond Words (2006); *Recreations* music, walking; *Style—* John Humphrys, Esq; ✉ BBC, News Centre, Wood Lane, London W12 7RJ

HUNGERFORD, John Leonard; s of Leonard Harold Hungerford (d 1979), and Violet Miriam, *née* Bickerstaff (d 2004); *b* 12 October 1944; *Educ* The Glyn Sch Epsom, Gonville & Caius Coll Cambridge, Charing Cross Hosp Med Sch (MA, MB BChir, DO); *m* 16 July 1987, Yvonne Carole, da of Sydney George Rayment (d 1962); 1 da (Miranda b 1988); *Career* Moorfields Eye Hosp: conslt surgn 1983–, dir Oncology Serv; St Bartholomew's Hosp: conslt ophthalmic surgn 1983–, dir Ocular Oncology Serv; author of pubns on ocular cancer; vice-pres Int Soc for Ocular Oncology 2001; FRCS 1978, FRCOphth 1988; *Recreations* travel, gardening, architecture; *Style—* John Hungerford, Esq; ✉ 8 Wimpole Street, London W1G 6LH (tel 020 7935 1565, fax 020 7224 1752)

HUNNIFORD, Gloria; *b* 10 April 1940; *Career* TV and radio personality; started singing at age of 9 in NI (appearing on all 3 TV networks and releasing 4 records), own weekly TV and radio music request show Ontario Canada 1969, worked on own 2 1/2 hour daily radio programme and weekly World Serv programme on Irish music for BBC NI, appeared on TV programmes such as Songs of Praise, Big Band specials and Queen's Jubilee Celebrations culminating in own daily one hour TV programme for Ulster TV, weekly broadcast for Br Forces Broadcasting to Germany 1969–81; host own daily radio show for BBC Radio 2 (first woman to do so) 1982–95, host chat show Sunday Sunday (LWT) 1982–91, host Gloria Live (Monday to Friday, BBC) 1990–93, stand in for Terry Wogan 1991, co-hosted (with Kenny Everett) That's Showbusiness (BBC), family affairs prog (with da Caron Keating, BBC) 1992–, reports for Holiday (BBC) 1993; pres TRIC 1999–2000 (first woman pres); other TV shows hosted: We Love TV (LWT), The Newly Wed Game (LWT), Gloria Plus (Saturday night chat show, UTV), Saturday Night Live (BBC), 6 O'Clock Show (LWT), BBC Pebble Mill Lunchtime Show, Good Fortune (BBC 1) 1994, Sunday Live (YTV) 1995–97, Sunday (LWT) 1995–, 'Time Off' With.... 1997– (BBC), Open House with Gloria Hunniford 1998–2002 (Open House Specials (Five) 2003); guest presenter This Morning (ITV) 2004, presenter and prodr Biography Channel (series of profiles) 2004–05; other TV credits (as singer): ten Royal Variety Performances, Val Doonican Show, Les Dawson Show, Children in Need Appeal, Paul Daniels Magic Show, Paul McKenna Show, Des O'Connor Show, Cannon & Ball Show, Bruce Forsyth's Show,

Noel Edmonds' Saturday Night Live Show, Noel's House Party and Xmas Presents, Freddie Starr Show; *Awards* incl: Variety Club Radio Personality of the Year 1982 and 1992, TV and Radio Indust Club Radio Personality of the Year 1983 and 1992, Panavista Britain's Best Dressed Woman 1985, TV Times TV Personality of the Year 1987, Spectacle Wearer of the Year 1991, Top Radio Personality (voted by readers of Chat magazine) 1991, Neighbour of the Year 1993, Comic Heritage Radio Personality 1997, Lifetime Achievement Award TRIC 2002, Irish World awards 2002; *Books* Gloria (autobiography, 1994), Gloria Hunniford's Family Cookbook (1995), Feel Fabulous Over Fifty (with Yan de Fries, 2000); *Style*— Miss Gloria Hunniford

HUNSDON OF HUNSDON, *see:* Aldenham (and Hunsdon of Hunsdon), Rt Hon Lord

HUNT, Alan Charles; CMG (1990); s of John Henry Hunt (d 1990), of Hounslow, and Nelly Elizabeth Hunt (d 1978); *b* 5 March 1941; *Educ* Latymer Upper Sch, UEA (BA); *m* 6 May 1978, Meredith Margaret, da of Reginald Claydon, of Sydney, Aust; 2 da (Charlotte Louise b 1980, Victoria Clare b 1982); *Career* clerical offr Miny of Power 1958; HM Dip Serv 1959–; vice-consul Tehran 1962–63, third sec Jedda 1964–65, floating duties Latin America 1965–67, second later first sec FCO 1970–73; first sec: Panama 1973–76, (commercial) Madrid 1977–81, FCO 1981–83; cnsllr (economic) Oslo 1983–87, head Br Interests Section (later Chargé d'Affaires) Buenos Aires 1987–90, cnsllr FCO 1990–91, consul gen Düsseldorf 1991–95, seconded to RCDS 1995, dir Trade and Investment Promotion FCO 1996–97, high cmmr to Singapore 1997–2001, overseas scholarships funding advsr FCO 2001–03, diplomatic dir Oxford Univ Foreign Serv Prog 2003–; *Recreations* golf, music, theatre, film, reading; *Style*— Alan Hunt, Esq, CMG; ✉ Oxford University Foreign Service Programme, Queen Elizabeth House, Oxford OX1 3TB

HUNT, Alannah Elizabeth; da of Humphrey Cecil Hunt (d 1965), of Curry Rivel, Somerset, and Molly Daphne Albury, *née* Hill (d 1979); *b* 22 March 1949; *Educ* Millfield, Taunton Tech Coll; *Career* selection conslt Webb Whitley Associates Ltd 1975–82, dir Overseas Link Ltd 1982–84; PricewaterhouseCoopers (formerly Price Waterhouse before merger): head of exec search and selection 1984–2002, ptnr 1990–2002; jt head of faculty CIPD Recruitment and Selection Cert 2001–03; author of various articles on recruitment and selection; ind memb Standards Ctee Avon and Somerset Policy Authy 2003–; memb Bd Somerset Coll of Arts and Technol 2002–06, govr Tanton Sch 2003–; FCIPD 1986; *Recreations* opera, theatre, gardening; *Style*— Miss Alannah Hunt; ✉ The Coach House, Cheddon Fitzpaine, Taunton, Somerset TA2 8JU (tel 01823 412824, e-mail alannah@alannah3.wanadoo.co.uk)

HUNT, Dr Anthony Blair (Tony); *b* 21 March 1944; *Educ* Birkenhead Sch, Worcester Coll Oxford (MA, BLitt), Univ of St Andrews (DLitt); *Career* reader in French Univ of St Andrews 1979–90 (temp lectr 1968–72, lectr 1972–79); Univ of Oxford: faculty lectr in medieval French lit 1990–, fell St Peter's Coll 1990–, lectr Worcester Coll 1993–, lectr Pembroke Coll 1995–; visiting prof of medieval studies Westfield Coll London 1986–88, R N Coe distinguished visitor Univ of Warwick 1987; research reader Br Acad 1986–88; dep warden Southgait Hall Univ of St Andrews 1975–79, dep warden John Burnet Hall 1979–80, warden Hamilton Hall 1980–90; advsy ed Arthurian Lit 1981–92, memb Advsy Bd Westfield Medieval Studies, former memb Editorial Bd Rhetorica and Cambridge Studies in Medieval Lit; memb Drama Panel Soc of West End Theatre Lawrence Olivier Awards London 1986–87; foreign memb Norwegian Acad of Sci Letters 1999; FSA 1986, FBA 1999; *Books* Rauf de Linham: Kalender (1983), Chrétien de Troyes: Yvain (Le Chevalier au Lion) (1986), Les Giupartiz des Eschez (1986), Plant Names of Medieval England (1989), Popular Medicine in Thirteenth-Century England: Introduction and Texts (1990), Teaching and Learning Latin in Thirteenth-Century England (1991), The Medieval Surgery (1992), Anglo-Norman Medicine 1 (1994), Le Livre de Catun (1994), Villon's Last Will: Language and Authority in the Testament (1996), Anglo-Norman Medicine 2 (1997), Anglo-Norman Sermons on Joshua (1998), Three Receptaria from Medieval England (2001), Les Paraboles Maistre Alain en Françoys (2005), Les Cantiques Salemon: The Song of Songs in MS Paris BNF fr 14966 (2006), Les Proverbez d'Alain (2007), Miraculous Rhymes: the Writing of Gautier de Coinci (2007); *Recreations* playing the double bass, opera, fell walking; *Style*— Dr Tony Hunt; ✉ St Peter's College, Oxford OX1 2DL (tel 01865 278852, fax 01865 278855, e-mail anthony.hunt@st-peters.ox.ac.uk)

HUNT, Prof Anthony James (Tony); s of James Edward Hunt (d 1976), and Joan Margaret, *née* Cassidy (d 2002); *b* 22 June 1932; *Educ* Salesian Coll Farnborough, Westminster Tech Coll; *m* 1, 1957 (m dis 1972), Patricia, *née* Daniels; 1 s (Julian b 12 Sept 1959), 1 da (Polly Leah b 27 July 1961); m 2, 1975 (m dis 1982), Patricia, *née* Daniels; m 3, 1985 (m dis 2007), Diana Joyce, *née* Collett; *Career* articled pupil Worshipful Co of Founders 1948–51, engr F J Samuely & Ptnrs 1951–59, engr Morton Lupton Architects 1960–62; Anthony Hunt Associates conslt engrs: fndr 1962, chm 1988–2002, conslt 2002–; chm YRM plc 1993–94; Graham Willis visiting prof Sch of Architecture Sheffield 1993–, Graham prof of architecture Univ of Pensylvania 2002, visiting prof Sch of Architecture Chinese Univ of Hong Kong 2004–, visiting prof Instituto Superior Téchnico (IST) Lisbon; projects incl: Hilton Hotel Heathrow, Waterloo Int Station, The Law Faculty Cambridge, West India Quay Bridge; recent projects incl: New HQ for Lloyds Register of Shipping, National Botanic Garden of Wales, Blackfriars Station for Thameslink, The Eden Project Cornwall, Barajas Airport Madrid; subject of a book by Angus MacDonald: Anthony Hunt - The Engineer's Contribution to Contemporary Architecture; Gold medal IStructE 1995; Hon DLitt Univ of Sheffield 1999, Hon DEng Univ of Leeds 2003; CEng, Hon FRIBA 1989, FIStructE, FRSA; *Awards* for: The Reliance Controls Factory Swindon, Willis Faber HQ Ipswich, Sainsbury Centre for the Visual Arts Norwich, Inmos Micro-electronics Factory Newport, Schlumberger Research Facility Cambridge, Don Valley Athletics Stadium Sheffield, Museum of Scotland, Nat Botanic Garden of Wales, Lloyds Register of Shipping, J C Decaux, Eden Project, Barajas Airport; *Books* Tony Hunt's Structures Notebook, Tony Hunt's Sketchbook and Second Sketchbook; *Recreations* music, sailing, food, wine, painting; *Clubs* Chelsea Arts, Oriental; *Style*— Prof Tony Hunt; ✉ The Studio, Box, Stroud GL6 9HD (tel 01453 834998, e-mail tony@huntprojects.co.uk)

HUNT, Bernard Andrew Paul; s of Sir Joseph (Anthony) Hunt (d 1982), and Hilde, *née* Pollitzer; *b* 24 March 1944; *Educ* Oundle, Magdalene Coll Cambridge (MA); *m* 1973, Florence, da of Alan White, of W Sussex; 1 da (Susanna b 1975), 1 s (Andrew b 1977); *Career* architect; ptnr Hunt Thompson Assocs 1969–98, md HTA Architects Ltd 1999–2003, chm HTA Architects Ltd 2004–; dir NHBC 1995–2001; chm: Housing Gp RIBA 1995–99, 2000 Homes 1997–2001, Architects in Housing 1999–2001, NHBC Services Ltd 1999–2001, Design for Homes 2001–; Coll of Estate Mgmnt Property Award 2001; hon memb Charter Soc; FRSA, RIBA 1969; *Recreations* cinema, theatre, reading, skiing, swimming, scuba diving; *Clubs* Reform, Architecture; *Style*— Bernard Hunt, Esq; ✉ 34 Fitzroy Road, London NW1; 79 Parkway, London NW1 (tel 020 7485 8555, fax 020 7485 1232, e-mail bh@hta-arch.co.uk)

HUNT, Dr Bernard Peter; s of William Branson Hunt, of Lincoln, and Ivy, *née* Hammond; *b* 30 July 1948; *Educ* Southend HS for Boys, St Catharine's Coll Cambridge (MA, MB); *m* 30 Sept 1972, June Elizabeth (Linda), da of George Syrnicki, of Buxton, Derbys; 2 s (Richard b 1976, Gareth b 1978), 1 da (Elizabeth b 1983); *Career* conslt rheumatologist United Lincolnshire Hospitals NHS Tst 1982–; FRCP 1993 (MRCP 1976); *Style*— Dr Bernard Hunt; ✉ Saddlers Mead, Northlands, Sibsey, Boston, Lincolnshire PE22 0UA (tel 01205 750165, e-mail bernard@saddlersmead.freeserve.co.uk)

HUNT, David Maitland; s of Bernard Wallis Hunt, and Doreen Margeret, *née* Shipp (d 1985); *b* 8 August 1948; *Educ* Radley, Guy's Hosp Med Sch London (MB BS); *m*; 2 s, 2 da; *Career* conslt orthopaedic surgn St Mary's Hosp 1983–; Oppenheimer travel award 1969, St Mary's Hosp short paper prize 1981 and 1982; pres Orthopaedic Section RSM 2001–02; pres Br Soc for Children's Orthopaedic Surgery 2004–; memb: BMA, Hunterian Soc, Br Orthopaedic Res Soc, Br Assoc for Surgery of the Knee, Med Defence Union; FRCS 1978, FRCSEd 1978, fell Br Orthopaedic Assoc; *Publications* Minimal Access Surgery (contrib chapters, ed R Rosin), Minimal Access Orthopaedics (ed), author of papers in various learned jls; *Recreations* fishing, sailing; *Clubs* RSM; *Style*— David M Hunt, Esq; ✉ 106 Harley Street, London W1N 1AF (tel 020 7935 6347, fax 020 7935 2788)

HUNT, David Malcolm; s of Albert Francis Hunt (d 1990), and Winifred Helena, *née* Pearce (d 1992); *b* 22 December 1941; *Educ* Owen's Sch, Univ of Warwick (MSc); *m* 24 Aug 1968 (m dis 1999), Betty, da of Maurice John Gifford Upchurch (d 1992); 3 s ((Jonathan) Mark b 5 Nov 1969, Patrick Simon, Wesley Paul (twins) b 26 March 1975); *Career* articled clerk Baker Sutton & Co 1961–68, auditor Arthur Andersen & Co 1968–70, Baker Sutton & Co 1971–75, ptnr Pannell Kerr Forster 1975–; visiting prof Nottingham Business Sch, dir and tstee Family First Ltd, chm CCAB, pres and tstee CAs Students Soc of London, pres AAT, pres Notts C of C, UK rep Educn Ctee Int Fedn of Accountants, nat treas Ramblers' Assoc, chm The Prince's Tst Notts, memb Cncl ICAEW (past chm Members' Directorate and memb Exec); FCA (ACA 1966), FIPD 1979, FRSA 1992, MAAT 2000; *Publications* On-The-Job Training (1980), Business Briefing: Doctors Accounts (with G Littlewood, 1984); *Recreations* walking, music, theatre, working for charities, watching cricket; *Style*— David Hunt, Esq; ✉ New Garden House, 78 Hatton Garden, London EC1N 8JA (tel 020 7831 7393, fax 020 7405 6736, mobile 077 8538 4846)

HUNT, David Roderic Notley; QC (1987); s of Dr Geoffrey Notley Hunt (d 1982), of Pembury, Kent, and Deborah Katharine Rosamund, *née* Clapham; *b* 22 June 1947; *Educ* Charterhouse, Trinity Coll Cambridge (MA); *m* 27 April 1974, Alison Connell, da of Lt-Col Arthur George Jelf (d 1958); 2 s (Thomas b 8 Feb 1976, Robert b 20 Feb 1979); *Career* called to the Bar Gray's Inn 1969 (bencher 1995); recorder 1991–; *Recreations* sailing, golf, skiing; *Clubs* Bar Yacht, Nevill Golf; *Style*— David Hunt, Esq, QC; ✉ Blackstone Chambers, Blackstone House, Temple, London EC4Y 9BW (tel 020 7583 1770)

HUNT, Dr Donald Frederick; OBE (1993); s of Albert Edward Hunt (d 1964), of Gloucester, and Dorothy, *née* Dixon (d 1959); *b* 26 July 1930; *Educ* King's Sch Gloucester; *m* 24 July 1954, Josephine Ann, da of Jack Benbow (d 1977), of Gloucester; 2 s (Thomas Christopher b 1957, Nicolas William b 1960), 2 da (Jacqueline Ann b 1955, Jane Elizabeth b 1958); *Career* asst organist Gloucester Cathedral 1948–53; dir of music: St John's Torquay 1953–56, Leeds Parish Church 1956–75; conductor: Halifax Choral Soc 1956–88, Leeds Philharmonic Soc 1962–75; chorus dir Leeds Festival 1962–75, Leeds City organist 1972–75, organist and master of the choristers Worcester Cathedral 1975–96; conductor Worcester Festival Choral Soc 1975–97, conductor and artistic dir Worcester Three Choirs Festival 1975–96, fndr dir the Elgar Chorale and Elgar Camerata 1980–, artistic dir Bromsgrove Festival 1981–91; princ Elgar Sch of Music Worcester 1997–; Hon DMus Univ of Leeds 1975; ARCM 1950, FRCO 1951; *Books* S S Wesley - Cathedral Musician (1990), Festival Memories (1996), Elgar and the Three Choirs Festival (1999); *Recreations* literature, travel, sport; *Style*— Dr Donald Hunt, OBE; ✉ 13 Bilford Avenue, Worcester WR3 8PJ (tel 01905 756329, e-mail dhunt2126@aol.com)

HUNT, James; s of Robert and Cynthia Hunt; *b* 19 October 1957; *Educ* Oakham Sch, Leicester Sch of Fine Art (BA); *m* 1985, Bryony Margaret, da of Robin Sellick; 1 da (Holly b 17 April 1986), 2 s (Freddie b 30 Sept 1987, Arthur b 11 June 1989); *Career* with Leicester Mercury 1980–85, journalist News Service Leicester 1985–87, prodr Central TV 1987–89; Granada TV: prodr This Morning 1989–92, ed This Morning 1992–94, exec prodr This Morning 1994–96, head of features Granada TV 1994–96; exec prodr Granada Sky Broadcasting 1996–97; controller: Granada Sky Broadcasting 1997–98, Lifestyle Progs GTV 1998–2001, Daytime and Lifestyle Progs Granada Content 2001–; dir: channel programming GTP 1998–, Moving Image Devpt Agency; memb RTS; *Awards* Team of the Year Award for This Morning RTS 1994, Outstanding Technical Achievement for Granada Sky Broadcasting 1997; *Style*— James Hunt, Esq

HUNT, Jeremy; MP; *b* 1967; *Educ* Charterhouse, Magdalen Coll Oxford; *Career* mgmnt conslt 1988–89, English teacher Japan 1990–91, fndr Profile PR, jt chief exec and co-fndr Hotcourses, fndr Hotcourses Fndn; MP (Cons) Surrey SW 2005–, shadow min for disabled people 2005–07, shadow sec of state for culture, media and sport 2007–; *Style*— Jeremy Hunt, Esq, MP; ✉ House of Commons, London SW1A 0AA (website www.localconservatives.org)

HUNT, John Brian; s of Peter Douglas Hunt, of Croxley Green, Herts, and Cynthia Mary, *née* Weatherilt; *b* 19 April 1951; *Educ* Rickmansworth GS, Harlow Tech Coll, Open Univ (BA); *m* 7 Feb 1986, Christine Elizabeth, da of Ronald Arthur Curl; 1 step s (Dean Keith Halls b 18 Feb 1970), 1 step da (Candice Margaret Halls b 30 Nov 1971); *Career* trainee journalist Doncaster Newspapers 1970–73, Sheffield Morning Telegraph 1973–79, dep chief sub ed Oracle Teletext 1979–84, scriptwriter and dep news ed 1984–89, sr news ed Channel Four News 1989–95, head ITN Resources ITN 1997– (resource mangr 1995–97); memb NUJ Nat Exec 1979, vice-chm NUJ Broadcasting Industrial Cncl 1988–89, chm ITN Jt Shops' Ctee 1989–93, tstee ITN Pension Fund 1989–95; *Recreations* cricket, football, photography, travel; *Clubs* Watford FC, Surrey CCC; *Style*— John Hunt, Esq; ✉ ITN, 200 Gray's Inn Road, London WC1X 8XZ (tel 020 7833 3000, e-mail john.hunt@itn.co.uk)

HUNT, Prof John David; s of Frederick John Hunt, and Doris Eleanor Hunt; *Educ* Wellington Sch, Christ's Coll Cambridge (BA, PhD); *Career* sr scientist Bell Telephone Labs Murray Hill NJ 1963–65, sr scientific offr UKAEA 1965–66; Univ of Oxford: lectr Dept of Metallurgy 1966–90, fell St Edmund Hall 1968–, reader in physical metallurgy 1990–96, prof of materials 1996–; hon prof The Key Solidification Lab of China NW Polytechnical Univ Xian 1996; Mathewson Gold Medal American Inst of Metallurgical Engrs 1967, Rosenhain Medal and Prize Inst of Metals 1981, Bruce Chalmers Medal American Inst of Metallurgical Engrs 1996, Royal Soc Armourers and Brasiers Medal and Prize 2001; FRS 2001; *Recreations* keeping livestock, growing ferns, walking; *Style*— Prof John Hunt; ✉ Department of Materials, University of Oxford, Oxford OX1 3PH (tel 01865 273712, fax 01865 273789, e-mail john.hunt@materials.ox.ac.uk)

HUNT, John Michael Graham; OBE (2000); s of Robert Graham Hunt, and Patricia Hunt (d 1989); *b* 5 February 1942; *Educ* Mill Hill Sch, Guy's Hosp Dental Sch Univ of London (BDS, LDS RCSEng); *m* Jill Mason, *née* Williams; 2 da (Jemma Lucy b 1 Oct 1969, Annabel Jane b 15 Sept 1971), 1 s (Edward Oliver Graham b 12 Aug 1976); *Career* resident dental house surgn Guy's Hosp 1965–66, clinical dental fell Eastman Dental Center Rochester NY (awarded Fulbright travelling scholarship) 1966–67, registrar in conservative dentistry London Hosp Dental Inst 1967–68, pt/t lectr in oral surgery London Hosp and pt/t in practice S London 1968–70, gen dental practice Torquay 1970–80, clinical dental surgn The Prince Philip Dental Hosp Univ of Hong Kong 1980–84, dental reference offr DHSS 1984–88, dental offr Dept of Health (on secondment from Dental Reference Serv to Dental Div) 1988–89, sr dental offr Dental Div Dept of Health 1989, hon lectr Dept of Child Dental Health London Hosp Med Coll 1989; chief exec BDA (former chm and sec Torquay Section, former sec Western Counties Branch, memb Gen Dental Servs Ctee) 1993–2000, dir Smile-on.com 2000–; memb: Cwlth Dental Assoc, Fedn Dental Internationale; Hon FFGDP (UK) 2001; *Recreations* sailing, hill walking, skiing; *Clubs* RSM, RSA; *Style*— John Hunt, Esq, OBE; ✉ Beaston, Broadhampston, Totnes, Devon TQ9 6BX (e-mail johnhunt@beaston.fsbusiness.co.uk)

HUNT, Jonathan Charles Vivian; OBE (1983), TD (1977, 3 clasps 1983, 1990 and 1994), DL (S Yorks 1981); s of Col George Vivian Hunt, OBE, TD (d 1979), and Sylvia Ann, *née* Tyzack (d 1985); *b* 6 March 1943; *Educ* Stowe; *m* 17 July 1971, Susan Aline, eld da of Francis Rawdon Crozier (d 2003); 2 s (James b 14 Sept 1973, Edward 6 June 1976); *Career* TA: cmmnd Queen's Own Yorks Yeo 1963, transferred B (Sherwood Rangers Yeo) Sqdn Royal Yeo (OC 1975–78), cmd Royal Yeo 1979–82, Dep Cdr 49 Inf Bde 1983–87, ADC (TA) to HM The Queen 1984–87, Project Offr Fast Track (TA compact commissioning course) 1987–91, TA Col RMA Sandhurst 1988–91, TA Col Ind Units MOD 1991–92, TA Col (Combat Arms) HQ UKLF 1992–95, Hon Col Sherwood Rangers Yeo 1994–2004; sr ptnr Wake Smith Slrs Sheffield 1988–2006 (ptnr 1967, conslt 2006–); dir Sheffield Training and Enterprise Cncl 1990–2001; chm: Sheffield Enterprise Agency Ltd 1986–2002, S Yorks Community Fndn 2005–, Rotherham Div SSAFA - Forces Help; memb Cncl Sheffield C of C 1999–; High Sheriff S Yorks 2007–08; memb Law Soc 1966; *Recreations* sailing, the countryside, golf, skiing, TA; *Clubs* Aldeburgh Yacht, Lindrick Golf, Aldeburgh Golf, Sheffield; *Style*— Jonathan C V Hunt, Esq, OBE, TD, DL; ✉ Wake Smith, 68 Clarkehouse Road, Sheffield S10 2LJ (tel 0114 266 6660)

HUNT, HE Rt Hon Jonathan Lucas; ONZ (2005); s of Henry Lucas Hunt (d 1967), and Alison Zora, *née* Pees; *b* 2 December 1938, Lower Hutt, NZ; *Educ* Univ of NZ (BA), Univ of Auckland NZ (MA); *Career* diplomat; teacher Kelston Boys HS West Auckland 1961–66, tutor in history Univ of Auckland 1964–66; MP NZ 1966–2005, dep speaker NZ Parl 1974–75, sr oppn whip 1980–84, Govt min 1984–90, sr oppn whip 1990–96, speaker NZ Parl 1999–2005; high cmmr to the UK 2005–; *Recreations* music, piano, opera, literature, art, wine appreciation, cricket; *Clubs* Wellington; *Style*— HE Rt Hon Jonathan Hunt, ONZ; ✉ 5B Park Lane Apartments, 68 Greys Avenue, Auckland 1, New Zealand; New Zealand High Commission, New Zealand House, 80 Haymarket, London SW1Y 4TQ (tel 020 7316 8961, e-mail jonathan.hunt@mfat.govt.nz)

HUNT, Neil Philip; s of Keith Hunt, of Devon, and Doreen Hunt; *b* 2 May 1954, London; *Educ* Univ of Sussex (BA), Goldsmiths Coll London (PGCE), Croydon Coll (CQSW); *Partner* Tracey Hassell; 2 s (Thomas, Oliver (twins) b 17 May 2001); *Career* sometime dir of child protection NSPCC, formerly with Home Office and Dept of Educn and Skills; chief exec Alzheimer's Soc 2003–; *Style*— Neil Hunt, Esq; ✉ Alzheimer's Society, Gordon House, 10 Greencoat Place, London SW1P 1PH (tel 020 7306 0840, fax 020 7306 0808, e-mail nhunt@alzheimers.org.uk)

HUNT, His Hon Judge (David) Peter; *b* 25 April 1951; *Educ* Grangefield GS Stockton, Keble Coll Oxford (MA); *m* 1 June 1984, Cherryl Janet, da of Alexander Hubert Nicholson, of Pinner, Middx; 2 s (James b 1985, Nicholas b 1987); *Career* called to the Bar Gray's Inn 1974; memb Bar Cncl 1981–84, jr NE circuit 1982, recorder 1993–97, circuit judge 1997–, designated family judge Leeds 2000–; memb Family Proceedings Rules Ctee 2001–; *Books* Distribution of Matrimonial Assets on Divorce (1990); *Style*— His Hon Judge Hunt; ✉ Leeds Combined Court, The Courthouse, 1 Oxford Row, Leeds LS1 3BG

HUNT, Peter Roland; MBE (1998); s of Roland George Hunt (d 1974), and Violet Hunt (d 1998); *Educ* Taunton's Sch Southampton; *m* 1955, Mary Elizabeth, da of late Arthur Davis, and late Henrietta Davis; 1 s (Roger Ian b 1958); *Career* successively reporter, feature writer then air reporter Southern Daily Echo Southampton 1944–53; Nat Serv RAF India/UK 1945–48; account exec John Webb Press Services London 1954–55, PR mangr Downtons Ltd Fleet St 1955–58; The Coca-Cola Company: joined Coca-Cola Export Corp London as PR mangr UK and Ireland 1958, subsequently head of PR Coca-Cola Northern Europe, dir of PR Coca-Cola Europe, dir of public affrs Coca-Cola Northwest Europe, exec asst to the Pres and dir of Govt and industry affrs, external affrs advsr Coca-Cola GB 1988–; co-fndr Dolphin Trophy Learn to Swim Awards Scheme (sponsored by Coca-Cola GB) 1963, author of first research paper on sports sponsorship for IPR 1966, recipient Olympic medal (awarded by Pres of Austria for originating the film Olympic Harmony) 1976, memb Ctee of Enquiry into Sports Sponsorship for CCPR (The Howell Report) 1981–83; IPR: chm Int Ctee 1974–77, pres IPR 1978, chm Benevolent Fund Tstees 1992–2002, chm Fellows' Forum Working Pty 1994–97, memb Govt Affrs Gp; BSDA: chm PR Ctee 1987–93, memb Exec Cncl and Bd 1987–95, pres 1988–90, chm Publishing Panel 1993–99, memb Europe Gp until 1995, hon life memb 1996; tstee The Soft Drinks Industry Benevolent Soc 1987–; Union of Euro Soft Drinks Assocs (UNESDA) Brussels: memb Nominations Ctee 1990, vice-chm Communications Ctee 1991–95; fndr and chm Coca-Cola Civil Serv/Industry Prog 1982–; memb: Mgmnt Ctee and Cncl Industry Cncl for Packaging and the Environment 1983–88, Food and Drink Fedn Key Issues Forum 1992–96; Tree Cncl: memb Fin and Gen Purposes Ctee 1990–2002, memb Funding Review Ctee 1992–94; memb: Charing Cross Club 1975–, Caxton Gp (co-fndr 1984); Freeman City of London 2000; fndr memb Guild of PR Practitioners 2001; MCAM (DipCAM), Hon FCIPR (MIPR 1959, FIPR 1977, Hon FIPR 1998); *Recreations* family, home, garden, watercolour painting; *Clubs* Travellers; *Style*— Peter R Hunt, Esq, MBE

HUNT, Simon Hugh d'Aquilar (Sam); s of Prof Hugh Hunt, CBE, of Criccieth, Gwynedd, and Janet Mary, *née* Gordon; *b* 4 January 1948; *Educ* Cranbrook Sch Australia, Abbotsholme Sch, Univ of Manchester (BA, post grad dip); *m* Anne, *née* Please; *Career* asst keeper Salford Museum and Art Gall 1972–73, sr curator Royal Albert Meml Museum Exeter 1975–78 (curator of decorative art 1973–75), curator Bath Museum Serv 1978–83, curator and asst dir of leisure Bath 1983–88, dir Area Museum Cncl for the SW 1988–2000, chief exec SW Museums Cncl 2000–05, assoc and sr conslt Kingshurst Gp 2005–; sec Bath Archaeological Trust 1978–88, tstee Dorset Archaeology and Natural History Soc, tstee Nat Maritime Museum Cornwall, memb SW Ctee Heritage Lottery Fund; FMA; *Books* Bath Camera (1987), West Country Silversmiths (1977); *Recreations* fly fishing, sketching, walking; *Style*— Sam Hunt, Esq; ✉ Longstone, Holford, Somerset TA5 1RZ (tel 01278 741345)

HUNT, Terence William (Terry); s of William Herbert Hunt, (d 1983), and Audrey, *née* Austen; *b* 8 June 1955; *Educ* Royal Liberty GS, UEA (BA); *Career* teacher N Africa 1977–78, graduate trainee Macmillan Publishers 1978–79, copywriter Smith Bundy Partners 1979–83, bd dir DDM Advertising 1986 (creative dir 1983–86), chm Evans Hunt Scott 1990 (founding ptnr 1986), chm EHSrealtime 2000–, chm EHS Brann 2002–; winner: over 50 creative and mktg awards, Most Creative Direct Marketer Campaign Poll 1989, Direct Marketer of the Year 1996, top of Marketing Direct Magazine Power 100 League 2005; memb Ctee: Direct Mktg Assoc (UK), Inst of Direct Mktg; memb Bd World Child Cancer Fndn; FIDM; *Books* Nationwide Book of Literary Quizzes (1979), Scoring Points: How Tesco Wins Customer Loyalty (2002); *Recreations* family, AFC Wimbledon, fishing, running, collecting books; *Clubs* Groucho, Shoreditch House; *Style*— Terry Hunt, Esq; ✉ 11 Granard Road, London SW12 8UJ; EHS Brann, 6 Briset Street, London EC1M 5NR (tel 020 7017 1000, e-mail terry.hunt@ehsbrann.com)

HUNT, Terry; CBE (1996); s of Thomas John Hunt (d 1976), of Taunton, Somerset, and Marie Louise, *née* Potter; *b* 8 August 1943; *Educ* Huish's GS Taunton; *m* 7 Jan 1967, Wendy Graeme, da of Dr Aldwyn Morgan George, MC (d 2000), of Perranwell Cornwall; 1 s (Philip Benjamin (Ben) b 1968), 1 da (Nicola Jane b 1969); *Career* hosp admin: Tone Vale Hosp 1963–65, NE Somerset Hosps 1965–67, Winchester Hosps 1967–69, Lincoln Co Hosp 1969–70; hosp sec Wycombe Gen Hosp 1970–73, dep gp sec Hillingdon Hosps 1973–74, area gen admin Kensington & Chelsea and Westminster AHA (T) 1974–76, dist admin NW Kensington & Chelsea and Westminster 1976–82, dist admin Paddington & N Kensington Health Authy 1982–84; gen mangr NE Thames RHA 1984–91; nat dir NHS Supplies Authy 1991– (chief exec 1996–2000); memb: Cncl of Govrs The London Hosp Med Coll 1985–91, Cncl UCL 1985–91, Steering Gp on Undergraduate Med and Dental Educn and Res 1987–91, Med Ctee Universities Funding Cncl 1989–93, Hosp Ctee of the EEC 1991–93, NHS Central R&D Ctee 1991–96; memb: Twyford & Dist Round Table 1975–84 (chm 1980–81, pres 1988), Ctee Reading Town Regatta 1983– (treas 1984–86, chm 1989), Rotary Club of Reading Maiden Erlegh 2004–; memb Inst of Health Serv Mgmnt; Liveryman Worshipful Co of Barbers 1998; CIMgt; Knight's Cross Order of the Falcon Iceland 2001; *Recreations* clock making, motor cycling; *Style*— Terry Hunt, Esq, CBE; ✉ 36 Old Bath Road, Charvil, Reading, Berkshire RG10 9QR (tel 01189 341062)

HUNT, Sir Tim; kt (2006); s of Richard Hunt (d 1979), and Kit, *née* Rowland (d 1977); *b* 19 February 1943; *Educ* Magdalen Coll Sch Oxford, Clare Coll Cambridge (MA, PhD); *m* Dr Mary Collins; 2 da (Celia Daisy b 27 Nov 1994, Agnes Beatrix b 7 May 1998); *Career* postdoctoral fell Dept of Med Albert Einstein Coll of Med 1968–70; Dept of Biochemistry Univ of Cambridge: joined as research fell 1971, Beit meml fell 1972–75, MRC sr asst in research 1975–76, Royal Soc research fell 1976–81, univ lectr 1981–90; Clare Coll Cambridge: research fell 1967–74, official fell 1975–2002, hon fell 2002–, princ scientist Cancer Research UK Clare Hall Labs South Mimms 1991–; jr proctor Univ of Cambridge 1982–83; summer course instr Marine Biological Lab Woods Hole: in embryology 1977 and 1979, in physiology 1980–83; chair Cncl EMBO 2006–; memb: EMBO Fund Ctee 1990–94, Cncl John Innes Inst 1991–93, BBSRC Cell and Molecular Biology Panel 1995–97, Scientific Advsy Bd IMP Vienna 1995–2001, Cncl Royal Soc 1996–97; tstee Brit Meml Fellowships 2004–; author of numerous articles in learned jls; memb Editorial Bd: Jl of Cell Sci, Molecular Biology of the Cell, Genes to Cells; Nina C Werblow lecture Cornell Univ Med Coll NY 1993; Abraham White Scientific Achievement Award George Washington Univ Dept of Biochemistry and Molecular Biology Washington DC 1993, Nobel Prize in Physiology or Medicine 2001 (jtly with Leland H Hartwell and Dr Sir Paul Nurse, FRS, *qv*); foreign hon memb American Acad of Arts and Sciences 1997, foreign assoc memb US Nat Acad of Sciences 1999, memb Academia Europaea 1999, memb EMBO 1979, FRS 1991, FMedSci 1998; offr Légion d'Honneur (France) 2002; *Style*— Sir Tim Hunt, FRS; ✉ Cancer Research UK, Clare Hall Laboratories, South Mimms, Hertfordshire EN6 3LD (tel 020 7269 3981, fax 020 7269 3804, e-mail tim.hunt@cancer.org.uk)

HUNT, William George; TD (1988, and Clasp 1994); s of Frank Williams Hunt, TD, and Mary Elizabeth Leyland Hunt, JP, *née* Orton; *b* 8 December 1946; *Educ* Liverpool Coll, Univ of Southampton (BA), Constance, Lausanne and Caen (Dip); *m* 26 Sept 1998, Michaela, da of Werner Wedel; 2 s; *Career* mentor Salem Sch 1967–69, audit mangr Arthur Young McClelland Moores 1970–83, fin controller and partnership sec Frere Cholmeley 1983–92, fin dir Hopkins & Wood 1993–95; Portcullis Pursuivant of Arms 1992–99, Windsor Herald of Arms 1999–; registrar Coll of Arms 2007–; clerk HM Cmmn of Lieutenancy for the City of London 1990–; dir Heraldry Soc 1997–2006; Maj and memb Ct of Assts HAC 1988–2000, treas HAC Biographical Dictionary (1537–1914) Tst 1993–; dep clerk City Livery Club 1998–2003 (clerk 1996–98), memb Ct of Common Cncl City of London 2004–; fndr memb Soc of Young Freemen of the City of London (treas 1976–78, chm 1978–79); Freeman City of London, Master Worshipful Co of Makers of Playing Cards 2000–01 (memb Ct of Assts 1996–); FCA; SBStJ 1999; *Books* Guide to the Honourable Artillery Company (1987), Dictionary of British Arms vol I (asst ed, 1992); *Recreations* orders and decorations; *Clubs* City Livery; *Style*— William Hunt, Esq, TD*, Windsor Herald; ✉ College of Arms, Queen Victoria Street, London EC4V 4BT (tel and fax 020 7329 8755)

HUNT-DAVIS, Brig Sir Miles Garth; KCVO (2003, CVO 1998), CBE (1990, MBE 1977); 2 s of Lt-Col Eric Hunt Davis, OBE, ED (d 1977), of Johannesburg, South Africa, and Mary Eleanor Turnbull, *née* Boyce (d 1964); *b* 7 November 1938; *Educ* St Andrew's Coll Grahamstown; *m* 11 Jan 1965, (Anita) Gay, da of Francis James Ridsdale; 1 da (Joanna b 2 June 1968), 2 s (Justin b 11 Sept 1970, Benedict b 15 March 1972); *Career* cmmnd 6 Queen Elizabeth's Own Gurkha Rifles 1962, active serv Borneo and Malaya 1964–66, student Canadian Land Forces Cmd and Staff Coll 1969–70, Brig Maj 48 Gurkha Infantry Brigade 1974–76, Cmdt 7 Duke of Edinburgh's Own Gurkha Rifles 1976–79, Instr Staff Coll Camberley 1982–83; Cdr: Br Gurkhas Nepal 1985–87, Bde of Gurkhas 1987–90 (ret 1991); private sec and treas to HRH The Prince Philip, Duke of Edinburgh 2000– (asst private sec 1991–92, private sec 1993–), Col 7 Duke of Edinburgh's Own Gurkha Rifles 1991–94; chm Gurkha Brigade Assoc 1991–2003; yr bro Trinity House 2004; *Recreations* golf, photography; *Clubs* Army and Navy, Hong Kong Golf, Beefsteak, Pratt's; *Style*— Brig Sir Miles Hunt-Davis, KCVO, CBE; ✉ Nottingham Cottage, Kensington Palace, London W8 4PY

HUNT OF CHESTERTON, Baron (Life Peer UK 2000), of Chesterton in the County of Cambridgeshire; Prof Julian Charles Roland Hunt; CB (1998); s of Roland Charles Colin Hunt, CMG (d 1999), and Pauline, *née* Garnett (d 1989); *b* 5 September 1941; *Educ* Westminster, Trinity Coll Cambridge (BA, PhD); *m* 1965, Marylla, *née* Shephard; 3 c (Jemima, Matilda, Tristram); *Career* res offr Fluid Dynamics Section Central Electricity Res Laboratories 1968–70; Univ of Cambridge: lectr in applied mathematics and engrg 1970–78, reader in fluid mechanics 1978, prof of fluid mechanics 1990–91, hon prof 1992–; chief exec Meteorological Office 1992–97, prof Arizona State Univ 1997–98, sr research fell Trinity Coll Cambridge 1998–99, visiting prof Delft Univ of Technol 1998–, prof of climate modelling UCL 1999–, dir Lighthill Inst for Mathematical Sciences UCL and Univ of London; pt/t lectr in fluid mechanics Lanchester Coll of Technol 1965, visiting lectr Univ of Cape Town 1967, res assoc Dept of Theoretical and Applied Mechanics Cornell Univ 1967, teaching fell Trinity Coll Cambridge 1970 (res fell 1966), visiting prof Dept of Civil Engrg Colorado State Univ 1975, visiting assoc prof Dept of Geosciences N Carolina State Univ 1977–79, visiting scientist CIRES Univ of Colarado Boulder 1980–86, memb UK Atmospheric Dispersion Working Gp 1980, visiting scientist Nat Center for Atmospheric Res Boulder Colorado 1983; asst (later assoc) ed Jl of Fluid Mechanics 1978–99; Inst of Mathematics and its Applications: chm Environmental Mathematics Gp 1978, hon sec and chm Prog Ctee and memb Cncl Fin and Gen Purposes Ctees 1983–, chair Prog Ctee of Int Congress of Industrial and Applied Mathematics 1986–, pres 1993–95; visiting lectr and res advsr Indian Inst of Technol Delhi 1984 and 1986, chm Turbulence Sub-Ctee Euro Mechanics Ctee 1984–92, memb Advsy Panel on Environmental Research Central Electricity Generating Bd 1985–91, visiting scientist Stanford Univ and NASA Ames 1987–90, gen sec Euro Res Community for Flow Turbulence and Combustion 1988 (chm Steering Ctee 1987–88), visiting scientist Japanese Soc for Visiting Scholars 1988; cncllr Cambridge City Cncl 1971–74 (ldr Lab Gp 1972–73); govr Chesterton Secdy Sch 1971–85 (chm 1979–85); chm Cambridge Environmental Research Consultants Ltd 2000– (dir 1986–91); L F Richardson medal Euro Geophysics Soc 2001; Hon Dr: Univ of Salford, Univ of Bath, UEA, Univ of Warwick, Univ of Grenoble, Univ of Uppsala; FRS 1989, Hon FIMA 2003, Hon FICE 2004; *Style*— The Lord Hunt of Chesterton, CB, FRS; ✉ Department of Earth Sciences, University College London, Gower Street, London WC1E 6BT

HUNT OF KINGS HEATH, Baron (Life Peer UK 1997), of Birmingham in the County of West Midlands; Philip Alexander Hunt; OBE; *b* 19 May 1949; *Educ* City of Oxford HS, Univ of Leeds (BA); *m* 1, 1974 (m dis); 1 da; m 2, 1988, Selina Ruth Helen, da of Prof John Stewart, *qv*; 3 s, 1 da; *Career* catering asst Mount Newman W Aust 1971–72, work study offr Oxford RHB 1972–74, hosp admin Nuffield Orthopaedic Centre 1974–75, sec Edgware/Hendon Community Health Cncl 1975–78; National Association of Health

Authorities: asst sec 1978–79, asst dir 1979–84, dir 1984–90; dir National Association of Health Authorities and Trusts 1990–97, chief exec NHS Confedn 1997; Lord in Waiting (Govt whip) 1998–99, Parly under sec of state for health 1999–2003, Parly under sec of state Dept for Work and Pensions 2005–; co-chair Assoc for Public Health 1994–97 (memb Cncl 1992–94), chair Nat Patient Safety Agy 2004–; pres Family Planning Assoc 1997–98; memb: Oxford City Cncl 1973–79, Oxon AHA 1975–77, Bd Volunteer Centre 1979–83, Birmingham City Cncl 1980–82, Home Office Devpt Gp on Voluntary Action 1980–82, Cncl Flouridation Soc 1981–93, Nat Advsy Ctee World Assembly on Ageing 1981–83, Cncl Int Hosp Fedn 1986–91, NHS Exec Advsy Gp on Patient's Charter 1992–93, Working Gp on Induction and Devpt of Chm and Bd Dirs NHS Exec 1993–94, Rail Users' Consultative Ctee (Midlands) 1994, External Advsy Study of Probity in the NHS Audit Cmmn 1994; *Publications* The Authority Member (with W E Hall, 1978), The Quango Debate (contrib), various articles in Health Service pubns (incl regular column in Health Services Jl); *Recreations* City of Birmingham Symphony Orchestra, cycling, swimming, football (Birmingham City), cricket (Warks CCC); *Style*— The Lord Hunt of Kings Heath, OBE; ✉ House of Lords, London SW1A 0PW

HUNT OF TANWORTH, Baron (Life Peer UK 1980), of Stratford-upon-Avon; John Joseph Benedict; GCB (1977, KCB 1973, CB 1968); s of Maj Arthur L Hunt, MC (d 1959), of Hale House, Churt, Surrey, and Daphne Hunt (d 1956); *b* 23 October 1919; *Educ* Downside, Magdalene Coll Cambridge; *m* 1, 1941, Hon Magdalen Mary (d 1971), da of 1 Baron Robinson (d 1952); 2 s (Hon Michael b 1942, Hon Martin b 1962), 1 da (Hon Charlotte (Hon Mrs Gill) b 1947 d 1995); m 2, 1973, Madeleine Frances (d 2007), da of Sir William Hume, CMG, and wid of Sir John Charles, KCB; *Career* RNVR 1940; Dominions Office 1946, attached Office of High Cmmr for UK in Ceylon 1948–50, memb directing staff IDC 1951–52, Office of High Cmmr for UK in Canada 1953–56, private sec to Sec of Cabinet 1956–58, private sec to Perm Sec to Treasy and Head of Civil Serv 1957–58, CRO 1958–60, Cabinet Office 1960–62, HM Treasy 1962, under-sec 1965–67, dep-sec 1968, first Civil Serv cmmr and dep sec CSD 1968–71, HM Treasy 1971, second perm sec Cabinet Office 1972, sec Cabinet 1973–79; chm Banque Nationale de Paris plc 1980–97, dir IBM UK 1980–90, advsy dir Unilever 1980–90; chm: Disaster Emergency Ctee 1981–89, Govt Inquiry into Cable Expansion and Broadcasting Policy 1982, Ditchley Fndn 1983–91, Tablet Publishing Co 1984–96 (dir 1984–99), Prudential Corp 1985–90 (dir 1980–92, dep chm 1982–85), European Policy Forum 1992–98; pres Local Govt Assoc 1997–2001; hon fell Magdalene Coll Cambridge; Hon DCL Univ of Northumbria 2003; Officier Légion d'Honneur (France) 1987–, Kt Cdr with Star Order of Pius IX 1997; *Style*— The Rt Hon the Lord Hunt of Tanworth, GCB; ✉ 8 Wool Road, Wimbledon, London SW20 0HW (tel 020 8947 7640, fax 020 8947 4879, e-mail madjon1919@hotmail.com)

HUNT OF WIRRAL, Baron (Life Peer UK 1997), of Wirral in the County of Merseyside; Rt Hon David James Fletcher Hunt; MBE (1973), PC (1990); s of late Alan Hunt, OBE; *b* 21 May 1942; *Educ* Liverpool Coll, Montpellier Univ, Univ of Bristol, Guildford Coll of Law; *m* 1973, Patricia Margery (Paddy), *née* Orchard; 2 s, 2 da; *Career* slr; Beachcroft Wansbroughs (now Beachcroft LLP): ptnr (also in predecessor firms) 1968–, sr ptnr 1996–2005, chm Financial Servs Div 2005–; chm YC Nat Advsy Ctee 1972–73, vice-chm Nat Union of Cons and Unionist Assocs 1974–76, oppn spokesman on shipping 1977–79, vice-chm Parly Youth Lobby 1978–80, pres Br Youth Cncl 1978–81 (chm 1971–74), chm Cons Gp for Europe 1981–82; MP (Cons): Wirral 1976–83, Wirral W 1983–97 (Parly candidate: Bristol S 1970, Kingswood 1974); PPS to: Trade Sec 1979–81, Def Sec 1981; jr Cons whip 1981–83, a Lord Cmmr of the Treasy (govt whip) 1983–84, vice-chm Cons Party 1983–85, Parly under-sec of state Dept of Energy 1984–87, treas HM Household (dep Govt chief whip) 1987–89, min for Local Govt and Inner Cities 1989–90, sec of state for Wales 1990–93, sec of state for Employment 1993–94, Chancellor of the Duchy of Lancaster (with responsibility for Public Service and Science) 1994–95; pres Tory Reform Gp 1991–97, pres All-Pty Parly Gp on Occupational Safety and Health 1999–; pres CMS UK 2005– (chm 2001–05); dir Slrs Indemnity Mutual Insurance Assoc Ltd 2000–, chm Assoc of Ind Fin Advsrs 2000–03, pres CII 2007– (dep pres 2006–07, chm Professional Standards Bd 2004–06); memb Cncl CBI; govr and chm ESU 2006– (dep chm 1999–2006); tstee Holocaust Educnl Tst 1998–; churchwarden Parish St Mary Magdalene Chewton Mendip 2007–; *Clubs* Hurlingham, Rotary; *Style*— The Rt Hon the Lord Hunt of Wirral, MBE, PC; ✉ Beachcroft LLP, 100 Fetter Lane, London EC4A 1BN (tel 020 7242 1011, fax 020 7894 6158, e-mail lordhunt@beachcroft.co.uk)

HUNTER, Andrew Lorimer; s of Eric Newton Hunter (d 1982), of Gairloch, Scotland, and Elizabeth Mary Anne, *née* Lorimer (d 1996); *b* 27 July 1946; *Educ* George Watson's Coll Edinburgh, Edinburgh Sch of Art; *m* 1, 1970 (m dis 1988), Patricia Thérèse O'Rourke; 1 s (Daniel b 1973), 1 da (Harriet b 1976); m 2, Alison Janet, da of Prof Ian Adair Silver, *qv*; 2 da (Emily b 1991, Freya b 1996), 1 s (Freddie b 1993); *Career* packaging designer trainee William Thyne Ltd 1966–70, dir Forth Studios 1973–79 (designer 1970–73), fndr and jt md Tayburn Design 1979–87; design dir: McIlroy Coates Design Consultants (later Tayburn McIlroy Coates) 1987–96 (md 1990–96), Redpath Design 1996–; maj design projects incl: identity for the new Scottish Parliament, corporate indentity Design Cncl (UK), identity and literature Edinburgh Int Festival, identity for NHS in Scotland; external assessor Scotvec Graphic Design courses 1987–92; chm: Design Business Assoc (Scotland), CSD (Scotland) 1991–2003; memb Advsy Bd Napier Univ Inst of Design Mgmnt; fndr memb Creative Forum, memb D & AD 1980, FCSD 1985 (MCSD 1966), FRSA; *Recreations* skiing, hill walking, fishing, tennis, cycling, travel, gardening, drawing and painting; *Style*— Andrew Hunter, Esq; ✉ Redpath Design Ltd, 5 Gayfield Square, Edinburgh EH3 9NW (tel 0131 556 9115, fax 0131 556 9116, e-mail ahunter@redpath.co.uk)

HUNTER, Dr Anthony Rex (Tony); s of Ranulph Rex Hunter (decd), of Great Chart, Kent, and Nellie Ruby Elsie, *née* Hitchcock; *b* 23 August 1943; *Educ* Felsted, Gonville & Caius Coll Cambridge (MA, PhD); *m* 1, 1969 (m dis 1974), Philippa Charlotte Marrack; m 2, 1992, Jennifer Ann Maureen Price; 2 s (Sean Alexander Brocas Price-Hunter b 17 Dec 1990, James Samuel Alan Hunter b 21 Dec 1996); *Career* research fell Christ's Coll Cambridge 1968–71 and 1973–75; Salk Inst La Jolla California: research assoc 1971–73, asst prof 1975–78, assoc prof 1978–82, prof 1982–; adjunct prof Univ of Calif San Diego 1983– (adjunct assoc prof 1979–83), research prof American Cancer Soc 1992–; memb Editorial Bd: Molecular and Cellular Biology 1982–88 (ed 1989–93), Jl of Virology 1982–98, Molecular Endocrinology 1987–91, Current Biology 1991–2001, Jl of Cell Biology 1997–2003; assoc ed: Cell 1980–, Virology 1982–93, Molecular Biology of the Cell 1996–2004, Molecular Cell 1997–, Proceedings Nat Acad of Sci 1999–, EMBO Jl 1999–; author of over 475 scientific pubns; memb Melbourne Branch Ludwig Inst for Cancer Research Scientific Review Ctee 1983–96, memb Sci Advsy Bd Burnham Inst 1984–; vice-chm Animal Cells and Viruses Gordon Conf 1988; dir Fndn for Advanced Cancer Studies 1989–; memb: Advsy Ctee Frederick Cancer Research Facility 1985–89, Scientific Review Bd Howard Hughes Med Inst 1989–97 and 2003–06, Bd Scientific Counselors Nat Cancer Inst 1996–99, Med Advsy Bd Howard Hughes Med Inst 1999–2002, Vollum Inst 2000–02, Biology Panel AAAS Project 2061, Ciba Novartis Fndn Scientific Advsy Panel; assoc memb European Molecular Biology Orgn 1992; foreign assoc National Acad of Scis (USA) 1998, memb Inst of Med 2004; American Business Fndn for Cancer Research Award 1988, Katharine Berkan Judd Award, Meml Sloan-Kettering Cancer Center 1992, General Motors Cancer Research Fndn Mott Prize 1994, Gairdner Fndn International Award 1994, Biochemical Soc Hopkins Meml Medal 1994, Bristol-Myers Squibb Cancer Grant Award 1997, Feodor Lynen Medal 1999, J Allyn Taylor Int Prize in Med 2000, Keio Med Sci Prize 2001, Sergio Lombroso Award in Cancer Research 2003, Medal of Honour American Cancer Soc 2004, Kirk A Landon American Assoc for Cancer Research Prize 2004, Louisa Gross Horowitz Prize 2004, Wolf Prize in Med 2005, Daniel Nathans Meml Award 2005, Pasarow Award in Cancer Research 2006; memb American Philosophical Soc 2006–; FRS 1987, FRSA 1989, FAAAS 1992; *Recreations* white water rafting, exploring Baja peninsula; *Style*— Dr Tony Hunter, FRS; ✉ Molecular and Cell Biology Laboratory, The Salk Institute,10010 North Torrey Pines Road, La Jolla, California, USA (tel 00 1 858 453 4100, fax 00 1 858 457 4765, e-mail hunter@salk.edu, website pingu.salk.edu/hunter)

HUNTER, Archibald Sinclair (Archie); DL (Renfrewshire, 1995); s of John Lockhart Hunter (d 1986), and Elizabeth Hastings, *née* Sinclair (d 1998); *b* 20 August 1943; *Educ* Queens' Park Sch Glasgow; *m* 6 March 1969, Patricia Ann; 1 da (Claire Patricia b 4 Feb 1973), 2 s (Stephen John b 4 July 1974, Craig Robertson b 25 Oct 1977); *Career* CA Mackie & Clark Glasgow 1966; Thomson McLintock: joined 1966, ptnr 1974, managing ptnr Glasgow Office 1983; KPMG Peat Marwick: managing ptnr 1987, Scottish sr ptnr 1992–99, memb UK Bd 1992–96; memb Bd: Macfarlane Group plc 1998– (chm 2003), Clydeport plc 1999–2003, Edinburgh US Tracker Tst 2003–, Royal Bank of Scotland 2004–, The Beatson Inst for Cancer Res; Convener of Ct Univ of Strathclyde; pres ICAS 1997–98; Hon Dr Univ of Strathclyde Univ 2006; *Recreations* golf, swimming, hill walking; *Clubs* Williamwood Golf (former capt), Western Gailes Golf; *Style*— A S Hunter, Esq; ✉ University of Strathclyde, McCance Building, 16 Richmond Street, Glasgow G1 1XQ

HUNTER, Dr (Charles) Christopher; s of Charles William Hunter (d 1972), of Nottingham, and Dorothy Mary, *née* Ward (d 1997); *b* 2 February 1950; *Educ* High Pavement GS Nottingham, Guy's Hosp Med Sch London (MB BS, MRCS, LRCP, Dip Psychological Med); *Career* Surgn Lt RN 1974–79 (med offr HMS Glamorgan 1974–76); conslt forensic psychiatrist and dep med dir Park Lane Hosp Liverpool 1982–89, conslt forensic psychiatrist and co-ordinator All Wales Forensic Psychiatric Serv 1989–2003, advsr in forensic psychiatry to Welsh Office 1989–2003, conslt forensic psychiatrist and clinical dir S Wales Forensic Psychiatric Serv 1992–2003; clinical teacher in forensic psychiatry Univ of Wales Coll of Med; memb: Nat Advsy Ctee on Mentally Disordered Offenders 1993–96, Mental Health Review Tbnl, Parole Bd; memb BMA, FRCPsych 1994 (MRCPsych 1980); *Recreations* reading, theatre, travel; *Style*— Dr Christopher Hunter

HUNTER, Dr Colin M; OBE (2000); s of Robert S Hunter (d 2002), and Elihzabeth G, *née* Moffat; *b* 28 April 1958, Stirling; *Educ* HS of Stirling, Univ of Aberdeen (MB CB); *m* 9 Sep 2000, Fiona S, *née* McKenzie; 1 da (Joanne b 6 Dec 1981), 1 s (Rory b 5 June 1984); *Career* princ gen medical practitioner Skene Med Gp 1986–; chm RCGP Scot 1996–2000, hon treas RCEP (UK) 2003–; nat coordinator primary care NHS Educn for Scot 1999–2005; Marinker Prize for Innovation in Primary Care 2000; memb: BMA 1981, RCGP Scot 1986; hon fell IHM 1996, FRCPEd 2000; *Recreations* singing, hill walking; *Style*— Dr Colin Hunter, OBE; ✉ 1 Craigstone Gardens, Westhill, Aberdeenshire AB32 6NL; Skene Medical Group, Discovery Drive, Westhill, Aberdeenshire, AB32 6FG (tel 01224 849400, e-mail colin.hunter@skene.grampian.scot.nhs.uk)

H

HUNTER, Ian Gerald Adamson; QC (1980); s of Gerald Oliver Hunter (d 1995), and June, *née* Brown (d 1979); *b* 3 October 1944; *Educ* Reading Sch, Pembroke Coll Cambridge (open scholar, Squire Univ law scholar, Trevelyan scholar, BA, MA, LLB), Harvard Law Sch (Kennedy Meml scholar, LLM); *m* 1, 22 March 1975 (m dis 1999), Maggie, da of Herbert Reed (d 1984); 2 s (James Elyot b 1977, Edward Iain b 1981); m 2, 8 July 2000, Jill van Vliet; *Career* called to the Bar Inner Temple 1967 (bencher 1986); sr counsel New South Wales 1994, avocat au barreau de Paris 1995; Bar Cncl: memb Int Rels Ctee 1982–90, memb Exec Ctee 1985–86; chm Consolidated Regulations and Transfer Ctee Senate of the Inns of Court 1986–87; Union Internationale des Avocats: pres 1989–90, dir of studies 1990–91; pres Anglo-Australian Lawyers Soc 1997–, memb CPR Panel of Distinguished International Mediators 1996–; accredited mediator CEDR 1998, accredited arbitrator 1998; hon memb Canadian Bar Assoc 1990, treas Bar Pro Bono Unit 1995, vice-pres Franco-Br Lawyers Soc 1996, pres Anglo-Australasian Lawyers Soc 1998; *Recreations* be-bop, French cuisine; *Clubs* Boodle's; *Style*— Ian Hunter, Esq, QC; ✉ Essex Court Chambers, 24 Lincoln's Inn Fields, London WC2A 3ED (tel 020 7813 8000, fax 020 7813 8080)

HUNTER, Ian William; s of William Gurnham Hunter, and Anna-Marie, *née* Faliescewska; *b* 17 March 1955; *Educ* Alleyn's Sch Dulwich, Univ of Surrey; *m* 1, 8 Nov 1986, Susan, da of James Edward Morris; m 2, 7 July 2006, Diana, da of Michael Lester; *Career* economist Bank of England 1975–79, fund mangr Swiss Bank Corp 1979–81, sr investment mangr Lazard Bros 1981–87, exec dir Far E div Midland Montagu Asset Mgmnt 1987–92, dir Martin Currie Investment Management 1992–94, dep md Daishin International (Europe) Ltd 1994–98, exec dir LG Securities Ltd 1998–99, dir and head of North Asian sales Nomura International plc 1999–; MSI, ACA; *Recreations* skiing, motor racing; *Clubs* 190, AMOC; *Style*— Ian Hunter, Esq; ✉ Lagness, 31 Keswick Road, London SW15 2JA (e-mail ianwilliamhunter@hotmail.com); Nomura International plc, Nomura House, 1 St Martin's-le-Grand, London EC1A 4NP (tel 020 7959 7310, fax 020 7959 7310)

HUNTER, Prof John Angus Alexander; OBE (1997); s of Dr John Craig Alexander Hunter (d 1992), of Holbeach, Lincs, and Alison Hay Shand, *née* Alexander, MBE (d 1998); *b* 16 June 1939; *Educ* Loretto, Pembroke Coll Cambridge (BA), Univ of Edinburgh (MB ChB, MD); *m* 26 Oct 1968, Ruth Mary, da of Douglas Verdun Farrow (d 1998), of Spalding, Lincs; 2 da (Rebecca Jean Alexander b 13 Sept 1970, Abigail Ruth Alexander b 24 Jan 1972), 1 s (Hamish John Alexander b 2 July 1973); *Career* med posts: Royal Infirmary Edinburgh, Inst of Dermatology London 1967, Univ of Minnesota 1968–69; Grant prof of dermatology Univ of Edinburgh 1981–99 (ret), prof emeritus Univ of Edinburgh 2000–; author dermatological papers in scientific jls; memb Med Appeal Tbnl; memb: BMA, Assoc of Physicians of GB and Ireland, Br Assoc of Dermatologists (pres 1998–99), Scottish Dermatological Soc (pres 1994–96); FRSM, FRCPE 1978; *Books* Common Diseases of the Skin (jtly, 1983), Clinical Dermatology (jtly, 1989, latest edn 2007), Skin Signs in Clinical Medicine (jtly, 1996), Davidson's Principles and Practice of Medicine (jtly, 1999, latest edn 2006); *Recreations* gardening, music, golf; *Clubs* Hon Co of Edinburgh Golfers, Hawks' (Cambridge); *Style*— Prof John Hunter, OBE; ✉ Sandy Lodge, Nisbet Road, Gullane, East Lothian EH31 2BQ (tel 01620 842 220, e-mail jaa.hunter@virgin.net)

HUNTER, John Garvin; CB (2004); s of Garvin Hunter (d 1970), and Martha, *née* McCracken (d 1976); *b* 9 August 1947; *Educ* Merchant Taylors', Queen's Univ Belfast (BA), Cornell Univ (MBA); *m* 20 March 1976, Rosemary Alison, *née* Haire; 2 da (Laurie Helen b 8 July 1979, Fiona Aileen b 14 May 1983), 1 s (Michael Garvin b 18 June 1981); *Career* asst princ N Ireland Office 1970–72, dep princ DHSS 1972–77, Harkness fell Cornell Univ 1977–79; asst sec: DHSS 1982–86 (princ offr 1979–82), Dept of Fin and Personnel 1986–89; dir General International Fund for Ireland 1987–89, under sec DHSS 1989–90, chief exec Health and Personal Social Servs Mgmnt Exec 1990–96, dir of personnel NI Civil Service 1997–99; perm sec Dept for Social Devpt 1999–2003, perm sec Dept for Finance and Personnel 2003–; *Recreations* tennis, camping, hill walking, swimming; *Style*— John Hunter, Esq, CB

HUNTER, Prof Sir Laurence Colvin; kt (1995), CBE (1987); s of late Laurence O Hunter, and late Jessie P, *née* Colvin; *b* 8 August 1934; *Educ* Hillhead HS Glasgow, Univ of Glasgow (MA), UC Oxford (DPhil); *m* 1958, Evelyn Margaret, *née* Green; 3 s (David Stuart b 1962,

Niall Laurence b 1964, Martin Alan b 1967), 1 da (Jennifer Ann b 1973); *Career* asst lectr Univ of Manchester 1958–59; 2 Lt Rifle Bde Nat Serv 1959–61; Walgreen post doctoral fell Univ of Chicago 1961–62; Univ of Glasgow: lectr 1962–66, sr lectr 1966–70, prof of applied economics 1970–2003, vice-princ 1982–86, dir of external relations 1987–92, dir Business Sch 1996–99, emeritus prof and hon sr research fell; treas Royal Soc of Edinburgh 1999–2004; visiting prof: Industry and Labour Relations Sch Cornell Univ 1973, Univ of Melbourne 2002 and 2004; memb: Cncl ACAS 1974–86, Scottish Economic Soc (pres 1993–96); chm Police Negotiating Bd 1986–2000 (dep chm 1979–86), ed Scottish Jl of Political Economy 1966–97; Hon DUniv Paisley 1999; FRSE, FRSA; *Recreations* golf, curling, painting; *Style*— Prof Sir Laurence Hunter, CBE, FRSE; ✉ University of Glasgow School of Business and Management, University of Glasgow, Glasgow G12 8QQ (tel 0141 330 6302, e-mail l.c.hunter@mgt.gla.ac.uk)

HUNTER, Margaret Steele; da of Thomas Hunter (d 2001), of Irvine, Ayrshire, and Norma, *née* Botley (d 1986); *b* 20 January 1948; *Educ* Irvine Royal Acad, James Watt Coll, Glasgow Sch of Art (1981–85), Hochschule der Künste Berlin (1985–87); *m* 1, 1969 (m dis 1982); 1 s (Thomas b 1969), 1 da (Alana b 1970); m 2, Joachim Gross (d 2003); *Career* artist; drawing office tracer/jr draughtswoman Skefko Ball Bearing Co 1964–68, masterclass Edinburgh Coll of Art Summer Sch 1996–2000; patron Edinburgh Sculpture Workshop; *Solo Exhibitions* incl: Rozelle House Gallery Ayr 1986, Berlin-Scotland-Transfer (Galerie IX Atelier) 1988, 369 Gallery Edinburgh 1988, Vanessa Devereux Gallery London 1988, touring exhbn (Maclaurin Gallery Ayr, 369 Gallery, Vanessa Devereux Gallery) 1990, Deutsche Industrie Bank Berlin 1990, touring exhbn Changing Places (Collins Gallery Univ of Strathclyde, Galerie M Berlin, Talbot Rice Gallery Univ of Edinburgh, Kunstverein Weinheim Germany, Vanessa Devereux London, Darlington Art Centre) 1992–93, Scratching the Surface (Rebecca Hossack Gallery) 1994, Portal Gallery Bremen 1995, Signs of Life (Art First London) 1995, Between the Lines (ATP-Expo 2000 Hanover) 1996, Vital Patterns (Art First, London) 1998, Tangents (International Cultural Centre, Cracow, Poland) 1998, Jean Bauscher's Vineyard Germany 1999, 10th Anniversary of the Fall of the Berlin Wall (Pentagon Centre Glasgow) 1999, Elemental Traces (Art First London) 2000, Paintings and Sculptures (Galerie im Gerstenboden, Hof, Germany), Holding Together (Paisley Museums and Art Gallery) 2001, Intercessions (Stathclyde Univ Glasgow, cat) 2001, Natural Adaptations (Art First NY) 2002, Lines of Continuity (Art First London) 2002, Malerei and Grafik (Kronacher Kunstverein eV Kronach Germany) 2003, Intonations (Art First London) 2004, Thinking Through the Body (Galerie der Umweltbundesamt Berlin) 2004, Paintings and Sculptures (Galerie Wichtendahl) 2006, Exerpts (Remise DEGEWO) 2006, Bunch of Person (Art First London) 2006; *Group Exhibitions* incl: Art in Exile (Mackintosh Museum Glasgow Sch of Art) 1987, The Franciscan Monastery Przemysl Poland 1988, jt venture at East Side Gallery painted on remainder of Berlin Wall 1990, Scottish Art Since 1900 (Scottish Nat Gallery of Modern Art and Barbican London) 1989–90, EAST Nat Open Art Expdn Norwich 1991, Festival Fourteen - Scottish Women Artists Exhbn (Dunfermline Museum) 1992, Through Women's Eyes (City Art Centre Edinburgh) 1992–93, Pendant Perdu (Gallery Dr Christiane Muller Berlin), Thursday's Child (Roger Billcliffe Gallery Glasgow) 1994, Paths of the Spirit The Artist as Shaman (Isis Gallery Leigh-on-Sea) 1995, The Continuing Tradition 75 Years of Painting at Glasgow Sch of Art 1920–95 (GSA Glasgow) 1995, Ausländische Kunstlerinnen in Berlin (Rote Rathaus Alexander Platz Berlin) 1997, REPERCUSSIONS - German Identities, Elastic Borders (Axiom Centre for the Arts Int Festival of Music Cheltenham) 1997, Ein Schöner Blick in dieser Zeit (Panzerhalle, Gross Glienicke, Germany) 1997, Great Britain in Brandenburg (Galerie Bauscher, Potsdam, Germany) 1997, Back to Nyk (Goethe Institute, Helsinki and the Gallery of Modern Art, Vaasa, Finland) 1998, Footsteps (initiated and coordinated artists exchange between Berlin Brandenburg and Scotland, Panzerhalle Gross Glienicke, Germany) 1998, 7 dones am Kunstmann (Galeria d'Art Joanna Kunstmann Santanyi, Mallorca) 1998, Restoration of Joint Venture (East Side Gallery on remaining part of the Berlin Wall) 2000, Bodies of Substance (Talbot Rice Gallery Univ of Edinburgh, cat) 2002, Skulptur Pur (Panzerhalle Gross Glinicke Germany) 2002, Between the 3rd and the 5th (Universitaet der Kuenste Berlin) 2002, Blue Hall Marktplatz Europa (Kunsthalle Arnstadt Gernamy), Sektor Panzerhalle (Atelier Panzerhalle Gross Glienicke Germany) 2005, Neue Mitglieder 2005 (BVBK Postdam) 2005, 12 x 12 Gallery Artists (Art First London) 2005, Scots Abroad (Open Eye Gallery Edinburgh) 2006, Thirty by Thirty (MacLaurin Gallery Ayr) 2006; *Public Collections* Scottish Nat Gallery of Modern Art Edinburgh, Graphothek Kunstamt Charlottenburg Berlin, Scottish Arts Cncl, Städtische Kunstsammlung Görlitz Germany, Niederschlesische Sparkasse Görlitz Germany, Univ of Strathclyde, Robert Fleming plc London, Harry and Margery Bosswell Art Collection, Beriner Hypo-Pfandbrief Bank AG Berlin, Chelsea and Westminster Hosp London, Evangelische Gesundbrunnen eV Steinbach Germany, Marienstift Arnstadt Germany, Hengeler Mueller Berlin Germany; *Awards and Residencies* Cargill Travel Scholarship 1985, Scottish Int Educn Tst 1985, Wilforge Fndn 1985, American Express Travel Prize 1985, Artists Bursary Scottish Arts Cncl 1987, prizewinner for painting exhbn Franciscan Monastery Przemysl Poland 1988, scholarship The Karl Hofer Gesellschaft Berlin 1993, artist-in-residence The Swedish Sch of Art Vaasa Finland 1997, artist-in-residence Atelier de Nigorra, Santanyi, Mallorca 1998, winner Arts Category European Woman of Achievement European Union of Women 1998, sculpture residency Lorbottle Hall Northumberland 2001 and 2006, ceramics summer workshop Verein Gebrannte Erde e V Glindow Germany 2002, Kunstbuch-Buchkunst artists and writers collaboration Brigitte-Reimann-Literaturhaus Neubrandenburg; *Style*— Ms Margaret Hunter; ✉ tel 00 49 30 302 7354

HUNTER, Mark; MP; *Career* ldr Stockport Cncl, MP (Lib Dem) Cheadle (by-election) 2005– (Parly candidate (Lib Dem) Stockport 2001); *Style*— Mark Hunter, Esq, MP; ✉ House of Commons, London SW1A 0AA

HUNTER, Prof (J) Martin Hugh; s of Colin Boorer Garrett Hunter (d 1958), of IOW, and Barbara Anne Crawford, *née* Cavendish (d 1962); *b* 23 March 1937; *Educ* Shrewsbury, Pembroke Coll Cambridge (MA), Coll of Law London; *m* 21 Jan 1972, Linda Mary, da of Francis Kenneth Ernest Gamble (d 1971); *Career* admitted slr 1964, ptnr Freshfields 1967–94 (asst slr 1964); called to the Bar Lincoln's Inn 1994, barr in private practice Essex Court Chambers 1994–; prof of int dispute resolution Nottingham Law Sch 1995–; hon dean of postgraduate studies Asser Inst The Hague 1991–, hon visiting fell Faculty of Law Univ of Edinburgh 1992–; visiting prof: Victoria Univ of Wellington NZ 1999, KCL 2004–; visiting lectr: Harvard Law Sch 2000–, Columbia Law Sch 2003, Univ of Cologne Summer Acad 2003–; chm Dubai Int Arbitration Centre 2004–, vice-chm DTI Ctee on Arbitration Law 1990–97; memb Editorial Bd: Arbitration International 1985–1997, American Review of International Arbitration 1989–, International Arbitration Law Review 1998–, Vindebona Jl 1999–; memb: Int Cncl for Commercial Arbitration 1988–, London Court of Int Arbitration 1985–2003, Int C of C Court of Arbitration 1988–90; Freeman: City of London, Worshipful Co of Arbitrators; FCIArb; *Books* Law & Practice of International Commercial Arbitration (with Alan Redfern, 1986, 4 edn 2004), The Freshfields Guide to Arbitration and ADR Clauses in International Contracts (with others, 1991), Arbitration Title, Butterworths Encyclopedia of Forms & Precedents (ed), The Internationalisation of International Arbitration (ed with others, 1995), The English Arbitration Act 1996: Text and Notes (with Toby Landau, 1998), Arbitration Title, Halsbury's Laws of England (ed with Ben Pilling, 2003); *Recreations* motor boat cruising, golf; *Clubs* Royal Cruising, Sunningdale Golf; *Style*— Prof Martin Hunter; ✉ Essex Court Chambers, 24 Lincoln's Inn Fields, London WC2A 3EG (tel 020 7813 8000, fax 020 7813 8080); Nottingham Law School, Belgrave Centre, Chancer Street, Nottingham NG1 5LP (tel 0115 948 6874, fax 0115 948 6989)

HUNTER, Paul Anthony; s of Gordon Nicholson Hunter (d 1985), of Leeds, and Kathleen Margaret, *née* Tyldesley (d 1991); *b* 22 November 1944; *Educ* The Leys Sch Cambridge, Univ of Cambridge (MA, MB BChir), Middx Hosp Med Sch; *m* 10 July 1971, Elizabeth Alex, da of Wing Cdr Jack Granville Pearse, of Harston, Cambs; 1 da (Rebecca b 1975), 1 s (Adam b 1978); *Career* res surgical offr Moorfields Eye Hosp 1976–80, conslt ophthalmic surgn KCH 1982–, hon lectr KCH Med Sch Univ of London 1982–; hon sec Ophthalmological Soc of the UK 1987–88, pres Royal Coll of Ophthalmologists 2000–03 (vice-pres 1996–2000); FRCP 2002, FRCS 1977, FRCOphth 1988; *Books* Atlas of Clinical Ophthalmology (jt ed 1985); *Recreations* gardening, travel, photography; *Style*— Paul Hunter, Esq; ✉ Ophthalmic Department, King's College Hospital, Denmark Hill, London SE5 9RS

HUNTER, Prof Richard Lawrence; s of John Lawrence Hunter, and Ruth Munro Hunter; *b* 30 October 1953; *Educ* Cranbrook Sch Sydney, Univ of Sydney (BA, univ medal), Pembroke Coll Cambridge (PhD); *m*; 1 s (b 22 July 1985), 1 da (b 12 March 1988); *Career* pt/t lectr Univ of Sydney 1975, actg asst prof of classics Univ of Virginia 1979 and 1984, acad dir Univ of Calif Cambridge programme 1982–85; Pembroke Coll Cambridge: fell 1977–2001, dir of studies in classics 1979–99 (coll lectr in classics 1981–87), asst tutor 1985–87, tutor for admissions (arts and social sciences) 1987–93; Univ of Cambridge: actg dir of studies in classics Girton Coll 1982–83, 1986 and 1993–94 (coll lectr in classics 1982–87), univ lectr in classics 1987–97, actg dir of studies New Hall 1996 and 1999, reader in Greek and Latin lit 1997–2001, regius prof of Greek 2001–, fell Trinity Coll 2001–, chm Faculty Bd of Classics 2003–04, chm Sch of Arts and Humanities 2007–; visiting sr fell Cncl of the Humanities and Old Dominion fell in classics Princeton Univ 1991–92, Brittingham visiting scholar Univ of Wisconsin 1998; T B L Webster meml lectr Stanford Univ 1999; jt ed Proceedings of the Cambridge Philological Soc 1985–93, ed Jl of Hellenic Studies 1995–2000, jt ed Cambridge Greek and Latin Classics 1999–; memb: Comitato Scientifico Materali e discussioni per l'analisi dei testi classici 1994–, Advsy Bd Hellenistica Groningana 1997–, Editorial Advsy Ctee and Mgmnt Ctee New Greek Lexicon Project 1998–, Comitato Scientifico Seminari Romani di Cultura Greca 1998–, Editorial Bd Cambridge Classical Studies 2001–; advsr in Greek lit and culture Int Visiting Ctee Centro de Estudos Clássicos Lisbon 1997–2003; pres Classical Assoc Cambridge 1997–2002 (memb Cncl 1992–95, chair Jls Bd 2001–), memb Cncl Soc for the Promotion of Hellenic Studies 1980–82, 1989–91 and 1994–96; jt sec Cambridge Greek Play Ctee 1987–95; memb Ctee Dover Fund 1995–; Hon PhD Univ of Thessaloniki; corresponding memb Acad of Athens, fell Australian Acad of the Humanities, Premio Anassilaos Regio Calabria 2006; *Books* Eubulus: The Fragments (1983), A Study of Daphnis & Chloe (1983), The New Comedy of Greece and Rome (1985), Apollonius of Rhodes: Argonautica III (1989), The 'Argonautica' of Apollonius: literary studies (1993), Jason and the Golden Fleece (The Argonautica) (trans, 1993), Theocritus and the Archaeology of Greek Poetry (1996), Studies in Heliodorus (ed, 1998), Theocritus - A Selection (1999), Theocritus - Encomium of Ptolemy Philadelphus (2003), Tradition and Innovation in Hellenistic Poetry (jtly, 2004), Plato's Symposium (2004), The Hesiodic Catalogue of Women (ed, 2005), The Shadow of Callimachus (2006); author of numerous articles in learned jls; *Recreations* sport, travel; *Style*— Prof Richard Hunter; ✉ Trinity College, Cambridge CB2 1TQ (tel 01223 338400, e-mail rlh10@cam.ac.uk)

HUNTER, Prof Robert; *b* 19 August 1953; *Educ* Univ of Glasgow (BSc, MB ChB, MD); *m* Eleanor Campbell; 1 s, 1 da; *Career* registrar in psychiatry West Scotland Psychiatric Trg Scheme 1982–85, clinical research scientist MRC Brain Metabolism Unit Dept of Pharmacology Univ of Edinburgh 1985–90, conslt psychiatrist Gartnavel Royal Hosp Glasgow 1990– (clinical servs mangr 1992–95), dir R&D NHS Gtr Glasgow and Clyde 1995– (chair R&D Mgmnt Gp 2003–), hon prof of psychiatry Univ of Glasgow 2004–, clinical dir Psychiatric Research Inst of Neuroscience Univ of Glasgow 2007–; research advsr Alzheimer's Scotland - Action on Dementia 1989–99; memb: various ctees RCPsych 1986–88, Working Gp on Mental Illness Clinical Resource and Audit Gp (CRAG) Scottish Office 1992–96, Panel Scot Health Advsy Service (SHAS) 1995–2002, Nat Projects Ctee CRAG 1997–98, Outcomes Measures in Mental Health Working Gp Scottish Exec 1997–2000, Clinical Effectiveness Sub-Gp CRAG 1998–2000, Mental Health Scoping Gp 1999–2000, Coll of Experts NHS R&D Nat Coordinating Centre for Health Technol Assessment 1999–, Scot R&D Dirs Gp 2000–, Examinations Bd RCPsych 2000–, Exec Ctee Nat Assoc of Psychiatric Intensive Care Units 2002–04, NHS R&D Advsy Gp of Chief Scientist Office 2002–, Int Gp for the Devpt and Use of HoNOS (Health of the Nation Outcome Scales) RCPsych 2003–, Scot Ethics Implementation Gp Chief Scientist Office 2006–; chair Scot Mental Health Research Network Steering Gp 1999–2002; second opinion doctor Mental Welfare Cmmn for Scotland 1995–2002, reviewer Cochrane Schizophrenia Gp Univ of Leeds 1996–; non-exec dir Bd of Mgmnt Scot Assoc for Mental Health 2000–06; memb: European Coll of Neuro-Psychopharmacology (ECNP) 1995–, Assoc of European Psychiatrists 2000–, Soc for Int Research on Schizophrenia (SIRS) 2005–, Soc for Biological Psychiatry 2006–; fell Collegium Internationalle Neuropsycho Pharmacologium 1997; FRCPsych 2002 (MRCPsych 1985); *Publications* Report on The Scottish Schizophrenia Outcomes Study (with R Cameron, 2006); author of over 100 scientific papers and contrib to numerous professional jls; *Style*— Prof Robert Hunter; ✉ Gartnavel Royal Hospital, 1055 Great Western Road, Glasgow G12 0XH (tel 0141 211 3600)

HUNTER, Robert John; s of Dr Henry Hunter, and Nora, *née* Sheehy (d 1993); *b* Bunbury, Western Aust; *Educ* Univ of York (BA), UCL (LLM); *m* 28 March 1987, Julie Raven; 2 s (Matthew Henry b 1991, Michael David b 1994); *Career* admitted slr 1984; Allen & Overy: slr 1984–90, ptnr 1990–, currently head Trust, Asset Tracing and Fraud Gp; sec and fndr memb Assoc of Contentious Tst and Probate Specialists (ACTAPS); *Recreations* flying, fishing; *Clubs* Reform; *Style*— Robert Hunter, Esq; ✉ Allen & Overy LLP, One Bishops Square, London E1 6AO (tel 020 3088 0000, fax 020 3088 0088, e-mail robert.hunter@allenovery.com)

HUNTER, Ross Buchanan; s of Ronald James McKinlay Hunter, and Agnes Rose, *née* Musk; *Educ* Dollar Acad, Alva Acad, Mackintosh Sch of Architecture (BArch, DipArch); *Career* designer; fndr Graven Images Ltd 1986; involved in graphic, interior and exhbn design; dir: Girvan Community Developments Ltd 2005–, 3Fold, Farm 7; ARCUK 1987, memb RIAS 1990; *Recreations* motorcycling; *Style*— Ross Hunter, Esq; ✉ Graven Images, 83A Candleriggs, Glasgow G1 1LF (tel 0141 552 6626, fax 0141 552 0433, e-mail ross@graven.co.uk)

HUNTER, Sally Elizabeth; da of Edward Ison Andrews (d 1986), of Woodbridge, Suffolk, and Elizabeth Margaret, *née* Hutchison (d 1992); *b* 20 March 1947; *Educ* Queenswood Sch, Cambridge Coll of Arts and Technol; *m* 1, 1970 (m dis 1978), Ian Hunter; m 2, 1990, Ian Richard Rosgate; *Career* ptnr Wills Lane Gallery St Ives Cornwall 1971–74, with Patrick Seale Gallery London 1978–83, fndr Sally Hunter Fine Art London (specialising in mid 20th Century Br paintings) 1984; *Recreations* theatre; *Style*— Ms Sally Hunter; ✉ Sally Hunter Fine Art, 54 Clarendon Road, London W11 2HJ (tel 07041 535001)

HUNTER, Tom; s of Ian Hunter of Durham, and Sheelagh, *née* Wilson; *b* 30 July 1965; *Educ* London Coll of Printing (BA), RCA (MA); *Career* photographer and artist; exhbns incl Living In Hell (Nat Gall); John Kobal Portrait Award 1997; *Publications* Tom Hunter (2004), Living in Hell (2005); *Style*— Tom Hunter, Esq; ✉ c/o White Cube Gallery, 48

Hoxton Square, London N1 6PB (tel 020 7930 5373, fax 020 7749 7480, e-mail irene@whitecube.com)

HUNTER, Sir Tom; kt (2005); *m* Marion; *Career* md Sports Division until 1998, co-fndr The Hunter Foundation 1998–, fndr West Coast Capital 2001–; former chm Entrepreneurial Exchange, dir Prince's Scottish Business Youth Tst, tstee Carnegie Tst; bequested Hunter Centre for Entrepreneurship Univ of Strathclyde; Hon Dr: Univ of Strathclyde 2001, Univ of Glasgow 2006, Univ of Aberdeen 2006; *Style*— Sir Tom Hunter; ✉ The Hunter Foundation, Marathon House, Olympic Business Park, Drybridge Road, Dundonald, Ayrshire KA2 9AE

HUNTER BLAIR, Sir Edward Thomas; 8 Bt (GB 1786), of Dunskey; s of Sir James Hunter Blair, 7 Bt (d 1985), and Jean Galloway MacIntyre (d 1953); *b* 15 December 1920; *Educ* Eton, Univ of Paris, Balliol Coll Oxford (BA); *m* 21 April 1956, Norma (d 1972), er da of Walter S Harris (d 1983), of Bradford, W Yorks; 1 adopted s (Alan Walter b 1961), 1 adopted da (Helen Cecilia (Mrs Watson) b 1963); *Heir* bro, James Hunter Blair; *Career* served WWII 1939–41 with KOYLI, discharged; temp civil servant Miny of Info 1941–43; journalist London Evening News (asst foreign ed) 1944–49; mangr and dir own co in Yorks 1950–63, landowner and forester SW Scotland 1964–; memb: Kirkcudbright CC 1970–71, Scottish Countryside Activities Cncl, Timber Growers UK SW Scotland Ctee until 1996, Cncl Wyndham's Tst 1992–2001, Ctee Scottish Assoc for Public Tport 1999–; *Books* Scotland Sings, A Story of Me (poems and autobiography, 1981), A Future Time, With An Earlier Life (poems, autobiography and prophecy), A Mission in Life (philosophy, religion, autobiography and poems, 1987), Nearing The Year 2000 (1990), Our Troubled Future (1993), Problems of Today (2002); *Recreations* gardening; *Clubs* Western Meeting (Ayr), Royal Over-Seas League; *Style*— Sir Edward T Hunter Blair, Bt; ✉ Parton House, Castle Douglas, Kirkcudbrightshire DG7 3NB (tel 01644 470234)

HUNTER GORDON, Christopher Neil (Kit); s of Maj Patrick Hunter Gordon, CBE, MC, JP, DL (d 1978), of Beauly, Inverness, and Valerie Margaret Frances, *née* Ziani de Ferranti; *b* 8 June 1958; *Educ* Ampleforth, Trinity Hall Cambridge (MA); *m* 29 Sept 1984, Georgina Mary, da of Capt Owen Varney, of Dedham, Essex; 2 s (Sam William b 5 March 1988, Ivan b 20 Sept 1989), 2 da (Ione Mary b 18 July 1992, Hebe Elizabeth b 9 Aug 1996); *Career* J Rothschild Holdings plc, and Aurit Serv 1983–85, md and co fndr The Summit Group 1985–, dir Comcap plc 1986–89, chief exec Anglo Leasing Holdings 1993–95; *Recreations* painting, architectural design, tennis; *Clubs* Brooks's, White's, Chelsea Arts; *Style*— Kit Hunter Gordon, Esq; ✉ The Summit Group Limited, 3 Broadgate, London EC2M 2QS (tel 020 7614 0000, fax 020 7614 0066)

HUNTER GORDON, Nigel; s of Maj Patrick Hunter Gordon, CBE, MC, JP (d 1978), of Beauly, Inverness-shire, and Valerie Margaret Frances, *née* de Ferranti; *b* 2 September 1947; *Educ* Ampleforth, Univ of St Andrews (MA); *m* 16 April 1977, Linda Anne, da of Brendan Robert Magill, of Eastbourne; 2 s (Kim b 23 March 1981, Bret b 19 March 1983); *Career* trained as CA Coopers & Lybrand 1970–76, James C Pringle & Co CA Inverness 1977–79; Ernst & Young: joined 1979, tax ptnr 1983–92, managing ptnr Highlands & Islands 1992–2000; dir Kinloch Damph Ltd 2001–04, dir Dunrobin Castle Ltd 2002–; Highland Area rep on Tax Practices Ctee, chm Highland Area Tax Ctee 1985–91 (memb Tech Sub Ctee); sec CBI Highland Area Gp, memb CBI Scotland Cncl, memb Chm's Ctee CBI Scotland 1992–98, memb IoD Scottish Ctee 1996–2000; FCA 1975 (ACA 1973), CTA 1979; *Recreations* skiing, gardens; *Style*— Nigel Hunter Gordon, Esq; ✉ Killearnan House, Muir of Ord, Ross-shire IV6 7SQ (tel 01463 870002)

HUNTER-PEASE, Charles E; *b* 1946; *m* 1984, Susan; 1 da (Alison b 1986), 1 s (Henry b 1988); *Career* articled clerk 1964–68, asst accountant in bldg industry 1968–69, branch mangr Autohall 1969–70, operational auditor, agency mangr then dist mangr Avis 1970–72, internal auditor Continental Oil 1972–73; Volvo 1973–: business mgmnt conslt 1973–75, dist planning mangr 1975, dealer representation mangr 1976–78, regnl mangr 1978–83, nat sales mangr 1983, field ops mangr 1984–86, UK bd dir 1986–97, dir of dealer ops 1986, sales and mktg dir 1987–92, dep chief exec 1990–92, chm VOCS Finance Ltd 1991–97, md Volvo Car UK Ltd 1992–96, sr vice-pres Volvo Car Corp Sweden 1993–98, chief exec Volvo Car UK Ltd 1996–98, vice-pres Network Volvo Cars Europe Mktg 1996–98, chm Benelux/UK Region 1996–98, sr advsr Volvo 1999–2006; RNLI: memb Fundraising Ctee 1991–2001, non-exec dir RNLI Sales 1995–2004, memb Cncl 1996–, chm Resources Ctee 1998–, tstee 1998–; *Recreations* sailing, antiques; *Style*— Charles Hunter-Pease, Esq

HUNTING, Richard Hugh; s of Charles Patrick Maule Hunting, CBE (d 1993), and Diana Margaret, *née* Pereira (d 1995); *b* 30 July 1946; *Educ* Rugby, Univ of Sheffield (BEng), Univ of Manchester (MBA); *m* 31 Oct 1970, Penelope Susan, da of Col L L Fleming, MBE, MC; 1 s (Rupert b 1974), 2 da (Joanna b 1976, Chloë b 1979); *Career* Hunting Group 1972–: Hunting Surveys and Consultants, Field Aviation, E A Gibson Shipbrokers, Hunting Oilfield Services, Hunting Engineering, chm Hunting Associated Industries 1989 (dir 1986–89), chm Hunting plc 1991– (dir 1989–), dir Yule Catto & Co plc 2000–; memb Cncl CBI 1992–97; chm: Geffrye Museum 2000– (tstee 1995–), Battle of Britain Meml Tst 2000– (tstee 1998–); tstee CORDA (Coronary Artery Disease Research Assoc) 2001–, cmmr Royal Hosp Chelsea 2002–, non-exec dir Royal Brompton and Harefield NHS Tst 2007–; memb Worshipful Co of Ironmongers (Master 1996–97); *Recreations* skiing, family history, arts; *Clubs* Boodle's, Chelsea Arts, Hurlingham, Travellers; *Style*— Richard Hunting, Esq; ✉ Hunting plc, 3 Cockspur Street, London SW1Y 5BQ (tel 020 7321 0123, fax 020 7839 0672, e-mail richard.hunting@hunting.plc.uk)

HUNTINGDON, Bishop of 2003–; Rt Rev Dr John Inge; s of Geoffrey Inge (d 1959) and Elsie, *née* Hill (d 1968); *b* 26 February 1955, Folkestone, Kent; *Educ* Kent Coll Canterbury, Univ of Durham (BSc, MA, PhD), Keble Coll Oxford (PGCE), Coll of the Resurrection Mirfield; *m* 8 July 1989, Denise, *née* Longenecker; 2 da (Eleanor b 17 Feb 1999, Olivia b 19 May 2004); *Career* ordained: deacon 1984, priest 1985; asst chaplain Lancing Coll 1984–86, sr chaplain Harrow Sch 1989–90 (jr chaplain 1986–89), vicar St Luke's Church Wallsend 1990–96, canon residentiary Ely Cathedral 1996–2003 (vice-dean 1999–2003); tstee Common Purpose 2005–; *Publications* A Christian Theology of Place (2003), Living Love (2007); *Style*— The Rt Rev the Bishop of Huntingdon; ✉ 14 Lynn Road, Ely, Cambridgeshire CB6 1DA (tel 01353 662137, fax 01353 669357, e-mail john.inge@ely.anglican.org)

HUNTINGDON, 16 Earl of (E 1529); William Edward Robin Hood Hastings-Bass; LVO (1999); s of Capt Peter Hastings-Bass (assumed additional name Bass 1954, d 1964), and Priscilla (b 1920, m 1947, dir Newbury Racecourse, memb Jockey Club), da of Capt Sir Malcolm Bullock, 1 Bt, MBE, and Lady Victoria Stanley, da of 17 Earl of Derby; suc kinsman, 15 Earl of Huntingdon 1990; *b* 30 January 1948; *Educ* Winchester, Trinity Coll Cambridge; *m* 1989, Susan Mary Gavin, da of John Jellico Pelham Francis Warner (d 1998), and gda of Sir Pelham Warner, MBE; *Heir* bro, Hon Simon Hastings-Bass; *Style*— The Rt Hon the Earl of Huntingdon, LVO; ✉ Hodcott House, West Ilsley, Newbury, Berkshire RG20 7AU

HUNTINGFIELD, 7 Baron (I 1796); Sir Joshua Charles Vanneck; 9 Bt (GB 1751); s of 6 Baron Huntingfield (d 1994), and Janetta Lois, *née* Errington; *b* 10 August 1954; *Educ* Eton, Magdalene Coll Cambridge (MA); *m* 1982, Arabella Mary, da of Maj Alastair Hugh Joseph Fraser, MC (d 1986), of Moniack Castle, Kirkhill, Inverness; 1 da (Hon Vanessa Clare b 1983), 4 s (Hon Gerard Charles Alastair b 1985, Hon John Errington b 1988, Hon Richard Fraser, Hon David Guise (twins) b 1990); *Heir* s, Hon Gerard Vanneck; *Career* Royal Scots Dragoon Guards; accountant: Deloitte Haskins & Sells Cambridge, NFU Cambridge; *Clubs* Pratt's; *Style*— The Lord Huntingfield

HUNTINGFORD, Richard Norman Legh; *b* 14 May 1956; *Educ* Radley; *m* 10 May 1996, Nicky, *née* Rice; 2 da, 1 s; *Career* with KPMG 1975–87; Chrysalis Gp plc: dir of corp devpt 1987–94, chief exec Radio Div 1994–99, gp ceo 1999–; non-exec dir Virgin Mobile Holdings plc 2005–06; FCA 1979; *Recreations* all sports especially tennis, restaurants; *Clubs* MCC, Queen's; *Style*— Richard Huntingford, Esq; ✉ Chrysalis Group plc, The Chrysalis Building, Bramley Road, London W10 6SP (tel 020 7221 2213, fax 020 7221 6341, e-mail ceos.office@chrysalis.com)

HUNTINGTON-WHITELEY, Sir Hugo Baldwin; 3 Bt (UK 1918), of Grimley, Worcester; DL (Worcs 1972); s of Capt Sir Maurice Huntington-Whiteley, 2 Bt, RN (d 1975), and Lady (Pamela) Margaret (d 1976), 3 da of 1 Earl Baldwin of Bewdley, KG, PC; *b* 31 March 1924; *Educ* Eton; *m* 1959, Jean Marie Ramsay, DStJ, da of late Arthur Francis Ramsay Bock; 2 da (Sophie Elizabeth (Mrs Zdatny) b 1964, Charlotte Anne (Mrs McAuliffe) b 1965); *Heir* bro, Miles Huntington-Whiteley, *qv*; *Career* RN 1942–47; ptnr Price Waterhouse 1963–83; High Sheriff Worcs 1971; memb Ct of Assts Worshipful Co Goldsmiths (Prime Warden 1989–90); FCA; *Recreations* music and travel; *Clubs* Brooks's; *Style*— Sir Hugo Huntington-Whiteley, Bt, DL; ✉ Ripple Hall, Tewkesbury, Gloucestershire GL20 6EY (tel 0168 459 2431)

HUNTINGTON-WHITELEY, (John) Miles; VRD (two clasps); s of Capt Sir Maurice Huntington-Whiteley, 2 Bt, RN (d 1975), and Lady (Pamela) Margaret (d 1976), 3 da of 1 Earl Baldwin of Bewdley, KG, PC; hp of bro, Sir Hugo Huntington-Whiteley, 3 Bt, DL, *qv*; *b* 18 July 1929; *Educ* Eton, Trinity Coll Cambridge; *m* 1960, HIllH Countess Victoria Adelheid Clementine Luise, da of late HIllH Count Friedrich Wolfgang zu Castell-Rüdenhausen (ka 1940) *see* Debrett's Peerage, Royal Family section; 2 da (Alice Louise Esther Margot b 1961, m 1985, Charles Percy Sewell, 3 s of late Maj Geoffrey Richard Michael Sewell by his wife Joan, 3 da of Sir Watkin Williams-Wynn, 8 Bt; Beatrice Irene Helen Victoria b 1962, m 1995, Andrew William Grant, of Bransford Manor, nr Worcester), 1 s (Leopold Maurice b 1965); *Career* Writer RN 1947–49, cmmnd RNVR 1949, recalled for Korean War and served Far East 1951–53, Lt Cdr RNR 1960; int investment portfolio mangr, ret; *Recreations* applied and fine arts, music, the paranormal; *Clubs* Naval; *Style*— Miles Huntington-Whiteley, Esq, VRD; ✉ 6 Matheson Road, London W14 8SW (tel and fax 020 7602 8484)

H

HUNTINGTOWER, Lord John Peter Grant of Rothiemurchus; DL (Inverness-shire 1986); 16 of Rothiemurchus; s of Lt-Col John Grant of Rothiemurchus, MBE (d 1987), and s and h of Countess of Dysart, *qv*; *b* 22 October 1946; *Educ* Gordonstoun; *m* 1971, Philippa, da of John Chance, of Llanvapley Court, Abergavenny; 1 s, 2 da; *Career* dir and chm Scottish Trout Ltd 1989–95; memb: Bd NE River Purification Bd 1990–96, Cairngorms Working Party 1991–92, Tourism Trg Scotland 1993–95, Native Woodlands Advsy Panel to the Forestry Cmmn 1993–96, Aviemore Partnership 1994–98, Cairngorm Partnership 1995–2003; dir Aviemore, Badenoch and Stratlspey Mktg Co 2003–; Nat Tst for Scotland: memb Cncl 1990–95, memb Countryside and Nature Conservation Ctee 1992–96, memb Exec Ctee 1994–98; vice-pres Scottish Landowners' Fedn 1991–2004, chm Tourism and Environment Task Force 1995–98; pres Royal Zoological Soc of Scotland 1996–2006; patron Highland Hospice; memb The Access Forum 1994–99; *Style*— Lord Huntingtower, DL; ✉ The Doune of Rothiemurchus, by Aviemore, Inverness-shire PH22 1QP

HUNTLY, 13 Marquess of (S 1599); Granville Charles Gomer Gordon; Premier Marquess of Scotland, also Earl of Aboyne, Lord Gordon of Strathavon and Glenlivet (both S 1660), and Baron Meldrum of Morven (UK 1815); Chief of the Clan Gordon; s of 12 Marquess of Huntly (d 1987), and his 1 w, Hon Pamela (d 1998), *née* Berry, da of 1 Viscount Kemsley; *b* 4 February 1944; *Educ* Gordonstoun; *m* 1, 1972 (m dis 1990), Jane Elizabeth Angela, da of late Lt-Col Alistair Monteith Gibb and Hon Yoskyl, *née* Pearson, da of 2 Viscount Cowdray, DL; 1 s (Alistair Granville, Earl of Aboyne b 1973), 2 da (Lady Amy Jane b 1975, Lady Lucy Yoskyl b 1979); m 2, 15 Feb 1991, Catheryn, da of Gay Kindersley, and formerly w of Robert Lennon Millbourn; 1 da (Lady Rose Marie-Louise b 1993); *Heir* s, Earl of Aboyne; *Career* patron Inst of Commercial Mgmnt, chm Cock of the North Liqueur Co Ltd; dir Ampton Investments Ltd; *Style*— The Most Hon the Marquess of Huntly; ✉ Aboyne Castle, Aberdeenshire (tel 01339 887778, fax 01339 886100, e-mail catheryn@catherynhuntly.com)

HUNTON, Christopher John (Chris); s of Thomas Hunton, of Bishop's Stortford, Herts, and Elsie, *née* Smith; *b* 12 August 1961, Enfield, Middx; *Educ* Univ of London (BA), Univ of Cambridge (PGCE); *m* 6 June 1992, Sara, da of Eric Finch; 1 s (Samuel George b 22 Nov 1992), 1 da (Amelie Louisa b 10 Jan 1995); *Career* teacher Knox Sch NY 1984–85, asst housemaster Wellingborough Sch 1985–86, account mangr Foote, Cone & Belding 1986–88, account dir Ayer Barker 1988–90, bd account dir Young & Rubicam 1990–94, gp account dir Lowe Howard-Spink 1994–98, chief exec McCann Erickson 1998–2004, md Lowe London 2005–06, global dir Rainey Kelly Campbell Roalfe Y&R 2007–; MIPA (elected to Cncl 2003); *Recreations* family, sport, musical theatre, fishing; *Style*— Chris Hunton, Esq

HUNWICKS, Trevor Alec; s of Alec Alfred Hunwicks, of Northampton, and Jean, *née* Brazier; *b* 22 September 1943; *Educ* Chislehurst and Sidcup GS, Braintree County HS, Univ of Greenwich (MA); *m* 14 Dec 1968, Zara, da of late Peter John Harris, and Valerie, *née* Harris (d 1998); 1 da (Victoria Louise b 21 August 1971), 1 s (William George b 7 Oct 1974); *Career* Nationwide Anglia Building Soc (formerly Anglia Building Soc) 1968–90: branch mangr 1968, London mangr 1971, London regnl mangr 1975, gen mangr mktg 1985, gen mangr corp devpt 1987; dir Benton Int (retail banking conslts) 1991–95, managing ptnr (UK) Strategic Futures Int (strategic forecasting and policy analysts) 1995–; chm of govrs Northampton Coll 1990–2005 (govr 2005–); FCIB 1977, FCIM 1981; *Recreations* theatre, music, painting, tennis; *Style*— Trevor Hunwicks, Esq; ✉ The Old Barn, Ecton, Northampton NN6 0QB (tel 01604 406203e-mail trevor.hunwicks@ukonline.co.uk)

HUPPERT, Prof Herbert Eric; s of Leo Huppert (d 1957), and Alice, *née* Neuman (d 1967); *b* 26 November 1943; *Educ* Sydney Boys' HS, Univ of Sydney (BSc), Aust Nat Univ (MSc), Univ of Calif San Diego (MS, PhD), Univ of Cambridge (MA, ScD); *m* 20 April 1966, Felicia Adina, da of Bernard David Ferster (d 1993), of Bellevue Hill, NSW; 2 s (Julian b 1978, Rowan b 1982); *Career* Univ of Cambridge: fell King's Coll 1970–, asst dir of research 1970–81, lectr 1981–88, reader in geophysical dynamics 1988–89, prof of theoretical geophysics and dir Inst of Theoretical Geophysics 1989–; prof of mathematics Univ of NSW 1991–96; assoc ed Jl of Fluid Mechanics 1971–90; memb Editorial Bd: Philosophical Transactions of the Royal Soc 1994–99, Reports on Progress in Physics 1997–2003; sr res fell BP Venture Unit 1983–89; co-chm Scientists for the Release of Soviet Refusniks 1987–91; memb Cncl: NERC 1993–99, Royal Soc 2001–03; Arthur L Day Prize and Lectureship US Nat Acad 2005, Israel Pollak distinguished lectr Technion (Israel Inst of Technol) 2005, William Hopkins Prize Cambridge Philosophical Soc 2005, Murchison Medal Geological Soc of London 2007; fell American Geographical Union 2002, fell American Physical Soc 2004; FRS 1987; *Recreations* my children, playing squash and tennis, walking, mountaineering, dreaming of a less hassled life in the sunshine; *Style*— Prof Herbert Huppert, FRS; ✉ 46 De Freville Avenue, Cambridge CB4 1HT (tel 01223 356071); Institute of Theoretical Geophysics, Department of Applied Mathematics & Theoretical Physics and Department of Earth Sciences, CMS, Wilberforce Road, Cambridge CB3 0WA (tel 01223 337853, fax 01223 765900, e-mail hehl@esc.cam.ac.uk)

HURD, Martyn Roy; s of late (Bernard) Roy Hurd, and Marjorie Sheila, *née* Burton; *b* 28 September 1948; *Educ* Blatchington Court, Open Univ (BA); *m* 31 Aug 1976, Philippa

Helen, da of late (John) Angus Beckett, CB, CMG; 2 da (Jane b 6 May 1979, Helen b 21 July 1981); *Career* planning offr W Midlands Central Independent TV until 1983; ITN: mangr of prodn planning 1983–91, head of studios programme and resource planning 1991–94, dir of human resources 1994–96, dir of resources 1997–2003; HR and industrial relations conslt; dir: GR Communications, Martyn Hurd & Assocs; chm nat educational registered charity Nonsuch (History and Dance) Ltd; dir Broadcast Journalism Trg Cncl (BJTC); govr Ravensbourne Coll of Design and Communication; memb: BAFTA, RTS; fell and pres Moving Image Soc (FBKSTS); *Recreations* walking, swimming, reading; *Style*— Martyn Hurd, Esq; ✉ 9 Roy Road, Northwood, Middlesex HA6 1EQ (tel 01923 826868, e-mail martyn.hurd@blueyonder.co.uk)

HURD, (Hon) Nicholas Richard (Nick); MP; s of Baron Hurd of Westwell, CH, CBE, PC (Life Peer), *qv*, and Tatiana Elizabeth Michelle, *née* Eyre; *b* 13 May 1962; *Educ* Univ of Oxford; *m* 1998, Kim; 2 s, 2 da; *Career* business dir, fndr Small Business Network 2002, formerly COS to Tim Yeo MP, *qv*, MP (Cons) Ruislip-Northwood 2005–; memb Funding Ctee Vote No to the EU Constitution Campaign, memb Environmental Audit Ctee House of Commons; dir Band-X Ltd; *Style*— Nick Hurd, Esq, MP; ✉ House of Commons, London SW1A 0AA (e-mail hurdn@parliament.uk, website www.nickhurd.com)

HURD OF WESTWELL, Baron (Life Peer UK 1997), of Westwell in the County of Oxfordshire; Douglas Richard Hurd; CH (1996), CBE (1974), PC (1982); eld s of Baron Hurd, sometime MP Newbury and agric corr The Times (Life Peer, d 1966; himself er s of Sir Percy Angier Hurd, sometime MP Frome and Devizes, ed Canadian Gazette and London ed Montreal Star; Sir Percy was er bro of Sir Archibald Hurd, also a journalist (Daily Telegraph) and formerly chm Shipping World Co), and Stephanie Frances, *née* Corner (d 1985); *b* 8 March 1930; *Educ* Eton, Trinity Coll Cambridge (MA); *m* 1, 1960 (m dis 1982), Tatiana Elizabeth Michelle, o da of (Arthur Charles) Benedict Eyre, MBE, of Bury, W Sussex; 3 s (Hon Nicholas Richard, *qv*, b 13 May 1962, Hon Thomas Robert Benedict b 20 Sept 1964, Hon Alexander Paul Anthony b 7 June 1969); m 2, 1982, Judy J, 2 da of Sidney Smart, of Chaddleworth, Berks; 1 s (Hon Philip Arthur b 1983), 1 da (Hon Jessica Stephanie b 1985); *Career* Dip Serv 1952–66 (Peking, UK Mission to UN, Rome, also private sec to perm under sec FO); CRD 1966–68 (head Foreign Affrs Section 1968); MP (Cons): Mid Oxon Feb 1974–1983, Witney 1983–97; private sec to Rt Hon Edward Heath as ldr of Oppn 1968–70, political sec to PM 1970–74, oppn spokesman on foreign affrs (with special responsibility for EEC) 1976–79; min of state: FCO 1979–83, Home Office 1983–84; sec of state for NI 1984–85, home sec 1985–89, sec of state for foreign and Cwlth affrs 1989–95; dir National Westminster Bank plc 1995–99, dep chm NatWest Markets 1995–98, chm British Invisibles 1997–2000 (dep chm 1996–97), dep chm Coutts & Co 1998–; chm: Prison Reform Tst 1997–2001 (hon pres 2001–), CEDR 2000–04 (currently chm Advsy Cncl), Canterbury Review Gp 2000; memb: Royal Cmmn on reform of House of Lords 1999, Appointments Cmmn 2000–; visiting fell Nuffield Coll Oxford 1978, fell Eton Coll 1981–96; chm of judges Booker Prize 1998; high steward Westminster Abbey 2000–; chm German-Br Forum 2000–05; co-pres RIIA 2001–; *Books* The Arrow War (1967), Truth Game (1972), Vote to Kill (1975), An End to Promises (1979); with Andrew Osmond: Send Him Victorious (1968), The Smile on The Face of the Tiger (1969), Scotch on the Rocks (1971), War Without Frontiers (1982); Palace of Enchantments (with Stephen Lamport, *qv*, 1985), Search for Peace (1997), Shape of Ice (1998), Ten Minutes to Turn the Devil (1999), Image in the Water (2001), Memoirs (2003), Sir Robert Peel (2007); *Clubs* Beefsteak, Travellers, Pratt's; *Style*— The Rt Hon Lord Hurd of Westwell, CH, CBE, PC; ✉ House of Lords, London SW1A 0PW

HURDLE, Michael William Frederick; s of Maurice Frederick Hurdle (d 1994), of Burton-on-Trent, and Mary Murielle Morton Wilson (d 1997); *b* 3 June 1941; *Educ* Uppingham, Keele Univ (BA); *Career* chm Marston Thompson and Evershed plc (Brewers); Liveryman Worshipful Co of Brewers; *Recreations* shooting, fishing, golf, horseracing; *Clubs* The Burton, The Oriental, Lloyds; *Style*— Michael Hurdle, Esq; ✉ Marston Thompson & Evershed plc, PO Box 26, Shobnall Road, Burton-on-Trent, Staffordshire DE14 2BW

HURFORD, Prof James Raymond (Jim); *b* 16 July 1941; *Educ* Exeter Sch, St John's Coll Cambridge (BA), UCL (PhD); *Career* assoc Dept of Germanic Languages UCLA 1963–64, postdoctoral res fell System Development Corporation Calif 1967–68, asst prof Dept of English Univ of Calif Davis 1968–71, sr lectr Dept of Linguistics Lancaster Univ 1976–79 (lectr 1972–76), prof of general linguistics Univ of Edinburgh 1979–; visiting res fell Univ of Melbourne 1989–90; visiting prof: Cairo Univ 1976, Univ of Calif 1982; memb of Faculty Linguistic Inst Linguistic Soc of America 1995; *Books* The Linguistic Theory of Numerals (1975), Semantics: a Coursebook (with B Heasley, 1983), Language and Number: the emergence of a cognitive system (1987), Grammar: a Student's Guide (1994); *Style*— Prof Jim Hurford; ✉ Department of Linguistics, University of Edinburgh, Adam Ferguson Building, Edinburgh EH8 9LL (tel 0131 650 3959/3960)

HURFORD, Sam; s of Alister Edwin Hurford, of Moorlands, East Winch Road, Ashwicken, Kings Lynn, Norfolk, and June Mary, *née* Kenny; *b* 9 September 1956; *Educ* Stanground Sch Peterborough, Peterborough Tech Coll, Trent Poly Nottingham (DipAD); *m* 5 Sept 1981, Christina Helen, da of Alojzy Brunon Gdaniec; 1 s (Max Michael b 28 April 1988), 1 da (Rosie Louise b 5 June 1990); *Career* typographer Boase Massimi Pollitt advtg agency 1979–81; art dir: Saatchi & Saatchi 1981–82, Gold Greenlees Trott 1982–85; art dir/gp head: Yellowhammer 1985–88, Publicis 1988–92; head of art/dep creative dir TBWA Holmes Knight Ritchie 1992–93, dep creative dir Young & Rubicam 1994–; awards incl: Creative Circle Gold, Silver and Bronze, Campaign Poster Silver and Bronze, D&AD Silver, Clio Gold, Euro Gold, Kinsale Grand Prix and 4 Golds, Cannes Silver 1992; memb 1991–98: D&AD, Creative Circle; *Recreations* skiing, sailing, running, football, cycling; *Style*— Sam Hurford, Esq

HURLEY, Elizabeth Jane; da of late Roy Leonard Hurley, and Angela Mary Hurley; *b* 10 June 1965; *Children* 1 s (Damian Charles b 4 April 2002); *Career* actress, prodr and model; spokeswoman and model for Estée Lauder; creative dir Elizabeth Hurley Beach; prodr Simian Films; Best Supporting Actress ShoWest Award 1997, Entrepreneur of the Year Glamour Magazine 2006; *Theatre* incl: The Cherry Orchard - A Jubilee (Russian & Soviet Arts Festival), The Man Most Likely To (Middle East tour); *Television* incl: title role in Christabel (BBC), The Orchid House (Channel 4), Rumpole (Thames), Inspector Morse (Zenith), The Young Indiana Jones Chronicles (Lucas Films Ltd), Sharpe's Enemy (Sharpe Films), The Job (ABC), The Human Face (BBC), presenter Project Catwalk (Sky One); *Film* incl: Aria, Rowing in the Wind, The Long Winter of 39, Passenger 57, Mad Dogs and Englishmen, Dangerous Ground, Samson and Delilah, Austin Powers: International Man of Mystery, Permanent Midnight, My Favourite Martian, Ed TV, Austin Powers: The Spy Who Shagged Me, Bedazzled, The Weight Of Water, Double Whammy, Serving Sara, Method; prodr: Extreme Measures, Mickey Blue Eyes; *Style*— Miss Elizabeth Hurley; ✉ Unit 3B, 101 Farm Lane, London SW6, 1QJ (tel 020 7386 2780, fax 020 7386 2781)

HURN, David; s of Stanley Hurn, of Cardiff, and Joan, *née* Maynard; *b* 21 July 1934, Redhill, Surrey; *Educ* Dorchester GS, RMA Sandhurst; *m* 1964 (m dis 1971), Alita Naughton; 1 da (Siân); *Career* photographer; asst photographer Reflex Agency London 1955–57, freelance for pubns incl The Observer, Sunday Times, Look and Life 1957–70, memb Magnum Photos 1967–; editorial advsr Album photographic magazine 1971; head Sch of Documentary Photography Gwent Coll of HE Newport 1973–90, distinguished visiting artist and adjunct prof Arizona State Univ Tempe 1979–80; memb: Photographic Ctee 1972–77, Arts Panel 1975–77, Cncl for Nat Academic Awards 1978–87, Arts Cncl of GB; Welsh Arts Cncl Award 1971, Kodak Special Photographic Bursary 1975, UK/USA Bicentennial Fellowship 1979–80, Imperial War Museum Arts Award 1987–88, Bradford Fellowship 1993–94, Arts Cncl Wales Bursary 1995; hon fell Univ of Wales Coll Newport; *Selected Solo Exhibitions* Serpentine Gallery London 1971, Bibliotheque Nationale Paris 1973, Nat Museum of Wales Cardiff 1974, The Photographers' Gallery London 1974, Recontres Internationales de Photographie Arles 1976, Centre d'Animation Culturelle Dovai 1976, Ecole Municipale des Arts Decoratifs Strasbourg 1976, FNAC Etoile Gallery Paris 1977, Arnolfini Gallery Bristol 1977, Ecole des Beaux Arts Angers 1977, Musée du Chateau d'Eau Toulouse 1977, Rheinisches Landesmuseum Bonn 1977, Rathaus Augsburg 1977, Stadtbucherei Stuttgart 1977, Stadtisches Museum Bochum 1978, Northlight Gallery Arizona State Univ Tempe 1978, Gemeentekijke Van Reekum Galerij Apeldoorn 1978, Culturele Raad Leeuwarden 1978, Openbare Bibliotheek Arnhem 1978, Culturee Centrum Winterswijk 1978, Canon Photo Galerij Amsterdam 1978, Univ of Idaho Moscow 1978, Galeria Spectrum Barcelona 1978, Galeria Spectrum Zaragosa 1978, San Carlos Opera House Lisbon 1979, Univ of Idaho Museum Moscow 1979, Univ of New Mexico Albuquerque 1979, Texas Christian Univ Fort Worth 1979, Midland Gp Gallery Nottingham 1979, Fifth Ave Gallery Scotsdale 1980, Sterling Coll of Art 1980, Les Recontres D'Olympus Paris 1981, Contrasts Gallery London 1982, Olympus Gallery London 1982, Malmo Museum 1982, Palais des Congres Lorient 1982, Olympus Gallery Tokyo 1983, Palais des Beaux Arts Charlerois 1983, Olympus Gallery Hamburg 1984, Ffotogalley Cardiff 1984, The Photographers' Gallery London 1985, Nat Museum of Photography Bradford 1985 and 1994, Cambridge Darkroom 1986, Axiom Gallery Cheltenham 1986, Stills Gallery Edinburgh 1986, Newport Museum 1994, Nat Museum and Gallery Cardiff 2000, Nat Library of Wales Aberystwyth 2000, Hay Literary Festival 2000, Int Eisteddfod Llangollen 2000, Aberystwyth Arts Centre 2007; *Selected Group Exhibitions* Personal Views 1850–1970 (touring) 1972, Images des Hommes (touring) 1978, Visitors to Arizona 1846–1980 (Phoenix Museum Arizona) 1980, British Photography 1955–1965 (The Photographers' Gallery London) 1983, Images of Sport (Ffotogallery Cardiff) 1983, Autographs (Cambridge Darkroom) 1983, Quelques Anglais (Centre National de la Photographie Paris) 1985, The Miners World (touring) 1985, Take One: British Film Stills (touring) 1985, Through the Looking Glass: Photographic Art in Britain 1945–89 (Barbican London) 1989, In Our Time: The world as seen by Magnum Photographers (touring) 1989, Distinguished visiting artists (Northlight Gallery Arizona State Univ Tempe) 1991, Revelations. Male and Female Nudes (John Jones Gallery London) 1994, A Positive View (The Saatchi Gallery London) 1994; *Work in Public Collections* incl: Welsh Arts Cncl, Contemporary Arts Soc for Wales, Arts Cncl of GB, Br Cncl, Bibliotheque Nationale Paris, FNAC Paris, Musée du Chateau d'Eau Toulouse, Int Center of Photography NY, Centre for Creative Photography Univ of Arizona Tucson, Univ of New Mexico Albuquerque, San Francisco MOMA, Calif Museum of Photography Univ of Calif Riverside, Int Museum of Photography George Eastman House Rochester, Nat Library of Wales, Nat Museum and Gallery Cardiff; *Books* David Hurn: Photographs 1956–76 (1979), A Day in the Life of London (1984), One Moment of The World (1984), Ireland. A week in the life of a nation (1986), History of Photography (1987), Bons Baisers (1987), In Our Time (1989), Music (1990), A L'Est de Magnum (1991), The Circle of Life (1991), L'Argot d'Eros (1992), Il Medico e il reportage (1992), Magnum Cinema (1994), Contemporary Photographers (1995), Magnum Landscape (1996), The Photo Book (1997), Magnum Photos, Photo Poche (1997), On being a photographer (with Bill Jay, 1997), 1968 Magnum throughout the world (1998), Young Meteors (1998), Hugs and Kisses (1998), On looking at pictures (with Bill Jay, 2000), Wales: Land of My Father (2000), Magnum (2000), Living in Wales (2003); *Recreations* collecting contemporary ceramics, exchanging photographs; *Style*— David Hurn, Esq; ✉ Prospect Cottage, Tintern, Gwent NP16 6SG (tel 01291 689358, e-mail hurn@tintern.u-net.com); Magnum Photos, Ground Floor, 63 Gee Street, Lonndon EC1V 3RS (tel 020 7490 1771, e-mail hurn@magnum.co.uk)

HURN, Sir (F) Roger; kt (1996); s of Francis James Hurn, and Joyce Elsa, *née* Bennett; *b* 9 June 1938; *Educ* Marlborough; *m* 1980, Rosalind Jackson; 1 da; *Career* Nat Serv 1959–61; engrg apprentice Rolls-Royce Motors 1956–58; Smiths Industries plc: export rep Automotive Business Europe and N America 1958–59 and 1961–65, export dir Motor Accessory Div 1969 (export mangr 1965–69), corp staff dir Overseas Ops 1969–74, md Int Ops 1974–76, exec dir 1976–78, md 1978–81, chief exec and md 1981–91, chm and chief exec 1991–96, chm 1991–98; chm: Marconi (formerly GEC) plc 1998–2001, Prudential plc 2000–02; non-exec dir: ICI plc 1993–2001, GlaxoSmithKline plc until 2003 (dep chm 1997–2003), Cazenove Group plc 2001–; chm of govrs Henley Management Coll until 2004; Liveryman Worshipful Co of Coachmakers and Coach Harness Makers 1979; *Style*— Sir Roger Hurn

HURN, Stanley Noel; s of Leonard Frederick Hurn (d 1973), of Colchester, and Kathleen Alice, *née* Frost (d 1984); *b* 24 December 1943; *Educ* Colchester Royal GS, Univ of Hull (BSc); *Career* mangr Standard Chartered Bank 1968–78, asst dir Orion Royal Bank Ltd 1978–82, dir Samuel Montagu & Co Ltd 1982–96, dir HSBC Loan Syndication 1996–98; memb Advsy Panel Railway Heritage Tst; FCIB 1995; memb Ct Guild of Int Bankers; Lord of the Manor of Thorpe Market Norfolk; *Books* Syndicated Loans - A Handbook for Banker and Borrower (1990); *Clubs* Cwlth; *Style*— Stanley Hurn, Esq; ✉ East Norfolk House, Thorpe Market, Norfolk NR11 8UD (tel 01263 833537, e-mail stan_hurn@hotmail.com)

HURST, Sir Geoffrey Charles (Geoff); kt (1998), MBE (1977); s of Charles Hurst, of Chelmsford, Essex, and Evelyn May, *née* Hopkins; *b* 8 December 1941; *Educ* Rainsford Secdy Modern Chelmsford; *m* 13 Oct 1964, Judith Helen, da of Jack Henry Harries; 3 da (Claire Helen b 30 Oct 1965, Joanne Louise b 16 March 1969, Charlotte Jane b 13 Feb 1977); *Career* former professional footballer and mangr; clubs: West Ham (500 appearances, 250 goals scored), Stoke City 1972–75 (128 appearances, 37 goals scored), West Bromwich Albion 1975–76 (12 appearances, 2 goals scored); player mangr Telford United 1976–79; mangr: Chelsea 1979–81, Kuwait 1982–84; England: debut v W Germany 1966, scored hat-trick in World Cup final 4–2 defeat of W Germany Wembley 1966, 49 caps, 24 goals, coach 1977–82; sales dir Motor-Plan Limited 1984–90, new business support mangr Ryan Insurance Group Europe 1992–93, dir i/c acquisitions London General Insurance 1998 (md Appliance Warranty Div 1993–98), conslt AON Warranty Gp 1998–; *Books* World Game (1967), 1966 and All That (2001); *Recreations* golf; *Clubs* Reform; *Style*— Sir Geoff Hurst, MBE; ✉ AON Warranty Group, 152–158 Northolt Road, Harrow, Middlesex KT12 1EQ (tel 020 8869 1758, fax 020 8869 1708)

HURST, George; *b* 20 May 1926, Edinburgh; *Educ* Sr Sch of the Royal Conservatory Canada (first graduate in composition); *Career* conductor and composer; prof of composition Peabody Inst Baltimore aged 21, conductor Peabody Conservatory Orch and Symphony Orch of York Pennsylvania 1950–55, London debut with London Philharmonic Orch 1953 (asst conductor 1955–57), princ conductor BBC Northern Symphony Orch (now BBC Philharmonic Orch) 1958–68; co-fndr Bournemouth Sinfonietta 1968, staff conductor Western Orchestral Soc (parent orgn of Bournemouth Sinfonietta and Bournemouth Symphony Orch) 1974–88 (artistic advsr 1969–74), princ guest conductor BBC Scot Symphony Orch 1986–89, first princ conductor RTE Nat Symphony Orch of Ireland 1990–93; conducting studies conslt Royal Acad of Music 1983–; conducted numerous other orchs incl: all major Br and Irish orchs, Nord Deutsch Rundfunk Symphony Orch, Orchestre National Paris, Orchestre Lamoureux Paris, Orchestre de la Suisse Romande, Royal Danish Orch, Hamburg Orch, Israel Philharmonic Orch; *Style*— George Hurst, Esq

HURST, John Edward; s of Edward Gostling Hurst (d 1964), of Weston Longville, Norwich, and Grace, *née* Holder (d 2000); *b* 10 October 1947; *Educ* Gresham's, Univ of London (LLB), Univ of Amsterdam (Post Grad Dip); *m* 19 Dec 1972, Julia, da of Hendrik Jan Engelbert van Beuningen, of Cothen (U), The Netherlands; 1 s (Robert Adriaan b 13 April 1979), 2 da (Olivia b 8 Sept 1974, Annette b 16 April 1977); *Career* admitted slr 1976; ptnr: Hurst van Beuningen (Farms) 1982–, Daynes Hill & Perks 1987–92, Eversheds Daynes Hill & Perks 1992–95, Eversheds 1995–2001; conslt Eversheds 2001–05, conslt Birketts LLP 2005–; nat chm Law Soc's Slr's Euro Gp 1987–88, lay chm Sparham Deanery Synod C of E 1987–96; memb: Law Soc 1976, NFU 1982; dir Briningham Farms Ltd 1998–2006; govr Taverham Hall Prep Sch 1996–; *Books* Legal Issues of European Integration: Harmonisation of Company Law in the EEC (1974); *Recreations* swimming, stalking and country pursuits; *Clubs* Norfolk; *Style*— John Hurst, Esq; ✉ Birketts, 16–18 Queen Street, Norwich NR2 4SQ (tel 01603 232300, fax 01603 626147, e-mail john-hurst@birketts.co.uk)

HURST, Kim Barbara; da of late Norman Campbell Hurst, of Sheffield, and late Elsie, *née* Hands; *b* 8 August 1956; *Educ* Ecclesfield Sch, Univ of Leicester (BA); *Career* trainee Grant Thornton 1978–81, Griffin Stone Moscrop 1982–83, under sec to the Auditing Practices Ctee ICAEW 1983–85, risk mgmnt and standards ptnr Mazars 1990– (joined 1985); vice-chair Investigations Ctee and memb Professional Standards Bd ICAEW, memb Bd Tearfund (chair Audit Ctee); FCA 1992 (ACA 1982); *Books* Tolley's Charities Manual; *Recreations* theatre, charity work, swimming; *Clubs* Virgin Active; *Style*— Ms Kim Hurst; ✉ Mazars, 24 Bevis Marks, London EC3A 7NR (tel 020 7220 3150, fax 020 7377 3107, e-mail kim.hurst@mazars.co.uk)

HURST, Lilla; da of John Hurst, of Petworth, West Sussex, and Anne, *née* Pendlebury; *b* 16 February 1973, Beaconsfield, Bucks; *Educ* Holy Cross Convent for Girls Chalfont St Peter, Framlingham Coll, De Montfort Univ (BA); *m* 16 Sept 2006, Jonathan Benton-Hughes; 1 s (Bertram b 16 Feb 2006); *Career* sales and devpt exec British Pathé 1997–1999, dir TVF Int 1999–2001, dir of acquisitions and co-production RDF Media 2001–04, head of co-prodn Channel Five 2004–; *Recreations* cooking, design, walking in the British countryside; *Clubs* Century; *Style*— Miss Lilla Hurst; ✉ Channel Five, 22 Long Acre, London WC2E 9LY (tel 020 7550 5674, fax 020 7550 5554, e-mail lilla.hurst@five.tv)

HURST, Peter Thomas; s of Thomas Lyon Hurst (d 1981), of Cheshire, and Norah Mary, *née* Delaney (d 1977); *b* 27 October 1942; *Educ* Stonyhurst, Univ of London (LLB, MPhil); *m* 1968, Diane, *née* Irvine; 2 da (Elizabeth b 1970, Catherine b 1972), 1 s (Charles b 1975); *Career* slr of Supreme Court 1967; ptnr: Hurst and Walker Slrs Liverpool 1967–77, Gair Roberts Hurst and Walker Slrs Liverpool 1977–81; Supreme Court Taxing Office: master 1981–90, chief master 1991–99; sr costs judge 1999–, judicial taxing offr House of Lords 2002–, judicial taxing offr Privy Cncl 2005–, Greffier subst Royal Court of Jersey 2005–, recorder; hon bencher Gray's Inn 2007; *Books* Butterworths Costs Service (1986–): Solicitors' Remuneration, Summary and Detailed Assessment; Cordery on Solicitors (contrib 8 edn, 1988); Legal Aid Practice (1996); Halsbury's Laws of England: Legal Aid (1994), Solicitor's Remuneration (1995), Civil Costs (1995, 4 edn 2007), Civil Procedure (The White Book, 2007), Criminal Costs (2007), The New Civil Costs Regime (jtly); *Clubs* Athenaeum; *Style*— Peter Hurst, Esq; ✉ Supreme Court Costs Office, Royal Courts of Justice, Cliffords Inn, Fetter Lane, London EC4A 1DQ

HURSTHOUSE, Roger Stephen; DL (Notts); *b* 20 June 1941; *Educ* Henry Mellish GS; *m* 1, (m dis), Janet; 2 s (James Roger b 1969, Andrew Stephen b 1972); m 2, 29 Feb 1996, Julia Gunn; *Career* articled clerk Harold T Hooley & Co Nottingham 1957–63; PKF Nottingham: mangr 1963–68, ptnr 1968–2003; co dir; pres: Nottingham Soc of CAs 1980–81, Notts C of C and Indust 1988–90; offr bro Order of St John, chm Cncl for Nottinghamshire; FCA; MCIArb; *Recreations* golf, cricket, music; *Clubs* 41; *Style*— Roger S Hursthouse, Esq, DL, FCA, MCIArb; ✉ 3 Elm Park, Gonalston Lane, Epperstone, Nottinghamshire NG14 6BE (tel 0115 966 3950, fax 0115 966 5400)

HURT, John Vincent; CBE (2004); s of Rev Father Arnould Herbert Hurt, and Phyllis, *née* Massey (d 1975); *b* 22 January 1940; *Educ* Lincoln Sch, St Martin's Sch of Art, RADA; *m* 1, 1984 (m dis 1990), Donna Lynn Peacock, da of Don Wesley Laurence (d 1986), of Texas USA; m 2, 1990 (m dis 1996), Jo Dalton; 2 s; m 3, 2005, Anwen Rees-Myers; *Career* actor; debut Arts Theatre London 1962; *Theatre* incl: Chips with Everything (Vaudeville) 1962, The Dwarfs (Arts, Critics Award for Most Promising Actor 1963) 1962, Inadmissible Evidence (Wyndhams) 1965, Little Malcolm and His Struggle Against The Eunuchs (Garrick) 1966, Belcher's Luck (Aldwych, RSC) 1966, The Caretaker (Mermaid) 1971, Travesties (Aldwych, RSC) 1973, The Shadow of a Gunman (Nottingham Playhouse) 1978, The Seagull (Lyric Hammersmith) 1985, London Vertigo (Gate Dublin) 1991, A Month in the Country (Albery) 1994, Krapps Last Tape (Barbican) 1999 and (Gate Theatre Dublin) 2001, Afterplay (Gate Theatre Dublin) 2002, Heroes (Wyndhams) 2005, Krapps Last Tape (Gate Theatre Dublin and Barbican) 2006; *Television* incl: The Playboy of the Western World (BBC) 1971, The Naked Civil Servant (Thames TV) 1975 (Br Acad Award for Best Actor 1978), I Claudius (BBC) 1976, Treats (YTV) 1977, Crime and Punishment (BBC) 1978, Fool in King Lear (with Olivier) 1982, The Storyteller (35 episodes) 1986, Poison Candy (BBC) 1987, Deadline 1988, Who Bombed Birmingham? (Granada) 1989, Journey to Knock 1991, Red Fox (LWT) 1991, Six Characters in Search of an Author (BBC) 1992, Enemy Within (BBC) 1995, Prisoner in Time (BBC) 1995, Krapp's Last Tape 2000, Bait 2001, The Alan Clark Diaries 2004; *Films* incl: A Man for All Seasons 1966, 10 Rillington Place 1970, East of Elephant Rock 1976, Spectre 1977, The Disappearance 1977, The Shout 1977, Watership Down 1977, Midnight Express 1977 (Oscar nomination 1978, Br Acad Award 1978, Golden Globe Award 1978, Variety Club Award 1978), Alien 1978, Heaven's Gate 1979, The Elephant Man 1980 (Oscar nomination, Br Acad Award, Variety Club Award), Night Crossing 1980, History of the World Part I 1982, Champions 1983 (Evening Standard Award for Best Actor 1984), Nineteen Eighty-Four 1984, The Hit 1984, Jake Speed 1986, Rocinante 1986, Aria 1987, White Mischief 1987, Bengali Night 1988, Scandal 1988, La Dame aux Chats 1988, Windprints 1989, Frankenstein Unbound 1989, The Field 1990, King Ralph 1990, Memory 1990, Dark at Noon 1991, Lapse of Memory 1991, Even Cowgirls get the Blues 1992, Great Moments in Aviation 1992, Crime & Punishment 1993, Wild Bill 1994, Rob Roy 1995, Saigon Baby 1995, Love and Death on Long Island 1998, The Commissioner 1998, All the Little Animals 1998, Night Train 1998, You're Dead 1998, New Blood 1999, Lost Souls 2000, Crime and Punishment 2000, Captain Corelli's Mandolin 2001, Harry Potter and the Philospher's Stone 2001, Tabloid 2001, Miranda 2002, Owning Mahowny 2003, Dogville 2003, Hellboy 2004, The Proposition 2004, Skeleton Key 2004, Shooting Dogs 2005, V for Vendetta 2005, Outlander 2006, Oxford Murders 2007, Lecture 21 2007, Indiana Jones IV 2007; *Recreations* riding, charity work; *Clubs* MCC, Garrick; *Style*— John Hurt, Esq, CBE; ✉ c/o ICM, 76 Oxford Street, London W1D 1BS

HUSBAND, Prof Dame Janet Elizabeth Siarey; DBE (2007, OBE 2002); da of Ronald Howard Siarey (d 1982), of Chinnor, Oxon, and Clarissa Marian Siarey (d 1987); *b* 1 April 1940; *Educ* Headington Sch, Guy's Hosp Med Sch (MB BS); *m* 1963, Peter Husband; 3 s (Matthew Bernard, Andrew Charles, Timothy Edward); *Career* prof of diagnostic radiology Inst of Cancer Res 1976–, conslt Royal Marsden Hospital 1980–, co-dir Clinical Magnetic Resonance Res Gp Cancer Res UK 1986–2005, med dir Royal Marsden NHS Fndn Tst 2003–06; pres: BIR 2003–04, RCR 2004–; vice-chair Acad of Med Royal Colls 2005–; Couch Award 1976; FRCR 1976, Hon FMedSci 2001, Hon FRCSI 2005; hon memb: Belgian Radiological Soc 1994, European Soc of Therapeutic and Radiation Oncology 1999; *Publications* Imaging in Oncology (jt ed, 2 vols 2004), author of over 270 pubns on imaging in oncology; *Recreations* walking, opera; *Clubs* RAC; *Style*— Prof Dame Janet Husband, DBE

HUSBAND, John; s of John Husband (d 1986), of Edgware, and Bridget Agnes Leahy; *b* 21 April 1945; *Educ* St Vincent's RC Sch Mill Hill, St James' RC HS Edgware, Univ of Hull (BSc); *Career* Daily Mirror: trainee reporter 1966–68, fin reporter 1968–74, dep City ed 1974–90 (and Sunday Mirror 1975–90), City ed 1990–93, Personal Finance ed 1993–, tstee Mirror Gp Newspaper Pension Scheme; memb: ABI Code Monitoring Ctee 1990–2001, FSA Treating Customers Fairly Consultative Ctee 2006–; Personal Fin Journalist of The Year 1990, Wincott Business Jl of the Year (for Sunday Mirror City column) 1991; ABI Lifetime Award for Achievements in Personal Finance, Bradford & Bingley Lifetime Award for Achievement in Personal Finance; chair of govrs: St Margaret Clitherow RC Primary Sch, St Catherine's RC Sch for Girls; treas Belvedere Community Forum; memb NUJ 1966; *Books* Money Mirror (1980), Daily Mirror Guide to Money (1993), Managing Your Money (1998); *Recreations* music, record collecting, walking, history; *Style*— John Husband, Esq; ✉ Mirror Group Newspapers, 1 Canada Square, Canary Wharf, London E14 5AP (tel 020 7293 3323, e-mail j.husband@mgn.co.uk)

HUSBAND, Prof Thomas Mutrie (Tom); s of Thomas Mutrie Husband, and Janet, *née* Clark; *b* 7 July 1936; *Educ* Shawlands Acad Glasgow, Univ of Strathclyde (BSc, MA, PhD); *m* 1, 1962, Pat Caldwell (d 2001); 2 s; m 2, 2003, Gwen Fox; *Career* Weir Ltd Glasgow: apprentice fitter 1953–58, engr/jr mangr 1958–62, sandwich degree student of mech engrg 1958–61; various engrg and mgmnt positions ASEA Ltd (Denmark, UK, South Africa) 1962–65, teaching fell Univ of Chicago 1966–67, lectr Univ of Strathclyde 1969–70, sr lectr Univ of Glasgow 1970–73, prof of mfrg orgn Loughborough Univ 1973–81; Imperial Coll London: prof of engrg manufacture 1981–90, dir Centre for Robotics 1982–90, head Dept of Mech Engrg 1983–90; vice-chllr Univ of Salford 1990–97; chm: Univ of Salford Holdings plc 1990–97, UK Educn and Research Networking Assoc 1997–2000, East and North Herts NHS Tst 2000–02; non-exec dir: Royal Exchange Theatre Manchester 1994–98, Univs and Colls Employers Assoc 1994–97; memb Engrg Cncl 1992–96; memb Bd Bournemouth Univ 2004–; FREng 1988, FIEE, FIMechE; *Publications* Work Analysis and Pay Structure (1976), Maintenance and Terotechnology (1977), Education and Training in Robotics (1986), author of articles in various jls; *Recreations* watching Arsenal FC, music, theatre; *Style*— Prof Tom Husband, FREng; ✉ 12 Roscrea Drive, Wick Village, Bournemouth BH6 4LU (tel 01202 433 585, e-mail focusfox@aol.com)

H

HUSKINSON, His Hon Judge (George) Nicholas Nevil; s of Thomas Leonard Bousfield Huskinson (d 1974), of Triscombe House, Somerset, and Helen Margaret, *née* Hales (d 1983); *b* 7 December 1948; *Educ* Eton, King's Coll Cambridge (MA); *m* 20 Dec 1972, Pennant Elfrida Lascelles, da of Thomas Lascelles Isa Shandon Valiant Iremonger (d 1998), of Milbourne Manor, Malmesbury, Wilts; 2 s (Thomas b 1978, Charles b 1981); *Career* called to the Bar Gray's Inn 1971 (Arden scholar 1972); in practice 1971–2003, recorder 1999–2003, circuit judge (SE Circuit) 2003–; a vice-pres Immigration Appeal Tbnl and subsequently sr immigration judge Asylum and Immigration Tbnl 2003–05, memb Lands Tbnl 2006–; memb Local Govt and Planning Bar Assoc; *Books* Woodfall's Law of Landlord and Tenant (asst ed 28 edn, 1978); *Recreations* tennis, cooking, family life, wine and food; *Clubs* MCC; *Style*— His Hon Judge Huskinson; ✉ Snaresbrook Crown Court, 75 Hollybush Hill, Wanstead, London E11 1QW (tel 020 8530 0000)

HUSKISSON, Dr Edward Cameron; s of Edward William Huskisson, of Northwood, Middx, and Elinor Margot, *née* Gibson; *b* 7 April 1939; *Educ* Eastbourne Coll, King's Coll London and Westminster Hosp (BSc, MB BS, MD); *m*; 3 s (Ian b 1971, Robert b 1990, Alexander b 1994), 1 da (Anna b 1974); *Career* rheumatologist in private practice; conslt physician Bart's until 1993, conslt rheumatologist King Edward VII Hosp for Offrs London; memb: BMA, RSM; MRCS, FRCP 1980 (MRCP 1967); *Books* Joint Disease All The Arthropathies (4 edn, 1988), Repetitive Strain Injury (1992); *Style*— Dr Edward Huskisson; ✉ 14A Milford House, 7 Queen Anne Street, London W1G 9HN (tel 020 7636 4278, fax 020 7323 6829, e-mail edwardhuskisson@aol.com)

HUSSAIN, Mukhtar; QC (1992); s of Karam Dad (d 1991), and Rehmi Bi (d 1955); *b* 22 March 1950; *Educ* William Temple Secdy Sch Preston; *m* 1972, Shamim Akhtar, *née* Ali; 3 da (Rukhshanda Jabeen b 30 March 1974, Farakhanda Jabeen b 12 Dec 1975, Mariam Sophia Rahmi b 20 May 1985); *Career* called to the Bar Middle Temple 1971 (bencher 2000), asst recorder 1987–90, recorder 1990–, head of chambers 1992–; Police Discipline Tbnl 1997–; memb: Criminal Injuries Compensation Bd (CICB) 1999, Mental Health Review Tbnl 2000, Bar Cncl 2000–01; *Recreations* reading, cricket, squash, bridge, golf; *Style*— Mukhtar Hussain, Esq, QC; ✉ Lincoln House, 5th Floor, 1 Brazennose Street, Manchester M2 5EL (tel 0161 832 5701)

HUSSAIN, Nasser; OBE (2002); s of Joe Hussain, of Brentwood, Essex, and Shireen, *née* Price; *b* 28 March 1968; *Educ* Highlands Sch Ilford, Forest Sch, Univ of Durham (BSc); *m* Karen, *née* Birch; 2 s (Jacob, Joel); *Career* professional cricketer; first class debut Essex CCC 1987, awarded county cap 1989, vice-capt 1995, capt 1999, ret 2004; England: 96 test matches (5,764 runs, 14 centuries, highest test score 207 v Aust Edgbaston 1997), 88 one-day ints (2,332 runs, 1 century), vice-capt 1998–99, capt 1999–2003 (incl World Cup SA and Zimbabwe 2003), memb touring squad India and WI 1990, WI 1993–94, Zimbabwe and NZ 1996–97, WI 1998, Aust 1998–99, SA 1999–2000, Pakistan and Sri Lanka 2000–01, Zimbabwe, India and NZ 2001–02, Aust 2002–03 and Bangladesh and Sri Lanka 2003, West Indies 2004, ret 2004 (ret from one day ints 2003); Vodafone England Cricketer of the Year 2001–02; currently cricket commentator Sky; *Recreations* golf, football; *Style*— Nasser Hussain, Esq, OBE

HUSSELBY, William Eric (Bill); OBE, DL (W Midlands 1991); s of late Eric Shaw Husselby, of Sandbanks, Dorset, and Betty, *née* Oubridge; *b* 7 July 1939; *Educ* Oundle; *m* 1968, Jillian Lyndon, da of Lyndon B Mills; 2 da (Francesca b 5 Aug 1969, Tania b 10 Dec 1971), 1 s (Marcus (twin) b 10 Dec 1971); *Career* md Cogent Elliott Limited 1967, chm Cogent Group 1973–; non-exec dir Marshalls plc 2005–; dir: WNO, Birmingham Opera; chm Birmingham NSPCC Centenary Appeal 1987–88, vice-chm Industry 96, tstee Think-Tank Birmingham Museum of Sci; chm Lady Katherine Leveson Tst, High Sheriff West Midlands 1986–87; FIPA 1990; *Style*— Bill Husselby, Esq, OBE, DL; ✉ Cogent Elliott Limited, Heath Farm, Meriden, West Midlands CV7 7LL (tel 0121 627 5040)

HUSSEY, Derek Robert; s of Robert Sidney Hussey, and Rachel *née* Maguire; *b* 12 September 1948; *Educ* Omagh Acad, Stranmillis Coll Belfast (CertEd); *m* Karen, *née* Vaughan; 2 s (Robert Samuel b 3 May 1984, Craig David Michael b 12 Jan 2003), 1 da (Rachel Rebecca Kate b 6 April 2000); *Career* head of business studies Castlederg HS 1972–98, publican 1992–; cncllr Strabane DC 1989–, memb NI Forum 1996–98; MLA (UU) W Tyrone 1998–2007; memb: UU Pty, Castlederg C of C, Orange Order, Apprentice Boys of Derry, Royal Black Inst; *Recreations* football, rugby, jogging, country and western music, church choir, skiing; *Clubs* Leeds United Supporters, NI Supporters, Dergview Football, Davy Crockett Country; *Style*— Derek Hussey, Esq

HUSSEY, Lady Susan Katharine; DCVO (1984, CVO 1971); 5 da of 12 Earl Waldegrave, KG, GCVO, TD (d 1995); *b* 1 May 1939; *m* 25 April 1959, Baron Hussey of North Bradley (d 2006); 1 s (Hon James Arthur b 1961, Page of Honour to HM The Queen 1975–76), 1 da (Hon Katharine Elizabeth (Hon Lady Brooke) b 1964); *Career* Lady-in-Waiting to HM The Queen 1960–; *Style*— Lady Susan Hussey, DCVO; ✉ Flat 15, 45–47 Courtfield Road, London SW7 4DB (tel 020 7370 1414)

HUSTLER, John Randolph; s of William Mostyn Collingwood Hustler (d 1976), and Angela Joan, *née* Hanson (d 1983); *b* 21 August 1946; *Educ* Eton; *m* 23 Sept 1978, Elizabeth

Mary, da of Andrew George Hughes-Onslow (d 1979); 2 s (Charles b 1982, Frederick b 1986), 1 da (Willa b 1983); *Career* chartered accountant; ptnr KPMG Peat Marwick 1983–93 (joined 1965); chm: Hustler Venture Partners Ltd 1993–, Northern 3 VCT plc 2001–; dir: Northern Venture Tst plc 1995–, Hygea VCT 2001–; FCA 1975; *Recreations* golf, tennis, gardening; *Clubs* Boodle's; *Style*— John Hustler, Esq; ✉ Ripsley House, Liphook, Hampshire GU30 7JH (tel 01428 727985, fax 01428 722793, e-mail john.hustler@btconnect.com)

HUSTLER, Dr Margaret Joan; da of Harry Hustler (d 1981), and Dorothy, *née* Kaye (d 2002); *b* 1 November 1949; *Educ* Noctorum HS Wirral, Marist Convent Fulham, Westfield Coll London (BSc), Royal Holloway Coll London (PhD); *m* 4 Aug 1976, David Thomas Wraight; 3 s (Peter Thomas b 16 Feb 1981, Christopher James 31 July 1986, Timothy David 23 Oct 1992), 5 da (Rebecca Ann b 10 Nov 1982, Elizabeth Louise b 20 March 1984, Katharine Mary b 5 May 1985, Daisy Harriet b 8 Sept 1988, Laura Jane b 10 Aug 1990); *Career* teacher Lady Eleanor Holles Sch Hampton 1977–85, dep head Atherley Sch for Girls Southampton 1985–89, headmistress St Michael's Sch Limpsfield 1989–96, headmistress Harrogate Ladies' Coll 1996–; govr Dover Coll; memb GSA 1989–; *Recreations* reading, walking, knitting, sewing, needlework; *Style*— Dr Margaret Hustler; ✉ Harrogate Ladies' College, Clarence Drive, Harrogate, North Yorkshire HG1 2QG (tel 01423 504543, fax 01423 568893, e-mail enquire@hlc.org.uk)

HUTCHEON, Dr Andrew William; s of George Hutcheon (d 1989), of Aberdeen, and Elsie Sophia, *née* Murison (d 1983); *b* 21 May 1943; *Educ* Robert Gordon's Coll, Univ of Aberdeen (MB ChB, MD); *m* 14 July 1966, Christine Gray, da of Francis Gray Cusiter, of Kirkwall, Orkney; 2 da (Louise b 1967, Wendy b 1973), 1 s (Barry b 1970); *Career* house offr med and surgery Aberdeen Royal Infirmary 1968–69, SHO and registrar gen med Glasgow Western 1969–72, research fell Western Infirmary Glasgow 1972–75, sr registrar Western Infirmary Glasgow and Royal Marsden London 1975–78, conslt physician and conslt med oncologist Aberdeen Hosps 1978–, sr lectr in med Univ of Aberdeen 1978–; memb: Cancer Research Campaign, ICRF, Br Assoc for Cancer Research; FRCP, FRCPEd, MRCP; *Books* Textbook of Medical Treatment (contrib, 1987); *Recreations* skiing, curling; *Clubs* Rubislaw Curling, Aberdeen; *Style*— Dr Andrew Hutcheon; ✉ Moreseat, 159 Midstocket Road, Aberdeen AB15 5LU (tel 01224 637204); Ward 17, Aberdeen Royal Infirmary, Foresterhill, Aberdeen AB25 2ZN (tel 01224 681818)

HUTCHIESON, Doris; da of Lawrence Willoughby (d 1956), and Sarah Willoughby (d 2007); *Educ* Glenlola Collegiate Sch Bangor, Queen's Univ Belfast (BA, PGCE); *m* 1970, Ron Hutchieson; *Career* asst lectr N Down FE Coll 1968–69, head Geography Dept and sr teacher Glenlola Collegiate Sch Bangor 1969–87, headmistress Coleraine HS 1987–2005; pres SHA NI 1998, chm NE Post Primary Heads' Assoc 2003–,05 memb Standing Conf for Secdy Educn NI 1995–2005; memb: Educnl Broadcasting Cncl BBC 1997–2001, Teaching Appts Ctee NE Educn and Library Bd (NEELB) 1998–2005, NI Regnl Standing Gp UCAS 1998–2005; external advsr for performance review and staff devpt for sch princs 2005–; High Sheriff Co Londonderry 1999; memb: Ct Univ of Ulster 1997–2005, Bd of Govrs Bangor GS 2006–, Bd of Govrs Rockport Sch 2006–; tstee Family Fund NI 2006–; FRSA; *Recreations* travel, gardening; *Clubs* Rotary Int, Royal Ulster Yacht; *Style*— Mrs Doris Hutchieson; ✉ September Cottage, 3 Main Street, Groomsport, Co Down, Northern Ireland BT19 6JR (tel 028 9147 8082)

HUTCHINGS, Graham Derek; s of William Hutchings, of Upper Beeding, W Sussex, and Beryl, *née* Bedwell; *b* 2 November 1951; *Educ* Imberhorne Co Secdy Modern Sch, Hatfield Poly, Ealing Coll of HE, SOAS Univ of London; *m* Elisabeth Marion, da of Cyril Leslie Judd (d 1987); 1 s (Nicholas Graham b 1978), 1 da (Anna Elisabeth b 1981); *Career* journalist; office jr JLP Denny Ltd fruit importers 1968–69, shop asst Forrest Stores 1969–70, telephone engr 1970–76, lectr in modern history Hatfield Poly 1983–85, research ed China Business Report 1985–86, dep ed Asian Electricity 1986–87; Daily Telegraph: China specialist 1987–89, Peking corr 1989–93, China corr 1993–98; writer on Chinese Affairs 1998–2000, ed Oxford Analytica Daily Brief 2000–; *Books* Modern China: A Companion To A Rising Power (2000); *Recreations* music; *Style*— Graham Hutchings, Esq; ✉ Oxford Analytica, 5 Alfred Street, Oxford OX1 4EH (tel 01865 261600, e-mail ghutchings@oxford-analytica.com)

HUTCHINGS, Gregory Frederick; s of Capt Frederick Garside Hutchings, and Edna May, *née* McQueen; *b* 22 January 1947; *Educ* Uppingham, Aston Univ (BSc), Aston Mgmnt Centre (MBA); *m* 14 June 1980 (m dis 2005), Caroline Jane; *Career* Hanson plc 1981–83, chm and chief exec Tomkins plc 1984–2000 (dir 1983–2000), chm Lupus Capital plc 2004–; dir NT 1996–2002 (memb RNTE and Devpt Bds 2002–05); memb Bd Museum of London 1999– (chm Archaeology Ctee); Hon DBA Univ of Sunderland; *Recreations* sport, music, literature; *Style*— Gregory Hutchings, Esq

HUTCHINGS, Prof Ian Michael; s of Douglas Gilbert Hutchings, of Wells, Somerset, and Sheila Margaret Hutchings; *b* 6 May 1950, Barnet, Herts; *Educ* Rugby, Trinity Coll Cambridge (MA, PhD, sr Rouse Ball student); *m* 1973, Jennifer Rosemary; 4 c; *Career* St John's Coll Cambridge: research fell 1975–78 (working in Cavendish Lab 1975–77), fell 1975–, coll lectr 1978–2001, tutor with responsibility for engrg students 1983–86, admissions tutor 1988–90, dir of studies in materials science and metallurgy 1990–2000; Dept of Materials Science and Metallurgy Univ of Cambridge: univ demonstrator 1977–82, univ lectr 1982–97, reader in tribology 1997–2000, dep head of dept 1998–2000; Dept of Engrg Univ of Cambridge: GKN prof of mfrg engrg 2001–, dep head of dept 2002–05; visiting research scientist Lawrence Berkeley Lab Univ of Calif 1980, visiting research scientist German Federal Materials Research Estab (BAM) Berlin 1992, visiting prof Xi'an Jiaotong Univ 2004; jt course ldr Annual Course on Tribology 1993–; pres Int Research Gp on Wear of Engrg Materials (IRG-OECD) 2007– (UK nat rep 1993–97) chm: Tribology Gp Inst of Physics 1993–95 (memb Ctee 1987–97, hon treas 1989–91), Prog and Pubns Ctee World Tribology Congress IMechE 1997, 2nd Int Conf on Erosive and Abrasive Wear Cambridge 2003; jt chm: 8th Int Conf on Erosion by Liquid and Solid Impact 1994, Int Conf on Abrasive and Erosive Wear 1998; memb: Peer Review Coll EPSRC 1995–, Ctee G2 on Friction Wear American Soc for Testing and Materials 1998–2004, Surface Engrg Divnl Bd Inst of Materials 1999–; memb Editorial Bd: Tribology Int 1992–, Wear 1993–98 (ed-in-chief 1998–), Tribology Letters 1994–; memb various ctees and working parties MOD Defence Scientific Advsy Cncl 1990–96 (working pty chm 1995–96); chm St John's Innovation Centre Ltd 1996– (memb Bd of Dirs 1993–); Toshiba/Design Cncl Year of Invention Award 1989, IMechE Tribology Silver Medal 1994, Univ of Cambridge Pilkington Teaching Prize 1996, Inst of Materials NPL Award for Materials Metrology 2000, IMechE Donald Julius Groen Prize 2000, ETH Zürich Staudinger-Durrer Prize 2007; hon prof China Univ of Mining and Technol Beijing 1999; memb American Soc for Testing and Materials 1991, memb Soc of Tribologists and Lubrication Engrs 1992; CEng, CPhys, FIM 1993 (MIM 1981), FInstP 1994 (MInstP 1978), FREng 2002; *Publications* Tribology: Friction and Wear of Engineering Materials (1992); more than 250 papers on tribology, surface engrg and related subjects; *Style*— Prof Ian Hutchings; ✉ University of Cambridge, Institute for Manufacturing, Mill Lane, Cambridge CB2 1RX

HUTCHINGS, Michael Balfour; OBE (2005); s of Benjamin Legh Balfour Hutchings (d 1981), and Ann, *née* Carter; *b* 8 November 1948; *Educ* Marlborough, Coll of William and Mary VA (BA); *m* m 1, 29 June 1974 (m dis 1987), Jane Elizabeth, *née* Bristow; 1 da (Anna b 4 July 1978), 1 s (William b 9 Jan 1981); m 2, 8 April 1992, Victoria, da of Arthur Trollope; 3 step s (Robin b 6 March 1979, Sholto b 16 Nov 1981, Dominic b 11 Aug 1985); *Career* articled clerk McKenna & Co 1970–72, admitted slr 1973, ptnr Lovell White Durrant 1981–95 (asst slr 1974–81); EU law conslt 1996–; memb: Law Soc, Br Inst of Int and Comparative Law; Liveryman Worshipful Co of Drapers; *Recreations* woodturning, golf; *Clubs* Travellers, St Enodoc Golf, Woking Golf; *Style*— Michael Hutchings, Esq, OBE; ✉ Sandhayes, Corsley, Warminster, Wiltshire BA12 7QQ (tel 01373 832480, e-mail mbh@dircon.co.uk)

HUTCHINSON, Anne-Marie; OBE (2002); da of Samuel Gerald Hutchinson, and Catherine, *née* Fitzgerald; *b* Ireland; *Educ* Univ of Leeds (BA), Nottingham Trent Law Sch; *children* 1 da (Catherine Louise b 1987), 1 s (Samuel Gerald b 1995); *Career* admitted slr 1985; slr specialising in matters relating to children (incl int custody disputes, child abduction and int adoption); ptnr Beckman & Beckman 1988–98, head Children's Law Dept Dawson Cornwell 1998–; chair Children's Interests Ctee Int Bar Assoc 2005–; memb: Working Gp on the Cross Border Movement for Children Inst of Advanced Legal Studies, Working Gp on Forced Marriages Home Office, Cwlth Working Gp on AIDS; int corr International Family Law; chair Bd of Tstees Reunite Int Child Abduction Centre; UNICEF Child Rights Lawyer of the Year 1999, Legal Aid Lawyer of the Year 2004; memb: Law Soc 1985, Int Soc of Family Law, Int Bar Assoc, Int Centre for Missing and Exploited Children; fell Int Acad of Matrimonial Lawyers; *Books* International Parental Child Abduction (jtly, 2003); *Publications* Children Law and Practice (conslt ed), International Parental Child Abduction (jt author); *Recreations* film, charitable work; *Style*— Ms Anne-Marie Hutchinson, OBE; ✉ Dawson Cornwell, 15 Red Lion Square, London WC1R 4QT (tel 020 7242 2556, fax 020 7539 4841, e-mail hutchinsona@dawsoncornwell.co.uk)

HUTCHINSON, Colman Joseph; s of William Joseph Hutchinson (d 2000), and Eileen Patricia, *née* Hogan (d 1985); *b* 10 July 1953, Dublin; *Educ* Christian Brothers' Coll Monkstown Park Dublin; *m* 3 June 1977, Sharon Elizabeth, *née* Leahy; 2 s (Aaron Patrick b 21 May 1978, Adam Joseph b 22 Dec 1979), 1 da (Ava Jean b 30 March 1983); *Career* researcher Gay Byrne's Late Late Show RTE Ireland 1977–85, prodr LWT 1985–95 (programmes incl Blind Date and Surprise Surprise); head of entertainment: Hat Trick Productions 1995–98, Celador 1998– (responsible for Who Wants to Be a Millionaire, nominee BAFTA Award 2000); *Style*— Colman Hutchinson, Esq; ✉ Celador Productions, 39 Long Acre, London WC2E 9LG (tel 020 7240 8101, mobile 07768 037473, e-mail chutchinson@celador.co.uk)

HUTCHINSON, (Edward) Graham; OBE (1997); s of Roger Hutchinson (d 1971), of Southport, Merseyside, and Katharine Norma, *née* Robinson (d 1984); *b* 11 January 1940; *Educ* Bryanston, King's Coll Cambridge (MA), Euro Inst of Business Admin Fontainebleau (MBA); *m* 7 Nov 1970, Diana Fair, da of William Fair Milligan, of Heswall, Merseyside; 2 da (Camilla b 1972, Christina b 1977), 1 s (Mark b 1974); *Career* dir and chief exec Neptun International Holding AG Basle 1972–80, md Dan-Air Servs Ltd 1981–91; dir: Davies and Newman Holdings plc 1980–90, Bowater Europe 1977–80, Air Scandinavia Ltd 1991–94, Ashford Hosp Trust 1991–98, Trusts in Partnership Ltd 1992–, Trustee Services Co Ltd 1997–, Yeldall Christian Centres Ltd 1979–2004 (chm 1979–97), Agapé Ministries Ltd 1980–96 (chm 1980–91); prop Thames Business Group 1993–; memb CBI London Regional Cncl 1983–89; MIEE 1966; *Recreations* leisure travel, music, family; *Clubs* Leander; *Style*— Graham Hutchinson, Esq, OBE; ✉ Silver Birches, Startins Lane, Cookham Dean, Berkshire SL6 9TS (tel 01628 481719, e-mail grahamhutchinson@thamesbusinessgp.demon.co.uk)

HUTCHINSON, Prof Gregory Owen; s of Rev J O Hutchinson, and Mrs D Hutchinson; *Educ* City of London Sch, Balliol Coll Oxford (scholar, MA, DPhil); *Career* Univ of Oxford: res lectr ChCh 1981–84, fell and tutor in classics Exeter Coll 1984–, reader in classical lit 1996–98, prof of Greek and Latin languages and lit 1998–; *Books* Aeschylus (1985), Septem Contra Thebas (1993), Hellenistic Poetry (1988), Latin Literature from Seneca to Juvenal: A Critical Study (1993), Cicero's Correspondence: A Literary Study (1998), Greek Lyric Poetry: A Commentary on Selected Larger Pieces (2001); *Recreations* playing the piano, reading literature (mostly English, French, German, Italian, Russian, Sanskrit); *Style*— Prof Gregory Hutchinson; ✉ Exeter College, Oxford OX1 3DP (tel 01865 279600, fax 01865 279630, e-mail gregory.hutchinson@exeter.ox.ac.uk)

HUTCHINSON, John; s of John Hutchinson, and Beatrice Hutchinson; *b* 5 August 1944; *Educ* King Charles I GS Kidderminster, Harvard Business Sch (Prog for Mgmnt Devpt, Managing Info System Resource course); *m* 1 April 1967, Elspeth Nanette; 1 da (Abigail Lucy b 5 November 1974); *Career* Lloyds Bank: various branch and Head Office positions 1960–80, corp devpt mangr 1980–82, dir and dep gen mangr Black Horse Agencies 1982–84, divnl mangr UK Retail Banking 1984–87, head of personal banking UK Retail Banking 1987–89, gen mangr support and devpt 1989–90; Nationwide Building Soc: main bd dir 1990–92, retail ops dir 1990–92, corp strategy dir 1992, exec chm Nationwide Property Services 1992; md Visa UK Ltd 1993–95; chief exec: The Performing Right Soc Ltd 1995–2005, Mechanical-Copyright Protection Soc 1996–2005; FCIB, CIMgt; *Recreations* skiing, swimming, travel, reading, theatre, ballet; *Style*— John Hutchinson, Esq; ✉ Ravenshead, School Lane, Great Wigborough, Colchester, Essex CO5 7RJ

HUTCHINSON, (John) Maxwell; s of Frank Maxwell Hutchinson (d 1977), and Elizabeth Ross Muir, *née* Wright (d 1987); *b* 3 December 1948; *Educ* Oundle, Scott Sutherland Sch of Architecture Aberdeen, AA Sch of Architecture (AADipl); *Career* chm: The Permarock Group Loughborough 1985–95, Hutchinson and Ptnrs Architects Ltd 1972–92, The Hutchinson Studio Architects 1992–2000; RIBA: memb Cncl 1978–93, sr vice-pres 1988–89, pres 1989–91; visiting prof of architecture Queen's Univ Belfast 1989–93, special prof of architectural design Univ of Nottingham 1992–96, visiting prof of architecture Univ of Westminster 1997–2001; chm: Industrial Building Bureau 1986–88, Br Architectural Library Tst 1991–, Schools of Architecture Validation Panel 1991–96, E Midlands Arts Bd 1991–94; vice-chm Construction Industry Cncl 1989–91; radio and TV broadcaster, compositions incl: The Kibbo Kift (Edinburgh Festival) 1976, The Ascent of Wilberforce III (Lyric Hammersmith) 1982, Requiem 1988, Christmas Cantata 1990; memb Cncl Royal Sch of Church Music 1997–2000; fndr and chm Architects for Aid (A4A) 2005–; Freeman City of London 1980, Freeman Worshipful Co of Chartered Architects 1988; hon fell Univ of Greenwich; hon fell Royal Soc of Ulster Architects, assoc memb PRS 1988; *Books* The Prince of Wales Right or Wrong? (1989), Number 57 - The Story of a House (2003); *Recreations* playing jazz piano, travel; *Clubs* Athenaeum, Blacks, Groucho; *Style*— Maxwell Hutchinson, Esq; ✉ e-mail maxwell@hutchinsonstudio.co.uk

HUTCHINSON, Prof Philip; DL (Oxfordshire 2003); s of George Hutchinson, of Bishop Auckland, Co Durham, and Edna Hutchinson; *b* 26 July 1938; *Educ* King James I GS Bishop Auckland, King's Coll Durham (BSc), Univ of Newcastle upon Tyne (PhD); *m* 1960, Joyce Harrison, da of Fred Harrison, of Bishop Auckland, Co Durham; 1 da (Barbara Helen b 1967), 1 s (John Paul b 1972); *Career* AERE Harwell: scientific offr rising to princ scientific offr Theoretical Physics Div 1962–69 and 1970–75, head Thermodynamics and Fluid Mechanics Gp Engrg Scis Div 1975–80, head Combustion Centre 1980–87, head Engrg Physics Branch Engrg Scis Div 1980–85, head Engrg Scis Div 1985–87; Cranfield Univ: head Sch of Mech Engrg 1987–2000, dep vice-chllr 1996–2003, pro-vice-chllr 1996–99, head Sch of Engrg 2000–02; princ Royal Mil Coll of Sci 1996–2006; visiting fell Dept of Chem Engrg Univ of Houston Texas 1969–70; visiting prof: Imperial Coll London 1980–85, Univ of Leeds 1985–; formerly chm: Exec Ctee on Fundamental Research in Combustion Int Energy Agency (1977–81), Combustion Physics Gp Inst of Physics (1985–89), Computational Fluid Dynamics Advsy Gp SERC; chm Bd European Research Community on Flow Turbulence and Combustion 1994–2000 (fndr memb, treas 2000–02); non-exec dir NUMECA Belgium 1998–2002; formerly Inst of

Physics rep then Combustion Inst (Br Section) rep on Watt Ctee Inst of Energy, memb Energy Panel Foresight Survey, UK memb COST (Co-operation in Sci and Technol) F1 Gp of CEC, Ed Advsy Bd Experiments in Fluids jl; Hon Dr Technol Univ of Lund Sweden 1999; MRI 1989, CPhys, CEng, FInstP, FREng 1997; *Publications* author of numerous articles in learned jls on statistical mechanics, fluid mechanics, spray and particle cloud disperson and combustion; *Recreations* squash, music, reading, Go, gadgets; *Clubs* Reform; *Style—* Prof Philip Hutchinson, DL, FREng; ✉ Cranfield University, Royal Military College of Science, Shrivenham, Swindon, Wiltshire SN6 8LA (tel 01793 7825436, fax 01793 782546)

HUTCHINSON OF LULLINGTON, Baron (Life Peer UK 1978), of Lullington in the County of East Sussex; Jeremy Nicolas Hutchinson; QC (1961); o s of St John Hutchinson, KC (d 1943), and Mary, o da of Sir Hugh Barnes, KCSI, KCVO; *b* 28 March 1915; *Educ* Stowe, Magdalen Coll Oxford (MA); *m* 1, 1940 (m dis 1966), Dame Peggy Ashcroft, DBE (d 1991); 1 da (Hon Eliza b 1941), 1 s (Hon Nicholas St John b 1946); m 2, 1966, June (d 2006), yr da of Capt Arthur Edward Capel, CBE (d 1919), and formerly wife of Franz Osborn; *Career* served RNVR 1939–46; called to the Bar Middle Temple 1939; recorder: Bath 1962–72, Crown Court 1972–76; sits as Lib Dem Peer in House of Lords (sat as Lab Peer until joining SDP 1981); vice-chm Arts Cncl 1977–79; tstee: Tate Gallery 1977–84 (chm 1980–84); prof of law RA 1988; *Clubs* MCC; *Style—* The Rt Hon Lord Hutchinson of Lullington, QC; ✉ House of Lords, London SW1A 0PW

HUTCHISON, David Alan; MBE (1976); s of Hector Donald Hutchison (d 1948), of Enfield, Middx, and Winifred, *née* Middlehurst (d 1986); *b* 13 January 1937; *Educ* Royal Masonic Sch Bushey, Bartlett Sch of Architecture UCL (BA); *m* 3 April 1961 (m dis 1989), Helen Elizabeth, da of Arthur George Penn (d 1981), of Pembury, Kent; 2 da (Gillian b 21 Jan 1962, Christine b 9 Aug 1965), 2 s (Michael b 1 Nov 1963, Peter b 24 Dec 1966); m 2, 18 May 1990, Audrey, da of Horace Scott, of Tolworth, Surrey; *Career* architect; worked with Powell & Moya 1960–64: chm: HLM (formerly Hutchison Locke & Monk) 1988–92 (fndr ptnr 1964), HLM Architects Ltd, HLM Planning Ltd, HLM Landscape Ltd; fndr and sr dir Moloney O'Beirne Hutchison Partnership Dublin 1977–, fndr and sr ptnr David Hutchison Partnership 1992– (architect St James Hosp Dublin, Royal London Hosp redevelopment, Barry Hosp, Chepstow Hosp, Hammersmith Hosp, Sixth Form Coll Farnborough, St John's Sch Marlborough, Broomfield Hosp Chelmsford, Royal London Hosp redevelopment, Royal Marsden Hosp, Princess Alexandra Hosp Harlow, Aldershot Hosp, Frenchay Hosp, Weston Hosp, Torbay Hosp, Nevill Hall Hosp, Monmouth Hosp); architect for major public sector cmmns in health and civic authorities 1964–88; health projects (hosps) incl: Bournemouth, Cheltenham, Ealing, Whipps Cross, Lister, Northern Gen Sheffield, Medway, Dunfermline West Fife, Liverpool Maternity, Royal Brompton London, Nottingham City, Guy's, N Middx; civic projects: Surrey Heath BC, Broxbourne BC, Daventry DC, Colchester BC, Waltham Forest Cncl, Macclesfield Cncl, Epsom and Ewell Cncl, Reigate and Banstead Cncl, Stoke-on-Trent Cncl, Stroud Cncl, North Staffs Cncl, schs in Redditch, Bristol and Bath; cmmns: Univs of Reading and Surrey, Smithfield Market Corp of London; winner: int competition (architecture) Paisley Civic Centre 1964, 7 Civic Tst Awards DOE Good Housing Award, RIBA Architecture Commendation, Redland Roof Tile Award, RIBA Energy Award, Concrete Soc Architecture Award; nat seat on Cncl RIBA 1987–93, assessor Civic Tst; Freeman: City of London 1977 (Liveryman 1990), Worshipful Co of Constructors 1977 (Master 2000), Worshipful Co of Arbitrators 1987; RIBA, ARIAS, FIA, FFB, AInst(Hosp)E, FIE, FRSA 1989; *Recreations* amateur theatre, local amenity soc; *Clubs* Arts (London), Camberley Soc (chm), Farnborough and RAE Operatic Soc, Camus Productions, Bath Light Operatic Gp, Gilbert and Sullivan Soc; *Style—* David Hutchison, Esq, MBE; ✉ 7 St Michael's Court, Monkton Combe, Bath BA2 7HA (mobile 07901 716866); Whittaker House, 2 Whittaker Avenue, Richmond upon Thames, Surrey TW9 1EH (tel 020 8822 6907); David Hutchison Partnership, Kelso Place, Upper Bristol Road, Bath BA1 3AU (tel 01225 303960, fax 01225 303985, e-mail architects@dhp-bath.co.uk)

HUTCHISON, Donald Colin Trevor; s of Brig Colin Ross Marshall Hutchison, DSO, MC (ka 1943), and Jovine Helen Trevor, *née* Williams (d 1957); *b* 12 March 1934; *Educ* Eton, Magdalene Coll Cambridge (MA); *Career* landowner; 2 Lt Oxon and Bucks LI 1952, served in Korean War 1953 and Egypt 1954 Durham LI; dir H C Stephens Ltd 1960–63, dir various property cos London, Paris and Nice 1964–79; *Recreations* landscaping, shooting; *Clubs* Brooks's; *Style—* D C T Hutchison, Esq; ✉ Heath House, Stockbridge, Hampshire SO20 6BX (tel 01264 810556)

HUTCHISON, Sir Peter Craft; 2 Bt (UK 1956), of Rossie, Co Perth, CBE (1992); s of Sir James Riley Holt Hutchison, 1 Bt, DSO, TD (d 1979), and Winefryde Eleanor Mary (Anne) (d 1988); *b* 5 June 1935; *Educ* Eton, Magdalene Coll Cambridge (BA); *m* 1966, Virginia, da of John Millar Colville, of Gribloch, Kippen, Stirlingshire; 1 s; *Heir* s, James Hutchison; *Career* former Lt Royal Scots Greys; chm Hutchison and Craft Ltd, former dir Stakis plc and other cos; memb Bd: Scottish Tourist Bd 1981–87, Deacon Incorporation of Hammermen 1984–85; Scottish Natural Heritage June-Dec 1994; chm Forestry Cmmn 1994–2001; vice-chm Bd Br Waterways Bd (memb 1987–98); chm of tstees Royal Botanic Garden Edinburgh 1985–94, dep convenor Loch Lomond and the Trossachs Nat Park 2002–; FRSE 1997; *Style—* Sir Peter Hutchison, Bt, CBE, FRSE; ✉ Broich, Kippen, Stirlingshire FK8 3EN

HUTCHISON, Sir Robert; 3 Bt (UK 1939), of Thurle, Streatley, Co Berks; s of Sir Peter Hutchison, 2 Bt (d 1998); *b* 25 May 1954; *Educ* Orwell Park Ipswich, Marlborough; *m* 7 Feb 1987, Anne Margaret, er da of Sir (Godfrey) Michael David Thomas, 11 Bt (d 2003); 2 s (Hugo Thomas Alexander b 16 April 1988, Guy Piers Giles b 30 April 1990); *Heir* s, Hugo Hutchison; *Career* with J & A Scrimgeour Ltd 1973–78, ind fin advsr 1978–; *Recreations* tennis, watching association football, family life, golf; *Clubs* Woodbridge Golf, Ipswich and Suffolk; *Style—* Sir Robert Hutchison, Bt; ✉ Hawthorn Cottage, Lower Road, Grundisburgh, Woodbridge, Suffolk IP13 6UQ (tel 01473 738199)

HUTCHON, Dr David James Riddell; s of James Hutchon (d 1971), and Alice Mary, *née* McIntosh; *b* 17 April 1945; *Educ* George Watson's Boys Coll Edinburgh, Univ of Edinburgh (BSc, MB ChB); *m* 12 June 1971, Rosemary Elizabeth, da of Dr Ronald Caile (d 1978), of Southport, Lancs; 2 s (Christopher b 1978, Andrew b 1995), 1 da (Fiona b 1979); *Career* govt med offr Grand Cayman BWI 1972–74, SHO Simpson Memorial Hosp Edinburgh 1974–76, registrar in obstetrics and gynaecology Ninewells Hosp Dundee 1976–78, res registrar Northwick Park Hosp London 1978–79, sr registrar in obstetrics and gynaecology Eastern Gen Hosp Edinburgh and clinical tutor Univ of Edinburgh 1979–81, conslt obstetrician and gynaecologist Darlington Health Authy 1981–; fell Edinburgh Obstetrical Soc, FRCOG; *Recreations* golf, skiing, sailing; *Clubs* Blackwell Grange Golf; *Style—* Dr David Hutchon; ✉ 9 Farr Holme, Blackwell, Darlington, Co Durham DL3 8QZ (tel 01325 358134); Department of Obstetrics and Gynaecology, Memorial Hospital, Darlington, Co Durham (tel 01325 380100, e-mail djrhutchon@postmaster.co.uk)

HUTH, Angela Maureen; da of Harold Edward Strachan Huth (d 1967), and Bridget, *née* Nickols (d 2004); *Educ* Guilsborough Lodge Sch, Lawnside Great Malvern, Beaux Arts Sch of Art Paris, Annigoni's Sch of Art Florence, Byam Shaw Art Sch London; *m* 1, 1961 (m dis 1970), Quentin Crewe (d 1998); 1 da (Candida Crewe, *qv*, b 1964); m 2, 1978, Dr James Howard-Johnston, s of late Rear Adm C D Howard-Johnston, CB, DSO, DSC; 1 da (Eugenie b 1981); *Career* memb Art Dept J Walter Thompson Advertising 1958–59, travel ed Queen Magazine 1959–61, woman's page Sunday Express 1962–63, reporter Man Alive (BBC) 1965–68, presenter How It Is (BBC) 1969–70, freelance journalist and reviewer 1965– (incl The Times, Sunday Times, Telegraph, Sunday Telegraph, Spectator, Guardian, Observer); FRSL 1975; *Publications* novels: Nowhere Girl (1970), Virginia Fly is Drowning (1972), Sun Child (1975), South of the Lights (1977), Monday Lunch in Fairyland and Other Stories (1978), Wanting (1984), Such Visitors (1989), Invitation to the Married Life (1991), Land Girls (1994), Another Kind of Cinderella and other stories (1996), Wives of the Fishermen (1998), Easy Silence (1999), Of Love and Slaughter (2002), The Collected Stories of Angela Huth (2003); non fiction: The English Woman's Wardrobe (1987), Island of the Children (ed, poetry anthology, 1987), Casting a Spell (ed, poetry anthology, 1991), Well Remembered Friends (ed, anthology of eulogies, 2004); stage plays: The Understanding (first performed 1981), The Trouble with Old Lovers (first performed 1995); TV plays incl: The Summer House (BBC, 1969), The Emperor's New Hat (BBC, 1971), Virginia Fly is Drowning (adaptation, BBC, 1975), The Understanding (YTV, 1987), Sun Child (YTV, 1988); radio plays incl Past Forgetting (2001); *Recreations* tap dancing, buying and selling paste jewellery; *Style—* Miss Angela Huth; ✉ c/o Caroline Michel, William Morris Agency Inc, Centrepoint, 103 New Oxford Street, London WC1A 1DD (tel 020 7534 6806)

HUTH, Johannes Peter; s of Prof Karl Huth, of Frankfurt, Germany, and Dr Brigitte, *née* Soergel; *b* 27 May 1960, Heidelberg, Germany; *Educ* LSE (BSc), Univ of Chicago (MBA); *m* 20 July 1991, Leili, *née* Persson; 2 s (Christopher b 18 April 1992, Nikolas b 7 Jan 1997), 3 da (Elisabeth b 1 June 1994, Susanna, Katrina (twins) b 5 April 1998); *Career* a vice-pres M&A Dept Salomon Brothers 1986–1991, memb Mgmnt Ctee Investcorp until 1999, with Kohlberg Kravis Roberts & Co 1999– (currently md and head London office); *Style—* Johannes Huth, Esq; ✉ Kohlberg Kravis Roberts & Co Limited, Stirling Square, 7 Carlton Gardens, London SW1Y 5AD (tel 020 7839 9800, fax 020 7839 9832)

HUTSON, Maurice Arthur; MBE (1998); s of William Arthur Hutson (d 1980), of S Yorks, and Ivy, *née* Roberts (d 1989); *b* 27 January 1934; *Educ* Gainsborough Tech Coll, Leeds Coll of Technol; *m* 1959, Janet, da of Arthur Edward Parkin, of S Yorks; 2 s (Mark Andrew b 1961, Jonathan Peter b 1970), 1 da (Helen Claire b 1963); *Career* chartered engr; apprentice Newell Ltd 1949–57, Nat Serv RAF 1957–59, design engr Pegson Ltd 1959–63, devpt engr Tarmac Roadstone Ltd 1963–71 (prodn and engrg mangr 1965, staff offr 1970); chm and md: Seaham Harbour Dock Co 1971–81 (dir 1981–87), Transport and Aggregates Ltd 1972–81, Mahcon Construction (Services) Ltd 1972–, Wath Quarries Ltd 1977–, Allerton Engrg Ltd 1983–2000, Naylor Sportscars Ltd 1986–93, Hutson Motor Co Ltd 1986–; exec chm: Parker Plant Ltd (chm and chief exec 1990–97 and 2003–), Templars of Rothley; chm: E Type Cars Ltd 1997, Canon Street Properties Ltd 1997, Park Hill Golf and Leisure Ltd 2000–; exec chm Universal Conveyors Co Ltd 1998–; dir: Necoast Ltd 1980–90, The Sundial Hotel Ltd Northallerton until 1996, The Seaham Harbour Dock Co 1981–87, Modern Air Systems Ltd 1992–, Leicestershire Engrg Trg Gp 1996–; memb: Cncl and vice-pres Fedn of Mfrs of Construction Equipment and Cranes (FMCEC) 1992–96, Lighthouse Club 1990–, Br Thai Business Gp, Asia Europe Meeting (ASEM); advsr Prince's Tst until 1997; CEng, MIMechE, MIEE, FIQ; *Recreations* grandchildren, advising people on new ventures and business set ups, motor sport, travel and walking, gardening, river and coastal cruising (motor boat), steam engines and vintage vehicles, golf, collecting antiques; *Clubs* Rotary (Stokesley), 41 (Guisborough); *Style—* Maurice A Hutson, Esq, MBE; ✉ West Acre, 25 The Ridgeway, Rothley, Leicestershire LE7 7LE (tel 0116 230 3230, fax 0116 230 2868); Parker Plant Ltd, Viaduct Works, Canon Street, Leicester LE4 6HD (tel 0116 266 5999, fax 0116 261 0745, telex 34542, e-mail mauriceahutson@parkerplant.com)

HUTSON, Robin; s of Derek Charles Hutson, of Whitsbury, Wilts, and Eileen Hilda, *née* Juniper; *b* 9 January 1957; *Educ* Haberdashers' Aske's Hatcham, Godalming GS, Brookland Tech Coll (OND); *m* 25 June 1983, Judith Alison, da of Douglas Hill; 2 s (Oliver Charles Westley b 10 Oct 1985, William Charles Westley b 3 Nov 1988); *Career* trainee Savoy Hotels Ltd 1975–81, front office mangr The Berkeley Hotel 1981–84, ops mangr Elbow Beach Hotel Bermuda 1984–86, md Chewton Glen Hotel Ltd 1990–94 (gen mangr 1986–90), md and chm Hotel du Vin Ltd 1994–2004; non-exec dir Richmond FC 1996–99, chm Soho House Ltd 1997–; memb: Bd of Friends Univ of Food & Wine Soc, Bd of Patrons Academy of Culinary Arts 2004–, Champagne Acad; Caterer and Hotelkeeper Hotelier of the Year 2003; MHCIMA 1990; *Clubs* Soho House; *Style—* Robin Hutson, Esq; ✉ Soho House Ltd, 3–5 Bateman Street, London W1D 4AG (tel 0207 851 1171)

HUTT, Ven David Handley; s of late Frank Handley Hutt, and Evelyn Violet Catherine, *née* Faarup; *b* 24 August 1938; *Educ* Brentwood Sch, RMA Sandhurst, KCL (AKC, Hanson Prize for Christian Ethics, Barry Prize for Theology); *Career* Reg Army 1957–64; ordained: deacon 1969, priest 1970; curate: Bedford Park London 1969–70, St Matthew Westminster 1970–73; priest vicar and succentor Southwark Cathedral 1973–78, sr chaplain King's Coll Taunton 1978–82; vicar: St Alban and St Patrick Birmingham 1982–86, All Saints' St Marylebone 1986–95, canon and steward Westminster Abbey 1995–2005 (canon emeritus 2005–), sub dean and archdeacon of Westminster 1999–2005, memb Bd Assoc of Leading Visitor Attractions (representing The Cathedrals' Gp) 2001 (memb Cncl 2000–05); fell and curator Sion Coll 2007– (pres 1996–97, memb Ct 2005–07), fndr ed Affirming Catholicism; patron London Parks and Gardens Tst 2003–, tstee United Westminster Schs Fndn 2006–, govr Sutton Valence Sch 2007–; MA (Lambeth) 2005; *Recreations* gardening, cooking, music, theatre; *Clubs* Reform; *Style—* The Ven David Hutt; ✉ 3CC Morpeth Terrace, London SW1P 1EW

HUTT, Sir Dexter Walter; kt (2004); Walter Hutt, of West Palm Beach, FL, and Binks Hutt (d 1948); *b* 25 July 1948, Georgetown, Guyana; *Educ* Mackenzie HS, Greenmore Coll, Univ of Birmingham (BSocSci); *m* Aug 1976, Rosemary Lyn; 1 da (Elizabeth b 23 June 1979), 2 s (Andrew b 7 Aug 1981, Steven b 16 July 1987); *Career* former teacher Handsworth and Coventry; head Ninestiles Sch Birmingham 1998–2004, exec headteacher Ninestiles Fedn of Schs, chief exec Ninestiles Plus; cmmr Cmmn for Racial Equality 2004–; *Style—* Sir Dexter Hutt; ✉ Ninestiles School, Hartfield Crescent, Acocks Green, Birmingham B27 7QG (tel 0121 693 1642, fax 0121 778 4234)

HUTT, Jane Elizabeth; AM; da of Prof Michael S R Hutt (decd), and Elizabeth, *née* Newton-Jones, of Crickhowell, Powys; *Educ* Highlands Sch Eldoret Kenya, Rosemead Sch Littlehampton, Univ of Kent (BA), LSE (CQSW), Univ of Bristol (MSc); *m* 14 July 1984, Michael John Hilary Trickey; 2 da (Jessica, Rachel); *Career* community worker: Impact (town planners and architects) 1972–74, Polypill Community Project Fndn 1975–77; co-ordinator Welsh Women's Aid 1975–88; dir: Tenant Participation Advsy Serv 1988–92, Chwarae Teg (equal opportunities) 1992–99; vice-chair Wales Cncl for Voluntary Action; memb: Common Purpose Advsy Ctee 1989–99, New Deal Wales Advsy Task Force 1996–99, New Opportunities Fund 1998–99; memb Nat Assembly for Wales (Lab) Vale of Glamorgan 1999–, min for health and social servs 1999–2005, min for assembly business, equal opportunities and children 2005–; hon fell Univ of Wales Inst Cardiff 1996; *Books* Opening the Town Hall: An Introduction to Local Government (2 edn, 1989), Making Opportunities: A Guide for Women and Employers (1992); *Recreations* reading, music; *Style—* Ms Jane Hutt, AM; ✉ National Assembly for Wales, Cardiff Bay, Cardiff CF99 1NA (tel 029 2082 5111, fax 029 2089 8229, e-mail j.hutt@wales.gov.uk)

HUTT, Peter Morrice; s of late Sqdn Ldr Harry Morrice Hutt, of Caversham, Berks, and late Joan Ethel Ludlow, *née* Whitmore; *b* 15 April 1945; *Educ* Leighton Park Sch Reading, Univ of Southampton (LLB); *m* 23 March 1974, Cynthia Anne, da of John Gauntlett Gubb (d 1988), of Uitenhage, South Africa; 1 s (Stephen b 1977); *Career* admitted slr 1969, Notary Public 1978; ptnr Brain & Brain 1973–97, conslt Field Seymour Parkes 1997–;

H

dep master Supreme Court Queen's Bench Div 1992–99; Rotherfield Peppard: chm Parish Cncl 1987–90, lay chm All Saints Parochial Church Cncl 1986–90, churchwarden All Saints Church 2005–; tstee Relief in Need Charity, clerk Polehampton Charities Twyford, former memb Caversham Round Table; memb: Law Soc 1967, Slr's Benevolent Assoc 1969, Notaries Soc 1978; *Recreations* music, walking, gardening, arts; *Style*— Peter Hutt, Esq; ✉ Rushton House, Church Lane, Rotherfield Peppard, Henley-on-Thames, Oxfordshire RG9 5JR (tel 01491 628335); Field Seymour Parkes, 1 London Street, Reading RG1 4QW (tel 0118 951 6200, fax 0118 950 2704, e-mail peter.hutt@fsp-law.com)

HUTTON, Alasdair Henry; OBE (1989, MBE 1986), TD (1977); s of Alexander Hutton (d 1954), and Margaret Elizabeth Hutton (d 1990); *b* 19 May 1940; *Educ* Gatehouse of Fleet Sch, Dollar Acad, Brisbane State HS Aust; *m* 1975, Dame Deirdre Mary Hutton, DBE, *qv*, da of Kenneth Alexander Home Cassels, of Wimbish Green, Essex; 2 s (Thomas b 1978, Nicholas b 1982); *Career* writer and narrator public events, audio, video; MEP (EDG) S Scot 1979–89; 2 i/c 15 Scot (Vol) Bn The Parachute Regt 1979–86, Watchkeepers Pool 1987–96; narrator: Edinburgh Military Tattoo 1992–, Berwick Military Tattoo 1994–2005, Queensland Tattoo 1996–2000; chm: Scot Cons Ctees on Environment and Europe 1989–93, Crime Concern Scot 1990–95, Disease Prevention Orgn 1990–; dir Scot Agric Coll 1990–95, pres Kelso Branch Royal Br Legion 2000–; hon pres Clydesdale Cons and Unionist Assoc 1991–95; cncllr Kelso and District (formerly Kelso Central) Scottish Borders Cncl 2002– (convener of the Cncl 2003–); chm John Buchan Soc 2000–06 (life memb 1985, vice-pres 2006–); chm (Scotland) Community Serv Vols 2002– (tstee 1985–); elder Church of Scotland 1985–; co sec and tstee Inst of Contemporary Scotland 2001–02; patron Borders Independent Advocacy Service (BIAS) 2001–; memb: Border Area Ctee Lowland RFCA 1990–, Int Rels Ctee Law Soc of Scot 1991–99, Bd UK 2000 Scotland 1991–96, Church & Nation Ctee Church of Scot 1992–96, Social Security Advsy Ctee 1996–99; memb Queen's Body Guard for Scotland (Royal Co of Archers) 1988–; patron ROKPA UK 1997–; chm Kelso Millennium Tst 2000–01; candidate (Cons) Scot Parl election 1999; Hon Col Lothian and Borders Battalion Army Cadet Force 2006–; fell Indust and Parl Tst; *Style*— Alasdair Hutton, Esq, OBE, TD; ✉ 4 Broomlands Court, Kelso, Roxburghshire TD5 7SR (tel 01573 224369, e-mail alasdairhutton@yahoo.co.uk)

HUTTON, Anthony Charles; CB (1995); s of late Charles James Hutton, and Athene Mary, *née* Hastie; *b* 4 April 1941; *Educ* Brentwood Sch, Trinity Coll Oxford (MA); *m* Sara, *née* Flemming; 2 s (Simon James b 1966, Nicholas Henry Coit b 1970), 1 da (Katharine Mary b 1968); *Career* civil servant; HM inspr of taxes 1962–64, princ Bd of Trade 1968–74 (asst princ 1964–68), PPS to Sec of State for Trade 1974–77; DTI: asst sec 1977–84, under sec 1984–91, dep sec and princ estab and fin offr 1991–96, DG Resources and Services 1996–97, DG Trade Policy 1997–2000; OECD Paris: dir Public Mgmnt Serv 2000–01, exec dir 2001–; *Clubs* Athenaeum; *Style*— Anthony Hutton, Esq, CB; ✉ OECD, 2 rue Andre-Pascal 75775, Paris Cedex 16, France (tel 00 33 1 45 24 84 44)

HUTTON, Baron (Life Peer UK 1997), of Bresagh in the County of Down; (James) Brian Edward Hutton; kt (1988), PC (1988); s of late James Hutton, and Mabel Hutton, of Belfast; *b* 29 June 1931; *Educ* Shrewsbury, Balliol Coll Oxford (BA), Queen's Univ Belfast; *m* 1, 1975, Mary Gillian (d 2000), da of James Murland, of Saintfield, Co Down; 2 da (Hon Louise b 1976, Hon Helen b 1978); m 2, 2001, Rosalind Anne Nickols, wid of Christopher Nickols; 2 step s (James b 1975, Hugo b 1981), 1 step da (Annabel b 1977); *Career* called to the Bar NI 1954, jr counsel to Attorney Gen NI 1969, QC (NI) 1970, sr crown counsel NI 1973–79, judge of the High Court of Justice (NI) 1979–88, Lord Chief Justice of NI 1988–97, a Lord of Appeal in Ordinary 1997–2004; chm Hutton Inquiry 2003–04; memb Jt Law Enforcement Cmmn 1974, dep chm Boundary Cmmn for NI 1985–88; pres NI Assoc for Mental Health 1983–90; visitor Univ of Ulster 1999–2004; *Style*— The Rt Hon the Lord Hutton, PC; ✉ House of Lords, London SW1A 0PW

HUTTON, Dame Deirdre Mary; DBE (2004, CBE 1998); da of Kenneth Alexander Home Cassels, of Wimbish Green, Essex, and Barbara Kathleen, *née* Alington; *b* 15 March 1949; *Educ* Sherborne Sch for Girls, Hartwell House; *m* 1 Nov 1975 (sep 2002), Alasdair Henry Hutton, *qv*, s of late Alexander Hutton; 2 s (Thomas Kennedy b 28 June 1978, Nicholas Alasdair b 27 Feb 1982); *Career* Anchor Housing Assoc Oxford 1973–75, res asst Glasgow C of C 1975–82; chm: Scot Consumer Cncl 1991–99 (memb 1986–90, vice-chm 1990–91), Rural Forum (Scotland) Ltd 1992–99, Ombudsman Cncl Personal Investment Authy 1997–2000 (chm 1994–96), Nat Consumer Cncl 2001–05 (memb Cncl 1991–, vice-chm 1997–2001), Steering Gp Food Chain Centre 2002–05, Food Standards Agency 2005–; vice-chm Scottish Environmental Protection Agency 1999–2002; memb: Scot Consultative Cncl on the Curriculum 1987–91, Ctee on Reporting 1989–91, Parole Bd for Scot 1993–96, Cabinet Office Better Regulation Task Force 1999–2005, Sustainable Devpt Cmmn 2000–01, Curry Cmmn on the Future of Agric and Food 2001; non-exec dir: FSA 1997– (dep chm Bd 2004–), Edinburgh City Theatres Tst 1998–99; lay memb for Scot of Gen Dental Cncl and memb Professional Misconduct Ctee 1988–94, memb Ctee to Review Curriculum Examinations in Fifth and Sixth Years of Scot Educn (Howie Ctee) 1990–92; memb, treas and chm Broomlands Sch Bd 1984–91, memb Music Ctee Scot Arts Cncl 1985–91, hon sec Kelso Music Soc 1985–95, chm Enterprise Music Scotland Ltd 1993–95; vice-chm Borders Local Health Cncl 1991–95, memb Bd Borders Health Bd 1996–2002; Hon DUniv Stirling 2000; *Recreations* gardening, music; *Style*— Dame Deirdre Hutton, DBE; ✉ Food Standards Agency, Aviation House, 125 Kingsway, London WC2B 6NH

HUTTON, His Hon Gabriel Bruce; s of late Robert Crompton Hutton, of Glos, and late Elfreda, *née* Bruce; fourth successive generation of judges living in Glos; *b* 27 August 1932; *Educ* Marlborough, Trinity Coll Cambridge (BA); *m* 1965, Deborah Leigh, da of Vivian Leigh Windus (d 1950), of Sussex; 2 da (Joanna b 1966, Tamsin b 1968), 1 s (Alexander b 1972); *Career* called to the Bar Inner Temple 1956; dep chm Gloucester Quarter Sessions 1971, recorder of the Crown Court 1972–78, circuit judge (Western Circuit) 1978–2003, liaison judge for Glos and res judge for Gloucester Crown Court 1987–2003; chm Criminal Justice Liaison Ctee for Glos and Wilts 1992–99, chm Criminal Justice Strategy Ctee for Glos 2000–03; chm Gloucester Branch CPRE 1992–2005; govr Barnwood House Tst 1999–2005; pres Friends of the Soldiers of Glos Museum 1999–; *Recreations* hunting (chm Berkeley 1973–2005), boating, shooting; *Style*— His Hon Gabriel Hutton; ✉ Chestal House, Dursley, Gloucestershire GL11 5AA (tel 01453 543285, fax 01453 549998)

HUTTON, Rt Hon John; PC (2001), MP; s of late George Hutton, and Rosemary Hutton; *b* 6 May 1955; *Educ* Westcliff HS Southend, Magdalen Coll Oxford (MA, BCL); *m* 1, 28 April 1978 (m dis 1993), Rosemary Caroline, *née* Little; 3 s (and 1 s decd), 1 da; m 2, 24 July 2004, Heather Rogers; *Career* legal asst CBI 1978–80, res fell Templeton Coll Oxford 1980–81, sr lectr in law Newcastle Poly 1981–92; Parly candidate (Lab) Penrith and the Border 1987, Euro Parly candidate Cumbria and N Lancs 1989, MP (Lab) Barrow and Furness 1992–; PPS: to Sec of State for Trade and Industry 1998, to Ldr of the House 1998; Parly under-sec of state Dept of Health 1998–99, min of state Dept of Health 1999–2005, Chllr of the Duchy of Lancaster 2005 sec of state for work and pensions 2005–07, sec of state for business and enterprise 2007–; chair All-Pty Gp: Welfare of Park Home Owners 1995–97, Br Latin Americal Gp 1997; memb: Select Ctee on Home Affrs 1994–97, Select Ctee on Unopposed Bills 1994–97; tstee Furness Animal Refuge; *Recreations* football, cricket, films, music, First World War history; *Clubs* Cemetary Cottages Working Men's (Barrow-in-Furness); *Style*— The Rt Hon John Hutton, MP; ✉ House of Commons, London SW1A 0AA (website www.johnhuttonmp.co.uk)

HUTTON, John Christopher; s of John Francis Hutton (d 1997), of Cardiff, and Elizabeth Margery Ethel, *née* Pugh (d 1998); *b* 7 June 1937; *Educ* Monmouth, Kingswood Sch Bath, ChCh Oxford (MA), Birmingham Coll of Technol (DMS), Coll of Aeronautics Cranfield; *m* 5 Aug 1963, Elizabeth Ann, da of Prof Eric Evans (d 1967); 2 da (Catrin b 1965, Bethan b 1968); *Career* Nat Serv RA Cyprus 1956–58; methods engr Tube Investments 1963–64 (graduate trainee 1961–63); Bristol and West Building Society: PA to Gen Mangr 1964–67, res mangr 1967–76, asst gen mangr 1976–88 (mktg and res 1976–86, corporate info and analysis 1986–88); fin mktg conslt 1988–2005; dir: Bristol & West Personal Pensions Ltd 1988–89, Wildscreen Trading Ltd 1991–94; conslt Money Which? 1971–2005; chm Housing Fin Panel Bldg Socs Assoc 1973–84 (memb 1967–), co-chm Tech Sub-Ctee of Jt Advsy Ctee on Mortgage Fin 1973–82; memb: Construction Industries Jt Forecasting Ctee NEDO 1978–89 (Housing Strategy Ctee 1975–77), Cncl Sub-Ctee on Reserves and Liquidity BSA 1981, Fin Advertising Sub-Ctee Advertising Standards Authy 1982–92; ldr BSA Netherlands Res Gp 1979; dir: Bristol Bldgs Preservation Tst Ltd 1984–2003, The Wildscreen Tst 1987–94; chm Kingsweston Preservation Soc 1993–97; FSS 1968, assoc IMS 1968; *Publications* author of many articles for the nat press; *Recreations* antiques, wine, countryside, journalism; *Style*— John Hutton, Esq; ✉ Ferns Hill, Kingsweston Road, Bristol BS11 0UX (tel 0117 982 4324); Wyevern, Aberedw, Builth Wells, Powys LD2 3UN (tel 01982 560439)

HUTTON, Matthew Charles Arthur; s of Capt Ronald David Hutton, MC (d 1984), of Loddon, Norfolk, and Rhodanthe Winnaretta, *née* Leeds (now Mrs Gerald Selous); *b* 10 September 1953; *Educ* Eton, ChCh Oxford (MA); *m* 6 Oct 1984, Anne Elizabeth Caroline, da of Leslie James Leppard, DFC, of Axminster, Devon; 2 da (Victoria b 1986, Alexandra b 1990), 1 s (David b 1988); *Career* chartered tax adviser, ptnr Daynes Hill & Perks (Slrs) Norwich 1987–89; ptnr in family farming business 1977–; govr St Felix Sch Southwold 1987–94, lay reader C of E 1992; tstee Norfolk and Norwich Families' House; FCInstT 1992 (ACInstT 1980); *Publications* Tax Planning for Private Residences (3 edn), Tolley's UK Taxation of Trusts (17 edn), Tottel's Trusts and Estates 2007/08, Post-death Rearrangements: Practice and Precedents (5 edn), Taxation of Farmers and Landowners (jtly, looseleaf), Stamp Duty - A Practical Guide (2 edn), Stamp Duty Land Tax (jtly); *Recreations* family life, country pursuits; *Clubs* Athenaeum, Boodle's, MCC, Norfolk (Norwich); *Style*— Matthew Hutton, Esq; ✉ Broom Farm, Chedgrave, Norwich NR14 6BQ (tel 01508 520775, fax 01508 528096, e-mail mhutton@paston.co.uk)

HUTTON, Prof Ronald Edmund; s of Geoffrey Edmund Hutton (d 1955), and Elsa Edwina, *née* Hansen (d 1978); *b* 19 December 1953, Ootacamund, India; *Educ* Ilford County HS for Boys, Pembroke Coll Cambridge (MA), St John's Coll Oxford (DPhil); *m* 1988, Lisa Radulovic; 1 da (Sophia Elisabeth b 19 March 1993); partner, Ana Adnan; *Career* Prize fell Magdalen College Oxford 1979–81; Univ of Bristol: lectr in history 1981–88, reader 1988–96, prof of history 1996–; Benjamin Franklin Prize Booksellers Assoc of America 1993; FRHistS 1981, FSA 1994; *Publications* author of 12 books, jt author of 2 books, author of 17 essays in academic jls and 20 in edited vols; *Recreations* travel with a view to adventure; *Style*— Prof Ronald Hutton; ✉ Department of Historical Studies, University of Bristol, 13 Woodland Road, Bristol BS8 1TB (tel 0117 928 7595, fax 0117 331 7933, e-mail r.hutton@bristol.co.uk)

HUTTON, Stuart Michael Colman; s of David S Hutton (d 1985), and Marjorie, *née* Colman; *b* 21 October 1946; *Educ* King's Sch Gloucester, Guildford and Lancaster Gate Colls of Law; *m* 25 July 1992, Clare Patricia, *née* Strowbridge; 1 da (Emelie Clare b 8 May 1993), 1 s (William Stuart b 11 April 1995); *Career* admitted slr 1975, slr advocate 1999; articled clerk Ingledew & Sons slrs Cardiff, ptnr Edwards Geldard 1977–86, fndr Hutton's Slrs Cardiff 1986–; fndr memb Child Care Panel Law Soc, pt/t chm Social Securities Appeal Tbnl 1986–89, past dir Slrs' Benevolent Assoc; lectr in professional legal studies and examiner Police and Criminal Evidence Act Centre for Professional Legal Studies Cardiff Univ; regular contrib on law and current affrs to radio and TV; past memb Cncl Cardiff & Dist Law Soc; chm Colwinston Village Hall Assoc; memb Law Soc 1975; *Publications* Jordan's Criminal Transaction Pack (1996); *Recreations* 16mm film collecting; *Style*— Stuart Hutton, Esq; ✉ The Old Parsonage, Colwinston, Vale of Glamorgan CF71 7NL (e-mail smch@o2email.co.uk); Hutton's Solicitors, 16 St Andrew's Crescent, Cardiff CF10 3DD (tel 029 2037 8621, fax 029 2038 8450, e-mail stuart.hutton@huttons-solicitors.co.uk)

HUTTON, Will; s of late William Thomas Hutton, and Dorothy Anne, *née* Haynes; *b* 21 May 1950; *Educ* Chislehurst & Sidcup GS, Univ of Bristol (BSocSci), INSEAD Fontainebleau (MBA); *Career* institutional account exec Phillips and Drew 1971–77; BBC: presenter various Panoramas, BBC2 series and radio documentaries, sr prodr The Financial World Tonight (Radio 4) 1978–81, prodr and dir The Money Programme (BBC2) 1981–83, economics corr Newsnight (BBC2) 1983–88; ed-in-chief European Business Channel Zürich 1988–90, economics ed The Guardian 1990–96 (asst ed 1995–96); The Observer: ed 1996–98, ed-in-chief 1998–99, contributing ed and columnist 2000–; memb Scott Tst 2004–; presenter: series on the City (Radio 4) 1995, series on The State We're In (Channel 4) 1996; chief exec The Work Fndn 2000–; memb: Editorial Bd New Economy, Bd LSE, New Life for Health ACHCEW Cmmn on NHS accountability; dir London Int Festival of Theatre; sr assoc memb St Antony's Coll Oxford summer 1993, hon fell Mansfield Coll Oxford 1997, visiting prof Manchester Univ Business Sch, visiting prof Sch for Public Policy UCL; Political Journalist of the Year What the Papers Say Awards 1993; govr LSE 1996–; Hon DLitt: Univ of Central England, Univ of Strathclyde, Kingston Univ 1995, De Montfort Univ 1996, Univ of Stafford 1999, Open Univ 2001, Univ of Bristol 2003, Univ of Glasgow 2003; *Books* The Revolution That Never Was (1986), The State We're In (1994), The State to Come (1997), The Stakeholding Society (1998), On the Edge (ed with A Gidden, 2000), The World We're In (2002), The Writing on the Wall: China and the West in the 21st Century (2007); *Style*— Will Hutton, Esq; ✉ The Observer, 119 Farringdon Road, London EC1R 3ER (tel 020 7713 4284, fax 020 7713 4794); The Work Foundation, 3 Carlton House Terrace, London SW1Y 5DG

HUXLEY, Prof Sir Andrew Fielding; OM (1983), kt (1974); s of Leonard Huxley (d 1933; 2 s of T H Huxley, the scientist and humanist), and his 2 w Rosalind, *née* Bruce (d 1994, aged 104); half-bro of Sir Julian Huxley, the biologist, and Aldous Huxley, the novelist; *b* 22 November 1917; *Educ* UC Sch, Westminster, Trinity Coll Cambridge; *m* 1947, Jocelyn Richenda Gammell (d 2003), JP, da of Michael Pease (whose paternal grandmother was Susanna, da of Joseph Fry, of the Bristol Quaker family of cocoa manufacturers, and 1 cous of Sir Theodore Fry, 1 Bt), and his w Hon Helen, *née* Wedgwood, JP, eldest da of 1 Baron Wedgwood; 5 da (Janet b 1948, Camilla b 1952, Eleanor b 1959, Henrietta b 1960, Clare b 1962), 1 s (Stewart Leonard b 1949); *Career* operational research for Anti-Aircraft Cmd and Admty WWII; Trinity Coll Cambridge: fell 1941–60 and 1990–, dir of studies 1952–60, hon fell 1967–90, master 1984–90; Univ of Cambridge: demonstrator Physiology Dept 1946–50, asst dir of research 1951–59, reader in experimental biophysics 1959–60; UCL: Jodrell prof of physiology and head of dept 1960–69, Royal Soc research prof 1969–83, emeritus prof of physiology 1983; Fullerian prof of physiology and comparative anatomy Royal Inst 1967–73; Cecil H and Ida Green visiting prof Univ of British Columbia 1980; memb ARC 1977–81; pres: British Assoc for Advancement of Science 1976–77, Int Union of Physiological Sciences 1986–93, Bath Inst of Med Engrg 1994–2000; tstee: British Museum of Natural History 1981–91, Science Museum 1984–88; memb: Nature Conservancy Cncl 1985–87, Animal Procedures Ctee (Home Office) 1987–95; hon memb: Royal Inst 1981, Royal Irish Acad 1986, Japan Acad of Science 1988; hon foreign memb: American Acad of Arts and Scis, Leopoldina Acad, Royal Danish Acad of Scis and Letters, American Physiological Soc, American

Philosophical Soc, Académie Royale de Belgique, Académie Royale de Médecine de Belgique, Dutch Soc of Scis, Indian Nat Sci Acad; hon fell: Inst of Biology, Darwin Coll Cambridge, Royal Soc of Canada, Royal Soc of Edinburgh, UCL, Imperial Coll London, Royal Acad of Engineering, Queen Mary & Westfield Coll London, Royal Holloway and Bedford Coll London; foreign assoc Nat Acad Sci USA; Nobel Laureate in Physiology or Medicine (jtly with A L Hodgkin and J C Eccles) 1963, Copley Medal Royal Soc 1973; 27 Hon Doctorates; FRS 1955 (memb Cncl 1960–62 and 1977–79, pres 1980–85), Hon FREng 1986, Hon FRCP, Hon FMedSci; Grand Cordon of the Sacred Treasure (Japan) 1995; *Books* Reflections on Muscle (1980); *Recreations* walking, designing scientific instruments; *Style*— Prof Sir Andrew Huxley, OM, FRS, Hon FREng; ✉ Manor Field, 1 Vicarage Drive, Grantchester, Cambridge CB3 9NG (tel and fax 01223 840207)

HUXLEY, Prof George Leonard; s of late Sir Leonard G H Huxley, and late Lady (Molly) Huxley; *b* 23 September 1932; *Educ* Blundell's, Magdalen Coll Oxford (BA); *m* 1957, Davina Best; 3 da; *Career* Mil Serv cmmnd RE 1951, Actg Ops Supt Longmoor Mil Rly 1951; fell All Souls Coll Oxford 1955–61, asst dir Br Sch at Athens 1956–58, visiting lectr Harvard Univ 1958–59 and 1961–62, prof of Greek Queen's Univ Belfast 1962–83, temp asst lectr St Patrick's Coll Maynooth 1984–85, hon research assoc TCD 1984–89, dir Gennadius Library American Sch of Classical Studies Athens 1986–89, hon prof of Greek Trinity Coll Dublin 1989–; memb: Exec NI Civil Rights Assoc 1971–72, Royal Irish Acad Dublin (sec for polite literature and antiquities 1979–86, sr vice-pres 1984–85 and 1999–2000, hon librarian 1990–94, special envoy 1994–97, vice-pres 1997–98), Irish Advsy Bd Inst of Irish Studies Univ of Liverpool 1996–2004; chm Organising Ctee 8th Int Congress of Classical Studies Dublin 1984, keynote speaker XVI Int Congress of Classical Archaeology Boston 2003; sr vice-pres Fédération Internationale des Sociétés d'Études Classiques 1984–89, Irish memb Standing Ctee for the Humanities Euro Sci Fndn Strasbourg 1978–86, memb: Managing Ctee American Sch of Classical Studies Athens 1990–, Int Komm Thesaurus Linguae Latinae (Munich) 1999–2001; visiting prof of history Univ of Calif San Diego 1990; hon pres Classical Assoc of Ireland 1999; Cromer Greek Prize 1963; Hon LittD Dublin, Hon DLitt Belfast; memb Academia Europaea 1990 (chm Classics subject gp 1995–96); FSA, MRIA; *Books* Achaeans and Hittites (1960), Early Sparta (1962), The Early Ionians (1966), Greek Epic Poetry from Eumelos to Panyassis (1969), Kythera, Excavations and Studies (ed with J N Coldstream, 1972), Pindar's Vision of the Past (1975), On Aristotle and Greek Society (1979), Homer and the Travellers (1988), author of various articles on Hellenic and Byzantine subjects; *Recreations* siderodromophilia; *Clubs* Athenaeum; *Style*— Prof G L Huxley; ✉ c/o School of Classics, Trinity College, Dublin 2, Ireland

HUXLEY, Prof Paul; s of late Ernest William Huxley, of London, and Winifred Mary, *née* Hunt; *b* 12 May 1938; *Educ* Harrow Sch of Art, Royal Acad Sch; *m* 1, Sept 1957 (m dis 1972), Margaret Doris, *née* Perryman; 2 s (Mark b 1961, Nelson b 1963); m 2, 18 May 1990, Susie Allen, *qv*, da of late Henry Francis Metcalfe; *Career* artist; prof of painting RCA 1986–98 (prof emeritus 1998–); memb Ctee Serpentine Gallery 1971–74, memb Arts Panel Arts Cncl GB 1972–76, tstee Tate Gallery 1975–82, treas Royal Acad 2000–; Harkness fell 1965–67, Lindbury Tst award 1977, Athena Arts award 1985, Nat Arts Collections Fund award 1989; RA 1991 (ARA 1987); *Group Exhibitions* incl: Whitechapel Gallery London 1964, Marlborough Gerson NY 1965, Galerie Milano Milan 1965, Pittsburgh Int Carnegie Inst Pittsburgh 1967, UCLA Art Galleries Los Angeles 1968, Tate Gallery London 1968, MOMA NY 1968, Museum am Ostwall Hanover 1969, Walker Art Gallery Liverpool 1973, Hayward Gallery London 1974, Royal Acad London 1977, Museo Municipal Madrid 1983, RCA London 1988, Mappin Art Gallery Sheffield 1988, Kettle's Yard Cambridge 1999; *Solo Exhibitions* Rowan Gallery London, Gillian Jason Gallery London, Galerie zur Alten Deutchen Schule Switzerland, Kornblee Gallery NY, Galleria da Emenda Lisbon, Forum Kunst Rotweil, Gardner Arts Centre Univ of Sussex, Jason & Rhodes Gallery London, Rhodes & Mann London, Pallant House Gall Chichester; *Commissions* incl: London Tport to design 22 ceramic murals for King's Cross Underground Station 1984, Rambert Dance Co to design sets and costumes for Cats Eye 1992; *Work in Public Collections* incl: Albright-Knox Gallery Buffalo NY, Art Gallery of NSW Aust, Leeds City Art Gallery, MOMA NY, Tate Gallery, V&A Museum, Whitworth Art Gallery Manchester, Ulster Museum Belfast, Art Gallery of Ontario Toronto, Arts Cncl of GB, Museum of Contemporary Art Sydney; *Books* Exhibition Road - Painters at The Royal College of Art (1988); *Style*— Prof Paul Huxley, RA; ✉ 2 Dalling Road, London W6 0JB (tel 020 8563 9495, e-mail paul@paulhuxley.com)

HYATT, Derek James; s of Albert James Hyatt (d 1972), of Ilkley, W Yorks, and Dorothy, *née* Sproat; *b* 21 February 1931; *Educ* Ilkley GS, Leeds Coll of Art (NDD), Norwich Coll of Art, RCA (ARCA); *m* 20 Feb 1960, Rosamond Joy, da of Sidney Rockey (d 1983), of Torquay, Devon; 1 da (Sally Jane b 27 June 1962); *Career* Nat Serv RAF Fighter Cmd 1952–54; artist, writer and teacher; visiting lectr Kingston Sch of Art 1959–64, lectr Leeds Coll of Art 1964–68, sr lectr Leeds Poly 1968–84 (head of illustration studies), visiting prof Cincinnati Univ 1980; life memb Nat Soc of Art Educn; *Solo Exhibitions* incl: New Art Centre London 1960, 1961, 1963 and 1966, Univ of York 1966, Goosewell Gallery Menston 1967, Arthur Gallery Tampa 1967, Scottish Gallery Edinburgh 1969, Compass Gallery Glasgow 1970, Waddington Gallery London 1975, Waddington and Tooths Gallery London 1977, Northern Arts Gallery 1980, Gillan Jason Gallery London 1988, Austin Desmond Gallery London 1989, Ruskin Gallery Sheffield 1990, Univ of Leeds 1990, Art Space Gallery London 1993, Mappin Gallery Sheffield 1995, major retrospective (70 works) Bradford Art Gallery 2001; *Work in Public Collections* work featured in 20 collections incl: Carlisle Art Gallery, Nuffield Fndn London, Balliol Coll Oxford, Yale Univ; *Books* The Challenge of Landscape Painting (1990), Ark Journal of RCA (ed nos 21, 22 and 23), The Alphabet Stone (1997), Stone Fires - Liquid Clouds: The Shamanic Art of Derek Hyatt (2001); various pubns in jls incl: Modern Painters, Contemporary Art; *Recreations* tennis, badminton, walking, looking, drawing; *Style*— Derek Hyatt; ✉ Rectory Farm House, Collingham, Wetherby, West Yorkshire LS22 5AS (tel 01937 572265)

HYATT, Peter Robin; s of Maj Arthur John Roach Hyatt (d 1987), of Send, Surrey, and Molly, *née* Newman (d 1983); *b* 12 May 1947; *Educ* Cheltenham Coll; *m* 1 (m dis 1984), Julie Ann, *née* Cox; 1 da (Gabriella Rosa b 1975), 1 s (Rafe James b 1978); m 2, 15 Jan 1988, Jenny Courtenay, da of Rt Rev John Bernard Taylor; *Career* gp mangr Coopers and Lybrand 1964–80; Mazars LLP (formerly Neville Russell): sr mangr 1980–82, ptnr 1983–2007, seconded as asst dir to the Serious Fraud Office 1991–94; hon treas and tstee S American Mission Soc 1997–; FCA 1978 (ACA 1971); *Recreations* cycling, watching cricket and rugby; *Style*— Peter Hyatt, Esq; ✉ Pippins, Vicarage Road, Potters End, Berkhamsted, Hertfordshire HP4 2QZ (tel 01442 873191, e-mail prhyatt@btinternet.com)

HYDE, Helen; da of Henry Seligman, and Tilly Seligman; *b* 11 May 1947; *Educ* Parktown Girls' HS Johannesburg, Univ of the Witwatersrand (BA 1965–67, BA 1969), Transvaal Teachers' Trg Coll (Dip), KCL (MA); *m* 4 Jan 1968, John Hyde; 2 da (Liza b 1 Aug 1973, Nicole b 27 Sept 1978); *Career* Acland Burghley Sch London: asst teacher 1970, second i/c Languages Dept 1972, head of modern languages 1978, primary liaison and PR offr 1979; dep head (pastoral) then dep head (curriculum) Highgate Wood Sch London 1983–87, headmistress Watford GS for Girls 1987–; chair Fndn and Aided Schs Nat Assoc 2006 (hon treas 2000–06), chair Voluntary Aided Ctee Nat Assoc of Headteachers 1999; *Books* Moving on Up (2003); *Recreations* reading, exercise, visiting art galleries; *Clubs* David Lloyd; *Style*— Mrs Helen Hyde; ✉ Watford Grammar School for Girls, Lady's Close, Watford, Hertfordshire WD18 0AE (tel 01923 223403, e-mail admin.watfordgirls@thegrid.org.uk)

HYDE, Jeremy Robin Powis (Jerry); s of Jesse Kay Hyde (d 1989), and Phyllis Irene Hyde (d 1995); *b* 16 January 1950; *Educ* Ashville Coll Harrogate, Univ of Hull (LLB); *m* 1984, Catherine Elizabeth, *née* Longrigg; 2 da (Caroline Sarah Kay b 24 May 1984, Anna Elisabeth b 23 Jan 1986); *Career* solicitor; CPS: asst chief crown prosecutor 1992–96, advocate and rep to N Wales Child Abuse Tbnl of Inquiry 1997–98, dep chief inspr 2000–; legal advsr Haringey Family Advice Centre 1973–80, treas Steering Gp Tottenham Law Centre 1976; memb: Law Soc 1974 (pres NE London Branch 1997), London Criminal Courts Slrs Assoc 1980; *Recreations* golf, riding, tennis; *Clubs* RAC, Limpsfield Chart Golf, Limpsfield Lawn Tennis, Whitsand Bay Golf; *Style*— Jerry Hyde, Esq; ✉ HM Crown Prosecution Service Inspectorate, 26–28 Old Queen Street, London SW1H 9HP (tel 020 7210 1183, fax 020 7210 1184, e-mail jerry.hyde@cps.gsi.gov.uk)

HYDE, Peter John; s of late Arthur Albert Hyde, of Harpenden, Herts, and Eileen, *née* Smith; *b* 21 July 1941; *Educ* Aldenham; *m* 19 Feb 1971, Jennifer Anne, da of Anne Gavina Venables, of Maresfield Park, Uckfield, E Sussex; 2 da (Henrietta b 24 May 1973, Gemma b 7 Nov 1979), 1 s (Nicholas b 5 Jan 1976); *Career* WS Crawford Ltd 1960–64; Hyde and Partners Ltd: dir 1966, md 1971, chm and chief exec 1976–95; md Hyde Marketing Services Ltd 1995–97, ptnr Hyde Business Partnership 1998–; vice-chm Arc Gp of Cos 1996–99; memb: Cncl Inst of Practitioners in Advertising 1974–2000, Membership Ctee Inst of Dirs 1977–88; pres Solus Club 1989 (hon treas 1983–2001), chm Bd of Govrs Epsom Sch of Art and Design 1989–94 (govr 1980), govr Surrey Inst of Art and Design 1994–2006; MCAM 1966, FIPA 1977 (MIPA 1966); *Recreations* golf, offshore sailing, skiing, scuba diving, swimming; *Clubs* Buck's; *Style*— Peter Hyde, Esq; ✉ Elmet House, Brimpton, Berkshire RG7 4TL (tel 0118 971 2977); Hyde Business Partnership (tel 020 7582 5956, fax 020 7820 1084, e-mail pjh@hydebusiness.co.uk)

HYDE PARKER, Sir Richard William; 12 Bt (E 1681), DL (Suffolk 1995); s of Sir William Stephen Hyde Parker, 11 Bt (d 1951); *b* 5 April 1937; *Educ* Millfield, RAC Cirencester; *m* 1972, Jean, da of late Sir Lindores Leslie, 9 Bt; 3 da (Beata, Margaret (twins) b 1973, Lucy b 1975), 1 s (William b 1983); *Heir* s, William Hyde Parker; *Career* High Sheriff Suffolk 1995–96; *Style*— Sir Richard Hyde Parker, Bt, DL; ✉ Melford Hall, Long Melford, Suffolk CO10 9AA

H

HYDON, Kenneth John; s of John Thomas Hydon (d 1966), and Vera Hydon (d 1972); *b* 3 November 1944; *m* Sylvia Sheila; 2 c; *Career* fin dir: Racal SES Ltd 1979–81, Racal Defence and Avionics Group 1981–85, Racal Millicom Ltd 1985–88, Racal Telecommunications Group Ltd 1985–88, Racal Telecom plc 1988–91, Vodafone Group plc 1991–99 and 2000–05, Vodafone AirTouch plc 1999–2000, Vodafone AirTouch International Holdings BV 1999–2000, Verizon Wireless USA 2000–05, Vodafone Europe Holdings 2000–03, Mannesmann AG 2000–03, Vodafone International 2 SARL 2003–05; non-exec dir: Reckitt Benckiser plc 2003–, Tesco plc 2004–, Royal Berks Hosp NHS Tst 2005–, Pearson Gp plc 2006–; FCMA, FCCA, FCT; *Recreations* badminton, sailing, golf, rugby, cricket; *Style*— Kenneth Hydon, Esq

HYETT, Paul David Etheridge; s of Derek James Hyett, of Breinton Common, Hereford, and Josephine Mable, *née* Sparks (d 1990); *b* 18 March 1952; *Educ* Hereford Cathedral Sch, AA Sch of Architecture (AADipl), Bartlett Sch of Planning (MPhil); *m* 1976, Susan Margaret, da of Richard Harry Beavan; 3 s (James b 1981, Benjamin b 1983, Peter b 1986); *Career* asst: Cedric Price Architects 1974–78, Alan Baxter Assocs 1978–80; ptnr: Arno Jobst and Paul Hyett Architects 1981–82, Nicholas Lacey Jobst and Hyett Architects 1982–87, Paul Hyett Architects 1987–97, Hyett Salisbury Whiteley Architects 1997–2000; chm: Ryder 2000–04, Ryder HKS Int 2005–; teacher: Canterbury Sch of Architecture 1986–87, Düsseldorf Sch of Architecture 1987–89, Bartlett Sch of Architecture and Planning 1994–; visiting prof Univ of Lincoln Sch of Architecture 2004–; columnist: Architects' Jl 1995–2000, RIBA Jl 2001–03; memb Governing Body AA Sch (hon treas 1993–98, vice-pres 1999–); tstee: Br Architectural Library Tst (BALT) 2003–, Civic Tst 2004–; dir Building Centre 2004–, chm Carbon Vision (Carbon Tst) 2004–; memb Expert Witness Inst; Hon DArt Univ of Lincoln; memb AA 1972, RIBA 1979 (vice-pres 1998–2000, pres 2001–03), MRTPI 1992, Hon FAIA, Royal Soc of Architects in Wales (RSAW); *Publications* In Practice (2000), Rough Guide to Sustainability (co-author, 2001), Architecture in the Anti-Machine Age (co-author, 2001); *Style*— Paul Hyett, Esq; ✉ Ryder HKS International, 7 Soho Square, London W1D 3QB (tel 020 7292 9494, e-mail phyett@ryderhks.com)

HYLAND, Paul Robert; s of Kenneth George Hyland (d 1979), and Hetta Grace, *née* Tilsley (d 2000); *b* 15 September 1947; *Educ* Canford Sch, Univ of Bristol (BSc); *m* 1, 21 Aug 1971 (m dis 1988), Noëlle Jean, da of James Houston Angus; m 2, 8 Dec 1990 (m dis 1998), Margaret Ann, da of Thomas William Ware; m 3, 27 Oct 2001, Susan Margaret, da of William Arthur Wilson, MBE; *Career* writer, broadcaster, teacher of creative writing, magician; memb: Dorset Natural History and Archaeological Soc, Poetry Soc, Soc of Authors, PEN, Int Brotherhood of Magicians, Magic Circle; broadcast work incl: plays, drama-documentaries, features, poetry; *Awards*: Eric Gregory Award for Poetry, Alice Hunt Bartlett Award, Authors' Fndn Award; *Books* Purbeck: The Ingrained Island (1978), Poems of Z (1982), Wight: Biography of an Island (1984), The Stubborn Forest (1984), The Black Heart: A Voyage into Central Africa (1988), Getting Into Poetry (1992), Indian Balm: Travels in the Southern Subcontinent (1994), Kicking Sawdust (1995), Backwards out of the Big World: a Voyage into Portugal (1996), Discover Dorset: Isle of Purbeck (1998), Ralegh's Last Journey (2003), Art of the Impossible (2004); *Style*— Paul Hyland, Esq; ✉ 32 Colliton Street, Dorchester, Dorset DT1 1XH (tel 01305 257593, e-mail write@paul-hyland.co.uk); c/o David Higham Associates Ltd, 5–8 Lower John Street, Golden Square, London W1F 9HA

HYLTON, 5 Baron (UK 1866); Sir Raymond Hervey Jolliffe; 5 Bt (UK 1821); s of Lt-Col 4 Baron Hylton (d 1967, whose mother was Lady Alice Hervey, da of 3 Marquess of Bristol), and Lady Perdita Asquith (d 1996), sis of 2 Earl of Oxford and Asquith and gda of 1 Earl, better known as HH Asquith, the Lib PM, by his 1 w); *b* 13 June 1932; *Educ* Eton, Trinity Coll Oxford (MA); *m* 1966, Joanna, da of Andrew de Bertodano, himself eldest s of 8 Marques de Moral (cr by King Charles III of Spain 1765), by Andrew's m to Lady Sylvia Savile (3 da of late 6 Earl of Mexborough, and sis of late Lady Agnes Eyston and late Lady Sarah Cumming-Bruce); 4 s (Hon William b 1967, Hon Andrew b 1969, Hon Alexander b 1973, Hon John b 1977), 1 da (Hon Emily b 1975); *Heir* s, Hon William Jolliffe; *Career* Lt Coldstream Gds Reserve; asst private sec to Govr-Gen Canada 1960–62; sits as independent peer in House of Lords (elected in 1999), memb All-Pty Parly Gps on: Human Rights, Penal Affairs, British-Palestinian, British-Russian, British-Philippines; pres NIACRO; vice-chm: Partners in Hope re Russia, MICOM re Moldova; tstee Forward Thinking re Peace in the Middle East; former chm: Catholic Housing Aid Soc, Nat Federation of Housing Associations, Housing Assoc Charitable Tst, Help the Aged Housing Tst; formerly tstee: Acorn Christian Healing Tst, ABCD (a tst for Palestinian children with disabilities); landowner, organic farmer and forester; govr Ammerdown Study Center; Hon DSocSc Univ of Southampton 1994; ARICS; *Style*— The Rt Hon the Lord Hylton; ✉ House of Lords, London SW1A 0PW (tel 020 7219 5353, fax 020 7219 5979)

HYMAN, Howard Jonathan; s of late Joe Hyman, of London, and late Corrine Irene, *née* Abrahams; *b* 23 October 1949; *Educ* Bedales, Univ of Manchester (BA); *m* 21 Sept 1972, Anne Moira, da of Capt Harry Sowden, of Ilkley, W Yorks; 2 s (Daniel b 1977, Sam b 1979), 1 da (Hannah b 1982); *Career* Price Waterhouse: ptnr 1984–94, specialist advsr on privatisation HM Treasy 1984–87, ptnr i/c Privatisation Servs Dept 1987–90, head Corporate Fin Europe 1990–94, memb E European Jt Venture Bd 1990–94, memb China Bd 1991–94, memb Euro Mgmnt Bd 1991–94, memb World Gen Cncl 1992–94, world head Corporate Fin 1994; dep chm Charterhouse Bank 1994–96, md Charterhouse plc 1994–96; chm Hyman Associates 1996–; Freeman City of London; FCA; *Books* Privatisation: The Facts (1988), The Implications of Privatisation for Nationalised Industries (1988); *Recreations* Chinese language and culture, walking, classical music, cricket, gardening; *Clubs* Reform, MCC, Cirencester Golf, Richmond Golf; *Style*— Howard Hyman, Esq; ⊠ 1 Cato Street, London W1H 5HG (tel 020 7258 0404, fax 020 7258 1424, e-mail howard@hymanassociates.com)

HYMAN, Robin Philip; s of Leonard Albert Hyman (d 1964), of London, and Helen Josephine, *née* Mautner (d 1991); *b* 9 September 1931; *Educ* Henley GS, Univ of Birmingham (BA); *m* 17 April 1966, Inge, *née* Neufeld; 2 s (James b 29 May 1967, Peter b 23 Nov 1968), 1 da (Philippa 13 March 1971); *Career* Nat Serv RAF 1949–51; ed Mermaid 1953–54, md Evans Bros Ltd 1972–77 (dep md 1967, dir 1964), chm Bell and Hyman Ltd 1977–86, chm and chief exec Unwin Hyman Ltd 1989–90 (md 1986–88), chm Laurence King Publishing Ltd (formerly Calmann & King Ltd) 1991–2004, dir Spiro Inst 1991–98, memb BBC Gen Advsy Cncl 1992–97; tstee ADAPT 1997–2006; memb Editorial Bd World Yearbook of Educn 1969–73, treas Educnl Publishers' Cncl 1972–75 (memb Exec Ctee 1971–76), memb first Br Publishers' Delgn to China 1978, pres Publishers' Assoc 1989–91 (memb Cncl 1975–92, treas 1982–84, vice-pres 1988–89 and 1991–92); FRSA; *Books* A Dictionary of Famous Quotations (1962), Boys and Girls First Dictionary (with John Trevaskis 1967); 11 children's books with Inge Hyman incl: Barnabas Ball at the Circus (1967), Runaway James and the Night Owl (1968), The Hippo Who Wanted to Fly (1973), The Greatest Explorers in the World (1978), The Treasure Box (1980); *Clubs* Garrick, MCC, Samuel Pepys; *Style*— Robin Hyman, Esq; ⊠ 101 Hampstead Way, London NW11 7LR (tel 020 8455 7055)

HYMAS, Charles Southern Albert; s of Peter David Hymas, of Northampton, and Margaret, *née* Southern; *b* 7 January 1961; *Educ* Harrow, Univ of Durham (BA), UC Cardiff (Postgrad Dip Journalism); *m* Sarah Elizabeth, da of Prof Michael Barbour; 1 da (Katharine Anna), 2 s (Tom, Luke); *Career* trainee journalist South Wales Argus Newport 1983–84 (educn corr 1984–85); Western Mail Cardiff: gen news reporter 1985–86, educn corr 1986–87, political corr 1987–88; political reporter Yorkshire Post 1988–90; The Sunday Times: educn corr 1990–95, dep ed Insight 1995–96, dep news ed 1996–97, news ed 1997–99, ed Focus 1999–2000, news ed 2000–; *Recreations* swimming, tennis and cooking; *Style*— Charles Hymas, Esq; ⊠ The Sunday Times, 1 Pennington Street, London E1 9XW (tel 020 7782 5210, fax 020 7782 5542)

HYND, Ronald; s of William John Hens (d 1991), of London, and Alice Louisa, *née* Griffiths (d 1994); *b* 22 April 1931; *Educ* Holloway Co Sch, Rambert Sch of Ballet; *m* 24 June 1957, Annette, da of James Lees Page (d 1979); 1 da (Louise b 20 April 1968); *Career* former ballet dancer, now dir and choreographer; Ballet Rambert 1949–51, Royal Ballet 1951–70 (princ dancer 1959), danced all major classical roles and many dramatic and romantic ballets; dir Bavarian State Ballet 1970–73 and 1984–86; choreographed full length ballets: The Nutcracker (London Festival Ballet, L'Opera de Nice 1976, La Scala 2000), Rosalinda (Johannesburg Ballet, Festival Ballet, Houston, Ljubljana, Santiago, Cincinnati, Bonn, Salt Lake City, Tulsa, Deutsche Oper Berlin 1997) 1978, Papillon (Houston, Sadlers Wells Royal Ballet, Johannesburg, Munich, Santiago) 1979, Le Diable a Quatre (Johannesburg, Santiago) 1984, Coppélia (Festival Ballet 1985, Santiago and Berlin 2000), The Merry Widow (Aust 1975, Canada 1986, Johannesburg 1993, Vienna 1994, Santiago and Houston 1995, La Scala Milan 1996, American Ballet Theatre 1997, Royal Danish Ballet 1998, Maggio Musicale Florence 2001, Pacific NW 2002, Hong Kong Ballet 2007), Ludwig II (Munich) 1986, Hunchback of Notre Dame (Houston) 1988, The Sleeping Beauty (English Nat Ballet 1993, Pacific N W 2001); one act ballets incl: Dvorák Variations, Le Baiser de la Fee, Mozartiana, Pasiphaë, La Chatte, Wendekreise, Das Telefon, Charlotte Brontë,

Liaisons Amoureuses, Marco Polo, Scherzo Capriccioso, The Seasons, The Sanguine Fan, Les Valses, In a Summer Garden, Fanfare, Valse Glacé and Winter 1850 for John Curry, Sylvia for Diana, Princess of Wales's 30 birthday; *Television* prodns incl: The Nutcracker (BBC), The Sanguine Fan (BBC), The Merry Widow (Canadian TV and Aust TV), Rosalinda (Slovenian TV); *Recreations* music, travel, gardens; *Style*— Ronald Hynd, Esq

HYPHER, David Charles; s of Harold Eldric Hypher, MBE (d 1971), of Byfleet, Surrey, and Marcia Evelyn, *née* Spalding (d 1992); *b* 24 July 1941; *Educ* Weybridge Tech Coll; *m* 1, March 1966 (m dis 1971), Jennifer, da of Robert Ingle; *m* 2, July 1978, Pamela Alison, da of Peter Rowland Craddock; 2 da (Nicola, Emma); *Career* stockbroker 1958–82; dir: INVESCO Asset Management Ltd (Britannia Asset Management) 1983–98, INVESCO Fund Managers Ltd 1984–98, various INVESCO International (offshore) Jersey and Luxembourg fund cos 1985–96, MIM International Management 1987–92, London Wall Britannia 1989–2002, INVESCO Luxembourg SA 1993–96, AMVESCAP Management Ltd 1998–99, David Hypher Consulting Ltd 1998–2002, Groupe Du Savoy 1998–; tstee: Rydes Hill Prep Sch Guildford 1989–, Surrey Community Devpt Tst 2000– (chair 2004–), High Sheriff of Surrey Youth Award Scheme 2005–; chm Surrey Cncl for Vol Youth Serv 2006–; govr Queen Elizabeth's Fndn 2006–; High Sheriff Surrey 2005–06; memb IIMR 1965–2005, memb Stock Exchange 1972–83; *Recreations* collecting antiques and cars; *Style*— David Hypher, Esq; ⊠ The Forge, Wood Street Village Green, Guildford, Surrey GU3 3DY (tel and fax 01483 234938, e-mail dhypher@aol.com)

HYTNER, Jim; *b* 22 July 1964; *Educ* Oxford Poly (BSc); *Children* 2 da (Molly, Lucy); *Career* marketeer; formerly: asst brand mangr on Bird's Trifle and Angel Delight, brand mangr on Lilt, Fanta and Sprite, mktg mangr Coca-Cola, Euro mktg mangr Sega, mktg dir BSkyB; dir of mktg and new business Channel 5 1998–2001, mktg and commerical dir ITV 2001–04, mktg dir Barclays 2004–; lectr Wharton Business Sch; tstee Comic Relief; nominated Marketeer of the Year by Marketing Week 1999; *Recreations* cajoling brother into journeys up the M6 to see their beloved reds; *Style*— Jim Hytner, Esq; ⊠ Barclays, 1 Churchill Place, London E14 5HP

HYTNER, Joyce Anita; OBE (2004); da of Bernard Myers (d 1979), of Altrincham, Cheshire, and Vera Myers, *née* Classick (d 1974); *b* 9 December 1935; *Educ* Withington Girls' Sch Manchester; *m* 19 Dec 1954, Benet Hytner, QC; 3 s (Nicholas Hytner, *qv*, b 1956, Richard b 1959, James b 1964), 1 da (Jennifer b 1958); *Career* dir Act IV; memb Bd: Manchester Royal Exchange Theatre 1989–, Royal Court Theatre 2002–, Nat Campaign for the Arts; memb Devpt Bd Historic Royal Palaces; *Recreations* theatre, music; *Style*— Mrs Joyce Hytner, OBE; ⊠ Act IV, 47 Frith Street, London W1D 4SE

HYTNER, Nicholas Robert; s of Benet Alan Hytner, QC, of London, and Joyce Hytner, OBE, *qv*, *née* Myers; *b* 7 May 1956; *Educ* Manchester Grammar, Trinity Hall Cambridge (MA); *Career* theatre, opera and film dir; prodns at Northcott Theatre Exeter and Leeds Playhouse; assoc dir Royal Exchange Theatre Manchester 1985–88, assoc dir NT 1989–2003, dir NT 2003–; *Theatre* dir: Measure for Measure (RSC) 1987, The Tempest (RSC) 1988, King Lear (RSC) 1990, Miss Saigon (Drury Lane Theatre and Broadway) 1989–91, The Importance of Being Earnest (Aldwych) 1993; prodns for NT incl: Ghetto 1989, Wind in the Willows 1990, The Madness of George III 1991, Carousel 1993 (Best Musical Direction Olivier Award 1993, Best Director of a Musical Tony Awards 1994), The Cripple of Inishmaan 1997, Mother Clap's Molly House 2001, Henry V 2003, The History Boys 2004 (Best Dir Olivier Award 2005, also Broadway NY (Best Dir Tony Awards 2006)), Henry IV Parts One and Two 2005, Southwark Fair 2006; *Opera* prodns incl: King Priam (Kent Opera) 1984, Rienzi (ENO) 1983, Xerxes (ENO) 1985, The Magic Flute (ENO) 1988, Julius Caesar (Paris Opéra) 1987, Le Nozze di Figaro (Opéra de Genève) 1989, La Clemenza di Tito (Glyndebourne) 1991, The Force of Destiny 1992, Xerxes (ENO) 2002 (Olivier Award for Best Opera Prodn, Evening Standard Opera Award); *Film* dir The Madness of King George 1995, The Crucible 1995, The History Boys 2006; *Style*— Nicholas Hytner, Esq; ⊠ National Theatre, Upper Ground, South Bank, London SE1 9PX (tel 020 7452 3333)

I

IAN, David; professional name of David Ian Lane; s of Reg Lane, of Loughton, Essex, and Jean, *née* Wiens (d 1997); *b* 15 February 1961, Ilford, Essex; *Educ* Ilford Co High GS for Boys; *m* 17 Sept 1994, Tracy, *née* Carter; 1 s (James William), 1 da (Emily Grace); *Career* actor until 1991, ind theatre prodr 1991–2000, joined Clear Channel Entertainment 2000, chm global theatre Live Nation (formerly Clear Channel Entertainment) 2005– (previously ceo); memb Bd Soc of London Theatre 1997–; West End credits as prodr incl: Saturday Night Fever (London Palladium), The King and I (London Palladium), Grease (Dominion, Cambridge and Victoria Palace), Defending the Caveman (Apollo), Ain't Misbehavin' (Lyric), Anything Goes (Theatre Royal), The Producers (Theatre Royal), Guys and Dolls (Piccadilly Theatre), The Sound of Music (London Palladium); touring prodns incl: Jesus Christ Superstar, Pirates of Penzance, Rocky Horror Show, Singin' in the Rain, Evita, Chess, Dr Dolittle, The King and I, West Side Story, Cats, Chicago, Starlight Express, My Fair Lady; other credits as prodr incl: Laurence Oliver Awards 1996–99, Phantom of the Opera (Venetian Hotel Las Vegas) 2006; winner Olivier Award 2000, 2005 and 2006; *Recreations* theatre, running (5 marathons); *Clubs* Garrick; *Style*— David Ian, Esq; ✉ Live Nation, 35–36 Grosvenor Street, London W1K 4QX (tel 020 7518 2820, fax 0870 749 0545, e-mail david.ian@livenation.co.uk)

IANNUCCI, Armando; s of Armando Iannucci (d 1982), and Gina, *née* Mignano; *b* 28 November 1963, Glasgow; *Educ* St Aloysius Coll Glasgow, Univ of Glasgow, UC Oxford (BA, DPhil); *m* 25 Aug 1990, Rachael, *née* Jones; 2 s (Emilio b 20 Jan 1994, Marcello b 1 July 1999), 1 da (Carmella b 23 Aug 2002); *Career* writer, producer, director, presenter; prodr BBC Radio Light Entertainment 1988–91; columnist: Daily Telegraph 2000–06, The Observer 2006–, Gramophone 2006–; memb BAFTA 2006; Award for Special Contribution to Comedy British Comedy Awards 1995; *Radio* BBC Radio 4 shows incl: On The Hour 1991–92 (Best Radio Comedy British Comedy Awards 1992), Knowing Me, Knowing You 1992–93 (Best Comedy Sony Radio Awards 1993, Best Radio Comedy British Comedy Awards 1993), Armando Iannucci Show (presenter) 1993–97, News Quiz (regular panellist); *Television* incl: The Day Today (BBC 2) 1994, Knowing Me, Knowing You With Alan Partridge (writer and prodr, BBC 2) 1994 (Best New TV Comedy British Comedy Awards 1995), Saturday Night Armistice (BBC 2) 1995, The Friday Night Armistice (BBC 2) 1996–99 (Bronze Rose of Montreux 1996), I'm Alan Partridge (writer and prodr, BBC 2) 1997 (Best Comedy BAFTA 1998, British Comedy Award 1998), The Armando Iannucci Shows (presenter and dir, Channel 4) 2001, The Thick of It (BBC 4) 2005–07 (Best Comedy BAFTA 2005, Best Comedy RTS 2005); *Publications* Facts and Fancies (1999); *Recreations* astronomy, classical music; *Style*— Armando Iannucci, Esq; ✉ c/o PBJ Management, 7 Soho Street, London W1D 3DQ (tel 020 7287 1112, e-mail jennifer@pbjmgt.co.uk)

IBBS, Sir (John) Robin; kt (1982), KBE (1988); o s of late Prof T L Ibbs, MC, and Marjorie, *née* Bell; *b* 21 April 1926; *Educ* West House Sch, Gresham's, Upper Canada Coll Toronto, Univ of Toronto, Trinity Coll Cambridge (MA); *m* 1, 1952, Iris Barbara (d 2005), da of late S Hall; 1 da; m 2, 2006, Penelope Ann, da of late Capt H C Buckland; *Career* Instr Lt RN 1947–49; called to the Bar Lincoln's Inn 1952 (hon bencher 1999); ICI: joined 1952, dir 1976–80 and 1982–88, seconded as head CPRS Cabinet Office 1980–82; Lloyds Bank plc: dir 1985–97, dep chm 1988–93, chm 1993–97; chm Lloyds TSB Group plc 1995–97; dep chm Lloyds Bank Canada 1989–90, chm Lloyds Merchant Bank Holdings 1989–92; Prime Minister's advsr on efficiency in govt (pt/t) 1983–88, ldr Review of House of Commons Services 1990, memb Advsy Ctee on Business Appts 1991–98, memb Sierra Leone Arms Investigation 1998; chm Cncl UCL 1989–95; tstee and dep chm Isaac Newton Tst 1988–99, memb Cncl Fndn for Science and Technol 1997–2002; BIM Special Award 1989; Hon DSc Univ of Bradford 1986, Hon LLD Univ of Bath 1993; hon fell UCL 1993; *Style*— Sir Robin Ibbs, KBE; ✉ c/o Lloyds TSB Group plc, 25 Gresham Street, London EC2V 7HN (tel 020 7626 1500)

IBRAHIMOV, HE Rafael; *b* 17 June 1965, Baku, Azerbaijan; *Educ* Azerbaijan State Univ (Dip Oriental Studies), Inst of Foreign Languages Baku, St Catharine's Coll Cambridge, Chartered Inst of Bankers; *m* Dinara; 1 s, 1 da; *Career* diplomat; linguistic trg secondment Northern Yemen 1985–86, MOD secondment Algeria 1987–90, with Baku Information Co and various commercial orgns 1990–93, State Protocol Dept and Int Economic Orgns Dept Miny of Foreign Affrs 1993–94, head Consular Section Embassy of the Republic of Azerbaijan London 1994–2001, ambass to the Ct of St James's 2001–; *Style*— HE Mr Rafael Ibrahimov; ✉ Embassy of the Republic of Azerbaijan, 4 Kensington Court, London W8 5DL

IDDON, Dr Brian; MP; s of John Iddon, and Violet, *née* Stazicker; *b* 5 July 1940; *Educ* Christ Church Boys' Sch Southport, Southport Tech Coll, Univ of Hull (BSc, PhD, DSc); *m* 1, 15 May 1965 (m dis 1989), Merrilyn Ann, *née* Muncaster; 2 da (Sally Jane, Sheena Helen); m 2, 16 Sept 1995, Eileen Harrison; 2 step s (Ian, Lee); *Career* sr demonstrator in organic chemistry Univ of Durham 1965–66 (temp lectr 1964–65); Univ of Salford: lectr in organic chemistry 1966–78, sr lectr 1978–86, reader 1986–97; visiting prof Chemistry Dept Univ of Liverpool; MP (Lab) Bolton SE 1997–,vice-pres Parly and Scientific Ctee, chm All-Pty Parly Drugs Misuse Gp, sec Br-Palestine Parly Gp, treas Parly Warm Homes Gp; chm All-Pty Chemical Industries Gp; memb Select Ctee on: Environmental Audit 1997–2000, Science and Technol 2000–; memb Lab Back Bench Ctee on: Educn and Skills, Tport, Local Govt and the Regions, Health and Social Services; memb: Commonwealth Parly Assoc, Inter-Parly Union, Friends of Remploy Gp of Lab MPs, Labour Middle East Cncl, Lab Parly Local Govt Assoc, Sigoma Local Authorities Gp, Trade Union Gp of Lab MPs; Bolton MDC: cncllr 1977–98, chm Housing Ctee 1986–96 (vice-chm 1980–82), former memb Mgmnt and Fin and Soc Servs Ctees, hon alderman 1998–; former dir Bolton City Challenge Ltd; chm Bd of Dirs Bolton Tech Innovation Centre; chm Care NOT Killing Alliance 2006–; patron: Soc of Registration Officers, The Friends of Lancashire (hon), Nat Assoc of Br Market Authorities (NAMBA), Catalyst Discovery Centre; memb: Amnesty Int, Arts for Lab, Lab Housing Gp, Co-op Pty; CChem, FRSC; *Publications* contrib various book chapters and author of numerous articles in learned jls; *Recreations* gardening, philately, cricket (as a spectator); *Clubs* Derby Ward Labour, Our Lady of Lourdes (Farnworth); *Style*— Dr Brian Iddon, MP; ✉ House of Commons, London SW1A 0AA (tel 020 7219 4064/2096, fax 020 7219 2653, e-mail iddonb@parliament.uk, website www.brianiddonmp.org.uk)

IDE, Christopher George; s of George Frederick Ide (d 2000), and Edith Harty, *née* Good (d 1998); *b* 25 September 1950; *Educ* Howard Sch Croydon, Heath Clark GS, Imperial Coll London (BSc); *m* 1, 1978 (m dis 1989), Elizabeth Mary Miller; 1 s (Edward Christopher b 1983); m 2, 2003, Barbara Jeanne Sorensen; 3 step s, 1 step da; *Career* actuarial student The English Insurance Co Ltd 1972–73; The Swiss Life Gp: joined 1973, asst actuary 1975–81, dep actuary 1982–86, UK actuary 1987–89, md Swiss Life (UK) Gp plc 1989–97, co-pres Swiss Life Insurance and Pension Co 1997–2000, chm Phillips & Drew Life 1997–2000; Royal London Gp: joined 2000, chief exec Royal London Retail 2002–04, dir School Fees Services Gp 2004–07; chm Pioneer Friendly Soc Ltd 2006–, vice-pres Sanderstead Hockey Club 2001–; memb: Trollope Soc 1990, Glyndebourne Festival Opera 1993; Freeman City of London 1982, Master Worshipful Co of Actuaries 2007 (Liveryman 1982), Liveryman Worshipful Co of Makers of Playing Cards 2007; FIA 1975; *Recreations* fell walking, bridge, opera, playing the tuba; *Clubs* Reform, Fellowship, Surrey CCC; *Style*— Christopher Ide, Esq; ✉ Haresfield, Packhorse Road, Sevenoaks, Kent TN13 2QR (tel 01732 460231, e-mail chris@haresfield.org.uk)

IDLE, Eric; *b* 29 March 1943, South Shields, Co Durham; *Educ* Royal Sch Wolverhampton, Pembroke Coll Cambridge (BA, pres Footlights); *m* 1 (m dis), Lyn Ashley; 1 s (Carey b 1973); m 2, Tania Kosevich; 1 da (Lily b 1990); *Career* actor, writer and film director; pres Prominent Features film co; *Stage* performances incl: Footlights '63 and '64 (Edinburgh Festival), I'm Just Wild About Harry (Edinburgh Festival) 1963, One For the Pot (Leicester Phoenix) 1965, First Farewell Tour (UK and Canada) 1973, Monty Python Live at Drury Lane 1974, Monty Python Live at City Centre 1976, Monty Python Live at the Hollywood Bowl 1980; writing incl: Pass the Butler (Globe) 1981, The Frog Prince (also dir, Faerie Tale Theatre), Seussical: A new musical based on the books of Dr Seuss 1998, Monty Python's Spamalot (Shubert Theater NY) 2005 (Best Broadway Musical Outer Critics Circle Awards, Best Musical Tony Awards); *Opera* Ko-Ko in Jonathan Miller's prodn of The Mikado (ENO 1987, Houston Opera House 1989); *Television* acting/performing incl: We Have Ways of Making You Laugh (LWT) 1968, Do Not Adjust Your Set (two series, BBC) 1968–69, Monty Python's Flying Circus (also writer, four series, BBC, winner Silver Rose Montreux) 1969–74, Monty Python's Fliegende Zirkus (Bavaria TV) 1971–72, Rutland Weekend Television (also writer, two series, BBC) 1975–76, Laverne and Shirley (ABC), Saturday Night Live (guest star twice, host four times, NBC), The Mikado (Thames TV) 1987, Nearly Departed (Lorimar Productions for NBC) 1989, Parrot Sketch Not Included (BBC) 1989, Suddenly Susan 1999–2000, House of Mouse 2001, The Scream Team 2002; writing also incl: Twice a Fortnight (BBC) 1967, The Frost Report (BBC, winner Golden Rose Montreux) 1967, The Two Ronnies (BBC), Marty Feldman (BBC) 1968–69; *Radio* performing incl: Radio Five (also writer, two series, BBC Radio 1) 1975, Behind the Crease (also writer, musical, BBC) 1990; writing also incl I'm Sorry I'll Read That Again (BBC); *Films* acting incl: Isadora The Biggest Dancer in the World (dir Ken Russell, BBC TV film) 1966, Alice in Wonderland (dir Jonathan Miller, BBC TV film) 1966, And Now For Something Completely Different (also writer) 1971, Monty Python and the Holy Grail (also writer) 1974, The Rutles - All You Need is Cash (also writer and dir, NBC TV film) 1978, Monty Python's Life of Brian (also writer) 1979, Monty Python Live at the Hollywood Bowl (also writer) 1980, Monty Python's The Meaning of Life (also writer, winner Cannes Jury Prize) 1983, Yellowbeard 1983, The Adventures of Baron Munchausen 1988, Nuns on the Run 1990, Too Much Sun 1990, Missing Pieces 1991, Splitting Heirs (also writer and prodr) 1993, Casper 1995, Burn Hollywood Burn 1998, The Quest for Camelot (voice of Devon) 1998, Dudley Do-Right 1999, South Park: Bigger Longer & Uncut 1999, Journey Into Your Imagination 1999, 102 Dalmatians 2000, Brightness 2000, Ella Enchanted 2004; *Recordings* incl: Monty Python's Flying Circus 1970, Another Monty Python Record 1970, Monty Python's Previous Record 1972, Matching Tie and Handkerchief 1973, Live at Drury Lane 1974, Monty Python's Instant Record Collection 1977, Monty Python's Contractual Obligation Album (prodr) 1980, The Final Ripoff Album 1987, Monty Python Sings 1989, Nearly Departed (theme song for TV series) 1989, One Foot in the Grave (theme song for TV series) 1990, Always Look on the Bright Side of Life (single, reached No2) 1991, The Quite Remarkable Adventures of The Owl and the Pussycat 1997; *Books* Monty Python's Big Red Book (contrib and ed, 1971), The Brand New Monty Python Bok (contrib and ed, 1973), The Monty Python Paperbok (1974), Hello Sailor (novel, 1975), The Rutland Dirty Weekend Book (1976), Monty Python and the Holy Grail (1977), Monty Python's Scrapbook/Life of Brian (contrib and ed, 1979), Pass the Butler (1981), Monty Python's Flying Circus - Just the Words (1989), The Road to Mars 1999; *Style*— Eric Idle, Esq

IDRISSOV, HE Erlan A; *b* 28 April 1959, Karkaralinsk, Kazakhstan; *Educ* Moscow State Inst of Int Rels Miny of Foreign Affrs USSR, Diplomatic Acad Miny of Foreign Affrs USSR; *m* Nurilla Anabekovna; 2 s (Daniar b 1983, Alzhan b 1998), 1 da (Aigerim b 1986); *Career* Kazakh diplomat; USSR State Ctee on Economic Co-operation Pakistan 1981–85, Miny of Foreign Affrs Kazakh Soviet Socialist Repub 1985–90, first sec Kazakhstan mission to the UN NY 1992–95, ambass-at-large and head America Dept Kazakhstan Miny of Foreign Affrs 1995–96, asst on int issues to Pres of Kazakhstan 1996–97, first vice-min of foreign affrs 1997–99 and 2002, min of foreign affrs 1999–2002, ambass to the Ct of St James's 2002–; *Recreations* lawn tennis, ice hockey, horse riding, travelling; *Style*— HE Mr Erlan A Idrissov; ✉ Embassy of the Republic of Kazakhstan, 33 Thurloe Square, London SW7 2SD (tel 020 7581 4646, fax 020 7584 8481, e-mail london@kazakhstan-embassy.org.uk)

ILES, Adrian; s of Arthur Henry Iles, of Loughton, Essex, and Joan, *née* Williams; *b* 19 September 1958; *Educ* Buckhurst Hill Co HS Essex, Jesus Coll Cambridge (MA); *m* 16 March 1985, Helen Marie, da of Frederick James Singleton, of Chelmsford, Essex; 2 da (Rosemary b 30 Aug 1989, Nancy b 13 July 1991); *Career* called to the Bar Inner Temple 1980, dep district judge 2000–; memb: SE Circuit, London Common Law and Commercial Bar Assoc, Professional Negligence Bar Assoc, Panel of Chairmen Disciplinary Ctee Milk Marketing Bd 1990–94; *Recreations* cricket, hockey, bell ringing; *Clubs* High Beach Cricket, Henley Royal Regatta, Old Loughtonians Hockey; *Style*— Adrian Iles, Esq

ILES, Ronald Alfred; s of George Iles (d 1966), of London, and Marie Elizabeth, *née* Kohl (d 1955); *b* 16 December 1935; *Educ* Raine's Fndn GS London; *m* Patricia Maud, da of John Alfred Hayes; 2 da (Sandra Gail (Mrs Delve) b 12 Sept 1962, Carol Ann (Mrs Markowski) b 18 Sept 1966); *Career* trainee surveyor British Rail 1952, finance position Metropolitan Water Bd 1952–53, Nat Serv RAF 1954–56; Alexander Howden: joined 1957, dir 1970, dep chm 1979, chm Alexander Howden Reinsurance Brokers Ltd 1981, sr vice-pres Alexander & Alexander Services Inc (US parent co) 1985, chm Alexander

& Alexander Services (UK) 1992–96, memb Mgmnt Exec Ctee Alexander & Alexander Services Inc 1992–96; chm: AON Re Worldwide Inc 1997–2000, AON UK Holdings Ltd 1997–2000; non-exec chm A101 Insurance Co Europe Ltd 2002–; non-exec dir: Nipponkoa Insurance Co Europe Ltd 2001–, Endurance Worldwide Holdings Ltd 2002–; memb Lloyd's, assoc Corpn of Insurance Brokers, FCII; *Style—* Ronald Iles, Esq; ✉ AON Re Worldwide Inc, 10 Devonshire Square, London EC2M 4LE (tel 020 7623 5500, fax 020 7621 1511)

ILEY, Malcolm; s of Thomas Iley (d 1980), and Barbara, *née* David; *b* 12 April 1949, Bradninch, Devon; *m* 29 May 1971, Joy, *née* Sharpe; 1 s (Lawson-Thomas b 1974), 1 da (Rachel b 1978); *Career* slr; various sr lawyer and exec positions in local govt (culminating in city slr and dep chief exec Plymouth City Cncl) and advsr to nat assocs 1970–94, head Public Sector Projects Dept Nabarro Nathanson 1997–2004, head Public Sector Commercial Gp Trowers and Hamlyns 2004–; chm and advsr Devon Environmental Business Tst 1992–95, dir BURA 1997–2001, non-exec dir and advsr Sutton Harbour plc 1989–2004, non-exec dir Sheffield Urban Regeneration Co, dir Prospects Ltd 1998–; memb Ministerial Advsy Gp DETR 2001–03; memb Bd and advsr: Plymouth Coll, Plymouth Arts Coll, Hammersmith and West London FE Corporation; chm Local Govt Chronicle regeneration awards; memb New Local Govt Network Ltd; Thomas Edis Prize Law Soc 1976; memb Law Soc; *Publications* incl: Local Government Act 1999: Best Value and Contracting, Local Government Contracting (contrib); author of articles in public sector press; *Recreations* sport, golf, skiing, tennis, walking on Dartmoor, music (listening and playing trumpet); *Style—* Malcolm Iley, Esq; ✉ Trowers & Hamlins, Sceptre Court, 40 Tower Hill, London EC3N 4DX (tel 020 7423 8345, e-mail miley@trowers.com)

ILIFFE, 3 Baron (UK 1933); Robert Peter Richard Iliffe; s of Hon William Henry Richard Iliffe (d 1959; yr s of 1 Baron Iliffe, GBE); suc uncle, 2 Baron Iliffe (d 1996); *b* 22 November 1944; *Educ* Eton, ChCh Oxford; *m* 1966, Rosemary Anne, da of Cdr Arthur Grey Skipwith, RN; 3 s (Hon Edward Richard b 1968, Hon George Langton b 1970, Hon Thomas Arthur b 1973), 1 da (Hon Florence Clare (twin) b 1973); *Heir* s, Hon Edward Iliffe; *Career* chm: Yattendon Investment Tst plc (parent co of Marina Developments Ltd, Cambridge Newspapers Ltd, Staffordshire Newspapers Ltd, Herts and Essex Newspapers Ltd, Yattendon Estates Ltd, Channel TV Hldgs Ltd); dir Scottish Provincial Press Ltd; former chm: Birmingham Post and Mail Ltd, Coventry Newspapers Ltd; memb Cncl RASE 1972– (chm 1994–98); warden Bradfield Coll 2001–06; High Sheriff Warks 1983–84; *Style—* The Rt Hon the Lord Iliffe; ✉ Yattendon Investment Trust plc, Barn Close, Yattendon, Thatcham, Berkshire RG18 0UX

ILLMAN, (Charles) John; s of Henry Alfred Charles Illman (d 2005), of Kirkby Fleetham, N Yorks, and Margaret Moorhouse (d 1975); *b* 22 September 1944; *Educ* King's Sch Ely; *m* 1975, Elizabeth Mary, da of Ronald Stamp; 2 s (James David Charles b 21 Dec 1979, Christopher George John b 12 June 1982); *Career* student actor Nottingham Playhouse 1963, asst stage mangr Southwold Repertory Company 1963; trainee reporter Hertfordshire Express 1964, reporter The Journal Newcastle upon Tyne 1968, features ed General Practitioner 1971; ed: New Psychiatry 1974, General Practitioner 1975; freelance journalist 1976–83, med corr Daily Mail 1983–88, health ed The Guardian 1989–96, med corr The Observer 1996–98; chm Med Journalists Assoc 1996–2003; Family Planning Assoc Award for reporting on women's health 1993, first prize Norwich Union Healthcare/Med Journalists' Assoc Awards 1994, Tony Thistlewaite Medical Journalists' Assoc Book Award 2005; md JIC Productions Ltd 2003; memb RSM 1987; *Books* Body Machine (jtly, 1981), Use Your Brain to Beat Depression (2004), Use Your Brain to Beat Panic and Anxiety (2005), Beat Panic and Anxiety (2006); *Recreations* family, cricket, running, reading, scuba diving; *Style—* John Illman, Esq; ✉ 9 Grand Avenue, London N10 3AY (tel 020 8365 3602, e-mail johnillman@blueyonder.co.uk)

ILLSLEY, Eric; MP; s of John Illsley, of S Yorks, and Maud, *née* Bassett; *b* 9 April 1955; *Educ* Barnsley Holgate GS, Univ of Leeds (LLB); *m* 1978, Dawn, da of Robert Charles Webb, of S Yorks; 2 da (Alexandra b 1980, Rebecca b 1982); *Career* chief offr Yorks Area NUM 1984–87; MP (Lab) Barnsley Central 1987–; memb Select Ctee: on Energy 1988–91, on Televising Proceedings of the House of Commons 1988–91, on Procedure 1991–, on Foreign Affrs 1997–, Chm's Panel 2000–; Lab Pty whip 1991–94, oppn spokesperson on health 1994–95, shadow min for local govt 1995, oppn spokesperson on NI 1995–97; vice-chm All-Pty Parly Occupational Pensions Gp, chair All Pty Parly Gp on Packaging Manufacturing Industry 2005–; memb Exec Ctee Inter Parly Union 1997–; memb CPA UK branch 1997–; treas Yorks Gp of Labour MPs; *Style—* Eric Illsley, Esq, MP; ✉ House of Commons, London SW1A 0AA (tel 020 7219 1543, fax 020 7219 0766); 18 Regent Street, Barnsley, South Yorkshire S70 2HG (tel 01226 730692, fax 01226 779429)

IMBERT, Baron (Life Peer UK 1999), of New Romney in the County of Kent; Sir Peter Michael Imbert; kt (1988), QPM (1980), JP (Greater London 1998); s of William Henry Imbert (d 1961), and Frances May, *née* Hodge (d 1985); *b* 27 April 1933; *Educ* Harvey GS Folkestone Kent; *m* 1956, Iris Rosina, da of Christopher Thomas Charles Dove (d 1983), of London; 1 s (Hon Simon b 1958), 2 da (Hon Elaine b 1960, Hon Sally b 1966); *Career* joined Met Police1953 (Detective Chief Supt until 1976), Asst then Dep Chief Constable Surrey Constabulary 1976–79, Chief Constable Thames Valley Police 1979–85, Cmmr Met Police 1987–93 (Dep Cmmr 1985–87); chm Capital Eye Security Ltd; advsr CDR International 1998–2000; memb Ministerial Advsy Bd Royal Parks 1993–2000; HM Lord Lt of Gtr London 1998–2008 (DL 1994–98); *Recreations* golf, bridge; *Style—* The Lord Imbert, QPM; ✉ Lieutenancy Office, 18th Floor, City Hall, PO Box 240, Victoria Street, London SW1E 6QP (tel 020 7641 3259)

IMBERT-TERRY, Sir Michael Edward Stanley; 5 Bt (UK 1917); s of Maj Sir Edward Henry Bouhier Imbert-Terry, MC, 3 Bt (d 1978), and Lady Sackville, *née* Garton, of Knole, Kent; suc bro, Sir Andrew Imbert-Terry, 4 Bt (d 1985); *b* 18 April 1950; *Educ* Cranleigh; *m* 1975, Frances Dorothy, 3 da of Peter Scott (d 1978), of Ealing; 2 da (Song b 1973, Bryony Jean b 1980), 2 s (Brychan Edward b 1975, Jack b 1985); *Heir* s, Brychan Imbert-Terry; *Style—* Sir Michael Imbert-Terry, Bt; ✉ Little Hennowe, St Ewe, Mevagissey, Cornwall (tel 01726 843893)

IMESON, Michael David; s of Terence Imeson, of Bradford, W Yorks, and Marian, *née* Glasby; *b* 26 October 1955; *Educ* Hanson GS Bradford, Univ of Bradford (BSc), LSE (MPhil); *m* 14 May 1988, Joanne Edwina, da of John Edward Simpson; 2 da (Sophia Rose b 8 June 1992, Olivia Mary b 12 Dec 1996), 1 s (Theodore David Robert b 27 Dec 2001); *Career* ed Export Times 1983–84 (reporter 1980–83); reporter: The Times 1984–86, London Daily News 1987; ed Maxwell Consumer Publishing and Communications 1987–92, publisher Financial and Business Publications 1992–, ed: Financial World (formerly Chartered Banker, Chartered Inst of Bankers magazine) 1995–2000, The Paper (Barclays Bank staff newspaper) 2000–01, Eclectic (Inst of Fin Servs magazine) 2000–05, Business Money Int 2005–07; contributing ed The Banker 2003–, assoc ed FT Global Events; memb: Communicators in Business, CPRE, CAMRA; *Books* Finance for Growth (ed, 1989), The Future of Building Societies (1999), Dangers in E-Banking (2001); *Recreations* running, skiing, five-a-side football, renovating old houses, antiques, cycling, photography, travel; *Style—* Michael Imeson, Esq; ✉ The Old Post House, Stanton, Broadway, Worcestershire WR12 7NE (tel 01386 584978, e-mail imeson@fbp.co.uk)

IMPALLOMENI, Dr Mario Giuseppe; s of Prof Col Rosario Impallomeni (d 1983), and Ada, *née* Ascarelli (d 1994); *b* 19 July 1937; *Educ* Scuole Pie Fiorentine Florence, Faculty of Med Univ of Florence (MD); *m* 10 March 1973 (m dis 2005), Madeleine Clare, da of Hugh Edward Blackburn (d 1964); 1 s (Tommaso Fergus b 11 Oct 1979), 1 da (Laura Chiara b 18 July 1982); *Career* jr lectr Dept of Clinical Med Univ of Florence 1961–66, registrar Queen's Hosp Croydon 1966–69, conslt physician Italian Hospital London 1969–90, sr registrar Central Middx Hosp & St Thomas' Hosp 1969–71, conslt geriatrician N Middx Hosp & St Anne's Hosp 1972–78, conslt gen and geriatric med and sr lectr Imperial Coll Sch of Med (formerly Royal Post Grad Med Sch) 1978–2002, conslt emeritus and hon sr lectr Dept of Med B Imperial Coll Sch of Med 2002–; hon physician Saracens RUFC 1992–2005; fndr memb and pres Italian Med Soc of GB 2002–04; contrib to several books on geriatric med, memb editorial bd of several med jls; chm NW Branch Br Geriatrics Soc 1985–89; FRCP 1985 (MRCP 1969); Commendatore dell'Ordine al Merito della Repubblica Italiana 2002; *Books* Textbook of Diagnostic Imaging in the Elderly (2002); *Recreations* history, chess, cycling, fell walking, classic music; *Style—* Dr Mario Impallomeni; ✉ Department of Medicine B, Faculty of Medicine, Imperial College, Hammersmith Hospital Campus, Du Cane Road, London W12 0HS (tel 020 8383 4290, fax 020 8383 3056, e-mail m.impallomeni@imperial.ac.uk)

IMRAY, Sir Colin Henry; KBE (1992), CMG (1983); s of Henry Gibbon Imray (d 1936), and Frances Olive, *née* Badman (d 1992); *b* 21 September 1933; *Educ* Highgate and Hotchkiss USA, Balliol Coll Oxford (MA); *m* 1957, Shirley Margaret, da of Ernest Matthews (d 1972); 1 s (Christopher), 3 da (Frances, Elizabeth, Alison); *Career* Nat Serv 2 Lt Seaforth Highlanders (Royal W African Force) 1952–54; CRO 1957, third (later second) sec UK High Cmmn Canberra 1958–61, first sec Nairobi 1963–66, Br Trade Cmmn Montreal 1970–73, cnsllr, head of Chancery and consul gen Islamabad 1973–77, RCDS 1977, commercial cnsllr Tel Aviv 1977–80, dep high cmmr Bombay 1980–84, dep chief clerk and chief inspr FCO 1984–85, high cmmr to the United Republic of Tanzania 1986–89, high cmmr to the People's Republic of Bangladesh 1989–93; High Steward Wallingford 2002–; Freeman City of London 1994; dir of overseas rels The Order of St John 1997–98 (sec gen 1993–97); chm Royal Over-Seas League 2000–05; KStJ 1993; *Recreations* gardening, travel; *Clubs* Travellers, Royal Over-Seas League (memb Central Cncl 1998–2005, memb Exec Cncl 1999–2005, vice-pres 2005–); *Style—* Sir Colin Imray, KBE, CMG; ✉ Holbrook House, Reading Road, Wallingford, Oxfordshire OX10 9DT

INCHBALD, Michael John Chantrey; s of Geoffrey Herbert Elliot Inchbald (sr ptnr City law firm Bischoff & Co, d 1982), and Rosemary Evelyn (d 1958), da of Arthur Ilbert, and niece of Sir Courtenay Peregrine Ilbert, GCB, KCSI, CIE (President of the Viceroy's Cncl and actg Viceroy of India, Clerk of the House of Commons for 18 years, he declined a peerage); *b* 8 March 1920; *Educ* Sherborne, Architectural Assoc Sch of Architecture; *m* 1, 31 Jan 1955 (m dis 1964), Jacqueline Bromley; 1 s (Courtenay Charles Ilbert b Dec 1958), 1 da (Charlotte Amanda b Feb 1960); m 2, June 1964 (m dis 1970), Eunice Haymes; *Career* architectural and interior designer; dir Michael Inchbald Ltd 1953–83, design conslt 1983–; co fndr Inchbald Sch of Design 1960; design projects for clients incl: Bank of America, Cncl of Industrial Design, Crown Estate Cmmrs, Cunard, Dunhill worldwide, Ferragamo, Forte (Post House, London Airport and several restaurants), Imperial Group, Justerini & Brooks, Law Soc, John Lewis, Manufacturers Hanover Bank, Manufacturers Hanover Trust Bank, John Player, Plessey Co, Pratt Bernard Engineering, Savoy Group (Berkeley, Claridges and Savoy Hotels, Stones Chop House complex), Scottish Highland Industries, Wolsey; other projects incl: ships (QE2, Carmania, Franconia, Windsor Castle), royal and private yachts and houses, projects for The Duc de la Rochefoucauld, 13 Duke of St Albans, 8 Marquess of Ailesbury, 6 Marquess of Bristol, 17 Earl of Perth, 9 Earl of Dartmouth, 2 Earl St Aldwyn, 3 Baron Gisborough, 6 Baron Kilmarnock, 7 Baron Latymer and 4 Baron St Levan; conslt to furniture and carpet manufacturers, consulted re changes at Buckingham Palace; work exhibited at: Triennale Milan, V&A, design centres in London, NY and Helsinki; winner of four out of four design competitions entered incl: Shapes of Things to Come 1946, National Chair Design Competition 1955; idFX/BIDA Award for Outstanding Contribution to Design 2005; subject of lecture at Courtauld Inst (chosen from all interior designers in Br); contrib: Architectural Review, Architectural Digest, Connaissance des Arts, Connoisseur, Country Life, Harpers & Queen, House & Garden, International Lighting Review, Tatler, Vogue, etc; Freeman Worshipful Co of Clockmakers 1984; FCSD; *Recreations* arts, travel, antiques, reading, music, walking; *Style—* Michael Inchbald, Esq; ✉ Stanley House, 10 Milner Street, London SW3 2PU (tel 020 7584 8832)

INCHCAPE, 4 Earl of (UK 1929); (Kenneth) Peter Lyle Mackay; also Baron Inchcape (UK 1911), Viscount Inchcape (UK 1924), and Viscount Glenapp (UK 1929); s of 3 Earl of Inchcape (d 1994), and his 1 w, Aline Thorn, *née* Pease; *b* 23 January 1943; *Educ* Eton; *m* 7 June 1966, Georgina, da of Sidney Cresswell Nisbet; 2 da (Lady Elspeth Pease (Lady Elspeth Hordern) b 1972, Lady Ailsa Fiona (Lady Ailsa Stonor) b 1977), 1 s (Fergus James Kenneth, Viscount Glenapp b 1979); *Heir* s, Viscount Glenapp; *Career* Lt 9/12 Royal Lancers served: Aden, Arabian Gulf, BAOR; formerly with Inchcape plc (20 years); dir: Inchcape Family Estates Ltd, The Glenapp Estate Co Ltd, Gray Dawes Travel Ltd, Assam Oil and Gas Co Ltd; pres Royal Alfred Seafarers Soc 1992–; memb Ct of Assts: Worshipful Co of Grocers (Master 1993–94), Worshipful Co of Shipwrights (Prime Warden 1998–99); Liveryman Worshipful Co of Fishmongers; AIB; *Recreations* shooting, fishing, golf, skiing, travel, farming; *Clubs* White's, Oriental, Pratt's, New, Prestwick, Royal Sydney Golf; *Style—* The Earl of Inchcape; ✉ Manor Farm, Clyffe Pypard, Wiltshire SN4 7PY; 63E Pont Street, London SW1 0BD

INCHIQUIN, 18 Baron (I 1543); Sir Conor Myles John O'Brien; 10 Bt (I 1686); The O'Brien, Chief of the name and the O'Brien Clan (one of the 20 recognised Irish bloodline Chiefs and Chieftains); s of Hon (Fionn) Myles Maryons O'Brien (yst s of 15 Baron Inchiquin); suc unc, 17 Baron Inchiquin, 1982; Lord Inchiquin is 13 in descent from the 3 s of 1 Baron Inchiquin, the latter being cr Earl of Thomond for life; the descendants of the eldest s of the 1 Baron held the Marquessate of Thomond 1800–55; The O'Briens descend from Brian Boroimhe, Prince of Thomond and High King of Ireland in 1002, who was k at the moment of victory against the Danes in the Battle of Clontarf 1014; *b* 17 July 1943; *Educ* Eton; *m* 1988, Helen O'Farrell, da of Gerald Fitzgerald Farrell, of Newtown Forbes, Co Longford; 2 da (Hon Slaney Alexandra Anne b 7 July 1989, Hon Lucia Josephine Mary b 27 May 1991); *Heir* cous, Conor O'Brien; *Career* late Capt 14th/20th King's Hussars; md Dromoland Development Company Ltd 1983–; *Clubs* Kildare Street and Univ (Dublin); *Style—* The Rt Hon the Lord Inchiquin; ✉ Thomond House, Dromoland, Newmarket-on-Fergus, Co Clare, Republic of Ireland (tel 061 368304, fax 061 368285, e-mail chiefob@iol.ie)

INCHYRA, 2 Baron (UK 1962), of St Madoes, Co Perth; Robert Charles Reneke Hoyer Millar; er s of 1 Baron Inchyra, GCMG, CVO (d 1989), and (Anna Judith) Elizabeth, da of Jonkheer Reneke de Marees van Swinderen, sometime Netherlands Min in London (d 1999); *b* 4 April 1935; *Educ* Eton, New Coll Oxford; *m* 1 Aug 1961, Fiona Mary, yr da of Edmund Charles Reginald Sheffield (d 1977), of Normanby Park, Scunthorpe, Lincs; 1 s (Hon (Christian) James Charles Hoyer b 12 Aug 1962), 2 da (Hon Henrietta Julia Hoyer (Hon Mrs Villanueva Brandt) b 21 Sept 1964, Hon Louisa Mary Hoyer (Hon Mrs Parladé) b 26 April 1968); *Heir* s, Hon James Millar; *Career* late Scots Gds; banker; local dir Barclays Bank Newcastle upon Tyne 1967–75, regnl gen mangr Barclays Bank 1976–81, dep chm Barclays Bank Tst Co Ltd 1982–85, gen mangr Barclays Bank plc 1985–87, dir UK Fin Services 1987–88, dir gen British Bankers Assoc 1988–94; dir Witan Investment Co plc 1979–2002, chm European Utilities Tst plc 1994–2005 (formerly Legg Mason Investors European Utilities Tst); chm Nat Assoc of Clubs for Young People (NACYP) 1994–2003, treas Multiple Sclerosis Int Fedn (MSIF) 2001–; memb Queen's

Body Guard for Scotland (Royal Co of Archers); *Clubs* White's, Pratt's; *Style—* The Rt Hon the Lord Inchyra; ✉ Rookley Manor, King's Somborne, Stockbridge, Hampshire SO20 6QX (tel 01794 388319)

IND, Dr Philip Waterloo; s of John Waterloo Ind, of San Juan, Spain, and Marjorie, *née* Hesketh; *b* 17 February 1950; *Educ* Haberdashers' Aske's, Gonville & Caius Coll Cambridge (BA, MA), UCH (MB BChir); *m* 30 June 1973, Dr Sally Ind, da of Dr Charles Hutcheon Thomson (d 1962), of Low Fell, Durham; 1 s (Robert b 3 Oct 1977), 2 da (Sarah b 25 April 1980, Kathryn b 28 Oct 1982); *Career* med registrar Edgware Gen Hosp 1975, hon sr registrar Hammersmith Hosp 1981 (registrar 1977), hon sr lectr and conslt physician Hammersmith and Ealing Hosp 1985–, currently sr lectr and actg head Dept of Respiratory Med NHLI Hammersmith Hosp; multiple academic papers and book chapters; FRCP 1991 (MRCP); *Recreations* reading, windsurfing, bridge, squash, tennis; *Style—* Dr Philip Ind; ✉ Respiratory Medicine, Clinical Investigation Unit, Imperial College School of Medicine at Hammersmith Hospital, Du Cane Road, London W12 0HS (tel 020 8740 3077, fax 020 8743 9733, e-mail p.ind@imperial.ac.uk)

IND, Rt Rev William; *see:* Truro, Bishop of

INESON, Dr Nigel Richard; s of Jeffrey Ineson, of Milton Keynes, and late Eileen, *née* Wood; *Educ* Watford GS, Guy's Hosp Med Sch London (MB BS, DRCOG, DFFP); *Children* 2 s (James Richard Mannakee b 8 Dec 1984, Andrew Nicholas Mannakee b 23 July 1986); *Career* various house jobs Hillingdon Hosp (med) and Wycombe Gen Hosp (surgical), subsequently on staff A&E Dept Hillingdon Hosp then SHO (gen surgical and orthopaedics rotation) Medway Hosp Gp Kent, SHO posts in med/geriatrics, psychiatry, paediatrics & obstetrics and gynaecology then gen practice trainee (vocational trg scheme) Watford 1981–84, ptnr in teaching practice Watford 1984–; princ Herts FHSA, company med offr DDD Ltd (mfr of ethical pharmaceuticals), med offr Watford FC; MAE, memb Expert Witness Inst, chm Beds & Herts Faculty RCGP; FRCGP; *Style—* Dr Nigel Ineson; ✉ Wentworth, 30 Green Lane, Oxhey, Hertfordshire WD1 4NH (tel 01923 233992); The Callowland Surgery, 141a Leavesden Road, Watford, Hertfordshire WD2 5EP (fax 01923 443143, mobile 078 3168 6531)

INFIELD, Paul Louis; s of Gordon Mark Infield, and Roda Molca, *née* Lincoln; *b* 1 July 1957; *Educ* Haberdashers' Aske's, The Peddie Sch Hightstown NJ, Univ of Sheffield (LLB); *m* 6 Feb 1987, Catharine Grace, da of Ancrum Francis Evans, of Clifton on Teme, Worcs, 1 s (Samuel b 1988), 1 da (Margery b 1991); *Career* called to the Bar Inner Temple 1980; memb Bd of Visitors HM Prison Wandsworth 1992–2000 (chm 1996–98), memb Exec Ctee Assoc of Membs of Bds of Visitors 1997–2000; tstee: The Suzy Lamplugh Tst 1999–, Prisoners' Educn Tst 1999–2000, Network for Surviving Stalking 2001–05; memb Ed Bd Community Safety Jl 2002–05; chm S London Liberal Synagogue 2002–07, offr Liberal Judaism 2005–; Freeman City of London 1979, Liveryman Worshipful Co of Plaisterers 1979; *Publications* The Prisons Handbook (contrib, 1997 and 1998), The Law of Harassment and Stalking (with Graham Platford, 2000), Stalking and Psychosexual Obsession (contrib, 2002); *Recreations* sailing, scuba diving; *Style—* Paul Infield, Esq; ✉ 34 Hillier Road, London SW11 6AU; 5 Paper Buildings, Temple, London EC4Y 7HB (tel 020 7815 3200, fax 020 7815 3201, e-mail paulinfield@5paper.com)

INGE, Charles; *b* 9 June 1961, Rugby, Warks; *Educ* Univ of Oxford (MA); *m* Jane; 3 da (Sarah, Emma, Laura); *Career* Lowe: joined 1986, various positions rising to creative dir 1999–2001; co-fndr Clemmow Hornby Inge 2001; winner numerous advtg industry awards incl: Cannes Grand Prix (for The Independent TV campaign) 1999, Cannes Grand Prix (for Stella Artois press campaign) 2000, IPA Effectiveness Grand Prix (for Tesco campaign) 2000; for Lowe: Campaign Agency of the Year 2000, Ad Age European Agency of the Year 2000, Br TV Advtg Agency of the Year 2001; for Clemmow Hornby Inge: Br TV Advtg Agency of the Year 2004, Creative Agency of the Year Marketing magazine 2004; *Style—* Charles Inge, Esq; ✉ Clemmow Hornby Inge, 7 Rathbone Street, London W1T 1LY (tel 020 7462 8514, fax 020 7462 8501, website www.chiadvertising.com)

INGE, Baron (Life Peer UK 1997), of Richmond in the County of North Yorkshire; Field Marshal The Rt Hon Peter Anthony Inge; KG (2001), GCB (1992, KCB 1988), PC (2004), DL (N Yorks 1994); s of Raymond Inge (d 1995), and Grace Maud Caroline, *née* Du Rose (d 1962); *b* 5 August 1935; *Educ* Wrekin Coll, RMA Sandhurst; *m* 26 Nov 1960, Letitia Marion, da of Trevor Thornton Berry (d 1967); 2 da (Hon Antonia b 17 May 1962, Hon Verity b 12 Oct 1965); *Career* cmmnd Green Howards 1954; served: Hong Kong, Malaya, Germany, Libya and N Ireland, ADC to GOC 4 Div 1960–61, Adj 1 Green Howards 1963–64, student Staff Coll 1966, MOD 1967–69, Co Comd 1 Green Howards 1969–70, student JSSC 1971, BM 11 Armd Bde 1972, instr Staff Coll 1973–74, CO 1 Green Howards 1974–77, Comdt Jr Div Staff Coll 1977–79, Comd 4 Armd Bde 1979–81, Chief of Staff HQ 1 (BR) Corps 1982–83, GOC NE Dist and Comd 2 Inf Div 1984–86, DGLP (A) MOD 1986–87, Comd 1 (BR) Corps 1987–89, C-in-C BAOR and Comd NORTHAG 1989–91, Col Comdt RMP 1987–92, ADC (Gen) to HM The Queen 1991–94; CGS 1992–94, CDS 1994–97, Field Marshal 1994; Constable HM Tower of London 1996–2001, pres Army Benevolent Fund 1997–2002, Pilgrims 2003–; Col The Green Howards 1982–94, Col Comdt APTC 1988–96; non-exec dir: Racal Electronics plc 1997–2000, Greenlys plc 1998–99; chm Cncl King Edward VII's Hosp Sister Agnes 2003–; memb: Cncl Marborough Coll 1998–2006, Cncl St George's House Windsor Castle 1999–; tstee: Royal Amouries 1996–2000, Historical Royal Palaces 1998–; Hon DCL Univ of Newcastle upon Tyne 1995; CIMgt 1993; *Recreations* cricket, walking, music, reading (especially military history); *Clubs* Army and Navy, MCC, Boodle's, Beefsteak; *Style—* Field Marshal the Lord Inge, KG, GCB, PC, DL; ✉ House of Lords, London SW1A 0PW

INGE, Rt Rev Dr John; *see:* Bishop of Huntingdon

INGHAM, Barrie Stanton; s of Harold Ellis Stead Ingham (d 1975), and Irene, *née* Bolton (d 1977); *b* 10 February 1932; *Educ* Heath GS Halifax; *m* 15 July 1957, Tarne, da of David Watkin Phillips, of Aust; 4 da (Catrin Marie b 7 March 1961, Liâne Jane b 12 March 1963, Francesca Shelley b 8 June 1964, Mali Terez b 5 Sept 1976); *Career* actor; 2 Lt RA 1951, TA offr 1953–; UK conslt to Int Theatre Arts Forum 1976, visiting prof Univ of Texas at Austin 1979, drama conslt to Baylor Univ 1980, hon assoc artist RSC 1989 (assoc artist 1974), artistic advsr to NY Shakespeare Soc 2001; dir Long Island Shakespeare Festival NY 2001; *Theatre* debut London in Hamlet, The Magistrate, Sganarelle, Tartuffe, A Midsummer Night's Drea, Measure for Measure, Mary Stuart, Julius Caesar, Henry VI, Henry VIII and King Lear (Old Vic) 1957–59; West End: Joie de Vivre 1959, The Happy Haven 1960, England Our England 1962, Virtue in Danger 1963, The Possessed 1963, The Bacchae 1964, The Bucksome Muse 1964, Pickwick 1964, On the Level 1966, Love, Love, Love 1972, Gypsy 1973, Snap 1974, Double Edge 1976, Aspects of Love 1990, Anything Goes 2003; RSC Stratford, London and world tours: Lalo in Criminals, Brutus in Julius Caesar, Leontes in Winter's Tale, Sir Andrew in Twelfth Night, Lord Foppington in the Relapse, Dazzle in London Assurance, Buffalo Bill in Indians, Pleasure and Repentance (all 1967–71), the Duke in Measure for Measure 1974, Beverly Carlton in the Man Who Came to Dinner 1989; National Theatre: The American Clock and the Bay at Nice 1986–87; NY: Ivor Novello in Waltz of my Heart 2003, Alfred Lunt on Noel, Alfred and Lynn 2002; Broadway: Claudio in Much Ado About Nothing 1959, Uriah Heep in Copperfield 1981, Pellimore in Camelot 1982, George in Aspects of Love 1991, Col Pickering in My Fair Lady 1994, Sir Danvers in Jekyll and Hyde 1997; US nat tours: Camelot 1982, Me and My Girl 1987, Aspects of Love 1992; int tours: Private Lives (Aust), Beatrice et Benedict (Canadian Opera), Love Love Love and The Actor (solo shows, worldwide) 1980–, Kind Lear in King Lear (Ludlow Festival) 1986; *Television* over 100 TV plays in USA and UK incl: The Victorians 1962, Ann Veronica 1965, The Caesars 1968, The Power Game 1970, title role in Hine 1971, Beyond a Joke 1972, Funny Man 1979, George Washington 1983, Time Warrior 1994, The Triangle 2005; *Films* incl: Dr Who and the Daleks 1964, title role in A Challenge for Robin Hood 1966, Day of the Jackal 1973, vioce of Basil in Disney's The Great Mouse Detective 1985; *Awards* Aust Theatre Most Distinguished Actor Award 1975, Freedom of City of Austin 1980, Drama Logue Award Best Performance in a Broadway Musical 1981, Southern Calif Motion Picture Cncl Award 1983; *Clubs* Groucho; *Style—* Barrie Ingham, Esq

INGHAM, Sir Bernard; kt (1990); s of Garnet Ingham (d 1974); *b* 21 June 1932; *Educ* Hebden Bridge GS; *m* 1956, Nancy Hilda, da of Ernest Hoyle (d 1944), of Halifax, W Yorks; 1 s (Dr John Bernard Ingham, *qv* b 16 Feb 1958); *Career* journalist: Hebden Bridge Times 1948–52, The Yorkshire Post and Yorkshire Evening Post 1952–59, The Yorkshire Post (northern industrial corr) 1959–62, The Guardian 1962–67 (Leeds 1962–65, Lab Staff London 1965–67); press advsr Nat Bd for Prices and Incomes 1967–68, head of info Dept of Employment and Productivity 1968–72; dir of info: Dept of Employment 1973, Dept of Energy 1974–78; under sec (Energy Conservation Div) Dept of Energy 1978–79, chief press sec to Prime Minister 1979–90; chm Bernard Ingham Communications 1991–; columnist: The Express 1991–98, PR Week 1994–2001 (winner Business and Professional Magazines Columnist of the Year PPA Awards 1995), The Yorkshire Post 2004–; non-exec dir Hill and Knowlton 1991–2001, non-exec dir McDonald's Restaurants Ltd 1991–2005, memb Advsy Bd McDonald's UK 2005–; pres Br Franchise Assoc 1993–; sec Supporters of Nuclear Energy 1998–; visiting fell Dept of Politics Univ of Newcastle upon Tyne 1989–2003, visiting prof Univ of Middlesex Business Sch 1998–; memb Cncl Univ of Huddersfield 1994–2000; hon fell Communication, Advertising and Marketing Educn Fndn 1998; Hon DLitt Univ of Buckingham 1997, Hon DUniv Middlesex 1999; Hon FINucE 1998; *Books* Kill the Messenger (1991), Yorkshire Millennium (1999), Yorkshire Castles (2001), Yorkshire Villages (2001), The Wages of Spin (2003), Yorkshire Greats (2005); *Recreations* walking, gardening, reading; *Clubs* Reform, Midgehole Working Men's, Hebden Bridge; *Style—* Sir Bernard Ingham; ✉ 9 Monahan Avenue, Purley, Surrey CR8 3BB (tel 020 8660 8970, e-mail bernardinghamcom@aol.com)

INGHAM, Prof Derek Binns; s of George Arthur Ingham (d 1967), and Fanny Walton, *née* Binns (d 1965); *b* 7 August 1942; *Educ* Univ of Leeds (BSc, PhD, DSc); *m* 22 Aug 1964, Jean, da of Tom Hirst (d 1963); 1 da (Catherine Gail b 30 Dec 1965), 1 s (Mark Andrew b 10 July 1967); *Career* Univ of Leeds: lectr in mathematics 1968–78 (1964–66), sr lectr 1978–83, reader 1983–86, prof 1986–, head Dept of Applied Mathematical Studies 1988–91; CLE Moore instr MIT 1966–68; hon grad Univ of Cluj Romania 2000; FIMA 1988; *Books* incl: Boundary Integral Equation Analyses of Singular, Potential and Biharmonic Problems (1984), The Mathematics of Blunt Body Sampling (1988), The Boundary Element Method for Solving Improperly Posed Problems (with Y Yuan, 1994), Boundary Element Methods in Fluid Dynamics II (ed with C A Brebbia and H Power, 1994), Boundary Elements XVIII (ed with C A Brebbia, J A Martins, M H Aliabadi, N Haie and M Power, 1996), Enhanced Sedimentation in Inclined Fracture Channels (with L Elliott and S McCaffery, 1997), Boundary Integral Formulations for Inverse Analysis (with L C Wrobel, 1997), Transport Phenomena in Porous Media (with I Pop, 1998, vol 2 2002), Convective Heat Transfer (with I Pop, 2001), Inverse Problems and Experimental Design in Thermal and Mechanical Engineering (ed with D Petit, Y Jarny and F Plourde, 2002), Proceedings of the First UK Conference on Boundary Integral Methods (ed with L Elliott and D Lesnic); *Style—* Prof Derek Ingham; ✉ 3 Fairfax Avenue, Menston, Ilkley, West Yorkshire LS29 6EP (tel 01943 875810); Department of Applied Mathematics, University of Leeds, Leeds LS2 9JT (tel 0113 343 5113, fax 0113 242 9925, telex 0113 255 6473, e-mail amt6dbi@amsta.leeds.ac.uk)

INGHAM, Graham; s of Alan Ingham, of Bacup, Lancs, and Marjorie, *née* White; *b* 30 September 1953; *Educ* Bacup and Rawtenstall GS, Thames Poly (BA), LSE (MSc); *Career* HM Treasy 1975–84: private sec to Sir Kenneth Couzens 1978–80, princ monetary policy 1980–81, princ Euro monetary affrs 1982–84; visiting fell and Fulbright scholar Princeton Univ 1981–82, economics specialist BBC World Serv 1984–88, economics corr BBC TV News and Current Affrs 1988–96, Guardian research fell Nuffield Coll Oxford 1995–96 (on leave from BBC), freelance broadcaster and journalist 1996–2000; dir of public affairs Centre for Economic Performance LSE 1995–2000; visiting prof of economics Univ of Greenwich 1992–93, visiting reader in economics Royal Holloway Coll London 1995–97; ed CentrePiece 1995–2001, with The Economist 2000–03, speechwriter and advsr (to Anne Krueger) Int Monetary Fund Washington DC 2003–06, advsr to the Pres Federal Reserve Bank of NY 2006–; *Books* Romance of the Three Empires (contrib, 1988), Managing Change: a guide to British economic policy (2000); *Recreations* opera, travel, reading; *Style—* Graham Ingham, Esq; ✉ c/o Federal Reserve Bank of New York, 33 Liberty Street, New York, NY 10045, USA (e-mail grahamingham@hotmail.com)

INGHAM, Dr John Bernard; s of Sir Bernard Ingham, *qv*, of Purley, Surrey, and Nancy Hilda, *née* Hoyle; *b* 16 February 1958; *Educ* Univ of Durham (BA, Fulbright scholar, PhD), Bowling Green State Univ of Ohio (MA); *m* 7 Sept 1985, Christine, da of James Yendley; 1 da (b 21 Sept 1991), 1 s (b 16 Sept 1994); *Career* visiting researcher Georgetown Univ Washington DC 1982–83, dep ed BNFL News 1984–87, ed Sellascene 1986–87, freelance sports reporter Sunday Express 1986–89; Northern Correspondent, Building Magazine, Chartered Surveyor Weekly 1987–89; news reporter Daily Express Manchester 1989–90; Daily Express: def and dip corr 1990–94, political corr 1994–96, environment corr 1996–99, environment and tport ed 1999–2002, environment, tport and def ed 2002–, columnist 2005–; *Recreations* travel, birdwatching, following cricket and soccer; *Style—* Dr John Ingham; ✉ Daily Express, The Northern & Shell Building, 10 Lower Thames Street, London EC3R 6EN (tel 0871 520 7108, fax 0871 434 2723, e-mail john.ingham@express.co.uk)

INGHAM, Prof Philip William; s of George Philip Ingham (d 1980), of Liverpool, and Dorothy, *née* Wensley; *b* 19 March 1955; *Educ* Univ of Cambridge (MA), Univ of Sussex (DPhil); *m* 1993, Anita, *née* Taylor; 2 da (Madeleine Philippa b 20 April 1994, Isabella Alexandria b 15 Sept 1998), 1 s (James William b 18 Sept 1995); *Career* research trg: Laboratoire de Génètique Moléculaire CNRS Gif-sur Yvette 1979, Laboratoire de Génètique Moléculaire des Eukaryotes Faculté de Médècine Strasbourg 1981–82, Developmental Genetics Laboratory ICRF London 1982–85; research scientist MRC Laboratory of Molecular Biology Univ of Cambridge 1986, research scientist rising to sr scientist ICRF Developmental Biology Unit Univ of Oxford 1986–94, princ scientist ICRF London 1994–96, prof of developmental genetics and dir Centre for Developmental and Biomedical Genetics Univ of Sheffield 1996–; visiting prof Nat Univ of Singapore 2005, investigator Inst of Molecular and Cell Biology Singapore 2006–; chm Br Soc for Developmental Biology 1999–2004 (pubns sec 1991–95), vice-chm MRC/Wellcome Tst Human Developmental Biology Resource Steering Ctee 2000–02; memb Ctee: Br Soc for Developmental Biology 1987–95, Genetics Soc of GB 1993–97; memb Scientific Advsy Bd: Ontogeny Inc 1995–99, MRC Centre for Developmental Neurobiology KCL 2002–; memb: Fellowship Review Panel Human Frontiers Science Prog 1996–98, Molecular and Cell Review Panel Wellcome Tst 1997–2001, Review Panel Yorks Cancer Research 1997–2001, Int Scientific Advsy Bd Max-Planck-Institut für Entwicklungsbiologie Tübingen 1999–, EMBO Courses and Workshops Ctee 2002–05; assoc ed: Developmental Biology 1995–2002, Molecular Cell 1999–2001; reviews ed Developmental Cell 2001–03; memb Editorial Advsy Bd: Current Topics in Developmental Biology 1990–, Genetical

Research 1991–96, Development 1991–98, Genes & Development 1991–2005, Mechanisms of Development 1991–, Current Biology 1993–, EMBO Jl 1999–, GeneScreen 1999–, Genome Biology 1999–, Comparative and Functional Genomics 1999–2005, EMBO Reports 2000–; author of 116 pubns in learned jls; Balfour Meml Prize Genetical Soc of GB 1991, Genetics Soc Medal 2005; Royal Soc European exchange fell 1980, EMBO long-term fell 1981, hon research lectr Univ of Oxford 1992; MA (by incorporation) Univ of Oxford 1987; memb EMBO 1995, FIBiol 2000, FMedSci 2001, FRS 2002; *Recreations* playing tennis, reading, listening to music (especially choral); *Style*— Prof Philip Ingham; ✉ Centre for Developmental Genetics, Department of Biomedical Science, University of Sheffield, Firth Court, Western Bank, Sheffield S10 2TN

INGILBY, Sir Thomas Colvin William; 6 Bt (UK 1866), of Ripley Castle, Yorkshire; s of Maj Sir Joslan William Vivian Ingilby, 5 Bt, JP, DL (d 1974), and Diana, *née* Colvin; *b* 17 July 1955; *Educ* Eton, RAC Cirencester (MRAC); *m* 25 Feb 1984, Emma Clare Roebuck, da of Maj Richard R Thompson, of Whinfield, W Yorks; 4 s (James William Francis b 1985, Joslan Richard Ryland b 1986, Jack Henry Thomas b 1990, Richard Joseph Frederick b 1994), 1 da (Eleanor Jane Pamela b 1989); *Heir* s, James Ingilby; *Career* teacher Springvale Sch Rhodesia 1973–74; asst land agent: Stephenson & Son York 1978–80, Strutt and Parker Harrogate 1981–83; mangr Ripley Castle Estates 1983– (Best Tourist Devpt RICS White Rose Awards, Silver Award for Best Small Visitor Attraction VisitBritain Enjoy Excellence in England Awards 2007–08); pres Nidderdale Amateur Cricket League 1979–; dir: N York TEC 1989–93, Yorkshire Tourist Bd 1997– (vice-chm 2005–); chm: Yorkshire's Great Houses, Castles and Gardens 1994–, The Great Inns of Britain 1996–; landowner (1000 acres) and hotelier Boar's Head Ripley; int hon citizen New Orleans 1979; ARICS, FAAV, FBII; *Books* Yorkshire's Great Houses - Behind the Scenes (2005); *Recreations* tennis, cricket; *Style*— Sir Thomas Ingilby, Bt; ✉ Ripley Castle, Ripley, Harrogate, North Yorkshire HG3 3AY (tel 01423 770152, fax 01423 771745, e-mail enquiries@ripleycastle.co.uk)

INGLE, Prof Stephen James; s of James Ingle (d 1991), and Violet Grace, *née* Stephenson (d 1997); *b* 6 November 1940; *Educ* The Roan Sch, Univ of Sheffield (BA, MA Econ, DipEd), Victoria Univ of Wellington NZ (PhD); *m* 5 Aug 1964, Margaret Anne, da of Henry James Hubert Farmer (d 1979), of Sutton Bridge, Lincs; 2 s (Jonathan James Stuart b 11 Oct 1970, Benedict John Stephen b 13 April 1972), 1 da (Cassie Louise b 8 June 1979); *Career* Cwlth scholar in NZ 1964–67, head of dept Univ of Hull 1985–90 (lectr in politics 1967–80, sr lectr 1980); Univ of Stirling: prof and head of Dept of Politics 1991–2002, vice-dean Faculty of Arts 1996–2002; visiting research fell Victoria Univ of Wellington NZ 1993; sec Political Studies Assoc UK 1987–88, chief examiner in politics Oxford, Cambridge and RSA Examinations Syndicate 1987–2002; memb E Yorks HA 1985–90; *Books* Socialist Thought in Imaginative Literature (1979), Parliament and Health Policy (1981), George Orwell: A Political Life (1993), British Party System (3 edn 1999), Narratives of British Socialism (2002), The Social and Political Thought of George Orwell: A Reappraisal (2006); *Recreations* music, theatre, hill walking; *Style*— Prof Stephen Ingle; ✉ The Ridings, Perth Road, Dunblane FK15 0HA (tel 01786 823372); University of Stirling, Stirling FK9 4LA (tel 01786 467593, e-mail s.j.ingle@stir.ac.uk)

INGLEBY, 2 Viscount (UK 1956); Martin Raymond Peake; s of 1 Viscount Ingleby (d 1966), and Lady Joan Rachel de Vere Capell (d 1979), da of 7 Earl of Essex; *b* 31 May 1926; *Educ* Eton, Trinity Coll Oxford; *m* 1, 1952, Susan (d 1996), da of Capt Henderson Russell Landale, of Ewell Manor, West Farleigh, Kent; 1 s (decd), 4 da; *m* 2, 2003, Dobnia, da of late Radomir Radovic; *Heir* none; *Career* late Lt Coldstream Gds; called to the Bar Inner Temple 1956; dir Hargreaves Gp Ltd 1960–80, CC N Riding Yorks 1964–67; landowner; *Recreations* forestry; *Style*— The Rt Hon the Viscount Ingleby; ✉ Snilesworth Lodge, Northallerton, North Yorkshire DL6 3QD

INGLEBY, Richard William; s of late William Ingleby, and Elizabeth Blackwood, *née* Craig; *b* 29 January 1967, Glasgow; *Educ* Trinity Coll Glenalmond, Univ of Durham (BA); *m* 22 Dec 1994, Florence; 3 da (Molly b 18 March 1996, Edie b 31 Oct 1998, Esme b 21 July 2002); *Career* Fine Art Soc 1990–97 (dir 1995–97), dir and prop Ingleby Gallery Edinburgh 1998–; art critic and columnist for various pubns 1996–2002; tstee: Arts Tst for Scotland, Edinburgh Art Festival, Little Sparta Tst; *Publications* Christopher Wood: An English Painter (1994), C R W Nevinson (1998), Alfred Wallis and James Dixon (1999), To the North: Jon Schueler (2003); *Recreations* arts, books, food, drink; *Clubs* Soho House, Hallion (Edinburgh); *Style*— Richard Ingleby, Esq

INGLESE, Anthony Michael Christopher; s of Angelo Inglese, and Dora, *née* Di Paola; *b* 19 December 1951; *Educ* Salvatorian Coll Harrow Weald, Fitzwilliam Coll Cambridge (MA, LLB); *m* 1974, Jane Elizabeth Kerry, *née* Bailes; 1 s, 1 da; *Career* called to the Bar Gray's Inn 1976, bencher 2003, Legal Adviser's Branch Home Office 1975–86, legal secretariat to Law Offrs 1986–88, Legal Adviser's Branch Home Office 1988–91, legal dir Office of Fair Trading 1991–95, legal advsr Treasy Slr's Dept Min of Defence 1995–97, dep Treasy slr 1997–2002, slr to DTI 2002–; *Recreations* organising theatricals; *Style*— Anthony Inglese, Esq; ✉ DTI, 1 Victoria Street, London SW1H 0ET

INGLETON, Diana Margaret; da of John Harston (d 1980), of Norfolk, and Freda Mary, *née* Boulton (d 1997); *b* 7 December 1957; *Educ* Havant GS, Havant Sixth Form Coll, Winchester Sch of Art, Norwich Sch of Art (BA); *m* 17 May 1986, William Simon Luke Ingleton, s of Richard William John Ingleton; *Career* graphic designer; formed design consultancy Design Motive Ltd specialising in brand identity and mgmnt 1993, currently jt md Grand Rapids brand consultancy; *Recreations* horse riding, conservation, sailing, walking; *Style*— Ms Diana Ingleton; ✉ The Hayloft, Rose Lane, Ripley, Surrey GU23 6NE

INGLEWOOD, 2 Baron (UK 1964); (William) Richard (Fletcher) Vane; DL (Cumbria); s of 1 Baron Inglewood, TD, DL (d 1989); *b* 31 July 1951; *Educ* Eton, Trinity Coll Cambridge (MA), Cumbria Coll of Agric and Forestry; *m* 29 Aug 1986, Cressida Rosa, yst da of late (Alan) Desmond Frederick Pemberton-Pigott, CMG, of Fawe Park, Keswick; 2 da (Hon Miranda Mary b 19 May 1987, Hon Rosa Katharine b 25 July 1989), 1 s (Hon Henry William Frederick b 24 Dec 1990); *Heir* s, Hon Henry Vane; *Career* called to the Bar Lincoln's Inn 1975; MEP (Cons): Cumbria and Lancs N 1989–94, NW England 1999–2004; Parly candidate (Cons): Houghton and Washington Gen Election 1983, Durham European election 1984; Cons spokesman on legal affrs European Parl 1989–94 and 1999–2004, Cons spokesman on constitutional affrs 2001–04, Cons chief whip European Parl 1994 (dep whip 1992–94), Lord in Waiting 1994–95; Capt Yeomen of the Guard 1995, Parly under sec of state Dept of National Heritage 1995–97, oppn spokesman on the environment House of Lords 1997–98, memb Sub-Ctee F European Communities Ctee of House of Lords 1997–99, elected memb House of Lords 1999–, memb Sub-Ctee A European Communities Ctee House of Lords 2004–; chm Reviewing Ctee on the Export of Works of Art 2003–; chm: C N Gp 2002– (dir 1997–), Carr's Milling Industries 2005– (dir 2004–); pres Cumbria Tourist Bd 2004–; memb: Lake Dist Special Planning Bd 1984–90, Regnl Land Drainage Ctee NWWA 1985–89, NWWA 1987–89; memb Ct Lancaster Univ 1985; Liveryman Worshipful Co of Skinners; MRICS, FSA; *Clubs* Travellers, Pratt's; *Style*— The Rt Hon Lord Inglewood, DL; ✉ Hutton-in-the-Forest, Penrith, Cumbria CA11 9TH (tel 017684 84500, fax 017684 84571)

INGLIS, Prof (James) Alistair Macfarlane; CBE (1984); s of Alexander Inglis (d 1948), and Dr Edith Marion Douglas, *née* Smith (d 1960); *b* 24 December 1928; *Educ* Fettes, Univ of St Andrews (MA), Univ of Glasgow (LLB); *m* 18 April 1959, (Mary) Elizabeth (d 2004), da of John Ronald Howie, JP (d 1982); 2 s (Alexander b 1960, Ronald b 1973), 3 da (Elspeth b 1962, Morag b 1963, Marion b 1966); *Career* Nat Serv RCS 1952–54, ret Capt

TA; ptnr McClure Naismith Glasgow 1956–93; Univ of Glasgow: prof of conveyancing 1979–93, prof of professional legal practice 1984–93, now emeritus prof; contrib to various jls incl Stair Meml Encyclopaedia: Laws of Scotland; pres Rent Assessment Panel Scotland 1976–87, memb Gtr Glasgow Health Bd 1975–83, dean Royal Faculty of Procurators Glasgow 1989–92, memb Ct of Patrons RCPSGlas 1995–; gen tstee Church of Scotland 1994–2004; memb Law Soc Scotland 1952; *Recreations* golf, gardening; *Clubs* Western (Glasgow); *Style*— Prof Alistair Inglis, CBE; ✉ Crioch, Uplawmoor, Glasgow G78 4DE (tel and fax 01505 850315)

INGLIS-JONES, Nigel John; QC (1982); s of Maj John Alfred Inglis-Jones (d 1977), and Hermione, *née* Vivian (d 1958); *b* 7 May 1935; *Educ* Eton, Trinity Coll Oxford (BA); *m* 1, 1965, Lenette (d 1986), o da of late Lt-Col Sir Walter Bromley-Davenport, and Lady Bromley-Davenport, of Cheshire; 2 da (Imogen b 1966, Cressida b 1967), 2 s (James b 1968, Valentine b 1972); *m* 2, 1987, Ursula Jane Drury, yr da of late Captain G D and Mrs Culverwell (now Lady Pile), of Sussex; 1 s (Sebastian b 1991); *Career* served as Ensign (Nat Serv) with Grenadier Gds 1953–55; called to the Bar Inner Temple 1954 (bencher 1981); recorder of the Crown Court 1977–92, gen cmmr for Income Tax 1992–2005, dep social security cmmr 1993–2002; *Books* The Law of Occupational Pension Schemes; *Recreations* fishing, gardening, collecting early English glass; *Clubs* MCC; *Style*— Nigel Inglis-Jones, Esq, QC; ✉ 21 Elms Crescent, London SW4 8QE (tel 020 7622 3043); Outer Temple Chambers, 222 The Strand, London WC2R 1BA (tel 020 7353 6381)

INGLIS OF GLENCORSE, Sir Roderick John; 10 Bt (NS 1703), of Glencorse, Midlothian (formerly Mackenzie of Gairloch, Ross-shire); s of Sir Maxwell Ian Hector Inglis, 9 Bt (d 1974); *b* 25 January 1936; *Educ* Winchester, Univ of Edinburgh (MB ChB); *m* 1, 1960 (m dis 1975), Rachel Evelyn, da of Lt-Col N M Morris, of Dowdstown, Ardee, Co Louth; 1 da (Amanda Fiona b 1963), 2 s (Ian Richard, Alexander Colin (twins) b 1965), and 1 s decd; *m* 2, 1975 (m dis 1977), Geraldine, yr da of R H Kirk, of Thaxted, Essex; 1 da (Harriet b 1977); *m* 3, 1986, Marilyn, da of A L Irwin, of Glasgow; 1 s (Harry Mackenzie b 1987); *Heir* s, Ian Inglis of Glencorse, yr; *Clubs* Country (Pietermaritzburg); *Style*— Sir Roderick Inglis of Glencorse, Bt; ✉ 18 Cordwalles Road, Pietermaritzburg, Natal, South Africa

INGOLD, Prof Timothy; s of Cecil Terence Ingold, of Wooler, Northumberland, and Leonora Mary, *née* Kemp (d 1998); *b* 1 November 1948; *Educ* Leighton Park Sch Reading, Churchill Coll Cambridge (BA, PhD); *m* 30 Dec 1972, Anna Kaarina, *née* Väli-Kivistö; 3 s (Christopher b 1975, Nicholas b 1977, Jonathan b 1981), 1 da (Susanna b 1994); *Career* Dept of Social Anthropology Univ of Manchester: lectr 1974–85, sr lectr 1985–90, prof 1990–95; Max Gluckman prof of social anthropology Univ of Manchester 1995–99, prof of social anthropology Univ of Aberdeen 1999–; pres Section H (Anthropology and Archaeology) BAAS 1998–99, chair of tstees Esperanza Tst RAI 1997–; Rivers Meml Medal RAI 1989, Award of Jean-Marie Delwart Fndn Royal Belgian Acad of Sciences 1994, Anders Retzius Gold Medal Swedish Soc for Anthropology and Geography 2004; FBA 1997, FRSE 2000; *Books* The Skolt Lapps Today (1976), Hunters, Pastoralists and Ranchers (1980), Evolution and Social Life (1986), The Appropriation of Nature (1986), The Perception of the Environment (2000), Lines (2007); *Recreations* music (playing cello and piano); *Style*— Prof Timothy Ingold; ✉ Department of Anthropology, School of Social Science, University of Aberdeen, Aberdeen AB24 3QY (tel 01224 274350, fax 01224 272552, e-mail tim.ingold@abdn.ac.uk)

INGRAM, Rt Hon Adam Paterson; PC (1999), MP; s of Bert Ingram, of Glasgow, and Louisa, *née* Paterson; *b* 1 February 1947; *Educ* Cranhill Secdy Sch; *m* 20 March 1970, Maureen, da of Leo McMahon, and Flora McMahon, of Glasgow; *Career* systems analyst SSEB 1970–77, trade union official NALGO 1977–87; MP (Lab): E Kilbride 1987–2005, E Kilbride, Strathaven and Lesmahagow 2005–; PPS to the Ldr of the Oppn Rt Hon Neil Kinnock 1988–92, memb Select Ctee on Trade and Industry 1992–93, front bench spokesman (Lab) on social security matters 1993–95, shadow min for sci & technol 1995–97; min of state NI Office 1997–2001, min of state for the armed forces 2001–; memb: Lab Pty, Co-op Pty; *Recreations* fishing, cooking, reading; *Style*— The Rt Hon Adam Ingram, MP; ✉ House of Commons, London SW1A 0AA (tel 020 7219 4093, e-mail adam_ingram@compuserve.com); constituency: (tel 01355 806016, fax 01355 265252)

INGRAM, Alexander Henry; s of Richard Irvine Ingram, of Kings Nympton, N Devon, and Peggy, *née* Ayers; *b* 25 September 1955; *Educ* St Paul's, Trinity Coll Cambridge (MA); *m* 19 Aug 1979, Caroline Rebecca, da of Dr Arnold Levene; 2 da (Zoë Abigail b 16 April 1984, Naomi Rose b 19 Dec 1986); *Career* conductor; Guildhall Sch of Music 1976–78, Nat Opera Studio 1978–79, WNO 1979–80, ENO 1980–83, asst md then md State Opera of S Australia 1983–85, Kiel Germany 1986–87, ENO 1987–2003 (resident conductor 1998–2003); *Style*— Alexander Ingram, Esq; ✉ e-mail alexanderingram@yahoo.co.uk

INGRAM, Christopher John (Chris); s of late Thomas Frank Ingram, of Southwick, W Sussex, and late Gladys Agnes, *née* Louttid; *b* 9 June 1943; *Educ* Woking GS; *m* 10 Oct 1964, Janet Elizabeth, da of late Charles Rye; 1 da (Kathryn Elizabeth b 30 March 1967), 1 s (Jonathan Devereux b 25 June 1969); *Career* md TMD 1972–76, fndr Chris Ingram Assocs 1976; Tempus Gp plc (formerly CIA Gp plc): chm and chief exec 1989–97, chm 1997–2002; ptnr Genesis Investments 2002–06, fndr Ingram 2003–; non-exec dir Vitesse Media plc; chm Centre for Creative Business; chm Woking FC Holdings 2002–, vice-pres Shelter 2002–; *Recreations* modern British art, theatre, travel in cold climates, eating out, football; *Clubs* Enterprise 100, Solus, Marketing Group; *Style*— Mr Chris Ingram; ✉ Ingram, 7–10 Beaumont Mews, London W1G 6EB (tel 020 7317 2902, fax 020 7317 2996, e-mail cingram@theingrampartnership.com)

INGRAM, Prof David Stanley; OBE (1999), VMH (2004); s of Stanley Arthur Ingram, of Birmingham, and Vera May, *née* Mansfield (d 1973); *b* 10 October 1941; *Educ* Yardley GS Birmingham, Univ of Hull (BSc, PhD), Univ of Cambridge (MA, ScD); *m* 28 July 1965, Alison Winifred, da of Spencer Thomas Graham (d 1975); 2 s (Michael b 27 Aug 1967, Jonathan b 14 Aug 1969); *Career* res fell: Univ of Glasgow 1966–68, Univ of Cambridge 1968–69; sr scientific offr Agric Res Cncl Cambridge 1969–74; Univ of Cambridge: lectr in botany 1974–88, fell Downing Coll 1974–90 (dean, tutor and dir of studies in biology, hon fell 2000–), reader in plant pathology 1988–90, master St Catharine's Coll 2000–06, chm Colls Ctee 2003–05, memb Cncl 2003–05; regius keeper (dir) Royal Botanic Garden Edinburgh 1990–98 (hon fell 1998), hon prof Univ of Edinburgh 1991– (advsr on Public Engagement with Science 1998–), visiting prof of plant pathology Univ of Glasgow 1991–, prof of horticulture RHS 1995–2000, visiting prof of environmental biology and horticulture Napier Univ 1998–2005; pres Br Soc of Plant Pathology 1998; chm Sci Ctee RHS 1994–2000; memb Bd Scot Nat Heritage 1998–2000; chm: Scot Sci and Plants for Schools Project 1990–98, Advsy Ctee on the Darwin Initiative for the Survival of Species DETR 1999–2005; memb Bd Jt Nature Conservation Ctee (JNCC) 1999 and 2002– (actg chair 2004, dep chair 2006–); memb Advsy Ctee ESRC Genomics Forum 2005–; RSE: prog convenor 2005–, chair Science and Soc Steering Gp 2006; tstee: Dynamic Earth 1998–2000, World Conservation Monitoring Centre 2000–04; hon pres Int Congress of Plant Pathology 1998; hon fell: Scot Geographical Soc 1998, Downing Coll Cambridge 2000, Myerscough Coll 2001, Worcester Coll Oxford 2003, St Catharine's Coll Cambridge 2006; Hon DUniv Open Univ 2000; hon prof Univ of Glasgow 2005; CBiol, FIBiol 1988, FIHort 1997, FRCPEd 1998; VMH 2004, Hon FRSE 2006 (FRSE 1993); *Books* Plant Tissue Culture (1974), Tissue Culture Methods for Plant Pathologists (1980), Advances in Plant Pathology (vols I-IX, 1982–93), Cambridge Encyclopaedia of Life Sciences (1985), Shape and Form in Plants and Fungi (1994), Molecular Tools for Screening Biodiversity: Plants and Animals (1997), Plant Disease: A Natural History (1999), Science and the Garden (2002 and 2007); *Recreations* literature, music, art, ceramics, gardening, travel, strolling around capital cities; *Clubs* New (Edinburgh); *Style*— Prof David Ingram, OBE, VMH, FRSE; ✉ c/o Royal Society of Edinburgh, 22–26 George Street, Edinburgh (tel 0131 240 5000, e-mail profdsi@waitrose.com)

INGRAM, Sir James Herbert Charles; 4 Bt (UK 1893), of Swineshead Abbey, Lincolnshire; s of (Herbert) Robin Ingram (d 1979, only s of Sir Herbert Ingram, 3 Bt, who d 1980), by his first w, Shiela, only da of late Charles Peczenik; *b* 6 May 1966; *Educ* Eton, Univ of Cardiff; *m* 5 December 1998, Aracea Elizabeth, da of Graham Pearce, of Cambs; *Heir* half-bro, Nicholas Ingram; *Style*— Sir James Ingram, Bt; ✉ Misthanger, Tally Ho, Guiting Power, Cheltenham, Gloucestershire GL54 5SX

INGRAM, Julian Andrew; s of Ernest Alfred Ingram, of Dawlish Warren, Devon and June Jamieson, *née* Ralph; *b* 17 April 1956; *Educ* Worthing GS for Boys, Worthing Sixth Form Coll, LSE (BSc, London Univ laurel); *m* 1, 19 July 1980 (m dis 1987), Jane, *née* Brockliss; m 2, 1 Oct 1994, Jennifer Lorraine, *née* Smith; 1 da (Alicia Imogen b 1 Sept 1995), 1 s (Edward Henry Alfred b 2 Oct 1997); *Career* bd dir and chm London Student Travel Ltd 1978–80, Saatchi & Saatchi Advertising 1980–86; Abbott Mead Vickers BBDO 1986–95; BBDO Europe: European dir 1995–97, business devpt dir 1998–2003; European dir and managing ptnr McCann Worldgroup 2005–; dir Brand2Brand Ltd; Party candidate (Lib Dem) 1983 and 1987 gen elections; memb Bd EACA 2000–03; memb: Lib Dems 1974, LSE Soc 1982, Mensa 1992, IPA 1992, Mktg Soc 1994; FIPA 2000; *Recreations* films, military history, cooking, gym; *Style*— Julian Ingram, Esq; ✉ McCann Worldgroup, 7–11 Herbrand Street, London WC1N 1EX (tel 020 7961 2026, e-mail julian.ingram@europe.mccann.com)

INGRAM, Kevin; s of Leonard Ingram, and Jennifer, *née* Lewis; *b* 7 August 1966, Cardiff; *Educ* St Cyres Comp Sch Penarth, UC Oxford (BA, BCL, Football blue); *m* 2 Sept 1995, Caroline, *née* Baggs; 1 s (James b 7 Feb 1998), 1 da (Katie b 26 July 1999); *Career* admitted slr 1991; Clifford Chance: trainee slr 1989–91, assoc slr 1991–98, ptnr 1998–, London head of securitisation 2003–; *Recreations* football, squash, cricket, writing poetry; *Clubs* Walton Casuals Jrs Football, East Molesey Cricket; *Style*— Kevin Ingram, Esq; ✉ Clifford Chance, 10 Upper Bank Street, London E14 5JJ (e-mail kevin.ingram@cliffordchance.com)

INGRAM, Prof Malcolm David; s of Arthur Ingram (d 1959), and Elsie May, *née* Cross (d 1993); *b* 18 January 1939; *Educ* Oldershaw GS, Univ of Liverpool (Sir W H Tate open scholar, BSc, PhD), Univ of Aberdeen (DSc); *m* 1967, Lorna, da of Thomas Hardman (d 1993); 1 da (Fiona Catherine b 1969), 1 s (Richard David b 1972); *Career* res assoc Rensselaer Poly Inst 1964–65; Univ of Aberdeen: lectr in physical chemistry 1965–78, sr lectr 1978–90, reader 1990–93, prof of chemistry 1993–2004, emeritus prof 2004–; visiting prof: Univ of Franche Comté 1992, Univ of Bordeaux 1994, Univ of Munster 2002–; chm RSC (Aberdeen) 1990–93; FRSC 1982, fell Soc of Glass Technol (FSGT) 2000, FRSA 2002; author of over 180 scientific papers on solid state electrochemistry, polymers and glass science; Humbolt Research Awardee 2002; *Publications* Physics and Chemistry of Glasses (ed); *Recreations* foreign travel, swimming in warm seas, gardening; *Style*— Prof Malcolm Ingram; ✉ Department of Chemistry, University of Aberdeen, Meston Walk, Aberdeen AB24 3UE (tel 01224 272943, fax 01224 272921, e-mail m.d.ingram@abdn.ac.uk)

INGRAM, Martin Alexander; s of late George Ingram, of Folkington, E Sussex, and late Joyce Mercia, *née* Jones; *b* 1 July 1945; *Educ* Charterhouse, King's Coll London (LLB); *m* 28 Feb 1970, Amanda Susanna, da of Stephen Alexander Lockhart, CMG, OBE (d 1989), of Milton Lockhart, Lanarks; 1 s (Bruce Richard b 14 July 1972), 1 da (Antonia Mary b 11 Aug 1976); *Career* with Hambros Bank 1968–72, ptnr Montagu Loebl Stanley 1972–76, ptnr Heseltine Moss & Co 1976–88, chm and md Brown Shipley Stockbroking Ltd 1988–91 (conslt 1991–92), conslt J M Finn & Co 1992–2005; memb Int Stock Exchange 1974–86; FSI (Dip); *Recreations* painting, tennis, wine; *Clubs* Brooks's, St Moritz Tobogganing, Rye Golf, City of London; *Style*— Martin Ingram, Esq; ✉ Domaine de Cazalas, Castelnavet 32290, Gers, France

INGRAM, Tamara; da of John Ingram, and Sonia, *née* Bolson; *b* 1 October 1960; *Educ* Queen's Coll Harley St London, UEA (BA); *m* Andrew Millington; 1 s (Max b 4 April 1991), 1 da (Anya Eve b 31 Dec 1992); *Career* prodr's asst working on various films incl A Private Function (with Dame Maggie Smith and Michael Palin) 1982–85; Saatchi & Saatchi: estab computer presentation dept 1985, account exec 1985–87, account supr 1987–88, account dir 1988–89, bd account dir 1990–93, gp account dir and memb Exec Bd 1993–95, jt ceo 1995–99, chief exec 1999–2001, exec chm 2001; ceo and chm McCann-Erickson UK & Ireland Gp 2001–03, pres Added Value, Fusion 5 and Henley Centre (all part of Kantar Gp) 2003–05, UK gp ceo Grey Gp 2005–07, exec vice-pres Grey Global Gp 2007–, pres team Proctor & Gamble 2007–; non-exec dir The Sage Gp plc 2004–; chair VisitBritain, chair Devpt Bd Royal Court Theatre; finalist Veuve Clicquot Business Woman of the Year Awards 1998; memb Mktg Soc, memb Mktg Gp of GB; FIPA 1995 (memb Cncl); *Recreations* theatre, opera, family and friends; *Clubs* Women in Advertising and Communications in London; *Style*— Ms Tamara Ingram

INGRAM, Timothy Charles William; s of Stanley Ingram, of Ibiza, Spain, and Sheila, *née* Angliss (d 1996); *b* 18 June 1947; *Educ* Harrow, Univ of Cambridge (MA), INSEAD Business Sch (MBA); *m* 30 Aug 1975, Christine; 3 s (Christopher Charles Sebastian b 7 March 1977, Jonathan James Angliss b 4 July 1978, Nicholas David Oliver b 1 Jan 1986); *Career* ANZ Grindlays Bank: trainee 1969–71, planning mangr 1972–73, md Banque Grindlay Internationale au Zaïre 1975–77, gen mangr (2 branches in Greece) 1977–79, gen mangr (30 branches in Cyprus) 1979–81, dir Eurocurrency Dept 1981–83, regnl dir (8 countries in Far East) 1983–84, regnl dir (7 countries in Middle East) 1984–87, gen mangr (UK & Europe) 1987–89, gen mangr Business Banking Australia 1989–91; gp fin dir First National Corp plc 1992–94, chief exec First National Finance Corp 1994–2002, exec dir Abbey National 1995–2002, chief exec Caledonia Investments 2002–; non-exec dir: Hogg Robinson 1999–2000, Sage plc 2002–, Savills plc 2002–; FCIB; *Recreations* opera, skiing; *Clubs* Reform, Hurlingham; *Style*— Timothy Ingram, Esq; ✉ Caledonia Investments, 30 Buckingham Gate, London SW1E 6NN (tel 020 7802 8080)

INGRAMS, Richard Reid; s of Leonard St Clair Ingrams (s of Rev William Smith Ingrams, MA), and Victoria Susan Beatrice (d 1997), da of Sir James Reid, 1 Bt, GCVO, KCB, MD, LLD; *b* 19 August 1937; *Educ* Shrewsbury, UC Oxford; *m* 1962 (sep), Mary Joan Morgan; 1 s (1 s and 1 da decd); *Career* ed Private Eye 1963–86 (chm 1974–), columnist The Observer 1988–, fndr and ed The Oldie magazine 1992–; *Books* Muggeridge - the biography (1995), The Life and Adventures of William Cobbett (2005); *Style*— Richard Ingrams, Esq; ✉ The Oldie Magazine, 45/46 Poland Street, London W1V 4AU (tel 020 7734 2225, fax 020 7734 2226)

INKSON, Prof John Christopher; s of George William Inkson, and Catherine Cynthia, *née* Laing (d 1988); *b* 18 February 1946; *Educ* Gateshead GS, Univ of Manchester (BSc), Univ of Cambridge (MA, PhD, ScD); *m* Pamela, da of William Henry Hepworth (d 1971); 1 s (Jonathan Allen), 2 da (Andrea Louisa, Beverley Jane); *Career* res physicist English Electric 1966–69, res fell Jesus Coll Cambridge 1972–85, demonstrator and lectr Univ of Cambridge 1975–85; Univ of Essex: prof of theoretical physics 1985–, head Dept of Physics 1989–, dep vice-chllr 1994–; memb PPARC 2002–; conslt to MOD; FInstP; *Publications* over 150 articles published on the theory of semiconductor physics; *Recreations* reading, walking; *Style*— Prof John Inkson; ✉ Department of Physics, University of Exeter, Exeter EX4 4QL (tel 01392 264148, fax 01392 264111, telex 42894 EXUNIV G)

INMAN, His Hon Judge Derek Arthur; s of Arthur William Inman (d 1978), and Majorie, *née* Knowles; *b* 1 August 1937; *Educ* Roundhay Sch Leeds, RNC Dartmouth (Queen's Sword of Honour, Queen's Telescope); *m* 1 (m dis 1979), Sarah, *née* Cahn; 2 da (Rachel b 20 Dec 1963, Chloe b 6 Oct 1968), 1 s (Benedick b 26 Dec 1965); m 2, June 1983, Elizabeth, *née* Dickenson, wid of Lt Col Colin Thomson, OBE; *Career* served RN 1957–73 (retired as Lt Cdr); called to the Bar Middle Temple 1968, in practice SE Circuit 1973–93, circuit judge (SE Circuit) 1993–; *Recreations* watching rugby and cricket, compulsory gardening; *Style*— His Hon Judge Inman; ✉ Middlesex Guildhall, Broad Sanctuary, London SW1P 3BB

INMAN, Edward Oliver; OBE (1998); s of John Inman, of Cumnor, Oxford, and Peggy Florence, *née* Beard; *b* 12 August 1948; *Educ* KCS Wimbledon, Gonville & Caius Coll Cambridge (MA), SSEES Univ of London (MA); *m* 1, 1971 (m dis 1982) Elizabeth *née* Douglas; 1 s, 1 da; m 2, 1984 (m dis 2005), Sherida Lesley, *née* Sturton; 1 da, 2 step da; *Career* Imperial War Museum: joined as res asst 1972, asst keeper 1974, dir Duxford Airfield 1978–2004, chief exec South Bank Employers' Gp 2004–; FRAeS 1999; *Style*— Edward Inman, Esq, OBE, FRAeS; ✉ South Bank Employers' Group, 103 Waterloo Road, London SE1 8UL (tel 020 7202 6900, fax 020 7202 6904)

INMAN, Melbourne Donald; QC (1998); s of Melbourne Alfred Inman; and Norah Freda Inman, *née* Thompson; *b* 1 April 1957; *Educ* Bishop Vesey's GS, Univ of Oxford (MA); *Career* called to the Bar 1979; asst recorder 1996–98, recorder 1998–; head of advocacy, trg and continuing professional devpt 1998–; *Recreations* skiing, listening to the piano; *Style*— Melbourne Inman, Esq, QC; ✉ St Philip's Chambers, 55 Temple Row, Birmingham B2 5LS (tel 0121 246 7000)

INNES, Callum; s of Donald Innes, of Edinburgh, and Christina Dow, *née* Charmichael (d 1968); *b* 5 March 1962; *m* 20 Sept 1990, Hyjdla Jadwiga Paula Kosaniuk; *Career* artist; *Solo Exhibitions* Artspace Gallery 1986, 369 Gallery Edinburgh 1988, Frith St Gallery London 1990, 1991, 1994, 1996 and 1998, Jan Turner Gallery LA 1990, Patrick de Brock Antwerpen 1991 and 1993, ICA London 1992, Galerie Nachst St Stephan Vienna 1992, Scottish Nat Gallery of Modern Art 1992, Bob Van Orsouw Galerie Zurich 1993, 1995 and 1998, Jan Turner Gallery LA 1993, Mackintosh Museum Glasgow Sch of Art 1995, Gilbert Brownstone and CIE Paris 1995, M & R Fricke Düsseldorf 1995 and 1997, Angel Row Gallery Nottingham 1995, Gentili Arte Contemporánea Florence 1995, The Turner Prize Tate Gallery 1995, Patrick De Brock Gallery Knokke 1996, Callum Innes (1990–1996) Inverleith House Royal Botanic Garden Edinburgh 50 Edinburgh Int Festival 1996, Galerie Slewe Amsterdam 1996, M & R Fricke Berlin 1997, Sean Kelly NY 1997, Kunsthaus Zurich (Zurich) 1997, M + R Fricke Berlin 1997, Frith Street Gallery London 1998, Galerie Bob Van Orsouw Zurich 1998, Brownstone & Correard Paris 1998, Sean Gallery NY 1998 and 2000, Ikon Gallery Birmingham 1998, Kunsthalle Bern 1999, Irish MOMA Dublin 1999, Jensen Gallery Auckland NZ 2000, Kerlin Gallery Dublin 2000, The Pier Arts Centre Stromness Orkney 2000; *Group Exhibitions* incl: Scottish Young Contemporaries 1985, Smith Biennial Stirling 1985 and 1989, Greenock Biennial Scotland 1988, 369 Gallery 1988 and 1989, Scatter (Third Eye Centre Glasgow) 1989, The Fruitmarket Gallery Edinburgh 1989, The Br Art Show 1990, Hayward Gallery London 1990, Resumé (Frith Street Gallery London) 1990, Painting Alone (The Pace Gallery NY) 1990, Kunst Europa (Br Cncl) 1991, Artisti Invitati Al Premio Internazionale (first prize) Milan, London, Rome and USA 1992, Abstrakte Malerei Zwischen Analyse und Synthese Galerie Nachst St Stephan Vienna, Galleria L'Attico Rome, Johnen & Scholte Cologne, Prospect 93 Frankfurt 1993, New Voices Br Cncl Touring Exhbn 1993, Callum Innes/Perry Roberts Frith Street Gallery 1993, John Moores 18 1993, Galerie Nachst St Stephen Vienna 1993, Wonderful Life Lisson Gallery London 1993, Coalition C C A Glasgow 1993, New Voices (Centre d'Art Santa Monica Barcelona, Museo de Bellos Artes Bilbao, touring to Murcia and Madrid) 1994, Delit d'inities (Gilbert Brownstone and Cie Paris) 1994, The Curator's Egg (Anthony Reynolds Gallery London) 1994, Lead and Follow: The Continuity of Abstraction (Robert Loader collection, Atlantis Gallery London) 1994, Paintmarks (Kettles Yard Cambridge, Southampton City Art Gallery, The Mead Gallery Univ of Warwick) 1994, Seeing and The Unseen (Peter Fleissig Collection, invisible Museum) 1994, (Collezione Agostino e Patrizia Re Rebaudengo Turin, La Galleria Civice di Modena Italy) 1994, Idea Europe (Palazza Publico Sienna Italy) 1994, The Mutated Painting (Galerie Martina Detterer Frankfurt) 1995, From Here (Waddington Galleries London) 1995, Architecture of the Mind (Galerie Barbara Farber Amsterdam) 1995, Busche Galerie Berlin 1995, Swarm (Scottish Arts Cncl travelling summer exhbn) 1995, New Paintings (Arts Cncl Collection travelling exhbn) 1995, New Voices (Br Cncl travelling exhbn) 1995, Jerwood Award for Painting (Royal Scottish Acad and RA) 1995, New Abstraction (Kohn Turner Gallery LA) 1995, The Punter's Art Show (The Orchard Gallery Derry) 1995, Kleine Welten (Galerie M & R Fricke Dusseldorf) 1996, Leoncavallo (Milan) 1996, MOMA (Oxford) 1996, Seattle Collects Paintings (Seattle Art Museum) 1997, About Vision - New British Paintings in the 1990's (The Fruitmarket Gallery Edinburgh) 1997, Magnetic - Drawings in Dialogue (Sean Kelly NY) 1997, Abstractions Provisoires Musee d'Art Moderne de St Etienne (John Moore's Walker Art Gallery Liverpool) 1997, Best of the Season (Aldrich Museum of Contemporary Art Ridgefield Connecticut) 1997, Inner Eye - Contemporary Art Marc and Livia Strauss Collection (Harn Museum Florida) 1998, Nat West Prize (First Prize, Lothbury Gallery London) 1998, Abstract Painting Once Removed (Contemporary Arts Museum Houston) 1998, Galerie Slewe Amsterdam 1998, Infra-Slim Spaces (Birmingham Museum of Art Alabama) 1998, Baltimore Collects, Four Corners Selections from the Collection of Michael and Ilene Salcman (Stevenson Maryland) 1998, Family (Inverleith House Edinburgh) 1998, Prime (Dundee Contemporary Arts Centre) 1999, New Work: Painting Today, Recent Acquistions (San Francisco MOMA) 1999, A Century of Innocence - the history of the white monochrome (Rooseum Centre for Contemporary Art Malmö) 2000, Expressions: Scottish Art 1976–1989 (Dundee Contemporary Arts Centre) 2000, The Tao of Painting: Principles of Monochrome (The McKinney Avenue Contemporary Dallas) 2000, Blue: borrowed and new (The New Art Gallery Walsall) 2000, On The Edge of The Western World (Invisible Museum London and San Francisco MOMA) 2000, Kevin Appel, Jeremy Dickinson, Callum Innes, Tom LaDuke, Linda Stark (Angles Gallery Santa Monica) 2000, Head and Hands (Washington Project for the Arts Washington DC) 2001; *Style*— Callum Innes, Esq; ✉ c/o Frith Street Gallery, 60 Frith Street, London W1V 5TA (tel 020 7494 1550, fax 020 7287 3733)

INNES, Brig David Robert ffolliott; s of Dr John Robert Faraday Innes, of Stradbroke, Suffolk, and Margaret Sheelagh, *née* ffolliott; *b* 9 February 1953; *Educ* Merchant Taylors' Northwood, RMA Sandhurst, RMCS Shrivenham (BSc); *m* 19 Aug 1978, Annemarie Lester, *née* Rigby; 1 da (Julia Lester b 7 July 1983), 1 s (Robert Charles ffolliott b 3 April 1985); *Career* student Army Staff Coll Camberley 1985, SO2 G2 HQ 1 (UK) Armd Div 1986, COS HQ RSME 1987–88, OC 29 Field Sqdn 1989–90, memb Directing Staff Army Staff Coll Camberley 1991–92, CO 22 Engr Regt 1992–95, ACOS G3/G4 HQ UKSC(G) 1995–96, RCDS 1997, dir Land Digitization MOD 1998–2001, Engr in Chief (Army) 2002–05; chief exec Canterbury Cathedral Devpt Ltd 2005–; FICE; *Recreations* golf, sailing, skiing; *Clubs* Royal Engr Yacht (Cdre 2000–01), Army and Navy; *Style*— Brig David Innes

INNES, Prof John Francis; s of Anthony Michael Innes, and Marguerite Mary, *née* Conway; *b* 7 February 1967, Walthamstow, London; *Educ* Ilford Co HS, Univ of Liverpool (BVSc),

I

Univ of Bristol (PhD); *m* July 1995, Caroline, *née* Bell; 1 da (Claudia Caitlin b 21 Jan 2006); *Career* lectr in vet surgery Univ of Bristol 1996–2001 (fell in vet surgery 1991–93), prof of vet surgery Univ of Liverpool 2001–; contrib to numerous papers published in academic jls; *Recreations* skiing; *Style*— Prof John Innes; ✉ University of Liverpool, Small Animal Teaching Hospital, Leahurst, Neston, Wirral CH64 7TE (tel 0151 795 6246, fax 0151 795 6101, e-mail j.f.innes@liv.ac.uk)

INNES, Dr (Norman) Lindsay; OBE (1994); s of Norman James Mackay Innes (d 1945), and Catherine Mitchell, *née* Porter (d 1992); *b* 3 May 1934; *Educ* Webster's Seminary Kirriemuir, Univ of Aberdeen (BSc, PhD), Univ of Cambridge, Univ of Birmingham (DSc); *m* 18 April 1960, Marjory Niven, da of William Farquhar (d 1938); 1 s (Neil b 1962), 1 da (Helen b 1964); *Career* sr cotton breeder Cotton Res Corpn: Sudan 1958–66, Uganda 1966–71; head Cotton Res Unit Uganda 1972, head Plant Breeding Section Nat Vegetable Res Station 1973–84 (dep dir 1977–84); Scot Crop Res Inst: head Plant Breeding Div 1984–89, dep dir 1986–94, hon prof 1994–; agricultural res conslt 1994–; hon prof: Univ of Birmingham 1973–84 (former hon lectr), Univ of Dundee 1988–95; chm: Governing Bd Int Potato Centre Peru 1991–95 (memb 1988–95), Governing Cncl Int Centre Insect Physiology and Ecology Kenya 1997–2000 (memb Governing Cncl 1995–2001); author of numerous pubns in sci jls on agriculture, horticulture, plant breeding and genetics; book review ed Experimental Agriculture 1997–; chm Br Assoc of Plant Breeders 1982–84, chm bd of tstees W Africa Rice Devpt Assoc Cote d'Ivoire 2000–03 (memb 1997–2004); memb: Bd of Euro Assoc of Plant Breeders 1981–86, Oxfam Cncl of Tstees 1982–84, Governing Bd Int Crop Res Inst for Semi-Arid Tropics India 1982–88 (chm Prog Ctee 1984–88), Cncl Royal Soc of Edinburgh 1996–99; pres Assoc of Applied Biologists 1993–94 (vice-pres 1990–92); FIBiol 1979, FRSE 1989; *Recreations* photography, travel; *Style*— Dr Lindsay Innes, OBE, FRSE; ✉ 14 Hazel Drive, Dundee DD2 1QQ (tel 01382 660064, fax 01382 562426, e-mail minnes1960@scri.sari.ac.uk)

INNES-HOPKINS, Robert; s of Colin Innes-Hopkins, of St Albans, Herts, and Judy, *née* Candy; *b* 4 May 1966; *Educ* Nottingham Trent Univ (BA); *Career* designer for theatre, opera, television and film; theatre designs for RSC, RNT and West Yorkshire Playhouse; opera designs for Opera North, WNO and Santa Fe Opera; *Awards* Critics Circle Designer of the Year 1996, TMA Barclays Designer of the Year 1997, nomination TMA Barclays Outstanding Achievement in Opera 1999; *Style*— Robert Innes-Hopkins, Esq; ✉ c/o Cruickshank Cazenove Ltd, 97 Old South Lambeth Road, London SW8 1XU (tel 020 7735 2933, fax 020 7820 1081, e-mail hjcruickshank@aol.com)

INNES OF BALVENIE, Sir Peter Alexander Berowald; 17 Bt (NS 1628), of Balvenie, Banffshire; s of Lt-Col Sir Berowald Innes of Balvenie, 16 Bt (d 1988), and his 1 w Elizabeth Haughton, *née* Fayle (d 1958); *b* 6 January 1937; *Educ* Prince of Wales Sch Nairobi, Univ of Bristol (BSc); *m* 18 July 1959, Julia Mary, yr da of late Alfred Stoyell Levesley; 2 s ((Alexander) Guy Berowald b 1960, Alastair John Peter b 1965), 1 da (Fiona Julie b 1963); *Heir* s, Guy Innes; *Career* conslt civil engr; dir Scott Wilson Kirkpatrick & Co Ltd, ret; *Recreations* travel, pointers; *Clubs* South Winchester Golf; *Style*— Sir Peter Innes of Balvenie, Bt

INNES OF COXTON, Sir David Charles Kenneth Gordon; 12 Bt (NS 1686), of Coxton, Co Moray; o s of Sir Charles Kenneth Gordon Innes of Coxton, 11 Bt (d 1990), and Margaret Colquhoun Lockhart, *née* Robertson (d 1992); *b* 17 April 1940; *Educ* Haileybury, Univ of London (BSc Eng); *m* 1969, Marjorie Alison, da of Ernest Walter Parker; 1 s (Alastair Charles Deverell b 1970), 1 da (Dione Elizabeth Colquhoun b 1974); *Heir* s, Alastair Innes; *Career* tech dir Peak Technologies 1972–78, md Peak Combustion Controls 1978–80, chief engr Combustion Controls Peabody Hamworthy 1983–92, conslt 1992–; ACGI; *Style*— Sir David Innes of Coxton, Bt; ✉ 28 Wadham Close, Shepperton, Middlesex TW17 9HT

INNES OF EDINGIGHT, Sir Malcolm Rognvald; KCVO (1990, CVO 1981), WS (1964), Orkney Herald of Arms Extraordinary (2001); s of Sir Thomas Innes of Learney, GCVO, LLD (d 1971), and Lady Lucy Buchan, 3 da of 18 Earl of Caithness; *b* 25 May 1938; *Educ* The Edinburgh Acad, Univ of Edinburgh (MA, LLB); *m* 19 Oct 1963, Joan, da of Thomas D Hay, CA, of Edinburgh; 3 s (John Berowald Innes of Edingight, yr b 1965, Colin William Innes of Kinnairdy b 1967, Michael Thomas Innes of Crommey b 1970); *Career* Lord Lyon King of Arms 1981–2001 (Falkland Pursuivant Extraordinary 1957–58, Carrick Pursuivant 1958–71, Lyon Clerk and Keeper of the Records 1966–81, Marchmont Herald 1971–81); Orkney Herald of Arms Extraordinary 2001; sec to Order of Thistle 1981–2001; KStJ 1981, Grand Offr of Merit SMO Malta; memb Queen's Body Guard for Scotland (Royal Co of Archers); *Recreations* reading; *Clubs* New (Edinburgh); *Style*— Sir Malcolm Innes of Edingight, KCVO, WS, Orkney Herald of Arms Extraordinary

INNES OF KINNAIRDY, Colin William; s of Sir Malcolm Innes of Edingight, KCVO, WS, and Joan, *née* Hay; *b* 1 December 1967, Edinburgh; *Educ* Edinburgh Acad, Univ of Aberdeen (LLB, DipLP, LLM); *m* 19 June 1993, Joanna, *née* Judge; 2 s (Thomas David b 19 Jan 1995, William James Maxim b 19 Jan 1997); *Career* slr; ptnr and head of planning and environmental law Shepherd + Wedderburn 1998– (trainee then asst assoc 1992–97); memb Cncl WS Soc; chm Scottish Cncl Salmon & Trout Assoc, life memb Nat Tst for Scotland, memb Cncl Edinburgh Academical Club; memb Law Soc of Scotland 1993, memb Law Soc 1997, legal assoc RTPI 2000; *Publications* Scottish Planning Encyclopaedia (case right ed, 1997), Scottish Human Rights Service (planning and environment section, 2004); *Recreations* fishing, shooting, historic buildings; *Clubs* 1790; *Style*— Colin Innes of Kinnairdy; ✉ 2A Wester Coates Gardens, Edinburgh EH12 5LT (tel 0131 337 2321); Shepherd + Wedderburn, Saltire Court, 20 Castle Terrace, Edinburgh EH1 2ET (tel 0131 473 5104, fax 0131 228 1222, e-mail colin.innes@shepwedd.co.uk)

INNES-WILKIN, David; s of Charles Wilkin (d 1978), and Louisa Jane, *née* Innes; *b* 1 May 1946; *Educ* Lowestoft GS, Univ of Liverpool Sch of Architecture (BArch, MCD); *m* 1, 10 April 1968, Beryl; 1 da (Thomasine b 1971), 2 s (Dylan b 1972, Matthew b 1974); m 2, 25 April 1987, Sarah, da of Rev Prof Peter Runham Ackroyd; 1 da (Emma Jane Louisa b 1989), 1 s (James Ackroyd b 1991); *Career* chartered architect; princ Innes-Wilkin Associates; chm SW Housing Assoc 1986–87, pioneered tenant participation in new housing estates designed 1979–; memb: RIBA Regnl Ctee, Community Architecture Gp 1983–84; visiting lectr Univs of Liverpool, Cardiff, Manchester and Bristol; memb Int Congress of Architects; design awards: RTPI Commendation 1983, Housing Centre Tst Jubilee Award for Good Design in Housing 1983, Times/RIBA Community Enterprise Awards 1986/87 (three), Energy Action Award 1990, Civic Soc 1991, Housing Project Design Award DOE 1997, Carpenters Award 1999; RIBA, MRTPI, MFB; *Publications* A Common Language (The Architects Jl, 1984), Among The Grass-Roots (RIBA Jl, 1983), Cuba: Universal Home Ownership (Roof, 1987), Shelter and Cities (Int Congress of Architects, 1987), Community Schools (Educn Research Unit, 1972); *Recreations* offshore sailing, painting, writing, the Renaissance; *Style*— David Innes-Wilkin; ✉ e-mail architects@inneswilkin.co.uk

INSALL, Donald William; CBE (1995, OBE 1981); s of William R Insall (d 1966), of Bristol, and Phyllis Irene, *née* Hill (d 1987); *b* 7 February 1926; *Educ* Univ of Bristol (LLD), Royal Acad Sch of Architecture, SPAB Lethaby scholar; *m* 13 June 1964, Libby, da of Malcolm H Moss, of Nanpantan, Leics; 2 s (Robert b 1965, Christopher b 1968), 1 da (Hilary b 1972); *Career* WWII Coldstream Gds (Regtl HQ Staff); fndr and dir Donald Insall Assocs Ltd 1958– (architects and planning conslts specialising in architectural conservation and new bldg in sensitive sites): conservation conslts to City of Chester 1970–87 and to Admin Tstees for reconstruction of Chevening House 1970–75, responsible for restoration of ceiling of Lords' Chamber in The Palace of Westminster 1981–84, co-ordinating architects for post-fire restoration at Windsor Castle 1993–97; over 100 awards, co awards incl Europa Nostra medals and Euro Architectural Heritage and Civic Tst awards, personal awards incl Queen's Jubilee medal 1977, APT International Harley McKee award 1999, RICS Medal for People in Conservation 1999, Europa Nostra Medal of Honour 2000 and Royal Warrant Holders Plowden medal 2001; visiting lectr RCA 1964–69, adjunct prof Univ of Syracuse 1971–81, visiting prof Coll of Europe Bruges and Catholic Univ of Leuven Belgium 1980–; conslt architect Worshipful Co of Goldsmiths 1982–2002; memb: Int Cncl of Monuments and Sites 1968–, Cncl RSA 1976–78, Historic Bldgs Cncl for England 1971–83, Ancient Monuments Bd for England 1980–83, Fabric Advsy Ctee Southwark Cathedral 1992–, Architectural Advsy Ctee Westminster Abbey 1993–98, Architectural Advsy Ctee Canterbury Cathedral 1997–, Royal Parks Advsy Bd 2000–02; fndr cmmr Historic Bldgs and Monuments Cmmn for England (English Heritage) 1984–89; fndn memb: Advsy Ctee Getty Grants Programme 1988–92, Architectural Advsy Ctee World Monuments Fund UK 1996–; life memb: SPAB (and memb Cncl), Georgian Gp, Victorian Soc, Royal Photographic Soc, Nat Tst, Rolls Royce Enthusiasts Club; hon memb Bath Preservation Tst, vice-chm Conf on Trg in Architectural Conservation 1989–99 (hon sec 1959–89); vice-pres: Bldg Crafts and Conservation Tst 1993–, City of Winchester Preservation Tst; pres Assoc for Studies in the Conservation of Historic Buildings 1995 (currently memb); patron: Richmond-upon-Thames Environmental Tst, The Kew Soc, Bedford Park Soc; academician Royal West of England Acad; Liveryman Worshipful Co of Goldsmiths, Hon Freeman City of Chester 2000; Hon LLD Univ of Bristol 2004; FRSA 1948, FRIBA 1948, FRTPI 1973, FSA 1975, RWA 1985; *Books* The Care of Old Buildings Today (1973), Chester: A Study in Conservation (1968), Conservation in Action (1982), Historic Buildings: Action to Maintain the Expertise for their Care & Repair (1974); contrib Encyclopaedia Britannica, contrib Buildings - Who Cares? (Arts Council Film for ITV); *Recreations* visiting, photographing, enjoying places, appreciating craftsmanship; *Clubs* Athenaeum; *Style*— Donald Insall, Esq, CBE; ✉ 73 Kew Green, Richmond, Surrey TW9 3AH; Donald Insall Associates Ltd, 19 West Eaton Place, Eaton Square London SW1X 8LT (tel 020 7245 9888, fax 020 7235 4370, e-mail architects@insall-lon.co.uk)

INSCH, Elspeth Virginia; OBE (1998); da of John Douglas Insch, and Isabella Elizabeth Campbell Brodie (d 1969); *b* 21 August 1949, Leicester; *Educ* Newarke Girls' Sch Leicester, Birkbeck Coll London (BSc), Univ of Edinburgh (MPhil, DipEd), Moray House Coll Edinburgh (CertEd), Open Univ; *Career* demonstrator Geography Dept Univ of Edinburgh 1970–73, conslt geomorphologist Springbank Sand and Gravel Co Ltd 1970–79, geography teacher Abington HS 1974–77, geography teacher (second in dept) Nottingham HS for Girls GDST 1977–84, first dep head Kesteven and Sleaford HS for Girls 1984–89, headmistress King Edward VI Handsworth Sch 1989–; pres Assoc of Maintained Girls' Schs 1999–2000, fndr Successful Girls' Schs, affiliate memb GSA; memb: SHA, Assoc of Heads of Grant Maintained Schs, Ctee Nat Grammar Schs' Assoc; RGS: chm Educn Ctee 1992–98 (memb 1998–), memb Cncl 1995–98, vice-pres (educn) 2003–06, chm RGS/Teacher Trg Agency working pty; Aston Univ: memb Univ Cncl 2002–, memb Estates Ctee 2003–, memb Personnel Ctee 2005; pres Leicester Caledonian Soc 1991–94, memb Lunar Soc; tstee: Grantham Yorke Tst, Frederick Soddy Tst; fell Winston Churchill Meml Tst 1980; Hon Dr Aston Univ 2006; CGeog 2002, FRGS, FRSA; *Recreations* walking in Austria and Switzerland, owner of large garden and a West Highland terrier; *Style*— Dr Elspeth Insch, OBE; ✉ King Edward VI Handsworth School, Rose Hill Road, Birmingham B21 9AR (tel 0121 554 2342)

INSHAW, Brig Timothy Gordon (Tim); s of Gordon Henry William Inshaw (d 1984), and Rita, *née* Holland (d 2004); *b* 14 August 1957; *Educ* Wilsthorpe Comp Sch, Welbeck Coll (head boy), RMCS, Army Staff Coll, RCDS; *m* 4 Sept 1982, Sally Patricia, *née* Roe; 3 s (Samuel b 23 Oct 1985, Benjamin b 13 Jan 1987, Jamie b 13 March 1990); *Career* CO 9 Signal Regt 1995–98, dep dir Defence Resources and Plans MOD 1998–2000, Cdr 1 Signal Bde and Rhine Garrison and Chief G6 HQ ARRC 2002–04, dir Capability Integration (Army) MOD 2004–; MIEE 1999; *Recreations* sport (cricket and hockey), amateur dramatics; *Style*— Brig Tim Inshaw; ✉ DCI(A), Floor 5, Zone M, Main Building, Ministry of Defence, London SW1A 2HB (tel 020 7218 7354)

INSKIP, Peter Thurston; s of Geoffrey Inskip (1959), and Lily Ethel, *née* Thurston; *b* 17 August 1944; *Educ* Bedford Sch, AA Sch of Architecture, Gonville & Caius Coll Cambridge (exhibitioner, scholar, Schuldham Plate, MA, DipArch); *Career* dir of studies in architecture Univ of Cambridge: Gonville & Caius Coll 1972–80, Newnham Coll 1973–82, Peterhouse 1975–82; jr bursar Newnham Coll Cambridge 1973–82; architect; fndr ptnr Peter Inskip + Peter Jenkins Architects 1972; princ works incl: restoration of Waddesdon Manor, Chastleton House, Stowe, Albert Meml, Gilbert Collection, Somerset House, Moggerhanger House, Chatsworth, Emmanuel Coll Chapel; awards: Oxford Preservation Tst 1983 and 2005, City Heritage Award 1993, Lighting Design Award 1996, Europa Nostra Medal 1998, Award for Architecture RIBA 1998, Civic Trust 1999, Royal Fine Art Cmmn Tst Building of the Year 2005 (specialist award); rep for Bedfordshire Nat Art Collections Fund 1992–2004; memb: Architectural Panel Nat Tst 1993–96 and 2000–, Expert Panel for Historic Buildings and Land Heritage Lottery Fund 1995–99, Architectural Panel World Monuments Fund in Britain 1996–, Historic Areas and Buildings Advsy Ctee English Heritage 1999–2001, Historic Built Environment Advsy Ctee English Heritage 2001–03; Georgian Gp Award 2005; RIBA 1972, FSA 1996; *Recreations* historic landscapes, gardening and sketching; *Style*— Peter Inskip, Esq; ✉ Peter Inskip + Peter Jenkins Architects, 19–23 White Lion Street, London N1 9PD (tel 020 7833 4002, fax 020 7278 5343)

INSTONE, Peter Duncan; s of Geoffrey Charles Instone (d 1999), and Kathleen Marjorie, *née* Hawkeswood (d 1960); *b* 31 October 1942; *Educ* Uppingham; *m* 6 May 1966, Anne Mary Instone, JP; 1 da (Amanda b 1966), 1 s (Dominic b 1969); *Career* slr; conslt Forsters; memb Law Soc; *Recreations* travel, gardening, visiting battlefields; *Clubs* Army and Navy; *Style*— Peter Instone, Esq; ✉ Forsters, 31 Hill Street, London W1J 5LS (tel 020 7863 8333, fax 020 7865 8444)

INVERARITY, James Alexander (Sandy); CBE (1997, OBE); s of William Inverarity (d 1978), and Alexina, *née* Davidson (d 1978); *b* 17 September 1935; *Educ* Loretto; *m* 8 March 1960, Jean Stewart (d 2006), da of James Rae Gellatly (d 1979); 2 da (Catherine b 1960, Alison b 1962), 1 s (Graeme b 1964); *Career* farmer, CA and co dir; pres NFU of Scot 1970–71; memb: Eggs Authy 1971–74, Farm Animal Welfare Cncl 1978–88, Panel of Agric Arbiters 1983–, Governing Body Scot Crop Research Inst 1984–97 (chm 1989–90), Dairy Produce Quota Tbnl for Scot 1984–85; dir: Scottish Agricultural Securities Corporation plc 1983– (chm 1987–), United Oilseeds Producers Ltd 1985–97 (chm 1987–97); chm Scottish Agric Coll 1990–98 (dir 1990–98); FRAgS, FInstD, FRSA; *Recreations* shooting, curling; *Clubs* Farmers'; *Style*— Sandy Inverarity, Esq, CBE; ✉ Cransley Fowlis, by Dundee DD2 5NP (tel 01382 580327)

INVERDALE, John Ballantyne; s of Capt J B Inverdale, CBE, RN and Stella Norah Mary Westlake, *née* Richards; *b* 27 September 1957; *Educ* Clifton, Univ of Southampton; *m* Jackie; 2 da (Josie, Juliette); *Career* with: Lincolnshire Echo 1979–82, BBC Radio Lincolnshire 1982–86; radio reporter BBC (Today Prog Radio 4 and Radio 2) 1986–88; presenter: Sport on 5 (previously Sport on 2, BBC Radio) 1988–94, Drivetime (Radio 5 Live), Rugby Special (BBC TV) 1994–97, Onside (BBC TV) 1997–, Grandstand (BBC TV) 1999–; Broadcaster of the Year Sony Awards 1997, Radio Personality of the Year Variety Club Awards 1997; *Recreations* rugby (mangr of Esher RFC), tennis, Lincoln City (pres Lincoln City Supporters Club), gardening, music, pubs; *Style*— John Inverdale, Esq;

✉ c/o Mike Burton Management Ltd, Bastion House, Brunswick Road, Gloucester GL1 1JJ (tel 01452 419666, fax 01452 309146)

INVERFORTH, 4 Baron (UK 1919); Andrew Peter Weir; only s of 3 Baron Inverforth (d 1982), and Jill Elizabeth Inverforth, *née* Thornycroft; *b* 16 November 1966; *Style*— The Rt Hon the Lord Inverforth

INVEST, Clive Frederick; s of Frederick Arthur Invest (d 1987), of Toddington, Beds, and Daphne Mary, *née* Bice; *b* 6 October 1940; *Educ* Southgate County GS, Royal Dental Hosp London (BDS, LDS RCS 1965), DGDP (UK); *m* 19 March 1966, Kirsten Elisabeth, da of Alfin Isaksen (d 1986), of Oslo; 2 s (James Clive Frederick b 27 Feb 1972, Robin Julian b 21 March 1975); *Career* pilot offr RAF 1963, qualified as dental surgn 1965, Flt Lt RAF Dental Branch 1965–70; in private practice: Geelong Aust 1970–71, Chichester Sussex 1971–74, Harley St London 1974–; teacher and clinical asst Guy's 1978–83; recognised specialist in prosthodontics (GDC) 2000; memb: BDA, Br Soc of Restorative Dentistry, Br Endodontic Soc; former memb Cncl Endo Soc; fell Pierre Fauchard Acad 1998; MFGDP; *Books* contrib one chapter in General Dental Practitioner's Handbook; *Recreations* skiing, swimming, photography, art, reading; *Clubs* RAF; *Style*— Clive Invest, Esq; ✉ 21 Hill Road, Haslemere, Surrey GU27 2JN (tel 01428 653457); 90 Harley Street, London W1N 1AF (tel 020 7935 5400, fax 020 7935 4185)

INWOOD, Rt Rev Richard Neil; *see:* Bedford, Bishop of

IONS, William Westbrook; s of William Westbrook Ions (d 1958), and Ethel Maud, *née* Skillen (d 1999); *b* 4 September 1941; *Educ* Rutherford GS Newcastle upon Tyne; *m* 3 July 1965, Patricia Louvain; 1 s (Adrian William b 30 Aug 1971), 1 da (Fiona Rosalind b 19 May 1973); *Career* fin controller: Dunlop Ltd, Rank Organisation, Wilkinson Sword; md Brown Bros (Polystyrene) Ltd; currently chm and md Lumsden Services Ltd; previously memb Cncl ICAEW; FCA 1974 (ACA 1964); *Recreations* all forms of sport (as a spectator); *Style*— William Ions, Esq; ✉ Lumsden Services Ltd, Hawks Road, Gateshead NE8 3BT (tel 0191 478 3838, fax 0191 490 0282)

IPSWICH, Archdeacon of; *see:* Gibson, Ven Terence Allen

IRANI, Dr Mehernoosh Sheriar; s of late Sheriar Ardeshir Irani, of London, and Banoo Sheriar; *b* 24 August 1949; *Educ* Chiswick County GS for Boys, KCH (BSc, LRCP, MRCS, MB BS); *m* 19 Sept 1987, Susan Clare, da of late Air Cdre Philip David Mallalieu Moore, of Fowey, Cornwall; 1 da (Jasmine b 1989), 2 s (Matthew b 1991, Beyrom b 1993); *Career* house physician KCH 1974, house surgn Kent and Sussex Hosp Tunbridge Wells 1974, registrar in nephrology and gen med Kent and Canterbury Hosp Kent 1977 (SHO 1975–76), registrar in rheumatology and gen med Radcliffe Infirmary Oxford 1977–79, hon sr registrar and res fell Dept of Rheumatology and Biochemical Pharmacology KCH 1979–81, sr registrar Westminster and Charing Cross Hosp 1981–85, currently conslt rheumatologist Ashford and St Peter's Hosps Middx; visiting physician: Princess Margaret Hosp Windsor, Lister Hosp, Runnymede Hosp, Clementine Churchill; MO Br Olympic team: Los Angeles 1984, Calgary 1988, Seoul 1988, Barcelona 1992; Int Weightlifting Fedn duty dr: Olympic Games Atlanta 1996, Olympic Games Athens 2004; MO England Cwlth games team: Edinburgh 1986, Auckland 1990, Victoria 1994; MO: Br Amateur Weightlifters Assoc 1986–, BCU 1986–, English Badminton Team World Championships Beijing China 1987, Br Dragon Boat Racing Assoc 1988–; dep MO Br Pistol & Rifle Assoc 1996–2002; sec-gen Int Assoc of Olympic MOs 1988–98; pres Med Ctee EWF 1994–99; memb: Med Ctee IWF, Medical Cmmn on Accident Prevention RCS 1992–99, Br Soc for Rheumatology, BOA; vice-chm Ethics Ctee NW Surrey, chm Ethics Ctee Ravenscourt 1997–2003, past med advsr Ind Tbnl Service; pres Sport Med Section RSM 2001–02 (sec 1996–98); examiner: RCS, RCP; hon sr lectr Charing Cross & Westminster Hospital Med Schs (recognised teacher in med Univ of London), lectr in basic sciences RCS; fell Inst of Sports Med 1996; Freeman City of London, Liveryman Worshipful Soc of Apothecaries; FRCP; *Books* contrib to Rheumatology and Rehabilitation (1984); *Recreations* family, cricket; *Clubs* Riverside; *Style*— Dr M S Irani; ✉ 20 Devonshire Gardens, Chiswick, London W4 3TN (tel 020 8994 0119); Department of Rheumatology, Ashford Hospital, London Road, Ashford, Middlesex TW15 3AA (tel 01784 884888, fax 01784 884240, e-mail mike.irani@asph.nhs.uk)

IRBY, Charles Leonard Anthony; s of Hon Anthony P Irby (d 1986), and Mary, *née* Apponyi (d 1952); *b* 5 June 1945; *Educ* Eton; *m* 23 Sept 1971, Sarah Jane, da of Col David G Sutherland, MC, of London; 1 s (Nicholas Charles Anthony b 10 July 1975), 1 da (Caroline Sarah (Viscountess Combermere) b 21 May 1977); *Career* dir: Baring Brothers & Co Ltd 1984–95, Baring Brothers International Ltd 1995–99 (dep chm 1997–99), ING Baring Group Holdings Ltd 1995–98, E C Harris 2001–05, QBE Insurance Gp Ltd 2001–, North Atlantic Smaller Companies Investment Tst plc 2002–, Great Portland Street Estates plc 2004–; md ING Barings 1995–99, sr UK advsr ING Baring 1999–2001; chm Aberdeen Asset Management plc 2000–; tstee and govr King Edward VII's Hosp Sister Agnes 2000–; FCA; *Recreations* travel, photography, skiing; *Clubs* Boodle's, City of London; *Style*— Charles L A Irby, Esq; ✉ 125 Blenheim Crescent, London W11 2EQ (tel 020 7221 2979); The Old Vicarage, Chieveley, Newbury, Berkshire RG20 8UX (tel 01635 248 117)

IREDALE, (John) Martin; s of John Leslie Iredale (d 1988), and Hilda, *née* Palfrey (d 1997); *b* 10 June 1939; *Educ* Abingdon Sch; *m* 14 Sept 1963, (Margaret) Anne, da of Reginald Walter Jewell (d 1968), of Reading; 3 s (Edward b 1 May 1965, Mathew b 3 Oct 1966, William b 18 May 1976), 1 da (Hannah b 30 March 1973); *Career* chartered accountant and licensed insolvency practitioner; ptnr: Cork Gully 1971–99, PricewaterhouseCoopers (formerly Coopers & Lybrand before merger) 1980–99; Royal Shakespeare Theatre: sec Tst 1970–91, memb Cncl of Mgmnt 1970–, govr 1981–2002 (hon govr 2002–), memb Bd 1991–2002, memb Audit Ctee 1997–2006; memb Hodgson Ctee on Profits from Crime and their Recovery 1981–82, memb ICAEW Investigation Ctee 1995–99; pres Old Abingdonian Club 1982–84, chm Cornhill Club 1985–86; Freemason 1973; Freeman City of London 1973; Liveryman Worshipful Co of Carmen 1978; FCA 1963–2005, FIPA 1985–2000; *Books* Receivership Manual (with C J Hughes, 1987); *Recreations* holidays, shooting clay and bird, waiting on my family; *Clubs* Leander, Cornhill, Reading Abbey Rotary 1988–2006, Burghfield Gun (sec 2006–); *Style*— Martin Iredale, Esq; ✉ Holybrook Farm House, Burghfield Bridge, Reading RG30 3RA (tel 0118 957 5108, fax 0118 950 4015, e-mail martin@iredale69.fsnet.co.uk)

IRELAND, John; s of Victor Edwin Ireland (d 1986), of Ipswich, Suffolk, and Mina Mary, *née* Bugler; *b* 14 July 1942; *Educ* Ipswich Sch, Westminster Hosp Med Sch; *m* 24 Sept 1972, Shahla Monireh, da of General A Samsami; 2 s (Michael b 1973, David b 1978), 1 da (Roya b 1974); *Career* formerly: sr registrar Royal Nat Orthopaedic Hosp, conslt surgn Dept of Orthopaedics King George Hosp Ilford Essex; currently conslt orthopaedic surgn Knee Surgery Unit Holly House Hosp Buckhurst Hill Essex; fndr and organiser New Knee Golf Soc; memb Int, Euro and Br Assocs for Surgery of the Knee; FRCS 1971; *Publications* author of scientific papers on knee surgery and arthroscopy; *Recreations* golf, music, wine, gardening; *Clubs* RAC; *Style*— John Ireland, Esq; ✉ 17 Kings Avenue, Woodford Green, Essex IG8 0JD (tel 020 8505 3211, fax 020 8559 1161); Royal National Orthopaedic Hospital, 45 Bolsover Street, London W1W 5AQ

IRELAND, Richard Henry; s of George Thomas Ireland (d 1970), of Eltham, London, and Irene Edith, *née* Lunt (d 1993); *b* 30 April 1946; *m* 30 Sept 1967, Joan Florence, da of William Thomas Smith (d 1958), of Lewisham, London; 1 s (Robert b 1972), 1 da (Suzanne b 1975); *Career* admitted slr 1978; Slaughter and May 1978; ptnr: Eaton & Burley 1982, Rowe & Maw 1984–94, Ireland & Associates 1994–97, conslt Park Nelson 1997–2004, md Warners Slrs Tonbridge 2004–; exec dir Lawyers In Mind Ltd 1994–97; dir: Virtual Management Group Ltd 1996–98, Intracels (Bexhill Mgmnt) Ltd 1998–2002; princ LIM Consultancy 1997–2004; Freeman: City of London, Worshipful Co of Slrs; memb: Law Soc 1978, Int Bar Assoc 1987; MInstD 1996; *Recreations* fly fishing, golf, music, reading; *Clubs* Royal Blackheath Golf; *Style*— Richard Ireland, Esq; ✉ Bank House, Bank Street, Tonbridge, Kent TN9 1BL (tel 01732 770660, fax 01732 362452, e-mail richard_ireland_uk@yahoo.co.uk)

IRETON, Barrie Rowland; CB (2000); s of Philip Thomas Ireton, CBE, and Marjorie Ireton; *b* 15 January 1944; *Educ* Trinity Coll Cambridge (MA), LSE (MSc); *m* 1965, June; 2 s (Paul b 1969 (decd), Stephen b 1976), 1 da (Helen b 1971); *Career* economic statistician to Zambian Govt Office of National Devpt and Planning 1965–69, economist Industrial Development Corporation Zambia 1968–69, LSE 1969–70, devpt sec Office of the President of The Gambia 1970–73; Dept for Int Devpt (formerly ODA): economic advsr on British Dependencies 1973–74, sr economic advsr Africa and ME aid; progs 1974–77, sr economic advsr Asia, Latin America, Caribbean and Pacific aid progs 1977–80, head Aid Policy Economists Gp 1980–84, head Aid Policy Dept 1984–88, princ fin offr and under sec Aid Policy and Fin Div 1988–93, under sec Africa Div 1993–96, dir gen programmes 1996–2003, special fin advsr 2003–; dir: Zambia Copper Investment, Konkola Copper Mines 2003–05; sr fell Inst of Cwlth Studies 2005–; FRA; *Style*— Barrie Ireton, Esq, CB; ✉ Department for International Development, 1 Palace Street, London SW1E 5HE (tel 020 7023 0480)

IRISH, John George Augustus; CBE (1989); s of Albert Edwin Irish (d 1986), of Hinton St George, Somerset, and Rosa Anna Elizabeth, *née* Norris (d 1963); *b* 1 August 1931; *Educ* Crewkerne Sch, LSE (BSc); *m* 1, 1953 (m dis 1967), Joan, *née* Hall; 1 da (Nicola (Mrs Cockroft) b 1962), 1 s (Timothy b 1964); m 2, 1968 (m dis 2006), Isabel Josephine, o da of Bernhard Berenzweig (d 1965), and Irma Berenzweig (d 1996), of Harrow-on-the-Hill, Middx; 4 s (Jonathan b 1970, Nicholas b 1972, Hugo b 1979, Charles b 1981); *Career* cmmnd Nat Serv 1952–54; exec Marks and Spencer 1954–65, retail dir David Greig 1965–70; chm: Eight Till Late Ltd 1981–91, Spar (UK) Ltd 1983–94 (md 1981–94), Spar Landmark Ltd 1993–94, Numark Ltd 1994–97, OSTA Ltd 1994–99, Burford Consultants Ltd 1995–2001, Assured British Meat Ltd 1997, Farm Assured British Beef and Lamb Ltd 1997–98; chief exec: Spar Landmark Services 1985–94, Landmark Cash and Carry Ltd 1986–91; dir: IGD (Amsterdam based trading co of International Spar) 1983–94, NAAFI 1989–99, Wessex Quality Meat Ltd 1996–98; hon pres Spar Nat Guild 1994– (vice-chm 1984–94); vice-pres Br Retail Consortium 1991–2001 (dep chm Retail Consortium 1981–91), memb Cncl Food from Britain 1991–98, conslt to Nat Fedn of Retail Newsagents (NFRN) 1999–2003; formerly: chm Voluntary Gp Assoc, memb Cncl Inst of Grocery Distribution, memb NEDC Distributive Trades, memb Cncl Nat Grocers' Benevolent Fund; Supermarketing Man of the Year 1986, Independent Grocer Gold Award 1987; govr Orley Farm Sch Middx 1980–, tstee One Plus One 1986–2000; FIGD 1985, FRSA 1989, fell Inst of European Business Suppliers (FIEBS) 1996; *Recreations* history, conservation, education; *Style*— John Irish, Esq, CBE; ✉ 50 Iverna Court, London W8 6TS (tel 020 7937 9544)

IRONS, Jeremy John; s of Paul Dugan Irons (d 1983), and Barbara Anne Brereton Brymer, *née* Sharpe (decd); *b* 19 September 1948; *Educ* Sherborne, Bristol Old Vic Theatre Sch; *m* 23 March 1977, Sinead Cusack, *qv*, da of late Cyril Cusack; 2 s (Samuel b 16 Sept 1978, Maximilian b 17 Oct 1985); *Career* actor; joined Bristol Old Vic Theatre Co 1971; Officier des Artes et Lettres 1996; *Theatre* incl: A Winter's Tale, What the Butler Saw, Hayfever, Godspell 1971, Wild Oats (RSC) 1975, Simon Gray's Rear Column (Clarence Derwent Award) 1976; RSC 1986–87 incl: A Winter's Tale, The Rover, Richard II, Embers 2006; Broadway: The Real Thing (Tony Award Best Actor, Drama League Distinguished Performance Award) 1984; *Television* incl: Brideshead Revisited 1982 (TV Times Best Actor Award), Elizabeth 1 2005 (Best Supporting Actor in a Miniseries or TV Movie Golden Globe Awards 2007); *Films* incl: French Lieutenant's Woman (Variety Club Best Actor Award), Moonlighting 1982, The Captain's Doll (BBC TV film) 1982, The Wild Duck (Aust film of Ibsen play) 1983, Betrayal 1983, Swann in Love 1983, The Mission 1985, Dead Ringers (Best Actor NY Critics Award, Best Actor Canada Genie Award) 1988, Chorus of Disapproval 1988, Danny Champion of the World 1988, Australia 1989, Reversal of Fortune (Golden Globe Best Actor Award, Academy Best Actor Award) 1990, Kafka 1991, Waterland 1992, Damage 1993, M Butterfly 1994, House of the Spirits 1994, voice of Scar in The Lion King 1994, Die Hard with a Vengeance 1995, Stealing Beauty 1995, The Man in the Iron Mask 1997, Lolita 1997, Longitude 1999, Dungeons & Dragons 2000, Fourth Angel 2000, And Now Ladies and Gentlemen 2001, Callas Forever 2001, Last Call 2001, Maltide 2002, Being Julia 2003, Merchant of Venice 2004, Kingdom of Heaven 2004, Casanova 2005, Eragon 2006; *Awards* European Film Acad Special Achievement Award 1998, French Cezan 2002; *Recreations* sailing, riding, skiing; *Clubs* West Carberry Hunt (jt MFH); *Style*— Mr Jeremy Irons; ✉ c/o Hutton Management Ltd, 4 Old Manor Close, Askett, Buckinghamshire HP27 9NA

IRONS, Keith Donald; s of Donald Henry Irons (d 1967), of Winchester, Hants, and Muriel, *née* Ridley-Kitt; *b* 16 November 1941; *Educ* Peter Symonds Coll Winchester, Eastleigh Coll, Royal Sch of Mines; *m* 8 June 1968, Diana Elizabeth, da of Stanley Frederick George Ransom (d 1992), of Warwick, and Dorothy, *née* Perceval; 2 s (Nicholas Guy b 6 Oct 1970, Rupert Charles b 24 May 1972); *Career* journalist: Hampshire Chronicle 1961–64, Evening Telegraph Coventry 1964–66, Birmingham Post 1966–69; PRO RST Ltd 1969–73, PR mangr RTZ Group 1973–76, dir of public affairs Blue Circle Industries plc 1976–87, public affairs conslt Charter Consolidated plc 1987–88, vice-pres Minorco SA 1988–90; chm and ceo: RMR Group Ltd 1990–91, Bankside Consultants Ltd 1991–; Parly candidate (Cons) Newham NW gen election 1983; FIPR 1993 (MIPR 1974); *Recreations* sailing; *Clubs* Little Ship (rear cdre, Sail and Power), Sea View Yacht; *Style*— Keith Irons, Esq; ✉ Bankside Consultants Ltd, 123 Cannon Street, London EC4N 5AX (tel 020 7220 7477, fax 020 7220 7211, e-mail keith@bankside.com)

IRONSIDE, 2 Baron (UK 1941); Edmund Oslac Ironside; s of Field Marshal 1 Baron Ironside, GCB, CMG, DSO (d 1959); *b* 21 September 1924; *Educ* Tonbridge; *m* 1950, Audrey Marigold, da of late Col the Hon Thomas George Breadalbane Morgan-Grenville, DSO, OBE, MC (3 s of late Lady Kinloss in her own right); 1 s, 1 da; *Heir* s, Hon Charles Ironside; *Career* Lt RN 1943–52; Marconi Co 1952–59, English Electric-Leo Computers 1959–64, Cryosystems Ltd 1964–68, International Research and Development Co Ltd 1968–84, NEI plc 1984–89, def conslt Rolls Royce Industrial Power Gp 1989–95; memb: Organising Ctee Br Library 1972–74, Select Ctee European Communities 1974–90; chm Sci Reference Library Advsy Ctee 1975–85; pres: Electric Vehicle Assoc of GB 1975–83, European Electric Road Vehicle Assoc 1980–82 (vice-pres 1978–80), Sea Cadet Corps Chelmsford 1959–88; vice-pres: Inst of Patentees and Inventors 1976–90, Parly and Scientific Ctee 1977–80 and 1983–86 (dep chm 1974–77); treas All-Pty Energy Studies Gp 1979–92, hon sec All-Pty Def Study Gp 1992–94 (chm 1994–99); memb: Privy Cncl of Ct City Univ 1975–94 (memb Cncl 1986–88), Ct Univ of Essex 1982– (memb Cncl 1984–87); memb Ct of Assts Worshipful Co of Skinners (Master 1981–82); Hon FCGI 1986; *Books* Highroad to Command (1972); *Clubs* Royal Ocean Racing; *Style*— The Rt Hon the Lord Ironside; ✉ Priory House, Old House Lane, Boxted, Colchester Essex CO4 5RB

IRONSIDE, Gordon Douglas; s of Douglas William Ironside (d 2002), and Doreen Grant, *née* King; *b* 11 August 1955, Workington, Cumbria; *Educ* Dame Allan's Sch Newcastle upon Tyne, Pembroke Coll Cambridge (open scholar, MA), UC Durham (PGCE); *m* 18 Aug 1979, Rachael Elizabeth Ann, *née* Golder; 2 s (Matthew Stuart b 8 June 1983,

I

Christopher William b 2 May 1989), 1 da (Jennifer Rachael b 2 Feb 1986); *Career* teacher: Strathallan Sch 1978–79, Alleyn's Sch Dulwich 1979–83; headmaster Sutton GS 1990– (teacher 1983–90); pres Sutton Rotary Club 1998–2000, tstee Spire Tst; CMath, FIMA 1990; *Style*— Gordon Ironside, Esq; ✉ Sutton Grammar School, Manor Lane, Sutton, Surrey SM1 4AS (tel 020 8642 3821, fax 020 8661 4500, e-mail gironside@aol.com)

IRRANCA-DAVIES, (Ifor) Huw; MP; s of Gethin Davies, and Anne Teresa Davies; *b* 22 January 1963; *Educ* Crewe and Alsager Coll (BA), Swansea Inst of HE (MSc); *m* 1991, Joanna Teresa Irranca; 3 s; *Career* recreation asst then duty mangr Lliw Valley BC 1986–89, mangr CLM Ltd and Serco Ltd 1989–92, facilities mangr Swansea Coll 1994–96, sr lectr Swansea Inst of HE 1996–2002, MP (Lab) Ogmore 2002–; asst Govt whip 2006–; *Recreations* hill walking, most sports; *Style*— Huw Irranca-Davies, Esq, MP; ✉ House of Commons, London SW1A 0AA (tel 020 7219 2952)

IRVIN, Albert Henry Thomas; s of Albert Henry Jesse Irvin (d 1947), of London, and Nina Lucy, *née* Jackson (d 1944); *b* 21 August 1922; *Educ* Holloway Co Sch, Northampton Sch of Art, Goldsmiths Coll London (NDD); *m* 1947, Beatrice Olive, da of John Wagner Nicolson; 2 da (Priscilla Jane b 24 July 1949, Celia Ann b 26 Feb 1959); *Career* artist; princ lectr in painting Goldsmiths Coll London 1962–83; memb London Gp 1965–; hon fell Goldsmiths Coll London 2002; RA 1998; *Solo Exhibitions* incl: 57 Gallery Edinburgh 1960, New Art Centre London 1963, 1965, 1971 and 1973, Skulima Berlin 1972 and 1978, Städtische Kunstsammlung Ludwigshafen 1974, Lüpke Frankfurt 1972, 1976, 1992 and 1995, Fleming Gallery Jeddah 1974, Berlin Opera House 1975, Aberdeen Art Gallery 1976 and 1983, Acme London 1980, Gimpel Fils London 1982, 1984, 1986, 1990, 1992, 1994, 1996, 1998, 2002, 2004 and 2007, Ikon Birmingham 1983, Coventry Sydney 1985, Kilkenny Castle 1985, Hendriks Dublin 1986, Campo Antwerp 1987, 1989 and 1993, Talbot Rice Edinburgh 1989, Gimpel and Weitzenhoffer New York 1988, Serpentine London 1990, Spacex Exeter 1990, Monochrome Brussels 1990, Welsh Arts Cncl 1990, Playhouse Harlow 1991, Lancaster Univ 1991, Punto Valencia 1992, Chapter Cardiff 1994, Wassermann Munich 1994 and 1997, RHA Dublin 1995, Oriel Theatr Clwyd 1996, Stühler Berlin 1997 and 2002, Centre D'Art Contemporain Meymac 1998, Dean Clough Halifax 1998, Works on Paper Touring German Museums 1998, RWA Gallery Bristol 1999, Orion Brussels 1999, Advanced Graphics London 2000, 2002 and 2005, West Cork Art Centre 2001, Storey Gallery Lancaster 2003, Peter Scott Gallery Lancaster Univ 2003, Peppercanister Gallery Dublin 2003 and 2006; *Group Exhibitions* incl: John Moores Liverpool 1961, 1980, 1982 (prize winner), 1987, 1989, 1991 and 1995, London Group (regularly), British Painting 74 (Hayward) 1974, British Art Show tour 1979, ROSC 84 Dublin 1984, Home and Abroad (Serpentine) 1985, Int Print Biennale Bradford (prize winner) 1986, Royal Acad Summer Exhibition 1987– (prize winner 1987 and 1989), Hoyland Beattie Irvin (Sunderland) 1988, Great British Art Show (Glasgow) 1990, Goldsmiths' Centenary Exhibition 1991, Courtauld Inst Loan Collection 1991–93, Design for Diversions Dance Co 1992, Here and Now (Serpentine) 1994, Recent Acquisitions (Irish MOMA Dublin) 1997, British Abstract Painting (Flowers East London) 2001, RWA Bristol 2001, Creative Quarters (Museum of London) 2001, RHA Dublin 2001 and 2003, 1979 (Bloomberg Space London) 2005, Réalitiés Nouvelles Paris 2006, Frost, Hoyland, Irvin (Chateau de Sours Bordeaux) 2006; *Work in Collections* of: Tate Gallery, Arts Cncl, Br Cncl, Royal Acad, private and public collections in Britain and abroad; *Commissions* incl: painting for Maternity Wing Homerton Hosp Hackney 1987, painting for Chelsea and Westminster Hosp 1995; *Awards* Arts Cncl Award (for visit to USA 1968, Major Award 1975, Purchase Award 1980), Gulbenkian Print Award 1983, Giles Bequest Prize from V&A and Br Museum at Int Print Biennale Bradford 1986; *Books* Albert Irvin Life to Painting (by Paul Moorhouse, 1998); *Recreations* music; *Clubs* Chelsea Arts, Arts; *Style*— Albert Irvin, Esq, RA; ✉ c/o Gimpel Fils, 30 Davies Street, London W1K 4NB (tel 020 7493 2488, fax 020 7629 5732, e-mail info@gimpelfils.com)

IRVINE, Sir Donald Hamilton; kt (1994), CBE (1987, OBE 1979); s of late Dr Andrew Bell Hamilton Irvine, and Dorothy Mary, *née* Buckley; *b* 2 June 1935; *Educ* King Edward VI GS Morpeth, Med Sch Univ of Newcastle upon Tyne (MB BS, MD); *m* 1, 16 July 1960 (m dis 1985), Margaret Mary, da of late Francis McGuckin of Ponteland, Northumberland; 2 s (Alastair b 1962, Angus b 1968), 1 da (Amanda b 1966); m 2, 28 June 1986 (m dis 2006), Sally, da of Stanley Arthur Day, of Bellingen, NSW; m 3, April 2007, Cynthia Rickitt, da of Brig Rymel Lymer, CBE, DSO, TD; *Career* princ GP Lintonville Med Gp Northumberland 1960–95, regnl advsr GP Regnl Postgrad Inst for Med and Dentistry Univ of Newcastle upon Tyne 1973–95; pres GMC 1995–2002 (memb 1979–); RCGP: memb Cncl 1968–95, hon sec 1972–78, chm of Cncl 1982–85; memb: Jt Ctee on Postgrad Trg for GP 1976–91 (chm 1988–91), UK Central Cncl for Nursing Midwifery and Health Visiting 1983–93; chm Bd of Govrs MSD Fndn 1983–89, memb The Audit Cmmn 1990–95; chm Picker Inst (Europe) 2002–, sr assoc Kings Fund 2002–04; chm Advsy Bd for Medicine Univ of Warwick 2003–, vice-chm Ethics Ctee of Dr Foster 2002–, memb Advsy Cncl Pfiyer Inc 2004–; 30th Sir William Oster lectr McGill Univ Montreal 2006; Hon DUniv York 1997; Hon DSc: Univ of Exeter 1997, Univ of Leicester 1998, Univ of Durham 2002; Hon DCL: Univ of Northumbria 2000, Univ of Newcastle upon Tyne 2002; fell BMA, FRSM, FRCGP 1972 (MRCGP 1965), Hon FRCP 1997, Hon FRCPEd 1997, Hon FRSH 1997, Hon FFPHM RCP 1998, Hon FFOM RCP 1998; *Books* The Future General Practitioner - Learning and Teaching (jtly, 1972), Managing for Quality in General Practice (1990), Making Sense of Audit (ed jtly with Sally Irvine, 1991, 2 edn 1997), A Practice of Quality Practice (with Sally Irvine, 1995), The Doctors' Tale: Professionalism and Public Trust (2003); *Recreations* gardening, walking, bird watching, theatre; *Style*— Sir Donald Irvine, CBE; ✉ Mole End, Fairmoor, Morpeth, Northumberland NE61 3JL (tel 01670 517546, fax 01670 510046, e-mail donald@donaldirvine.demon.co.uk)

IRVINE, Ian James; *b* 23 December 1957; *Educ* Robert Gordon's Coll Aberdeen, Pembroke Coll Oxford; *m* 1995, Laura Hermione, *née* Tennant; 2 s, 1 da; *Career* journalist; reviews ed Vogue 1979–81, dep ed The Literary Review 1982, arts ed Sunday Today 1985–86, asst arts ed The Independent 1987–89, dep ed Punch 1990, arts ed Evening Standard 1991–92, arts ed Harpers & Queen 1993, dep ed Sunday Telegraph Review 1994–98, features ed The Independent 1998–99, arts ed The Independent 1999–2002, ed Talk of the Town (Independent on Sunday's London magazine) 2003, asst ed Independent on Sunday 2004, assoc ed The Independent 2005, ed ABC Magazine Independent on Sunday 2006–07, freelance writer and publisher Tacit Hill Edns 2007–; *Clubs* Academy, Soho House; *Style*— Ian Irvine, Esq; ✉ e-mail ian.irvine@gmail.com

IRVINE, His Hon James Eccles Malise; yr s of Brig-Gen Alfred Ernest Irvine, CB, CMG, DSO, late DLI (d 1962), and Katharine Helen (d 1984), eld da of Lt-Gen H M C W Graham, CMG, late RMLI; *b* 10 July 1925; *Educ* Stowe (scholar), Merton Coll Oxford (MA, Postmaster); *m* 24 July 1954, Anne, eld da of Col Geoffrey Egerton-Warburton, DSO, TD, JP, DL (d 1961; ggs of Rowland Egerton-Warburton, bro of 8 and 9 Bts Grey-Egerton), of Grafton Hall, Cheshire, and Hon Georgiana Mary Dormer, MBE (d 1955), eld da of 14 Baron Dormer; 1 da (Susan Caroline Jane b 1961), 1 s (David Peter Gerard b 1963); *Career* WWII served Grenadier Gds 1943–46 (France and Germany Star, Hon Capt 1946); called to the Bar Inner Temple 1949 (Poland Prize in Criminal Law), prosecuting counsel for Inland Revenue on Oxford Circuit 1965–71, dep chm Glos QS 1967–71, circuit judge (Midland & Oxford Circuit) 1972–96; lay judge Court of Arches for Province of Canterbury and of Chancery Court of York for Province of York 1981–2000; pres: Grenadier Gds Assoc (Oxon) 1989–, Royal British Legion (Heyford and District Branch) 1999–; *Books* Parties and Pleasures - The Diaries of Helen Graham 1823–26 (1954); *Style*— His Hon James Irvine; ✉ 2 Harcourt Buildings, Temple, London EC4 9DB

IRVINE, Very Rev John Dudley; s of late Rt Hon Sir Arthur Irvine, QC, MP, and Lady Irvine; *Educ* Haileybury (head boy), Univ of Sussex (BA), Univ of Oxford (MA); *Career* called to the Bar Middle Temple 1973, in practice 1973–78; ordained: deacon 1981, priest 1982; curate Holy Trinity Brompton 1981–85, vicar St Barnabas Kensington 1985–2001, dean of Coventry 2001–; *Recreations* walking, film, theatre; *Style*— The Very Rev the Dean of Coventry; ✉ The Deanery, 11 Priory Row, Coventry CV1 5EX; Coventry Cathedral, 1 Hill Top, Coventry CV1 5AB (tel 024 7652 1227, fax 024 7652 1220, e-mail dean@coventrycathedral.org.uk)

IRVINE, Prof (John) Maxwell; s of John MacDonald Irvine (d 1977), of Edinburgh, and Joan Paterson, *née* Adamson (d 1982); *b* 28 February 1939; *Educ* George Heriot's Sch, Univ of Edinburgh (BSc), Univ of Michigan (MSc), Univ of Manchester (PhD); *m* 14 Sept 1962, Grace Irvine, da of Edward Ritchie, of Edinburgh; 1 s (Ritchie b 26 April 1971); *Career* res assoc Cornell Univ 1966–68, head Nuclear Theory Gp SERC Daresbury Laboratory 1974–76; Univ of Manchester: asst lectr 1964–66, lectr 1968–73, sr lectr 1973–76, reader 1976–82, prof 1983–91, dean of sci 1989–91, hon prof and higher educn conslt 2001–; princ and vice-chllr: Univ of Aberdeen 1991–96, Univ of Birmingham 1996–2001 (emeritus prof 2001–); vice-pres Inst of Physics 1983–87 (memb Cncl 1981–87 and 1988–92); chm: SERC Nuclear Structure Ctee 1984–88, Ctee of Scottish Univ Principals 1994–96, Cncl Assoc of Cwlth Univs 1994–97 (hon treas 1998–2004), Jt Info Servs Ctee for Higher Educn 1998–2003, chm 'Energy Issues for Scotland' ctee 2005–; memb: Cncl EPS 1989–92, SCDI 1992–96, Scottish Economic Cncl 1993–96, Scottish Ctee Br Cncl 1994–96, Scottish Forum BT 1994–96, Cncl CVCP 1995–98, Quality Management Panel European Univs Assoc (EUA) 2000–, Energy Steering Gp European Academics Sciences Advsy Ctee 2005–; dir: Grampian Enterprise Ltd 1992–96, Rowett Res Inst 1992–96, HEQC Ltd 1994–97, UCEA 1995–2001, UCAS 1995–2001, Barber Trust 1991–2001, COBUILD Ltd 1996–2001, Public Health Lab Serv 1998–2005, NERC 1998–2001, Cwlth Scholarship Cmmn 2002–06, Educnl Consultancy Service of Br Cncl (ECS) 2002–03; govr: English Speaking Union 1998–2005, Nursing and Midwifery Cncl 2005–06; advsr Oxford Round Table 2000–; DL (W Midlands) 1999–2002; Hon DSc William and Mary Coll, Hon DEd Robert Gordon Univ 1995, Hon DUniv Edinburgh 1995, Hon LLD Univ of Aberdeen 1997, Hon DUniv Birmingham 2001, Hon DSc Aston Univ 2002; FInstP 1971, FRAS 1986, Hon FRCSEd 1995, CIMgt 1995, FRSA 1993, FRSE 1993; *Books* Basis of Modern Physics (1967), Nuclear Structure Theory (1972), Heavy Nuclei, Super Heavy Nuclei and Neutron Stars (1975), Neutron Stars (1978); *Recreations* tennis, hill walking; *Clubs* Dartmouth House; *Style*— Prof Maxwell Irvine, FRSE; ✉ 27 Belfield Road, Manchester M20 6BJ; Schuster Lab, University of Manchester, Manchester M13 9PL (tel 0161 445 1434, e-mail j.m.irvine@man.ac.uk)

IRVINE, Michael Fraser; s of Rt Hon Sir Arthur James Irvine, QC, MP (d 1978), of London, and Eleanor, *née* Morris; *b* 21 October 1939; *Educ* Rugby, Oriel Coll Oxford (BA); *Career* called to the Bar Inner Temple 1964; Parly candidate (Cons) Bishop Auckland 1979, MP (Cons) Ipswich 1987–92, PPS to the Attorney Gen 1990–92; sr legal assessor Nursing and Midwifery Cncl 2004–; pres Ipswich Conservatinve Assoc 1998–; *Recreations* hill walking in Scotland; *Style*— Michael Irvine, Esq; ✉ 3 Hare Court, Temple, London EC4Y 7BJ (tel 020 7415 7800, fax 020 7415 7811, e-mail michaelirvine@3harecourt.com)

IRVINE, Lady; Sally Irvine; da of Stanley Arthur Day, of Bellingem, NSW, and Vera Marion, *née* Little; *b* 22 September 1944; *Educ* Univ of Cambridge (MA); *m* 1, 1973 (m dis), Alan Fountain; m 2, 1986 (m dis), Sir Donald Hamilton Irvine, CBE, *qv*; 3 step c; *Career* head Prog Office and asst to the DG GLC 1976–83; RCGP: gen admin 1983–94, conslt on mgmnt in gen practice 1994–97; ptnr Haman and Irvine Associates professional practice consultancy 1995–; non-exec dir Northern RHA 1993–94, non-exec chair Newcastle City Health (NHS) Tst 1994–99; vice-pres Assoc of Health Centre and Practice Admins (now Inst of Health Mgmnt) 1994–2003 (pres 1991–94); tutor and examiner Dip in Advanced Gen Practice Univ of Newcastle upon Tyne 1993–99, dir Practice Consultancy Trg Prog 1994–96, dir Pinning Down Partnership Kindling Ltd 1998–2000; non-exec advsr Civil Serv Occupational Health Agency 1995–96; ptnr Galbraith & Irvine Quality Improvement & Trg for Mental Health Act 1999–2001; GDC: memb 1999–, chair Standards Ctee 2003–05; JP Highgate Sessional Div 1977–95 (dep chair Juvenile Bench 1990–95); memb: Cncl Law Soc 2001–05, Slrs Regulations Authy 2005–, Ind Appt Selection Bd RICS; govr Univ of Northumbria 2002–04, memb Ct Univ of Newcastle Upon Tyne 2005–; arbitrator ACAS 1999–2001; vol guide Britten-Pears Library The Red House; Hon FRCGP, FAMGP, FRSA; *Books* Management Appreciation - the Book (with June Huntington, 1991), Balancing Dreams and Discipline - The Manager in Practice (1992), The Practice of Quality (with Donald Irvine, 1996), Making Sense of Personnel Management (with Hilary Haman, 2 edn 1997), Making Sense of Audit (ed jtly with Donald Irvine, 2 edn 1997), Spotlight on General Practice: reflections on quality management and governance in general practice (with Hilary Haman, 2001), Good Practice, Good People (with Hilary Haman, 2001), The Peer Appraisal Handbook for General Practitioners (with Hilary Haman and Di Jelley); also author of book chapters and published papers; *Recreations* travelling, cooking, walking, gardening; *Style*— Sally Irvine; ✉ Brick Kiln Cottage, Warren Hill Lane, Aldeburgh, Suffolk IP15 5QB (tel 01728 452510, e-mail sally.bkc@btinternet.com)

IRVINE OF LAIRG, Baron (Life Peer UK 1987), of Lairg in the District of Sutherland; Alexander Andrew Mackay Irvine; PC (1997); s of Alexander Irvine and Margaret Christina, da of late Alexander Macmillan; *b* 23 June 1940; *Educ* Inverness Royal Acad, Hutchesons' Boys' GS Glasgow, Univ of Glasgow (MA, LLB), Christ's Coll Cambridge (scholar, BA, LLB, George Long Prize in Jurisprudence); *m* 1974, Alison Mary, yst da of Dr James Shaw McNair, MD, and Agnes McNair, MA; 2 s (Hon David b 1974, Hon Alastair b 1976); *Career* lectr LSE 1965–69; contested (Lab) Hendon N (gen election) 1970; called to the Bar Inner Temple 1967 (bencher 1985); QC 1978, head of chambers 11 King's Bench Walk 1981–97, recorder 1985–88, dep judge of the High Court 1987–97, oppn spokesman on Legal and Home Affairs 1987–92, Lord Chllr 1997–2003 (shadow Lord Chllr 1992–97); pres Magistrates Assoc 1997–; jt pres: Industry and Parliament Tst 1997–, Br-American Parliament Gp 1997–, Inter-Parliamentary Union 1997–, Cwlth Parliamentary Assoc 1997–; church cmmr; memb Ctee Slade Sch of Fine Art 1990–; chm 2001 Ctee Univ of Glasgow 1998–; vice-patron World Fedn of Mental Health 1998–; fndn tstee Whitechapel Art Gallery 1990–97; tstee: John Smith Meml Tst 1992–97, Hunterian Collection 1997–; fell US Coll of Trial Lawyers 1998, hon bencher Inn of Court of NI 1998–, hon memb the Bar of Poland 2000; hon fell: Christ's Coll Cambridge 1996, Soc for Advanced Legal Studies 1997, LSE 2000–; Hon LLD Univ of Glasgow 1997, Hon Dr (Laurea hc) Univ of Siena 2000; *Recreations* collecting paintings, reading, theatre, cinema, travel; *Clubs* Garrick; *Style*— The Rt Hon Lord Irvine of Lairg, PC; ✉ House of Lords, London SW1A 0PW (tel 020 7219 3232)

IRVING, Dr Barrie Leslie; s of Herbert Leslie Irving (d 1998), and Joan Fletcher, *née* Robinson (d 1976); *b* 6 October 1942; *Educ* Stowe, Pembroke Coll Cambridge (BA), Grad Sch Univ of Calif Berkeley (MA), Univ of Cambridge (PhD); *m* 1 (m dis 1982), (Pamela) Jane, da of Capt Ronald Leese (ka 1943); 1 s (Dominic Paul b 26 May 1972), 1 da (Samantha Jane b 15 May 1968); m 2 (m dis 1997), Susan Margaret, da of Alec John Davey (d 1971); 1 s (Benjamin Alec James b 16 March 1985); m 3, (Patricia) Ann Carloss, da of T O Newbold; *Career* psychologist and criminologist; research staff Inst of Human Devpt Univ of Calif Berkeley 1965–66, professional staff (later memb Mgmnt Ctee)

Tavistock Inst of Human Relations London 1966–79; dir: The Police Fndn 1980–2005, Forensic Technology Ltd 1995–98; non-exec dir Security Industry Inspectorate 2002–05; visiting scholar Pembroke Coll Cambridge 2004–06, hon sr research fell Keele Univ 2005–, ptnr Matrix Research and Consultancy Ltd 2006–; special assignments incl: conslt to the official slr for Sir Henry Fisher's Inquiry into the Murder of Maxwell Confait 1977, res conslt to the Royal Cmmn on Criminal Procedure 1979, res conslt to the Royal Cmmn on Criminal Justice 1991; organised Police Fndn's Independent Inquiry into the Misuse of Drugs Act 1971 1997–2001; advsr to Nat Reassurance Policing Prog 2002–05; vice-chm Nat Stepfamily Assoc 1992–96; *Books* The Psychological Dynamics of Smoking (1968), Tied Cottages in British Agriculture (1975), Police Interrogation (1980), Regulating Custodial Interviews (1988), Police Interrogation (1989), Human Factors in the Quality Control of CID Investigations (1993), Hotspotting: turning policy theory into practice (2002); *Recreations* golf, piano; *Style*— Dr Barrie Irving

IRVING, (Edward) Clifford; CBE (1981); s of William Radcliffe Irving (d 1950), of Peel, IOM, and Mabel Henrietta, *née* Cottier (d 1920); *b* 24 May 1914; *Educ* Douglas HS, Chatham and Oshawa Collegiates Canada; *m* 11 Oct 1941, Norah Constance, da of Harold Page (d 1960), of Luton, Beds; 1 s (Paul Julian b 1949), 1 da (Caroline b 1953); *Career* cmmnd RA 1940, later at War Office responsible for economic matters in ex-Italian colonies under mil govt; dir Irvings Ltd 1950–84; chm: Bank of Wales (IOM) Ltd 1985–87, Etam (IOM) Ltd 1985–, Bank of Scotland (IOM) Ltd 1987–, Refuge (IOM) Ltd 1988–; memb House of Keys 1955–61, 1966–81 and 1984–87 (actg speaker 1971–81); memb IOM Govt Depts: Airports 1955–58, Assessment 1955–56, Social Security 1956, Local Govt 1956–62, Harbours 1985–87, Home Affairs 1985–86, Health 1985–86, Indust Advsy Cncl 1961–62 and 1971–81, Civil Serv Cmmn 1976–81, Indust Dept 1988–94; memb: Exec Cncl IOM Govt 1968–81, Legislative Cncl IOM 1987–95; chm: Exec Cncl 1977–81, IOM Tourist Bd 1971–81, IOM Sports Cncl 1971–81, IOM Harbours Bd 1985–87, IOM Govt TT Race Ctee 1971–81; pres: Douglas Angling Club, IOM Angling Assoc, Manx Parachute Club, Manx Nat Powerboat Club, Wanderers Male Voice Choir, Douglas Branch RNLI, Douglas Bay Yacht Club; *Recreations* powerboating, angling; *Style*— Clifford Irving, Esq, CBE; ✉ Highfield, Belmont Road, Douglas, Isle of Man IM1 4NR (tel 01624 673652)

IRVING, Dorothy (Dotti); da of Alexander Irving (d 1984), and Sheila, *née* McCaig; *b* 18 May 1950, Annan, Dumfriesshire; *Educ* Esdaile and St George's Sch for Girls, Univ of Edinburgh (MA), Moray House Coll of Educn (DipEd); *m* 31 Aug 1981; 1 da (Tess Riley b 6 March 1985 (d 2004)); *Career* Penguin Books 1974–86 (latterly PR dir), fndr and chief exec Colman Getty 1987–; *Clubs* Groucho; *Style*— Ms Dotti Irving; ✉ Colman Getty, 28 Windmill Street, London W1T 2JJ (tel 020 7631 2666, fax 020 7631 2699, e-mail dotti@colmangetty.co.uk)

IRVING, Dr Henry Charles; s of Dr Gerald Ian Irving, of Leeds, and Sonia Carol, *née* Sinson; *b* 6 October 1950; *Educ* Leeds GS, King's Coll and Westminster Med Sch London (MB BS); *m* 8 July 1973, (Alison) Jane, da of Peter Brackup, of Leeds; 2 da (Juliet b 1975, Georgina b 1978); *Career* conslt radiologist St James's Univ Hosp Leeds 1979–, sr clinical lectr radiodiagnosis Univ of Leeds 1979–; RCR regional postgrad educn advsr 1996–99; pres Br Med Ultrasound Soc 1994–96; memb Editorial Bd: British Jl of Radiology, Radiology Now, Radiography; author of various books on med ultrasound and radiography; RCR: memb Cncl, memb Examining Bd 1996–2000, treas 2000–05; FRCR 1978; *Recreations* golf, tennis; *Clubs* Moor Allerton Golf; *Style*— Dr Henry Irving; ✉ 24 Alwoodley Lane, Leeds LS17 7PX (tel 0113 261 1820, e-mail henry.irving@ntlworld.com)

IRVING, Prof Sir Miles Horsfall; kt (1995); s of Frederick William Irving (d 1953), of Southport, Lancs, and Mabel, *née* Horsfall (d 1988); *b* 29 June 1935; *Educ* King George V Sch Southport, Univ of Liverpool (MB ChB, MD, ChM), Univ of Sydney; *m* 13 Nov 1965, Patricia Margaret, da of Dr Richard Alexander Blaiklock, late Capt RAMC, of Alnwick, Northumberland; 2 da (Katherine Susan b 1966, Jane Elizabeth b 1967), 2 s (Peter Miles b 1970, Simon Richard b 1974); *Career* house physician then house surgn Broadgreen Hosp Liverpool 1959–60, Robert Gee fell in human anatomy Univ of Liverpool Med Sch 1961–62, Phyllis Anderson surgical res fell Univ of Sydney Med Sch 1965–67, reader in surgery and asst dir Professorial Surgical Unit Bart's London 1972–74, prof and head Univ Dept of Surgery Hope Hosp Salford 1974–99, chm Sch of Surgical Scis Univ of Manchester 1974–92, head Univ Dept of Surgery Manchester Royal Infirmary 1992–95, emeritus prof Univ of Manchester 1999–; regnl dir of res and devpt North Western RHA 1992–94, non-exec memb Salford HA 1992–94, dir NHS Health Technol Prog 1994–99, chm Newcastle Hosps NHS Tst 1998–2006, chm NHS Innovations (North) 2004–; visiting prof of surgery Univ of Newcastle upon Tyne 1998–; hon conslt surgn to the Br Army; numerous guest lectureships and external examinerships since 1974; Royal Coll of Surgns: former memb Cncl, former chm External Affrs Bd; Dept of Health: former memb Expert Advsy Gp on AIDS, former memb Trauma Centre Evaluation Advsy Gp, chm Standing Gp on Health Technologies 1993–99; tstee Imperial War Museum 2006–; past pres: Ileostomy Assoc of GB and I, Int Surgical Gp, Assoc of Surgns of GB and I, Section of Coloproctology RSM, Assoc of Coloproctology; memb GMC (and its Overseas and Educn Ctees) 1990–92, James IV Assoc of Surgns; past chm Fedn of Surgical Speciality Assocs; Guthrie Medal RAMC 2005; Hon Col 201 (Northern) Field Hospital 1998–2006; Hon DSc Univ of Salford 1996, Hon DUniv of Sibiu Romania 1997, Hon DCL Northumbria Univ 2007; Hon FFAEM, Hon FRCSGlas 1997, Hon FRCS (Canada) 1998, hon fell American Surgical Assoc 2000, Hon FACS 2000; fell Assocs of Surgeons of GB and I, fell Manchester Med Soc (hon fell 1995); FMedSci 1998; *Publications* Gastroenterological Surgery (1983), Intestinal Fistulas (1985), A B C of Colo Rectal Diseases (1993), Minimal Access Surgery (1996), 100 Years of the Royal Victoria Infirmary (2006); author of over 250 articles in surgical and other med jls; *Recreations* reading the Spectator, mountain climbing, opera; *Style*— Sir Miles Irving

IRWIN, Lt-Gen Sir Alistair Stuart Hastings; KCB (2002), CBE (1994, OBE 1987); s of Brig Angus Digby Hastings Irwin, CBE, DSO, MC (d 1997), and Elizabeth Bryson, *née* Cumming; *b* 27 August 1948; *Educ* Wellington, Univ of St Andrews (MA), RMCS Shrivenham, Pakistan Army Staff Coll Quetta; *m* 8 April 1982, Nicola Valentine Blomfield, *née* Williams; 2 da (Mary-Rose b 1975, Laura b 1978), 1 s (George b 1983); *Career* cmmnd Black Watch (RHR) 1970, Gen Staff Offr 2 (Weapons) MOD 1981–82, cmd mech inf co W Germany and NI 1982–83, second in command 1 Bn Black Watch 1983–84, promoted Lt-Col, Directorate of Command Control and Communications Systems (Army) MOD 1985, cmd 1 Bn Black Watch 1985–88 (despatches), tours of duty NI, Edinburgh and W Berlin, memb Directing Staff Camberley 1988–92, student then asst dir Higher Command and Staff Course Army Staff Coll Camberley, promoted Brig 1992, cmd 39 Inf Bde NI 1992–94, Dir Land Warfare 1994–95, project dir Procurement Exec 1996, promoted Maj-Gen, Cmdt RMCS Shrivenham 1996–99, Mil Sec 1999, promoted Lt-Gen, GOC NI 2000–03, Adj-Gen and memb Army Bd 2003–05, ret; Col The Black Watch 2003–06 (currently Rep Col The Black Watch 3 Bn Royal Regt of Scotland), Hon Col Tayforth Univs OTC 1997–, Col Cmdt Scottish Div 1999–2004; memb Queen's Body Guard for Scotland (Royal Co of Archers); pres: Army Angling Fedn 1997–2005, Tidworth Combined Services Polo Club 2003–05, Royal Br Legion Scotland 2006–, Earl Haig Fund for Scotland 2006–, Offrs Assoc Scotland 2006–, Army Offrs Assoc 2006–; memb Br Cmmn of Mil History, cncllr Army Records Soc; cmmr Cwlth War Graves Cmmn 2005–; author of numerous articles in military jls; chm Christina Mary Hendrie Tst 1993–, dir Queen Mother Meml Fund for Scotland 2003–; *Recreations* gardening, shooting, fishing; *Clubs* Boodle's, Caledonian, Royal Scots, Highland Bde; *Style*— Lt-Gen Sir Alistair Irwin, KCB, CBE; ✉ c/o Adam and Co plc, 22 Charlotte Square, Edinburgh EH2 4DF

IRWIN, Christopher Conran; s of John Conran Irwin (d 1997), and Helen Hermione, *née* Fletcher (d 2005); *b* 2 April 1948; *Educ* Bedales (scholar), Univ of Sussex; *m* Stephanie Jane, da of Hilary Noble Ball (d 1972); 2 da (Bryony b 12 Jan 1972, Tamsin b 25 April 1974), 1 s (John Phineas Hilary b 20 June 1978); *Career* freelance broadcaster BBC Radio Brighton 1968–69, Fed Tst for Educn and Res 1969–75, sr visiting fell Univ of Sussex 1971–72, Secretariat N Atlantic Assembly Brussels 1973–74, current affrs prodr BBC World Service 1975–77, sr res assoc IISS 1977–78; various BBC appointments incl: sec of BBC Scot 1978–79, head of radio BBC Scot 1979–82, gen mangr Satellite devpt 1982–84, chief exec Satellite Broadcasting Bd 1984–85; sold concept for Br Satellite Broadcasting to Pearson plc 1985; gen mangr new media devpt Pearson plc 1986–88, controller of resources and admin BBC World Service 1989–90, chief exec BBC World Service Television Ltd 1990–94, md Guinness World Records Ltd 1994–2001; chm TravelWatch SouthWest, dir Thamesdown Tport, vice-chm European Passengers Fedn; bd memb for passengers: European Railway Agency, European Rail Research Advsy Cncl; memb Exec SW Regnl Assembly 2001–, European policy advsr Passenger Focus, infrastructure advsr SW Regnl Devpt Agency; *Books* The Security of Western Europe (with Sir Bernard Burrows, 1972), Electing the European Parliament (1973), Towards a Peaceful Europe (1974); contrib to: International Affairs, Strategic Survey; *Recreations* gardening, historical topography, timetables; *Style*— Christopher Irwin, Esq; ✉ Bourton House, Bourton, Bishops Cannings, Devizes, Wiltshire SN10 2LQ (tel 01380 860252, mobile 07900 218290, e-mail christophercirwin@hotmail.com)

IRWIN, Flavia; da of Clinton Irwin, and Everilda, *née* Hatt-Cook; *b* 15 December 1916; *Educ* Hawnes Sch Ampthill, Chelsea Sch of Art (studied under Henry Moore and Graham Sutherland), Ruskin Sch of Art Oxford; *m* 2 May 1942, Sir Roger de Grey, KCVO (d 1995), s of Nigel de Grey; 2 s (Spencer de Grey, CBE, *qv*, Robert de Grey), 1 da (Emilia Crawford); *Career* teacher Medway Coll of Art and Design, head of decorative arts C&G London Art Sch; Hon ARWA (MRWA), sr RA; *Exhibitions* Andsdell Gallery (solo), People's Theatre (Newcastle upon Tyne), RA Summer exhbn (consistently), RA Friends Room (solo), Gallery 10 (London), Curwen Gallery, Phoenix Gallery, Business Art Galleries (Roya Acad of Arts), London Gp, Studio 3 Gallery; *Work in Collections* Westminster Conference Centre, Midland Montague Morgan Grenfell, Carlisle City Art Gallery, Manchester Walker Art Gallery, DOE, private collections in UK and USA; *Recreations* walking, swimming; *Style*— Flavia Irwin, RA; ✉ 5 Camer Street, Meopham, Kent (tel 01474 812327)

I

IRWIN, Prof George William; s of Charles James Irwin (d 1988); *b* 19 September 1950; *Educ* Sullivan Upper Sch Holywood, Queen's Univ Belfast (BSc, PhD, DSc); *m* 4 Aug 1976, Margaret Yvonne, *née* McFeeters; 1 s (Robin Charles b 29 April 1981); *Career* lectr Engrg Maths Dept Loughborough Univ of Technol 1976–80; Queen's Univ Belfast: lectr 1980–87, reader 1987–88, prof of control engrg (personal chair) Sch of Electrical and Electronic Engrg 1988–, dir Virtual Engrg Centre 2001–; non-exec dir Anex6 Ltd 1989–2004; author of 350 research pubns in the field of automatic control systems; chair UK Automatic Control Cncl; hon prof: Harbin Univ of Technol China 1999, Shanghai Univ China 2005, Shangfong Univ China 2005; IEE: Kelvin Premium 1985, Heaviside Premium 1987, Mather Premium 1991, Hartree Premium 1996; Inst of Measurement and Control: Honeywell Prize 1994, Honeywell Int Medal 2002; CEng 1992, FIEE 1992, FInstMC 1992, MRIA 2002, FREng 2002, FIEEE 2004; *Recreations* cottage in Portballintrae, swimming, reading, music, travel, popular culture; *Style*— Prof George W Irwin; ✉ Rosnaree, 49 Magheralave Grange, Lisburn, Co Antrim BT28 3BZ (tel 028 9258 6392); School of Electrical and Electronic Engineering, Queen's University Belfast, Ashby Building, Stranmillis Road, Belfast BT9 5AH (tel 028 9097 5439, fax 028 9066 4265, e-mail g.irwin@ee.qub.ac.uk)

IRWIN, (David) Gwyther Broome; s of Gwyther William Powell (d 1960), and Barbara Ethel, *née* Dallimore; *b* 7 May 1931; *Educ* Bryanston, Central Sch of Art & Design; *m* 10 April 1960, Elizabeth Anne, da of Robert Gowlett; 2 s (Brom Gwyther Giles b 1 Oct 1962, Capel Robert Powell b 10 April 1967), 1 da (Charlotte Alicia Estelle b 26 Dec 1963); *Career* artist; lectr: Bath Acad of Art 1963, Chelsea Sch of Art 1967–69; head of fine art Brighton Poly 1969–84; designed and cut Rectangular Relief for BP House 1965–68, large paintings cmmnd by Glaxo for Stevenage offices 1993; works embrace paper collages, construction, acrylic on canvas and watercolours; Greater London Arts Assoc Award 1978; *Solo Exhibitions* Gallery One 1957, AIA Gallery 1957, ICA 1958, Gimpel Fils (various years 1959–87), New Art Centre 1973, 1975, 1977, Newcastle Poly Gallery 1978, Kettle's Yard Cambridge 1981, John Jones Gallery 1992, The Sixties (Barbican) 1993, Redfern Gallery 1994, major retrospective (Royal Cornish Museum) 1995 and (Royal West of England Academy) 1996; *Group Exhibitions* incl: Young Contemporaries 1953, Paris Biennale 1960, Collage (MOMA NY) 1961, John Moores Liverpool Exhibitions 1961, 1963, 1978, British Kunst Denmark 1963, XXXII Venice Biennale 1964, Recent British Painting (Tate Gallery) 1967, Contemporary British Painting (Albright Knox Art Gallery) 1974, Three Decades of Artists (Royal Acad) 1983, Recalling the 50s (Serpentine Gallery) 1985, Print 86 (Barbican) 1986, Summer Show (Royal Acad) 1986–94; *Works in Public Collections* incl: Tate, Arts Cncl of GB, DOE, Peggy Guggenheim Venice, Yale; *Recreations* poker, chess, maritime activities; *Clubs* Chelsea Arts; *Style*— Gwyther Irwin, Esq; ✉ 21 Hillbury Road, London SW17 8JT (tel 020 8673 7930); 2 The Glyddins, Rock, Wadebridge, Cornwall PL27 6NW (tel 01208 863186)

IRWIN, Dr Michael Henry Knox; s of William Knox Irwin, FRCS, MD (d 1973), of Watford Heath, Herts, and Edith Isabel Mary, *née* Collins; descendant of John Knox; *b* 5 June 1931; *Educ* Merchant Taylors' Sch, St Bartholomew's Hosp London (MB BS), Columbia Univ NY (MPH); *m* 1958 (m dis 1982), Elizabeth, *née* Naumann; 3 da (Christina, Pamela, Diana); partner, Angela Farmer; *Career* physician; joined UN 1957, UN medical dir 1969–73, dir of personnel UN Devpt Programme 1973–76, UNICEF rep in Bangladesh 1977–80, sr advsr UNICEF 1980–82, medical dir UN, UNDP and UNICEF 1982–89, dir Health Servs Dept World Bank 1989–90; conslt American Assoc of Blood Banks 1984–90, advsr ActionAid 1990–91, dir Westside Action 1991–93, int health conslt 1993–95; pres World Fedn of Right-To-Die Socs 2002–05 (vice-pres 2000–02); chm UN Assoc 1996–98 (vice-chm 1995, vice-pres 1999–), chm Vol Euthanasia Soc 2002–04 (chm 1996–2000, vice-chm 2000–02), dir Doctors for Assisted Dying 1998–2001, fndr The Last Choice 2005, co-ordinator Secular Medical Forum 2006–; Parly candidate Kensington and Chelsea by-election (Living Will Campaign) 1999; initiated Secularist of the Year Award 2005; Offr Cross Int Fedn of Blood Donor Organisations 1984; *Books* Overweight: A Problem for Millions (1964), What Do We Know About Allergies? (1972), Nuclear Energy: Good or Bad? (1984), The Cocaine Epidemic (1985), Can We Survive Nuclear War? (1985), Talpa (1990), Peace Museums (1991), Double Effect (1997), Pro-Choice Living Will (2003), Psyche-Anima (2004), What Survives? (2005); *Recreations* windmills, writing, politics, metaphysics; *Style*— Dr Michael Irwin; ✉ 15 Hovedene, Cromwell Road, Hove, East Sussex BN3 3EH

IRWIN, Robert Graham; *b* 23 August 1946; *Educ* Epsom Coll, Merton Coll Oxford (postmaster, MA), SOAS; *m* 30 Sept 1972, Helen Elizabeth, *née* Taylor; 1 da (Felicity Anne); *Career* writer; lectr Dept of Mediaeval History Univ of St Andrews 1972–77; pt/t teacher 1977–: Arabic Dept Univ of Oxford, Arabic Dept Univ of Cambridge, History Dept SOAS, Islamic Art dip course Sotheby's, Morley Coll; dir Dedalus publishing, conslt ed TLS, conslt Time-Life Books History of the World; visiting lectr Arabic Dept Univ of St Andrews 1985, assoc Inst of Medieval Studies Univ of Nottingham 1991–, sr research assoc Dept of History SOAS 1997–; memb interview panel Wingate scholarships 2000–; numerous radio and TV broadcasts; Br Cncl: tour of Germany 1997, rapporteur Arabic Literary Trans Conf 2000, tour of Syria 2001; attended literary festivals incl: Antwerp 1997, Bath 1998, Edinburgh 1998, Turku Finland 2003, Lewes Live Literary Festival 2003, Prague Writers' Festival 2004, Hay-on-Wye Festival 2004, Edinburgh Literary Festival 2004; memb Inst of Historical Research Univ of London; patron Nat Acad of Writing; founding fell London Coll of Pataphysics; FRAS (former memb Cncl), FSA, FRSL (memb Cncl); *Non-Fiction* books incl: The Middle East in the Middle Ages: The Early Mamluk Sultanate 1250–1382 (1986), The Arabian Nights: A Companion (1994, 2 edn 2003), Islamic Art (1997), Night and Horses and the Desert: An Anthology of Classical Arabic Literature (1999), The Alhambra (2004), For Lust of Knowing: The Orientalists and Their Enemies (2006); author of numerous articles and reviews in books, newspapers and jls; *Fiction* novels: The Arabian Nightmare (1983, 5 edn 2002, trans into 13 other languages), The Limits of Vision (1986, 2 edn 1993), The Mysteries of Algiers (1988, 2 edn 1993), Exquisite Corpse (1995, nomination Best Novel Br Fantasy Soc 1995), Prayer-Cushions of the Flesh (novella, 1997, reprinted 2004), Satan Wants Me (1999); *Recreations* in-line skating, Times crossword; *Style—* Robert Irwin, Esq; ✉ c/o Juri Gabriel, 35 Camberwell Grove, London SE5 8JA (tel 020 7703 6186, e-mail jurigabriel@compuserve.com)

IRWIN, Hon Mr Justice; Sir Stephen John; kt (2006); s of John McCaughey Irwin (d 1993), of Co Down, NI, and Norma Gordon, *née* Cosgrove; *b* 5 February 1953; *Educ* Methodist Coll Belfast, Jesus Coll Cambridge (BA); *m* 29 July 1978, Deborah Rose Ann, da of Lawrence Spring (decd), and Katherine, *née* Ferguson; 2 da (Rachel b 8 Sept 1983, Ruth b 13 July 1992), 1 s (William b 18 August 1985); *Career* called to the Bar Gray's Inn 1976; QC 1997, recorder 1999–2006, judge of the High Court of Justice (Queen's Bench Div) 2006–; co-fndr Doughty St Chambers; memb Bar Cncl 1999–2004 (vice-chm 2003, chm 2004); specialist in medical and related litigation; *Books* Medical Negligence: Practitioner's Guide (lead author, 1995); *Recreations* walking, reading, Irish history, verse; *Style—* The Hon Mr Justice Irwin; ✉ Royal Courts of Justice, Strand, London WC2A 2LL

ISAACS, Dr Anthony Donald; s of David Isaacs (d 1995), of London, and Rosa, *née* Hockman (d 1998); *b* 18 January 1931; *Educ* Univ of London, Charing Cross Hosp Univ of London (MB BS, DPM); *m* 15 Dec 1963, Elissa, da of Isaac Cedar (d 1977); 1 da (Catharine b 28 Oct 1964), 1 s (Timothy b 13 Sept 1967); *Career* Nat Serv RAMC Lt to Capt 1955–57; conslt psychiatrist Bethlem Royal and Maudsley Hosp 1963–90; sub dean Inst of Psychiatry Univ of London 1982–90; vice-chm Grants Ctee King Edward's Hosp Fund for London; Freeman City of London 1962; FRSM, FRCP, FRCPsych; *Books* Studies in Geriatric Psychiatry (1978), Psychiatric Examination in Clinical Practice (1981, 3 edn 1990); *Style—* Dr Anthony Isaacs; ✉ Capio Nightingale Hospital, 11–19 Lisson Grove, London NW1 6SH (tel 020 7535 7906)

ISAACS, Dr Anthony John; s of Benjamin H Isaacs, of Finchley, and Lily, *née* Rogol; *b* 22 October 1942; *Educ* Wanstead County HS, Hertford Coll Oxford (BA), Westminster Med Sch (MA, BM BCh); *m* 1, 12 Dec 1971 (m dis), Jill, da of Paul Elek (d 1976), of Highgate; 3 s (Jeremy b 1973, Adrian, Nicholas (twins) b 1976); m 2, 24 Oct 1986, Edie Lynda, *née* Friedman; 1 da (Anna b 1988); *Career* Dept of Health: SMO Meds Div 1984–85, PMO Meds Div and assessor Ctee on Safety of Meds 1985–86, sr PMO, under sec and head of Med Manpower and Educn Div 1986–91; hon conslt endocrinologist Middx Hosp and UCH 1986–, on secondment to London Sch of Hygiene and tropical Med 1991–93, conslt endocrinologist Charing Cross Hosp 1993–95 and Chelsea & Westminster Hosp 1993–, conslt in clinical audit N Thames Regnl Health Authy 1993–95 and Barnet Health Authy 1995–2001, hon conslt physician Barnet, Enfield and Haringey Health Authy 2001–02; hon visiting prof Sch of Health and Social Sciences Middlesex Univ 2001–; diplomate memb Faculty of Public Health Med RCP 1999–; partnership govr Hendon Sch 1999– (parent govr 1987–92, first govr 1992–99); hon treas Section of Endocrinology Diabetes; memb: Soc for Endocrinology, BMA; MRCP 1971, MSc 1992, FRCP 1997, FRSM; *Books* Anorexia Nervosa (with P Dally and J Gomez, 1979); *Recreations* table tennis, music, cinema; *Style—* Dr Anthony Isaacs; ✉ Chelsea & Westminster Hospital, 369 Fulham Road, London SW10 9NH

ISAACS, Sir Jeremy Israel; kt (1996); s of Isidore Isaacs, and Sara, *née* Jacobs; *b* 28 September 1932; *Educ* Glasgow Acad, Merton Coll Oxford (MA, pres Oxford Union); *m* 1, 1958, Tamara (d 1986); 1 s, 1 da; m 2, 1988, Gillian Mary Widdicombe; *Career* TV prodr: Granada TV 1958–63 (progs incl What the Papers Say, All Our Yesterdays), Associated-Rediffusion 1963–65 (This Week), BBC 1965–67 (Panorama); Associated-Rediffusion (renamed Thames Television 1968): controller of features 1967–74, dir of progs 1974–78, prodr The World at War 1974, conslt Hollywood series; ind prodr: A Sense of Freedom (Scottish TV), Ireland - A Television History (13 part series BBC TV), Cold War (Turner Broadcasting) 1998, Millennium (Turner Broadcasting) 1999; chief exec Channel 4 1981–87, gen dir ROH 1988–97, chief exec Jeremy Isaacs Productions 1997–, chm Artsworld Channels Ltd 2000–03, chm IOCMS Advsy Panel European Capital of Culture 2001–03; awarded: Desmond Davis Award for outstanding contrib to TV 1972, George Polk Meml Award 1973, Cyril Bennett Award for outstanding contrib to TV programming (RTS) 1982, Peabody Award, Prix Italia 1999; govr BFI 1979, BFI fellowship 1986; pres RTS 1999–2001; Hon DLitt: Univ of Strathclyde 1984, CNAA 1987, Univ of Bristol 1988, Univ of Manchester 1999; fell British Acad of Film and TV 1985; RTS Hall of Fame 1996; Cdr Order of Arts and Letters (France) 1988, L'Ordre National du Mérite (France) 1992; *Books* Storm Over Four (1988), Cold War (jtly, 1998), Never Mind the Moon (1999), Look Me in the Eye (2006); *Recreations* walking, reading; *Style—* Sir Jeremy Isaacs; ✉ c/o PFD, Drury House, 34 Russell Street, London WC2B 5HA

ISAACS, Jeremy M; *Career* exec dir Goldman Sachs 1989–96; Lehman Brothers: co chief operating offr European Equities 1996, head of global equity derivative activities 1996, head of overall equity activities in Europe 1997, chief exec European activities 1999 (previously chief operating offr), responsible for Asian ops 2000–, currently ceo Europe and Asia, memb Exec Ctee and Mgmnt Ctee, chm Lehman Brothers Fndn (Europe); non-exec dir St Mary's Hosp NHS Tst; hon fell London Business Sch; *Style—* Jeremy M Isaacs, Esq; ✉ Lehman Brothers International (Europe), 25 Bank Street, London E14 5LE (tel 020 7102 1000)

ISAACS, Prof Neil; s of Lewis Thomas Isaacs (d 1981), and Nona, *née* Creedon; *b* 11 June 1945; *Educ* St Patrick's Coll Brisbane, Univ of Queensland (BSc, PhD); *m* 1966, Margaret, da of M J Bugler; 3 da (Rebecca b 26 Feb 1970, Anna b 22 Aug 1971, Ursula b 19 Feb 1973); *Career* research asst Chemical Labs Univ of Cambridge 1969–72, IBM jr research fell Balliol Coll Oxford 1972–75, IBM World Trade Research Fell T J Watson Research Center NY 1976, sr visiting fell Univ of York 1977, univ research fell Univ of Melbourne 1978, sr research fell St Vincent's Inst of Med Research (Nat Health and MRC) Melbourne 1979–88, Joseph Black prof of protein crystallography Univ of Glasgow 1989–; author of over 100 scientific pubns; FRSE 1997; *Recreations* walking, reading; *Style—* Prof Neil Isaacs, FRSE; ✉ Department of Chemistry, University of Glasgow, Glasgow G12 8QQ (tel 0141 330 5954, fax 0141 330 4888, e-mail n.isaacs@chem.gla.ac.uk)

ISAACSON, Laurence Ivor; CBE (1998); s of Henry Isaacson (d 1980), and Dorothy Hannah, *née* Levitt (d 1976); *b* 1 July 1943; *Educ* Quarry Bank GS Liverpool, LSE (BSc), Northwestern Univ Chicago (summer business course); *Career* restaurateur; various business traineeships 1962–64 (Commercial Bank of Italy Milan, Shell Italiana Genoa, Manpower Inc Milwaukee), mgmnt trainee rising to account exec Unilever plc 1964–67, account mangr Doyle Dane Bernbach advtg 1967–70, sr int account mangr Foote Cone & Belding advtg 1970–72; The Creative Business Ltd: fndr md 1974–81, dep chm 1981–83, chm 1986–90; dir Amis du Vin Group Ltd and fndr ptnr/dir Café des Amis Ltd 1972–83 (sold to Kennedy Brookes plc 1983), bd dir i/c mktg and gourmet restaurant gp Kennedy Brookes plc 1983–86, fndr ptnr/dep chm Groupe Chez Gérard plc (Chez Gérard, Bertorelli's, Café Fish, St Quentin, Soho Soho, Scotts and Livebait) 1986–2003, dir and ptnr Paris Commune Restaurant LLC USA 2004–; non-exec dir: Cullens Holdings plc 1984–87, Lazard Food & Drink Fund Ltd 1987–90, Katie's Kitchen Ltd 1988–91, Metabolic Services Ltd 1991–94, London Tourist Board Ltd 1994–2002, CRUSAID 1996– (memb Bd 1996–), Bd Arts and Business 1989–2002 (memb Cncl 1985–), Transaction Television plc 1998–2000, Berkley Adam Ltd 1998–, Ambassador Theatre Gp 2000–; chm MAP Travel (Canada) 2000–; Contemporary Dance Trust: tstee 1980–, govr 1982–, chm Fundraising Ctee 1983–88, chm Bd 1989–94; memb Bd Royal Shakespeare Co Fndn 1998–, chm Actors Circle RSC 2001–, Bd dir RSC 2003–, dir RSC America Inc 2004–; memb Covent Garden Forum of Representatives 1976 (hon treas 1978–80), chm Covent Garden Festival 1993– (fndr/dep chm 1990–93), patron Int Festival of Musical Theatre Cardiff 2002; MIAA (memb UK Branch Ctee 1979–, chm Activities Ctee 1982–83); tstee and dir World Cancer Research Fund (UK) 2003–; FHCIMA 1996, FRSA 1997; *Recreations* the arts, travel, food and drink; *Clubs* Groucho, Garrick, Home House; *Style—* Laurence Isaacson, Esq, CBE; ✉ The Loft, 30 Crosby Street, Soho, New York, NY 10013, USA (tel 001 212 431 8545); 5 Chalcot Crescent, London NW1 8YE (tel 020 7586 3793, e-mail laurencei@aol)

ISDELL-CARPENTER, Peter; s of Richard Isdell-Carpenter, OBE (d 1986), and Rosemary, *née* Ashworth (d 1995); *b* 18 November 1940; *Educ* Marlborough, St John's Coll Oxford (BA); *m* 28 Sept 1966, Antoinette, da of Louis Cass (d 1952), and Mary, *née* Whetherly; 1 s (Simon b 1968), 2 da (Katherine b 1968, Nicola b 1970); *Career* Birds Eye Foods Ltd 1964–69, Grey Advertising 1969–70, dir Young and Rubicam Advertising Ltd 1970–78, md Sea Tack Ltd 1978–81, dir Young and Rubicam Europe Ltd 1981–96; currently dir Peter Isdell-Carpenter & Assocs; *Recreations* sailing, Hebrides, golf, music, painting; *Clubs* Boodle's; *Style—* Peter Isdell-Carpenter, Esq; ✉ The Courtyard, Chawton, Hampshire GU34 1SJ

ISHAM, Sir Ian Vere Gyles; 13 Bt (E 1627), of Lamport, Northamptonshire; s of Lt-Col Vere Arthur Richard Isham, MC (d 1968); suc kinsman Sir Gyles Isham, 12 Bt (d 1976); *b* 17 July 1923; *Educ* Eton, Worcester Coll Oxford; *Heir* bro, Norman Isham, OBE; *Career* marketing analyst and cartographer; *Clubs* Overseas; *Style—* Sir Ian Isham, Bt; ✉ 50 Willow Court, Ackenden Road, Alton, Hampshire GU34 1JW (tel 01420 549193)

ISHERWOOD, Mark Allan; AM; s of Rodney Isherwood, and Pat McLean, *née* Curry; *b* 21 January 1959; *Educ* Stockport GS, Univ of Newcastle upon Tyne (BA); *m* 6 May 1985, Hilary, *née* Fleming; 4 da (Genevieve b 16 Nov 1985, Charlotte b 25 June 1987, Olivia b 24 Nov 1990, Meredith b 17 March 1993), 2 s (Myles b 13 Dec 1994, Henry b 17 June 1997); *Career* mgmnt trainee raising to branch mangr Cheshire Building Soc 1981–89, commercial business devpt mangr NWS Bank plc 1989–90, area mangr Cheshire Building Soc 1990–2003, memb Nat Assembly for Wales (Cons) N Wales 2003–; memb All Pty Gp on: Nat Assembly Sustainable Energy Gp (NASEG), Looked After Children, Disablity Gp, Funerals and Bereavement, Deaf Issues, Autism; memb Energywatch; founding memb CHANT Cymru; community cncllr Treddyn 1999–2004; patron Tyddyn Bach Tst Respite Centre, vice-pres N Wales Play and Playing Fields Assoc, memb Venture Housing Assoc (former Bd memb), memb Conwy Citizens Advice Bureau, former sch govr and chm Ysgol Parc y Llan, ambass Clwyd Girl Guiding; ACIB 1997; *Recreations* sailing, family, house, garden; *Clubs* S Caernarvonshire Yacht, Mold Round Table, Ruthin Conservative (hon memb); *Style—* Mark Isherwood, Esq, AM; ✉ National Assembly for Wales, Cardiff Bay, Cardiff CF99 1NA (tel 029 2089 8730, fax 029 2089 8323, e-mail mark.isherwood@wales.gov.uk)

ISHIGURO, Kazuo; OBE (1995); s of Shizuo Ishiguro, and Shizuko Michida; *b* 8 November 1954; *Educ* Woking Co GS, Univ of Kent (BA), UEA (MA); *m* Lorna Anne, da of Nicol Mackechnie MacDougall; 1 da (Naomi b 29 March 1992); *Career* author; work translated into 30 languages; memb: Soc of Authors 1989, PEN 1989; hon foreign memb American Acad of Arts and Sciences 1993; Hon DLitt: Univ of Kent 1990, UEA 1995, Univ of St Andrews 2003; FRSL 1989, FRSA 1990; Chevalier de l'Ordre des Arts et des Lettres (France) 1998; *Novels* A Pale View of Hills (1982, Winifred Holtby Award 1983), An Artist of the Floating World (1986, Whitbread Book of the Year 1986, Premio Scanno (Italy) 1995), The Remains of the Day (1989, Booker Prize 1989, Merchant-Ivory film 1993), The Unconsoled (1995, Cheltenham Prize 1995), When We Were Orphans (2000, shortlisted Man Booker Prize 2000), Never Let Me Go (2005, Corine Prize (Germany) 2006, Serono Prize (Italy) 2006, shortlisted Man Booker Prize 2005); *TV Plays* A Profile of Arthur J Mason (broadcast 1984), The Gourmet (broadcast 1987); *Film* The Saddest Music in the World (screenplay co-writer, 2003), The White Countess (original screenplay, 2005); *Recreations* playing musical instruments; *Style—* Kazuo Ishiguro, Esq, OBE, FRSL; ✉ c/o Rogers, Coleridge and White Ltd, 20 Powis Mews, London W11 1JN (tel 020 7221 3717, fax 020 7229 9084)

ISLAM, Runa; *b* 1970, Dhaka, Bangladesh; *Educ* Manchester Met Univ, Middx Univ, Rijksakademie van Beeldende Kunsten Amsterdam, Royal Coll of Art; *Career* artist; Campden Charities Scholarship 1997, NUFFIC Scholarship 1998, Univ of E London Richmix Cmmn 1999, Ford Motor Co and Breakthrough Nurture & Desire Cmmn 2000, Arena Sammling Fndn and NESTA Cmmn 2002–03, Public Art Strategy Artists Cmmn for Home Office Bldg 2004–2005; Fndn of Sports and Arts Award 1997, Rijksakademie van Beeldende Kunsten Acquisitions Prize 1998, Amsterdam Fonds voor de Kunst Aanmoedigings Prijs '99 1999, Fondazione Sandretto Re Rebaudengo Premio Regione Piemonte 2000, London Arts Visual Arts Award 2001; *Solo Exhibitions* incl: Screen Test/Unscript (Fig-1 London) 2000, Tschumi Pavillion Groningen 2000, Director's Cut (Fool for Love) (White Cube London) 2001, One day a day will come, when a day will not come any more (April in parking meters, Cologne) 2001, Rapid Eye Movement (MIT List Visual Arts Center Cambridge) 2003, Film and Video Works (Voralberger Kunstverein Bregenz) 2003, Director's Cut (Fool for Love) (Kunsthalle Wien Karlsplatz Project Space Vienna) 2003, Scale (1/16 inch = 1 foot) (ShugoArts Tokyo) 2004; *Group Exhibitions* Transit at Art Focus (Central Bus Station Tel Aviv) 1994, Lost Property (The Lost Goods Building London) 1995, Yerself is Steam (85 Charlotte Rd London) 1996, Big Blue (Coins London and Café Fix Berlin) 1997, The Road (Espace Culturel François Mitterand Beauvais) 1998, Martin (Catalyst Arts Belfast and Waygood Gallery Newcastle) 1998, The Vauxhall Gardens (Norwich Art Gallery) 1998, 000Zero, Zero, Zero (Whitechapel Art Gallery London) 1999, East International (Norwich Art Gallery) 1999, Dis-Locations (hARTware projekte Dortmund) 1999, And If There Were No Stories (Stephen Friedman Gallery London) 2000, The British Art Show 5 (Hayward Gallery touring exhbn) 2000, Haven Lodge (Haven Lodge Residential Home Ramsgate) 2000, Nurture and Desire (in aid of Breakthrough Breast Cancer, Hayward Gallery London) 2000, Century City (Tate Modern London) 2001, Whitechapel Centenary 1901–2001 (Whitechapel Art Gallery London) 2001, Please Disturb Me (Great Eastern Hotel London) 2001, Looking With/Out (Courtauld Inst London) 2001, A Haunted House of Art (Outline Amsterdam) 2002, Videodrome II (Zenith Media Lounge New Museum NY) 2002, Great Theatre of the World (Taipei Fine Arts Museum) 2002, Miradas Cómplices

(Accomplished Glances) (Centro Galego de Arte Contemporanea Santiago de Compostela) 2003, Sharjah Int Biennial 6 2003, Poetic Justice (8th International Istanbul Biennial) 2003, Love/Hate, Attempts at the Grand Emotion Between Art and the Theatre (Ursula Blickle Fndn Kraichal) 2003, In Movement: UNESCO Salutes Women in Video Art (UNESCO HQ Paris) 2004, Britannia Works (Ileana Tounta Contemporary Art Centre Athens) 2004, Párpados y Labios (Eyelids and Lips) (Antigua Fábrica de Tabascos Madrid) 2004, Lilith (Mot London) 2004, Eclipse, Towards the Edge of the Visible (White Cube London) 2004; *Collaborations* Life/Live (with David Medalla, Adam Nakervis and Peter Lewis, Musée d'Art Moderne de la Ville de Paris) 1996, Curator's Arse (with Peter Lewis, Catalyst Arts Belfast and Waygood Gallery Newcastle) 1997, Plaats (with J Daf, P Fillingham and J Isaacs, W139 Amsterdam) 1998, 'Alice in Bed' by Susan Sontag (with HZT and NY Theatre Workshop) 2000, History Lessons at Kunst en der Stadt 2000 (with Peter Lewis, Korn Theatre Bregenz) 2000, What's Wrong (with Peter Lewis, Trade Apartment London) 2001, Cité (with Roger Cremers, Institut Néerlandais Paris and Inst Hollandaise Paris) 2001; *Festivals, Events and Screenings* Hit and Run 1–4 (Arch 53 and The Ministry of Sound London) 1994, 1995 and 1996, Scope 2 International Film Festival (Artists Space NY) 1998, Runa Islam at Impakt Film Festival (Begane Grond Utrecht) 1999, World Wide Video Festival (Uitmarkt Stedlijk Museum Amsterdam) 1999, Devil Eats Out (Flag London) 2000, Idea Festival Video in the City (Centrum Hedendaagse Kunst Maastricht) 2001, Film and Video (Danish Film Inst) 2002, Rapid Eye Movement (Camden Arts Centre Off Centre Event, Everyman Cinema London) 2003; *Style—* Ms Runa Islam; ✉ White Cube, 48 Hoxton Square, London N1 6PB (tel 020 7930 5373, fax 020 7949 7480)

ISLE OF MAN, Archdeacon of the; *see:* Partington, Ven Brian Harold

ISRAEL, Rev Dr Martin Spencer; s of Elie Benjamin Israel (d 1980), of Johannesburg, South Africa, and Minnie, *née* Israel (d 1957); *b* 30 April 1927; *Educ* Parktown Boys HS Johannesburg, Univ of the Witwatersrand (MB ChB); *Career* RAMC 1955–57, Capt; registrar in pathology Royal Hosp Wolverhampton 1953–55; RCS: res fell in pathology 1957–60, lectr in microbiology 1961–66, sr lectr in pathology 1967–81, hon lectr 1982; curate St Michael Cornhill London 1974–76, asst priest Holy Trinity with All Saints S Kensington 1977–82 (priest i/c 1983–97, ret); pres Churches' Fellowship for Psychical and Spiritual Studies 1983–98; MRCP 1952, FRCPath 1975; *Books* General Pathology (with J B Walter, 1963), Summons to Life (1974), Precarious Living (1976), Smouldering Fire (1978), The Pain that Heals (1981), Living Alone (1982), The Spirit of Counsel (1983), Healing as Sacrament (1984), The Discipline of Love (1985), Coming in Glory (1986), Gethsemane (1987), The Pearl of Great Price (1988), The Dark Face of Reality (1989), The Quest for Wholeness (1989), Creation (1989), Night Thoughts (1990), A Light on the Path (1990), Life Eternal (1993), Dark Victory (1995), Angels (1995), Exorcism (1997), Doubt (1997), Happiness That Lasts (1999), Learning to Love (with Rev Neil Broadbent, 2001), The Devout Life (with Rev Neil Broadbent, 2001); *Style—* The Rev Dr Martin Israel; ✉ 21 Soudan Road, London SW11 4HH (tel 020 7652 0647, fax 020 7622 5756, website www.martinisrael.com)

ISSA, Moneim; s of Mustapha Issa (d 1987), of Alexandria, Egypt, and Zakeya, *née* Zaky; *b* 21 August 1939; *Educ* Alexandria Univ (BChD); *m* 1962, Christa Sylvia, da of Balthasar Sima (d 1973), of Marquartstein, Germany; 1 s (Thomas b 1963), 1 da (Alexandra b 1971); *Career* sr registrar Bart's 1969–73, conslt oral and maxillofacial surgn and postgrad tutor W Middx Univ Hosp 1973–79, conslt oral and maxillofacial surgn to Oxford RHA and NW Thames RHA 1973–2004, clinical dir Head and Neck Reconstructive Surgery Unit Heatherwood and Wexham Hosps Tst E Berks 1995–2000, clinical dir of urology 1996–2000; conslt to BA in oral and maxillofacial surgery 1986–; chm BDA Windsor Section 1984; memb: Windsor Med Soc, Hosp Conslts and Specialists Assoc 1974–; FFDRCSI 1968, FDSRCS 1969, fell Br Assoc of Oral and Maxillofacial Surgns 1973; *Books* Oral Surgery section in Hamlyn Medical Encyclopaedia (1978), Maxillo Facial Injuries section in Operative Plastic & Reconstructive Surgery (1980); *Recreations* tennis, skiing, waterskiing, chess; *Style—* Moneim Issa, Esq

ISSERLIS, Steven John; CBE (1998); s of George Isserlis, and Cynthia Saville; gs of Julius Isserlis, Russian composer and pianist; *b* 19 December 1958; *Educ* City of London Sch, Int Cello Centre (with Jane Cowan), Oberlin Coll Ohio (with Richard Kapuscinski); *m* Pauline Ann Mara; 1 s (Gabriel Mara b 26 April 1990); *Career* cellist; recitals and concerts all over Europe, N America, S America, Far East and Australia with maj worldwide orchs; worked with conductors incl: Sir Georg Solti, Christoph Eschenbach, Christopher Hogwood, Roger Norrington, Richard Hickox, John Eliot Gardiner, Gennadi Rozhdestvensky, Vladimir Ashkenazy, Philippe Herrweghe, Franz Brüggen, Ton Koopman, Lorin Maazel, Sakari Oramo, Daniel Harding; has played a leading role in many prestigious chamber music projects incl own festival Schumann and his Circle (Wigmore Hall London), Mendelssohn Series Salzburg Festival 1997, Brahms Series Salzburg Festival 2000, Brahms Frühling Series London, Berlin, Vienna 2000–01, Teneyev Series London 2002, Saint-Saëns Series London 2004; several television films incl Channel 4 films on Saint-Saëns 1993 and Schumann 1997; Royal Phiharmonic Award Piatgorsky Prize (1993), Schumann Preis City of Zwickau (2000); memb: Dvorâk Soc, Liszt Soc, Wilkie Collins Soc; Hon RAM, FRCM; *Recordings* incl: John Tavener The Protecting Veil and Threenos and Britten Suite no 3 (with LSO and Gennadi Rozhdestvensky, 1992, Gramophone Magazine Contemporary Music Award 1992, shortlisted for Mercury Prize and Grammy Award), Saint Saëns: Concerto no 1, Sonata no 1, The Swan and others (with LSO under Michael Tilson Thomas, with Dudley Moore, Pascal Devoyon and others, CD and video), Mendelssohn cello works (with Melvyn Tan, 1994), Fauré cello works (with Pascal Devoyon, 1995), Liszt, Grieg and Rubinstein cello works (with Stephen Hough, 1995), Shostakovich, Prokofiev and Janácek cello works (with Olli Mustonen, 1996), Barber Concerto (with St Louis Symphony Orch under Leonard Slatkin), John Tavener Svyati (with Kiev Chamber Choir, nomination Mercury Music Prize), Schumann cello works (with Deutsche Kammerphilharmonie, Eschenbach), Haydn concertos (with COE and Roger Norrington, Classic CD Concerto Award), Cello World (with Thomas Adès), Brahms, Schumann, Frühling clarinet trios (with Stephen Hough and Michael Collins), Saint Saëns: Cello Concerto no 2, La Muse et le Poète (with NDR Orchestra, Johua Bell and Pascal Devoyon, 2000), Strauss Don Quixote (with Maazel and Stephen Hough, 2001), Rachmaninov and Franck Cello Sonatas (with Stephen Hough, 2003), Brahms Sonatas, works by Dvorak and Suk (with Stephen Hough, 2005), Bach Cello Suites (2007); *Publications* music: Beethoven Mandolin Variations, Saint Saens - Complete Short Works for Cells and Piano, Steven Isserlis's Cello World, Unbeaten Tracks, various cello works for www.sheetmusicnow.com; Why Beethoven Threw the Stew (children's book, 2001), Why Handel Waggled His Wig (children's book, 2006); *Recreations* reading, sleeping, eating, talking, jetlag, panicking, dropping names, generally wasting time (my own and others'), finding excuses not to practise, scolding my son for making excuses not to practise, wondering why I don't have any interesting hobbies; *Style—* Steven Isserlis, Esq, CBE; ✉ c/o Harrison/Parrott Ltd, 12 Penzance Place, London W11 4PA (tel 020 7229 9166, fax 020 7221 5042, e-mail info@harrisonparrott.co.uk)

ISTED, Barrington James (Barry); s of James William Isted (d 1978), of Croydon, Surrey, and Gwendolyne Irene, *née* Fleetwood (d 1995); *b* 12 July 1935; *Educ* Wallington Co GS, Univ of Nottingham (BA); *m* 31 May 1963, Glenda Jeanne, da of Thomas Leonard Bunyan (d 1991), of Broxbourne, Herts; 2 s (Jonathan b 1964, Daniel b 1965); *Career* corporate ed: Pyrene Ltd 1957–58, Formica Ltd 1958–59; dir of personnel: Potterton International Ltd 1968–72, De La Rue Group 1977–88 (corp ed 1960–63, pubns mangr 1963–65, trg offr 1965–67, manpower controller 1973–77); co sec De La Rue plc 1985–88, dir Chandler Gooding Ltd 1993–2005; Br Assoc of Communicators in Business: nat chm 1967–68, chm of Senate 1981–84, vice-pres 1984–89 and 1996–, pres 1989–95; govr London Business Sch 1984–87 (chm Business Liaison Ctee); employment law conslt 1999–; memb: Employment Tbnls for England and Wales 1984–2005, London Bd Crimestoppers 1987–88; Fedn of European Industrial Eds Assoc Dip of Honour 1974; Freeman: City of London 1987, Worshipful Co of Makers of Playing Cards 1987; FCB 1968, FCMI (FIMgt 1980); *Books* Tolley's Employment Tribunals Handbook (jtly, 2002); *Recreations* writing, travel, food and drink; *Clubs* Reform; *Style—* Barry Isted, Esq; ✉ Pinnacles, Hatfield Broad Oak, Bishop's Stortford, Hertfordshire CM22 7HS (tel and fax 01279 718397, e-mail barry@hbo99.freeserve.co.uk)

ITALY AND MALTA, Archdeacon of; *see:* Reid, Ven Gordon

IVE, Jonathan; CBE (2006); *b* 1967, London; *Educ* Newcastle Polytechnic (BA); *Career* designer; with Tangerine 1990–92; Apple Computer Inc: joined 1992, dir of design 1996, vice-pres of industrial design 1998, sr vice-pres of design 2005–, designer iMac, iBook, PowerBook G4, iPod and iMac G5; Design Achievement Medal RSA 1999, Royal Designer for Industry RSA 2003, Designer of the Year Design Museum 2003, Benjamin Franklin Medal RSA 2004, Pres's Award D&AD 2005; Hon Dr Newcastle Poly; RDI 2003; *Style—* Jonathan Ive, Esq, CBE, RDI; ✉ Apple Computer Inc, 1 Infinite Loop, Cupertino, CA 95014, USA

IVEAGH, 4 Earl of (UK 1919); Sir Arthur Edward Rory Guinness; 4 Bt (UK 1885); also Baron Iveagh (UK 1891), Viscount Iveagh (UK 1905), and Viscount Elveden (UK 1919); er s of 3 Earl of Iveagh (d 1992), and Miranda Daphne Jane, *née* Smiley; *b* 10 August 1969; *m* 27 Oct 2001, Clare Georgina Hazell; 2 s (Arthur Benjamin Jeffrey, Viscount Elveden b 6 Jan 2003, Rupert Bertram Ralph b 4 June 2005); *Heir* s, Viscount Elveden; *Style—* The Rt Hon the Earl of Iveagh; ✉ The Estate Office, Elveden, Thetford, Norfolk IP24 3TQ

IVERSEN, Dr Leslie Lars; s of Svend Iversen, and Anna Caia Iversen; *b* 31 October 1937; *Educ* Heles Sch, Trinity Coll Cambridge (BA, MA, PhD, prize fellowship); *m* 1961, Susan Diana; 1 s, 1 da (and 1 da decd); *Career* Nat Serv Educn Branch RN 1956–58; Harkness fell of the Cwlth Fund Nat Inst of Mental Health Harvard Med Sch 1964–66, res fell Trinity Coll and Dept of Pharmacology Univ of Cambridge 1966–71, Locke res fell Royal Soc London 1967–71, dir MRC Neurochemical Pharmacology Unit Cambridge 1971–83, vice-pres Neuroscience Research Centre Merck Sharp & Dohme Research Laboratories Harlow 1987–95 (exec dir 1983–87), visiting prof Dept of Pharmacology Univ of Oxford 1995–, prof of pharmacology and dir Wolfson Centre for Age Related Diseases KCL 1999–2004; assoc of neurosciences Res Prog MIT USA 1975–84, foreign hon memb American Acad of Arts and Sciences 1981, Rennebohm lectr Univ of Wisconsin 1984, visiting prof Inst of Psychiatry Univ of London 1985, assoc memb Royal Coll of Psychiatrists UK 1986, foreign assoc memb Nat Acad of Sciences USA 1986, hon prof Beijing Med Univ China 1988; memb: Academia Europaea, American Coll of Neuropsychopharmacology, Bayliss and Starling Soc, Biochemical Soc UK, Br Pharmacological Soc, Collegium Internationale Neuro-Psychopharmacologicum, Euro Molecular Biology Orgn, Int Brain Res Orgn, Int Soc for Neurochemistry, Physiological Soc UK, Royal Acad of Med Belgium, Royal Soc of Med London, Save Br Science, Soc for Drug Res UK, Soc for Neuroscience USA; pres Euro Neuroscience Assoc 1980–82 (vice-pres 1978–80); FRS 1980; *Books* The Uptake and Storage of Noradrenaline in Sympathetic Nerves (1967), Behavioural Pharmacology (with S D Iversen, 1975), The Science of Marijuana (2000), Speed, Ecstasy, Ritalin: The Science of Amphetamines (2006); author of numerous articles in learned jls; *Style—* Dr Leslie Iversen, FRS; ✉ University Department of Pharmacology, University of Oxford, Mansfield Road, Oxford OX1 3QT (tel 01865 271850, fax 01865 271882, e-mail les.iversen@pharm.ox.ac.uk)

IVES, Charles John Grayston (Bill); s of Harold James Ives (d 1967), and Catherine Lilla, *née* Downing (d 2004); *b* 15 February 1948, Harleston, Norfolk; *Educ* King's Sch Ely, Selwyn Coll Cambridge (CertEd, MA); *m* 1, Bethan Eleri, *née* Jones; 1 da (Charlotte Angharad b 1977), 1 s (Nicholas Rhys b 1980); *m* 2, 20 Feb 1988, Janette Ann, *née* Buqué; *Career* asst dir of music Reed's Sch Cobham 1971–76, lay clerk Guildford Cathedral Choir 1971–75, music lectr Coll of FE Chichester 1976–78, tenor The King's Singers 1978–85, organist, informator choristarum and tutor in music Magdalen Coll Oxford 1991–; examiner Associated Bd of the Royal Schs of Music 1988–2006; memb: Br Acad of Composers and Songwriters 1975, Performing Rights Soc 1973; nominated Grammy Award 2005; *Choral Compositions* Canterbury Te Deum (cmmned for Archbishop George Carey's enthronement at Canterbury 1991),The Gift of Grace (cmmned for the Nat Commemoration Serv in Westminster Abbey 2007); Missa Brevis, Edington Service, Listen Sweet Dove; *Recreations* wine, films, football, England; *Style—* Bill Ives, Esq; ✉ 1 Cowley Place, Oxford OX4 1DX; Magdalen College, Oxford OX1 4AU (tel 01865 276007, e-mail bill.ives@magd.ox.ac.uk)

IVES, Prof Eric William; OBE (2001); s of Frederick Henry Ives (d 1981), of Trowbridge, Wilts, and Ethel Lily, *née* Halls; *b* 12 July 1931; *Educ* Brentwood Sch, Queen Mary Coll (BA, PhD); *m* 1 April 1961, Christine Ruth (d 2004), da of Norman Henry Denham (d 1971), of Dewsbury, W Yorks; 1 da (Susan b 1963), 1 s (John b 1967); *Career* res History of Parliament Tst 1957; Univ of Birmingham: fell Shakespeare Inst 1958–61, sr lectr in modern history 1972–83 (lectr 1968–72), prof of English history 1987–97 (reader 1983–87), dean Faculty of Arts 1987–89 (dept dean 1982–84), pro-vice-chllr 1989–93, head Dept of Modern History 1994–97, prof emeritus 1997–, dir Inst for Advanced Research in the Humanities 2002– (fell 1997); lectr in modern history Univ of Liverpool 1962–68 (asst lectr 1961–62); memb Cncl Hist Assoc 1968–77; govr: Warwick Schs Fndn 1980–2006 (chm Ctee Govrs Warwick Sch 1985–2003), Coventry Sch 1985–88, Westhill Coll 1991–99 (tstee and chm of Govrs); memb: Cncl Regents Park Coll Oxford 1988–, Ct Univ of Warwick 1989–, Cncl Selly Oak Colls 1993–96, Cncl Surgeons Coll 1993–2000 (Academic Bd 1987–); non-exec dir Birmingham Women's Health Care NHS Tst 1993–97; memb Bd Birmingham and Westhill Academic Alliance 1999–2001; tstee The King Henry VIII Endowed Tst Warwick 1996– (chm 2002–05), tstee Westhill Endowment Tst 2001–02; chm: Stratford-upon-Avon Choral Soc 1985–91 and 2007–, Coventry and Warwickshire Ecumenical Cncl 1996–; FRHistS 1963, FSA 1984; *Books* Letters & Accounts of William Brereton (1976), God in History (1979), Faction in Tudor England (1979, 2 edn 1986), The Common Lawyers of Pre-Reformation England (1983), The First Civic University (2000), The Life and Death of Anne Boleyn (2004); *Recreations* choral singing, lay preaching; *Style—* Prof E W Ives, OBE, FSA; ✉ School of History, University of Birmingham, Birmingham B15 2TT (tel 0121 414 5736, fax 0121 414 3656)

IVES, Kenneth Ainsworth; s of Lawrence George Ives (d 1956), and Margaret, *née* Walker (d 1978); *b* 26 March 1934; *Educ* Queen Mary's GS Walsall, Pembroke Coll Oxford (MA), RADA (Leverhulme scholar); *m* 1, Ann Brown; m 2, Imogen Hassall; m 3, 1985, Lynne Shepherd (the comedienne Marti Caine (d 1995)); *Career* Mil Serv Lt RN; director: over fifty plays for BBC TV, NT and West End, seven plays by Harold Pinter; latest theatre work The Philanthropist (by Christopher Hampton); called to the Bar Middle Temple 1993; *Recreations* cricket, opera, reading, walking; *Clubs* Garrick, MCC; *Style—* Kenneth Ives, Esq

IVORY, Sir Brian Gammell; kt (2006), CBE (1999); s of Eric James Ivory (d 1988), and Alice Margaret Joan (d 1984), da of late Sir Sydney Gammell; *b* 10 April 1949; *Educ* Eton,

I

Magdalene Coll Cambridge (MA); *m* 21 Feb 1981, Oona Mairi Macphie Ivory, DL, *qv*, da of Archibald Ian Bell-MacDonald (d 1987); 1 s (Euan b 1986), 1 da (Roseanna b 1989); *Career* CA; Highland Distillers plc: dir 1978–99, md 1988–94, gp chief exec 1994–97, exec chm 1997–99; chm Macallan Distillers Ltd 1996–99; non-exec dir: Rémy Cointreau SA 1991–, Bank of Scotland 1998–2007, The Scottish American Investment Co plc 2000– (chm 2001–), HBOS plc 2001–2007, Retec Digital plc 2001–, Orpar SA 2002–, Insight Investment Mgmnt Ltd 2003–, Synesis Life Ltd 2007–, Marathon Asset Management 2007–; chm Nat Galleries of Scotland 2000–, vice-chm Scottish Arts Cncl 1988–92 (memb Cncl 1983–92); memb: Arts Cncl of GB 1988–92, Scottish Economic Council 1996–98, treas Scotch Whisky Association 1998–99; fndr chm The Nat Piping Centre 1996–; memb Queen's Body Guard for Scotland (Royal Co of Archers) 1996; Freeman City of London 1996; FRSA 1993, FRSE 2001; *Recreations* the arts, farming, hill walking; *Clubs* New (Edinburgh); *Style*— Sir Brian Ivory, CBE; ✉ 12 Ann Street, Edinburgh EH4 1PJ

IVORY, James Francis; s of Capt Edward Patrick Ivory, US Army (d 1967), of Dinuba, California, and Hallie Millicent, *née* De Loney (d 1963); *b* 7 June 1928; *Educ* Univ of Oregon (BA), Univ of S Calif (MA); *Career* fndr Merchant Ivory Prodns (with Ismail Merchant and Ruth Prawer Jhabvala) 1963; Guggenheim fell 1975; memb: Dirs' Guild of America, Writers' Guild of America; *Films* incl: Shakespeare Wallah 1965, Savages 1972, Autobiography of a Princess 1975, Roseland 1977, Hullabaloo Over Georgie and Bonnie's Pictures 1978, The Europeans 1979, Quartet 1981, Heat and Dust 1983, The Bostonians 1984, A Room with a View (Best Dir nomination Acad Awards 1987) 1986, Maurice (Silver Lion Venice Film Festival) 1987, Slaves of New York 1989, Mr and Mrs Bridge 1990, Howards End (Best Dir nomination Acad Awards 1993) 1992, The Remains of the Day (Best Dir nomination Acad Awards 1994) 1993, Jefferson in Paris 1995, Surviving Picasso 1996, A Soldier's Daughter Never Cries 1998, The Golden Bowl 2000, Le Divorce 2003, The White Countess 2005; *Recreations* looking at pictures; *Style*— James Ivory, Esq; ✉ PO Box 93, Claverack, NY 12513, USA (tel 00 1 212 582 8049); Merchant Ivory Productions, 46 Lexington Street, London W1R 3LH (tel 020 7437 1200/020 7439 4335)

IVORY, Lady Oona Mairi MacPhie; DL (Edinburgh 1998); da of Archibald Ian Bell-MacDonald (d 1987), and Mary Rae, *née* Macphee (d 1983); *b* 21 July 1954; *Educ* Royal Scottish Acad of Music & Drama, King's Coll Cambridge (MA), Royal Acad of Music (ARCM); *m* 21 Feb 1981, Sir Brian Gammell Ivory, CBE, *qv*; 1 s (Euan b 1986), 1 da (Roseanna b 1989); *Career* dir RSAMD 1989–2001, chm Scottish Ballet 1995–97 (dir 1988–), fndr dir The Nat Piping Centre 1996–, tstee The Piping Tst 1996–; FRSA 1996; *Recreations* The Arts, sailing, wild places; *Style*— Lady Ivory, DL; ✉ 12 Ann Street Edinburgh EH4 1PJ (tel 0131 311 6903, fax 0131 311 6910)

IWANIEC, Prof Stanisława Dorota; *b* 20 April 1940; *Educ* Gimnazium Oleandry Kraków, Jagiellonian Univ Kraków (MA, DipEd), Univ of Leicester (CQSW, PhD); *m* 1, 1960, Zygfryd Iwaniec, s of Aleksander Iwaniec; 2 c (Zygmunt Witold b 16 Oct 1961, Andrzej Jan b 12 July 1966); m 2, 1993, Prof James Stevens Curl, *qv*, s of George Stevens Curl (d 1974); *Career* teacher Liceum Sienkiewicza Kraków 1959–60, generic social worker Leicester Social Servs Dept 1971–75, therapist/researcher Dept of Child Health Leicester Royal Infirmary and Univ of Leicester Med Sch 1977–82, dir Student Trg Unit Leicester 1982–89, team ldr Practice-Teaching Resource Centre Univ of Leicester/Social Servs Dept 1989–92; Queen's Univ Belfast: chair of Social Work 1992, head Sch of Social Work 1995–2002, dir Inst for Child-Care Res 1995–2005, currently emeritus prof; Science Award Women of Achievement Save the Children 2005; memb: Br Assoc of Behavioural and Cognitive Psychotherapists, Br Assoc of Social Workers; AcSS 2002, MRIA 2007; *Publications* Working with Children and Their Families (1987), Failure-to-thrive in Children, Emotional Abuse, Prediction of Child Abuse and Neglect (1989), The Emotionally Abused and Neglected Child: Identification, Assessment, and Intervention (1995), Making Research Work: Promoting Child-Care Policy and Practice (co-ed, 1998), Child and Welfare Policy Practice: Current Issues in Child-Care Research (co-ed, 2000), Emotional Abuse and Failure to Thrive: British and Polish Experiences (co-ed, 2003), Children Who Fail to Thrive: A Practice Guide (2004), The Emotionally Abused and Neglected Child - Identification, Assessment and Intervention: A Practice Handbook (2006), The Child's Journey through Care: Placement Stability, Care Planning, and Achieving Permanency (2006); *Recreations* walking, opera, theatre, food and wine, travel; *Clubs* Royal Over-Seas League; *Style*— Prof Stanisława Dorota Iwaniec; ✉ 15 Torgrange, Holywood, Co Down BT18 0NG (tel and fax 028 9042 5141, e-mail d.iwaniec@btinternet.com)

IZAT, (Alexander) John Rennie; OBE (2002), JP; s of Sir James Rennie Izat (d 1962), of Balliliesk, and Lady (Eva Mary Steen) Izat, *née* Cairns (d 1984); *b* 14 July 1932; *Educ* Trinity Coll Glenalmond, Oriel Coll Oxford (MA); *m* 12 April 1958, Frederica Ann, da of Colin Champness McNiel, of Hants; 2 da (Davina b 1959, Rosanna b 1963), 1 s (Alexander b 1960); *Career* stockbroker, farmer; ptnr Williams de Broë & Co London 1955–75; John Izat & Partners: Balliliesk and Naemoor 1961–87, High Cocklaw 1987–; former chm: Shires Income plc, Moredun Research Institute, U A Gp plc, U A Properties Ltd, U A Forestry Ltd, Fraser Tennant (Insurance Brokers) Ltd; former dir: Wiston Investment Co, Glasgow Investment Managers Ltd, Shires Smaller Companies plc; dir: Cromlix Estates Ltd, C Champness & Co, College Valley Estates Ltd; past pres: Fife-Kinross NFU, Kinross Agric Assoc; dir Royal Highland Agric Soc 1985–97 (hon treas 1992–96); fell Glenalmond Coll (memb Cncl 1975–95, chm Ctee 1989–95); FRAgS 2001; *Recreations* shooting, Suffolk sheep; *Clubs* Caledonian; *Style*— John Izat, Esq, OBE; ✉ High Cocklaw, Berwick-upon-Tweed TD15 1UZ (tel 01289 386591, fax 01289 386775)

J

JABALÉ, Rt Rev Mark; *see:* Menevia, Bishop of (RC)

JACK, Ian Grant; s of Henry Jack (d 1981), and Isabella, *née* Gillespie (d 2002); *b* 7 February 1945; *Educ* Dunfermline HS; *m* 1, 1979 (m dis 1992), Aparna Bhagat, da of Ganesh Bagchi; *m* 2, 1998, Rosalind Sharpe; 1 da (Isabella b 16 July 1992), 1 s (Alexander b 9 Oct 1993); *Career* trainee journalist 1965–66 (Glasgow Herald, Cambuslang Advertiser and East Kilbride News), Scottish Daily Express 1966–70; Sunday Times London 1970–86: chief sub-ed, ed Look pages and Atticus column, feature writer/foreign corr (newspaper and magazine) 1979–86; writer under contract Observer London and Vanity Fair NY 1986–89; Independent on Sunday: dep ed 1989–91, exec ed 1991–92, ed 1992–95; ed Granta magazine 1995–2007 (former contrib); also contrib to: New Statesman, Spectator, TLS and London Review of Books; *Awards* Journalist of the Year 1985, Magazine Writer of the Year 1985, Reporter of the Year 1988, Nat Newspaper Ed of the Year 1992; *Books* Before The Oil Ran Out (1987), The Crash That Stopped Britain (2001); *Recreations* reading, music, steam navigation, Indian history; *Clubs* India International Centre (New Delhi); *Style*— Ian Jack, Esq

JACK, Janet Marie; da of Albert Frederick Kaye (d 1951), and Ida, *née* Hancock (d 1951); *b* 5 June 1934; *Educ* Architectural Assoc Sch of Architecture (AADipl, GradDiplCons(AA)); *m* 8 Feb 1963, William Jack, s of Col Frank Weaver Jack, TD (d 1984); 1 s (Angus b 1963 d 1990), 1 da (Amy b 1965); *Career* architect; Architects Co-Partnership 1957–58, Harry Weesse Assocs Chicago 1958–59, IM PEI NY 1960, Planning and Devpt Ltd 1960–63, Dame Sylvia Crowe 1965–66, own landscape practice 1967–81; Building Design Partnership: joined 1981, ptnr 1986, sr ptnr 1988; own landscape practice 1991–; Landscape Inst: publicity offr 1984–88, memb External Affrs Ctee 1984–; memb Landscape Advsy Ctee on Trunk Roads Dept of Tport 1987–94; RIBA 1961, FRSA 1987, FLI 1994 (ALI 1973); *Books* The Design of Atria (contrib, 1983), The Design of Shopping Centres (contrib, 1989); *Recreations* art, architecture, the environment, organic gardening; *Style*— Mrs Janet Jack

JACK, Prof (James) Julian Bennett; *b* 25 March 1936; *Educ* Hamilton HS, Univ of Otago (MMedSc, PhD), Univ of Oxford (Rhodes scholar, BM, BCh); *Career* house offr Radcliffe Infirmary 1963–64; Univ of Oxford: fell, demonstrator, univ lectr, reader, prof 1968–; Physiological Soc: memb ctee 1982–90 and 1998–2002 (treas 1986–90); memb cncl Action Research 1988–91; Wellcome Tst: govr 1987–, dep chm 1994–99; Hon DSc Univ of Otago 1999; FRS 1997, FMedSci 1998, FRCP 1999, Hon MRCP 1994; FRSNZ (Hon) 1999; *Style*— Prof Julian Jack, FRS; ⊠ University Laboratory of Physiology, Parks Road, Oxford OX1 3PT (tel 01865 272537, e-mail julian.jack@physiol.ox.ac.uk)

JACK, Rt Hon (John) Michael; PC (1997), MP; s of Ralph Niven, of York, and Florence Edith, *née* Reed; mother's family Hewish of Devon said to have arrived with William the Conqueror; *b* 17 September 1946; *Educ* Bradford GS, Bradford Tech Coll, Univ of Leicester (BA, MPhil); *m* 1976, Alison Jane, da of Cncllr Brian Rhodes Musgrave; 2 s (Edmund b 1979, Oliver b 1981); *Career* formerly with Marks & Spencer and Procter & Gamble, sales dir L O Jeffs Ltd 1980–87; Parly candidate Newcastle Central Feb 1974, MP (Cons) Fylde 1987–; PPS to Rt Hon John Gummer as min of state for local govt then for agric fisheries and food 1988–90, Parly under sec Dept of Social Security 1990–92, min of state Home Office 1992–93, min of state MAFF 1993–95, fin sec to the Treasy 1995–97, shadow min MAFF 1997–98; currently chm: House of Commons Select Ctee for Environment Food and Rural Affrs (formerly Select Ctee on Agriculture) until 2005, Tax Law re-write Steering Ctee, 1922 Ctee 2000–03; jt sec Cons Tport Ctee 1987–88, chm Cons NW Membs Gp (sec 1988–90), vice-pres Think Green 1989–90; *Recreations* motor sport, dinghy sailing, growing vegetables, running, playing Boules; *Style*— The Rt Hon Michael Jack, MP; ⊠ House of Commons, London SW1A 0AA (tel 020 7219 3000, website www.michaeljackmp.org.uk)

JACK, Hon Mr Justice; Sir Raymond Evan Jack; kt (2001); s of late Evan Stuart Maclean Jack (d 1992), and Charlotte, *née* Fry (d 1993); bro of Roland Maclean Jack; *b* 13 November 1942; *Educ* Rugby, Trinity Coll Cambridge (MA); *m* 1 Oct 1976, Elizabeth Alison (Liza), da of Canon James Seymour Denys Mansel, KCVO (d 1995); 2 da (Katherine b 1979, Lucy b 1981), 1 s (Alexander b 1986); *Career* called to the Bar Inner Temple 1966; in practice in commercial work; QC 1982, recorder of the Crown Court 1989–91, circuit judge (Western Circuit) 1991–2001, liaison judge to Dorset magistrates 1991–94, first mercantile judge Bristol 1994–2001, judge of the High Court of Justice (Queen's Bench Div) 2001–; *Publications* Documentary Credits (1991, 3 edn 2001); *Style*— The Hon Mr Justice Jack; ⊠ c/o The Royal Courts of Justice, Strand, London WC2A 2LL

JACK, Prof Ronald Dyce Sadler; s of Muirice Jack (d 1982), of Ayr, and Edith Emily Sadler (d 1984); *b* 3 April 1941; *Educ* Ayr Acad, Univ of Glasgow (MA, DLitt), Univ of Edinburgh (PhD); *m* (Christabel) Kirsty Margaret, da of Rev Maj Angus Macdonald Nicolson, TD (d 1975), of Ayr; 2 da (Fiona b 1968, Isla b 1972); *Career* Dept of English Lit Univ of Edinburgh: lectr 1965, reader 1978, assoc dean 1971–73, prof of Scot and medieval lit 1987–2004, prof emeritus 2004–; visiting prof: Univ of Virginia 1973–74, Univ of Strathclyde 1993; Beinecke research fell Yale Univ 1992, visiting distinguished prof Univ of Connecticut 1998; memb Scot Consultative Ctee on the Curriculum 1987–89, dir UCAS (formerly UCCA) 1989–94; govr Newbattle Abbey Coll 1984–88; co-dir Bibliography of Scottish Literature in Translation; fell English Assoc (FEA), FRSE; *Books* The Italian Influence on Scottish Literature (1972), Scottish Prose 1550–1700 (ed, 1978), Choice of Scottish Verse 1560–1660 (ed, 1978), The Art of Robert Burns (co-ed, 1982), Alexander Montgomerie (1985), Scottish Literature's Debt to Italy (1986), Patterns of Divine Comedy (1989), The Road to the Never Land (1991), William Dunbar (1996), The Mercat Anthology of Early Scottish Literature (sr ed, 1997, revised edn 2000), New Oxford Dictionary of National Biography (assoc ed, 2004), Scotland in Europe (co-ed, 2006); *Recreations* golf; *Style*— Prof Ronald Jack; ⊠ 54 Buckstone Road, Edinburgh EH10 6UN (tel 0131 445 3498); Department of English Literature, University of Edinburgh, David Hume Tower, George Square, Edinburgh EH8 9JX (tel 0131 650 3620, fax 0131 650 6898, e-mail r.d.s.jack@ed.ac.uk)

JACK, His Hon Judge Simon Michael; s of Donald Fingland Jack (d 2003), and Hilary, *née* Gresham (d 2000); *b* 29 October 1951, Indore, India; *Educ* Winchester (scholar, head boy), Trinity Coll Cambridge (exhibitioner, BA); *m* (sep), Christine; 2 da (Kirsten Sarah b 8 July 1980, Zoë Alexandra b 5 Jan 1985), 1 s (Caspar Simon b 6 May 1982); partner, Sarah Fearon; *Career* called to the Bar Middle Temple 1974 (Harmsworth exhibitioner); practising barr 1975–2004, recorder 1996–2004 (asst recorder 1992–96), circuit judge

(North Eastern Circuit) 2004–; memb of chambers: 37 Park Square Leeds 1975–82, 38 Park Square (later Pearl Chambers then 9 Woodhouse Square) Leeds 1982–2001, Zenith Chambers Leeds 2001–04; *Recreations* skiing, flying (private pilot), cycling, running, sailing; *Style*— His Hon Judge Jack; ⊠ Kingston upon Hull Combined Court Centre, Lowgate, Hull HU1 2EZ (tel 01482 586161, fax 01482 588527, sjack@lix.co.uk)

JACK, Dr Timothy Michael (Tim); s of Michael Henry Fingland Jack (d 1990), of Teignmouth, Devon, and Margaret Joyce, *née* Baker (d 1978); *b* 5 July 1947; *Educ* King Edward's Sch Birmingham, Guy's Hosp (MB BS); *m* 20 Oct 1979, (Veronica) Jane, da of Richard Christopher Warde (d 1953), of Orpington, Kent; 2 s (Benjamin b 1983, Jonathan b 1986); *Career* anaesthetist Shanta Bhawan Hosp Kathmandu 1974–76, sr registrar Nuffield Dept of Anaesthetics Radcliffe Infirmary Oxford 1978–82, conslt anaesthetist Leeds Gen Infirmary and hon lectr Univ of Leeds 1982–90, conslt in pain relief and clinical dir Oxford Regnl Pain Relief Unit Oxford 1990–; chm Cancer Clinical Centre Oxford Radcliffe Hosp 1995–2001; memb: Exec Ctee Christian Med Fellowship 1987–95, Personnel Ctee Interserve (UK) 1978–98, Cncl The Pain Soc 1993–96; FFARCS 1977; *Recreations* sailing, mountain walking, gardening, bird watching; *Style*— Dr Tim Jack; ⊠ 46 Eaton Road, Appleton, Abingdon, Oxfordshire OX13 5JH (tel 01865 864900, fax 01865 226160)

JACKLIN, Walter William (Bill); s of Harold Jacklin (d 1964), of London, and Alice Mary, *née* Jones (d 1988); *b* 1 January 1943; *Educ* Walthamstow Sch of Art, Royal Coll of Art (MA, ARA); *m* 1, 1979 (m dis 1992), Lesley Sarina, da of Monty Berman; *m* 2, Janet Ann, da of Frank Russo; *Career* artist; teaching at various art colls 1967–75, artist in residence Br Cncl Hong Kong 1993–94; RA 1992; *Solo Exhibitions* Nigel Greenwood Inc London 1970, 1971 and 1975, Hester Van Royen Gallery London 1973 and 1977, Marlborough Fine Art London 1980, 1983, 1988, 1992, 1997, 2000, 2004 and 2008, Marlborough Gallery New York 1985, 1987, 1990, 1997, 1999, 2002, 2003 and 2007, Urban Portraits 1985–99 (retrospective, MOMA Oxford 1992, touring to Santiago Compostela Spain 1992–93), Urban Portraits Hong Kong (British Cncl, Hong Kong Arts Centre) 1995, Marlborough Graphics London 1996, L'Ecole de Londres Musée Maillol Paris 1998–99; included in numerous int gp exhibitions; *Work in Public Collections* Art Gallery of Sydney Aust, Arts Cncl of GB, Br Cncl London, Br Museum, Govt Arts Collection GB, Metropolitan Museum of Art, NY, Tate Gallery, V&A, Yale Center for Br Art; *Books* Monograph on Bill Jacklin (by John Russell-Taylor, 1997); *Recreations* walking, planting trees; *Clubs* Chelsea Arts; *Style*— Bill Jacklin, Esq, RA; ⊠ c/o Marlborough Fine Art, 6 Albermarle Street, London W1 (tel 020 7629 5161)

JACKMAN, Cassandra; MBE (2004); da of Michael Jackman, and Pat Jackman; *Career* squash player; Br jr champion 1989, 1990 and 1991, Euro jr champion 1989 and 1991, World jr champion 1991, Br ladies champion 1992, 1999, 2000, 2002, 2003 and 2004, Gold and Bronze medallist Cwlth Games 1998, women's World champion 1999, Silver and Bronze medallist Cwlth Games 2002, 73 England caps, most successful Br woman player; *Recreations* golf, Norwich City FC, movies, sport; *Clubs* Barnham Broom Country; *Style*— Mrs Cassandra Jackman, MBE

JACKMAN, Frederick Charles; s of Stanley Charles Jackman (d 1978), of Brentwood, Essex, and Lilian May, *née* Brassett (d 1991); *b* 29 February 1944; *Educ* Warren Sch Dagenham, Barking Coll of Technol, Borough Poly (HNC); *m* 14 June 1969, Zarene, da of Karim Gulam Husain (d 1973), of London; *Career* Stinton Jones & Ptnrs 1960–64, Costain Construction 1964–66, T P Bennett & Son 1966–69, Arup Assocs 1969–73, Upton Associates bldg servs consulting engrs 1973– (resident Dubai 1976, sr ptnr 1979–, Malaysia 1991); conslt to Scott Wilson Consulting Engrs 2007–; memb Soc of Light and Lighting (MSLL); CEng, FCIBSE, FIHEEM; *Recreations* travel, walking, fishing; *Style*— Frederick Jackman, Esq; ⊠ New House, Holyport Road, Maidenhead, Berkshire; Upton Associates, Pilot House, West Wycombe Road, High Wycombe, Buckinghamshire HP12 3AB (tel 01494 560740, fax 01494 450998)

JACKOWSKI, Andrzej Aleksander; s of Henryk Soplica Jackowski (d 1978), and Anne Biernaczak; *b* 4 December 1947; *Educ* Holland Park Sch, Camberwell Coll of Art, Falmouth Sch of Art (Dip AD), RCA (MA); *m* 1, 1 May 1970 (m dis 1989), Nicolette Tester; 1 da (Laura b 3 Feb 1972); partner, Eve Ashley; 1 s (Louis b 5 Oct 1990); *Career* artist; lectr 1977–86 (RCA, Byam Shaw Sch of Art Brighton); *Solo Exhibitions* Univ of Surrey 1978–79, Moira Kelly Fine Art 1982, Bluecoat Gallery Liverpool (touring) 1984, Marlborough Fine Art 1986, 1989 and 1990, Gardner Centre Gallery Brighton 1989, Castlefield Gallery Manchester transferred Nottingham Castle Museum 1989; *Group Exhibitions* incl: John Moores Exhbns (Walker Art Gallery Liverpool) 1976, 1980–81 and 1982–83, Narrative Painting (Arnolfini Bristol, travelling) 1979–80, Inner Worlds (Arts Cncl of GB, travelling), Eight in the Eighties (Britain Salutes New York Festival, NY) 1983, Interiors (Anne Berthoud Gallery) 1983–84, New Works on Paper (Br Cncl Travelling Exhibition) 1983–85, House and Abroad (Serpentine) 1984, The Image as Catalyst (Ashmolean Oxford) 1984, Human Interest, Fifty Years of British Art About People (Cornerhouse Manchester) 1985; Introducing with Pleasure: Star Choices from the Arts Cncl Collection (travelling exhibition, Gardner Centre Brighton) 1987; An Anthology: Artists who studied with Peter de Francia (Camden Arts Centre 1987; Cries and Whispers: New Works for the Br Cncl Collection (travelling exhibition Aust and NZ) 1988; 150 Anniversary Exhibition, Exhibition Road Painters at the RCA (RCA) 1988; Object and Image: Aspects of British Art in the 1980s (City Museum and Art Gallery, Stoke on Trent) 1988; The New British Painting (The Contemporary Arts Centre Cincinnati, travelling exhibition) 1988, The Tree of Life (South Bank Centre travelling exhibition Cornerhouse Gallery Manchester) 1989, School of London Words on Paper (Odette Gilbert Gallery) 1989, Now for the Future (South Bank Centre) 1990, Picturing People (Br Cncl travelling exhibition, Nat Art Gallery Kuala Lumpur, Hong Kong Museum of Art, The Empress Palace Singapore) 1990, On View (Marlborough) 1990, Tribute to Peter Fuller (Beaux Arts Bath) 1990; *Public Collections* incl: Arts Cncl of GB, Br Cncl, Contemporary Arts Soc, Euro Parl, RCA, SE Arts, Univ of Liverpool, Univ of Surrey; SE Arts fell Univ of Surrey 1978–79, Tolly Cobbold/Eastern Arts Major prize 1981; *Style*— Andrzej Jackowski, Esq; ⊠ c/o Purdy Hicks Gallery, 65 Hopton Street, London SE1 9GZ (tel 020 7237 6062)

JACKSON, Alan Francis; *b* 25 April 1935; *Educ* Westminster; *m* Jean Elizabeth; 1 da (Kate); *Career* J H Minet & Co Ltd 1955–58, worked in Canada 1958–62, underwriter Robert Bradford Ltd 1962–78, Alan Jackson Underwriting Agencies Ltd 1979–92 (merged with Wren Underwriting Agencies Ltd 1986); chm: Wren Syndicates Management Ltd, Wren

Holdings Ltd 1994, Wren Holdings Group plc 1995; non-exec dir Wren plc 1998–99, ret; sr dep chm Cncl of Lloyd's 1991; Freeman Worshipful Co of Goldsmiths; fell Ins Inst of Canada (FIIC), ACII; *Recreations* golf; *Style*— Alan Jackson, Esq

JACKSON, Alison Mary; da of George Hulbert Mowbray Jackson, and Catherine Mary, *née* Harvey Kelly; *b* 15 May 1960; *Educ* Chelsea Coll of Art, RCA; *Career* artist, photographer, film maker; *Exhibitions* incl: Richard Salmon Gallery London 1999, 2000 and 2003, Art London 2000, Jerwood Space London 2001, La Musée de la Photographie à Charleroi Brussels 2002, Paris Photo (Louvre Paris) 2002–05, Le Musée de la Photo Montreal 2003, Int Center of Photography (ICP) NY 2003, Photo London Pro-Gram Gallery 2004, Hayward Gallery London 2004, Julie Saul Gallery NY 2005, Kundst Forum Vienna 2005–06; *Television* DoubleTake (BBC2) 2001–03, Saturday Night Live USA 2004–05, The Royal Wedding (Channel 4) 2005, The Secret Election 2005, Tony Blair Rock Star 2005, Sven - The Coach, the Cash and his Lovers 2006, Blair: I'm a Straight Sorta Guy (Channel 4) 2007; *Advertising* Schweppes Campaign 2001–03; *Awards* Photographers' Gallery Award 1999, BAFTA Award for Innovation (for DoubleTake) 2002; for Schweppes: Creative Circle Award 2002, Campaign Awards 2002, Best of the Best Award IPA 2002 and 2003, Int Center of Photography Infinity Award 2004; *Publications* Private-Photographs (2003); *Recreations* tennis; *Style*— Alison Jackson; ✉ c/o Paul Stevens, ICM, 76 Oxford Street, London W1D 1BS (tel 020 7636 6565); c/o Kevin Cooper, CAA, 2000 Avenue of the Stars, Los Angeles, CA 90212, USA (tel 001 424 2884545)

JACKSON, Alison Muriel; *b* 24 September 1947; *Educ* St Anne's Coll Oxford (MA); *m*, 1 s; *Career* tutor and cnsllr Open Univ 1974–84, Civil Serv 1983–, Welsh Office 1986–1999 (local govt fin, private office, urban regeneration, agric), dir Wales Office 1999–; *Style*— Mrs Alison M Jackson; ✉ Wales Office, Gwydyr House, Whitehall, London SW1A 2ER (tel 020 7270 0558, fax 020 7270 0588, e-mail alison.jackson@walesoffice.gsi.gov.uk)

JACKSON, Andrew Graham; s of Thomas Armitage Geoffrey Jackson (d 1985), and Hilda Marion Jackson; *b* 5 May 1937; *Educ* Denstone Coll, Jesus Coll Cambridge (MA); *m* 1964, Christine Margaret, er da of Charles Edward Chapman, of Oundle; 2 da (Sarah Louise (Mrs Edwards) b 4 May 1967, Claire Elizabeth (Mrs Corrie) b 3 Sept 1969), 1 s (Matthew b 27 Dec 1971); *Career* Nat Serv 1955–57, Lt served Suez 1956; Stewarts & Lloyds Corby 1960–67; Denco Holdings Ltd: joined 1967, sales mangr 1967–69, sales dir and dep md 1972–77, gp md 1977–85; dir AMEC Projects Ltd 1985–86, chm and md Keg Services Ltd 1996–2003; pres: Hereford Dist Scouts Assoc, Hereford Sub-Aqua Club; Liveryman: Worshipful Co of Carmen, Worshipful Co of Engrs (Master 2001–02); CEng, FIMechE, FCMI; *Recreations* squash, water skiing, scuba diving; *Clubs* RAC; *Style*— Andrew Jackson, Esq; ✉ 330 Willoughby House, Barbican, London EC2Y 8BL (tel 020 7628 6183, e-mail agj@zenette.freeserve.co.uk); Cami de sa Cirvia enrocada 6, PO Box 28, Sant Lluis, Menorca 07710, Spain (tel 0034 971 359559)

JACKSON, Andrew Malcolm; s of Douglas MacGilchrist Jackson (decd), of Milford on Sea, Hants, and Mabel Pauline, *née* Brand; *b* 4 May 1945; *Educ* Marlborough, Middx Hosp Med Sch Univ of London (MB BS); *m* Anne Marie, da of Joseph Lucas, of Silksworth, Sunderland; 2 s (Charles b 1979, Adam Stuart b 1981); *Career* conslt orthopaedic surgn: UCH 1981–91, Hosp for Sick Children Gt Ormond St 1981–91, Queen Mary's Univ Hosp Roehampton 1991–94, St George's Hosp 1994–2001, King Edward VII Hosp 2000–; hon conslt Royal Nat Orthopaedic Hosp 1983; Freeman City of London 1981, Liveryman Worshipful Soc of Apothecaries; memb RSM, FRCS 1979; *Recreations* sailing, fishing; *Style*— Andrew Jackson, Esq; ✉ 107 Harley Street, London W1G 6AL (tel 020 7935 9521, fax 020 7486 0956)

JACKSON, Ashley Norman; s of Norman Valentine Jackson (POW Malaya, executed 1944/45), and Dulcie Olga, *née* Scott (Mrs Haigh); *b* 22 October 1940; *Educ* St Joseph's Singapore, Holyrood Barnsley, Barnsley Coll of Art; *m* 22 Dec 1962, (Patricia) Anne, da of Donald Hutchinson, of Barnsley, S Yorks; 2 da (Heather b 11 Nov 1968, Claudia b 15 Sept 1970); *Career* artist; exhibited: RI, RBA, RWS, Britain in Watercolour, UA; one man shows: Upper Grosvenor Gallery, Mall Gallery, Christina Foyle Gallery, Spanish Inst of Culture, London, New York, Chicago, San Francisco, Washington, Dallas, one-man exhibition in Huddersfield opened by HRH The Prince of Wales 1987, Huddersfield Art Gallery 1990, My Way - Art to the People (Rotherham Art Gallery) 1994, My Mistress and I - The Yorkshire Moors (touring) 1995, Here's to You, Dad (touring) 1995, From Yorkshire...with Love (touring) 1996, Earth, Wind and Fire (Salford Art Gallery) 1997, Twilight of the Twentieth Century (Cartwright Hall Bradford) 2000, Dawn's a New Day (Royal Armouries Leeds) 2000, Victoria Quarter Leeds 2002, Ashley Jackson's Yorkshire Moors: A Love Affair (Int Yorks Business Convention) 2003; works in the collections of: MOD, RN, NCB, British Gas, NUM, NATO HQ Brussels (original of The Day the World Changed - September 11th 2001) late Harold Wilson, Edward Heath, John Major, Pres Bill Clinton, Rudi Giuliani, George Robertson (Rt Hon Lord Robertson of Port Ellen); own TV series on: Yorkshire TV (A Brush with Ashley 1990, 1992, 1993, 1994, 1995, 1997, 1998, 1999 and 2000, A View with Ashley 1997 and 1998, In A Different Light 2001), BBC1, Channel 4 and PBS in America; supporter of and involved with Children in Crisis (Duchess of York's Charity) and the Woodland Trust; vice-pres Yorkshire Soc; Freeman City of London 2005; FRSA 1964; *Books* My Own Flesh and Blood (1981), The Artist's Notebook (1985), Ashley Jackson's World of Art 1 and 2 (1988), Painting in the Open Air (1992), A Brush With Ashley (1993), Painting the British Isles - a watercolourist's journey (1994), Ashley Jackson's Yorkshire Moors - a love affair (2000), 50 Golden Years with my Mistress and I - Yorkshire (2006); *Style*— Ashley Jackson, Esq; ✉ Ashley Jackson Galleries, 13–15 Huddersfield Road, Holmfirth, Huddersfield HD9 2JR (tel 01484 686460, fax 01484 681766, e-mail ashley@ashley-jackson.co.uk, website www.ashley-jackson.co.uk)

JACKSON, Sir Barry Trevor; kt (2001); s of late Arthur Stanley Jackson, of Chingford, and Violet May, *née* Fry; *b* 7 July 1936; *Educ* Sir George Monoux GS, King's Coll London, Westminster Med Sch (entrance scholar, MB MS); *m* 1962, Sheila May, *née* Wood, of Bollington Cheshire; 2 s (Simon, James), 1 da (Sarah); *Career* Serjeant Surgn to HM The Queen 1991–2001 (Surgn to HM's Household 1983–91); conslt surgn: St Thomas' Hosp 1973–2001, Queen Victoria Hosp East Grinstead 1977–98, King Edward VII Hosp for Offrs 1983–2002; hon conslt surgn to the Army 1990–2006; pres: Assoc of Surgns of GB and Ireland 1994–95 (hon sec 1986–91, vice-pres 1993–94), RCS 1998–2001 (memb Ct of Examiners 1983–89, memb Cncl 1991–2001), RSM 2002–04 (memb Cncl 1987–92, pres Section of Coloproctology 1991–92), Royal Medical Benevolent Fund 2002–, Medical Artists Assoc of GB 2004–, Br Acad Forensic Sciences 2005–07; memb Cncl Assoc of Coloproctology of GB and Ireland 1990–93; ed Annals RCS England 1992–97; memb Ct of Assts Worshipful Co of Barbers (Master 2003–04), Liveryman Worshipful Soc of Apothecaries; Hon DSc Univ of Hull; FRCS, FRCP, FRCS Glas, Hon FRCS Ed, Hon FRCS Ire, Hon FRACS, Hon FDSRCS, Hon FACS, Hon FRCSC, Hon FRSocMed; *Recreations* book collecting, reading, cryptic crosswords, opera, the arts generally; *Clubs* Athenaeum, Garrick; *Style*— Sir Barry Jackson; ✉ 7 St Matthew's Avenue, Surbiton, Surrey KT6 6JJ

JACKSON, Prof Bernard Stuart; s of Leslie Jackson (d 1989), of Liverpool, and Isabelle, *née* Caplan (d 1944); *b* 16 November 1944; *Educ* Liverpool Collegiate Sch, Univ of Liverpool (LLB), Univ of Oxford (DPhil), Univ of Edinburgh (LLD); *m* 1967, Rosalyn, *née* Young; 1 s (Iain Charles b 1970), 1 da (Judith Deborah b 1973); *Career* called to the Bar Gray's Inn 1966; lectr Dept of Civil Law Univ of Edinburgh 1969–76, princ lectr Div of Law Preston Poly 1976, prof of law Liverpool Poly 1980–85 (head Dept of Law 1977–85), prof of law Univ of Kent at Canterbury 1985–89, Queen Victoria prof of law Univ of Liverpool 1989–97, Alliance prof of modern Jewish studies and co-dir Centre for Jewish Studies Univ of Manchester 1997–; sr assoc fell Oxford Centre for Hebrew and Jewish Studies 1984–, pres The Jewish Law Assoc 1984–88 (chm 1980–84), sec-gen and treas Int Assoc for the Semiotics of Law 1987–93, chm BILETA Inquiry into Computer Provision in UK Law Schs 1989–91, pres Br Assoc for Jewish Studies 1993; memb Editorial Bd: Archivos Latinoamericanos de Metodologia y Filosofia, Advsy Bd Center for Semiotic Res in Law Govt and Economics Penn State Univ, Int Jl for the Semiotics of Law, International Jl of the Legal Profession, Zeitschrift für altorientalische und biblische Rechtsgeschichte, Law and Critique, Liverpool Law Review, Legal Ethics, Res Publica, Semiotic Crossroads; ed The Jewish Law Annual 1978–97; memb: Conseil d'administration Association Européenne pour la philosophie du droit 1989–2000, Soc for Old Testament Study 1974–, Br Assoc for Jewish Studies 1974–, Société d'Histoire du Droit 1975–, Soc for the Study of Theology 1976–, Mgmnt Ctee Nat Centre for Cued Speech 1985–89, Mgmnt Ctee UK Law Tech Centre 1989–92, Northern Circuit Ctee on Computer Support for Litigation 1991, Lord Chllr's Area Criminal Justice Advsy Ctee 1992–97, Liverpool Branch Soc for Computers and Law, Academic Advsy Bd Jews' Coll 1996–99; visiting appts: visiting asst prof Univ of Georgia Law Sch 1968–69, assoc fell Oxford Centre for Postgrad Hebrew Studies 1974 (Littman fell 1977), Br Cncl lectr Univ of Rotterdam and Univ of Amsterdam 1975, faculty lectr Faculty of Theology Univ Coll of N Wales 1980, Lady Davis visiting prof Dept of Bible Hebrew Univ of Jerusalem 1981, speaker's lectr in Biblical studies Univ of Oxford 1983–86, professeur invité Université de Paris-X Nanterre 1987–88, professore a contratto Università di Bologna 1988, Caroline and Joseph Gruss visiting prof in Talmudic legal studies Harvard Law Sch 1992, Gastprofessor Rechtstheorie Katholieke Universitet Brussels 1992–93 and 1994–, assoc prof University of Paris I (Panthéon-Sorbonne) 1994, professeur associé Université de Genève 2002; hon fell Soc for Advanced Legal Studies 1997–; DHL (hc) Hebrew Union Coll Jewish Inst of Religion 1998; *Books* Theft in Early Jewish Law (1972), Essays in Jewish and Comparative Legal History (1975), Semiotics and Legal Theory (1985), Law, Fact and Narrative Coherence (1988), Making Sense in Law (1995), Making Sense in Jurisprudence (1996), Studies in the Semiotics of Biblical Law (2000), Wisdom-Laws: A Study of the Mishpatim of Exodus 21:1–22:16 (2006), Essays on Halakhah in the New Testament (2007); ed of numerous legal books and jls; *Style*— Prof Bernard Jackson; ✉ Centre for Jewish Studies, School of Arts, Histories and Cultures, University of Manchester, Humanities (Lime Grove), Oxford Road M13 9PL (tel 0161 275 3607, fax 0161 275 3613, e-mail bernard.jackson@man.ac.uk)

JACKSON, Betty (Mrs David Cohen); CBE (2007, MBE 1987); da of Arthur Jackson (d 1977), and Phyllis Gertrude, *née* Rains (d 1983); *b* 24 June 1949; *Educ* Bacup and Rawtenstall GS, Birmingham Coll Art and Design; *m* 14 Jan 1986, David Cohen, s of Mansour Cohen (d 1977), of Marseille, France; 1 da (Pascale Phyllis b 1985), 1 s (Oliver Mansour b 1986); *Career* chief designer Quorum 1975, fndr Betty Jackson Ltd 1981, launched Betty Jackson for Men 1986; visiting prof RCA 1998; Cotton Designer of the Year 1983, Br Designer of the Year 1985, Fil D'Or award by International Linen 1985 and 1989, Viyella award by Coates Viyella 1987, Contemporary Designer of the Year 1999; tstee V&A 2005; hon fell: Univ of Birmingham 1988, RCA 1989, Univ of Central Lancashire 1992; RDI 1988; *Clubs* Groucho, Bluebird, Soho House; *Style*— Miss Betty Jackson, CBE; ✉ 311 Brompton Road, London SW3 2DY (tel 020 7589 7884, fax 020 7589 5924); Betty Jackson Ltd, 1 Netherwood Place, Netherwood Road, London W14 0BW (tel 020 7602 6023, fax 020 7602 3050, e-mail info@bettyjackson.com, website www.bettyjackson.com)

JACKSON, Bryan Alan; s of Michael Jackson, and Mildred, *née* Segal; *b* 26 February 1956; *Educ* Hutchesons GS, Glasgow Coll of Technol (Scottish HND in Accountancy); *m* 12 Aug 1980, Frances Lauren, da of Ronnie Freedman; 3 da (Leigh Sarah b 28 Jan 1982, Dawn Michele b 24 March 1985, Kara Nicole b 3 Aug 1987); *Career* articled clerk Ernst and Whinney Glasgow 1977–81; Pannell Kerr Forster: insolvency mangr 1981–85, ptnr (insolvency) 1985–94, managing ptnr 1995–, sr ptnr 2006–; lectr ICAS, spokesperson in insolvency to media, speaker on insolvency to professionals, govt agencies, Fraud Squad, Consumer Credit Assoc and debt counselling bodies; appointed on Motherwell, Clyde and Clydebank football clubs 2003–06; examiner in Scotland of the personal insolvency paper for the Jt Insolvency Examinations; treas Children's Aid (Scotland) Ltd; MICAS 1981; memb: Inst of Credit Mgmnt 1989, Insolvency Practitioners' Assoc 1989, Soc of Practitioners of Insolvency 1992; fell Assoc of Business Recoveries Specialists 2000; *Recreations* squash (rep GB Maccabiah Games Israel 1993, rep Scotland (silver medal) Euro Maccabi Games 1995), karate, skiing, football; *Style*— Bryan Jackson, Esq; ✉ PKF, 78 Carlton Place, Glasgow G5 9TH (tel 0141 429 5900, fax 0141 429 5901, mobile 07802 470 478)

JACKSON, Calvin Leigh Raphael; s of late Air Cdre John Arthur George Jackson, CBE, DFC, AFC, and Yolanda, *née* de Felice; *b* 13 August 1952; *Educ* Douai Sch, King's Coll London (LLB, LLM), CCC Cambridge (MPhil); *m* 14 Aug 1993, Caroline Mary, da of late Colin Herbert Clout; *Career* called to the Bar Lincoln's Inn 1975; in practice 1981–83, govt legal serv 1983–85, sr compensation conslt William M Mercer Ltd 1985–87, princ Coopers & Lybrand 1987–92, sr conslt Watson Wyatt Ltd 1992–; memb Hon Soc of Lincoln's Inn; *Clubs* Oxford and Cambridge; *Style*— Calvin Jackson, Esq; ✉ Watson Wyatt Limited, 21 Tothill Street, London SW1H 9LL (tel 020 7222 8033)

JACKSON, Dr Caroline Frances; MEP; *b* 5 November 1946; *Educ* Sch of St Clare Penzance, St Hugh's Coll Oxford (MA), Nuffield Coll Oxford (DPhil); *m* 1975, Robert Victor Jackson (MP for Wantage 1983–2005); 1 s (decd); *Career* res fell St Hugh's Coll 1972, memb Oxford City Cncl 1970–73, Parly candidate (Cons) Birmingham Erdington 1974; MEP (Cons): Wilts 1984–94, Wilts N and Bath 1994–99, SW England 1999–; dep chm Cons MEPs 1997–99, chm European Parl Ctee on Environment, Consumer Protection and Public Health 1999–2004; chm Inst European Environment Policy 2006–; dir Peugeot UK Ltd 1987–99; memb Nat Consumer Cncl 1982–84; *Books* A Student's Guide to Europe (1985 and 1996), Europe's Environment: A Conservative Approach (1989), The End of the Throwaway Society (1998), Playing by the Green Rules (2000), Britain's Waste: The lessons we can learn from Europe (2006); *Recreations* walking, painting, tennis; *Style*— Dr Caroline Jackson, MEP; ✉ ASP 14E 253, European Parliament, 60 rue Wiertz, B-1047 Brussels, Belgium

JACKSON, Charles Vivian; s of Louis Charles Jackson, MC, of E Sussex, and Sylvia, *née* Kerr; *b* 2 July 1953; *Educ* Marlborough, Magdalen Coll Oxford (MA), Stanford Univ (MBA); *m* 12 Feb 1982, Frances Miriam, da of Frederick Schwartzstein (d 1982), of NJ; 1 da (Rebecca b 1983), 1 s (David b 1985); *Career* Charter Consolidated 1974–76, Harkness fell 1976–78, NM Rothschild 1978–81, vice-pres Citibank 1981–85, md Mercury Asset Management Holdings 1987–90, dep chm Warburg Asset Management 1988–95, vice-chm Mercury Asset Management plc 1993–98, md Merrill Lynch Mercury Asset Management 1998–2000; dir: Warburg Investment Management 1985–87, Mercury Bond Fund 1985–98, Munich London 1986–90, Warburg Asset Management 1988–95, Mercury Asset Management plc 1990–98, Mercury Asset Management Group plc 1993–98, Govett European Enhanced Investment Tst 2003–04; sec Projects Ctee Nat Art Collections Fund 1979–84; memb Fin Ctee: Action Med Research 2002– (tstee 2006–), London Library 2003–; *Books* Active Investment Management (2003), Whither Active Management? (2005), Saving Savings: How to Promote Personal Investment (2005); *Clubs* Brooks's, Seaview Yacht; *Style*— Charles Jackson, Esq; ✉ Cottisford House, Brackley, Northamptonshire NN13 5SW (tel 01280 847675)

JACKSON, Christopher Murray; s of Rev Howard Murray Jackson (d 1955), and Doris Bessie Jackson (d 1995); *b* 24 May 1935; *Educ* Kingswood Sch Bath, Magdalen Coll Oxford (MA), Univ of Frankfurt, LSE; *m* 1971, Carlie Elizabeth, da of Bernard Sidney Keeling; 1 s (David), 1 da (Katie); *Career* Nat Serv cmmnd Pilot RAF; former: dir of corp devpt Spillers plc, sr mangr Unilever plc; MEP (Cons) Kent E 1979–94, Hon MEP 1994–; Cons Pty spokesman on: co-operation with developing countries 1981–86, agric 1987–89, foreign affrs and defence 1991, economics and monetary affrs and industrial policy 1992–94; dep chm and dep ldr Cons MEPs 1989–91; memb Cons Nat Union Exec 1995–98; dir: Westminster Communications Ltd 1988–95, Politics International Ltd 1995–98; dir and chm European Broadcasting Network plc 1997–2001, dir CJA Consultants Ltd 1995– (chm 1995–2003), dir and chm Natural Resources International Ltd 1997–2003; chm Cons Countryside Forum 1995–98; govr Ashford Sch 1998–2001, chm of govrs Bethany Sch 1999–; memb RIIA 1995–; *Books* Europe and the Third World (1985), Shaking the Foundations - Britain and the New Europe (1990), Your Watchdogs in Europe (1990), Careers in Europe (2 edn, 1991), The Maastricht Summit (with B Patterson, 1992), Whose Job Is It Anyway? - Subsidiarity in the EC (1992), Developing People (2007); *Recreations* music, gardening, travel, sailing; *Clubs* Athenaeum; *Style*— Christopher Jackson, Esq; ✉ Flackley Ash Farmhouse, Peasmarsh, Rye, East Sussex TN31 6TB (e-mail c.jackson@btinternet.com)

JACKSON, Colin Ray; CBE (2003, OBE, MBE); *b* 18 February 1967; *Career* athlete (110m hurdles); memb Brecon Athletics Club, UK int 1985–2002 (jr int 1984); honours incl: Silver medal Euro Jr Championships 1985, Gold medal World Jr Championships 1986, Silver medal Cwlth Games 1986, Silver medal Euro Cup 1987, Bronze medal World Championships 1987, Silver medal Olympic Games 1988, Silver medal World Cup 1989, Gold medal Euro Cup 1989, 1991 and 1993, Gold medal Cwlth Games 1990 and 1994, Gold medal World Cup 1992, Gold medal (and new world record) World Championships 1993 (Silver medal 4 x 100m relay), Gold medal European Championships 1998, Silver medal World Cup Johannesburg 1998, Gold medal World Championships Seville 1999, Silver medal Cwlth Games Manchester 2002, Gold medal European Championships Munich 2002; honours at 60m hurdles: Silver medal World Indoor Championships 1989 and 1993, Gold medal Euro Indoor Championships 1989 and 1994 (Silver medal 1987), new world record 1994; numerous Welsh, UK, Euro and Cwlth records; *Style*— Colin Jackson, Esq, CBE

JACKSON, David John; *b* 25 January 1953; *Educ* Univ of Bristol (LLB); *Career* articled clerk Grey Lloyd & Co slrs 1975–77, asst slr Barlow Lyde and Gilbert 1977–79, slr The Nestlé Company Ltd 1979–81, asst gp legal advsr Chloride Group plc 1981–87, head of legal Matthew Hall plc 1987–89, gen counsel and co sec PowerGen plc 1989–2002, co sec BP plc 2003–; *Recreations* rugby, tennis, sailing; *Clubs* Royal Ocean Racing, Seaview Yacht, Harlequins FC; *Style*— David Jackson, Esq

JACKSON, Prof Emily; da of Douglas Jackson, of Watford, Herts, and Lesley Jackson (d 1983); *b* 28 December 1966, London; *Educ* Univ of Oxford (MA); *Career* fell and lectr St Catharine's Coll Cambridge 1991–93, lectr Birkbeck Coll London 1993–98, sr lectr LSE 1998–2004, prof of medical law Queen Mary Univ of London 2004–07, prof of law LSE 2007–; memb: Human Fertilisation and Embryology Authy, Medical Ethics Ctee BMA, Ethics Ctee RCPath; *Publications* Regulating Reproduction (2001, Prize for Outstanding Legal Scholarship Soc for Legal Scholars 2002), Medical Law (2006); *Style*— Prof Emily Jackson; ✉ Law Department, London School of Economics, Houghton Street, London NC2A 2AE

JACKSON, Glenda; CBE (1978), MP; *b* 9 May 1936; *Educ* West Kirby Co GS for Girls, RADA; *Career* actress, former memb RSC; MP (Lab) Hampstead and Highgate 1992–; oppn spokesperson on tport 1996–97, Parly under sec of state DETR 1997–99; memb GLA Advsy Cabinet on Homelessness 2000; stood for mayor of London 2000; assoc memb RADA; *Theatre* incl: Marat/Sade 1966 (nominated Tony Award Best Supporting Actress), Rose 1981 (nominated Tony Award Best Actress), Strange Interlude 1985 (nominated Tony Award Best Actress), Macbeth 1988 (nominated Tony Award Best Actress); *Television* incl: Howards End 1970, Elizabeth R 1971, Strange Interlude 1988, A Murder of Quality 1991, The House of Bernarda Alba 1991, The Secret Life of Arnold Bax 1992, A Wave of Passion 1994; *Films* incl: Marat/Sade 1967, Women In Love 1969 (Oscar Best Actress), Mary, Queen of Scots 1971, Sunday Bloody Sunday 1971, A Bequest to the Nation 1973, A Touch of Class 1973 (Oscar Best Actress), Hedda 1975, Nasty Habits 1977, Stevie 1978, Lost and Found 1979, The Return of the Soldier 1982, Salome's Last Dance 1988, The Rainbow 1989; *Style*— Ms Glenda Jackson, CBE, MP; ✉ House of Commons, London SW1A 0AA

JACKSON, Gordon Ackroyd; s of Neville Ackroyd Jackson, of Guildford, Surrey, and Althea, *née* Landon (d 1993); *b* 25 March 1952; *Educ* Reeds Sch Cobham, Univ of Newcastle upon Tyne (Robinson prize, LLB); *m* 1975, Susan Mary, da of George Harry Pattinson, OBE (d 1997); 2 s (Christopher Ackroyd b 17 March 1980, Timothy George b 19 Jan 1982), 1 da (Rebecca Mary b 5 Nov 1985); *Career* slr; articled Bartlett & Gluckstein 1976–78, slr Bartlett & Gluckstein, Crawley & de Reya 1978–81, ptnr Bartletts de Reya 1978–88, ptnr and head of commercial dept Taylor Garrett 1988–89; Taylor Joynson Garrett (now Taylor Wessing): managing ptnr 1989–93, chm Int 1991–97, head Corporate 1997–98, head Technol and Life Sciences 1998–2005, chief operating offr 2002–; memb City of London Slrs' Co 1991; *Recreations* horse riding, gardening, steam boats, yachting, art, photography, walking; *Style*— Gordon Jackson, Esq; ✉ Taylor Wessing, Carmelite, 50 Queen Victoria Embankment, Blackfriars, London EC4Y 0DX (tel 020 7300 7000, fax 020 7300 7100, e-mail g.jackson@taylorwessing.com)

JACKSON, Graeme; s of Lewis Reginald Jackson, and Winifred Ivy Jackson; *b* 13 March 1943; *Educ* Brighton Coll; *m* 1, 22 Nov 1963, Elizabeth (decd); 1 s (Richard Andrew St John b 22 April 1964); m 2, 10 Aug 1972 (m dis 1980), Janet; *Career* jr surveyor Ibbet Moseley Card 1959–61, surveyor Donaldson & Co 1961–64, dir Central of Dist Properties plc 1966–71 (surveyor 1964–66), chm London and Manchester Securities plc 1971–83, chm and chief exec Warringtons plc 1986–91, chief exec BSS Ltd 1991–99, chm and chief exec Hampton Tst plc 1996–; *Recreations* ocean racing, real tennis, opera; *Clubs* RORC, Island SC, Queen's, Royal Berkshire; *Style*— Graeme Jackson, Esq

JACKSON, Helen; da of Stanley Price, and late Katherine Price; *b* 19 May 1939; *Educ* Berkhamsted Sch for Girls, St Hilda's Coll Oxford (MA, CertEd); *m* 1960 (m dis), Keith Jackson, s of Hugh Jackson; 2 s, 1 da; *Career* asst librarian The Queen's Coll Oxford 1960–61, asst teacher City of Stoke-on-Trent 1961–62, voluntary playgroup organiser and occasional researcher Liverpool City Cncl Social Servs 1962–70, teacher Lancs 1972–74, teacher Sheffield 1974–80; cncllr Huyton UDC 1973–74; Sheffield City Cncl: cncllr 1980–91, chm Public Works Ctee 1981–83, chm Employment and Econ Devpt Ctee 1983–91, chm and fndr memb Centre for Local Econ Strategies 1986–91, chm Sheffield Econ Regeneration Ctee 1987–91; MP (Lab) Sheffield Hillsborough 1992–2005; PPS to Mo Mowlam as sec of state for NI 1997, PPS to Peter Mandelson 1999, PPS to Dr John Reid as sec of state for NI 2001–05; memb: Select Ctee on the Environment 1992–97, Select Ctee on Modernisation 1997–2001, Select Ctee on Tport, Local Govt and the Regions 2001–02; chair: All-Pty Parly Water Gp 1992–97, Parly Environment Gp 1992–97, All-Pty Parly Steel Gp 2002–, Parly South Africa Gp; vice-chair All-Pty Parly Africa Gp; PLP: co-chair Women's Ctee 1992–97, vice-chair 1997–2002, memb Parly Ctee 2001–05; memb NEC Lab Pty 1999–2005; UK rep in AWEPA European Parliamentaries for Africa 1998; memb Sheffield Devpt Corp 1986–91; occasional tutor: Yorks Dist WEA, Northern Coll; tstee: Age Concern Sheffield 2005–, Fawcett Soc 2005–, Global Ptnrs 2006–, S Yorks Women's Devpt Tst; vol work on women and pensions Women's Pension Network EOC; *Recreations* walking, music; *Style*— Ms Helen Jackson; ✉ 2 Topside, Grenoside, Sheffield S35 8RD (tel 0114 246 3162, e-mail jacksonh5@btinternet.com)

JACKSON, Jane Therese (Tessa); *b* 5 November 1955; *Educ* Univ of E Anglia (BA), Univ of Manchester (Dip Museum Studies), Univ of Bristol (MA); *Career* museum asst Art Dept Castle Museum Norwich 1977–78, art ed Oxford University Press 1978–80, exhbns organiser Soc for the Protection of Ancient Bldgs London 1981–82, actg curator Eyemouth Museum Berwickshire 1982, curator Collins Gallery Univ of Strathclyde Glasgow 1982–88, seconded as visual arts offr Festivals Office Glasgow City Cncl 1988–91, dir Arnolfini Bristol 1991–99; dir Scottish Arts Cncl 1999–2001, conslt Int Cultural Devpt 2001–, Artistic Dir Artes Mundi Prize 2002–, chair Edinburgh Art Festival; memb Advsy Bd Tate Gallery St Ives Cornwall 1993–99; tstee Forest of Dean Sculpture Tst 1993–; external examiner: BA (Hons) Fine Art Winchester Sch of Art 1997–, BA (Hons) Fine Art Goldsmiths 1999–2001; govr Falmouth Coll of Arts Cornwall 1995–99; FRSA; *Style*— Ms Tessa Jackson; ✉ e-mail tessajackson@aol.com

JACKSON, (Henry) John; s of James William Jackson, and Annie Margaret, *née* Best; *b* 10 September 1937; *m* 17 Aug 1972, Jill Yvonne, da of Albert Horace Ireson, OBE, of Seaford, E Sussex; *Career* served regular army 1955–58; journalist Press Assoc 1952–54, The Scotsman 1954–55, Press Assoc 1958–62, Daily Telegraph 1962–66, Ilford Pictorial 1966–67, educn and Parly corr London Evening News 1967–75, Parly rep Press Assoc 1975–76, freelance 1976–79, Saudi Press Agency 1979–80, publishing dir Municipal Journal 1989–90 (ed 1980, dir 1986–89), ed Public Money 1990–91, ed Insurance Age 1992–98 (publisher and ed 1995–98), ed-in-chief CII Journal (Chartered Insurance Inst) 1998–2001, ed MQ (official pubn of United Grand Lodge of England) 2002–; Br Soc of Magazine Editors Business Editor of the Year 1995; memb Redbridge LBC 1968–74, Parly candidate (Cons) Erith Crayford 1970 and Hornchurch 1974; memb: Cromwell Assoc, Br Horse Soc, Inst of Advanced Motorists; Freeman City of London, Liveryman Worshipful Co of Loriners; *Publications* The Secret War of Hut 3 (ed, 2002), Ultra's Arctic War (2003), The Official History of British Sigint 1914–1945, Vol 1 (ed, 2004); *Recreations* photography, amateur radio; *Clubs* MCC; *Style*— John Jackson, Esq; ✉ Wingfield Farm, Wing, Leighton Buzzard LU7 0LD (tel 01296 688993, e-mail jjack10006@aol.com)

JACKSON, John David; CBE (1993); s of Cecil Jackson (d 1986), and Gwendoline Jackson (d 1976); *b* 7 December 1933; *Educ* Oundle, McGill Univ Montreal (BComm, LA); *m* 11 Dec 1966, Hilary Anne, da of Sir Rudolph Lyons, QC (d 1991), of Leeds; 4 da (Johanna b 1971, Julie b 1974, Jenny, Janie (twins) b 1976); *Career* dir: William Baird plc until 1997, Baird Textile Holdings Ltd until 1997, Mercedes-Benz N Yorks until 2006; chm Whitley Willows Ltd until 2004; vice-chm Br Clothing Industry Assoc until 1998 (chm Yorks and Humberside Region 1990–94), dir British Apparel and Textile Confedn until 1998; High Sheriff Yorks 2003–04; chm Leeds Western HA 1988–91, memb Bd Leeds HA 1991–96; memb Bd Leeds Development Corporation (UDC) 1988–95, dir Leeds City Development Co Ltd until 2003, pres Leeds C of C and Industry 1990–92; *Recreations* tennis, sailing, skiing, golf; *Style*— John D Jackson, Esq, CBE; ✉ Red Oaks, Manor House Lane, Wigton Moor, Leeds LS17 9JD (tel 0113 268 6359)

JACKSON, John Edgar; s of Wilfred Jackson JP (d 1965), of Burnley, and Sarah, *née* Duckworth (d 1956); *b* 11 December 1939; *Educ* Burnley GS, Kansas City CHS; *m* 1, 1963 (m dis 1987), Marilyn Cooper Jackson; 1 da (Rebekah b 1965), 1 s (Jonathan b 1967); m 2, 30 Sept 1988, Kathryn Lesley, da of Roland H Hughes, BEM, of Manchester; *Career* called to the Bar Middle Temple 1970; chm Burnley FC 1981–84 (dir 1976–84); *Recreations* soccer, sailing; *Style*— John E Jackson, Esq

JACKSON, Kenneth A; *Educ* Cannock HS, Birmingham Coll of Commerce; *Career* trained with Cannock Advertiser and Northern Mail, asst news ed The Journal Newcastle on Tyne 1962–64, business desk Express & Star Wolverhampton 1964–66, dep business ed/property ed Birmingham Post 1966–68, PR mangr Reliant Motor Company 1968–70, industrial ed/property ed Birmingham Evening Mail 1970–77; Tarmac plc: divnl mktg advsr Housing Div 1977–80, gp press advsr 1980–83, head of press and public affrs 1983–90 (led Tarmac's successful Channel Tunnel PR and mktg campaign), dir of corp affrs 1990–93; fndr Jackson-Brown & Associates media rels, public rels and corp affrs conslts 1993– (appointed conslt to Govt Inner Cities Initiative, Wolverhampton City Challenge, DOE Award for best City Challenge community newspaper in GB 1994 and 1997); chm Community Forum to Fight Drugs Abuse; audit chair (non-exec) Cannock Chase PCT 1999; chm Chase Voluntary Services; fndr memb: Wolverhampton Business Initiative, Partners in Progress; involved in various charity work; FRSA, FCIPR; *Clubs* Birmingham Press; *Style*— Kenneth A Jackson, Esq; ✉ Sandy Leys Farm, Sandon, Stafford, Staffordshire ST18 0D2 (tel 01889 508552)

JACKSON, Kenneth (Ken); s of Joseph Henry Jackson (d 1965), of Dewsbury, and Ada, *née* Smith (d 1981); *b* 23 September 1939; *Educ* Dewsbury Wheelwright GS, Batley Tech and Art Coll, Harvard Business Sch; *m* 25 Aug 1962, Elisabeth Joyce, da of David William Wilks (d 1975), of Dewsbury; 1 s ((Stephen) David b 8 Feb 1970); *Career* md Spencer & Halstead Ltd 1971 (personnel dir 1968–); vice-pres Bonded Abrasives Europe Carborundum & Co USA 1978, vice-pres (sales and mktg) Abrasives Carborundum Div Sohio 1981, gp md Carborundum Abrasives plc (became Carbo plc 1984), chief exec Carbo plc (formerly The Hopkinsons Gp plc) 1993–2002; non-exec chm: Ring plc 1997–2000, PMGroup plc 2002–; non-exec dir: Nightfreight plc 1996–2000, Kelda Gp plc 2000–05; *Recreations* travel, gardening; *Style*— Ken Jackson, Esq; ✉ Savile Ings Farm, Holywell Green, Halifax, West Yorkshire HX4 9BS (tel 01422 372608, fax 01422 378730, e-mail kenj@leglud.co.uk)

JACKSON, Len; OBE (2002); s of Eric Jackson (d 1981), and Katherine Jackson (d 1951); *b* 17 December 1948, Salford, Lancs; *m* Sept 1981, Angela Bayliss; 1 da (Elizabeth b Jan 1989); partner, Diana; 1 adopted s (Shaun b Oct 1975), 1 adopted da (Samantha b April 1978); *Career* md: Bowyers 1990–94, Pork Farms/Bowyers 1994–99, Amelca plc 2000–02; cmmr Ind Police Complaints Cmmn 2003–; memb Bd E Midlands Regnl Devpt Agency 1999–2001, chair E Midlands Regnl Sports Bd 2002–; chair: Nottingham Common Purpose 1994–98, Race for Opportunity E Midlands 1995–98, New Deal Employer Coalition 1997–98; *Recreations* theatre, sport; *Clubs* Flintham Cricket (chm 2006–); *Style*— Len Jackson, Esq, OBE; ✉ IPCC, Independent House, Whitwick Business Park, Stenson Road, Coalville, Leicestershire LE67 4JP (tel 01530 258751, e-mail len.jackson@ipcc.gsi.gov.uk)

JACKSON, Dr Michael; s of Stanley Jackson, and Maisie Joan Jackson; *b* 12 March 1948; *Educ* St Nicholas GS Northwood, Univ of Salford (BSc); *m* 1, 21 July 1973, Jacqueline Yvonne Doreen, da of Jesse Hudson; 1 s (Robert b 5 May 1976), 1 da (Helen Sara b 17 Oct 1978); m 2, 12 Aug 2001, Lynn Susan Killion, da of Arthur Price; *Career* industrial engr Hawker Siddeley 1970–73, fin controller Citibank NA 1975–76 (expense controller 1973–75), chief of staff Citifin Finanziaria 1976–82, consumer banking dir Citibank Savings 1985–86 (customer servs dir 1982–85), head of EMEA ops Bank of America 1988–90 (head of consumer loans 1986–88), chief exec Birmingham Midshires Building Society 1990–98, chm Results Plus Ltd 1998–2005, md Salans 2003–05, fndr and chm Shaping Tomorrow Ltd 2003–; non-exec dir Galliford Try plc 1997–2004; Hon DBA Univ of Wolverhampton 1997; FMS 1989, FRSA 1991, CIMgt 1993, FCIB 1994, FInstD 1995; *Recreations* model making, music, sport; *Style*— Dr Michael Jackson; ✉ mobile 07966 155912, e-mail mike.jackson@shapingtomorrow.com

JACKSON, Gen Sir Michael David (Mike); GCB (2005, KCB 1998, CB 1996), CBE (1992, MBE 1979), DSO (1999); s of Maj George Michael Jackson (d 1982), of Camberley, Surrey,

J

and Ivy, *née* Bower; *b* 21 March 1944; *Educ* Stamford Sch, RMA Sandhurst, Univ of Birmingham (BSocSc); *m* 2, 4 May 1985, Sarah Carolyn, da of Col Brian Jackson Coombe, GM; 2 s (Mark b 1973, Thomas b 1990), 1 da (Amanda b 1971); *Career* chief of staff Berlin Inf Bde 1977–78, Co Cdr 2 Para 1979–80, directing staff Staff Coll 1981–83, CO 1 Para 1984–86, sr directing staff Jt Serv Def Coll 1986–88, serv fell Wolfson Coll Cambridge 1989, Cdr 39 Inf Bde 1989–92, DG Personal Servs (Army) 1992–93, GOC 3 (UK) Div 1994–96, Cdr Multi-national Div South West (Bosnia) 1996, DG Development and Doctrine 1996–97, Cdr Allied Command Europe Rapid Reaction Corps 1997–2000, Cdr NATO Forces in Macedonia and Kosovo (KFOR) 1999, C-in-C UK Land Command 2000–03, CGS 2003–06; ADC Gen to HM The Queen 2001–06; chm: Benchmark Search Gp Ltd, Silk Route Resources Ltd; chair Defence Advsy Bd PA Consulting Gp 2007–, advsr Numis Securities, advsr Risk Advsy Gp; Hon Dr: Univ of Birmingham, Univ of Sheffield; Freeman City of London 1988; *Books* Central Region vs Out-of-Area: Future Commitments (Tri-Service Press, contrib, 1990); *Recreations* skiing, tennis, music; *Clubs* Garrick, St Moritz Tobogganing; *Style*— Gen Sir Mike Jackson, GCB, CBE, DSO; ✉ c/o RHQ Para Regt, Flagstaff House, Napier Road, Colchester, Essex CO2 7SW

JACKSON, Michael Edward Wilson; s of Sqdn Ldr Edward Grosvenor Jackson, of East Rigton, N Yorks, and Yvonne Brenda Jackson, OBE, *née* Wilson; *b* 16 March 1950; *Educ* The Leys Sch, Univ of Cambridge (LLB); *m* 1, 19 April 1980 (m dis), Prudence Elizabeth Robinson, da of Michael John Boardman, of White Howe, Norfolk; m 2, 18 Nov 1989, Harriet Leigh, da of Air Cdre Denis Wilson; *Career* dir The Guidehouse Group plc 1983–90; chm: Elderstreet Investments Ltd 1990– (also fndr), Sage Group plc 2000–06 (dir 1984–2006), Party Gaming 2005–, Planet Holdings plc, Computer Software Gp plc, Wetstone plc; FCA 1976; *Recreations* tennis; *Clubs* RAC, Annabel's; *Style*— Michael Jackson, Esq; ✉ Elderstreet Investments Ltd, 32 Bedford Row, London WC1R 4HE (tel 020 7831 5088)

JACKSON, Rt Rev Dr Michael Geoffrey St Aubyn; *see:* Clogher, Bishop of

JACKSON, Michael Richard; s of Ernest Jackson, and Margaret, *née* Kearsley; *b* 11 February 1958; *Educ* King's Sch Macclesfield, Poly of Central London (BA); *Career* organiser Channel Four Gp (pressure gp campaigning for independent access to fourth channel) 1979–81, freelance prodr 1981–82, fndr Beat Productions (progs for C4 incl The Media Show, Open the Box and Whose Town Is It Anyway?) 1983–87; BBC Television: joined 1987, ed The Late Show BBC2 1988–90, ed Late Show Productions (incl Naked Hollywood, Moving Picture, The Lime Grove Story) 1990–91, head of music and arts 1991–93, controller BBC2 1993–96, dir of television and controller BBC1 1996–97; chief exec Channel Four Television Corporation 1997–2001, chm Universal Television Gp USA 2002–04, pres of programming IAC/InterActiveCorp 2006–; non-exec dir EMI Gp plc 1999–2002; chm Photographer's Gallery London 2001–02; *Recreations* reading, walking, cinema; *Style*— Michael Jackson, Esq

JACKSON, Sir Nicholas Fane St George; 3 Bt (UK 1913), of Eagle House, Wimbledon, Surrey; s of Sir Hugh Nicholas Jackson, 2 Bt (d 1979), and Violet Marguerite Loftus, *née* St George (d 2001); the 1 Bt, Sir Thomas Graham Jackson, was the architect responsible for many buildings in Oxford incl Examination Schools, Brasenose, Hertford and Trinity Colls; *b* 4 September 1934; *Educ* Radley, Wadham Coll Oxford, Royal Acad of Music; *m* 1, 1961 (m dis 1968), Jennifer Ann, da of F A Squire, of Marylebone St, London; m 2, 1972, Nadia Françoise Genevieve, da of Georges Michard, of St Etienne, France; 1 s (Thomas Graham St George b 1980); *Heir* s, Thomas Jackson; *Career* organist, harpsichordist and composer; organist: St Anne's Soho 1963–68, St James's Piccadilly 1971–74, St Lawrence Jewry 1974–77; organist and master of the choristers St David's Cathedral 1977–84, musical dir and fndr St David's Cathedral Bach Festival 1979–85; concert tours: USA, France, Germany, Spain, Belgium, Croatia; dir Festival Bach at Santes Creus Spain 1987–89; dir Concertante of London 1987–; hon fell Hertford Coll Oxford 1995 (hon patron Music Soc); memb Ct of Assts Worshipful Co of Drapers (Master 1994–95), Liveryman Worshipful Co of Musicians; LRAM, ARCM; *Recordings* own organ works Chartres Cathedral 2000, Bach's Christmas Organ Music 2001, Bach's organ and harpsichord music 2001, own organ music at St Antoine des Quinze Uinets Paris 2004, own choral music Eton 2006, Bach's A Musical Offering 2007; also organ and harpsichord recordings for Decca, RCA, Abbey, Oryx and Priory Records; *Compositions* various (incl one opera) published by Boosey & Hawkes, Cardiff University Press, Anglo-American Publishers and Cathedral Music Chichester; *Publications* Recollections of Sir T G Jackson (edited and arranged, 2003); *Recreations* travel, architecture, sketching; *Style*— Sir Nicholas Jackson, Bt

JACKSON, (Kevin) Paul; s of late T Leslie Jackson, of Ealing, London, and late Jo, *née* Spoonley, of Caersws, Powys; *b* 2 October 1947; *Educ* Gunnersbury GS, Univ of Exeter (BA); *m* 21 Aug 1981, Judith Elizabeth, da of John Charles Cain, DSO, of Cowden, Kent; 2 da (Amy b 1981, Katie b 1984); *Career* formerly stage mangr: Marlowe Theatre Canterbury 1970, Thorndike Theatre Leatherhead 1971; prodr BBC TV 1971–82 (progs incl The Two Ronnies, Three of a Kind, Carrott's Lib, The Young Ones and Happy Families), freelance prodr and dir 1982–84 (progs incl Cannon and Ball and Girls on Top), prodr and chm Paul Jackson Productions 1984–86 (progs incl Red Dwarf, Don't Miss Wax and Saturday Live), md NGTV 1987–91, md Carlton Television Ltd 1993–94 (dir of progs 1991–92), md Carlton UK Productions 1995–96, freelance prodr/dir 1996–97, controller of entertainment BBC 1998–2000 (head of entertainment BBC 1997–98), ceo Granada Productions Aust 2000–02, ceo Granada America 2002–06, dir of entertainment and comedy ITV plc 2006–; memb ITV Broadcast Bd 1993–94; exec prodr Appointments of Dennis Jennings (winner Oscar for Best Live Action Short 1989), BAFTA Awards 1983 and 1984; chm: Comic Relief 1985–98, Charity Projects 1993–98 (vice-chm 1990–92), RTS 1994–96; memb: Bd of Dirs Nat Assoc of Television Prog Execs (NATPE) 2004–06, Bd of Dirs Int Acad of Television Arts and Sciences 2004–, Bd US Comedy Arts Festival Aspen 2004–; patron TimeBank 2000– (chm of tstees 1999–), chm of tstees Pilotlight 1996–2000; Stanford Exec Prog 1993; visiting prof Univ of Exeter 1999, Hon Dr Univ of Exeter 2004; FInstD 1992, FRTS 1993; *Recreations* theatre, rugby, travel, food and wine, friends and family; *Style*— Paul Jackson, Esq; ✉ c/o Capel and Land Ltd, 29 Wardour Street, London W1D 6PS; e-mail paul.jackson@itv.com

JACKSON, Paul Edward; s of George Edward Jackson, of Kington St Michael, Wilts, and Joan, *née* Barry; *b* 8 July 1953; *Educ* Taunton Sch, Watford Sch of Art, Canterbury Coll of Art (BA), Univ of Bradford; *m* 1, 8 May 1982, Jane Frances, da of Frank Haseler; 2 s (James Sims b 2 April 1980, Nicholas Edward Jackson b 16 Feb 1990); m 2, 4 Oct 2000, Elaine Claire, da of Bernard Adams; *Career* account exec Saatchi & Saatchi 1978–80, account exec Mathers 1980–81, account supr Fletcher Shelton Delaney 1981–83, account mangr Publicis 1983–85, bd dir BSB Dorland 1985–92, md Kevin Morley Marketing 1992–95, exec managing ptnr Ammirati Puris Lintas (following merger) 1995–97, client servs dir Citigate Dewe Rogerson (formerly Dewe Rogerson Ltd) 1997–99, chief exec Ogilvy & Mather London 2002–06 (exec mgmnt dir (Ford Europe) 1999–2002), md Int (American Express) Ogilvy Gp 2006–; non-exec dir Aga Foodservice 2006–; MInstD, MIPA, FRSA; *Recreations* sailing, painting, classical music, fly fishing; *Clubs* Little Ship; *Style*— Paul Jackson, Esq; ✉ Ogilvy & Mather, 10 Cabot Square, Canary Wharf, London E14 4QB (tel 020 7345 3066, fax 020 7345 9027)

JACKSON, Peter John; *b* 16 January 1947; *Educ* Univ of Leeds (BA); *m* Anne; 2 s (David b 1977, Andrew b 1983), 1 da (Rosemary b 1980); *Career* sr dir level appts Perkins Engines Gp 1976–87, chief exec British Sugar Group 1989–99 (exec dir 1987–88, dep md 1988–89), chief exec Associated British Foods plc 1999–2005 (dir 1992), non-exec chm Kingfisher plc 2006–; dir C Czarnikow Sugar Ltd 1993–2002, non-exec dir Smiths Gp plc 2003–; *Style*— Peter Jackson, Esq; ✉ Kingfisher plc, 3 Sheldon Square, London W2 6PX

JACKSON, Richard Anthony; s of Harold Reginald Jackson (d 1948), of Harrogate, N Yorks, and Irene Dallas, *née* Nelson (d 1968); *b* 31 March 1932; *Educ* Cheltenham; *Career* theatre producer; Nat Serv RE 1950–52; salesman Henry A Lane & Co Ltd 1953–56, merchandising asst Walt Disney Productions Ltd 1956–59, dir Richard Jackson Personal Management Ltd (actors representation) 1959–96; life memb BAFTA; Officier de l'Ordre des Arts et des Lettres (France) 1993; *Theatre* West End and Fringe incl: Madame de Sade (Kings Head) 1975, Charles Trenet in concert (Royal Albert Hall) 1975, The Bitter Tears of Petra Von Kant (New End) 1976, An Evening with Quentin Crisp (Duke of Yorks and Ambassadors) 1978, The Singular Life of Albert Nobbs, Alterations, Tribute to Lili Lamont (New End) 1978, Flashpoint (New End and Mayfair) 1978, A Day in Hollywood, A Night in The Ukraine (New End and Mayfair, Evening Standard Award for Best Musical and Plays and Players Award for Best Comedy) 1979, The Square, La Musica, Portrait of Dora (New End) 1979, Appearances (Mayfair) 1980, A Galway Girl (Lyric Studio) 1980, Bar and Ger (Lyric Studio) 1981, Latin (Lyric Studio) 1983, The Human Voice (with Susannah York, performed world-wide 1984–92), Swimming Pools at War (Offstage) 1985, Matthew, Mark, Luke and Charlie (Latchmere) 1986, I Ought to be in Pictures (Offstage) 1986, Pier Paola Pasolini (Offstage) 1987, Creditors, Latin (New End) 1989, Beached (Old Red Lion) 1990, Hamlet (Howarth Festival USA) 1990, Eden Cinema (Offstage, Peter Brook Empty Space Award) 1991, Noonbreak (French Inst) 1991, Beardsley (Offstage) 1992, Don't Play With Love (French Inst and Rudolf Steiner House) 1992, Play With Cocaine (New Grove) 1993, The Eagle has Two Heads (Lilian Baylis) 1994, Happy Days (French Institute) 1994, The Star-Spangled Girl (Latchmere) 1994, Suzanna Andler (BAC) 1995, Independent State, The First Years, Beginnings, Last Legs (Latchmere) 1995, This Wretched Splendour (Latchmere) 1998, Zastrozzi, The Master of Discipline (Cockpit) 1999, Onegin (White Bear) 1999, An Evening For Quentin Crisp (Drill Hall) 2000, Marry Me, You Idiot (Jermyn Street) 2002, Susannah York's The Loves of Shakespeare's Women (Jermyn Street) 2003; *Recreations* table tennis, crosswords; *Style*— Richard Jackson, Esq; ✉ 48 William Mews, London SW1X 9HQ (tel and fax 020 7235 3759)

JACKSON, Robert Kenneth; s of John Kenneth Jackson (d 1977), of Kendal, Cumbria, and Laura Theresa, *née* Rankin (d 1976); *b* 26 February 1933; *Educ* Heversham GS, Clare Coll Cambridge (MB BChir, MA), St Thomas' Hosp Med Sch London; *m* 21 June 1967, Margaret Elizabeth, da of Norman Dixon, of Aycliffe, Co Durham; 1 da (Emma Jane b 20 Feb 1968), 1 s (Robert Andrew b 2 April 1970); *Career* Surgn Spec RAF 1960–64; chief asst Orthopaedic Dept St Thomas' Hosp London 1966–71, conslt orthopaedic surgn Southampton Gen Hosp 1971–95; pres Br Scoliosis Soc 1993–94; chm: Med Advsy Ctee Southampton Health Authy 1991–94, Br Scoliosis Research Fndn 1998–2004, Lymington Vol Care Gp 2001–; chm of tstees League of Friends of Lymington Hosps 2002–05; fell Scoliosis Research Soc; FRCS 1964, FBOA; *Books* More Dilemmas in the Management of the Neurological Patient (1987); *Recreations* fishing, orienteering, mountaineering; *Clubs* RAF; *Style*— Robert Jackson, Esq; ✉ Well Cottage, Pilley, Lymington, Hampshire SO41 5QR

JACKSON, (Michael) Rodney; s of John William Jackson (d 1992), of E Yorks, and Nora, *née* Phipps (d 1984); *b* 16 April 1935; *Educ* King Edward VII Sch Sheffield, Queen Elizabeth GS Wakefield, Queens' Coll Cambridge (MA, LLM); *m* 1968, Anne Margaret, da of Prof Eric William Hawkins, CBE, of E Yorks; 2 s (Nicholas b 1969, Richard b 1972); *Career* admitted slr 1962, NP 1967, recorder of the Crown Ct 1985–2001, slr advocate (all Higher Cts) 1996–2005; sr ptnr Andrew M Jackson & Co Slrs 1992–94 (conslt 1994–2001), conslt Sandersons Slrs 2001–05; *Recreations* steam railway visits and rail travel in the UK and EU (particularly France); *Style*— Rodney Jackson, Esq; ✉ 11 The Paddock, Swanland, North Ferriby, East Yorkshire HU14 3QW (tel 01482 633278)

JACKSON, Sir (William) Roland Cedric; 9 Bt (UK 1869), of The Manor House, Birkenhead; s of Sir (William) Thomas Jackson, 8 Bt (d 2004); *b* 9 January 1954; *Educ* Wycliffe Coll, St Peter's Coll Oxford (MA), Exeter Coll Oxford (DPhil); *m* 1977, Nicola Mary, yr da of Prof Peter Reginald Davis, of St Mawes, Cornwall; 3 s (Adam William Roland b 1982, James Anthony Foljambe b 1984, Oliver Thomas Peter b 1990); *Heir* s, Adam Jackson; *Career* head of science Backwell Sch 1986–89, educn advsr ICI 1989–93, head of learning Science Museum 1993–2001 (actg head of museum 2001–02), chief exec BAAS 2002–; *Clubs* Athenaeum, Alpine; *Style*— Sir Roland Jackson, Bt; ✉ The BA, Wellcome Wolfson Building, Queen's Gate, London SW7 5HE (tel 020 7019 4926, e-mail roland.jackson@the-ba.net)

JACKSON, Hon Mr Justice; Sir Rupert Matthew Jackson; kt (1999); s of George Henry Jackson (d 1981), and Nancy Barbara, *née* May (d 1999); *b* 7 March 1948; *Educ* Christ's Hosp, Jesus Coll Cambridge (MA, LLB, pres Cambridge Union); *m* 20 Sept 1975, Claire Corinne, da of Harry Potter (d 1979); 3 da (Corinne b 1981, Chloe b 1983, Tamsin b 1985); *Career* called to the Bar Middle Temple 1972; QC 1987, practising SE Circuit, recorder 1990–98, head of chambers 1994–96, judge of the High Court of Justice (Queen's Bench Div) 1999–, judge i/c Technology and Construction Court 2004–; chm Professional Negligence Bar Assoc 1993–95; *Publications* conslt ed Jackson and Powell on Professional Negligence 2000– (gen ed 1982–99); *Clubs* Reform; *Style*— The Hon Mr Justice Jackson; ✉ Royal Courts of Justice, The Strand, London WC2A 2LL

JACKSON, Prof Stephen Philip (Steve); s of Philip George Jackson, and Marion Margaret, *née* Smith; *b* 17 July 1962; *Educ* Univ of Leeds (F Happold Prize, BSc), Univ of Edinburgh (PhD); *m* 21 Sept 1991, Teresa Margaret, *née* Clarke; 2 s (Alexander Stephen Jackson b 31 July 1997, Daniel Philip Jackson b 3 June 1999); *Career* postdoctoral res fell Univ of Calif 1987–91; Wellcome Tst/Cancer Research UK Gurdon Inst (formerly Wellcome/CRC Inst): gp ldr 1991–95, sr gp ldr 1996–, dep dir 2001–2004, head 2004–; Frederick James Quick prof of biology Dept of Zoology Univ of Cambridge 1996–; chief scientific offr KuDOS Pharmaceuticals Ltd; Biochemical Soc: memb 1993–, memb Cncl 1996–2000, memb Ctee Nucleic Acids and Molecular Biology Gp 1994–2001, 34th Colworth Medal 1997; memb: Cambridge Philosophical Society 1993–, EMBO 1997–, Acad Med Sci 2001; Tenovus Medal Tenovus-Scotland Symposia Ctee Univ of Glasgow 1997; Euro Young Scientist of the Year Eppendorf-Gmbl 1995, Anthony Dipple Carcinogenesis Young Investigator Award 2002; *Publications* author of over 130 primary scientific publications in international research jls, also various review articles and book chapters; *Recreations* my children, gardening, travel; *Style*— Prof Steve Jackson; ✉ Wellcome Trust/Cancer Research UK Gurdon Institute, University of Cambridge, Tennis Court Road, Cambridge CB2 1QN (tel 01223 334102, fax 01223 334089, e-mail s.jackson@gurdon.cam.ac.uk)

JACKSON, Stewart James; MP; s of Raymond Thomas Jackson and Sylvia Alice Theresa Jackson *née* Woodman; *b* 31 January 1965, London; *Educ* Chatham House GS Ramsgate, Royal Holloway Coll London (BA), Thames Valley Univ (MA); *m* 31 July 1999, Sarah O'Grady; 1 da (Isabel Ruby b 3 March 2005); *Career* business and personal banking mangr Lloyds TSB plc 1993–96, branch mangr Lloyds TSB plc 1996–98, HR mangr AZTEC Training and Enterprise Cncl SW London 1998–2000, HR business advsr Business Link for London 2000–05; Parly candidate (Cons): Brent S 1997, Peterborough 2001; MP (Cons) Peterborough 2005–; memb London Borough of Ealing Cncl 1990–98, memb Bd of Tstees London City YMCA 1993–98; memb Chartered Inst of Personnel and Devpt (MCIPD); *Recreations* family, biography, history, keep fit, travel; *Clubs* United & Cecil, Peterborough Cons; *Style*— Stewart Jackson, Esq, MP; ✉ House of Commons,

London SW1A 0AA (tel 020 7219 8286, e-mail jacksonsj@parliament.uk or mail@peterboroughconservatives.com, website www.stewartjackson.org.uk)

JACKSON, District Judge Susan; da of late Ronald Alfred Jackson, and Sheila Jackson; *Educ* Orme Girls' Sch Newcastle-under-Lyme, KCL (LLB), Coll of Law; *Career* admitted slr 1984, ptnr in private practice 1984–91, dir of Legal Servs Royal Borough of Kingston 1991–2001, district judge (Shoreditch County Ct) 2002–; memb: Law Soc, Assoc of District Judges; Rights of Audience Higher Ct 1996; foster carer providing respite care for disabled children; *Recreations* travel, entertaining, media; *Style*— District Judge Jackson; ✉ Shoreditch County Court, 19 Leonard Street, London EC2 4AL (tel 020 7253 0956)

JACKSON, (Francis) Sydney; s of Francis David Jackson, of Liverpool, and Edith Isobel Bold, *née* Butler; *b* 16 September 1926; *Educ* Liverpool Collegiate Sch, Univ of Sheffield (BSc), Univ of London (Dip); *m* Margaret Gillian, da of Sydney Alfred Hood White; 1 s (Nicholas David b 15 May 1962), 1 da (Sally Gillian b 1 April 1964); *Career* served Fleet Air Arm 1943–47; Esso: various tech and mgmnt positions Fawley Refinery 1951–65, supply mangr London 1965–67, marine ops mangr London 1967–74, transportation advsr Exxon Corp NY 1974–76, refinery mangr Milford Haven Refinery 1976–84, transportation mangr Esso Petroleum 1984–87; refinery mangr Rabigh Saudi Arabia 1990–91; chm: City Homes (UK) Ltd 1987–90, E Dorset Health Authy 1987–90, Royal Bournemouth and Christchurch Hosps NHS Trust 1991–95, ret; MInstD, FInstPet; *Recreations* gardening, walking, running church and village activities; *Clubs* Beaulieu River Sailing, Royal Southampton Yacht; *Style*— Sydney Jackson, Esq; ✉ Puffins, Bucklers Hard, Beaulieu, Hampshire SO42 7XD (tel 01590 616304)

JACOB, Nicholas Allen Swinton; s of Cdr John Jacob, and Rosemary Elizabeth Allen, *née* Shuter; *b* 25 June 1954; *Educ* Sherborne, Univ of Nottingham (BA, BArch); *m* 1979, Frederike Mathilde Maria Wilhelma, da of Theodorus Doreleijers; 1 s (Ian b 12 March 1983), 1 da (Philippa b 4 June 1985); *Career* Suffolk Co Architects' Dept 1979–81, joined Peter Cleverly (architect in Wetheringsett, Suffolk) 1981–84, ptnr Cleverly & Jacob Architects Stowmarket, ptnr Purcell Miller Tritton & Partners (following merger) 1985–96, established Nicholas Jacob Architects Ipswich 1996–; exec memb Ipswich Building Preservation Tst 1984–, memb Ipswich Conservation Advsy Panel 1986–; dir: Suffolk Building Preservation Tst 1990–, Suffolk Architectural Heritage Tst 1997–; RIBA 1980 (chm Eastern Region Conservation Gp 1998–99); *Recreations* choir of St Margaret's Church (Ipswich), walking, skiing, golf, sketching, painting; *Clubs* Rotary (Ipswich Wolsey); *Style*— Nicholas Jacob, Esq; ✉ Nicholas Jacob Architects, 89 Berners Street, Ipswich, Suffolk IP1 3LN (tel 01473 221150, fax 01473 255550, e-mail nicholas.jacob@njarchitects.co.uk)

JACOB, Prof (John) Peter; s of William Thomas Jacob (d 1960), and Doris Olwen, *née* Llewellyn (d 1991); *b* 13 May 1942; *Educ* Sir William Borlase's Sch, Univ of Durham (BA), Univ of Newcastle upon Tyne (BArch); *m* 21 July 1982, Lesley Diana, da of Alfred Charles Thomas James (d 1998); 1 da (Katharine b 1985); *Career* principal Peter Jacob Associates Architects 1967–; Kingston Univ (formerly Kingston Poly) Sch of Architecture and Landscape: princ lectr 1972–83, dep head 1983–87, head of sch 1987–2002, prof 1993–; chm Kingston Chapter RIBA 1980–82, memb Cncl RIBA 1983–89, memb Bd Architectural Educn Architect's Registration Cncl 1987–97, memb RIBA/ARB Joint Validation Panel 1995–2002, chm RIBA Publications Ltd 1989–94, dir RIBA Companies Ltd 1990–93, chm RIBA Educn Tst Funds Ctee 2003–; RIBA 1967, FRSA 1988; *Recreations* reading, swimming, motoring; *Style*— Prof Peter Jacob; ✉ Crackstone Mill House, Crackstone, Minchinhampton, Gloucestershire GL6 9BD (tel 01453 889684, fax 01453 889685, e-mail peterjacob@pjassociates.fslife.co.uk)

JACOB, Rt Hon Lord Justice; Rt Hon Sir Robert Raphael Hayim (Robin); kt (1993), PC (2004); s of Sir Jack I H Jacob, of London, and Rose Mary, *née* Samwell; *b* 26 April 1941; *Educ* Mountgrace Comp Sch, St Paul's, Trinity Coll Cambridge, (MA), LSE (LLB); *m* 1967, Wendy, da of Leslie Huw Thomas Jones; 3 s (Sam b 1970, Matthew b 1972, Oliver b 1975); *Career* called to the Bar Gray's Inn 1965 (bencher 1989, treas 2007); jr counsel to Treasury in patent matters 1976–81, QC 1981, QC (NSW) 1989, judge of the High Court of Justice (Chancery Div) 1993–2003, Chancery supervising judge Birmingham, Bristol and Cardiff 1997–2001, judge in charge of the Patents List 1994–97 and 2002–03, a Lord Justice of Appeal 2003–; dep chm Copyright Tbnl 1989–93, appointed to hear Trade Mark Appeals to Bd of Trade 1989–93; hon pres Assoc of Law Teachers 1999–; govr: LSE 1996–, Expert Witness Inst 1996–2006; hon fell St Peter's Coll Oxford 1998, hon prof Univ of Birmingham 1999–, distinguished judicial visitor UCL 2002–, hon fell LSE 2005; *Style*— The Rt Hon Lord Justice Jacob; ✉ Royal Courts of Justice, Strand, London WC2A 2LL (tel 020 7947 6771, e-mail lordjustice.jacob@judiciary.gsi.gov.uk)

JACOB, Ven Dr William Mungo; s of John William Carey Jacob (d 1982), of Ringstead, Norfolk, and Mary Marsters, *née* Dewar (d 1959); *b* 15 November 1944; *Educ* King Edward VII Sch King's Lynn, Univ of Hull (LLB), Linacre Coll Oxford (MA), Univ of Edinburgh (Dip), Univ of Exeter (PhD); *Career* asst curate Wymondham 1970–73, asst chaplain Univ of Exeter 1973–75, dir of pastoral studies Salisbury and Wells Theol Coll 1975–80 (vice-princ 1977–80), sec Ctee for Theol Educn Advsy Cncl for Church's Miny 1980–86, warden Lincoln Theol Coll and prebendary of Gretton in Lincoln Cathedral 1986–96, archdeacon of Charing Cross 1996–, rector St Giles-in-the-Fields 2000–; *Style*— The Ven the Archdeacon of Charing Cross; ✉ 15A Gower Street, London WC1E 6HG (tel 020 7323 1992)

JACOBI, Sir Derek George; kt (1994), CBE (1985); *b* 22 October 1938; *Career* actor; artistic dir Chichester Festival Theatre 1995–; narrator of The Iliad (talking book) 1993; *Theatre* RSC: Benedick in Much Ado About Nothing (tour to NY and Washington, Tony Award), title role in Peer Gynt, Prospero in The Tempest, title role in Cyrano De Bergerac (tour to NY and Washington), Macbeth 1993; Old Vic: title role in Hamlet (tour), Thomas in The Lady's Not for Burning, title role in Ivanov; Haymarket Theatre: Breaking The Code 1987, To Know, title role in Becket (UK tour); Octavius in Antony and Cleopatra (Cambridge Theatre Co), Apimantus in Timon of Athens (New Shakespeare Co), Charles Dyer in Staircase (Oxford Playhouse), Byron in The Lunatic, The Lover and The Poet (Lyric Hammersmith), Semyon in The Suicide (Anta Theatre NY), Breaking The Code (Neil Simon Theatre, nominated for Tony Award) 1987–88, Richard II/Richard III (Phoenix Theatre) 1988–89, Narrator in The Wedding Bouquet (Royal Opera House), title role in Kean (Old Vic Toronto), Frederick William Rolfe in Hadrian VII (Chichester Festival Theatre) 1995; *Television* BBC: Man of Straw, The Pallisers, title role in I Claudius, Richard II, Hamlet, The Vision Thing, Breaking the Code (nominated for Best Actor Br Academy TV Awards 1998); other credits incl: Skin (Anglia), The Stranger Left No Card (Anglia), Philby, Burgess and MacLean (Granada), Budgie (LWT), The Strauss Family (ATV), My Pye (Channel 4), In My Defence (Oyster TV), Wolves Are Howling (Yorkshire), Cadfael (Central), Jason and the Argonauts, The Gathering Storm, Inquisition, Mr Ambassador; *Films* incl: The Day of the Jackal, Blue Blood, The Odessa File, The Medusa Touch, The Human Factor, Charlotte, The Man Who Went Out In Smoke, The Hunchback of Notre Dame, Inside The Third Reich, Little Dorrit, The Tenth Man, Henry V, The Fool, Dead Again, Hamlet, Love is the Devil (Best Actor Evening Standard British Film Awards), Gladiator, Gosford Park, Two Men Who Went to War, Revengers Tragedy, Cloud Cuckoo Land; *Style*— Sir Derek Jacobi, CBE; ✉ c/o ICM Ltd, Oxford House, 76 Oxford Street, London W1D 1BS (tel 020 7636 6565, fax 020 7323 0101)

JACOBI, Hon Mary Jo; da of Lawrence John Jacobi (d 1999), and Delta M Jacobi (d 1993); *b* 7 December 1951, Bay St Louis, Mississippi; *Educ* Loyola Univ of New Orleans (BBA), George Washington Univ (MBA); *m* 31 Dec 2004, Patrick Jephson, LVO (former private sec to Diana, Princess of Wales); *Career* administrator US Senate Commerce Ctee 1973–76, public affrs Nat Assoc of Manufacturers 1977–79, public affrs 3M 1979–81, dir of business liaison US Dept of Commerce 1981–83, special asst to Pres Ronald Reagan 1983–85 (memb Advsy Ctee on Trade Negotiations 1986–90), public affrs Drexel Burnham Lambert 1985–90 (latterly exec dir), vice-pres gp public affrs USA Marine Midland Bank 1990–92, asst sec of commerce to Pres George Bush 1992–93; head of public affrs and advsr to the bd HSBC Hldgs 1993–2000, md Lehman Bros 2000–01, vice-pres Royal Dutch Shell 2001–05; currently memb Advsy Bd Pittacus; non-exec dir Tate & Lyle plc 1999–2004; UK Civil Serv cmmr 2005–, memb Wilton Park Advsy Cncl FCO, US-UK Fulbright cmmr; memb Advsy Bd: Center for Global Philanthropy Hudson Inst, Assoc of MBAs, Business Sch Univ of Oxford, Business Sch George Washington Univ; visiting fell Univ of Leeds Business Sch, lectr Moscow Sch of Political Studies; tstee: Sir Heinz Koeppler Tst, Educnl Tst for Russia; former memb Cncl: Congressional Mgmnt Fndn, Center for the Study of the Presidency, Industry and Parl Tst (also fell), Technol Colls Tst; non-exec dir American Cncl on Germany; non-exec dir Ladies European Golf Tour 1987–89, chair Ladies Professional Golf Assoc 1989–97; Good Housekeeping's 100 Young Women of Promise 1985, memb NY Acad of Women Achievers 1988; memb: Int Women's Forum UK and NY, Guild of Int Bankers, Guild of PR Practitioners, memb Worshipful Co of Fuellers; FRSA, MInstD, MRI; *Publications* America's New Women Entrepreneurs (contrib, 1986), Working with Americans (foreword, 2002); *Recreations* opera, golf; *Clubs* Reform, NY Economic; *Style*— The Honorable Mary Jo Jacobi; ✉ Pittacus, 83 Victoria Street, London SW1H 0HW (tel 020 3170 7180, e-mail mjjacobi@hotmail.com)

JACOBS, Brian David Lewis; s of John Barry Lewis Jacobs, of Chobham, Surrey, and Elizabeth, *née* Mendes; *b* 14 December 1949; *Educ* Charterhouse; *m* 26 Nov 1983, Rosalind Mary, da of late Leslie Jory; 2 da (Katherine Alice (Katie) b 3 Sept 1985, Emily Rose b 13 Dec 1988); *Career* messenger rising to research asst Horniblow Cox-Freeman 1968–71, media and market research exec Southern TV 1971–74, market research exec Access 1974, media research mangr Davidson Pearce 1974–80; Leo Burnett Advertising: assoc media dir 1980, media dir 1985, exec media dir 1986, international media dir 1990–95; media devpt dir Aegis Group plc 1995–96, md Carat International 1996–2001, regnl dir EMEA and head of worldwide accounts Universal McCann 2001–03, exec vice-pres Global Media Practice Millward Brown 2003–06, dir Brian Jacobs & Assocs 2006–; memb CAM, FIPA 1982; *Books* Spending Advertising Money (with Dr Simon Broadbent, 1984); *Recreations* golf, family, reading, the media, travel, theatre; *Clubs* Sunningdale Golf, The Hospital; *Style*— Brian Jacobs, Esq; ✉ 4 Holroyd Road, London SW15 6LN (tel 020 8785 1637)

JACOBS, Baron (Life Peer UK 1997), of Belgravia in the City of Westminster; Sir David Anthony Jacobs; kt (1998); s of Ridley and Ella Jacobs; *Educ* Clifton, Univ of London (BCom); *m* 1954, Evelyn Felicity Patchett; 1s, 1 da; *Career* chm: Nig Securities Gp 1957–72, Tricoville Gp 1961–90 and 1992–94, Br Sch of Motoring 1973–90; Parly candidate (Lib) Watford Feb and Oct 1974; jt treas Lib Pty 1984–87, vice-pres and fed exec Socialist and Lib Dem Pty 1988; FCA; *Recreations* golf, reading, theatre, opera, travel; *Clubs* Coombe Hill Golf, Palm Beach Country; *Style*— The Rt Hon the Lord Jacobs; ✉ 9 Nottingham Terrace, London NW1 4QB (tel 020 7486 6323)

JACOBS, David Lewis; CBE (1996), DL (Greater London 1983); s of late David Jacobs and late Jeanette Victoria, *née* Goldsmid; *b* 19 May 1926; *Educ* Belmont Coll, Strand Sch; *m* 1, 15 Sept 1949 (m dis 1972), Patricia Bradlaw; m 2, 1975, Caroline Munro (d 1975); m 3, 1979, Mrs Lindsay Stuart Hutcheson; 1 s (Jeremy (decd)), 3 da (Carol, Joanna, Emma), 1 step s (Guy); *Career* radio and television broadcaster; RN 1944–47; first broadcast Navy Mixture 1944, announcer Forces Broadcasting 1944–45, chief announcer Radio SEAC Ceylon 1945–47 (asst station dir 1947), newsreader BBC Gen Overseas Serv 1947, sometime commentator British Movietone News, freelance 1947–; numerous film appearances; dir: Duke of York's Theatre 1979–85, Man in the Moon UK Ltd 1986–, Video Travel Guides 1988–91; chm: Kingston FM 1995–96, Thames FM Radio 1996, Thames Radio 1997; chm Kingston Theatre Tst 1990–, formerly vice-chm RSPCA, chm Think Br Campaign 1985 (dep chm 1983–85), pres Kingston Branch Royal Br Legion, Kingston Alcohol Advsy Service, Wimbledon Girls Choir, SSAFFA & Forces Help Soc (SW London); vice-pres: Stars Orgn for Spastics (formerly chm), Royal Star and Garter Home Richmond, BA Cabin Staff Entertainment Soc, Soc of Stars; 6 Royal Command Performances; rep DL Royal Borough of Kingston upon Thames 1984–2001; High Steward of Kingston upon Thames 2001–; Hon Dr Kingston Univ 1994; *Radio* incl: Housewives' Choice, Journey into Space, BBC Jazz Club, Pick of the Pops, Any Questions?, Any Answers?, Melodies for You, The David Jacobs Show, Easy Does It, Soundeasy; *Television* incl: Make Up Your Mind, Tell The Truth, Juke Box Jury, Top of the Pops, David Jacobs Words and Music, Sunday Night With David Jacobs, Little Women, Where Are They Now?, What's My Line?, Miss World, Eurovision Song Contest, Come Dancing, Questions, Primetime, Countdown; *Awards* top disc jockey BBC and Radio Luxembourg 1947–53, TV Personality of the Year Variety Club of GB 1960, Personality of the Year BBC Radio 1975, Sony Gold Award 1984 (later admitted to Hall of Fame), Richard Martin Award RSPCA 1978, admitted to Radio Acad Hall of Fame 2005; *Books* Jacobs Ladder (1963), Caroline (1978), Any Questions? (with Michael Bowen, 1981); *Recreations* talking and listening, hotels; *Clubs* Chelsea Arts, Garrick, St James's; *Style*— David Jacobs, Esq, CBE, DL; ✉ Wyncombe Hill Cottage, The Fleet, Fittleworth, West Sussex RH20 1HN (tel 01798 865243)

JACOBS, Prof Howard Saul; s of Flt Lt Joseph Jacobs (d 2004), of London, and Florence Jacobs (d 1950); *b* 9 June 1938; *Educ* Malvern, Gonville & Caius Coll Cambridge (BA), Middx Hosp Med Sch (MB BChir), Univ of London (MD); *m* 15 July 1962, Sandra Rose, da of Mark Garelick; 3 da (Caroline, Susanna, Amber); *Career* asst prof UCLA 1969–74, sr lectr St Mary's Hosp Med Sch 1974–81, prof UCL and Middx Sch of Med 1983–98 (reader in gynaecological endocrinology 1981–83, emeritus prof 1998–), civilian conslt endocrinology RAF 1985–98; memb Ctee on Safety of Meds 1983–98; chm Biologicals Sub-Ctee Ctee on Safety of Meds 1993–98; pres: Endocrine Section RSM 1993–95, Br Fertility Soc 1998–2001 (chm 1993–95); FRCP, FRCOG; *Recreations* tennis, music, reading, theatre; *Style*— Prof Howard Jacobs; ✉ 169 Gloucester Avenue, London NW1 8LA (tel 020 7722 5593, fax 020 7722 5243, e-mail hsjacobs1@aol.com)

JACOBS, Michael Edward Hyman; s of Harry Ronald Jacobs, CC (d 1966), of London, and Edmonde, *née* London (d 1993); *b* 21 May 1948; *Educ* St Paul's, Univ of Birmingham (LLB); *m* 5 March 1973, Ruth; 2 s; *Career* admitted slr 1972; Nicholson Graham & Jones (now Kirkpatrick & Lockhart Preston Gates Ellis LLP): ptnr 1976–2004, head Tax Dept 1981–97, head Private Client Dept 1997–2004, conslt 2004–05; chm Jacobs Intrinsic Strategy 2005–; legal expert in employee benefits, share schemes and private client tax; ed Trust Law International (formerly Trust Law and Practice) 1989–95 (memb Editorial Bd 1986–89, conslt ed 1995–); author of articles on corporate and personal taxation; fndr memb and vice-chm Share Plan Lawyers Orgn 1989–2005, fndr memb Trust Law Ctee 1994– (sec 1994–97), chm Quoted Companies Alliance Share Schemes Ctee 1996–2002, dep chm Young Ctee on Investment and Corporate Governance for Voluntary Orgns ACEVO 2001–04; memb: Tax Working Pty ProShare 1992–96, Taxation Sub-ctee Quoted Companies Alliance 1993–97, VAT Practitioners Gp Trafalgar Chapter 1993–97, Private Tsts Ctee Assoc of Corp Tstees 1996–97, Exec Ctee Quoted Companies Alliance 1999–2002; Int Acad of Estate and Trust Law: memb 2002–04 memb Cncl 2005–, hon sec 2006–; memb Inland Revenue Ctee on the Simplification of Capital Gains Tax 2000–02; chm Child Welfare Scheme 2005–; memb: Law Soc 1972, Inst for Fiscal Studies 1984, Int Fiscal Assoc 1985–2002, Assoc of Pension Lawyers 1986–98, City of London Law Soc 1986, Charity Law Assoc 1992, Soc of Tst and Estate Practitioners 1993; Freeman City of London 1983, Liveryman Worshipful Co of Slrs 1987; AcSS 1999; FRSA 1993, fell Soc for Advanced Legal Studies (FSALS) 1998; *Books* Tax on Takeovers (1989, 6 edn 1994), Tolley's Tax on Takeovers (1990), Tolley's Tax Planning (contrib 1989, 7 edn 1994–95), Tolley's VAT Planning (contrib, 2 edn 1994–95), The Director's Guide to Employee Benefits (IOD, contrib 1991), Longman's Financial Precedents (contrib 1992), Rewarding Leadership (report on share schemes for key execs of smaller quoted cos, Quoted Companies Alliance, 1998); *Style*— Michael Jacobs, Esq; ✉ 6 Constable Close, London NW11 6TY (tel 020 8455 3243, e-mail mrjacobs@btinternet.com)

JACOBS, Nicholas; *b* 8 September 1959; *Educ* Univ of Buenos Aires (DipArch), Cornell Univ USA (MA); *Career* Skidmore, Owings & Merrill: joined 1988, elected assoc 1993, assoc dir 1995, New York office 1996, design dir 1998–; selected projects incl: St Giles Circus London 1989, Thames Poly Kent 1991, Sixt Hotel Germany 1992, Manchester Olympics 2000 1992, Olympia Halle Berlin 1992, Rehbrucke Germany 1993, Den Haag Central The Netherlands 1993, Apollo Museum Amsterdam 1993, Hilton Hotel Amsterdam 1994, Rembrandt Tower Amsterdam 1994, Broadgate Plaza London 1995, King's Hill Campus Greenwich Univ 1995, JFK Int Airport NY 1997, One Court Place Stanford Conn 1997, La Guardia Plaza Amsterdam 1998, Mahon Point Cork 1998, Torre Vasco de Gama Expo'98 1998, Atlantico Pavilion for Expo'98 Lisbon 1998 (winner of int design competitions), Shanakiel Residential Devpt Dublin 1999, Citibank Regnl HQ Bahrain 1999, Charrington Wharf London 2000, Arrowhead Quay London 2000, Paddington Basin St Mary's London 2000; Grand Offr Order of Merit Portugal 1999; *Style*— Nicholas Jacobs, Esq; ✉ Skidmore Owings & Merrill Inc, 30 Millbank, London SW1P 4SD (tel 020 7798 1000, fax 020 7798 1100, e-mail nicholas.jacobs@som.com)

JACOBS, Prof Patricia Ann; OBE (1999); da of Cyril Jacobs, and Sadie, *née* Jones; *b* 8 October 1934; *Educ* Univ of St Andrews (BSc, DSc, D'Arcy Thomson medal, Sykes medal); *m* 1972, Newton Ennis Morton; 3 step s, 2 step da; *Career* res asst Mount Holyoke Coll MA 1956–57, scientist MRC 1957–72, prof Dept of Anatomy and Reproductive Biology Univ of Hawaii Sch of Med 1972–85 (Regents medal 1983), prof and chief Div of Human Genetics Dept of Paediatrics Cornell Univ Med Coll NY 1985–87, dir Wessex Regional Genetics Lab 1988–2001; hon sr lectr Dept of Med Univ of Edinburgh 1966–72, hon prof of human genetics Univ of Southampton Med Sch 1988–; Allan Award American Soc of Human Genetics 1981, Premio Phoenix Anni-Verdi Award 1998, Euro Soc of Human Genetics Mauro Baschirotto Award 1999; fndr memb American Bd of Med Genetics 1979–82; memb Cncl: RCPath 1991–94, Royal Soc 1993–95, Acad Med Sci 1998–2001; author of over 250 articles; Hon DSc Univ of St Andrews 2002; FRSE 1977, FRCPath 1987, FRS 1993, FMedSci 1998, Hon FRCPEd 1999, Hon FRCOG 1999; *Recreations* botany, gardening, walking; *Style*— Prof Patricia Jacobs, OBE, FRS; ✉ Wessex Regional Genetics Laboratory, Salisbury District Hospital, Salisbury SP2 8BJ (tel 01722 429080, fax 01722 338095, e-mail wessex.genetics@salisbury.nhs.uk)

JACOBS, Paul Martin; s of Colin Alfred James Jacobs, of Ruthin, Clwyd, and Betty Mary, *née* Rowse; *b* 11 December 1951; *Educ* Oundle, The Queen's Coll Oxford (MA), Univ of Liverpool (MB ChB); *m* 1; m 2, 11 Feb 1989 (m dis 2001), Deborah Clare Josephine Smith; 1 s (Edmund Charles b 22 Nov 1991); m 3, 21 Feb 2004, Marie Colette McMahon; *Career* resident surgical offr Moorfields Eye Hosp 1982–85; conslt ophthalmic surgn: Univ Hosp Nottingham 1988–92, Borders Gen Hosp 1992–94, York District Hosp 1995–; FRCPSGlas 1984, FRCOphth 1988, FRCSEd 2000; *Recreations* music, skiing, running; *Clubs* RSM; *Style*— Paul Jacobs, Esq; ✉ Department of Ophthalmology, York Hospital, Wigginton Road, York YO31 8HE (tel 01904 631313)

JACOBS, Peter Alan; s of Cyril Jacobs (d 1971), and Sadie, *née* Jones (d 1973); *b* 22 February 1943; *Educ* Univ of Glasgow (BSc), Aston Univ (Dip Mgmnt Studies); *m* 30 May 1966, Eileen Dorothy, da of Dr Leslie Naftalin; 2 s (Andrew, Michael (twins) b 4 Feb 1969), 1 da (Katrina b 14 July 1972); *Career* prodn controller Toy Div Tube Investments Ltd 1968–70 (graduate trainee 1965–67), prodn mangr Pedigree Petfoods Ltd 1970–83 (prodn shift mangr 1970–72, Purchasing Dept 1972–81), sales dir Mars Confectionery 1983–86, chief exec Berisford International plc and chm subsid British Sugar Ltd 1986–91, chief exec BUPA 1991–98; chm: Hillsdown Holdings plc 1998–99, Healthcall Ltd 1998–2001, WT Foods 2002–05, abc Media 2005–, LA Fitness plc 1998–2005; non-exec dir: Allied Domecq plc 1998–2004, Bank Leumi UK plc 1998–2003, RAF Strike Command 2002–; *Recreations* reading, music, theatre, tennis, sailing; *Clubs* RAC; *Style*— Peter Jacobs, Esq; ✉ Garden Flat, 29 Daleham Gardens, London NW3 5BY (tel 020 7435 2646, fax 020 7443 9596, e-mail jacobs@peatonhouse.co.uk)

JACOBS, His Hon Judge Peter John; s of Herbert Walter Jacobs (d 1987), and Emma Doris, *née* Bull (d 1980); *b* 16 April 1943; *Educ* King Edward VII Sch Kings Lynn, UC Cardiff (BA); *m* 1975, Dr Ruth Edwards, da of Arthur Edwards; 2 s (Robin Edward b 1983, Edward Arthur b 1989); *Career* called to the Bar Gray's Inn 1973; recorder 1988–97 (asst recorder 1988–92), standing jr counsel to Inland Revenue 1995–97, circuit judge (Wales & Chester Circuit) 1997–2002, circuit judge (SE Circuit) 2002–, resident judge Norwich Crown Court 2004–; memb (Lib) Barry BC 1966–69; chm Llandaff Cathedral Choir Assoc 1993–96, pres Old Lennensians Assoc; *Recreations* fine art, music, Norfolk churches and railway history, watching Norwich City FC; *Clubs* Norwich City FC, Norfolk (Norwich), Norwich Wanderers Cricket (vice-pres); *Style*— His Hon Judge Jacobs

JACOBS, Richard David; QC (1998); s of Elliott Norman Jacobs (d 1998), and Ruth *née* Ellenbogen; *b* 21 December 1956; *Educ* Highgate Sch, Pembroke Coll Cambridge (MA); *m* 1990, Pamela, da of David and Joyce Fine; 2 da (Rebecca Maritza b 27 Dec 1991, Hannah Minnie b 14 May 1997), 1 s (Benjamin Alexander b 5 July 1994); *Career* called to the Bar Middle Temple 1979; recorder 2003–; visiting fell LSE 2003–07; *Books* Liability Insurance in International Arbitration: The Bermuda Form (2004); *Recreations* tennis, Arsenal FC, theatre, piano; *Clubs* MCC, RAC; *Style*— Richard Jacobs, Esq, QC; ✉ Essex Court Chambers, 24 Lincoln's Inn Fields, London WC2A 3ED (tel 020 7813 8000, fax 020 7813 8080)

JACOBSON, Prof Dan; s of Hyman Michael (d 1975), and Liebe, *née* Melamed (d 1961); *b* 7 March 1929; *Educ* Kimberley Boys' HS, Univ of the Witwatersrand (BA); *m* 1954, Margaret Dunipace, *née* Pye; 2 s (Simon Orde b 1955, Matthew Lindsay b 1958), 1 da (Jessica Liebe b 1966); *Career* writer; fell in creative writing Stanford Univ 1956–57, visiting prof Syracuse Univ NY 1965–66, visiting fell SUNY Buffalo NY 1972; UCL: lectr 1975–79, reader in English 1980–87, prof of English 1988–94 (emeritus prof 1994–); John Llewelyn Rhys Award 1958, W Somerset Maugham Award 1962, H H Wingate Award 1979, J R Ackerley Prize 1986, Mary Elinore Smith Poetry Prize 1992; Hon DLitt Univ of the Witwatersrand 1997; FRSL 1974–98; *Fiction* The Trap (1955), A Dance in the Sun (1956), The Price of Diamonds (1957), The Evidence of Love (1960), The Beginners (1966), The Rape of Tamar (1970), Inklings - Selected Stories (1973), The Wonderworker (1973), The Confessions of Jozef Baisz (1977, H H Wingate Award 1979), Her Story (1987), Hidden in the Heart (1991), The God-Fearer (1992), All for Love (2005); *Autobiography* Time and Time Again (1985); *Criticism* The Story of the Stories (1982), Adult Pleasures (1988); *Travel* The Electronic Elephant (1994), Heshel's Kingdom (1998); *Biography* A Mouthful of Glass (by Henk van Woerden, translated from Dutch 2000), Interview - Ian Hamilton in conversation with Dan Jacobson (2002); *Recreations* tennis, talking, walking; *Clubs* Athenaeum; *Style*— Prof Dan Jacobson; ✉ c/o A M Heath & Co, 79 St Martin's Lane, London WC2N 4AA (tel 020 8836 4271, fax 020 7497 2561)

JACOBSON, Howard; s of Max Jacobson, of Manchester, and Anita, *née* Black; *b* 25 August 1942; *Educ* Stand GS Whitefield, Downing Coll Cambridge (MA, Table Tennis half blue); *m* 1, 1964 (m dis 1972), Barbara, *née* Starr; 1 s (Conrad b 1968); m 2, 1978 (m dis 2004), Rosalin Joy, da of Allan Sadler, of Balnarring, Aust; m 3, 2005, Jenny De Yong, da of Dena De Yong, of London; *Career* lectr in Eng lit Univ of Sydney 1965–67, Eng tutor Selwyn Coll Cambridge 1969–72, sr lectr Wolverhampton Poly 1974–81, novelist and critic 1981–; reg contrib Modern Painters 1988– (currently memb Editorial Bd), weekly columnist The Independent 1998–; *Books* Shakespeare's Magnanimity (with Wilbur Sanders, 1978), Coming From Behind (1983), Peeping Tom (1984), Redback (1986), In The Land of Oz (1987), The Very Model of a Man (1992), Roots Schmoots (1993), Seriously Funny: An Argument for Comedy (1997), No More Mister Nice Guy (1998), The Mighty Walzer (1999), Who's Sorry Now? (2002), The Making of Henry (2004), Kalooki Nights (2006); *Television Films* Into the Land of Oz (1991), Yo, Mrs Askew (1991), Roots Schmoots (3 parts, 1993), Sorry, Judas (1993), Seriously Funny: An Argument for Comedy (5 parts, 1997), Howard Jacobson Takes on The Turner (2000), Why the Novel Matters (South Bank Show special, 2002); *Recreations* appearing on television; *Style*— Howard Jacobson, Esq; ✉ c/o Curtis Brown, Haymarket House, 28–29 Haymarket, London SW1Y 4SP (tel 020 7393 4400, fax 020 7393 4401/02, e-mail cb@curtisbrown.co.uk)

JACOBSON, Ivor Julian; s of Harry Jacobson (d 1980), and Rae, *née* Tatz (d 1950); *b* 6 May 1940; *Educ* King Edward VII Sch Johannesburg, Univ of the Witwatersrand (BComm); *m* 23 Dec 1963, Joan Yocheved, da of Isiah Adelson (d 1974); 1 s (Russell b 1965), 2 da (Lauren b 1968, Amanda b 1970); *Career* chief exec and controlling stockholder Trade and Industry Group (with subsids in many countries incl South Africa, UK, USA and Bermuda) 1968–; chm and pres Anglo African Shipping Co of New York Inc; md BayPond Investment Corp; CA (South Africa); *Recreations* squash, horse riding; *Style*— Ivor J Jacobson, Esq

JACOBSSON, (Ivar) Måns Gösta; *b* 14 January 1939; *Educ* Princeton Univ, Lund Univ Sweden; *Career* judge 1964–70, pres of div Stockholm Ct of Appeal 1985–2006; Swedish Miny of Justice: legal advsr 1970–81, asst under-sec and head Dept for Int Affrs 1982–84; dir: Int Oil Pollution Compensation Fund 1971 1985–2006, Int Oil Pollution Compensation Fund 1992 1996–2006, Int Oil Pollution Compensation Supplementary Fund 2005–06; visiting prof: World Maritime Univ Malmö Sweden, Shanghai Maritime Univ, Dalian Maritime Univ China; memb: Panel Singapore Maritime Arbitration Centre, Int Maritime Conciliation and Mediation Panel; head Swedish delgn to a number of int meetings (incl Int Maritime Orgn) 1970–1984; author of book on patent law and of numerous articles in various legal fields; Hon LLD Univ of Southampton; *Style*— Måns Jacobsson, Esq; ✉ e-mail mansjacobsson@hotmail.co.uk

JACOMB, Sir Martin Wakefield; kt (1985); s of Hilary Jacomb, and Félise Jacomb; *b* 11 November 1929; *Educ* Eton, Worcester Coll Oxford (MA); *m* 1960, Evelyn Helen, *née* Heathcoat Amory; 1 da, 2 s; *Career* called to the Bar Inner Temple 1955, practised at bar 1955–68; with Kleinwort Benson 1968–85, Commercial Union Assurance Co plc 1984–93 (dep chm 1987–93), dep chm Barclays Bank plc 1985–93; chm: Barclays de Zoete Wedd 1986–91, Postel Investment Management Ltd 1991–95, The British Cncl 1992–98, Delta plc 1993–2004, Prudential plc 1995–2000 (non-exec dir 1994–), Share plc 2003–; non-exec dir: Bank of England 1986–95, The Telegraph plc (formerly Daily Telegraph) 1986–95, Rio Tinto plc 1988–2000, Marks and Spencer plc 1991–2000, Canary Wharf Gp plc 1999– (actg chm 2003, chm 2004–); memb Nolan Ctee 1995–97; external memb Fin Ctee OUP 1971–95, tstee Nat Heritage Meml Fund 1982–97, chllr Univ of Buckingham 1998–; Liveryman Worshipful Co of Merchant Taylors; Hon Dr: Univ of Oxford, Univ of Buckingham, Humberside Univ; *Style*— Sir Martin Jacomb

JACQUES, Dr Martin; s of Dennis Arthur Jacques (d 1996), and Dorothy *née* Preston (d 1989); *b* 1 October 1945; *Educ* King Henry VIII Sch Coventry, Univ of Manchester (BA, MA), King's Coll Cambridge (scholar, PhD); *m* 1969 (m dis 1975), Brenda Simson; partner 1976–93, Philippa Anne, da of Sqdn Ldr Lloyd Norman Langton, RAF (decd); m 2, 1996, Harinder Kaur Veriah (d 2000); 1 s (Ravi Harinder b 1998); *Career* lectr in econ and social history Univ of Bristol 1971–77, ed Marxism Today 1977–91 (ed special issue 1998), dep ed The Independent 1994–96; writer for The Observer, The Guardian, The European and MSN online 1996–98; columnist: Sunday Times 1988–94, The Times 1990–91, L' Unità (Rome) 1990–93, The Guardian 2002–; also occasional contrib: The Independent, The Financial Times, Daily Mail, Daily Telegraph, The NY Times, Int Herald Tribune, Wall Street Journal, New Republic, South China Morning Post, Volkskrant, La Stampa, Corrière della Sera, Le Monde Diplomatique; writer and presenter of numerous TV progs incl The End of the Western World, Proud to Be Chinese, The Incredible Shrinking Politicians (BBC 2); visiting prof: Int Centre for Chinese Studies Aichi Univ Japan 2005, Ritsumaikan Univ Kyoto Japan 2005, Renmin Univ Beijing 2005–06; visiting research fell Asia Research Centre LSE 2003–, visiting sr research fell Asia Research Inst Nat Univ of Singapore 2006; memb Cncl European Policy Forum 1992–98; Demos: fndr, chm Advsy Cncl 1992–98, tstee 1994–99; memb Exec Ctee Communist Pty 1967–90 (memb Political Ctee 1978–80 and 1982–90); memb Econ History Soc 1971–77, fndr Harinder Veriah Tst 2003–; ambass for Coventry; winner (sports category) Race in the Media Award 2006; FRSA 1991; *Books* Forward March of Labour Halted (co-ed and contrib, 1981), The Politics of Thatcherism (co-ed and contrib, 1983), New Times (co-ed and contrib, 1989); contrib to various other books and publications; *Recreations* squash, tennis, skiing, running, motor racing, reading, cooking; *Style*— Dr Martin Jacques; ✉ 55 The Pryors, East Heath Road, London NW3 1BP (tel and fax 020 7435 7142, e-mail martinjacques1@aol.com)

JAFFA, Robert Harvey (Sam); s of Leslie Jaffa, and Dorothy, *née* Rakusen (d 1994); *b* 4 March 1953; *Educ* Allerton Grange Sch Leeds, Univ of Hull (BSc), Univ of Wales Coll of Cardiff (DipJour), Univ of London (pt/t MA); *m* 28 Aug 1988, Celia, da of Philip Barlow (d 1998); 2 s (Lewis b 28 Feb 1992, Torquil b 25 Oct 1996), 1 da (Lucy b 27 Jan 1995); *Career* trainee journalist Essex County Newspapers until 1980; BBC: reporter BBC Radio Humberside 1980–82, prodr BBC Radio Stoke 1982 (covered Ballykelly pub bombing while visiting N Ireland 1982), reporter National BBC Radio News 1984–91 (major assignments incl sinking of ferry Herald of Free Enterprise Zeebrugge, Bradford football stadium fire, Piper Alpha oil platform disaster), New York reporter 1991, reporter Business & Economics Unit 1992–95, N American business corr 1995–97, London 1997; head of media relations PricewaterhouseCoopers Europe, Middle East, Africa (formerly Price Waterhouse before merger) 1997–; memb Media Tst; *Books* Maxwell Stories (1992), Safe As Houses (1997); *Style*— Sam Jaffa, Esq; ✉ e-mail sam.jaffa@uk.pwcglobal.com

JAFFRAY, Sir William Otho; 5 Bt (UK 1892), of Skilts, Studley, Warks; s of Lt-Col Sir William Edmund Jaffray, 4 Bt, TD, JP, DL (d 1953), and his 2 w, Anne, *née* Paget; *b* 1 November 1951; *Educ* Eton; *m* 9 May 1981 (m dis 1997), Cynthia Ross, *née* Corrington, da of Mrs William M Geering, of Montreal, Canada; 3 s (Nicholas Gordon Alexander b 18 Oct 1982, Jack Henry William b 3 Aug 1987, William Lawrence Paget b 5 March 1990), 1 da (Alexandra Marina Ross b 1984); *Heir* s, Nicholas Jaffray; *Career* property conslt; *Style*— Sir William Jaffray, Bt

JAFFREY, Saeed; OBE (1995); s of Dr Hamid Hussain Jaffrey (d 1984), of Lucknow, Uttar Pradesh, India, and Hadia Imam (d 1987); *Educ* Wynberg-Allen Sch and St George's Coll Mussoorie UP India, Univ of Allahabad UP India (MA), RADA, The Catholic Univ of

America Washington DC (Fulbright scholar, MA); *m* 1, 1958 (m dis 1966), Madhur Jaffrey; 3 da (Zia b 1959, Meera Shameem b 1960, Sakina b 1962); m 2, 1980 Jennifer Irene, da of William Edward Sorrell, of Rustington, W Sussex; *Career* actor; formed own Eng theatre co Delhi, became first Indian actor to tour and perform Shakespeare across the US; joined Actors' Studio NY where played leads in: Lorca's Blood Wedding, Rashomon, Twelfth Night; Broadway debut as Prof Godbolé in A Passage to India, toured US in Brecht on Brecht, produced wrote and narrated the NY radio programme Reflections of India, recorded The Art of Love - A Reworking with Music of the Kama Sutra (new version released 1992); retrospective of work Birmingham Film and TV Festival 1996; *Theatre* West End incl: Brahma in Kindly Monkeys, On a Foggy Day (St Martin's), Captain Brassbound's Conversion (Cambridge), My Giddy Aunt (Churchill Theatre Bromley), A Touch of Brightness (Royal Court), The Mother Country (Riverside Studios), Oberon in A Midsummer Night's Dream (Regent's Park), Ibrahim in White Chameleon (RNT), Col Pickering in My Fair (Crucible Sheffield), The Kralahome in The King and I (London Palladium); *Television* incl: Jimmy Sharma in Tandoori Nights (Channel 4), Nawab in Jewel In The Crown (Granada), Frankie Bhoolabhoy in Staying On, Biju Ram in The Far Pavilions, leading role in A View From The Window (BBC2), three maj roles in Partition (Channel 4), Rafiq in Gangsters (BBC), Minder, Tales of the Unexpected, Callan, Destiny (Play for Today), Love Match (BBC2), A Killing on the Exchange (Anglia), Hard Cases (Central), Rumpole of the Bailey (Thames), Little Napoleons (Channel 4), Two Oranges and a Mango (BBC2), Common As Muck (BBC), Coronation Street (Granada); *Films* incl: Billy Fish in The Man Who Would Be King, The Guru, Hullabaloo Over Georgie and Bonnie's Pictures, Courtesans of Bombay, Hussein in The Deceivers, The Wilby Conspiracy, Nasser in My Beautiful Laundrette, Patel in Gandhi, Hamidullah in A Passage To India, three lead roles (incl Lord Krishna) in Masala 1992, lead in After Midnight, The Chessplayers (first film in India), Hermit of Amsterdam; *Radio* writer and broadcaster of hundreds of scripts in Hindi, Urdu and English, actor in numerous plays for BBC Radio 4 incl The Pump (played nine roles), other radio work incl: the Rajah in In The Native State (BBC Radio 3), Village By The Sea (BBC Radio, played all 39 characters), A Suitable Boy (20 episodes, BBC World Service, narrator and all 86 characters), Silver Castle (by Clive James, narrator and all 46 characters); *Awards* nominated for BAFTA Best Supporting Actor for My Beautiful Laundrette, winner Filmfare and Film World awards (India) for Best Actor in The Chessplayers, winner numerous awards in India for Best Actor for Ram Teri Ganga Maili, winner other awards for Dil and Henna, nominated for Canadian Academy Award (Genie) for Best Actor for Masala, selected for Norman Beaton Award for multi-cultural achievements; *Recreations* snooker, cricket, languages, cartooning, cooking, building cultural bridges; *Clubs* Littlehampton Constitutional, Ealing Snooker, The Br Legion; *Style*— Saeed Jaffrey, Esq, OBE

JAGGARD, Anthony John Thorrold; JP (1976); s of Rev Arthur William Percival Jaggard (d 1967), of Guilsborough Vicarage, Northamptonshire, and Isabel Louise May, *née* Capell (d 1972); *b* 5 June 1936; *Educ* Bedford Sch, Liverpool Sch of Architecture Univ of Liverpool; *m* 29 April 1961, (Elizabeth) Jane Jaggard, DL (pres Br Red Cross Soc Dorset Branch 1988–99), da of Col Sir Joseph William Weld, OBE, TD (d 1992, Ld-Lt Dorset 1964–84), of Lulworth Castle, Dorset; 3 da (Victoria (Mrs Nigel Beer) b 14 Jan 1962, Charlotte (Mrs David Swann) b 27 Jan 1964, Sarah (Mrs Robin Price) b 5 March 1968), 2 s (Oliver b and d 3 April 1970, Simon (twin) b 3 April 1970); *Career* Cheshire (Earl of Chester's) Yeomanry 1958–67 (Capt 1964, Adj 1967), RARO 1967–86; sr ptnr John Stark and Partners architects 1965–99, conslt John Stark and Crickmay 1999–; projects incl consultation on: Callaly Castle Northumberland, Hoddam Castle Dumfries, Lulworth Castle Dorset, Wardour Castle Wiltshire, Roman Town House Dorchester (Dorset Archaeological Award 2000, shortlisted Br Millennium Archaeological Award 2000), Ivington Park Herefordshire; new or remodelled houses incl: Ince Castle Cornwall, Gaston Grange Bentworth Hants, Longford House Sydling St Nicholas Dorset, Lulworth Castle House Dorset, Holywell Swanmore Hants, Bellamont House Long Bredy Dorset (nominated Country Life House of the Year 2002), Hedsor Wharf Bucks; contrib: Archaeological Journal, Dorset Natural History and Archaeological Soc Proceedings; memb Exec Cncl S Dorset Cons Assoc 1965–81; memb Cncl: Dorset Nat Hist and Archaeological Soc 1971–2006 (pres 1994–97), Dorset Cncl of St John 1978–81, Royal Archaeological Inst 1987–91, Salisbury Redundant Churches Ctee 1991–, British Archaeological Assoc 1997–2000; dir Dorset Bldgs Preservation Tst 1984–89, Liveryman Worshipful Co of Painter Stainers 1975; FRSA 1986; FSA 1990; *Recreations* old buildings, gardening, shooting; *Style*— Anthony Jaggard, Esq, JP, FSA; ✉ Eastfields, Sherborne, Dorset DT9 3DE (tel 01935 817695); John Stark and Crickmay Partnership, 13 and 14 Princes Street, Dorchester DT1 1TW (tel 01305 262636, fax 01305 260960, e-mail jscp@johnstark.co.uk)

JAGGER, Harriett Alexis; da of Philip Charles Upfill Jagger, of Warks, and Claudine, *née* Goodfellow (d 1996); *b* 30 October 1959; *Educ* King's HS for Girls Warwick, Marlborough, London Coll of Fashion (Dip Journalism); *m* 1984 (m dis 1999), Simon Gaul; 2 s (Hamilton John Alexander b 12 June 1992, Orlando Cory Rupert b 17 Feb 1997), 1 da (India Louisa Savannah b 17 Nov 1995); *Career* fashion asst The Observer 1982–85, fashion ed Elle magazine 1985–89, sr fashion ed Vogue magazine 1989–92, fashion and style dir Harpers & Queen magazine 1992–94, fashion dir Tatler magazine 1994–97, fashion dir Eve 2000, freelance stylist/conslt; *Recreations* theatre, cooking, tennis, travel, all aspects of design and photography; *Style*— Miss Harriett Jagger; ✉ Percy Lodge, 15 Christchurch Road, London SW14 7AB (e-mail harriettjagger@aol.com); agent: Joy Goodman, 3 Lonsdale Road, London NW6 6RA (website www.joygoodman.com)

JAGGER, Ven Ian; *b* 17 April 1955; *Educ* Huddersfield New Coll, King's Coll Cambridge, St John's Coll Durham; *m* Ruth, *née* Green; 1 s (Aidan b 1994); *Career* ordained: deacon 1982, priest 1983; asst curate St Mary the Virgin Twickenham 1982–85, priest in charge Willen Milton Keynes 1985–87, chaplain Willen Hospice Milton Keynes 1985–94, dir Milton Keynes Christian Trg Scheme 1986–94, team vicar Willen Milton Keynes 1987–94, team ldr Stantonbury Ecumenical Parish 1990–94, diocesan ecumenical offr 1994–96, team rector Holy Trinity with St Columba Fareham 1994–98, rural dean of Fareham 1996–98, canon residentiary Portsmouth Cathedral 1998–2001, archdeacon of Auckland 2001–06, archdeacon of Durham and canon residentiary of Durham Cathedral 2006–; *Recreations* reading, exploring new places; *Style*— The Ven the Archdeacon of Durham; ✉ 15 The College, Durham DH1 3EQ (tel 0191 384 7534, e-mail archdeacon.of.durham@durham.anglican.org)

JAGGER, Jade Jezebel; da of Sir Mick Jagger, and Bianca, *née* de Macias; *b* 21 October 1971, Paris; *Educ* St Mary's Sch Calne; *Family* 2 da (Assisi Jackson b 2 July 1992, Amba Jackson b 26 May 1995); *Career* artist and model 1990–95; fndr Jade Inc 1995–2000; creative dir: Garrard 2000–,Yoo 2005–; *Style*— Miss Jade Jagger; ✉ 24 Albemarle Street, London W1S 4TE (tel 020 7758 8951, e-mail jjezebel@mac.com)

JAGUSCH, Stephen Richard; s of Paul Franz Jagusch, of Auckland, NZ, and Eileen Marie, *née* Williamson (d 2003); *b* 31 May 1967, Auckland, NZ; *Educ* Auckland Univ (BCom, LLB, MComLaw); *m* 19 May 2001, Emma Katherine, *née* McVey; 2 da (Annabel Marie b 20 Dec 2005, Clara Louise b 1 May 2007); *Career* barr and slr NZ 1990, slr Eng and Wales 1995, slr advocate 1996; arbitrator specialising in int commercial and treaty arbitration; asst slr: Simpson Grierson Auckland 1989–94, Freshfields London 1994–96, Freshfields Paris 1996–2000; ptnr Allen & Overy LLP London 2002– (asst slr 2000–02); sr special fell UN Inst for Trg and Res 1998, alternate memb for NZ of the ICC Cmmn on Arbitration; memb: Swiss Arbitration Assoc, Int Arbitration Club, Int Arbitration Inst, LCIA, Panel of Neutrals (Arbitrators), American Arbitration Assoc; FCIArb; *Publications* Arbitration World (contrib, 1st edn 2003, 2nd edn 2005), Disputes (contrib, 2003), Towards a Uniform International Arbitration Law? (contrib, 2005), Evasive Problems in International Arbitration (contrib, 2006), Investment Arbitration and the Energy Charter Treaty (contrib, 2006); *Recreations* golf, skiing, holidaying in NZ; *Style*— Stephen Jagusch, Esq

JAIN, Dr Virendra Kumar (Viren); s of Trilok Chandra Jain (d 1974), and Roop Wati Jain (d 1995); *b* 3 August 1935; *Educ* Agra (BSc, MB BS); *m* 23 Nov 1960, Kamlesh, da of Jagdish Prashad Jain (d 1944); 2 da (Angela b 1964, Meena b 1977), 1 s (Sanjiv b 1965); *Career* sr registrar in psychiatry Powick Hosp Worcester 1966–68, lectr in psychiatry and sr registrar Professorial Unit Univ of Liverpool 1968–70, conslt psychiatrist Barnsley District Gen Hosp 1970–; Barnsley Community and Priority Servs NHS Tst: med dir 1991–, chm Med Staff Ctee; chm: Barnsley Div Br Med Assoc (memb Yorks Regnl Cncl), Barnsley Div Overseas Doctors' Assoc; cmmr Mental Health Act Cmmn; memb: Bd of Examiners RCPsych 1990–, Standing Conference of Asian Organisation UK Nat Cncl, Br Assoc of Med Mangrs, Assoc of Tst Med Dirs, BMA, Br Soc of Med and Dental Hypnosis, Br Assoc of Psychopharmacology; life memb Wakefield Civic Soc; FRCPsych, DPM RCP and RCS; *Books* A Short Introductory Guide to Clinical Psychiatry (1984); also several articles on depression and psychopharmacology; *Recreations* entertaining, playing tennis and golf, listening to Indian classical music; *Clubs* Sandal Lawn Tennis, Walton Hall Country, Waterton Park Golf; *Style*— Dr Viren Jain; ✉ Shantiniketan, 17 Beechfield, Sandal, Wakefield, West Yorkshire WF2 6AW (tel 01924 255207); Department of Psychological Medicine, Kendray Hospital, Doncaster Road, Barnsley, South Yorkshire S70 3RD (tel 01226 730000, fax 01226 296782)

JAINE, Tom William Mahony; s of William Edwin Jaine (d 1970), and Aileen, *née* Mahony (d 1943); *b* 4 June 1943; *Educ* Kingswood Sch Bath, Balliol Coll Oxford (BA); *m* 1983, Sally Caroline, da of late Andrew Agnew, of Crowborough, E Sussex, and Hon Joyce Violet, *née* Godber; 4 da (Harriet b 1974, Elizabeth b 1976, Matilda b 1985, Frances b 1987); *Career* restaurateur 1973–84; ed: Good Food Guide 1989–93, Journal of the International Wine and Food Society 1989–91; publisher Prospect Books 1993–; freelance writer (Sunday Telegraph and others) 1993–; Glenfiddich Award Wine and Food Writer of the Year 2001; *Recreations* baking; *Style*— Tom Jaine, Esq; ✉ Allaleigh House, Blackawton, Totnes, Devon TQ9 7DL (tel 01803 712269)

JAKES, Clifford Duncan; s of Ernest Thomas Jakes (d 1963), of Leigh on Sea, Essex; *b* 29 December 1942; *Educ* Westcliff HS Southend-on-Sea, Aston Univ; *Career* articled Wilkins Kennedy & Co London 1960–65, mgmnt trainee Tube Investments Ltd 1966–67, fin dir Raleigh Cycles (Malaysia) 1968–71, fin controller (Overseas Div) Raleigh Industries Ltd Nottingham 1971–73, fin dir and md Warren Plantation Holdings London 1974–81, md United Newspapers 1985–92, mgmnt conslt 1982; chm: Link House Publications 1983–Argus Press 1993–97, non-exec chm Indigo Int Publications 1999–; FCA; *Recreations* theatre, sport, preservation of wild life; *Clubs* City, Selangor (Malaysia), Bengal (Calcutta); *Style*— Clifford Jakes, Esq; ✉ Link House Publications plc, Robert Rogers House, New Orchard, Poole, Dorset (tel 0202 671171)

JAKOBER, Benedict Peter Benjamin (Ben); s of Henry Jakober (d 1975), of London, and Olga Jakober (d 1990); *b* 31 July 1930; *Educ* Mill Hill Sch, La Sorbonne Paris; *m* 1972, Yannick *née* Vu; 1 s (Reza b 1969), 1 da (Maima b 1973 d 1992); *Career* artist and sculptor; exhbns incl: Louisiana Museum Humlebaek 1985, XLII Bienal of Venice 1986, EXPO92 Seville 1992, Arnolfini Bristol 1993, Museum Moderner Kunst Vienna 1993, XLV Bienal of Venice 1993, Miro Fndn Palma 1994, Bienal XXII of São Paulo 1996, Mucsarnok Museum Budapest 1998, Castillo de Santa Barbara Alicante, Bienal de Valencia 2001; works in: Musee D'Art Moderne Brussels, Museum Moderner Kunst Vienna, Kunsthalle Bremen and Hamburg, Gabinetto Disegni Degli Uffizi Florence, Ludwig and Szépmûvészeti Múseum Budapest; Pilar Juncosa and Sothebys Special Prize 1993; FRBS; *Books* Ben Jakober / Yannick Vu (by Achille Bonito Oliva, 1996); *Style*— Ben Jakober, Esq; ✉ c/o Fundacion Yannick y Ben Jakober, Finca Sa Bassa Blanca, Apartado 10, 07400 Alcudia, Mallorca, Spain (tel 00 34 971 546915, fax 00 34 971 897163, e-mail bj.fuybjako@arrakis.es, website www.jakober-vu.com)

JAMAL, Dr Goran Atallah; s of Atallah Jamal (Talabani), of Iraq, and Nusrat Jamal (d 1987); *b* 19 July 1953; *Educ* Baghdad Univ (MB ChB), Univ of Glasgow (PhD, MD); *m* 15 Dec 1983, Vian, da of Maj-Gen Mohamad Salih Anber (ret), of Iraq; 1 da (Lazia b 23 May 1986), 1 s (Arie b 3 June 1992); *Career* sr registrar in neurology Bart's Med Sch 1986–88, conslt Dept of Neurology and sr clinical lectr Univ of Glasgow 1988–98 (research fell in neurology 1981–86), sr lectr in neurosciences Dept of Educn Strathclyde Region 1988–98, conslt and sr lectr Div of Neuroscience and Psychological Med Imperial Coll Sch of Med Univ of London 1998–; chm Kurdish Cultural Centre UK (a registered charity); memb: Assoc of Br Neurologists, EEG Soc, Assoc of Br Clinical Neuro-physiologists, Scottish Assoc of Neurosciences, New York Acad of Science, American Assoc of Electrodiagnostic Med, American EEG Soc; fell Assoc of Lawyers, memb: Inst of Expert Witnesses, Acad of Expert Witnesses; FRCPGlas; *Publications* author of over 150 articles, papers and book chapters; *Style*— Dr Goran Jamal; ✉ Department of Neurology, Central Middlesex Hospital, Acton Lane, London NW10 7NS (tel 020 8453 2247, fax 020 8453 2246, e-mail gji151283@aol.com)

JAMAL, Patricia Barbara; da of Lt Cdr John Enda Bernard Healy, RNVR (d 1967), and Barbara Maud, *née* Taylor; *b* 3 September 1943; *Educ* St Maur's Convent Weybridge, Ursuline Convent Wimbledon, Brooklands Coll Weybridge; *m* 16 Dec 1971, (Nizar) Ahmed Jamal, s of Abdulmalek Ahmed Jamal, of Vancouver, Canada; 3 da (Jenna b 1977, Sarah b 1980, Isabel b 1982); *Career* business devpt offr Bank of Montreal London 1983–87, chief dealer GTS Corp Servs Barclays Bank 1987–92, dir Barclays Metals Ltd 1992–95, md global money market sales Barclays Bank plc 1994–96, md financial instns Barclays Bank plc 1996–2001; non-exec dir: Anglo-Irish Bank 2003–06, Assurant Solutions 2007–; former dir Aston Charities Tst Ltd; *Recreations* family, reading, music, riding; *Style*— Mrs Patricia Jamal

JAMES, Prof Alan Morien; s of Willie James (d 1983), of Newport, Gwent, and Martha, *née* John (d 1990); *b* 20 January 1933; *Educ* Newport HS, LSE (BSc); *m* 1, 18 Aug 1956 (m dis 1980), Jean Valerie, da of Ernest Hancox, of Newport, Gwent; 4 s (Morien b 1958, Gwyn b 1962, Gareth b 1964, David b 1965), 3 da (Helen b and d 1959, Nesta b 1961, Ceri b 1969); m 2, 19 March 1981, Lorna, da of Frank Eric Lloyd, of Chester; *Career* Civil Serv 1955–57, successively asst lectr, lectr, sr lectr and reader LSE 1957–73, prof and head Dept of Int Rels Keele Univ 1974–91 (research prof 1990–98); Rockefeller research fell Inst of War and Peace Studies Columbia Univ 1968; visiting prof: Dept of Int Rels Univ of Ife Nigeria 1981, Sch of Int Studies Jawaharlal Nehru Univ New Delhi 1983, Nat Inst for Defense Studies Tokyo 1993; chm: Br Int Studies Assoc 1979–83, Br Int Studies Assoc Gp on Diplomacy 1994–96; memb Soc Studies Sub Ctee Univ Grants Ctee 1983–89, advsr in politics and int studies Univ Funding Cncl 1989–93, chm Int Law Section Int Studies Assoc (USA) 1992–93; *Books* The Politics of Peacekeeping (1969), The Bases of International Order (ed 1973), Sovereign Statehood - The Basis of International Society (1986), Peacekeeping in International Politics (1990), States in a Changing World - A Contemporary Analysis (co-ed 1993), Britain and the Congo Crisis, 1960–63 (1996), A Dictionary of Diplomacy (with G R Berridge, 2001, 2 edn 2003), Keeping the Peace in the Cyprus Crisis of 1963–64 (2002); *Recreations* hill and coast walking, golf, croquet, bowls, supporting Port Vale FC and Glamorgan CCC, music, food; *Style*— Prof Alan

James; ✉ 23 Park Lane, Congleton, Cheshire CW12 3DG (tel 01260 271801, e-mail alanmjames@waitrose.com)

JAMES, Albert (Alby); s of Albert Samuel James (d 1982), of London, and Florence Cassetta Renalda, *née* Thomas (d 1989); *Educ* St David's C of E Sch London, Southgate Tech Coll London, UEA (BA); *m* 5 Jan 1980, Vanessa Mary, da of Capt Christopher Simmonds; 2 s (William Marcus b 17 March 1980, Benjamin Andrew b 16 April 1982), 1 da (Eloïse Sarah b 4 Aug 1988); *Career* Arts Cncl trainee asst dir English Stage Co 1979–80, asst dir RSC (Barbican) 1982–83, artistic dir and chief exec Temba Theatre Co 1984–93, head of screenwriting and external devpt Northern Film Sch Leeds Met Univ 1999–2006, academic ldr for media and performance London Met Univ 2006–07, head of devpt Eon Screenwirters' Workshop 2007–; prodns incl: Meetings (Hampstead Theatre) 1982, Scrape off the Black (Temba) 1985, Porgy and Bess (assoc dir, Glyndebourne Festival Opera) 1986 and 1987 (also ROH, BBC TV and Primetime TV 1992), Fences (Liverpool Playhouse and Garrick Theatre London) 1990, Dona Rosita, The Spinster (RADA) 1990, Ghosts (Temba tour) 1991, A Killing Passion (Temba tour) 1992, The Constant Wife (RADA) 1992, King Lear and The Shelter (RADA) 1993, My Children, My Africa (Watermill Theatre) 1993, Mamma Decemba (BBC Radio 4) 1994, The Ramayana (BBC Radio 4) 1994, Taking Sides (BBC Radio 3) 1996, The Roads to Freedom (BBC Radio 4) 1994, Aman (BBC World Service) 1997, Short Stories from Southern Africa (Ulwazi for SABC) 1996, Nothing But The Truth (BBC Radio 3) 2002, exec prodr Dramatic Encounters a series of short films for SABC, report for Broadcasting Standards Cmmn (Cultural Diversity, Equality of Opportunity and Enterprise with Responsibility, for new regulatory structure for electronic media) 2003; conslt and trainer on cultural diversity and equal opportunity issues in the media and arts; specialist advsr for performing arts CNAA 1989–92, sr project ldr Sediba Script Devpt Prog South Africa 2004–; memb: Gen Advsy Cncl BBC 1987–91, Bd Screen Yorks Ltd 2002–07, Bd First Light Movies Ltd 2004–; *Recreations* listening to music, reading, photography, religion and politics, foreign travel; *Style*— Alby James, Esq; ✉ EON Screenwriters' Workship, EON House, 138 Piccadilly, London W1J 7NR (tel 0871 218 1007, fax 020 7408 1236, e-mail alby.james@eonworkshop.com)

JAMES, His Hon Judge Charles Edwin Frederic; s of Frederic Crockett Gwilym James (d 1970), formerly treas of the Great Universal Stores Ltd, and Marjorie Peggy, *née* Peace (d 1976); *b* 17 April 1943; *Educ* Trent Coll, Selwyn Coll Cambridge (MA); *m* 1968, Diana Mary Francis, da of James Francis Thornton (d 1977); 2 s (Daniel b 1971, Philip b 1973); *Career* called to the Bar Inner Temple 1965; jr Northern Circuit 1966, barr-at-law Northern Circuit 1965–93, recorder of the Crown Court 1982–93, circuit judge (Northern Circuit) 1993–; *Recreations* family pursuits; *Clubs* Cambridge Univ Cricket, Royal Liverpool Golf, Royal Mersey Yacht; *Style*— His Hon Judge Charles James

JAMES, His Hon Christopher Philip; s of Herbert Edgar James, CBE (d 1977), and Margaret James; *b* 27 May 1934; *Educ* Felsted, Magdalene Coll Cambridge (MA); *Career* cmmnd RASC 1953; called to the Bar Gray's Inn 1959, recorder of the Crown Court 1979, circuit judge (SE Circuit) 1980–97, ret; judge Woolwich County Court 1982–92, judge Lambeth County Court 1992–97; *Clubs* Oxford and Cambridge; *Style*— His Hon Christopher James

JAMES, Clive Vivian Leopold; s of late Albert Arthur James, and Minora May, *née* Darke; *b* 7 October 1939; *Educ* Sydney Tech HS, Univ of Sydney, Pembroke Coll Cambridge (pres Footlights); *Career* writer, TV presenter and entertainer; feature writer The Observer 1972– (TV critic 1972–82); fndr Watchmaker Productions 1994; *Television* presenter TV series: Cinema, Up Sunday, So It Goes, A Question of Sex, Saturday Night People, Clive James on Television, The Late Clive James, The Late Show with Clive James, Saturday Night Clive, The Talk Show with Clive James; TV documentaries: Shakespeare in Perspective - Hamlet 1980, The Clive James Paris Fashion Show 1981, Clive James and the Calendar Girls 1981, The Return of the Flash of Lightning 1982, Clive James in Las Vegas 1982, Clive James meets Roman Polanski 1984, The Clive James Great American Beauty Pageant 1984, Clive James in Dallas 1985, Clive James meets Katherine Hepburn 1986, Clive James on Safari 1986, Clive James and the Heroes of San Francisco 1987, Clive James in Japan 1987, Postcard from Rio 1989, Postcard from Chicago 1989, Postcard from Paris 1989, Clive James meets Jane Fonda, Clive James on the 80s 1989, Postcard from Miami 1990, Postcard from Rome 1990, Postcard from Shanghai 1990, Clive James meets Ronald Reagan 1990; *Music* record lyricist for Pete Atkin; albums incl: Beware of Beautiful Strangers, Driving through the Mythical America, A King at Nightfall, The Road of Silk, Secret Drinker, Live Lible, The Master of the Revels; song-book A First Folio (with Pete Atkin); *Non-fiction* incl: The Metropolitan Critic (1974), The Fate of Felicity Fark in the Land of the Media (1975), Peregrine Prykke's Pilgrimage through the London Literary World (1976), Britannia Bright's Bewilderment in the Wilderness of Westminster (1976), Visions Before Midnight (1977), At the Pillars of Hercules (1979), First Reactions (1980), Charles Charming's Challenges on the Pathway to the Throne (1981), Crystal Bucket (1981), From the Land of Shadows (1982), Glued to the Box (1982), Flying Visits (1984), Snakecharmers in Texas (1988), North Face of Soho (2006); autobiographies: Unreliable Memoirs (1980), Falling Towards England: Unreliable Memoirs II (1985), May Week Was in June: Unreliable Memoirs III (1990); *Fiction* Brilliant Creatures (1983), The Remake (1987), Brrm! Brrm! (1992), The Silver Castle (1996); *Verse* Fan-mail (1977), Poem of the year (1983), Other Passports: poems 1958–85; *Style*— Clive James, Esq

JAMES, (David) Colin; s of Wilfred John James (d 1996), and Gwyneth Mary, *née* Jenkins (d 1996); *b* 29 August 1941; *Educ* Bishop Gore GS Swansea, Welsh Sch of Architecture Univ of Wales Cardiff (BArch); *m* 18 February 1968, Catherine Mary, da of late Gibson Lynn; 2 da (Rachel b 23 June 1970, Helen b 27 January 1972); *Career* architect; project mangr/gp ldr Northampton Devpt Corp 1972–79, head Devpt Div West Midlands Metropolitan CC 1979–83, chief of architectural servs Oxfordshire CC 1983–92, in private practice 1992–2006; sometime: memb Visiting Bds Oxford and Portsmouth Polys, memb Bldg Advsy Ctee Heart of England TEC; hon treas RIBA 1997–2000, chm RIBA Southern Region 2001–2003; hon treas Br Architectural Library Tst 2000–06; memb (Lib Dem) West Oxfordshire DC (chm 1997–98); ARIBA 1968; *Recreations* family and friends, world travel, sailing, skiing, walking, cycling, theatre, photography, architecture; *Style*— Colin James, Esq; ✉ Colin James Architect, Pinsley Orchard, Main Road, Long Hanborough, Witney, Oxfordshire OX29 8JZ (tel and fax 01993 881395, e-mail colin.james@lineone.net)

JAMES, Dafydd Rhys; s of Philip Harrison James, and Kathryn, *née* Pritchard; *b* 24 July 1975, Mufulira, Zambia; *Educ* Brynteg Comp Sch, Bridgend Coll of Technol, Univ of Swansea; *Career* rugby union player; clubs: Llanelli, Bridgend, Pontypridd, Celtic Warriors, Harlequins, Llanelli Scarlets; Wales: 45 caps, debut v Aust 1996, memb squad World Cup 1999, also played for Wales A, Wales 7s, Wales under 21 and Welsh Students; memb Br Lions touring squad Aust 2001; *Recreations* golf, family; *Style*— Dafydd James, Esq; ✉ Llanelli Scarlets, Stradey Park, Llanelli SA15 4BT

JAMES, David Benjamin; *b* 1 August 1970, Welwyn Garden City, Herts; *Career* professional footballer; clubs: Watford 1990–92, Liverpool 1992–99, Aston Villa 1999–2001, West Ham United 2001–04, Manchester City 2004–06, Portsmouth 2006–; England: 35 caps, debut v Mexico 1997, memb squad World Cup 2002 and 2006, memb squad European Championships 2004; columnist The Guardian; *Style*— Mr David James

JAMES, Prof David Edward; s of Charles Edward James (d 1982), of Eastleigh, Hants, and Dorothy Hilda, *née* Reeves (d 1984); *b* 31 July 1937; *Educ* Peter Symonds Coll Winchester, Univ of Reading (BSc), Univ of Oxford (DipEd), Univ of London (Dip FE), Univ of Durham (MEd); *m* 30 March 1963, Penelope Jane, da of Lt Cdr Edward J Murray, of Bradford-on-Avon, Wilts; 1 da (Lucy b 1964), 2 s (Philip b 1966, Christopher b 1969); *Career* lectr in zoology and psychology City of Bath Tech Coll 1961–63, lectr in science and psychology St Mary's Coll of Educn Newcastle upon Tyne 1963–64; Univ of Surrey: lectr in educnl psychology 1964–68, res lectr in educn 1968–69, dir of adult educn 1969–80, prof of adult educn 1980–, prof and head Dept of Educnl Studies 1981–93, dean of assoc instns 1996–2002, special advsr to vice-chllr on regnl academic affrs 2002–05; md: Interactive Educational Systems International Ltd, IV Epoch Productions Ltd 1989–93; non-exec dir: Transnational Satellite Education Co Ltd 1991–94, ICON Productions Ltd 1993–95; chm: Cncl of Science and Technol Regnl Orgn for Surrey 1983–93, Surrey Retirement Assoc 1984–, Br Assoc for Educnl Gerontology 1986–99, High Coombe Tst for Midwife Educn 1990–, Moor Park Tst for Christian Adult Educn 1992–, Age Concern Waverley 1993–96; vice-chm: Br Assoc for Servs to the Elderly 1991–94, Cncl of Assoc of Business Execs 1994–98; pres: Preretirement Assoc of GB and NI 1993–02, Cmmn for Social Service Users and Carers (Surrey) 1998–02 (chm 1994–99); memb: Bd of Educn RCN 1980–92, Educn Ctee Royal Coll of Midwives 1986–91, Governing Body Centre for Int Briefing 1975–02, Gen Nursing Cncl 1972–80, UK Central Cncl for Nursing Midwifery and Health Visiting 1980–83, English Nat Bd for Nursing, Midwifery and Health Visiting 1983–88, Exec Ctee Guildford Branch English Speaking Union 1985–; CBiol, MIBiol 1963, CPsych, AFBPsS 1966, FRSH 1974, FRSA 1984, FITD 1991; *Books* A Students Guide to Efficient Study (1966), Introduction to Psychology (1968); *Recreations* farming; *Style*— Prof David James; ✉ 30 Glendale Drive, Guildford, Surrey GU4 7HZ

JAMES, Eirian; da of Dewi William James, of Cardigan, and Martha Ann, *née* Davies; *b* 7 September 1952; *Educ* Preseli Secdy Sch Crymych, Royal Coll of Music; *m* 29 Dec 1975 (m dis 1993), Alan Rowland Davies; 1 da (Sara Elen b 11 March 1990); *Career* soprano/mezzo-soprano; hosts own TV series on S4C featuring popular folk and operatic arias; *Roles* with Kent Opera incl: Olga in Eugene Onegin, title role in L'Incoronazione di Poppea, Rosina in The Barber of Seville, Nero in Agrippina, Dido in Dido and Aeneas, Cherubino in The Marriage of Figaro, Meg Page in Falstaff, Man Friday in Robinson Crusoe; with other cos incl: title role in La Perichole (Singers Co), Dorabella in Cosi fan Tutte (Singers Co, Aix-en-Provence), title role in Ariodante (Buxton Festival), Medea in Cavalli's Jason (Buxton Festival), Hänsel in Hänsel and Gretel (Geneva), Second Lady in The Magic Flute (Geneva), Cupid in Orpheus in the Underworld (Houston, ENO), Siebel in Faust (Houston), Sextus in Julius Caesar (Houston, Scottish Opera), Annina in Der Rosenkavalier (Covent Garden), Smeaton in Anna Bolena (Covent Garden), Nancy in Albert Hering (Covent Garden), Hermia in A Midsummer Night's Dream (Aix-en-Provence), Isolier in Count Ory (Lyon), Orlofsky in Die Fledermaus (WNO), Olga in Eugene Onegin (Covent Garden), Zerlina in Don Giovanni (Parma, Amsterdam, Ludwigsburg, London), Cherubino in Marriage of Figaro (Bordeaux, Bastille Paris), Despina in Cosi Fan Tutte (Garnier Paris), Diane in Hippolyte et Aricie (Garnier Paris), Cherubino in Figaro (Dresden Semperoper 1997 and Madrid 1998), Theatergarderobiere, Gymnasiast and Groom in Lulu (Bastille 1998), Meg Page in Falstaff (with John Eliot Gardiner, 1998, and recording), Falsirena in La Catena d'Adone (Innsbruck); *Recordings* Reuben in Christmas Rose (conducted by Howard Williams), Second Lady in The Magic Flute (conducted by Roger Norrington) 1990, Despina in Cosi Fan Tutte (conducted by John Eliot Gardiner), Zerlina in Don Giovanni (conducted by John Eliot Gardiner), Sextus in Julius Caesar (conducted by Jean-Claude Malgoire), Diane in Hippolyte et Aricie (conducted by William Christie), title role in Teseo (conducted by Mark Minkovsky), Christus Apollo (cantata composed and conducted by Jerry Goldsmith); *Recreations* gardening; *Style*— Ms Eirian James; ✉ The Vicarage, Tremain, Cardigan SA43 1SJ (tel and fax 01239 811 751, e-mail maesco.ejames@virgin.net)

JAMES, Elizabeth Sheila (Liz); (Mrs C Drummond Challis); da of Edward Leonard James, of Westerham, Kent, and Sheila Florence, *née* Jordan; *b* 24 August 1944; *Educ* Micklefield Sch for Girls Sussex, Ravensbourne Coll of Art and Design (BA); *m* 4 Oct 1984, (Christopher) Drummond Cremer Challis, s of Christopher George Joseph Challis; *Career* graphic designer: Crosby Fletcher Forbes 1965–66, Total Design Holland 1966–68, Pentagram 1968–74; freelance graphic designer Holland and London 1974–83, fndr ptnr Lambton Place Design 1983–87, design mangr Phaidon Press 1994–95, dir Liz James Design Consultancy 1987–; ret from graphic design, now practising in ceramics; PPL 1977; memb: D&AD 1983, DBA 1983 (dir 1992–93); FCSD 1986 (memb Cncl 1992–95), FRSA 1992; *Style*— Ms Liz Challis; ✉ Liz James Design Consultancy, Old Crebor Farm, Gulworthy, Tavistock, Devon PL19 8HZ (tel and fax 01822 618814)

JAMES, Erica Jane; da of Peter Joseph Sullivan, and Marie Ruby Sullivan; *Career* novelist; memb: Romantic Novelists' Assoc; Romantic Novel of the Year 2006 (four times shortlisted), finalist WH Smith Fresh Talent promotion 1996; *Books* A Breath of Fresh Air (1996), Time for a Change (1996), Airs & Graces (1997), A Sense of Belonging (1998), Act of Faith (1999), The Holiday (2000), Precious Time (2001), Hidden Talents (2002), Paradise House (2003), Love and Devotion (2004), Gardens of Delight (2005); *Recreations* travelling, reading, learning Italian; *Style*— Miss Erica James; ✉ Curtis Brown, Haymarket House, 28/29 Haymarket, London SW1Y 4SP (tel 020 7396 6600)

JAMES, Geraldine; OBE (2003); da of Gerald Thomas (d 1987), of Cornwall, and Annabella, *née* Doogan (d 1987); *b* 6 July 1950; *Educ* Downe House, Drama Centre London; *m* 28 June 1986, Joseph Sebastian Blatchley, s of John Blatchley (d 1994); 1 da (Eleanor b 20 June 1985); *Career* actress; worked in repertory theatre Chester, Exeter and Coventry 1972–75; numerous venues London Fringe; *Theatre* roles incl: Miss Julie, Desdemona, Raina, Annie Sullivan; other works incl: The White Devil (Oxford Playhouse) 1981, When I was a Girl I Used to Scream and Shout (Whitehall) 1987, Cymbeline (NT) 1988, Portia in The Merchant of Venice (Peter Hall Co London and Broadway, Drama Desk Award 1990, Tony Award nomination 1990) 1989, Death and the Maiden (Duke of York) 1992, Lysistrata (Old Vic) 1993, Hedda Gabler (Manchester Royal Exchange) 1993, Give Me Your Answer, Do (Hampstead Theatre) 1998, Faith Healer (Almeida Theatre) 2001, The Cherry Orchard (Oxford Stage Co) 2003, Home (Oxford Stage Co) 2004, The UN Inspector (NT) 2005; *Television* The Sweeney 1976, Dummy 1977 (Critics' Assoc Best Actress Award, BAFTA Best Actress nomination), Love Among The Artists 1978, The History Man 1980, The Jewel In The Crown (BAFTA Best Actress nomination), Blott on the Landscape 1984, Echoes 1987, Stanley and the Women 1991, A Doll's House 1991, Ex 1991, The Healer 1994, Band of Gold 1994 and 1995 (BAFTA Award nomination for Best Actress), Kavanagh QC 1994, 1995, 1997 and 1998, Over Here 1995, Rebecca 1996, Gold 1997, See Saw 1998, The Sins 2000 (BAFTA Best Actress nomination), Hans Christian Anderson 2001, Crime and Punishment 2001, White Teeth 2002, The Hound of the Baskervilles 2002, Hearts of Gold 2003, State of Play 2003, He Knew He Was Right 2003, Jane Hall's Big Bad Bus Ride 2004, Little Britain 2004, Poirot 2005, A Harlot's Tale 2006, The Amazing Mrs Pritchard 2006; *Film* incl: Sweet William 1978, Night Cruiser 1978, Gandhi 1981, The Wolves of Willoughby Chase 1988, The Tall Guy 1988, She's Been Away 1989 (Venice Film Festival Best Actress Award), If Looks Could Kill 1990, The Bridge 1990, Beltenebros 1991, Losing Track 1991, No Worries 1992, Doggin' Around 1994, Moll Flanders, The Man Who Knew Too Little 1998, Lover's Prayer 1999, Testimony of Taliesin Jones 1999, The Luzhin Defence 1999, Tom and Thomas 2001, An Angel for May 2001, Odour of Chrysanthemums 2002, Calendar Girls 2002, Hex 2004, The Fever 2005; *Recreations* music; *Style*— Miss Geraldine James, OBE; ✉ c/o Julian Belfrage Associates, Adam House, 14 New Burlington Street, London W1S 3BQ

JAMES, Glen William; s of Clifford Vizetelly James, of Long Ashton, Bristol, and Kathleen Mary Flora, *née* Doull; *b* 22 August 1952; *Educ* KCS Wimbledon, New Coll Oxford (MA); *m* 15 Aug 1987, Amanda Claire, da of Philip Dorrell, of Worcester; *Career* admitted slr 1976, ptnr Slaughter and May 1983–; Freeman Worshipful Co of Solicitors; memb Law Soc; MSI; *Recreations* music, reading, various sports; *Clubs* RAC; *Style*— Glen James, Esq; ✉ Slaughter and May, 1 Bunhill Row, London EC1Y 8YY (tel 020 7090 3050, fax 020 7090 5000, e-mail glen.james@slaughterandmay.com)

JAMES, Rt Rev Graham Richard; *see:* Norwich, Bishop of

JAMES, Helen; da of Peter Shaw, and Joan Mary, *née* Turner; *b* 29 March 1951; *Educ* Cheadle Hulme Sch, Girton Coll Cambridge (MA); *m* 30 August 1976, Allan James, s of Thomas Raymond James; 1 s (Peter Thomas b 26 March 1979), 2 da (Clare Elizabeth b 21 Oct 1980, Sarah Linda b 29 Sept 1985); *Career* actuary; Equity and Law 1972–74, ptnr Clay & Partners 1977–97 (joined 1975), ptnr Watson Wyatt 1997–2006, dir of law Debenture Pension Tst Corp 2006– (pension scheme ind tstee); *Style*— Mrs Helen James; ✉ 15 Church Avenue, Ruislip, Middlesex HA4 7HX (tel 01895 631 758); Law Debenture Pension Trust Corporation, 100 Wood Street, London (tel 020 7696 5255, e-mail helen.james@lawdeb.com)

JAMES, Prof Ioan Mackenzie; s of Reginald Douglas James (d 1966), of Heathfield, E Sussex, and Jessie Agnes, *née* Surridge (d 1982); *b* 23 May 1928; *Educ* St Paul's, The Queen's Coll Oxford; *m* 1 July 1961, Rosemary Gordon, da of William George Stewart (d 1953); *Career* Cwlth Fund fell (Princeton, Berkeley, Inst for Advanced Study) 1954–55, Tapp research fell Gonville & Caius Coll Cambridge 1956; Univ of Oxford: reader in pure mathematics 1957–69, sr research fell St John's Coll 1959–69, Savilian prof of geometry 1970–95 (emeritus prof 1995), hon fell St John's Coll 1987; New Coll Oxford: professorial fell 1987–95, hon fell, Leverhulme emeritus fell 1996–98; pres London Mathematical Soc 1985–86 (treas 1969–79), govr St Paul's Sch and St Paul's Girls' Sch 1970–99; hon prof Univ of Wales 1989; Hon DSc Univ of Aberdeen 1993; FRS 1968; *Books* The Topology of Stiefel Manifolds (1976), General Topology and Homotopy Theory (1984), Topological and Uniform Spaces (1987), Fibrewise Topology (1988), Introduction to Uniform Spaces (1990), Fibrewise Homotopy Theory (with Michael Crabb, 1998), Topologies and Uniformities (1998), History of Topology (1999), Remarkable Mathematicians (2002), Remarkable Physicists (2004), Asperger's Syndrome and High Achievement (2006), The Mind of the Mathematician (with Michael Fitzgerald, 2007); *Style*— Prof Ioan James, FRS; ✉ Mathematical Institute, 24–29 St Giles, Oxford OX1 3LB (tel 01865 735389)

JAMES, Prof James Roderick; s of James Henry James (d 1933), and Muriel May, *née* Trueman; *b* 20 June 1933; *Educ* Headlands GS Swindon, Univ of London (external student, BSc, PhD, DSc); *m* 5 March 1955, Pamela Joy, da of William Henry Frederick Stephens; 1 da (April Louise b 24 Feb 1956), 1 s (Julian Maxwell b 8 May 1962); *Career* Nat Serv RAF 1952–54; AERE Harwell 1950–52, radar devpt engr E K Cole Ltd 1954–58, applications engr Semiconductors Ltd 1958–61, demonstrator RMCS 1961–65, sr scientific offr AERE 1966; RMCS: sr lectr 1967, sr princ scientific offr and res prof 1976, dep chief scientific offr 1982, prof of electromagnetic systems engrg; dir Wolfson RF Engrg Centre 1984–98, chm Sch of Electrical Engrg and Science 1989, consltg engr; chm: Inst of Electronic and Radio Engrs Papers Ctee 1973–76, IEE Professional Gp on Antennas and Propagation 1980–83, IEE Int Conf on Antennas and Propagation 1983, Electronics Div IEE 1988–89; memb IEE Electronics Divnl Bd, pres Inst of Electronic and Radio Engrs 1984–85 (rep on Ctees of Engrg Cncl); emeritus prof Cranfield Univ 1999; visiting prof: Univ Teknologi Malaysia 1994, City Univ of Hong Kong 1999, Loughborough Univ 2000–; FIET, FIMA, FREng 1987; *Books* Handbook of Microstrip Antennas (co-author and ed, 1989), Mobile Antennas Systems Handbook (co-author and ed 1994, 2 edn 2001), Small Antennas (co-author and ed, 1987), Antenna Engineering Handbook (contrib, 4 edn 2007); ed of research studies books in antenna series; *Style*— Prof J R James, FREng; ✉ Royal Military College of Science (Cranfield University), Shrivenham, Swindon, Wiltshire SN6 8LA

JAMES, Sir Jeffrey Russell; KBE (2001), CMG (1994); *b* 13 August 1944; *Educ* Whitgift Sch Croydon, Keele Univ (BA); *m* 5 July 1965, (Carol) Mary, *née* Longden; 2 da (Alison b 7 Dec 1965, Lindsay b 4 April 1969); *Career* HM Dip Serv: joined 1967, Br Embassy Tehran 1969–70, second sec Br Embassy Kabul 1970–73, FCO 1973–78, dep political advsr Br Mil Govt Berlin 1978–82, FCO and Cabinet Office 1982–86, head of Chancery Br Embassy Pretoria/Cape Town 1986–88, head Economic and Commercial Dept Br High Cmmn New Delhi 1988–92, head Edinburgh European Council Unit 1992–93, chargé d'affaires Br Embassy Tehran 1993–97, high cmmr to Nairobi 1997–2001, UK special rep Nepal 2003–05; MRIIA; *Recreations* birding, hill walking, golf, tennis; *Clubs* Tandridge Golf (Oxted), Royal Cwlth Soc; *Style*— Sir Jeffrey James, KBE, CMG; ✉ 7 Rockfield Close, Oxted, Surrey RH8 0DN

JAMES, John Anthony; s of Charles Thomas James (d 1979), of Sutton Coldfield and Tenby, and Gwenith Aylwin, *née* Jones; *b* 15 July 1945; *Educ* King Edward VI GS Lichfield, Univ of Bristol (LLB); *m* 10 Sept 1973, Gwyneth Jane, da of Ambrose Elwyn Evans (d 1975), of Altrincham; 2 da (Harriet Lucy b 24 Sept 1975, Emily Jane b 22 Nov 1977); *Career* admitted slr 1969, ptnr Edge & Ellison 1974–93 (conslt 1993–), chief exec Birmingham City 2000, consIt Willis Corroon plc; dir: Remainders Ltd, Steel Plate and Sections Ltd, Quantum PR plc; sr jt hon sec Birmingham Law Soc 1987–91 (memb Cncl 1986–93), sec W Midlands Assoc of Law Socs 1991–93, memb Editorial Advsy Bd Law Soc Gazette; chm Lab Pty Fin and Industry Gp West Midlands; memb: Cncl Midlands Branch IOD, Ct Univ of Birmingham; dir Birmingham Repertory Theatre, chm Birmingham Press Club 1993–97; chm South Birmingham Coll 1998–; memb Law Soc 1970, FInstD 1985; *Recreations* reading, writing, theatre, jazz, opera; *Clubs* Solihull Sporting (chm), Moseley Rugby, Birmingham & Solihull Rugby, Avenue Bowling, Warwickshire Co Cricket; *Style*— John James, Esq; ✉ Birmingham City 2000, Rutland House, 148 Edmund Street, Birmingham B3 2JR (tel 0121 214 2515, fax 0121 214 1855, e-mail info@birminghamcity2000.co.uk)

JAMES, John Arthur William; s of Dr Peter Michael James (d 1971), and Eileen Mary, *née* Walters (d 1993); *b* 7 January 1942; *Educ* Douai Sch Berks; *m* 5 Aug 1967, Barbara, da of Maj William Nicholls (d 1955); 2 da (Jessica b 1968, Alice b 1970), 1 s (John-Leo b 1982); *Career* admitted slr 1967, sr ptnr Hand Morgan & Owen Stafford 1988; under sheriff Staffs and W Midlands 1983–2008, dep coroner S Staffs 1987, clerk to Cmmrs of Taxes Stafford and Cannock 1987, adjudicator on immigration 1986–91; chm Mid Staffs NSPCC 1976–95; memb Bd Stafford Prison 1975–93 (chm 1983–86); Cdr St John Ambulance Staffs 1994–2005; CStJ 2002; *Publications* The James Report (1996), The Walsall Suicide Review (2002); *Recreations* walking, shooting; *Style*— John James, Esq; ✉ Hand Morgan & Owen, 17 Martin Street, Stafford, Staffordshire ST16 2LF (tel 01785 211411, fax 01785 248573)

JAMES, John Christopher Urmston; OBE (2003); s of John Urmston James (d 1964), of Llandeilo, Carmarthenshire, and Ellen Irene, *née* Walker (d 2000); *b* 22 June 1937; *Educ* Hereford Cathedral Sch; *m* 1 (m dis 1982), Gillian Mary, *née* Davies; m 2, 20 Nov 1982, Patricia Mary, da of Arthur Leslie Walter White (d 1983), of Peckham, London; 2 s (David Henry Urmston b 3 Feb 1960, Christopher Hammond Urmston b 1 Jan 1961); *Career* trainee buyer Harrods 1954; rep: Jaeger 1961, Pringle 1972; sec LTA 1981–2003 (asst sec 1973–81, vice-pres 2003–), pres European Tennis Fedn 2003–, dir Br Tennis Fndn; chm British Olympic Fndn; pres Middx Tennis Assoc 2003–, vice-pres Cambridge Univ Tennis Club 2003–; dir Torch Trophy, tstee Dan Maskell Tst; memb: Nat Tst, Friends of Osterley Park, Ealing Nat Tst, Lib Dem Pty (pres Hounslow Lib Dem Pty), Int Tennis Hall of Fame Cncl; lay vice-chm St Mary's Church Osterley; *Recreations* tennis, rugby union, walking, architecture, topography, the countryside; *Clubs* All England Lawn Tennis and Croquet, Queen's, Llanelli Rugby, London Welsh, International Lawn Tennis Club of GB; *Style*— John James, Esq, OBE; ✉ Parkfield Cottage, Osterley Road, Isleworth, Middlesex TW7 4PF (tel 020 8232 8683)

JAMES, John Denis; s of Kenneth Alfred James, of Alvechurch, Worcestershire, and Pauline Audry, *née* Haymen; *b* 30 August 1950; *Educ* Bridley Moor GS Redditch; *m* 3 Sept 1975, Barbara Elizabeth, da of John Thorpe, of Birmingham; 1 s (Christopher John b 1975), 1 da (Emma Louise b 1978); *Career* trainee photographer Redditch Indicator 1965, sr photographer Birmingham Post and Mail 1972–2006, freelance photographer 2006–, co-fndr Midland Photographic Gp 2006; Midland Photographer of the Year 1981 and 1987, Midland News Photographer of the Year 1987 and 1991, Nat Br Press Award Photographer of 1987, Kodak News Photographer of 1987; memb Inst of Journalists; *Recreations* game fishing; *Style*— John James, Esq; ✉ website www.johnjames.net

JAMES, (David) Keith Marlais; OBE (2005); s of James Lewis James (d 1993), and Margaret Evelyn James (d 2001); *b* 16 August 1944; *Educ* Cardiff HS, W Monmouth Sch, Queens' Coll Cambridge (MA); *m* 4 Aug 1973, Kathleen Linda, da of Wilfred Lawson Marrs, OBE (d 1981), of Cyncoed, Cardiff; 2 da (Alys b 1978, Elizabeth b 1980), 1 s (Thomas b 1983); *Career* slr; ptnr Eversheds LLP 1969–2004 (chm 1995–2004); dir: various cos in Hamard Group 1977–86, Bank of Wales plc 1988–2001, AXA Insurance Co Ltd 1992–99, HTV Group 1997–98 and 1999–2006, Atlantic Venture Capital Ltd 2001–, Julian S Hodge Bank Ltd 2002–, Admiral Group plc 2002–, International Greetings plc; chm: Welsh Exec UN Assoc 1977–80, Welsh Centre for Int Affrs 1979–84; memb: UK Mgmnt Ctee Freedom from Hunger Campaign 1978–87, Welsh Mgmnt Ctee IOD 1985–94, Ct UWIST 1985–88, Cncl UWIST 1985–88, Advsy Panel Cardiff Business Sch 1986–, Cncl Univ of Wales Coll of Cardiff 1988–94, Editorial Bd Welsh Economic Review 1989–92, Representative Body of the Church in Wales 1989–95, Gen Advsy Cncl BBC 1991–92; vice-pres Cardiff Business Club 1987–, dep chm Inst of Welsh Affrs 1987–, non-exec memb Welsh Health Common Servs Authy 1991–95; dir The Int Festival of Musical Theatre in Cardiff 2001–04; memb Law Soc; CCMI, FRSA; *Recreations* golf; *Clubs* Cardiff and County, Oxford and Cambridge; *Style*— Keith James, Esq; ✉ Trehedyn Cottage, Peterston-Super-Ely, Vale of Glamorgan CF5 6LG

JAMES, Keith Royston; s of William Ewart Gladstone James (d 1990), of Birmingham, and Lilian Elizabeth James (d 1966); *b* 22 August 1930; *Educ* King Edward VI Camp Hill Sch Birmingham, Univ of Birmingham; *m* 6 May 1961, Venice Imogen, da of Maj Henry St John Murray Findlay (d 1954); 1 s (William b 1964), 3 da (Rohaise b 1966, Selina b 1968, April b 1971); *Career* admitted slr 1954; Needham & James: sr ptnr 1956–94, ptnr 1994–2001, conslt 2001–; dir Technology and Law 1980–97; chm Soc for Computers and Law 1988–90; pres Community Villacana Spain 2000–05, chm Michael Blanning Tst; *Books* A Guide to the Electronic Office for Practising Solicitors; author of articles on the application of technology to the law; *Recreations* shooting, walking, golf; *Clubs* Ingon Manor Golf, Welcombe Golf, El Paraiso Golf; *Style*— Keith R James, Esq; ✉ Welcombe House, 32 Avenue Road, Stratford-upon-Avon, Warwickshire CV37 6UN (tel 01789 261810); Needham & James, One Colmore Row, Birmingham B3 2BJ (tel 0845 630 8833, fax 0845 630 8822, e-mail keithjames@needhamandjames.com)

J

JAMES, Lesley; da of Albert Harry Showell (d 1978), of Birmingham, and Esme Kathleen, *née* Robinson; *b* 7 April 1949; *Educ* Lordswood Grammar Technical Sch, Open Univ (BA), Univ of Warwick (MA); *m* John William James; *Career* sec Joseph Lucas Ltd 1965–70, personnel mangr Delta Metal Co Ltd 1973–77 (PA 1970–73), personnel admin mangr Rank Hovis MacDougall Ltd 1977–79, mgmnt devpt mangr Sketchley Ltd 1979–80; Savacentre Ltd (subsid of J Sainsbury plc): personnel mangr 1980–83, checkout ops mangr 1983–85; Tesco Stores Ltd: regnl personnel mangr 1985–87, personnel dir (head office/distribution) 1987–89, personnel dir (retail) 1989–93, personnel and trg dir 1993–95; human resources dir Tesco plc 1995–99; non-exec dir: Selfridges plc 1998–2003, Care UK plc 2000–, West Bromwich Building Society 2001–, Liberty International 2004–; memb: Insolvency Service Steering Bd DTI, Governing Cncl Nat Coll for Sch Leadership, Cncl Open Univ; CCIPD, FRSA; *Style*— Mrs Lesley James

JAMES, Linda; *Educ* Univ of York; *m* Stephen Bayly; 1 da; *Career* television prodr; prodn asst TV commercials Sid Roberson Productions 1980, prodr Sgrin (82) Ltd (independent prodrs of progs for S4C) 1981–82 (prodr award-winning drama series Joni Jones with dir Stephen Bayly); Red Rooster Films Ltd (now subsid of Chrysalis plc): co-fndr with Stephen Bayly 1983, chief exec 1982–98; md Alibi Productions 1999–2003, dir Alibi Communications plc 1999–, md Sly Fox Films Ltd 2003–; investment fund mangr Wales Creative IP Fund 2005–; govr: BFI 1991–95, Nat Film and TV Sch 1991–98 (tstee 1998–2004 and 2006–), Childrens' Film and Television Fndn 1999–, Screen South 2001–; chair Edinburgh Int TV Festival 1992; memb: Br Screen Advsy Cncl 1993–96, Cncl BAFTA 2004–06, Kids' Ctee BAFTA, SE Media Network; memb awards juries for BAFTA, RTS, Int Emmys and BFI; *Programmes* Red Rooster prodns incl: And Pigs Might Fly (feature-length film for S4C, prodr) 1983, The Works (feature-length film, English/Welsh versions for S4C and Channel 4, prodr) 1984, Coming Up Roses (feature-length comedy for S4C and cinema release, prodr) 1985–86, Homing (for S4C, exec prodr) 1986, Just Ask for Diamond (feature film for Coverstop, Children's Film Fndn and British Screen, prodr) 1987–88, The Gift (series for BBC, prodr) 1989–90, The Diamond Brothers - South by South East (series for TVS, exec prodr) 1990–91, The Life and Times of Henry Pratt (comedy drama series for Granada, exec prodr) 1992, Body and Soul (drama series for Carlton, exec prodr) 1992–93, Smokescreen (drama series for BBC, exec prodr) 1993, Crocodile Shoes (drama series for BBC, exec prodr) 1994, The Sculptress (drama series for BBC, prodr), Wilderness (drama series for ITV, exec prodr), Heaven on Earth (drama series for BBC, exec prodr); Alibi prodns incl: Without Motive (drama series for ITV, exec prodr), The Safe House (drama series for ITV, prodr) 2000–01, Dead (comedy film for ITV, prodr) 2000–01, Sir Gadabout (children's series for ITV, exec prodr) 2001–03; Wales Creative IP Fund incl: Big Nothing (feature film for Pathe, exec prodr), The Restraint of Beasts (feature film for BBC films and UKFC, exec prodr), Mr Polly (TV film for ITV, exec prodr); *Awards* numerous incl: Chicago Children's Awards (for Joni Jones and And Pigs Might Fly), official selection Cannes Film Festival (Coming Up Roses), Golden Pierrot (first prize) for Best First Feature Vevey Int Festival of Comedy Film and Special Jury Prize Golden Plaque Chicago Int Film Festival (for Coming Up Roses), Best Adventure Film Moscow Film Festival (for Just Ask for Diamond), Welsh BAFTA for Outstanding Contributions to Children's Programmes, Indie Award (for Sir Gadabout); BAFTA nominations (for Body and Soul, Crocodile Shoes, The Sculptress and Sir Gadabout); *Style*— Ms Linda James

JAMES, Martin Jonathan; s of Kenneth Charles James, of Christchurch, NZ, and Beatrice Rose, *née* Dickson; *b* 22 September 1961; *Educ* NZ Sch of Dance; *m* 8 Feb 1985, Adrienne Jane Terehunga, da of Flt Lt James Matheson, DFC, of Christchurch, NZ; 1 da (Rachael Unaiki b 31 July 1990), 1 s (Marcus Sebastian Tane James b 20 Oct 1992); *Career* ballet dancer; Royal NZ Ballet 1981, awarded Queen Elizabeth II Arts Cncl Grant for study in America 1982; princ dancer: English Nat Ballet 1987–90 (joined 1985), Deutsche Oper Berlin (at invitation of Peter Schaufuss) 1990–94, Royal Danish Ballet 1994– (instr/ballet master 2002); guest teacher: Malmo 1997, Ballet Holstebro (with Peter Shaufuss) 1998, Rome 2003, Bartholin Int Ballet Seminar Copenhagen 2003; first one man graphic arts exhibition Molesworth Gallery NZ 1984, exhibition of paintings Denmark 1999; ARAD

1979, Solo Seal 1980; *Performances* incl: Albrecht and Hilarion in Giselle, Franz in Coppélia, Prince in The Nutcracker (with Lynn Seymour), Toreador in Petit's Carmen, Romeo and Paris in Ashton's Romeo and Juliet, The Poet in La Sylphide (Dame Alicia Markova's prodn), Blackamoor in Petrushka, world premiere Christopher Bruce's Symphony in 3 movements, Ben Stevenson's Three Preludes, Kevin Haigen's Meditation (cr role with Natalia Makarova) 1987, Spectre de la Rose 1987, Le Corsaire 1987, cr role of Benno in Makarova's Swan Lake 1987 (also role of Seigfried), title role in Cranko's Onegin 1987 (and with Ekaterina Maximova 1989), Oedipus in Glen Tetley's Sphinx, title role in Balanchine's Apollo 1987 and 1992, Balanchine's Symphony in C 1987, Christopher Bruce's Land 1987, Bull in Christopher Bruce and Lyndsey Kemp's Cruel Garden 1987 (and that ballet's German première 1992), leading soldier in Antony Tudor's Echoing Trumpets 1990, Donner and Hagen in Bejart's Ring um den Ring 1990, The Chosen One in Béjart's Sacre du Printemps and Firebird 1991, Tchaikovsky Pas de Deux (Kirov Theatre Leningrad) 1991, Albrecht in Peter Schaufuss' Giselle 1991, lead role in Kenneth Macmillan's Different Drummer 1991, James in Schaufuss' La Sylphide 1991, Prince in Valery Panov's Cinderella 1991 (Badische Zeitung Critics' Award), title role in Tales of Hoffman (Hong Kong Ballet) 1991, Albrecht in Paris Opera version of Giselle (with Inoue Ballet Fndn Japan) 1992, Le Corsaire Pas de Deux (with Sylvie Guillem, Paris Gala) 1992, Albrecht in Giselle (guest artist Kirov Theatre St Petersburg) 1993; roles with Royal Danish Ballet incl: world premiere of Anna Laekenson's Dromme 1994, Albrecht in Giselle 1994, Romeo, Paris and Benvolio in Ashton's Romeo and Juliet 1994, premiere of Marie Bronlin Tanis Dance Piece 1994, James and Gurn in Schaufuss' La Sylphide 1994, Paul Taylor's Aureole 1994, Kim Brandstrup's Mysteries 1994, Flower Festival of Genzano 1994, title role in Crankos' Onegin 1994, Oberon in Neumeier's Midsummer Night's Dream 1995, Dance Master in Conservatoire 1995, The King in Fleming Flint's Caroline Mathilde 1995, Peter Martin's Ash 1995, King in Peter Schaufuss' Hamlet 1996, Seigfried, Russian and Hungarian in Peter Martin's Swan Lake 1997, cr role of Amor in Kim Brandstrup's Amor and Psyche 1997, Juri Kylian's Return to a Strange Land (Brown pas de deux) 1997, James in Royal Danish Ballet version of La Sylphide 1997, Prince in Fleming Flint's Nutcracker 1997, White Pas de Trois of the Catalyst (choreographer Steven Baynes) 1998, Copain in Bejart's Gaite Parisienne 1998, Basilio in Nereyev's Don Quixote 1998, Camillo in Hynd's The Merry Widow 1998, Lifar's Suite en Blanc 1998, Husband in The Concert (choreographer Jerome Robins) 1999, Odysseus in John Neumiere's Odyssey 2002, Lescaut in Macmillan's Manon 2003; guest appearances in: Spain, London, France, Denmark, Russia, NZ, Berlin, Finland; film and TV performances incl: Gillian Lynne's Look of Love (princ role as Eros) 1989, Natalia Makarova's Swan Lake, James in La Sylphide (live, NZ) 1990; *Awards* Genée Awards 1988 and 1989, included amongst Five Hundred Leaders of Influence (ABI) 1996, Men of Achievement (IBC) 1997 and Int Directory of Distinguished Leadership (ABI) 1997, Golden Scroll of Excellence (IBC) 1997; *Recreations* painting, swimming, cooking, graphic arts, gardening; *Style—* Martin James, Esq; ✉ Royal Danish Ballet, Det Kongelige Teater Og Kapel, Postbox 2185, Copenhagen K, DK1017 Denmark; HM Contact Store, Kongensgade 71A, Copenhagen K, DK 1264 Denmark (tel and fax 45 3332 0667, e-mail martinjjames@yahoo.com)

JAMES, Dr Michael Leonard (Michael Hartland); s of late Leonard James, of Portreath, Cornwall; *b* 7 February 1941; *Educ* Latymer Upper Sch, Christ's Coll Cambridge; *m* 1975 (m dis 1992), Jill Elizabeth, da of late George Tarján, OBE, of Budapest; 2 da (Ruth, Susanna); *Career* writer and broadcaster 1983–; entered Br Govt Serv (GCHQ) 1963, private sec to Rt Hon Jennie Lee MP as Min for the Arts 1966–68, DES 1968–71, planning unit of Rt Hon Margaret Thatcher MP as Sec of State for Educn & Sci 1971–73, asst sec 1973, DCSO 1974, served Paris, Milan and London 1973–78, dir Int Atomic Energy Agency Vienna 1978–83, advsr on int rels Cmmn of the Euro Union Brussels 1983–85; feature writer and book reviewer for: The Times (thriller critic 1990–91, travel corr 1993–), Sunday Times, The Guardian, Daily Telegraph (thriller critic 1993–) 1986–; chm Wade Hartland Films Ltd 1991–2000; chm: Civil Serv Selection Bds 1983–93, GMC Professional Conduct Ctee 2000–06; memb: Asylum and Immigration Tbnl (formerly Immigration Appeal Tbnl) 1987–, Exec Ctee PEN 1997–2001; govr: E Devon Coll of FE Tiverton 1985–91, Colyton GS 1985–90, Sidmouth Community Coll 1988–2004 (chm of govrs 1998–2001); hon fell Univ of Exeter; FRSA; *Books* novels (as Michael Hartland): Down Among the Dead Men (1983), Seven Steps to Treason (1985, SW Arts Literary Award, dramatized for BBC Radio 4 1990), The Third Betrayal (1986), Frontier of Fear (1989), The Year of the Scorpion (1991), The Verdict of Us All (short stories, 2006), Masters of Crime: Lionel Davidson and Dick Francis (2006); (as Ruth Carrington) Dead Fish (1998); other publications (as M L James): Internationalization to Prevent the Spread of Nuclear Weapons (jtly, 1980); *Television and Radio* incl: Sonja's Report (ITV documentary, 1990), Masterspy (interviews with KGB defector Oleg Gordievsky, BBC Radio 4, 1991); *Clubs* Athenaeum, Detection, PEN, Devon and Exeter Institution; *Style—* Dr Michael James; ✉ Cotte Barton, Branscombe, Devon EX12 3BH

JAMES, Prof the Hon Oliver Francis Wintour; o s of Baron James of Rusholme (Life Peer, d 1992), and Cordelia Mary, *née* Wintour; *b* 23 September 1943; *Educ* Winchester, Balliol Coll Oxford (MA, BM BCh); *m* 4 Sept 1965, Rosanna, er da of Maj Gordon Bentley Foster (d 1963), of Sleightholme Dale, Fadmoor, York; 1 s (Patrick Esmond b 4 May 1967), 1 da (Helen b 26 Jan 1970); *Career* landowner (170 acres); Univ of Newcastle upon Tyne: prof of geriatric med 1985–, head Dept of Med 1994–, head Sch of Clinical Med Sciences 1995–; censor RCP, sr vice-pres RCP 1997–99; past pres Br Assoc for Study of the Liver; tstee: Sir James Knott Tst, Help the Aged 2002–; non-exec dir BUPA 1999–; FRCP 1981, FMedSci 1999; *Books* Liver Disease in the Elderly, Oxford Textbook of Clinical Hepatology (ed, 1999), Oxford Textbook of Medicine (contrib chapters, 2003); *Recreations* golf, gardening; *Style—* Prof the Hon Oliver James; ✉ Department of Medicine, Floor 4, Clinical Block, Medical School, Framlington Place, Newcastle upon Tyne NE2 4HH; Sleightholmedale Lodge, Kirbymoorside, York YO6 27JG (e-mail o.f.w.james@ncl.ac.uk)

JAMES, Dr Peter David; s of Thomas Geraint Illtyd James, of Ealing Common, London, and Dorothy Marguerite, *née* John; *b* 20 August 1943; *Educ* Mill Hill, Middx Hosp Med Sch and Univ of London (MB BS); *m* 14 Sept 1968, Angela Judith, da of William Robert Hearn, of Hovingham, N Yorks; *Career* lectr in pathology: Makerere Univ Kampala Uganda 1970–72, Bland-Sutton Inst Middx Hosp London 1972–73 (asst lectr 1967–70); conslt and hon sr lectr in histopathology Univ Hosp Nottingham 1973–; memb: BMA, Br Soc of Gastroenterology, Br Div Int Acad of Pathology; *Recreations* squash, shooting, horse riding; *Style—* Dr Peter James; ✉ Histopathology Department, University Hospital, Nottingham NG7 2UH (tel 0115 970 9175)

JAMES, Peter John; s of John Burnett James, and Cornelia, *née* Katz; *b* 22 August 1948; *Educ* Charterhouse, Ravensbourne Film Sch; *m* 21 April 1979 (m dis 1999), Georgina Valerie James, da of T D Wilkin, of Hove, E Sussex; *Career* dir: Quadrant Films Toronto 1972–77, Yellowbill Ltd 1977–85; co-fndr Pavilion Internet plc, former md of Movision Entertainment Ltd; film prodr: Dead of Night 1973, Spanish Fly 1976, Biggles 1985, Five Moon Square 2002, Jericho Mansions 2002, A Different Loyalty 2003, Head in the Clouds 2003, The Bridge of San Luis Rey 2003, The Statement 2003, The Last Sign 2003, The Merchant of Venice 2004, Bailey's Billions 2004, The River King 2004, Perfect Creatures 2004; former Royal Warrant Holder Queen's Warrant for Glove Mfrs; memb: Soc of Authors, Soc for Psychical Research; fell emeritus Hypnotherapy Soc; Freeman City of London 1980, Liveryman Worshipful Co of Glovers; author; *Books* Dead Letter Drop (1981), Atom Bomb Angel (1982), Billionaire (1983), Possession (1988), Dreamer (1989), Sweet Heart (1990), Twilight (1991), Prophecy (1992), Host (1993, floppy disk edn 1994, world's first electronic novel), Alchemist (1996), Getting Wired (1996), The Truth (1997), Denial (1998), Faith (2000), Dead Simple (2005), Looking Good Dead (2006), Not Dead Enough (2007); *Awards* Krimi Blitz (Crime Writer of the Year) Germany 2005, Le Prix Polar Int France 2006, Le Prix Coeur Noir France 2007, shortlisted Crime Thriller of the Year Br Galaxy Book Awards 2007; *Recreations* skiing, tennis, wine, motor racing, cars, restaurants; *Clubs* Groucho; *Style—* Peter James, Esq; ✉ c/o Carole Blake, Blake Friedmann, 122 Arlington Road, London NW1 7HP (tel 020 7284 0408, e-mail scary@pavilion.co.uk, website www.peterjames.com)

JAMES, Prof (William) Philip Trehearne; CBE (1993); s of Jenkin William James (d 1944), and Lilian Mary, *née* Shaw (d 1992); *b* 27 June 1938; *Educ* Ackworth Sch Pontefract, UCL (BSc), UCH London (MB, BSc, MD), Univ of Cambridge (MA), Univ of London (DSc); *m* 1961, Jean Hamilton, da of James Lingford Moorhouse (d 1977); 1 s (Mark), 1 da (Claire); *Career* asst dir MRC Dunn Nutrition Unit Cambridge 1974–82, dir Rowett Res Inst Aberdeen 1982–99, hon res prof Univ of Aberdeen; former memb DHSS Ctees on Medical Aspects of Food Policy and Novel Foods; memb: EU Scientific Ctee for Food 1992–95, EU Sci Steering Ctee 1997–2000, BSE Ctee 2001–02; chm: FAO Expert Consultation on Nat Energy Needs 1987, UK Nat Food Alliance 1987–90 (pres 1990–98), Coronary Prevention Group 1988–96 (pres 1999–), Int Obesity Task Force 1996–, UN Cmmn on Future Global Food and Health Issues 1997–99; formerly chm Working Pty on Nat Advsy Ctee of Nutrition Educn, vice-chm FAO/WHO/UNU Expert Consultation on Energy and Protein Requirement of Man 1981–85; memb Nutrition Advsy Ctee WHO Euro Region 1985–, chm Consultation on Nutrition and Health WHO 1989–91, special advsr to WHO DG 1989–; chm Scottish Working Pty on: Diet and Scottish Public Health 1992–93, Obesity Management 1994–98; chm Global Alliance for the Prevention of Chronic Diseases 2005–, pres-elect Int Assoc for the Study of Obesity 2006–; lectures: Cuthbertson Meml Lecture 1979, Peter Beckett Lecture Dublin 1983, Ames Meml Lecture 1985, Mehta Oration India 1985, Middleton Meml Lecture 1986, Davidson Meml Lecture 1987, Minshull Meml Lecture 1989, Hallberg Oration 1994, Gopalan Oration 1994; Sir Alister McIntyre Distinguished Award Univ of WI 2002; FRCP 1978, FRSE 1986, FIBiol 1987; *Books* incl: The Analysis of Dietary Fibre in Food (1981), Assessing Human Energy Requirements (1990), Human Nutrition and Dietetics for Doctors (10 edn, 1999); papers on nutrient absorption, energy and protein metabolism, health policy and food labelling incl: Food Standards Agency Report to PM, European Food Authority Report for EU Cmmn; author and chm UN ACC/SCN Millennium Cmmn on Ending Malnutrition by 2020; *Recreations* talking, writing government reports, eating; *Clubs* Athenaeum (London); *Style—* Prof Philip James, CBE, MD, FRSE; ✉ 1 Gatti's Wharf, 5 New Wharf Road, London N1 9RS; The International Obesity Task Force, 231–3, North Gower Street, London NW1 2NS (tel 020 7691 1900, fax 020 7387 6033, e-mail jeanhjames@aol.com, website www.iotf.org)

JAMES, Richard Daniel; *Educ* King's Coll; *Family* 3 s, 1 da; *Career* health authority administrator; charge nurse: Harris Hosp Texas 1973–74, Central Middlesex Hosp 1975–77; nursing offr: Harefield Hosp 1975–77, Hammersmith Hosp 1977–79; sr nursing offr Ham Green Hosp and Clevedon Hosp 1979–82, dir Nursing Services Hosp and Community Bristol and Weston HA 1983–85, unit gen mangr (gen community) Salisbury HA 1989–92 (unit gen mangr (acute community) 1986–89), chief exec Severn NHS Tst Gloucester 1992–2001, chief exec Cotswold and Vale Primary Care Tst 2001–07, ret; SRN 1972, RCNT 1975, NDN 1983; *Style—* Richard James, Esq; ✉ Pidgemore Farm, Nupend, Stonehouse, Gloucestershire GL10 3SU

JAMES, Rita; da of Harry James Butcher (d 1993), of Leiston, Suffolk, and May Gladys, *née* Songer (d 1999); *b* 18 March 1946; *Educ* Leiston GS, Hornsey Coll of Art (BA), RCA (MDesRCA); *m* 16 Dec 1967 (m dis), William David James; *Career* womenswear apparel fabric designer; freelance work for textile mfrs and fashion designers incl Br Wool Mktg Bd, Harris Tweed UK, Promostyl, Sekine, Daniel Hechter, Cacharel, Jean-Charles de Castelbajac France and Echo scarves USA until 1979, fashion co-ordinator (womenswear fabrics) Int Wool Secretariat 1979–84, in own consultancy Design Works (specialising in colour prediction and woven fabric design) 1985–; clients incl: TMG Fabrics Portugal, Marumasu Company Japan, Busan Textile Co S Korea, Taiwan Textile Fedn Taiwan, Wools of New Zealand; lectr in woven textiles at various colls/instns, external moderator in woven textiles Central Saint Martin's Coll of Art and Design; rep on many indust working ctees; Burton Group Design Award 1974; FRSA 1971, FCSD 1986, Design Cncl registered 1991; *Recreations* opera, hill walking; *Style—* Ms Rita James; ✉ Design Works, The Coach House, 121 Ipswich Road, Woodbridge, Suffolk IP12 4BY (tel 01394 380949)

JAMES, Russell; *see:* Logan, Russell James Vincent Crickard

JAMES, Siân; MP; *b* 24 June 1959, Morriston; *m*; 2 c; *Career* MP (Lab) Swansea E 2005–; dir Welsh Women's Aid; *Style—* Mrs Siân James, MP; ✉ House of Commons, London SW1A 0AA (e-mail sianjamesmp@parliament.uk)

JAMES, Dr Simon Robert; s of Alan William James (d 1994), and Dorothy Denise James; *b* 1 April 1952; *Educ* LSE (BSc Econ, MSc), Open Univ (MBA, MA), Univ of Leicester (LLM), Leeds Metropolitan Univ (PhD), CDipAF DipM; *Career* res asst LSE 1974–76, reader in economics Univ of Exeter 1996– (lectr 1976–88, sr lectr 1988–96); visiting research fell Curtin Univ WA 1997 and 1999, visiting fell ANU 1998 and 2003; specialist conslt to New Shorter Oxford English Dictionary 1990–93; FRSA 1990, CTA (fell) (FTII 1992), ACIM 1996; *Books* incl: Self Assessment for Income Tax (with N A Barr and Prof A R Prest, 1977), The Economics of Taxation (with Prof C W Nobes, 1978, Chinese edn 1988, Japanese edn 1996, 7 edn 1998), A Dictionary of Economic Quotations (1981, 2 edn 1984), Pears Guide to Money and Investment (1982), A Dictionary of Sexist Quotations (1984), A Dictionary of Legal Quotations (1987, Indian edn 1994), The Comprehensibility of Taxation (1987), A Dictionary of Business Quotations (jtly, 1990), Chambers Sporting Quotations (1990), Collins Dictionary of Business Quotations (jtly, 1991), Trapped in Poverty? (jtly, 1992), Putting the Family First: Identities, Decisions, Citizenship (jtly, 1994), Self-Assessment and the UK Tax System (1995), A Dictionary of Taxation (1998), Taxation: Critical Perspectives on the World Economy (ed, 4 vols, 2002); *Recreations* distance learning, cooking, St John Ambulance, quotations; *Style—* Dr Simon James; ✉ School of Business and Economics, University of Exeter, Streatham Court, Rennes Drive, Exeter EX4 4PU (tel 01392 263204, fax 01392 263242, e-mail s.r.james@exeter.ac.uk)

JAMES, Stephen Lawrence; s of Walter Amyas James (d 1978), of Clifton, Bristol, and Cécile Juliet, *née* Hillman (d 1970); *b* 19 October 1930; *Educ* Clifton, St Catharine's Coll Cambridge (BA); *m* 1, 1955 (m dis 1986), Patricia Eleanor Favell, da of Reginald Cave (d 1968), of Bristol; 2 s (Oliver, Benedict), 2 da (Gabrielle, Miranda); m 2, 1998, Monique Whittome, wid of Dr David Whittome; *Career* called to the Bar Gray's Inn 1953, admitted slr 1959; Simmons & Simmons: ptnr 1961–80, sr ptnr 1980–92, conslt 1992–; dir: Horace Clarkson plc; memb Law Soc 1959; *Recreations* yachting (yacht 'Jacobite'), gardening; *Clubs* Royal Yacht Sqdn, Royal Thames Yacht, Royal Lymington Yacht; *Style—* Stephen James, Esq; ✉ Widden, Shirley Holmes, Lymington, Hampshire SO41 8NL; Simmons & Simmons, CityPoint, One Ropemaker Street, London EC2Y 9SS (tel 020 7628 2020, fax 020 7628 2070)

JAMES, Tzena; da of Nesho Karaneshev (d 1958), of Sofia, Bulgaria, and Anna, *née* Vitanova (d 1991); *b* 22 February 1937; *Educ* Sofia HS, Architectural Faculty of Civil Engrg Sofia (Dip Architecture), RIBA; *m* 28 Feb 1965 (m dis 1986), Dennis Edward James;

1 da (Anna-Maria b 29 Nov 1972); *Career* architectural asst private practice Vienna 1963–64, project architect Miny of Trade Dept of Architecture Bulgaria 1964–65, architectural asst Dept of Architecture and Civic Design GLC 1965–75, freelance architect Bureau d'Étude Brussels 1976–77; sr architect: Architectural RES Partnership 1979–80, Dept of Architecture Royal Borough of Kingston 1980–83; princ architect Slough Corp Architects Div 1983–87, team ldr Tech Servs Dept London Borough of Ealing 1987; sr project architect: Broadway Malyan Chartered Architects 1987–88, Boyer Design Gp 1988–89; sr professional tech offr PSA Building Mgmnt South East Heritage Dept 1989–94, fndr own architectural practice 1995, princ architect TJ Chartered Architects; RIBA: memb Cncl 1993–1996 and 2001–, past chm SAG Ctee, memb Disciplinary Ctee, memb Int Relations Ctee, past chm Kingston/Richmond Dist Branch, memb London Regnl Cncl; awarded dip in project mgmnt RICS 1995; *Recreations* modern languages (Bulgarian, Russian, German, French), classical music, visual arts, politics, skiing, swimming; *Style*— Mrs Tzena James; ✉ 14 Temple Road, Kew, Richmond, Surrey TW9 2ED (tel and fax 020 8940 4068, e-mail tzena.james@virgin.net)

JAMES, Valerie Mary; da of Colin Alfred James Jacobs, of Llanbedr, Denbighshire, and Betty Mary, *née* Rowse; *b* 9 November 1954, Plymouth; *Educ* Penrhos Coll Colwyn Bay (maj scholar), Somerville Coll Oxford (BA); *m* 12 May 1979, Michael Frank James; 2 s (Samuel Charles b 18 May 1983, Jeffrey William b 26 Oct 1985); *Career* slr; articled clerk Bond Pearce 1976–79, slr Coward Chance 1980–83, assoc Malcolm Lynch Slrs 1992–2000; Wrigleys Solicitors LLP (formerly Wrigleys): asst slr 2000–02, ptnr 2002–; govr: Penrhos Coll (later Rydal Penrhos) 1990–98, David Young Community Acad 2006–; memb: Law Soc 1980 (nat chm Trainee Slrs Gp 1977–78), Charity Law Assoc 1992, Ecclesiastical Law Soc 1995; *Publications* Charities, Governance and the Law: The way forward (contrib, 2003); *Recreations* cooking, classical music, tennis, reading; *Style*— Mrs Valerie James; ✉ Wrigleys Solicitors LLP, 19 Cookridge Street, Leeds LS2 3AG (tel 0113 244 6100, fax 0113 244 6101, e-mail valerie.james@wrigleys.co.uk)

JAMES, Prof Vivian Hector Thomas; s of William Percy James (d 1970), of London, and Alice May James (d 1936); *b* 29 December 1924; *Educ* Latymer Upper Sch, Univ of London (BSc, PhD, DSc); *m* 20 April 1958, Betty Irene, da of Frederick Pike (d 1941), of London; *Career* joined RAF VR 1942, served as cmmnd pilot in UK and M East, released Flt Lt 1946; sci staff Nat Inst for Med Res 1952–56, reader in chemical pathology St Mary's Hosp Med Sch 1962–67 (lectr 1956–62), prof of chemical endocrinology Univ of London 1967–73, prof and head of Dept of Chemical Pathology St Mary's Hosp Med Sch Univ of London 1973–90 (currently emeritus prof of chemical pathology Imperial Coll Sch of Med at St Mary's Hosp following merger); chm Div of Pathology St Mary's Hosp 1981; ed Clinical Endocrinology 1972–74; memb Herts AHA 1967–72, sec Clinical Endocrinology Ctee MRC 1976–82, chm Human Pituitary Collection MRC, pres Section of Endocrinology RSM 1976–78, dep sec gen Int Soc of Endocrinology 1986–, sec gen Euro Fedn of Endocrine Socs 1987–94; hon memb Soc for Endocrinology 2003– (gen sec 1979–83, treas 1983–91); fndr ed Endocrine-related Cancer 1993–, editorial advsr Euro Jl of Endocrinology 1994–2003; chm UK Sport Expert Ctee 1999–; hon memb Italian Endocrine Soc 1980, Leverhulme emeritus fell 1991; Clinical Endocrinology Tst Medal 1990, Soc for Endocrinology Jubilee Medal 1992; Freedom of Haverfordwest, Fiorino D'Oro City of Florence 1977; FRSM 1960, FRCPath, Hon MRCP; *Books* Hormones in Blood (1983), The Adrenal Gland (1979, 2 edn 1992); *Recreations* languages; *Style*— Prof Vivian James; ✉ Unit of Metabolic Medicine, Imperial College School of Medicine at St Mary's Hospital, London W2 1PG

JAMES, William Stirling; s of Wing Cdr Sir Archibald William Henry James, KBE, MC (d 1980), and Eugenia, *née* Morris (d 1991); *b* 20 November 1941; *Educ* St George's Coll Rhodesia, Stonyhurst, Magdalene Coll Cambridge (MA); *Career* Morgan Grenfell & Co Ltd 1964–65; Touche Ross & Co: London 1965–68, NY 1968–69; dir: Hill Samuel & Co Ltd 1980–96 (joined 1969), LCF Rothschild 1997–; farmer; external memb Lloyd's; FCA 1978 (ACA 1968); *Recreations* shooting, bridge; *Clubs* Boodle's, Pratt's, Annabel's; *Style*— William James, Esq; ✉ 14 Queensberry Mews West, London SW7 2DU (tel 020 7584 6750); Champions Farm, Pulborough, West Sussex RH20 3EF

JAMES OF HOLLAND PARK, Baroness (Life Peer UK 1991), of Southwold in the County of Holland Park; Phyllis Dorothy James (P D James); OBE (1983); da of late Sydney Victor James, and late Dorothy May Amelia, *née* Hone; *b* 3 August 1920; *Educ* Cambridge HS for Girls; *m* 8 Aug 1941, Connor Bantry White (d 1964), s of Harry Bantry White, MC; 2 da (Hon Clare Bantry (Hon Mrs Flook) b 1942, Hon Jane Bantry (Hon Mrs McLeod) b 1944); *Career* admin NHS 1949–68, princ Serving Police and Criminal Policy Dept Home Office 1968–79; novelist; chm: Soc of Authors 1984–86 (pres 1997–), Booker Prize Judges 1987; memb Bd Br Cncl 1988–93, chm Lit Advsy Panel and memb Arts Cncl 1988–92, govr BBC 1988–93; hon fell: St Hilda's Coll Oxford 1996, Downing Coll Cambridge 2000, Girton Coll Cambridge 2000; Hon DLitt: Buckingham Univ 1992, Univ of Hertfordshire 1994, Univ of Glasgow 1995, Univ of Durham 1998, Univ of Portsmouth 1999; Hon DLit: Univ of London 1993; Hon DUniv Essex 1996; FRSL, FRSA; *Books* Cover her Face (1962), A Mind to Murder (1963), Unnatural Causes (1967), Shroud for a Nightingale (1971), The Maul and the Pear Tree (with T A Critchley, 1971), An Unsuitable Job for a Woman (1972), The Black Tower (1975), Death of an Expert Witness (1977), Innocent Blood (1980), The Skull Beneath the Skin (1982), A Taste for Death (1986), Devices and Desires (1989), The Children of Men (1992), Original Sin (1994), A Certain Justice (1997), Time to be in Earnest (1999), Death in Holy Orders (2001), The Murder Room (2003), The Lighthouse (2005); *Recreations* reading, exploring churches, walking by the sea; *Clubs* The Detection; *Style*— The Rt Hon Baroness James of Holland Park, OBE; ✉ c/o Greene and Heaton Ltd, Literary Agent, 37 Goldhawk Road, London W12 8QQ (tel 020 8749 0315)

JAMIESON, Prof Ian Miller; s of James Miller Jamieson (d 1959), and Winifred Emma Jamieson (d 1980); *b* 10 November 1944; *Educ* Brockley County GS, Hastings GS, Univ of Surrey (BSc, PhD), Univ of Leicester (PGCE); *m* 1975, Anne Emmery, da of Aksel Pedersen; 1 s (Erik b 15 June 1976), 1 da (Claire b 27 Oct 1984); *Career* Ealing Coll of HE (now Thames Valley Univ): variously lectr, sr lectr, head of sociology 1969–77; evaluator then co-dir Schs Cncl industry project Schs Cncl London 1978–84, reader in business and mgmnt Thames Valley Univ 1984–85; Univ of Bath: lectr in educn and industry 1985–89, prof of educn 1989–, head Dept of Educn 1990–93, auditor Quality Assurance Agency, pro-vice-chllr 1994–97 and 2003–, dean Faculty of Humanities and Social Sciences 1997–2005; non-exec dir UCAS 1999–2001; ed Jl of Educn and Work 1987–2001; memb AcSS 2003; FRSA 1991; *Books* Capitalism and Culture (1980), Schools and Industry (1982), Industry and Education (1985), Mirrors of Work: Work Simulations in Schools (1988), Rethinking Work Experience (1991), School Effectiveness and School Improvement (1996); *Recreations* tennis, theatre, opera, golf, writing; *Clubs* Cumberwell Park Golf, Combe Grove Manor; *Style*— Prof Ian Jamieson; ✉ 3 Rock Cottages, Combe Down, Bath BA2 5JP; University of Bath, Claverton Down, Bath BA2 7AY (tel 01225 386013, fax 01225 826113, e-mail I.M.Jamieson@bath.ac.uk)

JAMIESON, Dr Maybeth; da of John Alexander Jamieson, of Dumfries, and Andrena (Rena), *née* Waugh (d 1994); *b* 15 May 1953, Dumfries, Scotland; *Educ* Dumfries Acad, Univ of Aberdeen (BSc), Univ of Glasgow (PhD); *Career* cytogeneticist Duncan Guthrie Inst of Med Genetics 1975–86, conslt embryologist Glasgow Royal Infirmary 1986–; memb Human Fertilisation and Embryology Authy 2002–; fndr memb Assoc of Clinical Embryologists 1993; *Recreations* music, photography, travel; *Style*— Dr Maybeth Jamieson; ✉ Assisted Conception Service Suite, Glasgow Royal Infirmary, 10 Alexander Parade, Glasgow G31 2ER (tel 0141 211 5089, fax 0141 211 1139, e-mail maybeth.jamieson@northglasgow.scot.nhs.uk)

JANNER OF BRAUNSTONE, Baron (Life Peer 1997), of Leicester in the County of Leicestershire; Hon Greville Ewan Janner; QC (1971); s of Baron Janner (Life Peer, d 1982), and Elsie Sybil, CBE, JP, *née* Cohen (d 1994); *b* 11 July 1928; *Educ* Bishop's Coll Sch Canada, St Paul's Sch, Trinity Hall Cambridge, Harvard Law Sch USA; *m* 1955, Myra Louise, *née* Sheink (d 1996); 1 s (Hon Daniel), 2 da (Hon Marion, Hon Laura); *Career* called to the Bar 1955, author, journalist, broadcaster; MP (Lab): Leicester NW 1970–74, Leicester W 1974–97 (Parly candidate (Lab) Wimbledon 1955); chm Select Ctee on Employment 1992–96; chm All Pty Safety Gp, co-chm All Pty Employment Gp 1996–97, former vice-chm All Pty Parly Ctee for Release of Soviet Jewry; pres: Bd of Deputies of British Jews 1979–85, REACH 1980–, Cwlth Jewish Cncl (inaugural pres) 1982–, Inter-Parly Cncl Against Anti-Semitism 1990–, Maimonides Fndn 1993–2002; vice-pres World Jewish Congress 1981–, chm Holocaust Educnl Tst 1990–, jt pres Co-Existence Tst; former dir Jewish Chronicle Newspaper Ltd, non-exec dir Ladbroke plc 1986–95; Hon PhD Haifa Univ, Hon LLD De Montfort Univ; FIPD 1976; Kt Cdr Lithuanian Order of Grand Duke Gediminas 2002; *Books* 67 books incl: Janner's Complete Speechmaker (7 edn, 2003), One Hand Alone Cannot Clap (1998); *Recreations* Magic Circle, languages, swimming; *Style*— The Lord Janner of Braunstone, QC; ✉ House of Lords, London SW1A 0PW

JANSEN, N Elly; OBE (1980); da of Jacobus Gerrit Jansen, of Wisch, Holland, and Petronella Suzanna, *née* Vellekoop; *b* 5 October 1929; *Educ* Paedologisch Inst Free Univ Amsterdam, Boerhave Kliniek (SRN), Univ of London; *m* 1969, (Alan Brian Stewart) George Whitehouse; 3 da; *Career* fndr and dir Richmond Fellowship for Community Mental Health 1959–91, fndr and ceo Richmond Fellowship Int 1981–99, fndr and exec tstee Fellowship Charitable Fndn (now called Community Housing and Therapy) 1983–93; fndr Richmond Fellowship of: America 1968, Aust 1973, NZ 1977, Austria 1978, and subsequently of Barbados, Bangladesh, Bolivia, Canada, Costa Rica, France, Ghana, Grenada, Hong Kong, India, Israel, Jamaica, Malta, Mexico, Nigeria, Peru, Philippines, Trinidad & Tobago, Uruguay and Zimbabwe; fndr and ceo Richmond Fellowship Fndn Int 2006–; dep chm Richmond Fellowship Enquiry 1981–82; conslt to: Min of Social Affairs Holland 1969–73, Pan-American Health Organisation 1987–; advsr to many govts on community care legislation and servs; organiser of Int Confs on Therapeutic Communities 1973, 1975, 1976, 1979, 1984,1988 and 1999; fell German Marshall Meml Fund 1977–78; Templeton Award 1985; MInstD 1997; *Books* The Therapeutic Community Outside The Hospital (ed, 1980), Mental Health and the Community (contrib, 1983), Towards a Whole Society (contrib, 1985), R D Laing, Creative Destroyer (contrib, 1997); *Recreations* nature, reading, music, photography; *Style*— Mrs N Elly Whitehouse-Jansen, OBE; ✉ Clyde House, 109 Strawberry Vale, Twickenham TW1 4SJ (tel 020 8744 0374, fax 020 8891 0500)

JANSON-SMITH, (Peter) Patrick; s of John Peter Janson-Smith, of London, and Diana Mary, *née* Whittaker, of Dinant, Belgium; *b* 28 July 1949; *Educ* Cathedral Sch Salisbury, Cokethorpe Park Sch Witney; *m* 1, 22 April 1972 (m dis), Lavinia Jane, da of Robert Hugh Priestley, MBE; 1 da (Emma Mary b 12 Dec 1975), 1 s (Mark Robert b 19 July 1978); m 2, 12 June 1987 (m dis), Pamela Jean, da of Cdr Anthony William Gossage, RN; 2 s (Oscar William Patrick b 9 Jan 1989, Daniel Alexander b 15 Jan 1991); m 3, 20 March 2006, Mrs Anne-Louise Fisher; *Career* publisher; asst to export publicity mangr University of London Press Ltd (Hodder & Stoughton) 1967–69; Granada Publishing: asst to publicity mangr Panther Books Ltd 1969–70, ed Mayflower Books 1970–71 and 1973–74, press offr 1971–72; publicity mangr Octopus Books 1972; Transworld Publishers: ed Corgi Books 1974–78, assoc editorial dir Corgi Books 1978–79, editorial dir Nationwide Book Serv 1979–81, publisher Corgi & Black Swan Books 1981–95, publisher Transworld Publishers Adult Trade Div 1995–99, dep md (publishing) 1999–2001, jt md and publisher 2001–03, publisher 2003–06; agent Christopher Little Literary Agency 2006–; memb: Ctee Soc of Young Publishers 1969–71, Whitefriars Soc 1992–, Bd Edinburgh Book Festival 1994–99, Soc of Bookmen 1998–; *Recreations* book collecting, late 19th and early 20th century illustrations, wine and food; *Clubs* Garrick, Century; *Style*— Patrick Janson-Smith, Esq; ✉ The Christopher Little Literary Agency, 10 Eel Brook Studios, 125 Moore Park Road, London SW6 4PS

JANSONS, Mariss; s of Arvid Jansons, conductor; *b* 1943; *Educ* Leningrad Conservatory, Second Vienna Acad; *Career* conductor; trained with Prof Hans Swarowsky in Vienna and with Herbert von Karajan in Salzburg (winner Herbert von Karajan Competition 1971); Leningrad (now St Petersburg) Philharmonic: assoc princ conductor 1985, conducted orch on numerous tours to Europe, N America and Japan; Oslo Philharmonic: music dir 1979–2000, conducted orch at numerous international venues incl Salzburg Festival and Edinburgh Festivals, Carnegie Hall NY, Suntory Hall Tokyo, Vienna Musikverein and BBC Proms; princ guest conductor LPO 1992–98, prof of conducting St Petersburg Conservatoire 1993–2000, music dir Pittsburgh Symphony Orch 1997–2004, chief conductor Symphony Orch of Bavarian Radio 2003–, chief conductor Royal Concertgebouw Orch 2004–; conducted numerous other orchs incl: Boston, Chicago, Baltimore and Pittsburg Symphonies, Cleveland Orch, Philadelphia Orch, Los Angeles Philharmonic, Toronto and Montreal Symphonies, Vienna Symphony and Philharmonic, Berlin Philharmonic, Royal Concertgebouw Amsterdam, NDR Symphony Germany, Israel Philharmonic, LSO, LPO, The Philharmonia; recorded TV series Jansons Conducts for BBC Wales 1991; hon dr Univs of Oslo and Riga; hon memb Royal Acad of Music; EMI Classics' Artist of the Year 1996; awarded Anders Jahre Norwegian Culture Prize, Cdr with Star Royal Norwegian Order of Merit 1995, Three Star Medal of Latvia; *Recordings* with St Petersburg Philharmonic incl Shostakovich's 7th Symphony 1989 (winner Eddison Award Holland 1989); with Oslo Philharmonic incl: complete Tchaikovsky Symphonies (Chandos), numerous for EMI incl Sibelius and Prokofiev violin concertos (with Frank-Peter Zimmerman), Wagner overtures, Dvořák's Symphonies 5 (winner Penguin Award), 8 and 9, Saint-Saens Symphony No 3 (winner Spellemannsprisen Norway), other works by Bartók, Mussorgsky, Ravel, Respighi, Shostakovich and Svendsen; complete symphones of Shostakovich (Grammy Award for Symphony No 13); *Style*— Mariss Jansons, Esq; ✉ c/o Radmila Schweitzer, Symphonieorchester des Bayerischen Rundfunks, Runfunkplatz 1, 80335 Munich, Germany (tel 00 49 89 5900 4974)

JANTET, Georges Henry; s of Auguste Jantet (d 1955), and Renée, *née* Jacob (d 1978); *b* 5 October 1927; *Educ* Lycée Français de Londres, St Benedict's Sch Ealing, St Mary's Hosp Med Sch London (MB BS, Martin John Turner prize); *m* 4 June 1955, Alice, da of Jean-François Moulin, of St Etienne, France; 3 da (Martine (Mrs Cremer) b 4 March 1956, Blandine (Mrs Manière) b 24 March 1959, Nadine (Mrs Pistolesi) b 16 March 1963), 1 s (Bruno b 16 April 1957); *Career* Mil Serv with Serv de Santé des Armées Paris and Lyon 1952–53; house surgeon St Mary's Hosp then The Miller Hosp 1951–52, resident surgical offr Hôpital Français London 1953–54, sr house offr Royal Marsden Hosp 1954–55; St Mary's Hosp: prosector in anatomy and demonstrator Dept of Anatomy Med Sch 1953, resident casualty surgeon 1954, surgical registrar Surgical Professorial Unit 1955–57, sr registrar in surgery 1959–66 (also Regnl Hosp Bd NW Thames), assoc teacher Med Sch 1970–; lectr in surgery and research fell Surgical Professorial Unit St Thomas' Hosp and Med Sch 1957–59, research fell and asst in surgery Dept of Surgery Peter Bent Brigham Hosp Harvard 1961–62, conslt in gen and vascular surgery The Ealing Hosp and Assoc Hosps 1966–92; hon conslt surgeon: Dispensaire Français London 1967–, The Italian

Hosp London 1967–, Hammersmith Hosp and Royal Postgrad Med Sch 1974–92 (also sr lectr in surgery); RCS: surgical tutor 1973–77, regnl advsr 1977–88, memb Manpower Advsy Panel 1987–92, memb Euro Gp 1989–, chm Ct of Examiners 1986–87; memb numerous ctees NW Thames Regnl Health Authy (chm Surgeons' Ctee 1989–92); memb: BMA 1960, Cncl Assoc of Surgeons of GB & Ireland 1987–94 (fell 1966), Vascular Surgical Soc of GB & Ireland, Cncl Hunterian Soc 1975–90 (fell 1966, pres 1986–87), Société Clinique Française 1985– (pres 1987–90), Br Lymphology Interest Gp 1987–92; pres Union Internationale de Phlébologie 1995–99 (vice-pres 1992–95); memb Editorial Bd and Scientific Advsy Ctee various learned jls; FRCS 1955 (MRCS 1951), FRSM 1966; Chevalier Ordre National du Mérite, Chevalier de la Légion d'Honneur; *Books* New Trends In Basic Lymphology (co-ed, 1967), Phlebology 1985 (co-ed, 1986); author of chapters in various books; *Recreations* family and social life, tennis, sailing, fishing, skiing, travelling, history, current affairs, music; *Clubs* Surgical Specialists Soc, Roehampton; *Style*— Georges Jantet, Esq; ✉ 14 Rue Duroc, 75007 Paris, France (tel 00 33 1 47 34 46 28, e-mail jantet.georges@wanadoo.fr)

JANVRIN, Sir Robin Berry; GCB (2007, KCB 2003, CB 1997), GCVO (2007, KCVO 1998, CVO 1994, LVO 1983), PC (1998); s of Vice Adm Sir (Hugh) Richard Benest Janvrin, KCB, DSC (d 1993), and Nancy Edyth, *née* Fielding (d 1994); *b* 20 September 1946; *Educ* Marlborough, BNC Oxford; *m* 22 Oct 1977, Isabelle, da of Yann de Boissonneaux de Chevigny; 2 s, 2 da; *Career* RN: RNC Dartmouth 1964, HMS Devonshire 1965, HMS Lynx 1970, HMS Ganges 1973, HMS Royal Arthur 1974; Dip Serv: FCO 1975, 1978 and 1984, first sec UK Delgn NATO 1976, New Delhi 1981, cnsllr and dep head Personnel Dept 1985–87; private sec to HM The Queen 1999–2007 (press sec 1987–90, asst private sec 1990–95, dep private sec 1996–99); *Style*— The Rt Hon Sir Robin Janvrin, GCB, GCVO

JAQUES, Geoffrey Wilfred; s of Jack Kearsley Jaques, of Sevenoaks, Kent, and Yvette, *née* Hopkins; *b* 14 September 1942; *Educ* Downside, Univ of Manchester (LLB); *m* 18 Sept 1965, Marcia Hemming, da of late Norman Cowan Woodhead; 2 da (Sarah Lucy (Mrs Vavasour) b 17 June 1966, Sophie Victoria (Mrs Kaya) b 10 Oct 1970), 2 s (Charles Alexander Kearsley b 4 June 1968, Justin Geoffrey Kearsley b 10 March 1972); *Career* called to the Bar Lincoln's Inn 1963 (Mansfield scholar, bencher 1991), admitted to NSW Bar 1990, head of chambers 1991–98, registrar in bankruptcy Royal Courts of Justice 1998–; *Books* Butterworth's Encyclopedia of Forms and Precedents (co-ed, 4 edn, vols 18 and 19 sale of land, 1969); *Recreations* watching cricket; *Clubs* Athenaeum, MCC; *Style*— Geoffrey Jaques, Esq; ✉ Royal Courts of Justice, Strand, London WC2A 2LL

JARAY, Tess; da of Francis Ferdinand Jaray (d 1987), and Pauline, *née* Arndt; *b* 31 December 1937; *Educ* St Martin's Sch of Art, Slade Sch of Art; *Children* 2 da (Anna Vaux b 1964, Georgia Vaux b 1966); *Career* artist; teacher Hornsey Coll of Art 1964–68, teacher Slade Sch of Art 1968–99; *Solo Exhibitions* Grabowski Gallery 1963 (with Marc Vaux), Hamilton Gallery 1965 and 1967, Demarco Gallery Edinburgh 1967, Axiom Gallery London 1969, Graves Art Gallery Sheffield 1972, City Art Gallery Bristol 1972, Whitechapel Art Gallery 1973 (with Marc Vaux), Flowers Gallery 1976, Adelaide Festival Centre 1980, Whitworth Art Gallery Manchester 1984, Ashmolean Museum (Prints and Drawings) Oxford 1984, Serpentine Gallery 1988; *Group Exhibitions* Galleria Trastevere Rome 1962, John Moores Exhbn Liverpool 1963–78, Fine Art for Industry (RCA) 1969, 7 From London (Bern) 1973, British Painting 1974 (Hayward Gallery) 1974, Artists of the Sixties (Tate) 1977, 80 Prints by Modern Masters (Flowers Gallery) 1982, Platforms for Artists (BR/Gateshead Borough Cncl) 1987, and others; *Commissions* mural British pavilion Expo 1967 Montreal 1967, terrazzo floor Victoria Station London 1985, decorative paving Stoke-on-Trent Garden Festival 1986, decorative paving Midlands Art Centre 1987, Centenary Square Birmingham 1991, Cathedral Precinct Wakefield 1992, Hospital Square Leeds 1998 and others; *Work in Public Collections* Tate Gallery, Arts Cncl, Stadtisches Museum Leverkusen, British Cncl, Peter Stuyvesant Fndn Holland, UCL, Walker Art Gallery Liverpool, DOE, Univ of Warwick, Sundvalls Museum Stockholm, MOMA Belgrade, V&A, Graves Art Gallery Sheffield, Museum of Fine Art Budapest, Contemporary Art Soc, and others; *Style*— Ms Tess Jaray

JARDINE, Sir Andrew Colin Douglas; 5 Bt (UK 1916), of Godalming, Surrey; er s of Brig Sir Ian Liddell Jardine, 4 Bt, OBE, MC (d 1982), and Priscilla, *née* Scott-Phillips; *b* 30 November 1955; *Educ* Charterhouse, Royal Agric Coll/Univ of Reading 1993–96 (BSc); *m* 11 Oct 1997, Dr Claire Vyvien Griffith, da of Dr William Griffith, of Lyth Hill, Shrewsbury; 2 da (Iona Claire b 21 Feb 1999, Alexandra Scilla b 14 July 2001), 1 s (Guy Andrew b 15 March 2004); *Heir* s, Guy Jardine; *Career* served Royal Green Jackets 1975–78; C T Bowring & Co 1979–81, Henderson Administration Group plc 1981–92, dir Gartmore Investment Management Ltd 1992–93, Strutt & Parker 1996–99, resident land agent 2000–; memb Queen's Body Guard for Scotland (Royal Co of Archers); MSI 1993, MRICS 1998; *Style*— Sir Andrew Jardine, Bt; ✉ Comely Farm, Clapton, Berkeley, Gloucestershire GL13 9QX (tel 01453 511780)

JARDINE, Prof Nicholas; s of Michael James Jardine (d 1988), and Jean Caroline, *née* Crook (d 1997); *b* 4 September 1943; *Educ* Monkton Combe, King's Coll Cambridge (Trevelyan scholar, BA, PhD); *m* 1992, Marina, da of Mario Frasca-Spada; 4 c by previous marriages; *Career* Royal Society research fell 1968–73, sr research fell King's Coll Cambridge 1971–75 (jr research fell 1967–71); Univ of Cambridge: univ lectr in history and philosophy of science 1975–85, reader 1985–91, prof of history and philosophy of the sciences 1991–; fell Darwin Coll Cambridge 1975–; ed: Studies in History and Philosophy of Science 1982–, Studies in History and Philosophy of Biological and Biomedical Sciences 1998–; FBA; *Books* Mathematical Taxonomy (with R Sibson, 1971), The Birth of History and Philosophy of Science (1984, revised edn 1988), The Fortunes of Inquiry (1986), Romanticism and the Sciences (ed with A Cunningham, 1990), The Scenes of Inquiry (1991, revised edn 2000), Cultures of Natural History (ed with J Secord and E Spary, 1996), Books and the Sciences in History (ed with M Frasca-Spada, 2000); *Recreations* fungus hunting; *Style*— Prof Nicholas Jardine; ✉ Department of History and Philosophy of Science, University of Cambridge, Free School Lane, Cambridge CB2 3RH (tel 01223 334546)

JARDINE, Prof Richard James; s of Maj David Jardine (d 1987), and Dorothy, *née* Whitbread; *b* 15 May 1953; *Educ* Sir Roger Manwood's GS Sandwich, Imperial Coll London (BSc, MSc, DIC, PhD); *m* 1; 1 s (James Alexander b 5 Dec 1988), 1 da (Olivia Jane b 21 Jan 1991); m 2, Jayne Elizabeth, *née* Birch; 1 s (Alexander George b 2 Sept 2005); *Career* with Sir William Halcrow and Partners 1974–75, work on Thames tidal flood defences Southern Water Authy 1975–77, numerous major highways projects Kent CC 1977–81; Imperial Coll London: research asst 1981–84, lectr and reader 1984–98, prof of geotechnics 1998–; assoc Geotechnical Consulting Gp 1986–; ICE Telford Premium 1985, Unwin Prize Imperial Coll London 1985, Geotechnique Award 1988, American Soc for Testing Materials Hogentogler Award 1992, Japanese Ronbun Show Award 1993, Br Geotechnical Soc Prize 1996, Royal Acad of Engrg Medal 1998; FICE 2001 (MICE 1979), FREng 2002, FCGI 2007; *Publications* over 150 pubns on soil mechanics, geotechnics, fndns and offshore structures; *Recreations* tennis, diving, sailing, music; *Clubs* Iguales; *Style*— Prof Richard Jardine; ✉ Department of Civil and Environmental Engineering, Imperial College, London SW7 2BU (tel 020 7594 6083, fax 020 7225 2716, e-mail r.jardine@imperial.ac.uk)

JARDINE OF APPLEGIRTH, Sir Alexander Maule; 12 Bt (NS 1672), of Applegirth, Dumfriesshire; 23 Chief of Clan Jardine; s of Col Sir William Edward Jardine of Applegirth, 11 Bt, OBE, TD, JP, DL (d 1986), and Ann Graham Maitland (d 2006); *b* 24 August 1947; *Educ* Gordonstoun, Scottish Agric Coll Aberdeen (Dip Farm Business Orgn and Mgmnt); *m* 9 Oct 1982, Mary Beatrice, posthumous only child of Hon John Michael Inigo Cross (yst s of 2 Viscount Cross), and Sybil Anne, *née* Murray, who m subsequently Lt Cdr James Parker-Jervis, RN; 3 s (William Murray b 1984, John Alexander Cross b 1991, Douglas Edward b 1994), 2 da (Kirsty Sybil b 1986, Jean Maule b 1988); *Heir* s, William Jardine, yr of Applegirth; *Career* herb farmer, fuel saving and property mgmnt; memb Queen's Body Guard for Scotland (Royal Co of Archers); *Recreations* gardening, curling; *Style*— Sir Alexander Jardine of Applegirth, Bt; ✉ Ash House, Thwaites, Millom, Cumbria LA18 5HY (tel 01229 716331)

JARMAN, Andrew M; s of Basil Jarman (d 1999), of Petersfield, Hants, and Josephine Mary, *née* Lockyer (d 2000); *b* 16 May 1957; *Educ* Portsmouth GS, Hertford Coll Oxford (MA), Univ of Oxford (PGCE), NPQH; *m* 16 Aug 1980, Kerstin Maria, *née* Bailey; 1 s (Conrad William Anders b 24 April 1992), 2 da (Annika Elizabeth (twin) b 24 April 1992, Ella Louise b 15 June 1994); *Career* mathematics teacher: Aylesbury GS 1979–80, Portsmouth GS 1980–84, Haberdashers' Aske's Sch Elstree 1984–88; Cheltenham Coll: head of mathematics 1988–92, dir of studies 1992–2001; headmaster Lancaster Royal GS 2001–; memb ASCL, assoc memb HMC; memb Ct Lancaster Univ; *Recreations* cricket, golf, antique wineglasses; *Clubs* East India; *Style*— Andrew Jarman, Esq; ✉ Lancaster Royal Grammar School, East Road, Lancaster LA1 3EF (tel 01524 580600, fax 01524 847947, e-mail ajarman@lrgs.org.uk)

JARMAN, Prof Sir Brian; kt (1998), OBE (1988); *Educ* MB BS, MA, DIC, PhD; *Career* house physician St Mary's Hosp London 1969, house surgn St Bernard's Hosp Gibraltar 1970, resident in med Beth Israel Hosp Harvard Med Sch 1970, trainee GP London 1971, princ in GP Lisson Grove Health Centre London 1971–98, prof of primary health care and gen practice and head of dept Imperial Coll Sch of Med at St Mary's Hosp (St Mary's Med Sch until merger 1997)1984–98 (pt/t sr lectr 1973–83), head Primary Care and Population Health Sciences Div Imperial Coll Sch of Med 1997–98 (emeritus prof of primary health care 1998–); memb: MRC Health Servs Research Ctee 1987–89, English Nat Bd 1988–90, Kensington Chelsea and Westminster FHSA 1990–96, King's Fund Mgmnt Ctee 1994–97, London Strategic Review Panel Dept of Health 1997–98; medical memb Bristol Royal Infirmary Inquiry 1998–2001, sr fell Inst for Healthcare Improvement Boston USA, pres elect BMA 2002–; author of numerous papers in academic jls and research advsr to various bodies nationally and internationally; FRCGP 1984, FRCP 1988, FFPH 1999 (MFPHM 1994), FMedSci 1999; *Style*— Prof Sir Brian Jarman, OBE; ✉ Imperial College School of Medicine, Norfolk Place, London W2 1PG (tel 020 7594 3352, e-mail b.jarman@ic.ac.uk)

JARMAN, Nicolas Francis Barnaby; QC (1985); s of Archibald Seymour Jarman (d 1982), of Brighton, and Helen Marie Klenk; *b* 19 June 1938; *Educ* Harrow, ChCh Oxford (MA); *m* 1, 1973 (m dis 1977), Jennifer Michelle, da of Michael Lawrence Lawrence-Smith (d 1988), of Suffolk; 1 da (Jemima b 1975); m 2, Julia Elizabeth, da of Leonard Owen-John (d 1995), of Swansea; *Career* JUO Mons Offr Trg Sch 1957, cmmnd RA 1957, served Cyprus; called to the Bar Inner Temple 1965, in practice Midland & Oxford circuit, recorder of the Crown Ct 1982–, head of chambers 1989–2001; pres Mental Health Review Tbnl; jt chm Bucks Berks and Oxon Barristers-Slrs Jt Liaison Ctee 1985–96; *Recreations* fly fishing, France; *Style*— Nicolas Jarman, Esq, QC; ✉ Mas Terrier-Gibertes, 30700 Flaux, France (tel 00 334 6603 0308); 4 King's Bench Walk, Temple, London EC4 (tel 020 7822 7000)

JARMAN, Dr Paul Richard; s of Prof Sir Brian Jarman, OBE, *qv*; *b* 25 March 1964; *Educ* William Ellis Sch London, St Peter's Coll Oxford (exhibitioner, MA), UCL and Middx Hosp Sch of Med (MB BS), Inst of Neurology UCL (PhD); *Career* conslt neurologist Nat Hosp for Neurology and Neurosurgery, UC Hosps and Homerton Hosp London 2001–, hon sr lectr UCL 2001–; memb Fitness to Practice Ctee GMC; author of pubns on neurology and neurological genetics; *Style*— Dr Paul Jarman; ✉ National Hospital for Neurology and Neurosurgery, Queen Square, London WC1N 3BG (tel 020 7837 3611)

JARMAN, Richard Neville; s of Dr Gwyn Jarman (d 1995), of Herts, and Pauline, *née* Lane (d 2002); *b* 24 April 1949; *Educ* King's Sch Canterbury, Trinity Coll Oxford (MA); *Career* ENO: mktg mangr 1971–74, asst to admin dir 1974–76; dance touring offr Arts Cncl of GB 1976–77; Edinburgh Int Festival: artistic asst 1978–82, festival admin 1982–84; general admin English Nat Ballet 1984–90, general dir Scottish Opera 1991–97, interim general mangr Arts Theatre Cambridge 1997–98, artistic dir Royal Opera House 1998–2000, DG Britten-Pears Fndn and The Britten Estate 2002–; dir Scottish Opera; FRSA; *Books* History of Sadler's Wells/English National Opera (1974), History of the London Coliseum (1976), History of the New Opera Company (1978); *Recreations* gardening, music, theatre, food and drink; *Style*— Richard Jarman, Esq; ✉ 78 Riversdale Road, Highbury, London N5 2JZ (tel and fax 020 3227 0086, e-mail richard-jarman@btconnect.com)

JARRATT, Dr John Anthony; s of Leslie Jarratt (d 1958), and Lily, *née* Tweedie (d 1977); *b* 26 December 1939; *Educ* Spalding GS, Univ of Sheffield Med Sch (MB ChB); *m* 21 Feb 1970, Patricia Anne, da of Jack Madin, of Alford, Lincolnshire; 2 s (Mark b 24 Nov 1971, Paul b 5 Aug 1975); *Career* Nat Hosp for Nervous Diseases London: academic registrar 1969–70, MRC res fell 1970–72, registrar in clinical neurophysiology 1972; registrar in neurology Middx Hosp 1972, sr registrar Dept of Clinical Neurophysiology Rigshospitalet Copenhagen 1973, conslt in clinical neurophysiology Sheffield AHA 1976–, hon lectr in neurology Univ of Sheffield 1976–; author of numerous scientific pubns; pres Assoc of Br Clinical Neurophysiologists 1990–93 (sec 1984–88); memb Jt Neurosciences Ctee 1984–88, chm SAC on Higher Med Trg in Clinical Neurophysiology RCP 1988– (memb 1984–88), memb Expert Panel EEC 1989; memb: Assoc of Br Neurologists 1978, EEG Soc 1991; FRCP 1981; *Recreations* golf, photography, music, travel, technical innovation; *Style*— Dr John Jarratt; ✉ Department of Clinical Neurophysiology, Royal Hallamshire Hospital, Sheffield S10 2JF (tel 0114 271 2399)

JARRATT, Prof Peter; s of Edward Jarratt (d 1988), and Edna Mary Eliza, *née* Pearson (d 1976); *b* 2 January 1935; *Educ* Bingley GS, Univ of Manchester (BSc), Univ of Bradford (PhD); *m* 1 June 1971, Jeanette, da of Lucien Adrian Debeir (d 1946); 1 s (Robin Alexander Debeir b 1972), 1 da (Sophie Amanda Debeir b 1978); *Career* sr lectr Univ of Bradford 1963–72, dir of Computing Laboratory Univ of Salford 1972–75; Univ of Birmingham: prof of computer science 1975–2001, dir of Computer Centre 1975–90, dean Faculty of Science 1985–88, devpt advsr to Vice-Chllr 1991–98, exec chm for IT 1992–93, emeritus prof 2001–, memb Ct 2002–; dir: TV and Film Unit 1983–95, Birmingham Research Park 1985–88, Computer Based Learning Centre 1993–2001, Biss Ltd 1994–96, CARMA Ltd 1994–, Wang Ltd 1997–99, Wang Global Ltd 1998–2000; govr Royal Nat Coll for the Blind 1986–96; memb Exec Ctee Lunar Soc of Birmingham 1991–94, tstee Nat Fndn for Conductive Educn 1985–88, patron Henshaw's Soc for the Blind 1993–; author of numerous scientific pubns; FIMA 1968, FBCS 1968, FSS 1972, CEng 1990, CITP 2004; *Recreations* gardening, mountain walking, opera, chess, power boating; *Clubs* Athenaeum; *Style*— Prof Peter Jarratt; ✉ c/o Athenaeum, 107 Pall Mall, London SW1Y 5ER (tel 07773 666440, fax 020 798 8475, e-mail jarratt@risk-reward.com); The University of Birmingham, Edgbaston, Birmingham B15 2TT (tel 0121 414 3487, fax 0121 414 4281, e-mail p.jarratt@cs.bham.uk)

JARRETT, Rt Rev Martyn William; *see:* Beverley, Bishop of

JARRETT, Paul Eugene Marcus; s of Dr Maurice Eugene Decimus Jarrett (d 1987), of Woking, Surrey, and Doris Mabel Lake, of Cobham, Surrey; *b* 18 February 1943; *Educ* Queen Elizabeth's GS Blackburn, Downing Coll Cambridge (MA), St Thomas' Hosp London (MB BChir, DObstRCOG); *m* 1 April 1966, Ann, da of George Wilson (d 1982), of Blackburn, Lancs; 1 s (Michael b 1972); *Career* Kingston Hosp: conslt surgn 1978–2004, dir of surgical servs 1987–97; chm Healthcare Holdings plc 1993–94; former tstee Princess Alice Hospice Esher, former chm Br Assoc of Day Surgery, past pres Int Assoc of Ambulatory Surgery; FRCS 1972; *Recreations* medical antiques, golf; *Style—* Prof Paul Jarrett; ✉ Langleys, Queens Drive, Oxshott, Surrey KT22 0PB (tel 01372 842259, fax 01372 844257)

JARROLD, Kenneth Wesley; CBE (1997); s of William Stanley Jarrold (d 1981), and Martha Hamilton, *née* Cowan (d 1998); *b* 19 May 1948; *Educ* St Lawrence Coll Ramsgate, Sidney Sussex Coll Cambridge (Whittaker scholar, BA, pres Cambridge Union), Inst of Health Servs Mgmnt (Dip); *m* 1973 (sep 2007), Patricia, da of William Hadaway; 2 s (Luke b 28 Jan 1977, Paul b 6 April 1979); *Career* nat mgmnt trainee E Anglian Regnl Health Bd 1969–70, Briggs Ctee on Nursing 1970–71, dep supt Royal Hosp Sheffield 1971–74, hosp sec Derbyshire Royal Infirmary 1974–75, sector admin Nottingham Gen and Univ Hosps 1975–79, asst dist admin (planning) S Tees HA 1979–82, dist gen mangr Gloucester HA 1985–89 (dist admin 1982–84), chief exec Wessex RHA 1990–94; dir of human resourses NHS Executive 1994–97, chief exec Co Durham HA 1997–2002, chief exec Co Durham and Tees Valley Strategic HA 2002–05, dir Dearden Consulting 2007– (sr conslt 2006–); hon visiting prof: Univ of Salford 1998–2004, Univ of York 1998–, Univ of Durham 2005–; fell John Snow Coll Univ of Durham 2006–; pres Inst of Health Serv Mgmnt 1985–86 (memb Nat Cncl 1977–89); chm: MESOL Project Gp 1986–89 and 1991–93, Durham and Teeside Workforce Devpt Confedn 2001–02, Dept of Health Working Pty on Code of Conduct for NHS Mangrs 2002, NHS Reference Gp on Health Equalities 2003–05, Dept of Health Task Gp on Maximising the NHS contrib to Public Health 2004; memb: NHS Trg Authy 1984–87 (also chm Trg Ctee), Nat Advsy Bd NHS Leadership Centre 2002–04, Nat Mental Health Task Force 2003–05, HME Prog Bd on Health Inequalities 2004–05; non-exec dir Serious Organised Crime Agency 2005–; chair Co Durham Economic Partnership 2006–; Hon Dr Open Univ 1999; MHSM 1972, FIPD 1998; *Style—* Kenneth Jarrold, Esq, CBE; ✉ 20 Dunottar Avenue, Eaglescliffe, Stockton-on-Tees, Cleveland TS16 0AB

JARVIS, Anthony (Tony); s of Donald Anthony Jarvis (d 1997), and Ida, *née* Allmond (d 1998); *b* 1945; *Educ* City of Oxford HS, Univ of Sussex (BEd, MA); *m* Brigit Mary, *née* Convery; 1 s; *Career* dep princ St George's Sch Rome 1984–90, headmaster Sir Thomas Rich's Sch Gloucester 1990–94, headmaster St Olave's & St Saviour's GS Orpington 1994–; memb HMC 1996, headteacher memb Army Scholarship Bd; govr Hurstpierpoint Coll; fell and memb Bd of Dirs Woodward Corp; FRSA 1993; *Style—* Mr Tony Jarvis

JARVIS, David; s of Harold Jarvis (d 1945), and Phyllis Emma, *née* Hart; *b* 9 March 1941; *Educ* Gillingham GS, Maidstone Coll of Tech; *m* 9 Feb 1963, Williamina Bell, da of William Herbert Colby; 1 s (Julian David b 1966), 2 da (Andrea Claire b 1968, Nicola Emma b 1976); *Career* Anderson Clayton: controller and treas Milne and Cosa 1963–68, fin admin Peru 1968–70, gen mangr Consumer Prods Div Mexico 1970–78; gen mangr Int Business Devpt The Pillsbury Co USA 1978–81, vice-chm and chief fin offr Norwest Corp USA 1981–86, currently co-head Global Fin Instns Citigroup Global Markets (formerly Salomon Smith Barney); former tstee Fin Accounting Standards Bd USA; voyageur Outward Bound Sch MN; ACMA 1960; *Recreations* tennis, golf; *Clubs* Johns Island, Queen's, Annabel's; *Style—* David Jarvis, Esq; ✉ Citigroup Global Markets Ltd, 33 Canada Square, Canary Wharf, London E14 5LB (tel 020 7986 6000)

JARVIS, Gerald Joseph; s of Maurice Jarvis (d 1956), and Sarah, *née* Brown (d 1964); *b* 4 January 1947; *Educ* Pembroke Coll Oxford (BA), Univ of Oxford Sch of Med (BM, BCh); *m* 1 Oct 1977, Elizabeth Honor, da of Gordon Wilson Izatt, of Earlsferry, Fife; 2 s (Thomas Edward Maurice b 11 Sept 1979, Alexander James Patric b 11 Dec 1984), 1 da (Emma Elizabeth b 25 Feb 1982); *Career* conslt obstetrician and gynaecologist St James Univ Hosp Leeds 1981–2002, hon lectr in med Univ of Leeds 1981–2002; author of various publications on obstetrics and gynaecology; examiner RCOG 1989–, convenor of Nat Course on the Treatment of Female Urinary Incontinence; FRCSEd 1975, FRCOG 1989; *Books* Female Urinary Incontinence (1990), Obstetrics and Gynaecology (1994); *Recreations* playing piano, egyptology; *Style—* Gerald Jarvis, Esq; ✉ Beechwood House, Raby Park, Wetherby LS22 6SA (tel 01937 582218); St James's University Hospital, Beckett Street, Leeds LS9 7TF (tel 0113 243 3144); BUPA Hospital, Roundhay Hall, Jackson Avenue, Leeds LS8 1NT (tel 0113 269 3939)

JARVIS, Dr John Herbert; s of Herbert Henry Wood Jarvis (d 1982), and Mabel, *née* Griffiths (d 2001); *b* 16 May 1947, Purfleet, Essex; *Educ* Univ of Wales Swansea (BSc, PhD); *m* 20 June 1970, Jean Elizabeth Levy; 1 da (Louise Hannah Mary b 5 Oct 1976), 1 s (Robin Alexander Levy b 14 Dec 1985); *Career* post-doctoral research fell WNSM 1972–75, post-doctoral fell Univ of Bristol 1975–77, medical ed Elsevier Publishers 1977–79, medical ed then publishing dir Wiley Publishers 1979–92, md John Wiley & Sons Ltd 1992–, sr vice-pres Wiley Europe 1996–; chm Planning for Economic Prosperity; author of numerous scientific papers; dir Chichester Festival Theatre, govr Chichester Coll; memb Publishers' Assoc Cncl 1999–2005, dir Int Assoc of Scientific, Technical and Medical Publishers (STM) 1999–2005; *Recreations* boating, walking, music, daytrading; *Clubs* Groucho; *Style—* Dr John Jarvis; ✉ Wiley Europe, The Atrium, Southern Gate, Chichester, West Sussex PO19 8SQ (tel 01243 770222, e-mail jjarvis@wiley.co.uk)

JARVIS, John Manners; QC; s of Donald Edward Manners Jarvis, TD (d 1999), of Rockbourne, Hants, and Theodora Brixie, *née* Bryant (d 1991); *b* 20 November 1947; *Educ* KCS Wimbledon, Emmanuel Coll Cambridge (MA); *m* 5 May 1972, Janet Rona, da of Eric Cresswell Kitson, OBE (d 1975), of Mersham, Kent; 2 s (Christopher b 1974, Fergus b 1976); *Career* called to the Bar Lincoln's Inn 1970 (bencher); in practice at Commercial Bar, recorder of the Crown Court, dep judge of the High Court; chm Commercial Bar Assoc 1995–97; int ed Jl of Banking and Finance Law and Practice, conslt ed Jl of Int Banking and Finance Law; govr KCS Wimbledon; *Publications* Lender Liability (jtly, 1994), Banks, Liability and Risk (contrib 1991, 2 edn 1995); *Recreations* tennis, sailing, horse riding, skiing, cycling, music; *Clubs* Hurlingham; *Style—* John Jarvis, Esq, QC; ✉ 3 Verulam Buildings, Gray's Inn, London WC1R 5NT (tel 020 7831 8441, fax 020 7831 8479, e-mail jjarvis@3vb.com)

JARVIS, Martin; OBE (2000); s of Denys Jarvis, and Margot Jarvis; *b* 4 August 1941; *Educ* Whitgift Sch, RADA; *m* 1; 2 s; m 2, 23 Nov 1974, Rosalind Ayres, *qv*, da of Sam Johnson (d 1986); *Career* actor; first appearance Nat Youth Theatre 1960–62 (played Henry V Sadler's Wells 1962); dir Children's Film Unit 1993–99, currently prodr and dir of dramas for BBC Radio 4; contrib Comic Relief and Children in Need; *Theatre* NT incl: Importance of Being Earnest 1982, Victoria Station 1983, The Trojan War Will Not Take Place 1983, An Audience with Martin Jarvis 2003; other credits incl: Manchester Library Theatre 1962–63, Poor Bitos (Duke of York's) 1963, Man and Superman (Vaudeville) 1966, The Bandwagon (Mermaid) 1970, The Rivals (USA) 1973, title role in Hamlet (Festival of Br Theatre) 1973, The Circle (Haymarket) 1976, She Stoops to Conquer (Canada and Hong Kong Arts Festivals) 1977, Caught in the Act (Garrick) 1981, Woman in Mind (Vaudeville) 1986, The Perfect Party (Greenwich) 1987, Jerome in Henceforward (Vaudeville) 1989, Viktor in Exchange (Vaudeville) 1990 (also LA 1992), Sir Andrew Aguecheek in Sir Peter Hall's revival of Twelfth Night (Playhouse) 1991, title role in Leo in Love (Nuffield Theatre and nat tour) 1992, Dennis in the revival of Ayckbourn's Just Between Ourselves (Greenwich) 1992, starred in Make and Break (LA) 1993, starred in On Approval (Playhouse) 1994, starred in Ayckbourn's Man of the Moment (LA) 1994 and Table Manners (LA Theatre Works) 1995, concert performance of Peter and The Wolf (narrator, Barbican) 1997, The Doctor's Dilemma (Almeida) 1998, David Hare's Skylight (USA) 1999, Passion Play (Donmar Warehouse Theatre) 2000, Shadowlands (USA) 2001, By Jeeves (USA) 2001, Gielgud Centenary Gala 2004, Twelfth Night (Open Air Theatre Regent's Park) 2005; *Television* incl: The Forsyte Saga 1967, Nicholas Nickleby 1968, David Copperfield 1975, Rings on their Fingers 1978, Breakaway 1980, The Black Tower 1985, Chelworth 1988, Rumpole of the Bailey 1988–89, Countdown 1989–95, all voices in children's animated series Huxley Pig 1989–90, You Say Potato (USA) 1990–, all voices on animation series Fourways Farm (series) 1993–95, Scarlet and Black (film series) 1993, Touch of Love 1994, starred as Brillat Savarin 1994; other credits incl: Inspector Morse (Greeks Bearing Gifts, feature length TV film) 1991, Maurice Howling in Murder Most Horrid 1991, Woof 1992, Charles Longmuir in The Good Guys 1992, Boon 1992, Casualty 1992, Library of Romance 1993, Countdown 1993, Pebble Mill 1993, House Party 1993, Lovejoy 1994, Murder She Wrote 1995, A Touch of Frost 1995, Fantastic Mr Fox 1995, Space - Above and Beyond (USA) 1996, Walker - Texas Ranger (USA) 1996, Nation's Favourite Children's Book 1997, Supply and Demand 1998, Space Island One 1999, Sex 'n' Death 2000, Lorna Doone 2000, Micawber 2001, By Jeeves 2001, Inspector Lynley Mysteries 2002, Bootleg 2003, Psi-Kix (series, USA) 2003, Doctors 2004, Much Ado About Nothing 2005; commentaries for TV film documentaries and arts programmes; *Radio* numerous radio performances incl: Charles Dickens in The Best of Times, one-man series Jarvis' Frayn, Lord Illingworth in Wilde's A Woman of No Importance 1991, Speak After the Beep (also prodr), Dennis Potter Stories (also prodr) 1998, Colonel Clay (also prodr) 1998, M for Mother 1999, The Doctor's Dilemma (also prodr) 1999, Woman In Mind (also prodr) 2000, Spies 2001; as dir: Inappropriate Behaviour 2002, A Tribute to Finchie, Afternoons with Roger, The Trial of Walter Ralegh 2003, Forever Mine 2004, Teacher's Pet 2005; adapted and read over 120 of Richmal Crompton's William stories for radio, TV and CD; *Recordings* cassette recordings incl: Just William vols 1–5 (BBC), David Copperfield 1991, Jarvis's Frayn (CSA Telltapes) 1992, Tales From Shakespeare (LA) 1993, Honor Among Thieves (USA) 1993, narrator/host Concorde Playhouse 1994–95, Dick Francis series (Penguin) 1995–98, Oliver Twist 1996, Goodbye Mr Chips 1997, A Night to Remember 1997, The Third Man 1998, England Their England 1998, Hard Times 1998, Just William 6 1998, Jeffrey Archer Stories 1998, Ovid's Art of Love 1998, Fantastic Mr Fox 1998, A Tale of Two Cities 1999; *Film* incl: The Last Escape, Ike, The Bunker, Taste the Blood of Dracula, Buster, Emily's Ghost (CFU/Channel 4) 1993, Calliope 1993, Absence of War 1995, Titanic 1997, The X-Ray Kid 1998, Mrs Caldicot's Cabbage War 2001; *Awards* nominated Best Actor Sony Radio Awards 1991, NY Int Radio Award 1994, Peabody Award USA for Fourways Farm, Brit Talkies Award 1995, Audie Award (USA) 2001, Earphone Award 2002, Broadway Theatre World Award 2002; *Publications* Bright Boy (play, 1977), Just William Stories (ed, 1992), Meet Just William (1999), Acting Strangely (autobiography, 1999), Broadway, Jeeves? (2003); short stories for radio, articles in The Listener, Punch, Evening Standard, High Life, Daily Mail, Tatler, Sunday Telegraph; *Recreations* Beethoven, Mozart, people-watching, growing lemons; *Clubs* BBC; *Style—* Martin Jarvis, Esq, OBE; ✉ c/o Amanda Howard Associates, 21 Berwick Street, London W1F 0PZ (tel 020 7287 9277)

JARVIS, Peter Jack; CBE (1995); *b* 1 July 1941; *Educ* Christ's Coll Cambridge (MA); *Career* various sales and mktg appts with Unilever 1964–76; Whitbread plc: joined as sales and mktg dir Long John Int 1976, gp mktg dir 1978, main bd dir 1979–, int md (responsible for all overseas ops) 1981–83, md Trading Div 1983–85, gp md 1985–90, gp chief exec 1990–97; dep chm The Burton Group plc 1997–98, chm Debenhams plc (following demerger) 1998–; non-exec dir: Rank Group plc 1995–, Barclays Bank 1995–2001; *Style—* Peter Jarvis, Esq, CBE; ✉ Debenham's plc, 1 Welbeck Street, London W1A 1DF (tel 020 7408 4444, fax 020 7408 3366)

JARVIS, His Hon Judge (James) Roger; s of Douglas Bernard Jarvis, DFC, of Poole, Dorset, and Elsie Vanessa Jarvis; *b* 7 September 1944; *Educ* Latymer Upper Sch, Brockenhurst GS, Peter Symonds Coll Winchester; *m* 8 January 1972, Kerstin Marianne; 1 s (Simon Antony b 14 Sept 1973), 2 da (Marianne Susie b 23 Oct 1976, Sophie Emilia b 26 Dec 1981); *Career* admitted slr 1969; McQueen Yeoman (formerly Andrews McQueen): joined 1972, ptnr 1973–2000; circuit judge (Western Circuit) 2000–; *Recreations* jogging, walking, reading; *Style—* His Hon Judge Jarvis; ✉ c/o Bournemouth Crown and County Courts, Deansleigh Road, Bournemouth BH7 7DS (tel 01202 502800)

JARVIS, Sian Elizabeth; da of R A Jarvis and M Jarvis, *née* Owen; *Educ* Chelmsford HS for Girls, Loughborough Univ (BA); *Partner* John Sobey; 2 c (Georgina, Jack (twins) b 12 Jan 2006); *Career* trainee BBC News (regional) 1988–89, reporter/presenter BBC East 1989–92, political corr 1992–99, news presenter GMTV and Radio 5; Dept of Health: head of media 1999–2001, currently dir gen of communication; *Recreations* riding, opera, travel in Africa; *Style—* Ms Sian Jarvis; ✉ Department of Health, Richmond House, 79 Whitehall, London SW1A 2NS (tel 020 7210 5440, fax 020 7210 5134, e-mail sian.jarvis@dh.gsi.gov.uk)

JARVIS, William; s of W J Ryan Jarvis (d 1992), and Jean Marshall, *née* Hall (d 1984); *b* 14 October 1960; *Educ* Harrow; *m* (m dis); 2 s (Jack b 9 Nov 1988, Tom b 11 Sept 1990), 1 da (Lucinda b 16 May 1996); *Career* racehorse trainer Newmarket 1985–; trained winners at every English racecourse, trainer Grand Lodge (champion European 2 year old 1993 and winner of St James's Palace Stakes Royal Ascot 1994); vice-chm Newmarket Trainers Fedn; *Recreations* skiing and all sports; *Clubs* Turf, Jockey Club Rooms; *Style—* William Jarvis, Esq; ✉ Phantom House, Fordham Road, Newmarket, Suffolk CB8 7AA (tel 01638 662677, fax 01638 667328)

JARY, Michael Keith; s of Keith Jary, and Jacqueline Ann, *née* Pogue (d 2004); *b* 15 June 1963, Cambridge; *Educ* Berkhamsted Sch, Merton Coll Oxford (MA), INSEAD France (MBA); *Career* assoc Booz Allen & Hamilton 1985–87; OC&C Strategy Consultants: fndr memb 1987, managing ptnr London 2000–05, worldwide managing ptnr 2005–; *Books* Retail Power Plays (co-author, 1987), Markenpower (co-author, 1988); *Style—* Michael Jary, Esq; ✉ OC&C Strategy Consultants, The OC&C Building, 233 Shaftesbury Avenue, London WC2H 8EE (tel 020 7010 8024)

JASON, Sir David; kt (2005), OBE (1993); s of Arthur White, and Olwen, *née* Jones; *b* 2 February 1940; *Educ* Northside Secdy Sch; *m* 2005, Gill Hinchcliffe; 1 da (Sophie Mae b 26 Feb 2001); *Career* actor; first professional job with Bromley Repertory 1965; early work incl: 3 months in Crossroads, tour with Ron Moody in Peter Pan, Summer seasons with Bob Monkhouse and Dick Emery; fell BAFTA 2003; *Theatre* incl: Under Milk Wood (Mayfair), Bob Acres in The Rivals (Sadler's Wells), No Sex Please...We're British! (Strand) 1972, Darling Mr London 1975–76, Fancourt Babberley in Charley's Aunt, Norman in The Norman Conquests (Oxford Playhouse) 1976, Lord Foppington in The Relapse (Cambridge Theatre Co), Buttons in Cinderella, Tom Bryce in The Unvarnished Truth (Middle and Far East) 1983, Look No Hans! (Strand Theatre and tour) 1985–86; *Television* incl: Do Not Adjust Your Set 1967, The Top Secret Life of Edgar Briggs (LWT) 1973–74, Mr Stabbs (Thames) 1974, Blanco in Porridge (BBC) 1975, Lucky Feller (LWT) 1975, A Sharp Intake of Breath (ATV) 1978, Granville in Open All Hours (with Ronnie Barker, several series, BBC), Del Trotter in Only Fools and Horses (several series, BBC), Skullion in Porterhouse Blue (C4) 1986, Ted Simcock in A Bit of a Do (2 series, YTV) 1988–89, Single Voices: The Chemist (monologue by Roy Clarke, BBC) 1989, George in Amongst Barbarians (screenplay, BBC) 1989, Pa Larkin in The Darling Buds of May (YTV) 1990–2002, Inspector Jack Frost in A Touch of Frost (YTV) 1992–, The Bullion Boys (1993, Int Emmy for Best Drama 1994), Frank Beck in All the King's Men (BBC), The Ghostboat 2006, The Hogfather 2006; voice of many cartoon characters incl

Dangermouse and Count Duckula; dir The Quest 2002; *Film* Under Milk Wood, Royal Flash 1974, The Odd Job 1978, Only Fools and Horses (BBC), Toad in The Wind in the Willows; *Awards* Radio Times Funniest Actor, Variety Club Personality of the Year, Sony Radio Award, Water Rats Personality of the Year, TV Times Actor of the Year, TV Times Funniest Actor, BAFTA Award for Best Actor 1988, BAFTA Award for Best Light Entertainment Performer 1990, Nat Television Awards Special Recognition Award for Lifetime Achievement in Television 1996, Favourite Situation Comedy Performer at Aunties (BBC) 1996, BAFTA Award for Best Comedy Performance 1997, TV Quick Award for Best Actor 2000 and 2001, Nat TV Awards for Best Actor 2001, British Comedy Award for Lifetime Achievement 2001, BAFTA Fellowship Award 2003; *Recreations* helicopter pilot, gliding, restoration of old machines, work; *Style*— Sir David Jason, OBE; ✉ c/o The Richard Stone Partnership, 2 Henrietta Street, London WC2E 8PS (tel 020 7497 0849, fax 020 7497 0869)

JASON, Gillian Brett; da of A R F Bosworth (d 1963), of London, and Joan Lena, *née* Brett (d 2002); *b* 30 June 1941; *Educ* Dominican Covent Sch Brewood, Royal Ballet Sr Sch (Br Ballet Orgn award), London Opera Centre; *m* 21 March 1961, Neville Jason; 1 da (Elli b 1967), 1 s (Alexander b 1970); *Career* art gallery director; visual arts work 1973–79, private dealer 1980–81, dir Gillian Jason Gallery London 1981–94 (represented estates of: David Bomberg, Frank Dobson, John Tunnard, Bryan Wynter), dir Jason & Rhodes London 1994–99 (artists represented: Ansel Krut, Eduardo Paolozzi, Michael Sandle, Paul Storey, John Virtue), dir Gillian Jason Modern and Contemporary Art London 1999–; memb Soc of London Art Dealers 1995–; *Awards* incl: Vaughan-Williams Tst Bursary, Countess of Munster Tst Award 1966, finalist Kathleen Ferrier Meml Scholarship RAM 1966; *Recreations* music, theatre, literature; *Style*— Mrs Gillian Jason; ✉ Ormond House, 3 Duke of York Street, London SW1Y 6JP (e-mail art@gillianjason.com, website www.gillianjason.com)

JASPAN, Andrew; s of Mervyn Aubrey Jaspan (d 1974), and Helen, *née* Wright; *b* 20 April 1953, Manchester; *Educ* Beverley GS, Marlborough, Univ of Manchester (BA); *Career* founding ed New Manchester Review 1975–77; sub ed: Daily Telegraph 1978–80, Daily Mirror 1981; reporter Journalists in Europe (Paris) 1982, sub ed and reporter The Times 1983–85, asst news ed The Sunday Times 1985–88; ed: The Sunday Times Scotland 1988, Scotland on Sunday 1989–94, The Scotsman 1994–95, The Observer 1995–96; publisher and md The Big Issue 1996–98, business devpt exec Scottish Media Group plc 1997, ed The Sunday Herald 1998–2004, ed The Age (Aust) 2004–; *Recreations* reading, squash, psephology; *Clubs* Glasgow Art; *Style*— Andrew Jaspan, Esq

JAY, Sir Antony Rupert; kt (1988), CVO (1993); s of Ernest Jay (d 1957), of London, and Catherine Mary, *née* Hay (d 1981); *b* 20 April 1930; *Educ* St Paul's (scholar), Magdalene Coll Cambridge (major scholar, MA); *m* 15 June 1957, Rosemary Jill, da of Leslie Watkins, of Stratford-upon-Avon, Warks; 2 s (Michael b 1959, David b 1972), 2 da (Ros b 1961, Kate b 1964); *Career* Nat Serv Royal Signals 1952–54 (2 Lt 1953), Lt TA 1954; BBC 1955–64: ed Tonight 1962–63, head talks features 1963–64; freelance writer and prodr 1964–; ed A Prime Minister on Prime Ministers 1977; writer: Royal Family (1969), Yes Minister (3 series with Jonathan Lynn, 1980–82), Yes Prime Minister (2 series, 1985 and 1987), Elizabeth R (1992); chm Video Arts Ltd 1972–89; memb Annan Ctee on Future of Broadcasting 1974–77; BAFTA Writers' Award 1988; hon fell Magdalene Coll Cambridge 2001; Hon MA Univ of Sheffield 1987, Hon DBA Int Mgmnt Centre Buckingham 1988; FRSA, CIMgt 1991; *Books* Management and Machiavelli (1967), To England with Love (with David Frost, 1967), Effective Presentation (1970), Corporation Man (1972), The Complete Yes Minister (with Jonathan Lynn, 1984), Yes Prime Minister (1986, vol II 1987), Elizabeth R (1992), The Oxford Dictionary of Political Quotations (ed, 1996, 3 edn 2006), How to Beat Sir Humphrey (1997), Not In Our Back Yard (2005); *Style*— Sir Antony Jay, CVO; ✉ c/o Alan Brodie Representation Ltd, 211 Piccadilly, London W1V 9LD

JAY, John Philip Bromberg; s of Alec Jay (d 1993), and (Helena) June Jay (d 2005); *b* 1 April 1957; *Educ* UCS, Magdalen Coll Oxford (BA); *m* 1, 1987 (m dis 1992), Susy, *née* Streeter; m 2, 1992, Judi Bevan; 1 da (Josephine); *Career* reporter Western Mail 1979–81; city reporter: Thomson Regional Newspapers 1981–83, Sunday Telegraph 1984–86; city ed Sunday Times 1986 (dep business ed 1988), city and business ed Sunday Telegraph 1989–95, managing ed business news Sunday Times 1995–2001, currently devpt dir New Star Asset Management; *Recreations* skiing, reading, walking, cinema, theatre; *Style*— John Jay, Esq

JAY, Hon Martin; CBE (2000), DL; yr s of Baron Jay, PC (Life Peer, d 1996), and his 1 w, Margaret Christian, *née* Garnett; *Educ* Winchester, New Coll Oxford (MA); *m* 1969, Sandra, *née* Williams; 2 da (Claudia b 1971, Tabitha b 1972), 1 s (Adam b 1976); *Career* industrialist; with: GEC 1969–85 and 1987–89, Lewmar plc 1985; md and chief exec Vosper Thornycroft Holdings plc 1989–2002, chm VT Gp plc, chm Invensys plc 2003–, chm EADS UK Ltd; chm Tall Ships Youth Tst, tstee Mary Rose Tst; Hon LLD Univ of Portsmouth, Hon DBA Southampton Solent Inst; *Recreations* sailing, tennis, gardening; *Style*— The Hon Martin Jay, CBE, DL; ✉ Bishop's Court, Bishop's Sutton, Alresford, Hampshire SO9 5GR; Invensys plc, Portland House, Stag Place, London SW1E 5BF (tel 020 7821 3578, fax 020 7821 3505)

JAY, Hon Peter; er s of Baron Jay, PC (Life Peer, d 1996), and his 1 w, Margaret Christian, *née* Garnett; *b* 7 February 1937; *Educ* Winchester, ChCh Oxford (MA); *m* 1, 1961 (m dis 1986), Hon Margaret Ann Callaghan (now Baroness Jay of Paddington, *qv*, Life Peer), er da of Baron Callaghan of Cardiff, KG, PC (Life Peer, d 2005); 2 da (Hon Tamsin Margaret b 1965, Hon Alice Katharine b 1968), 1 s (Hon Patrick James Peter b 1971); m 2, Emma Bettina, da of Peter Kai Thornton; 3 s (Thomas Hastings b 1987, Samuel Arthur Maxwell b 1988, James William Hagen Thornton b 1992); issue by Jane Tustian (Nicholas James Tustian b 1980); *Career* Midshipman and Sub Lt RNVR 1956–57; former pres Oxford Union; HM Treasy: asst princ 1961–64, private sec to Jt Perm Sec 1964, princ 1964–67; economics ed The Times 1967–77, assoc ed Times Business News 1969–77, presenter Weekend World (London Weekend Television) 1972–77, ambass to USA 1977–79, conslt Economist Group 1979–81, dir Economist Intelligence Unit 1979–83, chm and chief exec TV-am plc 1980–83, chm Nat Cncl for Voluntary Orgns 1981–86, presenter A Week in Politics (Channel Four) 1983–86, ed Banking World 1983–86, chief of staff to Robert Maxwell 1986–89, economics ed BBC 1990–2001, presenter The Road to Riches (BBC) 2000; non-exec dir Bank of England 2003–, exec and prof of political economy Henley Mgmnt Coll 2006–; chm United Way (UK) Ltd 1982–83 and various United Way subsids; memb Cncl Cinema and TV Benevolent Fund 1982–83, govr Ditchley Fndn 1982–; dir New Nat Theatre Washington DC 1979–81; holder of various broadcasting honours and TV awards; visiting scholar Brookings Inst 1979–80, Wincott Meml lectr 1975, Copland Meml lectr 1980; *Books* The Road to Riches, or The Wealth of Man (2000); *Clubs* Garrick; *Style*— The Hon Peter Jay; ✉ Hensington Farmhouse, Woodstock, Oxfordshire OX20 1LH

JAY, Robert Maurice; QC 1998; s of Prof Barrie Samuel Jay, and Dr Marcelle Jay, *née* Byre; *b* 20 September 1959; *Educ* KCS Wimbledon, New Coll Oxford (open scholar, BA); *m* Deborah, *née* Trenner; 1 da (Hannah b 17 Feb 2000); *Career* jr counsel to the Crown (common law) 1989–98, recorder 1999–, former chm Administrative Law Bar Assoc; patron friend Wigmore Hall; *Recreations* opera, golf, chess, tennis, politics, music; *Clubs* RAC, Coombe Hill Golf; *Style*— Robert Jay, Esq, QC; ✉ 39 Essex Street, London WC2R 3AT (tel 020 7832 1111, fax 020 7353 3978, e-mail clerks@39essex.com)

JAY OF EWELME, Baron (Life Peer UK 2006), of Ewelme in the County of Oxfordshire; Sir Michael Hastings Jay; GCMG (2006, KCMG 1997, CMG 1993); s of Capt Alan David Hastings Jay, DSO, DSC, RN (d 1978), and Felicity, *née* Vickery, MBE; *b* 19 June 1946; *Educ* Winchester, Magdalen Coll Oxford, SOAS Univ of London; *m* 1975, Sylvia, *née* Mylroie; *Career* Miny of Overseas Devpt 1969–73, UK delgn to IMF and World Bank Washington 1973–75, Miny of Overseas Devpt 1975–78, first sec Br High Cmmn New Delhi 1978–81, FCO London 1981–85, cnsllr Cabinet Office 1985–87, cnsllr Br Embassy Paris 1987–90, asst under sec for EC affrs FCO 1990–94, dep under sec for EU and economic affrs 1994–96, Br ambass Paris 1996–2001, perm sec FCO 2002–06; non-exec dir: Associated British Foods plc 2006–, Valeo 2007–, Credit Agricole 2007–; sr assoc memb St Antony's Coll Oxford 1996; hon fell Magdalen Coll Oxford 2004; *Style*— The Rt Hon the Lord Jay of Ewelme, GCMG

JAY OF PADDINGTON, Baroness (Life Peer UK 1992), of Paddington in the City of Westminster; Margaret Ann Adler; PC (1998); er da of Baron Callaghan of Cardiff, KG, PC (Life Peer, d 2005); *b* 18 November 1939, 1939; *Educ* Blackheath HS, Somerville Coll Oxford (BA); *m* 1, 1961 (m dis 1986), as his 1 w, Hon Peter Jay; 2 da (Hon Tamsin Margaret b 1965, Hon Alice Katharine b 1968), 1 s (Hon Patrick James Peter b 1971); m 2, 26 March 1994, Prof Michael William Adler, *qv*; *Career* current and further educn depts BBC TV 1965–67, political res asst Senator John Tunney (Dem, Calif) 1969–70, freelance work for ABC TV and Nat Public Radio Washington DC 1977–82, memb Paddington and N Kensington DHA 1984–97, reporter Panorama and This Week BBC TV 1981–88, reporter and prodr Thames TV 1986–88, fndr dir Nat Aids Trust; oppn princ spokesperson on health House of Lords 1994–97, min of state Dept of Health 1997–98, Lord Privy Seal, ldr of the House of Lords and min for Women 1998–2001; non-exec dir: Carlton Television 1996–97, Scottish Power 1996–97, Independent News and Media 2001–, BT 2002–; non-exec memb Kensington Chelsea Westminster HA 1996–97; govr South Bank Univ 1995–97; chm Overseas Devpt Inst 2002– (memb Cncl 1994–97); memb Advsy Ctee Meteorological Office 1995–97; tstee Int Crisis Gp 1995–97; chm Nat Assoc of League of Hosp Friends 1994–97; patron: Help the Aged, REACTION Tst; *Books* Battered - The Story of Child Abuse (co-author 1986); *Style*— The Rt Hon Baroness Jay of Paddington; ✉ House of Lords, London SW1A 0PW

JAYAWANT, Prof Bhalchandra Vinayak; s of (Rao Saheb) Vinayak Laxman Jayawant (d 1971), of Nagpur, India, and Indira Jayawant (d 1948); *b* 22 April 1930; *Educ* Univ of Bombay (BE), Univ of Bristol (PhD), Univ of Sussex (DSc); *m* 3 Sept 1960, (Elizabeth) Monica, da of George William Bowdler (d 1985); 1 s (Richard Anthony b 4 April 1962), 1 da (Frances Rachael b 12 Aug 1964); *Career* jr engr Metropolitan Vickers Manchester 1956–60, lectr in electrical engrg Queen's Univ Belfast 1960–65; Sch of Engrg Univ of Sussex: reader in electrical engrg 1965–72, prof of electrical engrg 1972– (currently emeritus), dean 1985–90; IEE: chm Sussex Centre, chm Computing and Control Div, memb Cncl; Sir Harold Hartley medal 1988; FIEE, FInstMC, FRSA; *Books* Induction Machines (1968), Electromagnetic Suspension and Levitation Techniques; *Recreations* walking on the Downs, French wines; *Style*— Prof Bhalchandra Jayawant; ✉ The Department of Engineering & Design, School of Science and Technology, University of Sussex, Falmer, Brighton BN1 9QT

JAYSON, Prof Malcolm I V; *Educ* Middx Hosp Sch, Univ of London (MB BS), Univ of Bristol (MD); *m* 1 July 1962, Judith; 2 s (Gordon b 1963, Robert b 1966); *Career* lectr and sr lectr in med (rheumatology) Univ of Bristol and Royal Nat Hosp for Rheumatic Diseases Bath 1967–77, prof of rheumatology and dir of Rheumatism Res Laboratories Univ of Manchester 1977–99 (emeritus prof of rheumatology 1999–), dir Manchester and Salford Back Pain Centre 1993–2001; pres: Int Soc for Study of the Lumbar Spine, Section of Rheumatology and Rehabilitation RSM; sec gen Int Back Pain Soc; FRCP; *Books* Total Hip Replacement (1971), Stills Disease: Juvenile Chronic Polyarthritis (1976), Collagen In Health and Disease (1982), Locomotor Disability In General Practice (1983), Rheumatism and Arthritis (1991), Lumbar Spine and Back Pain (1992), Back Pain - The Facts (1992), Family Doctor Guide: Back Pain (2004); *Recreations* antiques, music, trout fishing; *Style*— Prof Malcolm I V Jayson; ✉ The Gate House, 8 Lancaster Road, Didsbury, Manchester M20 2TY (tel 0161 445 1729, fax 0161 448 8195)

JEANS, Christopher James Marwood; QC (1997); s of David Marwood Jeans (d 1966), and Rosalie Jean, *née* Whittle (d 2003); *b* 24 January 1956; *Educ* Minchenden Comp Sch, King's Coll London (LLB, Hickling Prize in Industrial Law), St John's Coll Oxford (BCL), Inns of Court Sch of Law; *m* 1998, Judith Mary, *née* Laws; 1 da (b 19 Aug 1999); *Career* called to the Bar Gray's Inn 1980, lectr in law City of London Poly 1981–83, in practice (specialising in employment law) 1983–, pt/t chm Employment Tbnls 1998–; memb The Times Law Panel 2005; FICPD 1998; *Recreations* football (Spurs), cricket, walking, swimming, theatre, cinema, Arctic and world travel; *Style*— Christopher Jeans, QC; ✉ 11 King's Bench Walk, Ground Floor, Temple, London EC4Y 7EQ (tel 020 7632 8500, fax 020 7583 9123 and 020 7583 3690, e-mail jeans@11kbw.com)

JEANS, Michael Henry Vickery; MBE (2006); s of Henry Tendron Wilson Jeans (d 1997), of Walton-on-Thames, Surrey, and Joan Kathleen, *née* Vickery (d 2003); *b* 14 March 1943; *Educ* St Edward's Sch Oxford, Univ of Bristol (BA); *m* 1, 27 June 1970 (m dis 1981), Iris Carla, da of Franco Dell'Acqua, of Milan, Italy; m 2, 12 Jan 1987 (m dis 2004), Paula Wendy, da of David Arthur Spraggs, of Thorpe Bay, Essex; 2 c (James, Rebecca (twins) b 25 Aug 1987); *Career* chartered accountant; trainee accountant KPMG (formerly Peat Marwick Mitchell) 1964–67, asst accountant Blue Circle Group 1967–70; KPMG: conslt 1970–81, ptnr 1981–94, memb Bd 1993–94, special advsr 1994–2003; ind mgmnt conslt 1994–; non-exec dir Ross Group plc 1995–2000; ind business advsr The Planning Inspectorate 1992–2003; lay memb Audit Ctee GMC 2004–; memb: St Matthew's Bayswater PCC 1990–2001, Bd Bath Festivals Tst 2002–06 (vice-chair 2003–06); non-exec dir: Gemserv plc 2004–, Bevan Brittan LLP 2004–, Human Insight Ltd 2007–; ind bd memb DTI Performance Monitoring Ctee 2005–07; memb Ct Cranfield Univ 2004–; Freeman City of London 1965; fndr memb Worshipful Co of Mgmnt Conslts (Master 2001–02); Liveryman: Worshipful Co of Haberdashers 1965 (memb Ct of Assts 1985, Master 2007–08), Worshipful Co of Chartered Accountants 1991; MBA (hc) Cranfield Univ 1996; FCA 1967, FCMC 1970 (pres 1990–91), FCMA 1971 (pres 2000–01), MMS 1984, FRSA 1990; *Publications* contrib chapters to: Activity Based Management (1992), Management Consultancy, A Handbook for Best Practice (1998), Success in Sight, Visioning (1998), The International Guide to Management Consultancy (2001); *Recreations* opera, theatre, Italy; *Clubs* RAC, Kingston Rowing, Mensa, Soc of London Ragamuffins; *Style*— M H V Jeans, Esq, MBE; ✉ 512 Balmoral Apartments, 2 Praed Street, London W2 1JL (tel 020 7087 4134, e-mail mike.jeans@kpmg.co.uk); Via Lanza 56/2, Celle Ligure, 17015 Savona, Italy (tel 00 390 19 993393)

JEANS, Royston (Roy); s of Ronald Henry Jeans, of Bordon, Hants, and Phyllis Margaret, *née* Kent; *b* 22 September 1956; *Educ* Heath End Sch, Farnham VI Form Coll, Univ of Sheffield (BA), Univ of Southern Calif (MA); *m* 15 Oct 1983, Amelia, da of Ubaldo Marini (d 1975); 2 da, 1 s; *Career* teaching asst Univ of Southern Calif 1979–81, classified rep Farnham Herald 1982–83; advtg exec: Regional Newpaper Advertising Bureau (RNAB) 1983–86, Advertising Media Representation Agency (AMRA) 1986–87; Cordiant plc (formerly Saatchi & Saatchi Co plc): regnl media mangr Saatchi & Saatchi Advertising 1987–88, regnl media dir Zenith Media 1988–90, md Zenith Outdoor 1989–90, TV buying dir Zenith Media 1990–91, exec dir of press Zenith Media 1991–94, gen mangr Zenith Media 1994–95; md AMRA 1995–97, dir Initiative Media London 1997–2004 (md 1998–2000, chief operating offr 2001–04), dir Initiative Media Paris 1999–2004, md

Unilever Europe 2001–03, md Magna Global UK 2003–, ceo Magna Outdoor 2004–; memb Editorial Bd Headlines magazine 1989–97, chm Regnl Press Club 1995–97, elected memb IPA's Media Policy Gp 1999, elected dir Postar 2000–02; winner Media Mind (jtly) 1991; FIPA 2007 (MIPA 1991); *Books* News from a Square World (with Alan Kamin, Unwin Paperbacks, 1986); *Recreations* travel, cinema, literature, modern art; *Style*— Roy Jeans, Esq; ✉ Magna Global, 7th Floor, Lynton House, 7–12 Tavistock Square, London WC1H 9SX (e-mail rjeans@ipm.co.uk)

JEBB, Lionel Richard; DL (2000, Shropshire); s of Richard Lewthwaite Jebb (d 1961), of Ellesmere, and Marjorie Joy, *née* Jacobs; *b* 21 December 1934; *Educ* Shrewsbury, Merton Coll Oxford (MA); *m* 28 May 1960, Corinna Margaret, da of late Charles Peter Elmhirst Hawkesworth, of Boroughbridge, N Yorks; 2 s (Richard b 1961, Andrew b 1966), 1 da (Sophie b 1963); *Career* farmer and landowner; cncllr Shropshire CC 1970–81; chm: Shropshire Conservation Devpt Tst 1981–88, Shropshire Ctee COSIRA 1982–91, Shropshire Branch CLA 1985–88, Shropshire Rural Devpt Forum 1985–96, Shropshire Heritage Tst 1996–2000; lay chm Ellesmere Deanery Synod 1970–74 and 1980–85, vice-chm Walford Coll of Agric 1981–88, chm Adcote Sch Shrewsbury 1989–2003; memb: Cncl CLA 1975–88, Rural Voice 1981–88, Shropshire Regnl Bd Prince's Youth Business Tst 1989–92, Shropshire Trg and Enterprise Cncl 1990–96; High Sheriff Shropshire 1991; *Recreations* conservation, shooting; *Clubs* Royal Over-Seas League; *Style*— L R Jebb, Esq, DL; ✉ The Lyth, Ellesmere, Shropshire SY12 0HR

JEBENS, Ana; da of Klaus-Peter Jebens, and Leonore Jebens; *Educ* Rudolph Steiner Sch Kings Langley, Central St Martins Coll of Art and Design (BA); *Career* designer; former resident designer Swan Theatre Worcester, asst designer to Hildegard Bechtler, *qv*, and Chloe Obolensky 1993–99; visiting lectr Middx Poly 1975–90; *Productions* Half Moon Theatre: Wizard of Oz, Who's a Hero, On the High Road, Guys and Dolls; Swan Theatre Worcester: California Suite, Way Upstream, Female Parts; Stadttheater Essen: The Robbers, As You Like It, Pal Joey; costume design: The Changing Room (Royal Court), Madame Butterfly (Opera Zuid Maastricht) 1998, Rheingold (Scottish Opera) 2000, War and Peace (ENO) 2001; other credits incl: Breach of the Peace (Pain's Plough), Destry Rides Again (Donmar Warehouse), Puntilla (Nat Theatre Mannheim), Guys and Dolls (Nat Theatre Mannheim), As You Like It (Stadttheater Essen), Pal Joey (Stadttheater Essen), The Glass Menagerie (tour), Can't Pay Won't Pay (Habima Theatre Tel Aviv), Behind a Painted Smile (Finborough and tour), Munera and Think of a River (both Black Women's Touring Co), A Bright Room Called Day (Bush Theatre), The Bugger's Opera (Trent Park), Passion Killers (Mecklenburg Opera) 1995, Walküre (Scottish Opera) 2001, Siegfried (Scottish Opera) 2002, War and Peace (Minnesota) 2003, Götterdämmerung from The Ring Cycle (Scottish Opera) 2003, Flying Dutchman (Opera Suid Holland) 2004; TV credits: Burning Embers (Channel 4), Killing Time (Channel 4); *Recreations* yoga, interior design; *Clubs* Iyengar Inst; *Style*— Ms Ana Jebens; ✉ c/o Loesje Sanders, Pound Square, North Hill, Woodbridge, Suffolk IP12 1HH (tel 01394 385260, fax 01394 388734, mobile 07747 603099)

JEENS, Robert Charles Hubert; s of John Rolfe Hinton Jeens (d 1982), and Mary Margaret, *née* Hubert (d 2004); *b* 16 December 1953; *Educ* Marlborough, Pembroke Coll Cambridge (MA); *m* 8 July 1978, Gillian Frances, da of (David) Gurney Arnold Thomas; 3 s (Richard b 6 Oct 1980, Henry b 2 May 1982, Edward b 15 Feb 1985); *Career* Touche Ross & Co 1975–87 (ptnr 1984–87), Kleinwort Benson Gp plc 1987–96 (gp finance dir 1992–96), finance dir Woolwich Building Society 1996–97, finance dir Woolwich plc 1997–99; chm: Causeway Technologies Inc 2001–05, 1st Credit (Hldgs) 2002–04, Protx Group 2002–06, m.a.partners 2002–06; non-exec dep chm: Hepworth plc 1999–2001, nCipher plc 2006–; non-exec dir: Dialight plc 2001–, TR European Growth Tst plc 2002–, The Royal London Mutual Insurance Society Ltd 2003–, Bank Insinger de Beaufort NV 2005–; FCA 1978, FRSA 1997; *Recreations* family life, skiing, wine, bridge, philately; *Style*— Robert Jeens, Esq; ✉ 2 Clement Road, London SW19 7RJ (tel 020 8946 9304, e-mail robertjeens@blueyonder.co.uk)

JEEVES, Prof Malcolm Alexander; CBE (1992); s of Alexander Frederic Thomas Jeeves (d 1977), and Helena May, *née* Hammond (d 1975); *b* 16 November 1926; *Educ* Stamford Sch, St John's Coll Cambridge (MA, PhD), Harvard Univ; *m* 7 April 1955, Ruth Elisabeth, da of Oscar Cecil Hartridge (d 1983); 2 da (Sarah b 1958, Joanna b 1961); *Career* Army 1945–48, cmmnd Royal Lincs Regt, served 1 Bn Sherwood Foresters BAOR; lectr Dept of Psychology Univ of Leeds 1956–59, fndn prof and head Dept of Psychology Univ of Adelaide S Aust 1959–69 (dean Faculty of Arts 1963–64); Univ of St Andrews: fndn prof of psychology 1969–93, vice-princ 1981–85, hon research prof 1993–; ed-in-chief Neuropsychologia 1990–93; pres: Int Neuropsychological Symposium 1985–91, Psychology Section BAAS 1988–89; memb: Cncl SERC 1985–89, Neuroscience and Mental Health Bd MRC 1985–89, Manpower Sub-Ctee ABRC 1990–93; pres RSE 1996–99 (vice-pres 1990–93, memb Cncl 1986–89); Hon Sheriff E Lothian and Tayside; memb Experimental Psychology Soc; Leverhulme emeritus fell 1994; Hon DSc: Univ of Edinburgh 1993, Univ of St Andrews 2000; Hon DUniv Stirling 1999; FRSE 1980, FBPsS 1958, FMedSci 1998; *Books* Thinking in Structures (with Z P Dienes, 1965), The Effects of Structural Relations upon Transfer (with Z P Dienes, 1968), The Scientific Enterprise and Christian Faith (1969), Experimental Psychology: an Introduction For Biologists (1974), Psychology and Christianity: the view both ways (1976), Analysis of Structural Learning (with G B Greer, 1983), Free to be Different (with R J Berry and D Atkinson, 1984), Behavioural Sciences: A Christian Perspective (1984), Psychology: Through the Eyes of Faith (with D G Myers, 1987, revised edn 2002), Mind Fields (1994), Callosal Agenesis: A Natural Split Brain? (with M Lassonde, 1994), Human Nature at the Millennium (1997), Science, Life and Christian Belief (with R J Berry, 1998), From Cells to Souls: and Beyond (ed and contrib, 2004), Human Nature (ed and contrib, 2006); *Recreations* fly fishing, music, walking; *Clubs* New (Edinburgh); *Style*— Prof Malcolm Jeeves, CBE, PPRSE; ✉ 7 Hepburn Gardens, St Andrews, Fife (tel 01334 473545); School of Psychology, University of St Andrews, St Andrews, Fife KY16 9JU (tel 01334 462072, fax 01334 477441, e-mail maj2@st-andrews.ac.uk)

JEFCOATE, Roger; CBE (1998); s of A G Jefcoate (d 1986), of Amersham; *b* 22 November 1940; *Educ* UCS London; *m* 31 Aug 1963, Jean Hammond; *Career* Stoke Mandeville Hospital:dep dir electronic lab Nat Spinal Injuries Centre 1962–72, developed Possum (world's first remote control system for disabled people, available through NHS since 1967); advsr on technology for disability 1973–; fndr: AbilityNet (adapted computers, vice-pres), Aidis Tst, Canine Partners (assistance dogs for disabled people, vice patron), Disability Aid Fund (electronic equipment for disabled people), ME Research UK (patron), Mobility Tst (wheelchairs for disabled people, vice-pres), National Assoc of Toy and Leisure Libraries; patron: Berks Bucks and Oxon Wildlife Tst, Charity Search, Design and Manufacture for Disability (DEMAND), MS Nat Therapy Centres, PACE special sch (Bucks), Raynaud's and Scleroderma Assoc, CEDA (Devon); vice-pres Buckinghamshire Youth Focus, first chm Prince's Tst Bucks 1990–97; tstee Golden Jubilee Tst 1999–; administrator Clare Milne Tst 2002–; helped to develop: Arkell Dyslexia Centre Surrey, Compaid Trust Kent, Neuromuscular Centre Cheshire, Pield residential special sch Uxbridge, St John's special sch Essex (oldest in UK), St Joseph's Centre London, initiated various disability equipment advice centres worldwide; Bucks ambass 2004; Unsung Heroes Award Celebrities Guild of GB 1986; Hon MA Open Univ 1980, Hon DSc Buckinghamshire Chilterns Univ 2005; Freeman City of London 1986, Liveryman Drapers' Co 1989; *Recreations* conservation, planting trees especially female black poplars (Britain's rarest native tree); *Style*— Roger Jefcoate, Esq, CBE; ✉ Willowbrook, Swanbourne Road, Mursley, Milton Keynes, Buckinghamshire MK17 0JA (tel 01296 720533)

JEFFCOAT, Rev Rupert Edward Elessing (baptised Robert); s of David Alan Jeffcoat, of Edinburgh, and Marilyn Annette, *née* Yeomans; *b* 23 June 1970; *Educ* St Mary's Music Sch Edinburgh (Episcopal Cathedral chorister), Glenalmond Coll (music scholar), St Catharine's Coll Cambridge (scholar and organ scholar, Ord travel grant); *m* 22 June 2001, Catherine Jane, *née* Corrigan; 2 da (Anastasia Catherine Eudora b 3 Feb 2003, Euphemia Catherine Aurelia b 27 June 2005); *Career* composer, arranger, conductor, organist, pianist, accompanist and writer; acting asst organist Guildford Cathedral 1989, church appts Northampton 1992, London 1994 and Pickering 1995, music asst Edinburgh Int Festival 1992–95, music teacher and tutor Ampleforth Coll 1993–95, asst organist St Philip's Cathedral Birmingham 1995–97, accompanist Birmingham Bach Choir 1995–97, music teacher Bluecoat Sch Birmingham 1995–97, musical dir Bournemouth Sinfonietta Choir 1996–99, dir of music Coventry Cathedral 1997–2005, dir of music St John's Cathedral Brisbane 2005–, memb of staff Birmingham Conservatoire, accompanist Nat Youth Orch; performer: piano duet and two-piano recitals (with bro Richard) 1976–, organ recitals UK and Europe 1988–; compositions incl: Missa Jacet Granum (for Canterbury Cathedral Choir) 1998, Here is my Servant 2000, The Prophet (words by Ted Hughes) 2000, Third Service 2000, Mass for Oakham 2001, Tabernacle of Peace 2001, Common Worship Psalter 2003–06; dir of music for various BBC progs, recorded and broadcast on BBC Radio 2, 3 and 4, appeared on German radio and Japanese and American TV, directed, played and produced several CDs; examiner Royal Sch of Church Music, tutor Guild of Church Musicians, leader cathedral choir tours and choral workshops, adjudicated at music festivals and sch competitions; memb: Cathedral Organists Assoc 1997–, Ctee ISM (Warks) 2001–, Performing Right Soc 2002–, Assoc of Ordinands 2002–, Coll of Preachers 2002–, Royal Philharmonic Soc 2003–, Anglican-Lutheran Soc 2003–, Fedn of Cathedral Old Choristers Assoc, Friends of Cathedral Music, Coventry and Warks Organists Assoc, Foleshill Multicultural Forum, Cncl for Music in Hospitals; fndr memb Mendelssohn on Mull Festival 1988; tstee Thomas Garratt Fund, involved with Live Music Now!; Prizewinner FRCO 1991; *Recreations* most European languages and literature, travelling, cooking; *Clubs* Scottish Arts; *Style*— The Rev Rupert Jeffcoat; ✉ tel 00 61 7 3835 2231, e-mail music@anglicanbrisbane.org.au

JEFFCOATE, Prof William James; s of Prof Sir (Thomas) Norman Arthur Jeffcoate (d 1992), and Josephine, *née* Lindsay (d 1981); *b* 31 May 1947; *Educ* Liverpool Coll, St John's Coll Cambridge (MA), Middx Hosp Med Sch (MB BChir); *Career* conslt physician and endocrinologist City Hosp Nottingham 1979–; MRCP; *Publications* Lecture Notes on Endocrinology (5 edn, 1993), The Diabetic Foot: An Illustrated Guide to Management (with R M Macfarlane, 1995); author of papers on diabetes and endocrinology; *Recreations* sailing; *Style*— Prof William Jeffcoate; ✉ Nottingham University Hospitals, City Hospital Campus, Hucknall Road, Nottingham NG5 1PB (tel 0115 969 1169, e-mail wjeffcoate@futu.co.uk)

JEFFCOTT, Prof Leo Broof; s of late Edward Ian Broof Jeffcott, and Pamela Mary, *née* Hull; *b* 19 June 1942; *Educ* Caius Sch Shoreham by Sea, Brighton Tech Coll, Royal Vet Coll Univ of London (BVetMed, PhD), Univ of Melbourne (DVSc), Univ of Cambridge (MA); *m* 14 June 1969, Tisza Jacqueline, *née* Hubbard; 2 da (Julie Marie b 9 Feb 1972, Michele Anne b 7 March 1978); *Career* Equine Res Station Animal Health Tst: asst pathologist 1967–71, radiologist and clinician 1972–77, head Clinical Dept 1977–82; prof of clinical radiology Vet Coll Swedish Univ of Agric Sciences 1981–82; Univ of Melbourne: prof of vet clinical sciences 1983–91, head Dept of Vet Clinical Sciences 1985–89, dep dean Faculty of Vet Science 1985, dir Vet Clinic and Hosp 1986–91; Univ of Cambridge: prof of vet clinical studies 1991–2004, dean Vet Sch 1992–2004, professorial fell Pembroke Coll 1993–2004; dean Faculty of Vet Science Univ of Sydney 2004–; official veterinarian Int Equestrian Fedn at: Olympic Games Seoul 1988, World Equestrian Games Stockholm 1990, Olympic Games Barcelona 1992, World Equestrian Games The Hague 1994, Olympic Games Atlanta 1996, World Equestrian Games Rome 1998, Olympic Games Sydney 2000, World Equestrian Games Jerez 2002, Olympic Games Athens 2004, Olympic Games Beijing 2008; chm Veterinary Ctee and memb Bureau of International Fedn (FEI) 1998–2006, int chm and convenor 5th Int Conf on Equine Exercise Physiology Japan 1998; Sir Frederick Hobday Meml Lecture 1977, Peter Hernquist Meml Lecture 1991, Share Jones Lectureship 1993; elected Univ of Kentucky Equine Res Hall of Fame 1991; G Norman Hall Medal 1978, Richard Hartley Clinical Prize 1980, Tierklinik Hochmoor Int Prize 1981, Open Award Equine Vet Jl 1982, John Hickman Orthopaedic Prize 1991, Animal Health Tst Outstanding Scientific Achievement Award 1994, Sefton Award for Servs to Equestrian Safety 1997, BVA Dalrymple-Champneys Cup and Medal 2001; memb: BVA, Br Equine Vet Assoc; hon memb: Societa Italiana di Ippologie 1977, Equine Section Swedish Soc for Vet Med 1992; Dr VetMed (hc) Swedish Agric Univ Uppsala; FRCVS 1978, Hon FRVC 1997; *Publications* Comparative Clinical Haematology (jt ed, 1977), Equine Exercise Physiology 3 (jt ed, 1991), Osteochondrosis in the 90's (jt ed, 1993), On to Atlanta '96 (jt ed, 1994), Thermoregulatory Responses During Competitive Exercise in the Performing Horse (jt ed, Vol 1 1995, Vol 2 1996), Equine Exercise Physiology 5 (ed, 1999), Osteochondrosis and Musculoskeletal Devolpment in the Foal under the Influence of Exercise (jt ed, 1999), A Tribute to Colonel John Hickman (jt ed, 2001); author of approx 300 articles in learned jls; *Recreations* photography, swimming, gardening; *Style*— Prof Leo Jeffcott; ✉ Faculty of Vetinary Science, University of Sydney, J D Stewart Building, Sydney, NSW 2006, Australia (tel 00 61 9351 6935, fax 00 61 9960 1548, e-mail leoj@vetsci.usyd.edu.au)

JEFFERIES, David George; CBE; s of George Jefferies (d 1981), of Upminster, Essex, and Emma, *née* Braybrook (d 1979); *b* 26 December 1933; *m* 12 Dec 1959, Jeanette Ann (Jean); *Career* chief engr Southern Electric (currently Scottish and Southern Energy plc) 1972–74, dir NW Region CEGB 1974–77, dir of personnel CEGB 1977–81, chm LEB 1981–86, dep chm Electricity Cncl 1986–90; chm: Electricity Pensions Ltd 1986–96, Electricity Pensions Trustees Ltd 1986–98, National Grid Company plc 1990–96, Viridian plc (formerly Northern Ireland Electricity) 1994–98, National Grid Group plc 1995–99, 24/Seven Utility Services 1999–2002, Smartlogik Ltd 2001–02, Costain Group plc 2001–, Geotrupes Energy 2003–07; pres Electrical and Electronic Industries Benevolent Assoc (EEIBA), co-chm Indo-Br Partnership 1999–2003, memb Bd Strategic Rail Authy 1999–2001, memb Bd Royal Instn 2000–; Freeman City of London 1982, Liveryman Worshipful Co of Wax Chandlers (Master 2005–06); Hon DTech, Hon LLD; FREng, FIEE (past pres), FInstE (past pres), CIMgt; *Recreations* golf, gardening, music; *Clubs* Athenaeum, RAC, Foxhills, Wentworth; *Style*— David Jefferies, Esq, CBE, FREng

JEFFERIES, Stephen; s of George Frederick Jefferies, of Birmingham, and Kitty Barbara, *née* Salisbury; *b* 24 June 1951; *Educ* Turves Green Sch Birmingham, Royal Ballet Sch; *m* 1972, Rashna, da of Homi B Minocher Homji; 1 da (Lara b 1982), 1 s (Christopher b 1985); *Career* ballet dancer; joined Sadler's Wells Royal Ballet 1969, character princ dancer 1993, sr princ dancer Royal Ballet 1979–93 (princ dancer 1973–76 and 1977–79); all maj roles with the Royal Ballet and Nat Ballet of Canada, over 25 roles created; rehearsal dir Rambert Ballet 1995, artistic dir Hong Kong Ballet 1996 (prodns choreographed for the Hong Kong Ballet incl: Swan Lake 1996, Giselle and the Nutcracker 1997, Tango Ballet Tango 2000, Sleeping Beauty 2002, The Legend of the Great Archer (designer) 2004), choreographer of Suzie Wong 2006, artistic dir and choreographer Suzhou Dance Co Suzhou Science and Arts Cultural Centre Co Ltd 2007–; Hon ARAD; *Recreations* golf; *Style*— Stephen Jefferies, Esq

J

JEFFERS, Prof John Norman Richard; s of Lt-Col J H Jeffers, OBE (d 1980), of Woodhall Spa, Lincs, and Emily Matilda Alice, *née* Robinson (d 1974); *b* 10 September 1926; *Educ* Portsmouth GS, Benmore Forestry Sch Dunoon; *m* 25 July 1951, Edna May, da of Ernest Reginald Parratt (d 1973), of Farnham, Surrey; 1 da (Ysanne b 11 July 1963); *Career* Forestry Cmmn: res forester 1944–53, princ statistician 1953–68, dir Merlewood Res Station Nature Conservancy 1968–73; Inst of Terrestrial Ecology (NERC): dep dir 1973–75, dir 1976–86; visiting prof: Maths Inst Univ of Kent 1988–2000, Dept of Chemical and Process Engineering Univ of Newcastle upon Tyne 1990–94, Dept of Mechanical, Materials and Mfrg Engrg Univ of Newcastle upon Tyne 1994–2001, Sch of Mathematics, Statistics and Computing Univ of Greenwich 1994–; DSc (hc) Lancaster Univ; memb Biometric Soc; CStat, CBiol, CIFor; *Books* Experimental Design and Analysis in Forestry (1953), An Introduction to Systems Analysis: with ecological examples (1978), Modelling (1982), Practitioner's handbook on the modelling of dynamic change in ecosystems (1988), Microcomputers in Environmental biology (1992), Research, Ecology and Environment (2003); *Recreations* military history; *Clubs* Athenaeum; *Style—* Prof John Jeffers; ✉ Glenside, Oxenholme, Kendal, Cumbria LA9 7RF (tel 01539 734375, fax 01539 734378)

JEFFERS, Raymond Jackson; s of George Dennis Jeffers, of Albany, Suffolk, and Jeannine, *née* Jacquier; *b* 5 August 1954; *Educ* Stanwell Sch Penarth, Aberystwyth UCW (LLB), Wadham Coll Oxford (BCL); *m* 4 Sept 1982, Carol Elizabeth, da of John Bernard Awty, of Freshwater, IOW; 3 da (Alice Elizabeth b 19 Aug 1994, Lara Victoria, Florence May (twins) b 27 Jan 1996); *Career* admitted slr 1980; Linklaters (formerly Linklaters & Paines): ptnr Corporate Dept 1986–, London head of employment 1990–2002, global head of employment 2002–; chm Employment and Industrial Rels Ctee Int Bar Assoc 2001–03; chm Employment Lawyers Assoc 2004–06 (dep chm 2003–04, chm Legislative and Policy Ctee 2000–03 (memb 1998–)); City of London Slrs' Co: memb Commercial Law Sub-Ctee 1986–1989, chm Employment Law Sub-Ctee 2001– (memb 1987–); memb Law Soc 1980; *Recreations* ornithology, badminton, golf, tennis; *Style—* Raymond Jeffers, Esq; ✉ Linklaters, One Silk Street, London EC2Y 8HQ (tel 020 7456 2000, fax 020 7456 2222)

JEFFERSON, Dr Ann; *Career* fell New Coll Oxford 1987–, CUF lectr in French Univ of Oxford; Leverhulme major research fell 2001–04; FBA 2004; *Books* The Nouveau Roman and the Poetics of Fiction (1980), Modern Literary Theory: A Comparative Introduction (jtly, 1982, revised edn 1986), Reading Realism in Stendhal (1988), Nathalie Sarraute, Fiction and Theory: Questions of Difference (2000); *Style—* Dr Ann Jefferson; ✉ New College, Oxford OX1 3BN

JEFFERSON, Sir George Rowland; kt (1981), CBE (1969); s of Harold Jefferson, and Eva Elizabeth Ellen; *b* 26 March 1921; *Educ* Dartford GS; *m* 1, 1943, Irene (d 1998), da of Frederick Watson-Browne; 3 s; m 2, 1999, Bridget Anne, da John Reilly; *Career* engrg apprentice Royal Ordnance Factory Woolwich 1937–42, cmmnd RAOC 1942, transferred REME 1942, served 1942–45 Anti-Aircraft Cmd on heavy anti-aircraft gun mounting devpt, subsequently memb Miny of Supply staff Fort Halstead until 1952; joined Guided Weapons Div English Electric Co Ltd 1952 (chief res engr 1953, dep chief engr 1958), dir English Electric Aviation (Guided Weapons) Ltd 1963 (dep md 1964, memb Bd 1965–77, md 1966–68, chm and md 1968–77); dir Br Aerospace and chm and md Dynamics Gp 1977–80 (memb Organising Ctee 1976–77); dir: British Aerospace (Australia) Ltd 1968–80, British Scandinavian Aviation AB 1968–80, Engineering Sciences Data Unit Ltd 1975–80, Hawker Siddeley Dynamics 1977–80, Babcock International 1980–87, Lloyds Bank 1986–89, AMEC plc 1988–92; chm BAC (Anti-Tank) 1968–78, dep chm Post Office 1980; chm: British Telecommunications plc 1981–87 (chief exec 1981–86), Matthew Hall plc 1987–88, City Centre Communications 1988, Videotron Holdings plc 1989–97; memb: NEB 1979–80, NICG 1980–84, NEDC 1981–84; Freeman City of London; Hon DSc Univ of Bristol 1984, Hon DUniv Essex 1985; FREng 1978, Hon FIMechE, FIEE, FRAeS, FRSA, CIMgt, FCGI; *Style—* Sir George Jefferson, CBE, FREng; ✉ 12 Ocean Shores Edge, Connolly, Joondalup, Perth, WA 6027, Australia

JEFFERSON, John Malcolm; s of Arthur Jefferson, of Driffield, E Yorks, and Gladys Evelyn Jefferson; *b* 26 June 1945; *Educ* Bridlington GS; *m* 30 March 1967, Gillian Mary, da of Joseph Healy; 2 s (Nathan b 28 Sept 1974, Daniel b 13 June 1978); *Career* news reporter Bridlington Free Press and Scarborough Evening News, chief reporter Redcar, industrial ed and dep news ed Evening Gazette Teesside; news prodr: BBC Radio Durham, BBC Radio Cleveland, BBC Radio Carlisle; prog organiser BBC Radio Humberside, station mangr and fndr BBC Radio York, managing ed BBC Radio Leeds 1988–95, memb BBC Ten Year Strategy Team 1995–96, media conslt and fndr JJ Media Projects 1996, dir em3media Ltd 2003–, memb Leeds Media; aid worker VSO Divine Word Univ Madang Papua New Guinea 1998; former memb: Carlisle Round Table, Holderness Rotary Club Hull; former chm York Branch Br Heart Fndn; memb: Radio Acad, Br Exec Services Oversea (voluntary work in Montenegro 1998, Moscow 1999, Nepal 2002 and Jasi Romania 2003 and 2004); *Books* Disasters and the Media - Managing Crisis Communications (contrib, 1999), Connecting in a Crisis - Working with the BBC in an Emergency (2002); *Clubs* York Vikings Rotary; *Style—* John Jefferson, Esq; ✉ JJ Media Projects, 41 Mile End Park, Pocklington, York YO42 2TH (tel and fax 01759 304875, e-mail johnjefferson@mediaprojects.clara.co.uk)

JEFFERSON, William Hayton; OBE (1986); s of Stanley Jefferson (d 1996), of Abbeytown, Cumbria, and Josephine, *née* Hayton (d 1985); *b* 29 July 1940; *Educ* Nelson-Thomlinson GS Wigton, Wadham Coll Oxford (MA); *m* 1, 1963 (m dis 1986), Marie-Jeanne, *née* Mazenq; 3 s (Jean-Marc b 1963, Jean-Michel b 1964, Vincent b 1970); m 2, 1986, Fadia George, *née* Tarraf; 1 s (William b 1986); *Career* Russian teacher 1963–66; British Council: Tripoli 1967–70, Kuwait 1970–72, Algeria 1972–75, dir Doha Qatar 1975–79, dir Overseas Cooperation London 1979–82, dir United Arab Emirates 1982–85, dir Algeria 1985–90, dir Czechoslovakia and cultural cnsllr British Embassy Prague 1990–96, dir Portugal and cnsllr British Embassy Lisbon 1996–98, borough cncllr Allerdale, Cumbria 1999–; chm N Allerdale Regeneration Partnership 2001–; chm Solway Coast Area of Outstanding Natural Beauty Cumbria; Czech Scientific Univ Gold Medal 1995, Charles Univ Prague Silver Medal 1996, Olomouc Univ Moravia Medal of Honour 1996, Masaryk Univ Brno Silver Medal 1996; *Recreations* bowls; *Style—* William Jefferson, Esq, OBE; ✉ 3 Marine Terrace, Silloth, Cumbria CA7 4BZ (tel 01697 332526, e-mail william.jefferson@allerdale.gov.uk)

JEFFERY, Prof Charles Adrian; s of Frank Bertram Jeffery (d 1969), and June Dorothy Addington, *née* Rouse; *b* 27 July 1964, Holcot, Northants; *Educ* Univ of Loughborough (BA, PhD); *m* 22 Aug 1998, Elke Lieve Versmessen; 2 da (Mieke Dot b 12 March 2002, Elsie Paul b 19 Sept 2005); *Career* lectr: N Staffs Poly 1988–89, Univ of Leicester 1989–94; Inst for German Studies Univ of Birmingham: sr res fell 1994, reader 1996–99, prof of German politics 1999–2004; prof of politics and co-dir Inst of Governance Univ of Edinburgh 2004–; ESRC: dir Res Prog on Devolution and Constitutional Change 2000–06, memb Cncl and chm Strategic Res Bd 2005–; advsr EU Ctee of the Regions 2002–05, advsr Ctee on Standards in Public Life 2002–07, specialist advsr House of Commons Select Ctee on the ODPM 2004–05; AcSS 2004, FRSE 2007; *Publications* German Federalism Today (co-ed, 1991), Federalism, Unification and European Integration (co-ed, 1993), Social Democracy in the Austrian Provinces, 1918–1934: Beyond Red Vienna (1995), The Regional Dimension of the European Union: Towards a 'Third' Level in Europe? (1997), Germany Today: A Student's Dictionary (co-ed, 1997), Recasting German Federalism: The Legacies of Unification (ed, 1998), Germany's European Diplomacy: Shaping the Regional Milieu (co-author, 2000), Verfassungspolitik und Verfassungswandel: Deutschland und Grossbritannien im Vergleich (co-ed, 2001), Devolution and Electoral Politics (co-ed, 2006); *Style—* Prof Charles Jeffery; ✉ 9 West Savile Road, Edinburgh EH16 5NG (tel 0131 478 0098); School of Social and Political Studies, University of Edinburgh, Adam Ferguson Building, George Square, Edinburgh EH8 9LL (tel 0131 650 4266, e-mail charlie.jeffery@ed.ac.uk)

JEFFERY, Christopher Paul; s of Dr David Jeffery, and Jennifer, *née* Hartree; *b* 23 April 1962, Bristol; *Educ* Bristol GS, Univ of York (BA), Univ of Exeter (PGCE); *m* 12 March 1988, Carol, *née* Buckley; 2 s (Thomas b 5 June 1992, Matthew b 28 Jan 1995), 1 da (Kate b 16 Aug 2000); *Career* clerical asst Dept of Employment 1980–81, teacher St Peter's Sch York 1984–85, songwriter and singer Mimic Theatrical Co 1986–87, admin Univ of Bristol 1988, history teacher Bristol GS 1988–96 (housemaster 1990–96), history teacher Perse Sch for Boys Cambridge 1996–2004 (head of middle sch 1996–2001, dep head 2001–04), headmaster Grange Sch Hartford 2005–; memb HMC 2005–; FRSA 2007; *Recreations* family life, published writer of contemporary church music, singer and performer of contemporary and choral music, memb St John's Church Hartford (sidesman), playing and watching sport, cinema, travelling and walking; *Style—* Christopher Jeffery, Esq; ✉ The Grange School, Bradburn's Lane, Hartford, Northwich, Cheshire CW8 1LU

JEFFERY, David John; CBE (2000); s of Stanley John Friend Jeffery (d 1972), and Sylvia May, *née* Mashford; *b* 18 February 1936; *Educ* Sutton HS Plymouth, RNC Greenwich, Croydon Coll of Technol, RCDS; *m* 28 March 1959, Margaret, da of George Yates (d 1983); 2 da (Karen b 6 Sept 1962, Susan b 22 July 1964), 1 s (Christopher b 6 Aug 1968); *Career* Nat Serv RAOC 1954–56; Admty MOD and Treasy, princ Treasy Centre for Admin Studies 1970–72, mgmnt sci trg advsr Malaysian Govt Kuala Lumpur 1972–74, Civil Serv Dept 1974–76, MOD 1976–80, asst sec 1980–84, dir Armaments and Mgmnt Servs RN Supply and Tport Serv 1984–86, advsr Kathmandu Volunteer Organisation Devpt (VSO) 2004–06; chief exec and memb Bd Port of London Authority 1986–99, chief exec Br Marine Equipment Cncl (BMEC) 2000–01; tstee dir Pilots National Pension Fund 1988–95; dir: British Ports Federation Ltd 1988–92, Estuary Services Ltd 1988–99 (chm 1988, 1991, 1993 and 1995–99), UK Major Ports Group Ltd 1993–99, British Ports Industry Training Ltd 1993–99 (chm 1998–99), Thames 2000 Ltd 1997–99; chm: Trade Facilitation Ctee, Int Assoc of Ports and Harbours (IAPH) 1992–96 (conference vice-pres 1995–97, memb Exec Ctee 1995–99), Euro Sea Ports Orgn 1993–99 (vice-chm 1993–96, chm 1997–99), DTI Port Sector Gp 1998–2001; memb Marine Foresight Panel 1997–2001; govr Selwood Middle Sch Frome 2001–04 (chm of govrs 2002–); chm Frome Citizens Advice Bureau 2001–03; Freeman: City of London 1987, Worshipful Co of Watermen and Lightermen of the River Thames 1987; *Style—* David Jeffery, Esq, CBE; ✉ The Old Coach House, Nunney, Frome, Somerset BA11 4LZ (tel 01373 836459)

JEFFERY, Jack; CBE (1995); s of Philip Jeffery (d 1973), and Elsie, *née* Carr (d 1999); *b* 10 March 1930; *Educ* Stanley GS Co Durham, King's Coll Durham (BSc, MSc); *m* 1 (m dis 1983); 3 da (Wyn b 1951, Carole b 1953, Jill b 1958); m 2, 1983, Deborah Mary, da of Kenneth Hyde; *Career* scientist NCB 1953–61, chemist and bacteriologist Southwest Suburban Water Co 1961–73 (asst gen mangr 1968–73); North Surrey Water: water quality controller 1973–77, gen mangr 1977–87, md 1987–95, chm 1990–2001; chm: General Utilities Projects Ltd 1990–2000, Tendring Hundred Water Services Ltd 1995–2000, Northumbria Larder 2006–; dep chm Three Valleys Water plc 2000–01; dir: WRC plc 1989–99, Tendring Hundred Water Services Ltd 1992–2002, Durham County Waste Management Ltd 1992–, East Surrey Holdings plc 1995–2000, County Durham Environmental Tst 2006–; chm Water Cos Assoc 1987–90; pres: Freshwater Biological Assoc 1988–95, Instn of Water Offrs 1991; chm Cncl of RIPH 2002–06 (dep chm 1993–2002); chm: Surrey First 1993–96, Careers Advsy Bd Univ of Newcastle upon Tyne 1995–2000, Convocation Univ of Newcastle upon Tyne 1999–, World Humanity Action Tst 2000–03 (tstee 1993–); hon memb: Instn of Water Offrs 1992, American Waterworks Assoc 1994; tstee: Univ of Newcastle upon Tyne Devpt Tst 1999–2004 and 2005–, Dementia North 2000–06; Distinguished Serv Certificate BSI 1995; author of various papers on water quality and treatment and water privatisation; Freeman City of London 1980, Liveryman, memb Ct of Assts and past Master Worshipful Co of Plumbers; FCIWEM 1987, FRIPH 1987, FRSA 1989, CCMI (CIMgt 1994); *Recreations* music, watching sport, books, wine; *Clubs* Lansdowne, MCC, Forty, Durham CCC, Lord's Taverners; *Style—* Jack Jeffery, Esq, CBE; ✉ Laleham House, Hedley on the Hill, Stocksfield, Northumberland NE43 7SW (tel 01661 843729, fax 01661 844058, e-mail j.jeffery@laleham.f9.co.uk)

JEFFERY, Paul Francis; s of Arthur Felgate Sinclair Jeffery (d 1998), of Storrington, W Sussex, and Muriel Carmen, *née* Privett (d 1992); *b* 27 January 1946; *Educ* Eastbourne Coll; *m* 13 March 1971, Patricia Ann Jeffery, OBE, da of Edward Frederick Emes; 1 s (Edward Paul b 21 Oct 1972); *Career* CA; articled clerk: Harry Price & Co Eastbourne 1964–66, Jones Avens Worley & Piper Chichester 1966–68; Thomson McLintock & Co: London office 1969–77, ptnr Norwich office 1977–87 (managing ptnr 1986–87), memb Quality Review Gp 1981–84, UK dir of quality review 1984–86; ptnr specialising in insolvency and restructuring KPMG (following merger of Thomson McLintock and Peat Marwick Mitchell in 1987): London office 1991–94, St Albans office 1994–2001; ptnr The Jeffery Partnership (governance advsr and mentor to business) 2001–; founding ptnr The Governance Consultancy 2002–; pres Norfolk and Norwich Soc of CAs 1982–83, chm Norwich Enterprise Agency Tst 1989–92 (memb Bd 1986–92), treas Mid Norfolk Cons Assoc 1993–96, treas Norfolk Cons Euro Constituency Cncl 1994–99, asst area treas (Norfolk) Cons Pty 1994–98; tstee Norfolk Archeological Tst 2004–; govr Eastbourne Coll 1992–2005 (vice-chm 1999–2005); FCA 1979 (ACA 1969), Insolvency Licence (ICAEW) 1987, memb Soc of Practitioners in Insolvency 1990; *Recreations* golf, swimming, travelling, reading, walking; *Style—* Paul Jeffery, Esq; ✉ Bilney House, East Bilney, Dereham, Norfolk NR20 4HW (tel 01362 860111)

JEFFERY, Timothy Arthur Rodney; s of Rodney Albert Jeffery, of Lymington, Hants, and Edith Rosina, *née* Meeks; *b* 13 June 1956; *Educ* Methodist Coll Belfast, Univ of Kent at Canterbury (BA); *m* 14 April 1984, (Margaret) Jennifer, da of Harold Gibson; 1 da (Kate Elizabeth Rosina b 4 Dec 1987); *Career* features ed Yachting World 1978–88, yachting corr The Daily Telegraph 1988–; former chm UKC Sports Fedn, memb Yachting Journalists' Assoc 1977; *Books* Sail of the Century (1983), Practical Sailing (1986), Sailing Year (1987), The Official History of The Champagne Mumm Admiral's Cup (1994), Beken of Cowes: Sailing Thoroughbreds (1998), Beken of Cowes: The America's Cup (1999), Alinghi America's Cup (2003); *Recreations* sailing, golf, skiing, tennis; *Clubs* Royal Thames Yacht, Royal Ocean Racing, Int Assoc of Cape Horners; *Style—* Timothy Jeffery, Esq; ✉ The Daily Telegraph, 1 Canada Square, Canary Wharf, London E14 5DT (tel 020 7538 5000, fax 020 7513 2507, e-mail mail@timjeffery.com)

JEFFORD, Nerys; *b* 25 December 1962; *Educ* Olchfa Comp Sch Swansea, Lady Margaret Hall Oxford (scholar, MA), Univ of Virginia (Fulbright scholar, LLM); *Career* called to the Bar Gray's Inn 1986 (Lord Justice Holker scholar, Karmel scholar, bencher); practising barr specialising in construction and engrg law and arbitration, memb Keating Chambers 1988–, recorder; chm Soc of Construction Law; memb: Technology and Construction Bar Assoc, Commercial Bar Assoc, London Common Law and Commercial Bar Assoc, Educn and Training Ctee Bar Standards Bd; memb Advsy Cncl Lady Margaret Hall; memb: Gray's Inn Chapel Choir, London Welsh Chorale, London Welsh Assoc, Racehorse Owners Assoc, Thoroughbred Breeders Assoc; *Recreations* flat racing, singing; *Style—* Miss Nerys Jefford; ✉ Keating Chambers, 15 Essex Street, London WC2R 3AA (tel 020 7544 2600, fax 020 7544 2700, e-mail njefford@keatingchambers.com)

JEFFREY, Nicholas; s of Manfred Jeffrey (d 1995), and Doris MacKay, *née* Spouge (d 1997); *b* 6 June 1942; *Educ* Ecclesfield GS, Univ of Sheffield (LLB); *m* 1965, Dianne Michelle, da of Cyril Cantor (d 1985); 2 s (Alexander b 1966, David b 1969), 2 da (Danya b 1968, Miranda b 1971); *Career* chm: United Industries plc (formerly Neepsend plc) 1994–2002, Coffee Republic plc 1998–, Channel Holdings plc 1999–2000, Eurocity Properties plc 2000–02, Halcyon Internet plc 2000–03, Mountain Warehouse 2002–, Maccess Ltd 2002–, Nightspeed Holding Ltd 2003–, Sheffield Hallam Univ 2003–; Liveryman: Worshipful Co of Furniture Makers, Worshipful Co of Cutlers in Hallamshire; *Recreations* shooting, sailing; *Style—* Nicholas Jeffrey, Esq

JEFFREY, Dr Robin Campbell; s of Robert Stewart Martin Jeffrey (d 1962), and Catherine Campbell McSporran (d 1995); *b* 19 February 1939; *Educ* Kelvinside Acad, Royal Coll of Science and Technol Univ of Glasgow (BSc), Pembroke Coll Cambridge (PhD), Templeton Coll Oxford; *m* 28 July 1962, Barbara Helen, da of Prof Sir Austin Robinson; 2 s (Alan b 17 Jan 1967, David b 9 Dec 1968), 1 da (Catherine b 19 Nov 1971); *Career* Babcock & Wilcox 1956–80; SSEB (now Scottish Power): engrg resources mangr 1964–79, tech servs mngr 1979–80, mangr Torness Project 1980–88, chief engr 1988–89, md Engrg Resources Business 1989–92; Scottish Nuclear Ltd: chief exec 1992–98, chm 1995–98; British Energy plc: exec dir North America and dep chm 1996–2001, chm and ceo 2001–02; chm Bruce Power 2001–02; visiting prof Univ of Strathclyde 1994; former memb: Bd London Transport, CBI Scot Cncl, SCDI Exec; FREng 1992, FIChemE 1992, FIMechE 1993; *Books* Open Cycle MHD Power Generation (co-author, 1969); *Recreations* squash, tennis, skiing, playing musical instruments; *Clubs* Cambridge Univ Royal Tennis, Glasgow Academical Squash, Queen's (Toronto); *Style—* Dr Robin Jeffrey, FREng

JEFFREY, William Alexander (Bill); CB (2001); s of Alexander Jeffrey (d 1979), and Joyce, *née* McCrindle; *b* 28 February 1948; *Educ* Allan Glen's Sch Glasgow, Univ of Glasgow (BSc); *m* 2 June 1979, Joan, da of Duncan MacNaughton; *Career* under sec (ops and resources) Immigration and Nationality Dept Home Office 1991–94 (various positions Home Office 1971–84 (incl private sec to the Perm Sec 1975–76), asst sec 1984–91), dep head Economic and Domestic Secretariat Cabinet Office 1994–98, political dir NI Office 1998–2002, DG Immigration and Nationality Directorate Home Office 2002–05, security and intelligence co-ordinator and perm sec Cabinet Office 2005, perm sec MOD 2005–; *Recreations* reading, hill walking, watching football; *Style—* Bill Jeffrey, Esq, CB

JEFFREY-COOK, John; *b* 5 January 1936; *Educ* Whitgift Middle (Trinity) Sch Croydon; *m* 12 May 1962, Gillian Audrey, da of Ronald Albert Kettle (d 1982), of Croydon, Surrey; 2 s (Richard Daniel b 1964, Malcolm John b 1970 d 1981), 1 da (Fiona Elizabeth b 1966); *Career* managing ed of taxation books Butterworth Law Publishers 1966–77, dir of pubns Deloitte Haskins & Sells 1977–85, ptnr Moores Rowland 1985–98; ed Moores Rowland's Yellow and Orange Tax Guides 1987–97, conslt ed Encyclopaedia of Forms and Precedents 1993–; memb Editorial Bd: Simon's Direct Tax Serv 1977–, Taxation 1989–2004, Taxation Practitioner 1992–99, Tax Adviser 2000–04; memb: Ctee London & Dist Soc of CAs 1966–77, Cncl Chartered Inst of Taxation 1977–90 (treas 1981–88), Cncl Assoc of Taxation Technicians 1989–2000, Addington Soc 1966– (chm 1993–95); Freeman City of London 1980, Liveryman Worshipful Co of Chartered Accountants 1980–, Liveryman Worshipful Co of Tax Advisers 1995 (clerk 1996–2001), memb Fellowship of Clerks 2001–; FCA 1958, FCIS 1959, fell CTA (FTII 1964), ATT 1989; *Books* Simon's Taxes (ed, 1970), de Voil's Value Added Tax (1973), Simon's Tax Intelligence and Cases (1973), Butterworths Orange Tax Handbook (1976), Foster's Capital Taxes Encyclopaedia (1976), Moores Rowland's Taxation of Farmers and Farming (1989); *Recreations* history, travel, theatre, cinema; *Style—* John Jeffrey-Cook, Esq; ✉ 18 Farncombe Close, Wivelsfield Green, Haywards Heath, West Sussex RH17 7RA (tel 01444 471751, e-mail john@jeffrey-cook.wanadoo.co.uk)

JEFFREYS, Alan Howard; QC (1996); s of Hugh Jeffreys (d 1988), and Rachel Mary, *née* Evans (d 1998); *b* 27 September 1947; *Educ* Ellesmere Coll, King's Coll London (LLB); *m* 1975, Jane Olivia, da of Richard Duncan Sadler; 1 da (Cerian Olivia Sophia b 7 July 1979), 1 s (Hugo Harri Richard b 8 July 1981); *Career* called to the Bar Gray's Inn 1970; in practice SE Circuit, recorder 1993–2004; memb: London Common Law and Commercial Bar Assoc, Personal Injuries Bar Assoc (memb Exec Ctee), Criminal Injuries Compensation Appeals Panel 1999–2002; *Recreations* fishing, chess, music; *Clubs* Hurlingham; *Style—* Alan Jeffreys, Esq, QC; ✉ Farrar's Building, Temple, London EC4Y 7BD (tel 020 7583 9241, fax 020 7583 0090)

JEFFREYS, Prof Sir Alec John; kt (1994); s of Sydney Victor Jeffreys, and Joan, *née* Knight (d 1994); *b* 9 January 1950; *Educ* Luton GS, Luton Sixth Form Coll, Merton Coll Oxford (MA, DPhil); *m* 28 Aug 1971, Susan, da of Frederick Charles Robert Miles (d 1975), of Luton, Beds; 2 da (Sarah Catherine b 1979, Elizabeth Jane b 1983); *Career* postdoctoral research fell European Molecular Biology Orgn Univ of Amsterdam 1975–77; Univ of Leicester: lectr 1977–82, Lister Inst research fell 1982–91, reader 1984–87, prof of genetics 1987–; Wolfson research prof of the Royal Soc 1991–; devpt of genetic fingerprinting system 1984–; memb: EMBO, Human Genome Orgn, Genetical Soc; hon memb: Int Soc for Forensic Haemogenetics 1997, American Acad of Forensic Sciences 1998, Biochemical Soc 2003; Hon DUniv Open Univ 1991; Hon DSc: Univ of St Andrews 1996, Univ of Strathclyde 1998, Univ of Hull 2004, Univ of Oxford 2004; hon fell: Merton Coll Oxford, Univ of Luton 1995; fell Forensic Sci Soc of India, fell Linnean Soc 1994, FRCPath 1991, Hon FRCP 1992, Hon FIBiol 1998, FMedSci 1998, Hon FRSM 2001, FRS; *Recreations* swimming, walking, postal history; *Style—* Prof Sir Alec Jeffreys, FRS; ✉ Department of Genetics, Adrian Building, University of Leicester, University Road, Leicester LE1 7RH (tel 0116 252 3435, fax 0116 252 3378)

JEFFREYS, 3 Baron (UK 1952); Christopher Henry Mark Jeffreys; s of 2 Baron Jeffreys (d 1986), and Mrs Sarah Clarke, of Lower Tredinnick, Cornwall; *b* 22 May 1957; *Educ* Eton; *m* 22 Aug 1985, Anne Elisabeth, da of Antoine Denarie, of Johannesburg, and Mrs Derek Johnson; 1 da (Hon Alice Mary b 1986), 1 s (Hon Arthur Mark Henry b 1989); *Heir* s, Hon Arthur Jeffreys; *Career* futures broker; Johnson Matthey & Wallace Ltd 1976–85, GNI Ltd 1985–90, stockbroker Raphael Zorn Hemsley 1992–2000, stockbroker and dir Savoy Investment Mgmt 2000–; *Recreations* country sports, sailing, skiing; *Clubs* Pratt's; *Style—* The Rt Hon the Lord Jeffreys; ✉ Manor Farmhouse, Edmondthorpe, Melton Mowbray, Leicestershire LE14 2JU (tel 01572 787397)

JEFFREYS, Prof Elizabeth Mary; da of Lawrence Brown (d 1995), of London, and Veronica, *née* Thompson (d 1987); *b* 22 July 1941; *Educ* Blackheath HS, Girton Coll Cambridge (entrance exhibition, MA), St Anne's Coll Oxford (BLitt); *m* 1965, Michael Jeffreys; 1 da (Katharine b 1974); *Career* res fell: Warburg Inst 1969–72, Dumbarton Oaks 1972–74, Univ of Ioannina 1974–76, Univ of Sydney 1976–95; Bywater and Sotheby prof of Byzantine and modern Greek language and literature Univ of Oxford 1996–2006 (emeritus prof 2006–); fell Aust Acad of the Humanities 1993; hon fell St Anne's Coll Oxford; *Books* Popular Literature in Late Byzantium (1983), The Chronicle of John Malalas (1986), Studies in John Malalas (1990), The War of Troy (1996), Digenis Akritis (1998), Through the Looking Glass (2000), Rhetoric in Byzantium (2003), The Age of the Dromon (2003); *Recreations* reading, walking; *Style—* Prof Elizabeth Jeffreys; ✉ Exeter College, Oxford OX1 3DP (tel 01865 270483, fax 01865 279630, e-mail elizabeth.jeffreys@exeter.ox.ac.uk)

JEFFREYS, Martyn Edward; s of William Herbert Jeffreys (d 1961), of Ealing, London, and Nora Emilie, *née* Crane (d 1995); *b* 20 January 1938; *Educ* St Clement Danes, Univ of Bristol (BSc); *m* 29 Oct 1960, Carol, da of Marcel Faustin Boclet (d 1964), of Twickenham, Middx; 2 s (Andrew b 1962, Adam b 1968), 1 da (Katy b 1965); *Career* operational res scientist BP 1961–63, sr mathematician and mangr Mathematical Programming Div SD-Scicon (formerly CEIR Ltd) 1964–67, chief mgmnt scis conslt and head professional servs SIA Ltd 1968–70, sr ptnr Wootton Jeffreys & Ptnrs 1971–84, exec chm Wootton Jeffreys Systems Ltd 1985–86, chm Jeffreys Systems plc 1987–2003 (ret); FBCS 1973, CEng 1990; *Style—* Martyn Jeffreys, Esq; ✉ 196 Epsom Road, Merrow, Guildford, Surrey GU1 2RR (tel 01483 539698, e-mail martyn.jeffreys@ntlworld.com)

JEFFREYS, Prof Paul William; s of George Lewis Jeffreys (d 1995), and Naomi Emily, *née* Williams; *b* 4 July 1954; *Educ* Drayton Manor GS London, Univ of Manchester (BSc), Univ of Bristol (PhD); *m* 23 Feb 1985, Linda Christine, *née* Pay; 2 s (Simon Richard Lewis b 20 April 1990, Oliver Samuel Fields b 23 July 1994), 1 da (Eleanor Lucy Clare b 10 March 1992); *Career* CERN fell Experimental Physics Div CERN Geneva 1979–82; Rutherford Appleton Laboratory: physicist on Large Electron Positron Collider experiment 1982–87, head Particle Physics Dept Computing Gp 1987–94, head Computing and Resource Mgmnt Div 1995–2001, ldr CLRC e-Science Centre 2000–01; Univ of Oxford: dir Computing Services 2001–, prof of computing 2003–, dir of ICT 2007 (actg dir 2005–07); professorial fell Keble Coll Oxford 2001– (tutor and hon memb SCR 1990–2001); dir Oxford Regnl e-Science Centre (OeSC) 2001–06, dir Oxford e-Research Centre (OeRC) 2006–; dir: Digitalspires 2004–, e-Horizons Inst James Martin 21st Century Sch 2005–; UK rep Plenary Ctee European Ctee for Future Accelerators 1996–2001, Research Cncl rep Jt Information Systems Ctee (JISC) for Networking 1997–, project ldr UK Particle Physics Grid 2000–01; chm IT Mgmnt Ctee Central Lab of the Research Cncls (CERN) 1999–2001, chair Proposal Mgmnt Bd UK Particle Physics Grid 2001; fndr memb: Int Ctee of Future Accelerators Networking Task Force 1997–2001, EU DataGrid Project 2000–02; memb: ESNet Working Ctee 1996–2001, Int Advsy Panel for Computing High Energy Physics Conf 1997 and 2000, High Energy Physics Central Computing Ctee 1999–2001, Int Advsy Ctee Topical Seminar on Global and Local Networks for Research and Educn Siena 2000, Informatics Ctee Office of Science and Technol 2000–01, Bioinfomatics Ctee Wellcome Tst 2000–01, Int Advsy Ctee for Computing High Energy Physics Conf 2001, Research Cncl Grid Opportunity Gp 2001, e-Science Steering Ctee ESPRC 2001, Dir of e-Science's Tech Advsy Gp 2001–06, e-Science Steering Ctee PPARC 2001–, e-Oversight Panel PPARC 2001–, e-Science Core Prog Grid Network Team 2001–03, Project Mgmnt Steering Ctee Nat Cancer Tissue Resource 2003–06, Bd Grid Ops Support Centre 2004, IBM World Community Grid Advsy Bd 2004–, NCeSS Nodes Commissioning Panel 2007–; author of numerous papers and articles in learned jls; CPhys, MInstP; *Recreations* family, active memb St Aldate's Church Oxford, sport (mainly squash, skiing, real tennis and running), photography; *Style—* Prof Paul Jeffreys; ✉ Keble College, Oxford OX1 3PG (tel 01865 273229, fax 01865 283346, e-mail paul.jeffreys@oucs.ox.ac.uk)

JEFFRIES, Prof Donald James; CBE (2007); s of Edmond Frederick Jeffries (d 1976), and Eileen Elizabeth, *née* Elton (d 1993); *b* 29 August 1941; *Educ* William Ellis GS, Royal Free Hosp Sch of Med London (BSc, MB BS); *m* 11 Aug 1966, Mary Millicent, da of Eric James Bray; 1 da (Caroline Mary b 1967), 2 s (Paul James b 1969, Richard Anthony b 1973); *Career* St Mary's Hosp Med Sch: sr registrar in microbiology 1970–72, head Div of Virology 1982–90, dir of clinical studies 1985–90, reader and hon conslt in clinical virology 1987–90 (lectr 1972–74, sr lectr 1974–87); Bart's and Royal London Sch of Med and Dentistry QMC: prof and head of virology 1990–2006, head Dept of Med Microbiology 1998–2006, emeritus prof of virology 2006–; Barts and the London NHS Tst: clinical dir of virology 1994–98, head of Microbiology and Virology Services 1998–2006; conslt in virology St John Ambulance 1994–, sr examiner Univ of London 1993–2000; visiting prof Riyadh 1988, C T Huang lectr Hong Kong 1991, Wellcome visiting prof Coll of Med South Africa 1993; vice-pres RCPath 1999–2002; chm: Panel of Examiners in Virology RCPath 1995–2000, Examinations Ctee RCPath 1999–2002, SAC in Microbiology RCPath 1999–2002, Jt Ctee on Infection and Tropical Med RCP/RCPath 1999–2002, ACDP Working Gp on Transmissible Spongiform Encephalopathies 1999–, HPA Steering Gp on Healthcare Associated Infections 2004–07, ABI Expert Working Gp on HIV 2005–; memb: Soc for General Microbiology 1970–, Hospital Infection Soc 1980– (memb Cncl 1980–83 and 1990–93), Advsy Ctee on Genetic Modification HSE 1988–99, Assoc of Profs of Med Microbiology 1991–2000, Expert Advsy Gp on AIDS 1992–2002 (actg chm 2003–05), UK Advsy Panel for Health Care Workers Infected with Blood Borne Viruses 1992–2002, Diagnostics and Imaging Panel Standing Gp on Health Technol NHS R&D Directorate 1993–98, Advsy Ctee on Dangerous Pathogens Dept of Health 1993–2002, Cncl RCPath 1996–2002, CJD Incidents Panel 2000– (actg chm 2003–05), Ctee on Safety of Med 2001–05 (memb Biologicals Sub-Ctee 1999–2005 (chm 2003–05)), Nat Expert Panel on New and Emerging Infections 2003–07; Ellison Nash Prize 2001; FRCPath 1986, FRCP 2001; *Publications* Lecture Notes on Medical Virology (1987), Current Topics in AIDS (Vol I 1987, Vol II 1989), Antiviral Chemotherapy (1995), Viral Infections in Obstetrics and Gynaecology (1999); *Recreations* hill walking, fly fishing, gardening; *Style—* Prof Donald Jeffries, CBE; ✉ 63 Manor Park Avenue, Princes Risborough, Buckinghamshire HP27 9AS (tel 01844 343821)

JEFFRIES, (Richard) Mark; s of David Vincent Jeffries, of Cottingham, E Yorks, and Margaret, *née* Pritchards; *b* 26 June 1957, Horsforth, Leeds; *Educ* Hymers Coll Hull, St John's Coll Cambridge (Master's prize, MA); *m* 17 Sept 1983, Catherine; 1 s (Timothy Richard b 13 Aug 1986), 1 da (Alice Louise b 9 Feb 1989); *Career* admitted slr 1981; Mills & Reeve: articled clerk 1979–81, slr 1981–85, ptnr 1985–, managing ptnr Norwich 1990–96, head Corporate Servs Gp 1996–99, nat managing ptnr 2001–07, sr ptnr 2007–; memb Law Soc; tstee Norfolk Community Fndn; *Recreations* skiing, cycling, horticulture; *Clubs* Cambridge Soc; *Style—* Mark Jeffries, Esq; ✉ 9 Judges Drive, Norwich NR4 7QQ (tel 01603 454622); Mills & Reeve, 1 St James Court, Whitefriars, Norwich NR3 1RU (tel 01603 693222, fax 01603 664670, e-mail mark.jeffries@mills-reeve.com)

JEFFRIES, Dr Michael Godfrey; *b* 16 April 1943; *Educ* Univ of Birmingham (BSc, MB ChB, DCCH), FRCGP; *m* 28 Aug 1965, Sheila; 2 s (Simon b 12 Dec 1967, Nick b 30 Dec 1975), 1 da (Clare b 28 Jan 1970); *Career* former med dir Clwyd Community Care NHS Tst (resigned 2000); RCGP: memb Cncl, currently chm Welsh Cncl 2002–; MRCGP 1984; *Style—* Dr Michael Jeffries; ✉ Meddygfa, Betws-y-Coed, North Wales LL24 0BD (tel 01690 710205, fax 01690 710051, e-mail mgj@pobox.com); RCGP Wales, Regus House, Falcon Drive, Cardiff Bay CF10 4RU

JEFFRIES, Michael Makepeace Eugene; s of William Eugene Jeffries (d 1975), of Port of Spain, Trinidad, and Margaret, *née* Makepeace (d 1995); *b* 17 September 1944; *Educ* Queens Royal Coll Port of Spain, Poly of North London (Dip Arch); *m* 10 Sept 1966, Pamela Mary, da of Sir Gordon Booth, KCMG, CVO, of Poole, Dorset; 2 s (Andrew b 1969, Simon b 1973), 2 da (Kathryn b 1971, Victoria b 1975); *Career* John Laing and Sons Ltd 1963–67, Deeks Bousell Partnership 1968–73, Bradshaw Gass and Hope 1973–75; ASFA Ltd (WS Atkins Gp) 1975–: dir 1978, chm and md 1979; dir WS Atkins Conslts 1979, chm W S Atkins plc 2001–05 (dir 1992–95, chief exec 1995–2001); chm: Wembley National Stadium Ltd 2002–, VT Gp plc 2005–, National Car Parks 2005–07; non-exec dir De La Rue plc 2000–07; chm Banstead Round Table 1980; RIBA 1973, FRSA 1987, FConsE 1998, FICE 2004; *Recreations* golf, sailing, skiing, water colours, antiquarian horology; *Clubs* RAC, Parkstone Golf; *Style—* Michael Jeffries, Esq; ✉ Hethfelton House, Hethfelton, Wareham, Dorset BH20 6HS (tel 01929 401609); VT House, Grange Drive, Hedge End Southampton SO30 2DQ (tel 01489 775212, fax 01489 775335 mobile 07860 366251, e-mail michael.jeffries@vtplc.com)

JEFFRIES, Neil; *b* 1959, Bristol; *Educ* St Martin's Sch of Art, Slade Sch of Fine Art; *Career* artist; artist in residence Kingston Poly 1984–85, artist in Schools Project Whitechapel 1986; pt/t lectr: Slade Coll of Art 1985–, Ruskin Sch 1985–; sculpture cmmn Scott Tallon & Walker; *Solo exhibitions* Arnolfini 1985, Blond Fine Art 1986, Flowers East 1990, Angela Flowers Gall 1992, Flowers East at London Fields 1992, Galeria Ray Gun 1994, Stadt Tuttlingen Stadtische Galerie Tuttlingen Germany 1995, Flowers East 1996, Riverside Studios London 1997, Drumcoon Wigan 1997, Flowers West Santa Monica 1999; *Group exhibitions* incl: Stowells Trophy Exhbn (RA) 1982, The New Contemporaries (ICA) 1982, The Best of 1982 (Christies) 1982, New Directions in Sculpture (Blond Fine Art) 1984, Artist of the Day (Angela Flowers Gall) 1984, Home and Abroad (Serpentine Gall) 1984, Summer Show (Blond Fine Art) 1984, Contemporary Art Society Fair (Five Dials Gall) 1984, Monstrous Craws (Actors Inst) 1984, A View From My Window (Angela Flowers Gall) 1984, Ten Painters (St Martin's Sch of Art) 1985, International Contemporary Art Fair (Olympia) 1985, Group Show (Blond Fine Art) 1985, In Their Circumstances (Usher Gall) 1985, Art for Ethiopia (Bonham's) 1985, Newbury Arts Festival 1985, Proud and Prejudiced (Twining Gall NY) 1985, Figures and Figures (Manchester Arts Centre) 1985, Peter Moores Project (Walker Art Gall) 1986, Living Art (Ideal Home Exhbn) 1986, Britain in Vienna (Künstlerhaus) 1986, Modern Art? It's a Joke! (Cleveland Gall) 1986, State of the Nation (Herbert Art Gall) 1987, Small Is Beautiful (Angela Flowers Gall) 1987, The Big Fight (Vanessa Devereux Gall) 1987, London (Royal Festival Hall) 1987, Contemporary Portraits (Flowers East) 1988, Small Is Beautiful - Part 6 (Flowers East) 1988, A Personal View (Nigel Greenwood Gall) 1988, Big Paintings (Flowers East) 1989, Ingenious Inventions (Harris Art Gall) 1989, 30 Tage (Galerie Siegart) 1990, Academicians Choice (Mall Galls) 1990, Summer Exhbn (RA) 1990 and 1991, Flowers East at Watermans Art Centre 1991, Artist's Choice Exhbn (Angela Flowers Gall) 1992, Decouvertes (Grand Palais Paris) 1993, But Big is Better (Flowers East) 1993, Inner Visions (Flowers East) 1994, The Twenty Fifth Anniversary Exhibition (Flowers East London Fields) 1995, Wheels on Fire, Cars in Art 1950–96 (Wolverhampton Art Gallery) 1996, Angela Flowers Gallery (Ireland) Inc Co Cork, Small is Beautiful Part XIV: Sex (Flowers East at London Fields) 1996, Angela Flowers Gallery 1997 (Flowers East at London Fields) 1997, Small is Beautiful XV: Death (Flowers East at London Fields) 1997, British Figurative Art Part 2: Sculpture (Flowers East London) 1998, Comic? (Oldham Art Gallery) 1998, Small is Beautiful Part XVI: Music (Flowers East at London Fields), Angela Flowers Gallery 30th Anniversary Exhbn (Flowers East London) 2000, Carnivalesque (Brighton Museum and Art Gallery, Univ of Brighton Gallery, Nottingham Castle Museum, Djanogly Gallery, Univ of Nottingham) 2000, Artist's Choice (Flowers East London) 2000; *Public Collections* Arts Cncl of GB, British Cncl; *Awards* Boise Travelling Scholarship 1984, Wollaston Award Summer Exhibition RA 1991, Arts Fndn Award for Drawing 1997; *Style*— Neil Jeffries, Esq; ✉ c/o Flowers East, 82 Kingsland Road, London E2 8DP (tel 020 8985 3333)

JEFFS, Dr Nicholas Graham; s of John Grahame Jeffs (d 1974), and Evelyn Maude, *née* Cattermole; *b* 20 November 1950; *Educ* Lycee Victor Hugo Marrakesh Morocco, Nottingham HS, Middx Hosp Med Sch (MB BS); *m* 18 Jan 1975, Jennifer Mary, da of Robert Herbert Rogers, of Colchester, Essex; 2 s (Richard b 1978, Thomas b 1983); *Career* anaesthetist; registrar London Hosp 1976–78, lectr Univ of London 1978–79, sr registrar St Mary's Hosp 1981–82, conslt Intensive Care Unit Luton and Dunstable Hosp 1982–2007, ret; hon physician Nat Rifle Assoc; fell Coll of Anaesthetics, FFARCS 1978; *Recreations* model engineering, shooting; *Clubs* N London Rifle, Br Cwlth Rifle; *Style*— Dr Nicholas Jeffs; ✉ 28 Ludlow Avenue, Luton, Bedfordshire LU1 3RW (tel 01582 451504, e-mail nick.jeffs@btinternet.com); Luton and Dunstable Hospital, Lewsey Road, Luton, Bedfordshire LU4 0DZ (tel 01582 497230)

JEHU, Jeremy Charles Rhys; s of Thomas Colin Jehu, of Pyrford, Surrey, and Betty Burrows, *née* Wilson; *b* 31 August 1955; *Educ* Royal GS Guildford, Univ Coll Durham (BA); *Career* journalist; Surrey Daily Advertiser: joined 1976, chief reporter main area office 1978–79, sub ed 1979; The Stage and Television Today: joined 1979, news ed 1986, dep ed 1986–92, ed 1992–94; freelance journalist and conslt 1995–; book critic/columnist Teletext (ITV and Channel 4) 1997–, book critic/presenter Literary Heroes Talk Radio 1998–99; fndr memb Arts Correspondent Gp 1981 (memb Ctee 1981–90), memb Broadcasting Press Guild 1989 (memb Ctee 1990–92); *Books* The Monday Lunchtime of the Living Dead (1999); *Recreations* shooting, classic car ownership, gossip, politics, all the usual cultural pursuits; *Clubs* Savage, Green Room (hon memb), London and Middx Rifle Assoc, Tennessee Squires Assoc, CAA (hon memb); *Style*— Jeremy Jehu, Esq; ✉ 11 Rita Road, London SW8 1JX (tel 020 7587 0423)

JELLICOE, Dr Jillian Ann; da of George Molyneux Jellicoe (d 1972), of Liverpool, and Ellen, *née* Fitzsimmons (d 1991); *b* 28 June 1947; *Educ* Holly Lodge HS for Girls Liverpool, KCH Med Sch; *m* 29 Sept 1973, Alan Fitzgerald, s of Raymond Charles Fitzgerald, of Brockenhurst, Hants; *Career* house surgn and house physician Hereford Hosps 1970–71; SHO in: obstetrics Royal Victoria Hosp Bournemouth 1972, anaesthetics Whiston Hosp 1972–73; GP Bournemouth 1973–77, registrar Liverpool RHA 1978–80, sr registrar Wessex Region 1981–84, conslt anaesthetist Shackleton Dept of Anaesthetics Southampton Gen Hosp 1985–, hon sr lectr Sch of Med Univ of Southampton 2002– (clinical sub-dean 1989–); memb: BMA, Assoc of Anaesthetists, Assoc of Cardio-Thoracic Anaesthetists; LRCP, MRCS 1970, DObstRCOG 1972, DA 1973, FFARCS 1980; *Recreations* reading, watching cricket, cats, church architecture; *Style*— Dr Jillian Ann Jellicoe; ✉ School of Medicine, Southampton General Hospital, Tremona Road, Southampton (tel 023 8079 6585, e-mail j.jellicoe@soton.ac.uk)

JENAS, Jermaine Anthony; *b* 18 February 1983, Nottingham; *Career* professional footballer; clubs: Nottingham Forest 1999–2002, Newcastle United 2002–05, Tottenham Hotspur 2005–; England: caps 15, debut v Australia 2003, memb squad World Cup 2006; PFA Young Player of the Year 2002; *Style*— Jermaine Jenas, Esq; ✉ c/o Tottenham Hotspur Football Club, White Hart Lane, Bill Nicholson Way N17 0AP

JENCKS, Charles Alexander; s of Gardner Platt Jencks (d 1989), and Ruth Dewitt, *née* Pearl; *b* 21 June 1939; *Educ* Brooks Sch, Harvard Univ (BA, MA), Univ of London (Fulbright scholar, PhD); *m* 1, Pamela Balding; 2 s (Ivor Cosimo b 1969, Justin Alexander b 1972); m 2, Maggie (d 1995), da of Sir John Henry Keswick, KCMG (d 1982); 1 s (John Keswick b 1979), 1 da (Lily Clare b 1980); *Career* writer on architecture 1966–, lectr and prof 1969–, TV writer and sometime participant 1971–, architect and designer 1976–, writer on art 1985–, garden designer 1989–, writer on non-architectural subjects 1989–; author of numerous books and articles on the subject of modern architecture and its successors; furniture and drawings exhibited; cmmns incl: Centre for Life Newcastle 2000, Landform Scottish Gallery of Modern Art Edinburgh 2002, Kew Gdns London 2003, Portello Park Milan 2003, DNA sculptures Cold Spring Harbor Labs Long Island; lectures at over 40 int univs; memb: AA, RSA; Nara Gold Medal for Architecture 1992, Country Life Gardener of the Year 1998; *Clubs* Groucho, Athenaeum, Chelsea Arts; *Style*—Charles Jencks, Esq; ✉ John Wiley and Sons, International House, Ealing Broadway Centre, London W5 5DB (tel 020 8326 3800, fax 020 8326 3801); c/o Frances Lincoln Ltd, Torriano Mews, 4 Torriano Avenue, London NW5 2RZ (tel 020 7284 4009, fax 020 7485 0490)

JENKALA, Adrian Aleksander; s of Georgius Ihorus Jenkala, and Olena, *née* Karpynec; *b* 21 May 1957; *Educ* Latymer Upper Sch, Univ of London (BSc, LLB); *Career* called to the Bar Middle Temple 1984; practising barr 1984–, lectr in law London Guildhall Univ 1985–92, instr Inns of Ct Sch of Law 1989–98; legal sec to Int Cmmn of Inquiry into 1932–33 Famine in Ukraine 1987–90 (report presented to UN in 1990); Sch of Slavonic and East European Studies (SSEES): chm Ukrainian Studies Tst Fund Ctee 1991–, hon res fell 1993–98; official international observer at the referendum and presidential elections in Ukraine 1991, advsr in legal affairs to the Ambass of Ukraine in GB 1998–; chm Assoc of Ukrainian Lawyers 1987–, memb Bd World Congress of Ukrainian Lawyers 1992– (vice-pres (Europe) 1994–2001); dep chm Br-Ukrainian Law Assoc 2001– (sec 1993–2001); visiting prof Cumberland Sch of Law Samford Univ Alabama 1994–; memb: Bd of Foreign Advisers Ukrainian Legal Fndn Kiev, Central and E European Sub-Ctee of the Int Practice Ctee of Bar Cncl, Hon Soc of the Middle Temple; Freeman City of London; ACIArb; *Books* Ukrainian Legal Dictionary (ed, 1994); *Recreations* squash, skiing, ski instructing; *Style*— Adrian Jenkala, Esq; ✉ Clarendon Chambers, 7 Stone Buildings, Lincoln's Inn, London WC2A 3SZ (tel 020 7681 7681, fax 020 7681 7684, e-mail jenkala@msn.com)

JENKIN, Hon Bernard Christison; MP; yr son of Baron Jenkin of Roding, PC, *qv*; *b* 9 April 1959; *Educ* William Ellis Sch Highgate, CCC Cambridge (pres Cambridge Union 1982); *m* 24 Sept 1988, Anne Caroline, da of late Hon Charles Strutt, and sis of 6 Baron Rayleigh, *qv*; 2 s (Robert Patrick Christison b 13 May 1989, Peter Andrew Graham b 29 July 1991); *Career* sales and mktg exec Ford Motor Co Ltd 1983–86, with 3i plc 1986–88, mangr Legal and General Ventures Ltd until 1989–92, advsr Legal & General Group plc 1992–95; Parly candidate Glasgow Central 1987; MP (Cons): Colchester N 1992–97, Essex N 1997–; memb Social Security Select Ctee 1993–97, PPS to Rt Hon Michael Forsyth, MP (sec of state for Scotland) 1995–97; oppn frontbench spokesman on constitutional affrs 1997–98, shadow min for tport 1998–2001 and London 1999–2001, shadow sec of state for defence 2001–03, shadow sec of state for regions 2003–05, shadow min for energy 2005, dep chm Cons Pty 2005–06, memb Defence Select Ctee 2006–; *Recreations* sailing, music (esp opera), fishing, family, DIY; *Clubs* Colchester Cons; *Style*— The Hon Bernard Jenkin, MP; ✉ House of Commons, London SW1A 0AA (tel 020 7219 4029, e-mail jenkinbc@parliament.uk, website www.bernardjenkinmp.com)

JENKIN OF RODING, Baron (Life Peer UK 1987), of Wanstead and Woodford in Greater London; (Charles) Patrick Fleeming Jenkin; PC (1973); s of Charles O F Jenkin (d 1939), of Gerrards Cross, Bucks; *b* 7 September 1926; *Educ* Clifton, Jesus Coll Cambridge; *m* 1952, Alison Monica, eldest da of late Capt Philip Skelton Graham, RN; 2 s (Rev Hon Charles Alexander Graham Jenkin b 1954, Hon Bernard Christison Jenkin MP, *qv*, b 1959), 2 da (Hon Nicola Mary b 1956, Hon Flora Margaret Christison b 1962); *Career* Queen's Own Cameron Highlanders 1945–48; called to the Bar Middle Temple 1952–57; Distillers Co Ltd 1957–70; memb Hornsey BC 1960–63; govr Westfield Coll London 1964–70; MP (Cons) Wanstead and Woodford 1964–87, jt vice-chm Cons Parly Trade and Power Ctee 1966, oppn front bench spokesman on Treasy, Trade and Econ Affrs 1965–70, fin sec to Treasy 1970–72, chief sec to Treasy 1972–74, min for Energy 1974, memb Shadow Cabinet and shadow spokesman on Energy 1974–76 and on Social Servs 1976–79; sec of state for: Social Servs 1979–81, Indust 1981–83, DOE 1983–85; memb House of Lords Select Ctee on Sci and Technol 1997–2001; dir Nat Econ Res Assocs Inc (UK office) 1986–98; chm Friends' Provident Life Office 1988–98; memb Supervisory Bd Achmea Holding NV Netherlands 1990–98; advsr: Sumitomo Tst and Bank Ltd; dir UK-Japan 21st Century Gp (chm 1986–90); chm: Forest Healthcare NHS Tst 1991–97, Westfield Coll Tst 1990–2000; tstee Monteverdi Choir and Orch Ltd 1990–2001; pres: Assoc for Sci Educn 2003, Fndn for Sci and Technol 2006 (vice-pres until 1997, chm 1998–2006); vice-pres: Nat Assoc of Local Cncls, Nat Federation of Housing Assoc, Local Govt Assoc; tstee Conservative Agents Superannuation Fund 1995–2000; jt pres London Cncls (previously Assoc of London Govt); chm Visual Handicap Gp 1991–98; memb Advsy Bd UK CEED 1987–2003; advsr Thames Estuary Airport Co Ltd; patron: St Clair Hospice Tst, Roding Conservation Gp, London NE Community Fndn; memb Cncl Royal Inst 2002–05; hon fell BAAS; fell QMC London; Hon FRSE, Hon FCOptom 2003; *Recreations* gardening, music, bricklaying, sailing, DIY; *Style*— The Rt Hon the Lord Jenkin of Roding, PC; ✉ House of Lords, London SW1A 0LP (tel 020 7219 6966, fax 020 7219 0759, e-mail jenkinp@parliament.uk)

JENKINS, Alan Dominique; s of Ian Samuel Jenkins, of Dorset, and Jeannette Juliette Jenkins; *b* 27 May 1952; *Educ* Clifton, New Coll Oxford (BA); *m* 30 June 1979, Caroline, da of Paul Treverton Jones (d 1983), of Monmouthshire; 1 s (Mark b 30 May 1982), 3 da (Claire b 13 April 1984, Alice 17 Oct 1989, Emily b 9 Nov 1991); *Career* admitted slr 1977, ptnr Frere Cholmeley Bischoff 1983–98 (managing ptnr 1996–98), ptnr Eversheds (following merger) 1998– (head of int 2002–04, chm 2004–); tstee: Int Inst for Environment and Devpt (vice-chm), Fndn for Int Environemntal Law and Devpt (vice-chm), GAP Activity Projects Ltd; memb: Law Soc, Int Bar Assoc, Union Internationale des Avocats; FRSA, FSALS; *Recreations* sport (rugby, golf, tennis, skiing), music, theatre, reading; *Clubs* MCC, Roehampton, Walbrook; *Style*— Alan Jenkins, Esq; ✉ Eversheds, Senator House, 85 Queen Victoria Street, London EC4V 4JL (tel 020 7919 4500, fax 020 7919 4919, e-mail alanjenkins@eversheds.com)

JENKINS, (Thomas) Alun; QC (1996); s of Seward Thomas Jenkins, of Abergavenny, and Iris Jenkins; *b* 19 August 1948; *Educ* Ebbw Vale Tech Sch, Univ of Bristol (LLB); *m* 1971, Glenys Maureen, da of Maj John Constant, of Abergavenny; 2 da (Clare Elizabeth b 19 Sept 1976, Katie Jane b 19 Dec 1982), 1 s (Christopher Alun b 7 Nov 1985); *Career* called to the Bar Lincoln's Inn 1972, in practice in Bristol and London 1972–, recorder of the Crown Court 2000–; *Recreations* opera, Shakespeare, literature, riding, point-to-point, rugby, motor cars, reading; *Style*— T Alun Jenkins, Esq, QC; ✉ Queen Square Chambers, 56 Queen Square, Bristol BS1 4PR; (tel 0117 921 1966, fax 0117 927 6493); 2 Bedford Row, London WC1R 4BU (tel 020 7440 8888)

JENKINS, Anne; da of Roy Dudley, of Blackpool, Lancs, and Georgina Ledlie, *née* McKeen (d 1996); *Educ* Elmslie Girls' Sch Blackpool, Univ of Manchester (BA); *m* 24 Sept 1988, Peter Lewis Jenkins, s of David Jenkins (d 1994); 1 da (Victoria Anne b 14 June 1993), 1 s (William Dudley b 23 April 1996); *Career* Mazars Neville Russell CAs Stockport (formerly Neville Russell) 1980–84 (ACA 1983), Peat Marwick CAs London 1984–85, The Financial Training Co 1986–90, ind trg conslt in fin 1990–97; dir ATC (CPD) Ltd 1997–2000, dir demist.com 2000–; ICAEW: memb Cncl 1993–, chm Recruitment and Promotion Ctee 1994–96, memb Educn and Trg Directorate 1994–97, memb Post Qualification Ctee 1998–99; pres Women in Accountancy 1998–99 (memb Ctee 1994–98), memb Business Law Ctee 1996–98, ldr Student Taskforce 1999; awarded FCA 1994; *Recreations* swimming, running, cycling, skiing, London Triathlon (Olympic) 1999, theatre; *Clubs* LA Fitness (Isleworth); *Style*— Mrs Anne Jenkins; ✉ 50 Beaconsfield Road, St Margarets, Middlesex TW1 3HU (tel 020 8287 4003, e-mail anne.jenkins@virgin.net)

JENKINS, Prof Aubrey Dennis; s of Arthur William Jenkins (d 1982), and Mabel Emily, *née* Street (d 1970); *b* 6 September 1927; *Educ* Dartford GS, Sir John Cass Tech Inst, King's Coll London (BSc, PhD, DSc); *m* 29 Dec 1987, Jitka, da of Josef Horský (d 1975); *Career* res chemist Courtaulds Fundamental Res Laboratory 1950–60, res mangr Gillette Fundamental Res Laboratory 1960–64, prof of polymer sci Univ of Sussex 1971– (joined 1964); sec: Macromolecular Div Int Union of Pure and Applied Chemistry 1985–93, Br High Polymer Res Gp 1991–2001; Nat Memb Cncl of the Royal Soc of Chemistry 2003–05; memb Brighton Health Authy 1983–90; Heyrovský Gold Medal for Chemistry Czechoslovak Acad of Sciences 1990; FRSC 1957; *Books* Kinetics of Vinyl Polymerization (1958), Polymer Science (1972), Reactivity Mechanism and Structure in Polymer Chemistry (1974), Properties of Liquids and Solutions (1994); *Recreations* music, travel; *Clubs* Br Czech and Slovak Assoc; *Style*— Prof Aubrey Jenkins; ✉ Vixen's, 22A North

Court, Hassocks, West Sussex BN6 8JS (tel and fax 01273 845410, e-mail polygon@vixens.eclipse.co.uk)

JENKINS, Brian; MP; *b* 19 September 1942; *Educ* state schs Staffs, Aston and Coventry Technical Colls, Coleg Harlech, LSE (BSc), Wolverhampton Poly (PGCE); *m* Joan; 1 s, 1 da; *Career* former lectr Tamworth Coll of FE; MP (Lab): Staffordshire SE (by-election) 1996–97, Tamworth 1997–; PPS to Home Office Min Joyce Quin 1997–98, PPS to Foreign Office Mins Joyce Quin, Derek Fatchett and Tony Lloyd 1998–2000, PPS to Joyce Quin MAFF 2000–01; memb Public Accounts Ctee 2001–; cncllr Tamworth BC 1985–96 (Cncl ldr 1995–96); *Style*— Brian Jenkins, Esq, MP; ✉ House of Commons, London SW1A 0AA (tel 020 7219 6622)

JENKINS, Sir Brian Garton; GBE (1991); s of Owen Garton Jenkins (d 1963), and Doris Enid, *née* Webber (d 1986); *b* 3 December 1935; *Educ* Tonbridge, Trinity Coll Oxford (MA); *m* 2 June 1967, (Elizabeth) Ann, da of John Philip Manning Prentice (d 1981), of Suffolk; 1 da (Julia b 1971), 1 s (Charles b 1973); *Career* 2 Lt RA 1955–57, served Gibraltar; ptnr Coopers & Lybrand 1969–95; chm Woolwich plc 1995–2000, dep chm Barclays plc 2000–04; pres ICAEW 1985–86; pres: London C of C 1996–98, Br Computer Soc 1997–98; pres Charities Aid Fndn 2003– (chm 1998–2003); Alderman City of London 1980– (Sheriff 1987–88); Lord Mayor of London 1991–92; Liveryman: Worshipful Co of CAs 1980– (Master 1990–91), Worshipful Co of Merchant Taylors 1984– (Master 1999–2000), Worshipful Co of Information Technologists 1985– (Master 1994–95); Hon Liveryman Worshipful Co of Cordwainers; hon bencher Inner Temple; hon fell: Trinity Coll Oxford, Goldsmiths Coll London; hon memb Baltic Exchange; Hon DSc City Univ, Hon DLitt London Guildhall Univ; FCA 1974 (ACA 1963), FRSA 1980; *Books* An Audit Approach to Computers (jtly, 4 edn 1992); *Recreations* garden construction, old books, large jigsaw puzzles, ephemera; *Clubs* Brooks's, City of London, City Livery; *Style*— Sir Brian Jenkins, GBE

JENKINS, Brian Stuart; s of Harold Griffith Jenkins (d 1970), of Christleton, Chester, and Ida Lily, *née* Stuart (d 1986); *b* 26 May 1934; *Educ* Shrewsbury; *m* 5 Sept 1959, Teresa Sheelagh, da of Stephen George Ronan (d 1980), of St Asaph, N Wales; 2 s (Nicolaus Stuart b 13 March 1961, Simon Spencer b 26 March 1962), 1 da (Vanessa Stephanie b 7 July 1965); *Career* RN 1952–54, Midshipman 1953 (served HMS Surprise, fleet despatch vessel Med Fleet), Mersey Div RNR, ret Lt 1960; chartered accountant; sr ptnr Haswell Bros 1970–93; chm: Wrexham Water plc 1987–2004 (dir 1969–2004), Dee Valley Water plc (now Dee Valley Group plc) 1994–2004; dir Mersey RHA 1990–94; former memb Wales Regnl Bd TSB Gp plc; FCA 1966; *Recreations* sailing, shooting, travel; *Clubs* Royal Yacht Sqdn, Royal Ocean Racing; *Style*— Brian Jenkins, Esq; ✉ Beeston House, Tarporley, Cheshire CW6 9ST (tel and fax 01829 260326, e-mail bsjenkins@beestonhouse.fsnet.co.uk)

JENKINS, Caroline Helen Clare; da of Daniel Jenkins, and Nell, *née* Cree; *b* 1952, Redhill, Surrey; *Educ* St Mary's Hall Brighton, KCL (BA); *m* 1975, Prof John Mack, *qv*; 1 da (Katherine Helen b 1985), 1 s (Samuel Thomas b 1989); *Career* admitted slr 1980; trainee slr Marcus Barnett, sr ptnr Parlett Kent 1986– (ptnr 1983–); memb: Clinical Negligence Panel Law Soc, Clinical Negligence Panel and Slrs Panel AVMA (Action against Medical Accidents); memb: Assoc of Personal Injury Lawyers, Assoc of Trial Lawyers of America; *Publications* Medical Accidents Handbook (contrib, 1997); *Style*— Ms Caroline Jenkins; ✉ Parlett Kent, Signet House, 49–51 Farringdon Road, London EC1M 3PP (tel 020 7430 0712, fax 020 7430 1796, e-mail cjenkins@parlettkent.co.uk)

JENKINS, Catrin Mary; da of Charles Bryan Jenkins, of Southerndown, Mid Glamorgan, and Anne, *née* Davies-Jones; *b* 22 December 1958; *Educ* Llanelli Girls GS, Univ Coll Cardiff (LLB); *m* 7 Sept 1996, Jonathan James; *Career* admitted slr 1983; ptnr: Eversheds Phillips & Buck 1988–95, Francis & Buck 1995–; *Style*— Ms Catrin Jenkins; ✉ 70 Ryder Street, Pontcanna, Cardiff; Francis & Buck, Celtic House, Cathedral Road, Cardiff CF11 9FB (tel 029 2034 4995, fax 029 2039 9646, e-mail enquiries@francisandbuck.co.uk)

JENKINS, Hon Charles Arthur Simon; s of Baron Jenkins of Hillhead (Life Peer, d 2003); *b* 25 March 1949; *Educ* Winchester, Holland Park Sch, New Coll Oxford; *m* 11 Sept 1971, Ivana Alexandra, da of Ing Ivo Vladimir Sertic (d 1986), of Zagreb, Croatia; 2 da (Alexandra Dorothea b 14 March 1986, Helena Harriet b 13 May 1988); *Career* European ed Economist Intelligence Unit 1975–, ed Euro Policy Analyst (quarterly magazine on European affairs); memb Exec Ctee Br Section European League for Economic Cooperation; memb Clapham Action on Tport; *Style*— The Hon Charles Jenkins

JENKINS, Prof David; s of Alfred Thomas Jenkins (d 1960), and Doris Cecilia, *née* Hutchings (d 1994); *b* 1 March 1926; *Educ* Marlborough, Royal Vet Coll (MRCVS), Univ of Cambridge (MA), Univ of Oxford (DPhil, DSc); *m* 8 April 1961, Margaret, da of James Wellwood Johnston (d 1958); 1 da (Fenella b 1967), 1 s (Gavin b 1969); *Career* vertebrate ecologist Nature Conservancy 1956–72; asst dir res Scotland NC 1966–72, Inst of Terrestrial Ecology 1972–86 (head Banchory Res Station), hon prof of zoology Univ of Aberdeen 1986–; memb NE Regnl Bd Nature Conservancy Cncl for Scotland and Scottish Natural Heritage 1992–98; chm: Sci Advsy Ctee World Pheasant Assoc 1976–94, Strathdee Music Club 1997–2002; FRSE 1986; *Publications* Population control in protected partridges (1961), Social behaviour in the partridge (1963), Population studies on red grouse in N E Scotland (with A Watson and G R Miller, 1963), Population fluctuations in the red grouse (with A Watson and G R Miller, 1967), Structure and regulation of a shelduck population (with M G Murray and P Hall, 1975), Of Partridges and Peacocks (2003); several papers on ecology of otters in Scotland and on monitoring woodland and moorland birds; *Recreations* international wildlife conservation, natural history, gardening; *Style*— Prof David Jenkins, FRSE; ✉ Whitewalls, 1 Barclay Park, Aboyne, Aberdeenshire AB34 5JF (tel 01339 886526, e-mail jenkinsdavid@talktalk.net)

JENKINS, Dr David Anthony Lawson; s of Phillip Ronald Jenkins (d 1969), of Folkestone, Kent, and Olive Lilian, *née* Lear (d 2000); *b* 5 December 1938; *Educ* Dauntsey's Sch West Lavington, Clare Coll Cambridge (BA, DPhil); *m* 13 Feb 1963, Evanthia, da of Spirithonos Nicolopoulou, of Patras, Greece; 2 s (Charles David b 19 June 1969, Anthony Phillip b 8 Aug 1970); *Career* BP: joined 1961, chief geologist Exploration 1979–82, sr vice-pres Exploration and Prodn Canada 1983–84, gen mangr Exploration 1985–88, chief exec Technol Exploration 1988–98, dir Exploration 1989–98, dir Canada 1989–91, ret 1998; dir: Chartwood Resources Ltd 1999–, Ranger Oil Ltd 1999–2000, GeoNet Energy Services Inc 1999–2001, BHP Billiton Ltd 2000–, Orion Energy Assocs Ltd 2005–; chm Oil Industry Int Exploration and Prodn Forum 1991–95; memb Advsy Cncl: BP Amoco Technol 1998–2000, Landmark Co 1999–2002, Science Applications Int Corp 1999–05, Halliburton Co 2000–03, Consort Resources Ltd 2000–03, Celerant Conslt 2000–05; FGS, AAPG; *Recreations* shooting, opera, gardening, current affairs; *Style*— Dr David Jenkins; ✉ Chartwood Resources Ltd, Ardennes, East Road, St George's Hill, Weybridge, Surrey KT13 0LB (tel 01932 847377, fax 01932 821703, e-mail jenkins@chartwood.com)

JENKINS, Maj-Gen David John Malcolm; CB (2000), CBE (1994); s of Brig M B Jenkins, DSO (d 1976), and Leslie Jean, *née* Perkin (d 1998); *b* 2 January 1945, Burton on Trent, Staffs; *Educ* Sherborne, Univ of Reading (BA), Magdalene Coll Cambridge (MPhil); *m* 5 July 1969, Ann Patricia, da of Gen Sir John Sharp, KCB, MC; 1 s (Mark), 2 da (Amanda, Kathryn); *Career* cmmnd QOH 1964, regtl serv 1974–75, RMCS and Staff Coll 1976–77, Allied Staff Berlin 1983–85, CO QOH 1985–87, COS 3 Armd Div 1988–90, Cdr Armd 1 (Bn) Corps 1990–91, dir Mil Ops 1991–3, Cmdt RMCS 1994–96, DG Land Systems MOD 1996–2000, Master Gen of the Ordnance 1998–2000; under treas Gray's Inn 2000–; Col Cmdt REME 1997–2002, Col QOH 1999–2004, Col Inns of Court and City Yeo 2003–; *Recreations* country sports, music, military history; *Clubs* Garrick, Beefsteak; *Style*— Maj-Gen David Jenkins, CB, CBE; ✉ The Honourable Society of Gray's Inn, 8 South Square, Gray's Inn, London WC1R 5ET (e-mail david.jenkins@graysinn.org.uk)

JENKINS, Ven David Thomas Ivor; s of Edward Evan Jenkins, and Edith Jenkins; *Educ* Maesteg GS, KCL (BD, AKC), Univ of Birmingham (MA); *Career* asst curate St Mark's Bilton 1953–56, vicar St Margaret's Wolston 1956–61, chaplain Carlisle City Cncl 1956–61, asst dir RE Dio of Carlisle 1961–63, vicar St Barnabas Carlisle 1963–72, vicar St Cuthbert's Carlisle 1972–91, diocesan sec 1984–95, canon residentiary Carlisle Cathedral 1991–95 (canon emeritus 2000–), archdeacon of Westmorland and Furness 1995–99 (now archdeacon emeritus); chm: Carlisle Marriage Guidance 1971–74, Mitre Housing Assoc 2000–; *Recreations* golf; *Clubs* Carlisle Golf; *Style*— The Ven David Jenkins; ✉ Irvings House, Sleagill, Penrith, Cumbria CA10 3HD (tel 01931 714400, fax 01931 714400, e-mail venjenks@globalnet.uk)

JENKINS, Derek William; s of William Jenkins (d 1961), of Burnley, Lancs, and Annie, *née* Haydock (d 1993); *b* 12 September 1934; *Educ* Burnley GS; *m* 3 June 1961, Hazel, da of late George Watson; 2 da (Fiona Louise (Mrs Fawcett) b 22 Dec 1962, Alison Helen (Mrs Winter) b 8 Feb 1966); *Career* articled clerk Proctor and Proctor CAs Burnley 1950–58 (Nat Serv 1952–54), various appts Binder Hamlyn & Co 1958–66, asst tax administrator Texaco UK Ltd 1966–68; RMC Gp plc: gp taxation mangr 1968–77, gp financial controller 1977–80, fin dir 1981–97; pres Cartophilic Soc of GB; Freeman City of London 1982, Liveryman Worshipful Co of Chartered Accountants in England and Wales 1982; FCA 1958, ATII 1962; *Recreations* cartophily, swimming, golf, family history, Burnley FC (past and present); *Clubs* Wentworth, Camberley Heath Golf; *Style*— Derek W Jenkins, Esq; ✉ The Pines, Springfield Road, Camberley, Surrey GU15 1AB (tel and fax 01276 671700)

JENKINS, (John) Emyr; s of Llywelyn Jenkins (d 1957), of Machynlleth, Powys, and Mary Olwen, *née* Jones (d 1967); *b* 3 May 1938; *Educ* Machynlleth Co Sch, Univ of Wales Aberystwyth (BSc); *m* 1964, Myra Bonner, da of Brynley Samuel; 2 da (Manon Bonner (Mrs Jeremy Huw Williams) b 1965, Ffion Llywelyn (Mrs William Hague) b 1968); *Career* BBC: trainee studio mangr BBC London 1961–62, asst studio mangr BBC Cardiff 1962–63, staff announcer and compere 1963–71, prog organiser BBC Wales 1971–77; dir Royal National Eisteddfod of Wales 1978–93, dir Welsh Arts Cncl 1993–94, chief exec Arts Cncl of Wales 1994–98; dep chm Welsh Coll of Music and Drama 2000–06 (govr 1998–2000), chm Bd Univ of Wales Press 2003–06 (memb 1999–2003), chm Welsh Music Information Centre 2000–05, chm Contemporary Theatre and New Writing Co 2007–; fndr chm MYM (Nat Assoc of Welsh-medium Playgroups) 1971–73; elder Crwys Welsh Presbyterian Church 1984–, hon memb Gorsedd of Bards 1982–; Hon MA Univ of Wales 1993; FRSA 1992, FWCMD 1997; *Recreations* music, theatre, sport, walking; *Style*— Emyr Jenkins, Esq

J

JENKINS, Graeme James Ewers; s of Kenneth Arthur Jenkins, of London, and Marjorie Joyce, *née* Ewers (d 1999); *b* 31 December 1958; *Educ* Dulwich Coll, Gonville & Caius Coll Cambridge (MA), Royal Coll of Music; *m* 19 July 1986, Joanna, da of Christopher Charles Cyprian Bridge, ERD, of E Sussex; 2 da (Martha Nancy b 18 May 1989, Isabella Dinah b 20 Dec 1991); *Career* conducted over 150 opera prodns of 100 different titles worldwide; music dir Glyndebourne Touring Opera 1985–91, music dir Dallas Opera 1993–, artistic dir Arundel Festival 1992–98, princ conductor Cologne Opera 1997–2002; has conducted at: Glyndebourne Festival Opera, ENO, Scottish Opera, Kent Opera, Opera North, Geneva Opera, Netherlands Opera, Paris Opera, Glimmerglass Opera, Canadian Opera, Australian Opera, Cologne Opera, Deutsche Oper Berlin, Danish Opera, Vienna State Opera (Billy Budd and Jenufa), Opera Theatre of St Louis, princ Br and several Dutch, German and French orchs (incl Orchestre de Lyon and Monte Carlo Philharmonique), Perth and Melbourne Symphony Orchs, Danish Radio Symphony Orch, Finnish Radio Symphony Orch, Göteborg Symphony Orch, Hungarian Radio Symphony Orch, New Zealand Int Festival 2004; conducted many American symphonic orchs: Utah, Houston, Dallas, San Antonio, Minnesota; recordings incl: Britten's Death in Venice, Picker's Therese Raquin; Freeman City of London 1989–, Freeman Worshipful Co of Goldsmiths 1989; ARCM; *Recreations* reading, cooking; *Style*— Graeme Jenkins, Esq; ✉ Philipston House, Winterborne Clenston, Blandford Forum, Dorset DT11 0NR (tel 01258 880100, fax 01258 880870)

JENKINS, Howard Max Lewis; s of Sqdn Ldr Lewis Max Jenkins, MBE (d 1981), of Bournemouth, and Georgina Ann, *née* Beasant (d 1989); *b* 30 July 1947; *Educ* Bournemouth Sch, Univ of London Middx Hosp (MB BS); *m* 20 Nov 1971, Carol Ann, da of Christopher Downs Hankinson (d 1958), of Southampton; 2 da (Catherine b 1976, Sarah b 1979); *Career* house surgn Middx Hosp 1972, registrar Professorial Unit Nottingham 1976–79; clinical teacher Univ of Nottingham 1985– (med res fell 1979–81, clinical lectr in obstetrics and gynaecology 1981–85, asst clinical sub dean 2003–), med dir Derby City Gen Hosp 1996–98 (conslt obstetrician and gynaecologist 1985–), med dir Southern Derbys Acute Hosps 1998–2002; author of many papers in professional jls and chapters in books; memb Examination Ctee and examiner RCOG, examiner Univ of Nottingham; memb: Nuffield Visiting Soc, Birmingham and Midland Obstetrics and Gynaecology Soc; DM Univ of Nottingham 1984; DObst RCOG 1973, FRCOG 1990 (MRCOG 1977); *Recreations* family and home, aeroplanes and other interesting machinery; *Style*— Mr Howard Jenkins; ✉ Derby City General Hospital, Uttoxeter Road, Derby DE22 3NE (tel 01332 340131); 14 Vernon Street, Derby DE1 1FT (tel 01332 347314)

JENKINS, Surgn Vice Adm Ian; CB (2006), CVO (1999); *Educ* Welsh Nat Sch of Med; *m*; 2 c; *Career* cmmnd RN 1975 (previously RNR), conslt urologist 1979; service incl: HMS Ark Royal, RNH Haslar, RNH Gibraltar, RM Surgical Support Team, HMY Britannia; prof of naval surgery 1988–91, MO in Cmd RNH Haslar 1991–96, defence postgrad med dean and Cmdt Royal Defence Med Coll 1996–99, Med DG (Naval) 1999–2002, Surgn-Gen to HM Armed Forces 2002–06; QHS 1994–2006; FRCS 1973; CStJ 1999; *Recreations* classical music, watercolour painting, photography, swimming, game fishing, travel; *Style*— Surgn Vice Adm Ian Jenkins, CB, CVO, FRCS; ✉ c/o Naval Secretary, Victory Building, HM Naval Base, Portsmouth PO1 3LS

JENKINS, Ian David Pearson; s of Norman Marsden Jenkins, of Emsworth, and Beryl Margaret Andrews, *née* Pearson; *b* 24 August 1946; *Educ* Denstone Coll, King's Coll London (LLB); *m* 6 Jan 1973, Judy Mary, da of John Ernest Middleton Rogers (d 1971), of Salisbury, Rhodesia; 2 s (Peter b 27 June 1979, David b 22 March 1982); *Career* sr ptnr Barlow Lyde & Gilbert 1989–2001; dir: Crowe Insurance Group Ltd 1990–, R J Kiln & Co Ltd 1993–, Kiln plc 1998–; *Recreations* sailing; *Clubs* Royal Thames Yacht, Ocean Cruising; *Style*— Ian Jenkins, Esq

JENKINS, Dr John Gordon; s of John Francis Jenkins (d 1992), and Eleanor Blair, *née* Gordon; *b* 30 November 1950; *Educ* Royal Belfast Academical Instn, Queen's Univ Belfast (Milroy Medal, MB BCh, BAO, MD); *m* 26 Oct 1974, Heather Caroline, *née* Harris; 2 s (Colin b 28 Nov 1976, Gareth b 17 Oct 1978), 1 da (Caroline b 9 Aug 1983); *Career* conslt paediatrician Northern Health and Social Services Bd NI (Waveney Hosp Ballymena then Antrim Hosp) 1982–, hon conslt paediatrician Royal Maternity Hosp Belfast 1999–, sr lectr in child health Queen's Univ Belfast 1999–; clinical dir Woman and Child Health Directorate United Hosps Gp 1994–96, med exec dir United Hosps Tst 1996–98; assessor GMC Performance Procedures 1998–2003, NI memb PMETB 2003–, NI rep GMC 2003–; DHSSPS: memb Central Med Advsy Ctee 1992– (chm 2003–), chm Implementation Support Gp/Advsy Gp on Jr Doctors' Hours 2000–; article reviewer: Archive of Diseases in Childhood, Biology of the Neonate, Irish Medical Jl, Ulster Med Jl; MRCP 1977, FRCPEd

1989, FRCPCH 1997, FRCPI 2003; *Style—* Dr John Jenkins; ✉ Paediatric Department, Antrim Hospital BT41 2RL (tel 028 9442 4510)

JENKINS, Mark Andrew; s of Prof George C Jenkins, and Elizabeth, *née* Welch; *b* 15 November 1957; *Educ* Forest Sch, Chelmer Inst, Inns of Court Sch of Law; *m* 1986, Susan Hilary; 2 da (Eloise b 1989, Tabitha b 1993), 1 s (Oscar b 1995); *Career* practised at the Bar 1980–85; asst co-sec MK Electric Gp plc 1985–87; co-sec: SKF (UK) Ltd 1987–92, PEEK plc 1992–98; legal dir and co-sec COLT Telecom Gp plc 1998–2004, gp co sec Signet Gp plc 2004–; memb Bar Assoc for Commerce Fin and Industry; *Recreations* music, books, Napoleonic history; *Style—* Mark Jenkins, Esq; ✉ Elba House, Goosey, Faringdon, Oxfordshire SN7 8PA (tel 01367 710156); Signet Group plc, 15 Golden Square, London W1F 9JG (tel 020 7317 9706, fax 020 7734 9376, e-mail mark.jenkins@signet.co.uk)

JENKINS, Sir Michael Nicholas Howard; kt (1997), OBE (1991); s of Maj Cyril Norman Jenkins (d 1985), and Maud Evelyn Sophie, *née* Shorter; *b* 13 October 1932; *Educ* Tonbridge, Merton Coll Oxford (BA); *m* 28 Sept 1957, Jacqueline Frances, da of Francis Jones (d 1979); 3 s (Howard Michael Charles b 1958, (Edward) Hugo b 1961, Oliver John b 1966); *Career* Nat Serv 2 Lt RA 1951–53; Shell-Mex and BP 1956–61, IBM UK 1961–67, ptnr Robson Morrow Management Consultants 1967–71, tech dir The Stock Exchange 1971–77, md European Options Exchange Amsterdam 1977–80, chief exec London International Financial Futures Exchange (LIFFE) 1981–92, non-exec chm London Commodity Exchange 1992–96, chm Futures & Options Assoc 1993–99, chm The London Clearing House 1996–2003 (dir 1990–2003), chm E-Crossnet 1999–2005; dir: Tradepoint Investment Exchange 1995–99, British Invisibles 1998–2001, EasyScreen 1999–2005; govr Sevenoaks Sch 1993–; tstee Brain and Spine Fndn 1993–; *Recreations* games, music, woodworking; *Clubs* Wilderness (Sevenoaks); *Style—* Sir Michael Jenkins, OBE

JENKINS, Sir Michael Romilly Heald; KCMG (1990, CMG 1984); s of Romilly James Heald Jenkins (d 1969), and Celine Juliette, *née* Haeglar; *b* 9 January 1936; *Educ* King's Coll Cambridge (BA); *m* 1968, Maxine Louise, da of Dudley Hodson (d 1982); 1 da (Catherine b 1971), 1 s (Nicholas b 1975); *Career* HM Dip Serv (Paris, Moscow, Bonn) 1959–93: dep sec-gen European Cmmn 1981–83, asst under-sec of state FCO 1983–85, min HM Embassy Washington 1985–87, ambass to the Netherlands 1988–93; vice-chm Kleinwort Benson (later Dresdner Kleinwort Wasserstein) 1997–2003 (dir 1993–2003), pres Boeing UK 2003–05, advsr The Boeing Co 2005–; chm WeComm 2002–; dir: Aegon NV 1995–2000, Sage International Ltd 1997–, EO 2000–02, Frontiers Capital 2005–, GeoPark Holdings 2006–; memb: Pres's Advsy Gp Atlantic Cncl 1994–, Br Gp Trilateral Cmmn 1996–2003, Advsy Cncl The Prince's Tst 2002–; *Books* Arakcheev, Grand Vizier of the Russian Empire (1969), A House in Flanders (1992); *Clubs* Brooks's, The Pilgrims, MCC (chm 1999–2001); *Style—* Sir Michael Jenkins, KCMG; ✉ The Boeing Company, 16 St James's Street, London SW1A 1ER

JENKINS, Neil Martin James; *b* 9 April 1945; *Educ* Westminster Abbey Choir Sch (chorister), Dean Close Sch Cheltenham (music scholar), King's Coll Cambridge (choral scholar, MA), RCM; *m* 1, 1969, Sandra, *née* Wilkes; *m* 2, 26 April 1982, Penny Maxwell, *née* Underwood; 5 c (Tom, Sam, Nicholas, Benjamin, Rosie); *Career* tenor; recital debut Kirckman Concert Series Purcell Rooms 1967, operatic debut Menotti's The Consul Israel Festival 1968; Geoffrey Tankard Lieder Prize 1967, Nat Fedn of Music Socs Award 1972; prof of singing RCM 1975–76, Cummins Harvey visiting fell Girton Coll Cambridge 2003; teacher various summer schs incl Dartington, Canford, Summer Music and Hereford 1989–; pres: Grange Choral Soc Hampshire, Haywards Heath Music Soc, Shoreham Oratorio Choir; vice-pres: Huntingdonshire Philharmonic, Brighton Competitive Music Festival; *Roles* incl: Ottavio in Don Giovanni (Kent Opera) 1971, Fenton in Falstaff (BBC) 1972, Ferrando in Cosi fan Tutte (Kent Opera) 1974, Almaviva in The Barber of Seville (WNO) 1974, Quint in Turn of the Screw (Eng Music Theatre 1977, Kent Opera 1979), title role in Return of Ulysses (Kent Opera) 1978 and 1990, Nadir in The Pearl Fishers (Scottish Opera) 1981–82, title roles in Peter Grimes (New Sussex Opera) 1981 and Robinson Crusoe (Kent Opera) 1983, Cat/Milkman in Higglety Pigglety Pop (Glyndebourne Festival Opera), Junger Diener in Elektra (Geneva) 1986 and 1990, Herod in Salome (WNO) 1991 and (Scottish Opera) 1993, Valzacchi in Der Rosenkavalier (WNO) 1994 and 2000, Sellem in Stravinsky's The Rake's Progress (WNO) 1996, Berg's Lulu (BBC Proms) 1996, Sir Philip Wingrave Owen Wingrave (Glyndebourne) 1997, Arnalta in The Coronation of Poppea 1998, Almoner in The Carmelites (WNO) 1999, Vitek in The Makropulos (Glyndebourne) 2001; *Recordings* incl: Rossini's Elisabetta Regina D'Ingilterra, Mozart's Le Nozze di Figaro, Bernstein's Candide, White House Cantata, Purcell's St Cecilia's Day Ode, Bach's St Matthew Passion and Cantata 131, Handel's Wedding Anthem, Schumann's Scenes From Faust, Henze's Kammermusik, Britten's Peter Grimes, Vaughan Williams' Hugh the Drover, Maxwell Davies' Resurrection; *Film Soundtracks* incl: Chariots of Fire, Revenge of the Pink Panther, SOS Titanic, Lion of the Desert; *Books* Carol Singer's Handbook, O Praise God, O Holy Night, Sing Solo Sacred, Bach St Matthew Passion and St John Passion, Christmas Oratorio, Magnificat, B Minor Mass, Easter Oratorio, Ascension Oratorio, Schütz The Christmas Story; *Recreations* visiting ancient monuments, 18th century music research; *Style—* Neil Jenkins, Esq; ✉ c/o Music International, 13 Ardilaun Road, London N5 2QR (tel 020 7359 5813)

JENKINS, Nicholas Garratt Primrose; s of Edward Adam Primrose (d 1965), and Betty, *née* Warburton; *b* 16 February 1939; *Educ* Bradfield Coll, Byam Shaw Sch of Art, St Martin's Sch of Art; *m* 1, 1959, Marie France Aries; 2 da (Nathalie b 1959, Carolyn b 1962); m 2, 1983, Jane Hiller; 2 da (Alys b 1985, Lucy b 1987); *Career* display designer Simpson's Piccadilly 1961–62, art dir New English Library 1963–64, sr tutor RCA 1965–75, co-fndr Guyatt/Jenkins (renamed The Jenkins Group) 1975; significant achievements incl: two solo exhibitions of poster designs (RCA and Univ of Marseilles), design of corporate identities for W H Smith, The Nat Gallery, HM The Queen's Silver and Golden Jubilees, Mowlem Construction and Macmillan Publishers, awarded first prize Israel Museum Book Design; visiting prof Nottingham Trent Univ 1994; chm Design Week Awards 1990, 1991 and 1992, chm Scottish Design Awards 1998, chm BTEC Advsy Bd on Design, co-fndr Design Business Assoc; pres CSD 1996–97 (resigned); FRCA, FCSD, FRSA; *Books* Photographics, David Hicks Living With Design, The Monarchy Book, The Business of Image; *Recreations* writing and jazz; *Style—* Nicholas Jenkins, Esq; ✉ Design Connection, 1 Adam & Eve Mews, London W8 6UG (tel 020 7376 1860)

JENKINS, (Graham) Nicholas Vellacott; s of Gwynne Jenkins (d 1988), of Radlett, Herts and Irene Lillan, *née* Vellacott; *b* 15 December 1945; *Educ* Radley; *m* 23 April 1977, Margaret Alice, *née* Bailey; 4 s (Nicholas Edward Vellacott b 9 May 1978, Jonathan William Vellacott b 16 July 1980, Edward Henry Vellacott b 20 March 1984, William Alexander Vellacott b 7 April 1987); *Career* CA; Whinney, Smith & Whinney (now Ernst & Young) London and Cardiff 1964–70; Moores Rowland: joined 1970, ptnr 1974–99; ptnr BDO Stoy Hayward 1999–; Freeman City of London, Liveryman Worshipful Co of Barbers; FCA (ACA 1969); *Recreations* fishing, golf; *Clubs* Hon Artillery Co, Flyfishers', Ashridge Golf, Royal Porthcawl Golf; *Style—* Nicholas Jenkins, Esq; ✉ BDO Stoy Hayward, 8 Baker Street, London W1U 3LL (tel 020 7486 5888, fax 020 7487 3686, e-mail nick.jenkins@bdo.co.uk)

JENKINS, Peter Sefton; s of John Harry Sefton Jenkins (d 1978), of Brackley, Northants, and Helen Summers, *née* Staveley; *b* 9 February 1948; *Educ* King's Sch Canterbury, St Edmund Hall Oxford (MA); *m* 1, 8 June 1972 (m dis 1991), Jacqueline, da of John Mills (d 1976); 2 s (Benjamin b 13 June 1975, Christopher b 7 April 1979); m 2, 9 Jan 1998, Emma Anne Elizabeth, da of Christopher Howard; 2 s (Thomas Christopher Howard b 24 Dec 1998, George Peter William Howard b 15 Aug 2000); *Career* HM Customs and Excise 1969–86: private sec to chm 1972–74, Cabinet Office 1974–77, involved in EC negotiations on customs duty harmonisations 1977–79, private sec to Chllr of Exchequer 1979, asst sec VAT Admin 1983–86; nat head Indirect Tax Ernst & Young 1990–2001 (Ernst & Whinney 1986–90), global head of indirect tax Ernst & Young 2001–; memb VAT Practitioners' Gp; *Recreations* music, opera, walking, windsurfing; *Clubs* Reform; *Style—* Peter Jenkins, Esq; ✉ Ernst & Young LLP, Becket House, 1 Lambeth Palace Road, London SE1 7EU (tel 020 7980 0477, e-mail pjenkins1@uk.ey.com)

JENKINS, Prof Rachel McDougall; da of Peter Osborne McDougall, of Durham, and Beryl, *née* Braddock; *b* 17 April 1949; *Educ* Monmouth Sch for Girls, St Paul's Girls' Sch, Girton Coll Cambridge (MA, MB BChir, MD); *m* 6 July 1974, (David) Keith Jenkins, s of Lt Cdr David Edward Jenkins, of Chesterfield; 1 da (Ruth b 1979), 1 s (Benjamin b 1983); *Career* registrar Maudsley Hosp 1975–77, conslt psychiatrist and sr lectr Bart's 1985–88, hon sr lectr Inst of Psychiatry 1985– (res worker and Wellcome fell 1977–82, sr lectr 1982–85), princ MO Mental Health, Elderly, Disability and Ethics Div Dept of Health 1988–96, dir WHO Collaborating Centre Inst of Psychiatry 1997–; 250 pubns in res jls; memb: Ctee of Mgmnt Inst of Psychiatry, Int Fedn of Psychiatric Epidemiologists, Cncl RCPsych; FRCPsych, FRIPHH, MFPH, FFOHM; distinguished fell American Psychiatric Assoc; *Books* Sex Differences in Minor Psychiatric Morbidity (1985), The Classification of Psychosocial Problems in Primary Care (1987), Post Viral Fatigue Syndrome (1991), Indicators of Mental Health in the Population (1991), Preventing Mental Ill Health at Work (1992), The Prevention of Depression and Anxiety - The Role of the Primary Care Team (1992), The Primary Care of Schizophrenia (1992), Promoting Mental Health Policies in the Workplace (1993), Prevention of Suicide (1994), Prevention in Psychiatry (1996), Mental Health Promotion and Prevention in Primary Care (1997), Management of Mental Disorders (2000), Developing a Mental Health Policy (2002), Social Inequalities in Mental Health (2004), Implementing Mental Health Promotion (2007); *Recreations* wild orchids, travel, walking, reading; *Clubs* Reform; *Style—* Prof Rachel McDougall Jenkins; ✉ 4 Roseway, Turney Road, London SE21 7JT; Le Fresse, Palluaud, St Severin, Charente, France; WHO Collaborating Centre, Institute of Psychiatry, Denmark Hill, London SE5 8AF (e-mail r.jenkins@iop.kcl.ac.uk)

JENKINS, His Hon Judge Richard Peter Vellacott; s of Gwynne Jenkins (d 1988), of Radlett, Herts, and Irene Lillian, *née* Vellacott; *b* 10 May 1943; *Educ* Edge Grove Sch Aldenham, Radley, Trinity Hall Cambridge (MA); *m* 5 April 1975, (Agnes) Anna Margaret, da of Howard Mullan (d 2003); 1 s (Daniel Gwynne b 1978), 1 da (Isobel Sarah b 1982); *Career* called to the Bar Inner Temple 1966; memb: Midland Circuit 1968–71, Midland & Oxford Circuit 1972–89 (asst treas and remembrancer 1985–89); recorder 1988–89, circuit judge (Midland Circuit) 2001– (Midland & Oxford Circuit 1989–2001); jt assigned judge: Lincs County Courts 1995–99, Humberside Probation Ctee 1996–2000, Lincs Probation Bd 2001–04; liaison judge Lincs Magistrates 1995–2005, designated family judge Lincoln Care Centre 1997–2007; vice-pres Lincs and S Humberside Magistrates' Assoc 1995–, chm Lincs Criminal Justice Strategy Ctee 2000–03, hon pres Lincs Family Mediation Serv 2003– (chm 1997–2002); ctee memb Cncl of Circuit Judges 2000– (chm Family Sub-Ctee 2003–); chm Advsy Bd Lincoln Univ Law Sch 2006–; Freeman City of London, Liveryman Worshipful Co of Barbers 1967; Hon Dr of Laws Univ of Lincoln 2004; *Clubs* MCC, Sleaford Music; *Style—* His Hon Judge Jenkins; ✉ Lincoln Combined Court Centre, 360 High Street, Lincoln LN5 7PS (tel 01522 883000, e-mail rjenkins@lix.compulink.co.uk)

JENKINS, (Sir) Simon David; kt (2004); s of Prof Daniel Jenkins (d 2002), and Agatha Helen Mary (Nell), *née* Cree (d 1992); *b* 10 June 1943; *Educ* Mill Hill Sch London, St John's Coll Oxford (BA); *m* 1978, Gayle Hunnicutt; 1 s (Edward Lloyd b 24 Feb 1982), 1 step s (Nolan); *Career* journalist; Country Life 1965, news ed Times Education Supplement 1966–68, columnist Evening Standard 1968–74, Insight ed Sunday Times 1974–75, ed Evening Standard 1976–78 (dep ed 1975–76), political ed The Economist 1979–86, columnist Sunday Times 1986–90 (ed Books Section 1988–89, Journalist of the Yr 1988); The Times: ed 1990–92, columnist 1992–2005 (Br Press Awards Columnist of the Year 1993); columnist: The Guardian 2005–, Sunday Times 2005–; memb: Bd BR 1979–90, Millennium Cmmn 1994–2000; dep chm English Heritage 1989–90, chm Buildings Books Tst 1995–; Hon Dr: UCE 1998, Univ of London 2000, City Univ 2001, Univ of Exeter 2002; Hon RIBA, FRSL, FSA; *Books* A City at Risk (1971), Landlords of London (1974), Insight on Portugal (ed, 1975), Newspapers: The Power and The Money (1979), The Companion Guide to Outer London (1981), The Battle for the Falklands (with Max Hastings, 1983), Images of Hampstead (1983), With Respect Ambassador (with Anne Sloman, 1985), The Market for Glory (1986), The Selling of Mary Davies and Other Writings (1993), Accountable to None (1995), England's Thousand Best Churches (1999), England's Thousand Best Houses (2003), Thatcher & Sons: A Revolution in Three Acts (2006); *Style—* Simon Jenkins, Esq

JENKINS, Dr (Bernard) Stephen; s of Bernard Pizzy Terence Jenkins (d 1952), and Jane, *née* Webb; *b* 21 December 1939; *Educ* Christ's Coll Cambridge (MA, MB BChir); *m* 1, 4 July 1964 (m dis 1983), Diana, da of Edward Farmer (d 1985), of Henley-on-Thames; m 2, 3 Nov 1995, Elizabeth, da of Eric Winder (d 1997), of Harrogate; *Career* conslt cardiologist: St Thomas' Hosp London 1971–2002 (emeritus 2002–), Cromwell Hosp London 2002–; dist gen mangr West Lambeth HA 1985–90, chief exec St Thomas' Hosp 1990–91; memb Br Cardiac Soc; FRCP; *Recreations* music; *Style—* Dr Stephen Jenkins; ✉ 13 Richborne Terrace, London SW8 1AS (tel 020 7587 1091, fax 020 7587 1799); Guy's & St Thomas' Foundation Hospital Trust, St Thomas' Hospital, London SE1 7EH (tel and fax 020 7261 1488)

JENKINS, Thomas Islwyn David (Tom); s of David Jenkins, of Dyfed, and Elizabeth, *née* Davies (d 1976); *b* 17 October 1950; *Educ* Ardwyn GS Aberystwyth, Craft Design and Technol Coll London (HND advtg and mktg); *m* 1983, Bridget Anne Sellers, step da of John Saunders; 2 da (Katherine Alice Myfanwy b 19 Aug 1985, Lydia Branwen b 4 Aug 1987); *Career* began advtg career as copywriter J Walter Thompson, later joined Davidson Pearce until 1981 (winner D&AD, Cannes, Br TV and Campaign Silvers for The Observer), Abbott Mead Vickers 1981–85 (award-winning work on Volvo, Olympus Sports stores, Waterstone's Bookshops, Paul Masson Wine and Sainsbury's); subsequently creative dir: Colman's (D&AD and Cannes Silvers for work on Citroën), Horner Collis Kirvan (awards for Peugeot and Majestic Wine Warehouses), Weiden and Kennedy US; currently sr copywriter/bd dir Abbott Mead Vickers BBDO Ltd; memb D&AD (memb Ctee 1991–92); *Recreations* reading, writing, watching rugby; *Clubs* Chelsea Arts; *Style—* Tom Jenkins, Esq; ✉ Abbott Mead Vickers BBDO Ltd, 151 Marylebone Road, London NW1 5QE (tel 020 7616 3500, fax 020 7616 3600)

JENKINSON, Prof Crispin; *b* 1962; *Educ* Bedford Coll London (BA), Univ of Oxford (MSc, DPhil); *m*; 1 s; *Career* Univ of Oxford: research fell Nuffield Coll until 1992, joined Health Services Research Unit 1992, currently prof of health services research, sr research fell Harris Manchester Coll; FFPH; *Books* Measuring Health and Medical Outcomes (ed, 1994), Assessment and Evaluation of Health and Medical Care: A Methods Text (ed, 1997), Health Status Measurement: A Brief but Critical Introduction (with Hannah McGee, 1998), Health Status Measurement in Neurological Disorders (ed with Ray Fitzpatrick and Damian Jenkinson, 2000); *Style—* Prof Crispin Jenkinson; ✉ Department of Public Health, Old Road Campus, Headington, Oxford OX3 7LF

JENKINSON, Dermot Julian; s of Julian Charles Lewis Jenkinson, and Diana Catherine, *née* Baird; *b* 2 December 1954; *Educ* Eton, Eurocentre (Lausanne and Cologne), Carnegie Mellon Univ Pittsburgh (GSIA); *m* 2 May 1979, Miranda Jane, da of John Maxwell Menzies; 1 da (Emily Lavinia b 1981), 1 s (Oliver John Banks b 1984); *Career* dir: John Menzies plc 1985–, Smith Hldgs 2003–; chm: Verine Ltd 1993–, beCogent Ltd 1999–; *Clubs* White's, New (Edinburgh); *Style*— Dermot J Jenkinson, Esq; ✉ Mersington House, Duns, Berwickshire TD10 6UL (tel 01890 840757); beCogent Ltd, Victoria Place, Airdrie ML6 9BY (tel 01236 628100)

JENKINSON, Eric; OBE (2003); s of Horace Jenkinson, and Bertha, *née* Fairclough (d 2003); *b* 13 March 1950; *m* 1 (m dis); 2 s (Michael James b 31 March 1980, Christopher Fraser b 18 Aug 1981); m 2, Márie Donnelly; *Career* diplomat; entered FCO 1967, Protocol Div FCO 1967–70, registry and communications offr UKREP Brussels 1971–73, immigration and entry clearance offr Islamabad 1973–76, full time language trg 1976–77, temp duty then third sec (commercial) Jedda 1978–80, second sec (commercial) Riyadh 1980–82, Science, Energy and Nuclear Dept FCO 1982–84, asst private sec Parly Under Sec's Office 1984–86, first sec (economic) Bonn 1986–90, dep consul-gen Frankfurt 1990–91, full time language trg 1991–92, dep head of mission Bahrain 1992–95, head Parly Relations Dept FCO 1995–98, first sec (commercial/economic) and later temp dep head of mission Tehran 1999–2002, high cmmr to The Gambia 2002–06; *Recreations* cooking, photography, rugby, cricket, reading, gardening; *Style*— Eric Jenkinson, Esq, OBE; ✉ c/o Foreign & Commonwealth Office, King Charles Street, London SW1A 2AH (tel 00 220 4496025, fax 00 220 4494986)

JENKINSON, Sir John Banks; 14 Bt (E 1661), of Walcot, Oxfordshire, and Hawkesbury, Gloucestershire; o s of Sir Antony Banks Jenkinson, 13 Bt (d 1989), and Frances, *née* Stremmel (d 1996); *b* 16 February 1945; *Educ* Eton, Univ of Miami; *m* 1979, Josephine Mary, da of late Samuel William Marshall-Andrew; 1 s (George Anthony Samuel Banks b 1980), 1 da (Samantha Emma b 1983); *Heir* s, George Jenkinson; *Style*— Sir John Jenkinson, Bt; ✉ Hawkesbury Home Farm, Hawkesbury, Badminton GL9 1AY

JENKINSON, Nigel; *b* 18 June 1955; *Educ* Univ of Birmingham (BSocSc), LSE (MSc); *m*; 2 s; *Career* Bank of England: joined 1977, past roles incl sr mangr reserves mgmnt Foreign Exchange Div and head Structural Economic Analysis Div, dep dir monetary analysis and statistics 1999–2003, exec dir financial stability 2003–; *Recreations* reading, theatre, football, cricket; *Style*— Mr Nigel Jenkinson; ✉ Bank of England, Threadneedle Street, London EC2R 8AH

JENKS, Prof Chris; s of late Arthur Jenks, and Alice Elizabeth Jenks; *b* 12 June 1947; *Educ* Westminster City Sch, Univ of Surrey, Univ of London; *m* Barbara Read; 2 da; *Career* sociologist; Goldsmiths Coll London: lectr, sr lectr then reader in sociology 1971–94, prof of sociology 1995–2004, pro-warden 1995–2000; Brunel Univ: prof of sociology and pro-vice-chllr 2004–06, vice-chllr and princ 2006–; ed Childhood jl 1995–; AcSS 2000, FRSA 2006; *Publications* Rationality, Education and the Social Organization of Knowledge (1976), Worlds Apart (1977), Towards a Sociology of Education (1977), The Sociology of Childhood (1982), Culture (1993, 2 edn 2005), Cultural Reproduction (1993), Visual Culture (1995), Childhood (1996, 2 edn 2005), Theorizing Childhood (1998), Core Sociological Dichotomies (1998), Images of Community: Durkheim, Social Systems and the Sociology of Art (2000), Aspects of Urban Culture (2001), Culture (4 vols, 2002), Transgression (2003), Urban Culture (4 vols, 2004), Subculture: The Fragmentation of the Social (2004), Childhood (3 vols, 2005), Qualitative Complexity (2006), Transgression (4 vols, 2006); author of articles in Br Jl of Sociology, Theory, Culture and Society, Cultural Values and others; *Recreations* cricket, art, literature; *Clubs* Athenaeum, Chelsea Arts, MCC; *Style*— Prof Chris Jenks; ✉ Brunel University, Uxbridge, Middlesex UB8 3PH

JENKYNS, Prof Richard Henry Austen; s of Henry Leigh Jenkyns, of Aldeburgh, Suffolk, and Rosalind Mary, *née* Home; *b* 18 March 1949; *Educ* Eton (King's scholar, Newcastle Scholar), Balliol Coll Oxford, CCC Oxford; *Career* writer and classicist; fell All Souls Oxford 1972–81, lectr in classics Univ of Bristol 1978–81, fell LMH Oxford 1981–; Univ of Oxford: lectr in classics 1981–96, reader in classical languages and literature 1996–99, prof of the classical tradition 1999–; *Books* The Victorians and Ancient Greece (1980, Arts Cncl Nat Book Award 1981, Yorkshire Post Book Award 1981), Three Classical Poets (1982), Dignity and Decadence (1991), Classical Epic: Homer and Virgil (1992), The Legacy of Rome (ed, 1992), Virgil's Experience (1998), Westminster Abbey (2004), A Fine Brush on Ivory (2004); *Recreations* playing the piano, looking at buildings, walking; *Style*— Prof Richard Jenkyns; ✉ Lady Margaret Hall, Oxford OX2 6QA (tel 01865 727237, fax 01865 511069, e-mail richard.jenkyns@lmh.ox.ac.uk)

JENNER, Prof Peter George; s of George Edwin Jenner (d 1948), and Edith, *née* Hallett (d 1995); *b* 6 July 1946; *Educ* Gravesend GS, Chelsea Coll London (BPharm, PhD, DSc); *m* 1 Dec 1973, Katherine Mary Philomena, da of Hilary David Harrison Snell (d 1958); 1 s (Terence Martin b 19 Oct 1977); *Career* postdoctoral fell Dept of Pharmacy Chelsea Coll London 1970–72; Univ of London Dept of Neurology Inst of Psychiatry: lectr in biochemistry 1972–78, sr lectr 1978–85, hon sr lectr 1983–85, reader in neurochemical pharmacology 1985–89; reader in neurochemical pharmacology KCH 1985–89 (hon sr lectr 1983–85), hon sr lectr Ins of Neurology 1988–2000, prof of pharmacology and head of dept KCL 1989–98, dir Neurodegenerative Diseases Research Centre KCL 1993–, prof of pharmacology Guy's King's and St Thomas' Sch of Biomedical Sciences 2005– (head Div of Pharmacology and Therapeutics 1998–2004); dir Parkinson's Disease Soc Experimental Res Laboratories 1988–99, dir Proximagen Ltd 2005–; vice-pres European Soc for Clinical Pharmacology 2001–; memb: Br Pharmacological Soc, Drug Soc, Movement Disorders Society; fell KCL 2006; FRPharmS 1994, FBrPharmS 2005; *Books* Dopamine Receptor Subtypes - From Basic Science to Clinical Application (co-ed with R Demirdamar, 1998), Beyond the Decade of the Brain - Neuroprotection in Parkinson's Disease Vol 3 (co-ed with C W Olanow, 1998), Cell Death and Neuroprotection in Parkinson's Disease (co-ed with M F Beal, 1998), Levodopa Induced Dyskinesias (co-ed with J Obeso, 2000); *Recreations* gardening, driving; *Style*— Prof Peter Jenner; ✉ Division of Pharmacology and Therapeutics, Guy's King's and St Thomas' School of Biomedical Sciences, Hodgkin Building, King's College, London SE1 1UL (tel 020 7848 6011, fax 020 7484 6034, e-mail peter.jenner@kcl.ac.uk)

JENNER, Air Marshal Sir Timothy Ivo (Tim); KCB (2000, CB 1996); s of Harold Ivo Jenner, and Josephine Dorothy Jenner; *b* 31 December 1945; *Educ* Maidstone GS, RAF Coll Cranwell; *m* 1968, Susan Lesley, da of Colin Stokes (d 1994); 2 da; *Career* with RAF; helicopter sqdn pilot UK, ME and Germany 1968–75, Puma pilot and instr 1976–78, desk offr Helicopter MOD 1979–80, Army Staff Coll Camberley 1981, OC 33 Sqdn 1982–84; mil asst to: ACDS (Commitments) 1985, DCDS (Progs & Personnel) 1986; OC RAF Shawbury 1987–88, RCDS 1989, dep dir Air Force Plans 1990–91, dir Def Progs 1992–93, AO Plans HQ Strike Cmd 1993, ACDS (Costs Review) 1993–95, Asst Chief of Air Staff 1995–98, COS and Dep C-in-C HQ Strike Command 1998–2000, NATO Cdr Combined Air Ops Centre 9 2000; dir European Air Gp 2000; strategic advsr Serco Gp 2001–, chm Serco Def and Aerospace 2003–05 (sr mil advsr 2005–), strategic advsr Atmaana 2006–; non-exec dir NATS 1996–98; pres Coventry branch RAeS 2002–; FRAeS 1997; *Recreations* gliding, old cars, photography, mountain walking; *Clubs* RAF; *Style*— Air Marshal Sir Tim Jenner, KCB; ✉ Holly Bank, Beech Hill, Hellidon, Northamptonshire NN11 6LH (tel 01327 261415)

JENNINGS, Alex Michael; s of Michael Thomas Jennings, of Shenfield, Essex, and Peggy Patricia, *née* Mahoney; *b* 10 May 1957; *Educ* Abbs Cross Tech HS Hornchurch, Univ of Warwick (BA), Bristol Old Vic Theatre Sch; *Partner* Lesley Moors; 1 s (Ralph Jennings Moors b 23 March 1990), 1 da (Georgia Jennings Moors b 14 April 1992); *Career* actor; assoc actor RSC, assoc RNT; Hon DLitt Univ of Warwick 1999; *Theatre* incl: The Scarlet Pimpernel (Her Majesty's) 1985, The Country Wife (Royal Exchange Manchester) 1986, Too Clever By Half (Old Vic) 1988, The Liar (Old Vic) 1989, The Wild Duck (Peter Hall Co) 1990, The Importance of Being Earnest (Aldwych) 1993, My Fair Lady (RNT, Theatre Royal Drury Lane) 2002; work for the RSC: Hyde Park, The Taming of the Shrew, Measure For Measure 1987–88, Richard II 1990–91, Peer Gynt (Young Vic), Oberon in A Midsummer Night's Dream (also US tour and Broadway) Measure for Measure 1995–96, Much Ado About Nothing, Hamlet (also US) 1996–98; work for RNT: Ghetto 1989, The Recruiting Officer 1992, Albert Speer 2000, The Winter's Tale 2001, The Relapse 2001, His Girl Friday 2003, Stuff Happens 2005, The Alchemist 2006, Present Laughter 2007; *Television* BBC incl: Smiley's People, The Franchise Affair, Alfonso Bonzo, Ashenden (with Kelso Films), Inspector Alleyn, Dread Poet's Soc, Hard Times, Too Much Sun (with Talkback), Riot and the Rite, Waking the Dead, Spooks, State Within, Cranford Chronicles; other credits incl: Inspector Morse - Sins of the Fathers (Central), Bye Bye Columbus (Channel Four), Liberty!, The American Revolution, CSS Hunley (TNT TV movie), Bad Blood (Carlton), A Very Social Secretary; *Film* War Requiem, A Midsummer Night's Dream, The Wings of the Dove, Joseph and his Amazing Technicolor Dreamcoat, Four Feathers, Five Children and It, Bridget Jones: The Edge of Reason, Babel, The Queen, The Calling; *Awards* for Too Clever By Half: Drama Magazine Best Actor Award 1988, Plays and Players Actor of the Year Award 1988, Olivier Award for Comedy Performance of the Year 1988; Olivier Award for Best Actor (for Peer Gynt) 1996, Helen Hayes Award for Best Actor (for Hamlet) Washington DC 1999; Evening Standard Drama Award for Best Actor (for The Winter's Tale and The Relapse) 2001, Olivier Award for Best Actor in a Musical (for My Fair Lady) 2002; *Style*— Alex Jennings, Esq; ✉ c/o ICM, Oxford House, 76 Oxford Street, London W1D 1BS (tel 020 7636 6565)

JENNINGS, Anthony; QC (2001); s of Robert Jennings, and Margaret (Irene), *née* Conlan (d 1993); *b* 11 May 1960; *Educ* St Patrick's Coll Belfast, Univ of Warwick, Inns of Court Sch of Law; *m* 3 July 1993, Louise Ethne, da of Michael McKeon; 1 s (Caolán b 3 March 1995), 1 da (Niam b 10 Jan 1999); *Career* called to the Bar 1983, recorder of the Crown Court 2002–; *Publications* Justice Under Fire: the abuse of civil liberties in Northern Ireland (ed, 1988); contrib Criminal Justice, Police Powers and Human Rights (Starmer et al); contrib ed Archbold 1996–; articles on crime and Human Rights for The Times, The Independent, The Guardian and numerous law jls; *Style*— Anthony Jennings, Esq, QC; ✉ Matrix Chambers, Griffin Building, Gray's Inn, London WC1R 5LN

JENNINGS, Rev Prof Barry Randall; s of Albert James Jennings (d 1981), of Worthing, W Sussex, and Ethel Victoria Elizabeth, *née* Randall (d 1983); *b* 3 March 1939; *Educ* St Olave's and St Saviour's GS Tower Bridge, Univ of Southampton (BSc, PhD, DSc), London South Bank Univ (DEng); *m* 1 Sept 1964, Margaret Penelope (Penny), da of Lionel Wall (d 1977), of Newport, Gwent; 2 da (Carolyn (Dr de Ferrars) b 1966, Samantha (Mrs Eveleigh) b 1969); *Career* res fell (maitre de recherches) Strasbourg Univ 1964–65, ICI fell Univ of Southampton 1965–66, lectr in physics Queen Elizabeth Coll London 1966–71; Brunel Univ: reader 1971–77, prof of experimental physics 1977–84, head of physics Brunel Univ 1982–84; estab prof of physics Univ of Reading 1984–89, res dir ECC International Ltd 1990–93, dir of res ECC plc group of companies 1994–97; visiting prof Univ of San Luis and Santa Rosa Argentina 1979, visiting prof of chemistry Univ of Bristol 1992–98, res prof of molecular optics Univ of Reading 1997–2001 (visiting prof of physics 1990–93 and 2001–), visiting prof of optoelectronics London South Bank Univ 1994–; chm: Plymouth Enterprise Partnerships 1997–2001, Univ of Plymouth Enterprise Ltd 2002–04; author of 240 scientific articles and holder of ten patents; vice-pres Minerals Industry Res Orgn 1991–97; ed: Int Jl of Biological Macromolecules 1979–84, Polymer Jl 1983–99, Semiconductor Sci and Technol 1986–87; hon ed Jl of Physics D (Applied) 1986–90; chm Int Ctee for Molecular Electro-optics 1988–94, chm Polymer Physics Gp Royal Soc of Chem 1981–87; pres Br Biophysical Soc 1982–83; memb: Ctee Standing Conf of Profs of Physics 1984–90, Scientific Ctee Assoc for Int Cancer Res 1984–90, Bd of Govrs Univ of Plymouth 1995–2001; Cowan-Keedy prize Univ of Southampton 1961, Soc of Chemical Industry Polymer prize 1969, Kerr medal Int Electro-Optics Gp 1994, Founders lectr Soc Chem Ind 1994; ordained: deacon C of E 1998, priest 1999; asst curate: benefice of St Germans with Hessenford & Tideford (Truro Diocese) 1998–2000, South Hill with Callington 2000–; chaplain to Caradon DC 2003–05; vice-pres Univs and Colls Christian Fellowship 1974–80, memb Bd of Govrs Cornwall Coll 2004–; pres Cornish Fedn of Male Voice Choirs 1991–; Freeman City of London 1997, Freeman Worshipful Co of Stationers 1997; FInstP 1970, CPhys 1985, CChem 1994, FRSC 1994; *Books* Atoms in Contact (with V J Morris, 1974), Electro-optics and Dielectrics of Macromolecules (1979), Colloid & Molecular Electro-optics (with S P Stoylov, 1992); *Recreations* swimming, long cased clocks, science and faith; *Style*— The Rev Prof Barry Jennings; ✉ Pitt Meadow, St Dominic, Saltash, Cornwall PL12 6SX (tel 01579 350940, e-mail barry@pittmeadow.fsnet.co.uk); J J Thompson Physical Laboratory, University of Reading, PO Box 220, Reading RG6 6AF (tel 0118 318571)

JENNINGS, Colin Brian; s of Brian Jennings, of Salisbury, and Jean, *née* Thomas; *b* 27 November 1952; *Educ* Hereford Cathedral Sch, Univ of Leicester (BA, MA); *m* 1978, Jane, da of Stanley Barfield, and Joan Barfield; *Career* various posts incl NATO nuclear and conventional def policy MOD 1976–83; FCO: Policy Planning Staff 1983–86, first sec (econ) Lagos 1986–89, dep head Central and Southern Africa Dept 1990–92, dep high cmmr Nicosia 1992–96, chief exec Wilton Park 1996–2006, special prof of diplomacy Univ of Nottingham 2006–; vice-chair Diplomatic Serv Appeal Bd 2007–; *Recreations* tennis, croquet, watching rugby, walking the fox terrier; *Style*— Colin Jennings, Esq; ✉ c/o Wilton Park Executive Agency, Wiston House, Steyning, West Sussex BN44 3DZ (tel 01903 817766, fax 01903 879647)

JENNINGS, Rt Rev David Willfred Michael; *see:* Warrington, Bishop of

JENNINGS, Sir John Southwood; kt (1997), CBE (1985); s of George Southwood Jennings (d 1978), of Crowle, Worcs, and Irene Beatrice, *née* Bartlett; *b* 30 March 1937; *Educ* Oldbury GS, Univ of Birmingham (BSc), Univ of Edinburgh (PhD, Shell res student), London Business Sch (Sloan fell); *m* 1961 (m dis), Gloria Ann, da of Edward Albert Griffiths (d 1985), of Hope Cove, Devon; 1 s (Iain), 1 da (Susan); m 2, Linda Elizabeth Baston, da of Frederick Zetter (d 1984), of Ipswich, Suffolk; *Career* chief geologist Shell UK Exploration and Production Ltd London 1968–70, exploration mangr Petroleum Development Oman Ltd 1971–75 (prodn mangr 1975–76), gen mangr and chief rep Shell Group of Companies Turkey 1976–79, md exploration and prodn Shell UK Ltd London 1979–84, exploration and prodn co-ordinator Shell International Petroleum Maatschappij BV The Hague 1984–89, md Royal Dutch Shell Group 1987–97, chm Shell Transport and Trading Co plc 1993–97 (dir 1987–2001); non-exec dir: Robert Fleming Holdings 1997–2000, Det Norske Veritas 1997–2001; dep chm MITIE Gp 1998–2007; dir Bechtel Gp Int 2002– (memb Bechtel Bd of Counsellors 1997); memb Int Advsy Bd Toyota Motor Corporation 1997; vice-pres Liverpool Sch of Tropical Med 1991–97, chllr Loughborough Univ 2003–; memb Cncl: RIIA 1994–97, Univ of Exeter 1997–99; govr: London Business Sch 1992–97, NIESR 1995–97; tstee Edinburgh Univ Devpt Tst 1996–98; memb Bd Open Europe 2006–; Hon DSc: Univ of Edinburgh 1991, Univ of Birmingham 1998; Commandeur de l'Ordre National du Mérite Gabon 1989; FGS, FRSE 1992; *Recreations* fly fishing, shooting; *Clubs* Flyfishers', Brooks's; *Style—* Sir John Jennings, CBE, FRSE; ✉ South Kenwood, Kenton, Exeter EX6 8EX

JENNINGS, Dr Kevin; s of Kevin Jennings, and Bridget, *née* Flynn; *b* 9 March 1947; *Educ* Downside, Bart's Med Sch (MB BS); *m* 24 June 1978, Heather Joanne, da of Ray Wolfenden; 2 s (Mark b 1979, Thomas b 1981), 1 da (Debra b 1987); *Career* registrar: KCL 1976–78, London Chest Hosp 1978–80; sr registrar Freeman Hosp Newcastle 1980–83, conslt cardiologist Aberdeen Royal Infirmary 1983–; vice-pres Br Cardiovascular Soc 2006–; memb Cncl: Br Heart Fndn, Br Cardiac Soc; FRCP 1988; *Publications* Acute Cardiac Care (1993), author of several articles on ischaemic heart disease and cardiac imaging; *Style—* Dr Kevin Jennings; ✉ Department of Cardiology, Royal Infirmary, Foresterhill, Aberdeen AB25 2ZN (tel 01224 553548, fax 01224 550692)

JENNINGS, Marie Patricia; MBE; da of Harold Robert Jennings, and Phyllis Hortense; *b* 25 December 1930; *Educ* Presentation Convent Coll Srinagar Kashmir; *m* 1 (m dis), Michael Keegan; 1 s (Michael Geoffrey b 18 July 1962); m 2, 3 Jan 1976, Eur Ing Prof (Harry) Brian Locke (d 2004), s of Harry Locke; m 3, 21 April 2007, Prof Walter Kurt Hayman, FRS, *qv*; *Career* md The Roy Bernard Co Ltd 1960–65; special advsr: Stanley Tools 1961–89, The Unit Trust Assoc 1976–90, The Midland Bank Gp (now HSBC) 1978–2002; dir: Lexington Ltd (JWT) 1971–75, PR Consultants' Assoc 1979–84, Cadogan Management Ltd 1984–90; fndr and pres: Money Management Cncl 1985–2004, Consumer Policy Inst 2000–03; vice-pres Nat Consumers Fedn (former chm); memb: Cncl Fin Int Mangrs and Brokers Regnl Assoc (FIMBRA) 1986–98, Exec Ctee Wider Share Ownership Cncl 1987–91, Consumer Panel Personal Investment Authy (PIA); Nat Assoc of Women's Clubs: pres 1993–98, patron 1998–; memb Cncl and dep chm Insurance Ombudsman Bureau (IOB) 1988–2001; Woman of the Year 1969; memb NUJ, MIPR, FInstD; *Books* Money Go Round (1977), The Money Guide (1983), Getting the Message Across (1988), Moneyspinner (1985), Women and Money (1988), A Guide to Good Corporate Citizenship (1990), Ten Steps to the Top (1992), Better Money Management (1994), Perfect PR (1995), Perfect Personal Finance (1996), Your Family and Money (1996), Perfect Insurance (1997), Diamonds & Pearls (2004); *Recreations* reading, writing; *Clubs* IOD, RAC; *Style—* Ms Marie Jennings, MBE; ✉ Cadogan Grange, Bisley, Stroud, Gloucestershire GL6 7AT (tel 01452 770003, fax 01452 770058)

JENNINGS, Nicholas David De Burgh; s of Robin Jennings, of London, and Diana, *née* Platt; *b* 28 November 1959, London; *Educ* Dulwich Coll, Haberdashers' Aske's Hatcham, Keble Coll Oxford (MA); *m* 30 Oct 1999, Jane; 1 da (Isabelle b 25 Jan 2001), 1 s (Alexander b 23 Dec 2002); *Career* Coopers & Lybrand 1982–87, Pentos plc 1987–88, Daily Mail and General Trust plc 1988– (co sec 1999–); FCA; *Clubs* MCC; *Style—* Nicholas Jennings, Esq; ✉ Daily Mail and General Trust plc, Northcliffe House, 2 Derry Street, London W8 5TT (tel 020 7938 6625, fax 020 7938 4626, e-mail nick.jennings@dmgt.co.uk)

JENNINGS, Prof Nicholas Robert (Nick); s of Robert George Jennings, of Dorchester, Dorset, and Valerie Ann Jennings; *b* 15 December 1966, London; *Educ* Univ of Exeter (BSc), QMC London (PhD); *m* 7 Aug 1993, Dr Joanne Marie, *née* Smith; 1 da (Anna Elizabeth b 25 June 1997), 1 s (Matthew James b 3 July 2000); *Career* Dept of Electronic Engrg QMC London: research asst 1988–89, lectr 1989–95, reader in intelligent systems 1995–98, prof of intelligent systems 1998–99; prof of computer science Univ of Southampton 1999–, chief scientific offr Lost Wax 2000–; dir BAE Systems/EPSRC Strategic Partnership project Decentralised Data and Info Systems 2005–; conslt: BHP Ltd, Defence Evaluation and Research Agency, Dept of Defense USA, DTI, Dresdner Kleinwort Benson, EDS, EU, General Dynamics, Hewlett Packard, IBM, London Underground, Mitsubishi Electric, Nat Science Fndn, QinetiQ; founding dir Int Fndn on Multi-Agent Systems 1998–; fndr ed-in-chief Int Jl of Autonomous Agents and Multi-Agent Systems 1998–2002 (memb Editorial Bd 2003–); memb Editorial Bd: The Knowledge Engrg Review 1994–, Int Jl of AI Communications 1996–2004, Jl of Logic and Computation 1998–, Int Jl of Electronic Commerce Research 2002–, Int Jl of Web Semantics 2002–, Int Jl of Applied Logic 2003–, Assoc for Computing Machinery (ACM) Transactions on Internet Technology 2003–, Computational Intelligence 2003–, Soc for the Study of AI and the Simulation of Behaviour (AISB) Jl 2004–, Jl of Computer Science and Technology 2004–; series ed Agent Technology series, memb Advsy Bd Cognitive Technologies series and Studies in Logic and Practical Reasoning series, memb Editorial Bd Multi-Agent Systems, Artifical Societies and Simulated Organizations series; memb Scientific Advsy Bd: Computer Science Lab Univ of Porto (LIACC) 1998–2002, German Research Centre for AI (DFKI) 2000–, Frictionless Commerce Inc 2000–03, ISheads! 2001–05, IBM Autonomic Computing 2002–05, Science Fndn Ireland Adaptive Information Cluster 2004–, Defence Technology Centre on Systems Engrg and Integrated Systems for Defence 2005–; memb OST Foresight Panel on: Cognitive Systems 2002–03, CyberTrust 2003–04, Intelligent Infrastructure Systems 2004; memb: IT Computing Coll EPSRC 1997–, Professional Gp Ctee on AI IEE 1999–2000, Mgmnt Bd AgentLink 1999–2002, IT Sector Panel IEE 2002–06, UK Computing Research Ctee (UKCRC) 2004; memb steering ctee and chair of numerous confs; external examiner for numerous UK and int univs; Computers and Thought Award 1999, Achievement Medal IEE 2000, ACM: Autonomous Agents Research Award 2003; CEng 2003, FBCS 2003, fell European Artificial Intelligence Assoc (ECCAI) 2003, CITP 2004, FIEE 2004 (sr memb 2003), FREng 2005; *Books* Cooperation in Industrial Multi-Agent Systems (1994), Intelligent Agents (jt ed, 1995), Foundations of Distributed Artificial Intelligence (jt ed, 1996), Intelligent Agents III (jt ed, 1997), Agent Technology: Foundations, Applications and Markets (jt ed, 1998), Intelligent Agents IV (jt ed, 2000), Multi-Agent Systems for Manufacturing Control (jtly, 2004); contrib to numerous academic jls and conf proceedings; *Recreations* cricket (treas Shedfield CC), football (mangr Waltham Wolves mini-soccer team), golf; *Style—* Prof Nick Jennings; ✉ School of Electronics and Computer Science, University of Southampton, Southampton SO17 1BJ (tel 023 8059 7681, fax 023 8059 2865, e-mail nrj@ecs.soton.ac.uk)

JENNINGS, Patrick Thomas; s of Charles Thomas Jennings (d 1983), of Witham, Essex, and Helen Joan, *née* Scorer; *b* 23 February 1948; *Educ* Forest Sch; *m* Jayne, da of Ronald Stanley Green; 3 da (Victoria Anne b 3 June 1977, Joanna Emily b 6 Oct 1979, Charlotte Joy b 16 Oct 1983), 1 s (Edward Thomas Patrick b 16 Aug 1990); *Career* articled clerk H Kennard & Son 1967–72; Slaughter and May: joined 1973, ptnr 1979–, head of property group; chm Building Contracts Ctee of the Construction Law Ctee Int Bar Assoc 1985–89; memb: Law Soc, Anglo-American Real Property Inst, City of London Slrs Co; *Publications* author of various articles and papers on construction law; *Style—* Patrick Jennings, Esq; ✉ Slaughter and May, 1 Bunhill Row, London EC1Y 8YY (tel 020 7600 1200, fax 020 7090 5000)

JENNINGS, Peter John Michael; s of Hugh Gerard Jennings (d 1995), and Marjorie, *née* Robinson (d 1997); *b* 4 December 1947; *Educ* St Columba's Coll, Greenmore Coll Birmingham; *m* 29 Oct 1977, Stella Mary, da of Leslie Mayes; 1 da (Sarah Anne Louise b 10 April 1983), 1 s (Joseph Francis Benedict b 22 March 1985); *Career* journalist, writer, broadcaster, photographer and PR and media conslt; specialist in religious, Irish and philatelic affrs; princ and fndr IMC International Media Contacts; pt/t press offr to Rt Rev Hugh Montefiore 1979–83; press sec: Jr Chamber Int World Congress 1989, Stamp '97 and Stamp '98 (both Wembley Conf Centre), Rare Stamps of the World 1997 and 1999 (Claridge's Hotel), Collect '97 (Olympia); launched Royal Mail: Saints' stamps 1997, Endangered Species' stamps 1998; stamp advsr: The Eden Project (Cornwall), Millennium Point (Birmingham); stamp conslt PA News 2000; co-fndr and chm Millennium Commemorative Covers Ltd; press sec to Archbishop of Birmingham and the Archdiocese of Birmingham 2000, press sec to Archbishop of Cardiff 2001, press sec to the Birmingham Oratory for the Cause of the Ven Cardinal John Henry Newman; ed Birmingham Catholic News 2002 (also special edn Pope John Paul II Silver Jubilee and Beatification of Blessed Mother Teresa of Calcutta 2003); concept, text and photograph World Youth Day Cologne miniature sheet IOM Post Office 2005; regular appearances on TV and radio incl interviews and commentary on the death of Pope John Paul II and the election of Pope Benedict XVI 2005; memb RUSI 2003; freelance memb Foreign Press Assoc; assoc IOD 2000; Lord of the Manor of Thremhall Priory Essex; Freeman City of London 1993, Liveryman Worshipful Co of Masons 1994; MCIPR; FRGS 2003; Knight of Merit with Star Sacred Military Constantinian Order of St George; *Publications* Aerogrammes (1973), Face to Face with the Turin Shroud (ed, 1978), The Pope in Ireland (1979), The Come Sunday Book (ed, 1979), The Church 2001 (ed, 1982), Pope John Paul II (1982), The Pope in Britain - The Official Record (1982), An End to Terrorism (1984, American edn 1985), Children of the Troubles (ed, 1986), The Wonderful World of Stamp Collecting in Universal Postal Union 125 years 1874–1999 (1999), The Queen Mother's Century Celebrated in Stamps (jtly with Tim Graham, *qv*, 2000), Benedict XVI and Cardinal Newman (ed, 2005); also author numerous newspaper and magazine contribs incl: The Times, stamp column The Universe (2001), The Queen Face to Face with her Stamp (2002, The Times Stamp Collecting Supplement), Atom Bomb Exploded above Tristan da Cumha during 1958: The Tristan da Cumha Post Office - Inland Post Inaugurated (2006, Gibbons Stamp Monthly), articles about Diana, Princess of Wales Royal Mail stamps (1998), interviews with HRH The Prince Philip (1998) and HRH The Princess Royal (2002); *Recreations* stamp collecting, aero-philately, watching sport (particularly Aston Villa and Warwickshire CCC), reading the works of The Ven Cardinal John Henry Newman; *Clubs* Royal Philatelic Society London, Birmingham Philatelic Society, East India; *Style—* Peter Jennings, Esq; ✉ IMC International Media Contacts, 47 Regent Road, Harborne, Birmingham B17 9JU (tel 0121 427 2780, mobile 07967 639556, e-mail imc@peterjennings.co.uk)

JEPHCOTT, Sir Neil Welbourn; 3 Bt (UK 1962), of East Portlemouth, Co Devon; s of Sir Harry Jephcott, 1 Bt (d 1978), suc bro, Sir Anthony Jephcott, 2 Bt (d 2003); *b* 3 June 1929; *Educ* Aldenham, Emmanuel Coll Cambridge (MA); *m* 1, 1951, Mary Denise (d 1977), da of Arthur Muddiman, of Abbots Mead, W Clandon, Surrey; 2 s (David Welbourn b 1952, Mark Lanwer b 1957), 1 da (Penelope Mary b 1955); m 2, 1978, Mary Florence, da of James John Daly (d 1950); *Heir* s, David Jephcott; *Career* professional engr; *Recreations* sailing; *Clubs* Royal Ocean Racing; *Style—* Sir Neil Jephcott, Bt; ✉ Thalassa, East Portlemouth, Salcombe, South Devon

JERMEY, Michael Francis; s of Clifford Jermey (d 2001), of London, and Patience, *née* Hughes; *b* 24 March 1964; *Educ* City of London Sch, BNC Oxford (MA); *m* 22 March 2003, Caroline, da of Dick Taverne; *Career* researcher Central Television 1985–86; ITN: grad trainee 1986–87, prodn journalist 1987–90, prog ed News at Ten 1990–91, head foreign news 1991–93, assoc ed ITV Progs 1993–95, dep ed ITN News on ITV 1995–99, exec prodr ITN progs for ITV2 1998–99, dir of development 1999–2004, launch managing dir ITN news channel 2000–01, md ITN International 2002–04, ed ITV Regnl News 2004–07, dir ITV Regions and Network News Ops 2007–; non-exec dir Parly Broadcasting Unit Ltd 2007–; tstee Rory Peck Tst 2002–; *Style—* Michael Jermey, Esq; ✉ ITV News, 200 Gray's Inn Road, London WC1 8XZ (tel 020 7430 4564)

JERRARD, Donald George; s of Harold George Jerrard, of Warsash, Hants, and Margaret Kathleen, *née* Pomeroy; *b* 21 March 1950; *Educ* Winchester (scholar), Emmanuel Coll Cambridge (MA, Rodwell prize for law), Coll of Law; *m* 10 Sept 1977, Susan Christine, da of John Henry Collett; 2 s (Peter George Eveleigh b 2 April 1984, Andrew David Eveleigh b 22 March 1987); *Career* admitted slr 1976; Lovell White & King: articled clerk 1974–76, asst slr 1976–77; Baker & McKenzie: joined as asst slr 1977, later ptnr, sr ptnr Intellectual Property and Information Technology Law Dept 1983–2000; memb Bd Fedn Against Software Theft 1988–91; memb Editorial Bd Computer Law and Security Report; memb Law Soc; *Books* Protecting Computer Technology (European ed, 1986); *Recreations* gardening, travel, watching sport of all kinds, swimming, scuba diving, underwater photography; *Style—* Donald Jerrard, Esq; ✉ The Coach House, Petersfield Road, Greatham, Liss, Hampshire GU33 6AB (tel 01420 538392)

JERSEY, 10 Earl of (E 1697); George Francis William Child Villiers; also Viscount Villiers of Dartford (E 1691), Viscount Grandison of Limerick (I 1620), and Baron Villiers of Hoo (E 1691); s of George Henry, Viscount Villiers (d 19 March 1998), and Sandra Jane Hubbard, *née* Hooper-Valpy; suc grandfather 9 Earl (d 9 Aug 1998); *b* 5 February 1976; *Educ* Mount House Tavistock, Canford, Birmingham Sch of Speech and Drama; *m* 16 Aug 2003, Marianne Simonne, da of Peter De Guelle, and Jeannette De Guelle, of Jersey; 1 da (Lady Mia Adriana Marie Rose b 28 Dec 2006); *Heir* half bro, Hon Jamie Child Villiers; *Career* actor; *Style—* The Rt Hon the Earl of Jersey

JERVIS, Simon Swynfen; s of Capt John Swynfen Jervis (ka 1944), and Diana Elizabeth, *née* Marriott (now Mrs Christopher Parker); *b* 9 January 1943; *Educ* Downside, Corpus Christi Coll Cambridge; *m* 19 April 1969, Fionnuala, da of Dr John MacMahon (d 1961); 1 da (Thalia Swynfen b 5 Jan 1971), 1 s (John Swynfen b 25 June 1973); *Career* student asst, asst keeper of art Leicester Museum and Art Gallery 1964–66; Dept of Furniture V&A: asst keeper 1966–75, dep keeper 1975–89, acting keeper 1989, curator 1989–90; dir Fitzwilliam Museum Cambridge 1990–95; dir of historic buildings Nat Tst 1995–2002 (memb Arts Panel 1982–95 (chm 1987–95), memb Properties Ctee 1987–95); guest scholar J Paul Getty Museum 1988–89 and 2003, Ailsa Mellon Bruce sr fell Center for Advanced Study in the Visual Arts (CASVA) Nat Gall of Art Washington DC 2006–07; dir The Burlington Magazine 1993– (tstee 1997–); pres Soc of Antiquaries 1995–2001 (memb Cncl 1986–88, memb Exec Ctee 1987–90); chm: Furniture History Soc 1998– (ed 1987–92), Walpole Soc 2003– (memb Cncl 1990–95), Leche Trust 2007– (tstee 1995–); tstee: The Royal Collection Tst 1993–2001, Leche Tst 1995–, Sir John Soane's Museum 1999–2002 (life tstee 2002–), Emery Walker Tst 2003–; memb: Advsy Cncl Nat Art Collections Fund 2002–, Reviewing Ctee on the Export of Works of Art 2007–; Iris Fndn Award for outstanding contribution to the decorative arts 2003–; FSA 1983; *Books* Victorian Furniture (1968), Printed Furniture Designs Before 1650 (1974), High Victorian Design (1983), Penguin Dictionary of Design and Designers (1984), Furniture from Austria and Hungary in the Victoria and Albert Museum (1986); *Recreations* tennis; *Clubs* Brooks's; *Style—* Simon Swynfen Jervis, Esq, FSA; ✉ 45 Bedford Gardens, London W8 7EF (tel 020 7727 8739, e-mail ss.jervis@btopenworld.com)

JERVOISE, John Loveys; DL (Hants 1994); s of Capt John Loveys, MC (d 1974), of Chudleigh, Devon, and Barbara Tristram Ellis (d 1992), o da of Arthur Tristram Ellis Jervoise (d 1942); descended maternally from Sir Thomas Jervoise, MP (d 1654) (*see* Burke's Landed Gentry, 18 edn, vol I, 1965); *b* 16 July 1935; *Educ* Hardye's Sch Dorchester, MacDonald Coll McGill Univ Montreal, Seale-Hayne Agric Coll; *m* 12 Aug 1961, Jane Elizabeth, eldest da of James Henry Lawrence Newnham (d 1975); 2 s (John Tristram b 3 May 1962, Anthony Richard b 2 Aug 1964), 2 da (Sarah Jane, Anne Elizabeth (twins) b 18 Nov 1965); *Career* Nat Serv Lt Devonshire Regt 1953–56, Capt 4/5 Bn Royal Hampshire Regt TA 1960–68; farmer and landowner; cncllr: Basingstoke Rural DC 1964–74, Basingstoke and Deane Borough Cncl 1974–78; dir Mid Southern Water Co 1974–91, chm Hampshire Branch Country Landowners' Assoc 1986–88, pres Black Welsh Mountain Sheep Breeders' Assoc 1980–82; High Sheriff of Hampshire 1989–90; *Recreations* hunting, shooting, walking; *Clubs* Naval and Military; *Style—* John Loveys Jervoise, Esq, DL; ✉ Grange Farmhouse, Herriard, Basingstoke, Hampshire RG25 2QB

JESS, Dr Digby Charles; *b* 14 November 1953; *Educ* Plymouth Coll, Aston Univ (BSc), Univ of Manchester (LLM, PhD); *m* 4 Aug 1980, Bridie Connolly; 1 s (Piers b 1988), 1 da (Francesca b 1999); *Career* called to the Bar Gray's Inn 1978; in practice 1981–, treasy counsel Northern Region 1990–2003, lectr in law (pt/t) Univ of Manchester 1986–87; pres Manchester Liability Soc 2006–; memb Ctee: NW Branch CIArb 1984–95 (chm 1992–93), Gtr Manchester and W Pennines Region BIIBA Liability Soc (dep chm 1992–93, chm 1993–99); legal assessor (pt/t) GMC Fitness to Practise Panels 2002–, memb ACCA Disciplinary and Licensing Ctees 2002–; memb: Northern Circuit Commercial Bar Assoc, Technology & Construction Ct Bar Assoc, Br Insurance Law Assoc; Chartered Arbitrator 1999, FCIArb 1992 (ACIArb 1984); *Books* The Insurance of Professional Negligence Risks: Law and Practice (1982, 2 edn 1989), The Insurance of Commercial Risks: Law and Practice (1986, 3 edn 2001), vol on Insurance in The Encyclopaedia of Forms and Precedents (vol 20, 1988), Butterworths Insurance Law Handbook (consulting ed, 3 edn 1992), Professional Indemnity Insurance Law (co-author, 2 edn 2007); numerous articles for various legal jls; *Recreations* family, walking, cinema; *Style*— Dr Digby C Jess; ✉ Exchange Chambers, 7 Ralli Courts, West Riverside, Manchester M3 5FT (tel 0161 833 2722, fax 0161 833 2789, e-mail jess@exchangechambers.co.uk)

JESSEL, Sir Charles John; 3 Bt (UK 1883), of Ladham House, Goudhurst, Kent; s of Sir George Jessel, MC, 2 Bt (d 1977); *b* 29 December 1924; *Educ* Eton, Balliol Coll Oxford, Northampton Inst of Agric (dip), Inst for Optimum Nutrition (dip); *m* 1, 1956, Shirley Cornelia (d 1977), da of John Waters, of Northampton; 2 s (George Elphinstone b 1957, Alastair John b 1959), 1 da ((Cornelia) Sarah b 1963); m 2, 1979 (m dis 1983), Gwendoline Mary, da of late Laurence Devereux, OBE, and wid of Charles Langer; *Heir* s, George Jessel; *Career* Lt 15/19 Hussars (despatches) WWII; farmer 1953–85, farmer in partnership with son 1985–, nutrition conslt 1987–; JP Kent 1960–78; chm: Ashford NFU 1963–64, Canterbury Farmers' Club 1972; pres: Kent Branch Men of the Trees 1979–83 and 1996–, Br Soc of Dowsers 1987–93 (life vice-pres 1993–); pres Psionic Med Soc 1996–2002 (hon fell 1977, vice-pres 2003–); memb: Br Inst for Allergy and Environmental Therapy 1990–, Br Assoc of Nutritional Therapists 1997–; assoc memb Parly Gp for Alternative and Complementary Med 1991–2001, govr Inst for Optimum Nutrition 1994–98 (chm 1997–98), patron Nutritional Cancer Therapy Tst 1998–2005; *Books* An Anthology of Inner Silence (1990); *Recreations* gardening, walking, planting trees, choral music, opera; *Clubs* Cavalry and Guards'; *Style*— Sir Charles Jessel, Bt; ✉ South Hill Farm, Hastingleigh, Ashford, Kent TN25 5HL (tel 01233 750325)

JESSEL, Christopher Robert; s of Robert William Albert Jessel, and Audrey Agnes, *née* Warburg; *Educ* Bryanston, Balliol Coll Oxford (MA); *Career* ptnr Farrer & Co 1979–; memb Law Soc 1970; *Books* The Law of the Manor (1998), Farms and Estates - A Conveyancing Handbook (1999), Development Land-Overage and Clawback (2001); *Style*— Christopher Jessel, Esq; ✉ Farrer & Co, 66 Lincoln's Inn Fields, London WC2A 3LH (tel 020 7242 2022, fax 020 7917 7556, e-mail crj@farrer.co.uk)

JESSEL, David Greenhalgh; s of Robert George Jessel (d 1954), and Penelope, *née* Blackwell (later Dame Penelope Jessel, DBE, d 1996); *b* 8 November 1945; *Educ* Eton (scholar), Merton Coll Oxford (exhibitioner, MA); *Children* 3 s (Benjamin Christian b 11 Jan 1978, Robert Ashton b 16 Dec 1980, James Edward Jackson b 22 April 1999), 1 da (Georgia Alessandra Jackson b 27 Nov 2003); *Career* reporter BBC Radio World at One (Paris riots) 1968, reporter/presenter World at One and World This Weekend 1969–72, reporter 24 Hours and Midweek (BBC TV) 1972–76; presenter: Morning Show (LBC) 1976, Newsweek (BBC TV) 1977–79; writer/presenter (for BBC TV): Heart of the Matter 1979–85, Out of Court 1980–86, Rough Justice 1987–88, Taking Liberties 1989; presenter: Trial & Error (Channel 4) 1992, BBC World News; fndr dir Just Television Ltd 1992–99; memb Criminal Cases Review Cmmn; memb Advtg Advsy Ctee; winner: RTS Int Current Affairs Award, UN Media Peace Prize, Bar Cncl Special Award, RTS Special Award; *Publications* Brainsex (with Anne Moir, 1989), Trial and Error (1994), A Mind to Crime (1995); *Clubs* Chelsea Arts; *Style*— David Jessel, Esq

JESSEL, Oliver Richard; er s of Cdr Richard Frederick Jessel, DSO, OBE, DSC (d 1988), of Marden, Kent; er bro of Toby Jessel, *qv*; *b* 24 August 1929; *Educ* Rugby; *m* 1950, Gloria Rosalie Teresa, *née* Holden; 1 s, 5 da; *Career* chm: numerous cos in Jessel Group 1954–89, London Australian & General Exploration Co 1960–75, Charles Clifford Industries (non-ferrous metals gp) 1978–81, Thomas Seager plc 1993–99; pioneer of specialised unit tsts, responsible for numerous mergers incl Johnson and Firth Brown and Maple Macowards; fndr: Castle Communications plc, New Issue and Convertible Issue Permanent Investment Trusts, Gold & General Unit Trust, 27 other quoted cos and tsts; *Style*— Oliver Jessel, Esq; ✉ Tilts House, Boughton Monchelsea, Maidstone, Kent ME17 4JE

JESSEL, Toby Francis Henry; yr s of Cdr Richard Jessel, DSO, OBE, DSC, RN (d 1988), and Winifred May (d 1977), da of Maj Walter Levy, DSO, and Hon Mrs Levy (later Hon Mrs Ionides), da of 1 Viscount Bearsted; bro of Oliver Jessel, *qv*; *b* 11 July 1934; *Educ* RNC Dartmouth, Balliol Coll Oxford (MA); *m* 1, 1967 (m dis); 1 da (decd); m 2, 1980, Eira Heath; *Career* Sub Lt RNVR 1954; memb GLC for Richmond-upon-Thames 1967–73; Parly candidate (Cons): Peckham 1964, Hull N 1966; MP (Cons) Twickenham 1970–97; chm: Indo-Br Parly Gp 1992–1997 (hon sec 1972–87, vice-chm 1987–92), Anglo-Belgian Parly Gp 1983–97, Cons Parly Arts and Heritage Ctee 1983–97 (vice-chm 1979–83); memb Cncl of Europe 1976–92, memb Select Ctee on Nat Heritage 1992–97; Liveryman Worshipful Co of Musicians; Order of Polonia Restituta (Polish Govt in Exile) 1975; Commander's Cross with Star of the Order of Merit Liechtenstein 1979; Chevalier de l'Ordre de la Couronne (Belgium) 1980; *Recreations* piano, gardening, skiing, swimming, croquet; *Clubs* Garrick, Hurlingham; *Style*— Toby Jessel, Esq; ✉ Old Court House, Hampton Court, East Molesey, Surrey KT8 9BW (fax 020 8979 4461)

JESSON, Paul; s of Peter Jackson (d 1999), and Silvia, *née* Locke; *b* 6 July 1946; *Educ* Hitchin Boys' GS, Guildhall Sch of Music & Drama (LGSM, John Clifford Pettican & Walter Rose prizes), Manchester Poly Sch of Theatre; *Career* actor; bd memb Out of Joint; Manchester Library Theatre 1971–73, Northcott Theatre Exeter 1973–74, first London appearance as Wally in Bingo (Royal Court) 1974, Birmingham Rep 1975 and 1976, Prospect Theatre Co 1977, Liverpool Everyman 1977–79; *Theatre* credits incl: Dan Poots in Flying Blind, title role in Richard III (Liverpool Everyman), Comings and Goings (Hampstead) 1978, The House (Joint Stock) 1979, Irving Gammon in Goosepimples (Hampstead and Garrick) 1981, Falkland Sound/Voces de Malvinas (Royal Court) 1983, Richard in Rents (Hammersmith) 1984, Tesman in Hedda Gabler and Schuffenecker in Mrs Gauguin (Almeida) 1984, Deadlines (Joint Stock) 1985, Felix in The Normal Heart (Royal Court and Albery) 1986, Tusenbach in Three Sisters (Greenwich) 1987, Mike in A Lie of the Mind (Royal Court) 1987, Poppy in Slavs! (Hampstead) 1994–95, Ryszard in The Flight into Egypt (Hampstead) 1996; RNT credits incl: Gooper in Cat on a Hot Tin Roof 1988, Alsemero in The Changeling 1988, Lovborg in Hedda Gabler 1989, Kruk in Ghetto 1989, Horatio in Hamlet 1989, Anderson in The Devil's Disciple 1994, Lord Burleigh in Mary Stuart 1996; RSC credits incl: Ulysses in Troilus and Cressida, John Ryder in Two Shakespearean Actors, Northumberland in Richard II 1990–91, Peachum in The Beggar's Opera, Oldrents in A Jovial Crew, Polixenes in The Winter's Tale, Enobarbus in Antony and Cleopatra 1992–93, Camillo in The Winter's Tale 1994, Prospero in The Tempest, Shakespeare in Bingo 1995–96, title role in Henry VIII 1996–98, First Gravedigger in Hamlet 1997–98; Cobett and Kell in Dreaming (Manchester Royal Exchange and the Queen's) 1999, Mr Braddock in The Graduate (Gielgud) 2000, Dad in Rita Sue and Bob Too 2001, Peter in A State Affair (Out Of Joint) 2001, Earl of Kent in King Lear (Almedia) 2002, Sir Toby Belch in Twelfth Night (Donmar and Brooklyn Acad) 2002–03, Sorin in The Seagull (Edinburgh Int Fest) 2003, Willy Loman in Death of a Salesman (Edinburgh Royal Lyceum) 2004, Leontes in The Winter's Tale (Shakespeare's Globe) 2005, Earl of Shrewsbury in Mary Stuart (Apollo) 2005–06, Pandarus in Troilus and Cressida (Edinburgh Int Festival and Stratford-upon-Avon) 2006, Shamrayer in The Seagull (Royal Court) 2007, Myron Berger in Awake and Sing! (Almeida) 2007; *Television and Film* numerous appearances incl: Clayhanger, The Winter's Tale, Richard III, Cymbeline, Widows, Love's Labour's Lost, Coriolanus, The Ploughman's Lunch, Pity in History, This Is History Gran, Interference, A Very Peculiar Practice, The Rivals, Quartermaine's Terms, Intimate Contact, War Poets of '39, The Gibraltar Inquest, Resnick, The Trial of Lord Lucan, Holding On, Midsomer Murders, A Touch of Frost, The Glass, All Or Nothing, Danielle Cable: Eyewitness, Vera Drake, Spooks, Rome, Slave Trader, Foyle's War, The Amazing Mrs Pritchard, Doctors; *Awards* Liverpool Actor of the Year 1978, Olivier Award for Best Supporting Actor (The Normal Heart) 1986; *Publications* contrib Players of Shakespeare 4 (Cambridge Univ Press, 1998); *Style*— Paul Jesson, Esq; ✉ c/o ICM, Oxford House, 76 Oxford Street, London W1D 1BS (tel 020 7636 6565, fax 020 7323 0101)

JESSOP, Sheriff Alexander Smethurst; s of Thomas Alexander Jessop (d 1953), of Montrose, and Ethel Marion, *née* Robertson (d 1998); *b* 17 May 1943; *Educ* Montrose Acad, Fettes Coll, Univ of Aberdeen (MA, LLB); *m* 16 Sept 1967, Joyce Isobel, *née* Duncan; 2 s (Graeme b 15 Nov 1969, Andrew b 14 Feb 1978), 1 da (Alison b 9 June 1972); *Career* apprentice then ptnr Campbell Middleton Burness & Dickson Montrose; depute procurator fiscal Perth 1976–78, asst slr Crown Office 1978–80, regnl procurator fiscal Aberdeen 1984–87, regnl procurator fiscal Glasgow 1987–90 (sr asst procurator fiscal 1980–84), Sheriff of Grampian Highland & Islands Aberdeen 1990–; external examiner Univ of Aberdeen; memb Scottish Legal Aid Bd; *Recreations* golf; *Clubs* Royal Montrose Golf; *Style*— Sheriff Alexander Jessop; ✉ Sheriff Court House, Castle Street, Aberdeen AB10 1WP (tel 01224 648316, e-mail sheriff.ajessop@scotcourts.gov.uk)

JEUNE, Reginald Robert; CBE (1996, OBE 1979); s of Reginald Valpy Jeune (d 1974), and Jessie Maud, *née* Robinson (d 1945); *b* 22 October 1920; *Educ* De La Salle Coll Jersey; *m* 1946, Monica Lillian, da of Hedley Charles Valpy, of Jersey; 2 s (Richard Francis Valpy b 1949 d 2005, Nicholas Charles b 1954), 1 da (Susan Elizabeth b 1958); *Career* slr Royal Court of Jersey 1945; conslt Mourant du Feu & Jeune (former sr ptnr); Senator of States of Jersey (pres Policy and Resources Ctee) 1962–96, chm Bd of Administrative Appeal States of Jersey 1997–2003; vice-chm of govrs De La Salle Coll Jersey, vice-pres Alliance Française Jersey, Methodist local preacher, life tstee Jersey Wildlife Preservation Tst; Freeman City of London 1996, Liveryman Worshipful Co of Glass Sellers; OStJ; Offr Ordre de Mérite Nationale, Chevalier Order of Orange Nassau; *Recreations* golf; *Clubs* RAC, MCC, Victoria (Jersey), Royal Jersey Golf, La Moye Golf; *Style*— Reginald R Jeune, CBE; ✉ 22 Grenville Street, St Helier, Jersey (tel 01534 609000, fax 01534 609333, telex 4192064)

JEWELL, Prof Derek Parry; s of Ralph Parry Jewell, of Bishopsteignton, Devon, and Eileen Rose, *née* Champion; *b* 14 June 1941; *Educ* Bristol GS, Pembroke Coll Oxford (MA, DPhil, BM BCh); *m* 6 July 1974, Barbara Margaret, da of late Leonard Pearson Lockwood; 1 s (Christopher b 1979), 1 da (Carolyn b 1981); *Career* visiting asst prof Stanford Univ Sch of Med 1973–74, sr lectr in med Royal Free Hosp 1974–80, conslt physician and prof in gastroenterology Univ of Oxford 1980–, fell Green Coll Oxford 1994–, sr tutor 2003–06; memb Res Ctee RCP 1978–87; memb Editorial Bds: Gut, Clinical Science, European Journal of Gastroenterology and Hepatology, Scandinavian Journal Gastroenterology, Canadian Journal of Gastroenterology; pres Br Soc of Gastroenterology 2001–02; ed Topics in Gastroenterology 1973 and 1984–89; FRCP 1979 (MRCP 1970), FMedSci 2000; *Books* Clinical Gastrointestinal Immunology (1979), Challenges in Inflammatory Bowel Disease (2000, 2 edn 2006); *Recreations* music, gardening; *Style*— Prof Derek Jewell; ✉ Madison, Brill Road, Horton-cum-Studley, Oxfordshire OX33 1BN (tel 01865 351315); Radcliffe Infirmary, Oxford (tel 01865 617176, fax 01865 790792, e-mail derek.jewell@ndm.ox.ac.uk)

JEWITT, (Anselm) Crispin; s of Vivian Henry Anselm Jewitt, of Edenbridge, Kent, and Helen Phyllis, *née* Charles (d 1986); *b* 30 July 1949; *Educ* The Skinners' Sch Tunbridge Wells, Poly of N London; *m* 1 July 1970, Mary *née* Lee; 1 da (Alexandra b 20 June 1977), 2 s (Michael b 23 Nov 1978, Henry b 6 May 1984); *Career* Br Library: joined 1974, curator Map Library 1980–83, dir Nat Sound Archive 1992–2003 (asst dir 1988–92), head Br Library Sound Archive 2003–07; pres Int Assoc of Sound and Audiovisual Archives 1999–2002, convenor Co-ordinating Cncl of Audiovisual Archives Assocs 2003–; tstee: Wildlife Sound Tst, Saga Tst; memb Kent Archaeological Soc; ALA 1974; *Books* Maps for Empire (1992); *Recreations* singing, travelling, whisky drinking; *Style*— Crispin Jewitt, Esq; ✉ The Bower, Mill Hill, Edenbridge, Kent TN8 5BU (e-mail crispinjewitt@hotmail.com)

JEWSON, Richard Wilson; s of Charles Boardman Jewson (d 1981), of Norfolk, and Joyce Marjorie, *née* Laws; *b* 5 August 1944; *Educ* Rugby, Pembroke Coll Cambridge (MA); *m* 1965, Sarah Rosemary, da of Henry Nevill Spencer, of Warks; 3 da (Henrietta b 1966, Charlotte b 1971, Camilla b 1977), 1 s (William b 1968); *Career* md Jewson Ltd 1974–86; Meyer International plc: dir 1984–93, md 1986, chm 1991–93; chm: InterX plc 1994–2002, Savills plc 1995–2004 (non-exec dir 1994), Archant Ltd (formerly Eastern Counties Newspaper Group Ltd) 1996– (dir 1982–96), Anglian Housing Group Ltd 1996–2001, Octagon Healthcare 1998–, EastPort Great Yarmouth Ltd 2000–, Queens Moat Houses plc 2002–03 (non-exec dir 1994), PFI Infrastructure plc 2004–; dir: Temple Bar Investment Tst plc 2001–, Lexi Holdings plc 2004–; non-exec dir: AWG plc (previously Anglian Water plc) 1991–2002 (dep chm 1994–2002), Grafton Group plc 1995–, Anglian Water Services Ltd 2002–04, Jarrold and Sons Ltd 2003–; chm East Anglia Arts Fund; pro-chllr UEA (memb Cncl 1980–2003); HM Lord-Lt Norfolk 2004– (DL); CIMgt; *Recreations* golf, tennis, sailing, eventing, visual arts; *Clubs* Boodle's, Royal W Norfolk Golf, Norfolk, Newmarket Real Tennis, RSA; *Style*— Richard Jewson, Esq; ✉ Dades Farm, Barnham Broom, Norfolk NR9 4BT (tel and fax 01603 757909 e-mail richard.jewson@archant.co.uk)

JHABVALA, Ruth Prawer; CBE (1998); da of Marcus Prawer (d 1948), and Eleonora, *née* Cohn (d 1983); *b* 7 May 1927; *Educ* Hendon Co Sch London, Univ of London (MA); *m* 16 June 1951, Cyrus Jhabvala, s of Shiavakshah Jhabvala (d 1973); 3 da (Renana b 1952, Ava b 1955, Firoza b 1957); *Career* authoress and screenwriter; collaborations with Ismail Merchant and James Ivory 1963–; Hon DLitt Univ of London, Hon LHD Hebrew Union Coll NY, Hon Dr of Arts Bard Coll NY; FRSL; *Films* incl: Shakespeare Wallah 1964, Autobiography of a Princess 1975, The Bostonians 1985, A Room With A View 1986 (Oscar for Best Screenplay Adaptation), Mr and Mrs Bridge 1990, Howards End 1992 (Oscar for Best Screenplay Adaptation), Jefferson in Paris 1995, The Golden Bowl 2000; *Books* To Whom She Will (1955), The Nature of Passion (1956), A Stronger Climate (1968), Heat and Dust (1975, winner Booker Prize), Out of India (1986), Three Continents (1987), Poet and Dancer (1993), Shards of Memory (1995), East Into Upper East (1998), My Nine Lives (2004); *Style*— Mrs Ruth Jhabvala, CBE; ✉ 400 East 52nd Street, New York, NY 10022, USA

JILLINGS, Godfrey Frank; s of Gerald Frank Jillings (d 1991), of Worcester Park, Surrey, and Dorothy Marjorie, *née* Smith (d 1996); *b* 24 May 1940; *Educ* Tiffin Boys' Sch Kingston upon Thames; *m* 1967, Moira Elizabeth, *née* McCoy (d 1986); 1 s (Simon Andrew b 1969); *Career* with S G Warburg & Co 1956–58; National Westminster Bank: joined 1958, head

Industrial Section 1983–85, sr project mangr 1985–86, chief exec NatWest Personal Financial Management Ltd 1986–89, dir County Unit Trust Managers Ltd 1986–87, dir NatWest Stockbrokers Ltd 1986–89, dir NatWest Stockbrokers Financial Services Ltd 1987–89, dir NatWest PEP Nominees Ltd 1988–89, sr exec Gp Chief Exec's Office 1989–90; chief exec FIMBRA 1990–94, dep chief exec Personal Investment Authy 1992–94; dir: DBS Management plc 1994–2001 (dep chm 1996–2001), Baronsmead VCT plc 1995–, Baronsmead VCT 2 plc 1998–, Financial Services Initiative Wales 1996–97, DBS Financial Management plc 1997–2001, Welsh Devpt Agency London Office 1997; dep chm Gladedale Holdings plc 2000–, chm Ma Potter's plc 2002–07, chm Spring Studios Ltd 2006– (non-exec dir 2004–); FCIB 2000 (ACIB 1961); *Recreations* travel, chess; *Clubs* RAC; *Style*— Godfrey Jillings, Esq; ✉ 47 Hurlingham Square, Peterborough Road, London SW6 3DZ (tel 020 7736 9083, fax 020 7736 9391, e-mail godfrey.jillings@btopenworld.com)

JIP, Dr James; s of Joseph Wing Jip (d 1980), of Liverpool, and Lai Jip (d 1977); *b* 10 July 1949; *Educ* Liverpool Collegiate Sch, Liverpool Univ Med Sch (MB ChB); *m* 20 Nov 1972, Margaret Victoria Ann, da of Victor Matthew Boulton (d 1970), of St Helens, Merseyside; 2 s (Edward James b 5 Jan 1976, Paul Francis b 13 Dec 1977), 1 da (Caroline Ann b 20 Aug 1981); *Career* house physician Whiston Hosp Merseyside 1972–73, house surgn St Helen's Hosp Merseyside 1973, registrar pathology Walton Hosp Merseyside 1974–75 (sr house offr pathology 1973–74), sr registrar haematology Mersey RHA 1975–80, conslt haematologist Royal Bolton Hospital 1980–; Br Soc Haematology, Br Blood Transfusion Soc, NW Regnl Haematology Sub-Ctee; FRCPath 1991 (MRCPath 1979); *Recreations* foreign travel, chess, piano; *Clubs* Bolton Chess; *Style*— Dr James Jip; ✉ The Department of Haematology, Royal Bolton Hospital, Minerva Road, Bolton, Lancashire BL4 0JR (tel 01204 390390)

JIRICNA, Eva Magdalena; CBE (1994); da of Josef Jiricny (d 1973), and Eva, *née* Svata; *b* 3 March 1939; *Educ* Tech Univ of Prague, Prague Acad of Fine Arts; *Career* architect; GLC's Sch Division 1968–69, Louis de Soissons Partnership 1969–78 (assoc architect), in practice with David Hodges 1978–82, freelance working for Richard Rogers Partnership 1982–84, own practice 1984–86, reformed co as Eva Jiricna Architects 1986–; clients incl: Amec plc, Time Products, Boodles, Harrods, Dubai Festival City, Accenture (formerly Andersen Consulting), Jubilee Line Extension, Prague Castle, Royal Acad of Arts, V&A, Canary Wharf Gp plc, Canary Wharf Mgmnt PTE, Selfridges, Millennium Dome Faith Zone; conslt Sir John Soanes Museum; lectr various venues; pres AA 2003–04; formerly memb Cncl RIBA; prof Univ of Applied Arts Prague 2002; Hon DTech Southampton Inst 2000, Hon DTech Technical Inst of Brno Czech Republic 2000, Hon DLitt Univ of Sheffield 2001; hon fell RCA 1990, Hon FSIA 1996, hon fell American Inst of Architects 2006; RDI 1991, RA 1997; *Style*— Ms Eva Jiricna, CBE, RA, RDI; ✉ Eva Jiricna Architects Ltd, 3rd floor, 38 Warren Street, London W1T 6AE (tel 020 7544 2400, e-mail mail@ejal.com, website www.ejal.com)

JOANNIDES, Prof Paul; s of Evdoros Joannides (d 1978), and Nancie, *née* Mayhow (d 2007); *b* 4 November 1945, London; *Educ* Haberdashers' Aske's, Trinity Coll Cambridge; *m* 1989, Marianne, *née* Sachs (d 2007); *Career* Dept of History of Art Univ of Cambridge: asst lectr 1973–78, lectr 1978–2002, reader in art history 2002–04, prof of art history 2004–; chargé de mission Musée du Louvre 1991–92; memb Société de l'Histoire de l'Art Français; *Books* The Drawings of Raphael (1983), Masaccio and Masolino (1993), Titian to 1518 (2001), Michel-Ange, Ecole, Copistes (2003), Drawing by Michelangelo and his Followers in the Ashmolean Museum (2007); *Recreations* cinema, theatre; *Style*— Prof Paul Joannides; ✉ Department of History of Art, 1–5 Scroope Terrace, Cambridge CB2 1PX (tel 01223 332975, fax 01223 332976, e-mail pej1000@cam.ac.uk)

JOB, Sir Peter James Denton; kt (2001); s of Frederick Job (d 1944), and Marion Pickard; *b* 13 July 1941; *Educ* Clifton, Exeter Coll Oxford (BA); *m* 1966, Christine, da of Frederick Cobley; 1 da (Laura (Mrs Christopher Braithwaite) b 21 May 1971), 1 s (Luke b 5 Sept 1973); *Career* Reuters: joined 1963, served as corr Paris, New Delhi, Kuala Lumpur, Jakarta 1963–71, mangr Buenos Aires 1971–73, mangr Reuters in Asia (mainly based Hong Kong) 1978–90, dir Reuters Holdings plc 1989–, chief exec 1991–2001; dir then chm Visnews Ltd 1989–92; non-exec dir: Grand Metropolitan plc 1994–97, Diageo plc (following merger between Grand Metropolitan plc and Guinness plc) 1997–99, Glaxo Wellcome plc 1997–2001, GlaxoSmithKline 2001–05, Schroders plc 1999– (sr ind dir 2003–), Shell Transport and Trading 2001–05, Instinet Inc NY 2001–05, Tibco Software Palo Alto 2001– (presiding dir 2007–), Supervisory Bd Deutsche Bank 2001–, Supervisory Bd Bertelsmann 2002–05, Royal Dutch Shell plc 2005–; chm Int Advsy Cncl NASDAQ 1998–99; memb: INSEAD UK Nat Cncl 1993–2001, DTI Japan Trade Gp 1994, HM Treasy City Promotion Panel 1995–96; hon fell Green Coll Oxford 1995, Hon DLitt Univ of Kent 1998, Hon LLD Univ of Exeter 2007; Cdr Order of the Lion of Finland 2001; *Recreations* theatre, classical music, boating, golf, country sports, tennis, gardening; *Style*— Sir Peter Job; ✉ 505 Rowan House, 9 Greycoat Street, London SW1P 2QD (tel 020 7592 9424, e-mail jobpeter@googlemail.com)

JOBSON, Anne Margaret; OBE (1992); da of late Colin Thomas Figgins Bell, of Fareham, Hants, and Margaret, *née* Porter; *b* 12 January 1952; *Educ* Purbrook Park Co GS, City of London Poly (BA); *m* 10 July 1976, (Stephen) Andrew Jobson (decd), s of Norman Jobson, of Walkden, Manchester; *Career* called to the Bar Gray's Inn 1975; barr-at-law (in practice as Anne Bell); Parly candidate (Cons) Exeter 2001; chm Exeter Cons Assoc 2001–; *Recreations* gardening, walking, theatre, watching cricket, keeping fit; *Style*— Mrs Anne Jobson, OBE; ✉ 26 Old Tiverton Road, Exeter, EX4 6LG (tel 01392 421420); Holborn Chambers, 6 Gate Street, Holborn, London WC2A 3HP (tel 020 7242 6060, fax 020 7242 2777, mobile 079 5873 9896, e-mail jobson@jobson.tory.org.uk)

JOBSON, Timothy Akers; s of Maj E O A Jobson (d 1965), and Joan, *née* Webb (d 1991); *b* 16 July 1944; *Educ* Bromsgrove Sch, Keble Coll Oxford (MA); *m* 1, 27 July 1970 (m dis 1980), L Bazeley; 1 s (Simon b 1973), 1 da (Annie b 1974); m 2, 7 April 1982 (m dis 2001), S Jeavons; m 3, 27 Aug 2004, Janice Ashwood; *Career* admitted slr 1968; ptnr: Lyon Clark & Co West Bromwich 1970–84, Keely Smith & Jobson Lichfield 1985–95, Oldham Rust Jobson Stafford 1995–2005, ORJ Solicitors LLP Stafford 2005–; co sec: Barnt Green Waters Ltd, British Business Parks, Chamber Member Services Ltd, United Leisure Ltd; dir PSL Coaching; dep chm West Bromwich & Dist YMCA; RYA club racing coach; *Recreations* sailing, swimming, gardening; *Clubs* Barnt Green Sailing, Oxford Univ Yacht; *Style*— Tim Jobson, Esq; ✉ Parkside Cottage, Ivetsey Road, Wheaton Aston, Stafford ST19 9QP (tel 01785 841146, e-mail tim.jobson@orj.co.uk)

JOFFE, Baron (Life Peer UK 2000), of Liddington in the County of Wiltshire; Joel Goodman Joffe; CBE (1999); s of Abraham Michael Joffe (d 1984), of Johannesburg, South Africa, and Dena, *née* Idelson (d 1984); *b* 12 May 1932; *Educ* Univ of the Witwatersrand (BCom, LLB); *m* 1 Nov 1962, Vanetta, da of François Pretorius (d 1975), of Port Elizabeth, South Africa; 3 da (Hon Deborah b 11 June 1963, Hon Lisa b 13 Aug 1964, Hon Abigail b 4 Sept 1969); *Career* human rights lawyer SA 1954–65; admin dir Abbey Life Assurance plc 1966–70, dep chm (formerly dir and md) Allied Dunbar Assurance plc 1971–91; chm: Swindon Cncl of Voluntary Servs 1973–80, Oxfam 1980–2001 (tstee, hon sec and chm), Swindon HA and NHS Tst 1988–94, The Giving Campaign 2000–04; memb Royal Cmmn for the Care of the Elderly 1997–99; *Recreations* tennis, cycling; *Style*— Lord Joffe, CBE; ✉ House of Lords, London SW1A 0PW

JOFFÉ, Roland Victor; *b* 17 November 1945, London; *m* 1, 1974 (m dis 1982), Jane Lapotaire, *qv*; 1 s (Rowan b 1973); m 2, (m dis) Cherie Lunghi, *qv*; 1 da (Nathalie-Kathleen b 26 Aug 1986); *Career* film dir and prodr; *Films* The Legion Hall Bombing 1978, The Spongers 1978, No Mama, No 1979, United Kingdom 1981, The Killing Fields 1984 (nomination Best Dir Academy Awards), The Mission 1986 (winner Palme D'Or Cannes Film Festival), Fat Man and Little Boy 1989, City of Joy 1992, Super Mario Bros 1993 (prodr), The Scarlet Letter 1995, Goodbye Lover 1997, Vatel 1999, Captivity 2007; *Style*— Roland Joffé, Esq

JOHANSON, Capt Philip; OBE (2002); s of Stanley Theodore Johanson (d 1991), and Betty Johanson (d 1984); *b* 10 April 1947; *Educ* Alderman Cogan C of E Sch Kingston upon Hull, Wilson Carlile Coll of Evangelism; *Career* Church Army: head of missions 1975–83, dir of evangelism 1983–90, chief sec 1990–2006, dir Bd; int sec Church Army International 2007–; memb: Partnership World Mission Ctee, Cncl Christian Enquiry Agency; patron African Pastor Fellowship; dir Bd of Mgmnt Portman House Tst; *Recreations* theatre, music, travel, reading; *Clubs* Royal Cwlth; *Style*— Capt Philip Johanson, OBE; ✉ 10 Ditton Lodge, 8 Stourwood Avenue, Bournemouth BH6 3PN (tel 01202 416917, e-mail p.johanson@churcharmy.org.uk)

JOHN, Daniel Howard; s of Michael Hanlon John, of London, and Patricia Ann, *née* Hawkes; *b* 6 June 1961; *Educ* Archbishop Tenison's GS London; *m* 1994, Tanya, *née* Allen; 2 s; *Career* trainee journalist West London Observer 1979–83, sr reporter West Kent Extra Series 1983–84, industrial reporter Kent Evening Post 1984–86, fin reporter Birmingham Post 1986–88, freelance reporter 1988–89 (The Guardian, Mail on Sunday, Daily Star), financial corr, tport corr and dep financial news ed The Guardian 1989, freelance Australian corr 1993, home news ed The Guardian 1993–96, managing ed (news) The Observer 1996–98, exec picture ed The Guardian and The Observer 1998–2001, exec ed Creative Dept Guardian 2001–02, picture ed The Sun-Herald Sydney Aust 2002–05, chief of staff photographic Sydney Morning Herald 2005–06, business reporter Sydney Morning Herald 2006; received Proficiency Test Cert from Nat Cncl for Trg of Journalists; NEC memb NUJ 1986–87; memb: Charter 88, Friends of the Earth; *Recreations* reading, current affairs, music, cooking, entertaining, cricket, golf; *Clubs* Ryde Hunters Hill Cricket; *Style*— Daniel John, Esq; ✉ c/o The Sunday Morning Herald, 201 Sussex Street, Sydney NSW 2111, Australia (tel +612 9282 2418, e-mail djohn@smh.com.au)

JOHN, Sir David Glyndwr; KCMG (1999); s of William Glyndwr John (d 1967), of Pontypridd, Mid Glamorgan, and Marjorie, *née* Gaze (d 1985); *b* 20 July 1938; *Educ* Llandovery Coll (Thomas Phillips Fndn scholar, Johnes scholar), Christ's Coll Cambridge (MA), Columbia Univ NY (NATO Research Studentship, MBA), Harvard Business Sch (Int Sr Mgmnt Prog); *m* 22 Aug 1964, Gillian, da of Henry J Edwards; 1 da (Emma Victoria b 7 July 1967), 1 s (Ceri David b 30 July 1968); *Career* graduate trainee then shift mangr United Steel Companies Sheffield 1962–64, mgmnt conslt then mktg dir subsid Hardman and Holden Ltd RTZ Corporation 1966–73; Redland Group plc: gen mangr Land Reclamation Co 1973–77, regnl dir Middle E and Far E Redland Industrial Services 1977–80, md Redland Purle 1980, md Cleanaway Ltd 1980–81; Inchcape plc: chief exec subsid Gray Mackenzie & Co Ltd Bahrain 1986–87 (devpt dir 1981–85), chief exec Inchcape Berhad Singapore 1987–90, main bd dir 1988–95, chm Inchcape Berhad 1990–95, exec chm Inchcape Toyota Motors 1994–95; chm: The BOC Group plc 1996–2002 (non-exec dir 1993–), Premier Oil plc 1998–, BSI Group 2002– (non-exec dir 2002–), Balfour Beatty plc 2003– (non-exec dir 2000–); non-exec dir: St Paul Cos Inc Minnesota USA 1996–2003, Welsh Development Agency 2001–02; chm External Funding Bd Dept Material Sciences Univ of Cambridge 1998–2001; memb CBI Int Advsy Bd 2002–; memb: CBI President's Ctee 1996–2002, Wilson Ctee on Review of Export Promotion, Cncl for Industry and Higher Educn 1996–2002, Panel 2000, Bd of Overseers Columbia Business Sch NY 1996–2001; govr SOAS Univ of London 1994–; *Recreations* sailing, skiing, reading; *Clubs* Oxford and Cambridge, Oriental, Travellers; *Style*— Sir David John, KCMG

JOHN, Sir Elton Hercules (né Reginald Kenneth Dwight); kt (1998), CBE (1996); s of Stanley Dwight, and Sheila, *née* Sewell; *b* 25 March 1947; *Educ* Pinner GS, Royal Acad of Music; *partner* David Furnish; *Career* pop singer and pianist; keyboard player with R&B band Bluesology 1965, first album Empty Sky released 1969, US debut at Troubadour Folk Club 1970, single Your Song first UK and US Top 10 record 1971, renowned during 1970s for outlandish costumes and ludicrous spectacles, albums Goodbye Yellow Brick Road, Captain Fantastic and The Brown Dirt Cowboy and Blue Moves confirmed worldwide stardom, toured Communist Bloc (played eight sell-out dates in Leningrad), album A Single Man 1978 and subsequent tour stripped away razzmatazz of early 1970s shows, album Two Low for Zero 1983 provided four worldwide hits, broadcast of Live in Australia album viewed by record Australian TV audience of six million 1987, stage costumes and memorabilia sold by Sotheby's 1988, 34th album Sleeping with the Past released 1989, No 1 in UK Album Charts July 1990, over 3 million copies sold worldwide, double A-Sided single Sacrifice/Healing Hands No 1 five weeks in UK (first UK No 1, all proceeds donated to AIDS related charities), No 1 double album The Very Best of Elton John released 1990 (over 9.5 million copies sold worldwide), album The One released 1992, album Duets released 1993, wrote music for film The Lion King (lyrics by Sir Tim Rice) 1994, album Made In England released 1995, album The Big Picture released 1997, single Candle in the Wind adapted as Candle in the Wind '97 (in memory of Diana, Princess of Wales, proceeds going to the Diana, Princess of Wales Memorial Fund) 1997, album Aida released 1999, album El Dorado released 2000, live album One Night Only released 2000, stage musical The Lion King playing at six theatres worldwide 2001, two US productions of Aida 2001, album Songs from the West Coast released 2001, album Greatest Hits 1970–2002 released 2002, single Are You Ready for Love? UK No 1 2003, album Goodbye Yellow Brick Road re-released 2003, residency The Red Piano (75 shows) The Colosseum Las Vegas 2004–, album Peachtree Road released 2004; as actor cameo role in Spiceworld The Movie 1997; significant achievements: record number of shows at Madison Square Gardens, first artist to enter Billboard US Album chart at No 1, seven consecutive No 1 US albums, writer of over 600 songs and has released over 30 albums, more weeks spent in UK chart than any other recording artist during 1970s, winner Best Male Artist BRIT Awards 1991, Lifetime Achievement award BRIT Awards 1995, Oscar for Can You Feel The Love Tonight? (from The Lion King) 1995, Polar Music Prize 1995, Freddie Mercury Award BRIT Awards 1998, Grammy Lifetime Achievement Award 2000, Tony Award Best Original Score for Aida 2000; chm Watford FC 1979–90; fndr Elton John Aids Fndn 1993; tstee The Wallace Collection 1999; involved in many charities incl: The Elton John Aids Fndn, Nordoff Robbins Music Therapy, Terrence Higgins Tst, London Lighthouse; *Recreations* Watford FC (life pres); *Style*— Sir Elton John, CBE

JOHN, Geraint Morton; s of Frederick William John (d 1977), of Swansea, and Gwladys Mary John (d 1970); *b* 2 April 1938; *Educ* Swansea GS, Bartlett Sch of Architecture UCL (DipArch); *m* Jan 1959, Jane Doreen, da of William Aurelius Williams; 2 da (Catrin Elizabeth b 1959, Betsan Sarah b 1961), 1 s (Dylan William b 1964); *Career* architect; articled to Sir Percy Thomas 1954–58; Maxwell Fry and Jane Drew 1961–63, Denys Lasdun 1963–64, Arup Associates 1964–65, Parkin Associates Toronto Canada 1965–66, Herts CC 1966–69, Architects and Bldgs Branch DES 1969–72, head Tech Unit for Sport and chief architect to Sports Council 1975–96 (joined 1972), sr advsr HOK Sport 1998–, sr advsr HOK Sport Architecture 2001–; visiting prof of architecture (sports building design) Faculty of Creative Art & Technology Univ of Luton 1998– (sr lectr 1996–98); corr on sports bldgs for Architects Jl 1978–82; memb: Arts Cncl Planning Bd 1988–93, Cncl Int Union of Architects 1990–93, RIBA Overseas Ctee 1985–93, Editorial Advsy Bd

Crowd Management magazine Int Assoc of Auditorium Managers, ILAM, Football Stadia Advsy Design Cncl 1989–93, Tech Ctee Sports Ground Initiative 1995–, Panel Design Cmmn for Wales (DCfW) 2003–, Cncl RIBA 2004–; chm RIBA/UIA Co-ordinating Ctee 1987–93, dir Sports and Leisure Prog Int Union of Architects 1996–, co-ordinator RIBA Client Forums on Spectator and Participation Facilities 1997–, hon advsr to Nat Playing Fields Assoc (NPFA) 1997–, client advsr RIBA 2007–; sec Sports and Leisure Work Gp Int Union of Architects 1985–96, chm Herts Assoc of Architects (HAA) 2004–; RIBA part 3 examiner Univ of Cambridge and London Met Univ 2002–; pres: Old Albanians RFC 1983–85, St Albans Welsh Soc 1980–83 and 2000–02; chm Old Albanian 948 Sports Fndn 2007–, chm Friends of Victoria Playing Field 2004–; Companion Inst of Sports and Recreation Management 1993–; hon memb Belgian Inst of Architects; RIBA (ARIBA 1962), FRSA; *Books* Handbook of Sports and Recreational Building Design (4 vols, jt ed 1981), Handbook of Sports and Recreation Design (revised edn, 3 vols, jt ed, 1994), Stadia Design (with Rod Sheard, *qv*, and Ben Vickery 1994, 4 edn 2007); *Recreations* water colours and sketching; *Style*— Prof Geraint John; ✉ 125 Verulam Road, St Albans, Hertfordshire AL3 4DL (tel 01727 857682, e-mail gmjohn@compuserve.com); HOK Sport Architecture, 14 Blades Court, Deodar Road, London SW15 2NU (fax 020 8874 7470)

JOHN, Dr Joshy; s of late Prof P V Ulahannan Mapilla, of Changanachery, Kerala, India, and late Mary, *née* Joseph; *b* 9 October 1940; *Educ* St Berchmans' HS, Kerala Univ (BSc, MB BS), Univ of Sheffield (MD); *m* 25 Jan 1970, Tresa, da of late K J Jacob, of Kerala, India; 2 s (Jason Joseph b 30 June 1974, James George b 7 Nov 1983), 1 da (Mary Anne b 14 March 1979); *Career* conslt physician genito-urinary med and HIV inf-AIDS; hon conslt HIV and AIDS Unit Chelsea and Westminster Hosp; former conslt physician genito-urinary med: HIV and AIDS Unit St Albans City Hosp, Derby Royal Infirmary, Chesterfield Royal Hosp, St Mary's Hosp Luton; former hon lectr Med Div Univ of Sheffield; memb: Br HIV Assoc, Indian Assoc Study of STIs and HIV/AIDS, Int Union Against VD and Treponematoses, Int Soc for AIDS, BMA, Hosp Conslts and Specialists Assoc; formerly: memb:Med Soc for the Study of VD, memb Herts HIV/AIDS and Sexual Health Working Pty, chm Clinical Sub-Gp on AIDS/HIV Infection St Albans and Hemel Hempstead NHS Tst, vice-chm NW Thames Regnl Specialist Gp; FRSM; *Books* papers on non-gonococcal urethritis therapy, asymptomatic gonorrhoea in male, abnormal forms of trichomonas vaginalis and genito-urinary trichomoniasis in male; *Recreations* gym, swimming, travel; *Style*— Dr Joshy John; ✉ Jostre, 30 Magnaville Road, Bushey Heath, Watford WD23 1PP (tel 07971 544574, fax 020 8386 9378); 104 Harley Street, London W1G 7JD; The Clementine Churchill Hospital, Sudbury Hill, Harrow HA1 3RX (tel 020 88722 3872, fax 020 8872 3836)

JOHN, Philip; *Career* princ King Williams' Coll IOM; *Style*— Philip John, Esq; ✉ King William's College, Castletown, Isle of Man IM9 1TP

JOHN, Simon; s of John Bedford, and Wendy Bedford; *b* 29 December 1966; *Educ* Mayfield Sch Portsmouth; *m* 22 July 1989, Victoria, da of John Richardson; 1 s (Charles b 6 Aug 1993), 1 da (Verity b 29 May 1996); *Career* photographer; prop Simon John Photographs Ltd; featured in exhbns at: Royal Albert Hall, Barbican, Dimbola Lodge; photography teacher, lectr Fuji Film; judge Int Photographic Awards, memb Admissions and Qualifications Ctee BIPP; contrib to various books on improving social photography; supporter Leukemia Busters Southampton; FBIPP 1996 (MBIPP 1987), hon fell Master Photographers Assoc 2002; *Awards* 10 Kodak Gold Awards, Best Overall Portrait Face 2000 Portrait Competition, various int awards for portrait and wedding photography; *Recreations* fencing, running, exercise, travel, music; *Clubs* Fedn of Small Businesses (FSB); *Style*— Simon John, Esq; ✉ Simon John Studios, 71 St Marys Road, Portsmouth, Hampshire PO1 5PG (tel 023 9286 1579, fax 023 9242 8080, e-mail simon@simonjohn.co.uk)

JOHN, Stewart Morris; OBE (1992); s of Ivor Morgan John (d 1989), and Lilian, *née* Morris (d 1989); *b* 28 November 1938; *Educ* Porth Co GS, N Staffs Tech Coll, Southall Tech Coll (HNC); *m* 3 July 1961, Susan Anne, da of William Alfred Cody; 1 s (Philip Andrew b 23 May 1964), 1 da (Sarah Margaret b 10 Nov 1967); *Career* BOAC apprentice aeronautical engr 1955–60, seconded as station engr to Kuwait Airways 1961–65, seconded as chief engr Borneo to Malaysia-Singapore Airlines E Malaysia 1965–67 (gen inspr and project engr Singapore 1963–66), engr Avionics Devpt London Airport 1967–70, asst to Gen Manager Maintenance 1970–71, works supt Mechanical Workshops 1972–73, aircraft maintenance supt 1973–74, maintenance mangr American Aircraft 1975–77, engrg dir Cathay Pacific Airways 1980–93 (dep dir engrg and maintenance Hong Kong 1977–80); dep chm Hong Kong Aircraft Engineering 1987–93 (dir 1982–93), chm Assoc Engineers Ltd Hong Kong 1990–93, ret; tech dir Aviation Exposure Management Ltd 1995–; dir of quality and memb Cncl Aviation Trg Assoc, pres RAeS 1997–98; memb: Bd Commercial Aero Engine Rolls-Royce 1993–98, Bd British Aerospace Aviation Services 1993–98, Bd Taikoo Aircraft Engineering Co Xiamen 1993–, Bd of Tstees Brooklands Museum Tst, Bd Hong Kong Aero Engine Service Limited (HAESL) 1996–98, Bd British Midland Aviation Services 1997–2000, Bd Aerospace North America 2000–02, Advsy Bd Kingfisher Airlines (India) 2006–; non-exec dir Green Dragon Gas (China) 2006–; pres Int Fedn of Airworthiness 1993–96, Selection Ctee François-Xavier Bagnond Aerospace Prize 2001–04; Gold medal Br Assoc of Aviation Conslts 1991; FREng 1990, FRAeS; *Recreations* golf, classic cars, rugger; *Clubs* The Hong Kong, Shek-o Country, Hong Kong Aviation, Burhill Golf, Bentley Drivers', Rolls Royce Enthusiast (chm Surrey section); *Style*— Stewart M John, Esq, OBE, FREng; ✉ Wychbury House, Warreners Lane, St George's Hill, Weybridge, Surrey KT13 0LH (tel 01932 847747, fax 01932 830777)

JOHNS, Prof Allan Thomas; s of William George Johns (d 1995), of Exeter, Devon, and Ivy Maud, *née* Camble; *b* 14 April 1942; *Educ* St Luke's Sch Exeter, Dartington Coll for the Performing Arts, Univ of Bath (BSc, PhD, DSc); *m* 23 Sept 1972, Marion, da of Charles Franklin (d 1952); 2 da (Louisa Anne b 1979, Victoria Helen b 1981); *Career* professional singer: cathedral lay vicar and clerk 1960–63, p/t concert baritone 1963–; asst dist engr SW Electricity Bd 1963–68, reader in power systems Univ of Bath 1976–84 (res fell 1968–69, lectr in electrical engrg 1969–76), head of Electrical Electronic and Information Engrg Dept and dir of Power and Energy Systems Research Centre City Univ 1988–91 (prof of electrical and electronic engrg 1984–88), prof of electrical engrg Univ of Bath 1991–2001 (head Sch of Electronic and Electrical Engrg 1992–98, dir Overseas Devpt 1998–2001), emeritus prof of electrical and electronic engrg 2001–; non-exec chm Intalec Int Electrical Engrg Consulting Engrs 1995–; chm SERC Electricity Research Co-Funding Ctee 1989–94, memb SERC Electromechanical Engrg Ctee (chm Electrical Power Industries Gp 1991–94), memb numerous national and int ctees incl Br nat memb CIGRÉ 2000–; conslt: GEC, NGC, British Technol Group; ed: IEE Power Engineering Series 1984–2005, IEE Power Engineering Jl 1989–99; govr Greendown Secdy Sch Swindon (sometime chm and vice-chm), ex-officio fndn govr Broad Hinton C of E Sch 2001– (chm 2003–); ind custody visiting co-ordinator Wilts Police Authy, memb Home Office Ind Monitoring Bd HMP Erlestoke; author of 4 books and over 200 res papers, awarded 4 learned soc premiums incl IEE Power Div and Crompton Awards (1968, 1982, 1988 and 1995); CEng, FIEE 1981, FRSA 1988, FIET 2006; *Recreations* ice-skating, bowls, walking, piano, singing (solo performer at major concerts), coaching promising young singers; *Clubs* Garrards; *Style*— Prof Allan T Johns; ✉ Faculty of Engineering and Design, University of Bath, Claverton Down, Bath (tel 01225 826052, fax 01225 826865, e-mail a.t.johns@bath.ac.uk)

JOHNS, Prof David John; CBE (1998); *b* 29 April 1931; *Educ* St Brendan's Coll Bristol, Univ of Bristol (BSc, MSc), Loughborough Univ of Technol (PhD, DSc); *Career* student apprentice (later tech offr section ldr) Br Aeroplane Co Ltd 1949–57, sr tech offr Sir W G Armstrong Whitworth A/C Ltd 1957–58; lectr Cranfield Coll of Aeronautics 1958–63; Loughborough Univ of Technol 1964–83: reader, prof, head of Dept of Tport Technol, dean of Sch of Engrg, sr pro-vice-chllr; fndn dir City Poly Hong Kong 1983–89; vice-chllr and princ Univ of Bradford 1989–98; pt/t exec dir Milton Keynes & N Bucks Lifelong Learning Partnership 1998–2000; memb: Aeronautical Res Cncl Dynamics Ctee 1970–80 (later chm), Cncl Inst of Acoustics 1979–83 (later vice-pres and pres-elect), Environmental Pollution Advsy Ctee Hong Kong 1984–89 (later chm), Vocational Trg Cncl (Hong Kong) 1984–89, Hong Kong Productivity Cncl 1984–89, Cncl Hong Kong Inst of Engrs 1984–89, Cncl Royal Acad of Engrg 1993–96, Funding Agency for Schools 1997–99, Br Bd of Agrément 1997–2006, Regl Ctee FEFC 1996–99; chm: Univs Assoc for Continuing Educn 1990–94, Prescription Pricing Authy 1998–2001, Strategic Health Authy (N and E Yorks and N Lincs) 2002–06, Genetics and Insurance Ctee 2002–; cmmr CWealth Scholarships Cmmn 2002–; CEng 1968, FRAeS 1969, FHKIE 1984, FAeSI 1986, FREng 1990; *Books* Thermal Stress Analyses (1965); *Recreations* theatre, bridge, music, art appreciation; *Clubs* RAF, Hong Kong, Hong Kong Jockey; *Style*— Prof David Johns, CBE, FREng, DSc; ✉ tel and fax 01423 502561, mobile 07703 621930, e-mail david@johnshg1.fsnet.co.uk

JOHNS, Derek; s of Oliver Johns, and Joan Johns; *Educ* Stratford GS Biggleswade; *Career* ed Random House NY 1983–86, publishing dir Harrap 1986–88, md The Bodley Head 1988–89, md Granta 1990–92, dir and literary agent A P Watt Ltd 1992– (jt md 1996–); pres Assoc of Authors 2003–06; tstee PEN; *Books* The Beatrice Mystery (1980), Wintering (2007); *Recreations* reading, music, walking; *Clubs* Soho House; *Style*— Derek Johns, Esq; ✉ A P Watt Ltd, 20 John Street, London WC1N 2DR (tel 020 7405 6774, fax 020 7831 2154, e-mail djohns@apwatt.co.uk)

JOHNS, Michael Alan; CB (2000); s of John William Johns, of Sevenoaks, Kent, and Kathleen Eva, *née* Hummerston (d 1982); *b* 20 July 1946; *Educ* Judd Sch Tonbridge, Queens' Coll Cambridge (MA); *Career* Inland Revenue 1967–79, Central Policy Review Staff 1979–80, Inland Revenue 1980–84, seconded Orion Royal Bank 1985; Inland Revenue: joined 1986, dir Business Ops Div 1993–97, chief exec Valuation Office Agency and cmmr of Inland Revenue 1997–; *Recreations* skiing, teaching (adults), moral philosophy; *Style*— Michael Johns, Esq, CB; ✉ Valuation Office Agency, New Court, Carey Street, London WC2A 2JE

JOHNS, Michael Charles; s of Arthur Charles Johns (d 1998), of Crediton, Devon, and Margaret Mary Johns (d 1986); *b* 20 December 1947; *Educ* Tiffin Sch, St Edmund Hall Oxford (BA, Cross-Country blue 1967 and 1968), Law Soc Finals (New Inn prize); *m* Sept 1970, Lucy Mary; 2 da (Kathryn Helen b 23 Oct 1973, Clare Louise b 16 April 1976); *Career* ptnr: Withers 1974–87 (joined 1970), Ashurst 1987–; *Style*— Michael Johns, Esq; ✉ Ashurst, Broadwalk House, 5 Appold Street, London EC2 (tel 020 7638 1111, fax 020 7638 1112, e-mail michael.johns@ashurst.com)

JOHNS, Michael Stephen Mackelcan; s of Jack Elliott Mackelcan Johns (d 1968), of Radlett, Herts, and Janet, *née* Price (d 1999); *b* 18 October 1943; *Educ* Marlborough; *m* 1, 20 Sept 1968 (m dis 1975), Joanna Turner, *née* Gilligan; 2 s (Alexander b 16 Sept 1971, Toby b 1 Sept 1973); m 2, 10 March 1979, Gillian, da of Geoffrey Duckett White (d 2004), of Perth, Western Aust; 1 da (Sophie b 2 Feb 1984); *Career* slr; sr ptnr K&L Gates (formerly Nicholson Graham & Jones) 2003– (ptnr 1973–); memb Law Soc, MInstD; *Recreations* golf, cricket, gardening, theatre; *Clubs* MCC, St George's Hill Golf, Royal Sydney Golf Australia; *Style*— Michael Johns, Esq; ✉ 22 Bowerdean Street, London SW6 3TW (tel 020 7731 7607); 110 Cannon Street, London EC4N 6AR (tel 020 7648 9000, fax 020 7648 9001, e-mail michael.johns@klgates.com)

JOHNS, Milton; né John Robert Milton; s of Arthur Wallace Milton (d 1956), and Olive Grace, *née* Trobridge (d 1968); *b* 13 May 1938; *Educ* Merrywood GS Bristol, Bristol Old Vic Theatre Sch; *m* 1961, Bella, da of Arthur Buckley Horsfield; 1 da (Leah b 1964), 1 s (Simeon Robert b 1969); *Career* actor; newspaper columnist The Stage 1992–95; Br Actors Equity: memb Cncl 1972–98, memb Exec 1972–92, hon treas 1975–92, hon life memb 2000; dir Equity Tst Fund 1988– (vice-chm 1995–), chm Acting Accreditation Bd Nat Cncl for Drama Trg 1991–95; vice-pres The Actors' Benevolent Fund 2003 (memb Exec Cncl 1992–, hon treas 1997–); pt/t racecourse announcer and auctioneer; *Theatre* various repertory incl: Sheffield, Coventry, Leicester and Farnham (also dir); various seasons incl: Bristol Old Vic 1961–62, Chichester Festival Theatre and Royal Exchange Manchester; credits incl: She Stoops to Conquer (debut, Theatre Royal Bristol) 1960, Swiss Cheese in Mother Courage 1961, Czar Alexander II in War and Peace (West End debut, Old Vic and Phoenix) 1962, Peter Shirley in Major Barbara (RSC, Aldwych) 1970, The Woman in Black (Fortune) 1991; *Television* Shop at Sly Corner (debut, BBC) 1960; began by playing various unsavoury characters in detective series; roles since incl: Parker in Pickwick Papers (BBC), William Potter in Death of a Ghost (BBC), Kistiacowski in Oppenheimer (BBC), Rev Horsley in Horseman Riding By (BBC), Griffiths in The Florence Bravo Mystery (BBC), Cassidy in Murphy's Mob (Central), Fred Mitchell in South Riding (Yorkshire), Arnold Haithwaite in The Intruder (Granada), Brendan Scott in Coronation Street (Granada), Adolf Eichmann in War and Remembrance (USA), Ernest Gilles in Born and Bred (BBC); *Recreations* horse racing, reading, music, cricket (full memb Assoc of Cricket Umpires); *Clubs* Garrick, Lord's Taverners, MCC; *Style*— Milton Johns, Esq; ✉ c/o Hilda Physick Agency, 78 Temple Sheen Road, London SW14 7RR (tel 020 8876 0073)

JOHNS, Peter Andrew; s of Lt John Francis, DSC, RNVR, of Porthcawl, Mid Glamorgan, and Megan, *née* Isaac; *b* 31 December 1947; *Educ* Bridgend GS, UCL (BSc); *m* 12 Aug 1985, Rosanne Helen Josephine, da of Capt William John Howard Slayter, RA, of Oxted, Surrey; 3 s (Jack b 1987, Robert b 1989, Harry b 1994), 1 da (Megan b 1996); *Career* md and head of banking NM Rothschild & Sons Ltd 2006– (dir 1987–), memb Mgmnt Ctee Rothschild Gp 2006–; dir Five Arrows Finance Ltd 1996–; memb Gen Assembly Univ of Manchester 2004–, chm of govrs Terra Nova Sch 2005–; ACIB 1975; *Recreations* golf, history, books; *Clubs* Alderley Edge Golf; *Style*— Peter Johns, Esq; ✉ NM Rothschild & Sons Ltd, New Court, St Swithin's Lane, London EC4P 4DU (tel 020 7280 5000, fax 020 7280 5560, e-mail peter.johns@rothschild.co.uk)

JOHNS, Prof Richard Bell; s of Charles Walter Johns (d 1962), and Cynthia, *née* Gamble (d 1986); *b* 10 August 1929; *Educ* St Paul's, Guy's Hosp London (LDSRCS, PhD); *m* 1954, Pamela Marie, da of Charles Henry Thurgood; 3 da (Susan b 1957, Katharine b 1958, Lucy b 1963), 2 s (Nicholas b 1961, Timothy b 1965); *Career* own NHS dental practice 1956–58; Guy's Hosp: lectr 1969–74, sr lectr 1974–79, reader 1979–81; Univ of Sheffield: prof of restorative dentistry 1981–93 (emeritus prof 1993), dean of dental studies Sch of Clinical Dentistry 1984–88; dir Inst for Dental Implants 1991–2003; memb Advsy Bd Denplan 1988–96, memb GDC 1989–94; RSM: pres Odontological Section 1994–95 (hon life memb), memb Cncl and tstee 1998–2003, hon treas 1999–2003; tstee Dental Implant Research Tst 1988–2002; ed Jl of the Br Endodontic Soc 1973–78; external examiner: Univs of Surrey, Tulane, Manchester, London, Dundee, Cork, Bristol, Liverpool, Edinburgh, Leeds, Birmingham and Hong Kong; ind rep to Standards Ctee Winchester City Cncl 2003–; hon life memb: Br Endodontic Soc (past pres), Br Soc for Restorative Dentistry (past pres), Acad of Osseointegration (USA), Euro Assoc of Osseointegration, BDA; *Books* contrib chapters: The Scientific Foundation of Dentistry (1976), General Dental Practice (1986), Dental Care for the Elderly (1986), A Companion to Dental Studies

(1986), The Brånemark Osseointegrated Implant (1989), The Osseointegration Book (2005); *Clubs* Royal Society of Medicine; *Style—* Prof Richard Johns; ✉ Manaccan, St Cross Road, Winchester SO23 9RX (tel 01962 622607, e-mail richard.johns@ntlworld.com)

JOHNS, Air Chief Marshal Sir Richard Edward; GCB (1997, KCB 1994, CB 1991), CBE (1984, OBE 1977), LVO (1972); s of late Lt-Col Herbert Edward Johns, of Emsworth, Hants, and Marjory Harley, *née* Everett; *b* 28 July 1939; *Educ* Portsmouth GS, RAF Coll Cranwell; *m* 23 Oct 1965, Elizabeth Naomi Anne, *née* Manning; 1 s, 2 da; *Career* cmmnd 1959; RAF, No 64 (F) Sqdn 1960–63, No 1417 (FR) Flt Aden 1965–67, flying instr duties 1968–71 (including tuition of HRH The Prince of Wales 1970–71), Staff Coll 1972, PSO/AOC in C NEAF 1973, No 3 (F) Sqdn as CO 1975–77, MOD Air Staff 1978–81, Station Cdr and Harrier Force Cdr RAF Gütersloh 1982–84, ADC to HM the Queen 1983–84, RCDS 1985, SASO HQ RAF Germany 1986–88, SASO HQ Strike Cmd 1989–91 (incl Dir of Operations for Op Granby at JHQ High Wycombe), AOC No 1 Gp 1991–93, COS/Dep C-in-C HQ Strike Cmd 1993–94, AOC-in-C Strike Cmd 1994, C-in-C Allied Forces Northwestern Europe 1994–97, Chief of Air Staff and Air ADC to HM The Queen 1997–2000; Hon Col 73 Engr Regt (V) 1994–2002, Hon Air Cdre RAF Regt 2001–; chm of tstees RAF Museum 2001–, tstee Prince Philip Tst 2001–; pres: Windsor Festival 2001–, Windsor and Eton Choral Soc 2001–, Royal Windsor Rose and Horticultural Soc 2001–; vice-pres Royal Windsor Horse Show 2001–; Constable and Governor of Windsor Castle 2000–; pres Hearing Dogs for Deaf People 2004–; Freeman City of London 1999, Liveryman GAPAN 1999; FRAeS 1997; *Recreations* military history, rugby, cricket, equitation; *Clubs* RAF; *Style—* Air Chief Marshal Sir Richard Johns, GCB, CBE, LVO, RAF; ✉ Norman Tower, Windsor Castle, Berkshire SL4 1NJ (tel 01753 868286)

JOHNSON, Rt Hon Alan Arthur; PC (2003), MP; s of Stephen Arthur Johnson and Lillian May Johnson; *b* 17 May 1950; *Educ* Sloane GS Chelsea; *m* 1 (m dis), Judith Elizabeth, *née* Cox; 1 s, 2 da; m 2, 1991, Laura Jane, *née* Patient; 1 s; *Career* postman 1968; UCW: branch official 1976, memb Exec Cncl 1981, nat offr 1987–93, gen sec 1993–95; jt gen sec Communication Workers Union (following merger with Nat Communication Union) 1995–97; MP (Lab) Hull West and Hessle 1997–; PPS to: fin sec to Treasury 1997–99, Paymaster General 1999; min for competitiveness DTI 1999–2001, min of state for Employment Relations, Industry and Regions 2001–03, min of state for Lifelong Learning, Further and Higher Educn 2003–04, sec of state for Work and Pensions 2004–05, sec of state for trade and industry 2005–06, sec of state for educn 2006–07, sec of state for health 2007–; memb: TUC Gen Cncl 1993–95, Nat Exec Lab Pty 1995–97, Postal, Telegraph & Telephone Int World Exec 1993–97; dir Unity Trust Bank plc 1992–97; govr Ruskin Coll 1991–97; Duke of Edinburgh Cwlth Study Conf 1992; *Recreations* music, tennis, reading, cooking, football, radio; *Style—* The Rt Hon Alan Johnson, MP; ✉ House of Commons, London SW1A 0AA (tel 020 7219 3000)

JOHNSON, Alan Michael Borthwick; s of Dennis Daniel Borthwick Johnson, OBE (d 1976), of Calderstones, Liverpool, and Nora, *née* MacLeod (d 1992); *b* 7 June 1944; *Educ* Liverpool Coll 1951–63, CCC Oxford (MA); *Career* called to the Bar Middle Temple (Harmsworth scholar) 1971, ad eundem Gray's Inn 1973; memb Criminal Bar Assoc; *Clubs* Oxford Society; *Style—* Alan Johnson, Esq; ✉ 1 Farm Place, London W8 7SX; 1 Gray's Inn Square, Gray's Inn, London WC1R 5AA (tel 020 7405 8946/8, fax 020 7405 1617, e-mail ajohnson@1gis.law.co.uk)

JOHNSON, Prof Anne Mandall; da of Dr Gordon Trevor Johnson (d 1979), of Hale, Cheshire, and Dr Helen Margaret Johnson, *née* Noble; *b* 30 January 1954; *Educ* Cheltenham Ladies' Coll, Newnham Coll Cambridge (MA), Univ of Newcastle upon Tyne (MB BS, MD), LSHTM (MSc); *m* 1996, Dr John Martin Watson, s of Robert Watson; 1 s (Oliver Mandall b 3 Aug 1993), 1 da (Sophie Mandall b 23 July 1995); *Career* various hosp posts and vocational trg in gen practice 1978–83, registrar in community med NE Thames Regnl HA 1983–84, lectr Middx Hosp Med Sch 1985–88; UCL Med Sch: sr lectr in epidemiology 1988–94, hon conslt in public health med 1998–, reader in epidemiology 1994–96; Royal Free and UCL Med Sch: prof of epidemiology 1996–, head Dept of Primary Care and Population Sciences 2002–; assoc Newnham Coll Cambridge 1996–2006, visiting prof LSHTM 1999–2006; dep chair Infection and Immunity Bd MRC 2004–06; non-exec dir Whittington Hosp NHS Tst 2005–; memb: Cncl Inst of Drug Dependency 1990–98, Physiological Med and Infections Bd MRC 2001–04, Specialist Advsy Ctee of Antimicrobial Resistance Dept of Health 2002–; ed AIDS 1994–2000; Royal Instn Australian science scholar 1971, Terrence Higgins Tst Award for social research in HIV 2002; FFPH 1993, FMedSci 2001, FRCGP 2002 (MRCGP 1982), FRCP 2004 (MRCP 1998); *Publications* Sexual Attitudes and Lifestyles (1994); numerous scientific papers on HIV, sexually transmitted infections and infectious diseases; *Recreations* singing; *Style—* Prof Anne Johnson; ✉ Department of Primary Care and Population Sciences, UCL Hampstead Campus, Rowland Hill Street, London NW3 2PF (tel 020 7472 6748, e-mail a.johnson@pcps.ucl.ac.uk)

JOHNSON, Dr (James) Barry; s of James Johnson, of Myerscough, Lancs, and Dorothea, *née* Tomlinson; *b* 2 June 1945; *Educ* Greaves Secdy Modern, Kirkham GS, Univ of Liverpool (BVSc); *m* 25 July 1976, Carolyn Ann, da of Tony Battersby; 6 s (John Robert James b 11 May 1974, David Barry b 4 Sept 1977, Michael Thomas b 11 Feb 1979, Andrew Peter b 30 July 1980, Paul Richard b 8 Dec 1981, Steven Tony b 16 July 1986); *Career* in vet practice: Kirkham Lancs 1969–71, Gloucester 1971–73, Myerscough then Goosnargh Lancs 1974– (currently sr ptnr); lectr Myerscough Coll 1974–2003; memb Cncl RCVS 1985–97 and 2000– (pres 1993–94); pres: Lancs Vet Assoc 1983, Farmers' Club, Kirkham GS Old Boys' 1999; govr Kirkham GS 1996, memb Cncl Animal Health Tst 1994; Freeman: City of Lancaster, City of London 1994; Hon DVSc Univ of Liverpool 1994; memb BVA, MRCVS; *Recreations* sports supporter, golf; *Clubs* Rotary; *Style—* Dr Barry Johnson; ✉ Brook House, Bilsborrow, Preston, Lancashire PR3 0RD (tel 01995 640952); J B Johnson and Partners, Oakhill Veterinary Centre, Langley Lane, Goosnargh, Preston, Lancashire PR2 2JQ (tel 01772 861300, fax 01772 862349, e-mail jbjohnson@talk21.com)

JOHNSON, (Alexander) Boris de Pfeffel; MP; s of Stanley Patrick Johnson, of Nethercote, Winsford, Minehead, Somerset, and Charlotte Mary Offlow, *née* Fawcett; *b* 19 June 1964, NY; *Educ* Eton, Balliol Coll Oxford (Brackenbury scholar, BA); *m* 1993, Marina, da of Charles Wheeler; 2 s, 2 da; *Career* reporter; LEK Management Consultants 1987; trainee reporter The Times 1987, reporter Wolverhampton Express & Star 1988; The Daily Telegraph: leader writer 1988, Euro community corr Brussels 1989–94, asst ed 1994–99, currently weekly columnist; ed The Spectator 1999–2005; MP (Cons) Henley 2001–; vice-chm (i/c campaigning) Cons Pty 2003–04, shadow min for arts 2004, shadow spokesman for higher educn 2005–; appearances on radio and TV; Political Commentator of the Year What The Papers Say Awards 1998, Nat Journalist of the Year Pagan Fedn of GB 1998, Eds' Ed of the Year 2003, Columnist of the Year British Press Awards 2004, Columnist of the Year What The Papers Say Awards 2005; *Books* The Oxford Myth (contrib, 1988), Friends, Voters and Countrymen (2001), Lend Me Your Ears (2003), Seventy Two Virgins (2004), The Dream of Rome (2006), Have I Got Views For You (2006); *Recreations* painting; *Style—* Boris Johnson, Esq, MP; ✉ House of Commons, London SW1A 0AA

JOHNSON, Prof Brian Frederick Gilbert; *b* 11 September 1938; *Educ* Univ of Nottingham (BSc, PhD), Univ of Cambridge (MA); *m*; 2 c; *Career* post-doctoral fell: MIT 1963–64, Univ of Manchester 1964–65; lectr in chemistry Univ of Manchester 1965–67, lectr UCL 1967–70, reader in inorganic chemistry Univ of Cambridge 1978–90 (lectr 1970–78); Fitzwilliam Coll Cambridge: fell 1970–90, steward 1972–77, asst dir of studies in chemistry 1975–90, fndn lectr 1984, dean 1987–90, pres 1989–90, acting master 1989–90, master 1999–; head Dept of Chemistry and Crum Brown chair of inorganic chemistry Univ of Edinburgh 1991–95, prof Dept of Chemistry and head of Inorganic Sector Univ of Cambridge 1995–; visiting prof: Simon Fraser Univ BC 1982, Univ of Wisconsin USA 1985, Texas A&M Univ USA 1986; RSC: Corday-Morgan medal and prize 1976, Chemistry and Electrochemistry of Transition Metals award 1982; memb RSC: Dalton Cncl 1984–87 and 1994–99 (pres 1997–99), Working Party 2000, Exempting Qualifications Panel; EPSRC: Cncl memb 1994–98, memb Tech Opportunities Panel 1994–98, chm PUSET; memb: Cncl of Senate Univ of Cambridge, Senate Univ of Edinburgh; chm Sch of Physical Scis 1999–2002; fell Academia Europaea 1994; FRS 1991, FRSC 1991, FRSE 1992; *Publications* Transition Metal Clusters (1982), author of over 1000 papers and review articles; *Style—* Prof Brian Johnson, FRS, FRSE; ✉ University of Cambridge, Department of Chemistry, Lensfield Road, Cambridge CB2 1EW (tel 01223 336337)

JOHNSON, Brian Joseph; s of Joseph Johnson, of Billinge, nr Wigan, and Margary, *née* Nichson; *b* 12 October 1953; *Educ* Grange Park Tech Sch St Helens, Univ of Manchester Sch of Architecture (BA, BArch); *m* 1 Sept 1979, Marie, da of John O'Brien; 1 da (Emma b 19 Sept 1986); *Career* student architect Gearey Blair Weed Dickenson Partners Liverpool 1976–77, architect Weightman and Bullen Partnership Liverpool 1979–81; Holford Associates 1982–: assoc 1984–88, salaried ptnr 1988–92, equity ptnr (i/c educnl sector) 1992–1999, ptnr Abbey Holford (following merger of Holford Associates and Abbey Hawson Rowe) 1999–2002, dir AEDAS AHR Architects Ltd (formerly Abbey Holford) 2002–; Civic Tst Award (for Lincoln House Manchester) 1987; memb ARUCK, RIBA; *Recreations* travel, squash, skiing; *Style—* Brian Johnson, Esq; ✉ Beacon Cottage, 17 Beacon Road, Billinge, Wigan, Lancashire WN5 7HE (tel 01744 601528); Abbey Holford Rowe, Sunlight House, Quay Street, Manchester M3 3JZ (tel 0161 828 7900, fax 0161 828 9730, mobile 0385 747328, e-mail brian.johnson@ahr.co.uk)

JOHNSON, Brian Michael; s of Frederick William Johnson, of Woking, and Helen Josephine, *née* Whitmarsh; *b* 1 May 1939; *Educ* Finchley GS, Univ of Sheffield (BEng); *m* 1, 24 Aug 1963 (m dis 1973), Jennifer Ann, da of Thomas Kenneth Derham (d 1989), of Earsham Hall, Norfolk; 3 s (Arawn b 1964, Jess b 1971, James b 1973), 2 da (Fiona b 1965, Emily b 1974); m 2, 31 March 1973, Maureen Patricia, *née* Haines (d 1981); m 3, 10 July 1982, Diana Victoria, *née* Armstrong; *Career* trainee engr Balfour Beatty & Co Ltd 1961–64, site agent Costain Civil Engrg 1964–70, contracts mangr Tilbury Gp 1970–73, chm and md Anglo Dutch Dredging Co Ltd 1973–; papers on engrg subjects and contract law; memb Central Dredging Assoc 1980–, assoc memb Hydraulics Res 1985–, chm Fedn of Dredging Contractors 1989–90 (memb 1973–, chm 1981–82 and 1996–97), memb Code of Practice Maritime Structures BSI (chm 1989–90); author papers on engrg subjects and contract law; chm Central Dredging Assoc 2001–2003 (memb 1990–, main Bd memb Europe 2001–); CEng 1967, FICE 1988 (MICE 1967); *Recreations* music, violin (Windsor & Maidenhead Symphony Orch), art-antiques, classic cars, historic rallying, tennis, cycling; *Clubs* Athenaeum; *Style—* Brian Johnson, Esq; ✉ Sunrise, Harvest Hill, Bourne End, Buckinghamshire SL8 5JJ

JOHNSON, Carlton (Carl); s of Ronald James Johnson (d 1990), and Margaret Ruth, *née* Vincent; *b* 3 November 1958; *Educ* Barton Peveril Coll Eastleigh Hampshire, Keble Coll Oxford (BA); *m* 29 Oct 1990, Linda Suzette; 4 s (Michael James b 16 Jan 1991, Christian Charles b 26 March 1993, Rory Alexander b 1 May 1995, Callum Luke b 1 Nov 1997); *Career* account exec Ogilvy & Mather advtg agency 1981–83, account mangr then dir Publicis 1983–85, account dir Gold Greenlees Trott 1985–88 (assoc bd dir 1987, bd dir 1988), gp md Simons Palmer Clemmow Johnson 1995–97 (md 1988–95), md TBWA Simons Palmer (following merger) 1997–98, chief exec TBWA GGT Simons Palmer (following merger) 1998–99, pres TBWA/Chiat/Day NY 1999–2002, chief operating officer TBWA Worldwide 2001–03; *Recreations* music, books, cinema, sport; *Style—* Carl Johnson, Esq

JOHNSON, Daniel Benedict; s of Paul Bede Johnson, of London, and Marigold E G Hunt, MBE; *b* 26 August 1957; *Educ* Langley GS, Magdalen Coll Oxford (BA); *m* 1988, Sarah Cynthia Charlotte, da of J W M Thompson, CBE; 2 s (Tycho b 1990, Leo b 1994), 2 da (Edith b 1992, Agatha b 1997); *Career* research student Peterhouse Cambridge 1978–81, Shakespeare scholar Berlin 1979–80, teaching asst in German history QMC London 1982–84, dir of pubns Centre for Policy Studies 1983–84; Daily Telegraph: leader writer 1986–87, Bonn corr 1987–89, Eastern Europe corr 1989–90, assoc ed 1998–2005; The Times: leader writer 1990–91, literary ed 1992–96, asst ed (comment) 1996–98; columnist New York Sun 2005–; contrib to pubns incl: The New Yorker, New Criterion, Commentary, American Spectator, TLS, Literary Review, Prospect, Wall St Jl; *Books* German Neo-Liberals and the Social Market Economy (co-ed, 1989), Death In Venice (Thomas Mann, introduction 1991), Collected Stories (introduction, 2001); *Recreations* chess; *Style—* Daniel Johnson, Esq; ✉ 46 Aldbourne Road, London W12 0LN (tel 020 8743 4995, e-mail danbjohn@aol.com)

JOHNSON, Darren; AM; s of Alan Johnson, and Joyce Reynolds, *née* Abram; *Educ* Goldsmiths Coll London (BA); *Career* memb Green Pty 1987– (princ speaker 2001–03), election co-ordinator on Nat Exec 1993–95, memb London Assembly GLA (Green) London (list) 2000–, cncllr (Green) London Borough of Lewisham 2002–, chair London Assembly Environment Ctee 2004–; *Recreations* walking, cycling; *Style—* Cllr Darren Johnson, Esq, AM

JOHNSON, David Bryan; s of Bernard Johnson, and Audrey, *née* Warrender; *b* 27 February 1957; *Educ* John Hunt Comp Sch Telford, Walker Tech Coll, Univ of Sheffield (BA); *m* Gillian; 1 s (Martyn b 4 Aug 1986); *Career* hosp porter Lodge Moor Hosp Sheffield 1978–79, housing offr Manchester City Cncl 1979–80, NHS Mgmnt Trg Scheme 1980–83 (asst hosp admin Birch Hill Hosp Rochdale), asst then dep hosp admin Manchester Royal Infirmary 1983–85, unit gen mangr Acute and Maternity Servs Pontefract HA 1985–90; chief exec: St James's Univ Hosp NHS Tst 1992–95 (dir of ops 1990–92, dep chief exec 1991–92), St James's and Seacroft Univ Hosps NHS Tst (following merger) 1995–98, Leeds Teaching Hosps NHS Tst 1998–2002, N and E Yorks and N Lincs Strategic HA 2002–07, ret; MHSM; *Recreations* golf, guitar, cycling, music, travel; *Style—* David B Johnson, Esq

JOHNSON, David Edward Dunn; DL (Staffs 1986); s of Frederick Shepard Johnson, CBE (d 1996), of Trentham, Staffs, and Barbara Crocker, *née* Dunn (d 1991); *b* 8 September 1937, Trentham, Staffs; *Educ* Stowe; *m* 22 May 1982, Virginia Wendy Hadden, *née* Todd; 1 da (Victoria Clare b 4 Nov 1972); *Career* cmmnd 7 Queen's Own Hussars Nat Serv 1956–58; joined family business Johnson Bros (later part of Wedgwood Gp) 1958 (rising to prodn dir 1968), md Midwinter Ltd 1975 (concurrently md: J&G Meakin 1976, Johnson Bros 1977), jt md Earthenware Div Wedgwood 1980, chm and owner Steelite Int plc (formerly Royal Doulton hotelware business) 1983–2002; chm of tstees Br Pottery Manufacturers' Fedn 1987–, pres Br Pottery Manufacturers' Fedn Club 1999–2002; chm: Willoughbridge Garden Tst 1986–99, Groundwork Stoke on Trent 1995–2005, Ptnrs Assuring a Safer Staffs 1999–2000, Fundraising Ctee for 30th Anniversary Douglas Macmillan Hospice 2001; High Sheriff Staffs 1999–2000; *Style—* David E D Johnson, Esq, DL; ✉ 4th Floor, Churchill House, 47 Regent Road, Stoke-on-Trent ST1 3RQ (tel 01782 219903, fax 01782 219912, e-mail dedj@chartleyestates.co.uk)

JOHNSON, David Gordon; s of Sidney Burnup Johnson, of Newcastle upon Tyne, and Pearl, *née* Jenkinson; *b* 13 December 1951; *Educ* Dame Allan's Boys' Sch Newcastle upon Tyne, Univ of Manchester (BSc); *m* 1 (m dis 1986), Lesley Annis Johnson; 2 s (James

Scott b 1981, Mark David b 1983); m 2, Judith Ann, da of Gerald Arthur Vernon Leaf, of Leeds; 2 s (Edward Matthew b 1989, William Charles b 1992), 1 da (Jessica Aimée b 1991); *Career* ptnr Duncan C Fraser and Co 1977, dir Mercer Human Resource Consulting Ltd 1986–2004; pres Soc of Pension Conslts 1990–92; Freeman: City of London 1989, Worshipful Co of Actuaries 1989, Guild of Air Pilots and Navigators 1991; FIA 1976; *Recreations* private aviation, motor racing, golf; *Clubs* Reform; *Style*— David G Johnson, Esq; ✉ Braybourne End, Kennel Lane, Kinsbourne Green, Harpenden, Hertfordshire AL5 3PZ

JOHNSON, David Leonard; s of Richard Lewis Johnson, of Las Palmas, Canary Islands, and Olive Mary, *née* Bellamy; *b* 2 February 1956; *Educ* Wellington, Univ of Durham; *m* 13 Dec 1986, Susan, da of James Fitzjohn, of Worksop, Notts; 1 s (Edward James b 1988), 2 da (Caroline Francesca b 1990, Cordelia Sarah b 1996); *Career* admitted slr 1981; Rowe & Maw 1979–87, ptnr D J Freeman (latterly Kendall Freeman) 1988–2006, ptnr Boodle Hatfield 2006–; memb: Law Soc, Soc for Construction Law, Adjudication Soc, City of London Law Soc; FCIArb; *Style*— David Johnson, Esq; ✉ Boodle Hatfield, 89 New Bond Street, London W1S 1DA (tel 020 7629 7411, e-mail djohnson@boodlehatfield.com)

JOHNSON, Diana; MP; da of late Eric Johnson, and Ruth Johnson; *b* 25 July 1966; *Educ* Northwich Co GS for Girls, Sir John Deane's Sixth Form Coll Cheshire, QMC (LLB), Cncl for Legal Educn; *Career* vol/locum lawyer Tower Hamlets Law Centre 1991–94, employment, immigration and educn lawyer N Lewisham Law Centre 1995–99, employment lawyer Paddington Law Centre 1999–2002; cncllr London Borough of Tower Hamlets 1994–2002 (chair Social Services 1997–2000, chair Social Services and Health Scrutiny Panel 2000–02), memb London Assembly (Lab) 2003–2004, MP (Lab) Hull N 2005– (Parly candidate (Lab) Brentwood and Ongar 2001); memb Public Accounts Select Ctee 2005, PPS to Rt Hon Stephen Timms, MP 2005–; legal visiting memb Mental Health Act Cmmn 1995–98; non-exec dir Tower Hamlets Primary Care Tst 2001–04, memb Met Police Authy 2003–04; nat offr FDA Trade Union 2002–03; memb: Co-operative Pty, Lab Women's Network, TGWU, Unison, Fawcett Soc, Amnesty Int, Fabian Soc; *Recreations* cinema, dog walking, theatre; *Style*— Ms Diana Johnson, MP; ✉ House of Commons, London SW1A 0AA (tel 020 7219 5647, fax 020 7219 0959, e-mail johnsond@parliament.uk, website www.dianajohnson.labour.co.uk),Constituency Office, Unit 8, Hull Business Centre, Guildhall Road, Hull HU1 1HJ (tel 01482 319135, fax 01482 319137)

JOHNSON, Digby Mark; s of Raymond William Johnson (d 2005), and Ella Margaret, *née* Blanksby; *b* 17 April 1960, Chesterfield, Derbys; *Educ* Tapton Mt Sch for the Blind, Tapton Comp Sch Sheffield, Univ of Cambridge (MA); *children* 1 da (Ursula Grace Downes b 1 Feb 1994), 1 s (Alfred Gregory Downes b 2 June 1996); *Career* slr; trainee slr Emsley Collins 1982–84, asst slr, slr then ptnr Truman & Appleby 1984–90, founding ptnr Johnson Partnership 1990–; nat chm Trainee Slrs Gp Law Soc 1982–84; tstee Rothwell Lab Club; involved in Royal Soc for the Blind; Notts Law Soc Slr of the Year 2003–04; memb Notts Law Soc 1984–; *Recreations* Nottingham Forest FC, Derbys CCC, wine of any colour; *Clubs* Victoria (Nottingham), Oxford & Cambridge; *Style*— Digby Johnson, Esq; ✉ Cherry Tree House, 6 Caythorpe Road, Lowdham, Nottinghamshire NG14 7EA (tel 07971 159003); The Johnson Partnership, Cannon Court Yard, Long Row, Nottingham NG1 6JE (tel 0115 941 9141, fax 0115 947 0178, e-mail mail@thejohnsonpartnership.co.uk)

JOHNSON, Dr Donald Arthur Wheatley; s of Arthur Edwin Johnson (d 1982), of London, and Ellen Victoria, *née* Wheatley (d 1983); *b* 18 April 1934; *Educ* Nat Univ of Ireland (MD), Univ of Manchester (MSC, DPM), Univ of London (DPM); *m* 3 Aug 1957, Dr Sheila MacDonald Johnson, da of Dr Hector MacDonald Walker (d 1969), of Manchester and Banff Scotland; 2 s (Ian James b 23 Nov 1960, Angus Howard b 9 June 1964); *Career* Capt RAMC 1960–63; lectr Univ of Manchester 1969–, res fell Oxford; conslt psychiatrist: N Manchester Gen Hosp 1971–74, Univ Hosp of S Manchester 1974–; magistrate in Manchester 1977–88, chm NW Div RCPsych 1986–90 (past sec, convener and exec memb), regnl advsr in psychiatry N W Health Authy 1987–, advsr Dept of Health, chm N W Mental Health Advsy Ctee, clinical dir Dept of Psychiatry Univ Hosp of S Manchester, former chm of N Manchester Med Soc, former sec and pres Psychiatry Section Manchester Med Soc, fndr memb Br Assoc for Psychopharmacology; DRCOG 1963, FRCPsych 1977 (MRCPsych 1972); *Books* New Perspectives in Treatment of Schizophrenia (1985), Causes and Management of Depression in Schizophrenia (1985), Maintenance Treatment of Chronic Schizophrenia (1989), Modern Trends in the Treatment of Schizophrenia (1991); *Recreations* walking, shooting, fishing; *Clubs* Lancashire CCC, Mere Golf and Country; *Style*— Dr Donald Johnson; ✉ Lyndhurst, Warrington Road, Mere, Cheshire WA16 0TE (tel 01565 830 188); Department of Psychiatry, University Hospital of South Manchester, West Didsbury, Manchester M20 8LR (tel 0161 445 8111)

JOHNSON, Emma Louise; MBE (1996); da of Roger George Johnson, of Petts Wood, Kent, and Mary, *née* Froud; *b* 20 May 1966; *Educ* Newstead Wood Sch, Sevenoaks Sch, Pembroke Coll Cambridge; *m* 1997, Christopher West; 1 da (Georgina Mary West); *Career* clarinettist and conductor; visiting prof of clarinet Royal Coll of Music 1997–2002; debuts: London (Barbican Centre) 1985, Austria (Konzerthaus Vienna) 1985, France (Montpellier Festival with the Polish Chamber Orch) 1986, Africa (tour of Zimbabwe) 1988, USA (Newport Festival) 1989, Tokyo 1990, USSR 1990, Australia 1996; tours with: Royal Philharmonic Orch, Bournemouth Sinfonietta, English Chamber Orch; concerts with Royal Liverpool Philharmonic, City of London Sinfonia, Halle, New Japan Philharmonic; Netherlands Radio Symphony, Warsaw Sinfonia (with Sir Yehudi Menuhin), LSO, London Mozart Players, Schubert Festival Hohenems (with Arleen Auger); various TV appearances; composed Variations on a Hungarian Folk Tune (for solo clarinet) 1988; hon fell Pembroke Coll Cambridge 1999; *Recordings* for ASV: Mozart Clarinet Concerto with the Eng Chamber Orch under Leppard 1985, Crusell Clarinet Concerto number 2, Weber, Baermann, Rossini with the Eng Chamber Orch with Eco/Groves 1986, Weber Clarinet Concerto number 1, Crusell, Tartini, Debussy with the Eng Chamber Orch under Tortelier 1987, La Clarinette Française 1988, Weber Concerto no 2, Crusell Concerto no 3, Spohr Concerto no 1 with Eco/Schwartz, A Clarinet Celebration 1990, Emma Johnson plays Weber 1991, Crusell Concerto no 1, Krommer Concerto, Kozeluh Concerto with RPO under Gunther Herbig 1991, Finzi Concerto and Stanford Concerto with Sir Charles Groves 1992, Encores with Piano and Harp 1992, Michael Berkeley Concerto 1993, Pastoral - British Music for Clarinet and Piano 1994, Encores II 1994, Complete Clarinet Works of Sir Malcolm Arnold 1995, Mozart and Weber Clarinet Quintets 2000; for Universal: Voyage 2004, The Mozart Album 2005; *Awards* winner BBC Young Musician of the Year 1984, Eurovision Young Musician of the Year Bronze award 1984, Wavenden award 1986, USA Young Concert Artists award 1991; *Books* Encore!, First Repertoire, Concert Repertoire; *Recreations* learning languages, literature, theatre, writing about music; *Style*— Miss Emma Johnson, MBE; ✉ c/o James Brown, Hazard Chase Ltd, 25 City Road, Cambridge CB1 1DP (tel 01223 312400, fax 01223 460827, e-mail emma@emmajohnson.co.uk, website www.emmajohnson.co.uk)

JOHNSON, Dr Gordon; s of Robert Johnson (d 1960), of South Shields, Co Durham, and Bessie, *née* Hewson (d 1956); *b* 13 September 1943; *Educ* Richmond Sch, Trinity Coll Cambridge (MA, PhD, Thirlwall Prize, Seeley Medal, Royal Cwlth Soc Walter Frewen Lord Prize); *m* 1973, Faith, da of Wilfred Sargent Lewis, of New Haven, CT, and North Haven, ME; 3 s (Timothy Foy b 14 May 1975, Nathaniel James b 10 May 1977, Orlando Benedict b 19 Jan 1980); *Career* Univ of Cambridge: fell Trinity Coll 1966–74, fell Selwyn Coll 1974–93 (tutor 1975–93, hon fell 1994), univ lectr in history of S Asia 1974–2005, sr proctor 1977–78, dir Centre of S Asian Studies 1983–2001, pres Wolfson Coll 1994– (pres elect 1993); Gates Cambridge Tst: provost 2000–, dep vice-chllr 2002–; chm Faculty of Oriental Studies 1984–87 (sec 1971–76); memb: Library Syndicate 1978–, Press Syndicate 1981– (chm 1993–), Gen Bd of the Faculties 1979–82 and 1985–90, Cncl of the Senate 1985–92 and 1999–2002, Syndicate of the Govt of the Univ (The Wass Syndicate) 1988–89; tstee: Cambridge Cwlth Tst, Cambridge Overseas Tst, The Nehru Tst for Cambridge Univ, The Hinduja Tst for Cambridge Univ, Malaysian Commonwealth Studies Centre; govr: Comberton Village Coll 1991–2002 (chm 1992–2001), Gresham's Sch Holt 2006–; preacher The Lady Margaret's Cambridge 2006; Liveryman Worshipful Co of Stationers and Newspaper Makers; *Books* Provincial Politics and Indian Nationalism (1973), University Politics: F M Cornford's Cambridge and his advice to the Young Academic Politician (1994), Cultural Atlas of India (1995), Printing and Publishing for the University, Three Hundred Years of the Press Syndicate (1999); The New Cambridge History of India (ed); ed Modern Asian Studies (CUP quarterly) 1971–; *Style*— Dr Gordon Johnson; ✉ The President's Lodge, Wolfson College, Cambridge CB3 9BB (tel 01223 35900)

JOHNSON, Graham Lee; s of Ronald Frank Johnson (decd), and June Rose Johnson; *Educ* Ringmer Co Secdy Sch, Brighton Coll of FE, Weymouth Coll (Dip Mgmnt Studies); *Career* prison govr; joined Prison Serv HMP Wakefield 1977, Leyhill Trg Coll 1977, HMP Lewes 1977–88, HMP Aldington 1988–92, HMP Highdown 1992–96 (head of residence 1994–96), dep govr HM Holding Centre Haslar 1996–97, dep govr HMP Guys Marsh 1997–2001, area project and devpt mangr SW Area Office 2001, govr HMP Dartmoor 2001–2003, Prison Serv performance improvement mangr 2003–05, seconded to EU as residential twinning advsr to Bulgarian Prison Serv (in preparation for Bulgaria's entry to the EU) 2005–; fell Inst of Leadership and Mgmnt (FInstLM), FCMI (MIMgt 2000); *Recreations* golf, reading, restoring classic cars; *Style*— Graham Johnson, Esq; ✉ Prison Service HQ, Abell House, John Islip Street, London SW1P 4LH (tel 020 7217 1847, e-mail graham.johnson2@hmps.gsi.gov.uk); Bulgarian Ministry of Justice, 1 Slavyanska Str, 1040 Sofia, Bulgaria (e-mail ganda625@msn.com)

JOHNSON, Graham Rhodes; OBE (1994); s of John Edward Donald Johnson (d 1986), and Violet May, *née* Johnson; *b* 10 July 1950; *Educ* Hamilton HS Bulawayo, Royal Acad of Music; *Career* concert accompanist; accompanied Elisabeth Schwarzkopf, Victoria de Los Angeles, Peter Shreier, Dame Margaret Price, Dame Janet Baker, Dame Felicity Lott, Ann Murray, Sarah Walker, Anthony Rolfe Johnson, Brigitte Fassbaender, Philip Langridge, Elly Ameling, Thomas Hampson, Christine Schäfer, Matthias Goerne; appeared as accompanist at numerous festivals incl: Aldeburgh, Bath, Edinburgh, Feldkirch (Hohenems), Munich and Salzburg; has taught various classes worldwide, prof of accompaniment at Guildhall Sch of Music; fndr The Songmakers' Almanac 1976, writer of BBC series for TV and radio, song advsr to the Wigmore Hall London 1992, chm of jury Wigmore Hall Song Competition 1997–99; recordings incl: a complete Schubert Lieder series for Hyperion beginning 1988, completed 2000, Hyperion French Song Edn beginning 1993, Hyperion Schumann Edn beginning 1996; recipient of Royal Philharmonic Soc award for instrumentalist of 1998; elected hon memb Swedish Royal Acad of Music 2000; FRAM 1985, FGSM 1988; Chevalier de l'Ordre des Arts et des Lettres (France) 2002; *Books* The Unashamed Accompanist by Gerald Moore (contrib, 1984), The Britten Companion (contrib, 1984), Song on Record (contrib, 1986), The Spanish Song Companion (contrib, 1992), The Songmakers Almanac 1976–96 (1996), A French Song Companion (2000), Britten, Voice and Piano (2003); *Recreations* restaurants and fine wine, book collecting; *Style*— Graham Johnson, Esq, OBE; ✉ c/o Askonas Holt Ltd, Lonsdale Chambers, 27 Chancery Lane, London WC2A 1PF

J

JOHNSON, Hugh Eric Allan; OBE (2007); s of Maj Guy Francis Johnson, CBE (d 1969), of London, and Grace Enid Marian, *née* Kittel; *b* 10 March 1939; *Educ* Rugby, King's Coll Cambridge (MA); *m* 13 March 1965, Judith Eve, da of Col Antony Gibbons Grinling, MBE, MC (d 1982), of Dyrham, Glos; 2 da (Lucy b 1967, Kitty-Alice b 1973), 1 s (Redmond b 1970); *Career* staff writer Vogue and House & Garden 1960–63, ed Wine & Food (sec Wine & Food Soc 1963–65), travel ed Sunday Times 1967 (wine corr 1962–67), ed Queen 1968–70, wine ed Gourmet Magazine 1971–72, editorial dir The Garden 1975–90 (conslt 1990–2005), gardening corr New York Times 1985–86; chm: The Movie Business, The Hugh Johnson Collection Ltd; dir Société Civile de Château Latour 1986–2001; wine conslt: Jardines Wine Tokyo 1986–2002, The Royal Tokaji Wine Co; pres: Sunday Times Wine Club 1973–, The Circle of Wine Writers 1997–; hon tstee American Center for Wine, Food and the Arts 2000–, hon pres The International Wine and Food Soc 2002–; churchwarden St James Great Saling 1971–98; fndr memb Tree Cncl 1974; Gold Veitch Meml Medal RHS 2000; Hon Dr Univ of Essex 1998; fell commoner King's Coll Cambridge 2001; Chevalier de l'Ordre Nationale du Mérite 2004; *Films* How to Handle A Wine (video 1984), Wine - A Users Guide (with KQED San Francisco, 1986), Vintage - A History of Wine (with WGBH Boston and Channel 4, 1989), Return Voyage (for Star TV Hong Kong, 1992); *Books* Wine (1966, revised 1974), Frank Schoonmaker's Encyclopedia of Wine (ed, 1967), The World Atlas of Wine (1971, revised 1977, 1985, 1994 and 5 edn 2001 with Jancis Robinson), The International Book of Trees (1973, revised 1984 and 1993, reissued 2000, new edn 2006), The California Wine Book (with Bob Thompson, 1976), Hugh Johnson's Pocket Wine Book (annually since 1977), The Principles of Gardening (1979, revised 1984, republished as Hugh Johnson's Gardening Companion 1996), Understanding Wine (1980), Hugh Johnson's Wine Companion (1983, revised 1987, 1991, 1997 and 5 edn 2003 with Stephen Brook), How to Enjoy Wine (1985, revised edn 1998), The Atlas of German Wines (1986, revised edn 1995), The Hugh Johnson Cellar Book (1986), The Wine Atlas of France (with Hubrecht Duijker, 1987, revised edn 1997), The Story of Wine (1989, new edn 2004), The Art & Science of Wine (with James Halliday, 1992), Hugh Johnson on Gardening (1993), Tuscany and its Wines (2000), Wine: A Life Uncorked (2005); many articles on gastronomy, gardening and travel incl Tradescant's Diary in The Garden (monthly since 1975); *Recreations* gardening, forestry, travel, pictures; *Clubs* Garrick, Saintsbury, Essex; *Style*— Hugh Johnson, Esq, OBE; ✉ Saling Hall, Great Saling, Essex CM7 5DT; 73 St James's Street, London SW1A 1PH

JOHNSON, Hugh Nicholas Tysilio; s of Basil Tysilio Johnson (d 1998), and Stella Gwendolen Johnson (d 1987); *b* 7 June 1958; *Educ* Lancing; *m* 21 Dec 1983, Hazel, da of Ian Francis and Ann Digby; 1 da (Camilla Henrietta b 18 March 1985), 1 s (Frederick Charles Tysilio b 19 March 1989); *Career* photographer, film dir Plunge Prodns; advertising and editorial photographer (specialising in still life, food, location, people, animals and cars) 1980–; clients incl: BP, Sony, BMW, VW, Volvo, IBM, Texaco, Br Govt, Bundesbank, Benson & Hedges, World of Interiors, Vogue, Silk Cut, ICI, Carling Black Label, Coca Cola, Harrods, Lego, Landrover; numerous pictures in various books; recipient: Grand Prize at NY Festival of Arts and Advertising, Gold Award Internationaler Druckschriften Wettbewerb 1993 and 1994, Bronze Award Art Dirs' Club Germany 1994, Gold Award Art Dirs' Club NY 1994; Silver Awards Assoc of Photographers; other awards from Assoc of Photographers, Campaign Posters, Campaign Press, D&AD, Creative Circle; work selected for special mention by George Roger (fndr memb of Magnum photographic agency), only living English photographer selected for Photography Now (V&A exhibition celebrating 150 year anniversary of photography); memb: AOP, SCCC, THFC; *Recreations* travelling, art, wildlife, sports; *Clubs* Chelsea Arts;

Style— Hugh Johnson, Esq; ✉ Hugh Johnson Studio, Studio 5, 2A Byam Street, Fulham, London SW6 2RD (tel 020 7731 3011, e-mail hugh@hughjohnson.co.uk, website www.hughjohnson.co.uk); Plunge Productions tel 020 3214 0000

JOHNSON, Ian Frederick; s of Alan Frederick Johnson, of Oswestry, Shropshire, and Betty, *née* Edwards; *b* 10 March 1960; *Educ* Oswestry Boys HS, Univ of Reading (LLB), Manchester Met Univ (PGCE), Liverpool John Moores Univ (LLM); *m* 18 March 1989, Hon Elizabeth Anne Cynlais, da of Baron Evans of Claughton (Life Peer, d 1992), of Claughton, Birkenhead; 2 da (Lucy Eva b 9 Oct 1995, Elise Claire b 19 April 1998); *Career* called to the Bar Gray's Inn 1982; memb Northern Circuit, barr at law 1983–; sr lectr in Law Manchester Metropolitan Univ 1998–; memb: Chancery Bar Assoc, Northern Chancery Bar Assoc; *Recreations* golf, sports cars, skiing; *Clubs* Allerton Park Golf (Liverpool); *Style*— Ian Johnson, Esq; ✉ Atlantic Chambers, 4–6 Cook Street, Liverpool L2 9QU (tel 0151 236 6757, fax 0151 227 3005); 5 Stone Buildings, Lincoln's Inn, London WC2A 3XT (tel 020 7242 6201, e-mail i.johnson@mmu.ac.uk)

JOHNSON, Prof Ian Richard; s of William Henry Johnson, of Eltham; *b* 14 July 1948; *Educ* Christ's Hosp, London Hosp Med Coll (BSc, MB BS), Univ of Nottingham (DM); *m* 1970, Jane, da of Frank Lewis Lockley (d 1984); *Career* sr house offr obstetrics and gynaecology Nottingham 1975–76 (house offr med and surgery 1974–75), registrar obstetrics and gynaecology Mansfield and Nottingham 1979–80, sr lectr and conslt North Staffs Med Centre Keele Univ 1983–87; Univ of Nottingham: lectr in physiology 1977–78, lectr in obstetrics and gynaecology 1980–83, prof of obstetrics and gynaecology 1987–, head Dept of Obstetrics and Gynaecology 1992–97 and 2002–, head Sch of Human Devpt 1997–2002; hon conslt: City Hosp Nottingham 1987–, Queen's Med Centre Nottingham 1987–; memb Gynaecological Visiting Soc; FRCOG 1988 (MRCOG 1978); *Books* MCQ's for Undergraduates in Obstetrics and Gynaecology (1985, 2 edn 1994), Obstetrics and Gynaecology Vade-Mecum (2000); *Recreations* gardening, antiques; *Clubs* Athenaeum; *Style*— Prof Ian Johnson; ✉ Department of Obstetrics and Gynaecology, University of Nottingham, Queen's Medical Centre, Nottingham (tel 0115 709 240)

JOHNSON, James North; s of Edwin Johnson (d 1987), of Harpenden, Herts, and Elizabeth Marjorie, *née* North (d 2004); *b* 13 November 1946; *Educ* Eastwood Sch Renfrewshire, Univ of Liverpool (MB ChB, MD); *m* 1, 1972 (m dis 2002), Dr Gillian Christine Markham, da of Harry Markham; 1 da (Katharine Sarah b 2 Oct 1987), 1 s (Charles Henry North b 15 Jan 1990); m 2, 6 May 2006, Fiona Helen, da of Maj William Simpson (d 1970); *Career* visiting prof in anatomy Univ of Texas 1973; Univ of Liverpool: lectr in anatomy 1973–74, Merseyside Assoc for Kidney Research fell 1974, clinical lectr in surgery 1987–, assoc postgrad dean 1990–93; sr registrar in surgery Royal Liverpool Hosp 1980–85, conslt vascular surgn Halton Gen Hosp Runcorn 1985– (dir of surgery 1993–97); BMA: memb Cncl 1975–80 and 1992–, chm Cncl 2003–, chm Hosp Jr Staff Ctee 1979–80, chm Central Conslts and Specialists' Ctee 1994–98 (dep chm 1990–94), chm Jt Conslts' Ctee 1998–2003 (vice-chm 1994–98), memb Standing Medical Advsy Ctee 1998–2004; memb: Cncl Liverpool Med Instn 1988–90, Mgmnt Ctee Nat Counselling Serv for Sick Doctors 1985–2004; author of articles on surgical, vascular surgical and NHS topics in various jls; FRCS, FRCP, FDSRCS; *Recreations* travel, fine wine, medical politics; *Clubs* Athenaeum; *Style*— James N Johnson, Esq; ✉ Talgarth, 66 View Road, Rainhill, Prescot, Merseyside L35 0LS (tel 0151 426 4306, fax 0151 426 6572); British Medical Association, BMA House, Tavistock Square, London WC1H 9JP (tel 020 7383 6100)

JOHNSON, (Helen) Jane; da of Donald Johnson, and Brenda Mary Johnson; *Educ* Liskeard GS, Goldsmiths Coll London (BA), Garnett Coll (Cert Higher and Further Educn), UCL (MA); *Career* George Allen & Unwin Publishers 1984, Harper Collins Publishers 1990– (publishing dir 1996–); authors incl: J R R Tolkien (publisher 1986–), Clive Barker, Brian Patten, Geoff Ryman, Stephen King and Peter Straub, David Eddings, Raymond E Feist, Robin Hobb; Euro Ed of the Year 1988; *Books* as Gabriel King: The Wild Road (1997), The Golden Cat (1998), The Knot Garden (1999), Nonesuch (2001); as Jude Fisher: The Lord of the Rings- The Fellowship of the Ring Visual Companion (2001), Sorcery Ring (2002); *Recreations* rock climbing, cinema, writing; *Style*— Ms Jane Johnson; ✉ Harper Collins Publishers, 77–85 Fulham Palace Road, London W6 8JB (tel 020 8307 4701, fax 020 8307 4656, e-mail jane.johnson@harpercollins.co.uk)

JOHNSON, Prof Dame Louise Napier; DBE (2003); *b* 26 September 1940; *Educ* Wimbledon HS GPDST, UCL (BSc), Royal Inst London (PhD); *m* Aug 1968; 1 s, 1 da; *Career* Univ of Oxford: lectr in molecular biophysics 1973–90, reader in molecular biophysics 1990, David Phillips prof of molecular biophysics 1990–, professorial fell Corpus Christi Coll 1990–, hon fell Somerville Coll 1991– (additional fell 1973–90); dir of life sciences Diamond Light Source 2003–; memb Cncl: European Molecular Biology Laboratory Scientific Advsy 1994–2000 (chm 1998–2000), Central Laboratories of the Research Cncls 1998–2001, Royal Soc 1998–2000; memb: EMBO 1991, Biochemical Soc, Biophysics Soc, Br Crystallographic Assoc, Wellcome Tst Infrastructure Ctee 1996–99; tstee Cambridge Crystallographic Data Base 1996–2003, govr Westminster Sch 1993–2001; Kaj Linderström-Lang Prize 1989, Royal Soc of Chemistry Award in Enzyme Chemistry (Charmian Medal) 1996, Fedn of European Biochemical Socs (Datta Medal) 1998; Hon DSc Univ of St Andrews 1992; fell UCL 1993, assoc fell Third World Acad of Sci 2000, fell Academia Europaea 2001; FRS 1990, FAAAS 2007; *Books* Protein Crystallography (with T L Blundell, 1976), Glycogen Phosphorylase (with K R Acharya, D I Stuart and K Varvill, 1991); also author of articles in learned jls; *Recreations* family, horses; *Style*— Prof Dame Louise Johnson, FRS; ✉ Laboratory of Molecular Biophysics, Rex Richards Building, University of Oxford, South Parks Road, Oxford OX1 3QU (tel 01865 275365, fax 01865 285353, e-mail louise.johnson@biop.ox.ac.uk)

JOHNSON, Dr Margaret Anne; da of Dr Frederick William Johnson, and Dr Margaret Rosemary Johnson, *née* Burke; *b* 7 February 1952; *Educ* Convent of the Sacred Heart Woldingham, Royal Free Hosp Med Sch London (MB BS, MD); *m* John William Winston Studd; 1 s (Thomas Joseph Benjamin b 16 Oct 1981), 2 da (Sarah Anne Victoria b 7 Dec 1984, Josephine Clare Francesca b 18 Feb 1992); *Career* house physician Royal Free Hosp 1976–77; SHO: postgrad trg scheme Whittington Hosp 1977–78, in thoracic med London Chest Hosp 1978, Nat Hosp for Nervous Diseases 1978–79; registrar rotation in gen med St Mary's Hosp Paddington 1979–81, research registrar Brompton Hosp 1981–83, sr registrar rotation in gen med and thoracic med Royal Free and Brompton Hosps 1983–89, conslt physician in gen med, HIV, AIDS and thoracic med Royal Free Hosp NHS Tst and hon sr lectr in virology Royal Free Hosp Sch of Med 1989–; med dir Royal Free NHS Tst; clinical dir Royal Free HIV/AIDS Unit; memb: Expert Advsy Gp on AIDS to the Dept of Health, AIDS Action Gp to Dept of Health, All Pty Parly Gp on AIDS, HIV Infection and AIDS Clinical Trials Working Pty MRC, Med Advsy Ctee to the Home Office on HIV/AIDS in Prisons, Med Advsy Ctee London Lighthouse; tstee, dir and memb Mgmnt Ctee Positively Women; FRCP 1993 (MRCP); *Books* HIV Infection in Women (jt ed with F Johnstone, 1993), An Atlas of HIV and AIDS: a Diagnostic Approach (with M C I Lipman and T A Gluck, 1994); numerous related articles in refereed jls; *Recreations* family, theatre, opera, tennis; *Style*— Dr Margaret Johnson; ✉ Medical Director, Royal Free Hospital, Pond Street, London NW3 2QG (tel 020 7794 0500 ext 4701, fax 020 7830 2201)

JOHNSON, Marlene; da of James and Catherine Johnson; *Educ* City of London Business Sch; *Career* fin dir Macdonald & Co Publishers 1971–81, gp controller Fitch & Co Design Consultants 1982–84, fin controller Leo Burnett Advtg 1984–86, fin dir rising to md Watts Publishing Gp Ltd 1986–2005, md Hachette Children's Books 2005–; FCCA 1980; *Recreations* yoga, theatre, reading, travel; *Style*— Ms Marlene Johnson; ✉ Hachette Children's Books, 338 Euston Road, London NW1 3BH

JOHNSON, Martin; s of Basil Johnson (d 1993), of Shipston-on-Stour, Warks, and Bridget Natalie, *née* Wilde; *b* 23 June 1949; *Educ* Rougemont Sch Newport, St Julian's HS Newport, Monmouth; *m* 1985, Teresa Mary, da of Reginald Victor Wright; 1 s (Andrew Joseph b 25 Nov 1984), 1 da (Charlotte Elizabeth b 25 Dec 1986); *Career* sports writer; trainee RG French Ltd advtg agency Liverpool 1967–68, steelworks labourer 1968–69, trainee journalist South Wales Argus Newport 1969–72; Leicester Mercury: sports writer and sub ed 1973–86, cricket corr 1974–86, rugby corr 1979–86; cricket corr The Independent 1986–95, Daily Telegraph sports feature writer 1995–; highly commended Br Sports Journalism Awards 1993 and 1994, Sports Feature Writer of the Year 1998; *Books* The Independent Book of 1987 World Cup India and Pakistan (anthology, 1987), David Gower: the Autobiography (co-author, 1992), Rugby and All That (2000); *Recreations* golf; *Clubs* Cosby Golf (Leics); *Style*— Martin Johnson; ✉ The Daily Telegraph, 1 Canada Square, Canary Wharf, London E14 5DT (tel 020 7538 5000, e-mail johnsonm@telegraph.co.uk)

JOHNSON, Prof Martin Hume; s of Reginald Hugh Ben Johnson, of Cheltenham, and Joyce Florence, *née* Redsell; *b* 19 December 1944; *Educ* Cheltenham GS, Christ's Coll Cambridge (scholar, MA, PhD); *Career* Univ of Cambridge: jr res fell Christ's Coll and MRC 1969–73, Elmore res studentship Physiological Lab 1973, sr res fell 1973–74, lectr Dept of Anatomy 1974–84, reader 1984–91, prof of reproductive sciences 1992– head Dept of Anatomy 1995–99, vice-master Christ's Coll 2007–; dir: Reproduction Research Information Service Ltd 1986–88, Company of Biologists Ltd 1986–94; co sec Cambridge Fertility Consultants 1989–91; inspr Human Fertilisation and Embryology Authy 1993– (memb 1994–99); Harkness fell Johns Hopkins Univ and Univ of Colorado 1971–73, Br Cncl fell Inst for Res in Reproduction Bombay and Indian Inst of Science 1979, Frank R Lillie fell Marine Biological Lab 1982, MRC res fell 1984–87, Albert Brachet Prize Belgian Royal Acad 1989, lectr CIBA Fndn Public Debate 1990, hon sr lectr UMDS 1991–95, Hammond lectr Soc for the Study of Fertility 1992, visiting fell La Trobe Univ Melbourne 1993 and 2006, annual public lectr Australasian Soc for Human Biology 1993, Halliburton lectr 1994, S T Huang meml lectr Hong Kong 1997, Anatomical Annual Review lectr 2000; visiting prof Univ of Sydney 1999–2004; memb: Soc for the Study of Fertility, Br Soc for Cell Biology, Euro Soc for Human Reproduction and Embryology, Soc of Scholars Johns Hopkins Univ 1993, Cambridge Philosophical Soc; chm Br Soc for Developmental Biology 1984–89, hon memb Stoke's Soc, hon sec Professional Advsy Gp for Infertility and Genetic Servs 1989–94; King's Fund prize for Innovation in Med Educn 1993; FRCOG (ad eundem) 2004; *Publications* Immunobiology of Trophoblast (jt ed, 1975), Physiological Consequences of Immunity to Reproductive Hormones (jt ed, 1976), Development in Mammals (ed, Vol 1 1976, Vol 2 1977, Vol 3 1978, Vol 4 1980, Vol 5 1983), Immunobiology of Gametes (jt ed, 1977), Essential Reproduction (jtly, 1 edn 1980, 6 edn 2007), Sexuality Repositioned (jt ed, 2004), Death Rites and Rights (jt ed, 2007); author of over 240 papers; *Recreations* opera, music, walking; *Style*— Prof Martin Johnson; ✉ Department of Physiology, Development and Neuroscience, Anatomy School, University of Cambridge, Downing Street, Cambridge CB2 3DY (tel 01223 333777, fax 01223 333786, e-mail mhj21@cam.ac.uk)

JOHNSON, Martin Osborne; CBE (2004, OBE 1998); *b* 9 March 1970, Solihull; *Educ* Welland Park Sch Market Harborough, Robert Smythe Upper Sch Market Harborough; *Career* rugby union player (lock); Leicester Tigers RUFC: capt 1997–2005, winners Pilkington Cup 1993, winners four successive Premiership titles 1999–2002, winners Heineken Cup 2001 and 2002, ret 2005; England: 84 caps, capt 1999–2003, debut v France 1993, winners Five Nations Championship 1995 (Grand Slam) and 1996, winners Six Nations Championship 2000, 2001 and 2003 (Grand Slam), memb squad World Cup 1995, 1999 and 2003 (champions 2003), ranked no 1 team in world 2003, ret 2004; memb Br Lions touring squads to NZ 1993, South Africa 1997 and Aust 2001 (only player ever to have captained Br Lions on two tours 1997 and 2001); also represented England Under 18 and NZ Under 21; Allied Dunbar Premiership Player of the Season 1998/99; exec dir Rhino Rugby 2006–; *Recreations* American football; *Style*— Martin Johnson, Esq, CBE

JOHNSON, Michael; s of Charles Beverley Johnson (d 1991), and Shirley Anne, *née* Fowler; *b* 26 April 1964; *Educ* Ecclesbourne Sch Duffield, Lancaster Univ (BA); *m* 1 July 1995, Lizzie, da of Arthur Schoon; 1 s (Joe b 20 Aug 1996), 1 da (Molly b 4 June 1998); *Career* jr conslt Wolff Olins London 1985–86, designer The Billy Blue Gp Sydney 1986–87, freelance designer Tokyo 1987, designer Emery Vincent Design Melbourne and Sydney 1988, art dir Omon Advtg Sydney 1988, sr designer Sedley Place Design London 1988–89, gp art dir Smith and Milton London 1990–92, estab johnson banks 1992; D&AD: memb 1991–, memb Ctee 1991–, educn chm 2001–02, pres 2003; chm Design Week Awards 1998 and 1999; memb Re-validation Ctee RCA (communications course) 1998; external examiner: Glasgow Sch of Art 2001–04, Kingston Univ 2006–; visiting tutor Central St Martins; visiting lectr: Kingston Univ (and visiting tutor), Univ of Nottingham, Univ of Northumbria, Middlesex Univ, Falmouth Coll of Art, Glasgow Sch of Art; 25 posters and designs in perm design selection V&A London; *Exhibitions* The Power of the Poster (contrib curator, V&A) 1999, Rewind - 40 Years of Design and Advertising (co-curator, V&A) 2002, Somewhere Totally Else, European Design Biennial (Design Museum) 2003, Communicate, Independent Graphic Design since the Sixties (Barbican) 2004, Creation Gallery Tokyo 2004 (solo poster exhibition); *Awards* D&AD Silver Awards 1991, 1993, 1997, 1999, 2002, 2003 and 2004 (nominated 1995, 1997 (twice), 1999, commendation 1991), Design Week Awards 1995, 1996, 1997, 1998, 1999 (three), 2002, 2004, 2007 and best of show 2004, NY Art Dirs Gold Award 1991, shortlisted BBC Design Awards 1996, D&AD Gold Award 2004, NY Art Dirs Silver Award 2004; *Publications* Problem Solved: a primer in design and communication (2002), Rewind - 40 years of design and advertising (contrib, 2002), featured in numerous design books, dictionaries and annuals; *Recreations* guitar playing/collecting, music, rollerblading; *Style*— Michael Johnson, Esq; ✉ johnson banks, Crescent Works, Crescent Lane, London SW4 9RW (tel 020 7587 6400, fax 020 7587 6411, e-mail michael@johnsonbanks.co.uk)

JOHNSON, Neil Anthony; OBE (Mil 1989), TD (1986); s of Anthony Johnson, of Glamorganshire, and Dilys Mabel Vera, *née* Smith; *b* 13 April 1949; *Educ* Canton Sch Cardiff, RMA Sandhurst; *m* 1, 1971 (m dis 1996); 3 da (Sarah b 1973, Amanda b 1975, Victoria b 1977); m 2, 1996, Mrs Elizabeth J Hunter Johnston, *née* Robinson; 1 da (Charlotte b 1998), 3 step da (Katharine, Lucy, Alice); *Career* exec dir British Leyland Ltd 1977–82, dir Jaguar Cars Ltd 1982–86, CO 4 Bn The Royal Green Jackets 1986–89, dir Rover Gp plc 1989–92, DG Engrg Employers Fedn 1992–94, ceo Royal Automobile Club 1994–98, chief exec RAC Holdings Ltd 1998–2000; chm: Hornby plc 2000–, Motability Finance Ltd 2001–, Cybit plc 2001–, Tenon plc 2003–06 (non-exec dir 2000–), Autologic plc 2006–; memb Royal Green Jackets TA Tst 1994–; Hon Col 157 Regt RLC (Pembroke Yeomanry) 1994–2001, Hon Col F Co (Royal Green Jackets) London Regt 2000–07, DL Greater London 1993–2007; memb Nat Employers Advsy Bd MOD 2006–; FIMI, FRSA, MInstM, CIMgt; *Recreations* country pursuits, fast British cars and slow Italian lunches; *Clubs* Army and Navy, Beefsteak, Cardiff & County, RAC, Royal Green Jackets, Arlberg Ski; *Style*— Neil Johnson; ✉ c/o Box 205, Royal Automobile Club, Pall Mall, London SW1Y 5HS

JOHNSON, Prof Newell Walter; s of Otto James Johnson, of Melbourne, and Lorna Dorothy Gardner, *née* Guy; *b* 5 August 1938; *Educ* Univ HS Melbourne, Univ of Melbourne

(MDSc), Univ of Bristol (PhD); *m* 1965 (m dis 1984), Pauline Margaret, *née* Trafford; 2 da (Sarah Kathryn b 1967, Nicola Dale b 1970); *Career* sr demonstrator in pathology and prosthetic dentistry Univ of Melbourne 1960–62, lectr in dental surgery UCL 1963–64, res scientist MRC Dental Res Unit Univ of Bristol 1965–67; London Hosp Med Coll: reader in experimental oral pathology 1968–76, prof of oral pathology 1977–83, hon dir MRC Dental Res Unit 1983–93; King's Coll Sch of Med and Dentistry: prof of oral pathology 1994–2003, dir Res and Univ Postgrad Educn 1994–95, visiting prof of oral health sciences 2003–; Nuffield res prof of dental sci RCS 1984–2003, extraordinary prof of oral and maxillofacial health Univ of Western Cape SA; hon prof: Univ of Nairobi, Tamilnadu Medical Univ; conslt: WHO, Pan American Health Orgn, Fédération Dentaire Internationale, USPHS, numerous health authys, univs and res cncls; hon conslt dental surgn Royal Hospitals Tst and King's Healthcare Tst; tstee and memb Cncl Br Soc of Peridontology 2001– (pres 1992–93); memb: RSM (pres Section of Odontology 1989–90, 2004–05), Fédération Dentaire Internationale, BDA, Int Assoc for Dental Res, Int Assoc of Oral Pathology, Pathological Soc; fell Royal Australasian Coll of Dental Surgeons, fell Faculty of Oral Pathology Royal Col of Pathologists of Australasia (FFOPRCPA) FDSRCS, FRCPath, FMedSci, ILTM; *Books* Oral Diseases in the Tropics (1991), Risk Markers for Oral Diseases (1991), Textbook of Oral Cancer (2003); author of over 300 scientific papers in jls; *Recreations* music, theatre, film, museums and art galleries; *Style*— Prof Newell Johnson; ✉ Guys, Kings and St Thomas' Dental Institute, King's College London, Caldecot Road, London SE5 9RW (tel 020 7346 3608, fax 020 7346 3624)

JOHNSON, Paul Bede; s of William Aloysius Johnson (d 1943), and Anne, *née* Hynes (d 1982); *b* 2 November 1928; *Educ* Stonyhurst, Magdalen Coll Oxford; *m* Marigold Edgerton Gigneac, da of Dr Thomas Hunt, of Upper Harley St, London W1 (d 1983); 3 s (Daniel Benedict b 1957, Cosmo James Theodore b 1958, Luke Oliver b 1961), 1 da (Sophie Jane Louise b 1963); *Career* Nat Serv Capt Army 1949–51; asst exec ed Realities Paris 1952–55, ed New Statesman London 1964–70 (asst ed then dep ed 1955–64), memb Bd New Statesman Publishing Co 1964–76; contrib: London Times, Daily Telegraph, Daily Mail, Wall Street Journal, New York Times, Washington Post, and various other newspapers and periodicals; frequently involved in broadcasting and the prodn of TV documentaries, int lectr to academic govt and business audiences; De Witt Wallace prof of communications American Inst for Public Policy Res Washington 1980; memb: Royal Commission on the Press 1974–77, Cable Authority 1984–90; winner numerous literary prizes incl: Yorkshire Post Book of the Year award 1975, Francis Boyer award for servs to public policy 1979, Krug award for excellence (literature) 1982; *Books* A History of Christianity (1976), A History of the Modern World (1983), A History of the Jews (1987), Intellectuals (1988), The Birth of the Modern World - World Society 1815–1830 (1992); *Recreations* hill walking, painting; *Clubs* Beefsteak; *Style*— Paul Johnson, Esq; ✉ The Coach House, Over Stowey, Bridgewater, Somerset (tel 01278 732 393); 29 Newton Road, London W2 5JR (tel 020 7229 3859, fax 020 7792 1676)

JOHNSON, Paula Joan; da of Grosvenor Marson Johnson (d 1981), and Diana Margery Joan, *née* Webb (d 1972); *b* 12 September 1953; *Educ* Atherley C of E Church Sch Southampton, Univ of Exeter (BA); *m* 20 April 1985, Lance Hamilton, s of John Harold Poynter, of Cowes, IOW; 1 s (Jago b 1994); *Career* asst literary ed: Now! Magazine 1979–81, Mail on Sunday 1982–83; literary ed Mail on Sunday 1983–; *Style*— Ms Paula Johnson; ✉ Mill Cottages, Donnington, Newbury, Berkshire RG14 2JP; Billing Place, London SW10 9UN

JOHNSON, Peter Alec Barwell; s of Oscar Ernest Johnson (d 1968), of Great Gransden, Cambs, and Marjorie, *née* Barwell (d 1991); *b* 26 July 1936; *Educ* Uppingham; *m* 3 July 1965, Gay Marilyn, da of Douglas Bennington Lindsay; 2 da (Juliet b 1966, Annabel b 1970); *Career* fndr: Br Sporting Art Tst, E Anglian Ctee and memb Exec Cncl Historic Houses Assoc; chm and md Arthur Ackermann & Peter Johnson Ltd; memb Cncl Br Antique Dealers' Assoc 1970–80; chm: Hans Town Ward Cons 1969–72, Cleaner Royal Borough 1989–91; govr Kimbolton Sch 1993–2000; memb Cromwell Museum Mgmnt Ctee, tstee Colvin Fire Prevention Tst 2000–; guide Chelsea Physic Garden, inventor (with John Barwell) of a weed-gathering hoe (Jo-hoe) 1994; *Books* The Nasmyth Family (with E Money, 1977), Good Gardens by Design (by Donald Chilvers, ed, 2005); *Recreations* gardening, riding, reading, learning to compose music for the piano, formed local group 'Millwrights' to compete for the Landmark East competition; *Clubs* Buck's, Hurlingham; *Style*— Peter Johnson, Esq; ✉ Rippington Manor, Great Gransden, Cambridge; Arthur Ackermann & Peter Johnson Ltd, 27 Lowndes Street, London SW1X 9HY (tel 020 7235 6464, fax 020 7823 1057)

JOHNSON, Peter Charles; s of Dr William Arthur Johnson (d 1993), and Suzanne Renee, *née* Roubitschek; *b* 12 November 1950; *Educ* Merchant Taylors', Pembroke Coll Cambridge (MA); *m* 27 July 1974, Judith Anne, da of Vincent Larvan, of Southport; 2 s (Matthew b 1980, Elliot b 1982), 2 da (Charlotte, Sophie (twins) b 1987); *Career* articled clerk Herbert Smith and Co 1973–75, admitted slr 1975, currently sr ptnr Alexander JLO; co sec Isle of Dogs Community Fndn, clerk Dame Henrietta Barnett Fund Hampstead Garden Suburb; Freeman City of London, Liveryman Worshipful Co of Distillers 1978; memb Law Soc; *Recreations* sailing; *Clubs* Oxford and Cambridge; *Style*— Peter Johnson, Esq; ✉ Alexander JLO, 11 Lanark Square, Glengall Bridge, Isle of Dogs, London E14 9RE (tel 020 7537 7000, fax 020 7538 2442, e-mail peter@london-law.co.uk)

JOHNSON, Prof Peter Malcolm; s of Ronald John Johnson (d 1968), and Beryl Mary, *née* Donaldson; *b* 20 April 1950; *Educ* Dulwich Coll, Jesus Coll Oxford (MA, DSc), Univ of London (PhD); *Family* 2 da (Katherine b 1976, Nicole b 1978); m 2001, Kay Eggleton; *Career* Royal Soc visiting fell Rikshospitalet Univ Hosp Oslo 1975–76, prof and head Div of Immunology Univ of Liverpool 1985– (lectr 1977–80, sr lectr 1980–82, reader 1982–85), dean Univ of Liverpool Faculty of Med 1997–2001 (dep dean 1994–97); dep dir Cancer Tissue Bank Res Centre Univ of Liverpool 1995–2003 (dir 1992–95), memb Steering Ctee WHO Task Force for Birth Control Vaccines 1985–90; co-fndr and chm Br Materno-Fetal Immunology Gp 1978–86, cncllr and sec-gen Int Soc of Immunology of Reproduction 1986–95, vice-pres American Soc of Immunology of Reproduction 1991–93, vice-pres Liverpool Med Instn 2005–; chm: Scientific Ctee of Br Soc for Rheumatology 1983–86 (memb Cncl 1981–86), Med Advsy Panel Nat Eczema Soc 1992–96, Cancer Res Ctee Univ of Liverpool 1992–96; memb: Ctee Br Soc of Immunology 1982–85, Ctee Br Transplantation Soc 1983–85, Cncl NW Cancer Res Fund 1992–96, Academic Ctee Univ of Liverpool 1991–2001, Liverpool HA 1997–2001, Cncl Euro Soc for Reproduction and Devpt Immunology 2000–, MRC Coll of Experts 2004–; chief ed Jl of Reproductive Immunology 1996–; author of over 200 papers and reviews concerning human immunology, notably the immunology of pregnancy; RYA nat umpire and nat judge 2002–, ISAF int judge 2005–, RYA NW regnl rules advsr 2007–; memb: Int Gp14 Class Ctee 1996–98, RYA Racing Rules Ctee 2002–, RYA Judges and Umpires Gp 2003– (chm 2006–); FRCPath 1993, Hon MRCP 2001; *Recreations* sailing, squash, football; *Clubs* West Kirby Sailing, Oxford and Cambridge Society Sailing; *Style*— Prof Peter Johnson; ✉ Division of Immunology, University of Liverpool Medical School, Duncan Building, Daulby Street, Liverpool L69 3GA (tel 0151 706 4354, fax 0151 706 5814, e-mail mq22@liv.ac.uk)

JOHNSON, Peter Michael; s of James Victor Johnson (d 1982), and Nancy Evelyn, *née* Taylorson (d 2001); *b* 3 July 1947; *Educ* Bromley GS, St Edmund Hall Oxford (Open exhibitioner, MA, BPhil); *m* 1972, Janet Esther, da of William Philip Ashman; 2 s (Simon Christopher b 1976, Timothy Paul b 1979), 1 da (Sarah Elizabeth b 1983); *Career* Unilever plc 1970–73; Redland: joined 1973, gp treas 1978–81, dir of planning 1981–84, md Redland Bricks 1984–89, exec dir Redland plc 1988–96; chief exec: The Rugby Group plc 1996–2000, George Wimpey plc 2000–06, non-exec chm D S Smith plc 2007– (non-exec dir 1999–); dir Home Builders Fedn 2005–; memb: Cncl Industry and Higher Educn (CIHE) 2001–, Supervisory Bd Wienerberger AE 2005–; pres: Tuiles et Briques Européennes (TBE) 1994–96, Nat Cncl of Bldg Material Prodrs 1998–2000; *Recreations* tennis, music, cricket; *Style*— Peter Johnson, Esq

JOHNSON, Peter Michael; s of Joseph William Johnson, of Abingdon, Oxon, and Dorothy, *née* Woolley; *b* 21 December 1947; *Educ* Bec GS, Mansfield Coll Oxford (MA, CertEd, Rugby blue, Judo blue); *m* 31 August 1969, Christine Anne, *née* Rayment; 2 s (Tom b 3 July 1973, James b 17 Feb 1978); *Career* cmmnd Parachute Bde 1971; 7 Parachute Regt RHA 1971–76, gen serv in UK, Cyprus, Malaya, Canada, Germany, emergency tours in Northern Ireland 1972–74; Radley Coll: asst master 1976–91, housemaster 1983–91, dir lower sch studies, games coach; headmaster Wrekin Coll 1991–98, headmaster Millfield 1998–; memb: HMC, SHA; capt Northampton Rugby Club 1978–79, Univ of Oxford rep RFU Cncl 1987–98, memb Exec Ctee England Rugby Football Schs Union; tstee Wells Cathedral; FRSA; *Recreations* golf, travel, music, oenology, classic cars; *Clubs* East India, Vincent's (Oxford), Free Foresters; *Style*— Peter Johnson, Esq; ✉ Millfield, Street, Somerset BA16 0YD (tel 01458 442291, fax 01458 841270)

JOHNSON, Peter William; s of Alfred Johnson (d 1989), and Emily, *née* Hall; *b* 2 November 1947; *Educ* Univ of Hull (BSc); *m* 10 Nov 1973, Ann Gillian, *née* Highley; 1 da (Rachael b 13 April 1974), 1 s (Simon b 19 March 1976); *Career* Rover Gp: mgmnt trainee 1969, sr mgmnt posts British Leyland 1970–79, sales dir Austin-Morris 1980–84, export dir Austin-Rover 1984–86, worldwide sales dir 1986–88; chief exec: Applied Chemicals 1988–90, Marshall Gp of Cos 1990–95; Inchcape plc: chief exec Inchcape Motor Retail 1995–96, chief exec Inchcape Motors Int 1996–98, main bd dir 1998–, gp chief exec 1999–2006 (gp chief exec designate 1998–99), non-exec chm 2006–; non-exec chm Rank Gp plc 2007–; non-exec dir: Wates Gp 2002–, Bunzl plc 2006–; chm Automotive Skills Cncl 2003–; vice-pres Inst of Motor Industry, memb Retail Motor Industries Fedn; Liveryman Worshipful Co of Coachmakers and Coach Harness Makers; FIMI 1984, MInstD 1989; *Recreations* golf, swimming, reading, travel; *Clubs* RAC, Redditch Golf; *Style*— Peter Johnson, Esq; ✉ Inchcape plc, 22A St James's Square, London SW1Y 5LP (tel 020 7546 8322, fax 020 7533 9110)

JOHNSON, Philip Robert; s of Robert Johnson, of Stockport, and Cicely, *née* Swalwell; *b* 12 October 1946; *Educ* Dialstone Sch Stockport; *m* 27 Aug 1969, Janette Anne, da of Arthur Gowling; 2 da (Clare Louise b 6 May 1976, (Nicola) Kate b 23 Sept 1978); *Career* articled clerk Pitt & Co Manchester 1964–69, qualified chartered accountant 1969, firm merged to become Mann Judd & Co 1970; ptnr: Mann Judd 1977, Touche Ross 1979– (following merger, now Deloitte & Touche LLP); head UK Audit Quality and Risk Mgmnt Gp Deloitte & Touche LLP; memb Deloitte UK Bd of Ptnrs 1988–93 and 1999–2004, chm Deloitte UK Audit Ctee 2002–04; memb Audit Registration Ctee ICAEW; vice-chm of Bd of Govrs Cheadle Hulme Sch; ACA 1970; *Recreations* travel, watching all forms of sport; *Style*— Mr Philip R Johnson; ✉ Deloitte & Touche LLP, 201 Deansgate, Manchester M60 2AT (tel 0161 832 3555 or 020 7007 0846)

JOHNSON, Sir Robert Lionel; kt (1989); s of Edward Harold Johnson (d 1986), and Ellen Lydiate Johnson (d 1989); *b* 9 February 1933; *Educ* Watford GS 1940–51, LSE (LLB); *m* 1957, Linda Mary, da of Charles William Bennie (d 1975), of Durham; 2 da (Melanie b 1961, Edwina b 1962 d 2006), 1 s (Robert b 1968 d 2007); *Career* served 5 Royal Inniskilling Dragoon Gds 1955–57 (Capt), ADC to GOC-in-C Northern Cmd 1956–57, Inns of Court Regt 1957–64; called to the Bar Gray's Inn 1957 (bencher 1986); recorder of the Crown Court 1977–89, QC 1978, judge of the High Court of Justice (Family Div) 1989–2004; jr counsel to Treasury in probate matters 1975–78, legal assessor GNC 1977–82; chm: Bar Fees and Legal Aid Ctee 1984–86, Family Law Bar Assoc 1984–86, Family Law Ctee of Justice 1990–94; memb: Bar Cncl 1981–88 (vice-chm 1987, chm 1988), Law Soc Legal Aid Ctee 1981–87, Supreme Court Procedure Ctee 1982–87, Judicial Studies Bd 1989–94; memb Nat Exec Ctee and tstee Cystic Fibrosis Res Tst 1964–, hon sec Int Cystic Fibrosis (Mucoviscidosis) Assoc 1984–90; *Recreations* gardening, charitable work; *Style*— Sir Robert Johnson; ✉ Forest Gate, Pluckley, Kent TN27 0RU

JOHNSON, Robert William Greenwood; s of Robert William Johnson (d 1960), and Susan, *née* Mills (d 1980); *b* 15 March 1942; *Educ* Licensed Victuallers' Sch Ascot, Univ of Durham (MB BS, MS); *m* 30 July 1966, Dr Carolyn Mary Johnson, da of Dr John Edmund Vooght (d 1997), of Newbury, Berks; 1 da (Melanie Jane b 16 June 1969), 1 s (Julian Robert Greenwood b 20 Aug 1972); *Career* asst prof of surgery Univ of Calif 1973–74 (Fulbright Scholar 1973), conslt surgn Manchester Royal Infirmary 1974–, hon conslt surgn Royal Manchester Children's Hosp; med dir Central Manchester and Manchester Children's Univ NHS Tst (CMMCT) 2000–02, former chm Med Exec Ctee Central Manchester Health Authy; hon reader in surgery Univ of Manchester, Hunterian prof RCS 1980; inter-collegiate examiner Royal Colleges of Surgery 1998–2003; pres: Br Transplant Soc 1996–99, Assoc of Surgeons of GB&I 2002–03, Fedn of Surgical Speciality Assoc 2003–; memb Senate of Surgery; Pybus Medal North of England Surgical Soc 1991, Hunterian Medal RCS; Freeman Worshipful Co of Innholders 1965; FRCS 1970, FRCSEd 1994; *Recreations* golf, tennis, skiing; *Clubs* Athenaeum, Royal Birkdale Golf; *Style*— Robert Johnson, Esq; ✉ Evergreen, Chapel Lane, Hale Barns, Cheshire WA15 0AJ (tel 0161 980 8840, e-mail rwgj@hotmail.com); Anson Medical Centre, 23–25 Anson Road, Victoria Park, Manchester M13 9WZ (tel 0161 248 2040, fax 0161 903 8452)

JOHNSON, Roy Arthur; s of Leonard Arthur Johnson (d 1974), of Hove, E Sussex, and Cicely Elsie, *née* Turner (d 1995); *b* 3 March 1937; *Educ* Lancing; *m* 31 July 1965, Heather Campbell, da of Alfred John Heald, of Hove, E Sussex; 2 s (Mark b 1967, Paul b 1968); *Career* chartered accountant 1960; ptnr: Coopers & Lybrand 1966–92, Cork Gully 1981–92; ICAS: moderator of Examination Bd 1975–87, memb Cncl 1984–90, convenor Fin and Gen Purposes Ctee 1986–90; dir Glasgow C of C 1988–98; Univ of Strathclyde: memb Ct 1992–2003 (chm 1997–2002), treas 1994–97, hon fell 2003–; dir Strathclyde Grad Business Sch 1992–98, govr Glasgow Acad 1996–2000; chm Prince's Tst Volunteers W of Scotland 1991–2002; gen cmmr of Income Tax 1993–; Deacon Incorporation of Cordiners of Glasgow 1976 (memb 1968), Deacon Convener Trades House of Glasgow 1990; Freeman City of London 1992; Hon DUniv Strathclyde 1998; MIPA 1986; *Recreations* golf, photography, gardening; *Clubs* Western (Glasgow); *Style*— Roy Johnson, Esq; ✉ 8 Hillcrest Drive, Newton Mearns, Glasgow G77 5HH (tel 0141 639 3800, fax 0141 616 0986, e-mail royjohnson@ntlworld.com)

JOHNSON, Stanley Patrick; s of Wilfred Johnson, and Irene Johnson; *b* 18 August 1940; *Educ* Sherborne, Exeter Coll Oxford (MA); *m* 1, 1963 (m dis 1979), Charlotte Offlow Fawcett; 3 s (Alexander, Leo, Joseph), 1 da (Rachel (Mrs Ivo Dawnay)); m 2, 1981, Mrs Jennifer Kidd; 1 s (Maximilian), 1 da (Julia); *Career* on staff: World Bank 1966–68, Int Planned Parenthood Fedn London 1971–73; conslt to UN Fund of Population Activities 1971–73, head of Prevention of Pollution and Nuisances Div EEC 1973–77, advsr to head of Environment and Consumer Protection Service EEC 1977–79, MEP (EDG) IOW and E Hants 1979–84, environmental advsr to EEC Cmmn Brussels; special advsr Coopers and Lybrand 1991, dir Environmental Resources Management 1992–94; Parly candidate (Cons) Teignbridge Gen Election 2005; Newdigate Prize for Poetry 1962, RSPCA Richard Martin Award, Greenpeace Prize 1984; *Books* Life Without Birth (1970), The Green Revolution (1972), The Population Problem (1973), The Politics of the Environment (1973), Antarctica - Last Great Wilderness (1984), World Population and the United

Nations (1988), The Earth Summit - the United Nations Conference on Environment and Development (1993), The Environmental Policy of the European Communities (2 edn, 1994), The Politics of Population (1995); *Novels* Gold Drain (1967), Panther Jones for President (1968), God Bless America (1974), The Doomsday Deposit (1980), The Marburg Virus (1982), Tunnel (1984), The Commissioner (1987), Dragon River (1989), Icecap (1998); *Recreations* writing, travel; *Style—* Stanley Johnson, Esq; ✉ 60 Regent's Park Road, London NW1 7SX

JOHNSON, Stuart Peter; s of Brian Fredrick Nelson Johnson, of Twyford, Berks, and Yvonne Knowles, *née* Walker; *b* 17 May 1957; *Educ* Willink Sch Reading, Westminster Coll; *m* Penelope Linda, da of Hugh Anthony Valentine; 1 da (Lucy Victoria b March 1988), 1 s (Edward Rory b Feb 1991); *Career* mgmnt trg scheme Savoy Hotel plc 1974–78, asst banqueting mangr Claridges Hotel 1978–80, mangr The Bishops Table Hotel Farnham 1980–82, personnel and purchasing mangr The Connaught Hotel London 1982–86, res mangr Cliveden 1986–90, hotel mangr The Savoy 1990–94, dir/gen mangr Cliveden (AA Five Red Stars, Egon Ronay 92%) 1994–98, ops dir St Andrews Int ltd 1999–; publishing dir Johansens Hotel Guides 2002–; Freeman City of London; Master Innholder 1995; FHCIMA 1995; *Recreations* riding, golf, squash, skiing; *Style—* Stuart Johnson, Esq; ✉ Johansens, Therese House, Glass House Yard, London EC1A 4JN (tel 020 7566 9700, fax 020 7490 2538, mobile 07768 131089)

JOHNSON, Prof William; eld s of James Johnson (d 1968), and Elizabeth, *née* Riley (d 1968); *b* 20 April 1922; *Educ* Manchester Central High GS, Manchester Coll of Technol (BSc Tech), Univ of London (BSc), Univ of Manchester (DSc); *m* 6 April 1946, Heather Marie (d 2004), da of John and Mildred Thornber; 3 s (Philip James b 5 May 1948, Christopher John b 19 July 1951, Jeremy William b 16 June 1954), 2 da (Helen b 23 April 1953, Sarah b 6 Feb 1959); *Career* HM Forces 1943–47: cmmnd REME 1944, served UK, Italy and Austria; admin grade Civil Serv 1948–50; lectr in mechanical engrg: Northampton Poly (now City Univ) 1950–51, Univ of Sheffield 1952–56; sr lectr Univ of Manchester 1956–60, prof and head of Dept of Mechanical Engrg UMIST 1960–75, prof of mechanics Univ of Cambridge 1975–82 (now prof emeritus); visiting prof Industrial Engrg Dept Purdue Univ USA 1983–85, United Technologies distinguished prof of engrg 1988 and 1989, various visiting professorships overseas; fndr and ed: Int Jl Mechanical Sciences 1960–87, Int Jl Impact Engineering 1983–87; memb Hon Research Bd of Advsrs American Biographical Inst 2007; Lord Austin Essay Prize IProdE 1943; IMechE: T Bernard Hall Prize 1965 and 1966, James Clayton Fund Prize 1972 and 1977, Best Paper for Safety 1980 and 1991, James Clayton Prize (for Educn and Research) 1987, Silver medal Inst of Sheet Metal Engrg, Gold medal Adv Mats Proc Tech Dublin 1995, ASME Engineer Historian Award 2000; Hon DTech Univ of Bradford 1976; Hon DEng: Univ of Sheffield 1986, UMIST 1995; fell UCL 1981; foreign fell: Acad of Athens 1982, Russian Acad of Sciences (Urals Branch) 1993, Indian Nat Acad of Engrg 1999; FIMechE 1960, FRS 1982, FREng 1983; *Books* Mechanics of Metal Extrusion (with H Kudo, 1962), Plasticity for Mechanical Engineers (with P B Mellor, 1962), Plane Strain Slip Line Fields (with J B Haddow and R Sowerby, 1968), Crashworthiness of Vehicles (with A G Mamalis, 1968), Engineering Plasticity (with P B Mellor, 1973, 1982 and 1985), Impact Strength of Materials (1972), Engineering Plasticity: Metal Forming Processes (Vol II, with A G Mamalis, 1976), A Source Book of Plane Strain Fields for Metal Deformation Processes (with R Sowerby and R D Ventner, 1982), Collected Works on B Robins and C Hutton (2001), Record and Services, Satisfactory (2003); *Recreations* historical reading, music; *Style—* Prof William Johnson, FRS, FREng

JOHNSON-FERGUSON, Sir Ian Edward; 4 Bt (UK 1906), of Springkell, Co Dumfries, Kenyon, Newchurch-in-Culcheth, Co Palatine of Lancaster, and Wiston, Co Lanark; s of Sir Neil Edward Johnson-Ferguson, 3 Bt, TD, JP, DL (d 1992), and Sheila Marian, *née* Jervis (d 1985); *b* 1 February 1932; *Educ* Ampleforth, Trinity Coll Cambridge (BA), Imperial Coll London (DIC); *m* 9 April 1964, Rosemary Teresa, yr da of Cecil John Whitehead (d 1989), of Edenbridge, Kent; 3 s (Mark Edward b 14 Aug 1965, Paul Duncan b 20 Aug 1966, Simon Joseph b 23 July 1967); *Heir* s, Mark Johnson-Ferguson; *Style—* Sir Ian Johnson-Ferguson, Bt; ✉ Littlefield House, Webbs Lane, Abbotts Ann, Andover, Hampshire SP11 7DD

JOHNSON-GILBERT, Christopher Ian; s of Thomas Ian Johnson-Gilbert (d 1998), and Gillian June, *née* Pool; *b* 28 January 1955; *Educ* Rugby, Worcester Coll Oxford (BA); *m* 25 July 1981, Hon Emma Davina Mary, da of Baron Terrington, DSO, OBE, FRSL (d 2001); 3 da (Cordelia b 14 June 1983, Jemima b 24 July 1985, Imogen b 11 Jan 1990), 1 s (Hugh b 22 Oct 1991); *Career* admitted slr 1980; ptnr Linklaters 1986–2002; memb Int Bar Assoc; assoc Inst of Wine and Spirits; *Clubs* MCC, Hurlingham, Vincent's (Oxford), Rye Golf; *Style—* Christopher Johnson-Gilbert, Esq; ✉ 79 Thurleigh Road, London SW12 8TY

JOHNSON-HILL, Nigel; s of Kenelm Clifton Johnson-Hill, JP (d 1977), and Joyce Wynne, *née* Booth (d 1994); *b* 8 December 1946; *Educ* Rugby; *m* 23 Oct 1971, Catherine, da of Edward Sainsbury, TD; 2 da (Chloe b 1976, Anna b 1981), 1 s (Sam b 1978); *Career* Hongkong & Shanghai Banking Corp 1965–73, W I Carr (Overseas) 1973–78, Hoare Govett 1978–87, Hoenig & Co Ltd 1988–2002; chm: Liv-Ex Ltd, Mundane Asset Management, The Vintry Wine Co, Bedlam Asset Mgmnt; FSI (memb Stock Exchange 1979); *Recreations* wine, skiing; *Clubs* Hong Kong, Turf; *Style—* Nigel Johnson-Hill, Esq; ✉ Park Farm, Milland, Liphook, Hampshire, GU30 7JT (tel 01428 741389, fax 01428 741368, e-mail nigel@vintry.co.uk)

JOHNSON-LAIRD, Dr Philip Nicholas; s of Frederick Ryberg Johnson-Laird (d 1962), of Middlesbrough, and Dorothy, *née* Blackett (d 1947); *b* 12 October 1936; *Educ* Culford Sch, UCL (BA, PhD); *m* 1 Aug 1959, Maureen Mary Bridget, da of John Henry Sullivan (d 1948); 1 s (Benjamin b 1966), 1 da (Dorothy b 1971); *Career* asst lectr in psychology UCL 1966–67 (lectr 1967–73), visiting memb Inst for Advanced Study Princeton 1971–72, reader in experimental pyschology Univ of Sussex 1973–78 (prof 1978–82), visiting fell Cognitive Science Prog Stanford Univ Spring 1980; visiting prof in psychology: Stanford Univ Spring 1985, Princeton Univ Spring 1986 and 1987; asst dir MRC Applied Psychology Unit Cambridge 1983–89 (fell Darwin Coll Cambridge 1986–89), prof of psychology Princeton Univ 1989– (Stuart prof 1994–); memb: Psychology Ctee SSRC 1975–79, Linguistics Panel SSRC 1980–82, Advsy Cncl Int Assoc for Study of Attention and Performance 1984; memb: Linguistics Assoc 1967, Experimental Psychology Soc 1968, Cognitive Sci Soc 1980, Assoc for Computational Linguistics 1981, Br Psychology Soc, American Philosophical Soc 2006, Nat Acad of Sci 2007; Fyssen Int Prize 2002; Hon DPhil Göteborg Sweden 1983, Hon Laurea (hc) Padua 1997, Hon DSc Trinity Coll Dublin 2000, Hon DPsych UNED Madrid 2000, Hon Dr Ghent 2002, Hon Laurea Univ of Palermo 2005; FBA 1986, FRS 1991, fell Assoc of Psychological Sci 2007; *Books* Thinking and Reasoning (ed jtly, 1968), Psychology of Reasoning (with P C Wason, 1972), Language and Perception (with G A Miller, 1976), Thinking (ed jtly, 1977), Mental Models (1983), The Computer and the Mind (1988), Deduction (with R M J Byrne, 1991), Human and Machine Thinking (1993), How We Reason (2006); *Style—* Dr Philip Johnson-Laird, FRS, FBA; ✉ Department of Psychology, Princeton University, Princeton, NJ 08544, USA (tel 00 1 609 258 4432, fax 00 1 609 258 1113, e-mail phil@princeton.edu)

JOHNSTON, Rt Hon Lord; Alan Charles Macpherson; PC (2005); s of Hon Lord Dunpark (d 1991), and Katherine Margaret, *née* Mitchell (d 1982); *b* 13 January 1942; *Educ* Loretto, Jesus Coll Cambridge (BA), Univ of Edinburgh (LLB); *m* 30 July 1966, Anthea Jean, da of John Blackburn (d 1985); 3 s (Alexander b 1969, Charles b 1971, Nicholas b 1974); *Career* advocate 1967, standing jr counsel Scottish Home and Health Dept 1972–78, QC 1980, dean Faculty of Advocates 1989–94 (treas 1978–89, advocate depute 1979–82), senator of the Coll of Justice 1994–; chm: Industrial Tbnl 1982–88, Med Appeal Tbnl 1984–89; Hon DUniv Heriot-Watt 2001; *Recreations* fishing, golf, shooting; *Clubs* New (Edinburgh), Pitt (Cambridge); *Style—* The Rt Hon Lord Johnston; ✉ 3 Circus Gardens, Edinburgh EH3 6TN (tel 0131 225 1862); Advocates' Library, Parliament House, Edinburgh EH1 1RF (tel 0131 226 5071)

JOHNSTON, Alastair John Carmichael; OBE (1990); s of Harry Scott Johnston (d 1973), of Tayport, Fife, and Jean Carmichael (d 1966); *b* 16 September 1928; *Educ* Harris Acad Dundee, Univ of St Andrews (BSc); *m* 7 Sept 1953, Morag Elizabeth, da of Robert Campbell (d 1956), of Tayport, Fife; 2 s (Malcolm b 1957, Scott b 1963); *Career* North British Rubber Co 1953–59, plant mangr Armstrong Cork Co 1960–70, dir Wm Briggs & Sons Ltd 1970–74; md: Permanite Ltd 1974–77, Trident Equipment Ltd 1977–81; dir Uniroyal Ltd 1982–85, md The Gates Rubber Co Ltd 1986–91, chm Duncan Honeyman Ltd 1992–95; memb Scottish Cncl CBI 1983–91, dep chm Dumfries and Galloway Enterprise Co 1990–92; *Recreations* hill walking; *Style—* Alastair Johnston, Esq, OBE; ✉ Dunalistair House, 7 Dunalistair Gardens, Broughty Ferry, Dundee DD5 2RJ (tel 01382 739076)

JOHNSTON, Alexander David; s of Sir Alexander Johnston, GCB, KBE (d 1994), and Betty Joan Johnston, CBE, *née* Harris (d 1994); *b* 3 September 1951; *Educ* Westminster, Corpus Christi Coll Cambridge (MA); *m* 1980, Jackie Barbara, da of Ernie Stephenson (d 2001); 2 s (Mark b 29 June 1987, George b 1 March 1990); *Career* Lazard London: joined 1973, dir 1986–2003, md 1999–2003; non-exec chm BMS Associates Ltd, external memb Fin Ctee Univ of Cambridge; memb: Competition Cmmn, Utilities Panel Competition Cmmn; *Recreations* classical music, reading, skiing, walking; *Style—* Alexander Johnston

JOHNSTON, Alexander Dewar Kerr (Alistair); s of Kerr Johnston (d 1999), and Elizabeth Alexandra Johnston; *b* 28 June 1952, Glasgow; *Educ* LSE (Stern scholarship, BSc); *Partner* Christina Maria Nijman; *Career* KPMG (formerly Peat Marwick Mitchell): joined 1973, sector specialist leasing and finance San Francisco 1977–79, US specialist Tech Advsy Gp 1979–83, departmental sr mangr 1983–86, ptnr 1986–, estab KPMG int HQ Amsterdam 1987–89, head of UK mktg 1990–94, head of UK insurance practice 1994–98, gen ptnr 1996, vice-chm UK Fin Servs Practice 1997–98, int vice-chm global markets 1998–2003, fndr memb Int Exec 1998–2003, memb UK Bd 2002–, vice-chm UK 2004–, global vice chm 2007; dir British American Business Inc; visiting prof and memb Int Advsy Bd Cass Business Sch; memb: London Ctee Scottish Cncl for Devpt and Industry, Bd FCO; chm Int Advsy Bd ICAEW; FCA; *Clubs* Athenaeum, RAC; *Style—* Alistair Johnston, Esq; ✉ KPMG, 8 Salisbury Square, London EC4Y 8BB (tel 020 7311 4923, fax 020 7311 4242, e-mail alistair.johnston@kpmg.co.uk)

JOHNSTON, Andrew Ian; s of Maurice Johnston, of Harrogate, and Pauline Mary, *née* Teasdale; *b* 10 January 1956; *Educ* Harrogate GS, St Edmund Hall Oxford (open exhibitioner, MA); *m* 9 April 1988, Sara Lesley (d 1997), da of late Geoffrey R T Lewis; 1 da (Harriet Louise b 26 Jan 1990); *Career* Government Actuary's Dept: trainee actuary (public sector pensions) 1978–82, actuary (social security income and expenditure forecasting) 1982–91, chief actuary (public serv pensions) 1991–2005, dep govt actuary 2005–; FIA; *Style—* Andrew Johnston, Esq; ✉ Government Actuary's Department, Finlaison House, 15–17 Furnival Street, London EC4A 1AB (tel 020 7211 2651, fax 020 7211 2660, e-mail andrew.johnston@gad.gov.uk)

JOHNSTON, Barrie Colin; OBE (1994); s of Alfred John Johnston, OBE (d 1964); *b* 7 August 1925; *Educ* Epsom Coll; *m* 1952, Cynthia Anne, *née* Clark; 1 s (Alastair John), 1 da (Nicola Mary); *Career* Lt RM Far East; merchant banker (ret); dir: Charterhouse Japhet Ltd 1973–84, T H White Ltd 1981–87, Mornington Building Society 1988–91; memb: Mgmnt Ctee The Pension Fund Property Unit Trust 1966–89, Mgmnt Ctee Charities Property Unit Trust 1967–88, Cncl Barnardo's 1980–95, Cncl King George's Fund for Sailors 1982–2001 (hon treas 1985–96), Fin Ctee The Spastics Soc (now Scope) 1984–88, Cncl Hearing Dogs for Deaf People 1993–2002, Fin Ctee Royal Assoc for Disability and Rehabilitation (RADAR) 1995–98; hon treas Royal Marines Assoc 1972–99; Charities Aid Fndn: tstee 1989–98, chm Investment Ctee 1976–96, chm and tstee Common Investment Funds 1990–2000, tstee Abbeyfield Cheam Soc Ltd 2000–03 (chm 2000–02); tstee Royal Marines Museum 1989–97; memb Ct of Assts Worshipful Co of Turners (Master 1990–91); Hon FRCR, FPMI, FRSA, ASIP; *Books* Life's a Lottery - or is it? (2001); *Recreations* sport, travel; *Style—* Barrie C Johnston, Esq, OBE; ✉ Yew Cottage, 8 The Green, Ewell, Surrey KT17 3JN (tel 020 8393 2920)

JOHNSTON, Catherine Elizabeth; CB (2000); da of Sir Alexander Johnston, GCB, KBE (d 1994), and Betty Johnston, CBE *née* Harris (d 1994); *b* 4 January 1953; *Educ* St Paul's Girls' Sch, St Hugh's Coll Oxford (scholar, BA); *m* 5 Aug 1989, Brendan Patrick Keith; 1 s, 1 da; *Career* with the office of the Parly Counsel 1980– (seconded to Parly Counsel Office Canberra 1987–88), Parly counsel 1994–; *Style—* Miss Catherine Johnston, CB; ✉ Office of the Parliamentary Counsel, 36 Whitehall, London SW1A 2AY (tel 020 7210 6612)

JOHNSTON, David Lawrence; OBE (1997); s of Herbert David Johnston (d 1983), and Hilda Eleanor, *née* Wood (d 1998); *b* 12 April 1936; *Educ* Lancastrian Sch Chichester, King's Coll Durham (BSc); *m* 8 July 1959, Beatrice Ann, da of John Turnbull Witten (d 1973); 3 da (Fiona b 1959, Pauline b 1960, Kate b 1970); *Career* apprentice electrical fitter Portsmouth Dockyard 1951–56, Lt RN 1959–62, electrical offr HMS Eastbourne 1960–62; MOD: overseeing Wallsend 1962–63, warship switchgear design Bath 1963–66, prodn and project mgmnt Devonport Dockyard 1966–73, dockyard policy Bath 1973–76, warship electrical system design Bath 1976–79, prodn and planning Portsmouth Dockyard 1979–81, mgmnt systems, planning and prodn Devonport Dockyard 1981–84, asst under sec of state and md Devonport Dockyard 1984–87; chm DDL (mgmnt buy out co) 1985–87, dep chm DML 1987, mgmnt conslt 1988, DG Nat Inspection Cncl for Electrical Installation Contracting (NICEIC) 1989–2001, chm and chief exec National Quality Assurance Ltd (NQA) 1993–2001 (dir 1989–2001), dep chm National Quality Assurance USA Inc 1998–2001 (dir 1993–2001); dir: NSCIA Ltd 1989–90, NACOSS Ltd 1990–1996; HSE: memb Electrical Equipment Certification Mgmnt Bd 1990–2002, chm BASEEFA Advsy Cncl 1990–2002, chm Advsy Bd BASEEFA (2001) Ltd 2002–; dir UK Accreditation Serv (UKAS) 2000–06, memb Open Govt Appeals Panel 1995–2002, memb Wiring Regulations Policy Ctee IEE 2001–04; CEng, FIEE 1980, FIMgt 1982, RCNC; *Recreations* novice golf, home, hearth and gardening, watercolour painting; *Style—* David Johnston, Esq, OBE, CEng; ✉ Chinley House, 1 Eaton Park Road, Cobham, Surrey KT11 2JG (tel 01932 588269, fax 01932 864472, e-mail david.johnston@elmquay.freeserve.co.uk)

JOHNSTON, Prof Derek Iain; s of John Johnston, and Anna, *née* Howitt; *b* 31 May 1943; *Educ* Collyers Sch, Queens' Coll Cambridge (MA, MD, BChir); *m* 19 April 1969, Heather Christine, da of Donald Stuart; 3 s (Andrew b 1971, Robert b 1976, James b 1979), 1 da (Emily b 1972); *Career* conslt paediatrician and endocrinologist 1976–2005, ret; FRCP 1982 (MRCP 1970), FRCPCH 1997; *Books* Essential Paediatrics (4 edn 1999); *Recreations* sailing; *Style—* Prof Derek Johnston

JOHNSTON, Frederick Patrick Mair; CBE (1993); s of Frederick Mair Johnston (d 1973), of Falkirk, and Muriel Kathleen, *née* Macbeth (d 1994); the Johnston family have had a major interest in Johnston Press plc and its predecessor since 1767; *b* 15 September 1935; *Educ* Lancing, New Coll Oxford (MA); *m* 1961, Elizabeth Ann, da of Robert Thomas Jones (d 1998); 2 s (Michael b 1962, Robert b 1964); *Career* cmmnd Royal Scots Fusiliers, served East Africa 4 Uganda Bn KAR 1955–56; chm Dunn & Wilson Group 1976–97; dir: Johnston Press plc (F Johnston & Co Ltd until 1988) 1959– (chm 1973–2001), Scottish

Mortgage & Trust plc 1991–2002, Lloyds TSB Scotland plc 1996–2003, Press Assoc 1997–2001; pres: Young Newspapermen's Assoc 1968–69, Forth Valley C of C 1972–73, Scottish Newspaper Proprietors' Assoc 1976–78, Newspaper Soc 1989–90; memb: Press Cncl 1974–88, Royal Commonwealth Soc 1999–; chm: Central Scot Manpower Ctee 1976–83, Edinburgh Int Book Festival 1996–2001, Scotland in Europe 2001–04; treas: Soc of Master Printers of Scotland 1981–86, Cwlth Press Union 1987–91; regent RCSEd 2001–; Liveryman Worshipful Co of Stationers and Newspaper Makers 2004; FRSA 1992; *Recreations* reading, travelling; *Clubs* New (Edinburgh), Caledonian; *Style—* Frederick P M Johnston, Esq, CBE; ✉ Johnston Press plc, 53 Manor Place, Edinburgh EH3 7EG (tel 0131 225 3361)

JOHNSTON, Geoffrey Edward Forshaw; s of Ronald Douglas Graham Johnston (d 1985), of Fenwick, Ayrshire, and Nancy Forshaw, *née* Price; *b* 20 June 1940; *Educ* Loretto, Univ of St Andrews (LLB); *m* 21 Dec 1964, Elizabeth Anne, da of Maj William C Lockhart, of Irvine; 2 da (Susannah b 12 May 1968, Victoria b 14 Aug 1969); *Career* trained as CA Wilson Stirling & Co 1959–65; Arbuckle Smith Group: joined 1965, md 1972, MBO 1984, gp md 1984–99; vice-chm Scottish Friendly Assurance Society Ltd; dir Glasgow C of C 1980–2001 (pres 1994–95), chm Scottish Chambers of Commerce 1996–2000, chm Central Coll of Commerce Glasgow 1999–2005; memb Scot Valuation Advsy Cncl 1982–2001; nat chm BIFA 1990–91; memb Merchants' House City of Glasgow; hon Belgian consul for W of Scot 1988–94; FCIT, FILT; *Recreations* sailing, skiing, hill walking, golf; *Style—* Geoffrey Johnston, Esq; ✉ Upper Dunard, Station Road, Rhu, Dunbartonshire G84 8LW (e-mail geoffrey@dunard.demon.co.uk)

JOHNSTON, Sheriff (Alexander) Graham; WS (1971); s of Hon Lord Kincraig, and Margaret Joan, *née* Graham; *b* 16 July 1944; *Educ* Edinburgh Acad, Strathallan Sch, Univ of Edinburgh (LLB), UC Oxford (BA, Golf blue); *m* 1, 1972 (m dis 1982), Susan Gay Horne; 2 s (Robin Graham b 30 Nov 1973, Paul Mark b 20 Oct 1975); m 2, 6 Feb 1982, Dr Angela Astrid Synnove Anderson, da of Mayer Olsen, of Newport-on-Tay; *Career* ptnr Hagart & Burn-Murdoch WS 1972–82; Sheriff: Grampian Highlands & Islands Aberdeen 1982–85, Glasgow & Strathkelvin at Glasgow 1985–2005; ed Scottish Civil Law Reports 1987–92; hon fell Inst of Professional Investigators 1979; *Recreations* photography, information technology, computers, puzzles, bridge, cooking; *Clubs* Vincent's (Oxford); *Style—* Sheriff Graham Johnston, WS; ✉ 3 North Dean Park Avenue, Bothwell, Lanarkshire G71 8HH (tel 01698 852177, e-mail grahamjohnston1@tiscali.co.uk); Kincraig, 1 Elie House, Elie, Fife KY9 1ER

JOHNSTON, Dr Ian Alistair; CB (1995), DL (2004); s of Donald Dalrymple Johnston (d 1985), and Muriel Joyce Johnston (d 1994); *b* 2 May 1944; *Educ* Royal GS High Wycombe, Univ of Birmingham (BSc, PhD); *m* 1973, Mary Bridget, da of Francis Patrick Lube (d 1985); 1 s (Donald b 1979), 1 da (Claire b 1981); *Career* Dept of Employment: asst princ 1969, princ 1973, asst sec 1978, under sec 1984, private sec to Sir Denis Barnes 1972–74, first sec Br Embassy Brussels 1975–78, Advsy Conciliation Serv 1978–84, dir Planning and Resources MSC 1984–85, chief exec VET Gp 1985–87, dep dir gen Dept of Employment Trg 1987–92, dir Resources and Strategy Directorate Dept of Employment 1992, DG Dept for Educn and Employment 1992–95; dep to Vice-Chllr and Princ Sheffield Hallam Univ 1995–98 (dep chm 1991–94), vice-chllr and princ Glasgow Caledonian Univ 1998–2006; study gp expert educn and trg strategy DG XXII Euro Cmmn 1995–99; non-exec dir: Qualifications for Industry 1996–99, CAPITB plc 1998–2003, Glasgow C of C 1998–2004; hon treas Industrial Soc 1992–2002; chief exec University for Industry 1998 (vice-chm 1998–2003); dir: Scottish Enterprise Glasgow 2004–, Lifelong Learning UK Sector Skills Cncl 2004–; tstee Carnegie Tst for the Univs of Scotland 1998–; memb: Cncl Ind and Higher Educn 2000–, Cncl EDEXCEL 1995–98, Goodison Gp Educn Think Tank 2000–; memb Bd Universities and Colleges Employers Assoc (UCEA) 2001–, CCMI, FCIPD; *Publications* author of book chapters on virtual univs, urban regeneration and application of CIT to learning; *Recreations* bird watching, fishing, tennis; *Style—* Dr Ian Johnston, CB, DL; ✉ Glasgow Caledonian University, Cowcaddens Road, Glasgow G4 0BA (tel 0141 331 3113, fax 0141 331 3174)

JOHNSTON, Prof Ian Alistair; *b* 13 April 1949; *Educ* Univ of Hull (BSc, PhD); *Career* NERC postdoctoral research fell Univ of Bristol 1973–76; Univ of St Andrews: lectr 1976–84, reader in physiology 1984–85, dir Gatty Marine Lab 1985–, prof of comparative physiology (personal chair) 1985–97, Chandos prof of physiology 1997–, fndr chm Dept of Biological and Preclinical Med 1987–91, head Sch of Biological and Med Scis 1991–92, chm Research Div of Environmental and Evolutionary Biology 1992–97, head Sch (later Div) of Environmental and Evolutionary Biology 1997–2002, dir of research Sch of Biology 2002–; visiting scientist to various outside orgns, numerous research visits abroad; memb: Bd Scottish Assoc of Marine Scis 1991–97 (memb Cncl 1994–97), Antarctic Research Ctee Royal Soc 1993–; vice-pres Soc for Experimental Biology 2005–, memb NERC (chm Marine Science and Technology Bd 1995–2000); memb Editorial Bd Jl of Comparative Physiology; Royal Soc John Murray travelling studentship in oceanography and limnology 1983, Scientific Medal Zoological Soc of London 1984, Silver Medal 8th Plymouth Marine Sci lectr USA 1994; memb Physiological Soc 1982, scientific fell Zoological Soc of London 1985, FRSE 1987, FIBiol 1997; *Books* Essentials of Physiology (jtly, 3 edn 1991, trans Spanish 1987, Italian 1989, French 1990), Phenotypic and Evolutionary Adaptation of Animals to Temperature (jt ed, 1996), Environmental Physiology of Animals (2000); various book chapters, numerous reviews and original refereed papers; *Style—* Prof Ian Johnston, FRSE; ✉ Gatty Marine Laboratory, School of Biology, University of St Andrews, St Andrews, Fife KY16 8LB (e-mail iaj@st-andrews.ac.uk)

JOHNSTON, (William) Ian Ridley; CBE (2001), QPM (1993); s of late William Johnston, and late Alice, *née* Ridley; *b* 6 September 1945; *Educ* LSE (BSc); *m* 18 May 1968, Carol Ann, da of late George Smith; 2 s (Mark Daniel, Paul Matthew); *Career* Staff Offr to Cmmr Met Police 1988–89, Asst Chief Constable Kent 1989–92, Asst Cmmr Met Police 1994–2001, Chief Constable Br Tport Police 2001–; chm Orpington Rovers Boys FC; Freeman City of London; ACPO; *Recreations* jogging, football, tennis, squash, walking; *Clubs* Orpington Rovers FC; *Style—* Ian Johnston, Esq, CBE, QPM; ✉ British Transport Police, 25 Camden Road, London NW1 9LN (tel 020 7830 8811, e-mail ian.johnston@btp.pnn.police.uk)

JOHNSTON, Prof Ivan David Alexander; s of David Johnston, and Mary, *née* Clarke; *b* 4 October 1929; *Educ* Royal Belfast Acad, Queen's Univ Belfast (MB Bch, MCH); *m* 1, 3 Sept 1959, Elizabeth (d 1987); 2 s (Stephen Robert David b 29 Nov 1961, Philip Ivan b 11 Dec 1962); m 2, 16 Dec 1989, Annette, *née* Elphinstone; *Career* lectr in surgery Queen's Univ 1954–59, res asst Mayo Clinic USA 1959–61, sr lectr and conslt surgn Royal Postgrad Med Sch London 1963–66, prof and head of Dept of Surgery Univ of Newcastle 1966–, sr surgn Royal Victoria Infirmary 1966–; pres: Int Surgical Gp 1991–92, Travelling Surgical Soc of GB 1992–95, Int Assoc Endocrine Surgns 1993–95; Hon Col 201 NGen Hosp RAMC 1989; memb: Northumberland Health Authy, Cncl RCS; FRSM, FRCS 1959, Hon FACS 1985, FRCSEd 1987; *Books* Metabolic Basis of Surgical Care (1968), Advances in Parenteral Nutrition (1980), Modern Trends in Surgical Endocrinology (1986); *Recreations* gardening, photography; *Clubs* 1942, Grey Turner Surgical; *Style—* Prof Ivan Johnston; ✉ The Old Farmhouse, Ebrington, Chipping Campden, Gloucestershire GL55 6NL

JOHNSTON, Dr Leland Herries (Lee); s of Henry Johnston (d 1966), and Freda Johnston (d 2000); *b* 11 June 1944; *Educ* Milton HS Bulawayo, Univ of Cape Town (BSc, MSc), Univ of Oxford (Rhodes scholar, DPhil); *m* 19 Dec 1970, Margaret, *née* Caldwell; *Career* Damon Runyon cancer research fell Univ of Calif Berkeley 1971–73, Fulbright fell 1971–73, research fell Max Planck Soc Tubingen 1974–75, staff scientist Nat Inst for Med Research 1975–88, head Div of Yeast Genetics Nat Inst for Med Research 1988–; author of many papers in scientific jls; rep Rhodesia, All South African Univs and Univ of Oxford at waterpolo; fell EMBO 1995, FMedSci 2000; *Recreations* reading, hiking, worrying, music, art, scuba diving; *Clubs* Bushey and Borehamwood Sub Aqua; *Style—* Dr Lee Johnston; ✉ Division of Genetics, National Institute for Medical Research, The Ridgeway, Mill Hill, London NW7 1AA (tel 020 8816 2234, fax 020 8816 2523)

JOHNSTON, Mark Steven; s of Ronald Johnston, of Gartmore, by Stirling, Scotland, and Mary Woods, *née* Nicol; *b* 10 October 1959; *Educ* McLaren HS Calander, Univ of Glasgow; *m* 8 June 1985, Deirdre Munro, da of Dr Duncan Ferguson, of Bearsden, Glasgow; *Career* veterinary practice 1983–86; racehorse trainer 1987–; horses trained incl: Mister Baileys, Double Trigger, Bijon D'Inde, Princely Heir, Lend a Hand, Pearl of Love, Royal Rebel, Yavana's Pace, Attraction, Shamardal; races won incl: Two Thousand Guineas 1994, Ascot Gold Cup 1995, 2001 and 2002, St James Palace Stakes 1996, Phoenix Stakes 1997, Gran Criterium 1997 and 2003, Credit Suisse Private Banking Pokal 2002, One Thousand Guineas 2004, Irish One Guineas 2004, Coronation Stakes 2004, Sun Chariot Stakes 2004, Dewhurst Stakes 2004, Matron Stakes 2005; MRCVS 1983; *Style—* Mark Johnston, Esq; ✉ Kingsley House, Middleham, Leyburn, North Yorkshire DL8 4PH (tel 01969 622237, fax 01969 622484, mobile 07802 339670)

JOHNSTON, Peter William; s of William Johnston (d 1974), and Louisa Alice, *née* Pritchard (d 2001); *b* 8 February 1943; *Educ* Larbert HS, Univ of Glasgow (MA, LLB); *m* 1967, Patricia Sandra, da of late Alexander Yates Macdonald; 1 da (Wendy Ann b 7 May 1969), 1 s (Alasdair Peter b 10 Dec 1970); *Career* ptnr MacArthur & Co Slrs 1971–76 (asst 1968–76), procurator fiscal Procurator Fiscal Service 1978–86 (sr legal asst 1976–78), Crown Office 1986–89 (latterly asst slr), chief exec and sec ICAS 1989–99, chief exec Int Fedn of Accountants (IFAC) 1999–; memb Law Soc of Scotland 1967; FRSA 1990; *Recreations* music, sailing, languages; *Clubs* New (Edinburgh); *Style—* Peter Johnston, Esq; ✉ 10 East 29th Street, Apt 40G, New York, NY 10017, USA (tel 00 1 212 679 3401); The International Federation of Accountants (IFAC), 535 Fifth Avenue 26th Floor, New York, NY 10017, USA (tel 00 1 212 286 9344, e-mail peterjohnston@ifac.org)

JOHNSTON, Robert; s of F P M Johnston, of Edinburgh, and E A Jones; *b* 6 November 1964; *Educ* Edinburgh Acad, UEA (BA); *Career* journalist; ed Style Sunday Times 2000–2002 (dep ed 1999–2000), editorial conslt Evening Standard 2002, exec ed Wallpaper* 2003–; *Recreations* reading, travel, feuds and food; *Clubs* Soho House; *Style—* Robert Johnston, Esq; ✉ 16 West Square, London SE11 4SN (tel 020 7771 1393)

JOHNSTON, Prof Ronald John (Ron); s of Henry Louis Johnston (d 1989), and Phyllis Joyce, *née* Liddiard (d 2006); *b* 30 March 1941; *Educ* Commonweal Co GS Swindon, Univ of Manchester (BA, MA), Monash Univ (PhD); *m* 16 April 1963, Rita, *née* Brennan; 1 s (Christopher Martin b 18 Sept 1964), 1 da (Lucy Carolyn b 30 July 1966); *Career* Monash Univ: teaching fell 1964, sr teaching fell 1965, lectr 1966; Dept of Geography Univ of Canterbury: lectr 1967–69, sr lectr 1969–73, reader 1973–74; Univ of Sheffield: prof Dept of Geography 1974–92, pro-vice chllr for academic affairs 1989–92; vice-chllr Univ of Essex 1992–95, prof of geography Univ of Bristol 1995–; Inst of Br Geographers: sec 1982–85, vice-pres 1988–89, pres 1990; honors award for scholarly distinction Assoc of American Geographers 1991; Prix Vautrin Lud 1999; Hon DUniv Essex, Hon LLD Monash Univ, Hon DLitt Univ of Sheffield, Hon DLitt Univ of Bath; FRGS (Murchison award 1985, Victoria medal 1990), FBA 1999, memb Acad of Social Scis (AcSS) 1999; *Books* author of 50, ed of over 40; *Recreations* bell-ringing (pres Yorks Assoc of Change Ringers 1989–92, pres Central Cncl of Church Bellringers 1993–96 (vice-pres 1990–93)); *Style—* Prof Ron Johnston; ✉ School of Geographical Sciences, University of Bristol, Bristol BS8 1SS (tel 0117 928 9116, fax 0117 928 7878, e-mail r.johnston@bristol.ac.uk)

JOHNSTON, Sir Thomas Alexander; 14 Bt (NS 1626), of Caskieben, Aberdeenshire; only s of Sir Thomas Alexander Johnston, 13 Bt (d 1984), and Helen Torrey, *née* Du Bois; *b* 1 February 1956; *Heir* kinsman, William Johnston; *Style—* Sir Thomas A Johnston, Bt

JOHNSTONE, Dr Adrian Ivor Clive; *b* 14 January 1960; *Educ* St Dunstan's Coll London, Royal Holloway Coll London (BSc, PhD); *Career* Royal Holloway Coll London (now Royal Holloway Univ of London): research fell 1984–86, lectr 1986–97, dean Faculty of Science 1994–97, sr lectr 1997–; visiting lectr in VLSI design: Curtin Univ of Technol Perth Australia 1991, King's Coll London 1991–92; tech dir Soroban Ltd 1987–91, visiting industrial fell Image Inspection Ltd 1990–93; memb/chm various Coll and Univ ctees and bds; assoc memb: Inst of Electrical and Electronic Engrs (USA), Assoc for Computing Machinery (USA); govr St Anne's Heath Junior Sch 1998–; MBCS, MIEE; *Books* LATEX, concisely (1992, revised edn and trans into Japanese 1994); also author of numerous articles and papers in learned jls; *Style—* Dr Adrian Johnstone; ✉ Faculty of Science, Royal Holloway, University of London, Egham, Surrey TW20 0EX (e-mail a.johnstone@rhul.ac.uk)

JOHNSTONE, Alexander; MSP; *b* 31 July 1961; *m* 7 Nov 1981, Linda; 1 s (Alexander b 21 March 1983), 1 da (Christine b 19 May 1987); *Career* self-employed farmer; MSP (Cons) Scotland NE 1999–; *Style—* Alex Johnstone, Esq, MSP; ✉ The Scottish Parliament, Edinburgh EH99 1SP (tel 0131 348 5649, fax 0131 348 5934, mobile 07802 190833); 25 Evan Street, Stonehaven, Kincardineshire AB39 2EQ (tel and fax 01569 765826)

JOHNSTONE, Iain Gilmour; s of Jack Johnstone (d 1990), of Perth, Scotland, and Gillie Gilmour (d 1979); *b* 8 April 1943; *Educ* Campbell Coll Belfast, Univ of Bristol (LLB, slrs finals); *m* Maureen, da of Robert Watson; 2 da (Sophie b 22 June 1981, Holly b 28 Aug 1983), 1 s (Oliver b 1 March 1990); *Career* newscaster ITN 1966–67, reporter The Times 1967, prodr BBC TV 1968–74 (devised Ask Aspel, Film '71 and Friday Night Saturday Morning), visiting prof Univ of Boston 1975, presenter Film 83 and Film 84 (BBC), film critic The Sunday Times 1983–93; chm Screenplay BBC Radio 4 1986–95, UK host Academy Awards (Sky) 1991 and 1992; BAFTA nomination for best documentary (Snowdon on Camera) 1981; accredited mediator 2004; *Books* The Arnhem Report (1976), The Man With No Name (1978), Dustin Hoffman (1980), Cannes: The Novel (1990), Wimbledon 2000 (1992), The James Bond Companion (2000), Tom Cruise: All the World's a Stage (2007), Richard Whiteley (2007); *Screenplays* Fierce Creatures (with John Cleese, *qv*, 1997), The Evening News (2001), The Bank of San Benedetto (2002), Glenn and Sebastian (2008); *Recreations* lawn tennis, skiing, poetry; *Clubs* Garrick, Queen's; *Style—* Iain Johnstone, Esq; ✉ c/o Sheil Land Associates Limited, 52 Doughty Street, London WC1N 2LS (e-mail iain.j@uk.com)

JOHNSTONE, Patricia Anne (Pat); da of John Johnstone (d 2006), and Catherine (Kitty), *née* McGirr; *b* 17 March 1955, Dumfries; *Educ* Dumfries Acad, Univ of Glasgow (MA), Univ of Central Eng; *partner* Gilles Crawford; *Career* admitted slr 1986; Eversheds (formerly Eversheds & Tomkinson): joined as trainee slr 1984, slr Corp Dept 1986, banking ptnr 1994–; memb Advsy Bd Aston Business Sch; MInstB; *Recreations* house renovation, riding, ballet; *Style—* Ms Pat Johnstone; ✉ Long Marston Grounds, Long Marston, Stratford on Avon, Warwickshire CV37 8RP; Eversheds LLP, 115 Colmore Row, Birmingham B3 3AL (tel 0845 497 1083, e-mail patjohnstone@eversheds.com)

JOHNSTONE, Sir (John) Raymond; kt (1993), CBE (1988); o s of Capt Henry James Johnstone, RN (d 1947, fourth in descent from John Johnstone, who commanded the artillery at the Battle of Plassey, to which victory he substantially contributed, and who was s of Sir James Johnstone, 3 Bt), of The Myretoun, Menstrie, Clackmannanshire, and Margaret Alison McIntyre (d 1984); *b* 27 October 1929; *Educ* Eton, Trinity Coll Cambridge (BA); *m* 1979, Susan Sara, da of Christopher Gerald Gore (d 1955), widow of Peter

Quixano Henriques (d 1974), and of Basil Ziani de Ferranti; 5 step s, 2 step da; *Career* chm: Dominion Insurance Ltd 1978–95, Scottish Amicable Life Assurance Soc 1983–85 (dir 1971–97), Scottish Opera 1983–86 (hon pres 1986–98), Murray Johnstone Ltd 1984–92 (md 1968–88, hon pres 1992–2001), Yamaichi-Murray Johnstone Ltd 1986–96, Scottish Financial Enterprise 1989–92, Forestry Commission 1989–94, Summit Group plc 1989–98, Atrium Underwriting plc (formerly Lomond Underwriting plc) 1993–2003, The Historic Bldgs Cncl for Scotland 1995–2002; dir: Murray Ventures plc 1984–98, Murray Income Trust plc 1989–99, Murray Global Return Trust plc 1989–2000, Murray Enterprise plc 1989–2000, Murray International Trust plc 1989–2005, Kiln plc 1995–2002, The Nuclear Liabilities Fund Ltd 1996– (chm 1995–2002), Loch Lomond Tst 1999–2002, The Patrons of the Nat Galleries of Scotland 1999–2003 (chm 1995–99), The Nuclear Tst (chm 1996–2003); CA 1955; *Recreations* fishing, music, farming; *Style—* Sir Raymond Johnstone, CBE; ✉ 20 Ann Street, Edinburgh EH4 1PJ (tel 0131 311 7100, fax 0131 311 7101)

JOHNSTONE, Sir (George) Richard Douglas; 11 Bt (NS 1700), of Westerhall, Dumfriesshire; s of Sir Frederic Allan George Johnstone, 10 Bt (d 1994); *b* 21 August 1948; *Educ* Magdalen Coll Oxford (MA); *m* 1976, Gwyneth, da of Arthur Bailey, of Hastings; 1 s (Frederic Robert Arthur b 18 Nov 1981), 1 da (Caroline Anne b 1983); *Heir* s, Frederic Johnstone; *Career* md Moat House Conslts Ltd, FIMC; *Style—* Sir Richard Johnstone, Bt

JOHNSTONE, William Neill (Bill); s of Harry McCall Johnstone (d 1985), of Forfar, and Ethel Mary Neill; *b* 16 May 1938; *Educ* Forfar Acad, Edinburgh Acad, Univ of Edinburgh, Scottish Coll of Textiles, RCA; *m* 1 (m dis); 2 da (Catriona Mhairi b 14 Dec 1964, Lilian MacDonald b 14 March 1966); m 2, 14 Dec 1991, Mara Lukic; 1 s (James Ilya Neill b 27 Oct 1993), 1 da (Louise Jelena b 20 Aug 1995); *Career* designer then design dir R G Neill & Son 1961–70, md and design dir Neill of Langholm 1970–85, design dir Illingworth Morris Group and co-ordinator trg programme 1982–85; fndr: Neill Johnstone Ltd 1986 (specialises in providing seasonal collections for int apparel fabric markets), Fabric Design Consultants International Ltd 1989; IWS design conslt 1978–90; memb C B W T Steering Ctee 1981–85 (chm 1982–85); indust on selection panel S D A/S W I Designer Graduate Attachment Scheme; RDI 1989, FRSA 1991; *Recreations* climbing, hill walking, collecting inuit carvings; *Style—* Bill Johnstone, Esq; ✉ Neill Johnstone Ltd, William Street, Langholm DG13 0BN (tel 01387 381122, fax 01387 381106, e-mail neilljohnstone@neilljohnstoneltd.com)

JOICEY, 5 Baron (UK 1906); Sir James Michael Joicey; 5 Bt (UK 1893); s of 4 Baron Joicey, DL (d 1993), and Elisabeth Marion, *née* Leslie Melville; *b* 28 June 1953; *Educ* Eton, ChCh Oxford; *m* 16 June 1984, Agnes Harriet Frances Mary, yr da of Rev William Thompson, of Jedburgh, Roxburghshire; 2 da (Hon Hannah Elisabeth b 25 June 1988, Hon Claire Vida b 1 Dec 1994), 2 s (Hon William James b 21 May 1990, Hon Richard Michael b 17 Feb 1993); *Heir* s, Hon William Joicey; *Style—* The Rt Hon the Lord Joicey; ✉ Etal Manor, Berwick-upon-Tweed TD15 2PU

JOICEY-CECIL, James David Edward; s of Edward Wilfrid George Joicey-Cecil (d 1985), gs of 3 Marquess of Exeter, and Rosemary Lusia, *née* Bowes-Lyon (d 1989), gd of 14 Earl of Strathmore and Kinghorne, and of 5 Earl of Portarlington; *b* 24 September 1946; *Educ* Eton; *m* 1975, Jane Susanna Brydon, da of Capt P W B Adeley (d 1968); 2 da (Katherine Mary b 1978, Susanna Maud b 1981); *Career* Whinney Murray & Co (now Ernst & Young) 1965–72; James Capel & Co 1972–96 (pnr 1978–86), HSBC Investment Bank plc (formerly James Capel & Co) 1996–98; dir: HSBC Financial Services (Middle East) Ltd 1995–98, Sutherlands Ltd 1998–2000, Charterhouse Securities Ltd 2000; fund dir Cazenove 2000–02, Credit Suisse Private Banking 2004–; memb London Stock Exchange 1978–92, dir Milton Abbey School Services Ltd; FCA 1979, FSI 2001; *Clubs* Annabel's, Boodle's, City of London, HAC; *Style—* James Joicey-Cecil, Esq; ✉ 24 Clapham Mansions, Nightingale Lane, London SW4 9AQ (tel 020 8675 0265); Keeper's Cottage, Delcombe, Milton Abbas, Blandford, Dorset DT11 0BT (tel 01258 880292)

JOLL, Christopher Andrew; s of Sqdn Ldr Ian K S Joll, DFC, AE, RAuxAF (d 1978), and Eileen Mary Sassoon Sykes; *b* 16 October 1948; *Educ* Oundle, RMA Sandhurst (Armorers and Braziers Co young offrs prize), Mansfield Coll Oxford (MA); *Career* served Br Army: joined RMA Sandhurst 1966, cmmnd 2 Lieut Life Gds 1968, served NI 1969, 1970, 1972 and 1974, ret 1975; gen mangr Michael Peters & Partners Ltd 1978 (joined 1977), dir corp affrs United Scientific Holdings 1988 (joined 1978), chief exec Charles Barker City Ltd 1989 (dir 1988), dir Charles Barker Ltd 1989, chief exec Georgeson & Co Ltd 1991–93, dep chm GCI Financial Ltd (formerly GCI Focus Ltd) 1996–2001; chm: The Silver Fund plc 2001–04, MJ2 Ltd 2002–; dir: Kleinwort Benson Securities Ltd 1993–95, Butler Kelly Ltd 2001–, Dragon Retail Ltd 2002–, Bisichi Mining plc 2001–; memb Steering Ctee Household Cavalry Museum Tst 2002–; dir Br Youth Opera 1993–2000; *Recreations* field sports, bridge, collecting; *Clubs* Brooks's; *Style—* Christopher Joll, Esq; ✉ Sham Castle, Acton Burnell, Shropshire SY5 7PE; MJ2 (tel 07721 330730)

JOLLES, Bernard Nathan; s of Dr Benjamin Jolles (d 1985), of Northampton, and Miriam, *née* Blake; *b* 23 August 1949; *Educ* Bedford Sch, St John's Coll Cambridge (MA), Balliol Coll Oxford (MSc), London Business Sch (MSc); *m* 1 Dec 1986, Pamela, da of Horace Knight (d 1973), of Hastings; 1 da (Antonia Sarah b 21 Jan 1989); *Career* dir: Samuel Montagu & Co Ltd 1982–87, Henry Ansbacher & Co Ltd 1988–94, Campbell Lutyens & Co Ltd 1995–2001, Wilmington Gp plc 2001–05 (chm 2003–05); *Recreations* golf, skiing, tennis; *Style—* Bernard N Jolles, Esq; ✉ 110 Regent's Park Road, London NW1 8UG (tel 020 7722 5522)

JOLLIFFE, John Anthony; s of Donald Norman Jolliffe (d 1967), of Dover, Kent, and Edith Constance Mary, *née* Lovegrove (d 1993); *b* 1 August 1937; *Educ* Dover Coll; *m* 1, 5 June 1965 (m dis 1983), Jacqueline Mary, *née* Smith, 1 da (Jenny b 1966), 1 s (Jeffrey b 1968); m 2, 3 Aug 1984 (m dis 1986), Irmgard Elizabeth, *née* Melville; 1 s (Andrew b 1985); m 3, 11 Aug 1990 (m dis 1994), Dorothy Jane, *née* Saul; *Career* Nat Serv RAF 1955–57; ptnr R Watson & Sons 1967–91 (joined 1957), princ J A Jolliffe & Co 1991–; examiner in pension funds Inst of Actuaries 1970–75 (tutor 1965–70), memb UK Steering Ctee for Local Govt Superannuation 1975–95, chm ACA Local Govt Superannuation Ctee 1975–95, treas Assoc of Consulting Actuaries 1980–84; dir: London Aerial Tours Ltd 1983–, Highverse Ltd 1991–; chm: Capital Pension Trustees Ltd 1992–2002, Pentrust Ltd 2002–; memb Cncl Nat Assoc of Pension Funds 1983–91; chm: NAPF Int Ctee 1986–88, Euro Fedn of Retirement Provision 1988–91; Freeman City of London, Liveryman Worshipful Co of Actuaries; FIA 1964, FPMI 1977; *Recreations* flying, tennis, travel; *Style—* John Jolliffe, Esq; ✉ Hurst House, Clay Lane, Redhill, Surrey RH1 4EG (tel 01737 779997, fax 01737 778478, e-mail johnjolliffe@lineone.net)

JOLLY, Michael Gordon; CBE (2001); *b* 21 September 1952; *Career* The Tussauds Group (incl Alton Towers, Chessington World of Adventures, Warwick Castle, Madame Tussaud's London, The London Planetarium, London Eye, Madame Tussaud Scenerama Amsterdam, Thorpe Park, Madame Tussaud's Las Vegas, New York and Hong Kong): exec dir 1987–92, chief operating offr 1992–94, chm and chief exec 1994–2000, chm 2001; chief exec Penna Consulting plc 2001–03, chm Star Parks Europe (incl 7 European theme parks) 2004–06, chm Cinque Ports Leisure 2006–; chm CBI Tourism Gp 1997–2000, tstee Tourism and Hospitality Tst 1997–2000, advsr to New Millennium Experience Co Bd 1999, cmmr English Heritage; *Recreations* golf, the arts; *Style—* Michael Jolly, Esq, CBE

JOLLY, (Robert) Miles; s of John Jolly (d 1990), and Lucy, *née* Bradley (d 1968); *b* 2 September 1937, Walton, Yorks; *Educ* Trent Coll; *m* 6 July 1963, Gillian, *née* Robson; 1 s (Marcus James Miles b 26 Sept 1967), 1 da (Fiona Claire b 31 Aug 1970); *Career* fin dir GEC Electronics 1969–71, md Britpack Ltd 1972–75, md Humberoak Group 1976–80, chm and md Limes Gp of Cos 1980–; canon Lincoln Cathedral (also memb Governing Chapter and chm of finance); FCA; *Clubs* Army and Navy; *Style—* Miles Jolly, Esq; ✉ Limes House, Burton-by-Lincoln LN1 2RB

JOLLY, Nicholas John; s of Michael Harvey Jolly, and Anne Margaret, *née* Saunders; *b* 11 March 1962; *Educ* St Francis Xavier's Coll Liverpool, Worthing Sixth Form Coll, W Sussex Coll of Art, Glos Coll of Art (BA), Royal Acad Schs (postgrad dip); *Career* artist, co-fndr and art dir The Chap Magazine; television animator Jack Dee's Happy Hour; awarded Elizabeth Greenshields Fndn Grant 1989, Susan Kasen Travel Scholarship (6 Months in Connecticut) 1993, Pollock-Krasner Fndn Grant 1995; *Solo Exhibitions* Paton Gallery London 1991 and 1993, Beaux Arts London 1996; *Group Exhibitions* John Player Portrait Awards (Nat Portrait Gallery) 1984, Young Masters - Ten Young Painters (Solomon Gallery London) 1985, Young Masters (Kunsthaus im Welserhof Augsburg) 1988, New Faces II (Paton Gallery) 1989, Royal Over-Seas League Annual Exhbn 1989, 1990 and 1991, Threshold - Two Man Exhbn (Plymouth City Museum and Art Gallery) 1990, The Bridge Show (Lannon Gallery NY) 1994, The Kasen Summer Collection (touring exhbn Glasgow and London) 1994–95, Osaka Triennale (Japan) 1996, BP Portrait Awards (Nat Portrait Gallery) 1997, Arnot Art Museum Elmira NY 1997, René Magrite and Contemporary Art Ostend Belgium 1998, Figure Eight (Newarts Gallery CT) 1999; Hunting Art Prizes RCA 1998, Osaka Triennale 2001; *Public Collections* Metropolitan Museum of Art NY, Durban Museum of Art SA; *Books* The Chap Manifesto (2001), The Chap Almanac (2002), Around the World in Eighty Martinis (2003), The Lost Art of Travel (2006); *Recreations* intemperance and torpidity; *Style—* Nicholas Jolly, Esq; ✉ Holmcroft, High Street, Findon, West Sussex BN14 0SZ (tel 020 7916 1694, e-mail nick@artfink.demon.co.uk)

JOLLY, Sir (Arthur) Richard; KCMG (2001); s of late Arthur Jolly, and Flora Doris, *née* Leaver; *b* 30 June 1934; *Educ* Brighton Coll, Magdalene Coll Cambridge (BA, MA), Yale Univ (MA, PhD); *m* 1963, Alison Bishop; 2 s, 2 da; *Career* community devpt offr Baringo Dist Kenya 1957–59, sec Br Alpine Hannibal Expedition 1959, research fell Makerere Coll Uganda 1963–64, research offr Dept of Applied Economics Univ of Cambridge 1964–66, advsr Parly Select Ctee on Overseas Aid and Devpt 1974–75; Univ of Sussex: professorial fell 1971–, dir Inst of Devpt Studies 1972–81; dep exec dir UNICEF 1982–95, special advsr UNDP 1996–2000; memb: Founding Ctee Euro Assoc of Devpt Insts 1973–75, Editorial Bd World Devpt 1973–, UK Cncl on Int Devpt 1974–78, Triennial Review Gp Cwlth Fund for Tech Co-operation 1975–76, Governing Cncl for Society for Int Devpt 1976–85 (vice-pres 1982–85), UN Ctee for Devpt Planning 1978–81; chm North-South Round Table 1988–96 (memb 1978–); Master Worshipful Co of Curriers 1977–78; Hon DLitt: UEA 1988, Univ of Sussex 1992; *Publications* Cuba: The Economic and Social Revolution (jtly, 1964), Planning Education for African Development (1969), Redistribution with Growth (jtly, 1974), The Impact of World Recession on Children (ed jtly, 1984), Adjustment with a Human Face (ed jtly, 1987), Human Development Report (jtly, 1996–2000), UN Contributions to Development Thinking and Practice (2004); author various articles in professional jls; *Recreations* billiards, croquet, nearly missing trains and planes; *Style—* Sir Richard Jolly, KCMG; ✉ Institute of Development Studies, University of Sussex, Brighton, East Sussex BN1 9RE (tel 01273 606261)

JOLOWICZ, Prof John Anthony (Tony); QC (1990); s of Prof Herbert Felix Jolowicz (d 1954), and Ruby Victoria, *née* Wagner (d 1963); *b* 11 April 1926; *Educ* Oundle, Trinity Coll Cambridge (MA); *m* 8 Aug 1957, Poppy, da of Norman Stanley; 2 da (Kate (Mrs Little) b 4 May 1959, Sophie b 26 June 1961), 1 s (Nathaniel Herbert b 20 July 1963); *Career* Lt RASC 1944–48; called to the Bar Inner Temple 1952, bencher Gray's Inn 1978; Univ of Cambridge: asst lectr 1955, lectr 1959, reader 1972, prof of comparative law 1976–93, chm Faculty of Law 1984–86, fell Trinity Coll 1952–; prof associé Univ de Paris II 1976, Lionel Cohen lectr Univ of Jerusalem 1983; pres SPTL 1986–87, a vice-pres Int Acad of Comparative Law 1994–2006; ed of various law jls and author of various legal works; HonD Universidad Nacional Autónoma de México 1985, Hon LLD Univ of Buckingham 2000; memb Academia Europaea; Chevalier de la Légion d'Honneur 2002; *Recreations* reading, music, travel; *Clubs* Leander, RAC; *Style—* Prof J A Jolowicz, QC; ✉ West Green House, Barrington, Cambridge CB22 7SA (tel 01223 870495, fax 01223 872852); La Truffière, 47120 St Jean-de-Duras, France; Trinity College, Cambridge CB2 1TQ (tel 01223 338400, fax 01223 338564, e-mail jaj1000@cam.ac.uk)

JOLY, Dom; *b* 1967, Beirut, Lebanon; *Educ* Haileybury, SOAS Univ of London; *Career* comedian; intern European Cmmn Prague 1991–92, researcher Roth's Parly Profiles 1993–94, asst prodr then prodr Around Westminster (BBC) and House to House (ITN) 1995–96, political researcher The Mark Thomas Comedy Product (Channel 4) 1996, asst prodr Man-Made News (Paramount Comedy Channel) 1997, prodr and performer War of the Flea (Paramount Comedy Channel) 1998, co-writer, co-prodr and performer Trigger Happy TV (Channel 4) 1998–2002 (Silver Rose of Montreux 2000, Best Entertainment Show BBC2 Awards 2000), Trigger Happy (Comedy Central USA) 2003, prodr and performer This Is Dom Joly (2 series, BBC3) 2003, co-writer, co-prodr and performer World Shut Your Mouth (BBC1) 2005; columnist Independent on Sunday, travel writer Sunday Times; *Books* Look At Me, Look At Me! (2004); *Style—* Dom Joly; ✉ c/o PBJ Management, 7 Soho Street, London W1D 3DQ (tel 020 7287 1112, fax 020 7287 1191)

JOLY, Simon Michael Bencraft; 2 s of Richard Bencraft Joly (d 1956), and Joan Letitia Brooke, *née* Parnell (d 1993); *b* 14 October 1952; *Educ* Christ's Hosp, CCC Cambridge (MA); *Career* conductor; music staff WNO 1974–78, asst then assoc chorus master ENO 1978–80, conductor BBC Singers 1989–95 (asst conductor 1980–89); asst to Pierre Boulez with BBC Singers Paris, Berlin and London; FRCO; *Performances* BBC Singers' concerts incl: 70th Anniversary Concert (music by Britten, Messiaen, Ligeti, Poulenc and Xenakis), Berio Coro (with London Sinfonietta, La Scala Milan); BBC Proms: Stravinsky Les Noces, Giles Swayne CRY, Steve Reich The Desert Music; work with BBC Symphony Orch incl: Hindemith Cello Concerto, Martinu Symphony No 6, Charles Ives Three Places in New England, Gavin Bryars The War in Heaven (premiere, Royal Festival Hall), Debussy La Damoiselle Élue and Le Martyre de St Sebastien, Stravinsky Canticum Sacrum, Messiaen Le Tombeau Resplendissant and L'Ascension, David Bedford 1st Symphony, Henze The Raft of the Medusa; work with other orchs incl: London Sinfonietta, Bournemouth Sinfonietta, City of London Sinfonia, BBC Philharmonic, Ulster Orch, Endymion Ensemble, New London Orch; *Operas* several Wexford Festivals, Smetana The Bartered Bride (ENO), Mozart Cosi Fan Tutte and Le Nozze di Figaro (Irish National Opera), Britten Peter Grimes (Irish and Royal Danish Opera), Gluck La Contesa de Numi (Royal Danish Opera), Bizet Carmen (with José Carreras, Berlin), rare operas by Max Brand, Wagner-Regeny and Weber (Radio 3); *Recordings* incl major choral music of Sir P Maxwell Davies, Sir John Tavener and Granville Bantock; *Recreations* theatre, films; *Style—* Simon Joly, Esq, FRCO; ✉ 49B Disraeli Road, Putney, London SW15 2DR (tel 020 8785 9617, e-mail simonjoly@tiscali.co.uk)

JONAS, Christopher William; CBE (1994); s of Philip Griffith Jonas, MC (d 1982), and Kathleen Marjory, *née* Ellis (d 2000); *b* 19 August 1941; *Educ* Charterhouse, Coll of Estate Mgmnt, London Business Sch; *m* 1, 1968 (m dis 1997), Penny, *née* Barker; 3 s ((Leslie) Peter b 16 April 1970, Toby Philip b 10 Nov 1971, Max Christopher b 2 Feb 1977), 1 da (Freya Josephine Wendy b 4 Feb 1981); m 2, 2003, Dame Judith Mayhew, DBE; *Career* TA Inns of Court Regt 1959–66; Jones Lang Wootton 1959–67; Drivers Jonas: ptnr 1967–82, managing ptnr 1982–87, sr ptnr 1987–95; fndr Christopher Jonas/Strategy for Corporate Property 1995–2005; pres RICS 1992–93; property advsr Staffs CC 1982–2005; chm Economics Res Assoc (USA) 1987–93; fndr ProHelp 1989; dir: Securities and Futures

Authy 1988–91, British Rail Property Bd 1991–94, Railtrack Group plc 1994–2001, Canary Wharf Gp plc 1994–2004, Sunrise Senior Living International 1998–, England Bd Bank of Scotland 1998–2000, Business in the Community 1999–2006; memb: Port of London Authy 1985–99, Further Educn Funding Cncl 1992–98 Bd British Railways 1993–94; chm: Education Capital Finance 2000–, Glasgow Harbour 2001–03, Ethics Standards Bd Accountancy Fndn 2001–03, Henderson Global Property Companies Ltd 2006–; sr advsr Lazard & Co 2007–; tstee Westminster Abbey Pension Fund 2001–; chm second stage devpt Tate Modern 2006– (chair original devpt 1997–2000); dir ENO 1999–2007; govr: Charterhouse 1995–2006, UCL 1997–2005 (vice-chm 2000–04); chm Cncl: Roedean 2004–, Goldsmiths Univ of London 2006–; memb Counselors of Real Estate USA (Gold medal 2007); Hon DSc De Montfort Univ 1997; Liveryman Worshipful Co of Clothworkers (Master 2007–08); FInstD, FRSA; *Recreations* lieder, church music, opera, playing tennis; *Clubs* Queen's, Toronto (Toronto); *Style—* Christopher William Jonas, Esq, CBE; ✉ 25 Victoria Square, London SW1W 0RB (tel 020 7828 9977, e-mail cwj@kingslodge.com)

JONAS, Sir Peter; kt (2000), CBE (1993); s of Walter Adolf Jonas (d 1965), of Hamburg and London, and Hilda May, *née* Ziadie, of Kingston, Jamaica; *b* 14 October 1946, London; *Educ* Worth Sch, Univ of Sussex (BA), Royal Northern Coll of Music (LRAM), Royal Coll of Music (CAMS), Eastman Sch of Music, Univ of Rochester; *m* 22 Nov 1989 (m dis 2001), Lucy, da of Christopher Hull, and Cecilia, *née* Pollen; *Career* Chicago Symphony Orch: asst to music dir 1974–76, artistic admin 1976–85; dir of artistic admin Orchestral Assoc of Chicago 1977–85 (Chicago Symphony Orch, Civil Orch of Chicago, Chicago Symphony Chorus, Allied Arts Assoc, Orchestra Hall), gen dir ENO 1985–93, staatsintendant (gen dir) Bavarian State Opera Munich 1993–2006 (now hon life memb); lectr and faculty memb Univ of St Gallen 2003–, lectr Univ of Zürich 2004–, visiting lectr Bavarian Theatre Acad Munich; chm German Speaking Opera Intendants Conf 2001–05; memb: Bd of Mgmnt Nat Opera Studio 1985–93, Cncl of Mgmnt London Lighthouse 1990–93, Kuratorium Richard Strauss Gesellschaft 1993–, Beirat (Advsy Bd) Hypovereinsbank Munich 1994–2004, Rundfunkrat (Bd of Govrs) Bayerische Rundfunk (Bavarian Radio and TV) 1999–2006; memb: Assoc Internationale de Directeurs de L'Opera 1985–2006, Deutsche Bühnenverein 1993–2006, Bavarian Acad of Fine Arts 2005–, Deutsche Opernkonferenz 1993–2006, Stiftungsrat (Bd of Tstees) Berlin Opera and Ballet cos 2005–, Advsy Bd Carl Linde Acad Tech Univ Munich; Hon DMus Univ of Sussex 1994; FRCM 1989 (memb Cncl 1988–95); FRSA 1989, FRNCM 2000; Bayerische Verdienstorden 2001, Bavarian Constitutional Medal 2001; *Publications* Powerhouse, The English National Opera Experience (jtly, 1993), Eliten and Demokratie (jtly, 1999); *Recreations* mountain and long-distance hiking, cinema, cricket, 20th century architecture, old master paintings; *Clubs* Athenaeum, Surrey CCC, Munich CC; *Style—* Sir Peter Jonas, CBE; ✉ Einsiedlerstrasse 15a, 8820 Wädenswil, Switzerland (tel 0041 43 477 9871, fax 0041 43 477 9872, e-mail sirpeterjonas@hispeed.ch and sirpeterjonas@t-online.de)

JONATHAN, Mark; s of John Francis Boyle, and Josephine, *née* Harper (d 2000); *b* 2 January 1956; *Educ* Oxted Co Sch; *Career* lighting designer; chief electrician Nat Youth Theatre 1973–78, technical dir Nat Youth Theatre 1980–81, dep lighting mangr Glyndebourne Festival Opera 1978–92, head of lighting RNT 1993–2003, freelance lighting designer 2003–; lighting designs incl prodns for: RNT, Royal Ballet, Birmingham Royal Ballet, LA Opera, Israeli Opera, Bavarian State Opera, Washington Nat Opera, Opera du Rhin, Vlammse Opera, Scottish Ballet, Berlin Staats Ballett, Scottish Opera, Northern Ballet Theatre, Stuttgart Ballet, American Ballet Theatre, Royal Court London, Chichester Festival; various West End and Broadway prodns; lectr in lighting for dirs, designers and lighting designers on BA, postgrad and specialist courses; professional and exec memb Assoc of Lighting Designers, memb Assoc of Br Theatre Technicians; memb: SBTD, United Scenic Artists, Br Actors Equity; nomination Outstanding Lighting Design Drama Desk NY 2007; ski teacher, memb Br Assoc of Snowsport Instructors; *Recreations* classical music, theatre, winter sports; *Style—* Mark Jonathan, Esq; ✉ 103 Bellenden Road, London SE15 4QY (tel 020 7639 7815, mobile 07802 769376, e-mail mj@markjonathan.com, website www.markjonathan.com)

JONES, Alan Wingate; s of Gilbert Victor Jones (d 1971), of Kingswood, Surrey, and Isobel Nairn Wilson; *b* 15 October 1939; *Educ* Sutton Valence, King's Coll Cambridge (MA); *m* 6 July 1974, Judith Ann, da of George William Curtis (d 1952); 1 s (Mark b 1975), 1 da (Sophie b 1980); *Career* dir Plessey Co plc 1985–89, md Plessey Electronic Systems 1987–89, chm and chief exec Westland Gp plc 1989–95, dir GKN plc 1994–95, chief exec BICC plc 1995–99; chm: British International 2000–05, Britax 2001–04, Manchester Airports Gp 2004–; non-exec dir: Fisons plc 1995–96, Witan Investment Company Ltd 1997–, AgustaWestland NV 2005–; memb: Pres Ctee CBI 1997, Fin Reporting Cncl 1998; Companion CIM 1989; FREng 1989, FIEE, FRAeS 1992; *Recreations* shooting, opera; *Clubs* Mark's; *Style—* Alan W Jones, Esq, FREng; ✉ Manchester Airports Group, Olympic House, Manchester Airport M90 1QX

JONES, Alec Norman; s of Norman Albert Jones, of Birmingham, and Iris Doreen, *née* Philips; *b* 23 December 1951; *Educ* West Bromwich GS, Univ of Nottingham (BA); *m* Mary Cherie; 2 da (Nicola Cherie b 21 July 1982, Sophie Elizabeth b 23 March 1984); *Career* ptnr PricewaterhouseCoopers (formerly Price Waterhouse before merger) 1981– (joined 1972); ACA 1975; *Recreations* all sports especially golf; *Style—* Alec Jones, Esq; ✉ PricewaterhouseCoopers LLP, Cornwall Court, 19 Cornwall Street, Birmingham B3 2DT (tel 0121 200 3000, fax 0121 265 5780)

JONES, Prof Allan Robert; s of Robert Douglas Jones (d 1989), and Gladys May, *née* Stuckey; *b* 12 August 1951, Wimbledon, London; *Educ* Univ of Southampton (BSc, PhD); *m* 28 June 1975, Janet; 3 s (Matthew Allan b 19 March 1979, Christopher Robert b 29 Sept 1980, David Nicholas b 13 Aug 1982); *Career* gp head (combustion and fuel technol) CEGB Marchwood Engrg Labs 1988 (research offr 1975); Powergen plc: section mangr (combustion) Ratcliffe Technol Centre1989, mangr (environment and combustion) Power Technol 2000; E.ON UK: mangr Environment and Combustion Business Stream Power Technol 2002–07, head of R&D 2007–; dir and vice-pres British Coal Utilisation Research Assoc; memb: DTI Advsy Ctee on Carbon Abatement Technols, Generation Cncl Electric Power Research Inst (EPRI; USA); former: dir British Flame Research Ctee, chair Coal Research Forum, chair Combustion Physics Gp Inst of Physics; special prof in low carbon technologies for power generation Univ of Nottingham 2006; author of numerous articles, research papers and conf proceedings; Royal Soc Esso Energy Award 1988, Inst of Energy Caleb Brett Award 1997; CEng 1989, FInstP 1996 (MInstP 1977), FREng 2004, CSci 2004; *Recreations* badminton, golf, travel; *Style—* Prof Allan Jones; ✉ E.ON UK, Power Technology, Ratcliffe on Soar, Nottingham NG11 0EE (tel 0115 936 2390, fax 0115 936 2205, e-mail allan.r.jones@eon-uk.com)

JONES, Allen; s of William Jones, and Madeline, *née* Aveson; *b* 1 September 1937; *Educ* Ealing GS for Boys, Hornsey Sch of Art, RCA; *m* 1, 1964 (m dis 1978), Janet, *née* Bowen; 2 da (Thea, Sarah (twins) b 1967); m 2, 1994, Deirdre Morrow; *Career* artist; teacher of lithography Croydon Coll of Art 1961–63, teacher of painting Chelsea Sch of Art 1966–68; tstee Br Museum 1990–99; first int exhbn Paris Biennale 1961; RA 1986 (ARA 1981); *Solo Exhibitions* incl: Arthur Tooth & Sons London, Neuendorf Hamburg, Zwirner Cologne, Galeria Milano Milan, Crispolti Rome, Bischofberger Zurich, Ariadne Vienna, Von Wentzel Cologne, Springer Berlin, Thorden Wetterling Gothenburg, Heland Wetterling Stockholm, C Cowles NY, Richard Feigen Gallery NY, Chicago and LA, Marlborough Fine Art London, Waddington Galleries London, James Corcoran Gallery LA, Galerie Patrice Trigano Paris, Barbican Art Gallery London, Thomas Gibson Fine Art London, Br Cncl Print Retrospective Norway, Czechoslovakia, Cyprus and Brazil, Levy Hamburg, Trussardi Milan, Steinrötter Münster, Ars Nova Museum of Contemporary Art Turku, Forsblom Helsinki, Galleria d'Arte Maggiore Bologna, Galerie Terminus Munich, Palazzo dei Sette Orvieto, Nordeutscher Landesbank Hannover, Landeshauptstadt Schwerin, Galerie Hilger Vienna; *Museum and Group Exhibitions* incl: 40 Years of Modern Art (Tate Gallery) 1986, British Art in the Twentieth Century (Royal Acad then Stuttgart) 1987, Pop Art (Tokyo) 1987, Picturing People (Br Cncl exhbn touring Hong Kong, Singapore and Kuala Lumpur) 1990, Br Art since 1930 (Waddington Gallery) 1991, Br Museum 1991 and 1997, Pop Art (Royal Acad, Museum Ludwig Cologne, Renia Sofia Madrid and Museum of Fine Arts Montreal) 1991–93, The Portrait Now (National Portrait Gallery) 1993, Treasure Island (Gulbenkian Fndn Lisbon) 1997, Augenlust (Kunsthaus Hannover) 1998–99, Pop Impressions (MOMA NY) 1999, Pop Art US/ UK Connections 1956–66 (Menil Foundation Houston) 2001, Les années pop (Centre Georges Pompidou Paris) 2001, Pop Art (Kunsthalle Villa Kobe Halle) 2002, Eurpa im Beeld (Den Haag Sculptur) 2002, Blast to Freeze (Wafsburg) 2002 (also at Les Abattoirs Toulouse 2003), Thinking Big: Concepts for 21st Century British Sculpture (The Peggy Guggenheim Collection Venice) 2002, Phantom der Lust (Stadtmuseum Graz) 2002, ...from little acorns... Early Works by Academicians (Royal Acad) 2002–03, Editions Alecto: A Fury for Prints (Whitworth Art Gallery Manchester and Bankside London) 2003, Mike Kelley - The Uncanny (Tate Liverpool) 2004, Art and the Sixties - This was Tomorrow (Tate Britain) 2004 (also at Birmingham Museum and Art Gallery 2004–05), The Human Figure in British Art from Moore to Gormley (Graves Art Gallery Sheffield) 2005, Small is Beautiful (Flowers Central) 2005, Newby Hall Sculpture Park 2005, British Pop Art Exhibition: The 1960s (Museum of the Arts Bilbao) 2005, Royal Academicians in China (China National Museum of the Arts Beijing) 2005 (also Shanghai 2006); *Commissions* incl sculptures for: Cottons Atrium London Bridge City 1987, Heathrow Sterling Hotel 1990, Chelsea and Westminster Hosp 1993, LDDC 1994, Sir Terence Conran's Mezzo restaurant 1995, Swire Properties Hong Kong 1997 and 2002, Goodwood 1998, Chatsworth Derbys 2000 and 2007, GlaxoSmithKline London 2001, Yuzi Paradise Sculpture Parks Guilin and Shanghai 2005 and 2006; *Designs* designer of sets for TV and stage in UK and Germany (incl sets and costumes for Rambert Dance Co 1989 and Royal Ballet 1996); *Books* Allen Jones Figures (1969), Allen Jones Projects (1971), Waitress (1972), Sheer Magic (1979), Allen Jones (monograph, 1993), Allen Jones Prints (1995), Allen Jones (1997), Allen Jones Works (2005); *Recreations* gardening; *Clubs* Chelsea Arts, Garrick; *Style—* Allen Jones, Esq, RA; ✉ 41 Charterhouse Square, London EC1M 6EA (fax 020 7600 1204, e-mail aj@ajstudio.demon.co.uk)

JONES, (Robert) Alun; QC (1989); *Educ* Oldershaw GS Wallasey, Univ of Bristol (BSc); *Career* called to the Bar Gray's Inn 1972; recorder of the Crown Court 1992–96; memb: Bar Cncl, Criminal Bar Assoc; *Publications* Jones on Extradition and Mutual Assistance (2 edn, 2001); *Style—* Alun Jones, Esq, QC; ✉ 3 Raymond Buildings, Gray's Inn, London WC1R 5BH (tel 020 7831 3833, fax 020 7242 4221)

JONES, Dr Alun Denry Wynn; OBE (2001); s of Thomas D Jones (d 1982), of Penygroes, Carmarthenshire, and Ray, *née* Morgan (d 1994); *b* 13 November 1939; *Educ* Amman Valley GS Ammanford, ChCh Oxford (MA, DPhil); *m* 22 Aug 1964, Ann, da of Brinley Edwards (d 1955), of Betws, Carmarthenshire; 2 da (Helen b 1966, Ingrid b 1969); *Career* sr student Cmmn for the Exhibition of 1851 1964–66, sr res fell UKAEA 1966–67, Lockheed Missiles and Space Co Calif 1967–70, tutor Open Univ 1971–82, dep ed Nature (Macmillan Journals) 1972–73 (joined 1971), BSC 1974–77, British Steel Overseas Services 1977–81, asst dir Tech Change Centre 1982–85, dir and sec Wolfson Fndn 1987–90 (dep dir 1986–87), chief exec Inst of Physics 1990–2002; BAAS: sec Working Pty on Social Concern and Biological Advances 1972–74, memb Section X Ctee 1981–92, memb Cncl 1999–, memb Exec Ctee 2001–05, memb Audit Ctee 2005–; Br Library: memb Advsy Cncl 1983–85, Document Supply Centre Advsy Ctee 1986–89; memb Cncl Nat Library of Wales 1987–94 (govr 1986–94), govr UCW Aberystwyth 1990–92 and 2002–05 (memb Cncl 2002–05), govr City Univ 1991–2000; dir Science Cncl (formerly Cncl for Science and Technol Inst) 1990–2002, assessor Science Bd SERC 1991–94, chm Registration Authy Science Cncl 2005–; memb Cncl Assoc for Schs Science Engrg and Technol (formerly Standing Conf on Schs' Science and Technol) 1992–2000 (dep chm 1997–2000), govr Sir William Perkins's Sch Chertsey 2003– (chm 2005–); fell Univ of Wales Aberystwyth 2000; fell American Physical Soc 2003; FInstP 1973, CDipAF 1977, CPhys 1987; *Books* Our Future Inheritance: Choice or Chance (jtly, 1974); *Recreations* Welsh culture, gardening, theatre; *Style—* Dr Alun Jones, OBE; ✉ 4 Wheatsheaf Close, Woking, Surrey GU21 4BP

JONES, Alun Ffred; AM; *Educ* UCNW Bangor; *Career* early career as Welsh teacher and head of dept Mold Alun Sch, journalist and presenter HTV Cardiff 1980–82, dir, prodr, author and co dir Nant Films 1982; cncllr Arfon BC 1992, ldr Gwynedd Cncl 1996–2003; memb Nat Assembly for Wales (Plaid Cymru) Caernarfon 2003–, chair Environment Planning and Countryside Ctee, Plaid Cymru spokesperson for economic devpt 2006–; chair Antur Nantlle 1992–, chm Nantlle Vale FC; *Style—* Alun Ffred Jones, Esq, AM; ✉ National Assembly for Wales, Cardiff Bay, Cardiff CF99 1NA

JONES, Alun Richard; s of Howell Jones (d 1993), and Olive Kathleen, *née* Williams; *b* 9 March 1948; *Educ* Kingston GS, St Catharine's Coll Cambridge (British Steel scholar, MA); *m* 18 Sept 1971, Gail Felicity; 1 da (Hannah Clare Rhys b 2 June 1979); *Career* PricewaterhouseCoopers (formerly Price Waterhouse before merger): joined 1970, transferred to Century City Calif 1975–77, ptnr 1981, sr client ptnr 1993; non-exec dir Primary Health Properties plc 2007–; FCA 1973; *Recreations* golf, tennis, opera, concerts, living in France; *Clubs* Effingham Golf; *Style—* Alun Jones, Esq

JONES, Andrew Bryden; s of David Jones (d 1998), of Stirling, Scotland, and Ellen Milne, *née* Rennie (d 1983); *b* 31 March 1948; *Educ* HS of Stirling; *m* 9 Feb 1974, Rosemary Ann, da of Norman Thomas Clarke, of Buckhurst Hill, Essex; 2 s (Alasdair David b 1975, Douglas Ian b 1976); *Career* chartered accountant; apprentice Dickson Middleton & Co Stirling 1965–70, qualified 1970, sr accountant in tax Arthur Andersen Glasgow 1970–71, mangr in tax Edward Moore & Co London 1971–74, supervisor to mangr Whinney Murray London 1974–79; Ernst & Whinney: ptnr 1979, ptnr i/c tax London 1984–88, nat tax ptnr 1988, coordinating ptnr of firms exec 1988; Ernst & Young: ptnr i/c int tax 1989–90, nat tax ptnr 1990–95, memb Firm's Exec 1992–, managing ptnr UK 1995–98, vice-chm Tax and Legal Serv 1998–; MICAS 1970; *Recreations* golf, reading; *Style—* Andrew B Jones, Esq

JONES, Ann; AM; da of Charles Sadler (d 1978), and Helen (d 1999); *b* 4 November 1953; *Educ* Rhyl HS; *m* 1973, Adrian Jones; 1 da (Victoria b 1975), 1 s (Vincent b 1981); *Career* official Fire Brigades' Union Nat 1982–99, memb North Wales Fire Authy 1995–99; agent Lab Pty 1983–99, memb Nat Assembly for Wales (Lab) Vale of Clwyd 1999–; Rhyl: town cncllr 1991–99, mayor 1996–97; Denbighshire co cncllr 1995–99, local co-ordinator Jubilee 2000; *Style—* Ms Ann Jones, AM; ✉ National Assembly for Wales, Cardiff Bay, Cardiff CF99 1NA (tel 029 2082 5111, e-mail ann.jones@wales.gov.uk); 25 Kinmel Street, Rhyl LL18 4AG (tel 01745 332813, fax 01745 369038)

JONES, Prof Anne; da of Sydney Joseph Pickard (d 1987), and Hilda Everitt, *née* Bird (d 1999); *b* 8 April 1935; *Educ* Harrow Weald Co Sch, Westfield Coll London (BA), King's Coll London (PGCE), Univ of London (DipSoc); *m* 9 Aug 1958 (m dis 1988), Cyril Gareth Jones, s of Lyell Jones (d 1936); 1 s (Christopher Lyell b 24 July 1962), 2 da (Catherine Rachel b 8 Aug 1963, Rebecca Madryn b 15 March 1966); *Career* asst mistress: Malvern

J

Girls Coll 1957–58, Godolphin & Latymer Sch 1958–62, Dulwich Coll 1964; sch cnsllr Mayfield London 1965–71, dep head Thomas Calton Sch London 1971–74; head: Vauxhall Manor Sch 1974–81, Cranford Community Coll 1981–87; under sec (dir of educn) Employment Dept 1987–91, visiting prof of educn Univ of Sheffield, educn and training conslt 1991–; Brunel Univ: prof of continuing educn 1991–, dir Centre for Lifelong Learning 1995–2000, prof emeritus 2001–; ceo and dir Lifelong Learning Systems Ltd (LLS) 2001–; dir: West London Leadership 1995–99, Business Link London NW 1995–99; chair: Assoc of Child Psychology and Psychiatry 1979–80, Area Manpower Bd for London South and West 1983–87; ind lay chair Complaints NHS 1996–2005; conslt EDGE 2005–; former memb: Schools' Broadcasting Cncl, Home Office Advsy Ctees on Drugs and on Sexual Offences; former memb Cncl: CRAC, NICEC, Grubb Inst, W London Inst of HE, RSA; tstee: The Westfield Tst 1992–, Menerva Educnl Tst 1993–2004 (chair 1993–99); govr The Abbey Sch 2004–; chm: Henley Choral Soc 2005–, Boathouse Reach Mgmnt 2005–; hon memb City and Guilds Inst; Hon FCP 1990; fell Queen Mary & Westfield Coll London 1992 (memb Cncl 1992–2002), FRSA (former memb Cncl 1992–2002), FCMI (chm Reading Branch), FICPD; *Books* Counselling Adolescents: School and After (1986), Leadership for Tomorrow's Schools (1987); *Recreations* walking, gardening, boating; *Clubs* Phyllis Court (Henley-on-Thames); *Style*— Prof Anne Jones; ✉ 8 Boathouse Reach, Henley-on-Thames RG9 1TJ (tel 01491 578672, e-mail anne.jones@lls.co.uk, website www.lls.co.uk)

JONES, Arfon; *b* 21 April 1943; *Educ* Bristol GS, Clare Coll Cambridge (MA); *m* 27 Sept 1970, Janet Myra Hoskins Lloyd; 2 s (Rupert b 8 April 1971, Oliver b 18 April 1976), 1 da (Victoria b 28 Nov 1972); *Career* admitted slr 1968; sr corp ptnr CMS Cameron McKenna (formerly Cameron Markby Hewitt) (ptnr 1970–); non-exec dir Camford Engineering plc 1976–86; chm of govrs Rokeby Sch 1996–; memb: Law Soc 1968, City of London Slrs' Co; *Recreations* golf, skiing, hockey; *Clubs* Royal Wimbledon Golf; *Style*— Arfon Jones, Esq; ✉ CMS Cameron McKenna, Mitre House, 160 Aldersgate, London EC1A 4DD (tel 020 7367 3000, fax 020 7367 2000, e-mail arfon.jones@cmck.com)

JONES, Prof (Norman) Barrie; s of Leslie Robert Jones, of Bebington, Merseyside, and Edith, *née* Morris; *b* 3 January 1941; *Educ* Liverpool Inst, Univ of Manchester (BSc), McMaster Univ (MEng), Univ of Sussex (DPhil); *m* 13 July 1963, Sandra Mary, da of George Albert Potts (d 1976), of Liverpool; 1 da (Victoria Mary b 21 Oct 1965), 1 s (Geoffrey Stephen b 7 May 1968); *Career* Univ of Sussex: lectr 1968–73, reader 1973–84, dir Centre for Med Res 1982–84; Univ of Leicester: prof of engrg 1985–, head Dept of Engrg 1988–95; recorder Med Sciences Section Br Assoc; CEng 1978, FIEE 1984; *Style*— Prof N Barrie Jones; ✉ Department of Engineering, The University, Leicester LE1 7RH (tel 0116 223 1300, telex 347250, fax 0116 252 2619)

JONES, Prof Barry Edward; s of Frederick Edward Jones (d 1994), of Winchcombe, Glos, and Margaret Alice, *née* Redwood (d 1975); *b* 11 March 1940; *Educ* Cheltenham GS, N Gloucestershire Tech Coll, Univ of Manchester (BSc, MSc, PhD, DSc); *m* 7 Dec 1963, Julie, da of William Pritchard (d 1993), of Torquay, Devon; 2 da (Ruth Gillian Sarah b 1966, Jennifer Claire b 1969); *Career* scientific asst Govt Communications Headquarters Cheltenham 1956–60, lectr in electrical engrg Univ of Manchester 1964–81, pt/t tutor Faculty of Technol Open Univ 1972–84, sr lectr Dept of Instrumentation and Analytical Sci UMIST 1981–86; Brunel Univ: dir The Brunel Centre for Mfrg Metrology (BCMM) 1986–2006, Hewlett Packard prof of mfrg metrology 1986–91, prof of mfrg metrology 1991–2003 (now emeritus); chm: IEE Professional Gp on Fundamental Aspects of Measurement 1980–81, IEE Professional Network Measurement, Sensors, Instrumentation and NDT 2001–04; vice-chm IEE Science Educn and Technol Div 1998–2000; directorships of two univ spinout companies: Advanced Acoustic Emission Systems Ltd 2003–07, Forcesensys Ltd 2005–; dir AMAKA Beautiful Child Ltd 2006–07; hon ed Jl of Physics E Sci Inst 1983–87, sensors series sr ed: Inst of Physics Publishing 1987–2005, CRC Press Taylor and Francis Gp 2005–; memb: CNAA 1983–85, DTI Measurement Advsy Ctee Working Parties 1992–2006, IEE Cncl 2004–06, IEE Knowledge Services Bd 2004–, UK Sensors Forum Steering Bd; Metrology award for World Class Manufacturing 1995; Dr (hc) Technical Univ of Sofia 2001; CEng 1970, FInstMC 1979, FInstP 1982, FIEE 1984, CPhys 1986, fell SPIE 1992, EurIng 1992, FRSA 1992; *Books* Instrumentation, Measurement and Feedback (1977), Instrument Science and Technology (ed and contrib vol 1 1982, vol 2 1983, vol 3 1985), Current Advances in Sensors (ed and contrib, 1987); *Recreations* music, gardening, Methodist local preacher; *Style*— Prof Barry E Jones; ✉ Stancombe House, 38 Moorlands Road, Great Malvern, Worcestershire WR14 2UA (tel and fax 01684 893005, e-mail barryedwardjones@hotmail.com)

JONES, Baron (Life Peer UK 2001), of Deeside in the County of Clwyd; (Stephen) Barry Jones; PC (1999); s of Stephen Jones (d 1988), and Grace Jones (d 1944); *b* 1937; *m* Janet, da of F W Davies; 1 s (Hon Stephen); *Career* head Eng Dept Deeside Secdy Sch, regnl offr NUT, Parly candidate (Lab) Northwich Cheshire 1966; MP (Lab): Flint East 1970–83, Alyn and Deeside 1983–2001; PPS to the Rt Hon Denis Healey 1972–74, Parly Under Sec of State for Wales 1974–79, Oppn spokesman on employment 1980–83, chief Oppn spokesman on Wales 1983–92, memb Lab Shadow Cabinet 1983–87 and 1988–92; chm Political Parties Ctee 1999–2001; chm Welsh Grand Ctee; memb Intelligence and Security Ctee 1993–97 and 1997–2001; formerly memb Welsh Exec Ctee WEU and Cncl of Europe; memb Speaker's Panel of Chairmen; chm Diocesan Bd of Educn St Asaph; pres Deeside Hosp; pres Flintshire Alzheimers Soc; govr: Nat Library of Wales, Nat Museum of Wales; life memb Royal Liverpool Philharmonic Soc; fell Industry and Parliament Tst; friend: Royal Acad of Arts, Tate Gallery, Merseyside Museums & Galleries; *Style*— The Rt Hon the Lord Jones

JONES, Barry Malcolm; s of Albert George Jones (d 1980), and Margaret Eileen, *née* Clark; *b* 4 April 1951; *Educ* Battersea GS, Charing Cross Hosp Med Sch Univ of London (MS, MB BS, LRCP); *m* 12 May 1973, Janine Diane, da of Laurence Henry Gilbey, of London; 1 s (Huw b 1984), 1 da (Georgina b 1986); *Career* sr registrar in plastic surgery Mount Vernon Hosp 1982–85, fell in craniofacial surgery Hôpital des Enfants Malades Paris 1985, currently conslt plastic and cranio-facial surgn The Hosp for Sick Children Gt Ormond St London; Hunterian prof RCS; memb: Br Assoc Plastic Surgns, Br Assoc Aesthetic Plastic Surgns (pres 1999–2001), Int Soc of Aesthetic Plastic Surgns, Int Soc of Craniomaxillofacial Surgns, Euro Craniofacial Soc, Euro Assoc Plastic Surgns, Craniofacial Soc of GB, Int Microsurgical Soc; Freeman: City of London 1982, Worshipful Soc of Apothecaries; FRCS (MRCS); *Recreations* exercise, golf, classical and contemporary guitar, literature, culinary arts, oenology; *Clubs* RAC, Moor Park Golf; *Style*— Barry M Jones, Esq; ✉ 14A Upper Wimpole Street, London W1G 6LR (tel 020 7935 1938, fax 020 7935 6607, e-mail bmj@barrymjones.co.uk); The Hospital for Sick Children, Great Ormond Street, London WC1

JONES, Dr (Robert) Brinley; CBE (2000); s of John Elias Jones, and Mary Ann, *née* Williams; *b* 27 February 1929; *Educ* Tonypandy GS, Univ of Wales Cardiff (BA, DipEd), Jesus Coll Oxford (DPhil), Int Inst for Advanced Studies Clayton MO (MA); *m* 1971, Stephanie Avril Hall; 1 s (Aron Rhys); *Career* educn offr RAF Kidlington and Bicester 1955–58 (cmmnd 1955); asst master Penarth GS 1958–60, lectr UC Swansea 1960–66, asst registrar Univ of Wales 1966–69, dir Univ of Wales Press 1969–76, Warden Llandovery Coll 1976–88, memb Broadcasting Standards Council 1988–91; pres: Nat Library of Wales 1996–, Univ of Wales Lampeter 2007–; chm: Cathedrals and Churches Cmmn Wales 1994–2003, Mgmnt Ctee Univ of Wales Centre for Advanced Welsh and Celtic Studies 2002–; memb: Literature Ctee Welsh Arts Cncl 1968–74 and 1981–87, Bd Br Cncl 1987–96 (chm Welsh Ctee 1987–96), Court and Cncl Nat Library of Wales 1974–82, Cncl St David's Univ of Wales Lampeter 1977–95 (hon fell 1987), Governing Body Church in Wales 1981–2005, Welsh Acad 1981–, Electoral Coll Church in Wales, Ct Univ of Wales Swansea 1983– (hon fell 2002), Cncl Trinity Coll Carmarthen 1984–2003 (vice-chm 1997–2003); chm: Dinefwr Tourism Gp 1988–96, Carmarthenshire Tourism Forum 1998–2002; managing tstee St Michael's Theol Coll 1982–94, hon memb Druidic Order Gorsedd of Bards 1979–, vice-pres Llangollen Int Musical Eisteddfod 1989–98; ed The European Teacher 1964–69; Hon DD Columbia Evangelical Seminary 1992, Hon DLitt Greenwich Univ USA 1997, Hon DUniv Wales 2006; fell Univ of Wales Cardiff, hon fell Trinity Coll Carmarthen 2003; FSA 1971, FCP 1982, FRCS 1988; *Books* The Old British Tongue (1970), Writers of Wales (ed with M Stephens, 1970–), Anatomy of Wales (contrib and ed, 1972), Astudiaethau ar yr Hengerdd: studies in old Welsh poetry (ed with R Bromwich, 1978), Introducing Wales (1978, 3 edn 1988), Certain Scholars of Wales (1986), Songs of Praises (1991, 2 edn 1995), Prize Days (1992), William Salesbury (1994), 'A Lanterne to their Feete' (1994), Floreat Landubriense (1998), The Particularity of Wales (2001), World-Wide Wales (2005); *Recreations* walking, farming, music; *Style*— Dr R Brinley Jones, CBE, FSA; ✉ Drovers Farm, Porthyrhyd, Llanwrda, Dyfed SA19 8DF (tel 01558 650649)

JONES, Carey Frederick; s of Clifford William Jones (d 1990), of Bonvilston, S Glam, and Mary Gwendoline, *née* Thomas; *Educ* Llandovery Coll Univ of Wales Aberystwyth (BSc), Selwyn Coll Cambridge (MA); *m* 2 Dec 1979, Bernadette Marie, da of Anthony Fulgoni; 1 s (Alexander Anthony b 10 Feb 1985), 1 da (Mariclare Dominique b 2 July 1981); *Career* graduate surveyor MAFF 1975–79, surveyor Mid Glam CC 1979–80, sr surveyor Cardiff City Cncl 1980–82 (surveyor 1980–81), sole princ Crown & Co Chartered Surveyors 1982; chief exec Royal Life Estates West 1988–92, dir and gen mangr Crown and Company Estate Agents 1993–94, md Knights Chartered Surveyors 1994–; FRICS 1991 (ARICS 1979); *Recreations* equine pursuits, classic cars; *Clubs* Pitt; *Style*— Carey Jones, Esq; ✉ Knights Chartered Surveyors, 70 Albany Road, Cardiff CF2 3RS (tel 029 2045 5550, fax 029 2045 5551)

JONES, Carwyn Howell; AM; s of Caron Wyn Jones, and Katherine Janice, *née* Howells, of Bridgend; *b* 21 March 1967; *Educ* Brynteg Comp Bridgend, Univ of Aberystwyth (LLB), Inns of Court Sch of Law (Judge Fricker Prize, Ede & Ravenscroft Prize); *m* 3 Dec 1994, Lisa Josephine, da of Edward Michael Murray, and Stella Therese; 1 da (Seren Hâf b 20 July 2000), 1 s (Ruari Wyn b 18 Sept 2002); *Career* barrister; professional tutor Centre for Professional Legal Studies Cardiff 1997–99; cncllr (Lab) Bridgend Co BC 1995–2000, chair Bridgend County Borough Lab Gp 1998–99; memb Nat Assembly for Wales (Lab) Bridgend 1999–, min for Rural Affairs 2000–02, min for Open Govt 2002–03, min for Environment, Planning and the Countryside 2003–; memb: Amnesty Int, Fabian Soc, Railway Devpt Soc; *Recreations* sport, travel, reading; *Clubs* Brynaman Rugby, Musselburgh Rugby, Bridgend Rugby; *Style*— Mr Carwyn Jones, AM; ✉ Constituency Office, 12 Queen Street, Bridgend CF31 1HX (tel 01656 664320, e-mail carwyn.jones@wales.gov.uk)

JONES, Prof Charles; s of Charles Jones (d 1962), of Glasgow, and Margaret, *née* Fagan; *b* 24 December 1939; *Educ* St Aloysius Coll Glasgow, Univ of Glasgow (MA, BLitt, DLitt); *m* 12 Aug 1966, Isla, da of Alexander Shennan (d 1989); *Career* lectr Dept of English: Univ of Hull 1964–67, Univ of Edinburgh 1967–78; prof Sch of English Univ of Durham 1978–90, Forbes prof of English language Univ of Edinburgh 1990–2005 (emeritus 2005); Leverhulme major research fellowship 2001–2003; chm: Scots Language Resource Centre 1992–96, Educn Ctee Saltire Soc 1994–96, Mgmnt Ctee Scots Language Project Scottish Consultative Cncl on the Curriculum 1994–96; memb Ct Univ of Edinburgh 1993–96, memb Cncl Saltire Soc 1995; memb Merchant House of Glasgow 2005–; FRSE 1995, FRSA 2001; *Books* Introduction to Middle English (1973), Phonological Structure and the History of English (1974), Grammatical Gender in English (1988), A History of English Phonology (1989), A Treatise on the Provincial Dialect of Scotland (Sylvester Douglas (Lord Glenbervie), ed 1991), Historical Linguistics: Problems and Perspectives (ed, 1993), A Language Suppressed (1995), The Edinburgh History of the Scots Language (ed, 1997), The English Language in Scotland: An Introduction to Scots (2003), English Pronunciation in the Eighteenth and Nineteenth Centuries (2005); *Recreations* breeding Soay sheep; *Clubs* Edinburgh New; *Style*— Prof Charles Jones, FRSE; ✉ Laggan Cottage, Faladam, Midlothian EH37 5SU (tel 01875 833652); Department of English Language, University of Edinburgh, 14 Buccleuch Place, Edinburgh EH8 9LN (tel 0131 650 3602, e-mail charles.jones@ed.ac.uk)

JONES, Charlotte Elizabeth; da of Lindsey William Jones, of Worcester, and Carol, *née* O'Keefe; *b* 6 February 1968; *Educ* St Mary's Convent Worcester, Balliol Coll Oxford (BA); *m* 11 July 1998, Paul Bazely, s of Maurice Bazely, of Madras, India; 1 s (Daniel Sean b 22 July 2002), 1 da (Molly Gwendoline b 13 Feb 2005); *Career* playwright; stage plays: Airswimming (Battersea Arts Centre) 1998 (also broadcast on BBC Radio 4), In Flame (Bush Theatre, New Ambassador's Theatre) 1999–2000, Martha, Josie and the Chinese Elvis (Octagon Theatre Bolton, Everyman Theatre Liverpool and Palace Theatre Watford) 1999–2001 (Pearson TV Best New Play Award 1998, Best New Play Award Manchester Evening News 1999), Humble Boy (RNT, Gielgud Theatre, Manhattan Theatre Club NY) 2001–02 (Susan Smith Blackburn Award 2000, Critic's Circle Award for Best New Play 2001), The Dark (Donmar Warehouse), The Woman in White (book, Palace Theatre London and Marquis Theatre NY) 2005, The Lightning Play (Almeida Theatre) 2006; screenwriting for TV: Bessie and the Bell (Carlton) 2000, Mother's Ruin (Carlton) 2001; radio plays for BBC Radio 4: Mary Something Takes the Veil, Future Perfect, A Seer of Sorts, Sea Symphony for Piano and Child, Blue Air Love and Flowers; writer Dogstar (film) 2000; Critics' Circle Most Promising Playwright Award 1999; *Style*— Ms Charlotte Jones; ✉ c/o St John Donald, PFD, Drury House, 34–43 Russell Street, London WC2B 5HA (tel 020 7344 1050, fax 020 7836 9539, e-mail sdonald@pfd.co.uk)

JONES, Christopher Ian Montague (Chris); s of Brian Montague Jones, of Oxford, and Madeleine, *née* Housham; *b* 14 July 1955; *Educ* St Edward's Sch Oxford (scholar), Selwyn Coll Cambridge (scholar); *m* 1, 1979, Valerie Smith; 1 da (Laura Rose b 5 July 1983); m 2, 1989, Sara Everett; 1 s (Augustus (Gus) Peter Montague b 27 Feb 1994); *Career* J Walter Thompson Co Worldwide: ceo 1997, chm 1998, ret 2001; currently operating ptnr and memb Bd Cognetas LLP (formerly Electra Ptnrs Europe); non-exec dir: Xenogen, FastChannel, EFinancial Gp, De Beers LV, Results Business Consulting; sr advsr Marakon Associates; memb Health Advsy Bd Bloomberg Sch of Public Health Johns Hopkins Univ; memb Exec Ctee IISS; govr: St Edward's Sch Oxford, Dragon Sch Oxford; FIPA, FRSA; *Recreations* recovering from jet-lag, cooking; *Clubs* Hurlingham, National Arts (NY); *Style*— Chris Jones, Esq

JONES, Christopher Kenneth; s of William Henry Jones (d 1942), and Dorothy Irene, *née* Tonge (d 1990); *b* 22 March 1939; *Educ* Sir Roger Manwood's GS Sandwich, Univ of Southampton Sch of Navigation; *m* 29 June 1963, (Moira) Jane, da of Gp Capt David Fowler McIntyre, AFC (d 1957), of Troon, Ayrshire; 2 s (Mark b 1964, Neil b 1965), 1 da (Amanda b 1967); *Career* third offr Union-Castle Mail SS Co Ltd 1957–62, merchandise dir Peter Robinson/Top Shop Ltd 1964–72, dep md Richard Shops Ltd 1972–76, md Bally London Shoe Co Ltd 1976–80, chief exec Lillywhites Ltd 1980–84, md retail activities Seaco Inc 1984–86, sr ptnr Sunningdale Marketing Management 1986–, dir Orebus Ltd 2000–03, dir Sport Retail Management Ltd 1993–2001; parish cncllr Grayshott; Freeman City of London; FRSA 1974; *Recreations* skiing, golf; *Clubs* Hindhead

Golf; *Style*— Christopher Jones, Esq; ✉ Pook's Hill, Headley Road, Grayshott, Surrey GU26 6DL (e-mail chrisjones234@hotmail.com)

JONES, Christopher Michael Stuart (Chris); s of Flt Lt Richard Leoline Jones, RAFVR, of Witney, Oxon, and Elizabeth Margaret, *née* Cook; *b* 1 January 1944; *m* 1 Sept 1966, Jennifer Amy, da of Leonardus Franciscus Aarts, of Wolverhampton, W Midlands; 1 s (Richard b 3 June 1970), 1 da (Victoria b 16 Oct 1973); *Career* sales mangr RH Macy NY USA 1964; James Beattie: buyer Wolverhampton 1965, gen mangr Birkenhead 1972; gen mangr Solihull 1974, gp merchandise controller 1977, merchandise dir 1979, jt md 1984, currently chm and md James Beattie plc; non-exec dir HSBC Bank plc 2001–; *Style*— Chris Jones, Esq

JONES, Christopher William; s of John Clayton Jones, and Ann, *née* Emsley; *b* 23 February 1953; *Educ* Fulneck Sch for Boys Pudsey, Univ of Nottingham, Chester Coll of Law (LLB); *m* 1975 (m dis), Caroline; 2 s (Oliver b 1980, Max b 2002); *Career* admitted slr 1977; licensed insolvency practitioner; Sampson Wade & Co 1975–84 (slr and latterly ptnr), Hammond Suddards 1984–2006 (latterly managing ptnr); chm Clarity Credit Mgmnt Solutions Ltd 2004–; dir: Britannia Building Soc 2003–, Agenda Mgmnt Servs Ltd 2003–; memb: Soc for Practitioners of Insolvency, Inst of Credit Mgmnt, Insolvency Lawyers Assoc, Insolvency Practitioners Assoc; fell Inst of Continuing Professional Devpt, FRSA, fell R3; *Recreations* tennis, skiing, cycling, wine, cars, rock music; *Clubs* Leeds United 100, Moortown Golf, Ilkley Rugby, Ilkley Lawn Tennis & Squash; *Style*— Christopher Jones, Esq

JONES, Clive William; CBE (2007); s of Kenneth David Llewellyn Jones, of Pontllanfraith, Gwent, S Wales, and Joan Muriel, *née* Withers; *b* 10 January 1949; *Educ* Newbridge GS, LSE (BSc Econ); *m* 1, 1971 (m dis 1987), Frances Jones; 2 s (Paul Dafydd b 24 Oct 1973, Samuel Alun b 7 Sept 1975), 1 da (Angharad Elizabeth Louisa b 7 May 1979); m 2, 12 Nov 1988 (m dis 2000), Fern Mary Philomena Britton, *qv*, da of Tony Britton, the actor, of London; 2 s (Harry, Jack (twins) b 14 Dec 1993), 1 da (Grace Alice Bluebell b 27 April 1997); m 3, 2004, Vikki Heywood, *qv*; *Career* journalist Yorkshire Post Group 1970–73, news ed and asst ed Morning Telegraph 1973–78, prodr Yorkshire TV 1978–82, managing ed then ed TV-am 1982–84; Television South: joined 1984, dep md and dir of regnl progs and dir TVS Entertainment Ltd and TVS Television Ltd until 1992; md London News Network 1992–94 (dir LNN Ltd 1992–), md Central Independent Television 1994–95 (dir 1994–2004), md Carlton UK Broadcasting (following t/o of Central by Carlton) 1995, chief exec Carlton Television 1996–2004 (dir 1994–2004), chm YCTV 2002–, jt md ITV 2002–04, chief exec ITV News Gp 2004–07 (advsr ITN 2007–), chm GMTV 2005–; chm Skillset 2002–; dir: Young Vic 2005–, SSDA 2006–, S4C 2007–; FRTS 1995; *Recreations* books, films, rugby; *Clubs* Reform; *Style*— Clive Jones, Esq, CBE

JONES, Dafydd; s of Glyn Price Jones, and Elsie, *née* Griffiths; *b* 1 February 1958; *Educ* Oxford Boys' GS, Winchester Sch of Fine Art (BA); *m* 1983, Linzi Noelle, da of Brig Peter Ellis, OBE; 1 da (Poppy b 29 June 1985), 1 s (Lewis b 14 July 1987); *Career* photographer; Tatler magazine 1981, Vanity Fair magazine 1989, staff photographer The New York Observer 1992–93, guest photographer Paper magazine 1995, Talk magazine 1999, photographer Sunday Telegraph magazine 2001–06, photographer TheFirstPost.com; photographs appeared in various pubns incl: The Sunday Times, Connoisseur, Evening Standard magazine; *Exhibitions* incl: The Party is Over (Opsis Gallery NY) 1992, High Society(?) (Proud Gallery London) 2002, New York Stories (Hotwell Gallery Bristol); *Clubs* Dangerous Sports; *Style*— Dafydd Jones, Esq; ✉ e-mail dafyddj@btinternet.com, website www.dafjones.com

JONES, David Alan Freeborn; s of Daniel Edward (d 1966), of King's Norton, Birmingham, and Winnifred Kate, *née* Freeborn (d 1990); *b* 28 March 1943; *Educ* King's Norton GS, Univ of Nottingham (LLB); *m* 1, 15 Feb 1969 (m dis 1995), Mavis, da of John Douglas (d 1961), of Northumbria; 1 s (Nicholas 1971), 2 da (Rachel b 1973, Hannah b 1980); m 2, 31 Jan 2000, Patricia Anne, da of Jack Alan Shelley (d 1954), of London; *Career* law lectr Birmingham Coll of Commerce 1965–68, called to the Bar Gray's Inn 1967, in practice Birmingham 1969–, head of chambers 1985, recorder of the Crown Court 1994– (asst recorder 1990–94); organiser, deliverer and publisher of annual lecture to the Birmingham Bar and Midland Circuit on criminal law 1986–96; memb Criminal Bar Assoc; *Recreations* cricket, golf, ornithology, gardening, tennis; *Clubs* Alvechurch CC, Fulford Heath and Aberdovey Golf, RSPB, Worcs Nature Conservancy Tst; *Style*— David Jones, Esq; ✉ 12 Cherry Hill Avenue, Barnt Green, Birmingham B45 8LA (tel and fax 0121 445 1935, e-mail dafjones@btinternet.com); 5 Fountain Court, Steelhouse Lane, Birmingham B4 6DR (tel 0121 606 0500, fax 0121 210 7315)

JONES, Prof David Alwyn; s of late Trefor Jones, of London, and Marion Edna, *née* Miles (d 1997); *b* 23 June 1934; *Educ* St John's Sch Leatherhead, Corpus Christi Coll Cambridge (BA), Magdalen Coll Oxford (DPhil); *m* 29 Aug 1959, Prof Hazel Cordelia Jones, da of Dan Lewis, FRS, of London; 1 da (Catherine b 26 Dec 1961), 2 s (Edmund b 6 June 1963, Hugh b 2 Sept 1965); *Career* lectr in genetics Univ of Birmingham 1961–73, prof of genetics Univ of Hull 1973–89, prof Dept of Botany Univ of Florida 1989–2003 (chm 1989–98); BAAS: memb Ctees of Sections D and K 1974–89, chm Co-ordinating Ctee for Cytology and Genetics 1974–87; chm Membership Ctee Inst of Biology 1982–87; co-ed Jl of Chemical Ecology 1994–2000; pres Int Soc of Chemical Ecology 1987–88 (Distinguished Serv Award 2001); memb: Gamma Sigma Delta, Linnean Soc, Sigma Xi (pres Univ of Florida chapter 2000–01), Genetics Soc (formerly Genetical Soc); FIBiol 1974; *Books* Variation and Adaptation in Plant Species (with D A Wilkins, 1971), Analysis of Populations (with T J Crawford, 1976); *Recreations* Morris Minors, gardening, native plants, habitat restoration; *Style*— Prof David Jones; ✉ Gagle Brrok House, Bignell House, Chesterton, Bicester, Oxfordshire OX26 1UF (tel 01869 243614, e-mail djones@botany.ufl.edu)

JONES, Prof David Emrys Jeffreys; *b* 4 September 1963; *Educ* Bradford GS, Jesus Coll Oxford (BA, Jesus Coll Prize (twice)), Green Coll Oxford (BM BCh, Oxford Graduates' Med Club Essay Prize, George Pickering Prize), Univ of Newcastle upon Tyne (PhD); *Career* house surgn then house physician Freeman Hosp Newcastle upon Tyne 1988–89; SHO: Newcastle Gen Hosp 1989–90, Royal Victoria Infirmary Newcastle upon Tyne 1990 and 1991, Freeman Hosp Newcastle upon Tyne 1990–91; MRC trg fell Med Molecular Biology Gp Dept of Med Univ of Newcastle upon Tyne and hon registrar Liver Unit Freeman Hosp Newcastle upon Tyne 1991–94, registrar in gastroenterology Regnl Liver Unit Freeman Hosp Newcastle upon Tyne 1994, registrar in gen med and gastroenterology N Tyneside Gen Hosp 1995–96 (sr registrar 1996); Centre for Liver Research Univ of Newcastle upon Tyne: MRC clinician scientist 1996–99, hon lectr 1996–99, hon sr lectr 1999, sr lectr in hepatology 1999–2003; hon conslt hepatologist Freeman Hosp Newcastle upon Tyne 1999–; Univ of Newcastle upon Tyne: prof of liver immunology 2003–, postgrad tutor Sch of Clinical Med Sciences, memb Jt Research Exec Scientific Ctee, memb Sch Research Ctee, memb Sch Grad Ctee; sec NE Immunology Club, govr Liver North (memb Scientific Ctee); memb: Med Ctee Primary Biliary Cirrhosis (PBC) Fndn, Steering Ctee Euro-PBC Trial Gp, Refereeing Panel European Assoc for the Study of the Liver (EASL) Annual Meeting, Cncl Br Soc of Immunologists; memb Editorial Bd Jl of Hepatology; faculty lectureships: Netherlands Gastroenterological Assoc 2002, American Gastroenterological Assoc 2002 and 2003, Br Assoc for the Study of the Liver 2002, Falk Liver Week 2003; Mayo Fndn Travel Award 1994, Soc for Mucosal Immunology Travel Award 1995, finalist Med Research Soc Young Investigator Award 1996, Br Assoc for Study of the Liver Travel Award 1998, Br Assoc for the Study of the Liver Young Investigator Award 2001, RCP Goulstonian Lectureship 2002; memb Assoc of Physicians of GB and I; FRCP 2001 (MRCP 1991); *Publications* author of numerous book chapters, articles and peer-reviewed editorials; *Recreations* scuba diving, skiing, classic cars, Art Deco and Art Nouveau glassware and ceramics; *Style*— Prof David E J Jones; ✉ Centre for Liver Research, 4th Floor William Leach Building, The Medical School, Framlington Place, Newcastle upon Tyne NE2 4HH (tel 0191 222 5784, fax 0191 222 0723, e-mail d.e.j.jones@ncl.ac.uk)

JONES, David Ian; MP; *b* 22 March 1952; *Educ* Ruabon GS, UCL; *m* Sara; 2 s; *Career* sr ptnr David Jones & Co 1985–2005; memb Nat Assembly for Wales 2002–03, MP (Cons) Clwyd W 2005– (Parly candidate (Cons): Conwy 1997, City of Chester 2001); *Style*— David Jones, Esq, MP; ✉ House of Commons, London SW1A 0AA

JONES, David Lewis; CBE (2005); s of Gwilym Morgan Jones (d 1975), of Aberaeron, and Joyce, *née* Davies (d 1999); *b* 4 January 1945; *Educ* Aberaeron County Sch, Jesus Coll Oxford (MA), Coll of Librarianship Wales (ALA); *Career* asst librarian Int of Historical Research 1970–72, law librarian Univ of Aberystwyth 1972–77, dep librarian House of Lords 1977–91, librarian House of Lords 1991–2006; tstee Cross Inn Sch 1975–; sec David Lloyd George Statue Appeal Tst 1998–; hon sec Hon Soc of Cymmrodorion 1994–96, Gorsedd y Beirdd (Aelod er Anrhydedd) 1996; Freeman City of London 1993, Liveryman Stationers' and Newspapermakers' Company 1994; FSA, FRHistS, FRSA 2006; *Publications* Paraguay: A Bibliography (1979), Debates and Proceedings of the British Parliaments: A Guide to Printed Sources (1986), Peers, Politics and Power: The House of Lords 1603–1981 (jt ed, 1986), A Parliamentary History of the Glorious Revolution (1988), Eirene: A Tribute (2001); *Clubs* Beefsteak; *Style*— David Jones, Esq, CBE; ✉ House of Lords Library, House of Lords, London SW1A 0PW (tel 020 7219 3240, fax 020 7219 6396)

JONES, Dr David Martin; *b* 14 August 1944; *Educ* Univ of London (BSc, BVetMed); *m* Janet Marian; 3 s (Mark b 1976, Simon b 1978, Thomas b 1980); *Career* The Zoological Soc of London: vet offr Whipsnade Park Zoo 1969–75, sr vet offr and head Dept of Vet Science 1975–84, asst dir of zoos 1981–84, dir of zoos 1984–91, gen dir 1991–92, dir Conservation & Consultancy 1992–94; dir North Carolina Zoological Park 1994–; overseas conslt, fund-raiser, author of scientific papers and articles; chm: Brooke Hosp for Animals, North Carolina Rural Heritage Forum, Yadkin Pee-Dee Lakes Project, Uwharrie Heritage LLC; memb Cncl: WWF (USA), WWF (UK); memb Bd: Uwharrie Capital Corps, Audubon North Carolina, Environmental Defense North Carolina; MRCVS, FIBiol; *Style*— Dr David Jones; ✉ North Carolina Zoological Park, 4401 Zoo Parkway, Asheboro, NC 27205, USA (tel 00 1 336 879 7102, fax 00 1 336 879 2891)

JONES, David Morris; s of Capt Morris Jones, MN (ka 1941), of Beaumaris, Anglesey, and Menna Lloyd, *née* Evans; *b* 24 March 1940; *Educ* Beaumaris GS, Univ Coll Bangor (BA, DipEd); *m* 3 Dec 1971, Patricia Jones; 2 da (Sian b 24 Nov 1976, Eira b 17 Feb 1980); *Career* journalist Liverpool Daily Post and Echo Ltd 1962–63; BBC News: journalist 1963–64, sr news asst 1964–67, chief news asst 1967–71, TV news prodr 1971–82, managing ed news and current affrs Wales 1982–85, head of news and current affrs BBC Wales 1985–89; controller of news and current affrs TVS Television Ltd 1989–92, head of prog devpt HTV plc 1994–96, currently md Merlin Broadcast Ltd, NewsNet UK Ltd; currently dir: The Radio Corporation Ltd, Capital TV Ltd (formerly md), Swansea TV Ltd, City TV Ltd; memb: RTS, Radio TV News Dirs' Assoc (USA), Inst of Welsh Affrs, BAFTA, ESU, Community Media Assoc, Local Independent Television Network, Advsy Cncl The Documentary Channel (USA); *Recreations* sailing; *Style*— David Morris Jones, Esq; ✉ 21 Uppercliff Close, Penarth, South Glamorgan CF64 1BE (tel 029 2070 7018); Newsnet UK Ltd, Aquaplan House, Burt Street, Cardiff Bay CF10 5FZ (tel 02920 488500, fax 02920 250703, e-mail dmj@newsnet.co.uk)

JONES, Della Louise Gething; da of Cyril Vincent Jones (d 1982), and Eileen Gething Jones; *Educ* Neath Girls' GS, Royal Coll of Music (LRAM, ARCM, GRSM); *m* 2 April 1988, Paul Anthony Hooper Vigars, s of Norman Vigars; 1 s (Raphael b 1989); *Career* mezzo-soprano; soloist ENO 1977–82, sung with all maj Br opera cos and at opera houses and concert halls throughout Europe, USA, USSR and Japan (specializing in Rossini, Handel and Mozart); Dido in Les Troyens (WNO) 1987, Ramiro in Finta Giardiniera and Cecilio in Lucio Silla (Mostly Mozart Festival NY), Sorceress in Dido and Aeneas (Buckingham Palace tercentenary celebration of William and Mary) 1988, Rosina in Il Barbier di Siviglia (Covent Garden) 1990, Handel's Riccardo Primo (in Cyprus and Covent Garden, to celebrate 800th anniversary of Richard I's arrival in Cyprus) 1991, Sesto in Mozart's La Clemenza de Tito (with Acad of Ancient Music, Japan) 1991; Laurence Olivier Award nomination for Rosina in The Barber of Seville ENO 1988; extensive recordings (incl Recital of Rossini arias 1990, and Spanish and French songs), frequent radio and TV broadcasts incl soloist Last Night of the Proms 1993 and Hong Kong Handover Celebrations; hon fell Welsh Coll of Music and Drama 1995, hon fell Univ of Wales Swansea 1999; *Recreations* collecting elephants, visiting Venice for Bellini, writing cadenzas, animal welfare, reading, writing; *Style*— Miss Della Jones; ✉ c/o Music International, 13 Ardilaun Road, Highbury, London N5 2QR (tel 020 7359 5183)

JONES, Denis Raymond; s of Joseph David Jones (d 1981), of Marton, Cleveland, and Gladys Margaret, *née* Lennox; *b* 24 September 1950; *Educ* Eston Co Modern Sch; *m* 15 June 1990, Linda, da of Czeslaw Dworowski; 1 s (Samuel Joseph b 6 Feb 1989); *Career* press photographer; trainee marine engr 1966–70, maintenance engr London Zoo 1970–72, photographer Fleet St News Agency 1972–74, freelance photographer (Daily Express, Evening News, Sun) 1974–76; staff photographer: Evening News (mainly fashion assignments) 1976–80, Evening Standard 1985– (freelance 1980–85); *Recreations* video photography, collecting nostalgia, mountain trekking, country walks; *Clubs* Marylebone Rifle and Pistol; *Style*— Denis Jones, Esq; ✉ Evening Standard, Northcliffe House, 2 Derry Street, London W8 5EE (tel 020 7938 7562 mobile 078 3624 1158)

JONES, Denise Idris; AM; da of James Woodrow of Johnstown Wrexham, and Rhona, *née* Jones; *b* 7 December 1950, Rossett, Wrexham; *Educ* Univ of Liverpool (BEd); *m* John Idris Jones; 2 s (William Idris Jones b 14 Nov 1988, James Aled Jones b 13 Sept 1981); *Career* English and French teacher: Rainford HS Merseyside 1971–72, Grango Sch Rhos 1972–2003; memb Nat Assembly for Wales (Lab) Conwy 2003–; memb: CWU, Amicus; *Recreations* travelling, reading, golf; *Style*— Mrs Denise Idris Jones, AM; ✉ National Assembly for Wales, Cardiff Bay, Cardiff CF99 1NA (tel 029 2089 8381, fax 029 2089 8384, e-mail deniseidris.jones@wales.gov.uk)

JONES, Derek William; s of William Jones, and Patricia Mary, *née* Gill; *b* 8 December 1952; *Educ* Univ Coll Wales Cardiff (BA); *m* 1976, Fiona Christine Anne Laidlaw; 2 s; *Career* worked on regnl policy, company law and privatisation DTI 1977–82; HM Treasury: Public Expenditure Control 1982–84, head Financial Instns and Markets 1984–87; head Japan Desk and Overseas Trade Policy Div DTI 1987–89; Welsh Office: asst sec 1989, head Industrial Policy Div 1989–92; Finance Progs Div: head 1992–94, under sec 1994; dep sec dir of econ affrs 1999, sr dir Policy 2003; *Recreations* family life, reading, blues guitar; *Style*— Derek Jones, Esq; ✉ National Assembly for Wales, Cathays Park, Cardiff CF10 3NQ (tel 029 2082 3325)

JONES, Diana Wynne; da of Richard Aneurin Jones (d 1953), of Thaxted, Essex, and Marjorie, *née* Jackson; *b* 16 August 1934; *Educ* Friends' Sch Saffron Walden, St Anne's Coll Oxford (BA); *m* 1956, Prof John Anthony Burrow, s of William Burrow; 3 s (Richard William b 1958, Michael Peter b 1961, Colin John b 1963); *Career* author (mainly of children's books) 1942–, completed first book 1946; books published USA, Japan, Germany, Holland, France, Scandinavia, Finland, Israel, Poland, Spain, Brazil, Italy, Hungary and Greece; winner: Guardian award for Children's Books 1978, Boston

J

Globe/Horn Book (Honours) award 1984 and 1986, Mythopaeic Soc of Calif award for Juvenile Fantasy 1995 and 1999, The Karl Wagner Fantasy Award 1999, Phoenix Award 2006; judge: Guardian Award Panel 1979–81, Whitbread Award Panel (Children's Section) 1988; Hon DLitt Univ of Bristol 2006; memb Soc of Authors; *Books* Changeover (1970), Wilkin's Tooth (1973, US version Witches' Business)), The Ogre Downstairs (1974), Eight Days of Luke (1975), Cart and Cwidder (1975), Dogsbody (1975), Power of Three (1976), Drowned Ammet (1977), Charmed Life (1977), Who Got Rid of Angus Flint? (1978), The Spellcoats (1979), The Magicians of Caprona (1980), The Four Grannies (1980), The Homeward Bounders (1981), The Time of the Ghost (1981), Witch Week (1982), Warlock at the Wheel and other stories (1984), The Skivers' Guide (1984), Archers' Goon (1984, televised BBC 1992), Fire and Hemlock (1985), Howl's Moving Castle (1986, animated film by Haio Miyazaki 2005), A Tale of Time City (1987), The Lives of Christopher Chant (1988), Chair Person (1989), Wild Robert (1989), Hidden Turnings (1989), Castle in the Air (1990), Black Maria (1991, US version Aunt Maria), Yes Dear (1992), A Sudden Wild Magic (1992), The Crown of Dalemark (1993), Hexwood (1993), Fantasy Stories (1994), Everard's Ride (1995), The Tough Guide to Fantasyland (1996), Minor Arcana (1996), Deep Secret (1997), Dark Lord of Derkholm (1998), Puss in Boots (1999), Mixed Magics (2000), Year of the Griffin (2000), The Merlin Conspiracy (2003), Unexpected Magic (2004), Conrad's Fate (2005), The Pinhoe Egg (2006), The Game (2007); *Style*— Ms Diana Wynne Jones; ✉ 9 The Polygon, Bristol BS8 4PW (tel 0117 927 7845); c/o Laura Cecil, 17 Alwyne Villas, London N1 2HG (tel 020 7354 1790)

JONES, Dylan; s of Michael John Jones, and Audrey Joyce, *née* Wilshire; *Educ* Chelsea Sch of Art, St Martins Sch of Art; *Career* journalist; ed i-D 1984, contrib ed The Face 1987, ed Arena 1988, associate ed The Observer Magazine 1992, associate ed The Sunday Times Magazine 1993, gp ed The Face, Arena, Arena Homme Plus 1996, ed-at-large The Sunday Times 1997, ed GQ 1999–; *Books* Dark Star (1990), True Brit (1995), Meaty, Beaty, Big & Bouncy (1996), Sex, Power & Travel (1996), iPod, Therefore I Am (2004), Mr Jones' Rules (2006); *Clubs* Groucho; *Style*— Dylan Jones, Esq; ✉ GQ Magazine, Vogue House, Hanover Square, London W1R 0AD (tel 020 7499 9080, e-mail djones@condenast.co.uk)

JONES, Edward Bartley; QC (1997); s of Meurig Bartley Jones, of Yarnton, nr Oxford, and Ruby, *née* Morris; *b* 24 December 1952; *Educ* Cardiff HS, Balliol Coll Oxford (BA); *Career* called to the Bar Lincoln's Inn 1975, in practice Chancery and Commercial Bar in Liverpool 1976–, head Commercial Dept Exchange Chambers Liverpool 1994–, asst recorder 1997–; memb: Northern Circuit Commercial Bar Assoc, Chancery Bar Assoc, Northern Chancery Bar Assoc; pt/t lectr Univ of Liverpool 1977–81; *Recreations* opera, skiing, horses, golf; *Clubs* Oxford and Cambridge, Portal; *Style*— Edward Bartley Jones, Esq, QC; ✉ Exchange Chambers, 1st Floor, Pearl Assurance House, Derby Square, Liverpool L2 9XX (tel 0151 236 7747, fax 0151 236 3433)

JONES, Prof Edward David Brynmor; s of David Jones, and Margot, *née* Derricourt; *b* 20 October 1939; *Educ* Haileybury, AA Sch of Architecture (AADip); *m* 1 (m dis); 1 s, 2 da; m 2, Margot, *née* Griffin; 1 s, 2 da; *Career* architect; princ in private practice 1973–89, in partnership with Jeremy Dixon 1989–2003, Dixon Jones Ltd 2003–; cmmns incl: Royal Opera House 1983–99, Henry Moore Fndn Perry Green 1989–, Henry Moore Inst Leeds 1989–93, Darwin Coll Cambridge 1989–93, Robert Gordon Univ Aberdeen 1991–93, superstore for J Sainsbury plc Plymouth, Univ of Portsmouth 1993, luxury housing New Delhi, Nat Portrait Gallery London 1994–2000, Saïd Business Sch Univ of Oxford 1996–2001, second phase Centre for Executive Educn 2007–; master planners: Somerset House 1998–2001, Nat Gallery 1998–2006, Magna Carta project Salisbury Cathedral 2001, Student Centre Queen's Univ Belfast 2001–, Panoptican building UCL 2001–, offices Kings Cross 2002, Portrait Gall of Canada 2003–, house in Provence 2003, Exhibition Road Project 2004, offices Regents Palace 2005, 5/6 St James's Square 2006; tutor AA, Poly of Central London and UC Dublin 1968–72, sr tutor RCA Sch of Environmental Design 1973–83, adjunct prof Univ of Toronto 1983–89 (visiting prof 1973–82); visiting prof: UC Dublin 1971–73, Cornell, Rice, Harvard, Yale, Princeton Univs USA and Syracuse (NY-based) Univ in Florence 1973–; RIBA external examiner: AA 1985, Kingston Univ, Univ of Portsmouth and Heriot-Watt Univ 1990–93, Univ of Wales 1994–97, Caribbean Sch of Arch 1997–2000, MacKintosh Sch Glasgow 2007–; RIBA: memb President's Gold Medal Ctee 1993 and 1994, memb Stirling Prize Ctee 2003–; memb jury for architectural competition: Laban Dance Centre Deptford 1998, Diana, Princess of Wales Meml Fountain London 2002, Barbara Hepworth Gallery Wakefield 2002, Parliamentary building Ottawa 2003, Univ Boulevard competition Univ of Br Columbia 2005, Victoria Embankment Competition 2005; memb Cncl AA 1993–99 (vice-pres 1995–97); Hon DLitt Univ of Portsmouth 2001, hon fell Univ of Wales Cardiff 2001, hon prof Univ of Wales 2003; tstee Portsmouth Naval Base Property Tst 2005; RIBA, RAIC *Awards* first prize: Northampton County Offices 1973, Mississauga City Hall Canada 1982 (Govr General's Award for Architecture 1988), Bus Station Venice 1990, Venice Biennale 1991; *Books* A Guide to the Architecture of London (with Christopher Woodward, 1983, 3 edn 2000), Jeremy Dixon and Edward Jones: Buildings and Projects 1959–2002; contrib to architectural jls; *Recreations* cooking, walking, drawing, looking out of the window, Staffordshire Bull Terriers; *Style*— Prof Edward Jones; ✉ Dixon Jones Ltd, Unit 6C, 44 Gloucester Avenue, London NW1 8JD (tel 020 7483 8888, fax 020 7483 8899, e-mail edwardjones@dixonjones.co.uk)

JONES, Elin; AM; *Educ* Lampeter Comp Sch, Univ of Wales Cardiff (BSc), Univ of Wales Aberystwyth (MSc); *Career* devpt mangr Welsh Devpt Agency 1991–99; memb Nat Assembly for Wales (Plaid Cymru) Ceredigion 1999–, shadow agric min 1999–2002, shadow econ devpt min 2002–06, shadow environment min 2006–; memb Aberystwyth Town Cncl 1992–99, mayor of Aberystwyth 1997–98; chair Plaid Cymru 2000–02; *Style*— Ms Elin Jones, AM; ✉ National Assembly for Wales, Cardiff Bay, Cardiff CF99 1NA

JONES, Prof Emrys Lloyd; s of Peter Jones (d 1984), and Elizabeth Jane, *née* Evans; *b* 30 March 1931; *Educ* Neath GS, Magdalen Coll Oxford (BA, Violet Vaughan Morgan scholarship, Charles Oldham Shakespeare prize); *m* 1 Sept 1965, Barbara Maud, da of Leonard Everett; 1 da (Hester b 1967); *Career* Univ of Oxford: fell and tutor Magdalen Coll 1955–77, reader in English 1977–84, Goldsmiths' prof of English lit 1984–98, fell New Coll 1984–; FBA 1982; *Books* Scenic Form in Shakespeare (1971), The Origins of Shakespeare (1977), Poems of Henry Howard, Earl of Surrey (ed 1964), Antony and Cleopatra (1977), New Oxford Book of Sixteenth-Century Verse (1991); *Recreations* looking at buildings, opera; *Style*— Prof Emrys Jones, FBA; ✉ New College, Oxford OX1 3BN

JONES, Dr Emyr Wyn; s of Evan Walter Jones (d 2003), of Bodelen, Ffordd Caerdydd, Pwllheli, Gwynedd, and Buddug Morwenna Jones; *b* 23 February 1950; *Educ* Pwllheli GS, Univ of Nottingham (DM), Univ of Liverpool (MB ChB); *m* 19 April 1974, Patricia Anne, da of Crowley Hammond (d 1989), of Walton-on-the-Naze, Essex; 3 da (Anne-Mair b 11 May 1976, Rhiannon Clare b 27 July 1978, Sioned Patricia b 17 March 1980), 1 s (Dafydd Benjamin b 28 Nov 1981); *Career* registrar in med Royal Liverpool Hosp 1976–78, clinical res fell and hon sr registrar Dept of Med Univ Hosp Queen's Med Centre Nottingham 1979–86, conslt physician specialising in diabetes mellitus and endocrinology 1986–, clinical tutor Doncaster Postgrad Med Fedn (former), med dir Doncaster and Bassetlaw Hosps NHS Fndn Tst; memb UK Cncl Caldicott Guardians, memb Professional and Educnl Section Diabetes UK, memb Bd and tstee Br Assoc of Med Mangrs, chair Clinical Ldrs Network of the Fndn Tst Network; author of papers on: platelets, thrombosis, diabetes; memb BMA; FRCP 1992 (MRCP 1978); *Publications* An Illustrated Guide for the Diabetic Clinic (1998); *Recreations* playing guitar in a rock 'n' roll band, all sorts of music, ornithology; *Style*— Dr Emyr Jones; ✉ 16 St Eric's Road, Bessacarr, South Yorkshire DN4 6NG (tel 01302 531059, e-mail emyr@winder-house.fsnet.co.uk); Doncaster Royal Infirmary, Armthorpe Road, Doncaster, South Yorkshire DN2 5LT (tel 01302 366666, e-mail emyr.jones@dbh.nhs.uk)

JONES, (David) Gareth; *m*; 1 s, 1 da; *Career* Abbey National plc: joined as asst gen mangr and treas 1989, dir of retail ops until 1993, exec dir and treas 1993–2001, also i/c Europe 1994–95, md Wholesale Banking 1996–2001; chm Paterson Enterprises Ltd; advsr Terra Firma Capital Ptnrs; non-exec dir Kensington Gp plc 2002–, non-exec dir and ptnr Prytania LLC 2005–; formerly dir: Somerfield plc, TBI plc, Management Consulting Gp plc, Orbis Capital Ltd, Marley plc; former chm Assoc of Corporate Treasurers; memb: ESRC Centre for Business Research, Accountancy Review Bd; FCA, FCT; *Recreations* steam engines, model engineering, politics, opera, reading; *Clubs* RAC; *Style*— D Gareth Jones, Esq

JONES, Dr Gareth; s of Lyell Jones (d 1937), and Ceridwen, *née* Jenkins (d 1992); *b* 28 May 1933; *Educ* Nantyglo GS, Christ's Coll Cambridge (MA), Birkbeck Coll London (PhD); *m* 1, 9 Aug 1958 (m dis 1988), Anne, da of Sidney Pickard (d 1987), of Bampton, Oxon; 1 s (Christopher b 24 July 1962), 2 da (Katy b 8 Aug 1963, Becky b 15 March 1966); m 2, 7 April 1989, Helen Patricia Rahming; *Career* RAF 1954–56; Stationers' Company's Sch 1957–59, Dulwich Coll 1959–63, Esso Petroleum Co 1963–69, Booz Allen and Hamilton mgmnt conslts 1969–85 (vice-pres 1973, managing ptnr UK 1974), dir Booz Allen & Hamilton Inc 1981–84, managing ptnr Ernst & Whinney mgmnt conslts UK 1985–89; chm Nevill Hall & Dist NHS Tst 1994–99; dir WNO 1990–94; chm Mansel Thomas Tst 1996–2005; dir: Inst of Welsh Affairs, Shaw Healthcare 1996–; memb: Powys CC 1999–2004, Brecon Beacons Nat Park Authy 1999–2004, Doctors and Dentists Pay Review Body 1999–2005, Community Devpt Fndn 2002–05; govr Univ of Glamorgan 1992–2002; FIAM 1987; *Books* Wales 2010: Creating Our Future (jtly, 1993), Welsh Roots and Branches (1994 and 2005), The Aneurin Bevan Inheritance: the story of the Nevill Hall & District NHS Trust (1998); *Recreations* travel, walking, opera; *Style*— Dr Gareth Jones; ✉ 2 Rue de la Tour, 16130 Segonzac, France

JONES, Gareth; OBE (1991), AM; s of Thomas Jones, and Catherine Jones; *Educ* Ffestiniog Co Sch, UC Swansea (BA); *Career* head of geography: Ffestiniog Co Sch 1963, Ysgol Dyffryn Nanille 1964–74; dep princ Snowdonia Nat Park Centre 1975, headmaster Ysgol John Bright Llandudno 1976–93, ind educnl conslt 1994–99; AM (Plaid Cymru): Conwy 1999–2003, Aberconwy 2007–; chair Educn Ctee Nat Assembly for Wales 2002–03; *Recreations* cycling, golf; *Clubs* Conwy Golf; *Style*— Prof Gareth Jones, AM

JONES, Gary David; s of Charles William Jones (d 1997), and Myra Elizabeth, *née* Walton; *b* 14 August 1965; *Educ* Pensby Secdy Sch for Boys Wirral, Carlett Park Catering Coll Wirral, Oxford Coll of FE; *m* 8 Dec 1996, Caroline, da of Cdre John Burton Hall; 3 da (Holly Louise Isobel b 8 March 1999, Charlotte Annabel Lucy b 5 May 2001, Isobel Rose Clemmie b 15 March 2003); *Career* chef de partie saucier rising to jr sous chef Mountbatten Hotel Seven Dials 1986–88, chef de partie poissonier and saucier Waterside Inn 1988–90, sous chef Le Manoir aux Quat'Saisons 1990–93, resident exec chef to Richard Branson Necker Island Br Virgin Islands 1993–95, chef conslt Soneva Fushi Resort BAA ATOL Maldives 1995, head chef Homewood Park Hotel Hinton Charterhouse 1996–98 (four AA Rosettes 1997, first Michelin Star 1998, 7 out of 10 Good Food Guide 1998), head chef Cliveden House's Waldos Restaurant 1998–99 (four AA Rosettes 1998, 8 out of 10 Good Food Guide 1999, Michelin Star 1999), exec head chef Le Manoir aux Quat'Saisons 1999– (5 AA Rosettes 1999–, 2 Michelin Stars 2000–, 9 out of 10 Good Food Guide 2000–, RAC Guide Gold Ribbon and 4 Stars 1999, Zagat Guide Best Restaurant In and Around London 2000, 19 out of 20 Gault Millau and 4 Toques 2000, Readers' First Choice Restaurant Caterer and Hotelkeeper 2000, Best Restaurant in the UK with Rooms Tatler magazine 2000, placed 28th in Restaurant magazine's Best 50 Restaurants in the World 2005); *Recreations* scuba diving, water-skiing; *Style*— Gary Jones, Esq; ✉ Le Manoir aux Quat'Saisons, Church Road, Great Milton, Oxfordshire OX44 7PD (tel 01844 277205, fax 01844 278847, e-mail lemanoir@blanc.co.uk, website www.manoir.com)

JONES, George Quentin; s of John Clement Jones, CBE (d 2002), and Marjorie, *née* Gibson (d 1991); *b* 28 February 1945; *Educ* Highfield Sch Wolverhampton; *m* 1, April 1972 (m dis 1989), Diana, *née* Chittenden; 1 da (Jennifer Lucy b 2 Jan 1976), 1 s (Timothy Edward b 13 Jan 1979); m 2, 29 Dec 1990, Teresa Grace, da of John Lancelot Rolleston; *Career* trainee journalist Eastern Daily Press 1963–67, journalist South Wales Argus and Western Mail 1967–69, Reuters London 1969, Parly staff The Times 1969–73, Parly and political corr The Scotsman 1973–82; political corr: The Sunday Telegraph 1982–85, The Sunday Times 1985–86, The Daily Telegraph 1986–88; political ed The Daily Telegraph 1988–, regular broadcaster BBC and independent radio; chm Journalists Parly Lobby 1987–88, chm Parly Press Gallery 1996–97; *Style*— George Jones, Esq; ✉ The Daily Telegraph, Room 10, Press Gallery, House of Commons, London SW1A 0AA (tel 020 7538 5000, e-mail george.jones@telegraph.co.uk)

JONES, Prof George William; OBE (1999); s of George William Jones (d 1973), of Wolverhampton, and Grace Annie, *née* Cowmeadow (d 1982); *b* 4 February 1938; *Educ* Wolverhampton GS, Jesus Coll Oxford (MA), Nuffield Coll Oxford (DPhil); *m* 14 Sept 1963, Diana Mary, da of Henry Charles Bedwell (d 1982), of Kidlington; 1 da (Rebecca b 1966), 1 s (Maxwell b 1969); *Career* lectr Univ of Leeds 1965–66 (asst lectr 1963–65); LSE: lectr 1966–71, sr lectr 1971–74, reader 1974–76, prof of govt 1976–2003 (emeritus prof 2003–), chm LSE Graduate Sch 1990–93, vice-chm Appts Ctee 1996–99; Layfield Ctee on Local Govt Fin 1974–76, vice-chm Political Sci and Int Rels Ctee of SSRC 1978–81 (memb 1977–81); memb: Nat Consumer Cncl 1991–99, DOE Jt Working Pty on the Internal Mgmnt of Local Authorities in England 1992–93, DETR Beacon Cncls Advsy Panel 1999–2003, DETR Motorists Forum Consultation Working Gp 2000; hon fell Univ of Wolverhampton 1986; hon prof: Univ of Birmingham 2003–, Queen Mary Univ of London 2004–; hon memb: Soc of Local Authy Chief Execs (SOLACE) 2003–, Chartered Inst of Public Fin and Accountancy 2003–; FRHistS 1980, memb RIPA 1963 (memb Cncl 1984–90); *Books* Borough Politics (1969), Herbert Morrison (co-author, 1973 and 2001), Political Leadership in Local Authorities (jt ed, 1978), New Approaches to the Study of Central-Local Government Relationships (ed, 1980), The Case for Local Government (jt author, 1985), Between Centre and Locality (jt ed, 1985), West European Prime Ministers (ed, 1991), The Government of London (co-author, 1991), The Impact of Population Size on Local Authority Costs and Effectiveness (co-author, 1993), Local Government: The Management Agenda (1993), Joint Working Between Local Authorities (jt author, 1995), The Role of the Local Authority Chief Executive in Local Governance (jtly, 1996), The New Local Government Agenda (1997), At the Centre of Whitehall (jtly, 1998), Regulation Inside Government (jtly, 1999); *Recreations* cinema, eating, reading, dancing; *Clubs* National Film, Beefsteak; *Style*— Emeritus Prof G W Jones, OBE; ✉ Department of Government, London School of Economics and Political Science, Houghton Street, London WC2A 2AE (tel 020 7955 7179, fax 020 7831 1707, e-mail g.w.jones@lse.ac.uk)

JONES, Geraint Martyn; s of Robert Kenneth Jones, of Luton, Beds, and Frances Elizabeth, *née* Mayo; *b* 15 July 1948; *Educ* St Albans Sch, Christ's Coll Cambridge (MA, LLM), Inns of Court Sch of Law; *m* 29 July 1978, Caroline Mary Jones, da of Lt Peter Edwin Cecil Eyres, RNVR (d 1975); 1 s (Robert b 1980), 1 da (Louisa b 1982); *Career* called to the Bar Gray's Inn 1972; in practice (principally in commercial, property and planning law): London 1972–74, SE Circuit (mainly in Cambridge) 1974–; memb Chancery Bar Assoc, chm Rent Assessment Ctees 1985–, chm Leasehold Valuation Tribunals 1998–; Cambridge Bar Mess: chm 1999; memb SE Circuit Ctee 1991–94; asst cmmr Parly Boundary Cmmn 1992–95 and 2000–; chm Madingley Sch Tst 1988–91, chm of govrs Bourn Sch 1993–99; churchwarden Longstowe 2003–; memb: RYA, RNLI, Game Conservancy Tst, Cruising Assoc, BASC; Liveryman Worshipful Co of Glaziers 1992; *Recreations* sailing, shooting, jazz, carpentry, cooking; *Clubs* Little Ship, Royal Norfolk and Suffolk Yacht, Grafham Water Sailing; *Style*— Geraint Jones, Esq; ✉ Fenners Chambers, 3 Madingley Road, Cambridge CB3 0EE (tel 01223 368761, fax 01223 313007, e-mail geraint.jones@fennerschambers.co.uk); 8–12 Priestgate, Peterborough PE1 1JA (e-mail geraintmjones@hotmail.com)

JONES, Geraint Owen; MBE (2006); s of Emrys Jones, and late Carol Jones; *b* 14 July 1976, Kundiawa, Papua New Guinea; *Educ* Harristown State HS Toowoomba Aust, MacGregor State HS Brisbane; *Partner* Jennifer Evans; *Career* cricketer (wicketkeeper); grade cricket Aust 1995–98, club cricket UK 1998–2001, Kent CCC 2001–; England: 34 test caps, 49 one day appearances, test debut v WI Antigua 2004, one day debut v WI Trent Bridge 2004, memb Ashes-winning team 2005; *Style*— Mr Geraint Jones, MBE; ✉ Kent County Cricket Club, St Lawrence Ground, Old Dover Road, Canterbury, Kent CT1 3NZ

JONES, Geraint Stanley; CBE (1993); s of Rev David Stanley Jones (d 1974); *b* 26 April 1936; *Educ* Pontypridd GS, UCNW Bangor (BA, DipEd); *m* 1961, Rhiannon, da of Emrys Williams (d 1971); 2 da (Sioned b 1965, Siwan b 1966); *Career* served RAEC, Sgt; BBC Wales: studio mangr 1960–62, TV prodn asst Current Affrs 1962–65, TV prodr Current Affrs 1965–69, prodr Features and Documentaries 1969–73, asst head of progs Wales 1973–74, head of progs Wales 1974–81, controller BBC Wales 1981–85, dir of public affrs 1986–87; md BBC Regnl Broadcasting 1987–89, chief exec S4C (Welsh Fourth Channel Authy) 1989–94; broadcasting conslt and prodr 1994–; visiting prof Int Acad of Broadcasting (IAB) Montreux; dir: WNO 1985–94, Wales Millennium Centre 1998–2005; memb: Ct and Cncl UCW Aberystwyth 1990–96, Arts Cncl of Wales 1995–2000, BT Wales Forum 1995–2001, Ct Univ of Wales 1998–2000, Br Cncl Film and TV Advsy Ctee 1995–2002; chm: Royal Welsh Coll of Music and Drama 1989–2000 (vice-pres 2000–), TV Prog Ctee Euro Broadcasting Union 1990–96, Nat Language Centre 1994–97, Sgrin Welsh Med Agency 1999–2004, Ryan Davies Tst; vice-pres: Cardiff Business Club, Pendyrus Male Choir; memb UK Freedom from Hunger Ctee 1978–97; tstee: UNA Welsh Centre 1999–2005, Wales Video Gallery 2001–, Pendyrus Tst 2001–; Clwyd Theatr Cymru Devpt Tst 2004–; memb Bd Clwyd Theatr Cymru 2006–; hon fell UCNW Bangor 1988, Hon LLD Univ of Wales 1998, Hon DLitt Univ of Glamorgan 2000; FRSA, FRTS, FRWCMD 2000; *Recreations* music, painting, horse riding; *Clubs* Cardiff and County, Royal Over-Seas League; *Style*— Dr Geraint Stanley Jones, CBE

JONES, Prof (Walton) Glyn; s of Emrys Jones, and Dorothy Ada, *née* North; *b* 29 October 1928; *Educ* Manchester Grammar, Pembroke Coll Cambridge (MA, PhD); *m* 1, 12 June 1953 (m dis 1981), (Karen) Ruth, da of Vilhelm Olaf Fleischer; 2 s (Stephen b 1 Dec 1956, Olaf b 11 June 1958), 2 da (Monica b 9 June 1962, Anna b 29 June 1965); m 2, 30 Nov 1981, Kirsten, da of Christen Gade; *Career* reader in Danish UCL 1966–73 (Queen Alexandra lectr in Danish 1956–66), visiting prof of Danish Univ of Iceland 1971, prof of Scandinavian studies Univ of Newcastle upon Tyne 1973–86, prof of literature Faroese Acad 1979–81, prof of European literature UEA 1986–94 (emeritus prof 1994); hon memb Swedish Literary Soc Finland 1985, fell Royal Norwegian Acad of Sciences 1988; corresponding memb Danish Soc of Authors 1989, memb Faroese Acad of Letters 1996; Knight Royal Danish Order of the Dannebrog 1994; *Books* Johannes Jørgensens modne År (1963), Johannes Jørgensen (1969), Denmark (1970), William Heinesen (1974), Faerø og Kosmos (1974), Danish - A Grammar (with Kirsten Gade, 1981), Tove Jansson (1984), Vägen Från Mumindalen (1984), Denmark - A Modern History (1986), Georg Brandes Selected Letters (1990), Blue Guide to Denmark (with Kirsten Gade, 1992, 2 edn 1997), Faroese Literature chapter in A History of Danish Literature (ed S H Rossel, 1992), Colloquial Danish (with Kirsten Gade, 1993, 2 edn 2003), Colloquial Norwegian (with Kirsten Gade and Kari Bråtveit, 1994), Institutionsnavne Dansk-Engelsk (with Arne Juul and Jens Axelsen, 2001); *Translations* The Black Cauldron (William Heinesen) 1992, Days with Diem (Svend Aåge Madsen) 1994, The Lost Musicians (William Heinesen) 2006; *Recreations* music, Danish church architecture; *Style*— Prof W Glyn Jones; ✉ c/o School of Literature, Language and Translation, University of East Anglia, Norwich NR4 7TJ (tel 01603 456161, fax 01603 250599, e-mail kgjones@paston.co.uk or kgjones@mail.tele.dk)

JONES, Rev Canon Glyndwr; s of Bertie Samuel Jones (d 1965), of Birchgrove, Swansea, and Elizabeth Ellen Jones (d 2001); *b* 25 November 1935; *Educ* Dynevor Sch Swansea, St Michael's Theol Coll Llandaff (DipTheol), Univ of Wales (MA); *m* 1, 13 Dec 1961, Cynthia Elaine Jenkins (d 1964); m 2, 23 July 1966, (Marion) Anita, da of David Morris (d 1969), of Plasmarl, Swansea; 1 da (Susan b 30 June 1968), 1 s (Robert b 11 Aug 1970); *Career* Nat Serv 1954–56, RAPC attached 19 Field Regt RA, served Korea, Hong Kong, demobbed Sgt AER; ordained Brecon Cathedral: deacon 1962, priest 1963; curate: Clydach 1962–64, Llangyfelach 1964–67, Sketty 1967–70; rector: Bryngwyn with Newchurch and Llanbedr, Painscastle with Llandewi Fach 1970–72; Missions to Seamen: port chaplain Swansea and Port Talbot 1972–76, sr chaplain Port of London 1976–81, sec gen The Missions to Seamen 1990–2000 (aux ministries sec 1981–85, asst gen sec 1985–90); memb Cncl: Marine Soc 1990–2000, Partnership for World Mission 1990–2000, Int Christian Maritime Assoc 1990–2000, Merchant Navy Welfare Bd 1990–99; hon chaplain Royal Alfred Seafarers Soc 1987–93, hon canon St Michael's Cathedral Kobe Japan 1988–; chaplain: Worshipful Co of Information Technologists 1989–2000, Worshipful Co of Innholders 1990–2002, Worshipful Co of Farriers 1990–2004, Worshipful Co of Carmen 1990–2004; chaplain to HM The Queen 1990–2005, chaplain to the Lay Sheriff of London 1993–94 and 1999–2000; commissary to bishop of Cyprus and the Gulf 1996–2000; tstee Eddie Baird Meml Tst 2002– (treas 2007); co-chm Orsett Churches Centre 2003–04, hon sec to the tstees Orsett Churches Centre 2004; memb: Batti Wallah's Soc (pres 2006–07), Thurrock Probus Club (pres 2005–06), Rotary Club of Grays Thurrock 2003 (vice-pres 2006–07, pres 2007–08); Freeman City of London 1990, Hon Liveryman Worshipful Co of Carmen 1995, Hon Liveryman Worshipful Co of Farriers 1999; *Recreations* sport, music, reading, theatre, travel; *Clubs* Thurrock Rugby (chaplain), Grays Thurrock Rotary; *Style*— The Rev Canon Glyndwr Jones; ✉ 5 The Close, Grays, Essex RM16 2XU (tel 01375 375053, e-mail glynita.tomdavey@blueyonder.co.uk)

JONES, (David) Graham; s of Mrs Dorothy Hartley, of Wakefield, W Yorks; *b* 16 June 1951; *Educ* Queen Elizabeth GS Wakefield, Keble Coll Oxford (MA), UCW Cardiff; *m* 1, 23 March 1977, Lynne Francis (d 1996); m 2, 5 March 2007, Virginia Frances Tooley; *Career* leader writer Glasgow Herald 1973–74; reporter: Sheffield Star 1973, The Sun 1974–79; Now! Magazine 1979–81 (reporter, dep foreign ed), Foreign Desk Daily Mail and Mail On Sunday 1981–83, Daily Telegraph 1983–89 (reporter, political staff, asst news ed, chief asst news ed, dep news ed), news ed Daily Star 1989–94, asst ed (news) Sunday Express 1994–96, ed News and Business CNNText 1996–98, sr ed CNNI Text 1998–2000, dep ed CNN.com Europe 2000–01, sr writer CNN.com International 2001–; *Books* Forked Tongues (1984), Own Goals (1985), The Forked Tongues Annual (1985), Plane Crazy (1986), I Don't Hate Men But.../I Don't Hate Women But... (1986), Boat Crazy (1987), The Official Candidate's Book of Political Insults (1987), I Love Sex/I Hate Sex (1989), The Book of Total Snobbery (1989); *Recreations* writing, current and international affairs, travel, gardening, photography, journalism training (seminars/workshops for Thomson Fndn and UNICEF in Ghana, Romania, Malaysia, Ukraine, Belarus, Russia, Pakistan, Mongolia and Papua New Guinea); *Style*— Graham Jones, Esq; ✉ 4 Dennis Road, East Molesey, Surrey KT8 9ED (tel 020 8979 4198); CNN.com, CNN House, 16 Great Marlborough Street, London W1F 7HS (tel 020 7693 1717, e-mail graham.jones@cnn.com)

JONES, His Hon Judge (Anthony) Graham Hume; s of Sir Edward Warburton Jones (d 1993), of Co Down, and Margaret Anne Crosland Smellie (d 1953); *b* 16 August 1942; *Educ* Trinity Coll Glenalmond, Trinity Coll Dublin (BA); *m* 5 Nov 1966, Evelyn Ann, da of W Brice Smyth (d 1998); 2 s (Hume Riversdale b 26 July 1968, Benjamin Brice b 4 March 1972), 1 da (Katharine Ann Crosland b 22 May 1975); *Career* mgmnt trainee Mardon Son & Hall Bristol 1966–71, called to the Bar Gray's Inn 1971, in practice Western Circuit 1971–93, circuit judge (Western Circuit) 1993–, resident judge Taunton Crown Court 2003–; dep judge Sovereign Base Area Cyprus 1999–; memb Cncl RNLI 2003–; Master Antient Soc of St Stephens Ringers 1999–2000; *Recreations* sailing, golf; *Clubs* Royal Co Down Golf, Burnham and Berrow Golf, Holyhead Golf, Royal Ocean Racing, Trearddur Bay Sailing (Cdre 1995–96); *Style*— His Hon Judge Graham Hume Jones; ✉ c/o Western Circuit Office, Bridge House, Sion Place, Clifton, Bristol BS8 4BN

JONES, His Hon Graham Julian; s of David John Jones, CBE (d 1974), and Edna Lillie Jones, *née* Marshall (d 2002); *b* 17 July 1936; *Educ* Porth Co GS, Univ of Cambridge (MA, LLM); *m* 30 Aug 1961, Dorothy, da of James Smith Tickle (d 1980), of Abergavenny; 2 s (Nicholas David Julian b 1963, Timothy James Julian b 1968), 1 da (Sarah Elizabeth b 1965); *Career* ptnr Morgan Bruce & Nicholas (slrs Cardiff) 1961–85; dep circuit judge 1975–78, recorder 1978–85; Wales & Chester Circuit: circuit judge 1985–2002, sr circuit judge 2002–05, circuit official referee 1993–2005, assigned and designated family judge Cardiff Co Court 1994–98, designated civil judge Civil Justice Centre Cardiff 1998–2000, South and West Wales 2000–05; pres Assoc Law Soc of Wales 1982–84; memb: Lord Chllr's Legal Aid Advsy Ctee 1980–85, Ct Univ of Wales Coll of Cardiff 1996–, Mgmnt Ctee Centre for Professional Legal Studies Cardiff Law Sch 1996–, Civil Justice Cncl 2004–; govr Univ of Glamorgan 1999–2006; vice-pres RNLI 2007– (memb Cncl 2002–07); *Recreations* golf, boats; *Clubs* Cardiff and County, Radyr Golf (Cardiff), Royal Porthcawl Golf; *Style*— His Hon Graham Jones

JONES, Rev Prof Gwilym Henry; s of John Lloyd Jones (d 1971), and Jennie, *née* Roberts (d 1973); *b* 16 July 1930; *Educ* Pwllheli GS, Univ Coll of N Wales Bangor (BA, PhD, DD), Jesus Coll Oxford (MA); *m* 28 March 1959, Mary Christabel, da of Owen Tudor Williams (d 1972); 2 s (Rhys b 18 May 1966, Huw b 24 Jan 1969), 1 da (Ruth b 13 April 1975); *Career* min Presbyterian Church of Wales 1956–61, prof of Hebrew Theological Coll Aberystwyth 1961–66; Univ Coll of N Wales Bangor: lectr 1966, sr lectr 1979, reader 1984, prof of religious studies 1987–95, emeritus prof 1995–, dean of arts 1988–91; dean Bangor Sch of Theology 1980–83 and 1992–95, dean of divinity Univ of Wales 1987–90; dir New Welsh Bible 1994–; pres Soc for Old Testament Study 1995; Hon DLitt Univ of Wales 2004; *Books* Arweiniad i'r Hen Destament (1966), Gwirionedd y Gair (1974), Cerddi Seion (1975), Gramadeg Hebraeg y Beibl (1976), Diwinyddiaeth yr Hen Destament (1979), 1 and 2 Kings (New Century Bible) (1984), Y Gair Ddoe a Heddiw: Eseia o Jerwsalem (1988), The Nathan Narratives (1990), 1 and 2 Chronicles (Old Testatment Guides) (1993), Hen Destament 1988 (1995), 1 and 2 Samuel (2001), O Sgrepan Teithiwr (2001); *Recreations* walking, gardening, music; *Style*— The Rev Prof Gwilym Jones; ✉ Afallon, Holyhead Road, Menai Bridge, Ynys Mon LL59 5RH (tel 01248 712226)

J

JONES, Gwyn; s of Edgar Jones (d 1994), and Laura, *née* Davies (d 1993); *b* 22 July 1960, Trawsfynydd; *Educ* Ysgol y Moelwyn Blaenau Ffestiniog, Liverpool Poly (BA), Coll of Law Chester; *m* 30 Aug 1986, Margaret, *née* MacMillan; 1 s (Mathew Gwyn b 21 Jan 1990), 1 da (Ruth Mererid b 17 Dec 1991); *Career* slr specialising in gen crime; Leo Abse & Cohen Cardiff: articled clerk 1982–84, asst slr 1984–86, ptnr 1986–96; ptnr Gamlins Slrs Rhyl 1996–; dep dist judge 2001–; chair Llamau Housing Soc Ltd 1989–92; chair Ctee and chair of tstees Bod Alaw PTA 1999–2001; author of various articles on current legal issues in Western mail and Daily Post; regular participant with BBC radio and TV progs; memb Law Soc; *Recreations* gardening, mountain biking, eating out; *Style*— Gwyn Jones, Esq; ✉ Gamlins Solicitors & Notaries, 31–37 Russell Road, Rhyl LL18 3DB (tel 01745 357355, fax 01745 343616, e-mail gwyn.jones@gamlins.co.uk)

JONES, Dame Gwyneth; DBE (1986, CBE 1976); da of late Edward George Jones, and late Violet, *née* Webster; *b* 7 November 1936; *Educ* Twmpath Secdy Modern Sch Pontypool, Royal Coll of Music, Accademia Chigiana Siena, Zürich Int Opera Studio; *Children* 1 da; *Career* principal dramatic soprano: ROH Covent Garden 1963–, Vienna Staatsoper 1966–, Bavarian State Opera 1966–, Deutsche Oper Berlin 1966–; guest artiste: Paris, Met Opera NY, La Scala Milan, Zürich, Hamburg, Barcelona, Buenos Aires, Tokyo, San Francisco, Chicago, Rome, Madrid, Oslo, Moscow, Geneva, Bayreuth Festival, Salzburg Festival, Verona Festival, Edinburgh Festival, Hong Kong, Peking, Tokyo, Seoul; debut as dir Der Fliegender Holländer (new prodn, Deutsches Nat Theatre Weimar); hon memb Vienna State Opera; Kammersängerin Austria and Bavaria, Shakespeare Prize FRG 1987, Bundesverdienstkreuz FRG 1988, Premio Puccini Award Torre del Lago 2003, Cymry for the World Award 2004, Golden Medal of Honor Vienna, Osterreichische Ehren Kreuz fur Wissenschaft und Kunst (1 Klasse), Hon DMus: Univ of Wales, Univ of Glamorgan; Hon RAM 1980, fell Royal Welsh Coll of Music and Drama 1992, FRCM (ARCM); Commandeur de l'Ordre des Artes et des Lettres France 1992; *Roles* incl: Ariadne in Ariadne auf Naxos, Octavian and Die Feldmarschallin in Der Rosenkavalier, Brünnhilde in Die Walküre, Siegfried and Götterdämmerung, Isolde in Tristan und Isolde, Elisabeth and Venus in Tannhäuser, Senta in Der Fliegende Holländer, Leonore in Fidelio, Lady Macbeth in Macbeth, Desdemona in Otello, Kostelnicka in Jenufa, La Voix Humaine, Farberin and Kaiserin in Die Frau ohne Schatten, title roles in Elektra, Salome, Helen of Egypt, Aida, Tosca, Madame Butterfly, Turandot and Norma, Kabanicha in Katia Kabanowa; film, CD recordings and television roles incl: Isolde, Aida, Turandot, Brünnhilde, die Feldmarschallin, Leonore, Poppea in L'Incoronazione di Poppea, La Voix Humaine and Erwartung, title role in The Merry Widow; *Style*— Dame Gwyneth Jones, DBE; ✉ PO Box 2000, CH 8700 Küsnacht, Switzerland

JONES, Gwyneth Ann; da of Desmond James Jones, and Mary Rita, *née* Dugdale; *b* 14 February 1952; *Educ* Notre Dame Convent Sch Manchester, Univ of Sussex (BA); *m* 1976, Peter Wilson Gwilliam; 1 s (Gabriel Jimi Jones b 4 Sept 1987); *Career* author; children's books under own name: Water In The Air (1977), The Influence of Ironwood (1978), The Exchange (1979), Dear Hill (1980), Seven Tales and a Fable (1995); children's books under name of Ann Halam: Ally Ally Aster (1981), The Alder Tree (1982), King Death's Garden (1986), The Daymaker (1987), Transformations (1988), The Skybreaker (1990), Dinosaur Junction (1992), The Haunting Raven (1994), The Fear Man (1995, winner Children of the Night Award Dracular Soc 1995); novels under own name: Divine Endurance (1984), Escape Plans (1986), Kairos (1988), The Hidden Ones (1988), White Queen (1991, winner of James Tiptree Jr award), Flowerdust (1993), North Wind (1994, short listed Arthur C Clarke Award), Seven Tales And a Fable (two World Fantasy Awards, 1996), Phoenix Cafe (1997), Bold as Love (2001, Arthur C Clarke Award), Castles Made of Sand (2002); memb: SE Arts Literature Panel 1988–94, Science Fiction Foundation 1986–; Richard Evans Meml Award for Science Fiction 2001; *Recreations* walking, gardening, book reviewing; *Style*— Ms Gwyneth Jones; ✉ c/o David Higham Associates, 5–8 Lower John Street, Golden Square, London W1R 4HA (tel 020 7437 7888, fax 020 7437 1072, e-mail gwyneth.jones@ntlworld.com, websites www.boldaslove.co.uk and http://homepage.ntlworld.com/gwynethann/)

JONES, Prof Hamlyn Gordon (Lyn); s of Douglass Gordon Jones (d 1978), and Mary Elsie, *née* Hoadley (d 1966); *b* 7 December 1947; *Educ* St Lawrence Coll Ramsgate, St John's

Coll Cambridge (MA, Lister entrance scholarship, Wright Prize), Australian National Univ (PhD, ANU scholarship); *m* 1972, Amanda Jane, da of Sir James Perowne Ivo Myles Corry; 2 da (Katherine Myleta Gordon b June 1974, Julia Patricia Gordon b Nov 1976); *Career* res scientist Plant Breeding Inst Cambridge 1972–76, Title A res fellow St John's Coll Cambridge (Henry Humphreys Prize) 1973–76, lectr in botany Univ of Glasgow 1977–78, ldr Stress Physiology Gp East Malling Res Station 1978–88; Horticulture Research International: dir Crop Science Res 1988–95, dir Res Strategy 1995–97; prof of plant ecology Univ of Dundee 1997–; special prof Univ of Nottingham 1992–97, hon prof Univ of Birmingham 1995–98; visiting prof: Univ of Toronto 1981, Univ of Basilicata 1989–90; memb: Cncl Soc of Experimental Biology 1986–90, Scientific Advsy Ctee Scottish Nat Heritage 2005–; govr S Warks Coll of FE 1988–89, hon lectr Univ of Glasgow 1978–90, hon research prof Scot Crop Research Inst Invergowrie 1998–; author of over 200 scientific pubns; FIHort 1993; *Books* Plants and Microclimate (1983, last edn 1992) and joint ed of 4 books; *Recreations* squash, tennis, mountains, lounging; *Style*— Prof Lyn Jones; ✉ 1 Hazel Drive, Dundee DD2 1QQ; Department of Biological Sciences, University of Dundee, Dundee DD1 4HN (tel 01382 562731, fax 01382 344275)

JONES, Heather; da of Harold Bentham Gledhill (d 1975), of Coventry, Warks, and Bessie, *née* Johnson; *b* 24 April 1941; *Educ* Stoke Park GS for Girls Coventry, Bedford Coll London (BSc, postgrad DES scholarship); *m* 8 Aug 1964, Ivan Arthur Francis Jones; 2 s (Alexander Francis b 19 Oct 1966, Matthew Bentham b 21 March 1969); *Career* teacher: biology, botany and zoology Camden Sch for Girls London 1963–66, pt/t science HM Borstal Usk 1967–68, pt/t biology and chemistry Henley Coll of FE Coventry 1969–70, pt/t human biology and English for foreign students Brooklyn Tech Coll Birmingham 1970–73, pt/t biology and chemistry Boldmere HS Sutton Coldfield 1972–74, pt/t biology and gen science Coleshill Secdy Sch 1973–74, pt/t Latin and science Chetwynd House Prep Sch Sutton Coldfield 1974, biology, chemistry and environmental studies then head of science and dir of studies (sr teacher) Handsworth Wood Girls' Sch Birmingham 1974–80; dep head Bournville Sch 1980–87, headteacher Yardleys Sch Birmingham 1987–2003 (commended HM Sch Inspectorate 1992, Independent Parents' Choice selection 1992, winner of numerous regnl and nat environmental awards incl DfES Sch Improvement Award 2003); fndr sch conservation project - 22 acre abandoned allotments site Acocks Green 1992 (exhibited Green Show 1992); currently educn and PFI conslt; memb Professional Assoc of Teachers 1975–91, memb NAHT 1992–; fndr memb Rotary Club of Birmingham Breakfast; *Recreations* foreign travel, conservation work, horticulture, listening to classical music, reading, tapestry; *Style*— Mrs Heather Jones; ✉ 103 Hamstead Hill, Birmingham B20 1BX (tel and fax 0121 551 5479, e-mail heatherjonesconsultancy@hotmail.com)

JONES, Helen; MP; *b* 24 December 1954; *Educ* UCL, Univ of Liverpool, Manchester Metropolitan Univ (MEd); *m*; 1 s; *Career* former: teacher, devpt offr MIND, slr; MP (Lab) Warrington N 1997–; memb Chester City Cncl 1984–91; *Style*— Ms Helen Jones, MP; ✉ House of Commons, London SW1A 0AA (tel 020 7219 4048); Constituency: Gilbert Wakefield House, 67 Bewsey Street, Warrington WA2 7JQ (tel 01925 232480, fax 01925 232239)

JONES, Helen Mary; AM; da of John Merfyn Jones (d 2004), and Daphne André Helen, *née* Lyle Stuart (d 1994); *b* 29 June 1960; *Educ* Colchester Co HS for Girls, Llanfair Caereinion HS, UCW Aberystwyth (BA); *Children* 1 da (Catrin Rhian Elen b 17 May 1996); *Career* memb Nat Assembly for Wales (Plaid Cymru): Mid and West Wales 2003–07, Llanelli 2007–; shadow health min Nat Assembly for Wales; formerly: sr devpt mangr Equal Opportunities Cmmn (Wales), memb Nat Assembly Advsy Gp, positions with UNISON and TGWU; vol Welsh Women's Aid; *Style*— Ms Helen Mary Jones, AM; ✉ National Assembly Office, Bres House, Bres Road, Llanelli SA15 1UA (tel 01554 774393, fax 01554 759174, e-mail helen-mary.jones@wales.gov.uk)

JONES, Helen Mary; *b* 28 April 1955; *Educ* chartered secretary 1976; *Career* grad trainee (Finance) Coventry Climax 1976–77, co secretarial asst Ernst and Whinney 1977–79, asst co sec rising to legal advsr corp fin Guinness plc 1979–87; Kingfisher plc: asst co sec and gp mangr fin ops 1987–91, successively mktg mangr Home, head of buying then logistics mangr Stationery and mangr Range Mgmnt Woolworths plc 1991–95, gp co sec 1995–, dir of governance and corp servs 2002–; chair Primary Markets Gp London Stock Exchange; memb: Co Secs Forum ICSA, European Retail Round Table Business Gp, Bd of Mgmnt BRC (also memb Fin and Gen Purposes Gp), Europe Ctee CBI (also memb London Regnl Cncl 1996–2002), Advsy Bd HM CPS Inspectorate 2001–; ICSA, FCIS 1996; *Style*— Ms Helen Jones; ✉ Kingfisher plc, 3 Sheldon Square, Paddington, London W2 6PX (tel 020 7644 1051, fax 020 7644 1245)

JONES, His Hon Hugh Duncan Hitchings; DL (Mid Glamorgan); s of Norman Everard Jones (d 1971), of Mountain Ash, and Ann, *née* Hitchings (d 1991); *b* 25 May 1937; *Educ* Mountain Ash GS (state scholar), UCL (LLB); *m* 1966, Helen Margaret, da of Norman Kingsley Payne; 3 da (Gweno Elizabeth, Siriol Ann (twins) b 19 April 1967, Rhian Margaret b 30 May 1970); *Career* admitted slr 1961, registrar Cardiff Co Court 1978–91, recorder 1988–91, circuit judge (Wales & Chester Circuit) 1991–2004 (dep circuit judge 2004–); memb: Law Soc 1961–, Ctee of Registrars' Assoc 1985–91, Co Court Rules Ctee 1994–98; *Recreations* gardening, cricket, golf, holidays; *Clubs* Mountain Ash Golf; *Style*— His Hon Hugh Jones, DL; ✉ c/o Wales & Chester Circuit Office, Churchill House, Churchill Way, Cardiff CF1 4HH

JONES, Huw; s of Idris Jones (d 1993), and Olwen, *née* Edwards; *b* 5 May 1948; *Educ* Cardiff HS for Boys, Jesus Coll Oxford (MA); *m* 29 Aug 1972, Siân Marylka, da of Kazimierz Miarczynski; 2 c (Owain Elidir b 1973, Siwan Elenid b 1977); *Career* pop singer, recording artist and TV presenter 1968–76, dir/gen mangr Sain Recording Company 1969–81, chm Barcud Cyf (TV Facilities) 1981–93, md/prodr Teledu'r Tir Glas Cyf (ind prodn co) 1982–93, first chm Teledwyr Annibynnol Cymru (Welsh ind prodrs) 1984–86, chief exec S4C 1994–2005; dir: Sgrin Cyf 1996–2005, S4C Masnachol Cyf 1999–2005, SDN Ltd 1999–2005; dir Skillset Ltd 2001–05 (patron 2006–), chm Skillset Cymru Cyf 2002–05; currently: chair Portmeirion Ltd, chair Cyfle Cyf, dir StrataMatrix Cyf, dir Nant Gwrtheyrn Cyf, conslt Univ of Wales Bangor; memb: Gorsedd of Bards, National Eisteddfod of Wales, Welsh Language Bd, RSPB Advsy Ctee for Wales; hon fell Univ of Wales Aberystwyth 1997; FRTS 1999; *Recreations* reading, cycling, skiing; *Style*— Huw Jones, Esq

JONES, Hywel Ceri; CMG (1999); s of Gwilym Ceri Jones (d 1963), and Mary Symmons (d 1970); *b* 22 April 1937; *Educ* Pontardawe GS, Univ of Wales Aberystwyth (BA, DipEd, John and Elizabeth Williams scholar); *m* Morwenna, da of late Wilfred Carnsew Armstrong; 1 da (Hannah Ceri b 29 Aug 1967), 1 s (Gwilym Ceri b 5 May 1970); *Career* Univ of Sussex: asst registrar 1962–65, dep dir Centre for Educnl Technol and Curriculum Devpt 1965–69, special asst to vice-chllr for planning and devpt 1969–73, visiting fell in educn and contemporary European studies 1973–80; EC: head Dept for Educn and Youth Policies 1973–79, dir Educn, Vocational Trg and Youth Policy 1979–88, dir Task Force for HR, Educn, Trg and Youth 1989–93, actg DG then dep DG Employment, Social Policy, Employment and Industrial Rels 1993–98; advsr to George Soros on the Open Soc's Network of Fndns 1998–99, European advsr to Welsh Office and chm Ctee on Wales and Europe 1998–99, chm Governing Bd of European Policy Centre Brussels 1999–2007; chm European Inst for Educn and Social Policy Paris 2000–04, dir Network of European Fndns (NEF); visiting prof Univ of Glamorgan 1999–2001; author of numerous articles on educn and trg and social policy in Europe; chm: prog ctees on educn and trg EU, Advsy Ctee for Vocational Trg EC, European Social Dialogue Ctee, European Social Fund Ctee, task force to prepare the social dimension to the enlargement of the EU; vice-chm: European Centre for Vocational Trg (CEDEFOP), European Fndn for Living and Working Conditions Dublin; govr European Cultural Fndn 1999–2007; govr: NE Wales Inst of HE 2003–, Federal Tst for Educn and Research 2004–, Bd ECORYS 2006–; memb Bd Nat Playing Fields Assoc for Wales 2002–, memb Bd Franco-Br Inst 2003–; Winston Churchill fell 1967, Eisenhower fell 1978; Hon DUniv: Sussex 1991, Leuven 1992, Open Univ 2000; Hon LLD Nat Cncl for Educnl Awards of Ireland 1992, Hon Dr Free Univ of Brussels 2002; hon fell: Educn Inst of Scot 1988, Univ of Westminster 1990, Univ of Wales Aberystwyth 1990, NE Wales Inst of HE 1993, Univ of Glamorgan 1994, Univ of Swansea 1995; Gold Medal of the Republic of Italy 1987; *Style*— Hywel Ceri Jones, CMG

JONES, Ian; s of Reginald Sampson Jones (d 1977), of Birmingham, and Florence, *née* Lees (d 2000); *b* 3 July 1947; *Educ* Queensbridge Sch Birmingham, Hall Green Tech Coll Birmingham, Birmingham Poly Sch of Fine Art (BA), RCA (MA); *m* 2 July 1966, Carole Ann, da of Albert Percival Holmes (d 1984); 2 s (Antony Ian b 27 Dec 1966 d 2001, Stuart Timothy b 12 Oct 1968); *Career* artist; apprentice toolmaker W H Doherty Co Ltd 1963–69; toolmaker: Aero Coldform Co Ltd 1969–72, Producit Co Ltd 1972–75; teacher of art: Limerick Coll of Art & Design, Birmingham Sch of Fine Art, St Martin's Coll of Art London, Kingston Poly, Canterbury Art Coll, Brighton Poly Sch of Fine Art, Univ of E London; *Major Works* Head (Father) 1982, Drinking & Smoking 1982, The Engineer 1982, The Life Raft 1985, Tightrope Walker 1986, A Quick Trip to Ireland 1987, Hi Heel Sneakers 1987, There'll Be a Bit of a Breeze Tonight 1987, The Wedding 1988, Shoes on a Custard Carpet 1989, Celebrating the Buff Envelope 1989, The Karin B 1989, Brummagem 1989, Sweet Smell of Success 1989, Reflections 1989, Money Talks 1990, Big Legs Tight Skirts 1990, Eight Hour Stay 1991, Yates's 1991, Northfied Girls 1991, Swimmer 1991, Stare 1991, Traffic 1992, Obsession III and IV 1992, Hot Hatch Six Pack 1993, Fast Ford 1993, Move It On Over 1993, Any Road Up 1993, Female Heads I, II, III, IV, V 1995; *Solo Exhibitions* Chapter Art Centre Cardiff 1984, 21 Days Work (Leamington Spa 1985, Stratford upon Avon 1986), Recent Paintings and Drawings (Consort Gallery ICST) 1987, Some New Work (Vortex Gallery London) 1987, Recent Paintings (Camden Arts Centre London) 1988, Anderson O'Day Gallery London 1989–91 and 1995, Big Paintings for the Barbican (Concourse Gallery Barbican) 1993, Cornhill Exhibition 1995 and 1996, Earl of Smith Gallery Leamington Spa 1997; *Group Exhibitions* incl: Drawings (Foyle Gallery Birmingham) 1975, 5 Painters (Consort Gallery) 1981, New Contemporaries (ICA Gallery) 1982, New Blood on Paper (MOMA Oxford) 1983, Gallery 24 London 1984, Open Studios (Fish Island Artists London) annually 1985–91, Print Show (The Grannery Limerick) 1986, Mead Gallery Warwick Univ 1987, Athena Awards (Barbican) 1988, The Falklands Factor (Manchester City Art Gallery and tour) 1988, Jumping Ship (Vortex Gallery London) 1989, Images of Paradise (Harewood House, Yorks) 1989, Contemporary London (Transart Cologne) 1989, Salon de la Jeune Peinture Grand Palais Paris 1990, Summer Exhibition (Anderson O'Day Gallery London) 1990 and 1991, Art Frankfurt 1991, The Discerning Eye (Mall Galleries) 1991, Dieppe-Brighton Exchange (Dieppe) 1992, Chelsea Arts Club London 1995, Royal Acad Summer Show 1995, Absolout Secret (RCA) 1995 and 1996, The Motor Show (Herbert Museum and Art Gallery Coventry and tour) 1996, Wheels on Fire (Wolverhampton Art Gallery and tour) 1996; *Work in Public Collections* Unilever, Nordstern Cologne, WEA, Guinness Brewing Worldwide, Pepsi Cola, Br Airports Authy, EMI Worldwide, Glaxo Holding; *Awards* Whitworth Wallis prize 1976, John Minton award 1982, major award Greater London Arts award 1983, short list prize Athena Awards 1988, Unilever prize Portobello Festival 1989; *Recreations* music; *Clubs* Chelsea Arts; *Style*— Ian Jones, Esq; ✉ Anderson O'Day Gallery, 5 St Quintin Avenue, London W10 6NX

JONES, Prof Ian; *b* 13 June 1947; *Educ* Univ of Cambridge (MA), Univ of Birmingham (PhD); *Career* Univ of Birmingham: SRC res fell Dept of Physical Metallurgy 1972–74, res fell Dept of Metallurgy and Materials 1974–81, lectr Dept of Metallurgy and Materials 1981–86, sr lectr 1986–92, reader in the electron microscopy of materials 1992–96, prof of physical metallurgy 1996–; visiting prof Dept of Metallurgy and Materials Engrg Ohio State Univ Columbus 1992–1998, visiting prof Dept of Metallurgy and Mining Engrg Univ of Illinois Urbana-Champaign 1973 and 1984, visiting fell Theoretical Physics Div Atomic Energy Research Establishment 1973, distinguished foreign visitor fellowship Nagoya Inst of Technol Japan 1989; MIM CEng, FInstP; *Books* Chemical Microanalysis Using Electron Beams (1992), Materials Science for Electrical and Electronic Engineers (2000); also author of over 160 academic papers; *Style*— Prof Ian Jones; ✉ Department of Metallurgy & Materials, The University of Birmingham, Edgbaston, Birmingham B15 2TT (tel 0121 414 5184, fax 0121 414 5232, e-mail i.p.jones@bham.ac.uk, website www.bham.ac.uk/metallurgy/staff/academic/ipjones.html)

JONES, Ian Geoffrey; s of Geoffrey Frederick Jones, and Ann Elizabeth, *née* Taylor; *b* 18 August 1965; *Educ* Bolton Sch, West Glamorgan Inst of Higher Educn (HND), Bournemouth Art Coll (PQE); *m* 21 Oct 1995, Elizabeth Caroline Hare; 1 s (Angus Ian b 28 March 1998), 1 da (Iona Elizabeth b 26 April 2000); *Career* chief photographer Skishoot 1987–91, freelance 1991–, Daily Telegraph photographer 1992–; projects incl maj home and world news assignments and Royal foreign tours; memb: Newspaper Publishers' Assoc, Old Boltonians' Assoc; *Awards* highly commended Martini Royal Photographer Awards 1992, winner Canon News Photographer of the Year 1992 and Fuji News Photographer of the Year 1992, Martini Royal Photographer of the Year 1993 and 1994, Martini Royal Photographer of the Decade 1996; *Recreations* skiing, fishing; *Style*— Ian Jones, Esq; ✉ c/o The Daily Telegraph, 111 Buckingham Palace Road, London SW1W 0DT (mobile 07850 329349, e-mail ian.jones@telegraph.co.uk)

JONES, (Charles) Ian McMillan; s of Wilfred Charles Jones (d 1986), of Wroxham, Norfolk, and Bessie, *née* McMillan (d 1998); *b* 11 October 1934; *Educ* Bishop's Stortford Coll, St John's Coll Cambridge (MA, PGCE, capt Cambridge Univ Hockey XI 1958–59); *m* 9 Aug 1962, Jennifer Marie, da of Alec Potter (d 1980), of Hertford; 2 s (William Ian b 18 Jan 1964, Robert Andrew b 28 Jan 1970); *Career* Nat Serv 1953–55, cmmnd RA, Subalt 45 Field Regt in BAOR, regtl motor tport offr, TA 1955–57, Lt Herts Yeomanry; head Geography Dept Bishop's Stortford Coll 1960–70 (asst to headmaster 1967–70), vice-princ King William's Coll IOM 1971–75, headmaster Bedford Sch 1975–86, dir studies Britannia RNC Dartmouth 1986–88, project dir The Centre for Br Teachers Negara Brunei Darussalam 1988–91, Malaysia 1990–91, educnl advsr Kolej Tuanku Ja'afar Malaysia 1988–91, dir CfBT Educn Servs SE Asia 1992–94, grants and awards administrator CfBT Educn Servs 1995–97, educn conslt 1995–, tutor for Nat Professional Qualification for Head Teachers 1998–; played for: England Hockey XI 1959–64, GB Hockey XI 1959–64; competed in Olympic Games Rome 1960 and Tokyo 1964, mangr/coach England Hockey XI 1967–69; English Schoolboy Hockey Assoc: chm 1976–86, pres 1980–88; mangr England Schoolboy Hockey XI 1967–77; memb: Ctee of Headmasters' Conf 1981–83, IOM Sports Cncl 1972–75; chm ISIS Central 1981–83; contributed feature articles: on hockey to The Guardian 1969–72, on educn and travel to The Borneo Bulletin 1990–94, on education to The Officer and RAF In-Flight; conslt ed Hobsons Guide to UK Boarding Schools 1995–; govr: Bishop's Stortford Coll 1995–2004, Thorpe House Sch Norwich 1999–; non-exec dir Norwich Community Health Partnership 1995–97; FCMI 1981, FRSA 1981; *Recreations* hockey, cricket, squash, golf; *Clubs* MCC, Hawks' (Cambridge), Pantai Mentiri Golf (Brunei), Royal Norwich Golf; *Style*— Ian Jones, Esq; ✉ 9 Phillipa Flowerday Plain, Norwich, Norfolk NR2 2TA (tel and fax 01603 661443, e-mail cianmjones@aol.com)

JONES, Ian Quayle; WS; s of Arnold Bates Jones (d 1977), of Poynton, Cheshire, and Lilian Quayle Jones (d 1989); *b* 14 July 1941; *Educ* Strathallan Sch, Univ of Edinburgh (MA, LLB); *m* 24 Feb 1968, Christine Ann, da of Kenneth Macrae, WS (d 1984), of Edinburgh; 1 da (Stephanie Margaret b 1974), 2 s (Simon Quayle b 1977, Richard Ian b 1980); *Career* ptnr Cowan and Stewart WS 1968–72, fund mangr Ivory & Sime 1972–74, dir Br Linen Bank Ltd 1974–83 (mangr, asst dir and dir), chief exec Quayle Munro Holdings plc 1983– (exec chm 1999– (pt/t 2001–)); *Recreations* golf, skiing, fishing; *Clubs* Hon Co of Edinburgh Golfers; *Style*— Ian Jones, Esq, WS; ✉ Quayle Munro Ltd, 8 Charlotte Square, Edinburgh EH2 4DR (tel 0131 226 4421, fax 0131 225 3391)

JONES, Rt Rev Dr Idris; *see:* Glasgow and Galloway, Bishop of

JONES, Ieuan; s of David Edward Humphries Jones, of Mathrafal, Powys, and Beryl Elizabeth Mary, *née* Proudlove; *b* 24 January 1963; *Educ* Llanfair Caereinion Sch, Royal Coll of Music (Most Distinguished Student award, Tagore Gold medal, winner Royal Over-Seas League music competition, runner-up Israel Harp contest); *m* 18 June 1992, Penny Gore Browne, *née* Thomson; 1 step s (Edward), 1 step da (Alexandra); *Career* harpist; prof of harp RCM 1996–; appointed harpist to the House of Commons 1984–97; London debut Purcell Room 1985, Wigmore Hall debut 1987; recitals given and appearances with orchs in various countries incl: USA, Argentina, Uruguay, Mexico, Spain, Italy, Switzerland, Germany, Austria, France, Belgium, Netherlands, China, Philippines, Australia, Israel and Ireland; private appearance before HRH Queen Elizabeth The Queen Mother at the Royal Lodge Windsor 1986, guest appearance St James' Palace 1988 and Holyrood House 1989, world premiere Concerto for Harp and Marimba World Harp Festival 1994, cmmnd and premiered work by Jean-Michel Damase Wigmore Hall 1994, Concertgebouw debut with Ginastera Concerto 1995, Hong Kong, Phillippines and Australia solo debut tour 1995, Far East tour (Bangkok, Hong Kong, Brunei, Australia, Philippines) 1997 and 1999; jury memb for int competitions incl Israel, Japan, Spain and London; recordings: The Uncommon Harp (1987), The Two Sides of Ieuan Jones (1988), ...In The French Style (1990), Mozart in Paris (1990), All Through the Night (1992), French Chamber Music (1994), William Alwyn (1994), Concerto D'Aranjuez/Batiz (1995), The Liszt of the Harp (1999), Rodrigo - Concierto De Aranjuez (2003); memb Chelsea Arts Club 1997; ARCM 1981, DipRCM 1985; *Recreations* health and fitness, travel; *Style*— Ieuan Jones, Esq

JONES, Ieuan Wyn; AM; s of Rev John Jones (d 1977), of Gwynedd, and Mair Elizabeth Jones, *née* Pritchard; *b* 22 May 1949; *Educ* Pontardawe GS, Ysgol-Y-Berwyn Y Bala Gwynedd, Liverpool Poly (LLB); *m* 1974, Eirian Llwyd, da of John Nefydd Jones, of Clwyd; 2 s (Gerallt b 1975, Owain b 1978), 1 da (Gwenllian b 1977); *Career* admitted slr 1973, ptnr William Jones & Talog Davies Ruthin Clwyd 1974 (ptnr Llangefni Branch 1985–); MP (Plaid Cymru) Ynys Mon 1987–2001; memb Select Ctee: on Welsh Affairs 1989–92, on Agric 1992–2001; memb Nat Assembly for Wales (Plaid Cymru) Ynys Mon 1999–, ldr of the oppn Nat Assembly for Wales; Plaid Cymru: nat chm 1980–82 and 1990–92, pres 2000–03, ldr Plaid Cymru Gp Nat Assembly for Wales; sponsored Hearing Aid Cncl (Amendment) Act 1989 private members bill; *Books* Europe: The Challenge for Wales (1996), Biography of Thomas Gee (1998); *Recreations* sport, local history; *Style*— Ieuan Wyn Jones, Esq, AM; ✉ Ty Newydd Rhosmeirch, Llangefni, Gwynedd LL77 7RZ (tel 01248 722261, 01248 723599)

JONES, Rt Rev James Stuart; *see:* Liverpool, Bishop of

JONES, Jenny; AM; da of Percy Jones, and Christine Heasman; *Educ* Westlain GS Brighton, Inst of Archaeology, UCL (BSc); *Career* archaeologist, formerly fin controller; memb Green Party (chm 1994–97); GLA: memb London Assembly (Green) London (list) 2000–, dep mayor 2003–04, Mayor's road safety ambass, Mayor's Green transport advsr; memb: Met Police Authy, memb Budget Ctee, Business Mgmnt and Appts Ctee; chair London Food 2003–; cncllr S Camberwell ward Southwark Cncl 2006–; *Recreations* cinema, reading; *Style*— Cncllr Jenny Jones, AM; ✉ London Assembly, City Hall, Queens Walk, Southwark, London SE1 2AA (tel 020 7983 4358, fax 020 7983 4398, e-mail jenny.jones@london.gov.uk)

JONES, Prof (William) Jeremy; s of Thomas John Jones (d 1975), of Llandeilo, Dyfed, and Margaret Jeremy (d 1958); *b* 15 August 1935; *Educ* Llandeilo GS, UCW Aberystwyth (BSc, MSc), Trinity Coll Cambridge (PhD); *m* 29 June 1963, (Margaret) Anne, da of Dr Frederick Greystock Robertson, of Cobourg, Ontario; 2 s (Jeremy b 18 May 1964 d 1987, Michael b 28 March 1968), 1 da (Suzanne b 19 June 1970); *Career* Univ of Cambridge: external research student Trinity Coll 1958–60, title A research fell Trinity Coll 1960–64, demonstrator in physical chemistry 1965–70, lectr 1970–78, tutor Trinity Coll 1973–78 (fell and dir studies 1964–78); research student Courtaulds 1958–61, fell Nat Research Cncl of Canada 1962–64, prof and head Dept of Chemistry UCW Aberystwyth 1978–88; Univ of Wales Swansea: prof of chemistry 1988–2000 (emeritus prof 2000–), dean Faculty of Science 1992–96; memb Optical Soc of America 1978; FRSC 1978; *Recreations* golf, gardening, walking; *Style*— Prof Jeremy Jones; ✉ Department of Chemistry, University of Wales Swansea, Singleton Park SA2 8PP (e-mail w.j.jones@swansea.ac.uk)

JONES, John Elfed; CBE (1987), DL; s of Urien Maelgwyn Jones (d 1978); *b* 19 March 1933; *Educ* Blaenau Ffestiniog GS, Denbighshire Tech Coll, Heriot-Watt Coll; *m* 1957, Mary Sheila, da of David Thomas Rosser; 2 da (Bethan, Delyth); *Career* Flying Offr RAF; chartered electrical engr CEGB 1949–1969, dep md Anglesey Aluminium Metal Ltd 1969–79, under-sec (industry) Welsh Office 1979–82; chm: Welsh Water Authy 1982–89, Welsh Water plc 1989–93, HTV Wales/Cymru 1992–97, International Greetings plc 1996–; dep chm HTV (Group) plc 1992–97; chm: Bwrdd Yr Iaith Gymraeg (Welsh Language Bd) 1988–93, Nat Assembly Advsy Gp (set up by sec of state for Wales) 1997–98, Exec Ctee Nat Eisteddfod of Wales 1998; pres: UCW Lampeter (St David's Univ) 1992–98, Campaign for the Protection of Rural Wales 1995–2001, Côr Bro Ogwr 1999–, The Miners Rest Porthcawl 2000–, Princess of Wales Hosp Scanner Appeal 2000–; chm Menter Mantis Cyf 1999–2004; fell: Univ of Wales Aberystwyth 1991, NE Wales Inst 1996; Hon DUniv Glamorgan 1997, Hon LLD Univ of Wales 2000; CEng, CIMgt, FIET, FRSA; *Recreations* fishing (salmon and trout), attending Eisteddfodau, golf; *Clubs* RAF, Cardiff & County, Royal Porthcawl Golf, Cotterell Park Golf; *Style*— John Elfed Jones, Esq, CBE, DL; ✉ Ty Mawr, Coety, Penybontarogwr, Morgannwg Ganol CF35 6BN (tel 01656 653039, fax 01656 667204)

JONES, John Maurice; s of late Maurice Parry Jones, of Llwynderw, Bala, N Wales, and Armorel Winifred, *née* Adams; *b* 6 March 1943; *Educ* Llandovery Coll, Middx Hosp Univ of London (MB BS); *m* 17 Feb 1968, Valerie Patricia; 2 da (Katie b 1970, Vanessa b 1971), 1 s (Richard b 1973); *Career* surgical registrar Edinburgh 1970–74, orthopaedic registrar St George's Hosp London 1974–76, sr registrar Cardiff 1976–80, orthopaedic conslt Leicester 1980–2005; formerly examiner RCS(Ed); fell Presbyterian St Luke's Chicago; memb BSSH, FRCSEd; *Style*— John Jones, Esq; ✉ 8 Knighton Drive, Leicestershire LE2 3HB (tel 0116 270 6961, mobile 07860 553135)

JONES, Prof Jonathan Dallas George; s of George Ronald Jones (d 1987), and Isabel Dallas Orr, *née* Pinkney; *b* 14 July 1954, London; *Educ* Hampton GS, Peterhouse Cambridge (BA), Univ of Cambridge (PhD); *m* 22 July 1991, Caroline Dean; 1 s (William George b 8 Feb 1992), 1 da (Philippa Susan b 23 April 1994), 1 other da (Gillian b 6 March 1983); *Career* postdoctoral research Harvard Univ 1981–82, Advanced Genetic Sciences Oakland CA 1983–88, Sainsbury Lab John Innes Centre Norwich 1988–; memb EMBO 1998; FRS 2003; *Recreations* sailing, music, children; *Clubs* Waverley and Oulton Broad Yacht; *Style*— Prof Jonathan Jones; ✉ The Sainsbury Laboratory, John Innes Centre, Colney Lane, Norwich NR4 7UH (tel 01603 450327, fax 01603 450011, e-mail jonathan.jones@bbsrc.ac.uk)

JONES, Jonathan Guy; s of Leonard Martell Jones (d 1993), and Margaret Eleanor, *née* Jones (d 2006); *b* 21 May 1962; *Educ* Llandovery Coll, St Chad's Coll Durham (Horsfall scholar, organ scholar, BA), Inns of Court Sch of Law; *Career* called to the Bar: Middle Temple 1985, NI 2006; Legal Dept OFT 1989–93, Legal Advsr's Office Dept of Tport 1993–94, legal secretariat to the Law Officers Attorney-Gen's Chambers 1994–98, dep legal advsr HM Treasy 1998–2002, legal advsr DfES and dir Treasy Slr's Dept 2002–04, DG Attorney-Gen's Office 2004–; *Style*— Jonathan Jones, Esq; ✉ Attorney General's Office, 20 Victoria Street, London SW1H 0NB (tel 020 7271 2400)

JONES, Karen Elisabeth Dind; CBE (2006); da of Eric Jones (d 1992), and Margaret, *née* Dind; *b* 29 July 1956; *Educ* UEA (BA), Wellesley Coll Mass; *m* Hamish Easton; 2 da (Rose b 16 June 1990, Molly b 3 Sept 1995), 1 s (Max b 2 Jan 1993); *Career* co-ed Straight Lines Magazine 1978–80, account planner Boase Massimi Pollitt 1980–81, operations dir Theme Holdings plc 1981–88; md: The Pelican Gp plc 1989–99, Punch Gp Ltd; chief exec Spirit Gp Ltd 1999–2006, co-fndr Food & Fuel 2006–; non-exec dir: EMAP plc 1997–, Gondola Holdings plc 2005–, HBOS plc 2006–; memb Bd Royal National Theatre Enterprises; memb Industrial Devpt Advsy Bd DTI 2004–; finalist Veuve Clicquot Business Woman of the Year 1995; FRSA; *Recreations* my children, food and wine, theatre, interior design, contemporary American and English literature; *Style*— Ms Karen Jones, CBE

JONES, Kate; da of Mark Jones, and Shirley, *née* Tebbutt; *m* 31 July 1996, John Tackaberry, QC; 1 da (Molly b 15 Feb 2000); *Career* literary agent: Tessa Sayle Literary Agency, Penguin Books 1989–2001, Ian Fleming Pubns Ltd 2001–03, ICM Books 2003–; *Style*— Ms Kate Jones; ✉ ICM Books, 4–6 Soho Square, London W1D 3PZ (tel 020 7432 0800, fax 020 7432 0808)

JONES, Kathleen; MBE (2006); da of David Edward Edwards (d 1992), and Sheila Edwards; *b* 31 July 1953, Wrexham; *Educ* Grove Park Girls GS Wrexham, Univ of Wales Bangor (DipN, BN, PGCE); *m* 21 Feb 1976, Alun Charles Jones; 1 da (Bethan Sian b 3 April 1981), 1 s (Gareth Edward b 14 Nov 1983); *Career* student nurse Northwick Park Hosp Harrow 1971–74, staff nurse Univ Hosp of Wales Cardiff 1974–75; Wrexham Maelor Hosp: pupil midwife 1975–76, staff midwife 1976–79, community midwife 1979–; lectr practitioner Univ of Wales Bangor 1993–94; Royal Coll of Midwives: steward 1996–97, memb Cncl 2001–; SRN 1974, SCM 1976; *Publications* Essential Midwifery (with C Henderson, 1997); *Style*— Mrs Kathleen Jones, MBE; ✉ 3 Park View, Old Wrexham Road, Gresford, Wrexham LL12 8UB (tel 01978 854033, e-mail kathjonesmw@aol.com); Wrexham Maelor Hospital, Croesnewydd Road, Wrexham LL13 7TD (tel 01978 725021)

JONES, Very Rev Keith Brynmor; s of John Brynmor Jones (d 1970), and Mary Emily, *née* Evans (d 1980); *b* 27 June 1944; *Educ* Univ of Cambridge (MA); *m* 1973, Viola Mary, da of Henry Leigh Jenkyns; 3 da (Sophia b 27 Dec 1974, Olivia b 6 June 1977, Isabel b 3 July 1980); *Career* curate Limpsey with Titsey Dio of Southwark 1969–72, dean's vicar Cathedral and Abbey Church of St Albans 1972–76, vicar (subsequently team vicar) St Michael's Boreham Wood Team Miny Herts 1976–82, vicar St Mary le Tower Ipswich 1982–96, rural dean of Ipswich 1992–96, hon canon St Edmundsbury Cathedral 1993–96, dean of Exeter 1996–2004, dean of York 2004–; gen synod 1999–2005; chm The Pilgrims Assoc 2001–; *Recreations* gardening, music, theatre, wool-gathering; *Style*— The Very Rev Keith Jones, Dean of York; ✉ The Deanery, York YO1 7JN

JONES, Dr Keith Howard; CB (1997); s of Arthur Leslie and Miriam Jones; *b* 14 October 1937; *m* 1962, Dr Lynne *née* Pearse; 3 s; *Career* various posts in clinical med and research at teaching hosps in Cardiff, Edinburgh and Cambridge 1960–67, chief toxologist Agrochemical Div Fisons 1967–70, head of safety assessment and clinical pharmacology Beecham Pharmaceuticals 1970–79, exec dir (medical affairs) Merck Sharp & Dohme Research Laboratories 1979–1989, chief exec Medicines Control Agency 1992–2002 (dir 1989–92); former adjunct prof of med Thomas Jefferson Med Sch 1979–89, visiting prof of pharmacology Univ of London 1995–2002; UK Rep: EC Ctee for Pharmaceutical Med Products 1989–95, EC Pharmaceutical Ctee 1989–2002; chm Scientific Ctee Medical Products and Medical Devices 1997–2000, scientific advsr to EU, memb Scientific Steering Ctee 1997–2002, chm Mgmnt Bd European Medicines Evaluation Agency 2001–03 (memb 1995–2002); author of numerous pubns on clinical and metabolic med, pesticide and drug toxicology and clinical pharmacology and drug devpt; FFPM 1989, FRCPE 1990, FRCP 1993; *Recreations* sailing, tennis; *Style*— Dr Keith Jones, CB

JONES, Kelly; *Career* musician; vocalist and guitarist Stereophonics 1996–; *Albums* incl: Word Gets Around 1997, Performance and Cocktails 1999, Just Enough Education to Perform 2001, You Gotta Go There To Come Back 2003, Language.Sex.Violence.Other? 2005, Live from Dakota 2006; *Style*— Kelly Jones, Esq; ✉ c/o Nettwerk Management, Clearwater Yard, 35 Inverness Street, Camden, London NW1 7HB (tel 020 7424 7500, fax 020 7424 7501, e-mail natalie@nettwerk.com)

JONES, Kevan; MP; *b* 25 April 1964; *Educ* Portland Comp, Newcastle upon Tyne Poly, Univ of Southern Maine; *Career* memb Lab Pty 1982–; GMB Northern Region: political offr 1989–2001, regnl organiser 1992–99, sr organiser 1999–2001; memb Newcastle City Cncl 1990–2001 (chief whip, chair Public Health Ctee, cabinet memb for devpt and tport), MP (Lab) Durham N 2001–; memb: Co-op Pty, NE Tourism Advsy Bd; *Style*— Kevan Jones, Esq, MP; ✉ House of Commons, London SW1A 0AA

JONES, Laura Anne; AM; da of John Dilwyn Jones, and Penelope Anne, *née* Haining; *b* 21 February 1979, Newport, Gwent; *Educ* Caerleon Comp Sch, Univ of Plymouth (BSc); *Career* memb Nat Assembly for Wales (Cons) S Wales E 2003–; supporter: NSPCC, Cancer Research UK, Br Heart Fndn, Leukaemia Research, Red Cross; ambass Girl Guides; *Recreations* swimming, hockey, skiing, horse riding, cycling; *Clubs* Usk Conservative, Caerphilly Conservative; *Style*— Miss Laura Anne Jones, AM; ✉ Llanusk Cottage, Llanbadoc, Monmouthshire NP15 1TA; National Assembly for Wales, Cardiff Bay, Cardiff CF99 1NA (tel 029 2089 8713, fax 029 2089 8272, e-mail laura.jones@wales.gov.uk or laura.jones@lauraannejonesam.com)

JONES, Laurance Aubrey; s of Aubrey Joseph Goldsmid Jones (d 1990), of Godmanchester, Huntingdon, and Frances Laura, *née* Ward (d 1997); *b* 7 April 1936; *Educ* King's Sch Rochester; *m* 8 July 1961, Joan, da of Douglas Stanley Sargeant (d 1997), of Staplehurst, Kent; *Career* Nat Serv RAF 1954–56; Royal Insurance Group 1953–54 and 1956–57, National Employers Mutual General Insurance Association Ltd 1957–58, co sec Marchant & Tubb Ltd 1959–67, jt sec Tollemache & Cobbold Group Cambridge 1967–70, dep sec International Timber Corporation Ltd 1970–77, gp sec Land Securities plc 1977–98, memb and chm Land Securities Charities Ctee 1998–2007, tstee Land Securities Gp Pension Scheme 1999–; tstee Harold Samuel Educnl Tst 1998–; Freeman: Maidstone 1957, City of London 1981; Liveryman: Worshipful Co of Chartered Secretaries and Administrators 1981, Worshipful Co of Masons 1998; FCIS 1972 (ACIS 1968); *Recreations* tennis, golf, travel, bridge; *Clubs* City Livery, Broad Street Ward, United Wards' (City of London), RAC; *Style*— Laurance Jones, Esq; ✉ 242 Cromwell Tower, Barbican, London EC2Y 8DD; Les Terrasses de l'Esterel, Domaine du Grand Duc, 4 Avenue Maurice Utrillo D9, 06210 Maudelieu, France

JONES, Lucy Katharine; da of Anthony Tom Brett-Jones, CBE, and Ann, *née* Fox; *b* 21 February 1955; *Educ* Byam Shaw Sch of Art, Camberwell Sch of Art (BA), RCA (MA, Cubitt award for painting, Anstruther award for painting), Br Sch in Rome (Rome scholar in painting); *m* Peter Leach; *Career* self employed artist and painter; formerly visiting tutor at various art colls incl: Ruskin Sch of Art, Byam Shaw Sch of Art, West Surrey Coll of Art and Design, Winchester Sch of Art; currently pt/t tutor Chelsea Coll of Art and Slade Sch of Art; *Solo Exhibitions* Angela Flowers Gallery London 1986, 1987, and 1989, Spitalfields Health Centre in assoc with Whitechapel Art Gallery 1987, Drumcroon Art Educn Centre Wigan 1990, Flowers East London 1991, 1993, 1995, 1997, 1999 and 2000, Flowers Graphics London 1998 and 2001, Flowers West Santa Monica Calif 1999; *Group Exhibitions* incl: Royal Acad Summer Exhibition 1981, 1990, 2000, 2001 and 2002, The Pick of Graduate Art (Christies Inaugural) 1982, 10 Artisti della Accademia Britannica (Palazzo Barberini Rome) 1984, Canvas-New British Painters (John Hansard Gallery and Milton Keynes City Art Gallery) 1986, Artist of the Day (Angela Flowers Gallery) 1986, Young Masters (The Solomon Gallery London) 1986, Whitechapel Open 1987 and 1992, Passage West (Angela Flowers Ireland Co Cork) 1987, The Subjective City (The Small Mansion Arts Centre London) 1988, London Glasgow NY: New Acquisitions (Metropolitan Museum of Art NYC) 1988, Contemporary Portraits (Flowers East) 1988, Big Paintings (Flowers East) 1989, XXI International Festival of Painting Cagnes-sur-Mer-France 1989, Flowers at Moos (Gallery Moos NYC) 1990, The Subjective City (Cleveland Gallery Middlesbrough and tour) 1990, Rome 1980–90 (RCA) 1990, Rome scholars 1980–90 (RCA) 1990, Drumcroon The First Ten Years (Drumcroon Educn Art Centre) 1990, Anglo/Soviet Landscapes (Peterborough and Leningrad) 1991, Foregrounds and Distances (Galleria de Serpenti Rome) 1992, The Discerning Eye (Mall Galleries) 1992, But Big is Better (Flowers East) 1993, Overcoming Obstacles: Women Artists in NW Collections (Blackburn Museum and Art Gallery) 1993, featured artist Art 24 '93 (Basel) 1993, Two Women Artists (with Eileen Cooper, Collyer Bristow London) 1993, Inner Visions (Flowers East) 1994, Downeen Decade (Angela Flowers Gallery) 1994, Ireland Small is Beautiful Park XII: Night and Day (Flowers East) 1994, The Twenty Fifth Anniversary (Flowers East) 1995, John Moore's Exhbn (Walker Art Gallery) 1995, Small is Beautiful Part XIII: Food and Drink (Flowers East) 1995, In the Looking Glass: Contemporary Self Portraits by Women Artists (Usher Gallery Lincoln and touring) 1996, The Whitechapel Open (Whitechapel Art Gallery) 1998, The Hunting Art Prize Exhbn (RCA) 2001, Art-Tube 01 (42 artists on one Piccadilly Line tube train London Underground) 2001; *Work in Public Collections* Sheffield City Art Gallery, Univ of Reading, Arts Cncl, Security Pacific, Metropolitan Museum of Art, Rugby Museum, Drumcroon Education Art Centre Wigan, Unilever plc, Contemporary Art Soc, Arthur Andersen, Clifford Chance, Deutsche Bank AG London, Harris Museum and Art Gallery Preston, Procter & Gamble London, Univ of Hull, Univ of Southampton, Westminster and Chelsea Hosp; *Awards* Oppenheim-John Downes Meml Tst 1986, Daler-Rowney award (best work in oil) Royal Acad Exhibition 1989, John Moore's Exhbn prize winner Walker Art Gallery Liverpool 1995, Grand Award Young Print Royal Acad Summer Exhibition; *Recreations* swimming, music, opera, cooking, sailing; *Style*— Ms Lucy Jones; ✉ Angela Flowers Gallery plc, Flowers East, 82 Kingsland Road, London E2 8DP (tel 020 8985 3333, e-mail gallery@flowerseast.com, website www.lucyjones.com)

JONES, Dr Lynne Mary; MP; da of late Stanley Stockton, and Jean Stockton; *b* 26 April 1951; *Educ* Univ of Birmingham (BSc, PhD), Birmingham Poly (Dip Housing Studies); *Children* 2 s; *Career* research fell Univ of Birmingham 1972–86, housing assoc mangr 1987–92; MP (Lab) Birmingham Selly Oak 1992–; memb: Sci and Technol Select Ctee 1992–2001, Environment, Food and Rural Affrs Select Ctee; *Style*— Dr Lynne Jones, MP; ✉ House of Commons, London SW1A 0AA (tel 0121 486 2808, 020 7219 4190, e-mail jonesl@parliament.uk, website www.lynnejones.org.uk)

JONES, Prof Malcolm Vince; s of Reginald Cross Jones (d 1986), and Winifred Ethel, *née* Vince (d 1992); *b* 7 January 1940; *Educ* Cotham GS Bristol, Univ of Nottingham (BA, PhD); *m* 27 July 1963, Jennifer Rosemary, da of Frederick Walter Durrant (d 1987); 1 s (Alexander b 30 May 1967), 1 da (Helen b 5 Dec 1968); *Career* asst lectr in Russian Sch of Euro Studies Univ of Sussex 1965–67; Univ of Nottingham: lectr 1967–73, sr lectr 1973–80, prof Dept of Slavonic Studies 1980–97, dean Faculty of Arts 1982–85 (vice-dean 1976–79), pro-vice-chllr 1987–91, prof emeritus 1997–; memb Editorial Bd Birmingham Slavonic Monographs 1976–, gen ed Cambridge Studies In Russian Literature 1985–96; hon pres: Assoc of Teachers of Russian 1985–86, Br Universities Assoc of Slavists 1986–88 (hon sec 1974–76), Co-ordinating Cncl for Area Studies Assoc 1991–93 (hon vice-pres 1988–91), Univ of Nottingham Convocation 1992–97; hon vice-pres Br Assoc For Soviet, Slavonic and E European Studies 1988–90, memb Humanities Research Bd British Acad 1994–97; pres Int Dostoyevsky Soc 1995–98; *Books* Dostoyevsky The Novel of Discord (1976), New Essays On Tolstoy (ed, 1978), New Essays On Dostoyevsky (jt ed, 1983), Dostoyevsky after Bakhtin (1990), Cambridge Companion to the Classic Russian Novel (jt ed, 1998), Dostoyevsky and the Dynamics of Religious Experience (2005); *Recreations* painting; *Clubs* Univ (Nottingham); *Style*— Prof Malcolm Jones; ✉ University of Nottingham, Department of Russian and Slavonic Studies, University Park, Nottingham NG7 2RD (e-mail malcolmvjones@btinternet.com)

JONES, Mark; s of David Jones, and Jean, *née* Wallet; *b* 10 May 1960; *Educ* John Cleveland Coll Hinckley, Trinity Coll Cambridge; *m* 1990, Annie, da of Bryson Ross; *Career* journalist; ed Londoner's Diary Evening Standard 1986–97, ed Campaign magazine 1989–90, exec features ed Evening Standard 1994–96, ed High Life magazine 1996–2003, editorial dir Cedar Communications 1997–; BSME Ed of the Year (Consumer Magazines) 1997, Travelex Travel Writer of the Year (Magazines) 1999; *Books* Invasion of the Rubbernecks (1990); *Recreations* football, cricket, Andalucia, gazing at rivers; *Clubs* Groucho, BSME, Racing Club de Blackheath; *Style*— Mark Jones, Esq; ✉ Cedar Communications, Pegasus House, 37–43 Sackville Street, London W1S 3EH (e-mail mark.jones@cedarcom.co.uk)

JONES, Mark Ellis Powell; s of John Ernest Powell-Jones, of Cranleigh, Surrey, and Ann Elizabeth, *née* Murray; *b* 5 February 1951; *Educ* Eton, Univ of Oxford, Courtauld Inst of Art; *m* Dr Ann Camilla, da of Stephen Toulmin; 2 da (Sarah b 9 Oct 1974, Agnes b 7 Feb 1987), 2 s (Luke b 27 Aug 1985, William b 31 Dec 1988); *Career* keeper Dept of Coins and Medals British Museum 1990–92 (asst keeper 1974–90), dir National Museums of Scotland 1992–2001, dir V&A 2001–; fndr dir SCRAN 1995; hon prof Univ of Edinburgh 1996; memb Advsy Ctee Royal Mint 1994–2004, sec British Art Medal Soc 1982–94 (pres 1998–2004), pres Fédération Internationale de la Médaille 1994–2000; ed The Medal 1983–95, memb Bd: Resource/MLA 2000–05, Crafts Cncl 2001–06, Ct RCA 2001–, Chllr's Forum Univ of Arts London 2002–06; tstee: Nat Tst 2005–, Pilgrim Tst 2006–; chm Nat Museum Dirs Conference 2006–; memb Advsy Bd DCMS 2007–; Liveryman Worshipful Co of Goldsmiths; Hon DLitt Royal Holloway Coll London 2001; FRSE 1999; *Publications* The Art of the Medal (1977), Impressionist Paintings (1979), Catalogue of French Medals in the British Museum (Vol I 1982, Vol II 1988), Fake: The Art of Deception (ed, 1990), Why Fakes Matter (ed, 1992), Designs on Posterity (ed, 1994); *Clubs* Scottish Arts, Athenaeum; *Style*— Mark Jones, Esq; ✉ 5 Corbetts Wharf, 87 Bermondsey Wall East, London SE16 4TU; Victoria & Albert Museum, Cromwell Road, London SW7 2RL (tel 020 7938 8500, e-mail mark.jones@vam.ac.uk)

JONES, Prof Martin Kenneth; s of John Francis Jones, and Margaret Olive, *née* Baldwin; *b* 29 June 1951; *Educ* Eltham Coll, Peterhouse Cambridge (Frank Smart prize); *m* 29 June 1985, Lucienne Mary, da of Clive Walker; 1 s (Alexander b 20 Dec 1987), 1 da (Leonie b 6 Aug 1990); *Career* environmental archaeologist Oxford Archaeological Unit 1973–78, res asst Botany Sch Univ of Oxford 1978–81, sr lectr Univ of Durham 1989–90 (lectr 1981–89), George Pitt-Rivers prof of archaeological science Univ of Cambridge 1990–; Hon DUniv Stirling 1999; FSA 1990; *Books* Environment of Man: The Iron Age to the Anglo Saxon Period (1981), Integrating the Substance Economy (1983), England before Domesday (1986), Archaeology and the Flora of the British Isles (1988), Molecular Information and Prehistory (1999), The Molecule Hunt (2001), Conflict (2006), Feast: Why Humans Store Food (2007); *Recreations* walking, sketching, cooking and eating; *Style*— Prof Martin Jones, FSA; ✉ Department of Archaeology, Downing Street, Cambridge CB2 3DZ (tel 01223 333507, fax 01223 333503, e-mail mkj12@cam.ac.uk)

JONES, Martyn David; MP; s of Vernon Pritchard Jones, of Wrexham, and Violet Gwendoline Jones, *née* Griffiths; *b* 1 March 1947; *Educ* Grove Park GS Wrexham, Trent Poly; *m* 1974 (m dis 1991), Rhona, da of Roger Bellis, of Wrexham; 1 da (Linzi b 1974), 1 s (Nicholas b 1984); *Career* MP (Lab): Clwyd SW 1987–97, Clwyd S 1997–; an oppn whip 1988–92, oppn frontbench spokesperson on food agriculture and rural affairs 1994–95, memb Agric Select Ctee 1988–94 and 1995–97, chm Welsh Affrs Select Ctee 1997–2005, memb Speaker's Panel of Chairmen 2005–; county cncllr 1981–89; MIBiol; *Recreations* backpacking, target shooting, sailing; *Style*— Martyn Jones, Esq, MP; ✉ Cnstituency Office, Foundry Buildings, Gutter Hill, Johnstown, Wrexham LL14 1LU; House of Commons, London SW1A 0AA (tel 020 7219 3417)

JONES, Martyn Eynon; s of Cledwyn Jones, and Megan, *née* Eynon; *b* 22 July 1951; *Educ* Dynevor GS, Denbigh GS, UC Swansea (BSc); *m* 15 Sept 1973, Doreen Judith, da of late Russell, and Muriel Long, of Carlisle; 2 s (Alistair b 1979, Christopher b 1985); *Career* chartered accountant; Robson Rhodes and Deloitte Haskins & Sells 1972–77, Accountancy Tuition Centre 1977–81, under sec then sec Auditing Practices Ctee 1981–84, UK and Ireland advsr to Int Auditing Practices Ctee 1983–84; Deloitte & Touche LLP (formerly Touche Ross & Co): sr mangr 1984–87, nat audit tech ptnr 1987–; memb: City Regulatory Panel CBI 1993–96, Corp Law Panel CBI 1996, Companies Ctee CBI 2003–; ICAEW: memb Cncl 2006–, memb Business Law Ctee 1993–2006, chm Special Reports of Accountants Sub-Ctee and Panel 1993–2000, and on Investment Custodians 1997, memb Research Bd 1995–99, vice-chm Tech and Practical Auditing Ctee 1995–2006, advsr on Handbook 1995, chm Working Party on Guidance on Audit Ctees 2001, chm Centre for Business Performance 2002–06, chm Int Standards on Auditing Implementation Sub-Gp 2003–, memb Corp Governance Ctee 2005–06, chm Ethics Standards Ctee 2006–, memb Tech Strategy Bd; chm: Task Force on future mission of audit and governing principles of auditing 1994, Working Party on reporting on prospective fin info 1996–2000, Audit Quality Forum 2004–, Ethics Standards Gp Consultative Ctee of the Accountancy Bodies 2006–; memb: Audit Procedures Task Force Deloitte Touche Tohmatsu International 1990–97, Int Sub-Ctee Auditing Practices Bd 1991–, DTI Working Party on revision of company law 1993, Working Party on Statements on Investment Circular Reporting Standards 1997–99, Knowledge Task Force Deloitte Touche Tohmatsu 1998, Assurance and Advsy Services Deloitte Touche Tohmatsu 1998–99, Deloitte Touche Tohmatsu Global Service Innovation Bd 1999–2002, Audit Strategy Forum of the Consultative Ctee of Accountancy Bodies 1999–2003, Deloitte Touche Tohmatsu Technical Policy and Methodology Gp 1999–; FCA 1981, FRSA 1997; *Books* Safely past the perils - the new investment business accounting requirements (jtly, 1987), The Audit Committee and its Chairman (jtly, 1993), the Finance Director and the Audit Committee (jtly, 1993), Progress Reports on the Financial Aspects of Corporate Governance (jtly, 1993–), Corporate Governance Handbook (conslt ed, 1996–2003), Taking Fraud Seriously (jtly, 1996), Audit Committees - a framework for assessment (jtly, 1997), Avoiding Corporate Governance Overload (jtly, 1997), Implementing Turnbull (jtly, 1999), The Effective Audit Committe- a Challenging Role (2001); *Recreations* gardening, appreciating Georgian architecture, watching rugby, relaxing in Gower, South Wales; *Style*— Martyn E Jones, Esq; ✉ Deloitte, Hill House, 1 Little New Street, London EC4A 3TR (tel 020 7007 0861, fax 020 7007 0158, e-mail mjones@deloitte.co.uk)

JONES, Medwyn; s of Capt Ieuan Glyn Du Platt Jones, of Llandbedr Duffryn, N Wales, and Margaret, *née* Owen; *b* 13 September 1955; *Educ* Scorton Sch, Chester GS, Univ of Sheffield (LLB), The Coll of Law; *m* 1990, Rita, da of Raymond Bailey; 1 s (George Thomas b 1992), 1 da (Harriet Rhys b 1994); *Career* slr Theodore Goddard 1980–81 (articled clerk 1978–80), ptnr Walker Martineau 1983–92 (slr 1981–83); ptnr: Cameron Markby Hewitt 1992–94, Harbottle & Lewis LLP 1994–; memb: Law Soc 1980, RTS 1994, BAFTA 2001; Freeman City of London; *Recreations* skiing; *Style*— Medwyn Jones, Esq; ✉ Harbottle & Lewis LLP, Hanover House, 14 Hanover Square, London W1S 1HP (tel 020 7667 5000, fax 020 7667 5100, DX 44617 Mayfair)

JONES, Prof (Richard) Merfyn; s of John E Jones, of Llanfrothen, Gwynedd, and Elen Jones, *née* Roberts; *b* 16 January 1948, Tremadog, Gwynedd; *Educ* Ysgol Gynradd Llanfrothen, Ysgol Ardudwy, Univ of Sussex (BA), Univ of Warwick (MA, PhD); *m* 30 Jan 2004, Nerys, *née* Thomas; 2 c from previous m (Rhodri b 1978, Steffan b 1981); *Career* sr researcher Univ of Wales Swansea 1971–74; Univ of Liverpool: lectr 1975–80, memb Senate 1981–89, dir Dept of Continuing Educn 1982–85 (sr lectr 1980), actg dean Faculty of Educn 1985 and 1988–89, dir Centre for Community and Educnl Policy Studies 1986–89, memb Cncl 1988–89, fell Dept of Economic and Social History 1989–92, memb Ct 2002–; Univ of Wales Bangor: head Sch of History and Welsh History 1993–96, memb Senate and Cncl 1994–, prof of Welsh history 1995, dean Faculty of Arts and Social Sciences 1996–98, memb Bd of Celtic Studies 1998–, pro-vice-chllr 1998–2003, vice-chllr 2004– (actg vice-chllr 2003); visiting lectr: Univ of Paris VIII 1987–89, Univ of Tubingen 1997 (memb Advsy Bd Welsh Studies Centre 1996–), Univ of Chemnitz Germany 1998; external examiner for numerous educnl insts; BBC: nat govr for Wales 2003–07, memb Bd of Govrs 2003–; memb: Advsy Bd N American Assoc for the Study of Welsh Culture and History 1995–, Mgmnt Bd Univ of Wales Press 2001–03, Hon Degree Ctee Univ of Wales 2003–; chair Broadcasting Cncl for Wales 2003–07, memb Broadcasting Standards Cmmn 2002–03; BAFTA Cymru Award 2000; memb: Bd of Dirs Ymddiriedolaeth Hybu Gwyddoniaeth (Sci Promotion Tst) 2002–06, Gorsedd of Bards Nat Eistedfodd of Wales 2004; FRHistS 1995; *Publications* North Wales Quarrymen 1874–1922 (1981), Hanes Cymru Yn Yr Ugeinfed Ganrif (History of Wales in the Twentieth Century, 1999), contrib to numerous articles; *Recreations* mountaineering, cooking; *Clubs* Athenaeum; *Style*— Prof Merfyn Jones; ✉ University of Wales, Bangor, Gwynedd LL57 2DG (tel 01248 382001, e-mail merfyn.jones@bangor.ac.uk)

JONES, Dr Miah Gwynfor (Gwyn); s of Robert Jones (d 1979), of Porthmadog, Gwynedd, and Jane Irene, *née* Evans (d 1981); *b* 2 December 1948; *Educ* Ysgol Eifionydd Porthmadog, Univ of Manchester (BSc), Univ of Essex (PhD); *m* 10 Jan 1976, Maria Linda, da of Kenneth Johnson (d 1984), of Swansea; 2 da (Victoria Rachel Sian b 1980, Holly Alexandra Jane b 1982); *Career* British Steel 1975–77, ICL 1977–81, chm and chief exec Corporate Technology Group plc 1981–87, chm Welsh Devpt Agency 1988–93; non-exec dir: Tesco plc 1992–98, ACT Group plc 1989–95, Invesco English and Int Tst 1993–, Welsh Water Enterprises Ltd 1990–93; memb Cncl Univ of Wales 1990–95; nat govr for Wales BBC 1992–97, memb S4C Authy 1992–97, HBO & Co (UK) Ltd 1995–97; chm Corporate Technologies 1995–, dep chm Agenda Television Ltd 1997–2000, chm Agenda Online 1999–, exec chm Agenda Multimedia Ltd 2000–, dir Real Radio Ltd 2000–; hon fell Univ of Glamorgan (formerly Poly of Wales) 1991; FBCS; *Recreations* travel, boats, walking, opera; *Style*— Dr Gwyn Jones

JONES, Prof Michael Christopher Emlyn; s of late Reginald Luther Jones, and Megan Bevan Jones; *b* 5 December 1940; *Educ* Rugeley GS, Univ of Leicester, Trinity Coll Oxford (MA, DPhil, DLitt); *m* 1966, Elizabeth Marjorie, *née* Smith; 1 s; *Career* tutor in medieval history Univ of Exeter 1966–67; Univ of Nottingham: asst lectr 1967–69, lectr 1969–81, sr lectr 1981–84, reader in medieval history 1984–91, prof of medieval French history 1991–2002, emeritus prof 2002–; sr scholar Wolfson Fndn 1975, Euro fell Leverhulme Tst 1977, visiting fell All Souls Coll Oxford 1984–85; jt ed Renaissance and Modern Studies 1986–89, ed Nottingham Medieval Studies 1989–; author of numerous papers and reviews in hist jls; jt literary dir Royal Hist Soc 1990–97; FRHistS 1971, FSA 1977, Correspondant de l'Institut de France 2006; *Books* Ducal Brittany 1364–1399 (1970, French edn 1998), Philippe de Commynes - Memoirs, the Reign of Louis XI (trans, 1972, internet edn 1999), Recueil des actes de Jean IV, duc de Bretagne (3 vols, ed, 1980–2001), Philippe Contamine - War in the Middle Ages (trans, 1984), John Le Patourel - Feudal Empires Norman and Plantagenet (ed, 1984), Gentry and Lesser Nobility in Later Medieval Europe (ed, 1986), The Family of Dinan in England in the Middle Ages (1987), The Creation of Brittany (collected papers, 1988), England and her Neighbours 1066–1453 - Essays in Honour of Pierre Chaplais (ed with Malcolm Vale, 1989), The Bretons (with Patrick Galliou, 1991, also French, Italian and Czech edns), Aimer les Châteaux de Bretagne (with Prof Gwyn Meirion-Jones, 1991, also English and German edns), Les Châteaux de Bretagne (with Prof Gwyn Meirion-Jones, 1992), Manorial Domestic Buildings in England and Northern France (ed with Prof Gwyn Meirion-Jones, 1993), Recueil des actes de Charles de Blois et Jeanne de Penthièvre, duc et duchesse de Bretagne (1341–1364) (1996), La Ville de Cluny et ses maisons XIe-XVe siècles (with Pierre Garrigou Grandchamp, Gwyn Meirion-Jones and Jean-Denis Salvèque, 1997), Catalogue sommaire des Archives du Fonds Lebreton, Abbaye Saint-Guénolé, Landévennec (1998), The Charters of Duchess Constance of Brittany and her Family, 1171–1221 (with Judith Everard, 1999), New Cambridge Medieval History, vol vi, c.1300–c.1415 (ed, 2000), Handbook of Dates for Students of British History (ed C R Cheney, 1945, revised edn 2000), The Seigneurial Residence in Western Europe AD c 800–1600 (ed with Prof Gwyn Meirion-Jones and Edward Impey, 2002), Between France and England: Politics, Power and Society in Late Medieval Brittany (2003), Letters, Orders and Musters of Bertrand du Guesclin, 1357–1380 (2004), Le Premier Inventaire du Trésor des Chartes des Ducs de Bretagne (1395): Hervé le Grant et les Origines du Chronicon Briocense (2007); *Recreations* browsing in book shops, gardening, philately, photography; *Clubs* MCC, Athenaeum; *Style*— Prof Michael Jones, FSA; ✉ Parr's Cottage, Main Street, Norwell, Nottinghamshire NG23 6JN (tel 01636 636365, e-mail michael.jones@nottingham.ac.uk)

JONES, Michael Lynn Norman; s of Lynn Daniel Jones (d 2002), of Rhiwbina, Cardiff, and Mary Hannah, *née* Edwards (d 1992); *b* 14 January 1943; *Educ* Neath Boys GS, Jesus Coll Oxford (MA), Coll of Law; *m* 16 April 1974, Ethni, da of Gwynfryn Morgan Daniel (d 1960), of Llandaff, Cardiff; 1 s (Garmon b 1975), 3 da (Mererid b 1976, Gwenfair b 1979, Rhiannon b 1982); *Career* slr; ptnr C Hugh James & Ptnrs Cardiff 1966–2003, sr ptnr Hugh James Jones & Jenkins Cardiff 1970–97, conslt Hugh James Cardiff 2003–; slr-advocate (Higher Courts Civil) 1994–; memb: Wales & Chester Circuit Advsy Ctee 1971–77, Curriculum Cncl Wales 1988–91, Standing Orders Cmmn for National Assembly for Wales 1998–99; Cardiff and Dist Law Soc: asst sec 1969–91, vice-pres 1991–92, pres 1992–93, memb Cncl 1993–; memb Cncl Univ of Wales Coll of Med 2001–; govr: Coed-y-Gof Welsh Primary Sch 1985–96 (chm 1989–92), Glantaf Welsh HS 1988– (chm 1996–98); elder Salem Presbyterian Church of Wales Canton Cardiff 1988 (sec 2003–); memb Law Soc 1966; CIArb 1987; *Recreations* gardening, walking; *Clubs* Cardiff & County, Oxford Union; *Style*— Michael Jones, Esq; ✉ Hugh James, Hodge House, 114–116 St Mary Street, Cardiff CF10 1DY

JONES, Milton; s of Dr Colin Jones, and Isabel, *née* Wiesener; *b* 16 May 1964; *Educ* Latymer Upper Sch, Middx Poly; *m* 13 Sept 1986, Caroline, *née* Church; 5 c; *Career* stand up comic 1989–; involved with Christians in Comedy; Perrier Best Newcomer Edinburgh Fringe Festival 1996 (nominated 1997), Time Out Best Comedy Performer 2003; *Television* The Stand Up Show (BBC), The Comedy Store (five), The Strangerers (Sky); *Radio* The Very World of Milton Jones (BBC Radio 4) 1998, 1999 and 2001 (nomination Comedy Award 1999, Sony Bronze 2000), The House of Milton (BBC Radio 4) 2003; *Recreations* football; *Style*— Milton Jones, Esq; ✉ c/o Vivienne Clore, The Richard Stone Partnership, 2 Henrietta Street, London WC2E 8PS (tel 020 7497 0849, fax 020 7497 0869)

JONES, His Hon Judge Nicholas Graham; s of Albert William Jones, and Gwendolen Muriel Taylor-Jones, *née* Phillips; *b* 13 August 1948; *Educ* Latymer Upper Sch, St Catherine's Coll Oxford (MA); *m* 25 Sept 1976, Shelagh Ann, da of Robert Maitland Farror; 1 s (Benjamin Nicholas Farror b 1986); *Career* film ed and prodr BBC 1969–73; called to the Bar Inner Temple 1975; recorder SE Circuit 1994–2001, circuit judge (SE Circuit) 2001–; *Recreations* sailing, walking, music; *Clubs* Royal London Yacht, Royal Ocean Racing, Bar Yacht (vice-cdre 2003–05); *Style*— His Hon Judge Nicholas Jones; ✉ Kingston Crown Court, 6–8 Penrhyn Road, Kingston upon Thames, Surrey KT1 2BB (tel 020 8240 2500, fax 020 8240 2675)

JONES, Nicholas Keith Arthur (Nick); s of Keith Jones, and Anna, *née* Martin (d 2002); *b* 22 September 1963; *Educ* Shiplake Coll; *m* 1 (m dis); 1 da (Natasha b 2 June 1993), 1 s (Oliver b 8 April 1995); m 2, 30 Sept 1999, Kirsty Young, *qv*, da of John Young; 2 da (Freya b 15 Feb 2001, Iona b 5 April 2006); *Career* restaurateur; md: Cafe Boheme London 1992–, Soho House London 1995–, Babington House Somerset 1998–, Boheme Kitchen Bar London 1999–, Electric Cinema, House and Brasserie London 2002–, Soho House NY 2003–, Balham Kitchen and Bar London 2003–, Cecconi's London 2005–, Cowshed Clarendon Cross London 2005–, High Road House and Brasserie Chiswick 2006–, Shoreditch House 2007–; patron: PAC Project Frome, Cheeky Chops London; tstee The Roundhouse; *Recreations* cooking, eating, drinking, napping; *Style*— Nick Jones, Esq; ✉ Soho House, 3–5 Bateman Street, London W1D 4AG (tel 020 7851 1171, 020 7851 1198, e-mail nickjones@sohohouse.com)

JONES, Nicholas Michael Houssemayne; s of Henry J E Jones, of Glos, and Patricia Rose, *née* Holland; *b* 27 October 1946; *Educ* Winchester, London Business Sch (MSc); *m* 1, 25 March 1971 (m dis 1999), Veronica Anne, da of Brig the Hon R G Hamilton-Russell, DSO, LVO, DL; 1 da (Rowena Rose b 5 Sept 1975), 1 s (Oliver Mark b 5 April 1977); m 2, 2 Feb 2002, Cherry Victoria Richardson, da of Sidney Smart; *Career* Peat Marwick Mitchell 1965–73, dir J Henry Schroder Wagg & Co 1975–87, vice-chm Lazard & Co 1999– (md 1987–); dir: Hilton Group plc 2002–06, Ladbrokes plc 2006–; chm The National Stud 1991–2000; govr: James Allens Girls' Sch 1989–93, Birkbeck Coll London 1995–99; memb London Business Sch Advsy Bd 1996–, memb Devpt Cncl Winchester Coll 2002–; FCA 1969; *Recreations* racing, tennis, stalking, bridge, gardening; *Clubs* Turf; *Style*— Nicholas Jones, Esq; ✉ The Manor, Coln St Dennis, Cheltenham, Gloucestershire GL54 3JU; Lazard, 50 Stratton Street, London W1J 8LL (tel 020 7187 2000, fax 020 7072 6401, e-mail nicholas.jones@lazard.com)

JONES, Nigel Glanville Ollerton; s of David Jones, and Gill Jones; *b* 6 May 1958, Rustington, W Sussex; *Educ* St Edward's Sch Oxford; *m* 14 Aug 1982, Alyson, *née* Cuckney; 1 da (Katie b 25 Sept 1987), 1 s (Oliver b 13 Nov 1992); *Career* CA; Ernst & Young: joined as trainee, head of assurance UK 2003–, head of assurance Northern Europe, Middle East, India, Africa 2006–; *Recreations* rugby, tennis, sailing; *Style*— Nigel Jones, Esq; ✉ Ernst & Young, 1 More London, London SE1 2AF (tel 020 7951 4203, e-mail njones@uk.ey.com)

JONES, Nigel Michael; s of Ralph Michael Jones, of Wolverhampton, and Patricia May, *née* Phelps; *b* 23 September 1960; *Educ* Wolverhampton GS, Keble Coll Oxford (exhibitioner, BA); *m* 27 June 1987, Gillian Hazel, da of Eric Keith Philpot; 2 s (Louis Frederick Bramley, Ethan Alexander Bramley), 1 da (Iona Nancy Bramley); *Career* grad trainee rising to head of account planning and bd dir BMP DDB 1984–98, fndr/managing ptnr Jones Mason Barton Antenen 1999–2000, chief exec Claydon Heeley Jones Mason 2000–05, chief exec DraftFCB Gp UK 2005–; *Awards* US TV and Radio Commercials Festival Mobius award 1987, 1st prize IPA Advertising Effectiveness Awards 1988, 1st prize and grand prix IPA Advertising Effectiveness Awards 1990; *Recreations* music, playing guitar, chess, golf, Wolverhampton Wanderers; *Style*— Nigel Jones, Esq; ✉ Draft FCB Group UK, 55 Newman Street, London, W1T

JONES, Prof Norman; s of Edward Valentine Jones, and Mary Alice, *née* Collins; *b* 18 March 1938; *Educ* Evered HS, UMIST (BScTech, MScTech, PhD), Univ of Manchester (DSc); *m* 11 July 1964, Jenny, da of Fred Schofield (d 1946); 2 da (Alison Elizabeth b 29 Aug 1967, Catherine Ann b 8 March 1971); *Career* pt/t lectr Dept of Mech Engrg Manchester Coll of Sci and Technol 1961–63, James Clayton fell IMechE 1962–63, asst lectr Faculty of Technol Univ of Manchester 1963–65; asst prof: Dept of Mech Engrg Georgia Inst of Technol USA 1965–66, Dept of Engrg Brown Univ USA 1966–68; Dept of Ocean Engrg MIT USA: asst prof 1968–70, assoc prof 1970–77, prof 1977–79; Univ of Liverpool: prof of mechanical engrg (A A Griffith prof of mechanical engrg since 1993) 1979–2005 (emeritus prof 2005–), head Dept of Mech Engrg 1982–90, dir Impact Research Centre 1985–2005; ed-in-chief Int Jl of Impact Engineering 1988– (ed 1982–87), assoc ed Applied Mechanics Reviews 1995–; memb Editorial Bd: Jl of Ship Research 1972–80, Int Jl of Mechanical Sciences 1975–, Acta Mechanica Sinica 1991–, Dymat Jl 1992–96, Latin American Jl of Solids and Structures 2003–; memb: Ductile Collapse Ctee 3.1 Int Ship Structures Congress 1985–88, Safety in Mines Res Advsy Bd 1985–2005, Hull and Machinery Ctee Def Scientific Advsy Cncl 1989–95, Man-made Hazards Ctee Inter-Engrg Inst Hazards Forum 1990–99 (chm 1991–95), Solid Mechanics Conf Ctee Euro Mechanics Cncl 1990–2000 (chm 1995–2000), Euromech Cncl 1992–2000; hon prof: Huazhong Univ of Sci and Technol Wuhan China 1987, Taiyuan Univ of Sci and Technol Shanxi China 1988; IMechE William Sweet Smith Prize 1989, Ludwig Mond Prize 1992, Eminent Scientist Award Wessex Inst of Technol 1998, Bronze Medal RINA 1998; memb ASME 1966 (fell 1990), PEng Massachusetts 1972, foreign fell Indian Nat Acad of Engrg 2005; FIMechE 1980, FRINA 1980, FREng 1998; *Books* Structural Crashworthiness (with T Wierzbicki, 1983), Structural Failure (with T Wierzbicki, 1989), Structural Impact (1989 and 1997), Structural Crashworthiness and Failure (with T Wierzbicki, 1993); *Recreations* walking, classical music; *Style*— Prof Norman Jones, FREng; ✉ Department of Engineering (Mechanical), The University of Liverpool, Brownlow Hill, Liverpool L69 3GH (tel 0151 794 4858, fax 0151 794 4848, e-mail norman.jones@liv.ac.uk)

JONES, His Hon Norman Henry; QC (1985); s of Warrant Offr Henry Robert Jones, DFM (d 1992), and Charlotte Isabel Scott, *née* Davis; *b* 12 December 1941; *Educ* Bideford GS, N Devon Tech Coll, Univ of Leeds (LLB, LLM); *m* 28 March 1970, Trudy Helen, da of Frederick George Chamberlain (d 1974), of Werrington, Cambs; 2 s (Gareth b 22 Dec 1977, Nicholas b 14 April 1981), 1 da (Helena b 6 April 1983); *Career* called to the Bar Middle Temple 1968 (Harmsworth scholar); recorder 1987–92 (asst recorder 1984–87), circuit judge (NE Circuit) 1992–2001, sr circuit judge (NE Circuit) 2001–07, resident judge Bradford Combined Court 2000–01, resident judge Leeds Combined Court 2001–07; hon recorder of Leeds 2001; *Recreations* boats, walking; *Style*— His Hon Norman Jones, QC

JONES, Olwen Elizabeth; da of William Jones (d 1991), of Rowhedge, Colchester, and Margaret Olwen Jones (d 1995); *b* 1 March 1945; *Educ* Harrow Sch of Art (NDD), Royal Acad Schs (silver medal in drawing, bronze medal in painting, David Murray travelling scholar); *m* 1970, Charles Bartlett, s of late Charles Henry Bartlett; *Career* artist; pt/t lectr: Putney Sch of Art 1966–71, Harrow Coll of Art 1970–86, City & Guilds of London Art Schs 1993–94; RE 1982, RWS 1992 (vice-pres 2004); *Exhibitions* solo exhbns incl: Zaydler Gallery London 1971, Oldham Art Gallery 1971, Dudley Museum and Art Gallery 1972, Halesworth Gallery 1973, travelling exhbn (Oldham Art Gallery, Wrexham Library and Art Centre, Lewes Art Centre) 1975, Craftsman Gallery Colchester 1977, Bohun Gallery Henley 1979, 1985, 1988 and 2002, travelling exhbn (Minories Colchester, Usher Gallery Lincoln, Univ of Durham, Oriel Theatre Clkwyd, Towner Art Gallery Eastbourne, Anthony Dawson Gallery London) 1984, Coach House Gallery Guernsey 1989, Printworks Colchester 1991 and 1993, Royal Exchange Theatre Manchester 1994, Hayletts Gallery Colchester 1994, Chappel Galleries Essex 1999, John Russell Gallery Ipswich 2002; gp exhbns incl: RA regularly 1996–, RE regularly 1968–, Barbican Centre London 1985 and 1987, Modern English Graphics Moscow; *Collections* work in numerous private and public collections incl: Dept of the Environment, Beecroft Art Gallery Southend, Bradford City Art Gallery, Graves Art Gallery Sheffield, Norwich Castle Museum, Nat Museum of Wales, Greenwich Library, Dudley Museums and Art Gallery, Reading Museums and Art Gallery, Usher Art Gallery Lincoln, art galleries of Huddersfield, Salford, Plymouth, Bolton, Keighley and Oldham; *Style*— Ms Olwen Jones

JONES, Paul Adrian; né Pond; s of Norman Henry Pond, of Worthing, W Sussex, and Amelia Josephine, *née* Hadfield; *b* 24 February 1942; *Educ* Portsmouth GS, Edinburgh Acad, Jesus Coll Oxford; *m* 1, 1963, Sheila MacLeod; 2 s (Matthew b 21 Oct 1963, Jacob b 10 Jan 1965); m 2, Fiona Jayne, da of Hugh Holbein Hendley; *Career* singer, musician, composer, actor, writer and presenter; *Music* gp lead singer Manfred Mann 1962–66 (composer The One in the Middle, 5–4–3–2–1 for TV pop show Ready Steady Go! and others), solo singer 1966–; memb: The Blues Band 1979–, The Manfreds 1994–; songs recorded by numerous artists incl Helen Shapiro and Eric Clapton, has played harmonica for other recording artists, TV and TV advertisements, Royal Ballet Sinfonia featured soloist Street (world premiere) 1993; composer of theme music incl: BBC TV series The Wednesday Play and Fighting Back, films Privilege, The Committee and Intimate Reflections, BBC documentary The Last Vacation; *Theatre* incl: debut as Jack Argue in Muzeeka (Open Space Theatre) 1969, Conduct Unbecoming (Queen's Theatre 1969–70, Ethel Barrymore Theatre NY 1970–71), The Banana Box (Apollo Theatre) 1973, Pippin (Her Majesty's Theatre) 1973–74, Hamlet (Ludlow Festival) 1976, Drake's Dream (Shaftesbury and Westminster Theatres) 1977–78, Cats (New London Theatre) 1982, The Beggar's Opera/Guys and Dolls (Nat Theatre) 1982–83, The Pyjama Game (Leicester Haymarket and tour) 1985–86, Kiss Me Kate (RSC Stratford and tour, Old Vic) 1987, Julius Caesar (Ludlow Festival) 1989; *Films* Privilege 1966, The Committee 1968, Demons of the Mind 1971, The Blues Band 1980; *Television* incl: Top of the Pops, Ready Steady Go! (and other pop shows), A Bit of Discretion (Yorkshire TV) 1968, Square One (LWT) 1971, Z-Cars (BBC) 1972, The Protectors 1973, A Different Kind of Frost, Jackanory, The Sweeney, Space 1999, Great Big Groovy Horse, Twiggy Show (BBC), A Matter of Taste (BBC), The Songwriters (BBC) 1978, The Beggar's Opera (Channel 4) 1983, Weekend (Granada) 1983–84, A Plus 4 (Thames and Channel 4) 1984–85, Beat the Teacher 1985–86, John Lennon - A Journey in the Life 1985, A Royal Celebration 1985, Lyrics by Tim Rice 1985, Live from the Palladium 1988, Uncle Jack series 1990–95; author of play They Put You Where You Are (BBC) 1966; *Radio* Paul Jones on Music (Radio 4) 1983, Counterpoint (BBC World Serv) 1982–92, BBC Radio 2 1985–, GLR 1988–90, Jazz FM 1990–; *Recordings* incl: The Andrew Lloyd Webber Collection (Pickwick Records), The Blues Band: Fat City (RCA Records), Groovin' With The Manfreds (EMI Records); *Awards* UK Male Vocalist Br Blues Connection Awards 1990 and 1991, Scroll of Honour (Outstanding Contribution to the Blues) 1993, Gold Badge Award Br Acad of Songwriters, Composers and Authors 1996; memb: Br Actors' Equity, Musicians' Union, Br Acad of Songwriters, Composers and Authors; *Recreations* music, books, walking, food, conversation; *Style*— Paul Jones, Esq; ✉ c/o Chatto and Linnit, 123a King's Road, London SW3 4PL (tel 020 7352 7722, fax 020 7352 3450)

JONES, Peter David; s of David Jones, and Eileen Jones; *b* 18 March 1966; *Partner* Tara Capp; 4 da (Annabelle, Natalia, Talulah, Isabella), 1 s (William); *Career* entrepreneur; estab tennis acad at local club 1982, estab computer business 1984, head of PC business

J

Siemens Nixdorf 1994, prop, chm and ceo Phones Int Gp 1998–, prop Peter Jones TV 2006–, chm and dir of numerous cos incl Red Letter Days, wines4business.com and celcius.co.uk; TV appearances: Dragons' Den (BBC 2, 5 series) 2005– (investor in cos incl mymarina.com, Wonderland Magazine, The Generating Co and Reggae Reggae Sauce), Tycoon (ITV) 2007; Emerging Entrepreneur of the Year The Times/Ernst & Young 2001, 10th in Britain's Top Entrepreneurs under 40 Daily Telegraph 2006; *Style*— Peter Jones, Esq; ✉ website www.peterjones.tv; Phones International Group, Network House, Globe Park, Marlow, Buckinghamshire SL7 1LY

JONES, His Hon Judge Peter Henry Francis; s of Eric Roberts Jones, MBE, of Swansea (d 2004), and Betty Irene, *née* Longhurst (d 1981); *b* 25 February 1952; *Educ* Bishop Gore GS Swansea, Newport HS Gwent, Balliol Coll Oxford (MA); *m* 3 June 1978, Anne Elizabeth, da of David Jones, DFC (d 1995), of Cheadle; 2 da (Clare b 14 May 1980, Eleanor b 14 July 1982); *Career* admitted slr 1977; ptnr: Darlington & Parkinson Slrs London 1979–87, John Howell & Co Slrs Sheffield 1987–95; stipendiary magistrate then District Judge (Magistrates' Court) S Yorks 1995–2001, recorder 1997–2001, circuit judge 2001–; memb: Lord Chllr's Legal Aid Advsy Ctee 1983–92, Legal Aid Bd 1992–95, Sentencing Advsy Panel 1999–2005, Magistrates' Courts Rules Ctee 2001–04; *Recreations* tennis, watching rugby union, books; *Clubs* Dethreau Boat, Scorpions Cricket, Druidstone (Dyfed); *Style*— His Hon Judge Peter Jones; ✉ Sheffield Combined Court Centre, 50 West Bar, Sheffield S3 8PH

JONES, Prof Peter Howard; s of Thomas Leslie Jones (d 1963), of London, and Hilda Croesora, *née* Parkinson (d 1982); *b* 18 December 1935; *Educ* Highgate Sch, Queens' Coll Cambridge; *m* 8 Oct 1960, (Elizabeth) Jean, da of Robert James Roberton, JP (d 1972), of Morebattle, Roxburghshire; 2 da (Rachel (Mrs Michael Groves) b 1964, Laura b 1969); *Career* Br Cncl 1960–61, res scholar Univ of Cambridge 1961–63, asst lectr in philosophy Univ of Nottingham 1963–64, prof of philosophy Univ of Edinburgh 1984–98 (lectr then reader 1964–84, emeritus prof 1998–), dir Inst for Advanced Studies in the Humanities Edinburgh 1986–2000; visiting prof of philosophy: Rochester Univ NY 1969–70, Dartmouth Coll NH 1973 and 1983, Carleton Coll MN 1974, Oklahoma Univ 1978, Baylor Univ TX 1978, Univ of Malta 1993, Belarusian State Univ 1997, Jagiellonian Univ Cracow 2001, 2002 and 2004–; visiting fell: Humanities Res Centre ANU 1984 and 2002, Calgary Inst for the Humanities 1992; Lothian lectr 1993, Gifford lectr Univ of Aberdeen 1994–95, Loemker lectr Emory Univ GA 1995–96; tstee: Nat Museums of Scotland 1987–99 (chm Client Ctee 1991–99), Univ of Edinburgh Devpt Tst 1990–98, Morrison's Acad 1984–98, Fndn for Advanced Studies in Humanities 1997–2002, Fettes Tst 1995–2005, Scots at War, MBI Al Jaber Fndn, Policy Inst; memb: Ct Univ of Edinburgh 1987–90, Cncl Royal Soc of Edinburgh 1992–95, UNESCO forum on tolerance Tblisi 1995–, UNESCO dialogue on Europe and Islam 1997–, Spoliation Advsy Panel 2000–; FRSE 1989, FRSA, FSA Scot; *Books* Philosophy and the Novel (1975), Hume's Sentiments (1982), A Hotbed of Genius (1986, 2 edn 1996), Philosophy and Science in The Scottish Enlightenment (ed, 1988), The Science of Man in the Scottish Enlightenment (ed, 1989), Adam Smith Reviewed (ed, 1992), James Hutton: Investigation of the Principles of Knowledge (ed, 1999), The Enlightenment World (ed, 2004), Henry Home, Lord Kames: Elements of Criticism (ed, 2005), The Reception of David Hume in Europe (ed, 2005), Ove Arup Masterbuilder of the Twentieth Century (2006); *Recreations* opera, chamber music, architecture, arts, travel; *Clubs* New (Edinburgh); *Style*— Prof Peter Jones, FRSE; ✉ 6 Greenhill Terrace, Edinburgh EH10 4BS (tel and fax 0131 447 6344)

JONES, Peter Ivan; s of Glyndwr Jones (d 1995), of Bridport, and Edith Evelyn, *née* Whittaker; *b* 14 December 1942; *Educ* Gravesend GS, LSE (BScEcon); *m* 1 (m dis 1969), Judith, *née* Watson; 1 da (Claire Amanda Markham b 1964), 1 s (Nicholas Francis Markham b 1968); m 2, 15 Aug 1970, Elizabeth, da of Raymond Gent; 1 da (Victoria Louise b 1975), 1 s (Matthew Alexander b 1978); *Career* dir Boase Massimi Pollitt Partnership 1968–75, chief exec Boase Massimi Pollitt plc 1989 (non-exec dir 1983–88), chm BBDO Ltd 1989–90, dir Omnicom Inc 1989–94, chief exec Omnicom UK plc 1989–94, pres Diversified Agency Services (DAS) 1994–97; pres Racehorse Owners' Assoc 1990–93, memb Br Horseracing Bd 1992–96, memb Horserace Betting Levy Bd 1993–95 and 1997–, chm Horserace Totalisator Bd 1997– (memb 1995–); chm Dorset Police Authy 1997–2003 (memb 1995–2003); MIPA 1971; *Publications* Trainers Record (1973–87); *Recreations* watching all sport, computer programming; *Style*— Peter Jones, Esq; ✉ Melplash Farmhouse, Melplash, Bridport, Dorset DT6 3UH (tel 01308 488383, fax 01308 488650); 34 Rossetti Garden Mansions, Flood Street, London SW3 5QX (tel 020 7352 8977); Horserace Totalisator Board, Tote Park, Westgate House, Chapel Lane, Wigan WN3 4HS (tel 01942 617500)

JONES, Prof Philip Douglas; s of Douglas Idris Jones, and Peggy Rita Yvonne, *née* Cleave; *b* 22 April 1952, Redhill, Surrey; *Educ* Glyn GS Ewell, Lancaster Univ (BA), Univ of Newcastle upon Tyne (MSc, PhD); *m* 4 Aug 1973, Ruth Anne; 1 da (Hannah Megan b 21 March 1977), 1 s (Matthew David b 14 Aug 1978); *Career* UEA: prof Sch of Environmental Sciences, dir Climatic Research Unit 1976–; memb Editorial Ctee Int Jl of Climatology until 1995, memb Editorial Bd Climatic Change; author of 200 scientific papers in peer-review jls; Hugh Robert Mill Medal Royal Meteorological Soc 1995 (jtly), Outstanding Scientific Paper Award Environmental Research Labs/NOAA 1997, Hans Oeschger Medal European Geophysical Soc 2002, Int Jl of Climatology Prize Royal Meteorological Soc 2002; memb: Academia Europaea 1998, American Meteorological Soc 2001; FRMetS 1992; *Books* Climate Since AD 1500 (co-ed, 1992), Climatic Variations and Forcing Mechanisms of the Last 2000 Years (co-ed, 1996), History and Climate: Memories of the Future (co-ed, 2001), Improved Understanding of Past Climatic Variability from Early European Instrumental Sources (co-ed, 2002); *Style*— Prof Philip Jones; ✉ Climatic Research Unit, School of Environmental Sciences, University of East Anglia, Norwich NR4 7TJ (tel 01603 592090, e-mail p.jones@uea.ac.uk)

JONES, Dr Philip Edward; s of Edward Thomas Jones (d 1946), and Stella Mary, *née* Coën (d 1992); *b* 5 October 1945; *Educ* Manchester Grammar, Univ of Birmingham Med Sch; *m* 2 Sept 1972, Bernadette Catherine, da of John Terence Cain (d 1978); 3 da (Nina b 1980, Stephanie b 1984, Sarah b 1988); *Career* house physician Dudley Rd Hosp Birmingham 1968–69, registrar Univ Coll Hosp and Whittington Hosp 1972–75, registrar and res fell Hammersmith Hosp 1975–77, sr registrar Manchester Royal Infirmary 1977–82, conslt physician Wythenshawe Hosp 1982–, med dir S Manchester Univ Hosp Tst 1996–99; memb: Br Soc of Gastroenterology, N W Gastroenterology Soc, Manchester Med Soc; FRCP 1989 (MRCP); *Recreations* swimming, music; *Style*— Dr Philip Jones; ✉ Wythenshawe Hospital, Department of Gastroenterology, Southmoor Road, Wythenshawe, Manchester M23 9LT (tel 0161 291 2394)

JONES, Philip Gwyn; s of Gwynfryn Jones, and Beatrice Evelyn Jones; *Educ* Bishop of Llandaff Sch, Univ of York; *Career* rights asst Aladdin Books Ltd 1988–89; Collins Publishers (later Harper Collins Publishers): ed 1989–92, sr ed 1992–94, ed dir Fontana Press 1994–96, publishing dir Flamingo 1996–2004; fndr Portobello Books 2005; *Recreations* reading to my son, Italy, eating well; *Style*— Philip Gwyn Jones, Esq

JONES, Rhidian Huw Brynmor; s of Rev Preb Ivor Brynmor Jones, RD (d 1982), and Elizabeth Mary, *née* Morris (d 1996); *b* 13 July 1943; *Educ* Queen Mary's GS Walsall, Keble Coll Oxford (MA); *m* 8 Aug 1970, Monica Marianne, da of Bror Eric Sjunne Sjöholm (d 1957), of Halmstad, Sweden; 1 da (Anna b 1978), 1 s (Gavin b 1982); *Career* trainee sec asst Selection Tst Ltd 1966–68, legal asst Total Oil GB Ltd 1968–69, co sec J E Lesser (Hldgs) Ltd 1969, asst sec Granada Group Ltd 1970–76, articled clerk and asst slr Herbert Smith and Co 1976–80, sr asst slr Kenneth Brown Baker Baker (sic) 1980–81, ptnr Turner Kenneth Brown 1981–2002 (merged with Nabarro Nathanson May 1995), head of corporate dept Nabarro Nathanson 1999–2002, conslt Grundberg Mocatta Rakison LLP 2003–; non-exec dir: Mornington Building Society 1986–91, Serco Group Plc 1987–94 and 1996–2004, The Mortgage Agency plc 1988–93, Britannia Building Society 1993–2003 (dep chm 2000–2002), Ealing Hosp NHS Tst 2004–, Unity Tst Bank plc 2004–; vice-pres Ealing FC (RU), tstee and hon legal advsr Middx Co RFU Youth Tst 1994–2003; tstee: Middx Co RFU Memorial Fund 1996–2007, Wavell Wakefield and Middx Sports Fndn, The Second World War Experience Centre (chm 2007–); former memb Cncl Anglo Swedish Soc, memb Swedish BV Soc 1997 (Viking 1998, Berserk 1999, Hirdman 2002); Freeman City of London Slrs' Co 1979, memb Ct of Assts Worshipful Co of Turners 2002 (Freeman 1992, Liveryman 1993); FCIS 1976, memb Law Soc 1978, FCMI 1987, FInstD 1998 (MInstD 1987); *Recreations* rugby, skiing, military history, Celtic and Scandinavian studies; *Clubs* Rotary (London); *Style*— Rhidian Jones, Esq; ✉ Roseleigh, 80 Elers Road, Ealing, London W13 9QD (tel 020 8579 9785, fax 020 8579 9892, mobile 07768 171475, e-mail rhidian.j@ukonline.co.uk)

JONES, Richard; *Career* director; *Theatre* Too Clever by Half (Old Vic, Olivier Award), The Illusion (Old Vic, Evening Standard Award), Into the Woods (Phoenix Theatre London, Olivier Award, Evening Standard Award), A Flea in the Ear (Old Vic), Le Bourgeois Gentilhomme (RNT), Black Snow (American Rep Theatre), All's Well That Ends Well (Public Theatre NY), Holy Mothers (Ambassadors/Royal Court Theatre), La Bête (Broadway), Titantic (Broadway), Wrong Mountain (Broadway), Six Characters Looking for an Author (Young Vic), A Midsummer's Night Dream (RSC), Hobson's Choice (Young Vic), Tales from the Vienna Woods (RNT); *Opera* The Queen of Spades (WNO, Barclays/TMA Award 2001, nominated South Bank Show Award), Hansel and Gretel (WNO, Olivier Award), The Love for Three Oranges (ENO), Die Fledermaus (ENO), Der Ring des Nibelungen (ROH, Evening Standard Award), Pelleas and Melisande (Opera North and ENO, Olivier Award Nomination), Der Fliegende Holländer (Amsterdam), Jenufa (Amsterdam), Julius Caesar (Munich, Opernwelt Prodn of the Year), The Midsummer Marriage (Munich), L'enfant et les sortilèges (Paris), Der Zwerg (Paris), Un ballo in maschera (Bergenz Festival, Designer of the Year Award 2000 with Antony McDonald), La Boheme (Bregenz Festival), Flight (Glyndebourne), From Morning till Midnight (ENO), Wozzeck (WNO, Royal Philharmonic Soc Award), Lulu (ENO), The Trojans (ENO, Olivier Award), The Bitter Tears of Petra von Kant (ENO), Lady Macbeth of Mtsensk (ROH, Olivier Award); *Style*— Richard Jones, Esq; ✉ c/o Judy Daish Associates Ltd; 2 St Charles Place, London W10 6EG (tel 020 8964 8811, fax 020 8964 8966)

JONES, Richard Colwyn; s of late William Meirion Jones, and Doris, *née* Hill; *b* 24 June 1950; *Educ* Penlan Comp Sch, Bournemouth Coll (HND Business Studies); *m* 1973, Angela, da of Hugh Scriven; 1 s (Andrew Stephen b 1974), 1 da (Karen Elizabeth b 1978); *Career* trainee accountant BP 1972–74, Aluminium Co of America 1974–85 (successively devpt accountant, chief mgmnt accountant, fin controller, fin dir & co sec, mangr ops accounting Euro Region, md); with PricewaterhouseCoopers (formerly Coopers & Lybrand before merger) 1985–2002 (successively sr conslt, managing conslt, assoc dir, currently ptnr i/c World Class Fin Service Gp), vice-pres IBM Business Consulting Services 2002–; former pres Swansea & W Wales Dist ACCA; FCCA, MCIS, MIMC; *Recreations* tennis, badminton, gardening, reading, walking; *Clubs* National Liberal, Congresbury Tennis (chm); *Style*— Richard Jones, Esq; ✉ Beech Hay, Wrington Road, Congresbury, Bristol BS49 5AR (tel 01934 832413); IBM UK Limited, Upper Ground, South Bank, London (tel 020 7219 3935)

JONES, Richard Henry; QC (1996); s of Henry Ingham Jones (d 1993), of Teignmouth, Devon, and Betty Marian, *née* Allison; *b* 6 April 1950; *Educ* Moseley GS Birmingham, St Peter's Coll Oxford (MA); *m* 1989, Sarah Jane, da of Peter Wildsmith; 1 s (Christopher b 12 March 1991), 1 da (Bryony Alice b 21 July 1994); *Career* called to the Bar Inner Temple 1972, in practice 1972–80 and 1986–, asst recorder 1999–2000, recorder 2000–; legal advsr: Crown Life Insurance Gp 1980–82, Financial Times Gp 1982–86; panel memb Accountancy Investigation and Disciplinary Bd, chm Editorial Bd Counsel; fell Soc of Advanced Legal Studies; *Publications* Investigations and Enforcement (2001); *Recreations* cricket and rugby (as spectator); *Clubs* MCC, RAC, London Scottish FC; *Style*— Richard Jones, Esq, QC; ✉ 5 Fountain Court, Steelhouse Lane, Birmingham B4 6DR (tel 0121 606 0500)

JONES, Robert; s of Robert Aldwyn Jones, of Sanderstead, Surrey, and Joyce Margaret, *née* Madley; *b* 21 November 1956; *Educ* Trinity Sch of John Whitgift Croydon, Royal Coll of Music (jr exhibitioner in piano), ChCh Oxford (music scholar, MA), Univ of London (Music Teacher's Cert); *m* 23 May 1981, Eleanor Anne, da of Kenneth Michael Harre; 4 s (Edward b 12 Nov 1984, Henry b 4 Feb 1987, Alexander b 16 June 1990, Orlando b 19 June 1999); *Career* organist Trinity Sch 1972–75, organist and choirmaster St Mary's Church Addington 1973–75, academical clerk (choral scholar) ChCh Oxford and conductor Steeple Aston Choral Soc and Nuova Cappella of Oxford 1975–78, asst organist Hampstead Parish Church and St Clement Danes 1978–79, lay clerk St George's Chapel Windsor Castle and organist/choirmaster All Saints Windsor 1979–83, also visiting tutor Eton Coll and pt/t music teacher Tiffin Girls' Sch 1979–83, dir of music Putney Parish Church and conductor Feltham Choral Soc and Thames Voyces 1983–85, lay clerk Westminster Cathedral 1985–88, dir of music St Bride's Fleet St 1988–; memb Cte Church Music Soc 1997–2001; fndr memb Tallis Scholars; freelance organ recitalist in venues incl St Paul's Cathedral and Sydney Cathedral, regular oratorio soloist; numerous broadcasts and recordings with choir of St Bride's, Tallis Scholars (Gramophone Record of the Year 1987), Orlando Consort (Gramophone Early Music Award 1996) and Gabrieli Consort; examiner Associated Bd Royal Sch of Music 2004–; ARCM 1974, FRCO 1975 (chm), ADCM 1979, LRAM 1979; *Recreations* watching cricket, current affairs, good food, real ale; *Style*— Robert Jones, Esq; ✉ 15 Addington Close, Windsor, Berkshire SL4 4BP (tel and fax 01753 853573); St Bride's Church, Fleet Street, London EC4Y 8AU (tel 020 7427 0133, fax 020 7583 4867, e-mail roberthjones@supanet.com)

JONES, Prof Robert Maynard; s of Sydney Jones (d 1956), of Cardiff, and Edith Jones (d 1981); *b* 20 May 1929; *Educ* Univs of Wales and Ireland (MA, PhD, DLitt); *m* 27 Dec 1952, Anne Elizabeth, da of John James (d 1979), of Clunderwen; 1 s (Rhodri Siôn), 1 da (Lowri Gwenllian); *Career* former head Dept of Welsh Language and Literature Univ of Wales Aberystwyth 1980 (lectr and sr lectr 1955–77, reader 1978, prof 1980, now emeritus prof); memb Editorial Bd Welsh Nat Dictionary; Welsh Arts Cncl Prizes 1956, 1959, 1971, 1987, 1990 and 1998; fell Yr Academi Gymreig 1965; FBA 1993; *Books* Nid Yw Dŵr yn Plygu (1958), I'r Arch (1959), Cyflwyno'r Gymraeg (1964), Ci Wrth y Drws (1968), System in Child Language (1970), Traed Prydferth (1973), Tafod y Llenor (1974), Llên Cymru a Chrefydd (1977), Seiliau Beirniadaeth (1984–88), Selected Poems (1987), Casgliad o Gerddi (1988), Crio Chwerthin (1990), Dawn Gweddwon (1992), Cyfriniaeth Gymraeg (1994), Canu Arnaf (1995), Epistol Serch a Selsig (1997), Ysbryd y Cwlwm (1998), Ynghylch Tawelwch (1998), O'r Bedd i'r Crud (2000), Mawl a'i Gyfeillion (2000), Mawl a Gelynion ei Elynion (2002), Ol Troed (2003), Dysgu Cyfansawdd (2003), Beirniadaeth Gyfansawdd (2003), Rhy Iach (2004), Y Fadarchen Hudol (2005), Meddwl y Gynghanedd (2005); *Style*— Prof Emeritus Robert Jones, FBA; ✉ Tandderwen, Heol Llanbadarn, Aberystwyth, Dyfed SY23 1HB (tel 01970 623603)

JONES, (James) Roger; s of Albert James Jones (d 1999), and Hilda Vera, *née* Evans (d 1989); *b* 30 May 1952; *Educ* Shrewsbury, St Catharine's Coll Cambridge (sr scholar, MA); *Career* called to the Bar Middle Temple 1974 (Lloyd Jacob Meml exhibitioner, Astbury scholar), practised Oxford and Midland Circuit 1975–83, Office of the Parliamentary Counsel 1983–94, with Law Commission 1988–91, dep parliamentary counsel 1991–94; head Antique Dept Colefax & Fowler 1994–; *Recreations* walking the dog; *Style*— Roger Jones, Esq; ✉ Sibyl Colefax & John Fowler, 39 Brook Street, London W1K 4JE

JONES, Ronald Fitzgerald; OBE (1989); s of Henry Fitzgerald Jones (d 1941), of Liverpool, and Margaret Chisholm, *née* Mackenzie (d 1964); *b* 16 February 1926; *Educ* Skerry's Coll Liverpool, Wallasey Catering Coll (CGLI Diplomas 150 and 151); *m* 1, 1951, Jeanette Pamela (d 1975), da of Samuel Wood; 2 s (Graham Stuart b 1955, Russell Brent b 1959); m 2, 1978, Eve Helen Hunter Macpherson, da of David Warren; *Career* WWII RN 1944–46; trainee hotel mangr 1946–53, gen mangr Dornoch Hotel Scotland 1956–57, sr asst mangr Midland Hotel Manchester 1957–58; gen mangr: Turnberry Hotel Ayrshire 1958–61, Station Hotel Hull 1961–64, Queen's Hotel Leeds 1964–67, Central Hotel Glasgow 1967–69, Royal Garden Hotel London 1969–72, Athenaeum Hotel London 1972–84; dir and gen mangr Claridge's London 1984–94, dir Dormy House Hotel Broadway 1995–, ptnr Jones and Jones Hotel Management Services 1995–; visiting fell Oxford Brookes Univ 1997; Master Innholder 1979, Hotelier of the Year 1988; Freeman City of London 1979, Hon Citizen City of New Orleans 1979, Liveryman Worshipful Co of Innholders 1996; Hon DUniv Derby 1999; FHCIMA 1979 (memb 1969); *Books* Grand Hotelier (1997), Gastromania (2001), World On A Plate (2004), The Log Of The Seafaring Bears (2005); *Recreations* painting, music, travel, theatre; *Style*— Ronald Jones, Esq, OBE; ✉ 714 Willoughby House, Barbican, London EC2Y 8BN (e-mail jonesandjones@hotmail.com)

JONES, Prof Ronald Mervyn; s of Cdr Glyn Owen Jones, MBE, OStJ (d 1987), and Doris, *née* Woodley (d 1983); *b* 24 April 1947; *Educ* Devonport HS Plymouth, Univ of Liverpool (MD); *m* 1, 1970 (m dis 1988), Angela Christine, *née* Parsonage; 1 da (Emily b 1976), 1 s (Alex b 1979); m 2, 1989, Caroline Ann, da of Dr Neill Wordsworth Marshall; 2 da (Catherine Elizabeth b 17 Feb 1992, Lucy Clare b 21 Jan 1995); *Career* memb Faculty: Karolinska Inst Stockholm 1978, Univ of Michigan 1979–80; conslt Nottingham Hosps 1981–82, sr lectr and conslt Guy's Hosp 1982–90, prof of anaesthetics Imperial Coll London and conslt anaesthetist St Mary's Hosp 1990–99; memb: Advsy Ctee on NHS Drugs Dept of Health 1990–99, Cncl Royal Coll of Anaesthetists 1997–2002 (dir of continuing educn and professional devpt); civilian advsr to RN; academician Euro Acad of Anaesthesiology; hon life memb Aust Soc of Anaesthetists; FFARCS; *Books* Medicine for Anaesthetists (1989), Clinical Anaesthesia (1995); *Recreations* music, history, sailing; *Clubs* Royal Naval Sailing Association; *Style*— Prof Ronald Jones

JONES, Prof Ronald Samuel; OBE (1998), JP; s of Samuel Jones (d 1974), of Oswestry, Shropshire, and Gladys Jane, *née* Philips (d 1953); *b* 29 October 1937; *Educ* Oswestry Boys' HS, Univ of Liverpool (BVSc); *m* 21 April 1962, Pamela, da of Wilfred Evans, of Pant Oswestry, Shropshire; 2 da (Rachel Mary Patricia b 1963, Alison Jane b 1966); *Career* Univ of Glasgow: house surgn 1960–61, univ asst 1961–62; Univ of Liverpool: lectr 1962–77, sr lectr 1977–86, reader 1986–89, prof 1990–, emeritus prof 2001; RCVS: memb Cncl 1986–98, treas 1993–95, pres 1996–97; John Henry Steele Medal RCVS 1989, Coll Medal RCA 1996; FRSM, FRCVS 1981 (MRCVS 1960), FIBiol 1988, Hon FRCA 2001, DVSc Pretoria 1992; *Recreations* gardening, horse racing, philately, fly fishing; *Clubs* Farmers; *Style*— Prof Ronald S Jones, OBE; ✉ 7 Birch Road, Oxton, Prenton, Merseyside CH43 5UF (tel 0151 653 9008, fax 0151 653 7551)

JONES, Rupert James Livingston; s of Walter Herbert Jones (d 1982), and Dorothy Jocelyn, *née* Dignum (d 1989); *b* 2 September 1953; *Educ* KCS Wimbledon, Univ of Birmingham (LLB); *m* 24 June 1978, Sheila Carol, da of Andrew Kertesz (d 1993); 3 s (Oliver b 10 June 1984, Stephen b 13 Sept 1989, Michael b 20 Feb 1994), 1 da (Philippa b 31 Jan 1987); *Career* admitted slr 1978; ptnr: Allen and Overy 1985–97 (articled clerk 1976–78, asst slr 1978–85), Sonnenschein Nath & Rosenthal 1997–99, Buchanan Ingersoll 2000–02; counsel Weil, Gotshal & Manges 2002–; chm London Young Slrs Gp 1987–88 (Ctee 1984–89), memb Nat Ctee Young Slrs Gp 1986–89; chm: Whittington Ctee City of London Slrs Co 1992–94 (memb 1988–94), Planning and Environmental Law Ctee City of London Law Soc 2005– (memb 1997–); Liveryman Worshipful Co of Slrs 1998 (memb 1985); memb Law Soc 1976; *Recreations* gardening, cinema, motoring, computing; *Style*— Rupert Jones, Esq; ✉ Weil, Gotshal and Manges, One South Place, London EC2M 2WG (tel 020 7903 1000, fax 020 7903 0990, e-mail rupert.jones@weil.com)

JONES, Russell Alan; *b* 26 May 1960; *Educ* Greenshaw HS Sutton, Univ of Kent at Canterbury (BA); *Career* orch personnel mangr Royal Liverpool Philharmonic Soc 1981–86, concerts mangr Scottish Chamber Orch 1986, chief exec and co sec Nat Fedn of Music Socs 1987–97, head of Business in the Arts ABSA 1997–99, dir of Prog Arts and Business 1999, dir of Operations Arts and Business 2000–01, dir of Policy and Public Affrs 2001–02; dir Assoc of Br Orchs 2002–07, vice-pres for mktg and membership devpt American Symphony Orch League NY 2007–; admin Haydn Orch 1986–, jt fndr/admin/co sec Southwark Music Festival 1988–90; vice-pres Nat Fedn of Music Socs 1998, vice-pres Acad of Live and Recorded Arts 2000–04, chm Nat Music Cncl of GB 1995–2000 (memb Exec Ctee 1987–95), hon treas and sec Voluntary Arts Network 1991–97; memb: Cncl Amateur Music Assoc 1987–89, Cncl London Symphony Chorus 1987–89, 1991–94 and 1996–98, Steering Ctee Nat Music Day 1992–94, Musicians Benevolent Fund, Nat Campaign for the Arts, Nat Tst; past master Billingsgate Ward Club; Freeman City of London 2003, Liveryman Worshipful Co of Musicians 2003; FRSA; Chevalier Order of Champagne; *Recreations* music, singing, piano, violin, current affairs, Br and American politics, cooking and entertaining, wine, badminton; *Style*— Russell Jones, Esq; ✉ c/o American Symphony Orchestra League, 33 West 60th Street, Fifth Floor, New York NY 10023–7905, USA

JONES, Sarah; *Educ* Univ of Leeds (MBA); *m*; 1 s; *Career* BAE Systems: joined 1990, dir RG Ammunition (div of RO Defence business unit) 2002–05; chief exec Ufi/learndirect 2005–; former vol cnsllr prison service, sch govr; *Style*— Mrs Sarah Jones; ✉ Ufi Limited, Dearing House, 1 Young Street, Sheffield S1 4UP

JONES, Sir Simon Warley Frederick Benton; 4 Bt (UK 1919), of Treeton, W Riding of Yorks; s of Lt-Col Sir Peter Fawcett Benton Jones, 3 Bt, OBE (d 1972), and Nancy, *née* Pickering; *b* 11 September 1941; *Educ* Eton, Trinity Coll Cambridge (MA); *m* 14 April 1966, Margaret Fiona, OBE, DL, eldest da of David Rutherford Dickson, of Bury St Edmunds, Suffolk; 2 da (Fiona Charlotte Farquharson b 1967, Fleur Alexandra Collins b 1970), 3 s (James Peter Martin b 1973, David William Anthony b 1975, Alastair Frederick Malcolm b 1981); *Heir* s, James Benton Jones; *Career* farmer; High Sheriff Lincs 1977–78; JP Lincs 1971–2000, chm Lincs Magistrates Courts Ctee 1996–2000; *Recreations* shooting, fishing; *Style*— Sir Simon Benton Jones, Bt; ✉ Irnham Hall, Grantham, Lincolnshire NG33 4JD; Sopley, Christchurch, Dorset BH23 7BE

JONES, Stephen; s of Joseph Jones, of Manchester, and Constance, *née* Potter; *b* 15 November 1962, Ashton-under-Lyne, Lancs; *Educ* Manchester Grammar, Queen's Coll Cambridge (MA), Manchester Met Univ; *partner* Maria O'Malley; 3 s (Ocean b 16 Feb 1998, Macdara b 16 June 1999, Holden b 10 May 2004), 1 da (Pebbles b 17 April 2003); *Career* admitted slr 1986; Goldberg Blackburn & Howards (now Pannone LLP): trainee slr 1984–86, slr 1986–91; slr Russell Jones & Walker 1991–92, ptnr Pannone LLP 1992–; slr to Royal Liverpool Children's Inquiry 2000, slr to Redfern Inquiry into tissue sampling in UK nuclear facilities 2007; memb: Clinical Negligence Panel Law Soc, Slrs' Referral Panel Action Against Medical Accidents (AvMA), MIND Legal Network; memb Law Soc 1984; *Recreations* following Manchester City FC home and away; *Style*— Stephen Jones, Esq; ✉ Pannone LLP, 123 Deansgate, Manchester M3 2BU (tel 0161 909 3000, fax 0161 909 4444, e-mail stephen.jones@pannone.co.uk)

JONES, Stephen John Moffat; s of Gordon Jones, of Marlow, Bucks, and Margaret, *née* Moffat; *b* 31 May 1957; *Educ* Liverpool Coll, St Martin's Sch of Art (BA); *Career* model millinery designer 1981–, estab diffusion range Miss Jones/Jones Boy 1989; first British milliner to work for French designer collections (clients incl Marc Jacobs, John Galliano, Comme des Garçons, Claude Montana and Christian Dior); designer of hats for film and music business; work in perm collections of: V&A London, Australian Nat Gallery Canberra, Brooklyn Museum NY, Kyoto Costume Inst; references of work included in Status, Style, Glamour (Colin McDowell, Thames and Hudson, 1992); *Recreations* painting, sculpture; *Style*— Stephen Jones, Esq; ✉ Stephen Jones Millinery Ltd, 36 Great Queen Street, Covent Garden, London (tel 020 7242 0770, fax 020 7242 0796, website www.stephenjonesmillinery.com)

JONES, Stewart Elgan; QC (1994); s of Gwilym John Jones (d 1987), of Flecknoe, Warwickshire, and Elizabeth, *née* Davies; *b* 20 January 1945; *Educ* Cheltenham Coll, The Queen's Coll Oxford (MA); *m* 21 July 1979, Jennifer Anne, da of Maj James Ian Leonard Syddall (d 1963), of Riseley, Berks; 2 da (Eleanor b 1980, Clementine b 1981), 2 step c (Katherine b 1969, James b 1971); *Career* called to the Bar Gray's Inn 1972 (bencher 2002); memb Western Circuit, recorder of the Crown Court 1990–; *Recreations* home, hearth, the great outdoors; *Clubs* Athenaeum; *Style*— Stewart E Jones, Esq, QC; ✉ 3 Paper Buildings, Temple, London EC4Y 7EU (tel 020 7583 8055, fax 020 7353 6271)

JONES, Terence Graham Parry (Terry); s of late Alick George Parry Jones, and Dilys Louise, *née* Newnes (d 1971); *b* 1 February 1942; *Educ* Royal GS Guildford, St Edmund Hall Oxford; *m* 20 June 1970, Alison, da of James Veitch Telfer; 1 da (Sally Louise Parry b 1974), 1 s (William George Parry b 1976); *Career* writer and performer; *Television* Monty Python's Flying Circus (BBC TV) 1969–74, Ripping Yarns (dir and co-writer) 1978, More Ripping Yarns (dir and co-writer) 1980, Dr Fegg's Encyclopaedia (sic) of All World Knowledge (dir and co-writer) 1984, So This Is Progress (writer and presenter) 1991, Crusades (writer and presenter) 1994/95, Ancient Inventions (presenter, Discovery Channel) 1997, Longitude (screenplay writer) 1997, Gladiators - The Brutal Truth (presenter, BBC) 1999, Python Night anniversary (dir, BBC 2) 1999, narrator in Boy in Darkness (BBC Choice) 1999, The Hidden History of Ancient Egypt (Discovery/BBC) 2003, The Hidden History of Ancient Rome (Discovery/BBC) 2003, TheSurprisingHistory of Sex and Love (Discovery/BBC) 2003, Terry Jones' Medieval Lives (presenter and writer, BBC) 2004, The Story of One (presenter and writer) 2005, Terry Jones' Barbarians (presenter and writer) 2006; *Film* Monty Python and the Holy Grail (dir, actor and co-writer) 1974, Monty Python's Life of Brian (dir, actor and co-writer) 1978, Monty Python's Meaning of Life (dir, actor and co-writer) 1981, Personal Services (dir) 1986, Erik the Viking (dir, writer and actor) 1989, The Wind in the Willows (dir, writer and actor) 1996, Asterix and Obelix (writer and dir, English version) 1999, BFI signature film for IMAX Theatre (writer and dir) 1999, BFG (sreenplay writer) 2003; *Theatre* Evil Machines (musical); *Publications* Chaucer's Knight (1980), Fairy Tales (1981), The Saga of Erik the Viking (1983), Nicobobinus (1986), The Curse of the Vampire's Socks (1988), Attacks of Opinion (1988), Fantastic Stories (1992), Crusades (jtly, 1994), Lady Cottington's Book of Pressed Fairies (jtly, 1994), Fairy Tales and Fantastic Stories (1997), The Lady and the Squire (2000), The Image of Chaucer's Knight (essay, 2000), Who Murdered Chaucer? (jtly, 2003), Terry Jones' Medieval Lives (jtly, 2004); published: The Knight and the Squire (1997), The Starship Titanic (with Douglas Adams, 1997), Terry Jones' War on the War on Terror (2005), Terry Jones' Barbarians (jtly, 2006); *Style*— Terry Jones, Esq; ✉ c/o Casarotto & Co, National House, 60–66 Wardour Street, London W1V 4ND (tel 020 7287 4450, fax 020 7287 9128)

JONES, Thomas Henry (Tom); OBE (1996); s of Cadwaladr Jones (d 1986), and Olwen Ellyw, *née* Humphreys (d 1993); *b* 8 February 1950; *Educ* Tywyn Sch Merioneth, UCW Aberystwyth (BA); *m* 20 Sept 1980, Dr Margaret Elizabeth Jones, da of John Wyn Jones, of Welshpool, Powys; 2 s (Owain b 1 Sept 1985, Steffan b 24 Nov 1991), 1 da (Siwan b 12 Jan 1988); *Career* farmer; former vice-pres Farmers' Union of Wales, former pres Young Farmers' Clubs of Wales; former chm: Wales Ctee Nat Lottery Charities Bd, Berwyn Local Access Forum; chm Millennium Stadium Charitable Tst; memb: Richard's Cmmn on the Powers of the National Assembly for Wales, Legal Services Cmmn; formerly memb: S4C Authy, National Parks Review Panel, Agric Trg Bd; memb Countryside Cncl for Wales until 2002, govr Welsh Agricultural Colls, vice-pres Wales Cncl for Voluntary Action; FRAgS; *Books* Brain Yn Y Brwyn (1976), Dyddiadur Ffarmwr (1985); *Style*— Tom Jones, Esq, OBE; ✉ Plas Coch, Dolanog, Welshpool, Powys (tel 01938 810553)

JONES, Dr (David) Timothy (Tim); s of David Percy Jones (d 1993), and Elvair Jones (d 1990); *b* 21 August 1944; *Educ* Queen Elizabeth GS Carmarthen, Univ of Salford, Univ of Leeds (PhD), INSEAD (MBA), MRSC; *m* 30 March 1968, Jean Margaret; 4 da; *Career* British Petroleum 1969–93 (succession of posts in S Yemen, Germany, France, UK and Belgium, latterly dir BP Oil Europe based Brussels); Lloyd's Register of Shipping: dep chm 1993–2000, ceo 1996–2000; chm: DTI Foresight Panel on the Marine Industry 1999–2002, SE Regnl Ctee Educn and Learning Wales (ELWa) 2001–; non-exec chair InnovOx; *Recreations* golf, squash, watching rugby; *Style*— Dr Tim Jones

JONES, Timothy Aidan; s of Dr Derek Hugh Powell Jones, and Thelma Ann, *née* Gray; *Educ* Bexhill GS, Bexhill VI Form Coll, Christ's Coll Cambridge (BA); *m* 30 April 2001, Dr Christin Marschall; 1 da (b 2005); *Career* FCO: joined 1984, second sec The Hague 1988–92, EU Admin of Mostar 1995–96, dep head of mission Tehran 1996–99, ambass to Armenia 1999–2003, FCO 2003–; *Recreations* reading, swimming, cycling; *Style*— Timothy Jones, Esq

JONES, Timothy Arthur; s of Canon Idwal Jones, of Birdingbury, Warks, and Jean Margaret, *née* Shuttleworth; *b* 20 April 1951; *Educ* Christ's Hosp (Almoners' nominee open scholar), Jesus Coll Cambridge, LSE, Coll of Law Chancery Lane; *Children* 1 da (Harriet b 1980); *Career* called to the Bar: Inner Temple 1975, King's Inn Dublin 1990, NI 1998; practising Midland Circuit (specialising in planning, local govt, and environment law); memb: Planning and Environmental Bar Assoc, Admin Law Bar Assoc, Bar Human Rights Ctee; Parly candidate (Lib later Lib Dem): Warwick and Leamington 1974, Mid Staffordshire 1983, 1987 and 1990; memb Lib Dem Federal Policy Ctee 1990–92, memb Brereton and Ravenhill Cncl (chm Planning Ctee 2003–); pres Cambridge Univ Liberal Club 1970, memb Standing Ctee Cambridge Union 1971; vice-chm League of Friends Rugeley Hosp 1985–89; FCIArb, FRGS, FRSA; *Publications* chapter on Town and Country Planning in Travellers and the Law (2004), chapter on The Impact of European Law on the UK in Criteria of Copenhagen; *Recreations* theatre, walking, ornithology, opera; *Style*— Timothy Jones, Esq; ✉ No 5 Chambers (Birmingham, London & Bristol), Fountain Court, Steelhouse Lane, Birmingham B4 6DR (tel 0870 203 5555, fax 0121 606 1501, e-mail planning@no5.com, website www.no5.com); Arden Chambers, 2 John Street, London WC1N 2ES (tel 020 7242 4244, fax 020 7242 3224, e-mail clerks@arden-chambers.law.co.uk, website www.arden-chambers.law.co.uk)

JONES, Sir Tom, *né* Thomas Jones Woodward; kt (2006), OBE (1999); *b* 7 June 1940; *m*; *Career* singer; formed first band Tommy Scott & The Senators 1963; released first solo single Chills and Fever 1964; hit singles incl: It's Not Unusual (1965, reached UK no 1), Thunderball (from film, 1966), Green Green Grass of Home (1966, UK no 1), Detroit City (1967, UK no 8), I'll Never Fall in Love Again (1967, UK no 2), I'm Coming Home (1967, UK no 2), Delilah (1968, UK no 2), 'Til (1971, UK no 2), A Boy From Nowhere (1987,

UK no 2), Kiss (with Art of Noise, 1988, UK no 5); albums incl: Along Came Jones (1965, UK no 11), From The Heart (1966, UK no 23), Green Green Grass of Home (1967, UK no 3), Live At the Talk of the Town (1967, UK no 6), Delilah (1968, UK no 1), Help Yourself (1969, UK no 4), This Is Tom Jones (1969, UK no 2), Tom Jones Live In Las Vegas (1969, UK no 3), Tom (1970, UK no 4), She's A Lady (1971, UK no 9), 20 Greatest Hits (1975, UK no 1), I'm Coming Home (1978, UK no 12), Matador (musical soundtrack, 1987, UK no 26), Under Milk Wood (with George Martin, 1988), Carrying A Torch (with Van Morrison, 1991, UK no 44), The Lead and How to Swing It (1994), Reload (with 17 guest artists, UK no 1) 1999; TV shows incl: Billy Cotton Band Show 1965, The Ed Sullivan Show 1965, Call In On Tom 1965, Sunday Night At The London Palladium, Spotlight 1967, This Is Tom Jones 1969, Comic Relief 1991, Tom Jones - The Right Time 1992, Amnesty International 40th Anniversary Special 2001, Pavarotti and Friends 2001, Prince's Trust Party in the Park 2001; Mars Attacks (film) 1996; Nordhoff Robbins Silver Clef Award 2001; fell Welsh Coll of Music and Drama 1994; *Style*— Sir Tom Jones, OBE

JONES, Trevor; s of John Jones (d 1995), of New Penshaw, Tyne & Wear, and Florence Mary, *née* Rogerson (d 1978); *b* 23 December 1950; *Educ* New Coll Durham, Washington GS; *m* Hazel, da of Robert Oliver; *Career* served local govt 1969–78, regnl auditor then head of financial policy and planning Northern RHA 1978–83, dep treas S Manchester HA 1983–86, gen mangr Waltham Forest HA 1989–91 (dir of fin and dep gen mangr 1986–89), chief exec Forest Healthcare NHS Tst 1991–95, chief exec Lothian Health Board 1995–2000, head Health Dept Scottish Exec 2000–, chief exec NHS Scotland 2000–; chm NHS Bd 1998–2000; CIPFA 1973, FCCA 1981, FCIS 1982, CCMI 2004 (MIMgt 1979); *Recreations* golf, Durham CCC, photography, Sunderland AFC; *Style*— Trevor Jones, Esq; ✉ Scottish Executive Health Department, St Andrew's House, Regent Road, Edinburgh EH1 3DG

JONES, Prof Trevor Mervyn; CBE (2003); s of Samuel James Jones (d 1992), of Finchampstead, Berks, and Hilda May, *née* Walley (d 1978); *b* 19 August 1942; *Educ* Wolverhampton Sch, King's Coll London (BPharm, PhD); *m* 9 April 1966, Verity Ann, da of Richard Bates (d 1963), of Emsworth, Hants; 1 da (Amanda Melissa (Mrs Lawrence Richard Kerr) b 1968), 1 s (Timothy Damian b 1971); *Career* formerly: lectr Univ of Nottingham, head of devpt The Boots Co Ltd, dir of R&D and med Wellcome plc, DG Assoc of the British Pharmaceutical Industry; currently dir: Allergan Inc, BAC BV, Next Pharma Technologies Ltd, People in Health; chm Dept of Health Advsy Gp for Genetics Research; memb: Advsy Bd MRC Social and Genetic Developmental Psychiatric Research Centre Inst of Psychiatry, WHO Cmmn on Intellectual Property Rights, Innovation and Public Health (CIPIH) 2004–06; Fédération Internationale Pharmaceutique: pres Int Cmmn on Technol 1979–83, memb Bd of Pharmaceutical Scis 1980–84; pres Bd Maurice-Marie Janot Int Ctee, memb Bd of Hon Advsrs The Glynn Research Fndn, memb Bd Euro Fedn of Pharmaceutical Industry; currently chm ReNeuron Holdings Ltd, Kinetique Ltd; non-exec memb Bd Merlin Ventures Ltd; former memb Bd: Medidesk Ltd, Datapharm Communications Ltd; sometime visiting prof: KCL, Univ of Strathclyde, Univ of N Carolina; author of various pubns; memb Editorial Bd: Jl of Pharmacy and Pharmacology, Drug Development and Industrial Pharmacy, Int Jl of Pharmaceutics, Drugs and the Pharmaceutical Sciences; memb UK Medicines Cmmn 1982–94; former memb: Nuffield Cncl on Bioethics Expert Gp on the Use of Human Tissue, Cabinet Office Advsy Ctee on the Human Genome, Bd UK Sci Policy Support Gp, Cncl London Medicine, Advsy Bd MRC; tstee: Aviation Health Inst 1996–98, The Epilepsy Research Fndn 1996–2002, Northwich Park Inst for Med Research 1998–2004, Medicines for Malaria Venture 1999–, Br Urological Fndn 2005–; dep chm Cncl KCL 2003–; govr Croydon HS; Freeman: Worshipful Soc of Apothecaries 1988, City of London 1994; Hon PhD Univ of Athens 1993; Hon DSc: Univ of Strathclyde 1994, Univ of Nottingham 1998, Univ of Bath 2000, Univ of Bradford 2003; Harrison Meml Medal 1987, Gold Medal Comenius Univ 1992, Charter Gold Medal Royal Pharmaceutical Soc of GB 1996, SCRIP BTG Lifetime Achievement Award 2006; Hon FFPM (RCP) 1995, hon fell London Sch of Pharmacy 1998, FRPharmS, CChem, FRCS, FCPP, FKC, hon fell Br Pharmacological Soc 2005, Hon FRCP 2005; *Books* Drug Delivery to the Respiratory Tract (1987), Advances in Pharmaceutical Sciences (1992); *Recreations* gardening, opera, golf, Welsh rugby; *Clubs* Athenaeum; *Style*— Prof Trevor Jones, CBE; ✉ Woodhyrst House, 18 Friths Drive, Reigate, Surrey RH2 0DS

JONES, Ven Trevor Pryce; s of John Pryce Jones (d 1997), of Rhuddlan, N Wales, and Annie, *née* Jepson (d 1991); *b* 24 April 1948; *Educ* St Luke's Coll Exeter (CertEd), Univ of Southampton (BEd, BTh, ACP), Salisbury/Wells Theol Coll, Univ of Wales, Cardiff Law Sch (LLM); *m* Susan Diane, da of Rev Peter John Pengelley; 1 da (Anna Catherine b 5 June 1982), 1 s (David Richard Pryce b 4 March 1985); *Career* asst teacher and lay chaplain Shaftesbury GS 1969–73; ordained: deacon 1976, priest 1977; asst curate Gloucester St George Lower Tuffley Glos 1976–79, warden Bishop Mascall Centre Ludlow 1979–84, memb Hereford Diocesan Educn Team 1979–84, diocesan communications offr Hereford 1981–86, team rector Hereford South Wye Team Miny 1984–87, officiating chaplain to the Forces 1985–97, prebendary of Hereford Cathedral 1993–97, archdeacon of Hertford 1997–, hon canon Cathedral and Abbey Church of St Albans 1997–, chm St Albans and Oxford Miny Course 1998–2007; bishops' selector 2001–, memb Gen Synod C of E 2000–05 and 2006–, memb C of E Legal Advsy Cmmn 2006–; chm St Albans Diocese Reach Out projects 1997–2002, chair Rural Strategy Advisory Gp (RUSTAG) 2001–, chair Hockerill Educnl Fndn 2005–, vice-chair East Anglia Ministerial Course 2005–; memb: Ecclesiastical Law Soc 1997, Canon Law Society of GB and I 2003; *Recreations* country walks, vintage buses and trains; *Clubs* Royal Commonwealth; *Style*— The Ven the Archdeacon of Hertford; ✉ St Mary's House, Church Lane, Stapleford, Hertfordshire SG14 3NB (tel 01992 581629, fax 01992 558745, e-mail archdhert@stalbans.anglican.org)

JONES, Prof Tudor Bowden; s of Idris Jones (d 1961), of Ystradgynlais, S Wales, and Tydvil Ann, *née* Bowden (d 1978); *b* 8 November 1934; *Educ* Univ of Wales, UC Swansea (BSc, PhD, DSc); *m* 16 Aug 1960, Patricia (Pat); 2 s (Owen Bowden b 14 Jan 1968, Hywel Bowden b 11 Sept 1970); *Career* sr research assoc US Nat Acad of Sci 1971–72, conslt on ionospheric radiowave propogation to UK, US and Canadian Govt Agencies; Univ of Leicester: former lectr, sr lectr and reader, prof of ionospheric physics 1980, head Dept of Physics and Astronomy 1993–98 (emeritus prof 1998–); Leverhulme emeritus fell 2001–02; memb various ctees SERC; national coordinator of Solar Terrestial Physics at Particle Physics and Astronomy Research Cncl 1998–2000; awarded: Appleton Prize Royal Soc 1993, Charles Chree Prize Inst of Physics 1994; IEE Appleton Lecture 1996/97; FInstP, FIEE, CEng, FRAS; *Books* Ionospheric Radiowave Propagation (1969); *Recreations* classical music, rugby football; *Style*— Prof Tudor Jones; ✉ Physics and Astronomy Department, University of Leicester, University Road, Leicester LE1 7RH (tel 0116 252 3561, fax 0116 252 3555, e-mail tbj@ion.le.ac.uk)

JONES, Vincent Peter (Vinnie); s of Peter Jones, and Glenda, *née* Harris; *b* 5 January 1965; *Educ* Langleybury Sch, Bedmond Sch, Chancellors, Brookmans Park; *m* Tanya; 1 s (Aaron b 29 May 1991), 1 step da (Kaley b 15 April 1987); *Career* professional footballer; formerly amateur player Wealdstone; Wimbledon 1985–89 (debut v Nottingham Forest), Leeds United 1989–90 (joined for £650,000), Sheffield United 1990–91 (joined for £700,000), Chelsea 1991–92 (joined for £575,000), Wimbledon 1992–98 (rejoined for £700,000), player-coach QPR 1998, ret from football 1999; honours: 9 international caps for Wales (one as capt), FA Cup winners Wimbledon 1988, Div 2 Championship winners Leeds United 1990; currently actor; *Films* Lock, Stock and Two Smoking Barrels (Comedy Film of the Year 1998) 1998, Gone in Sixty Seconds 2000, Snatch 2000 (Best Actor Empire Film Awards 2001), Mean Machine 2002, A Night at the Golden Eagle 2002 (Best Supporting Actor New York Film Awards 2003), The Big Bounce 2004, Tooth 2004, Eurotrip 2004, Johnny Was (2005), She's the Man (2005), XMen 3 (2006), The Riddle (2006); *Television* presenter The 100 Greatest Sporting Moments (Channel 4) 2001; *Recreations* shooting, fishing, golf, charitable work; *Style*— Vinnie Jones, Esq; ✉ c/o Classic Management Ltd, 5th Floor, 140 Brompton Road, London SW3 1HY (tel 020 7808 0233, fax 020 7584 7933, e-mail info@classicmanagement.biz)

JONES, William George Tilston; s of Thomas Tilston Jones (d 1976), and Amy Ethel, *née* Millar (d 1991); *b* 7 January 1942; *Educ* Portsmouth GS, Portsmouth Poly (BSc); *m* 18 Dec 1965, Fiona Mary; 1 da (Zoë Samantha b 1966); *Career* PO: exec engr 1965–69, head of gp 1969–75, head of section 1975–78, head System X Devpt Div 1978–80; British Telecommunications: dep dir System X 1980–83, dir System Evolution and Standards Div 1983–84, chief exec (technol) 1984–86, dir of technol studies 1988–90; engrg conslt 1990–; exec in residence Int Mgmnt Inst Geneva 1987; hon fellowship Portsmouth Univ (formerly Portsmouth Poly) 1989; FIEE; *Recreations* theatre, debating society, camping; *Style*— William Jones, Esq; ✉ Cornerways, Lordings Road, Newbridge, Billingshurst, West Sussex RH14 9JA (tel 01403 780331)

JONES, Wynne Melville; s of Rev John Melville Jones (d 1972), and Eirlys, *née* Davies; *b* 7 August 1947; *Educ* Co Secondary Sch Tregaron, Swansea Coll of Art, Trinity Coll Carmarthen; *m* 1971, Linda Rees, da of John Verdun Rees; 2 da (Meleri Wyn, Manon Wyn); *Career* head of PR Welsh League of Youth 1975 (co organiser Carmarthenshire 1969, publicity offr headquarters 1971), fndr Strata Public Relations Aberystwyth 1979, exec dir and also chm Strata Matrix 1989– (result of merger between Strata and Cardiff Design & Advertising Co); fndr ptnr Deli Cymru Aberystwyth (delicatessen specialising in fine food from Wales and the rest of the world) 1994–98; hon pres and tstee Welsh League of Youth 1997–, memb Bd of Dirs Golwg (Welsh language current affrs magazine); fell Welsh PR Assoc (fndr memb); *Publications* Am Cymru - A week by week account of the Welsh Assembly (1999); *Recreations* art appreciation, swimming, hill walking, rural activities; *Style*— Wynne Melville Jones, Esq; ✉ 25 North Parade, Aberystwyth, Ceredigion SY23 2JN (tel 01970 625552, fax 01970 612774, e-mail wynne@stratamatrix.co.uk)

JONES-DAVIES, Henry Ellis; s of late Dr Thomas Ellis Jones-Davies; *b* 30 March 1949, Caerfyrddin; *Educ* Rugby, St Peter's Coll Oxford (MA); *m* Frances Dorothy Roden; 3 s (Edward Owain Ellis b 1991, Tomos Llywelyn Ellis b 1993, Rhidian Glyndwr Ellis b 2000); *Career* dep leader archaeological expdn to Iran 1969 (memb 1968 expdn), dep leader expdn to N Afghanistan 1970, English teacher Hamburg 1974–75, worked PR co London 1975–78, exec asst to ceo of an industrial corp Jeddah Saudi Arabia 1978–80, fndr tourism business (expanded into PR, advtg and publishing) Turkey 1981–88, co-fndr (with Nigel Havers, *qv*) Pegasus Pictures London 1983–93, political risk analyst and relationship-builder BP Algiers 1993–96, fndr and ed Cambria - The Nat Magazine for Wales 1997–; Wales co-ordinator Anrhydedd Cymry'r Cyfanfyd (Worldwide Welsh Award), hon vice-pres Wales Heritage Campaign, dir Nat Welsh-American Fndn; frequent lectr in USA; FRGS; Hadhrami Medal of Honour; *Publications* I owe my life to... 125 Year of the International Red Cross (contrib), various articles and reviews; *Recreations* Welsh, European and political history, Celtic folk, classical, Christian and Islamic liturgical music, calligraphy, painting, running, mountaineering; *Style*— Henry Jones-Davies, Esq; ✉ Cambria Magazine, PO Box 22, Carmarthen SA32 7YH (tel 01267 290188, e-mail editorial@cambriamagazine.com)

JONES-LEE, Prof Michael Whittaker; s of Lt-Col Walter Whittaker Jones-Lee (d 1977), of Leybourne, Kent, and Christina, *née* Hamilton (d 1985); *b* 3 April 1944; *Educ* Prince Rupert Sch Wilhelmshaven, Bishop Wordsworth's Sch Salisbury, Univ of Sheffield (BEng), Univ of York (DPhil); *m* 20 Dec 1969, Hazel, da of Arthur Stephen Knight (d 1999); 2 s (Rupert b 1974, Ben b 1976), 1 da (Sarah b 1979); *Career* sr lectr Dept of Political Econ Univ of St Andrews 1971–72; Univ of York: Esmée Fairbairn lectr in fin 1967–71, sr lectr Dept of Econs 1972–76, reader Dept of Econs 1976–77; Univ of Newcastle upon Tyne: prof Dept of Econs 1977–, head of dept 1984–95, dean Faculty of Social Science 1984–88; conslt: DfT, DEFRA, TRL, HSE, NICE, London Underground, Railtrack, New Zealand Land Tport Safety Authy, Rail Safety Standards Bd; specialist advsr to House of Lords Select Ctee on Economic Affrs Inquiry into Govt Policy on the Mgmnt of Risk 2005–06; adjunct prof of risk mgmnt Univ of Stavanger 2007–; *Books* The Value of Life: An Economic Analysis (1976), The Value of Life and Safety (ed, 1982), The Economics of Safety and Physical Risk (1989), Economic Valuation with Stated Preference Techniques: A Manual (co-author, 2002); *Recreations* shopping and old sports cars; *Style*— Prof Michael Jones-Lee; ✉ Business School - Ecomonics, University of Newcastle upon Tyne, Newcastle upon Tyne NE1 7RU (tel 0191 222 6549, fax 0191 222 6548, e-mail michael.jones-lee@ncl.ac.uk)

JONES OF BIRMINGHAM, Baron (Life Peer UK 2007), of Alvechurch and of Bromsgrove in the County of Worcestershire; Sir Digby Marritt Jones; kt (2005); s of late Derek Jones, of Bromsgrove, Worcs, and Bernice, *née* Marritt; *b* 28 October 1955; *Educ* Bromsgrove Sch (head boy 1974), UCL (LLB), Chester Coll of Law; *m* 1 November 1990, Patricia Mary; *Career* Edge & Ellison Slrs: articled clerk 1978–80, asst slr 1980–81, assoc ptnr 1981–84, ptnr 1984–, head of corp 1987–, dep sr ptnr 1990–, sr ptnr 1995–98; vice-chm corp fin KPMG 1998–99, DG CBI 2000–06, chm Industries Gp and sr advsr Deloitte 2006–; non-exec dir: iSOFT plc, ALBA plc, Aggregate Industries; Govt's skills envoy 2006–, min of state for trade and investment Dept for Business, Enterprise and Regulatory Reform 2007–; dir Business in the Community; memb Bd VisitBritain, memb Nat Learning and Skills Cncl, cmmr Cmmn for Racial Equality; vice-pres Birmingham Hospice, vice-pres UNICEF, corp ambass Royal Br Legion; patron: Cancer BACUP, Why My Child Appeal, Canning House Library Appeal, Hospice of Hope Romania; memb Law Soc 1980–, memb City of Birmingham Symphony Orch Devpt Tst; fell UCL, hon fell Cardiff Univ; Hon DUniv: Univ of Central England, Univ of Birmingham, UMIST; CCMI, FRSA, fell Royal Inst; *Recreations* skiing, rugby, theatre, military history, recreational cycling; *Style*— The Lord Jones of Birmingham; ✉ Deloitte, Stonecutter Court, 1 Stonecutter Street, London EC4A 4TR

JONES OF CHELTENHAM, Baron (Life Peer UK 2005), of Cheltenham in the County of Gloucestershire; Nigel David Jones; s of late A J Jones, and late Nora Jones; *b* 30 March 1948; *m* 21 May 1981, Katy, *née* Grinnell; 1 s, 2 da (twins); *Career* computer operator Westminster Bank Ltd 1965–67, computer programmer ICL Computers 1967–70, systems analyst Vehicle and General Insurance 1970–71, systems programmer Atkins Computing 1971, systems designer rising to project mangr ICL Computers 1971–92; cncllr (Cheltenham Park) Glos CC 1989–93; MP (Lib Dem) Cheltenham 1992–2005; exec memb: Cwlth Parly Assoc, Inter-Parly Union; chair Botswana Gp; Lib Dem spokesman on: England, Local Govt and Housing 1992, Sci and Technol 1993–, Consumer Affrs 1995–97, Sport 1997–99, Int Devpt 1999–; memb Select Ctee on: Standards and Privileges 1995–97, Sci and Technol 1997–99, Int Devpt 1999–2002, Public Accounts 2002–05; *Recreations* watching Cheltenham Town FC and Swindon Town FC, cricket, gardening; *Clubs* Reform, National Liberal; *Style*— The Rt Hon the Lord Jones of Cheltenham

JONES PARRY, Sir Emyr; GCMG (2007, KCMG 2002, CMG 1992); s of Hugh Jones Parry (d 1992), and Eirwen, *née* Davies; *b* 21 September 1947, Carmarthen; *Educ* Gwendraeth GS, Cardiff Univ (BSc), Univ of Cambridge (PhD); *m* 30 July 1971, Lynn, *née* Noble; 2 s (Mark b 1977, Paul b 1979); *Career* various diplomatic serv postings 1973–97, dir EU

FCO 1997–98, political dir FCO 1998–2001, ambass North Atlantic Cncl 2001–03, ambass and perm rep UN NY 2003–07; author of various scientific pubns 1973; fell Cardiff Univ 2003; Hon LLD Univ of Wales; Hon FInstP; *Recreations* sport, theatre, reading; *Style*— Sir Emyr Jones Parry, GCMG

JONES-PARRY, Tristram; s of Sir Ernest Jones-Parry (d 1993), and Lady Mary Jones-Parry, *née* Powell (d 1997); *b* 23 July 1947; *Educ* Westminster, ChCh Oxford (exhibitioner); *Career* operational research NCB 1968–69, maths lectr and head of computing Dulwich Coll 1969–72; sometime head of maths, housemaster and undermaster Westminster Sch 1973–94, headmaster Emanuel Sch 1994–98, headmaster Westminster Sch 1998–2005; *Recreations* cycling, travelling, walking, reading; *Style*— Tristram Jones-Parry, Esq

JOPLING, Jay; s of Baron Jopling, PC, DL (Life Peer), *qv*, and Gail, *née* Dickinson; *Educ* Eton, Univ of Edinburgh; *m* 1997, Sam Taylor-Wood , *qv*; 1 da (Angelica b April 1997); *Career* opened White Cube 1993; *Style*— Jay Jopling, Esq; ✉ White Cube, 48 Hoxton Square, London N1 6PB (tel 020 7749 7491, fax 020 7749 7480)

JOPLING, Baron (Life Peer UK 1997), of Ainderby Quernhow in the County of North Yorkshire; (Thomas) Michael Jopling; PC (1979); s of late Mark Bellerby Jopling; *b* 10 December 1930; *Educ* Cheltenham Coll, King's Coll Newcastle, Univ of Durham (BSc); *m* 1958, Gail, da of late Ernest Dickinson; 2 s; *Career* farmer; memb Nat Cncl NFU 1962–64; MP (Cons): Westmorland 1964–83, Westmorland and Lonsdale 1983–97 (Parly candidate (Cons) Wakefield 1959); PPS to Min of Agric 1970–71, asst Govt whip 1971–73, a Lord Cmmr of the Treasy (Govt whip) 1973–74, oppn whip 1974, oppn spokesman on Agric 1974–79, shadow min for agric 1975–76, Parly sec to Treasy and Govt chief whip 1979–83, min of agric, fisheries and food 1983–87; memb: Foreign Affrs Select Ctee 1987–97, Int Exec Cwlth Parly Assoc 1988–89 (memb UK Exec 1974–79 and 1987–97, vice-chm 1977–79), Select Ctee on Sittings of the House (Jopling Report, chm 1991–92); pres EEC Cncls of Agric and Fishery Ministers 1986; hon sec Br American Parly Gp 1987–2001; memb UK Delegation NATO Parly Assemby 1987–97 and 2001–, ldr UK delegation OSCE Parly Assembly 1991–97; House of Lords: Select Ctee on EU Legislation 2000–03, Sub-Ctee D (Agriculture) 1997–99, Sub-Ctee C (Foreign Affrs and Defence) 2000–04 (chm 2001–04), Select Ctee on the Merits of Statutory Instruments 2004–, Sub-Ctee F (Home Office) 2006–; memb UK Exec Inter Parly Union 1997–; pres Auto Cycle Union 1988–2003; Hon DCL Univ of Newcastle 1992; DL: Cumbria 1991–97, N Yorks 1998–2005; *Style*— The Rt Hon Lord Jopling; ✉ Ainderby Hall, Thirsk, North Yorkshire YO7 4HZ; House of Lords, London SW1A 0PW

JORDAN, Andrew; s of Andrew Jordan (d 2003), of Belfast, and Bessie, *née* Gray (d 1977); *b* 12 March 1950; *Educ* Queen's Univ Belfast (BSc), Darwin Coll Cambridge (Dip Mathematical Statistics), Cranfield Sch of Mgmnt (MBA); *Career* statistician Unilever Research Ltd 1974–77, statistician Overseas Devpt Admin 1977–79, investment controller 3i 1980–84, ptnr PricewaterhouseCoopers (formerly Coopers & Lybrand before merger) 1985–2002; called to the Bar 2007; memn Hon Soc of the Inner Temple; chm of tstees The Migraine Tst 1996–; FRSS; *Recreations* skiing, waterskiing, opera, Cresta Run; *Clubs* St Moritz Tobogganing; *Style*— Andrew Jordan, Esq; ✉ 22 Northumberland Place, London W2 5BS (tel 020 7229 0546, e-mail andrew@ajordan.net)

JORDAN, Prof Dame Carole; DBE (2006); da of Reginald Sidney Jordan, and Ethel May, *née* Waller; *b* 19 July 1941; *Educ* Harrow Co GS for Girls, UCL (BSc, PhD); *Career* res assoc Jt Inst for Laboratory Astrophysics Univ of Colorado 1966, post doctoral appt UKAEA Culham Laboratory 1966–69; SRC's Astrophysics Res Unit Culham Laboratory: post doctoral res asst 1969–71, sr scientific offr 1971–73, princ scientific offr 1973–76; Univ of Oxford: former univ lectr Dept of Theoretical Physics, reader in physics 1994–96, prof of physics 1996–; fell and tutor in physics Somerville Coll Oxford 1976–; RAS: sec 1981–90, vice-pres 1990–91 and 1996–97, pres (first female to hold position) 1994–96; memb SERC 1985–90, memb PPARC 1994–97; FRAS 1966, memb IAU 1967, FInstP 1973, FRS 1990; *Recreations* gardening; *Style*— Prof Dame Carole Jordan, DBE, FRS; ✉ Department of Physics (Theoretical Physics), University of Oxford, 1 Keble Road, Oxford OX1 3NP (tel 01865 273980, fax 01865 273947)

JORDAN, Eddie; *b* 30 March 1948, Dublin; *m* Marie; 4 c (Zoe, Miki, Zak, Kyle); *Career* clerk Bank of Ireland 1967–70; racing driver: initially go-kart racing (winner Irish Kart Championship 1971), Formula Ford 1600 1974, Formula Atlantic 1977 (winner Irish Formula Atlantic Championship 1978), subsequently raced in Br Formula 3 series (as memb Team Ireland), world sport car champion (in a Porsche 908), then Formula 2 and test driver McLaren Formula 1 1979; fndr: Eddie Jordan Racing 1980 (raced in Britain (winners championship 1987, driver Johnny Herbert), European Formula 3 and Formula 3000 (champion 1989, driver Jean Alesi)), Jordan Grand Prix 1990–2005 (entered Formula 1 1991, one of only 5 teams to have won multiple Grands Prix in that time); *Publications* An Independent Man (autobiography, 2007); *Recreations* football, horse racing, rock and roll music, playing drums in band V10; *Style*— Eddie Jordan, Esq

JORDAN, (Michael) Guy; s of Maj Michael Edward Jordan, of Plymouth, Devon, and Elizabeth Marcia Dermot, *née* Harris; *b* 10 June 1955; *Educ* Downside, Univ of Durham; *m* 12 July 1980, Helena Mary, *née* Moore; 2 s (Adam b 11 Oct 1986, Miles b 20 April 1991), 1 da (Lucy b 13 Dec 1988); *Career* admitted slr 1980; ptnr Masons 1986–2004, ptnr Forsters 2004–; memb Law Soc 1980; *Recreations* field sports, sheep farming; *Clubs* Army and Navy; *Style*— Guy Jordan, Esq; ✉ Forsters, 31 Hill Street, London W1J 5LS (tel 020 7863 8333, e-mail mgjordan@forsters.co.uk)

JORDAN, Dr Michael John; s of Dr John Jordan (d 1963), of Kidderminster, Worcs, and Margaret Tuer Jordan, MBE, *née* Harper (d 1992); *b* 26 May 1949; *Educ* Malvern Coll, Trinity Hall Cambridge, St Thomas' Hosp Med Sch; *m* 12 May 1984, (Gena) Rosamund, da of Alan Rigby Horler; 3 da (Camilla b 1986, Olivia b 1988, Isobel b 1991); *Career* Anaesthetics Dept St Thomas' Hosp: SHO 1976, registrar 1977, sr registrar 1979; visiting asst prof of anaesthesiology Univ of Texas Dallas 1981–82; conslt anaesthetist Bart's 1983–95, clinical dir of anaesthesia St Peter's Hosp Chertsey 1999–2003 (conslt anaesthetist 1995–); FFARCS 1978; memb: Anaesthetic Res Soc, BMA, Assoc of Anaesthetists; *Recreations* photography, music, cinema, theatre; *Clubs* Athenaeum, Sette of Odd Volumes; *Style*— Dr Michael Jordan; ✉ North Down, 2 Fort Road, Guildford, Surrey GU1 3TB (tel 01483 567510, fax 01483 827489, e-mail mike_jordan@ntlworld.com); Department of Anaesthesia, St Peter's Hospital, Chertsey, Surrey KT16 0PZ (tel 01932 872000, mobile 07802 312244)

JORDAN, Terence Frank; s of Frank William Jordan, of Papworth Everard, Cambridge, and Morfydd Enid Jordan; *b* 16 October 1941; *Educ* Leicester Coll of Art and Design (DipArch); *m* 1, 1963 (m dis 1976), Christine Ann; 1 s (Simon David b 23 April 1972), 1 da (Elizabeth Ann b 25 March 1964); *m* 2, 7 April 1978, Anita Lesley, da of Douglas Richard Reed, of Cambridge; 1 s (Daniel Thomas b 24 Nov 1981), 1 da (Sarah Louise b 7 Sept 1986); *Career* fndr ptnr Clark and Jordan 1973–76, md Covell Matthews Wheatley 1985–92 (fndr dir 1976), dir CMW Group plc 1990–92, fndr ptnr T Jordan Assoc 1993–96, md Corp Services Arlington Securities plc 1997–2006, dir T Jordan Assoc Ltd 2007–; former memb Mgmnt Ctee Cambridge Preservation Soc, former chm Fin and Property Ctee 1978–84; RIBA, FRSA; *Recreations* music, golf, gardening; *Style*— Terence Jordan, Esq; ✉ Grove Cottage, 40 Church Street, Haslingfield, Cambridge CB3 7JE (tel 01223 872346, fax 01223 871432)

JORDAN, Baron (Life Peer UK 2000), of Bournville in the County of West Midlands; William Brian (Bill); CBE (1992); s of Walter Jordan (d 1974), and Alice, *née* Heath; *b* 28 January 1936; *Educ* Barford Rd Secdy Modern Birmingham; *m* 8 Nov 1958, Jean Ann, da of Ernest Livesey; 3 da (Pamela, Lisa, Dawn); *Career* former machine tool fitter GKN; pres AEEU 1986–95, gen sec Int Confedn of Free Trade Unions 1995–2001; formerly: memb NEDC, memb Gen Cncl and major ctees TUC, chair Euro-Strategy Ctee TUC, memb Exec Ctee and chair Engrg Ctee CSEU, pres Euro Metalworkers Fedn, memb Exec Cncl Int Metalworkers Fedn, memb Engrg Trg Authy, memb ACAS, memb UK Skills Cncl, memb Fndn for Mfrg and Industry, memb National Trg Task Force, NACETT, Duke of Edinburgh Conf Cncl; govr BBC 1988–98; currently: memb UN High Level Panel on Youth Employment, memb UN Global Compact Advsy Cncl, memb Cncl Industrial Soc, memb Cncl VSO, memb Br Overseas Trade Bd, memb Cncl Action Resource Centre, memb Invest in Br Campaign, vice-pres W Midland Productivity Assoc, govr LSE, Ashridge Mgmnt Coll, vice-pres Involvement and Participation Assoc (IPA), memb English Partnerships, memb Advsy Bd Victim Support, memb Cncl Winston Churchill Tst; chm English Partnerships Pension Scheme 2003; memb RIIA; tstee: Parly Tst, ReAction Tst; fell World Employment Forum; Hon Dr: Univ of Central England, Cranfield Univ; City and Guilds Insignia Award (hc); Hon FCGI; *Recreations* reading, most sports (particularly football, supporter Birmingham City FC); *Style*— The Rt Hon the Lord Jordan, CBE

JOSEPH, Bernard Michael; s of Harry Toby Joseph (d 1989), of London, and Esther, *née* Markson (d 1999); *b* 27 September 1948; *Educ* Bede GS for Boys; *m* 12 Oct 1980, Ruth Lesley-Ann, *née* Trent; 1 da (Danielle Natasha b 20 May 1983), 1 s (Darren Paul b 2 Sept 1985); *Career* CA; trainee Jennings Johnson 1971–75, Peat Marwick & Mitchell 1975–77, Nash Broad & Co 1977–79, sole practitioner 1979–88, ptnr Johnsons 1988–90, sr ptnr Joseph & Co 1990–; Freeman: City of London, Worshipful Co of CAs; FICA 1975; *Clubs* 41 (chm); *Style*— Bernard Joseph, Esq; ✉ 3 Hillersdon Avenue, Edgware, Middlesex HA8 7SG (tel 020 8905 3721); Joseph & Co, PO Box 199,Edgware, Middlesex HA8 7SG (tel 08707 104245, fax 0870 710 4245)

JOSEPH, His Hon Judge (Thomas John) Cedric; s of Thomas Rhees Joseph (d 1979), of St Dogmaels, Pembrokeshire, and Catherine Ann, *née* Davies (d 1997); *b* 25 August 1938; *Educ* Cardigan GS, LSE (LLB); *m* 12 Oct 1960, Mary, da of Harry Weston; 3 da (Sarah Jane, Catherine Mary, Emma Fiona); *Career* called to the Bar Gray's Inn 1960, crown counsel Malawi 1962–64, recorder 1992–94 (asst recorder 1987–92), circuit judge (South Eastern Circuit) 1994–, resident judge Croydon Crown Court 1998–2006; *Recreations* music, travel, collecting antique glass, wine, good food; *Clubs* Travellers; *Style*— His Hon Judge Joseph; ✉ Lewes Combined Court Centre, The Law Courts, High Street, Lewes BN17 1YB (tel 01273 485205)

JOSEPH, Derek Maurice; s of late Eugene Joseph, of London, and late Gertrude, *née* Enoch; *b* 10 December 1949; *Educ* Kilburn GS, Univ of Leeds (BCom); *m* 1980, Elizabeth, da of Charles Long; 1 da (Rosamond Amy b 6 June 1981), 1 s (Thomas Reuben b 24 April 1985); *Career* fin dir and sec Circle 33 Housing Tst 1975–79, md HACAS Group plc 1980–2003, dir Tribal Treasury Services 2003–; non-exec chm Wadharma Investment plc 2001–07; non-exec dir: Tilfen Land Ltd 2000–, Basepoint plc 2001–, General Industries plc 2003–; voluntary dir Homeless International, voluntary worker Preset; FCIS 1985, AIS 2005; *Publications* various books and articles incl: Private Finance Initiatives for Affordable Rental Housing (1997); *Recreations* theatre, travel, ardent supporter of Watford FC; *Style*— Derek Joseph, Esq; ✉ Tribal Treasury Services, The Clove Building, 4 Maguire Street, London SE1 2NQ (tel 020 7378 3030, fax 020 7378 3040, e-mail derek.joseph@tribalhch.co.uk)

JOSEPH, (Hon Sir) James Samuel Joseph; 3 Bt (UK 1943), of Portsoken, City of London; o s of Baron Joseph, CH, JP (Life Peer and 2 Bt; d 1994), and his 1 w, Hellen Louise, *née* Guggenheimer; *b* 27 January 1955; *Educ* Harrow; *Heir* s, Sam Joseph; *Style*— James Joseph, Esq

JOSEPH, Jane; da of Leonard Joseph (d 1989), and Hannah Joyce, *née* Stern; *b* 7 June 1942; *Educ* Downe House, Camberwell Sch of Arts and Crafts (NDD, Leverhulme travelling award); *Career* painter and printmaker; teacher principally at Morley Coll London; Abbey Award in Painting British Sch at Rome 1991 and 1995; *Solo Exhibitions* Morley Gallery London 1973, 1997 and 2000, The Minories Colchester 1982, Angela Flowers Gallery 1987, Flowers East 1989 and 1992, Edinburgh Printmakers 1994, Scarborough Art Gallery 1999, Hebrew Union Coll NY 2000, Italian Cultural Inst London 2000, Worcester City Art Gallery 2001, Victoria Art Gallery Bath 2002, Sch of Art Gallery Aberystwyth 2004; *Group Exhibitions* S Wales Gp 1971, Air Gallery 1981, Gardner Centre Univ of Sussex 1984, Imperial Coll London 1985, 100 Years - Artists and Morley (Morley Coll) 1990, Gardner Centre Univ of Sussex 1992, Artists Market, Cleveland Int Drawing Biennale, Int Print Biennale Bradford, London Gp, RA Summer Exhbns, Cheltenham Open Drawing Exhbns (Award winner 1998), Eagle Gallery London 2002, Artspace Gallery London 2004, Biennal of Graphic Arts Ljubljana 2005; *Work in Public Collections* Br Museum, Br Library, Castle Museum Norwich, Chelsea and Westminster Hosp, Govt Art Collection, Imperial Coll London, Univ of Northumbria at Newcastle, Unilever House, Brecknock Museum and Art Gallery Brecon, Paintings in Hosps, Ben Uri Gallery, New Hall Coll Cambridge, Fitzwilliam Museum Cambridge, Hebrew Union Coll NY, Worcester City Art Gallery, Lindley Library London, Nat Art Library, V&A, Yale Center for Br Art New Haven, Ashmolean Museum Oxford, Birmingham City Museum and Art Gallery, Sch of Art Gallery Aberystwyth; *Publications* A Little Flora of Common Plants (text by Mel Gooding); etchings accompanying If This is a Man and The Truce by Primo Levi; *Recreations* walking for observation; *Style*— Miss Jane Joseph; ✉ 6A Eynham Road, London W12 0HA (e-mail jane_joseph@yahoo.co.uk)

JOSEPH, Jenny; da of Louis Joseph (d 1979), and Florence Ethel, *née* Cotton (d 1989); *b* 7 May 1932; *Educ* Badminton Sch, St Hilda's Coll Oxford (scholar, BA); *m* Charles Anthony Coles (decd); 1 s (Martin Louis b 1961), 2 da (Penelope Clare b 1963, Rebecca Ruth b 1965); *Career* poet, writer, broadcaster and lectr; newspaper reporter: Bedfordshire Times, Oxford Mail, Drum Publications (Johannesburg, South Africa); awarded travelling scholarship Soc of Authors 1995, FRSL; *Books* The Unlooked-for Season (1960, Gregory Award), Rose in the Afternoon and Other Poems (1974, Cholmondeley Award), The Thinking Heart (1978), Beyond Descartes (1983), Persephone: A Story (1986, James Tait Black Meml Award for Fiction), The Inland Sea (1989), Beached Boats (with photographs by Robert Mitchell, 1991), Selected Poems (1992), Ghosts and Other Company (1995), Extended Similes (1997), Warning (1997), Led by the Nose (2002), Extreme of Things (2006); for children (with Katherine Hoskyns): Boots (1966), Wheels (1966), Wind (1967), Water (1967), Tea (1968), Sunday (1968), All the Things I See (2000); *Style*— Miss Jenny Joseph; ✉ 17 Windmill Road, Minchinhampton, Gloucestershire GL6 9DX; c/o Johnson and Alcock Ltd, Clerkenwell House, 45–47 Clerkenwell Green, London EC1R 0HT

JOSEPH, Joe; *b* 20 May 1955; *m* Jane Louise, *née* Winterbotham; 2 s (Thomas Daniel b 20 Nov 1989, Charles Benjamin b 2 Dec 1992), 1 da (Eliza Rose b 6 March 1995); *Career* formerly with Reuters News Agency (London, NY), chief TV critic, feature writer and columnist The Times (formerly Tokyo corr); *Books* The Japanese: Strange but not Strangers (1993); *Style*— Joe Joseph, Esq; ✉ The Times, 1 Pennington Street, London E98 1TT (tel 020 7782 5000)

JOSEPH, Julian; *b* 1966; *Educ* Interchange's Weekend Arts Course Kentish Town, Berklee Sch of Music Boston (ILEA scholar, BA); *Career* pianist, composer; fndr: own quartet 1990, Julian Joseph Trio, Forum Project (8 piece), Electric Project; int tours of USA, Canada, Bermuda, India, Australia, Europe and Caribbean as a soloist and with Branford Marsalis, Wynton Marsalis, Bobby McFerrin, Joe Williams, George Coleman, Chico Freemen, Arthur Blyth, Gary Bartz, Courtney Pine; festival appearances incl: Montreaux Jazz, North Sea, Nancy, Tourcoin, Brecon, Glasgow, Aldeburgh, City of London,

J

Cheltenham, Bermuda, Audi Munich Piano Summer, House of Culture of the World (Berlin), St Lucia Jazz, Arundel; projects incl: The Two Sides of Julian Joseph Weekend Barbican 1994 (Classics meets Jazz with Royal Philharmonic Concert Orch, Total Jazz with Julian Joseph Big Band), Julian Joseph Jazz Series Wigmore Hall 1994 with Johnny Griffin, Eddie Daniels, Andy Sheppard and Jason Rebello, Ronnie Scott's Club, Jazz Café, Sweet Basils NY, BBC Proms Royal Albert Hall 1995, Concertgebouw Amsterdam 1996, Queen Elizabeth Hall (premier performance of Electric Project) 1996, City of London Festival concert series with London Symphony (performing Gershwin's Rhapsody in Blue), concert series with Residence Orkest Hague 1996 (performance of Gershwin's Second Rhapsody), recital at Bridgwater Hall 1997; presenter eight-part television series Jazz with Julian Joseph (Meridian) 2000; writer and presenter Jazz Legends (BBC Radio 3) 2000–; *Recordings* The Language of Truth 1991, Reality 1993, Julian Joseph in Concert at the Wigmore Hall 1995, Universal Traveller 1996; patron Jazz Devpt Tst 1998–; *Style—* Julian Joseph, Esq; ✉ c/o James Joseph Music Management, 85 Cicada Road, Wandsworth, London SW18 2PA (tel 020 8874 8647, fax 020 8877 1678, e-mail jj3@jamesjoseph.co.uk, website www.jamesjoseph.co.uk)

JOSEPH, Michael Peter; s of Edward Albert Joseph (d 1959), and Eleonore Cecilie Therese, *née* Seffers; *b* 28 May 1941; *Educ* Michaelhouse Balgowan, London Coll of Printing and Graphic Arts; *m* Julia Lillian, da of George Mallison Hogg (ka 1944); 2 da (Joanna Victoria b 22 Oct 1971, Justine Samantha b 14 Nov 1972), 1 s (Jay Edward Jonathon b 14 June 1974); *Career* advtg and portrait photographer; early career experience as reportage photographer; cmmnd by Town magazine to cover shark fishing in Ireland, the primative painters Chesher, Lloyd and Holzhandler 1963 and to cover the Vietnam War 1964 (photos bought by Paris Match, Sunday Times, The Guardian and The Mirror); subsequent advtg cmmns for clients incl: Aer Lingus, Benson & Hedges, Ford Cars, White Horse Whiskey; other assignments incl Beggars Banquet album cover (Rolling Stones); co-fndr TV prodn co Joseph Dixon Hogg, estab photographic studio Clapham Common 1980; numerous D&AD awards for advtg campaigns; memb Assoc of Photographers (vice-chm 1968); *Exhibitions* Faces of the Century (National Portrait Gall) 2000, The Stones Collection (Atlas Gall London), Rolling Stones Iris Prints (Govinda Gall Washington), Rock and Roll Images (San Francisco Art Exchange); *Books* The World of Children (main contrib, 1966), Complete Photography Course (1993), Illustrated Hitchhiker's Guide to the Galaxy (1994); *Recreations* sailing, tennis and primarily photography; *Style—* Michael Joseph, Esq

JOSEPH, Richard Lewis; s of Alfred Joseph (d 1967), of London, and Rose Sarah, *née* Melzack; *b* 24 July 1949; *Educ* Algernon Road Sch, Haberdashers' Aske's Sch; *m* March 1974, Linda Carol, da of Frank Hyams; 1 da (Danielle Frances b July 1978), 1 s (Mark Alan b Nov 1981); *Career* articled clerk: Lewis Bloom, Blick Rothenberg & Noble; qualified chartered accountant 1972, Stoy Hayward & Co 1972, Elliott Woolfe & Rose 1977–78, fin controller Unit Tst Gp 1978–82, private practice 1978–; fndr Micro Computer Gp of N London, chm Ctee N London Soc of CAs 1990–91 (joined 1986); London Soc of Chartered Accountants: chm 2000–01, chm Communications Ctee 1998–99, hon sec 2004–; chm LSCA Ed Bd 1992–96, memb Support Task Force ICAEW 1995–96, memb Ctee Edgware and Burnt Oak C of C; FCA (ACA 1972); *Recreations* golf, music, cricket, football, rock and blues guitarist; *Clubs* Elstree Golf; *Style—* Richard Joseph, Esq; ✉ Richard Joseph & Co, 2nd Floor, 65 Station Road, Edgware, Middlesex HA8 7HX (tel 020 8952 5407, fax 020 8951 0779, e-mail rlj@richardjoseph.co.uk)

JOSEPH, Wendy Rose; QC 1998; da of Norman Joseph (d 1969), and Carole Esther, *née* Marks (d 2005); *Educ* Cathays HS for Girls, Westridge Sch for Girls Pasadena CA, New Hall Cambridge; *Career* called to the Bar Gray's Inn 1975 (bencher 2004); recorder 1999 (asst recorder 1995); pres Mental Health Review Tbnl 2001; *Recreations* literature, classical music; *Style—* Ms Wendy Joseph, QC; ✉ 6 King's Bench Walk, Temple, London EC4Y 7DR (tel 020 7583 0410, fax 020 7353 8791)

JOSHI, Prof Heather Evelyn; OBE (2002); da of Guy Malcolm Spooner, MBE (d 1989), and Molly Florence Spooner, MBE (d 1997); *b* 21 April 1946; *Educ* Tavistock Sch, St Hilda's Coll Oxford (MA), St Antony's Coll Oxford (MLitt); *m* 1, 26 June 1969 (m dis 1977), Vijay Ramchandra Joshi; m 2, 14 Oct 1982, Gregory Martin; 1 da (Julia Florence b 11 July 1982), 1 s (Benjamin William Malcolm b 8 Nov 1985); *Career* asst res offr Inst of Economics and Statistics Univ of Oxford 1969–73, economic advsr Govt Economic Serv 1973–79, sr res fell Centre for Population Studies LSHTM 1979–87, sr research fell Dept of Economics Birkbeck Coll London 1987–89, sr lectr Centre for Population Studies LSHTM 1990–93, sr lectr then prof Social Statistical Research Unit City Univ 1993–98; Inst of Educn Univ of London: prof 1998–, dir Centre for Longitudinal Studies 2003– (dep dir 1998–2003); dir ESRC Millennium Cohort Study; pres: Euro Soc for Population Economics 1996 (memb 1985–), Br Soc for Population Studies 2000 (memb 1976–); memb Royal Economic Soc 1970 (chair Ctee on Women in Economics 2001–04); AcSS 2000, FBA 2000; *Books* The Changing Population of Britain (ed, 1989), The Tale of Mrs Typical (jtly, 1996), Unequal Pay (jtly, 1998), Women's Incomes over the Lifetime (jtly, 2000), Children of the Twenty-First Century (jtly, 2005); *Recreations* walking, listening to music; *Style—* Prof Heather Joshi, OBE; ✉ Institute of Education, 20 Bedford Way, London WC1H 0AL (tel 020 7612 6874, fax 020 7612 6880, e-mail h.joshi@ioe.ac.uk)

JOSHI, Sanjay; s of R K Joshi and Kirin Joshi; *b* 2 May 1961; *Educ* Univ of Kent at Canterbury (BA(Econ), MA(Econ)); *m* Ranmali Deepika, *née* Ratnatunga; 1 s (Ravi), 1 da (Selina); *Career* research offr and lectr City Univ Business Sch 1984–86, sr economist CBI 1986–87, sr economist Baring Bros 1987–90, chief economist and head of bond research Daiwa Europe Ltd 1990–98, sr strategist SPP Investment Management 1998, currently head of fixed income London & Capital; regular pubns: Quarterly Fixed Income Strategy, Yen Weekly, Relative Value Perspective; regular portfolio selection The Economist 1990–; also contrib: CBI Economic Situation Report, Euromoney, IFR; memb: Nat Assoc for Business Economists, UK Soc for Business Economists (SBE), Harlequins RFC, memb Brentham CC; ECB level 1 coach; *Style—* Sanjay Joshi, Esq

JOSHUA, Rosemary; *Educ* Royal Coll of Music; *Career* soprano; *Performances* incl: Blonde in Die Entführung aus dem Serail (Buxton Festival), Zerlina in Don Giovanni (Scottish Opera), Adele in Die Fledermaus (ENO), Yum Yum in The Mikado (ENO), Norina in Don Pasquale (ENO), title role in Princess Ida (ENO), Pamina in The Magic Flute (Covent Garden Festival and Opera N Ireland, Brussels), Angelica in Orlando (Aix-en-Provence Festival), Sophie in Der Rosenkavalier (ENO, Deutsche Opera Berlin), Poussette in Manon (Royal Opera House), Poppea in Agrippa (Cologne Opera, Brussels and Paris), Susanna in Marriage of Figaro (Cologne Opera), Ilia in Idomeneo (Lisbon), Calisto title role in La Monnaie (Brussel), title role in Semele (BBC Proms1996, Aix-en-Provence, Innsbruck Festival, Flanders Opera and ENO), Gianetta in The Gondoliers (BBC Proms) 1997, Susanna in Le Nozze di Figaro, Susanna and Anne Trulove (Glyndebourne Festival), Cleopatra in Giulio Cesare (Florida), Juliet in Romeo and Juliet (San Diego), title role in The Cunning Little Vixen (Flanders Opera and the Theatre des Champs Elysées; future roles incl: Adele in Die Fledermaus (Metropolitan Opera New York), Euridice in Orfeo et Euridice, Micael in Saul, Sophie and Susanna (all at the Bavarian State Opera Munich) *Recordings* Orlando (with Les Arts Florissants and William Christie), Venus and Adonis (with René Jacobs), Sophie in Der Rosenkavalier, Sandman in Hansel und Gretel, Dido et Aeneas (with René Jacabs); *Awards* winner: Van Der Beugel Opera Prize, Royal Philharmonic Soc Debut Award 1992, Gold medal RCM; nominated for Laurence Olivier Award for Outstanding Achievement in Opera; *Style—* Ms Rosemary Joshua; ✉ c/o Askonas Holt, Lonsdale Chambers, 27 Chancery Lane London WC2A 1PF

JOSIPOVICI, Prof Gabriel David; s of Jean Josipovici, and Sacha Elena, *née* Rabinovitch; *b* 8 October 1940; *Educ* Victoria Coll Cairo, Cheltenham Coll, St Edmund Hall Oxford; *Career* prof Univ of Sussex 1984– (formerly lectr and reader), Lord Weidenfeld prof of comparative literature Univ of Oxford 1996–97; author; FRSL 1998, FBA 2001; *Plays* for the stage incl: Dreams of Mrs Fraser (Theatre Upstairs) 1972, Flow (Edinburgh Lyceum) 1973, Marathon (ICA) 1978; radio plays incl: Playback (1972), AG (1977), Vergil Dying (1980), Mr Vee (1989); *Books* The Inventory (1968), The World and The Book (1971), Mobius the Stripper (1975), Migrations (1977), Conversations in Another Room (1984), Contre-Jour (1986), In the Fertile Land (1987), The Book of God: A Response to the Bible (1988), Steps: Selected Fiction and Drama (1990), The Big Glass (1991), Text and Voice: Essays 1981–91 (1992), In a Hotel Garden (1993), Moo Pak (1994), Touch (1996), Now (1998), On Trust (1999), A Life (2001), Goldberg: Variations (2002), The Singer on the Shore: Essays (2006), Everything Passes (2006); *Style—* Prof Gabriel Josipovici; ✉ University of Sussex, Arts Building, Falmer, Brighton, East Sussex BN1 9SH (tel 01273 606755)

JOSLIN, Paul; s of Edgar Alfred (d 1958), and Mary Elizabeth Elsie, *née* Buckeridge; *b* 20 November 1950; *Educ* City of Portsmouth Tech HS, Royal Coll of Music (GRSM, LRAM, ARCM), Univ of Reading (MMus); *m* 2 August 1975, Gwenllian Elfyn, da of Rev Ifor Elfyn Ellis (d 2001), of St Asaph, N Wales; *Career* organist and dir of music St Paul's Onslow Sq London 1972–77; Holy Trinity Brompton London: associate dir of music 1977–79, organist and dir 1979–92; organist and dir: St Luke's Redcliffe Sq SW10 1992–97, St Jude Courtfield Gdns 1997–98; organist St Marylebone Crematorium London 2005– (actg organist 2004); asst conductor Brompton Choral Soc 1977–81, actg dir of music St Catherine Sch Twickenham 1993; solo and organ accompanist; continuo work with London Bach Orch, Thames Chamber Orch and English Chorale, concerto soloist with and memb of English Chamber Orch, choral and orchestral conductor BBC Radio and TV (team organist and dir Daily Service 1989–94, organist Rome Pilgrimage Daily Service Tour 1992, Songs of Praise 2004–05, Sunday Worship 2004–05); dir of music (St Paul's Cathedral): Let's Celebrate 1993–96, London Bridges 1997, Feast of the Kingdom 1998, Partners in Mission 2000; vice-pres London Organist Guild 1994–, visiting lectr Univ of Reading 1994–95; memb Cncl Br Inst of Organ Studies 1997–2001 (co-ordinator Historic Organ Scheme 2003–); recordings for Historic Organ Sound Archive Chelmsford Birchanger 2006; *Recreations* architecture, swimming, 35mm photography, collection 78rpm classical records; *Style—* Paul Joslin, Esq; ✉ 109 Hanover Road, London NW10 3DN (tel 020 8459 5547)

JOSS, Timothy Hans (Tim); *b* 27 June 1955; *Educ* Harrow, The Queen's Coll Oxford, Univ of Grenoble, RAM; *m* 1983, Elizabeth Morag, *née* Wallace; 1 da (Hannah b 18 May 1987); *Career* Live Music Now! 1980–82, music and dance offr NW Arts 1982–89, concerts dir Bournemouth Sinfonietta rising to sr mangr Bournemouth Orchs 1989–93, dir Bath Festivals Tst 1993–2003; chm: Cmmn for Community Music Int Soc for Music Educn 1992–94, Br Arts Festivals Assoc 1998–; dir Rayne Fndn 2005–; memb Bd: London Sinfonietta 2003–, Richard Feilden Fndn 2005–; FRSA; Chevalier dans l'Ordre des Arts et des Lettres 2007; *Books* Directory of Community Music (1993); *Style—* Tim Joss; ✉ The Rayne Foundation, Carlton House, 33 Robert Adam Street, London W1U 3HR (tel 020 7487 9650, fax 020 7935 3737, e-mail tjoss@raynefoundation.org.uk)

JOSSE, Dr (Silvain) Edouard; OBE (1983); s of Albert Josse (d 2001), of London, and Charlotte, *née* Karolicki (d 2000); *b* 8 May 1933; *Educ* Highgate Sch, Middx Hosp Med Sch, Univ of London (MB BS, MRCS, LRCP); *m* 1, 15 May 1960 (m dis 1983), Lea, da of Alter Majer Ber (d 1977); 2 s (David b 22 July 1961, Jeremy b 14 July 1968), 1 da (Anna b 19 Sept 1964); m 2, 27 Oct 1991, Yvonne, da of Harry Levine (d 1970); *Career* gen med practitioner 1962 (ret 1996), princ forensic med examiner Metropolitan Police 1965, Tst Respiratory Physician Noth Middx Hosp, former regnl advsr in gen practice and assoc dean of postgrad med N Thames (E) Region Br Postgrad Med Fedn Univ of London 1974–95, former GP memb NE Thames RHA; former chm: Enfield and Haringey Local Med Ctee, Jt Ctee on Postgrad Training for Gen Practice; former memb: Standing Ctee on Postgrad Med and Dental Educn, Enfield and Haringey Family Practitioners' Ctee; sec gen UEMO 1982–86; memb Expert Witness Inst, Soc of Expert Witnesses (memb Cncl); pres RSM Section for GP 2001–02; Liveryman Worshipful Soc of Apothecaries; MA London 1989; memb RSM 1978 (Cncl 1997–2001); fell BMA 2002 (memb 1956–); FRCGP 1977, DMJ 1970, FACBS 2004, FFFLM 2005, FZS, AFP (pres 1998–2000), MLS, BAFS (memb Cncl 2003–05), MAE; *Recreations* skiing, gardening, history, good wine and malt whisky tasting; *Clubs* MCC, Middx CC, RAC; *Style—* Dr Edouard Josse, OBE; ✉ 2 Shirehall Gardens, London NW4 2QS (tel 020 8202 7740, fax 020 8903 9891, mobile 07966 531334, e-mail eddiejosse@aol.com)

JOST, Professor H Peter; CBE (1969); s of Leo Jost (d 1941); *b* 25 January 1921; *Educ* Liverpool Tech Coll, Manchester Coll of Technol; *m* 1948, Margaret Josephine, da of Michael Kadesh (d 1952); 2 da; *Career* planning engr D Napier & Son Ltd 1943, methods engr K & L Steelfounders & Engrs Ltd 1946–55, gen mangr and dir Trier Bros Ltd 1955–60, lubrication conslt August Thyssen Hutte AG 1963–66; chm: Bright Breezing Ltd 1969–76, Peppermill Brass Foundry Ltd 1970–76, Centralube Ltd 1974–77 (md 1955–77), K S Paul Group 1973–2000 (md 1955–89), Associated Technology Group Ltd 1977–, Engrg and Gen Equipment Ltd 1977–2006, Eley Estate Co Ltd 1989–2001; dir: Williams Hudson Ltd 1967–75, Stothert & Pitt plc 1971–75, Fuchs Lubritech Int 2000–03; Lord President's nominee for Ct Univ of Salford 1971–87 (memb Cncl 1974–84), chm Manchester Technol Assoc in London 1976–87; Parly and Scientific Ctee: memb 1976–, memb Cncl 1983–, hon sec 1990–93, vice-pres 1993–95 and 1998–2001, vice-chm 1995–98, life memb 2002; pres: Int Tribology Cncl 1973–, Inst of Prodn Engrs 1977–78 (chm Tech Policy Bd 1974–76, vice-pres 1975–77), Manchester Technol Assoc 1984–85 (dep pres 1983); vice-pres Inst of Mech Engrs 1987–92 (memb Cncl 1974–92, chm Fin Bd 1988–90); memb Bd and Exec Ctee Cncl Engrg Instns 1977–84 (chm Home Affrs Ctee 1980–83), memb FCO Consultative Gp on Science and Technol 1994–; life fell Soc of Mfrg Engrs (USA) 1988 (life memb 1977), memb Ct Univ of Middlesex 1996–; hon industrial prof Liverpool John Moores Univ (formerly Liverpool Poly) 1983–, hon prof of mech engrg Univ of Wales 1986–; chm: Lubrication Educn and Res Working Gp Dept of Educn and Sci 1964–65, Ctee on Tribology Miny of Technol DTI 1966–74, Industrial Technologies Mgmnt Bd DTI 1972–74; memb: Advsy Cncl on Technol Miny of Technol and DTI 1968–70, Ctee on Terotechnology DTI 1971–72 (fndr), Fndn for Sci and Technol 1985–89, Parly Gp for Engrg Devpt 1986–, Sci and Technol Consultitative Gp FCO 1994–; chm of tstees Michael John Tst 1986–; Liveryman Worshipful Co of Engrs 1984, Freeman City of London 1984; hon memb: Inst of Plant Engrs 1969, Societe Tribologique de France 1972, Gesellschaft für Tribologie (FGR) 1972, Chinese Mechanical Engrg Soc 1986 (one of first eight foreign membs), Nat Tribology Cncl of Bulgaria 1991, Japanese Soc of Tribologists 1992, Slovak Tribology Soc 1993, Ukranian Acad of Tport 1994, Polish Tribological Soc 1995; hon foreign memb: Russian Acad of Engrs 1991 (first hon foreign memb), Belarus Acad of Engrg and Technology 1996; hon life memb STLE (USA) 1997; hon fell Univ of Central Lancs 2003; Hon DSc Univ of Salford 1970, Hon DTech CNAA 1987, Hon DSc Slovak Univ 1987, Hon DEng Univ of Leeds 1989, Hon DSc Univ of Bath 1990, Hon DSc Tech Univ Budapest 1993, Hon DSc Belarus Acad of Sciences 2000, Hon DEng UMIST 2004; Hon FIEE 1980 (life memb Cncl), Hon FASME 1986; State Legislative Commendation of State of California (USA) 1978, Gold Insignia of Order of Merit of Polish People's Republic 1986, Offr Cross of Order of Merit Fed Republic of Germany 1992, Officier de l'Ordre des Palmes Académique (France) 1995, Austrian Decoration of

Hon for Sci and Art (1st class) 2001; *Awards* Hutchinson Meml Medal for best paper by a graduate IProdE 1952, Silver Medal for best paper by a member IProdE 1952, Derby Medal Liverpool Engrg Soc 1955, Tribute for Scientific Achievement Polisch Cncl of Engrg Institutions 1977, Merit Medal Hungarian Scientific Soc of Mech Engrs 1983, Gold Medal Slovak Tech Univ 1984, Georg Vogelpohl Insignia German Tribology Soc 1979, 1st Nuffield Medal IProdE 1981, Entry in Roll of Honour Belarussian Acad of Sci 1989, Colclough Medal and Prize Inst of Materials 1992, Louw Alberts Award South African Inst of Tribology 1992, Int Award Soc of Tribologists and Lubrication Engrs USA 1997; *Recreations* music, gardening; *Clubs* Athenaeum; *Style*— Professor H Peter Jost, CBE; ✉ Hill House, Wills Grove, Mill Hill, London NW7 1QL (tel 020 8959 3355); Angel Lodge Chambers, 57 London Road, Enfield, Middlesex EN2 6DU (tel 020 3213 1030, fax 020 3213 1040)

JOURDAN, Martin Henry; s of Henry George Jourdan (d 1990), of Dumfries, Scotland, and Jocelyn Louise, *née* Courtney (d 1962); *b* 7 October 1941; *Educ* Bishopshalt GS, Guy's Hosp Med Sch (MB BS, BSc, LRCP, PhD, MS); *m* 22 Oct 1966, May, da of John McElwain (d 1960), of Glasgow; 2 s (Iain Campbell b 1967, Adam Ramsay b 1985), 2 da (Anthea b 1969, Gabrielle b 1970); *Career* conslt surgn Guy's Hosp 1978–, external examiner in surgery to Univs of Bristol and W Indies 1978–87, reader in surgery Univ of London 1982, sub-dean Guy's Hosp Med Sch 1984–89, sr examiner in surgery Univ of London 1984–, memb Ct of Examiners RCS 1986–; Freeman City of London, Master Worshipful Soc of Apothecaries of London (memb Ct of Assts 2001–02); memb BMA, Surgical Res Soc Assoc of Surgns; FRSM, FRCS; *Recreations* tennis, reading, opera; *Clubs* Athenaeum; *Style*— Martin Jourdan, Esq; ✉ 55 Shirlock Road, Hampstead, London NW3 2HR (tel 020 7267 1582); Department of Surgery, St Thomas' Hospital, London SE1 7EH (tel 020 7928 9292 ext 1003, private room 020 7403 3817)

JOWELL, Prof Jeffrey Lionel; Hon QC (1993); s of Jack and Emily Jowell, of Cape Town, SA; *b* 4 November 1938; *Educ* Univ of Cape Town (BA, LLB), Hertford Coll Oxford (MA, pres Oxford Union 1963), Harvard Law Sch (LLM, SJD); *m* 8 Dec 1963, Frances Barbara, da of Dr Moses Suzman, of Johannesburg, South Africa, and Helen Suzman, DBE; 1 da (Joanna b 2 Sept 1967), 1 s (Daniel b 11 June 1969); *Career* called to the Bar Middle Temple 1965; res asst Harvard Law Sch 1966–68, fell Jt Centre Urban Studies Harvard and MIT 1967–68, assoc prof of law and admin studies York Univ Toronto 1968–71; LSE: Leverhulme fell in urban legal studies 1972–74, lectr in law 1974–75; UCL: prof of public law 1975–2006, dean Faculty of Law 1979–89 and 1998–2002 (head of dept 1982–89 and 1998–2002), vice-provost and head Grad Sch 1992–99, prof of law 2006–; Venice Cmmn (European Cmmn for Democracy Through Law): UK memb 2000–, memb Governing Bd 2001–, vice-pres 2003–06; memb Royal Cmmn on Environmental Pollution 2003–, non-exec dir Office of Rail Regulation 2004–, chair Br Waterways Ombudsman Ctee 2005–; Lionel Cohen lectr in Hebrew Univ of Jerusalem 1986; visiting prof: Univ of Paris 1991, Univ of Aix-Marseilles 2002, Columbia Law Sch NY 2002; hon prof Univ of Cape Town 1999–2006; non-exec dir: UCL Press 1994–95, Camden and Islington Community Health Tst 1994–97; SSRC: chm Social Science and Law Ctee 1981–84, vice-chm Govt and Law Ctee 1982–84; memb: Nuffield Ctee Town and Country Planning 1983–86, Bd Inst of Cwlth Studies 1994–99, Cncl Justice 1997–, Bd Chancellor's Ctee to review Crown Office List 1999; chm Ctee of Heads Univ Law Schs 1984–86; Br delegate CSCE Conf Oslo 1991; chm Inst of Philanthropy 2000–04; tstee: John Foster Meml Tst 1986–, Int Centre for Public Law 1993–97, Prince of Wales's Inst of Architecture 1997–99, Prince of Wales's Fndn for Architecture and the Urban Environment 1998–99; chair Friends of the South African Constitutional Court Tst 2003–; memb editorial bds of various jls, convenor of numerous int workshops and confs on constitutional law and democratic principles, assisted with the drafting of various nat constitutions; hon fell UCL 1997, hon bencher Middle Temple 1999; Hon DJur Univ of Athens 1987, Hon LLD Univ of Ritsumeikan 1988, Hon LLD Univ of Cape Town 2000; *Books* Law and Bureaucracy (1975), Lord Denning: The Judge And The Law (jt ed, 1984), The Changing Constitution (jt ed, 1985, 1989, 1994, 2000, 2004 and 2007), Judicial Review of Administrative Action (jt author, 1995 and 2007), Principles of Judicial Review (jt author, 1999), Understanding Human Rights Principles (jt ed, 2001), Delivering Rights (jt ed, 2003); numerous articles and reviews on public law, human rights and planning law; *Recreations* tennis, Exmoor and London; *Style*— Prof Jeffrey Jowell QC; ✉ Blackstone Chambers, Middle Temple, London EC4Y 9BW (tel 020 7583 1770)

JOWELL, Rt Hon Tessa; PC (1998), MP; da of Dr Kenneth Palmer, and Rosemary Palmer; *b* 17 September 1947; *Educ* St Margaret's Sch Aberdeen, Univ of Aberdeen, Univ of Edinburgh, Goldsmiths Coll London; *m* 17 March 1979, David Mills; 1 s, 1 da, 3 step c; *Career* child care offr London Borough of Lambeth 1969–71, psychiatric social worker The Maudsley Hosp Camberwell 1972–74, asst dir MIND 1974–86, dir Community Care Special Action Project Birmingham 1987–90, dir Joseph Rowntree Fndn Community Care Programme 1990–92; Parly candidate Ilford N 1979; MP (Lab): Dulwich 1992–97, Dulwich and West Norwood 1997–; min of state for public health Dept of Health and spokesperson for Women in the Commons 1997–1999, min of state for employment DfEE 1999–2001, sec of state for Culture, Media and Sport 2001–07, min for women 2005–06, min for the Olympics and London 2005–, currently min with responsibility for humanitarian assistance; cmmr for Mental Health Act 1985–90; cncllr London Borough of Camden 1971–86, vice-chm then chm Social Servs Ctee Assoc of Met Authorities 1978–86, govr Nat Inst for Social Work 1985–97; visiting fell Nuffield Coll Oxford 1993–2002, visiting sr fell Policy Studies Inst 1986–90, visiting sr fell King's Fund 1990–92; *Style*— The Rt Hon Tessa Jowell, MP; ✉ House of Commons, London SW1A 0AA

JOWITT, Prof Paul William; s of late Stanley Jowitt, of Thurcroft, S Yorks, and late Joan Mary, *née* Goundry; *b* 3 August 1950; *Educ* Maltby GS, Imperial Coll London (BSc, PhD); *m* 11 Aug 1973, Jane Catriona, da of late Lt Ronald George Urquhart, of Romford, Essex; 1 s (Christopher b 17 Feb 1978), 1 da (Hannah b 29 June 1980); *Career* lectr in civil engrg Imperial Coll 1974–86 (warden Falmouth Hall 1980–86), chm Tynemarch Systems Engineering Ltd 1984–86 (dir 1984–91), ed Journal of Civil Engineering Systems 1985–; Heriot-Watt Univ: prof 1987–, head Dept of Civil Engrg 1988–91, head Dept of Civil and Offshore Engrg 1991–99; vice-pres ICE 2004, dir Scottish Inst of Sustainable Technol, memb Scotland Water; author of various specialist tech pubns and jl articles; memb various nat and local assoc ctees ICE; CEng 1988, FICE 1994 (MICE 1988), FRSA 1996, FRSE 2005, FCGI 2006; *Recreations* painting, Morgan 3-wheelers, restoring old houses; *Clubs* Chaps, Links, MTWC; *Style*— Prof Paul Jowitt; ✉ 14 Belford Mews, Edinburgh EH4 3BT; SISTech, Heriot-Watt University, Edinburgh EH14 4AS (tel 0131 451 3143, fax 0131 451 8150, e-mail p.w.jowitt@hw.ac.uk)

JOWITT, Peter John Russell; s of Harold John Duncan Mackintosh Jowitt (d 1999), of Southwell, Notts, and Kathleen Joyce, *née* Clark (d 2005); *b* 30 July 1942; *Educ* Bryanston, Univ of Nottingham (BEd), Univ of Cambridge (Cert ICT); *Career* asst master Cheltenham Coll 1979–82, dep headmaster Cokethorpe Sch 1982–84, head of modern languages Claire's Court Sch 1985–89, dir Monksoft Ltd 1988–91, researcher Language Centre Univ of Buckingham 1989–91, head of modern languages St Edmund's Sch Hindhead 1991–96, head of ICT Thomas's Prep Battersea 1996–2000; memb Ctee Nat Sch's Regatta 1973–, selector GB Jr Rowing Team 1974–76, chm Jr Rowing Ctee and memb Exec Ctee Amateur Rowing Assoc 1978–79, memb Jr Cmmn FISA 1979–84 (holder umpire's licence 1971–2007); chef de mission Moscow 1979, chm Kitchin Soc 1989–91 (sec 1986–89); LRPS 1993; *Recreations* photography, ocean racing, rowing administration; *Clubs* Lloyd's Yacht, Leander, London Rowing; *Style*— Peter Jowitt, Esq; ✉ 27 Woodfield Gardens, Belmont, Hereford HR2 9RN (tel 01432 360612, e-mail pj@jowitt.org.uk)

JOYCE, Prof Dominic; *b* 8 April 1968; *Educ* Queen Elizabeth's Hosp Bristol, Merton Coll Oxford (postmaster, sr scholar, Jr Mathematical Prize, Sr Mathematical Prize, Johnson Univ Prize, DPhil); *m* Jayne; 2 da (Matilda b 28 Aug 2000, Katharine b 2 July 2003); *Career* jr research fell ChCh Oxford 1992–95, research memb Inst for Advanced Study Princeton 1993–94 (year abroad, also worked at Mathematical Sciences Research Inst (MSRI) Berkeley); Univ of Oxford: lectr in pure mathematics 1995–, prof of mathematics 2002–; tutorial fell in mathematics Lincoln Coll Oxford 1995–2006; EPSRC advanced research fell 2001–06; author of numerous conf proceedings, papers and articles in books and learned jls; second prize British Mathematical Olympiad 1986, Silver medal Int Mathematical Olympiad Warsaw 1986 (memb British team), Bronze medal Int Physics Olympiad London 1986 (memb British team); Jr Whitehead Prize London Mathematical Soc 1997, prize for young European mathematicians European Mathematical Soc 2000, Adams Prize 2004; *Books* Compact Manifolds with Special Holonomy (2000), Calabi-Yau Manifolds and Related Geometries (jtly, 2003), Riemannian Holonomy Groups and Calibrated Geometry (2007); *Style*— Prof Dominic Joyce; ✉ Lincoln College, Oxford OX1 3DR; Mathematical Institute, 24–29 St Giles', Oxford OX1 3LB

JOYCE, Eric Stuart; MP; s of Leslie Joyce (d 1977), and Sheila McKay, *née* Christie; *b* 13 October 1960; *Educ* Univ of Stirling (BA), Perth Acad (PGCE), Univ of Bath (MA), Keele Univ (MBA); *m* 1, 1978 (m dis 1982), Christine Louise, *née* Guest; m 2, 1991, Rosemary Anne, da of John Gwydon Morris Jones; 2 da (Megan Frances, Angharad Grace (twins) b 5 Nov 2001); *Career* served in ranks Black Watch 1978–81, cmmnd offr 1987–99 (GSM NI); Cmmn for Racial Equality 1999–2000; MP (Lab) Falkirk W 2000– (by-election); exec memb Fabian Soc; *Publications* Arms and the Man - Renewing the Armed Services (1997), Now's the Hour: New Thinking for Holyrood (ed, 1999); *Recreations* climbing, running, judo, most sports; *Clubs* Camelon Labour; *Style*— Eric Joyce, Esq, MP; ✉ Constituency Office, 2 Lint Riggs, Falkirk FK1 1DG (tel 01324 638919, fax 01324 679449, mobile 07631 150469, e-mail joyceе@parliament.uk)

JOYCE, Peter Stuart Langford; QC (1991); s of Dr Horace Langford Joyce (d 1984), of Porthmadog, Gwynedd, and Nancy, *née* Dryden (d 1997); *b* 5 February 1946; *Educ* Oundle, Coll of Law; *m* 1971, Helen Christina, da of John Lazenby; 2 s, 2 da; *Career* called to the Bar Inner Temple 1968 (bencher 2001), recorder Midland Circuit 1986–, currently head of chambers 1 High Pavement Nottingham; *Recreations* golf, sailing, gardening, reading; *Style*— Peter Joyce, Esq, QC

JOYCE, Rosemary; da of J G M Jones, of West Sussex, and V M Jones, *née* Fletcher; *b* 18 September 1963, Bromsgrove, Worcs; *Educ* Univ of Stirling (BA), Inst of Educn Univ of London (MA, PGCE); *m* 1991; 2 da (Megan, Angharad (twins) b 5 Nov 2001); *Career* teacher: Millais Sch Horsham 1987–90, Aylesbury HS 1990–92, The Clarendon Sch Trowbridge 1993–2000; dep headteacher Nonsuch HS for Girls Cheam 2000–05, headteacher Tonbridge GS 2005–; NPQH; *Style*— Rosemary Joyce; ✉ Tonbridge Grammar School, Deakin Leas, Tonbridge, Kent TN9 2JR (tel 01732 365125, fax 01732 359417, e-mail headteacher@tgs.kent.sch.uk)

J

JOYNER, Prof Richard William; s of late Stanley William Joyner, of Carrickfergus, Co Antrim, and late Jenny Kane, *née* Hagan; *b* 20 December 1944; *Educ* Belfast HS, Queen's Univ Belfast (BSc, DSc), Univ of Bradford (PhD); *m* 1, 1 Sept 1967 (m dis), (Ann) Jenepher, da of late George Wilson Grange, of Belfast; 2 da (Clare b 24 July 1970, Carol b 9 Dec 1974); m 2, 29 March 2006, Elizabeth (Liz) Lines, da of late John Caie, of Leamington Spa; *Career* res fell Univ of Calif Berkeley 1970–71, memb Staff Chemistry Dept Univ of Bradford 1971–80, head Fundamentals of Catalysis Res Gp and Res Assoc BP Res Sunbury-on-Thames 1980–87, dir Leverhulme Centre for Innovative Catalysis and prof of chemistry Univ of Liverpool 1987–94, dean of res Nottingham Trent Univ 1994–2004 (prof emeritus 2004–); hon prof Queen's Univ Belfast 2004–; memb: Editorial Bd Catalysis Letters, Research Careers Initiative Steering Gp 1998–2000; chm Ctee Surface Reactivity and Catalysis Gp Royal Soc of Chemistry 1990–94 (sec 1982–86), chm Exec Ctee Save British Science 1996–2006; former chm Br Vacuum Cncl; memb E Bridgford Parish Cncl 2007–; FRSC 1989; *Publications* approx 250 scientific publications in international journals, 2 books and several book chapters; *Recreations* music, wine, biographies, Italy, bridge, choral singing; *Style*— Prof Richard Joyner; ✉ 53 Kneeton Road, East Bridgford, Nottinghamshire NG13 8PG (e-mail richard.joyner@ntu.ac.uk)

JOYNES, Stephen Frederick (Steve); MBE (2006); s of Stephen Sidney Joynes (d 1988), and Doris Winifred, *née* Thurling; *b* 24 February 1935, Walsall, W Midlands; *Educ* Blue Coat Secdy Modern and the academy of life; *m* 8 July 1978, Janet Lesley, *née* Cook; 1 s (Steven Earl b 8 Jan 1969); *Career* early career in building trade 1950–53; Nat Serv RAF 1953–56; fndr and prop: mobile fish and chip van 1956, Golden Grill Restaurant Wylde Green 1958, Midland Hotel Walsall 1961, County Hotel Walsall 1965, Chateau Impney Hotel Droitwich 1970, Barons Court Hotel Walsall Wood 1973, Hoar Cross Hall Spa Resort Hotel Hoar Cross 1989, Eden Hall Spa Newark 2002; memb of Midland Assoc of Restaurants, Caterers and Hoteliers; Salesman of the Year Autobar Vending Machines 1965, Most Excellent Spa Johansonns Award for Excellence, Best Health Spa Good Housekeeping, Lifetime Achievement Award and 3 Crystal Awards Thalgo, England's Leading Resort World Travel Awards 2005 and 2006; *Books* Take Action; *Recreations* health, happiness, fitness, creating successful businesses and helping others to do the same; *Style*— Steve Joynes, Esq, MBE; ✉ Hoar Cross Hall Spa Resort, Hoar Cross, Staffordshire DE13 8QS (tel 01283 575671, fax 01283 575224, e-mail marketing@hoarcross.co.uk)

JUBB, Brian Patrick; s of Charles Patrick Jubb (d 1992), and Patricia Elizabeth, *née* Parry (d 1968); *b* 25 August 1948; *Educ* The King's Sch Canterbury, Inns of Court Sch of Law; *m* 1, 16 Nov 1974 (m dis 1982), Susan Patricia Taylor; 1 da (Alexandra b 10 June 1978); m 2, 13 Sept 1985, Susan Elizabeth Lunn; 1 da (Lucy b 13 July 1988); *Career* called to the Bar Gray's Inn 1971, head of chambers 1994–; *Recreations* general aviation, scuba diving, reading; *Style*— Brian Jubb, Esq; ✉ Renaissance Chambers, Gray's Inn, London WC1R 5JA (tel 020 7404 1111, fax 020 7430 1522 and 020 7430 1050)

JUBB, David; *Educ* Bedford Modern Sch, Bretton Hall Coll (BA), Univ of Bristol (MA), Central Sch of Speech and Drama (MA); *Career* theatre director; sch drama teacher 1992–95, lectr in performing arts Chippenham Coll 1995–96, project dir then venue dir Central Sch of Speech and Drama 1997–99, artistic dir Economical Truth Theatre 1997–2001, devpt prodr Battersea Arts Centre (BAC) 1999–2001 (assoc prodr 2001–04), fndr and dir Your Imagination 2001– (chair 2004–), artistic dir BAC 2004–; chair Bd of Tstees Lion & Unicorn Theatre 2001–02; *Style*— David Jubb, Esq; ✉ BAC, Lavender Hill, London SW11 5TN (tel 020 7326 8219, fax 020 7978 5207, e-mail davidjubb@bac.org.uk)

JUCKES, Robert William Somerville; QC (1999); s of Dr William Renwick Juckes, and Enid Osyth Juckes; *b* 1 August 1950; *Educ* Marlborough, Univ of Exeter; *m* 14 Sept 1974, Frances Anne, *née* MacDowell; 3 s (Timothy b 24 Aug 1979, Daniel b 22 May 1982, David b 30 Dec 1986); *Career* called to the Bar 1974, asst recorder 1992, recorder 1995; *Recreations* tennis, golf, cricket, Georgian history, historical novels particularly the works of Patrick O'Brien; *Style*— Robert Juckes, Esq, QC

JUDA, David; s of Paul Juda, and Annely Juda, CBE; *Educ* Ibstock Place Froebel Sch, John Kelly Secdy Modern, Kilburn Poly; *m* March 1983, Yuko Shiraishi, *qv*, da of Masahiro Shinoda; *Career* dir Annely Juda Fine Art 1978 (joined 1967); memb Exec Ctee Fine Art and Antiques Export Ctee 1971–96; vice-chm Soc of London Art Dealers 1986–90 and

1995–2001 (memb 1970–); *Recreations* skiing; *Clubs* Groucho; *Style—* David Juda, Esq; ✉ Annely Juda Fine Art, 23 Dering Street, London W1S 1AW (tel 020 7629 7578, fax 020 7491 2139, e-mail ajfa@annelyjudafineart.co.uk)

JUDD, Baron (Life Peer UK 1991), of Portsea in the County of Hampshire; Frank Ashcroft Judd; s of Charles W Judd, CBE (d 1974), of Surrey, and Helen Osborn Judd, JP, *née* Ashcroft (d 1982); *b* 28 March 1935; *Educ* City of London Sch, LSE (BScEcon); *m* 1961, Christine Elizabeth Louise, da of Frederick Ward Willington (d 1966), of Kent; 2 da (Hon Elizabeth b 1967, Hon Philippa b 1969); *Career* F/O RAF 1957–59; sec gen Int Voluntary Serv 1960–66; MP (Lab): Portsmouth W 1966–74, Portsmouth N (following boundary change) 1974–79; memb Public Accounts Ctee 1966–69, chm PLP Overseas Aid and Devpt Gp 1967–70, PPS to Min for Housing and Local Govt 1967–70, jt sec All-Pty Parly Gp for UN 1967–72, memb Commons Select Ctee on Overseas Devpt 1969–74, jt PPS to Rt Hon Harold Wilson as Ldr of Oppn 1970–72, memb Br Parly Delgn to Cncl of Europe and WEU 1970–73 and 1997–2005, jr oppn def spokesman 1972–74, Parly under sec of state for def (RN) 1974–76, Parly sec Miny for overseas devpt 1976, min for Overseas Devpt 1976–77, min of state FCO 1977–79; assoc dir Int Defence & Aid Fund for Southern Africa 1979–80, dir VSO 1980–85, chm Centre for World Devpt Educn 1980–85, dir Oxfam 1985–91, chm Int Cncl of Voluntary Agencies 1985–90, memb House of Lords Oppn front bench foreign affrs team 1991–92; House of Lords princ front bench spokesman on: educn 1992–94, overseas devpt co-operation 1992–97; memb House of Lords oppn front bench defence team 1995–97; chm Geneva World Economic Forum Conf on future of Southern Africa 1990 and 1991, memb Governing Cncl Nat Housing and Tenant Resource Centre 1992–94; chm: Oxford Diocesan Bd for Social Responsibility 1992–95, Selly Oak Colls Birmingham 1994–97, European-Atlantic Gp 1997–99, Refugee Sub-Ctee of Ctee on Migration Refugees and Demography Parly Assembly of the Cncl of Europe 1998–2001; advsr on security matters, educn and community rels to The Forbes Tst 1992–2000, conslt World Humanity Action Tst 1993–96, advsr De Montfort Univ 1993–; memb: Int Cmmn on Global Governance 1992–2001, WHO Task Force on Health and Devpt 1994–98, Justice Goldstone's Int Working Gp on Human Duties and Responsibilities in the New Millennium 1997–99, Sub-Ctee on Environment, Agriculture, Public Health and Consumer Protection of Lords Ctee on European Communities 1997–2001, Procedure Ctee House of Lords 2001–, Ecclesiastical Ctee House of Lords 2001–, Jt Ctee on Human Rights 2003–, Advsy Bd Centre for Human Rights LSE 2007–; non-exec dir Portsmouth Harbour Renaissance Bd 1998–2006; memb: Labour Pty 1951–, Fabian Soc (former chm), Br Cncl, Amicus, GMB, Governing Body Queen Elizabeth House Univ of Oxford 1989–94, NW Regnl Ctee Nat Tst 1996–2005, Oxfam Assoc 1997–2004, Royal Cwlth Soc, RIIA, Advsy Bd Centre for Human Rights LSE 2007–; pres: YMCA (England) 1996–2005, European Atlantic Gp 1999–2001, Friends of the Lake District 2005–; hon vice-pres: Cncl for Nat Parks 1998–, UN Assoc, Intermediate Devpt Technol Gp, Lakeland Housing Tst; govr: LSE, Westminster Coll Oxford 1992–98; convenor Social Responsibility Forum of Churches Together Cumbria 1999–2005; memb Cncl: Lancaster Univ, Univ of Newcastle; tstee: International Alert 1994–2000 (chm 1997–2000), Ruskin Fndn 2002–, Saferworld 2002–; freedom of the City of Portsmouth 1995; hon pres Friends of the Royal Navy Museum 2002–, hon fell Selly Oak Colls Birmingham, hon fell and Hon DLitt Univ of Portsmouth, Hon DLitt Univ of Bradford, Hon DLitt De Montfort Univ, Hon LLD Univ of Greenwich 1999; FRSA; *Books* Radical Future (jtly, 1967), Fabian International Essays (jtly, 1970), Purpose in Socialism (jtly, 1973), Imagining Tomorrow: Rethinking the Global Challenge (jtly, 2000); *Recreations* enjoying Cumbria, family holidays, listening to music; *Clubs* Cwlth Tst; *Style—* The Lord Judd; ✉ House of Lords, London SW1A 0PW

JUDD, James; s of Eric Judd (d 1986), and Winifred Judd (d 1997); *b* 30 October 1949; *Educ* Hertford GS, Trinity Coll of Music; *m* 25 Sept 1993, Valerie; *Career* conductor; music dir Florida Philharmonic 1988–2001, music dir New Zealand Symphony Orch 1999–, Florida Grand Opera 1993–96; princ guest conductor Orchestre National de Lille; fndr memb Chamber Orch of Europe; has conducted numerous other major orchs incl: English Chamber Orch, Hallé Orch, Royal Philharmonic Orch, LSO, LPO, Royal Scottish National Orch, Vienna Symphony Orch, Prague Symphony Orch, Berlin Philharmonic, Orchestre National de France, Zurich Tonhalle, Orchestre de la Suisse Romande; also conducted numerous operas incl: Il Trovatore, La Traviata, The Barber of Seville, Rigoletto and The Marriage of Figaro (all with ENO), La Cenerentola (Glyndebourne Festival) 1985, Don Giovanni (US operatic debut, Miami) 1988; *Recordings* incl: Mahler Symphony No 1 (with Florida Philharmonic Orch), Elgar Symphony No 1 (with Hallé Orch) 1992, live recordings of Mahler Symphonies No 9 and 10, complete recordings of Meyerbeer and Donizetti operas on Opera Rara, various others with Euro Community Youth Orch, Gustav Mahler Youth Orch, English Chamber Orch, Hallé Orch and Chamber Orch of Europe; *Recreations* almost anything; *Style—* James Judd, Esq; ✉ Columbia Artists Management, New York (tel 001 212 841 9560, website www.cami.com)

JUDD, Lionel Henry; s of John Basil Thomas Judd (d 1983), and Cynthia Margaret Georgina, *née* White-Smith; *b* 24 October 1945; *Educ* The Leys Sch Cambridge, Downing Coll Cambridge (MA); *m* 19 Sept 1970, Janet Elizabeth, da of Arthur Boyton Fraser (d 1966), of Stansted, Essex; 1 s (Edward b 1972), 1 da (Alexandra b 1975); *Career* admitted slr 1972; Cumberland Ellis Peirs (formerly Darley Cumberland): ptnr 1975–, managing ptnr 1997–2001, sr ptnr 2001–04, conslt 2005; memb Exec Ctee Abbeyfield Soc Bucks 1980– (vice-chm 2005, chm 2006–); tstee: Downing Coll Boathouse Centenary Tst 1995–, Game Conservancy Ctee (Bucks branch) 1999–, and various private charities; tstee Aylesbury Cons Assoc 1999–, pres Wendover Cons Assoc 2005–; *Recreations* rowing, country pursuits, travel; *Clubs* Leander, Caledonian; *Style—* Lionel Judd, Esq; ✉ Little Coombe, Wendover, Buckinghamshire HP22 6EQ

JUDD, Very Rev Peter Somerset Margesson; s of William Frank Judd, of Monkton, Kent; *b* 20 February 1949, Calgary, Canada; *Educ* Charterhouse, Trinity Hall Cambridge (MA), Cuddeson Coll Oxford (CertTheol); *m* Judith Margaret; 1 s (Tom b 17 Dec 1981), 1 da (Alice b 29 Dec 1983); *Career* ordained: deacon 1974, priest 1975; curate St Philip with St Stephen Salford 1974–76; Clare Coll Cambridge: chaplain 1976–81, elected fell 1980, actg dean 1980–81; team vicar Hitcham and Dropmore Burnham Team Miny 1981–88, vicar of St Mary the Virgin Iffley 1988–97, rural dean of Cowley 1995–97, rector and provost of Chelmsford 1997–2000, dean of Chelmsford 2000–; *Recreations* architecture and art, listening to music, literature, drawing, fell walking, cooking; *Style—* The Very Rev the Dean of Chelmsford; ✉ The Dean's House, 3 Harlings Grove, Waterloo Lane, Chelmsford CM1 1YQ; The Cathedral Office, Guy Harlings, New Street, Chelmsford CM1 1TY (tel 01245 294492, fax 01245 294499, e-mail dean@chelmsfordcathedral.org.uk)

JUDGE, Lady; Barbara; *see:* Thomas, Hon Barbara S

JUDGE, Ian; s of John Judge, of Southport, Merseyside, and Marjorie Judge; *b* 21 July 1946; *Educ* King George V GS, Guildhall Sch of Music and Drama; *Career* stage director; *Theatre* joined RSC 1975; Stratford: Henry IV Parts 1 and 2, Henry V and Coriolanus (asst dir); assoc dir Poppy (Barbican, re-worked for the Aldephi), The Wizard of Oz (Stratford and Barbican) 1987 and 1988, The Comedy of Errors (UK and Asia/Aust tour) 1990, Love's Labour's Lost (UK and Japan) 1993, Twelfth Night (UK and world tour) 1994, The Relapse 1995, A Christmas Carol, Troilus and Cressida 1996, The Merry Wives of Windsor 1997; other directing credits incl: The Rivals and King Lear (Old Vic), The Orchestra (King's Head Theatre Club), Rookery Nook (Barbican Centre), Musical Chairs (Chichester Festival Theatre Studio), Friends of Dorothy and How Lucky Can You Get (Donmar Warehouse), Banana Ridge and Peter Pan (Shaw Festival Canada), Henry the Eighth and Love for Love (Chichester Festival Theatre), Macbeth (Sydney Theatre Co); *Musicals* incl: Oh Kay! (Chichester Festival Theatre, The Swan-Down Gloves (RSC)), Merrily We Roll Along (Guildhall Theatre Barbican, Arts Theatre Cambridge and Bloomsbury Theatre London), Bitter Sweet (New Sadler's Wells Opera), A Little Night Music (Chichester Festival Theatre and Piccadilly Theatre), Show Boat (RSC, Opera North and London Palladium), D'Oyly Carte in The Mikado (Savoy Theatre), West Side Story (Aust); *Opera* Ariodante (Buxton Festival), Faust (ENO and Opera North), The Merry Widow, Cavalleria Rusticana, Pagliacci, Don Quixote, La Belle Vivette, Mephistopheles, and Sir John in Love (all ENO), Macbeth, Tosca, Acis and Galatea, Boris Godunov and Attila (Opera North), Falstaff (Bremer Theatre Germany, Scottish Opera), Eugene Onegin (Grange Park Opera), Lohengrin (Wiesbaden Germany), The Tales of Hoffmann and Don Quixote (Victoria State Opera), Faust (Sydney Opera), Macbeth (Cologne Opera), The Flying Dutchman and Simon Boccanegra (ROH), The Tales of Hoffmann (Houston Grand Opera), Norma (Scottish Opera), Cosi Fan Tutte (Garsington Opera), Falstaff (Baden Baden Opera, Royal Albert Hall, Theatre du Chatelet Paris), Simon Boccanegra (Washington Opera and Dallas Opera), Mefistofele (Teatro Colon Buenos Aires), La Boheme (Kirov Opera St Petersburg), Ernani (National Reisopera Holland), Salome (NYC Opera), Tosca, Madama Butterfly, Le Nozze di Figaro, Roméo et Juliette, Don Carlo, Tannhäuser (all Los Angeles Opera); *Awards* Best Musical Revival Olivier Awards (for Show Boat), Green Room Theatre Best Dir Awards Victoria Aust (for Faust, The Tales of Hoffman, West Side Story); *Style—* Ian Judge, Esq; ✉ e-mail judge1@mac.com, website www.ianjudge.com

JUDGE, Prof Kenneth Franklin (Ken); *b* 1 January 1948; *Educ* Sidney Sussex Coll Cambridge (MA, PhD, Essay prize); *Career* lectr in social policy: Univ of Bristol 1974–79, Civil Service Coll 1979–80; sr res fell and dep dir Personal Servs Res Unit Univ of Kent 1980–85, dir King's Fund Policy Inst 1986–97, prof of social policy Univ of Kent at Canterbury 1997–2000, prof of health promotion policy Univ of Glasgow 2000–; Harkness fell advsr Commonwealth Fund; FFPH; *Books* Rationing Social Services, Charging for Social Care, Tackling Inequalities in Health, Caring for Older People; author of numerous books and reports in learned pubns; *Style—* Prof Ken Judge; ✉ Public Health and Health Policy, Faculty of Medicine, University of Glasgow, 1 Lilybank Gardens, Glasgow G12 8RZ (tel 0141 330 5008, e-mail k.judge@clinmed.gla.ac.uk)

JUDGE, Sir Paul Rupert; kt (1996); s of Rupert Cyril Judge (d 1986), and Betty Rosa Muriel, *née* Daniels; *b* 25 April 1949; *Educ* Christchurch Sch Forest Hill, St Dunstan's Coll Catford, Trinity Coll Cambridge (MA), Wharton Business Sch Univ of Pennsylvania (MBA); *m* 25 June 1983; 2 s (Christopher Paul, Michael James); *Career* Cadbury Schweppes plc: fin analyst then fin planning mangr Overseas Gp 1973–76, internal memb Gp Strategic Planning Project 1976–77, gp dep fin dir 1977–79, planning dir N American Region 1980, md Cadbury Schweppes Kenya Ltd 1980–82, md Cadbury Typhoo 1982–84, gp planning dir and memb Gp Exec Ctee 1984–85; Premier Brands Ltd: led MBO of food business of Cadbury Schweppes 1986, md 1986–87, chm 1987–89, co sold to Hillsdown Hldgs plc 1989; chm Food From Britain 1990–92, DG Cons Pty 1992–95, special advsr to Rt Hon Roger Freeman as Chllr of the Duchy of Lancaster 1995–96; non-exec dir: Grosvenor Development Capital plc 1989–93, Boddington Gp plc 1989–93, Strategy Ventures plc 1989–2002, WPP Gp plc 1991–97, Schroder Income Growth Fund plc 1995– (chm 2005–), Standard Bank Gp Ltd (Johannesburg) 2003–, Tempur-Pedic Int Inc (Kentucky) 2004–; pres Chartered Mgmnt Inst 2004–, vice-pres The Mktg Cncl 2001–; memb: Cncl Food and Drink Fedn 1988–89, Milk Mktg Bd 1989–92, Cncl RASE 1991–96, Cncl Assoc of MBA 1992– (pres 1997–); chm: Advsy Bd Cambridge Univ Inst of Mgmnt Studies 1991–2002, Br-N American Ctee 2001–, Bd of Companions Inst of Mgmnt 2001–04; tstee: Cambridge Fndn 1991–, Br Food Tst 1997–2007, Enterprise Education Tst 1998– (chm 1999–), Royal Instn 1999–2005, American Mgmnt Assoc 2000– (dep chm), Wharton European Bd (chm 2000–), Teachers' TV 2005– (chm); treas Imperial Soc of Knights Bachelor 1999–2006 (registrar 2006–); dep chm Globe Theatre Devpt Cncl 2000–06; chm RSA 2003–06; govr: Bromsgrove Sch 1990–96, St Dunstan's Coll Catford 1997– (chm 2001–); listed in Business Magazine Top 40 under 40 1986, food industry personality of the year Food Processing Awards 1992; Freeman City of London 1970, Liveryman Worshipful Co of Marketors 1993 (Master 2005); Hon LLD Univ of Cambridge 1995, Hon DLitt Univ of Westminster 2006, Hon DSc City Univ 2007; FRSA 1971, FInstD 1988, fell Mktg Soc 1991, CIMgt 1994; *Recreations* family, travel; *Clubs* Athenaeum, Carlton, Mombasa (Kenya); *Style—* Sir Paul Judge; ✉ 152 Grosvenor Road, London SW1V 3JL

JULIUS, Dr Anthony Robert; s of Morris and Myrna Julius; *b* 16 July 1956; *Educ* City of London Sch, Jesus Coll Cambridge (MA), Coll of Law, UCL (PhD); *m* 1, 1979 (m dis 1998), Judith, *née* Bernie; 2 s (Max Yoram b 8 December 1981, Theo Raphael b 6 September 1992), 2 da (Laura Yael b 12 July 1983, Chloe Anna b 10 February 1990); m 2, 1999, Dina, *née* Rabinovitch; 1 s (Elon Lev b 12 Aug 2001); *Career* slr; ptnr Mishcon de Reya 1984–98 (head of litigation 1988–98); tstee Diana, Princess of Wales Meml Fund 1997– (chm 1997–99, vice-pres 2002–), chair Law Panel Inst of Jewish Policy Research 1997–; *Books* T S Eliot Anti-Semitism and Literary Form (1995), Law & Literature (contrib, 1999), Idolising Pictures (2001), Transgressions (2002); *Recreations* cooking, writing; *Style—* Dr Anthony Julius; ✉ Mishcon de Reya, Summit House, 12 Red Lion Square, London WC1R 4QD (tel 020 7440 7000, fax 020 7404 8171, e-mail anthony.julius@mishcon.co.uk)

JULIUS, Dr DeAnne; CBE (2002); da of Marvin G Julius, of Iowa, USA, and Maxine M, *née* Meeske; *b* 14 April 1949; *Educ* Iowa State Univ (BSc), Univ of Calif (MA, PhD); *m* 21 Nov 1976, Ian Alexander Harvey, *qv*, s of Dr Alexander Harvey (d 1987), of Cardiff; 1 da (Megan b 28 March 1979), 1 s (Ross b 9 Dec 1980); *Career* econ advsr World Bank 1975–82, md Logan Associates Inc 1982–86, dir of economics RIIA 1986–89; chief economist: Royal Dutch/Shell 1989–93, British Airways 1993–97, Monetary Policy Ctee Bank of England 1997–2001; non-exec dir: Ct of the Bank of England 2001–04, Lloyds TSB 2001–, BP 2001–, Serco 2001–, Roche 2002–; chm Banking Consumer Codes Review Gp 2000–01, chm RIIA 2003–; *Books* Global Companies and Public Policy: The Growing Challenge of Foreign Direct Investment (1990), The Economics of Natural Gas (1990), The Monetary Implications of the 1992 Process (1990); *Clubs* IOD; *Style—* Dr DeAnne Julius, CBE; ✉ Royal Institute of International Affairs, Chatham House, 10 St James's Square, London SW1Y 4LE

JULIUS, Rosamind; da of Maurice Hille (d 1968), of London, and Ray Hille (d 1986); *Educ* North London Collegiate Sch Canons, Regent St Poly, St Martin's Sch of Art; *m* 20 Feb 1944, Leslie Julius (d 1989), s of late Harold Julius; 1 da (Corinne); *Career* WRNS 1943–45; trainee surveyor George Wimpey & Son; Hille International Ltd: joined 1945, various appts in sales and mktg, fndr Contract Div, dir Design Unit 1950–84; fndr Julius International Design Consultants 1984–; Int Design Conference Aspen USA: advisor to Bd, programme chm 1986, presented Insight and Outlook (views of Br design) with Kenneth Grange; Gold Medal RSA bicentennial 1972; Hon FRIBA, Hon FCSD, Hon FRSA, Sr FRCA 1998; *Recreations* tennis, skiing, sailing, art, architecture; *Clubs* Arts; *Style—* Mrs Rosamind Julius; ✉ Julius International Design Consultants, 15 Ulster Terrace, Regents Park, London NW1 4PJ (tel 020 7487 4832, fax 020 7935 2994)

JUNG, Prof Roland Tadeusz; *b* 8 February 1948; *Educ* St Anselm's Coll Birkenhead, Pembroke Coll Cambridge (exhibitioner, fndn scholar, MA, MB BChir, MD), St Thomas' Hosp London (LRCP); *m* 1974, Felicity Helen, da of Prof J O L King; 1 da (b 1987); *Career* MRC clinical research scientific offr Dunn Nutrition Unit Cambridge 1977–79, sr registrar in endocrinology and diabetes Hammersmith Hosp and Royal Postgrad Med Sch London 1980–82, conslt physician/specialist in endocrinology and diabetes Ninewells Hosp Dundee 1982–, hon reader in med Ninewells Hosp and Med Sch Dundee 1991–, clinical director of med Dundee Teaching Hosps NHS Tst 1991–94, dir for res devpt Tayside NHS Consortium 1997–2001; hon prof of medicine 1998–; chief scientist for Scottish Exec Health Dept 2001–; Card Medal Western Gen Hosp Edinburgh 1987; memb: Scottish Soc of Physicians 1984, Assoc of Physicians of UK and I 1987, Scottish Hosp Endowments Tst 1998–2001; chm Scottish Hosp Endowments Tst 2000–01; FRCPEd, FRCP (London), MRCP (UK), MRCS; *Books* Endocrine Problems in Cancer (jt ed, 1984), Colour Atlas of Obesity (1990); *Recreations* gardening, walking, reading; *Style*— Prof Roland Jung; ✉ Diabetes Centre, Ninewells Hospital and Medical School, Dundee, Tayside

JUNGELS, Dr Pierre Jean Marie Henri; Hon CBE (1989); s of Henri Jungels, and Jeanne Jungels; *b* 18 February 1944; *Educ* Univ of Liège (Ing Civ), Caltech (PhD); *m* 2, 1988, Caroline, da of Dr Z Benc, of Worcester; 2 step c and 2 c from previous m; *Career* gen mangr and chief exec Fina Petroleos (Angola) 1977–80, md and chief exec Fina plc (UK) 1980–89, exec dir Petrofina Gp 1989–95, md BG plc 1996, chief exec Enterprise Oil plc 1997–2001; chm OHM plc, chm Oxford Catalysts plc, exec chm Rockhopper Exploration plc; non-exec dir: Imperial Tobacco Gp plc, Woodside Petroleum Ltd, Baker Hughes Inc; pres Inst of Petroleum 1987–89 and 2002, co-chm Energy Inst 2002–03; *Recreations* tennis, skiing, shooting; *Style*— Dr Pierre Jungels, CBE

JUNIPER, Anthony Thomas (Tony); s of Austin Wilfred Juniper (d 1984), of Oxford, and Constance Margaret, *née* Eliston (d 2002); *b* 24 September 1960; *Educ* Oxford Sch, Oxford Coll of FE, Univ of Bristol (BSc), UCL (MSc); *m* Dec 1990, Susan Sparkes; 1 da (Madeleine b 1991), 2 s (Aneurin b 1994, Samuel b 1997); *Career* various posts: S Oxfordshire Countryside Educn Tst 1984, Nat Cmmn for Wildlife Conservation and Devpt Saudi Arabia 1988; freelance researcher 1988–89, contract worker UCL 1989, parrot conservation offr Int Cncl for Bird Preservation (now BirdLife Int) 1989–90; Friends of the Earth: sr campaigner (tropical rainforests) 1990–93, sr campaigner (biodiversity) 1993–95, dep campaigns dir 1995–97, campaigns dir 1997–98, policy and campaigns dir 1998–2003, vice-chair Friends of the Earth Int 2000–, exec dir Friends of the Earth England, Wales and NI 2003–; memb World Parrot Tst Scientific Ctee, founding bd memb Stop Climate Chaos 2005; *Publications* Threatened Planet (1996), Parrots (with Parr, 1998, UK Library Assoc Reference Book of the Year 1999), Spix's Macaw - the race to save the world's rarest bird (2002), How Many Light Bulbs Does It Take to Change a Planet? (2007), Saving Planet Earth (2007); also author of book chapters, scientific papers and magazine articles; contrib: BBC Wildlife magazine, The Ecologist, Bird Conservation International, Oryx, The Guardian, FT, The Independent, The Times; *Recreations* family, natural history (especially ornithology), walking in wild places, all kinds of fishing, keeping fit, drawing and painting, gardening; *Style*— Tony Juniper, Esq; ✉ Friends of the Earth, 26–28 Underwood Street, London N1 7JQ (tel 020 7490 0336, fax 020 7490 0881, e-mail tonyj@foe.co.uk)

JUNOR, Brian James Ross; s of Donald Junor, MBE (d 1986), of Dundee, and Ann Russell, *née* Mackie (d 1985); *b* 10 February 1946; *Educ* Dundee HS, Univ of St Andrews (MB ChB), Univ of Dundee (MD); *m* 1, 4 Feb 1972, Sheena MacLeod (d 1972), da of Sir Donald Douglas, of White House, Nevay Newtyle; *m* 2, 19 Jan 1979, Elizabeth Jane, da of John Fotheringham, OBE, of St Helen's, Fife; 1 s (Malcolm b 1980), 1 da (Katherine b 1982); *Career* sr registrar of medicine Aberdeen Royal Infirmary 1976–78, Aust Kidney Res Fndn fell Univ of Melbourne 1978–79, hon clinical lectr Univ of Glasgow 1979–, conslt nephrologist Gtr Glasgow Health Authy 1979–; currently sec Specialty Section in Nephrology Union of Euro Med Specialists; former memb Jt Ctee for Higher Med Training, former chm Specialist Advsy Ctee in Renal Diseases; memb BMA 1970, FRCPS 1982, FRCPE 1987; *Recreations* skiing, gardening, golf; *Style*— Brian Junor, Esq; ✉ The Barn, Ballagan, Strathblane, Glasgow (tel 01360 770767); Renal Unit,

Western Infirmary, Dunbarton Road, Glasgow (tel 0141 211 2000, e-mail brian.junor@northglasgow.scot.nhs.uk)

JUNOR, Penelope Jane (Penny); da of Sir John Junor (d 1997), and Pamela Mary, *née* Welsh; *b* 6 October 1949; *Educ* Benenden, Univ of St Andrews; *m* 8 Sept 1970, James Stewart Leith; 3 s (Sam b 1 Jan 1974, Alexander b 23 July 1976, Jack b 17 Jan 1985), 1 da (Peta b 31 Dec 1987); *Career* trainee IPC Young Magazine Gp 1969–70, feature writer 19 Magazine 1970–71, writer Londoners' Diary Evening Standard 1971–73, freelance journalist 1974–, columnist Private Eye 1974–81, reporter Collecting Now (BBC) 1981, presenter 4 What It's Worth (Channel 4) 1982–89, co-presenter The Afternoon Show 1984–85, presenter The Travel Show (BBC) 1988–97, Paper Tigers (Radio Scotland) 2006, In the Footsteps of Fame (Radio Scotland) 2007; gen ed John Lewis Partnership 1994–99; patron Women's Health Concern 2002–, tstee beat (formerly Eating Disorders Assoc); *Books* Newspaper (1980), Babyware (1982), Diana, Princess of Wales (1982), Margaret Thatcher, Wife, Mother, Politician (1983), Burton - The Man Behind the Myth (1985), Charles (1987), Charles and Diana - Portrait of a Marriage (1991), Queen Elizabeth - Pictorial Celebration of Her Reign (1991), The Major Enigma (1993), Charles: Victim or Villain? (1998), Home Truths: Life Around My Father (2002), The Firm: The Troubled Life of the House of Windsor (2005), Wonderful Today: The Autobiography with Pattie Boyd (2007); *Recreations* walking, tennis; *Clubs* Groucho, Century; *Style*— Ms Penny Junor; ✉ c/o Jane Turnbull, Barn Cottage, Veryan, Truro, Cornwall TR2 5QA (tel 01872 501317); c/o Hilary Knight (tel 01604 781818, e-mail hilary@hkmanagement.co.uk)

JUPP, Jeffrey Addison; s of Leonard James Jupp (d 1988), and Elizabeth, *née* Addison (d 1984); *b* 31 December 1941; *Educ* Enfield GS, Queens' Coll Cambridge (MA); *m* 1965, Margaret Elizabeth, da of Ronald Peatchey; 1 da (Elizabeth Jane b 1971), 1 s (Richard James b 1974); *Career* Aerodynamics Dept Hawker Siddeley Aviation (subsequently British Aerospace) Hatfield: aerodynamicist 1964–73, head Fluid Motion Section 1973–80, type aerodynamicist Airbus and head Airbus Section 1980–84, asst chief aerodynamicist Devpts 1984; British Aerospace Airbus Ltd Filton: asst chief engr Airbus 1984–87, chief engr A330/A340 (BAe), chief engr Airbus 1988–92, dir Engrg 1993–98, dir Tech 1998–2001, ret; non-exec dir Cranfield Aerospace Ltd 2002–; chm: ARB Tech Ctee 1999–2004, Tech Bd SBAC 2000–2001, DTI Aerospace Innovation and Growth Team Environment, Safety and Security Working Gp 2003–06; former memb: Tech Dirs Ctee Airbus Industrie, Industry Advsy Ctee to Supervisory Bd of Euro (Cryogenic) Transonic Windtunnel Cologne; memb: ARB CAA 1995–2004, RAeS Medals and Awards Ctee; author of numerous published lectures and papers; visiting prof Mechanical Engrg Dept Univ of Bath; jt winner Esso Energy Award Royal Soc Gold Medal 1987, Br Bronze Medal Royal Aeronautical Soc 1992, Gold Medal Royal Aeronautical Soc 2002; FRAeS 1990, FREng 1996; *Recreations* coastal sailing, listening to classical music, choral singing; *Style*— Jeffrey Jupp, Esq, FREng, FRAeS; ✉ 21 Bloomfield Park, Bath BA2 2BY (tel 01225 311390, e-mail jeff@jupp248.fsnet.co.uk)

JURY CRAMP, Felicity; da of Cecil Walter Cramp (d 2007), of Horsham, W Sussex, and Hilary, *née* Napper (d 1971); *b* 9 July 1961; *Educ* Sir John Cass London (dip), Royal Coll of Art (MA); *Career* watch, eyewear and jewellery designer; early design experience with Alain Mikli Paris 1985–86, Optyl Vienna 1987, IDC Paris 1989–90, Betty Jackson 1990–91, Katharine Hamnett 1991–2000, Patrick Cox 1997–2000, Gucci 2000–; fndr memb The New RenaisCAnce (multi media co specialising in fashion and accessory design, display, styling and video prodn) 1991–; exhbns incl: Fouts and Fowler Gallery London 1991, The World of The New RenaisCAnce (Royal Festival Hall and Parco Gallery Tokyo) 1992, Court Couture (Kensington Palace) 1992, Vision Gallery London 1992, Spectacles: A Recent History (Crafts Cncl) 1997; TV and video work incl title sequences for BBC1, Channel 4 and Carlton, window design for Liberty and Harvey Nichols London; *Style*— Ms Felicity Jury Cramp; ✉ tel 07775 782684

K

KABERRY, Hon Sir Christopher Donald (Kit); 2 Bt (UK 1960), of Adel cum Eccup, City of Leeds; s of Baron Kaberry of Adel, TD, DL (Life Peer and 1 Bt, d 1991), and Lily Margaret, *née* Scott (d 1992); *b* 14 March 1943; *Educ* Repton; *m* 25 March 1967, Gaenor Elizabeth Vowe, yr da of Cecil Vowe Peake, MBE, of Tunbridge Wells, Kent; 2 s (James Christopher b 1970, Angus George b 1972), 1 da (Claire Elizabeth b 1974); *Heir* s, James Kaberry; *Career* chartered accountant; fin dir: Union Railways (North) Ltd, CTRL (UK) Ltd, Channel Tunnel Rail Link Ltd; FCA 1967; *Style*— The Hon Sir Kit Kaberry, Bt; ✉ Rock View, Chiddingstone Hoath, Kent TN8 7BT (tel 01892 870539)

KADO, Sven Alexander; s of Leonhardt Kado (d 1953), and Livia, *née* Kablitz; *b* 10 October 1944, Bad Mergentheim; *Educ* schooling in Germany, USA and France, Univ of Cologne, INSEAD Fontainebleau (MBA); *m* 9 Aug 1969, Suzanne Poensgen; 3 c (Carlos b 1980, Jeannette b 1982, Pascal b 1982); *Career* Orion Bank 1972–74; chief financial offr: Heimbach 1975–83, Nixdorf Computer 1984–90, Dyckerhoff 1991–97; sr advsr Principal Finance 1998–2000, chm MMC Germany 2000–; non-exec dir Compass Gp plc; memb Int Cncl INSEAD; *Recreations* field sports, skiing; *Clubs* Rotary; *Style*— Sven A Kado, Esq; ✉ Pienzenauerstrasse 31A, D-81679 Munich, Germany (tel 00 49 89 9988 8875, fax 00 49 89 9988 8876); Marsh & McLennan Germany, Marstallstrasse 11, D-80539 Munich, Germany (tel 00 49 89 2905 6641, fax 00 49 89 2905 6649, e-mail svenalexander.kado@mmc.com)

KADRI, Sibghatullah; QC (1989); s of Alhaj Maulana Firasatullah Kadri (d 1990), and Begum Tanwir Fatima, *née* Hamidi (d 1986); *b* 23 April 1937; *Educ* Christian HS Budaun UP India, SM Sci Coll Karachi Univ Pakistan, Inns of Court Sch of Law London; *m* 1963, Carita Elisabeth da of Ole Idman (d 1973), of Helsinki; 1 s (Sadakat b 1964), 1 da (Maria Fatima b 1965); *Career* BBC External Serv 1965–68, prodr and presenter BBC Home Serv, visiting lectr in Urdu Holborn Coll 1966–68; called to the Bar Inner Temple 1969 (bencher 1997); head of chambers 1973–, memb Midland & Oxford Circuit; Pakistan Students Fedn in Britain: gen sec 1961–62, vice-pres 1962–63; pres Inner Temple Students Assoc 1968–69; Standing Conference of Pakistani Orgn: gen sec 1975–78, pres 1978–84; convener Asian Action Ctee 1976, vice-chm Jt Ctee Against Racism, chm Soc of Black Lawyers 1981–83, sec Br Lawyers Ctee for Human Rights and Justice in Pakistan 1984–, chm Asian Lawyers Conference, memb Bar Cncls Race Rels Ctee 1982–85, 1988 and 1989; FRSA 1991; *Style*— Sibghatullah Kadri, Esq, QC; ✉ 6 Kings Bench Walk, Temple, London EC4Y 7DR (tel 020 7353 4931/2, 020 7583 0695/8, fax 020 7353 1726)

KAFETZ, Dr Kalman Meir; s of Vivian Kafetz (d 1969), of Regent's Park, London, and Rose, *née* Gilbert (d 1982); *b* 3 December 1947; *Educ* Eton (King's Scholar), St Thomas' Hosp Med Sch (BSc, MB BS); *m* 11 Oct 1972, Marion Linda, da of Gerald Singer, of Mill Hill, London; 2 s (Alexander b 1976, Sebastian b 1980), 1 da (Cordelia b 1983); *Career* conslt physician Dept of Medicine for Elderly People Whipps Cross Univ Hosp London 1982–2007, hon sr clinical lectr Bart's and Royal London 1994–2007 (hon lectr 1987–94); pres-elect Section of Geriatrics and Gerontology RSM; examiner RCP; memb: Br Geriatrics Soc, Old Etonian Med Soc, Jewish Medical Soc UK; FRCP 1994 (MRCP 1976); *Books* Clinical Tests - Geriatric Medicine (1986); *Recreations* short walks to country pubs; *Clubs* RSM; *Style*— Dr Kalman Kafetz; ✉ 22 Offham Slope, London N12 7BZ (tel 020 8922 5642); Old Court Cottage, Kenegie Manor, Gulval, Penzance, Cornwall TR10 8YW (e-mail kalmankafetz@hotmail.com)

KAHN, Meyer; s of Ben Kahn (d 1966) and Sarah Kahn (d 1995); *b* 29 June 1939; *Educ* Univ of Pretoria (BA, MBA); *m* 1968, Lynette Sandra; 2 da (Deanne b 1969, Hayley b 1972); *Career* md Amrel 1972–77, exec chm OK Bazaars (1929) Ltd 1980–83 (md 1977–80); SAB Ltd/plc: gp md 1983–90, exec chm 1990–97; chief exec SA Police Service 1997–99; chm SAB Ltd/plc (now SABMiller plc) 1999–; pres SA Fndn 1995–96, prof extraordinaire Univ of Pretoria 1989, chm Miracle Drive 1990–2000; Top Five Businessmen SA 1983, Mktg Man of the Year SA 1987, Businessman of the Year SA 1990, Award for Business Excellence Univ of the Witwatersrand 1991, SA Police Star for Outstanding Service 2000; Hon Dr in Commerce Univ of Pretoria 1990; FInstM 1988; *Recreations* golf; *Clubs* Houghton Golf, The River; *Style*— Meyer Kahn, Esq; ✉ SABMiller plc, PO Box 1099, Johannesburg 2000, South Africa (tel 011 407 1800/1, fax 011 403 1857, mobile 082 809 5483, e-mail meyer.kahn@sabmiller.com)

KAHN, Paula; da of Cyril Maurice Kahn, and Stella, *née* Roscoe; *b* 15 November 1940; *Educ* Chiswick Co HS, Univ of Bristol (BA); *Career* teacher and admin 1962–66; Longman Group: ed then publisher, publishing dir, divnl md 1966–79, md ELT Div, Dictionaries Div and Trade and Reference Div 1980–85, md Int Sector 1986–88, chief exec of publishing 1988–89, chm and chief exec 1990–94; project dir World Learning Network 1995–96, md Phaidon Press 1996–97, chm Equality Works 1998–, chm Islington Primary Care Tst 2002–, chm Cripplegate Fndn 2005–; vice-chair Bd Inst of Int Visual Arts; CIMgt, FRSA; *Recreations* cinema, theatre, France, books; *Style*— Ms Paula Kahn; ✉ 4 Mica House, Barnsbury Square, London N1 1RN (tel 020 7609 6964, e-mail paulakahn@micahouse.co.uk)

KAHRMANN, Rainer Thomas Christian; s of Dr Johannes Wilhelm Karl Kahrmann, of Germany, and Therese, *née* Gillrath; *b* 28 May 1943; *Educ* Neusprachliches Gymnasium Erkelenz, Univ of Fribourg (LicRerPol, DrRerPol); *m* 8 Dec 1972, Christiane Jeanne Maria, *née* De Muller; 2 da (Louise b 27 Sept 1979, Alice b 19 Nov 1981); partner, Hilary Harrison-Morgan; 2 s (Frederic Johannes Christian, Maximilian Henry Thomas (twins) b 19 Oct 2001); *Career* apprenticeship Commerzbank AG Germany 1963–64, Dow Chemical Co (Dow Banking Corp) 1969–88, md EBC Amro Bank Ltd 1974–89, chm EBC Asset Mgmnt Ltd 1989–, sole md CBB Holding AG i L Cologne; *Recreations* work, family, antiquarian horology; *Style*— R C Kahrmann, Esq; ✉ c/o EBC Securities Services Limited, 9 Long Road, Canvey Island, Essex SS8 9JA (tel 01268 514274, fax 01268 514027)

KAIN, Prof Roger James Peter; CBE (2005); s of Peter Albert Kain (d 1981), and Ivy, *née* Sharp; *b* 12 November 1944; *Educ* Harrow Weald Middx Co GS, UCL (BA, PhD, DLit); *m* 1970, Annmaree, da of Sidney Frank Wallington; 2 s (Simon Peter Wallington b 1986, Matthew James Wallington b 1991); *Career* tutor Bedford Coll London 1971; Univ of Exeter: lectr 1972–91, prof of geography 1991–, head Sch of Geography and Archaeology 1999–2001, dep vice-chllr 2002–; Gill Meml Award RGS 1990, McColvin Medal Library Assoc 1996; treas Br Acad 2001–; fell UCL 2002; FBA 1990, FSA 1992; *Books* The Tithe Surveys of England and Wales (1985), Atlas and Index of the Tithe Files (1986), Cadastral Maps in the Service of the State (1992), The Tithe Maps of England and Wales (1995), Historical Atlas of SW England (1999), English Maps: A History (1999), Tithe Surveys for Historians (2000), Historic Parishes of England and Wales (2001), Enclosure Maps of England and Wales (2004), England's Landscape: South-West England (2006); *Recreations* mountain walking, gardening; *Clubs* Geographical; *Style*— Prof Roger Kain, CBE, FBA, FSA; ✉ Northcote House, University of Exeter, Exeter EX4 4QJ (tel 01392 263333, fax 01392 263008, e-mail r.j.p.kain@exeter.ac.uk)

KAKKAD, Sunil Shantilal; s of Shantilal Kalyanji Kakkad (d 1996), of London, and Usha Shantilal, *née* Kanani; *b* 19 May 1959; *Educ* Alder Sch, Barnet Coll, Univ of Hull (LLB); *m* 23 Aug 1984, Darshna Sunil, da of Kantilal Vithaldas Hindocha, of Harrow, Middx; 1 s (Rajiv Sunil b 1990), 1 da (Radhika Sunil b 1996); *Career* admitted slr 1984; slr Hill Dickinson & Co 1984–89, ptnr Hill Taylor Dickinson 1989–2000, ptnr Lawrence Graham 2000–; memb Law Soc; *Recreations* music, cinema, food; *Style*— Sunil Kakkad, Esq; ✉ Lawrence Graham LLP, 4 More London Riverside, London SE1 2AU (tel 020 7379 0000, fax 020 7379 6854, e-mail sunil.kakkad@lg-legal.com)

KALE, Stuart Guy; s of Ernest Guy Kale (d 1989), of Skewen, Swansea, and Eileen Beryl, *née* Ward (d 1983); *b* 27 October 1944; *Educ* Neath GS, Guildhall Sch of Music, London Opera Centre; *m* 4 Sept 1989, Deborah Ann, da of Derek Raymond Wellbrook; 2 s (Adam Nicholas Ward b 23 July 1990, Simon Edward Henry b 12 Oct 1991), 1 da (Sophie Alexandra Rose b 6 April 1996); *Career* tenor; with WNO 1972–73, princ tenor ENO 1975–87, freelance 1987–; *Roles* int debut in Albert Herring (Phoenix Opera) 1972, ENO debut Beppe in I Pagliacci 1972; roles with WNO incl: Don Ottavio in Don Giovanni, Red Whiskers in Billy Budd, The Prince in Lulu; with ENO incl: Don Ottavio, Michel in Julietta, Pierre in War and Peace, Nanki-Poo in The Mikado, title role in Orpheus in the Underworld, Don Basilio in The Marriage of Figaro, Guillot de Morfontaine in Manon, Valzacchi in Der Rosenkavalier, Zinovy in Lady Macbeth of Mtsensk, Vogelgesang in Die Meistersinger, Spoletta in Tosca, Menelaus in La Belle Hélène, Truffaldino in The Love for Three Oranges 1990, Peter Quint in The Turn of the Screw (Coliseum and Russian tour) 1990; others incl: The Captain in Wozzeck (Strasbourg 1987, Parma 1989, Canadian Opera Co 1989, San Francisco 1990, Geneva and Bologna 1995), Mephistopheles, Jacob Glock and Agrippa in The Fiery Angel (Adelaide), Podesta in La Finta Giardiniera (Drottningholm), Guillot de Morfontaine in Manon (Royal Opera House Covent Garden), Drum Major in Wozzeck (Turin) 1989, Lucano in L'Incoronazione di Poppea (Paris) 1989, Bob Boles in Peter Grimes (Covent Garden 1989, Munich 1992), High Priest in Idomeneo (Covent Garden) 1989, Shursky in Boris Godunov (Strasbourg 1990, Bordeaux 1992–93), Zinovy in Lady Macbeth of Mtsensk (Toulouse) 1991, title role in Idomeneo (Drottningholm) 1991, The Prince/Manservant/Marquis in Lulu (Le Châtelet Paris) 1991, Aegisthe in Elektra (Karlsruhe) 1991, Vogelgesang in Die Meistersinger (Trieste) 1992, Don Eusebio in L'Occasione fa il Ladro (Schwetzingen/Cologne) 1992, Dormont in Scala di Seta (Cologne) 1992, Alfred in Die Fledermaus (Opera Durhin) 1992–93, Captain Vere in Billy Budd (Cologne) 1992–93, Valzacchi in Der Rosenkavalier (Le Châtelet) 1993–94, Albert Gregor in The Makropulos Case (Opera Durhin, Lisbon) 1993–94, Herod in Salome (Lisbon, Strasbourg) 1994, title role in Peter Grimes (Regersburg) 1996, Prince Shuisky in Boris Godunov (Montpellier) 1996, Prologue/Peter Quint in The Turn of the Screw (Barcelona) 1996, title role in La Clemenza di tito (Rennes) 1996, Baron Zarandelle in Venus (by Othmar Schoeck, Geneva) 1997, Gafforio in Il Re Teodoro in Venezia (by Paisiallo, Ludwigshafen/Dresden) 1997, Bob Boles in Peter Grimes (Genoa) 1997; *Recordings* incl: Rodrigo in Otello (under Mark Elder, EMI), title role in Orpheus in the Underworld (under Mark Elder, TER), Brother II in The Seven Deadly Sins (under Michael Tilson Thomas, Philips), Dr Suda in Osud (under Sir Charles Mackerras), Mr Bumble in Oliver (under John Owen Edwards, TER), Bob Boles in Peter Grimes (under Bernard Haitink, EMI), The Mayor in Albert Herring (under Steuart Bedford, Collins Classics); *Recreations* reading, golf, fine wines; *Style*— Stuart Kale, Esq

KALETSKY, Anatole; s of Jacob Kaletsky (d 1989), and Esther, *née* Feinsilber; *b* 1 June 1952; *Educ* King's Coll Cambridge (hon sr scholarship, BA, DipEcon), Harvard Univ Graduate Sch (Kennedy memorial scholarship, MA); *m* 5 Dec 1985, Fiona Elizabeth, da of Christopher Murphy; 2 s (Michael b 10 Dec 1988, Jacob Alexander Christopher (Sasha) b 27 Feb 1992), 1 da (Katherine b 2 Nov 1986); *Career* fin writer The Economist 1976–79; The Financial Times: ldr and feature writer 1979–81, Washington corr 1981–84, int economics corr 1984–86, chief New York Bureau 1986–90, Moscow corr 1990, sr features writer April-Sept 1990; The Times: economics ed 1990–, assoc ed 1992–; Specialist Writer of the Year Br Press Awards 1980 and 1992, BBC Press Awards Commentator of the Year 1995; conslt: UN Devpt Ctee, UN Conf on Trade and Devpt, Twentieth Century Fund; memb Advsy Bd UK Govt Know-How Fund for Eastern Europe; numerous television and radio appearances; *Books* The Costs of Default (1985); *Style*— Anatole Kaletsky, Esq; ✉ The Times, 1 Pennington Street, London E1 9XN (tel 020 7782 5000, fax 020 7782 5229)

KALICHSTEIN, Joseph; s of Isaac Kalichstein (d 1959), of Tel Aviv, Israel, and Mali, *née* Bendit (d 1995); *b* 15 January 1946; *Educ* The Juilliard Sch NY; *m* 1971, Rowain, da of late Edward Schultz; 2 s (Avshalom b 1974, Rafael b 1977); *Career* pianist; recital debut NY 1967, London debut LSO (conductor André Previn) 1969, formed Kalichstein-Laredo-Robinson trio 1976; chamber music advsr to Kennedy Center; appearances with major orchestras incl: Berlin, Israel, London, LA, NY and Oslo Philharmonics, Baltimore, Boston, Chicago, Cincinnati, London, Pittsburgh, San Francisco and St Louis Symphony Orchestras, Cleveland Orchestra, Minnesota Orchestra, Nat Symphony Orchestra Washington; conductors worked with: Barenboim, Boulez, Conlon, De Priest, De Waart, Dohnányi, Dutoit, Foster, Herbig, Leinsdorf, Lopez-Cobos, Macal, Mata, Mehta, Previn, Sanderling, Schwarz, Slatkin, Szell, Zinman; solo recordings incl: Bartók and Prokofiev 1968, Chopin 1973, Brahms 1975, Schumann and Schubert 1990, Schubert, Brahms, Mendelssohn and CPE Bach 1998; recordings with trio incl: Mendelssohn Trios, Brahms Trios, Beethoven Triple with ECO, two Beethoven Trios, Shostakovich's music for piano, violin, cello and viola, Ellen Taaffe Zwilich concertos; various Mendelssohn concerto recordings incl No 1 with LSO 1971 and No 1 and No 2 with Scot Chamber Orch 1987; first prize Leventritt Int Piano Competition 1969; *Recreations* chess, books, acrostic puzzles; *Style*— Joseph Kalichstein, Esq; ✉ c/o Harrison/Parrott Ltd, 12 Penzance Place, London W11 4PA (tel 020 7229 9166, fax 020 7221 5042)

KALKHOF, Peter Heinz; s of Heinz Emil Kalkhof (d 1945), and Kate Ottilie, *née* Binder (d 1976); *b* 20 December 1933; *Educ* Sch of Arts and Crafts Braunschweig, Acad of Fine Art Stuttgart, Slade Sch of Fine Art London, École des Beaux Arts Paris; *m* 1962, Jeanne The Soen Nio (d 1996); 1 s (Peter T L b 1964); *Career* artist; Slade Sch travel grant Br Isles 1961; lectr in painting Univ of Reading 1970–99 (pt/t lectr in lithography and etching 1964–70); artist in residence: Osnabruck Germany 1985, Künstlerhaus Schieder-Schwalenberg Germany 1995 (six months); memb Br Museum Soc; friend: Royal Acad, V&A, Tate Gallery; *Solo Exhibitions* Galerie in der Garage Stuttgart 1964, Oxford Gallery 1970, Annely Juda Fine Art London 1970, 1974, 1977, 1979, 1990, 1997 and 2002, Wellmann Galerie Düsseldorf 1973, Galerie HS Erkelenz 1974, Royal Shakespeare Theatre 1975, Oliver Dowling Gallery Dublin 1976, Kulturgeschichtliches Museum Osnabruck 1977, Hertfordshire Coll of Art and Design St Albans 1978, Kunstverein Marburg 1979, Goethe Inst London 1981, Juda Rowan Gallery London 1983, Galerie Altes Rathaus Worth am Rhein 1987, Landesmuseum Oldenburg 1988, Camden Arts Centre London 1989, Ostpreussisches Landesmuseum Luneburg 1989, Galerie Rösch Neubrunn 1993, Galerie Rösch Karlsruhe 1994, Rathaus Galerie Balingen Germany 1995, Prignitz Museum am Dom Havelberg Germany 1996, Stadt Museum Galerie Schieder-Schwalenberg Germany 1996, Galerie 'Planie' Reutlingen Germany 1998, St Hugh's Coll Oxford 1998, Gallery Rösch Houston TX 2000, t1+2 artspace London 2004, Annely Juda Fine Art London 2007; *Group Exhibitions* incl: Spectrum 1971 (Alexandra Palace London) 1971, International Biennale of Drawing Middlesbrough 1973 and 1979, British Painting 74 (Hayward Gallery London) 1974, Celebrating 8 Artists (Kensington and Chelsea Arts Cncl Exhibition) 1977, Six Painters (Univ of Reading Art Gallery) 1984, Three Decades of Contemporary Art (Juda Rowan Gallery) 1985, From Prism to Paint Box (Welsh Arts Cncl touring exhbn) 1989–90, A Centenary Exhibition (Univ of Reading Art Gallery) 1992, Konstruktiv Tendens Gallery Stockholm 2002, Open Secret (Imperial War Museum) 2004, Summer Exhibition (Royal Acad) 2004 and 2007; *Recreations* travelling, reading, listening to music, seeing films, visiting museums, exhibitions, art galleries etc; *Style*— Peter Kalkhof, Esq; ✉ c/o Annely Juda Fine Art, 23 Dering Street, London W1R 9AA (e-mail p.kalkhof@virgin.net)

KALKHOVEN, Ir Paul; *b* 25 May 1955; *Educ* Triniteits Lyceum Haarlem The Netherlands, Dept of Architecture and Town Planning Tech Univ Delft The Netherlands (Ingenieur); *Career* architect; MacCormac Jamieson & Prichard 1980–85, Foster & Partners 1986– (currently st ptnr); ARB 1984; *Style*— Ir Paul Kalkhoven; ✉ Foster and Partners, Riverside 3, 22 Hester Road, London SW11 4AN (tel 020 7738 0455)

KALLAKIS, Achilleas Michalis; *b* 3 September 1968; *Educ* St Paul's, Univ of Buckingham (BSc); *m* Pamela Anne, *née* Stachowsky; 1 da (Erinoula b 12 July 1997), 2 s (Michalis, Aristotlelis (twins) b 7 Oct 1998); *Career* fndr chm and ceo Pacific Gp of Cos 1990–; chm Pacific Vending Gp 1998–, chm and ceo Atlas Alliance Gp 2000–; dir: Global Transport Inc 1989–, Ocean Gp 1989–, Bernouli Tst Corp 1994–, US C of C London 1997–, Pacific Coffee Corp 1998–, British American Business Inc; chm South Pacific Advsy Bd 1994–; memb US C of C Japan; dir Friends of Florence 1997–; memb: Royal Opera House, National Tst, Navy League, Soc for Protection of Ancient Buildings (SPAB), Landmark Tst, Metropolitan Opera Guild NY, Devpt Bd Nat Portrait Gallery; involved with various children's, educnl, royal and cancer-related charities; FInstD; *Books* Maritime Registries of the World (1994), The Wonders of Italy (1996); *Recreations* tennis, travel, Italian studies, backgammon; *Clubs* Cliveden, Queen's, Metropolitan (NY); *Style*— Achilleas Kallakis, Esq; ✉ Pacific Group of Companies, 8 Carlos Place, Mayfair, London W1K 3AS (tel 020 7495 5252)

KALMS, Baron (Life Peer UK 2004), of Edgware in the London Borough of Brent; Sir Stanley Kalms; kt (1996); s of Charles Kalms (d 1978), and Cissie, *née* Schlagman (d 1990); *b* 21 November 1931; *Educ* Christ's Coll Finchley; *m* 28 Feb 1954, Pamela Audrey, da of Morris Jimack (d 1968), of London; 3 s (Hon Richard b 10 March 1955, Hon Stephen b 3 Dec 1956, Hon Paul b 6 March 1963); *Career* Dixons Group plc: joined 1948, chm 1971–2002, pres 2002–; non-exec dir British Gas plc (now BG plc) 1987–97; chm King's Healthcare NHS Tst 1993–96, memb Funding Agency for Schs 1994–97 (chm Fin Ctee 1994–97); non-exec dir Centre for Policy Studies 1991–2001; visiting prof Univ of N London Business Sch 1991; govr: Dixons Bradford City Technol Coll, NIESR 1995–2003; tstee: Industry in Education Ltd 1993–2002, The Economic Education Trust 1993–2002; dir Business for Sterling 1998–2001; pty treas Cons Pty 2001–03; Hon DLitt: CNAA/Univ of London 1991, Univ of Sheffield 2002; Hon Dr Univ of N London 1994, Hon DEcon Richmond 1996, Hon Degree Univ of Buckingham 2002; hon fell London Business Sch 1995; Hon FCGI 1988; *Publications* A Time for Change (1992); *Recreations* communal educnl activities, sailing, opera; *Clubs* Carlton, Savile, Portland; *Style*— The Rt Hon the Lord Kalms; ✉ 84 Brook Street, London W1K 5EH (tel 020 7499 3494, fax 020 7499 3436)

KALMUS, Prof George Ernest; CBE (2000); s of Hans Kalmus (d 1988), and Anna, *née* Rosenberg (d 1997); *b* 21 April 1935; *Educ* St Albans Co GS, UCL (BSc, PhD); *m* 15 June 1957, Ann Christine, da of Ernest Henry Harland (d 1984); 3 da (Susan Jane b 1960, Mary Elisabeth b 1962, Diana Christine b 1965); *Career* Lawrence Radiation Laboratory Univ of Calif Berkeley: res assoc 1962–63 and 1964–67, sr physicist 1967–71; UCL: res assoc 1959–62, lectr Physics Dept 1963–64, visiting prof 1984–; Rutherford Appleton Laboratory: gp ldr Bubble Chamber and Delphi Gps 1971–86, dir Particle Physics 1986–97, sr physicist 1998–2000, hon scientist 2000–; FRS 1988; *Recreations* skiing, reading, cycling; *Style*— Prof George Kalmus, CBE, FRS; ✉ 16 South Avenue, Abingdon, Oxfordshire OX14 1QH (tel 01235 523340); Rutherford Appleton Laboratory, Chilton, Didcot, Oxfordshire OX11 0QX (tel 01235 445443, fax 01235 446733, e-mail george.kalmus@rl.ac.uk)

KALSI, Amarjit; s of Mohinder Singh Kalsi, and Savitri Rani, *née* Bhogal; *b* 30 May 1957; *Educ* Little Ilford Comp London, Architectural Assoc; *m* 18 Dec 1982, Giurjeet Kaur Kalsi; 4 c (Mangla b 15 May 1984, Anju b 28 June 1987, Noorie b 29 July 1990, Mira b 4 Sept 2000); *Career* architect; Richard Rogers Partnership: joined 1981, co-dir 1988–; lectr: Kingston Univ, Univ of Nottingham, Univ of Newcastle, Architectural Assoc, Univ of Edinburgh, Univ of Westminster, Michigan Univ; memb judging panel Design Sense Competition Deisgn Museum 2000; guest speaker: Indian Stainless Steel Assoc Delhi 1999, German Stainless Steel Assoc Berlin 2000, Italian Stainless Steel Assoc Milan 2000; *Projects* incl: Lloyd's Bldg, Pump House, Reuter's Data Centre, Port Aupec, European Ct of Human Rights Strasbourg, Bordeaux Judiciare, Learning Resource Thames Valley Univ, SmithKline Beecham, Heathrow Airport Terminal 5, Daiwa II 88 Wood Street, Millennium Dome, Montevetro Battersea London, Antwerp Ct House, Lurven Station Competition, Amano Labs Japan; *Style*— Amarjit Kalsi, Esq; ✉ Richard Rogers Partnership, Thames Wharf, Rainville Road, London W6 9HA

KAMDAR, Batookrai Anopchand; s of Anopchand Keshavlal Kamdar, and Lilavati, *née* Shah; *b* 29 October 1939; *Educ* Gujarat Univ (MB BS), FRCS (tutor); *m* 27 May 1964, Dr Beni Kamdar, da of Dr Chandulal Chhotalal Shah, of Baroda, India; 1 s (Neel b 1965), 1 da (Sujata b 1967); *Career* orthopaedic registrar: Hammersmith Hosp 1970–71, Heatherwood Hosp Ascot Berks 1971–72; sr orthopaedic registrar Royal Free Hosp London 1973–75, conslt orthopaedic surgn Dartford and Gravesham Health Dist 1975–; memb Br Orthopaedic Assoc; FRCSEd, FRCSEng; *Publications:* Complications Following Total Knee Replacement (1974), Soft Tissue Calcification Following Total Hip Replacement (1976), Early Soft Tissue Release in CTEV (1977), Lat Popliteal N Palsy in Unicompartmental Knee Replacement (2003); *Recreations* reading, music, philately, cricket, skiing, golf; *Clubs* MCC, London Golf; *Style*— Batookrai Kamdar, Esq; ✉ 7 Liskeard Close, Chislehurst, Kent BR7 6RT (tel 020 8467 9851, mobile 07050 113619, e-mail batukkamdar@aol.com); Fawkham Manor Hospital, Fawkham, Kent (tel 01474 879900)

KAMIL, His Hon Judge Geoffrey Harvey; s of Peter Kamil, of Leeds, and Sadie, *née* Morris; *b* 17 August 1942; *Educ* Leeds GS, Univ of Leeds (LLB); *m* 17 March 1968, Andrea Pauline, da of Gerald Ellis, of Leeds; 2 da (Sharon b 1969, Debra b 1971); *Career* admitted slr of the Supreme Court 1968, ptnr J Levi Leeds 1974–87; stipendiary magistrate: W Midlands 1987–90 (dep 1985), W Yorks 1990–93; recorder of Crown Court 1991–93 (asst recorder 1986–91), circuit judge (NE Circuit) 1993–; liaison judge Pontefract and Wakefield Magistrates' Court 1997–, ethnic minority liaison judge 1998–; dep chm Immigration Appeals Tbnl 1998–2000; memb: Magisterial Ctee Judicial Studies Bd 1991–93, W Yorks Race Issues Advsy Gp 1998–, Equal Treatment Advsy Ctee of Judicial Studies Bd 2000–, Race Issues Advsy Gp NACRO 2003–, Family Ctee Judicial Studies Bd 2004–; judicial memb Parole Bd 2000–; memb Centre for Criminal Justice Studies Univ of Leeds; sec Stonham's Kirkstall Lodge Hostel Leeds 1974–87; *Recreations* gardening, gym, walking, classic cars; *Clubs* David Lloyd Tennis, The Bradford; *Style*— His Hon Judge Kamil; ✉ The Law Courts, Exchange Square, Drake Street, Bradford, West Yorkshire BD1 1JA

KAMPFNER, John; *Career* journalist; foreign corr Daily Telegraph, chief political corr Financial Times, political commentator Today Programme (BBC Radio 4), ed New Statesman 2005– (previously political ed); *Books* Inside Yeltsin's Russia: Corruption, Conflict, Capitalism (1994), Robin Cook (1998), Blair's Wars (2003); *Style*— John Kampfner, Esq; ✉ New Statesman, 52 Grovesnor Gardens, London SW1W 0AU

KANABUS, Annabel; da of Sir Robert Sainsbury, and Lisa, *née* Van den Bergh; *b* 22 January 1948; *Educ* Francis Holland Sch, UEA (BSc); *m* 13 March 1975, Peter John Kanabus, s of Edward Kanabus; 2 s (Jason b 9 June 1976, Adrian b 15 Feb 1978); *Career* fndr and tstee of the charity Avert 1986–; *Recreations* gardening; *Style*— Mrs Annabel Kanabus; ✉ Avert, 4 Brighton Road, Horsham, West Sussex RH13 5BA (tel 01403 210202, fax 01403 211001, e-mail info@avert.org)

KANDER, Nadav; *b* 1961; *Career* photographer, established studio London working freelance on major advertising campaigns 1986– (incl Amnesty International, Dr Barnardos, Heals, Levis, Nike, Adidas and Stella Artois; *Exhibitions* Nat Portrait Gallery, V&A, Tate Liverpool, Royal Photographic Soc Bath, Photographers' Gallery London, Shine Gallery London, Leeds Met Univ Gallery, Acte II Gallery paris, Palais de Tokyo Paris, Shanghai Art Museum, Yancey Richardson Gallery NY, Fahey Klein Gallery LA, Peter Fetterman Gallery LA; *Awards* 2 Gold and 11 Silver Awards Assoc of Photographers, 7 Awards of Excellence Communication Arts, 2 Silver Awards D&AD, 2 Gold and 4 Silver Awards Art Director's Club of NY, Creative Review Annual, IPA Lucie Advtg Photographer of the Year; *Publications* Nadav Kander - Night (2001), Beauty's Nothing (2001); articles, reviews and editorial in various publications incl: Sunday Times Magazine, NY Times Magazine, Details, Dazed & Confused, Creative Review; *Style*— Nadav Kander; ✉ c/o Nadav Kander, Unit D, Imperial Works, Perren Street, London NW5 3ED (tel 020 7485 6789, fax 020 7485 4321, e-mail mail@nadavkander.com)

KANE, Archie Gerard; s of Archie Kane (d 1990), and Rose Anne McGhee (d 1982); *b* 16 June 1952, Bellshill, Lanarkshire; *Educ* St Aloysius Coll Glasgow, Univ of Glasgow (BAcc), City Univ (MBA), Harvard Business Sch (AMP); *m* 26 Sept 1986, Diana Muirhead; 2 da (Rebecca b 3 Sept 1990, Brodie b 11 Nov 1992); *Career* asst mangr Price Waterhouse 1978–80, sr mgmnt auditor rising to finance dir General Telephone & Electronics Corporation 1980–85, finance dir British Telecom Yellow Pages Sales Ltd 1986, gp finance controller TSB Commercial Holdings Ltd 1986–89; TSB Bank plc: financial controller then dir of financial control Retail Banking Div 1989–91, dir of financial control then ops dir Retail Banking and Insurance 1991–94, gp strategic devpt dir 1994–96; Lloyds TSB Gp plc: project dir (post merger integration) 1996, retail financial servs dir 1996, dir of gp IT and ops 1997–99, gp exec dir IT & Ops 2000–03, gp exec dir Insurance and Investments 2003–, chief exec Scottish Widows plc 2003–, chm Lloyds TSB General Insurance Ltd 2003–, chm Scottish Widows Investment Partnership Gp Ltd 2003–; chm Assoc of Payment Clearing Systems (APACS) 1991–93, memb Bd ABI 1994–; MICAS, FCIBS 2005; *Recreations* golf, tennis, skiing; *Style*— Mr Archie Kane; ✉ Lloyds TSB Group plc, 25 Gresham Street, London EC2V 7HN (tel 020 7356 1409, fax 020 7356 1195)

KANE, Martin Christopher; s of Bernard Kane, of Milngavie, Glasgow, and Rosina, *née* Maguire; *b* 3 June 1958; *Educ* St Andrew's HS Clydebank Glasgow, Edinburgh Coll of Art (BA); *m* 17 Oct 2002, Sharon, *née* Goodlet; 1 s (Christopher b 13 June 2003); *Career* artist; *Solo Exhibitions* Artist of the Day (Angela Flowers Gallery) 1988, Memory and Imagination (Jill George Gallery London) 1990, Reflections (Jill George Gallery London) 1992, Beyond the Wall (Jill George Gallery) 1993, New Paintings (Beaux Arts Gallery London) 1996, Both Sides of the Wall (Studio One Child Graddon Lewis London) 2002; *Group Exhibitions* incl: student annual exhibition (Royal Scottish Acad) 1986 and 1987, New Generation (Compass Gallery Glasgow) 1987, Obsessions (Raab Gallery London) 1987, Two Scottish Artists (Boundary Gallery) 1988, Int Art Fair (LA with Thumb Gallery) 1989, 1990, 1991 and 1992, Art 90, Art 91, Art 92, Art 93, Art 94, Art 95, Art 96, Art 99, Art 2000 and Art 2001 (Design Centre London), London to Atlanta (Thumb Gallery Atlanta) 1990, Lineart 95 (Gent) 1995, Small Paintings (Beaux Arts), 1st Int Art Fair New York 1998, Cabnet Paintings (Glasgow Print Studio) 2001, New Work 2003 (Seagull Gallery Gourock Scotland) 2003, Finding the Sacred in the 21st Century (Church of St John Edinburgh Festival) 2005, Glasgow Boys (Gatehouse Gallery Glasgow) 2006, Six Scottish Artists (Lyme Art Gallery Old Lyme CT) 2007; *Public Collections* Glasgow District Cncl, Cleveland Museum Middlesbrough, CBS Collection, Scottish Devpt Agency Glasgow, Unilever plc Collection London, Gartmore Investments, Glasgow Museums Collection, Harry Taylor of Ashton; *Recreations* music, classic cars; *Clubs* Glasgow Art, Mercedes-Benz; *Style*— Martin Kane, Esq

KANIS, Prof John Anthony; s of Max Kanis (d 1957), of London, and Elizabeth Mary, *née* Mees (d 2003); *b* 2 September 1944; *Educ* Univ of Edinburgh (MB ChB); *m* 1, 11 April 1966 (m dis 1984), Patricia Sheila, *née* Mclaren; 4 da (Lisa b 13 Dec 1967, Emma b 24 Sept 1969, Sarah b 4 July 1971, Rebecca b 2 Jan 1975); m 2, 19 June 1989, Monique Nicole Christiane, da of Georges Marie Benéton (d 1997); 1 step da (Natalie Beresford b 10 Dec 1978); *Career* Wellcome sr research fell Univ of Oxford 1976–79; conslt: Royal Hallamshire Hosp 1979–, Miny of Health France 1981–; prof of human metabolism Univ of Sheffield 1982–2003 (now emeritus); pres Euro Fndn for Osteoporosis and Bone Disease 1987–90, tstee Int Osteoporosis Fndn 1987–, advsr on osteoporosis WHO 1988–, dir WHO Collaborating Centre for Metabolic Bone Disease Sheffield; chm Strakan Gp Ltd 1997–2005; ed Bone jl, author of 600 scientific pubns on bone disease; MRCPath 1982, FRCP 1984, MD 1985, FRCPE 1986; *Books* Paget's Disease of the Bone, Osteoporosis; *Recreations* antiques restoration, genealogy; *Style*— Prof John Kanis; ✉ WHO Collaborating Centre for Metabolic Bone Diseases, University of Sheffield Medical School, Beech Hill Road, Sheffield S10 2RX (tel 0114 285 1109, fax 0114 285 1813, e-mail mbeneton@compuserve.com)

KANTOROWICZ-TORO, Donald; s of Rodolph Kantorowicz, and Blanca Livia, *née* Toro; *b* 4 August 1945; *Educ* Jesuit Sch Cali Colombia, Hochschule für Welthandel Vienna (MBA), Faculté de Droit et Sciences Economiques Paris (DEconSc); *m* 1, 12 Sept 1973 (m dis 1986); 2 da (Melanie Tatiana b 1976, Johanna Joy b 1978); m 2, 16 July 1999 (m dis

K

2006), Laura Puyana-Bickenbach; *Career* Banque de L'Union Européenne Paris 1969–71, vice-pres and mangr Bank of America Paris and Madrid 1972–79, md and chief exec Consolidado UK/Vestcor Partners Ltd 1980–94, first vice-pres Merrill Lynch 1995–; memb French Fin Assoc Paris; *Recreations* skiing, sailing, classical music, history; *Clubs* Overseas Bankers, Cercle Interallie Paris; *Style*— Donald Kantorowicz-Toro, Esq; ✉ 11 South Terrace, London SW7 2BT (tel 020 7584 8185); Houston Palace, 7 Boulevard Princesse Grace, Monaco 98000; Merrill Lynch, 2 King Edward Street, London EC1A 1HQ (tel 020 7996 8124, fax 020 7996 8520, e-mail donald_kantorowicz@ml.com); Merrill Lynch, Le Prince de Galles, 5 Avenue des Citronniers, BP 163, MC 98003, Monaco

KAPADIA, Asif; *b* 1973, Hackney, London; *Educ* RCA; *Career* film dir; work incl commercials for AMV BBDO and 180 Amsterdam; *Film* dir: The Waiting Room (screened at British and Munich short film festivals) 1996, The Sheep Thief (graduation film, screened Channel 4, and London, Clermont-Ferrand, NY, Texas and Cork Film Festivals) 1997, Hot Dog (short film for Channel 4/Ideal World's Spotlight Series) 1998, The Warrior 2001 (also co-writer), Cinema16 2003, The Return 2006; *Awards* for The Waiting Room: RTS Student Award; for The Sheep Thief: Grand Jury Prize Cannes Int Film Festival 1998, Grand Prix European Short Film Festival Brest, Direction Prize Poitiers Film Festival; for The Warrior: BAFTA Alexander Korda Award (for Outstanding Br Film of the Year) 2003; BAFTA Carl Foreman Award (for special achievement by a dir, screenwriter or prodr in their first feature film) 2003; *Style*— Asif Kapadia, Esq; ✉ c/o Paul Weiland Film Company, 14 Newburgh Street, London W1F 7RT (tel 020 7287 6900, fax 020 7434 0146)

KAPLICKY, Jan; s of Josef Kaplicky (d 1962), and Jirina, *née* Florova (d 1984); *b* 18 April 1937; *Educ* Coll of Applied Arts and Architecture Prague (DipArch); *m* 1991, Amanda Levete, *qv*; 1 s (Josef b 18 April 1995); *Career* architect; private practice Prague 1964–68, Denys Lasdun & Partners 1969–71, Piano & Rogers 1971–73, Spencer & Webster 1974–75, Louis de Soissons 1975–77, Foster Assocs 1977–83; fndr Future Systems 1979; teacher/unit master Architectural Assoc 1982–88, sometime lectr UK, Europe, USA and Australia; Hon FRIBA *Projects* incl: Comme des Garçons New York and Tokyo, Natwest Media Centre Lord's Cricket Ground, West India Quay Bridge Canary Wharf, Hauer-King House London, MOMI Tent, Manni shops London, Milan, Tokyo, Paris and NY, Selfridges Birmingham 2003; *Exhibitions* incl: Jan Kaplicky Projects (Art-Net) 1978, Future Systems (RIBA) 1982 (also at The Graham Fndn Chicago 1987, Architectural Assoc 1987, The Cube Manchester 1999), Nouvelles Tendances (Pompidou Centre Paris) 1987, Bibliothèque de France (Institut Français d'Architecture) 1989, Royal Acad Summer Show 1990, 1993, 1995 and 1996, Future Systems: Architecture (RIBA) 1991, Future Systems: Recent Work (Store-Front NYC) 1992, Permanent Collection (Pompidou Centre Paris) 1993, Contemporary British Architecture (LA and Chicago) 1995, Cities of the Future (Hong Kong) 1997, ICA 1998, National Gallery Prague 1998, New Urban Environments (Tokyo) 1998, Future Systems (Cube Gallery Manchester) 1999, Future Systems Originals (Faggionato Fine Arts Gallery London) 2001, La Biennal di Venezia (Venice) 2002 and 2004, La Triennale di Milano (Milan) 2003 and 2004, A Blueprint for Life (National Portrait Gallery) 2004, Royal Academy Summer Show 2005 and 2006; profiles and coverage of buildings on TV; *Awards* first prize: Industrial Estates Competition Newcastle 1976, Liverpool Focus on the Centre Competition 1978, Landmark Competition Melbourne 1979, AJ/Bovis Royal Acad 1993, Aluminium Imagination Architectural Award 1995 and 1999, Civic Tst Award 1996 and 1997; jt first: Design Week (Product Design) 1992, British Construction Industry 1992 and 1997; second prize: Bridge of the Future Competition Tokyo 1987, Int Competition Bibliothèque de France Paris 1989; other awards incl: Graham Fndn Chicago 1986, NASA Certificate of Recognition 1989, finalist Designer of the Year The Prince Philip Prize 1991, Geoffrey Gribble Meml Conservation Award, RIBA Award Wild at Heart flower shop 1998, Millennium Product Natwest Media Centre 1999, Stirling Prize 1999, Designer of the Year FX Int Interior Design Awards 2003; *Books* Future Systems: The Story of Tomorrow (by Martin Pawley, 1993), For Inspiration Only (1996), Hauer-King House (by Martin Pawley, 1996), More For INspiration Only (1999), Future Systems (1999, by Marcus Field), Unique Building by Future Systems (2001), Confessions (2002), Czech Inspiration (2004), Jan Kaplicky Album (2005), Future Systems (by Deyan Sudjic, 2006); *Recreations* history of modern architecture; *Clubs* Architecture; *Style*— Jan Kaplicky, Esq; ✉ Future Systems, The Warehouse, 20 Victoria Gardens, London W11 3PE (tel 020 7243 7670)

KAPOOR, Anish; CBE (2003); *b* Bombay, India; *Educ* Hornsey Coll of Art London, Chelsea Sch of Art; *Career* artist, sculptor; teacher Wolverhampton Poly 1979, artist in residence Walker Art Gallery Liverpool 1982; subject of numerous books, articles and reviews; memb Arts Cncl of England 1998–; hon dr London Inst 1997, Hon FRIBA 2001; *Solo Exhibitions* incl: Patrice Alexandre Paris 1980, Lisson Gallery 1983, 1985, 1988, 1989–90 and 1993, Walker Art Gallery Liverpool 1982 and 1983, Barbara Gladstone Gallery NY 1984, 1986, 1989–90 and 1993, Stedelijk Van Abbemuseum Erndhoven 1986, Anish Kapoor: Recent Sculpture and Drawings (Univ Gallery Massachusetts) 1986, Anish Kapoor: Works On Paper 1975–87 (Ray Hughes Gallery) 1987, Kohji Ogura Gallery Japan 1989, Br Pavilion Venice 1990, Anish Kapoor Drawings (Tate Gallery) 1990–91, Centre National d'Art Contemporain Grenoble 1990–91, Palacio de Velazquez Madrid 1991, Kunstverein Hannover 1991, Feuerle Köln 1991, The Sixth Japan Ushimado Int Art Festival Japan 1991, Galeria Soledad Lorenzo Madrid 1992, San Diego Museum of Contemporary Art 1992–93, Designs for a Dance (South Bank Centre London) 1993, Tel Aviv Museum of Art 1993, Mala Galerija Moderna Galerija Ljubljana 1994, Echo (Kohji Ogura Gallery) 1994, Anish Kapoor (Tillburg Nishimura Gallery Tokyo) 1995, Prada Milanoarte Milan and also Lisson Gallery London 1995–96, Anish Kapoor. Sculptures (Aboa Vetus & Ars Nova Finland) 1996, Anish Kapoor: Two Sculptures (Kettle's Yard Cambridge) 1996, Galleria Massimo Minini Brescia 1996, Gourd Project 1993–95 (Freddie Fong Contemporary Art San Francisco) 1996, Kunst-Station Sankt Peter Cologne 1996, Hayward Gallery London 1998, Lisson Gallery London 1998, Barbara Gladstone Gallery NY 1998, CAPC Bordeaux 1998, Baltic Centre for Contemporary Art Gateshead 1999, Scai The Bathhouse Tokyo 1999, Museé d'Art Contemporain de Bordeaux 1999, Blood (Lisson Gallery London) 2000, The Edge of the World (installation, Axel Vervoordt Kanal Wijnegem Belgium) 2000, Blood Solid (fig-1 London) 2000, Taratantara (installation, Baltic Centre Gateshead and Piazza del Plebiscito Naples) 2000, Taidehalli Helsinki 2001, Barbara Gladstone NY 2001, Marsyas (installation, Tate Modern) 2002, Painting (Lisson Gallery London) 2003, Kukje Gallery Seoul 2003, Galleria Continua San Gimignano Italy 2003, Idomeneo (set design, Glyndebourne) 2003, My Red Homeland (Kunsthaus Bregenz) 2003, Nat Archaeological Museum Naples 2003, Whiteout (Barbara Gladstone Gallery NY) 2004, Cloud Gate (Chicago Millennium Park) 2004, Massimo Minini Gallery Brescia 2004, Melancholia (MAC Grand-Hornu Belgium) 2004, Japanese Mirrors (SCAI Tokyo) 2005, My Red Homeland (CAC Malaga) 2006, Regen Projects LA 2006, Ascension (BBCC Rio de Janeiro and Brasilia) 2006 and (Sao Paulo) 2007, Sky Mirror (Rockefeller Center NY) 2006, Lisson Gallery London 2006, Works on Paper (Gladstone Gallery NY) 2007; *Group Exhibitions* incl: Art Into Landscape 1 (Serpentine Gallery London) 1974, Young Contemporaries (Royal Academy London) 1975, London/New York 1982 (Lisson Gallery London) 1982, Paris Biennale (Paris) 1982, India: Myth and Reality (MOMA Oxford) 1982, Finland Biennale (Helsinki) 1983, Sculpture 1983 (Van Krimpen Gallery Amsterdam) 1983, New Art (Tate Gallery) 1983, An International Survey of Recent Painting and Sculpture (MOMA NY) 1984, Nouvelle Biennale de Paris (Paris) 1985, Europa oggi/Europe now (Museo d'Arte Contemporánea Italy) 1988, Starlit Waters, British Sculpture: An International Art 1968–88 (Tate Gallery Liverpool) 1988, Heroes of Contemporary Art (Galerie Saqqarah Switzerland) 1990–91, British Art Now (touring) 1990–91, Gallery Shirakawa Kyoto 1991, Feuerle Gallery 1991, Anish Kapoor and Abstract Art in Asia (Fukuoka Art Museum Japan) 1991–92, Whitechapel Open 1992, British Sculpture from the Arts Cncl Collection (Derby Museum and Art Gallery) 1993, Punti Dell'Arti (Italian Pavilion Venice Biennale) 1993, Art Against Aids (Venice Biennale) 1993, Sculpture (Leo Castelli Gallery NY) 1993, Sculptors' Drawings (Tate Gallery) 1994, Re Rebaudengo Sandretto Collection Turin 1994, Ars 95 Helsinki (Museum of Contemporary Art Helsinki) 1995, Ideal Standard Summertime (Lisson Gallery London) 1995, British Abstract Art Part II: Sculpture (Flowers East Gallery London) 1995, Fémininmasculin. Le sexe de l'art (Centre Georges Pompidou Paris) 1996, New Art on Paper 2 (Philadelphia Museum of Art) 1996, Un siècle de sculpture anglaise (Jeu de Paume Paris) 1996, Anish Kapoor, Barry X Ball (Angles Gallery Santa Monica USA) 1996, 23rd Int Biennial of Sao Paolo 1996, Moderner Galerija Ljubljana (MOMA Sarajevo Ljubljana Slovenia) 1996, Betong (Malmö Konsthall) 1996, entgegen (Mausoleum am Dom Graz) 1997, Arte Continua (Chiesa di San Guisto and Pinacoteca Civica Volterra Italy) 1997, Belladonna (ICA London) 1997, Changing Spaces (Detroit Inst of Arts) 1997/98, Wounds: Between Democracy and Redemption in Contemporary Art (Moderna Museet Stockholm) 1998, Then and Now (Lisson Gallery London) 1998, Prime (Dundee Contemporary Art Dundee) 1999, Shape of the Century (Salisbury Festival) 1999, Den Haag Sculptuur (The Hague) 1999, Art Worlds in Dialogue (Museum Ludwig Cologne) 1999, Together: Artists in Support for the Homeless (The Passage House London) 1999, Beauty - 25th Anniversary (Hirschhorn Museum and Sculpture Garden Washington DC) 1999, Retrace Your Steps: Remember Tomorrow (Soane Museum London, curated by Hans Ulrich Obrist) 1999, Blue (New Walsall Museum Walsall) 2000, Groenningen Exhibition 2000 (Charlottenborg Copenhagen) 2000, Sinn und Sinnlichkeit (Neues Museum Weserburg Bremen) 2000, La Beauté (Papal Palace Avignon) 2000, Lyon Biennale (Lyon) 2000, 1951–2001 Made in Italy (triennale, Palazzo dell'Arte Milan) 2001, BO01 (Concepthaus Malmo) 2001, Drawings (Regen Projects LA) 2001, Field Day: Sculpture form Britain (Tapei Fine Art Museum Japan) 2001, Homage to Rudolf Schwarzkogler (Galerie Krinzinger Vienna) 2002, Kaash (touring collaborative dance prodn) 2002, this ain't no tupperware (Kunststof, Kortrijk and Herford Belgium) 2002, Colour White (De La Warr Pavilion) 2002, No Object, No Subject, No Matter... (Irish MOMA) 2002, Remarks on Colour (Sean Kelly Gallery NY) 2002, Blast to Freeze (Kunstmuseum Wolfsburg) 2002–03, Retrospectacle: 25 Years of Collecting Modern and Contemporary Art (Denver Art Museum) 2002–03, Mind Space Ho-Am Art Gallery Seoul 2003, Beaufort 2003 (Ostend) 2003, Himmelschwer Graz 2003, Ineffable Beauty (Kunsthalle Erfurt) 2003, In Good Form (Longside Gallery Yorks Sculpture Park) 2003, Longside Gallery Yorks Sculpture Park 2003, Saved! (Hayward Gallery) 2003–04, Pain: passion Companssion Sensibility (Science Museum London) 2004, Lustwarande 04 (Tilburg) 2004, Gwangju Biennale Korea 2004, Arts and Architecture 1900–2000 (Genova Palazzo Ducale) 2004, Kanazawa Museum 2004, Universal Experience (MCA Chicago) 2005, Colour after Klein (Barbican) 2005, British Sculpture Show (Kunsthalle Würth) 2005, God is Great (Venice) 2005, Museo Madre Naples 2005, Arte all'Arte (San Gimignano) 2005, Sixty Years of Sculpture (Arts Cncl Collection) 2006, The Sublime is Now (Museum Franz Gertsch Switzerland) 2006, Sculpture (Thaddaeus Ropac Salzburg) 2006, The Expanded Eye (Kunsthaus Zurich) 2006, Surprise, Surprise (ICA London) 2006, How to Improve the World (Hayward Gallery London) 2006, Super Vision (ICA Boston) 2006, Asia Pacific Triennial of Contemporary Art (Queensland Art Gallery) 2006–07, One Colour (Galleria Continua Beijing) 2007, Timer (Milan) 2007, Contrepoint III (Louvre Paris) 2007; *Works in Collections* incl: Tate Gallery London, Hirshhorn Museum and Sculpture Park Washington DC, MOMA NY, Art Gallery of New South Wales Sydney, Rijksmuseum Kroller-Muller Otterlo, Moderna Museet Stockholm, Tel Aviv Museum of Art Israel, Vancouver Art Gallery and San Diego Museum of Contemporary Art; *Awards* Premio Duemila Venice Biennale 1990, Turner Prize 1991; *Style*— Anish Kapoor, Esq, CBE; ✉ Lisson Gallery (London) Ltd, 67 Lisson Street, London NW1 5DA (tel 020 7724 2739, fax 020 7724 7124)

KAPOSI, Dr Agnes Aranka; da of Imre Kristof (d 1962), and Magda Csengeri; *b* 20 October 1932; *Educ* Kossuth Zsuzsa Girls' Sch Budapest, Tech Univ of Budapest (Dipl Ing), PhD (UK); *m* 1952, Janos Ferenc Kaposi, s of Ernö Kaposi; 2 da (Esther Julia b 1959, Anna Jane b 1963); *Career* sr res engr and head of Digital Systems Gp Ericsson Telephones Beeston 1957–60, princ res engr and head of Storage Electronics ICL Research Laboratories Stevenage 1960–64, lectr Cambridgeshire Coll of Arts and Technol 1964–67, princ lectr and dir of res and postgrad studies Kingston Poly (now Univ of Kingston upon Thames) 1967–77, head Dept of Electrical and Electronic Engrg South Bank Poly (now South Bank Univ) 1977–88; formerly: ptnr Polytechnic Consultants, dir ARC Consultants Ltd; ptnr Kaposi Associates 1986–; visiting prof Engrg Design Centre City Univ 1990–95, academic govr Richmond The American Int Univ in London 1992–, memb Nat Bd Academic Accreditation of the Hungarian Govt 1994–97; former memb WSET Ctee Office of Sci and Technol; Instn of Electrical Engrs: memb Cncl, memb Int Bd, memb Accreditation Ctee, memb Pool of Accreditors, former memb Public Affrs Bd, chair London Branch 1994–95; memb Nominations Ctee Engrg Cncl 1986–96; EPSRC (formerly SERC): memb, memb Electromechanical Engrg Ctee, memb Info Technol Liaison Ctee 1989–93; memb Cncl Women's Engrg Soc 1990–94; FIEE 1977 (MIEE 1958), FREng 1992; *Books* Systems, Models and Measures, Systems for computer systems professionals, A first systems book (with M Myers, 1994); *Recreations* reading, music, walking, debating, bridge; *Style*— Dr Agnes Kaposi, FREng; ✉ Kaposi Associates, 3 St Edwards Close, London NW11 (tel 020 8458 3626, fax 020 8458 0899)

KAPP, Carlo David; s of Robert Scope Kapp (d 1975), of Hayling Island, Hants, and Paola Luisa, *née* Putoto; *b* 31 July 1947; *Educ* Ladybarn Sch Manchester; *m* 1, 28 March 1970 (m dis 1978), Jean Gillian, da of Aubrey Charles Overington (d 1980), of Richmond, Surrey; 1 da (Kelli Anne b 4 July 1977); m 2, 30 Oct 1979, Basia Evelyn, da of Dr Abraham Seinwel Bardach (d 1988), of London; 1 s (Daniel Joseph Scope b 5 Oct 1980), 1 da (Pippa Luisa b 25 Feb 1983); *Career* creative servs mangr Estée Lauder Group (UK) 1974–81; chm and md: Dawson Kapp Overseas 1981–88, The DKO Group plc 1988–; chm The Best Group Ltd 1988–; govr RNLI; memb: The Little Ship Club, Greenpeace; *Recreations* shooting, golf, skiing, marathon running, sailing; *Clubs* RAC, LSC, Wimbledon Park Golf; *Style*— Carlo Kapp, Esq; ✉ 145 Kensington Church Street, London W8 7LP

KAPPLER, David; s of Alec Kappler (d 1995), and Hilary, *née* Coleman; *b* 24 March 1947; *Educ* Lincoln Sch; *m* 1970, Maxine; 3 da (Suzanne b 1973, Isabel b 1975, Sally b 1981); *Career* fin dir: Jeyes Gp 1977–84, Trebor Gp 1984–89; Cadbury Schweppes plc: fin dir (Cadbury Ltd) 1990–91, fin dir confectionary 1991–93, corp fin dir 1994–95, gp fin dir 1995–2004; non-exec chm Premier Foods plc 2004–; non-exec dir: Camelot plc 1997–2004, HMV Gp plc 2002–, Shire Pharmaceuticals plc 2004–, InterContinental Hotels Gp plc 2004–; Leverhulme Prize (CIMA) 1968; FCIMA 1970; *Recreations* watching sports, playing golf; *Clubs* Harewood Downs Golf, RAC; *Style*— David Kappler, Esq

KARAT, David Spencer; s of Lt Rene Karat, and Frances, *née* Levy; *b* 1 August 1951; *Educ* Merchant Taylors, Univ of Leicester (LLB); *m* 1, 1 Sept 1976 (m dis 2003), Shirley Lessels; 2 da (Florence Louisa b 22 Sept 1980, Emma Rachel b 21 May 1985); m 2, 19 July 2005, Aurore L'Heritier; 1 s (Joshua b 30 Sept 2006); *Career* slr Slaughter & May 1976, gp counsel Royal Bank of Canada 1980; Merrill Lynch: assoc dir 1984, exec dir 1986, md 1989, head Fin Instns Gp; md and head of capital mkts Salomon Brothers International Limited 1990–96, md and co-head Fin Instns BZW 1996–97, md Fin Instns Barclays Capital 1997, ptnr Deloitte & Touche 1998–2003, founding ptnr Clarat Ptnrs 2003–; memb Law Soc; *Recreations* classic cars, motorbikes, running, theatre, jazz and classical music; *Clubs* RAC; *Style*— David S Karat, Esq; ✉ Clarat Partners, 56 Queen Anne Street, London W1G 8LA (tel 020 7317 3143)

KARIM, Sajjad Haider; MEP; s of Fazal Karim, and Shamshad Karim; *b* 11 July 1970; *Educ* Mansfield HS, Nelson and Colne Coll, London Guildhall Univ, Coll of Law Chester; *m* 17 Aug 1997, Zahida; 2 c (Bilal Haider b 24 Jan 2000, Rabia Iman b 27 Sept 2002); *Career* ptnr: SFN Slrs 1995–2001, Marsdens Slrs 2001–; MEP (Lib Dem) NW England 2003–; cncllr Pendle BC 1994–2002; memb Law Soc 1997; *Style*— Sajjad Karim, Esq, MEP; ✉ Marsdens Solicitors, 20A-22A Manchester Road, Nelson, Lancashire BB9 7EG (tel 01282 611899, fax 01282 611988, e-mail sajjad.karim@marsdens.uk.com)

KARLWEIS, Georges Joseph Christophe; s of Oskar Karlweis, and Ferdinanda Gabrielle, *née* Coulon; *b* 25 January 1928; *Educ* Univ of Paris (LLB); *m* 6 June 1986, Brigitte, da of Robert Camplez; *Career* economics corr AGEFI Paris 1946–52, sec gen Société Industrielle des Huiles au Maroc Casablanca Morocco 1952–55; former memb of various international Groupe Edmond de Rothschild cos, vice-chm Banque Privée Edmond de Rothschild SA Geneva, non-exec dir N M Rothschild & Sons Ltd; *Clubs* Golf of Geneva, Golf of Mortefontaine (Paris), Maxim's Business (Paris and Geneva); *Style*— Georges Karlweis, Esq; ✉ La Petite Pommeraie, 3 Chemin Palud, 1292 Pregny-Geneva, Switzerland (tel 00 41 22 758 2479); Lyford Cay Club, Nassau, Bahamas; Banque Privée Edmond de Rothschild SA, 18 rue de Hesse, 1204 Geneva, Switzerland (tel 00 41 22 818 9111, fax 00 41 22 818 9128)

KARMILOFF-SMITH, Prof Annette Dionne; CBE (2004); da of late Jack Smith, and Doris Ellen Ruth, *née* Findlay; *b* 18 July 1938; *Educ* Edmonton Co GS, Inst Français de Londres, Univ of Lille (Certificat d'Etudes Bilingues), Holborn Coll of Law and Languages (Dip Int Conf Interpreting), Univ of Geneva (Diplôme Général de Psychologie de l'Enfant, Licence en Psychologie, Diplôme de Spécialisation en Psychologie Génétique, Doctorat en Psychologie Génétique et Expérimentale); *m* 1, 1966 (m dis 1991), Igor Alexander Karmiloff; 2 da; *m* 2, 2001, Mark Henry Johnson; *Career* int conf interpreter UN 1966–70, research conslt UNWRA/UNESCO Inst of Educn Beirut 1970–72, research collaborator Int Centre for Genetic Epistemology Geneva 1972–76, chargé du cours Faculty of Med Univ of Berne 1977–79, dir of studies Univ of Geneva 1979, visiting research assoc Max-Planck Inst Nijmegen 1978–82, special appointment career scientist Cognitive Devpt Unit MRC 1988–98 (sr scientist 1982–88), hon prof of psychology UCL 1982–98, head Neurocognitive Devpt Unit Inst of Child Health 1998–2006, professorial research fell Birkbeck Univ London 2007–; visiting lectr: Free Univ of Brussels 1985, Max-Planck Inst Munich 1986, Univ of Chicago 1987, Univ of Barcelona 1988, Carnegie Mellon Univ Pittsburgh 1991–92, Univ of Aix-Marseilles 1995, Univ of Madrid 1995; Sloan fell: Yale Univ 1978, Univ of Calif Berkeley 1981; hon professorial fell in cognitive science Univ of Sussex 1979–81; memb and former memb editorial bds on numerous learned jls 1982–, author of numerous book chapters and of articles in learned journals; memb: Soc for the Study of Behavioural Phenotypes, Br Psychological Soc (memb Cncl 1988–91), US Soc for Philosophy and Psychology, US Cognitive Science Soc; memb Academia Europaea 1991, FBA 1993, FRSA 1996, FMedSci 1999; *Books* A Functional Approach to Child Language (1979, 2 edn 1981), Child Language Research in ESF Countries (jtly, 1991), Beyond Modularity: A Developmental Perspective on Cognitive Science (1992, British Psychological Society Book Award 1995), Baby It's You: A unique insight into the first three years of the developing baby (1994), Rethinking Nativism: Connectionism in a Developmental Framework (jtly, 1996), Everything Your Baby Would Ask (jtly, 1999); *Recreations* antique collecting, working out, going on multiple diets, writing/reading poetry; *Style*— Prof Annette Karmiloff-Smith, CBE, FBA, FMedSci

KARNEY, (Eur Ing) Andrew Lumsdaine; s of Rev Gilbert Henry Peter Karney (d 1996), and Celia Finch Wigham, *née* Richardson (d 1994); gf Rt Rev Arthur B L Karney, First Bishop of Johannesburg; *b* 24 May 1942; *Educ* Rugby, Trinity Coll Cambridge; *m* 1969, Beryl Fleur Goldwyn, MRAD, prima ballerina of Ballet Rambert 1950–60, da of late Louis Goldwyn, of Australia; 1 s (Peter John b 1972); *Career* staff memb UN Relief and Works Agency Beirut and Gaza 1963–64, devpt engr for STC (now Nortel) London and Paris 1965–68, sr scientist GEC Hirst Res Centre (now Marconi) 1968–71, planning engr communications Gas Council (now BG Gp) 1972–73; Logica plc (now Logica CMG plc) 1973–94: chm Logica Space and Communications Ltd 1984–94, fndr dir Logica General Systems Spa (Italy) 1984–94, fndr dir Logica Ltd (Hong Kong) 1986–94, corp devpt dir Logica plc 1986–94, dir Logica Data Architects Inc (USA) 1988–90, dir Logica Aerospace and Defence Ltd 1989–91, fndr dir Speedwing Logica Ltd 1990–94; fndr dir Cable London plc 1984–86; non-exec chm Language Line Ltd 1996–99 and 2003–06, non-exec chm Conclusive Logic Ltd 2000–02, non-exec dep chm Communicandum Ltd 1999–2003; non-exec dir: Integrated Micro Products plc 1995–96, Guardian Media Gp plc 1997–2006, Shreeveport Ltd 1997–, ViewGate Networks Ltd 1997–2001, Telematix Ltd 2000–01, Netcentric Systems Ltd 2000–01, Guardian Newspapers Ltd 2001–06, Baronsmead VCT3 plc 2001– (sr ind dir); ind conslt to various UK and int companies; memb Ctee Nat Electronics Cncl 1989–99, chm Tiri (int integrity NGO); Freeman City of London, Liveryman Worshipful Co of Info Technologists; memb: Royal Photographic Soc, Chatham House; CEng, Eur Ing, FIET, FInstD, FRSA; *Recreations* travel, photography, scuba diving; *Style*— Mr Andrew Karney; ✉ The Old Rectory, Credenhill, Herefordshire HR4 7DJ (tel 01432 761655, mobile 07956 366086, e-mail andrew@karney.com, website www.karney.com)

KARSTEN, His Hon Judge Ian George Francis; QC (1990); s of late Dr Frederick Karsten, and late Edith Karsten; *b* 27 July 1944; *Educ* William Ellis Sch Highgate, Magdalen Coll Oxford (MA, BCL); *m* 25 May 1984 (m dis 2002), Moira Elizabeth Ann, da of Wing Cdr Laurence O'Hara; 2 da (Lucy Caroline Jane b 9 Oct 1985, Emma Catherine Louise b 17 June 1988), 1 s (Charles Frederick Laurence b 9 Feb 1993); *Career* called to the Bar Gray's Inn 1967, in practice Midland & Oxford Circuit 1970–, recorder of the Crown Court 1994–, head of chambers, circuit judge (SE Circuit) 1999–; lectr in law: Univ of Southampton 1966–70, LSE 1970–88; delegate to Hague Conf on Private Int Law 1973–77 (Convention on the Law Applicable to Agency, appointed rapporteur), ldr UK Delegation to Unidroit Conf (Convention on Agency in the Int Sale of Goods) Bucharest 1979 and Geneva 1983; diplomé Hague Acad of Int Law; *Books* Conflict of Laws - Halsbury's Laws of England (co-author 4 edn, 1974); *Recreations* opera, travel, chess; *Style*— His Hon Judge Ian Karsten, QC; ✉ Crown Court at Blackfriars, 1–15 Pocock Street, London SE1 0BJ

KASER, Prof Michael Charles; s of Charles Joseph Kaser (d 1983), of St Albans, Herts, and Mabel Lucina, *née* Blunden (d 1976); *b* 2 May 1926; *Educ* Gunnersbury Catholic GS, Wimbledon Coll, King's Coll Cambridge (MA), Univ of Oxford (MA, DLitt); *m* 13 May 1954, Elizabeth Ann Mary, da of Cyril Gascoigne Piggford (d 1956), of Springs, South Africa; 4 s (Gregory b 1955, Matthew b 1956, Benet b 1959, Thomas b 1962), 1 da (Lucy b 1968); *Career* economist; chief sci advsr div Miny of Works 1946–47, Economic Intelligence Dept FO 1947–51, second sec HM Embassy Moscow 1949, economic affrs offr UN Economic Cmmn for Europe Geneva 1951–63, visiting prof Graduate Inst of Int Studies Univ of Geneva 1959–63; Univ of Oxford: Leverhulme res fell St Antony's Coll 1960–62, faculty fell St Antony's Coll 1963–72, faculty lectr in Soviet economics 1963–72, professorial fell St Antony's Coll 1972–93 (emeritus fell 1993–), reader in economics 1972–93 (reader emeritus 1993–), assoc fell Templeton Coll 1983–, dir Inst of Russian Soviet and East Euro Studies 1988–93, memb Inst of Slavonic Studies 1997–2004, memb Ctee Programme on Contemporary Turkey 2000–05, memb Steering Ctee SE European Studies 2005–; princ Charlemagne Inst Edinburgh 1993–94; chm: Advsy Cncl for Adult Educn Oxford 1972–78, RIIA Central Asian and Caucasian Advsy Bd 1993–2004; Latin preacher Univ Church of St Mary the Virgin 1982; visiting faculty Henley Mgmnt Coll 1986–2002; sec Cwlth Assoc of Geneva 1956–63; memb: Königswinter Steering Ctee 1969–90, Cncl Royal Economic Soc 1976–86 and 1987–90, Royal Inst of Int Affrs 1979–85 and 1986–92, Exec Ctee Int Economic Assoc 1974–83 and 1986–2007 (gen ed 1986–2007), Int Social Sciences Cncl (UNESCO) 1980–90, Cncl SSEES Univ of London 1981–87, Advsy Bd Inst for East-West Security Studies NY 1989–90, HEFCE Advsy Gp on Former Soviet and E European Studies 1995–2000, E Europe Ctee CAFOD 2001–06, Project Evaluation Gp Univ of Halle 2002–04; chm: Co-ordinating Cncl of Area Studies Assocs 1986–88 (memb 1980–93 and 1995), Wilton Park Acad Cncl (FCO) 1986–92 (memb 1985–2001), Sir Heinz Koeppler Tst 1992–2001 (tstee 1987–2001), Acad Ctee Fndn of King George VI & Queen Elizabeth 1992–2001 (memb 1975–2001, tstee 1987–2006), Keston Inst Oxford 1994–2002; pres: Br Assoc for Soviet Slavonic and East Euro Studies 1988–91 (previously first chm and memb Ctee Nat Assoc for Soviet and East Euro Studies 1964–88, vice-pres 1991–93), Albania Soc of Britain 1992–95, Br Assoc of Former UN Civil Servants 1994–2001; sec Br Acad Ctee for SE Euro Studies 1988–93 (memb 1970–75); govr Plater Coll Oxford 1968–95 (emeritus govr 1995–2006); special advsr House of Commons Foreign Affairs Ctee 1985–87; hon fell Univ of Edinburgh 1993–96, hon prof Univ of Birmingham 1994–; Hon DSocSc Univ of Birmingham 1994; KSG 1990, Order of Naim Frashëri Albania 1995, Order of Merit Knight's Cross Poland 1999; *Books* Comecon - Integration Problems of the Planned Economies (1965 and 1967), Soviet Economics (1970), Planning in Eastern Europe (jtly, 1970), The New Economic Systems of Eastern Europe (jtly, 1975), The Soviet Union since the Fall of Khrushchev (jtly, 1975), Health Care in the Soviet Union and Eastern Europe (1976), Soviet Policy for the 1980s (jtly, 1982), The Cambridge Encyclopaedia of Russia and the Soviet Union (jtly, 1982 and 1994), The Economic History of Eastern Europe 1919–75 (ed, 3 vols 1985–86), The Central Asian Economies after Independence (jtly, 1992 and 1996), Privatization in the CIS (1995), The Economies of Kazakstan and Uzbekistan (1997); *Clubs* Reform; *Style*— Prof Michael Kaser; ✉ 31 Capel Close, Oxford OX2 7LA (tel and fax 01865 515581, e-mail michael.kaser@economics.ox.ac.uk)

KASKI, Prof Juan Carlos; s of Moises Kaski, and Ofelia, *née* Fullone; *b* 3 May 1950, Mar del Plata, Argentina; *Educ* Universidad del Salvador Buenos Aires (Gold Medal, MD, DM), Univ of London (DSc); *m* 19 Sept 1975, Dr Marta Carpani; 2 s (Juan-Pablo b 3 June 1977, Diego b 3 Oct 1979), 1 da (Maria-Cecilia b 16 Feb 1984); *Career* med intern Universidad del Salvador Buenos Aires 1974–75, resident (internal med) Rawson Hosp Buenos Aires 1975–78; Ramos Mejia Hosp Buenos Aires: chief resident 1978–79, cardiology fell and registrar 1979–82, head of coronary disease research 1986–88; sr registrar and lectr in cardiology Hammersmith Hosp London 1988–91 (research fell 1982–86); St George's Hosp London: lectr in cardiology 1991–95, sr lectr and hon conslt cardiologist 1995–97, Br Heart Fndn Sugden sr lectr 1996–98, Br Heart Fndn Sugden reader in cardiology 1998–99, prof of cardiovascular science and hon conslt 1999–, head Cardiological Sciences, dir Coronary Artery Disease Research Unit; head Cardiovascular Biology Res Centre SEUL London 2003, dep head Div of Cardiac and Vascular Sciences SEUL London 2004; scientfic advsr Miny for Health São Paulo 1992–, advsr St Pau Hosp Directorate Univ of Barcelona 1999–, external advsr Argentine Fund for Promotion of Science and Technol (FONCYT) 2000–; chm Working Gp on Microcirculation European Soc of Cardiology 1994–96 (vice-chm 1992–94); memb: Steering Ctee Cardiovascular Research Gp R&D Ctee St George's Hosp Med Sch 1997–, Educn and Trg Prog Ctee European Soc of Cardiology 1997–, Project Grants Ctee 1 Br Heart Fndn 2002–; UK govr Int Soc of Cardiovascular Pharmacotherapy 2005; chm CEM Ctee Int Soc of Cardiovascular Pharmacotherapy 2006; assoc ed Cardiovascular Drugs and Therapy 2006; memb: Br Cardiac Soc, Argentine Soc of Cardiology, Atherosclerosis and Coronary Circulation Cncl, American Heart Assoc; Distinguished Cardiologist Award Fukushima Univ 2002, Gold Medal Spanish Soc of Cardiology 2003; hon prof Univ of São Paulo 1998, prof (hc) Universidad del Salvador Buenos Aires 1998, scientiae magistri Univ of Rome 1998; fell NY Acad of Sciences 1993, fell Societa Medico-Chirurgica Univ of Bologna 1994; FACC 1990, FESC 1991, FRCP 1999; *Publications* author of three books, 60 book chapters, 300 abstracts and 400 papers in peer-reviewed jls; *Recreations* collecting illuminated manuscripts, photography, tennis; *Style*— Prof Juan Carlos Kaski; ✉ St George's Hospital Medical School, Cranmer Terrace, London SW17 0RE (tel 020 8725 5901, fax 020 8725 3328, e-mail jkaski@sghms.ac.uk)

KASPSZYK, Jacek; *b* 1952; *Career* conductor; debut aged 14, studied in Warsaw, Warsaw Opera debut 1975, international debut Düsseldorf Opera 1976, US debut NY 1978, UK debut Royal Festival Hall 1980; princ conductor Polish Nat Radio Symphony Orch 1977–82 (music dir 1980–82), princ conductor Wren Orch 1983–91, princ conductor and artistic advsr North Netherlands Orch 1991–, princ guest conductor English Sinfonia 1992–; worked with orchs incl: Berlin Philharmonic, French National, Stockholm Philharmonic, Bavarian Radio Symphony, Rotterdam Philharmonic, Czech Philharmonic, Hallé, Bournemouth Symphony, Scottish Nat, Ulster Orch, BBC Scottish and Welsh Symphony Orchs, Northern Sinfonia, Scottish Chamber, Cincinnati Symphony, San Diego Symphony, Calgary Philharmonic, Oslo Philharmonic, Orchestre National de France, Spanish Nat, Danish Radio, New Swiss Philharmonic (incl 1987 Euro tour), Vienna Symphony, Berlin Radio Symphony, Yomiuri Nippon, London Philharmonic, Philharmonia, London Symphony Orch, Royal Philharmonic Orch; appeared at venues incl: La Scala Milan, various London venues, Paris, Linz, Musikverein Vienna, the Netherlands, Australia, Japan, N America, Scandinavia; *Opera* work incl: A Midsummer Night's Dream (Lyons Opera), Eugene Onegin (Bordeaux), The Magic Flute (Opera Comique Paris, Stockholm Opera), The Seven Deadly Sins (Lyons), Die Fledermaus (Scottish Opera), The Flying Dutchman (Opera North), The Barber of Seville (ENO); *Recordings* incl: Il Signor Bruschino (with Warsaw Chamber Opera, first complete recording in Italian), various with London Philharmonic, London Symphony Orch, Royal Philharmonic Orch, Philharmonia; *Style*— Mr Jacek Kaspszyk; ✉ c/o English Sinfonia, 1 Wedgewood Court, Stevenage, Hertfordshire SG1 4QR (tel 01438 350990, fax 01438 350930)

KATIN, Dr Peter Roy; s of Jerrold Katin (d 1991), and Gertrude Kate May (d 1976); *b* 14 November 1930; *Educ* Royal Acad of Music; *Career* pianist; musical talent evident at age of four, admitted to Royal Acad of Music at age of twelve; debut: Wigmore Hall 1948, Henry Wood Promenade Concert (with Tchaikovsky's second Concerto) 1952; first postwar Br artist to make a solo tour of the USSR 1958; early influences incl: Clifford Curzon, Claudio Arrau, Myra Hess; recordings incl: complete Mozart Sonatas, Chopin Nocturnes and Impromptus, complete Chopin Waltzes and Polonaises, complete Grieg Lyric Pieces, Clementi, Schubert and Chopin (on square pianos), works by Schubert, Liszt, Tchaikovsky, Schumann, Rachmaninov, Brahms, Scarlatti and Mendelssohn; composer of various piano pieces and songs, the song cycle Sequence (words by Charlotte Morrow) and various cadenzas to Beethoven and Mozart Concertos; series of subscription recitals and master classes for young artists 1968–78, prof Royal Acad of Music 1956–60, visiting prof Univ of W Ontario 1978–84, prof Royal Coll of Music 1992–2001; writer of

K

articles on various aspects of music-making and composing, currently writing autobiography; Eric Brough Meml Prize 1944, Chopin Arts Award 1977; Hon DMus 1994; ARCM 1952, FRAM 1960; *Recreations* theatre, literature, writing, photography, record collections; *Style—* Dr Peter Katin; ✉ 41 First Avenue, Bexhill-on-Sea, East Sussex TN40 2PL (tel 01424 211167, e-mail peter.katin@btinternet.com)

KATZ, Alan Jacob; s of Berl Katz, and Edith Lena, *née* Seidel; *b* 29 September 1945; *Educ* Salford GS, LSE (BSc); *m* Susan Ernesta, *née* Rees; 2 da (Nicola b 6 March 1977, Joanna b 8 Dec 1979); *Career* chartered accountant; Arthur Andersen: articled clerk 1966–69, mangr 1972–78, ptnr 1978–98, conslt 1998–; res fell ICRA Lancaster Univ 1999–; memb ICA 1969, MIPA 1989, MSPI 1991, MABRP 2000; *Recreations* walking, swimming, theatre; *Clubs* St James (Manchester); *Style—* Alan Katz, Esq; ✉ International Centre for Research in Accounting, Lancaster University, Lancaster LA1 4YX (tel 01524 593976, fax 01524 594334)

KATZ, Andrew James Stewart; s of Stewart Katz, and Janet, *née* McDonnell (d 2004); *b* 13 April 1966, Melton Mowbray, Leics; *Educ* Uppingham (entrance scholar), Churchill Coll Cambridge (entrance scholar, MA), Inns of Court Sch of Law; *m* 1 April 1996, Lucy, *née* Pollard; 1 s (Oscar Guy b 17 Oct 1999), 1 da (Isabelle Lucy b 21 May 2002); *Career* called to the Bar Inner Temple 1990, admitted slr 1993; barr Winward Fearon & Co 1991–93; slr: Brethertons 1993–99 (ptnr 1996), Moorcrofts LLP 2000– (ptnr 2001); memb: Bd Telecommunications Industry Assoc 2001–03, Ctee Open Source Specialist Gp BCS; supporter Open Rights Gp, UK Licence contrib Creative Commons; memb Law Soc 2003; *Books* A Manager's Guide to IT Law (contrib, 2004); *Recreations* reading, wine, food, web 2.0, music; *Style—* Andrew Katz, Esq; ✉ Moorcrofts LLP, James House, Dedmere Road, Marlow, Buckinghamshire SL7 1KJ (tel 01628 470003, fax 01628 470001, e-mail andrewk1@moorcrofts.com, website www.moorcrofts.com)

KAUFMAN, Rt Hon Sir Gerald Bernard; kt (2004), PC (1978), MP; s of Louis Kaufman, and Jane Kaufman; *b* 21 June 1930; *Educ* Leeds GS, The Queen's Coll Oxford; *Career* political staff Daily Mirror 1955–64, political corr New Statesman 1964–65, Lab Pty press liaison offr 1965–70; MP (Lab): Manchester Ardwick 1970–83, Manchester Gorton 1983–; Parly under sec Environment 1974–75, Parly under sec Industry 1975, min of state Dept of Industry 1975–79; oppn front bench spokesman and memb Shadow Cabinet: Environment 1980–83, Home Affrs 1983–87, Foreign and Cwlth Affairs 1987–92; memb Labour Party NEC 1991–92; chm House of Commons: Nat Heritage Ctee 1992–97, Culture, Media and Sport Ctee 1997–2005, All-Pty Dance Gp 2006–; memb Royal Cmmn into reform of House of Lords 1999; chm Booker Prize judges 1999; *Style—* The Rt Hon Sir Gerald Kaufman, MP; ✉ 87 Charlbert Court, Eamont Street, London NW8 7DA (tel 020 7219 3000)

KAUFMANN, Julia Ruth; OBE (1997); da of Felix Kaufmann, of Fort Lauderdale, FL, and Ruth Armley, *née* Arnold; *Educ* Ursuline Convent Wimbledon, St George's Hosp London (SRN), Sidney Webb Coll London (BEd), Brunel Univ (Dip Social Policy and Admin); *m* (m dis); 2 s (Luke Kelly b 1962, Oisin Kelly b 1965), 1 da (Tara Kaufmann b 1964); *Career* primary sch teacher Croydon Educn Authy 1974–76, pt/t advsy teacher ILEA 1976–79, pt/t co-dir Social Educn Unit Centre for Human Rights and Responsibilities 1976–78, chief exec Gingerbread (association for one parent families) 1979–87 (press and info offr 1978–79), dir BBC Children in Need Appeal 1987–2000; pt/t cmmr Postcomm 2000–06, memb Employment Relations Advsy Panel on Public Appointments 2001–05; chair Whizz-Kidz 2006–, vice-pres Deafax, tstee Community Network 1999–, memb Advsy Cncl Charities Aid Fndn 2005–, memb Bd Capacity Builders 2006–; *Style—* Ms Julia Kaufmann, OBE; ✉ 2 Carberry Road, Upper Norwood, London SE19 3RU (tel 020 8653 3877, e-mail julia.kaufmann@btinternet.com)

KAUKAS, Bernard Aloysius; MBE (1984); s of Joseph Kaukas (d 1964), of Stamford Hill, and Ethel Mary, *née* Morgan-Adlam (d 1979); *b* 30 July 1922; *Educ* St Ignatius Coll Stamford Hill, Northern Poly London (DipArch); *m* 23 May 1945, Pamela Dora (d 1998), da of David Widdowson, MBE (d 1980), of Hampstead Garden Suburb; 1 s (Christopher David b 6 Sept 1946), 1 da (Amanda Mary (Mrs Burroughs) b 18 June 1954); *Career* RN 1941–46; MCC 1952–54, LCC 1954–56, private practice 1956–59, Br Tport Cmmn 1959–64; BR Bd: planning offr 1964–68, chief architect 1968–74, devpt dir Property Bd 1974–77, dir of environment 1977–84; planning conslt to Michael Burroughs Assoc 1984–; memb Int Cncl on Monuments and Sites; fell Science Museum 1984–89; ARIBA 1952, FRSA 1977; *Recreations* painting, writing, collecting; *Clubs* Savage; *Style—* Bernard Kaukas, Esq, MBE; ✉ 13 Lynwood Road, Ealing, London W5 1JQ (tel 020 8998 1499)

KAUR, Pervinder; da of Sarwan Singh (d 1988), and Surjit Kaur; *b* 28 November 1971, Nottingham; *Educ* Fernwood Comp Sch Nottingham, Bilborough Sixth Form Coll, Univ of Sheffield (LLB), Coll of Law Chester (Dip); *Career* admitted slr 1996; Addleshaw Goddard: trainee slr 1994–96, slr 1996–2004, legal dir 2004–; memb: Charity Law Assoc, Law Soc 1996; *Recreations* photography, tennis, fashion, travel; *Style—* Miss Pervinder Kaur; ✉ Addleshaw Goddard, Sovereign House, Sovereign Street, Leeds LS1 1HQ (tel 0113 2092381, fax 0113 2092060, e-mail pervinder.atcha@addleshawgoddard.com)

KAVADZE, HE Amiran; *b* 21 April 1951, Tbilisi, Georgia; *Educ* Inst of Social and Political Studies Baku, Bakh Biochemistry Inst, USSR Acad of Sciences Moscow, Georgian State Agric Univ; *Career* Georgian diplomat; jr scientist Dept of Wine Processing and Microbiology Georgian State Agric Univ 1973–74, scientist Dept of Bioorganic Chemistry Georgian State Agric Univ 1978–79, various leading positions in local admin and activities in industry, economy, science and educn 1979–81, private business activities 1991–92, dep head of section rising to head of div and dep dir Int Economic Relations Dept Miny of Foreign Affrs 1992–94, dir Int Economic Relations Dept Miny of Foreign Affrs 1994–97, ambass to Swiss Confedn 1997–2003, ambass to the Holy See 2001–03, perm rep to UN Office and other int orgns at Geneva 1997–2003, dep min of Foreign Affrs 2003–04, ambass to the Ct of St James's 2004– (concurrently ambass to Ireland); *Publications* Georgia's Path to the Multilateral Trading System (2003); also author of researches and articles in the field of int economic relations and trade; *Style—* HE Mr Amiran Kavadze; ✉ Embassy of Georgia, 4 Russell Gardens, London W14 8EZ (tel 020 7603 7799, fax 020 7603 6682, e-mail kavadze@geoemb.plus.com)

KAVANAGH, Prof Dennis Anthony; s of Patrick Joseph Kavanagh, and Agnes, *née* Campbell; *b* 27 March 1941; *Educ* St Anselm's Coll, Univ of Manchester (BA, MA); *m* 13 Aug 1966, Monica Anne, *née* Taylor; 3 da (Jane b 24 July 1968, Catherine b 4 Nov 1972, Helen b 3 Jan 1981), 1 s (David b 20 Nov 1970); *Career* prof of politics Dept of Politics Univ of Nottingham 1982–95, prof of politics Dept of Politics Univ of Liverpool 1996–2006, now research fell Univ of Liverpool; visiting prof: European Univ Inst Florence 1977, Stanford Univ 1985; memb ESRC Cncl, Liverpool Democracy Cmmn; RSA; *Books* Constituency Electioneering, The British General Election of February 1974 (with Dr David Butler, *qv*), The British General Election of 1979 (with David Butler), British Politics Today (with W Jones), New Trends in British Politics (ed, with Prof Richard Rose, FBA, *qv*), The Politics of the Labour Party (ed), Political Science and Political Behaviour, The British General Election 1983 (with David Butler), Thatcherism and British Politics, The British General Election of 1987 (with David Butler), Consensus Politics from Attlee to Thatcher (with Peter Morris), The Thatcher Effect (ed, with Anthony Seldon), Comparative Government and Politics, Personalities and Politics, The British General Election of 1992 (with David Butler), The Major Effect (with Anthony Seldon), Electoral Politics, The New Marketing of Politics, The British General Election of 1997 (with David Butler), The Reordering of British Politics, Oxford Dictionary of Political Biography, The Powers Behind the Prime Minister (with Anthony Seldon), British Politics: Continuities and Change, The British General Election of 2001 (with David Butler), The British General Election of 2005 (with David Butler), The Blair Effect II (with Anthony Seldon); *Recreations* running, tennis, music, obituaries; *Style—* Prof Dennis Kavanagh; ✉ Lynston, Belgrave Road, Bowdon, Cheshire WA14 2NZ (e-mail dennis@kavanagh41.fsnet.co.uk)

KAVANAGH, Giles; s of Joseph Kavanagh, of Belfast, and Bernadette, *née* Kelly; *b* 2 May 1959, Belfast; *Educ* St Malachy's Coll Belfast, St John's Coll Cambridge (Mellon Fndn scholar, pres Cambridge Union); *m* 1996 (m dis); 2 da (Tierney Rose b 7 April 1998, Erin Aoire Bernadette b 9 July 2001), 1 s (Conall Joseph b 22 March 2000); *Career* called to the Bar Middle Temple 1984 (scholar); barr 1984–98, ptnr Barlow Lyde & Gilbert 1998– (head of aerospace 2004–); chm Air Law Gp Ctee RAeS; *Recreations* golf, swimming, tennis; *Clubs* RAC, Woodcote Park; *Style—* Giles Kavanagh, Esq; ✉ Barlow Lyde & Gilbert, Beaufort House, 15 St Botolph Street, London EC3A 7NJ (tel 020 7643 8008, e-mail gkavanagh@blg.co.uk)

KAVANAGH, Patrick Joseph; s of H E (Ted) Kavanagh (d 1958), and Agnes O'Keefe (d 1985); *b* 6 January 1931; *Educ* Douai Sch, Lycée Jaccard, Merton Coll Oxford (MA); *m* 1, 1956, Sally (d 1958), da of Hon Mrs R N Philipps (Rosamond Lehmann), and Wogan Philipps (2 Baron Milford); m 2, 1965, Catherine, da of Sir John Guthrie Ward, GCMG; 2 s (Cornelius b 1966, Bruno b 1969); *Career* writer; actor 1959–70, columnist The Spectator 1983–96, columnist TLS 1996–2002; FRSL; *Poetry* One and One (1960), On the Way to the Depot (1977), About Time (1970), Edward Thomas in Heaven (1974), Life Before Death (1979), Selected Poems (1982), Presences (1987), An Enchantment (1991), Collected Poems (1992, Cholmondley Prize for Poetry), Something About (2004); *Novels* A Song and Dance (1968, Guardian Fiction Prize), A Happy Man (1972), People and Weather (1979), Only by Mistake (1986), The Perfect Stranger (autobiography, Richard Hillary Prize 1966); *Children's books* Scarf Jack (1978), Rebel for Good (1980); *Anthologies* ed: Collected Poems of Ivor Gurney (1982), The Essential G K Chesterton (1985), Oxford Book of Short Poems (with James Michie), A Book of Consolations (1992), Voices in Ireland - A Literary Companion (1994); *Essays* People and Places (1988), A Kind of Journal (2003); *Travel* Finding Connections (1990); *Style—* P J Kavanagh, FRSL; ✉ c/o PFD, Drury House, 34–43 Russell Street, London WC2B 5HA

KAVANAGH, Peter Richard Michael; s of Patrick Bernard Kavanagh, CBE, QPM, of Epsom, Surrey, and Beryl Annie, *née* Williams (d 1984); *b* 20 February 1959; *Educ* Wimbledon Coll, Gonville& Caius Coll Cambridge (MA); *m* 16 Nov 1985, Vivien Mary, da of Gordon Samuel Hart, of Bromham, Beds; 1 da (Emma b 1988); *Career* admitted slr 1984; ptnr Theodore Goddard 1989–2002, ptnr Hunton & Williams 2002–; memb Law Soc; *Style—* Peter Kavanagh, Esq; ✉ Hunton & Williams, 30 St Mary Axe, London EC3A 8EP (tel 020 7220 5764, fax 020 7220 5772, e-mail pkavanagh@hunton.com)

KAVANAGH, Trevor Michael Thomas; s of Bernard George Kavanagh (d 1978), and Alice Rose, *née* Thompson; *b* 19 January 1943; *Educ* Reigate GS; *m* 1967, Jacqueline Gai, da of John Swindells; 2 s (Benjamin b 14 June 1969, Simon John b 20 March 1971); *Career* political ed The Sun until 2006; chm The Lobby House of Commons Westminster 1990–91, chm Parly Press Gall 2000–01; Journalist of the Year and Specialist Reporter of the Year British Press Awards 1997; *Recreations* golf, swimming; *Clubs* RAC, Pall Mall; *Style—* Trevor Kavanagh, Esq

KAWCZYNSKI, Daniel; MP; *b* 1972; *Educ* Univ of Stirling; *Career* MP (Cons) Shrewsbury and Atcham 2005– (Parly candidate (Cons) Ealing Southall 2001); *Style—* Daniel Kawczynski, Esq, MP; ✉ House of Commons, London SW1A 0AA

KAY, Prof (Anthony) Barrington (Barry); s of Anthony Chambers, and Eva Gertrude, *née* Pearcey (later Mrs Kay, now Mrs Reuben); *b* 23 June 1939; *Educ* King's Sch Peterborough, Univ of Edinburgh (MB ChB, DSc), Jesus Coll Cambridge (MA, PhD), Harvard Med Sch; *m* 1966, Rosemary Margaret, da of Hugh Johnstone; 3 da (Emma Rosalind b 21 Sept 1968, Rebecca b 13 May 1975, Eleanor Elizabeth b 19 Nov 1976); *Career* various posts as house physician and surgn City and Eastern Gen Hosps Edinburgh 1963; student Univ of Cambridge 1964–65; house physician City Hosp Edinburgh 1965–66; post grad student Dept of Pathology Univ of Cambridge and hon registrar Addenbrooke's Hosp Cambridge 1966–69; research fell Harvard Med Sch at Robert B Brigham Hosp Boston 1969–71; Univ of Edinburgh: lectr in respiratory diseases 1971–74, pt/t sr lectr 1974–76, sr lectr in experimental pathology 1977–79, reader Dept of Pathology 1979–80; dep dir and conslt Immunology Div SE Scot Regnl Blood Transfusion Serv Royal Infirmary Edinburgh 1974–76; prof of clinical immunology and dir Dept of Allergy and Clinical Immunology Nat Heart and Lung Inst London 1980–2004, prof emeritus of allergy and clinical immunology and sr research investigator NHLI Div Imperial Coll 2004–; hon conslt physician Royal Brompton and Nat Heart and Lung Hosp 1980–, conslt physician (allergy) The London Clinic 2005–, scientific advsr House of Lords Select Ctee on Allergy 2006–07; co-fndr and dir Circassa Ltd; pres: European Acad of Allergology and Clinical Immunology 1989–92, Br Soc of Allergy and Clinical Immunology 1993–; T K Stubbins research fell RCP 1969–71; scientific achievement award Int Assoc of Allergology and Clinical Immunology 1991, Citation Superstar of the UK ISI Web of Science 1999, seventh most-cited UK biomedical researcher of decade Science Watch 2000, ISI Highly Cited researcher 2000, Paul Ehrlich Medal European Acad of Allergology and Clinical Immunology 2005; hon fell American College of Allergy 1986; hon memb: American Assoc of Physicians 1988, Hungarian Soc of Allergology and Clinical Immunology 1990, Swiss Soc of Allergology and Clinical Immunology 1991; Hon DUniv (laurea honris causa) Univ of Ferrara Italy 2000; FRCPE 1975, FRCP 1980, FRCPath 1989, FRSE 1993, FMedSci 1999; *Books* Clinical and Experimental Allergy (co-ed, since 1984), Asthma: Clinical Pharmacology and Therapeutic Progress (ed, 1986), Allergy and Inflammation (ed, 1987), Allergic Basis of Asthma (ed, 1988), Allergy and Asthma: New Trends and Approaches to Therapy (ed, 1989), Eosinophils, Allergy and Asthma (ed, 1990), Eosinophils in Allergy and Inflammation (ed, 1993), Allergy and Allergic Diseases (ed, 1997); also numerous scientific articles on asthma and allergy; *Recreations* Baroque and modern bassoon, tennis, country walks; *Clubs* Hurlingham, Chelsea Arts; *Style—* Prof Barry Kay, FRSE; ✉ Stamford Brook House, 12 Stamford Brook Avenue, London W6 0YD (tel 020 8741 5899, fax 020 8400 7766); Room 374, Sir Alexander Fleming Building, Leukocyte Biology Section, Imperial College, NHLI Division, South Kensington Campus, London SW7 2AZ (tel 020 7594 3174, fax 020 7594 1475, e-mail a.b.kay@imperial.ac.uk)

KAY, Benedict James (Ben); MBE (2004); s of Rt Hon Lord Justice Kay (d 2004), and Jeffa Kay; *b* 14 December 1975, Liverpool; *Career* rugby union player (lock); clubs: Waterloo RUFC, Leicester Tigers RUFC 1999– (winners four successive Premiership titles 1999–2002, winners Heineken Cup 2001 and 2002); England: 47 caps, debut v Canada 2001, ranked no 1 team in world 2003, winners Six Nations Championship 2003 (Grand Slam), winners World Cup Aust 2003, memb squad World Cup France 2007; memb squad Br & I Lions tour to NZ 2005; *Style—* Ben Kay, Esq, MBE; ✉ c/o Leicester Tigers, Aylestone Road, Leicester LE2 7TR

KAY, Brian Christopher; s of Noel Bancroft Kay (d 1980), of York, and Gwendoline, *née* Sutton (d 2004); *b* 12 May 1944; *Educ* Rydal Sch, King's Coll Cambridge (choral scholar), New Coll Oxford; *m* 1, 1970, Sally, *née* Lyne; 1 s (Jonathan b 22 June 1973), 1 da (Charlotte Joanna b 24 Feb 1975); m 2, 1983, Gillian Elizabeth Fisher, *qv*; *Career* conductor, singer, radio and TV presenter; fndr memb and bass The King's Singers 1968–82, chorus master Huddersfield Choral Soc 1984–93, freelance singer various vocal gps incl John Alldis Choir, London Voices and BBC Singers; conductor: Cecilian Singers of Leicester 1987–91, Cheltenham Bach Choir 1989–97, Mary Wakefield Westmorland Festival 1996–2003,

Leith Hill Musical Festival 1996–, Bradford Festival Choral Soc 1998–2002, Burford Singers 2002–, The Really Big Chorus 2005–; presenter various BBC progs incl: Cardiff Singer of the World (BBC TV), Choir of the Year (BBC TV), Mainly for Pleasure (Radio 3) 1983–91, Music in Mind (weekly prog Radio 4) 1989–96, arts prog Radio 2, Record Review (World Serv), Brian Kay's Sunday Morning (Radio 3) 1992–2001, Classics with Kay (weekly prog World Serv) 1996–98, Comparing Notes (Radio 4) 1996–98, Friday Night is Music Night (Radio 2) 1998–, Choirworks (Radio 3) 1998–99, Brian Kay's Light Programme (Radio 3) 2002–07, Melodies for You (Radio 2) 2003–04; Music Presenter of the Year Award Sony Radio Awards 1996; appeared in feature film Amadeus as voice of Schickenaeder; lay vicar Westminster Abbey 1968–71; pres: Harrogate Choral Soc, Market Harborough Singers, Nottingham Choral Tst, Derbyshire Singers, Bristol Bach Choir; vice-pres: Assoc of Br Choral Dirs, Royal Sch of Church Music; *Recreations* reading, gardening, the local pub; *Style—* Brian Kay, Esq

KAY, Dr Clifford Ralph; CBE (1977); s of Maurice Witt Kay (d 1971), of Chester, and Fay Celia Kay (d 1992); *b* 17 October 1927; *Educ* King's Sch Chester, Univ of Liverpool (MB ChB, MD), Univ of Manchester (PhD); *m* 1950, Yvette Adele, da of Maurice Hytner; 1 s (Roger Neil b 1952), 1 da (Alison Jane b 1954); *Career* Nat Serv Sqdn Ldr RAF Med Branch 1952–53; fndr of gen practice Didsbury 1955–95 (became Barlow Med Centre 1971), md Bd of Mgmnt Barlow Med Centre 1990–95; travelling lectr in gen practice research Canada 1970; pt/t sr research fell Dept of Gen Practice Univ of Manchester 1971– (hon sr research fell 1992–), conslt NHS Exec for pilot trial of barcoded prescription printing in gen practice 1994–; WHO temp conslt on contraceptive research Indian Cncl for Med Research 1972, (Br Cncl) advsr Danish Med Research Cncl on the initiation of a Gen Practice Research Unit in Denmark 1978, expert advsr to Chief Scientist DHSS 1973–76; memb: UK Health Servs Research Bd 1973–76, Clinical Research Advsy Ctee NW RHA 1972–82, MRC Advsy Ctee on Hormone Replacement Therapy 1977–82, Research Ctee World Orgn of Nat Colls and Academies of Gen Practice 1979–83, MRC Contraceptive Clinical Research Ctee 1983–87, NHS Exec Info Mgmnt and Technol Forum 1985–97; non-exec dir Stockport Healthcare NHS Tst 1996–98; RCGP: memb NW England Faculty Bd 1953–95 (provost 1991–92), pt/t dir Manchester Research Unit 1968–94 (conslt 1994–97), memb Cncl 1970–95, memb Scientific Fndn Bd 1970–82, chm Research Ctee 1973–82, exec dir Meds Surveillance Orgn 1981–97; author of numerous original papers in academic jls; Sir Charles Hastings Research Prize BMA 1961, Mackenzie Medal RCPEd 1975, travelling lectr in gen practice research SA 1975, Fndn Cncl Award RCGP 1978, Mackenzie lectr RCGP 1979, Gregory Pincus Meml Lecture Detroit USA 1982, Jane Berry Meml Lecture Southampton 1984, visiting professorship Univs of Edmonton and Calgary 1987, Hippocrates Medal (Societas Internationalis Medicinae Generalis for outstanding contrib to gen practice in Europe) 1990, George Swift Meml Lecture Portsmouth 1992; pres Manchester Med Soc 1988–89; FRCGP 1971 (MRCGP 1958); hon fell Faculty of Family Planning and Reproductive Health RCOG 1994; *Recreations* photography, gardening, sailing; *Style—* Dr Clifford Kay, CBE; ✉ 12 Dene Park, Didsbury, Manchester M20 2GF (tel 0161 445 9686, fax 0161 434 2040, e-mail cliffordkay@talktalk.net)

KAY, Jason (Jay Kay); *b* 1969; *Career* lead singer with Jamiroquai; albums: Emergency On Planet Earth (debut, UK no 1) 1993, Return of the Space Cowboy (UK no 2) 1994, Travelling Without Moving (UK no 2) 1996, Synkronized (UK no 1) 1999, A Funk Odyssey 2001, Late Night Tales 2003, Dynamite 2005; top ten singles: Too Young To Die, Blow Your Mind, Return of the Space Cowboy, Virtual Insanity, Cosmic Girl, Deeper Underground, Canned Heat; winner numerous industry awards; *Recreations* classic cars; *Style—* Jason Kay, Esq

KAY, (Robert) Jervis; QC (1996); s of late Philip Jervis Kay, VRD, of Suffolk, and late Pamela, *née* Carter; *Educ* Wellington, Univ of Nottingham (LLB); *m* 1, 1975 (m dis 1986), Rosemary, da of late Dr Arthur Pollard; m 2, 1988, Henrietta Kathleen, da of late Maj Guy Ward, RA, and Elizabeth Ward; 3 da (Pamela Felicity Iona b 1988, Katherine Elizabeth Skye b 1993, Lucinda Valentine Ailsa b 1995), 1 s (Philip-Alexander Guy Jervis b 1990); *Career* called to the Bar Lincoln's Inn 1972, called to the Bar of NSW 1984, called to the Bar of Antigua and Barbuda 1998, specialist in admiralty, commercial shipping and yachting; memb: London Common Law & Commercial Bar Assoc, Br Maritime Law Assoc, Commercial Bar Assoc, London Maritime Arbitrators' Assoc (supporting); *Books* Atkins Court Forms (ed Vol 3, Admiralty, 1979, 1990, 1994, 2000 and 2004); *Recreations* sailing, golf, cricket, reading; *Clubs* Turf, MCC, Royal Ocean Racing, Bar Yacht; *Style—* Jervis Kay, Esq, QC; ✉ Stone Chambers, 4 Field Court, Gray's Inn, London WC1R 5EF (tel 020 7440 6900)

KAY, Prof John Anderson; s of James Scobie Kay (d 1983), of Edinburgh, and Allison, *née* Anderson; *b* 3 August 1948; *Educ* Royal HS Edinburgh, Univ of Edinburgh (MA), Nuffield Coll Oxford (MA); *m* 1986 (m dis 1995), Deborah, da of Raymond Freeman; *Career* Univ of Oxford: fell St John's Coll Oxford 1970–, univ lectr in economics 1971–79; Inst for Fiscal Studies: research dir 1979–82, dir 1982–86; London Business Sch: prof of economics 1986–96, dir Centre for Business Strategy 1986–91; dir Saïd Business Sch Univ of Oxford 1997–99; chm Clear Capital Ltd 2004–; dir: Govett Strategic Investment Trust plc 1982–95, London Economics 1986–2000 (chm 1986–96), Investors' Compensation Scheme 1988–95, Halifax Building Society (now Halifax plc) 1991–2000, Foreign & Colonial Special Utilities Investment Trust plc 1993–2003, Undervalued Assets Trust plc 1994–2005, Value and Income Trust plc 1994–, Law Debenture Corporation 2004–; memb Bd Social Market Fndn 1992–94; FBA 1997, FRSE 2007; *Books* Concentration in Modern Industry (with L Hannah, 1977), The Reform of Social Security (with A W Dilnot and C N Morris, 1984), The Economic Analysis of Accounting Profitability (with J Edwards and C Mayer, 1987), The British Tax System (with M A King, 1989), Foundations of Corporate Success (1993), The Business of Economics (1996), The Truth about Markets (2003), Culture and Prosperity (2004), Everlasting Light Bulbs (2004), The Hare and the Tortoise (2006); *Recreations* travelling, walking; *Style—* Prof John Kay, FBA; ✉ The Erasmus Press, PO Box 4026, London W1A 6NZ (tel 020 7224 8797, fax 020 7402 1368, e-mail johnkay@johnkay.com, website www.johnkay.com)

KAY, Rt Hon Lord Justice; Sir Maurice Ralph; kt (1995), PC (2004); s of Ralph Kay (d 1981), of Knutsford, and Hylda Jones; *b* 6 December 1942; *Educ* William Hulmes GS Manchester, Univ of Sheffield (LLB, PhD), De Montfort Univ (MA); *m* 24 July 1968, Margaret Angela, da of Joseph Bernard Alcock, of Formby (d 1985); 4 s (Jonathan b 1969, Dominic b 1971, Oliver b 1975, Tristan b 1982); *Career* lectr: Univ of Hull 1967–72, Univ of Manchester 1972–73; prof of law Keele Univ 1973–83; called to the Bar Gray's Inn 1975 (bencher 1995), QC 1988, recorder of the Crown Court 1988–95 (asst recorder 1987–88), a judge of the High Court of Justice (Queen's Bench Div) 1995–2003, a judge of the Employment Appeal Tbnl 1995–2003, a presiding judge of the Wales & Chester Circuit 1996–99, nominated judge Crown Office 1998–2003, judge in charge Admin Court 2002–03, a Lord Justice of Appeal; dep chm Boundary Cmmn for Wales 1996–2000; Hon LLD 2003; *Publications* ed and contrib legal text books; *Recreations* music, theatre, sport; *Clubs* Reform; *Style—* The Rt Hon Lord Justice Kay; ✉ c/o Royal Courts of Justice, Strand, London WC2A 2LL

KAY, Steven Walton; QC (1997); s of Maj John Kay, of Epsom, Surrey, and Eunice May; *b* 4 August 1954; *Educ* Epsom Coll, Univ of Leeds (LLB); *m* 1, (m dis); 1 s (Alexander b 1991); m 2, 14 Feb 2000, Valerie, *née* Logan; 1 da (Madeleine Lily b 2000); *Career* called to the Bar Inner Temple 1977; recorder of the Crown Court 1997–, specialist in criminal law, war crimes (def counsel before UN War Crimes Tribunal for former Yugoslavia and Rwanda), assigned defence counsel in trial of ex-Pres Slobodan Milosevic at ICTY The Hague 2001; memb Working Party on Efficient Disposal of Business in the Crown Court 1992, sec Criminal Bar Assoc 1993–95 and 1995–96; memb: Bail Issues Steering Gp 1993, Legal Servs Ctee Bar Cncl 1993, Nat Steering Gp for Recommendation 92 1993, Bar Standards Review Body 1994; organiser of numerous confs and deliverer of various lectures on criminal law; frequent commentator on radio, TV and in press on criminal judicial system; memb: South Eastern Circuit, Criminal Bar Assoc; *Recreations* golf, counting crows, works of pg; *Clubs* Hurtwood Park Polo; *Style—* Steven Kay, QC; ✉ 9 Bedford Row, London WC1R 4AZ (tel 020 7489 2727, fax 020 7489 2828)

KAY, Susan Elaine; da of Donald Jackson Hodgson, of Manchester, and Joyce, *née* Martyn; *b* 24 June 1952; *Educ* Brookway HS Manchester, Mather Coll of Educn (Cert in Teaching), Univ of Manchester (BEd); *m* 1974, Norman Kay, s of Norman Kay (d 1975); 1 s (Tristan Andrew b 18 Feb 1979), 1 da (Sarah Elizabeth b 23 April 1982); *Career* author; infant sch teacher until 1979; *Books* Legacy (1985, Historical Novel prize in memory of Georgette Heyer 1985, Betty Trask Award for a first novel 1985), Phantom (1990, winner Romantic Novel of the Year Award 1991, ALA Best Book for Young Adults Award 1991); *Recreations* theatre, craft work, writing; *Style—* Mrs Susan Kay; ✉ c/o Heather Jeeves Literary Agency, 9 Kingsfield Crescent, Witney, Oxfordshire OX8 6JB (tel 01993 700253)

KAY, Vernon; s of Norman Kay, of Bolton, and Gladys Kay; *b* 28 April 1974, Bolton; *Educ* St Joseph's RC Sch Horwich, St John Rigby Coll Orrell, Manchester Met Univ; *m* 12 Sept 2003, Tess Daly; 1 da (Phoebe Elizabeth b 2004); *Career* TV and radio presenter; former model; supporter NCH; pres Bolton FC Jr Whites, memb Br Model Flying Assoc; *Television* as presenter incl: T4 (Channel 4) 2000–, Celebrities Under Pressure (ITV) 2003, Boys and Girls (Channel 4) 2003, Head Jam (BBC2 and BBC3) 2004, Wife for William (E4) 2004, Hit Me Baby One More Time (ITV and NBC) 2005; *Radio* sometime presenter Xfm, presenter BBC Radio 1 2004–; *Clubs* Fifty, Soho House, Union; *Style—* Vernon Kay, Esq; ✉ c/o Princess Talent Management, Whiteleys Centre, 151 Queensway, London W2 4SB (tel 020 7985 1985, fax 020 7985 1989, e-mail talent@princesstv.com)

KAY, William John; s of William Jarvie Kay (d 1988), and Agnes Sutherland Walker (d 2002); *b* 12 September 1946; *Educ* Westminster City Sch, The Queen's Coll Oxford (open scholar, MA); *m* 1968 (m dis 1986); 2 s (Andrew James b 15 Aug 1972, Benjamin William Matthew b 3 Nov 1973); partner Lynne Elizabeth Bateson; *Career* fin journalist: London Evening News 1968–72, London Evening Standard 1972–77, Daily Telegraph 1977–79; features ed Financial Weekly 1979, dep business ed Now magazine 1979–81, fin writer The Sunday Times Business News 1981–84, City ed The Times 1984–86, freelance journalist (The Times, The Sunday Times, The Sunday Telegraph, The Independent, Independent on Sunday and Mail on Sunday) 1986–95, fin ed Independent on Sunday 1995, City ed Mail on Sunday 1995–99, personal fin ed The Independent 2001–05, money ed The Sunday Times 2005–06, freelance writer LA 2006–; Wincott Personal Financial Journalist 2002, Headlinemoney Columnist of the Year 2005, Assoc of Br Insurers Lifetime Achievement Award 2005; *Books* A-Z Guide to Money (1983), Tycoons (1985), Big Bang (1986), The Stock Exchange: A Marketplace for Tomorrow (The Stock Exchange, ed, 1986), Battle For the High Street (1987), Nightmare - The Ernest Saunders Story (ghosted, by-line James Saunders, 1989), Modern Merchant Banking (ed, 1990), The City and the Single European Market (ed, 1991), Charity Appeals (ghosted, by-line Marion Allford, 1993), The Bosses (1994), Lord of the Dance - The Story of Gerry Robinson (1999); *Recreations* cricket, Chelsea FC, travel, good food; *Clubs* MCC; *Style—* William Kay, Esq

KAYE, *see also:* Lister-Kaye

KAYE, Dr Georges Sabry; s of Dr Georges Kaye, of Beirut, The Lebanon, and Claire, *née* De las Case; *b* 21 May 1949; *Educ* Villa St Jean, Fribourg, Ratcliffe, KCL (BSc), Westminster Hosp Med Sch (MB BS); *Career* physician i/c Occupational Health Dept Cromwell Hosp 1982–; Euro med dir to General Electric Co 1982–; currently co med dir to: Citigroup, Pendragon Capital Mgmnt Ltd, Air France, Hill Samuel Financial Services; memb International Commission on Occupational Health; memb BMA and RSM 1974, AFOM 1986; *Books* La Soif (The Thirst) (1976), Musings upon a Busy Doctor's Life (2000), The Tortured Wounded Healer that is Today's Patient (2000); *Recreations* French literature, lute playing; *Clubs* The Reform; *Style—* Dr Georges Kaye; ✉ 4 Manson Mews, South Kensington, London SW7 5AF (tel 020 7370 0920, e-mail GSK@georgeskaye.com); Braco Castle, Perthshire

KAYE, Jeremy Robin; s of Kenneth Brown Kaye (d 1985), of Doncaster, and Hannah Eleanor Christabel, *née* Scott (d 1991); *b* 25 September 1937; *Educ* Eastbourne Coll, Worcester Coll Oxford (MA); *Career* Nat Serv Bombardier RA 1956–58; called to the Bar Inner Temple 1962; asst sec Limmer and Trinidad Lake Asphalt Co Ltd 1962–67, chief legal offr and asst sec Limmer Holdings Ltd 1967–72; sec: Arbuthnot Latham Holdings Ltd 1975–81, Dow Scandia Holdings Ltd 1982–86, Arbuthnot (formerly Secure Trust) Banking Gp plc 1987–, Arbuthnot Fund Mangrs Ltd 1987–; dir: Arbuthnot Latham Bank Ltd 1984–91 (sec 1973–91); lay chm East Grinstead Deanery 1977–87 (sec 1967–77, treas 1993–); Diocese of Chichester: memb Synod 1970–73 and 1988–, memb Bd of Fin 1992–, treas 2002–; FCIS; *Recreations* gardening, cricket, golf; *Clubs* MCC, Holtye Golf; *Style—* Jeremy Kaye, Esq; ✉ Mallards, 52 Moat Road, East Grinstead, West Sussex RH19 3LH (tel 01342 321 294); Arbuthnot House, 20 Ropemaker Street, London EC2Y 9AR (tel 020 7012 2430, fax 020 7012 2401)

KAYE, Laurence Martin; s of Moss Kaye, and Beatrice, *née* Herman; *b* 1 September 1949; *Educ* Haberdashers' Aske's, Sidney Sussex Coll Cambridge (Whittaker scholar, MA); *m* 1 July 1976, Lauren Merrill, *née* Shaymow; 1 s (David Benjamin b 22 Sept 1978), 1 da (Debra Ann b 16 Oct 1981); *Career* admitted slr 1975; ptnr: Brecher & Co 1977 (articled clerk 1972–75), Saunders Sobell Leigh & Dobin 1980–94, The Simkins Partnership (head of publishing and new media) 1994–98, Paisner & Co (head of e-commerce) 1998–2000, Andersen Legal (head of technology and e-business) 2000–02; slr in private practice (Laurence Kaye Slrs) 2002–; legal advsr to Euro Publishers' Cncl; former chm: Mount Vernon Cleft Lip and Palate Assoc Ltd, Meher Baba Assoc Ltd; memb: Law Soc, Int Bar Assoc; *Recreations* tennis, golf, theatre, music, yoga; *Clubs* Radlett Lawn Tennis; *Style—* Laurence Kaye, Esq; ✉ Wisley House, Gills Hill Lane, Radlett, Hertfordshire WD7 8DD (tel 01923 352117, e-mail laurie@laurencekaye.com, website www.laurencekaye.com)

KAYE, Maj Sir Paul Henry Gordon; 5 Bt (UK 1923), of Huddersfield, Co York; s of Sir David Alexander Gordon Kaye, 4 Bt (d 1994), and his 2 w, Adelle Frances, *née* Thomas; *b* 19 February 1958; *m* 1, 1984 (m dis 2000), Sally Ann Louise, *née* Grützner; m 2, 2005 (m dis 2007), Ma Bonita, *née* Yang; *Heir* bro, John Kaye; *Career* cmmnd RAE 1982, Maj Aust Intelligence Corps (ret 2001); *Recreations* rugby union, horse riding, motorcycles; *Style—* Maj Sir Paul Kaye, Bt

KAYE, His Hon Judge Roger Godfrey; TD (1980, 1985), QC (1989); s of Anthony Harmsworth Kaye (d 1971), and Heidi Alice, *née* Jordy (d 1984); *b* 21 September 1946; *Educ* King's Sch Canterbury, Univ of Birmingham (LLB); *m* 15 April 1974, Melloney Rose, da of Rev H Martin Westall (d 1994); *Career* called to the Bar Lincoln's Inn 1970 (bencher 1997); jr Treasy counsel in Insolvency Matters 1978–89, dep High Court bankruptcy registrar 1984–2001, dep High Court judge 1990–, recorder 1995–2005, specialist chancery and mercantile circuit judge (NE Circuit) 2005–; chm: Bar Cncl Fees Collection Ctee 1990–93, Bristol and Cardiff Chancery Bar Assoc 1990–95; memb Bar Cncl Professional Conduct Ctee 1995–97; dep chllr: Dio of St Albans 1995–2002, Dio of Southwark 1995–99, Dio of Hereford 1997–2000; chllr: Dio of Hertford 2000–, Diocese of

St Albans 2002–; Hon Col 3 (V) MI Bn 1998–; Freeman City of London 1997; FRSA 1995, FCIArb 2001; *Recreations* going home; *Clubs* Athenaeum, RAC, Army and Navy, Special Forces; *Style*— His Hon Judge Kaye, TD, QC

KAYE, Simon; s of Isaac Kaye (d 1964), of London, and Dora, *née* Libovitch (d 1964); *b* 22 July 1935; *Educ* Wycombe Sch; *m* 8 Sept 1957, Sylvia Adrienne, da of Michael Kagan (d 1982); 2 s (Jeremy b 22 Oct 1959, Trevor b 6 May 1966), 1 da (Elaine b 24 Sept 1962); *Career* film sound recordist; entered film industry 1953, sound mixer 1962, dir Siren Sound 1967–89, recorded over 100 Br and American films; winner of Oscars (for Platoon and Last of the Mohicans), 2 other Oscar nominations (for Reds and Gandhi), 3 BAFTA Awards (for Oh! What a Lovely War, A Bridge Too Far and Cry Freedom), 10 Br Acad Award nominations (for The Charge of the Light Brigade, The Lion in Winter, Oh! What a Lovely War, Sunday Bloody Sunday, A Bridge Too Far, Reds, Ghandi, Indiana Jones and the Temple of Doom, Cry Freedom and Last of the Mohicans), Cinema Audio Soc Best Sound Award 2004 (for The Life and Death of Peter Sellers); other credits incl: Shadowlands, Lost in Space, The Bone Collector, Under Suspicion, Spy Game, Tomb Raider II, Life and Death of Peter Sellers, Being Julia, Fateless; memb: BAFTA, Acad Motion Pictures Arts and Sciences, Cinema Audio Soc, Assoc Motion Picture Sound; *Style*— Simon Kaye, Esq; ✉ 39 Belfield Avenue, Harrow Weald, Middlesex HA3 6ST (tel 020 8428 4823)

KAYE, Prof Stanley Bernard; *b* 5 September 1948; *Educ* Roundhay Sch Leeds, Charing Cross Hosp Med Sch London (BSc, MB BS, MD); *Career* jr hosp posts in med oncology and gen med 1972–79, acting staff specialist in med oncology Ludwig Institute for Cancer Research Sydney 1980–81, prof of med oncology Univ of Glasgow 1985–2000 (sr lectr 1981–85), prof of med oncology Inst of Cancer Research and Royal Marsden Hosp 2000–; Cancer Research UK: memb Scientific Exec Bd 2002–, chm Clinical and Translational Research Ctee 2004–; non-exec dir North Glasgow Univ Hosp NHS Trust 1999–2000; memb MRC Cancer Therapy Ctee 1986–93, memb Gynaecological Cancer Working Pty 1990, memb Working Parties on Lung and Gynaecological Cancer 1986–90; memb: Scottish Cancer Coordinating and Advsy Ctee 1992, Scottish Cancer Therapy Network 1993; clinical ed British Jl of Cancer 1993; memb Editorial Bd: Prescribers Jl, European Jl of Cancer, Int Jl of Oncology, Current Drugs, Current Clinical Cancer, Anti Cancer Research; author of various med pubns; FRCP 1989, FRCPGlas 1992, FRCR 1993, FRSE 2001, FMedSci 2004; *Recreations* playing several sports badly; *Style*— Prof Stanley Kaye; ✉ Royal Marsden Hospital, Sutton, Surrey SM2 5PT (e-mail stan.kaye@icr.ac.uk)

KEABLE, Nicholas Simon Phillip-James (Nick); s of John Todhunter Keable (d 1996), of Sanderstead, Surrey, and Norma Sybil, *née* Norton; *b* 6 June 1966; *Educ* Ratcliffe Coll, RMA Sandhurst; *m* 1998, Tanya Towhidi; *Career* cmmnd Grenadier Gds 1986–94, latterly Capt (ops offr); Euro Parl 1994–96, with PPS Group 1997–2005 (latterly md), vice-pres TSCG 2005–; cnclIr (Cons) London Borough of Croydon 1998–2002; MInstD; *Style*— Nick Keable, Esq; ✉ TSCG, 18 Buckingham Gate, London SW1E 6LB

KEAL, Anthony Charles (Tony); s of Maj Kitchener Keal, of Thornton Dale, N Yorks, and Joan Marjorie, *née* Ayling; *b* 12 July 1951; *Educ* Stowe, New Coll Oxford (BA); *m* 24 Nov 1979, (Janet) Michele, da of late John Charles King, of Javea, Spain; 4 s (Julian Charles b 1982, Jonathan David b 1986, Christopher James b 1987, Alexander Anthony b 1989); *Career* slr Allen & Overy 1976, slr and co sec Libra Bank plc 1976–78, ptnr Allen & Overy 1982–2005 (slr 1978–82), ptnr Simpson Thacher & Bartlett LLP 2005–; memb Worshipful Co of Slrs; memb Law Soc; *Recreations* sailing, travel, skiing, family, opera; *Style*— Tony Keal, Esq; ✉ Simpson Thacher & Bartlett LLP, Citypoint, One Ropemaker Street, London EC2Y 9HU

KEALEY, Gavin Sean James; QC (1994); s of Paul E Kealey, and Evelyn, *née* Fegali; *b* 2 September 1953; *Educ* Charterhouse, UC Oxford (Fletcher scholar, BA); *m* 28 Feb 1981, Karen Elizabeth, da of Robert Nowak; 3 da (Alexandra Louise b 22 March 1983, Eleanor Victoria b 26 March 1986, Rowena Charlotte Ambrosiana b 19 Feb 1992); *Career* lectr in laws KCL; called to the Bar Inner Temple 1977; recorder 2000–, head of chambers 2001–, dep judge of the High Court (Queen's Bench Div Commercial Court) 2002–; *Style*— Gavin Kealey, Esq, QC; ✉ 7 King's Bench Walk, Temple, London EC4Y 7DS (tel 020 7910 8300, fax 020 7910 8400)

KEANE, Dillie; da of Dr Francis Keane, of Portsmouth, and Miriam, *née* Slattery; *b* 23 May 1952; *Educ* Portsmouth HS, Convent of the Sacred Heart Woldingham, TCD, LAMDA; *Career* songwriter, chanteuse, actress and writer; fndr memb Fascinating Aïda with Marilyn Cutts and Adèle Anderson (nominated for Perrier Award 1984, City Limits Most Popular Cabaret Act Award 1985, Olivier Award nomination for Best Entertainment 1995, 2000 and 2004); one woman shows: Single Again (nominated for Perrier Award 1990), Citizen Keane 1991, Back With You 2000–2001 (Möers Comedy Festival Award 2001); nominated Best Actress Manchester Evening News for Maggie in Dancing at Lughnasa, Sony Radio Award Best Documentary for Call me When You're in Something; *Recordings* with Fascinating Aïda: Sweet FA 1985, A Load of Old Sequins 1988, Live at the Lyric 1995, It, Wit, Don't Give a Shit Girls 1997, Barefaced Chic 1999, One Last Flutter 2003; solo recordings: Back With You 2001; *Books* Fascinating Who? (1987), The Joy of Sequins (1994); *Recreations* cooking, gardening, golf, pretending not to be middle aged; *Clubs* Chelsea Arts; *Style*— Miss Keane; ✉ c/o Gavin Barker Associates, 2D Wimpole Street, London W1M 7AA (tel 020 7499 4777, fax 020 7499 3777); website www.fascinating-aida.co.uk

KEANE, Fergal Patrick; OBE (1997); s of Eamon Brendan Keane (d 1990), and Mary, *née* Hasset; *b* 6 January 1961; *Educ* Terenure Coll Dublin, Presentation Coll Cork; *m* 11 July 1986, Anne Frances, da of Frank Coleman Flaherty; *Career* trainee reporter Limerick Leader 1979–82; reporter: Irish Press Group Dublin 1982–84, Radio Telefis Éireann Belfast 1986–89 (Dublin 1984–86); BBC Radio: Northern Ireland corr 1989–91, Southern Africa corr 1991–94, Asia corr 1994–; BBC special correspondent 1997–; presenter Fergal Keane's Forgotten Britain (BBC TV) 2000; Hon DLitt Univ of Strathclyde 2001 *Awards* Reporter of the Year Sony Silver Award 1992 and Sony Gold Award 1993, Amnesty International Press Awards Int Reporter of the Year 1993, RTS Journalist of the Year 1994, BAFTA 1998, James Cameron Prize 1998; *Books* Irish Politics Now (1987), The Bondage of Fear (1994), Season of Blood: A Rwandan Journey (1995), Letter to Daniel: Despatches from the Heart (1996), Letters Home (1999), A Strangers Eye (2000), All of these People (2005); *Recreations* fishing, golf, poetry; *Style*— Fergal Keane, Esq, OBE; ✉ c/o BBC News and Current Affairs, Radio, Television Centre, London W12 7RJ

KEANE, Sheriff Francis Joseph; s of Thomas Keane (d 1967), of W Lothian, and Helen Flynn; *b* 5 January 1936; *Educ* Blairs Coll Aberdeen, Gregorian Univ Rome (PHL), Univ of Edinburgh (LLB); *m* 19 April 1960, Lucia Corio, da of John Morrison (d 1983), of Glasgow; 2 s (Paul b 1963, Mark b 1965), 1 da (Lucy b 1961); *Career* slr; ptnr McCluskey Keane & Co Edinburgh 1959; depute procurator fiscal: Perth 1961, Edinburgh 1963; sr depute procurator fiscal Edinburgh 1971, sr legal asst Crown Office Edinburgh 1972, procurator fiscal Airdrie 1976, regnl procurator fiscal S Strathclyde, Dumfries and Galloway 1980; pres Procurators' Fiscal Soc 1982–84; Sheriff Glasgow and Strathkelvin 1984–93, Sheriff Lothians and Borders 1993–98, Sheriff Tayside Central and Fife 1998–2004; *Recreations* music, tennis, painting, Italian; *Style*— Sheriff Francis Keane; ✉ 1/1 West Cherrybank, Stanley Road, Edinburgh EH6 4SW

KEANE, (Mary) Georgina; da of Dr Henry Anthony Keane, of Eire and S Wales, and Patricia Josephine, *née* Nolan; *b* 3 February 1954; *Educ* Convent of the Sacred Heart Woldingham; *m* 21 Dec 1978, Dr Saad Al-Damluji, s of Prof Salem Al-Damluji, of Abu Dhabi, UAE; 2 s (Salem b 1981, Hassan b 1982); *Career* barr 1975–84 (chambers in London, Colchester Ipswich and Norwich), legal advsr Employment Affrs Directorate CBI 1984–86, conslt barr Titmuss Sainer & Webb 1986–88; admitted slr 1988; ptnr and head employment unit: Titmuss Sainer Dechert (formerly Titmuss Sainer & Webb) 1988–96, Richards Butler 1996–2000, Lawrence Graham 2000–01, ptnr Keane & Co 2001–; memb Law Soc, Employment Lawyers Assoc, American Bar Assoc; *Recreations* theatre, avoiding domestic chores; *Style*— Miss Georgina Keane; ✉ Keane & Co, 107–111 Fleet Street, London EC4A 2AB (tel 020 7936 9975, fax 020 7936 9128, e-mail gk@keanelaw.co.uk)

KEANE, Prof John Charlick; s of Ronald Melville Keane (d 1974), of Adelaide, and Mavis Matilda, *née* Charlick (d 1978); *b* 3 February 1949; *Educ* King's Coll Adelaide, Univ of Adelaide (Tinline scholar, BA, Archibald Grenfell Price prize, Charles Fenner prize), Univ of Toronto (Canadian Cwlth scholar and fell, MA, PhD); *m* Kathleen Margaret, *née* O'Neil; 4 c (Rebecca Allison b 1974, Leo Lawson-O'Neil b 1980, George b 1991, Alice b 1992); *Career* prof of politics Univ of Westminster 1988– (dir Centre for the Study of Democracy 1989–); Nuffield fell King's Coll Cambridge 1979–80, visiting lectr Inter-Univ Centre of Dubrovnik Yugoslavia 1982, 1983 and 1985, Social Scis Research Cncl fell Freie Universität Berlin FRG 1983, DAAD research fell Universität Bielefeld FRG 1984, overseas teaching and research fell Griffith Univ Aust 1984, research fell Zentrum für Interdisziplinäre Forschung Universität Bielefeld FRG 1987, visiting sr fell Dept of Politics and Soc Scis Euro Univ Inst Florence 1990, visiting prof Depts of Political Sci and Communications Univ of Calif San Diego 1990 and 1994, visiting prof Central Euro Univ Prague 1990, Andrew Mellon sr fell American Philosophical Soc Philadelphia 1991–92, Karl Deutsch prof Wissenschftszentrum Berlin 2001, sr fell IPPR London 2002–03; Anglo-German Br Cncl Research Award Universität Bremen and Freie Universität Berlin FRG 1991, PCFC Award Europe in the Twenty-First Century 1992–93, Univ of Westminster Euro Awareness Fund 1992, Br Cncl travel grant 1993, DEVR/QR Research Assessment Exercise Award CSD 1993–, Deutsch-Englische Gesellschaft fell 1994; memb: Governing Bd Institutum Studium Humanitatis Ljubljana Slovenia 1992–, Assoc Thomas Paine (Paris) 1990–, Editorial Bd The Political Quarterly 1989–, Jan Hus Educnl Fndn (with frequent contribs to parallel university lectrs and seminars in Brno and Prague) 1984–89; Superdon Award The Times (London) 1994; FRSA 1992, FBA 1998–99; *Books* Public Life and Late Capitalism: Towards a Socialist Theory of Democracy (1984), Contradictions of the Welfare State (ed and translator, 1984), The Power of the Powerless: Citizens Against the State in Central-Eastern Europe (ed, 1985), Disorganized Capitalism (ed and co-translator, 1985), After Full Employment (co-author with John Owens, 1986), Nomads of the Present: Social Movements and Individual Needs in Contemporary Societies (co-ed with Paul Mier, 1988), Civil Society and the State: New European Perspectives (ed and translator, 1988), Democracy and Civil Society (1988), The Media and Democracy (1991), Tom Paine: A Political Life (1995), Reflections on Violence (1996), Civil Society: Old Images, New Visions (1998), Václav Havel: A Political Tragedy in Six Acts (1999), On Communicative Abundance (2000), Whatever Happened to Democracy? (2002), Global Civil Society (2003); *Recreations* walking, running, gardening, journalism, film, theatre, cooking; *Style*— Prof John Keane; ✉ Centre for the Study of Democracy, 100 Park Village East, London NW1 3SR (tel 020 7911 5138, fax 020 7911 5164, e-mail csd@westminster.ac.uk)

KEANE, John Granville Colpoys; s of Granville Keane (d 1990), and Elaine Violet Meredith Doubble (d 2004); *b* 12 September 1954; *Educ* Wellington, Camberwell Sch of Art (BA); *m* June 1996, Rosemary Anne McGowan (television prodr); 1 da (Calypso McGowan b 7 April 1997), 1 s (Theodore Granville Peter b 28 June 2002); *Career* artist; official Br war artist Gulf Crisis 1991; work in several public collections incl: Imperial War Museum, Ulster Museum, Nat Army Museum, Nat Portrait Gallery, Wolverhampton Museum, The Lowry Salford; artist in residence Whitefield Sch London 1985–86, visiting prof Univ of the Arts London, res fell Camberwell Coll of Arts, artist in residence Independent on Sunday 2000–01; FRSA 2005; *Solo Exhibitions incl* Peking, Moscow, Milton Keynes (Minsky's Gallery London) 1980, Some of it Works on Paper (Centre 181 London) 1982, War Efforts (Pentonville Gallery London) 1984, Conspiracy Theories (Angela Flowers Gallery London) 1985, Perspective '85 (Basel Art Fair Switzerland) 1985, Work Ethics (Angela Flowers Gallery London) 1986, Bee Keeping in the War Zone (Angela Flowers Gallery) 1988, Against the Wall (Turnpike Gallery Leigh Gtr Manchester) 1988, The Accident (cmmnd painting and screenprint for Greenpeace, Flowers East London) 1988, Divided States (Terry Dintenfass Gallery NY) 1989, Forum (Hamburg Germany) 1989, The Other Cheek? (Flowers East London) 1990, Cloth Caps and Hang-Gliding (cmmnd exhibition about Ollerton Mining Community, Angel Row Gallery Nottingham) 1991, Before the War (Kelvingrove Art Gallery Glasgow) 1991, Gulf (Imperial War Museum London) 1992, Fairytales of London (Lannon Cole Gallery Chicago) 1992, Burden of Paradise, Paintings of Guatemala (Flowers East) 1992, The Struggle for the Control of the Television Station (Terry Dintenfass Gallery, Flowers East) 1993, Gulf (Norton Gallery of Art Florida) 1993, Graham Greene and the Jungle of Human Dilemma (Flowers East) 1995, Truth, Lies and Super-8 (Flowers East) 1997, Conflicts of Interest Touring Retrospective (Wolverhampton City Art Gallery, Ulster Museum, Belfast & Laing Gallery, Newcastle upon Tyne) 1998, Trading Flaws and Sporting Mistakes, Flowers West (Los Angeles), Making a Killing (Flowers East) 2000, Exchange Rates (Gwenda Jay Addington, Chicago) 2000, Saving the Bloody Planet (in assoc with Greenpeace), Flowers East 2001, Recent Events (Flowers Central) 2002, The Inconvenience of History (The London Inst Gallery, in assoc with Christian Aid) 2004, Back to Fundamentals (Flowers East, Ferens Art Gallery Hull) 2004, Fifty Seven Hours in the House of Culture (Flowers East, Sakharov Museum Moscow) 2006, Guantanamerica (Flowers NY) 2006; *Books* Conflicts of Interest (by Mark Lawson, 1995); *Clubs* Groucho, Chelsea Arts; *Style*— John Keane, Esq; ✉ Flowers East, 82 Kingsland Road, London E2 8DP (tel 020 920 7777, fax 020 920 7770)

KEANE, Philip Vincent; s of Bernard Vincent Keane (d 1983), of London, and Brenda Ellen Margaret, *née* Ford; *b* 11 August 1940; *Educ* Wimbledon Coll GS, LSE (BSc); *m* 18 Sept 1965, (Kathleen) Winifred, da of William Aloysius Thomson (d 1987), of London; 2 da (Angelina Teresa b 14 Sept 1968, Noelle Francesca b 16 Dec 1969); *Career* sr investment analyst Esso Pension Tst 1967–71, head of investment res Mercantile & General Reinsurance 1971–75, equity fund mangr Prudential Pensions 1976–77, investment mangr Rea Bros Ltd 1977–81; dir: Wardley Investment Mgmnt Ltd, HK Unit Tst Managers Ltd 1981–82, Rea Bros (Investment Mgmnt) Ltd 1982–89, CS Investment Mgmnt Ltd 1989–91; assoc dir IBJ Asset Management International Ltd (subsid of the Industrial Bank of Japan, and formerly IBJ International plc) 1991–; AIIMR; *Recreations* travel, photography, skiing, literature; *Style*— Philip Keane, Esq; ✉ 70 Pine Grove, off Lake Road, Wimbledon, London SW19 7HE; IBJ Asset Management International Ltd, Bracken House, 1 Friday Street, London EC4M 9JA (tel 020 7236 1090)

KEANE, Sir Richard Michael; 6 Bt (UK 1801), of Cappoquin, Co Waterford; s of Lt-Col Sir John Keane, 5 Bt, DSO (d 1956), and Lady Eleanor Hicks Beach (d 1960), da of 1 Earl St Aldwyn; *b* 29 January 1909; *Educ* Sherborne, ChCh Oxford; *m* 1939, Olivia Dorothy, da of Oliver Hawkshaw, TD, of Chisenbury Priory, Wilts; 1 da (Vivien Eleanor (Mrs Simon Pleydell-Bouverie) b 1940), 2 s (John Charles b 1941, David Richard b 1950); *Heir* s, John Keane; *Career* served with Co of London Yeo and 10 Royal Hussars 1939–44, liaison offr (Maj) with HQ Vojvodina Yugoslav partisans 1944, attached British Military Mission Belgrade 1944–45; diplomatic corr: Reuters 1935–37, Sunday Times 1937–39 (also asst ed); publicity conslt to ICI Ltd 1950–62; farmer; *Books* Germany - What Next?

(1939); *Recreations* fishing, forestry; *Clubs* Kildare Street; *Style*— Sir Richard Keane, Bt; ✉ Cappoquin House, Cappoquin, Co Waterford, Ireland

KEANE, Roy Maurice; *b* 10 August 1971, Cork; *Career* professional footballer and coach; clubs: Cobh Ramblers until 1990, Nottingham Forest 1990–93 (154 first team appearances, 33 goals, Full Members' Cup winner 1992), Manchester United 1993–2005 (over 400 first team appearances, club capt 1998–2005, Premier League Champions 1994, 1996, 1997, 1999, 2000, 2001 and 2003, FA Cup winners 1994, 1996, 1999 and 2004 (finalists 2005), Charity Shield winners 1993, 1996 and 1997, European Champions League winners 1999), Celtic FC 2005–06, ret 2006; Republic of Ireland: 61 full caps, 9 goals, debut v Chile 1991, memb squad World Cup USA 1994, original memb squad (left squad before start of tournament) World Cup Japan/Korea 2002; mangr Sunderland FC 2006– (winners Championship 2007); *Publications* Keane: The Autobiography (with Eamonn Dunphy, 2002); *Style*— Roy Keane, Esq

KEARNS, Hon Mr Justice Nicholas J; s of William Kearns (d 1995), and Joan, *née* Welland; *b* 13 April 1946, Dublin; *Educ* St Mary's Coll Rathmines, UCD, King's Inns Dublin; *m* 18 Sept 1971, Eleanor; 4 s (Stephen, Daniel, Simon, Nicholas); *Career* called to the Bar: King's Inns Dublin 1968, England and Wales 1980; sr counsel 1982–98, judge of the High Court of Ireland 1998–2004, judge of the Supreme Court of Ireland 2004–; subst/alternate judge European Court of Human Rights 2001, judge Permanent Court of Arbitration The Hague 2005; chair Referendum Cmmn (on citizenship) 2004; co-fndr Assoc of European Competition Law Judges; *Recreations* reading, writing, walking, golf; *Style*— The Hon Mr Justice Nicholas Kearns; ✉ Supreme Court of Ireland, Four Courts, Inns Quay, Dublin 7, Ireland

KEATES, Jonathan Basil; s of Richard Herbert Basil Keates (d 1949), and Sonia Evangeline, *née* Wilcox; *b* 7 November 1946; *Educ* Bryanston (scholar), Magdalen Coll Oxford (MA), Univ of Exeter (PGCE); *Career* author; asst English master City of London Sch 1974–; regular contrib to: The New York Times, The Spectator, The Literary Review, TLS; Hawthornden Prize 1984, James Tait Black Prize 1984; judge Booker Prize 1991; FRSL 1993; *Books* The Companion Guide to Shakespeare Country (1979), Allegro Postillions (1983), Handel: the man and his music (1985), The Stranger's Gallery (1986), Tuscany (1988), Umbria (1991), Italian Journeys (1991), Stendhal (1994), Purcell (1995), Soon To Be A Major Motion Picture (1997), Smile Please (2000), The Siege of Venice (2005); *Recreations* music, travel, libraries, friendship; *Clubs* Athenaeum; *Style*— Jonathan Keates, Esq, FRSL; ✉ c/o Felicity Bryan, 2A North Parade, Banbury Road, Oxford OX2 6PE (tel 01865 513816, fax 01865 310055)

KEATING, David George Michael; s of George Francis Keating (d 1989), and Una Rosalie, *née* Metters (d 1990); *b* 31 January 1943; *Educ* UCS London, King's Coll Durham (LLB); *m* 1, 18 Dec 1965, Alicia Gay, da of Frederick Johnson (d 1978); 2 da (Ruth b 31 Oct 1967, Rebekah b 21 July 1973), 1 s (Daniel b 30 Dec 1968); m 2, 5 July 1980, Jane, da of Dr Henry Thistlethwaite; *Career* admitted slr: Eng & Wales 1967, Western Pacific High Cmmn 1969 (also barr 1969), Republic of Ireland 1992; advocate Jt Tbnl New Hebrides 1971; NP 1973; vice-pres PECO Ctee of CCBE; former sec and pres Hartlepool Law Soc, former pres Durham & N Yorks Law Soc; chm Br Albanian Law Assoc; former chm: Easington CAB, NE Legal Servs Ctee; hon memb: Bucharest Bar, Union of Advocates Ukraine; Freeman City of London 2003, Liveryman Worshipful Co of Woolmen 2003; *Recreations* walking, postal history, the Balkans; *Clubs* East India; *Style*— David Keating, Esq; ✉ South Mall, Lismore, Co Waterford, Ireland

KEATING, Henry Reymond Fitzwalter (Harry); s of John Hervey Keating (d 1950), and Muriel Marguerita, *née* Clews (d 1986); *Educ* Merchant Taylors', TCD (BA); *m* 3 Oct 1953, Sheila Mary, da of William Ford Mitchell, ISO (d 1968); 3 s (Simon b 1955, Piers b 1960, Hugo b 1964), 1 da (Bryony b 1957); *Career* Army 1945–48; journalist 1952–63; chm: Crime Writers' Assoc 1970–71, Soc of Authors 1982–84; pres The Detection Club 1986–2001; FRSL 1990; *Books* Death and the Visiting Firemen (1959), The Perfect Murder (1964), The Murder of the Maharajah (1980), The Lucky Alphonse (1982), Under A Monsoon Cloud (1986), Dead on Time (1988), Inspector Ghote - His Life and Crimes (1989), The Rich Detective (1993), Doing Wrong (1994), The Good Detective (1995), The Bad Detective (1996), Asking Questions (1996), The Soft Detective (1997), Bribery, Corruption Also (1999), The Hard Detective (2000), Breaking and Entering (2001), A Detective in Love (2001), The Dreaming Detective (2003), A Detective at Death's Door (2004), One Man and His Bomb (2006), Rules, Regs and Rotten Eggs (2007); *Style*— H R F Keating, FRSL; ✉ 35 Northumberland Place, London W2 5AS (tel 020 7229 1100)

KEATING, John David; s of Peter Steven Keating (d 1944, war casualty), of York, and Muriel Emily Alice Lamport; *b* 18 June 1943; *Educ* King Edward VI Chelmsford, Highbury Coll Portsmouth; *m* 28 Aug 1970, Linda Margaret, da of Sidney Reginald Hall, of London; 1 s (Matthew b 1971), 1 da (Sarah b 1973); *Career* seagoing purser with P&O 1960–70, Lt Reserve Serv RN 2 Submarine Div 1970–71; asst to md CWS 1972–74, UK divnl accountant Borden Chemical Corp 1975–81, fndr dir and proprietor WRA Ltd 1982–; dir: WRA Holdings Ltd 1984–, WRA (Offshore) Ltd (Sub-Sea Devpt) 1985–, Russell Square Management Co Ltd 1991–, Martel-Wessex Composites Ltd 1991–, Euro-Maritime Ltd 1992–, The Halsey Arms Co Ltd 2000–; md Wessex Resins & Adhesives Ltd; elected memb for Ringwood South Ward of New Forest DC 1987–; FCCA 1977 (ACCA), MHCIMA; *Recreations* sailing, skiing; *Clubs* Naval, Royal Naval Sailing Assoc, Royal Lymington Yacht, Ski Club of GB; *Style*— John Keating, Esq; ✉ Greenways, Hightown Hill, Ringwood, Hampshire BH24 3HG (tel 01425 475446); Chalet Florence, Le Villard, Méribel les Allues, France (tel and fax 00 334 79 00 37 28); Wessex Resins & Adhesives Ltd, Cupernham House, Cupernham Lane, Romsey, Hampshire SO51 7LF (tel 01794 521111, fax 01794 517779, e-mail john.keating@wessex-resins.com)

KEATING, Prof Michael James; s of Michael Joseph Keating (d 1974), and Margaret Watson, *née* Lamb (d 2001); *b* 2 February 1950, Hartlepool, Co Durham; *Educ* Univ of Oxford (BA, MA), CNAA (PhD); *m* 22 Feb 1975, Patricia Ann, *née* McCusker; 1 s (Patrick David b 24 Feb 1979); *Career* pt/t lectr Glasgow Coll of Technol 1972–75, sr res offr in govt Univ of Essex 1975–76, lectr in politics North Staffordshire Poly 1976–79, lectr and sr lectr Univ of Strathclyde 1979–88, prof of political science Univ of Western Ontario 1988–99, prof of politics Univ of Aberdeen 1999, prof of political science European Univ Inst Italy 2000–; FRSE; *Books* Labour and Scottish Nationalism (jtly, 1979), Regional Government in England (jt ed, 1982), The Government of Scotland (jtly, 1983), Labour and the British State (jtly, 1985), Regions in the European Community (jt ed, 1985), Decentralisation and Change in Contemporary France (jtly, 1986), Remaking Urban Scotland: Strategies for Local Economic Development (jtly, 1986), The City that Refused to Die: Glasgow - The Politics of Urban Regeneration (1988), State and Regional Nationalism: Territorial Politics and the European State (1988), Politics and Public Policy in Scotland (jtly, 1991), Comparative Urban Politics: Power and the City in the United States, Canada, Britain and France (1991), The Politics of Modern Europe: The State and Political Authority in the Major Democracies (1993, 2 edn 1999), The European Union and the Regions (jt ed, 1995), Nations against the State: The New Politics of Nationalism in Quebec, Catalonia and Scotland (1996, 2 edn 2001), The Political Economy of Regionalism (jt ed, 1997), The New Regionalism in Western Europe: Territorial Restructuring and Political Change (1998), Remaking the Union: Devolution and British Politics in the 1990s (jt ed, 1998), Paradiplomacy in Action: The External Activities of Subnational Governments (jt ed, 1999), Plurinational Democracy: Stateless Nations in a Post-Sovereignty Era (2001), Minority Nationalism and the Changing International Order (jt ed, 2001), The Dynamics of Decentralization: Canadian Federalism and British Devolution (jt ed, 2001), Culture, Institutions and Economic Development: A Study of Eight European Regions (jtly, 2003), The Regional Challenge in Central and Eastern Europe: Territorial Restructuring and European Integration (jt ed, 2003), The Government of Scotland: Public Policy Making after Devolution (2005), European Integration and the Nationalities Question (jt ed, 2006), Devolution and Public Policy: A Comparative Perspective (jt ed, 2006), Scottish Social Democracy (ed, 2007); *Recreations* traditional music, sailing, hiking, cooking; *Style*— Prof Michael Keating; ✉ Middleton of Dudwick, Ellon, Aberdeenshire AB41 8EG; European University Institute, Badia Fiesolana, 5001 4 San Domenico di Fiesole, Italy (tel 00 39 055 4685 250, fax 00 39 055 4685 201, e-mail keating@eui.eu)

KEATING, Roly; *b* 5 August 1961; *Educ* Balliol Coll Oxford; *Career* BBC gen trainee incl attachments to Radio Ulster, Kaleidoscope, Everyman and Newsnight 1983, prodr and dir Bookmark, Omnibus, Arena and numerous music and arts programmes incl Made in Ealing and Philip Roth - My True Story 1985, fndr prodr The Late Show 1988, ed The Late Show 1990 (winner BP Arts Journalism Award), ed Bookmark 1992 (winner BAFTA Best Documentary award and Int Emmy nomination), exec prodr series incl A History of British Art, The House Detectives and How Buildings Learn 1993, devised and launched heritage magazine One Foot in the Past for BBC2, head of devpt music and arts with special responsibility for New Services BBC 1995, seconded to BBC Broadcast to develop factual channel propositions for BBC Worldwide/Flextech joint venture, head of programming UKTV 1997, overseer all new services incl BBC Choice and BBC Knowledge, controller Digital Channels BBC 1999, controller arts commissioning for all BBC TV channels 2000, controller BBC4 2001–04 (Channel of the Year MediaGuardian Edinburgh Int TV Festival), controller BBC2 2004–; *Style*— Roly Keating; ✉ c/o BBC, Television Centre, Wood Lane, London W12 7RJ (tel 020 8225 6621, e-mail roly.keating@bbc.co.uk)

KEATINGE, Richard Arthur Davis; *b* 30 August 1947; *Educ* Portora Royal Sch, Trinity Coll Dublin (BA), UC Dublin (MBA), Wharton Business Sch (AMP); *m* 1970, Athene; 2 s (Benjamin b 17 Aug 1973, Douglas b 5 May 1976), 1 da (Rebecca b 4 Sept 1979); *Career* fin journalist: Reuters Ltd 1969–71, The Irish Times 1971–78; Bank of Ireland: dir and corp fin exec 1978–83, head of gp strategy 1983–86, chief exec UK 1986–90, exec dir Britain 1990–91; chm NCB Corporate Finance 1991–92, dir NCB Group 1991–92; dir Hardwicke Ltd Dublin 1992–93, former chm and md IBI Corporate Finance Ltd; non-exec dir Heiton Holdings 1999–; *Recreations* golf, fishing, tennis; *Clubs* Kildare Street and Univ, Royal St George Yacht, Connemara Golf, Carrickmines Golf; *Style*— Richard Keatinge, Esq

KEATINGE, Prof William Richard; s of Sir Edgar Keatinge (d 1998), of Salisbury, Wilts, and Katherine Lucille Keatinge; *b* 18 May 1931; *Educ* Upper Canada Coll, Rugby, Univ of Cambridge (MA, MB BChir, PhD); *m* 15 Oct 1955, Margaret Ellen Annette (d 2000), da of David Hegarty (d 1973); 1 s (Richard), 2 da (Claire, Mary); *Career* RNVR seconded for res at Univ of Cambridge 1956–58; dir of studies in med and jr res fell Pembroke Coll Cambridge 1958–60, fell Cardiovascular Res Inst San Francisco 1960–61, MRC post and fell Pembroke Coll Oxford 1961–68, head Physiology Dept London Hosp Med Coll 1981–90 (reader 1968–71, prof 1971–), head Physiology Dept Queen Mary & Westfield Coll London 1990–96 (emeritus prof 1996–); memb: Physiological Soc 1959, RSM; FRCP 1990 (MRCP 1984); *Books* Survival In Cold Water, Local Mechanisms Controlling Blood Vessels; *Recreations* archaeology, sailing; *Style*— Prof William Keatinge; ✉ 39 Shawfield Street, London SW3 4BA

KEATLEY, (Robert) Bryan; TD (1961); s of James Walter Stanley Keatley (d 1978), of Royston, Herts, and Helen Rankin Thompson; *b* 21 March 1930; *Educ* Aldenham, St Catharine's Coll Cambridge (MA); *m* 14 Sept 1957, Diana, da of Frank Harvey, of Bishop's Stortford, Herts; 2 da (Georgina b 1960, Rebecca (Mrs Meyrick) b 1962), 2 s (Robert b 1967, Richard (twin) b 1967 d 2000); *Career* landowner, chartered surveyor and land agent; Nat Serv 1949–50; conslt Humberts London 1990–95 (ptnr 1962–90, sr ptnr 1980–85); TA Cambs Regt (16 Airborne Div), Maj & OC Herts Regt; memb Nat Tst: Fin Ctee 1983–88, Estates Panel 1983–96, Enterprise Bd 1984–88; dir: Landplan Ltd 1974–90, Glen Rinnes Ltd 1990–, BK Underwriting Ltd 1998–; chm: Formfield (BES) 1984, Rural Assets 1987–; cmmr of taxes 1960–95; chm Herts (Hadhams Branch) Royal Br Legion 1984–95, govr Wellington Coll 1992–2001; tstee Keatley Tst 2002–; Freeman City of London 1978, Liveryman Worshipful Co of Farmers; FRICS, FRSA; *Recreations* shooting, conservation, gardens, browsing; *Clubs* Boodle's, Farmers', Royal Over-Seas League; *Style*— Bryan Keatley, Esq, TD; ✉ Bonjedward Hill, Jedburgh, Roxburghshire TD8 6SF (tel 01835 863636); Estate Office (tel and fax 01835 864626, e-mail rbkeatley@aol.com)

KEATLEY, John Rankin Macdonald; s of James Walter Stanley Keatley (d 1978), of Royston, and Helen Rankin Thompson; *b* 20 August 1933; *Educ* Aldenham, RAC Cirencester; *m* 1964 (m dis 1980), Carolyn Margaret, da of Rodney Telford Morell, of Melbourne, Aust; 1 s (James b 1965), 1 da (Arabella b 1967); *Career* 2 Lt Duke of Wellington's Regt, Korea 1952–53, Capt Hertfordshire Regt TA 1953–60; Parly candidate (Cons) Hemsworth 1964; leader Cambridge CC 1967–69; dir REA Holdings plc 1978–; chm: The Keatley Tst 1968–, Lansdowne Club 1979–97; fndr tstee Cambridge Museum of Technol 1970–, patron Decorative Arts Soc 1990–; pres: SW Cambridgeshire Cons Assoc 1987, S Cambridgeshire Cons Assoc 1999–2002, Arts Cncl of North Hertfordshire 1991–2000, Guild of Glass Engravers 2001–; chm S Cambridgeshire Cons Fedn 2001–03; memb: Ctee Contemporary Art Soc 1989–95 (buyer 1990), Syndicate Fitzwilliam Museum Cambridge 1990–, Crafts Advsy Ctee Br Library Oral History Project; hon fell Guild of Designer Bookbinders 1989; *Publications* Commonplace Reflections (2002), A Keatleian Miscellany (2006); *Recreations* art, music, gardening; *Style*— J R M Keatley, Esq; ✉ Melbourn Lodge, Royston, Hertfordshire SG8 6AL (tel 01763 260680)

KEBEDE, HE Berhanu; *b* 11 April 1956, Addis Ababa; *Educ* Haile Selassie I Secdy Sch, Addis Ababa Univ, Free Univ of Brussels (MA); *m*; 3 c; *Career* Ethiopian diplomat; joined Miny of Foreign Affrs as Ethiopian-EEC rels desk offr 1978, economist Ethiopian Mission Brussels 1983, head Western European Div Miny of Foreign Affrs 1992–93, DG Int Orgn and Economic Cooperation Miny of Foreign Affrs 1992–2000, charge d'affaires Ethiopian embassy Russian Fedn 2000–02, ambass to Sweden, Norway, Denmark, Finland and Iceland 2002–06, ambass to Ct of St James's 2006–; *Style*— HE Mr Berhanu Kebede; ✉ Ethiopian Embassy, 17 Princes Gate, London SW7 1PZ (tel 020 7838 3888)

KECK, Colleen; *b* 23 October 1958; *Educ* Univ of Saskatchewan (BA, LLB), Univ of London (LLM); *Career* corp lawyer specialising in IT and intellectual property (commercial) law; admitted slr and called to the Bar Alberta Canada 1983, admitted slr England and Wales 1988; articled student Bennett Jones Barristers and Solicitors Canada 1982–83, barr and slr Home Oil Co Ltd 1983–88, ptnr Allen & Overy 1992– (asst 1988–92); frequent publisher/lectr on pharmaceutical, intellectual property, IT and media topics; Ctee memb: Int Trade Marks Assoc, Licensing Execs Soc; memb: Law Soc of England and Wales, Law Soc of Alberta, Canadian Bar Assoc; *Style*— Ms Colleen Keck; ✉ Allen & Overy, One New Change, London EC4M 9QQ (tel 020 7330 3000, fax 020 7330 9999)

KEE, Prof (Alexander) Alistair; s of Robert Kee (d 1983), and Agnes Stevenson Kee (d 1963); *b* 17 April 1937; *Educ* Clydebank HS, Univ of Glasgow (MA, BD, Dickson prize, DLitt), Union Theological Seminary NY (Scots fell, STM, PhD); *m* 1961, Anne Mary Paterson (d 1992); 2 s (David Graeme b 1967 d 1968, Colin Cameron b 1969), 1 da (Hilary Moira b 1970); *Career* lectr Dept of Theology UC Rhodesia 1964–67, lectr Dept of Theology Univ of Hull 1967–76, reader Univ of Glasgow 1983–88 (sr lectr 1976–83), prof Dept of

K

Theology and Religious Studies Univ of Edinburgh 1991–2002 (reader 1988–91, prof emeritus 2002–); Karl Jaspers lectureship Ripon Hall Oxford 1975, Ferguson lectureship Univ of Manchester 1986; memb: Soc for the Study of Theology, Br Assoc for the Study of Religion; ed Studies in World Christianity 2002–; *Books* The Way of Transcendence (1971), Seeds of Liberation (1973), A Reader in Political Theology (1974), The Scope of Political Theology (1978), Constantine Versus Christ (1982), Domination or Liberation (1986), Being and Truth (1986), The Roots of Christian Freedom (1988), Marx and the Failure of Liberation Theology (1990), From Bad Faith to Good News (1991), Nietzche Against the Crucified (1999), The Rise and Demise of Black Theology (2006); *Clubs* New (Edinburgh), Bruntsfield Links Golfing Soc; *Style*— Prof Alistair Kee; ✉ 24 Colinton Road, Edinburgh EH10 5EQ (tel 0131 447 0209); School of Divinity, University of Edinburgh, New College, Mound Place, Edinburgh EH1 2LX (tel 0131 650 8921, e-mail alistair.kee@ed.ac.uk)

KEE, Robert; CBE (1998); s of Robert Kee (d 1958), and Dorothy Frances, *née* Monkman (d 1964); *b* 5 October 1919; *Educ* Rottingdean Sch, Stowe (scholar), Magdalen Coll Oxford (exhibitioner, MA); *m* 1, 1948, Janetta, da of G H J Woolley; 1 da (Georgiana); m 2, 1960, Cynthia Charlotte, da of Edward Judah; 2 s (Alexander, Benjamin (decd)), 1 da (Sarah); m 3, 1990, Hon Catherine Mary Trevelyan, OBE, da of Baron Trevelyan, KG, GCMG, CIE, OBE (Life Peer, d 1985); *Career* served RAF 1940–46, Picture Post 1948–52; author, translator journalist and broadcaster, TV interviewer, presenter and documentary maker BBC and ITV 1958–; radio broadcaster 1946–; Richard Dimbleby Award 1976, Jacobs Award (Dublin) for BBC Ireland 1981; memb: BECTU, Equity; *Publications* A Crowd is not Company (1947, republished 1982 and 2000), The Impossible Shore (1949), A Sign of the Times (1956), Broadstrop in Season (1959), Refugee World (1961), The Green Flag (1972), Ireland: A History (1981, updated paperback 2003), The World We Left Behind (1984), The World We Fought For (1985), Trial and Error (1986), Munich: The Eleventh Hour (1988), The Picture Post Album (1989), The Laurel and The Ivy: C S Parnell and Irish Nationalism (1993); *Clubs* Reform; *Style*— Robert Kee, Esq, CBE; ✉ c/o Rogers Coleridge and White, 20 Powis Mews, London W11 1JN (tel 020 7221 3717)

KEEBLE, Giles; s of Thomas Whitfield Keeble (d 1994), and Ursula, *née* Scott-Morris; *b* 12 November 1949; *Educ* The King's Sch Canterbury, St John's Coll Cambridge (MA); *m* 1, 1981 (m dis 1988), Gillian, *née* Perry; 2 s (Nicholas, Sam); m 2, 1992, Caroline, *née* de Méric; 1 da (Hannah), 2 step da (Polly, Chlöe); *Career* account handler JWT 1971–73, account mangr BMP 1973–75, sr account mangr and account planner FGA 1975–76; copywriter: FGA 1976–77, Abbott Mead Vickers 1978–81, WCRS 1981–88 (dir 1984); creative ptnr Leo Burnett 1994–95 (exec creative dir 1988–94), exec creative dir The Open Agency (Abbott Mead Vickers advertising and design subsid) 1996–99, gp creative dir Publicis Ltd 1999–2001, regnl creative dir Lowes Asia Pacific 2001–02, strategic and creative brand consultancy 2002–; winner various advertising industry awards; *Recreations* sport, music, reading, friends; *Clubs* Hawks' (Cambridge), Groucho; *Style*— Giles Keeble, Esq; ✉ e-mail giles.keeble@btinternet.com

KEEBLE, John Francis; s of Frank Edward Keeble (d 1989), and Lilith Louise Keeble (d 1993); *b* 26 April 1933; *Educ* Slough GS, Acton Tech Coll (BSc); *m* 29 March 1958, Vivienne, da of Reginald William Anderson; 1 s (Peter b 1960), 1 da (Elizabeth b 1964); *Career* 2 Lt RCS 1954–56; methods study asst Pharmaceutical Co 1956–60 (res asst 1950–54), sr admin BBC TV 1968–83 (orgn and methods conslt 1960–66, asst to head TV drama 1966–68), sr admin dir business admin and dep chief exec BBC Enterprises Ltd 1983–92; dir: BBC Telecordiale 1988–92, BBC Sub TV Ltd 1990–92, Twin Network Ltd 1990–92, BBC World Service Television Ltd 1991–92; company sec UK Gold Television Ltd and UK Living Ltd 1992–97; FRTS (memb 1970–); *Recreations* theatre, ballet, travel; *Style*— John Keeble, Esq; ✉ 4 Turner Road, Slough, Berkshire SL3 7AN (tel 01753 533850)

KEEBLE, Sally Curtis; MP; da of Sir Curtis Keeble, GCMG, and Margaret Ellen Stephenson Stuart, *née* Fraser; *b* 13 October 1951; *Educ* Cheltenham Ladies' Coll, St Hugh's Coll Oxford (exhibitioner, BA), Univ of South Africa (BA); *m* 9 June 1990, Andrew Porter; 2 c (Eleanor b 8 June 1994, Lewis b 15 April 1996); *Career* journalist 1974–83, press offr Lab Pty, head communications GMB 1986–90, ldr Southwark Cncl 1990–93, MP (Lab) Northampton N 1997–; Parly under-sec of state: DTLR 2001–02, Dept for Int Devpt 2002–; memb: Fabian Soc, NUJ; sch govr; hon fell South Bank Univ 1992; *Publications* Conceiving Your Baby, How Medicine Can Help (1995); *Recreations* antique glass, walking, gardening; *Style*— Ms Sally Keeble, MP; ✉ House of Commons, London SW1A 0AA (tel 020 7219 4039)

KEEFE, Prof Terence (Terry); s of Wilfrid Patrick Keefe (d 1979), and Laura Clara, *née* Mitchell; *b* 1 February 1940; *Educ* Five Ways GS Birmingham, Univ of Leicester (BA, MA), Univ of London (BA); *m* 30 June 1962, Sheila Roberta, da of John Parkin (d 1975), of Great Yarmouth; 1 s (Simon Patrick b 24 Dec 1968), 1 da (Rosanna Jancis b 24 April 1971); *Career* asst master Lincoln City GS 1963–65, asst lectr then lectr then sr lectr in French Univ of Leicester 1965–88, prof of French studies Lancaster Univ 1988–; *Books* Simone De Beauvoir: A Study of Her Writings (1983), French Existentialist Fiction (1986), Zola and the Craft of Fiction (co-ed, 1990), Beauvoir: Les Belles Images, La Femme Rompue (1991), Autobiography and the Existential Self (ed, 1994), Simone de Beauvoir (1998); *Recreations* golf, birdwatching, canoeing; *Style*— Prof Terry Keefe; ✉ Department of European Languages and Cultures, Lonsdale College, Lancaster University, Lancaster LA1 4YN (tel 01524 592667, e-mail t.keefe@lancaster.ac.uk)

KEEFFE, Barrie Colin; s of late Edward Thomas Keeffe, and late Constance Beatrice, *née* Marsh; *b* 31 October 1945; *Educ* East Ham GS; *m* 1, 1969 (m dis 1979), Dee Sarah Truman; m 2, 1981, Verity Eileen Proud, *née* Bargate (d 1981); 2 step s; m 3, 1983 (m dis 1993), Julia Lindsay; *Career* actor Nat Youth Theatre, journalist, writer in residence Shaw Theatre, resident playwright Royal Shakespeare Co 1978, assoc writer Theatre Royal Stratford East 1986–91; also theatre and radio plays dir; memb Bd of Dirs: Soho Theatre Co 1978–89, Theatre Royal Stratford 1989–91; tutor City Univ 2002–05; Judith E Wilson fell Christ's Coll Cambridge 2003–04; UN ambass 1995; *Theatre* Only a Game 1973, A Sight of Glory 1975, Scribes 1975, Here Comes the Sun 1976, Gimme Shelter 1977, A Mad World My Masters 1977, Barbarians 1977, Gotcha 1977, Frozen Assets 1978, Sus 1979, Bastard Angel 1980, She's So Modern 1980, Black Lear 1980, Chorus Girls 1981, Better Times 1985, King of England 1988, My Girl 1989, Not Fade Away 1990, Wild Justice 1990, I Only Want to be With You 1995, The Long Good Friday 1996, Shadows on The Sun 2001 *Television* plays: Nipper 1977, Champions 1978, Hanging Around 1978, Waterloo Sunset 1979, King 1984; TV series No Excuses 1983, Paradise 1991; *Films* The Long Good Friday 1981; *Awards* French Critics Prix Revelation 1978, Giles Cooper Best Radio Plays 1980, Mystery Writers of America Edgar Allan Poe Award 1982; *Novels* Gadabout (1969), No Excuses (1983); *Recreations* origami; *Style*— Barrie Keeffe, Esq; ✉ 110 Annandale Road, Greenwich, London SE10 0JZ

KEEGAN, Dr Donal Arthur John; OBE (1999); s of Daniel McManus Keegan, of Balliniska, Co Londonderry, and Geraldine, *née* Halpin (d 1979); *b* 8 October 1938; *Educ* St Columb's Coll Londonderry, Queen's Univ Belfast (BSc, MB BCh, BAO); *m* 5 March 1973, Elizabeth, *née* Nelson; 1 da (Rosemary Elizabeth Catriona b 6 Nov 1974); *Career* conslt physician Altnagelvin Hosp Londonderry 1975–2003 (now emeritus); chm: Regnl Advsy Ctee on Cancer 1997–, Central Med Advsy Ctee 1999–2003, NI Cncl for Postgrad Med and Dental Educn 1999–2004; med dir Med Distinction and Meritorious Serv Awards Ctee 2002–04; fndr memb Scottish Rehabilitation Gp 1971–75, memb Br Soc for Rheumatology 1970, memb BMA 1975; WHO Fellowship 1975; Hon Col 204 (N Irish) Field Hosp (V); jt vice-pres RFCA NI; HM Lord-Lt Londonderry 2002–; FRCPI 1973, FRCP 1989, FRCPEd 1990; *Publications* various papers on internal med and rheumatology; *Recreations* fishing, shooting; *Clubs* RSM; *Style*— Dr Donal Keegan, OBE; ✉ Auskaird, 5 Greenwood, Culmore, Londonderry BT48 8NP (tel 028 7135 1292); Altnagelvin Hospital, Londonderry BT47 6SB (tel 028 7134 5171)

KEEGAN, Sir John Desmond Patrick; kt (2000), OBE (1991); s of Francis Joseph Keegan (d 1975), of London, and Eileen Mary, *née* Bridgman (d 2001); *b* 15 May 1934; *Educ* King's Coll Taunton, Wimbledon Coll, Balliol Coll Oxford (MA); *m* 10 Dec 1960, Susanne Ingeborg, da of Dr Thomas Everett, of Horsington, Somerset (d 1974); 2 da (Lucy Newmark b 1961, Rose Keegan b 1965), 2 s (Thomas b 1963, Matthew b 1965); *Career* sr lectr in war studies RMA Sandhurst 1960–86, defence ed Daily Telegraph 1986–; Lees Knowles lectr in mil history Cambridge 1986–87; cmmr Cwlth War Graves Cmmn 2001–; visitor Sexey's Hosp Bruton Somerset, tstee Nat Heritage Meml Fund 1999–2000; fell Princeton Univ 1984, Delmas distinguished prof of history Vassar Coll 1997; Reith lectr 1998; hon fell Balliol Coll Oxford 1999, Hon LLD Univ of New Brunswick 1997, Hon DLit Queen's Univ Belfast 2000, Hon DLitt Univ of Bath 2002, FRHistS, FRSL; *Books* The Face of Battle (1976), World Armies (1978), Six Armies in Normandy (1982), The Mask of Command (1987), The Price of Admiralty (1988), The Second World War (1989), A History of Warfare (1993, Duff Cooper prize 1993), Warpaths (1995), The Battle for History (1995), War and Our World, the Reith Lectures (1998), The First World War (1998, Westminster Medal), Intelligence in War (2003), The Iraq War (2004); *Clubs* Garrick, Beefsteak, Pratt's, The Brook (NY); *Style*— Sir John Keegan, OBE, FRSL; ✉ The Manor House, Kilmington, Warminster, Wiltshire BA12 6RD (tel 01985 844856); The Daily Telegraph, 1 Canada Square, Canary Wharf, London E14 5DT (tel 020 7538 5000)

KEEGAN, Dame (Elizabeth) Mary; DBE (2007); da of Michael Keegan (d 1991), of Upminster, Essex, and Elizabeth, *née* Sarginson; *b* 21 January 1953; *Educ* Brentwood Co HS for Girls, Somerville Coll Oxford (Caroline Haslett meml scholar, Coombs exhibitioner, MA, Rowing blue); *Career* PricewaterhouseCoopers (formerly Price Waterhouse before merger): articled London 1974, Paris 1979, Chicago 1982, ptnr 1985–2001, nat tech ptnr 1991–96, dir Professional Standards Europe 1994–98, head Global Corp Reporting Gp 1998–2001; chm Accounting Standards Bd 2001–04 (memb Urgent Issues Task Force 1993–99, ex officio memb Fin Reporting Cncl), md Govt Financial Mgmnt HM Treasy and head Govt Finance Profession 2004–; vice-pres, memb Cncl and chm Auditing Working Pty Fédération des Experts Comptables Européens (FEE) 1997–2001; memb: Cncl ICAEW 1994–97 (chm Fin Reporting Ctee 1994–97), Standing Interpretations Ctee Int Accounting Standards Ctee 1997–2001, Int Forum on Accountancy Devpt 1999–2001, Supervisory Bd European Financial Reporting Advsy Gp 2001–04; FCA 1983 (ACA 1977), FRSA; *Publications* The ValueReporting Revolution: moving beyond the earnings game (jtly, 2001); frequent contrib to professional jls; *Recreations* classical music, sailing; *Style*— Dame Mary Keegan, DBE

KEEGAN, Nicholas Francis; s of J P Keegan (d 1977), of IOM, and C H Keegan, *née* Glynn (d 1993); *b* 16 September 1955, Solihull; *Educ* Douai Sch Woolhampton, CCC Oxford (MA); *m* 10 Oct 1992, Sally Anne, *née* Woodburn; 2 da (Louise Harriet b 2 Aug 1993, Caroline Vivien b 18 Apr 1995); *Career* Price Waterhouse London 1978–82, Hill Samuel & Co Ltd 1982–87, Barclays de Zoete Wedd Ltd 1987–92 (dir corp fin 1990–92); gp fin dir: Newman Tonks Gp plc 1992–97, Frederick Cooper plc 1997–2001, Evenser Gp Ltd 2001–04; chief fin offr CompAir Holdings Ltd 2005–; non-exec dir: Interserve plc 2003–, Staffline Recruitment Gp plc 2005–; FCA 1991; *Recreations* opera, swimming, tennis; *Clubs* Oxford and Cambridge; *Style*— Nicholas Keegan, Esq; ✉ Alderminster Lodge, Stratford-upon-Avon, Warwickshire CV37 8NY (tel 01789 450493, fax 01789 450148, e-mail nick.keegan@btinternet.com); Interserve House, Ruscombe Park, Twyford, Berkshire RG10 9JU (tel 01527 838218)

KEEGAN, William James Gregory; s of William Patrick Keegan (d 1995), of Durham, and Julia Sheila, *née* Buckley (d 1976); *b* 3 July 1938; *Educ* Wimbledon Coll, Trinity Coll Cambridge (MA); *m* 1, 7 Feb 1967 (m dis 1982), Tessa, *née* Young (wid of John Ashton); 2 s, 2 da; m 2, 24 Oct 1992, Hilary Stonefrost , *qv*, da of Maurice Stonefrost, CBE, DL, and Audrey Stonefrost; 2 da (Caitlin Clare b 5 Sept 1994, Lucinda Grace Julia b 18 Dec 1997), 1 s (James Patrick William (twin) b 18 Dec 1997); *Career* Nat Serv 5 Royal Tank Regt RASC (cmmnd 1958) 1957–59; journalist: Financial Times 1963–64, Daily Mail 1964–67; economics corr Financial Times 1967–76, worked Econ Intelligence Dept Bank of England 1976–77, economics ed The Observer 1977–2003 (assoc ed 1982–2003, sr economics commentator 2003–); memb: BBC Advsy Ctee on Business and Industrial Affrs 1981–88, Cncl Employment Inst 1987–92, Advsy Bd Dept of Applied Economics Univ of Cambridge 1988–92, Nat Cncl The Catalyst Forum; visiting prof of journalism Univ of Sheffield 1989– (hon res fell 1990–), memb CNAA (memb Ctee for Social Sci 1991–92); govr NIESR 1998–; Hon DLitt: Univ of Sheffield 1995, City Univ 1998; *Books* fiction: Consulting Father Wintergreen (1974), A Real Killing (1976); non-fiction: Who Runs The Economy (jtly, 1978), Mrs Thatcher's Economic Experiment (1984), Britain Without Oil (1985), Mr Lawson's Gamble (1989), The Spectre of Capitalism (1992), 2066 And All That (2000), The Prudence of Mr Gordon Brown (2003); *Clubs* Garrick, MCC; *Style*— William Keegan, Esq; ✉ 76 Lofting Road, Islington, London N1 1JB (tel 020 7607 3590); The Observer, 3–7 Herbal Hill, London EC1R 5EJ (tel 020 7278 2332)

KEELEY, Barbara; MP; da of Edward Keeley (d 2003), of Leeds, and Joan Keeley (d 1995); *Educ* Mount St Mary's Coll Leeds, Univ of Salford (BA); *m* Colin Huggett; *Career* systems engr IBM until 1989 (latterly field systems engrg mangr), ind conslt in community regeneration and orgn devpt 1990–94 and 1995–2001, area mangr Business in the Community 1994–95, conslt and advsr to Princess Royal Tst for Carers 2001–05, MP (Lab) Worsley 2005–, PPS to Rt Hon Harret Harman QC, MP (as Min for Women) 2007–, memb Finance and Servs Ctee 2006–, chair Women's PLP Ctee; cncllr Trafford MBC 1995–2004; dir Pathfinder Children's Tst Trafford 2002–04; memb: GMB, Fabian Soc, Amnesty Int; *Recreations* jogging, swimming, listening to live music; *Style*— Ms Barbara Keeley, MP; ✉ House of Commons, London SW1A 0AA (tel 020 7219 2303, website www.barbarakeeley.co.uk); Constituency Office tel 0161 799 4159

KEELING, Christopher Anthony Gedge; s of Sir Edward Keeling, MC, MP, DL (d 1954), of London, and Martha Ann, *née* Darling (d 1988); *b* 15 June 1930; *Educ* Eton, RMA Sandhurst; *m* 1, 20 Sept 1955 (m dis 1972), Veronica, da of Alec Waugh, writer (d 1980), of Edringtonr, Berks; 2 s (Simon Alexander Edward d 1982, Julian James), 1 da (Nicola Sara); m 2, 1974, Rachael Macdonald; *Career* Capt Grenadier Gds 1948–56; dir and chm various Lloyd's Agency Cos; Freeman City of London, Liveryman Worshipful Co of Fishmongers 1955; ACII; *Recreations* shooting, reading, watching cricket; *Clubs* White's, MCC, Beefsteak, City of London; *Style*— Christopher Keeling, Esq; ✉ Leyden House, Thames Bank, London SW14 7QR (tel 020 8876 7375); Hampden Agencies Limited, 85 Gracechurch Street, London EC3V 0AA (tel 020 7863 6542, fax 020 7863 6728, e-mail christopher.keeling@hpcgroup.co.uk)

KEELING, Dr John David; s of David Keeling, of Worthing, W Sussex, and Helen, *née* Weir; *b* 31 October 1958, Aberdeen; *Educ* Trinity Sch Croydon, Guy's Hosp Med Sch, KCH Med Sch (MB BS); *m* 2 Aug 1980, Catherine, *née* Tanguy; 1 da (Elizabeth Helen Moncur b 31 Dec 1983), 1 s (James Edward David b 3 April 1985); *Career* SMO ATR Pirbright 1993–97, CO 22 Field Hosp 1997–99, SO1 Med NATO Surgn Gens Dept 1999–2000, SMO ATR Pirbright 2000–01, clinical servs dir Army Primary Healthcare Serv 2003–07, DACOS Med HQ LAND 2007–; memb Cncl BMA 2000–, chm BMA Pension Tstees Ltd

2003– (dir 2002–); DRCOG 1990, FRCGP 2004 (MRCGP 1988); *Recreations* reading, wine, music, fly fishing; *Style—* Dr John Keeling; ✉ HQ, Army Primary Healthcare Service, The Former Army Staff College, Slim Road, Camberley, Surrey GU15 4NP (tel 01276 412922, fax 01276 412919)

KEEMER, Peter John Charles; s of Frederick George Keemer (d 1973), and Queenie Ellen, *née* Gaston (d 1972); *b* 27 January 1932; *Educ* Price's Sch Fareham, City of London Coll, Univ of Bath (MPhil); *m* 5 Aug 1954, Yvonne (d 2002), da of late Henry Griffin; 2 s (Jeremy b and d 1958, Nigel Richard b 1962), 1 da (Caroline Jane b 1959); *Career* Nat Serv Sgt Royal Army Educn Corps 1950–52; Exchequer and Audit Dept: asst auditor then auditor 1952–62, private sec to Comptroller and Auditor Gen 1962–65, seconded to Office of Parly Cmmr for Admin as ceo 1966–70, chief auditor 1970–74, dep dir 1974–77, dir 1978, seconded to Euro Ct of Auditors as dir 1978–86; Nat Audit Office (formerly Exchequer and Audit Dept): dir 1986–89, asst auditor gen 1989–93; external auditor European Univ Inst Florence 1994–98, memb Conciliation Ctee for the clearance of Agric Accounts EC 2001–06; hon treas Inst of Cancer Research 1996–2000 (dir 1994–2000), dir and tstee Breakthrough Breast Cancer Ltd 2001– (chm 1997–2001); memb CIPFA 1982; *Clubs* Royal Anglo-Belgian; *Style—* Peter Keemer, Esq; ✉ How Green Cottage, How Lane, Chipstead, Coulsdon CR5 3LL (tel 01737 553711, e-mail keemer@globalnet.co.uk)

KEEN, Alan; MP; s of late Jack Keen, and Gladys Keen; *b* 25 November 1937; *Educ* Sir William Turner's Sch Redcar; *m* 21 June 1980, Ann Lloyd Keen, MP, *qv*; 2 s, 1 da; *Career* various industrial and commercial positions 1963–92, pt/t tactical scout Middlesbrough FC 1969–85, sometime fire protection conslt; cnCllr London Borough of Hounslow 1986–90; MP (Lab/Co-op) Feltham and Heston 1992–; memb Culture, Media and Sport Select Ctee 1997–, chm All Pty Football Gp 2001–; *Recreations* music, football, athletics; *Style—* Alan Keen, MP; ✉ House of Commons, London SW1A 0AA

KEEN, Ann Lloyd; MP; *Educ* Univ of Surrey; *m* Alan Keen, MP, *qv*; 2 s (Mark Lloyd, David), 1 da (Susan); *Career* former nurse, gen sec Community & District Nursing Assoc; MP (Lab) Brentford and Isleworth 1997– (Parly candidate (Lab) Brentford and Isleworth 1987 and 1992); PPS to: Rt Hon Frank Dobson, MP 1999–2000, Rt Hon Gordon Brown, MP 2000–; memb Departmental Ctees on: Home Affrs, Trade & Industry, Int Devpt; chair All Pty Theatre Gp; former vice-chair Trade Union Gp of MPs; hon prof of nursing Thames Valley Univ 1997; patron: Hounslow Youth Conselling Serv, Bereavement Servs, Shooting Star Tst, Action for Sick Children; *Recreations* Brentford FC, classic cars, theatre, film; *Style—* Ann Keen, MP; ✉ House of Commons, London SW1A 0AA (tel 020 7219 3000, e-mail annkeenmp@parliament.uk)

KEEN, Maurice Hugh; OBE (2004); s of Harold Hugh Keen (d 1974), and Catherine, *née* Cummins; *b* 30 October 1933; *Educ* Winchester (scholar), Balliol Coll Oxford (BA); *m* 20 July 1968, Mary Agnes, da of Francis Keegan; 3 da (Catherine b 1969, Harriet b 1971, Clare b 1973); *Career* Nat Serv 2 Lt Royal Ulster Rifles 1952–54; Univ of Oxford: jr res fell The Queen's Coll 1957–61, fell and tutor in medieval history Balliol Coll 1961–2000, clerk of the market 2002–06; govr Blundell's Sch 1970–89, fell Winchester Coll 1989–2002; FSA 1987, FBA 1990; *Books* The Outlaws of Medieval Legend (1961), The Laws of War in the Later Middle Ages (1965), Pelican History of Medieval Europe (1968), England in the Later Middle Ages (1973), Chivalry (1984), English Society in the Later Middle Ages (1990), Origins of the English Gentleman (2002); *Recreations* fishing, shooting; *Style—* Maurice Keen, Esq, OBE, FSA, FBA; ✉ 4 Walton Street, Oxford OX1 2HG

KEEN, Nigel John; s of Peter John Keen (d 1985), and Margaret Alice, *née* Peach; *b* 21 January 1947; *Educ* Charterhouse, Peterhouse Cambridge (MA); *m* 2 Sept 1972, Caroline Jane, *née* Cumming; 2 s (Dominic John b 22 March 1977, Thomas Christopher b 30 Jan 1990); *Career* auditor Touche Ross & Co 1968–74, dir European Banking Co Ltd 1974–83; chm: Cygnus Gp of Cos 1983–2001, Oxford Instruments plc 1999–, Axis-Shield plc 1999–, Deltex Medical Gp plc 2000–, The Laird Group plc 2000–; dir Channel Islands Development Corp Ltd 1998–; tstee David Shepherd Wildlife Fndn 1999–; FCA 1979; *Recreations* opera, golf; *Clubs* HAC; *Style—* Nigel Keen, Esq; ✉ The Laird Group plc, 100 Pall Mall, London SW1Y 5NQ (tel 020 7468 4040, fax 020 7930 6853, e-mail n.keen@laird-plc.com)

KEEN, Richard Sanderson; QC (Scot 1993); s of Derek Michael Keen, of Wester Balgedie, Kinross-Shire, and Jean, *née* Sanderson; *b* 29 March 1954; *Educ* King's Sch Rochester, Univ of Edinburgh (Beckman scholar, LLB); *m* 7 April 1980, Jane Carolyn, da of Dr William Marr Anderson; 1 s (Jamie Marr Sanderson b 29 Sept 1983), 1 da (Sophie Jane b 29 Sept 1985); *Career* admitted Faculty of Advocates 1980, standing jr counsel DTI Scotland 1986–93; treas Faculty of Advocates 2006–; tstee Nat Library of Scotland; *Recreations* opera, golf, shooting, skiing; *Clubs* New (Edinburgh), Bruntsfield Links Golfing Soc, Golf House (Elie); *Style—* Richard Keen, Esq, QC; ✉ Advocates Library, Parliament House, Parliament Square, Edinburgh EH1 1RF; 39 Ann Street, Edinburgh EH4 1PL; The Castle, Elie, Fife KY9 1DN

KEEN, His Hon Judge (Kenneth) Roger; QC (1991); s of Kenneth Henry Keen, of Hickleton, S Yorks, and Joan Megan, *née* Weatman; *b* 13 May 1946; *Educ* Doncaster GS for Boys; *m* Lorraine; c from previous marriage: 1 s (Kenneth Matthew b 15 Aug 1975), 1 da (Charlotte Jane b 19 Oct 1977); *Career* solicitor 1968, barrister 1976, recorder 1986, head of chambers 1994, circuit judge (NE Circuit) 2001–; *Recreations* golf, walking, travel; *Style—* His Hon Judge Keen, QC

KEENE, Bryan Richard; s of Edward Stanley William Keene (d 1963), of Weybridge, Surrey, and Sybil White, *née* Holmes (d 1991); *b* 14 September 1937; *Educ* St James' Boys Sch Weybridge, LLB; *Career* Securities Agency Ltd and Drayton Corp Ltd 1963–74, asst dir Samuel Montagu & Co Ltd 1974–84; dir: Elliot Assocs Ltd 1984–, Anglo-Scottish Securities Ltd 1986–, Staple Investment Tst Ltd 1986–, Invesco Tstee Corp 1986–, Anglo-Scottish Amalgamated Corp Ltd 1993–, Invesco Pension Tstees Ltd 1994–; FCIS 1968, CTA (ATII 1977); *Style—* Bryan Keene, Esq; ✉ Woodside, Winterbourne Grove, Weybridge, Surrey (tel 01932 841708, e-mail bryanrk@aol.com)

KEENE, Rt Hon Lord Justice; Rt Hon Sir David Wolfe; kt (1994), PC (2000); s of Edward Henry Wolfe Keene (d 1987), and Lilian Marjorie, *née* Conway; *b* 15 April 1941; *Educ* Hampton GS, Balliol Coll Oxford (Eldon scholar, BA, BCL, Winter Williams prize), Inner Temple (Public Int Law prize); *m* 1965, Gillian Margaret, da of Geoffrey Lawrance; 1 da (Harriet Margaret b 1968), 1 s (Edward Geoffrey Wolfe b 1970); *Career* called to the Bar Inner Temple 1964 (bencher 1987, treas 2006); QC 1980–94, recorder of the Crown Court 1989–94, judge of the High Court of Justice (Queen's Bench Div) 1994–2000 (dep High Ct judge 1993); judge Employment Appeal Tbnl 1994–2000; Lord Justice of Appeal 2000–; visitor Brunel Univ 1995–2000; chm Examination-in-Public Cumbria Structure Plan 1980, inspector County Hall (London) Public Inquiry 1987, chm Planning Bar Assoc 1994, sometime memb Final Selection Bd Planning Inspectorate DOE; hon fell Soc for Advanced Legal Studies 1998– (chm Planning Law Reform Gp), chm Judicial Studies Bd 2003–07 (memb 1998–, chm Equal Treatment Advsy Ctee 1998–2003), memb Bowman Ctee on the Crown Office 1999–2000; memb Exec Ctee Amnesty International (Br section) 1965–68; Hon LLD Brunel Univ 2000, hon fell Balliol Coll Oxford 2004; *Books* The Adult Criminal (co-author 1967); *Clubs* Athenaeum; *Style—* The Rt Hon Lord Justice Keene; ✉ Royal Courts of Justice, Strand, London WC2A 2LL

KEENE, Gareth John; s of Victor Horace Keene (d 1993), and Muriel Olive, *née* Whitehead (d 2002); *b* 31 March 1944; *Educ* Tonbridge, St John's Coll Cambridge (Choral scholar, MA, LLM); *m* 1, 1969 (m dis 1983), Georgina Garrett Thomas; 3 s (Timothy b 1973, David b 1975, Jonathan b 1979); m 2, 1983, Charlotte Louise, da of Peter Frank Lester (d 1985), of Devon; *Career* called to the Bar Gray's Inn 1966; sec Allen & Hanburys Ltd 1968–73, admin Dartington Coll of Arts 1973–78 (govr 1989–, vice-chm 2001–), sec The Dartington Hall Tst 1978–83; dir: TSW Television South West Holdings plc 1980–92, Gamida for Life BV Netherlands 1989–; chm: Gamidor Technical Services Ltd 1994–, Evans Estates (1956) Ltd 2007–; chm: EU Chamber Orchestra Tst 1995–, Beaford Arts Centre 1987–2002 (tstee 1980–2002), Dartington N Devon Fndn 2002– (tstee 1991–), TSW Film and Television Archive 2006– (tstee 1992–); govr Judd Sch 2007–; Freeman City of London 1971, Liveryman Worshipful Co of Skinners 1974; FRSM; *Books* Sacred and Secular (with Adam Fox, 1975); *Recreations* singing, small holding, golf; *Style—* Gareth Keene, Esq; ✉ Buttermead, Manaton, Newton Abbot, Devon TQ13 9XG (tel and fax 01647 221208, e-mail gareth@gckeene.plus.com); Windy Edge, Concordia, Tobago, West Indies (tel and fax 001 868 639 5596)

KEENE, Martin Elliott; MVO (2007); s of John Keene, and Pamela, *née* Richards; *b* 8 September 1957; *Educ* Felsted, Sidney Sussex Coll Cambridge (BA); *Career* photographer: Torquay Herald Express 1978–82, Torbay News Agency 1982–87; The Press Association: joined as staff photographer 1987, special responsibility for royal coverage 1990, chief photographer 1992–95, picture ed 1995, currently head of pictures; *Books* Practical Photojournalism - a professional guide (1993); *Style—* Martin Keene, Esq, MVO; ✉ The Press Association, 292 Vauxhall Bridge Road, London SW1V 1AE

KEENE, Raymond Dennis; OBE (1985); s of Dennis Arthur Keene (d 1992), of Worthing, W Sussex, and Doris Anita, *née* Leat (d 1969); *b* 29 January 1948; *Educ* Dulwich Coll, Trinity Coll Cambridge (MA); *m* 1974, Annette Sara, da of Walter Goodman; 1 s (Alexander Philip Simon b 21 March 1991); *Career* chess corr: The Spectator 1977–, The Times 1985–, Thames Television 1986–90, Channel 4 TV 1993–, Classic FM Radio 1993–, Sunday Times 1996– International Herald Tribune 2001–; The Times: daily columnist 1997–, weekly IQ columnist 1997–; chess contrib to Encyclopaedia Britannica; memb Eng Olympic chess team 1966, 1968, 1970, 1972, 1974, 1976, 1978 and 1980, Br Chess Champion 1971, Olympic Bronze medal 1976, Bronze medal Cwlth Chess Championship Melbourne 1983; dep chm Braingames Asia 2002–, dir Hardinge/Simpole Publishing 2002–; winner various int chess tournaments: Johannesburg 1973, Camagüey (Cuba) 1974, Alicante 1977, Sydney 1979, Dortmund 1980, London (Lloyds Masters) 1981, Adelaide 1983, Valletta 1985; chess grandmaster 1976 (life title); chief organiser: World Chess Championship between Kasparov and Karpov London 1986, World Memory Championship London 1991, World Draughts Championship London 1992, second World Memory Championship London 1993, World Chess Championship between Kasparov and Short London 1993, World Draughts Championship Human v Computer Boston 1994, third World Memory Championship London 1994, World Chess Championship between Kasparov and Kramnik London 2000; organiser: First Mind Sports Olympiad Royal Festival Hall 1997, Second Mind Sports Olympiad London 1998, Third Mind Sports Olympiad London 1999, seven Brighton Int Chess Tournaments (with Julian Simpole); ceo Mind Sports Olympiad 1998, fndr IMPALA London Ltd (Int Media Prodn and Literary Activities) 2005, fndr and sole prop Impala Films 2006; Freeman City of London (2001); *Books* author of over 130 books on chess (world record) incl: Duels of the Mind, Kingfisher Pocket Book of Chess, Batsford Chess Openings (with Garry Kasparov), Buzan's Book of Genius (co-author); *Recreations* attending ballet, theatre, opera, collecting modern British art; *Clubs* St Stephen's Westminster, RAC, Garrick, Arts; *Style—* Raymond Keene, Esq, OBE; ✉ 86 Clapham Common North Side, London SW4 9SE (tel 020 7228 7009, fax 020 7924 6472); The Times, News International, 1 Virginia Street, London E1 9XN (e-mail rdkobe@aol.com)

KEENS, David Wilson; s of Wilson Leonard Keens (d 1959), and Olive Ivy, *née* Collins; *b* 16 August 1953; *m* Shirley Ann, da of Cyril Charles Cardnell; 1 s (Benjamin David b 17 Nov 1983), 1 da (Emma Louise b 15 Oct 1985); *Career* Gale Brown & Co Essex: articled clerk 1970–75, chartered accountant 1975–77; successively chief fin offr (Tunis), fin controller (Liverpool), fin dir (Lancs) and planning dir and treas (Berks) RJR Nabisco Inc 1977–86, dir of treasy then gp fin dir Next plc 1986–; FCCA, MCT; *Style—* David Keens, Esq; ✉ Next plc, Desford Road, Enderby, Leicestershire LE19 4AT (tel 0845 456 7777, fax 0116 286 7178, mobile 07710 533666, e-mail david_keens@next.co.uk)

KEETCH, Paul Stuart; MP; s of John Norton Keetch (d 1988), and Agnes Keetch (d 1996); *b* 21 May 1961; *Educ* The Boys' HS Hereford, Hereford Sixth Form Coll; *m* 21 Dec 1991, Claire Elizabeth, da of Gordon Baker; 1 s (William Stuart Norton b 11 Feb 1995); *Career* Midland Bank 1978, with various water hygiene companies 1979–95, political and media advsr to Lithuanian and Bosnian political parties 1995–96, OSCE monitor Albanian elections 1996, dir MarketNet 1996–; MP (Lib Dem) Hereford 1997–; Lib Dem Parly spokesman on: health 1997, employment and trg 1997–99; Lib Dem shadow defence sec 2001–05; memb: Select Ctee on Educn and Employment 1997–99, Environmental Audit Ctee 1999–, Armed Forces Bill Select Ctee 2001–, Foreign Affrs Select Ctee 2005–, Quadrapartite Select Ctee 2005–; chm All-Pty Cider Gp 1997–, vice-chm All-Pty Childcare Gp 1998–, sec All-Pty Albanian Gp 1997–, memb All-Pty Defence Studies Gp 1997–; hon pres Staffordshire Univ Lib Dem Gp, chair Lib Int 2005–; memb: Cwlth Parly Assoc, Cncl Electoral Reform Soc, Inter Parly Union, IISS, IPMS Trade Union 1998–, RUSI 1999–; patron St Michael's Hospice Hereford; pres: Hereford Hosp Radio 1998–, Pegasus Juniors FC; vice-pres: Westfields FC Hereford, Hereford Amateur Dramatic Soc, Nat Child-Minding Assoc 1998–, Ross-on-Wye HS, Hereford Heartstart 2004–; *Recreations* swimming, entertaining, building model warships; *Clubs* National Liberal, Herefordshire CC, Herefordshire Farmers'; *Style—* Paul Keetch, Esq, MP; ✉ House of Commons, London SW1A 0AA (tel 020 7219 2419, fax 020 7219 1184, e-mail info@paulkeetch.org.uk)

KEEYS, Geoffrey Foster; s of Richard Kipling Foster Keeys, and Joan, *née* Anderson; *b* 29 October 1944; *Educ* Abingdon Sch, Univ of Manchester (LLB); *m* 4 April 1970, Christine Mary (Donna), da of Henry Albert Lavers, of Newbury, Berks; 1 da (Georgia Ellen b 22 May 1974), 1 s (Henry Foster b 16 April 1976); *Career* graduate trainee Mobil Oil 1966–68, various personnel positions to dir of personnel and industrial relations (Euro and world export) Massey Ferguson 1968–82, dir gp personnel Chubb & Son plc 1982–84, dir of Personnel and Business Servs Prudential Corporation plc 1984–95, md Strategic Thinking Group 1995–, dir Resistance Media 2004, dir Incite Solutions Ltd; non-exec memb Bd HM Prison Service until 1995; FIPM; *Recreations* golf, national hunt horse racing, cricket; *Clubs* Broadway Golf; *Style—* Geoffrey Keeys; ✉ Strategic Thinking Group, 211 Piccadilly, London W1V 9LD (tel 020 7917 2867, fax 020 7917 2868, e-mail gfkeeys@strategicthinker.com)

KEFFER, John W; s of James Morgan Keffer (d 1935), and Dove, *née* Douglas (d 1934); *b* 5 June 1923; *Educ* Texas Technol Univ (BA), The Univ of Texas (JD), Johns Hopkins Univ (MA); *m* 25 Aug 1954, Natalia (d 1997), da of Baron Giulio Blanc (d 1978), of Le Château, Tolochenaz, Switzerland; 2 s (Charles b 1955 d 1959, John b 1957); *Career* ensign USNR 1943; served Europe 1944–45: Normandy Invasion 1944, Invasion Southern France 1944, Lt (JG); served Pacific 1945–46: Okinawa, Philippines, occupation of Japan; lawyer 1950–53: Schuster & Davenport NY, Travieso Paul Caracas Venezuela; gen counsel: Esso Standard Oil Havana Cuba 1954–60, Coral Gables Florida 1960–63, Creole Petroleum Corp Caracas Venezuela 1964–73, Esso Europe London 1973–85; counsel Fulbright & Jaworski London 1986–97; chm of tstees American Museum in Britain 1982–2001 (tstee 1979–), memb Advsy Bd Royal Acad 1987–97; memb: Int Bar Assoc, American Bar Assoc, Texas Bar; *Recreations* photography, collecting paintings, drawings, watercolours, antiques; *Clubs* Garrick, Brooks's, Circolo Della Caccia (Rome); *Style—* John Keffer, Esq

KEIGHLEY, Dr Brian Douglas; s of Jeffrey Torrance Keighley (d 2004), of Bishopbriggs, Glasgow, and Alice Winifred, *née* North; *b* 21 May 1948; *Educ* Glasgow Acad, Univ of Glasgow (MB ChB, DFM); *m* 11 Sept 1976 (m dis 2002), Ruth Patricia, da of James Kevin Maguire; 2 s (Douglas John b 31 Aug 1978, Andrew James b 5 May 1981); *Career* house offr: in gen med Law Hosp Lanarkshire 1972–73, in gen surgery Stobhill Hosp Glasgow 1973; SHO: in obstetrics and gynaecology Robroyston Hosp Glasgow 1973–74, in paediatrics Falkirk Royal Infirmary Falkirk 1974; trainee GP 1974–75, princ in gen practice 1975–; police surgn 1975– (dep 1975–83), GP trainer 1978–94, MO Ballikinrain Sch 1983–; GMC: memb 1994–, memb Educn Ctee 1998–2003, medical screener 2000–04, memb Fin and Estab Ctee 2001–, chm Governance Working Gp 2000–03, dep treas 2003–, chm GMC Staff Pension Tstees 2005–; memb: Scottish Gen Med Servs Ctee 1978– (chm 1995–98), Forth Valley Area Med Ctee (chm 1989–92), Forth Valley Local Med Ctee (chm 1986–89), Scottish Rural Practices Fund Ctee 1986– (chm 1989–95), Scottish Cncl BMA 1992–, Gen Med Servs Ctee UK 1992–, Private Practice and Professional Fees Ctee BMA 1992–94, Jt Ctee on Postgrad Trg for Gen Practice 1990– (chm 1997–2000), Scottish Cncl for Postgrad Med and Dental Educn 1993–2002 (chm Audit Ctee, vice-chm 1999), BMA Cncl 1998–2002 and 2006–, Clinical Standards Bd for Scotland 1999–2002, BMA Fin Audit Ctee 2000–; treas and dir General Practitioners Defence Fund Ltd 2003–, non-exec dir British Med Jl Publications Ltd 2003– (dep chm 2006–); memb Assoc of Police Surgns 1975; FRSM 1988, FRCGP 1990; *Recreations* angling, jogging, squash; *Clubs* RSM, Western Medical (Glasgow); *Style*— Dr Brian Keighley; ✉ Hector Cottage, Bankers Brae, Balfron, Stirlingshire G63 0PY (tel 01360 440520, fax 01360 440829); The Clinic, Buchanan Street, Balfron, Stirlingshire G63 0TS (tel 01360 440515, fax 01360 440831, car 078 3117 4139, e-mail bkeighley@aol.com)

KEIGHLEY, Prof Michael Robert Burch; s of Rev Dr R A S Keighley, TD (d 1988), and Dr J V Keighley, *née* Burch (d 2000); *b* 12 October 1943; *Educ* Monkton Combe Sch, Bart's Med Coll London (MB BS, MS); *m* 27 Sept 1969, Dr D Margaret Keighley, da of J H Shepley (d 1985); 1 da (Helen Louise b 28 Oct 1971), 1 s (Nicholas John Alexander b 23 Jan 1974); *Career* Univ of Birmingham: prof of gastrointestinal surgery 1985–88, Barling prof and head Dept of Surgery 1988–2004, emeritus prof Nowlton Faculty (also prof CMC Vellore Studia); Hunterian prof RCS 1976, Jacksonian prize RCS 1980, Boerhaave prof of surgery Univ of Leiden 1985, Eybers visiting prof Univ of Bloemfontein 1988, visiting prof Harvard Univ 1990, Penman visiting prof Univ of Cape Town 1991, Alan Parks visiting prof St Marks' London 1995, Turnbull visiting prof Univ of Washington 1997, Henry Bacon prof Indian Surgical Assoc 1997, visiting prof Hong Kong and China 1999, visiting prof Karolinska Inst Stockholm 2001; chm: Public Affairs Ctee United European Gastroenterology Fedn (UEGF), PR and Ethics Ctee Assoc of Coloproctology of GB & I (ACPGBI); treas and memb Cncl Br Jl of Surgery; memb: American Soc of Colorectal Surgns, Br Soc of Gastroenterology (formerly memb Cncl), Coloproctology Section RSM (formerly pres and memb Cncl), Cncl Surgical Res Soc, Assoc of Surgns of GB & I; hon fell Brazilian Coll of Surgns, hon fell Royal Australasian Coll of Surgns, hon memb Portuguese Soc of Surgery; FRSC (Edinburgh) 1970, FRCS 1971; *Books* Antimicrobial Prophylaxis in Surgery (1980), Inflammatory Bowel Diseases (1983, 1990 and 1997), Gastrointestinal Haemorrhage (1985), Textbook of Gastroenterology (1986 and 1993), Surgery of the Anus, Rectum & Colon (1993, 1999 and 2006), Atlas of Colorectal Surgery (1996), Flesh and Bones: Surgery; *Recreations* painting, music, writing, travel, botony, walking, sailing; *Clubs* RSM, Athenaeum; *Style*— Prof Michael Keighley; ✉ Whalebone Cottage, Vicarage Hill, Tanworth in Arden, Warwickshire B94 5AN (tel 01564 741885, fax 01564 742705, e-mail keighleycolo@btinternet.com)

KEIGHTLEY, Maj-Gen Richard Charles; CB (1987); s of Gen Sir Charles F Keightley, GCB, GBE, DSO (d 1974), and Joan Lydia (d 1998), da of Brig-Gen G N T Smyth-Osbourne, CB, CMG, DSO (d 1942); *b* 2 July 1933; *Educ* Marlborough, RMA Sandhurst; *m* 21 Oct 1958, Caroline Rosemary, da of Col Sir Thomas Butler, 12 Bt, DSO, OBE, MVO (d 1994); 3 da (Charlotte (Mrs Jenkinson) b 4 March 1961, Arabella (Mrs O'Connell) b 31 July 1962, Victoria (Mrs Cross) b 3 Dec 1965); *Career* cmmnd 5 Royal Inniskilling Dragoon Gds 1953; served Suez Canal Zone, Far East, Cyprus, Libya, NI and Germany, Cdr 1972–75; Cdr: Task Force E 1978–79, Western Dist 1982–83; Cmdt RMA Sandhurst 1983–87, Col 5 Royal Inniskilling Dragoon Gds 1986–91; chm: Combined Servs Polo Assoc 1982–87, Dorset HA 1988–95 and 1998–2001, Dorset Healthcare NHS Tst 1995–98, Southampton Univ Hosps NHS Tst 2002–; pres: Dorset Co Royal Br Legion 1992–, Relate Dorset 2000–; *Recreations* equitation, field sports, cricket, farming; *Clubs* Cavalry and Guards; *Style*— Maj-Gen Richard Keightley, CB; ✉ Kennels Farmhouse, Tarrant Gunville, Blandford, Dorset DT11 8JQ (tel 01258 830418), fax 01258 830651, e-mail crkeightley@clara.co.uk); Southampton General Hospital, Tremona Road, Southampton SO16 6YD (tel 023 8079 4494)

KEIL, Charles George; *b* 7 March 1933; *Educ* St Bartholomew's GS Newbury, QMC London (BSc(Eng)); *m* 23 April 1960, Janette Catherine; 1 da (Fiona b 1962), 2 s (Duncan b 1963, Ewan b 1964); *Career* fighter pilot RAF 1951–55, Flt Lt; served Canada, Germany, France, Cyprus; ed of monthly aviation jl Aircraft Engineering 1959–65, assoc ed (London) Indian Aviation 1963–66, gp ed Thomas Reed Pubns Ltd 1965–66, dir John Fowler & Ptnrs Ltd (PR conslts) 1966–73, md Harrison Cowley PR Birmingham Ltd 1974–94, chm Harrison Cowley Ltd 1988–2001, chm Brumhalata Storytelling Co 1995–99, chm Tindal Street Press 2000–02; dir Nat Acad of Writing 1998–2003; chm Birmingham Readers' and Writers' Festival 1992–96, mktg dir Birmingham Centre for Drama 1994–95, dir Birmingham Rep Theatre 2001–; mktg advsr Business in the Arts 1992–2002, session ldr Understanding Industry 1992–2000, memb Servs Ctee Birmingham City 2000 1995–98, memb New Partners Ctee Arts and Business 2001–05; judge RTS Midlands Centre Awards 1996–2004; govr St George's Sch Edgbaston 2006–; MRAeS, CEng; *Books* Aerodynamics (jt ed and trans with Janette C Loder, textbook); *Recreations* reading, golf, theatre-going, music, aviation; *Clubs* RAF; *Style*— Charles Keil, Esq; ✉ Illyria, 536 Streetsbrook Road, West Midlands B91 1RD (tel 0121 705 0773, e-mail charlesgkeil@aol.com)

KEILL, (William Richard) Ian; s of Cdre W J D Keill (d 1980), and Annie Mavis, *née* Dash; *b* 11 May 1937; *Educ* Liverpool Coll, RADA (Dip); *m* 1, 1963 (m dis 1977), Carole Ann, *née* Bishop; 1 s (Jeremy William Richard b 8 Oct 1964); m 2, 1990, Enid Averil, *née* Musson; *Career* former actor, subsequently director, producer and writer; BBC TV 1962–68 and 1970–72; prodr and dir of many progs for Late Line Up (especially features on film incl a subjective Drama Someone in the Lift and a surreal documentary Waking Dreams), dir 3 documentaries in the series Yesterday's Witness (I Have Flown and it's Marvellous, The Narrow Boatmen, and First War in the Air) 1968, dir 4 documentaries in the series The Curious Character of Britain 1969, prodr and dir Up Sunday 1971–73, prodr and dir 30 documentaries in the One Man's Weeks series 1971–74, prodr and dir The End of the Pier Show 1974, prodr In The Looking Glass (series of experimental comedy dramas with John Wells, John Fortune and John Bird) 1977, prodr and co-dir 2 series of Rutland Weekend Television (starring Eric Idle) 1977, prodr and co-dir 3 series of The Innes Book of Records (featuring Neil Innes) 1979 and 1981; pioneered electronic fantasy on TV with: The Snow Queen 1976, The Light Princess 1978, The Mystery of the Disappearing Schoolgirls 1980, The Ghost Downstairs 1982; prodr strip cartoon Jane, dir and prodr two schoolgirl dramas 1982–83, prodr A Question of Fact (Hitler spoof prog) and the drama The Pyrates 1986, prodr History of Westerns 1987, dir children's ghost serial 1988, prodr Lucinda Lambton in Desirable Dwellings (Forty Minutes) 1988, prodr Frederic Raphael in Frontiers 1989; currently freelance; dir 3 progs in Dream Gardens (series for BBC 2) 1991, dir Gardener's World 1992, prodr and dir Quest for the Rose (TV documentary series in Britain, America and China) 1993; currentlt advising cos in Wales and Provence on film and TV techniques; *Recreations* acquiring far too many books and classical CDs/cassettes and LPs, photography; *Style*— Ian Keill, Esq; ✉ Dovedale Cottage, Moor End Common, Lane End, Buckinghamshire HP14 3EZ (tel 01494 881541, e-mail ian.keill@virgin.net)

KEITH, Hon Mr Justice; Sir Brian Richard Keith; kt (2001); s of Alan Keith, OBE (d 2003), and Pearl, *née* Rebuck; *b* 14 April 1944; *Educ* UCS, Lincoln Coll Oxford (MA), Harvard Law Sch; *m* 16 Nov 1978, Gilly Mary, da of late Air Cdre Ivan James de la Plain, CBE; 1 da (Joanna b 22 Oct 1980), 1 s (Benjamin b 15 March 1982); *Career* called to the Bar Inner Temple 1968 (bencher 1996); in practice 1969–91, asst recorder 1988, QC 1989, a judge of the High Court Hong Kong 1991–2001 (judge of the Court of First Instance 1997–99, justice of appeal 1999–2001), recorder of the Crown Court 1993–, presiding judge Constitutional and Admin Law List High Court of Hong Kong 1997–99, judge of the High Court of Justice (Queen's Bench Div) 2001–; chm Zahid Mubarek Inquiry 2004–06; *Recreations* travel, tennis, cinema; *Clubs* The Hong Kong; *Style*— The Hon Mr Justice Keith

KEITH, Penelope Anne Constance; CBE (2007, OBE 1989), DL; da of Frederick Arthur William Hatfield, and Constance Mary, *née* Nutting; *b* 2 April 1940; *Educ* Webber Douglas Acad; *m* 1978, Rodney Timson; *Career* actress; worked in repertory Chesterfield, Lincoln, Manchester and Salisbury, seasons with RSC; pres Actors' Benevolent Fund 1989; govr Queen Elizabeth's Fndn for the Disabled People 1990, govr Guildford Sch of Acting; tstee Yvonne Arnaud Theatre Guildford; memb HFEA 1990; High Sheriff Surrey 2002–03; *Theatre* roles incl: Maggie Howard in Suddenly at Home (Fortune) 1971, Sarah in The Norman Conquests (Greenwich and Globe) 1974, Lady Driver in Donkey's Years 1976, Orinthia in The Apple Cart (Chichester and Phoenix) 1977, Epifania in the Millionairess (Haymarket) 1982, Sarah in Moving (Queen's) 1981, Maggie in Hobson's Choice (Haymarket) 1982, Lady Cicely Waynflete in Captain Brassbound's Conversion (Haymarket) 1982, Judith Bliss in Hayfever (Queen's) 1983, The Dragon's Tail (Apollo) 1985, Miranda (Chichester) 1987, The Deep Blue Sea (Haymarket) 1988, Dear Charles (Yvonne Arnaud Theatre) 1990, The Merry Wives of Windsor (Chichester) 1990, The Importance of Being Earnest 1992, On Approval, Glyn and It (all Yvonne Arnaud Theatre) 1994, Good Grief (Theatre Royal Bath) 1998, Monsieur Amilcar (Chichester), Star Quality (Apollo) 2001–02, Time and the Conways (Theatre Royal Bath) 2003–04, Blithe Spirit (Savoy) 2004–05; dir: Relatively Speaking 1992, How the Other Half Loves 1994, Mrs Warren's Profession (Yvonne Arnaud Theatre) 1997; *Television* Six Shades of Black, Kate, The Pallisters, Jackanory, Saving it for Albie, The Morecambe and Wise Christmas Show, Tickle on the Tum, Woof, The Good Life, To the Manor Born, Law and Disorder, Sweet Sixteen, Executive Stress, No Job for a Lady, Next of Kin, Coming Home; former presenter: What's My Line, Capability Brown, Growing Places, Behind the Scenes; *Film* The Priest of Love; *Awards* BAFTA 1976 and 1977, SWET 1976, Variety Club of GB 1976 and 1979, Pye Female Comedy Star 1977, Radio Industries 1978 and 1979, Daily Express 1979/80/81/82, BBC TV Swap Shop 1977–78 and 1979–80, TV Times 1976, 1977–78, 1979–80, 1983 and 1988, United States TV and Radio Mobius 1988; *Style*— Miss Penelope Keith, CBE, DL; ✉ c/o Actors' Benevolent Fund, 6 Adam Street, London WC2N 6AD (tel 020 7836 6378, fax 020 7836 8978)

KEITH-LUCAS, Peter; s of Prof Bryan Keith-Lucas, and Mary Keith-Lucas; *Educ* Bradfield Coll, The Queen's Coll Oxford (MA); *Career* admitted slr 1976; chief exec Medina BC 1988–89, dir of central servs Swansea CC 1989–96, dir of legal and admin servs City and Co of Swansea 1996–97, ptnr (local govt) Wragge & Co 1997–; lectr on local govt law, constitutions and probity; Society of Town Clerks Prize for Local Govt Law 1976; pres Assoc of Cncl Secs and Slrs 1996–97; *Books* The Monitoring Officer, Facilitating Executive Government (2002); *Recreations* tennis, sailing; *Clubs* Swansea Lawn Tennis and Squash Racquets, Priory (Edgbaston); *Style*— Peter Keith-Lucas, Esq; ✉ 50 Greenfield Road, Harborne, Birmingham B17 0EG (tel 0121 244 3472); Wragge & Co, 55 Colmore Row, Birmingham B3 2AS (tel 0121 214 1084, fax 0121 214 1099, mobile 07767 256566)

KELJIK, Christopher Avedis; OBE (2006); s of Garbis Keljik (d 1984), and Suzanne, *née* Zambakjian; *b* 1 October 1948; *Educ* Merchant Taylors', Univ of Kent (BA), Stanford Univ (Sr Exec Prog); *m* 18 Nov 1978, Doreen, *née* Markaryan; 2 s (James Stephen Charles b 26 May 1984, Edward Christopher Gerald b 12 July 1987); *Career* CA; Ball Baker Deed 1970–74, Deloitte Haskins and Sells 1974–76; Standard Chartered plc: various mgmnt positions (London, Singapore, NYC and Hong Kong) 1976–99, gp exec dir 1999–2005; non-exec dir: Foreign & Colonial Investment Trust plc 2005–, Jardine Lloyd Thompson Gp plc 2005–, Millennium & Copthorne Hotels plc 2006–; Freeman City of London, Liveryman Worshipful Co of Merchant Taylors; FCA 1979; *Recreations* family, music, theatre, reading, walking, travel; *Clubs* Travellers; *Style*— Christopher Keljik, Esq, OBE

KELLAWAY, Prof Ian Walter; s of Leslie William Kellaway (d 1975), and Margaret Seaton, *née* Webber; *b* 10 March 1944; *Educ* King Edward VI GS Totnes, Univ of London (BPharm, PhD, DSc); *m* 2 Aug 1969 (m dis 1995), Kay Elizabeth, da of Raymond Cyril Downey, of Ystrad Mynach; 1 s (Robert b 5 July 1972), 1 da (Jane b 21 May 1974); *m* 2, 4 Sept 1998, Sally Elizabeth Partridge, da of Jack Carter (d 1990), of Cardiff; *Career* lectr in pharmaceutics Dept of Pharmacy Univ of Nottingham 1969–79, prof of pharmaceutics Welsh Sch of Pharmacy Univ of Cardiff 1979–2000, prof of pharmaceutics Sch of Pharmacy Univ of London 2000–04 (prof emeritus 2004–); fell American Assoc of Pharmaceutical Scientists 1993; FRPharmS 1969; *Recreations* gardening, travel; *Style*— Prof Ian Kellaway; ✉ The School of Pharmacy, University of London, London WC1N 1AX (tel and fax 020 7753 5944)

KELLEHER, Patricia Mary (Tricia); *b* 17 March 1962; *Educ* Grays Convent RC Comp Sch, Palmer's Sixth Form Coll Grays, Lady Margaret Hall Oxford (MA), Univ of Nottingham (PGCE), Univ of Sussex (MA); *Career* history teacher Haberdashers' Aske's Sch for Girls Elstree 1985–88; Brighton & Hove GDST: asst history teacher 1988–92, head of year 7 1990–97, head of history 1992–97; dep headmistress Brentwood Sch 1997–2001, headmistress Perse Sch for Girls Cambridge 2001–; *Recreations* theatre, cinema, music, travel, walking; *Style*— Miss Tricia Kelleher; ✉ Perse School for Girls, Union Road, Cambridge CB2 1HF

KELLETT, Sir Stanley Charles; 7 Bt (UK 1801), of Lota, Cork; s of Sir Stanley Everard Kellett, 6 Bt (d 1983), and Audrey Margaret, *née* Phillips; *b* 5 March 1940; *m* 1, 1962 (m dis 1968), Lorraine May, da of F Winspear; m 2, 1968 (m dis 1974), Margaret Ann, da of James W Bofinger; m 3, 1982, Catherine Lorna, da of W J C Orr; 1 da (Leah Catherine Elizabeth, b 1983); *Heir* unc, Charles Kellett; *Style*— Sir Stanley Kellett, Bt; ✉ 58 Glad Gunson Drive, Eleebana, Newcastle, NSW 2280, Australia

KELLETT-BOWMAN, Edward Thomas; JP (Middx 1966); s of Reginald Edward Bowman (d 1934), and Mabel Bowman (d 1997); *b* 25 February 1931; *Educ* Reed's Sch, Slough Coll of Technol (DMS), Cranfield Univ (MBA); *m* 1, 1960, Margaret Blakemore (d 1970); 3 s, 1 da; m 2, 1971, (Mary) Elaine Kellett (Dame Elaine Kellett-Bowman); *Career* MEP (EDG): Lancs E 1979–84, Hampshire Central 1988–94, Itchen, Test and Avon 1994–99; Liveryman Worshipful Co of Wheelwrights; FIMgt; *Recreations* shooting, tennis, swimming; *Style*— Edward Kellett-Bowman, Esq; fax 01794 367845

KELLEY, John Victor; s of William Kelley (d 1988), and Beatrice, *née* Armitage (d 1984); *b* 20 February 1947; *Educ* Harold Hill GS; *m* 1974 (sep), Anne; 1 s (John William b 28 Feb 1980), 1 da (Rosemary Anne b 26 June 1982); *Career* jr art dir Brunning Advertising

1963–66; copywriter: Foote Cone & Belding 1966–69, PKL (later BBDO) 1969–75, Collett Dickensen Pearce 1976–81 (rising to gp head); fndr ptnr Lowe Howard Spink 1981–82, copywriter/bd dir Abbott Mead Vickers 1982–83, creative dir Geers Gross 1983–85, vice-chm and exec creative dir Abbott Mead Vickers 1985–93, creative dir Publicis 1993–95, vice-chm and sr creative TBWA 1996–97, jt creative dir TBWA Simons Palmer 1997–98, exec creative dir (Ford Europe) Ogilvy & Mather 1998–; D&AD Silver Awards for: best 15 sec TV commercial (Great Northern Bitter) 1973, most outstanding direction of TV campaign (Daily Express) 1977, most outstanding 45 sec TV commercial (Heineken) 1981, most outstanding typography in an advertisement (Long John Whisky) 1981, most outstanding direction of cinema commercial (Benson & Hedges) 1982; other awards incl: Br TV ITV Award for best commercial (EMI Records) 1978, Film & TV Festival of NY Gold Award (Bass Charrington) 1984, Br Cinema Advtg Awards Gold Award (Britvic Corona) 1988, NY One Show Merit Awards (Cow & Gate) 1990 and 1991, Gold Award APG (Hula Hoops) 1996, Gold Award APG (Ford Transit) 1999; former memb Exec Ctee D&AD; *Style—* John Kelley, Esq; ✉ Ogilvy & Mather, 10 Cabot Square, Canary Wharf, London E14 4QB (tel 020 7345 3000)

KELLIE, Ian; s of Lionel Kellie (d 1996), and Doris, *née* Stead; *b* 7 July 1950, Surrey; *Educ* Queen Elizabeth GS Hexham, Univ of Durham (BSc), St John's Coll York (PGCE), Univ of Bristol (MEd); *m* 1979 (m dis 2002); 2 s (Simon b 8 Jan 1982, Peter b 2 Jan 1984); *Career* chemistry master St Bees Sch Cumbria 1972–75, second in chemistry dept Cotham GS Bristol 1975–82, head of science Ashton Park Sch Bristol 1982–88; Sir Thomas Rich's Gloucester: dep headmaster 1988–94, headmaster 1994–; *Recreations* walking, cycling, table tennis; *Style—* Ian Kellie, Esq; ✉ Sir Thomas Rich's School, Oakleaze, Longlevens, Gloucester GL2 0LF (tel 01452 338400, fax 01452 338401, e-mail iankellie@strs.org.uk)

KELLNER, Peter Jon; s of Michael Kellner (d 1991), and Lily, *née* McVail (d 2004); *b* 2 October 1946, Lewes, Sussex; *Educ* Minchenden GS London, Royal GS Newcastle upon Tyne, King's Coll Cambridge (BA); *m* 1, 1972, Sally, *née* Collard; 2 da (Tara b 1977, Katherine b 1979), 1 s (Michael b 1981); m 2, 1988, Catherine Margaret Ashton (Rt Hon Baroness Ashton of Upholland), *qv*; 1 s (Hon Robert b 1989), 1 da (Hon Rebecca b 1992); *Career* journalist Sunday Times 1969–80, political ed New Statesman 1980–87; political columnist: The Independent 1986–92, Sunday Times 1992–96, The Observer 1996–97, London Evening Standard 1997–2003; political analyst BBC2 Newsnight 1990–97; YouGov plc: chm 2001–07, pres and non-exec dir 2007–; visiting prof Univ of Hertfordshire 2006; Journalist of the Year British Press Awards 1978; Hon DLitt Univ of Hertfordshire 1998; *Publications* co-author: Callaghan: The Road to Number 10 (1976), The Civil Servants: An Inquiry into Britain's Ruling Class (1980), The New Mutualism (1998); *Clubs* Cwlth; *Style—* Peter Kellner, Esq; ✉ YouGov plc, 50 Featherstone Street, London EC1Y 8RT (tel 020 7012 6000, e-mail peter.kellner@yougov.com)

KELLS, Ronald David (Ronnie); OBE (1999), DL; *b* 14 May 1938; *Educ* Bushmills GS, Sullivan Upper Sch Holywood, Queen's Univ Belfast (BSc (Econ)), Babson Coll Boston Mass; *m* 30 July 1964, Elizabeth; 1 da (Louise), 1 s (Jeremy); *Career* formerly with Wm F Coates and Co and Wm Patterson and Co stockbrokers Belfast; Ulster Bank: joined 1964, investment mangr 1969, dep head of related banking servs 1976–79, head of planning and mktg 1979–82, seconded to National Westminster Bank plc 1982–84, dir and head Branch Banking Div (later Retail Servs Div) 1984–94, chief exec 1994–98; currently chm United Drug plc, dir Readymix plc and number of other cos; founding chm NI Film Cmmn 1997–2002, govr BFI 1998–2003; dep chm Irish Inst for European Affrs 1996–2000; dir Men Against Cancer, hon memb Cncl NSPCC; FCIS; *Recreations* golf, winter sports, gardening, walking; *Style—* Ronnie Kells, Esq, OBE, DL

KELLY, Dame Barbara Mary; DBE (2007, CBE 1992), DL (Dumfriesshire 1998); da of John Maxwell Prentice, JP, (d 1990), of Dalbeattie, Stewartry of Kirkcudbright, and Barbara Bain, *née* Adam (d 1989); *b* 27 February 1940; *Educ* Dalbeattie HS, Kirkcudbright Acad, Moray House Edinburgh; *m* 28 July 1960, Kenneth Archibald Kelly, s of Thomas Archibald Grant Kelly (d 1960); 3 s (Hamish Grant b 1961 d 1961, Neil Grant b 1963, Jonathan Ormiston b 1965, d 1985), 2 da (Joanna Barbara b 1970, Christian Maxwell b 1972); *Career* ptnr in mixed farming enterprise; memb Scottish Bd BP plc 1990–2004, dir Clydesdale Bank plc 1994–98; chair Scottish Consumer Cncl 1985–90, memb Nat Consumer Cncl 1985–90, pres Rural Forum Scotland 1992–99 (chair 1988–92), former chair Dumfries and Galloway Area Manpower Bd, cmmr in Scotland for EOC 1991–95; memb: Scottish Enterprise 1990–95, Scottish Econ Cncl 1992–98, Scottish Tourist Bd 1992–97, Priorities Bd MAFF 1990–93, BBC Scotland Rural Affairs Advsy Ctee 1992–97, Scottish Nat Heritage Bd 1995–2002, Scottish Post Office Bd 1997–2003, Broadcasting Cncl for Scotland BBC 1997–2002; chair Architects Registration Bd 1997–2002; convenor: Millennium Forest for Scotland Tst, Crichton Fndn; tstee: Robertson Tst 2002–, Royal Botanic Garden Edinburgh 2002–; memb UK Advsy Ctee Duke of Edinburgh Award 1981–85 (former chm Scottish Advsy Ctee); Hon LLD: Univ of Strathclyde, Univ of Aberdeen, Univ of Glasgow 2002, Queen Margaret UC 2005, Bell Coll 2006; Freeman City of London 2002; *Recreations* family, music, the pursuit of real food, gardening of necessity; *Style—* Dame Barbara Kelly, DBE, DL; ✉ Barncleugh, Irongray, Dumfries, Dumfries and Galloway DG2 9SE (tel 01387 730210)

KELLY, Prof (Thomas) Bernard; s of Joseph Harold Kelly (d 1989), and Ada Eileen, *née* Dolan (d 1981); *b* 14 August 1948; *Educ* West Park GS St Helens, UMIST (BSc); *m* 13 Feb 1971, Catherine Patricia, da of Albert Reginald Spencer; 1 s (Matthew James b 3 Aug 1975), 1 da (Dr Gemma Louise b 15 July 1978); *Career* formerly: plant mangr Laporte, process engr Unilever Research Labs, process engr ICI; BNFL: joined as memb THORP Front End Design Team 1981, asst chief engr 1986–87, chief process engr 1987–89, gen mangr BNFL Engrg 1989–94, md BNFL Instruments Ltd 1994–2000, ceo BNFL Instruments Inc USA 1997–2000, head of engrg technol BNFL Engrg 2000–03, head of effluent strategy Site Remediation Gp 2003–07, prof of nuclear decommissioning engrg Dalton Inst Univ of Manchester 2007–; regnl organiser Opening Windows on Engrg scheme (sch careers advice) 1977–82; Dip Co Direction IOD 1997; CEng 1974, FIChemE 1987, FREng 2001; *Recreations* walking, reading, music, languages; *Style—* Prof Bernard Kelly; ✉ University of Manchester, Pariser Building, PO Box 88, Sackville Street, Manchester M60 1QD

KELLY, Bernard Noel; s of Sir David Kelly, GCMG, MC (d 1959), of Co Wexford, and Comtesse Renée Marie Noële Ghislaine de Vaux (d 1995); *b* 23 April 1930; *Educ* Downside; *m* 11 July 1952, Lady Mirabel Magdalene Fitzalan Howard; 7 s, 1 da; *Career* Capt 8 Queen's Royal Irish Hussars incl reserves 1948–60; admitted slr 1956; ptnr Simmons and Simmons 1958–62; banker; md Compagnie Monegasque de Banque SAM 1976–80; dir: S G Warburg & Co 1963–76, Barnes Gp Inc USA 1975–91, Insilco USA 1978–89, Lazard Bros and Co Ltd 1980–90 (vice-chm and md 1981–85), PXRE USA 1988–2002, American Phoenix Investment Ltd 1990–99, Société Générale Investissement (LUX) 1990–, Campbell Lutyens & Co Ltd (chm 1990–92); chm: Langbourne Income Growth & Property Unit Trust 1984–, International Select Fund Ltd 1989–96, LET Ventures plc 1990–95, Nexus Structured Finance Ltd 1993–, Discovery Gp of Funds 1997–2003, First Equity Ltd 2000–; dir: Gen Med Clinic 1998–, PXP International Ltd 2000–03; *Clubs* Athenaeum, Brooks's, Kildare Street and Univ (Dublin), United Arts (Dublin); *Style—* Bernard Kelly, Esq; ✉ 45 Fernshaw Road, London SW10 0TN (tel 020 7352 8272)

KELLY, Prof Catriona Helen Moncrieff; da of Alexander Kelly (d 1996), and Margaret Moncrieff Kelly; *b* 6 October 1959; *Educ* Godolphin & Latymer Sch, St Hilda's Coll Oxford (BA), Univ of Oxford (DPhil); *m* 1993, Prof Ian Thompson; *Career* ChCh Oxford: sr scholar 1983–87, jr research fell 1987–90, Br Acad fell 1990–93; lectr in Russian language and literature SSEES Univ of London 1993–96; Univ of Oxford: lectr 1996–, reader 1997–2002, prof of Russian 2002–, tutorial fell New Coll; *Publications* Petrushka, the Russian Carnival Puppet Theatre (1990), An Anthology of Russian Women's Writing 1777–1992 (ed, 1994), A History of Russian Women's Writing, 1820–1992 (1994), Constructing Russian Culture in the Age of Revolution (co-ed, 1998), Russian Cultural Studies: An Introduction (co-ed, 1998), Utopias: Russian Modernist Texts 1905–1940 (ed, 1999), Russian Literature, Modernism, and the Visual Arts (co-ed, 2000), Refining Russia: Advice Literature, Polite Culture, and Gender from Catherine to Yeltsin (2001), Russian Literature: A Very Short Introduction (2001), Comrade Pavlik: The Rise and Fall of a Soviet Boy Hero (2005), Children's World: Growing Up in Russia 1890–1991 (2007); also author of book chapters, chapters in specialised volumes and articles in professional jls; reviews published in jls incl: The Guardian, TLS, Evening Standard, Jl of Modern History, American Historical Review; *Recreations* visual arts, travel, slash and burn gardening; *Style—* Prof Catriona Kelly; ✉ New College, Oxford OX1 3BN (tel 01865 279555, fax 01865 279590, e-mail catriona.kelly@new.ox.ac.uk)

KELLY, Sir Christopher William; KCB (2001); s of Dr Reginald Edward Kelly (d 1990), and Peggy Kathleen, *née* Stone; *b* 18 August 1946; *Educ* Beaumont Coll, Trinity Coll Cambridge (MA), Univ of Manchester (MA); *m* 1970, Alison Mary Collens, da of Dr Henry Durant (d 1982), and Peggy Durant; 2 s (Jake b 1974, Toby b 1976), 1 da (Rachel b 1980); *Career* HM Treasy: asst princ 1970, private sec to Fin Sec 1971–73, sec to Wilson Ctee of Inquiry into Fin Instns 1978–80, asst sec 1981, under sec Pay and Industrial Relations Gp in Treasy 1987–90, under sec Social Servs and Territorial Gp 1990–92, under sec Gen Expenditure Policy Gp 1992–94, dir of fiscal and monetary policy 1994–95, dir of budget and public fins 1995; head Policy Gp Dept of Social Security 1995–97, perm sec Dept of Health 1997–2000; memb Bd Nat Consumer Cncl 2001–, chm NSPCC 2002–, chm Financial Ombudsman Serv 2005– (non-exec dir 2002–); *Recreations* narrow boating, walking; *Style—* Sir Christopher Kelly, KCB; ✉ 22 Croftdown Road, London NW5 1EH (tel 020 7485 3739)

KELLY, Crispin Noel; s of Bernard Kelly, *qv*, of London, and Lady Mirabel, *née* Fitzalan Howard; *b* 21 October 1956; *Educ* Magdalen Coll Oxford (MA), AA Sch of Architecture (Dip); *m* 9 July 1982, Frances, da of Charles Pickthorn; 4 c (Alex b 9 Aug 1984, Christian b 18 Jan 1987 d 1987, Jessica b 12 July 1988, Rowan b 28 Aug 1998); *Career* architect; fndr and md Baylight Properties plc 1982; pres AA 2001–03; RIBA 1994; *Books* Building More Homes (with R Ehrman, 2003); *Style—* Crispin Kelly; ✉ Baylight Properties plc, 50 Sulivan Road, London SW6 3DX (tel 020 7731 1303, fax 020 7731 5644)

KELLY, Dr David Roy; s of Roy Alfred Kelly, and Marie Rose Kelly; *b* 16 April 1955; *Educ* Univ of Salford (BSc, PhD), Univ of Waterloo Canada, Univ of Maryland, Univ of Oxford; *m* 13 Sept 1980, Judith Wendy, da of Eric Hadfield, of Marsden, W Yorks; 1 da (Lauren Rachael Olivia b 14 July 1990); *Career* post doctoral fell: Univ of Waterloo 1979–80, Univ of Maryland 1980–81, Univ of Oxford 1981–84; New Blood lectr in organic chem Cardiff Univ (formerly UC Cardiff) 1984– (dir of external liaison 2006–), speaker The Chemistry of Sexual Attraction; over 85 pubns in jls; broadcaster (several TV and radio appearances); sec: Gregynog Symposium for Young Chemists 1987–, Agriculture Sector Ctee RSC 1998–; treas Bioorganic Subject Gp Ctee RSC 1996–, memb: Chemical Senses in Vetebrates Steering Ctee 1999–, Editorial Bd Archives in Organic Chemistry (ARKIVOC) 1999–, Research Panel Faraday Pro-Bio Partnership 2001–05, ECLAIR 209; MACS, MSCI, MRSC (CChem) 1979; *Books* Biotransformations in series Biotechnology (ed, vol 8a 1998, vol 8b 2000); *Recreations* cabinet making; *Style—* Dr David R Kelly; ✉ Department of Chemistry, Cardiff University, PO Box 912, Cardiff CF10 3TB (tel 029 2087 4063, fax 029 2087 4030, mobile 07971 240448)

K

KELLY, Dr Desmond Hamilton Wilson; s of Norman Wilson Kelly, OBE (d 1976), and Anne Elizabeth, *née* Megarry (d 1976); *b* 2 June 1934; *Educ* King's Sch Canterbury, St Thomas' Hosp London (Crawford Exhibitioner, MB BS, Plank Prize in psychiatry), DPM, MD; *m* 6 Feb 1960, Angela Marjorie, da of Stuart Way Shapland; 2 s (Jonathan Desmond b 6 Jan 1963, Simon James 16 Nov 1965); *Career* St Thomas' Hosp: med casualty offr 1958, house surgn 1959, psychiatric house physician 1959; RAMC 1960–63; St Thomas' Hosp: res registrar 1963–65, sr registrar 1965–67, chief asst psychiatry 1968–69; registrar The Maudsley Hosp 1965, Nuffield Fndn Med Fellowship Johns Hopkins Hosp USA 1967–68, conslt psychiatrist St George's Hosp 1971–79 (sr lectr and hon conslt 1969–71), med dir The Priory Hosp 1980–97; visiting prof of psychiatry UCL 1991–; lectr in USA & ME; Pavlovian Award and Medal Soc of N America 1971, physician of the year 1981; gp med dir the Priory Hosps Gp 1993–99 (dir 1981–99, chm 1988–93); memb: Assoc of Univ Teachers of Psychiatry 1970, Int Ctee for the Prevention and Treatment of Depression UK (chm 1976), Cncl Psychiatric Section of RSM 1977–80; pres UK Branch Int Stress and Tension Control Soc 1985–88, pres Int Stress Mgmnt Assoc 1988–92, hon pres Priory Healthcare 1999–2003; FRSM 1963, FRCPsych 1975 (MRCPsych 1971), FRCP 1977 (MRCP); *Books* Anxiety and Emotions: physiological basis and treatment (1980), A Practical Handbook for the Treatment of Depression (co-ed,1987), Kelly's Burma Campaign (2003); author of over 50 papers; *Recreations* tennis, skiing, windsurfing, gardening; *Clubs* Roehampton; *Style—* Dr Desmond Kelly; ✉ Clare Cottage, 19 Hertford Avenue, London SW14 8EF (tel 020 8876 8261, fax 020 8876 7230, e-mail desmond.kelly@blueyonder.co.uk)

KELLY, Desmond Hugh; OBE (2005); s of Fredrick Henry Kelly (d 1973), of Salisbury, Southern Rhodesia, and Mary Josephine, *née* Bracken; *b* 13 January 1942; *Educ* Christian Brothers Coll Bulawayo, Elaine Archibald Ballet Sch Bulawayo, Ruth French Dance Acad London; *m* 4 Jan 1964, Denise Jeanette, da of Henri Charles le Comte; 1 da (Emma Louise b 30 Dec 1970), 1 s (Joel Henry b 1 June 1973); *Career* dancer; princ London Festival Ballet 1964 (joined 1959), Zurich Ballet 1966–67, ballet master teacher and princ dancer New Zealand Ballet 1967–68, Nat Ballet of Washington 1968–70 (most notable role James in La Sylphide with Margot Fonteyn), The Royal Ballet 1970–76 (ballets incl Swan Lake, Giselle and Romeo and Juliet); Sadler's Wells Royal Ballet: princ dancer 1976–78, ballet master 1978–, asst to dir 1988, currently asst dir and int guest teacher; roles incl: Thomas in La Fille Mal Gardée, Dr Coppélius in Coppélia, Dago in Façade, Mr Hobson in David Bintley's Hobson's Choice; various TV appearances; *Recreations* theatre, gardening, cooking, reading; *Style—* Desmond Kelly, Esq, OBE; ✉ Birmingham Royal Ballet, Birmingham Hippodrome, Thorp Street, Birmingham B5 4AU (tel 0121 245 3500, fax 0121 245 3570, e-mail desmondkelly@brb.org.uk)

KELLY, (Reay) Diarmaid Anthony; s of Capt Edward Raymond Anthony Kelly (d 1991), of Belgrave Mews North, London, and Bridget Ramsay, *née* Hornby; *b* 8 July 1959; *Educ* Ampleforth; *m* 18 April 1991, Candida, eld da of Peter Meinertzhagen; 2 s (Barnaby b 15 Jan 1993, Augustus b 15 June 1995); *Career* sales exec Henderson Crosthwaite & Co 1981–84, dir Baring Securities Ltd (later ING Baring Securities Ltd) 1984–96, fndr dir CrossBorder Capital 1996–; *Recreations* racing; *Clubs* Boodle's, Pratt's, Turf; *Style—* Diarmaid Kelly, Esq; ✉ CrossBorder Capital, Marcol House, 289–293 Regent Street, London W1 (tel 020 7535 0400, fax 020 7535 0435, e-mail dk@liquidity.com)

KELLY, Prof Francis Patrick (Frank); s of Francis Kelly, and Margaret, *née* McFadden; *b* 28 December 1950; *Educ* Van Mildert Coll Durham (BSc), Emmanuel Coll Cambridge (PhD); *m* 1972, Jacqueline Pullin; 2 s; *Career* operational res analyst Scicon Ltd 1971–73; Univ of Cambridge: asst lectr in engrg 1976–78, lectr Statistical Laboratory 1978–86, Nuffield Fndn sci res fell 1986–87, reader in mathematics of systems 1986–90, prof of the mathematics of systems 1990–, dir Statistical Laboratory 1991–93, Royal Soc Leverhulme Tst sr research fell 1994–95; chief scientific advsr Dept for Transport 2003–06, master

Christ's Coll Cambridge 2006– (fell 1976–); Rollo Davidson Prize 1979, Guy Medal in silver RSS 1989, Lanchester Prize Operation Res Soc of America 1992, Clifford Paterson lectr Royal Soc 1995, Blackett lectr Operational Res Soc 1996, Naylor Prize London Mathematical Soc 1997, IEEE Koji Kobayashi Award 2005; chm Lyndewode Research Ltd 1987–; assoc ed: Stochastic Models 1983–86, Annals of Probability 1984–90, Jl of the Royal Statistical Soc 1986–90, Probability in the Engineering and Informational Scis 1986–96, Combinatorics, Probability and Computing 1991–95, Queueing Systems 1995–, Mathematics of Operations Research 2003–; Hon DSc Heriot-Watt Univ 2001; FRS 1989; *Books* Reversibility and Stochastic Networks 1979, numerous articles in mathematical & statistical jls; *Recreations* skiing, golf; *Style*— Prof Frank Kelly, FRS; ✉ Statistical Laboratory, Wilberforce Road, Cambridge CB3 0WB (tel 01223 337963, fax 01223 337956)

KELLY, James; MSP; s of Frank Kelly, and Lilian, *née* Reid; *b* 23 October 1963, Glasgow; *Educ* Glasgow Coll of Technol (BSc); *m* 12 June 1992, Alexandra, *née* Mullan; 2 da (Carys b 9 Jan 1998, Erin b 18 July 2000); *Career* analyst programmer Argyll and Clyde Health Bd 1985–88, computer auditor and fin officer Scottish Power 1988–99, sr analyst Scottish Electricity Settlements 1999–2004, business analyst SAIC 2004–07; MSP (Scot Lab) Glasgow Rutherglen 2007–; CIMA 1994; *Recreations* half marathons, five-a-side football, golf; *Style*— James Kelly, Esq, MSP; ✉ The Scottish Parliament, Edinburgh EH99 1SP

KELLY, Jane Maureen; da of Adrian Morgan Kelly (d 1995), of Bristol, and Monica Dallas, *née* Edwards; *b* 20 September 1948; *Educ* Notre Dame HS Sheffield, Univ of Birmingham (LLB); *m* 1, 1975, (m dis 1981); m 2, 1 July 1994, Michael Randolph Peter Blanckenhagen, s of John Stanley Blanckenhagen (d 1974); *Career* admitted slr 1971; slr in private practice in Eng and Far East 1971–79; AMI Healthcare Group plc 1979–90: legal advsr 1979, co sec 1983, dir of corporate health servs 1988; dir AMI Healthcare Group plc 1987–90; independent mgmnt conslt 1990–; chm: W Middx Univ Hosp NHS Tst 1992–2002, NW London SHA 2002–03, regnl cmmr London NHS Appts Cmmn 2003–; hon visiting fell Dept of Health Studies Univ of York 1996–; non-exec dir A Big Smile Ltd 2000–02; lay memb Gen Cncl and Register of Osteopaths 1990–95; chm Women in Mgmnt 1987–89, chm Jt Cncl of the Lay and Monastic Communities of Worth Abbey 1991–95, tstee Lifecare Charitable Tst 1992–2003, memb Cncl English Nature 1992–2000, memb Cncl Nat Tst 1994–98, fndr patron The Mulberry Centre Appeal; *Style*— Miss Jane Kelly; ✉ NHS Appointments Commission, Cheapside House, 138 Cheapside, London EC2V 6BB (tel 020 7615 9300)

KELLY, John Anthony Brian; RD (1974); s of Lt Cdr Brian John Parmenter Kelly, DSC (d 1994), of Bangor, Co Down, and Ethne Mary, *née* Ryan (d 1977); *b* 21 August 1941; *Educ* Bangor GS, Fort Augustus Abbey Sch, Queen's Univ Belfast (LLB); *m* 28 March 1971, Denise Anne, da of Ronald James Circuit, of St Albans; 2 da (Katrina b 1973, Joanna b 1975), 2 s (Christopher b 1977, Nicholas b 1982); *Career* Lt Cdr RNR 1959–84; Price Waterhouse and Co 1963–68 (qualified 1967), exec Old Broad St Securities 1968–70, exec and assoc Laurie Milbank and Co 1971–78, dir Brown Shipley and Co Ltd 1982–92 (mangr 1978); dir: Close Brothers Ltd 1992–96, Close Securities Ltd 1997–; non-exec dir: Cosalt plc 1986– (chm 2005–), SEP Industrial Holdings plc 1996–2001, Clugston Group Ltd 1997–, iRevolution Gp plc 2001–02; Liveryman Worshipful Co of Founders; FCA; *Recreations* walking, reading, poetry, golf; *Clubs* The Naval, Royal Ulster Yacht; *Style*— John Kelly, Esq, RD; ✉ Cherrytrees, Penn Road, Beaconsfield, Buckinghamshire HP9 2LW (e-mail kellycherrytrees@hotmail.com); Close Securities Ltd, 10 Crown Place, London EC2A 4FT (tel 020 7426 4000)

KELLY, Prof John Stephen; s of Michael Kelly (d 1982), and Joan, *née* Trebble; *b* 4 February 1942; *Educ* Trinity Coll Dublin (fndn scholar, univ prize in Old and Middle English, Henry Hutchinson Stewart literary scholarship, vice-chllr's prize for English prose, BA, univ research exhbn), St Catharine's Coll Cambridge (Gardiner meml scholar, PhD); *m* 1966, Christine Juliet, eld da of Capt Michael Rahilly, RN; 1 da (Katharine Sophia b 1971), 2 s (Tom Michael b 1974, Ned b 1978); *Career* lectr in English Univ of Kent at Canterbury 1968–76; St John's Coll Oxford: fell and tutor in English 1976, sr English fell 1980, tutor for admission 1982–85, vice-pres 1991, prof of English 1997–; Lamont visiting prof Union Coll Schenectady NY 1990, Donnelly visiting prof of Irish studies Notre Dame Univ 1999; dir Yeats Summer Sch 1971–76; founding memb Int Assoc for the Study of Anglo-Irish Literature (IASAIL) 1969 (treas 1969–71); Leverhulme Fellowship 1972–73, sr research fell Univ of Leicester 1973–74, Br Acad Readership 1988–90; O'Donnell lectr Univ of Oxford 1991, Churchill lectr Univ of Bristol 1992; curator Oxford Playhouse (univ theatre) 1978–83, sr memb Experimental Theatre Club Univ of Oxford 1978–87; hon fell Trinity Coll Dublin 1998; *Books* The Collected Letters of W B Yeats (ed, vol I 1986, vol II 1997, vol III 1994, vol IV 2005), The Spirit of the Nation (ed, 1999), Poems and Ballads of Young Ireland (ed, 2000); ed of editions: James Joyce, John Mitchel, James Fintan Lalor, James Clarence Mangan, Gerald Griffin, John Banim, Thomas Davis, William Allingham, Samuel Ferguson, Charles Kickham; *Recreations* theatre, cinema, running; *Style*— Prof John Kelly; ✉ St John's College, Oxford OX1 3JP (tel 01865 277300, fax 01865 277435, e-mail john.kelly@sjc.ox.ac.uk)

KELLY, Rt Hon Sir John William (Basil); kt (1984), PC (1984), PC (NI 1969); s of Thomas William Kelly (d 1955), of NI, and Emily Frances, *née* Donaldson (d 1966); *b* 10 May 1920; *Educ* Methodist Coll Belfast, Trinity Coll Dublin (BA, LLB); *m* 1957, Pamela, da of Thomas Colmer Colthurst (d 1960), and Marjorie Colthurst; 1 da; *Career* called to the Bar: NI 1944, Middle Temple 1970 (bencher 2002); QC 1958, MP NI 1964–72, attorney gen NI 1968–72, judge of the High Court NI 1973–84, Lord Justice of Appeal Supreme Court of Judicature NI 1984–95; chm: Bar Cncl of NI 1968–70, Cncl of Legal Educn NI 1989–93, Judicial Studies Bd NI 1993–95; memb Legal Advsy Ctee British Cncl 1983–93; UK judicial representative Int Assoc of Judges 1982–94; *Recreations* golf, travel, music; *Style*— The Rt Hon Sir Basil Kelly; ✉ c/o Royal Courts of Justice, Belfast BT1 3JF

KELLY, Judith Pamela (Jude); OBE (1997); da of John Kelly, of Wimbledon, London, and Ida Kelly; *b* 24 March 1954; *Educ* Calder HS Liverpool, Univ of Birmingham; *m* Michael Bird (professionally known as Michael Birch); 1 da (Caroline b 21 Oct 1986), 1 s (Robbie b 4 Sept 1989); *Career* director; began career as freelance folk and jazz singer 1970–75, actress with Michael Bogdanov's Co (Leicester Phoenix Theatre) 1975–76, fndr dir Solent People's Theatre Hampshire (over 42 community shows) 1976–80, artistic dir BAC 1980–85 (also co-fndr BAC based General Theatre Co 1983), freelance dir Nat Theatre of Brent 1982–85, artistic dir York Festival and Mystery Plays 1988 (joined pt/t 1985–88), chief exec West Yorkshire Playhouse 1993–2002 (artistic dir 1988–2002), fndr artistic dir Metal (artists' lab) 2002–05 (chair 2005–), artistic dir South Bank Centre 2005–; BAC prodns incl: rodns incl: Fascinating Aida 1983, Second from Last in the Sack Race (also tour) 1983, The Devil Rides Out - A Bit (also Lyric Hammersmith and tour) 1984; Nat Theatre of Brent prodns incl Harvey and the Wallbangers (3 nat tours, 2 TV shows); other prodns incl: The Pink Briefcase (Lyric Hammersmith and tour) 1985, Lynchville (RSC festival, joined as asst dir) 1986, Sarcophagus 1987 (The Pit, transferring to Mermaid (two nominations Olivier Awards)), Affairs in a Tent 1988, A Garden Fête 1988 (both Bristol Old Vic); West Yorkshire Playhouse prodns incl: Wild Oats, Safe in our Hands, Getting Attention, The Pope and the Witch, Second from last in the Sack Race, Pratt of the Argus, The Revenger's Tragedy, Wicked Old Man, Happy Days, The Taming of the Shrew, Comedians, Gypsy, The Merchant of Venice, Mail Order Bride, Call in the Night, King Lear, Beatification of Area Boy, World Goes 'Round, A Perfect Ganesh, Odysseus Thump, Queen, Blast from the Past, Macbeth, Singin' in the Rain (transferred to RNT, Olivier Award for Outstanding Musical Production 2001), Half a Sixpence; freelance prodns incl: When We Are Married, Othello (for Shakespeare Theatre Washington DC), The Elixir of Love (for ENO), Saturday Sunday and Monday; formed resident ensemble company at West Yorkshire Playhouse led by Sir Ian McKellen (prodns incl: The Seagull, The Tempest); fndr memb Noroc 1992 (cultural exchange initiative between Br and Romania); visiting prof: Univ of Leeds 2002–, Kingston Univ 2002–; chair: Common Purpose Charitable Tst 1997–, Qualifications and Curriculum Authy Advsy Gp on the Arts 2001, Arts, Educn and Culture Ctee London 2012 Olympic Games Bid 2004–05, Culture, Ceremonies and Educn London Organising Ctee of the Olympic Games 2005–; dep chair NACCCE (National Advsy Ctee on Creative and Cultural Educn) 1998–2000, represents UK for UNESCO on cultural matters 1998–2000; memb: Leeds Initiative, Cncl and Ct Univ of Leeds, Arts Cncl Drama Panel 1995–97, Cncl RSA 1998–99, Bd RJC Reggae, Jazz, Contemporary Dance Co 2001–, Bd Br Cncl 2002–; awarded Br Jr C of C Outstanding Young Person's Cultural Achievement 1993; Hon Dr: Leeds Met Univ 1995, Univ of Bradford 1996, Univ of Leeds 2000, Univ of York 2001, Open Univ 2001; *Recreations* windsurfing; *Style*— Ms Jude Kelly, OBE; ✉ Metal, 198A Broadhurst Gardens, London NW6 3AY (e-mail jude@metalculture.com)

KELLY, Laurence Charles Kevin; s of Sir David Kelly, GCMG, MC (d 1959), and Comtesse Renée Marie Noële Ghislaine de Vaux (d 1995); *b* 11 April 1933, Brussels; *Educ* Downside, New Coll Oxford (MA); *m* 1963, Linda, da of Maj R G McNair Scott (d 1995), and Hon Mrs Scott (d 1996), of Old Basing, Hants; 1 s, 2 da; *Career* Lt Life Gds 1949–52; served FO (Northern Dept) 1955–56, Guest Keen and Nettlefolds 1956–72; Helical Bar plc: non-exec dir 1972–93, dep chm 1981–84, chm 1984–88, vice-chm 1988–93; dir: GKN Int Trading 1972, Morganite Int Ltd 1984–92, KAE Mintel Int Ltd 1985–2003; chm Queenborough Steel Co 1980–89; vice-chm British Steel Consumers' Cncl 1974 (res 1985); memb: Bd NI Devpt Agency 1972–78, Monopolies and Mergers Cmmn 1982–88; tstee Carmelite Church Choir Tst 1997–; sr assoc memb St Antony's Coll Oxford 1985–92; FRGS, FRSL 2003; *Books* Lermontov - Tragedy in the Caucasus (1978), Travellers' Companion to St Petersburg (1981), Travellers' Companion to Moscow (1983), Travellers' Companion to Istanbul (1987), Proposals (with A L Kelly, 1989), Diplomacy and Murder in Tehran: Alexander Griboyedov and Imperial Russia's Mission to the Shah of Persia (2001); *Recreations* swimming, opera; *Clubs* Brooks's, Turf, Beefsteak, Univ (Dublin); *Style*— Laurence Kelly, Esq; ✉ 44 Ladbroke Grove, London W11 2PA (tel 020 7727 4663); Lorton Hall, Low Lorton, Cockermouth, Cumbria CA13 7UP (tel 01900 85252)

KELLY, Linda; da of Ronald McNair Scott (d 1995), and Hon Mary McNair Scott *née* Berry (d 1996); *b* 1 October 1936; *Educ* Southover Manor, Byam Shaw Sch of Art; *m* 20 April 1963, Laurence Kelly, s of Sir David Kelly, GCMG, MC; 2 da (Rosanna b 21 May 1964, Rachel b 19 Sept 1965), 1 s (Nicholas b 24 Nov 1967); *Career* copywriter Condé Nast Pubns 1956–60, travel ed Vogue 1960–63; tstee: London Library 2001–04, Wordsworth Tst 2001–; FRSL; *Books* The Marvellous Boy (1971), The Young Romantics (1976), The Kemble Era (1980), Women of The French Revolution (1987), Juniper Hall (1991), Richard Brinsley Sheridan (1997), Susanna, the Captain and the Castrato (2004), Ireland's Minstrel (2006); anthologies: Feasts (with Christopher Bland, 1986), Proposals (with Laurence Kelly, 1989); *Recreations* reading, opera-going, family life; *Style*— Ms Linda Kelly; ✉ 44 Ladbroke Grove, London W11 2PA (tel 020 7727 4663)

KELLY, Linda Mary; da of late John Nicholl Millar, and Vicenta Amy Gibson, *née* Smith; *b* 2 January 1955; *m* 24 April 1987, Brian James Kelly; 2 da (Natasha Vicenta b 4 Dec 1987, Kirsty Marion b 6 Aug 1998); *Career* hosp pharmacist Royal Free Hosp and Oldchurch Hosp 1977–78, various mktg and product devpt posts Merck Sharp and Dohme Pharmaceuticals 1978–87, new product planning mangr rising to mktg dir Smith Kline Beecham 1988–91, sales and mktg dir then md (UK and Ireland) Bristol Myers Squibb Pharmaceuticals 1991–95, pres (UK) Astra Pharmaceuticals Ltd (now Astra Zeneca) 1995–99 (also chm Pension Fund and tstee Astra Fndn), full time study at Christies Educn 1999–2000, chief exec Parkinson's Disease Soc 2001–05, chief exec Lloyds TSB Fndn 2006–; MRPharmS, FRSA; *Recreations* walking, the arts; *Clubs* Riverside (Chiswick); *Style*— Mrs Linda Kelly

KELLY, (Richard) Martin; s of Norman Keith Kelly, of Bishop Burton, and Gwendoline, *née* Fisher; *b* 25 April 1954; *Educ* Beverley GS, Leeds Poly (Dip Landscape Architecture), Oxford Poly (Dip Urban Design, MA); *m* 10 May 1986 (m dis), Anna Acton-Stow; 1 da (Victoria Grace b 1987); *Career* asst planning offr Landscape and Reclamation Section Sheffield Met Dist Cncl until 1979; currently md Derek Lovejoy Partnership London (joined 1979, ptnr 1986); landscape infrastructure work undertaken for public and private sector clients; expert witness at public enquiries; dir Derek Lovejoy Touchstone Ltd; memb SE Chapter Landscape Ctee; author various articles and book reviews for tech press; FLI 1990, FIHT 1990; *Style*— Martin Kelly, Esq

KELLY, Matthew David Alan; s of Ronald Nugent Kelly, and Olive Hilda, *née* Rixon; *b* 9 May 1950; *Educ* Urmston GS, Manchester Poly (DipEd), Open Univ (BA); *m* 1970, Sarah Elizabeth, *née* Gray; 1 s (Matthew David (stage name Matthew Rixon) b 1970), 1 da (Ruth Emma b 1972); *Career* actor and television presenter; theatre 1967–, TV 1977–; early leading TV role as Fitz in sitcom Holding the Fort (LWT) 1979–82; credits incl: Game for a Laugh (LWT) 1981–83, You Bet! (LWT) 1990–95, Stars in their Eyes (Granada) 1990–2004, City Hospital (BBC) 2002–04, Bleak House (BBC) 2005, The Great Belzoni (BBC) 2005, Cold Blood (Granada) 2005 and 2006, Where the Heart Is 2006, Marple 2006; recent theatre performances incl: Rough Crossing, Kafka's Dick, Of Mice and Men, The Taming of the Shrew, Of Mice and Men (Olivier Award Best Actor 2004), Season's Greetings, Don Quixote, Twelfth Night, Mirandolina (Manchester Royal Exchange Theatre) 2006; pres Neuromuscular Centre Cheshire 1990–; hon memb Stretford and Urmiston Rotary; Paul Harris fell 2003; *Style*— Matthew Kelly, Esq

KELLY, Matthias John; QC (1999); s of Ambrose Kelly (d 2001), of Dungannon, Co Tyrone, and Anne, *née* McKiernan (d 1973); *b* 21 April 1954; *Educ* St Patrick's Secdy Sch Dungannon, St Patrick's Acad Dungannon, Trinity Coll Dublin (BA, LLB), Cncl of Legal Educn London; *m* 5 May 1979, Helen Ann, da of Peter Joseph Holmes (d 1974), of Longford, Ireland; 1 s (Peter b 1986), 1 da (Anne b 1987); *Career* called to the Bar: Gray's Inn 1979 (bencher 2002), NI 1983, Repub of Ireland 1983; admitted attorney: NY 1986, USA Federal Bar 1987; recorder of the Crown Court 2002–, SC Repub of Ireland 2005; conslt EU Cmmn Health and Safety UK 1994–96; chm: Bar Conference Eng and Wales 2001, Personal Injuries Bar Assoc 2001–02 (sec 1994–2000, vice-chm 1999–2001), Bar Cncl of Eng and Wales 2003 (memb 1997–2004, chm Policy Ctee 1999–2000, chm Public Affrs Gp 2001–, vice-chm 2002); memb: Mgmnt Ctee Gray's Inn 1993–95, Ogden Working Pty 1997–2003, Blackwell Ctee on non-legally qualified claims handlers 1999–2000; chm: EVA Campaign 1989–93, Children Act Housing Action Gp 1990–94, Mgmnt Ctee Alcohol Recovery Project 1993–96; dir Allied Irish Bank (GB) Gp 2004–; hon life memb Br Soc of Criminology 1986; FRSA; *Publications* Personal Injury Handbook (jt ed, 1997, 2 edn 2000), Munkman on Employers Liability (jt ed, 13 edn 2001); also on ed panel for Specialist Research papers on Personal Injury (1996–2000); *Recreations* walking, cycling, reading; *Style*— Matthias Kelly, Esq, QC; ✉ 39 Essex Street, London WC2 (tel 020 7832 1111, fax 020 7353 3978)

KELLY, Dr Michael; CBE (1983), JP (Glasgow 1973), DL (1983); s of David Kelly (d 1972); *b* 1 November 1940; *Educ* Univ of Strathclyde (BSc, PhD); *m* 1965, Zita, da of Hugh Harkins; 3 c; *Career* economics lectr Univ of Aberdeen and Univ of Strathclyde 1967–84, md Michael Kelly Associates 1983–; columnist The Scotsman 2000–; chm RSSPCC 1987–96, pres Strathclyde Branch Inst of Mktg 1986–89, dir Celtic FC 1990–94; chm Glasgow Central CLP 2004–; memb: Scottish ABSA 1986–90, Scottish Ctee Nat Art Collections Fund 1990–94, External Relations Advsy Gp ESRC 2001–05; Lord Provost of Glasgow (and ex officio Lord-Lt) 1980–84, Lord Rector Univ of Glasgow 1984–87; Hon LLB Univ of Glasgow 1983; FIM 1989; OStJ 1984, Knight's Cross Order of Merit (Poland) 1998; *Books* Paradise Lost, The Struggle for Celtic's Soul (1994), London Lines: The Capital by Underground (1996); *Recreations* golf, photography, philately, sking; *Style*— Dr Michael Kelly, CBE, DL; ✉ 50 Aytoun Road, Glasgow G41 5HE (e-mail kellymkelly1@aol.com)

KELLY, Prof Michael Howard; s of Kenneth Howard Kelly (d 2004), of Hull, and Kathleen Mary, *née* Lucas (d 1994); *b* 19 November 1946; *Educ* Hull GS, Univ of Warwick (BA, PhD), Univ of Southampton Mgmnt Sch (MBA); *m* 3 Jan 1975, Josephine Ann, da of Patrick Joseph Doyle, of Dublin; 2 s (Thomas Doyle b 1980, Paul Doyle b 1983); *Career* lectr in French UC Dublin 1972–86, prof of French Univ of Southampton 1986– (head Sch of Humanities); dir HE Acad Subject Centre for Languages, Linguistics and Area Studies, dir Routes into Languages Prog; sec Euro Language Cncl; memb: Steering Ctee Thematic Network in Languages, Advsy Bd Language and Intercultural Communication, Editorial Bd Arts and Humanities in HE, Advsy Bd Modern and Contemporary France; assoc ed French Cultural Studies; formerly: pres Assoc of Univ Profs of French, chm Irish Cncl for Civil Liberties, chair Univ Cncl of Modern Languages, memb Nuffield Languages Inquiry; FRSA; *Books* Pioneer of the Catholic Revival: Emmanuel Mounier (1979), Modern French Marxism (1982), Hegel in France (1992), French Cultural Studies: An Introduction (1995), Pierre Bourdieu: Language, Culture and Education (1999), French Culture and Society (2001), Third Level, Third Space (2001), A New Landscape for Languages (2003), The European Language Teacher (2003), Cultural and Intellectual Rebuilding of France (2004); *Recreations* tennis, choir, cinema; *Style*— Prof Michael Kelly; ✉ School of Humanities, University of Southampton, Highfield, Southampton SO17 1BF (tel 023 8059 2191, fax 023 8059 3868, e-mail m.h.kelly@soton.ac.uk)

KELLY, Prof Michael Joseph; s of Steve Kelly (d 1988), and Mary Constance, *née* Powell (d 1987); *b* 14 May 1949; *Educ* Francis Douglas Meml Coll NZ, Victoria Univ of Wellington (scholar, MSc, DSc), Univ of Cambridge (MA, PhD, DSc); *m* 1 June 1991, Ann Elizabeth, da of Dr Daniel Brumhall Cochrane Taylor (d 2003); 1 da (Constance Frances b 12 Feb 1993); *Career* res fell Trinity Hall Cambridge 1974–77, IBM res fell Univ of Calif 1975–76, SRC advanced fell Cavendish Laboratory and staff fell Trinity Hall Cambridge 1977–81, res asst GEC 1981–92; Univ of Surrey: prof of physics and electronics 1992–96, head Electronic and Electrical Engrg Dept 1996–97, head Sch of Electronics, Computing and Mathematics 1997–2001, visiting prof 2002–; Prince Philip prof of technol Univ of Cambridge 2002–05, dep head Dept of Engrg Univ of Cambridge 2002–04, exec dir Cambridge-MIT Inst 2003–05, chief scientific advsr to the Dept for Communities and Local Govt 2006–; visiting prof MIT 2004–06; dir: Centre for Solid State Electronics, Advanced Technol Inst Sch of Electronics, Computing and Mathematics 2001–02; conslt GEC Marconi 1992–93, visiting researcher Cavendish Laboratory 1988–92, non-exec dir Laird Gp plc 2006–; Rutherford Meml lectr Royal Soc 2000; Paterson Medal and Prize Inst of Physics 1989, Nelson Gold Medal GEC 1991, Royal Acad of Engrg Silver Medal 1999, Hughes Medal of the Royal Soc 2006; holder of 13 patents on semiconductor devices, author of 200 papers, review articles and book chapters in refereed jls; memb: American Inst of Physics, Cncl of Univ of Surrey 1996–2001, Cncl Royal Soc 2001–02; fell Trinity Hall 1989–92 and 2002–, Erskine fell Univ of Canterbury NZ 1999; Hon DSc Victoria Univ of Wellington 2002; CPhys, FInstP 1988 (memb Cncl 1997–2001, vice-pres 2001–05), FIEE 1989, FRS 1993, FREng 1998, Hon FRSNZ 1999, SMIEEE 2003 (MIEEE 1998); *Books* The Physics and Fabrication of Microstructures and Microdevices (ed, 1986), Low Dimensional Semiconductors: Physics, Materials, Technology, Devices (1995); *Recreations* music, literature; *Style*— Prof Michael Kelly, FRS, FREng; ✉ Electrical Engineering Division, Centre for Advanced Photonics and Electronics, 9 JJ Thomson Avenue, Cambridge CB3 0FA (tel 01223 748303, fax 01223 748348, e-mail mjk1@cam.ac.uk)

KELLY, Neil; WS; s of Neil Kelly, and Bridget, *née* Morgan; *b* 28 June 1961, Bellshill, Lanarkshire; *Educ* St Patrick's HS Coatbridge, Univ of Aberdeen (LLB, DipLP); *m* 3 Sept 1994, Alison, *née* Whyte; 2 s (Nicholas, Christopher), 1 da (Elizabeth); *Career* ptnr MacRoberts slrs 1991– (joined as trainee 1983); NP; cmmr Scottish Cncl for Int Arbitration, convener Scottish region Adjudication Soc; ed Scottish Construction Law Review; memb Law Soc of Scotland; *Publications* MacRoberts on Scottish Building Contracts (contrib, 1999); *Recreations* travel, opera, classical music; *Style*— Neil Kelly, Esq, WS; ✉ 64 Pentland Terrace, Edinburgh EH10 6HE (tel 0131 445 1148, e-mail njkopera@blueyonder.co.uk); MacRoberts, 30 Semple Street, Edinburgh EH3 8BL (tel 0131 229 5046, fax 0131 229 0849, e-mail neil.kelly@macroberts.com)

KELLY, Patricia Mary (Pat); MBE (1977); da of Edward James Kelly (d 1941), of Newbury, Berks, and Elizabeth Lilian, *née* Hyde (d 1956); *b* 6 January 1938; *Educ* Newbury Girls' GS, UCL (BA); *m* 21 May 1994, William Eduard (Bob) Drysdale, s of Charles Drysdale (d 1963); *Career* joined Govt Serv 1964, Dept of Economic Affrs 1964–66, asst private sec to Sec of State for Foreign Affrs 1966–68, third sec Singapore 1968–71, Hong Kong Dept FCO 1972–74, second later first sec (info) The Hague 1974–78, first sec Personnel Dept FCO 1978–80, consul Rio de Janeiro 1981–82, seconded to private sector London 1982–83, first sec (commercial) Caracas 1984–88, dep head Commercial Mgmnt and Exports Dept FCO 1988–90; consul gen: Rio de Janeiro 1990–93, Naples 1993–97, ret; hon citizen State of Rio de Janeiro Brazil 1993; memb London Business Sch Alumni Assoc; *Style*— Miss Pat Kelly, MBE; ✉ Greystones, Dovedale End, Blockley, Gloucestershire GL56 9HQ

KELLY, Peter; *b* 1931; *Educ* Loxford Central Sch Ilford, West Ham Sch of Art and Technol, Central Sch of Art and Design; *Career* artist; Nat Serv Royal Signals 1950–52; graphic designer 1952–57, painter and illustrator 1957–; cmmns from numerous British and foreign companies and galleries; RBA 1982 (ARBA 1980); *Solo Exhibitions* Hallam Gallery London, John Adams Fine Art London; *Two-Man Exhibitions* Llewelyn Alexander Gallery London, John Adams Fine Art London, Adam Gallery Bath; *Group Exhibitions* incl: Waterman Fine Art, Mall Gallery, Westminster Central Hall, Roy Miles Gallery, RA Summer Exhbn, Royal Soc of Portrait Painters; *Awards* Laing Competition (5 times), Berol Drawing Prize, painting prize Beecroft Gallery Essex, Pro Arte Brush Award, RBA Daler Rowney Award, Higgs & Hill Bursary, Artist Magazine Drawing Prize, De Lazlo Medal 1997, Jeffrey Archer Prize; *Style*— Peter Kelly, Esq; ✉ c/o Llewellyn Alexander Ltd, 124–126 The Cut, London SE1 8LN

KELLY, Philip John; s of William Kelly (d 1979), of Crosby, Merseyside, and Mary Winifred, *née* Ellison (d 2006); *b* 18 September 1946; *Educ* St Mary's Coll Crosby, Univ of Leeds (BA); *m* 12 Nov 1988, Dorothy Margaret Jones; 2 s (Matthew b 1980, Robert b 1986); *Career* freelance journalist and PR conslt 1970–87; co-fndr: Leveller 1976, State Research 1977; ed Tribune 1987–91; advsr and press offr to Michael Meacher, MP (Shadow Sec of State for Social Security) 1991; journalist and political conslt 1992–98, dir Butler Kelly Ltd 1998–; chm London Freelance Branch NUJ 1983; cncllr (Lab) London Borough of Islington 1984–86, 1990–98 and 2006–; Parly candidate (Lab) Surrey SW 1992; *Recreations* railways, model railways; *Clubs* Red Rose; *Style*— Philip Kelly, Esq; ✉ 56 Windsor Road, London N7 6JL (tel 020 3008 8527, e-mail philk@butlerkellyltd.co.uk)

KELLY, Ruth Maria; PC (2004), MP; da of Bernard James Kelly, and Gertrude Anne Kelly; *b* 9 May 1968; *Educ* Sutton HS, Westminster, The Queen's Coll Oxford (BA), LSE (MSc); *m* 1 June 1996, Derek John Gadd, s of late Frederick Gadd; 1 s (Eamonn Frederick b 26 May 1997), 3 da (Sinéad Maria Constance b 10 July 1998, Roisin Joyce Maud b 13 Aug 2000, Niamh Anne Kathleen b 20 May 2003); *Career* econs writer The Guardian 1990–94, economist Bank of England 1994–97 (dep head Inflation Report Div 1994–96, mangr financial stability 1996–97); MP (Lab) Bolton W 1997–; PPS to Rt Hon Nicholas Brown MP, *qv*, 1998–2001, econ sec to HM Treasy 2001–02, fin sec to HM Treasy 2002–04, min of state Cabinet Office 2004, sec of state for educn 2004–06, sec of state for the community and local govt 2006–07, min for women 2006–07, sec of state for tport 2007–; elected to the Royal Economic Soc Cncl 1999–2001, memb House of Commons Treasy Select Ctee 1997–98; memb: Fabian Soc, Cncl of Mgmnt Nat Inst for Econ and Social Research 1998–2001; Minister to Watch Zurich/Spectator Parly Awards 2001; *Publications* Taxing the Speculator (1993), Hedging your Futures (co-author, 1994), The Wrecker's Lamp (co-author, 1994), The Case for a Universal Payment - chapter 3 in Time Off With The Children: Paying For Parental Leave (1999), Europe - chapter 8 in Beyond 2000: Long-Term Policies for Labour (1999), Reforming the Working Family Tax Credit: How an Integrated Child Credit Could Work for Children and Families (2000), New Gender Agenda (contrib chapter, 2000), The Progressive Century (contrib chapter, 2001); *Recreations* walking, family; *Style*— The Rt Hon Ruth Kelly, MP; ✉ House of Commons, London SW1A 0AA (tel 020 7219 3000)

KELLY, Dr William Francis; s of William Francis Kelly (d 1951), of Wolverhampton, and Lilian Rose, *née* Foister (d 1986); *b* 16 June 1942; *Educ* Royal Wolverhampton Sch, Univ of London (BSc), St Mary's Med Sch London (MB BS, MD); *m* 21 Aug 1971, Miranda Jane, da of Leonard Oscar Goddard, of Wonersh, Surrey; 1 s (Adam John William b 1974), 1 da (Juliet Miranda b 1977 d 1995); *Career* qualified CA 1964 (resigned 1972); consult physician S Tees Acute Hosps 1983–2006 (chm Sr Med Staff Ctee 1990–93); clinical lectr Univ of Newcastle 1988 (hon sr lectr 1998–), hon lectr Univ of Durham 2006–; author of articles in endocrine and diabetic jls, editorial asst Clinical Endocrinology 1986–93, memb Editorial Bd Cinical Endocrinology 1994–97; chm Northern Region Advsy Gp for Diabetes 1993–96; examiner RCP 1998; memb: Br Diabetic Assoc 1976 (pres S Tees Branch), Endocrine Section RSM 1978–98, FRCP 1989 (MRCP 1975), FRCP(Ed) 1996; *Recreations* walking, literature, photography; *Style*— Dr William Kelly; ✉ tel 01287 624192

KELMAN, Alistair Bruce; s of James Bruce Edward Kelman (d 1983), of London, and Florence Gwendoline, *née* Cutts (d 1987); *b* 11 August 1952; *Educ* Haberdashers' Aske's, Univ of Birmingham (BSc); *m* 2 Sept 1978, Diana Elizabeth, da of Prof Joseph Tinsley, of Aberdeen; *Career* called to the Bar Middle Temple 1977; specialist in computer law 1979–2000; litigation: R v Bedworth (computer addiction defence) 1993, McConville v Barclays and others (group action against UK banks over phantom withdrawals from automatic teller machines) 1993, IBCOS v Poole and Barclays (software copyright in the UK) 1994; currently working and advising on computer related problems, electronic commerce, distance learning and broadband satellite technol; visiting fell LSE Computer Security Research Centre 1994–; head of legal content to Epoq Software Ltd 2002; reviewer ESPRIT multimedia projects for EC 1989–96; fndr memb Parly Info Technol Ctee House of Commons; AMBCS 1982, ACIArb 1986; *Books* The Computer in Court (with R Sizer, 1982), Computer Fraud in Small Businesses (1985), E-Commerce: Law and Practice (with M Chissick, 1999, 3 edn 2001); *Recreations* writing; *Style*— Alistair Kelman; ✉ 37 Station Road, Hendon, London NW4 4PN (tel 020 8202 8215, fax 0870 706 0458, e-mail ali.kelman@gmail.com)

KELNAR, Prof Christopher John Harvey; s of Dr John Kelnar (d 1979), of London, and Rose, *née* Stoller (d 1992); *b* 22 December 1947; *Educ* Highgate Sch, Trinity Coll Cambridge (MA, MB BChir, MD), Bart's Med Coll London (DCH); *m* Alison Frances, da of Dr Ernst Adolf Schott (d 1984); 2 da (Clare Deborah Rosemary b 5 April 1976, Rachel Catherine Ruth b 9 May 1978), 1 s (David John Samuel b 12 June 1981); *Career* successively registrar in paediatrics rising to research fell in paediatric endocrinology Middx Hosp London, sr paediatric registrar Hosp for Sick Children Great Ormand St, clinical tutor Inst of Child Health London 1976–83, conslt paediatrician, endocrinologist and diabetologist Royal Hosp for Sick Children Edinburgh, prof Dept of Child Life and Health Univ of Edinburgh 1983–; vice-chm Scottish Intercollegiate Guideline Network (SIGN) 2002–, chm Clinical Fellowship Programme Euro Soc for Paediatric Endocrinology 2002–; post doctoral fell in Edocinology: Human Reproductive Sciences Unit Edinburgh, Oregon Health Sciences Univ USA 1999–2000; memb: Educn, Audit, Research and Symposium Ctees RCPEd, Exec Ctee Surveillance Unit Royal Coll of Paediatrics and Child Health; Sydney Watson Smith and Charles McNeil lectr RCPEd; pres-elect and memb Cncl European Soc for Paediatric Endocrinology (also chair Clinical Fellowship Ctee, memb Scientific Ctee 1995); memb Scientific Ctees: Euro Soc for Paediatric Research Edinburgh 1993, Int Colloquium on Growth and Growth Disorders Pisa 1994; memb: Br Soc for Paediatric Endocrinology and Diabetes; FRCPEd 1985, FRCP, FRCPCH; *Books* The Sick Newborn Baby (with D R Harvey, 1981, 3 edn 1995), Childhood and Adolescent Diabetes (ed, 1995), Growth Disorders - Pathophysiology and Treatment (2 edn 2007); contrib chapters to other med books and author of over 100 reviews and original scientific papers; *Recreations* music, gardening; *Style*— Prof Christopher Kelnar; ✉ 9 Easter Belmont Road, Edinburgh EH12 6EX (tel 0131 337 3195); Department of Child Life and Health, University of Edinburgh, 20 Sylvan Place, Edinburgh EH9 1UW (tel 0131 536 0611, fax 0131 536 0821, e-mail chris@kelnar.com)

KELNER, Simon; *b* 9 December 1957; *Educ* Bury GS, Preston Poly; *Career* trainee reporter Neath Guardian 1976–79, sports reporter Extel 1979–80, sports ed Kent Evening Post 1980–83, asst sports ed The Observer 1983–86, dep sports ed The Independent 1986–89; sports ed: Sunday Correspondent 1989–90, The Observer 1990–91; ed Observer Magazine 1991–93 (Magazine of the Year 1992), sports ed Independent on Sunday 1993–95 (launched first national sports section); The Independent: night ed 1995, features ed 1995–96; ed Night & Day magazine Mail on Sunday 1996–98, ed-in-chief The Independent 1998–; hon fell Univ of Central Lancashire; *Awards* Editor of the Year What the Papers Say Awards 1999 and 2003, The Edgar Wallace Award 2000, Newspaper of the Year Br Press Awards 2004, Newspaper of the Year What the Papers Say Awards 2004, GQ Editor of the Year GQ Awards 2004, Media Achiever of the Year Campaign Media Awards 2004, Marketeer of the Year Marketing Week Effectiveness Awards 2004. Newspaper of the Year London Press Club 2004; *Publications* To Jerusalem and Back (1996); *Style*— Simon Kelner, Esq; ✉ The Independent, Independent House, 191 Marsh Wall, London E14 9RS (tel 020 7005 2000, fax 020 7005 2022)

KELSALL, John Arthur Brooks; s of Joseph Brooks Kelsall, of Broome, Suffolk, and Dorothy, *née* Bee; *b* 18 June 1943; *Educ* Royal GS Lancaster, Emmanuel Coll Cambridge (MA); *m* 7 Aug 1965, Dianne Scott, da of Rev William Woodward; 1 s (Jeremy Scott b 24 March 1967), 1 da (Rebecca Jane b 25 July 1969); *Career* head of economics King Edward VII Sch Lytham St Annes 1965–68, head of geography Whitgift Sch Croydon 1968–78; headmaster: Bournemouth Sch 1980–87 (dep headmaster 1978–80), Arnold Sch Blackpool 1987–93, Brentwood Sch 1993–2004; Freeman City of London, Liveryman Worshipful Co of Needlemakers; *Recreations* hill walking, opera, ornithology, golf; *Clubs* Royal Lytham & St Annes Golf; *Style*— John Kelsall, Esq; ✉ Hill View House, Laxfield Road, Fressingfield, Suffolk IP21 5PY (tel 01379 588099)

KELSALL, Prof Malcolm Miles; s of Alec James Kelsall, and Hetty May, *née* Miles; *b* 27 February 1938; *Educ* William Hulme's GS Manchester, Brasenose Coll Oxford (state scholar, MA, Sr Hulme scholar, BLitt); *m* 5 Aug 1961, Mary Emily, da of George Hurley Ives (d 1978); *Career* staff reporter The Guardian 1961, asst lectr Univ of Exeter 1963–64, lectr Univ of Reading 1964–75, prof and head English Dept UC Cardiff 1975–88, prof Univ of Wales Cardiff 1988–2005 (emeritus prof 2005–); visiting prof: Univ of Paris 1978,

K

Univ of Hiroshima 1979, Univ of Wisconsin 1996; visiting scholar in residence Int Center for Jefferson Studies 1997; advsy ed: The Byron Journal, Litteraria Pragensia; memb: Mgmnt Ctee Welsh Nat Drama Co 1976–77, Int Advsy Bd Messolonghi Byron Soc; *Books* Sarah Fielding's David Simple (ed, 1969), Thomas Otway's Venice Preserved (ed, 1969), William Congreve's Love for Love (ed, 1969), Joseph Trapp's Lectures on Poetry (ed, 1973), JM Synge's The Playboy of the Western World (ed 1975), Christopher Marlowe (1981), Congreve: The Way of the World (1981), Joseph Trapp's The Preface to the Aeneis (ed 1982), Studying Drama (1985), Byron's Politics (1987, awarded Elma Dangerfield prize, 1991), Encyclopedia of Literature and Criticism (ed, 1990), The Great Good Place: The Country House and English Literature (1992), British Academy Warton Lecture (1992), Jefferson and the Iconography of Romanticism (1999), Literary Representations of the Irish Country House (2003), Marchand Lecture (2005); *Recreations* theatre, long distance walking; *Style*— Prof Emeritus Malcolm Kelsall; ✉ 17 Withyholt Park, Charlton Kings, Gloucestershire GL53 9BP (tel 01242 530335)

KELSEY, Alan Howard Mitchell; s of Emanuel Kelsey (d 1985), of London, and Dorothy Mitchell, *née* Smith; *b* 10 April 1949; *Educ* KCS Wimbledon, Oriel Coll Oxford (MA); *m* 12 March 1977, Sarah D'Oyly, da of Robin Carlyle Sayer, of Little Walsingham, Norfolk; 1 da (Keziah b 19 Jan 1978), 2 s (Guy b 22 Feb 1980, William b 27 July 1981); *Career* Kitcat & Aitken: tport investment analyst 1975–88, head of res 1987–89, head of corp fin 1989–90; dir: RBC Dominion Securities International 1988–91, RBC Dominion Securities Inc 1989–91, Merrill Lynch International (formerly Smith New Court) 1992–96; gp dir of corporate devpt National Express Group plc 1996–98; md and global head of Tport Industry Gp WestLB Panmure 1999–, co-head corp broking WestLB Panmure 2001–; chm local Cons Assoc 1985–88, memb Cncl Soc of Investment Analysts 1986–88; assoc IIM, MSI (dip), FCIT; *Recreations* fishing; *Clubs* Brooks's; *Style*— Alan Kelsey, Esq; ✉ The Priory, Little Waldingfield, Suffolk CO10 0SW (tel 01787 247335); Flat 19, Tennyson House, 7 Culford Gardens, London SW3 2XS (tel 020 7584 4238); WestLB Panmure Limited, New Broad Street House, 35 New Broad Street, London EC2M 1SQ (tel 020 7444 6410)

KELSEY, Linda; da of Samuel Cohen, and Rhona, *née* Fox, of London; *b* 15 April 1952; *Educ* Woodhouse GS, Univ of Warwick; *m* 1972 (m dis 1980); partner Christian Testorf; 1 s (Thomas Testorf b 1988); *Career* trainee sub ed Good Housekeeping 1970–72, sub ed, asst features ed then features ed Cosmopolitan 1972–78; dep ed Company Magazine 1978–81, dep ed Options Magazine 1981–82, ed Cosmopolitan 1985–89 (dep ed 1982–85), ed SHE Magazine 1989–95, ed-at-large Nat Magazine Co 1996–; chair Br Soc of Magazine Editors 1987 (memb), memb Women's Financial Forum 1993; Editor of the Year award for Cosmopolitan Periodical Publishers Assoc 1989, Women's Magazine Editor of the Year award for SHE Br Soc of Magazine Editors 1990; *Recreations* family, reading, trekking, walking; *Clubs* Groucho, RAC; *Style*— Ms Linda Kelsey; ✉ c/o National Magazine Co, 72 Broadwick House, London W1F 9EP

KELSEY-FRY, John; QC (2000); s of Dr Ian Kelsey-Fry, and Mary Josephine, *née* Fitzpatrick-Casey; *m* 29 July 2000, Sally Halkerston, da of Rod Muddle; *Career* called to the Bar Gray's Inn 1978; sr treasury counsel Central Criminal Court 1997–2000 (jr 1992–97); *Recreations* horseracing, golf; *Style*— John Kelsey-Fry, Esq, QC; ✉ Cloth Fair Chambers, 39–40 Cloth Fair, London EC1A 7NR (tel 07875 012444)

KELTON, Michael John St Goar; s of Gerald St Goar Kelton (d 1972), and Beatrice Millicent (d 1993), da of J B Body (md S Pearson & Co, responsible for many engrg devpts in Mexico *ca* 1900 incl: draining of Valley of Mexico, construction of Vera Cruz harbour, founding Mexican Eagle Oil Co); *b* 25 March 1933; *Educ* Stowe, Queens' Coll Cambridge (MA); *m* 19 June 1958, Joanna Elizabeth, da of Sir (William) John Peel, MP (Cons) Leicester SE 1957–74; 3 s (Jeremy b 1960, Andrew b 1961, Simon b 1966); *Career* Capt 3 Carabiniers (now Royal Scots Dragoon Gds); merchant banker Lazard Bros and Co Ltd 1957–; dir: Lazard Securities until 1971, Raphael Zorn Hemsley Ltd 1976–98, Matheson Investment Ltd 1998–99, Prudential Bache Ltd 1999–2004; ret; *Recreations* shooting, fishing, golf; *Clubs* Cavalry and Guards', Flyfishers', Hankley Common Golf; *Style*— Michael Kelton, Esq; ✉ Pipers Well, Churt, Farnham, Surrey GU10 2NT (tel 01428 713194)

KEMBALL, Christopher Ross Maguire; MBE (Mil 1973); s of John Patrick Gerard Kemball (d 2003), of Vila Praia De Ancora, Portugal, and Rachel Lucy, *née* Vernon; *b* 29 December 1946; *Educ* Ampleforth, Pembroke Coll Cambridge (BA); *m* 3 Feb 1979, Frances Maria, da of Flt Lt Richard Peter Monico, RAF (d 1945); 1 s (Charles b 1983); *Career* Regular Army Capt (actg Maj) Royal Green Jackets 1968–75, Sultan's Armed Forces, Maj Northern Frontier Regt 1972–73; dir Kleinwort Benson Ltd 1975–86, vice-chm Kleinwort Benson Hldgs Inc 1984–86, md Dillon Read & Co Inc 1986–91, exec md and co-head Dillon Read Ltd 1987–91, head of corp fin (emerging markets Euro region) and dir Baring Brothers & Co Ltd (now ING Barings) 1992–98, md corp fin ING Barings 1999–2000, vice-chm Hawkpoint Partners Ltd 2000–, chm The Davis Service Gp plc 2005– (non-exec dir 1998–); non-exec dir: Control Risks Gp Ltd 1998–; *Recreations* opera, swimming, skiing, shooting, sailing, beekeeping; *Clubs* Royal Green Jackets, Brooks's, RAC; *Style*— Christopher Kemball, Esq, MBE; ✉ Hawkpoint Partners Ltd, 41 Lothbury, London EC2R 7AE (tel 020 7665 4500)

KEMBALL, Air Marshal Sir John; KCB (1990), CBE (1981), DL (Suffolk 1999); s of Richard Charles Kemball (d 1983), of Suffolk, and Margaret James, *née* Robson (d 1987); *b* 31 January 1939; *Educ* Uppingham, Open Univ (BA, 1990); *m* 1962, Valerie Geraldine, da of Maj Albert John Webster, RA (d 1998); 2 da (Katherine b 1964, Samantha b 1966); *Career* cmmnd RAF 1957, served UK, France, Middle East, USA, cmd No 54 Sqdn 1976–78, RAF Laarbruch 1978–81, Cmdt RAF Central Flying Sch 1983–85, Cdr Br Forces Falkland Islands 1985–86, Chief of Staff and dep C-in-C Strike Cmd 1989–93, ADC to HM The Queen 1984–85, co-ordinator Br-American Community Rels MOD 1994–2004; chief exec Racing Welfare 1995–2004, pres Corp of Commissionaires; memb ICL Def Advsy Bd 1996–2000; chm Essex Rivers NHS Healthcare Tst 1993–96; pres RAF Assoc 1995–98 (life vice-pres); Hon Col 77 Regt RE (V) 1993–96; High Sheriff Suffolk 2007–08; Freeman City of London 1995; FRAeS 2003; *Recreations* riding, gardening; *Clubs* RAF; *Style*— Air Marshal Sir John Kemball, KCB, CBE, DL, FRAeS

KEMBERY, John Philip; s of Alec George Kembery, of Keynsham, Somerset; *b* 6 October 1939; *Educ* Queen Elizabeth's Hosp Bristol, Univ of Surrey; *m* 1964, Marjorie Carolyn, da of Gilbert James Bowler, of Much Cowarne, Herefords; 2 s (Jonathan Alexander b 1967, Nicholas Philip b 1969); *Career* md: Alcan Extrusions 1975–80, Alcan Metal Centres 1980–81; chm: McKechnie Metals non-ferrous metal mfrs (md 1981–87), PSM Int plc, EADIE IND Ltd 2001–; dir and chm Metals and Engrg Divs McKechnie plc 1986–92, business conslt and chm MW Technologies 1992–95; exec chm Belgravium Technologies plc (formerly Eadie Holdings plc) 1997– (dir 1996–); non-exec chm: Wheelpower International 1993–94, Black and Luff Holdings Ltd 1994–98, Sunleigh plc 1995–98; non-exec dir: Trigon Cambridge Ltd 1993–95, Europower plc (formerly Brasway plc) 1994–2000, Crosrol Ltd 1995–, Trigon Packaging Systems (Europe) Ltd, Trigon Packaging Systems (UK) Ltd; pres Br Non-Ferrous Metals Fedn 1988–90; CEng, FIM, FInstD; *Recreations* golf, shooting, good food; *Style*— John Kembery, Esq; ✉ 12 Parkfields, Arden Drive, Dorridge, West Midlands B93 8LL (tel 01564 730168, fax 01564 778057, mobile 07770 731021, e-mail john@kembery.net)

KEMM, John Robert; s of Rupert St John Kemm (d 1979), and Katherine Morva Kemm (d 1983); *b* 12 March 1944; *Educ* Blundell's, Sidney Sussex Coll Cambridge (MA), St Thomas' Hosp Med Sch (MD); *m* 1969, Catherine Mary Gaze; 1 da (Emma Jane b 1972), 1 s (Jeremy Robert b 1974); *Career* lectr in physiology Univ of Newcastle upon Tyne 1969–75, reader in physiology Univ of Khartoum Sudan 1975–77, lectr in community health Univ of Nottingham 1977–83, sr lectr in public health and epidemiology Univ of Birmingham and hon conslt in public health med Central Birmingham HA 1983–94, conslt in Public Health Med S Birmingham HA 1994–96, dir of public health Health Promotion Wales 1996–99, conslt in public health med Gwent HA 1999–2000, conslt in public health med Govt Office for the W Midlands, dep regnl dir of public health, currently dir W Midlands Public Health Observatory; memb: Bd Alcohol Concern, Alcohol Educn and Research Cncl; FFCM 1988 (MFCM 1982), FRCP 1992 (MRCP 1973); *Books* Alcohol and the Public Health (1991), Promotion of Healthier Eating (with D Booth, 1992), Health Promotion Principles and Practice (with A Close, 1995), Health Impact Assessment: Concept, Theory, Techniques and Applications (with J Parry and S Palmer, 2004); *Style*— Dr John Kemm; ✉ West Midlands Public Health Observatory, Birmingham Research Park, Vincent Drive, Edgbaston, Birmingham B15 2SQ (tel 0121 414 8190, e-mail john.kemm@wmpho.org.uk)

KEMP, Alan Scott; s of Alexander Scott Kemp (d 1968), of Edinburgh, and Christina Margaret, *née* Stocks (d 1965); *b* 2 April 1944; *Educ* George Heriot's Sch Edinburgh; *m* 9 Dec 1967, June, da of John Christie (d 1986), of Edinburgh; 2 s (Graeme, Martin); *Career* dep mangr The Edinburgh Investment Trust plc 1974–84, dep chief exec Dunedin Fund Managers Ltd 1990–95 (investment dir 1985–90); currently dir Aberdeen Asian Smaller Cos Investment Tst plc; memb Murrayfield and Cramond Rotary Club; MICAS; *Recreations* golf; *Style*— Alan Kemp, Esq

KEMP, Prof Bruce Ernest; s of Norman Beck Kemp (d 1956), and Mary Frances, *née* Officer; *b* 15 December 1946, Sydney, Aust; *Educ* Univ of Adelaide (BAgrSc), Flinders Univ (PhD); *m* 23 Jan 1970, Alison Virginia; 3 s (Robert E S b 18 May 1977, William E B b 12 March 1980, Charles E F b 9 March 1983); *Career* postdoctoral fell Sch of Med Univ of Calif Davis 1974–76, Nat Heart Fndn fell Flinders Med Centre 1977–78; Univ of Melbourne: Queen Elizabeth II fell Howard Florey Inst 1979, sr research fell Howard Florey Inst 1980–84, sr research fell Repatriation Gen Hosp Heidelberg Victoria 1984–88, fed fell CSIRO Health Science and Nutrition, Pehr Edman fell St Vincent's Inst of Med Research 1989–2003, currently professorial assoc St Vincent's Hosp Victoria; research collaboration with Agen Biomedical 1987–99, memb Scientific Advsy Bd Besagen (formerly Bresatec Pty Ltd) 1993–2003, co-fndr and memb Scientific Advsy Bd Mercury Therapeutics Inc 1999–; memb Bd Genomic Disorders Research Centre (GDRC, formerly Mutation Research Centre) 1996–2003, memb Scientific Advsy Bd and Mgmnt Ctee Nat Serology Reference Lab (NSRL) 1997–; memb Editorial Bd: Cellular Signalling 1988–, Biochim Biophys Acta 1992–97, Biochemistry Jl 1994–96, Jl of Biological Chemistry 1998–; memb: Aust Soc for Biochemistry and Molecular Biology, Aust Soc for Med Research, Aust Soc for Microbiology, AAAS; Selwyn Smith Prize for Med Research 1988, Newman Award for Excellence in AIDS Research (jtly) 1989, AIDS Tst of Aust Award 1989, Wellcome Aust Medal for Med Research and Technol Devpt 1990, Wellcome Rapid Diagnostics Award 1991, Lemberg Medal Aust Soc for Biochemistry and Molecular Biology 1996, Royal Soc of Victoria Research Medal 1996, Max Planck Award 2000, Centenary Medal 2003; FAAS 2000, FRS 2002, Fedn fell 2003; *Publications* Peptides and Protein Phosphorylation (ed, 1990); author of over 250 articles in jls and contribs and chapters to books; *Recreations* tennis; *Clubs* North Kew Tennis, Univ House (Melbourne); *Style*— Prof Bruce Kemp, FRS; ✉ St Vincent's Institute of Medical Research, 41 Victoria Parade, Fitzroy, Victoria 3065, Australia (tel 00 61 3 9288 2480, fax 00 61 3 9416 5676, e-mail bkemp@svi.edu.au)

KEMP, His Hon Judge Charles James Bowring; s of Capt Michael John Barnett Kemp, ERD (d 1982), of Winchcombe, Glos, and Brigid Ann Vernon-Smith, *née* Bowring; *b* 27 April 1951; *Educ* Shrewsbury, UCL (LLB); *m* 21 Dec 1974, Fenella Anne, da of Harry Herring (d 1995), of Cropwell Butler, Notts; 1 da (Sophie b 11 Feb 1977), 1 s (Marcus b 28 Feb 1979); *Career* called to the Bar Gray's Inn 1973; recorder 1991–98, circuit judge 1998–; memb: Sussex Probation Bd 2001–07, Sussex Courts Bd 2004; *Recreations* tennis, swimming, cricket, golf, country pursuits, music; *Style*— His Hon Judge Kemp; ✉ Lewes Combined Court Centre, 182 High Street, Lewes, East Sussex BN7 1YB (tel 01273 480400, fax 01825 724106, e-mail ckemp@lix.compulink.co.uk)

KEMP, Fraser; MP; s of William and Mary Kemp, of Washington; *b* 1 September 1958; *Educ* Washington Comp Sch; *m* 1989 (m dis), Patricia Mary, da of Patrick Joseph Byrne; 2 s (Matthew b 1992, Alexander b 1995), 1 da (Katie b 28 May 1993); *Career* civil servant 1975–81; Lab Pty: organiser Leicester 1981–84, asst regnl organiser E Midlands 1984–86, regnl sec W Midlands 1986–94, nat general election co-ordinator 1994–96; MP (Lab) Houghton and Washington E 1997–; asst Govt whip 2001–05, Lab election campaign spokesperson 2005; memb Select Ctee on Public Admin 1997–99, chair PLP Cabinet Office Ctee; *Recreations* people; *Style*— Fraser Kemp, Esq, MP; ✉ House of Commons, London SW1A 0AA (tel 020 7219 5181, constituency office 0191 584 9266, fax 0191 584 8329)

KEMP, Gene; da of Albert Rushton, of Tamworth, Staffs, and Alice Anne, *née* Sutton; *Educ* Wigginton C of E Sch, Tamworth Girls' HS, Univ of Exeter (BA); *m* 1 (m dis), Norman Charles Pattison, s of Charles Pattison; m 2, Allan William Kemp, s of late William Kemp; 1 s (Richard William), 2 da (Judith Eve, Chantal Jennifer); *Career* author; teacher: Wychbury HS Hagley, Drewsteignton CP Sch, St Sidwell's Combined Sch Exeter, Rolle Coll; govr: Central and Middle Schs Exeter 1975–85, Montgomery Sch Exeter 1994–96, St Sidwell's Sch Exeter 2001–04; memb: Lab Pty, Soc of Authors; Hon MA Univ of Exeter 1984; *Awards* The Other Award 1977, Carnegie Medal 1978; shortlisted: Whitbread Award 1985, Smarties Award 1986 and 1990; *Books* incl: Tamworth Pig Stories, Cricklepit Combined School Stories (incl The Turbulent Term of Tyke Tiler, Gowie Corby Plays Chicken and Just Ferret), The Well, Dog Days and Cat Naps (short stories), Mr Magus is Waiting for You (TV drama), Ducks and Dragons (poetry, ed), The Mink War (narrative poem), Roundabout, Puffin Book of Ghosts and Ghouls, The Wacky World of Wesley Baker, Zowey Corby's Story (fiction), Goosey Farm, Rebel, Rebel (anthology), Goosey Farm: The Wishing Tower, Bluebeard's Castle, Snaggletooth's Mystery, Seriously Weird, Haunted Piccolo, Nothing Scares Me; *Recreations* gardening, politics, reading, grandchildren; *Style*— Mrs Gene Kemp; ✉ c/o Philippa Milnes-Smith, Lucas Alexander Whitley Ltd, 14 Vernon Street, London W14 0RJ (tel 020 7471 7900); c/o Faber & Faber Ltd, 3 Queen Square, London WC1N 3AU (tel 020 7465 0045, fax 020 7465 0034); c/o Puffin, 27 Wrights Lane, London W8 5TZ (tel 020 7416 3000, fax 020 7416 3099); c/o Orchard Books, 96 Leonard Street, London EC2A 4XD (tel 020 7739 2929); e-mail genekemp6@aol.com

KEMP, (Edmund) Jeremy James; s of Edmund Reginald Walker (d 1994), of Felixstowe, Suffolk, and Elsa May, *née* Kemp (d 1983); *b* 3 February 1935; *Educ* Abbotsholme Sch, Central Sch of Speech and Drama (Dip Dramatic Art); *Career* actor; Nat Serv 1953–55, served Duke of Wellington Regt, cmmnd 2 Lt 1 Bn Gordon Highlanders; memb of Br Actors Equity Cncl for 5 years; *Theatre* Old Vic 1958–60, Nottingham Playhouse, West End, NT; plays incl: Celebration, Arthur Miller's Incident at Vichy, Simon Gray's Spoiled, Richard III (Buckingham); *Television* incl: Bob Steele in Z-Cars (original cast), Sqdn Ldr Shaw in Colditz, Warwick in St Joan, Leontes in The Winters Tale, Norfolk in Henry VIII, Peter the Great, Winds of War, War and Remembrance (US TV); *Films* over thirty films incl: Operation Crossbow, The Blue Max, Darling Lili; *Recreations* course games, cricket, golf, skiing, walking, natural history; *Style*— Jeremy Kemp, Esq; ✉ 29 Britannia Road, London SW6 2HJ; 17025 Empanada Drive, Encino, California 91436, USA (tel 00

1 818 981 3707); c/o French & Gordon, 12–13 Poland Street, London W1V 3DE (tel 020 7734 4818, fax 020 7734 4832)

KEMP, Kit; da of William Henry Thomas (d 1982), and Stella Gould (d 1999); *b* 29 November 1956, Southampton; *m* 6 July 1983, Timothy J R Kemp; 3 da (Tiffany b 28 Feb 1986, Willow b 19 Oct 1987, Araminta b 26 July 1990); *Career* interior designer; early career working in architectural practice, then started own design co; opened (with Tim Kemp) Dorset Square Hotel London 1985, co-fndr (with Tim Kemp) Firmdale Hotels 1986–; hotels incl: The Soho Hotel, Charlotte Street Hotel, Covent Garden Hotel, The Pelham Hotel, Knightsbridge Hotel, Number Sixteen, Haymarket Hotel; numerous design and hotel awards, Queen's Award 2000 and 2006, Crown Estate Urban Business Award 2007; *Recreations* riding, horses; *Style*— Mrs Kit Kemp; ✉ Firmdale Hotels, 18 Thurloe Place, London SW7 2SP (tel 020 7581 4045, e-mail kitk@firmdale.com)

KEMP, Prof Martin John; s of Frederick Maurice Kemp (d 1990), of Watton, Norfolk, and Violet Anne, *née* Tull; *b* 5 March 1942; *Educ* Windsor GS, Downing Coll Cambridge (MA), Courtauld Inst of Art London; *m* 27 Aug 1966 (m dis 2005), Jill, da of Dennis William Lightfoot, of Bisham, Bucks; 1 da (Joanna b 1972), 1 s (Jonathan b 1976); *Career* lectr in history of western art Dalhousie Univ Nova Scotia 1965, lectr in fine arts Univ of Glasgow 1966–81; Univ of St Andrews: prof of fine arts 1981–90, memb Ct 1988–91, prof of the history and theory of art 1991–95, provost St Leonard's Coll 1991–94; prof of history of art Univ of Oxford 1995–; memb Inst for Advanced Study Princeton 1984–85, Slade prof Univ of Cambridge 1987–88, Benjamin Sonenberg visiting prof Inst of Fine Arts NYU, Wiley prof Univ of N Carolina Chapel Hill 1993, Br Acad Wolfson research prof 1993–98, visiting scholar Getty Research Inst LA 2002–, Mellon research fell Canadian Centre for Architecture Montreal 2004; tstee: Nat Galleries of Scotland 1982–87, V&A 1986–89, Br Museum 1995; hon prof of history Royal Scottish Acad 1985–, pres Leonardo da Vinci Soc 1987–96, chm Assoc of Art Historians 1989–92, memb Exec Scottish Museums Cncl 1990–96, dir and chm Graeme Murray Gallery 1990–92; dir: Interalia Bristol 1992–, Museums Training Inst 1993–99, Wallace Kemp/Artakt 2001–; memb Cncl Br Soc for the History of Science 1994–97; fell Downing Coll Cambridge 1999; Hon DLitt Heriot-Watt Univ 1995; hon memb American Acad of Arts and Sciences 1996; FRSA 1983–98, HRSA 1985, FRIAS 1988, FBA 1991, FRSE 1992; *Books* incl: The Science of Art - Optical Themes in Western Art from Brunelleschi to Seurat, Behind The Picture - Art and Evidence in the Italian Renaissance, The Oxford History of Western Art, Visualizations, The 'Nature' Book of Art and Science, Spectacular Bodies (with Marina Wallace), Leonardo; *Recreations* sport (especially hockey); *Style*— Prof Martin Kemp, FBA, FRSE; ✉ Trinity College, Oxford OX1 3BH

KEMP, (Bernard) Peter; s of William Gordon Kemp, of Chorley, Lancs, and Teresa, *née* Howarth; *b* 16 October 1942; *Educ* Thornleigh Coll Bolton, King's Coll London (BA, MPhil); *Career* lectr in English Middx Poly 1968–88; regular book reviewer: The Listener 1978–91, TLS 1980– (weekly TV and radio column 1982–86); fiction ed and chief fiction reviewer Sunday Times 1995– (regular fiction reviewer 1987–95); theatre reviewer The Independent 1986–90; regular broadcaster on: Front Row, Saturday Review, Night Waves, Open Book; *Books* Muriel Spark (1974), H G Wells and The Culminating Ape (1982, 2 edn 1996), The Oxford Dictionary of Literary Quotations (ed, 1997, 2 edn 2003); *Recreations* travel, art galleries, music, gardening; *Style*— Peter Kemp, Esq; ✉ The Sunday Times, 1 Pennington Street, London E1 9XW (tel 020 7782 5777, fax 020 7782 5798, e-mail peter.kemp@sunday-times.co.uk)

KEMP, Richard Harry; s of Thomas Kemp, and Audrey, *née* Withers (d 1965); *b* 7 July 1956, Romford, Essex; *Educ* Oakham Sch, St Catharine's Coll Cambridge (MA), Université Libre de Bruxelles; *m* 20 June 1987, Margaret, *née* Wade; 2 s (Christopher b 26 Feb 1988, Nicholas b 6 May 1990); *Career* admitted slr 1980; with Clifford-Turner 1978–84, with Hopkins & Wood 1984–91 (ptnr 1985), ptnr and co-fndr London office Hammond Suddards 1992–95, ptnr Garretts 1995–97 (first head European intellectual property/IT practice 1996), fndr and managing ptnr Kemp & Co 1997–2001 (ldr Legal Business Technol Team of the Year 2002), fndr Kemp Little LLP 2001; memb Bd Computer Law Assoc 2002–06; memb Law Soc; *Clubs* Hurlingham; *Style*— Richard Kemp, Esq; ✉ Kemp Little LLP, Cheapside House, Cheapside, London EC2V 6BR (tel 020 7710 1610, fax 020 7600 7878, e-mail richard.kemp@kemplittle.com)

KEMP, Prof Roger John; s of late Ivor Kemp, and Audrey, *née* Hobbs; *b* 18 December 1945; *Educ* Hitchin GS, Univ of Sussex (BSc); *m* 3 Aug 1968, Joan Caroline, da of Kenneth and Winifred Walker (both decd); 1 da (Deborah Rachael b 29 Oct 1971), 1 s (Nicholas Ian b 15 Dec 1972); *Career* electrical and mechanical engr; science teacher Malaysia VSO 1964–65, various engrg appts 1969–85, engrg dir GEC Transportation Projects Ltd Manchester 1985–89, directeur des Études d'Ensemble GEC Alsthom SA Paris 1989–91, project dir Eurostar Paris 1991–93, safety dir ALSTOM Transport 2000–03, prof of engrg Lancaster Univ 2003– (visiting prof 1998–2003); memb various professional ctees and author of numerous papers in various professional jls; CEng, FIEE, FIMechE, FREng 1995; *Recreations* playing double bass, music, theatre; *Style*— Prof Roger Kemp, FREng; ✉ Engineering Department, Lancaster University, Lancaster LA1 4YW (e-mail r.kemp@lancaster.ac.uk)

KEMP, Ross; s of John Kemp, of Norfolk, and Jean Kemp; *b* 21 July 1964, Essex; *Educ* Webber Douglas Theatre Sch; *m* 11 June 2002, Rebekah Wade, *qv*; *Career* actor; *Theatre* early career at Westcliffe-on-Sea Rep Theatre; roles incl Petruchio in Taming of the Shrew; *Television* incl: Emmerdale Farm 1986–87, Birds of a Feather 1989, EastEnders (as Grant Mitchell) 1990–99 and 2005 (Best Actor Br Soap Awards 1999), City Central 1998, Hero of the Hour 2000, Without Motive 2000, In Defence 2000, A Christmas Carol 2000, Ultimate Force I, II and III 2002 and 2005, The Crooked Man 2003, A Line in the Sand 2004, Spartacus 2004, Lethal Attraction 2004; *Clubs* Chelsea Arts; *Style*— Ross Kemp, Esq; ✉ c/o Michael Foster, ARG, 4 Great Portland Street, London W1W 8PA

KEMP, Prof Terence James; s of Thomas Brynmor Kemp (d 1978), and Emily Maud, *née* Spriggs (d 1982); *b* 26 June 1938; *Educ* Cardiff HS, Watford GS, Jesus Coll Oxford (MA, DPhil, DSc); *m* 8 April 1961, Sheila Therese, da of Henry Francis Turner (d 1972); 1 s (Jeremy b 1964), 2 da (Celia b 1966, Penelope b 1969); *Career* Univ of Warwick: asst lectr 1965, lectr 1966, sr lectr 1970, reader 1974, prof 1980– (emeritus 2006–), pro-vice-chllr 1983–89, seconded pt/t to Quality Assurance Agency 1995–; specialist subject assessor HEQC 1993–95; memb Evaluation Ctee: Univ of Malta 1990, Univ of Namibia 1993, Univ of Qatar 2001; CChem, FRSC 1969, FRSA 1986; Order of Merit Polish Repub 1985; *Books* Introductory Photochemistry (1971), Dictionary of Physical Chemistry (1992); *Recreations* philately, cinema, walking; *Style*— Prof Terence Kemp; ✉ 93 Leamington Road, Coventry CV3 6GQ (tel 024 7641 4735); Department of Chemistry, University of Warwick, Coventry CV4 7AL (tel 024 7652 3235, fax 024 7652 4112, e-mail sheila@kemp.ac.uk)

KEMP-GEE, Mark Norman; s of Bernard Kemp-Gee (d 1993), and Ann, *née* MacKilligin; *b* 19 December 1945; *Educ* Marlborough, Pembroke Coll Oxford (MA); *m* 26 July 1980, Hon Lucy Lyttelton, 3 da of 10 Viscount Cobham, KG (d 1977); *Career* chm Greig Middleton & Co Ltd (stockbrokers); dir Gerrard Group plc 1975–99, chief exec Exeter Investment Gp plc 1999–2004; memb Hants CC 2005–; *Recreations* point-to-points; *Style*— Mark Kemp-Gee, Esq

KEMP-WELCH, Sir John; kt (1999); s of Peter Wellesbourne Kemp-Welch, OBE (d 1964), and Peggy Penelope, *née* Hunter; *b* 31 March 1936; *Educ* Winchester; *m* 1964, Diana Elisabeth, da of Dr A W D Leishman (d 1978); 1 s, 3 da; *Career* Hoare & Co 1954–58, Cazenove & Co 1959–94 (jt sr ptnr 1980–94); chm: Lowland Investment Co 1993–97 (dir 1963–97), Scottish Eastern Investment Trust 1994–99 (dir 1993–99), London Stock Exchange 1994–2000 (memb 1959–86, dir 1991–2000), Claridges Hotel 1995–97, Martin Currie Portfolio Investment Tst plc 1999–2000; dir: Savoy Hotel plc 1985–98, British Invisibles 1994–98, Royal & Sun Alliance Insurance Group (formerly Sun Alliance Group) 1994–99, Pro Share 1995–97, HSBC Holdings 2000–06; dep chm Financial Reporting Cncl 1994–2000, dir SFA 1994–97, dir Accountancy Fndn 2000–01; memb: City Capital Markets Ctee 1989–94, Panel on Takeovers and Mergers 1994–2000, (Lord Mayor of London's) City No 1 Consultancy 1994–2000; pres Investor Rels Soc 1994–2000, pres Securities Industry Mgmnt Assoc 1994–2000, vice-pres Fedn of European Stock Exchanges 1996–98, memb Exec Ctee Fedn Internationale des Bourses de Valeurs 1994–98; memb: Cncl London First 1994–96, Advsy Cncl PYBT 1996–2000; chm: Lucy Kemp-Welch Meml Tst 1965–, King's Med Research Tst 1991–2006 (tstee 1984–2006) tstee: Stock Exchange Benevolent Fund 1980–2000, KCH Special Tstees 1997–99, KCH Charitable Tst 1998–99, Game Conservancy Tst 1990–94 (also memb Cncl, hon research fell 1998–), Sandford St Martin Tst 1994–99, Dulverton Tst 1994– (dep chm (finance) 2001–), Farmington Tst 2002–, St Paul's Knightsbridge Fndn 2002–; vice-pres Reed's Sch 2005– (pres Financial Appeal 2003–04); govr: North Foreland Lodge Sch 1980–92, Ditchley Fndn 1980–; pres Cazenove Assoc 2005–; memb: Courtauld Inst of Art Tst, Highland Soc of London 1992–; memb Guild of Int Bankers 2004–; Joseph Nickerson Heather Award Joseph Nickerson Heather Improvement Fndn 1998; Hon DBA London Guildhall Univ 1998; CCMI (CBIM 1984), FRSA 1989, Hon FSI 1996 (MSI 1992, FSI 1996); *Recreations* the hills of Perthshire, country life, City of London history, cricket nostalgia, champagne and claret, Lucy Kemp-Welch paintings, heather moorland management; *Clubs* White's, City of London, Pilgrims, MCC, Essex; *Style*— Sir John Kemp-Welch; ✉ 4 Park Place, St James's, London SW1A 1LP

KEMSLEY, Arthur Joseph; s of Joseph Alfred Kemsley (d 1966), of Stepney, London, and Ivy Elizabeth Everet; *b* 21 May 1936; *Educ* Nicholas Gibson Secdy Sch; *m* 1967, Maureen (d 1989); 1 da (Gemma Louise b 29 Sept 1983); *Career* SAC RAF 1953–58; photographer; copy boy Advertising Dept Kemsley Newspapers 1951–52, gen asst Pathe Pictorial 1952–53; BAA (formerly Heathrow Airport Ltd): joined 1958, chief photographer 1965–89, TV prodr/dir 1989–; R&D on video-visual imaging system for recording condition and quality of runway approach lights at airports (first of its kind) 1993–95, currently working on range of aviation safety progs covering all aspects of airport ops incl digital imaging and computer based interactive trg for airport staff; dir Airside Training Co 2001; developing immersive learning for aviation airside ops using DVD interactive technol; aviation trg with Aircraft Service Int Gp 2002; trg conslt Air France Services Ltd 2005–; 2 Gold and 3 Silver Medals World Airports Photographers competition 1988, Bronze Medallion USAF (for photographing the space shuttle Discovery); memb Professional Photographers of America; MBKS, FRPS, FBIPP; *Recreations* research and development for future aviation trg; *Style*— Arthur Kemsley, Esq; ✉ Air France Services Ltd, Room 229, Terminal Two Office Block, Heathrow Airport, Middlesex TW6 1RR

KEMSLEY, 3 Viscount (UK 1945); Sir Richard Gomer Berry; 3 Bt (UK 1928); Baron Kemsley (UK 1936); s of Hon Denis Gomer Berry, TD, DL (d 1983), and his 2 w, Pamela, *née* Wellesley (d 1987); suc uncle 2 Viscount Kemsley (d 1999); *b* 17 April 1951; *Educ* Eton; *m* 1, 1981 (m dis 1988), Tana-Marie, er da of Clive William Lester, of Beaulieu, Hants; m 2, 17 Sept 1994, Elizabeth J, da of Dennis Barker, of Brockenhurst, Hants; 1 s (Hon Luke Gomer b 2 Feb 1998, Hon Jake Edward b 26 July 1999); *Heir* s, Hon Luke Berry; *Style*— The Rt Hon the Viscount Kemsley

KENCH, Eric Arthur; s of Joseph Peter Kench (d 2005), of Oxon, and Ethel Catherine, *née* Younger; *b* 30 September 1952; *Educ* Henley GS; *m* 20 July 1974, Kathleen Jennifer, da of Philip Hague (d 1980); 1 s (David b 1979), 2 da (Caroline b 1981, Sarah b 1982); *Career* chartered accountant; fndr E A Kench & Co 1982–; former chm Thames Valley Young Chartered Accountants Gp; ICAEW: memb Smaller Practitioners' Ctee 1984–90, memb Gen Practitioner Bd 1990–2000 (vice-chm 1998–2000), vice-chm Gen Practitioner Panel 2000–2003, chm Practice Soc 2004–, memb Cncl 2004–; pres Thames Valley Soc of Chartered Accountants 1987–88; FCA; *Recreations* squash, long distance cycling, flying (private pilot), reading, working; *Style*— Eric Kench, Esq; ✉ E A Kench & Co, 10 Station Road, Henley-on-Thames, Oxfordshire RG9 1AY (tel 01491 578207, e-mail erickench@kench.co.uk)

KENDAL, Felicity Anne; CBE (1995); da of Geoffrey Kendal (d 1998), of Chelsea, London, and Laura May, *née* Liddell (d 1992); *Educ* convents in India; *m* 1, 1969 (m dis 1976), Drewe Henley; 1 s (Charles b 23 Jan 1973); m 2, 1983 (m dis 1991), Michael Edward Rudman, s of Duke Rudman, of Dallas, Texas; 1 s (Jacob Henry b 1 Oct 1987); *Career* grew up touring and acting with parents' theatre co in India and Far East, London debut in Minor Murder (Savoy) 1967; *Theatre* Henry V and The Promise (Leicester) 1968, Back to Methuselah (NT) 1969, A Midsummer Night's Dream and Much Ado About Nothing (Regents Park) 1970, Kean (Oxford 1970 and London 1971), Romeo and Juliet,' Tis Pity She's a Whore 1972, The Three Arrows 1972, The Norman Conquests (Globe) 1974, Once Upon a Time (Bristol) 1976, Arms and the Man (Greenwich) 1978, Clouds (Duke of York's) 1978, Amadeus (NT) 1979, Othello (NT) 1980, On the Razzle (NT) 1981, The Second Mrs Tanqueray (NT) 1981, The Real Thing (Strand) 1982, Jumpers (Aldwych) 1985, Made in Bangkok (Aldwych) 1986, Hapgood (Aldwych) 1988, Much Ado About Nothing and Ivanov (Strand) 1989, Hidden Laughter (Vaudeville) 1990, Tartuffe (Playhouse) 1991, Heartbreak House (Yvonne Arnaud Guildford and Haymarket) 1992, Arcadia (RNT) 1993, An Absolute Turkey (Globe) 1994, Indian Ink (Aldwych) 1995, Mind Millie for Me (Haymarket) 1996, Waste (Old Vic) 1997, The Seagull (Old Vic) 1997, Alarms and Excursions (Gielgud Theatre) 1998, Fallen Angels (Apollo) 2000, Humble Boy (Gielgud Theatre) 2002, Happy Days (Arts Theatre) 2004, Amy's View (Garrick Theatre) 2006; *Television* Barbara in The Good Life 1975–77, Twelfth Night 1979, Solo 1980 and 1982, The Mistress 1985, The Camomile Lawn 1992, Honey for Tea 1994, How Proust Can Save Your Life 1999, Rosemary and Thyme 2003–05; *Films* Shakespeare Wallah 1965, Valentino 1976, Parting Shots 1998; *Awards* Variety Club Most Promising Newcomer 1974, Best Actress 1979, Clarence Derwent Award 1980, Variety Club Best Actress Award 1984, Evening Standard Best Actress Award 1989, Actress of the Year Sony Radio Awards 1992, Variety Club Best Actress Award 2000; *Books* White Cargo (autobiography, 1998); *Style*— Miss Felicity Kendal, CBE; ✉ c/o Chatto & Linnit, 123a Kings Road, London SW3 4PL (tel 020 7352 7722)

KENDALL, Bridget; MBE (1994); da of David George Kendall, and Diana Louise, *née* Fletcher; *b* 27 April 1956; *Educ* Perse Sch for Girls Cambridge, Lady Margaret Hall Oxford (BA), Harvard Univ (Harkness fell), St Antony's Coll Oxford, Voronezh Univ (Br Cncl scholar), Moscow State Univ (Br Cncl postgrad scholar); *Career* BBC: prodr and reporter BBC World Service, BBC Radio 4 and Newsnight 1983–89, Moscow corr 1989–93, made series of special reports on Russia for Newsnight and Panorama 1993–94, Washington corr 1994–98, diplomatic corr 1998–; James Cameron Meml Award for Journalism 1992, Voice of the Listener and Viewer Award for Excellence in Broadcasting 1993; memb Advsy Bd on Russia and Eurasia RIIA; hon fell St Antony's Coll Oxford; Hon DUniv Univ of Central England in Birmingham 1997, Hon LLD Univ of St Andrews 2001, Hon LLD Univ of Exeter 2002; *Recreations* literature, music, theatre and film; *Style*— Ms Bridget Kendall, MBE; ✉ BBC World Affairs Unit, Room 2505, Television Centre, Wood Lane, London W12 7RJ (tel 020 8624 8550, fax 020 8743 7591, e-mail bridget.kendall@bbc.co.uk)

KENDALL, David Richard; s of Frederick Richard Kendall, of Lutterworth, Leics, and Gwendoline Florence, *née* Blackwell; *b* 17 September 1955; *Educ* Lutterworth GS, Univ of Birmingham (LLB), City of London Poly (MA), Sprachen und Dolmetsch Institut Munich (Dip); *m* 28 June 1980, Marsha Alexa, da of Allan Rothenberg; 1 da (Sarah Louise b 13 Feb 1982), 2 s (Ralph Alexander b 14 Sept 1984, Ian William b 1 April 1986); *Career* Messrs Hedleys: articled clerk 1979–81, asst slr 1981–85, ptnr 1985–88; head Insurance Dept D J Freeman 1991–2003 (ptnr 1988–), sr ptnr Kendall Freeman 2003–; panel arbitrator Lloyd's 1993–; memb: Law Soc 1977, Fedn of Insurance and Corp Counsel 1993; ARIAS; *Recreations* tennis, woodwork; *Style*— David Kendall, Esq; ✉ Kendall Freeman, One Fetter Lane, London EC4A 1JB (tel 020 7583 4055, fax 020 7353 7377, e-mail davidkendall@kendallfreeman.com)

KENDALL, (Gilbert) John; s of Arthur Charles Kendall (d 1983), of Crickhowell, Powys, and Hilda Mary, *née* Morgan (d 2001); *b* 31 May 1950; *Educ* Rugby (scholar), New Coll Oxford (exhibitioner, MA), KCL; *m* 4 Oct 1986, Jennifer Lynne, da of Peter Owen Watton; *Career* slr; articled clerk Stephenson Harwood 1973; Allen & Overy: slr 1977–, ptnr 1985–98, specialist in litigation, arbitration and construction law, managing ptnr Litigation Dept 1994–97; ind mediator 1998–; registered mediator; chm Alternative Dispute Resolution Sub-Ctee Int Bar Assoc 1993–96; Freeman City of London; *Publications* Expert Determination (3 edn, 2001), Russell on Arbitration (co-author, 21 edn 1997), author of numerous articles; *Recreations* walking, opera; *Style*— John Kendall, Esq; ✉ The Manor House, St David's Street, Presteigne, Powys LD8 2BP (tel 01544 260019, fax 01874 547310, e-mail jkendall@btinternet.com)

KENDALL, John Melville; s of Capt Charles Edward Kendall (d 1978), of Benenden, Kent, and Cara Honoria, *née* Pelly (d 1996); *b* 1 September 1931; *Educ* Ampleforth; *m* 23 Feb 1971, Anthea Diana, da of Col T D Partridge; 1 s (Mark b 12 Jan 1972), 1 da (Sophia b 4 July 1973); *Career* Lt RN 1952–56 (served as pilot Fleet Air Arm); chm Charles Kendall Gp of Cos 1978–; Grand Order of Renaissance of Oman, Order of Sultan Qaboos First Class, Knight of Honour and Devotion SMOM; *Recreations* hunting recollections, sailing, skiing, opera; *Clubs* Brooks's; *Style*— John Kendall, Esq; ✉ Pelyn, Lostwithiel, Cornwall PL22 0JE; Charles Kendall Group, 7 Albert Court, Prince Consort Road, London SW7 2BJ (tel 020 7589 1256, fax 020 7581 4112)

KENDALL, Prof Kevin; Cyril Kendall (d 1960), of Accrington, Lancs, and Margaret, *née* Swarbrick (d 1950); *b* 2 December 1943; *Educ* St Marys Coll Blackburn, Univ of London (BSc), Cavendish Lab Cambridge (PhD), Monash Univ; *m* 1969, Patricia Jennifer, da of Jim Heyes; 1 da (Michaela b 21 Aug 1970), 1 s (Alexander b 8 Nov 1971); *Career* researcher Joseph Lucas 1961–66, scientist BR 1969–71, fell Monash Univ 1972–74, fell Univ of Akron 1974, scientist ICI Runcorn 1974–93, prof of materials science Keele Univ 1993–2000, prof of formulation engrg Univ of Birmingham 2000–; FRS 1993; *Publications* Molecular Adhesion and its Applications (2001), High Temperature Solid Oxide Fuel Cells (2003); numerous papers in learned journals 1971–2005; *Recreations* squash; *Style*— Prof Kevin Kendall, FRS; ✉ Chemical Engineering, University of Birmingham, Edgbaston, Birmingham B15 2TT (tel 0121 414 2739, fax 0121 414 5377); Wycherley, Tower Road, Ashley Heath, Market Drayton, Shropshire TF9 4PY (tel 01630 672665, e-mail k.kendall@bham.ac.uk)

KENDALL, Nicholas John (Nick); s of Leonard and Barbara Kendall; *b* 29 September 1959; *Educ* Manchester Grammar, ChCh Oxford (BA); *m* 23 Sept 1989, Patrice Rosanna, da of Roy Charlton Chasteau; *Career* account exec Sharps Advertising 1981–82, account planner Burkitt Weinreich Clients & Co 1982–87; Bartle Bogle Hegarty: account planner 1987–93, bd dir 1989–, head of planning 1993–; Gold IPA Effectiveness Awards 1992; memb Effectiveness Ctee IPA 1993, convenor of judges IPA Effectiveness Awards 1998, designer and chief examiner IPA Dip professional qualification 2006 and 2007; memb MRS; *Recreations* work, my wife; *Style*— Nick Kendall, Esq; ✉ Bartle Bogle Hegarty, 60 Kingly Street, London W1R 6DS (tel 020 7734 1677, fax 020 7437 3666)

KENDALL-TAYLOR, Prof Pat; da of Kendall-Taylor, CBE (d 1999), of Wimbledon, London, and Dorothy, *née* Lawton (d 1958); *b* 17 February 1937; *Educ* RCM (ARCM), Royal Free Hosp Univ of London (MD); *Career* lectr in med Univ of Sheffield 1968–74, conslt physician Royal Victoria Infirmary Newcastle upon Tyne 1978–2001, prof of endocrinology Univ of Newcastle upon Tyne 1985–2001 (sr lectr and reader in med 1980–85, emeritus prof 2001–); sr ed Clinical Endoncrinology 1988–2002; past pres Br Thyroid Assoc; memb Assoc Physicians 1973, FRCP; *Publications* numerous chapters and papers on endocrinology and medicine; *Recreations* fell walking, gardening, bird watching, music; *Style*— Prof Pat Kendall-Taylor; ✉ e-mail pat.kendall-taylor@ncl.ac.uk

KENEALLY, Thomas Michael (Tom); AO (1983); *m*, Judith; 2 da (Margaret, Jane); *Career* author and playwright; contrib to numerous magazines and newspapers incl: New York Times Book Review, Boston Globe, Washington Post, The Times, The Guardian, The Independent, Observer Colour Magazine, Time, Newsweek, The Australian, Sydney Morning Herald, Medical Journal of Australia; work translated into over 15 languages incl: French, German, Spanish, Hebrew, Czechoslovakian, Flemish, Japanese; distinguished prof Dept of English Creative Writing Sch Univ of Calif Irvine 1991–95 (prof 1985–), visiting prof and Berg prof Dept of English Creative Writing Sch New York Univ 1988; inaugural memb Australia-China Cncl 1978–83; pres: Aust Nat Book Cncl 1985–89, Aust Soc of Authors 1990 (cncl memb 1981–, chm 1987–90); dir Australian Republican Movement Movement 1993– (inaugural chairperson 1991–93); memb: Lit Bd Aust Cncl 1985–, Advsy Panel Aust Constitutional Cmmn 1985–88, Aust Writers' Guild, US Screenwriters' Guild; Hon DLit: Queensland Univ 1993, Nat Univ of Ireland 1994, Fairleigh Dickenson Univ USA 1994, Rollins Coll USA 1995; Dr (hc) Univ of W Sydney 1997; Univ Medal Univ of Calif Irvine 1995; FRSL, FAAAS 1993; *Books* incl: Bring Larks and Heroes (1967, Miles Franklin Award), Three Cheers for the Paraclete (Miles Franklin Award 1968), The Survivor (1969, Captain Cook Bi-Centenary Prize 1970), The Chant of Jimmie Blacksmith (1972, Booker McConnell shortlisted, RSL Prize 1973, later filmed), Gossip from the Forest (1975, The Age Fiction Prize, Booker McConnell shortlisted 1977, filmed 1979), Ned Kelly and the City of Bees (for children, 1978), Confederates (1979, Booker McConnell shortlisted), Schindler's Ark (1982, Booker McConnell Prize, Los Angeles Times Prize for Fiction 1983, titled Schindler's List in US), A Family Madness (1985), The Playmaker (1987), Towards Asmara (1989), Flying Hero Class (1991), Now And In Time To Be (1991), Place where Souls are Born (1992), Woman of the Inner Sea (1992), Jacko (1993), A River Town (1995), Bettany's Book (2000), The Office of Innocence (2002), The Tyrant's Novel (2004), The Widow and Her Hero (2007); *Non-Fiction* The Utility Player (1993), Our Republic (1993), Homebush Boy - A Memoir (1995), The Great Shame (1999), American Scoundrel (2002), Lincoln (2004), The Commonwealth of Thieves: The Story of the Founding of Australia (2006); *Plays* incl: Childermas (1968), An Awful Rose (1972), Gossip from the Forest (1983), The Playmaker (adapted from novel, 1988); *Film and Television scripts* incl: Too Many People are Disappearing, Silver City (Critics' Circle award for Best Screenplay 1985), Libido, Catalpa - The Australian Break, Corroboree; *Style*— Tom Keneally, Esq, AO, FRSL

KENILWORTH, 4 Baron (UK 1937); (John) Randle Siddeley; only s of 3 Baron Kenilworth (d 1981); *b* 16 June 1954; *Educ* Northease Manor, London Coll of Furniture; *m* 1, 1983 (m dis 1990), Kim, only da of Danie Serfontein, of Newcastle upon Tyne; m 2, 15 Aug 1991, Mrs Kiki McDonough, *née* Axford; 2 s (Hon William Randle b 24 Jan 1992, Hon Edward Oscar b 4 Feb 1994); *Heir* s, Hon William Siddeley; *Career* dir: Siddeley Landscape Designs, Randle Siddeley Assocs; *Style*— The Rt Hon the Lord Kenilworth; ✉ e-mail randle@randlesiddeley.co.uk

KENNA, Michael; s of Walter Kenna, and Eva, *née* Sherrington (d 1968); *b* 20 November 1953, Widnes, Cheshire; *Educ* St Joseph's Coll Upholland, Banbury Sch of Art, London Coll of Printing (HND Photography); *m* 1991, Camille, *née* Solyagua; 1 da from prev m (Olivia Morgan b 1985); *Career* photographer/master printer since 1978 (specialising in the interaction between the natural landscape and urban structures); advertising clients 1990– incl: Adidas, Audi, Bank of America, BMW, British Rail, British Airways, Isuzu, Jeep Chrysler, Landrover, Mazda, Mazerati, Moët et Chandon, RAF, Rolls Royce, Saab, Spanish Tourist Bd, Toshiba, Volvo; Hon MA Brooks Inst Santa Barbara CA; Chevalier de l'Ordre des Artes et des Lettres 2000; *Solo Exhibitions* incl: Stephen Wirtz Gallery San Francisco 1984, 1987, 1990, 1995, 1997. 1999, 2000, 2002, 2003 and 2004, Weston Gallery Carmel CA 1985, 1988, 1991, 1992, 1994, 1995, 1998, 2000 and 2002, Madison Art Center Madison WI 1985, Zur Stockeregg Gallery Zurich 1986, 1994 and 2000, Gallery MIN Tokyo 1987 and 1990, Fox Talbot Museum Lacock Wilts 1987, Halsted Gallery Birmingham MI 1988, 1990, 1992, 1994, 1995, 1996, 1997, 1999, 2000, 2001, 2002, 2003 and 2004, National Centre for Photography Bath Avon 1988, Long Beach Museum of Art CA 1988, Tampa Museum of Art FL 1988, Germans Van Eck Gallery NY 1989 and 1993, Hamiltons Gallery London 1989 and 1992, Fuerte Gallery Tokyo 1990, Catherine Edelman Gallery Chicago IL annually 1990–, G Gibson Gallery Seattle WA 1991, 1993, 1994, 1995, 1996, 1997, 2000, 2001, 2002 and 2003, Jackson Fine Art Atlanta GA 1991, 1994, 1996, 2001 and 2003, Robert Klein Gallery Boston MA 1992, 1993, 1997, 1999 and 2004, Cleveland Art Museum OH 1992, University Art Museum Ann Arbor MI 1992, Int Center for Photography NY 1993, Photo Picture Space Osaka Japan 1994, Craig Krull Gallery LA 1995, 1996, 1998, 2000 and 2003, Il Tempo Gallery Tokyo 1995, 1999, 2000, 2002 and 2003, Industrial Relations - The Rouge and other sites (Detroit Inst of Arts) 1995, Marly le Roi (Clark Humanities Museum Claremont) 1997, Les Notre's Gardens (Huntingdon Library Pasadena) 1997, Musée Marly-le-Roi (Louveciennes France) 1997, Robert Mann Gallery NY 1997, 2000 and 2003, Le Notre's Gardens (Musée Jean de la Fontaine France) 1999, Point Light Gallery Haymarket NSW 2000, Galerie Laurent Herschritt Paris 2001, Michael Kenna: Photographs (Albright-Knox Art Gallery Buffalo NY) 2001, Night Work (Friends of Photography San Francisco) 2001, Zelda Cheatle Gallery London 2002, Gallery Lelassi Italy 2002, SK Josefsberg Gallery Portland OR 2002, Point Light Gallery Sydney 2002 and 2003, Jospeh Bellows Gallery La Jolla CA 2002, Galerie Laurent Herschritt Paris 2002, Easter Island (Center for Photographic Art Carmel CA and Cornell Museum Delray Beach FL) 2002, Calais Lace (Musée des Beaux Arts Calais) 2002, Japan (Chateau d'Eau Museum Toulouse) 2003, Ralls Collection Washington DC 2003, Terrence Denley Gallery AL 2003, Japan (Museum of Glass Int Centre for Contemporary Art WA 2003, Whitewall Gallery Seul 2003, Michael Kenna (Tokyo Photographic Cultural Centre Tokyo) 2003, Impossible to Forget (Houston Holocaust Museum TX) 2003, John Cleary Gallery Houston TX 2003, Joseph Bellows Gallery La Jolla CA 2004; *Group Exhibitions* incl: Architecture: Subject, Object or Pretext? (Musee des Beaux-Art Argen) 1983, Lay of the Land (Palo Alto Cultural Center Palo Alto CA) 1985, Museotrain Les Collections Photographiques des FRAC (France) 1986, Silver Image Exhibition (Gallery MIN Tokyo) 1988, The Landscape at Risk (Houston Center for Photography Texas) 1989, La Conversation - Recent Acquisitions (MOMA Strasbourg) 1990, Galerie Michele Chomette Paris 1991, Le Desert de Retz (Palace of the Legion of Honor San Francisco) 1991, Selenographie (Observatoire Astronomique Strasbourg) 1991, Le Mois de la Photographie 1992 (Pavillon des Arts Paris) 1992, Recent Acquisitions (San Francisco Museum of Art) 1993, Sites/Fragile Ecologies (Smithsonian travelling exhbn, Washington DC) 1993, Contemporary Photographs from the Museum Collection (The Art Museum Princeton Univ) 1994, Latent August: The Legacy of Hiroshima and Nagasaki (Fort Mason Center San Francisco) 1995, Water (Robert Klein Gallery Boston) 1995, Trees (Galerie zur Stockeregg Zurich) 1995, Now and Then: The first eight years (Catherine Edelman Gallery Chicago) 1996, A Centennial Exposed (Jackson Fine Art Atlanta) 1996, Musee Matisse Nice 1997, Jackson Fine Art Atlanta 1998, New Work (John Cleary Gallery Houston) 1998, Catherine Edelman Gallery Chicago 1998, Braga Photography Festival Portugal 1998, Halstead Gallery Minneapolis 1998, Intimate Landscapes (Tacoma Art Museum) 2000, Desirs de Rivages (Musée National de la Marine Palais de Chaillot Paris) 2000, Elton John Collection (High Museum of Art Atlanta) 2000, Beyond Boundaries: Contemporary Photography in California (travelling exhbn) 2000–01, Depicting Absence/Implying Presence (San José ICA) 2001, Between Light and Shadow: Photographs and Prints from the Gary Bettis Collection (Boise Art Museum Indiana) 2001, Ce qui a été (Museum of Modern Liege) 2002, What were you Thinking? (Catherine Edelman Gallery Chicago) 2003, Artists of Nazraeli Press (Whitewall Gallery Seul Korea) 2003, Enchanted Evening (Yancey Richardson Gallery NY) 2003, Reflecting Buddha (Pasadena Museum for California Art) 2003, Twelfth Anniversary Show (Ralls Collection Washington DC) 2003, Homage aux Donnateurs (Musee Carnavalet Paris) 2004, Recent Acqyuisitions (Amon Carter Museum Fort Worth TX) 2004, Vagues 2 - Hommages et Digressions (Musee Malraux France) 2004; *Selected Collections* work included in the permanent collections of numerous museums incl: Australian Nat Gallery Canberra, Bibliothèque Nationale Paris, Fine Arts Museums San Francisco, Los Angeles County Museum of Art CA, Musee National d'Art Moderne Paris, National Gellery Washington DC, Rijksmuseum Amsterdam, The Museum of Decorative Arts Prague, The San Francisco MOMA, Tokyo Fuji Art Museum, Yale Univ Art Gallery New Haven Connecticut, V&A London; *Awards* Imogen Cunningham Award (San Francisco) 1981, Art in Public Buildings Award (California Arts Cmmn Sacramento) 1987, The Inst for Aesthetic Devpt Award (Pasadena) 1989, Golden Saffron Award (Consuegra Spain) 1996; *Selected Books and Catalogues* The Hound of the Baskervilles (photographic illustrations, 1985), Michael Kenna 1977–1987 (1987), Night Walk (1988), Le Desert de Retz (1990), Michael Kenna (1990), The Elkhorn Slough and Moss Landing (photographic illustrations, 1991), Michael Kenna - A Twenty Year Retrospective (1994), The Rouge (1995), Les Notre's Gardens (1997), Monique's Kindergarten (1997), Night Work (2000), L'Impossible Oubli (2001), Easter Island (2002), Et la Dentelle (2003), Ratcliffe Power Station (2004), Retrospective Two (2004); *Style*— Michael Kenna, Esq; ✉ c/o Maconochie Photography, 4 Meard Street, London W1VF 0EF (tel 020 7439 3159, fax 020 7439 2552)

KENNAIR, William Brignall; s of Joseph Terry Kennair, of Newcastle upon Tyne, and late Nancy, *née* Neasham; *b* 6 June 1956; *Educ* Royal GS Newcastle upon Tyne, UCL (LLB); *m* 2 Aug 1980, Karen Elizabeth, da of Keith John Williams, of Cardiff; *Career* sr ptnr John Venn & Sons London 1999– (ptnr 1986–), Scrivener Notary (John Venn & Sons, Scrivener Notaries and Translators); co-chm Task Force on Security and Authentication of ICC Cmmn on E-Business, IT and Telecoms; dir Cybernotary Assoc UK; Freeman City of London 1983–; Liveryman Worshipful Co of Scriveners 1983– (memb Ct of Assts 2000–, Upper Warden), Freeman Worshipful Co of Information Technologists 1993–; assoc memb American Bar Assoc 1994–; chm Soc of Scrivener Notaries London (representative to the Union Internationale du Notariat (UINL)), memb Permanent Cncl UINL, pres UINL Informatics and Judicial Security Cmmn, Chargé d'Affaires for UINL to UN Cmmn for Int Trade Law (UNCITRAL); *Books* contrib section on Notaries in Halsbury's Laws of England 4 edn vol 33, General Usage of International Digitally Ensured Commerce (GUIDEC) for ICC (2 edn, 2001); *Recreations* informatics, cuisine, wine, travel; *Style*— William Kennair, Esq; ✉ John Venn & Sons, 95 Aldwych, London WC2B 4JF (tel 020 7395 4300, fax 020 7395 4310, e-mail kennair@johnvenn.co.uk, website www.johnvenn.co.uk)

KENNARD, Dr Olga (Lady Burgen); OBE (1988); da of Joir Weisz (d 1990), and Catherina, *née* Sternberg (d 1988); *b* 23 March 1924; *Educ* Prince Henry VIII GS, Univ of Cambridge (ScD); *m* 1, 1948 (m dis 1961), Dr David William Kennard; 2 da (Susanna Clare b 1955, Julia Sarah b 1958); m 2, 1993, Sir Arnold Stanley Vincent Burgen, FRS; *Career* res asst Cavendish Laboratory Cambridge 1944–48; MRC: memb Scientific Staff Vision Res Unit 1948–51, Nat Inst for Med Res 1951–61, Chem Laboratory Univ of Cambridge 1961–, special appt 1971–89; scientific dir Cambridge Crystallographic Data Centre 1965–97, visiting prof Univ of London 1988–90; author of scientific papers and books on scientific data; memb numerous ctees of scientific socs; tstee British Museum 2004–; Hon LLD Univ of Cambridge 2003; FRS 1987 (memb Cncl 1995–97); *Recreations* swimming, modern architecture, reading; *Style*— Dr Olga Kennard, OBE, FRS; ✉ Keelson, 8A Hills Avenue, Cambridge CB1 7XA (e-mail ok10@cam.ac.uk)

KENNARD, Peter; *b* 1949, London; *Educ* Byam Shaw Sch of Art, Slade Sch of Art, RCA; *Career* artist/photographer; pt/t lectr Byam Shaw Sch of Art, pt/t lectr NE Londom Poly 1980–82, lectr West Surrey Coll of Art and Design 1989–94, sr lectr RCA 1994–; photomontages used for varied film and video work incl: Lab Pty election broadcast 1983, State of Emergency - South Africa (Bandung File Channel 4) 1986, Heartfield - The Father of Photomontage (Granada TV) 1991; work published in newspapers and jls incl: The Guardian (regular contrib), The Listener, Time Magazine, Washington Post, New Scientist, Sunday Times; book covers cmmnd by: Penguin, Pluto Press, Paladin, Verso; work in the collections of: Magdalen and St Catherine's Colls Oxford, V&A, Imperial War Museum, Arts Cncl of GB, Saatchi Collection London; *Exhibitions* one man incl: St Catherine's Coll Oxford 1968, Gardner Arts Centre Univ of Sussex (artist in residence) 1971, Photographers Gallery Univ of Southampton 1973, A Document of Chile (Half Moon Gallery London and touring) 1978, Images for Disarmament (ICA London and Arnolfini Gallery Bristol) 1981, Despatches from an Unofficial War Artist (opening GLC Peace Year County Hall London and touring) 1982–83, Images Against War 1965–85 (Barbican Centre London) 1985, Photomontages for Peace (UN Palais des Nations Geneva) 1989, Images for the End of the Century (Gimpel Fils Gallery London and Imperial War Museum London) 1990, Reading Room (Gimpel Fils Gallery) 1996, Zelda Cheatle London 1997, Dazed and Confused Gallery London 1997; group incl: Photographer as Printmaker (Arts Cncl touring) 1981, Art of the Comic Strip (Gimpel Fils Gallery London) 1984, Whitechapel Open 1985–88, Invention D'un Art (Pompidou Centre Paris) 1989, Shocks to the System (Festival Hall London and touring) 1991, Photomontage Now (Manchester City Art Gallery) 1991, The Cutting Edge (Barbican Art Gallery London) 1992, Do You Speak English? (Int Artists' Centre Poznan Poland), Where is Home? (Kent Gallery New York) 1994, No More Hiroshimas (Phoenix Gallery Brighton) 1995, Gimpel Fils Gallery London 1996, The Power of the Poster (V&A Museum London) 1998, Art in Exile (Brixton Art Gallery London) 1999, Housing and Homelessness (Candid Gallery London) 1999; curator Look Out (Wolverhampton City Art Gallery and touring) 2000; work in public collections incl: Antwerp Art Gallery, Arts Council of Britain, Gallery of Modern Art Glasgow, Imperial War Museum London, Oxford National Museum of Photography, Film and Television Bradford, Science Museum London, University College London, V&A Museum London; *Books* No Nuclear Weapons (jtly, 1981), Jobs for a Change (1983), Keep London out of the Killing Ground (jtly, 1983), Target London (1985), About Turn (jtly, 1986), Images for the End of the Century (1990); *Style*— Peter Kennard, Esq

KENNEDY, Dr Alexander; s of late Alexander Kennedy, and late Florence Edith, *née* Callin; *b* 20 April 1933; *Educ* Merchant Taylors', Univ of Liverpool (MB ChB, MD); *m* 6 Aug 1960, Marlene Joan Campbell, da of Alfred Beveridge (d 1939), of Edinburgh; 1 da (Fiona b 1963), 1 s (Alistair b 1969); *Career* RAF Med Branch, Flt Lt pathologist RAF Hosp Wroughton 1958–61; lectr in pathology Univ of Liverpool 1961–67, visiting asst prof Dept of Pathology Univ of Chicago 1968, sr lectr Dept of Pathology Univ of Sheffield 1968–77, hon conslt pathologist Sheffield Area HA 1969–77, formerly conslt histopathologist Northern Gen Hosp NHS Tst Sheffield, hon clinical lectr Univ of Sheffield 1977–1997; pres Sheffield Medico-Chirurgical Soc 1997–98; memb: Pathological Soc of GB and Ireland, Int Acad of Pathology, British Thoracic Soc; Tport Campaign, Peak District and S Yorks Branch CPRE 1999–; formerly churchwarden St Andrew's Sharrow; FRCPath 1985 (MRCPath 1966); *Books* Essentials of Surgical Pathology - A Programmed Instruction Text (with A C Daniels and F Strauss, 1974), Basic Techniques in Diagnostic Histopathology (1977); articles on heart disease and medical aspects of cycling; *Recreations* cycling, walking, music, gardening, genealogy; *Style*— Dr Alexander Kennedy; ✉ 16 Brincliffe Gardens, Sheffield S11 9BG (e-mail sandy.kennedy@care4free.net)

KENNEDY, Alison Louise; da of Prof R Alan Kennedy, and Edwardine Mildred, *née* Price; *b* 22 October 1965; *Educ* HS of Dundee, Univ of Warwick (BA); *Career* writer; co-ordinator of creative writing for Project Ability 1989–94, writer in residence SAC/Strathclyde Regnl Social Work Dept 1990–92; judge on Booker Prize 1996, memb Granta Best Young British Novelists list 2003; FRSL, FRSA; *Awards* Social Work Today Special Award 1990, Scottish Arts Cncl Book Award 1991, Saltire First Book Award 1991, Mail on Sunday/John Llewelyn Rhys Prize 1991, Best of British Young Novelist list Granta 1993, Edinburgh Festival Fringe First 1993, Scottish Arts Cncl Book Award 1994, Somerset Maugham Award 1994, Saltire Best Book Award 1995, Scottish Arts Council Book Award 1995, 1997 and 1999, Encore Award 1996; *Film* Stella Does Tricks 1997; *Books* Night Geometry and the Garscadden Trains (1991), Looking for the Possible Dance (1993), Now That You're Back (1994), So I am Glad (1995), Original Bliss (1997), The Life And Death of Colonel Blimp (1997), Everything You Need (1999), Indelible Acts (2002), Paradise (2004), Day (2007); *Recreations* cinema, banjo; *Style*— Miss A L Kennedy; ✉ c/o Antony Harwood, Antony Harwood Ltd, 103 Walton Street, Oxford OX2 6EB (tel 01865 559615, fax 01865 310660)

KENNEDY, Dr Cameron Thomas Campbell; s of Thomas Kennedy (d 1981), and Dorian, *née* Talbot; *b* 30 January 1947; *Educ* Forest Sch, Queens' Coll Cambridge and UCH (MA, MB BChir); *m* 19 May 1973, Dr Rosalind Penolope, da of Raymond Whittier Baldwin, of Alderley Edge, Cheshire; 3 s (Nicholas b 5 June 1979, Thomas b 3 March 1981, Stephen b 29 Jan 1984); *Career* registrar in dermatology London Hosp 1973–75, sr registrar St George's Hosp 1975–80; Bristol Royal Infirmary: conslt dermatologist 1981–, postgrad clinical tutor 1985–89; conslt dermatologist: Southmead Hosp Bristol 1981–, Bristol Children's Hosp 1981–; memb Bd Br Jl of Dermatology 2005–; hon chm Br Soc of Paediatric Dermatology 1994–97 (hon treas/sec 1991–94), pres Section of Dermatology RSM 2001–02; memb Br Assoc of Dermatologists, non-resident fell American Acad of Dermatology; FRCP 1986, FRSM; *Recreations* gardening, reading, squash, badminton; *Clubs* Bristol Savages; *Style*— Dr Cameron Kennedy; ✉ 16 Sion Hill, Clifton, Bristol BS8 4AZ (tel 0117 974 1935, e-mail camkennedy@doctors.org.uk); Bristol Royal Infirmary, Department of Dermatology, Marlborough Street, Bristol BS2 8HW (tel 0117 928 2520)

KENNEDY, Rt Hon Charles Peter; PC (1999), MP; yr s of Ian Kennedy and Mary MacVarish, *née* MacEachen, of Fort William; *b* 25 November 1959; *Educ* Lochaber HS Fort William, Univ of Glasgow (MA), Univ of Indiana (Fulbright Scholarship); *m* 20 July 2002, Sarah Gurling; 1 s (Donald James b 12 April 2005); *Career* broadcaster and journalist BBC Highland Inverness 1982, graduate student/lecturer (speech communications and British politics) Univ of Indiana USA 1982–83; MP (SDP until 1987, now Lib Dem): Ross, Cromarty and Skye 1983–97, Ross, Skye and Inverness W 1997–2005, Ross, Skye and Lochaber 2005–; chm SDP Cncl for Scotland 1985–87, Alliance spokesman on social security 1987; SDP spokesman on Scotland, health and social security 1983–87, SLD spokesman on trade and industry 1988–89; Lib Dem spokesman on: health 1989–92, Europe 1992–97, agriculture and rural affrs 1997–99; pres Lib Dem Pty 1990–94; ldr Lib Dem Pty 1999–2006; hon dr Univ of Glasgow 2001; FRSA 2005; *Publications* The Future of Politics (2000); *Recreations* journalism, lecturing, broadcasting, music, reading, writing; *Clubs* National Liberal, Royal Cwlth; *Style*— The Rt Hon Charles Kennedy, MP; ✉ House of Commons, London SW1A 0AA (tel 020 7219 0356, fax 020 7219 4881, e-mail kennedyc@parliament.uk)

KENNEDY, Prof Clive Russell; s of Thomas Kennedy (ka 1941), of Paisley, Renfrewshire, and Victoria Alice, *née* Russell; *b* 17 June 1941; *Educ* Liverpool Coll, Univ of Liverpool (BSc, PhD, DSc); *m* 1, 23 Feb 1963, Beryl Pamela (d 1978), da of David Redvers Jones (d 1979), of Nantgaredig, Carmarthen; 1 s (Aidan b 1970), 1 da (Kate b 1971); m 2, 5 May 1979 (m dis 1998), Margaret Hilary, da of Bernard Wise (d 1973), of Oxford; m 3, 4 Sept 1999, Patricia Frances, da of Huw Jones, of Reading; *Career* asst in zoology UC Dublin 1963–64, asst lectr in zoology Univ of Birmingham 1964–65; Univ of Exeter: lectr in biological sci 1965–76, reader in zoology 1976–86, prof of parasitology 1986–2001, dean of sci 1990–93, head Sch of Biological Sci 1996–2000, emeritus prof 2001–; visiting prof: King's Coll London 1986–90, Univ Roma Tor Vergata 1996–2001; memb: Regnl Fisheries Advsy Ctee Nat Rivers Authy, Fisheries Soc of the Br Isles 1969, Ctee NERC 1984–88; hon memb: Br Soc of Parasitology (memb 1968, vice-pres 1992–94, pres 1994–96), Russian Parasitology Soc, Scandinavian Soc for Parasitology; *Books* Ecological Animal Parasitology (1975), Ecological Aspects of Parasitology (1976), Ecology of the Acanthocephala (2006), numerous papers in sci jls; *Recreations* walking, churches, glass, rugby; *Style*— Prof Clive Kennedy; ✉ School of Biological Sciences, The University, Exeter EX4 4PS (tel 01392 263757, fax 01392 263700, telex 42894 EXUNIVG, e-mail c.r.kennedy@exeter.ac.uk)

KENNEDY, Danny; MLA; s of John Trevor Kennedy, and Mary Ida, *née* Black; *b* 6 July 1959; *Educ* Newry HS; *m* 26 March 1988, Karen Susan, da of Robert McCrum; 2 s (Stephen Daniel b 17 March 1990, Philip Robert b 7 Oct 1992), 1 da (Hannah Ruth b 30 Nov 1997); *Career* BT NI 1978–98; cncllr Newry and Mourne DC 1985– (chair 1994–95), memb Newry and Mourne Dist Policing Partnership Bd, memb Newry and Mourne Local Strategic Partnership; memb UUP 1974–; MLA (UUP) Newry and Armagh 1998–, chm Educn Ctee 2001–03; memb NI Tourist Board 1996–98; govr: Bessbrook Primary Sch, Newry HS; *Recreations* family, church activities, sports (as a spectator), reading; *Style*— Danny Kennedy, Esq, MLA; ✉ Northern Ireland Assembly, Parliament Buildings, Stormont Estate, Belfast BT4 3XX (tel 028 9052 1336, fax 028 9052 1757, e-mail danny.kennedy@niassembly.gov.uk); Advice Centre, 107 Main Street, Markethill, Co Armagh BT60 1PH (tel 028 3755 2831, fax 028 3755 2832)

KENNEDY, Jane; *b* 28 February 1953; *Educ* Sch of Architecture Univ of Manchester, Sch of Architecture Manchester Poly (DipArch); *m* John Maddison, artist and writer; 2 s; *Career* asst in Historic Buildings Gp Planning Dept Gtr Manchester Cncl 1974–75, Manchester Poly 1975–78, architect with Br Waterways Bd Rugby 1978–80, asst to David Jeffcoate Architect London 1980–81, pt/t work (due to family) 1981–86, historic buildings architect Planning Dept Norwich City Cncl 1986–88; Purcell Miller Tritton and Partners: joined Norwich Office as asst 1988, assoc 1989, ptnr Ely Office 1992–; cmmr English Heritage 2006– (conslt inspecting architect 1994–2001); surveyor to the Fabric of Ely Cathedral 1994– (asst surveyor 1990), memb Cncl for the Care of Churches 1996–2003; occasional lectr at Univs of York, Cambridge and Edinburgh; tstee and chm Church and Community Tst 1992–2003 (chm 1999–2003), sec Cathedral Architects Assoc 1999–2006, architect to St Nicholas Cathedral Newcastle upon Tyne 2006–; memb: The Victorian Soc (ctee memb Manchester and E Anglia), Soc for the Protection of Ancient Buildings, National Tst; RIBA 1979; memb: ARCUK 1979, IHBC 1997; FRSA 1994; *Recreations* walking and family life; *Style*— Ms Jane Kennedy; ✉ Purcell Miller Tritton, 46 St Mary's Street, Ely, Cambridgeshire CB7 4EY (tel 01353 660660, fax 01353 660661, e-mail janekennedy@pmt.co.uk)

KENNEDY, Jane; PC (2003), MP; da of Clifford Hodgson, and Barbara Hodgson; *b* 4 May 1958; *Educ* Haughton Comp Sch, Queen Elizabeth Sixth Form Coll, Univ of Liverpool; *m* 14 Dec 1977 (m dis 1998), Malcolm Kennedy; 2 s; *Career* residential child care offr Liverpool City Cncl 1979–83, care asst Liverpool Social Servs 1984–88, area organiser NUPE 1988–92 (branch sec 1983–88); MP (Lab): Liverpool Broadgreen 1992–97, Liverpool Wavertree 1997–; memb: Social Security Select Ctee 1992–94, Environment Select Ctee 1995; oppn whip Oct 1995–97, asst govt whip 1997–98, a Lord Cmmr (Govt whip) 1998–99, Parly under sec of state Lord Chllr's Dept 1999–2001, min of state for Security, Prisons and Policing NI Office 2001–04, min of state Dept for Work and Pensions 2004–05, min of state Dept of Health 2005–06; chair Labour Friends of Israel 1997–98 and 2006–; memb Governing Body: Liverpool Poly 1986–88, Oldham Sixth Form Coll 1990–92; memb: Lab Pty 1978–, Ramblers' Assoc, Belgian Shepherd Dog Assoc; *Style*— The Rt Hon Jane Kennedy, MP; ✉ Threlfall Building, Trueman Street, Liverpool L3 2EX (tel 0151 236 1117, fax 0151 236 0067); House of Commons, London SW1A 0AA

KENNEDY, Joanna Alicia Gore; OBE (1995); da of Capt Gerald Anthony Gore Ormsby, DSO, DSC, RN (d 1992), and Nancy Mary (Susan), *née* Williams (d 1974); *b* 22 July 1950; *Educ* Queen Anne's Sch Caversham, Lady Margaret Hall Oxford (MA); *m* 21 July 1979, Richard Paul Kennedy, *qv*; 2 s (Peter b 1985, David b 1988); *Career* Ove Arup & Ptnrs consltg engrs: design engr 1972, sr engr 1979, assoc 1992, assoc dir 1994, dir 1996–; dir Engrg and Technol Bd 2002–05; memb: Engrg Cncl 1984–86 and 1987–90, Cncl ICE 1984–87, Advsy Cncl RNEC Manadon 1988–94, Engrg Bd SERC 1990–93, Engrg and Technol Bd SERC 1993–94, EPSRC 2002–06 (memb Tech Opportunities Panel 1994–97); dir Port of London Properties Ltd 2001–05; cmmr Royal Cmmn for the Exhbn of 1851 2003–; memb: Cncl Univ of Southampton 1996–99, Bd Port of London Authy 2000–, Cncl RCA 2001–; tstee Science Museum 1992–2002; Hon DSc Univ of Salford 1994; FICE, MCIArb, FRSA, FREng 1997; *Style*— Mrs Joanna Kennedy, OBE, FREng; ✉ Ove Arup & Partners, 13 Fitzroy Street, London W1T 4BQ (tel 020 7755 2003, fax 020 7755 2143, e-mail joanna.kennedy@arup.com)

KENNEDY, Rt Rev Monsignor John; s of James Kennedy (d 1961), and Alice, *née* Bentham (d 1978); *b* 31 December 1930; *Educ* St Joseph's Coll Upholland, English Coll Rome (PhL, STL), Campion Hall Oxford (MPhil); *Career* curate: St John's Wigan 1956–64, St Austin's St Helens 1964–66, St Edmund's Waterloo Liverpool 1966–68; lectr Christ's Coll Liverpool 1968–83 (head Dept of Theology 1975–83), rector English Coll Rome 1984–91, parish priest Southport Merseyside 1991–; *Books* Priest & People (contrib, 1968); *Recreations* golf, cricket; *Clubs* Royal Birkdale Golf (Southport), Royal Over-Seas League; *Style*— The Rt Rev Monsignor Kennedy; ✉ Holy Family, 1 Brompton Road, Southport, Merseyside PR8 6AS (tel 01704 532613)

KENNEDY, John Maxwell; s of George Steel Kennedy (d 1979), of Cardiff, and Betty Gertrude, *née* Bennett (d 1983); *b* 9 July 1934; *Educ* UCL (LLB); *m* 1958, Margaret Joan, da of Dr Trevor Davies; 4 s (Simon b 1959, Alexander b 1960, David b 1964, Hamish b 1965); *Career* slr; Allen & Overy: joined 1954, ptnr 1962–94, sr ptnr 1986–94; chm The Law Debenture Corporation plc 1994–2000; dir: Nuclear Liabilities, Amlin plc 1993–2004 (chm 1996–98); memb Bd FSA (formerly SIB) 1993–98; Freeman City of London; *Recreations* music, reading, sport; *Clubs* City of London, City Law, Hurlingham, Royal Wimbledon Golf; *Style*— John Kennedy, Esq; ✉ 16 Kensington Park Road, London W11 3BU (tel 020 7727 6929, fax 020 7727 3262)

KENNEDY, Louise; da of James Kennedy, of Tipperary, Ireland, and Margaret, *née* McCormack (d 1984); *b* 28 June 1960; *Educ* St Annes Mount Merrion Ave Dublin, Coll of Mktg & Design Dublin, Grafton Acad of Design Dublin; *Career* fashion designer (under own label) 1984–; designer of inauguration outfit for Mary Robinson (first female pres of Ireland) 1989, selected to join Br Designer Gp and exhibit at London Designer Show 1990, elected Tipperary Person of the Year (for outstanding achievements in Irish fashion 1992), opened flagship retail outlets in Dublin and London, launched Crystal Collection in conjunction with Tipperary Crystal 1999; other Irish fashion awards incl: Best Irish Coat Collection 1985, Irish Designer of the Year 1989 and 1990, Best Suit and Best Coat Award 1991, Best Irish Designer Collection (Fashion Oscar Award) 1992, Best Coat and Suit Collection Designer of the Year Awards 1993, first female designer to receive award for Outstanding Achievements in Fashion from Irish Clothing Industry 1994; Veuve Clicquot Irish Business Woman of the Year 2003; *Style—* Ms Louise Kennedy

KENNEDY, Sir Ludovic Henry Coverley; kt (1994); s of Capt Edward Kennedy, RN (ka 1939; ggs of Hon Robert Kennedy, bro of 1 Marquess of Ailsa and 3 s of 11 Earl of Cassillis), and Rosalind, da of Sir Ludovic Grant, 11 Bt of Dalvey; *b* 3 November 1919; *Educ* Eton, ChCh Oxford; *m* 1950, Moira Shearer (d 2006), formerly ballerina with Sadler's Wells Ballet, actress (incl The Red Shoes), and writer, da of Harold King; 1 s, 3 da; *Career* writer and broadcaster; served WWII, Lt RNVR; private sec and ADC to Govr of Newfoundland 1943–44; librarian Ashridge Coll 1949, lectr British Cncl 1955–56; Parly candidate (Lib) Rochdale: 1958 by-election, 1959 gen election; columnist: Newsweek International 1974–75, Sunday Standard 1981–82; chm Royal Lyceum Theatre Co of Edinburgh 1977–84, Voltaire meml lectr 1985, dir The Spectator 1988–89; pres Nat League of Young Liberals 1959–61, memb Lib Party Cncl 1965–67; pres Voluntary Euthanasia Soc 1995–; Hon LLD: Univ of Strathclyde 1985, Univ of Southampton 1993; Hon DUniv: Edinburgh 1990, Stirling 1991; FRSA 1974–76, FRSL 1998; West German Cross of Merit First Class 1979; *Television and Radio Work* incl: newscaster Independent Television News 1956–58; introducer: This Week (AR) 1958–59, Time Out (BBC) 1964–65, World at One 1965–66; commentator Panorama (BBC) 1960–63; presenter: Lib Party's Gen Election TV Broadcasts 1966, The Middle Years (ABC) 1967, The Nature of Prejudice (ATV) 1968, Face the Press (Tyne-Tees) 1968–69 and 1970–72, Against the Tide (Yorkshire TV) 1969, Living and Growing (Grampian TV) 1969–70, 24 Hours (BBC) 1969–72, Ad Lib (BBC) 1970–72, Midweek (BBC) 1973–75, Newsday (BBC) 1975–76, Tonight (BBC) 1976–78, A Life with Crime (BBC) 1979, Change of Direction (BBC) 1979, Lord Mountbatten Remembers 1980, Did You See? 1980–88, Timewatch 1984, Indelible Evidence 1987 and 1990, A Gift of the Gab 1989, Portrait 1989; *TV Films* incl: The Sleeping Ballerina, The Singers and the Songs, Scapa Flow, Battleship Bismarck, Life and Death of the Scharnhorst, U-Boat War, Target Tirpitz, The Rise of the Red Navy, Lord Haw-Haw, Coast to Coast, Who Killed the Lindbergh Baby, Elizabeth - The First Thirty Years, Happy Birthday, dear Ma'am, Consider the End, Murder in Belgravia: The Lucan Affair; *Awards* Rockefeller Fndn Atlantic Award in Literature 1950, winner Open Finals Contest English Festival of Spoken Poetry 1953, Richard Dimbleby BAFTA Award 1988; *Books* Sub-Lieutenant (1942), Nelson's Band of Brothers (1951), One Man's Meat (1953), Murder Story (play, 1956), Ten Rillington Place (1961), The Trial of Stephen Ward (1964), Very Lovely People (1969), Pursuit - The Chase and Sinking of the Bismarck (1974), A Presumption of Innocence - The Amazing Case of Patrick Meehan (1975), The British at War (gen ed, 1973–77), Menace - The Life and Death of the Tirpitz (1979), The Portland Spy Case (1979), Wicked Beyond Belief (1980), A Book of Railway Journeys (ed, 1980), A Book of Sea Journeys (ed, 1981), A Book of Air Journeys (ed, 1982), The Airman and the Carpenter (1985), On My Way to the Club (autobiography, 1989), Euthanasia - The Good Death (1990), Truth to Tell (collected writings, 1991), In Bed with an Elephant: A Journey Through Scotland's Past and Present (1995), All in the Mind: A Farewell to God (1999), Thirty-Six Murders and Two Immoral Earnings (2002); *Clubs* Brooks's, Army and Navy; *Style—* Sir Ludovic Kennedy, FRSL; ✉ c/o Rogers, Coleridge & White, 22 Powis Mews, London W11 1JN

KENNEDY, Dr Malcolm William; CBE (2000); s of William Kennedy (d 1970), of Gosforth; *b* 13 March 1935; *Educ* Univ of Durham (BSc), Univ of Newcastle upon Tyne (PhD); *m* June 1962, Patricia Ann, da of George Arthur Forster; 1 da (Clare Rachel b 10 Oct 1967); *Career* apprentice to C A Parsons & Co Ltd; Merz and McLellan: joined 1964, ptnr 1981, sr ptnr 1988–91, first chm and md (following incorporation) 1991–94, chm 1995–; non-exec dir Port of Tyne Authy 1994–2001, chm PB Power Ltd 1999–2002, chm NEA 2001–, dir New and Renewables Energy Centre 2003–; advsr Dept of Energy on privatisation of electricity indust 1987–90; memb: Electricity Panel MMC 1992–98; IEE: vice-pres 1989–92 and 1994–97, dep pres 1997–99, pres 1999–2000; CEng 1967, FIEE 1974, FREng 1986, FRSE 2002; *Recreations* Methodist local preacher, cricket, railways; *Clubs* National; *Style—* Dr Malcolm Kennedy, CBE, FREng, FRSE

KENNEDY, (William) Michael Clifford; s of Dr Clifford Donald Kennedy (d 1989), and Isobel Sinclair Kennedy (d 1984); *b* 29 October 1935; *Educ* Rugby, Merton Coll Oxford (BA); *m* 1962, Judith Victoria, da of Kenneth Fulton Gibb, of Fife; 1 s (Niall b 1964), 1 da (Tessa b 1965); *Career* chartered accountant; former chm and chief exec Martin Currie Investment Mgmnt Ltd; *Recreations* shooting, fishing, golf, gardening, music; *Clubs* New (Edinburgh), Hon Co of Edinburgh Golfers; *Style—* Michael Kennedy, Esq; ✉ Oak Lodge, Inveresk, Midlothian EH21 7TE (tel 0131 665 8822)

KENNEDY, His Hon Michael Denis; QC (1979); s of Denis George Kennedy (d 1970), of London, and Clementina Catherine, *née* MacGregor; *Educ* Downside, Gonville & Caius Coll Cambridge; *m* 1964, Elizabeth June, *née* Curtiss; 2 s (Laurence James Denis b 8 Oct 1965, Benedict Michael b 24 March 1969), 2 da (Rachel Mary Helen b 6 June 1967, Alice Catherine Elizabeth b 12 Feb 1971); *Career* called to the Bar Inner Temple 1961; recorder 1979–84, circuit judge (SE Circuit) 1984–2004 (dep circuit judge 2004–), designated civil judge Lewes 1998–2004; memb Ct Univ of Sussex 1980–90; Univ of Brighton: chm Students' Appeals Ctee 1992–98, memb Bd of Govrs 1993–2002; *Recreations* music (tstee The Cardinall's Musick 1998–), hedge-laying, flint-walling, fishing; *Clubs* S of England Hedge-Laying Soc, Schola Gregoriana (Cambridge); *Style—* His Hon Michael Kennedy, QC

KENNEDY, Sir Michael Edward; 8 Bt (UK 1836), of Johnstown Kennedy, Co Dublin; s Lt-Col Sir (George) Ronald Derrick Kennedy, 7 Bt, OBE (d 1988), and Noelle Mona, *née* Green; *b* 12 April 1956; *Educ* Rotherfield Hall Sussex; *m* 1984 (m dis 2005), Helen Christine, da of Patrick Lancelot Rae, of Nine Acres, Halstead, Kent; 3 da (Constance Andrea Rae b 4 Aug 1984, Josephine Jennifer Rae b 6 Dec 1986, Katherine Colleen Rae b 2 Jan 1997), 1 s (George Matthew Rae b 9 Dec 1993); *Heir* s, George Kennedy; *Career* memb Standing Cncl of the Baronetage; *Style—* Sir Michael Kennedy, Bt; ✉ 48 Telston Lane, Otford, Kent TN14 5LA

KENNEDY, Nigel Alan; s of Alan Ridsdale Kennedy (d 1980), of Claygate, Surrey, and Joan, *née* Mellows; *b* 2 February 1956; *Educ* Ardingly, Trinity Coll Oxford (MA); *m* 11 Sept 1982, Nicola Helen, da of Christopher Maurice Spencer; 2 da (Rachel b 21 Dec 1985, Rosalind b 16 Feb 1988), 2 s (Michael b 4 June 1990, Rory b 16 June 1997); *Career* public affrs offr: Mobil Oil Co Ltd London 1979–81, Total Oil Great Britain Ltd London 1981–84, co-ordinator (Northern Europe) Total Compagnie Française des Pétroles Paris 1984–86, dir The Communication Group plc 1986–93, gp chief exec Grayling 1999– (md 1993–1999); *Recreations* soccer, cricket, tennis, squash, travel; *Style—* Nigel Kennedy; ✉ Grayling, 1 Bedford Avenue, London WC1B 3AU (tel 020 7255 1100, fax 020 7255 5455, e-mail nigel.kennedy@uk.grayling.com, website www.grayling.com)

KENNEDY, Nigel Paul; s of John Kennedy, and Scylla, *née* Stoner; *b* 28 December 1956; *Educ* Yehudi Menuhin Sch, Juilliard Sch of Performing Arts; *Career* solo violinist; debut at Festival Hall with Philharmonia Orch 1977, Berlin debut with Berlin Philharmonia 1980, Henry Wood Promenade debut 1981, New York debut with BBC Symphony Orch 1987, tour of Hong Kong and Aust with Hallé Orch 1981, extensive tours USA and Europe; recordings incl: Tchaikovsky, Sibelius, Vivaldi (Double Platinum Disc), Elgar Violin Concerto (Record of the Year 1985, Gold Disc), Bruch and Mendelssohn (Gold Disc), Walton Violin and Viola, Let Loose, Kafka, Classic Kennedy, The Kennedy Experience; *Style—* Nigel Kennedy, Esq; ✉ c/o Ellie Page, First Floor, No 5, 119 Church Street, Malvern, Worcestershire WR14 2AJ (tel 01684 560040, fax 01684 561613)

KENNEDY, Rt Hon Sir Paul Joseph Morrow; kt (1983), PC (1992); s of late Dr Joseph Morrow Kennedy, of Sheffield, and late Bridget Teresa Kennedy; *b* 12 June 1935; *Educ* Ampleforth, Gonville & Caius Coll Cambridge; *m* 1965, Hon Virginia, da of late Baron Devlin; 2 s, 2 da; *Career* called to the Bar Gray's Inn 1960 (bencher 1982, vice-treas 2001, treas 2002); recorder of the Crown Court 1972, QC 1973, judge of the High Court of Justice (Queen's Bench Div) 1983–92, presiding judge NE Circuit 1985–89, a Lord Justice of Appeal 1992–2005, vice-pres Queen's Bench Div of the High Court 1997–2002; main bd memb Judicial Studies Bd 1993–96 (chm Criminal Ctee 1993–96), chm Advocacy Studies Bd 1996–99; hon fell Gonville & Caius Coll Cambridge 1998; Hon LLD Univ of Sheffield 2000; *Style—* The Rt Hon Sir Paul Kennedy

KENNEDY, Prof Paul M; CBE (2000); *b* 1945; *Educ* Univ of Newcastle upon Tyne (BA), Univ of Oxford (DPhil); *m* 1, Catherine (d 1998); 3 s; m 2, Cynthia Farrar, 2001; *Career* UEA: lectr 1970–75, reader 1975–82, prof 1982–83; J Richardson Dilworth prof of history Yale Univ 1983– (dir of int security studies); co-dir of the Secretariat to the Int Advsy Gp Report - The UN in its Second Half Century; res awards from British Acad, Leverhulme Fndn, Alexander von Humboldt Fndn, Beit Fund Oxford, Social Science Res Cncl, German Academic Exchange Serv; Hon MA Yale Univ, Hon DLitt Univ of Newcastle, Hon DHL Long Island Univ, Hon DHL Univ of New Haven, Hon LLD Ohio Univ, Hon DLitt UEA, Hon Doctorate Univ of Leuven; supernumary fell St Antony's Coll Oxford; fell: Inst for Advanced Study Princeton 1978–79, American Philosophical Soc, Soc of American Historians, Alexander von Humboldt Fndn; FRHS, FAAAS, FBA; *Books* Pacific Onslaught 1941–43 (1972), Conquest: The Pacific War 1943–45 (1973), The Samoan Tangle: A Study in Anglo-German-American Relations 1878–1900 (1974), The Rise and Fall of British Naval Mastery (1976), The Rise of the Anglo-German Antagonism 1860–1914 (1980), The Realities Behind Diplomacy: Background Influences on British External Policy 1865–1980 (1981), Strategy and Diplomacy, 1870–1945: Eight Essays (1983), The Rise and Fall of the Great Powers: Economic Change and Military Conflict from 1500–2000 (1988), Preparing for the Twenty-First Century (1993), The Parliament of Man: The Past, Present and Future of the United Nations (2006); reg contrib to numerous jls and publications incl The New York Times, The Los Angeles Times, The Atlantic and others; *Recreations* hawk watching, old churches, helping to run local soup kitchen; *Style—* Prof Paul Kennedy, CBE, FBA; ✉ Department of History, Yale University, New Haven, Connecticut, USA (tel 00 1 203 432 6246, fax 00 1 203 432 6250)

KENNEDY, Dr Peter Francis; s of Maurice Joseph Kennedy (d 1980), of Bradford, W Yorks, and Mary Josephine, *née* Benson; *b* 31 May 1941; *Educ* St Bede's GS Bradford, Univ of Leeds (MB ChB, DPM), Univ of Edinburgh (MD); *m* 1965, Sarah Elizabeth, da of Lawrence Arthur Inman; 2 s (John b 1966, Andrew b 1971), 1 da (Juliette b 1967); *Career* med houseman York 1965–68, scientist MRC Epidemiology Unit Edinburgh 1968–71, sr lectr in psychiatry and hon conslt psychiatrist Univ of Edinburgh 1973–80 (lectr 1971–73), gen mangr Mental Health Servs York 1985–88, dist gen mangr York HA 1988–92, chief exec York Health Servs NHS Tst 1992–99, Northern Centre for Mental Health 1999–2005, chm St Leonard's Hospice York 2005–; visiting prof Univ of York 2002–04; conslt in mental health WHO: Burma 1975, India 1978, Athens 1982, Qatar 1989 and 1990; FRCPsych 1982 (vice-pres 2005–); *Books* Trends in Suicide and Attempted Suicide in Europe (WHO) 1982; *Recreations* sailing; *Style—* Dr Peter Kennedy; ✉ 10 St George's Place, York YO2 2DR (tel 01904 621636, e-mail peter@kennedy89.freeserve.co.uk)

KENNEDY, Prof Peter Graham Edward; s of Philip Kennedy, of London, and Trudie Sylvia, *née* Summer; *b* 28 March 1951; *Educ* UCS London, UCL and UCH (MB BS, MD, PhD, DSc), Univ of Glasgow (MPhil, MLitt); *m* 6 July 1983, Catherine Ann, da of Christopher King; 1 s (Luke b 1988), 1 da (Vanessa b 1991); *Career* hon res asst MRC Neuroimmunology Project UCL 1978–80, sr registrar (formerly registrar) in neurology Nat Hosp London 1981–84, asst prof of neurology Johns Hopkins Univ Sch of Med 1985, Burton prof and head Dept of Neurology Univ of Glasgow 1987– (sr lectr in neurology and virology 1986–87), conslt neurologist Inst of Neurological Sciences Glasgow 1986–; visiting fell in med Jesus Coll Cambridge 1992, Fogarty int scholar-in-residence Nat Insts of Health USA 1993–94; memb Med Res Advsy Ctee Multiple Sclerosis Soc 1987–98, chm Med Res Advsy Ctee Scot Motor Neurone Disease Assoc 1987–97, chm Scientist Panel on Infections incl AIDS of the Euro Fedn of Neurological Societies 2000–06; sr assoc ed Jl of Neurovirology; memb Editorial Bds: Neuropathology and Applied Neurobiology 1986–92, Brain 1997–2004, Jl of Neuroimmunology, Jl of the Neurological Sciences; BUPA Med Fndn Doctor of the Year Res Award 1990; Fleming Lecture RCPSGlas 1990, Linacre Medal and Lecture RCP 1991, T S Srinivasan Endowment Lecture and Gold Medal 1993, J W Stephens Lecture Denver Colorado 1994, Brain Bursary Lecture King's College Hosp 1999, Livingstone Lecture RCPSGlas 2004; pres Int Soc for Neurovirology 2004– (pres elect 2004–), sec Int Soc for Neurovirology 2000–03; memb: Assoc of Br Neurologists, American Neurological Assoc, Soc for Gen Microbiology, Assoc of Clinical Profs of Med, Euro Neurological Soc, Scottish Assoc of Neurological Sciences, Scottish Soc of Physicians, Royal Medico-Chirurgical Soc Glasgow, Assoc of Physicians of GB and I; fell Br Astronomical Assoc; FRCP 1988, FRCPG 1989, FRSE 1992, FRCPath 1997 (MRCPath 1988), FMedSci (fndr) 1998, FRAS 2004, FRSM; *Books* Infections of the Nervous System (ed with R T Johnson, 1987), Infectious Diseases of the Nervous System (ed with L E Davis, 2000), The Fatal Sleep (2007); author of numerous papers on neurology, neurovirology and sleeping sickness; *Recreations* astronomy, philosophy, walking in country, tennis, music, cycling; *Style—* Prof Peter Kennedy, FRSE; ✉ 23 Hamilton Avenue, Pollokshields, Glasgow G41 4JG (tel 0141 427 4754); Glasgow University Department of Neurology, Institute of Neurological Sciences, Southern General Hospital, Glasgow G51 4TF (tel 0141 201 2474, fax 0141 201 2993, e-mail p.g.kennedy@clinmed.gla.ac.uk)

KENNEDY, Richard Paul; s of late David Clifton Kennedy, of Southampton, and Evelyn Mary Hall, *née* Tindale; *b* 17 February 1949; *Educ* Charterhouse (foundation scholar), New Coll Oxford (exhibitioner, MA); *m* 21 July 1979, Joanna Alicia Gore Kennedy, OBE, FREng, *qv*, da of late Capt Gerald Anthony Gore Ormsby, DSO, DSC, RN; 2 s (Peter Michael Andrew b 1985, David Anthony James b 1988); *Career* asst master: Shrewsbury Sch 1971–77, Westminster Sch 1977–84; dep headmaster Bishop's Stortford Coll 1984–89, headmaster Highgate Sch 1989–2006; HMC: memb Sports Sub-Ctee 1992–95, memb Ctee 1995–96, chm London Div 1996; memb: Fin Steering Gp 2001, Bd Architectural Educn 1992–96; govr: The Hall Sch Hampstead 1989–2006, Wycombe Abbey Sch 1992–2002; GB int athlete 1973–76; memb Acad of St Martin-in-the-Fields Chorus 1977–2000;

Recreations choral music; *Clubs* East India, Devonshire, Sports and Public Schs, Vincent's (Oxford); *Style*— Richard Kennedy, Esq; ✉ Luscombe Hall, 9 Luscombe Road, Poole, Dorset BH14 8ST (tel 01202 466810)

KENNEDY, Tessa Georgina; da of late Geoffrey Farrer Kennedy, and Daska McLean, *née* Ivanovic; *b* 6 December 1938; *Educ* Oak Hall Haslemere, Ecole des Beaux Arts Paris; *m* 1, 27 Jan 1958 (m dis 1969), Dominick Evelyn Bede Elwes, s of Simon Elwes (d 1975); 3 s (Cassian b 1959, Damian b 1960, Cary b 1962); m 2, 26 June 1971, Elliott Kastner; 1 s (Dillon b 1970), 1 da (Milica b 1972); *Career* interior designer; former clients incl: John Barry, Sam Spiegel, Richard Burton, De Beers, BUPA Hosps, HM King Hussein of Jordan, Michael Winner, Candice Bergen, Rudolf Nureyev, George Harrison, Pierce Brosnan, Claridges, Berkeley Hotels, Port Lympne Zoo, Aspinalls Casino, Ritz Bar, Ritz Casino; current clients incl Bibi's Restaurant and private residences in Moscow; D&D Designer of the Year 2003, D&D Best Traditional Commerical Design 2003; fell Int Interior Design Assoc (IIDA), memb Br Int Design Assoc (BIDA); *Recreations* tennis, movies, watching American football; *Clubs* Vanderbilt, Harbour; *Style*— Miss Tessa Kennedy; ✉ Tessa Kennedy Design Ltd, Studio 5, 2 Olaf Street, London W11 4BE (tel 020 7221 4546, fax 020 7229 2899, e-mail info@tessakennedydesign.com)

KENNEDY OF THE SHAWS, Baroness (Life Peer UK 1997), of Cathcart in the City of Glasgow; Helena Ann Kennedy; QC (1991); da of late Joshua Patrick Kennedy, of Glasgow, and Mary Veronica, *née* Jones; *b* 12 May 1950; *Educ* Holyrood Secdy Sch Glasgow, Cncl of Legal Educn; *m* 1986, Dr Iain Louis Hutchison; 1 s (Hon Roland), 1 da (Hon Clio); 1 s (Keir) from previous partner Roger Ian Mitchell; *Career* called to the Bar Gray's Inn 1972 (bencher 1999–); in practice: Garden Court 1974–84, Tooks Court 1984–90, Doughty Street Chambers 1990–; specialises in criminal law (acted in Brighton Bombing Trial and Guildford Four Appeal); broadcaster and journalist on law and women's rights; chair: London Int Festival of Theatre 1993–2002, Br Cncl, Human Genetics Cmmn; memb Advsy Cncl of the World Bank Inst; chllr Oxford Brookes Univ 1994–2001; contrib to: The Bar on Trial (1982), Child Sexual Abuse Within the Family (1985), Balancing Acts (1989); created Blind Justice (BBC, 1987); presenter: Heart of the Matter (BBC, 1987), Raw Deal (1989), The Trial of Lady Chatterley's Lover (1990), Time Gentleman, Please (BBC Scotland, awarded TV Prog Award Industrial Journalism Awards 1994), Hypotheticals; vice-pres Haldane Soc; chair: Standing Ctee for Youth Justice, Charter 88 until 1997, Br Cncl 1998–, London Int Festival Theatre 1993–2002; patron Liberty; memb Cncl Howard League for Penal Reform; pres National Children's Bureau 1998–; vice-pres Nat Assembly of Women; cmmr Nat Cmmn on Educn; pres: North of England Educn Conf 1994;18 Hon LLD from Br Univs; hon memb Academie Universelle des Cultures Paris; hon fell: Inst of Advanced Legal Studies, Univ of London; fell City and Guilds London Inst; FRSA; *Awards* Women's Network Award 1992, UK Woman of Europe Award 1995, Campaigning and Influencing Award Nat Fedn of Women's Institutes 1996, The Times Newspaper Lifetime Achievement Award in the Law 1997; *Publications* incl: Eve Was Framed (1992), Learning Works (report for the Further Educn Funding Cncl, 1997), Just Law: The Changing Face of Justice (2004); *Style*— Helena Kennedy, QC; ✉ c/o Hilary Hard, 12 Athelstan Close, Harold Wood, Essex RM3 0QJ (tel and fax 01708 379482, e-mail hilary.hard@btinternet.com)

KENNEDY-SANIGAR, Patrick; s of William Adrian George Sanigar, of Ely, Cambs, and Patricia Anne, *née* Kay; *b* 27 September 1957; *Educ* Soham GS, Soham Village Coll, Gordonstoun, Canterbury Coll of Art Sch of Architecture (BA, DipArch); *m* 12 Oct 1989, Melena Kay, da of Alan Mark Kennedy; 3 da (Courtney Oneka b 24 July 1991, Ottilie Fabien b 6 April 1993, Sydney Camille b 27 Aug 1995); *Career* head of design Townscape Homes Ltd 1981 (site agent 1979); fndr: Townscape Designs Ltd (dir and head of design) 1982, Townscape Interiors Ltd 1984, Harbour Studios 1986 (having resigned all directorships of the Townscape Group); head of design 691 Promotions Ltd 1991–95, head of design servs Faithdean Interiors Ltd Chatham 1995–97 (design conslt 1991–95); dir: Domus Estates Ltd 1992–99, Honeywood Forestry Ltd 1993, Space Shuffle Ltd 2001; projects incl: The Tube shoe retail chain 1985 (featured Designers Journal 1986), restoration in assoc with Lionel March The How House (LA) 1986, The Cocoon concert bldg 1991, Swedish Knotty Timber project 1991–92 and 1994–95, The Penguin Café Canterbury, The Kent Bio-power Renewable Energy Project 1993–95, The Millennium Underground Dwelling Project 2000, Earth Studio Three Project 2006; memb Visiting Bd Panel RIBA 1987–89; FCSD 1988 (co chm of Interiors Gp and memb Cncl 1990), fell Br Inst of Interior Design 1988; *Recreations* qualified gymnasium instructor, swimming, earth sheltered housing; *Style*— Patrick Kennedy-Sanigar, Esq; ✉ Wolverton, 95 The Street, Boughton-under-Blean, Faversham, Kent ME13 9BG (tel 01227 750639, e-mail p.kennedysanigar@btinternet.com)

KENNELLY, Brendan; *b* 1936; *Educ* St Ita's Coll Co Kerry, TCD (BA, MA, PhD), Univ of Leeds; *Career* poet, dramatist and lectr; lectr TCD 1963–71, Guidersleeve prof Barnard Coll NYC 1971, Cornell prof of literature Swarthmore Coll Penn 1971–72, prof of modern literature TCD 1973–2004; hon doctorate Trinity Coll Conn 1992; *Publications* The Real Ireland (text, photos by Liam Blake, 1984), Ireland Past and Present (ed, 1985), Landmarks of Irish Drama (1988); *Poetry* My Dark Fathers (1964), Collection One - Getting Up Early (1966), Good Souls to Survive (1967), Dream of a Black Fox (1968), A Drinking Cup (1970), Selected Poems (1969), The Penguin Book of Irish Verse (ed, 1970, 2 edn 1981), Selected Poems (1971), Love Cry (1972), The Voices (1973), Shelley in Dublin (1974), A Kind of Trust (1975), New and Selected Poems (1976), Islandman (1977), A Small Light (1979), The Boats Are Home (1980), The House That Jack Didn't Build (1982), Moloney Up and At It, Cromwell (1983 Eire, 1987 UK), Selected Poems (1985), Mary (1987), Love of Ireland - Poems from the Irish (trans, 1989), A Time for Voices - Selected Poems 1960–90 (1990), The Book of Judas (1991, Sunday Independent/Irish Life Award for Poetry), Joycechoyce: The poems in verse and prose of James Joyce (ed jtly with A N Jeffares, 1992), Breathing Spaces (1992), Poetry My Arse (1995), The Man Made of Rain (1998), Begin (1999), Glimpses (2001), The Little Book of Judas (2002), Martial Art (2003), Familiar Strangers: New and Selected Poems 1960–2004 (2004), Now (2006); *Novels* The Crooked Cross (1963), The Florentines (1967); *Plays* Antigone (1983, Peacock Theatre Dublin), Medea (1988, Dublin Theatre Festival), Cromwell (1986, Damer Hall Dublin), Trojan Women (1993, Peacock Theatre Dublin), Blood Wedding (1996, Newcastle Playhouse); *Style*— Brendan Kennelly, Esq; ✉ Department of English, Trinity College, Dublin 2, Ireland (tel 00 353 1 896 2301 or 00 353 1 896 1111, fax 00 353 1 677 2694)

KENNERLEY, Prof James Anthony Machell (Tony); s of late William James Kennerley, of Hale, Cheshire, and late Vida May, *née* Machell; *b* 24 October 1933; *Educ* Altrincham GS, Rhyl GS, Univ of Manchester (BSc), Imperial Coll London (MSc); *m* 12 Jan 1978, Dorothy Mary, da of George Paterson Simpson; 2 c (David James, Elizabeth Lindsay (twins) b 20 Nov 1978); *Career* Univ and RAF Pilot Training 1952–55; aerodynamicist: AV Roe & Co Manchester 1955–58, Pratt & Whitney USA 1958–59; Flying Offr RCAF 1959–62; asst prof of mathematics Univ of New Brunswick 1962–67, dir of graduate studies Manchester Business Sch 1967–69, assoc prof of business mathematics Columbia Univ Business Sch NY 1969–70, sr lectr in mktg and quantitative methods London Business Sch 1970–73, dir and prof Strathclyde Univ Business Sch 1973–83; exec dir Business Graduates' Assoc 1983–86, dir Intermatrix Ltd (Mgmnt Consits) 1984–89, ind mgmnt conslt 1983–97, visiting prof City Univ 1991–95, prof of health mgmnt Univ of Surrey 1993–97; arbitrator ACAS 1976–, memb Advsy Bd Meta Generics 1991–96, chm W Surrey and NE Hants HA 1986–93, chm Cncl for Professions Supplementary to Med 1990–96, chm NW Surrey HA 1993–95, chm W Surrey Health Cmmn 1995–96; dir First Step Housing Co Waverley BC 1990–93; memb: Legal Aid Advsy Ctee 1991–93, Monopolies and Mergers Ctee 1991–99, Cncl Inst of Mgmnt 1991–98, Competition Cmmn 1999–2001; Complaints Cmmr for Channel Tunnel Rail Link 1997–; Crossrail referee 2005–; CEng, CMath, AFIMA, MIMechE, AFRAeS, CIMgt; *Books* Guide To Business Schools (1985), Arbitration, Cases in Industrial Relations (1994); *Recreations* flying, travelling; *Clubs* Reform, Caledonian; *Style*— Prof Tony Kennerley; ✉ 15 Stonelodge Lane, Ipswich IP2 9PF (tel 01473 603127)

KENNERLEY, Peter Dilworth; TD (1989); s of John Dilworth Kennerley, and Margery, *née* Dugard (d 1977); *b* 9 June 1956; *Educ* Collyers Sch, Sidney Sussex Coll Cambridge (MA); *m* 1989, Hon (Anne Marie) Ghislaine du Roy, da of late Hon Sir Thomas Galbraith, KBE, MP; 2 da (Sarah Marie Louise b 30 Jan 1991, Julia Anne Delphine b 13 Feb 2002), 1 s (Samuel John Maximilian b 21 July 1992); *Career* TA Maj Royal Yeo 1986; Simmons & Simmons: joined 1979, admitted slr 1981, ptnr 1986–99; co sec and gen counsel Scottish & Newcastle plc 1999–; sec Panel on Takeovers and Mergers 1986–88; cncllr London Borough of Wandsworth 1994–98; Parly candidate (Cons) Doncaster N 1997; memb Law Soc; *Clubs* Cavalry and Guards'; *Style*— Peter Kennerley, Esq; ✉ Scottish & Newcastle plc, 28 St Andrew Square, Edinburgh EH2 1AF (tel 0131 203 2100, fax 0131 203 2323, e-mail peter.kennerley@s-n.com)

KENNET, 2 Baron (UK 1935); Wayland Hilton Young; s of 1 Baron Kennet, GBE, DSO, DSC, PC (d 1960), and Kathleen, da of Rev Canon Lloyd Stewart Bruce (3 s of Sir James Bruce, 2 Bt) and widow of Capt Robert Falcon Scott, CVO, RN, the Antarctic explorer; Lady Kennet was a sculptor whose works include the statue of her first husband in Waterloo Place, London; *b* 2 August 1923; *Educ* Stowe, Trinity Coll Cambridge (MA), Univ of Perugia; *m* 24 Jan 1948, Elizabeth Ann, da of Capt Bryan Fullerton Adams, DSO, RN; 1 s, 5 da; *Heir* s, Hon Thoby Young; *Career* sat as Lab and Social Dem peer in House of Lords 1960–99; RN 1942–45, FO 1946–47 and 1949–51, delg Parly Assemblies WEU and Cncl of Europe 1962–65, Parly sec Miny of Housing and Local Govt 1966–70, Labour oppn spokesman Foreign Affrs and Science Policy 1971–81; chm: Advsy Ctee on Oil Pollution of the Sea 1970–74, CPRE 1971–72, Int Parly Conferences on the Environment 1972–78; MEP 1978–79, SDP chief whip in House of Lords 1981–88, SDP spokesman on Defence and Foreign Affrs 1981–90; vice-chm: Parly Office of Sci and Technol 1990–98; vice-pres: Parly and Sci Ctee 1988–96, Chartered Inst of Environmental Health 1984–, Arboricultural Assoc 1977; pres: Architecture Club 1983–93, Avebury Soc 2002–, Stonehenge Alliance 2006– (former chm); patron Action for the River Kennet 2005– (former pres); memb Bd of Advsrs Centre for Medical Law and Ethics KCL 1990; memb North Atlantic Assembly 1997–2000; writer; Hon FRIBA; *Books* novels: The Deadweight, Now or Never, Still Alive Tomorrow; non-fiction: The Italian Left, Strategy for Survival, The Montesi Scandal, The Profumo Affair, Eros Denied, Thirty Four Articles, Preservation, The Futures of Europe (ed), The Rebirth of Britain (ed), Parliaments and Screening (ed); jtly (with wife Elizabeth Young): Old London Churches, London's Churches, Northern Lazio: An Unknown Italy (first prize Euro Fedn of Tourist Press 1990); *Recreations* sailing, music, walking; *Style*— Lord Kennet; ✉ 100 Bayswater Road, London W2 3HJ (e-mail waylandkennet@gn.apc.org)

KENNETT, Ronald John (Ron); s of William John Kennett (d 1980), of Thornhill, W Yorks, and Phyllis Gertrude, *née* Whipp (d 1972); *b* 25 March 1935; *Educ* Bishopshalt Sch, Bradford Tech Coll (HNC in electrical engrg); *m* 16 March 1957, Sylvia, da of Tom Barstow (d 1976), of Thornhill, W Yorks; 1 s (Andrew Martyn b 1958), 3 da (Julie Elizabeth b 1959, Stephanie Louise b 1964, Ruth Victoria b 1967); *Career* Lucas Aerospace Ltd: various engrg appts Bradford 1956–78, chief engr Power Systems Div 1978–86, quality assurance mangr Power Systems Div 1986–88; dir Royal Aeronautical Soc 1988–98; non-exec dir NHS 2000–06; memb Ct Univ of Herts 2004–06, vice-chair of govrs Aldbury VC Primary Sch, churchwarden St John the Baptist Church Aldbury; FRAeS 1981; *Recreations* reading, music, photography, Persian cat, golf; *Clubs* Stocks Golf; *Style*— Ron Kennett, Esq; ✉ Greenbanks, Toms Hill Road, Aldbury, Tring, Hertfordshire HP23 5SA (tel 01442 851268, e-mail ron.kennett@virgin.net)

KENNEY, Anthony; s of Eric Alfred Allen Kenney (d 1992), of West Mersea, Essex, and Doris Winifred, *née* Dollwood (d 1995); *b* 17 January 1942; *Educ* Brentwood Sch, Gonville & Caius Coll Cambridge (MA), The London Hosp Med Coll (MB BChir); *m* 1, 1966 (m dis 1973), Elizabeth Dain Fielding; 2 s (Christopher Julian b 1967, Nicholas Charles b 1970); m 2, 1973, Patricia Clare, da of Maj Rafe Trevor Newbery, MBE (d 1981); 2 s (Alexander William b 1974, Simon Rafe b 1977), 1 da (Louise Clare b 1980); *Career* formerly: sr registrar Westminster and Kingston Hosps, sr house surgn Queen Charlotte's and Chelsea Hosp for Women, res accoucheur The London Hosp, conslt obstetrician and gynaecologist St Thomas' Hosp London 1980–2002; former examiner RCOG and Univs of Cambridge, London and Liverpool; tstee: Tommy's Campaign, Quit, Med Soc of London; FRCS 1970, FRCOG 1987 (MRCOG 1972); *Recreations* canal cruising, foreign travel; *Clubs* RSM; *Style*— Anthony Kenney, Esq; ✉ Perching Sands Farmhouse, Edburton Road, Fulking, West Sussex BN5 9LS (tel 01273 857171)

KENNEY, Edward John; s of George Kenney, and Emmie Carlina Elfrida, *née* Schwenke; *b* 29 February 1924; *Educ* Christ's Hosp, Trinity Coll Cambridge (Craven scholar, Craven student, Chancellor's medallist, MA); *m* 18 June 1955, (Gwyneth) Anne, da of late Henry Albert Harris; *Career* served WWII: Royal Signals UK and India 1943–46, cmmnd 1944, Lt 1945; asst lectr Univ of Leeds 1951–52; Univ of Cambridge: res fell Trinity Coll 1952–53, asst lectr 1955–60, lectr 1966–70, reader in Latin lit and textual criticism 1970–74, Kennedy prof of Latin 1974–82; Peterhouse Cambridge: fell 1953–91, dir of studies in classics 1953–74, librarian 1953–82, tutor 1956–62, sr tutor 1962–65, Perne librarian 1987–91, domestic bursar 1987–88; jt ed: Classical Quarterly 1959–65, Cambridge Greek and Latin Classics 1970–; Sather prof of classical lit Berkeley 1968, Carl Newell Jackson lectr Harvard Univ 1980 (James C Loeb fell in classical philology 1967–68); author of articles and reviews in classical jls; pres: Jt Assoc of Classical Teachers 1977–79, Classical Assoc 1982–83, Horatian Soc 2002–07; treas and chm Cncl of Almoners Christ's Hospital 1984–86; FBA 1968, foreign memb Royal Netherlands Acad of Arts and Scis 1976; *Books* P Ouidi Nasonis Amores etc (ed, 1961, 2 edn 1995), Ovidiana Graeca (ed with Mrs P E Easterling, 1965), Appendix Vergiliana (ed with W V Clausen, F R D Goodyear, J A Richmond, 1966), Lucretius De Rerum Natura III (ed, 1971), The Classical Text (1974, Italian trans 1995), Cambridge History of Classical Literature II (ed and contrib, 1982), The Ploughman's Lunch (1984), Ovid, Metamorphoses (introduction and notes, 1985), Ovid, The Love Poems (introduction and notes, 1990), Apuleius, Cupid & Psyche (ed, 1990), Ovid, Sorrows of an Exile (introduction and notes, 1992), Ovid, Heroides XVI-XXI (ed, 1996), Apuleius, The Golden Ass (trans, introduction and notes, 1998); *Recreations* cats, books; *Style*— Prof E J Kenney, FBA; ✉ Peterhouse, Cambridge CB2 1RD

KENNICUTT, Prof Robert Charles; s of Robert Charles Kennicutt (d 1996), and Joyce Ann, *née* Laird; *b* 4 September 1951, Baltimore, MD; *Educ* Rensselaer Poly Inst NY (BS), Univ of Washington (MS, PhD); *Family* 1 da (Laura b 18 Sept 1982); *Career* adjunct research fell California Inst of Technol and Carnegie postdoctoral fell Hale Observatories 1978–80, asst prof then assoc prof Dept of Astronomy Univ of Minnesota 1980–88; Univ of Arizona: astronomer Steward Observatory 1988–2005 (memb Cncl 1989–2005), assoc prof 1988–92, dep head Dept of Astronomy 1991–98 (academic dir 1990–98), prof 1992–2005; Plumian prof of astronomy and experimental philosophy Univ of Cambridge 2005–, professorial fell Churchill Coll Cambridge 2006–; visiting positions and lectureships incl: visiting fell Leiden Observatory 1982, Beatrice M Tinsley centennial visiting prof Univ of Texas 1994, Adriaan Blaauw visiting prof Univ of Groningen 2001, Whitford lectr Univ of Wisconsin 2002, Caroline Hershel distinguished visitor Space Telescope Science Inst Baltimore 2006–07, Lyman Spitzer lectr Princeton Univ 2007; ed-in-chief The Astrophysical Jl 1999–2006, memb Int Advsy Ctee Chinese Jl of Astronomy and Astrophysics 2002–, memb Editorial Bd Cambridge Univ Press Astrophysics Series 2007–; memb of numerous professional ctees incl: Nat Acad of Sciences/Nat Research Cncl Ctee on Astronomy and Astrophysics 1998–2001, Hubble Space Telescope Science Inst Cncl 2000–04, Advsy Ctee Nat Science Fndn Nat Virtual Observatory 2002–06, NASA Science Mission Directorate Evaluation Team 2004–05, Astrophysics Sub-Ctee NASA Advsy Cncl 2006–, Scientific Advsy Ctee European Virtual Observatory Project 2006–, Wissenschaftlicher Beirat Astrophysikalishe Inst Potsdam 2006–; Alfred P Sloan fell 1983–87; Dannie Heineman Prize American Inst of Physics/American Astronomical Soc 2007; memb: Nat Acad of Sciences (USA) 2006, IAU, American Astronomical Soc (vice-pres 1998–2001, memb Exec Ctee 1999–2001), Astronomical Soc of the Pacific; FRAS, fell American Acad of Arts and Sciences 2001; *Recreations* rock collecting; *Style*— Prof Robert C Kennicutt; ✉ 55 Carlyle Road, Cambridge CB4 3DH (tel 01223 328558); Institute of Astronomy, Madingley Road, Cambridge CB3 0HA (tel 01223 765844, fax 01223 766658, e-mail robk@ast.cam.ac.uk)

KENNY, Sir Anthony John Patrick; kt (1992); s of John Kenny, and Margaret, *née* Jones; *b* 16 March 1931; *Educ* St Joseph's Coll Upholland, Gregorian Univ Rome, St Benet's Hall Oxford (DPhil); *m* 2 April 1966, Nancy Caroline, da of Henry T Gayley Jr, of Ithaca, NY, USA; 2 s (Robert b 1968, Charles b 1970); *Career* master Balliol Coll Oxford 1978–89, warden and sec Rhodes Tst Oxford 1989–99, pro-vice-chllr Univ of Oxford 1995–2001, pres Univ of Oxford Devpt Prog 1999–2001; chm Br Library Bd 1993–96; Hon DLitt: Bristol 1982, Liverpool 1988, Glasgow 1990, Lafayette PA 1990, Trinity Coll Dublin 1992, Hull 1993, Warwick 1995, Sheffield 1995, London 2002; Hon DHL Denison OH 1986, Hon DCL: Oxford 1987, Belfast 1994; hon bencher Lincoln's Inn 1999; FBA 1974 (vice-pres 1986–88, pres 1989–93); *Books* Action, Emotion and Will (1963 and 2003), Descartes (1968), Wittgenstein (1973), Will, Freedom and Power (1975), Freewill and Responsibility (1978), The God of the Philosophers (1979), A Path from Rome (1986), The Road to Hillsborough (1986), The Heritage of Wisdom (1987), Reason and Religion (1987), The Metaphysics of Mind (1989), Aristotle on the Perfect Life (1992), What is Faith? (1992), Aquinas on Mind (1992), The Oxford Illustrated History of Western Philosophy (ed, 1994), Frege (1995), A Life in Oxford (1997), A Brief History of Western Philosophy (1998), Essays on the Aristotelian Tradition (2000), Aquinas on Being (2002), A New History of Western Philosophy, Vol I (2003), Arthur Hugh Clough: A Poet's Life, The Unknown God (2004), A New History of Western Philosophy, Vol II (2005), A New History of Western Philosophy, Vol III (2006), What I Believe (2006), Life, Liberty and the Pursuit of Utility (jtly, 2006), A New History of Western Philosophy, Vol IV (2007); *Clubs* Oxford and Cambridge, Athenaeum; *Style*— Sir Anthony Kenny, FBA; ✉ St John's College, Oxford OX1 3JP

KENNY, Julie Ann; CBE (2002), DL (S Yorks 2005); da of Cyril Bower (d 1992), of Sheffield, and H J Johanna, *née* Klement; *b* 19 August 1957, Sheffield; *m* (m dis); 2 s (Oliver James Paul b 19 Jan 1989, Laurence Jason Peter b 6 Jan 1992), 1 da (Charlotte Louise b 20 Nov 1993); *Career* litigation lawyer in private practice and with local authorities until 1989, md Pyronix Ltd and chief exec Secure Holdings Ltd 1989–; chm: Regnl Industrial Devpt Bd 1996–2002, Rotherham New Deal Employers' Coalition 2000–02, S Yorks Steel Task Force 2000–02, Business Link S Yorks 2001–05, S Yorks New Deal Employers' Coalition 2002–05, Rotherham Partnership 2002–05, Small Business Cncl 2005–07; memb Bd: Br Security Industry Assoc 1992– (chm Security Equipment Manufacturers' Section 1998–2000 and 2002–04), S Yorks Investment Fund 2000–05, S Yorks Learning and Skills Cncl 2001–02, Yorks Forward 2003–, S Yorks Partnership 2004–, Creative Sheffield 2005–; hon dir Rotherham C of C 2004– (memb Bd and pres 2000–04); tstee Rudston Prep Sch 2002–05; fell Inst of Legal Execs 1983, FRSA 2002; *Style*— Mrs Julie Kenny, CBE, DL; ✉ Pyronix Ltd, Pyronix House, Braithwell Way, Hellaby, Rotherham, South Yorkshire S66 8QY (tel 01709 535218, fax 01709 700101, e-mail juliek@pyronix.com)

KENNY, Prof Phillip Herbert; s of Robert Kenny, of King's Lynn, and Moira, *née* Davies; *b* 9 August 1948; *Educ* Univ of Bristol (LLB), Univ of Cambridge (Dip Criminology), Columbia Univ (LLM); *m* 7 Aug 1970, Ann Mary, da of Harold Langley (d 1970), of Winchester; 1 s (Stephen b 1982), 3 da (Julia b 1975, Angharad b 1977, Helen b 1979); *Career* slr; head of Law Dept Univ of Northumbria at Newcastle (formerly Newcastle Poly) 1980–, former univ and poly lectr, legal dir Educn Assets Bd; conslt Messrs Dickinson Dees Slrs Newcastle upon Tyne; *Publications* Conveyancing Law, Study of Law, Conveyancing Law and Practice, Licensed Conveyancers the New Law, Sweet and Maxwell's Law Files, Mines and Minerals in Conveyancing, Property Law Statutes, Leasehold Reform Housing and Urban Development Act 1994, Covenants for Title, Trusts of Land and Appointment of Trustees, Mobile Homes an Occupiers Guide (Shelter); *Recreations* shooting, walking, sailing, golf; *Clubs* Keswick Golf; *Style*— Prof Phillip Kenny; ✉ 105 Kenton Road, Gosforth NE3 4NL; University of Northumbria at Newcastle, Ellison Building, Ellison Place, Newcastle upon Tyne NE1 8ST (tel 0191 232 6002, fax 0191 235 8017)

KENRICK, Martin John; s of William Edmund Kenrick (d 1981), of Birmingham, and Elizabeth Dorothy Magdalen, *née* Loveday (d 1999); family non-conformists who settled with others in Midlands; *b* 5 February 1940; *Educ* Newlands, Rugby, TCD (MA, BComm), Cranfield Inst of Technol (MSc); *m* 21 Feb 1970, Christine Mary, da of Charles Ronald Wingham (d 1972), of St Albans, Herts; 2 da (Tanya b 1972, Helen b 1973), 1 s (Hilgrove b 1977); *Career* guardian Birmingham Assay Office 1971–2007, cmmr of taxes 1972–, chm Archibald Kenrick & Sons Ltd 1978–91 (md 1973–78); dir: Birmingham R&D Ltd 1985–2003 (chm 1985–87), Rote Public Relations 1991–92, Jones & Barclay Ltd 1991–93, Martin Kenrick Associates 1991–2004, Turnock Ltd 2001–02, Swan Laundry Ltd 2001–02, Cape Instruments Ltd 2001–04; managing conslt Directormatch 1993–2004; Univ of Birmingham: hon life memb Ct of Govrs 1978, memb Cncl 1981–96, memb Fin and Gen Purpose Ctee 1987–88; memb Mgmnt Ctee W Midlands Regnl Mgmnt Centre 1978–82; Birmingham C of C and Industry: memb Cncl 1981–98, memb Gen Purposes Ctee 1982–93, chm Educn Ctee 1985–89, memb Working Pty for Industry Year 1985–86, vice-pres 1988–90, pres 1990–91; dir: Birmingham Chamber Training Ltd 1986–87, Black Country Museum Tst 1987–2003; chm: Policy Gp Birmingham Local Employer Network 1987–89, W Midlands Region Industry Matters 1987–90, Birmingham Educn Business Partnership 1989–93, Police Advsy Ctee Birmingham City Centre 1995–2000; govr Fndn for Schs of King Edward VI Birmingham 1990–93; chm W Midland Bird Club 2007–; FInstD; *Recreations* ornithology, skiing, tennis, gardening; *Style*— Martin J Kenrick, Esq; ✉ September House, Woodrow, Chaddesley Corbett, Worcestershire DY10 4QE (tel 01562 777415, e-mail martin@kenrick.co.uk)

KENSINGTON, 8 Baron (I 1776 and UK 1886); Hugh Ivor Edwardes; s of Capt Hon Owen Edwardes (d 1937, 2 s of 6 Baron Kensington, CMG, DSO, TD, JP, DL); suc unc, 7 Baron, 1981; *b* 24 November 1933; *Educ* Eton; *m* 1961, Juliet Elizabeth Massy, da of Capt Alexander Massy Anderson (d 1943); 1 da (Hon Amanda b 1962), 2 s (Hon Owen b 1964, Hon Rupert b 1967); *Heir* s, Hon Owen Edwardes; *Career* farmer and thoroughbred breeder; *Recreations* horse breeding, shooting; *Clubs* Boodle's, Victoria Country (Pietermaritzburg); *Style*— The Rt Hon the Lord Kensington; ✉ Friar Tuck, PO Box 549, Mooi River, 3300 Natal, South Africa (tel 00 27 33 2666323)

KENSINGTON, Bishop of 1996–; Rt Rev Michael John Colclough; s of Joseph Colclough, of Stoke-on-Trent, Staffs, and Beryl, *née* Dale (d 1969); *b* 29 December 1944; *Educ* Stanfield Tech HS 1957–65, Univ of Leeds (BA), Cuddesdon Theol Coll; *m* 24 Sept 1983, Cynthia Flora Mary, da of Joseph Christopher de Sousa, MBE; 2 s (Edward Joseph, Aidan Michael); *Career* curate: St Werburgh Burslem 1971–75, St Mary S Ruislip 1975–79; vicar of St Anselm Hayes 1979–86, area dean of Hillingdon 1985–92; priest-in-charge St Margaret and St Andrew Uxbridge and St John Uxbridge Moor 1986–88, team rector of Uxbridge 1988–92, archdeacon of Northolt 1992–94, personal asst to the Bishop of London 1994–96, priest-in-charge St Vedast-alias-Foster London 1994–96, priest-in-charge St Magnus the Martyr London 1995–96, dep priest in Ordinary to HM The Queen 1995–96; dean of univ chaplains 1994–96; chair Dioceses of London and Southwark Penal Concerns Gp 1996–, vice-pres Everychild 1998–2002; patron: Micro-Loan Fndn 1999–, London Care Connections 2003–, Shooting Star Tst 2004, West London Action for Children 2005–, Hoffman Fndn 2005–; *Recreations* English countryside, family, reading; *Style*— The Rt Rev the Bishop of Kensington; ✉ Dial House, Riverside, Twickenham, Middlesex TW1 3DT (tel 020 8892 7781, fax 020 8891 3969, e-mail bishop.kensington@london.anglican.org)

KENSWOOD, 2 Baron (UK 1951); John Michael Howard Whitfield; does not use title; s of 1 Baron Kenswood (d 1963); *b* 6 April 1930; *Educ* Trinity Coll Sch Ontario, Harrow, Grenoble Univ, Emmanuel Coll Cambridge; *m* 1951, Deirdre Anna Louise, da of Colin Malcolm Methven, of Errol, Perthshire; 4 s (Hon Michael b 1955, Hon Anthony b 1957, Hon Steven b 1958, Hon Benjamin b 1961), 1 da (Hon Anna Louise b 1964); *Heir* s, Hon Michael Whitfield; *Style*— (preferred style) John Whitfield; ✉ La Gavotte, 84400 Rustrel, France

KENT, Brian Hamilton; s of Clarence Kent (d 1946), of Hyde, Cheshire, and Edyth Kent (d 1963); *b* 29 September 1931; *Educ* Hyde GS, Univ of Salford (BSc Eng); *m* 15 May 1954, Margery, da of Laurence Foulds (d 1974), of Bredbury, Cheshire; 1 s (Peter Hamilton b 15 April 1958), 2 da (Wendy Susan (Mrs Martin) b 13 July 1960, Linda Anne (Mrs Lynch) b 10 Oct 1961); *Career* Lt RN(t) 1954–57; mangr Mather and Platt Contracting Ltd 1960, mktg dir Morganite Carbon Ltd 1965, md Alfa Laval UK Ltd 1970; chm: Staveley Industries plc 1987–94 (chief exec and gp md 1980), Wellington Holdings plc 1994–2005, BPC Ltd 1996–98, Hallmark Industries Ltd 2006–; dir and dep chm I.A.C Ltd 2000–; former tstee Industry and Parliamentary Tst, past cncl memb CBI, pres IMechE 1994, past memb Cncl Bd of Engrg Profession 1995–98; govr Kingston Univ 1996–2003 (chm Fin Ctee); Hon DSc Univ of Salford 1995; FIMechE, FIEE, FREng 1995; *Recreations* boating, bridge, tennis; *Clubs* RAC, Directors; *Style*— Brian Kent, Esq, FREng; ✉ Collingwood, 16 Woodlands Road, Surbiton, Surrey KT6 6PS; c/o Mezzanine Management, 1 Southampton Street, London WC2R 0LR (tel 020 7665 5000, fax 020 7665 5001)

KENT, Michael Harcourt; QC (1996); s of late Capt Barrie Harcourt Kent, RN, of Petersfield, Hants, and Margaret, *née* Wightman; *b* 5 March 1952; *Educ* The Nautical Coll Pangbourne, Univ of Sussex (BA); *m* 1977, Sarah Ann, da of Alan John Ling; 2 s (Rupert Haworth Harcourt b 2 April 1982, Leo Jonathan Harcourt b 2 Feb 1985); *Career* called to the Bar Middle Temple 1975; memb Supplementary Panel of Jr Counsel to the Crown (Common Law) 1988–96, recorder 2000– (asst recorder 1999–2000); asst boundary cmmr 2001–; *Recreations* sailing; *Style*— Michael Kent, Esq, QC; ✉ Crown Office Chambers, 2 Crown Office Row, Temple, London EC4Y 7HJ (tel 020 7797 8100, fax 020 7797 8101, e-mail kent@crownofficechambers.com)

KENT, Dr Paul Welberry; JP (1972); s of Thomas William Kent (d 1975), of Doncaster, and Marion, *née* Cox (d 1954); *b* 19 April 1923; *Educ* Doncaster GS, Univ of Birmingham (BSc, PhD), Jesus Coll Oxford (MA, DPhil, DSc); *m* 23 Aug 1952, Rosemary Elizabeth Boutflower, da of Maj Charles Herbert Boutflower Shepherd, MC, TD (d 1980), of Oxford; 3 s (Anthony b 1955, Richard b 1961, Peter b 1964), 1 da (Deborah b 1957); *Career* asst lectr subsequently ICI fell Univ of Birmingham 1946–50, visiting fell Princeton Univ NJ 1948–49, demonstrator in biochemistry Univ of Oxford 1950–72, tutor and Dr Lees reader ChCh Oxford 1955–72 (emeritus student 1972–, censor of degrees 2000–), master Van Mildert Coll Durham 1972–82 (res dir 1972–82); biochemical conslt, visiting prof Windsor Univ Ontario 1971 and 1980; memb: Oxford City Cncl 1964–72, Ctee Biochemical Soc 1963–67, Chemical Cncl 1965–70, Advsy Ctee Cystic Fibrosis Res Cncl 1977–82; govr: Oxford Coll of Technol (subsequently Oxford Poly) 1964–72 and 1983–88 (vice-chm 1966–69, chm 1969–71), St Chad's Coll Durham 1976–88, Pusey House Oxford 1983–2000 (registrar 1993–96, vice-pres 2004); memb Oxford Poly (now Oxford Brookes Univ) Higher Educn Corp 1988–97; Rolleston Prize 1952, Medal of the Société de Chemie Biologique Paris 1969, hon fell Canterbury Coll Ontario 1974, Hon DLitt Drury Univ 1973, Hon DSc CNAA 1991; author of articles in scientific jls and jt author of scientific monographs; FRSC 1950; Order of Merit (Germany) 1970; *Books* Biochemistry of the Amino Sugars (with M W Whitehouse, 1955), International Aspects of the Provision of Medical Care (1976), Some Scientists in the Life of Christ Church Oxford (2001), Robert Hooke and the English Renaissance (with A Chapman, 2005); *Recreations* travel, flute and organ music; *Clubs* Athenaeum; *Style*— Dr Paul Kent; ✉ 18 Arnolds Way, Cumnor Hill, Oxford OX2 9JB (tel 01865 862087)

KENT, Pauline; da of Roy Kent, of Felmingham, Norfolk, and Irene, *née* Rimes; *b* 30 June 1961; *Educ* Orme Girls' Sch Newcastle-under-Lyme, Univ of Birmingham (BA); *m* 1992, Jeremy Budden, s of Michael Budden; 1 da (Olivia Clementine b 4 Oct 1994), 1 s (Matthew b 10 Sept 1996); *Career* copywriter/account exec Lynne Franks PR 1982–84, account mangr Grant Spreckley Williams 1984–87, account mangr then account dir VandenBurg PR 1987–90, dir VandenBurg Kent 1990–93, creative dir Countrywide Porter Novelli 1993–; PRCA awards for: Reed Employment 1989, launch of first UK Disney Store 1990, Nivea/Fashion Targets Breast Cancer Campaign 1996; author of various articles in the trade and nat press; memb Business in the Community Task Force; *Recreations* walks by the sea, writing children's stories (for own children), cycling, relaxing with friends and family; *Style*— Ms Pauline Kent

KENT, Roderick David; s of Dr Basil Stanley Kent (d 1991), of Ramsdell, Hants, and Vivien Margaret, *née* Baker (d 2006); *b* 14 August 1947; *Educ* King's Sch Canterbury, CCC Oxford (MA), INSEAD (MBA); *m* 12 Aug 1972, Belinda Jane, da of W H Mitchell (d 1983), of Grouville, Jersey; 3 da (Sophie b 1974, Nicola b 1976, Tiffany b 1978); *Career* with J Henry Schroder Wagg & Co Ltd 1969–71, Banque Blyth (Paris) 1971, Triumph Investment Tst 1972–74; Close Brothers Gp: dir Close Brothers 1974–84, md Close Brothers 1975–84, md Close Brothers Gp plc 1984–2002, non-exec dir 2002–, non-exec chm 2006–; chm Bradford & Bingley 2002–; non-exec dir: Wessex Water plc 1989–98, English and Scottish Investors plc 1989–98, M & G Group plc 1995–99 (chm), Whitbread plc 2002–; chm Grosvenor Ltd 2000–, non-exec dir Grosvenor Gp Ltd 2000–; tstee Esmee Fairbairn Fndn; Liveryman of Worshipful Co of Pewterers; *Recreations* sport; *Style*— Roderick Kent, Esq

KENT, Sarah Ann; da of Hugh Kent (d 1989), of Cornwall, and Joan Eileen, *née* Mather (d 1972); *b* 19 November 1941; *Educ* Haberdashers' Aske's Sch for Girls, Slade Sch of Fine Art (Dip Fine Art, Painting and Printmaking), UCL (MA), Univ of London Inst of Educn (Advanced Dip Art Educn); *m* 1961 (m dis 1965), John Howard Drane; 1 s (Matthew Pendarell); *Career* artist, exhibition curator, lectr, broadcaster, writer and magazine ed; pt/t lectr various art schs 1965–77 (incl Hornsey, London Coll of Printing, Harrow and Byam Shaw); lectr in art history and criticism: City Literary Inst London 1965–76, Extra-mural Dept Univ of London 1967–75; visiting lectr: Tate Gallery, Hayward Gallery,

Courtauld Inst, Serpentine Gallery, Nat Portrait Gallery, Whitechapel, RCA, South London Gallery; visual arts ed: Time Out magazine 1976–, 20/20 magazine 1989–90; dir of exhibitions ICA London 1977–79; *Exhibitions as curator* since 1979: Br section of Lichtbildnisse (historical survey of portrait photography Bonn) 1982, Problems of Picturing (Serpentine Gallery) 1984, Retrospective of Elisabeth Frink's Sculpture, Drawings and Prints (Royal Acad) 1985, Br section of Sydney Biennale (Art Gallery of NSW) 1986, Peripheral States (Benjamin Rhodes London), Photo 94 (Photographers' Gallery), Artist of the Day (Flowers East Gallery) 1995, Whistling Women (Royal Festival Hall) 1995, Critic's Choice (FACT Gallery) 2005; *Exhibitions as artist* solo: Redmark Gallery London 1968, Design Progression London 1970; mixed: Young Contemporaries 1965, Arts Cncl Touring 1965, Slade/Royal Coll Show 1966, Free Painters and Sculptors 1966, Ben Uri Gallery 1966, Reeves Bicentennial Exhibition 1966, Survey '67 (Camden Arts Centre) 1967, Lancaster Arts Festival 1967, Arts Cncl Touring Exhibition 1969–71, Cleveland Int Drawing Biennale 1973 (prizewinner), Cleveland Int Drawing Biennale Touring Exhibition 1979–80, Aspects of Drawing (House Gallery London) 1981, Fully Exposed - The Male Nude in Photography (Photographers' Gallery London) 1990, Artists in the Arts (John Jones Gallery London) 1992; work in collections incl: Arts Cncl of GB, Camden Arts Cncl, Cleveland BC, numerous private collections; *as writer and broadcaster* numerous contribs to TV and radio incl: Art and Technology, Arena, The South Bank Show, The Late Show, J'Accuse, Private View, Critics' Forum, Third Ear, Third Opinion, After Eight, Kaleidoscope, Meridian, Nightwaves; numerous contribs to art jls and magazines incl: Studio International, Art Monthly, Flash Art, Artscribe, Arte, Tema Celeste, Art in America, Time Out, Dance Now; memb Jury: Turner Prize Tate Gallery 1992, Gulbenkian New Horizons Award 1992, Barclay Young Artists Awards 1993, SE Arts Purchasing Award 1993, British Tport Painting Competition 1993, Arts Fndn Fellowship 1995, Northern Graduates Fine Arts Prizes 1996, John Kobal Photographic Portrait Award Nat Portrait Gallery 1998, Bloomberg New Contemporaries 2000, Schweppes Photographic Portrait Award (Nat Portrait Gallery) 2004, Emerging Artist Award British Oxygen Co 2004 and 2005; external examiner: Chelsea Sch of Art (Sculpture MA) 1986–90, Trent Poly (MA Fine Art) 1982–86, Staffs Poly (Sculpture BA) 1990–93, Univ of Nottingham (Contemporary Art Practice BA) 1993–95, Glasgow Sch of Art (Fine Art MA) 1993–97; *Publications* Berlin a Critical View: Ugly Realism 20's-70's (with Eckhart Gillen, 1978), Elisabeth Frink: Sculpture (1985), Women's Images of Men (with Jacqueline Morreau, 1985 and 1990), Shark Infested Waters (1994), Composition (1995), Stephen Balkenhol (1996); contrib to: Fotografie als Kunst: Kunst als Fotografie (by Floris M Neususs, 1979), Lichtbildnisse (by Klaus Honeff, 1982), Drawings and Graphics (by Jacqueline Morreau, 1986), Nudes in Budapest (by James Cotier, 1992), Paula Rego: Dancing Ostriches (1996), The Saatchi Decade (1999), London from Punk to Blair (2003), Flowers: Jo Self (2003); photographs published in: The Naked and the Nude (by Jorge Lewinski, 1987), Fully Exposed: the Male Nude in Photography (by Emmanuel Cooper, 1990), Running Scared (by Peter Lehman, 1993), The Boy (by Germaine Greer, 2003); *Recreations* walking, travelling, singing, sleeping, reading; *Style*— Ms Sarah Kent; ✉ Time Out Magazine, Universal House, 251 Tottenham Court Road, London W1T 7AB (tel 020 7813 3000, fax 020 7813 6193, e-mail sarahkent@timeout.com)

KENT, Trevor Lincoln; s of Ernest George Kent (d 1987), and Evelyn Gertrude Mary Kent (d 1999), of Gerrards Cross, Bucks; *Educ* Thorpe House Sch, Denstone Coll, London Coll of Commerce; *m* 7 July 1979, Angela Christine (d 1996), da of Gp Capt John Thornhill Shaw, DSO, DFC, AFC (d 1975), and Doreen Lilian Shaw (d 2004), of Berwick upon Tweed; 4 s (Toby d 1980, Lincoln b 1982, Warwick b 1983, Leicester b 1987); *Career* princ Trevor Kent & Co estate agents and auctioneers 1971–; freelance writer and broadcaster specialising in residential property and related finance; co-presenter: Moving and Improving, Housebuying Explained, Hot Property, Only Follies and Houses; specialist commentator BBC, GMTV, LWT, ITN, Sky News, IRN, Jeremy Vine Show BBC Radio 2; columnist: International Property, Estate Agency News, English Homes, The Negotiator; former media spokesman Nat Assoc of Estate Agents (pres 1989–90); memb Govt's Inter-Professional Working Pty on the Transfer of Residential Property 1989–90; dist cncllr South Bucks DC 1978–82; licensed asst C of E; FNAEA, hon memb Du Page Assoc of Realtors Chicago USA; *Recreations* cricket, watching the garden grow, auctioneering for charities, not dieting; *Clubs* Middlesex and Bucks County Cricket; *Style*— Trevor Kent, Esq; ✉ Kent House, Oxford Road, Gerrards Cross, Buckinghamshire SL9 7DP (tel 01753 885522, fax 01753 887777, website www.trevorkent.com)

KENTFIELD, Graham Edward Alfred; s of Edward Leonard Harvey Kentfield (d 1984), and Frances Elfrida May, *née* Tucker (d 2000); *b* 3 September 1940; *Educ* Bancroft's Sch, St Edmund Hall Oxford (BA); *m* 29 April 1965, Ann Dwelley, da of James Préaud Hewetson; 2 da; *Career* Bank of England: joined 1963, Economic Intelligence Dept 1964–66, seconded to Dept of Applied Economics Univ of Cambridge 1966–67, Foreign Exchange Operations 1967–69, Overseas Dept 1969–74 (a mangr 1972–74), mangr Monetary Policy Forecasting 1974–76, Govrs speechwriter 1976–77, ed Bank of England Quarterly Bulletin 1977–80, sr mangr Financial Statistics Div 1980–84, advsr Banking Dept 1984–85, dep chief Banking Dept 1985–91, chief Banking Dept and chief cashier 1991–94, dep dir and chief cashier 1994–98; chm: Insolvency Practices Cncl 2000–04, Building Societies Tst Ltd 2002–; memb: Building Societies Investor Protection Bd 1991–2001, Financial Law Panel 1994–98, Cncl London Univ 2000–; tstee Chartered Inst of Bankers Pension Fund 1994– (chm 2000–06); tstee Overseas Bishoprics Fund 1999– (chm 2005–); hon treas Soc for the Promotion of Roman Studies 1991–; FCIB; *Recreations* Roman history, genealogy, philately; *Style*— Graham Kentfield, Esq; ✉ 27 Elgood Avenue, Northwood, Middlesex HA6 3QL (tel 01923 825401)

KENTON, Jeremy Martin; s of Dr Ralph J Kenton (d 1988), of Westcliff-on-Sea, Essex, and Veronica Maisie, *née* Field (d 1994); *b* 11 December 1955; *Educ* Chigwell Sch, Br Coll of Naturopathy and Osteopathy (Dip Osteopathy, Dip Naturopathy); *m* 21 July 1990, Sharon Anna, da of Reginald Eric Calder; 1 da (Claudia Elizabeth b 7 Oct 1992), 1 step da (Katrina Anna b 12 July 1986); *Career* osteopath; lectr Br Coll of Naturopathy and Osteopathy London 1979–, private osteopath London and Essex 1979–; sr clinician Br Coll of Naturopathy and Osteopathy Teaching Clinic 1981–92, Br delegate to Euro Osteopathic Liaison Ctee Brussels 1983–87, fndr Ctee Cncl for Complimentary and Alternative Med 1984; pres Br Naturopathic and Osteopathic Assoc 1988–90 (memb 1979–); memb: Gen Cncl and Register of Osteopaths 1987– (memb Cncl 1989–92, pres 1990), memb Gen Osteopathic Cncl 1998–; regular broadcaster on nat and local radio and TV 1980–, author of numerous of articles in newspapers and magazines; advsr on osteopathy to All-Pty Gp; expert witness; DO 1979, ND 1979; *Publications* Competence in Osteopathic Practice (1994); *Recreations* family, patients, horse riding, motor racing, music, theatre; *Clubs* East India, New Cavendish; *Style*— Jeremy M Kenton, Esq; ✉ 148 Harley Street, London W1G 7LG (e-mail jmkostl@aol.com)

KENTRIDGE, Sir Sydney; KCMG (1999), QC (1984); s of Morris Kentridge (d 1964), of Johannesburg, South Africa, and May, *née* Shafner (d 1971); *b* 5 November 1922; *Educ* King Edward VII Sch Johannesburg, Univ of the Witwatersrand (BA), Univ of Oxford (MA); *m* 15 Jan 1952, Felicia, da of Max Geffen (d 1977), of Johannesburg, South Africa; 2 s (William, Matthew), 2 da (Catherine, Elizabeth); *Career* WWII Lt SA Forces served E Africa, Sicily, Italy; admitted Johannesburg Bar 1949, sr counsel South Africa 1965, called to the Bar Lincoln's Inn 1977 (bencher 1986); sometime judge of the Courts of Appeal of Jersey, Guernsey and Repub of Botswana, actg justice of the Constitutional Court of South Africa 1995–96; Roberts lectr Univ of Pennsylvania 1979, Granville Clark prize USA 1978; hon fell Exeter Coll Oxford; Hon LLD: Seaton Hall (New Jersey) 1978, Univ of Leicester 1985, Univ of Cape Town 1987, Univ of Natal 1989, Univ of London 1995, Univ of Sussex 1997, Univ of the Witwatersrand 2000; hon memb Bar Assoc of City of NY 2001; *Recreations* theatre, concerts, opera-going; *Clubs* Athenaeum; *Style*— Sir Sydney Kentridge, KCMG, QC; ✉ Brick Court Chambers, 7–8 Essex Street, London WC2R 3LD (tel 020 7379 3550, fax 020 7379 3558)

KENWAY, Prof Richard Donovan; s of Alfred Bertram Kenway, and Sheila Ethel Donovan (d 1994); *b* 8 May 1954; *Educ* Univ of Exeter (BSc), Jesus Coll Oxford (grad scholar, DPhil); *m* 11 Feb 1981, Anna Cass; 3 c (Owain Alfred b 11 March 1982, Angharad Sonia b 9 April 1985, Carys Sheila b 23 Oct 1986); *Career* research assoc Brown Univ USA 1978–80, postdoctoral fell Los Alamos Nat Lab USA 1980–82; Univ of Edinburgh: SERC postdoctoral fell 1982–83, lectr in physics 1983–90, reader 1990–94, chm Edinburgh Parallel Computing Centre 1997– (dir 1993–97), Tait prof of mathematical physics 1994–, head Dept of Physics and Astronomy 1997–2000, asst princ 2002–05, vice-princ 2005–; chm UK Nat e-Science Centre 2001–; chm Particle Physics Theory Ctee PPARC 1997–2000, sr res fell PPARC 2001–04, memb American Physical Soc 1976; FInstP 2001 (MInstP 1982), FRSE 1997; *Publications* author of 120 publications in Elementary Particle Physics, High Performance Computing, and Condensed Matter Physics; *Recreations* munroing, running; *Style*— Prof Richard Kenway, FRSE, FInstP; ✉ School of Physics, University of Edinburgh, The King's Buildings, Edinburgh EH9 3JZ (tel 0131 650 5245, fax 0131 651 4048, e-mail r.d.kenway@ed.ac.uk)

KENWORTHY, Jonathan Martin; s of Alexander Kenworthy, and Joan, *née* Copper; *b* 23 June 1943; *Educ* Kingston GS, RCA, Royal Acad Schs; *m* 8 Sept 1989, Kristina Louise, *née* Wethered; 1 da (Maia Alexandra b 18 Jan 1991), 1 s (William Adam Jonathan b 15 March 1993); *Career* sculptor; cmmns incl: Ernest Hemingway Memorial Cmmn 1969, The Leopard in the City of London 1985, Lioness and Lesser Kudu London 2000; numerous exhibitions in London, New York and Africa; twice winner Landseer Travelling Scholarship, Royal Acad President's Prize for Craftsmanship, four Royal Acad Silver Medals for sculpture, Royal Acad Gold Medal and Travelling Scholarship for Sculpture, Greenshield Fndn Award Montreal 1969; FRBS 1984; *Style*— Jonathan Kenworthy, Esq

KENWORTHY-BROWNE, (Bernard) Peter Francis; s of Bernard Evelyn Kenworthy-Browne (d 1979), and Margaret Sibylla (d 1985), da of late Sir George Hadcock, KBE, FRS; *b* 11 May 1930; *Educ* Ampleforth, Oriel Coll Oxford (MA); *m* 1, 1975 (m dis 1982), Jane Elizabeth, da of late Denis Malcolm Mackie; m 2, 1989, Elizabeth Anne, da of late Dr J A Bowen-Jones; *Career* Nat Serv 2 Lt Irish Guards 1949–50; called to the Bar Lincoln's Inn 1955, Oxford and Midland & Oxford circuits 1957–82, recorder of the Crown Court 1981–82, registrar of the Family Div of High Court of Justice 1982–91, district judge of the Principal Registry of the Family Div 1991–2002; *Recreations* music, field sports, photography; *Clubs* Cavalry and Guards; *Style*— Peter Kenworthy-Browne, Esq; ✉ The Old Vicarage, Staverton, Daventry, Northamptonshire NN11 6JJ (tel 01237 704667)

K

KENWRIGHT, Bill; CBE (2001); s of Albert Kenwright, of Liverpool, and Hope, *née* Jones; *b* 4 September 1945; *Educ* Liverpool Inst HS for Boys; *m* (m dis) Anouska Hempel (Lady Weinberg); *Career* stage and film producer; actor 1964–70, theatre prodr 1970–; exec prodr Theatre Royal Windsor chm and prodr Olivier Awards Soc of London Theatres; chm Everton FC 2004– (dep chm 1999–2004); Hon Dr John Moores Univ Liverpool 1994; *Theatre* current West End productions: Blood Brothers (Phoenix), Ghosts (Comedy), The Female Odd Couple (Apollo); recent West End productions incl: Fallen Angels, Long Day's Journey Into Night (Lyric), Brief Encounter (Lyric), Miss Julie (Theatre Royal Haymarket), The Chiltern Hundreds (Vaudeville), Song at Twilight (Gielgud), 4 Steps to Heaven (Piccadilly), An Ideal Husband (Globe, Haymarket, Gielgud, Old Vic, Albery, Lyric, Barrymore NY), Stepping Out - The Musical (Albery), Hurlyburly (Queen's), Pygmalion (Albery), The Mysterious Mr Love (Comedy), Lady Windermere's Fan (Theatre Royal Haymarket), The School for Wives (Picadilly and Comedy), A Streetcar Named Desire (Theatre Royal Haymarket), Shakespeare For My Father (Theatre Royal Haymarket), The Aspern Papers (Wyndham's), The Odd Couple (Theatre Royal Haymarket), Elvis the Official Musical (Prince of Wales), Passion (Queen's), Company (Albery), Present Laughter (Globe and Aldwych), Chapter Two (Gielgud), Design for Living (Gielgud), The Roy Orbison Story (Piccadilly and Whitehall), Rupert Street Lonely Hearts Club (Criterion), The Miracle Worker (Comedy and Wyndham's), No Man Land (Comedy), Moonlight (Comedy), Dead Guilty (Apollo), In Praise of Love (Apollo), The Deep Blue Sea (Apollo), The Winslow Boy (Globe), Travels With My Aunt (Wyndham's and Minetta Lane Theatre NY, winner Drama Desk Award), Dancing at Lughnasa (Garrick and Plymouth Theatres Broadway, winner Tony award), Medea (Wyndham's and Longacre Theatre NY, winner Tony Award), Funny Money (Playhouse), My Night With Reg (Playhouse), Jane Eyre (Playhouse), Up'n'Under (Playhouse); Broadway productions: Blood Brothers (Music Box Theatre) 1993–95, A Doll's House (Belasco Theatre) 1997, The Chairs (Theatre de Complicite, Golden Theatre) 2000; prodr Peter Hall Co season (Picadilly): Waiting for Godot, The Misanthrope, Major Barbara, Filumena, Kafka's Dick; prodr (dir by Sir Peter Hall, *qv*): Mind Millie for Me (Theatre Royal Haymarket), The Master Builder (Theatre Royal Haymarket and Toronto), Hamlet (Gielgud), An Absolute Turkey (Globe), The Gift of the Gorgon (Wyndham's), Lysistrata (Old Vic, Athens and Wyndham's), Separate Tables (Albery), She Stoops To Conquer (Queen's); *Films* as exec prodr incl: Stepping Out 1991, The Day After the Fair, Zoe; *Awards* winner numerous awards incl: Tony Awards, Olivier Awards, Evening Standard Awards, Scouser of the Year 1991 and 1992, gold badge BASCA; *Recreations* football; *Style*— Bill Kenwright, Esq, CBE; ✉ Bill Kenwright Ltd, 106 Harrow Road, London W2 1RR (tel 020 7446 6200, fax 020 7446 6222)

KENYON, Guy Stuart; s of Horace Stuart Kenyon (d 1997), of Hunstanton, Norfolk, and Katherine Mary, *née* Chapman; *b* 6 January 1948; *Educ* Perse Sch Cambridge, Univ of Edinburgh (BSc, MB ChB, MD), Univ of Surrey (MBA); *m* 30 Sept 1989, Judith Elizabeth, da of Edward Meirion Morgan, of Kettering, Northants; 2 s (James Edward Stuart b 1 Feb 1991, Benjamin Raymond Guy b 20 Dec 1993); *Career* RNR 1979–88, Surgn Lt Cdr; training in gen surgery United Bristol and Royal Northern Hosps 1977–80, registrar and sr registrar in otolaryngology London Hosp, Royal Free Hosp and Royal Surrey County Hosp Guildford 1981–87; conslt surgn in otolaryngology: London Hosp 1987–, Hosps for Sick Children London 1987–92, conslt surgn St Luke's Hosp for the Clergy 1987–; contrib papers on neuro-otology and head and neck cancer; memb: Med Soc of London, The Otorhinolaryngological Res Soc 1983, The Joseph Soc 1987; FRCSEd 1980, FRCS 1982; *Books* Hutchinson's Clinical Examination (1984 and 1994), Textbook of Otolaryngology (contrib, 1988), many articles in medical journals; *Recreations* skiing, swimming, music, reading; *Clubs* RSM, Royal Naval Medical, Blizzard; *Style*— Guy Kenyon, Esq; ✉ Pentlands, East Common, Harpenden, Hertfordshire AL5 1DG (tel 01582 767593, fax 01582 767751)

KENYON, Ian Peter; s of Peter Kenyon (d 1986), and Barbara, *née* Thirlby; *b* 23 September 1961, Wimbledon; *Educ* Bradfield Coll, Univ of Nottingham (BSc); *m* 1989, Louise, *née* Tucker; 2 da (Alice b 23 Oct 1994, Fiona b 5 Sept 1996) 1 s (Richard b 26 Feb 2001); *Career* Price Waterhouse 1983–89, St Ives plc 1989–94, Kingfisher plc 1994–2002, dir financial reporting Sainsburys 2002–05, gp finance dir Carpetright plc 2005–; Liveryman Worshipful Co of Glovers; ACA 1986; *Recreations* church, tennis; *Style*— Ian Kenyon, Esq

KENYON, Dr Julian N; s of Dr Joseph Bernard Kenyon, of Worsthorne, Lancs, and Marie Therese, *née* Rudant; *b* 8 March 1947; *Educ* Lancaster Royal GS, Univ of Liverpool Med Sch (scholar, MB ChB, MD); *m* 1, 1970 (m dis 1985), Margaret Angela, *née* O'Connor; 2 da (Rachel b 31 March 1973, Abigail b 28 Feb 1984), 2 s (Benjamin b 21 Nov 1974, Rupert b 18 Jan 1978); m 2, 1987, Rachel Staveley Jessel (m dis 1999), da of Dr Thomas Bonsor Staveley Dick; 1 da (Meri Barbara b 9 June 1989), 1 s (Micha Tom b 26 Sept 1993); m 3, 2000, Tanya Cartwright, da of Norman Armitage, and Lois Armitage; *Career* house surgn Broadgreen Hosp Liverpool 1971 (house physician 1970–71), demonstrator Dept of Anatomy Univ of Liverpool Med Sch 1971–72, lectr in child health Univ of Liverpool 1972–74, princ in gen practice Crosby Liverpool 1974–76, full-time private practice in med alternatives 1976–82; currently dir: The Dove Healing Tst, The Dove Clinic for Integrated Med; former co-dir The Centre for the Study of Complementary Med Southampton; hon specialist Pain Relief Fndn Clinic Walton Hosp Liverpool 1980–82, visiting prof Calif Inst for Human Sci; pres Int Assoc of Auricular Therapy; memb: Ctee Br Holistic Med Assoc, Bd of Advsrs Findhorn Holistic Health Centre Forres Scotland, Br Soc for Clinical Ecology, Br Med Acupuncture Soc (fndr chm 1980); pres Int Auricular Med Soc, fndr chm Br Soc of Integrated Med 2002; FRCSEd 1972; *Publications* contrib, author or ed of numerous books and booklets on acupuncture and related subjects; *Recreations* playing violin, gardening; *Style*— Dr Julian N Kenyon; ✉ The Dove Clinic for Integrated Medicine, Hockley Mill Stables, Church Lane, Twyford, Winchester, Hampshire SO21 1NT (tel 01962 718000, fax 01962 718011, website www.doveclinic.com); 97 Harley Street, London W1G 6AG (tel 020 7486 5588, fax 020 7487 4442)

KENYON, 6 Baron (GB 1788); Sir Lloyd Tyrell-Kenyon; 6 Bt (GB 1784); eldest s of 5 Baron Kenyon, CBE, DL (d 1993), and Leila Mary, *née* Cookson; *b* 13 July 1947; *Educ* Eton, Magdalene Coll Cambridge (BA); *m* 1971, Sally Carolyn, da of Jack Frank Page Matthews, of Thurston, Bury St Edmunds; 2 s (Hon Lloyd Nicholas b 9 April 1972, Hon Alexander Simon b 29 Nov 1975); *Heir* s, Hon Lloyd Tyrell-Kenyon; *Career* High Sheriff Clwyd 1986; memb: Wrexham Maelor BC 1991–96, Wrexham CBC 1996–, EU Ctee of the Regions 1994–97; *Style*— The Rt Hon the Lord Kenyon; ✉ Gredington, Whitchurch, Shropshire SY13 3DH (tel 01948 830305)

KENYON, Nicholas; CBE (2001); *b* 1951; *Educ* Balliol Coll Oxford (BA); *m*; 4 c; *Career* English Bach Festival 1973–76, Music Div BBC 1976–79; music critic: The New Yorker 1979–82, The Times 1982–85; music ed The Listener 1982–87, ed Early Music 1983–92; music critic The Observer 1985–92, prog advsr Mozart Now Festival South Bank Centre 1991; BBC Radio: controller Radio 3 1992–98, BBC Proms 1996–, controller millennium progs 1998–2000, controller BBC Proms, live events and TV classical music 2000–07; md Barbican Centre 2007–; *Publications* The BBC Symphony Orchestra - The First 50 Years, Simon Rattle: From Birmingham to Berlin, Authenticity and Early Music (ed), BBC Proms Pocket Guide to Great Symphonies, BBC Proms Guide to Great Concertos (ed), BBC Proms Guide to Choral Works (ed), BBC Proms Guide to Great Orchestral Works (ed), The Faber Pocket Guide to Mozart (2005); *Style*— Nicholas Kenyon, Esq, CBE; ✉ Barbican Centre, Silk Street, London EC2Y 8DS

KENYON, Ronald James; s of Fletcher Kenyon (d 1981), of Penrith, Cumbria, and Isabella, *née* Winter; *Educ* Queen Elizabeth's GS Penrith, Trent Poly; *m* 27 April 1985, Anne Christine, da of William Eckersall; 1 s (Michael Fletcher b 14 Oct 1990), 1 da (Catherine Sarah b 31 Oct 1993); *Career* chartered accountant; articled clerk F T Kenyon and Son (founded by gf), ptnr Saint and Co (formerly F T Kenyon and Son then Kyle Saint and Co) 1980–; dir Penrith Building Soc 1993–2003; pres Penrith Chamber of Trade 2006–; chm: Cumberland Dist Soc of CAs 1991, Penrith Civic Soc 1989–91, Eden Climbing Wall 1992–, Eden Sports Cncl 1996–, Penrith Partnership 1999, Penrith Running Track Gp 2004–; treas: Penrith Amateur Savoyards 1981–84, Eden Valley Visitors Assoc 1983–2000, Penrith Agric Soc 1986–, Penrith Lions 1988–90, Greenpeace Eden Valley Support Gp 1991–93, Juniper Tst 1996–2002, Penrith Partnership 1998–; memb: Penrith Mountain Rescue Team 1967–92 (pres 1992–2002), Tibet Support Gp; winner Penrith Sports Superstar 1976; FCA (ACA 1975); *Books* Rock Climbers' Guide - North of England (1978), Rock Climbers' Guide - Borrowdale (1986 and 1990), Recent Developments of Rock Climbs in the Lake District (1984, 1986, 1988, 1990 and 1996); *Recreations* rock climbing, fell running; *Clubs* Eden Valley Mountaineering, Fell and Rock Climbing (vice-pres 1992–94, sec Guidebook Ctee 1998–), Borderliners Orienteering, Eden Runners (jrs treas and coach 2003–); *Style*— Ronald Kenyon, Esq; ✉ 30 Wordsworth Street, Penrith, Cumbria CA11 7QY (tel 01768 864728); Saint and Company, Poets Walk, Penrith, Cumbria CA11 7HJ (tel 01768 865189, fax 01768 891003, mobile 07775 768569, e-mail ron@jaggedlakes.plus.com)

KEOGH, Colin Denis; s of John Denis Keogh, and Hillary Joan, *née* Campbell; *b* 27 July 1953; *Educ* St John's Coll, Eton, UC Oxford (MA), INSEAD (MBA); *m* 26 Aug 1978, Joanna Mary Martyn, da of John Frederick Leapman; 2 s (Thomas b 27 March 1983, William b 6 May 1987), 2 da (Kate b 6 Nov 1984, Georgina b 10 Aug 1990); *Career* Arthur Andersen & Co 1978–82, INSEAD 1982–83, Saudi Int Bank 1983–85; Close Brothers Gp plc: joined 1985, dir Close Brothers Ltd 1986–95, gp dir 1995, chm Close Brothers Corporate Finance Ltd 1995–98, gp chief exec 2002–; *Recreations* sport, theatre; *Style*— Colin Keogh, Esq; ✉ Close Brothers Group plc, 10 Crown Place, London EC2A 4FT

KER, David Peter James; s of Capt David John Richard Ker, MC, DL, JP (d 1997), of Aldworth, Reading, Berks, and Virginia Mary Eloise, *née* Howard, of Suffolk and Berks; *b* 23 July 1951; *Educ* Eton; *m* 27 June 1974, Alexandra Mary, da of Vice Adm Sir Dymock Watson, KCB, CBE, DL (d 1987), of Trebinshwyn, Powys; 1 da (Clare Rose (m Donald Rice, s of Sir Tim Rice, *qv*) b 23 Nov 1977), 2 s (David Edward Richard b 18 Dec 1979 d 1980, David Humphry Rivers b 11 Oct 1982); *Career* fndr and sole proprietor David Ker Fine Art 1980–; dir: Parc St Roman SA 1977–79, Oceanic Development Co (Bahamas) Ltd 1979–80, Ker Management Ltd 1980–, Belgrave Frames Ltd 1986–92, John Paravicini Ltd 1988–92, James Roundell Ltd 1995–, Dickinson Roundell Inc USA 1998–, Humphrey Butler Ltd 2001–; md Simon C Dickinson Ltd; memb Soc of London Art Dealers 1986 (memb Ctee 2001–); *Recreations* shooting, fishing, collecting fine art, racing; *Clubs* White's, Turf, Beefsteak, Pratt's, The Brook (NY); *Style*— David Ker, Esq; ✉ 58 Jermyn Street, London SW1Y 6LX (tel 020 7493 0340, fax 020 7493 0796, mobile 07899 668972, e-mail ker@simondickinson.com)

KEREVAN, Austin James (Jim); s of James Kerevan (d 1983), of Lincoln, and Olive, *née* Stroud (d 1998); *b* 18 May 1935; *Educ* City Sch Lincoln; *m* 14 May 1966, Yvonne, da of John Burns (d 1985); 2 s (Mark James b 22 July 1968, Thomas James b 19 Sept 1984), 1 da (Emily Jane b 4 Nov 1971); *Career* RAF 1959–61; KPMG Peat Marwick: joined Peat Marwick Mitchell 1961, London office 1961–75, Reading 1975–92; currently chm Marbaix (Holdings) Ltd pension scheme; chm: W Berks Priority Care NHS Tst 1992–99; chm of govrs: St Andrew's Sch Pangbourne 2001–05 (govr 1996–2005), Rhos-y-Gwalian Outdoor Educn Centre, Abbey Sch Reading; govr Bradfield Coll 1998–2005; FCA (ACA 1959); *Recreations* family, golf, reading (all sorts), bridge, studying railways; *Clubs* West Hill Golf, Huntercombe Golf, Trevose Golf; *Style*— Jim Kerevan, Esq

KERMODE, Prof Sir (John) Frank; kt (1991); s of John Pritchard Kermode (d 1966), and Doris Pearl, *née* Kennedy (d 1967); *b* 29 November 1919; *Educ* Douglas HS, Univ of Liverpool; *Career* lectr: Univ of Durham 1947–49, Univ of Reading 1950–58; prof: Univ of Manchester 1955–65, Univ of Bristol 1965–67, UCL 1967–74, Univ of Cambridge 1974–82, Harvard Univ 1977–78, Columbia Univ 1983 and 1985; memb Arts Cncl of GB 1969–71; Hon Dr: Chicago Univ, Univ of Amsterdam, Yale Univ, Univ of Newcastle upon Tyne, Univ of Liverpool, Wesleyan Univ, Univ of London, Univ of the South Sewanee, Columbia Univ, Harvard Univ; FRSL 1957, FBA 1973, fell American Acad of Arts and Letters 1999; *Books* author of numerous works incl: Romantic Image (1957), The Sense of an Ending (1967), The Genesis of Secrecy (1979), Forms of Attention (1985), The Uses of Error (1990), Not Entitled (memoirs, 1996), Shakespeare's Language (2000), Pleasing Myself (2001), Pieces of my Mind (2003), The Age of Shakespeare (2004), Pleasure and Change (2004); *Style*— Sir Frank Kermode, FBA, FRSL; ✉ 9 The Oast House, Grange Road, Cambridge CB3 9AP (tel 01223 357931, e-mail frankkermode@lineone.net)

KERNAGHAN, Paul Robert; CBE (2005), QPM (1998); s of Hugh Kernaghan, of Belfast, and Diane, *née* Herdman; *b* 27 December 1955; *Educ* Methodist Coll Belfast, Queen's Univ Belfast (LLB), Univ of Ulster (Dip Personnel Mgmnt), Univ of Leicester (MA), RCDS; *m* 6 May 1983, Mary, *née* McCleery; 1 da (Catherine Victoria b 24 May 1988); *Career* pt/t serv UDR 1974–77 (cmmnd 2 Lt 1976); grad entrant RUC 1978, operational and staff appts Belfast, Londonderry, Strabane and Warrenpoint; Chief Constable Hants Constabulary 1999–; memb UN Int Policing Advsy Cncl 2006–; ACPO portfolio holder on int affrs; MCIPD 1991; *Recreations* reading, family, strong interest in international security issues; *Style*— Mr Paul Kernaghan, CBE, QPM; ✉ Police Headquarters, West Hill, Winchester, Hampshire SO22 5DB (tel 01962 871002, fax 01962 871201)

KERR, Alan Grainger; OBE (2000); s of Joseph William Kerr (d 1974), and Eileen, *née* Allen (d 1989); *b* 15 April 1935; *Educ* Methodist Coll Belfast, Queen's Univ Belfast (MB BCh, BAO, DRCOG); *m* 14 April 1962, Patricia Margaret (d 1999), da of Edward Stewart McNeill; 2 s (Jonathan Richard b 5 June 1963, Anthony Michael b 16 Oct 1965), 1 da (Rosalind Patricia b 18 Dec 1966); *Career* basic med trg Belfast Hosps, otolaryngology trg Belfast Hosps and Harvard Med Sch, conslt otolaryngologist Royal Victoria Hosp and Belfast City Hosp 1968–2003; prof of otorhinolaryngology Queen's Univ Belfast 1979–81; Harrison prize RSM, Jobson Horne prize BMA, Howells prize Univ of London 1988 and 1998; past pres: Section of Otology RSM, Otorhinolaryngological Res Soc, Int Otopathology Soc, Br Assoc of Otorhinolaryngologists, Irish Otolaryngological Soc, Int Soc for Otologic Surgery; FRCS 1964, FRCSEd 1987; *Books* Scott-Brown's Otolaryngology (ed, 5 edn 1987, 6 edn 1996); *Recreations* tennis, skiing, bowling; *Clubs* RSM; *Style*— Alan Kerr, Esq, OBE; ✉ 6 Cranmore Gardens, Belfast BT9 6JL (tel 028 9066 9181, fax 028 9066 3731, e-mail agkerr@unite.net)

KERR, Andy; MSP; s of William Kerr, of East Kilbride, and May Kerr, *née* Palmer; *b* 17 March 1962; *Educ* Claremont HS East Kilbride, Glasgow Coll (BA); *m* 10 April 1992, Susan, da of James Kealy; 3 da (Sophie b 9 May 1993, Lucy b 17 Oct 1995, Katherine b 18 Oct 1995); *Career* res offr Strathkelvin Dist Cncl 1987–90, quality assurance conslt Achieving Quality 1990–93, quality and environmental mangr Glasgow City Cncl 1993–99; MSP (Lab) East Kilbride 1999–, min for fin and public services 2001–04, min for health and community care 2004–; chm Tport and Environment Ctee Scot Parl 1999–; *Recreations* football, family, reading, running (10km races and half marathons); *Style*— Andy Kerr, Esq, MSP; ✉ The Civic Centre, East Kilbride G74 1AB (tel 01355 806223, fax 01355 806343, e-mail andy.kerr.msp@scottish.parliament.uk)

KERR, Lord Chief Justice of Northern Ireland; Rt Hon Sir Brian Francis; kt (1993); s of James William Kerr (d 1959), of Lurgan, Co Armagh, and Kathleen Rose, *née* Murray (d 1996); *b* 22 February 1948; *Educ* St Colman's Coll Newry, Queen's Univ Belfast (LLB); *m* 31 Oct 1970, Rosemary Gillian Owen, da of John Owen Widdowson; 2 s (John James b 6 May 1977, Patrick Brian b 11 Jan 1980); *Career* called to the Bar NI 1970 (England and Wales 1974), QC (NI) 1983, sr crown counsel NI 1988–93 (jr crown counsel 1978–83), bencher Inn of Court NI 1990–, judge of the Supreme Court of NI 1993–2004, Lord Chief Justice of NI 2004–; chm: Mental Health Cmmn NI 1988–, Distinction and Meritorious Servs Awards Ctee 1997–2001; memb: Br-Franco Judicial Cooperation Ctee 1995–2001, Judical Studies Bd for NI 1995–2004; Eisenhower fell for NI 1999; hon bencher: Gray's Inn 1997, King's Inn Dublin 2004; *Style*— The Rt Hon Sir Brian Kerr; ✉ The Royal Courts of Justice, Chichester Street, Belfast BT1 3JF

KERR, Caroline; da of John Joseph Kerr, of Co Donegal, and Maureen, *née* McNulty; *b* 27 May 1962; *Educ* St Catherine's Sr Sch Strawberry Hill, Newnham Coll Cambridge (BA); *m* 5 Feb 1994, Gerard Harvey, s of Patrick Harvey; 1 s (Patrick John Harvey b 21 March 1996), 1 da (Anna Caroline Harvey b 16 Feb 1999); *Career* ITN: trainee 1984–86, prodr 1986–89, reporter Channel 4 Daily 1989–92 (assignments incl fall of Berlin Wall and subseq end of communist rule in Eastern Europe, Gulf War from Jordan, Israel and liberated Kuwait), gen reporter ITN 1992–94 (assignments incl Bangkok riots 1992, Bombay bombings 1993), Asia corr 1994–96, sr reporter 1996–98, business and economics ed 1998–; *Style*— Ms Caroline Kerr

KERR, Prof David James; CBE (2002); s of Robert James Andrew Kerr (d 1986), and Sarah Pettigrew, *née* Hogg (d 1976); *b* 14 June 1956; *Educ* Univ of Glasgow (BSc, MB ChB, MD, MSc, PhD, DSc, Bellahouston Prize); *m* 11 July 1980, Annie, *née* Young; 1 s (Stewart), 2 da (Sarah, Fiona); *Career* hon sr registrar Beatson Inst for Cancer Research Glasgow 1986–88; Cancer Research Campaign (CRC) Dept of Med Oncology Univ of Glasgow: CRC sr research fell and hon sr registrar 1988–89 (CRC research fell and hon registrar 1984–86), CRC sr fell, sr lectr in med oncology, hon conslt physician and ldr Pharmacology Gp 1989–92; prof of clinical oncology and clinical dir CRC Inst for Cancer Studies Univ of Birmingham 1992–2001, hon conslt physician Birmingham Oncology Centre Queen Elizabeth Hosp and City Hosp Birmingham 1992–2001, Rhodes prof of cancer therapeutics and clinical pharmacology and head Dept of Clinical Pharmacology Univ of Oxford 2001–, hon conslt in med oncology Radcliffe Hosps Tst Oxford 2001–; fell CCC Oxford 2001–; visiting scientist Chronobiology Labs Univ of Minnesota 1986, hon prof Univ of Strathclyde 1990–, visiting prof of med oncology Univ of Belgrade 1998–; dir Nat Translational Cancer Research Network 2001–, founding cmmr Cmmn for Health Improvement 1999–2001 (memb Advsy Gp 1998); chm: Scientific Ctee European Soc for Med Oncology 1998, Dept of Health Audit on Cancer Waiting Times 1999, Nat Cancer Servs Collaborative 1999–2003, Adjuvant Colorectal Cancer Trials Gp Nat Cancer Research Inst 2003–; memb: Clincal Trials Ctee CRC 1998–2001, Gastro-Intestinal Study Gp European Orgn for the Research and Treatment of Cancer (EORTC) 1998–, Int Working Pty on Colorectal Cancer 1999–, Nat Cancer Task Force 2000–, Nat Colorectal Cancer Task Force 2003–, Nat Framework B NHS in Scotland Advsy Gp 2004–05, Thyroid Study Gp EORTC, Thyroid Medullary Cancer Study Gp CRC, Drug Pharmacology and Metabolism Gp EORTC; memb Research for Patient Benefits Working Pty 2003–05; memb MRC: Colorectal Cancer Working Pty 1992–2003, Clinical Fellowships Panel 1993–96, Ctee A Molecular and Cell Med Bd 1993–97, LINK with Industry Panel 1995, Realising Our Potential Awards Ctee 1995–96; ed-in-chief Annals of Oncology 1999–; memb Editorial Bd: Gastrointestinal Cancer, In Vivo, Int Jl of Oncology, S American Jl of Cancer Research, Br Jl of Cancer, Japanese Jl of Clinical Oncology; delivered lectures at confs and symposia worldwide; memb: Br Oncology Assoc, Royal Medico-chirugical Soc of Glasgow, Caledonian Endocrine Soc, Br Assoc for Cancer Research, Scottish Radiological Soc, European Soc of Med Oncology, Assoc of Cancer Physicians, European Assoc for Cancer Research, UK Assoc of Pharmaceutical Scientists, NY Acad of Sciences, Int Soc of Regnl Cancer Therapy, American Assoc for Cancer Research, American Soc for Clinical Oncology, European Sch of Oncology Alumni Club; Graham Wilson travelling fell 1985, 1986, 1987 and 1988; Jean M MacKintosh Research Fellowship 1985, CRC Travel Fellowship 1986, Nat Cancer Inst Travelling Fellowship 1987, RCPSGlas Travelling Fellowship 1987, Br Assoc for Cancer Research

Fellowship 1988, Int Union Against Cancer Cancer Research Fellowship Int Cancer Research Exchange Technol Transfer Grant 1989; Alexander Fletcher Meml Prize RCPSGlas 1987, European Sch of Oncology Int Award 1987, May and Baker Prize RCPSGlas 1991, Int Prize for Excellence in the field of colorectal cancer research and treatment Int Drug Devpt Centre and European Assoc for Research into Gastrointestinal Cancer 1999 (second recipient), Nye Bevan Award for Innovation NHS 2000 (first recipient); Pauline TSU Meml Lecture RCPEd 1992, Zeneca Lecture Int Soc of Geriatrics 1995, Annual Lecture Royal Soc of Art 1995, 100th Erasmus Darwin Lecture 1996; advsr Cwlth Scholarships and Fellowships 1999–; memb Scottish Astronomical Soc; memb Br Tandem Soc; MA (by incorporation) Univ of Oxford 2002; FRCPGlas 1995, FRCP 1996 (MRCP 1983), FMedSci 2000; *Publications* incl: New Molecular Targets for Cancer Chemotherapy (jt ed, 1994), Regional Chemotherapy: Principles and Practice (jt ed, 1998), Clinical Textbook of Colorectal Cancer (jt ed, 2000), ABC of Colorectal Cancer (jt ed, 2001); also author of numerous papers in learned jls; *Recreations* playing drums in a rock 'n' roll band; *Clubs* Reform, Partick Thistle Supporters; *Style*— Prof David Kerr, CBE; ✉ University of Oxford, Institute of Cancer Medicine, Department of Clinical Pharmacology, Radcliffe Infirmary, Woodstock Road, Oxford OX2 6HE (tel 01865 224482, fax 01865 224538, e-mail david.kerr@clinpharm.ox.ac.uk)

KERR, Prof David Nicol Sharp; CBE (1992); s of William Sharp Kerr (d 1972), and Elsie May Ransted (d 1989); *b* 27 December 1927; *Educ* George Watson's Boys Sch Edinburgh, Univ of Edinburgh (MB ChB), Univ of Wisconsin (MSc); *m* 2 July 1960, Mary Eleanor Jones, da of Capt John Roberts, of Holyhead, Gwynedd; 1 da (Jane b 1961), 2 s (Gordon b 1963, Ian b 1965); *Career* RNVR Surgn Lt 1953–55, RNR Surgn Lt Cdr 1963; prof of med Univ of Newcastle upon Tyne 1968–83, dean Royal Postgrad Med Sch 1984–91, prof of renal med Univ of London 1986–93 (prof emeritus 1993–); postgraduate med advsr NW Thames RHA 1991–97, med awards admin Cwlth Scholarships Cmmn 1993–97; Br Heart Fndn: memb Cncl 1991–97, chm Fellowships Ctee 1992–97; RCP: Goulstonian lectr 1968, Lumleian lectr 1983, censor 1982–84, sr censor 1990–91, ed 1994–98, Watson Smith lectr 1997; non-exec dir Ealing Hosp NHS Tst 1991–95; vice-pres Kidney Research UK (formerly Nat Kidney Research Fund) 2003– (tstee 1999–, chm 2000–02); formerly: pres Renal Assoc UK, conf pres Euro Renal Assoc, memb Cncl Int Soc of Nephrology; memb MRC Systems Bd; Hon DSc Univ of Khartoum 2005; FRCP 1968 (MRCP 1955), FRCPE 1967 (MRCPE 1955), FCMSA 1992; *Books* Short Textbook of Renal Disease (1968), Oxford Textbook of Clinical Nephrology (edns, 1992 and 1997), sections in med textbooks; *Recreations* fell walking; *Style*— Prof David Kerr, CBE; ✉ 22 Carbery Avenue, London W3 9AL (tel and fax 020 8992 3231, e-mail dnskerr@aol.com)

KERR, Rev Fergus Gordon Thomson; OP (1956); s of George Gordon Kerr (d 1967), of Banff, and Jean, *née* Smith (d 2000); *b* 16 July 1931, Banff; *Educ* Banff Acad, Univ of Aberdeen (MA), Le Saulchoir Paris (STL); *Career* Flying Offr RAF 1953–55; prior: Blackfriars Oxford 1969–78, Blackfriars Edinburgh 1988–94; regent Blackfriars Oxford 1998–2004; ed New Blackfriars 1992–; Hon DD Univ of Aberdeen 1995; FRSE 2003; *Books* Theology after Wittgenstein (1986), Immortal Longings (2001), After Aquinas (2003); *Recreations* walking, reading fiction; *Style*— The Rev Fergus Kerr, OP; ✉ 24 George Square, Edinburgh EH8 9LD (tel 0131 650 0901, e-mail fergus.kerr@english.op.org)

KERR, Dr Finlay; DL (Inverness 2000); s of Robert Cunningham Kerr (d 1979), and Mary MacKay, *née* McCaskill (d 2000); *b* 8 August 1941; *Educ* Keil Sch (head boy 1958–59), Univ of Glasgow (MB ChB, pres MacBrayne Hall 1962–63); *m* 1968, Margaret Ann Carnegie, da of Samuel Allan; 3 da (Fiona Mary Allan b 4 Oct 1964 d 1983, Joanna Margaret b 1 Nov 1973, Marsaili Barbara Carnegie b 8 May 1979), 1 s (Finlay b 3 Oct 1970); *Career* jr house offr: Western Infirmary Glasgow 1965–66, Ruchill Hosp Glasgow 1966–67, Queen Mother's Hosp Glasgow 1967; SHO Western Infirmary Glasgow 1967–68, fell Univ of Southern California 1968–70, lectr Dept of Med Univ of Edinburgh 1970–73, sr registrar Edinburgh Hosps 1973–75, conslt physician/cardiologist Raigmore Hosp Inverness 1976–2005, ret; RCPEd: regional advsr 1992–98, memb Cncl 1994–2000; memb: Exec Ctee Scottish Soc of Physicians 1989–94, Cncl Scottish Cardiac Soc 1993–96; chm: Bd of Dirs Highland Hospice 1986–87, Highlands and Western Isles Hosp Med Servs Ctee 1979–82, Hosp Sub-Ctee Area Med Ctee 1987–88, Hosp Med Staff Assoc 1987–88, Highland Area Med Ctee 1993–96, Highland Discretionary Awards Ctee 1999–2000; pres Highland Med Soc 1997–98; clinical dir Raigmore NHS Tst 1998–99; clinical dir Highland Acute Hosp Tst 1999–2001, non-exec dir NHS Highland Bd 2001–03; pres Scot Cardiac Soc 2001–03; memb: BMA, Br Cardiac Soc, Scot Soc of Physicians; memb Ctee Highland Discretionary Points Awards 1999–2000 and 2003–04, regnl advsr Scottis Advsy Ctee Distinction Awards 2003–04; FRCPGlas, FRCPEd, FFCS 2001; *Recreations* piping, skiing, sailing, windsurfing, golf; *Style*— Dr F Kerr, DL; ✉ The Birks, 2 Drummond Place, Inverness IV2 4JT (tel 01463 234779)

KERR, Glynn; *Educ* Coventry Univ; *Career* motorcycle designer and conslt; former bodywork designer TVR; BMW Munich: exterior designer 1982–84, sr designer motorcycle division 1984–87; chief designer Global Design Amsterdam (now GK Design Europe) 1987–90, ind conslt 1990– (clients incl: Ducati, Triumph, Aprilia, Honda, Bajaj, Kymco, Kawasaki, Yamaha), creative dir Motovisions California 2006–; co-fndr and pres Motorcycle Design Assoc 2001–; former lectr Art Center Coll of Design Europe, reg speaker on bike design and rendering techniques, columnist in motorcycle magazines worldwide; *Style*— Glynn Kerr, Esq; ✉ 8521 St Germaine Court, Roseville, CA 95747, USA (e-mail glynnkerr@yahoo.com, website www.glynnkerr.com)

KERR, Jim; *b* 9 July 1959; *m* 1, 5 May 1984, Chrissie Hynde; 1 da (Yasmin Paris b 1985); m 2, 1992 (m dis 1996), Patsy Kensit; 1 s (James b 4 Sept 1992); *Career* singer; memb Johnny & the Self Abusers 1977, co fndr Simple Minds 1977; albums with Simple Minds: Life In A Day (1979, reached UK no 30), Real To Real Cacophony (1980), Empires And Dance (1980, UK no 41), Sons And Fascinations/Sister Feelings Call (two albums released as one double, 1981, UK no 11), Celebration (1982, UK no 45), Themes for Great Cities (1982), New Gold Dream (81, 82, 83, 84) (1982, UK no 3), Sparkle In The Rain (1984, UK no 1), Once Upon A Time (1985, UK no 1), Live In The City of Light (live, 1987, UK no 1), Street Fighting Years (1989, UK no 1), Themes - Vol 1–4 (compilation discs, 1990), Real Life (1991, UK no 1), Glittering Prizes 81/92 (Best of) (1992), Good News from the Next World (1995, UK no 2), Néapolis (1998), Neon Lights (2001), Cry (2002), The Best of Simple Minds (2002), Our Secrets are the Same (2003); performances incl: Live Aid (Philadelphia) 1985, Amnesty Conspiracy of Hope 1985, Nelson Mandela 70th Birthday 1988; *Style*— Jim Kerr, Esq; ✉ c/o Simple Minds Ltd, 26a Alva Street, Edinburgh EH2 4PY (tel 0131 225 1707)

KERR, John Neilson; WS (1980); s of John Kerr (d 2000), of Edinburgh, and Helen, *née* Clark (d 2000); *b* 23 September 1956, Edinburgh; *Educ* John Watson's Sch Edinburgh, Univ of Edinburgh (LLB); *m* 12 Oct 1991, Adrienne, *née* Thompson; 2 s (Struan b 17 Feb 1994, Moray b 7 April 1996); *Career* slr; NP 1980; ptnr Anderson Strathern (formerly Strathern & Blair WS) 1984– (apprentice 1978–80); *Publications* Stair Memorial Encyclopaedia (Fire Services section); *Recreations* sport; *Clubs* Stewart's Melville Rugby; *Style*— John Kerr, Esq; ✉ Anderson Strathern, 1 Rutland Court, Edinburgh EH3 8EY (tel 0131 625 7240, fax 0131 270 7704, e-mail john.kerr@andersonstrathern.co.uk)

KERR, Rear Adm Mark William Graham; s of Capt M W B Kerr, DSC, RN (d 1986), and Coralie Erskine (Pat), *née* Clark; *b* 18 February 1949, Malta; *Educ* Marlborough, New College Oxford (BA); *m* 16 Sept 1978, Mary Louisa; 1 da (Eleanor b 3 Feb 1980), 2 s (Harry b 21 Oct 1981, Robert b 29 Sept 1983); *Career* cmd HMS Alert 1976, RN staff course 1981–82, cmd HMS Beachampton 1982–84, RN Schs Presentation Team 1984–85, exec offr HMS Ariadne 1985–88, cmd HMS Broadsword 1988–90, MOD 1990–94, cmd HMS Cumberland 1994–95, RN Presentation Team 1996, Dep Flag Offr Sea Trg 1997–99, Cdre Britannia RNC Dartmouth 1999–2002, Naval Sec and DG HR (Navy) 2002–04, chief exec Powys CC 2004–; memb: Naval Review 1977, Assoc of Local Authy Chief Execs (ALACE), Soc of Local Authy Chief Execs (SOLACE) 2004–; Hon Col Powys Army Cadet Force 2006–; FCIPD 2002; *Recreations* skiing, gardening, reading, hill walking; *Clubs* Naval and Military; *Style*— Rear Adm Mark Kerr; ✉ Powys County Council, County Hall, Llandrindod Wells, Powys LD1 5LG (tel 01597 826370, fax 01597 826220, e-mail chief.executive@powys.gov.uk)

KERR, Lord Ralph William Francis Joseph; DL (Derbyshire 2005); s of 12 Marquess of Lothian, KCVO; *b* 7 November 1957; *Educ* Ampleforth; *m* 1, 1980 (m dis 1987), Lady Virginia Mary Elizabeth, da of 11 Duke of Grafton, KG; m 2, 5 March 1988, Marie-Claire, yr da of (Michael) Donald Gordon Black, MC, of Cupar, Fife; 4 s (John Walter Donald Peter b 8 Aug 1988, Frederic James Michael Ralph b 23 Oct 1989, Francis Andrew William George b 5 Sept 1991, Hugh Alexander Thomas Joseph b 15 Aug 1999), 2 da (Amabel Mary Antonella b 5 Jan 1995, Minna Alice Priscilla Elizabeth b 31 March 1998); *Career* political researcher, currently estate mangr, songwriter, Sotheby's rep; dir Grange Estates (Newbattle) Ltd, pres of tstees Treetops Hospice 1988–, county pres St John Ambulance 1994–2000 (vice-pres Derbys 2000–), pres Melbourne Male Voice Choir, patron Castle Donington Museum Tst; memb Queen's Body Guard for Scotland (Royal Co of Archers); Knight of Honour and Devotion SMOM; *Recreations* playing the piano, reading, walking; *Style*— The Lord Ralph Kerr, DL; ✉ Melbourne Hall, Melbourne, Derby DE73 8EN (tel 01332 862163, e-mail melbhall@globalnet.co.uk); 20 Upper Cheyne Row, London SW3 5JN (tel 020 7352 7017)

KERR, Rose; da of William Antony Kerr, of Almeley, Herefordshire, and Elizabeth, *née* Rendell; *b* 23 February 1953; *Educ* Convent of Sacred Heart Hammersmith, Belmont Abbey Hereford, SOAS Univ of London (BA), Languages Inst of Beijing; *m* Stephen Charles Lord; *Career* fell Percival David Fndn of Chinese Art 1976–78; V&A Far Eastern Dept: res asst 1978, asst keeper 1979, keeper 1987; dep keeper V&A Asian Dept, ret 2003; memb: Exec Cncl GB-China Assoc 1989, Cncl Oriental Ceramic Soc (pres), Br Assoc for Chinese Studies, GB-China Educational Tst 1995 (chm); *Books* Kiln Sherds of Ancient China (with P Hughes-Stanton, 1980), Guanyin - A Masterpiece Revealed (with John Larson, 1985), Chinese Ceramics - Porcelain of the Qing Dynasty (1986), Later Chinese Bronzes (1990), Chinese Art and Design (The T T Tsui Gallery of Chinese Art) (ed and contrib, 1991), Ceramic Evolution in the Middle Ming Period (with Rosemary E Scott, 1994), Chinese Qing Dynasty Ceramics in the Collection of England's Victoria & Albert Museum (1996), Blanc de Chine: Porcelain from Dehua (jtly, 2001), Ceramics of the Song Dynasty (2004), Science and Civilisation in China vol 13 no 5: Ceramic Technology (jtly, 2004); *Recreations* walking, reading, gardening; *Style*— Ms Rose Kerr

KERR, Timothy Julian (Tim); QC (2001); s of Sir Michael Kerr (d 2002), and Julia, *née* Braddock; *b* 15 February 1958; *Educ* Westminster (Doncaster scholarship), Magdalen Coll Oxford; *m* 4 Aug 1990, Nicola, da of late Dominic Croucher; 3 s (Gavin Michael b 22 June 1989, George Alfred b 27 Oct 1998, Marcel Robert Shyam b 26 Jan 2001); *Career* called to the Bar Gray's Inn 1983 (Holt scholar, Birkenhead scholar); pt/t chm Employment Tbnls 2001–06; sec Bar Sports Law Gp 1997–2003, memb Ctee Br Assoc for Sport and Law 1999–2005, memb Panels of Arbitrators (Chm) and Assoc Mediators Sports Dispute Resolution Panel; memb Editorial Bd Int Sports Law Review 2000–; *Books* Sports Law (jtly, 1999); *Style*— Tim Kerr QC; ✉ 11 King's Bench Walk, Temple, London EC4Y 7EQ (tel 020 7632 8500, fax 020 7583 9123, e-mail kerr@11kbw.com)

KERR-DINEEN, Michael Norman Colin; s of Frederick George Kerr-Dineen (d 1988), and Hermione Iris, *née* Macdonald; *b* 14 July 1952; *Educ* Marlborough, Univ of Edinburgh (MA); *m* 1, 1976 (m dis 1981), Catharine, da of Alexander McCrindle; 1 s (Robert Crockford b 4 Oct 1979); m 2, 1988 (m dis 1995), Sally, da of Raymond Leonard; 1 s (Luke Giles b 26 Feb 1989), 1 da (Iris Sophie b 20 May 1992); m 3, 1997, Jacqui, da of Donald Graham; 2 s (Edward Graham b 22 Feb 1997, Thomas Michael b 14 July 1998), 1 da (Natasha Marie b 14 Oct 2000); *Career* Economic Intelligence Dept Bank of England 1975–79, PA to chm and chief exec British National Oil Corporation 1979–81, exec Alastair Morton & Co 1981–82; md: Guinness Peat Group 1982–88, Cambridge International Partners NY 1988–89; chief exec: UBS Laing & Cruickshank Investment Management (formerly Laing & Cruickshank Investment Management) 1989–2006, Cheviot Asset Mgmnt Ltd 2006–; *Recreations* horse racing, golf, skiing, opera; *Clubs* Athenaeum, Derby, Turf, MCC; *Style*— Michael Kerr-Dineen, Esq; ✉ Cheviot Asset Management Limited, 90 Long Acre, London WC2E 9RA (tel 020 7845 6150, fax 020 7845 6155)

KERR-MUIR, James; *Educ* Univ of Oxford (BA), Harvard Business Sch (MBA); *Career* formerly vice-pres fin Redpath Industries Toronto, md UK Div Tate & Lyle 1987–91 (gp fin dir 1984–88), fin dir Kingfisher plc 1992–95; chm: The Outdoor Gp Ltd 1996–99, Freeport plc 1996–2001, Ehrmanns Holdings Ltd 2000–03, Davenham Gp plc 2000–, Senior plc 2001– (non-exec dir 1996–, dep chm 2000–01), Hardys Hansons plc 2004–; dep chm Birmingham Midshires 1997–2001; dir Wilson Connolly Holdings plc 2003; non-exec dir: Graseby plc 1992–97, The Boddington Gp plc 1993–95, Gartmore Fledgling Tst plc 1994–, Yates Gp plc 1998–2004; *Style*— James Kerr-Muir, Esq; ✉ jkerrmuir@ukonline.co.uk

KERR OF KINLOCHARD, Baron (Life Peer UK 2004), of Kinlochard in Perth and Kinross; Sir John Olav Kerr; GCMG (2001, KCMG 1991, CMG 1987); s of Dr and Mrs J D O Kerr; *b* 22 February 1942; *Educ* Glasgow Acad, Pembroke Coll Oxford; *m* 1965, Elizabeth Mary, da of Wilfrid George Kalaugher, of Marlborough, Wilts; 2 s, 3 da; *Career* HM Dip Serv: joined 1966, served FO, Moscow, Rawalpindi, FCO and HM Treasy, princ private sec to Chancellor of the Exchequer 1981–84, head of Chancery Washington 1984–87, asst under sec of state FCO 1987–90, ambass and UK perm rep to EC 1990–95, ambass Washington 1995–1997, perm under-sec of state and head of the Diplomatic Serv 1997–2002; sec-gen European Convention 2002–; dir: Shell Transport and Trading Co 2002–, Rio Tinto plc 2003–, Scottish American Investment Tst; tstee: Nat Gallery, Rhodes Tst; *Style*— The Rt Hon the Lord Kerr of Kinlochard, GCMG; ✉ 175 Rue de la Loi, B1048 Brussels, Belgium

KERRIDGE, Jeremy Robert Owst; s of Hugh and Rosemary Kerridge; *b* 14 December 1962; *Educ* Royal Ballet Sch; *Children* 1 da (Emma-Jayne b 10 Oct 1988), 1 s (Sebastian Joe b 23 June 1992); *Career* ballet dancer; with Northern Ballet Theatre 1981–2003; freelance ballet teacher 2003–; solo and princ roles incl: L S Lowry in A Simple Man (Lynne) 1987, Sancho Panza in Don Quixote (Pink) 1988, The Gentleman in Liaisons Amoureuses (Hynd) 1989, Soldier in Strange Meeting (Pink) 1989, The Teacher in The Lesson (Flindt) 1990, Mercutio in Romeo and Juliet (Moricone) 1991 (Best Dancer in a Character Role Dance and Dancers Magazine), Scrooge in A Christmas Carol (Moricone) 1992, The Tutor in Swan Lake (Pink/Gable) 1993, Renfield in Dracula (Pink/Gable) 1996, Gringoire in The Hunchback of Notre Dame (Pink) 1998, The Barman in Carmen (Veldman) 1999, Steve in A Streetcar Named Desire (Veldman) 2001, Goro in Madame Butterfly (Nixon) 2002; *Television* A Simple Man (BBC) 1987, Royal Variety Performance, Mercutio in Romeo and Juliet (BBC) 1992, Scrooge in A Christmas Carol (BBC) 1993); *Film* The Magic Toyshop; *Recreations* music, film; *Style*— Jeremy Kerridge, Esq; ✉ Northern Ballet Theatre, West Park Centre, Spen Lane, Leeds LS1 5BE (tel 0113 274 5355)

KERRIGAN, Greer Sandra; CB (2006); da of Wilfred McDonald Robinson (d 1998), of Trinidad, and Rosina, *née* Ali (d 1964); *b* 7 August 1948; *Educ* Bishop Anstey HS

Trinidad, Coll of Law Cncl of Legal Education; *m* 11 May 1974, Donal Brian Matthew Kerrigan, s of Daniel Patrick Kerrigan, QC; 1 s (Dylan Brian Rum b 25 April 1976), 1 da (Lanra Lee Gin b 24 Jan 1979); *Career* legal advsr to Public Utilities Cmmn Trinidad 1972–74, various positions DSS 1974–96, formerly legal dir Dept of Health, currently legal dir Law, Governance and Special Policy Gp Dept for Work and Pensions; *Recreations* bridge, reading, travelling; *Style*— Mrs Greer Kerrigan, CB; ✉ Department for Work and Pensions, Richmond House, 79 Whitehall, London SW1A 2NS

KERRIGAN, Prof John Francis; s of late Stephen Francis Kerrigan, and Patricia, *née* Baker; *b* 16 June 1956; *Educ* St Edward's Coll Liverpool, Keble Coll Oxford (BA); *Children* 1 da; *Career* jr research fell Merton Coll Oxford 1979–82 (Domus sr scholar 1977–79); Univ of Cambridge: lectr in English 1986–98 (asst lectr 1982–86), reader in English lit 1998–2001, prof of English 2001–, chair Bd English Faculty 2003–06; fell St John's Coll Cambridge 1982– (dir of studies in English 1987–97); visiting prof Meiji Univ Tokyo 1986; tstee Dove Cottage Wordsworth Tst 1984–2001; Br Acad research readership 1998–2000; Chatterton lectr Br Acad 1988, J A W Bennett meml lectr Perugia 1998, Acad lectr Acad for Irish Cultural Heritage Derry 2003, F W Bateson lectr Oxford 2004, Gareth Roberts lectr Exeter 2007; Charles Oldham Shakespeare Prize 1976, Matthew Arnold Meml Prize Univ of Oxford 1981, Truman Capote Award for Literary Criticism 1998; fndn fell English Assoc 1999, fell Wordsworth Tst 2001; *Publications* Shakespeare: Love's Labour's Lost (ed, 1982), Shakespeare's Sonnets and A Lover's Complaint (ed, 1986, 2 edn 1995), Hugh Sykes Davies: Wordsworth and the Worth of Words (ed with J Wordsworth, 1987), Motives of Woe: Shakespeare and Female Complaint (1991), English Comedy (jt ed, 1994), Revenge Tragedy: Aeschylus to Armageddon (1996), The Thing About Roy Fisher: critical studies (ed with P Robinson, 2000), On Shakespeare and Early Modern Literature: essays (2001), Archipelagic English (2007); reviewer and article contrib to jls incl: Critical Quarterly, Essays in Criticism, Shakespeare Quarterly, Yale Jl of Criticism, London Review of Books, TLS; *Recreations* music; *Style*— Prof John Kerrigan; ✉ St John's College, Cambridge CB2 1TP (tel 01223 338620, e-mail jk10023@cam.ac.uk)

KERSHAW, Andrew (Andy); s of Jack Kershaw, of Blackpool, and Eileen, *née* Acton; *b* 9 November 1959; *Educ* Univ of Leeds; *Partner* Juliette Banner; 1 s (Sonny Banner b 23 August 1997), 1 da (Dolly Banner b 2 March 1999); *Career* broadcaster, presenter and journalist; radio presenter: Andy Kershaw Programme (BBC Radio 1) 1985–2000, Andy Kershaw's World of Music (BBC World Service) 1985–, Break for the Border (Br Forces Broadcasting) 1987–90, Space 5 (BBC Radio 5) 1991–92, Down Your Way (BBC Radio 4) 1992, Antique Records Roadshow (BBC Radio 1) 1993, Four Corners (BBC Radio 4) 1993–95, Kershaw in South Africa & Africa's Greatest Hits (BBC Radio 1) 1995, Andy Kershaw Programme (BBC Radio 3) 2001–; occasional radio presenter Pick of the Week (BBC Radio 4) 1987–, guest radio presenter Start the Week (BBC Radio 4) 1988–; radio contrib to: Kaleidoscope (BBC Radio 4), Loose Ends (BBC Radio 4), Archive Feature (BBC Radio 4), Fourth Column (BBC Radio 4) 1994–96; radio reporter: From Our Own Correspondent (BBC Radio 4) 1990–96, Today Programme (BBC Radio 4) 1994 and 1996, The World Tonight (BBC Radio 4) 1996; several radio documentaries for BBC Radio 1, 4 and 5 1988–95; TV presenter: Whistle Test (BBC 2) 1984–87, Live Aid (BBC TV) 1985, New Country, Getting Tough (BBC 2) 1987, Great Journeys of the World (BBC 2) 1989, Big World Cafe (Channel 4 TV) 1989; TV reporter: As It Happens (Channel 4 TV) 1990–92, Travelog (Channel 4 TV) 1990–95, Newsnight (BBC 2) 1991, Alien Nations (Channel 4 TV) 1994; contrib to: The Guardian, The Independent, Observer Magazine, The Oldie, Daily Telegraph, Punch, Vogue, Q, Mojo, The Listener, London Daily News, 20/20, Time Out, Radio Times, Literary Review, Motor Cycle News, Sunday Correspondent, South China Morning Post, New Musical Express; memb: Sony Radio Awards Ctee 1990–95, Strategy Review Ctee BBC (Music and Arts) 1993; patron Mines Advsy Gp; Hon DMus: UEA 2004, Univ of Leeds 2005; *Awards* Best Specialist Music Programme Sony Radio Awards 1987, 1989 and 1996, Most Outstanding Contribution to Radio Broadcasting Press Guild's Awards 1990, Without Whom.....Award Folk Roots Magazine Annual Reader's Poll 1987–92, three Sony Radio Awards 2002; *Recreations* motorcycle racing, travels to extreme countries, music, fishing, boxing; *Clubs* The Academy; *Style*— Andy Kershaw; ✉ c/o Sincere Management, Flat B, 6 Bravington Road, London W9 3AH (tel 020 8960 4438, fax 020 8968 8458)

KERSHAW, David Andrew; s of Lawrence Morris Kershaw (d 1991), of Malaga, Spain, and Rona, *née* Levy; *b* 26 February 1954; *Educ* Bedales, Univ of Durham (BA), London Business Sch (MBA); *m* 1993, Clare Elizabeth, *née* Whitley; 1s (Tom b 1997), 1 da (Emma b 1998); *Career* advtg exec; account exec Wasey Campbell Ewald 1977–80, London Business Sch 1980–82; Saatchi & Saatchi Advertising: account dir 1982–86, gp account dir 1986–90, md 1990–94, chm and ceo 1994–95, resigned; ptnr M&C Saatchi 1995–; memb Mktg Soc, FIPA; *Recreations* Arsenal, music (playing clarinet), opera, golf, tennis; *Clubs* RAC, Groucho; *Style*— David Kershaw, Esq; ✉ M&C Saatchi Ltd, 34–36 Golden Square, London W1F 9EE (tel 020 7543 4510, fax 020 7543 4502, e-mail davidk@mcsaatchi.com)

KERSHAW, David Robert; s of late Noel Ernest Kershaw, TD, and Dorothy Anne, *née* Cheyne, b 1953; *Educ* Urmston GS Manchester, Trinity Coll Cambridge (MA); *m* 1978, Christine Anne, da of John Spear Sexton (d 1986); 3 s (Oliver James b 1979, Toby Thomas b 1984, Charles Henry Alexander b 1986), 1 da (Isabelle Alice Katharine b 1989); *Career* admitted slr 1978; specialist in corporate fin, mergers and acquisitions and equity capital markets; ptnr Ashurst 1986–; memb City of London Law Soc; memb Ctee Trinity Law Assoc, chm Trinity Coll Alumni Advsy Bd; Freeman City of London Slrs' Co; *Recreations* classical guitar, violin, windsurfing, tennis, literature; *Clubs* Bewl Valley SC, The Nevill LTC; *Style*— David Kershaw, Esq; ✉ Ashurst, Broadwalk House, 5 Appold Street, London EC2A 2HA (tel 020 7638 1111, fax 020 7638 1112, e-mail david.kershaw@ashurst.com)

KERSHAW, Elizabeth Ann (Liz); da of Lawrence Colin Ward Kershaw, and Grace Elizabeth, *née* Milburn; *b* Sheffield; *Educ* Cheltenham Ladies' Coll, King Edward VII Sch Sheffield, Univ of Sheffield (BA); *Children* 1 s (Oliver Patrick Lawrence b 27 Oct 2001); *Career* National Magazine Co: publisher Harpers & Queen 1990–93, publishing dir Good Housekeeping 1993–98, memb Bd 1993–, publishing dir Cosmopolitan Gp 1998–2000, exec gp publishing dir Harpers & Queen, Esquire, Country Living and Focus 2000–02, exec gp publishing dir Good Housekeeping and Country Living Gp 2002–; emeritus dir Cosmetic Executive Women (CEW), memb Advsy Bd Fragrance Fndn; memb: IOD, Marketing Soc, Womens' Advtg Club of London; PPA Publisher of Year 1995; Freeman City of London, Liveryman Worshipful Co of Gunmakers; *Style*— Ms Liz Kershaw; ✉ National Magazine Company, 72 Broadwick Street, London W1F 9EP (tel 020 7439 5279)

KERSHAW, Prof Sir Ian; kt (2002); s of Joseph Kershaw (d 1969), and Alice, *née* Robinson; *b* 29 April 1943, Oldham, Lancs; *Educ* Univ of Liverpool (BA), Merton Coll Oxford (DPhil); *m* 29 Oct 1966, Betty, *née* Gammie; 2 s (David b 7 Oct 1970, Stephen b 22 Jan 1973); *Career* Univ of Manchester: lectr in medieval history 1971–74 (asst lectr 1968–71), lectr then sr lectr in modern history 1974–87 (reader-elect 1987); prof of modern history Univ of Nottingham 1987–89, prof of modern history Univ of Sheffield 1989–; actg prof of contemporary European history Ruhr-Univ Bochum 1983–84; Deutscher Akademischer Austauschdienst (DAAD) Scholarship 1974, Alexander von Humboldt-Stiftung Fellowship 1976–77 (continuation 1985, 1997 and 1999), Br Acad-Akademie der Wissenschaften der DDR Exchange Scholarship 1981, Leverhulme Fellowship 1982, Br Acad-Polish Acad of Sciences Exchange Scholarship 1989, Wissenschaftskolleg zu Berlin Fellowship 1989, Leverhulme Tst Research Award 1991, Br Acad-Leverhulme Fndn Sr Scholarship 1994–95, Leverhulme Major Research Fellowship 2002–; keynote lectures incl: Commemoration of Reichskristallnacht Paulskirche Frankfurt 2000, Remembering the Future: Oxford Int Conf 2000, 1st Glasgow Holocaust Meml Lecture 2001, 1st London Holocaust Meml Lecture 2002, Trevelyan Lecture Cambridge 2002, Sir Frank Stenton Meml Lecture 2002, 1st BBC-Open Univ Televised History Lecture 2005, Ramsay Murray Lecture Cambridge 2005; conslt for BBC documentaries: The Nazis. A Warning from History (series) 1994–97, Hitler's War in the East (series) 1997–99, Timewatch: Operation Sealion 1998, Timewatch: Himmler 2001, Timewatch: The Making of Adolf Hitler 2002; conslt and academic advsr to ZDF (Zweites Deutsches Fernsehen); newspaper contrib, various TV and radio broadcasts; Hon Dr: Univ of Manchester 2004, Univ of Stirling 2004, Queen's Univ Belfast 2007; hon fell Merton Coll Oxford 2005; FRHistS 1991 (also 1972–74), FBA 1991; Bundesverdienstkreuz (Germany) 1994; *Publications* Bolton Priory Rentals and Ministers' Accounts, 1473–1539 (ed, 1969), Bolton Priory: The Economy of a Northern Monastery (1973), Der Hitler-Mythos: Volksmeinung und Propaganda im Dritten Reich (1980, revised edn 1999), Popular Opinion and Political Dissent in the Third Reich: Bavaria, 1933–1945 (1983, revised edn 2002), The Nazi Dictatorship: Problems and Perspectives of Interpretation (1985, 4 edn 2000), The 'Hitler Myth': Image and Reality in the Third Reich (1987), Weimar: Why did German Democracy Fail? (ed, 1990), Hitler: A Profile in Power (1991, 2 edn 2001), Stalinism and Nazism: Dictatorships in Comparison (ed with Moshe Lewin, 1997), Hitler, 1889–1936: Hubris (1998, revised edn 2001), Hitler, 1936–1945: Nemesis (2000, revised edn 2001), The Bolton Priory Compotus 1286–1325 (ed with David M Smith, 2001), Making Friends With Hitler: Lord Londonderry, the Nazis and the Road to War (2004), Fateful Choices: Ten Decisions That Changed the World (2007); regular reviewer and author of 75 articles in learned jls; *Awards* Bruno-Kreisky Prize (Austria) for Political Book of the Year 2000, Wolfson Literary Award for History 2000, Damals Book of the Year 2000, Br Acad Book Prize 2001; shortlisted: Samuel Johnson Prize 1999, Whitbread Biography Prize 1999 and 2002, Los Angeles Times Book Prize 2000, WH Smith Prize 2001, James Tait Black Meml Prize 2002, Norton Medlicott Medal Historical Assoc 2004, Elizabeth Longford Prize for Historical Biography 2005; *Recreations* rugby league, cricket, football, classical music, opera, jazz, wine, real ale; *Style*— Prof Sir Ian Kershaw; ✉ Department of History, University of Sheffield, Sheffield S10 2TN (tel 0114 222 2550, fax 0114 278 8304)

KERSHAW, His Hon (Philip) Michael; QC (1980); s of His Honour Philip Charles Stones Kershaw (d 1986), and Michaela, *née* Raffael (d 1993); *b* 23 April 1941; *Educ* Ampleforth, St John's Coll Oxford (MA); *m* 30 Dec 1980, Anne; 1 s (Francis Edward b 23 Aug 1984); *Career* called to the Bar Gray's Inn 1963, recorder 1980–90, commercial circuit judge Northern Circuit 1990–92, mercantile circuit judge Northern Circuit 1992–97, mercantile judge 1997–2006; fell Soc for Advanced Legal Studies; FCIArb 1991; *Clubs* Athenaeum (Liverpool); *Style*— His Hon Michael Kershaw, QC; ✉ The Crown Court, Crown Square, Manchester M60 9DJ

KERSHAW, Nicholas John; s of Henry Kershaw (d 1995), and Daphne Kershaw; *b* 16 November 1963; *Educ* Bolton Sch, KCL (LLB), Inns of Court Sch of Law; *m* 1994, Karen; 2 da (Lucy b 21 June 1997, Natalya b 3 April 2004); *Career* called to the Bar Eng and Wales 1988, advocate Jersey 1996; sr offr UBS 1987–89, lawyer Clifford Chance 1990–93, ptnr Ogier 1997– (joined 1993, currently managing ptnr Jersey); *Recreations* golf, skiing, running, tennis; *Style*— Nicholas Kershaw, Esq; ✉ Ogier, Whiteley Chambers, Don Street, St Helier, Jersey JE4 9WG (tel 01534 504263, fax 01534 504444, e-mail nick.kershaw@ogier.com)

KERSHAW, Stephen; s of John Bertram Kershaw, of Ashington, Egley Road, Mayford, Woking, Surrey, and Joyce Mary, *née* Robson; *b* 24 April 1955; *Educ* Dr Challoner's GS Amersham Bucks; *m* 1978, Alison Deborah, da of Thomas Charles Garrett, of 10 Brushwood Drive, Chorleywood; 1 da (Deborah Stephanie b 12 Dec 1982), 1 s (Carl Thomas b 15 Sept 1985); *Career* salesman Cavenham Foods 1973–75; Wilkinson Sword Ltd: salesman 1975–76, mktg asst 1977–78, product mangr 1978; Cadbury Ltd: product mangr 1978–79, sr product mangr 1980–82, product gp mangr 1983–84; head of mktg Britvic Ltd 1984–86; Bartle Bogle Hegarty advtg: successively account dir, business devpt dir/mgmnt rep, then bd dir/team ldr 1986–98, md 1998–; memb Mktg Soc; *Style*— Steve Kershaw; ✉ Bartle Bogle Hegarty, 60 Kingly Street, London W1B 5DS (tel 020 7734 1677, fax 020 7437 3666, e-mail steve.kershaw@bbh.co.uk)

KERSHAW, Walter; s of Walter Kershaw (Flt Sgt RAF 19 Sqdn Duxford Battle of Britain, d 1998), and Florence, *née* Ward; *b* 7 December 1940; *Educ* De La Salle Coll Salford, Univ of Durham (BA); *Career* war artist King's Regt NI 1976; artist and pioneer of large external mural painting; UK work: Manchester Trafford Park 1993, Science Museum, Manchester United FC, CEGB, Univ of Salford 1979–89, Br Aerospace and Granada TV 1984–88, Wensum Lodge Norwich 1985, Italian Consulate Manchester 1991, P&O Manchester Arndale 1996; work abroad: Brazil, São Paulo and Recife 1983–95, Sarajevo Int Arts Festival 1996, Briggs of Burton 1999, Airtours 1999, Leonard Cheshire Homes 2002; works exhibited: V&A, Tate Gallery, Nat Portrait Gallery, Gulbenkian Fndn, Arts Cncl and Br Cncl Berlin, Brazil and Edinburgh; in conversation BBC Radio Four with Sue MacGregor 1984; *Recreations* travel, cricket, photography; *Clubs* Littleborough Cricket; *Style*— Walter Kershaw, Esq; ✉ Studio, Todmorden Road, Littleborough, Lancashire OL15 9EG (tel 01706 379653)

KERSLEY, Dr Jonathan Bernard; s of Edward Kersley (d 1976), of London, and Hilda, *née* Stone; *b* 4 March 1942; *Educ* Christ's Coll Finchley, St Bartholomew's Hosp Med Coll Univ of London (MB BS); *m* 13 April 1969, Susan Esther, da of Prof William W Mushin, CBE, of Cardiff; 2 da (Deborah Anne b 26 March 1971, Sarah Rebecca b 16 Dec 1976), 1 s (Benjamin Alexander b 8 Aug 1973); *Career* SHO Luton and Dunstable Hosp 1971–72, registrar in surgery St Bartholomew's Hosp 1973 (house surgn to Professorial Surgical Unit 1967 and Thoracic Unit 1968), registrar in surgery Portsmouth Hosp 1972–74 (house physician 1967), sr orthopaedic registrar Addenbrooke's Hosp Cambridge 1974–78; conslt orthopaedic surgn: Birmingham Heartlands Hosp 1978–95, Birmingham Orthopaedic Service 1995–, Royal Orthopaedic Hosp Birmingham 1998–; memb: Int Soc of Arthroscopy Knee Surgery and Orthopaedic Sports Med, Euro Soc of Knee Surgery and Arthroscopy, Br Assoc for Surgery of the Knee, BMA; MB BSLRCP, DObstRCOG, FBOA, FRCS; *Recreations* gardening, ornithology, aviculture, photography; *Style*— Dr Jonathan B Kersley; ✉ Trevalsa, Churchtown, St Levan, Penzance, Cornwall TR19 6JS (tel 01736 810401); Birmingham Nuffield Hospital (tel 0121 456 2000, e-mail jonathanbkersley@knees.fsbusiness.co.uk)

KERWIN, Prof David George; s of late William George Kerwin, and Winifred Margaret, *née* Bowger; *b* 26 May 1948, Liverpool; *Educ* Sir John Deane's GS Northwich, Keele Univ (CertEd, BEd), Univ of Leeds (MA), Loughborough Univ (PhD); *m* 15 Aug 1972, Linda Anne; 2 s (Thomas David b 1977, Samuel John William b 1980); *Career* school teacher Cheshire LEA 1970–72, lectr Stockport Coll 1972–75, sr lectr Bedford Coll of HE 1976–81; Loughborough Univ: lectr 1982–90, sr lectr 1990–99, head of sports science 1996–99; prof and head of sport and exercise science Univ of Bath 1999–; memb: Scientific Cmmn Fedn Internationale Gymnastique (FIG), Scientific Advsy Bd NZ Sports Cmmn, Scientific Advsy Bd British Gymnastics Med Cmmn; biomechanics ed Jl of Sports Sciences until 2002, author of numerous articles and papers in learned jls; fell British Assoc of Sport and Exercise Sciences (BASES) 1999 (memb 1976); *Recreations* golf, sport, theatre, television; *Clubs* Cumberwell Park Golf; *Style—* Prof David Kerwin

KESLER, Steven Bogdan (Steve); s of Czeslaw Kesler (d 1982), of Brighton, and Josefa, *née* Karas; *b* 8 April 1951; *Educ* Imperial Coll London (BSc Eng, ARSM, PhD, DIC, Ernest Edward Glorney Prize), Grad Sch of Business Cape Town, Templeton Coll Oxford; *m* 29 Sept 1979, Jennifer, da of Johannes Burger; *Career* general mangr Rossing Uranium Ltd Namibia 1989–91, vice-pres Minera Escondida Ltd Chile 1991–94, chief exec Cia Minera Doña Ines de Collahuasi Chile 1994–96, pres Philnico Philipines 1996–97, chief exec Pacific Nickel Ltd Australia 1996–97, exec dir Billiton plc 1997–2001, dir MIRO 2001–02, exec vice-pres Washington Gp Int; CEng 1979, FIMM 1989; *Recreations* golf, music, travel; *Clubs* Wentworth; *Style—* Steve Kesler, Esq; ✉ 7 Alan Crescent, Scunthorpe, Lincolnshire DN15 7PL (e-mail skesler@attglobal.net)

KESSELER, Dr Michael Edward; s of Sydney Joseph Kesseler (d 1989), and Edith Maud, *née* Smith (d 1978); *b* 18 December 1946; *Educ* King Edward's Sch Five Ways Birmingham, Univ of Birmingham (MB ChB); *m* 15 April 1978, Gale, da of Clifford Narbett, of Snitterfield, Warks; *Career* sr registrar in dermatology Royal S Hants Hosp 1978–83, consIt dermatologist and hon sr clinical lectr Univ of Sheffield 1983–, govr Rotherham NHS Fndn Tst, dep med dir Rotherham Gen Hosp 1999–2006 (clinical dir 1991–98); pres N of England Dermatological Soc 2005–06, past chm Rotherham BMA; FRCP 1989 (MRCP 1978), FRSM; *Recreations* wine, theatre; *Style—* Dr Michael Kesseler; ✉ The Beeches, Doncaster Road, Thrybergh, Rotherham, South Yorkshire S65 4NU (tel 01709 850307); Rotherham General Hospital, Moorgate Road, Oakwood, Rotherham, South Yorkshire S60 2UD (tel 01709 304161, fax 01709 304481)

KESSLER, George Bernard; CBE (2001); s of William Kessler, of London, and Joanna, *née* Rubner; *b* 17 August 1953; *Educ* City of London Sch, Univ of Nottingham (BSc); *m* 25 Oct 1986, Deborah Susan, da of Beni Baltfried Jaffe, of London; 2 da (Madeleine b 1987, Flora b 1988); *Career* consIt Logica 1974–77, various positions Kesslers Int 1977–90, dir Kesslers Int Ltd 1988–, ops dir Kesslers Gp 1990–, md Kesslers Manufacturing 1990–, md Kesslers Int Ltd 2000–; dir: Bridgewater Distribution & Mgmnt Ltd 1989–, Newham Schools & Industry Liaison Ctee 1989–91, Kesslers Investment Ltd 1989–, Newham Educn Employer Partnership 1991, Kesslers Int Holding Co Ltd 1991–, Carpenters Road Properties Ltd 1991–, Brand Technology Ltd 1991–, Tower Hamlets Educn Business Partnership 1993–95, Roegate Ltd 1994–2002, Point Topic Ltd 1998, London First 1999– (memb Educn Advsy Gp 1995–96), Business Educators 2001–04, Loopweave Ltd 2003–, Kesslers Properties North Ltd 2005–, Kesslers Properties South Ltd 2005–, Kesslers Int Gp Ltd 2005–, Carpenters Road Hldgs Ltd 2005–; chm: Newham Compact 1988–95 (fndr), Newham Community Coll 1992–93 (chm of govrs 1994–95), London Regnl Competitiveness Gp 1995–98, Educn & Employability Gp 1996–97, LDP Business Support Task Force 1998–2000, London TEC Cncl 1999–2001 (memb 1996–1999), London Devpt Agency Prodn Industry Cmmn 2002–, 3H 2005–; dep chm London E TEC 1994–2001 (fndr memb 1990, chm Educn Advsy Gp 1991–96, memb Ethnic Minorities Focus Gp 1996–98), London Innovation and Knowledge Transfer Strategy 2001–, vice-chm London Section Britain in Europe 2002–, dep chm London Devpt Agency Business Competitiveness Agency 2001–04; fndr memb Campaign for Learning 1995–97 (memb Steering Ctee 1994–97); memb: Royal Inst 1978–, Bd E London Strategic Forum 1992–96, RSA Learning Soc Exchange 1993–95, London Regnl Ctee FE Funding Cncl 1993–99, RSA Learning Advsy Gp 1994–98, Industry Forum 1994–, Bd Futures 1995–96, Fndn for Sci and Technol 1995–2000, CBI Educn and Trg Advsy Gp 1996–98, Bd Business Link London 1996–2001, Bd London Mfrg Gp 1996–, Ind Review Panel Cncl Membs' Allowances 1997–98, Steering Ctee EU Presidency Life Long Learning Conf 1997–98, Newham & Tower Hamlets Steering Ctee on Welfare to Work 1997–98, Task Force to Advise on Mfrg in London 1998–99, Bd London Devpt Partnership (LDP) 1998–2000, LDP Skills Strategy Task Force 1998–2000, TEC Nat Cncl 1998–2001 (memb Trg and Educn Ctee 1997–98), London Mfrg Task Force 2000–01, Bd London European Prog Ctee 2000–01, Bd London and SE Regnl Industrial Devpt Bd 2001–02, Bd N London LSC 2001–03, Bd Cultural Strategy Gp 2001–03, Bd London Int Festival of Theatre 2001–04, London Devpt Agency People's Educn and Trg Ctee 2001–04, Made in London SRB Steering Gp 2000–, Bd London Devpt Agency 2000–, Gordon Brown's Task Force to review Modern Apprenticeships 2003–, Advsy Bd Britain in Europe, London Devpt Agency Corp Affrs Ctee 2004–, London Devpt Agency Regeneration and Devpt Ctee 2004–, London Regional Ctee Prince's Tst 2005–, judging panel RCA design competition 2005–; memb Advsy Cncl: New Voice for London 1999–2000, E London Business Alliance 1999–2001, Employment Cmmn for London 1999–2002, London Borough Grants Reference Gp 2000–02; princ sponsor NIACE Learning Works Award 1999–2003; chair Steering Gp to select Regnl Centre for Mfrg Excellence 2001–02; memb judging panel: London Smart Awards 1999–2000, DTI Design & Mfrg Task Force 1999–2000; govr Stratford Sch 1996–97; Hon Dr Univ of East London 2005–; MRI 1975, FRSA 1994, CIMechE 2001; *Recreations* contemporary art, reading, theatre; *Clubs* Savile; *Style—* George Kessler, Esq, CBE; ✉ 22 Tanza Road, London NW3 2UB; Kesslers International Ltd, No 1 International Business Park, Rick Roberts Way, Stratford, London E15 2NF (tel 020 8522 3000, fax 020 8522 3129, e-mail kesslerg@kesslers.com)

KESTENBAUM, Jonathan Andrew; s of Ralph Kestenbaum, of Switzerland, and Gaby, *née* Schwalbe; *b* 5 August 1961; *Educ* Hasmonean GS, LSE (BA), Univ of Cambridge (post grad research, Soccer half blue), Hebrew Univ Jerusalem (MA), City Univ Business Sch (MBA); *m* 9 Dec 1984, Deborah Jane, da of Barry Zackon; 4 c (Gilad b 1987, Michal b 1989, Avishai b 1992, Yoav b 1994); *Career* chief exec Office of Chief Rabbi 1991–96, chief exec United Jewish Israel Appeal, COS to Sir Ronald Cohen, *qv* (chm Apax Partners Ltd) and chief exec Portland Tst until 2005, chief exec NESTA 2005–, chm Quest Ltd; dir: Design Cncl, Enterprise Insight; tstee: Rowley Lane Recreational Tst, London Community Centre, Holocaust Educn Tst, Planning Gp World Econ Forum; memb Bd of Advsrs: Club of Three, Assoc of MBAs; *Recreations* soccer, tennis; *Style—* Jonathan Kestenbaum, Esq

KESTER, Prof Ralph Charles; s of John David Kester, of Peterborough, Canada, and Christine Petronella, *née* Miller; *b* 16 February 1938; *Educ* Univ of Cape Town (MB ChB, MD, ChM); *m* 19 Sept 1964, Ilse Helga, da of John Phillip Meyer (d 1969), of Knysna, South Africa; 1 da (Anthea b 1966), 1 s (Bruce b 1967); *Career* sr surgical registrar Dundee Teaching Hosps 1970–74, sr Fulbright travel scholar and res fell Univ of Calif San Diego 1971–72, sr surgical lectr Univ of Leeds, hon surgn St James's Univ Hosp Leeds 1974–80, Hunter prof of surgery 1982, Arris and Gale lectr RCS 1974; prof of vascular surgery Univ of Leeds 1995–, ret as consIt and vascular surgn St James's Univ Hosp Leeds 2003; hon surgn to Yorkshire Rugby Union, pres Yorks RFU 2005–06; past pres elect Vascular Surgical Soc of GB and I; memb: Surgical Res Soc, Assoc of Surgns of GB and I; FRCS 1965; *Books* A Practice of Vascular Surgery (1981), Handbook of Infections in Surgery (2000); *Recreations* rugby union football; *Style—* Prof Ralph Kester

KESWICK, Hon Mrs (Annabel Térèse (Tessa)); *née* Fraser; yr da of 15 Lord Lovat, DSO, MC, TD (d 1995); *b* 15 October 1942; *Educ* Woldingham, French Baccalaureat Course (Paris); *m* 1, 1964 (m dis 1978), 14 Lord Reay; 2 s, 1 da; m 2, 1985, Henry Neville Lindley Keswick, *qv*, eld s of Sir William Johnston Keswick (d 1990); *Career* early career with J Walter Thompson and journalist on Telegraph and Spectator, London ed Business and Energy International 1974–78, dir Cluff Investments and Trading 1981–95 (also fndr memb Cluff plc 1973), special advsr to Rt Hon Kenneth Clarke QC, MP (as Sec of State for Health then Educn and Sci, Home Sec and Chllr of the Exchequer) 1989–95, exec dir Centre for Policy Studies 1995–; Parly candidate (Cons and Unionist) Inverness, Nairn and Lochaber 1987; reg contrib to pubns incl: The Times, Daily Telegraph, FT; cncllr Queensgate Ward RBK&C 1982–86; former memb City of London and Westminster Assoc (former memb Ctee St James's Ward); *Publications* incl: A Conservative Agenda (co-author, 1996), Conservative Women (1999), Second Amongst Equals (2000); *Recreations* collecting antiques, horses and travel; *Clubs* Reform; *Style—* The Hon Mrs Keswick; ✉ 6 Smith Square, London SW1P 3HT; The Centre for Policy Studies, 57 Tufton Street, London SW1P 3QL (tel 020 7222 4488)

KESWICK, Sir (John) Chippendale Lindley (Chips); kt (1993); s of Sir William Johnston Keswick (d 1990), and Mary, *née* Lindley; bro of Henry Neville Lindley Keswick *qv*, and Simon Lindley Keswick *qv*; *b* 2 February 1940; *Educ* Eton, Univ of Aix Marseilles; *m* 1966, Lady Sarah Ramsay, da of 16 Earl of Dalhousie, KT, GCVO, GBE, MC (d 1999); 3 s (David b 1967, Tobias b 1968, Adam b 1973); *Career* Hambros Bank Ltd: chief exec 1985–95, chm and chief exec 1986–95, non-exec chm 1995–98; chief exec Hambros 1995–98 (jt dep chm 1990–95, chm 1997–98); non-exec dir: Persimmon plc 1984–, The Edinburgh Investment Trust plc 1992–2001, De Beers Consolidated Mines Ltd 1993–, Bank of England 1993–2001, IMI plc 1994–2003, Anglo American plc 1999–2001, Investec Bank (UK) 2000–; memb Queen's Body Guard for Scotland (Royal Co of Archers); *Recreations* bridge, country pursuits; *Clubs* White's, Portland; *Style—* Sir Chips Keswick; ✉ 1 Charterhouse Street, London EC1N 6SA (tel 020 7421 9823, fax 020 7242 6277)

KESWICK, Henry Neville Lindley; s of Sir William Johnston Keswick (d 1990), and Mary, *née* Lindley; bro of Sir (John) Chippendale Lindley (Chips) Keswick, *qv* and Simon Lindley Keswick *qv*; *b* 29 September 1938; *Educ* Eton, Trinity Coll Cambridge (MA); *m* 1985, Annabel Thérèse (Tessa), *qv*, da of 15 Lord Lovat; *Career* Nat Serv cmmnd Scots Guards 1956–58; prop The Spectator 1975–80; dir: Jardine Matheson & Co Ltd 1967 (chm 1972–75), Sun Alliance & London Insurance 1975–96, Royal & Sun Alliance Insurance Group plc 1989–2001 (dep chm 1993–96), Robert Fleming Holdings 1975–2000, Mandarin Oriental Ltd, Dairy Farm Int Ltd, The Telegraph Gp Ltd 1990–2004, Rothschilds Continuation Holdings AG 2006–; chm: Matheson & Co Ltd 1975–, Jardine Matheson Holdings Ltd, Jardine Strategic Holdings Ltd; chm National Portrait Gallery 1994–2001, jt vice-chm Hong Kong Assoc (chm 1988–2001); *Recreations* country pursuits; *Clubs* White's, Turf, Portland, Third Guards'; *Style—* Henry Keswick, Esq; ✉ Matheson & Co Ltd, 3 Lombard Street, London EC3V 9AQ (tel 020 7816 8100, fax 020 7623 5024)

KESWICK, Simon Lindley; s of Sir William Johnston Keswick (d 1990), and Mary, *née* Lindley; bro of Sir (John) Chippendale Lindley (Chips) Keswick, *qv* and Henry Neville Lindley Keswick *qv*; the firm of Jardine Matheson was founded in 1832 by William Jardine and James Matheson; the Keswicks of Dumfries married into the Jardine family in the mid-nineteenth century; *b* 20 May 1942; *Educ* Eton, Trinity Coll Cambridge; *Career* dir: Jardine Matheson Holdings Ltd 1972– (chm 1983–89), Matheson & Co 1982–, Jardine Strategic Hldgs Ltd 1987– (chm 1987–89), Jardine Lloyd Thompson Group plc 2001–; chm: Hong Kong Land Hldgs Ltd 1983–, Mandarin Oriental Int Ltd 1984–, Dairy Farm Int Hldgs Ltd 1984–, Trafalgar House plc 1993–96, Kwik Save Group plc 1990–98; dir: HSBC 1983–88, Fleming Mercantile Investment Tst 1988–2007 (chm 1990–2003), Hanson plc 1991–2005, Wellcome plc 1995–96; tstee: Br Museum 1989–99, Henry Moore Fndn 2003–; *Style—* Simon Keswick, Esq; ✉ Matheson & Co, 3 Lombard Street, London EC3V 9AA

KETTELEY, John Henry Beevor; s of John Joseph Beevor Ketteley (d 1975), and Violet, *née* Robinson (d 1995); *b* 9 August 1939; *Educ* Brentwood Sch, Hackley Sch Tarrytown NY; *m* 15 April 1967, Susan Elizabeth, da of Robert Charles Jay Gordon, of Great Wakering, Essex; 2 da (Sara b 11 July 1969, Alexandra b 15 Nov 1970), 2 s (Stephen b 13 Nov 1973, Thomas b 20 Aug 1985); *Career* exec dir S G Warburg & Co Ltd 1972–81, md Rea Bros plc 1981–83, exec dir Barclays De Zoete Wedd Ltd 1983–87; non-exec dep chm Sutcliffe Speakman plc 1991–95; non-exec dir: Boosey & Hawkes plc 1987–98, Throgmorton Preferred Income Trust plc 1993–95, Calorex Heat Pumps plc 1995–2005, Clariant UK Ltd 2000–02; non-exec chm: BTP plc 1994–2000, Prolific Income plc 1994–2000, Country Casuals Holdings plc 1997–98; exec chm Eleco plc 1997–, memb Advsy Bd HawkPoint Ptnrs 1998–2001; memb Bd COROUS Open Univ 2002–03; Freeman City of London 1978, Liveryman Worshipful Co of CAs 1978; FCA 1970; *Recreations* sailing, golf, tennis; *Clubs* Royal Burnham Yacht, Royal Thames; *Style—* John Ketteley, Esq; ✉ Keeway, Ferry Road, Creeksea, Burnham-on-Crouch, Essex CM0 8PL (tel 01621 783748, fax 01621 784966, car 07785 238585, e-mail john@ketteley.com)

KETTLE, Martin James; *b* 7 September 1949; *Educ* Leeds Modern Sch, Balliol Coll Oxford; *m* Alison Hannah; 2 s; *Career* journalist and writer; asst ed and chief leader writer The Guardian; *Books* Policing the Police (with Peter Hain 1980), Uprising (with Lucy Hodges 1982); *Style—* Martin Kettle, Esq; ✉ The Guardian, 119 Farringdon Road, London EC1R 3ER (tel 020 7278 2332)

KETTLEY, John Graham; s of Harold Kettley (d 2005), of Littleborough, Lancs, and Marian, *née* Greenwood; *b* 11 July 1952; *Educ* Todmorden GS, Lanchester Poly Coventry (BSc); *m* 12 Sept 1990, Lynn Nicola; 2 s (Charles William b 19 Sept 1992, George Kit b 26 Sept 1994); *Career* Meteorological Office 1970–2000 (Meteorological Res Flight Farnborough then Fluid Dynamics Dept Bracknell 1970–79), television weatherman for BBC and ITV Nottingham Weather Centre 1980–85, forecaster BBC Television and Radio 1985–2000, resident weather expert The Travel Show BBC 2 1988–90, weather and sports features presenter BBC Radio 5Live 2001–; currently freelance presenter and weather consIt John Kettley Enterprises; ptnr British Weather Services; guest appearances on Blankety Blank (BBC), Telly Addicts (BBC), Through the Keyhole (BBC and ITV), Style Challenge (BBC) 1997, Call My Bluff (BBC), Watchdog (BBC), Test the Nation (BBC); subject of song John Kettley is a Weatherman (Tribe of Toffs) 1988; ambass Cricket World Cup England 1999, presenter and host Triangular NatWest One-Day Int cricket: England, Australia and Pakistan 2001, England, India and Sri Lanka 2002; consIt to Dick Francis for novel Second Wind (1999); corporate video presenter for cos incl: Boots, Crown Paints, North Herts Dist Cncl; FRMetS; *Recreations* cricket, horse racing, photography, fell walking, gardening, cycling; *Clubs* Lord's Taverners; *Style—* John Kettley, Esq; ✉ Ambition Management, Carina Marina, Nottingham (tel 0115 950 2010)

KEVILL, Siân Louise; da of David Kevill, of Kent, and Frances, *née* Davies; *b* 29 January 1961; *Educ* Southgate Comp Sch, Newnham Coll Cambridge (BA); *m* (m dis 2002), Peter Jukes; 1 s (Alexander Jukes b 4 May 1990), 1 da (Katherine Jukes b 12 October 1992); *Career* BBC: news trainee 1986–88, prodr Newsnight 1988–92, day ed Newsnight 1992–94, dep ed On the Record 1994–95, ed of foreign progs BBC Radio 1995–97, dep head of political progs 1997–98, ed Newsnight 1998–2002, headed BBC New Politics Initiative 2002, currently editorial dir BBC World Ltd; Echo Radio Awards 1996 and 1997, Race in the Media Awards (RIMA) Award 2001, Women in Film and TV (WIFT) Award for contrib to news and current affairs; BAFTA nomination 1999, RTS nominations 1999, 2000 and 2001; assoc Newnham Coll Cambridge 2001; *Books* China and the Soviet Union (1985); *Recreations* reading, cinema, socialising, swimming; *Style—* Ms Siân Kevill

KEY, Geoffrey George Bamford; s of George Key (Sgt RA, d 1967), and Marion, *née* Bamford; *b* 13 May 1941; *Educ* Manchester High Sch of Art, Manchester Regnl Coll of Art (NDD, Dip of Associateship of Manchester, Postgrad in Sculpture); *Career* painter and sculptor; major exhibitions: Salford Art Gallery 1966, Univ of Manchester 1969, Erica Bourne Gallery London 1974, Salon d'Automne Clermont Ferrand France 1974, Nancy France 1974, Gallery Tendenz Germany 1977, Lausanne Switzerland 1980, Madison

K

Avenue NY 1980, Solomon Gallery Dublin 1983, Solomon Gallery London 1985, Damme Belgium 1990, Moret-sur-Loing France 1991, Hong Kong 1992, 1993 and 1994, Art 95 London, Arley Hall Cheshire 1995–97, Joshua Fine Art Kuala Lumpur Malaysia 1997, Harrods Knightsbridge 1999, Rotunda Hong Kong 2000, Oriel Gallery Dublin 2003; work incl in the collections of: Salford Art Gallery, Manchester City Art Gallery, Bolton Art Gallery, NW Arts Assoc, Univ of Manchester, Wigan Corp, Granada TV, Chateau de St Oven France, Jockey Club Hong Kong, Mandarin Hotel Hong Kong, Perrier, Chateaux Relais, Nat West Bank, Nat Art Library V&A; memb Cncl Friends of Salford Art Gallery; *Books* G Key A Book of Drawings and Interview (1975), Daydreams (1981), Clowns (2001), Geoffrey Key Twentieth Century Drawings (2002), Images (2004); *Recreations* collecting African art; *Style—* Geoffrey Key, Esq; ✉ 59 Acresfield Road, Pendleton, Salford, Lancashire M6 7GE (tel 0161 736 6014, website www.geoffreykey.com)

KEY, (Simon) Robert; MP; s of Rt Rev John Maurice Key (d 1984), and (Agnes) Joan Dence (d 1995); Rt Rev Maurice Key (d 1984) was Bishop of Sherborne (1946–60) and Bishop of Truro (1960–73); *b* 22 April 1945; *Educ* Salisbury Cathedral Sch, Sherborne, Clare Coll Cambridge (MA), Cert Ed; *m* 1968, Susan Prisilla Bright, da of Very Rev Thomas Thurstan Irvine, former Dean of St Andrews; 2 s (James (decd), Adam b 1974), 2 da (Sophy b 1977, Helen b 1979); *Career* asst master: Loretto Sch Edinburgh 1967–69, Harrow Sch 1969–83; MP (Cons) Salisbury 1983–; PPS to: Rt Hon Sir Edward Heath, KG, MBE 1984–85, min of state for energy 1985–87, Rt Hon Chris Patten, CH, *qv*, 1987–90; Parly under sec of state: DOE 1990–92, nat heritage 1992–93, transport 1993–94; oppn frontbench spokeman on: defence 1997–2001, trade and industry 2001–02; shadow min for: int devpt 2002–03, energy 2003–04, science 2004–05; memb House of Commons Select Ctee on: Educn, Sci and the Arts 1983–86, Defence 1995–97, Science and Technol 2003–05, Information 2004–05 (chm), Defence 2005–; chm Cncl for Educn in the Cwlth 1984–87; memb: UK Nat Cmmn for UNESCO 1985–86, MRC 1989–90, Cncl Winston Churchill Meml Tst 2004–07, Cncl Salisbury Cathedral 2003–, Gen Synod C of E 2005–; tstee and memb Bd Wessex Tst for Archaeology 2004–; *Style—* Robert Key, Esq, MP; ✉ House of Commons, London SW1A 0AA (tel 020 7219 3000, e-mail rob@robertkey.com)

KEYES, Marian; da of Ted Keyes, and Mary, *née* Cotter; *Educ* UC Dublin (BCL); *m* 29 December 1995, Tony Baines; *Career* writer; books translated into 30 languages; Irish Tatler Literary Award 2001, Irish World Literary Award 2002, Popular Fiction Book of the Year Br Book Awards 2007; *Books* Watermelon (1995), Lucy Sullivan is Getting Married (1996), Rachel's Holiday (1998), Last Chance Saloon (1999), Sushi for Beginners (2000), Under the Duvet (2001), Angels (2002), The Other Side of the Story (2004), Further Under the Duvet (2005), Anybody Out There? (2006); *Style—* Ms Marian Keyes; ✉ c/o J Lloyd, Curtis Brown, 28–29 Haymarket, London SW1Y 4SP (tel 020 7396 6600)

KEYES, Timothy Harold (Tim); s of Edward Keyes (d 1999), and Mary, *née* Mylchreest; *b* 15 December 1954; *Educ* Christ's Hosp, Wadham Coll Oxford, Univ of Exeter (PGCE); *m* 1979, Mary Anne, da of Robert Lucas; 2 s (Samuel b 6 Sept 1986, William b 26 April 1989); *Career* teacher Tiffin GS Kingston upon Thames 1979–83, teacher Whitgift Sch Croydon 1983–88, head of classics Perse Sch Cambridge 1988–93, dep head Royal GS Guildford 1993–98, headmaster King's Sch Worcester 1998–; *Recreations* church bellringing, choral singing, Yorkshire cricket; *Clubs* East India; *Style—* Tim Keyes, Esq; ✉ The King's School, 5 College Green, Worcester WR1 2LH (tel 01905 721700, fax 01905 721710, mobile 07753 681211, e-mail headmaster@ksw.org)

KEYNES, Prof Simon Douglas; s of Prof Richard Darwin Keynes, CBE, ScD, FRS, and Hon Anne Pinsent Keynes, da of 1 Baron Adrian, OM, FRS; *b* 23 September 1952; *Educ* King's Coll Choir Sch Cambridge, Leys Sch Cambridge, Trinity Coll Cambridge (BA, PhD, LittD); *Career* res fell Trinity Coll Cambridge 1976–79; Univ of Cambridge: asst lectr Dept of Anglo-Saxon, Norse, and Celtic 1978–82, lectr 1982–92, reader in Anglo-Saxon history 1992–99, Elrington and Bosworth prof of Anglo-Saxon 1999–, head of dept 1999–2006; Liveryman Worshipful Co of Goldsmiths; FRHistS 1982, FSA 1985, FBA 2000; *Books* incl: The Diplomas of King Aethelred the Unready 978–1016 (1980), Alfred the Great (1983), Facsimiles of Anglo-Saxon Charters (1991), The Liber Vitae of the New Minster Winchester (1996); *Clubs* Roxburghe; *Style—* Prof Simon Keynes; ✉ Trinity College, Cambridge CB2 1TQ (tel 01223 338421, e-mail sdk13@cam.ac.uk)

KEYS, David Chaloner; s of John Henry Keys (d 1982), of Sussex, and Jean Winifred, *née* Glover (d 1970); *b* 12 February 1934; *Educ* Merchant Taylors', St John's Coll Oxford (MA); *m* 20 June 1959, Pamela Helen, da of Philip Henry Megson (d 1984), of Cheshire; 3 da (Charlotte b 1962, Harriet b 1965, Rebecca b 1973); *Career* Nat Serv cmmnd RAF 1953–55; private sec to Dep Govr Bank of England 1963 (joined 1958), seconded to UK Treasy Delgn Washington 1964–66, seconded as md Bank of Mauritius 1968–70, with Morgan Grenfell 1971–88; dir: Morgan Grenfell and Co Ltd 1973–88, A De Gruchy and Co Ltd 1982–99 (chm 1988–99), Morgan Grenfell Gp plc 1987–88, Norwich Union Insurance Gp 1988–2001, Robert M Douglas Holdings plc 1989–91, Interserve plc (formerly Tilbury Douglas plc) 1991–2003 (dep chm 1996–2003); chm: HFC Bank plc 1989–98 (dir 1982–98), Beneficial Bank plc 1998–99; dir: Maples Holdings Ltd (later chm) 1975–80, Thomas Borthwick and Sons plc 1981–84, Target Gp plc 1986–87, Merchant Retail Gp plc 1999–2002; chm E Surrey HA 1988–90; memb Mole Valley DC 1973–92 (chm 1991–92), memb Cncl RSPB 1999–; *Recreations* reading, travelling, ornithology; *Clubs* Oxford and Cambridge, Norfolk; *Style—* David Keys, Esq; ✉ Cley Old Hall, Cley next the Sea, Norfolk NR25 7RY (tel 01263 740549)

KEYS, Richard John; s of Henry John Keys, of Rustington, W Sussex, and Bessie, *née* Taylor (d 1995); *b* 10 April 1951; *Educ* Lewes Co GS for Boys; *m* 5 Oct 1974, Helen Kathryn, da of Alan Herbert Jackson; 2 da (Emily Sarah b 19 Feb 1986, Letitia Mary b 2 March 1990); *Career* articled clerk Singleton Fabian Derbyshire 1969–73; PricewaterhouseCoopers (formerly Coopers & Lybrand before merger): joined Cooper Bros & Co 1973, ptnr 1984–, seconded to Dept of Environment (water finance) 1983–84, memb Energy Water and Tport Market Bd 1989–98 (chm 1989–96), memb Audit Bd 1993–96; professional standards and risk mgmnt leader UK Assurance 2004–07, global ldr accounting consltg services 2007–; memb Tech Ctee ICAEW 1988–90; Freeman Worshipful Co of Glaziers & Painters of Glass 2003; FCA (ACA 1973); *Recreations* shooting, opera, fly fishing; *Clubs* Reform; *Style—* Richard Keys, Esq; ✉ PricewaterhouseCoopers, 1 Embankment Place, London WC2N 6RH (tel 020 7583 5000, fax 020 7213 2112, e-mail richard.j.keys@uk.pwc.com)

KEYTE, Malcolm William; s of William Keyte (d 1977), of Sandsgate, Devon, and Grace Mary, *née* Bocking (d 1983); *b* 23 February 1944; *Educ* Tonbridge (athletics and 1st VIII cross country); *m* May 1983, Nicola Anne, da of Arthur Leonard Spiller; 3 da (Sophie Victoria b 30 March 1985, Charlotte Mary b 10 Jan 1987, Alice Joanna b 18 Dec 1990), 1 s (Thomas William b 25 March 1993); *Career* princ Keyte & Co Chartered Accountants 1973– (articled clerk 1961–67); Croydon and Dist Soc of Chartered Accountants: memb 1968–, pres 1991–92, chm Gen Practitioner Bd 1994–2001; memb: Gen Practitioner Bd/Panel ICAEW 1994–2002, Cncl Small Firms Lead Body 1995–98; chm S London HMRC Working Together Ctee 2000–; treas Tonbridge Sch Parents Arts Soc 2007–; capt Purley Squash Club 1981–84; fell WWF 1985–; FCA 1979 (ACA 1968); *Recreations* gardening, tennis, walking; *Style—* Malcolm W Keyte, Esq; ✉ Keyte & Co, Coombe Avenue, Croydon CR0 5SD (tel 020 8688 6551, fax 020 8760 1951)

KHALILI, Nasser David; *b* 18 December 1945, Iran; *Educ* schooling in Tehran, Queens Coll NY (BA), SOAS Univ of London (PhD); *m* 1978, Marion Easton; 3 s (Daniel b 5 Aug 1981, Benjamin, Raphael (twins) b 2 May 1984); *Career* scholar, art collector and philanthropist; army medic Iranian military 1967–67; art collector 1967–; fndr: Khalili Family Tst 1970, Nour Fndn (Khalili Collection of Islamic Art) 1982, Mobarak Fndn (Khalili Collection of Enamels of the World) 1986, Kibo Fndn (Khalili Collection of Japanese Art) 1988, Khalili Collection of Spanish Damascene Metalwork 1988, Khalili Collection of Swedish Textile Art 1988; estab Khalili Chair of Islamic Art at the Sch of Oriental and African Studies Univ of London 1989; fndr and chm Favermead Ltd and subsids 1992–, restored 18–19 Kensington Palace Gardens London; estab Khalili Research Centre for Art and Material Culture of the Middle East Univ of Oxford 2005; numerous lectures on art in UK and abroad; numerous pubns covering all five collections; memb: Governing Body SOAS Univ of London 1992, Advsy Cncl London Middle East Inst 1994, Bd of Govrs NAIMA Jewish Prep Sch 1995, Int Bd of Overseers Tufts Univ USA 1997; tstee Boston Univ 2003, assoc res prof SOAS Univ of London 2003; estab Nasser David Khalili Charitable Settlement 1992, fndr and chm Maimonides Fndn 1995–; memb Elias Ashmole Gp Ashmolean Museum Oxford 2000, memb Chancellors Ct of Benefactors Oxford 2006, co-fndr and tstee Iran Heritage Fndn 1995, hon patron Graymatters Mehran David Fndn 2001, founding patron Jewish Arts Festival 2001, patron Arts in the Vatican Museums 2002, founding patron Multi-Faith Secondary Sch 2002, memb Ctee Jewish Arts Cncl 2002, memb Bd of Tstees Moroccan-Br Soc 2003, cultural patron Asia House 2004, friend Duke of Edinburgh Award 2005, tstee Br Edutrust Fndn 2006; High Sheriff of London Award 2007; hon fell: SOAS Univ of London 1991, Wolfson Coll Oxford 2005; Hon Dr: Boston Univ 2003, Univ of the Arts London 2005; tstee City of Jerusalem 1996; Knight Cdr Royal Order of Francis I, Knight Equestrian Order of Pope St Sylvester 2004; *Style—* Professor Nasser D Khalili; ✉ c/o Sue Bond Public Relations, Hollow Lane Farmhouse, Hollow Lane, Thurston, Bury St Edmunds, Suffolk IP31 3RQ

KHALSA, Guru Dharam Singh; s of Richard Hinchcliffe Ainley (d 1966), of London, and Dr Rowena Woolf (d 1967); *b* 7 January 1956; *Educ* UCS London, Diss GS Norfolk, Park Lane Coll of FE Leeds, London Sch of Acupuncture and Traditional Chinese Med (Dip), London Coll of Chinese Herbal Med (Dip); *Career* teacher of Kundalini yoga and meditation 1982–, vice-princ London Acad of Oriental Med 1988–96, fndr dir Lotus Healing Centre 1990–, tutor in Chinese med London Acad of Chinese Herbal Med 1991–, dir Sch of Kundalini Yoga 1997–, chm Universal Yoga Centre NY 2002–; expert speaker Assoc of Chief Execs (ACE) 2002–; memb: Kundalini Yoga Fedn of GB 1987–, Br Acupuncture Cncl 1989–, Register of Chinese Herbal Med 1991–; assoc dir Inst of Med Yoga Stockholm 2001–; min of Sikh Dharma; *Books* Kundalini - Essence of Yoga (2002); *Recreations* nature, music; *Style—* Guru Dharam Khalsa, Esq; ✉ Lotus Healing Centre Ltd, 30A Wimpole Street, London W1G 8YA (e-mail gurudharam@kunalinilotus.com)

KHAN, Akram Hossain; MBE (2005); *b* 29 July 1974; *Educ* Rutlish HS Merton Park, Prayag Sangeet Samati (Dance Bd of India, Sr Dip), De Montfort Univ (BA), Northern Sch of Contemporary Dance Leeds (BPA); *Career* choreographer and dancer; teacher: Bangladesh Centre London 1986, Leicester Cncl 1994–95, Merton Adult Inst London 1992–, Acad of Indian Dance London 1994–96, Wakefield Arts Centre 1996; Jonathan Burrows Co: Freiburg Residency 1998, Kevin Volans Evening 1999; choreographer in residence Royal Festival Hall 2001–03, assoc artist Royal Festival Hall 2003–, assoc artist Sadler's Wells Theatre 2005–; Hon Dr Arts De Montfort University 2004; *Performances* nat performances incl: Bangladesh Festival (Cwlth Inst) 1983–86, Bangladesh Festival of Freedom London 1984–86, Ora Kadam Ali (Cwlth Inst) 1985, Makhon Churi-Krishna (Trevini Co) 1985, Jungle Book (Br Arts Cncl, touring) 1984–85, Treveni Co 1986, Round House 1986, Mahabharata (RSC, world tour) 1988, solo performance tour 1992, solo performance (Cwlth Inst and Bhavan) 1992, Treveni (tour) 1992, Merton Festival 1993–95, vision prodn (The Place Theatre) 1995, Indian Dance Festival (Phoenix Theatre) 1995, Homage to the Four Tops (Glasgow Festival) 1996, Dance Umbrella Festival (Cochrane Theatre) 1996, X-10–DED (Woking Dance Umbrella) 1996, Ross-on-Wye Int Festival 1997, Purush (Birmingham) 1997, Watermans Arts Centre 1998, Interface (Interface Festival) 1998, Choreolab 1999, Per4mance (short film) 1999, Saint (CADMAD Cardiff) 1999, Desert Steps (QEH London) 1999, Saint (Greenwich and Docklands Int Festival) 1999, No Male Egos (Purcell Room London) 1999, Loose in Flight 2000, Fix 2000, Rush 2000 (added to A-level syllabus 2004), Related Rocks 2001, kaash 2002, ma 2004, zero degrees (Sadler's Wells) 2005 (nominated Best New Dance Prodn Laurence Olivier Awards 2006), sacred monsters 2006, variations for vibes, strings & pianos 2006; int performances incl: Mahabharata (int tour) 1987–89, solo performance (India and Bangladesh) 1990, Lucknow and TV interview (Bombay) 1993, solo performance (Divya Drishti Indian TV), vision prodn Bangladesh 1995, X-10–DED (Oriental Festival Germany) 1997; *Awards* Jerwood Choreography Award 1999, Outstanding Newcomer to Dance Dance Critics Circle 2000, Outstanding Newcomer Time Out Live Award 2001, Best Choreography (modern section) Critics' Circle National Dance Awards 2003, Most Promising Newcomer in Dance International Movimentos Tanzpreis Berlin 2004, Outstanding Male or Female Artist (modern) Critics' Circle National Dance Awards 2005, South Bank Show Dance Award 2005 (nominated 2000); *Style—* Akram Khan, Esq, MBE; ✉ website www.akramkhancompany.net

KHAN, Prof Geoffrey Allan; s of Clive Khan, and Diana Margaret Hodson; *b* 1 February 1958; *Educ* SOAS Univ of London (BA, PhD); *m* 21 Jan 1984, Colette Winefride Mary, da of Alfred A Alcock; 1 da (Hannah Maryam b 26 Feb 1987), 1 s (Jonathan Anthony b 24 Oct 1989); *Career* research assoc Taylor-Schechter Genizah Research Unit 1987–93 (research asst 1983–87); Univ of Cambridge: lectr in Hebrew and Aramaic (Semitic languages) 1993–99, prof of Semitic philology 2002– (reader 1999–2002); Lidzbarski Gold Medal for Semitic Philology 2004; fell Inst for Advanced Studies Jerusalem 1990–91; FBA 1998; *Books* Studies in Semitic Syntax (1988), Karaite Bible Manuscripts from the Cairo Genizah (1990), Arabic Papyri: Selected material from the Khalili Collection (1992), Arabic Legal and Administrative Documents in the Cambridge Genizah Collections (1993), Bills, Letters and Deeds. Arabic Papyri of the Seventh-Eleventh Centuries (1993), A Grammar of Neo-Aramaic (1999), The Early Karaite Tradition of Hebrew Grammatical Thought (2000), Early Karaite Grammatical Texts (2001), Exegesis and Grammar in Medieval Karaite Texts (2002), The Neo-Aramaic Dialect of Qaraqosh (2002), The Karaite Tradition of Hebrew Grammatical Thought in its Classical Form (2003), The Jewish Neo-Aramaic Dialect of Sulemaniyya and Halabja (2004), Arabic Documents from Early Islamic Khurasan (2007); also author of numerous articles and reviews in learned jls; *Recreations* mountain walking; *Style—* Prof G Khan, FBA; ✉ Faculty of Oriental Studies, Sidgwick Avenue, Cambridge CB3 9DA (tel 01223 335114, fax 01223 335110, e-mail gk101@cam.ac.uk)

KHAN, (Mohammed) Ilyas; s of Mohammed Yasin Khan (d 1970), of Gillingham, Kent, and Hafiza Begum; *b* 14 October 1945; *Educ* Duke of Gloucester Sch Nairobi Kenya; *m* 14 April 1972, Amtul Naseer, da of Abdul Rehman Qureshi (d 1965); 1 da (Maham Hina b 1988), 1 s (Shamail Ahmed Nadeem b 1992); *Career* Cncl of Legal Educn 1965–68, called to the Bar Lincoln's Inn 1969, res magistrate Kenya 1977–80, immigration adjudicator 1992– (pt/t 1983–92), special asylum adjudicator 1993–, dep regnl adjudicator 2003–05, designated immigration judge 2005–; recorder of the Crown Ct 1996– (asst recorder 1991); *Recreations* cricket, squash; *Style—* Ilyas Khan, Esq; ✉ 12 Halfway Close, Great Barr, Birmingham B44 8JL

KHAN, Irene Zubaida; *b* 24 December 1956, Bangladesh; *Educ* Univ of Manchester, Harvard Law Sch; *Career* fndr memb Concern Universal 1977, human rights activist Int Cmmn of Jurists 1979; UNHCR: joined 1980, various positions at HQ and in field ops, sr exec offr to UN High Cmmr 1991–95, chief of mission India 1995–98, dep dir of int protection 1999–2001; sec gen Amnesty Int 2001–; hon dr: Ferris Univ Japan, Ghent Univ, Staffordshire Univ, Univ of London; Ford Fndn fell; Pilkington Woman of the Year Award 2002, City of Sydney Peace Prize 2006, John Owens Distinguished Alumni Award Univ of Manchester; *Style*— Dr Irene Khan; ✉ Amnesty International, 1 Easton Street, London WC1X 0DW (tel 020 7413 5994, e-mail secgen@amnesty.org)

KHAN, Rosemarie; OBE (1999); *b* 29 July 1947; *Educ* GDC (Dip Dental Hygiene), Univ of Manchester (BEd, MEd); *m* Mohammad Aslam; 1 s (Alexander b 24 Nov 1965), 1 da (Sophia b 5 June 1973); *Career* formerly dental hygienist Dental Dept St Mary's Hosp Whitworth Park Manchester, dental hygienist in gen dental practice 1971–, tutor dental hygienist Univ of Manchester Dental Hosp 1971–98, oral health promotion mangr Sheffield Primary Dental Care Serv 1998–2004, tutor dental hygienist Gtr Manchester Sch for Professionals Complementary to Dentistry (PCDs) 2004–; nat pres Br Dental Hygienists Assoc (BDHA) 1984–86 (memb Cncl 1981–84), UK dir Int Dental Hygienists Fedn 1986–89; memb: Central Examining Bd for Dental Hygienists 1976–98, Panel of Examiners Central Examining Bd for Dental Hygienists 1982–99; elected memb GDC 1991– (memb Dental Auxiliaries Ctee 1985–98); BDHA Leatherman 1995, BDA Roll of Distinction 1999; *Recreations* family, reading, travel; *Style*— Mrs Rosemarie Khan, OBE; ✉ Greater Manchester PCD School, 4th Floor, St James's House, Pendleton Way, Salford M6 5FW

KHAN, Sadiq; MP; s of Amanullah Ahmed Khan (d 2003), and Sehrun Nisa Khan; *b* 8 October 1970, Tooting, London; *Educ* Ernest Bevin Secdy Comp Tooting, Univ of N London (LLB), Coll of Law Guildford (Sweet & Maxwell Law Prize, Windsor fell, Esso Law Award); *m* 1994, Saadiya Ahmad; 2 da; *Career* solicitor; ptnr: Christian Fisher Slrs 1998–2000 (trainee slr 1993–95, slr 1995–98), Christian Fisher Khan Slrs 2000–02, Christian Khan Slrs 2002–04 (also co-fndr); MP (Lab) Tooting 2005–; cncllr (Lab) Wandsworth BC 1994–2006 (dep ldr Lab gp 1996–2001); chair: Liberty 2001–04, Legal Affrs Ctee Muslim Cncl of Britain (MCB) 2004–05; vice-chair Legal Action Gp (LAG) 1999–2004; fndr Human Rights Lawyers Assoc; memb: Unison, Co-op, GMB, CWU, Fabian Soc, Friends of the Earth, Law Soc 1993–; govr Fircroft Primary Sch 1993–, chair of govrs Gatton Primary Sch 2004–; Newcomer of the Year Spectator Parly Awards 2005; *Publications* Challenging Racism (2003), Police Misconduct (2005); author of articles in various pubns on variety of matters; *Recreations* playing and watching sports, cinema, family, friends, local community, lifelong supporter of Liverpool FC; *Style*— Sadiq Khan, Esq, MP; ✉ House of Commons, London SW1A 0AA (tel 020 7219 6967, fax 020 7219 6477, e-mail sadiqkhanmp@parliament.uk); Tooting Labour Party, 58 Trinity Road, London SW17 7RH (tel 020 8767 9660, fax 020 8772 4593, e-mail tooting@email.org.uk, website www.sadiqkhan.org.uk)

KHARITÔNOV, Dimitri; s of Anatolij Ivanovich Kharitônov, and Valentina Nikolaievna, *née* Loboda; *b* 18 October 1958; *Educ* Rimsky-Korsakov Coll of Music Leningrad State Conservatoire, Odessa State Conservatoire; *m* Nicoletta; 2 s (Vadim b 9 April 1987, Georgij b 13 Oct 1994); *Career* baritone; princ baritone Odesa State Philharmonie Sociaty 1982–84, princ baritone Odessa State Opera 1983–85, leading baritone Bolshoi Theatre 1985–89, leading baritone Bolshoi Theatre Moscow, corso di perfezionaniento La Scala Milan, based in UK/Italy 1989–; winner: Zolotaja Osen all-Ukrainian Competition for Concert Interpretation Kiev 1983, all-Ukrainian Lysenko Competition for Opera Singers Odessa 1984, all-USSR Michail Ivanovich Glinka Competition 1984 (with special prize for best interpretation of Rimsky-Korsakov works), Grand Prix Verviers Int Opera Competition Belgium 1987, gold medal Bastianini Int Competition Siena Italy 1988, Voci Verdiane Competition Busseto Italy 1988, Carlo Alberto Cappelli Competition Arena di Verona for winners of international competitions; *Performances* regular roles with Bolshoi incl: title role in Eugene Onegin, Prince Yeletsky in Queen of Spades, Duke Robert in Iolanta, Silvio in I Pagliacci, Ferdinando in Duenna, Giorgio Germont in La Traviata, Figaro in Il Barbiere di Siviglia; with Odessa State Opera: most of the above, also Seaman Zarev in Semion Kotko, Matveev in Po to storonu 1980/81; others incl: Bill in Mahagonny (Maggio Musicale Fiorentino) 1990, Shchelkalov in Boris Godunov (Maggio Musicale Fiorentino) 1991, Jokanaan in Salome (UK debut role at Edinburgh Festival 1989, ENO 1991), Giorgio Germont in La Traviata (Liège, Dublin Grand Opera), Orbazzano in Tancredi (Buxton Festival), Sonora in La Fanciulla del West (Chicago Lyric Opera 1990–91), Prince Andrei Bolkonsky in War and Peace and Escamillo in Carmen (San Francisco War Meml Opera House 1991), Prince Yeletsky in The Queen of Spades (Barcelona Liceum Opera 1992, Glyndebourne Festival 1992 recorded on BBC Video), Enrico in Lucia di Lammermoor and Renato in Un Ballo in Maschera (both at LA Music Center), title role in Nabucco (Teatro Communale Carlo Felice Genoa) 1994, Renato in Un Ballo in Maschera (Dresden Semperoper and Sächische Staatsoper) 1994, Sharpless in Madama Butterfly (Teatro Colon Buenos Aires) 1994; gala concert at Palais des Beaux Arts Brussels 1992, recitals (with pianist Leif Ove Andsens) Olympic Games Cultural Prog Oslo, Lillehammer and Hamer 1994, recitals at Royal Opera House, Hamburg Symphony Hall, Ceseria Teatro Alessandro Bonei, Buxton Festival and Bergamo; *Style*— Dimitri Kharitônov, Esq

KHASRU, Ameer; s of Abdur Rahman Khasru, of Bangladesh, and Saleha Khasru; *b* 28 January 1942; *Educ* Collegiate Sch Chittagong, Univ of Dhaka (BCom); *m* 4 March 1965 (m dis 1997), Chantal Berthe, da of Andre Faucher (d 1979), of France; 1 s (Stephane Reza b 1966), 1 da (Ambreen Joy b 1970); *Career* sr ptnr Khasru & Co London; chm Thai Pavilion Restaurants; chief accountant: Burmah Eastern Ltd, Chittagong Bangladesh 1968–71; sr lectr Business Studies SW London Coll 1971–74, trg mangr 1974–78; FCA; *Recreations* swimming, tennis, theatre, reading, good food; *Style*— Ameer Khasru, Esq; ✉ Khasru & Co, 121 Kennington Road, London SE11 6SF (e-mail mak@thaipavilion.com)

KHAW, Prof Kay-Tee; CBE (2003); da of Kai-Boh Khaw (d 1972), of Kuala Lumpur, and Chweegeok, *née* Tan; *b* 14 October 1950; *Educ* Victoria Inst Kuala Lumpur, Univ of Cambridge (MA, MB BChir), LSHTM (MSc); *m* 1980, Dr James William Fawcett; 1 da (Nicola b 21 Dec 1981), 1 s (Andrew b 14 Feb 1984); *Career* house physician and surgn St Mary's Hosp 1975–76, SHO Whittington Hosp 1977–78, registrar KCH 1978–79; Wellcome Tst res fell: St Mary's Hosp and LSHTM 1980–82, Univ of Calif 1982–84; asst prof Univ of Calif 1985–89; Univ of Cambridge: sr registrar (community med) 1986–89, prof of clinical gerontology 1989–; fell Gonville & Caius Coll Cambridge 1992–; FRCP, FFPHM, FMedSci; *Style*— Prof Kay-Tee Khaw, CBE; ✉ Clinical Gerontology Unit, University of Cambridge, Addenbrooke's Hospital, Cambridge CB2 2QQ (tel 01223 217292, fax 01223 336928)

KHAYAT, His Hon Judge Georges Mario; QC (1992); s of Fred Khayat (d 1973), of Israel and USA, and Julie, *née* Germain (d 1990); *b* 15 August 1941; *Educ* Terra Sancta Coll Nazareth, Prior Park Coll Bath; *Career* called to the Bar Lincoln's Inn 1967, pupillage with K Zucker (now His Hon Judge Zucker, QC), mixed practice later specialising in prosecution and defence in criminal cases, recorder 1987–2002, dep head of chambers 1992–99, head of chambers 1999–2002, circuit judge SE Circuit 2002–; chm Surrey and S London Bar Mess 1995–98; *Recreations* music, reading, boating, riding and travelling; *Style*— His Hon Judge Khayat, QC

KHERAJ, Naguib; *b* 15 July 1964, London; *Educ* Dulwich Coll, Robinson Coll Cambridge; *m* Nazira Jiwan Hirji; 1 s (Ali Hirj b 21 Dec 2002); *Career* Salomon Bros 1986–96 (joined Investment Banking Div, appointed chief financial offr 1993), co-head of global capital markets and memb Exec Ctee Robert Fleming 1996–97, joined Barclays 1997, successively chief operating offr then global head of investment banking Barclays Capital and dep chm Barclays Global Investors, chief exec Barclays Private Clients 2003–04, gp finance dir Barclays plc 2004–07, memb Barclays Gp Exec Ctee, Bd Barclays plc and Bd Barclays Bank plc 2004–07; memb: Bd of Govrs Inst of Ismaili Studies, Devpt Bd Prince's Tst; *Style*— Naguib Kheraj, Esq

KHIYAMI, HE Dr Sami; *b* 28 August 1948, Damascus, Syria; *Educ* American Univ of Beirut (BE), Univ of Claude Bernard Lyon (DEA, PhD); *m* Amina; 1 s, 2 da; *Career* Syrian diplomat; head Electronics Dept, chief researcher and dir of research Higher Int of Applied Sciences and Technol (HIAST) Nat Research Centre 1980–95, prof of computer engrg and electronic measurements Damascus Univ 1980–95; visiting prof Inst Nat Poly Grenoble 1993; telecom and technol conslt; project co-ordinator for design and implementation of software projects in Syria incl: Tport Directorate 1995, Central Bank 1995, investment cert lottery 1995, Popular Credit Bank 1995–96, Damascus Univ admin 1996–98, Agriculture Bank 1998–2000, Miny of Tourism 1998–99, civil registration nat project 2000– (also pilot project 1998–99); memb Bd and conslt Spacetel 2004–, memb Bd Syrian Arab Airlines 2004, conslt Systems Int; ambass to the Ct of St James's 2004–; key negotiator of the projected Syrian European partnership agreement 2003–04; author of numerous papers in scientific reviews, seminars and computer confs; co-fndr and memb Bd Syrian Computer Soc 1989–; *Recreations* philately, gardening, music; *Style*— HE Dr Sami Khiyami; ✉ Embassy of the Syrian Arab Republic, 8 Belgrave Square, London SW1X 8PH (tel 020 7245 9012, fax 020 7235 4621)

KHMELNITSKII, Prof David; s of Ephraim A Khmelnitskii (d 1984), and Ida S, *née* Borodyanskaya (d 1998); *b* 5 December 1944; *Educ* Landau Inst for Theoretical Physics Moscow (PhD, DSc); *m* 20 Jan 1981, Ellen, da of Pietr Kaminskii; 2 da (Anna b 22 Aug 1981, Eugenia b 28 Nov 1984); *Career* grad student and researcher L D Landau Inst Moscow 1969–84 (gp leader 1989), gp leader Inst for Solid State Physics 1985–89, sr research fell Trinity Coll Cambridge 1991–; hon prof Univ of Cambridge 2002; Hewlett-Packard Europhysics Prize 1993, Landau-Weizmann Award 1995; *Style*— Prof David Khmelnitskii; ✉ Cavendish Laboratory, University of Cambridge, Cambridge CB3 0HE (tel 01223 337289, fax 01223 337356, e-mail dek12@cam.ac.uk)

KHOO, Francis Kah Siang; s of late Teng Eng, and late Swee Neo, *née* Chew; *b* 23 October 1947; *Educ* Univ of Singapore (LLB), Univ of London (MA); *m* 29 Jan 1977, Dr Swee Chai Ang, da of late Peng Liat Ang; *Career* advocate and slr Singapore 1971–77, business, political journalist and cartoonist London 1980–87, gen sec War on Want London (Br Devpt Aid Agency) 1988–89, slr Law Soc of England and Wales 1998–; vice-chm and fndr memb Medical Aid for Palestinians 1984–; chm, tstee and sec Radicle 2000–; memb: NUJ 1979–, Singapore Law Soc 1971–; *Books* Bungaraya Blooms All Day (1978), The Rebel and the Revolutionary (1994); *Recreations* song-writing, swimming, camera designing; *Style*— Francis Khoo, Esq; ✉ 285 Cambridge Heath Road, Bethnal Green, London E2 0EL (tel 020 7729 3994, e-mail fkhoo@compuserve.com)

KHOURY, Dr Ghassan George; s of George Sammaan Khoury, of Amman, Jordan, and Margaret, *née* Rizik; *b* 14 July 1954; *Educ* Bryanston, UCL, UCH; *m* 7 Aug 1984, Sonia, da of Jubran Khoury, of Jifna, Ramallah, Israel; 2 s (George Ghassan b 1986, Timothy b 1993), 2 da (Genevieve b 1996, Emma b 1997); *Career* lectr in radiotherapy and oncology Univ of Leeds 1986–89, conslt and head Radiotherapy and Oncology Dept Portsmouth 1989–; memb radiotherapy co-op gp EORTC; memb: BMA 1978, British Oncological Assoc 1987, Faculty of Clinical Oncology RCR 1998; MRCP 1981, FRCR 1985, FRCP 1998; *Recreations* swimming, riding, skiing; *Style*— Dr Ghassan Khoury; ✉ St Mary's Hospital, Milton Road, Portsmouth PO3 6AD (tel 023 9228 6000, fax 023 928 66313)

KIBAZO, Joel Serunkuma; s of Godfrey Serunkuma Lule, and Margaret Mary, *née* Namusisi; *b* 24 June 1961; *Educ* HS for Boys Swindon, Kingsbury HS London, Sunderland Poly (BA), Univ of Reading (MA), Univ of Bradford (MBA); *Career* trainee reporter New Life 1986–87, political corr The Voice 1987–88, Financial Times 1988–2000, dir of communications and public affairs The Commonwealth Secretariat 2000–06, ptnr JK Associates 2007–; memb Policy Ctee Centre for the Study of African Economies Univ of Oxford; fell of Africa Research Gp Univ of Bradford; *Recreations* swimming, African history, Third World development issues; *Style*— Joel Kibazo, Esq; ✉ JK Associates, 33 Downs Hill, Beckenham, Kent BR3 5ET (tel 020 8658 2821, mobile 07887 788566, e-mail joel@joelkibazo.com)

KIBBLE, Richard David; s of David John Kibble, of Lewes, E Sussex, and Maureen Carol, *née* Scott; *b* 14 February 1968, Cuckfield, Sussex; *Educ* New Coll Oxford (BA); *m* 20 March 1993, Alison Caroline, *née* Mitchell; 1 s (Zachary David b 31 July 2003); *Career* Marakon Assocs: joined 1990, ptnr 1999–, managing ptnr 2005–; memb Regeneration Ctee Business in the Community; *Recreations* squash, tennis, cycling, bridge, chess; *Clubs* RAC; *Style*— Richard Kibble, Esq; ✉ Marakon Associates, 1–3 Strand, London WC2N 5HP (tel 020 7321 3629, fax 020 7930 9716, e-mail rkibble@marakon.com)

KIDBY, Robert James; s of late James Clarence Kidby, and Myrtle Eileen, *née* Wright; *b* 27 February 1951; *Educ* Steyning GS, Univ of London (LLB); *m* 3 Dec 1977, Stephanie Elizabeth Mary, da of Morris Shipley (decd); 1 s (Samuel Robert b 4 Aug 1985), 1 da (Harriet Elizabeth Cynthia b 6 Nov 1988); *Career* admitted slr 1977; ptnr: Durrant Piesse 1985–88, Lovells (previously Lovell White Durrant) 1988– (currently head of real estate); dir Br Property Fedn; appeal steward Br Boxing Bd of Control; Freeman Worshipful Co of Slrs 1984; memb Law Soc 1978; *Recreations* electric guitar, Antarctic memorabilia; *Clubs* City of London, MCC; *Style*— Robert Kidby, Esq; ✉ Lovells, Atlantic House, Holborn Viaduct, London EC1A 2FG (tel 020 7296 2000, e-mail robert.kidby@lovells.com)

KIDD, Andrew Nicholson; s of Albert Kidd, of Santa Fe, NM, and Elizabeth, *née* White; *b* 18 September 1968, Houston, TX; *Educ* American Sch London, Brown Univ Providence (AB); *m* 9 July 1993, Solange, *née* Weinberger; 2 s (Nicolas b 13 June 1997, Oliver b 12 Feb 2001); *Career* editorial dir Penguin 1994–2002, publisher Picador and Pan Macmillan 2002–; *Style*— Andrew Kidd, Esq; ✉ Pan Macmillan, 20 New Wharf Road, London N1 9RR (tel 020 7014 6000, e-mail a.kidd@macmillan.co.uk)

KIDGELL, John Earle; CB (2003); s of Maj Gilbert James Kidgell, TD, RA and TA (d 1989), and Cicely Alice Whitfield, *née* Earle (d 1982); *b* 18 November 1943; *Educ* Eton House Sch Southend, Univ of St Andrews (MA), LSE (MSc); *m* 30 March 1968, Penelope Jane, da of Kenneth Tarry (d 1970); 2 da (Clare Louise b 1972, Alexandra Frances b 1981), 1 s (James Kenneth b 1974); *Career* NIESR 1967–70, Gallup Poll 1970–72, statistician Central Statistical Office and Treasury 1972–79, chief statistician DOE and PSA 1979–88, under sec (grade 3) Office for National Statistics (formerly Central Statistical Office) 1988– (dir Macro-Economic Statistics and Analysis Gp 1994–99, dir Economic Statistics 1999–2002); *Recreations* tennis, hill walking, golf, reading; *Style*— John Kidgell, Esq, CB

KIDNER, Michael James; s of Norman William Kidner (d 1931), of Kettering, and Kathleen Kidner (d 1976); *b* 11 September 1917; *Educ* Bedales, Univ of Cambridge (MA); *m* 24 Feb 1951, Marion, da of Morton Frederick (d 1975), of NY, USA; 1 s (Simon Morton b 15 Sept 1962, d 10 March 1982); *Career* Nat Serv Royal Canadian Signal Corps 1942–46; artist and sculptor; one man shows incl: ACGB Expo Serpentine Gallery London 1984, Museum of Contemporary Art Łódź Poland 1985, Joszefvarosi Kaillito Teerem Gallery Budapest Hungary 1986, Amos Anderson Museum Helsinki Finland 1987, The Wave: Concepts in Construction (Galerie Hubert Winter Vienna Austria) 1990 and 1992, At-tension to the Wave (CICA NYC) 1990, Galerie Bismarck Bremen 1992, Galerie Schlege Zurich 1991, Critics' Choice (Cowling Gallery) 1992, Michael Kidner 1958–93 (Galerie Hoffmann Friedberg Germany) 1993–94, Michael Kidner (Gallerie Emilia Sucico

Ettlingham Germany) 1995, Science in the Arts Art in the Science (Budapest) 1999, Fine Gallery London 1999, Nantes France 1999, Michael Kidner Works 1959–2001 Galerie Hubert Winter Vienna Austria 2001; numerous gp expos worldwide; public collections incl: Tate Gallery, MOMA NY, Nat Gallery of Aust Canberra, Amos Anderson Museum Helsinki, Manchester City Art Gallery, Victoria and Albert Museum, Sainsbury Collection; cmmns incl: sculpture for the Museo Internazionale di Scultura all'Aperto Citta di Portofino Italy 1988, sculpture in Vissingen Holland 1989, sculpture in Dresdner Bank Merseburg Germany 1995; *Books* Elastic Membrane (1980); *Style*— Michael Kidner; ✉ 18 Hampstead Hill Gardens, London NW3 2PL (tel 020 7435 9630, fax 020 7431 5105, e-mail mail.kidner@virgin.net)

KIDNEY, David Neil; MP; s of Neil Bernard Kidney (d 2000), and Doris, *née* Booth (d 1994); *b* 21 March 1955; *Educ* Longton HS, City of Stoke on Trent Sixth Form Coll, Univ of Bristol (LLB); *m* Elaine; 1 s (Robert b 15 Aug 1985), 1 da (Katherine b 11 Sept 1987); *Career* slr in private practice 1979–97, MP (Lab) Stafford 1997–; pres Stafford & District Law Soc 1991–92, patron of ASIST (Advocacy Servs in Staffs), memb Law Soc; *Recreations* bridge, chess, cycling/swimming with family; *Style*— David Kidney, Esq, MP; ✉ 6, Beechcroft Avenue, Stafford, Staffordshire ST16 1BJ; House of Commons, London SW1A 0AA (tel 020 7219 6472, fax 020 7219 0919, e-mail kidneyd@parliament.uk, website www.davidkidney.com)

KIDSTON, Cath; da of Archibald Kidston (d 1978), and Susan, *née* Pease (d 1991); *b* 6 November 1958, London; *Educ* West Heath Girls Sch Sevenoaks, Southover Sch Lewes; *partner* Hugh Padgham; *Career* interior designer; asst to Nicky Haslam, 1984–87, jt prop Curtainalia & Interior Design store 1987–92, fndr and creative dir Cath Kidston Ltd (11 UK and 2 US stores) 1992–; memb RSA 2002; *Publications* Vintage Style (1999), Tips for Vintage Style (2004), Cath Kidston In Print (2005); *Recreations* family, car boot sales, art exhibitions, travel; *Style*— Miss Cath Kidston; ✉ Cath Kidston Ltd, 1 & 8 The People's Hall, 2 Olaf Street, London W11 4BE (tel 020 7221 4248, fax 020 7313 3743, e-mail cath@cathkidston.co.uk)

KIELY, John Andrew; s of Nicholas Joseph Kiely (d 1989), and Maureen, *née* O'Neill; *b* 12 December 1961; *Educ* Stonyhurst, UCL (BA); *m* 1 June 1991, Sarah, da of Maj Peter Challen; 1 s (Alexander Fergus), 2 da (Georgia Francesca, Eloise India); *Career* Broad Street Associates PR 1986–88, fndr dir Square Mile Communications 1988–95, dir Bell Pottinger Financial (formerly Lowe Bell Financial) 1995–98, md Smithfield Financial 1998–; *Recreations* most sports; *Clubs* Queen's, Rye Golf, Royal Worlington and Newmarket Golf, Worplesdon Golf; *Style*— John Kiely, Esq; ✉ Smithfield, 10 Aldersgate Street, London EC1A 4HJ

KIERNAN, Peter Anthony; s of Joseph Patrick Kiernan (d 1980), and Mary (Molly) Kiernan (d 1989); *b* 11 September 1960, Watford, Herts; *Educ* St Michael's Sch Garston, Downing Coll Cambridge (MA); *m* 20 April 1991, Felicity Ann, *née* Pearce; 1 da (Mary Grace Elizabeth b 9 Nov 1996); *Career* Peat Marwick Mitchell & Co 1982–86, md Corp Finance Div S G Warburg & Co Ltd (and successor orgns) 1986–2000, md Investment Banking Div Goldman Sachs Int 2000–03, md Lazard 2004–; tstee Ireland Fund of GB; ACA 1985; *Recreations* family and friends, golf, tennis, skiing, reading; *Style*— Peter Kiernan, Esq; ✉ Lazard, 50 Stratton Street, London W1J 8LL

KILBANE, Dr (Mary) Paula Jane; CBE (2003); da of Dr Mathew Clement Kelly (d 1971), of Warrenpoint, and Dr Margot Kelly, *née* King; *b* 17 May 1950; *Educ* Trinity Coll Dublin, Queen's Univ Belfast (MB BCh), London Sch of Hygiene and Tropical Med (MSc), RCP (MFCM); *m* 3 Nov 1979, James Kilbane, s of James Kilbane; 1 da (Caroline b 23 Feb 1981), 1 s (James Patrick b 24 March 1983); *Career* jr doctor posts Royal Victoria Hosp Belfast 1973–76, registrar then sr registrar LSHTM and City and East London Area Health Authy 1976–80, conslt in public health med NE Thames RHA 1980–84, jt conslt and lectr LSHTM Islington 1982–86, conslt Eastern Health and Social Servs Bd Belfast 1986–90, chief exec Southern Health and Social Servs Bd 1993–95 (dir of public health 1990–93), chief exec Eastern Health and Social Servs Bd 1995–; memb: Health Economics Gp, Soc of Social Med, NI Higher Educn Cncl 1993–; FFPH (memb Bd 1991–93), FRCP 1997; *Books* AIDS Responding to the Challenge - A Comparative Study of Local AIDS Programmes in the UK (jtly, 1989), Oxford Textbook of Public Health (contrib, 1991); author of numerous published papers in learned periodicals; *Recreations* France, food and wine; *Clubs* Reform; *Style*— Dr Paula Kilbane, CBE; ✉ Eastern Health and Social Services Board, Champion House, 12/22 Linenhall Street, Belfast, Co Antrim BT2 8BS (tel 028 9032 1313, fax 028 9032 1520, e-mail pkilbane@ehssb.n-i.nhs.uk)

KILBORN, Dr John Robert; s of Charles James Kilborn (d 1995), of Desborough, Northants, and Winifred Jane, *née* Fenton; *b* 22 April 1939; *Educ* Kettering GS, Univ of Durham, Univ of Newcastle upon Tyne (BSc, PhD, MB BS); *m* 3 July 1965, Jean Margaret (Jan), da of Stewart Allen (d 1966), of Newcastle upon Tyne; 3 s (David John b 1970, Andrew James b 1973, Christopher Richard b 1975); *Career* physician Royal Victoria Infirmary Newcastle 1969–71, clinical res physician Hoffman la Roche 1971–73, SMO Glaxo Group 1973–77, cardiovascular clinical res leader then med dir UK Laboratories d'Études et de Recherche Synthélabo Paris and London 1977–83; md: Lorex Pharmaceuticals Ltd 1983–88, Eurocetus UK Ltd 1988–93; Worldwide Clinical Trials Ltd: med dir 1995–97, vice-pres Euro operations 1997–; md Worldwide Clinical Trials SARL 1997–1998; Kyowa Hakko UK Ltd: med dir Europe 1998–2000, dir Drug Devpt Europe 2001–04; md Clinical Devpt Ptnrs Ltd 2004–; author of various publications on clinical pharmacology and therapeutics; FFPM, FInstD; *Style*— Dr John Kilborn; ✉ CDP Ltd (e-mail johnkilborn@doctors.org.uk)

KILBURN, Alan Edward; OBE (1990); s of Edward Kilburn (d 1979), and Ethel, *née* Doidge (d 1997); *b* 15 April 1936; *Educ* Wellfield A J Dawson GS Wingate; *m* 27 July 1963, Doreen, da of Richard Edward Gratton; 1 s (Matthew Charles b 24 Nov 1970), 1 da (Jessica b 9 Jan 1974); *Career* Peterlee Devpt Corp 1952–63; housing mangr: Ashington UDC 1963–65, Knottingley UDC 1965–66, Felling UDC 1966–69; asst dir of housing Newcastle upon Tyne City Cncl 1969–73, regnl dir N Br Housing Assoc Ltd 1973–74, dep dir of housing Nottingham City Cncl 1974–76, chief exec Home Housing Assoc 1976–98; int housing advsr 1998–; non-exec dir Barratt Developments plc 1998–2006; memb Inquiry into Br Housing 1985 and 1991; tstee William Sutton Housing Assoc 2002– (chm 2003–); fell Inst of Housing 1972 (pres 1982–83); *Recreations* sport: assoc football, rugby football, cricket, golf; theatre and music; *Style*— Alan Kilburn, Esq, OBE

KILCLOONEY, Baron (Life Peer UK 2001), of Armagh in the County of Armagh; John David Taylor; PC (NI 1970); s of George David Taylor (d 1979), of Armagh, and Georgina, *née* Baird (d 1986); *b* 24 December 1937; *Educ* Royal Sch Armagh, Queen's Univ Belfast (BSc); *m* 1970, Mary Frances, da of Ernest Leslie Todd (d 1985); 1 s (Jonathan), 5 da (Jane, Rachel, Rowena, Alex, Hannah); *Career* memb (UU): NI Parliament Stormont (memb for S Tyrone) 1965–72 (min of Home Affrs 1970–72), NI Assembly (memb for Fermanagh and S Tyrone) 1973–74, NI Constitutional Convention (memb for N Down) 1975–76, NI Assembly (memb for N Down) 1983–86, New NI Assembly 1997–2007; MEP NI 1979–89; MP (UUP) Strangford 1983–2001; memb Parly Assembly WEU 1996–; chartered engr; dir: West Ulster Estates Ltd 1968–, Bramley Apple Restaurant Ltd 1974–, Ulster Gazette (Armagh) Ltd 1983–, Gosford Housing Assoc (Armagh) Ltd 1978–, Carrickfergus Advertiser Ltd 1992–, Cerdac Print (Belfast) Ltd, Tyrone Printing Ltd, Tyrone Courier Ltd, Tyrone Constitutions Ltd, Sovereign Properties (NI) Ltd, Tontine Rooms Holding Co Ltd, Ulsternet (NI) Ltd, Outlook Press Ltd, Coleraine Chronicle Ltd, Northern Constitution Ltd, Northern Newspapers Ltd, Guardian Newspapers, Midland Tribune Ltd 2004–, Alpha Publications Ltd 2004–, Athlone Voice Ltd 2005–, Seven FM Radio Ltd 2005–, Six FM Radio Ltd 2006–, Q 102.9 FM Ltd 2006–, Q 101.2 FM Ltd 2006–, Q 97.2 FM Ltd 2006–, Q Internet Ltd 2006–, Northern Media Gp Ltd 2006–, Five FM Radio Ltd 2007–; memb Bd: Charles Sheils Houses, Gosford Voluntary Housing Assoc, Royal Sch Armagh; memb: RHS, Inst of Civil Engrs of Ireland, Inst of Highway Engrs; Hon PhD Eastern Mediterranean Univ 1998; *Publications* Ulster: The Economic Facts (1971); *Recreations* gardening, foreign travel; *Clubs* Armagh County (Armagh City), Farmers'; *Style*— The Rt Hon the Lord Kilclooney, PC; ✉ Mullinure, Armagh BT61 9EL (tel and fax 028 3752 2409); House of Lords, London SW1A 0PW (tel 020 7931 7211, fax 020 7219 0575)

KILFOYLE, Peter; MP; s of Edward Kilfoyle, and Ellen Kilfoyle; *b* 9 June 1946; *Educ* St Edward's Coll Liverpool, Univ of Durham, Christ's Coll Liverpool; *m* 27 July 1968, Bernadette, *née* Slater; 2 s, 3 da; *Career* building labourer 1965–70 and 1973–75, student 1970–73, teacher 1975–85, Lab Pty organiser 1985–91, MP (Lab) Liverpool Walton July 1991–; Parly sec Office of Public Serv 1997–1999, under-sec of state for defence 1999–2000; *Recreations* reading, music, spectator sports; *Style*— Peter Kilfoyle, Esq, MP; ✉ House of Commons, London SW1A 0AA

KILGALLON, William (Bill); OBE (1992); s of William Kilgallon (d 1984), of Co Mayo and Leeds, and Bridget Agnes, *née* Earley; *b* 29 August 1946; *Educ* St Michael's Coll Leeds, Ushaw Coll Durham, Gregorian Univ Rome (STL), London Sch of Economics (DSA), Univ of Warwick (MA), Lancaster Univ (MSc); *m* 20 Jan 1978, Stephanie, da of Benjamin Martin; 2 s (Stephen b 1979, Michael b 1980); *Career* RC priest Dio of Leeds 1970–77: asst priest St Anne's Cathedral 1970–74, fndr chm St Anne's Shelter and Housing Action 1971–74, social work trg 1974–76, social worker Leeds Catholic Children's Soc 1976–77; returned to lay state 1977, mangr St Anne's Day Centre 1977–78, chief exec St Anne's Shelter and Housing Action 1978–2002, chief exec Social Care Inst for Excellence 2003–; memb (Lab) Leeds City Cncl 1979–92: chm Housing Ctee 1984–88, chm Social Serv Ctee 1988–90, Lord Mayor of Leeds 1990–91, chm Environment Ctee 1991–92; NHS: memb Leeds Family Practitioner Ctee 1978–80, memb Leeds AHA 1980–82, memb Leeds Eastern District HA 1982–86, non-exec dir and vice-chm Yorkshire RHA 1990–92 (memb 1986–90), chm Leeds Community and Mental Health Servs Teaching NHS Tst 1992–98, chm Leeds Teaching Hosps NHS Tst 1998–2002; ldr of inquiry into: abuse in children's home Northumberland 1994–95, community health care North Durham NHS Tst 1997–98; memb: Cncl NHS Confedn 1997–2002 (vice-chm 1998–2000), Independent Reference Gp on Mental Health Dept of Health 1997–99, Reference Gp on Nat Health Serv Framework for Mental Health 1998–99, CCETSW 1998–2001, Nat Task Force on Learning Disability 2001–04; non-exec dir Places for People Gp 2004–05; Hon LLD Univ of Leeds 1997, Hon DUniv Leeds Metropolitan Univ 2000; FRSA 1992; *Recreations* reading, walking, travel, sport - Rugby League and cricket; *Style*— Bill Kilgallon, OBE; ✉ Chief Executive's Office, Social Care Institute for Excellence, Goldings House, 2 Hays Lane, London SE1 2HB (tel 020 7089 6840, fax 020 7089 6841)

KILKENNY, Alan; OBE (1990); s of John Patrick Kilkenny (d 1970), and Florence Sybil, *née* Coole (d 2001); *b* 17 March 1950; *Educ* Devizes GS, LSE (BSc(Econ)); *m* 1, 10 July 1971 (m dis 1990), Carmelinda, *née* Freelance; m 2, 3 Nov 1990, Denise Mary Acton Davis, da of Michael Kelleher; 1 da (Charly b 6 July 1992); *Career* various PR appts in consultancy and industry 1971–81, dir Public Affrs Sony (UK) 1981–84, chief exec The Grayling Group 1984–89, ind PR conslt in assoc with Bell Pottinger Communications 1989–; chm Publicity Ctee Wishing Well Appeal Gt Ormond St 1986–89, tstee Gt Ormond St Hosp For Sick Children 1992–; memb Devpt Bd The Cardinall's Musick 2003–; *Recreations* skiing, gardening, fly fishing, enjoying France, music and the contemporary arts; *Clubs* Flyfishers', Ocean Reef (Key Largo); *Style*— Alan Kilkenny, Esq, OBE; ✉ The Fishing Cottage, Nether Wallop, Hampshire SO20 8ET (tel 01264 781228, fax 01264 781971, e-mail alankilkenny@btconnect.com); 14 Curzon Street, Mayfair, London W1J 5HN (tel 07836 311639)

KILLANIN, 4 Baron (UK 1900); (George) Redmond Fitzpatrick Morris; s of 3 Baron Killanin, MBE, TD (d 1999); *b* 26 January 1947; *Educ* Gonzaga Coll Dublin, Ampleforth, TCD; *m* 1972 (m dis 1999), Pauline, da of Geoffrey Horton, of Cabinteely, Co Dublin; 1 s (Hon Luke), 1 da (Hon Olivia); m 2, 2000, Sheila Elizabeth, da of Patrick and Mary Lynch, of Dublin; 1 da (Hon Hannah), 1 s (Hon George); *Heir* s, Hon Luke Morris; *Career* film prodr; *Style*— The Rt Hon the Lord Killanin

KILLEARN, 3 Baron (UK 1943); Sir Victor Miles George Aldous Lampson; 4 Bt (UK 1866); s of 1 Baron Killearn, GCMG, CB, MVO, PC (d 1964), by his 2 w Jacqueline Aldine Leslie, da of late Marchese Senator Sir Aldo Castellani, KCMG; suc half-bro, 2 Baron Killearn (d 1996); *b* 9 September 1941; *Educ* Eton; *m* 1971, Melita Amaryllis Pamela Astrid, da of Rear Adm Sir Morgan Charles Morgan-Giles, DSO, OBE, GM, DL, (MP Winchester 1964–79); 2 da (Hon Pamela Camilla Roxana b 1973, Hon Miranda Penelope Amber b 1975), 2 s (Hon Miles Henry Morgan b 1977, Hon Alexander Victor William b 1984); *Heir* s, Hon Miles Lampson; *Career* late Capt Scots Gds; ptnr Cazenove & Co 1979–2002, non-exec dir AMP Ltd 1999–2003, non-exec chm Henderson Global Investors Hldgs Ltd 2001–05, non-exec dir: Maxis Communications Berhad 2002–06, Shanghai Real Estate Ltd 2003–07, Ton Poh Emerging Thailand Fund 2005, Vietnam Dragon Fund 2005; *Clubs* White's, Pratt's, City of London, Hong Kong; *Style*— The Rt Hon the Lord Killearn

KILLEN, Fiona Mary; da of Thomas Killen, of Scotland, and Anne, *née* Thomas, of Wales; *b* 24 February 1969, Hamilton; *Educ* Univ of Leeds (BA), Univ of Edinburgh (LLB, LLM, DipLP); *m* 7 June 2003, Lloyd Quinan; *Career* slr and NP; political researcher UK Parl and US Senate 1990–92, asst dir RICS Scotland 1994–96; Univ of Edinburgh: co-ordinator Scottish Univs Research Consortium 1996–98, tutor in public law 1999–2003; legal researcher Scottish Law Cmmn 1998–99, sr legal research specialist Scot Parl 1999–2001; Anderson Strathern: joined 2002–, head of parly and public law 2005–, ptnr 2006–; memb: Br Assoc for Sport and the Law (BASL), Erin Tst; former memb Bd: Scottish Human Rights Centre, Scot Civic Forum; memb: Law Soc of Scot 2003, Assoc of Regulatory and Disciplinary Lawyers 2005; jt winner Specialist Client Team of the Year Scottish Legal Award 2006; *Publications* University Research in Scotland: Developing a Policy Framework (co-author, 1997), Inter-disciplinary Research: Process, Structures and Outcome (co-author, 1998); *Recreations* running, football, travel, music, reading; *Style*— Ms Fiona Killen; ✉ Anderson Strathern, 1 Rutland Court, Edinburgh EH3 8EY (tel 0131 270 7700)

KILLEN, Prof John Tyrrell; s of John Killen (d 1975), and Muriel Caroline Elliott, *née* Bolton (d 1975); *b* 19 July 1937; *Educ* The High Sch Dublin, Trinity Coll Dublin (fndn scholar, vice-chllr's Latin medallist, BA), St John's Coll Cambridge (Robert Gardiner meml scholar, PhD); *m* 1964, Elizabeth Ann, da of J W Ross; 1 s (Richard James b 3 April 1966), 2 da (Sheelagh Margaret b 22 Feb 1968, Nicola Jane b 25 Feb 1971); *Career* Univ of Cambridge: asst lectr in classics 1967–70, lectr 1970–90, chm Faculty Bd of Classics 1984–86, reader in Mycenaean Greek 1990–97, prof of Mycenaean Greek 1997–99, emeritus prof 1999–; Churchill Coll Cambridge: Gulbenkian research fell 1961–62, fell and librarian 1962–69; Jesus Coll Cambridge: lectr 1965–97, fell 1969–, actg bursar 1973, sr bursar 1979–89, dir Quincentenary Devpt Appeal 1987–90; tstee All Saints Charities Cambridge; FBA 1995; *Publications* Corpus of Mycenaean Inscriptions from Knossos (with J Chadwick et al, 1986–98), The Knossos Tablets (with J-P Olivier, 5 edn 1989); also author of numerous articles in learned jls; *Recreations* golf, watching sport on TV, reading the FT, music; *Clubs* Gog Magog Golf (Cambridge); *Style*— Prof John Killen, FBA; ✉ Jesus College, Cambridge CB5 8BL (tel 01223 339424, fax 01223 339300)

KILLICK, Dr Stephen Robert; s of Herbert Percy Killick, of Poulton-le-Fylde, Lancs, and Lois Margaret, *née* Richardson (d 1985); *b* 30 December 1952; *Educ* Univ of London Guy's Hosp Med Sch (BSc, MB BS, MD); *m* 25 May 1985, Diane, da of George Hall Billings (d 1980); 2 da (Georgina b 15 Oct 1987, Harriet b 10 Nov 1990); *Career* SE England jr hosp dr 1976–79, surgical registrar Soweto SA 1979–80, SE England jr hosp dr qualifying in gynaecology 1980–82, res fell Univ of Manchester 1982–87, conslt obstetrician and gynaecologist and sr lectr Univ of Manchester 1987–92, currently prof of reproductive med and surgery Univ of Hull; numerous articles in med pubns; FRCOG; *Recreations* rugby, badminton, gardening; *Style*— Prof Stephen Killick; ✉ Department of Obstetrics and Gynaecology, University of Hull, Hull HU6 7RX (tel 01482 382757, fax 01482 382781, e-mail s.r.killick@hull.ac.uk)

KILMAINE, 7 Baron (I 1789); Sir John David Henry Browne; 13 Bt (NS 1636); s of 6 Baron Kilmaine, CBE (d 1978); *b* 2 April 1948; *Educ* Eton; *m* 1982, Linda, yr da of Dennis Robinson; 1 s (Hon John b 1983), 1 da (Hon Alice b 1985); *Heir* s, Hon John Browne; *Career* dir: Fusion (Bickenhill) Ltd 1969–97, Whale Tankers Ltd 1974–2001; *Style*— The Rt Hon the Lord Kilmaine

KILMARNOCK, 7 Baron (UK 1831); Alastair Ivor Gilbert Boyd; s of 6 Baron Kilmarnock, MBE, TD (d 1975), and Hon Rosemary Guest (d 1971), da of 1 Viscount Wimborne. Lord Kilmarnock's f (6 Baron) changed his family name from Hay to Boyd 1941, having succeeded his bro, the 22 Earl of Erroll (in the UK Barony only) the same year; 5 in descent from the 18 Earl of Erroll cr 1 Baron Kilmarnock who m (1820) Elizabeth FitzClarence, a natural da of William IV by the actress Mrs Jordan; *b* 11 May 1927; *Educ* Bradfield, King's Coll Cambridge; *m* 1, 1954 (m dis 1969), Diana Mary (d 1975), da of D Grant Gibson; m 2, 1977, Hilary Ann, da of Leonard Sidney Bardwell; 1 s (James Charles Edward Boyd b 27 Jan 1972); *Heir* bro, Hon Robin Boyd; *Career* Lt Irish Gds, serv Palestine 1947–48; joined SDP 1981, chief SDP whip in House of Lords 1983–86, dep ldr SDP peers 1986–87, chm All-Pty Parly Gp on AIDS 1986–96, gen sec Euro Public Health Fndn 1994–98; ed conslt Social Market Fndn; chief of Clan Boyd, page to Lord High Constable of Scotland at Coronation of HM King George VI; *Books* as Alastair Boyd: Sabbatical Year (1958), The Road from Ronda (1969), The Companion Guide to Madrid and Central Spain (1974); as Alastair Kilmarnock: The Radical Challenge (1987), The Essence of Catalonia (1988), The Sierras of the South (1992), The Social Market and the State (1999); *Clubs* Pratt's; *Style*— The Lord Kilmarnock; ✉ Social Market Foundation, 11 Tufton Street, London SW1P 3QB

KILMISTER, (Claude Alaric) Anthony; OBE (2005); s of Dr Claude Emile Kilmister (d 1951), of Swansea; *b* 22 July 1931; *Educ* Shrewsbury; *m* 24 May 1958, Sheila Harwood (d 2006); *Career* Nat Serv 1950–52, cmmnd Army; with NCB 1952–54, Cons Pty Orgn 1954–60; gen sec Cinema and TV Benevolent Fund 1962–72 (asst sec 1960–61), exec dir Parkinson's Disease Soc 1972–91, fndr memb Ctee Action for Neurological Diseases 1987–91, pres Prostate Research Campaign UK 2004– (fndr 1994–); pres Anglican Assoc 2007– (memb Exec Ctee 1976–); memb: Int Cncl for the Apostolic Faith 1987–93, Standing Ctee Assoc for the Apostolic Ministry 1989–96, Cncl Forward in Faith 1996–, St Alban's Diocesan Synod 2006–; Prayer Book Soc: fndr memb and dep chm incl BCP Action Gp (its forerunner) 1972–89, chm 1989–2001, vice-pres 2001–, pres St Alban's Branch 2006–; Freeman City of London 2003–; MA (Lambeth) 2002; *Books* The Good Church Guide (1982), When Will Ye be Wise? (1983), My Favourite Betjeman (1985), The Prayer Book and Ordination: A Prayer Book View of Women Bishops (2006); *Recreations* writing, walking; *Style*— Anthony Kilmister, Esq, OBE; ✉ 36 The Drive, Northwood, Middlesex HA6 1HP (tel 01923 824278)

KILMISTER, Lemmy; s of Rev Sidney Kilmister (d 2000), and Jessica Maud Simpson; *Children* 1 s (Paul Inder b 1967); *Career* musician and songwriter; memb: Rev Black and the Rocking Vickers 1965–67, Sam Gopal 1968–69, Hawkwind 1971–75, Motörhead 1975–; Classic Songwriter Award Kerrang! 1998, Lifetime Achievement Award Rock City News 1998, Lifetime Achievement Award Kerrang! 2000, Best Metal Performance (for Whiplash) Grammy Awards 2005; supporter of various charities; *Albums* with Hawkwind: Space Ritual Alive 1972 (Gold disc), Hall of the Mountain Grill 1973 (Gold disc); with Motörhead: On Parole 1976, Motörhead 1977, Overkill 1979 (Silver disc), Bomber 1979 (Silver disc), Ace Of Spades 1980 (Gold disc), No Sleep 'Til Hammersmith 1981 (Gold disc), Iron Fist 1982, Another Perfect Day 1983, No Remorse 1984 (Silver disc), The Birthday Party 1985, Orgasmatron 1986, Rock 'n' Roll 1987, No Sleep At All 1990, 1916 1991, March Or Die 1992, Bastards 1993, Sacrifice 1995, Overnight Sensation 1996, Snake Bite Love 1998, Everything Louder Than Everyone Else 1999, We Are Motörhead 2000, The Best of Motörhead 2000, Hammered 2002, Inferno 2004; *Singles* Silver Machine 1972 (with Hawkwind, Silver disc), You'll Never Walk Alone (with The Crowd, Silver disc); with Motörhead: Leaving Here 1977, Motörhead 1977, Louie Louie 1978, No Class 1979, Bomber 1979, The Golden Years Live EP 1980, Ace Of Spades 1980 (Silver disc), Beer Drinkers and Hell Raisers 1980, St Valentine's Day Massacre EP 1981, Motörhead (Live) 1981, Iron Fist 1982, Stand By Your Man 1982, I Got Mine 1983, Shine 1983, Killed By Death 1984, Deaf Forever 1986, Eat The Rich 1986, Ace Of Spades (live) 1988, The One To Sing The Blues 1990, Hellraiser 1992, Ace Of Spades 1993, Don't Let Daddy Kiss Me 1993, Born To Raise Hell 1994, God Save The Queen 2000; *Books* White Line Fever (autobiography, 2002); *Recreations* pursuit of opposing gender, conversation, self-improvement; *Style*— Lemmy Kilmister, Esq

KILMORE, Bishop of (RC) 1998–; Most Rev Philip Leo O'Reilly; s of Terence O'Reilly (d 1973), of Cootehill, Co Cavan, and Maureen, *née* Smith (d 1951); *b* 10 April 1944; *Educ* St Patrick's Coll Cavan, St Patrick's Coll Maynooth, Gregorian Univ Rome (BSc, BD, Higher DipEd, STD); *Career* St Patrick's Coll Cavan 1969–76, Irish Coll Rome 1976–81, Bailieborough Community Sch 1981–88, Dio of Minna Nigeria 1988–90, St Paul's Missionary Seminary Abuja Nigeria 1990–95, Parish of Castletara Kilmore 1995–97, coadjutor bishop of Kilmore 1997–98; *Books* Word and Sign in the Acts of the Apostles. A Study in Lucan Theology (1986); *Recreations* reading, walking, golf; *Style*— The Most Rev the Bishop of Kilmore; ✉ Bishop's House, Cullies, Cavan, Republic of Ireland (tel 00 353 49 4331496, e-mail bishop@kilmorediocese.ie)

KILMOREY, 6 Earl (I 1822); Sir Richard Francis Needham; kt (1997), PC (1994); also Hereditary Abbot of the Exempt Jurisdiction of Newry and Mourne, Viscount Kilmorey (I 1625) and Viscount Newry and Morne (I 1822); s of 5 Earl of Kilmorey (d 1977), and Helen, da of Sir Lionel Faudel-Phillips, 3 and last Bt; *b* 29 January 1942; *Educ* Eton; *m* 1965, Sigrid Juliane, da of late Ernst Thiessen, and Mrs John Gairdner; 2 s (Robert, Viscount Newry and Morne b 1966, Hon Andrew b 1969), 1 da (Lady Christina b 1977); *Heir* s, Viscount Newry and Morne, *qv*; *Career* PA to Rt Hon James Prior MP (oppn spokesman on employment) 1974–79; MP (Cons): Chippenham 1979–83, Wilts N 1983–97; memb Public Accounts Ctee 1982–83; PPS to: Rt Hon James Prior as sec of state for NI 1983–84, Rt Hon Patrick Jenkin as sec of state for environment 1984–85; min of health for NI 1985–89, min of environment for NI 1985–92, min for the economy for NI 1989–92, min of trade DTI 1992–95; chm: Gleneagles Hospital UK Ltd 1995–2001, Biocompatibles Int plc 2000–06, Avon Rubber plc; dir Dyson Ltd, vice-chm NEC Europe Ltd; exec dir GEC plc 1995–97, non-exec dir Meggitt plc 1997–2002; advsr AMEC plc; pres Br Exporters Assoc, patron Mencap NI; govr Br Inst of Florence 1983–85; fndr memb: Anglo-Japanese 2000 Gp, Anglo-Korean Forum for the Future; formerly cncllr (Cons) Somerset CC; Order of the Rising Sun (Gold and Silver Star) Japan; *Publications* The Honourable Member (1983), Battling for Peace (1998); *Clubs* Pratt's; *Style*— The Rt Hon the Earl of Kilmorey, PC

KILPATRICK OF KINCRAIG, Baron (Life Peer UK 1996), of Dysart in the District of Kirkcaldy; Sir Robert Kilpatrick; kt (1986), CBE (1979); s of Robert Kilpatrick (d 1974), and Catherine Sharp, *née* Glover (d 1944); *b* 29 July 1926; *Educ* Buckhaven HS, Univ of Edinburgh (MB ChB, MD); *m* 28 Oct 1950, Elizabeth Gibson Page, da of Alexander Sharp Forbes, of East Wemyss, Fife; 1 da (Hon Katherine b 9 Aug 1951), 2 s (Hon Neil b 25 March 1956, Hon John b 28 May 1959); *Career* Univ of Sheffield: lectr 1955–56, prof of clinical pharmacology and therapeutics 1966–75, dean Faculty of Med 1970–73; Univ of Leicester: dean Faculty of Med 1975–89, prof and head Dept of Clinical Pharmacology and Therapeutics 1975–83, prof of med 1984–89; pres: GMC 1989–95, BMA 1997–98; Hon DUniv Edinburgh 1987, Hon LLD Univ of Dundee 1992, Hon DSc Univ of Hull 1994, Hon DSc Univ of Leicester 1994, Hon LLD Univ of Sheffield 1995; memb Physiological Soc 1960; Hon FRCPath 1994, Hon FRCS 1995, Hon FRCP(Dublin) 1995, Hon FRCSEd 1996; FRCPE 1963, FRCP 1975, FRCPGlas 1991, FRSE 1998; *Recreations* idling; *Clubs* New (Edinburgh), Royal and Ancient; *Style*— The Rt Hon Lord Kilpatrick of Kincraig, CBE, FRSE; ✉ 12 Wester Coates Gardens, Edinburgh EH12 5LT (tel 0131 337 7304)

KILROY, Thomas; s of Thomas Kilroy, of Callan, Co Kilkenny, Ireland, and Mary, *née* Devine; *b* 23 September 1934; *Educ* St Kieran's Coll Kilkenny, Univ Coll Dublin; *m* 1, 1963 (m dis 1980), Patricia, *née* Cobey; 3 s; m 2, 1981, Julia Lowell, *née* Carlson; 1 da; *Career* writer; lectr in Eng Univ Coll Dublin 1965–73, prof of modern Eng Univ Coll Galway 1979–89 (now emeritus); Guardian Fiction Prize 1971, short listed for Booker Prize 1971, Heinemann Award for Literature 1972, AIB Literary Prize 1972, American-Irish Fndn Award 1975; memb: Irish Acad of Letters, Aosdána; FRSL; *Novels* The Big Chapel 1971; *Plays* The Death and Resurrection of Mr Roche 1968, The O'Neill 1969, Tea and Sex and Shakespeare 1976, Talbot's Box 1977, Double Cross 1986, The Madame MacAdam Travelling Theatre 1991, Gold in the Streets 1993, The Secret Fall of Constance Wilde 1997, The Shape of Metal 2003, My Scandalous Life 2004, Blake 2004; *Adaptations* The Seagull 1981, Ghosts 1989, Six Characters in Search of An Author 1996, Previous Relations 2001; *Style*— Thomas Kilroy, Esq, FRSL; ✉ Kilmaine, County Mayo, Ireland (tel 00 353 93 33361); c/o Alan Brodie Representation, 211 Piccadilly, London W1J 9HF (tel 020 7917 2871, fax 020 7917 2872, website www.alanbrodie.com)

KILROY-SILK, Robert; MEP; s of William Silk (d 1943); *b* 19 May 1942; *Educ* Secdy Modern Sch, Sparkhill Commercial Sch, Saltley GS, LSE; *m* 1963, Jan, da of William Beech; 1 s, 1 da; *Career* lectr Univ of Liverpool 1966–74, govr Nat Heart and Chest Hosp 1974–77; MP (Lab): Ormskirk Feb 1974–83, Knowsley North 1983–86; PPS to Min of Arts 1975–76, memb Select Ctee on Race Relations and on Wealth Tax 1974–75, vice-chm PLP Home Affrs Gp 1976–79, chm PLP Civil Liberties Gp 1979–84, chm Parly Penal Affrs Gp 1979–86, memb Select Ctee Home Affrs 1979–84, chm PLP Home Affrs Gp 1983–84, frontbench spokesman Home Affrs 1984–86; TV presenter Kilroy! 1986–2004; MEP (UKIP until 2005 then Veritas) E Midlands 2004–; columnist: The Times 1987–90, The Daily Express 1990–96, The Sunday Express 2001–; chm The Kilroy Television Co 1989–; *Publications* Socialism since Marx (1973), The Ceremony of Innocence (novel, 1984), Hard Labour: The Political Diary of Robert Kilroy-Silk (1986); *Recreations* gardening; *Style*— Robert Kilroy-Silk, Esq, MEP

K

KILSHAW, David Andrew George; OBE (1999); s of George Arthur Kilshaw (d 1963), and Margaret Annie, *née* Bridgwater (d 1991); *b* 18 March 1953; *Educ* Keil Sch Dumbarton; *m* 17 June 1976, Judith Margaret, da of John Sydney Milner; 3 s (Ross David b 26 May 1980, Craig John b 18 Feb 1982, Iain George b 21 Oct 1985); *Career* qualified asst Messrs Brunton Miller, Alexander & Martin Slrs Glasgow 1979–80 (legal apprenticeship 1974–79), slr Borders Regnl Cncl 1980–82, NP 1982, ptnr Messrs Cullen Kilshaw Slrs Galashiels, Melrose and Peebles 1982–; chm Borders Health Bd 1993–2001 (non-exec memb 1991–93); memb Law Soc of Scotland 1979; *Recreations* golf, fishing, listening to music; *Style*— David Kilshaw, Esq, OBE; ✉ Cullen Kilshaw, Solicitors and Estate Agents, 27 Market Street, Galashiels TD1 3AF (tel 01896 758311, fax 01896 758112)

KIMBALL, Baron (Life Peer UK 1985), of Easton in the County of Leicestershire; Marcus Richard Kimball; kt (1981), DL (Leics 1984); s of late Maj Lawrence Kimball, JP, DL, sometime MP Loughborough, by his 1 w, Kathleen Joan, only surviving da of Richard Ratcliff, of Stanford Hall, Loughborough, by his w Christine, 3 da of Vaughan Hanning Vaughan-Lee, JP, DL, sometime MP W Somerset; *b* 18 October 1928; *Educ* Eton, Trinity Coll Cambridge; *m* 1956, June Mary, only da of Montagu John Fenwick (whose mother Millicent was da of Rt Hon Lord Robert Montagu, 2 s of 6 Duke of Manchester), of Great Stukeley Hall, Huntingdon; 2 da (Hon Mrs Gibbs, Hon Mrs Straker); *Career* Lt Leics Yeo (TA) 1947, Capt 1952, Maj 1955; MP (Cons) Gainsbrough Div of Lincs 1956–83, CC Rutland 1955–63, PC rep Cncl of RCVS 1969–82 (Hon ARCVS 1982); external memb Cncl Lloyd's 1982–91; chm: South East Assured Tenancies 1988–96, Fire Arms Consultative Ctee 1989–94, Univ of Cambridge Vet Sch Tst 1989–97, British Greyhound Racing Fund Ltd 1993–96; pres: Hunters Improvement Soc 1989, Olympia Int Show Jumping Championships 1991–99, British Inst of Innkeeping 1992–97, Br Field Sports Soc 1995–98 (chm 1966–82); vice-pres Countryside Alliance 1998–; *Recreations* fox hunting, past jt master of FitzWilliam and Cottesmore; *Clubs* White's, Pratt's; *Style*— The Rt Hon the Lord Kimball, DL; ✉ Great Easton Manor, Great Easton, Market Harborough, Leicestershire LE16 8TB (tel 01536 770333, fax 01536 770453)

KIMBER, Sir Charles Dixon; 3 Bt (UK 1904), of Lansdowne Lodge, Wandsworth, Co London; s of Sir Henry Dixon Kimber, 2 Bt (d 1950); *b* 7 January 1912; *Educ* Eton, Balliol Coll Oxford (BA, Dip Social Anthropology); *m* 1, 1933 (m dis 1950), Ursula (d 1981), da of late Ernest Roy Bird, MP; 2 s (Timothy Roy Henry b 1936, Robert b 1941) and 1 s (decd); m 2, 1950 (m dis 1965), Margaret, o da of late Francis John Bonham, of Wimbledon; 1 da (Rhys Catherine (Mrs Michael Fox) b 1951); *Heir* s, Timothy Kimber, DL; *Style*— Sir Charles Kimber, Bt; ✉ Lower End Farm, Great Comberton, Pershore, Worcestershire WR10 3DU (e-mail charleskimber@onetel.net.com)

KIMBERLEY, 5 Earl of (UK 1866); Sir John Armine Wodehouse; 12 Bt (estab 1611); also 7 Baron Wodehouse (GB 1797); s of 4 Earl of Kimberley (d 2002); *b* 15 January 1951; *Educ* Eton, UEA (BSc, MSc); *m* 1973, Hon Carol Lylie, 2 da of 3 Baron Palmer (d 1990); 1 da (Lady Katherine b 1976), 1 s (David Simon John, Lord Wodehouse b 1978); *Heir* s, Lord Wodehouse; *Career* systems programmer with Glaxo 1979–95 (joined as res chemist 1974), advanced technology and informatics specialist GlaxoSmithKline (formerly Glaxo Wellcome) 1996–2000, sr internet analyst GlaxoSmithKline 2001–; chm: UK Info Users Gp 1981–83, UIS Users Gp 1991–93; fell Br Interplanetary Soc 1984 (assoc fell 1981–83); FRSA, MBCS CITP 1988, CEng 1993; *Recreations* photography, computing, running; *Style*— The Rt Hon the Earl of Kimberley; ✉ The Vicarage, Great Hormead, Buntingford, Hertfordshire SG9 0NT; GlaxoSmithKline, Medicines Research Centre, Gunnels Wood Road, Stevenage, Hertfordshire SG1 2NY (tel 01438 763222, e-mail w0400@bigfoot.com)

KIMMINS, Malcolm Brian Johnston; CVO (2002); s of Lt-Gen Sir Brian Charles Hannam Kimmins, KBE, CB, DL (d 1979), and Marjory, *née* Johnston (d 1992); *b* 12 February 1937; *Educ* Harrow, Grenoble Univ; *m* 1968, Jane, da of Thomas Douglas Pilkington; 2 da (Katie b 1969, Mary-Anne b 1974), 1 s (Charles b 1971); *Career* 15/19 King's Royal Hussars 1955–57; chm and md William Sanderson & Son Ltd, chm Corney & Barrow Gp Ltd; dir: Shepherd Neame Ltd, Newbury Racecourse plc, Laurent Perrier UK; tstee Ascot Authy 1989–2002; High Sheriff Royal Co of Berkshire 2003–04; *Recreations* horse racing, golf, shooting; *Clubs* White's, Jockey, Swinley Golf, Royal St George's Golf; *Style*—

Malcolm Kimmins, Esq, CVO; ✉ Wick Lodge, Hoe Benham, Newbury, Berkshire RG20 8EX (tel 01488 608368, fax 01488 608595)

KINCH, Christopher Anthony; QC (1999); s of Anthony Kinch, CBE (d 1999), and Barbara, *née* Paton Walsh (d 1992); *b* 27 May 1953; *Educ* Bishop Challoner Sch Bromley, ChCh Oxford (MA); *m* 14 May 1994, Carol Lesley, *née* Atkinson; 1 s (Samuel George b 1998), 2 da (Eleanor Kathleen b 2001, Martha Rose b 2004); *Career* called to the Bar Lincoln's Inn 1976, in practice 1977–, recorder of the Crown Court 1998, head of chambers 23 Essex Street 2006–; chm Kent Bar Mess 2001–04; stagiaire EC Cmmn 1976–77; dir of educn Criminal Bar Assoc 2005–, chair Bar Nat Mock Trial for Schs Competition Working Pty 1999–; *Style—* Christopher Kinch, Esq, QC; ✉ 23 Essex Street, London WC2R 3AA (tel 020 7413 0353)

KINCLAVEN, Hon Lord; Alexander Featherstonhaugh Wylie; s of Ian Hamilton Wylie (d 1991), and Helen Jane, *née* Mearns (d 1993); *b* 2 June 1951; *Educ* Univ of Edinburgh (LLB); *m* 12 July 1975, Gail Elizabeth Watson, da of Winifred and William Duncan; 2 da (Claire Elizabeth b 4 Aug 1981, Nicola Jane b 1 April 1985); *Career* admitted slr Scotland 1976, admitted Faculty of Advocates 1978, in practice 1978–2005, standing jr counsel to Accountant of Ct 1986–89, advocate depute 1989–92, QC (Scot) 1991, senator Coll of Justice 2005–; called to the English Bar Lincoln's Inn 1990; jt chm Discipline Ctee ICAS 1994–2005, memb Scottish Cncl of Law Reporting 2001–05, pt/t chm Police Appeals Tribunal 2001–05, pt/t memb Scottish Legal Aid Bd 1994–2002; pt/t sheriff 2000–05; FCIArb 1991 (ACIArb 1977); *Style—* The Hon Lord Kinclaven; ✉ Parliament House, Edinburgh EH1 1RQ

KINDER, John Russell; s of Herbert Kinder, of Leicester, and Kathleen Margaret, *née* Sarson; *b* 10 November 1937; *Educ* Wyggeston GS Leicester, CCC Oxford (MA); *m* 1964, Diana Christine, da of Frederick Gordan Evans (d 1984); 4 s (Mark Russell b 1966, Andrew John b 1967, Stephen James b 1970, Jonathan Charles b 1974); *Career* RAF 1956–58; dir William Brandts Sons & Co Ltd 1975–77, jt md Warwick Engineering Investment Ltd 1978–80, md CH Industrials plc 1980–90, chief exec Kinder Consultants mgmnt conslts 1992–, financial dir Reflec plc 2005–; chief exec Westminster Fndn for Democracy 2002–03; dir: Aston Martin Lagonda 1980–83, Aston Martin Tickford 1981–90; chm of tstees Priors Court Sch 2002–; FCA; *Recreations* tennis, sailing, christian youth work; *Clubs* National, Hurlingham, Oxford Kilburn (pres 2001–); *Style—* John Kinder, Esq; ✉ Kinder Consultants, 23 Woodville Gardens, Ealing, London W5 2LL (tel 020 8932 3744, fax 020 8723 3672, e-mail john@jkinder.co.uk)

KINDERSLEY, 3 Baron (UK 1941); Robert Hugh Molesworth Kindersley; s of 2 Baron Kindersley, CBE, MC (d 1976), and Nancy Farnsworth (d 1977); *b* 18 August 1929; *Educ* Eton, Trinity Coll Oxford, Harvard Business Sch; *m* 1, 4 Sept 1954 (m dis 1989), Venice Marigold (Rosie), da of late Capt Lord (Arthur) Francis Henry Hill (yr s of 6 Marquess of Downshire); 3 s (Hon Rupert John Molesworth b 11 March 1955, Hon Hugh Francis b 22 June 1956 d 1991, Hon Dickon Michael b 9 March 1962), 1 da (Hon Anna Lucy b 19 June 1965); m 2, 1989, Patricia Margaret (Tita), o da of late Brig Hugh Ronald Norman, DSO, MC, of St Clere, Kemsing, Kent, and former w of Henry Colum Crichton-Stuart; *Heir* s, Hon Rupert Kindersley; *Career* Lt Scots Gds served Malaya 1949; dir: London Assurance 1957–96, Witan Investment Co Ltd 1958–85, Steel Co of Wales 1959–67, Lazard Bros and Co Ltd 1960–91, Marconi Co Ltd 1963–68, Sun Alliance & London Insurance Group 1965–96, English Electric Co Ltd 1966–68, GEC Ltd 1968–70, British Match Corporation Ltd 1969–73, Swedish Match Co 1973–85, Maersk Co Ltd 1986–2001, Maersk India 1990–2001; chm: Cwlth Devpt Corpn 1980–89, Siam Selective Growth Trust 1990–2000, Brent Walker Group plc 1991–92; dep chm Advsy Cncl ECGD 1975–80; fin advsr Export Gp for the Constructional Industries 1961–85; chm BBA 1976–78, pres Anglo-Taiwan Trade Ctee 1976–86; memb Inst Int d'Études Bancaires 1971–85; chm Smith's Charity 1990–97; memb Ct of Assts Worshipful Co of Fishmongers 1973– (Prime Warden 1989–90); *Recreations* all sports, painting, gardening; *Clubs* All England Lawn Tennis and Croquet, Queen's, MCC, Vincent's (Oxford), Pratt's; *Style—* The Rt Hon The Lord Kindersley; ✉ West Green Farm, Shipbourne, Kent TN11 9PU (tel 01732 810293, fax 01732 810799); 5A Crescent Grove, London SW4 7AF (tel and fax 020 7622 1198)

KING, Alastair John; s of Bernard Frank Beaumont King, and Jean, *née* Ferguson; *b* 22 December 1967; *Educ* Bath Coll of HE (BA), Univ of Birmingham (MA), Univ of Kansas (MMus); *m* 12 Oct 2002, Claire, *née* Holyoake; 1 s (Harry Francis b 30 Jan 2004), 1 da (Ella Sophia b 17 Sept 2006); *Career* composer; orchestrator and conductor on films incl: Thunderpants 2001, The Heart of Me 2002, What a Girl Wants 2003, Goose 2005, King Arthur 2004, The Magic Roundabout 2005, Kingdom of Heaven 2005, The Island 2005, Wallace and Gromit: The Curse of the Were-Rabbit 2005, Curious George 2006, Pirates of the Caribbean: Dead Man's Chest 2006, Over the Hedge 2006, Harry Potter and the Order of the Phoenix 2007; TV compositions incl: The Last Detective 2003 and 2007, The Br Book Awards 2004, 2005, 2006 and 2007; memb Performing Right Soc 1991, memb Br Acad of Composers and Songwriters 1999; *Compositions* concert works incl: In Just 1997, Irpy 1998, Straight on Til Morning 1999, Hit the Ground (Running, Running, Running) 2000 (finalist Masterprize 2001), Time Let Me Play 2001, Dance Marathon ($1000 Stake) 2001, Three Dance Miniatures 2002, The Games We Play (written for Evelyn Glennie, *qv*) 2003, Hints of Immortality 2004, Concerto for Youth Orchestra 2004, Volante 2005; *Recreations* football; *Style—* Alastair King, Esq; ✉ Chester Music, 14–15 Berners Street, London W1T 3LJ (tel 020 7612 7400)

KING, Prof Andrew John; s of Neville Douglas King (d 1999), and Audrey Kathleen, *née* Manix (d 2001); *b* 8 April 1959, Greenford, Middx; *Educ* Eliot's Green GS, KCL (BSc), Nat Inst for Med Research and KCL (PhD); *partner* Dr Scott Thomas Bryan; *Career* Univ of Oxford: Douglas McAlpine jr research fell in neurology Green Coll 1983–86, SERC postdoctoral fell 1984–86, E P Abraham Cephalosporin jr research fell in med scis Lincoln Coll 1986–89, research fell Lister Inst 1986–91, Wellcome Tst sr research fell 1991–2006, univ research lectr 1996, reader in auditory physiology 2000, sr research fell in med scis Merton Coll 2002–, prof of neurophysiology 2004–, Wellcome Tst princ research fell 2006–; visiting scientist Eye Research Inst of Retina Fndn Boston USA 1998; author of pubns in academic jls and chapters in books; memb Nat Ctee Br Neuroscience Assoc; Layton Science research award KCL 1980, Wellcome Prize medal and lecture in physiology 1990; *Recreations* travel, cooking; *Style—* Prof Andrew King; ✉ Department of Physiology, Anatomy and Genetics, Sherrington Building, University of Oxford, Parks Road, Oxford OX1 3PT (e-mail andrew.king@dpag.ox.ac.uk)

KING, Andy; *b* 14 September 1948; *Educ* Hatfield Poly, Nene Coll (CQSW, CMS); *m*; 1 da; *Career* sometime labourer, apprentice motor mechanic, postal offr, and unit mangr Northampton Soc Servs; MP (Lab) Rugby and Kenilworth 1997–2005; chair All-Pty Gp on Sewers and Sewerage, treas All-Pty Cable and Satellite Gp, memb House of Commons Deregulation Select Ctee, memb Social Security Select Ctee, memb All-Pty Gp on ME, memb Parly Liaison for Golf; cncllr: Warwickshire CC 1989–98, Rugby BC 1995–98; memb Warwickshire Police Authy 1989–97; *Recreations* golf, dominoes, football; *Style—* Andy King, Esq; ✉ Constituency Office, 12 Regent Place, Rugby, Warkwickshire CV21 2PN (tel 01788 575504, fax 01788 575506, e-mail kinga@parliament.uk)

KING, Prof Anthony Stephen; s of Harold Stark King (d 1949), and Marjorie Mary, *née* James (d 1982); *b* 17 November 1934; *Educ* Queen's Univ Kingston Ontario (BA), Univ of Oxford (BA, DPhil); *m* 1, Vera Korte (d 1972); m 2, Janet Frances Mary, da of Adm of the Fleet Sir Michael Pollock, KGCB, DSO, of Churchstoke, Powys; *Career* fell Magdalen Coll Oxford 1961–65; Univ of Essex: sr lectr in govt 1966–67, reader 1967–69, prof 1969–, academic pro-vice-chllr 1986–89; fell Center for Advanced Study in the Behavioral Scis Stanford Calif 1977–78, visiting prof of public int affrs Princeton Univ 1984, hon foreign memb American Acad of Arts and Sciences 1993–; memb: Ctee on Standards in Public Life 1994–98, Royal Cmmn on Reform of House of Lords 1999; *Books* Westminster and Beyond (with Anne Sloman, 1973), British Members of Parliament (1974), Why is Britain Becoming Harder to Govern? (ed, 1976), Britain Says Yes: The 1975 Referendum on the Common Market (1977), The British Prime Minister (ed, 2 edn 1985), The New American Political System (ed, 2 edn 1990), Britain at the Polls (ed, 1992), SDP: The Birth, Life and Death of the Social Democratic Party (with Ivor Crewe, 1995), Running Scared: Why America's Politicians Campaign Too Much and Govern Too Little (1997), New Labour Triumphs (ed, 1997), British Political Opinion 1937–2000: The Gallup Polls (ed, 2001), Does the United Kingdom Still Have a Constitution? (2001), Britain at the Polls 2001 (ed, 2001), Leaders' Personalities and the Outcomes of Democratic Elections (ed, 2002), Britain at the Polls, 2005 (ed, 2005), The British Constitution (2007); *Recreations* music, holidays, walking; *Clubs* Royal Cwlth Soc; *Style—* Prof Anthony King; ✉ Department of Government, University of Essex, Wivenhoe Park, Colchester, Essex CO4 3SQ (tel 01206 873393, fax 01206 873234)

KING, Prof Bernard; CBE (2004); *b* 4 May 1946; *Educ* Synge St Christian Brothers Sch Dublin, Coll of Technol Dublin, Aston Univ (MSc, PhD); *m* 29 July 1970, Maura Antoinette, da of Mathew Collinge; 2 da (Madge b 5 Feb 1973, Sinead b 26 June 1977); *Career* pt/t lectr in microbiology Birmingham Poly 1970–72, research fell Aston Univ 1971–76; Dundee Coll of Technol: lectr in microbiology 1976–79, sr lectr 1979–83, head Dept of Molecular and Life Scis 1983–91, prof 1985–91, dean Faculty of Sci 1987–89; asst princ Robert Gordon Inst of Technol 1991–92, princ Dundee Inst of Technol 1992–94, princ and vice-chllr Univ of Abertay Dundee 1994–; memb: Universities UK (formerly CVCP), Ctee of Euro Rectors, Bd Scottish Leadership Fndn, Higher Educn Acad; chm Scottish Crop Research Inst, govr Unicorn Preservation Soc; FIWSc 1975, CBiol, FIBiol 1987, CCMI (CIMgt 1999); *Recreations* sailing, late medieval music, opera, reading; *Style—* Prof Bernard King, CBE; ✉ University of Abertay Dundee, Kydd Building, Bell Street, Dundee DD1 1HG (tel 01382 308012, fax 01382 308011, e-mail b.king@abertay.ac.uk)

KING, Prof Christine Elizabeth; CBE (2007), DL (Staffs); da of William Edwin King, and Elizabeth, *née* Coates; *Educ* Univ of Birmingham (BA, MA), Cncl for National Academic Awards (PhD); *Career* teacher Southampton Sixth Form Coll 1967–70, lectr Preston Poly 1970–74, staff tutor Open Univ 1974–75; Univ of Central Lancs (formerly Lancs Poly): research asst 1975–78, successively lectr, sr lectr, princ lectr then head of history 1978–85, head Sch of Historical and Critical Studies 1985–87, dean Faculty of Arts 1987–90; Staffordshire Univ (formerly Staffordshire Poly): asst dir and dean Faculty of Business Humanities and Social Sciences 1990–92, pro-vice-chllr 1992–95, vice-chllr 1995–; pres Nat Inst for Adults Continuing Educn (NIACE); Hon DLitt: Univ of Birmingham 1998, Univ of Portsmouth 2001; Hon DUniv: Derby 2001, Portsmouth 2001; Hon Dr (hc) Univ of Edinburgh 2005, Mensión de Honor Consejo Superior Europeo de Doctores ESERP Barcelona-Madrid 2007; hon fell Univ of Central Lancs 2001; CIMgt, FRSA, FRHistS; *Publications* author of numerous articles and chapters in books and learned jls incl: Resistance in Nazi Germany (Bulletin of John Rylands Library, Vol 70, No3, 1988), The Jehovah's Witnesses (chapter in A Mosaic of Victims: Non-Jews persecuted and murdered by the Nazis, 1990), His Truth Goes Marching On (chapter in Popular Culture and Pilgrimage, 1992), Through the Glass Ceiling: Effective Management Development for Women (ed 1993), The Student Experience (chapter in The Changing University, 1995), Making Things Happen (chapter in Managing Innovation and Change in Universities and Colleges, 1995), The Death of a King (chapter in The Changing Face of Death, 1997), Networking and Mentoring (chapter in Women as Leaders in Higher Education, 1997); *Style—* Prof Christine King, CBE, DL; ✉ Staffordshire University, Beaconside, Stafford ST18 0AD (tel 01785 353200, fax 01785 245441, e-mail c.e.king@staffs.ac.uk)

KING, Christopher John; s of Kavan John King, of New Malden, Surrey and Gwendoline June, *née* Kent (d 1985); *b* 15 October 1959; *Educ* KCS Wimbledon, Univ of Edinburgh; *m* 1989, Gayle Shiona, da of John Thomson, of Dollar, Clackmannanshire; 2 s (James Alexander b 4 Oct 1990, Thomas William b 20 July 1997), 1 da (Georgie Louisa b 10 Feb 1992); *Career* cmmnd Royal Regt of Fus 1978–; brand mangr Procter & Gamble Ltd 1982–84, account supervisor Ted Bates Advertising 984, account dir Grey Advertising Ltd 1985–87, bd dir Jenner Keating Becker Reay 1989–91 (account dir 1987–88), Reay Keating Hamer 1991–94; Grey Advertising (formerly Mellors Reay and Ptnrs): joined as bd dir 1994, subsequently vice-chm, gp md 1998–; MIPA; *Style—* Christopher King, Esq; ✉ Grey Advertising, 215–227 Great Portland Street, London W1N 5HD (tel 020 7636 3399)

KING, Prof Sir David Anthony; kt (2003); s of Arnold Tom Wallis King, of Johannesburg, South Africa, and Patricia Mary Bede, *née* Vardy; *b* 12 August 1939; *Educ* St John's Coll Johannesburg, Univ of the Witwatersrand (BSc, PhD), UEA (ScD), Univ of Cambridge (ScD); *m* 5 Nov 1983, Jane Margaret Lichtenstein (uses maiden name), da of Hans Lichtenstein, of Llandrindod Wells, Wales; 3 s (Benjamin Tom b 11 Nov 1973, Tobias Alexander b 15 Sept 1975, Zachary Adam b 17 Sept 1986), 1 da (Emily Sarah b 20 Feb 1984); *Career* Shell scholar Imperial Coll London 1963–66, lectr in chemical physics UEA 1966–74, Brunner prof of physical chemistry Univ of Liverpool 1974–88; Univ of Cambridge: 1920 prof of physical chemistry 1988–2005, head Dept of Chemistry 1993–2000, dir of research 2005–; fell St John's Coll Cambridge 1988–95, master Downing Coll Cambridge 1995–2000, fell Queens' Coll Cambridge 2001–; chief scientific advsr to UK Govt and head Office of Sci and Innovation 2000–; pres AUT 1976–77; chm Leverhulme Tst Res Awards Advsy Ctee 1995–2000, memb Direction Ctee Fritz Haber Inst Berlin 1981–93; ed Chemical Physics Letters 1989–2001, chm Kettle's Yard (House and Art Gallery) Cambridge 1989–2000; Br Vac Cncl medal and award for research 1991, Greenpeace Business Lectr 2004, World Wildlife Fund Awareness Award 2004; FInstP 1977 (MInstP 1967), FRSC 1974 (medal and award for surface chem 1978, Tilden lectr 1988–89, Liversidge lecture and medal 1997), FRS 1991 (Rumford medal and prize 2002), foreign fell American Acad of Arts and Sciences 2002; *Publications* numerous scientific pubns on the chemical physics of solid surfaces and gas/surface interactions; *Recreations* art, photography; *Clubs* Chelsea Arts; *Style—* Prof Sir David King, FRS; ✉ 20 Glisson Road, Cambridge CB1 2HD; Department of Chemistry, University of Cambridge, Lensfield Road, Cambridge CB2 1EW (tel 01223 336338, fax 01223 762829); 1 Victoria Street, London SW1H 0ET (tel 020 7215 3820, fax 020 7215 0314)

KING, Frances; da of Sir Colin Imray, of Wallingford, Oxon, and Shirley, *née* Matthews; *b* 26 September 1960, Aust; *Educ* Ashford Sch for Girls, St Hilda's Coll Univ of Oxford (MA), Univ of London (MA), Univ of Hull (MBA); *m* 24 July 1982, Timothy King; 1 da (Emily b 6 Dec 1988), 1 s (Henry b 29 April 1993); *Career* head of religious educn: Lady Eleanor Holles Sch 1984–85, Francis Holland Sch 1985–90, Guildford County Sch 1990–93, Tormead Sch 1993–2000 (head of upper sch 1997–2000); dep headmistress St Mary's Sch Ascot 2000–03, headmistress Heathfield Sch Ascot (latterly Heathfield St Mary's) 2003–; *Recreations* travel, walking; *Clubs* Royal Over-Seas League; *Style—* Mrs Frances King; ✉ Heathfield St Mary's School, London Road, Ascot, Berkshire SL5 8BQ (tel 01344 898341, e-mail headmistresspa@heathfieldstmarys.net)

KING, Francis Henry; CBE (1985); s of Eustace Arthur Cecil King (d 1937), and Faith Mina, *née* Read (d 1992); *b* 4 March 1923; *Educ* Shrewsbury, Balliol Coll Oxford (MA); *Career* author; Br Cncl offr 1950–63; lectr: Florence 1950–51, Salonica and Athens 1951–57; asst rep Finland 1957–58, regnl dir Kyoto 1958–63; drama critic Sunday Telegraph 1976–88;

int vice-pres PEN 1989– (int pres 1986–89); FRSL 1958; *Books* The Dividing Stream (1951, Somerset Maugham Award), The Man on the Rock (1957), The Custom House (1961), The Needle (1975), Act of Darkness (1983), Voices in an Empty Room (1984), The Woman Who Was God (1988), The Ant Colony (1991), Secret Lives (1991), Yesterday Come Suddenly (autobiography, 1993), The One and Only (1994), Ash on an Old Man's Sleeve (1996), A Hand at the Shutter (1996), Dead Letters (1997), Prodigies (2001), The Nick of Time (2003), The Sunlight on the Garden (2006), With My Little Eye (2007); *Recreations* gossiping and grumbling; *Style*— Francis King, Esq, CBE; ✉ 19 Gordon Place, London W8 4JE (tel 020 7937 5715, e-mail fhk@dircon.co.uk)

KING, Ian Ayliffe; s of Jack Edward King (d 1990), of Henley-on-Thames, Oxon, and Hilda Bessie King (d 2002); *b* 25 April 1939; *Educ* Bromsgrove Sch; *m* 1, 1963 (m dis 2004), Rosemary, *née* Wolstenholme; 4 c (Joanna b 1965, Giles b 1966, Oliver b 1972, Philippa b 1977); m 2, 2004, Jane Margaret FitzGibbon, *née* Liddington; *Career* chartered accountant; ptnr Baker Tilly (formerly Chalmers Impey) 1968–2004 (nat chm HLB Kidsons 1992–2002); dir: E Walters (Ludlow) Ltd 1968–85, Baker & Sons (Margate) Ltd 1975–, Beoley Hall (1992) Ltd 2004–, V-Viz Ltd 2005–, The All England Lawn Tennis Ground Ltd 1991–96, LTA Tst Ltd 1991–94, The Queen's Club Ltd 1993–2007, The South Birmingham Mental Health NHS Tst Ltd 1994–97, The Int Tennis Hall of Fame 1995–2005, ITF Ltd 1995–2005 (memb Fin Ctee, chm Women's Circuit Ctee, chm Constitutional Ctee, hon life cnsllr 2006–); tstee: Sir Barry Jackson Tst, The Jack Kendall Tennis Tst; govr Whitford Hall Sch 1973–90; LTA: memb Cncl 1981–87 (representing Herefordshire and Worcestershire LTA), memb Bd of Mgmnt 1984–2004 (chm 1991–93), dep pres 1988–90, pres 1991–93, int rep 1995–2004, dir Int and Professional Tennis Div Bd, chm Anti-Doping Ctee; memb Ctee of Mgmnt of the Championships Wimbledon 1987–2005; pres Herefordshire and Worcestershire LTA 2002– (memb Ctee 1969–, chm 1980–2002); Liveryman Worshipful Co of Chartered Accountants in England and Wales 1991; FCA 1962; *Recreations* tennis, cricket, theatre, travel; *Clubs* All England Lawn Tennis, Queen's, Barnt Green Tennis, Edgbaston Priory Tennis, The International Lawn Tennis Clubs of GB and Aust, Bromsgrove Tennis, Worcs CCC; *Style*— Ian King, Esq; ✉ 2 Beoley Hall, Beoley, Redditch, Worcestershire B98 9AL (tel 01527 591548, fax 01527 597823, e-mail ian_a_king@hotmail.com)

KING, Ian Charles; *b* 28 December 1934; *Educ* UCS Hampstead, Bartlett Sch of Achitecture Univ of London (Dip Arch); *m* 1 (m dis); m 2, 5 Feb 1980, Nathalie Wareham, *née* Singh; *Career* architect in private practice 1964–, Ian C King Associates Architects; Freeman City of London 1981; Liveryman: Worshipful Co of Glass Sellers 1982, Worshipful Co of Chartered Architects 1988; RIBA 1960; *Recreations* lawn tennis, theatre, veteran cars; *Clubs* All England Lawn Tennis and Croquet, Hurlingham (past chm), Athenaeum; *Style*— Ian C King, Esq; ✉ Flat 28, Sherwood Court, Riverside Plaza, Chatfield Road, London SW11 3UY; 5 St George's Court, 131 Putney Bridge Road, London SW15 2PA (tel 020 8871 2022, fax 020 8871 2989, e-mail ian@iancking.co.uk)

KING, Jeremy Richard Bruce; s of Charles Henry King (d 2003), and Molly, *née* Chinn; *b* 21 June 1954, Taunton, Somerset; *Educ* Christ's Hosp; *m* 9 Jan 1982, Debra Hauer; 2 da (Hannah b 16 April 1991, Margot b 1 June 1993), 1 s (Jonah b 30 May 1995); *Career* restaurateur; dir and prop (with Chris Corbin, *qv*) Caprice Holdings Ltd 1981–2003; restaurants opened incl: Le Caprice 1981, The Ivy 1990, J Sheekey 1998; dir and prop (with Chris Corbin) The Wolseley 2003–, St Alban 2007; Caterer and Hotelkeeper Restaurateur of the Year 1993 (jtly); chm Tate Catering, memb Cncl Tate Modern, dir Tate Enterprises Ltd 2006–; *Clubs* Garrick, RAC; *Style*— Jeremy King, Esq; ✉ Rex Restaurant Associates, 170 Piccadilly, London W1J 9EJ (tel 020 7647 1810, fax 020 7439 0420, e-mail jeremy.king@rexra.com)

KING, John Arthur Charles; *b* 7 April 1933; *Educ* Sir Joseph Williamson's Mathematical Sch Rochester, Univ of Bristol (BSc); *m*; 2 s; *Career* IBM 1956–70, UK md Telex Computer Products 1971–73, dir UK Data Processing Div Metra Consulting 1974–75, UK dir of mktg rising to Euro dir of business and market devpt ITT Business Systems and Communications Group 1976–81, commercial dir Philips International Business Communications Systems 1981–83, md Overseas Div and main bd dir BT plc 1983–88; chm: Quotron International Citicorp Information Business 1988–91, Analysys Ltd 1991–2001, Olsy UK Ltd (previously Olivetti UK Ltd) 1995–98 (non-exec dir 1991–), Superscape plc 1998–2003; vice-chm Leeds Permanent Building Society 1995–96 (non-exec dir 1991–); dir: Science Research Associates Ltd 1992–93, Knowledge Support Systems Ltd 1997–2001 (chm 1998–2001), TTP Capital Ptnrs Ltd 1999–2003; sec gen European Fndn for Quality Management 1993–94; memb Restrictive Practices Court 1995–2000, non-exec memb Bd Child Support Agency 1996–98, memb Supervisory Bd Fugro NV 1997–2003; vol advsr Enterprise First 2004–; Liveryman Worshipful Co of Info Technologists 1992; FBCS, FInstD, FRSA; *Recreations* golf, bridge, music; *Clubs* Wisley Golf; *Style*— J A C King, Esq; ✉ e-mail jacking33@btinternet.com

KING, John B; *Educ* MB BS, LRCP; *Career* hon sr lectr and hon conslt in orthopaedic and trauma surgery Sch of Med and Dentistry St Bartholomews, Royal London Hosp, Queen Mary Coll London, former dir Academic Dept of Sports Med The London Hosp Med Coll, hon conslt Sports Clinic The London Hosp; former chm Br Assoc of Sports Med, former sr examiner in sports med Worshipful Soc of Apothecaries, former external advsr to Bath Distance Learning Course for Doctors in Sports Med, former orthopaedic conslt to Nat Sports Centre Crystal Palace London; academic assoc The Univ of London Interdisciplinary Research Centre in Biomedical Materials, former memb Editorial Bd Int Jl of Orthopaedic Trauma; Robert Milne prize in orthopaedic and related subjects 1977, Br Orthopaedic Assoc Euro travelling fell 1977; memb: Br Assoc for Surgery of the Knee (fndr memb), BMA, RSM, Br Orthopaedic Assoc, Int Soc of Arthroscopy, Knee Surgery and Orthopaedic Sports Medicine (ISAKOS), Euro Soc of Sports Traumatology, Knee Surgery and Arthroscopy; FRCS, FISM; *Publications* author of more than 80 pubns in learned jls and books; *Clubs* Athenaeum; *Style*— John B King, Esq; ✉ The London Independent Hospital, Beaumont Square, London E1 4NL

KING, Sir John Christopher; 4 Bt (UK 1888), of Campsie, Stirlingshire; s of Sir James Granville Le Neve King, 3 Bt, TD (d 1989), and Penelope Charlotte, *née* Cooper-Key (d 1994); *b* 31 March 1933; *Educ* Eton; *m* 1, 3 Oct 1958 (m dis 1972), Patricia Monica, o da of late Lt-Col Kingsley Osbern Nugent Foster, DSO, OBE; 1 s, 1 da; m 2, 1984 (m dis 2000), Mrs (Aline) Jane Holley, er da of Col Douglas Alexander Brett, GC, OBE, MC; *Heir* s, James King; *Career* Sub Lt RNVR, 1 Lt Berkshire Yeo TA; memb Stock Exchange 1958–73; *Recreations* sailing, shooting; *Clubs* Brooks's; *Style*— Sir John King, Bt

KING, Prof Julia Elizabeth; CBE (1999); da of Derrick King (d 1997), and Jane, *née* Brewer; *b* 11 July 1954; *Educ* Godolphin & Latymer Sch, New Hall Cambridge (MA, Posener scholar, PhD); *m* 4 Aug 1984, Dr Colin William Brown; *Career* Rolls-Royce research fell Girton Coll Cambridge 1978–80, lectr Univ of Nottingham 1980–87; Univ of Cambridge: British Gas/Fellowship of Engrg sr research fell 1987–92, teaching fell Churchill Coll 1987–94 and 2002–, lectr 1992–94, asst dir Technol Centre for Ni-Base Superalloys 1993–94; head of materials Rolls-Royce Aerospace Group 1994–96, dir of advanced engrg Rolls-Royce Industrial Power Group 1997–98, md Fan Systems Rolls-Royce plc 1998–2000, dir of engrg and technol Marine Rolls-Royce plc 2000–02; chief exec Inst of Physics 2002–04, princ Faculty of Engrg Imperial Coll London 2004–06, vice-chllr Aston Univ 2006–; chair MOD DSAC 2003–07; hon sec for educn and trg Royal Acad of Engrg 2003–06; memb: Foresight Panel for Defence & Aerospace 1994–97, Foresight Panel for Materials 1994–96, Materials Bd DSAC 1996–98, Tech Opportunities Panel EPSRC 1997–99, Link/TCS Bd 1998–2001, EPSRC Cncl 2000–03, Cncl Royal Acad of Engrg 2002–06, Engrg and Technol Bd 2003–, Technol Strategy Bd DTI 2004–; memb Editorial Bd: Int Jl of Fatigue 1989–96, Fatigue and Fracture of Engrg Materials and Structures 1990–97; author of numerous papers on fatigue and fracture in structural materials; memb Women's Engrg Soc; Grunfeld Medal Inst of Materials 1992, Japan Soc for Promotion of Sci Fellowship 1993, Bengough Medal (jtly) Inst of Materials 1995, Kelvin Medal 2001; hon chair: Univ of Swansea 1995–, Univ of Newcastle upon Tyne 1997–; hon fell: New Hall Cambridge 2003, Univ of Cardiff 2003; Hon DSc Queen Mary Univ of London 2008; Liveryman Co of Goldsmiths 1998, Freeman City of London 1998; FREng 1997, FIMMM, FRAeS, FIMarEST, FInstP, CPhys, FCGI; *Recreations* collecting modern prints (particularly of plants and places), photography, walking; *Style*— Prof Julia King, CBE, FREng; ✉ Aston University, Aston Triangle, Birmingham B4 7ET

KING, Justin Matthew; s of Alan Sydney King, of Alton, Hants, and Elaine, *née* Adams; *b* 17 May 1961; *Educ* Tudor Grange Sch Solihull, Solihull Sixth Form Coll, Univ of Bath (BSc); *m* 12 May 1990, Claire Andrea, da of Neville Simmons; 1 da, 1 s; *Career* univ sponsorship to Lucas Electrical Birmingham 1979–83; various positions Mars Confectionery incl: mfrg mangr 1983–84, servs buyer 1984–85, nat account mangr 1986–89; various positions Pepsi Cola International incl: sales devpt mangr Cyprus 1989–90, sales and mktg dir Egypt 1990; md Haagen-Dazs UK Ltd 1990–93, mktg dir Allied Maples (Div of Asda plc) 1993–94, product devpt dir Asda 1997–98 (dir of drinks and kiosks 1994–97), dep trading dir Asda plc 1998–2000, head of foods M&S 2000–03, chief exec J Sainsbury plc 2004–; *Recreations* sailing; *Clubs* Hayling Island Sailing; *Style*— Justin King, Esq

KING, Laurence Richard; s of (Cecil) Francis Harmsworth King, of London, and Jenifer Mary, *née* Beckett; *b* 28 July 1955; *Educ* Winchester, Jesus Coll Cambridge (BA); *m* Caroline Monica Elizabeth Ann, *née* Schofield; *Career* Calmann & King Ltd (formerly John Calmann & Cooper Ltd until 1983): asst ed 1976–80, sales dir 1980, md 1983–2001; fndr Laurence King Publishing Ltd 1991; *Style*— Mr Laurence King; ✉ 26b Sekforde Street, London EC1R 0HH; Laurence King Publishing, 361–373 City Road, London EC1V 1LR (tel 020 7841 6900, fax 020 7841 6910, e-mail enquiries@laurenceking.co.uk)

KING, Malcolm James Geoffrey; s of late Douglas James Edward King; of Hadley Wood, Herts, and Betty Alice, *née* Martin; *b* 10 April 1945; *Educ* Harrow, Coll of Estate Mgmnt, Univ of Western Ontario (MBA); *m* 1, 6 June 1970 (m dis 2001), Jennifer Kate, da of Arthur Charles Rose; 1 da (Annabel Kate b 11 Jan 1973), 1 s (Oliver James b 25 March 1975); m 2, 2 May 2003, Dr Josephine Angela Emery, da of Jack Thomas; *Career* chartered surveyor Gerald Eve 1963–68; King & Co: joined 1968, head Investment Dept 1970, assoc 1972–75, ptnr 1975–88, jt sr ptnr 1988–94, sr ptnr 1994–2005, int chm 2005–; Freeman City of London; Liveryman: Worshipful Co of Wheelwrights, Worshipful Co of Chartered Surveyors; FRICS; *Recreations* fly fishing, golf, shooting, stalking, flying, gardening; *Clubs* Flyfishers', The Machrie, Hadley Wood Golf, Piscatorials; *Style*— Malcolm King, Esq; ✉ King Sturge, 7 Stratford Place, London W1C 1ST (tel 020 7318 4300, fax 020 7409 0635)

KING, Martina; *née* Doyle; *b* 7 March 1961; *Educ* Bonus Pastor RC Sch Bromley Kent; *m* 1995, Simon King; *Career* personnel exec GLC 1980–82, telephone sales canvasser The Observer 1982–84; The Guardian 1984–93: classified sales exec 1984–86, display sales exec 1986–88, gp head (Display Sales) 1988–89, display sales mangr 1989–93; Capital Radio 1993–99: client sales dir Jan-Aug 1993, sales dir Aug 1993–94, station dir 1994–97, md 1997–99; md TSMS Gp Ltd 1999, md Yahoo! UK & Ireland 1999–2003, md country ops Yahoo! Europe 2003–04; non-exec dir: Johnston Press plc 2003–, Capita Gp plc 2005–; memb Mayor's Cmmn on the Creative Industries London Devpt Agency; tstee Help a London Child; *Recreations* watersports, music, family life and friends; *Style*— Mrs Martina King

K

KING, Mary Elizabeth; da of late Lt Cdr Michael Dillon Harding Thomson, RN, and Patricia Gillian, *née* Hole; *b* 8 June 1961; *Educ* King's GS Ottery St Mary, Evendine Court Malvern (cordon bleu coll); *m* 1995, (Alan) David Henry King; 1 da (Emily Maria b Jan 1996), 1 s (Fredrick Arthur b Nov 1998); *Career* three day eventer; began with Axe Vale Pony Club, trained with Sheila Willcox 1977–80, fndr own yard 1981; achievements incl: winner Windsor Horse Trials 1988, 1989 and 1992, Br Open champion 1990, 1991 and 1996, team Gold medal European Championships 1991, winner Badminton Horse Trials 1992 and 2000 (runner-up 1989 and 1997), winner Althorp Maverick Championships 1993, team Gold medal and individual fourth place World Equestrian Games 1994, winner Punchestown and Compiègne Int Events 1995, team Gold medal and individual Bronze medal European Championships 1995, winner Burghley Horse Trials 1996, team Gold medal European Open Championships 1997, team Silver medal Olympic Games Athens 2004, team Silver medal World Equestrian Games 2006; GB rep Olympic Games: Barcelona 1992, Atlanta 1996, Sydney 2000, Athens 2004; ranked no 1 British event rider 1993, 1994 and 1997, holds world record for consecutive three day event wins (5 in 1991–92); Sun Systems Outstanding Rider of the Year 1990, Animal Health Tsts Equestrian Personality of the Year 1991, The Times/Minet Supreme Award 1992; watch leader on the Sir Winston Churchill tall ship 1980, chalet girl Zermatt 1980–81; *Books* Mary Thomson's Eventing Year (1993), All the King's Horses (1997), William and Mary (1998); *Video* Mary Thomson - Rider of the World (1995); *Recreations* tennis, snow and water skiing, deep sea diving; *Style*— Mrs David King; ✉ Matford Park Farm, Exminster, Exeter, Devon EX6 8AT (tel 01392 273887, fax 01392 258846)

KING, Prof Mervyn Allister; s of Eric Frank King, and Kathleen Alice, *née* Passingham; *b* 30 March 1948; *Educ* Wolverhampton GS, King's Coll Cambridge (MA); *Career* jr res offr Dept of Applied Economics (memb Cambridge Growth Project) 1969–73, Kennedy scholarship Harvard Univ 1971–72; Univ of Cambridge: res offr Dept of Applied Economics 1972–76, fell and dir studies St John's Coll 1972–77, lectr Faculty of Economics 1976–77; Esmée Fairbairn prof of investment Univ of Birmingham 1977–84, prof of economics LSE 1984–95; Bank of England: chief economist 1991–98, exec dir 1991–98, dep govr 1998–2003, govr 2003–; visiting prof of economics: Harvard Univ 1982–83 and 1990, MIT 1983–84; visiting fell Nuffield Coll Oxford 2002–; pres Euro Economic Assoc 1993, pres IFS 1999–2003; memb: Prog Ctee Econometric Soc Congress 1974, 1979, 1985, Meade Ctee on Taxation (sec) 1975–78, CLARE Gp 1976–85, Editorial Bd Jl of Industrial Economics 1977–83, Economics Ctee ESRC 1980–82, Cncl and Exec Ctee Royal Economic Soc 1981–86, Res Ctee ENSAE Paris 1985–88, Economic Policy Panel 1985–86 and 1990–91, Bd The Securities Assoc 1987–89, City Capital Markets Ctee 1989–91; res assoc NBER 1978–, co-dir ESRC Res Prog on Taxation Incentives and Distribution of Income LSE 1979–89, research fell Centre for Economic Policy Res 1984–, co-dir (with C Goodhart) Financial Markets Gp LSE 1987–91; asst ed Economic Jl 1974–75, managing ed Review of Economic Studies 1978–83, assoc ed Jl of Public Economics 1982–98, memb Editorial Bd American Economic Review 1985–88, chm Soc of Econ Analysis 1984–86; Walras-Bowley lectr Econ Soc 1987, Review of Economics lectr Cambridge 1986, assoc memb Inst of Fiscal and Monetary Policy Miny of Fin Japan 1986–91; conslt: NZ treasy 1979, OECD 1982, Royal Cmmn on Distribution of Income and Wealth 1975; tstee Kennedy Meml Tst 1990–2000; res fell INSEE Paris 1977, hon res fell UCL 1977–79; Helsinki Univ medal 1982; hon degrees: London Guildhall Univ 2001, City Univ 2002, Univ of Birmingham 2002, LSE 2003, Univ of Wolverhampton 2003, Univ of Edinburgh 2005, Univ of Helsinki 2006; FBA 1992; *Books* Indexing for Inflation (ed with T Liesner, 1975), Public Policy and the Corporation (1977), The British Tax System (with J A Kay, 1978, 5 edn 1990), The Taxation of Income from Capital: A Comparative Study of the US, UK, Sweden and West Germany (with D Fullerton et al,

1984), author of numerous articles; *Clubs* Brooks's, Garrick, Athenaeum; *Style*— Prof Mervyn King; ✉ Bank of England, Threadneedle Street, London EC2R 8AH (tel 020 7601 4444, fax 020 7601 4953)

KING, Prof Michael Bruce; s of Bruce Eugene King, of Napier, NZ, and Patricia Alfredith, *née* Maxwell; *b* 10 February 1950; *Educ* Univ of Canterbury Christchurch (sr scholar in zoology, BSc), Sch of Med Univ of Auckland (sr scholar in med, Sims travelling Cwlth scholar, BSc, MB ChB, MD, sr prize for med), Univ of Aberdeen (Dip Health Economics), Univ of London (PhD); *Career* pre-registration/physicians trg Auckland 1976–77, GP trg Hammersmith Hosp 1978–81, trg in psychiatry Royal Bethlem and Maudsley Hosps 1981–84; Inst of Psychiatry: res worker/hon sr registrar 1984–86, clinical lectr/hon sr registrar 1986–88, sr lectr/hon conslt 1988–89, hon sr lectr 1989–; Dept of Psychiatry Behavioural Sciences Royal Free and UC Med Sch: sr lectr and hon conslt 1989–94, reader, hon conslt and head of dept 1994–96, prof and head of dept 1996–; memb: Dept of Health's Expert Advsy Gp on AIDS 1992–98, AIDS Working Pty RCGP 1994–98, Cncl Section of Psychiatry RSM (past pres); memb: Educn Ctee RCPysch 1992–95, Steering Gp for the Mental Health Fndn/Dept of Health Sr Educnl Fellowship in Mental Health and Gen Practice 1993–97, Public Health and Health Services Research Bd MRC 1998–2002, Standing Ctee Assoc of Univ Teachers of Psychiatry, Primary Care Working Pty Mental Health Fndn, Nat Panel of Referees for the Nat Mental Health R&D Prog (NHS Mgmnt Exec); asst ed Jl of Psychosomatic Research 1990–93; memb Editorial Bd: Br Jl of General Practice 1993–99, Br Jl of Psychiatry; memb Int Editorial Bd AIDS Care; author of numerous original papers in learned jls; Dennis Hill Prize Maudsley Hosp/Inst of Psychiatry 1983; FRCGP 1991 (MRCGP), FRCP 1996 (MRCP), FRCPsych 2000 (MRCPsych); *Books* Male Victims of Sexual Assault (ed and jt author, 1992, 2 edn 2000), AIDS, HIV and Mental Health (1993); contrib: Eating Disorders and Disordered Eating (1988), The Scope of Epidemiological Psychiatry (1989), Epidemiology and the Prevention of Psychiatric Disorder (1989), The Public Health Impact of Mental Disorder (1990), Principles of Social Psychiatry (1993), Recent Advances in Clinical Psychiatry (1993), The Medical Annual 1993/94 (1993), Psychiatry and General Practice (1994), Research Foundations for Psychotherapy Research (1995), Assessment of Parenting (1995), Evidence Based Counselling and Psychological Therapies (2000), The Trauma of Sexual Assault: Treatment, Prevention and Policy (2002), Identity and Health (2004), Textbook of Men's Mental Health (2007); *Recreations* swimming, languages; *Style*— Prof Michael King; ✉ Hampstead Campus, Department of Mental Health Sciences, Royal Free and University College Medical School, Rowland Hill Street, London NW3 2PF (tel 020 7830 2397, fax 020 7830 2808, e-mail m.king@medsch.ucl.ac.uk)

KING, (Austin) Michael Henry; s of Gerald King (d 1970), of Bath, and Pauline King, MBE, *née* Gillow; *b* 9 February 1949, Bath; *Educ* Stonyhurst Coll; *m* 18 Oct 1975, Frances-Anne, *née* Sutherland; 3 s (Edward John b 16 July 1978, Dominic Henry b 27 March 1982, Piers Michael Hugo b 27 Nov 1987); *Career* articled clerk Stone King & Wardle and Charles Russell & Co 1969–74, admitted slr 1974; Stone King (Bath and London): ptnr 1975–, opened London office 1990, head Charity Unit 1993–, sr ptnr 1996–; memb Exec Ctee Charity Law Assoc 1993–2006 (chm 1997–2000), pres Bath Law Soc 2001–02; chm Catholic Charity Conf 1991–; several appts as tstee of charitable orgns and govr of schs incl tstee and hon sec Bath Royal Literary and Scientific Inst 1992–97, current positions incl chm British Hospitalité Tst, chm Kilmersdon Rural Housing Assoc, vice-chm of tstees Holburne Museum Bath, govr Royal HS Bath; *Publications* The Charities Act Explained (2000), Charities Act 2006: A Guide to the New Law (2007); *Recreations* sailing, shooting, tennis, watching rugby; *Clubs* Lansdowne; *Style*— Michael King, Esq; ✉ Stone King, 13 Queen Square, Bath BA1 2HJ (tel 01225 337899, fax 01225 335437, e-mail michaelking@stoneking.co.uk); 28 Ely Place, London EC1A 7JQ (tel 020 7796 1007)

KING, Eur Ing Prof Michael Stuart; s of Edward Roy King (d 1963), of Thornham, Norfolk, and Jessie Margaret, *née* Davis (d 1994); *b* 2 June 1931; *Educ* St Edward's Sch Oxford, Univ of Glasgow (BSc), Univ of Calif (MS, PhD); *m* 1, 9 June 1962 (m dis 1983), Margaret Helen Hoeschen, da of Theodore de Vassily Bujila (d 1979), of Montreal, Canada; 1 da (Sarah Bernadine Margaret b 1966), 2 s (Bernard John Edward b 1967, David Matthew Stuart b 1971); m 2, 21 Oct 1989, (Shirley) Georgina King, OBE, da of Dr the Hon Walter Symington Maclay (d 1963), of Newbury, Berks; *Career* prof of geological engrg Univ of Saskatchewan 1966–81, prof of mechanical engrg Univ of Calif Berkeley 1981–86, Phoebe Apperson Hearst distinguished prof 1986, oil industry prof of petroleum engrg Imperial Coll London 1986–96 (prof emeritus 1996, sr research fell 2001); FIMechE 1985, FGS 1985, Eur Ing 1991; *Recreations* field sports, music; *Style*— Eur Ing Prof Michael King; ✉ Cedar House, Hellidon, Daventry, Northamptonshire NN11 6GD (tel 01327 261919, e-mail m.s.king@debrett.net); Department of Earth Science and Engineering, Imperial College London, London SW7 2AZ (e-mail m.s.king@imperial.ac.uk)

KING, Mike; *b* 22 September 1962; *Educ* St Benedict's Ealing; *Career* photographer; progressively: jr in small sports photographic agency, with Allsport agency, chief sports photographer The Observer; currently with The Daily Telegraph; Sports Cncl Black and White Photographer of the Year 1989, Nikon Sports Photographer of the Year 1989 and 1990, IAF Athletics Photographer of the Year, Sport England Sports Photographer of the Year 1999; Sport England Sports Picture of the Year 2001; *Recreations* cycling; *Style*— Mike King, Esq; ✉ 28 Beauval Road, London SE22 8UQ (tel 020 8299 0484)

KING, Neil Gerald Alexander; QC (2000); s of Joseph King (d 2005), and Leila, *née* Saxton; *b* 14 November 1956, London; *Educ* Harrow, New Coll Oxford (MA); *m* 15 July 1978, Matilda, *née* Oppenheimer; 4 da (Dorothy b 2 April 1987, Hannah b 2 Dec 1988, Elsa b 17 April 1990, Lily b 2 Aug 1993); *Career* called to the Bar 1980; practising barr, currently memb Landmark Chambers; memb Planning and Environment Bar Assoc; dir: Garsington Opera Ltd, Harrison Housing Ltd, Scarista House Hotel; *Recreations* golf, walking, opera (especially Verdi), pianism; *Clubs* Isle of Harris, Royal Jersey Golf, Huntercombe Golf, RAC, Army and Navy; *Style*— Neil King, Esq, QC; ✉ The White House, Whitchurch-on-Thames, Reading RG8 7HA (tel 0118 984 2800, fax 0118 984 1264, e-mail neil_ga_king@msn.com); Landmark Chambers, 180 Fleet Street, London EC4A 2HG (tel 020 7421 1330, e-mail nking@landmarkchambers.co.uk)

KING, Prof Phillip; CBE (1974); s of Thomas John King (d 1973), and Gabrielle Laurence, *née* Liautard (d 1975); *Educ* Mill Hill Sch, Univ of Cambridge (MA); *m* 1 (m dis); 1 s (Anthony Thomas b 1965 d 1984); m 2, 1991, Judith Corbalis; *Career* prof of sculpture: RCA 1981–90 (emeritus prof 1990–), Royal Acad Schs 1990–99; memb Arts Cncl, tstee Tate Gallery 1967–69; Hon Dr Kingston Univ 2004; PRA 1999 (RA 1987, ARA 1977); *Recreations* travelling, swimming, music, windsurfing; *Style*— Prof Phillip King, CBE, PRA

KING, Prof Preston Theodore; s of Clennon King (d 1975), of Albany, GA, and Margaret, *née* Slater (d 1990); *b* 3 March 1936; *Educ* Fisk Univ (BA), Univ of Vienna, Univ of Strasbourg, Univ of Paris, LSE (MSc, PhD); *m*; 2 s (Slater, Akasi Peter), 1 da (Oona King); *Career* tutor: LSE 1958–60, Univ of Maryland 1961; lectr: Keele Univ 1961–62, Univ of Ghana 1963–66, Univ of Sheffield 1966–68; reader Univ of E Africa Nairobi 1968–70, sr res assoc Acton Soc Tst 1970–72; Univ of Nairobi: prof 1972–76, chm of dept 1972–74, founded Diplomacy Training Prog for Anglophone Africa 1972–73, dir DTP 1973–74; prof of political sci Univ of NSW 1976–86 (head of sch 1978–80), prof of politics Lancaster Univ 1986–2001 (head of dept 1986–87), prof Emory Univ and Morehouse Coll 2002–05; visiting prof: Univ of Dar es Salaam 1973, Institut des Relations Internationales Univ of Cameroun 1976, McGill Univ 1981, Philosophy Dept LSE 1983 (Politics Dept 1979), Univ of Auckland 1995; external examiner: Makerere Univ 1973, Univ of Khartoum 1974–75, Univ of the S Pacific Fiji 1977–83, Univ of Liverpool 1988–91, Univ of Reading, LSE; gen ed: Aust Nat Univ Monograph Series in Social and Political Thought 1977–80, Int Series in Social and Political Thought 1980–; ed CRISPP (Critical Review of International Social and Political Philosophy); author of numerous articles and reviews on socio-political related topics published in nat and int jls; broadcaster; memb Exec Ctee Conference for the Study of Political Thought, chair Research Ctee for Political Philosophy (IPSA); former memb: Bd of Tstees Nat Museums and Galleries on Merseyside, Advsy Ctee Centre for Res in Ethnic Relations Univ of Warwick; involvement in various int political orgns and conferences; *Books* incl: Fear of Power (1967), The History of Ideas (1983), The Ideology of Order (1974), Toleration (1976), Federalism and Federation (1982), An African Winter (1986), Thomas Hobbes: Critical Assesments (4 vols, 1993), Socialism and The Common Good: New Fabian Essays (1996), Thinking Past A Problem: Essays on the History of Ideas (2000), Trusting in Reason (2003), Black Leaders and Ideologies in the South (2005), Friendship in Politics (2007); *Style*— Prof Preston King; ✉ Leadership Center, Morehouse College, 830 Westview Drive SW, Atlanta, GA 30314, USA (tel 00 1 404 614 8565, e-mail pking@morehouse.edu)

KING, Robert John Stephen; s of Stephen King, of Wolverhampton, and Margaret Digby; *b* 27 June 1960; *Educ* Radley, St John's Coll Cambridge (MA); *Career* conductor and harpsichordist; dir The King's Consort (Baroque orch) 1980–; conductor and dir on over 95 records on Hyperion (exclusive contract); artistic dir ION Festival Nürnberg 2003–; guest dir: Aarhus Symphony Orchestra, Real Filharmonica de Galicia, Orquesta de Cadaques, English Chamber Orchestra, Uppsala Chamber Orchestra, Orquesta Sinfonica Euskadi, RTL Symphony Orchestra, Netherlands Chamber Orchestra and Chamber Choir, Koninklijke Filharmonisch Orkest van Vlaanderen, Atlanta Symphony Orchestra, Houston Symphony Orchestra, Nat Symphony Orchestra (Washington), Seattle Symphony Orchestra, Detroit Symphony Orchestra, Minnesota Symphony Orchestra, Danish Radio Symphony Orchestra, Stavanger Symphony Orchestra, Norrkoping Sinfoniorkester, Orquestra Ciudad de Granada; concert tours: France, Holland, Belgium, Spain, Finland, Italy, Japan, Hong Kong, Mexico, Taiwan, Turkey, S America, USA; TV and radio appearances throughout Europe and the UK, ed of much 1600–1750 music (publisher Faber Music); *Recreations* skiing, cricket, lupin growing; *Style*— Robert King, Esq; ✉ c/o The King's Consort, The Old Rectory, Alpheton, Suffolk CO10 9BT (e-mail info@tkcworld.com)

KING, Prof Roger Patrick; *b* 31 May 1945; *Educ* St Anselm's GS Birkenhead, St George's GS Hong Kong and Singapore, Wimbledon Coll, Univ of London (external BSc), Univ of Birmingham (MSc); *m*; *Career* exec offr Miny of Housing & Local Govt London 1963–64, sales mangr United Glass Ltd 1964–65, sales mangr Marley Tiles Ltd 1965–66; lectr then sr lectr in social science Manchester Poly 1970–75; princ lectr Dept of Behavioural Sciences Huddersfield Poly 1976–82 (head of dept 1982–85); Univ of Lincs and Humberside (Humberside Poly until 1992): dep dir (resources) 1985–89, dir and chief exec 1989–92, vice-chllr 1992–2000, personal professorship 1992–; visiting research prof Open Univ 2003–, visiting research fell Assoc of Cwlth Univs 2003–; chm Inst for Learning and Teaching 1997–2001; Br Cncl: memb Ctee for Asia and the Oceans 1991–95, memb Ctee for Int Co-operation in Higher Educn 1991–; memb Funding Gp PCFC 1988–89, memb Libraries and Learning Resources Review Gp and chm Managing Libraries Sub-Gp HEFCE 1993–94, memb HEFCE Ctee on Learning and Teaching 1998–; Ctee of Dirs of Polys: memb Funding of Teaching Gp 1991–, memb Student Issues Gp 1992–; CVCP: memb Fin Ctee 1992–, memb European Ctee 1992–, memb Student Affairs Ctee 1992–; memb Exec Bd Poly and Colls Employers Forum 1992–, memb Cncl Humberside TEC 1991–; chm Int Centre for Mgmnt Educn Singapore 1992–; CNAA: memb Combined Studies (Social Sciences) Sub-Ctee 1985–88, memb Sociological Studies Bd 1984–88; memb: Political Studies Assoc, Soc for Research into HE; author of numerous res papers and pubns; *Style*— Prof Roger King; ✉ Telham Lodge, Telham Lane, Battle, East Sussex TN33 0SN (tel and fax 01424 830056)

KING, Ronald Gordon; s of Basil Frederick Gordon King (d 1991), and Jacqueline Marie Catherine, *née* Timmermans (d 1994); *b* 31 December 1946; *Educ* Jesuit Coll Antwerp; *Career* ed: Viewpoint 1965–, The Keys of Peter 1969–, Warfare 1972–; librarian: The Times 1969–86, Today 1986–92, CSO Research 1992–; dir Christian Social Order; sec: Christian Centre Pty, Napoleon Soc, Pugin Gild; librarian Army and Navy Club 1969–99; *Books* Catholicism and European Unity (1980), Zionism and the Vatican (1981), Napoleon and Freemasonry (1985), NATO's First War (1999), Beria Was on Our Side (2001); *Style*— Ronald King, Esq; ✉ 157 Vicarage Road, London E10 5DU (tel and fax 020 8539 3876, e-mail keys@fsmail.net)

KING, (Derek) Ross; s of David Johnston King, of Glasgow, and Isabel Moore McLeod, *née* Ross; *b* 21 February 1964; *Educ* Victoria Drive Secdy Sch Glasgow; *m* 30 May 1999, Helen Way; *Career* actor, radio and TV presenter; *Theatre* Frankfurter in The Rocky Horror Show, Wallace Spencer in Summer Holiday, Toby McWiry in Dick Whittington (Sadlers Wells), Fancourt Babberly in Charleys Aunt; others incl: She Stoops to Conquer, Guys and Dolls, Joseph, Butterfly Children, Life and Limb (LA, dir); pantomimes incl: Cinderella, Dick Whittington, Snow White, Jack and the Beanstalk, Mother Goose, Babes in the Wood; *Film* She Said I Love You, Do it for Uncle Manny, Comfort and Joy, The Girl in the Picture, Half Past Dead, The Day After Tomorrow; *Television* for BBC: Pebble Mill, The Ross King Show, The 8.15 from Manchester, Holiday, King of the Road, Summer in the City, Hot Chefs, Newshound, Pop Goes Summer, The Wetter the Better, CTV1; for ITV: Run the Gauntlet, My Secret Desire, Young Krypton, Quiz Night, Pick of the Week, Auto TX, Who's Into, Living It Up, The Calendar Fashion Show, Mini Champions; American Juniors (Fox TV); Living TV: Charmed: Behind the Magic, Will & Grace: Access All Areas, According to Jim: Access All Areas; *Radio* Ross King Show (Capital Radio), Ross King Show (Radio Clyde), Sportsbeat and various others incl Olympics (Radio 5), The Eurochart (ILR Network), Ok to Talk (Talk Radio), Ross King's Sportstars (Talk Radio), The King in LA; *Awards* Local Radio DJ of the Year Sony Radio Awards and Smash Hits, Sony Radio Award for outstanding sports presentation of Barcelona Olympics; *Recreations* sport, theatre, cinema; *Clubs* Ham Polo; *Style*— Ross King, Esq; ✉ website www.rossking.com

KING, Prof Roy D; s of Leonard Stanley King (d 1991), of Potters Bar, Herts, and Helena, *née* Loe (d 1978); *b* 1 January 1940, Potters Bar; *Educ* Stationers' Co's Sch, Univ of Leicester (BA), Univ of Cambridge (DipCrim), LSE (PhD); *m* 20 Feb 1965, Janet MacDonald, *née* Price; 2 s (Simon Henry b 1970, Matthew David b 1974); *Career* res offr Inst of Social Psychiatry 1963–64, res offr Inst of Educn London 1964–67, lectr Univ of Southampton 1967–72, visiting fell Yale Law Sch 1972–73, sr lectr Univ of Southampton 1974–79, prof of social theory and instns Univ of Wales Bangor 1979–83, visiting prof Univ of Wisconsin 1983–84, prof of criminology and criminal justice Univ of Wales Bangor 1984–2004, sr res fell Inst of Criminology Cambridge 2004–; memb Parole Bd for Eng and Wales 1968–72 and 2001–07; conslt: Amnesty Int, Netherlands Helsinki Ctee, Cncl of Europe; memb: Br Soc of Criminology, American Soc of Criminology; *Books* Patterns of Residential Care (1970), Albany: Birth of a Prison - End of an Era (1977), Future of the Prison System (1981), Prisons in Context (1994), The State of Our Prisons (1995), Doing Research on Crime and Justice (2007); *Recreations* Wagner; *Style*— Prof Roy King

KING, Stephen Daryl; s of Harold King, and Joan, *née* Squire; *b* 19 November 1963; *Educ* Vyners GS Ickenham, New Coll Oxford (BA); *m* 1991, Yvonne Miriam, da of Maurice Nathan; 3 da (Helena Rachel b 1993, Olivia Esther b 1995, Sophie Leah b 1997); *Career*

economist HM Treasy 1985–88; James Capel: Euro economist 1988–89, Japanese economist 1989–92, dep chief economist 1992–96, chief Euro economist 1996–98; HSBC plc: md economics 1998–2006, group chief economist 2006–; memb Shadow Cncl European Central Bank 2007–; columnist The Independent 2001–; first place Extel Survey Euro Econ 1996–99; *Books* EMU: Four Endings and a Funeral (1996), Strainspotting: Moving to a Single European Interest Rate (1997), Bubble Trouble: The US Bubble and How It Will Burst (1999), Decline and Fall: Bubbles, Busts and Deflation (2002), The Consumer Takes it All (2002), Thinking the Unthinkable (2003), The Lucky and the Losers (2004), China, the Renminbi and the World Financial Order (2005), Global Imbalances: Economic Myth and Political Reality (2006), Money Makes the World Go Round (2007); *Recreations* music, playing clarinet and piano, cooking, travelling; *Style*— Stephen King, Esq; ✉ 1 Glenmore Road, Belsize Park, London NW3 4BY (tel 020 7483 1233); HSBC Bank plc, Corporate, Investment Banking and Markets, Level 10, 8 Canada Square, London E14 5HQ (tel 020 7991 6700, fax 020 7992 4864, e-mail stephen.king@hsbcib.com)

KING, Stephen James (Steve); s of Joseph Henry King, of Leicester, and Jean, *née* Bond; *b* 11 September 1956; *Educ* Bosworth Upper Sch, Charles Keene Coll Leicester (OND); *m* 14 July 1984, Philippa Jane, da of George Walter Lay; 1 s (James b 21 May 1992); *Career* presenter and prodr: Loughborough Hosp Broadcasting 1978–81, University Radio Loughborough 1978–81, Centre Radio Leicester 1981–83; Viking Radio Hull: joined as presenter 1984, head of music Viking Radio 1985–88, presentation controller 1988–89, prog controller 1989–91, also gen mangr Viking FM 1990–91; prog controller Hallam FM Sheffield, Yorks regnl prog controller Metro Radio Group plc (parent co of Viking Radio and Radio Hallam, and others) 1993–, prog dir Radio Hallam Ltd 1993–96, md Radio Aire Ltd (parent co of 96.3 Aire FM and magic 828, pt of Emap Radio Ltd) 1996–; dir GE Digital Ltd 1998–; *Recreations* national economics, football, cycling; *Style*— Steve King, Esq; ✉ Radio Aire Ltd, 51 Burley Road, Leeds LS3 1LR (tel 0113 245 2299, fax 0113 244 0445)

KING, Stephen William Pearce; s of William Raymond Pearce King, CBE (d 1980), and Edna Gertrude, *née* Swannock (d 1971); *b* 21 January 1947; *Educ* King Edward's Sch Birmingham; *m* 22 Sept 1973 (m dis 2004), Angela Denise, da of Dennis George Gammon, of Worcester; 2 s (Alexander b 1976, Jeremy b 1978); *Career* admitted slr 1973; princ Stephen King & Co slrs (specialists in child care, criminal and matrimonial law) 1974–97, dealer in fine art (princ Phoenix Fine Art) and freelance journalist and writer 1997–, princ health and nutrition business 1998–, princ travel business 2004–; *Recreations* sport, music, charity work, writing, theatre, travelling, meeting interesting people, art, conservation; *Style*— Stephen W P King, Esq; ✉ Natural Health Company, 34 South Drive, Sutton Coldfield, West Midlands B75 7TF

KING, Dame Thea; DBE (2001, OBE 1985); da of Henry Walter Mayer King, MBE, and Dorothea Louise King; *b* 26 December 1925; *Educ* Bedford HS, RCM; *m* Jan 1953, Frederick Thurston, CBE (d Dec 1953); *Career* clarinettist; Sadler's Wells Orch 1950–52, Portia Wind Ensemble 1955–68, London Mozart Players 1956–84, Vesuvius Ensemble 1965–76, Melos Ensemble of London 1974–93; currently memb: English Chamber Orch, Robles Ensemble; frequent soloist broadcaster and recitalist; prof: RCM 1962–87, Guildhall Sch of Music 1988–; recordings: music by Mozart and Brahms, lesser-known 19th-century works and 20th-century works by Lutoslawski, Finzi, Ireland, Maconchy, Britten and other British composers; pubns: Clarinet Solos (Chester Woodwind series, 1977), arrangement of J S Bach Duets for Two Clarinets (1979), Schumann For The Clarinet (1991), Mendelssohn for the Clarinet (1993), The Romantic Clarinet - A Mendelssohn Collection (1994), Tchaikovsky (1995); FRCM, ARCM, FGSM; *Recreations* skiing, cows, pillow-lace; *Style*— Dame Thea King, DBE; ✉ 16 Milverton Road, London NW6 7AS (tel 020 8459 3453)

KING, Thomas George (Tom); s of Thomas Herbert King (d 1974), of Cambridge, and Cecilia Edith, *née* Tromp (d 1986); *b* 21 May 1938; *Educ* Perse Sch Cambridge, Royal Sch of Mines Imperial Coll London (BSc, ARSM, Inst of Petroleum Prize 1958); *m* Jan 1960, Judith Mary Clarke; 2 s (Aivars Thomas b Feb 1961, Warwick Ralph b July 1962), 1 da (Tania Ann b Nov 1963); *Career* Shell Group of Cos 1960–66; Gulf Oil Corp 1966–82: Kuwait Oil Co 1966–74, gen mangr Zaïre Gulf Oil 1974–78, mangr planning 1978–79, vice-pres and gen mangr Cabinda Gulf Oil 1979–82; dir of ops Burmah Oil 1984–86 (gen mangr UK 1982–84), pres and chief exec Trafalgar House Oil and Gas Inc 1986–87; LASMO plc: dir Prodn 1988–89, dir Exploration and Prodn 1990–93, dir New Business 1993–97, non-exec dir 1997–99; non-exec chm: Pipeline Engineering plc 1997–2004, Metoc plc 1997–; memb Soc of Petroleum Engrs, FGS, FInstPet, FInstD; Chevalier Ordre National du Zaïre; *Recreations* rugby, cricket, boating; *Style*— Tom King, Esq; ✉ mobile 07753 608942, e-mail thomas_king@tiscali.co.uk

KING, Hon Mr Justice; Sir Timothy Roger Alan; kt (2007); s of Harold Bonsal King (d 1992), of Liverpool, and Dorothy, *née* Watts; *b* 5 April 1949; *Educ* Liverpool Inst (Margaret Bryce scholar), Lincoln Coll Oxford (MA, BCL); *m* 7 June 1986, Bernadette Tracy, *née* Goodman; *Career* called to the Bar Lincoln's Inn 1973 (bencher 2000), practising barr Northern Circuit 1973–2007, QC 1991, recorder 1991–2007, judge of the High Court of Justice (Queen's Bench Div) 2007–; *Recreations* travel; *Clubs* Liverpool Athenaeum; *Style*— The Hon Mr Justice King; ✉ Royal Courts of Justice, Strand, London WC2A 2LL

KING, His Hon Judge Timothy Russell; s of Charles Albert King (d 1988), and Elizabeth Lily, *née* Alexander (d 1996); *b* 4 June 1946; *Educ* St Mary's Coll Southampton, Inns of Court Sch of Law; *m* 1, 1973 (m dis 1979); 2 s (Anthony Laurence b 25 Nov 1973, Gregory James b 14 Oct 1974); m 2, 1989, Rotraud (Jane) Webster-King, da of Wilhelm Karl Oppermann (d 1994), of Hannover, Germany; *Career* HM Dip Service (Colonial Office) 1966–67; called to the Bar Gray's Inn 1970; in practice 1971–86, dep judge advocate 1986–90, asst judge advocate-gen 1990–95, asst recorder 1989–93, recorder of the Crown Court 1993–95, circuit judge (South Eastern Circuit) 1995–; legal memb Mental Health Review Tbnl 2002–; pres St Leonard's Soc 1998–2006; *Recreations* sailing, skiing, classical music, reading, walking, cooking and (occasional) golf; *Clubs* Royal London Yacht (Cowes), Island Sailing (Cowes), Osborne Golf; *Style*— His Hon Judge Timothy King; ✉ The Crown Court at Snaresbrook, Hollybush Hill, London E11 1QW (tel 020 8530 0000)

KING, Sir Wayne Alexander; 8 Bt (UK 1815), of Charlestown, Roscommon; s of Sir Peter Alexander King, 7 Bt (d 1973), and Jean Margaret, *née* Cavell (d 2001); *b* 2 February 1962; *Educ* Sir Roger Mawood's Sch Sandwich, Algonquin Coll Ontario; *m* 1, 1984 (m dis 1990), Laura Ellen, da of Donald James Lea, of Almonte, Ontario; 1 s (Peter Richard Donald b 1988); m 2, 2003, Deborah Lynn, da of Doug MacDougall, and Marilyn MacDougall, of Sydney, Nova Scotia; *Heir* s, Peter King; *Style*— Sir Wayne King, Bt; ✉ 146 High Street, Almonte, Ontario, Canada K0A 1A0

KING, William Lawrence; s of Ian Lawrence King (d 1974), and Maisie, *née* Cooke (d 1988); *b* 29 December 1947; *Educ* Oundle, Trinity Hall Cambridge (MA); *m* 24 May 1975, Jane, da of Philip George Wrixon, of Norton Canon, Herefords; 2 s (Edward b 1979 d 1997, Tom b 1981); *Career* ptnr Macfarlanes slrs 1979–2000 (joined 1970); chm Maresfield PC 2003–; Master Worshipful Co of Slrs 1996–97; *Recreations* golf, beagling; *Style*— William King, Esq; ✉ tel 01825 713798, e-mail w@wlking.com

KING-FARLOW, Charles Roderick; s of Roderick Sydney King-Farlow (d 1988), and Alice Frances Joan, *née* Ashley (d 1988); *b* 16 February 1940; *Educ* Eton, Trinity Coll Oxford (MA); *m* 1965, Tessa, da of Robert Lawrence Raikes (d 1989); 1 da (Alice Caroline 1968), 1 s (Joshua Michael b 1971); *Career* admitted slr 1965; ptnr Pinsent Curtis (formerly Pinsent & Co) 1969–2001; dir ISS UK Ltd 1969–2001; conslt Martineau Johnson; pres Birmingham Law Soc 1991–92; vice-pres Fedn of European Bars 1992–93; Law Soc: hon auditor 1995–97, memb Audit Ctee 1997–99; chm Midlands Arts Centre 1985–89, chm Clent Hills Ctee of the Nat Tst 2000–; memb: CBSO Cncl of Mgmnt 1972–80, Taxation Ctee of Historic Houses Assoc 1980–, Friends of Birmingham Museums and Art Gallery Ctee 1972–78 and 1983–88, Bd Birmingham Opera Co 1987–92 and 1999–, Public Art Cmmns Agency 1990–2000; tstee The Wye and Usk Fndn 1997–; *Recreations* gardening, fishing, skiing; *Clubs* Oriental; *Style*— Charles King-Farlow, Esq

KING OF BRIDGWATER, Baron (Life Peer UK 2001), of Bridgwater in the County of Somerset; Thomas Jeremy (Tom) King; CH (1992), PC (1979); s of John H King, JP, of Langford, Somerset; *b* 13 June 1933; *Educ* Rugby, Emmanuel Coll Cambridge; *m* 1960, (Elizabeth) Jane, 3 and yst da of late Brig Robert Tilney, CBE, DSO, TD, DL, Lord of the Manor of Sutton Bonington (maternal gs of Sir Ernest Paget, 1 Bt); 1 s, 1 da; *Career* Nat Serv Somerset LI and King's African Rifles (Tanganyika and Kenya), formerly with E S & A Robinson Ltd Bristol (rising to div gen mangr), chm Sale Tilney & Co 1971–79 (dir 1965–79); MP (Cons) Bridgwater 1970–2001; PPS: to Min of Posts and Telecommunications 1970–72, to Min for Industrial Devpt 1972–74; vice-chm Cons Parly Industry Ctee 1974; oppn front bench spokesman on: industry 1975–76, energy 1976–79; min of state for local govt and environmental servs DOE 1979–83; sec of state for: environment Jan-June 1983, transport June-Oct 1983, employment Oct 1983–85, Northern Ireland 1985–1989, defence 1989–1992; chm Intelligence and Security Ctee 1994–2001; memb Ctee on Standards in Public Life 1994–97; chm London Int Exhbn Centre (Excel), non-exec dir Electra Private Equity plc; *Style*— The Rt Hon the Lord King of Bridgwater, CH, PC

KING OF WEST BROMWICH, Baron (Life Peer UK 1999), of West Bromwich in the County of West Midlands; Tarsem King; JP (West Bromwich 1987); s of Ujagar Singh, of Kultham, Punjab, India, and Dalip Kaur; *b* 24 April 1937; *Educ* Khalsa HS Dosanjh Kalan, Univ of India (BA), Nat Foundry Coll (Dip Foundry Technol and Mgmnt), Aston Univ (Postgrad Dip Mgmnt Studies), Teacher Trg Coll Wolverhampton (Teacher's Cert), Univ of Essex (MSc); *m* 1957, Mohinder Kaur, da of Gurdev Singh, and Satwant Kaur; 1 s (Hon Rajinder Singh b 1972); *Career* lab asst 1960–62, foundry trainee 1964–65, teacher 1968–74 (dep head of mathematics 1974–90), md Sandwell Polybags Ltd 1990–; sits as Labour Peer in House of Lords; dep ldr Sandwell Cncl 1992, ldr Sandwell MBC 1997–2000, mayor of Sandwell 2001 (dep mayor 1982); chm West Bromwich Town Ctee 2002–; tstee S Staffs Water Disconnections Charitable Tst, vice-pres West Bromwich and District YMCA; *Recreations* reading, music; *Style*— The Rt Hon the Lord King of West Bromwich; ✉ House of Lords, London SW1A 0PW (tel and fax 0121 532 5688)

KING-SMITH, Ronald Gordon (Dick); s of Capt Ronald King-Smith, DSO, MC (d 1980), of Bitton, Glos, and Gay, *née* Boucher (d 1980); *b* 27 March 1922; *Educ* Marlborough, Univ of Bristol (BEd); *m* 1, 6 Feb 1943, Myrle (d 2000), da of Gp Capt Tom Harry England, DSC, AFC (d 1975), of Malta; 1 s (Giles b 1953), 2 da (Juliet b 1945, Elizabeth (Mrs Rose) b 1948); m 2, 11 April 2001, Zona Bedding; *Career* WWII serv Lt Grenadier Gds 1941–46 (wounded Italy 1944, despatches); farmer 1947–67, teacher 1976–82, writer of children's books 1978–; *Books* incl: The Fox Busters (1978), Daggie Dogfoot (1980), The Mouse Butcher (1981), Magnus Powermouse (1982), The Queen's Nose (1983), The Sheep-Pig (1983), Harry's Mad (1984), Saddlebottom (1985), Noah's Brother (1986), Tumbleweed (1987), The Toby Man (1988), Martin's Mice (1988), George Speaks (1988), Dodos are For Ever (1989), Paddy's Pot of Gold (1990), The Water Horse (1990), Alphabeasts (1990), Jungle Jingles (1990), and a great many more; *Recreations* writing children's books; *Style*— Dick King-Smith, Esq; ✉ Diamond's Cottage, Queen Charlton, Keynsham, Bristol BS31 2SJ

KINGARTH, Rt Hon Lord; Hon Derek Robert Alexander Emslie; PC (2006); 2 s of Baron Emslie, MBE, PC (Life Peer) (d 2002); bro of Hon Nigel Hannington Emslie (Hon Lord Emslie) and Dr the Hon Richard Emslie, *qqv*; *b* 21 June 1949; *Educ* Edinburgh Acad, Trinity Coll Glenalmond, Gonville & Caius Coll Cambridge (BA, history scholar), Univ of Edinburgh (LLB); *m* 1974, Elizabeth Jane Cameron, da of Andrew Maclaren Carstairs; 3 c; *Career* advocate, QC (Scot 1987); standing jr counsel DHSS 1979–87, standing jr counsel MDDUS 1980–87, advocate depute 1985–88, pt/t chm Pension Appeal Tbnl 1988–95, pt/t chm Medical Appeal Tbnl 1990–95; vice-dean Faculty of Advocates 1995–97, senator of the Coll of Justice 1997–; *Style*— The Rt Hon Lord Kingarth; ✉ Supreme Courts, Edinburgh EH1 1RQ

KINGDOM, David; s of Eric Kingdom, of Scarborough, N Yorks, and Patricia Anne Kingdom; *b* 26 May 1955; *Educ* Riley HS Hull, Hull Sch of Architecture (DipArch), Leeds Met Univ (Dip Arbitration and Construction Law); *m* 1987 (m dis); 1 s (Louis Michael Alexander b 25 March 1990); *Career* architect: Br Rail Chief Architect's Dept York 1974–84, Deutsche Bundesbahn Architekten Frankfurt 1984–85, Fitzroy Robinson Partnership 1985–87, Abbey Hanson Rowe Huddersfield 1987–99; ptnr Abbey Holford Rowe Manchester 1999–2002, dir Aedas Architects Manchester and London 2002– (ptnr 1994–); memb Interact Construction Club (past chm); RIBA 1982, MAPM 1994, ACIArb 1999, MCMI; *Recreations* fell walking, horse riding; *Clubs* Manchester Interact Soc; *Style*— David Kingdom, Esq; ✉ 30 North Road, Kirkburton, Huddersfield, West Yorkshire HD8 0RH (tel 01484 606555, e-mail alpujarra26@hotmail.com); Aedas Architects, 5–8 Hardwick Street, London EC1R 4RB (tel 020 7837 9789, fax 020 7837 9676, e-mail david.kingdom@aedas.com)

KINGHAM, Richard; s of James Richard Kingham (d 1977), and Loretta Catherine Kingham; *b* 2 August 1946, Lafayette, IN; *Educ* Woodward Sch Washington DC, George Washington Univ (BA, tstee scholar), Univ of Virginia Sch of Law (JD, Order of the Coif); *m* 6 July 1968, Justine, *née* McClung; 1 s (Richard Patterson b 4 Nov 1987); *Career* memb DC Bar 1973, registered foreign lawyer England & Wales 1993; editorial asst Washington Star 1964–68 and 1969–70; US Army 1968–69; Virginia Govr's Cncl on the Environment 1971; Covington & Burling: assoc Washington 1973–81, ptnr 1981–, coordinator Food and Drug Practice Gp Washington 1981–84, managing ptnr London office 1996–2000, memb Mgmnt Ctee 2000–04, coordinator Life Sciences Industry Gp 2001–, coordinator Industry, Regulatory and Legislative Umbrella Gp 2005–; lectr Univ of Virginia Sch of Law 1977–90, lectr in grad prog of pharmaceutical med Univ of Wales and Cardiff Univ 1998–, adjunct prof Georgetown Univ Law Centre 2003–; memb Ctee: Inst of Med Nat Acad of Sciences USA, Nat Advsy Allergy and Infectious Diseases Cncl Nat Insts of Health USA, Dean's Cncl and Business Advsy Cncl Univ of Virginia Sch of Law; treas and memb PCC and pres American Friends St Peter's Church Eaton Sq; author of numerous articles in professional jls; *Recreations* vertebrate palaeontology; *Clubs* Reform; *Style*— Richard Kingham, Esq; ✉ Covington & Burling, 265 Strand, London WC2R 1BH (tel 020 7067 2000, fax 020 7067 2222, e-mail rkingham@cov.com)

KINGHAM, Tess; *b* 4 May 1963; *Educ* Dartford GS for Girls, Univ of London (BA), UEA (PGCE); *m* 1991, Mark Luetchford; 2 da (Rosa b June 1995, Natasha b Jan 2000), 1 s (Karl b Jan 2000); *Career* Norfolk liaison offr Br Tst for Conservation Volunteers 1985, nat appeals offr War on Want 1985–90, mktg and communications dir Blue Cross 1990–92, ed Youth Express (Daily Express/Crime Concern Publication) 1992–94, communications exec Oxfam 1994–96, head of fund-raising War on Want 1996–97, MP (Lab) Gloucester 1997–2001; memb: House of Commons Int Devpt Select Ctee 1997–2001, All Pty Parly Human Rights Gp 1997–2001, All Pty Parly Gp on Cuba; sec All Pty Gp on Rwanda, the Great Lakes Region and the Prevention of Genocide, chm All Pty Western Sahara

Parly Gp 1997–2001; contested (Lab) Cotswolds Euro elections 1994; memb Cncl Overseas Devpt Inst; currently writer and conslt: World Bank Inst, Amnesty International, Oxfam, id21; *Publications* e-Parliaments (for the World Bank Institute, 2003); *Style*— Ms Tess Kingham

KINGHAN, Neil; CB (2005); s of Derek Kinghan (d 1991), and Esmé, *née* Webb; *b* 20 August 1951; *Educ* Brentwood Sch, Hertford Coll Oxford (MA, MPhil); *m* 1994, Dr Lilian Pusavat; *Career* DOE: private sec to Parly Under Sec 1978–80, princ 1980–87, private sec to Mins of Housing Ian Gow then John Patten 1984–87, head Sport and Recreation Div 1987–90, head Homelessness Policy Div 1990–92, dir Housing Policy and Private Sector 1992–94, dir Departmental Task Force 1994–96, dir Local Govt Fin Policy 1996–97; Local Govt Assoc: dir of local govt fin 1997–2001, dir Econ and Environmental Policy Div 2002–03; DG Local and Regnl Governance Gp Dept for Communities and Local Govt (formerly ODPM) 2003–; *Recreations* cricket, skiing, buying books; *Clubs* Surrey CC; *Style*— Neil Kinghan, Esq, CB; ✉ Eland House, Bressenden Place, London SW1E 5DO

KINGHORN, Prof George Robert; s of Alan Douglas Kinghorn, of Allendale, Northumberland, and Lilian Isobel, *née* Henderson; *b* 17 August 1949; *Educ* Royal GS Newcastle upon Tyne, Univ of Sheffield (MB ChB, MD); *m* 14 July 1973, Sheila Anne, da of Haydn Wilkinson Littlewood, of Sheffield; 1 s (Robert b 1978), 1 da (Joanne b 1982); *Career* trg in gen med Royal Hosp and Royal Infirmary Sheffield 1972–76, sr registrar in genito-urinary med Royal Infirmary Sheffield 1976–78, conslt in genito-urinary med General Infirmary Leeds 1979–; Univ of Sheffield: sr clinical lectr i/c Sub-Dept of Genito-Urinary Med 1979–2005, hon prof of genito-urinary med 2005–; Sheffield Teaching Hosps NHS Fndn Tst: conslt physician in genito-urinary med 1979–, clinical dir of communicable diseases 1991–; WHO conslt: Sri Lanka 1985, Tunisia 1987; EEC conslt Kenya 1988; chm Advsy Sub-Ctee on Genito-Urinary Med Trent Region 1989–93 (memb 1978–, vice-chm 1985–89), memb Trent Regnl Med Ctee 1989–93; chm: Special Advsy Ctee in Genito-Urinary Med 1986–87 (memb 1981–84, sec 1984–86), Regnl Educn Ctee Genito-Urinary Med 1993–97, Ctee on Genito-Urinary Med RCP 1991–95 (memb 1983–86, hon sec 1986–90), Herpes Simplex Panel 2003–; hon sec Br Co-operative Clinical Gp 1983–93 (chm 1996–99); memb: Clinical Medicine Bd RCP 1994–95, PHLS STI/HIV Ctee 1996–, Nat Ctee Providers of AIDS Care and Treatment (PACT) 1996–, MRC Ctee on Epidemiological Studies in AIDS (CESA) 1998–2002, Exec Ctee Br HIV Assoc 1999–2001, Jt Liaison Ctee on GU Med RCP 1999–2001, Nat Sexual Health and HIV Strategy Working Gps 1999–2001, MRC Sexual Health and HIV Research Ctee 2003–, Ind Advsy Gp in Sexual Health and HIV 2003–, Coll of Experts 2006–; tstee: Med Fndn for AIDS and Sexual Health (MedFASH) 2002–, Br Assoc for Sexual Health and HIV (BASHH) 2003–; memb Editorial Bd: Int Jl of STD and AIDS 1990–, Sexually Transmitted Infections 1990–; memb: Med Soc for Study of Venereal Diseases 1976– (pres 1999–2001, tstee 1999–2003), E Midlands Soc of Physicians 1979–, Assoc of Genito-Urinary Medicine; MRCP 1986, FRCP 1988; *Publications* author of 3 books, 44 book chapters and over 250 peer reviewed publications; *Recreations* travel, gardening, home computers, sport; *Style*— Prof George Kinghorn; ✉ Department of Genitourinary Medicine, Royal Hallamshire Hospital, Glossop Road, Sheffield S10 2JF (tel 0114 271 3524, fax 0114 271 3408, e-mail g.r.kinghorn@virgin.net or g.r.kinghorn@sheffield.ac.uk or g.r.kinghorn@sth.nhs.uk)

KINGHORN, Myra; da of Alan Douglas Kinghorn (d 1993), and Lilian Isobel Kinghorn (d 1994); *b* 24 January 1951; *Educ* La Sagesse HS Newcastle upon Tyne, UCW Aberystwyth (BLib); *m* 1986, Richard John Haycocks; 2 s (Thomas b 20 May 1987, James b 20 Aug 1990); *Career* mgmnt trainee National Westminster Bank 1973–74, audit mangr Deloitte Haskins & Sells 1974–81, mangr financial servs Uniroyal Ltd 1981–82, audit mangr Binder Hamlyn 1982–84, exec mangr Ernst & Young 1984–88, chief exec and dir Investors Compensation Scheme Ltd 1988–2001; non-exec dir Serious Fraud Office 2001–04, memb Occupational Pensions Regulatory Authy (OPRA) 2003–04, chief exec Pension Protection Fund 2004–06; chartered dir IOD 2000; FCA 1978; *Recreations* French, music, theatre, cooking, gardening; *Style*— Miss Myra Kinghorn

KINGSALE, 31 Baron (I c 1340, precedence 1397); (Nevinson) Mark de Courcy; Premier Baron of Ireland; s of Nevinson Russell de Courcy (d 1999), and Nora Lydia, *née* Plint (d 1994); ggggs of Adm Hon Michael de Courcy, 3 s of 25(20) Baron Kingsale; suc kinsman, 30 Baron Kingsale, 2005; *b* 11 May 1958; *Style*— The Lord Kingsale; ✉ 22 Armadale Road, Remuera, Auckland 1050, New Zealand (e-mail nmdecourcy@clear.net.nz)

KINGSDOWN, Baron (Life Peer UK 1993), of Pemberton in the County of Lancashire; Sir Robert (Robin) Leigh-Pemberton; KG (1994), PC (1987); s of Capt Robert Douglas Leigh Pemberton, MBE, MC, JP (d 1964), of Torry Hill, Sittingbourne, Kent, and Helen Isabel, *née* Payne-Gallwey (d 1985); bro of Jeremy Leigh Pemberton, CBE, DL, *qv*; *b* 5 January 1927; *Educ* Eton, Trinity Coll Oxford; *m* 8 July 1953, Rosemary Davina, OBE (1995), da of Lt-Col David Walter Arthur William Forbes, MC (ka 1943), of Callander, Falkirk, and Diana (d 1982; who m 2, 1946, 6 Marquess of Exeter who d 1981, gda of 1 Baron Faringdon); 4 s (1 decd) (Hon John b 16 March 1955, Hon James b 10 Dec 1956, Hon Edward b 10 Jan 1959, Hon William b 20 March 1964); *Career* Lt Grenadier Gds, served Palestine 1946–48; Hon Col: Kent and Sharpshooters Yeo Sqdn 1979–92, 265 (Kent County London Yeo) Signal Sqdn (V) 1979–92, 5 (Vol) Bn The Queen's Regt 1987–93; pres: SE TA&VR Assoc 1986–95, Kent SSAFA - Forces Help until 2002; hon pres Kent Wing Air Trg Corps until 2002; called to the Bar Inner Temple 1954, practised London and SE Circuit 1954–60, hon bencher 1983; dir: Birmid Qualcast 1966–83 (dep chm 1970, chm 1975–77), University Life Assurance Society 1967–78, Redland Ltd 1972–83, Equitable Life Assurance Society 1979–83 (vice-pres 1982–83); chm: National Westminster Bank 1977–83 (dir 1972–83, dep chm 1974), Ctee of London Clearing Bankers 1982–83; govr Bank of England 1983–93; non-exec dir: Glaxo Welcome plc 1993–96, Hambros plc 1993–98, Redland plc 1993–97, Foreign and Colonial Investment Trust plc 1993–98; memb NEDC 1982–92; tstee: Royal Acad of Arts Tst 1982–87 (now tstee emeritus), Kent CCC, Kent Co Playing Fields Assoc, Kent Co Agric Soc (pres 1984–85 and 2001–05), Rochester Cathedral Tst (until 2002), The Kent Fndn (until 2002), RASE 1993–2002 (pres 1989–90, hon tstee 2002–); pres E of England Agric Soc 1986–87; sometime pres: Kent Rural Community Cncl, St John Cncl for Kent; former patron Red Cross for Kent; pro-chllr Univ of Kent 1977–83; co cnclr Kent 1961–77 (chm Cncl 1972–75); JP 1961–75, HM Lord-Lt Kent 1982–2002 (DL 1970, Vice Lord-Lt 1972–82); chm Canterbury Cathedral Tst 1983–, seneschal of Canterbury Cathedral 1983–; hon fell Trinity Coll Oxford 1984; Liveryman Worshipful Co of Mercers; Hon DCL Univ of Kent 1983; Hon DLitt: City of London Univ 1988, Loughborough Univ 1989, City Poly 1990; memb RSA, Hon FCIB, KStJ 1983; *Recreations* country life; *Clubs* Brooks's, Cavalry and Guards'; *Style*— The Rt Hon Lord Kingsdown, KG; ✉ Torry Hill, Sittingbourne, Kent ME9 0SP

KINGSHOTT, (Albert) Leonard; s of Albert Leonard Kingshott, of Ingatestone, Essex, and Katherine Bridget, *née* Connelley; *b* 16 September 1930; *Educ* LSE (BSc); *m* 10 Aug 1957, Valerie, da of Ronald Simpson (d 1964); 1 da (Nicola b 1958), 2 s (Adrian b 1960, Brendan b 1962); *Career* RAF (FO) 1952–55; fin analyst BP Corp 1955–59, economist British Nylon Spinners 1960–62, fin mangr Iraq Petroleum Co 1963–65; treas 1965–70: Ford of Europe, Ford Motor Co, Ford of Britain; fin dir Whitbread Group 1970–72, md (fin) British Steel Corp 1972–77; Lloyds Bank plc: dir Merchant Banking Div 1977, dir Int Banking Div 1977–89, exec dir Europe 1980, exec dir Marketing & Planning 1983, dep chief exec Marketing & Planning 1985 and dir several assoc cos; exec dir (banking) The Private Bank and Tst Co Ltd 1989–91, exec dir Rosehaugh plc 1991 (chm 1992–93); appointed Crown Agent 1989–91, memb Monopolies and Mergers Cmmn 1990–96; dir Mutual Management Services 1993–96, md MicroTrace Ltd 1996–; chm Delamas Properties Ltd 1997–; md Trace Tag Ltd 2001–; non-exec dir: Shandwick IPR (formerly Shandwick International plc) 1993–99, New Markets Foods Ltd 1994–97; chm Oakbridge Counselling Gp 1990–96; govr and assoc memb Faculty Ashbridge Mgmnt Coll; FCIS; *Books* Investment Appraisal (1967); *Recreations* reading, chess, golf; *Style*— Leonard Kingshott, Esq; ✉ 4 Delamas, Beggar Hill, Fryerning, Ingatestone, Essex

KINGSLAND, Charles Richard; s of Richard Alan Kingsland, of Nottingham, and Noreen Monica, *née* Hayes; *b* 29 October 1957; *Educ* Mundella GS Nottingham, Univ of Liverpool (MB ChB, MD, DRCOG); *m* Catharine Anne, da of Peter O'Neill; 1 s (Joseph Edward), 2 da (Charlotte Alexandra, Lucy Elizabeth); *Career* house offr Royal Liverpool Hosp 1982–83, registrar Liverpool Hosps 1983–87, res fell Middx Hosp 1987–89, sr lectr in obstetrics and gynaecology Univ of Liverpool 1992–93 (lectr 1989–92), conslt 1993–; memb: BMA 1982, American Fertility Soc 1992, Br Fertility Soc (memb Ctee 1992–); FRCOG; *Recreations* soccer, hiking; *Style*— Charles Kingsland, Esq; ✉ The Women's Hospital, Crown Street, Liverpool L8 7SS (tel 0151 708 9988, fax 0151 702 4137, e-mail ckingsland@yahoo.com)

KINGSLAND, Baron (Life Peer UK 1994), of Shrewsbury in the County of Shropshire; Sir Christopher James Prout; PC (1994), kt (1990), TD (1987), QC (1988), DL (Shropshire 1997); s of Frank Yabsley Prout, MC and bar (d 1980), and Doris Lucy, *née* Osborne (d 1983); *b* 1 January 1942; *Educ* Sevenoaks Sch, Univ of Manchester (BA), The Queen's Coll Oxford (BPhil, DPhil); *Career* TA Offr (Maj) OU OTC 1966–74, 16/5 The Queen's Royal Lancers 1974–82, 3 Armd Div 1982–88, RARO 1988–97; called to the Bar Middle Temple 1972 (bencher 1996, master of the garden 1999–); recorder (Wales & Chester Circuit) 2000– (asst recorder 1997–99), dep High Court judge 2005–; ESU fell Columbia Univ NYC 1963–64, staff memb Int Bank for Reconstruction and Devpt (UN) Washington DC 1966–69, Leverhulme fell and lectr in law Univ of Sussex 1969–79; MEP (Cons) Shropshire and Stafford 1979–94; dep whip Euro Democratic Gp (EDG) 1979–82, chief whip of the EDG 1983–87, chm Parly Ctee on Legal Affrs 1987, ldr of Cons MEPs Euro Parl 1987–94, chm and ldr of the EDG 1987–92, vice-chm EPP Parly Gp 1992–94, chm Sub-Ctee F Select Ctee on European Communities House of Lords 1996–97; shadow Lord Chllr 1997–; chm: Plymouth Marine Lab 2002–, Jersey Competition and Regulatory Authy 2004–; pres Shrops and W Midlands Agric Soc 1993; hon fell The Queen's Coll Oxford 2006; Master Shrewsbury Drapers Co 1995; La Grande Médaille de la Ville de Paris 1988; Schuman Medal 1995; *Books* Market Socialism in Yugoslavia (1985), Halsbury's Laws of England (contrib Vols 8, 51 and 52, 4 edn); author of misc lectures, pamphlets, chapters and articles; *Recreations* boating, gardening, musical comedy, the turf; *Clubs* White's, Pratt's, Beefsteak, Buck's (hon), Royal Ocean Racing, Royal Yacht Squadron; *Style*— The Rt Hon Lord Kingsland, PC, TD, QC, DL; ✉ House of Lords, London SW1 (tel 020 7219 3000)

KINGSLEY, Sir Ben; kt (2002); s of Rahimtulla Harji Bhanji, and Anna Lyna Mary, *née* Goodman; *b* 31 December 1943; *Educ* Manchester Grammar; *Career* actor; associate artist RSC; patron and affiliated memb of many charitable organisations; Hon MA Univ of Salford 1984; memb: BAFTA 1983, American Acad of Motion Picture Arts and Sciences; Padma Sri (India) 1985; *Theatre* incl: RSC 1967–86 (title roles incl Hamlet and Othello), Nat Theatre 1977–78 (leading roles incl Mosca in Volpone), Waiting for Godot (Old Vic) 1997; *Film* incl: Gandhi, Betrayal, Turtle Diary, Harem, Silas Marner, Maurice, Slipstream, Testimony, Pascali's Island, Without a Clue, Murderers Amongst Us, Fifth Monkey, The Children, Bugsy, Sneakers, Searching for Bobby Fischer, Dave, Schindler's List, Death and the Maiden, Species, Twelfth Night, The Assignment, Photographing Fairies, Sweeney Todd, Weapons of Mass Distraction, The Confession: Crime & Punishment, Alice in Wonderland, Spookey House, Sexy Beast, Rules of Engagement, What Planet are you From, The Triumph of Love, Anne Frank: The Whole Story, Artifical Intelligence: AI, Suspect Zero, Sound of Thunder, House of Sand and Fog, Thunderbirds, Oliver Twist; *Awards* incl: Oscar, BAFTA (twice), Golden Globe (twice), NY Critics', LA Critics', Grammy, Simon Wiesenthal Humanitarian, Berlin Golden Camera, Evening Standard Best Actor Award (for Schindler's List) 1995, European Film Acad Best Actor Award 2001, Br Ind Film Award for Best Actor 2001, Screen Actor's Guild Best Actor Award 2002, Broadcast Critics' Award for Best Actor 2002; *Style*— Sir Ben Kingsley; ✉ c/o ICM Ltd, Oxford House, 76 Oxford Street, London W1D 1BS (tel 020 7636 6565, fax 020 7323 0101)

KINGSLEY, David John; OBE (2006); s of Walter John Kingsley, and Margery, *née* Walden; *b* 10 July 1929; *Educ* Southend HS for Boys, LSE (BSc(Econ)); *m* 1, July 1955 (m dis), Enid Sophia, da of Thomas Jones, MBE (d 1985), of Llandeilo; 2 da (Nichola Sophia b 1962, Nadia b 1964); m 2, May 1968 (m dis), Gillian (d 2000), da of George Leech (d 1978); 2 s (Andrew John b 1966, Paul David b 1967); m 3, 25 Oct 1988, Gisela Irene, *née* Reichardt; *Career* dir Benton and Bowles Advertising Agency 1961–64, fndr and ptnr Kingsley Manton & Palmer Advertising Agency 1964–78, dir and chm Kimpher Group Communications Group 1969–78, ptnr and chm Kingsley & Kingsley Business Consultancy 1974–, dir Francis Kyle Gallery 1978–, chair Worldaware - the centre for world devpt educn, chm Cartoon Arts Tst 1994–2001, chair Discover 1997–2006; dir: Mediawise 2003–06, Fun Radio UK 2004–; advsr Institute of Global Ethics 2002–; memb Devpt Ctee RCM; tstee: The Ireland Fund (UK) 1986–2002, @Bristol 1995–2003, Royal Philharmonic Orch; Lab Parly candidate East Grinstead 1952–54; advsr to: Lab Pty and Govt on Communications 1962–70, Govt of Zambia 1974–82, Govt of Mauritius 1977–81, SDP 1981–87; organiser and creator: The Greatest Children's Party in the World for the Int Year of the Child 1980, HM The Queen's 60th Birthday Celebration, the Creative Summit 1999; hon doctorate Soka Univ Tokyo; LSE: govr LSE (memb Cncl) 1966–2006 (now emeritus govr), hon fell, chair LSE Alumni Assoc; hon memb RCM; FRSA, FIPA, MCSD; *Books* Albion in China (1979), How World War II was Won on the Playing Fields of LSE; *Recreations* music, books, creating happy public events, travel, art; *Clubs* Reform; *Style*— David J Kingsley, Esq, OBE; ✉ Kingsley & Kingsley, 81 Mortimer Road, London N1 5AR (tel 020 7275 8889, e-mail kingsleydavid@btconnect.com)

KINGSLEY, Nicholas William; s of Philip Francis Kingsley (d 2004), and Joan Rosamond, *née* Holliday (d 2004); *b* 14 September 1957, London; *Educ* St Paul's, Keble Coll Oxford (MA); *m* 14 June 1980, Susan Mary, *née* Summerhayes; *Career* archive trainee Bodleian Library Oxford 1978–79, modern records archivist Glos Record Office 1982–89 (asst archivist 1979–82), city archivist Birmingham CC 1989–96, mangr Birmingham Central Library 1996–2000, county and diocesan archivist Glos Record Office 2000–05, head Nat Advsy Servs and sec Historical Manuscripts Cmmn Nat Archives 2005–; Nat Cncl of Archives: memb 1991–, sec 1993–99, vice-chm 2000–01, chm 2001–05; author of articles for Country Life and professional jls; chm Victoria County History Nat Ctee 2005–, chm DLM Forum EU 2006; Hon DLitt Univ of Birmingham 2006; memb Soc of Archivists 1979, FSA 2003; *Books* The Country Houses of Gloucestershire: 1500–1660 (1989, 2 edn 2001), The Country Houses of Gloucestershire: 1660–1830 (1992), The Country Houses of Gloucestershire: 1830–2000 (jtly, 2001); Handlist of the Contents of the Gloucestershire Record Office (1988, 4 edn 2002), Archives Online (1998), Changing the Future of the Past (2003); *Recreations* visiting historic buildings, historical research, photography, food, genealogy; *Style*— Nicholas Kingsley, Esq; ✉ The National Archives, Kew, Richmond, Surrey TW9 4DU (tel 020 8392 5330, e-mail nick.kingsley@nationalarchives.gov.uk)

KINGSLEY, Stephen Michael; s of Ernest Robert Kingsley, of Cheadle, Cheshire, and Ursula Renate, *née* Bochenek (d 1972); *b* 1 June 1952; *Educ* Cheadle Hulme Sch, Univ of Bristol (BSc); *m* 18 March 1982, Michelle, da of Oscar Solovici (d 1983), of Paris; 1 da (Natalie b 1984); *Career* Arthur Andersen: joined 1973, mangr 1979–86, ptnr 1986–2002, head London Capital Markets Gp 1987–92, dir Euro regnl capital mkts 1988–93, dir Euro regnl banking and capital mkts 1993–2002, dir Euro Financial Risk Mgmnt Practice 1995–2002; managing pntr Global Financial Services Industry 2001–02, ptnr DiamondCluster International 2002–04, ceo sales and business devpt Aon Europe 2004–06, head of UK financial servs practice BearingPoint Inc 2006–07, dir LECG London 2007–; memb Tech Panel Securities and Investments Bd 1985–87; visiting lectr Coll of Petroleum Studies Oxford; FCA; *Books* Managing A Foreign Exchange Department (contrib, 1985), Currency Options (contrib, 1985), European Banking and Capital Markets - a strategic survey; *Recreations* travel, ballet, classical music, current affairs; *Style*— Stephen Kingsley, Esq; ✉ 23 Gloucester Walk, London W8 4HZ (tel 020 7937 4525); LECG Limited, Davidson Building, 5 Southampton Street, London WC2E 7HA (e-mail skingsley@lecg.com)

KINGSNORTH, Andrew Norman; s of John Norman Kingsnorth, of Eynsford, Kent, and Kathleen Dorothy, *née* Bassett; *b* 20 November 1948; *Educ* Sevenoaks Sch, Royal Free Hosp Sch of Med (BSc, MB BS, MS); *m* 1 June 1974, Jane Mary, da of Mervyn Bryant Poulter; 2 s (Edward Anthony b 1 July 1977, Peter John b 27 March 1982), 1 da (Bryony Jane b 30 June 1980); *Career* house surgn Addenbrooke's Hosp Cambridge 1974–75, sr house offr Norwich Hosps 1976–77, registrar John Radcliffe Hosp Oxford 1977–80, res fell Harvard Univ Boston 1980–81, lectr in surgery Univ of Edinburgh 1982–86, jr conslt Groote Schuur Hosp Cape Town SA 1986–87, sr lectr and reader in surgery Univ of Liverpool 1987–96, prof of surgery Plymouth Postgrad Med Sch 1996–2002, conslt surgeon Derriford Hosp Plymouth 2002–, hon prof Peninsula Medical Sch 2003–, clinical dir of surgery; RCS: Arris and Gale lectr 1984, memb Ct of Examiners 1994–2000, tutor in Telemedicine 1999–2002; Rodney Smith prize Pancreatic Soc 1993; FACS, FRCS; *Books* Fundamentals of Surgical Practice (jtly, 1998 2 edn 2005) Incisional Hernia (jtly, 2000), Principles of Surgical Practice (jtly, 2001), Advanced Surgical Practice (jtly, 2002), Management of Abdominal Hernias (jtly, 2003); also author of over 140 articles in scientific jls; *Recreations* bell ringing, fell walking, duplicate bridge; *Clubs* Travelling Surgical Soc; *Style*— Andrew Kingsnorth, Esq; ✉ Rowden House, Stoke Road, Noss Mayo, Plymouth PL8 1JG; Department of Surgery, Level 7, Derriford Hospital, Plymouth PL6 8DH (tel 01752 763017, fax 01752 763007, e-mail andrew.kingsnorth@phnt.swest.nhs.uk)

KINGSTON, Jeremy Henry Spencer; s of William Henry Kingston (d 1989), of Brighton, E Sussex, and Elsie, *née* Cooper (d 1980); *b* 5 August 1931; *Educ* Reigate GS; *m* 1967 (m dis 1996), Meg, da of James Ritchie, of Dumbarton; 2 s (Benjamin James b 1968, Rufus William b 1970); *Career* Nat Serv 2 Lt Royal Signals; casually employed Chelsea 1951–55 (coffee houses, sculpture model, barr's clerk's clerk), sec to John Lehmann 1955–57; playwright: No Concern of Mine (Westminster) 1958, Signs of the Times (Vaudeville) 1973, Oedipus at the Crossroads (King's Head) 1977, Making Dickie Happy (Rosemary Branch) 2004; theatre critic: Punch 1964–75, The Times 1985–; *Books* Love Among The Unicorns (1968), and three children's books; *Recreations* long conversations over meals; *Style*— Jeremy Kingston, Esq; ✉ 65 Romulus Court, Brentford Dock, Middlesex TW8 8QL (tel 020 8568 4714, e-mail jhskingston@aol.com); The Times, Pennington Street, London E98 1TA

KINGSTON, (William) Martin; QC (1992); s of William Robin Kingston, of Bishops Frome, Worcs, and Iris Edith, *née* Grocott; *b* 9 July 1949; *Educ* Middlewich Secdy Modern Sch, Hartford Coll of Further Educn, Univ of Liverpool (LLB); *m* 9 Sept 1972, Jill Mary, da of Robert Philip Sidney Bache; 2 da (Joanna Jessie b 3 Feb 1976, Emma Rachel b 9 Dec 1980), 1 s (Thomas Henry Robin b 22 June 1978); *Career* called to the Bar Middle Temple 1972, recorder 1991–99 (asst recorder 1987–91); dep chm Agricultural Lands Tbnl 1985–, asst cmmr Parly Boundary Cmmn for England 1992–; *Recreations* fly fishing, skiing, reading, holidays; *Style*— Martin Kingston, Esq, QC; ✉ No 5 Chambers, Steelhouse Lane, Birmingham B4 6DR (tel 0121 606 0500, fax 0121 606 1501)

KINGSTON, Bishop of 2002–; Rt Rev Dr Richard Ian Cheetham; s of John Brian Margrave Cheetham, and Mollie Louise, *née* Cannell; *b* 18 August 1955; *Educ* Kingston GS, CCC Oxford (MA, PGCE), Ripon Coll Cuddesdon (CertTheol), KCL (PhD); *m* 1977, Felicity Mary; 1 s (Michael b 1979), 1 da (Sarah b 1981); *Career* sci teacher Richmond Sch Yorks 1978–80, physics teacher Eton Coll 1980–83, investment analyst Legal & Gen London 1983–85; ordinand 1985–87, asst curate Holy Cross Newcastle upon Tyne 1987–90, vicar St Augustine Luton 1990–99, rural dean of Luton 1995–98, archdeacon of St Albans 1999–2002; *Publications* Collective Worship: Issues and Opportunities (2004); *Recreations* hockey, squash, tennis, walking, cinema, theatre; *Style*— The Rt Rev the Bishop of Kingston

KINGSTON, (John) Simon; s of (Laurence Henry) Leonard James Kingston (d 1981), and (Patricia) Elisabeth Archer, *née* Clay (d 2000); *b* 29 May 1949, London; *Educ* Highgate Sch, Oxford Poly; *m* 19 Dec 1970, Anna Mary, *née* Latham; 2 s ((John Louis) James b 1973, Charles Edward b 1974); *Career* ed: Faber and Faber 1969–70, Routledge 1971–72, Blandford Press 1973–74, G Bell and Sons 1974–79, variously ed, head of London office and head of editorial, mktg and admin Gordon Fraser 1980–89, gen mangr Marshall Cavendish Books 1989–93, dir of publishing SPCK 1993, gen sec and ceo SPCK 2007 (sr exec offr 2006–); dir Read For Your Life, educn bd advsr Trinity Fndn for Christianity and Culture, chair Religious Publishers Gp Publishing Assoc 2001–; MInstD 2004; Freeman City of London, Liveryman Worshipful Co of Vintners; *Recreations* music, poetry and photography, the year 1762; *Style*— Simon Kingston, Esq; ✉ 135 Gordon Road, London W13 8PL; SPCK, 36 Causton Street, London SW1P 4ST (tel 020 7592 3900, e-mail skingston@spck.org.uk)

KINGTON, Miles Beresford; s of William Beresford Nairn Kington, of Vrondeg Hall, nr Wrexham, and Jean Ann, *née* Sanders; *b* 13 May 1941; *Educ* Glenalmond, Trinity Coll Oxford (BA); *m* 1, 29 Feb 1964 (m dis), Sarah, da of Robert Paine, of Canterbury, Kent; 1 da (Sophie b 1966), 1 s (Thomas b 1968); m 2, 6 June 1987, Caroline, da of Nick Carter, of Knysna, South Africa; 1 s (Adam b 1987); *Career* freelance writer and radio presenter; former asst gardener in Ladbroke Square, former jazz corr The Times, double bass player with Instant Sunshine, literary ed Punch (cr Let's Parler Franglais column) 1973–80; journeyed through Andes for BBC's Great Train Journeys of The World Series (Three Miles High) 1980; humorous columnist for: The Times (cr Moreover) 1981–87, The Independent 1987–; translator of Alphonse Allais (French humorist); *Radio* incl: co-presenter (with Edward Enfield) Double Vision (BBC Radio 4), presenter Reading Music (BBC Radio 2), documentaries on General De Gaulle, General Franco and Django Reinhardt (BBC Radio 4); *Plays* Waiting for Stoppard (Bristol New Vic) 1995, The Death of Tchaikovsky - a Sherlock Holmes Mystery (Edinburgh Festival) 1996; *Books* incl: Let's Parler Franglais!, Let's Parler Franglais Again!, Parlez vous Franglais?, Let's Parler Franglais One More Temps, The Franglais Lieutenant's Woman, Un Four-Pack de Franglais, Miles and Miles, Moreover, Moreover Two, Nature Made Ridiculously Simple, Steaming Through Britain, The Jazz Anthology, Miles Kington's Motorway Madness; *Recreations* bicycling, drinking, trying to remember if I have signed the Official Secrets Act; *Clubs* Ronnie Scott's; *Style*— Miles Kington, Esq; ✉ 40 Lower Stoke, Limpley Stoke, Bath BA2 7FR (tel 01225 722262, fax 01225 723894); c/o The Independent, Independent House, 191 Marsh Wall, London E14 9RS

KININMONTH, James Wyatt; s of Peter Wyatt Kininmonth, of Ashmore, Dorset, and Priscilla Margaret, *née* Sturge; *b* 26 September 1952; *Educ* Harrow, RMA Sandhurst; *m* 19 March 1977, Susie, da of Richard William Griffin, of Albemarle, USA; 2 da (Annabel b 1980, Harriet b 1983), 1 s (Charles b 1985); *Career* 5 Royal Inniskilling Dragoon Gds 1973, Capt 1977, trans to Reserve 1978; dir Kininmonth Holdings 1982–85; md Kininmonth Lambert North America 1987–91 (dir 1985–); dir: Lowndes Lambert North America Ltd 1990–92, Cooper Gay & Co Ltd 1992–; memb Lloyd's since 1983; govr Haberdashers' Aske's Schs Elstree 2003–; Freeman City of London; Liveryman Worshipful Co of Haberdashers 1982; *Recreations* shooting, skiing, golf; *Clubs* City of London, Royal & Ancient, Piltdown, Annabel's; *Style*— J W Kininmonth, Esq; ✉ Old Mill Barn, Isfield, East Sussex TN22 5XJ (tel 01825 750732, e-mail james@kininmonth.com); Cooper Gay & Co Ltd, 52 Leadenhall Street, London EC3A 2EB (tel 020 7480 7322, fax 020 7481 4695)

KINKEAD-WEEKES, Prof Mark; s of Lt-Col Alfred Bernard (Bill) Kinkead-Weekes, MC (d 1960), and Vida May, *née* Kinkead (d 1946); *b* 26 April 1931; *Educ* Potchefstroom Boys HS, Univ of Cape Town (Rhodes scholar), BNC Oxford; *m* March 1959, (Margaret) Joan, da of Benjamin Irvine (d 1966); 2 s (Paul b 1962, Timothy Guy b 1963); *Career* lectr Univ of Edinburgh 1958–65 (asst lectr 1956–58); Univ of Kent at Canterbury: lectr 1965–66, sr lectr 1966–74, prof of English and American literature 1974–84 (emeritus prof 1984–), pro-vice-chllr 1974–77; sometime govr Contemporary Dance Tst; FBA 1992; *Books* William Golding: A Critical Study (with I Gregor, 1967, 2 edn 1984), Samuel Richardson: Dramatic Novelist (1973), D H Lawrence: The Rainbow (ed, 1989), D H Lawrence: Triumph to Exile (1996), William Golding: A Critical Study of the Novels (2002); *Recreations* walking, music; *Style*— Prof Mark Kinkead-Weekes

KINLOCH, Prof Anthony James; *b* 7 October 1946; *Educ* Queen Mary Coll London (PhD), Univ of London (DSc); *m* 1969, Gillian Patricia; 2 s (Ian Anthony b 1975, David Michael Robert b 1981), 1 da (Elizabeth Sarah b 1978); *Career* Royal Armaments R&D Establishment MOD 1972–84; Imperial Coll London: sr lectr 1984–85, reader in engrg adhesives 1985–90, prof of adhesion 1990–; visiting appts: Nat Bureau of Standards Washington DC 1982, Ecole Polytechnique Fédérale de Lausanne 1986, Univ of Utah 1988; UK ed Jl of Adhesion 1985–; US Adhesion Soc Award 1992, Griffith Medal and Prize Inst of Materials 1996; Thomas Hawksley Meml Lectr (Adhesives in Engrg) IMechE 1996, Thomas Hawksley Gold Medal IMechE 1998, Wake Meml Medal Inst of Materials 2002; chair Soc Adhesives Inst of Materials 2000–02; memb: Cncl Inst of Materials 1997–02, EPSRC Coll for Structural Materials 1994–; fell US Adhesion Soc 1995 (pres 2002–04), CChem 1982, FRSC 1982, FIM 1982, CEng 1988, FREng 1997, FCGI 2001, FRS 2007; *Publications* author of two books and more than 200 scientific papers in the field of composite materials, adhesion and adhesives; *Recreations* opera, tennis, walking; *Style*— Prof Anthony J Kinloch, FREng; ✉ Department of Mechanical Engineering, Imperial College of Science, Technology and Medicine, Exhibition Road, London SW7 2BX (tel 020 7594 7802, fax 020 7823 8845, e-mail a.kinloch@imperial.ac.uk)

KINLOCH, Sir David; 13 Bt (NS 1686), of Gilmerton, East Lothian; s of Maj Sir Alexander Davenport Kinloch, 12 Bt (d 1982), and his 2 w, Hilda Anna (d 1986), da of Thomas Walker, of Edinburgh; *b* 5 August 1951; *Educ* Gordonstoun; *m* 1, 1976 (m dis 1986), Susan, da of Arthur Middlewood, of North Side Farm, Kilham; 1 da (Alice b 1976), 1 s (Alexander b 1978); m 2, 1987, Maureen, da of Robert Carswell; 2 s (Christopher Robert b 1988, Matthew Carswell b 20 July 1990); *Heir* s, Alexander Kinloch; *Career* civil engr; *Style*— Sir David Kinloch, Bt; ✉ Gilmerton House, Athelstaneford, North Berwick, East Lothian (tel 01620 880207, fax 01620 880276, e-mail reception@gilmertonhouse.com)

KINLOCH, Sir David Oliphant; 5 Bt (UK 1873), of Kinloch, Co Perth; s of Sir John Kinloch, 4 Bt (d 1992), and Doris Ellaline, *née* Head (d 1997); *b* 15 January 1942; *Educ* Charterhouse; *m* 1, 1968 (m dis 1979), Susan Minette, da of Maj-Gen Robert Elliott Urquhart, CB, DSO; 3 da (Katherine Cecilia b 1972, Emily Nicole b 1974, Nicola Marjorie b 1976); m 2, 1983, Sabine, da of Philippe de Loës, of Geneva, Switzerland; 1 s (Alexander Peter b 1986), 1 da (Sophie b 1994); *Heir* s, Alexander Kinloch; *Career* chartered accountant; dep chief exec Caledonia Investments plc; dir: British Empire Securities and General Trust plc, Sterling Industries plc, Amerindo Internet Fund plc; chm: ISIS Asset Management plc, JPMorgan Fleming Chinese Investment Trust plc, Radio Investments Ltd, Wallem Group Ltd; *Style*— Sir David Kinloch, Bt; ✉ House of Aldie, Fossoway, Kinross-shire KY13 0QH; 29 Walpole Street, London SW3 4QS

KINLOCH ANDERSON, *see:* Anderson

KINLOSS, Lady (S Lordship 1602); Beatrice Mary Grenville; *née* Morgan-Grenville; da of Rev the Master of Kinloss (2 s of Lady Kinloss, 11 holder of title, but he suc er bro in courtesy title); suc grandmother as 12 holder of title 1944; *b* 18 August 1922; *Educ* Ravenscroft Sch Eastbourne; *m* 1950, Dr Greville Stewart Parker Freeman-Grenville (d 2005), s of Rev Ernest Charles Freeman (changed name with husb to Freeman-Grenville, recognised by Lord Lyon King of Arms 1950); 1 s, 2 da; *Heir* s, Master of Kinloss, *qv*; *Career* sat as Ind peer in House of Lords 1964–99; memb House of Lords Ctee on European Communities (Sub Ctee C) 1990–92, has sat on numerous Select Ctees; special interests: disabled persons (especially deaf-blind), water transport, local govt; FRAS 1997; *Recreations* music, gardening, travel in Africa and the Middle East; *Style*— The Rt Hon Lady Kinloss; ✉ North View House, Sheriff Hutton, York YO60 6ST (tel and fax 01347 878447)

KINLOSS, Master of; Hon Bevil David Stewart Chandos Freeman-Grenville; s and h of Lady Kinloss, *qv*; *b* 20 June 1953; *m* 6 Oct 2001, Marie-Thérèse, da of late William Driscoll, and wid of Stuart Sturrock; *Style*— The Master of Kinloss; ✉ Orchard House, 6 Warwick Close, Sheriff Hutton, York YO60 6QW (tel 01347 878346, e-mail bevilkinloss@aol.com)

KINMONTH, Prof Ann Louise; CBE (2002); da of Maurice Henry Kinmonth, of East Langton, Leics, and Gwendolyn Stella, *née* Phillipps; *b* 8 January 1951; *Educ* Market Harborough GS, New Hall Cambridge (exhibitioner, MB BChir, MA, MD), LSHTM (MSc), St Thomas' Hosp London (exhibitioner); *Career* res fell Univ Dept of Paediatrics Oxford 1978–81, vocational trg for gen practice Berinsfield Oxon 1981–82, princ in gen practice Aldermoor Health Centre Southampton 1983–96, prof of primary med care Univ of Southampton 1992–96 (reader 1990–92), prof of gen practice Univ of Cambridge 1997–; James Mackenzie Prize for contribs to research and practice RCGP, William Pickles lectr 2001; author of pubns on the orgn and delivery of diabetes care in childhood and adult life, on preventive med and gen practice; memb: British Diabetic Assoc, Norfolk Naturalists Tst; FZS, FRCP, FRCGP, FRCPCH, FMedSci; *Recreations* walking, sailing wooden boats, reading and talking; *Style*— Prof Ann Louise Kinmonth, CBE; ✉ General Practice and Primary Care Research Unit, Institute of Public Health, University Forvie Site, Robinson Way, Cambridge CB2 0SR (tel 01223 763830, fax 01223 762515, e-mail alk25@medschl.cam.ac.uk)

KINNAIRD, Nicky; *Educ* Victoria Coll Belfast, Univ of Reading (BSc); *Career* chartered surveyor 1987–92; fndr Space NK Ltd lifestyle concept store Covent Garden 1993, fndr Space NK Apothecary luxury skincare and make-up boutiques (now trading at 54 UK locations) 1996, opened SPAce NK day spa Notting Hill 2000; Space NK signature products launched internationally 2001, launched Space NK online store 2004, opened first Space NK Apothecary store in US 2007, launched Space NK US online store 2007; *Books* Awaken Your Senses, Change Your Life (2002); *Recreations* running, yoga, pilates, tennis, cinema, art, books; *Style*— Ms Nicky Kinnaird; ✉ Space NK Ltd, 5th Floor,

K

Shropshire House, 11–20 Capper Street, London WC1E 6JA (tel 020 7299 4999, fax 020 7299 4998, e-mail nk@spacenk.com)

KINNIMENT, Prof David John; s of Herbert John Kinniment (d 1974), and Iris Henrietta, *née* Vivaudou (d 1987); *b* 10 July 1940; *Educ* Haberdashers' Aske's, Univ of Manchester (BSc, MSc, PhD); *m* 11 Aug 1962, Anne, da of James Lupton, of Burnley, Lancs; 2 da (Michelle Jane b 19 Aug 1964, Sarah Lynne b 15 Sept 1966); *Career* Univ of Manchester: lectr in electrical engrg 1964, lectr in computer sci 1964–71, sr lectr in computer sci Univ of Manchester 1971–79; Univ of Newcastle upon Tyne: prof of electronics 1979–98 (emeritus prof 1998–), head Dept of Electrical and Electronic Engrg 1982–90 and 1995–97; author of over 100 articles in professional and academic jls; SERC: memb Sub-Ctee Solid State Devices 1979–83 and Microelectronics Facilities 1982–86, memb Ctee Alvey Industrial and Academic Liaison Ctee 1984–87; memb: Cncl Microelectronics Application Res Inst 1983–90, Devices Ctee EPSRC 1988–91, Peer Review Coll for IT (electronics and photonics tech) 1995–2000 and 2006–, IEE Awards and Prizes Working Pty 2002–04; MIEE 1966, MIEEE 1970; *Recreations* walking, history; *Style*— Prof David Kinniment; ✉ School of Electrical, Electronic and Computer Engineering, The University, Newcastle upon Tyne NE1 7RU (tel 0191 222 7338, fax 0191 222 8180, e-mail david.kinniment@ncl.ac.uk)

KINNOCK, Lady Glenys Elizabeth; MEP (Lab) Wales; *b* 7 July 1944, Roade, Northampton; *Educ* Holyhead Comprehensive Sch, Univ Coll Cardiff (BA, DipEd); *m* 25 March 1967, Baron Kinnock (Life Peer), *qv*; 1 s (Hon Stephen Nathan), 1 da (Hon Rachel Nerys Helen); *Career* sec Socialist Soc UC Cardiff 1964–66, chm NUS Cardiff 1965–66, sch teacher 1966–93; MEP (Lab): South Wales East 1994–99, Wales 1999–; co-pres ACP/EU Jt Parly Assembly 2002–; memb: Devpt and Cooperation Ctee European Parl, Foreign Affairs Ctee; European Parl Lab Pty spokesperson on Int Devpt; pres: One World Action, Wales Cncl for Voluntary Action, Coleg Harlech; vice-pres Parliamentarians for Global Action, SE Wales Racial Equality Cncl, St David's Fndn, Special Needs Advsy Project (SNAP) Cymru, UK Nat Breast Cancer Coalition Wales, Community Enterprise Wales, Charter Housing, UK Women of the Year Lunch and Assembly; patron: Saferworld, Drop the Debt Campaign, Welsh Woman of the Year, Burma Campaign UK, Crusaid, Elizabeth Hardie Ferguson Tst, Med Fndn for Victims of Torture, Nat Deaf Children's Soc; memb Cncl: VSO, Br in Europe; memb Bd World Parliamentarian Magazine; memb Advsy Bd Int Research Network on Children and Armed Conflict; hon fell: Univ of Wales Coll Newport, Univ of Wales Coll Bangor Hon Dr: Thames Valley Univ, Brunel Univ, Kingston Univ; FRSA; *Publications* Voices for One World (1997), Eritrea - Images of War and Peace (1989), Namibia - Birth of a Nation (1991), Could Do Better - where is Britain in the European league tables?, By Faith & Daring (1993), Zimbabwe: On the Brink (2003); *Recreations* theatre, cooking, grandchildren, reading; *Style*— Lady Kinnock, MEP; ✉ c/o European Parliament, 13G302, Rue Wiertz, Brussels, Belgium; Labour European Office, The Coal Exchange, Mount Stuart Square, Cardiff CF10 6EB (tel 029 2048 5305, fax 029 2048 4534, e-mail gkinnock@welshlabourmeps.org.uk, website www.glenyskinnock.org.uk)

KINNOCK, Baron (Life Peer UK 2005), of Bedwellty in the County of Gwent; Neil Gordon Kinnock; PC (1983); s of late Gordon H Kinnock, steelworker and former coalminer, and Mary, *née* Howells, nurse; *b* 28 March 1942; *Educ* Lewis Sch Pengam, UC Cardiff (BA, DipEd); *m* 25 March 1967, Glenys Elizabeth (Lady Kinnock, MEP, *qv*), da of Cyril Parry; 1 s (Hon Stephen Nathan), 1 da (Hon Rachel Nerys Helen); *Career* UC Cardiff: pres Socialist Soc 1963–66, pres Union 1965–66, hon fell 1982; tutor organiser WEA 1966–70, memb Welsh Hosp Bd 1969–71, former memb BBC Gen Advsy Cncl; MP (Lab): Bedwellty 1970–83, Islwyn 1983–95. PPS to Sec of State for Employment 1974–75, memb Nat Exec Lab Party 1978–94, princ oppn front bench spokesman on educn 1979–83 (memb Shadow Cabinet 1980–92), leader Lab Pty and HM Oppn 1983–92, chm Lab Party 1987–88; EC: tport cmmr 1995–99, vice-pres for reform and cmmr for Audit, Personnel and Admin, Languages and Logistics 1999–2004; chair Br Cncl 2004–; pres Univ of Cardiff 1998–; memb TGWU; Alexis de Tocqueville Prize European Inst of Public Admin 2003, Danish Shipowners' Cncl Prize 2004; Hon LLD: Univ of Wales 1992, Univ of Glamorgan 1996; *Publications* Wales and the Common Market (1971), Making Our Way - Investing in Britain's Future (1986), Thorns and Roses (1992); *Recreations* music (esp male voice choral work and opera), the theatre, rugby and association football, cricket, being with family; *Style*— The Rt Hon the Lord Kinnock; ✉ British Council, 10 Spring Gardens, London SW1A 2BN

KINNOULL, 15 Earl of (S 1633); Arthur William George Patrick Hay; also Viscount Dupplin and Lord Hay (S 1627, 1633, 1697), Baron Hay (GB 1711); s of 14 Earl of Kinnoull (d 1938); *b* 26 March 1935; *Educ* Eton; *m* 1961, Gay Ann, da of Sir Denys Colquhoun Flowerdew Lowson, 1 Bt (d 1975); 1 s, 3 da; *Heir* s, Viscount Dupplin, *qv*; *Career* sats as Cons in House of Lords, jr Cons whip House of Lords 1966–68; FRICS; sr ptnr Langley Taylor Scotland; memb Agricultural Valuers' Assoc; pres: National Cncl on Inland Tport 1964–76, Scottish Clans Assoc 1970; vice-pres Nat Assoc of Parish Cncls 1971; chm Property Owners' Building Society, non-exec dir Woolwich Building Society (now Woolwich plc); memb Cncl Royal Nat Mission to Deep Sea Fishermen 1978–; Cons delg Cncl of Europe 1983–92; co-chm Regents Bd Harris Manchester Coll Oxford 2000–; memb Queen's Body Guard for Scotland (Royal Co of Archers) 1965–; govr St John's Sch Leatherhead 1985–; *Clubs* Turf, Pratt's, White's, MCC; *Style*— The Rt Hon the Earl of Kinnoull; ✉ 15 Carlyle Square, London SW3 6EX; Pier House, Seaview, Isle of Wight

KINROSS, 5 Baron (UK 1902); Christopher Patrick Balfour; WS; s of 4 Baron Kinross, OBE, TD, DL, and his 2 w, Helen (d 1969), da of Alan Hog and formerly w of Lt-Col Patrick Perfect; *b* 1 October 1949; *Educ* Eton, Univ of Edinburgh (LLB); *m* 1, 1974 (m dis 2004), Susan Jane, da of Ian Robert Pitman; 2 s (Hon Alan Ian b 1978, Hon Derek Andrew b 1981); m 2, May 2004, Catherine Taylor, da of late Stanislav Ostrycharz; *Heir* s, Hon Alan Balfour; *Career* slr and WS; ptnr HBJ Gateley Wareing Edinburgh; memb Queen's Body Guard for Scotland (Royal Co of Archers); hon memb James IV Assoc of Surgns; Queen's Golden Jubilee Medal 2002; Grand Baili of the Bailiwick of Scotland Mil and Hospitaller Order of St Lazarus of Jerusalem; *Recreations* shooting, motorsport; *Clubs* New (Edinburgh); *Style*— The Rt Hon the Lord Kinross, WS; ✉ 27 Walker Street, Edinburgh EH3 7HX

KINSELLA, Paul; *b* 11 August 1947; *Educ* Beaumont Coll, Trinity Hall Cambridge (BA); *m* Karin, *née* Riechers; 1 da (Antoinette); *Career* Lawrence Graham: qualified 1974, ptnr and head of Commercial Property (Mgmnt Gp) 1978, head Commercial Property Dept 1985–90, also head of Int Property; fndr memb: Steering Ctee for NY Assocs Rosenman & Colin, Jt Ctee of ABLE (Associated Business Lawyers in Europe, now LG International); memb: Govt Affrs Ctee, Urban Task Force Br Cncl of Shopping Centres, Investment Property Forum, ICSC (Europe) Legal Gp; hon memb St Petersburg-London Assoc; *Recreations* travel, gardening, reading, conversation, retired cricketer; *Style*—Paul Kinsella, Esq; ✉ Lawrence Graham, 4 More London Riverside, London SE1 2AU (tel 020 7759 6531, fax 020 7173 8531, e-mail paul.kinsella@lg-legal.com)

KINSELLA-BEVAN, Col Richard Dennis; s of late Lt Col Richard Bevan, of Bowelk House, Co Monaghan, and Margot, *née* Kinsella; *b* 5 January 1943; *Educ* Brighton Coll, King's Coll Cambridge (MA); *m* 1971, Kitty, da of late Capt A B B J Gor, KRRC, and Judith Bloomfield; 1 s (Desmond b 1 Oct 1975), 2 da (Emma-Louise b 16 March 1977, Edwina b 6 Sept 1979); *Career* cmmnd 5th Royal Inniskilling Dragoon Gds 1965; served: N Africa, Cyprus, Oman, Dhofar War (Sultan's Commendation), BAOR, Iraq; psc, Cmd Sultan's Armoured Regt 1984–87 (Sultan's Commendation Medal and Order of the Special Emblem); Head Secretariat National Employers' Liaison Ctee for the Reserve Forces 1992–95; Sr Br Loan Serv Offr (Army) Sultanate of Oman 1996–99 (DSM); registrar Med Soc of London 1999–, exec sec Harveian Soc 1999–; dir St George's Court Pimlico; author of articles in mil jls; Freeman City of London, Liveryman Worshipful Co of Farriers (memb Ct of Assts 2003–, Master 2007), memb Farriers' Registration Cncl 2004–; FRGS 1985 (Baram-Rejang Expdn 1961, Kinabalu 1962); *Recreations* field sports (MH Shrivenham Beagles 1987–88); *Clubs* Cavalry and Guards', Kildare Street and University (Dublin); *Style*— Col Richard Kinsella-Bevan; ✉ Knockbrack Grange, Oldcastle, County Meath, Ireland; Medical Society of London, 11 Chandos Street, Cavendish Square, London W1G 9EB (tel 020 7580 1043, fax 020 7580 5793)

KINSEY, Julian; s of Tom Kinsey, of Solihull, and Ruth, *née* Owen-Jones; *b* 8 October 1959, Birmingham; *Educ* Solihull Sch, Univ of Sheffield (LLB), Chester Coll of Law; *m* 1 July 1989, Amanda *née* Cundy; 1 s (George b 1 Oct 1992); *Career* admitted slr 1984; trainee Rigby Loose & Mills 1982–84, Linklaters 1984–86, Harbottle & Lewis 1986–88, Bond Pearce 1988– (ptnr 1993–, currently head of banking); *Recreations* family, cricket, music; *Clubs* Tideford Cricket (tstee); *Style*— Julian Kinsey, Esq; ✉ Bond Pearce LLP, 3 Temple Quay, Temple Back East, Bristol BS1 6DZ (tel 0845 415 0000, e-mail julian.kinsey@bondpearce.com)

KINSMAN, Prof Rodney; s of John Thomas Kinsman, and Lilian, *néa* Bradshaw; *b* 9 April 1943; *Educ* Mellow Lane GS, Central Sch of Art (NDD); *m* Lisa Sau-Yuk, *née* Ngai; 1 s (Brandon Lee b 19 June 1968), 2 da (Charlie Sam b 24 Nov 1973, Chloe Jessica b 4 Jan 1975); *Career* furniture designer; chm and md OMK Design Ltd (fndr 1966), Kinsman Assoc 1981; work in exhibitions incl: The Way We Live Now (V&A Museum) 1979, Sit (RIBA) 1980, The Modern Chair (ICA) 1989, The Review (Design Museum London) 1989, Evolution of the Modern Chair (Business Design Centre London) 1989, BBC Design Awards (Design Centre London) 1990, In Focus OMK The Designs of Rodney Kinsman (Design Museum) 1992; also chosen to represent Britain in numerous foreign exhibitions; designs featured in: various Museum permanent collection UK and abroad incl V&A, numerous publications, TV and radio broadcasts; awards incl: Observer Design award UK 1969, Design Council award 1984, Resources Cncl Inc 1987, Product Design award USA 1987, Industrial Design Designers Choice USA 1988, D&AD Silver award for most outstanding Br product design for the home UK 1989, The British Design award 1991, Design Cncl Millennium Product 1998; prof: The London Inst 1996, Univ of the Arts London 2005; visiting prof: RCA 1985–86 (external examiner 1987–89), St Martin's and Central Sch of Art; memb BA Advsy Cncl St Martin's and Central Sch of Art 1989–90; govr Univ of the Arts; Hon FRCA 1988; FCSD 1983, FRSA 1991, RDI 1990; *Publications* Rodney Kinsman - The Logical Art of Furniture (monograph, 1992); *Recreations* polo, skiing; *Clubs* Reform, Chelsea Arts, Groucho; *Style*— Prof Rodney Kinsman, RDI; ✉ OMK Design Ltd, Stephen Building, 30 Stephen Street, London W1P 1QR (tel 020 7631 1335, fax 020 7631 3227, e-mail enquiries@omkdesign.com, website www.omkdesign.com)

KIRBY, (Bernard William) Alexander (Alex); s of Frederic William Kirby (d 1953), and Vera Beryl, *née* Crawshaw (d 1989); *b* 11 July 1939; *Educ* King's Coll Taunton, Keble Coll Oxford; *m* 8 April 1972, Belinda Anne, da of Hugh Alfred Andrews (d 1991); 2 s (Edmund b 29 Dec 1978, Thomas b 14 April 1982); *Career* asst curate Isle of Dogs 1965–66, community relations offr London Borough of Newham 1967–70, ed Race Today magazine 1970–73, co-ordinator Br Volunteer Prog Burkina Faso and Niger 1974–75, researcher Prog to Combat Racism World Cncl of Churches 1976–78; BBC: journalist World Service News 1978–83, stringer N Africa 1983–84, actg bureau chief and Cairo corr 1986, reporter BBC Radio News 1986–87, agric and environment corr 1987–96, religious affairs corr 1996–98, presenter Costing the Earth (BBC Radio 4) 1998–2005; environment corr BBC News Online 1998–2005; hon vice-chm Wildlife and Countryside Link 1996–, chm World Water Forum of Journalists 2006–, advsr UN Environment Prog 2004–, assoc Conservation Fndn, tstee Lewes Railway Land Wildlife Tst; tstee ChildHope UK; hon visiting fell Green Coll Oxford; memb Royal Inst; *Recreations* walking, drinking beer, marathon running; *Style*— Alex Kirby; ✉ 28 Prince Edward's Road, Lewes, East Sussex BN7 1BE (tel 01273 474935, e-mail alexkirby_uk@yahoo.co.uk)

KIRBY, Prof Anthony John; s of Samuel Arthur Kirby, and Gladys Rosina, *née* Welch; *b* 18 August 1935; *Educ* Eton, Gonville & Caius Coll Cambridge (MA, PhD); *m* 1962, Sara Sophia Benjamina Nieweg; 1 s, 2 da; *Career* Nat Serv RCS 1954–55; NATO postdoctoral fell: Univ of Cambridge 1962–63, Brandeis Univ 1963–64; Univ of Cambridge: univ demonstrator 1964–68, lectr and reader in organic chemistry 1985–95 (lectr 1968–85), prof of bioorganic chemistry 1995–2002, coll lectr Gonville & Caius Coll 1965–2002 (tutor 1966–74, fell 1962–), dir of studies in natural sciences 1968–96; visiting prof: Univ of Paris Orsay 1970, Université Pierre et Marie Curie Paris 1987, The Technion Haifa 1991, Queen's Univ Kingston Ontario 1996, Univ of Toronto 1997, Univ of Western Ontario 1997; res fellowship Japan Soc for the Promotion of Res 1986, visiting scholar Univ of Cape Town 1987, invited lectr in numerous countries; co-ordinator Euro Networks on Antibody Catalysis 1993–96, Gemini Surfactants 1997–2001, Artificial Nucleases 2000–04; memb: Mgmnt Ctee Organic Reaction Mechanisms Gp RSC 1983–86 and 1999–2003 (chm 1986–90), Perkin Editorial Bd RSC 1983–87, Organic Chemistry Sub-Ctee SERC 1986–89, Chemistry Ctee SERC 1988–91, Hooke Ctee Royal Soc 1988–91, Advsy Ctee Salters Advanced Chemistry Project 1989–, Panel of Experts Univ of London 1989–; elector to 1702 chair of chemistry Univ of Cambridge 1987; RSC Ingold lectr 1996–97, Backer lectr Univ of Groningen 2003; RSC Award in Organic Reaction Mechanisms 1983; PhD (hc) Univ of Turku 2006; FRS 1987; *Publications* The Organic Chemistry of Phosphorus (with S G Warren, 1967), The Anomeric Effect and Related Stereoelectronic Effects at Oxygen (1983), Stereoelectronic Effects (1996), numerous papers and review articles; *Recreations* chamber music, walking; *Style*— Prof Anthony J Kirby, FRS; ✉ University Chemical Laboratory, Cambridge CB2 1EW (tel 01223 336370, fax 01223 336362, e-mail ajkl@cam.ac.uk)

KIRBY, John Patrick; s of Robert Kirby, of Liverpool, and Matilda, *née* Carroll (d 1976); *b* 2 February 1949; *Educ* Cardinal Godfrey Tech Sch Liverpool, St Martin's Sch of Art (BA), Royal Coll of Art (MA); *Career* artist; shipping clerk American Express Company Liverpool 1965–67, book salesman Burns & Oates 1967–69, voluntary social worker Boy's Town of Calcutta India 1969–71, asst warden Sydney House Hostel 1971–72, probation offr London and Plymouth 1972–77, asst stage doorman Royal Opera House 1977–78, market stall holder Kensington High St 1978–79, probation offr Brixton 1979–82, mothers' help London 1985, hosp porter London 1986; *Solo Exhibitions* incl: Other People's Lives (Angela Flowers Gallery Ireland) 1988, Still Lives (Flowers East London) 1989, New York and Related Works (Flowers East) 1991, Homeland (Lannon Cole Gallery Chicago) 1991 and (Flowers East) 1992, The Sign of the Cross (Angela Flowers Gallery London) 1993, The Company of Strangers (Flowers East) 1994, The Company of Strangers (Ferens Art Gallery Hull) 1995, Art Basle 27 Switzerland 1996, John Kirby (Il Polittico Rome) 1997, In the Dark (Flowers East) 1997, Lost Children (Flowers West Santa Monica CA) 1998, Lost Children (Flowers East) 1999, Il Polittico Rome 2000, New Prints and Monoprints (Flowers Graphics) 2000; work displayed in numerous group exhibitions and public collections; *Recreations* watching TV, contemplating suicide; *Clubs* Copacabana; *Style*— John Kirby, Esq; ✉ c/o Flowers East, 82 Kingsland Road, London E2 8DP (tel 020 8985 3333, fax 020 8985 0067)

KIRBY, Maj-Gen Norman George; OBE; s of George William Kirby (d 1978), and Laura Kirby (d 1980); *Educ* King Henry VIII Sch Coventry, Univ of Birmingham (MB ChB);

m 1 Oct 1949, Cynthia Maire, da of Thomas Ian Bradley (d 1954); 1 s (Robert b 22 June 1954), 1 da (Jill b 11 Nov 1958); *Career* regtl MO 10 Parachute Regt TA 1950–51, offr i/c 5 Parachute Surgical Team 1956–59 (served Suez landing 1956), offr i/c Surgical Div BMH Rinteln 1959–60, OC and surgical specialist BMH Tripoli 1960–62, OC and conslt surgn BMH Dhekelia 1967–70, chief conslt surgn Cambridge Mil Hosp 1970–72, conslt surgn HQ BAOR 1973–78; 1978–82: dir of Army surgery, conslt surgn to the Army, hon surgn to the Queen; Hon Col: 308 Gen Hosp RAMC TA 1982–87, 144 Para Field Sqdn RAMC TA 1985–96; Col Cmdt RAMC 1987–92; surgical registrar: Plastic Surgery Unit Stoke Mandeville Hosp 1950–51, Birmingham Accident Hosp 1953–55, Postgrad Med Sch Hammersmith 1964; hon conslt surgn Westminster Hosp 1979–; Guy's Hosp: conslt A&E surgn 1982–93, dir Clinical Servs, Accidents, Emergencies and Admissions 1985–93, conslt A&E surgn Nuffield House Guy's Hosp 1993–; chm: A&E Ctee SE Thames RHA 1983–88, Army Med Dept Working Pty Surgical Support for BAOR 1978–80; memb Med Ctee Defence Scientific Advsy Cncl 1979–82, examiner in anatomy RCS Edinburgh 1982–90, memb Ct of Examiners RCS 1988–94; pres: Br Assoc for A&E Med 1990–93, Mil Surgical Assoc 1991–92; vice-pres: Br Assoc of Trauma in Sport 1982–88, Faculty of A&E Med 1993–94; hon librarian RSM 1993–98; memb Cncl: ICS 1980, Royal Coll of Surgns 1989–94; McCombe lectr RCS Edinburgh 1979, Mitchener medal RCS 1982, memb Editorial Bd Br Jl of Surgery and Injury 1979–82, librarian Med Soc of London 1988–92 (pres 1992–93); memb HAC; Freeman City of London 1980, Liveryman Worshipful Soc of Apothecaries of London; OStJ; Hon FACEP, FRCS, FICS, FRCSEd, FCEM (FFAEM), DMCC, fndr memb Inst of Expert Witnesses; *Books* Field Surgery Pocket Book (1981), Baillieres First Aid (1985), Accidents and Emergencies (pocket reference, 1991), Medical Care of Catastrophies (handbook, co-ed, 1996); *Recreations* travel, reading, archaeology; *Clubs* Surgical Travellers'; *Style*— Maj-Gen Norman Kirby, OBE; ✉ Nuffield House, Guy's Hospital, London SE1 1YR (tel 020 7955 4752, fax 020 7955 4754)

KIRBY, Richard Charles; s of Charles Neil Vernon Kirby (d 1970), and Nora Helena, *née* Corner (d 1997); *b* 18 September 1946; *Educ* Sevenoaks Sch, Jesus Coll Oxford (MA); *m* 18 May 1985, Jill Christine, da of Kenneth Fernie, of Rugby, Warwicks; 3 s (Thomas Charles b 1986, James Edward b 1988, Robert Alexander b 1992 d 2004); *Career* admitted slr 1971; ptnr Speechly Bircham 1973– (managing ptnr 1989–91); memb Ctee London Young Slrs 1973–74; cncllr Tonbridge and Malling Borough 1971–84 (ldr 1979–82); memb: Exec Tonbridge and Malling Cons Assoc 1978–84 (vice-chm and treas 1979–84), Exec SE region Nat Housing and Town Planning Cncl 1980–83, Cncl Together Working for Wellbeing (formerly Mental After Care Assoc) 1982– (hon treas 1987–); dir Hortons' Estate Ltd 1996– (dep chm 2002–); slr Worshipful Co of Pewterers 1981– (Hon Freeman 1991, Liveryman 2000); Freeman City of London 1992; *Recreations* reading, theatre, walking; *Clubs* Carlton; *Style*— Richard C Kirby, Esq; ✉ Yerdley House, Long Compton, Warwickshire CV36 5LH (tel 01608 684923); Speechly Bircham, 6 St Andrew Street, London EC4A 3LX (tel 020 7427 6400, fax 020 7427 6600, e-mail richard.kirby@speechlys.com)

KIRDAR, Nemir Amin; s of Amin Jamil Kirdar (d 1958), and Nuzhet Mohammed Ali Kirdar (d 1982); *b* 28 October 1936; *Educ* Coll of the Pacific Calif (BA), Fordham Univ (MBA), Harvard Univ; *m* 1 Feb 1967, Nada, da of Dr Adnan Shakir; 2 da (Rena b 1968, Serra b 1975); *Career* Allied Bank International NY 1969–73, Nat Bank of N America NY 1973–74, Chase Manhattan Bank NY 1974–81, fndr pres and ceo Investcorp Bank EC Bahrain 1982–; fndr memb World Business Cncl World Econ Forum; memb: Bd of Int Cncllrs Center for Strategic and Int Studies Washington DC, Bd of Visitors Edmund A Walsh Sch of Foreign Serv Georgetown Univ Washington DC, Advsy Bd Sch of Int and Public Affairs Columbia Univ NYC, Bd of Tstees Eisenhower Exchange Fellowship Philadelphia, Bd of Dirs Georgetown Univ Washington DC, Advsy Bd Judge Business Sch Univ of Cambridge, Int Advsrs Cncl Brookings Instn Washington, UN Investments Ctee (overseeing UN Pension Fund), Ctee on Univ Resources Harvard Univ Bd of Overseers, Bd of Dirs Qatar Financial Center Authy; author of several articles in leading business and fin magazines; *Recreations* reading, skiing, tennis, golf, architecture, antiques; *Clubs* Metropolitan (Washington DC), Knickerbocker (NY); *Style*— Nemir Kirdar, Esq; ✉ Investcorp, 48 Grosvenor Street, London W1K 3HW (tel 020 7629 6600, fax 020 7887 3333, e-mail nkirdar@investcorp.com)

KIRK, Prof David; s of Herbert Arthur Kirk (d 1969), of Sutton Coldfield, Warks, and Constance Florence, *née* Mortimer; *b* 26 May 1943; *Educ* King Edward's Sch Birmingham, Balliol Coll Oxford, Clinical Med Sch Oxford (MA, BM BCh, DM); *m* 7 Aug 1965, Gillian Mary, da of Maj Wilson Bell Wroot, of Sutton Coldfield, Warks; 2 da (Tonya b 1969, Lucy b 1975), 1 s (Robert b 1971); *Career* res med appts Radcliffe Infirmary Oxford 1968–69, univ demonstrator Univ of Oxford 1969–70; SHO appts 1970–72: Radcliffe Infirmary, Churchill Hosp Oxford, Bristol Royal Infirmary; surgical registrar 1973–75: Royal Infirmary Sheffield, Children's Hosp; res asst in surgery Univ of Sheffield 1975–76; sr surgical registrar 1976–78: Bristol Royal Infirmary, Royal Devon and Exeter Hosp; sr urological registrar 1978–82: Bristol Royal Infirmary, Southmead Hosp; conslt urological surgn Gtr Glasgow Health Bd (latterly N Glasgow Hosps) 1982–2005, hon prof Univ of Glasgow 1995–2005 (hon clinical lectr/sr lectr 1982–94, lead urologist 1995–), urological advsr Nat Med Advsy Ctee Scottish Office 1996–2004; Arris and Gale lectr RCS 1980–81; memb Cncl: Section of Urology RSM 1984–87, Br Assoc of Urological Surgns 1988–91; chm: Scot Urological Oncology Gp 1985–88 (sec 1983–85), Prostate Forum 1991–94 (memb Steering Ctee 1995–2000), Intercollegiate Bd in Urology 1994–97, Working Pty on Early Prostate Cancer Br Assoc of Urological Surgns, Cruse Bereavement Care Scotland Central Scotland Region 2007– (chm Forth Valley branch 2004–07); memb: Scientific Ctee Br Urological Fndn 1995–2000, Nat Cancer Research Inst (NCRI, formerly UKCCCR, memb prostate and testis working parties) until 2003; memb Specialist Advsy Ctee in Urology 1999–2004; memb/study coordinator Prostate Cancer Working Pty MRC; contrib to multi-author books on mgmnt of urological cancer, memb Editorial Ctee Br Jl of Urology 1997–2002; pres Scottish Urology Soc 2004–, memb Urological Club of GB; FRCS 1973, FRSM 1981, FRCPS 1989, FRCSEd 1997; *Publications* Understanding Prostate Disorders, International Handbook of Prostate Cancer (ed), Managing Prostate Disease; *Recreations* skiing, hill walking, classical music, woodwork; *Style*— Prof David Kirk; ✉ 1 The Biggins, Keir, Dunblane FK15 9NX (tel 01786 820291, e-mail dkirk70683@aol.com)

KIRK, (Alistair) Graham; s of Alexander Charles Tansley Kirk, of Stokeholy Cross, Norfolk, and Dulce Marjory, *née* Ewins; *b* 10 May 1935; *Educ* Windsor GS, Berks Coll of Art and Design (NDD); *m* July 1986, Gillian Ruth, da of Mark Cresswell Bostock; 2 da (Catherine Elizabeth b 26 Oct 1987, Alexandra Claire b 30 May 1989); *Career* art dir various London advertising agencies until 1967, set up own photographic studio London 1968, visiting lectr in photography London Coll of Printing 1969; portfolio incl: location, still life and food photography for advertising and editorial publications, stamp edn series of photographs for PO (Food and Farming Year) 1989 (D&AD award 1989), photography for various internationally renowned chefs; contrib to Sunday Times and Observer magazines, numerous books (especially on French, Italian and Oriental cuisine); fndr memb AFAEP (now Assoc of Photographers), FCSD 1986; *Recreations* music and gardening; *Style*— Graham Kirk, Esq; ✉ tel and fax 01797 230345

KIRK, Matthew J L; s of Sir Peter Kirk (d 1977), and Elizabeth, *née* Graham; *b* 10 October 1960; *Educ* Felsted, St John's Coll Oxford (MA), Ecole Nationale d'Adminstration Paris (Diplome International d'Administration Publique); *m* 20 May 1989, Anna Thérèse, *née* Macey; 2 da (Georgina b 1995, Alexandra b 1998); *Career* joined HM Dip Serv 1982; served: UK mission to UN NY 1982, FCO 1983–84, Br Embassy Belgrade 1984–87, Office of the Gov of Gibraltar 1988, FCO 1988–92, Br Embassy Paris 1992–97, FCO 1997–98, Cabinet Secretariat 1998–99, FCO 1999–2002; ambass to Finland 2002–06; dir of external relationships Vodafone Gp plc 2006–; FRGS 1988; *Recreations* music, reading, walking, tennis; *Clubs* Brooks's, Beefsteak; *Style*— Matthew Kirk, Esq

KIRK, Raymond Maurice; *b* 31 October 1923; *Educ* County Secdy Sch W Bridgford Nottingham, Univ of London (MB BS, MS); *m* 2 Dec 1952, Margaret; 1 s (Jeremy), 2 da (Valentine, Louise); *Career* Lt RN 1942–46; hon consulting surgn Royal Free Hosp (conslt surgn 1964–89), hon prof of surgery Royal Free and UCL Sch of Med Scis 2004–; RCS: memb Ct of Examiners 1975–81, memb Cncl 1983–91, ed Annals 1985–92, former dir Overseas Doctors Trg Scheme; examiner: Univ of London, Univ of Kuwait, Univ of Liverpool, Univ of Bristol, Univ of Khartoum, Univ of Malta, Univ of Colombo, RCPSG; former pres Surgical Section RSM; past pres: Med Soc London, Hunterian Soc; memb: Soc of Academic and Res Surgery, British Soc of Gastroenterology, Assoc of Surgns of GB and Ireland, Soc of Authors (memb Cncl Med Section 1996–2000); hon fell: Assoc of Surgeons of Poland, Coll of Surgeons of Sri Lanka; FRCS, FRSM; *Books* A Manual of Abdominal Operations (1967), Surgery (jtly, 1973), Basic Surgical Techniques (1973, 5 edn 2002), General Surgical Operations (1978, 5 edn 2006), Complications of Surgery of the Upper Gastrointestinal Tract (jtly, 1986), A Career in Medicine (1998), Clinical Surgery in General (jt ed, 1993, 4 edn 2004), Essential General Surgical Operations (2001, 2 edn 2007); *Recreations* squash, cycling, opera, travel; *Style*— Professor Raymond Kirk; ✉ 10 Southwood Lane, Highgate Village, London N6 5EE (tel 020 8340 8575); Royal College of Surgeons of England, 35–43 Lincoln's Inn Fields, London WC2A 3PN (tel 020 7405 3474), Royal Free and University College Medical School, Royal Free Campus, Rowland Hill Street, London NW3 2PF (tel 020 7794 0500 ext 35412, fax 020 7472 6444, e-mail r.kirk@medsch.ucl.ac.uk)

KIRK, Séamus; TD; s of John Kirk, and Bridget, *née* Boylan; *b* 26 April 1945, Co Louth, Ireland; *Educ* Drumsinnot Nat Sch, Christian Bros Secdy Sch; *m* Sept 1974, Mary, *née* McGeough; 3 s (Ciaran b 19 March 1976, Colm b 8 Jan 1979, Kevin b 14 May 1982), 1 da (Gráinne (twin) b 14 May 1982); *Career* memb Louth CC 1974–85, TD (Fianna Fáil) Louth 1982–, min of state 1987–92; memb Br-Irish Inter-Parly Body; chm Fianna Fáil Parly Party; memb: GAA, local community groups; *Clubs* St Bride's Gaelic Football; *Style*— Siamus Kirk, Esq, TD; ✉ Rathiddy, Knockbridge, Dundalk, Co Louth, Ireland (tel 00 353 42 9331032, fax 00 353 42 9355680, e-mail skirk@mail.com)

KIRKBRIDE, Julie; MP; da of late Henry Raymond Kirkbride, and Barbara, *née* Bancroft; *b* 5 June 1960; *Educ* Highlands Sch Halifax, Girton Coll Cambridge (MA, vice-pres Cambridge Union), UC at Berkeley (Rotary Fndn scholar); *m* 1997, Andrew MacKay, *qv*; 1 s (Angus Robert b 12 Oct 2000); *Career* successively 1983–96: journalist Yorkshire Television, prodr BBC News and Current Affrs, journalist ITN, political corr The Daily Telegraph, social affrs ed The Sunday Telegraph; MP (Cons) Bromsgrove 1997–; *Recreations* walking, travelling, opera; *Style*— Miss Julie Kirkbride, MP; ✉ House of Commons, London SW1A 0AA (tel 020 7219 1101)

KIRKBY, Maurice Anthony (Tony); s of George Sydney Kirkby (d 1972), of Southwell, Notts, and Rose, *née* Marson (d 1958); *b* 12 April 1929; *Educ* Trent Coll, King's Coll Cambridge; *m* 2 Aug 1954, Muriel Beatrice, da of Robert Longmire; 1 s (Peter Michael b 13 Dec 1955), 1 da (Susan Margaret b 5 June 1958); *Career* Bruntons (Musselburgh) Ltd 1952–54 (chief engr 1954); Anglo-Iranian Oil Co (later British Petroleum): trainee petroleum engr 1954–56, service in Iraq, Kuwait, Tanganyika, Iran, dist supt Iran 1964–67, regnl petroleum engr London 1967–69, chief petroleum engr London 1969–74, gen mangr BP Petroleum Devpt Aberdeen 1974–76, gen mangr Exploration & Prodn London 1976–80, sr vice-pres Oil & Gas Standard Oil Co Ohio 1980–82, pres and chief exec BP Canada Inc 1983–88, chm and chief exec Hope Brook Gold Inc 1986–88, ret from BP 1988; dep chm North American Gas Investment Tst 1989–95; dir: Ensign Oil & Gas Inc Denver 1989–2001, Intera Information Technology Corporation Calgary 1992–96, Atlantis Resources Ltd Calgary 1992–94; vice-chm: UK Offshore Operators' Assoc 1974–76, IX World Petroleum Congress (PD 16); chm X World Petroleum Congress (PD 8), memb Business Cncl on Nat Issues Ottawa 1983–88; memb Soc of Petroleum Engrs (dir 1980 and 1981–83); MIMechE 1955, FIMM (memb Cncl 1990), FREng 1980; *Recreations* skiing, golf, gardening, beekeeping; *Clubs* Ranchmen's (Calgary, 1983–88); *Style*— Tony Kirkby, Esq, FREng; ✉ e-mail tony@makirby.demon.co.uk

KIRKBY, Prof Michael John (Mike); s of John Lawrence Kirkby (d 1989), of London, and Hilda Margaret, *née* Potts (d 1974); *b* 6 May 1937; *Educ* Radley, Univ of Cambridge (BA, PhD); *m* 1, 24 July 1963 (m dis 1975), Anne Veronica Tennant, da of Philip Whyte (d 1983), of Bedford; 1 s (David b 1967), 1 da (Clare b 1970); m 2, 15 May 1976, Fiona Elizabeth, da of Donald Weston Burley; 2 s (John b 1978, Nicholas b 1982); *Career* Nat Serv 2 Lt REME 1955–57; lectr in geography Univ of Bristol 1967–72, prof of physical geography Univ of Leeds 1973–2002, emeritus prof 2002–; author of numerous scientific pubns; memb BGRG 1966; chartered geographer 2003; RGS Founders' Medal 1999; FRGS 1963, fell AGU 2004; *Books* Hillslope Form and Process (with M A Carson, 1972), Hillslope Hydrology (ed, 1978), Soil Erosion (ed with R P C Morgan, 1980), Computer Simulation in Physical Geography (jtly, 1987 and 1993), Channel Network Hydrology (ed with K J Beven, 1993), Process models & theoretical geomorphology (ed, 1994), Dryland Rivers (ed with L J Bull, 2002); managing ed Earth Surface Processes and Landforms 1976–; *Recreations* hill walking, photography; *Style*— Prof Mike Kirkby; ✉ School of Geography, University of Leeds, Leeds LS2 9JT (tel 0113 343 3310, fax 0113 343 6758, e-mail m.j.kirkby@leeds.ac.uk)

KIRKHAM, Donald Herbert; CBE (1996); s of Herbert Kirkham (d 1987), and Hettie, *née* Trueblood (d 1999); *m* 17 Sept 1960, Kathleen Mary, da of Christopher Lond (d 1999); 1 s (Richard b 1963), 1 da (Sarah b 1966); *Career* Nat Serv Army 1954–56; The Woolwich Building Society: joined Lincoln Branch 1959, branch mangr Worcester 1963, gen mangr's asst 1967, business prodn mangr 1970, asst gen mangr of ops 1972, gen mangr 1976, appointed to Local Bd for Scotland and NI 1979–84, dep chief gen mangr 1981, memb Main Bd 1982, chief exec 1986–95, non-exec dir 1996–97; vice-pres Chartered Building Societies Inst 1986 (pres 1981–82), pres Cncl ICSA 1991; chm: Met Assoc of Building Societies 1988–89, Building Societies Assoc 1994–95 (dep chm 1993–94), Banque Woolwich SA 1995–2001, Banca Woolwich SpA 1995–2002, Woolwich Insurance Services Ltd 1995–96; memb Bd: Horniman Museum 1989–2004 (chm 1996–2004), Gresham Insurance Co Ltd 1995–96, Building Societies Investor Protection Bd 1995–97, Bexley and Greenwich HA 1996–98, and 1999–2001, Ranyard Meml Charitable Trust 2001–, Oxleas NHS Fndn Tst 2006–; Freeman City of London, Liveryman Worshipful Co of Chartered Secretaries and Administrators (memb Ct of Assts, Master 2003–04); Hon DBA 1991; FCIS 1973, FCIB 1993; *Recreations* boating; *Clubs* Christchurch Sailing; *Style*— Donald Kirkham, Esq, CBE; ✉ 2 Chaundrye Close, The Court Yard, Eltham, London SE9 5QB (tel and fax 020 8859 4295, e-mail donaldhk@aol.com)

KIRKHAM, Her Hon Judge Frances Margaret; da of Brian Llewellyn Morgan Davies, and Natalie May Davies; *b* 29 October 1947; *Educ* KCL (BA, AKC, Merchant Taylor's Prize and Edward Jones medal and exhbn); *m* 27 March 1971, Barry Charles Kirkham, s of Stanley Edward Kirkham; *Career* Bank of England 1969–73, Lloyds Bank Int 1973–74; admitted slr 1978; Pinsent & Co 1976–84, Bettinsons 1984–87, Edge & Ellison 1987–95, Dibb Lupton Alsop 1995–2000, circuit judge (Midland Circuit) 2000–, designated judge Technol and Construction Court 2000–; cmmr Parly Boundary Cmmn 2000; memb:

Working Pty on Civil Justice Reform 1992–93, Law Soc Civil Litigation Ctee 1988–92, Birmingham Law Soc Civil Litigation Ctee 1992–93, Cncl CIArB 1992–97 and 2000, W Midlands Branch CIArb (chm 1994–97), Advsy Bd for Centre for Advanced Litigation Nottingham Law Sch 1992–97, Judicial Appointments Cmmn 2006–; fndr chm W Midlands Assoc of Women Slrs 1983, sec UK Assoc of Women Judges 2003–06, tstee A-CET 2002–; hon memb: Technol and Construction Slrs Assoc (TeCSA) 2005, Arbrix; chm of govrs Heathfield Sch Pinner 1984–91 (govr 1981–91); memb Law Soc; FCIArb, chartered arbitrator; *Recreations* time with friends, sailing, skiing, walking, music, theatre, gardening; *Clubs* Bank of England Sailing, Univ Women's; *Style—* Her Hon Judge Kirkham; ✉ Birmingham Civil Justice Centre, The Priory Courts, 33 Bull Street, Birmingham B4 6DW (tel 0121 681 3181, fax 0121 250 6730)

KIRKHAM, John Squire; s of Squire Wilfred Kirkham (d 1989), and Una Mary, *née* Baker (d 2001); *b* 20 September 1936; *Educ* Gonville & Caius Coll Cambridge (MA, MB BChir, MChir), Westminster Hosp; *m* 19 Sept 1969, Charlotte, da of Paul Giersing (d 1981), of Aalborg, Denmark; 1 s (Alexander), 1 da (Sophie); *Career* ships surgn Union Castle Line MN 1962–63; house surgn Westminster Hosp; sr house offr: Birmingham Accident Hosp, The Hosp for Sick Children Gt Ormond St; surgn registrar Aberdeen Royal Infirmary, sr surgical registrar St James's Hosp SW12 and Charing Cross Hosp; conslt surgn St George's Hosp London and St James's Hosp London 1971–90, hon sr lectr St George's Hosp Med Sch, Queen Mary's Univ Hosp Roehampton 1991–96 (conslt in gen surgery, surgical gastroenterology and digestive endoscopy); examiner: Univ of London, Khartoum, Basra; visiting prof: Khartoum, Basra, Cairo, Melbourne, Alexandria; author papers on: surgical aspects of gastroenterology, gastro-intestinal bleeding, endoscopy, various surgical topics, chapters in surgical textbooks; memb: Save Br Sci, Int Dendrology Soc, Pancreatic Soc of GB and Ireland, Br Soc of Gastroenterology, Assoc of Surgns of GB and Ireland, Int Gastro-Surgical Club, Surgical Specialists Soc; FRSM, FRCS, FRCSEd; *Books* contrib to Maingot's Adbominal Operations (1984), Surgery of Obesity (1984), British Surgical Progress (1990); *Recreations* reading, dendrology, sailing, travelling, fishing; *Clubs* Athenaeum; *Style—* John Squire Kirkham, Esq; ✉ Flat 18, Millicent Court, 31 Marsham Street, Westminster, London SW1P 3DW

KIRKHILL, Baron (Life Peer UK 1975), in District of City of Aberdeen; John Farquharson Smith; s of Alexander Findlay Smith; *b* 7 May 1930; *Educ* Robert Gordon's Colls Aberdeen; *m* 1965, Frances Mary Walker Reid; 1 step da; *Career* Lord Provost of the City and Royal Burgh of Aberdeen 1971–75, min of state Scottish Office 1975–78, chm North of Scotland Hydro-Electric Bd 1979–82; delg to Parly Assembly Cncl of Europe and WEU 1987–01, chm Ctee on Legal Affrs and Human Rights 1991–95; Hon LLD Univ of Aberdeen 1974; *Style—* The Rt Hon the Lord Kirkhill; ✉ 3 Rubislaw Den North, Aberdeen AB15 4AL (tel 01224 314167)

KIRKHOPE, Timothy John Robert; MEP (Cons) Yorkshire & the Humber; s of John Thomas Kirkhope (d 1991), of Newcastle upon Tyne, and Dorothy Buemann Kirkhope, *née* Bolt (d 1973); *b* 29 April 1945; *Educ* Royal GS Newcastle upon Tyne, Coll of Law Guildford; *m* 1969, Caroline, da of Christopher Thompson Maling (d 1975), of Newcastle upon Tyne; 4 s (Justin b 1970, Rupert b 1972, Dominic b 1976, Alexander 1979); *Career* slr; ptnr with Wilkinson Maughan Newcastle upon Tyne (now Eversheds) 1977–87, conslt 1987–90; MP (Cons) Leeds NE 1987–97; House of Commons: PPS to David (now Sir David) Trippier as Min of State for the Environment and Countryside 1989–90, asst Govt whip 1990–92, Lord Cmmr to the Treasy (Govt whip) 1993–95, vice-chamberlain HM's Household 1995, under sec of state Home Office 1995–97; slr and business conslt 1997–; dir Bournemouth and West Hampshire Water Co 1999–; MEP (Cons) Yorkshire & the Humber 1999–; European Parl: Cons chief whip 1999–2001, Cons spokesman on Justice and Home Affairs 1999–2007, Cons spokesman on Transport and Tourism 2007–, ldr Cons in European Parl 2004–; memb: Bd Cons Party 2005–, Northern Bd Cons Party 2007–; memb 'Future of Europe' Constitutional Convention 2002–03; chm: Kirkhope Cmmn on Asylsum 2003, Kirkhope Cmmn on Immigration 2004; vice-chm Constitutional Affairs Ctee 2007–; memb: Newcastle Airport Controlling Bd 1981–85, Northern Region HA 1982–86, Mental Health Act Cmmn 1983–86; cncllr Northumberland CC 1981–85; govr Newcastle upon Tyne Royal GS 1986–99, dep chm Governing Bodies Assoc for Ind Schs 1990–98; *Recreations* swimming, tennis, flying (holds private pilot's licence); *Clubs* Northern Counties (Newcastle upon Tyne), Dunstanburgh Castle Golf (Northumberland), IOD; *Style—* Timothy Kirkhope, Esq, MEP; ✉ ASP 14E 246, European Parliament, Rue Wiertz, B-1047 Brussels, Belgium (tel 0032 2284 7321, fax 0032 2284 9321, e-mail timothy.kirkhope@europarl.europa.eu or timothy.kirkhope@btinternet.com)

KIRKLAND, Prof Angus Ian; s of Hugh Thomson Kilpatrick Kirkland, of Rayleigh, Essex, and Kathleen Theresa, *née* Doherty; *b* 29 August 1965, Rochford, Essex; *Educ* Univ of Cambridge (MA, PhD), Univ of Oxford (MA, DPhil); *partner* Keiren Towlson; *Career* Univ of Cambridge: Br Ramsay fell 1991–93, sr res fell 1993–2003; Univ of Oxford: Leverhulme sr res lectr 2003–05, prof of materials 2005–; fell: Fitzwilliam Coll Cambridge 1992–2003, Linacre Coll Oxford 2003–; memb Inst of Physics, FRSC 2000 (MRSC 1989), CChem 2000, fell Royal Microscopical Soc (FRMS); *Publications* over 200 papers in scientific jls; *Recreations* horse racing; *Clubs* Hawkes; *Style—* Prof Angus Kirkland; ✉ University of Oxford, Dept of Materials, Parks Road, Oxford OX1 3PH

KIRKPATRICK, Prof David Lawson Irwin; s of John Finlay Kirkpatrick (d 1981), of Belfast, and Mabel Ireland, *née* Irwin (d 1992); *b* 25 July 1939; *Educ* Royal Belfast Acad Inst, Queen's Univ Belfast (BSc), Univ of Virginia (MSc), Univ of Southampton (PhD), Birkbeck Coll London (MSc); *m* 1965, Carol Gillian Eveline, da of Robert Harold Evelyn Gladstone; 1 s (John Finlay Evelyn b 1966), 1 da (Alison Jacqueline Jean b 1968); *Career* various positions rising to Grade 5 Scientific Civil Service MoD 1962–95; attache on Br Defence Staff USA 1985–88; Grade 5 head Aerodynamic Dept RAE and dir Project Time and Cost Analysis MoD (PE) 1988–95; prof of defence analysis UCL 1999–2004 (sr lectr 1995–99); assoc fell RUSI 1996, memb American Civil War Round Table (UK); FRAeS 1989; *Publications* numerous publications on aerodynamics, aircraft design, defence procurement, defence economics, operational analysis, and military history; *Recreations* reading, bridge; *Style—* Prof David Kirkpatrick; ✉ Woodside, Broad Oak, Odiham, Hook, Hampshire RG29 1AQ

KIRKPATRICK, Sir Ivone Elliott; 11 Bt (NS 1685), of Closeburn, Dumfriesshire; s of Sir James Alexander Kirkpatrick, 10 Bt (d 1954), and Ellen Gertrude, *née* Elliott; *b* 1 October 1942; *Educ* Wellington, St Mark's Coll Adelaide Univ; *Heir* bro, Robin Kirkpatrick; *Style—* Sir Ivone Kirkpatrick, Bt; ✉ PO Box 181, Kent Town, S Australia 5071, Australia

KIRKPATRICK, Prof Janice Mary; da of James Burns Kirkpatrick, and Jane Henry Copeland Borthwick Kirkpatrick; *b* 16 April 1962; *Educ* Dumfries Acad, Glasgow Sch of Art (BA, MA); *Career* designer; creative dir and fndr Graven Images Ltd 1985–; visiting lectr Glasgow Sch of Art 1993–96, external examiner Kingston Univ 1997–, visiting prof Univ of Glasgow 1999–; dir and chair: The Lighthouse Tst 1998–, Glasgow Sch of Art 1999–; tstee Nat Endowment for Sci, Tech and the Arts; memb D&AD; FSCD, FRSA; *Awards* RSA 1983, Scottish Film Cncl 1983, Newberry Medal 1984, commended finalist Prince Philip Designer of the Year Award 1994, Conran Fndn Archive Collector 1996; *Publications* contrib magazines incl: Creative Review, Design Review, Architectural Journal, Scottish Homes and Interiors; delivered numerous papers on design issues; *Recreations* motorcycling, breeding saddleback pigs; *Style—* Prof Janice Kirkpatrick; ✉ Graven Images Ltd, 83A Canderiggs, Glasgow G1 1LF (tel 0141 552 6626, fax 0141 552 0433, e-mail janice@graven.co.uk)

KIRKPATRICK, Jennifer Augustine (Jenny); da of Richard Arthur Seckerson (d 1973), of Wallasey, Merseyside, and Olive Frances Maude, *née* O'Connor; *b* 7 August 1946; *Educ* Oldershaw GS Wallasey, Cheshire Coll of Educn, Keele Univ (BEd); *Career* teacher 1968–79; gen sec Nat Assoc of Probation Offrs 1979–85; dir: Electricity Consumers' Cncl 1985–88, The Paul Hamlyn Fndn 1988–89, Burson-Marsteller 1989–92, Venture Link Investors 1991–93, LS Research Ltd 1994–, The Strategic Partnership (London) Ltd 1996–; chm: Oxfordshire Community Health NHS Trust 1993–99, Gas Consumers' Cncl 1995–2000; ceo Electricity Assoc 2002; memb: Consultative Ctee European Coal and Steel Community 1998–2002, Pensions Protection and Accreditation Bd 2000–; *Recreations* written and spoken word, public policy, anything obsessional - crosswords, bridge, puzzles, horses; *Style—* Jenny Kirkpatrick

KIRKUP, Prof James Falconer; s of James Harold Kirkup (d 1958), and Mary Johnson (d 1973); descendant of Seymour Stocker Kirkup (DNB), Thomas Kirkup (DNB), William Falconer (DNB); *b* 23 April 1918; *Educ* South Shields Secdy Sch, King's Coll Durham (BA); *Career* lectr and prof at various univs in Britain, Europe, USA and Far East, prof of comparative lit Kyoto Univ of Foreign Studies 1976–88, composer An Actor's Revenge (opera); sponsor Inst of Psychophysical Res Oxford 1970; named Ollave Order of Bards, Ovates and Druids 1974; pres Br Haiku Soc 1990–; British Centre for Literary Translation 1995; FRSL 1964; *Books* volumes of poetry incl: The Sense of the Visit (1985), Throwback: Poems towards an Autobiography (1992), Shooting Stars: Haiku (1992), Words for Contemplation: Poems (1993), Look at it This Way: Poems for Young People (1993), Short Takes: One-Line Senryu and Haiku (1993), Blue Bamboo (1994), The Genius of Haiku (1994), Formulas for Chaos (1994), Strange Attractors (1995), An Extended Breath: Collected Longer Poems (1995), Selected Shorter Poems: Omens of Disaster Vol 1 (1995), A Certain State of Mind (1995), How to Cook Women: Selected Poems and Stories of Takagi Kyozo (1996), Burning Giraffes: An Anthology of Modern and Contemporary Japanese Poets (1996), A Book of Tanka (1996), Utsusemi, tanka (1996), Broad Daylight: Poems East and West (1996), Child of the Tyne (reprint of The Only Child and Sorrows, Passions and Alarms in 1 vol, 1996), Measures of Time: Collected Longer Poems Vol II (1996), Once and for All Vol II (1996), The Patient Obituarist: New Poems (1996), Collected Shorter Poems (2 vols, 1997), A Book of Tanka (winner of Japan Festival Fndn Prize, 1997), He Dreamed He Was a Butterfly: tanka (1997), Tanka Tales (1997), The Signing (1998), Pikadon: An Epic (1998), One-Man Band: Poems Without Words (1999), Tokonoma: Haiku and Tanka with woodprints by Naoko Matsubara (1999), Tanka Alphabet: Tanka Illustrated, An Island in the Sky: Poems for Andorra, A Tiger In Your Tanka: Songs and Narratives (2001), In Thickets of Memory: 700 Tanka Poems by Saito Fumi (trans with Tamaki Makoto, 2002), Pages from the Seasons: A Journal of Tanka Poems by Professor Emeritus Fumiko Miura (trans with Fumiko Miura, 2002), Shields Sketches (with illustrations by George McVay, 2002), No More Hiroshimas (revised edn, 2004), Myself as an Anatomical Lovemaking Chart and Other Poems by Takahashi Mutsuo (trans with Tamaki Makoto, bilingual edn, 2004), Andorra: An Island in the Sky (poems, essays, translations, 2005), The Authentic Touch (2006), We of Zipangu: Poems of Takahashi Mutsuo (2006), A Pilgrim in Hell: Poems by Iwan Gilkin (poems in translation, 2006); translator of Kawabata, Takahashi Mutsuo, Simone de Beauvoir, Schiller, Kleist and Pasolini (internet poetry translations at www.brindin.com and www.beineke.com); winner Scott-Moncrieff Prize for Translation 1993 for Painted Shadows by Jean-Baptiste Niel, Blindsight (trans Hervé Guibert, 1995), Paradise (trans Hervé Guibert, 1996); A Poet Could Not But Be Gay (autobiography), I of All People (autobiography), Gaijin On The Ginza (novel), Me All Over: Memoirs of a Misfit (autobiography, 1993), Queens have Died Young and Fair (novel, 1993); *Recreations* reading, music (jazz and classical), cinema, travel; *Style—* Prof James Kirkup; ✉ Atic D, Edifici les Bons, Avinguda de Rouillac 7, Les Bons, Encamp, Principality of Andorra

KIRKWOOD, Hon Mr Justice; Sir Andrew Tristram Hammett Kirkwood; kt (1993); s of Maj Tristram Guy Hammett Kirkwood, RE (ka 1944), and Margaret Elizabeth Montague Brown (who m 2, Rt Rev Arthur Groom Parham, MC, Bishop of Reading, and 3, Sir Neville Major Ginner Faulks, MBE, TD) (d 1982); *b* 5 June 1944; *Educ* Radley, Christ Church Oxford (MA); *m* 13 July 1968, Penelope Jane, *née* Eaton; 1 da (Sophie b 25 Oct 1969), 2 s (Tristram b 2 Jan 1972, Edward b 19 June 1977); *Career* called to the Bar Inner Temple 1966 (bencher 1993); recorder of the Crown Court 1987–93, QC 1989, judge of the High Court of Justice (Family Div) 1993–; chm Leicestershire Inquiry 1992, memb Judicial Studies Bd 1994–99 (co-chm Civil and Family Ctee 1994–98, chm Family Ctee 1998–99), judge Employment Appeal Tbnl 1996–98; liaison judge Family Div: Midland & Oxford Circuit 1999–2001, Midland Circuit 2001–06; *Recreations* the countryside; *Clubs* MCC; *Style—* Hon Mr Justice Kirkwood; ✉ Royal Courts of Justice, Strand, London WC2A 2LL

KIRKWOOD, Colin Bennie; s of Matthew Chrystal Kirkwood (d 1991), of Killearn, Stirlingshire, and Charlotte Margaret, *née* Bennie (d 1993); *b* 6 December 1951; *Educ* Glasgow Acad, Napier Coll of Science and Technol Edinburgh (Dip Book and Periodical Publishing); *m* 4 April 1987, Isabel Mary, da of David Gordon Johnstone (d 1976); 1 s (Matthew David b 1989), 1 da (Rosanna Mary b 1991); *Career* The Aberdeen University Press Ltd 1990–92, publishing conslt 1992–93, publishing dir Times Books/Bartholomew Div HarperCollins Publishers Ltd 1993–94, publishing and mktg conslt 1994–95, mktg dir Colin Baxter Photography Ltd 1995–2006, mktg conslt 2006–; chm Scot Young Publishers Soc 1979, chm Scot Publishers Assoc 1984–86, dir Tuckwell Press 1994–95, memb Bd Edinburgh Book Festival 1984–89, ed Charles Rennie Mackintosh Soc Newsletter 1976–84; *Books* The National Book League (1972); *Recreations* golf, walking, cooking, architecture; *Style—* Colin B Kirkwood, Esq; ✉ Easter Coulnakyle, Nethy Bridge, Inverness-shire PH25 3EA (tel 01479 821393)

KIRKWOOD, 3 Baron (UK 1951); David Harvie Kirkwood; s of 2 Baron Kirkwood (d 1970, s of 1 Baron, PC, JP, MP Dumbarton Burghs 1922–50, who as David Kirkwood was deported for being the ringleader in a protest against rent increases); *b* 24 November 1931; *Educ* Rugby, Trinity Hall Cambridge (MA, PhD); *m* 1965, Judith, da of John Hunt, of Leeds; 3 da (Hon Ruth b 17 Sept 1966, Hon Anne b 24 April 1969, Hon Lucy b 28 July 1972); *Heir* bro, Hon James Stuart Kirkwood; *Career* warden Stephenson Hall 1974–79, sr lectr Sheffield Univ 1976–87, hon sr lectr 1987–; memb AUT; CEng; *Clubs* Nat Liberal; *Style—* The Lord Kirkwood; ✉ 56 Endcliffe Hall Avenue, Sheffield S10 3EL (tel 0114 266 3107)

KIRKWOOD, The Rt Hon Lord; Ian Candlish Kirkwood; PC (2000), QC (1970); s of John Brown Kirkwood OBE (d 1964), and Constance Kirkwood (d 1987); *b* 8 June 1932; *Educ* George Watson's Boys' Coll Edinburgh, Univ of Edinburgh (MA, LLB), Univ of Michigan (LLM); *m* 1970, Jill, da of Lt-Cdr Trevor P Scott, RN (ret), of Torquay; 2 s (Jonathan b 1973, Richard b 1975); *Career* chm Medical Appeal Tribunal (until 1987); memb Parole Bd for Scotland 1994–97; senator Coll of Justice Scotland 1987; *Recreations* tennis, golf, chess; *Style—* The Rt Hon Lord Kirkwood, PC; ✉ 58 Murrayfield Avenue, Edinburgh EH12 6AY (tel 0131 477 1994); Knockbrex House, Borgue, Kirkcudbrightshire DG6 4UE (tel 01557 870269)

KIRKWOOD OF KIRKHOPE, Baron (Life Peer UK 2005), of Kirkhope in Scottish Borders; Sir Archibald Johnstone (Archy) Kirkwood; kt (2002); s of David Kirkwood, of Glasgow, and Jessie Barclay (d 1980); *b* 22 April 1946; *Educ* Heriot-Watt Univ (BSc); *m* 1972, Rosemary Jane, da of Edward John Chester; 1 s, 1 da; *Career* slr; MP (Lib until 1988, now Lib Dem) Roxburgh and Berwickshire 1983–2005; House of Commons: Lib spokesman on health and social security 1985–87, Alliance spokesman on overseas devpt

1987, Lib spokesman on Scotland 1987–88, SLD spokesman on welfare, health and educn 1988–89, Lib Dem convenor and spokesman on welfare and social security 1989–94, Lib Dem chief whip 1992–97 (dep 1989–92), Lib Dem spokesman on community care 1994–97, spokesman House of Commons Cmmn 1997–2005, chm Social Security Select Ctee 1997–2001, chm Work and Pensions Select Ctee 2001–05, sponsored Private Member's Bills leading to Access to Personal Files Act 1987 and Access to Medical Reports Act 1988; chm Lib Dem Campaigns Ctee 1989–92; chm Rowntree Reform Tst 1985–2007; former memb Bd of Govrs Westminster Fndn for Democracy; *Recreations* music; *Style*— The Lord Kirkwood of Kirkhope

KIRSCHEL, Laurence Grant; s of Eric Kirschel, and Ruth, *née* Novak; *b* 17 December 1962, Middlesex; *Educ* Franklin House London, Carmel Coll Wallingford; *Children* 1 s (Davar Ethan b 3 Aug 2000); *Career* property developer; estab main company 1983; tstee Kirschel Fndn; FRICS; *Style*— Laurence Kirschel, Esq; ✉ 26 Soho Square, London W1D 4NU (tel 020 7437 4372, fax 020 7437 3800, e-mail laurence@26sohosq.com)

KIRSTEIN, Prof Peter Thomas; CBE (2003); s of Walter Kirstein (d 1983), of London; *b* 20 June 1933; *Educ* Highgate Sch, Gonville & Caius Coll Cambridge (BA), Stanford Univ (MSc, PhD), Univ of London (DSc); *m* 5 July 1958, Gwen Margaret Oldham; 2 da (Sarah Lynn b 1964, Claire Fiona b 1971); *Career* res assoc and lectr W W Hansen Laboratory of Physics Stanford Univ 1957–58, accelerator physicist Centre of European Nuclear Research Geneva 1959–63, scientific rep Europe General Electric Company of USA 1963–67, prof of computer systems Univ of London 1970–73 (reader in information processing 1967–70); UCL: prof 1973–, head Dept of Computer Science 1980–95, dir of research 1995–, hon fell 2006; Sr Award IEE 1999, ComSoc Award IEEE 1999, Postel Award 2003, Life Achievement Award RAE 2006; foreign hon memb AAAS 2002; FIEE 1965, FInstP 1965, SMIEEE 1975, FREng 1985, distinguished FBCS 2003 (FBCS 1964); *Books* Space Charge Flow (1967); *Recreations* skiing, tennis, bridge; *Clubs* Alpine Ski; *Style*— Prof Peter Kirstein, CBE, FREng; ✉ 31 Bancroft Avenue, London N2 0AR (tel 020 8340 3154); Department of Computer Science, University College London, Gower Street, London WC1E 6BT (tel 020 7679 7286, fax 020 7387 1397, e-mail kirstein@cs.ucl.ac.uk)

KISSACK, Nigel Euan Jackson; s of Maj Henry Jackson Kissack, RE (ret), of Sydney, Aust, and formerly Isle of Man, and Ethel Valerie, *née* Kneen; *b* 8 April 1955; *Educ* King William's Coll IOM, Univ of Sheffield (LLB); *m* 11 Oct 1980, Kathryn Margaret, da of Thomas Lloyd-Jones, of Hale, Cheshire; 1 da (Annabel Laura Jayne b 4 Aug 1982), 1 s (Richard Lloyd b 2 Aug 1984); *Career* admitted slr 1979; articled clerk Foysters Manchester, Alsop Wilkinson 1979–1996, ptnr DLA 1996–97, ptnr and nat head of litigation Pinsent Masons1997–, managing ptnr Leeds 2000–03; author of various professional articles; *Recreations* rugby, cricket, cycling, reading, golf, skiing; *Style*— Nigel Kissack, Esq; ✉ Pinsents Masons, Citypoint, One Ropemaker Street, London EC2Y 9AH (tel 020 7667 0110)

KISSMANN, Edna; da of Karl Kissmann (d 1983), of Jerusalem, and Frieda Mosser Kissmann, of Tel Aviv; *b* 20 December 1949; *Educ* Hebrew Univ HS, Hebrew Univ (BA), Univ of Boston Sch of Public Communications (MSc); *Career* asst press sec PM's Office Govt of Israel 1975, md Ruder and Finn PR Ltd Israel 1976–77 (assoc dir 1973–75); Burson-Marsteller Inc NY: account exec 1978–79, account supervisor 1979–80, client servs mangr 1980–82, gp mangr 1982–85, vice-pres then sr vice-pres, exec vice-pres and unit mangr i/c healthcare communications practice 1985–88; Burson-Marsteller London: EUP/unit mangr of healthcare and mktg 1988–89, jt md 1989–92; chief Burson-Marsteller Germany 1992–93; Burson-Marsteller London: global head of healthcare practice 1994–97, chief knowledge offr worldwide 1997–99; winner of several internal Burson-Marsteller awards; vice-chm Europe 1993; memb Bd: Business in the Community, London First Centre; fndr memb Israel PR Assoc 1974 (memb London 1990); *Recreations* music, theatre, travel, people, good food and wine; *Clubs* The Reform; *Style*— Miss Edna Kissmann

KISZELY, Lt-Gen Sir John Panton; KCB (2004), MC (1982); s of Dr John Kiszely (d 1995), and Maude, *née* Panton; *b* 2 April 1948; *Educ* Marlborough, RMAS; *m* 28 July 1984, Hon Arabella Jane, da of 3 Baron Herschell, *qv*; 3 s (Alastair b 17 Feb 1986, Matthew b 27 Nov 1987, Andrew b 28 April 1990); *Career* CO 1 Bn Scots Guards 1986–88 (mentioned in despatches 1988), Cdr 22 Armd Bde 1991–93, Cdr 7 Armd Bde 1993, Dep Cmdt Staff Coll Camberley 1993–96, GOC 1 (UK) Armd Div 1996–98, ACDS (Programmes) MOD 1998–2001, Dep Cdr NATO Force Bosnia 2001–02, Cdr Regnl Forces 2002–04, Dep Cdr Multinational Force Iraq 2004–05, dir Defence Acad 2005–; Regtl Lt Col Scots Gds 1995–2001, Col Comdt The Intelligence Corps 2000–, Hon Col Univ of London Offr Trg Corps 2003–; Queen's Commendation for Valuable Service 1996; CRAeS 2006; Offr Legion of Merit (USA) 2005; *Publications* contrib: The Science of War: Back to First Principles (1983), Military Power: Land Warfare in Theory and Practice (1997), The Falklands Conflict Twenty Years On (2004), The Past as Prologue: History and the Military Profession (2006); author of numerous articles in military jls; *Recreations* sailing, fishing, music, chess; *Clubs* Royal Yacht Squadron, Royal Solent Yacht, Cavalry and Guards'; *Style*— Lt-Gen Sir John Kiszely, KCB, MC; ✉ c/o HQ Scots Guards, Wellington Barracks, Birdcage Walk, London SW1E 6HQ (tel 020 7930 4466)

KITAJ, R B (Ronald); s of Dr Walter Kitaj (d 1982), and Jeanne Brooks Kitaj; *b* 29 October 1932; *Educ* Royal Coll of Art; *m* 15 Dec 1983, Sandra Fisher; 2 s (Lem b 1958, Max b 1984), 1 da (Dominie b 1964); *Career* artist; US Army 1955–57; pt/t teacher: Camberwell Sch of Art 1961–63, Slade Sch 1963–67; visiting prof: Univ of Calif Berkeley 1968, UCLA 1970; Hon DLitt London 1982; Hon Dr: RCA 1991, Calif Coll of Art & Craft 1995, Durham 1996; memb US Inst of Arts and Letters NY 1982, Nat Acad of Design NY 1987; RA 1991 (ARA 1984); Chevalier de l'Ordre des Arts et des Lettres (France) 1996; *Solo Exhibitions* Marlborough New London Gallery 1963 and 1970, Marlborough Gallery NY 1975 and 1974, LA Co Museum of Art 1965, Stedelijk Museum Amsterdam 1967, Museum of Art Cleveland 1967, Univ of Calif Berkeley 1967, Galerie Mikro Berlin 1969, Kestner Gesellschaft Hanover 1970, Boymans-van-Beuningen Museum Rotterdam 1970, Cincinnati Art Museum Ohio (with Jim Dine) 1973, Marlborough Fine Art 1977, 1980 and 1985; *Retrospective Exhibitions* Hirshhorn Museum Washington 1981, Cleveland Museum of Art Ohio 1981, Kunsthalle Düsseldorf 1982, Tate Gallery 1994 and 1996, Los Angeles County Museum 1995, Metropolitan Museum NY 1995, Golden Lion (painting) Venice Biennale 1995; *Style*— R B Kitaj, Esq, RA; ✉ c/o Marlborough Fine Art Ltd, 6 Albemarle Street, London W1X 3HF (tel 020 7629 5161)

KITCHEN, Mervyn John; s of Hubert John Kitchen, and Phyllis Elizabeth, *née* Webber; *b* 1 August 1940; *Educ* Backwell Comp Sch Bristol; *m* Anne, *née* Mathias; 1 da (Faye b 30 Sept 1975), 1 s (Jody b 6 March 1977); *Career* cricket umpire; laboratory asst Long Ashton Res Centre 1955–56; professional cricketer Somerset CCC: joined 1957, debut v Middx at Lord's, awarded county cap 1966, testimonial 1973, ret 1979; first class cricket umpire: appointed 1982, test debut Eng v NZ Lord's 1990, one day int debut v India Trent Bridge 1990; honours as player: John Player League winners 1979, runners-up Gillette Cup (Man of the Match award), awarded best batting performance BBC TV Sunday Cricket 1966; jobs during off-seasons whilst player incl: orchard technician, DIY asst, lorry driver, photographic printer, bookmaker's clerk; *Style*— Mervyn Kitchen, Esq; ✉ c/o England and Wales Cricket Board, Lord's Cricket Ground, London NW8 8QN (tel 020 7286 4405)

KITCHEN, Michael; s of Arthur Kitchen, and Betty, *née* Allen; *b* 31 October 1948; *Educ* City of Leicester Boys GS, RADA; *Children* 2 s (Jack b 7 Oct 1988, James b 25 Nov 1995); *Career* actor; writer of two screenplays and short stories; *Theatre* work incl: Nat Theatre 1974–84, RSC 1987 (roles incl Hogarth, Mercutio, Bolingbroke), Lenny in The Homecoming (West End); *Television* numerous appearances incl: Caught on a Train, Brimstone and Treacle, Home Run, Benefactors, The Brontës, Freud, No Man's Land, Savages, Chancer, The Justice Game, Bedroom Farce, King Lear, A Comedy of Errors, School Play, Love Song, Ball Trap at the Côte Sauvage, To Play the King, Dandelion Dead, Buccaneers, The Hanging Gale, Reckless, Wilderness, Oliver Twist, The Secret World of Michael Fry, Foyle's War, Alibi, Falling, Mobile; *Film* incl: Out of Africa, The Russia House, Fools of Fortune, The Dive, Pied Piper, Unman Wittering and Zigo, The Bunker, The Enchanted April, Hostage, The Guilty, The Trial, Mrs Dalloway, Goldeneye, The Last Contract, The World is Not Enough, Proof of Life; *Recreations* music, guitar, piano, composition, pilot's licence, riding, tennis, skiing, swimming; *Style*— Michael Kitchen, Esq; ✉ c/o ICM Ltd, Oxford House, 76 Oxford Street, London W1N 0AX (tel 020 7636 6565, fax 020 7323 0101)

KITCHENER, Prof Henry Charles; *b* 1 July 1951; *Educ* Eastwood HS, Univ of Glasgow (MB ChB, MD); *m* 12 June 1977, Valerie Anne, 1 da (Sophie); *Career* Florence and William Blair-Bell res fell 1980–82, lectr in obstetrics and gynaecology Univ of Singapore 1983–84, William Blair-Bell meml lectr RCOG 1985, conslt obstetrician and gynaecologist specialising in gynaecological oncology Aberdeen Royal NHS Tst 1988–96, prof of gynaecological oncology Univ of Manchester 1996–; pres Br Soc for Colposcopy and Cervical Pathology (BSCCP) 2000–03 (vice-pres 1997–99), memb Gynaecological Visiting Soc of GB and I; FRCSGlas 1989, FRCOG 1994 (MRCOG 1980); *Recreations* golf, hill walking; *Clubs* Prestbury Golf, Royal Dornoch Golf; *Style*— Prof Henry Kitchener; ✉ Southlands, Bridge End Drive, Prestbury, Cheshire SK10 4DL (e-mail hckitchener@aol.com); Department of Obstetrics and Gynaecology, St Mary's Hospital, Whitworth Park, Manchester M13 0JH (tel 0161 276 6461, fax 0161 273 6134)

KITCHENER-FELLOWES, *see:* Fellowes

KITCHENER OF KHARTOUM AND OF BROOME, 3 Earl (UK 1914); Henry Herbert Kitchener; TD, DL (Cheshire 1972); s of Viscount Broome (d 1928, s of 2 Earl and n of the Field Marshal who won his reputation at the recapture of Khartoum); suc gf 1937; *b* 24 February 1919; *Educ* Winchester, Trinity Coll Cambridge; *Heir* none; *Career* Maj RCS (TA), ret; pres Lord Kitchener Nat Meml Fund, pres Henry Doubleday Res Assoc; *Clubs* Brooks's; *Style*— The Rt Hon the Earl Kitchener of Khartoum, TD, DL; ✉ Westergate Wood, Eastergate, Chichester, West Sussex PO20 3SB (tel 01243 545797, e-mail ekk@talk21.com)

KITCHIN, Alan William Norman; s of Norman Tyson Kitchin (d 1995), and Shirley Boyd, *née* Simpson; *Educ* Oundle, Univ of Cambridge (Squire univ scholar, BA, Tapp postgrad scholar, MA); *Career* admitted slr 1978; Ashurst Morris Crisp (now Ashurst): ptnr 1986–, ptnr in charge Tokyo office 1991–2003, managing ptnr Asia 1998–2003, head worldwide Japanese practice 2003–; chm Infrastructure and Privatisation Ctee Law Asia; *Books* International Trade for the Nonspecialist (co-author); *Recreations* golf, tennis; *Clubs* Walton Heath Golf, Luffenham Heath Golf, Reform, Kasumigaseki Golf Tokyo; *Style*— Alan Kitchin, Esq; ✉ Ashurst, Broadwalk House, 5 Appold Street, London EC2A 2HA (tel 020 7638 1111, fax 020 7972 7990, e-mail alan.kitchin@ashursts.com)

KITCHIN, Hon Mr Justice; Sir David James Tyson; kt (2005); s of Norman Tyson Kitchin (d 1995), and Shirley Boyd, *née* Simpson (d 2002); *b* 30 April 1955; *Educ* Oundle, Fitzwilliam Coll Cambridge (MA); *m* 28 Oct 1989, Charlotte, da of Cdr David Jones; 1 da (Lara b 16 June 1991), 1 s (James b 2 July 1993); *Career* called to the Bar Gray's Inn 1977 (bencher 2003), QC 1994, judge of the High Court of Justice (Chancery Div) 2005–; chm Vet Code of Practice Ctee Nat Office of Animal Health 1995–2001; chm Intellectual Property Bar Assoc 2004–05, memb Bar Cncl 2004–05; *Recreations* golf, tennis; *Clubs* Walton Heath, Leander, Hawks' (Cambridge); *Style*— The Hon Mr Justice Kitchin; ✉ Royal Courts of Justice, Strand, London WC2A 2LL

KITCHING, Alan; *b* 29 December 1940; *m* 1962, Rita, *née* Haylett (d 1984); 2 s; *Career* compositor to J W Brown & Son Darlington 1956–61, fndr (with Anthony Froshaug) Experimental Printing Workshop Sch of Art Watford Coll of Technol 1964 (first year work exhibited ICA 1965), freelance design practice working in magazine and book design 1971–78, fndr (with Derek Birdsall) Omnific Studios Partnership Covent Garden 1978–86, subsequently estab letterpress studio Islington 1986, fndr/designer The Typography Workshop Clerkenwell 1989–; pt/t teacher of typography Central Sch of Art & Design London 1968–72, visiting lectr in typography RCA 1988–2006, visiting prof London Inst 2001, visiting prof Univ of the Arts London 2001; estab letterpress workshops RCA 1992, subsequent workshops at Univs of Brighton and Middx and Glasgow Sch of Art, workshop/lecture tour Norway 1997, Germany 1999, Denmark and Holland 2000; designer millennium stamp for Royal Mail 1999; memb AGI 1994, RDI 1994; FRCA 1998; *Exhibitions* Pentagram Gall London (first exhbn of letterpress work) 1992, RCA (retrospective exhbn of typography and printing) 1993, Type Art '98 (Coningsby Gallery) 1998, Pentagram Gall London (solo) 2002; *Books and Publications* Typography Manual (Watford Sch of Art, 1970), Broadside (occasional pubn devoted to the typographic arts, 1 edn 1988); *Clubs* Chelsea Arts; *Style*— Alan Kitching, RDI; ✉ The Typography Workshop, 19 Cleaver Street, London SE11 4DP

KITCHING, John; s of Douglas Eric Kitching, of Barwell, Leics (d 1992), and Dorothy Violet, *née* Mellors (d 2005); *b* 7 July 1950, Surrey; *Educ* Davidson HS Croydon; *m* 1, 16 March 1973; 1 da (Sarah Elaine b 16 May 1975); m 2, 15 May 1982, Elaine, *née* Flint; 1 da (Elizabeth Elzine b 24 March 1983); *Career* early career as building services engr then various sr mgmnt roles Harris Queensway; Carpetright plc: joined 1988, sales dir 1992, md 1996, chief exec Europe 2005–; MInstD; *Recreations* authy on the life and times of Queen Victoria, classic 20th century Br cars; *Style*— John Kitching, Esq; ✉ Carpetright plc, Amberley House, New Road, Rainham, Essex RM13 8QN (tel 01708 527738, fax 01708 557047)

KITCHING, Paul; s of William Kitching (d 1968), and Angela Ainslie (d 2002); *b* 23 March 1961; *Educ* Dryden Rd HS Gateshead, Newcastle Coll of Art & Technol; *Career* commis chef: Viking Hotel 1981–83, Middlethorpe Hall York 1983–84; sous chef: Restaurant 74 Canterbury (joined as commis chef) 1984–87, Gidleigh Park 1987–90 (joined as 3 chef); head chef Nunsmere Hall Hotel 1990–96, head chef and owner Juniper 1996–; *Awards* for Nunsmere Hall Hotel: 3 stars Good Food Guide and Co Restaurant of the Year 1993 and 1995, 3 AA rosettes 1993–96, 3 AA red stars (for hotel), Egon Ronay 77% (for hotel); for Juniper: Cheshire Life Newcomer of the Year, City Life Best Restaurant, Manchester Evening News Best Dinner, 3 stars Good Food Guide and Co Restaurant of the Year 1997, Cheshire Life Restaurant of the Year 1998, 7 out of 10 Good Food Guide (annually) 1998–2007, Michelin rosette (annually) 1998–2007, Highest Rated Restaurant in Manchester, Gtr Manchester, Lancashire, and Cheshire 1996–99, Highest Rated Restaurant in the North West, placed 17th in top 50 Restaurants 2000–2001, 4 AA rosettes (annually) 2002–07, Good Food Guide Restaurant of the Year 2003, Guardian Weekend 18.5/20 and Restaurant of the Year 2003, Metro News Restaurant of the Year 2003; Life Magazine: Northwest Chef of the Year 2003, Restaurant of the Year (Cheshire) 2007; *Recreations* history of the American Civil War 1861–65; *Style*— Paul Kitching, Esq; ✉ Juniper, 21 The Downs, Altrincham, Greater Manchester WA14 2QD (tel 0161 929 4008, fax 0161 929 4009)

KITNEY, Prof Richard Ian; OBE (2001); s of Leonard Walter Richard Kitney, and Gladys Simpson, *née* Byrne; *b* 13 February 1945; *Educ* Enfield GS, Univ of Surrey (DipEE, MSc), Imperial Coll London (PhD, DIC) Univ of London (DSc); *m* 7 May 1977, Vera Theresa; 2 s (Andrew John b 18 March 1978, Paul David b 30 July 1980); *Career* electronics engr

K

Thorn EMI 1963–72, lectr in biophysics Chelsea Coll London 1972–78; Imperial Coll London: lectr 1978–85, reader 1985–89, prof 1989–, dir Centre of Biological and Med Systems 1991–97, head of dept 1997–2001, dean Faculty of Engrg 2003–; visiting prof: Georgia Inst of Technol 1981–90, MIT 1991–; govr Imperial Coll London 1995–98, govr Royal Post Grad Med Sch 1995–98; tech dir Intravascular Research Ltd 1987–94, dir St Mary's Imaging plc 1991–96, dep chm and tech dir ComMedica Ltd 1999–; tstee: Smith and Nephew Fndn 1996, Dennis Rosen Tst 2001–; regular contrib to BBC radio progs, also occasional film and TV work; Freeman City of London 1996, Liveryman Worshipful Co of Engrs 1995; FIEE 1993, FRSM 1994, FRCPEd 1996, FREng 1999, fell World Technology Network 2000, FRSA 2001; *Publications* Recent Advances in the Study of Heart Rate Variability (with O Rompelman, 1980), The Beat-by-Beat Investigation of Cardiac Function (with O Rompelman, 1987), The Coming of the Global Healthcare Industry (with N Bosenquet, 1998); over 100 papers in learned jls and 120 conf papers; *Recreations* history, cooking, France; *Clubs* Athenaeum; *Style*— Prof Richard Kitney, OBE; ✉ Department of Bioengineering, Imperial College, London SW7 2AZ (tel 020 7594 6226, fax 020 7584 4297, mobile 07785 341922, e-mail r.kitney@imperial.ac.uk)

KITSON, Prof Alison Lydia; da of James Robert McClelland (d 1993), and Winifred Elizabeth, *née* Wortley (d 1992); *b* 23 March 1956, Portadown, Co Armagh; *Educ* Portadown Coll, Univ of Ulster (BSc, RN, PhD); *m* 1, 1979, Kenneth James Kitson; m 2, 1990, Dr Paul Henry Yerrell; 1 s (Joshua Henry b 18 Nov 1989), 1 da (Lydia Florence Winifred b 1 June 1992), 1 step da (Kathryn Lucy b 16 Nov 1971), 1 step s (Matthew Paul b 16 Aug 1973); *Career* staff nurse and research nurse Ulster Hosps Dundonald and DHSS 1979–82, lectr in nursing studies Univ of Ulster 1982–85, dir RCN Standards of Care Prog 1985–92 (also RCN advsr for standards of care 1985–89), head of evaluation and research Inst of Nursing 1989–92, dir Nat Inst for Nursing 1992–96, dir RCN Inst 1996–2002, exec dir of nursing RCN 2002–; supernumerary fell Green Coll Oxford 1993– (jr research fell 1989–92); visiting prof Oxford Brookes Univ 1992–97, distinguished nurse lectr Johns Hopkins Hosp Univ of Baltimore 1996, Rosenstadt visiting prof of nursing Univ of Toronto 1999, visiting prof Univ of Adelaide 2000; memb Editorial Bd Quality and Safety in Health Care 1990– (former assoc ed), author of articles in learned jls; memb: Health Technol Assessment Commissioning Gp 1998–2002, Research Advsy Bd Parkinsons Disease Soc 2002–04, Widening Participation Working Gp HEFCE 2003–, Health Advsy Bd IPPR 2005–, Health Advsy Bd Health Fndn 2005–, Bd Skills for Health 2005–, Bd Nat Collaborating Centre for Nursing and Supportive Care 2006–; tstee Brendoncare Tst 1998–; memb Cncl Henley Mgmnt Coll 2006–; Distinguished Grad of the Year Univ of Ulster 2002, Florence Nightingale Leadership Award 2004; hon prof: Univ of Ulster 2002–, City Univ 2002–, Univ of Leicester 2002–; FRCN 1991; *Recreations* reading, opera, jazz, running, mountain biking, entertaining, travel, family; *Style*— Prof Alison Kitson; ✉ Royal College of Nursing, 20 Cavendish Square, London W1M 0AB (tel 020 7647 3652, e-mail alison.kitson@rcn.org.uk)

KITTEL, Gerald Anthony (Gerry); s of Francis William Berthold Kittel (d 2000), of Pinner Hill, Middx, and Eileen Winifred, *née* Maybanks (d 1973); *b* 24 February 1947; *Educ* Merchant Taylors', Univ of Poitiers (Dip), Ealing Poly; *m* 26 April 1975, Jean Samantha, *née* Beveridge; 2 s (Christian b 1969, Ashley b 1976), 1 da (Natalie b 1979); *Career* currently chm City Road Communications Ltd; dir: KML Ltd, The 3 Amigos Mktg Ltd (promotions and bar accessories specialists, manufacturers of Bar-Star); chief exec The Invention Shop Ltd, chm Open Internet Solutions Ltd (specialist developer of software using open source derived platforms), chief exec Osmatic Systems (manufacturers of on-license beer dispense and control systems and CO2 recyclers), chm Osmatic Systems LLC (US agents); memb Country Gentleman's Assoc; MIPA, MCIM, MInstD; *Recreations* riding, squash, tennis; *Clubs* Old Merchant Taylors' Soc; *Style*— Gerry A Kittel, Esq; ✉ Valence End, Hosey Hill, French Street, Westerham, Kent TN16 1PN (tel 01959 564009); City Road Communications Ltd, 42–44 Carter Lane, London EC4V 5EA (tel 020 7248 8010, e-mail gerry.kittel@inventionshop.com)

KITZINGER, Uwe; CBE (1980); *b* 12 April 1928; *Educ* Watford GS, Balliol Coll and New Coll Oxford (MA, MLitt, pres Oxford Union 1950); *m* 1952, Sheila Helena Elizabeth, *née* Webster; 5 da; *Career* Cncl of Europe 1951–56, fell Nuffield Coll 1956–76 (emeritus fell 1976–), fndr ed Journal of Common Market Studies 1961–; visiting prof: Harvard Univ 1969–70, Paris Univ 1970–73; advsr to vice-pres of EC Cmmn i/c external rels Brussels 1973–75, dean Euro Inst of Business Admin INSEAD Fontainebleau 1976–80 (hon alumnus 1980–), dir Oxford Centre for Mgmnt Studies 1980–84, fndr pres Templeton Coll Oxford 1984–91 (hon fell 2001–), visiting scholar Harvard Univ 1993–2003 (affiliate 2003–), sr res fell Atlantic Cncl 1993–; fndr chm: Ctee on Atlantic Studies 1967–70, Major Projects Assoc 1981–86; fndr pres Int Assoc of Macro-Engr Socs 1987–92 and 1996–; chm Oxfordshire Radio Ltd 1988, co-fndr Lentils for Dubrovnik 1991–93; pres Fedération Britannique des Alliances Francaises 1999–2004; patron Asylum Welcome 2004–; memb Br Univs Ctee of the Encyclopedia Brittanica 1967–98; memb Int Bds: Conflict Mgmnt Gp Cambridge MA 1997–, Inst for Transition to Democracy Zagreb 1997–, Asian Disaster Preparedness Center Bangkok 2000–; memb Cncl: RIIA 1973–85, European Movement 1974–76, Oxfam 1981–85, Fondation Jean Monnet 1990–, Tufts Inst for Global Leadership 2006–; Hon LLD 1986; Order of the Morning Star (Croatia) 1997; *Books* German Electoral Politics (1960), The Challenge of the Common Market (1961), Britain, Europe and Beyond (1964), The Second Try (1968), Commitment and Identity (1968), Diplomacy and Persuasion (1973), Europe's Wider Horizons (1975), The 1975 Referendum (with D Butler, 1976, republished 1996), Macro-Engineering and the Earth (with E Frankel, 1998); *Recreations* sailing (ketch 'Anne of Cleves'); *Clubs* Royal Thames Yacht, Oxford and Cambridge; *Style*— Uwe Kitzinger, Esq, CBE; ✉ Standlake Manor, Witney, Oxfordshire (tel 01865 300266 or 01865 300702); La Rivière, 11100 Bages, France (tel and fax 00 33 468 41 70 13, e-mail uwe_kitzinger@yahoo.com)

KLASSNIK, Robin; s of Dr Benjamin Klassnik, and Leila Fabian, *née* Hammerschalg; *b* 28 January 1947; *Educ* Haverstock Comprehensive Sch, Hornsey Coll of Art, Leicester Coll of Art (BA); *m* 1 Dec 1979, Kathryn, da of Henry Halton; 1 s (Tomas b 2 Jan 1981), 1 da (Zoë b 9 Oct 1983); *Career* artist, lectr, gallery owner; fndr, owner and dir Matts Gallery 1979–; gp ldr Fndn Course London Coll of Printing 1979–82, head Complementary Studies Byam Shaw Sch of Art 1982– (visiting lectr 1977–82), res asst (sculpture theory) Statens Kunstakademie Oslo Norway 1990–91; guest lectr: Poznan Acad of Fine Art, Maidstone Sch of Art, Camberwell Sch of Art, Brighton Poly, Slade Sch of Fine Art, Statens Kunstakademie Oslo, Goldsmiths Coll London, RCA London, Valands Konsthogskola Göteborg Sweden, Bath Coll of HE, Chelsea Coll of Art & Design (external examiner sculpture MA); dir New Contemporaries; publisher of artists books and bookworks; *Solo Exhibitions* incl: Walk Through Painting (Pavilions in the Park Croydon) 1969, Nine Till Four (Acland Burghley Sch) 1969, Postal Sculpture (Boyd Inst and James Carters Bookshop) 1970, 34'3" x 57' x 11'6" (New Gallery) 1970, Galeria Dois Porto Portugal 1974, Open Studio Martello St 1974, Galeria Akumulatory 2 Poznan Poland 1975, Space Open Studios 1976, Nearly a Sculpture (Galeria Akumulatory 2, Galeria Pawilon Kraków, Whitechapel Art Gallery) 1978–79, Five Pheromones The Incomplete Documentation (Matts Gallery) 1980, Three Works (Spectro Art Gallery Newcastle upon Tyne) 1981, To Be Or Not To Be Original That is The Question (Galeria Akumulatory 2, Piwna 20/26 Warsaw Poland) 1983; *Recreations* cricket; *Clubs* Burger King; *Style*— Robin Klassnik, Esq; ✉ Matt's Gallery, 42–44 Copperfield Road, London E3 4RR

KLEEMAN, David George; s of Jack Kleeman (d 1984), and Ruth, *née* Stephany (d 1981); *b* 20 August 1942; *Educ* St Paul's, Trinity Hall Cambridge (MA); *m* 1968, Manuela Rachel, da of Edouard Cori, of Paris; 4 da (Susanna b 1970, Nicole b 1973, Julie b 1974, Jenny b 1978); *Career* md Daman Financial Services Ltd; chm: Fayrewood plc, Computerlinks AG; dir of other public and private cos; sr ptnr Pickering Kenyon Slrs 1971–84; chm Enfield & Haringey HA 1991–95, dep chm NHS Logistics Authy 1995–2001; non-exec dir Housing Corp (responsible for Merseyside and the NW) 1990–98; chm Springboard Housing Assoc 2000–07; *Recreations* fly fishing, reading, opera; *Clubs* MCC; *Style*— David Kleeman, Esq; ✉ 15 St Stephens Close, London NW8 6DB (tel 020 7449 9371); Daman Financial Services Ltd, 4th Floor, 74 Chancery Lane, London WC2A 1AD (tel 020 7430 9329)

KLEIN, Gillian; da of Harry Falkow (d 1980), of Johannesburg, South Africa, and Enid, *née* Ash (d 1985); *Educ* Univ of the Witwatersrand (BA, Dip Library and Info Sci), Univ of Central England Birmingham (PhD); *Children* 1 s (Graeme b 31 Dec 1961), 1 da (Leanne b 20 March 1964); *Career* info offr private indust 1960–61, sch librarian 1967–74, librarian ILEA Centre for Urban Educnl Studies 1974–81, teacher fell Inst of Educn Univ of London 1981–82, resources librarian ILEA 1982–90; visiting lectr: Brighton Poly 1986–89, Poly of N London 1987–90, Univ of Warwick 1989–95, SOAS Univ of London 1996–2000; fndr and ed Race Equality Teaching Jl 1982–, editorial dir Trentham Books Ltd 1984–; rapporteur Cncl of Europe Multicultural Studies in Higher Educn 1983–86; conslt: Children's Book Project of Thailand 1991–, ANC Centre for Educnl Policy and Devpt Kwa-Zulu and Transvaal 1994–; chair Anne Frank Tst 2003–06 (tstee 1993–); FRSA 1993; *Publications* incl: Fancy Dress Party (1981), Resources for Multicultural Education (1982), Scrapbooks (1983), School Libraries for Cultural Awareness (1985), Reading into Racism (1985), Agenda for Multicultural Teaching (jtly, 1986), Education towards Race Equality (1993), A Vision for Today - John Eggleston's Writings on Education (jtly, 2003), Equal Measures (jtly, 2004); *Recreations* family and friends, travel, theatre, art and architecture, swimming, reading, food; *Style*— Dr Gillian Klein; ✉ Trentham Books, Westview House, 734 London Road, Stoke on Trent ST4 5NP

KLEIN, Michael Stuart; s of Bernard Howard Klein, and Leah, *née* Shapiro; *b* 12 November 1963, NY; *Educ* Wharton Sch of Business; *m* 16 Jan 1999, Beth Robin, *née* Neckman; 1 da (Kathryn Barret b 10 July 2000), 1 s (Jack Winston b 31 July 2002); *Career* early career with M&A Gp Salomon Bros; Citigroup: responsible for Global Financial Entrepreneurs and Private Equity Gps 1987, ceo Corporate and Investment Bank EMEA and co-head of global investment banking 2000–03, ceo Global Banking 2004–, currently chm and co-ceo Citi Markets & Banking (chm Planning Gp) and memb Citi Business Heads, Operating Ctee and Mgmnt Ctee; memb: Bd London Investment Banker's Assoc (LIBA), Bd IHS Inc, Bd General Motors Acceptance Corporation LLC, Investment Advsy Bd of PM of Turkey; co-chair Trans-Atlantic Business Dialogue; memb: Int Advsy Bd British American Business Inc, Bd Peter G Peterson Inst for Int Economics, Dean's Cncl Woodrow Wilson Sch of Public and Int Affrs Princeton Univ, Bd American Acad in Berlin, Int Advsy Bd Grad Sch of Mgmnt St Petersburg Univ; memb: Advsy Bd Nat Football League (NFL), Bd Mount Sinai Med Center; involved with: Make-A-Wish Fndn Metro NY Inc, Farms for City Kids, Children's Defence Fund, Endeavor Global, Bd of Tstees Prep for Prep; Investment Banker of the Year Investment Dealers Digest 2001, Global Ldr to Watch Fortune Magazine; memb Guild of Int Bankers; ✉ 388 Greenwich Street, New York, NY 10013, USA; Citigroup Centre, 33 Canada Square, Canary Wharf, London E14 5LB

KLEIN, Roland; s of Fernand Klein (d 1982), and Marguerite, *née* Meyer (d 1987); *b* 3 July 1938; *Educ* CEC, BEPC and Beaux Arts Rouen France, Ecole de la Chambre Syndicale de la Haute Couture Parisienne and CAP Paris France; *Career* designer; Nat Serv France 1959–60; asst tailor Jean Patou Paris 1958–59, asst designer Christian Dior Paris 1960–61, asst designer Jean Patou and Karl Lagerfeld 1961–63, designer Nettie Vogue London 1963–66, design dir Marcel Fenez London 1970–88 (designer 1966–70), designer Roland Klein Ltd London and Tokyo 1988–, interior designer 2001–; major projects incl: conslt designer British Airways corporate image clothing 1986, Max Mara and Marina Rinaldi Italy 1988–, British Telecom corporate image clothing 1991, Halifax Building Society 1992, Midland Bank plc 1993, Russell & Bromley 1993; memb Br Interior Designer Assoc 2007–; Fil D'or 1987; *Style*— Roland Klein, Esq; ✉ Roland Klein Ltd, 16 Bolton Gardens, London SW5 0AJ (tel and fax 020 7373 9267, e-mail rmklondon@aol.com)

KLEINPOPPEN, Prof Hans Johann Willi; s of Gerhard Kleinpoppen (d 1985), and Emmi, *née* Maass (d 1997); *b* 30 September 1928; *Educ* HS Germany, Univ of Giessen Germany, Univ of Heidelberg Germany, Univ of Tübingen Germany; *Career* Privat-Dozent Univ of Tübingen 1967, visiting fell and prof Univ of Colorado Boulder and Columbia Univ NY 1967–68; Univ of Stirling: prof of experimental physics 1968–96, head of Physics Dept 1972–74, dir Inst of Atomic Physics 1974–81, head of Atomic and Molecular Physics Res Unit 1981–96, prof emeritus 1996–; fell Center for Theoretical Studies Univ of Miami 1973, visiting prof Univ of Bielefeld 1978–89; guest research scientist Fritz-Haber-Inst of the Max-Planck-Soc Berlin 1990–; emeritus fell Leverhulme Tst 1998–2000; chm and co-dir various nat and int confs and summer schs on atomic, molecular and optical physics; CPhys, FInstP 1969, FAmPhysSoc 1970, FRAS 1974, FRSE 1987, FRSA 1990; *Publications* Monograph Series on Physics of Atoms and Molecules (ed jtly with P G Burke, CBE), Festschrift for the occasion of 60th birthday: Coherence in Atomic Collision Physics (ed H J Beyer, K Blum and R Hippler, 1988), Hans Kleinpoppen Symposium on Complete Scattering Experiments (1998), Proceedings of the Symposium (contrib (ed U Becker and A Crowe), 2001); jt ed-in-chief Springer series on Atomic, Optical and Plasma Physics 2006–; ed of 15 books on atomic and molecular physics, author of over 200 scientific research papers in int jls of physics and comprehensive articles on physics of atoms in advanced German and English textbooks; *Recreations* music, fine art; *Style*— Prof Hans Kleinpoppen, FRSE

KLEINWORT, Sir Richard Drake; 4 Bt (UK 1909), of Bolnore, Cuckfield, Sussex; DL (West Sussex 2005); s of Sir Kenneth Drake Kleinwort, 3 Bt (d 1994), and his 1 w, Lady Davina Rose Pepys (d 1973), da of 7 Earl of Cottenham; *b* 4 November 1960; *Educ* Stowe, Univ of Exeter (BA); *m* 29 Nov 1989, Lucinda, da of William Shand Kydd, of Bucks; 3 s (Rufus Drake b 16 Aug 1994, Tristan William b 10 July 1997, Ivo John b 24 June 1999), 1 da (Heloise b 28 Feb 1996); *Heir* s, Rufus Kleinwort; *Career* Kleinwort Benson Geneva 1979, Banco General de Negocios Buenos Aires 1983, banker corp fin Deutschebank AG Hamburg and Frankfurt 1985–88, Biss Lancaster plc 1988–89, Grandfield Rork Collins Financial 1989–91, dir Cardew & Co 1994–2000 (ptnr 1991–94), head of financial PR Ogilvy 2000–01, chm The Richard Kleinwort Consultancy Gp 2001–; patron The Cuckfield Soc; pres The Little Black Bag Housing Assoc; fell World Scout Fndn Geneva; chm Knepp Castle Polo Club 1997–2006; govr Stowe Sch 1999–2004, chm The Stowe Sch Fndn, chm The Campaign for Stowe until 2004; dir Steppes East Ltd; vice-pres Chichester Cathedral Millennium Endowment Appeal; memb: The Sussex Club, Royal Horticultural Soc, S of England Agric Soc, The Countryside Alliance, Inst King Edward VII Hosp Midhurst, Compagnie Internationale de la Chasse (CIC), Cncl of Ambassadors WWF UK; ambassador Study Support Prog Prince's Tst; tstee: The Ackroyd Tst, The Ernest Kleinwort Charitable Tst; *Recreations* my family, laughter, travel, sports (in general), watching England win; *Clubs* MCC, Turf, WWF (1001), White's, The Benedicts; *Style*— Sir Richard Kleinwort, Bt, DL; ✉ Heaselands, Haywards Heath, West Sussex RH16 4SA

KLEMPERER, Prof Paul David; s of late Hugh G Klemperer, and Ruth, *née* Jordan; *b* 15 August 1956; *Educ* King Edward's Sch Birmingham, Peterhouse Cambridge (BA), Stanford Univ (MBA, top student award, PhD); *m* 1989, Margaret, *née* Meyer; 2 s (David b 1995, William b 1997), 1 da (Katherine b 1997); *Career* conslt Andersen Consulting (now Accenture) 1978–80, Harkness fell of the Cwlth Fund 1980–82; Univ of Oxford: lectr in operations research and mathematical economics 1985–90, reader in economics 1990–95, Edgeworth prof of economics 1995–, John Thomson fell and tutor St Catherine's Coll 1985–95, fell Nuffield Coll 1995–; memb Competition Cmmn 2001–05; visiting positions: MIT 1987, Univ of Calif Berkeley 1991 and 1993, Stanford Univ 1991 and 1993, Yale Univ 1994, Princeton Univ 1998; conslt US Federal Trade Cmmn 1999–2001, princ auction theorist UK 3G auction UK Radiocommunications Agency 2000; advsr to EU, US, UK and other govts and private firms; ed RAND Jl of Economics 1993–99; assoc ed or memb Editorial Bd: Oxford Economic Papers 1986–2000, Review of Economic Studies 1989–97, Jl of Industrial Economics 1989–96, International Jl of Industrial Organization 1993–, European Economic Review 1997–, Review of Economic Design 1997–2000, Economic Policy 1998–99, Economic Jl 2000–04, Frontiers in Economics 2000–, BE Jl of Economic Analysis and Policy 2001–, Jl of Competition Law and Economics 2004–; memb Cncl: Econometric Soc 2001–, Royal Economic Soc 2001–05 (also memb Exec Ctee), European Economic Soc 2002–; hon fell ESRC Centre for Economic Learning and Social Evolution (ELSE) 2001, fell European Econ Assoc 2004, foreign hon memb American Acad of Arts and Sciences 2005, hon memb Argentine Econ Assoc 2006; fell Econometric Soc 1994; FBA 1999; *Publications* The Economic Theory of Auctions (2000), Auctions: Theory and Practice (2004); author of articles in economics jls on industrial organization, auction theory, and other economic theory; *Style*— Prof Paul Klemperer, FBA; ✉ Nuffield College, Oxford OX1 1NF (tel 01865 278588, e-mail paul.klemperer@economics.ox.ac.uk, website www.paulklemperer.org)

KLIMENTOVA, Daria; da of Zdenek Kliment, of Prague, and Ludmila Klimentova; *b* 23 June 1971; *Educ* Sch of Music and Dance Prague State Conservatory; *m* Ian Comer; 1 da (Sabrina b 6 Nov 2000); *Career* ballet dancer; studied with Prof Dr Olga Paskova and Prof Jaroslav Slavicky; soloist Nat Theatre Ballet Prague 1989–92, princ Capab/Kruik Ballet Cape Town 1992–93, princ Scottish Ballet 1993–96, princ English Nat Ballet 1996–; appeared with: Prague Festival Ballet Portugal and USA, Nat Theatre Ballet of Brno Germany tour; guested in ballet galas all over the world; subject of profile on Czech TV 1998; *Roles* with Nat Theatre Ballet of Prague incl: Aurora in Sleeping Beauty, Margarita in Lady with Camellias, Kitri in Don Quixote, title role in Sylvia, solo in Paguita, solo in Return to a Strange Land, Princess in From Tale to Tale, Diverttimento m 15, Double Concerto, Concerto, A Million Kisses to my Skin; with Capab/Kruik Ballet incl: solo in Walpurgisnacht, solo in Four Last Songs, Titania in A Midsummer Night's Dream, Sugar Plum Fairy/Snow Queen in The Nutcracker, title role in Raymonda, Ophelia in Hamlet; with The Scottish Ballet incl: Swanilda in Coppélia, Solo Navy in Bruch Violin Concerto No 1, Wendy in Peter Pan, title role in Anna Karenina, Odette/Odile in Swan Lake, title role in La Sylphide, A Fond Kiss, Haydn Pieces, The Scotch Symphony; with English Nat Ballet incl: title role in Giselle, title role in Paguita, Mazurka in Les Sylphides, Ballerina in Eludes, Dream Alice in Alice in Wonderland, Ben Stevenson's 3 Preludes, Cut to the Chase, Nikya in La Bayadere, Sphinx Voluntaries, Tchaikovsky pas de deux; *Film* Lady with Camellias (Czech Republic, 1992), A Midsummer Night's Dream (South Africa, 1993), Daria Klimentova (documentary), Daria Klimentova Masterclasses (Czech Republic, 2003), Terra Musica - Daria's Masterclasses (2006), Daria Klimentova - Portrait (2006); *Awards* second prize nat ballet competition Brno Czech Republic 1987, Prize of Paris Dance Fndn 1989, Prix de Lausanne Tokyo 1989, winner int ballet competition Pretoria 1991; *Publications* ballet calenders 2003–07, incl: Ballet Calendar 2003, English Nat Ballet Calendar 2004; *Recreations* photography, nature and animals, art, computers; *Style*— Miss Daria Klimentova; ✉ English National Ballet, Markova House, 39 Jay Mews, London SW7 2ES (tel 020 7581 1245, fax 020 7225 0827, e-mail daria@ntlworld.com)

KLINOWSKI, Prof Jacek Maria; s of Dr Czeslaw Klinowski (d 1984), of Krakow, Poland, and Dr Julia Klinowska, *née* Penkala; *b* 11 October 1943, Krakow, Poland; *Educ* Jagiellonian Univ Krakow (MSc, Dr rer nat), Univ of London (DIC, PhD), Univ of Cambridge (MA, ScD); *m* 11 May 1967, Dr Margaret Klinowska, *née* Townsend; 1 da (Dr Teresa Klinowska b 30 July 1969); *Career* lectr in chemistry Jagiellonian Univ 1965–68, res fell Univ of Aberdeen 1968–69, res fell Imperial Coll London 1969–79; Univ of Cambridge: sr res assoc 1980–85, asst dir of res 1985–98, reader in chemical physics 1998–2000, prof of chemical physics 2000–, professorial fell Peterhouse; visiting prof: Univ of Krakow, Univ of Poznan, Univ of Aveiro, Univ of Cagliari; ed-in-chief Solid State Nuclear Magnetic Resonance; author of over 480 scientific pubns; Marie Curie Medal Polish Chemical Soc; hon memb Polish Chemical Soc 1994, foreign memb Polish Acad of Arts and Sciences 1993, presidential prof Repub of Poland 1988; *Books* incl: Cinema, the Magic Vehicle: A Guide to Its Achievement: The Cinema Through 1949 Journey 1 (with Adam Garbicz, 1980), Cinema, the Magic Vehicle: A Guide to Its Achievement: The Cinema in the Fifties Journey 2 (with Adam Garbicz, 1980), Fundamentals of Nuclear Magnetic Resonance (with Jacek W Hennel, 1993), A Primer of Magnetic Resonance Imaging (with Jacek W Hennel and Teresa Kryst-Widzgowska, 1997), New Techniques in Solid-State NMR (ed, 2004); *Recreations* cinema (sometime film critic), music; *Style*— Prof Jacek Klinowski; ✉ Peterhouse, Cambridge CB2 1RD (tel 01223 338228, e-mail jk18@cam.ac.uk)

KLUG, Sir Aaron; OM (1995), kt (1988); s of Lazar Klug (d 1971), of Durban, South Africa, and Bella, *née* Silin (d 1932); *b* 11 August 1926; *Educ* Durban HS, Univ of the Witwatersrand (BSc), Univ of Cape Town (MSc), Univ of Cambridge (PhD, ScD); *m* 8 July 1948, Liebe, da of Alexander Bobrow (d 1983), and Annie Bobrow, of Cape Town; 2 s (Adam Brian Joseph b 1954 d 2000, David Rupert b 1963); *Career* Nuffield research fell Birkbeck Coll London 1954–57, ldr virus research project 1958–61; Univ of Cambridge: fell Peterhouse 1962–93, dir of natural sci studies Peterhouse 1962–85, memb staff MRC Laboratory of Molecular Biology 1962–, jt head structural studies 1978–86, dir of laboratory 1986–96, hon prof 1989–96; awards: Heineken prize Royal Netherlands Acad 1979, Louisa Gross Horwitz prize Columbia Univ 1981, Nobel prize for chemistry 1982; Hon DSc: Chicago 1978, Witwatersrand 1984, Hull 1985, St Andrews 1987, Western Ontario 1991, Warwick 1994, Cape Town 1997, London 2000, Oxford 2001; Hon Dr Columbia 1978, Dr (hc) Strasbourg 1978, Hon Dr Stockholm 1980, Hon PhD Jerusalem 1984, Hon DLitt Cambridge 1998, Hon DUniv Stirling 1998; hon fell: Trinity Coll Cambridge 1983, Peterhouse Cambridge 1993; hon memb: Worshipful Co of Salters 1995, Biochem Soc (Harden medal 1985); foreign assoc: American Acad of Arts and Sciences 1969, Nat Acad of Sciences of USA 1984, Max-Planck-Gesellschaft FRG, Académie des Sciences Paris 1989, American Philosophical Soc 1998, Japan Acad 2001; Hon FRCP 1986 (Baly medal 1987), Hon FRCPath 1991, FRS 1969 (Copley medal 1985, pres 1995–2000); *Recreations* reading, ancient history; *Style*— Sir Aaron Klug, OM, PPRS; ✉ MRC Laboratory of Molecular Biology, Hills Road, Cambridge CB2 2QH (tel 01223 248011, fax 01223 412231)

KNAGG, John Worsley; OBE (1996); s of Albert Knagg, and Ivy, *née* Worsley; *b* 22 September 1953, Manchester; *Educ* Bury GS, Worcester Coll Oxford (MA), UCNW Bangor (PGCE), Univ of Edinburgh (MSc), Henley Mgmnt Coll; *Children* 2 s (Alex b 9 July 1995, Martin b 14 Aug 1996), 1 da (Emily b 29 June 1998); *Career* British Cncl: dir Porto 1987–90, dep dir Singapore 1993–98, dir Ecuador 1998–2001, dir Chile 2001–; chair Educn Ctee British Sch Quito 1999–2001; *Style*— John Knagg, Esq; ✉ British Council, Eliodoro Yañez 832, Providencia, Santiago, Chile (tel 00 56 2 410 6900, fax 00 56 2 410 6929)

KNAPMAN, Paul Anthony; s of Frederick Ethelbert Knapman, of Torquay, Devon, and Myra, *née* Smith; *b* 5 November 1944; *Educ* Epsom Coll, King's Coll London, St George's Hospital Medical Sch (MB BS, DMJ, MRCS, LRCP), Inns of Court Sch of Law (barrister, Gray's Inn); *m* 1970, Penelope Jane, da of Lt Cdr Michael Cox, of Torquay, Devon; 1 s, 3 da; *Career* medical practitioner and barrister; Surgn Lt RNR 1970; HM Coroner Inner West London at Westminster Coroner's Ct 1980–; hon lectr in med jurisprudence St George's Hosp Med Sch, hon clinical teacher in forensic med UCH and Royal Free Hosp Med Sch, hon sr lectr in public health Imperial Coll of Sci Technol and Med; Langdon-Browne Lectr RCP 1998, Christmas lectr Imperial Coll of Sci, Technol and Medicine 1999; memb: Clinical Forensic Med Section RSM (pres 1997), Br Acad of Forensic Scis (memb Cncl 1982–86), Medicolegal Soc, Soc of Doctors of Law (memb Cncl 1996–), Coroners Soc (memb Cncl 1985–), SE England Coroners Soc (pres 1980); govr London Nautical Sch 1978– (chm of Govrs 1997–99); Liveryman Worshipful Soc of Apothecaries (memb Ct 1993–); FRCS, FRCP; *Books* The Law and Practice on Coroners (jtly, 3 edn 1985), Medicine and the Law (1989), Casebook on Coroners (1989), Sources on Coroners Law (1999); *Recreations* beagling, boats and shooting; *Clubs* Athenaeum, Garrick, Royal Torbay Yacht, Royal Naval Volunteer Reserve Yacht; *Style*— Paul Knapman, Esq; ✉ c/o Westminster Coroner's Court, Horseferry Road, London SW1P 2ED (tel 020 7834 6515)

KNAPMAN, Roger Maurice; MEP; s of Harry Arthur Blackmore Knapman (d 1996), of North Tawton, Devon and Joan Margot, *née* Densham (d 1970); *b* 20 February 1944; *Educ* St Aubyn's Sch Tiverton, All Hallows Sch Lyme Regis, RAC Cirencester; *m* 25 March 1967, Carolyn Trebell, da of Sidney George Eastman (d 1993), of Appledore, N Devon; 1 s (William b 1970), 1 da (Rebecca b 1971); *Career* chartered surveyor; MP (Cons) Stroud 1987–97, PPS to Rt Hon Archie Hamilton as Min of State for the Armed Forces 1990–92 (resigned); memb: Agric and Food Research Cncl 1991–94, Select Ctee on Agric 1994–95; asst govt whip 1995–96, a Lord Cmmr HM Treasy (Govt whip) 1996–97, vice-chm Cons European Affrs Ctee 1989–90; ldr UKIP 2002–06 (political advsr 2000–02), MEP (South West) UKIP 2004–; FRICS 1967; *Recreations* fishing, snooker; *Style*— Roger Knapman, Esq, MEP; ✉ Coryton House, Coryton, Okehampton, Devon EX20 4PA

KNEALE, Prof (Robert) Bryan Charles; s of William Thomas Kneale (d 1963), of Douglas, IOM, and late Lilian, *née* Kewley; *b* 19 June 1930; *Educ* Douglas HS IOM, Douglas Sch of Art IOM, Royal Acad Schs (Rome scholar); *m* 1956, Doreen, da of Clifford Lister; 1 da (Katherine b 1957), 1 s (Simon Benedict b 1960, d 1996); *Career* painter until 1959; first exhibition of paintings Redfern Gallery 1954, recipient Daily Express Young Painters prize 1955; sculptor (mainly in bronze) 1960–, regular exhibitor Redfern Gallery until 1986; head of sculpture Hornsey Coll of Art and Design 1968, prof of sculpture Royal Acad 1980–87; RCA: tutor 1963–80, sr tutor 1980–85, head of sculpture 1985–90, prof of drawing 1990–95; Leverhulme prize 1952, Arts Cncl purchase award 1969; RA 1974 (ARA 1971, tstee Royal Acad), sr fell RCA; *Exhibitions* incl: John Moores 1961, Sixth Congress of Architects Union (Southbank) 1961, Art d'Aujourd'hui Paris 1963, Battersea Park Sculpture Int 1963–66, Profil 2 Bochom 1964, Retrospective (Whitechapel Gallery) 1966, English Eye 1965, British Sculpture of the 60's (Tate Gallery) 1966, City of London Open Air Sculpture 1968, British Sculptors Winter Exhibition (Royal Acad) 1972 (also curator), Holland Park 1973, New Art (Hayward Gallery) 1975, Silver Jubilee Exhibition of British Sculpture (Battersea Park) 1977 (also curator), Monumental Sculpture (Manx Millenium) 1979, Serpentine Gallery 1979, Royal Acad 1985, Retrospective (Henry Moore Gallery) 1986, Fitzwilliam Museum 1987, Sal Uno Rome 1988, Drawing Retrospective (Natural History Museum) 1991, Sculpture and Drawing (bone drawings and sculpture retrospective Manx Museum and National Tst) 1992, Chelsea Harbour sculpture 1993, Retrospective (Royal West of England Acad) 1995, Discerning Eye 1995–96, Goodwood Sculpture Park 1996–99, Sculpture for Manx Government Building 1996, Lewes Festival 1997, Bronze Doors for Portsmouth Cathedral 1997, sculpture for Westminster Cathedral 1998 and 1999, Angela Flowers East Figurative Arts 1998, Holland Park Sculpture Exhbn Bronze 2000, New Arts Centre Roche Court 2000, Eye of the Storm Mandria Park Turin 2000, Hart Gallery 2002 and 2004, Cass Sculpture Fndn Gallery 2005, sculpture for Nobles Hosp IOM 2005, sculpture for Castletown Hosp IOM 2005, sculpture for Malew Church IOM 2006, sculpture for Tower Bridge House London 2007, sculpture for RTZ Building Paddington 2007; *Clubs* Chelsea Arts, Arts; *Style*— Prof Bryan Kneale, RA; ✉ Hart Gallery, 113 Upper Street, London N1 1QN (tel 020 7704 1131, fax 020 7288 2922)

KNEALE, David Arthur; *b* 20 August 1954; *Educ* Douglas HS IOM, Univ of Nottingham (BA); *m* 13 May 1996, Jacqueline Sylvia, da of Sylvia Agnes Paterson; *Career* treas Student Union Univ of Nottingham 1975–76; The Boots Company 1976–99: asst expense controller 1976–77, pet food buyer 1978–80, leisure gp mangr 1980–82, cosmetics gp mangr 1982–83, asst merchandise controller (med merchandise) 1983–85, asst mktg controller (food and own brand meds) 1985–86, buying controller (personal care business centre) 1986–89, gen mangr (personal care) 1989–92, gen mangr (beauty and personal care) 1992–95, dir of merchandise and mktg 1995–97, md int retail devpt 1997–99; md Waterstone's Booksellers Ltd 1999–2001; dir of trading Boots UK and Ireland 2002–; *Recreations* reading, cinema, travel; *Style*— David Kneale, Esq; ✉ tel 020 7351 9631

KNEALE, Matthew Nicholas Kerr; s of Nigel Kneale, of London, and Judith Kerr; *b* 24 November 1960; *Educ* Latymer Upper Sch, Magdalen Coll Oxford (BA); *m* 2000, Shannon Lee, da of Gary Russell; 1 s (Alexander b 2001), 1 da (Tatiana b 2004); *Career* writer; former English teacher Japan; *Books* Mr Foreigner (1988, Betty Trask Award 1987, Somerset Maugham Award 1988), Inside Rose's Kingdom (1989), Sweet Thames (1992, John Llewellyn Rhys Award 1993), English Passengers (2000, shortlisted Booker Prize 2000, Whitbread Book of the Year Award 2000, shortlisted Miles Franklin Award (Australia) 2001, Relay Prix d'Evasion (France) 2002), Small Crimes in an Age of Abundance (2005); *Recreations* mountain walking, cycling, photography, travel (85 countries and 7 continents); *Style*— Matthew Kneale, Esq; ✉ c/o Rogers, Coleridge & White, 20 Powys Mews, London W11 1JN (tel 020 7221 3717, e-mail matthew.kneale@attglobal.net)

KNECHT, Prof Robert Jean; s of Jean Joseph Camille Knecht (d 1970), and Odette Jeanne Eugenie Juliette, *née* Mioux (d 1983); *b* 20 September 1926; *Educ* Lycée Français London, Salesian Coll Farnborough, KCL (BA, MA), Univ of Birmingham (DLitt); *m* 1, 8 Aug 1956, Sonia Mary Fitzpatrick (d 1984), da of Dr Hubert Hodge; *m* 2, 28 Aug 1986, Maureen Joan, *née* White; *Career* Univ of Birmingham: asst lectr in modern history 1956–59, lectr 1959–68, sr lectr 1968–78, reader 1978–85, prof of French history 1985–92, emeritus prof and hon sr res fell in modern history 1992–97, fell Inst for Advanced Research in Arts and Social Scis 1998–; chm: Soc for Renaissance Studies 1989–92, Bd of Govrs Wroxall Abbey Sch Warwick 1989–92; co fndr Soc for Study of French History (chm 1995–98); memb Société de l'Histoire de France; FRHistS; Chevalier dans l'Ordre des Palmes Académiques 2001; *Books* The Voyage of Sir Nicholas Carewe (1959), Francis I (1982), French Renaissance Monarchy (1984), The French Wars of Religion (1989), Richelieu (1990), Renaissance Warrior and Patron (1994), The Rise and Fall of Renaissance France (1996), Catherine de' Medici (1998), Un Prince de la Renaissance: François 1er et son royaume (1998), The French Civil Wars (2000), The French Religious Wars (2002), The Valois (2004); *Recreations* travel, art, music, photography; *Style*— Prof

K

Robert Knecht; ✉ 79 Reddings Road, Moseley, Birmingham B13 8LP (tel and fax 0121 449 1916, e-mail r.j.knecht@btinternet.com)

KNIBB, Prof Michael Anthony; s of Leslie Charles Knibb (d 1987), and Christian Vera, *née* Hoggar (d 1978); *b* 14 December 1938; *Educ* Wyggeston Sch Leicester, KCL (BD, PhD), Union Theol Seminary NY (STM), CCC Oxford; *m* 30 Dec 1972, Christine Mary, da of John Henry Thomas and Patricia Mary Burrell, of Leicester; *Career* Old Testament studies KCL: lectr 1964–82, reader 1982–86, prof 1986–97, Samuel Davidson prof 1997–2001; head Theology and Religious Studies Dept KCL 1989–93 and 1998–2000; Sch of Humanities KCL: dep head 1992–97, head 2000–01, prof emeritus 2001–; Schweich lectr British Acad 1995; memb SOTS 1965–, ed SOTS Book List 1980–86; hon sec Palestine Exploration Fund 1969–76; memb: Studiorum Novi Testamenti Societas 1980– (jt convener of seminar on early Jewish writings and the New Testament 1986–91), Cncl British Acad 1992–95, Humanities Research Bd 1995–98 (chm Postgraduate Ctee 1996–98); memb Governing Body: Watford GS for Girls 1993–2002, SOAS Univ of London 2000– (vice-chair 2006–); FBA 1989, FKC 1991; *Books* The Ethiopic Book of Enoch (1978), Commentary on 2 Esdras (1979), Het Boek Henoch (1983), The Qumran Community (1987), Translating the Bible: The Ethiopic Version of The Old Testament (1999); *Recreations* hill walking; *Clubs* Athenaeum; *Style—* Prof Michael A Knibb, FBA; ✉ 6 Shootersway Park, Berkhamsted, Hertfordshire HP4 3NX (tel 01442 871459)

KNIGHT, Prof Alan Sydney; s of William Henry Knight (d 1998), and Eva Maud, *née* Crandon (d 1979); *b* 6 November 1946; *Educ* Christ's Hosp, Balliol Coll Oxford (BA), Nuffield Coll Oxford (DPhil); *m* 1, 1969 (m dis), Carole, da of Gordon Jones; 1 da (Katharine b 1974); m 2, 1985, Lidia, da of Juan Lozano Martin; 2 s (Alexander b 1980, Henry b 1982); *Career* res fell Nuffield Coll and lectr in politics Balliol Coll Oxford 1971–73, lectr in modern history Univ of Essex 1973–85, visiting prof Centre for US-Mexican Studies Univ of Calif San Diego 1986; Univ of Texas: Worsham Centennial prof of history 1986–90, C B Smith sr prof of history 1990–92; Univ of Oxford: prof of Latin America history and dir Latin American Centre 1992–, fell St Antony's Coll 1992–; memb: Soc for Latin American Studies 1982–, Latin American Studies Assoc 1986–; Bolton prize Conf on Latin American History 1987, Beveridge prize American Historical Soc 1987, Guggenheim fell 1990–91; FBA 1998; *Books* The Mexican Revolution (1986), US-Mexican Relations 1910–40: An Overview (1987), The Mexican Petroleum Industry in the Twentieth Century (ed, 1992); *Recreations* kayaking; *Style—* Prof Alan Knight, FBA; ✉ St Antony's College, Oxford OX2 6JF (tel 01865 274490, fax 01865 274489)

KNIGHT, Very Rev Alexander Francis; OBE (2006); s of Benjamin Edward Knight, of Bridport, and Dorothy Mary, *née* Sherwood; *b* 24 July 1939; *Educ* Taunton Sh, St Catharine's Coll Cambridge (MA), Wells Theol Coll; *m* 23 June 1962, Sheelagh Elizabeth, *née* Desmond Faris; 3 da (Catharine Mary b 2 April 1964, Susannah Elizabeth b 8 June 1966, Helen Clare b 31 Dec 1968), 1 s (William Benjamin James b 22 Jan 1971); *Career* asst curate Hemel Hempstead 1963–68, chaplain Taunton Sch 1968–74, dir The Bloxham Project 1975–81, dir of studies Aston Trg Scheme 1981–83, priest-in-charge Easton and Martyr Worthy 1983–91, archdeacon of Basingstoke 1990–98, canon residentiary of Winchester Cathedral 1991–98, dean of Lincoln 1998–2006 (now emeritus); Hon DLitt Univ of Lincoln; *Recreations* gardening, theatre, walking; *Style—* The Very Rev Dr Alec Knight, OBE; ✉ Shalom, Clay Street, Whiteparish, Salisbury, Wiltshire SP5 2ST (tel 01794 884402)

KNIGHT, Andrew Stephen Bower; s of M W B Knight, and S E F Knight; *b* 1 November 1939; *m* 1, 1966 (m dis), Victoria Catherine Brittain; 1 s (Casimir); m 2, 1975 (m dis 1991), Sabiha Rumani Malik; 2 da (Amaryllis, Afsaneh); *Career* ed The Economist 1974–86; Daily Telegraph plc: chief exec 1986–89, ed-in-chief 1987–89; exec chm News International plc 1990–94 (non-exec chm 1994–95), dir News Corporation 1991–; dep chm Home Counties Newspapers Holdings plc 1996–98; non-exec dir RIT Capital Partners 1996–, Templeton Emerging Markets Investment Tst plc; Stanford Univ: memb Advsy Bd Centre for Econ Policy Res 1981–, memb Advsy Cncl Inst of Int Studies; govr Ditchley Fndn 1981– (memb Mgmnt Cncl 1982–), dir Anglo Russian Opera & Ballet Tst; *Clubs* Brooks's, Beefsteak, RAC, Tadmarton Heath; *Style—* Andrew Knight, Esq; ✉ Compton Scorpion Manor, Shipston-on-Stour, Warwickshire CV36 4PJ

KNIGHT, Angela; CBE (2007); da of Andrew McTurk Cook, and late Barbara Cook; *b* 31 October 1950; *Educ* Sheffield Girls HS, Univ of Bristol (BSc); *m* 7 Feb 1981 (m dis), David George Knight; 2 s; *Career* devpt engr Air Products Ltd 1972–77, fndr and md engrg co specialising in heat treatment of metals 1977–92; cncllr Sheffield City Cncl 1987–92 (spokesman on educn, planning and industry), MP (Cons) Erewash 1992–97; memb Educn Select Ctee 1992–93, sec Backbench Environment Ctee 1992–93, PPS DTI 1993–94, PPS to Chllr of the Exchequer 1994–95, economic sec to the Treasy 1995–97; chief exec Assoc of Private Client Investment Managers and Stockbrokers (APCIMS) 1997–2006, chief exec British Bankers Assoc (BBA) 2007–; non-exec dir: Scottish Widows 1997–2006, South East Water 1998–2004, LogicaCMG plc 1999–, Port of London Authy 2002–, Lloyds TSB 2003–06; *Clubs* London Capital; *Style—* Mrs Angela Knight, CBE

KNIGHT, Dr Anthony Harrington; s of Dr Bryant William Knight (d 1982), and Gladys Irene, *née* Eldridge (d 2000); *b* 29 April 1940; *Educ* Univ Coll Sch, St Bartholomew's Hosp Med Sch (MB BS); *m* 24 Aug 1963, Sheila Mary, da of Alfred Stanley Brewer (d 1989); 2 s (Jonathan Clive b 1965, Christopher Harrington b 1968); *Career* conslt physician Stoke Mandeville and Royal Bucks Hosps 1974–2005, fndr and physician in charge Aylesbury Diabetes Educn and Treatment Centre 1978–2005, dist clinical tutor Univ of Oxford 1979–86, vice-chm Aylesbury Vale HA 1982–89; memb Br Diabetic Assoc Med Scientific and Educn Sections (sec Educn Section 1986–89, chm 1991–94), pres Aylesbury Dist Br Diabetes UK 1976–2005, fndr and leader Ridgeway and Vale Diabetes Club, memb Stoke Mandeville Hosp Post Grad Med Soc; MRCS 1963, FRCP 1980 (MRCP 1968); *Recreations* hill and mountain walking, oil painting; *Style—* Dr Anthony Knight; ✉ The Old Vicarage, 101 Aylesbury Road, Bierton, Buckinghamshire HP22 5BT (tel 01296 489701, e-mail tktheoldvic@btinternet.com)

KNIGHT, Prof Bernard Henry; CBE (1993), GSM (Malaya) 1956; s of Harold Ivor Knight (d 1984), of Cardiff, and Doris, *née* Lawes (d 1995); *b* 3 May 1931; *Educ* St Illtyd's Coll Cardiff, Welsh Nat Sch of Med (MD BCh), DMJ (Path); *m* 11 June 1955, Jean Gwenllian, da of Charles Ogborne (d 1947), of Swansea; 1 s (Huw David Charles b 1964); *Career* Short Serv Cmmn Capt RAMC specialist in pathology Malaya 1956–59; called to the Bar Gray's Inn; lectr in forensic med Univ of London 1959–62, sr lectr Univ of Newcastle 1965–68, prof of forensic pathology Univ of Wales 1980–96 (sr lectr 1968–76, reader 1976–80, now emeritus prof), Home Office pathologist 1965–96, conslt pathologist Cardiff Royal Infirmary, dir Wales Inst of Forensic Med 1989–96, pathology ed Forensic Sci Int; memb GMC 1979–94, vice-pres Int Acad of Legal Med 1982–86, pres Forensic Sci Soc 1987–89, memb Cncl RCPath, memb Home Office Policy Advsy Bd on forensic pathology, pres Br Assoc of Forensic Med 1991–93 (former sec), hon memb Finnish, Hungarian and German Socs of Forensic Med; Hon DSc Univ of Glamorgan 1996, Hon LLD Univ of Wales 1998, Hon DM Univ of Turkh Finland, Hon PhD Univ of Tokyo; Hon FRSM; MRCP, FRCPath; *Books* crime novels: The Lately Deceased (1963), The Thread of Evidence (1965), Russian Roulette (1968), Policeman's Progress (1969), Tiger at Bay (1970), Deg Y Dragwyddoldeb (1972), The Expert (1976); historical novels: Lion Rampant (1974), Madoc Prince of America (1977), The Sanctuary Seeker (1998), The Poisoned Chalice (1998), Crowner's Quest (1999), The Awful Secret (2000), The Tinner's Corpse (2001), The Grim Reaper (2002), Fear in the Forest (2003), Brennan (2003), The Witch Hunter (2004), Figure of Hate (2005), The Tainted Relic (2005), The Elixir of Deth (2006), The Sword of Shame (2006), The Noble Outlaw (2007); Autopsy: The Memoirs of Milton Helpern (biography, 1977); popular non-fiction: Murder Suicide or Accident (1971), Discovering the Human Body (1980); textbooks: Legal Aspects of Medicine (5 edn, 1992), Sudden Death In Infancy (1982), Coroner's Autopsy (1983), Lawyer's Guide to Forensic Medicine (1983, 2 edn 1998), Essentials of Forensic Medicine (with Polson and Gee, 1985), Forensic Medicine (1986), Forensic Pathology (1991, 3 edn 2004), Simpson's Forensic Medicine (11 edn, 1996), Estimation of Time Since Death (2 edn, 2002); *Recreations* writing: crime and history novels, biography, radio and TV drama; *Style—* Prof Bernard Knight, CBE, GSM; ✉ 26 Millwood, Lisvane, Cardiff CF14 0TL (e-mail knight.j4@sky.com)

KNIGHT, Beverley; MBE (2006); *b* 22 March 1973, Wolverhampton, Staffs; *Career* singer, songwriter and record producer; top 20 singles incl: Made it Back 99 1999, Greatest Day 1999, Get Up 2001, Shoulda Woulda Coulda 2002, Come As You Are 2004, Keep This Fire Burning 2005, Piece of My Heart 2006; albums: The B-Funk 1995, Prodigal Sista 1998, Who I Am 2002, Affirmation 2004, Voice - The Best of Beverley Knight 2006 (platinum); collaborations incl: Hard Times (Courtney Pine) 2000, Main Vein, A Foolsophy (Jamiroquai) 2001, Do They Know It's Christmas (Band Aid 20) 2004, Where in the World (Jools Holland) 2005; resident singer Just the Two of Us (BBC1 series) 2006, host Beverley's Gospel Nights BBC Radio 2; ambass: Christian Aid, Stop AIDS Campaign, Terrence Higgins Tst, Rainbow Tst, Elton John Aids Fndn; Best R&B Artist and Best Producer Black Music Awards 1996, Best R&B Act MOBO Awards 1998 and 1999, Best Album MOBO Awards 1999, Best Br Music Act EMMA Awards 1999, Trailblazing Artist BBM/BMC Awards 2003, Lifetime Acheivement Urban Music Awards 2004; *Style—* Ms Beverley Knight; ✉ c/o The Outside Organisation Limited, Butler House, 177–178 Tottenham Court Road, London W1T 7NY (tel 020 7436 3633, fax 020 7436 3632); DWL Limited, 53 Goodge Street, London W1T 1TG (tel 020 7436 5529, fax 020 7637 8776)

KNIGHT, Brien Walter; s of Edward Alfred Knight (d 1993), of Sussex, and Winifred, *née* Stolworthy (d 1976); *b* 27 June 1929; *Educ* Woodhouse GS, Sir John Cass Coll London; *m* 1, 1955, Annette, da of Alfred Scotten (d 1964), of Barnet; 4 da (Carolyn b 1961, Judith b 1964, Emma b 1966, Sophie b 1966), 1 s (Darrell b 1963); m 2, Maria Antoinette (Rita), da of Abraham Van Der Meer (d 1958), of Holland; *Career* dir: Knight Strip Metals Ltd 1951 (chm 1970–), Sterling Springs Ltd 1952–, Knight Precision Wire Ltd 1979– (chm 1979–); Precision Metals NV (Belgium) 1973–; chm: Knuway Investment Ltd 1973–, Arenastock Ltd 1998–; FInstD; *Recreations* DIY; *Style—* Brien Knight, Esq; ✉ Sherborne, Nightingales Lane, Chalfont St Giles, Buckinghamshire HP8 4SR; Linkside, Summit Road, Cranborne Road, Potters Bar, Hertfordshire EN6 3JL (e-mail brien.knight@knight-group.co.uk)

KNIGHT, Charles Henry; s of Robert W S Knight, DL (d 2004), and Susan M, *née* Ball; *b* 30 March 1966, Southerndown, Glamorgan; *Educ* Radley, South Bank Univ (BSc); *m* 1993, Lalley, *née* Usher-Smith; 2 da (Ophelia b 1997, Anastasia b 1999), 1 s (Henry b 2007); *Career* investment surveyor Grimley J R Eve 1989, assoc ptnr GVA Grimley 1993, fndr shareholder and dir Mansford Wales Ltd 1997, main bd dir Mansford Hldgs plc 2001–; memb Investment Property Forum; Commercial Devpt of the Year (Old Brewery Quarter Cardiff) Western Mail Welsh Property Awards 2005; memb CLA; High Sheriff Mid Glamorgan 2007–08; MRICS 1991; *Recreations* golf, shooting, boating; *Clubs* Royal Porthcawl Golf, Seaview Yacht, Cardiff & County; *Style—* Charles Knight, Esq; ✉ Tythegston Court, Mid Glamorgan CF32 0NE (tel 01656 773366); Mansford Holdings plc, 15 Bury Walk, London SW3 6QD (tel 020 7838 0111, e-mail cknight@mansford.com)

KNIGHT, Dr Charles James; s of Alfred Charles James Knight, and Janet Elizabeth Knight; *Educ* Canford Sch, Magadalene Coll Cambridge (MA, MD), Merton Coll Oxford (BM BCh); *Career* hon sr registrar and Br Heart Fndn research fell Royal Brompton Hosp 1994–96, sr registrar St George's Hosp 1996–99, conslt cardiologist London Chest Hosp and King George's Hosp 1999–, hon sr lectr Queen Mary London 2001–; memb Br Cardiac Soc 1994; FRGS, FRCP 2003 (MRCP 1992); *Recreations* bridge, gardening; *Style—* Dr Charles Knight; ✉ London Chest Hospital, Bonner Road, London E2 9JX (tel 020 8983 2248, fax 020 8983 2278)

KNIGHT, Dominic John Gerard; s of Kenneth Alexander Knight (d 1999), of Broadstairs, Kent, and Irene Elaine Clements, *née* Robey (d 1992); *b* 15 November 1954; *Educ* Chatham House Sch Ramsgate, Exeter Coll Oxford (open scholar, MA); *m* Jane Nina, *née* Askew; 2 s (Sebastian Alexander John b 3 April 1990, Rupert Charles Guy b 19 May 1993); *Career* vice-pres Stockton Press New York 1984–88; Macmillan Press Ltd (re-named Palgrave Macmillan, 2001): gp marketing dir 1989–91, publishing dir 1992–94, md 1994–; exec dir Macmillan Ltd 2000–; dir: Publishers Licensing Soc 2000–, Copyright Licensing Soc 2004–; *Recreations* playing the violin, piano and mandolin, golf and walking in the local hills; *Style—* Dominic Knight, Esq; ✉ Palgrave Macmillan, Brunel Road, Houndmills, Basingstoke RG21 6XS (tel 01256 329242)

KNIGHT, Rt Hon Gregory (Greg); PC (1995), MP; s of late Albert George Knight, of Leicester, and late Isabella, *née* Bell; *b* 4 April 1949; *Educ* Alderman Newton's GS Leicester, Coll of Law Guildford; *Career* admitted slr 1973, practising until 1983 and 2000–06; Leicester City cncllr 1976–79, Leicestershire co cncllr 1977–83; former chm Public Protection Ctee; MP (Cons): Derby N 1983–97, Yorkshire E 2001–; PPS to Rt Hon David Mellor, QC, *qv*, 1987–89, asst Govt whip 1989, a Lord Cmmr of the Treasury (Govt whip) 1990–93, Treasurer HM Household (dep chief whip) 1993–96, min of state DTI 1996–97; oppn spokesman for Shadow Ldr of the House 2001–02; shadow min for: Culture 2002–03, Railways and Aviation 2003–05, Roads 2005–06; chm House of Commons Select Ctee on Procedure 2006–; business exec 1997–2001; former dir Leicester Theatre Tst Ltd (former chm of Fin Ctee); memb Law Soc 1973; *Books* Westminster Words (1988), Honourable Insults (1990), Parliamentary Sauce (1993), Right Honourable Insults (1998), Naughty Grafitti (2005); *Recreations* arts (especially music), classic cars; *Style—* The Rt Hon Greg Knight, MP; ✉ House of Commons, London SW1A 0AA (e-mail secretary@gregknight.com)

KNIGHT, Henrietta Catherine; da of Maj Hubert Guy Broughton Knight (d 1994), and Hester, *née* Loyd (d 2001); *b* 15 December 1946, London; *Educ* Didcot Girls' GS, Westminster Coll of Educn (BEd), Berks Coll of Agric; *m* 1995, Terrence Walter (Terry) Biddlecombe; *Career* racehorse trainer; biology and history teacher St Mary's Wantage Sch 1970–74; chm Horse Trials Sr Selection Ctee 1984–88, licenced racehorse trainer 1989– (horses trained incl Best Mate (winner Cheltenham Gold Cup 2002, 2003 and 2004)); Lanson Lady of the Year 2002, Timeform Personality of the Year (jtly with Terry Biddlecombe) 2003, 7 Guinness Awards Cheltenham Festival 2002, 2003 and 2004, Horseracers Writers and Photographers Assoc Nat Hunt Trainer of the Year 2002 and 2004, Channel 4 Racing Personality of the Year 2003; *Publications* Best Mate: Chasing Gold (2003), Best Mate: Triple Gold (2004); *Recreations* breeding Connemara ponies, judging at major horse shows and county shows, farming; *Style—* Miss Henrietta Knight; ✉ West Lockinge Farm, Wantage, Oxfordshire OX12 8QF (tel 01235 833535, fax 01235 820110, e-mail hen@westlockinge.co.uk)

KNIGHT, James Philip (Jim); MP; s of late Philip John Knight, and Hillier, *née* Howlett; *b* 6 March 1965; *Educ* Eltham Coll, Fitzwilliam Coll Cambridge; *m* 1989, Anna, *née* Wheatley; 1 da (Ruth Bridget b 31 Aug 1988), 1 s (Fergus James b 26 Sept 1990); *Career* actor and theatre mangr 1987–91, publisher of telephone directories Dentons Directories Ltd 1991–2001 (co dir 1998–2001); MP (Lab) S Dorset 2001– (Parly candidate (Lab) S Dorset 1997, European Parly candidate (Lab) SW England 1999), memb House of Commons

Defence Ctee 2001–03, Parly sec DEFRA 2005–06, min of state DfES 2006–; memb Frome Town Cncl 1995–2001 (mayor 1998–99), memb Medip DC 1997–2001 (dep ldr 1999–2001); *Style—* Jim Knight, Esq, MP; ✉ House of Commons, London SW1A 0AA

KNIGHT, (William) Jeremy Jonathan; s of Richard Beatty MacBean Knight, of Brighton, and Yvonne Stephanie, *née* Searles; *b* 27 May 1951; *Educ* Brighton Coll; *m* 15 March 1975, Marian Margaret, da of Albert Edward Hoare; 2 s (Richard Andrew b 6 Feb 1978, Simon Peter Edward b 7 July 1979); *Career* CA/insolvency practitioner; articled clerk Graves Goddard & Horton-Stephens 1969–73, National Trading Co Johannesburg 1973–74, Peat Marwick Mitchell 1974–76; ptnr: Chater Spain Brothers 1978–88 (joined 1976), Moores Rowland (following merger) 1988–89; sole practitioner specialising in insolvency Jeremy Knight & Co Brighton and Croydon 1989–; pres SE Soc of CAs 1991–92, memb Cncl ICAEW 1995–2005; FCA 1975, MIPA 1987; *Recreations* flying, motor racing; *Style—* W J J Knight, Esq; ✉ 48 Welbeck Avenue, Hove, East Sussex BN3 4JN (tel 01273 558045); Jeremy Knight & Co, 68 Ship Street, Brighton, East Sussex BN1 1AE (tel 01273 203654 or 020 8680 4274, fax 01273 206056, mobile 07887 931322)

KNIGHT, Dr Lorna A; da of Gerald A Knight (d 1991), and Sybil E, *née* Cole (d 1999); *b* 12 February 1949, Taunton, Somerset; *Educ* Bedford Coll Univ of London (BA, PhD); *m* 1, 15 Sept 1973, Ian M Sinclair; 2 s (Simon J b 11 July 1977, Christopher M b 17 Feb 1981); m 2, 28 Aug 2004, Ian S McTier; *Career* lectr in French Univ of Strathclyde 1973–77; Dictionaries Div HarperCollins Publishers: lexicographer 1979–85, managing ed 1985–89, publishing mangr 1989–95, publishing dir 1995–2002, md Collins Dictionaries 2002–; princ flautist Glasgow Orchestral Soc 1973–; *Publications* main contrib to numerous Collins Dictionaries 1975–, Collins-Robert French-English Dictionary (co-author, 1978), Collins German-English Dictionary (co-author, 1980); *Recreations* classical music, dance, keeping fit; *Style—* Dr Lorna Knight; ✉ HarperCollins Publisher, Dictionaries Division, Westerhill Road, Glasgow G64 2QT (tel 0141 306 3679, e-mail lorna.knight@harpercollins.co.uk)

KNIGHT, Matthew; s of Nicholas Knight, and Patricia Knight; *Educ* Eltham Coll, Univ of Newcastle upon Tyne, Coll of Law Guildford; *Career* articled clerk Farrer & Co 1981–83, asst slr Sinclair Roche & Temperley 1983–85, ptnr Cripps Harries Hall 1986–94 (asst slr 1985–86), sr ptnr Knights Slrs 1994–; slr: Business for Sterling (memb Southern Cncl), Reform Britain, Countryside Alliance (also memb); memb: Law Soc 1981–, Tunbridge Wells, Tonbridge & Dist Law Soc 1994–, Kent Law Soc 1994–, City of Westminster and Holborn Law Soc 2002–; Liveryman Worshipful Co of Broderers; *Recreations* hunting, shooting, skiing, sailing, running, reading, riding; *Style—* Matthew Knight, Esq; ✉ Knights, Regency House, 25 High Street, Tunbridge Wells, Kent TN1 1UT (tel 01892 537311, fax 01892 526141, e-mail matthew.knight@knights-solicitors.co.uk)

KNIGHT, Michael James; s of Charles Knight (d 1988), of London, and Ellen, *née* Murphy (d 1997); *b* 29 August 1939; *Educ* St Bonaventures Sch London, King's Coll London, St George's Hosp London (MB BS, MS); *m* 1981, Phyllis Mary, da of William Ansel Purcell; 1 s (William Robert Charles b 1981), 1 da (Ellen Harrison b 1983); *Career* surgical registrar: Royal Hampshire County Hosp Winchester 1965–69, St George's Hosp 1969–71 (surgical res fell 1971–72); surgical res fell Washington Univ St Louis MO 1972–73, sr surgical registrar St George's Hosp London 1973–78, Hunterian prof RCS 1975, hon sr lectr St George's Hosp Med Sch; conslt surgn: St James's Hosp London 1978–88, St George's Hosp London 1978–, Royal Masonic Hosp London 1979–97; ind advsr to the Health Servs Cmmr for England 1998–2006; memb: Pancreatic Soc of GB and I (pres 1987), RSM, Euro Soc of Surgical Res, Ct of Examiners RCS 1988–98; examiner in surgery Univ of London, external examiner RCS in I, Edinburgh and Univ of Colombo; author of numerous pubns on gastroenterology, hepatic, pancreatic and biliary tract diseases; FRCS 1967 (MRCS 1963), LRCP; *Recreations* music; *Style—* Michael Knight, Esq; ✉ 1 St Aubyn's Avenue, Wimbledon, London SW19 7BL

KNIGHT, Sir Michael William Patrick; KCB (1983, CB 1980), AFC (1964); s of William and Dorothy Knight; *b* 23 November 1932; *Educ* Univ of Liverpool (BA); *m* 1967, Patricia Ann, *née* Davies; 1 s (Richard), 2 da (Gillian, Lisa); *Career* Sqdn pilot/Flt Cdr Nos 30, 53, 216, 139 and 249 Sqdns 1955–61, OC 32 Sqdn (RAF Akrotiri) 1961–63, RAF Staff Coll 1964, Miny of Aviation 1965–66, OC Far East Strike Wing (RAF Tengah) 1966–68, OC Flying Tengah 1968–69, head AOC-in-C's Secretariat RAF Strike Cmd 1969–70, princ mil asst to Chm NATO Mil Ctee 1970–73, OC RAF Laarbruch 1973–74, RCDS 1975, dir of ops Air Force Dept MOD 1976–77, SASO RAF Strike Cmd 1977–80, AOC No 1 Gp RAF Strike Cmd 1980–82, Air Memb for Supply and Orgn 1983–86, UK Mil Rep NATO 1986–89, Air ADC to HM The Queen 1986–89 (ADC 1973–74), ret as Air Chief Marshal 1989; Flying Offr RAFVR(T) 1989–; Hon Air Cdre 7630 Int Sqdn RAuxAF 2000–; chm: Cobham plc 1995–2001 (dep chm 1994–95), Page Group Holdings Ltd 1997–2000, Cranfield Aerospace 2000–03; dir: Craigwell Research 1989–97, FR Group plc 1990–94, Page Group Ltd 1991–96, Smiths Industries Aerospace & Defence Systems Group 1992–95, RAFC Co Ltd 1993–2003, SBAC (Farnborough) Ltd 1996–99; life vice-pres Air League 2004– (chm 1992–98, pres 1998–2004), pres Cncl NAAFI 1984–86, vice-pres Atlantic Cncl of UK 1993–, chm of tstees VTS 2002–; vice-pres: RAF Club 1983–2003, The Youth Trust 1994–98; Exmoor Calvert Tst: tstee 1998–, chm of tstees 1999–; adj prof Carnegie Mellon Univ Pittsburgh 1989–93; chm: Northern Devon Healthcare NHS Tst 1990–94, N Devon Cheshire Fndn FSS 1989–91, RAF Charitable Tst 2005–; sr pres Offrs' Assoc 1997–2000 (Air Force pres 1991–97); patron: Vulcan Restoration Appeal 1999–2002, Guild of Aviation Artists 2005– (vice-pres 1995–2005); pres: Aircrew Assoc 1991–96, Buccaneer Aircrew Assoc 1994–, Royal Int Air Tattoo 2005– (vice-pres 1991–2005); hon vice-pres RAF Allied Air Forces Memorial Ctee 1996–; pres: RAF Lawn Tennis Assoc 1984–86, RAF Rugby Union 1986–90 (chm 1975–78), Combined Servs RFC 1986–88 (chm 1976–78); memb Ctee RFU 1977–92, vice-pres Crawshays Welsh RFC 1999–, vice-pres Penguin Int RFC 2001–; Devon Co rep RAF Benevolent Fund 1990–; memb: Cncl RUSI 1984–87, Cncl Taunton Sch 1987–2000, Cncl RGS 1995–97, Cncl SBAC 1995–99, Cncl Calvert Tst 1999–; tstee RAF Museum 1983–86, tstee RAF Central Fund 1983–86, vice-patron Yorkshire Air Museum 1996–; Liveryman Guild of Air Pilots and Air Navigators 1993 (Upper Freeman 1989), Freeman City of London 1989; Hon DLitt; FRAeS, FRGS, FRSA; *Publications* War in the Third Dimension (contrib, 1986), Strategic Offensive Air Power & Technology (1989); author of articles in numerous professional pubns 1975–; *Recreations* flying, rugby, other sports, music, writing, lecturing; *Clubs* RAF, Colonels (fndr memb); *Style—* Sir Michael Knight, KCB, AFC, FRAeS; ✉ c/o Nat West Bank plc, 24 Derby Street, Leek, Staffordshire ST13 5AF

KNIGHT, Nicholas David Gordon (Nick); s of Michael Anthony Gordon Knight, and Beryl Rose Knight; *b* 24 November 1958; *Educ* Hinchingbrooke Sch Huntingdon, Huntingdon Tech Coll, Chelsea Coll London, Bournemouth and Poole Coll of Art (PQE DipAD); *m* 1995, Charlotte Esme, *née* Wheeler; 2 da (Emily Ruby b 1993, Ella May b 1994), 1 s (Calum Kingsley b 1997); *Career* photographer; commissioning picture ed i-D Magazine 1990, contracted photographer for Vogue 1995–; dir SHOWStudio Ltd; dir NK Image Ltd; lectr: V&A, RCA, Manchester Coll of Art; prof Univ of the Arts London 2007–; fashion and advtg campaigns incl: Yves Saint Laurent, Lancôme, Guerlain, Christian Dior, Levis, Yohji Yamamoto, Jil Sander, Alexander McQueen, Mercedes, Royal Mail, Royal Ballet; record covers for: David Bowie, George Michael, Rolling Stones, Bjork, Massive Attack; *Exhibitions* Photographers Gallery 1982, 20 For Today (Nat Portrait Gallery) 1986, 14–21 Youth Culture Exhbn (V&A) 1986, Out of Fashion (Photographers Gallery) 1989, Ils Annoncent la Colour (Les Rencontres d'Arles) 1989, Vanités (Paris) 1993, Plant Power (permanent exhbn cmmnd by Nat History Museum) 1993, Biennale di Firenze - Art/Fashion (with Alexander McQueen) 1996, JAM (Barbican Art Gallery) 1997, Contemporary Fashion Photography (V&A) 1997, Look at Me - Fashion Photography 1965 to Present (travelling) 1998, Shoreditch Biennale 1998, Addressing the Century: 100 Years of Art & Fashion (Hayward Gallery) 1998, Silver & Syrup (V&A) 1999, Century City Tate Modern 2001; *Awards* Kodak 1985 and 1987, D&AD Award 1985, Magazine Publishing Award 1986, Club des Directors Artistique Award 1988, Expansion Magazine Awards 1988, Halina Award 1989, Gold Award USA 1989, Int Festival de la Photo de Mode 1991 and 1992, voted by GQ magazine as one of Britain's best dressed men 1992, 2002 and 2006, Int Festival de la Photo de Mode Award 1994, voted most influential fashion photographer in the world Face Magazine 1995, Royal Mail Innovation Award 1996, D&AD Silver Award 1997, The Power of Photography Award 1998, Total Publishing 'Best Front Cover of the Year' for Dazed & Confused Magazine 1999, D&AD Silver Award for Best Music Poster for Massive Attack album 'Mezzanine' 1999, Design Distinction Award from Int Design Magazine for front cover of Visionaire Magazine, Fashion Tribute Moet & Chandon 2006; Hon MA Anglia Polytechnic Univ 2000; hon fell Bournemouth and Poole Coll of Art and Design 1998; *Books* Skinheads (1982), NICKNIGHT (retrospective by Schirmer Mosel, 1994), Flora (Herbarium samples from the Nat History Museum, 1997); *Recreations* architecture, natural history; *Style—* Nick Knight, Esq; ✉ tel 020 8940 1086, fax 020 8948 8761, e-mail info@nkimage.com

KNIGHT, Dr Peter Clayton; CBE (1995); s of Norman Knight, and Vera, *née* Jordan; *b* 8 July 1947; *Educ* Bishop Vesey GS, Univ of York (BA, DPhil); *m* 2 April 1978, Catherine Mary, da of Raymond Ward; 1 s (Andrew b 5 March 1979), 1 da (Gail b 29 Aug 1981); *Career* asst dir Plymouth Poly 1979–82, dep dir Lancashire Poly 1982–85, dir Birmingham Poly 1985–92, vice-chllr Univ of Central England Birmingham 1992–; memb: Burnham Further Educn Ctee 1976–81, Ctee on Mgmnt Public Sector Higher Educn 1977, Nat Advsy Body for Local Authy Higher Educn 1981–84, Polys and Colls Funding Cncl 1988–, Armed Forces Pay Review Bd 2004–; chm: Polys and Colls Employers Forum 1992–, Teacher Training Agency 1995–; nat pres NATFHE 1978–79, chm Soc for Research into Higher Educn 1990–92, awarded 'Maverick of the Year' 2000; Hon DUniv York, Hon DSc Aston Univ; FRAS, CPhys, MInstP; *Style—* Dr Peter Knight, CBE; ✉ University of Central England, Perry Barr, Birmingham B42 2SU (tel 0121 331 5555, fax 0121 356 5436)

KNIGHT, Peter John; s of William Knight (d 1974), of Ware, Herts; *b* 16 April 1950; *Educ* Trinity Hall Cambridge (MA); *m* Aug 1975, Jennifer Joan, da of late Wilfred Walter Townsend; 4 s (Jonathan William b May 1979, Robert Peter b Dec 1980, Oliver James b July 1984, Christopher Richard b Feb 1987); *Career* admitted slr England and Wales, Hong Kong and NSW Aust; Baker & McKenzie: slr London 1975–76 and 1979–82, slr Sydney 1976–79, managing ptnr Singapore 1987–90 (ptnr 1983–87), ptnr London 1990–; chm Br Assoc of Singapore 1989–90; memb Ctee: Asia Pacific Advsy Gp (DTI) 1992–98, London C of C 1993–; memb Bd of Advsrs Japanese and SE Asian Studies, chm Cambridge in the Capital 1995–98; govr Tanglin Tst Schs 1987–90; memb: Law Soc of England and Wales, Law Soc of Singapore; *Recreations* tennis, sailing, golf, early music, opera, theatre; *Style—* Peter J Knight, Esq; ✉ Baker & McKenzie LLP, 100 New Bridge Street, London EC4V 6JA (tel 020 7919 1000, fax 020 7919 1999)

K

KNIGHT, Prof Sir Peter Leonard; kt (2005); s of Joseph Knight (decd), of Bedford, and Eva Lillian Knight; *b* 12 August 1947; *Educ* Bedford Modern Sch, Univ of Sussex (BSc, DPhil); *m* 1965, Christine Mary, *née* Huckle; 2 s (David b 1965, Phillip b 1967), 1 da (Victoria b 1971); *Career* res assoc Univ of Rochester NY 1972–74, SRC res fell Univ of Sussex 1974–76, Jubilee res fell Royal Holloway Coll London 1976–78; Imperial Coll London: SERC advanced fell 1978–83, lectr 1983–87, 1987–88, prof 1988–, head of laser optics and spectroscopy 1991–2000, head of quantum optics and laser science 2001–02, head Physics Dept 2002–05, princ Faculty of Natural Sciences 2005– (actg princ 2004–05); chief scientific advsr Nat Physical Lab 2002–05; co-ordinator SERC Initiative in Non-Linear Optics 1988–92 (chm 1992–93), chm Quantum Electronics Div Euro Physical Soc 1988–92, pres Physics Section of BAAS 1994–95, dir Optical Soc of America 1999–2005; ed: Jl of Modern Optics 1987–2006, Jl of Contemporary Physics 1993–; Alexander von Humbolt Res Award 1993, European Physical Soc lectr 1998–99, Einstein Medal and Prize for Laser Sci Soc of Optical and Quantum Electronics 1996, Parsons Medal Inst of Physics and Royal Soc 1997, Thomas Young Medal and Prize Inst of Physics 1999; memb: Mexican Acad of Scis 2000, Academia Europaea 2001; Dr (hc): INAOE Mexico 1998, Slovak Acad of Sciences 2000; fell Optical Soc of America (vice-pres 2002, pres 2004); FInstP, FRS 1999; *Publications* Principles of Quantum Optics (1983), Introductory Quantum Optics; also author of over 400 articles in scientific literature; *Recreations* traditional music; *Style—* Prof Sir Peter Knight, FRS; ✉ Faculty of Natural Sciences, Imperial College, London SW7 2AZ (tel 020 7594 5477, fax 020 7594 7504, e-mail p.knight@ic.ac.uk)

KNIGHT, Prof Roger John Beckett; s of Lt Cdr John Beckett Knight (d 1983), of Bromley, Kent, and Alyson Yvonne Saunders, *née* Nunn; *b* 11 April 1944; *Educ* Tonbridge, Trinity Coll Dublin (MA), Univ of Sussex (PGCE), UCL (PhD); *m* 1, 3 Aug 1968 (m dis 1980), Helen Elizabeth, da of Dr William Magowan (d 1980), of Hawkhurst, Kent; 2 s (William b 1973, Richard b 1976); m 2, 31 Jan 1998, Jane Hamilton-Eddy, *née* Coffey; *Career* National Maritime Museum: custodian Manuscripts 1977–81 (dep 1974–77) dep head Books and Manuscripts 1981–84, head Info Project Gp 1984–86, head Documentation Div 1986–88, head Collections Div and chief curator 1988–93, dep dir and head Display Div 1993–95, dep dir and head Information Div 1995–97, dep dir 1997–2000; prof of naval history Univ of Greenwich 2006– (visiting prof 2000–06); memb: Ctee Greenwich Soc 1988–90, Cncl Soc for Nautical Res 1975–79 (vice-pres 1992–2006), Cncl Navy Records Soc 1975–; tstee National Maritime Museum Cornwall 1998–2002; FRHistS; *Books* Guide to the Manuscripts in the National Maritime Museum (1977, 1980), The Journal of Daniel Paine, 1794–1797 (with Alan Frost, 1983), Portsmouth Dockyard in the American War of Independence, 1774–1783 (1986), British Naval Documents 1204–1960 (jt ed, 1993), The Pursuit of Victory: The Life and Achievement of Horatio Nelson (2005, Mountbatten Maritime Prize Br Maritime Charitable Fndn 2005, Duke of Westminster's Medal RUSI 2006); *Recreations* sailing, music; *Clubs* Athenaeum, Royal Naval Sailing Assoc; *Style—* Prof Roger Knight; ✉ Greenwich Maritime Institute, University of Greenwich, Old Royal Naval College, Greenwich, London SE10 9LS (tel 020 8331 7688, fax 020 8331 7690, e-mail r.j.b.knight@gre.ac.uk)

KNIGHT, Dr Ronald Kelvin; s of Walter Leonard Knight, and Kathleen Elizabeth, *née* Langran; *b* 12 October 1945; *Educ* Latymer Upper Sch, Gonville & Caius Coll Cambridge (MA), St Bart's Med Coll London (MB BChir); *m* 31 March 1984, Clare Louise, da of Donald Scott, of Wrexham; 3 da (Olivia b 26 Feb 1985, Georgia b 18 Feb 1988, Imogen b 9 Sept 1989); *Career* currently conslt physician in gen and respiratory med at Frimley Park, Farnham and Royal Brompton and Nat Heart Hosps; has researched into and contributed several chapters to reference books on respiratory diseases and runs a clinic for patients with cystic fibrosis referred on a nat level; chm Dept of Med and dir Knight Centre for Cystic Fibrosis Frimley Park Hosp; med advsr Camberley and Dist Asthma Soc, memb Thoracic Assoc; FRCP (MRCP); *Books* contrib chapters to a number of reference books on respiratory disease; *Recreations* children, running, association football; *Style—* Dr Ronald Knight; ✉ Brambley Wood, Snowdenham Links Road, Bramley, Guildford GU5 0BX (tel 01483 894392); Frimley Park Hospital, Portsmouth Road, Frimley, Camberley, Surrey GU16 7UJ (tel 01276 692777); Royal Brompton and National Heart Hospital, Fulham Road, Chelsea, London SW3 6HP (tel 020 7352 8121)

KNIGHT, Stephen Charles; s of Reginald Frank Knight (decd), of Street, Somerset, and Sheila Ethel Clarice, *née* Jones (decd); *b* 25 November 1954; *Educ* Colfe's Sch, Bromley Coll; *m* 30 July 1977, Lesley Joan, da of Harold Leonard Davison, of Petts Wood, Kent; 2 s (Timothy David Stephen b 1988, Joshua James Stephen b 1990); *Career* gen mangr mktg and devpt Newcross Building Society 1983–84, vice-pres Citibank 1984–87, chm Private Label Mortgage Services Ltd 1987–, chm GMAC RFC Ltd 2000–; FCIB 1977, MCIM 1979, FRSA 2007; *Publications* The Art of Marketing Mortgages (1997), Creator and Trader: A Vision for Growth in the UK Mortgage Market (2006); *Recreations* sport, writing; *Clubs* IOD, RSA; *Style*— Stephen Knight, Esq; ✉ GMAC RFC Ltd, 90 Long Acre, London WC2E 9RA (tel 020 7420 7660, fax 020 7420 7661, e-mail stephen.knight@gmacrfc.co.uk)

KNIGHT, Tina Patricia; da of Jack Leonard King (d 1983), of London, and Nellie Irene, *née* Baxter (d 1999); *Educ* Walthamstow Co HS for Girls, SW Essex Tech Coll; *Career* mgmnt conslt and trouble-shooter until 1978, md GSC (UK) Ltd 1978–84, mgmnt conslt Scientific Staff Consultants 1984–85, prop Nighthawk Enterprises 1985– (prop and md Nighthawk Electronics Ltd 1985–2002, md Nighthawk Traders Ltd 1986–2002); non-exec dir Essex TEC 1990–2000, chm Millbrook Bakeries Ltd 2002–03, dep chm EWP 2002–, chief exec Entrepreneurial Exchange 2002–, chm CHA 2003–, dir PSA 2004–, dir Northern Cyprus Property Centre Ltd 2005–, dist cncllr Uttlesford 2005–; numerous TV and radio appearances incl: Election Special (Channel 4), Question Time (BBC 1) and various regnl broadcasting appearances; also professional after-dinner and conf speaker incl: Nat Conf Small Business Bureau, Women in Business Int Conf; memb: Bd Prince's Youth Business Tst 1990, Ctee China-Britain Trade Gp 1990, Ctee Advsy Unit Small Business Bureau 1991, Bd TAVRA 1992, Bd East of England Industry Devpt Bd (EEIDB) 1999–2002; chm Women Into Business 1995 (dep chm 1992–95), vice-chm London Businessmen's Network 1994, vice-pres Small Business Bureau; runner-up TSB/Options Magazine Women Mean Business 1988, TOBIE Award 1989, runner-up Veuve Clicquot Business Woman of the Year 1989, Starr Award Top Entrepreneur of the World 1998, Global Summit of Women Award UK BusinessPioneer 1998, Br Assoc of Women Entrepreneurs (BAWE) Award for Br Entrepreneur of the Year 1999, BAWE Joyce Award; chm Addenbrooke's Hosp Food Chain Appeal, tstee Galapagos Conservation Tst 2005–, hon pres Tang Ting Twinning Assoc; FInstD 1987, FRSA 1992, fell PSA 1999; *Recreations* bridge, theatre, opera, bookbinding, fishing, art galleries, needlepoint; *Clubs* Wig & Pen, Mosimann's, Univ Women's; *Style*— Tina Knight; ✉ Nighthawk Enterprises, PO Box 44, Saffron Walden, Essex CB11 3ND (tel 01799 540881, fax 01799 541713, e-mail tpk@nighthawk.co.uk)

KNIGHT, (Christopher) William; s of Claude Knight (d 1993), and Hon Priscilla (d 1995), da of 2 Baron Monk Bretton, CB; *b* 10 April 1943; *Educ* Eton; *m* 6 Sept 1969, Jonkvrouwe Sylvia Caroline, da of Jonkheer Emile van Lennep (d 1996); 2 da (Alexa b 9 Nov 1971, Louisa b 15 Oct 1977), 1 s (Christopher b 20 Oct 1973); *Career* princ mangr Portugal The Bank of London and S America 1982–84; dir: Lloyds Merchant Bank 1985–91, Lloyds Investment Mangrs 1987–91; md Lloyds Bank Fund Mgmnt 1988–91, fndr William Knight and Associates 1991; chm: Thai-Euro Fund Ltd, European Growth Fund Ltd, Abingworth Bioventures II, Siberia Investment Co plc; dir: J P Morgan Fleming Chinese Investment Tst, Fidelity Asian Values Tst, L G India Fund Ltd, KASB Capital Ltd, Evolvence India Hldgs plc; advsr: Clearwater Capital, Campbell Lutyens & Co; *Recreations* cricket, opera, travel writing, wine, contemporary global politics; *Clubs* Boodle's, Shek-O, Hurlingham; *Style*— William Knight, Esq; ✉ 82 Lansdowne Road, London W11 2LS (tel 020 7221 3900, fax 020 7221 2178, e-mail william.wknight@gmail.com)

KNIGHT, William John Langford (Bill); s of William Knight, and Gertrude Alice, *née* Wallage; *b* 11 September 1945; *Educ* Sir Roger Manwood's Sch Sandwich, Univ of Bristol (LLB); *m* 21 April 1973, Stephanie Irina, da of Lt-Col Edward Jeffery Williams; 1 da (Sarah b 1977), 1 s (Sam b 1980); *Career* admitted slr 1969; Simmons & Simmons Slrs: joined 1967, ptnr 1973–2001, i/c Hong Kong office 1979–82, head Corp Dept 1994–96, sr ptnr 1996–2001; dep chm Cncl of Lloyd's 2003– (memb 2000–); former chm Standing Ctee on Co Law for Law Soc; chm: London Weighting Advsy Panel for GLA 2001–02, Enforcement Ctee Gen Insurance Standards Cncl 2002–04, Financial Reporting Review Panel 2004–; memb: Financial Reporting Cncl 2004–, Gaming Bd for GB 2004–05; gambling cmmr 2005–; Liveryman City of London Slrs' Co (memb Ct of Assts 2002–, Master 2007); FRSA; *Books* The Acquisition of Private Companies and Business Assets (1975, 7 edn 1997); *Recreations* photography, Arsenal; *Clubs* Travellers, Hong Kong; *Style*— Bill Knight, Esq

KNIGHT OF COLLINGTREE, Baroness (Life Peer UK 1997), of Collingtree in the County of Northamptonshire; Dame (Joan Christabel) Jill Knight; DBE (1985, MBE 1964); da of A E Christie (d 1933); *b* 1927; *Educ* Fairfield Sch, King Edward GS for Girls Birmingham; *m* 1947, Montague Knight (decd), s of Leslie Knight of Harpole Hall, Northampton; 2 s; *Career* MP (Cons) Birmingham Edgbaston 1966–97 (Parly candidate (Cons) Northampton 1959 and 1964); memb: Race Relations and Immigration Select Ctee 1969–72, Home Affrs Select Ctee 1980–84 and 1992–97, Privileges and Standards Select Ctee 1993–97; chm Cons Backbench Ctee Health and Social Services 1981–97, memb Cncl Europe 1977–88 and 1999–, chm Lords and Commons All Pty Child Protection Gp 1983–97, pres W Midlands Cons Political Centre 1980–83, vice-chm 1922 Ctee 1992–97, chm Inter-Parliamentary Union 1994–97 (memb Exec Ctee 1992–97), vice-chm Assoc of Cons Peers 2002–06, chm All Pty Parly Gp for Northern Cyprus 2004–; dir Computeach International Ltd 1990–2002, dir Heckett Multiserv 1999–2002; memb Northampton Borough Cncl 1956–66; lectr and broadcaster; vice-pres Br Fluoridation Soc 1994–; Hon DSc Aston Univ 1998; *Publications* About the House (1997); *Style*— The Rt Hon Baroness Knight of Collingtree, DBE; ✉ House of Lords, London SW1A 0PW

KNIGHTLEY, Keira; da of Will Knightley, and Sharman MacDonald; *b* 1985; *Career* actress; *Films* incl: Star Wars: Episode I - The Phantom Menace 1999, The Hole 2001, Bend It Like Beckham 2002, Pirates of the Carribean: The Curse of the Black Pearl 2003, Love Actually 2003, King Arthur 2004, The Jacket 2005, Pride & Prejudice 2005, Domino 2005, Pirates of the Caribbean: Dead Man's Chest 2006, Pirates of the Caribbean: At World's End 2007, Atonement 2007; *Awards* London Critics Circle Award for Best Newcomer 2003, Best Int Actress Irish Film and TV Festival 2004, Breakthrough Award Hollywood Film Festival 2004, nomination Golden Globe Awards and Oscars (for Pride & Prejudice) 2006; *Style*— Ms Keira Knightley; ✉ c/o PFD, Drury House, 34–43 Russell Street, London WC2B 5HA

KNIGHTON, Vicky; da of Robert Gibbs, of France, and Theodora (Theo) Campbell, of Spain; *b* 16 November 1950; *Educ* Holy Trinity Convent Bromley, Bedgebury Park Kent; *Children* 1 da (Hannah Theodora Edith b 18 Jan 1987); *Career* Independent Television News Ltd: sec 1971–72, editorial asst House of Commons 1972–73, news desk asst 1973–77, asst news ed 1977–82, news ed 1982–90, foreign ed 1990–92; sr news ed London News Network 1992–93; ITN: rejoined as sr foreign ed 1994, head of foreign news 1996–; *Style*— Ms Vicky Knighton; ✉ ITN Ltd, 200 Gray's Inn Road, London WC1X 8XZ (tel 020 7430 4411)

KNIGHTS, Baron (Life Peer UK 1987), of Edgbaston in the County of West Midlands; Philip Douglas Knights; kt (1980), CBE (1976, OBE 1971), QPM (1964), DL (1985); s of Thomas James Knights (d 1978), of Ottershaw, Surrey, and Ethel Ginn (d 1963); *b* 3 October 1920; *Educ* East Grinstead Co Sch, King's Sch Grantham, Police Staff Coll; *m* 1945, Jean, da of James Henry Burman (d 1971); *Career* served WWII with RAF; police cadet Lincolnshire Constabulary 1937, all ranks to Chief Supt 1937–57, Dep Cmdt Police Staff Coll 1963–66, Dep Chief Constable Birmingham City Police 1970–72 (Asst Chief Constable 1959–70); Chief Constable: Sheffield and Rotherham 1972–74, S Yorks 1974–75, W Midlands Police 1975–85; pres ACPO 1978–79; memb: Cncl Aston Univ 1985–98, Ctee Warks CCC 1985–89; tstee Police Fndn 1979–98, memb Advsy Cncl Cambridge Inst of Criminology 1986–2003; winner Queen's Police Gold Medal Essay Competition 1965; Hon DSc Aston Univ 1996; CCMI 1977; *Recreations* sport, travel, reading; *Clubs* Royal Over-Seas League; *Style*— The Rt Hon the Lord Knights, CBE, QPM, DL; ✉ House of Lords, London SW1A 0PW

KNILL, Sir Thomas John Pugin Bartholomew; 5 Bt (UK 1893), of The Grove, Blackheath, Kent; s of Sir John Kenelm Stuart Knill, 4 Bt (d 1998); *b* 23 August 1952; *m* 1977, Kathleen Muszynski; *Heir* bro, Jenkyn Knill; *Style*— Sir Thomas Knill, Bt

KNOBEL, Lance; s of Lawrence Roy Knobel (d 1990), and Gladys, *née* Smith (d 1994); *b* 6 November 1956; *Educ* New Trier East HS Winnetka Illinois, Princeton Univ (BA), Worcester Coll Oxford (MA); *Career* asst ed The Architectural Review 1980–82; ed: Designer's Journal 1983–87, Management Today 1987–89; md New International Media Milan Italy 1989–90, editorial dir Haymarket Marketing Publications 1990 (publishing devpt dir 1991–92), md and ed-in-chief World Link Publishing 1992–2000, head of prog World Economic Forum's Annual Meeting Davos 2000, advsr PM's Strategy Unit 2001–02, currently co-fndr and ed-in-chief Q Network Inc; *Books* Faber Guide to Twentieth Century Architecture (1985), Office Furniture (1987), International Interiors (1989); *Recreations* scuba diving, trumpet playing, tennis, skiing; *Style*— Lance Knobel, Esq; ✉ website www.davosnewbies.com

KNOLLYS, 3 Viscount (UK 1911); David Francis Dudley Knollys; also Baron Knollys (UK 1902); s of 2 Viscount Knollys, GCMG, MBE, DFC (d 1966), and Margaret (d 1987), da of Sir Stuart Coats, 2 Bt; *b* 12 June 1931; *Educ* Eton; *m* 1959, Hon Sheelin Virginia, DL (Norfolk 1996), da of Lt-Col the Hon Somerset Arthur Maxwell, MP (d 1942), and sis of 13 Baron Farnham; 3 s, 1 da; *Heir* s, Hon Patrick Knollys; *Career* late 2 Lt Scots Gds; *Style*— The Rt Hon the Viscount Knollys; ✉ The Bailiff's House, Bramerton Hall Farm, Norwich, Norfolk NR14 7DN

KNOPF, His Hon Judge Elliot Michael; s of Harry Knopf (d 1976), and Clara Renée, *née* Weingard; *b* 23 December 1950; *Educ* Bury GS, UCL (LLB); *m* 8 Feb 1976, Elizabeth Carol, da of Eugene Lieberman; 1 s (Anthony Martin b 17 Dec 1979), 1 da (Marcelle Rebecca b 4 Feb 1983); *Career* articled clerk Conn Goldberg Slrs Manchester 1974–76; Pannone March Pearson Slrs Manchester: admitted slr 1976, asst slr 1976–79, equity ptnr 1979–91; dep district registrar of the High Court and dep registrar of Co Court (Northern Circuit) 1987–91, district judge of the High Court and Co Court 1991–2002, asst recorder of Crown Court (Northern Circuit) 1996–2000, recorder of Crown Court (Northern Circuit) 2000–02, circuit judge (Northern Circuit) 2002–; memb Law Soc 1976–; *Recreations* reading, swimming, walking, theatre, foreign travel, the family; *Style*— His Hon Judge Knopf; ✉ Bolton Combined Courts, Blackhorse Street, Bolton BL1 1SU (tel 01204 392881)

KNOPFLER, Mark; s of Erwin Knopfler (d 1993), and Louisa Knopfler; *b* 12 August 1949; *Career* musician; former journalist Yorkshire Evening Post and teacher; fndr Dire Straits 1977; has produced: Bob Dylan, Randy Newman and others; albums with Dire Straits: Dire Straits (1978, reached UK no 5), Communique (1979, UK no 5), Making Movies (1980, UK no 4), Love Over Gold (1982, UK no 1), Alchemy - Dire Straits Live (live, 1984, UK no 3), Brothers In Arms (1985, UK no 1, formerly best ever selling UK album), Money For Nothing (compilation, 1988, UK no 1), On Every Street (1991, UK no 1), On the Night (1993), Live at the BBC (1995), Sultans of Swing: The Very Best of Dire Straits (compilation, 1998), Private Investigations: The Best of Dire Straits and Mark Knopfler (2005); solo soundtrack albums: Local Hero (1982, UK no 14), Cal (1984, UK no 65), Comfort and Joy (1984), The Princess Bride (1987), Last Exit to Brooklyn (1989), Wag the Dog (1998), Metroland (1999), Shot at Glory (2002); other albums: Stay Tuned (with Chet Atkins, 1986), Missing...Presumed Having A Good Time (as Notting Hillbillies, 1990, UK no 2), Neck And Neck (with Chet Atkins, 1990, UK no 41), Golden Heart (1996), Sailing to Philadelphia (2000), The Ragpicker's Dream (2002), Shangri-La (2004), All the Roadrunning (with Emmylou Harris, 2006); has won Ivor Novello, BRIT, MTV and Grammy awards; *Style*— Mark Knopfler, Esq

KNOPS, Prof Robin John; s of Joseph Nicholas Jean Toussaint Knops (d 1978), of Weymouth, Dorset, and Rita Josephine, *née* Colombo (d 1997); *b* 30 December 1932; *Educ* Thames Valley GS Twickenham, Univ of Nottingham (BSc, PhD); *m* 2 Sept 1965, Margaret Mary, da of Michael McDonald (d 1977), of Newcastle upon Tyne; 4 s (Andrew b 10 June 1966, Peter b 4 May 1968, Joseph b 12 April 1970, Robert b 22 Oct 1971), 2 da (Geraldine b 9 Aug 1974, Catherine b 9 Jan 1980); *Career* lectr in mathematics Univ of Nottingham 1959–62 (asst lectr 1956–59), reader in continuum mechanics Univ of Newcastle upon Tyne 1968–71 (lectr in applied mathematics 1962–68); Heriot-Watt Univ: prof of mathematics 1971–98, head of dept 1971–83, dean of science 1984–87, vice-princ 1988–95, special advsr to princ 1995–97, sr research fell 1997–98, prof emeritus 1998–; memb Bd of Govrs Scottish Coll of Textiles 1992–98; pres: Edinburgh Mathematical Soc 1974–75, Int Soc for the Interaction of Mechanics and Mathematics 1991–95 (vice-pres 1995–99); Leverhulme emeritus fell 2000–02, Hon DSc Heriot-Watt Univ 1999; FRSE 1975 (memb Exec Ctee 1982–92, memb Cncl 1982–87, meeting sec 1982–87, curator 1987–92), FRSA 1989–2000; *Books* Uniqueness Theorems in Linear Elasticity (with L E Payne, 1971); *Recreations* walking, travel, reading; *Style*— Prof R J Knops, FRSE; ✉ Heriot-Watt University, Edinburgh EH14 4AS (tel 0131 451 3363, fax 0131 449 5153, e-mail r.j.knops@hw.ac.uk)

KNOTT, Herbert Espenett (Herbie); s of Lt-Col Roger Birbeck Knott, OBE, MC (d 1960), of Wilmslow, Cheshire, and Eva, *née* Conroy (d 1995); *b* 11 March 1949; *Educ* Rugby, UC Oxford (MA); *Career* mgmnt trainee Atlas Express Ltd 1972–73; photojournalist: London Evening Standard 1977–80, Now! magazine 1980–81, The Sunday Times 1981–86, The Independent 1986–96, freelance 1996–; visiting lectr London Sch of Photojournalism 1998–2000; contrib exhibitions: Br Press Photographers Assoc Exhibitions 1986–89, World Press Photo Exhibitions 1987, 1989 and 1998, Telegraph Magazine 25th Anniversary Exhibition, Witness Exhibition (NT) 1990, Politicians (Impressions Gallery York) 1992 (also at Stills Gallery Edinburgh 1993 and Battersea Arts Centre London 1994), Fashion Exposures (London) 1993–2002, London Exhibition (Zwemmer Gallery London) 1994, The Oblique View - 10 Years of The Independent (Visa pour l'Image Perpignan) 1997, Ilford Printers' Exhibition (RPS Bath) 1998, Royal Acad Eden Project 2001 (with Nicholas Grimshaw), Redesign - Sustainability in New British Design (Br Cncl Norway, China and Kenya) 2001, Skin - Surface, Substance and Design (Cooper-Hewitt Nat Design Museum NY) 2002; music CD illustrations: Miss Chatelaine (k d lang, 1993), Up All Night (Dark Blues, 1998), What Do You Think of it So Far (Nik Kershaw, 1999), One Wild Night (Bon Jovi, contrib, 2001), Six by Six (Dark Blues, 2002); book covers: Precious Little Sleep (Wayne Sleep, 1996), The Lost Gardens of Heligan (Tim Smit, 1997), The Heligan Vegetable Bible (Tim Smit, 2000), Kinnock (Martin Westlake, 2001), New Architecture in Britain (Kenneth Powell, 2003), Stitching (Anthony Neilson, 2002); contrib illustrations to books: The Words of Gilbert & George (1997), Heligan - The Complete Works (Tim Smit, 1999), Eden (Tim Smit, 2001), High Tech Para High Tech (ed Paco Asensio, 2001), Blow Up (Sean Topham, 2002), Skin (Ellen Lupton, 2002), The Architecture of Eden (Hugh Pearman and Andrew Whalley, 2003), Heligan - Portrait of the Lost Gardens (Tom Petherick and Melanie Eclare, 2004), Heligan: Fruit Flowers and

Herbs (Philip McMillan Browse, 2005), Venice Biennale Catalogue (Gilbert and George, 2005); *Awards* Nikon Photographer of the Month June 1983 and Dec 1990, Nikon Photographer of the Election 1987; *Books* Carol Thatcher's Diary of an Election (illustrations, 1983), How They Made Piece of Cake (with Robert Eagle, 1988), Black and White (1990), Glasmoth - Moscow and Back by Tiger Moth (with Jonathan Elwes, 1990), Spitfire: The Biography (illustrations, by Jonathan Glancey, 2006); *Recreations* gardening, tennis, supporting AFC Wimbledon; *Style*— Herbie Knott, Esq; ✉ c/o Rex Features Ltd, Vine Hill, London EC1R 5DZ (tel 020 7278 7294, mobile 07905 105009)

KNOTT, Prof John Frederick; OBE (2004); s of Fred Knott, of Bristol, and Margaret, *née* Chesney; *b* 9 December 1938; *Educ* Univ of Sheffield (BMet), Univ of Cambridge (PhD); *m* 1, 16 April 1963 (m dis 1986), Christine Mary, da of William Roberts; 2 s (William Frederick b 28 April 1965, Andrew John b 10 May 1966); m 2, 15 Sept 1990, Susan Marilyn (formerly Mrs Cooke), da of William Jones; 2 step s (Paul Antony b 6 Dec 1966, James Daniel b 21 April 1981); *Career* res offr Central Electricity Res Laboratories Leatherhead 1962–66; Univ of Cambridge: lectr Dept of Materials Sci and Metallurgy 1967–81, univ reader in mechanical metallurgy 1981–90; Churchill Coll Cambridge: Goldsmiths' fell 1967–91, vice-master 1988–90, extra-ordinary fell 1991–2006; Univ of Birmingham: prof and head of Sch of Metallurgy and Materials 1990–96, Feeney prof 1994–, dean of engrg 1995–98; hon prof Beijing Univ of Aeronautics and Astronautics 1992–, hon prof Xian Jiaotong Univ 1995–; pres Int Congress on Fracture 1993–97 (hon fell 1984); chm Materials, Manufacturing and Structures Advsy Bd (formerly Materials and Processing Advsy Bd) Rolls-Royce 2000– (memb 1987–); memb: Tech Assessment Gp on Structural Integrity 1988–, Research Bd of the Welding Inst 1989–, EPSRC/DTI LINK Ctee (EEM) 1992–99, Nuclear Safety Advsy Ctee 1992–2005 (actg chm 2003–04, chm Sub Ctee on Research 2000–05), EPSRC Prog Mgmnt Ctee for Structural Integrity 1998–2001, MOD Research Prog Gp 2003–, Graphite Tech Advsy Gp 2004–, Defence Nuclear Safety Ctee 2006–; foreign memb Acad of Sciences of the Ukraine 1992; foreign assoc US Nat Acad of Engrg 2003; visiting fell Japan Soc for the Promotion of Sci 1980; gave Royal Soc/Royal Acad of Engrg lecture at the Royal Soc 1999; Sheffield Soc of Engrs and Metallurgists prize 1958, Mappin medal 1959, Nesthill medal 1959, L B Pfeil prize for Physical Metallurgy 1973, Rosenhain medal for Physical Metallurgy 1978, Leslie Holliday prize (Materials Sci Club) 1978, Inst of Materials Griffith Medal 1999, Robert Franklin Mehl award Minerals, Metals & Materials Society 2005, Hatfield lectr IMMM 2006; ScD (Cantab) 1991; Hon DEng Univ of Glasgow 2004; hon memb Inst of Metals Japan 2005, foreign fell Indian Nat Acad of Engrg 2006; FIM 1974 (AIM 1963), CEng 1978, FWeldI 1985, FRSA 1985, FREng 1988, FRS 1990, FIMechE 1994; *Books* Fundamentals of Fracture Mechanics (1973), Worked Examples in Fracture Mechanics (with Dr David Elliott, 1979), Fracture Mechanics - Worked Examples (with Dr Paul Withey, 1993); *Publications* author of more than 300 technical publications in jls and conference proceedings; *Recreations* bridge, cryptic crosswords, listening to traditional jazz (preferably in live performance), playing the tenor recorder with enthusiasm rather than skill; *Style*— Prof John Knott, OBE, FRS, FREng; ✉ 5 Mildmay Close, Stratford upon Avon CV37 9FR (tel 01789 261977); The University of Birmingham, School of Engineering (Metallurgy and Materials), Edgbaston, Birmingham B15 2TT (tel 0121 414 6729, e-mail j.f.knott@bham.ac.uk)

KNOTT, Malcolm Stephen; s of Eric Stephen Knott (d 1999), of Framlingham, Suffolk, and Grace Lilley, *née* Smith; *b* 22 August 1940; *Educ* Mercers' Sch Holborn; *m* 15 Sept 1962, Eileen Margaret (Meg), da of Ernest William Smith-Lane (d 1969), of Potters Bar, Middx; 1 s (Mungo b 1964), 1 da (Nancy b 1967); *Career* slr 1962–67, called to the Bar 1968; head of chambers Lincoln's Inn 1980–85, Bar Cncl 1985–89, in practice Queen's Bench and Chancery Divs London, recorder Crown and Co Courts; sr lecturer Coll of Law 2001–05; Freeman City of London 1959; *Books* The Soldier's Daughter (1996), Drafting Service Agreements for Senior Employees (1999), The Woodbridge Solicitor (2000), The Endell Street Mystery (2001), The Ottoman Saloon (2004), The Norfolk Baronet (2007); *Recreations* philately, toy soldiers, family history; *Style*— Malcolm Knott, Esq; ✉ Westward View, Low Street, Badingham, Woodbridge, Suffolk IP13 8JS (tel 01728 638728, e-mail malcolm.knott@btinternet.com)

KNOWLAND, Raymond Reginald (Ray); CBE (1992); s of Reginald George Knowland (d 1945), and Marjorie Doris, *née* Alvis; *b* 18 August 1930; *Educ* Bristol GS, Sir John Cass Coll; *m* 1 Sept 1956, Valerie Mary, da of Norman Wintour Higgs (d 1969); 3 s (Paul b 1961, Peter b 1963, Jeremy b 1967); *Career* Nat Serv RAF 1955–57; BP Chemicals: works gen mangr Barry Works S Wales 1969–75 (various appts 1957–69), works gen mangr Baglan Bay Works S Wales 1975–78, md BP Chemicals Belgium Antwerp 1978–80, ceo BP Chemicals London 1983–89 (dir 1980–83); md BP Co plc until 1992, non-exec dir Br Standards Inst 1992–99; pres: Br Plastics Fedn 1985–86, Assoc of Petrochemical Prodrs Europe 1985–88, Chemical Industries Assoc 1990–92; vice-pres Soc of Chemical Industry 1992–96, chm Bd Chemical Industry Ecology and Toxicology Centre 1986–90; Freeman City of London, Master Worshipful Co of Horners 2000; FRSC 1958, CIMgt 1987 (MIMgt 1958); *Recreations* sailing, photography, rugby football; *Clubs* Athenaeum, Savage; *Style*— Ray Knowland, Esq, CBE; ✉ Herons Wake, Flowers Hill, Pangbourne, Reading, Berkshire RG8 7BD (tel 0118 984 4576)

KNOWLES, Sir Charles Francis; 7 Bt (GB 1765), of Lovell Hill, Berkshire; s of Sir Francis Gerald William Knowles, 6 Bt, FRS (d 1974), and Ruth, *née* Brooke-Smith; *b* 20 December 1951; *Educ* Marlborough, Oxford Sch of Architecture (DipArch); *m* 1979, Amanda Louise Margaret, da of Lance Lee Bromley, Esq, MChir, FRCS, of London; 2 s ((Charles) William Frederick Lance b 1985, Edward Francis Annandale Bromley b 7 April 1989); *Heir* s, William Knowles; *Career* dir: Charles Knowles Design Ltd (architects), Richmond Knowles Architects; works incl: new Battersea Dogs Home London and Old Windsor, refurbishment of Bank of England, historic country houses and listed London properties; RIBA 1978, FRSA 1984; *Recreations* flying, shooting, architecture, countryside; *Style*— Sir Charles Knowles, Bt; ✉ Wyndham Croft, Turners Hill, West Sussex RH10 4PS

KNOWLES, Evelyn; *Educ* Coborn GS for Girls, Ealing Coll of HE (BA); *m* (m dis); 1 s (William), 2 da (Louise, Gillian); *Career* administrator and fundraiser SOS Childrens Villages Int 1981–86, trg co-ordinator Cambridge Training and Devpt 1988–90, trg consltt Women Returning to Work and Women Undergraduates 1987–, dir Victoria Road Community Centre Cambridge 1990–98; 300 Group: memb 1983–, memb Nat Exec for several years, chm 1991–92; former rep for: National Alliance of Women's Organisations, Opportunity 2000; memb Fawcett Soc, regular speaker on radio and to groups; cncllr (Lib Dem) City of Cambridge 1987–2003, hon cncllr 2003–; dep mayor Cambridge City 1995–96, mayor of Cambridge 2000–2001; non-exec memb Bd Cambridge City Primary Care Tst (lay memb Cambridge City Primary Care Gp 1998–2002); former City Cncl rep for: Cambridge Community Health Cncl (chm 1994–96), Cambridge City Police Local Consultation Gp; Parly candidate NW Norfolk 1997, memb Exec IOW Lib Dems 2006–; pres Cambridge MS Soc 2000–03, tstee Cambridge CAB (chm 1998–2000); memb Sports Hall Bd Kelsey Kerridge Tst 1988–2000; FRSA; *Recreations* family, movies, travel, music, books, dining out, photography, cycling, walking; *Style*— Ms Evelyn Knowles; ✉ Carisbrooke, 1B Madeira Road, Ventnor PO38 1QP (tel 01983 855 193, e-mail evelynk@uwclub.net)

KNOWLES, Rt Rev Graeme Paul; *see:* Sodor and Man, Bishop of

KNOWLES, Rev John; s of Geoffrey Knowles, and Jean Knowles; *b* 12 June 1948; *Educ* St Bees Sch Cumbria, Univ of Manchester (BSc), Worcester Coll Oxford (PGCE), Univ of London (MSc), Queen's Coll Birmingham (Dip Christian Miny); *m* July 1974, Roey, *née* Wills; 3 da (Hannah b 11 Oct 1975, Louise b 2 Dec 1978, Amy b 2 Nov 1980); *Career* teacher: Mill Hill Sch 1970–75, Wellington Coll 1975–76; head of physics Watford GS 1976–84, vice-master Queen Elizabeth's GS Blackburn 1984–90, headmaster King Edward VI Five Ways Sch Birmingham 1990–99, rector Hutchesons' GS 1999–2005, warden of readers Dio of Chester and priest-in-charge Woodford 2005–; chief examiner A Level Nuffield Physics 1984–99; SHA 1996–99: memb Grant Maintained Ctee, memb Birmingham Exec Ctee; chm of govrs Kingsmead Sch Hoylake 1988–93, chm Assoc of Heads of Grant Maintained Schools 1998–99; chm IMPACT (SW Birmingham Educn and Business Partnership); ordained C of E 1998; memb The Elgar Soc (formerly treas and vice-chm); FRSA; *Publications* Elgar's Interpreters on Record (2 edn, 1984), Elgar Studies (contrib, 1990), This is the Best of Me (contrib, 1999); author of sleeve notes for records and CDs, record reviewer for various jls and newspapers; *Recreations* music; *Style*— The Rev John Knowles

KNOWLES, Peter Francis Arnold; CB (1996); s of Sidney Francis Knowles, and Patricia Anette Knowles; *b* 10 July 1949; *Educ* Whitgift Sch, UC Oxford (open scholar, MA); *m* 2 Sept 1972, Patricia Katharine, da of W H M Clifford; 2 s (Henry b 14 July 1977, Toby b 12 March 1980); *Career* called to the Bar Gray's Inn 1971; practised as barr Lincoln's Inn 1973–75, Parliamentary Counsel Office 1975–93 and 1996– (appointed Parliamentary Counsel (grade 2) 1991), seconded as draftsman in charge Law Commission 1993–96 (head drafting team Tax Law Rewrite Project 2001–03); *Style*— Peter Knowles, Esq, CB; ✉ Office of the Parliamentary Counsel, 36 Whitehall, London SW1A 2AY

KNOWLES, Robin; CBE (2006), QC (1999); s of Norman Richard Knowles, of Alkham, Kent, and Margaret Mary, *née* Robinson; *b* 7 April 1960; *Educ* Sir Roger Manwood's GS, Trinity Coll Cambridge; *m* 1987, Gill, *née* Adams; 1 da (Emma Kathleen b 26 April 1991); *Career* called to the Bar 1982, asst recorder 1998, recorder 2000; tstee and memb Mgmnt Ctee Bar Pro Bono Unit 1996–, tstee RCJ Advice Bureau 1999–, chm N American Ctee of the Commercial Bar Assoc 2000–, tstee Bar in the Community 2001–, tstee Slrs Pro Bono Gp 2001–, memb Exec of the Commercial Bar Assoc 1999–, memb various Bar Cncl, Commercial Bar Assoc and Inn ctees and working parties; memb: Middle Temple, Gray's Inn, Commercial Bar Assoc, Chancery Bar Assoc, S E Circuit; *Recreations* the East End of London; being with family and friends; *Style*— Robin Knowles, CBE, QC; ✉ 3–4 South Square, Gray's Inn, London WC1R 5HP (tel 020 7696 9900, fax 020 7696 9911, e-mail robinknowles@southsquare.com)

KNOWLSON, Prof James Rex; s of Francis Frederick Knowlson (d 1972), of Ripley, Derbys, and Elizabeth Mary, *née* Platt; *b* 6 August 1933; *Educ* Swanwick Hall GS, Univ of Reading (BA, DipEd, PhD); *m* Elizabeth Selby, da of Thomas Albert Coxon (d 1985); 2 s (Gregory Michael b 1960, Richard Paul b 1963), 1 da (Laura Elizabeth b 1968); *Career* asst master Ashville Coll Harrogate 1959–60, lectr in French Univ of Glasgow 1963–69 (asst lectr 1960–63); Univ of Reading: lectr 1969–75, Leverhulme research fell 1975–76, sr lectr 1975–78, reader 1978–81, prof of French 1981–98, emeritus prof 1998–; fell Nat Humanities Center USA 2002–03, Leverhulme emeritus fell 2003–04; memb Soc of Authors 1987; Hon DLitt Univ of Reading; *Books* Samuel Beckett: An Exhibition (1971), Light and Darkness in the Theatre of Samuel Beckett (1972), Universal Language Schemes in England and France 1600–1800 (1975), Happy Days/Oh les beaux jours (ed, 1978), Frescoes of the Skull: The Later Prose and Drama of Samuel Beckett (with John Pilling, 1979), Samuel Beckett's Krapp's Last Tape (ed, 1980), Happy Days (ed, 1985), The Theatrical Notebooks of Samuel Beckett Vol III - Krapp's Last Tape (ed, 1992), Waiting for Godot Vol I (ed, 1993), Damned to Fame: The Life of Samuel Beckett (1996), Images of Beckett (with John Haynes, 2003), Beckett Remembering, Remembering Beckett (with Elizabeth Knowlson, 2006); *Recreations* badminton, cricket, theatre; *Style*— Prof James Knowlson; ✉ Rivendell, 259 Shinfield Road, Reading, Berkshire RG2 8HF (tel 0118 962 1587); Department of French, The Faculty of Letters and Social Sciences, The University of Reading, Whiteknights, Reading, Berkshire RG6 6AE (tel 0118 931 8776, e-mail j.r.knowlson@reading.ac.uk)

KNOX, Anthony Douglas (Tony); s of William Trevor Knox, of Bournemouth, Dorset, and Jean, *née* Calder; *b* 23 March 1945; *Educ* St Dunstan's Coll, ChCh Oxford (MA); *m* 3 Feb 1990, Adele Josephine, *née* Penny; 1 da (Camilla Rose b 26 June 1990), 1 s (Alexander George Douglas b 26 Nov 1992); *Career* memb Business Bd Compass Partners Private Equity; non-exec dir Financial Dynamics Ltd; *Recreations* tennis, skiing; *Clubs* Hurlingham, Woking Lawn Tennis and Croquet; *Style*— Tony Knox, Esq; ✉ Financial Dynamics Limited, Holborn Gate, 26 Southampton Buildings, London WC2A 1PB (tel 020 7831 3113, fax 020 7405 8007)

KNOX, Bernadette Marie; da of Joseph Chapman Knox (d 1979), and Theresa, *née* Birney; *b* 22 October 1954; *Educ* Sacred Heart GS Newcastle upon Tyne, St Anne's Coll Oxford (MA); *Career* J Walter Thompson Co Ltd: joined 1976, UK bd dir 1989, global planning dir 1997–; *Recreations* books, cinema, listening to music, following Newcastle United; *Style*— Ms Bernadette Knox; ✉ 1 Knightsbridge Green, London SW1 (tel 020 7656 7000, e-mail bernadette.knox@jwt.com)

KNOX, Ian Campbell; s of Eric Campbell Knox, and Mary Fyfe, *née* Beattie; *b* 18 January 1954; *Educ* Royal HS Edinburgh, Waid Acad Anstruther, Edinburgh Coll of Art, Br Cncl scholarship to Budapest, Nat Film Sch; *Career* freelance writer and director 1980–; many British TV drama series credits, currently working on feature film Fergus; film credits incl: The Stronger, The Privilege, Shoot for The Sun, Down Where The Buffalo Go, The Police; *Awards* BAFTA Award for Best Short film (for The Privilege), Bilbao Film Festival Award for Best Short Fiction (The Privilege), Scottish Radio and TV Awards for Best Play (for Workhorses); *Recreations* music, motor cycling; *Style*— Ian Knox, Esq; ✉ 22 Ruston Mews, London W11 1RB (tel 020 7792 0101, e-mail sonsy@dircon.co.uk)

KNOX, Jack; s of Alexander Knox (d 1986), of Kirkintilloch, and Jean Alexander Gray, *née* Graham (d 1988); *b* 16 December 1936; *Educ* Lenzie Acad, Glasgow Sch of Art; *m* 5 July 1960, Margaret Kyle, da of Walter Duncan Sutherland (d 1963), of Linlithgow; 1 s (Kyle Alexander b 1964), 1 da (Emily Barbara b 1967); *Career* collections incl: Scottish Nat Gallery of Modern Art, Glasgow Art Galleries, Scottish Nat Portrait Gallery, Aberdeen Art Gallery, Arts Cncl of GB, Contemporary Art Soc, Edinburgh City Arts Centre, Univ of Glasgow, Hunterian Museum Glasgow, City Art Gallery Manchester, Royal Scottish Acad Collection, Scottish Arts Cncl, Scottish Television; head of Painting Glasgow Sch of Art 1981–92; memb: Scottish Arts Cncl 1974–79, Tstees Ctee Scottish Nat Gallery of Modern Art 1975–81, Bd of Tstees Nat Gallery of Scotland 1982–87; sec Royal Scottish Acad 1990–91; external examiner Univ of Dundee 1990; Hon DLitt Univ of Glasgow 2004; RSA 1979, RGI 1981, RSW 1987, Hon FRIAS 1997; *Exhibitions* solo incl: 57 Gallery Edinburgh 1961, The Scottish Gallery Edinburgh 1966, Richard Demarco Gallery Edinburgh 1969, Serpentine Gallery London 1971, Buckingham Gallery London 1972, Civic Arts Centre Aberdeen 1972, Retrospective (Edinburgh, Fruit Market Glasgow, Third Eye and touring) 1983, The Scottish Gallery Edinburgh 1989, Kelvingrove Art Gallery and Museum Glasgow 1990, Open Eye Gallery Edinburgh 1991, Festival Exhbn Open Eye Gallery Edinburgh 1993 and 1995, Compass Gallery 1998, Gerber Fine Art Glasgow 1998; group incl: Scottish Art Now (Fruitmarket Gallery Edinburgh) 1982, Six Scottish Painters (Graham Gallery NY) 1983, Arte Escozia Contemporea (Nat Gallery of Brazil) 1985, Moorehead State Univ Minnesota 1987, The Compass Contribution (Tramway Glasgow) 1990, Scottish Art since 1900 (The Barbican London) 1990, The Sunday Times Watercolour Competition (Singer & Friedlander) 1997; *Style*— Dr Jack Knox, RSA, RGI, RSW, Hon FRIAS; ✉ 66 Seafield Road, Broughty Ferry, Dundee DD5 3AQ (tel 01382 770411)

K

KNOX, Lesley Mary; da of Prof Eric Samuel, CBE, of SA, and Vera Eileen; *b* 19 September 1953; *Educ* Cheltenham Ladies' Coll, Univ of Cambridge (MA); *m* 1, 1983 (m dis); m 2, 1991, Brian Knox; 1 da (Fenella Megan b 27 June 1994); *Career* slr Slaughter & May 1979, attorney Shearman & Sterling USA 1980; Kleinwort Benson: joined 1981, dir 1986, head of institutional asset mgmnt 1991; non-exec directorships incl: Alliance Tst plc 2001– (chm 2004–), Hays plc 2002–, HMV Gp 2002–; memb Bd of Govrs Museum of London 1999–; *Recreations* fly fishing, family, collector of contemporary art; *Style*— Mrs Lesley Knox

KNOX, (John) Robert; s of John Arthur Knox, and Rosalind, *née* Kingscote; *b* 4 June 1946; *Educ* Univ of Victoria Canada (BA), Univ of Cambridge (MA); *m* 1 Aug 1981, Helen Elizabeth Irène, da of Arnold Zarb; 3 da (Alexandra, Catherine, Antonia); *Career* British Museum: keeper Dept of Oriental Antiquities 1994–2003 (asst keeper 1978–92, dep keeper 1992–94), keeper Dept of Asia 2003–; memb: Percival David Fndn, Britain-Nepal Acad Cncl; tstee Gurkha Museum; *Books* India, Past into Present (with B Durrans, 1982), Explorations and Excavations in Bannu District (jtly, 1991), Amaravati, Buddhist Sculpture from the Great Stupa (1992), Akra The First Capital of Bannu (jtly, 2000); *Recreations* walking, music, 78s; *Style*— Robert Knox, Esq; ✉ Department of Asia, The British Museum, Great Russell Street, London WC1B 3DG (tel 020 7323 8359, fax 020 7323 8561)

KNOX, Robert William (Bob); s of Jack Dallas Knox (d 1983), of Claygate, Surrey, and Margaret Meikle, *née* Elder (d 2001); *b* 15 December 1943; *Educ* Cranleigh Sch; *m* 10 Feb 1968, Susan Mary, da of Cyril Joseph O'Bryen (d 1991), of Weybridge, Surrey, and Gertrude, *née* Foulsham (d 1999); 2 da (Julie b 1970, Katharine b 1972); *Career* Baker Tilly (formerly HLB Kidsons) CAs: ptnr 1972–2003, managing ptnr London office 1993–97, exec (fin) London office 1997–2002, conslt 2003–; memb London (W End) Dist Trg Bd ICAEW 1984–94, practising memb Acad of Experts 1995–2001, memb Jt Disciplinary Scheme Tbnl ICAEW 2005–06; FCA 1966; *Books* Statements of Source and Application of Funds (1977); *Recreations* croquet, bridge, blue and white ceramics, philately, family history; *Style*— Robert W Knox, Esq; ✉ Baker Tilly, 2 Bloomsbury Street, London WC1B 3ST (tel 020 7413 5100, fax 020 7413 5101)

KNOX-JOHNSTON, Sir William Robert Patrick (Robin); kt (1995), CBE (1969), RD (1978, and Bar); s of David Robert Knox-Johnston (d 1970), and Elizabeth Mary, *née* Cree (d 2004); *b* 17 March 1939; *Educ* Berkhamsted Sch; *m* 1962, Suzanne (d 2003), da of Denis Ronald Singer; 1 da (Sara b 1963); *Career* yachtsman; first person to circumnavigate the world non-stop and single handed 14 June 1968–22 April 1969, Br Sailing Trans Atlantic Record (10 days 14 hours 9 mins) 1986, World Champion Class II multihulls 1985, co-skipper Enza NZ (world's fastest circumnavigation under sail, 74 days 22 hours 17 mins 22 secs) 1994, fourth Velux 5 Oceans solo around the world race 2007; tstee: Greenwich Maritime Museum 1992–2002, National Maritime Museum Cornwall 1997–; pres Sail Trg Assoc 1993–2001; memb: Lottery Panel Sports Cncl 1995–2000, Cncl Sport England 2000–02; RIN Gold medal 1992; Younger Bro Trinity House 1973–; Freeman: City of London, London Borough of Bromley; Hon DSc Maine Maritime Acad, Hon DTech Southampton Inst of Technol 1993; FRIN 1994; *Books* World of my Own (1969), Sailing (1975), Twilight of Sail (1978), Last but not Least (1978), Bunkside Companion (1982), Seamanship (1986), The BOC Challenge (1986–87), The Cape of Good Hope (1989), The History of Yachting (1990), The Columbus Venture (1991, Book of the Sea Award), Sea, Ice and Rock (with Sir Christian Bonington, CBE, *qv*, 1992), Cape Horn (1994), Beyond Jules Verne (1995); *Recreations* sailing; *Clubs* Royal Yacht Sqdn (hon), Little Ship (hon pres), RNSA (Hon Rear Cdre); hon memb Yacht Clubs: Royal Irish, Royal NI, Royal Harwich, Royal Southampton, Royal Western, National (Dublin), Royal Bombay (India), Fremantle Sailing (Aust), Berfleet, Brixham, Hawth (Ireland), Liverpool; *Style*— Sir Robin Knox-Johnston, CBE, RD; ✉ St Francis Cottage, Torbryan, Newton Abbot, Devon TQ12 5UR

KNOX-PEEBLES, Brian Philip; s of Lt-Col George Edward Knox-Peebles, RTR, DSO (d 1969), and Patricia, *née* Curtis-Raleigh (d 2002); *b* 19 June 1936; *Educ* Wellington, Göttingen Univ W Germany, BNC Oxford (MA); *m* 20 Aug 1960, Rose Mary, da of Capt Cyril Telford Latch; 3 da (Nina b 16 Nov 1962, Fleur b 3 Feb 1964, Bryonie b 16 Nov 1967), 1 s (Brendan b 21 Sept 1965); *Career* Daily Mail 1963–64, Evening Standard 1964–65, The Times 1965–67, United Newspapers plc 1967–89; dir: Punch Publications 1969–86 (publisher 1984–1986) Bradbury Agnew Ltd 1979–82, United Provincial Newspapers 1981–89, Webster & Horsfall 1987–; gp mktg dir United Newspapers plc 1974–89; fndr and chm Consultants in Media; fndr memb and first pres Int Newspaper Mktg Assoc (Europe); former Euro dir Int Circulation Managers' Assoc; *Books* The Fleet Street Revolution; *Recreations* cinema, walking, swimming, reading, writing; *Clubs* Hurlingham; *Style*— Brian Knox-Peebles, Esq; ✉ Farm Cottage, Farm Place, London W8 7SX (tel 020 7727 9595, e-mail brian@knox-peebles.co.uk)

KNUTSFORD, 6 Viscount (UK 1895); Michael Holland-Hibbert; DL (1977 Devon); also Baron Knutsford, of Knutsford, Co Chester (UK 1888), and 7 Bt (UK 1853); o s of Hon Wilfrid Holland-Hibbert (d 1961; 2 s of 3 Viscount), and Isabel Audrey, *née* Fenwick; suc cous, 5 Viscount, 1986; *b* 27 December 1926; *Educ* Eton, Trinity Coll Cambridge (BA); *m* 8 May 1951, Hon Sheila Constance Portman, er da of 5 Viscount Portman (d 1942); 1 da (Hon Lucy Katherine b 27 June 1956), 2 s (Hon Henry Thurstan b 6 April 1959, Hon James Edward b 19 May 1967); *Heir* s, Hon Henry Holland-Hibbert; *Career* SW regnl dir Barclays Bank 1956–86; memb various ctees Nat Tst 1965–99; High Sheriff Devon 1977–78; *Clubs* Brooks's; *Style*— The Rt Hon the Viscount Knutsford, DL; ✉ Broadclyst House, Exeter, Devon EX5 3EW (tel 01392 461244)

KOBBORG, Johan; s of Martinus Vedel Kobborg, and Käthe Kobborg; *Career* dancer; joined Royal Danish Ballet 1988 (princ dancer 1994), princ dancer Royal Ballet 1999–; performances incl: Swan Lake, Giselle, La Bayadere, Don Quixote, Coppélia, La Sylphide, Hamlet, Romeo and Juliet, Nutcracker, La Fille Mal Gardee, Onegin, Paquita, Napoli, The Dream, Le Corsaire, Agon, Etudes, Flowerfestival in Genzano, In the Middle Somewhat Elevated, Vestris, Songs of the Earth, Rendezvous, The Concert; TV and video performances incl: Hamlet, Don Quixote, Bournonville Ballet Technique, Sleeping Beauty, Mime Matters; galas incl: Stars of the 21st Century (Paris, NY, Canada), Nijinsky Gala (Germany), John Cranka Gala (Stuttgart), Stars of American Ballet (Italy); guest appearances with companies incl: Bolshoi Ballet, La Scala, Nat Ballet of Canada, Teatro San Carlo, Stuttgart Ballet, Hamburg Ballet, Finnish Nat Ballet, Scottish Ballet, Nat Ballet of Japan, Hanover Ballet; prodr: The Bournonville Gp Italy 1999, Johan Kobborg and Friends Copenhagen 2001; Gold Medal Erik Bruhn Competition 1993, Grand Prix and Gold Medal Nureyev Int Ballet Competition 1994, Grand Prix and Gold Medal Jackson Int Ballet Competition 1994, Best Male Dancer Critics Circle Award 2001; *Style*— Johan Kobborg, Esq; ✉ Royal Ballet, Covent Garden, London WC2E 9DD (tel 020 7240 1200)

KOCEN, Dr Roman Stefan; TD (1973); s of late Dr Mieczyslaw and Mrs Lisa Kocen; *b* 20 March 1932; *Educ* Roundhay Sch Leeds, Leeds Sch of Med (MB ChB, various prizes); *m* 1, 1963 (m dis 1971), Anna Louise, *née* Derer; 2 da; m 2, 1974, Elisabeth Ann, *née* Glover; 2 s; *Career* house physician then house surgn in neurosurgery Gen Infirmary Leeds 1956–57; Nat Serv Actg Maj/Offr i/c Med Div Br Mil Hosp Kamunting Malaya RAMC 1958–60, neurologist Mobile Neurosurgical Team RAMC AER 1960–75; registrar then sr registrar Nat Hosp Queen Square 1963–68; conslt neurologist: Brook Gen Hosp 1968–70, Nat Hosp Queen Square 1970–97 (emeritus 1997–); hon civil conslt neurologist to RAF 1997–; formerly hon conslt neurologist: British Airways, St Luke's Hosp for the Clergy; sub-dean Inst of Neurology Univ of London 1976–81, chm Med Ctee Nat Hosp 1991–93; formerly sec: Neurology Section RSM, Ctee on Neurology RCP; Freeman City of London; memb: Assoc of Br Neurologists, Br Neuropathological Soc; FRCP 1974 (MRCP); *Recreations* reading, music, walking, skiing, cooking; *Clubs* Garrick; *Style*— Dr Roman Kocen, TD; ✉ National Hospital for Neurology and Neurosurgery, Queen Square, London WC1N 3BG (tel 020 7837 3611, fax 020 7833 8658); home (tel 020 8455 9000, fax 020 8201 8486)

KOCHHAR, Prof Ashok Kumar; s of Sansar Chand Kochhar (d 1997), and Satya, *née* Vohra; *b* 31 January 1949; *Educ* India, Univ of London (BSc Engrg), Univ of Bradford (PhD); *m* 1987, Dr Rupa Mehta; *Career* graduate engr Rolls Royce 1970–71 (engrg apprentice 1966–70); Univ of Bradford: researcher 1971–74, postdoctoral research fell 1974–76, lectr 1976–83, reader 1983–86, prof of mfrg systems engrg 1986–92; UMIST: Lucas prof of mfrg systems engrg and head Mfrg Div 1992–98, head Dept of Mechanical Engrg 1997–98; Aston Univ: head Sch of Engrg and Applied Sciences 1999–2007, exec dean Engrg and Applied Science 2007–; dir Birmingham Technol Ltd 2001–; memb Editorial Bd: Jl of Engrg Manufacture, Int Jl of Advanced Mfrg Technol, Integrated Mfrg Systems, Int Jl of Mfrg Systems Design; memb: Int Fedn of Info Processing Gp on Computer-Aided Prodn Mgmnt, DTI/Br Cncl sponsored missions to Japan, Korea, China, Hong Kong and India, Design and Integrated Prodn Coll EPSRC; memb Global Research Awards Panel Royal Acad of Engrg 2001–; conslt to several mfrg companies; author of over 150 papers in jls and conf proceedings; memb Ct Cranfield Univ 1997–98; FIEE 1989 (memb Cncl 2000–), FIMechE 1992, FREng 1997; *Awards* Donald Julius Groen Prize IMechE 1988, Joseph Whitworth Prize IMechE 1988 and 1998, Nat Mfrg Intelligence Award DTI, A M Strickland Prize IMechE 1999; *Books* Development of Computer-Based Production Systems (1979), Micro-Processors and Their Manufacturing Applications (with N D Burns, 1983), Integrating Micro-Processors into Product Design (with N D Burns, 1983), Proceedings of the 30th International MATADOR Conference (ed, 1993), Proceedings of the 31st International MATADOR Conference (ed, 1995), Proceedings of the 32nd International MATADOR Conference (ed, 1997), Managing By Projects For Business Success (with John Parnaby and Stephen Wearne, 2003); *Recreations* reading, current affairs, music; *Style*— Prof Ashok Kochhar, FREng; ✉ School of Engineering and Applied Science, Aston University, Aston Triangle, Birmingham B4 7ET (tel 0121 204 3658, fax 0121 204 3678, e-mail a.k.kochhar@aston.ac.uk)

KOEFOED-NIELSEN, Kester Carl (Kes); *see:* Kes Nielsen

KOERNER, Prof Joseph Leo; s of Henry Koerner, the artist (d 1991), and Joan Frasher Koerner; *b* Pittsburgh, PA; *Educ* Yale Univ (BA), Univ of Cambridge (MA), Univ of Heidelberg, Univ of Calif Berkeley (MA, PhD); *Family* 1 s (Benjamin Henry Anders b 2 Oct 1991), 1 da (Sigrid Anna Gunhild b 6 May 1995); m, 28 June 2003, Margaret Koster; 1 s (Leo Anselm b 3 June 2004), 1 da (Lucy Willa b 16 Jan 2006); *Career* Soc of Fellows Harvard Univ 1986–89, prof of history of art and architecture Harvard Univ 1989–99, prof of modern art history Univ of Frankfurt 1999–2000, prof UCL 2000–04, prof Courtauld Inst of Art London 2004–; curator Henry Koerner retrospective Austrian Nat Gallery 1997; presenter Northern Renaissance (BBC TV) 2006; Jan Mitchell Prize for the History of Art 1992; Phi Beta Kappa 1979; memb American Acad of Arts and Sciences 1995; *Books* Die Suche nach dem Labyrinth (1983), Paul Klee: Legends of the Sign (with Rainer Crone, 1991), Caspar David Friedrich and the Subject of Landscape (1990), The Moment of Self-Portraiture in German Renaissance Art (1993), The Reformation of the Image (2004); *Recreations* mountaineering, cycling, piano; *Clubs* Savile; *Style*— Prof Joseph Leo Koerner; ✉ Courtauld Institute of Art, Somerset House, Strand, London WC2R 0RN

KOHNER, Prof Eva Maria; OBE (1994); da of Baron George Nicholas Kohner, of Szaszberek (d 1945), of Hungary, and Andrea Kathleen, *née* Boszormenyi (d 1985); *b* 23 February 1929; *Educ* Baar-Madas Presbyterian Boarding Sch for Girls, Royal Free Hosp Sch of Med Univ of London (BSc, MB BS, MD); *m* 26 April 1961 (m dis 1979), Steven Ivan Warman; *Career* med registrar med ophthalmogy Lambeth Hosp 1963–64, res fell Royal Postgraduate Med Sch Hammersmith Hosp London 1965–68, MRC Alexander Wernher Piggott Meml fell NY 1968–69; Moorfields Eye Hosp and Hammersmith Hosp: sr registrar and lectr 1970–77, conslt med ophthalmologist 1977–88, prof med ophthalmology (first full-time prof in Britain) 1988–; worked in field of treatment of diabetic eye disease by laser (in part instrumental in this treatment now being available to all patients in Britain) and pathogenic mechanisms in diabetic eye disease; FRCP 1977 (MRCP 1963), FRCOphth 1991; *Books* over three hundred publications in field of retinal vascular disease; *Recreations* art, travel; *Style*— Prof Eva Kohner, OBE; ✉ 32 Monckton Court, Strangways Terrace, London W14 8NF

KOK, Nicholas Willem; s of Felix Kok, and Ann, *née* Steel; *b* 30 December 1962; *Educ* King's Sch Worcester, New Coll Oxford (organ scholar, BA, ARCO, FRCO), RCM (Lofthouse Memorial Prize, Countess of Munster Award); *m* 19 Sept 1992, Sarah, *née* Hickson; *Career* conductor; music dir Janet Smith and Dancers 1985–87, asst conductor/repetiteur ENO and music advsr Contemporary Opera Studio 1989–93, princ conductor and artistic dir ViVA: the orchestra of the east midlands 1996–; involved in setting up Almeida Opera; conductor: ENO, Opera North, Stuttgart Opera, Köln Opera, English Touring Opera, Opera Rara, Opera Factory, Dublin Grand Opera, The Opera Co, The Philharmonia, London Philharmonic, Royal Scottish Nat Orch, London Sinfonietta, Scottish Chamber Orch, Ulster Orchestra, Halle, CBSO, Bournemouth Sinfonietta, Endymion Ensemble, Premiere Ensemble, Trinity Coll of Music Sinfonia, London Pro Arte Orch, Philippines Philharmonic, Alvin Ailey Dance Theater London Coliseum, Orch of St John's, Nash Ensemble; television and radio incl: The Return of Ulysses, The Fairy Queen, Arion and the Dolphin, The Soldier's Tale, The Carnival of the Animals, Reginald Smith Brindle's Journey Towards Infinity, Erollyn Wallen's Mondrial, A Man For All Seasons and other broadcasts of several operas; interviewer/commentator: Cardiff Singer of the World, Sainsbury's Choir of the Year, BBC Proms; *Style*— Nicholas Kok, Esq; ✉ c/o Andrew Rosner, Allied Artists, 42 Montpelier Square, London SW7 1JZ (tel 020 7589 6243)

KOKOSALAKI, Sophia; da of Vasilios Kokosalakis, and Stella, *née* Leonidaki; *b* 3 November 1972, Athens, Greece; *Educ* Univ of Athens (BA), Central St Martins Sch of Art (MA); *Career* fashion designer; first catwalk show autumn/winter 1999–2000 London Fashion Week, catwalk show for Ruffo Research spring/summer 2001 and autumn/winter 2001–02, debut catwalk presentation thirteenth collection (spring/summer 2005) Paris Fashion Week; chief designer Olympic Games 2002–04 (design for opening ceremony and officials uniforms Athens 2004); guest designer Fendi 2002; creative dir for relaunch of Vionnet 2006–07; Sophia Kokosalaki Ltd (jt venture with Staff Int Spa) 2007; Best New Designer Elle Style Awards 2001, Arts Fndn Award 2002, Best New Designer Lycra Awards 2003; voted on of Britain's 'cool brand leaders' 2004; *Style*— Miss Sophia Kokosalaki; ✉ Unit 7, 47–49 Tudor Road, London E9 7SN (tel 020 8986 6001, e-mail sophia@sophiakokosalaki.com)

KOLBERT, His Hon Colin Francis; s of Arthur Richard Alexander Kolbert (d 1992), of Barnet and Barnstaple, and Dorothy Elizabeth, *née* Fletcher (d 1996); *b* 3 June 1936; *Educ* Queen Elizabeth's Barnet, St Catharine's Coll Cambridge (MA, PhD), St Peter's Coll Oxford (MA, DPhil); *m* 12 Sept 1959, Jean Fairgrieve, da of Stanley Hutton Abson (d 1964), of Friern Barnet; 2 da (Julia Catharine b 1963, Jennifer Sally b 1965); *Career* RA 1954–56, Cambridge Univ OTC (TAVR) 1969–74; called to the Bar Lincoln's Inn 1961 (bencher 2005); fell and tutor in jurisprudence St Peter's Coll Oxford 1964–68, fell Magdalene Coll Cambridge 1968– (tutor 1969–88), lectr in law Dept of Land Economy Cambridge

1968–88; recorder SE Circuit 1985–88; circuit judge: SE Circuit 1988–90, NE Circuit 1990–95; ind bd memb and tbnl chm SFA 1995–2001, dep chm Regulatory Decisions Ctee FSA 2001–06; asst surveillance cmmr 2001–; Freeman City of London 1997, Liveryman Wax Chandlers' Company 1999; FCIArb 1997; *Clubs* Hawks' (Cambridge), MCC, Farmers', Cambridge Univ Rugby (tstee 1988–), Leeds; *Style—* His Hon Colin Kolbert; ✉ Magdalene College, Cambridge CB3 0AG (tel 01223 332158, fax 01223 276735); Outer Temple Chambers, 222 Strand, Temple, London WC2R 1BA

KOLTAI, Ralph; CBE (1983); s of Dr Alfred Koltai (d 1970), and Charlotte, *née* Weinstein (d 1987); *b* 31 July 1924; *Educ* Berlin, Central Sch of Arts and Crafts London (DipAD); *m* 29 Dec 1954 (m dis 1976), Mary Annena, da of late George Stubbs, of Liverpool; *Career* stage designer and director; RASC attached Intelligence Corps, served Nuremberg War Crimes Trial and War Crimes Interrogation Unit 1944–47; assoc designer RSC 1963–66 and 1976–; first prodn Angelique for London Opera Club 1950; Retrospective Exhibition (London) 1997; designs for: Royal Opera House, Sadler's Wells, Scottish Opera, Nat Welsh Opera, Ballet Rambert; RDI 1984; hon fell The London Inst 1996; fell: Acad of Performing Arts Hong Kong 1994, Rose Bruford Coll; FRSA; *Theatre* RSC prodns incl: The Caucasian Chalk Circle 1962, The Representative 1963, The Birthday Party 1964, The Jew of Malta 1964, Timon of Athens 1965, Little Murders (Drama Critics Award) 1967, Major Barbara 1970, Old World 1976, Wild Oats 1977, The Tempest 1978, Hamlet 1980, The Love Girl and The Innocent (Drama Critics Award) 1981, Molière 1982, Much Ado About Nothing 1982, Cyrano de Bergerac (SWET Award) 1984, Troilus and Cressida 1985, Othello 1986; NT prodns incl: As You Like It (Drama Critics Award) 1967, Back To Methuselah 1969, State of Revolution 1977, Brand (SWET Award) 1978, Richard III 1979, Man and Superman 1981; other prodns incl: Wagner's complete Ring Circle (ENO) 1973, Tannhauser (Sydney) 1973 and Geneva 1986, Fidelio (Munich) 1974, Bugsy Malone 1983, Pack of Lies 1983, Metropolis 1989, dir and designer of The Flying Dutchman 1987 and La Traviata (Hong Kong Arts Festival) 1990, The Planets (Royal Ballet) 1990, The Makropulos Affair (Norwegian Opera) 1992, Hair (Old Vic) 1993, La Traviata (Swedish Opera) 1993, Otello (Essen Opera) 1994, Madam Butterfly (Tokyo) 1995, Twelfth Night (Copenhagen) 1996, Carmen (Royal Albert Hall) 1997, Simon Boccanegra (WNO) 1997, Dalibor (Edinburgh Festival) 1998, A Midsummer Night's Dream (Copenhagen) 1998, Don Giovanni (Kirov Opera) 1999, Genoveva (Edinburgh Festival, Prague and Venice) 2000–01; has worked throughout Europe and in Argentina, USA, Canada, Aust and Japan; retrospective exhibitions in London 1997, Beijing 1998, Hong Kong, Taipei and Prague 1999; *Awards* incl: co-winner Individual Gold Medal Prague Quadrienal 1975, Golden Triga 1979 and 1991, Individual Silver Medal 1987; *Publications* Ralph Koltai - Designer for the Stage (1997); *Recreations* wildlife photography; *Style—* Ralph Koltai, Esq, CBE; ✉ c/o London Management, 2–4 Noel Street, London W1V 3RB (tel 020 7287 9000, fax 020 7287 3436)

KONDRACKI, Henry Andrew; s of Pawel Kondracki (d 1986), of 12 Union St, Edinburgh, and Boyce Matilda, *née* Hills (d 1988); *b* 13 February 1953; *Educ* Bellevue Secdy Sch Edinburgh, Byam Shaw Sch of Art London, Slade Sch of Fine Art (BA, Sir William Coldstream prize for best figurative work, Slade prize for Fine Art 1985 and 1986); *m* 2 Oct 1985, Sara, da of Dr Mohamed Gawad Elsarrag; 3 s (Patrick, Miles, Edward); *Career* artist; *Solo Exhibitions* Traverse Theatre Club Edinburgh 1979, The Artist's Collective Gallery Edinburgh 1984 and 1992, Vanessa Devereux Gallery London 1987 and 1989, Michael Wardell Gallery Melbourne Aust 1988, William Jackson Gallery London 1991 and 1994, Flowers East Gallery London 1995, 1996, 1998 and 2001, Bellevue Gallery Edinburgh 1997, Flowers West Gallery Los Angeles 2000; *Group Exhibitions* Royal Scottish Acad Edinburgh 1984 and 1988, The Peter Moores Exhibition (Walker Gallery Liverpool) 1986, Royal Acad Summer Show 1989, 1990 and 2000 (invited artist 1993 and 1994), Polish Roots British Soil (Edinburgh City Art Centre touring show) 1993, John Moores Liverpool Exhibition 19 1995 (prizewinner), Contemporary Painting Scotland (The Rotunda Hong Kong) 1996, Flowers West Gallery Los Angeles 1998; *Work in Public Collections* Granada Fndn Manchester, Br Arts Cncl, Br Cncl, UCL, Manchester City Art Gallery, Guildhall London, Glasgow Art Galleries and Museums, City Art Centre Edinburgh; *Prizes and Awards* incl: South Bank Bd Prize 1987, Spectator Art Prize 1991, John Moores Exhibition 2nd Prize 1995, Noble Grossard Scotland on Sunday 3rd Prize 1997, Cheltenham Drawing Competition Prize 1999, Hunting Group Regnl Prize 2000, Hunting Gp Prize 2004; *Style—* Henry Kondracki, Esq

KONSTANT, The Rt Rev David Every Konstant; s of Antoine Konstant (d 1985), and Dulcie Marion Beresford Leggatt (d 1930); *b* 16 June 1930; *Educ* St Edmund's Coll Ware, Christ's Coll Cambridge (MA), Univ of London Inst of Education (PGCE); *Career* priest Diocese of Westminster 1954, Cardinal Vaughan Sch Kensington 1959, diocesan advsr on religious educn 1966, St Michael's Sch Stevenage 1968, dir Westminster Religious Educn Centre 1970, auxiliary bishop of Westminster (bishop in Central London) 1977–85; chm Nat Bd of Religious Inspectors and Advisers 1970–75; bishop of Leeds (RC) 1985–2004 (bishop emeritus 2004–); episcopal advsr: Catholic Teachers' Fedn 1980–88, Catholic Inst for Int Relations 1982–2004; chm: Oxford and Cambridge Catholic Educn Bd 1984–96, Dept of Catechetics Bishops Conf 1978–84, Dept of Catholic Educn 1984–98, W Yorks Ecumenical Cncl 1986–87 and 2000, Dept Int Affairs Bishops' Conf 1998–2004; Hon LLD Met Univ of Leeds 2005, Hon DUniv Bradford 2006; Freeman City of London 1984; FRSA 1996; author of various books on religious educn and liturgy; *Recreations* music, watching sport of most kinds, jam making, computers; *Style—* The Rt Rev David Konstant; ✉ Ashlea, 62 Headingley Lane, Leeds LS6 2BU (tel and fax 0113 261 8002)

KOOPS, Eric Jan Leendert; LVO (1997); s of Leendert Koops (d 1990), of Hellingly, E Sussex, and Daphne Vera, *née* Myhill (d 1998); *b* 16 March 1945; *Educ* Eastbourne Coll, Lancaster Univ (BA); *m* 1, 1968 (m dis 1985); 1 da (Amanda Charlotte b 25 Sept 1972), 1 s (Mark Alexander b 20 Feb 1975); m 2, 1987, Hon Mrs Justice Hogg, DBE, *qv*, da of Baron Hailsham of St Marylebone, KG, CH (d 2001); 1 da (Katharine Mary b 17 March 1989), 1 s (William Quintin Eric b 21 Dec 1991); *Career* TA 2 Lt 4/5 KORR 1964–67; corporate advsr and co dir; Parly candidate (Cons) Wakefield 1974; fdnr and chm Friends of Africa Fndn 2000–, chm Friends of Kenya Ltd 2003–; vice-pres Political Ctee Carlton Club 1988– (chm 1984–88); hon chm: The Duke of Edinburgh's Award, World Fellowship 1987–97; tstee: The Duke of Edinburgh's Award Int Fndn 1994–97, Inst for Policy Research, Winnicott Clinic of Psychotherapy Charitable Tst; FCA 1971; *Publications* Money for our Masters (1970), Airports for the Eighties (1980); *Recreations* travel, cricket, biographies; *Clubs* Buck's, Carlton, MCC; *Style—* Eric Koops, Esq, LVO; ✉ Forest Lodge, Wych Cross, Forest Row, East Sussex RH18 5JP (tel 01342 824096)

KOPELMAN, Prof Peter Graham; s of Dr Harry Kopelman, of Essex, and Joan, *née* Knowlman (d 1995); *b* 23 June 1951; *Educ* Felsted, St George's Hosp Med Sch London (MB BS, MD, Prize for Pathology); *m* 1981, Susan Mary, *née* Lewis; 2 da (Sarah b 22 Oct 1981, Claire b 3 May 1983), 1 s (Thomas b 25 Sept 1989); *Career* St George's Hosp London: hon registrar in gen med 1978, research registrar Dept of Med 1978–79, registrar in gen med 1979–80; conslt physician Newham Healthcare NHS Tst London 1986–95, sr lectr in med The London Hosp 1986–96 (lectr in gen med, metabolism, diabetes and endocrinology 1980–86); Bart's and The London Queen Mary's Sch of Med and Dentistry Univ of London: sr clinical tutor 1990–97, reader in med 1996–98, prof of clinical med 1998–2006, dep warden 2001–06, vice-princ 2003–06; chm Med Studies, memb Cncl Univ of London 2001–06, assoc non-exec dir NE London SHA 2004–06; dean Faculty of Health UEA 2006–; memb: Scientific Advsy Ctee on Nutrition; RCP: chm Clinical Nutrition Ctee 1998–2004, chm Working Pty on Management of Obesity and med Aspects of Nutrition, former NE Thames specialty advsr; former chm NE Thames (dep chm N Thames) Specialty Ctee for Diabetes and Endocrinology, currently pres Euro Assoc for the Study of Obesity; memb: GMC, Med Def Union, BMA, RCP, Diabetes UK, MRS, Assoc for the Study of Med Educn, Assoc of Physicians; tstee Int Assoc for the Study of Obesity 2002–; FRCP 1992, FFPH 2005; *Publications* author of numerous scientific papers and book chapters on metabolism and obesity; *Recreations* all sports (with enthusiastic son), music (with daughters), painting and drawing, reading modern literature, political biographies; *Clubs* Athenaeum; *Style—* Prof Peter Kopelman; ✉ Institute of Health, University of East Anglia, Norwich NR4 7TJ (tel 01603 593681, fax 01603 593233, e-mail p.kopelman@uea.ac.uk)

KOPPEL, Jessica Esther (Jess); da of Heinz Koppel (d 1980), of Cwmerfyn, Aberystwyth, and Renate Hanni, *née* Fischl; *b* 4 April 1963; *Educ* Penglais Aberystwyth, Cardiff Coll of Art (Higher Nat Dip Photography); *Career* photographer; asst to Bryce Attwell 1984–85, freelance photographer 1985– (specialising in food and still life); numerous exhibitions incl: Stages Photographers Gallery 1988, Assoc of Photographers Gallery, F45 Womens Exhibition every year; winner: Silver award Assoc of Photographers, Clio Gold award Int Food Packaging 1988, award of Excellence Mead Show 1989; memb Assoc of Photographers 1985; *Books* incl: Sophie Grigson's Ingredients Book, 10 Minute Cuisine, Henrietta Green's Country Kitchen, Sophie Grigson's Eat Your Greens, Sophie Grigson's Meat Course, Sophie Grigson's Taste of the Times; *Style—* Ms Jess Koppel; ✉ Jess Koppel Studio, 71 White Lion Street, London N1 9PP (tel 020 7837 8374)

KOPS, Bernard; *b* 28 November 1926; *m* 1956, Erica, *née* Gordon; 4 c; *Career* writer; lectr in drama: The Spiro Inst 1985–86, Surrey Educn Authy, Ealing Educn Authy, ILEA, Arts Educnl Schs 1989–90, City Literary Inst 1990–94, The Paines Plough Co 1992–94; Arts Cncl bursary 1957, 1979, 1985, 1990, and 2002, C S Lewis fellowship 1981, 1982, 1983 and 1992; *Novels* incl: Awake for Mourning (1958), The Dissent of Dominick Shapiro (1966), The Passionate Past of Gloria Gaye (1972), Partners (1975), On Margate Sands (1978); *Non-Fiction* Neither Your Honey Nor Your Sting - An Offbeat History of the Jews (1985), The World is a Wedding (autobiography, 1963, 1975), Collected Plays: Vol 1 (1998) Vol 2 (2000), Vol 3 (2002), Shalom Bomb (autobiography, 2000), Bernard Kops East End, The World is a Wedding (2007); *Poetry* Poems (1955), Poems and Songs (1958), Anemone for Antigone (1959), Erica, I Want You to Read Something (1967), For the Record (1971), Barricades in West Hampstead (1988), Grandchildren and Other Poems (2000); *Stage Plays* incl: The Hamlet of Stepney Green (1956), The Dream of Peter Mann (1959), Enter Solly Gold (1961, televised 1968), Stray Cats and Empty Bottles (1967, televised 1967), Ezra (1981, on radio 1980), Simon at Midnight (1985, on radio 1982), More Out Than In (1980, on radio 1985), Kafe Kropotkin (1988, also on radio), Sophie! the Last of the Red Hot Mamas (1990), Moss (1991, on radio 1983, televised 1976), Playing Sinatra (1992), Dreams of Anne Frank (1992, winner London Fringe Awards 1993), Who Shall I Be Tomorrow (1992), Call in the Night (1995), Golem (1996), Jacob and the Green Rabbi (1997), Houdini (1999), Cafe Zeitgeist (1999), Riverchange (2000), The Opening (2001), I am Isaac Babel (2002), Returning we hear the Larks (2004), Knocking on Heaven's Door (2005); *Radio Plays* incl: Return to Stepney Green (1957), Home Sweet Honeycomb (1962), Israel Pt 1 (1963), Israel Pt 2 (1964), I Grow Old, I Grow Old (1979), Over the Rainbow (1981), Trotsky was My Father (1984), Congress in Manchester (1990), Soho Nights (serial, 1993), Sailing With Homer (1994, Writer's Guild Award 1994/95), The Jericho Players (1996), Rogues and Vagabonds (1998), Monster Man (1999), Falling in Love Again (2000), The Lost Love of Phoebe Myers (2006); *Television Drama/Documentary* incl: I Want to Go Home (1963), The Lost Years of Brian Hooper (1965), It's A Lovely Day Tomorrow (1975), The Geese that Shrieked and The Boy Philosopher (adaptions from Isaac Bashevis Singer 1975), Rocky Marciano is Dead (1977), Nightkids (1983); *Style—* Bernard Kops, Esq

KORALEK, Paul George; CBE (1984); s of Ernest Koralek (d 1983), and Alice, *née* Muller (d 1989); *b* 7 April 1933; *Educ* Aldenham, AA Sch of Architecture (AADipl); *m* 13 Dec 1958, (Audrey) Jennifer, da of Capt Arthur Vivian Chadwick (d 1980); 2 da (Catherine b 16 March 1961, Lucy b 19 Dec 1962), 1 s (Benjamin b 14 July 1967); *Career* ptnr and dir Ahrends Burton & Koralek Architects 1961–; princ works incl: Trinity Coll Dublin (Berkeley Library 1972, Arts Faculty bldg 1979), residential bldg Keble Coll Oxford 1976, Templeton Coll Oxford 1969–88, Nebenzahl House Jerusalem 1972, warehouse and showroom for Habitat Wallingford, factory for Cummins Engines Shotts, J Sainsbury supermarket Canterbury 1984, WH Smith retail HQ Swindon 1985, John Lewis dept store Kingston 1990, St Mary's Hosp Newport IOW 1991, Heritage Centre Dover 1991, stations for extension Docklands Light Railway 1992, new Br Embassy Moscow 1999, Techniquest Science Centre Cardiff 1995, LRC for Selly Oak Colleges 1997, Dublin Dental Hosp and Sch 1998, Insts of Technology Tralee and Waterford 1999, Inst of Technology Blanchardstown 2002, Offaly CC civic offices 2002, Tipperary CC civic offices 2005, current projects John Wheatley Coll Glasgow, Cork civic offices, Arts Faculty Bldg Extension TCD and TCD Enterprise Centre Dublin Docklands; RIBA 1957, RA 1986, fell Royal Inst of Architects of I (FRIAI) 2002; *Style—* Paul Koralek, Esq, CBE, RIBA, FRIAI, RA; ✉ Ahrends Burton & Koralek, Unit 1, 7 Chalcot Road, London NW1 8LH (tel 020 7586 3311, fax 020 7722 5445, e-mail abk@abklondon.com, website www.abk.co.uk)

KORLIPARA, Dr Krishna Rao; s of Laxminarayana Korlipara, of Denduluru, India, and Krishnaveni, *née* Kodali; *b* 14 September 1938; *Educ* Kasturba Med Coll Karnatak Univ Mangalore S India (MB BS); *m* 4 May 1963, Uma Devi Korlipara, da of Rajendra Vara Prasad Veeramachaneni; 3 da (b 1964, 1965 and 1968), 1 s (b 1970); *Career* sr house offr in gen med: Manor Park Hosp Bristol 1965–66, Huddersfield 1967, Mansfield Hosp Notts 1967–68; registrar in gen med Bolton Gen Hosp 1969–72, princ in gen practice Horwich 1972–, pt/t clinical asst in cardiology Wythenshawe Hosp Regional Cardiac Centre Univ of S Manchester 1977–99, trainer in gen practice 1984–94; fndr chm: Bolton Dist Med Services Ltd (first GP co-operative in UK) 1977–2002 (pres 2002–), Nat Assoc of GP Co-Operatives 1981–97 (pres 1997–2003); chief exec and pres CMEDS (Bolton) Ltd 2005–; chm: Bharatiya Vidya Bhavan (Manchester) Ltd (Indian Inst of Culture in Britain) 1996–99, Rivington View Ltd; GMC: memb 1984–, med screener for professional conduct and performance, memb Registration Ctee, memb Ctee on Professional Performance 2001–, former chm GP Consultative Gp on Revalidation, former memb Revalidation Steering Gp, former memb Professional Conduct Ctee, Overseas Ctee and Health Ctee; chm NW Regnl Steering Gp NHS Direct 1999–2001; memb: Bolton Local Med Ctee 1993–, Exec Ctee PCD-UK (Primary Care Diabetes in UK, a section of Br Diabetic Assoc) 1997–99; gen sec Overseas Doctors Assoc UK 1979–84; memb: Med Protection Soc 1965, Bolton Med Soc 1972 (pres 1992–93), BMA 1978; FInstD 1994, MRCGP 2001; *Publications* contrib numerous articles in learned jls incl: Int Jl of Clinical Practice, Cardiology News, Br Jl of Cardiology, Br Jl of Gen Practice; *Recreations* reading, meditating; *Style—* Dr Krishna Korlipara; ✉ Pike View Medical Centre, Albert Street, Horwich, Bolton BL6 7AN (tel 01204 699311, fax 01204 668387, mobile 07867 503559, e-mail kkorlipara@hotmail.com (personal)); Rivington View Ltd, Albert Street, Horwich, Bolton BL6 7AW; CMEDS (Bolton) Ltd, Landmark House, 12 Chorley New Road, Bolton BL1 4AP (tel 01204 546760)

KORN, Jacqueline; da of Harry Korn (d 1989), of London, and Essie, *née* Simmons (d 2002); *b* 15 April 1938; *Educ* Harrow Weald Co GS; *m* 14 March 1965, Ralph Glasser (d 2002); 1 s (Roland b 5 Feb 1973), 1 da (Miranda b 29 Sept 1975); *Career* authors' agent; became jt owner David Higham Associates 1972 (joined 1958); *Recreations* music, theatre, reading, walking; *Clubs* Groucho; *Style—* Miss Jacqueline Korn; ✉ David Higham

K

Associates Ltd, 5–8 Lower John Street, Golden Square, London W1F 9HA (tel 020 7434 5900, fax 020 7437 1072, e-mail jacquelinekorn@davidhigham.co.uk)

KORNBERG, Prof Sir Hans Leo; s of Max Kornberg; *b* 14 January 1928; *Educ* Queen Elizabeth GS Wakefield, Univ of Sheffield; *m* 1, 1956, Monica King (d 1989); 2 s (Jonathan, Simon (twins)), 2 da (Julia, Rachel); m 2, 28 July 1991, Donna, da of William B Haber, of Los Angeles; *Career* prof of biochemistry Univ of Leicester 1960–75, Sir William Dunn prof of biochemistry Univ of Cambridge 1975–95, fell Christ's Coll Cambridge 1975– (master 1982–95), univ prof and prof of biology Boston Univ 1995–, dir The Univ Profs 2002–05; a managing tstee Nuffield Fndn 1973–93, chm Royal Cmmn on Environmental Pollution 1976–81, chm Sci Advsy Ctee and chm Kuratorium Max-Planck Inst Dortmund 1979–89, memb AFRC 1981–85, memb Advsy Cncl for Applied Res & Devpt 1982–85, chm Advsy Ctee for Genetic Modification 1986–95, memb Priorities Bd for Res in Agric and Food 1985–90, dir UK Nirex 1987–95, memb Advsy Ctee Harkness Fellowships 1989–94, govr Wellcome Tst 1990–95; pres: Br Assoc 1984–85, Biochemical Soc 1990–95, Int Union of Biochemistry and Molecular Biology 1991–94, Assoc Sci Educn 1991–92; memb various int acads; Hon DSc: Cincinnati, Warwick, Leicester, Sheffield, Bath, Strathclyde, South Bank, Leeds, La Trobe Univ Melbourne; Hon DUniv Essex, Hon MD Leipzig, Hon LLD Univ of Dundee; FIBiol, FRSA, Hon FRCP 1989, FRS 1965; *Style—* Prof Sir Hans Kornberg, FRS; ✉ The University Professors, Boston University, 745 Commonwealth Avenue, Boston, MA 02215, USA (tel 00 1 617 353 1691, fax 00 1 617 353 5084, e-mail hlk@bu.edu)

KORNER, Joanna Christian Mary; CMG (2004), QC (1993); da of John Hugh George Korner, of House of Elrig, Portwilliam, and Martha Maria Emma, *née* Tupay von Isertingen; *b* 1 July 1951; *Educ* Queensgate Sch London, Inns of Court Sch of Law; *Career* called to the Bar Inner Temple 1974 (bencher 1996); tenant in chambers 1975, recorder of the Crown Court 1995– (asst recorder 1992–95); sr prosecuting counsel Int Criminal Tbnl for the Former Yugoslavia The Hague 1999–2004, conslt to chief prosecutor Bosnia and Herzegovina 2004–05; chair Advocacy Trg Cncl Int Ctee; memb: SE Circuit, Criminal Bar Assoc, Crown Court Rules Ctee 1994–2000, Advocacy Trg Cncl 2004, Professional Practice Ctee of Bar Cncl; co-opted memb Gen Cncl of the Bar 1994–97; *Recreations* collecting books and porcelain, tennis, cinema; *Style—* Miss Joanna Korner, CMG, QC; ✉ 6 King's Bench Walk, Temple, London EC4Y 7DR (tel 020 7583 0410, fax 020 7353 8791)

KORNICKI, Prof Peter Francis; s of Sqdn Ldr F Kornicki, of Worthing, W Sussex, and P C Kornicki; *b* 1 May 1950; *Educ* St George's Coll Weybridge, Lincoln Coll Oxford (BA, MSc), St Antony's Coll Oxford (DPhil); *m* 1, 1975, C O Mikolaski (d 1995); 1 s (Martin b 15 July 1985), 1 da (Alice b 24 Sept 1990); m 2, 1998, Dr F Orsini; *Career* lectr in Japanese Univ of Tasmania 1978–82, assoc prof Univ of Kyoto 1982–84; Univ of Cambridge: lectr 1985–95, chm Faculty of Oriental Studies 1993–95, reader 1995–2001, prof 2001–; author of numerous articles and reviews; pres European Assoc for Japanese Studies 1997–2000, chm African and Oriental Studies Section Br Acad 2006–; Special Prize Japan Fndn 1992; tstee Corbridge Tst, tstee Bell Tst; FBA 2000; *Books* Early Japanese Books in Cambridge University Library (1991), The Book in Japan: A Cultural History (1998); *Recreations* languages, cooking, hiking; *Style—* Prof Peter Kornicki; ✉ Faculty of Asian and Middle Eastern Studies, Sidgwick Avenue, Cambridge CB3 9DA (tel 01223 335106, fax 01223 335110, e-mail pk104@cam.ac.uk)

KOSCIUSZKO, Stefan Henry; s of Konstanty Kosciuszko (d 1985), and Elizabeth, *née* Havelock; *b* 2 June 1959, NYC; *Educ* Gordonstoun, Divine Mercy Coll, Univ of Keele (BA, Josiah Wedgwood Meml Prize Award); *m* 15 Jan 1985, Takako, *née* Yamaguchi; 2 da (Krystyna Midori Havelock b 18 May 1989, Rachel Sayaka Havelock b 7 Aug 1991); *Career* National Westminster Bank 1980–82, Sumitomo Bank London and Tokyo 1982–85, Chemical Bank London and Tokyo 1985–88; Schroders: gen mangr Tokyo 1988–91, London 1992–95, dir 1995–98, head of Asia Pacific equity capital markets 1995–97, head of corp fin Indonesia 1997–98; md Gavin Anderson 1999–2000, dir Credit Suisse First Boston 2000–02, chief exec Asia House 2000–; exec dir Pakistan Britain Trade & Investment Forum 2003–, sec Indo British Partnership Network 2005–07, exec dir UK-Korea Forum for the Future 2007–; govr Gainsborough House Museum 2002–06, sec Sudbury Soc 2002–06; FRSA 2006; *Recreations* sports, chess, fine wine, antiques, Asian culture and history; *Clubs* Naval and Military; *Style—* Stefan Kosciuszko, Esq; ✉ Abbas Hall, Cornard Tye, Great Cornard, Sudbury, Suffolk CO10 0QD (tel 01787 881015, e-mail stefan@kosciuszko.com)

KOUMI, Margaret (Maggie); da of Yiasoumis Koumi (d 1982), and Melexidia Paraskeva (d 2002); *b* 15 July 1942; *Educ* Buckingham Gate London; *m* 8 Aug 1980, Ramon Sola; *Career* sec Thomas Cook 1957–60; sub ed and feature/fiction writer Visual Features Ltd (incl Boyfriend, Top Boys, Big Beat and Boyfriend Annual) 1960–66, sub ed TV World 1966–67, ed 19 Magazine (concurrently ed Hair Magazine (bi-annual then quarterly)) 1969–86 (prodn ed 1967–69), managing ed Practical Parenting, Practical Health and Practical Hair & Beauty 1986–87, sole ed Hello! 1993–2001 (jt ed 1988–93); conslt ed 2001–; awards for Hello!: Consumer Magazine of the Year PPA and Media Week 1990, Magazine of the Year Br Press Circulation Awards 1991, Eds of the Year for gen interest magazine BSME 1991, Consumer Magazine of the Year Media Week 1992, Int Consumer Magazine of the Year PPA 1999; *Books* Beauty Care (1981); *Recreations* travel, reading; *Style—* Ms Maggie Koumi; ✉ Flat 8, 8 Mercer Street, London WC2H 9QB (tel 020 7836 5989, fax 020 7379 8295)

KOUVARITAKIS, Prof Basil; s of Alexander Kouvaritakis (d 1984), and Xanthippi, *née* Vasileiou (d 1988); *b* 19 December 1948; *Educ* Varvakeios Model Sch Athens, Atlantic Coll S Wales (Schilizzi Fndn scholar), UMIST (BSc, IEE Prize, MSc, PhD); *m* 14 Sept 1974, Sheila, *née* Kennedy; 2 s (Philip, Nicholas); *Career* demonstrator UMIST 1972–74, asst researcher Univ of Cambridge 1974–78, lectr Univ of Bradford 1978–80, fell St Edmund Hall Oxford 1981–, prof of engrg sci Univ of Oxford 1998– (lectr 1981–96, reader 1996–98); MIEE 1980; *Books* Nonlinear Predictive Control: Theory and Practice (jt ed, 2001); author of over 200 articles in scientific jls; *Recreations* memb various orchestras, chamber music and duet performances, cycling, walking; *Style—* Prof Basil Kouvaritakis; ✉ Huggins Cottage, Old Road, Headington, Oxford OX3 8SZ; Department of Engineering Science, University of Oxford, Parks Road, Oxford OX1 3PJ (tel 01865 765876, e-mail basil.kouvaritakis@eng.ox.ac.uk)

KOVACEVICH, Stephen; s of Nicholas Kovacevich, and Loretta, *née* Zuban; *b* 17 October 1940; *Educ* Berkeley HS Calif; *Career* concert pianist and conductor; studied with Dame Myra Hess, worldwide concert tours, Kimber Award California 1959, Hertz Scholar 1959–61, Mozart Prize London 1962, Edison Award for Bartók Piano Concerto no 2, Gramophone Award and Stereo Review Record of the Year for Brahms Piano Concerto no 1 (with London Philharmonic/Wolfgang Sawallisch) 1993; int chair piano studies RAM; exclusive recording contract with EMI 1991–; *Books* Schubert Anthology; *Recreations* tennis, films, chess, Indian food; *Style—* Stephen Kovacevich, Esq; ✉ c/o Van Walsum Management, 4 Addison Bridge Place, London W14 8XP (tel 020 8371 4343, fax 020 8371 4344, e-mail vwm@vanwalsum.co.uk)

KOVAR, Dr Ilya Zdenek; s of Victor Kovar (d 1971), and Nina, *née* Klein; *b* 17 March 1947; *Educ* Sydney Boys' HS Aust, Univ of Sydney (MB BS); *m* 29 Dec 1974, Cynthia Rose, da of Norbert Sencier; 3 s (Simon b 10 Oct 1976, Benjamin b 23 March 1979, David b 31 May 1984), 1 da (Sarah b 5 Aug 1981); *Career* formerly sr lectr in child health at Charing Cross and Westminster Schs and conslt paediatrician Charing Cross Hosp London, currently conslt in paediatrics and perinatal med Chelsea and Westminster Hosp London; author of med, scientific, clinical articles and med texts; Lt Col RAMC(V); FRCPCH, FRCP, FRCP(C), FAAP, DRCOG, RAMC (V); *Books* Textbook for DCH (1984, 1991), Make it Better (1982); *Recreations* riding, reading, music; *Style—* Dr Ilya Kovar; ✉ Neonatal Unit, Chelsea and Westminster Hospital, London SW10 9NH (tel 020 8846 7195, fax 020 8846 7998, e-mail i.kovar@imperial.ac.uk)

KOWALSKI, Gregor; s of Mieczeslaw Kowalski (d 1986), and Jeannie Hutcheson, *née* MacDonald (d 2002); *b* 7 October 1949; *Educ* Airdrie Acad, Univ of Strathclyde (LLB); *m* 4 July 1974, Janet McFarlane, da of Andrew McWilliam Pillatt (d 1976); 2 s (Gavin Gregor b 1978, Giles McFarlane b 1980); *Career* asst slr Levy and McRae Glasgow 1973–74 (legal apprentice 1971–73), depute procurator fiscal Glasgow 1974–78; Lord Advocate's Dept London: asst then dep parly draftsman for Scotland 1978–87, seconded legal draftsman Govt of Seychelles 1982–83, Scottish parly counsel 1987–99, Scottish parly counsel to UK Govt 1999–2000, dep parly counsel to Office of the Parly Counsel 2000–05, parly counsel 2005–; memb Law Soc of Scotland 1973, fndr sec Soc of Scottish Lawyers in London 1987 (pres 1991–92); *Recreations* music, singing; *Style—* Gregor Kowalski, Esq; ✉ 36 Whitehall, London SW1A 2AY

KRAEMER, (Thomas Wilhelm) Nicholas; s of Dr William Paul Kraemer (d 1982), of London, and Helen, *née* Bartrum; *b* 7 March 1945; *Educ* Lancing, Dartington Coll of Arts, Univ of Nottingham (BMus, ARCM), Guildhall Sch of Music; *m* 22 April 1984, Elizabeth Mary, da of John Anderson; 2 da (Emma b 1986, Chlöe b 1993), 3 s (Dominic b 1988, Matthew b and d 1990, Daniel b 1991); *Career* conductor and harpsichordist: Monteverdi Orchestra and English Baroque Soloists 1970–80, Acad of St Martin in the Fields 1972–80; musical dir: Unicorn Opera Abingdon 1971–75, West Eleven Children's Opera 1971–88; fndr and dir Raglan Baroque Players 1978–2003, musical dir Opera 80 1980–83, princ conductor Divertimenti 1980–95, assoc conductor BBC Scottish Symphony Orchestra 1983–85, artistic dir London Bach Orchestra 1985–93, artistic dir Irish Chamber Orch 1985–90, princ conductor Manchester Camerata 1992–95 (perm guest conductor 1995–); guest conductor: Music of the Baroque Chicago (princ guest conductor 2003–), Manchester Camerata, Collegium Musicum, Winterthur and Kanazawa Orchestra Japan, Halle Orchestra, Scottish Chamber Orchestra, St Paul Chamber Orchestra, Manchester Camerata and Music of the Baroque Chicago, Berlin Philharmonic, ENO, Northern Sinfonia, Bergen Philharmonic, BBC NOW, Chicago Symphony Orch, Detroit Symphony Orch, Toronto Symphony Orch; prog dir Bath Festival 1994; memb Royal Soc of Musicians; *Recreations* watching football, active fatherhood; *Style—* Nicholas Kraemer; ✉ c/o Caroline Phillips Management, The Old Brushworks, Pickwick Road, Corsham, Wiltshire SN13 9BX (tel 01249 716716, fax 01249 716717)

KRAMER, Prof Matthew Henry; s of Alton Kramer (d 2007), and Eunice Bixon Kramer (d 1993); *b* 9 June 1959, Boston, MA; *Educ* Cornell Univ (BA), Harvard Univ (JD), Univ of Cambridge (PhD, LLD); *Career* fell and dir of studies in law Churchill Coll Cambridge 1994–, prof of legal and political philosophy Univ of Cambridge 2002–; dir Cambridge Forum for Legal and Political Philosophy 2001–; subject ed Routledge Encyclopedia of Philosophy 2000–; vice-pres UK Assoc for Legal and Social Philosophy 1998–99; Br Acad Research Leave Award 1998, Guggenheim Fndn Fellowship 2001–02, Leverhulme Tst Major Research Fellowship 2005–07; *Books* In the Realm of Legal and Moral Philosophy (1999), In Defense of Legal Positivism (1999), Rights, Wrongs, and Responsibilities (2001), The Quality of Freedom (2003), Where Law and Morality Meet (2004), Objectivity and the Rule of Law (2007); *Recreations* Shakespearean drama, Bible commentary, long-distance running; *Style—* Prof Matthew Kramer; ✉ Churchill College, Cambridge CB3 0DS (tel 01223 336231, fax 01223 336180, e-mail mhk11@cam.ac.uk)

KRAMER, His Hon Judge Stephen Ernest; QC (1995); s of Frederic Kramer, of Peterborough, and Lotte Karoline, *née* Wertheimer; *b* 12 September 1947; *Educ* Hampton GS, Keble Coll Oxford (Open exhibitioner, MA), Coll of Law, Université de Nancy; *m* 12 March 1978, Miriam, da of Siegfried Leopold (d 1992), and Charlotte Leopold (d 1997); 1 da (Joanna Louise b 13 Sept 1981), 1 s (Robert Paul b 13 Oct 1982); *Career* called to the Bar Gray's Inn 1970 (bencher 2001); standing counsel (Crime) Customs and Excise SE Circuit 1989–95, recorder of the Crown Court 1991–2003 (asst recorder 1987–91), circuit judge (SE Circuit) 2003–05, sr circuit judge (sitting at Central Criminal Court) 2005–; chm Liaison Ctee Bar Cncl/Inst of Barristers Clerks 1996–99; memb: Bar Cncl 1993–95, Ctee Criminal Bar Assoc 1993–98 (actg vice-chm 1998–99, vice-chm 1999–2000, chm 2000–01), Ctee SE Circuit 1997–2000; Parly candidate (Lib) Twickenham 1974 (both elections); *Recreations* theatre, music, swimming, walking, watching rugby union; *Style—* His Hon Judge Stephen Kramer, QC

KRAMER, Susan; MP; *Educ* St Paul's Girls' Sch, St Hilda's Coll Oxford, Univ of Illinois (MBA); *Career* former vice-pres Citibank, MP (Lib Dem) Richmond Park 2005–; memb: Women Lib Dems Exec 1997–2000, London Regnl Exec 1997–2003, Lib Dem Fed Exec 2001–04; fndr Future Water Int, memb Bd Tport for London 2000–05; *Style—* Ms Susan Kramer, MP; ✉ House of Commons, London SW1A 0AA

KREBS, Baron (Life Peer UK 2007), of Wytham in the County of Oxfordshire; Prof Sir John Richard Krebs; kt (1999); s of Sir Hans Krebs (d 1981), of Oxford, and Margaret Cicely, *née* Fieldhouse (d 1993); *b* 11 April 1945; *Educ* City of Oxford HS, Pembroke Coll Oxford (MA, DPhil); *m* 3 Aug 1968, Katharine Anne, da of John Fullerton (d 1973), of Newport, Gwent; 2 da (Emma Helen b 1977, Georgina Clare b 1980); *Career* asst prof Inst of Animal Resource Ecology Univ of British Columbia 1970–73, lectr in zoology UCNW Bangor 1973–75, fell Wolfson Coll Oxford 1975–81, lectr in zoology Edward Grey Inst Oxford 1975–88 (demonstrator in ornithology 1970), Royal Soc research prof and fell Pembroke Coll 1988– (EP Abraham fell 1981–88), chief exec Natural Environment Research Cncl 1994–99, chm UK Food Standards Agency 2000–05, princ Jesus Coll Oxford 2005–; sr scientific conslt AFRC 1991–94; memb: Max Planck Soc 1985–, AFRC 1988–94, Cncl Zoological Soc of London 1991–92, Academia Europaea 1995; hon memb Br Ecological Soc 1999; foreign memb American Philosophical Soc 2000; fell American Acad of Arts and Sciences 2000, foreign memb US Nat Acad of Sci 2004; Hon DSc: Univ of Sheffield 1993, Univ of Wales 1997, Univ of Birmingham 1997, Univ of Exeter 1998, Univ of Stirling 2000, Univ of Warwick 2000, Cranfield Univ 2001, Univ of Kent 2001, Univ of Plymouth 2001, Queen's Univ Belfast 2002, Heriot-Watt Univ 2002, South Bank Univ 2003, Lancaster Univ 2005, Univ of Guelph 2006; hon fell Univ of Cardiff 1999, hon fell German Ornithologists' Soc 2003; Zoological Soc of London: Scientific Medal 1981, Frink Medal 1996; Linnean Soc Bicentenary Medal 1983; American Ornithologists Union: Elliot Coues Award 1999, Assoc Study Animal Behaviour Medal 2000; Royal Soc of the Promotion of Health Benjamin Ward Richardson Gold Medal 2002, Woodridge Medal British Veterinary Assoc 2003, Croonian Lecture Royal Soc 2004, Harbel Gold Medal RIPH 2006; hon fell Univ of Wales Inst Cardiff 2006; Hon Freeman City of London, hon memb Salters' Co 2007; FRS 1984, FMedSci 2004, hon FZS 2006; *Books* Behavioural Ecology (with N B Davies, 1978, 1984, 1991 and 1997), Introduction to Behavioural Ecology (with N B Davies, 1981, 1987 and 1993), Foraging Theory (with D W Stephens, 1986); *Recreations* running, violin, gardening, travel, walking, cooking; *Style—* The Rt Hon the Lord Krebs, FRS; ✉ tel 01865 279701, e-mail principal@jesus.ox.ac.uk

KREINCZES, Gerald Michael; s of Maurice Kreinczes (d 1985), of London, and Alice, *née* Baker; *b* 28 October 1951; *Educ* Kingston GS, Lancaster Univ (BA); *m* 1976, Catherine, da of Francis J Cronin (d 1993); 1 da (Nicola Catherine b 17 Aug 1985), 1 s (Christopher Gerald b 22 April 1988); *Career* graduate trainee AGB Market Research 1974–75, Findus Ltd 1975–79, dir/head of mktg Allen Brady & Marsh Ltd 1979–84, dir Mgmnt and Mktg Servs Publicis Ltd 1984–86, planning dir Dorlands 1986–89, exec planning dir Allen

Brady & Marsh 1989–90, ptnr The Kreinczes Partnership 1990–92, exec planning dir Kevin Morley Marketing 1992–96, planning dir Lintas i 1996, vice-chm Ammirati Puris Lintas 1996–99, chm Occam Insight 2000–; memb: Mktg Soc, IOD; MCIM; *Recreations* sailing, music, reading; *Style—* Gerald Kreinczes, Esq; ✉ Occam Insight, 21 Roupell Street, London SE1 8SP (tel 020 7928 8199, fax 020 7928 0895)

KRIEGER, Ian Stephen; s of Sid Krieger, and Raie, *née* Dight; *b* 2 February 1952; *Educ* Christ's Coll Finchley, Univ of Kent (BA); *m* Caron Meryl, *née* Gluckstein; 3 s (James Michael b 1990, Elliott Charles b 1992, Ben Scott b 1995); *Career* Arthur Andersen: articled clerk 1973–76, CA 1976, ptnr 1985–2002; vice-chm Deloitte & Touche LLP 2002–; FCA 1981; *Books* Management Buy-Outs (1990); *Style—* Ian Krieger, Esq; ✉ Deloitte, Hill House, 1 Little New Street, London EC4A 3TR (tel 020 7936 3000, fax 020 7007 0155)

KRIKLER, Dennis Michael; s of Barnet Krikler (d 1992), and Eva Krikler (d 1986); *b* 10 December 1928; *Educ* Muizenberg HS, Univ of Cape Town (MB ChB); *m* 3 July 1955, Anne, da of August Winterstein; 1 da (Shirley Jean b 1957), 1 s (Paul Alan b 1961); *Career* fell Lahey Clinic Boston 1956, C J Adams Meml Travelling Fell 1956, sr registrar Groote Schuur Hosp 1957–58 (house physician and registrar 1952–55); conslt physician: Salisbury Central Hosp Rhodesia 1958–66, Prince of Wales Hosp London 1966–73; conslt cardiologist Hammersmith and Ealing Hosps 1973–94, sr lectr in cardiology Royal Postgrad Med Sch 1973–94, expert clinicien en cardiologie Ministère des Affaires Sociales Santé France 1983, int lectr American Heart Assoc 1984 (Paul Dudley White Citation for int achievement); visiting prof: Baylor Univ, Indiana Univ and Univ of Birmingham 1985, Boston, Kentucky, and UCLA 1988; Joseph Welker lectr Univ of Kansas, George Burch lectr Association of Univ Cardiologists USA 1989, Henri Denolin lectr Euro Soc of Cardiology, Hideo Ueda lectr Japan Soc of Electrocardiology 1990, visiting prof Univ of Minnesota and H B Burchell lectr 1991; author of papers on cardiology in nat and int jls; ed British Heart Journal 1981–91 (ed emeritus 1992–); memb Editorial Ctee: Cardiovascular Res 1975–91, Archives des Maladies du Coeur et des Vaisseaux 1980–; hon memb: Soc di Cultura Medica Vercellese Italy, Soc de Cardiologia de Levante Spain, Soc Française de Cardiologie 1981–; memb Scientific Cncl Revista Portuguese de Cardiologia 1982–, hon fell Cncl on Clinical Cardiology American Heart Assoc 1984; McCullough prize 1949, Sir William Osler Award Miami Univ 1981, medal of Honour Euro Soc of Cardiology; Freeman: Worshipful Soc of Apothecaries 1989, City of London 1990; memb Br Cardiac Soc 1971 (Silver medal 1991); Chevalier Ordre National de la Légion d'Honneur (France) 1999; FACC 1971, MD 1973, FRCPE 1970, FRCP 1973; *Books* Cardiac Arrhythmias (with J F Goodwin, 1975), Calcium Antagonism in Cardiovascular Therapy (with A Zanchetti, 1981), Amiodarone and Arrhythmias (with D A Chamberlain and W J McKenna, 1983), Workshop on Calcium Antagonists (with P G Hugenholtz, 1984), British Cardiology in the 20th Century (jtly, 2000); *Recreations* photography, history; *Style—* Dr Dennis Krikler; ✉ 2 Garden Court, Grove End Road, London NW8 9PP (tel 020 7286 1440, e-mail dennis_krikler@btconnect.com)

KROLL, Nicholas James; CB (2002); s of Alexander Kroll, and Maria, *née* Wolff; *b* 23 June 1954; *Educ* St Paul's, CCC Oxford; *m* 1981, Catherine Askew; 2 da (1 decd), 1 s; *Career* joined Civil Serv 1977, Dept of Environment and Tport 1977–82, Dept of Tport 1982–86; HM Treasy: head Banking Policy Branch 1986–90, head European Community Budget Div 1990–93; DCMS (formerly Dept of Nat Heritage): head Arts Div 1993–95, head Broadcasting Policy Div 1995–96, dir Creative Industries, Media and Broadcasting Gp 1996–2000, corp services dir 2000–03 (acting perm sec 2001), dir chief operating offr and dep to Perm Sec 2002–04; dir of governance BBC 2004–06, dir BBC Tst 2007–; memb Bd Nat Youth Orchestra 2005–; *Style—* Nicholas Kroll, Esq, CB; ✉ BBC Trust, 35 Marylebone High Street, London W1U 4AA

KROTO, Prof Sir Harold Walter (Harry); kt (1996); *b* 7 October 1939; *Educ* Bolton Sch, Univ of Sheffield (BSc, PhD); *Career* postdoctoral fell NRC Ottawa 1964–66, memb tech staff Bell Telephone Laboratories 1966–67; Univ of Sussex: tutorial fell 1967–68, lectr 1968–78, reader 1978–85, prof 1985–91, Royal Soc research prof 1991–; Tilden lectr 1981–82; currently Eppes prof of chemistry Florida State Univ; visiting prof: Univ of Southern Calif 1981, UCLA 1988–93, Univ of Calif Santa Barbara (UCSB) 1994–; visiting scientist NRC Ottawa 1976 and 1978; memb Editorial Bd: Chemical Soc Reviews 1986–96, Zeitschrift für Physik D 1992–, Carbon 1992–; chm Vega Science Tst; memb various SERC Ctees; author of 300 research papers in scientific jls and numerous pubns; Hon Degree: Univ of Stockholm, Limburg Univ Brussels, Univ of Sheffield, Kingston Univ, Univ of Sussex, Helsinki, Univ of Nottingham, Yokohama City Univ, Sheffield Hallam Univ, Univ of Aberdeen, Univ of Leicester, Univ of Patras, City Univ of Hong Kong, Manchester Metropolitan Univ, Univ of Liverpool, Univ of Manchester, Univ of Surrey; memb Academia Europaea 1992, hon foreign memb Korean Acad of Sci and Technol 1997, foreign memb Accademia delle Scienze di Termo 2005; Hon FRMS 1998, Hon FRSE 2000; FRS 1990; *Awards* Sunday Times Book Jacket Design Award 1964, Int Prize for New Materials American Physical Soc 1992, Italgas Prize for Innovation in Chemistry 1992, Longstaff Medal RSC 1993, Hewlett Packard Europhysics Prize 1994, Moët Hennessy/Louis Vuitton Science pour L'Art Prize 1994, jt winner Nobel Prize for Chemistry 1996, Royal Soc Faraday Award 2002, Copley Medal Royal Soc 2004; *Style—* Prof Sir Harold Kroto, FRS; ✉ Deparment of Chemistry and Biochemistry, Dittmer Building, Florida State University, Tallahassee, FL 32306-4390, USA (e-mail kroto@chem.fsu.edu)

KRUT, Ansel Jonathan; s of Dr Louis Harold Krut, and Rhoda, *née* Robinson; *b* 19 March 1959; *Educ* Univ of the Witwatersrand (BA), RCA (MA); *Career* artist; Cité International des Arts Paris 1982–83, Rome prize Br Sch Rome 1986–87, subsequently lived and worked in Rome 1987–90, returned London 1990; *Exhibitions* Fischer Fine Art London (one man) 1989 and 1990, Gillian Jason Gallery London (one man) 1994, Royal Acad Summer Show 1985, John Moores 14 Liverpool 1985, 12 British Artists (Künstlerhaus Vienna) 1986, The Human Touch (Fischer Fine Art London) 1986, Artists at the Br Sch at Rome (Rome) 1987, The Self Portrait (Bath and touring) 1988, 3 Ways (Budapest and touring Eastern Europe) 1989, 10 Years of the Br Sch at Rome (RCA London) 1990, The Discerning Eye (Mall Galleries London) 1991, A View of the New (Royal Over-Seas League London) 1991, 20th Century British Art Fair (London) 1992, Contemporary Portraits, Real and Imagined (Gillian Jason Gallery) 1993, Jason and Rhodes Gallery (one man) 1996 and 1998, George Adams Gallery (One Man) 2000; work in public collections: Arts Cncl of GB, Br Cncl London, Contemporary Art Soc London, Johannesburg Art Gallery, Govt Art Collection London, The Harris Museum and Art Gallery Preston Lancs, Mercer Art Gallery Harrogate; *Style—* Ansel Krut, Esq; ✉ George Adams Gallery, 41 West 57th Street, New York 10019 NY (tel 212 644 5665)

KUENSSBERG, Nicholas (Nick); OBE (2004); s of late Dr Ekkehard von Kuenssberg, CBE, and late Constance, *née* Hardy; *b* 28 October 1942; *Educ* Edinburgh Acad, Wadham Coll Oxford (BA), Manchester Business Sch; *m* 27 Nov 1965, Sally, da of Hon Lord Robertson (Lord of Session); 1 s (David b 1971), 2 da (Joanna b 1973, Laura b 1976); *Career* worked in Europe and Latin America 1965–78; chm: Dynacast International Ltd 1978–91, David A Hall Ltd 1996–98, GAP Gp Ltd 1996–2005, Stoddard International plc 1998–2000, Canmore Partnership Ltd 1999–, iomart gp plc 2000–, Keronite Ltd 2005– (dir 2004), eTourism Ltd 2007–; md Dawson International plc 1994–95 (dir 1991–); dir: J & P Coats Ltd 1978–91, West of Scotland Bd Bank of Scotland 1984–88, Scottish Power plc (formerly South of Scotland Electricity Bd) 1984–97, Coats Patons plc 1985–91, Coats Viyella plc 1986–91, Standard Life Assurance Co 1988–99, Baxi Partnership Ltd 1996–99, Sanmex Int plc 1998–2003, Chamberlain & Hill plc 1999–2006, Ring Prop plc 2002–06, Amino Technologies plc 2004–07; chm: Assoc of Mgmnt Educn & Trg in Scotland 1996–98, IoD Scotland 1997–99, Scottish Networks International 2001–, ScotlandIS 2001–03, Scotland the Brand 2002–; memb: Scottish Legal Aid Bd 1996–2004, Advsy Gp to Sec of State on Sustainable Devpt 1996–99, Scottish Environment Protection Agency 1999– (dep chm 2003–), Scottish Ctee Br Cncl 1999–, Quality Assurance Agency Scotland 2004–; visiting prof Strathclyde Business Sch 1988–91 (visiting fell 1986–87), govr Queen's Coll Glasgow 1989–91, chm The Glasgow Sch of Art 2003– (dir 2001–); dir Citizens Theatre Glasgow 2000–03; FCIS 1977, CCIMgt 1989, FRSA 1993, FInstD 1996; *Recreations* travel, languages, opera, sport; *Clubs* New (Edinburgh); *Style—* Nick Kuenssberg, Esq, OBE; ✉ 6 Cleveden Drive, Glasgow G12 0SE (tel 0141 339 8345, fax 0141 334 9730)

KUHN, Prof Annette; *Educ* Univ of Sheffield, Univ of London (PhD); *Career* various posts incl writer, ed, lectr and TV prodr; reader in film and TV studies Univ of Glasgow 1991–98 (lectr 1989–91), reader in cultural research Lancaster Univ 1998–2000, prof of film studies Lancaster Univ 2000–; Fulbright sr research scholar Mount Holyoke Coll; visiting appts: Humanities Research Centre ANU, Stockholm Univ; co-ed Screen; memb Editorial Bd: Secuencias: revista de historia del cine, Int Jl of Cultural Studies, Jl of British Cinema, Intensities: Online Jl of Cult Media, Visual Studies, Visual Culture in Britain; FBA 2004; *Publications* Six Years After (jtly 1970), Graduates (jtly, 1972), Feminism and Materialism (jt ed, 1978), Ideology and Cultural Production (jt ed, 1979), Women's Pictures: Feminism and Cinema (1982, 2 edn 1994), The Power of the Image: Essays on Representation and Sexuality (1985), Cinema, Censorship and Sexuality (1988), The Women's Companion to International Film (ed, 1990), Alien Zone: Cultural Theory and Contemporary Science Fiction Cinema (ed, 1990), Family Secrets: Acts of Memory and Imagination (1995, revised edn 2002), Queen of the Bs: Ida Lupino Behind the Camera (ed, 1995), Screen Histories: A Screen Reader (jt ed, 1998), Alien Zone II: The Spaces of Science Fiction Cinema (ed, 1999), An Everyday Magic: Cinema and Cultural Memory (2002), Screening World Cinema (jt ed, 2006), Locating Memory: Photographic Arts (jt ed, 2006); also author of book contribs, academic articles and reviews; *Style—* Prof Annette Kuhn

KUHRT, Ven Dr Gordon Wilfred; s of Wilfred Nicholas Henry Kuhrt, and Doris Adeline, *née* Goddard (d 2002); *b* 15 February 1941; *Educ* Colfe's GS, Univ of London (BD), Oakhill Theol Coll, Middx Univ (Dr of Professional Studies); *m* 31 Aug 1963, Olive Margaret, da of Raymond Frank Alexander Powell; 3 s (Martin b 1966, Stephen b 1969, Jonathan b 1972); *Career* religious educn teacher 1963–65, vicar Shenstone Dio of Lichfield 1973–79, vicar Emmanuel Croydon Dio of Southwark 1979–89, rural dean Croydon Central 1981–86, hon canon Southwark Cathedral 1987–89, biblical studies lectr Univ of London 1984–89, memb Gen Synod C of E 1986–96, archdeacon Lewisham Dio of Southwark 1989–96 (now archdeacon emeritus), chief sec Advsy Bd for Ministry 1996–98, dir of miny C of E 1999–2006, assoc min Tredington Dio of Coventry 2006–, pt/t tutor in preaching Wycliffe Hall Oxford 2006–; *Books* Handbook for Council and Committee Members (1985), Believing in Baptism (1987), The Church and its Unity (contrib, 1992), Doctrine Matters (ed, 1993), Growing in Newness of Life - Christian Initiation in Anglicanism Today (contrib, 1993), To Proclaim Afresh (ed, 1995), Issues of Theological Education and Training (1997), Clergy Security (1998), Introduction to Christian Ministry (2000), Ministry Issues for the Church of England: Mapping the Trends (2001), Bridging the Gap - Reader Ministry Today (ed, 2002); *Style—* The Ven Dr Gordon Kuhrt; ✉ The Rectory, Tredington, Shipston-on-Stour CV36 4NG (tel 01608 661264, e-mail omkuhrt@tiscali.co.uk)

KULUKUNDIS, Sir Eddie; kt (1993), OBE (1988); s of George Elias Kulukundis (d 1978), and Eugenia, *née* Diacakis (d 1993); 5th generation shipping family; *b* 20 April 1932; *Educ* Collegiate Sch NYC, Salisbury Sch Connecticut, Yale Univ; *m* 4 April 1981, Susan Hampshire, OBE, *qv*, da of George Kenneth Hampshire (d 1964); *Career* theatrical producer and co-producer of over 80 shows in the West End and NY 1969–1996; chm: Knightsbridge Theatrical Productions Ltd 1970–, London Coaching Fndn 1990–, Sport Aid Fndn 1988–93, Ambassadors Theatre Gp 1992–, Br Athletic Charitable Tst (previously Br Athletics Field Events Charitable Tst) 1996–; vice-chm Royal Shakespeare Theatre Tst 1984–88 (dir 1968); vice-pres: Traverse Theatre Club 1988–, UK Athletics 1998–2003; tstee: Salisbury Sch Connecticut 1983–, Sports Aid Fndn Trust 1987–, Theatre Trust 1976–April 1995; govr: Royal Shakespeare Theatre 1976–2003, The Raymond Mander & Joe Mitchenson Theatre Collection Ltd 1981–2001, Sports Aid Fndn 1977–; dir: Rethymnis & Kulukundis Ltd 1964–, Rethymnis & Kulukundis (Chartering) Ltd 1969–, London & Overseas Freighters plc 1980–85 and 1989–97, Soc of London Theatre 1973–2003, Hampstead Theatre Ltd 1969–2004, Hampstead Theatre Trust 1980–2003; memb: Baltic Exchange 1959–2001, Lloyd's 1964–95 (memb Cncl 1983–89), Richmond Theatre Tst 2001–; hon vice-pres SOLT 2003 (memb Bd 1973–2003); *Productions* London prodns incl (some jtly): Enemy 1969, The Happy Apple 1970, Poor Horace 1970, The Friends 1970, How the Other Half Loves 1970, Tea Party and the Basement (double bill) 1970, The Wild Duck 1970, After Haggerty 1971, Hamlet 1971, Charley's Aunt 1971, Straight Up 1971, London Assurance 1972, Journey's End 1972, Small Craft Warnings 1973, A Private Matter 1973, Dandy Dick 1973, The Waltz of the Toreadors 1974, Life Class 1974, Pygmalion 1974, Play Mas 1974, The Gentle Hook 1974, A Little Night Music 1975, Entertaining Mr Sloane 1975, The Gay Lord Quex 1975, What the Butler Saw 1975, Travesties 1975, Lies 1975, The Seagull 1975, A Month in the Country 1975, A Room with a View 1975, Too True to be Good 1975, The Bed Before Yesterday 1975, Dimetos 1976, Banana Ridge 1976, Wild Oats 1976, Candida 1977, Man and Superman 1977, Once a Catholic 1977, Privates on Parade 1978, Gloo Joo 1978, Bent 1979, Outside Edge 1979, Last of the Red Hot Lovers 1979, Beecham 1980, Born in the Gardens 1980, Tonight at 8.30 1981, Steaming 1981, Arms and the Man 1981, Steafel's Variations 1982, Messiah 1983, Pack of Lies 1983, Of Mice and Men 1984, The Secret Diary of Adrian Mole Aged 13–3/4 1984, Camille 1985, The Cocktail Party 1986, Curtains 1987, Separation 1989, South Pacific 1989, Married Love 1989, Over My Dead Body 1989, Never the Sinner 1990, King and I 1991, Carmen Jones 1991, Noel & Gertie 1992, Slip of the Tongue 1992, Shades 1992, Annie Get Your Gun 1992, Making it Better 1992, The Prime of Miss Jean Brodie 1994, The Killing of Sister George 1995; NY prodns (jtly): How the Other Half Loves, Sherlock Holmes, London Assurance, Travesties, The Merchant, Players, Once a Catholic; *Recreations* theatre, athletics; *Clubs* Garrick; *Style—* Sir Eddie Kulukundis, OBE; ✉ c/o The Ambassador Theatre Group, 39–41 Charing Cross Road, London WC2H 0AR (tel 020 7854 7000)

KUMAR, Dr Ashok; MP; s of Mr J R Saini, and Mrs S Kumari (d 1991); *b* 28 May 1956; *Educ* Rykneld Sch for Boys, Derby Coll for FE, Derby Coll of Art and Technology, Aston Univ (BSc, MSc, PhD); *Career* research offr British Steel Technical 1978–79, research fell Imperial Coll London 1982–84, sr research offr British Steel Technical Teesside Technology Centre 1984–97; MP (Lab): Langbaurgh 1991–92, Middlesbrough S and E Cleveland 1997–; cncllr (Lab) Middlesbrough BC 1987–97; FIChemE 1978; *Recreations* reading history and philosophy, listening to jazz, badminton and cricket; *Clubs* Marton CC; *Style—* Dr Ashok Kumar, MP; ✉ House of Commons, London SW1A 0AA (tel 020 7219 3000); constituency office: 8 Wilson Street, Guisborough, TS14 6NA (tel 01287 610878, fax 01287 631894, e-mail ashokkumarmp@parliament.uk)

KUMAR, Prof Parveen June; CBE (2001); da of Cyril Proshuno Fazal Kumar (d 1982), and Grace Nazira, *née* Faiz (d 2001); *b* 1 June 1942; *Educ* Lawrence Sch Sanawar N India,

Maida Vale HS, Bart's Med Coll (BSc, MB BS, MD); *m* Dr David G Leaver, s of Frances Joseph Leaver; 2 da (Rachel Nira b 28 March 1972, Susannah Kiran b 22 July 1974); *Career* house physician Bart's 1966–67, house surgn Royal Berks Hosp Reading 1968, research registrar in bacteriology Bart's 1968–69, house physician Royal Postgrad Med Sch 1969–70, registrar, sr registrar then lectr Bart's 1970–85, conslt physician St Leonard's and Hackney Hosps 1983, sr lectr in gastroenterology and hon conslt physician Bart's and Homerton Hosps (City and Hackney HA) 1985–94, currently prof of clinical med educn and hon conslt physician and gastroenterologist Bart's and The London Queen Mary Sch of Medicine and Dentistry Univ of London, hon conslt physician Homerton Hosp; coll tutor RCP 1988–93, clinical tutor BPMF 1988–96, dir of postgraduate med educn Royal Hosps Tst 1993–96, undergraduate sub-dean Bart's & London Sch of Med and Dentistry 1996–98; RCP: procensor then censor 1996–98, dir Continuing Medical Educn 1998–2002, vice-pres (academic) 2003–05, currently sr examiner; non-exec dir: Nat Inst for Clinical Excellence 1999–2002, Barts and the London NHS Tst 1999–2003; chm Medicines Cmmn UK 2001–05; pres BMA 2006–07; tstee: Med Coll of St Bartholomews, Cancer Backup; examiner of univ degrees; author of published papers and lectr at home and abroad; memb: Br Soc of Gastroenterology (elected memb Cncl 2001–04), Br Soc of Immunology; Hon DM Univ of Nottingham; FRCP, FRCPE, FICG; *Books* Gastrointestinal Radiology (jtly, 1981), Kumar and Clark's Clinical Medicine (jtly 1987, 6 edn 2005), Kumar and Clark's Acute Clinical Medicine (co-ed, 2 edn 2006); series co-ed of several other books; *Recreations* opera, skiing; *Style—* Prof Parveen Kumar, CBE; ✉ St Bartholomew's Hospital, West Smithfield, London EC1A 7BE (tel 020 7882 7191, fax 020 7882 7192, e-mail p.j.kumar@qmul.ac.uk)

KUNKLER, Dr Ian Hubert; s of Dr Peter Bertrand Kunkler, of Las Fuentes, Spain, and Pamela, *née* Hailey (d 1988); *b* 22 July 1951; *Educ* Clifton, Univ of Cambridge (MA, MB BChir), St Bartholomew's Hosp London; *m* 18 July 1981, Dr (Alison) Jane Kunkler, da of late Ronald George Pearson, of Kenya; *Career* house offr Univ of Leicester Med Sch 1978–79, sr house offr in gen med Nottingham City Hosp 1979–81, sr registrar Western Gen Hosp Edinburgh 1984–88 (registrar 1981–83), EEC and French Govt clinical res fell Inst Gustave Roussy Paris 1986–87; conslt in radiotherapy and oncology: Sheffield 1988–92, Edinburgh 1992–; author of papers on bone scanning in breast cancer, radiotherapy in breast and laryngeal cancer and the value of clinic follow-up in cervical cancer; pres London Med Gp 1977, convener annual conference Pain - A Necessity? Charing Cross Med Sch; pres British Oncological Assoc 2000–02; memb BMA 1978, DMRT Edinburgh 1983, FRCR 1985, FRSM 1989, FRCPE 1994, FRSA 1996; *Books* Cambridge University Medical Journal (ed, 1974), Walter and Miller's Textbook of Radiotherapy (jt author, 6 edn, 2002); *Recreations* fly fishing; *Style—* Dr Ian Kunkler

KUNZELMANN, C Dixon; s of Fabian W Kunzelmann, of Old Bennington, VT, and Helen Dixon; *b* 19 December 1941; *Educ* St Paul's Sch Concord NH, Univ of Freiburg, Hobart Coll Geneva NY, Amos Tuck Hanover NH; *m* 3 Feb 1968, Joan, da of Rawson Atwood, of Rumson, NJ; 1 s (Christopher Ely b 1970), 1 da (Laura Rawson b 1973); *Career* JP Morgan: joined 1965, sr vice-pres Personnel London 1982–89, sr vice-pres Securities Gp NYC 1989–90, sr vice-pres Central Personnel NYC 1990–91, md Private Banking NYC 1991–93, md Global Asset Management London 1993–98; tstee Hobart Coll NY 1990–, former pres American Friends of Georgian Gp 1989–94, human resources advsr Russell Reynolds Associates 1999–, vice-chm America Rugby 2000, Appeal 1991–93, non-exec dir Roxton Bailey Robinson Hungerford 1990–, chm Bowdoin Coll Parents' Ctee 1993–; *Recreations* shooting, fishing, driving; *Clubs* Piscatorial Soc, Queen's, Pilgrims, Links (NY), Union (NY), Rockaway Hunt (NY), Mt Lake (FL); *Style—* C Dixon Kunzelmann, Esq; ✉ 1220 Park Avenue, New York City, NY 10128, USA (tel 00 1 212 722 8409); Russell Reynolds Associates, 24 St James's Square, London SW1Y 4HZ (tel 020 7830 8051, e-mail dkunzelmann@russellreynolds.com)

KUPER, Prof Adam Jonathan; s of Simon Meyer (d 1963), of Johannesburg, and Gertrude, *née* Hesselson (d 1987); *b* 29 December 1941; *Educ* Parktown Boys HS Johannesburg, Univ of the Witwatersrand Johannesburg (BA), King's Coll Cambridge (PhD); *m* 16 Dec 1966, Jessica Sue, da of Sidney Cohen (d 1986), of Johannesburg; 2 s (Simon b 1969, Jeremy b 1971), 1 da (Hannah b 1974); *Career* lectr in social anthropology Makerere Univ of Kampala 1967–70, lectr in anthropology UCL 1970–76, prof of African anthropology and sociology Univ of Leiden 1976–85, prof of social anthropology Brunel Univ 1985–; visiting appts: asst prof Univ of Calif 1969, planner Nat Planning Agency Office of PM Jamaica 1972, prof Univ of Gothenburg 1975; fell Centre for Advanced Study in the Behavioural Sci Calif 1980–81, memb Inst for Advanced Study Princeton 1994–95; chm Euro Assoc of Social Anthropologists 1989–90; Hon Dr Univ of Gothenburg 1978; memb Academia Europaea, FBA 2000; *Books* Kalahari Village Politics (1970), Councils in Action (ed, 1971), The Social Anthropology of Radcliffe-Brown (ed, 1977), Wives for Cattle: Bridewealth and Marriage in Southern Africa (1982), Anthropology and Anthropologists: The Modern British School (1983), The Social Science Encyclopaedia (ed, 1985), South Africa and the Anthropologist (1987), The Invention of Primitive Society: Transformations of an Illusion (1988), Conceptualizing Society (ed, 1992), The Chosen Primate (1994), Culture: The Anthropologists' Account (1999), Among the Anthropologists (1999), The Reinvention of Primitive Society (2005); *Style—* Prof Adam Kuper; ✉ 16 Muswell Road, Muswell Hill, London N10 2BG (tel 020 8883 0400); Brunel University, Department of Human Sciences, Uxbridge, Middlesex UB8 3PH (tel 01895 56461, fax 01895 32806, telex 261173 Brunel G, e-mail kuper@ajkuper.freeserve.co.uk)

KUPFERMANN, Jeannette Anne; da of Nathan Weitz (d 1988), and Eva Tarnofsky (d 2000); *b* 28 March 1941; *Educ* Hendon Co GS, LSE (BA), UCL (MPhil); *m* 25 June 1964, Jacques H Kupfermann (d 1988), s of Elias Kupfermann (k ca 1940); 1 s (Elias Jonathan b 16 April 1965), 1 da (Mina Alexandra b 10 May 1967); *Career* res librarian Wenner-Gren Fndn Anthropological Res NY 1963–65, actress Woodstock Playhouse NY 1964–67, res asst Univ of London 1976–77; broadcasting 1972–; writer: Man and Myth (Radio 3, award for best radio documentary series 1976), An Introduction to Social Anthropology (1980); presenter and contrib LWT and Thames TV 1970–, panelist on Tomorrow's Child; writer of documentaries Channel 4 and five; tech advsr to film dirs: Fred Zinnemann (The Dybbuk) 1972, Barbra Streisand (Yentl) 1982; journalist: Woodstock Times 1965–67, Sunday Times 1984–88, Daily Telegraph 1987; TV critic and feature writer: Daily Mail 1984–, Sunday Times Magazine, You, She, New Woman, The Mail on Sunday, Aspire magazine; memb Br Broadcasting Press Guild 1988; *Books* The Mistaken Body (1978), When The Crying's Done - A Journey Through Widowhood (1992), The American Madonna (2002); *Recreations* dancing (flamenco), choreography, gardening, walking, painting (water colours), studying cosmology; *Clubs* Whitefriars; *Style—* Ms Jeannette Kupfermann; ✉ Features Department, Daily Mail, Northcliffe House, 2 Derry Street, London W8 5EE (tel 020 7583 8000)

KURBAAN, Dr Arvinder Singh; s of Meherban Singh Kurbaan, and Satinder Pal Kurbaan; *b* 17 January 1966; *Educ* UMDS London (BSc, MB BS), Nat Heart and Lung Inst and Imperial Coll Sch of Med London, Univ of London (MD); *Career* trg posts: Guy's and associated hosps London 1990–93, Bart's 1993–94, Harefield Hosp Middx 1994–95, Imperial Coll London 1995–96, Royal Brompton Hosp 1995–98, Chelsea & Westminster Hosp 1996–98, St Mary's Hosp London 1998–2000; conslt cardiologist London Chest Hosp and Homerton Hosp 2000–; memb: RSM, BMA, Br Cardiac Soc, Br Cardiovascular Intervention Soc, Br Pacing and Electrophysiology Gp; memb Amnesty Int; FRCP 2003 (MRCP 1993); *Publications* author of numerous papers, book chapters, abstracts and presentations; *Recreations* tennis, cricket, skiing, watching films; *Style—* Dr Arvinder Kurbaan; ✉ St Bartholomew's Hospital, West Smithfield, London EC1A 7HE (tel 020 7487 9541, fax 020 7487 9549)

KUREISHI, Hanif; *b* 5 December 1954, Kent; *Educ* KCL; *Career* novelist and scriptwriter; writer in residence Royal Court Theatre 1982; Chevalier de l'Ordre des Arts et des Lettres (France); *Plays* Outskirts (George Devine Award 1981), Sleep With Me (1999), When Night Begins (2004); *Fiction* The Buddha of Suburbia (1990, Whitbread First Novel Award, also televised), The Black Album (1995), Love in a Blue Time (short stories, 1997), Intimacy (1998), Midnight All Day (short stories, 1999), Gabriel's Gift (2001), The Body (2002); *Non-Fiction* Dreaming and Scheming (essays, 2002), My Ear at His Heart (2004); *Screenplays* My Beautiful Laundrette (1984, Oscar nomination), Sammy and Rosie Get Laid (1988), London Kills Me (1991, also dir), My Son the Fanatic (1998), The Mother (2003), Venus (2006); *Style—* Hanif Kureishi, Esq; ✉ c/o Deborah Rogers, Rogers, Coleridge & White Ltd, 20 Powis Mews, London W11 1JN (tel 020 7221 3717, fax 020 7229 9084, e-mail hannahw@rcwlitagency.co.uk)

KURTZ, Prof Donna Carol; *Educ* Univ of Cincinnati (BA), Yale Univ (MA), Univ of Oxford (DPhil); *Career* Univ of Oxford: Beazley archivist Ashmolean Museum, prof of classical art, fell Wolfson Coll, memb Mgmnt Ctee Oxford Internet Inst; *Books* incl: The Iconography of the Athenian White-Ground Lekythos (1968), Greek Burial Customs (with John Boardman, 1971), Athenian White Lekythoi: Patterns and Painters (1975), The Man-Eating Horses of Diomedes in Poetry and Painting (1975), The Eye of Greece: Studies in the Art of Athens (ed with Brian Sparkes, 1982), Mr Hattatt's Painter (1982), The Berlin Painter (1983), Gorgo's Cup: An Essay on Connoisseurship (1983), Vases for the Dead: An Attic Selection 750–400 BC (1984), The Achilles Painter's Early White Lekythoi (1990), Studies in Greek Vases and their Paintings: An Introduction to Classical Archaeology (1992), The Reception of Classical Art in Britain: An Oxfird Story of Plaster Casts from the Antique (2000), Reception of Classical Art: An Introduction (ed, 2004); *Style—* Prof Donna C Kurtz; ✉ Wolfson College, Linton Road, Oxford OX2 6UD

KUSHNER, Her Hon Judge Lindsey Joy; QC (1992); da of Harry Kushner, of Manchester, and Rita, *née* Alexander; *b* 16 April 1952; *Educ* Manchester HS for Girls, Univ of Liverpool (LLB); *m* 15 Aug 1976, David Norman Kaye; 1 s (Alexander Lewis b 8 Sept 1979), 1 da (Tamara Ruth b 21 July 1981); *Career* called to the Bar 1974, pupilled to His Hon Judge Charles Bloom, QC, *qv*, recorder 1993–2000 (asst recorder 1989–93), circuit judge (Northern Circuit) 2000–; legal chm: Medical Appeal Tbnl 1989–2000, Disablement Appeal Tbnl 1992–99; former memb Ethnic Minorities Advsy Ctee Judicial Studies Bd; *Recreations* cooking, cinema; *Style—* Her Hon Judge Kushner, QC; ✉ Courts of Justice, Crown Square, Manchester M3 3PL

KUTAPAN, Nicola Annette; da of Peter Kutapan (d 1965), and Molly Grace, *née* Hawkins; *b* 21 April 1958; *Educ* Greycoat Hosp Sch; *Children* 1 s (b 1995); *Career* dir Seven Dials Monument Co 1986–; 300 Group (all-pty campaign for more women in Parliament and public life): chair 1992–94, treas 1994–95; head of admin CPSA 1992–95, chair Opportunity 2000 Women's Advsy Panel 1993; Lab Pty: Parly candidate Solihull 1992, vice-chair Holborn and St Pancras CLP, sec London Central Euroconstituency; London Borough of Camden: cncllr 1986–90, vice-chair Planning Ctee and chair Planning Sub-Ctee, vice-chair Employment Ctee, chair Public Control Sub-Ctee; dir Fitzrovia Trust 1989–92, govr St Joseph's Sch 1989–91; *Style—* Miss Nicola Kutapan; ✉ 11 Hunter House, King James Street, London SE1 0AG (tel 020 7928 6403)

KVERNDAL, Simon Richard; QC (2002); s of Ole Sigvard Kverndal (d 2003), of Colgates, Halstead, Kent, and Brenda, *née* Skinner; *b* 22 April 1958; *Educ* Haileybury, Sidney Sussex Coll Cambridge (MA); *m* 1997, Sophie Rowsell; *Career* called to the Bar Middle Temple 1982, practising barr in commercial and maritime law 1983–; Lloyd's (LOF) salvage arbitrator 2006–; Liveryman Worshipful Co of Shipwrights 1983 (memb Ct of Assts 1999); *Recreations* real tennis, rackets, squash, wine tasting, opera, the Church of England; *Clubs* Hawks' (Cambridge), Queen's, MCC, Garrick, Mjolnirs Rackets; *Style—* Simon Kverndal, Esq, QC; ✉ 17 Heathfield Terrace, London W4 4JE; Quadrant Chambers, 10 Fleet Street, London EC4Y 1AU (tel 020 7583 4444, fax 020 7583 5544, e-mail simon.kverndal@quadrantchambers.com)

KWEI-ARMAH, Kwame (né Ian Roberts); *b* 1967, Tottenham, London; *Educ* London Coll of Printing; *m* (m dis); 3 c; *Career* actor, playwright and singer; writer in residence Bristol Old Vic 1999–2001; *Theatre* as writer incl: Blues Brother, Soul Sister (also actor, Bristol Old Vic) 1999, Big Nose (also actor, Belgrade Coventry) 1999, A Bitter Herb (Bristol Old Vic) 2001 (Peggy Ramsay Award), Elmina's Kitchen (also actor, NT and Garrick Theatre) 2003 (Evening Standard Most Promising Playwright Award 2003, nominated Best New Play Laurence Olivier Awards 2003, nominated Best New Writer for screen adaptation BAFTA Awards), Fix Up (NT) 2004; *Television* incl: The Latchkey Children 1980, Casualty 1999–2004 (Favourite TV Actor Screen Nat Film and TV Awards 2003), Comic Relief Does Fame Academy (winner) 2003, Pride 2004; *Films* incl: Cutthroat Island 1995, My West 1998, The 3 Kings 2000; *Albums* Kwame 2003; *Style—* Kwame Kwei-Armah, Esq; ✉ c/o Lou Coulson Associates, 1st Floor, 37 Berwick Street, London W1F 8RS (tel 020 7734 9633, fax 020 7439 7569)

KYLE, James; CBE (1989); s of John Kyle (d 1978), and Dorothy Frances, *née* Skillen (d 1967); *b* 26 March 1925; *Educ* Ballymena Acad, Queen's Univ Belfast (MB BCh, MCh, DSc); *m* 31 July 1950, Dorothy Elizabeth, da of Alexander Galbraith (d 1945); 2 da (Frances b 1952, Maureen b 1956); *Career* lectr in surgery Univ of Liverpool 1957, sr lectr Univ of Aberdeen 1959, sr surgn Aberdeen Royal Infirmary; chm: Grampian Health Bd 1989–93, Raigmore Hosp NHS Tst Inverness 1993–97; chm: BMA Rep Body 1984–87, Scot Ctee for Hosp Med Servs 1977–81, Scot Jt Conslts Ctee 1984–89; memb: Exec Int Soc of Surgery 1971–88, Surgical Research Soc 1972–74, GMC 1979–94, Cons Med Soc 1988–92; patron Royal Scot Nat Orch; regnl rep War Memls Tst; Burgess of Guild of the City of Aberdeen; MInstD; FRCS 1954, FRCSI 1954, FRCSEd 1964, FRAS, FRPSL; *Books* Peptic Ulceration (1960), Pye's Surgical Handicraft (1962), Scientific Foundations of Surgery (1967), Crohn's Disease (1972); *Recreations* astronomy, amateur radio (callsign GM4CHX), philately; *Clubs* Royal Northern, University; *Style—* James Kyle, Esq, CBE; ✉ Grianan, 7 Fasaich, Strath, Gairloch, Ross-shire IV21 2DH (tel 01455 712398)

KYLE, Dr Peter McLeod; s of late Andrew Brown Kyle, of Ravens Court, Thorntonhall, and late Janet, *née* McLeod; *b* 19 August 1951; *Educ* Glasgow HS, Univ of Glasgow (MB ChB); *m* 25 March 1982, Valerie Anne, da of late James Steele, of Mairi Lodge, Hamilton; 1 s (Alasdair McLeod b 23 Jan 1983), 2 da (Catriona Jane b 20 Dec 1984, Gillian Fiona b 16 Feb 1989); *Career* clinical dir of ophthalmology Southern Gen Hosp Glasgow 1993–98 (conslt 1982), memb Med Appeal Tbnl 1985–, hon clinical sr lectr Univ of Glasgow 1985 (lectr in ophthalmology 1980–84), ophthalmology convenor RCPSGlas; memb Gen Optical Cncl; memb Trades Houses of Glasgow 1997–, Deacon Incorporation of Barbers of Glasgow 1998–99; FRCS (Glasgow and Edinburgh), FRCOphth; *Books* Current Ophthalmic Surgery (1990); *Clubs* Glasgow Art, Golf House (Elie); *Style—* Dr Peter Kyle; ✉ 36 Sutherland Avenue, Glasgow G41 4ES; The Stables, Earlsferry, Fife

KYNOCH, George Alexander Bryson; s of late Gordon Kynoch, and late Nesta Kynoch; *b* 7 October 1946; *Educ* Glenalmond Coll, Univ of Bristol (BSc (MechEng)); *m* 2 Sept 1971, Dr Rosslyn Margaret McDevitt (d 2002); 1 s, 1 da; *Career* plant engr ICI Silicones 1968–71; G & G Kynoch plc: joined 1971, fin dir 1975–77, jt md 1977–81, chief exec 1981–90, dir of restructured gp 1990–95; MP (Cons) Kincardine and Deeside 1992–97; PPS to: Alastair Goodlad as Min of State at FO 1992–94, Gillian Shephard as Sec of State for Educn 1994–95; Parly under-sec of state Scottish Office (min for industry and local govt) 1995–97; memb Scottish Affairs Select Ctee 1992–95; chm Scottish Woollen

Publicity Cncl 1983–90, pres Scottish Woollen Industry 1990–91; non-exec chm: Silvertech Int plc 1997–2000, London Marine Gp Ltd 1998–2004, Benson Gp Ltd 1998–2005, Muir Matheson Ltd 1998–, Jetcam Int Holdings Ltd 1999–2003, TEP Exchange Gp plc 2001–, RDF Gp plc (formerly Eurolink Managed Services) 2003–06, Toluna plc 2005–, OCZ Technology Gp Inc 2006–, Madwaves (UK) Ltd 2006–, Mercury Gp plc 2007–; non-exec dir: PSL Holdings Ltd 1998, Midmar Energy Ltd 1998–99, Premisys Technols plc (formerly WML Gp plc) 1998–2001, TECC-IS plc 2003–04, Talent Gp plc 2003–; memb Aberdeen and Dist Milk Mktg Bd 1988–92, chm Laurence J Smith Ltd 1989, dir Moray Badenoch and Strathspey Local Enterprise Co 1991–92; chm Moray Cons and Unionist Assoc 1990 (various offices 1980–92), vice-chm Northern Area Scottish Cons and Unionist Assoc 1991; *Recreations* golf; *Clubs* Carlton; *Style*— George Kynoch, Esq

KYTE, Peter Eric; QC (1996); s of Eric Frank Kyte (d 1980), and Cicely Evelyn Leslie, *née* Watts; *b* 8 May 1945; *Educ* Dragon Sch Oxford, Wellington, Trinity Hall Cambridge (MA Law); *m* 7 Oct 1969, Virginia Cameron, da of Athelstan Claud Muir Cornish-Bowden; 1 da (Atlanta Rose b 17 Feb 1975), 1 s (William Simon b 19 March 1980); *Career* mangr Charter Consolidated Ltd 1968–73, account exec Merrill Lynch New York 1973–74; called to the Bar Gray's Inn 1970, recorder 1991– (asst recorder 1988); memb Criminal Bar Assoc 1976; *Recreations* tennis, motorcycling, scuba diving, watching England perform on the sports field; *Clubs* Aula (Cambridge); *Style*— Peter Kyte, Esq, QC; ✉ Hollis/Whiteman Chambers, Queen Elizabeth Building, Temple, London EC4Y 9BS (tel 020 7583 5766, fax 020 7353 0339)

KYTE, Thomas Peter (Tom); *b* 4 June 1947; *m* 1970, Lynn Dora Harding; 2 da, 1 s; *Career* HM Inland Revenue 1963–65, investment commentator Financial Times 1970–77 (statistician 1966–70), writer Questor column Daily Telegraph 1977–86, City ed The Independent 1987–88 (dep City ed 1986–87), ptnr Brunswick Group Ltd 1988– (consulting ptnr 2001–); *Recreations* sports, literature, cooking; *Style*— Tom Kyte, Esq; ✉ Brunswick Group Ltd, 15–17 Lincoln's Inn Fields, London WC2A 3ED (tel 020 7404 5959, fax 020 7831 2823)

L

LA TROBE-BATEMAN, Richard George Saumarez; s of John Saumarez La Trobe-Bateman (d 1996), of Sark, CI, and Margaret Jane, *née* Schmid; *b* 17 October 1938; *Educ* Westminster, St Martin's Sch of Art, RCA (MDesRCA); *m* 26 April 1969, Mary Elizabeth, OBE (2001), da of Arthur Jolly, JP (d 1984), of Hove, E Sussex; 2 da (Emily b 1971, Alice b 1976), 1 s (Will b 1973); *Career* studied sculpture under Anthony Caro at St Martin's Sch of Art 1958–61, studied furniture under David Pye at RCA 1965–68; exhbns at UK Design Centre, Crafts Cncl, V&A, Br Craft Centre and Contemporary Applied Art and in Belgium, Holland, Denmark, Austria, France, USA and Japan; works in public collections incl: V&A, Crafts Cncl, Leeds City Art Collection, Tyne & Wear Art Collection (Shipley Art Gallery), Portsmouth Museum and Art Gallery, Craft Study Centre Bath, Contemporary Arts Soc, Cheltenham Art Gallery; public footbridges in Britain (Cumbria, Essex and Kent) incl bridge at Nat Pinetum Kent, Swing-Lift Bridge Quenington Glos 2002 (winner Wood Awards 2003), Parrett Bridge Somerset 2005–06; memb Crafts Cncl 1982–86 (work presented to HRH Prince of Wales by Craft Cncl 1984); prof of furniture San Diego State Univ 1986–87; *Clubs* Contemporary Applied Arts; *Style*— Richard La Trobe-Bateman, Esq; ✉ Elm House, Batcombe, Shepton Mallet, Somerset BA4 6AB (tel 01749 850442)

LAAJAVA, HE Jaakko Tapani; CMG (1995); s of Erkki Laajava (d 1986), and Aune, *née* Varis (d 1976); *b* 23 June 1947, Joensuu, Finland; *Educ* Univ of Stockholm (BA), Univ of Helsinki (MA); *m* 1972, Pirjoriitta, *née* Väyrynen; 2 da (Minna b 1974, Milla b 1978), 1 s (Mikko b 1977); *Career* Finnish diplomat; entered Finnish Foreign Miny as attaché 1972; second sec: Finnish Delgn to Conf on Security and Co-operation in Europe (CSCE) Geneva 1973–75, Warsaw 1975–77, Belgrade 1977–78; Foreign Miny Helsinki 1978–80, first sec and cnsllr Madrid 1980–82, head of arms control Helsinki 1982–85, fell Harvard Univ 1985–86, min-cnsllr Washington 1986–90, dep DG for political affairs and DG Helsinki 1990–96, ambass to Washington DC 1996–2001, under-sec Helsinki 2001–05, ambass to the Court of St James's 2005–; memb IISS; Freeman City of London 2006, Hon Liveryman Worshipful Co of Glass Sellers; Cdr First Class Order of Lion of Finland 2004; *Recreations* music, golf; *Clubs* Harvard Club of Finland, RAC, Travellers, Athenaeum; *Style*— HE Mr Jaakko Laajava, CMG; ✉ The Embassy of Finland, 38 Chesham Place, London SW1X 8HW (tel 020 7838 6200, fax 020 7838 9500)

LACE, Garry Marc; s of John Cresswell Lace (d 1989), and Carole Anne, *née* Harrison; *b* 8 May 1967; *Educ* Thomas Rotherham Sixth Form Coll, Univ of Manchester (BA); *m* 12 July 1997, Katherine; 1 s (Thomas Cresswell b 27 May 1998), 1 da (Eleanor Daisy b 27 April 2003); *Career* grad trainee Saatchi & Saatchi 1990, bd dir Euro RSCG 1995, TBWA: jt md 1999, ceo 2001; ceo Grey London 2002–04, ceo Lowe London 2005–; memb Cncl IPA 1999–; patron: Sparks, NCH; MInstD, FIPA 2002 (MIPA 1999); *Recreations* tennis, skiing, opera; *Clubs* Solus; *Style*— Garry Lace, Esq; ✉ Lowe, Bowater House, 68–114 Knightsbridge, London SW1X 7LT

LACEY, Prof (John) Hubert; s of Percy Hubert Lacey, of Leics, and Sheila Margaret, *née* Neal; *b* 4 November 1944; *Educ* Loughborough GS, Univ of St Andrews (MB ChB), Univ of London (MPhil), Univ of Dundee (MD), RCOG (DipObst); *m* 7 Feb 1976, Susan Millicent, da of late Richard England Liddiard, CBE, of Wimbledon; 1 da (Emma Louise Susan b 1978), 2 s (Ben William Hubert b 1979, Jonathan Rupert Neal b 1982); *Career* jr hosp appts Dundee, St Thomas' and St George's Hosps London 1969–78, prof Univ of London 1991– (sr lectr 1978–86, reader 1987–91); hon conslt psychiatrist: Middx Hosp 1978–80, St George's Hosp London 1980–; dir and conslt i/c Eating Disorders Service 1980–, head of psychiatry St George's Hosp Med Sch London 1987– (chm Dept of Psychiatry 1991–93); clinical dir: Pathfinder Hosp Tst 1993–2000, SW London St Georges NHS Tst 2000–; dir: Yorks Centre for Eating Disorders Leeds NHS Tst 2004–07, Peninsular Eating Disorders Unit Exeter and Devon NHS Tst, Newbridge Healthcare Systems 2007–; conslt and dir Capio Nightingale Hosp London 2007–, conslt and med advsr Priory Hospital Gp; non-exec dir Merton Sutton and Wandsworth HA 1994–96; pres Euro Cncl on Eating Disorders, patron Eating Disorders Assoc; past pres Int Coll of Psychosomatic Med, elector Ct of Electors RCPsych 2001– (memb Cncl, former chm gen psychiatry); NHS Modernisation Award 2003; Freeman: City of London 1986, Worshipful Co of Plaisterers 1986 (memb Ct of Assts 2007–); memb RSM, FRCPsych 1985 (MRCPsych 1974); *Books* Psychological Management of the Physically Ill (1989), Overcoming Anorexia (2007); *Recreations* reading, interior decoration, hill walking; *Clubs* Athenaeum; *Style*— Prof J Hubert Lacey; ✉ 5 Atherton Drive, Wimbledon, London SW19 5LB (tel 020 8947 5976, e-mail jhubertlacey@hotmail.com); Department of Psychiatry, Jenner Wing, St George's University of London, Tooting, London SW17 0RE (tel 020 8725 5528/5529, fax 020 8725 3350, e-mail hlacey@sghms.ac.uk); Eating Disorders Unit, Nightingale Hospital, 11–19 Lisson Grove, London NW1 6SH (tel 020 7563 6604); Eating Disorders Unit, Priory Hospital, Priory Lane, Roehampton, London SW15 5JJ (tel 020 8392 4227, fax 020 8392 4321, e-mail jhubertlacey@prioryhealthcare.com)

LACEY, Nicholas Stephen; s of John Stephen Lacey (d 2005), of Highgate, London, and Norma, *née* Hayward (d 1995); *b* 20 December 1943; *Educ* Univ Coll Sch, Emmanuel Coll Cambridge (MA), Architectural Assoc London (AADip); *m* 1, 1965 (m dis 1976), Nicola, da of Dr F A Mann (d 1991); 2 s (Joshua b 1968, William b 1973), 1 da (Olivia b 1970); m 2, 1981, Juliet, da of Dr Wallace Aykroyd, CBE (d 1979); 2 da (Laetitia b 1978, Theodora b 1980); *Career* ptnr: Nicholas Lacey & Assoc Architects 1971–83, Nicholas Lacey & Ptnrs Architects 1983–; dir ContainerSpace Ltd 2003; winner: Wallingford Competition 1972, Crown Reach 1977; jt winner Arunbridge 1977, prize winner Paris Opera House Competition 1983; *Recreations* music, theatre, sailing; *Clubs* Athenaeum, Royal Dorset Yacht; *Style*— Nicholas Lacey, Esq; ✉ Nicholas Lacey & Partners, Reeds Wharf, Mill Street, London SE1 2AX (tel 020 7231 5154, fax 020 7231 5633); home (tel 020 7237 6281)

LACEY, Prof Nicola Mary; da of John McAndrew (d 1995), and Gillian, *née* Wroth; *b* 3 February 1958; *Educ* Malvern Girls' Coll, UCL (LLB, Hurst prize, Maxwell law prize, Maxwell medal), UC Oxford (BCL); *m* 1991, David Soskice; *Career* lectr Faculty of Laws UCL 1981–84, fell and tutor in law New Coll Oxford 1984–95 (tutor for admissions 1988–91), CUF lectr Univ of Oxford 1984–95, prof of law Birkbeck Coll London 1995–97 (head Dept of Law 1996–97), prof of criminal law LSE 1998– (dir doctoral prog Law Dept 2000–02); visiting scholar Stanford Law Sch 1992, guest prof Law Faculty Humboldt Univ Berlin 1996, fell Wissenschaftskolleg zu Berlin 1999–2000, visitor Global Law Sch NY Univ 2001 and 2003, prof Programme in Ethics, Politics & Economics Yale Univ 2004; ANU: visiting prof Law Sch 1992, visiting fell Dir's Section Res Sch of Social Sciences 1995–96, adjunct prof Law Prog Res Sch of Social Sciences 1999–2001, adjunct prof Social and Political Theory Prog Res Sch of Social Sciences 2002–; Univ of Oxford: memb Working Pty on Sexual Harrassment 1988, memb Rules Ctee Panel Disciplinary Ct 1988–91, memb Gen Purposes Ctee Law Bd 1989–91, memb Proctors' Advsy Panel on Sexual Harrassment 1991–94, memb Grad Studies Ctee in Law 1993–95; articles co-ed Modern Law Review 2001–; assoc ed: Int Jl of the Sociology of Law 1988–91, Social and Legal Studies 1991–; memb Editorial Bd: Law and Philosophy series of monographs 1988–, New Community 1993–94, Clarendon Studies in Criminology 1994–95, Oxford Jl of Legal Studies 1994–95, Current Legal Problems 1994–, Policy Studies 1995–, Cambridge Studies in Law and Society 1996–, Economy and Society 1997–2001, Modern Law Review 1998–; memb: Advsy Gp on draft bill of rights for Inst of Public Policy Res (published 1991), Advsy Bd Law in Context series 1995–, Int Editorial Advsy Bd Buffalo Criminal Law Review 1996–; memb Criminal Justice Ctee Justice 1993–95, memb Ctee on Women's Imprisonment Prison Reform Tst 1998–2000; memb Planning Ctee 14th World Congress of the Int Assoc for Philosophy of Law and Social Philosophy Edinburgh 1988–89; tstee and memb Cncl Charter 88 1989–91; FBA 2001; *Publications* State Punishment: Political Principles and Community Values (1988), Reconstructing Criminal Law: Critical Perspectives on Crime and the Criminal Process (jtly, 1990, 3 edn 2003), The Politics of Community: A Feminist Analysis of the Liberal-Communitarian Debate (jtly, 1993), Criminal Justice: A Reader (ed, 1994), Unspeakable Subjects: Feminist Essays in Legal and Social Theory (1998); author of numerous articles in learned jls and contributions to books; *Style*— Prof Nicola Lacey, FBA; ✉ Law Department, London School of Economics and Political Science, Houghton Street, London WC2A 2AE (tel 020 7955 7254, fax 020 7955 7366, e-mail n.lacey@lse.ac.uk)

LACEY, Peter; s of Ernest Lacey, of Ipswich, Suffolk, and Elsie, *née* Bolt; *b* 11 August 1946; *Educ* St Joseph's Coll Ipswich, Balliol Coll Oxford (MA, DipEd); *m* 1969, Naomi Ruth; 3 s (Jonathan b 25 June 1975, Timothy b 10 Nov 1977, Jeremy b 9 Dec 1981); *Career* teacher The Leys Sch Cambridge 1972–92, headmaster The King's Sch Gloucester 1992–; memb HMC 1994; memb Area Child Protection Ctee; FRCA; *Recreations* sport, golf, wine writing; *Clubs* MCC; *Style*— Peter Lacey, Esq; ✉ King's School House, College Green, Gloucester GL1 2BG (tel 01452 524260); The King's School, Gloucester GL1 2BG (tel 01452 337337, fax 01452 337319, e-mail headmaster@thekingsschool.co.uk)

LACEY, Peter William; s of Maj Eric Oliver Lacey (d 1947), of Moseley, Birmingham, and Edna Joyce Annie (Joy), *née* Bennett (d 1986); *b* 13 November 1945; *Educ* The Old Hall Wellington, Solihull Sch; *m* 22 Nov 1969, Pamela Muriel, da of Neville Nicholl (d 1981), of Musbury, Devon; 3 s (David b 1972, Guy b 1975, Benjamin b 1980); *Career* chartered accountant; articled clerk Chas Richards & Co Birmingham 1964–68, Goodland Bull & Co Taunton, Robson Rhodes Taunton, Apsleys Wellington 1969–90; dir Community Cncl for Somerset 1990–2001, co sec Somerset Assoc of Local Cncls 1990–; dir Somerset TEC 1997–; memb County Ctee Rural Devpt Cmmn, former chm Somerset Customer Consultative Ctee Wessex Water, chm Somerset Assoc of Local Cncls 1986–89, memb Regnl Bd Wessex and chm Regnl Rivers Advsy Ctee NRA 1989–96, memb Regnl Environmental Protection Advsy Ctee 1996–97, chm N Wessex Area Environment Gp Environment Agency 1996–97; former chm West Buckland Parish Cncl; memb Cannington Coll Corp 1997–2000; FCA 1979 (ACA 1969); *Recreations* gardening; *Clubs* Old Silhillians; *Style*— Peter Lacey, Esq; ✉ The Old Forge, West Buckland, Wellington, Somerset TA21 9JS (tel 01823 662376); Somerset Association of Local Councils, Victoria House, Victoria Street, Taunton, Somerset (tel 01823 252515, fax 01823 289967, e-mail peter.lacey@somerset.gov.uk)

LACEY, Air Vice-Marshal Richard Howard; CBE (2004); s of Henry Howard Lacey (d 1996), of Croydon, Surrey, and Mary Elliott Lacey; *b* 11 December 1953; *Educ* Peterhouse Cambridge, RAF Coll Cranwell; *m* 30 May 1980, Cate; 1 da (Alexandra b 23 June 1981), 1 s (Gregory b 7 May 1984); *Career* advanced flying trg RAF Shawbury 1978 (qualified helicopter pilot), ops 72 and 28 Sqdns UK, NI and Hong Kong 1978–83, trg as helicopter flying instr 1984–85, Flight Cdr 72 Sqdn NI 1985–87, RAF Staff Coll 1989, Personal Staff Offr to COS RAF Strike Command then C-in-C Gulf War 1989–91, promoted Wing Cdr 1991, cmd 33 Sqdn RAF Odiham 1992–94, served Air Plans and Progs MOD 1994–97, promoted Gp Capt, asst dir Jt Warfare Commitments Area MOD, cmd RAF Benson 1997–99, RCDS 2000, promoted Air Cdre, dir NATO Policy MOD 2000–03, Cdr Br Forces Falkland Islands 2003–05, UK Nat Mil Rep SHAPE Belgium 2005–06, Cdr Br Forces Cyprus 2006–; *Recreations* industrial archaeology, photography, model engineering; *Clubs* RAF; *Style*— Air Vice-Marshal Richard Lacey, CBE; ✉ e-mail cateandrichlacey@gmail.com

LACEY, Prof Richard Westgarth; s of Jack Lacey, and Sybil Lacey; *b* 11 October 1940; *Educ* Felsted, Jesus Coll Cambridge (BA, MB BChir, MD, PhD), The London Hosp (DCH); *m* Fionna; 2 da (Miranda, Gemma); *Career* The London Hosp 1964–66, Bristol Royal Infirmary 1966–68, reader Univ of Bristol 1973–74 (lectr 1968–73), conslt in infectious diseases King's Lynn E Anglia RHA 1974–83, conslt in chemical pathology King's Lynn Queen Elizabeth Hosp 1975–83, prof of clinical microbiology Univ of Leeds 1983–98 (emeritus prof 1998–); numerous pubns in jls; memb Pathological Soc of GB, conslt to WHO; FRCPath; *Books* Poison on a Plate (1998), Hard to Swallow (1994), Mad Cow Disease (1994); *Recreations* gardening, antique restoration (intermittently); *Style*— Prof Richard Lacey; ✉ Carlton Manor, Carlton, Yeadon, Leeds LS19 7BE (tel 0113 2507696)

LACHELIN, Dr Gillian Claire Liborel; da of Pierre Joseph Augustin Lachelin (d 1977), and Joan Kathleen Moncaster, *née* Hilbery (d 1963); *b* 5 February 1940; *Educ* Princess Helena Coll Sch for Girls, Girton Coll Cambridge (MA, MB BChir), Univ of London (MD); *Career* registrar in obstetrics and gynaecology UCH London 1969–72, lectr and hon sr registrar Univ Coll Med Sch and UCH 1972–77, reader and hon conslt in obstetrics and gynaecology UCL Sch of Med 1977–2000, emeritus reader and conslt 2000–; memb Ctee on Safety of Meds Jan 1993–Dec 1995; advsr to Ctee on Safety and Medicines 1996–2001; memb: Blair Bell Res Soc 1975, Soc for Endocrinology 1979, Br Fertility Soc 1981, Soc for Gynecologic Investigation USA 1982; FRCOG 1982 (MRCOG 1969); *Books* Miscarriage: The Facts (1985, 2 edn 1996), Practical Gynaecology (with D T Y Liu, 1989), Clinical Reproductive Endocrinology (1991); *Recreations* archaeology, travel, photography, gardening; *Style*— Dr Gillian C L Lachelin; ✉ Obstetric Unit, 88–96 Chenies Mews, London WC1E 6HX (tel 020 7679 6056, fax 020 7383 7429)

LACHMANN, Prof Sir Peter Julius; kt (2002); s of Heinz Ulrich Lachmann (d 1971), of London, and Thea Emilie, *née* Heller (d 1978); *b* 23 December 1931; *Educ* Christ's Coll Finchley (state scholar, HSC), Trinity Coll Cambridge (scholar), UCH (Goldsmid scholar, MA, MB BChir, PhD, ScD (Cantab), Fellowes Silver medal, Tuke Silver medal, Liston Gold medal); *m* 7 July 1962, Sylvia Mary, da of Alan Stephenson; 2 s (Robin b 20 June 1965, Michael b 20 Aug 1970), 1 da (Helen b 16 Sept 1967); *Career* house surgn Newmarket General Hosp 1956–57, house physician Med Unit UCH and Rheumatism Unit Canadian Red Cross Meml Hosp 1957–58, John Lucas Walker student, res scholar and BMA science res scholar Trinity Coll Cambridge 1958–60, visiting investigator and asst physician Rockefeller Univ 1960–61; Dept of Pathology Univ of Cambridge: Arthritis and Rheumatism Cncl fell 1962–64, asst dir of res Immunology Div 1964–71; dir of med studies Christ's Coll Cambridge 1969–70 (fell 1962–71), prof of immunology RPMS Univ of London 1971–75; Univ of Cambridge: fell Christ's Coll 1976–, Sheila Joan Smith prof of immunology 1977–99, emeritus prof 1999–, hon dir MRC Molecular Immunopathology Unit 1980–97; conslt WHO 1968, hon conslt pathologist Hammersmith Hosp 1971–75, hon conslt clinical immunologist Cambridge HA 1976–99; visiting investigator: Basel Inst for Immunology 1971, Scripps Clinic and Res Fndn 1975, 1980, 1986 and 1989; SmithKline and French visiting prof Aust 1984, Mayerhoff visiting prof Dept of Chemical Immunology Weitzmann Inst 1989; visiting prof: Dept of Med RPMS 1986–90, College de France 1993; memb: Medical Advsy Ctee British Council 1983–97, Gene Therapy Advsy Ctee Dept of Health 1993–96, Int Bioethics Ctee UNESCO 1993–98, Scientific Advsy Bd SmithKline Beecham 1995–2000, Exec Ctee Inter-Acad Med Panel 2000–06; chm: Int Archive Advsy Gp DEFRA 2002–, Research Advsy Ctee CORE 2003–; non-exec dir Adprotech plc 1997–2000 (chm Scientific Advsy Bd 1997–2004); RCPath: memb Cncl 1982–85 and 1989–93, pres 1990–93; biological sec and vice-pres Royal Soc 1993–98; pres: Fedn of European Academies of Med 2004–05 (vice-pres 2002–03), Henry Kunkel Soc 2003–05; nat patron Lupus (UK) 1996–; tstee: Darwin Tst 1991–2001, Arthritis Research Campaign 2000–06; assoc ed Clinical and Experimental Immunology 1990–2001, pres Cncl and memb Bd of Dirs Int Jl of Experimental Pathology 1991–; memb Editorial Bd Gene Screen; memb: Br Soc for Immunology 1959 (memb Ctee 1966–69), Gold medallist European Complement Network 1997, Med and Europe Sr Prize Inst des Sciences de la Santé 2003; fell Royal Postgrad Med Sch 1995, fndr fell UCL Hosp 1999, fell Imperial Coll London 2001, hon fell Trinity Coll Cambridge 2007; Hon DSc Univ of Leicester 2005; American Assoc of Immunologists 1966, Norwegian Acad of Science and Letters 1991, Academia Europaea 1992; foreign fell Indian Nat Sci Acad 1996; hon memb: Societé Française d'Immunologie 1986, Assoc of Physicians 1999; hon fell Faculty of Pathology RCPI 1993; FRSM, FRS 1982, fndr fell and pres Acad of Med Sci 1998–2002; FRCP 1973, FRCPath 1981, FRS 1982, FMed Sci 1998; *Publications* Clinical Aspects of Immunology (co-ed, 5 edn 1993); author of numerous papers in professional jls on complement and immunopathology; *Clubs* Athenaeum; *Style*— Prof Sir Peter Lachmann, FRS, FMedSci; ✉ Conduit Head, 36 Conduit Head Road, Cambridge CB3 0EY (tel 01223 354433, fax 01233 300169); Department of Veterinary Medicine, Madingley Road, Cambridge CB3 0ES (tel 01223 766242, fax 01223 766244, e-mail pjl1000@cam.ac.uk)

LACK, Dr (John) Alastair; s of Prof Charles Hansard Lack (d 1991), of Salisbury, Wilts, and Janet Doreen, *née* Steele (d 2003); *b* 1 September 1942; *Educ* Westminster, UCH (MB BS), Imperial Coll London (DIC); *m* 2 July 1966, (Patricia) Margaret, da of Alec Reynolds; 2 da (Juliette b 14 March 1970, Katherine b 18 May 1973), 1 s (Christopher b 7 Jan 1975); *Career* asst prof of anaesthesia Stanford Calif 1971–73, conslt anaesthetist Salisbury Hospitals 1974–2003 (dir resource mgmnt 1990–95); memb Cncl Royal Coll of Anaesthetists 1997–2003; pres Soc for Computing & Technology in Anaesthesia 1995–98, pres World Fedn of Socs for Technology in Anaesthesia 1997–2000, chair European Soc Technology in Anaesthesia & Intensive Care 1992–96; chair Professional Standards Ctee RCA 2000–03; ret 2003; author of books and articles on the quality of medicine, computing and technology in anaesthesia and resource mgmnt; FRCA 1968; *Recreations* music, wine, golf, computing science, classic cars, gardening, genealogy; *Style*— Dr Alastair Lack; ✉ The River House, Coombe Bissett, Salisbury, Wiltshire SP5 4LX (tel 01722 718303, e-mail jal@lackfamily.net)

LACON, Sir Edmund Vere; 8 Bt (UK 1818), of Great Yarmouth, Norfolk; s of Sir George Vere Francis Lacon, 7 Bt (d 1980), by his 1 w Hilary; *b* 3 May 1936; *Educ* Woodbridge Sch Suffolk; *m* 1963, Gillian, o da of Jack Henry Middleditch, of Wrentham, Suffolk; 1 da (Anna Kathryn b 1965), 1 s (Edmund Richard Vere b 1967); *Heir* s, Edmund Lacon; *Clubs* Naval and Military; *Style*— Sir Edmund Lacon, Bt

LACY, Sir Patrick Bryan Finucane; 4 Bt (UK 1921), of Ampton, Suffolk; s of Sir Maurice John Pierce Lacy, 2 Bt (d 1965); suc bro, Sir Hugh Maurice Pierce Lacy, 3 Bt, 1998; *b* 18 April 1948; *Educ* Downside; *m* 1971, Phyllis Victoria, da of Edgar P H James; 1 s, 1 da; *Heir* s, Finian Lacy; *Style*— Sir Patrick Lacy, Bt

LADDIE, Prof Sir Hugh Ian Lang; kt (1995); s of Bertie Daniel Laddie, and Rachel, *née* Cohen; *b* 15 April 1946, London; *Educ* Aldenham Sch Elstree, St Catharine's Coll Cambridge; *m* 2 April 1970, Stecia Elizabeth, *née* Zamet; 2 s (James Matthew Lang b 25 Oct 1972, Gideon Mark Lang b 19 Nov 1973), 1 da (Joanna Ruth Lang b 3 Nov 1976); *Career* called to the Bar Middle Temple 1969 (bencher 1993); jr counsel to HM Treasy in patent matters 1981–86, QC 1986, judge of the High Court of Justice (Chancery Div) 1995–2005 (latterly sr judge of the Patents Court); conslt and head intellectual property arbitration and mediation practice Rouse & Co International 2005–; visiting professorial fell Queen Mary Univ of London 2005–, prof of intellectual property law UCL 2006–; chm Vet Code of Practice Ctee Nat Office of Animal Health 1991–92, dep chm Copyright Tbnl 1993–95; vice-pres Intellectual Property Inst London 2000–; dep ind chm London Theatre Cncl and Provincial Theatre Cncl 1993–95, memb Cncl Queen Mary Univ of London 2000–06 (vice-chm 2005–06); *Publications* The Modern Law of Copyright (1980, 3 edn 2000); *Recreations* fishing, family, music; *Style*— Prof Sir Hugh Laddie; ✉ Rouse & Co International, 11th Floor, Exchange Tower, 12 Harbour Exchange Square, London E14 9GE

LADDS, Rt Rev Robert Sidney; *see:* Whitby, Bishop of

LADENBURG, Michael John Carlisle; s of John Arthur George Ladenburg (d 1990), of W Sussex, and Yvonne Rachel Bankier, *née* Carlisle (d 1968); *b* 2 February 1945; *Educ* Charterhouse, ChCh Oxford (MA); *m* 1971, Susan Elizabeth, da of Dr George Denys Laing, of Surrey; 2 da (Harriet b 1975, Olivia b 1977), 1 s (William b 1980); *Career* merchant banker; dir: J Henry Schroder Wagg & Co Ltd 1979–88, Robert Fleming & Co Ltd 1988–91; head of corp fin Saudi International Bank 1992–98, chief exec Br Occupational Health Research Fndn 1998–2001, gp banking dir Leopold Joseph Holdings plc 2001–04, head of corp banking Nat Bank of Abu Dhabi 2004–; *Recreations* music, sailing, golf, skiing, reading, tennis; *Clubs* Hurlingham, Tandridge Golf; *Style*— Michael Ladenburg, Esq; ✉ National Bank of Abu Dhabi, PO Box 4, Abu Dhabi, UAE (tel 00 9 712 611 1119, fax 00 9 712 627 4903, e-mail michael.ladenburg@nbad.ae)

LADENIS, Nicholas Peter (Nico); s of Peter Ladenis (d 1960), of Kenya, and Constance, *née* Antoniadis (d 1976); *b* 22 April 1934; *Educ* Prince of Wales Sch Nairobi, Regent St Poly, LSE, Univ of Hull (BSc(Econ)); *m* 29 June 1963, Dinah-Jane, da of Theodore Zissu (d 1942); 2 da (Natasha Nicole b 29 April 1964, Isabella Therese b 28 June 1966); *Career* restaurateur; various appointments incl: Caltex Kenya, Ford Motor Company, Sunday Times; first entered catering 1971; fndr chef and patron: Chez Nico (with wife Dinah-Jane as ptnr) 1973–2003, Simply Nico 1989 (since sold), Nico Central 1992 (since sold), Chez Nico at Ninety Park Lane 1992–2003, Incognico 2000–03, DECA 2002–03; first distinction Good Food Guide 1976, Chef of the Year 1988, third Michelin Star 1995 (first 1981, second 1984), 5 out of 5 Good Food Guide 1996 and 1997, 10 out of 10 Good Food Guide 1998, 1999 and 2000; Hon DSc(Econ) Univ of Hull 1997; *Books* My Gastronomy (1987), Nico (1996); *Recreations* food, travelling, family; *Style*— Nico Ladenis, Esq

LADER, Prof Malcolm Harold; OBE (1996); s of Abe Lader (d 1979), of Liverpool, and Minnie, *née* Sholl (d 1998); *b* 27 February 1936; *Educ* Liverpool Inst HS, Univ of Liverpool (BSc, MB ChB, MD), Univ of London (PhD, DPM, DSc), Open Univ (LLB); *m* 16 April 1961, Susan Ruth, da of Louis Packer (d 1990), of Hendon, Middx; 3 da (Deborah b 1966, Vicki b 1969, Charlotte b 1972); *Career* memb external scientific staff MRC 1966–2001, conslt Bethlem Royal and Maudsley Hosp 1970–2001, prof of clinical psychopharmacology Univ of London 1978–2001 (emeritus prof 2001–); tstee Psychiatry Res Tst 2001–; memb Advsy Cncl Misuse of Drugs 1981–2000; hon fell American Coll of Psychiatrists 1994; FRCPsych 1971, FMedSci 1999; *Books* Psychiatry on Trial (1977), Dependence on Tranquillizers (1984), Biological Treatments in Psychiatry (1996); *Recreations* antiques, English watercolours; *Clubs* RSM; *Style*— Prof Malcolm Lader, OBE; ✉ 16 Kelsey Park Mansion, 78 Wickham Road, Beckenham, Kent BR3 6QH; Addiction Sciences Building, Inst of Psychiatry, De Crespigny Park, London SE5 8AF (tel 020 7848 0372, fax 020 8650 0366)

LADER, Philip; *Educ* Duke Univ Durham N Carolina (Phi Beta Kappa), Univ of Michigan (MA), Pembroke Coll Oxford, Harvard Law Sch (JD); *m* Linda LeSourd Lader; 2 da (Mary-Catherine, Whitaker); *Career* businessman and educator, diplomat of the USA; formerly: pres Sea Pines Company (developer/operator award-winning large-scale recreation communities), exec vice-pres US holding co of late Sir James Goldsmith, pres univs in S Carolina and Aust; one-time chm South Carolina Cncl on Small and Minority Business and fndr dir South Carolina Jobs-Economic Devpt Authy, candidate govr S Carolina 1986, subsequently joined Govt Serv, becoming White House dep chief of staff/asst to Pres Clinton and dep dir for mgmnt Office of Mgmnt and Budget, then administrator US Small Business Admin and memb Pres Clinton's Cabinet; American ambass to the Ct of St James's 1997–2001; non-exec chm WPP Gp plc 2001–, sr advsr Morgan Stanley Int 2001–; non-exec dir: WPP Gp, AES Corp, Marathon Oil Corp, RAND Corp, RUSAL Corp, Lloyd's Cncl; memb: Cncl on Foreign Rels, Chief Execs Orgn, American Assoc of Royal Acad of Arts Tst; tstee: Smithsonian Museum of American History, Salzburg Seminar, St Paul's Cathedral Fndn; former tstee: Br Museum, Windsor Leadership Tst; memb: Advsy Bd Br-American Business Cncl, The Prince's Tst; memb: Int Advsy Bd Columbia Univ, Bd of Visitors Harvard Law Sch, Bd of Visitors Yale Divinity Sch; formerly: pres Business Execs for Nat Security, memb Bds American Red Cross and Duke Univ's Public Policy Inst; fndr Renaissance Weekends (family retreats for innovative ldrs) 1981; hon fell: Pembroke Coll Oxford, London Business Sch, John Moore's Univ; recipient hon doctorates from 14 univs; *Style*— The Hon Philip Lader

LADYMAN, Dr Stephen John; MP; s of late Frank Ladyman, and late Winifred, *née* Lunt; *b* 6 November 1952; *Educ* Liverpool Poly (BSc), Univ of Strathclyde (PhD); *m* 1, 1975 (m dis 1994): m 2, 1995, Janet Ann; 1 da (Sam b 31 May 1994), 2 step s (Karl, Joseph), 1 step da (Jessica); *Career* research scientist MRC Radiobiology Unit Harwell 1979–84, head of computing Kennedy Inst of Rheumatology London 1984–90, head of computer support Pfizer Central Research Kent 1990–97; Thanet DC: cncllr 1995–99, chm Fin and Monitoring 1995–97; Parly candidate Wantage 1987, MP (Lab) Thanet S 1997–; PPS to Rt Hon Adam Ingram, MP, *qv* 2001–03, Parly under Sec Dept of Health 2003–05, min of state Dept for Tport 2005–; chm All-Pty Parly Gp on Autism 2000–03, memb Environment, Tport and Regions Select Ctee and Tport Sub-Ctee 1999–2001; memb: GMB, USDAW, Fabian Soc, CWS Retail Soc; *Recreations* watching soccer, occasional golf; *Style*— Dr Stephen Ladyman, MP; ✉ 28 Newington Road, Ramsgate, Kent CT12 6EE; House of Commons, London SW1A 0AA (tel 01843 852696, fax 01843 852689, e-mail stephenladymanmp@souththanetlabour.org.uk, website www.steveladyman.labour.co.uk)

LAGDEN, Ronald Gordon; s of Reginald Bousfield Lagden, OBE, MC (d 1944), and late Christine, *née* Haig; *b* 4 September 1927; *Educ* Marlborough, RMC Sandhurst (Sword of Honour), Harvard Univ, AMP; *m* 1951, Elizabeth Veronica, da of John Kenneth Mathews (d 1972); 2 s, 1 da; *Career* Lt Queen's Own Cameron Highlanders serv Italy; Maconochie Foods 1947–53, Bowater Scott Corp 1953–63, md Findus Ltd 1963–68, chm and md Quaker Oats Ltd 1968–71 (chm and pres (Europe) Quaker Oats Co 1971–85, non-exec dir 1985–93); dir Pagepine Ltd, non-exec dir SFS Gp Ltd; *Books* Principles and Practices of Management (jtly); *Recreations* golf, gardening, reading, bridge, family; *Clubs* R&A, Sunningdale Golf, Royal Golf de Belique, Worthing Golf, W Sussex Golf (pres 2005–), MCC; *Style*— Ronald Lagden, Esq; ✉ Spear Hill Cottage, Ashington, West Sussex RH20 3BA

LAIDLAW, Charles David Gray; s of George Gray Laidlaw, and Margaret Orr, *née* Crombie; *b* 23 January 1954; *Educ* Strathallan Sch, Univ of Edinburgh (LLB); *m* 27 June 1986, Lucy Elizabeth, *née* Brookes; 2 s (Robert Gray b 27 June 1989, Douglas John b 8 May 1991); *Career* political writer D C Thompson Group 1977–79 (reporter 1975–77), reporter Sunday Express 1980, def intelligence analyst MOD 1980–83, exec Good Relations 1983–85, mangr PA Consulting Group 1985–87, gp mangr Reginald Watts Associates 1987–88; dir: Burson-Marsteller and Burson-Marsteller Financial 1988–90, TMA Group 1990, Citigate Scotland 1991–96; chief exec Scottish and Westminster Communications 1992–96, head of media and public relations Scottish Rugby Union 1996–98, sec Club Scotland 1998–2001, md David Gray PR 2002; Freeman City of Glasgow (hereditary); memb Grand Antiquary Soc; MIPR 1986; *Recreations* rugby, running, writing; *Clubs* London Scottish, N Berwick RFC; *Style*— Charles Laidlaw, Esq; ✉ Gullane Business Centre, 12A Lammermuir Terrace, Gullane, East Lothian EH31 2HB (e-mail info@davidgraypr.com)

LAIDLAW, Sir Christophor Charles Fraser; kt (1982); s of late Hugh Alexander Lyon Laidlaw; *b* 9 August 1922; *Educ* Rugby, St John's Coll Cambridge; *m* 1952, Nina Mary Prichard; 1 s, 3 da; *Career* BP Co Ltd: dir of ops 1971–72, md 1972–81, dep chm 1980–81; chm BP Oil 1977–81; exec chm ICL plc 1981–84; dir: Commercial Union Assurance 1978–83, Barclays Bank Int 1980–87, Barclays Bank plc 1981–88, Amerada Hess Corporation 1983–94, Dalgety plc 1984–92, Redland plc 1984–92, Mercedes Benz (UK) 1985–93, Daimler-Benz (UK) 1994–99, Daimler Chrysler UK Holdings 1999–; chm Bridon plc 1985–90; pres German Chamber of Industry and Commerce in UK 1983–84, dir INSEAD 1987–94 (chm UK Advsy Bd 1987–93); memb Ct of Assts Worshipful Co of Tallow Chandlers (Master 1988–89); hon fell St John's Coll Cambridge 1996; Hon FRSA 1997; *Style*— Sir Christophor Laidlaw; ✉ 49 Chelsea Square, London SW3 6LH

LAIDLAW, Baron (Life Peer UK 2004), of Rothiemay in Banffshire; Irvine Alan Stewart Laidlaw; s of late Roy Alan Laidlaw, of Keith, Scotland; *Educ* Merchiston Castle Sch Edinburgh, Univ of Leeds (BA), Columbia Univ (MBA); *m* 1, 1965 (m dis 1985), Anne Marie, da of late Knut Bakkevig; m 2, 1987, Christine, da of late Francis O'Day; *Career* fndr and chm Inst for Int Research Ltd 1974–2005; memb Global Advsy Bd Wall St 2000–; fndr Laidlaw Youth Project 2003; Hon DL St Andrew's Univ 2002; *Clubs* Royal Thames Yacht, NY Yacht; *Style*— The Lord Laidlaw

LAIDLAW, James Robertson; s of James Laidlaw (d 1969), of Edinburgh, and Margaret, *née* Craig (d 1991); *b* 23 July 1935; *Educ* George Watson's Coll, Sch of Architecture

L

Edinburgh Coll of Art (Andrew Grant travelling scholar, DA); *m* 17 June 1961, Pauline, da of Walter Peckham, of Bury St Edmunds; 1 s (Quentin James b 29 July 1963), 1 da (Julia Margaret b 12 Nov 1966); *Career* architect; with A H Mottram Architects 1958–60; Bamber Gray Partnership (previously Fairbrother Hall & Hedges): joined 1960, ptnr 1965, sr ptnr 1975–93, conslt 1993–97; high-tech industrial, scientific and educnl buildings in UK; chm Caledon House Investments (Scotland) Ltd 1970–2004, dir Stafford Catering Services Ltd 1971–77; memb Cncl: RIAS 1979–86 (pres 1993–95), RIBA 1982–87 and 1993–95; memb: Bd Chord Housing Assoc 1969–74, Bd Fire Prevention Cncl Scot 1974–84, ARCUK 1987–94, Bd of Architectural Educn 1987–94, Bd of Dirs ABS 1997–2002; govr Edinburgh Coll of Art 1987–99 (also memb Scholarships and Awards Ctee 1989–99, memb Audit Ctee 1995–97, chm Estates Ctee 1998–2000); High Constable City of Edinburgh 1986; ARIBA 1958, FRIAS 1970 (ARIAS 1958, PRIAS 1993), FRSA 1988; *Recreations* swimming, sailing and sitting in the sun; *Clubs* New (Edinburgh), Westwoods (Edinburgh); *Style*— James R Laidlaw, PPRIAS, Chartered Architect; ✉ 34 Colinton Grove, Edinburgh EH14 1DB

LAIDLAW, Jonathan James; *b* 28 February 1960; *Educ* Univ of Hull (LLB); *Career* called to the Bar Inner Temple 1982; jr Treasy counsel Central Criminal Court 1995–2001, recorder 1998–, sr Treasy counsel 2001–; *Style*— Jonathan Laidlaw, Esq; ✉ 2 Hare Court, Temple, London EC4Y 7BH (tel 020 7353 5324)

LAIDLAW, (Henry) Renton; s of Henry Renton Laidlaw (d 1989), of Broughty Ferry, Dundee, and Margaret McBeath, *née* Raiker (d 2004); *b* 6 July 1939; *Educ* James Gillespie's Edinburgh, Daniel Stewart's Coll Edinburgh; *Career* golf corr Evening News Edinburgh 1957–68, news presenter Grampian TV Aberdeen 1968–70, news presenter and reporter BBC Scotland Edinburgh 1970–73, golf corr Evening Standard London 1973–98; golf presenter 1973–95: BBC Radio, ITV, TWI, Eurosport, Screensport; presenter BBC Sport on 2 1985–88; currently golf presenter: PGA European Tour Productions, The Golf Channel USA; Meml Tournament Journalism Award 2001, Lifetime Achievement Award in Journalism PGA of America 2003; Freeman Worshipful Co of Scriveners; *Books* Play Golf (with Peter Alliss), Tony Jacklin - The First 40 Years (with Tony Jacklin), Play Better Golf, Golfing Heroes, Ryder Cup 1985, 1987 and 1989, Captain at Kiawah (with Bernard Gallacher), Wentworth - 70 Years, The Golfers' Handbook (ed), The Sunningdale Centenary (ed); *Recreations* theatre-going, playing golf, travelling; *Clubs* Caledonian, Sunningdale Golf, Wentworth Golf, Royal Burgess Golf, Ballybunion Golf (hon), R&A; *Style*— Renton Laidlaw, Esq; ✉ c/o Kay Clarkson, 10 Buckingham Place, London SW1E 6HX (tel 020 7233 9055, fax 020 7233 9155)

LAIDLAW, (William) Samuel Hugh (Sam); s of Sir Christophor Laidlaw, *qv*, of Chelsea, London, and Nina Mary, *née* Prichard; *b* 3 January 1956, London; *Educ* Eton, Gonville & Caius Coll Cambridge (MA), INSEAD Fontainebleu (MBA); *m* 15 April 1989, Deborah Margaret, *née* Morris-Adams; 3 s (Arthur Charles Hugh b 12 May 1990, Humphrey Thomas Christopher b 27 Aug 1992, Fergus Richard Playfair b 1 Dec 1995), 1 da (Clementine Selina b 29 Sept 1998); *Career* admitted slr 1980; formerly: exec vice-pres Chevron Corporation, ceo Enterprise Oil, pres and chief operating offr Amerada Hess; ceo Centrica plc 2006–; non-exec dir Hanson plc; dir Business Cncl for Int Understanding; tstee RAFT; *Recreations* sailing; *Clubs* Royal Thames Yacht; *Style*— Sam Laidlaw, Esq; ✉ Centrica plc, Millstream, Maidenhead Road, Windsor, Berkshire SL4 5GD (tel 01753 494000, fax 01753 494955, e-mail sam.laidlaw@centrica.com)

LAINE, Dame Clementine Dinah (Cleo); (Lady Dankworth); DBE (1997, OBE 1979); da of Alexander Campbell, and Minnie, *née* Bullock; *b* 28 October 1927; *m* 1, 1947 (m dis 1958), George Langridge; 1 s; m 2, 1958, Sir John Philip William Dankworth, CBE, *qv*; 1 s, 1 da; *Career* vocalist; with The Dankworth Orchestra 1953–58; has appeared on television numerous times and made guest appearances with symphony orchestras in England and abroad; fndr Wavendon Stables Performing Arts Centre (with John Dankworth) 1970; jt 70 birthday tribute (with John Dankworth) BBC Proms 1997; Hon MA Open Univ 1975; Hon DMus: Berklee Coll of Music, Univ of York, Univ of Cambridge; Freeman Worshipful Co of Musicians 2002; *Theatre* incl: lead in Seven Deadly Sins (Edinburgh Festival and Sadler's Wells) 1961, A Time to Laugh, Hedda Gabler 1966, The Women of Troy 1967 (both Edinburgh Festival), lead in Showboat 1972; Colette 1980, The Mystery of Edwin Drood 1986 (winner of Theatre World Award, nominated for a Tony Award and Drama Desk Award), Into The Woods (US tour) 1989; *Film* Last of the Blonde Bombshells 2000; *Recordings* albums incl: Cleo Laine Jazz 1991, Nothing Without You 1992, Blue and Sentimental 1994, Solitude 1995, The Very Best of Cleo Laine 1997; Gold records incl: Feel the Warm, I'm a Song, Live at Melbourne; Platinum records incl: Best Friends, Sometimes When We Touch; *Awards* incl: Golden Feather Award LA Times 1973, Edison Award 1974, Variety Club 1977, Singer of the Year (TV Times) 1978, Grammy Award (best female jazz vocalist) 1985, Theatre World Award 1986, Presidential Lifetime Achievement Award (Nat Assoc of Recording Merchandisers (NARM)) 1990, Vocalist of the Year (British Jazz Awards) 1990, Lifetime Achievement Award (USA) 1991, Distinguished Artists award (Int Soc for the Performing Arts Fndn (ISPA)) 1999, Back Stage Bob Harrington Lifetime Achievement Award (with John Dankworth) 2001, BBC British Jazz Awards Lifetime Achievement Award (with John Dankworth) 2002; *Books* Cleo (autobiography, 1994), You Can Sing if You Want To (1997); *Style*— Dame Cleo Laine, DBE; ✉ The Old Rectory, Wavendon, Milton Keynes, Buckinghamshire MK17 8LU (tel 01908 583151, fax 01908 584414)

LAING, Christopher Maurice; OBE (2000), DL (Herts 2000); s of Sir Kirby Laing, JP, DL, FREng, and Joan Dorothy, *née* Bratt (d 1981); *b* 1 May 1948; *Educ* St Lawrence Coll Ramsgate, Herts Coll of Building St Albans; *m* 15 May 1971, Diana Christina, *née* Bartlett; 2 s, 2 da; *Career* with John Laing Services Ltd 1971–2002, dir John Laing Construction Ltd 1986–2001, md Grosvenor Laing Urban Enterprise Ltd 1987–97; dir: Crofton Country Centre Ltd 1989–98, Crofton Trust Ltd 1989–98, Br Sch of Osteopathy 1992–98, Tyringham Foundation Ltd 1993–, Chartered Inst of Building Benevolent Fund Ltd 1994–2002, Construction Industry Relief and Assistance for the Single Homeless Ltd 1996–2004, Laing Construction plc 1998–2001; non-exec dir: NPFA Services Ltd 1987–2000, Eskmuir Properties plc 1990–98 and 2000– (chm 2005–), Englemere Ltd 1992–; pres Chartered Inst of Building 1992–93 (vice-pres 1989–92); chm: Nat Playing Fields Assoc 1993–2000 (memb Cncl 1985–2000), Herts Groundwork Tst 1998–2006, N London Leadership Team 1993–95, Upper Lee Valley Partnership SRB Gp 1995–97; memb Cncl: Tidy Britain Gp 1993–2002, Euro Cncl for Building Professionals 1993–2002; tstee: Global Action Plan 2001–04, Groundwork UK 2003–04, Herts In Trust 2003–, Herts Community Fndn 2003–; High Sheriff Herts 2001–02; Lord's Taverners: pres St Albans Chapter 2000–, treas 2004–, tstee 2005–, chm of fndn 2006–; memb Ct of Assts Worshipful Co of Paviors 1993– (Liveryman 1971); *Recreations* golf, shooting, tennis, swimming; *Clubs* RAC, Brocket Hall Golf, Royal Cinque Ports Golf, NRA, North London Rifle; *Style*— Christopher Laing, Esq, OBE, DL; ✉ Abbotshay Farm, Ayot St Lawrence, Welwyn, Hertfordshire AL6 9BS

LAING, Eleanor; MP; da of Matthew Pritchard (d 1995), and Betsy, *née* McFarlane (d 1999); *Educ* Univ of Edinburgh (BA, LLB, first woman pres of union); *m* (m dis 2003), Alan Laing, s of Alan and Margaret Laing; 1 s (b 14 June 2001); *Career* lawyer Edinburgh, City of London and industry 1983–89; special advsr to Rt Hon John MacGregor, MP as: sec of state for educn 1989–90, Ldr of the House of Commons 1990–92, sec of state for Tport 1992–94; MP (Cons) Epping Forest 1997– (Parly candidate Paisley N 1987); oppn whip 1999, oppn front bench spokesman on constitutional affrs 2000–01, oppn frontbench spokesman on educn and skills 2001, shadow min for women and equality 2004–, shadow sec of state for Scotland 2005; *Recreations* music, theatre, golf; *Style*— Mrs Eleanor Laing, MP; ✉ House of Commons, London SW1A 0AA (tel 020 7219 3000)

LAING, Gerald; *see:* Ogilvie-Laing, Gerald

LAING, Jennifer Charlina Ellsworth; da of James Ellsworth Laing, FRCS (d 1983), of Salisbury, Wilts, and Mary McKane, *née* Taylor; *Educ* Godolphin, North Western Poly; *m* (m dis); *Career* bd dir: Saatchi & Saatchi Garland Compton 1977, Leo Burnett 1978; Saatchi & Saatchi Advertising: dep chm 1981–87, jt chm 1987–88; chm and chief exec Aspect Hill Holliday 1988, mgmnt buyout to form Laing Henry Limited 1990–95 (merged with Saatchi & Saatchi Advertising 1995), chairman Saatchi & Saatchi Advertising (London) 1995–96, memb Exec Bd Saatchi & Saatchi Advertising Worldwide 1996–2000, chief exec N American ops Saatchi & Saatchi (New York) 1996–2000; assoc dean of external rels London Business Sch 2002–; non-exec dir: Remploy Ltd, Great Ormond Street Hosp for Children NHS Trust, Hudson Highland Gp Inc 2003–, InterContinental Hotels Gp plc 2005–; dir London First; fell Mktg Soc, FIPA; *Recreations* racing, ballet, opera; *Style*— Miss Jennifer Laing

LAING, Sir (John) Martin Kirby; kt (1997), CBE (1991), DL (Herts 1987); s of Sir (William) Kirby Laing, and Joan Dorothy, *née* Bratt (d 1981); *b* 18 January 1942; *Educ* St Lawrence Coll Ramsgate, Emmanuel Coll Cambridge (MA); *m* 6 Nov 1965, Stephanie Stearn, da of Leslie Worsdell; 1 s, 1 da; *Career* John Laing plc: joined gp 1966, dir 1980, chm 1985–2002, non-exec dir 2002–04, hon pres 2004–; memb Bd Parsons Brinckerhoff Inc 2002, non-exec dir Eskhuir Properties Ltd 2002, memb Corp Finance Advsy Bd PricewaterhouseCoopers 2002; chm: Nat Contractors Gp of Building Employers' Fedn 1987, Br Urban Devpt 1988–90, CBI Overseas Ctee 1989–96, Br Overseas Trade Bd 1995–99, Construction Industry Employers Cncl 1995–2000; pres Construction Confederation 1997–2000; vice-chm Br Trade Int 1999; chm Worldwide Fund for Nature (WWF) UK 1990–97 (tstee 1988–97, now tstee emeritus), memb Bd WWF Int 1990–97; memb: Ctee for Middle E Trade 1982–86, UK Advsy Ctee Br American C of C 1985–2002, Cncl CBI 1986–2002, Cncl World Economic Forum 1986–2000, Business in the Community 1986–2002, Archbishops' Cncl Church Urban Fund 1987–94, Ct Univ of London 1987–95, Home Office Parole Review Ctee 1987–88, UK-Japan 2001 Gp 1988–2002, World Business Cncl for Sustainable Devpt 1991–, Cncl United World Coll of the Atlantic 1996, Cncl BESO 1999; dir: Herts Groundwork Tst 1986–91, City of London Sinfonia 1988–95; tstee National Energy Fndn 1988–99, govr St Lawrence Coll Ramsgate 1988–95, govr NIESR 1999–; Hon DSc: City Univ 1996, Univ of Birmingham 2003; Hon DEng Univ of W England 1997; Master Worshipful Co of Paviors 1995–96 (Freeman 1964, Upper Warden 1994, Master 1995); FRICS 1984, FIEx 1987, FICE 1993, FCIOB 1995; *Recreations* gardening, music, travel, the environment; *Style*— Sir Martin Laing, CBE, DL; ✉ John Laing plc, Page Street, London NW7 2ER (tel 020 8959 3636, fax 020 8906 5297)

LAING, Sir (John) Maurice; kt (1965); s of Sir John William Laing, CBE (d 1978), of Mill Hill, London, and Beatrice, *née* Harland (d 1972); *b* 1 February 1918; *Educ* St Lawrence Coll Ramsgate; *m* 20 March 1940, Hilda Violet, da of William Tom Steeper Richards (d 1946), of Ramsgate; 1 s (John Hedley b 1959); *Career* WWII RAFVR 1941–45 (seconded Glider Pilot Regt for Rhine crossing 1945); dir: John Laing plc 1939–87 (jt md 1947–54, md 1954–76, chm 1976–82), Bank of England 1963–80; pres: Br Employers' Confedn 1964–65, CBI 1965–66 (first pres), Export Gp for the Constructional Industries 1976–80, Fedn of Civil Engrg Contractors 1977–80, RYA 1983–87; memb: Export Guarantees Advsy Cncl 1959–63, Econ Planning Bd 1961, NEDC 1962–66, NIESR 1964–82, Admin Staff Coll 1965–70; pres London Bible College 1993–99; tstee RYS 1995–; adm Royal Ocean Racing Club 1976–82, adm Island Sailing Club 1997–2000; Insignia Award CGLI 1978; Hon LLD Strathclyde 1967, Hon DSc Univ of Exeter 1996; FCIOB 1981, Hon FCGI; *Recreations* sailing, swimming; *Clubs* Royal Yacht Sqdn, Royal Ocean Racing; *Style*— Sir Maurice Laing; ✉ Laing Family Trusts, 33 Bunns Lane, Mill Hill, London NW7 2DX (tel 020 8238 8890)

LAING, HE (John) Stuart; s of late Dr Denys Laing, and Dr Judy Laing, *née* Dods; *b* 22 July 1948; *Educ* Rugby, CCC Cambridge; *m* 12 Aug 1972, Sibella, da of Sir Maurice Dorman, GCMG, GCVO, of West Overton, Wiltshire; 1 s (James b 1974), 2 da (Catriona b 1979, Hannah b 1985); *Career* diplomat; entered HM Dip Serv 1971, FCO 1971–72, MECAS Lebanon 1972–73, Jeddah 1973–75, UK Perm Representation to EC 1975–78, FCO 1978–83, Cairo 1983–87, FCO 1987–89, Prague 1989–92, Riyadh 1992–95, head Know How Fund for Central Europe (FCO and later DFID) 1995–98, high cmmr to Brunei 1998–2002, ambass to Oman 2002–05, ambass to Kuwait 2005–; *Recreations* music, hill walking; *Clubs* Athenaeum; *Style*— HE Mr Stuart Laing; ✉ c/o Foreign & Commonwealth Office (Kuwait), King Charles Street, London SW1A 2AH

LAING, Susan Anne (Sue); da of Angus Murray Laing (d 1984), and Anne Catherine, *née* Wilson-Walker; *b* 6 March 1954; *Educ* Wycombe Abbey, St Hugh's Coll Oxford; *m* 17 March 1984, Wolfgang Bauer; 2 s (Georg b 11 Sept 1985, Angus b 31 Oct 1987), 1 da (Ruth b 7 Dec 1990); *Career* admitted slr 1978; Boodle Hatfield: asst slr 1978–81, ptnr 1981–, head Tax and Fin Planning Dept 2001–; memb: Law Soc, Soc of Tst & Estate Practitioners; *Recreations* playing piano, sailing, walking; *Style*— Miss Sue Laing

LAING OF DUNPHAIL, Baron (Life Peer UK 1991), of Dunphail in the District of Moray; Sir Hector Laing; kt (1978); s of Hector Laing, of Edinburgh; *b* 12 May 1923; *Educ* Loretto, Jesus Coll Cambridge; *m* 1950, Marian Clare, da of Maj-Gen Sir John Emilius Laurie, 6 Bt, CBE, DSO (d 1983); 3 s (Hon Mark Hector b 1951, Hon Robert John b 1953, Hon Anthony Rupert b 1955); *Career* WWII served Scots Gds 1942–47 (despatches 1944), demobbed Capt; joined McVitie & Price 1947 (chm 1963), dir United Biscuits 1953 (md 1964, chm United Biscuits (Holdings) plc 1972–90); chm: Food and Drink Industries Cncl 1977–79, Scottish Business in the Community 1982–90, City and Industrial Liaison Cncl 1985–90, Business in the Community 1987–91; dir: Bank of England 1973–91, Exxon Corp Inc 1984–94, Hakluyt Fndn; pres: Goodwill 1983–92, The Weston Spirit 1989–93; treas Cons Pty 1988–93, jt chm The Per Cent Club 1986–90, chm the tstees The Lambeth Fund 1983–1995, govr Wycombe Abbey Sch 1981–94, pres Trident 1992–94; Hon DUniv: Univ of Stirling, Heriot-Watt Univ, FRSE 1989; *Recreations* gardening, walking; *Clubs* White's; *Style*— The Lord Laing of Dunphail, FRSE; ✉ High Meadows, Windsor Road, Gerrards Cross, Buckinghamshire SL9 8ST

LAIRD, Baron (Life Peer UK 1999), of Artigarvan in the County of Tyrone John Dunn; s of Dr Norman Davidson Laird, OBE, JP, MP (d 1970), of Belfast, and Margaret, *née* Dunn (d 1983); *b* 23 April 1944; *Educ* Royal Belfast Academical Instn; *m* 24 April 1971, Caroline Ethel, da of William John Ferguson, of Dromore, Derrygonnelly, Co Fermanagh; 1 da (Alison Jane b 24 March 1976), 1 s ((John) David b 18 Oct 1977); *Career* Belfast Saving Bank: bank official 1963–67, bank inspr 1967–68, computer programmer 1968–73; memb (UU): St Anne's Div Belfast NI House of Commons 1970–73, W Belfast NI Assembly 1973–75, NI Convention 1975–76; hon treas Ulster Unionist Pty 1974–76; chm John Laird Public Relations 1976–2001; chm NI Branch Inst of PR 1989–92, visiting prof of PR Univ of Ulster 1993–; pres NI European Network 2002–; chm Ulster Scots Agency 1999–2004; FCIPR 1991; *Videos* Trolleybus Days in Belfast (1992), Swansong of Steam in Ulster (1993), Waterloo Sunset (1994), Rails on the Isle of Wight (1994), The Twilight of Steam in Ulster (1994); *Recreations* transport, travel, cricket, history; *Style*— The Rt Hon Lord Laird; ✉ House of Lords, London SW1A 0PW

LAIRD, Robert Edward; s of Robert Laird (d 1975), of Seaford, E Sussex, and Esther Margaret, *née* Stoney (d 1976); *b* 25 December 1940; *Educ* Aldenham, Harvard Univ; *m* 8 Aug 1964, Mary Theresa, da of Martin Cooke (d 1969), of Galway, Ireland; 2 s (Robert

Richard Martin b 1964, Julian Alexander b 1968), 1 da (Caroline b 1971); *Career* various appts Unilever Ltd 1959–76, dir Carnation Foods 1977–80, md Vandemoortele 1980–86, chm Polar Entertainment Gp 1986–88, dir Keith Butters Ltd 1988–89, head of mktg Tate & Lyle Sugars 1989–96; behavioural conslt 1996–; memb Sugar Bureau Ctee 1991–96; Advtg Assoc: memb Int Working Pty 1992–95, chm Food Advtg Ctee 1992–96 (memb 1991), chm Public Affrs Prog Gp 1993–95, memb Exec Ctee 1995–96; memb Cncl Coronary Prevention Gp; memb: Astrological Lodge of London 1999–, Astrological Soc of GB 2000–, Co Donegal Historical Soc 2003–; Freeman: City of London 1984, Worshipful Co of Upholders 1984; MInstM 1978, FIMgt 1980, MInstD 1982; *Recreations* golf, jogging, reading, genealogy, horse racing, astrology; *Clubs* Carlton, Old Aldenhamians, Harvard Business Sch Club of London, The Sportsman; *Style—* R E Laird, Esq; ✉ Suite 262, 22 Notting Hill Gate, London W11 3JE (tel 07973 262012, e-mail lboblaird@aol.com)

LAIT, Jacqui; MP; da of late Graham Lait, and late Margaret Lait; *b* 16 December 1947; *Educ* Paisley GS, Univ of Strathclyde; *m* 1 June 1974, Peter Jones; *Career* PR exec Jute Industries Ltd 1968–70, with Visnews Ltd 1970–74, Govt Info Serv 1974–79, Parly advsr Chemical Industries Assoc 1980–84, independent Parly conslt 1984–92; MP (Cons): Hastings and Rye 1992–97, Beckenham (by-election) 1997–; former PPS to Sec of State for Wales, asst Govt whip (first female Tory whip) 1996–97, whip 1999–2000, Cons spokesman on pensions 2000–01, shadow sec of state for Scot 2001–03 shadow home affrs min 2003–05, shadow min for London 2005–; chm: City and E London Family Health Servs Authy 1987–91, Br Section Euro Union of Women 1990–92; *Style—* Mrs Jacqui Lait, MP; ✉ House of Commons, London SW1A 0AA

LAITY, Mark Franklyn; s of Frank Laity, of Cornwall, and Pamela, *née* Dunn; *b* 18 December 1955; *Educ* Redruth County GS, Univ of York (MA); *m* 6 Oct 1990, Sarah Lisa, da of Edward Thomas Parker-Gomm; *Career* trainee and reporter Western Mail 1978–81, news prodr BBC Radio Wales 1981–83; prodr BBC Radio 4: Today 1983–86, Analysis 1986–88; dep ed The World This Weekend Radio 4 1988–89, defence corr BBC 1989–2000; NATO: dep spokesman and special advsr to Sec Gen 2000–03, special advsr on strategic communications to Supreme Allied Cdr Europe (SACEUR) 2004–05, chief of public information Supreme HQ Allied Powers Europe (SHAPE) 2005–06, NATO spokesman Kabul 2006–07, chief of strategic communications SHAPE 2007–; *Recreations* sailing, reading military and maritime history literature; *Clubs* RAF, Thames Sailing; *Style—* Mark Laity, Esq; ✉ 35 Cherry Orchard Road, West Molesey, Surrey KT8 1QZ (tel 00 32 65 444513, fax 0871 247 0962, e-mail markflaity@hotmail.com or mark.laity@shape.nato.int)

LAKE, Sir (Atwell) Graham; 10 Bt (GB 1711), of Edmonton, Middx; s of Capt Sir Atwell Henry Lake, 9 Bt, CB, OBE, RN (d 1972); *b* 6 October 1923; *Educ* Eton; *m* 1983, Mrs Katharine Margaret Lister, da of late D W Last; *Heir* bro, Edward Lake; *Career* serv in Gilbert & Ellice Mil Forces 1944–45, Col Admin Serv 1945–55, sec to Govt of Tonga 1950–53, Br High Cmmn New Delhi 1966–68, FCO 1969–72; sr tech advsr MOD to 1983, ret; hon sec Abbeyfield Epping Soc 1987–96, chm 1996–97; *Recreations* bridge, chess, landscape gardening; *Clubs* Lansdowne; *Style—* Sir Graham Lake, Bt; ✉ 9 Bay Tree Close, Iffley, Oxford OX4 4DT

LAKE, Dr Lionel Malcolm; s of Colin Frank Lake (d 1962), of Brockworth, Glos, and Marie Moss, *née* Gay (d 2001), of Harrow, Middx; *b* 5 July 1934; *Educ* Acton Tech Sch, Acton Tech Coll, Chelsea Poly, Birkbeck Coll London (BSc Geology (pt/t)), Imperial Coll London (MSc(Eng), DIC), Univ of Surrey (PhD (pt/t)); *m* 2, 1986, Pamela Margaret, *née* Howe; 2 s (Nicholas Lionel b 1988, Alexander Henry b 1990); 2 da by previous m (Kathryn Maria b 1958, Heather Jane b 1963); *Career* Nat Serv cmmnd 60 HAA Regt RA 1953–55; soil mechanics and foundations technician/engr Ground Explorations Ltd 1955–63, dep chief civil engr Le Grand Sutcliffe & Gell Ltd 1967–71 (geotechnical engr 1963–66), chief engr Soil Mechanics Ltd (John Mowlem & Co) 1971–73; Mott MacDonald (formerly Mott, Hay & Anderson): divnl head 1973–75, assoc dir 1975–77, md Fndn & Geotechnical Div 1977–87, md MOTT YARD Ltd 1987–94, Main Bd dir 1992–94, conslt 1994–2002, now ret; major projects with Mott MacDonald: Tyne & Wear Metro, Channel Tunnel 1973–76, 1978–79 and 1986–94, Lantau Suspension Bridge and New Airport Hong Kong; conslt Environmental Servs Gp John Mowlem & Co 1995–; visiting prof in geotechnical engrg Univ of Newcastle upon Tyne 1987–90, external examiner (postgrad) Dept of Engrg, Geology & Geotechnics Imperial Coll London 1987–91, Royal Acad of Engrg visiting prof in civil engrg design Univ of Brighton 1993–2002; memb Nominations & Audit Ctee Engrg Cncl (former memb Senate), memb Cncl Fndn for Sci and Technol; former memb Environmental and Civil Engrg Ctee SERC, fndr memb and former Ctee memb Assoc of Geotechnical Specialists, former memb Advsy Panel Geotechnique and CIRIA Advsy Ctee on Earthworks and Foundations; govr Valley End CE Sch 2000–; author of 29 published papers in public domain and numerous papers and reports with restricted access, numerous lectures to univs, colls, instns and socs; memb: Société des Engenieurs et Scientifiques de France, British Geotechnical Soc, Int Soc of Rock Mechanics, Br Ground Freezing Soc; MACE, MIMM 1966, fell Geological Soc 1966, CEng 1971, FICE 1991 (MICE 1971); *Recreations* sailing, modelling, music, walking, badminton, rugby spectator; *Clubs* Cruising Assoc, Royal Yachting Assoc, Hawley Lake Sailing; *Style—* Dr Lionel Lake; ✉ Arden, Snows Ride, Windlesham, Surrey GU20 6PE (tel 01276 471672, fax 01276 471672)

LAKE, (Charles) Michael; CBE (1996); s of Stanley Giddy, and late Beryl, *née* Heath; step s of late Percival Redvers Lake; *b* 17 May 1946; *Educ* Humphry Davy GS Penzance, RMA Sandhurst; *m* 1970, Christine, *née* Warner; 3 da (Catherine b 26 Jan 1972, Anna b 25 Feb 1974, Victoria b 25 Oct 1978); *Career* cmmnd RCT 1965, various regtl appts in Germany, Hong Kong, NI and Oman 1965–77, attached Cmdt-Gen RM 1977–78, directing staff Staff Coll 1982–83, Cmd 1st Div Tport Regt 1983–86, Cdr Tport HQ British Forces Riyadh Gulf War 1990–91, Regtl Col Royal Logistic Corps 1992–96, ret 1997; DG Help the Aged 1996–; memb: Bd HelpAge Int 1996–2004, Cncl Occupational Pensions Advsy Serv 1997–2001, Benevolent and Strategy Ctee Royal Br Legion 1997–2005, Bd Network Housing Assoc 1999–2001, Cncl Disasters Emergency Ctee 1999–, Cncl Oxford Inst of Ageing 2000, Advsy Bd Oxford Centre for Population Ageing Univ of Oxford 2000–; lay memb Lord Chllr's Advsy Ctee on Conscientious Objectors 2002; vice-chair Air Ambulance Fndn (AAF) 2003–04, chm Br Gas Energy Tst 2004–; tstee: Disasters Emergency Ctee 1999–, Pensions Policy Inst 2001–; Chelsea Arts Club: dir and memb Bd 1997, currently chm Mgmnt Bd; Freeman City of London 1995, Liveryman Worshipful Co of Carmen 1995; FILog 1995; *Recreations* all sports, avid golfer, declining cricketer, rugby, post impressionist art; *Clubs* Sloane, Chelsea Arts, Fadeaways, Penguin Int Rugby, West Cornwall Golf, North Hants Golf, MCC; *Style—* Michael Lake, Esq, CBE; ✉ Help The Aged, 207–221 Pentonville Road, London N1 9UZ (tel 020 7278 1114, fax 020 7239 1809)

LAKE, Richard Lawrence Geoffrey; s of Albert Lake (d 1968), and Elsie Lake (d 1995); *b* 11 November 1939; *m* 17 Oct 1964, Sheila June, da of Charles Douglas Marsh; 2 da (Amanda b 18 April 1967, Katharina b 1 May 1980), 1 s (Martyn b 24 April 1985); *Career* chartist Laurie Milbank 1969–72; ptnr: Zorn and Leigh-Hunt 1972–76, Grieveson Grant 1976–84, Raphael Zorn 1984–86; dir Swiss Bank Corp 1986–89, chm World Stockmarket Analysis 1989–90, dir Hoare Govett Securities 1991–92, dir and head of technical analysis SBC Warburg 1992–97, dir and head of institutional sales Brewin Dolphin 1997–; deacon Duke St Baptist Church Richmond; memb: Securities Inst, Inst of Investment Mgmnt and Research; fell Soc of Technical Analysts; *Recreations* family life, music and walking; *Style—* Richard Lake; ✉ 285 Petersham Road, Petersham, Richmond, Surrey TW10 7DA (tel 020 8940 3795); Brewin Dolphin, 12 Smithfield Street, London EC1A 9BD (tel 020 7246 1137, e-mail richard.lake@brewin.co.uk)

LAKE, Tony; QPM; *Educ* Univ of Cambridge (MA); *Career* joined Met Police 1972 (latterly Chief Inspr New Scotland Yard), with West Yorkshire Police 1992–94, Asst Chief Constable then Actg Dep Chief Constable Sussex Police 1994–2000, Dep Chief Constable Br Transport Police 2000–03, Chief Constable Lincolnshire Police 2003–; chair: ACPO Forensic Science Portfolio, Nat DNA Database Strategy Bd; *Style—* Tony Lake, Esq, QPM; ✉ Lincolnshire Police Headquarters, PO Box 999, Lincoln LN5 7PH

LAKER, Dr Michael Francis; s of Sqdn Ldr Walter John Laker (d 2001), of Ledbury, and Joyce, *née* Ashill; *b* 9 June 1945; *Educ* Newport HS, Univ of London (MD, BS, Dip BioChemistry); *m* 13 Dec 1969, Alison Jean, da of Thomas Borland (d 1986), of Tunbridge Wells; 2 da (Hannah b 1974, Bethan b 1977), 2 s (Christopher b 1981, Jonathan b 1983); *Career* lectr in chemical pathology and metabolic disorders St Thomas' Hosp Med Sch 1973–80, res fell Dept of Med Univ of Calif San Diego 1979–80, sr lectr in clinical biochemistry and metabolic med Univ of Newcastle upon Tyne and conslt chemical pathologist Newcastle HA 1980–89, reader in clinical biochemistry and metabolic med Univ of Newcastle upon Tyne 1989–2006 (sub dean for Admissions The Med Sch 1990–98), conslt in clinical biochemistry Royal Victoria Infirmary and Associated Hosps NHS Tst 1989–2006, med dir Newcastle upon Tyne Hosps NHS Trust 1998–2006, med advsr N E Stretegic Health Authy 2006–; memb Ctee Br Hyperlipidaemia Assoc; FRCPath 1988; *Books* Short Cases in Clinical Biochemistry (1984), Cholesterol Lowering Trials - Advice for the British Physicians (1993), Clinical Biochemistry for Medical Students (1995), Multiple Choice Questions in Clinical Pathology (1995), Understanding Cholesterol (2003); *Recreations* music, computing, gardening; *Style—* Dr Michael Laker; ✉ 9 Campus Martius, Heddon-on-the-Wall, Northumberland NE15 0BP (e-mail mike.laker@northeast.nhs.uk)

LAKEY, Prof John Richard Angwin; s of late William Richard Lakey, and late Edith; *b* 28 June 1929; *Educ* Morley GS, Univ of Sheffield (BSc, PhD); *m* 22 Dec 1955, Dr Pamela Janet Lakey, JP, da of late Eric Clifford Lancey; 3 da (Joanna Margaret, Philippa Mary (Mrs Lewry), Nicola Janet (Dr King)); *Career* res posts Simon Carves Ltd, secondment to AERE Harwell and GEC 1953–60; RNC Greenwich: asst prof 1960–80, prof of nuclear sci and technol 1980–89, dean 1984–86 and 1988–89; reactor shielding conslt DG Ships 1967–89, radiation conslt WHO 1973–74, hon visiting lectr Harvard Univ 1984–2004, hon visiting prof Univ of Surrey 1988–95, radiation protection conslt John Lakey Assocs 1989–2000, visiting prof in radiological protection Univ of Greenwich 1997–2004; memb CNAA Physics Bd 1973–82, pubns dir Int Radiation Protection Assoc 1979–88, external examiner Univ of Surrey 1980–86, memb Editorial Bd Physics in Med and Biology 1980–83, news ed Health Physics 1980–88, memb Medway HA 1981–90, regnl scientific advsr No 5 Region 1984–93, chm UK Liaison Ctee for Scis Allied to Med and Biology 1984–87, pres Inst of Nuclear Engrs 1988–90 (vice-pres 1983–87), pres Int Radiation Protection Assoc 1988–92, vice-pres London Int Youth Sci Forum 1988–, vice-pres Euro Nuclear Soc 1989–95; G William Morgan Award US Health Physics Soc 1997; Freeman City of London 1988, Liveryman Worshipful Co of Engineers 1988; memb: Soc for Radiological Protection, US Health Physics Soc; Eur Ing, CEng, FIE, CPhys, FInstP, Hon FSRP 1992, CSci 2004; *Books* Protection Against Radiation (1961), Radiation Protection Measurement: philosophy and implementation (1975), ALARA principles and practices (1987), IRPA Guidelines on Protection Against Non-Ionizing Radiation (1991), Off-site Emergency Response to Nuclear Accidents (1993), Radiation and Radiation Protection (1994), Radiation Protection for Emergency Workers (1997), papers on nuclear safety, radiological protection and management of emergencies; *Recreations* photography, conversation; *Clubs* Athenaeum, RNSA; *Style—* Prof John Lakey; ✉ 5 Pine Rise, Meopham, Gravesend, Kent DA13 0JA (tel 01474 812551)

LAKHANI, Prof Mayur Keshavji; CBE (2007); s of Keshavji V Lakhani (d 1989), and Shantaben K, *née* Moijaria (d 2002); *b* 20 April 1960, Uganda; *Educ* Univ of Dundee (MB ChB); *m* 3 July 1988, Mayuri M, *née* Jobanputra; 2 da (Sonam b 15 Feb 1991, Priyanka b 19 June 1992), 1 s (Rahul b 13 Feb 1995); *Career* princ in gen practice Highgate Medical Centre Loughborough 1991; visiting prof Dept of Health Sciences Univ of Leicester Medical Sch 2006; chm Cncl RCGP 2004–; DFFP; FRCGP (MRCGP 1991), FRCPEd, FRCP; *Publications* incl: A Celebration of General Practice (ed, 2003), Recent Advances in General Practice (jt ed, 2005); *Recreations* tennis; *Style—* Prof Mayur Lakhani, CBE; ✉ Royal College of General Practitioners, 14 Princes Gate, London SW7 1PU (tel 020 7581 3232, fax 020 7589 3145, e-mail mlakhani@rcgp.org.uk)

LAKIN, Sir Michael; 4 Bt (UK 1909), of The Cliff, Borough of Warwick; s of Sir Henry Lakin, 3 Bt (d 1979); *b* 28 October 1934; *Educ* Stowe; *m* 1, 1956 (m dis 1963), Margaret, da of Robert Wallace, of Mount Norris, Co Armagh; m 2, 1965, Felicity, da of Anthony Denis Murphy, of Londiani, Kenya; 1 da (Mary Jane b 1966), 1 s (Richard Anthony b 1968); *Heir* s, Richard Lakin; *Style—* Sir Michael Lakin, Bt; ✉ Little Sherwood, Tunley, Gloucestershire GL7 6LW

LAKIN, His Hon Judge Peter Maurice; s of Ronald Maurice Lakin (d 1985), of Coventry, and Dorothy Kathleen, *née* Cowlishaw; *b* 21 October 1949; *Educ* King Henry VIII GS Coventry, Univ of Manchester (LLB); *m* 11 Dec 1971, Jacqueline, da of John Alexander Jubb; 1 s (Michael John b 25 May 1975), 1 da (Emma Jane b 14 May 1977); *Career* asst slr Conn Goldberg Solicitors 1974–76 (articled clerk 1971–74), ptnr (i/c Forensic and Criminal Litigation) Pannone and Partners Solicitors 1976–95; recorder of the Crown Court 1993–95, circuit judge (Northern Circuit) 1995–; memb Law Soc 1974; *Recreations* fell walking, gardening, opera; *Style—* His Hon Judge Lakin; ✉ Manchester Crown Court, Minshull Street, Manchester M1 3FS (tel 0161 954 7500)

LAL, Prof Deepak Kumar; s of Nand Lal (d 1984), of New Delhi, India, and Shanti, *née* Devi; *b* 3 January 1940; *Educ* Doon Sch Dehra Dun, Stephen's Coll Delhi (BA), Jesus Coll Oxford (MA, BPhil); *m* 11 Dec 1971, Barbara, da of Jack Ballis (d 1987), of New York, USA; 1 da (Deepika b 17 March 1980), 1 s (Akshay b 18 Aug 1981); *Career* Indian Foreign Serv 1963–65, lectr ChCh Oxford 1966–68, res fell Nuffield Coll Oxford 1968–70, reader political econ UCL 1979–84 (lectr 1970–79), prof of political econ Univ of London 1984–93 (emeritus 1993), James S Coleman prof of devpt studies UCLA 1990–; conslt Indian Planning Cmmn 1973–74, res admin World Bank Washington DC 1983–87; conslt since 1970: ILO, UNCTAD, OECD, UNIDO, World Bank, Miny of Planning South Korea and Sri Lanka; co-dir: Trade Policy Unit Centre for Policy Studies London 1993–96, Trade and Devpt Unit Inst of Econ Affrs 1997–2002; Wincott Meml Lecture 1989, Ohlin Meml Lecture 1995, Shenoy Meml Lecture 1996, Peking Univ Centennial Lecture 1998, Hal Clough Lecture 1998, Julian Simon Meml Lecture 2000, Sven Rydenfeldt Meml Lecture 2001, The Wendt Lecture 2002, The Snape Meml Lecture 2006; *Books* Wells and Welfare (1972), Methods of Project Analysis (1974), Appraising Foreign Investment in Developing Countries (1975), Unemployment and Wage Inflation in Industrial Economies (1977), Men or Machines (1978), Prices for Planning (1980), The Poverty of Development Economics (1983, 3 edn 2002), Labour and Poverty in Kenya (with P Collier, 1986), Stagflation, Savings and the State (ed with M Wolf, 1986), The Hindu Equilibrium (1988 and 1989, revised and abridged edn 2005), Public Policy and Economic Development (ed with M Scott, 1990), Development Economics, 4 vols (ed 1992), The Repressed Economy (1993), Against Dirigisme (1994), The Political Economy of Poverty, Equity and Growth (with H Myint, 1996), Unintended Consequences (1998), Unfinished Business (1999), Trade, Development and Political Economy (ed with R Snape, 2001), In Praise of Empires (2004), Reviving the Invisible Hand (2006); *Recreations* opera, theatre, golf; *Clubs* Reform; *Style—*

Prof Deepak Lal; ✉ 2 Erskine Hill, London NW11 6HB (tel and fax 020 8458 3713); A 30 Nizamuddin West, New Delhi 110013, India (tel 00 9111 24359465); 213 Park Wilshire, 10724 Wilshire Boulevard, Los Angeles, CA 90024, USA (tel and fax 00 1 310 474 6624); Department of Economics, 8369 Bunche Hall, UCLA, 405 Hilgard Avenue, Los Angeles, CA 90024, USA (tel 00 1 310 825 4521, fax 00 1 310 825 9528, e-mail dlal@ucla.edu)

LALANDI-EMERY, Lina Madeleine; OBE (1975); da of late Nikolas Kaloyeropoulos, and late Toula, *née* Gelekis; *Educ* Athens Conservatoire (prizewinner), privately in England; *m* Ralph Emery; *Career* first appeared as harpsichord soloist Royal Festival Hall 1954, int career in concert radio and TV, dir Eng Bach Festival Trust 1963– (fndr 1962, specialising in baroque opera and dance); appearances incl Covent Garden, Versailles and numerous festivals of music (Granada, Athens, Monte Carlo, Madrid); Officier de l'Ordre des Arts et des Lettres (France) 1978, Gold Cross of the Phoenix (Greece); *Recreations* cooking, reading, astrophysics, knitting; *Style—* Mrs Lina Lalandi-Emery, OBE; ✉ English Bach Festival Trust, 15 South Eaton Place, London SW1W 9ER (tel 020 7730 5295, fax 020 7730 1456, e-mail info@ebf.org.uk, website www.ebf.org.uk)

LALVANI, Gulu; s of Tirach Singh Lalvani (d 1972), and Dharam Kaur Devi (d 1973); *b* 9 March 1939, Karachi, Pakistan; *Educ* Bombay Univ, Univ of Leeds; *m* 1, Vimla; 1 s (Dinesh b 27 March 1973), 1 da (Divia b 26 March 1976); m 2, Semiramis; 1 s (Zoran b 10 June 1988); *Career* prop Binatone Telecom Gp 1958–; developer Royal Phuket Marina Thailand; *Recreations* golf, sailing; *Clubs* Hurlingham, Annabel's, Mark's, Harry's Bar, George; *Style—* Gulu Lalvani, Esq; ✉ Binatone Telecom plc, Unit 1, Ponders End Industrial Estate, East Duck Lees Lane, Enfield, Middlesex EN3 7SP; Binatone Electronics International, Floor 23A, 9 Des Voeux Road West, Hong Kong (tel 00 852 2802 7388, fax 00 852 2802 8138)

LAMB, Adrian Frank; OBE (2005); s of Frank Lamb (d 1981), and Mary Elizabeth Graham, *née* Chambers (d 1977); *Educ* Gateshead GS; *m* 4 May 1974, Jane, da of William Moore, of Blyth, Notts; 3 da (Katharine b 1976, Amy b 1978, Jennifer b 1982), 1 s (Richard b 1982); *Career* CA; Richard Ormond Son & Dunn 1960–65, ptnr PricewaterhouseCoopers (formerly Coopers & Lybrand before merger) 1975–2001, seconded to Civil Serv Dept 1970; hon treas RIIA; FCA 1966 (Gold medal); *Books* Analysed Reporting (1977), Internal Audit in the Civil Service (jtly, 1971); *Recreations* tennis, bridge, music, gardening; *Style—* Adrian Lamb, OBE; ✉ Lynbury House, Burtons Way, Chalfont St Giles, Buckinghamshire HP8 4BP (tel 01494 764810)

LAMB, Sir Albert Thomas (Archie); KBE (1979, MBE 1953), CMG (1974), DFC (1945); s of Reginald Selwyn Lamb (d 1970), and Violet, *née* Haynes (d 1980); *b* 23 October 1921; *Educ* Swansea GS; *m* 8 April 1944, Christina Betty, da of Albert Henry Wilkinson (d 1960); 2 da (Elizabeth b 1945, Kathryn b 1959), 1 s (Robin b 1948); *Career* RAF 1941–46; FO 1938–41, Rome Embassy 1947–50, Genoa Consulate 1950, Bucharest Legation 1950–53, FO 1953–55, MECAS 1955–57, Bahrain (political residency) 1957–61, FO oil desk 1961–65, Kuwait Embassy 1965, political agent Abu Dhabi 1965–68, chief inspr Dip Serv 1968–74; ambass: Kuwait 1974–77, Norway 1978–80; memb Bd BNOC 1981–82, dir Britoil plc 1982–88, memb Bd Samuel Montagu & Co Ltd 1981–85 (advsr 1985–88), sr assoc Conant & Associates Ltd Washington DC 1985–94; clerk of Parish Cncl of Zeals 1991–97, memb Bd National Bank of Kuwait (International) plc 1994–; hon fell Swansea Inst of Higher Educn 2004, hon fell Univ of Wales Swansea 2005; *Publications* A Long Way From Swansea (A Memoir Of A Diplomatic Career) (2003), Abu Dhabi 1965–68 (2003), The Last Voyage of S S Cronsay (2004); *Recreations* gardening; *Clubs* RAF; *Style—* Sir Albert Lamb, KBE, CMG, DFC; ✉ White Cross Lodge, Zeals, Wiltshire BA12 6PF (tel 01747 840321, e-mail atlamb@zealswilts.demon.co.uk)

LAMB, Dr Andrew Martin; s of late Harry Lamb, and late Winifred, *née* Emmott; *b* 23 September 1942; *Educ* Werneth Sch Oldham, Manchester Grammar, CCC Oxford (MA, DLitt); *m* 1 April 1970, Wendy Ann, da of Frank Edward Davies (decd); 1 s (Richard Andrew b 1976), 2 da (Helen Margaret b 1972, Susan Elizabeth b 1973); *Career* investment mangr then asst gen mangr MGM Assurance 1976–88, chief investment mangr Friends Provident Life Office 1988–98, dir (operational projects) Friends Ivory & Sime plc 1998–2000; music historian; FIA 1972; *Books* Jerome Kern in Edwardian London (1985), Gänzl's Book of the Musical Theatre (with Kurt Gänzl, 1988), Light Music from Austria (1992), Skaters' Waltz: The Story of the Waldteufels (1995), An Offenbach Family Album (1997), Shirley House to Trinity School (1999), 150 Years of Popular Musical Theatre (2000), Leslie Stuart - Composer of Florodora (2002), Leslie Stuart's My Bohemian Life (ed, 2003), Fragson: The Triumphs and the Tragedy (with Julian Myerscough, 2004), The Merry Widow at 100 (2005), A Life on the Ocan Wave: The Story of Henry Russell (2007); contrib to: Gramophone, Opera, The New Grove Dictionary of Music & Musicians, The Oxford Dictionary of National Biography; *Recreations* cricket, music, family; *Clubs* Lancashire CCC; *Style—* Dr Andrew Lamb; ✉ 12 Fullers Wood, Croydon, CR0 8HZ (tel 020 8777 5114, e-mail andrewmlamb@googlemail.com)

LAMB, Dave; s of Jim Lamb and Shirley, *née* Hopson; *b* 17 January 1969; *Educ* Univ of Warwick (BA); *m* 17 July 2004, Nicola Dowbiggin; *Career* comic actor, writer and voice over artist; founding dr Top Dog Prodns; >i<Film>r< Hunting the Beast 2005, Send in the Clowns 2006; >i<Theatre>r< Caught in the Net (Vaudeville Theatre) 2002, Finding Bin Laden (Gilded Balloon) 2003; >i<Television>r< Goodness Gracious Me 1997–2001, Armstrong & Miller 1997–2001, People Like Us 1997, Barking 1998, How Do You Want Me? 1998–99, Hippies 1999, Dark Ages 1999, Rhona 2000, 2DTV 2001–05, Dr Terrible's House of Horrible 2001, Fun At The Funeral Parlour 2001, We Know Where You Live 2001, My Parents Are Aliens 2003 and 2005, French and Saunders 2004, EastEnders 2004, Doc Martin 2004, Comedy Connections 2005, Bromwell High 2005, The Smoking Room 2005, Broken News 2005, The Late Edition 2006, City Lights 2007, The Life and Times of Vivienne Vyle 2007–; writer: Spitting Image 1996, The Russ Abbot Show 1996, Oddballs 1996, Saturday Live 1996, The Cheese Shop 1996–97, The End of the Year Show 1997, The Jack Docherty Show 1997–98, Barking 1998, The Outlaw 1998, Terry and John 1999, 2DTV 2001–05, Live with Christian O'Connell 2003; voice overs: Come Dine With Me 2004–; >i<Rado>r< Weekending 1994–97, The Game's Up 1995–96, You Cannot Be Serious 1995–97, The Cheeseshop 1997–2000, The Alan Davies Show 1997–98, Rent 1997–98, The Way It Is 1997–2002, Another Case of Milton Jones 1998–99, The Dominic Holland Show 2000, The Bigger Issues 2000–03, At Home with the Snails 2001–02, Whole Nother Story 2001–03, The Hudson & Pepperdine Show 2001–05, All The Young Dudes 2002, Artists 2003, Double Income No Kids Yet 2003, Wild Things 2003, Baggy Trousers 2003, London Europe 2003–04, The Rapid Eye Movement 2004, Fifteen Minute Musical 2004–, The Very World of Milton Jones 2005–, Be Prepared 2005, Bearded Ladies 2005, Life In London 2006–, Vent 2006–, Look Away Now 2007–; writer: Weekending 1994–97, News Huddlines 1994–98, The Game's Up 1995–96, You Cannot Be Serious 1995–97 (Radio Light Entertainment Peter Titheridge Award 1996–97), The Cheeseshop 1997–2000, The Way It Is 1997–2002, The Bigger Issues 2000–03, London Europe 2003–04, Look Away Now 2007–; *Style—* Dave Lamb, Esq; ✉ c/o Joe Hutton, BWH, Barley Mow Business Centre, 10 Barley Mow Passage, London W4 4PH (tel 020 8996 1661)

LAMB, Elspeth; da of John Cunningham Lamb (d 1961), and Margaret Paterson Lyon (d 1988); *b* 28 March 1951; *Educ* Glasgow Sch of Art, Manchester Poly (post grad in printmaking), Ruskin Sch of Drawing Oxford; *Partner* Malcolm Gray; *Career* lectr in etching Glasgow Sch of Art 1975–76, lectr Printmaking, Drawing and Painting Dept Edinburgh Coll of Art 1978– (actg head of dept 1995–99); visiting lectr: Glasgow Sch of Art 1988, 1991, 1993, 1994 and 1995, Univ of Ulster 1991, 1993, 1994 and 1996, Grays Sch of Art Aberdeen 1991, Univ of Newcastle 1991 and 1992, Queens Univ Kingston Ontario 1992, Canberra Sch of Art Aust 1993, Monash Univ Gippsland Aust 1993, Ballarat Univ Art Sch Victoria Aust 1993, Slade Sch of Art UCL 1994, The Joan Miro Fndn Spain 1994, 1996 and 1997, Hornsea Sch of Art Middx Univ 1995 and 1996; artist in res: Grafikan Paja Jyvaskyla Finland 1991, Open Studio Toronto 1992, Canberra Sch of Art 1993, Malasplna Printmakers Vancouver 1995; fndr Bon a Tirer Editions (first ind lithography workshop in Scotland) 1986; appeared various arts progs television and radio, subject of various jl and newspaper articles; memb Visual Arts Awards Panel Scottish Arts Cncl 1994–; ARSA 1991, RGI 1992; *Solo Exhibitions* Glasgow Sch of Art 1974, Univ of Glasgow 1975, Glasgow Print Studio Gallery 1986, Taller Galeria Fort (Spain) 1986, Int Festival Exhbn Scottish Gallery (Edinburgh) 1987, Mercury Gallery (London) 1988 and 1990, Touchstones (City of Culture exhbn Glasgow Print Studio) 1990, Edinburgh Printmakers Gallery 1990, Cornerstones (Mayfest exhbn Compass Gallery Glasgow) 1992, Edinburgh Coll of Art Int Festival 1992, Electra Fine Art Gallery (Toronto) 1992 and 1995, Foyer Gallery (Canberra Sch of Art) 1993, Malaspina Gallery (Vancouver) 1995; *Group Exhibitions* incl: Glasgow Print Studio Gallery 1981, Corners Gallery (Glasgow) 1983, Grease and Water (Arts Cncl tour) 1983, Etching (Ats Cncl tour) 1983, New Scottish Prints (NY and tour of N America) 1983, Wenniger Gallery (Boston) 1984, Print Exhibition (Cadaques Spain) 1984, Printmakers Drawings (Mercury Gallery Edinburgh) 1987, Ravensdale Gallery (London) 1987, New Scottish Art (Turberville-Smith London) 1987, Culture City Prints (Amsterdam) 1987, The Lillie Art Gallery (Glasgow) 1987, With an Eye to the East (Scottish Arts Cncl travelling gallery) 1989, Critic's Choice (Bohun Gallery London) 1989, Grafika Creativa (Aalto Museum Jyvaskyla Finland) 1990, Union of Artists Gallery (Red Square Moscow) 1991, Henry Moore Gallery (RCA) 1991, Xian Acad of Fine Arts (China) 1994, Celtic Connections (Glasgow) 1995, Exhibition Costillo de Soutomaior (Pontevedra Spain) 1995, Brought to Book (Collins Gallery Glasgow) 1995, Scottish Art Gallery Shek-O (Hong Kong) 1996, Otra Vez Gallery (LA) 1996; Int Print Biennales: Ljubljana 1985, Bradford 1985 and 1990, Berlin 1987, Varna Bulgaria 1989, Kochi-Chi Japan 1990, Kanagawa Japan 1990, Cracow 1991 and 1994, La Louviere Belgium 1992, Katowice Poland 1992 and 1994, Beograd 1997, Portland USA 1997; various art fairs 1981–; *Work in Public Collections* Br Cncl London, Japanese Consular Collection London, Scottish Arts Cncl, BBC, Glasgow Museums and Art Galleries Kelvingrove, Leeds Art Galleries, Inverness Art Galleries, The Arts in Fife, City Arts Centre Edinburgh, Perth Art Galleries and Museums; *Awards* RSA Meyer Oppenheim Award 1973, Scottish Young Contemporaries Prize 1973, Scottish Arts Cncl Award 1975 and 1979, SSA Educational Inst of Scotland Award 1983, Mini-print Int Prize Spain 1983, Edinburgh Coll of Art res bursary (to study at Tamarind Inst of Lithography Univ of New Mexico) 1985, Scottish Print Open IV Rives Arches Mill Award 1987, RSA W&J Burness Award 1989, Hope Scott Tst Award 1989, 1992 and 1995, Lady Artists Club Tst Award 1989, Scottish Arts Cncl bursary (for USA project) 1989, Int Print Biennale Gerhardt & Leimar Award Bradford 1990, RGI Bank of Scotland Award 1990, Scotland on Sunday Paper Boat Award (for Cornerstones exhbn Glasgow Mayfest) 1992, RSA Satire Soc Award 1993, RSA Gillies Award (to study in New Mexico) 1995, Portland Museum Oregon Int Print Exhbn Purchase Award 1997; *Publications* The Best of British Women (1995), Best of Printmaking (1997); various edns of lithographs; *Recreations* travel, hill walking, swimming, badminton, aerobics; *Clubs* Western Baths (Glasgow); *Style—* Ms Elspeth Lamb; ✉ Bon a Tirer Editions, 15 East Campbell Street, Glasgow G1 1DG (tel 0141 552 7250)

LAMB, Air Vice Marshal George Colin; CB (1977), CBE (1966), AFC (1947); s of George Lamb (d 1958), of Hornby, Lancs, and Bessie Lamb; *b* 23 July 1923; *Educ* Lancaster Royal GS; *m* 1, 1945, Nancy Mary, da of Ronald Godsmark, of Norwich, Norfolk; 2 s; m 2, 1981, Mrs Maureen Margaret Mepham, da of Thomas Bamford (d 1967), of Hounslow, Middx; *Career* asst cmdt RAF Coll Cranwell 1964–65, dep cdr Air Forces Borneo 1965–66, Air Cdre 1968, OC RAF Lyneham 1969–71, RCDS 1971–72, dir of control (ops) Nat Air Traffic Serv 1972–74, Cdr Southern Maritime Air Region 1974–75, COS No 18 Gp 1975–78, RAF vice-pres Combined Cadet Forces Assoc 1978–94; chm Yonex UK Ltd 1995–97 (md 1990–95); int rugby football referee 1967–72, chief exec Badminton Assoc of England 1978–89, memb Sports Cncl 1983–90; chm: Lilleshall Nat Sports Centre 1983–2005, Sports Ctee Prince's Tst 1985–2005, Br Int Sports Devpt Aid Tst 1995–2005; memb Sports Cncl Drug Abuse Advsy Gp 1984–92, privilege memb RFU 1985 (memb Ctee 1973–85), gen sec London Sports Med Inst 1989–90, Br Int Sports Ctee 1989–97; pres: St George's Day Club 1994–, Assoc of Lancastrians in London 1999; vice-pres British Berlin Airlift Assoc 1998–; FIMgt; *Recreations* rugby union football, gardening; *Clubs* RAF; *Style—* Air Vice Marshal George Lamb, CB, CBE, AFC; ✉ Hambledon, 17 Meadway, Berkhamsted, Hertfordshire HP4 2PN (tel and fax 01442 862583)

LAMB, John Tregea; s of late Roger Craven Lamb, of Scaynes Hill, W Sussex, and Katherine Honor Lamb; *b* 1 August 1952; *Educ* Felsted, Poly of N London (BA); *Children* 2 da (Mary Jane b 14 March 1973, Naomi b 26 Oct 1987), 2 s (Jamie b 25 Nov 1974, Max b 4 April 1984); *Career* trainee exec Richmond Towers PR 1970–71, trainee reporter Camberley News Surrey 1971–73, sub ed National Newsagent 1976–77, reporter Computing magazine 1977–78, news ed Computer Talk 1978–80, freelance journalist covering computer and electronics field 1980–88, ed Computer Weekly 1988–96, ed Computer Age supplement Sunday Business 1996, ed-in-chief Information Week 1998–99, ed Butler Gp Review 2002–04, ed IT Strategy, ed Information Economics Jl 2003–04, publisher Ability magazine 2004; dir IT Media Conferences 1999; Liveryman Worshipful Co of Info Technologists; MBCS; *Recreations* gardening, sailing; *Style—* John Lamb, Esq; ✉ Pellingbrook, Lewes Road, Scaynes Hill, Haywards Heath, West Sussex RH17 7NG

LAMB, Prof Jonathan Robert; s of Henry Arthur Patrick Lamb, of Modbury, Devon, and Edna Carol, *née* Parkins; *b* 13 October 1952; *Educ* Kelly Coll Tavistock, Univ of Edinburgh (BDS, DSc), Brasenose Coll Oxford (MA), Univ of London (PhD); *m* 15 Jan 1977, Deborah Mary, da of John Keith Batey; 2 da (Rachel Alice b 12 Oct 1986, Eleanor Francis b 1 Sept 1989); *Career* dental house surgn Guy's Hosp 1976, MRC trg fell Guy's Hosp 1977–80, research asst prof Georgetown Univ Med Sch 1980–82, research fell ICRF UCL 1982–85, MRC scientist Royal Postgrad Med Sch 1988–90, prof of immunology Imperial Coll London 1990–97, prof of respiratory science Univ of Edinburgh 1997–2003, head of immunology Translational Medicine and Technol GlaxoSmithKline 2003–07, prof of veterinary clinical immunology Sch of Veterinary Studies Univ of Edinburgh 2007–; Bradley sr scholar in biomedicine Univ of Wisconsin 1987; hon prof: Imperial Coll London, Univ of Edinburgh, Hong Kong Univ, Univ of Oxford; FRCPath 1996, FRSE 2002, FMedSci 2002; *Publications* author of more than 250 articles and review in the field of immunology and inflammation; *Recreations* classical music, art, reading, gardening; *Style—* Prof Jonathan Lamb; ✉ 7 Mansionhouse Road, Edinburgh EH9 1TZ (tel 0131 667 5038); Department of Veterinary Clincal Studies, Royal (Dick) School of Veterinary Studies, University of Edinburgh, Easter Bush Veterinary Centre, Roslin, Midlothian EH25 9RG (tel 0131 650 6280, mobile 07874 039257, e-mail j.r.lamb@ed.ac.uk)

LAMB, Prof Joseph Fairweather; s of Joseph Lamb (d 1972), of Balnacake, Brechin, Angus, and late Agnes May, *née* Fairweather; *b* 18 July 1928; *Educ* Auldbar Public Sch, Brechin HS, Univ of Edinburgh (MB ChB, BSc, PhD); *m* 1, 10 Sept 1955 (m dis 1989), Olivia Jane, da of Robert Horne (d 1960), of Uganda; 1 da (Angela Gail b 1956), 5 s (Joseph William b 1958, John Robert b 1962, Andrew Noel b 1964, James Gerald b 1985, William Finlay b 1987); m 2, 21 April 1989, Bridget Cecilia, da of John Kingsley Cook (d 1994), of London; *Career* Nat Serv RAF 1947–49, house offr appts 1955–56, lectr Royal (Dick) Vet Coll

Univ of Edinburgh 1958–61, lectr then sr lectr in physiology Univ of Glasgow 1961–69, Chandos prof of physiology Univ of St Andrews 1969–93 (emeritus 1993); sec Physiological Soc 1982–85, chm and fndr memb Save Br Sci 1986–97 (chm Scottish Section 1997–2003); chm and organiser Gas Greed campaign 1994–95, govr Rowett Research Inst Aberdeen 1998–2003; FRCPE 1984, FRSE 1986; *Books* Essentials of Physiology (1980); *Recreations* sailing; *Clubs* Sceptre Sailing; *Style*— Prof Joseph Lamb, FRSE; ✉ Kenbrae, 53 Darnell Road, Trinity, Edinburgh EH5 3PH; School of Biological & Medical Sciences, Bute Medical Buildings, University of St Andrews, Fife KY16 9TS (e-mail jfl@st-and.ac.uk)

LAMB, Martin James; s of Dr Trevor A J Lamb, of Knowle, W Midlands, and Shirley, *née* Hubbard; *b* 7 January 1960, Leeds; *Educ* Bradford GS, Solihull Sixth Form Coll, Imperial Coll London (BSc), Cranfield Business Sch (MBA); *m* 13 Aug 1983, Jayne Louise, *née* Bodenham; 4 da (Charlotte b 13 Dec 1989, Rebecca b 15 Aug 1991, Georgia b 23 Feb 1994, Victoria b 29 April 1996); *Career* grad trainee IMI Cornelius Inc USA 1982–83, project engr IMI Air Conditioning UK 1983–85, R&D mangr Coldflow Ltd 1985–87, md IMI Cornelius (UK) Ltd 1991–96 (mktg dir 1987–91), chief exec IMI plc 2001– (exec dir 1996–2000); non-exec dir Spectris plc 1999–2006, tstee City Technol Coll Birmingham 1997–; Hon Dr Univ of Central Eng 2006; CCMI 2002; *Recreations* family, tennis, golf; *Style*— Martin Lamb, Esq; ✉ IMI plc, Lakeside, Solihull Parkway, Birmingham Business Park, Birmingham B37 7XZ (tel 0121 717 3700, fax 0121 717 3801)

LAMB, Prof Michael Ernest de Lestang; s of Francis B W Lamb (d 1979), and M M Michelle, *née* Nageon de Lestang; *b* 22 October 1953, Lusaka, Zambia; *Educ* Univ of Natal Durban (BA), Johns Hopkins Univ (MA), Yale Univ (MPhil, MS, PhD); *m* 22 Oct 2005, Hilary S Clark; 3 s (Damon b 8 April 1982, Darryn b 21 Aug 1986, Philip b 12 Aug 1996), 1 da (Jeanette b 13 May 1992), 4 step da (Aya b 10 Oct 1982, Amy b 21 May 1990, Kate b 9 Nov 1992, Lily b 23 Sept 1995); *Career* Univ of Wisconsin 1976–78, Univ of Michigan 1978–80, Univ of Utah 1980–87, Nat Inst of Child Health and Human Devpt 1987–2004, Univ of Cambridge 2004–; Young Psychologist Award American Psychological Assoc 1976, Boyd McCandless Young Scientist Award 1978, Univ of Utah Superior Res Award 1985, Univ of Utah Distinguished Res Award 1986, Hammer Award US Govt 1998, Cattell Award for Lifetime Achievement and Contributions American Psychological Soc/Assoc for Psychological Science 2003–04; PhD (hc) Univ of Goteburg Sweden 1995, DCL (hc) UEA 2006; fell Assoc for Psychological Science, memb Soc for Res in Child Devpt; author of several hundred articles in learned jls; *Books* The Role of the Father in Child Development (ed, 1976, 4 edn 2004), Social and Personality Development (ed, 1978), Social Interaction Analysis: Methodological Issues (co-ed, 1979), Advances in Developmental Psychology, (co-ed, Vol 1 1981, Vol 2 1982, Vol 3 1983, Vol 4 1986), Infant Social Cognition: Empirical and Theoretical Considerations (co-ed, 1981), Child Psychology Today (jtly, 1982, 2 edn 1986), Development in Infancy: An Introduction (jtly, 1982, 4 edn 2002), Socialization and Personality Developmment (jtly, 1982), Non-Traditional Families (ed, 1982), Sibling Relationships: Their Development and Significance Across the Lifespan (co-ed, 1982), Fatherhood and Family Policy (co-ed, 1983), Developmental Psychology: An Advanced Textbook (co-ed, 1984, 5 edn 2005), Infant-Mother Attachment (jtly, 1985), Adolescent Fatherhood (co-ed, 1986), The Father's Role: Applied Perspectives (ed, 1986), The Father's Role: Cross-Cultural Perspectives (ed, 1987), Infant Development: Perspectives from German-Speaking Countries (co-ed, 1991), Child-Care in Context: Cross-Cultural Perspectives (ed, 1992), Adolescent Problem Behavior: Issues and Research (co-ed, 1994), Images of Childhood (co-ed, 1996), Investigative Interviews with Children: A Guide for Helping Professionals (jtly, 1998), Parenting and Childhood in 'Nontraditional' Families (ed, 1999), Conceptualizing and Measuring Father Involvement (co-ed, 2004), Hunter-Gatherer Childhoods: Evolutionary Developmental and Cultural Perspectives (co-ed, 2005), Child Sexual Abuse: Disclosure, Delay and Denial (co-ed, 2007); *Style*— Prof Michael Lamb; ✉ Faculty of Social and Political Sciences, University of Cambridge, Free School Lane, Cambridge CB2 3RQ (tel 01223 334523, fax 01223 334550, e-mail mel37@cam.ac.uk)

LAMB, Norman Peter; MP; s of Hubert Horace Lamb (d 1997), of Holt, Norfolk, and Beatrice Moira, *née* Milligan; *b* 16 September 1957; *Educ* Univ of Leicester (LLB); *m* 14 July 1984, Mary Elizabeth Lamb; 2 s (Archie b 9 Feb 1988, Edward b 30 May 1991); *Career* trainee slr then sr asst slr Norwich CC 1982–86, slr then ptnr Steele & Co Slrs 1986–2001; cncllr Norwich CC 1987–91; MP (Lib Dem) Norfolk N 2001–; dep spokesman for int devpt 2001–03, memb Treasy Select Ctee 2003–05, Lib Dem shadow spokesman for Trade and Industry 2005–06, chief of staff to Sir Menzies Campbell 2006, Lib Dem shadow sec of state for Health 2006–; memb: Law Soc 1982–; *Publications* Remedies in the Employment Tribunal (1998); *Recreations* art, Norwich City FC season ticket holder; *Style*— Norman Lamb, Esq, MP; ✉ House of Commons, London SW1A 0AA (tel 020 7219 8480, e-mail normanlamb@hotmail.com)

LAMB, Hon Timothy Michael (Tim); 2 s of 2 Baron Rochester, *qv*; *b* 24 March 1953; *Educ* Shrewsbury, The Queen's Coll Oxford (MA); *m* 23 Sept 1978, Denise Ann, da of John Buckley, of Frinton-on-Sea, Essex; 1 da (Sophie b 15 Sept 1983), 1 s (Nicholas b 9 Nov 1985); *Career* professional cricketer with: Middlesex CCC 1974–77, Northants County Cricket Club 1978–83; sec/gen mangr Middlesex CCC 1984–88; ECB (formerly TCCB): cricket sec 1988–96, chief exec 1996–2004; chief exec Central Cncl of Physical Recreation (CCPR) 2005–; *Recreations* golf, travel, watching sport, walking, photography; *Style*— The Hon Tim Lamb

LAMB, Timothy Robert; QC (1995); s of Stephen Falcon Lamb (d 1992), and Pamela Elizabeth, *née* Coombes; *b* 27 November 1951; *Educ* Brentwood Sch, Lincoln Coll Oxford (MA); *m* 1978, Judith Anne, da of Francis Ryan; 1 s (Jonathan Francis b 31 Aug 1981), 1 da (Victoria Josephine b 8 Aug 1983); *Career* called to the Bar Gray's Inn 1974 (bencher 2003); recorder 2000–, jt head of chambers 3 Paper Bldgs Temple 2004–; Western Circuit rep Bar Cncl and memb Law Reform Ctee 2005–, legal assessor to Gen Dental Cncl; legal advsr: RPSGB, General Optical Cncl; chartered arbitrator, accredited mediator, accredited adjudicator; memb: LCLCBA, TECBAR, PIBA; *Recreations* family, travel, watersports, gliding; *Style*— Timothy Lamb, Esq, QC

LAMB, Dr Trevor Arthur John; s of Arthur Bradshaw Lamb, and Ruth Ellen, *née* Eales; *b* 7 December 1929; *Educ* Wanstead GS, QMC London (BSc, PhD); *m* 1952, Shirley Isabel, da of Sidney Charles Hubbard (d 1971); 2 s (John b 1957, Martin b 1960), 2 da (Susan b 1960, Karen b 1964); *Career* pt/t lectr Univ of London 1950–52, section ldr Bristol Aeroplane Co Engine Div 1952–56, section head (engrg res) Imperial Chemical Industries 1956–58, factory mangr then gen mangr Leeds Plant Marston Excelsior Ltd (subsid of ICI Metals Div, became Imperial Metal Industries Ltd, styled IMI Ltd) 1958–62, md then exec chm Radiator Gp IMI Ltd 1962–74; IMI plc: main bd dir of overseas and mktg 1974–87, exec chm Australasian, Refinery and Fabrication Gps 1974–77, exec chm Valve Gp 1977–89, exec chm Fluid Power Gp 1981–91, conslt 1992–94; non-exec dir: W Canning plc 1980–96, Richard Burbidge Ltd 1992–96; business conslt 1992–; govr The City Technol Coll Kingshurst 1989–93; Eur Ing, CEng, FIMechE; *Recreations* music, golf, tennis, swimming; *Style*— Dr Trevor Lamb; ✉ Heronbrook House, 75 Bakers Lane, Knowle, Warwickshire B93 8PW (tel 01564 773877, fax 01564 779428, e-mail drtrevorlamb@aol.com)

LAMBERT, Air Cdre Andrew; *Educ* Wellington, RAF Coll Cranwell, Univ of Cambridge (MPhil); *m*; 1 s, 1 da; *Career* flying trg as navigator, completed tours 54(F), 31 and 23(F) Sqdns, memb Weapons Instr Staff Phantom Operational Conversion Unit 1979, promoted Sqdn Ldr 1981, Weapons Ldr 23 Sqdn 1981, Flight Cdr 23 Sqdn Falkland Islands 1983, cmd Phantom Weapons Instr Sch 1983–85, RAF Staff Coll 1986, promoted Wing Cdr 1988, posted Plans Branch HQ Strike Command 1988, Sqdn Cdr 23 Sqdn 1991–93 (cmd Operation Deny Flight Bosnia), Dir of Defence Studies RAF 1995–97, Air Cdr and COS Br Forces Falkland Islands 1997–98, Cdr Br Forces Warden 1999, Dep Cdr CAOC3 Reitan 2000–01, Asst Cmdt (Air) Jt Services Command and Staff Coll 2001–03; lectr and advsr on coercive techniques, published several monographs; Nicolson Trophy for Best Qualified Weapons Instr 1978, Wilkinson Battle of Britain Meml Sword, QCVSA; fell commoner Downing Coll Cambridge; MRIN, MRUSI; *Recreations* sailing, sub aqua diving, ancient history; *Style*— Air Cdre Andrew Lambert; ✉ c/o RAF Club, 128 Piccadilly, London W1J 7PY; tel and fax 01363 83150, e-mail andrewlambert99@hotmail.com

LAMBERT, Prof Andrew David; s of David George Lambert, of Beetley, Norfolk, and Nola, *née* Burton; *b* 31 December 1956; *Educ* Hamond's Sch Swaffham, City of London Poly (BA), King's Coll London (MA, PhD); *m* 27 Nov 1987, Zohra, da of Mokhtar Bouznat, of Casablanca, Morocco; 1 da (Tama-Sophie b 29 May 1990); *Career* lectr modern int history Bristol Poly 1983–87, conslt Dept of History and Int Affrs RNC Greenwich 1987–89, sr lectr in war studies RMA Sandhurst 1989–91; KCL: lectr 1991–96, sr lectr in war studies 1996–99, prof of naval history 1999–2001, Laughton Prof of naval history 2001–; memb Cncl SS Great Britain Project 1989–, hon sec Soc Navy Records 1996–2005; writer and presenter War at Sea (BBC 2) 2004; FRHistS 1990; *Books* Battleships in Transition: The Creation of the Steam Battlefleet 1815–1960 (1984 and 1985), The Crimean War: British Grand Strategy Against Russia 1853–56 (1990), The Last Sailing Battlefleet: Maintaining Naval Mastery 1815–1850 (1991), The Foundations of Naval History (1998), War at Sea in the Age of Sail (2000), Nelson: Britannia's God of War (2004); *Recreations* running, motorcycling; *Clubs* Vintage Motorcycle; *Style*— Prof Andrew Lambert; ✉ Department of War Studies, King's College London, Strand, London WC2R 2LS (tel 020 7848 2179, fax 020 7848 2026)

LAMBERT, Angela Maria; da of late John Donald Helps, of Sherborne, Dorset, and Ditha, *née* Schroeder; *b* 14 April 1940; *Educ* Wispers Sch, St Hilda's Coll Oxford (BA); *m* 1962 (m dis 1966), Martin John Lambert; 1 da (Carolyn Ruth (Mrs Butler) b 1963), 1 s (Jonathan Martin Andrew b 1964); partner 1986–, Tony Price; 1 da from previous ptnr (Marianne Jane Colette b 1971); *Career* author and journalist; PPS to Lord Longford House of Lords 1965–68, freelance journalist 1968–72, TV reporter for News at Ten, LWT and Thames TV 1972–88; feature writer: The Independent 1988–96, The Daily Mail 1996–2000, The Sunday Telegraph 2000–; *Books* Unquiet Souls (1984), 1939: The Last Season of Peace (1989); novels: Love Among The Single Classes (1989), No Talking After Lights (1990), A Rather English Marriage (1992), The Constant Mistress (1994), Kiss and Kin (1997), Golden Lads and Girls (1999), The Property of Rain (2001), The Lost Life of Eva Braun (2006); *Recreations* eating, drinking and travelling, seven grandchildren; *Style*— Ms Angela Lambert; ✉ tel 020 7244 9762, fax 020 7244 8297, e-mail angelambert@compuserve.com; L'Escarcelle, au lieu dit Gaudemagne, 24250 Groléjac, France (tel 00 33 5 53 28 14 85)

LAMBERT, David George; *b* 7 August 1940; *Educ* Barry GS, UC Wales Aberystwyth (LLB); *m* 1966, Diana Mary, *née* Ware; 1 s (Nicholas David b 1976), 1 da (Julia Mary b 1978); *Career* admitted as slr 1964; slr and legal advsr (grade 3) Welsh Office 1991–99 (joined 1966), legal advsr to the Presiding Office of the Nat Assembly for Wales 2000–04; research fell: Cardiff Law Sch, UC Cardiff; registrar Diocese of Llandaff, provincial registrar Church in Wales, dep chapter clerk Llandaff Cathedral; NP, memb Law Soc (memb Wales Ctee); *Recreations* ecclesiastical law, baroque music; *Style*— David Lambert, Esq; ✉ 9 The Chantry, Llandaff, Cardiff CF5 2NN (tel 029 2056 8154); Cardiff Law School, Cathays Park, Cardiff CF1 3NQ (tel 029 2087 4644)

LAMBERT, Eva Margaret; da of Frank Holroyd (d 1978), and Elsie Irene, *née* Fearnley; *b* 17 September 1946; *Educ* Elland GS; *m* 1; 1 s (Terry Graham b 16 Dec 1966), 1 da (Justine Louise b 30 July 1968); m 2, 17 April 1982, Robert Stephen Lambert, s of Robert Lambert; 1 da (Jemma Louise b 13 April 1983); *Career* NHS: health service administrator 1973–83, fin accountant 1983–85, mgmnt accountant 1985–86, dep fin mangr 1986–90, dep unit gen mangr 1990–91, divnl gen mangr 1991–92, chief exec Huddersfield NHS Tst 1992–97, ret; ind conslt Freshstart Consulting 1997–, chief exec Pennell Initiative for Women's Health 1999–2004; co sec R Lambert Transport Ltd; chair Huddersfield Mencap 2005–, tstee Kirklees Active Leisure Tst 2002–, govr Greenhead Coll Huddersfield; FIMgt, AAT 1982, FCCA 1993 (ACCA 1987), FRSA 2002; *Recreations* tennis, squash, handicrafts; *Clubs* Huddersfield Lawn Tennis and Squash (fin dir (vol)); *Style*— Mrs Eva Lambert; ✉ 3 Easedale Gardens, Lindley, Huddersfield, West Yorkshire HD3 3UR (tel 01484 641543, mobile 07932 409065, e-mail eva17lambert@hotmail.co.uk)

LAMBERT, Dr Hannah Eva; *Educ* St Mary's Hosp Med Sch Univ of London (MB BS, DObstRCOG, DMRT); *Career* various house posts in surgery, med, paediatrics, obstetrics and gynaecology 1957–60, registrar obstetrics and gynaecology Edgware Gen Hosp and W Middx Hosp 1961–63, instr of obstetrics and gynaecology Univ of Pittsburgh PA 1963–65, res asst Dept of Obstetrics and Gynaecology Hammersmith Hosp 1965–69, med offr MRC 1969–70, registrar then sr registrar in radiotherapy and oncology Middx Hosp 1971–75, sr registrar in oncology Mount Vernon Hosp 1975–79, conslt clinical oncologist Hammersmith Hosp 1979–95; hon conslt St Mary's Hosp Paddington 1983–; hon sr lectr: Imperial Coll Sch of Med at Hammersmith Hosp (Royal Postgraduate Med Sch until merger 1997) 1979–, Inst of Obstetrics and Gynaecology 1983–; memb: N Thames Ovary Gp (fndr), MRC Gynaecological Cancer Working Pty, Breast Cancer Diagnostic and Screening Services Gp, PMB Gp, Portland Gynaecological Oncology Gp, Int Gynaecological Cancer Soc, British Gynaecological Cancer Soc, British Oncological Assoc, Rad Soc; FRCR 1976, FRCOG 1981 (MRCOG 1962); *Books* Gynaecological Oncology (with Dr P Blake, 1992), An Introduction to Gynaecological Oncology (1997); author of numerous pubns, book chapters and papers in med jls; *Style*— Dr Hannah Lambert

LAMBERT, Jean; MEP; da of Frederick Archer, and Margaret, *née* McDougall; *b* 1 June 1950; *Educ* Palmer's Girls GS, St Paul's Coll Cheltenham, Univ Coll Cardiff (BA), (PGCE, ADB Ed); *m* 1977, Stephen Lambert; 1 s, 1 da; *Career* secdy sch teacher 1972–89, pt/t teacher 1992–99; Green Pty: memb 1977–, princ speaker 1984 and 1998–99, political liaison with Green Gp in Euro Parl 1989–92, chair Pty Exec 1994; MEP (Green) London 1999–, vice-pres Green/EFA Gp 2001–06, memb European Parl Ctee on Employment and Social Affrs, memb EP Delgn to India and SAARC; memb: Charter 88, Waltham Forest Race Equality Cncl, Cncl Liberty, Mgmnt Ctee Make Votes Count; patron East London Out Project; *Publications* No Change? No Chance! Green Politics Explained (1997), Research into Women and Decision-Making in EP Green Parties (1995); *Recreations* dancing, detective fiction; *Style*— Mrs Jean Lambert, MEP; ✉ Green MEP Office, Suite 58, The Hop Exchange, 24 Southwark Street, London SE1 1TY (tel 020 7407 6269, fax 020 7234 0183, e-mail jeanlambert@greenmeps.org.uk)

LAMBERT, Nigel Robert Woolf; QC (1999); s of Dr E Vivian Lambert, MB, BS, MRCS, LRCP (d 1970), and Sadie, *née* Woolf (d 1966); *b* 5 August 1949; *Educ* Cokethorpe Sch Oxford, Coll of Law; *m* 1975, Roamie Elisabeth, da of late Philip Sado, and Mrs Renée Sado; 1 s (David Vivian Robin b 11 Dec 1978), 1 da (Talia Susanna b 15 April 1981); *Career* called to the Bar Grays Inn 1974 (bencher 2003), add eundem memb Inner Temple 1986; recorder 1996– (asst recorder 1993–96), dep head of chambers 2004; memb: Bar Cncl 1993–2000, Professional Standards Ctee 1993–95 and 1997–99, Public Affairs Ctee 1994, Fin Ctee 1994, Legal Aid and Fees Ctee 1996, South Eastern Circuit Ctee 1992–, Criminal

L

Bar Assoc Ctee 1993–2000, Criminal Bar Assoc, Justice, South Eastern Circuit Exec Ctee 2001–07, Inner Temple Bar Liaison Ctee 2002–03, Inner Temple Circuit Ctee 2002–03; chm: North London Bar Mess 2001–07 (jr 1992–99), South Eastern Circuit/Inst of Barristers' Clerks Ctee 2001–07; govr Cokethorpe Sch 1971–78, life vice-pres Cokethorpe Old Boys' Assoc; *Recreations* supervising, organising, gossiping; *Clubs* Garrick; *Style*— Nigel Lambert, Esq, QC; ⊠ Carmelite Chambers, 9 Carmelite Street, London EC4Y 0DR (tel 020 7936 6300, e-mail nlambert@carmelitechambers.co.uk)

LAMBERT, Sir Peter John Biddulph; 10 Bt (GB 1711), of London; o s of John Hugh Lambert (d 1977), and Edith, *née* Bance (d 1988); suc kinsman Sir Greville Foley Lambert, 9 Bt (d 1988); *b* 5 April 1952; *Educ* Upper Canada Coll, Trent Univ Peterborough (BSc), Univ of Manitoba Winnipeg (MA), Univ of Toronto (BEd); *m* 2 Sept 1989, Leslie Anne, da of Richard Welkos Lyne; 1 da (Maeve Edith Jean *b* 7 Oct 1992), 1 s (Thomas Hugh John *b* 14 March 1999); *Heir* s, Thomas Lambert; *Style*— Sir Peter Lambert, Bt

LAMBERT, Stephen; s of Roger Lambert, of London, and Monika, *née* Wagner; *b* 22 March 1959; *Educ* Thames Valley GS, UEA, Univ of Oxford; *m* 8 April 1988, Jenni, da of Martin Russell, of South Africa; 1 da (Jessica *b* 1988), 1 s (Harry *b* 1992); *Career* BBC TV: joined 1983, Documentary Dept prodr/dir 40 Minutes 1987–90 and Inside Story 1991–92, series prodr/dir True Brits 1994, exec prodr BBC1 and BBC2 series 1996–99, series ed Modern Times (BBC2) 1994–98; RDF Media: dir of progs 1998–2005, chief creative offr 2005–; ed Real Life (ITV) 1999–2001; Commissioning Ed of the Year Broadcast Prodn Awards 1997; memb BAFTA, FRSA; *Books* Channel Four (1982); *Recreations* sailing, skiing; *Style*— Stephen Lambert, Esq; ⊠ RDF Media, Gloucester Building, Kensington Village, Avonmore Road, London W14 8RF (tel 020 7013 4440, e-mail stephen.lambert@rdfmedia.com)

LAMBERT, Verity Ann; OBE (2002); da of Stanley Joseph Lambert, and Ella Corona Goldburg; *b* 27 November 1935; *Educ* Roedean, Sorbonne; *Career* prodr BBC TV 1963–74, controller Drama Dept Thames TV 1974–76, chief exec Euston Films 1976–82, dir of prodn and exec prodr Thorn EMI Screen Entertainment 1982–85, ind film prodr 1985– (co name Cinema Verity Ltd), prodr A Cry in the Dark; exec prodr TV films and series incl: Sleepers (BBC), GBH (Channel Four), Boys from the Bush (BBC), Coasting (Granada), Sam Saturday (LWT), Eldorado (BBC), Class Act (Carlton), Comics (Channel Four), She's Out (Carlton), Capital Lives (Carlton), Heavy Weather (BBC), A Perfect State (BBC), Jonathan Creek (BBC), The Cazalets (BBC), Love Soup (BBC); memb RTS, fell BFI; *Recreations* good books, good food; *Style*— Ms Verity Lambert, OBE; ⊠ Cinema Verity Productions Ltd, 11 Addison Avenue, London W11 4QS

LAMBERTY, Mark Julian Harker; s of Dr G B Lamberty (d 1982), of Rossendale, Lancs, and Dr D S Lamberty; *b* 17 August 1947; *Educ* Rugby, Keble Coll Oxford (MA), Univ of Oxford (postgrad BCL); *m* 17 Aug 1991, Pamela Jean Wilson; *Career* called to the Bar Gray's Inn 1970; practising barr specialising in serious crime; former head of chambers; *Recreations* cricket; *Clubs* Norden Cricket (tstee); *Style*— Mark Lamberty, Esq; ⊠ St Johns Buildings, 24a-28 St John Street, Manchester M3 4DJ

LAMBIE, James (Jim); s of Robert Lambie, and Cecilia, *née* Blair; *b* 28 April 1964, Bellshill, N Lanarkshire; *Educ* Glasgow Sch of Art (BA); *Family* 1 c (Van); *Career* installation artist; Paul Hamlyn Award 2000, nominated Turner Prize 2005; *Solo Exhibitions* Ultralow (Carnival Soho) 1998, ZOBOP (The Showroom Gallery London) 1999, Voidoid (Transmission Gallery Glasgow) 1999, Weird Glow (Sadie Coles HQ London) 1999, Sonia Rosso (Pordenone Italy) 2000, Triangle Paris 2000, Konrad Fisher Dusseldorf 2000 and 2004, Blank Generation (Jack Hanley San Francisco) 2001, The Modern Institute Glasgow 2001, Sadie Coles HQ London 2001, Boy Hairdresser (Anton Kern NY) 2001, Salon Unisex (Sadie Coles HQ London) 2002, The Breeder projects (Athens) 2002, Acid Trails (Basel/Miami Beach Art Fair and The Modern Institute) 2002, Kebabylon (Inverleith House Edinburgh) 2003, Male Stripper (Museum of Modern Art Oxford) 2003, Mars Hotel (Franco Noero and Sonia Rosso Turin) 2004, Grand Funk (OPA Mexico) 2004, Mental Oyster (Anton Kern NY) 2004, My Boyfriend's Back (Konrad Fischer Galerie Dusseldorf) 2004, Concentrations 47: Jim Lambie (Dallas Museum of Art) 2005, Shoulder Pad (Sadie Coles HQ London) 2005, The Byrds (The Modern Institute Glasgow) 2005, P.I.L. (Mizuma Art Gallery Tokyo) 2006, Directions - Jim Lambie (Hirshhorn Museum & Sculpture Garden Washington DC) 2006; *Style*— Jim Lambie, Esq; ⊠ c/o The Modern Institute, Suite 6, 73 Robertson Street, Glasgow G2 8QD (tel 0141 248 3711, e-mail mail@themoderinstitute.com)

LAMBIE-NAIRN, Martin John; *Career* asst graphic designer BBC 1965, graphic designer Rediffusion 1966, freelance graphic designer 1967, art dir Conran Associates 1968, dep sr designer ITN 1968, graphic designer LWT 1970–76, chm and creative dir Lambie-Nairn & Company (brand identity for TV and commercials prodns) 1990–97, creative dir Lambie-Nairn (The Brand Union Ltd) 1997–; work incl: Channel 4 TV corp identity 1982, Anglia TV corp identity 1988, review of on-screen presentation for BBC1 and BBC2 1989, TFI corp identity 1989, BBC1 and BBC2 channel identities 1991, RTSI corp identity 1992, Carlton TV corp identity 1992–97, ARTE (France & Germany) 1995, ITN corp identity 1995, BBC corp identity 1997, Millennium Experience corp identity 1998, O2 corp identity 2002; prof Faculty of Design, Architecture and Fine Art Lincoln Univ 2005; devisor of Spitting Image (ITV); chm Graphics Jury BBC Design Awards 1987; pres D&AD 1990 (memb Exec Ctee 1985, chm Corporate Identity Jury 2000); memb: BAFTA, RTS; hon fell Kent Inst of Art and Design 1994; Hon DA Lincoln Univ 2004; FCSD 1982, RDI 1987, FRTS 2004; *Awards* winner (with Daniel Barber) BAFTA Award for BBC2 identity 1992, recipient RTS Judges' Award for 30 years of creativity 1995, Lambie-Nairn & Co recipient of Queen's Award for Export Achievement 1995, President's Award D&AD 1997, Prince Philip Designers Prize 1998; *Books* Brand Identity for Television with Knobs On (1997); *Style*— Martin Lambie-Nairn, Esq; ⊠ Greencoat House, Francis Street, London SW1P 1DH

LAMBIRTH, Andrew Gordon; s of Gordon Frank Trevallion Lambirth, of Ottery St Mary, Devon, and Adelaide Harriet, *née* Betteridge; *b* 2 January 1959; *Educ* St John's Sch Leatherhead, Univ of Nottingham (BA); *Career* porter Sotheby's London 1981–82, freelance researcher and writer 1983–, ed and collaborator on Eileen Agar's autobiography A Look At My Life (1988) 1985–88, cataloguer and conslt on papers of Malcolm Muggeridge 1987–88, contrib ed Royal Academy Magazine 1990–2002; currently art critic The Spectator; *Monographs* incl: Allen Jones (1997 and 2005), Josef Herman (1998), Aubrey Beardsley (1998), Kitty North (1998), William Shakespeare (1999), W B Yeats (1999), Ken Kiff (2001), Ron King (2002), Craigie Aitchison (2003), R B Kitaj (2004), Maggi Hambling (2006), Roger Hilton (2007); *Recreations* reading, walking and looking; *Style*— Andrew Lambirth, Esq; ⊠ c/o The Spectator, 56 Doughty Street, London WC1N 2LL

LAMBIRTH, Mark Nicholas; s of Peter Mabson Lambirth (d 2001), of St Albans, and Jean Margaret, *née* Barber; *b* 30 May 1953; *Educ* St Albans Sch, Queens' Coll Cambridge (BA); *m* 7 June 1986, Anne Catherine, da of George Wood; *Career* civil servant; Price Cmmn 1975–77; Civil Service 1977–: princ 1982, Shipping Policy 1982–85, Ports Div 1985–88, sr princ 1988, ministerial speech writer and dep head Info Div 1988–89, asst sec 1989, head Public Tport London Div 1989–92, head Central Fin Div 1992–95, under sec 1995, dir Planning and Tport Directorate Govt Office for London 1995–98, dir Local Government Fin Directorate DETR 1998–2002, dir Rail Delivery Directorate 2002–; *Recreations* poetry, cooking, wine; *Clubs* MCC; *Style*— Mark Lambirth, Esq

LAMBTON, (Lady) Lucinda; eld da of Antony Lambton (6 Earl of Durham who disclaimed peerage 1970); does not use courtesy title of Lady; *b* 10 May 1943; *m* 1, 16 Jan 1965, Henry Mark Harrod, s of Sir (Henry) Roy Forbes Harrod; 2 s (Barnaby, Huckleberry); m 2, 11 Jan 1986 (m dis), Sir Edmund Fairfax-Lucy, 6 Bt, of Charlecote Park, Warwick; m 3, 11 May 1991, as his 2 w, Sir Peregrine Gerard Worsthorne, *qv*; *Career* photographer, writer and broadcaster; broadcaster many progs for BBC Radio 4; hon FRIBA; *Television* programmes: On The Throne, Animal Crackers, Cabinet of Curiosities, The Great North Road, Desirable Dwellings, Hurray for Today (on modern architecture, six part series), Hurray for Today USA (six part series), The Alphabet of Britain (24 part series), One Foot in the Past (thirteen contribs), The Other House of Windsor, Travels with Pevsner, Old New World (3 part series), Sublime Suburbia (4 part series and part series), Treasures of Jamaica; *Books* Vanishing Victoriana, Temples of Convenience (1978, 1995 and 2007), Chambers of Delight, Beastly Buildings (1985, republished as Palaces for Pigs 2008), Album of Curious Houses, Magnificent Menagerie, Lucinda Lambton's A-Z of Britain, Old New World; *Style*— Lucinda Lambton; ⊠ The Old Rectory, Hedgerley, Buckinghamshire SL2 3UY (tel 01753 646167, fax 01753 646914, e-mail lucinda.lambton@virgin.net)

LAMING, Baron (Life Peer UK 1998), of Tewin in the County of Hertfordshire; Sir (William) Herbert Laming; kt (1996), CBE (1985), DL (Herts 1999); s of William Angus Laming, and Lillian, *née* Robson; *b* 19 July 1936; *Educ* Univ of Durham (DSocSci); *m* 1962, Aileen Margaret, *née* Pollard; *Career* probation offr then sr probation offr Nottingham Probation Serv 1961–68, asst chief probation offr Nottingham City and Co Probation Serv 1968–71, deputy dir then dir Hertfordshire CC Social Servs 1971–91, chief inspr Social Servs Inspectorate DHSS 1991–98; chair: Ind Inquiry into Care and Treatment of Mr Justice Cummins 2000, Review of the Mgmnt of Prison Serv 2000, Victoria Climbiè Inquiry 2001–03; pres Assoc of Dirs of Social Servs 1982–83; *Style*— The Lord Laming of Tewin, CBE, DL; ⊠ House of Lords, London SW1A 0PW

LAMMER, Peter; s of Alfred Ritter von Lammer (d 2000), and Benedicta, *née* Gräfin Wengersky; *b* 18 December 1958; *Educ* Alleyn's Sch Dulwich, Univ of Warwick (BSc), St John's Coll Oxford (DPhil); *Career* co-fndr and jt ceo (with Dr Jan Hruska, *qv*) Sophos plc 1985–2005 (non-exec dir 2006–); KM; *Recreations* forestry, stalking, bridge, skiing, old sports cars; *Clubs* Travellers; *Style*— Peter Lammer, Esq; ⊠ Sophos plc, The Pentagon, Abingdon Science Park, Abingdon OX14 3YP (tel 01235 559933, fax 01235 544181)

LAMMY, David; MP; s of Rosalind Lammy; *b* 19 July 1972; *Educ* King's Sch Peterborough, Univ of London (LLB), Inns of Court Sch of Law, Harvard Law Sch (LLM); *Career* barr 3 Serjeant's Inn 1994–98, attorney Howard Rice USA 1997–98, barr DJ Freeman 1998–2000; GLA (Lab) 2000; MP (Lab) Tottenham 2000– (by-election); PPS to Rt Hon Estelle Morris, MP 2001–02, Parly under sec of state Dept of Health 2002–03, Parly under sec of state DCA 2003–06, Parly under sec of state DCMS 2006–; memb Select Ctee: Public Admin 2000–01, Procedure 2000–01; memb All-Pty Gp: Rwanda and the Prevention of Genocide, Br-Caribbean, Aids; memb Parly Cwlth Assoc; memb: Soc of Lab Lawyers, Christian Socialist Movement; tstee Action Aid 2001–06 (hon ambass 2006–); *Recreations* film, live music, Spurs FC; *Style*— David Lammy, Esq, MP; ⊠ House of Commons, London SW1A 0AA (tel 020 7219 0767, fax 020 7219 0357)

LAMONT, (Archibald) Colin (Neil); s of Archie and Christabel; *b* 20 June 1956; *Educ* Greenock Acad, Univ of Glasgow (BA), Royal Scottish Acad of Music & Drama (Dip Speech & Drama, winner Duncan Macrae Meml Competition), Jordanhill Coll of Educn Glasgow (PGCE); *Career* media conslt, actor, writer and broadcaster; secdy teacher, mgmnt trainee Clydesdale Bank Ltd 1973–77; Scottish Opera: touring mangr and presenter 1980, dir educn prog 1981–84, mktg offr 1983; asst mangr Pitlochry Festival Theatre 1981; announcer/newscaster: Grampian Television Aberdeen 1984–85, Scottish Television Glasgow 1985–88, Border Television Carlisle 1985–89, gen mangr and controller of programmes CentreSound Radio (now Central FM) Stirling 1989–90, mgmnt conslt 1990–91; sr prodr/presenter: Red Rose Radio Preston 1992–94, Central Scotland Radio Edinburgh, Scot FM Leith 1994–97, EMAP Radio, Hallam FM Sheffield, TFM Middlesbrough, Magic AM Liverpool, Leeds and Hull 1997–98, Century Radio Manchester, Nottingham and Newcastle 1998–2000, The Wireless Gp 96.3 QFM Glasgow and AM NW Yorks and the Midlands 2000–02, EMAP Radio, Sheffield, Leeds and Hull and Magic AM Yorks, Lincs and the Midlands 2002–04, SRH (Scottish Radio Holdings) Radio Forth Edinburgh, 2003–05, SRH Radio Clyde Glasgow 2004–05; UTV Radio: Q96 Glasgow 2006, Talk 107 Edinburgh 2006–; guest appearances: BBC Radio 4, BBC World Serv, BBC Radio Scotland, Talk Radio London, conductor Hallé orch Manchester Arena, The Chieftain Bearsden Milngavie Highland Games 2007; columnist: Daily Record, The Sun; visiting lectr: Stevenson Coll Edinburgh, Univ of Salford; memb: Equity, Exec Ctee Sea Corps 1975–80, Soc of Friends and Descendants of the Knights of the Garter St George's Chapel Windsor 1977–; *Publications* An Audience With Scottie McClue (video, 1996); *Recreations* music, conversation, working field-trials labradors, classic motoring (owner/driver), classic coastal cruising (owner/master/skipper); *Clubs* Royal Over-Seas League; *Style*— Colin Lamont, Esq; ⊠ Scottie McClue, UTV Radio, Talk 107, 9 South Gyle Crescent, Edinburgh Park, Edinburgh EH12 9EB (tel 0131 316 3107, e-mail bigtalkman@btinternet.com, www.scottie-mcclue.com)

LAMONT, John Robert; MSP; s of Robert Lamont, and Elizabeth, *née* Wilson; *b* 15 April 1976, Irvine, Ayrshire; *Educ* Kilwinning Acad, Univ of Glasgow (LLB), Coll of Law Chester; *Career* trainee slr then assoc Freshfields 2002–04, assoc Bristows 2004–05, sr slr Brodies 2005–07; MSP (Cons) Roxburgh and Berwickshire 2007–; memb Law Soc of Eng and Wales 2002; *Recreations* swimming, tennis; *Style*— John Lamont, Esq, MSP; ⊠ Scottish Parliament, Edinburgh EH99 1SP (tel 0131 348 6532)

LAMONT, Prof William Montgomerie; s of Hector Lamont (d 1985), of Harrow, London, and Hughina Carmichael, *née* MacFadyen (d 1982); *b* 2 February 1934; *Educ* Harrow Weald County GS, Univ of London (BA, PGCE, PhD); *m* 5 April 1961, Linda Mary, da of Lionel Stanley Cuthbert Murphy; 3 da (Catriona *b* 1 Jan 1962, Ailsa *b* 10 May 1963, Tara *b* 26 June 1965); *Career* schoolmaster Hackney Downs Secdy Sch 1959–63, lectr Aberdeen Coll of Educn 1963–66; Univ of Sussex: lectr 1966, reader 1970, prof of history Univ of Sussex 1966–99, dean Sch of Cultural and Community Studies 1981–86, research prof of history 1999–2002, emeritus prof 2003–; dir Centre for the History of Br Political Thought Folger Library Washington 1985; FRHistS 1969; *Books* Marginal Prynne (1963), Godly Rule (1969), The Realities of Teaching History (ed, 1972), Politics Religion and Literature in the 17th century (jtly, 1975), Richard Baxter and the Millennium (1979), The World of the Muggletonians (jtly, 1983), Richard Baxter A Holy Commonwealth (ed, 1994), Puritanism and Historical Controversy (1996), Historical Controversies and Historians (ed, 1998), Last Witnesses: The Muggletonian History 1652–1979 (2006); *Recreations* watching Arsenal; *Style*— Prof William Lamont; ⊠ 4 East Street, Lewes, East Sussex BN7 2LJ (tel 01273 470940)

LAMONT OF LERWICK, Baron (Life Peer UK 1998), of Lerwick in the Shetland Islands; Rt Hon Norman Stewart Hughson Lamont; PC (1986); s of Daniel Lamont and Irene Lamont; *b* 8 May 1942; *Educ* Loretto (scholar), Fitzwilliam Coll Cambridge (pres Cambridge Union); *m* 1971 (m dis 2000), Alice Rosemary, da of Lt-Col Peter White; 1 s, 1 da; *Career* PA to Duncan Sandys 1965, Cons Res Dept 1966–68, merchant banker N M Rothschild & Sons 1968–79 (dir Rothschild Asset Management); Parly candidate (Cons) Hull E 1970, MP (Cons) Kingston upon Thames 1972–97, Parly candidate (Cons) Harrogate and Knaresborough 1997; chm: Coningsby Club 1970–71, Bow Gp 1971–72; PPS to Arts Min 1974; oppn spokesman: on consumer affairs 1975–76, on industry 1976–79; under-sec of state Dept of Energy 1979–81; Min of State: DTI 1981–85, for Defence Procurement

1985–86; Financial Sec to Treasy May 1986–July 1989, Chief Sec to the Treasy July 1989–Nov 1990, Chancellor of the Exchequer Nov 1990–May 1993, memb House of Lords Select Ctee on Euro Union Affairs 1999–2003; non-exec dir N M Rothschild & Sons Ltd 1993–95, chm and dir of various investment tsts 1995–; dir: Balli plc 1995–, Compagnie Internationale de Participations Bancaires et Financieres 1999–, RAB Capital 2004–; chm: Jupiter Adria 2006–, Advsy Bd Uniastrum Bank Russia 2006–; advsr to the Romanian Govt 1997–98, advsr to the Western Union Co 2006–, pres Br-Romanian C Of C 2002–, chm Br Iranian C of C 2004–, chm Clan Lamont Soc 2006–; vice pres Bruges Gp 2006–; awarded Star of Merit (Chile) 2000; *Books* In Office (1999), Sovereign Britain (1994); *Style—* The Rt Hon the Lord Lamont of Lerwick, PC; ✉ c/o Balli plc, 5 Stanhope Gate, London W1Y 5LA

LAMPARD, Clive; s of Roy Lampard (d 1978), of Maidstone, and Renee Lampard; *b* 25 May 1959; *Educ* Oakwood Park GS Maidstone, Westfield Coll London (BA, MA); *m* 1984, Julia Catherine, da of James Bernard Carr; 1 da (Sarah b 13 Jan 1987), 2 s (Daniel b 22 March 1989, Luke b 12 June 1992); *Career* articled clerk Slaughter and May 1983–85; ptnr Macfarlanes 1991– (joined 1989, currently head Corporate Real Estate Practice); author of various articles; govr The Hall Sch Hampstead; memb Law Soc; *Recreations* family, wine, sport, church; *Style—* Clive Lampard, Esq; ✉ Macfarlanes, 10 Norwich Street, London EC4A 1BD (tel 020 7831 9222, fax 020 7831 9607, e-mail clive.lampard@macfarlanes.com)

LAMPARD, Frank James; s of Frank Lampard, the West Ham and England footballer; *b* 21 June 1978, Romford, Essex; *Partner* Elen Rives; 2 da (Luna Patricia b 2005, Isla b 2007); *Career* professional footballer; clubs: West Ham United FC 1995–2001 (Swansea City (on loan) 1995–96), Chelsea FC 2001– (winners FA Premiership 2005 and 2006 (runners-up 2004 and 2007), League Cup 2005 and 2007, FA Cup 2007 (finalists 2002)); England: 56 caps, 11 goals, debut v Belgium 1999, memb squad European Championships 2004 and World Cup 2006; runner-up PFA Player of the Year 2004 and 2005, England Footballer of the Year 2004 and 2005, Football Writers Footballer of the Year 2005 (runner-up 2004), runner-up European Footballer of the Year and World Player of the Year 2005; *Style—* Mr Frank Lampard; ✉ c/o Chelsea Football Club, Fulham Road, London SW6 1HS

LAMPERT, Catherine Emily; da of Lt Cdr Chester Graham Lampert (d 1981), of Washington DC, USA, and Emily Schubach Lampert; *b* 15 October 1946; *Educ* Brown Univ (BA), Temple Univ (MA); *m* 22 Dec 1971 (m dis 1994), Robert Keith Mason; 1 da (Susana b 1990); *Career* sr exhibition organiser Arts Cncl of GB 1973–88, dir Whitechapel Art Gallery 1988–2001; organiser of several exhibitions incl retrospectives of: Frank Auerbach, Lucian Freud, Michael Andrews, Henri Matisse, Drawings and Sculpture, Auguste Rodin, In the Image of Man, Euan Uglow, Richard Diebenkorn, Juan Gris, Francisco Toledo, Nan Goldin; memb Charles Wallace India Tst; memb ICOM, CIMAM; *Books* The Drawings and Sculpture of Auguste Rodin (1987), Lucian Freud: Recent Work (1993), Frank Auerbach, Paintings and Drawings 1954–2001 (2001), The Prophet and the Fly: Francis Alÿs (2003), Rodin (2006), Uglow (2007), Lucian Freud (2007); *Style—* Mrs Catherine Lampert; ✉ 92 Lenthall Road, London E8 3JN (tel 020 7241 2065, e-mail clampert@dial.pipex.com)

LAMPL, Sir Frank William; kt (1990); s of Dr Otto Lampl (d 1934), and Olga, *née* Jellinek (d Auschwitz 1944); *b* 6 April 1926; *Educ* Faculty of Architecture and Engrg Tech Univ Brno Czechoslovakia; *m* Wendy Dianne, da of Robert Scarborough (d 1980); 1 s (Thomas b 1950); *Career* various construction industry appts rising to md in Czechoslovakia before emigrating to UK 1968; Bovis Construction Group: project mangr then construction dir Bovis Ltd 1971, md Bovis Construction Southern Ltd and exec dir Bovis Construction Ltd 1974, chief exec and md Bovis International Ltd 1978, dir Bovis Ltd 1979, chm Bovis Construction Ltd and Bovis International Ltd 1985–89, exec dir Peninsular and Oriental Steam Navigation Co (P&O, parent co of Bovis) 1985–99, chm Bovis Construction Group 1986–99, dir Lehrer McGovern Bovis Inc NY 1986–, chm Bovis (Far East) Ltd 1987–, chm P&O Developments Ltd 1987–89, pres Bovis Lend Lease Holdings 2001– (chm 1999–2001); dir Mills Corporation Washington DC 2004–; chllr Kingston Univ 1994–2000; Pres's Medal Chartered Inst of Bldg 1993, Bldg Award for Lifetime Achievement 2002; hon doctorates: Brno Tech Univ 1993, Kingston Univ 1994, Univ of Reading 1995, Univ of Middx; CIMgt, FCIOB; *Clubs* RAC, Athenaeum; *Style—* Sir Frank Lampl

LAMPORT, Sir Stephen Mark Jeffrey; KCVO (2002, CVO 1999), DL (Surrey 2006); s of Eric George Lamport, of Horsted Keynes, W Sussex, and Jeanne Helen, *née* Jeffries; *b* 27 November 1951; *Educ* Dorking Co GS, CCC Cambridge (MA), Univ of Sussex (MA); *m* 1979, Angela Vivien Paula, da of Peter De La Motte Hervey; 2 s (Edward b 1983, William b 1985), 1 da (Alexandra b 1990); *Career* HM Dip Serv: joined 1974, third later second sec Br Embassy Tehran 1975–79, private sec to Douglas Hurd as minister of state 1981–83, private sec to Malcolm Rifkind as min of state 1983–84, first sec Br Embassy Rome 1984–88, FCO 1988–93 (appointed counsellor 1990), private sec and treas to HRH The Prince of Wales 1996–2002 (dep private sec 1993–96); gp dir for public policy and govt affrs Royal Bank of Scotland 2002–, non-exec dir Brewin Dolphin Holdings plc 2007–; tstee: Queen Mother Meml Fund 2003–06, Surrey Community Fndn 2006–; memb: Cncl Arvon Fndn 2004, Cncl of Guildford Cathedral 2006–, Scottish Nat Ballet Tramway Appeal 2007–; memb Ct Royal Fndn of St Katharine 2004; *Books* The Palace of Enchantments (with Douglas Hurd, *qv*, 1985); *Clubs* RAC, Grillions; *Style—* Sir Stephen Lamport, KCVO, DL; ✉ Elm Tree Cottage, Downside, Cobham, Surrey KT11 3NQ

LAN, David; *b* 1 June 1952; *Educ* Univ of Cape Town (BA), LSE (BSc, PhD); *Career* playwright, translator, social anthropologist, theatre dir; writer in residence Royal Court Theatre 1995–97, artistic dir Young Vic Theatre 2000–; *Theatre* prodns at Young Vic incl: 'Tis Pity She's a Whore 1999, Julius Caesar 2000, A Raisin in the Sun 2001, Doctor Faustus 2002, The Daughter in Law 2002, The Skin of our Teeth 2004, A Raisin in the Sun 2005; other prodns incl: The Glass Menagerie (Watford) 1998, As You Like It (Wyndhams) 2005; *Film* for BBC: The Sunday Judge 1985, Welcome Home Comrades 1986, Dark City (writer) 1996, Artist Unknown 1996, Royal Court Diaries (dir) 1997; *Plays* incl: Painting a Wall (Almost Free) 1974, Bird Child (Royal Court) 1974, The Winter Dancers (Royal Court) 1977, Sergeant Ola (Royal Court) 1979, Flight (RSC) 1986, Desire (Almeida) 1990, The Ends of the Earth (NT) 1996; *Translations* Ghetto 1989 (NT), Hippolytos (Almeida) 1991, Ion (RSC) 1994, Uncle Vanya (RSC/Young Vic) 1998, La Lupa (RSC) 1999, The Cherry Orchard (NT) 2000; *Libretti* Tobias and the Angel (music J Dove) 1999, Ion (music Param Vir) 2000 and 2003; *Books* Guns and Rain: Guerrillas and Spirit Mediums in Zimbabwe (1985); *Style—* David Lan, Esq; ✉ c/o Young Vic Theatre, 66 The Cut, London SE1 8LZ

LANCASTER, His Hon Judge Anthony Trevor; s of Thomas William Lancaster (decd), and Jean Margaret, *née* Grainger; *b* 26 June 1948; *Educ* Austin Friars Sch Carlisle, Univ of Leeds (LLB); *Family* 3 s (Philip James b 23 Dec 1974, John Andrew b 7 May 1977, David Francis b 29 March 1981), 1 da (Helen Alice b 4 Aug 1991); m 11 May 1997, Beverley Anne, *née* Conlon; 1 s (Matthew Charles b 31 Oct 1998), 1 da (Rebecca Niamh b 10 Nov 2000); *Career* admitted slr 1973; registrar County Court 1988–91, district judge 1991–2001, recorder of the Crown Court 1999–2001 (asst recorder 1995–99), circuit judge (NE Circuit) 2001–; pres Assoc District Judges 2000–01, pt/t chm Social Security Appeals Tbnl 1985–88; memb Law Soc 1973; *Style—* His Hon Judge Lancaster; ✉ c/o Law Courts, Quayside, Newcastle upon Tyne NE1 1EE (tel 0191 201 2000, fax 0191 201 2001)

LANCASTER, Graham; s of Eric Lancaster, of Salford, Gtr Manchester, and Edna, *née* Butterworth; *b* 24 February 1948; *Educ* Salford GS, Mid Cheshire Coll (HND), Open Univ (BA); *m* 10 Oct 1971, Lorna Mary, da of William Thomas White (d 1982); *Career* Hawker Siddeley Aviation 1968–69, asst to Dir of Information and Educn The Textile Cncl 1969–70, trg devpt offr Corah Ltd 1971, policy coordinator to Pres CBI 1972–77, head of public affrs ABTA 1977, chm Euro RSCG Biss Lancaster plc 1978–, EMEA chm Euro RSCG Worldwide PR 2006–; memb Bd PRCA (chm 2001–03), tstee Br Lung Fndn 2005–; FCIM, FIPR, FRSA; *Books* The Nuclear Letters (1979), Seward's Folly (1980), The 20 Percent Factor (1987 and 1989), Gravesong (1996), Payback (1997); *Recreations* writing; *Clubs* Groucho, Travellers; *Style—* Graham Lancaster, Esq; ✉ Euro RSCG Biss Lancaster plc, Cupola House, 15 Alfred Place, London WC1E 7EB (tel 020 7467 9200, fax 020 7467 9201)

LANCASTER, Mark; TD (2002), MP; s of Rev Ron Lancaster, MBE; *Educ* Univ of Buckingham (BSc, PhD), Univ of Exeter (MBA); *m* Katie; *Career* offr Queens Gurkha Engineers (served Hong Kong), Maj TA (served Kosovo and Bosnia as part of UN peacekeeping force); md Kimbolton Fireworks; Parly candidate (Cons) Nuneaton 2001, MP (Cons) Milton Keynes NE 2005–; *Style—* Mark Lancaster, TD, MP; ✉ House of Commons, London SW1A 0AA (tel 020 7219 8414, fax 020 7219 6685, e-mail lancasterm@parliament.uk); Constituency Office, 13A High Street, Newport Pagnell, Buckinghamshire MK16 8AR (tel 01908 615757, website www.lancaster4mk.com)

LANCASTER, Bishop of (RC) 2001–; Rt Rev Patrick Augustine O'Donoghue; s of Daniel O'Donoghue (d 1970), of Mallow, Co Cork, and Sheila, *née* Twomey (d 1985); *Educ* Patrician Acad Mallow, Campion House Coll Osterley, St Edmund's Coll Ware; *Career* ordained RC priest 1967; Dio of Westminster: memb Diocesan Mission Team 1970–73, rector Allen Hall Diocesan Seminary Chelsea 1985–90, admin Westminster Cathedral 1990–93, aux bishop of Westminster with responsibility for the West Area 1993–2001; involvement with other orgns incl: The Passage Day Centre for the Poor, Cardinal Hume Centre for Young Homeless, The Lillie Road Centre for Children in Care, Acton Homeless Concern, Christian Arts Tst; *Recreations* walking (in countryside), travel, theatre, football (spectator); *Style—* The Rt Rev the Bishop of Lancaster; ✉ Bishop's Apartment, Cathedral House, Balmoral Road, Lancaster LA1 3BT (tel 01524 384830, fax 01524 596053, e-mail bishop@lancasterrcdiocese.org.uk)

LANCASTER, Roger; *b* 4 February 1951; *Educ* Univ of Leicester (LLB); *m* Margaret; 2 s, 1 da; *Career* admitted slr 1975; former sr ptnr and head of planning and environmental law Halliwell Landau; called to the Bar, practising fom King's Chambers Manchester; *Recreations* cricket, squash; *Style—* Roger Lancaster, Esq; ✉ Kings Chambers, 40 King Street, Manchester M2 6BA (tel 0161 832 9082)

LANCASTER SMITH, Dr Michael John; s of late Ronald Lancaster Smith, of Hastings, E Sussex, and Marie, *née* Wright; *b* 4 September 1941; *Educ* Hastings GS, London Hosp Med Sch (BSc, MB BS, MD); *m* 11 April 1964, Susan Frances Bayes, da of Lt Arthur Bannister (d 1946); 2 da (Catherine b 1966, Naomi b 1971), 1 s (Daniel b 1969); *Career* registrar and sr registrar The London Hosp 1969–73 (house physician and surgn 1966–68), sr lectr Bart's London 1973–74, conslt physician Queen Mary's Univ Hosp Sidcup 1974–; vice-chm Bexley HA 1986–89, formerly chm South Thames Regnl Gastroenterology Trg Ctee, South Thames Regnl Gastroenterology advsr RCP, assessor Nat Clinical Assessment Authy 2003; memb: Br Soc of Gastroenterology (memb Cncl 1993–95), BMA, RSM; FRCP; *Books* Problems in Practice - Gastroenterology (1982), Problems in Management - Gastroenterology (1985), Ulcer and Non Ulcer Dyspepsia (1987), Dyspepsia - Fast Facts (2003), Gastrointestinal Problems (2004); *Recreations* cricket, music, theatre, bloodstock; *Clubs* MCC; *Style—* Dr Michael Lancaster Smith; ✉ Stableside House, 36 Southborough Road, Bickley, Bromley, Kent BR1 2EB (tel 020 8467 4184); Queen Mary's University Hospital, Sidcup, Kent DA14 6LT (tel 020 8302 2678 ext 423); Blackheath Hospital, London SE3 9UD; The Sloane Hospital, Beckenham, Kent BR3 5HS; Chelsfield Park Hospital, Kent BR6 7RG

LANCE, Prof (Edward) Christopher; s of F Nevill Lance (d 1987), and Elizabeth, *née* Bagnall (d 1989); *b* 17 January 1941; *Educ* Dulwich Coll, Trinity Coll Cambridge (MA, PhD); *m* 9 April 1966, Mary Margaret, *née* Hall; 1 s (Stephen b 1969), 1 da (Elizabeth b 1971); *Career* lectr in pure maths Univ of Newcastle 1965–73, reader Univ of Manchester 1973–78, prof of mathematics Univ of Leeds 1980–; visiting prof Univ of Pennsylvania USA 1971–72, 1978–80 and 1992–93; vice-pres London Mathematical Soc 1988–90, sec Euro Mathematical Soc 1990–94; *Recreations* hill walking, music; *Style—* Prof Christopher Lance; ✉ School of Mathematics, The University of Leeds, Leeds LS2 9JT (tel 0113 233 5142, fax 0113 233 5145, e.c.lance@leeds.ac.uk)

LANCELEY, Ian Kenneth; s of Thomas Peter Kenneth Lanceley, of Paignton, Devon, and Barbara Doreen, *née* Allen; *b* 12 February 1946; *Educ* Blundell's, Coll of Law; *m* 12 Dec 1980, Valerie, da of Frederick William Kay (d 1987), of Richmond, North Yorks; 2 s (Adam b 1981, Charles b 1983); *Career* admitted slr (with hons)1971; ptnr Freeborough Slack & Co 1977–85, sr ptnr Freeboroughs 1985–98, ptnr WH Matthews and Co (incorporating Freeboroughs) 1998–; dep magistrate Metropolitan Stipendiary 1985–90; memb Law Soc; *Recreations* family, golf, tennis, wine drinking; *Clubs* Roehampton, Royal Wimbledon Golf; *Style—* Ian K Lanceley, Esq; ✉ 19 Penrhyn Road, Kingston upon Thames KT1 2BZ (tel 020 8549 0264, e-mail ikl@whmatthews.com and ikl@debrett.net)

LANCELOT, James Bennett; s of Rev Roland Lancelot (d 1983), and Margaret, *née* Tye (d 1998); *b* 2 December 1952; *Educ* St Paul's Cathedral Choir Sch, Ardingly, RCM, King's Coll Cambridge (Organ scholar, MA, MusB); *m* 31 July 1982, Sylvia Jane, da of Raymond Hoare, of Cheltenham; 2 da (Rebecca b 1987, Eleanor b 1989); *Career* asst organist Hampstead Parish Church and St Clement Danes Church 1974–75, sub-organist Winchester Cathedral 1975–85, master of the choristers and organist Durham Cathedral 1985–, conductor Univ of Durham Choral Soc 1987–, organist Univ of Durham 2002–, fell St Chad's Coll Durham 2006–; numerous recordings; lay canon Durham Cathedral 2002–; pres Cathedral Organists' Assoc 2001–03, pres Darlington and District Organists' and Choirmasters' Assoc 2004–05; hon fell Guild of Church Musicians 2002; FRCO (chm 1969), ARCM 1970; *Books* Durham Cathedral Organs (co-author with Richard Hird, 1991), The Sense of the Sacramental (contrib, 1995); *Recreations* railways; *Style—* Canon James Lancelot; ✉ 6 The College, Durham DH1 3EQ (tel 0191 386 4766)

LAND, (John) Anthony; *b* 21 September 1939; *Educ* Westminster (Queen's scholar), Trinity Coll Cambridge (minor scholar, BA); *m* Deborah Lucy Irene; 2 c; *Career* asst mangr (special pubns) The Times 1962–65; Readers' Digest London: asst then dep ed (magazines) 1965–71, managing ed (magazines) 1971–74, exec dir (books) 1974–77; Consumers' Assoc: head of publishing 1977–91, asst dir 1987–91; freelance consit (Thames and Hudson, Joseph Rowntree Fndn, The Planning Exchange, Asia Inc) 1991–93; Design Cncl: dir of publishing 1991–94, resources dir and sec to the Cncl 1994–2000; mgmnt and editorial conslt 2001– (Equal Opportunities Cmmn, Gen Social Care Cncl, Social Care Inst for Excellence, Royal Soc, Kensington and Chelsea PCT); non-exec chm Dr Foster Intelligence 2006–; non-exec dir: Book Tst London 1989–96, Health and Social Care Information Centre Leeds 2005–; chm Campden Hill Residents' Assoc 1994–2001; memb Parly and Legal Ctee PPA 1989–94; Hon DLitt Univ of Brighton; ACCA (Charterd Dip Accounting and Fin); *Recreations* swimming, walking, opera, travel, history; *Style—* Anthony Land, Esq; ✉ Edlins, Aston Upthorpe, Oxfordshire OX11 9EF (tel 01235 850051, e-mail anthony@murdochland.net)

LAND, (Harold) Brook; s of David Land (d 1995), of London, and Zara, *née* Levinson; *b* 12 March 1949; *Educ* St Paul's; *m* 7 Dec 1975, Anita Penny, da of Leslie Grade; 1 da (Lesley Olivia b 19 Jan 1981), 1 s (Daniel Edward b 30 April 1983); *Career* Nabarro Nathanson Solicitors: articled clerk 1967–72, asst slr 1972–74, ptnr 1974–96, conslt 1996–; memb

L

Law Soc 1972; non-exec chm: RPS Gp plc 1997–, Medal Entertainment and Media plc 2001–; non-exec dir: JLI Gp plc 1989–98, Signet Gp plc 1995–2008, Brown Lloyd James Ltd 1997–2006, Crown Personnel plc 1998–2005; chm Theatre Royal Brighton Ltd 1996–99; *Recreations* reading, family, Arsenal; *Style*— Brook Land, Esq; ✉ 10 Wyndham Place, London W1H 2PU (tel 020 7723 2456, fax 020 7723 7567, e-mail brook@brookl.co.uk)

LAND, Dr John Melville; s of Ernest G E Land (d 1979), and Joyce Land; *b* 19 February 1950; *Educ* Hymers Coll Hull, Univ of London (BSc, PhD), London Business Sch (MBA), Merton Coll Oxford (BM BCh); *Career* jr med positions 1980–81, Hammersmith Hosp London 1981, Brompton Hosp London 1982, John Radcliffe Hosps Oxford 1982–92, conslt Neurometabolic Unit National Hosp London 1992–, clinical head of service Biochemical Med UCLH Tst 2002–; Salters fell Univ of Pennsylvania 1974–75, Brian Johnson Prize in pathology Univ of Oxford 1979, NHS Exec Bursary 1994–97; corresponding memb American Soc of Neurochemistry 2003; FRSM 1985, MRCPath 1999; *Publications* author of many pubns in med and biochemical jls; *Recreations* cricket, walking, cooking; *Clubs* Savile; *Style*— Dr John Land; ✉ Neurometabolic Unit, National Hospital, Queen Square, London WC1N 3BG (tel 020 7829 8768, e-mail john.land@uclh.org)

LAND, Prof Michael Francis; s of Prof Frank William Land (d 1990), and Nora Beatrice, *née* Channon (d 1985); *b* 12 April 1942; *Educ* Birkenhead Sch, Jesus Coll Cambridge (BA, Frank Smart Prize in zoology), UCL (PhD); *m* 1 (m dis 1980), Judith Drinkwater; 1 s (Adam Michael b 1969); m 2, 10 Dec 1980, Rosemary, da of James Clarke; 2 da (Katharine Rosemary b 1981, Penelope Frances b 1983); *Career* asst prof Univ of Calif Berkeley 1969–71 (Miller fell 1967–69); Sch of Biological Sciences Univ of Sussex: lectr 1972–78, reader 1978–84, prof 1984–; sr visiting fell Aust Nat Univ Canberra 1982–84; memb Cncl of the Marine Biological Assoc 1995–; memb Editorial Bd Jl of Comparative Physiology; Frink Medal Zoological Soc of London 1994; FRS 1982; *Publications* Animal Eyes (2002); author of 150 publications on aspects of animal and human vision in learned jls and popular sci jls; *Recreations* gardening, music; *Style*— Prof Michael Land, FRS; ✉ White House, Cuilfail, Lewes, East Sussex BN7 2BE (tel 01273 476780); Department of Biology and Environmental Science, University of Sussex, Brighton BN1 9QG (tel 01273 678505, fax 01273 678535)

LAND, Ralph Richard; CBE (1996, OBE 1985); s of Louis Landsberger (d 1976), of London, and Sofia, *née* Weinberger (d 1999); *b* 24 October 1928, Berlin; *Educ* Willesden Co GS, LSE (BSc (Econ)); *m* 3 April 1954, Jacqueline-Marie, da of Gustave Bourdin; 2 s (Bryan Christopher b 23 July 1959, Anthony Michael b 6 July 1960); *Career* mgmnt accountant J Lyons & Co Ltd 1952–59, Leo Computers, English Electric Computers and ICL 1959–76 (gen mangr Eastern Europe Div ICL 1964–72, mktg dir Western European Div ICL 1972–74, md ICL Deutschland GMBH 1974–76), gen mangr Eastern Export Ops Rank Xerox Ltd 1976–91, dir of Eastern European affrs Rolls-Royce plc 1991–94 (advsr to the Bd 1994–96), chm Cyberaction Ltd 1997–2000, dir Financial Information Technology Ltd 1999–, chm PCG Worldwide Ltd 2002–05; non-exec dir Int Advsy Bd ICL plc 1991–2001, memb Int Advsy Bd American Phoenix Life and Reassurance Co 1998–2001, dir Co of the Far Countries 2003–; chm Russo-British C of C 1995–2004; UNICE Working Gp on Eastern and Central Europe and Taskforce on Enlargement 1995–2000, E European Trade Cncl (EETC)/DTI; co-chm British Romanian C of C, dep chm Westminster Fndn for Democracy 1993–97; memb: Advsy Bd British Know How Fund 1991–99, Eastern European Trade Cncl, Int Ctee London C of C, Russian Studies Advsy Bd Chatham House; frequent lectr at confs and seminars on Eastern Europe, TV and radio commentator on Eastern European business matters; chm Br Consultancy Charitable Tst 2006–, tstee Healthprom; former tstee: Hamlet Tst, BBC World Serv Tst, BESO; memb: Lab Pty, Serge Prokofiev Soc, Br Computer Soc, RIIA; FRSA 1992; *Publications* Leo: The Incredible Story of the World's First Business Computer (contrib, 1997); author of numerous articles; *Recreations* travel, opera and music, photography, food and drink; *Clubs* Reform, Rotary; *Style*— Ralph Land, Esq, CBE; ✉ 27 Alder Lodge, London SW6 6NP (tel 020 7385 3054, fax 020 7610 1116, mobile 07785 257388, e-mail r.land@btinternet.com)

LAND, Sonia; da of Tan Peng Liat (d 1965), and Md Lioh Ta Fan; *b* 29 January 1948, Singapore; *Educ* Singapore Chinese Girls' Sch, Raffles Inst, Univ of Singapore (BAcc); *m* 27 Sept 1975, Nicholas Charles Edward Land; 1 s (Christopher Mark Nicholas b 30 Dec 1983); *Career* Ernst & Young 1971–75, mgmnt accountant Trust Houses Forte 1975–76, financial and mgmnt accountant BB Mason Ltd 1976–77, financial dir Granada Publishing Ltd 1977–83, gp finance dir William Collins Plc 1983–88, exec dir Newmarket Venture Capital Plc 1988, dir of planning News International plc 1988–90, ceo HarperCollins Publishing Gp UK and Europe 1989–90, ceo Sheil Land Assocs Ltd 1990–; non-exec dir: Mirror Gp 1993–98, Waterford Wedgewood Gp 1994–98; fell Certified and Corporate Accountants 1974; *Recreations* tennis, gardening, travel, cooking; *Style*— Mrs Sonia Land; ✉ Sheil Land Associates Ltd, 52 Doughty Street, London WC1N 2LS (tel 020 7405 9351, fax 020 7831 2127, e-mail sland@sheilland.co.uk)

LANDALE, Sir David William Neil; KCVO (1993), DL (Nithsdale and Annandale (Dumfriesshire) 1984); s of David Fortune Landale (d 1970), and Louisa Mary Dorothy Charlotte, *née* Forbes, (d 1956), yst da of Charles Forbes of Falkirk; *b* 27 May 1934; *Educ* Eton, Balliol Coll Oxford (MA); *m* 1961, Melanie, da of Sir Harold Roper, CBE, MC, MP (Cons) for N Cornwall 1949–59 (d 1971); 3 s (Peter b 1963, William b 1965, Jamie b 1969); *Career* Black Watch Royal Highland Regt 1952–54; Jardine Matheson & Co Ltd: joined 1958, dir 1967–75, worked in Hong Kong, Thailand, Taiwan and Japan; dir: Matheson & Co Ltd 1975–98, Pinneys Holdings Ltd 1982–87; chm: T C Farries & Co Ltd 1982–96, Timber Growers UK Ltd 1985–87; appointed sec and keeper of records of The Duchy of Cornwall 1987–93, dir Dumfries & Galloway Enterprise Co 1993–95; pres Royal Highland Agric Soc of Scotland 1994–95; chm: Royal Highland Agric Soc Ingliston Devpt Tst 1995–97, Royal Scottish Forestry Soc Tst Co (Cashel) 1996–, Malcolm Sargent Cancer Care for Children for Scotland 1996–99 (also tstee), Maggie Keswick Jenks Cancer Caring Centre Tst 1996–99; convenor Chrichton Fndn 1998–2001 (chm 1998–2000); *Recreations* all countryside pursuits, theatre, reading (history); *Clubs* Boodle's, Pratt's, New (Edinburgh); *Style*— Sir David W N Landale, KCVO, DL; ✉ Bankhead, Dalswinton, Dumfries DG2 0XY

LANDAU, Dr David; Hon CBE (2007); s of Aharon Landau, of Jerusalem, and Evelyne, *née* Conti, of Italy; *b* 22 April 1950, Tel Aviv, Israel; *Educ* Liceo Berchet Milan (Maturitá Classica), Pavia Univ (MD), Wolfson Coll Oxford (MA); *m* 2001, Marie-Rose *née* Kahane; 1 s (Max b 2004), 1 da (Mia b 2004 (twin)); *Career* curator Mantegna exhbn Oxford 1979, print curator The Genius of Venice 1500–1600 exhbn Royal Acad 1983, chm Steering Ctee Andrea Mantegna exhbn Royal Acad and Met Museum NYC 1986–92; co-fndr Italian ice cream business 1983–86; Loot (classified listings paper): fndr and jt md 1985–95, chm 1995–2000; fndr of other jls: Print Quarterly 1984 (ed 1984–), Via Via (Holland) 1986, Modern Painters 1988; chm Saffron Hill Ventures 2000–; fndr treas and chm Free Ad Paper Int Assoc 1986–91 (ctee offr 1991–93), jt fndr and treas Young British Friends of the Art Museums of Israel charity 1988–95 (ctee offr 1995–), tstee Nat Gallery 1996–2003, tstee Nat Gallery Tst 1996–, dir Nat Gallery Co 1995–98 (chm 1998–2003), memb Ctee Nat Art Collections Fund 1996–, treas Venice in Peril Fund 1997– (tstee 1996–); fell Worcester Coll Oxford 1980–; FRSA; *Books* Il Catalogo Completo dell'Opera Grafica di Georg Pencz (catalogue of the prints of Georg Pencz, 1978), Federica Galli - Catalogo Completo delle Acqueforti (1982), The Renaissance Print (with Prof Peter Parshall, 1994); numerous articles in jls incl: The Burlington Magazine, Master Drawings, Print Collector, Print Quarterly, Art International, Oxford Art Jl; *Recreations* looking at and collecting art, opera; *Style*— Dr David Landau, CBE; ✉ 51 Kelso Place, London W8 5QQ (tel 020 7795 4989, fax 020 7795 4988, e-mail dlandau@saffronhill.com)

LANDAU, Sir Dennis Marcus; kt (1987); s of late Michael Landau, metallurgist; *b* 18 June 1927; *Educ* Haberdashers' Aske's; *m* 2 Dec 1992, Mrs Pamela Garlick; *Career* chief exec Co-operative Wholesale Society Ltd 1980–92, dep chm Co-operative Bank plc 1989–92; vice-chm Enterprise plc (formerly Lancashire Enterprises plc) 1989–97; chm: Unity Trust Bank plc 1992–2000, Social Economy Forum; pres Lancashire CCC 2003–07 (hon treas 1997–2003); CIMgt, FRSA; *Style*— Sir Dennis Landau; ✉ c/o Lancashire CCC, Old Trafford, Manchester M16 0PX

LANDAU, Lawrence; JP; s of Erwin Landau (d 1970), of London, and Flora, *née* Caplan (d 1972); *b* 16 December 1929; *Educ* Kilburn GS; *m* 1, 12 Oct 1958 (m dis 1985), Janet, *née* Wise; 2 da (Carolyn b 30 Aug 1960, Joanna b 7 May 1972), 1 s (David b 13 Dec 1962); m 2, 3 March 1994, Carole, *née* Lyman; *Career* chartered shipbroker; head legal dept Hellenic Lines 1952–60, chm Dolphin Maritime Services Ltd 1960–96; Hon Consul of Benin 1969–, pres Consular Corps 1984–90 and 1997–2001; ACIArb, FICS; *Recreations* snooker, chess, music; *Clubs* RAC; *Style*— Lawrence Landau, Esq; ✉ Benin Consulate, Millennium House, Humber Road, London NW2 6DW (tel 020 8830 8612, fax 020 7435 0665, e-mail l.landau@btinternet.com)

LANDAU, Toby Thomas; s of Dr Thomas L Landau (d 1991), and Marianne, *née* Samson; *b* 9 October 1967, London; *Educ* Univ Coll Sch London, Merton Coll Oxford (MA, BCL, Eldon law scholar, Slaughter & May Prize, coll exhibitioner, Fowler Prize), Inns of Ct Sch of Law, Harvard Law Sch USA (Kennedy scholar, LLM); *m* Sept 1998, Nudrat B Majeed; 1 da (Zakiya Marianne b 4 Sept 2002); *Career* called to the Bar: Eng and Wales 1993, NI 2000; admitted attorney and cnsllr-at-law NY 1994; lawyer Civil Appeals Office Court of Appeal 1991, law tutor Univ of London 1991–92, memb Essex Ct Chambers 1993–, practising barr specialising in int and commercial law and arbitration; dir of studies, lectr and legal conslt Miny of Justice Thailand 1993–94; visiting sr lectr in arbitration law KCL; visiting lectr: Chulalongkoun Univ and Judge's Inst 1993, Asser Inst The Hague 1995–2004, Int Devpt Law Orgn Rome 2003 and 2004, Pakistan Coll of Law Lahore 2005; memb Govt's Standing Ctee on Private Int Law 1997–; memb: Bd London Ct of Int Arbitration, Int Arbitration Inst, Swiss Arbitration Assoc, American Soc of Int Law, Commercial Bar Assoc, Int Law Assoc; FCIArb (also tstee); *Publications* incl: The English Arbitration Act 1996: Texts and Notes (jtly, 1998), The English Arbitration Act 1996: An Approach to Harmonisation (1999), Commentary on WIPO Arbitration Rules (2000), The Written Form Requirement for Arbitration Agreements: When 'Written' Means 'Oral' (2002); *Clubs* Harvard (NYC); *Style*— Toby Landau, Esq; ✉ Essex Court Chambers, 24 Lincoln's Inn Fields, London WC2A 3EG

LANDER, Geoffrey Ian; s of Victor Lander; *b* 11 January 1951; *m* Lynn; *Career* Nabarro Nathanson: joined as trainee slr 1973, ptnr 1980–2002, head Property Dept 1995–2002; princ Tricore Equity Ptnrs LLP 2002–; non-exec dir: Dolphin Square Tst Ltd 1999–, Plato Enterprises 2005–, TTA Gp 2006–; featured in Euromoney Guide to World's Leading Real Estate Lawyers; past chm CoreNet Global UK (formerly NACORE, also past chm European Advsy Bd), pres Br Cncl for Offices 1998–99; memb Exec Ctee and Bd UK Branch American C of C; memb Law Soc 1976; *Recreations* watching Manchester Utd, bridge, golf; *Style*— Geoffrey Lander, Esq

LANDER, John Hugh Russell; s of Hugh Russell Lander, of IOW, and Maude Louise, *née* Ellis; *b* 25 February 1944; *Educ* Sandown GS, Univ of Sheffield (BSc), Imperial Coll London (MSC, DIC); *m* 1, 1972 (m dis); 2 da (Melody b 1975, Annabel b 1982), 2 s (Robert b 1976, Edward b 1983); m 2, 1995, Alexandra Margaret, *née* Waldron; *Career* exploration dir RTZ Oil & Gas Ltd 1983–89, md PICT Petroleum plc 1989–95, dir British Borneo Petroleum plc 1996–97, md Tuskar Resources plc 1998–1999, UK business unit md Tullow Oil plc 2000–04, non-exec chm Alkane Energy and Medoil plc 2004–; *Recreations* sailing, squash, tennis; *Clubs* RAC, Cannons, Lagos Yacht; *Style*— John Lander, Esq; ✉ Camelot, 26 The Island, Thames Ditton, Surrey KT7 0SH

LANDER, Sir Stephen James; KCB (2000, CB 1995); *b* 1947; *Educ* Bishop's Stortford Coll, Queens' Coll Cambridge (open exhibitioner, MA, PhD); *m* Felicity Mary, *née* Brayley; 1 s (decd), 1 da; *Career* Inst of Historical Research 1972–75, DG Security Service (MI5) 1996–2002 (joined 1975); non-exec dir: HM Customs and Excise 2002–05, Northgate Information Solutions 2004–, Steamshield Networks Ltd 2004–; ind cmmr to Law Soc 2002–05, chair Serious Organised Crime Agency 2004–, memb Slr's Regulation Authy 2006–; Hon LLD Hertfordshire Univ 2005; *Style*— Sir Stephen Lander, KCB

LANDERS, Dr John Maxwell; s of William Maxwell Landers (d 2003), and Muriel, *née* Wilkinson (d 2007); *b* 25 January 1952; *Educ* Southgate Tech Coll, Hertford Coll Oxford (MA), Churchill Coll Cambridge (PhD), Univ of Oxford (LittD); *m* 1991, Diana Parker; *Career* oil demand analyst Shell UK Oil 1979–80, lectr in biological anthropology UCL 1980–90 (tutor Human Scis Interdisciplinary Prog 1984–87, departmental tutor Anthropology Dept 1987–90); Univ of Oxford: fell All Souls Coll and univ lectr in historical demography 1991–2005, princ Hertford Coll 2005–, univ assessor 1994–95, academic sec All Souls Coll 1994–98, memb Jt Ctee Hon Sch of Human Sci 1996–2000, memb Hebdominal Cncl and Gen Bd of the Faculties 1997–2000, chm of curators Examination Schs 1998–2000, memb Communications and IT Ctee 1998–2000, convenor of MSt grad degree and memb Grad Studies Ctee Modern History Faculty 2002–05, chm Mgmnt Ctee Wellcome Unit for the History of Medicine 2003–05; chm Gen Bd Review Ctee Dept of Statistics 1998; memb: Ctee Soc for the Study of Human Biology 1988–92, Advsy Ctee Centre for Metropolitan History Inst of Historical Research Univ of London 1988–95, Review Panel ESRC Cambridge Gp for the History of Population and Social Structure 1993, Ctee Pitt-Rivers Museum 1996– (chm 1999–), History of Medicine Ctee Wellcome Tst 1995–2001 (vice-chm 2000–01); hon sec Br Soc for Population Studies 1990–94, sr treas Oxford Union Soc 1996–98; memb Int Union for the Scientific Study of Population 1987–; FRHistS 2002; *Publications* Death and the Metropolis (1993), The Field and the Forge (2003); author of numerous articles in learned jls and chapters in books incl Jl of Historical Geography, Population Studies, Fertility and Resources, Social History of Medicine, Medical History, Darwinism and Historical Demography, Historical Epidemiology and the Health Transition; *Style*— Dr John Landers; ✉ Hertford College, Catte Street, Oxford OX1 3BW

LANDON, Prof John; s of Charles Landon, and Ellen, *née* Hutton; *b* 2 December 1931; *Educ* King William's Coll Isle of Man, St Mary's Hosp Med Sch (MD); *m* Mary Ursula; 2 s (Ewan, Mark), 1 da (Bridget); *Career* prof of chemical pathology Bart's Med Coll 1968–95, chm and research dir MicroPharm Ltd 1998–; FRCP; *Style*— Prof John Landon; ✉ Reproductive Physiology Laboratories, 48–53 Bartholomew Close, London EC1A 7BE (tel 020 7606 0686)

LANDON, Theodore Luke Giffard; s of Rev Sylvanus Luke Landon (d 1979), formerly vicar of Marldon, Devon, and Florence Faith Loetitia Trelawny, *née* Lowe (d 1972; her mother was Eleanor Salusbury-Trelawny, *see* Sir John Salusbury-Trelawny 13 Bt), Mr Landon is the head of the French Huguenot family of Landon, founded in England by Samuel Landon in 1683; *b* 10 October 1926; *Educ* Blundell's, Univ of London; *m* 1956, Joan, da of Frederic Archibald Parker (d 1977), of Alresford, Hants (s of Rev Hon Archibald Parker, sometime rural dean of Wem, Salop, and Hon Maud Bateman-Hanbury, da of 2 Baron Bateman; the dean was 9 s of 6 Earl of Macclesfield); 3 s (Mark b 1958, Philip b 1962, Benjamin b 1967), 2 da (Felicity b 1960, Rohais b 1964); *Career* dep chm and md Terra Nova Insurance Co Ltd 1970–79, dep chm C T Bowring Underwriting Holdings

Ltd 1979–83; dir: English and American Insurance Co Ltd 1982–89, Murray Lawrence Corporate Ltd 1987–99, La Providence (The French Hosp) 1992–; chm English and American Pension Tst 1994–99 (dir 1984–94); memb Lloyd's 1961–; govr Kelly Coll Tavistock 1969–; tstee Huguenot Soc 1973– (pres 1989–92); *Recreations* history, music, genealogical research; *Clubs* East India; *Style*— Theodore Landon, Esq; ✉ Great Bromley House, Great Bromley, Colchester, Essex CO7 7TP (tel 01206 230385)

LANDSHOFF, Prof Peter Vincent; *b* 22 March 1937; *Educ* Univ of Cambridge (wrangler, Smith's prize, PhD); *m*; 3 c; *Career* Univ of Cambridge: research fell St John's Coll 1961–63, fell Christ's Coll 1963– (vice-master 1999–2002), asst lectr 1964–65, lectr 1965–74, reader in mathematical physics 1974–94, prof of mathematical physics 1994–2004; instr Princeton Univ 1961–62, visiting assoc prof Univ of Calif Berkeley 1966, scientific assoc CERN 1970, 1975–76, 1984–85 and 1991–92; SERC: chm Nuclear Theory Sub-Ctee 1979–82 (memb 1978–82), memb Particle Physics Experiments Selection Panel 1978–79, memb Nuclear Physics Bd 1979–82, memb Postgraduate Trg Ctee 1981–82; chm: Mgmnt Ctee Cambridge eScience Centre 2001–04, Mgmnt Ctee Nat Inst for Environmental eScience 2002–04, Computational Biology Inst Cambridge 2003–04; dir of research Cambridge-MIT Inst 2004–06; memb: Rutherford Lab Experiments Selection Panel 1975, European Ctee for Future Accelerators 1979–82, Ctee Isaac Newton Inst for Mathematical Scis Management (chm 1990–94 and 2001–06); ed Physics Letters B 1982–2005; FInstP, FRSA; *Books* The Analytic S-Matrix (jtly, 1966), Simple Quantum Physics (with A J F Metherell, 1979), Essential Quantum Physics (with A J F Metherell and W G Rees, 1997); *Style*— Prof Peter Landshoff; ✉ Centre for Mathematical Sciences, Wilberforce Road, Cambridge CB3 0WA (tel 01223 337880, fax 01223 766883, e-mail pvl@damtp.cam.ac.uk)

LANDSMAN, Dr David Maurice; OBE (2001); s of Sidney Landsman (d 1998), and Miriam, *née* Cober; *b* 23 August 1963; *Educ* Chigwell Sch, Oriel Coll Oxford (MA), Clare Coll Cambridge (MPhil, PhD); *m* 1990, Catherine Louise, da of Geoffrey Holden; 1 s (Henry Francis Hugh b 1992); *Career* Univ of Cambridge Local Examinations Syndicate 1988–89; joined FCO 1989, second sec Athens 1991–94, dep head of mission Belgrade 1997–99, head Br Embassy Office Banja Luka and concurrently first sec Budapest 1999–2000, head Br Interests Section Belgrade then charge d'affaires 2000–01, ambass Tirana 2001–03, head Counter Proliferation Dept 2003–06, seconded as int affrs advsr De La Rue Identity Systems 2006–; *Publications* author of articles on Greek and Balkan languages; *Recreations* travel, languages, music, food, wildlife; *Clubs* Athenaeum, Commonwealth; *Style*— Dr David Landsman, OBE; ✉ De La Rue Identity Systems, De La Rue House, Jays Close, Basingstoke RG22 4BS (e-mail david.landsman@uk.delarue.com)

LANE, Abigail; *b* 1967, Penzance, Cornwall; *Educ* Bristol Poly, Goldsmiths Coll London (BA); *Career* artist; *Solo Exhibitions* Abigail Lane: Making History (Karsten Schubert Gallery London, collaboration with Interim Art) 1992, Emi Fontana Milan 1994, Skin of the Teeth (ICA London) 1995, 25 Watt Moon (Ridinghouse Editions London) 1996, Bonnefanten Museum Maastricht 1996–97, Another Time, Another Place (Galerie Chantal Crousel Paris) 1997, Andréhn-Schiptjenko Stockholm 1997, Never, never mind (Victoria Milo Gallery London) 1998, Whether the roast burns, the train leaves or the heavens fall (Museum of Contemporary Art Chicago) 1998, Inspirator (Andréhn-Schiptjenko Gallery Stockholm) 2001, Tomorrow's World, Yesterday's Fever (Mental Guests Incorporated) (Milton Keynes Gallery and Victoria Miro Gallery London) 2001; *Group Exhibitions* Freeze (Surrey Docks London) 1988, The New Contemporaries (ICA London) 1989, Home Truths (Castello di Rivara Turin) 1989, Modern Medicine (Building One London) 1990, Show Hide Show (Anderson O'Day Gallery London) 1991, Group Show (Emi Fontana Milan) 1992, Etats Spécifiques (Musée des Beaux-Arts Le Havre) 1992, Group Show (Kunsthalle Luzern) 1992, 20 Pièces Fragiles (Galerie Barbara et Luigi Polla Geneva) 1992, Group Show (Barbara Gladstone Gallery and Stein Gladstone Gallery NY) 1992, Group Show (Galerie Tanja Grünert Cologne) 1992, Privacy (Documentario Milan) 1992, Visione Britannica (Valentina Moncada & Pino Casagrande Rome) 1993, Displace (Cohen Gallery NY) 1993, Ha - Ha (Killerton House Gardens and Spacex Gallery Exeter) 1993, Peccato di Novita (Emi Fontana Milan) 1993, Recent British Sculpture from the Arts Council Collection (nat touring exhbn) 1993–94, photo 94 (The Photographers' Gallery London) 1994, Punishment + Decoration (Hohenthal und Bergen Cologne) 1994, Cyberintimismo (Erotica Bologna) 1994, Domestic Violence (Gio Marconi Milan) 1994, Not Self-Portrait (Karsten Schubert Gallery London) 1994, Some Went Mad, Some Ran Away... (Serpentine Gallery London) 1994, Ars Lux (billboard project, various sites Bologna) 1994, Fiction/Non-Fiction (Galleria Bonomo Rome) 1994, Some Went Mad, Some Ran Away... (Nordic Arts Centre Helsinki, Kunstverein Hannover, MCA Chicago and Portalen Copenhagen) 1995, Corpus Delicti (Kunstforeningen Copenhagen) 1995, Here and Now (Serpentine Gallery London) 1995, Karaoke: 4 for 4 and 2 to 2 Too (South London Gallery) 1995, Group Show of Young British Artists (Shoshana Wayne Gallery Santa Monica) 1995, Brill: works on paper by "Brilliant!" artists (Montgomery Glasoe Fine Art Minneapolis) 1995, 4th International Istanbul Biennial 1995, Images of Masculinity (Victoria Miro Gallery London) 1995–96, Brilliant! New Art from London (Walker Art Center Minneapolis) 1995–96, Brilliant! New Art From London (Contemporary Arts Museum of Houston) 1996, #10 (Rhona Hoffman Gallery and Gallery 312 Chicago) 1996, Chaos, Madness. Permutations of Contemporary Art (Kunst Halle Krems) 1996, An exhibition of young British artists (Roslyn Oxley Gallery Sydney and RMIT Gallery Melbourne) 1996, From Figure to Object (Karsten Schubert Gallery and Frith Street Gallery London) 1996, Painting - The Extended Field (Magasin 3 Stockholm Konsthall) 1996–97, Intérieurs - Fischli & Weiss - Clay Ketter - Abigail Lane (Galerie Chantal Crousel Paris) 1996–97, Full House (Kunstmuseum Wolfsburg) 1996–97, Painting - The Extended Field (Rooseum Center for Contemporary Art Mälmo) 1997, L'Empreinte (Centre Pompidou Paris) 1997, Material Culture: The Object in British Art of the 1980's and 1990's (Hayward Gallery London) 1997, Gothic (ICA Boston touring to Portland Art Museum) 1998, Apocalyptic Wallpaper (Wexner Center for the Arts Columbus) 1997, L'Autre (4e Biennale de Lyon Halle Tony Garnier Lyon) 1997, Sensation. Young British Artists from the Saatchi Collection (Royal Acad of Arts London) 1997, Minor Sensation (Victoria Miro Gallery London) 1997, Art from the UK: Abigail Lane, Mona Hatoun, Rachel Whiteread, Douglas Gordon (Sammlung Goetz Munich) 1997–98, Exterminating Angel (Galerie Ghislaine Hussenot Paris) 1998, Close Echoes. Public Body & Artificial Space (City Gallery Prague and Kunst Halle Krems) 1998, London Calling (Br Sch at Rome) 1998, Fotografie als Handlung 4. Internationale Foto-Triennale Esslingen (Galerien der Stadt Esslingen Esslingen am Neckar) 1998, Trance (Philadelphia Museum of Art) 1998–99, Emotion - Junge britische und amerikanische Kunst in der Sammlung Goetz (Deichtorhallen Hamburg) 1998–99, Sensation. Yonug British Artists from the Saatchi Collection (Hamburger Bahnhof Berlin) 1998–99, Moving Images without Tears (Galerie Vera Munro Hamburg) 1998–99, Graphic! British Prints Now! (Yale Center for British Art New Haven) 1999, Mayday (Centre d'Art Neuchâtel) 1999–2000, De Schreeuw/The Scream (Galerij 't Leerhuys Bruges) 1999–2000, Raw (Victoria Miro Gallery London) 2000, Close Up (Kunstverein Freiburg im Marienbad, Kunsthuas Baselland and Kunstverein Hannover) 2000–01, Uncovered (The Gallery Univ of Essex) 2001, Summer Exhibition (Royal Acad of Arts London) 2001, Works on paper: from Acconci to Zittel (Victoria Miro Gallery London) 2001; *Style*— Ms Abigail Lane; ✉ c/o Victoria Miro Gallery, 16 Wharf Road, London N1 7RW

LANE, Maj-Gen Barry Michael; CB (1984), OBE (1974, MBE 1965); *b* 10 August 1932; *Educ* Dover Coll, RMA Sandhurst; *m* 1, 1956, Eveline Jean (d 1986), da of Vice Adm Sir Harry Koelle, KCB; 1 da (Juliet b 1959), 1 s (Anthony b 1962); m 2, 1987, Shirley Ann, da of E V Hawtin; *Career* cmmnd Somerset LI 1954; cmd: 1 LI 1972–75, II Armd Bde 1977–78; RCDS 1979, DAQ 1981–82, Vice-QMG 1982–83, GOC S W Dist 1984–87, Col LI 1982–87, Hon Col 6 LI (V) 1987–97, Hon Col Bristol Univ OTC 1987–99; chief exec Cardiff Bay Devpt Corp 1987–92; chm of govrs Taunton Sch 1997–2001, vice-pres St Margarets Somerset Hospice; *Recreations* cricket, gardening, architecture, wines; *Clubs* Army and Navy; *Style*— Maj-Gen Barry Lane, CB, OBE; ✉ c/o Army and Navy Club, London SW1Y 5JN

LANE, Prof Christel; da of Erich Noritzsch (d 1985), of Flensburg, Germany, and Paula, *née* Lessman (d 1995); *b* 10 December 1940, Flensburg, Germany; *Educ* Univ of Essex (BSocSci), LSE (PhD); *m* 1962, David Lane, 1 s (Christopher b 1964), 1 da (Julie b 1973); *Career* post-doctoral research fell Univ of Cambridge 1976–79, lectr Univ of Aston 1981–90, lectr, reader and prof Univ of Cambridge 1990–, fell St John's Coll Cambridge 1990–; pres Soc for Advancement of Socio-Economics 2006; *Books* Christian Religion in the Soviet Union (1976), Rites of Rulers (1981), Management and Labour in Europe (1989), Industry and Society in Europe (1995), Trust Within and Between Organisations (1998); *Recreations* walking, contemporary novels, travel; *Style*— Prof Christel Lane; ✉ 3 Barrow Road, Cambridge CB2 2AP (tel 01223 359113); Faculty Office, Social and Political Sciences, Free School Lane, Cambridge CB2 3RQ (tel 01223 330521, fax 01223 334550, e-mail col21@cam.ac.uk)

LANE, David Goodwin; QC (1991); s of James Cooper Lane (d 1981), of Gloucester, and Joyce Lilian, *née* Goodwin; *b* 8 October 1945; *Educ* Crypt Sch Gloucester, KCL (LLB, AKC); *m* 31 Aug 1991, Jacqueline Elizabeth, da of Kenneth Frank Cocks (d 1989); *Career* called to the Bar Gray's Inn 1968, recorder of the Crown Court; *Style*— David Lane, Esq, QC

LANE, David Ian; *see:* David Ian

LANE, Prof Sir David Philip; kt (2000); *b* 1 July 1952; *Educ* John Fisher Sch, UCL (BSc, PhD); *Career* post doctoral res fell 1976–77, lectr Zoology Dept Imperial Coll of Science and Technol London 1977–81, Robertson res fell and CRI fell Cold Spring Harbor Laboratories USA 1978–80, lectr Biochemistry Dept Imperial Coll London 1981–85, princ scientist ICRF 1988–90 (sr head scientist 1985–88), dir Cell Transformation Res Gp Cancer Research Campaign 1990–; Gibb fell CRC 1990; fndr dir and chief scientific offr Cyclacel 1997–; memb: EMBO 1990, CRC Scientific Ctee 1995– (former memb Grants Ctee), Cncl Royal Soc of Edinburgh 1995–; author of over 160 papers; Charles Rodolphe Brupbacher Fndn Prize 1993, Howard Hughes Int Scholar Award 1993–98, Joseph Steiner Prize 1993, Jan Waldenstrom Lecture 1994, Yvette Mayent Prize 1995, Lennox Black Prize 1995, Mayenberg Prize 1995, Paul Erlich Prize 1998; FRSE 1992, FRS 1996; *Style*— Prof Sir David Lane, FRS, FRSE; ✉ Cancer Research Campaign, Laboratories, Department of Surgery and Molecular Oncology, Dundee University Medical School, Dundee DD1 9SY

LANE, David Stuart; *Educ* King Edward's Camp Hill GS Birmingham, Univ of Birmingham (BSocSc), Nuffield Coll Oxford (DPhil), Univ of Cambridge (PhD, by incorporation); *m* Christel, *née* Noritzsch; 1 s (Christopher), 1 da (Julie); *Career* Univ of Birmingham: lectr Faculty of Commerce and Social Sci 1962–64, lectr Centre for Russian and E Euro Studies 1964–67, prof of sociology 1981–90; Univ of Essex: lectr 1967–71, reader 1971–73, chm Sociology Dept 1972–73; Emmanuel Coll Cambridge: univ lectr 1974–80 and 1990–92, reader 1992–2000, fell 1974–80 and 1990–2000; sr research assoc: Univ of Cambridge 2001–, Leverhulme project on transformation of Russia and Ukraine 2004–07; research supported by ESRC on new economic and political elites in Russia and political economy of Russian oil and financial system; memb New Modes of Governance within the European Union inter-univs consortium EU; visiting scholar Woodrow Wilson Centre Washington DC 1982, 1986 and 1995; visiting prof: Cornell Univ USA 1987, Univ of Graz Austria 1991 and 1996, Harvard Univ 1993 and 2001, Sabanci Univ Istanbul 2000–02; chm W Midlands Branch Campaign for Mentally Handicapped People 1982–83, sec W Midlands Cncl for Disabled People 1983–86, exec ed Disability, Handicap and Society jl 1985–89, vice-chm Birmingham Elfrida Rathbone Assoc 1986–90, memb Exec Br Sociological Assoc 1987–92, jt chm and fndr first Euro Sociological Conf 1992, memb Exec Euro Sociological Assoc, memb Exec Ctee Euro Sociological Assoc 1999–2001, memb Exec Ctee European Sci Fndn Network on Transition 1994–98; memb Editorial Bd Mir Rossii (Moscow); holder Br Acad Network Award supporting Network for Studies of Strategic Elites and European Enlargement 2004–09; *Books* incl: The Roots of Communism (1969), Politics and Society in the USSR (1970), The Socialist Industrial State - Towards a Political Sociology of State Socialism (1976), Current Approaches to Down's Syndrome (jt ed, 1985), Soviet Economy and Society (1985), Soviet Labour and the Ethic of Communism - Employment and the Labour Process in the USSR (1987), Soviet Society under Perestroika (1991), Russia in Flux (ed, 1992), Russia in Transition (ed, 1995), The Rise and Fall of State Socialism (1996), The Transition from Communism to Capitalism: Ruling Elites from Gorbachev to Yeltsin (jtly, 1998), The Political Economy of Russian Oil (ed and contrib, 1999), The Legacy of State Socialism and the Future of Transformation (ed and contrib, 2002), Russian Banking: Evolution, Problems and Prospects (ed and contrib, 2002), Pod"em i upadok gosudarstvennogo sotsialisma (2006), Varieties of Capitalism in Post-Communist Countries (jt ed and contrib, 2006), The Transformation of State Socialism: System Change, Capitalism or Something Else? (ed and contrib, 2007); author of articles in pubns incl: European Societies, Jl of Post-Communist and Transition Studies, Political Studies, Sociology, Competition and Change, Mir Rossii; *Recreations* playing squash, cinema, theatre, supporting Arsenal FC; *Style*— David Lane; ✉ Emmanuel College, Cambridge CB2 3AP (tel 01223 359113, fax 01223 334550, e-mail dsl10@cam.ac.uk)

LANE, (Sara) Elizabeth; da of Rt Hon Sir Lionel Heald, QC, MP (d 1981), and Daphne Constance Heald, CBE; *b* 30 April 1938; *Educ* Heathfield Sch Ascot, Paris; *m* 15 May 1963, George Henry Lane, MC, s of Ernest Lanyi, of Budapest, Hungary; *Career* dir Seek & Find Ltd 1963–68, advsr on works of art and assoc Baron Martin von Koblitz 1968–78, dir Christie Manson & Woods Ltd 1978–; *Recreations* country pursuits; *Style*— Mrs George Lane; ✉ 12 Petersham Place, London SW7 5PX (tel 020 7584 7840); Christie Mansion & Woods Ltd, 8 King Street, St James's, London SW1Y 6QT (tel 020 7839 9060, fax 020 7839 1611, e-mail elane@christies.com)

LANE, Mark Alastair; *b* 18 March 1950; *Educ* Cranleigh Sch Surrey, Trinity Coll Cambridge (Keasby award), Coll of Law Guildford; *m* Judy West; 1 s (Benjamin), 1 da (Sarah); *Career* admitted slr: England and Wales 1975, Hong Kong 1984; trainee slr Stephenson Harwood 1973–75; slr Macfarlanes 1975–76, lectr Coll of Law London 1976–79; slr: A G Qarooni Iliffe & Edwards (Bahrain) 1979–81, Cameron McKenna 1982–85; Pinsent Masons (formerly Masons): slr 1986–88, ptnr 1988–, head Water Sector Gp 1995–, ed-in-chief Pinsent Masons Water Yearbook; former chair Water Ctee Int Bar Assoc, co-vice-chair elect Int Construction Projects Ctee Int Bar Assoc; memb Exec Ctee European Construction Inst; memb Worshipful Co of Water Conservators; FRSA; *Recreations* tennis, running, gardening, sculpting, collecting antiques; *Style*— Mark Lane, Esq; ✉ Pinsent Masons, 30 Aylesbury Street, London EC1R 0ER (e-mail mark.lane@pinsentmasons.com)

LANE, Dr Nancy Jane; OBE (1994); da of Temple Haviland Lane (d 1994), of Nova Scotia, and Frances de Forest, *née* Gilbert (d 1967); *Educ* Dalhousie Univ Canada (Allan Pollock scholar, Khaki Univ scholar, Ross Stewart Smith scholar, B'nai B'rith prize, Eugene Harris prize in zoology, BSc, Univ Gold medal, MSc), LMH Oxford (DPhil), Univ of Cambridge (PhD, DSc); *m* 22 Dec 1969, Prof R N Perham, FRS, *qv*; 1 da (Temple Helen Gilbert b 8 Oct 1970), 1 s (Quentin Richard Haviland b 14 Oct 1973); *Career* res asst prof Dept of Pathology Albert Einstein Coll of Med NY 1964–65, res staff biologist Dept of Biology Yale Univ 1965–68; Univ of Cambridge: research fell Girton Coll 1968–70, official fell and lectr in cell biology Girton Coll 1970–, tutor Girton Coll 1975–98, sr princ scientific offr ARC Unit of Invertebrate Chemistry and Physiology (later AFRC Unit) Zoology Dept 1982–90 (sr scientific offr 1968–73, princ scientific offr 1973–82), sr res assoc Zoology Dept 1990–, project dir Women in Sci, Engrg and Technol Initiative (WiSETI) 1999–2007; visiting prof: Siena Univ 1990–93, Padua Univ 1991–94; memb: PM's Advsy Panel for the Citizen's Charter 1991–93; chair: BTEC's Advsy Bd for Science and Caring 1991–94, Working Pty for Women in Science and Engrg (OST) Cabinet Office 1993–94, Athena Project 2003– (vice-chair 1998–2003, chair 2004–); dir WOYLA 1997–2004, ptnr Women Resource Centre DTI 2004–; ed-in-chief Cell Biology International 1995–98, chair Editorial Ctee Science and Public Affairs (SPA) 2001–, co-author Set Fair Greenfield Report 2002, assoc ed 5 learned jls; non-exec dir: Smith and Nephew plc 1991–2000, Peptide Therapeutics plc 1995–98; memb: science GNVQ Advsy Ctee NCVQ 1993, Forum UK 1994–, Cmmn on Univ Career Opportunities CVCP 1996–2000, Exec Cncl Bioscience Fedn 2002–06, Scientific, Engrg and Environment Advsy Ctee Br Cncl (SEEAC) 2003–07; Scientific Ctee for Women in Sci and Technol UNESCO; chair UK Experts Database 2005; ptnr UK Resource Centre for Women in Sci 2005–; elected to Nova Scotia Hall of Fame for Science (Canada) 2006; Hon LLD Dalhousie Univ 1985, Hon DSc Univ of Salford 1994; Hon ScD: Sheffield Hallam Univ 2002, Oxford Brookes Univ 2003, Univ of Surrey 2005; pres Inst of Biology 2002–04 (pres elect 2001–02); memb: Soc for Experimental Biology 1962, American Soc for Cell Biology 1965, Histochemical Soc 1965, American Assoc for the Advancement of Science 1965, Br Soc for Cell Biology 1980 (sec 1982–90), Br Soc for Developmental Biology 1980; fell Royal Microscopical Soc 1965; MRI 1987, MInstD 1991, FZS 1986 (memb Cncl 1998–2001, vice-pres 1999–2001), FIBiol 1991, FRSA 1992, Hon Fell BAAS 2005; *Publications* author of over 190 scientific papers; *Recreations* theatre, dance and opera, 20th Century art, travelling; *Clubs* IOD, Oxford and Cambridge; *Style*— Dr Nancy J Lane, OBE; ✉ Master's Lodge, St John's College, Cambridge CB2 1TD (tel and fax 01223 765615); Department of Zoology, Downing Street, Cambridge CB2 3EJ (tel 01223 330116/336600, fax 01223 330116, e-mail njl1@cam.ac.uk)

LANE, (Alan) Piers; s of Peter Alan Lane, of Brisbane, Aust, and Enid Muriel, *née* Hitchcock; *b* 8 January 1958; *Educ* Kelvin Grove HS Brisbane, Queensland Conservatorium of Music, RCM London; *Career* concert pianist; prof Royal Acad of Music, writer and presenter BBC Radio 3 (54 programmes The Piano 1998–99), presenter of Legends series (BBC) 2000–03; artistic dir Australian Festival of Chamber Music 2007–; critic CD Review; appeared with orchs incl: Royal Philharmonic, London Philharmonic, the Philharmonia, Hallé Orch, BBC Welsh, BBC Scottish, BBC Concert, BBC Symphony, BBC Philharmonic, Scottish Chamber Orch, Australian Chamber Orch, New Zealand Symphony Orch, Bombay Chamber Orch, Adelaide Symphony Orch, American Symphony, Ensemble Kanazawa, Cape Town Symphony, Transvaal Philharmonic, Natal Philharmonic, Royal Liverpool Philharmonic, RTE Orch, Queensland Symphony, W Aust Symphony, Tasmanian Symphony, Melbourne Symphony, Queensland Philharmonic, Auckland Philharmonic, Christchurch Symphony, Montpellier Philharmonic Orch, Royal Oman Symphony, Brabants Orkester, Noorhollands Philharmonisch Orkest, Gothenburg Philharmonic, Aarhus Philharmonic, Romanian Radio Orch, CBSO, Orchestre National de France, Bournemouth Symphony, Australian Chamber Orchestra, Prague Chamber Orchestra, Janacek Philharmonic; toured extensively in UK, Ireland, Aust, NZ, S America, Western and Eastern Europe, USA, Africa, Japan, India, Sweden, Denmark, Norway, Canada; special prize Bartók-Liszt Int Competition Budapest 1976, best Australian pianist Sydney Int Piano Competition 1977, winner Royal Over-Seas League Competition 1982; dir and tstee The Hattori Fndn; patron: European Piano Teachers' Assoc, Queensland Music Teachers' Assoc, Accompanists' Guild Queensland; memb jury Int Piano Competition in Tbilisi 2001 and Sydney 2004; memb: Liszt Soc, Delius Soc; vice-pres Putney Music Club, patron The Old Granary Studio, patron Youth Music Fndn Aust; Churchill fell 1979; Hon DUniv Griffith Univ 2007; Hon RAM 1994; *Recordings* Moszowski and Paderewski Concertos (with BBC Scottish Symphony Orch and Jerzy Maxymiuk, 1991), Complete Études of Scriabin 1992, works by Mussorgsky, Balakirev and Stravinsky 1992, Piano Quintet by Brahms (New Budapest Quartet) 1992, Violin Virtuoso (with Tasmin Little) 1992, Sonatas by Shostakovich, Prokofiev, Schnittke and Rachmaninoff (with cellist Alexander Baillie), Franz Waxman Rhapsody (with Queensland Symphony Orch and Richard Mills), d'Albert Concertos (with BBC Scottish Orch and Alun Francis) 1994, Busch Concerto (with Royal Philharmonic and Vernon Handley) 1994, Vaughan-Williams and Delius Concertos plus Finzi Eclogue (with RLPO and Vernon Handley) 1994, Piano pieces by Alan Bush 1994, Elgar Piano Quintet (with Vellinger String Quartet) 1994, Virtuoso Strauss Transcriptions 1995, Concertos by Parry and Stanford 1995, French Violin Sonatas by Ravel, Debussy and Poulenc (with Tasmin Little) 1995, Delius Violin Sonatas (with Tasmin Little) 1997, d'Albert Solo Piano Works 1997, Saint-Saëns Complete Etudes 1998, Kullak & Dreyschock Concertos (with BBCSO and Niklas Willen) 1999, Complete Scriabin Preludes 2000, Carninal of the Animals (with Kathryn Stott, BBCCO and Barry Wordsworth) 1999, Grainger Piano Transcriptions 2001, Bach Transcriptions by Grainger, Friedman and Murdoch 2002, Finzi Eclogue (with Eng Chamber Orchestra and Nicholas Daniel) 2002, Moscheles Concert Etudes 2003, Hensett Concert Etudes 2004, Stanford Piano Quintet (with Vanburgh String Quartet) 2004, Alnaes and Sinding Concertos (with Bergen Philharmonic and Andrew Litton) 2006, Delius Songs (with Yvonne Kenny) 2006, Bloch Piano Quintets (with Goldner String Quartet) 2007; *Style*— Piers Lane, Esq; ✉ Georgina Ivor Associates, 28 Old Devonshire Road, London SW12 9RB (tel 020 8673 7179, fax 020 8675 8058, e-mail info@giamanagement.com, website www.giamanagement.com)

LANE, Robert Charles; CBE (2001); s of Sidney Arthur Lane, of Wanstead, London, and Eileen Ethel Anna, *née* Cleave (d 1991); *b* 29 August 1958, London; *Educ* Buckhurst Hill HS, UCL (LLB), Coll of Law; *m* 26 April 1986, Margaret Enid, da of Rev Stanley Peter Handley Stubbs, of London; 2 s (Edward b 2 Aug 1988, William b 20 May 1990), 1 da (Alice b 28 Aug 1991); *Career* articled clerk then slr Slaughter and May 1980–86; Cameron McKenna LLP (formerly McKenna & Co): slr 1986–90, ptnr 1990–, currently head Regulated Industries Gp; chm Power Sector Advsy Gp UK Trade & Investment (DTI and FCO), exec memb Parly Gp for Energy Studies, exec memb Br Energy Assoc, former chm Utilities Ctee Int Bar Assoc; memb Kensington Soc; Freeman City of London 1987, Liveryman Worshipful Co of City of London Slrs 1988; memb Law Soc 1982; *Recreations* opera, cricket, family; *Clubs* City of London, RAC, Bentham; *Style*— Robert Lane, Esq, CBE; ✉ CMS Cameron McKenna LLP, Mitre House, 160 Aldersgate Street, London EC1A 4DD (tel 020 7367 3000, fax 020 7367 2000, e-mail robert.lane@cmck.com)

LANE, Prof Stuart N; *Educ* Fitzwilliam Coll Cambridge, City Univ London; *Career* fell, tutor and dir of studies in geography Fitzwilliam Coll Cambridge 1994–2000, asst univ lectr then univ lectr in geography Univ of Cambridge 1994–2000, prof of physical geography Univ of Leeds 2000–04, prof of physical geography Univ of Durham 2004–; adjunct prof INRS-Georesources Quebec 2001–; visiting scientist: Nat Inst for Water and Atmospheric Research NZ 1998, Dept of Geography Univ of Montreal 1998; memb: Photogrammetric Soc 1993–, European Geophysical Soc 1995–, American Geophysical Union 1995–, Int Assoc of Hydraulics Research 1997–; refereeing ed and memb Int Editorial Bd Photogrammetric Record 2002–, memb Editorial Advsy Bd Jl of River Basin Mgmnt 2003–; memb Editorial Bd: Transactions of the Inst of British Geographers 2003–, Earth Surface Processes and Landforms 2004–; tstee Yorkshire Dales Rivers Tst; Jan de Ploey Award Int Assoc of Geomorphologists 1997, Harold J Schoemaker Award Int Assoc of Hydraulics Research 2001 (jtly), President's Prize Remote Sensing and Photogrammetry Soc 2001, Philip Leverhulme Prize Leverhulme Tst 2002; FRGS 1991; *Style*— Prof Stuart N Lane; ✉ Department of Geography, Science Laboratories, South Road, Durham DH1 3LE

LANE FOX, Robin James; s of James Henry Lane Fox, of Middleton Cheney, Oxon, and Anne, *née* Loyd; *b* 5 October 1946; *Educ* Eton, Magdalen Coll Oxford (MA); *m* 26 June 1970 (m dis 1993), Louisa Caroline Mary, da of Maj Charles Farrell, MC, of Watlington, Oxon; 1 da (Martha b 10 Feb 1973), 1 s (Henry b 19 Oct 1974); *Career* fell Magdalen Coll Oxford 1970–73, lectr in classics Worcester Coll Oxford 1974–76, res fell classical and Islamic history Worcester Coll Oxford 1976–77, fell and tutor New Coll Oxford 1977–, univ reader in ancient history Univ of Oxford 1990–; gardening columnist Financial Times 1970–, Br Press Award Leisure Journalist of Year 1988; garden master New Coll Oxford 1979–; FRSL 1974; *Books* Alexander The Great (1973), Variations On A Garden (1974), Search for Alexander (1980), Better Gardening (1982), Pagan and Christians (1986), The Unauthorised Version (1991), The Long March (2004), The Making of Alexander (2004), The Classical World: From Homer to Hadrian (2005); *Recreations* gardening, hunting, travelling; *Clubs* Beefsteak; *Style*— Robin Lane Fox, Esq, FRSL; ✉ c/o New College, Oxford OX1 3BN (tel 01865 279 555)

LANE OF HORSELL, Baron (Life Peer UK 1990), of Woking in the County of Surrey; Sir Peter Stewart Lane; kt (1984), JP (Surrey 1976); s of Leonard George Lane (d 1950); *b* 29 January 1925; *Educ* Sherborne; *m* Doris Florence (d 1969), da of Robert Simpson Botsford (d 1955); 2 da (Hon Rosalie (Baroness Trefgarne) b 1946, Hon Alexandra (Hon Mrs (Jeremy) Cresswell b 1956); *Career* Sub Lt RNVR 1943–46; sr ptnr BDO Binder Hamlyn 1979–92; chm: Brent International plc 1985–95, Attwoods plc 1994, Automated Security (Holdings) plc 1994–96; dep chm More O'Ferrall plc 1985–97; chm: Air Travel Tst Ctee 1989–2000, Nuffield Hospitals 1993–96; pres Bd of Gen Purposes United Grand Lodge of England 1991–95; Nat Union of Cons and Unionist Assocs: chm 1983, chm Exec Ctee 1986–91; FCA; *Clubs* Boodle's, Beefsteak, MCC; *Style*— The Rt Hon Lord Lane of Horsell; ✉ House of Lords, London SW1A 0PW

LANE-SMITH, Roger; s of Harry Lane-Smith (d 1979), of Cheshire, and Dorothy, *née* Shuttleworth; *b* 19 October 1945; *Educ* Stockport GS, Guildford Coll of Law (Robert Ellis Memorial prizeman); *m* 1969, Pamela Mary, da of Leonard Leigh; 1 s (Jonathan Roger b 10 Nov 1973), 1 da (Zoe Victoria b 21 June 1971); *Career* admitted slr 1969; ptnr David Blank & Co Manchester 1973–77; Alsop Wilkinson: managing ptnr Manchester Office 1977–88, managing ptnr London Office 1988–92, chm 1992–96; DLA Piper Rudnick Gray Cary (formerly Dibb Lupton Alsop): dep sr ptnr 1996–98, sr ptnr and chm 1998–2005, conslt 2005–; non-exec chm JJB Sports plc 2005– (non-exec dir 1998–); non-exec dir: MS Int plc, Timpsons plc, Civica plc 2007–; memb Cncl CBI; winner Robert Ellis Meml prize; memb Law Soc; *Recreations* golf, tennis, shooting, deep-sea fishing; *Clubs* Mark's, St James'; *Style*— Roger Lane-Smith, Esq; ✉ JJB Sports plc, Martland Park, Challenge Way, Wigan, Lancashire WN6 0LD

LANG, Belinda Lucy; da of Jeremy Hawk, of London, and Joan, *née* Heal; *b* 23 December 1955; *Educ* Lycee Français de Londres, Central Sch of Speech and Drama; *m* 15 Oct 1988, Hugh Munro, s of John Hugh Munro Fraser (d 1987); 1 da (Lily Irene b 1990); *Career* actress; co-fndr Haig-Lang Productions 2004; *Theatre* incl: Present Laughter (Vaudeville) 1981, Hobsons Choice (Haymarket) 1982, Antigone and Tales from Hollywood (NT) 1983–84, Clandestine Marriage (Albery) 1984, Mrs Klein (Apollo) 1989, Thark (Lyric Hammersmith) 1989, Dark River (Orange Tree) 1992, On Approval (Peter Hall Co) 1994, Dead Funny (Savoy and tour) 1996, Blythe Spirit (Chichester Festival) 1997, My Boy Jack (Hampstead Theatre) 1997, Things We Do for Love (Duchess Theatre) 1999, Life x Three (Savoy Theatre) 2002, Three Sisters Two (Orange Tree) 2002, The Secret Rapture (Lyric Theatre) 2003, My Boy Jack (tour, Haig-Lang Prodns) 2004, What the Butler Saw (Hamsptead Theatre) 2005, Hay Fever (Haymarket Theatre) 2006; *Television* incl: To Serve Them All My Days (BBC) 1980, Dear John (BBC) 1985, The Bretts (Central) 1986, Bust (LWT) 1988, Alleyn Mysteries (BBC) 1990 and 1993–94, Second Thoughts (LWT) 1991–94, 2 Point 4 Children (BBC) 1991–99, Justice in Wonderland (BBC) 2000; *Recreations* walking, reading; *Style*— Miss Belinda Lang

LANG, Dr Brian Andrew; s of Andrew Ballantyne Lang, and Mary Bain, née Smith; *b* 2 December 1945; *Educ* Royal High Sch Edinburgh, Univ of Edinburgh (MA, PhD); *m* 1, 1975 (m dis 1982); 1 s; m 2, 1983 (m dis 2000); 1 s, 1 da; m 3, 2002, Tari Hibbitt, *qv*, da of late Suwondo Budiardjo, and Carmel Budiardjo; *Career* social anthropological field res Kenya 1969–70, lectr in social anthropology Aarhus Univ Denmark 1971–75, scientific staff SSRC 1976–79, sec Historic Bldgs Cncl for Scotland (Scottish Office) 1979–80, sec Nat Heritage Meml Fund 1980–87, dir of public affairs National Trust 1987–91, chief exec and dep chm The British Library 1991–2000; chm Euro Nat Libraries Forum 1993–2000, chair Heritage Image Partnership 2000–02, memb Cncl National Trust Scotland 2001–04, tstee Hopetoun House Preservation Trust 2001–05, chm Newbattle Abbey Coll Tst 2004–; princ and vice-chllr Univ of St Andrews 2001–; bd memb Scottish Enterprise Fife 2003–, memb Scottish Exec Cultural Cmmn 2004–05; Pforzheimer lectr Univ of Texas 1998, visiting prof Napier Univ Edinburgh 1999–, visiting scholar Getty Inst LA 2000; memb: Library and Information Services Cncl (England) 1991–94, Library and Information Cmmn 1995–2000, Cncl St Leonards Sch St Andrews 2001–; tstee: 21st Century Learning Initiative 1995–99, Nat Heritage Meml Fund 2004–; chair Ctee for Scotland Heritage Lottery Fund 2005–; pres Inst of Info Scientists 1993–94 (hon fell 1994); Hon FLA 1997, FRSE 2006; *Publications* numerous articles, contribs to professional jls; *Recreations* music, museums and galleries, pottering; *Clubs* R&A, New (Edinburgh); *Style*— Dr Brian Lang; ✉ Office of the Principal, College Gate, University of St Andrews, North Street, St Andrews, Fife KY16 9AJ (tel 01334 462545)

LANG, Rt Rev Declan; *see:* Clifton, Bishop of (RC)

LANG, Hugh; ERD (1967); s of Hugh Lang (d 1981), of Holmwood, Surrey, and Lilian Maydee, *née* Mackay; *b* 22 December 1934; *Educ* Harrow; *m* 11 March 1961, Rosanne Auber, da of Lt-Col Richard Quentin Charles Mainwaring (d 1983), of Kells, Co Meath; 2 s (Alistair Hugh b 15 July 1963, James Richard b 13 March 1966); *Career* 2 Lt 5 Royal Inniskilling Dragoon Gds cmmnd 1954, RARO (AER) 1955–67; ptnr: John Prust & Co 1963–70, Laurence Prust & Co 1970–80; conslt Wallace Smith Trust Co Ltd 1985–92; MSI (memb Stock Exchange 1962), chief exec and sec The Stock Exchange Benevolent Fund 1980–94; govr Crossways Trust Ltd 1980–94, tstee Poyle Charity 1968–94; Offrs' Assoc: memb Exec and Fin Ctee 1985–94, memb Cncl 1995–2005; govr and hon fin advsr Royal Nat Coll for the Blind 1990–97, dir RNC Enterprises plc 1992–97, memb Investment and Fin Ctee DGAA 1991–92, tstee Marine Quay Property Co Ltd 1995–; govr: St Edmund's Sch Tst Ltd 1992–2003, Bridewell Royal Hosp and King Edward's Sch Witley 1992–2004 (dep treas 1996); chm Friends King Edward VII Hosp Midhurst 1996–2001; Freeman City of London 1956, Liveryman Worshipful Co of Skinners 1956; *Recreations* shooting, fishing, gardening, wine; *Clubs* Sloane, MCC; *Style*— Hugh Lang, Esq, ERD; ✉ Durfold Hatch Cottage, Fisher Lane, Chiddingfold, Surrey GU8 4TF (tel and fax 01428 684286)

LANG, Prof Tim; s of Robert Anthony Lang (d 1996), and Katharine Margaret, *née* Alcock (d 2004); *b* 7 January 1948, Lincoln; *Educ* Uppingham, Univ of Leeds (BA, PhD); *m* 2 April 2004, Valerie Elizabeth Castledine, *née* Boon; *Career* dir: London Food Cmmn 1984–90, Parents for Safe Food 1990–94; prof of food policy: Thames Valley Univ 1994–2002, City Univ 2002–; conslt WHO 1996–2003, advsr House of Commons Health and Agric Ctees (inquiries incl: Food Standards Agency Bill 1998–99, Food Standards Agency 2000, Globalisation 2000, Obesity 2003–04), tech advsr to French Presidency of the European Cmmn Food and Nutrition Initiative 1999–2000, chair Sustain 1999–; tstee: Food Cmmn (UK) 1990–, Friends of the Earth 1994–2001; memb Bd The Rodale Inst USA 1997–; vice-pres Chartered Inst of Environmental Health 1999–; Caroline Walker Award 2002, BBC Radio 4 Food & Farming Derek Cooper Award 2003; FRSA, FFPH 2001, fell Faculty of Public Health RCP; *Publications* More than we can Chew (jtly, 1982), Food Irradiation: the Myth and the Reality (jtly, 1990), P is for Pesticides (jtly, 1991), The New Protectionism (jtly, 1993), The Unmanageable Consumer: Contemporary Consumption and its Fragmentation (jtly, 1995), The Atlas of Food (jtly, 2003, André Simon Food Book of the Year Award 2003), Food Wars: The Battle for Mouths, Minds and Markets (jtly, 2004); *Recreations* reading the papers; *Style*— Prof Tim Lang; ✉ City University, Northampton Square, London EC1V 0HB (tel 020 7040 8798, e-mail t.lang@city.ac.uk)

LANG OF MONKTON, Baron (Life Peer 1997), of Merrick and the Rhinns of Kells in Dumfries and Galloway; Rt Hon Ian Bruce Lang; PC (1990), DL (Ayrshire & Arran 1998); s of late James Fulton Lang, DSC; *b* 27 June 1940; *Educ* Lathallan Sch, Rugby, Sidney Sussex Coll Cambridge (BA); *m* 1971, Sandra Caroline, da of John Alastair Montgomerie, DSC; 2 da; *Career* MP (Cons): Galloway 1979–83, Galloway and Upper Nithsdale 1983–97 (Parly candidate (Cons): Central Ayrshire 1970, Glasgow Pollok 1974); asst govt whip 1981–83, a Lord Cmmr of the Treasy 1983–86; Parly under-sec of state: Dept of Employment 1986, Scottish Office 1986–87; min of state Scottish Office 1987–90, sec of state for Scotland 1990–95, pres Bd of Trade (sec of state for Trade and Industry) 1995–97; memb House of Lords Constitution Ctee 2001–; chm: Second Scottish National Trust plc 1997–2004, Thistle Mining Inc 1998–, US Special Opportunities Tst plc 2001–; dir: Marsh & McLennan Companies Inc 1997–, Lithgows Ltd 1997–, Charlemagne Capital Ltd; chm Patrons of Nat Galleries of Scotland 1999–; govr Rugby Sch 1999–; memb Queen's Body Guard for Scotland (Royal Co of Archers) 1974; OStJ 1974; *Publications* Blue Remembered Years (2002); *Clubs* Prestwick Golf, Pratt's, Athenaeum; *Style*— The Rt Hon Lord Lang of Monkton, PC, DL; ✉ House of Lords, London SW1A 0PW

LANGDON, (Richard) Benedict (Ben); s of David Langdon, OBE, of Prestwood, Bucks, and April Yvonne Margaret, *née* Sadler-Phillips; *b* 28 August 1963; *Educ* Royal GS High Wycombe, Jesus Coll Oxford (BA); *m* 21 Oct 1989, Vicky, da of George Henderson; 1 s (Max David b 25 Sept 1992), 1 da (Ruby Louise b 25 April 1994); *Career* account mangr: Allen Brady & Marsh advtg agency 1985–87, Lowe Howard Spink 1987–88; Still Price Court Twivy D'Souza Lintas: account dir 1989–90, bd/gp account dir 1990, new business dir 1991–93; md Addition Marketing Jan-June 1993, client servs dir McCann-Erickson Advertising 1993, chief-exec Collett Dickenson Pearce 1995–96 (md 1993–95), chief-exec and md McCann-Erickson Advertising 1996–1999, ceo and chm McCann-Erickson UK & Ireland 1999–2003, regional dir McCann-Erickson EMEA 2000–03, co-fndr Ben Mark Orlando Jan-Mar 2004, chm Euro RSCG Worldwide UK and Euro RSCG London 2004–05, ceo Digital Marketing Group plc 2006–; non-exec dir Hay & Robertson plc 1999–2001; *Recreations* golf, soccer; *Clubs* Harewood Downs Golf (Little Chalfont); *Style*— Ben Langdon, Esq; ✉ Digital Marketing Group plc, Couching House, Couching Street, Watlington, Oxfordshire OX49 5PX

LANGDON, Prof John Dudley; s of Jack Langdon (d 1984), of London, and Daphne Irene Heloise, *née* Liebsch (d 1988); *b* 24 March 1942; *Educ* Highgate Sch, London Hosp Med Coll (BDS, MB BS, MDS, Med, Surgery and Pathology prize, London prize, Annual Award of Merit American Soc of Dentistry for Children, Harold Fink prize, Charrington prize, James Anderson prize), RCS (LDS); *Career* house surgn Royal London Hosp 1965, sr house surgn Dept of Oral Surgery Royal Dental and St George's Hosp 1965–66, SHO Dept of Oral Surgery Eastman Hosp 1966; registrar: Dept of Oral Surgery Royal London Hosp 1967 (Oral Surgery and Conservative Dentistry 1966–67), Oral Surgery and Maxillofacial Unit Honey Lane Hosp 1967–68; pt/t demonstrator Dept of Dental Anatomy London Hosp Med Coll 1968–69, locum registrar Dept of Oral Surgery St Thomas' Hosp 1969, pt/t lectr London Hosp Med Coll 1970–73, house physician Harold Wood Hosp 1974 (house surgn 1973), locum conslt oral surgn Oldchurch Hosp 1974; sr registrar Dept of Oral and Maxillofacial Surgery: Royal London Hosp 1974–76, KCH 1976–77; tutor RCS 1977, conslt oral and maxillofacial surgn Queen Mary's Hosp 1977–83 (hon conslt 1983–90), sr lectr/conslt Dept of Oral and Maxillofacial Surgery King's Coll Sch of Med and Dentistry 1983–92, special lectr in oral surgery Dental Sch Univ of Bristol 1987–93, prof of oral and maxillofacial surgery King's Coll Sch of Med and Dentistry 1992–2004 (vice-dean Faculty of Clinical Dentistry 1987–90), exec dir of patient servs King's Dental Inst 1994–; hon conslt: St George's Healthcare NHS Tst 1984–2000, Royal Surrey and St Luke's NHS Tst 1993–2000, Epsom Healthcare NHS Tst 1994–2003; chm Intercollegiate Bd in Oral & Maxillofacial Surgery 1998–2001; pres: Section of Odontology RSM 1998–99, Br Assoc of Head and Neck Oncologists 1998–2001, Inst of Maxillofacial Prosthetists & Technologists 1999–2001; memb: Cncl Assoc of Head and Neck Oncologists of Great Br 1981–84, Academic Advsy Ctee Oral and Maxillofacial Surgery 1989–97, SAC in oral surgery and oral med 1989–94, Speciality Advsy Bd in oral and maxillofacial surgery RCS (Ed) 1990–98 (chm), Bd Faculty of Dental Surgery RCSE 1994–, BDA, BMA, Br Soc of Dental Res, Craniofacial Soc of Great Britain, Euro Assoc for Cranio-Maxillo-Facial Surgery; hon treas Br Assoc of Oral and Maxillofacial Surgns 1992–2004; fndr memb Maxillofacial Study Gp, hon sec (Odontology) RSM 1993–95; fndn fell Asian Assoc of Oral and Maxillofacial Surgns; ed (Oncology Section) Int Jl of Oral and Maxillofacial Surgery 1988–, conslt ed (Oral Oncology) Euro Jl of Cancer 1991–; fell: Br Assoc of Oral and Maxillofacial Surgns, Int Assoc of Oral and Maxillofacial Surgns, Acad of Med Science (fndr fell), Int Acad of Oral Oncology (fndr fell); FKC 2002, FDS 1972, FRCS 1985; *Books* Malignant Tumours of the Oral Cavity (with J M Henk, 1985), Cancer of the Mouth, Jaws and Salivary Glands (with J M Henk, 1994), Surgical Pathology of the Mouth and Jaws (with R A Cawson and J Eveson, 1995), Surgical Anatomy of the Infratemporal Fossa (with B K B Berkovitz and B J Moxham, 2003), Operative Maxillofacial Surgery (with M F Patel, 1998); *Recreations* gardening, opera, antiques, cooking; *Style*— Prof John Langdon; ✉ The Old Rectory, Limington, Somerset BA22 8EQ (tel and fax 01935 840127)

LANGFORD, 9 Baron (I 1800); Col Geoffrey Alexander Rowley-Conwy; OBE (mil 1943), DL (Clwyd 1977); s of Maj Geoffrey Seymour Rowley-Conwy (ka 1915, himself ggs of 1 Baron, who in his turn was 4 s of 1 Earl of Bective, the Earldom of the same now forming one of the subsidiary dignities of the Marquesses of Headfort), of Bodrhyddan, Rhuddlan, Clwyd; suc 2 cous once removed, 8 Baron Langford, 1953; *b* 8 March 1912; *Educ* Marlborough, RMA Woolwich, Staff Coll Quetta; *m* 1, 1939 (m dis 1956), Ruth St John (d 1991), da of late Albert St John Murphy; m 2, 1957, Grete (d 1973), da of late Col E T von Freiesleben, Danish Army; 3 s; m 3, 1975, Susan, da of C Denham; 1 s, 1 da; *Heir* s, Hon Owain Rowley-Conwy; *Career* cmmnd RA 1932, Lt 1935, Capt 1939, Maj 1941, Lt-Col 1945, serv 1939–45, with RA in Singapore (POW escaped), with Indian Mountain Artillery in Burma (Arakan, Kohima), CO 25 Mountain Regt 1945, DAQMG Berlin Airlift, Fassberg 1948–49, GSO1 42 Inf Div TA 1949–52, CO 31 Regt RA 1954–57, ret 1957, Hon Col 1967; constable of Rhuddlan Castle, lord of the manor of Rhuddlan; Freeman City of London; *Clubs* Army and Navy; *Style*— Col The Rt Hon the Lord Langford, OBE, DL; ✉ Bodrhyddan, Rhuddlan, Clwyd LL18 5SB

LANGFORD, Prof Paul; s of Frederick Wade Langford, of Cinderford, Glos, and Olive Myrtle, *née* Walters; *b* 20 November 1945; *Educ* Monmouth, Hertford Coll Oxford (MA, DPhil); *m* 1970, Margaret Veronica, *née* Edwards; 1 s (Hugh b 1984); *Career* Univ of Oxford: tutorial fell in history Lincoln Coll 1970 (jr res fell 1969), lectr in history 1971–94, reader in modern history 1994–96, prof of modern history 1996–, rector Lincoln Coll 2000–; visiting fell: Huntington Library 1973, American Antiquarian Soc 1974; Ford's lectr in English history Univ of Oxford 1990, Ralegh lectr Br Acad1996; memb Humanities Research Bd 1995–98, chm and chief exec AHRB 1998–2000; chm Oxford Inspires 2002–; hon fell Hertford Coll Oxford 2000, sr fell RCA 2001; Hon DLitt Univ of Sheffield 2002; FRHistS 1979, FBA 1993; *Books* A Polite and Commercial People 1727–83: New Oxford History of England (1989), Public Life and the Propertied Englishman 1689–1798 (1991), Englishness Identified: Manner and Character 1650–1850 (2000); *Recreations* gardening; *Clubs* Athenaeum; *Style*— Prof Paul Langford, FBA; ✉ Lincoln College, Oxford OX1 3DR (tel 01865 279795, fax 01865 279802, e-mail paul.langford@lincoln.ox.ac.uk)

LANGFORD, Philip Baber; s of Percy Norman Langford (d 1968), and Elizabeth Ellen, *née* Jones (d 1987); *b* 23 March 1934; *Educ* Bromsgrove Sch, BNC Oxford (MA), Univ of London (LLB); *m* 10 March 1987, Catherine Judith, da of late William Arthur Gibbon; 2 step s (Edward b 1977, Richard b 1979); *Career* Nat Serv 2 Lt RAEC attached to 2 Bn Coldstream Guards 1959–61; admitted slr 1959; asst slr Kent CC 1961–63, ptnr Thomson Snell & Passmore 1965–92 (joined 1963), dep district judge 1992–99; chm: SE Area Legal Aid Ctee 1985, SE Rent Assessment Panel 1992–; pres Tunbridge Wells Tonbridge and Dist Law Soc 1986; memb Law Soc; Ordre des Chevaliers Bretvins; *Recreations* golf and cricket (as a spectator), reading, travel, wine; *Style*— Philip Langford, Esq; ✉ Baber House, Ticehurst, Wadhurst, East Sussex TN5 7HT (tel 01580 200978)

LANGHAM, John Michael; CBE (1976); s of George Langham (d 1951); *b* 12 January 1924; *Educ* Bedford Sch, Queens' Coll Cambridge (MA), Admin Staff Coll; *m* 1949, Irene Elizabeth, *née* Morley; 2 s, 1 da; *Career* served RN 1944–46; joined J Stone & Co 1947, divnl chm Stone-Platt Industries plc 1967–81, exec chm Stone Manganese Marine Ltd 1967–; chm: Bruntons Propellers Ltd 1960–, Stone Marine Canada Ltd 1967–2000, Stone Marine Singapore Pte Ltd 1969–, Vacu-Lug Traction Tyres Ltd 1973–95, Winters Marine Ltd 1975–, Stone Marine SA Pty Ltd 1977–, Langham Industries Ltd 1981–, Langham Overseas Ltd 1981–, Stone Marine Overseas Ltd 1981–, Stone Fasteners Ltd 1982–, Stone Foundries Ltd 1982–89, Weardale Steel (Wolsingham) Ltd 1983–2002, Tridan Engineering Ltd 1988–89, Appledore Shipbuilders Ltd 1989–2003, Langham Farms Ltd 1990–, Portland Port Ltd 1995–, Portland Harbour Authority Ltd 1996–; dir: BPB Industries plc 1976–92, Barclay Curle Ltd 1985–, Appledore land Ltd 1989–, James Robertson Ltd 1992–2003, Mashford Brothers Ltd 1999–2003; memb: Cncl CBI 1967–79 (chm Prodn Ctee 1970–79), Exec Bd BSI 1969–76 (dep chm Quality Assurance Cncl 1971–79), Gen Cncl Engrg Employers' Fedn 1974–82 (memb Mgmnt Bd 1979–82); Br Foundry Medal and Prize 1954, Award of the American Foundrymen's Soc 1962; Liveryman Worshipful Co of Shipwrights; CEng, CIMgt, FIMechE, FIMarE; *Recreations* skiing, sailing, farming; *Clubs* Brooks's, Leander, RMYC, Hawks' (Cambridge); *Style*— John Langham, Esq, CBE; ✉ Bingham's Melcombe, Dorchester, Dorset DT2 7PZ

LANGHAM, Sir John Stephen; 16 Bt (E 1660), of Cottesbrooke, Northampton; s of Sir James Michael Langham, 15 Bt (d 2002); *b* 14 December 1960; *m* 1991, Sarah Jane, da of late John Denis Verschoyle-Greene; 1 s (Tyrone Denis James b 13 Aug 1994), 2 da (Phoebe Tara b 9 Jan 1999, Isabella Hay b 3 Oct 2000); *Style*— Sir John Langham, Bt; ✉ Tempo Manor, Tempo, Enniskillen, Co Fermanagh BT94 3PA

LANGHAM, Tony; s of Trevor Langham, and Margaret, *née* Harris; *b* 4 June 1961; *Educ* Holgate Comp, Univ of Birmingham (BA); *m* 1993, Clare, da of Anthony Parsons (d 1964); 2 s ((Charles) Alexander b 10 Jan 1994, Theodore Maximilian b 14 Oct 1996); *Career* sr researcher MORI 1982–84, jt head of retail fin PR Dewe Rogerson 1984–89; Lansons Communications: co-fndr (with Clare Parsons) 1989, chief exec 2001–; memb MRS 1986, MIPR 1989, FCIPR 2007; *Recreations* playing and watching sport, contemporary music, history, mountains; *Style*— Tony Langham, Esq; ✉ Lansons Communications, 24a St John Street, London EC1M 4AY (tel 020 7490 8828, fax 020 7490 5460, e-mail tonyl@lansons.com)

LANGHORNE, Richard Tristan Bailey; s of Eadward John Bailey Langhorne, MBE (d 1995), of Chichester, and Rosemary, *née* Scott-Foster; *b* 6 May 1940; *Educ* St Edward's Sch Oxford, St John's Coll Cambridge (MA); *m* 18 Sept 1971, Helen Logue (d 2005), da of William Donaldson, CB (d 1988); 1 s (Daniel b 22 Nov 1972), 1 da (Isabella b 29 Aug 1975); *Career* lectr in history Univ of Kent 1966–75 (master Rutherford Coll 1971–74), fell St John's Coll Cambridge 1975– (steward 1975–79, bursar 1975–87), dir Centre of Int Studies Univ of Cambridge 1987–93, dir and chief exec Wilton Park FCO 1993–96, prof of political science and dir Grad Div of Global Affrs Rutgers Univ 1996–; visiting prof: Sch of Int Rels Univ of Southern Calif 1986, Canterbury Christchurch Univ 2005; hon prof of int rels Univ of Kent at Canterbury 1994, hon prof of global affrs Univ of Buckingham 2006– (also prog co-dir MA in global affrs); chm Br Int History Assoc 1988–93; FRHistS 1985; *Books* The Collapse of the Concert of Europe 1890–1914 (1982), Diplomacy and Intelligence during the Second World War (ed, 1985), The Practice of Diplomacy (with K A Hamilton, 1994), The Coming of Globalization (2000), Guide to International Relations and Diplomacy (ed, 2002), Diplomacy (ed, 3 vols, 2004), Diplomacy and Governance (2004), The Essentials of Global Politics (2006); *Recreations* cooking, music, railways; *Clubs* Athenaeum; *Style*— Richard Langhorne, Esq; ✉ Carleton House, King Street, Fordwich, Canterbury, Kent CT2 0DA (tel 01227 712454); 123 Washington Street, #510, Newark, NJ 07102, USA

LANGLANDS, Sir (Robert) Alan; kt; *b* 29 May 1952; *Educ* Allan Glen's Sch Glasgow, Univ of Glasgow (BSc), Inst of Health Service Mgmnt; *m* 1977, Elizabeth McDonald; 1s, 1 da; *Career* with Argyll and Clyde Health Bd 1976–78, with dist maternity services S Lothian 1978–82, unit admin Middx Hosp 1981–82, with Middx Hosp, UCH and Soho Hosp for Women 1982–85, dist gen mangr Harrow HA 1985–89, healthcare mgmnt conslt in private practice 1989–90, regnl gen mangr NW Thames RHA 1990–93; Dept of Health NHS Exec: dep chief exec 1993–94, chief exec 1994–2000; princ and vice-chllr Univ of Dundee 2000–; chair: Cmmn on Good Governance in the Public Servs 2004–05, Gateways to the Professions 2004–05, UK Biobank Ltd 2004–; memb Advsy Bd: INSEAD 1999–2003, Johns Hopkins Univ Bioethics Inst 2000–04; hon prof Warwick Business Sch; Hon DUniv Glasgow 2001; Hon FFPH (Hon FFPHM 1994), FIA 1999, FCGI 2000, CCMI (CIMgt 2000), Hon FRCP 2001, Hon FRCGP 2001, Hon FRCSE 2001, Hon FRCPSGlas 2002, FRSE; *Recreations* living and walking in Scotland and Yorkshire; *Style*— Sir Alan Langlands, FRSE; ✉ University of Dundee, Dundee DD1 4HN (tel 01382 345555, fax 01382 229948)

LANGLEY, Hon Mr Justice; Sir (Julian Hugh) Gordon Langley; kt (1995); s of Gordon Thompson Langley (d 1943), and Marjorie, *née* Burgoyne (d 2000); *b* 11 May 1943; *Educ* Westminster, Balliol Coll Oxford (MA, BCL); *m* 20 Sept 1968, Beatrice Jayanthi, da of Simon Tennakoon (d 1986), of Colombo, Sri Lanka; 2 da (Ramani Elizabeth b 1969, Sharmani Louise b 1972); *Career* called to the Bar Inner Temple 1966 (bencher 1996); QC 1983–95, recorder 1986–95, judge of the High Court of Justice (Queen's Bench Div)

L

1995–; *Recreations* music, sport; *Style*— The Hon Mr Justice Langley; ✉ Royal Courts of Justice, Strand, London WC2A 2LL

LANGLEY, Kenneth William; s of William Thomas Charles Langley (d 1984), of Wanstead, London, and Ada Winifred, *née* Looke (d 1979); *b* 13 January 1932; *Educ* East Ham Tech HS, East Ham Tech Coll; *m* 16 March 1957, Daisy Rosina, da of Frederick Charles Parsons (d 1956), of Essex; 3 da (Gillian b 1959, Susan b 1961, Elizabeth b 1964); *Career* Nat Serv Sgt RE Egypt and Jordan; non-exec chm Bryen & Langley Ltd (building contractors) until 2004 (ret); former memb Construction Industry Res and Info Assoc, past chm Kent Branch Jt Consultative Ctee for Bldg Industry; govr emeritus Lewisham Coll (past chm of govrs), memb Rotary Club Poole Bay; Freeman City of London 1972, Liveryman Worshipful Co of Basketmakers 1977; FCIOB 1957, FRICS 1960, ACIArb 1966; *Recreations* music, reading; *Clubs* City Livery; *Style*— Kenneth Langley, Esq; ✉ Wentworth, 26 Bingham Avenue, Poole, Dorset BH14 8NE (tel 01202 701506)

LANGLEY, Peter James; *b* 18 February 1942; *Educ* Brighton Hove and Sussex GS, Courtauld Inst of Art London (MA); *m* 1970 (m dis 1993), Ann Christine Williams; 1 s (James William b 1973), 1 da (Catherine Jane b 1975); *Career* articled clerk Mileham Scatliff and Allen Brighton 1960–65, admitted slr 1965; ptnr C F Snow & Co Littlehampton 1966–70 (asst slr 1965–66), ptnr Slaughter and May London 1975–99 (asst slr 1970–75); memb Law Soc; *Recreations* history of art, collecting fine bindings, golf; *Clubs* MCC, RAC, Wisley Golf; *Style*— Peter Langley, Esq; ✉ c/o Slaughter and May, 1 Bunhill Row, London EC1Y 8YY (tel 020 7600 1200, fax 020 7090 5000, e-mail pjl@madpursuit.com)

LANGMAN, Prof Michael John Stratton; *b* 30 January 1935; *Educ* St Paul's, Guy's Hosp Med Sch (BSc, MB, MD); *m* Rosemary Ann Langman, JP; 2 s (Nicholas, Benjamin), 2 da (Suzannah, Victoria); *Career* conslt physician, sr lectr, then reader in med Nottingham Teaching Hosps 1968–73, Boots prof of therapeutics Univ of Nottingham Med Sch 1974–87; Univ of Birmingham Med Sch: William Withering prof of med 1987–2000, dean 1992–97, hon prof of med 2000–05, emeritus prof 2005–; hon prof Univ of Warwick 2005–; pres Br Soc of Gastroenterology 1997–99; chm: Expert Gp on Vitamins and Mineral Supplements Food Standards Agency 2000–03, Coventry and Warwick Ambulance NHS Tst 2000–05, Jt Ctee on Vaccination and Immunization of the UK 2000–05; memb: Ctee on Review of Meds 1980–86, Ctee on Safety of Meds 1987–2005; FRCP 1974 (MRCP 1960), FFPM 1990, FMedSci 1998; *Recreations* tennis, cricket, opera-going; *Clubs* MCC, Athenaeum; *Style*— Prof Michael Langman; ✉ Faculty Office, Medical School, University of Birmingham, Edgbaston, Birmingham B15 2TT (tel 0121 414 3780)

LANGMEAD, Jeremy John; s of John Sambrook, and Juliet Langmead, *née* Popplewell; *b* 3 November 1965; *Educ* St Joseph's Coll Ipswich, Central St Martin's Sch of Art London (BA); *m* 1992 (sep), India Knight, da of Michel Aertsens; 2 s (Oscar Augustus b 8 Dec 1992, Archie Jack b 8 Nov 1995); *Career* journalist; previous appts with Tatler, Elle Decoration and Mirabella magazines and freelance contrib to various newspapers incl Sunday Times, Evening Standard and The Guardian; Style ed The Sunday Times 1995–2000 (dep Style ed 1994–95), ed Nova 2000–01, Life and Style ed Evening Standard 2001–02, ed-in-chief Wallpaper* 2002–; *Recreations* travelling, cycling and socialising; *Style*— Jeremy Langmead, Esq

LANGRIDGE, Edward James; s of Edward Victor Langridge (d 1977), of Eastbourne, E Sussex, and Edith Mabel, *née* Blair; *b* 7 August 1946; *Educ* Eastbourne GS; *m* 1, 1967 (m dis 1983), Margaret Dally, *née* Scott; 1 s (Stuart Edward b 12 Oct 1973), 1 da (Nicola Ann b 7 March 1972); m 2, 1982, Judith Anne, da of Stanley Frederick Hammersley; 1 s (Alexander James b 2 July 1988), 1 da (Sophie Clare Henrietta b 9 Feb 1990); *Career* prodn mangr Gordon Scott & Barton Ltd 1966–72 (prodn trainee 1963–66); Smedley McAlpine Ltd: prodn mangr 1972, assoc dir 1975, dir 1980, dep md 1983, md 1987–91; jt md Bastable Hazlitt Partnership (formerly Bastable Advertising and Marketing) 1991–95, exec mktg dir McCarthy & Stone (Developments) Ltd 1996–97, md Langridge Hammersley Advertising Ltd 1998–; FInstM; *Recreations* classic cars, golf; *Clubs* Jaguar Drivers', Villa Golf; *Style*— Edward Langridge, Esq; ✉ Byeways, Gipps Cross Lane, Langton Green, Tunbridge Wells, Kent TN3 0DH (tel 0189 286 2006)

LANGRIDGE, Philip Gordon; CBE (1994); s of Arthur Gordon, and Elsie Kate, *née* Underhill; *b* 16 December 1939; *Educ* Maidstone GS, Royal Acad of Music; *m* 1, 2 Aug 1962, (Margaret) Hilary, da of Rev George Davidson; 1 s (Stephen Maitland b 28 May 1962), 2 da (Anita Jane (Mrs Keith McNicoll) b 11 June 1966, Jennifer Mary (Mrs Richard Strivens) b 19 Dec 1970); m 2, 6 June 1981, Ann Murray, the mezzo soprano, da of Joseph Eugene Murray, of Dublin; 1 s (Jonathan Philip b 20 Oct 1986); *Career* concert and opera singer (tenor); Glyndebourne Festival debut 1964, BBC Proms debut 1970, Edinburgh Festival debut 1970; served on Music Panel for Arts Cncl of GB; LRAM, GRSM, FRAM, ARAM; *Performances* Glyndebourne incl 1977–97: Idomeneo, Don Giovanni, Titus, King Kong; Royal Opera House 1983–2001: Boris Godunov, Jenufa, Idomeneo, Death in Venice, Semele, Das Rheingold, Peter Grimes (video), Palestrina, The Tempest, Figaro; The Met New York 1985–99: Cosi Fan Tutte, Das Rheingold, Billy Bud, Peter Grimes, Boris, Moses und Aron; ENO: Mask of Orpheus (world première) 1986, new prodn of Billy Budd 1988, Peter Grimes 1991; Salzburg Festival: Moses und Aron 1987 and 1988, Idomeneo 1990, Poppea, Boris, House of the Dead; Munich State Opera: Titus, Midsummer Marriage, Das Rheingold, Peter Grimes; other prodns incl: Idomeneo Angers 1975, Idomeneo La Scala, Boris Godunov (with Claudio Abbado) La Scala 1979, Rake's Progress La Scala, Peter Grimes La Scala, Hamburg and Los Angeles; *Awards* Grammy Award: for Moses und Aron (Schonberg) under Solti 1986, Peter Grimes 1997; Olivier Award for Osud (Janácek) 1984, winner of RPS Charles Heidsieck Singer of the Year 1988–89, Making Music/Sir Charles Grove Prize (for contrib to Br music) 2001; *Recordings* over 100 recordings of early, baroque, classical, romantic and modern music; *Recreations* collecting watercolours; *Style*— Philip Langridge, Esq, CBE

LANGRISH, Rt Rev Michael Laurence; *see:* Exeter, Bishop of

LANGRISHE, Sir James Hercules; 8 Bt (I 1777), of Knocktopher Abbey, Kilkenny; s of Sir Hercules Ralph Hume Langrishe, 7 Bt (d 1998); *b* 3 March 1957; *m* 1985, Gemma Mary Philomena, eldest da of Patrick O'Daly, and Rita, *née* Hickey, of Kiltale, Co Meath; 1 da (Victoria Anna Jean b 1986), 1 s (Richard James Hercules b 8 April 1988); *Heir* s, Richard Langrishe; *Style*— Sir James Langrishe, Bt; ✉ Arlonstown, Dunsany, Co Meath, Republic of Ireland

LANGSLOW, Dr Derek Robert; CBE (2000); s of Alex Langslow (d 1993), and Beatrice, *née* Wright (d 1992); *b* 7 February 1945; *Educ* Ashville Coll Harrogate, Queens' Coll Cambridge (MA, PhD); *m* 1969, Helen Katherine Addison; 1 s (Ian b 1975), 1 da (Sarah b 1980); *Career* res fell Univ of Cambridge 1969–72, lectr in biochemistry Univ of Edinburgh 1972–78; Nature Conservancy Cncl: sr ornithologist 1978–84, asst chief scientist 1984–87, dir policy planning and servs 1987–90; chief exec English Nature 1990–2000, memb Agric and Environment Biotechnol Cmmn 2000–05; dir Br Waterways 2000–06, dep chm Harwich Haven Authy 2001–; chm E of Eng Tourist Bd 2006–; memb: Rail Passengers Eastern Eng 2000–05, Rail Passengers Cncl 2005–; tstee Heritage Lottery Fund 2002–; author of more than 50 scientific pubns; *Style*— Dr Derek Langslow, CBE; ✉ 4 Engaine, Orton Longueville, Peterborough PE2 7QA (tel 01733 232153, e-mail derek.langslow@btinternet.com)

LANGSTAFF, Hon Mr Justice; Sir Brian Frederick James; kt (2005); s of Frederick Sydney Langstaff, of Boxted, Essex, and Muriel Amy Maude, *née* Griffin; *b* 30 April 1948; *Educ* George Heriot's Sch Edinburgh, St Catharine's Coll Cambridge (BA); *m* 19 July 1975, Deborah Elizabeth, da of Samuel James Weatherup (d 1953), of NI; 1 da (Kerry b 1978), 1 s (Nicholas b 1980); *Career* called to the Bar Middle Temple 1971 (bencher 2002), called to the Bar of NI 1999; sr lectr in law Chelmer Coll 1971–75 (formerly lectr), Harmsworth scholar 1975, in practice 1975–2005, QC 1994, recorder 1995–2005 (asst recorder 1991–95), judge Employment Appeal Tbnl 2000–03, head of chambers 2002–05, judge of the High Court of Justice (Queen's Bench Div) 2005–; leading counsel Bristol Royal Infirmary Inquiry 1998–2001; memb Exec Ctee: Personal Injury Bar Assoc 1995–2002 (chm 1999–2001), Industrial Law Soc 1997–2005 (hon vice pres 2005–), Bd of Govrs local primary sch; chm: Law Reform Ctee of Bar Cncl 2001–2002 (vice-chm 1999–2001), working pty on structured settlements for Master of Rolls 2001–02, Serious Personal Injury and Clinical Negligence Ctee Civil Justice Cncl 2003–; advsy ed OHS&E 1997–2000; *Books* Concise College Casenotes Series: Equity & Trusts (1975); contrib Health and Safety at Work (Halsbury's Laws, 4 edn), Bullen & Leake's Precedents of Pleading (conslt ed, 1999, 15 edn 2003), Munkman on Employers' Liability (contrib, 2000 and 2006), Personal Injury Handbook (ed and contrib, 2001 and 2006), Personal Injury Schedules (2002 and 2005); *Recreations* sport, tennis, swimming, walking, travel, watching TV, mowing the lawn; *Style*— The Hon Mr Justice Langstaff; ✉ Royal Courts of Justice, Strand, London WC2A 2LL

LANGSTAFF, Rt Rev James Henry; *see:* Lynn, Bishop of

LANGTON, Simon Guy Charles; s of David Langton (d 1994), of Stratford-upon-Avon, Warks, and Mona Rosemary, *née* Copeman (d 1972); *b* 5 November 1941; *Educ* Bloxham Sch; *m* 1, 1971 (m dis 1973), Victoria Master; partner since 1985, Jan Child; *Career* director; asst stage mangr Folkestone Repertory Theatre 1959, stage mangr Theatre Royal Windsor 1960–62, BBC TV 1963–71, freelance dir 1971–; memb: Dirs' Guild of GB 1980, Dirs' Guild of America 1983; *Television and Film* credits incl: Microbes & Men (BBC) 1972, Love For Lydia (LWT) 1973, Upstairs Downstairs (LWT) 1974, Duchess of Duke Street (BBC) 1976, Gate of Eden (YTV) 1977, Danger UXB (Euston Films) 1978, Rebecca (BBC) 1979, Therese Raquin (BBC) 1980, Nelson (ATV) 1980, Smiley's People (BBC) 1981, Lost Honour of Katherine Beck (CBS) 1982, Casanova (ABC) 1984, Anna Karenina (CBS) 1985, Laguna Heat (HBO) 1986, Dos Destinos (corporate film for BA) 1986, Whistle Blower (feature) 1987, Out of Darkness (ABC/Robert Halmi) 1987, Mother Love (BBC) 1988, Jeeves & Wooster II (Carnival Films) 1990, Good Guys (Havahall Pictures) 1991, Headhunters (BBC) 1992, The Cinder Path (YTV) 1993, Pride and Prejudice (BBC) 1994, Stanley's Search for Dr Livingstone (Hallmark Films) 1997, Nancherrow (Portman Prodns/Telemunchen) 1998, Scarlet Pimpernel (BBC) 2000 Murder Rooms (BBC) 2001, Agatha Christie's The Hollow (LWT) 2003, Poirot 2003, The Old Masters (co-prod) 2004, Rosemary and Thyme 2004 and 2005; *Awards* Peabody Award (for Smiley's People), Tric Award (for Mother Love), Best Drama RTS Award (for Scarlet Pimpernel) 2002; for Pride and Prejudice 1996: Tric Award for Best Drama, Broadcasting Press Guild Award for Best Drama Serial, Banff Television Festival Award for Best Mini Series and Grand Prize for Best Programme; nominations incl: BAFTA 1972 (for Microbes & Men), BAFTA 1979 (for Therese Raquin), BAFTA (Mother Love), BAFTA for Best Serial 1996 (for Pride and Prejudice); nominations for Smiley's People: BAFTA, Emmy, Peoples Award; *Recreations* natural history; *Clubs* Garrick; *Style*— Simon Langton, Esq; ✉ Newnham Hill Farmhouse, Newnham Hill, Henley-on-Thames, Oxfordshire RG9 5TP; c/o Ben Hall, Curtis Brown Group Ltd, 28–29 Haymarket, London SW1Y 4SP (tel 020 7396 6600, fax 020 7396 0110)

LANKESTER, Sir Timothy Patrick (Tim); KCB (1994); s of Robin Prior Archibald Lankester, and Jean Dorothy, *née* Gilliat; *Educ* Monkton Combe Sch, St John's Coll Cambridge (BA), Jonathan Edwards Coll Yale Univ (Henry fell, MA), St John's Coll Oxford (Fereday fell); *m* 1968, Patricia, *née* Cockcroft; 3 da (Alexandra Kim b 30 April 1970, Olivia Mary b 28 Sept 1971, Laura Camilla b 9 Oct 1981); *Career* economist World Bank 1966–73 (Washington until 1969 and New Delhi until 1973); HM Treasy: princ 1973–77, asst sec 1977, private sec to Rt Hon James Callaghan 1978–79, private sec to Rt Hon Margaret Thatcher 1979–81, seconded to S G Warburg and Co Ltd 1981–83, under sec 1983–85, econ minister Washington (and exec dir World Bank and IMF) 1985–88, dep sec (and dir European Investment Bank) 1988–89; perm sec: ODA 1989–94, Dept for Educn 1994–95; dir SOAS Univ of London 1996–2000, pres Corpus Christi Coll Oxford 2001–; dep chm British Cncl 1998–2003; non-exec dir Mitchell & Butlers plc 2003–; *Style*— Sir Tim Lankester, KCB; ✉ Corpus Christi College, Merton Street, Oxford OX1 4JF (tel 01865 276740, fax 01865 276769, e-mail tim.lankester@ccc.ox.ac.uk)

LANNON, Dr Frances; da of Martin Lannon, and Margaret, *née* O'Hare; *b* 22 December 1945, Newcastle upon Tyne; *Educ* Sacred Heart GS Newcastle upon Tyne, Lady Margaret Hall Oxford (MA), St Antony's Coll Oxford (DPhil); *Career* lectr in history Queen Mary Coll London 1975–77; Lady Margaret Hall Oxford: fell and tutor in modern history 1977–2002, princ 2002–; visiting prof Univ of South Carolina 1986, fell Woodrow Wilson Center Washington DC 1992; FRHistS 1986; *Publications* Privilege, Persecution and Prophecy: The Catholic Church in Spain 1875–1975 (1987), Elites and Power in Twentieth-Century Spain: Essays in Honour of Sir Raymond Carr (ed with Paul Preston,1990), The Spanish Civil War (2002), Lady Margaret Hall, Oxford: The First 125 Years 1879–2004 (2004); *Clubs* Reform; *Style*— Dr Frances Lannon; ✉ Lady Margaret Hall, Oxford OX2 6QA (tel 01865 274302, fax 01865 274294, e-mail frances.lannon@lmh.ox.ac.uk)

LANSDOWNE, 9 Marquess of (GB 1784) Charles Maurice Petty-Fitzmaurice; LVO (2002), DL (Wilts 1990); also Baron Kerry and Lixnaw (I 1295), Earl of Kerry, Viscount Clanmaurice (both I 1723), Viscount FitzMaurice, Baron Dunkeron (both I 1751), Earl of Shelburne (I 1753), Lord Wycombe, Baron of Chipping Wycombe (GB 1760), Earl Wycombe, and Viscount Calne and Calston (both GB 1784); assumption of additional surnames of Petty-Fitzmaurice recognised by decree of Lord Lyon 1947; s (by 1 m) of 8 Marquess (d 1999), and Barbara Stuart Chase (d 1965); *b* 21 February 1941; *Educ* Eton; *m* 1, 1965 (m dis 1987), Lady Frances Eliot (d 2003), da of 9 Earl of St Germans; 2 da (Lady Arabella Helen Mary (Lady Arabella Unwin) b 1966, Lady Rachel Barbara Violet (Lady Rachel Spickernell) b 1968), 2 s (Simon Henry George, Earl of Kerry b 1970, Lord William Nicholas Charles b 1973); m 2, 1987, Fiona Mary, da of Donald Merritt; *Heir* s, Earl of Kerry; *Career* page of honour to HM The Queen 1956–57; served: Kenya Regt 1960–61, Wiltshire Yeomanry (TA), amalgamated with Royal Yeomanry Regt 1963–73; cncllr: Calne and Chippenham RDC 1964–73, Wilts CC 1970–85, N Wilts DC (chm 1973–76); memb: SW Econ Planning Cncl 1972–77 (chm Working Ctee on Population and Settlement Pattern), Historic Bldgs and Monuments Cmmn 1983–89, Cncl Duchy of Cornwall 1990–2002; pres: Wilts Playing Fields Assoc 1965–75, Wilts Assoc of Boys' Clubs and Youth Clubs 1976–2003, NW Wilts Dist Scout Cncl 1977–88, HHA 1988–93 (dep pres 1986–88), South West Tourism 1989–2006, Wiltshire Historic Buildings Tst 1994–, The Wilts and Berks Canal Partnership 2001–; Parly candidate (Cons) Coventry NE 1979; Liveryman Worshipful Co of Fishmongers; *Clubs* Turf, Brooks's; *Style*— The Most Hon the Marquess of Lansdowne, LVO, DL; ✉ Bowood House, Calne, Wiltshire SN11 0LZ (tel 01249 812102)

LANSLEY, Andrew David; CBE (1996), MP; s of Thomas Stewart Lansley, OBE, of Hornchurch, Essex, and Irene, *née* Sharp; *b* 11 December 1956; *Educ* Brentwood Sch, Univ of Exeter (BA, pres Guild of Students); *m* 1, 1985 (m dis); 3 da (Katherine Elizabeth Jane b 1987, Sarah Isabel Anne b 1989, Eleanor Rose Amy b 1993); m 2, 2001, Sally Anne, da of Donald Low, of Cheshire; 1 da (Martha Rose Low b 2003), 1 s (Charles Frederick Low b 2004); *Career* private sec to Sec of State for Trade and Industry 1984–85 (joined DOI 1979), princ private sec to Chancellor of the Duchy of Lancaster Cabinet

Office 1985–87, dep DG Assoc of British Chambers of Commerce 1989–90 (dir policy and progs 1987–89), dir Conservative Research Dept 1990–95, dir Public Policy Unit 1995–97; MP (Cons) S Cambridgeshire 1997–; a vice-chm Cons Pty 1998–99; shadow min for the Cabinet Office 1999–2001, shadow chllr of the Duchy of Lancaster 1999–2001, shadow sec of state for health 2003–; memb: Health Select Ctee 1997–98, Trade and Industry Select Ctee 2001–03; memb Exec Ctee Nat Union of Cons and Unionist Assocs 1990–95; *Publications* A Private Route (1988), Conservatives and the Constitution (with R Wilson, 1997), Extending the Reach (2003); *Recreations* history, political biographies, travel, cricket; *Style*— Andrew Lansley, CBE, MP; ✉ House of Commons, London SW1A 0AA (tel 020 7219 3000, e-mail lansleya@parliament.uk)

LANTOS, Prof Peter Laszlo; s of Sandor Leipniker (d 1945), and Ilona, *née* Somlo (d 1968); *b* 22 October 1939; *Educ* Med Sch Szeged Univ Hungary (MD), Univ of London (PhD, DSc); *Career* Wellcome research fell 1968–69, sr lectr and hon conslt in neuropathology Middx Sch of Med 1976–79 (research asst 1969–73, lectr in neuropathology 1974–75), prof of neuropathology Inst of Psychiatry 1979–2001 (prof emeritus 2001–); hon consult in neuropathology: Bethlem Royal and Maudsley Hosps 1979–2002, KCH 1985–2002, St Thomas' Hosp 1992–2002; dir Neuropathology Serv King's Neuroscience Centre 1995–2002; chm: Scientific Advsy Panel Brain Research Tst 1985–91, Neuropathology Sub-Ctee RCPath 1986–89 (chm Panel of Examiners in Neuropathology 1983–89), Academic Bd Inst of Psychiatry 1988–91; cncllr Int Soc of Neuropathology 1995–, advsr German Federal Miny for Educn and Research 2000–02; tstee: Psychiatry Research Tst 1996–, Alzheimer Research Tst 2001–; memb: Pathologic Soc of GB and I 1971, Br Neuropathological Soc 1972 (pres 1995–97), Samantha Dickson Research Tst 2003–, Med Advsy Ctee Multiple Sclerosis Soc; FRCPath 1987 (MRCPath 1975), FMedSci 2001; *Books* Parallel Lines (2006); Greenfield's Neuropathology (ed, 1997 and 2002); contrib: Brain Tumours: Scientific Basis, Clinical Investigation and Current Therapy (1980), Histochemistry in Pathology (1983), Scientific Basis of Clinical Neurology (1985), Schizophrenia: The Major Issues (1988), Systemic Pathology (3 edn, 1990), Oxford Textbook of Pathology (1992), WHO Tumours of the Nervous System (2000), Dementia (2000), Early-onset Dementia (2001), Neurodegeneration (2003); *Recreations* travel, theatre, fine arts; *Clubs* Athenaeum; *Style*— Prof Peter Lantos

LANYON, Prof Lance Edward; CBE (2001); s of Harry Lanyon (d 1947), of London, and Heather Gordon, *née* Tyrell; *b* 4 January 1944; *Educ* Christ's Hosp, Univ of Bristol (BVSc, PhD, DSc, MRCVS); *m* 1, 15 April 1972 (m dis 1997), Mary, da of Harold Kear (d 1966), of Sevenoaks, Kent; 1 s (Richard b 1975), 1 da (Alice b 1977); m 2, 6 Sept 2003, Joanna, da of John Price, of Goodwick, Pembrokeshire; *Career* reader in veterinary anatomy Univ of Bristol 1980–83 (lectr 1967–79), prof Tufts Sch of Veterinary Med Boston Mass USA 1983–84 (assoc prof 1980–83); The Royal Veterinary Coll London: prof of veterinary anatomy 1984–89, head Dept of Veterinary Basic Sci 1987–88, princ 1989–2004, prof emeritus 2004–; pro-vice-chancellor Univ of London 1997–99; FBOA; memb: Bone and Tooth Soc, American Soc for Bone and Mineral Res; author of numerous chapters in books on orthopaedics, osteoporosis and athletic training, and various scientific articles in orthopaedic and bone related jls; *Recreations* building, home improvements, sailing; *Style*— Prof Lance Lanyon, CBE; ✉ The Royal Veterinary College, Royal College Street, London NW1 0TU (tel 020 7468 5000)

LAPOTAIRE, Jane Elizabeth Marie; da of Louise Elise Burgess Lapotaire; *b* 26 December 1944; *Educ* Northgate GS Ipswich, Bristol Old Vic Theatre Sch; *m* 1, 1965 (m dis 1967), Oliver Wood; m 2, 1974 (m dis 1982), Roland Joffé, *qv*; 1 s (Rowan b 1973); *Career* actress; pres Bristol Old Vic Theatre Club 1985–, memb Marie Curie Meml Fndn Appeals Ctee 1986–88, hon pres Shakespeare's Globe Friends 1986–2003, hon assoc artist RSC 1993, visiting fell Univ of Sussex 1986–2001, visiting artist in residence Univ of Washington St Louis 1999; Hon DLitt: Univ of Bristol 1997, UEA 1998, Univ of Warwick 2000, Univ of Exeter 2004; hon fell Univ of Exeter 2006; *Theatre* RSC various periods 1974–94 incl: Viola in Twelfth Night, Sonya in Uncle Vanya, Rosaline in Love's Labour's Lost 1978–79, Misalliance 1986, Archbishop's Ceiling 1986, Gertrude in Kenneth Branagh's Hamlet 1993, Mrs Alving in Ghosts 1993 & 1994, Katherine of Aragon in Henry VIII 1996–98; NT various periods 1967–84 incl: Measure for Measure, Flea in Her Ear, Dance of Death, Way of the World, Merchant of Venice, Oedipus, The Taming of the Shrew, Eileen in Kick for Touch 1983, Belvidera in Venice Preserv'd, Antigone 1984; other credits incl: Bristol Old Vic Co 1965–67, Vera in A Month in the Country, Lucy Honeychurch in A Room with a View (both Prospect Theatre Co West End) 1975–76, Rosalind in As You Like It (Edinburgh Festival) 1977, title role in Piaf (The Other Place, RSC, Aldwych, Wyndhams and Broadway) 1978–81, title role in St Joan (Compass Co) 1985, Double Double (Fortune) 1986, Greenland (Royal Court) 1988, Joy Davidman in Shadowlands (Queen's) 1990; *Television* freelance 1971–74 and 1976–78; credits incl: Marie Curie (Emmy and BAFTA nomination) 1977, Antony and Cleopatra 1981, Macbeth 1983, Seal Morning 1985, Napoleon and Josephine 1987, Blind Justice (BAFTA nomination) 1988, The Dark Angel 1989, Love Hurts (series 1 and II, BBC) 1991–92, Big Battalions 1992; *Films* Eureka 1983, Lady Jane 1986, Surviving Picasso (Merchant Ivory) 1996; *Awards* incl: Emmy and BAFTA nominations 1976 for Marie Curie, Helen Hayes Award USA for Katharine of Aragon 1999; awards for performance in Piaf: SWET Award 1979, London Critics' Award 1980, Variety Club Award 1980, Broadway Tony Award 1981; for Blind Justice: Br Press Guild Best Actress Award 1988, Variety Club Award 1989 for Shadowlands; *Books* Grace and Favour (autobiography, 1989), Out of Order (1999), Time Out Of Mind (2003), Everybody's Daughter Nobody's Child (2007); *Recreations* walking, cooking; *Style*— Ms Jane Lapotaire; ✉ Lou Coulson Associates, 37 Brewer Street, London W1F 8RS

LAPPERT, Prof Michael Franz; s of late Julius Lappert, of Brno, Czechoslovakia, and late Kornelie, *née* Beran; *b* 31 December 1928; *Educ* Wilson's GS London, Northern Poly London (BSc, PhD, DSc); *m* 14 Feb 1980, Lorna, da of David McKenzie (d 1974), of Seaton, Workington; *Career* sr lectr N London Poly 1955–59 (asst lectr 1952–53, lectr 1953–55), sr lectr UMIST 1961–64 (lectr 1959–61), prof Univ of Sussex 1969– (reader 1964–69); sr SERC fell Univ of Sussex 1980–85; author of more than 750 papers on organometallic and inorganic chemistry; pres Dalton Div RSC 1989–91; RSC Awards: Main Gp Element 1970, Tilden lectr 1972, Organometallic Chemistry 1978, Nyholm lectr 1994, Sir Edward Frankland lectr 1999; Kipping Award ACS 1976; Hon Doctorate München 1989; FRS 1979, FRSC, MACS; *Books* Metal and Metalloid Amides: Syntheses, Structures and Physical and Chemical Properties (with P P Power, A R Sanger, R C Srivastava, 1980), Chemistry of Organo-Zirconium and Hafnium Compounds (with D J Cardin, C L Raston, 1986); *Recreations* theatre, opera, art, tennis, walking; *Style*— Prof Michael Lappert, FRS; ✉ 4 Varndean Gardens, Brighton BN1 6WL (tel 01273 503661); John Dalton Cottage, Eaglesfield, Cockermouth, Cumbria CA13 0SD; Department of Chemistry, School of Life Sciences, University of Sussex, Brighton BN1 9QJ (tel 01273 678316, fax 01273 677196, e-mail m.f.lappert@sussex.ac.uk)

LAPPING, Anne Shirley Lucas; CBE (2005); da of Frederick Stone, and Dr Freda Lucas Stone; *b* 10 June 1941; *Educ* City of London Sch for Girls, LSE; *m* 1963, Brian Michael Lapping, *qv*; 3 da (Harriet, Claudia, Melissa); *Career* journalist: New Society 1964–68, London Weekend Television 1970–73, The Economist 1974–82; md: Brook Lapping Productions 1982–, Scott Tst 1995–; non-exec dir: Channel 4 TV 1989–95, NW London Mental Health Tst 1993–98; vice-chair Central and NW London Mental Health Tst 2000–04; govr LSE 1995– (memb Governing Cncl 2004–); memb: Nat Gas Consumers Cncl 1978–79, Social Science Research Cncl 1978–82; *Recreations* literature, cooking; *Style*— Anne Lapping, CBE; ✉ 61 Eton Avenue, London NW3 3ET (tel 020 7586 1047); Brook Lapping Productions, 6 Anglers Lane, Kentish Town, London NW5 3DG (tel 020 7428 3100, fax 020 7284 0626)

LAPPING, Brian Michael; CBE (2005); *m* 1963, Anne Shirley Lucas Lapping, *qv*; 3 da (Harriet, Claudia, Melissa); *Career* early career as journalist on Daily Mirror, Guardian, Financial Times and New Society until 1970; Granada Television 1970–88: exec prodr World in Action 1976–79, End of Empire 1985, creator Hypotheticals current affrs format (30 progs produced for Granada); fndr Brian Lapping Associates (independent prodn co) 1988–, merged with Brook Assocs to form Brook Lapping Prodns 1997; Brian Lapping Associates progs incl: further Hypotheticals series (annually on BBC 2), Countdown to War (ITV) 1989, The Second Russian Revolution (BBC2, Discovery US, NHK Japan) 1991 (RTS and Broadcasting Press Guild Best Documentary Series Awards, Silver Medal Int Film and TV Festival NY 1992), Question Time (BBC1) 1991–94, The Washington Version (BBC2 and Discovery US) 1992, Woolly Al Walks the Kitty Back (BBC2 and Discovery US) 1992, Off the Back of a Lorry (BBC1) 1993, Watergate (BBC2 and Discovery US) 1994, Fall of the Wall (BBC2, Spiegel TV and Discovery US) 1994, The Death of Yugoslavia (BBC2, ORF Austria, Discovery US, Canal Plus France) 1995 (RTS Judges' Award 1996, Best Ind Prodn and Best News and Current Affrs Prodn Indie Awards 1996, Broadcasting Press Guild Best Documentary Series 1996, George Foster Peabody Award Univ of Georgia 1996, BAFTA Best Documentary 1996, duPont Gold Baton Columbia Univ 1996), The 50 Years War: Israel and the Arabs (BBC 2, PBS) 1998, The Money Changers (a history of European Monetary Union) 1998, Hostage (C4, PBS, Canal Plus) 1999, Playing the China Card (C4, PBS) 1999 (George Foster Peabody Award Univ of Georgia 2000), Endgame in Ireland (BBC2, PBS) 2000, Avenging Terror (C4, PBS, France 2, ZDF, NHK) 2002, The Fall of Milosevic (BBC2, Discovery) 2003, Israel and the Arabs: Elusive Peace (BBC2, Arte, PBS) 2005 (RTS Journalism Programme of the Year 2004–05, duPont Gold Baton Columbia Univ 2007); chm Teachers' TV Dep of Educn 2003–08; *Awards* incl: various for World in Action, RTS Best Documentary Series for The State of the Nation 1979, Silver Medal Int Film and TV Festival NY for Hypotheticals prog Kidnapped 1984, Broadcasting Press Guild Best Documentary Series for Apartheid 1984, Gold Medal Int Film and TV Festival NY for Breakthrough at Reykjavik 1988 (also finalist Prix Italia) and for Countdown to War 1989; News World First Documentary Award 2003, BAFTA Personal Award for Creative Contribution to Television 2003, Broadcasting Press Guild Award for Outstanding Contribution to Broadcasting 2003; *Style*— Brian Lapping, Esq, CBE; ✉ Brook Lapping Associates Ltd, 6 Angler's Lane, London NW5 3DG (tel 020 7428 3100, fax 020 7284 0626)

LAPSLEY, (Alastair Gourlay) Howard; s of Rev Claude William Lapsley (d 1976), and Florence Lapsley; *b* 20 May 1940; *Educ* Dulwich, Coll of Law; *m* 5 June 1965, Susan Elizabeth, da of Charles Henry Bassingthwaighte (d 1988), of Diss, Norfolk; 1 s (Angus b 1970), 1 da (Catriona b 1972); *Career* admitted slr 1964; dir JA Gadd Ltd 1975–; memb Br Motor Sports Cncl 1984–; Br Rally Champion (1300 cc) 1983; memb Law Soc; *Recreations* motor sport, music, travel; *Clubs* RSAC; *Style*— Howard Lapsley, Esq

LAPTHORNE, Richard Douglas; CBE (1997); *b* 25 April 1943; *Educ* Calday Grange GS, Univ of Liverpool (BCom); *m* 1967, Valerie, *née* Waring; 2 s, 2 da; *Career* trainee Unilever Audit UCMDS 1965–67, fin accountant Lever Brothers (Zambia) Ltd 1967–69, accountant Unilever Pensions 1969–71, chief accountant Food Industries Ltd 1971–74, commercial offr Urachem Div Unilever Holland 1974–75; commercial dir: Synthetic Resins Ltd 1975–77, Sheby SA Paris 1977–80, Urachem Div 1980–81, Crosfields Chemicals Ltd 1981–83; Courtaulds plc: gp fin controller 1983–86, gp fin dir 1986–92, pres Courtaulds United States Inc 1986–92; British Aerospace plc: fin dir 1992–98, vice-chm 1998–99; non-exec chm: Amersham International plc 1996–97 (non-exec dir 1988–2003), Nycomed Amersham (following merger, now Amersham plc) 1999–2003 (dep chm 1997–99), Morse Group Ltd 1998–, Avecia 1999–2005, TI Automotive 2001–03, Cable and Wireless plc 2003–, New Look 2005–; non-exec dir: Orange plc 1996–99, Robert Fleming Holdings Ltd 1998–2002, Oasis International Leasing Ltd (Abu Dhabi) 1997–2006; tstee: Royal Botanic Gardens Kew 1998– (HM The Queen's rep 2004–), Calibre (books for the blind) 1999–, Tommys Campaign 2002–; memb: Industry Devpt Advsy Bd 1996–2000, Advsy Bd Cancer Research Campaign 1998–2001; FCCA, FCMA, FCTA, CIMgt; *Recreations* gardening, opera, travel; *Style*— Richard Lapthorne, CBE

LARCOMBE, Brian; *Career* 3i Group plc: joined 1974, local dir 1982, regnl dir 1988, fin dir 1992–97, chief exec 1997–2004; non-exec dir: Smith & Nephew plc 2002–, Party Gaming plc 2005–06, Gallaher Gp plc 2005–06, F&C Asset Mgmnt plc 2005–; chm Br Venture Capital Assoc 1994–95; *Style*— Brian Larcombe, Esq

LARDER, Phillip John; MBE (2004); s of Maurice Larder (d 1992), and Edith, *née* Walker; *Educ* Hulme GS Oldham, Loughborough Coll; *m* 1988, Anne Margaret; 2 s (Matthew, David), 1 da (Anna); *Career* head of PE Saddleworth Sch 1966–82; *Rugby League* dir of coaching Rugby Football League 1982–92; coach: Widnes RLFC 1992–94 (runners-up League 1992/93, runners-up Cup Challenge 1993), Keighley RLFC 1994–96 (winners League and Premiership 1994/95, runners-up League and Premiership 1995/96), Sheffield Eagles 1996–97; coach: England 1995 (runners-up World Cup 1995), GB 1996 (asst coach 1985–92); *Rugby Union* defensive coach Leicester Tigers 1998– (winners League 1998/99, 1999/2000, 2000/01 and 2001/02, Premiership 2000/01 and European Cup 2000/01 and 2001/02); defensive coach: England 1997–2006 (winners Six Nations Championship 2000, 2001 and 2003 (Grand Slam), winners World Cup Aust 2003), British and Irish Lions Aust tour 2001 and NZ tour 2005; inducted into Sports Coach Hall of Fame Nat Coaching Fndn 2004; *Publications* The Rugby League Skills Manual (1986), The Rugby League Coaching Manual (1988, 2 edn 1990); *Recreations* reading, travel; *Style*— Phillip Larder, Esq, MBE

LAREDO, Jaime; *b* 1940; *Career* violinist; pupil of: Antonio de Grassi, Frank Houser, Josef Gingold, Ivan Galamian; debut recital 1948, orchestral debut 1951, youngest winner ever (age 17) Queen Elizabeth competition Brussels 1959; festival appearances with major orchestras worldwide incl: Spoleto, Tanglewood, Hollywood Bowl, Mostly Mozart, Ravinia, Blossom, Marlboro, Edinburgh, Harrogate, The Proms; guest soloist and/or conductor with orchestras inl: Chicago Symphony, Boston Symphony, Philadelphia Orch, NY Philharmonic, London Symphony; dir Chamber Music at the 92nd Street Y series NY, memb Kalichstein/Laredo/Robinson Trio (Musical America's Ensenble of the Year 2002), memb Ax, Stern, Laredo Ma Quartet (Grammy Award for piano quartets), teacher Artist Faculty Curtis Inst, chamber musician, dir and soloist with int chamber orchestras incl: Scottish Chamber, English Chamber Orchestra, Orchestra of St Luke's; holds post as Distinguished Artist with St Paul Chamber Orchestra; numerous tours worldwide, numerous recordings incl The Complete Cycle of Beethoven Trios with Kalichstein/Laredo/Robinson Trio; awarded Handel medallion NY; *Style*— Jaime Laredo; ✉ c/o Askonas Holt, Lonsdale Chambers, 27 Chancery Lane, London WC2A 1PF (tel 020 7400 1751, e-mail info@askonasholt.co.uk)

LARGE, Sir Andrew McLeod Brooks; kt (1996); s of Maj-Gen Stanley Eyre Large, MBE (d 1991), of Dalbeattie, Kirkcudbrightshire, and Janet Mary, *née* Brooks; *b* 7 August 1942; *Educ* Winchester, CCC Cambridge (MA), INSEAD Fontainebleau (MBA); *m* 17 June 1967, Susan Mary, da of Sir Ronald Melville, KCB (d 2001); 2 s (Alexander b 1970, James b 1972), 1 da (Nina b 1976); *Career* British Petroleum Ltd 1964–71, md Orion Bank Ltd 1971–79; Swiss Bank Corp Int 1980–87: md 1980–83, chief exec and dep chm 1983–86, gp chief exec and dep chm 1986–87; memb Exec Bd Swiss Bank Corp (Zurich) 1988–89; chm: Large Smith & Walter Ltd 1990–92, Securities and Investments Bd (SIB) 1992–97,

Euroclear 1998–2000; dep chm Barclays Bank plc 1998–2002, dep govr Bank of England 2002–06; non-exec dir: Nuclear Electric plc 1990–94, Ranks Hovis McDougall plc 1990–92, Phoenix Securities Ltd 1990–92, Dowty Group plc 1991–92, ECC Group plc 1991–96; non-exec chm Luthy Baillie Dowsett Pethick & Co Ltd 1990–92; chm Int Orgn of Securities Cmmns (IOSCO) 1992; dep chm Int Securities Regulation Orgn (ISRO) 1985–86, memb Cncl Stock Exchange 1986–87; non-exec chm: The Securities Assoc 1986–87, London Futures and Options Exchange Ltd (London FOX) 1991–92; chm UK Cncl INSEAD 1997–2002 (memb Bd INSEAD 1998–); memb Bd Inst of Int Finance Washington 1998–2001; govr: Winchester Coll 1998– (warden 2003–), Christ Coll Brecon 1998–, Abingdon Sch 1991–98; pres Marcher Apple Network 2003–; *Recreations* skiing, walking, photography, music, weather, gardening, old apple trees; *Clubs* Brooks's; *Style*— Sir Andrew Large

LARKEN, Anthea; CBE (1991); da of Frederick William Savill (d 1993), of Winchester, Hants, and Nance, *née* Williams (d 1993); *b* 23 August 1938; *Educ* Stafford Girls' HS; *m* 19 Dec 1987 (m dis 1997), Rear Adm (Edmund Shackleton) Jeremy Larken, DSO, *qv*; *Career* range assessor WRNS 1956, cmmnd 1960, qualified photographic interpreter 1961, qualified WRNS Sec Offr 1967, i/c WRNS offrs trg BRNC Dartmouth 1977–79, RN Staff Coll 1978–79, NATO Mil Agency for Standardisation Brussels 1981–84, Chief Staff Offr (admin) to Flag Offr Plymouth 1985–86, Royal Coll of Def Studies 1987, Dir WRNS and ADC to HM The Queen 1988–91, ret Cmdt; dir and co sec Operational Command Training Organisation Ltd 1991–96; Hon LLD Univ of Greenwich 2000; *Recreations* theatre, music, reading, home, family and friends; *Clubs* Army and Navy; *Style*— Mrs Anthea Larken, CBE; ✉ c/o HSBC, 8 Market Square, Stafford ST16 2JP

LARKEN, Rear Adm (Edmund Shackleton) Jeremy; DSO (1982); s of Rear Adm Edmund Thomas Larken, CB, OBE (d 1965), and Eileen Margaret, *née* Shackleton; *b* 14 January 1939; *Educ* Bryanston, BRNC Dartmouth; *m* 1, 1963 (m dis 1987), Wendy Nigella, *née* Hallett; 2 da (Juliet b 1963, Henrietta b 1968); m 2, 1987 (m dis 1997), Anthea Larken, CBE, *qv*; m 3, 1997, Helen Denise, da of Bernard Barry Shannon (d 1977), of Mold; 1 s (Thomas b 1996), 1 da (Isobel b 1999); *Career* joined RN 1957, specialised in submarines 1961, navigation 1964, exchange with USN Submarine Force 1971–73; cmd: HMS Osiris 1969–70, Glamorgan 1975, Valiant 1976–77, Third Submarine Sqdn 1979–81, HMS Fearless 1981–83 (incl Falklands Campaign); Naval Plans 1983–84, Dir Naval Staff Duties 1985, Cdre Amphibious Warfare and Cmd UK/NL Amphib Force 1985–87; Rear Adm 1988, ACDS (Overseas) 1988–90; md Operational Command Training Organisation Ltd (OCTO) 1991–; govr Bryanston Sch 1988–99; MRUSI, FInstD; *Recreations* crisis management, leadership, maritime and aviation interests, history and strategy, theatre, reading, home, family and friends; *Clubs* Reform; *Style*— Rear Admiral Jeremy Larken, DSO; ✉ OCTO, Caerlleon House, 142 Boughton, Chester CH3 5BP (e-mail jeremy.larken@octo.uk.com)

LARKIN, Colin; *b* 15 December 1949; *m* 1, 1982 (m dis 1994), Laura McLachlan; 3 s (Ben b 1975 d 1993, Tom b 1983, Dan b 1986), 1 da (Carmen b 1989); m 2, 2000 (m dis 2003), Kelly Harte-Harris; m 3, 2003, Jenny Rastall; *Career* writer, musician, broadcaster and editor; apprentice commercial artist/graphic designer 1966, founded book publishing company 1976, freelance music writer; NBL (Nat Book League) design award 1976; *Publications* compiled or written over 55 books on popular music incl: Virgin Music Encyclopedias series, The Encyclopedia of Popular Music (1992, 4 edn 2006), The All Time Top 1000 Albums (1994, 4 edn 2003); ed-in-chief Muze UK Ltd; regular contrib to BBC Radio and music magazines; *Style*— Colin Larkin, Esq; ✉ e-mail colinmuze@mac.com

LARKIN, Judith Mary; da of Patrick John Larkin, and Sylvia May, *née* Silverthorne; *b* 22 May 1952; *Educ* The North London Coll Sch, City of London Poly; *Career* trainee Unilever plc 1971, corporate PR specialist in IT, telecommunications and electronics industries, head of corporate PR Logica plc 1979–84; dir: Traverse-Healy & Regester 1984–87, Charles Barker 1987; md Fleishman-Hillard UK Ltd 1990–94, fndr ptnr Regester Larkin Ltd 1994, fdnr ptnr Risk Principals Ltd 2006; chm Br Gp Int PR Assoc; memb Bd Issue Mgmnt Cncl 1997; FIPR 1997 (MIPR 1985); *Books* Risk Issues and Crisis Management (with Michael Regester, 1997); *Style*— Ms Judith Larkin

LARLHAM, Christopher; s of Maj Percival Edward Larlham (d 1968), of London, and Cecelia Louise, *née* Farrell (d 2001); *b* 8 November 1949; *Educ* Dulwich Coll; *m* 1, 3 May 1973 (m dis 1984), Caroline Jane Godfrey; 3 s (Edward b 1976, Guy b 1978, George b 1980); m 2, 1 Oct 1994, Cecily, da of Robin Hazell, of Bodmin, Cornwall; 1 s (Sam b 30 June 1996); *Career* admitted slr 1975; ptnr CMS Cameron McKenna (and predecessor firms) 1976–98 (managing ptnr 1990–94); memb Law Soc; capt Cambs and Hunts CBA and Saffron Walden Bridge Club, hon sec The Primary Club; Liveryman Worshipful Co of Slrs; *Recreations* cricket, bridge, wine; *Clubs* MCC; *Style*— Christopher Larlham, Esq; ✉ Apple Cottage, Hempstead, Saffron Walden, Essex CB10 2NU (tel 01799 586507, fax 01799 586064, e-mail secretary@primaryclub.org)

LARNER, Gerald; s of Clifford Larner (d 1968), of Leeds, and Minnie, *née* Barraclough (d 1985), of Leeds; *b* 9 March 1936; *Educ* Leeds Modern Sch, New Coll Oxford (sr scholarship, BA); *m* 1, 1959 (m dis 1988), Celia Ruth Mary, da of late Harry Gordon Norman White; 2 da (Alice Elizabeth b 1960, Melissa Ruth b 1962); m 2, 1989, Lynne Catherine Telfer, da of late Stuart George Cameron Walker; *Career* asst lectr German Dept Univ of Manchester 1960–62; The Guardian: music critic and features sub ed 1962–64, dep features ed 1964–65, regnl music and opera critic 1965–93, freelance music critic associated mainly with The Times 1993–2001; specialist writer of prog and sleeve/liner notes, occasional lectr on music and opera; tv and radio broadcaster; memb: NW Arts Music Panel 1975–80, Hallé Orch Advsy Ctee 1990–92; artistic dir Bowden Festival 1980–84; Officier de l'Ordre des Arts et des Lettres (France) 2001; *Books* Wolf's Der Corregidor (trans, 1966), McCabe's The Lion The Witch and the Wardrobe (librettist, 1971), The Glasgow Style (1979), The New Grove (contrib, 1980), Opera Grove (contrib, 1992), Maurice Ravel (1996); *Stage productions* Peter and the Women (Royal Exchange Theatre Manchester and Buxton Festival, 1993), A Chabrier Cabaret (Edinburgh Int Festival, 1994), Ravel Unravelled (Wooburn Festival, 1998, Mananan Festival 1999); *Recreations* visual arts incl decorative arts and design, theatre, literature, wine; *Style*— Gerald Larner, Esq; ✉ 38 Heyes Lane, Alderley Edge, Cheshire SK9 7JY (tel 01625 585378, fax 01625 590175)

LARRECHE, Prof Jean-Claude; s of Pierre Albert Alexis Larreche, of Pau, France, and Odette Jeanne Madeleine, *née* Hau-Sans; *b* 3 July 1947; *Educ* Lyon (INSA), Univ of London (MSc), INSEAD (MBA), Stanford Univ (PhD); *m* 10 Sept 1971, Denyse Michèle Joséphine, da of Michel Francis Henri Gros, of Besancon, France; 1 da (Sylvie b 1975), 1 s (Philippe b 1978); *Career* INSEAD: prof of mktg 1974–, dir Euro Strategic Mktg Inst 1985–89, Alfred H Heineken chair 1993–, dir Competitive Fitness of Global Firms Initiative 2000–02; non-exec dir: Reckitt and Colman plc (London) 1983–99, Reckitt Benckiser (London) 1999–2001; chm StratX Paris France 1985–, memb Bd The Mac Group Boston 1986–89; memb: America Mktg Assoc 1973, Inst of Mgmnt Sci 1975; FInstD; *Recreations* tennis, golf; *Style*— Prof Jean-Claude Larreche; ✉ 85 Rue Murger, 77780, Bourron Marlotte, France (tel 00 33 1 64 45 62 00, fax 00 33 1 64 45 98 76); INSEAD, 77305, Fontainebleau, France (tel 00 33 1 60 72 41 51, fax 00 33 1 60 74 55 00, e-mail jean-claude.larreche@insead.edu)

LARVIN, Prof Michael (Mike); s of John Larvin, of Marske by the Sea, Redcar, and Mary, *née* Cairns; *b* 13 September 1956; *Educ* Sir William Turner's Sch Coatham, Guy's Hosp Med Sch Univ of London (BSc, MB BS), Univ of Leeds (MD), Inst of Educn Univ of London (MA); *m* 25 July 1981, Keyna, *née* O'Donnell; 3 da (Elizabeth b 31 August 1982, Catherine b 18 March 1984, Abigail b 24 Feb 1996), 2 s (Christopher b 19 Dec 1985, David b 12 Nov 1990); *Career* jr surgical trg Guy's Hosp and Northwick Park Hosp 1981–85, research fell Univ of Leeds 1985–88, registrar Guy's Hosp 1989, lectr St James's Univ Hosp Leeds 1990–93, conslt surgn Univ Hosp Lewisham 1993–96, conslt surgn and sr clinical lectr Leeds 1996–2002, prof of surgery Univ of Nottingham at Derby 2002–; American gastroenterology int fell 1988, Pancreatic Soc travelling fell 1988, Hunterian prof of surgery RCS 1996–97, Rovsing medal Denmark 1998; author of more than 100 pubns in medical and educnl literature; patron Pancreatitis Supporters' Network 1997–, supporter Chernobyl Children's Tst 1998–; pres Pancreatic Soc of GB & I 2002, tutor RCS Soc of Trust and Estate Practitioners 2002–, helath clinical leader NHS Nat Library 2007–; memb: BMA 1981, Pancreatic Soc 1985, Pancreas Club USA 1987, Br Soc of Gastroenterology 1989, Soc for Surgery of the Alimentary Tract USA 1997, Int Assoc of Pancreatology 1997, American Pancreatic Assoc 2004; FRCSGlas 1986, FRCS 2001; *Recreations* swimming, reading, electronics and computing; *Style*— Prof Mike Larvin; ✉ Medical School, Derby City General Hospital, Derby DE22 3DT (tel 01332 724703, fax 01332 724697, e-mail mike.larvin@nottingham.ac.uk)

LASCELLES, Angela Marion; da of James Anthony Greig (d 1967), of Mersham, Kent, and Juliet Felicia, *née* Colvile; *Educ* Ashford Sch, Univ of London (BA); *m* 8 June 1974, Richard Lascelles, s of Dr William Lascelles; 2 s (Edward b 1975, Simon b 1978), 1 da (Rosalind b 1981); *Career* private clients Phillips & Drew Stockbrokers 1968–70, investment analyst Spencer Thornton Stockbrokers 1970–72, investment mangr Dawnay Day (Merchant Bank) 1972–74, Associated British Foods Pension Fund 1975–79, Courtaulds Pension Fund 1979–86, exec dir OLIM Ltd 1986–; jt investment dir Value & Income Trust plc 1986–2007; govr: The London Inst 1989–92, West Heath Sch 1996–97; churchwarden; AIIMR; *Recreations* tennis, music; *Style*— Mrs Angela Lascelles; ✉ OLIM Ltd, Pollen House, 10–12 Cork Street, London W1X 1PD (tel 020 7439 4400, fax 020 7734 1445)

LASK, Prof Bryan; s of Dr Aaron Lask, and Rita, *née* Flax (d 1989); *b* 18 February 1941; *children* 2 s (Gideon, Adam); *Career* conslt psychiatrist and prof St George's Univ of London, former ed Jl of Family Therapy; former ed Clinical Child Psychology and Psychiatry; fell Int Coll of Psychosomatic Medicine, FRCPsych, FRCPCH; *Books* Child Psychiatry & Social Work (1981), Children's Problems (1985), Childhood Illness - The Psychosomatic Approach (1989), Eating Disorders in Childhood and Adolescence - A Parent's Guide (1999), Childhood - Onset Anorexia Nervosa and Related Eating Disorders (2000), Psychosocial Aspects of Cystic Fibrosis (2000), Practical Child Psychiatry (2003, 2 edn 2007); *Recreations* sports, theatre, music; *Style*— Prof Bryan Lask; ✉ St George's University of London, Department of Psychiatry, London SW17 0RE (tel 07808 580858, e-mail blask@sgul.ac.uk)

LASKEY, Ronald Alfred; *b* 26 January 1945; *Educ* The Queen's Coll Oxford (open major scholar, MA, DPhil); *Career* scientific staff: Dept of Molecular Virology ICRF 1970–73, MRC Lab of Molecular Biology Cambridge 1973–83; professorial fell Darwin Coll Cambridge 1982–, Charles Darwin prof of embryology Univ of Cambridge 1983–, Cancer Research Campaign (CRC) dir Wellcome/CRC Inst Univ of Cambridge 1991–2001, hon dir MRC Cancer Cell Unit 2000–; vice-chm MRC Cell Bd 1989–1992, convenor Cell and Devpt Biology Academia Europaea 1991–96, tstee Strangeways Research Lab Cambridge 1993–; pres Br Soc for Cell Biology 1995–99; ed Current Opinion in Genetics and Devpt 1990–99, assoc ed: Cell 1982–, Current Biology 1991–99, Molecular Cell 1997; memb Editorial Bd Current Opinion in Genetics and Development 1999–; memb: EMBO 1982, Academia Europaea 1988; memb Cncl: Royal Soc 1988–90, ICRF 2000–02; memb Scientific Ctee: Cancer Research Campaign 1993–2001, EMBL Heidelberg 1999–2004, Max Planck Inst for Biochemistry 2000– (chair 2002–08); memb: Scientific Advsy Bd Cytosystems 2006–, UK Panel for Research Integrity 2006–; tstee Inst of Cancer Research 2007–; hon foreign memb Japanese Biochemical Soc, hon memb Dept of Biochemistry Univ of Oxford 1997–; FRS 1984, FMedSci 1998; *Awards*: Colworth Medal Biochemical Soc 1979, Alkis Seraphim meml lectr 1984, L'Institut Jacques Monod Medal 1986, Runnström lectr, Medal and Prize Univ of Stockholm 1991, Earl King meml lectr Royal Postgrad Med Sch 1991, Frank Rose meml lectr Br Assoc Cancer Research 1997, Biochemical Soc CIBA Medal 1997, Bidder lectr Soc of Experimental Biology 1998, Feldberg Prize for Med Research Germany 1998, Louis-Jeantet Prize for Med Switzerland 1998, Univ Medal Charles Univ Prague 1999, BBC Tomorrow's World Health Innovation Award 2000, Croonian lectr Royal Soc 2001, Wenner Gren lectr Univ of Stockholm 2001, Kettle lectr RCPath 2003, Mühlbock lectr European Assoc of Cancer Research 2006; *Style*— Prof Ronald A Laskey, FRS; ✉ MRC Cancer Cell Unit, Hutchison/MRC Research Centre, Hills Road, Cambridge CB2 2XZ (tel 01223 334106/7, fax 01223 763293, e-mail ral@hutchison-mrc.cam.ac.uk or ral19@mole.bio.cam.ac.uk)

LASOK, Dr (Karol) Paul Edward; QC (1994); s of Prof Dominik Lasok, QC (d 2000), and Sheila May, *née* Corrigan; *b* 16 July 1953; *Educ* Jesus Coll Cambridge (MA), Univ of Exeter (LLM, PhD); *m* 23 Feb 1991, Karen Bridget Morgan, da of Rev Dr Hugh Griffith, HCF (d 1991); 2 da (Frances Katharine Marina b 10 June 1993, Anna Zofia Christina b 18 June 1997); *Career* called to the Bar Middle Temple 1977 (bencher 2002); legal sec Court of Justice of European Communities 1980–84 (locum tenens March-May 1985); private practice: Brussels 1985–87, London 1987–; memb Editorial Bd: European Competition Law Review, Law and Justice; Tax Lawyer of the Year 2005; *Books* The European Court of Justice Practice and Procedure (2 edn, 1994), Law & Institutions of the European Union (7 edn, 2001); contrib: Halsbury's Laws of England 4 edn vols 51 and 52 (1986), Stair Memorial Encyclopaedia of the Laws of Scotland, Weinberg & Blank on Take-overs and Mergers (1989); *Recreations* walking, music, amusing daughters; *Style*— Dr Paul Lasok, QC; ✉ 57 Ellington Street, London N7 8PN (tel 020 7607 5874); Monckton Chambers, 1 & 2 Raymond Buildings, Gray's Inn, London WC1R 5NR (tel 020 7405 7211, fax 020 7405 2084)

LASSEN-DIESEN, David Peter; s of Sigurd Lassen-Diesen (d 1986), and Mary Margaret, *née* Wright; *b* 30 January 1938; *m* 7 Sept 1968, Valerie Jane, da of Joseph John Ive (d 1964); 1 da (Karen b 1971), 2 s (David b 1974, Piers b 1977); *Career* property investor/developer; fndr ptnr Diesen Property Co 1967; dir: Frost Holdings 1972–74; MInstD; *Recreations* yachting; *Style*— David P Lassen-Diesen, Esq; ✉ Heath Grove, Kingswood, Surrey KT20 6JE (tel 01737 830920, fax 01737 833393, website www.lassen-diesen.com)

LAST, Andrew John; s of Prof John William Last, CBE *qv*, of Llannerch Hall, Clwyd, and Susan Josephine, *née* Farmer; *b* 2 January 1969; *Educ* Birkenhead Sch, Trinity Coll Oxford (MA); *m* 14 June 1997, Sarah Jane, da of Giles Bartleet; 2 s (Henry Jack b 16 July 1998, Jordan Michael b 12 Jan 2001); *Career* account exec Pettifor Morrow & Associates Ltd 1990–92, account mangr Nexus Public Relations 1992–96, conslt Bell Pottinger Consultants 1996–99, founding dir salt 2000–; Freeman City of London 1997; assoc memb IPR 1998; *Recreations* football, golf; *Clubs* RAC; *Style*— Andrew Last, Esq; ✉ salt, Park House, 14 Northfields, London SW18 1DD (tel 020 8870 6777, fax 020 8870 6837, e-mail andrew@saltlondon.com)

LAST, Prof John William; CBE (1989); s of late Jack Last (d 1986), and Freda Edith, *née* Evans (d 1976); *b* 22 January 1940; *Educ* Sutton GS, Trinity Coll Oxford (MA); *m* 1967, Susan Josephine, da of late John Holloway Farmer, of Knaresborough, N Yorks; 3 s (Andrew John Last, *qv*, b 2 Jan 1969, Philip James b 12 June 1971, Peter Charles b 7 June 1973); *Career* corp affrs advsr Littlewoods Orgn (joined 1969), dir of public affrs United Utilities plc (North West Water plc) 1993–98; fndr Merseyside Maritime Museum;

chm: Walker Art Gallery Liverpool 1977–81, Royal Liverpool Philharmonic Orch 1977–92; memb: Arts Cncl 1980–84, Press Cncl 1980–86, Museums Cmmn 1983–95, Dernier Property Gp 1999, Bute Communications Ltd; non-exec dir Spares Finder Ltd 1999–2002; tstee: Theatre Museum 1983–86, V&A 1983–86 (memb Advsy Cncl), Nat Museum of Wales 1994–97 and 2003–; vice-pres Museums Assoc 1983–84, chm Museums Trg Inst 1990–97; visiting prof in arts admin City Univ 1985–, vice-chm NE Wales Inst Univ of Wales 2001–, Christie lectr 1990, vice-chm Northern Ballet Theatre; dep treas Lib Dem Pty 2003–06, memb Federal Exec Lib Dem Pty 2007–; Merseyside Gold Medal for Achievement 1991; Freeman City of London 1985, Liveryman Worshipful Co of Barber Surgns 1986 (joined Ct of Assts 1999, Middle Warden 2003, Master 2005–06); Hon DLitt City Univ 1995; hon fell Liverpool John Moores Univ 1989; *Recreations* memorabilia of Edward VIII, music, swimming; *Clubs* Garrick; *Style—* Prof John Last, CBE; ✉ Llannerch Hall, St Asaph, Denbighshire LL17 0BD

LASZLO, *see:* de Laszlo

LATCHMAN, Prof David Seymour; *b* 22 January 1956; *Educ* Haberdashers' Aske's, Queens' Coll Cambridge (entrance scholar, fndn scholar, BA, coll prizes), Univ of Cambridge (bachelor scholar, MA, PhD), Univ of London (DSc); *Career* postdoctoral research fell Eukaryotic Molecular Genetics Gp Cancer Research Campaign Dept of Biochemistry Imperial Coll London 1981–84, lectr in molecular genetics Dept of Biology (formerly Zoology) UCL 1984–88, dir Medical Biology Unit Dept of Biochemistry and Molecular Biology UCL and Middx Sch of Med 1988–91 (reader 1990); UCL: prof of molecular pathology (established chair) and head Dept of Molecular Pathology 1991–99, chm Div of Pathology 1995–99, dir Windeyer Inst of Med Scis 1996–99, dep head UCL Grad Sch 1998–99, dean and prof of human genetics Inst of Child Health Gt Ormond Street Hosp UCL 1999–2002 (non-exec dir Gt Ormond Street Hosp for Children NHS Tst 2001–02), master Birkbeck Coll London and prof of genetics Birkbeck Coll and UCL 2003–; chm Science Expert Advsy Ctee Univ of London; memb Univ of London: Central Equipment and Scholarships Fund, Examinations and Assessment Cncl Advsy Bd, Examinations Bd and Biological Subjects Advsy Panel; chair London Ideas Genetics Knowledge Park 2002–, chm London Higher, memb Bd London Devpt Agency; chm Scientific Advsy Bd Nat Inst for Biological Standards, vice-chm Med Advsy Panel Parkinson's Disease Soc; memb: Br Heart Fndn Project Grants Ctee, Advsy Bd MRC, Biological Standards Bd Nat Inst for Biological Standards, Examining Panel in Genetics RCP, Health Protection Agency, Genetics and Insurance Ctee, HEFCE Research Strategy Ctee, UUK Research Strategy Ctee, Cncl Lifelong Learning UK, Biochemical Soc, Soc for General Microbiology, AAAS, American Soc for Microbiology, NY Acad of Scis; pres The Maccabeeans; FRCPath; *Books* Gene Regulation - a eukaryotic perspective (1990, 5 edn 2005), Eukaryotic Transcription Factors (1991, 4 edn 2004), Transcription Factors: a practical approach (ed, 1993, 2 edn, 1999), From Genetics to Gene Therapy (ed, 1994), PCR Applications in Pathology (ed, 1994), Genetic Manipulation of the Nervous System (ed, 1996), Landmarks in Gene Regulation (ed, 1997), Basic Molecular and Cell Biology (ed, 1997), Stress Proteins (ed, 1999), Viral Vectors for Treating Diseases of the Nervous System (ed, 2003); *Recreations* book collecting, opera; *Clubs* Athenaeum; *Style—* Prof David Latchman; ✉ Birkbeck College, Malet Street, London WC1E 7HX (tel 020 7631 6274, fax 020 7631 6259, e-mail master@bbk.ac.uk)

LATCHMORE, Andrew Windsor; s of Arthur John Craig Latchmore, MBE, FRCS (d 1998), and Joyce Mary Latchmore, JP, *née* Raper (d 1993); *b* 9 February 1950; *Educ* Oundle, Univ of Leeds (LLB); *m* 1 (m dis 1989), Jillian Amanda, da of Victor Hugo Watson, of East Keswick, W Yorks; 1 da (Lucy Emma 1979), 1 s (Jolyon Guy 1981); m 2, Clarissa Mary, da of Maj Peter J Orde (d 2001); 1 da (Chloe Roseanna b 1991), 1 s (Max Andrew b 1993); *Career* admitted slr 1975; Eversheds: (formerly Hepworth and Chadwick): ptnr 1978–2004, chm of commercial property 1991–98, nat managing ptnr Client Servs 1998–2000; ptnr Shulmans 2004–; memb Exec Bd Br Cncl for Offices 2001–05 (chm Northern Chapter 1999–2005); govr Gateways Sch 1992–94 (sec to govrs 1977–92), chair of govrs of Queen Mary's Sch Baldersly 2004–; hon sec Leeds Law Soc 1986–90; memb Law Soc; *Recreations* music, opera, golf, tennis, skiing, walking, travel; *Clubs* Alwoodley Golf; *Style—* Andrew Latchmore, Esq; ✉ Shulmans, 120 Wellington Street, Leeds LS1 4LT (tel 0113 245 2833, fax 0113 246 7326, e-mail alatchmore@shulmans.co.uk)

LATHAM, Rt Hon Lord Justice; Rt Hon Sir David Nicholas Ramsay; kt (1992), PC (2000); s of Robert Clifford Latham, CBE (d 1995), of Cambridge, and Eileen Frances, *née* Ramsay (d 1969); *b* 18 September 1942; *Educ* Bryanston, Queens' Coll Cambridge (MA); *m* 6 May 1967, Margaret Elizabeth, *née* Forrest; 3 da (Clare Frances (Mrs Jonathan Speight) b 2 Aug 1969, Angela Josephine (Mrs Ian Taylor) b 23 Jan 1972, (Rosemary) Harriet (Mrs Charles Waggett) b 10 Dec 1974); *Career* called to the Bar Middle Temple 1964 (bencher 1989); jr counsel to the Crown Common Law 1979–85, jr counsel to Dept of Trade in export credit guarantee matters 1982–85, QC 1985, recorder of the Crown Court 1983–92, judge of the High Court of Justice (Queen's Bench Div) 1992–2000, presiding judge Midland & Oxford Circuit 1995–99, Lord Justice of Appeal 2000–; vice-pres Court of Appeal Criminal Div 2006–; memb: Gen Cncl of the Bar 1986–92, Judicial Studies Bd 1988–91, Cncl Legal Education 1988–96, Sentencing Guidelines Cncl 2006–; vice-chm Cncl for Legal Educn 1992–96; *Recreations* reading, music, food, drink; *Clubs* Travellers, Leander; *Style—* The Rt Hon Lord Justice Latham; ✉ Royal Courts of Justice, Strand, London WC2A 2LL

LATHAM, Derek James; s of James Horace Latham, DFC (d 1996), of Newark-on-Trent, and Mary Pauline, *née* Turner (d 1974); *b* 12 July 1946; *Educ* King Edward VI GS Retford, Leicester Sch of Architecture, Trent Poly Nottingham (DipArch, DipTP, DipLD); *m* 14 Sept 1968, Pauline Elizabeth, OBE, da of Philip George Tuxworth, of Lincs; 1 da (Sarah Jane b 1972), 2 s (Benjamin James b 1974, Oliver James b 1981); *Career* Clifford Wearden & Assocs (architects and planners) London 1968–70, housing architect and planner Derby CC 1970–73, design and conservation offr Derbyshire CC 1974–78, tech advsr Derbyshire Historic Bldgs Tst 1978–, princ Derek Latham and Assocs 1980–89, chm Derek Latham and Company 1989–; md Michael Saint Developments Ltd 1984–96; dir: Acanthus Associated Architectural Practices Ltd 1984–98 (chm 1987–89), Omega Two Ltd (artworks advsrs) 1990–, Acanthus Europe 1993–98, Church Converts Ltd 1996–; chm Opun (Architecture and Built Environment Centre for the East Midlands) 2002–05, chm Regeneration E Midlands 2005–; memb Exec Ctee Cncl for Care of Churches 1985–91, architectural advsr Peak Park Tst 1986–, concept co-ordinator Sheffield Devpt Corp 1987–89; master planner Derby City Challenge 1992–94; memb Regnl Ctee HLF 2001–06; memb: Soc for the Protection of Ancient Buildings 1974 (memb Ctee 1993–2001), Ancient Monument Soc 1975, Assoc of Heritage Interpretation 1976, EASA 1991, Urban Design Gp 1991, RSA 1989 (chm RSA Dean Clough 1995–98), Inst of Historic Bldg Conservation 1997, Inst of Environmental Mgmnt and Assessment; regnl ambass CABE 2001– (educn enabler 2002–), client deisgn advsr RIBA 2005–; external examiner: Leicester Sch of Architectural Conservation Studies 1983–86, Leicester Sch of Architecture 1988–92, Sch of Architecture Univ of Nottingham 1996–99; govr Nottingham Sch of Interior Design 1986–90, memb Ct Univ of Derby 1995–; memb Register of Architects Accredited in Building Conservation 2001; RIBA 1971, MRTPI 1974, ALI 1978; *Publications* Creative Re-use of Buildings: Donhead 2000; *Recreations* squash, sailing, rambling, cycling, swimming; *Clubs* Duffield Squash and Lawn Tennis, Little Eaton Lawn Tennis (pres 1991–2003); *Style—* Derek J Latham, Esq; ✉ Hieron's Wood, Vicarage Lane, Little Eaton, Derby DE21 5EA (tel 01332 832371); Latham Architects, St Michaels, Derby DE1 3SU (tel 01332 365777, fax 01332 290314, e-mail derek@lathamarchitects.co.uk)

LATHAM, 2 Baron (UK 1942); Dominic Charles Latham; er (twin) s of Hon Francis Charles Allman Latham (d 1959), and his 3 w Gabrielle Monica, *née* O'Riordan (d 1987), and gs of 1 Baron Latham (d 1970); *b* 20 September 1954; *Educ* NSW Univ (BEng, MEngSc); *Heir* bro, Anthony Latham; *Career* civil engr with Electricity Cmmn of New South Wales 1979–88; structural engr with Rankine & Hill consulting engrs 1988–91; sr structural engr with Gerard Barry Assocs 1992; social dancing teacher 1993–; *Recreations* tennis, squash, snooker, electronics, sailboarding; *Style—* The Rt Hon the Lord Latham

LATHAM, (John) Martin; s of William John Lawrence Latham, of Leatherhead, Surrey, and late Kathleen Louise, *née* Ward; *b* 28 July 1942; *Educ* Bradfield Coll, Fitzwilliam Coll Cambridge (MA); *m* 7 June 1997, Barbara Joy Ruth, yr da of late Air Vice-Marshal Michael Lyne, CB, AFC, DL; *Career* Peat Marwick Mitchell & Co London 1965–74; James Capel & Co: corp fin exec 1974–76, co sec 1976–87, head of secretariat 1987–92, compliance dir 1992–96; gp compliance dir HSBC Investment Bank plc 1996–97; FSI (memb Stock Exchange 1978), FCA 1979; *Recreations* tennis, golf, yachting; *Clubs* MCC, Roehampton; *Style—* Martin Latham, Esq; ✉ 53 Abbotsbury Close, Holland Park, London W14 8EQ (tel 020 7603 2591, fax 020 7602 2518)

LATHAM, Sir Michael Anthony; kt (1993), DL (Leics 1994); s of Wing Cdr S H Latham (d 1993); *b* 20 November 1942; *Educ* Marlborough, King's Coll Cambridge, Dept of Educn Univ of Oxford; *m* 1969, Caroline Susan (d 2006), da of Maj T A Terry, RE (d 1971); 2 s; *Career* housing and local govt offr CRD 1965–67, co-opted memb GLC Housing Ctee 1967–73, memb Westminster City Cncl 1968–71, dir and chief exec House Builders Fedn 1971–73; MP (Cons): Melton 1974–83, Rutland and Melton 1983–92; memb: Select Ctee on Energy 1979–82, Public Accounts Ctee 1983–92; advsr on economic and political issues 1993–95; pres: Br Flat Roofing Cncl 1995–99, Flat Roofing Alliance 2000–, Euro Construction Inst 2002–; chm: Construction Industry Bd 1995–96, Jt Major Contractors' Gp 1996–, Jt Industry Bd for the Electrical Contracting Industry 1998–, Willmott Dixon Ltd 1999–2002 (non-exec dir 1996–99, dep chm 2002–), Partnership Sourcing Ltd 2000–05, Construction Skills (formerly Construction Industry Trg Bd) 2002–, Roofing Industry Alliance 2003– (dep chm 1997–2003), Collaborative Working Centre Ltd 2003–, E C Harris Public Sector Exec 2004–; dep chm BIW Technologies Ltd 2000–05; non-exec dir James R Knowles construction conslts 1997–2003; consIt on partnering Inspace plc 2005–; visiting prof: Univ of Northumbria 1995–2000, The Bartlett Sch of Architecture UCL 1997–2000, Univ of Central Eng 2001–; reviewer Jt Govt/Indust Review on Procurement/Contractual Problems in the Construction Indust 1993–94; hon vice-pres Anglo-Israel Assoc 1994– (pres 1990–94), vice-pres Cncl of Christians and Jews 2000– (jt hon treas 1996–2000); tstee Oakham Sch 1987–2001; Anglican lay reader 1988–; hon fell: Chartered Inst of Building Services Engineers 2002, Chartered Inst of Purchasing and Supply 1994, ICE 1995, CIOB 1995, Landscape Inst 1997, Royal Acad of Engrg 1997, Royal Incorporation of Architects in Scotland 1998, RIBA 2000; hon memb RICS 1996; Hon LLD Nottingham Trent Univ 1995, Hon DEng Univ of Birmingham 1998, Hon DCL Univ of Northumbria 1999, Hon DTech Loughborough Univ 2004; FRSA 1992; *Recreations* cricket, fencing, gardening, listening to classical music; *Clubs* Carlton; *Style—* Sir Michael Latham, DL; ✉ 508 Hood House, Dolphin Square, London SW1V 3NH

LATHAM, (Edward) Michael Locks; DL (Cornwall 1995); s of Edward Bryan Latham, CBE (d 1980); *b* 7 January 1930; *Educ* Stowe, Clare Coll Cambridge; *m* 1955, Joan Doris, da of Charles Ellis Merriam Coubrough (d 1967); 1 s, 2 da; *Career* chm: James Latham plc 1973–87 (dir 1957–91), Bloomsbury Properties 1997–2004 (dir 1991–), Trebartha Estates Ltd 1984–2001, The Lanlivery Tst 1989–2005; non-exec dir Royal Cornwall Hosp Tst 1991–97; pres: Sandringham Assoc of Royal Warrant Holders 1982–83, Timber Trade Fedn 1984–85; memb Exec Ctee Nat Cncl of Bldg Material Prodrs 1985–91; govr St Dunstan's Abbey Sch 1988–93, pres Royal Cornwall Agric Assoc 1992, chm Duchy Opera 1994–99; High Sheriff Cornwall 1992; Co Cdr St John Ambulance Cornwall 1993–97; *Recreations* tennis, the countryside, languages, books, stamp collecting; *Clubs* St Mellion Int; *Style—* E Michael Latham, Esq, DL; ✉ Trebartha Lodge, Launceston PL15 7PD

LATHAM, Richard Brunton; QC (1991); s of Frederick Latham, and Joan Catherine, *née* Glover; *b* 16 March 1947; *Educ* Farnborough GS, Univ of Birmingham (LLB); *m* 1 Jan 1972, Alison Mary, da of John Llewellyn Goodall; 3 s (Thomas Richard b 6 Jan 1977, Nicholas John b 30 Aug 1979, Peter James b 5 Feb 1982); *Career* called to the Bar Gray's Inn 1971 (bencher 1999), recorder Midland & Oxford Circuit 1987–, standing counsel Inland Revenue 1987–91; *Recreations* sailing, opera, photography; *Style—* Richard Latham, Esq, QC; ✉ 7 Bedford Row, London WC1R 4BS (tel 020 7242 3555, fax 020 7242 2511)

LATHAM, Sir Richard Thomas Paul; 3 Bt (UK 1919), of Crow Clump, Walton-upon-Thames, Co Surrey; s of Sir (Herbert) Paul Latham, 2 Bt (d 1955); *b* 15 April 1934; *Educ* Eton, Trinity Coll Cambridge (MA); *m* 1958, (Marie-Louise) Patricia, da of late Frederick Hooper Russell, of Vancouver, Canada; 2 da (Nicola Patricia (Mrs Colin D Jones) b 1959, Alison Kathleen b 1965); *Heir* none; *Style—* Sir Richard Latham, Bt; ✉ 2125 Birnam Wood Drive, Santa Barbara, California 93108, USA

LATIMER, Dr Raymond Douglas (Ray); s of Kenneth Eric Latimer, MBE (d 1975), of London, and Doris Evelyn, *née* Friend; *b* 15 August 1941; *Educ* City of London Sch, Univ of Cambridge (MA), Middlesex Hosp Med Sch (LRCP, MB BS); *m* 15 May 1965, Patricia Mary, da of Frank Theodore Page; 3 s (Paul b 1968, Mark b 1970, Andrew b 1978), 1 da (Sarah b 1971); *Career* cardiothoracic anaesthetist Papworth Hosp, assoc lectr Univ of Cambridge, ed Jl of Cardiothoracic Anaesthesia; guest lectr: China 1987, Iran 1989, India and China 1991, Romania 1994; fndr Assoc of Cardiothoracic Anaesthetists of GB and I, sec and treas Euro Assoc of Cardiothoracic Anaesthesiologists, memb Cncl World Assoc of Cardiothoracic and Vascular Anaesthesia; memb Queens' Coll Cambridge; tstee St Stephens Hosp Delhi; Lifetime Achievement Award Indian Assoc of Cadriovascular Thoracic Anaesthesioligists 2004; hon prof of anaesthesia SCT Inst for Med Sci Trivandrum India; academician European Acd of Anaesthesia; MRCS; FRCA; *Books* Thoracic Anaesthesia - Principles and Practice (with S Ghosh, 1999); author of chapters in pubns on endotoxaemia in cardiac surgery, anaesthesia for heart and lung transplantation, selective phosphodieterase inhibitors in treatment of heart failure and inhaled nitric oxide in pulmonary hypertension; *Recreations* sailing, Christian Youth Leader (Pathfinders); *Clubs* Christian Med Fellowship; *Style—* Dr Ray Latimer; ✉ Oaksway, 15 Braggs Lane, Hemingford Grey, Huntingdon, Cambridgeshire PE28 9BW (tel 01480 463582); Papworth Hospital, Papworth Everard, Cambridge CB3 8RE (tel 01480 364406, fax 01480 364936)

LATTIMORE, Colin Reginald; OBE (2005), JP (Cambridgeshire 1983); s of George Edward Lattimore (d 1957), and Margaret Fee, *née* Mackie (d 1984); *b* 28 March 1934; *Educ* Kingston HS Hull, UCL (MB BS), RCS (Dip Anaesthetics); *m* 11 Feb 1961, Mary Isobel, da of Charles Ramsay of Sunderland; 2 da (Fiona Mary b 7 July 1963 d 1988, Angela Jane b 19 May 1967), 1 s (Iain William b 6 April 1973); *Career* various pre registration house offr posts (surgery and obstetrics) 1959–60, SHO in anaesthetics Lister Hosp Hitchin 1960–62, registrar in anaesthetics Bedford Hosp 1962–64, locum conslt anaesthetist Grantham Hosp 1964–66, asst anaesthetist Dumfries and Galloway Hosp 1966–70, asst sr admin MO East Anglian RHA (EARHA) 1970–76, conslt Public Health Med EARHA 1976–82, dir Public Health Huntingdon HA 1982–94, dep coroner Huntingdon 1993–, dep coroner Cambridge 1999–, assoc mangr (Mental Health) Huntingdon Healthcare Tst 1995–; chm Hunts Rural Tport Initiative 1994–97; chm:

L

Cambridgeshire Probation Serv 1991–2001, Cambridge Area Nat Probation Serv 2001–04; memb and past pres Cambridge Med Soc; memb: Heraldry Soc, Huntingdon Decorative and Fine Arts Soc; past pres Cambridgeshire Numismatic Soc, life pres Comberton Antiquarian Soc; chm Bookplate Soc; lectr Nat Assoc of Decorative and Fine Art Socs; licentiate Br Horological Inst (pres 1999), hon keeper of Clocks and Watches Fitzwilliam Museum Cambridge 1999–; Liveryman and memb Ct of Assts Worshipful Co of Clockmakers (Master 1999, keeper of the Co's silver); FFPHMI 1988 (MFPHMI 1978), MFPHM (by distinction) 1991, FSA Scot; *Publications* English Nineteenth Century Press Moulded Glass (1979), Bookplates and Heraldry, The Bookplate Soc Jl (1987), An Introduction to Erotic Bookplates (1990), A Short History of the Worshipful Company of Clockmakers (private edn, 1995); *Recreations* lecturing on English decorative and applied fine arts; *Style*— Dr Colin Lattimore, OBE, JP; ✉ Caxton Court, Caxton, Cambridge CB3 8PG (tel and fax 01954 719310)

LATYMER, 9 Baron (E 1431–32); Crispin James Alan Nevill Money-Coutts; eldest s of 8 Baron (d 2003); *b* 8 March 1955; *Educ* Eton, Keble Coll Oxford; *m* 1, 1978 (m dis 1995), Hon Lucy Rose Deedes, yst da of Baron Deedes (Life Peer); 2 da (Hon Sophia Patience b 1985, Hon Evelyn Rose b 1988), 1 s (Hon Drummond William Thomas b 11 May 1986); m 2, 1995, Shaunagh Anne Henrietta, former w of Thomas Peter William Heneage, and da of (George Silver) Oliver Annesley Colthurst; *Heir* s, Hon Drummond Money-Coutts; *Career* E F Hutton, Bankers Trust International, European Banking Co, Coutts & Co 1986 (latterly head of int private banking and memb Gp Exec Ctee), Cazenove & Co 2000– (currently dir Cazenove Capital Mgmnt); non-exec dir: Manek Investment Mgmnt, Throgmorton Tst plc 2007–; *Clubs* Mark's, Beefsteak, House of Lords Yacht; *Style*— The Rt Hon the Lord Latymer; ✉ 28 Chelsham Road, London SW4 6NP

LAUDERDALE, 17 Earl of (S 1624); Sir Patrick Francis Maitland; 13 Bt (NS 1680); also Lord Maitland of Thirlestane (S 1590), Viscount of Lauderdale (S 1616), Viscount Maitland, and Lord Thirlestane and Boltoun (both S 1624); Hereditary Bearer of National Flag of Scotland by Decrees of Lord Lyon King of Arms (1790 and 1952); s of Rev Hon Sydney George William Maitland (d 1946; 2 s of 13 Earl); suc bro, 16 Earl 1968; *b* 17 March 1911; *Educ* Lancing, BNC Oxford; *m* 1936, Stanka (d 2003), da of Prof Milivoje Lozanitch, of Belgrade Univ; 2 s, 2 da (1 of whom Lady Olga Maitland, *qv*); *Heir* s, Viscount Maitland, *qv*; *Career* sat as Cons in House of Lords until 1999; journalist 1933–59, fndr and sometime ed Fleet Street Letter Service, sometime ed The Whitehall Letter; war corr: The Times (Central and Eastern Europe) 1939–41, News Chronicle (Pacific) 1941–43; MP (Cons) Lanarkshire (Lanark Div) 1951–59 (resigned whip 1956–58 in protest at withdrawal from Suez); fndr and chm Expanding Cwlth Gp at House of Commons 1955–59 (re-elected chm 1959), fndr and first chm All-Pty Parly Gp on Energy Studies, chm House of Lords Sub-Ctee on Energy Tport and Res 1974–79; conslt Elf Exploration (UK) plc 1980–2000; pres The Church Union 1956–61, memb (emeritus) Coll of Guardians Nat Shrine of Our Lady of Walsingham 1955–; FRGS; *Books* European Dateline (1945), Task for Giants (1957); *Clubs* New (Edinburgh); *Style*— The Rt Hon the Earl of Lauderdale

LAUE, Prof Ernest Douglas; *b* 18 August 1955; *Educ* RSC, CNAA (PhD); *Career* Univ of Cambridge: demonstrator then lectr Dept of Biochemistry 1985–99, fell St John's Coll 1987– (coll lectr in biochemistry 1987–2000), reader in structural biology 1999–2000, prof of structural biology 2000–; memb: Biochemistry and Biophysics Sub-Ctee SERC 1987–91, Advsy Ctee on NMR MRC 1994–98, Review of Structural Biology BBSRC 1996, BMS Ctee Network Gp BBSRC 1997–2004, Infrastructure Panel Wellcome Tst 1997–99, Advsy Bd MRC 2002–, Tools and Resources Strategy Panel BBSRC 2004–; author of numerous research papers and articles in learned jls particularly on the structure and function of macromolecules; conslt: Dupont Pharmaceutical Co 1991–2001, Mitotix Inc 1996–2000; *Style*— Prof Ernest Laue; ✉ University of Cambridge, Department of Biochemistry, 80 Tennis Court Road, Old Addenbrooke's Site, Cambridge CB2 1GA (tel 01223 333677, fax 01223 766002)

LAUGHTON, Prof Michael Arthur; s of William Arthur Laughton (d 1986), of Barrie, Ontario, Canada, and Laura, *née* Heap (d 1987); *b* 18 December 1934; *Educ* King Edward Five Ways Birmingham, Etobicoke Collegiate Inst Toronto, Univ of Toronto (BASc), Univ of London (PhD, DSc(Eng)); *m* 1960 (m dis 1994), Margaret Mary, yr da of Brig George Vincent Leigh Coleman, OBE (QVOCG Indian Army, d 1970); 2 da (Joanna Margaret (Mrs Brogan-Higgins) b 28 June 1963, Katherine Alice (Dr Gardner) b 22 Nov 1965), 2 s (Mark Michael b 30 July 1968, Thomas George b 16 May 1971); *Career* graduate apprentice GEC Witton Birmingham 1957–59, project engr GEC Engineering Computer Services 1959–61; QMC London (later Queen Mary & Westfield Coll London, now Queen Mary Univ of London): DSIR res student 1961–64, lectr Dept of Electrical Engrg 1964–72, reader in electrical engrg 1972–77, prof 1977–2000, emeritus prof 2000–, dean Faculty of Engrg 1983–85 and 1990–94, pro-princ QMC 1985–89; visiting prof: Univ of Purdue USA 1966, Univ of Tokyo Japan 1977, Imperial Coll 2002–; external examiner numerous univs UK and abroad 1970–; co-ed and fndr Int Journal of Electrical Power and Energy Systems 1978–; chm: Tower Shakespeare Company Ltd 1985–93, Queen Mary College Industrial Research Ltd 1988–91 (dir 1979); organising sec Power Systems Computation Confs 1963–81 (chm Exec Ctee 1981–); chm Working Gp on Renewable Energy 1986–90 (Watt Ctee Exec 1986–); memb: Info Ctee Royal Society 1988–92, British Scholars Selection Ctee Fulbright Cmmn 1991–, House of Lords Select Ctee on the Euro Communities (specialist advsr to Sub Ctee B (Energy, Tport and Technol) on Inquiries into Renewable Resources 1988 and Efficiency of Electricity Use 1989), Cncl IEE 1990–94, House of Commons Welsh Ctee (specialist advsr on Inquiry on Wind Energy) 1994, Energy Policy Advsy Gp Royal Soc 2001–, Int Ctee Royal Acad of Engrg 2002–06; memb Ct Cranfield Inst of Technol 1991–96; IEE Career Achievement Medal 2002; Freeman City of London 1990, Liveryman Worshipful Co of Barbers 1995; MRI 1973–91, FIEE 1977 (MIEE 1968), FREng 1989; *Publications* Electrical Engineers Reference Book (with: M G Say 1985, G R Jones 1993, D G Warne 2002), Expert System Applications in Power Systems (ed with T S Dillon, 1990), Renewable Energy Sources (ed 1990); author of numerous papers on electrical power and energy systems, control and computation; *Recreations* music, following rugby and cricket; *Clubs* Athenaeum; *Style*— Prof M A Laughton, FREng; ✉ 28 Langford Green, Champion Hill, London SE5 8BX (tel 020 7326 0081, e-mail michael.laughton1@btinternet.com)

LAUGIER NAIM, Carole; da of Augustin Raymond Laugier, and Helen Capanidou Laugier, of Houston, Texas; *b* 17 June 1963; *Educ* Univ of Notre Dame South Bend Indiana (BFA), Parson's Sch of Design Paris, Central St Martin's Coll of Art and Design (MA); *m* 10 June 1995, HRH Nadir Naim, s of Mohammed Aziz Naim, of Afghanistan; *Career* designer Barron Hoffar Studio Chicago Illinois 1985–86, art dir Spiegel Inc Chicago Illinois 1986–88; designer: Sampson Tyrrell London 1990–91, Lamb & Shirley London 1991–92; creative dir and ptnr Identica London 1992–; Communication Arts Award 1994, Rockport Digital Design Award 1998; *Recreations* yoga, running, music, painting, cooking; *Style*— Mrs Carole Laugier Naim; ✉ Identica, 45 Notting Hill Gate, Newcombe House, London W11 (tel 020 7569 5600, fax 020 7569 5656, e-mail carole.l@identica.com)

LAUNDER, Prof Brian Edward; s of Harry Edward Launder (d 1997), of Manchester, and Elizabeth Ann, *née* Ayers (d 2003); *b* 20 July 1939; *Educ* Enfield GS, Imperial Coll London (BSc(Eng), Bramwell Medal, Unwin Premium, ACGI), MIT (SM, ScD), Univ of London (DSc(Eng), Victoria Univ of Manchester (DSc), UMIST (DEng); *m* 20 Sept 1968, Dagny, da of Svend Simonsen; 1 da (Katya Jane b 18 July 1970), 1 s (Jesper David b 12 May 1973); *Career* res asst MIT 1961–64, reader in fluid mechanics Imperial Coll London 1972–76 (lectr in mech engrg 1964–72), prof of mech engrg Univ of Calif Davis 1976–80; UMIST (now Univ of Manchester): prof of mech engrg 1980–98, head of Thermodynamics & Fluid Mechanics Div 1980–90, head of Mech Engrg Dept 1983–85 and 1993–95, res prof 1998–, chm Environmental Strategy Gp 1998–2004; adjunct prof Pennsylvania State Univ 1984–88; assoc ed ASME Fluids Engrg Jl 1978–81, ed-in-chief Int Jl of Heat & Fluid Flow 1987–; regnl dir Tyndall Centre for Climate Change Res 2000–06; hon prof Nanjing Univ of Aeronautics and Astronautics PRC 1993; Hon DUniv INP Toulouse 1999, DSc (hc) Aristotle Univ of Thessaloniki 2005; FIMechE 1981, FASME 1983, FRS, FREng 1994, FRAeS 1996, FCGI 2003; *Books* Mathematical Models of Turbulence (with D B Spalding, 1972), Turbulence Models and their Application (with W C Reynolds and W Rodi, 1985), Closure Strategies for Turbulent and Transitional Flows (with N Sandham, 2002); also author of over 200 scientific articles on turbulence and turbulent flow; *Recreations* photography, country walking, cycling; French life, literature, culture, food and wine; *Style*— Prof Brian Launder, FRS, FREng; ✉ Department of Mechanical, Aerospace and Manufacturing Engineering, University of Manchester, PO Box 88, Manchester M60 1QD (tel 0161 200 3700, fax 0161 200 3723, e-mail brian.launder@manchester.ac.uk)

LAUNER, Dr Michael Andrew; s of Ellis Launer (d 1978), of Manchester, and Sylvia Launer, *née* Cohen (d 1985); *b* 29 May 1947; *Educ* Manchester Grammar, Univ of Leeds (DPM), Open Univ (BA), Liverpool John Moores Univ (MA); *m* Nov 1972, Hilary Elizabeth, da of Herbert Frederick Coates (d 1955), of Milford Haven, Wales; 1 s (Jack Simon b 1974); *Career* conslt psychiatrist Burnley Healthcare Tst 1977–2004, fndr Psychonutritional Unit for the Treatment of Eating Disorders Burnley 1984, currently med dir and conslt psychiatrist NW Services Partnerships in Care; pioneer in use of Clozapine for schizophrenia; freelance contrib: Hospital Doctor, local radio, TV and newspapers; hon conslt: NW, Samaritans, Relate; hon conslt advsr: Rethink, SANE (memb Nat Advsy Bd), MIND; advsr Health Care Cmmn; Law Society approved expert witness; memb Advsy Cncl Jewish Assoc for mentally ill; memb Nat Ctee for Sick Doctors, assessor for: conslt appts RCPsych; opinion ldr on schizophrenia; LRCP, MRCS 1970, MRCPsych 1975, memb BMA; FRSA 1996; *Recreations* writing, sport as a spectator, aspiring novelist and communicator; *Style*— Dr Michael Launer; ✉ The Spinney, Everest Road, Atherton, Manchester M46 9NT (tel 01942 885584, e-mail mikelauner@yahoo.co.uk or mlauner@partnershipsincare.co.uk)

LAURANCE, Anthony John (Tony); CBE (2005); s of Dr Bernard Laurance (d 1994), and Audrey, *née* Kidner (d 1968); *Educ* Bryanston, Clare Coll Cambridge (exhibitioner, MA); *m* 1981, Judith, *née* Allen; 2 da (Rachel b 13 March 1982, Miriam b 23 May 1986); *Career* trainee BBC News 1975, various policy jobs DHSS 1975–85, princ private sec to Sec of State for Social Servs 1985–87, Newcastle Central Office DSS 1987–90, territorial dir Benefits Agency 1990–95, regnl dir SW NHS Exec 1995–2002, prog dir NHSU 2002–; *Recreations* tennis, poker, fiction; *Style*— Tony Laurance, Esq, CBE

LAURANCE, Ben James; s of David Laurance (d 1970), and Helen, *née* Young; *b* 27 May 1956; *Educ* Oakham Sch, Trinity Coll Cambridge (BA); *Career* Eastern Counties Newspapers 1977–82, business corr then energy ed Lloyd's List 1982–86, dep City ed Daily Express 1986–88, fin reporter then dep fin ed The Guardian 1988–94, investment analyst Smith New Court/Merrill Lynch 1994–96, business ed The Observer 1996–98, contributing ed 1999–2000; ed Financial Mail on Sunday 2000–; Financial Journalist of the Year British Press Awards 1998 and 2000, Joint Business Journalist of the Year 2002, Business Journalist of the Year Awards 2002; *Recreations* sailing, cycling, beachcombing; *Style*— Ben Laurance, Esq; ✉ Financial Mail on Sunday, 2 Derry Street, Kensington, London W8 5TS (tel 020 7938 6000)

LAURENCE, Andrew David; s of Kenneth Gordon Laurence (d 2003), of Northants, and Vera, *née* Gilbert; *b* 1 October 1957; *Educ* Wellingborough Sch, Univ of Reading (LLB), Inns of Court Sch of Law, Webber Douglas Acad of Dramatic Art; *m* 1982, Priscilla, da of Donald C Bergus; 2 da (Elizabeth Emma b 1991, Katherine Louisa b 1993); *Career* called to the Bar Middle Temple 1981; actor, writer and prodr 1981–84, press and PR for West End and provincial theatre 1984–86, PR mangr LDDC 1986–89; Hill & Knowlton (UK) Ltd: joined 1989, main bd dir and md Corp Communications Div 1993–99, jt chief exec 1999–2001, chm EMEA 2001–03, chm and ceo EMEA 2004–; memb Br Actors' Equity; MInstD, MCIPR; *Recreations* theatre, film, music, swimming, scuba, travel; *Clubs* Middle Temple, Home House; *Style*— Andrew Laurence, Esq; ✉ Hill & Knowlton (UK) Ltd, 20 Soho Square, London W1A 1PR (tel 020 7413 3005, fax 020 7973 4445, mobile 07768 034000, e-mail alaurence@hillandknowlton.com)

LAURENCE, George Frederick; QC (1991); s of Dr George Bester Laurence (d 1993), of SA, and Anna Margaretha, *née* Niemeyer; *b* 15 January 1947; *Educ* Pretoria Boys HS, Univ of Cape Town (Smuts Meml scholar, BA), UC Oxford (Rhodes scholar, MA); *m* 1, 27 Aug 1976, (Ann) Jessica (d 1999), da of John Gordon Chenevix Trench; 1 da (Catherine Ann b 28 Aug 1978), 1 s (Benjamin George b 24 Oct 1981), 1 step s (Thomas James Yardley b 14 Sept 1974); m 2, 25 July 2000 (Anne) Jacqueline, da of Dr Hugh Baker; 1 da (Claire Elizabeth b 29 Oct 2001), 1 s (Edward Stephen b 3 March 2003); *Career* called to the Bar Middle Temple 1972 (Harmsworth scholar, bencher 1999); memb Editorial Bd Rights of Way Law Review; memb: Administrative Law Bar Assoc, Parly Bar Mess, Planning and Environmental Bar Assoc, Chancery Bar Assoc, Justice, Amnesty International; rep foreign membs on Cncl of the South African Inst of Race Relations; fell Soc of Advanced Legal Studies 1999–; *Recreations* cricket, tennis, theatre; *Clubs* Grannies Cricket; *Style*— George Laurence, Esq, QC; ✉ 12 New Square, Lincoln's Inn, London WC2A 3SW (tel 020 7419 8000, fax 020 7419 8050, e-mail clerks@newsquarechambers.co.uk)

LAURENCE, Michael; s of Jack Laurence, MBE (d 1960), of London, and Eveleen, *née* Lewis (d 1988); *b* 18 June 1930; *Educ* Stonyhurst, St Mary's Hosp Med Sch, Univ of London (MB BS); *m* 12 Sept 1967, Parvin, da of Jamshid Faruhar (d 1969), of Iran; 1 s (Arian b 1968), 2 da (Nicola b 1970, Hotessa b 1972); *Career* RAMC Capt specialist anaesthetics MELF 1955–57; orthopaedic surgn and conslt: Guy's Hosp, St Olave's Hosp, New Cross Hosp and Lewisham Hosp 1970–94, Hosp of St John and St Elizabeth and Royal London Hosp 1995–; conslt orthopaedic surgn: Hammersmith Hosp 1968–70, Royal Nat Orthopaedic Hosp Stanmore 1968–70; sr lectr Inst of Orthopaedics London Univ 1968–70, lectr Dept of Surgery Royal Post Grad Med Sch 1968–70; conslt orthopaedic surgn: Royal London Hosp 1995–97 and 2001–02, UCH 1997–, St Mary's Hosp 2000; chm Med Staff Ctee Hosp of St John & St Elizabeth 1982–88; assoc ed Jl of Bone and Joint Surgery, author of many articles, papers and chapters in books on the subject of Reconstructive Joint Surgery in Chronic Arthritis; pres Rheumatical Arthritis Surgical Soc 1978–79 and 1988–89, chm Bd of Affiliated Socs Cncl Br Orthopaedic Assoc 1989–94, hon treas NHS Support Fedn 1990–92, pres Hampstead Med Soc 1991–93, pres Hunterian Soc 2002–03; RSM: pres Orthopaedic Section 1993–94, pres Sports Med Section 1999–2000; FRCS 1960; *Recreations* sailing, golf, skiing; *Clubs* Highgate Golf; *Style*— Michael Laurence, Esq; ✉ 2 Lyndhurst Terrace, Hampstead NW3 5QA; Billingham Manor, Newport, Isle of Wight PO30 3HE; 106 Harley Street, London W1G 7JE (tel 020 7435 6682)

LAURENCE, Vice Adm Timothy James Hamilton; CB (2007), MVO (1989); yr s of Cdr Guy Stewart Laurence, RN (d 1982), and Barbara Alison, *née* Symons; *b* 1 March 1955; *Educ* Sevenoaks, RNC Dartmouth, UC Durham; *m* 12 Dec 1992, HRH The Princess Royal (*see* Royal Family section); *Career* cmmnd RN 1979, Cdr 1988, Capt 1995, Cdre 1998, Rear Adm 2004, Vice Adm 2007; asst navigating offr HM Yacht Britannia 1979, cmd HMS Cygnet 1981–82 (despatches), equerry to HM The Queen 1986–89, cmd HMS Boxer 1990–91, MOD 1992–95, cmd HMS Cumberland 1995–96, cmd HMS Montrose and Capt

Sixth Frigate Sqdn 1996–97, MOD 1997–98 and 2001–, JSCSC (Asst Cmdt (Maritime)) 1999–2001, ACDS (Resources and Plans) 2004–07, chief exec Defence Estates 2007–; ADC 2004; Hudson fell St Antony's Coll Oxford 1998–99; memb Cncl RNLI; memb: RUSI, IISS; memb Ct of Assts Worshipful Co of Coachmakers & Coach Harness Makers; FRGS, AMNI; *Style—* Vice Adm Timothy Laurence, CB, MVO, ADC; ✉ c/o Buckingham Palace, London SW1A 1AA; Defence Estates, Kingston Road, Sutton Coldfield, West Midlands B75 7RL

LAURENSON, James Tait; s of James Tait Laurenson (d 1986), of Seal, Kent, and Vera Dorothy, *née* Kidd (d 1968); *b* 15 March 1941; *Educ* Eton, Magdalene Coll Cambridge (MA); *m* 13 Sept 1969, Hilary Josephine, da of Alfred Howard Thompson, DFC (d 1991), of Chatton, Northumberland, and Josephine, *née* Armstrong (d 1997); 3 da (Emily b 1972, Marianne b 1974, Camilla b 1978), 1 s (Fergus b 1976); *Career* Ivory & Sime Investment Managers 1968–83, dep chm and md Adam & Company Group plc 1984–93; dir: I & S UK Smaller Companies Trust plc 1983–2005, Hiscox Investment Management Ltd 1992–2004, Fidelity Special Values plc 1994–2005; chm Hopetoun House Preservation Tst 1998–2003; FCA 1967; *Recreations* golf, travel, gardening; *Clubs* Boodle's, Hon Co of Edinburgh Golfers; *Style—* James Laurenson, Esq; ✉ PO Box 69, Helensville, New Zealand (tel 00 64 9 420 7195)

LAURIE, Sir (Robert) Bayley Emilius; 7 Bt (UK 1834), of Maxwelton; s of Maj-Gen Sir John Emilius Laurie, 6 Bt, CBE, DSO (d 1983), and Evelyn, *née* Richardson-Gardner (d 1987); *b* 8 March 1931; *Educ* Eton; *m* 1968, Laurelie Meriol Winifreda, da of Sir Reginald Lawrence William Williams, 7 Bt, MBE, ED (d 1971); 2 da (Clare Meriol b 1974, Serena Catherine b 1976); *Heir* kinsman, Andrew Laurie; *Career* Capt 11 Bn Seaforth Highlanders (TA) 1951–67; Samson Menzies Ltd 1951–58, CT Bowring & Co Ltd 1958–88, dir CT Bowring (Underwriting Agencies) Ltd 1967–83, chm Bowring Membs Agency Ltd 1983–88, dir Murray Lawrence Membs Agency Ltd 1988–92; memb Lloyd's 1955–; *Style—* Sir Bayley Laurie, Bt; ✉ The Old Rectory, Little Tey, Colchester, Essex (tel 01206 210410)

LAUTENBERG, HE Alexis P; s of Anatole A Lautenberg (d 1958), and Nelly C, *née* Schnapper (d 1983); *b* 28 October 1945, Zürich, Switzerland; *Educ* Lausanne Univ (BA); *m* Gabrielle; 10 June 1972, Gabrielle; 2 da (Aline b 20 Nov 1975, Jeanne b 11 Oct 1980), 1 s (Philippe b 1 Dec 1976); *Career* Swiss diplomat; Gen Defense Staff 1970–74, served CSCE Geneva and Stockholm 1974–75, dep chief of mission Warsaw 1976–77, dep chief of mission Swiss delgn to EFTA-GATT Geneva 1977–81, head economic section Bonn 1981–85, min and head Financial Div Dept of Foreign Affrs 1985–93, ambass and head of mission EC Brussels 1993–2000, ambass to Italy 2000–04, ambass to the Ct of St James's 2004–; chm: Negotiating Gp on Financial Services GATT 1990–91, Financial Action Task Force on Money Laundering 1991–92; memb Bd Coll of Europe Bruges 1994–99; author of various pubns in learned jls; *Clubs* Travellers, Athenaeum, London Capital; *Style—* HE Mr Alexis P Lautenberg; ✉ Swiss Embassy, 16–18 Montagu Place, London W1H 2BQ (tel 020 7616 6030, fax 020 7723 0039, e-mail alexis.lautenberg@eda.admin.ch)

LAUTERPACHT, Prof Sir Elihu; kt (1998), CBE (1989), QC (1970); s of Sir Hersch Lauterpacht, QC (d 1960), and Rachel, *née* Steinberg (d 1989); *b* 13 July 1928; *Educ* Harrow, Trinity Coll Cambridge (MA, LLM); *m* 1, 1955, Judith Maria (d 1970), er da of Harold Hettinger; 1 s (Michael), 2 da (Deborah, Gabriel); m 2, 1973, Catherine Josephine, da of Francis Daly (d 1960); 1 s (Conan); *Career* international lawyer; called to the Bar Gray's Inn 1950 (bencher 1983); Univ of Cambridge: dir Res Centre for Int Law 1983–95, hon prof of int law 1994–; judge (ad hoc) Int Court of Justice 1993–; pres: Eastern Regn UN Assoc 1991–2001, World Bank Admin Tbnl 1979–98, Perm Court of Arbitration; chm: Asian Devpt Bank Admin Tbnl 1993–95, Dispute Settlement Panel N American Free Trade Agreement 1996, World Bank Center for the Settlement of Investment Disputes Arbitration Panels 1997–, UN Compensation Cmmn 1998–99, Eritrea-Ethiopia Boundary Cmmn 2001–; hon memb American Soc of Int Law; govr Westminster Sch 1990–2001; *Clubs* Garrick; *Style—* Prof Sir Elihu Lauterpacht, CBE, QC; ✉ 20 Essex Street, London WC2R 3AL (tel 020 7583 9294, fax 020 7583 1341)

LAVAN, Hon Mr Justice Vivian; s of late Patrick Lavan, and Sarah Lavan; *Educ* UC Dublin Law Sch, King's Inns Dublin; *m* 10 Aug 1974, Dr Una Lavan, *née* McCullough; 2 s (Myles, Vivian), 2 da (Naomi, Sarah); *Career* called to the: Irish Bar King's Inns Dublin 1969 (bencher), English Bar 1975, Inner Bar 1982; judge of the High Court of Ireland 1989–, pres Law Reform Cmmn of Ireland 1998–2000; memb Gen Cncl of the Bar of Ireland 1970–82 (treas 1976–80); co-fndr Free Legal Advice Centres 1969, memb bd that implemented civil legal aid in Ireland 1979, chm Mining Bd of Ireland 1982, Irish delg European Assoc of Judges and Int Assoc of Judges 1996, jurist-in-residence Syracuse Univ NY 1998; memb Arbitration Sub-Ctee Int C of C 1986–89, memb Panel of Conciliators and Panel of Arbitrators Int Centre for Investment Disputes 1988; assoc CIArb, memb Int Acad of Trial Lawyers US 1980, hon memb American Bar Assoc 1980; *Clubs* Pipers, Cumann na bPiobairi Uilleann, UC Dublin RFC; *Style—* The Hon Mr Justice Vivian Lavan; ✉ The High Court, Four Courts, Inns Quay, Dublin 7, Ireland

LAVELLE, Richard John; s of Alexander Joseph Lavelle (d 1970), of Shrewsbury, and Suzanne Mai, *née* Townley (d 1996); *b* 25 February 1936; *Educ* Shrewsbury, St Mary's Hosp Med Sch London (scholar, MB BS, MRCS, LRCP); *m* 22 July 1961, Anne Christine, da of late Tom Sims, of Sonning, Berks; 3 s (Jonathan Richard b 5 May 1962, Edward Charles b 5 Aug 1964, Alexander James b 8 May 1971), 1 da (Emma Charlotte b 16 April 1973); *Career* formerly house surgn Royal Nat Throat Nose and Ear Hosp London, sr registrar St Mary's Hosp London (casualty offr 1964) and Royal Marsden Hosp London 1969–71, conslt ENT surgn London Chest Hosp 1973–78, conslt i/c ENT Dept and clinical dir in surgical specialities Bart's London, ENT surgn King Edward VII Hosp for Offrs 1984–2000; memb Ct of Examiners RCS, past pres Chelsea Clinical Soc; author of numerous articles on diseases of the ears, nose and throat; FRCS 1967, FRSM; *Recreations* golf, racing; *Clubs* Berkshire Golf (capt 1973, pres 1994–99), Royal & Ancient Golf, Swinley Forest Golf, Kempton Park (memb Race Ctee), Jockey Club Rooms; *Style—* Richard Lavelle, Esq; ✉ Kingsmead, Hatchet Lane, Windsor Forest, Berkshire SL4 4RJ (tel 01344 882669); Princess Margaret Hospital, Windsor, Berkshire SL4 3SJ (tel 01753 743312)

LAVENDER, Justin; s of late Alexander Desmond Lavender, of Christchurch, Dorset, and Hilary May, *née* Coleman; *b* 4 June 1951; *Educ* Bedford Modern Sch, QMC London, Guildhall Sch of Music and Drama; *m* 1; 1 s (William b 4 May 1982), 1 da (Catherine b 21 Jan 1984); m 2, Louise, da of Derek William Crane; *Career* tenor; has performed with all major Br orchs; *Performances* professional debut as Nadir in The Pearl Fishers (Sydney Opera House) 1980; other debuts incl: Arnold in Rossini's Guillaume Tell (Royal Opera House) 1990, Tamino in Die Zauberflöte (Vienna State Opera) 1990, title role in Rossini's Le Comte d'Ory (La Scala Milan) 1991, Demodokos in Dallapiccola's Ulisse (Salzburg Festival) 1993; concert performances incl: Schubert's Mass in E Flat (Giulini and Berlin Philharmonic) 1988, Bartók's Cantata Profana (Solti and London Philharmonic) 1988, Schnittke's Faust Cantata (Abbado and Vienna Symphony) 1991 (Slatkin and BBC) 2001, Gerontius (Slatkin and Philharmonia) 1996, title role in Gounod's Faust (Royal Opera House) 2004; appeared in The Life of David Gale (film) 2002; *Recordings* incl: videos of Oedipus Rex 1983 and Mitridate 1993, audio of La Noche Triste 1989, La Favorite 1991, Messiah 1993, I Puritani 1993, The Wreckers 1994, Rossini and Donizetti arias 1994, Britten Song Cycles 1996, Bomtempo Mattutina dei Morti 1996, Mozart Arias 1997, Alceste 1998, War and Peace 1999, Schnittke Faust Cantata 2004, Elgar Dream of Gerontius 2006; *Recreations* rowing, sailing, railway modelling; *Style—* Justin Lavender, Esq; ✉ c/o Athole Still International Management, Forresters Hall, 25–27 Westow Street, London SE19 3RY (tel 020 8771 5271, fax 020 8771 8172)

LAVER, Prof John David Michael Henry; CBE (1999); s of Harry Frank Laver (d 1985), and Mary, *née* Brearley (d 1994); *b* 20 January 1938; *Educ* Churcher's Coll Petersfield, Univ of Edinburgh (MA, DipPhon, PhD, DLitt); *m* 1, 29 July 1962 (m dis 1974), Avril Morna Anel Macqueen, *née* Gibson; 2 s (Nicholas b 1963, Michael b 1965), 1 da (Claire b 1968); m 2, 1 Aug 1974, Sandra, da of Alexander Traill, of Bonnyrigg, Midlothian; 1 s (Matthew b 1972); *Career* lectr in phonetics Univ of Ibadan 1964–66 (asst lectr 1963–64); Univ of Edinburgh: lectr in phonetics 1966–76, sr lectr 1976–80, reader 1980–85, personal chair in phonetics 1985–2000, chm Centre for Speech Technol Res 1989–94 (dir 1984–89), research prof in the Faculty of Arts 1994–2000, vice-princ 1994–97; res chair in speech sciences Queen Margaret Univ Edinburgh 2001–04 (vice-princ 2002–03, dep princ 2003–04), prof emeritus 2004–; pres Int Phonetic Assoc 1991–95 (memb Cncl), memb Bd Euro Speech Communication Assoc 1988–93; Hon DLitt: De Montfort Univ 1999, Univ of Sheffield 1999, Queen Margaret Univ 2006; FIOA 1988–2001, FBA 1990 (chm Humanities Research Bd 1994–98, memb Cncl 1998–2001), FRSE 1994 (vice-pres 1996–99, fellowship sec 1999–2002, Bicentenary medal 2004, Royal Medal 2007), FRSA 1995, hon fell Royal Coll of Speech and Language Therapists (Hon FRCSLT) 2003; *Books* The Phonetic Description of Voice Quality (1980), The Gift of Speech (1991), Principles of Phonetics (1994); *Recreations* lexicography, bird watching; *Style—* Prof John Laver, CBE, FBA, FRSE; ✉ Queen Margaret University, Clerwood Terrace, Edinburgh EH12 8TS (tel 0131 317 3165, e-mail jlaver@qmu.ac.uk)

LAVERICK, David John; s of Wilfred Henry Laverick (d 1992), of Redcar, Cleveland, and (Ivy Mabel) Doreen, *née* Lockhart; *b* 3 August 1945; *Educ* Sir William Turner's Sch Redcar, KCL (Halliday Prize), Coll of Law Lancaster Gate; *m* 5 Oct 1968, Margaret Elizabeth, da of Gerald Myatt; 3 s (John Lockhart b 23 Feb 1971, Andrew Duncan b 16 Oct 1972, Benjamin Ian b 9 Aug 1975); *Career* asst slr: Beds CC 1970–72, Lincs (Lindsey) CC 1972–74; dir of admin and slr E Lindsey DC 1973–75, dir Cmmn for Local Admin in England 1975–95 (local govt ombudsman), chief exec Family Health Serv Appeal Authy 1995–2001, pensions ombudsman 2001–07; pres Adjudication Panel for England 2001–; formerly: legal memb Mental Health Review Tbnl, regnl chm Anchor Housing Assoc, hon sec Tuke Housing Assoc; memb Law Soc 1970 (Beds Law Soc prizewinner); *Recreations* Scottish country dancing, digital photography; *Style—* David Laverick, Esq; ✉ 23 Victoria Avenue, Harrogate, North Yorkshire HG1 5RD (tel 01423 538783, fax 01423 525164, mobile 07798 667226, e-mail davidlaverick@adjudicationpanel.org.uk)

LAVERICK, Peter Michael; s of Lt Peter Laverick, and Joyce Margaret Carpenter; *b* 7 June 1942; *Educ* Canford Sch, Sch of Law; *m* 25 Feb 1972, Elaine Ruth, da of Leopold Steckler; 2 da (Helen Tanya b 1973, Elise Mary b 1975); *Career* Capt GS (attached Coldstream Guards) 1968–71; slr 1966, Notary Public 1985, sr ptnr Bennett Griffin Worthing, pres Worthing Law Soc 1995; *Recreations* playing the tuba, sailing and skiing, rowing, punting and skiffing; *Clubs* Leander, Thames Rowing, Thames Punting, Thames Valley Skiff; *Style—* Peter M Laverick, Esq; ✉ North Barn, Poling, West Sussex (tel 01903 883205); Bennett Griffin, 23 Warwick Street, Worthing, West Sussex (tel 01903 229910, fax 01903 229160, e-mail peter@laverick.net)

LAVERS, Richard Douglas; s of D A Lavers, of Nairobi, Kenya, and Edyth, *née* Williams; *b* 10 May 1947, Nairobi; *Educ* Hurstpierpoint Coll, Exeter Coll Oxford (MA); *m* 24 May 1986, Brigitte Anne Julia Maria, da of late Robert Moers, of Turnhout, Belgium; 2 s (Anthony Robert Douglas b 1988, Jonathan Richard Oliver b 1989); *Career* joined FCO 1969, with S Asian Dept FCO 1969–70, third sec Buenos Aires 1970–1972, second later first sec Wellington 1972–76, with News Dept then S Asian Dept FCO 1976–1981, first sec (political/economic) Brussels 1981–1985, seconded to Guinness Mahon & Co 1985–1987, asst head Hong Kong Dept then Def Dept FCO 1987–89, NATO Def Coll Rome 1989, dep head of mission and consul-gen Santiago 1990–93, ambass to Ecuador 1993–97, FCO 1997–99, head of research analysts FCO 1999–2001, ambass to Guatemala 2001–06 (concurrently non-resident ambass to El Salvador and Honduras), ret; *Recreations* golf, fishing, travel, books, pictures; *Clubs* Oxford and Cambridge; *Style—* Richard Lavers, Esq

LAVERY, Bryony Mary; da of Harold Shepherd (d 1997), of Scarborough, N Yorks, and Kathleen Betty Shepherd (d 1996); *b* 21 December 1947, Wakefield, W Yorks; *Educ* Wheelwright GS for Girls, Univ of London (BA); *m* 13 Sept 1969, Paul Lavery (d 1991); *Career* playwright; dir Performing Arts Labs, former artistic dir Gay Sweatshop and Les Oeufs Malades, former writer in residence Unicorn Theatre for Children, former tutor Univ of Birmingham; Hon Dr Arts De Montfort Univ; FRSL 2002; *Stage Plays* incl: Last Easter, Smoke, Wicked, Her Aching Heart (Pink Paper Play of the Year 1991), More Light, Illyna, Discontented Winter, House Remix, Adaptations, Magic Toyshop, A Doll's House, Behind The Scenes at The Museum, Precious Bane, Frozen (Best New Play TMA 1998, Eileen Anderson Best New Play Award 1998), A Wedding Story; *Radio Plays* incl: No Joan of Arc (nominated Sony Award), Velma and Therese, The Smell of Him, Requiem, Wuthering Heights (adaptation), Lady Audley's Secret (adaptation), Wise Children (adaptation); *Style—* Ms Bryony Lavery; ✉ c/o PFD, Drury House, 34–43 Russell Street, London WC2B 5HA (tel 020 7344 1000, e-mail sdonald@pfd.co.uk)

LAVIN, Deborah Margaret; da of George E Lavin (d 1987), of Johannesburg, South Africa, and Laura Kathleen Lavin (d 1987); *b* 22 September 1939; *Educ* Roedean Sch Johannesburg, Rhodes Univ Grahamstown, Lady Margaret Hall Oxford (MA, DipEd); *Career* lectr Dept of History Univ of Witwatersrand SA 1962–64, lectr then sr lectr Dept of History Queen's Univ Belfast 1965–80; Univ of Durham: princ Trevelyan Coll 1980–95, dep dean of colleges 1990–93, pres Howlands Trust Univ of Durham 1993–97, princ-elect the new coll 1995–97, co-dir Research Inst for Study of Change 1995–97; non-exec dir and tstee Westlakes Research Ltd 1994–2002; sr assoc memb St Antony's Coll Oxford 2001–; memb: Cncl Benenden Sch 1998–, Corporation Truro Coll 2005–; hon life memb Nat Martimime Museum Falmouth 2004–; assoc fell RIIA 1997–99; FRSA 1996; *Clubs* Reform; *Style—* Miss Deborah Lavin; ✉ Hickmans Cottages, Cat Street, East Hendred, Wantage, Oxfordshire OX12 8JT (tel and fax 01235 833408)

LAVIN, John Jeffrey; OBE (2001); s of Cynthia, *née* Gledhill; *b* 11 September 1953; *Educ* Scarborough HS for Boys, Tal Handaq Services Sch Malta, King Richard's Services Sch Cyprus; *Career* Dept of Energy: joined as exec offr 1973, various policy posts until 1983, private sec to Under Sec of State for Energy 1983–85, head trg and devpt 1985–88, head indust section Energy Efficiency Office 1988–89; dir of operations Royal Botanic Gardens Kew 1989–97 (dep dir 1998–2002); bd dir: RBG Enterprises 1993–, Assoc of Leading Visitor Attractions (ALVA) 1992–, Chelsea Physic Garden Trading Co 1995–; *Recreations* golf, tennis, squash, football, gardening, cycling, eating out, writing poetry; *Style—* John Lavin, Esq, OBE

LAVINGTON, Prof Simon Hugh; s of Edgar Lavington (d 1982), of Wembley Park, London, and Jane, *née* Nicklen (d 2004); *b* 1 December 1939; *Educ* Haileybury and ISC, Univ of Manchester (MSc, PhD); *m* 6 Aug 1966, Rosalind Margaret, da of Rev George Charles William Twyman, ISO (d 1991), of Herstmonceux, E Sussex; 2 s (Damian b 25 Aug 1968, Dominic b 9 April 1970), 2 da (Hannah b 7 Sept 1971, Tamsin b 9 May 1973); *Career* sr lectr Univ of Manchester 1974–86 (lectr 1965–74); prof Univ of Ife Nigeria 1976–77, prof Univ of Essex 1986–2002 (emeritus prof 2002–); memb various BCS ctees; UN tech expert 1975; CEng, FBCS 1978, FIEE 1985, FRSA 1988; *Books* Logical Design of Computers (1969), History of Manchester Computers (1975), Processor Architecture (1976), Early British Computers (1980), Information Processing 80 (1980), Emerging

Trends in Database and Knowledge - Base Machines (1995), Mining Very Large Databases with Parallel Processing (1998), The Pegasus Story: a history of a vintage British computer (2000); *Recreations* sailing, walking; *Style*— Prof Simon Lavington; ✉ Lemon Tree Cottage, High Street, Sproughton, Suffolk IP8 3AH (tel 01473 748478, e-mail lavis@essex.ac.uk)

LAW, Andrew Jonathan Parker (Andy); s of Peter Leslie Law, and Audrey Iris, *née* Potter; *b* 25 May 1956; *Educ* Portsmouth GS, Univ of Bristol (BA); *m* 12 April 1986, Amanda Mary, da of Ronald Ernest Southey; 1 s (Thomas Andrew Peter (Tom) b 27 Dec 1988), 2 da (Olivia Rosie Jean b 31 Jan 1993, Venetia Elizabeth b 25 Sept 1997); *Career* account supervisor Wasey Campbell-Ewald advtg 1980 (trainee 1978, asst account exec 1979), account dir Foote Cone & Belding 1981–83 (account supervisor 1980), account dir Collett Dickenson Pearce & Partners 1983–90 (London bd dir 1985, int bd dir 1988); Chiat/Day: business devpt dir 1990–92, client servs dir 1992–93, md London 1993–95, managing ptnr Chiat/Day Inc 1994–95; fndr, chm and ceo St Luke's Holdings Ltd (after MBO of Chiat/Day London) 1995–; worldwide chm and fndr The Law Firm Global Advertising Network 2005; Entrepreneur of the Year 2002; FRSA 2003; *Publications* Open Minds: 21st Century Business Lessons and Innovations from St Luke's, Experiment at Work; *Recreations* family, reading and translating the classics; *Style*— Andy Law, Esq; ✉ e-mail andy@thelawfirmgroup.com

LAW, Charles Ewan; s of Robert Charles Ewan Law, DSO, DFC (ret Gp Capt), of Constantine Bay, Cornwall, and Norah, *née* Eaden (d 1998); *b* 12 August 1946; *Educ* Wrekin Coll, Univ of Nottingham (BSc), Manchester Business Sch (MBA); *m* 5 Sept 1970, Clodagh Susan Margaret, da of Col Eric Steele-Baume, CBE (d 1968); 1 da (Angharad b 1972), 2 s (Huw b 1974, Henry b 1980); *Career* metallurgist British Steel Corp 1969–71, mangr United International Bank 1973–79, vice-pres Merrill Lynch International Bank 1979–81, exec dir First Interstate Ltd 1984–87, non-exec dir Continental Illinois Ltd 1987–94 (exec dir 1981–84), md Continental Bank 1988–94, md Bank of America 1994–; *Recreations* sailing, theatre; *Style*— Charles Law, Esq; ✉ 5 Canada Square, London E14 5AQ (tel 020 7174 4368, fax 020 7174 6444)

LAW, (David) Jude; s of Peter Law, and Maggie Law; *b* 29 December 1972, Lewisham, London; *Career* actor; *Theatre* incl: Les Parent Terribles (RNT and Broadway) 1994–95, Death of a Salesman (West Yorkshire Playhouse) 1994, 'Tis Pity She's a Whore (Young Vic) 1999, Dr Faustus (Young Vic) 2002; *Film* incl: Wilde 1997, Gattaca 1997, Midnight in the Garden of Good and Evil 1997, The Wisdom of Crocodiles 1998, The Talented Mr Ripley 1999, Existenz 1999, Love, Honour and Obey 2000, Enemy at the Gates 2001, A.I. 2001, The Road to Perdition 2002, Cold Mountain 2003, I Heart Huckabee's 2004, Closer 2004, Alfie 2004, The Aviator 2004, Sky Captain and the World of Tomorrow 2004, All the King's Men 2006, The Holiday 2006; *Style*— Jude Law, Esq

LAW, Leslie; MBE (2005); *b* 5 May 1965; *Career* three day eventer; achievements incl: team Silver medal Olympic Games Sydney 2000, team Gold medal European Championships 2001, team Bronze medal World Equestrian Games 2002, team Gold medal European Championships 2003, team Silver medal and individual Gold medal Olympic Games Athens 2004; *Books* Cross Country Masterclass (with Debby Sly, 1995); *Recreations* football, National Hunt racing; *Style*— Leslie Law, Esq, MBE

LAW, Richard Alastair; *b* 29 April 1953; *Educ* Rendcomb Coll, Exeter Coll Oxford (MA); *m* Monique Ratcliffe; *Career* CA; ptnr Ernst & Young LLP; FCA, ATII; *Recreations* National Hunt racing; *Style*— Richard A Law, Esq; ✉ Ernst & Young LLP, 1 More London Place, London SE1 2AF (tel 020 7951 2000, fax 020 7951 1345)

LAW, Richard Arthur; *b* 1943; *Educ* Tettenhall Coll Wolverhampton, RAC Cirencester; *m*; 2 c; *Career* sr ptnr BK Bruton Knowles Gloucester and branches 1986–; RICS: past pres Rural Practice Faculty, memb Gen Cncl 1988–92, pres Rural Practice Div 1989–90 (memb Divnl Cncl 1983–91), fndr memb Pres's Advsy Gp on Arbitrations; memb Lord Chllr's Panel of Arbitrators; fndr memb Agricultural Law Assoc, sr managing agent Crown Estate Cmmrs Taunton and Dunster Estates 1987–2006; chm Three Counties Agric Soc 1993–2005, memb Central Assoc of Agricultural Valuers; vice-chm of govrs RAC Cirencester 1992–2005; FRICS 1976; *Recreations* travel, rural pursuits, farming, sailing, good food, wine; *Clubs* Oriental; *Style*— Richard Law, Esq; ✉ Bisley House, Green Farm Business Park, Bristol Road, Gloucester GL2 4LY (tel 01452 880000, fax 01452 880199, e-mail richard.law@brutonknowles.co.uk)

LAW, Roger; s of George Law, and Winifred Law; *b* 6 September 1941; *Educ* Littleport Secdy Modern Sch, Cambridge Sch of Art; *m* 2 March 1960, Deirdre Amsden; 2 c (Shem b 26 July 1962, Sophie b 15 Sept 1965); *Career* cartoonist and illustrator; The Observer 1962–65, Sunday Times 1965–67, artist in residence Reed Coll Oregon USA 1967, first puppet film The Milkman 1967, freelance illustrator Pushpin Studios NY 1968–69, caricaturist and features ed Sunday Times 1971–75; Luck and Flaw: formed with Peter Fluck 1976, BBC Arena Art Documentary Luck and Flaw Show 1979; Spitting Image: co-fndr 1982, creative dir Spitting Image Productions 1983–97, first series televised 1984, first American show (NBC TV) 1986, final (18) series 1996; The Win'gin Pom (TV puppet series) 1991; Potshots Film (Ceramic Millennium Amsterdam) 1999; elected memb Alliance Graphic Int (AGI) 1993; memb: RDI, Royal Soc for the Encouragement of Arts Manufacturing and Commerce 1999; Hon DLitt Loughborough Univ 1999; fell of Int Specialised Skills Australia 1997, hon FRCA 2004; *Exhibitions* Cutting Edge Major Installation (Barbican Art Gallery) 1992, Seven Deadly Sins (with Janice Tchalenko, V&A) 1993, Teapot Mania (with Janice Tchalenko, Norwich Castle Museum) 1995, Modern Antiques (with Janice Tchalenko, Richard Dennis Gallery) 1996, Puppet Installation (Royal Acad of Art) 1997, Aussie Stuff (Rebecca Hossack Gallery) 2000, Risk Takers and Pioneers (Ceramic Exhibition Centenary Gallery) 2001, The Land of Oz (The Fine Art Soc) 2005, Still Spitting at Sixty (Newsroom Archive and Visitor Centre) 2005; *Awards* D&DA award Magazine Illustration 1967 (Roger Law); for Luck and Flaw: Assoc of Illustrators awards Consistent Excellence 1984, D&DA award 1984; for Spitting Image: BPG TV award Best Light Entertainment Prog 1984, Emmy award 1984 and 1986, Grammy award 1987, Int Film and TV award NY 1989, BAFTA award 1989; Gold award NY Film and TV Festival 1991, Emmy award 1994 (Peter and the Wolf Puppets), Lifetime Achievement award Cartoon Art Tst 1998, Political Satire award Political Studies Gp 2000; *Publications* Synthetic Fun (with Jeremy Sandford, 1965), A Christmas Carol (with Peter Fluck, 1979), The Appallingly Disrespectful Spitting Image Book (1985), Treasure Island (with Peter Fluck, 1986), Spitting Images (1987), The Spitting Image Giant Komic Book (1988), Goodbye Magazine (1992), A Nasty Piece of Work (with Lewis Chester, 1992), Thatcha The Real Maggie Memoirs (1993), Aussie Stuff (exhibition catalogue, 2000), The Land of Oz (exhibition catalogue, 2005), Still Spitting at Sixty (autobiography, 2005); *Recreations* making mischief; *Style*— Roger Law; ✉ Saltwater Barn, Croft Yard, Wells-next-the-Sea, Norfolk NR23 1JS (tel and fax 01328 712045)

LAWDEN, James Anthony Henry; s of Maj Henry Tipping Lawden, MC (d 1981), of Roehampton, and Claire Phyllis, *née* Berthoud (d 1962); *b* 10 August 1955; *Educ* Winchester, New Coll Oxford (MA); *Career* admitted slr 1981; Freshfields Bruckhaus Deringer (formerly Freshfields): joined 1979, seconded with Aoki, Christensen & Nomoto Tokyo 1984–85, ptnr 1988, resident ptnr Tokyo Office 1992–95, resident ptnr Bangkok Office 1995–2001 (managing ptnr 1998–2001), currently managing ptnr Tokyo Office; memb: Law Soc, First Tokyo Bar Assoc; *Recreations* tennis, golf, squash, travelling; *Clubs* Naval and Military, Roehampton, Tokyo American, Tokyo Lawn Tennis, Bangkok, Bangkok British; *Style*— James Lawden, Esq; ✉ Freshfields Bruckhaus Deringer, Whitefriars, 65 Fleet Street, London EC4Y 1HS (tel 020 7936 4000, fax 020 7832 7001, telex 889292, e-mail james.lawden@freshfields.com)

LAWLER, Geoffrey John; s of Maj Ernest Lawler (d 2004), and Enid Florence Lawler (d 1998), of Richmond, N Yorks; *b* 30 October 1954; *Educ* Colchester Royal GS, Richmond Sch, Univ of Hull (BSc); *m* 1989 (m dis 1998), Christine Roth, da of C Roth, of Wyoming, USA; *Career* Cons Res Dept 1980–82, PR exec 1982–83, md The Public Affairs Company (GB) Ltd 1987–, dir Democracy International Ltd 1995–, vice-pres International Access Inc 1987–95; FCO observer Russian elections 1993, 1995 and 1996, UN observer South African elections 1994, EC observer Liberia 1997; MP (Cons) Bradford N 1983–87; vice-pres Bradford N Cons Assoc 1987–2001; pres: Univ of Hull Students' Union 1976–77, Br Youth Cncl 1984–87, W Yorks Youth Assoc 1995–2004 (vice-pres 1986–95); chm Aromatherapy Regulation Gp 2001; memb Cncl UKIAS 1987–93; Freeman City of London; *Recreations* cricket, travel; *Style*— Geoffrey Lawler, Esq; ✉ The Public Affairs Company, Castlehill House, Otley Road, Leeds LS6 3AA (tel 0113 278 0211, fax 0113 278 0214, e-mail geoff@glawler.com)

LAWLER, His Hon Judge Simon William; QC (1993); s of Maurice Rupert Lawler, of W Yorks, and Daphne Lawler; *b* 26 March 1949; *Educ* Winchester Secdy Modern, Peter Symonds' Sch Winchester, Univ of Hull (LLB); *m* 7 Jan 1985, Josephine Sallie, da of Norman Hanson Day; 2 s (Rupert Hanson b 28 June 1986, Toby William b 3 June 1988); *Career* called to the Bar Inner Temple 1971, memb chambers 6 Park Square Leeds 1971–2002, recorder 1989–2002 (asst recorder 1983–89), circuit judge (NE Circuit) 2002–; *Recreations* opera, gardening, cricket; *Style*— His Hon Judge Lawler, QC; ✉ Sheffield Crown Court, 50 West Bar, Sheffield, South Yorkshire S3 8PH (tel 0114 281 2400)

LAWLEY, Susan (Sue); OBE (2001); da of Thomas Clifford Lawley (d 1972), and Margaret Jane Lawley; *b* 14 July 1946; *Educ* Dudley Girls' HS, Univ of Bristol (BA); *m* 1, David Arnold Ashby; 1 s (Thomas David Harvey b 1976), 1 da (Harriet Jane b 1980); *m* 2, Roger Hugh Williams; *Career* trainee reporter and sub ed Western Mail and South Wales Echo 1967–70, BBC Plymouth 1970–72 (freelance reporter, sub ed, TV presenter); govr Nat Film & TV Sch 1990–95; Hon LLD: Univ of Bristol 1989, Univ of Wolverhampton 1995; Hon MA Univ of Birmingham 1989; *Television* presenter BBC: Nationwide 1972–75 and 1977–81, Tonight 1976, Budget and general election progs Nine O'Clock News 1981–82, Six O'Clock News 1982–86, chat shows and other special series incl: News '45, Hospital Watch, Here and Now, general election progs; *Radio* presenter Desert Island Discs BBC Radio Four 1988–; *Recreations* eating, biographies, bridge; *Style*— Ms Sue Lawley; ✉ c/o Desert Island Discs, BBC

LAWRENCE, Andrew; *b* 23 April 1954; *Educ* Univ of Edinburgh (BSc), Univ of Leicester (PhD); *Partner* Debbie Capel; 4 c (Zoë, Kit, Dylan, Jake); *Career* exchange scientist Centre for Space Research MIT 1980–81, sr research fell Royal Greenwich Observatory 1981–84; Queen Mary & Westfield Coll London: SERC postdoctoral research asst Sch of Mathematical Scis 1984–87, SERC advanced fell Sch of Mathematical Scis 1987–89, lectr Dept of Physics 1989–94; regius prof and head Sch of Physics Univ of Edinburgh 2004–; former memb: Cncl PPARC, ESO Survey Working Gp, Astronomy Ctee PPARC; former chm Space Sci Advsy Ctee BNSC/PPARC; FRSE, FRAS; *Publications* author of over 120 articles, reports etc in scientific jls; *Recreations* drama, literature, art and music; *Style*— Prof Andrew Lawrence, FRSE; ✉ Institute for Astronomy, Royal Observatory, University of Edinburgh, Blackford Hill, Edinburgh EH9 3HJ (tel 0131 668 8356, fax 0131 668 8416, e-mail al@roe.ac.uk)

LAWRENCE, Dr Clifford Maitland; s of Ronald Douglas Lawrence, and Irene Rose Emma, *née* Abell; *b* 29 November 1950; *Educ* East Ham GS, Univ of Sheffield Med Sch (MB ChB, MD); *m* 2 April 1977, (Patricia) Anne; 3 s (Thomas b 12 Sept 1981, Christopher b 22 June 1986, James b 29 Jan 1991), 1 da (Joanna b 23 Feb 1984); *Career* dermatologist N Staffs Hosp Centre and Royal Victoria Infirmary Newcastle; chm British Soc for Dermatological Surgery; author of papers on: skin surgery, psoriasis, dithranol inflammation; FRCP 1993 (MRCP 1978), MD 1988; *Books* Physical Signs in Dermatology - A Color Atlas and Text (with N H Cox, 1993, 2 edn 2002), Diagnostic Picture Tests in Dermatology (with N H Cox, 1995), An Introduction to Dermatological Surgery (1996, 2 edn 2002), Diagnostic Problems in Dermatology (with N H Cox, 1998); *Recreations* gardening; *Style*— Dr Clifford Lawrence; ✉ Department of Dermatology, Royal Victoria Infirmary, Newcastle upon Tyne NE1 4LP (tel 0191 282 4548)

LAWRENCE, David Charles; s of Charles Alfred Lawrence, of Kingsbridge, Devon, and Muriel Betty, *née* Fife; *b* 11 October 1961; *Educ* Reading Sch, Univ of Newcastle upon Tyne (BA, BArch); *m* 22 Aug 1987, Ingrid, da of Malcolm Bell; 2 da (Harriet Kristina b 17 July 1993, Flora Anna b 28 Dec 1996); *Career* architect; assoc dir Fitzroy Robinson London 1986–96, sr assoc Abbey Hanson Rowe London 1996–97, dir Hamilton Associates London 1997–; ARB 1996, RIBA 1996; *Recreations* rugby, cricket, football, music, art; *Style*— David Lawrence, Esq; ✉ Hamilton Associates Architects Ltd, 280 Kings Road, London SW3 5AW (tel 020 7351 5432, fax 020 7352 7361, e-mail d.lawrence@hamilton-assoc.com)

LAWRENCE, 5 Baron (UK 1869); Sir David John Downer Lawrence; 5 Bt (UK 1858); s of 4 Baron Lawrence (d 1968) by his 1 w, Margaret Jean, *née* Downer (d 1977); *b* 4 September 1937; *Educ* Bradfield; *Style*— The Rt Hon the Lord Lawrence

LAWRENCE, Edward George; s of Capt Edward Sear Lawrence (d 1964), of Southgate, London, and Ethel May, *née* Lambert (d 2002); *b* 26 February 1927; *Educ* Edmonton Co GS, Latymer's Sch; *Career* dir Lawrence Bros (Transport) Ltd 1949–77, ret; memb Heraldry Soc 1952–, life govr Royal Soc of St George 1953 (memb Exec Cncl for eight years), silver staff usher Jubilee HM Queen Elizabeth II 1977, wandsman St Paul's Cathedral London 1977–88, usher at wedding of TRH The Prince and Princess of Wales 1981; memb Ctee Middx Fedn of Old Grammarian Socs 1955–64, dep dir of ceremonies of Most Venerable Order of St John 1994–97 (asst dir 1980); Freeman City of London 1959; Liveryman: Worshipful Co of Carmen 1960, Worshipful Co of Scriveners 1983; memb: Guild of Freemen of London, Walbrook Ward Club; AMInstTA 1947, FFCS 1954, FInstD 1955, FRSA 1963, FCIL 2001; KStJ 1989 (CStJ 1979); *Recreations* heraldry, deipnosophism, ceremonial, official and academic dress; *Clubs* City Livery, Wig & Pen; *Style*— Edward Lawrence, Esq; ✉ 33 Woodmere Court, Avenue Road, Southgate, London N14 4BW

LAWRENCE, Francine; *Educ* Twickenham Art Sch; *m* Jan 1998, Malcolm Macalister Hall; *Career* won Thames TV Design bursary and travelled Caribbean, exhibition of photographs on return, worked with several design gps, asst art dir Fontana and freelance work for Virago Books, art ed Woman's Journal, art dir and assoc ed Living, ed Country Living 1989–95 (art dir 1985), freelance journalist and photographer 1995–, conslt ed Heritage Today magazine English Heritage 2003–, lectr in magazine journalism City Univ London 2003–; contrib to various magazine titles; UK co-ordinator FOSCO (charity for street children in Colombia); Designer of The Year Award Periodical Pubns Assoc 1988, Marc Boxer Award for Art Editors 1989; chair Br Soc of Magazine Eds 1991; *Recreations* photography, cats, gardening, travel, The Archers; *Style*— Ms Francine Lawrence

LAWRENCE, Gordon Charles; s of Alfred Charles Lawrence, and Gertrude Emily, *née* Frost; *b* 2 March 1931; *Educ* Isleworth GS; *m* 17 July 1954, Barbara Mary Rees, da of Francis Charles Rees Deacon, MBE (d 1983); 2 s (Simon b 1957, Jonathan b 1963), 1 da (Catriona b 1959); *Career* financial consultant; dir: Schreiber Industries Ltd 1967–70, Helena Rubinstein Ltd 1970–74; National Trust: dir of fin 1977–88, memb Wessex Regnl Ctee 1988–96; dir Heritage Educn Trust 1992–; FCA, FCMA, JDipMA; *Recreations* music, sailing; *Clubs* Royal Malta Yacht; *Style*— Gordon Lawrence, Esq; ✉ Walnut Tree House, Bromham, Wiltshire SN15 2HF (tel 01380 850294)

LAWRENCE, Sir Ivan John; kt (1992), QC (1981); s of Leslie Lawrence; *b* 24 December 1936; *Educ* Brighton Hove and Sussex GS, ChCh Oxford (MA); *m* 1966, Gloria Helene; 1 da; *Career* Nat Serv RAF 1955–57; called to the Bar Inner Temple 1962 (Yarborough-Anderson scholar, bencher 1990), in practice SE Circuit, recorder of the Crown Court 1985–2002 (asst recorder 1983–85), head of chambers 1997–2000, visiting prof of law Univ of Buckingham 2004, memb Gen Cncl of the Bar 2005–; MP (Cons) Burton 1974–97; memb: Expenditure Select Ctee 1974–79, Foreign Affrs Select Ctee 1983–92; chm: Cons Parly Legal Ctee 1987–97, All-Pty Jt Parly Barristers Gp 1987–97, Cons Parly Home Affrs Ctee 1988–97, Home Affrs Select Ctee 1992–97, Exec Ctee UK Branch Cwlth Parly Assoc 1994–97; promoted Nat Lottery as private members bill (1990) leading to introduction of Nat Lottery following Govt bill (1992); vice-chm Cons Friends of Israel 1994–97; memb: Board of Deputies of British Jews 1979–, Exec 1922 Ctee 1988–89 and 1992–97, Cncl of Justice 1989–95, Exec Ctee Soc of Cons Lawyers 1989–95 and 1998– (chm Criminal Justice Ctee 1997–); chm Burton Breweries Charitable Tst 1979–97; contrib to newspapers and magazines on political and legal subjects, also broadcaster, lectr and after dinner speaker; Freeman of City of London 1993; fell Soc of Advanced Legal Studies; *Recreations* piano, squash, travel, friends; *Clubs* Carlton, Burton, Pratt's; *Style*— Sir Ivan Lawrence, QC; ✉ Clarendon Chambers, 1 Plowden Buildings, Temple, London EC4Y 9BU (tel 020 7353 0003, fax 020 7353 9213)

LAWRENCE, Jeffrey; s of Alfred Silver (d 1957), and Sylvia, *née* Fishgold; *b* 28 March 1946; *Educ* Carmel Coll, London Business Sch; *m* 8 April 1971, Vivienne Lesley, da of Clifford Arch (d 1987); 2 da (Faith b 1973, Sarah b 1975); *Career* Merrill Lynch 1969–94 (md Merrill Lynch Asset Management 1989–94), dir of sales and mktg American Express Bank Ltd 1994–96, md Elan Asset Management Ltd (formerly Lawrence Oliver Ltd) corp fin and asset mgmnt 1996–2004, conslt to Dawnay Day 2004–; *Recreations* golf, racehorse owner; *Clubs* RAC; *Style*— Jeffrey Lawrence, Esq

LAWRENCE, Jill; *b* 17 April 1947; *Educ* Loughborough Univ (BA); *m*; *Career* designer and conslt; industrial design and devpt conslt to global int corporations; BA and MA course conslt and examiner; FRSA 1982; *Style*— Ms Jill Lawrence; ✉ JLD Intl, No 2, 64 Southwood Lane, London N6 5DY (tel 020 8340 9122, fax 020 8340 9244, e-mail jill@jldintl.com)

LAWRENCE, John Wilfred; s of Wilfred James Lawrence, and Audrey Constance, *née* Thomas; *b* 15 September 1933; *Educ* Salesian Coll Cowley Oxford, Hastings Sch of Art, The Central Sch of Art and Design; *m* 14 Dec 1957, Myra Gillian, da of Dr George Douglas Hutton Bell, CBE, FRS; 2 da (Emma b 26 July 1958, Kate b 6 Feb 1960); *Career* book illustrator; lectr in illustration: Brighton Poly 1960–68, Camberwell Sch of Art 1960–92; visiting prof in illustration: London Inst, Anglia Ruskin Univ Cambridge Sch of Art 2001–; external assessor of illustration: Bristol Poly 1978–82, Brighton Poly 1982–85, Exeter Coll of Art 1986–89, Duncan of Jordanstone Coll of Art 1986–89, Kingston Poly 1990–93, Edinburgh Coll of Art 1991–94; work represented in: Ashmolean Museum, V&A, Nat Museum of Wales, Manchester Metropolitan Univ, collections abroad; memb Art Workers' Guild 1972 (Master 1990), RE 1987, Soc of Wood Engravers; *Books* The Giant of Grabbist (1968), Pope Leo's Elephant (1969), Rabbit and Pork Rhyming Talk (1975), Tongue Twisters (1976), George His Elephant and Castle (1983), Good Babies Bad Babies (1987), This Little Chick (2002, New York Times Certificate of Excellence), Tiny's Big Adventure (by Martin Waddell, *qv*, 2004), Lyra's Oxford (by Philip Pullman, *qv*, 2003), Secret Seahorse (by Chris Butterworth, 2006); illustrator of more than 200 books; *Clubs* Double Crown; *Style*— John Lawrence, Esq; ✉ 6 Worts Causeway, Cambridge CB1 8RL (tel 01223 247449)

LAWRENCE, Michael John; s of Geoffrey Frederick Lawrence, of London, and Kathleen, *née* Bridge (d 1981); *b* 25 October 1943; *Educ* Wembley County GS, Univ of Exeter (BSc), Univ of Bristol (PhD); *m* 1967, Maureen, da of Terence Henry Blennerhassett; 3 c; *Career* postgrad research in solid state physics Univ of Nottingham 1965–66, research fell Univ of Bristol 1966–69; Price Waterhouse: joined 1969, qualified CA 1972, ptnr 1978–88; gp fin dir Prudential Corporation plc 1988–93, chief exec London Stock Exchange 1994–96; non-exec dir: Port of London Authy 1983–89, London Transport Bd 1994, Yattendon Investment Tst 1998–; external memb Cncl Defence Research Agency 1990, chm Hundred Gp of Fin Dirs 1992–93; memb Bow Gp 1970–74, cncllr London Borough of Hillingdon 1974–79 (chm Fin Ctee 1978–79); Freeman City of London 1974, memb Ct of Assts Worshipful Co of Tin Plate Workers; FCA; *Recreations* flying, sailing, bridge, tennis; *Style*— Michael Lawrence, Esq

LAWRENCE, Sir (John) Patrick (Grosvenor); kt (1988), CBE (1983), DL (W Midlands 1993); s of Ernest Victor Lawrence, and Norah Grosvenor, *née* Hill; *b* 29 March 1928; *Educ* Denstone Coll; *m* 1954, Anne Patricia, da of Dr Charles Auld; 1 s (decd), 1 da; *Career* RNVR 1945–48; admitted slr 1954; sr ptnr Wragge & Co Birmingham 1982–93 (ptnr 1959–82); chm Nat Union of Cons and Unionist Assocs 1986–87 (vice-pres 1986–1994), pres W Midlands Cons Cncl 1988–89; chm: W Midlands Rent Assessment Panels 1971–99, Kidderminster Healthcare NHS Tst 1993–96, Enterprise VCT plc 1995–2004; vice-pres Br Shooting Sports Cncl 2002– (chm 1995–2002); chm Birmingham Cathedral in Need Appeal 1990–92; memb: Bromsgrove RDC 1967–74, Admin Chapter Birmingham Cathedral 1995–2002; memb Cncl: Denstone Coll 1989–99, Aston Univ 1990–2001, White Ensign Assoc 1995–; Freeman City of London; Hon DSc Aston Univ 1996; *Clubs* Law Soc Yacht, Bean (Birmingham), Royal Over Seas League; *Style*— Sir Patrick Lawrence, CBE, DL; ✉ c/o Wragge & Co, 55 Colmore Row, Birmingham B3 2AS

LAWRENCE, Dr Peter Anthony; s of Instr Lt Ivor Douglas Lawrence (d 1990), of Swanage, Dorset, and Joy Frances, *née* Liebert (d 1999); *b* 23 June 1941; *Educ* Wennington Sch Wetherby, Univ of Cambridge (MA, PhD); *m* 9 July 1971, (Ruth) Birgitta, da of Prof Ake Haraldson (d 1985), of Uppsala, Sweden; *Career* Cwlth (Harkness) fell 1965–67, Genetics Dept Univ of Cambridge 1967–69, MRC Lab of Molecular Biology Cambridge 1969–, Zoology Dept Univ of Cambridge 2006–; FRS 1983; *Books* Insect Development (ed, 1976), The Making of a Fly (1992); *Recreations* Ascalaphidae, fungi, gardening, golf, theatre, trees; *Style*— Dr Peter Lawrence, FRS; ✉ 9 Temple End, Great Wilbraham, Cambridge CB21 5JF (tel 01223 880505); MRC Laboratory Molecular Biology, Hills Road, Cambridge CB2 2QH (tel 01223 402282, fax 01223 411582, e-mail pal@mrc-lmb.cam.ac.uk)

LAWRENCE, Sandra Elizabeth; da of Brig Roderick Gwynne Lawrence, OBE (d 1976), and Gillian Winifred, *née* Bishop (d 1994); *Educ* St Mary's Sch Wantage, St Martin's Sch of Art London, Byam Shaw Sch of Art London, Simi's Acad Florence; *Career* painter (chiefly wild life, still life and portraits); exhibited Royal Acad, Francis Kyle, Fischer Fine Art, Pastel Soc, Grosvenor Gallery, Royal Inst of Oil Painters, Inst of Fine Arts Glasgow, Tryon and Swann Gallery, New York, Caracas, Palm Beach, Singer & Friedlander Sunday Times Watercolour Competition 1997–98, Hunting Art Prizes 1997–2002; designed: Overlord Embroidery D-Day Museum Portsmouth 1968–72, 275ft of cartoons which hang in the Pentagon Washington DC; ROI 1980; *Recreations* travel, music, reading; *Clubs* Chelsea Arts; *Style*— Sandra Lawrence; ✉ 12 Paultons House, Paultons Square, London SW3 5DU (tel 020 7352 0558, website www.sandralawrence.co.uk)

LAWRENCE, Stephen Richard; s of Richard Lawrence, of Thrussington, Leics, and Joyce, *née* Howarth; *b* 6 September 1951; *Educ* Longslade Coll; *Children* 1 s (Alexander Guy b 16 Jan 1993); *Career* pilot offr cadet RAF 1971; Civil Service 1969–71, advtg mangr Loughborough Monitor 1971–72, reporter and features writer Leicester Mercury 1972–76, ed Leicester Shopwindow 1976–78, chief sub ed Gulf Mirror Bahrain 1978–79, sr ed Daily Nation Nairobi Kenya 1979–82, fndr Media Management Kenya 1983–86 and London 1986–87, ptnr Raitt Orr & Associates Public Relations 1988–90, press and PR mangr BP Chemicals 1990–96, communications mangr (Europe) BP 1997–99, dir govt and public affairs BP Azerbaijan 1999–2001, dir public affrs BP China and Asia Pacific 2002–05, fndr Crutial Communications - reputation management in crisis Phuket 2005; memb British Business Assoc of Phuket; MIPR 1986; *Books* The Complete Guide To Amboseli National Park (1983), The Total Guide To Nairobi National Park (1986), The Total Guide To Amboseli National Park (1986); *Recreations* sailing, diving, snowboarding, mountaineering, microlight flying, music; *Clubs* Royal Yachting Assoc (yachtmaster),Cruising Assoc; *Style*— Stephen Lawrence, Esq; ✉ Post Net PO Box 138 (Box No 10), Muang, Phuket 83000, Thailand (tel 00 66 0 6270 9968, e-mail stevelawrence@csloxinfo.com)

LAWRENCE, Susanne; da of Julian Lawrence, and Irene Leah Esme, *née* Conn (d 1980); *b* 15 December 1944; *Educ* Brondesbury & Kilburn HS for Girls, City of London Coll (Dip), Inst of Public Relations City of London Coll (Cert), Coll for the Distributive Trades; *Career* PR consultancy with Wilcox Press & PR, International News Service and Good Relations 1963–68, editorial asst, asst ed then dep ed Personnel Management 1968–74, ed Personnel Management monthly jl of IPM 1974–94, co-fndr, editorial dir and dep md Personnel Publications Ltd 1981–93, dep chm Personnel Publications Ltd 1993–, chief exec Indigo Publishing Ltd 1996–; launched: Transition magazine for Br Assoc for Commercial & Industrial Educn 1985, Personnel Management Plus mid-monthly magazine for IPM 1990, Human Resource Management Journal as jt publisher 1990–2005, Newsline for Nat Fedn of Retail Newsagents 1994, People Management for Inst of Personnel and Devpt 1995, Supply Management for Chartered Inst of Purchasing and Supply 1996, newsletters for Employers Forum on Age and Employers Forum on Disability 1996; published Charity magazine for Charities Aid Fndn 1996–98, relaunched and ed Worldlink and website for World Fedn of Personnel Management Assocs 1998–; memb Editorial Bd Vision (magazine of Br WIZO) 1997–2003; awards incl: Specialist Journalist of the Year Blue Circle Awards for Industrial Journalism 1980, Best Specialist Columnist Magazine Publishing Awards 1983, highly commended Ed of the Year Award PPA 1993; fndr and hon sec: Equal Pay and Opportunity Campaign 1974–87, David Wainwright Equal Opportunity Devpt Tst 1987– (chair of tstees); has served as judge in advtg awards, WIZO Short Story Competition, Personnel Mangr of Year Awards, Parents at Work Employer Awards and in trade union jl awards; chartered fell Chartered Inst of Personnel and Devpt; MIPR 1968, FCIPD 1992, FRSA 1998; *Recreations* cinema, theatre, travel; *Style*— Ms Susanne Lawrence; ✉ Personnel Publications Ltd, 17a Manchester Street, London W1U 4DJ (tel 020 7299 9911, fax 020 7299 9912, e-mail susanne.lawrence@ppltd.co.uk)

LAWRENCE, His Hon Timothy; s of late Alfred Whiteman Lawrence, MBE, and Phyllis Gertrude, *née* Lloyd-Jones; *b* 29 April 1942; *Educ* Bedford Sch, Coll of Law; *Career* Slrs' Dept New Scotland Yard 1967–70, ptnr Claude Hornby and Cox 1970–86 (sr ptnr 1976), recorder 1983, circuit judge (SE Circuit) 1986–2006; memb: Criminal Law Ctee Law Soc 1978–86, No 13 Area Legal Aid Ctee 1983–86, Judicial Studies Bd 1984–87 (Criminal Ctee until 1988), Tbnls Ctee 1991–96, Parole Bd 1998–2004 and 2005–; chm: No 14 Area Duty Slr Ctee 1984–86, Exec Ctee of Br Acad of Forensic Sciences 1991– (pres 1992–93); dep chm Advsy Ctee on Conscientious Objectors 2003–; legal memb Mental Health Review Tbnls 1989–; pres: London Criminal Cts Slrs' Assoc 1984–86 (sec 1974–84), Industrial Tbnls for England and Wales 1991–97 (as sr circuit judge); FRSA; *Clubs* Hurlingham, Reform; *Style*— His Hon Timothy Lawrence; ✉ 8 Slaidburn Street, London SW10 0JP

LAWRENCE, Timothy Gordon Roland (Tim); s of Lionel Arthur Lawrence (d 1975), and Patricia Mary Young (d 1992); *b* 22 August 1936; *Educ* Wimbledon Coll, St George's Coll Weybridge; *m* 19 Sept 1964, (Mabyn) Ann, da of Robert Hugh Shuttleworth Petherbridge; 1 s (Stephen Robert Anthony b 3 April 1966), 2 da (Katherine Ann b 15 July 1967, Joanna Frances b 22 Feb 1972); *Career* Nat Serv 1958–60 (cmmnd Royal Irish Fusiliers); articled clerk Wilson de Zouche & Mackenzie (later Wilson Davis & Co) 1953–58, CA 1958 (won Gold medal of ICAEW for first place in final examination); Coopers & Lybrand (formerly Cooper Brothers & Co): joined 1960, ptnr 1967–96, memb Governing Bd 1975–90, vice-chm 1988–90; chm Professional Asset Indemnity Ltd 1993–96; chm London Soc of Chartered Accountants 1984–85, dir Solicitors Indemnity Fund Ltd 1997–, treas St Francis Leprosy Guild 1990–; FCA; *Recreations* bridge, golf; *Clubs* MCC, Gerrards Cross Golf, Austenwood Bridge; *Style*— Tim Lawrence, Esq; ✉ Whitethorn, Collinswood Road, Farnham Common, Slough, Berkshire SL2 3LH (tel 01753 647454, fax 01753 647445, e-mail tim@timlawrence.co.uk)

LAWRENCE, Dr Vanessa Vivienne; da of Leonard Walter Sydney Lawrence (d 1972), and Margaret Elizabeth, *née* Summers; *b* 14 July 1962, Beaconsfield, Bucks; *Educ* St Helen's Sch Northwood, Univ of Sheffield (BA), Univ of Dundee (MSc); *Career* Longman Gp UK Ltd: publisher 1985–89, sr publisher 1989–91, publishing mangr 1991–93; dir GeoInformation Int Pearson Gp Ltd 1993–96; Autodesk Inc: regnl business devpt mangr EMEA West Region 1996–2000, global mangr strategic mktg and communications GIS Solutions Div 2000; DG and ceo Ordnance Survey 2000–; chair UK Agency Chief Executives' Assoc (ACE) 2003–, non-exec dir ODPM 2002–06; memb: Cncl Remote Sensing Soc 1991–94, Cncl Inst of Br Geographers 1994–95, Research Resources Bd ESRC 1995–99, Cncl Assoc for Geographical Info 1996–2001 (chair 1999–2000), Cncl RGS 2002–, Bd Open Geospatial Consortium 2005–; visiting prof: Univ of Southampton 2000–, Kingston Univ 2003–; Univ of Southampton: memb Ct 2001–, memb Cncl 2002–, memb Bd of Advsrs Sch of Mgmnt 2005–; hon research assoc Dept of Geography Univ of Manchester 1990–; hon vice-pres Geographical Assoc 2006–; patron: Coastin' 2002–06, MapAction 2006–, Cure Parkinson's Tst 2007–; Hon DSc: Univ of Sheffield 2001, Nottingham Trent Univ (on behalf of Southampton Inst) 2002, Kingston Univ 2002, Univ of Glasgow 2005; Hon DUniv Oxford Brookes 2001, Hon LLD Univ of Dundee 2003; hon fell UCL 2003; CGeog 2002, CCMI 2003, assoc fell Remote Sensing and Photogrammetry Soc 2001, Hon FInstCES 2001, FRICS 2003; *Recreations* scuba diving, sailing, walking, collecting antique maps, tennis; *Clubs* Rickmansworth Sailing; *Style*— Dr Vanessa Lawrence; ✉ Ordnance Survey, Romsey Road, Southampton SO16 4GU (tel 023 8079 2559, fax 023 8079 2660)

LAWRENCE, Sir William Fettiplace; 5 Bt (UK 1867), of Ealing Park, Middx; OBE (2003); s of Maj Sir William Lawrence, 4 Bt (d 1986), and Pamela Mary, *née* Gordon; *b* 23 August 1954; *Educ* King Edward VI Sch Stratford-upon-Avon; *m* 2005, Tamar Bubashvili, da of Revaz Bubashvili, and Mariam, *née* Khizanishvili, of Tbilisi, Georgia; *Heir* cous, Peter Lawrence; *Career* asst fin accountant: W B Bumpers Ltd, Rockwell International 1980–81; gen mangr Newdawn & Sun Ltd 1981–98; proprietor William Lawrence Wines; dir: Unicorn Tourism Ltd 1994–98, South Warwickshire Business Partnership 1995–, Stratford-upon-Avon & District Marketing Ltd 1995–97, Stratford-upon-Avon Crossroads Care Attendant Scheme Ltd 1996–99, Midland Music Festivals 1996–98; cncllr Stratford-on-Avon DC 1982– (chm 1990–91); memb S Warks Health Authy 1984–92, non-exec/assoc dir S Warks General Hospitals NHS Tst 1993–2003; non-exec dir Orchestra of the Swan; memb W Midlands Arts 1984–91, chm Heart of England Tourist Bd 1991– (non-exec dir 1989–); chm: Tourism for All 2002–, Br Toilet Assoc; exec memb Stratford District Cncl for Voluntary Serv 1986–91; pres: Stratford and Dist MENCAP, Stratford-upon-Avon Chamber Music Soc, Birmingham Symphonic Wind; tstee Holiday

Care Serv 2001–; memb: Warks Branch Rural Devpt Cmmn 1995–98, W Midlands Life 1999–, W Midlands Business Cncl 2002–, W Midlands Regnl Assembly 2003–, Local Govt Assoc Tourism Exec Culture and Sport; conslt to The Insite Consultancy on Disability Awareness Training 1995–2000; membCt Univ of Birmingham 1990–; former govr Royal Shakespeare Theatre; formerly: pres Action Unlimited Tst, dir Cncl for the Advancement of the Arts Recreation and Education, memb Corporation Stratford-upon-Avon Coll, govr King Edward VI Sch Stratford-upon-Avon, govr Stratford-upon-Avon GS for Girls, tstee Live Music Now 2006; Hon MA Univ of Worcester 2006; fell Tourism Soc 2003, FRSA 2005; *Recreations* wine; *Style*— Sir William Lawrence, Bt, OBE; ✉ The Knoll, Walcote, Alcester, Warkwickshire B49 6LZ (tel 01789 488303, mobile 07836 636932, e-mail sirwlawrence@cix.co.uk)

LAWRENCE-JONES, Sir Christopher; 6 Bt (UK 1831), of Cranmer Hall, Norfolk; suc uncle, Sir Lawrence Evelyn Jones, 5 Bt, MC, TD (d 1969); *Educ* Sherborne, Gonville & Caius Cambridge, St Thomas' Hosp (MA, MB BChir, DIH); *m* 1967, Gail, da of Cecil Arthur Pittar, FRACS (d 1976), of Auckland, NZ, and Helen Miller, *née* Finlay (d 1973); 2 s (Mark Christopher b 1968, John Alexander b 1971); *Heir* s, Mark Lawrence-Jones; *Career* med advsr to various organisations 1967–; gp chief med offr ICI Gp HQ London 1985–93, chm Medichem 1986–92; pres Section of Occupational Med RSM 1990–91; FRCP, FFOM; *Clubs* Royal Cruising, Royal Cornwall Yacht; *Style*— Sir Christopher Lawrence-Jones, Bt

LAWRENSON, Prof Peter John; s of John Lawrenson (d 1949), of Prescot, and Emily, *née* Houghton (d 1979); *b* 12 March 1933; *Educ* Prescot GS, Univ of Manchester (BSc, MSc, DSc); *m* 5 April 1958, Shirley Hannah, da of Albert Edward Foster, of Macclesfield; 1 s (Mark b 1958), 3 da (Ruth b 1960, Rachel b 1963, Isobel b 1965); *Career* res engr GEC 1956–61; Univ of Leeds: lectr 1961, reader 1965, prof 1966–91, head Dept of Electrical and Electronic Engrg 1974–84, chm Faculty of Sci and Applied Sci 1978–80, chm Faculty of Engrg 1980–81; Switched Reluctance Drives Ltd: chm 1980–97, non-exec dir 1997–2002; conslt Rolls-Royce plc 2000–02; author of over 120 papers for various sci jls; awards: Inst Premium IEE 1981, Alfred Ewing Gold Medal Royal Soc and Inst of Civil Engrs 1983, Esso Energy Gold Medal Royal Soc 1985, Faraday Medal IEE 1990; pres IEE 1992–93; memb Cncl Univ of Buckingham 1987–93; FIEE 1974, FIEEE 1975, FREng 1980, FRS 1982; *Books* Analysis and Computation of Electric & Magnetic Fields (with K J Binns, 1963 and 1973), Per Unit Systems (with M R Harris & J M Stephenson, 1970), The Analytical and Numerical Solution of Electric and Magnetic Fields (with K J Binns and C W Trowbridge) 1992; *Recreations* chess, bridge, tennis, gardening, walking; *Style*— Prof Peter Lawrenson, FREng, FRS; ✉ Switched Reluctance Drives Ltd, East Park House, Otley Road, Harrogate HG3 1PR (tel 01423 845200, fax 01423 845201)

LAWRIE, Paul; MBE (2000); *b* 1 January 1969; *m* 1991, Marian; 2 s (Craig, Michael); *Career* professional golfer; turned professional 1986; tournament victories: Catalonian Open Spain 1996, Qatar Masters 1999, Open Championship at Carnoustie 1999, Dunhill Links Championship 2001, Wales Open 2002; memb European Ryder Cup Team 1999; *Style*— Paul Lawrie, Esq, MBE; ✉ c/o IMG, McCormack House, Chiswick, London W4 2TH (tel 020 8233 5300, fax 020 8233 5301)

LAWS, David Anthony; MP; s of D A Laws, and Mrs M T Savidge; *b* 30 November 1965; *Educ* St George's Coll Weybridge, King's Coll Cambridge (scholar, BA); *Career* vice-pres JP Morgan & Co 1987–94, md Barclays de Zoete Wedd 1992–94; Lib Dems: econ advsr 1994–97, dir of policy and research 1997–99; MP (Lib Dem) Yeovil 2001–, memb Treasy Select Ctee 2001–03; spokesman for defence 2001–02, Lib Dem shadow chief sec 2002–05, Lib Dem spokesman on work and pensions 2005–; Observer Mace Nat Debating Champion 1984; *Style*— David Laws, Esq, MP; ✉ Spring Cottage, Lydmarsh, Chard, Somerset TA20 4AA; House of Commons, London SW1A 0AA (tel 020 7219 8413); Constituency Office: 94 Middle Street, Yeovil BA20 1LT (tel 01935 423284)

LAWS, Rt Hon Lord Justice; Hon Sir John Grant McKenzie; kt (1992), PC (1999); s of Dr Frederic Laws (d 1961), and Dr Margaret Ross Laws, *née* McKenzie; *b* 10 May 1945; *Educ* Durham Sch (King's scholar), Exeter Coll Oxford (Sr open classical scholar, BA, MA); *m* 1973, Sophie Susan Sydenham Cole, *née* Marshall; 1 da (Margaret Grace McKenzie b 1980); *Career* called to the Bar Inner Temple 1970 (Marshall Hall scholar), recorder 1985–92 (asst recorder 1983–85), first jr counsel to the Treasy in Common Law 1984–92, bencher Inner Temple 1985, judge of the High Court of Justice (Queen's Bench Div) 1992–97, Lord Justice of Appeal 1999–; called to the Bar: New South Wales 1987, Gibraltar 1988; pres Bar Euro Gp 1994–; hon fell: Robinson Coll Cambridge, Exeter Coll Oxford; judicial visitor UCL 1997–; *Recreations* Greece, living in London, philosophy; *Clubs* Garrick; *Style*— The Rt Hon Lord Justice Laws; ✉ c/o Royal Courts of Justice, Strand, London WC2A 2LL

LAWS, Stephen Charles; CB (1996); s of late Dennis Arthur Laws, and Beryl Elizabeth, *née* Roe; *b* 28 January 1950; *Educ* St Dunstan's Coll Catford, Univ of Bristol (LLB); *m* 1, Angela Mary (d 1998), da of John William Deardon; 3 da (Clare Theresa b 10 Aug 1976, Mary Veronica b 20 May 1980, Philippa Jane b 24 Nov 1982), 2 s (Michael Benedict b 11 Feb 1978, Patrick Joseph b 30 July 1985); m 2, Elizabeth Ann Owen, da of Robert Williams; 1 step s (Matthew Thomas David Owen b 16 Jan 1978), 1 step da (Katherine Louise Owen b 26 Nov 1979); *Career* asst lectr Univ of Bristol 1972–73; called to the Bar Middle Temple 1973; pupil of Michael Hutchison then Andrew Longmore 1973–74, legal asst Home Office 1975–76; Parly Counsel: asst 1976–82, seconded to Law Cmmn 1980–82 and 1989–91, sr asst 1982–85, dep parly counsel 1985–91, parly counsel 1991–2006, first parly counsel 2006–; *Books* Halsbury's Laws: Statutes Title (1983); *Recreations* Italy, history, family life; *Style*— Stephen Laws, Esq, CB; ✉ Office of the Parliamentary Counsel, 36 Whitehall, London SW1A 2AY (tel 020 7210 6629, e-mail stephen.laws@cabinet-office.x.gsi.gov.uk)

LAWSON, Anthony Raymond; s of Alexander Lawson (d 1965), of Redcroft, Whitefield, Manchester, and Jeanne Alexandra Lawson (d 1968); *b* 26 August 1931; *Educ* Repton; *m* 1, 1955, Anne, da of Dr Walter Martin, MC, of Bury, Lancs; 1 s, 1 da; m 2, 1980, Patricia Jane, da of Dr F Lascelles, MC, of Formby, Lancs; *Career* chm and chief exec Hollas Group plc 1970–94; currently chm: Irwell Bridge Mills Ltd, Doctor Insomniac (UK) Ltd; FRSA, FIMgt; *Recreations* tennis; *Style*— Anthony Lawson, Esq; ✉ Churn Cottage, Budworth Road, Aston-By-Budworth, Cheshire CW9 6LT (tel 01565 777530, fax 01565 777546)

LAWSON, Sir Charles John Patrick; 4 Bt (UK 1900), of Weetwood Grange, Headingley-cum-Birley, W Riding of Yorks; s of Sir John Charles Arthur Digby Lawson, 3 Bt, DSO, MC (d 2001); *b* 19 May 1959; *Educ* Harrow, Univ of Leeds, RAC Cirencester; *m* 18 Sept 1987, Lady Caroline Lowther, da of 7 Earl of Lonsdale; 1 da (Tess b 30 Aug 1988), 3 s (Jack William Tremayne b 6 Dec 1989, Thomas Charles Lancelot b 5 May 1992, Ralph Hugh Arthur b 7 Sept 1995), 1 step s (George Hunt b 8 Nov 1982); *Heir* s, Jack Lawson; *Career* Jackson-Stops and Staff: ptnr Exeter 1992–, ptnr Truro 2000–05, ptnr Barnstaple 2004–; MRICS; *Recreations* children, kite flying, shooting, gardening, fell walking (and too infrequently running), wine; *Style*— Sir Charles Lawson, Bt; ✉ Heckwood, Sampford Spiney, Yelverton, Devon PL20 6LG (tel 01392 214222, e-mail lawson@brandan.co.uk)

LAWSON, Prof Colin James; s of Eric William Lawson (d 1998) and Edith Mary, *née* Pounder (d 1998); *b* 24 July 1949, Saltburn-by-the-Sea, Cleveland; *Educ* Keble Coll Oxford (MA), Univ of Birmingham (MA), Univ of Aberdeen (PhD), Univ of London (DMus); *m* 16 April 1982, (Aileen) Hilary, *née* Birch; 1 s (Oliver James b 10 Jan 1985); *Career* lectr in music Univ of Aberdeen 1973–77, successively lectr, sr lectr and reader in music Univ of Sheffield 1978–97, prof of performance studies Goldsmiths Coll 1998–2001, pro-vice-chllr Thames Valley Univ 2001–05, dir Royal Coll of Music 2005–; princ clarinet: English Concert, London Classical Players, King's Consort; solo appearances worldwide incl Carnegie Hall and Lincoln Center NY; FLCM 2005, FRCM 2005; *Publications* Cambridge Companion to the Clarinet (ed, 1995), Mozart Clarinet Concerto (1996), Brahms Clarinet Quintet (1998), Historical Performance of Music (1999), The Early Clarinet (2000), Cambridge Companion to the Orchestra (ed, 2003); *Recreations* travel, acquisition of early clarinets; *Clubs* Athenaeum; *Style*— Prof Colin Lawson; ✉ Royal College of Music, Prince Consort Road, London W7 2BS (tel 020 7591 4363, e-mail clawson@rcm.ac.uk)

LAWSON, Prof David Hamilton; CBE (1993); s of David Lawson (d 1956), of East Kilbride, and Margaret Harvey, *née* White (d 1982); *b* 27 May 1939; *Educ* HS of Glasgow, Univ of Glasgow (MB ChB, MD); *m* 7 Sept 1963, Alison (d 1996), da of William Diamond (d 1974), of Sale; 3 s (Derek b 1965, Iain b 1967, Keith b 1970); *Career* visiting conslt Univ Med Center Boston Mass 1972–90; conslt physician: Royal Infirmary Glasgow 1973–2003, Dental Hosp Glasgow 1984–2003; visiting prof Sch of Pharmacy Univ of Strathclyde 1976–2006, hon prof of med Univ of Glasgow 1993–; chm Scottish Medicines Consortium 2001–04; hon conslt physician Glasgow Royal Infirmary 2003–; advsr on adverse drug reactions WHO Geneva 1984–89, external assessor Scientific Branch Civil Serv Cmmn 1986–99; Dept of Health London: chm Ctee on Review of Med 1987–91 (memb 1979–91), memb Ctee on Safety of Med 1987–93, chm Medicines Cmmn 1994–2001, vice-pres RCPE 1998–99; memb: Br Pharmacological Soc 1976, Assoc of Physicians GB & Ireland 1979, Scottish Soc of Physicians 1975; HonDSc Univ of Herts 2000, DSc (hc) Univ of Strathclyde 2001; FRCP, FRCPEd, FRCPGlas, FFPM, FFPHI, fell American Coll of Clinical Pharmacology; *Books* Clinical Pharmacy & Hospital Drug Management (with R M E Richards, 1982), Current Medicine - 2 (1990), Current Medicine - 3 (1991), Current Medicine - 4 (1994); *Recreations* hill walking, photography, bird-watching; *Clubs* Royal Commonwealth Soc, London; *Style*— Prof David Lawson, CBE; ✉ 25 Kirkland Avenue, Blanefield, Glasgow G63 9BY

LAWSON, Hon Dominic Ralph Campden; s of Baron Lawson of Blaby, PC (Life Peer), *qv*, and his 1 w, Vanessa Mary Addison, *née* Salmon (d 1985); bro of Nigella Lucy Lawson, *qv*; *b* 17 December 1956; *Educ* Westminster, ChCh Oxford; *m* 1, 11 Sept 1982, Jane Fiona, da of David Christopher Wastell Whytehead, of W Dulwich, London; m 2, 30 Dec 1991, Hon Rosamond Mary Monckton (Hon Mrs Lawson, *qv*), only da of 2 Viscount Monckton of Brenchley, CB, OBE, MC, DL, FSA; 2 da (Savannah Vanessa Lucia b 23 Dec 1992, Domenica Marianna Tertia b 1 June 1995); *Career* res The World Tonight Radio 4 1979–81; The Financial Times: joined staff 1981, energy corr 1983–86, columnist Lex 1986–87, columnist 1991–94; ed: The Spectator 1990–95 (dep ed 1987–90), The Sunday Telegraph 1995–2005; columnist: The Sunday Correspondent 1990, Daily Telegraph 1994–95, The Independent 2006–; memb Press Complaints Cmmn 1998–2002; Harold Wincott Prize for financial journalism 1987; *Books* Korchnoi - Kasparov: The London Contest (with Raymond Keene, 1983), Britain in the Eighties (contrib, 1989), The Inner Game (1994, published in US as Endgame); *Recreations* chess; *Clubs* Garrick, MCC; *Style*— The Hon Dominic Lawson

LAWSON, Edmund James; QC (1988); s of late Donald Edmund Lawson, of Norwich, and Veronica, *née* Clancy; *b* 17 April 1948; *Educ* City of Norwich Sch, Trinity Hall Cambridge (BA); *Career* called to the Bar Gray's Inn 1971 (bencher), head of chambers 1989–98, fndr memb Cloth Fair Chambers 2006–; *Recreations* music; *Style*— Edmund Lawson, Esq, QC; ✉ 39–40 Cloth Fair, London EC1A 7NT (e-mail edmundlawson@clothfairchambers.com)

LAWSON, Elizabeth Ann; QC (1989); da of Alexander Edward Lawson (d 1995), of Croydon, Surrey, and Helen Jane, *née* Currie (d 1989); *b* 29 April 1947; *Educ* Croydon HS for Girls, Univ of Nottingham (LLB); *Career* called to the Bar Gray's Inn 1969; currently head of chambers 1 Pump Court; recorder 1997–, dep High Court judge, dep district judge; chair Leeways Inquiry London Borough of Lewisham 1985, counsel Tyra Henry Inquiry 1987, represented social workers Sharon Campbell Inquiry 1987, chair Liam Johnson Inquiry London Borough of Islington 1989, counsel Victoria Climbie Inquiry 2001–02; chair Mental Health Review Tbnls; memb: Ctee Family Law Bar Assoc 1983– (sec 1994–95, chm 1995–97), Remuneration Ctee Bar Cncl, Review Ctee London Legal Services; sec St Paul's Bayswater United Reformed Church; The Times Woman Lawyer of the Year 2000; *Publications* 1 Pump Court, London EC4Y 7AB; *Recreations* knitting, cake decoration; *Style*— Miss Elizabeth Lawson, QC

LAWSON, Lesley (Twiggy); da of William Norman Hornby, and Nell Helen, *née* Reeman; *b* 19 September 1949; *m* 1, 1977, Michael Whitney Armstrong (d 1983); 1 da (Carly); m 2, 1988, Leigh Lawson, the actor; *Career* actress and singer; came to prominence in modelling career 1966–71; has been the recipient of many awards and honours; launched Twiggy Skin Care range 2001; *Theatre* incl: Cinderella 1976, Elvira in Blithe Spirit (Chichester) 1977, Captain Beaky 1982, My One And Only 1983–84, Noel & Gertie (Bay St Theatre NY) 1998, If Love Were All (Lucille Lortel Theatre NY) 1999, That Play I Wrote (Wyndhams Theatre London) 2002, Mrs Warren's Profession 2003; *Television* incl: Twiggy Series 1978, Twiggy And Friends 1980, Pygmalion 1981, Captain Beaky 1982, Little Match Girl 1986, Sun Child 1988, Sophie's World, The Young Charlie Chaplin 1989, Princesses (US pilot) 1991, Something Borrowed Something Blue (CBS) 1998; *Films* incl: The Boyfriend 1971, W 1975, There Goes The Bride 1979, Blues Brothers 1981, The Doctor And The Devils 1985, Club Paradise 1986, Madame Sousatzka 1988, Harem Hotel Istanbul 1988, Woundings 1998; *Recordings* incl: Here I Go Again, Please Get My Name Right, London Pride (Songs from the Brit Musicals), If Love Were All, Midnight Blue 2003; *Books* Twiggy (autobiography, 1975), An Open Look (1985), Twiggy in Black & White (autobiography, 1997); *Recreations* music, design, dressmaking; *Style*— Ms Twiggy Lawson; ✉ c/o PFD, Drury House, 34–43 Russell Street, London WC2B 5HA (tel 0202 7344 1000, fax 0202 7836 9539, e-mail postmaster@pfd.co.uk)

LAWSON, Mark Gerard; s of Francis Lawson, of Harpenden, Herts, and Teresa, *née* Kane; *b* 11 April 1962; *Educ* St Columba's Coll St Albans, UCL (BA); *m* 1990, Sarah Gillian Jane, da of Alan John Gilbert Bull; 2 s (William Mark b 25 July 1992, Benjamin Gilbert Francis b 18 March 1999), 1 da (Anna Sarah b 15 March 1995); *Career* journalist; jr reporter and TV critic The Universe 1984–85, TV previewer The Sunday Times 1985–86, asst arts ed and TV critic The Independent 1986–89 (Parly sketchwriter 1987–88), chief feature writer The Independent Magazine 1988–95, TV critic The Independent on Sunday 1990–91; columnist and feature writer: The Independent 1993–95, The Guardian 1995–; freelance contrib to numerous pubns since 1984 incl: The Times, Time Out, The Listener, Mirabella, Vogue, New Statesman, The Tablet; writer and presenter of TV documentaries: Byline: Vote For Ron (BBC) 1990, J'Accuse: Coronation Street (Channel 4) 1991, The Secret Life of The Pope (BBC 2) 1996, The Clinton Complex (BBC 2) 1998; writer and presenter TV and radio progs: The Late Show (BBC 2) 1993–95, Late Review/Newsnight Review (BBC 2) 1994–2005, The Big Question (BBC 1) 1996–99, Vice or Virtue (BBC Radio 4) 1996–98, Burning for Atlanta (BBC Radio 4) 1996, A Brief History of The Future 1997, Front Row (BBC Radio 4) 1998–, Mark Lawson Talks To... (BBC 4) 2004–; script-writer: The Vision Thing (BBC TV) 1993, The Man who had 10,000 Women (BBC Radio 4) 2002, St Graham and St Evelyn, Pray for Us (BBC Radio 4) 2003, Absolute Power (BBC TV) 2003–05, The Third Soldier Holds his Thighs (BBC Radio 4) 2005, London, this is Washington (BBC Radio 4) 2006, Expand This (BBC Radio 4) 2007; *Awards* British Press Award 1987, BP Arts Journalism Awards 1989, 1990 and 1991, TV-am Critic of the Year 1989, TV-am Broadcast Journalist of the Year 1990, Sony Radio Silver Award 1999; *Books* Bloody Margaret: Three Political Fantasies (1991), The Battle for Room Service (1993), Idlewild (1995), Conflicts of Interest: The Art of John Keane (1995), Going Out Live (2001), Enough is Enough (2005); contrib: House of Cards: A Selection of Modern Political Humour (1988), Fine Glances: An anthology of cricket writing (1990); *Recreations* television, watching football and cricket, red wine, reading; *Style—* Mark Lawson

LAWSON, His Hon Judge Michael Henry; QC (1991); s of Dr Richard Pike Lawson, MC (d 2005), of Calne, Wilts, and Margaret Haines, *née* Knight (d 1990); *b* 3 February 1946; *Educ* Monkton Combe Sch Bath, Univ of London (LLB); *m* Ann Pleasance Symons, da of late John Guy Brisker, CBE, RD, RN; 2 da (Kate Alexandra b 13 Oct 1971, (Antonia) Sophia Louise b 27 Feb 1974); *Career* called to the Bar Inner Temple 1969 (bencher 1993); primarily in criminal advocacy practice, recorder of the Crown Court 1987 (asst recorder 1983–87), ldr SE Circuit 1997–2000, circuit judge (SE Circuit) 2004–; memb Bar Cncl 1997–2003; Liveryman Worshipful Co of Curriers 1982 (Master 2007); *Clubs* Garrick; *Style—* His Hon Judge Michael Lawson, QC; ✉ The Crown Court, Barker Road, Maidstone, Kent ME16 8EQ

LAWSON, Nigella Lucy; da of Lord Lawson of Blaby, PC (Life Peer), *qv*, and Vanessa Mary Addison, *née* Salmon (d 1985); sis of Hon Dominic Ralph Campden Lawson, *qv*; *b* 6 January 1960; *Educ* Godolphin & Latymer Sch, Lady Margaret Hall Oxford (BA); *m* 1, Sept 1992, John Diamond (d 2001); 1 da (Cosima Thomasina b 15 Dec 1993), 1 s (Bruno Paul Nigel b 28 June 1996); m 2, Sept 2003, Charles Saatchi, *qv*; *Career* journalist and broadcaster; ed Quartet Books 1982–84; Sunday Times: asst on Arts & Review section 1984–86, dep literary ed 1986–88, arts writer 1988–89; restaurant columnist The Spectator 1985–96; columnist: Evening Standard 1989–94, The Times 1995–98, The Observer 1998–2001; food writer Vogue 1996–2002; Channel 4 television broadcast: Nigella Bites 2000 and 2001 (won Television Broadcast of the Year at Guild of Food Writers Awards 2001), Forever Summer 2002; Author of the Year British Book Awards 2001; *Books* How to Eat (1998), How to be a Domestic Goddess (2000), Nigella Bites (2001), Forever Summer (2002), Feast (2004); *Style—* Nigella Lawson; ✉ c/o Ed Victor Limited, 6 Bayley Street, Bedford Square, London WC1B 3HB (tel 020 7304 4100, fax 020 7304 4111)

LAWSON, Roger Hardman; *b* 3 September 1945; *m* Jeni; 3 da (Sarahjane, Annabel, Louise); *Career* Directors Resource (handling substantial investments) 3i plc 1993–2002 (head Int Dept until 1993); dir Zotefoams plc and a number of UK unlisted companies; tstee: Thalidomide, St Paul's Staff Fund; memb ICAEW (former pres); FCA; *Recreations* golf, food, family; *Clubs* Royal Wimbledon Golf, Rye Golf; *Style—* Roger Lawson, Esq; ✉ 62 Thurleigh Road, London SW12 8HD

LAWSON, Hon Mrs (Rosamond Mary); only da of 2 Viscount Monckton of Brenchley, CB, OBE, MC, DL, FSA; *b* 26 October 1953; *Educ* Ursuline Convent Tildonk Belgium; *m* 30 Dec 1991, as his 2 w, Dominic Ralph Campden Lawson, *qv*, s of Baron Lawson of Blaby, PC (Life Peer), *qv*; 2 da; *Career* asst md Cartier London 1979, sales and exhibition mangr Tabbah Jewellers (Monte Carlo) 1980, promotions mangr Asprey 1982–85, md Tiffany London 1986–97 (pres 1997–2000), non-exec chm Asprey & Garrard 2002–04 (chief exec 2000–02); pres KIDS 2003– (chm 1999–2003); patron: Acorn Hospice, Downside Up, Downs Ed; tstee Gilbert Collection 2003–; Liveryman Worshipful Co of Goldsmiths 2000 (Freeman 1982); *Recreations* books, dogs, voyages; *Style—* The Hon Mrs Lawson

LAWSON, Hon (Sarah Jane); da of (Lt-Col) 5 Baron Burnham, JP, DL (d 1993); *b* 7 October 1955; *Educ* Heathfield Sch Ascot; *m* 1, 1982 (m dis 1991), Michael Ian Grade, CBE, *qv*; m 2, 1992, David Patrick Maher; 1 s (Edward James Lawson b 16 June 1997), 1 da (Lucy Sarah Beatrice b 24 Nov 2000); *Career* slr Macfarlanes 1976–80, agent Curtis Brown 1980–82, vice-pres Devpt TV D L Taffner Ltd 1982–84, pres Taft Entertainment/Lawson Group 1985–87; md: Lawson Productions Ltd 1987–95 and 1996–, Anglia Television Entertainment Ltd 1995–96, Wicklow Films 1996–; *Style—* The Hon Sarah Lawson; ✉ 6 Wellington Gardens, Oakley Road, Dublin 6, Ireland

LAWSON, Sonia; da of Frederick Lawson (d 1968), of Castle Bolton, North Yorks, and Muriel Mary, *née* Metcalfe (both artists); *b* 2 June 1934; *Educ* RCA (MA, postgrad travelling scholarship); *m* 14 Jan 1969, Charles William Congo; 1 da (b 29 May 1970); *Career* artist; currently visiting lectr Royal Acad Schs; Rowney Drawing Prize 1984, Lorne Award 1987, Eastern Arts drawing prize (first prize 1984 and 1989); RWS 1987 (Assoc 1984), RA 1982, Hon RWA 2005; *Solo Exhibitions* incl: Zwemmer Gallery London 1960, New Arts Centre London 1963, Queens Square Gallery Leeds 1964, Trafford Gallery London 1967, Billingham/Middlesbrough 1973, Harrogate Art Gallery 1979, retrospective Shrines of Life touring exhbn 1982–83, Central Art Gallery Milton Keynes 1982, Mappin Gallery Sheffield 1982, Cartwright Bradford 1982, Leicester Kimberlin and Hull Ferens 1983, Midnight Muse (City Art Gallery Manchester) 1987, Wakefield City Art Gallery 1988, Bradford Cartwright 1989, Boundary Gallery London 1989, 1995, 1998, 2000, 2003 and 2005, Univ of Birmingham 1994 and 2006, retrospective Dean Clough Halifax 1996, Shirehall Stafford 1999, Royal West of England Acad Bristol 2000, Carlow Arts Festival Eire 2001, Vertigo London 2002, Aylesbury Art Gallery & Museum 2006; *Group Exhibitions* incl: London Gp, Royal Acad, RWS, 25 Years of British Art (Royal Acad Jubilee) 1977, Fragments Against Ruin (Arts Cncl tour) 1981–82, Moira Kelly Fine Art (London 1982 and NY 1983), Tolly Cobbold Tour 1982–83 and 1985–86, Leeds Poly 'New Art' 1987, Manchester City Art Gallery 1988, London RCA Centenary 1988, Olympia, Islington, RCA and Bath Festivals 1989–2000, China Br Cncl Touring Exhbn 1989–90, Royal Inst of Fine Art Glasgow 1990, The Infernal Method etchings, Royal Acad London 1990, John Moores Liverpool 1991, Nielson & Wuethrich Inter Fine Art Thun Switzerland 1992, Mercury Gallery Duncan Campbell London 1992, Lamont, Connaught Brown 1994–97; *Work in Collections* incl: Imperial War Museum London (BAOR cmmnd 1984), Arts Cncl GB, Sheffield Graves, Belfast Art Gallery, Univ of Leeds, Middlesbrough Art Gallery, Miny Works, Royal Acad and RCA Collections, Bradford, Huddersfield, Wakefield, Carlisle, Bolton and Rochdale Galleries, Univ Centre Birmingham (cmmnd 1994), St Peter's Oxford, various educn authorities and corp collections, Vatican Rome (cmmnd 1989), Lambeth Palace (cmmnd 1989), Chatsworth House collection, private collections in Europe, USA, Canada and Aust; *Publications* illustrator for: book of poems by James Kirkup (1993), short story by Fay Weldon (1995); *Clubs* Royal Over-Seas League; *Style—* Sonia Lawson, RA, RWS; ✉ Royal Academy of Arts, Piccadilly, London W1 (tel 020 7300 5680, fax 020 7300 0837, e-mail art@sonialawson.co.uk, website www.sonialawson.co.uk)

LAWSON OF BLABY, Baron (Life Peer UK 1992), of Newnham in the County of Northamptonshire; Nigel Lawson; PC (1981); s of Ralph Lawson, and Joan Elisabeth, *née* Davis; *b* 11 March 1932; *Educ* Westminster, ChCh Oxford; *m* 1, 1955 (m dis 1980), Vanessa Mary Addison (d 1985), 2 da of Felix Addison Salmon, of Ham Common, Surrey; 1 s (Hon Dominic Ralph Campden, *qv*, b 1956), 3 da ((Hon) Nigella Lucy, *qv*, b 1960, Hon Thomasina Posy (Hon Mrs Hill) b 1961 d 1993, Hon Horatia Holly b 1966); m 2, 1980, Thérèse Mary Maclear, da of Henry Charles Maclear Bate, of Putney, London; 1 s (Hon Thomas Nigel Maclear b 1976), 1 da (Hon Emily Hero b 1981); *Career* Sub-Lt RNVR 1954–56; memb editorial staff Financial Times 1956–60, city ed Sunday Telegraph 1961–63, ed The Spectator 1966–70; Parly candidate (Cons) Eton and Slough 1970, MP (Cons) Blaby 1974–92; oppn whip 1976–77, oppn spokesman on Treasy and Economic Affrs 1977–79, fin sec to the Treasy 1979–81, Energy sec 1981–83, Chancellor of the Exchequer 1983–1989 (resigned); dir Barclays Bank 1990–98, chm Central Europe Trust 1990–, chm Oxford Investment Ptnrs 2006–; pres Br Inst of Energy Economics 1994–2003; special advsr Cons HQ 1973–74; hon student ChCh Oxford 1996; *Books* The Power Game (with Jock Bruce-Gardyne, 1976), The View From No 11 (memoirs, 1992), The Nigel Lawson Diet Book (1996); *Style—* The Rt Hon the Lord Lawson of Blaby, PC; ✉ House of Lords, London SW1A 0PW

LAWSON ROGERS, (George) Stuart; QC (1994); s of George Henry Roland Rogers, CBE (d 1983), of Bournemouth, Dorset, and Mary Lawson (d 1983); *b* 23 March 1946; *Educ* Buckingham Coll Harrow, LSE (LLB); *m* 19 July 1969, Rosalind Denise, da of Lt Dennis Ivor Leach, of Bournemouth, Dorset; 1 s (Dominic b 1971), 1 da (Lucy b 1972); *Career* called to the Bar Gray's Inn 1969; recorder of the Crown Court 1990– (asst recorder 1986–89); asst boundary cmmr Boundary Cmmn (Parly) for England and Wales 1981, ad hoc appt asst boundary cmmr Local Govt Boundary Cmmn for England and Wales 1983, appt to Panel of Chairmen of Structure Plan Examinations in Public Dept of Environment 1984, appt to Panels of Legal Assessors to GMC and Gen Dental Cncl 1988, inspector Dept of Transport (Merchant Shipping Act 1988 investigations) 1989, inspector DTI (insider dealing investigation) 1989, Standing Counsel to HM Customs and Excise (Criminal SE Circuit) 1989–94; dir Watford AFC 1990–96; fell Soc for Advanced Legal Studies 1998; *Recreations* theatre, music, gardening, reading; *Clubs* Athenaeum; *Style—* Stuart Lawson Rogers, Esq, QC; ✉ 7 Harrington Street, Liverpool L2 9YH (tel 0151 2420707, fax 0151 2362800, e-mail clerks@harringtonstreet.co.uk); 23 Essex Street, London WC2R 3AS (tel 020 7413 0353, fax 020 7413 0374)

LAWSON-TANCRED, Sir Henry; 10 Bt (E 1662); s of Maj Sir Thomas Selby Lawson-Tancred, 9 Bt (d 1945); *b* 1924; *Educ* Stowe, Jesus Coll Cambridge; *m* 1, 1950, Jean Veronica (d 1970), da of Gerald Robert Foster (d 1962); 5 s, 1 da; m 2, 1978, Susan Dorothy Marie-Gabrielle, da of late Sir Kenelm Cayley, 10 Bt, and formerly w of Maldwin Drummond; *Heir* s, Andrew Lawson-Tancred; *Career* served with RAFVR 1942–46, JP West Riding 1967–94; *Style—* Sir Henry Lawson-Tancred, Bt; ✉ 17 Hungate, Brompton-by-Sawdon, Scarborough, North Yorkshire YO13 9DW

LAWTON, Commodore Alan Frederick; s of Frederick Lawton (d 1974), of Berkhamsted, and Ivy, *née* Parker (d 1989); *b* 14 February 1939; *Educ* Berkhamsted Sch, Britannia RNC Dartmouth, Royal Naval Engrg Coll, Univ of London (BSc), RCDS; *m* 21 Jan 1967, Susan Russell, da of John Torrie Johnston (d 1978), of Glasgow; 2 da (Tina b 1967, Jennifer b 1970); *Career* RNC Dartmouth 1957, Cdr 1975, Trg Cdr HMS Caledonia 1976–78, Dir Marine Engrg RNZN 1978–79, Chief Tech Servs RNZN 1979–80, Marine Engr Offr HMS Bristol 1980–82, Offr i/c Machinery Trials Units 1982–83, Capt 1984, Offr i/c Fleet Maintenance Falklands Is 1984, Asst Dir Naval Plans and Progs 1985–87, memb Royal Coll of Def Studies 1988, Cdre 1992, Dir Naval Logistic Planning 1989–92, Dir Naval Logistic Staff 1992–93; Head of Logistics Engrg (LE) Systems and Servs Div British Aerospace Defence 1993–96, Horizon IJVC 1996–99, LE Dir Type 45 Destroyer 1999–2000; non-exec dir Scottish Ambulance Service 2000–; FIMgt 1991, FInstD 1992, FIMechE 1993; *Recreations* golf, sailing, tennis, watching cricket and rugby; *Style—* Alan Lawton

LAWTON, (Frederick) Anthony (Tony); s of Rt Hon Sir Frederick Horace Lawton (d 2001), and Doreen, *née* Wilton; *b* 9 July 1940, Bodmin, Cornwall; *Educ* Stonyhurst, Univ of Bordeaux (Certificat d'Études), CCC Cambridge; *m* 5 Sept 1964, Catherine Andrée, *née* Bellet; 3 da (Emilie b 18 June 1965, Marie-Josèphe b 11 Aug 1968, Sébastienne Agnès b 21 April 1970); *Career* articled to chief slr Br Railways Bd 1963–66; Grays Slrs: ptnr 1967–2006, conslt 2006–; tstee Trustee Savings Bank of Yorkshire & Lincoln 1975–89; memb Ctee Conf of Slrs for Catholic Charities 1967– (memb 1967, chm 1998–2007); memb: Law Soc 1966, Yorks Law Soc 1967; *Recreations* history, gardening, travel; *Clubs* Yorkshire; *Style—* Tony Lawton, Esq; ✉ The Old Rectory, The Village, Skelton, York YO30 1XY (tel 01904 470301, e-mail falawton@gotadsl.co.uk); Messrs Grays, Solicitors, Duncombe Place, York YO1 7DY (tel 01904 634771, fax 01904 610711, e-mail tony.lawton@grayssolicitors.co.uk)

LAWTON, Charles Henry Huntly; s of Philip Charles Fenner Lawton, CBE, DFC (d 1993), and Emma Letitia Gertrude, *née* Stephenson; *b* 17 April 1946; *Educ* Westminster; *m* 21 April 1979, Sarah Margaret, da of Rev Christopher Lambert; 1 s (Timothy b 1982), 1 da (Hermione b 1984); *Career* admitted slr 1970; legal advsr and head Legal Dept Rio Tinto plc 1985–; *Recreations* walking, reading, fishing; *Clubs* RAC; *Style—* Charles Lawton, Esq; ✉ Rio Tinto plc, 6 St James's Square, London SW1Y 4LD (tel 020 7930 2399, fax 020 7930 3249)

LAWTON, Jeffrey; s of Harold Lawton (d 1975), of Oldham, and Edna, *née* Penney (d 1978); *b* 11 December 1938; *Educ* Greenhill GS, Royal Manchester Coll of Music; *m* 26 Sept 1959, Ann Barbara, da of Alan Whitehead; 2 s (Andrew David b 19 Sept 1966, Robert Jeffrey b 7 May 1969), 1 da (Sara Jane b 17 Oct 1971); *Career* tenor; princ WNO 1982–87 (chorus 1981), freelance 1987–, artistic dir Civit Hills Opera Theatre 1995–2000, dir Mananan Opera Isle of Man 1995, dir of vocal studies and opera La Tour de France Festival 1995–99, prof Vocal Studies Dept RSAMD 1995–99, sr lectr RNCM (head of Sch of Vocal and Opera Studies 1999–2000); has sung with various major Br orchs and conductors; appeared at various major festivals incl: Edinburgh, Llangollen, Salisbury, York, BBC Proms; *Performances* with WNO incl: Ringmaster in The Bartered Bride 1982, Tichon in Katya Kabanova 1982, Judge in Un Ballo in Maschera 1982, Large Prisoner in House of the Dead 1982, Laca in Jenufa 1984, Manolious in The Greek Passion 1984, title role in Siegfried 1985 and 1986, Siegfried in Götterdämmerung 1985, title role in Otello (in Brussels, Nancy and Paris) 1987 and 1990, Don José in Carmen 1987, Emperor in Die Frau ohne Schatten 1989, Luka in House of the Dead 1991, Aegisthus in Elektra 1992 and 1995, Tristan in Tristan und Isolde 1993; other operatic roles incl: Florestan in Fidelio (Opera North) 1988, Siegmund in Die Walküre (Cologne) 1988, Siegfried in Götterdämmerung (Cologne) 1989, Erik in Der Fliegende Holländer (Opera North) 1989, title role in Otello (Lisbon) 1989 and (Covent Garden) 1990, Radames in Aida (Den Bosch Holland) 1991, Prince Shuisky in Boris Godunov (Opera North) 1992, Laca in Jenufa (New Israeli Opera) 1993, Captain in Wozzeck (Opera North) 1993, Aegisthus in Elektra (Covent Garden) 1994, Tristan in Tristan und Isolde (Scottish Opera, Lisbon and Mainz) 1994, Wird in Der Rosenkavalier (Covent Garden), Apollo in Daphne (Garsington) 1995, Aegisthus in Elektra (Canadian Opera Co) 1996, Laca in Jenufa (New Israeli Opera) 1996, Pedro in Indes de Castro (world premiere, Scottish Opera) 1996, title role in Tannhäuser (Opera North) 1997, President Mendez in Der Kuhhandel (Opera North) 2006, title role in Peter Grimes (Scottish opera); concert performances incl: Das Lied von der Erde (Paris, under Janovski, also broadcast on radio, BBC Proms 1995), Mahler Symphony No 8 (Turin, also televised), Tristan (Stuttgart 1997, Scottish Opera 1998, WNO 1999), Siegmund (Prague State Opera) 1998, Tristan (Lyric Opera Chicago) 1999, Tristan (Buenos Aires) 2000, Das Lied von der Erde (Buenos Aires) 2000, Siegmund in Die Walküre (BBC Scottish Symphony Orch) 2004, Zorn in Die Meistersinger von Nünberg (Edinburgh Festival) 2006; *Recordings* incl: The Greek Passion (under Sir Charles Mackerras) 1982, Panait and Adonis, Supraphon (with Brno State Philharmonic Orch); *Clubs* Oldham Athletic FC; *Style—* Jeffrey Lawton, Esq; ✉ c/o Music International, 13 Ardilaun Road, London N5 2QR (tel 020 7359 5183, fax 020 7226 9792)

LAWTON, Prof Sir John Hartley; kt (2005), CBE (1997); s of Frank Hartley Lawton (d 1982), of Leyland, Lancashire, and Mary, *née* Cuerden; *b* 24 September 1943; *Educ* Balshaw's GS Leyland, UC Durham (BSc, PhD); *m* 22 Oct 1966, Dorothy, da of Harold Grimshaw (d 1960), of Leyland Lancs; 1 da (Anna Louise b 1968), 1 s (Graham John b 1969); *Career* Univ of Oxford: departmental demonstrator in zoology 1968–71, lectr in zoology Lincoln Coll 1970–71, lectr in zoology St Anne's Coll 1970–71; Dept of Biology Univ of York: lectr 1971–78, sr lectr 1978–82, reader 1982–85, prof 1985–89; prof of community ecology

L

and dir Centre for Population Biology Imperial Coll of Sci Technol and Med Univ of London 1989–99, adjunct scientist Inst of Ecosystem Studies Millbrook NY 1992–2000, chief exec NERC 1999–2005, chm Royal Cmmn on Environmental Pollution 2005–; memb NERC (chm Terrestrial and Freshwater Sci and Technology Bd) until 1999, vice-pres RSPB 2000– (chm Cncl until 1998), vice-pres Br Tst for Ornithology 2000–, pres Br Ecological Soc 2005–07; formerly memb: Cncl Freshwater Biological Assoc, Royal Cmmn on Environmental Pollution, Br Ecological Soc; tstee WWF UK 2002–; Hon DSc: Lancaster Univ 1993, Univ of Birmingham 2005, Univ of York 2005, Univ of Aberdeen 2006, UEA 2006; fell ICSTM 2006; hon fell Royal Entomological Soc; FRS; *Books* Insects on Plants: Community Patterns and Mechanisms (1984), Blackwell Scientific Oxford (with T R E Southwood and D R Strong), The Evolutionary Interactions of Animals and Plants (ed with W G Chaloner and J L Harper, 1991), Linking Species and Ecosystems (ed with C G Jones, 1994), Extinction Rates (ed with R M May, 1995), Community Ecology in a Changing World (2000); *Recreations* bird watching, gardening, photography, running, hill walking, travel; *Style—* Prof Sir John Lawton, CBE, FRS; ✉ The Hayloft, Holburns Croft, Heslington, York YO10 5DP

LAWTON, Julie Grace; da of Arthur Barber, of Stourbridge, W Midlands, and Audrey, *née* Vann; *b* 2 April 1958; *Educ* Solihull HS for Girls, Solihull Sixth Form Coll, Univ of Hull (BA, PGCE), Univ of Birmingham (MEd); *m* 11 Aug 1979, Mark Lawton; *Career* teacher of French and German: Newland HS for Girls Hull 1980–83, Parkfield Sch Wolverhampton 1983–86 (also teacher i/c German); head of modern languages Kingswinford Sch Dudley 1987–94, vice-princ and dir of sixth form studies St Peter's Collegiate Sch Wolverhampton 1995–2003 (actg princ 2000), headmistress Wolverhampton Girls' HS 2004–; memb Assoc for Language Learning; *Recreations* walking, travelling abroad; *Style—* Mrs Julie Lawton; ✉ Wolverhampton Girls' High School, Tettenhall Road, Wolverhampton WV6 0BY (tel 01902 312186, fax 01902 312187, e-mail jglawton@girlshigh.biblio.net)

LAWTON, District Judge; Peter Edward; s of Frank Edward Lawton (d 1997), of Nottingham, and Ida Hook, *née* Rayner (d 1986); *b* 4 June 1946; *Educ* Henry Mellish GS Nottingham, Univ of Leeds (LLB); *m* 22 May 1976, Joy Ann, da of David John Reavill (d 2006); 1 s (Mark Edward b 15 June 1977); *Career* admitted slr 1971, ptnr J H Milner & Son Solicitors Leeds 1972–91 (articled clerk 1968–70), dep registrar 1986, district judge 1991–; chief examiner part I slrs' qualifying exam torts 1977–82; attorney at law State of Texas 1980; *Recreations* amateur radio, walking, gardening; *Style—* District Judge Lawton; ✉ Bradford County Court, The Law Courts, Exchange Square, Drake Street, Bradford, West Yorkshire BD1 1JA (tel 01274 840274, fax 01274 840275, e-mail districtjudge.lawton@judiciary.gsi.gov.uk)

LAWTON, Robert Noyes; CBE (1997), DL (2002); *Educ* Porchester Sch, Dorset Coll of Agric (NCA), Shuttleworth Coll of Agric (NDA), Wye Coll Centre for Euro Studies (advanced farm mgmnt); *Career* asst to Maj J B Schuster reorganising family estate in Oxon 1960–62, VSO asst mangr of large mechanised farming scheme in Basutoland Protectorate 1962–64, devpt offr and farm mgmnt conslt ICI Ltd 1964–69; chm Wessex Regnl Panel 1988–97 (advsr to min of agriculture); past chm Wiltshire Farming and Wildlife Advsy Gp; memb numerous agric ctees and advsy gps 1982–; govr: Royal Agric Coll 1996–, Silsoe Res Inst 1996–2002; High Sheriff Wilts 2000; Joseph Nickerson Husbandry Award 1982, Farmer of the Year 1993; FRAgS 1993, FIAgrE 2002; *Recreations* fly fishing, shooting, cross-country skiing, watercolour painting, military history, bee-keeping, book collecting (especially early agric publications); *Style—* Robert Lawton, Esq, CBE, DL

LAX, Prof Alistair; s of John Lax (d 1993), of Glasgow, and Isobel, *née* Coutts; *b* 30 March 1953, Glasgow; *Educ* Univ of Glasgow (BSc), ICRF (PhD); *m* 1 Sept 1975, Pauline, *née* Smith; 3 s; *Career* staff scientist Inst for Animal Health BBSRC 1979–96; King's Coll London: sr lectr 1996–2002, prof of cellular microbiology 2002–; *Books* Cellular Microbiology (jtly, 1999), Bacterial Protein Toxins (ed, 2005), Toxin (2005); *Style—* Prof Alistair Lax; ✉ King's College London Dental Institute, Guy's Tower, King's College London, Guy's Hospital, London SE1 9RT

LAXTON, Robert (Bob); MP; s of Alan and Elsie Laxton; *b* 7 September 1944; *Educ* Woodlands Secdy Sch, Derby Coll of Art and Technology; *m* (m dis); *Career* with British Telecom plc 1961–97 (branch sec/negotiator Post Office Engrg Union/Nat Communications Union/Communication Workers Union 1974–97); MP (Lab) Derby N 1997–; PPS to Alan Johnson, MP, *qv*; vice-chair: Trade Union Gp of Labour MP's, PLP Trade and Indust Departmental Ctee; Derby City Cncl: cncllr 1979–97, ldr 1986–88 and 1994–97; chm East Midlands Local Govt Assoc 1996–97; *Recreations* hill walking; *Style—* Bob Laxton, MP; ✉ House of Commons, London SW1A 0AA (tel 020 7219 4096, e-mail laxtonb@parliament.uk); constituency office: 1st Floor, Abbots Hill Chambers, Gower Street, Derby DE1 1SD (tel 01332 206699, fax 01332 206444, website www.boblaxton.org.uk)

LAY, David John; s of Walter Charles Frederick Lay (d 1984), and June Barbara, *née* Cadman (d 2003); *b* 15 August 1948; *Educ* Magdalen Coll Sch Oxford, CCC Oxford (MA); *m* 1 Sept 1973, Tamara Said, da of Said Pasha Mufti (d 1989), former PM of Jordan; 3 da (Sima b 1977, Maya b 1980, Lana b 1982), 1 s (Taimour b 1982); *Career* BBC radio news reporter 1974–79, presenter Twenty-four Hours BBC World Serv 1979–91, ed Oxford Analytica 1988–2000; American Int Gp (AIG): chief ed Exec Briefing Book 2000–, vice-pres global risk assessments 2006–; sr assoc memb St Antony's Coll Oxford 1997–98, memb Sr Common Room CCC Oxford 1997–; *Recreations* foreign travel, Middle East politics; *Style—* David Lay, Esq; ✉ 90 Coombe Lane West, Kingston upon Thames, Surrey KT2 7DB (tel 020 8336 1325, e-mail davidjlay@hotmail.com); 2 Gold Street, Apartment 5108, New York, NY 10038, USA (tel 00 212 430 5799)

LAY, Richard Neville; CBE (2001); s of late Edward John Lay, of Banstead, Surrey, and Nellie, *née* Gould; *b* 18 October 1938; *Educ* Whitgift Sch; *m* Jan 2003, Veronica Anne Jones, *née* Hamilton-Russell; 2 c by previous m (Melanie St Clair b 1965, Martin Richard Forbes b 1969); *Career* chartered surveyor; pres Royal Instn of Chartered Surveyors 1998–99; ptnr Debenham Tewson & Chinnocks 1965–87, chm DTZ Holdings plc and subsid cos 1987–2000; chm Central London Bd Royal & Sun Alliance and London Insurance Group; tstee Tate Gallery Fndn 1988–94; chm: Market Requirements Ctee RICS (The Lay Report, 1991), Commercial Market Panel RICS 1992–96; chm and tstee Portman Estate 1999–; dir Nat House Building Cncl 2000–07; co-chair Corby Regeneration Co Ltd 2003–06, chm North Northants Devpt Co Urban Regeneration Cos; memb: Cncl Br Property Federation 1992–99, Bank of England Property Forum 1994–2000, Advsy Panel on Standards in the Planning Inspectorate 1996–2001, Bd of Coll of Estate Mgmnt 2000–04; chm Dept of Communities and Local Govt Commercial Property Gp 2004–; chm London Underwriting Centre 2005–; surveyor to the Worshipful Co of Armourers & Brasiers 1983–98 (memb Ct 1998–, Master 2003–04); Property Personality of the Year 1999; FRICS; *Recreations* gardening; *Clubs* RAC; *Style—* Richard Lay, Esq, CBE, FRICS; ✉ 12 Paultons Street, London SW3 5DR (tel mobile 07767 613529, e-mail richard.lay@portmanestate.co.uk)

LAYARD, Adm Sir Michael Henry Gordon; KCB (1993), CBE (1983); s of Edwin Henry Frederick Layard (d 1972), of Colombo, Sri Lanka, and Doris Christian Gordon, *née* Spence (d 1965); *b* 3 January 1936; *Educ* Pangbourne Coll, BRNC Dartmouth; *m* 17 Dec 1966, Elspeth Horsley Fisher, da of late Rev L C Fisher; 2 s (James Henry Gordon b 1967, Andrew Charles Gordon b 1969); *Career* RN: Seaman Offr 1954–58, flying trg 1958–60, fighter pilot 1960–70, air warfare instr 1964; Cmd: 899 Naval Air Sqdn (Sea Vixens) 1970–71, HMS Lincoln 1971–72; NDC 1974, Directorate Naval Air Warfare MOD 1975–77, Cdr (Air) HMS Ark Royal 1977–78, CSO (Air) to Flag Offr Naval Air Cmd 1979–82, SNO SS Atlantic Conveyor Falklands conflict 1982; Cmd: RNAS Culdrose 1982–84, HMS Cardiff 1984–85 (ldr Task Force to Persian Gulf); Dir Naval Warfare (Air) MOD 1985–88, Flag Offr Naval Air Command 1988–90 (latterly Flag Offr Naval Aviation), DG Naval Manpower and Trg 1990–92, head RN Offr Study Gp 1992–93, Second Sea Lord, Chief of Naval Personnel and Adm Pres RNC Greenwich 1993–94, Second Sea Lord and Cdr in Chief Naval Home Command and Flag ADC to HM The Queen 1994–95; Gentleman Usher to the Sword of State 1997–2005; memb Cncl: White Ensign Assoc 1991–2006, Royal Patriotic Fund; non-exec dir Taunton & Somerset NHS Tst 1996–2000; pres RN Golfing Soc 1988–94; tstee: Fleet Air Arm Museum 1988– 2006, Falkland Islands Meml Chapel Tst 1992–2007; govr Pangbourne Coll 1995–, memb Cncl King's Coll and King's Hall Taunton 1997–2005; memb: RN Sailing Assoc, Fleet Air Arm Offrs' Assoc, RUSI; Ordre de Chevalier Bretvin; *Recreations* music, history, painting, sailing, collecting experiences; *Clubs* Army and Navy, Royal Navy Club of 1765 & 1785; *Style—* Adm Sir Michael Layard, KCB, CBE; ✉ Harwood House, Aller, Langport, Somerset TA10 0QN

LAYARD, Baron (Life Peer UK 2000), of Highgate in the London Borough of Haringey; Prof (Peter) Richard Grenville; s of John Willoughby Layard (d 1974), and Doris, *née* Dunn (d 1973); *b* 15 March 1934; *Educ* Eton, Univ of Cambridge (BA), LSE (MSc); *m* 1991 Molly, *née* Reid; *Career* 2 Lt 4 RHA 1953–54, RA 1952–54; sch teacher LCC 1959–61, sr res offr Robbins Ctee of Higher Educn 1961–64; LSE: dep dir Higher Educn Res Unit 1964–74, lectr 1968–75, head Centre for Lab Economics 1974–90, reader 1975–80, prof of economics 1980–, dir Centre for Econ Performance 1990–2003 (dir Well-being Prog 2003–); econ conslt Govt of Russian Fedn 1991–97; memb Univ Grants Ctee 1985–89, chm Exec Ctee Employment Inst until 1986 and chm 1987–91; conslt Dept for Educn and Employment 1997–2001; fell Econometric Soc, FBA; *Books* Microeconomic Theory (with A Walters, 1978, reissued 1987), How to Beat Unemployment (1986), Unemployment: Macroeconomic Performance and the Labour Market (with S Nickell and R Jackman, 1991), What Labour Can Do (1997), Tackling Unemployment (1999), Tackling Inequality (1999), What the Future Holds (ed, 2002), Happiness: Lessons from a New Science (2005); *Recreations* walking, tennis; *Style—* Prof Lord Layard; ✉ London School of Economics and Political Science, Houghton Street, London WC2A 2AE (tel 020 7955 7281, fax 020 7955 7595, e-mail r.layard@lse.ac.uk)

LAYDEN, Anthony Michael; s of Sheriff Michael Layden, SSC, TD, and Eileen Mary Layden; *b* 27 July 1946; *Educ* Holy Cross Acad Edinburgh, Univ of Edinburgh (LLB); *m* 1969, Josephine Mary, *née* McGhee; 3 s, 1 da; *Career* Lt 15 Scottish Volunteer Bn, Parachute Regt 1966–69; HM Dip Service: FCO 1968, MECAS Lebanon 1969, Jedda 1971, Rome 1973, FCO Middle East, Rhodesia, Personnel Ops Depts 1977–82, head of chancery Jedda 1982–85, FCO Hong Kong Dept 1985–87, cnsllr and head of chancery Muscat 1987–91, cnsllr (Econ and Commercial) Copenhagen 1991–95, dep head of mission Copenhagen 1994–95, head of W Euro Dept FCO 1995–99, ambass Morocco 1999–2002 (concurrently non-resident ambass to Mauritania), ambass to Libya 2003–06, ret; *Recreations* sailing, walking, music, bridge; *Clubs* Travellers; *Style—* Anthony Layden, Esq; ✉ c/o Foreign & Commonwealth Office, King Charles Street, London SW1A 2AH

LAYE, Michael George (Mike); s of George Edward Laye (d 2002), of North Lancing, W Sussex, and Audrey, *née* Ford; *b* 16 May 1948; *Educ* Henley GS Henley-on-Thames, Univ of Manchester (BA); *m* 1, 1968 (m dis 1972), Helen, *née* Capewell; m 2, 1982 (m dis 2006) Emily Louise, *née* Goodrum; 2 da (Maybelle Evelyn b 22 Aug 1983, Agnes Annie Webb b 23 May 1986), 1 step da (Selena Cleo b 8 Aug 1978); m 3, 1 July 2006, Sandra Ross; 1 s (Sam George Thomas Ross-Laye b 5 Sept 1994); *Career* actor/dir 1972–75, dir ICA Theatre 1975–77, freelance photographer 1977–2000; AFAEP: Merit Award 1987, Gold, Silver and Merit Awards 1988; chm Assoc of Photographers 1990 (memb Cncl 1987–90); fndr memb and communications offr The Digital Communications Group (UK) 1996–98; new media dir Contact Design and Mktg 1996–99; founded image-access.net 2000; *Recreations* walking, jazz, technology; *Style—* Mike Laye; ✉ Le Bourg, Monsac 24440, France (tel and fax 08707 605020); image-access.net, Kings House, 14 Orchard Street, Bristol BS1 5EH (tel and fax 0870 760 5020, e-mail mail@image-access.net)

LAYTON, Alexander William; QC (1995); s of Paul Henry Layton (d 1989), of London, and Frances Evelyn, *née* Weekes (d 1996); *b* 23 February 1952; *Educ* Marlborough, BNC Oxford (MA), Ludwig-Maximilians-Univ Munich; *m* 1988, Sandy Forshaw, *née* Matheson; 2 da; *Career* called to the Bar Middle Temple 1976 (bencher 2004), asst recorder 1998–2000, recorder 2000–; chm: Br German Jurists' Assoc 1988–93, Bar European Gp 2005–; chm of tstees Inst of Int and Comparative Law 2005–; memb Commercial Bar Assoc (COMBAR); FCIArb 2000; *Books* The Bar on Trial (contrib, 1977), European Civil Practice (co-author, 1989, 2 edn 2004), Practitioners Handbook of EC Law (contrib, 1998); *Style—* Alexander Layton, Esq, QC; ✉ 20 Essex Street, London WC2R 3AL (tel 020 7842 1200, fax 020 7842 1270, e-mail alayton@20essexst.com)

LAYTON, Hon Christopher Walter; s of 1 Baron Layton, CH, CBE (d 1966); *b* 31 December 1929; *Educ* Oundle, King's Coll Cambridge; *m* 1, 1952 (m dis 1957), Anneliese Margarethe, da of Joachim von Thadden, of Hanover; 1 s, 1 da; m 2, 1961 (m dis), Margaret Ann, da of Leslie Moon; 3 da; m 3, 1995, Wendy Daniels, da of Kenneth Bartlett; 1 da; *Career* Intelligence Corps 1948–49; ICI Ltd 1952, The Economist Intelligence Unit 1953–54, editorial writer Euro affairs The Economist 1954–62; contested (Lib) Chippenham Parly election 1962, 1964 and 1966; econ advsr to Liberal Party 1962–69, personal asst to Jo Grimond, Liberal Party ldr 1962–64; dir Centre for European Industrial Studies Bath Univ 1968–71; Cmmn of Euro Communities: Chef de Cabinet to Cmmr Spinelli 1971–73, dir Computer Electronics, Telecommunications and Air Transport Equipment Manufacturing, Directorate-General of Internal Market and Industrial Affairs 1973–81, hon dir-gen EEC 1981–; dir World Order Project Federal Tst 1987–90; ed Alliance 1982–83, assoc ed New Democrat 1983–85; contested (SDP) London W Euro Parly Election 1984; fndr memb Grimstone Community 1990–; chm: Action for a Global Climate Community, Peace Building UK; *Publications* Transatlantic Investment (1966), European Advanced Technology (1968), Cross-frontier Mergers Europe (1970), Industry and Europe (jtly, 1971), Ten Innovations - International Study on Development Technology and the Use of Qualified Scientists and Engineers in Ten Industries (jtly, 1972), Europe and the Global Crisis (1987), A Step Beyond Fear (1989), The Healing of Europe (1990), A Community of the Willing: How Europe can lead the world's response to climate change (2001); *Recreations* painting, sculpture, music; *Style—* The Hon Christopher Layton

LAYTON, 3 Baron (UK 1947); Geoffrey Michael Layton; o s of 2 Baron Layton (d 1989), and Dorothy Rose, *née* Cross (d 1994); *b* 18 July 1947; *Educ* St Paul's, Stanford, Univ of Southern Calif; *m* 1, 1969 (m dis 1970), Viviane, da of François P Cracco, of Louvain, Belgium; m 2, 1989 (m dis 1999), Caroline Jane, da of William Thomas Mason, of Fairford, Glos, and formerly w of Adm Spyros Soulis, of Athens; *Heir* unc, Lt-Col the Hon David Layton, MBE; *Style—* The Rt Hon the Lord Layton

LAZAREV, Alexander; *Educ* St Petersburg Conservatory, Moscow Conservatory; *Career* conductor; fndr Ensemble of Soloists Bolshoi Theatre 1978, chief conductor and artistic dir Bolshoi Theatre 1987–95, chief conductor Royal Scottish Nat Orch 1997–2005 (princ guest conductor 1994–97); princ guest conductor BBC Symphony Orchestra 1992–95; Bolshoi debut 1973, UK debut with Royal Liverpool Philharmonic Orch 1987; worked with orchs incl: St Petersburg Philharmonic, USSR State Symphony, Berlin Philharmonic, Bavarian Radio Symphony, Royal Concertgebouw, Munich Philharmonic, Netherlands

Radio Philharmonic, Rotterdam Philharmonic, Orchestre National de France, Orchestra Sinfonica del Teatro alla Scala Milan, Orchestra Sinfonica dell'Accademia Nazionale di Santa Cecilia Rome, London Philharmonic, The Philharmonia, NHK Symphony Orch, Cleveland Orch, Montreal Symphony, Orchestre de la Suisse Romande; venues incl: Barbican Hall, Royal Festival Hall, Royal Albert Hall (BBC Proms annually 1991–), La Scala Milan, Edinburgh Festival, Metropolitan Opera NY, Theatre Royal de la Monnaie Brussels, Arena di Verona, Bavarian State Opera; various recordings on Melodiya, Virgin Classics, Sony Classical, Hyperion and Erato record labels; first prize USSR nat competition for conductors 1971, first prize and Gold medal Karajan Competition 1972; *Style*— Alexander Lazarev, Esq; ✉ c/o Tennant Artists, Unit 2, 39 Tadema Road, London SW10 0PZ (tel 020 7376 3758, fax 020 7351 0679)

LAZARIDIS, Stefanos; s of Nicholas Lazaridis (d 1982), and Alexandra, *née* Cardovillis; *b* 28 July 1942; *Educ* Greek Sch Addis Ababa, Ecole Internationale Geneva, Byam Shaw Sch of Art London, London Central Sch of Speech and Drama; *Career* stage designer and director; conslt designer for the film Testimony, dir and designer Duran Duran's 1993 North American tour, work has been featured in numerous exhibitions; worked with many leading dir incl: David Pountney, Graham Vick, Jonathan Miller, Steven Pimlott, Yuri Lyubimov, Nicholas Hytner, John Copley, Patrick Garland, John Cox, Colin Graham, Keith Warner, Tim Albery, Phyllida Lloyd; artistic dir and gen mangr Greek Nat Opera 2006–; RDI 2003; *Theatre* prof debut Eccentricities of A Nightingale (Yvonne Arnaud Theatre) 1967; other credits incl: The Possessed (London, Paris, Milan Bologna), Little Tragedies (Bologna and Rome), Moscow Gold (RSC), The Taming of The Shrew (RSC Stratford and Barbican), The Mitford Girls (London and Chichester Festival), Enemy of the People (Chichester Festival), A Doll's House (Watford Palace Theatre); *Opera* since 1970 over 30 prodns for ENO incl: Rusalka, Doctor Faust, Lady Macbeth of Mtsensk, Hansel and Gretel, Macbeth, Wozzeck, The Adventures of Mr Broucek, Madam Butterfly, The Mikado, Werther, Italian Season 2000; designs for Royal Opera House incl: Le nozze di Figaro, Idomeneo, Wozzeck, Der Ring des Nibelungen; opera credits abroad incl: Fidelio (Stuttgart), Rigoletto and Tosca (Maggio Musicale, Florence), Tristan und Isolde (Bologna), Ariane et Barbe-Bleue (Krefeld), Don Carlos (San Francisco), La fanciulla del West (Milan, Turin, Tokyo and Zurich), The Turn of the Screw (Brussels), Rigoletto and Lucia di Lammermoor (Tel Aviv), The Nose (Amsterdam), Carmen (arena prodn, Tokyo, Melbourne, Sydney, Berlin, Munich, Zurich), Cavalleria rusticana and I pagliacci (Staatsoper Berlin), Moïse et Pharaon (1997 Rossini Festival Pesaro), Julietta (Opera North and Prague), Macbeth (Zurich), A Midsummer Night's Dream (Venice); prodns for Bregenz Festival incl: Der fliegende Holländer, Nabucco and Fidelio (all lake stage), The Greek Passion (indoor stage and ROH); Katya Kabanova, Faust (Bayerische Staatsoper), Lohengrin (Bayreuth Festival); dir and designer credits incl: Oedipus Rex (Opera North), Maria Stuarda, Oedipus Rex, Bluebeard's Castle (all Scottish Opera), Orphée et Eurydice (Aust Opera), Dimitriadis's The Ark of Life (Athens); overall concept and individual design Italian opera season (ENO); *Ballet* for Royal Ballet incl: El Amor Brujo (choreographer Peter Wright, *qv*), Knight Errant (choreographer Antony Tudor); *Awards* incl: Soc of West End Theatre Best Designer for The Mitford Girls 1981, Doctor Faust and The Mikado 1986, German Critics' Award for Ariane et Barbe-Bleue 1986, Olivier Award nomination for The Coronation of Poppea 2001, Olivier Award nomination for Outstanding Achievement in Opera for Italian Season; jt winner Evening Standard Opera Award and Olivier Award to ENO prodn of Lady Macbeth of Mtsensk & Hansel and Gretel 1987, Designer of the Year Opernwelt Germany for Julietta and The Turn of the Screw 1998, Dip of Honour Int Exhibition of Stage Design (Prague) for The Turn of the Screw and Katya Kabanova 1999, winner special medal from the Martinu Fndn 2000, Olivier Award for the Greek Passion 2001 and Wozzeck 2002; *Recreations* travel, reading; *Style*— Stefanos Lazaridis, Esq, RDI; ✉ 9 Kydathinaion Str, 10558 Athens, Greece (e-mail stefanos_lazaridis@hotmail.com); Greek National Opera, Olympia Theatre, 59 Akidimias Str, 10679 Athens, Greece (e-mail artisticdirector@nationalopera.gr)

LAZAROWICZ, Mark; MP; *b* 8 August 1953, Romford, Essex; *Educ* Univ of St Andrews (MA), Univ of Edinburgh (LLB); *m*; 4 c; *Career* MP (Lab) Edinburgh N and Leith 2001–; memb: Regulatory Reform Select Ctee, Environment, Food and Rural Affrs Select Ctee, Modernisation Ctee 2005–; chair All Pty Debt and Personal Fin Gp 2003–, memb Co-op Pty; *Style*— Mark Lazarowicz, Esq, MP; ✉ House of Commons, London SW1A 0AA

LAZENBY, David William; CBE (2002); s of George William Lazenby, of Walton-on-Thames, Surrey, and Jane, *née* Foster; *b* 13 October 1937; *Educ* Canford Sch, Battersea Coll of Technol, Imperial Coll London (DIC), City Univ London (Dip, CU); *m* 2 Sept 1961, Valerie Ann, da of Lewis Edward Kent, OBE (d 1972); 1 s (Jonathan b 22 Jan 1965), 1 da (Andrea b 23 Feb 1968); *Career* dir Andrews Kent & Stone Ltd consulting engrs 1983–97 (joined 1962, ptnr 1972, chm 1983); dir BSI 1998–2003 (memb Bd 1997–2003); memb Cncl ISO 1998–2004, vice-pres European Standards Body CEN 1999–2003; civil and structural engrg work includes: Nat Library of Wales, Merchant Navy Coll, East Sussex Co Hall; Eur Ing, Hon FCGI, FICE, FIStructE (past pres); *Books* Cutting for Construction (1978), Structural Mechanics for Students (1984), 1936/85 Structural Steelwork for Students (jtly, 1985); *Recreations* travel, tennis, opera, good food and wine; *Style*— Eur Ing David Lazenby, CBE; ✉ Pond Cottage, 28 Sanger Drive, Send, Woking, Surrey GU23 7EB (tel 01483 223104, fax 01483 225880, e-mail davidwlazenby@aol.com)

LAZENBY, Terence Michael (Terry); s of Ernest Lazenby (d 1990), and Joyce, *née* Spice (d 1987); *b* 29 November 1942; *Educ* King's Sch Macclesfield, Univ of Swansea (BSc), Stanford Univ (MSc), Cert Dip of Fin and Accounting; *m* 1971, Eleanor Jane, da of James Livingston Ritchie; 1 s (Simon James b 1975), 1 da (Sarah Jane b 1977); *Career* BP plc (formerly British Petroleum Co plc before merger 1998): univ apprentice 1961–64, technologist 1964–71, process engr 1971–77, engrg mangr Sullom Voe Project 1979–81, tech div mangr BP Developments Aust 1981–84, works gen mangr BP Chemicals Grangemouth 1984–88, dir of mfrg and supply BP Oil UK Ltd 1988–90, gen mangr BP Engrg 1990–92, mangr BP Research and Engrg Site 1993, chief engr BP Int 1994–99; chm: Br Pipeline Agency 1988–98, ACTIVE 1996–2002, Railtrack/Jarvis Alliance 2000–01, NTO Gp for Engrg 2000–, UMITEK Ltd 2001–05, Portsmouth Water Ltd 2002–, Engineering Construction Industry Trg Bd 2005–; non-exec dir: Expo Int Group plc 2003–, MTL Instruments Group plc; assurance mangr Br Museum 2000–02; visiting prof of process integration UMIST; memb Senate Engrg Cncl 1996–98; Lt-Col (ELSC); FInstPet 1991, FIChemE 1992, FREng 1995; *Recreations* golf, swimming, gardening; *Style*— Terry Lazenby, Esq, FREng; ✉ Seamab, Woodland Drive, East Horsley, Surrey KT24 5AN (tel 01483 284232, e-mail terrylazenby@terrylazenby.plus.com)

LE BRUN, Christopher Mark; s of John Le Brun, BEM, QSM, RM (d 1970), of Portsmouth, Hants, and Eileen Betty, *née* Miles; *b* 20 December 1951; *Educ* Southern GS Portsmouth, Slade Sch of Fine Art (DFA), Chelsea Sch of Art (MA); *m* 31 March 1979, Charlotte Eleanor, da of Gp Capt Hugh Beresford Verity, DSO, DFC, of Richmond, Surrey; 2 s (Luke b 1984, Edmund b 1990), 1 da (Lily b 1986); *Career* artist; prof of drawing Royal Acad Schs 2000–02; awards and cmmns: prizewinner John Moores Liverpool Exhibitions 1978 and 1980, Calouste Gulbenkian Fndn Printmakers Commission Award 1983, designer Ballet Imperial Royal Opera House Covent Garden 1985; DAAD Fellowship Berlin 1987–88, Jerusalem Tst Commn Liverpool Cathedral 1996; tstee: Tate Gallery 1990–95, Nat Gallery 1996–2003, Dulwich Picture Gallery 2000–05, Prince's Drawing Sch 2004–; RA 1997; *Solo Exhibitions* incl: Nigel Greenwood Gallery London 1980, 1982, 1985 and 1989, Gillespie-Laage-Salomon Paris 1981, Sperone Westwater NY 1983, 1986 and 1988, Fruitmarket Gallery Edinburgh 1985, Arnolfini Gallery Bristol 1985, Kunsthalle Basel 1986, DAAD Galerie Berlin 1988, Galerie Rudolf Zwirner Cologne 1988, Art Center Pasadena 1992, LA Louver Los Angeles 1992, Marlborough Fine Art London 1994, 1998 and 2001, Astrup Fearnley MOMA Oslo 1995, Fitzwilliam Museum Cambridge 1995, Courtauld Gallery 1997, Marlborough Chelsea New York 2004; *Group Exhibitions* incl: Nuova Imagine Milan Triennale 1980, Sydney Biennale 1982, New Art (Tate Gallery London) 1983, An Int Survey of Recent Painting and Sculpture (MOMA NY) 1984, The British Show (toured Australia and NZ) 1985, Paris Biennale 1985, San Francisco Biennale 1986, Venice Biennale 1982 and 1984, Falls the Shadow (Recent Br and Euro Art Hayward Gallery London) 1986, British Art of the 1980's (MOMA0: Oxford, Budapest, Warsaw, Prague) 1987, Avant Garde in the Eighties (LA County Museum) 1987, Br Art of the 1980's (Liljevalchs Museum Stockholm) 1987, The Br Picture (Louver Gallery LA) 1988, New Br Painting (Cincinnati Museum and American tour) 1988–89, Br Art Now (Setagaya Art Museum and Japanese tour) 1990–91, Contemporary Br Art in Print (Scottish Nat Gallery of Modern Art and American tour) 1995–96, Encounters (Nat Gallery London) 2000, Contemporary Voices (MOMA NY) 2005; *Style*— Christopher Le Brun, Esq, RA; ✉ c/o Royal Academy of Arts, Piccadilly, London W1J 0BD

LE CARPENTIER, Francis Stewart; s of Frank Henry Le Carpentier (d 2001), of Worthing, W Sussex, and Elizabeth, *née* Stafford (d 1961); *b* 26 February 1949; *Educ* Royal Wolverhampton Sch; *m* 2 July 1976 (m dis 1991), Nicole Madeleine Fischer Corderior, da of Willey Fischer, of Brussels; 1 s (Phillipe Alexandre), 1 da (Mercedes Elizabeth); *Career* offr US Armed Forces 1969–74, served Europe and Far East; retail mangr until 1969, gp sales dir Int Property Developers 1974, chm and chief exec Paramount Group 1975–91; chief exec TFL Defence Gp of cos based in UK, North America, Africa1991–; FInstD 1989 (MInstD 1988); *Recreations* skiing, shooting (not animals), motorsports and powercraft racing; *Clubs* Annabel's (London), various in rest of world; *Style*— Francis Le Carpentier, Esq; ✉ El Morapio, Calle 15D, Casa 6D, Las Brisas, Nueva Andalucia, Marbella, Malaga, Spain (tel 00 34 95 281 2627, fax 00 34 95 281 3505, e-mail francistfl@aol.com)

LE CARRÉ, John (pen name of David John Moore Cornwell); s of Ronald Thomas Archibald Cornwell, and Olive, *née* Glassy; *b* 19 October 1931; *Educ* Sherborne, Univ of Berne, Lincoln Coll Oxford (BA); *m* 1, 1954 (m dis 1971), Alison Ann Veronica Sharp; 3 s; m 2, 1972, Valerie Jane Eustace; 1 s; *Career* novelist; schoolmaster Eton 1956–58, British Foreign Serv 1960–64 (serv as second sec Bonn then political consul Hamburg); Grand Master Award Mystery Writers of America, Malaparte Prize Italy, Crime Writers' Assoc Diamond Dagger Award 1988; subject of Time and Newsweek cover stories and work subject of many books; Hon DLitt: Univ of Exeter 1990, Univ of St Andrews 1996, Univ of Southampton 1997, Univ of Bath 1998; hon fell Lincoln Coll Oxford 1984; Commandeur d l'Ordre des Arts et des Lettres 2005; *Books* Call for the Dead (1961, filmed as the Deadly Affair 1967), A Murder of Quality (1962, TV film prize winner at Venice Prix Italia 1991), The Spy Who Came in From the Cold (1963, film, Somerset Maugham Award, Crime Writers' Assoc Golden Dagger Award, Best Mystery of the Year Mystery Writers of America Inc), The Looking Glass War (1965, film), A Small Town in Germany (1968), The Naïve and Sentimental Lover (1971), Tinker, Tailor, Soldier, Spy (1974, BBC TV series), The Honourable Schoolboy (1977, James Tait Black Meml Prize, Crime Writers' Assoc Golden Dagger Award), Smiley's People (1980, BBC TV series), The Little Drummer Girl (1983, Warner Bros film), A Perfect Spy (1986, BBC TV series), The Russia House (1989, film, Nikos Kasanzakis Prize 1991), The Secret Pilgrim (1990), The Night Manager (1993), Our Game (1995), The Tailor of Panama (1996, film 2000), Single and Single (1999); The Karla Trilogy (Smiley's People, Tinker, Tailor, Soldier, Spy and The Honourable Schoolboy) published in one volume as The Quest for Karla, The Constant Gardener (2001, film 2005), Absolute Friends (2004); *Style*— John le Carré, Esq; ✉ c/o David Higham Associates, 5–8 Lower John Street, Golden Square, London W1F 9HA (tel 020 7434 5900, fax 020 7437 1072)

LE FANU, Mark; OBE (1994); s of Adm of the Fleet Sir Michael Le Fanu (d 1970), and Prudence, *née* Morgan (d 1980); *b* 14 November 1946; *Educ* Winchester, Univ of Sussex (BA), Coll of Law; *m* 1976, Lucy Rhoda, da of John Cowen (d 1982), of Bisley, Glos; 3 s (Thomas b 1980, Matthew b 1982, Caspar b 1986), 1 da (Celia b 1985); *Career* Lt RN 1964–73; slr McKenna & Co 1973–78; Soc of Authors 1979– (gen sec 1982–); *Recreations* sailing, golf; *Style*— Mark Le Fanu, Esq, OBE; ✉ 25 St James's Gardens, London W11 4RE (tel 020 7603 4119); Society of Authors, 84 Drayton Gardens, London SW10 9SB (tel 020 7373 6642)

LE FLEMING, Sir David Kelland; 13 Bt (E 1705), of Rydal, Westmorland; elder s of Sir Quentin John le Fleming, 12 Bt (d 1995), and Judith Ann, *née* Peck; *b* 12 January 1976; *Educ* Queen Elizabeth Coll Palmerston North, Wellington Poly (BA, VCDN); *Heir* bro, Andrew le Fleming; *Career* freelance graphic designer and artist; *Recreations* sculpting, oil painting, fishing; *Style*— Sir David le Fleming, Bt; ✉ 250 Colyton Road, RO 5, Feilding, Manawatu, New Zealand

LE GALLAIS, Brig Charles Lyle; CBE (2001, OBE 1994); s of Sir Richard Le Gallais (d 1983), and Juliette, *née* Forsythe; *b* 11 February 1953; *Educ* Sherborne, RMA Sandhurst, RMCS Shrivenham; *m* 12 June 1976, Jacqueline, *née* Emerson; 2 s (James b 29 Dec 1979, Richard b 13 April 1982); *Career* regtl duties 1972–92 (despatches 1986), CO 15 Signal Regt NI 1992–94, Central Staff MOD 1995–96, cmd Royal Sch of Signals 1997–98, RCDS 1999, Dir Jt Mil Affrs Bosnia 2000, cmd 11 Signal Bde 2001–04; with Westland Helicopters Ltd 2004–; *Recreations* hill walking, rural conservation; *Clubs* Special Forces; *Style*— Brig Charles Le Gallais, CBE; ✉ The Old Vicarage, Isle Abbotts, Taunton, Somerset TA3 6RH

LE GOY, Raymond Edgar Michel; s of Jean Andre Stanhope Nemorin Michel Le Goy (d 1966), of Mauritius, and May, *née* Callan (d 1976); *b* 20 April 1919; *Educ* William Ellis Sch, Gonville & Caius Coll Cambridge (MA, sec Cambridge Union); *m* 27 Aug 1960, (Silvia) Ernestine, da of Philip Luther Burnett (d 1947), of Trelawny, Jamaica; 2 s (Keith b 1962, Mark b 1964); *Career* Br Army: joined 1940, cmmnd 1941, Staff Capt HQ E Africa 1943–45, Maj 1945; London Passenger Transport Bd 1947, UK civil servant 1947–, princ 1948, asst sec 1958, under sec 1968; dir-gen for Transport EEC 1973–81, a dir-gen Cmmn of the EU 1982–; chm Union of Univ Liberal Soc 1939–40; FCIT; *Books* The Victorian Burletta (1953); *Recreations* theatre, music, race relations; *Clubs* Oxford and Cambridge, National Liberal; *Style*— Raymond Le Goy, Esq

LE GRAND, Julian Ernest Michael; s of Roland John Le Grand (d 1976), of Taunton, Somerset, and Eileen Joan, *née* Baker (d 2006); *b* 29 May 1945; *Educ* Eton, Univ of Sussex (BA), Univ of Pennsylvania (PhD); *m* 19 June 1971, Damaris May, da of Rev Nigel Robertson-Glasgow, of Fakenham, Norfolk; 2 da (Polly b 1978, Zoe b 1981); *Career* lectr in economics: Univ of Sussex 1971–78, LSE 1978–85; sr res fell LSE 1985–87, prof of public policy Univ of Bristol 1987–92, Richard Titmuss prof of social policy LSE 1993–; sr policy advsr 10 Downing Street 2003–05; memb Avon Family Health Serv Authy 1990–95, non-exec dir Avon HA 1994–95, vice-chm Frenchay NHS Healthcare Tst 1996–99, cmmr Cmmn for Health Improvement 1999–2003; conslt: OECD, Euro Cmmn, WHO, World Bank, NAO, Dept of Health, HM Treasy, BBC; chm Health England Dept of Health 2006–, chm Social Care Practices Working Gp DfES 2006–07; ESRC: memb Social Affrs Ctee 1982–86, memb Research Grants Bd 1988–92; sr assoc Kings Fund; Hon DLitt Univ of Sussex; founding AcSS; Hon FFPHM; *Books* The Economics of Social Problems (with R Robinson, 1976, 3 edn 1992), The Strategy of Equality (1982), Privatisation and the Welfare State (ed with R Robinson, 1984), Not Only the Poor (with R Goodin, 1987), Market Socialism (ed with S Estrin, 1989), Equity and Choice (1991),

Quasi-Markets and Social Policy (ed with W Bartlett, 1993), Evaluating the NHS Reforms (ed with R Robinson, 1994), Learning from the NHS Internal Market (ed with N Mays and J Mulligan, 1998), Health Care and Cost Containment in the European Union (ed with E Mossialos, 1999), Motivation, Agency and Public Policy (2003); *Recreations* drawing, reading; *Style*— Mr Julian Le Grand; ✉ 31 Sydenham Hill, Cotham, Bristol BS6 5SL (tel and fax 0117 944 2476); London School of Economics and Political Science, Houghton Street, London WC2A 2AE (tel 020 7955 7353, fax 020 7955 7415, e-mail j.legrand@lse.ac.uk)

LE GRICE, (Andrew) Valentine; QC (2002); s of Charles Le Grice (d 1982), of Penzance, Cornwall, and Wilmay, *née* Ward (d 2007); *b* 26 June 1953; *Educ* Shrewsbury, Collingwood Coll Durham (BA); *m* 1, 17 Dec 1977 (m dis 2000), Anne Elizabeth, da of Philip Moss, of Great Bookham, Surrey; 2 s (Charles b 8 Oct 1984, Philip b 16 Aug 1986), 1 da (Alexandra b 24 Nov 1989); m 2, 1 May 2001, Jayne Elizabeth, da of late Dr Brian Sandford-Hill, and Eira Sandford-Hill, of Cardiff; 1 da (Blanche b 9 Oct 2002); *Career* called to the Bar Middle Temple 1977; *Recreations* watching sport, throwing things away; *Clubs* Travellers; *Style*— Valentine Le Grice, Esq, QC; ✉ 1 Hare Court, Temple, London EC4Y 7BE

LE MARCHANT, Sir Francis Arthur; 6 Bt (UK 1841), of Chobham Place, Surrey; s of Sir Denis Le Marchant, 5 Bt (d 1987), and Elizabeth Rowena, *née* Worth; *b* 6 October 1939; *Educ* Gordonstoun, Royal Acad Schs; *Heir* kinsman, Michael Le Marchant; *Career* farmer and painter; solo exhibitions include Agnews, Sally Hunter Fine Art, Roy Miles 1996, Evansville Museum of Art Indiana 1998, Baring Asset Mgmnt at ING Bank 2005; mixed exhibitions include Royal Academy Summer Exhibitions, Leicester Galleries, Bilan de l'Art Contomerain Paris, Spink & Co "Ten at Spink"; *Clubs* Savile; *Style*— Sir Francis Le Marchant, Bt; ✉ c/o Midland Bank, 88 Westgate, Grantham, Lincolnshire

LE MAY, Malcolm John; s of John Francis Le May, and Janet Bill; *b* 24 July 1958, Kent; *Educ* St Olave's and St Saviour's GS for Boys, UCNW Bangor; *m* 10 Sept 1983, Sarah, *née* McCormack; 3 s (Alexander Gilmour, Henry Graham, Oliver William); *Career* Arthur Andersen & Co 1979–83, Morgan Grenfell plc 1983–86, Drexel Burnham Lambert 1986–90, BZW Ltd 1990–95, UBS AG 1995–98, ING 1998–2001, Morley plc 2001–03, JER Partners 2003–; non-exec dir: Royal & Sun Alliance plc, Pendragon plc; ACA 1982; *Recreations* shooting, tennis, golf, bridge; *Style*— Malcolm Le May, Esq; ✉ JER Partners, Clarges House, 6–12 Clarges Street, London W1J 8AD (tel 020 7518 4350)

LE MÉTAIS, Dr Joanna Petra Fransisca Maria; da of Peter Joseph Bevers, of St Agnes, S Aust, and Geertruda Petronella, *née* van der Zanden; *b* 2 January 1949; *Educ* Loreto Abbey Victoria Aust, Croydon Tech Coll, Gipsy Hill Coll Kingston upon Thames (CertEd, BEd), Université de Caen (Diplôme d'Études Françaises), Inst of Linguists (final level French), Brunel Univ (MA, PhD); *m* 2 Sept 1972 (m dis 1980), Michel Philippe Alfred Le Métais, s of Alfred Le Métais, of Vimoutiers, France; *Career* dep head Modern Languages Dept Redstone Sch Surrey 1974–76 (French teacher 1973–76), head Languages Dept Raynes Park HS 1976–82, pt/t adult educn teacher 1978–79, professional asst Educn Dept London Borough of Hounslow 1982–84; Nat Fndn for Educnl Research: dep head Info Dept and dir EPIC Europe (Educn Policy Info Centre for Europe) 1984–97, head Nat Unit EURYDICE (educn policy info network in the European Community) 1984–97, dir Int Centre 1997–2000, head Int Project Devpt 2000–04, dir Le Metais Consltg 2004–; external examiner: Univ of London 1977–81, SE Regnl Examination Bd 1977 and 1978; pres Merton Branch Nat Assoc of Schoolmasters Union of Women Teachers 1980 (vice-pres 1979), tstee Inst of Linguists Educnl Tst 1988–90, memb Int Ctee Soc of Educn Offrs 1991–98, memb Exec Ctee UK Forum for Int Educn and Trg 1994–2004, memb Advsy Gp Teacher Mobility, Brain Drain, Labour Markets and Educnl Resources in the Cwlth 2003–, quality assessor HEFCE 1995–96, project dir Int Review of Curriculum and Assessment Frameworks 1996–, memb Exec Ctee Br Assoc for Int and Comparative Educn 1998–2004; memb Editorial Advsy Bd Int Electronic Jl for Leadership in Learning 1997–; overseas expert Visiting Cmmn Netherlands 1992, attended UNESCO Int Forum for solidarity against intolerance Tbilisi Georgia 1995; life memb Sail Trg Assoc 1990–; Hon DEd Brunel Univ 2000; MIMgt 1985–89, MInstD 1989–95, FRSA 1979, FIL 1986 (MIL 1978, memb Cncl 1987–90, chm Cncl 1988–90); *Publications* Communication and Culture: Foreign Languages in and out of the Curriculum (ed, 1988), The Impact on the Education Service of Teacher Mobility (1990), The Search for Standards (contrib, 1992), Performance-related Pay in Education (contrib, 1992), The Supply and Recruitment of Teachers (contrib, 1993), Teachers' Salaries in France, Germany and Scotland (1994), Effective Governors for Effective Schools (contrib, 1995), Legislating for Change: School Reforms in England and Wales 1979–1994 (1995), Values and Aims in Curriculum and Assessment Frameworks (1997), INCA: The International Review of Curriculum and Assessment Frameworks Archive (CD-Rom, jtly, 1998, published online 2000, 4 edn 2004), Values and Aims in Curriculum and Assessment Systems: a 16 nation review (in Curriculum in Context, 1998), Approaches to Comparology (1999), Strategic Market Research: A Study of Overseas Services (jtly, 1999), The Democratic Curriculum: Developments in England 1944–1999 (2000), School Curriculum Differences across the UK: Report to the British Broadcasting Corporation (jtly, 2001, also published online), International Developments in Upper Secondary Education: Context, Provision and Issues (2002, also published online), A Europe of Differences: Educational Responses for Interculturalism (ed, 2002), International Trends in Primary Education (2003, also published online), Secondary Education at the Crossroads: International Perspectives Relevant to Asia-Pacific Region (contrib, 2006), Learning and Teaching for the 21st Century (contrib, 2007); *Recreations* people, travel, pottery; *Style*— Dr Joanna Le Métais; ✉ Le Metais Consulting, 19 Geffers Ride, Ascot, Berkshire SL5 7JY (tel 01344 622910, e-mail joanna@lemetais.co.uk)

LE PARD, Geoffrey; s of Desmond Allen Le Pard, of Sway, Lymington, and Barbara Grace, *née* Francis; *b* 30 November 1956; *Educ* Purley GS, Brockenhurst GS, Univ of Bristol (LLB); *m* 19 May 1984, Linda Ellen, da of Leslie Jones, of Costessey, Norwich; 1 s (Samuel William b 23 April 1990), 1 da (Jennifer Grace b 8 Feb 1993); *Career* slr specialising in commercial property law, property devpt, and landlord and tenant law; articled clerk Corbould Rigby & Co 1979–81, ptnr Freshfields 1987– (asst slr 1981–87); memb: City of London Slrs Co, Anglo American Real Property Inst; *Recreations* cycling, walking long distance footpaths, watching any sport, theatre, good food, gardening, being a dad; *Style*— Geoffrey Le Pard, Esq; ✉ Freshfields, 65 Fleet Street, London EC4Y 1HS (tel 020 7936 4000)

LE ROUX, François; s of Pierre Le Roux, and Claudie, *née* Blanchard; *b* 30 October 1955; *Educ* Madagascar, Univ of Tours; *Career* baritone; studied with François Loup then Opera Studio Paris with Vera Rosza and Elizabeth Grümmer, winner Maria Canals competition Barcelona 1978 and Rio de Janeiro 1979; memb Lyon Opera Co 1980–85, given numerous recitals at various international venues; given masterclasses at: Atelier de l'Opera and Conservatoire Superieur Lyon, Cleveland Inst of Music Ohio 1992, Helsinki Sibelius Acad Finland 1994, 1995 and 1996; *Performances* with Lyons Opera incl: Papageno in The Magic Flute, Figaro in The Barber of Seville, Lescaut in Manon, Pelléas in Pelléas et Mélisande; at Royal Opera House Covent Garden incl: Lescaut 1987, Papageno 1988, Dandini in La Cenerentola 1989 and 1994, Figaro in The Barber of Seville 1991, world premiere of Birtwistle's Gawain 1991 (also in 1994), Dr Malatesta in Don Pasquale 1992, Pelléas 1993, Mercutio in Gounod Romeo and Juliet 1994; others incl: Pelléas (Paris 1985, La Scala Milan 1986, Edinburgh 1986, Vienna Staatsoper 1988, LA 1995, Venice 1995), Ramiro in L'Heure Espagnole (Glyndebourne debut) 1987, title role in Don Giovanni (Paris 1987 for which awarded Critics' Union Prize, Zurich 1989), Count Almaviva in Le Nozze di Figaro (Trieste) 1986, Marcello in La Bohème (Hamburg) 1987, Oreste in Iphigenie en Tauride (Frankfurt) 1987 and (Athens) 1993, Der Prinz von Homburg (Munich 1992 and 1993, Antwerp and Ghent 1995), John Ruskin in world premiere of David Lang's Modern Painters (Santa Fe Opera) 1995; *Recordings* incl: Debussy Pelléas et Mélisande (under Claudio Abbado, DGG), Chabrier L'Étoile (under John Eliot Gardiner, EMI), Poulenc Dialogues of the Carmelites (under Kent Nagano, Virgin), Cimarosa Il Matrimonio Segreto (under Jesus Lopez-Cobos, Cascavelle), Duparc complete songs (REM), Fauré complete songs (REM), La Fontaine Fables in Music (EMI, winner French Academy Award), L'Invitation au Voyage (French songs with orch under John Nelson, EMI), Poulenc songs with ensemble (under Charles Dutoit, DECCA); *Style*— M François Le Roux; ✉ website www.francoisleroux.net

LEA, Anthony William (Tony); s of George Frederick Lea (d 1995), and Elaine Constance, *née* Oman (d 1996); *b* 30 November 1948, Johannesburg, South Africa; *Educ* Michaelhouse Natal, Univ of the Witwatersrand Johannesburg (BA); *m* 2 Aug 1986, Clare, da of William Frederick Harries; 1 s (James Frederick b 1988), 1 da (Camilla Rose b 1990); *Career* Anglo American Gp: joined 1972, dir Anglo American Corporation of SA 1987–, fin dir Minorco SA, 1988–91, exec dir Minorco SA 1992–98, fin dir Anglo American plc 1998–2005, chm Merrill Lynch World Mining Tst plc 2006–; *Recreations* country pursuits; *Clubs* Reform, Inanda (Johannesburg); *Style*— Tony Lea, Esq

LEA, Prof Peter John; s of Dr Alan Joseph Lea (d 1983), of Tamworth, and Jessie, *née* Farrall (d 1997); *b* 1 December 1944; *Educ* Arnold Sch Blackpool, Univ of Liverpool (BSc, PhD, DSc); *m* 30 July 1965, Christine, *née* Shaw; 1 da (Julia b 5 Dec 1966); *Career* res fell Royal Soc 1972–75, princ scientific offr Rothamsted Experimental Station Harpenden Herts 1978–84 (sr scientific offr 1975–78); Lancaster Univ: prof of biology 1985–, head Div of Biological Scis 1988–91, dean 1994–96; chm Phytochemical Soc Europe 1988–94 (sec 1982–87), sec Soc Experimental Biology 1998–2001, pres Assoc of Applied Biologists 2006–; FIBiol; *Books* incl: The Genetic Manipulation of Plants and its Application to Agriculture (with G R Stewart, 1984), The Biochemistry of Plant Phenolics (with C F van Sumere, 1986), Biologically Active Natural Products (with K Hostettmann, 1987), Methods in Plant Biochemistry (1989, 1993), The Biochemistry of Plants (with B J Miflin, 1990), Plant Biochemistry and Molecular Biology (with R C Leegood, 1993, 1998), Plant Nitrogen (with J F Morot-Gaudry, 2001); *Recreations* cricket, collecting wedgwood pottery; *Style*— Prof Peter Lea; ✉ The Old School, Chapel Lane, Ellel, Lancaster LA2 0PW (tel 01524 751156); Lancaster University, Division of Biological Sciences, Bailrigg, Lancaster LA1 4YQ (tel 01524 592104, fax 01524 843854, e-mail p.lea@lancaster.ac.uk)

LEA, Ruth Jane; da of Thomas Lea, of Warburton, Cheshire, and Jane, *née* Brown (decd); *b* 22 September 1947; *Educ* Lymm GS, Univ of York (BA), Univ of Bristol (MSc); *Career* HM Treasy 1970–73, lectr in economics Thames Poly (now Univ of Greenwich) 1973–74, Civil Serv Coll 1974–77, HM Treasy 1977–78, CSO 1978–84, DTI 1984–87, Invest in Britain Bureau DTI 1987–88, Mitsubishi Bank 1988–93 (rising to chief economist), chief UK economist Lehman Brothers 1993–94, economics ed ITN 1994–95, head Policy Unit IOD 1995–2003, dir Centre for Policy Studies 2004–, dir Global Vision 2007–; non-exec dir Arbuthnot Banking Gp 2005–; memb: RPI Advsy Ctee 1992–94, Nat Consumer Cncl 1993–96, Rowntree Fndn Income and Wealth Inquiry Gp 1993–94, Nurses' Pay Review Body 1994–98, Research Centres Bd ESRC 1996, Research Priorities Bd 1996–97, Statistics Advsy Ctee Office of Nat Statistics 1996–97, Nott Cmmn on the £ Sterling 1999; judge numerous awards on econ and business issues; author numerous research papers and articles on econ and business issues; memb Cncl Univ of London 2001–06, govr LSE 2003–; Hon DBA Univ of Greenwich; memb: Soc of Business Economists 1988, Royal Economic Soc 1994 (memb Cncl 1995–2000); FRSA 1993, FSS 1996; *Recreations* music, natural history and countryside, heritage, philately; *Clubs* Reform; *Style*— Miss Ruth Lea; ✉ 25 Redbourne Avenue, Finchley, London N3 2BP (tel 020 8346 3482); Centre for Policy Studies, 57 Tufton Street, London SW1P 3QL (tel 020 7222 4488, fax 020 7222 4388)

LEA, Sir Thomas William; 5 Bt (UK 1892), of The Larches, Kidderminster, Worcestershire, and Sea Grove, Dawlish, Devon; eldest s of Sir (Thomas) Julian Lea, 4 Bt (d 1990), and Gerry Valerie, o da of late Capt Gibson Clarence Fahnestock, USAF; *b* 6 September 1973; *Educ* Uppingham; *Heir* bro, Alexander Lea; *Style*— Sir Thomas Lea, Bt

LEA OF CRONDALL, Baron (Life Peer UK 1999), of Crondall in the County of Hampshire; David Edward Lea; OBE (1978); s of Edward Cunliffe Lea, of Tyldesley, Lancs; *b* 2 November 1937; *Educ* Farnham GS, Christ's Coll Cambridge (MA); *Career* asst gen sec TUC 1978–99; *Style*— The Lord Lea of Crondall, OBE

LEACH, Clive William; CBE (2000); s of Stanely Aubrey Leach, of Kessingland, Suffolk, and Laura Anne, *née* Robinson; *b* 4 December 1934; *Educ* Sir John Leman Sch Beccles, Univ of Birmingham; *m* 1, 25 Oct 1958; 3 s (Christopher b 1959, Stuart b 1961, Adrian b 1964); m 2, 25 Sept 1980, Stephanie Miriam, da of Patrick McGinn, of Sidmouth, Devon; 1 s (Damian b 1981); *Career* gen sales mangr Tyne Tees Television 1968–74, dir of sales and mktg Trident Television 1979–82 (sales dir 1974–79), md Link Television 1982–85; Yorkshire Television Ltd: dir of sales and mktg 1985–88, md 1988–93, chm Yorkshire Television Enterprises Ltd 1988–94 (md 1985–88), chm Yorkshire Television International Ltd 1988–94; Yorkshire-Tyne Tees Television Holdings: gp chief exec 1992–94, gp chm 1993–94; dir: ITN 1988–93, New Era Television 1988–93; chm: Leeds TEC Ltd 1991–2000, Yorkshire Enterprise Gp Ltd 1995–, Leeds HA 1996–2000, Gabriel Communications Ltd 1997–, Yorkshire Cultural Consortium 2001–, West Yorkshire LSC; played first class cricket for Warks 1955–57, also for Durham and Bucks counties; MCIM, FRSA; *Recreations* golf, travel, entertaining; *Clubs* Warks County Cricket, MCC, Alwoodley Golf, Reform; *Style*— C W Leach, Esq, CBE; ✉ The White House, Barkston Ash, Tadcaster, North Yorkshire LS24 9TT

LEADBETTER, Dr Alan James; CBE (1994); s of Robert Pickavant Leadbetter (d 1989), and Edna, *née* Garlick; *b* 28 March 1934; *Educ* Univ of Liverpool (BSc, PhD), Univ of Bristol (DSc); *m* 23 Oct 1957, (Jean) Brenda, da of Percy Williams (d 1966); 1 s (Andrew Robert b 1 Aug 1964), 1 da (Jane b 22 Dec 1966); *Career* postdoctoral research fell Nat Res Cncl Canada Ottawa 1957–59; Univ of Bristol Sch of Chemistry: research asst 1959–62, lectr 1962–72, reader in physical chemistry 1972–74; prof of physical chemistry Univ of Exeter 1975–82; SERC: assoc dir Science Bd and head Neutron Div 1982–87, assoc dir and head Science Dept (Rutherford Appleton Lab) 1987–88, dir Daresbury Lab 1988–94, dir adjoint Institut Laue-Langevin 1994–99, pres Int Advsy Ctee Commisariat à l'Energie Atomique France (CEA) 2002–06, Evaluation Panels for Research Infrastructures and Marie-Curie actions of Framework Programme (FP)6 of the EC 2003–; memb: Review Ctee Los Alamos Nat Lab USA 1999–2003, Tech Advsy Ctee Australian Nuclear Science and Technol Orgn (ANSTO) 2000–06; visiting prof De Montfort Univ 1994–2001, hon visiting prof Univ of Exeter 2002–05, Hon DSc De Montfort Univ 2000; FRSC, FInstP; *Publications* author of numerous articles in scientific jls; *Recreations* cooking, walking, gardening; *Style*— Dr Alan Leadbetter, CBE; ✉ e-mail a.j.leadbetter@exeter.ac.uk

LEAF, Robert Stephen; s of Nathan Leaf, and Anne, *née* Feinman; *b* 9 August 1931; *Educ* Univ of Missouri (Bachelor of Journalism, MA); *m* 8 June 1958, Adele Renee; 1 s (Stuart b 4 June 1961); *Career* Burson-Marsteller International: joined 1957, vice-pres 1961, exec vice-pres 1965, pres 1968, chm 1985; chm Robert S Leaf Consultants Ltd 1997–; writer in various trade and business pubns for USA, Europe and Asia; speaker on PR mktg and communications in W and E Europe (incl Russia), Asia (incl China), Australia, N and S America; memb: PR Consltg (former memb Bd), Int Advertising, Foreign Press;

FIPR 1984 (MIPR 1973); *Recreations* tennis, travel, theatre; *Clubs* Hurlingham; *Style—* Robert Leaf, Esq; ✉ 3 Fursecroft, George Street, London W1H 5LF (tel 020 7262 4846)

LEAH, Chris; *Career* dir Safety and Environment Railtrack Group plc 1999–; *Style—* Chris Leah, Esq; ✉ Railtrack Group plc, Railtrack House, Euston Square, London NW1 2EE

LEAHY, Sir John Henry Gladstone; KCMG (1981, CMG 1973); s of William Henry Gladstone Leahy (d 1941), and Ethel, *née* Sudlow (d 1967); *b* 7 February 1928; *Educ* Tonbridge, Clare Coll Cambridge (BA), Yale Univ (MA); *m* 1954, Elizabeth Anne, da of John Hereward Pitchford, CBE; 2 s, 2 da; *Career* served RAF 1950–52; entered FO 1952, head of chancery Tehran 1965–68, FCO 1968, head of personnel servs FCO 1969, head News Dept FCO 1971–73, cnsllr and head of chancery Paris 1973–75, asst under sec state on loan to NI Office 1975–77, asst under sec state FCO 1977–79, ambass SA 1979–82, dep under sec state (Africa and ME) FCO 1982–84, high cmmr Aust 1984–88; dir The Observer 1989–93, non-exec dir Lonrho plc 1993–98 (chm 1994–97); chm Britain-Australia Soc 1994–97, memb Franco-Br Cncl (chm 1989–93); pro-chllr City Univ 1991–97; memb Ct of Assts Worshipful Co of Skinners (master 1993–94); Hon DCL City Univ 1997; Officier de la Légion d'Honneur (France) 1996; *Books* A Life of Spice (2006); *Recreations* golf; *Style—* Sir John Leahy, KCMG; ✉ 16 Ripley Chase, The Goffs, Eastbourne, East Sussex BN21 1HB (tel 01323 725368, e-mail johnleahy@dsl.pipex.com)

LEAHY, Michael J; OBE (2004); *b* 7 January 1949, Pontypool; *m* Irene; 2 s (Sean, Greg); *Career* chargehand Cold Rolling Dept Panteg Works Richard Thompson & Baldwins Ltd 1965–77; Community (formerly Iron and Steel Trades Confedn (ISTC)): memb 1965–, organiser 1977–86, sr organiser 1986–92, asst gen sec 1993–98, gen sec 1999–, sec ISTC Superannuation Soc Ltd 1999–2004, sec ISTC Staff Pension Fund 2004–; pres Gen Fedn of Trade Unions 2001–02 (vice-pres 1999–2001, memb Exec Cncl 1996–2002, memb and tstee Educnl Tst), memb Gen Cncl TUC 1999– (memb Exec Ctee 2000–); memb Sheet Trade Bd 1966–77, memb Sandwell and Dudley Area Trg Bd Manpower Servs Cmmn 1986–88, memb Nat Trades Union Steel Co-ordinating Ctee 1992– (chm 1998–), memb Exec Cncl Confedn of Shipbuilding and Engrg Unions 1994–99, memb Euro Coal and Steel Community Consultative Ctee 1995–2002 (memb Sub-Ctee for Markets and Forward Studies 1995–2002), memb Nat Jt Industrial Cncl for the Slag Industry 1995–99, memb Exec Ctee Euro Metalworkers' Fedn 1999– (memb Industrial Policy Ctee 1999–, memb Steel Ctee 1999–), pres Iron, Steel and Non-Ferrous Metals Dept Int Metalworkers' Fedn 1999– (hon sec Br Section 1999–); Br Steel (now Corus Gp plc): memb Strip Trade Bd 1995–2000 (employees' sec 1998–2000), memb Long Products Jt Standing Ctee 1995–2000 (employees' sec 1998–2000), memb Jt Accident Prevention Advsy Ctee 1995–99, memb Advsy Ctee for Educn and Trg 1995–99, employees' sec Euro Works Cncl 1998–; memb Bd Unions Today Ltd 1999–2002, chm KSP (formerly Steel Partnership Trg Ltd) 2000–, memb European Economic and Social Ctee Consultative Cmmn on Industrial Change 2002–, memb Central Arbitration Ctee UK Steel Enterprise 2002– (memb Bd 2003–); Bevan Fndn: chm 2000–02, memb Bd of Dirs 2002–, chm of tstees 2002–; memb Lab Pty 1966– (memb NEC 1996, memb Nat Policy Forum 1996–99); pres Welsh Abuse Tst 2005–; FRSA 2005; *Recreations* golf, rugby; *Style—* Michael Leahy, Esq, OBE; ✉ Community, Swinton House, 324 Gray's Inn Road, London WC1X 8DD (tel 020 7239 1200, fax 020 7278 8378, e-mail mleahy@community-tu.org)

LEAHY, Sir Terence Patrick (Terry); kt (2002); s of late Terence Leahy, and Elizabeth Leahy; *b* 28 February 1956; *Educ* St Edward's Coll Liverpool, UMIST (BSc); *m* Aug 1985, Alison; 2 s (Tom b 9 Nov 1988, David b 1 June 1992), 1 da (Katie (twin) b 9 Nov 1988); *Career* Tesco: joined as mktg exec 1979, mktg mangr 1981, mktg dir Tesco Stores Ltd 1984–86, commercial dir fresh foods 1986–92, mktg dir 1992–95 (appointed to Bd Tesco plc), dep md 1995–97, chief exec Tesco plc 1997–; dir Liverpool Vision Regeneration Bd; chllr UMIST 2002–04, co-chllr Univ of Manchester 2004–; European Businessman of the Year Fortune Magazine 2004; Freeman City of Liverpool; *Recreations* sport, reading, theatre, architecture; *Style—* Sir Terry Leahy; ✉ Tesco plc, Tesco House, PO Box 18, Delamare Road, Cheshunt, Hertfordshire EN8 9SL (tel 01992 646628, fax 01992 644962, e-mail terry.leahy@tesco.com)

LEAKE, Prof Bernard Elgey; s of Norman Sidney Leake (d 1963), and Clare Evelyn, *née* Walgate (d 1970); *b* 29 July 1932; *Educ* Wirral GS Bebington, Univ of Liverpool (BSc, PhD), Univ of Bristol (DSc), Univ of Glasgow (DSc); *m* 23 Aug 1955, Gillian Dorothy, da of Prof Charles Henry Dobinson, CMG; 5 s (Christopher b 1958, Roger b 1959, Alastair b 1961, Jonathan b 1964, Nicholas b 1966); *Career* Leverhulme res fell Univ of Liverpool 1955–57, res assoc Berkeley California 1966, reader in geology Univ of Bristol 1968–74 (lectr 1957–68); Univ of Glasgow: prof 1974–97 (prof emeritus 1997), head Dept of Geology 1974–92, head Dept of Applied Geology 1989–92, hon keeper of geological collections Hunterian Museum 1974–97; currently hon res fell Cardiff Univ; author of over 150 res papers and maps, especially of Connemara Western Ireland; treas: Geological Soc London 1980–85 and 1989–96 (pres 1986–88), Geologists' Assoc 1997–; pres Mineralogical Soc of GB 1998–2000; Lyell Medal 1978; Gledden sr fell Univ of WA 1985, Erskine fell Univ of Canterbury NZ 1999, Leverhulme emeritus fell 2000–02, hon life memb Liverpool Geological Soc 2007; FGS 1956, FRSE 1976; *Books* Catalogue of Analysed Calciferous Amphiboles (1968), The Geology of the Dalradian and associated rocks of Connemara, Western Ireland (1994), The Life of Frank Coles Phillips (1902–1982) and his role in the Moine petrofabric controversy (2002); *Clubs* Geological Soc; *Style—* Prof Bernard Leake, FRSE; ✉ School of Earth, Ocean and Planetary Sciences, Cardiff University, Main Building, Park Place, Cardiff CF10 3YE (tel 029 2087 4337, fax 029 2087 4326, e-mail leakeb@cardiff.ac.uk)

LEAKE, Christopher Jonathan Piers; s of Kenneth Piers Leake (d 1988), of Frodsham, Cheshire, and Sheila Mary, *née* Salt; *b* 17 May 1951; *Educ* St Olave's Sch York, St Peter's Sch York; *m* 1976, Carol Joan, da of Lawrence Miveld, of Hartford, Cheshire; 1 da (Claire Louise b 21 Oct 1978), 1 s (Gerard William b 13 Dec 1982); *Career* journalist; reporter W Cheshire Newspapers 1970–74, Express and Star Wolverhampton 1974–79 (reporter, industrial corr), The Daily Telegraph 1979–82 (Scottish corr, memb industrial staff), industrial and consumer affrs ed Mail on Sunday 1982–2001, UK communications dir Tesco Stores 2001–02, defence and home affrs ed Mail on Sunday 2002–; *Recreations* cycling, running, people, films; *Style—* Christopher Leake, Esq; ✉ The Mail on Sunday, Associated Newspapers plc, Northcliffe House, 2 Derry Street, Kensington, London W8 5TS (tel 020 7938 7061, fax 020 7937 3829)

LEAKEY, Dr David Martin; s of Reginald Edward Leakey (d 1969), of Redhill, Surrey, and Edith Doris, *née* Gaze (d 1974); *b* 23 July 1932; *Educ* Imperial Coll London (BSc, PhD, DIC); *m* 1, 31 Aug 1957, Shirley May (d 2003), da of George Clifford Webster (d 1968), of Bridlington, E Yorks; 1 da (Pamela Susan b 1961), 1 s (Graham Peter b 1967); m 2, 3 June 2006, Betty Ethel, da of Richard James Marks (d 1985), of Northwood, Middx, and former w of Cedric Walter Garland (d 2000); *Career* tech dir GEC Telecoms Ltd 1969–84; dir: Fulcrum Telecommunications Ltd 1985–92, Mitel Inc Canada 1986–92; British Telecom (BT): dep engr-in-chief 1984–86, chief scientist 1986–91, gp technical advsr 1991–92, ret 1992; conslt telecommunications services, systems and networks 1992–; dir: BABT (Br Approvals Bd Telecommunications) 1990–2000, Wireless Systems International Ltd 1995–2000; chm BSI/DISC 1996–2002; visiting prof Univ of Bristol 1985–; tstee IEE Benevolent Fund 2001–; Liveryman Worshipful Co of Engrs, Freeman City of London; Hon DEng Univ of Bristol 1995; FREng 1979, FIEE, FCGI; *Recreations* horticulture; *Style—* Dr David Leakey, FREng

LEAMAN, Adrian John; s of Robert Edgar Leaman, and Rita, *née* Fricker; *b* 20 October 1946; *Educ* Tiffin Sch Kingston upon Thames, Univ of Sussex (BA); *m* Rita Harland, *née* Russell; 2 step c (Joseph Harland, Katie Harland (now Mrs Kelly)); *Career* researcher Science Policy Research Unit Univ of Sussex 1969–71, with RIBA 1971–78 (worked in Research Unit and ed Journal of Architectural Research), sometime teacher and researcher Bartlett Sch of Architecture and Unit for Architectural Studies UCL (co-fndr Space Syntax research programme), lectr Poly of N London 1978–86, md Building Use Studies Ltd (studying human behaviour in buildings) 1987– (joined 1986), dir of research Inst of Advanced Architectural Studies Univ of York 1993–97, sec and dir of educn The Usable Buildings Tst 2002–; visiting prof Univ of Delft Netherlands 1998, visiting fell School of Architecture Victoria Univ Wellington NZ 2002; FRGS 1983, FRSA 1994; *Style—* Adrian Leaman, Esq; ✉ Building Use Studies Ltd tel 01904 671280, e-mail adrianleaman@usablebuildings.co.uk, website www.usablebuildings.co.uk

LEAMAN, Rear Adm Richard Derek; OBE (1993); s of late Derek Leaman, of Torquay, Devon, and Jean, *née* Chapman; *b* 29 July 1956; *Educ* Torquay Boys' GS; *m* 1; 2 s (Adrian b 1977, Nicholas b 1980); m 2, Suzy, *née* Clarke; *Career* cmmnd RN 1975, early trg Baltic, Pacific and Caribbean, navigator HMS Crichton and HMS Birmingham, instr BRNC Dartmouth, Princ Warfare Offr Course 1982 (Edgerton Prize), Gunnery Offr HMS Glasgow, Anti-Air Warfare Course, operational duties HMS Birmingham and HMS Glasgow, staff appt trg offrs in air defence 1987, cmd HMS Dumbarton Castle 1988, Sr Warfare Offr HMS Ark Royal, promoted Cdr 1991, cmd HMS Cardiff 1991, served MOD 1995, promoted Capt 1996, cmd HMS Cumberland 1996, cmd RN Presentation Team, Higher Command and Staff Course 2000, dep dir responsible for warship procurement MOD, promoted Cdre 2000, dir of corp communications (Navy) 2000–02, Cdr UK Task Gp 2003–04, dir Higher Command and Staff Course 2004–05, promoted Rear Adm 2005, COS to CC MAR Naples 2005–07, DCOS NATO HQ Norfolk VA 2007–; MIPR 2001; *Recreations* swimming, fly fishing, playing classical guitar; *Style—* Rear Adm Richard Leaman, OBE; ✉ DCOS(T), HQ SACT BFPO 63 (e-mail richardleaman@hotmail.com)

LEAN, Prof Michael Ernest John; s of Maj John Holman Lean, of Suffolk and Cornwall, and Estelle Flower, *née* Oulton; *b* 16 March 1952; *Educ* Trinity Coll Glenalmond, Downing Coll Cambridge (MA), St Bart's Hosp Med Sch (MB BChir, MD (Cantab)); *Career* prof of human nutrition Univ of Glasgow, hon conslt physician Glasgow Royal Infirmary, dir Health Educn Bd for Scotland 1995–2003; chm Food Standards Agency Advsy Ctee on Res; memb: Diabetes UK, Nutrition Soc, Scottish Fiddle Orch, Le Clan des Gueux; weekly columnist Sunday Herald 2001–02; André Mayer prize 1986; FRCPEd, FRCPGlas; *Publications* over 200 scientific papers on nutrition and diabetes; *Recreations* violin, Scottish music, cross-country and hill running (winner Barmekin Hill Race 1991, 1992 and 1993, and Glenisla Games Hill Race 1996), fishing and mountaineering; *Style—* Prof Michael Lean; ✉ Hatton Castle, Newtyle, Angus PH12 8UN (tel 01828 650404); Department of Human Nutrition, University of Glasgow, Glasgow Royal Infirmary, Glasgow (tel 0141 211 4686, fax 0141 211 4844, e-mail lean@clinmed.gla.ac.uk)

LEAPER, David John; s of David Thomas Leaper, of Leeds, and Gwendoline, *née* Robertson; *b* 23 July 1947; *Educ* Leeds Modern GS, Univ of Leeds (MB ChB, MD, ChM); *m* Francesca Anne; 1 s (Charles David Edward), 1 da (Alice Jane Sophia); *Career* Univ of Leeds: house offr 1970–71, MRC res fell 1971–73, registrar in surgery 1973–76; Univ of London: CRC res fell, sr registrar in surgery 1976–81; conslt sr lectr in surgery Univ of Bristol 1981–95, prof of surgery at North Tees Gen Hosp 1995–2004; Hunterian prof of surgery RCS 1981–82, Zachary Cope lectr 1998, prof of surgery Hong Kong Univ 1988–90, emeritus prof of surgery Univ of Newcastle upon Tyne 2004–; visiting prof: Univ of Cardiff 2004, Univ of Southampton 2006–08, Imperial Coll London 2006–; dir Wound Research Centre Salisbury NHS Fndn Tst 2006–; medical advsr: Renovo (UK) 2005–, Arizant (USA), Inditherm plc (UK) 2004–06; memb Cncl and vice-pres RSM (surgery) 1982–88, fndr memb (pres 1999) Surgical Infection Soc of Europe, fndr memb European Wound Mgmnt Assoc 1990 (pres 1994), memb Ct of Examiners RCS 1992–98, memb Ctee Surgical Res Soc (UK) 1987–88, professorial memb Specialist Advsy Ctee, prog dir Higher Training Northern Deanery 2000–04, memb Bd European Tissue Repair Soc 2006–, chair Guidelines Devpt Gp (NICE) Surgical Site Infection 2007–08, expert memb Advsy Gp Antimicrobial Resistance and Healthcare Associated Infections 2007–; FRCS 1975, FRCSEd 1974, FICA 1984, FRCS Glas 1998, FACS 1998; *Publications* Your Operation (series), International Surgical Practice, Wounds: Biology and Management Oxford Handbooks Clinical Surgery, Operative Surgery and Operative Complications, Complete Revision for the Intercollegiate FRCS, An Introduction to Wounds, Wound Management: Changing Ideas on Antiseptics, Hospital Infection Control, Guidance on the Control of Infection in Hospitals; memb Editorial Bd: Br Journal of Surgery, Surgery Research Cmmn, International Wound Jl, Wounds UK, Turkish Medical Jl; *Clubs* Rotary Int (past chm 647 Round Table Br and Ireland 1987–88); *Style—* Prof David Leaper; ✉ 33 Peverell Avenue East, Poundbury, Dorchester, Dorset DT1 3RH

LEAPMAN, David; *Educ* St Martin's Sch of Art, Goldsmiths Coll; *Career* artist; *Solo Exhibitions* Journeying in Search of Hidden Treasures (Ikon Gallery Birmingham) 1988, Galerie Raph Debarrn Paris 1993, Todd Gallery London 1988, 1990, 1992, 1994 and 1995, Hales Gallery London 1997, One in the Other (London) 1998, Beaux Arts London 2000, Habitat King's Road London 2000; *Group Exhibitions* Young Blood (Riverside Studios London) 1983, Problems of Picturing (Serpentine London) 1984, Between Identity & Politics - A New Art (Gimpel Fils tour) 1996, Unheard Music (Stoke-on-Trent Museum) 1986, Small Scale (Lidewij Edelkoort Gallery Paris) 1986, Nature Morte (Edward Totah Gallery London) 1986, Impulse 8 (Galerie Lohrl Monchengladbach) 1986, Figuring Out the 80s (Laing Art Gallery & Museum Newcastle upon Tyne) 1988, New Paintings by David Leapman and Roy Voss (Curwen Gallery London) 1989, New Contemporaries (Institute of Contemporary Arts London) 1981, 1989, Aperto 90 (Venice Biennale Venice) 1990, Hyunsoo Choi et David Leapman (Galerie Gutharc Ballin Paris) 1993, Pet Show (Union Street Gallery London) 1993, In House Out House (Unit 7 Camberwell) 1993, Strictly Painting (Cubitt Street Gallery London) 1993, Moving into View (Arts Council touring exhbn) 1993–96, XXVIe Festival International de la Peinture (British Council) 1994, LandEscapes (Turin) 1994, Exhibition 19 (Walker Art Gallery Liverpool, 1st prize winner) 1995–96, Being There II (Centrun Beeldende Kunst Rotterdam) 1996–98, Whitechapel Open (Whitechapel Art Gallery London) 1985, 1986, 1990, and 1996, The East Wing Collection (Courthauld Institute of Art London) 1996–98, WHAT (Trinity Buoy Wharf London) 1997, John Moores Liverpool Exhibition 20 (prize winner), The Art Works (Riverside California) 1998, The Jerwood Painting Prize (London) 1998, Recent Acquisitions (Beaux Arts London) 1999, Simmer (Beaux Arts London) 1999, Work on Paper (Stalke Gallery Copenhagen) 1999; *Style—* David Leapman, Esq; ✉ c/o Beaux Arts, 22 Cork Street, London W1X 1HB

LEAPMAN, Edwina; da of Charles Morris Leapman (d 1962), of London, and Hannah, *née* Schonfield (d 1988); *b* 21 October 1931; *Educ* Farnham Sch of Art, Slade Sch of Fine Art, The Central Sch of Art; *m* Dec 1957 (m dis 1969), John Saul Weiss; *Career* artist; *Solo Exhibitions* The New Art Centre London 1974, Annely Juda Fine Art London 1976, 1980, 1993 and 1998, Gallerie Loyse Oppenheim Nyon Switzerland 1979, Gallery Artline The Hague Holland 1979, Juda Rowan Gallery London 1987, Galerie Konstrucktiv Tendens Stockholm Sweden 1990, The Serpentine Gallery London 1991, ACP Viviane Ehrli Galerie Zurich Switzerland 1996 and 1998, Annely Juda Fine Art London 2002, Galerie Konstruktiv Tendens Stockholm 2002; *Group Exhibitions* incl: Signals Gallery London 1956, Four Abstract Painters (ICA, London) 1967, Survey '67 (Camden Art Centre, London) 1967, Silence (Camden Art Centre) 1971, John Moores Exhibition Liverpool 1972, 1974 and 1976, Post Minimal Painting (Scottish Arts Cncl, Edinburgh) 1974, Rini Dippel:

A Selection of Six Painters (Air Gallery, London) 1976, Gallerie Loyse Oppenheim Nyon Switzerland 1977, Hayward Annual '78 (Hayward Gallery, London) 1978, A Free Hand (Arts Cncl Touring Exhibition) 1978, The Arts Cncl Collection (Hayward Gallery) 1980, Masters of the Avant-Garde & Three Decades of Contemporary Art (Annely Juda/Juda Rowan) 1986, A Disquieting suggestion (John Hansard Gallery Southampton) 1988, The Presence of Painting: Aspects of British Abstraction (South Bank Touring Exhibition) 1989, The Experience of Painting: Eight Modern Artists (Laing Art Gallery Newcastle, S Bank Touring Exhibition) 1989, From Picasso to Abstraction (Annely Juda Fine Art) 1989, The Arts Cncl Collection (Festival Hall) 1993, Lead and Follow: the continuity of abstraction (Atlantis Gallery) 1994, British Abstract Art: Painting (Flowers East London) 1994, New Painting (Arts Cncl Collection Newlyn) 1995, Mostly Monochrome (Green on Red Gallery Dublin) 1996, New Paintings (Arts Cncl Collection Bath Museum) 1996, British Abstract Art - Works on Paper (Flowers East London) 1996, Geometrisk Abstraktion XV (Galerie Konstruktiv Tendens Stockholm) 1996, John Moores Exhibition Liverpool 1997, Geometrisk Abstraktion XVI (Galerie Konstruktiv Tendens Stockholm) 1997, Jerwood Painting Prize 1998, A Line in Painting (Gallery Fine London) 1999, White Out (Gallery Fine London) 1999, An Exemplary Life (Bury St Edmunds Art Gallery) 2000, In a Marine Light (The Customs House South Shields) 2000, Underlying Perfection (Gallery Fine London), Blan bei Kemper (Galerie Kemper Munich Germany) 2000, British Abstract Painting (Flowers East London) 2001, Geometrisk Abstraktion XX (Galerie Konstruktiv Tendens Stockholm) 2001, Drawings (Sarah Myerscough Fine Art at Reid Minty London) 2002, Geometrisk Abstraktion XXI (Galerie Konstruktiv Tendens Stockholm) 2002, Eagle Gallery London 2002, Thirty years at Annely Juda Fine Art 2006; *Style—* Ms Edwina Leapman; ✉ c/o Annely Juda Fine Art, 23 Dering Street, London W1R 9AA (tel 020 7722 5311)

LEARY, Brian Leonard; QC (1978); s of late A T Leary, and late M C Leary, *née* Bond; *b* 1 January 1929; *Educ* King's Sch Canterbury, Wadham Coll Oxford (MA); *m* 14 April 1965, Myriam Ann, da of late Kenneth Bannister, CBE, of Mexico City; *Career* called to the Bar Middle Temple 1953 (bencher 1986); sr prosecuting counsel to Crown 1971–78 (jr 1964–71); chm Br Mexican Soc 1989–92; FCIArb 1999; *Recreations* travel, sailing, growing herbs; *Style—* Brian Leary, Esq, QC; ✉ c/o 5 Paper Buildings, Temple, London EC4Y 9AR

LEASK, Annie Carol; da of Kenneth Roy Leask, of Hatfield, S Yorks, and Marion Gladys, *née* Dixey; *b* 23 July 1965; *Educ* Thorne GS, Univ of Kent Canterbury (BA), Nat Cncl for Training Journalists Proficiency Cert; *Career* trainee Croydon Advertiser Newspaper Group 1986–89, presenter and reseacher daily news bulletins Croydon Cable TV 1987–88, freelance journalist 1989 (Thames TV, Sunday Mirror, Evening Standard); The Express: showbusiness reporter and music critic 1989–91, dep showbusiness ed 1991–97, special projects ed 1992–97, showbusiness ed 1997–98; dep features ed The Sun 1998, commissioning ed Weekend Magazine Daily Mail 1998–; *Recreations* horse riding, squash, skiing, reading; *Style—* Ms Annie Leask; ✉ Weekend Magazine, Daily Mail, Northcliffe House, 2 Derry Street, London W8 5TT (tel 020 7938 6000 ext 6554, mobile 07971 517284)

LEATES, Margaret; da of Henry Arthur Sargent Rayner, and Alice, *née* Baker; *b* 30 March 1951; *Educ* Lilley and Stone Girls' HS Newark, King's Coll London (LLB, LLM, AKC), Univ of Kent (MA); *m* 26 May 1973, Timothy Philip Leates; 1 s (Benjamin b 15 April 1982), 1 da (Lydia b 14 July 1983); *Career* admitted slr 1975; Parliamentary Counsel Office 1976–90, Parliamentary draftsman and conslt 1990–; memb Law Soc; *Recreations* other people's gardens, hermeneutics; *Clubs* Whitstable Yacht; *Style—* Mrs Margaret Leates; ✉ Crofton Farm, 161 Crofton Lane, Orpington, Kent BR6 0BP (tel 01689 820192, fax 01689 878441); Mumford House, Kingsnorth, Ashford, Kent TN23 3EG (tel 01233 610269); Nyanza, 87 Bennells Avenue, Whitstable, Kent CT5 2HR (tel 01227 272335, e-mail ml@leates.org.uk)

LEATHAM, Lady Victoria Diana; *née* Cecil; DL (1993 Cambs); da of 6 Marquess of Exeter, KCMG (d 1981), and 2 w, Diana (d 1982), da of Hon Arnold Henderson, OBE (d 1933, 5 s of 1 Baron Faringdon, CH); *b* 1947; *m* 1967, Simon Patrick Leatham; 1 s, 1 da; *Career* dir: Preservation Tst, Burghley House; dir and co-owner Ancestral Collections Ltd; presenter of tv progs on stately homes; lectr on antiques UK and overseas; Hon Dr of Arts De Montfort Univ Leicester 1994; Hon Col 158 (Royal Anglian) Regt 1996–2002; The Royal Logistics Corps (Volunteer); Hon DLitt Bishop Grosseteste Coll Lincoln 1999; *Books* Burghley - The Life of a Great House (1992); *Style—* The Lady Victoria Leatham, DL; ✉ Burghley House, Stamford, Lincolnshire (tel 01780 763131)

LEATHER, Dame Susan Catherine (Suzi); DBE (2006, MBE 1994); da of Hugh Moffat Leather, and Catherine Margaret, *née* Stephen; *Educ* St Mary's Sch Calne, Tavistock Sch, Univ of Exeter (BA, BPhil), Univ of Leicester (MA); *m* 1986, Prof Iain Hampsher-Monk; 1 s, 2 da; *Career* sr res offr Consumers in Europe Gp 1979–84, trainee probation offr 1984–86, freelance consumer conslt 1988–97, chair Exeter and Dist NHS Tst 1997–2001, dep chair Food Standards Agency 2000–02, chair Human Fertilisation and Embryology Authy 2002–06, ex officio memb Human Genetics Cmmn 2002–06, chair Charity Cmmn for England and Wales 2006–; chair: St Sidwell's Project Healthy Living Centre 1998–2001, School Food Tst 2005–06; Caroline Walker Tst Award (consumer category) 1993; Hon DLitt Univ of Exeter 2003, Hon DCL Univ of Huddersfield 2005, Hon LLD Univ of Leicester 2007, Dr (hc) Univ of Aberdeen 2007; FRCOG ad eundem 2004, Hon FRSH 2006; *Publications* articles on consumer, food and health policy incl: Food and Low Income: a practical guide for advisers and supporters working with families and young people on low incomes (1994), Budgeting for Food on Benefits (1995), The Making of Modern Malnutrition (1996); *Recreations* keeping fit, sailing, walking, running; *Style—* Dame Suzi Leather, DBE; ✉ Charity Commission for England and Wales, Harmsworth House, 13–15 Bouverie Street, London EC4Y 8DP

LEATHERBARROW, Prof William John; s of William Leatherbarrow (d 1996), and Lily, *née* Halliday (d 1986); *b* 18 October 1947, Liverpool; *Educ* Liverpool Inst HS for Boys, Univ of Exeter (BA, MA); *m* 19 Oct 1968, Vivien Jean, *née* Burton; 1 s (James William b 28 April 1970), 1 da (Corin Jean (Mrs Robertson) b 15 Jan 1972); *Career* Univ of Sheffield: lectr in Russian 1970–89, sr lectr in Russian 1990–94, prof of Russian 1994–, dean Faculty of Arts 1997–99, chair Sch of Modern Languages 2001–04; memb Br Assoc for Slavonic and East European Studies; *Books* incl: Fedor Dostoevsky (1981, CD-ROM 1993), A Documentary History of Russian Thought: From the Enlightenment to Marxism (jtly, 1987), Fedor Dostoevsky: A Reference Guide to the Literature (1990), Dostoevsky: The Brothers Karamazov (1992), Dostoevskii and Britain (ed, 1995), Dostoevsky's The Devils: A Critical Companion (ed, 1999), The Cambridge Companion to Dostoevsky (ed, 2002), A Devil's Vaudeville: The Demonic in Dostoevskii's Major Fiction (2005); also ed of critical edns of Dostoevsky; *Recreations* wine collecting, cricket, walking, astronomy; *Style—* Prof William Leatherbarrow; ✉ Department of Russian and Slavonic Studies, University of Sheffield, Sheffield S10 2TN (tel 0114 222 7404, e-mail w.leatherbarrow@shef.ac.uk)

LEATHERDALE, Dr Brian Anthony; s of Dennis Hector Leatherdale, and Mary Ann, *née* Sheilds (d 1984); *b* 30 November 1942; *Educ* St Joseph's Coll Birkfield, London Hosp Med Coll (BSc, MD, DipObst); *m* 27 April 1968, Salliebelle, da of Joseph Gilley Dathan (d 1987); 2 s (Anthony Stephen b 15 May 1971, Daniel Brian b 23 March 1973); *Career* sr med registrar King's Coll Hosp 1972–75, conslt physician Dudley Rd Hosp Birmingham 1975–81, conslt physician Southampton Univ Hosp Tst 1981–2007 (post grad tutor 1983–88); regnl advsr Wessex RCP 1988–94; memb BMA, memb RSM, FRCP 1985; *Recreations* cricket, golf, assoc football; *Clubs* Brockenhurst Manor Golf; *Style—* Dr Brian Leatherdale; ✉ Hewers Orchard, Newtown, Minstead, Lyndhurst, Hampshire SO43 7GD (tel 023 8081 2789, fax 023 8081 3184); F Level, Southampton General Hospital, Tremona Road, Southampton SO16 6YD (tel 023 8079 4391)

LEATHERS, 3 Viscount (UK 1954); Christopher Graeme Leathers; JP; also Baron Leathers (UK 1941); s of 2 Viscount Leathers (d 1996), and his 1 w, Elspeth Graeme, *née* Stewart (d 1985); *b* 31 August 1941; *Educ* Rugby, Open Univ (BA); *m* 1964, Maria Philomena, da of Michael Merriman, of Charlestown, Co Mayo; 1 da (Hon Melissa Maria (Hon Mrs Wesley) b 22 April 1966), 1 s (Hon James Frederick b 27 May 1969); *Heir* s, Hon James Leathers; *Career* with Wm Cory & Son Ltd 1961–83, Mostyn Docks Ltd 1984–86, civil servant Dept for Tport, Local Govt and the Regions (formerly Dept of Tport and Environment, Tport and the Regions) 1988–2003, ret; memb Inst of Chartered Shipbrokers, MIMgt; Liveryman Worshipful Co of Shipwrights; *Style—* The Rt Hon the Viscount Leathers; ✉ e-mail christopher.leathers@talk21.com

LEAVER, Sir Christopher; GBE (1981), JP (Inner London); s of Dr Robert Leaver, and Audrey Kerpen; *b* 3 November 1937; *Educ* Eastbourne Coll; *m* 1975, Helen Mireille Molyneux Benton; 1 s (Benedict), 2 da (Tara, Anna); *Career* cmmnd RAOC 1956–58, Hon Col 151 (Gtr London) Tport Regt RCT (V) 1983–88, Hon Col Cmdt RCT 1988–91; chm Thames Line plc 1987–89, vice-chm Thames Water plc 1994–2000 (dep chm 1983–93, chm 1993–94); dir: Bath & Portland Group plc 1983–85, Thermal Scientific plc 1985–88, Unionamerica Holdings plc 1994–97; cncllr RBK&C 1971–74, Alderman Ward of Dowgate City of London 1974–2002 (memb Ct of Common Cncl 1973), Sheriff City of London 1979–80, Lord Mayor of London 1981–82; memb: Bd Brixton Prison 1975–78, Cmmn of Lt for City of London 1982–2002, Fin Ctee London Diocesan Fund 1983–86, Cncl Mission to Seamen 1983–93, Advsy Gp Royal Parks 1993–96; govr: Christs' Hosp Sch 1975–2002, City of London Girls' Sch 1975–78, City Univ 1978–2002 (chllr 1981–82), City of London Freemen's Sch 1980–81, Music Therapy Tst 1981–89; chm: Young Musicians' Symphony Orchestra Tst 1979–81, London Tourist Bd 1983–89, Eastbourne Coll 1988–; tstee London Symphony Orchestra 1983–90; vice-pres: Nat Playing Fields Assoc 1983–99, Bridewell Royal Hosp 1983–89; church warden St Olave's Hart St 1975–89, church cmmr 1982–93 and 1996–99; hon memb GSM 1982; Hon DMus City Univ 1982; Freeman Co of Watermen and Lightermen, Liveryman Co of Water Conservators; Hon Liveryman: Worshipful Co of Farmers, Worshipful Co of Environmental Cleaners; Master Worshipful Co of Carmen 1987–88; KStJ 1982; *Style—* Sir Christopher Leaver, GBE; ✉ tel and fax 020 7352 2273

LEAVER, Prof Christopher John; CBE (2000); s of Douglas Percival Leaver (d 1978), and Elizabeth Constance, *née* Hancock; *b* 31 May 1942; *Educ* Lyme Regis GS, Imperial Coll London (BSc, ARCS, DIC, PhD), Univ of Oxford (MA); *m* 8 Oct 1971, Anne, da of Prof Hastings Dudley Huggins (d 1970); 1 s (Tristan), 1 da (Anya); *Career* Fulbright scholar Purdue Univ 1966–68, scientific offr ARC Plant Physiology Unit Imperial Coll London 1968–69; Univ of Edinburgh: lectr 1969–80, reader 1980–86, SERC sr res fell 1985–90, prof of plant molecular biology 1986–89; Univ of Oxford: fell St John's Coll 1989–, Sibthorpian prof of plant sciences 1990–, head Dept of Plant Sciences 1991–; visiting prof Univ of Western Aust 2002–; memb: Cncl AFRC 1990–94, Priorities Bd MAFF 1990–94, Cncl Euro Molecular Biology Orgn 1991–97 (chm 1997), ACOST 1992–93, Cncl Royal Soc 1992–94, External Scientific Advsy Bd Inst of Molecular and Cell Biology Univ of Oporto (chair 1999–), Exec Ctee Biochemical Soc (vice-chair 2002–05, chair 2005–07), ITQB Advsy Ctee Univ of Lisbon 2000–07, GM Sci Review Panel DTI 2002–03, Sci Advsy Panel Royal Instn of GB 2002–, Scientific Advsy Bd Inst of Molecular and Cell Biology Singapore 2002–06, Exec Ctee Sense about Sci 2002– (also tstee), Ctee for Sr Academic Promotions in Biology, Sci and Clinical Med Univ of Cambridge 2003–, Int Advsy Panel A*Star Grad Acad Singapore 2003–07, Ctee for Scientific Planning and Review Int Cncl for Science 2005–, Scientific Advsy Bd Plant Energy Biology ARC Centre of Excellence Univ of WA Perth 2006–, Int Advsy Panel Nat Univ of Singapore 2006–; BBSRC: memb IMP Panel 1996–2005, memb Cncl 2000–03, chair Personal Merit Promotion Panel 2005–; delg OUP 2002–07; tstee: John Innes Fndn 1987–, Nat History Museum London 1997–2006; T H Huxley Gold Medal Imperial Coll 1970, Tate and Lyle Award Phytochem Soc of Europe 1984, Humboldt Prize (Germany) 1997; memb EMBO 1982, FRS 1986, FRSE 1987, memb Academia Europaea 1988, hon fell Royal Instn of GB 2002, corresponding memb American Soc of Plant Biologists 2003; *Recreations* walking and talking in Upper Coquetdale; *Style—* Prof Christopher Leaver, CBE, FRS, FRSE; ✉ Department of Plant Sciences, South Parks Road, Oxford OX1 3RB (tel 01865 275143, fax 01865 275144, e-mail chris.leaver@plants.ox.ac.uk)

LEAVER, Colin Edward; s of Edward Roy Leaver, of West Wittering, W Sussex, and Freda Eleanor, *née* Toogood; *b* 25 May 1958; *Educ* Haywards Heath GS, Lincoln Coll Oxford (MA); *m* 10 May 1986, Maria Victoria, da of John Hutton Simpkins, of Alicante, Spain; 2 da (Christina b 1987, Mónica b 1991), 1 s (James b 1989); *Career* Simmons & Simmons: articled clerk 1980–82, asst slr 1982–86, ptnr 1986–, based Hong Kong 1989–96, based London 1996–; *Recreations* sailing, philately, aviation; *Clubs* Royal Hong Kong Yacht; *Style—* Colin Leaver, Esq; ✉ Simmons & Simmons, CityPoint, One Ropemaker Street, London EC2Y 9SS (tel 020 7628 2020, fax 020 7628 2070, e-mail colin.leaver@simmons-simmons.com)

LEAVER, Peter Lawrence Oppenheim; QC (1987); s of Marcus Isaac Leaver (d 1966), of London, and Lena, *née* Oppenheim (d 1984); *b* 28 November 1944; *Educ* Aldenham, Univ of Dublin; *m* 2 June 1969, Jane Rachel, o da of Leonard Pearl (d 1983), of London; 3 s (Marcus, James, Benjamin) 1 da (Rebecca); *Career* called to the Bar Lincoln's Inn 1967 (bencher 1995); recorder 1994–, dep judge of the High Court 1994–; memb Gen Cncl Bar 1987–90; chm: Bar Ctee 1989 (vice-chm 1988–89), Int Practice Ctee 1990; memb: Ctee on Future of Legal Profession 1986–88, Cncl Legal Educn 1986–90; dir Investment Mgmnt Regulatory Organisation Ltd 1994–2000, dep chm FSA Regulatory Decisions Ctee; chief exec FA Premier League 1997–99; memb Football Task Force 1997–99; memb Court of Arbritation for Sport; former tstee The Free Representation Unit; *Recreations* sport, wine, theatre, opera; *Clubs* Garrick, Groucho, MCC; *Style—* Peter Leaver, Esq, QC; ✉ 13 Clifton Gardens, London W9 1AL (tel 020 7286 0208); 1 Essex Court, Temple, London EC4Y 9AR (tel 020 7583 2000, fax 020 7583 0118, e-mail pleaver@oeclaw.co.uk)

LECCA, Marie-Jeanne; da of Mircea Lecca (d 1970), and Mona *née* Beller Cantacuzino; *b* 31 January 1960; *Educ* Beaux Arts Inst Bucharest; *m* 2 Oct 1982, Dan Mihai Sandru, s of Vasile Sandru; *Career* set and costume designer; memb SBTD; patron Pro Patrimonio; *Theatre* incl: Yvonna, Princess of Burgundy (Mic Theatre Bucharest) 1984 (Best Scene Designer Assoc of Romanian Artists Prize), La Bete Humaine (Nottingham Playhouse) 1993, The Taming of the Shrew (RSC Stratford and Barbican) 1995, As You Like It (Nottingham Playhouse) 1997, Napoleon (Shaftesbury Theatre) 2000; *Opera* designs for ENO: The Stone Guest 1987, Pacific Overtures 1987, Falstaff 1989, Pelleas & Melisande 1990, The Adventures of Mr Brouček 1992 (transferred to Bayerische Staatsoper Munich 1995), Der Freischutz 1999, Nabucco 2000, Verdi Requiem 2000; other designs incl: Le Pre-aux-Clercs (John Lewis Partnership Music Soc) 1985, La Wally (Wexford Opera Festival) 1985, Iolanthe (Scottish Opera Glasgow) 1986, La Boheme (Eng Touring Opera) 1986, The Pirates of Penzance (d'Oyly Carte Opera Co London, UK and US tour) 1989, Carmen (Minnesota Opera) 1991 (transferred to Houston Grand Opera 1994, Seattle Opera 1995 and Teatro Regio Turin 1996), The Barber of Seville (Glimmerglass Opera) 1993–94, Cavalleria Rusticana and I Pagliacci (Berlin State Opera) 1996, The Nose (De Nederlandse Opera Amsterdam) 1996, La Maison des Morts (Opera du Rhin Strasbourg) 1996, Julietta

(Opera North Leeds) 1997 (Martinu Fndn Medal, nomination Barclays Theatre Award 1998), Rienzi (Vienna State Opera) 1997, The Turn of the Screw (La Monnaie Brussels) 1998, Angel Magick (BBC Proms and Salisbury Playhouse) 1998, Salammbo (Bastille Opera Paris) 1998–2000, Katya Kabanova (Bayerische Staatsoper Munich) 1999, The Greek Passion (Bregenzer Festspiele and ROH) 1999–2000 (jt winner Olivier Award), Faust (Bayerische Staatsoper Munich) 2000, La Clemenza di Tito (Opera Nat du Rhin Strasbourg) 2001, Macbeth (Opernhaus Zurich) 2001, Therese Raquin (Dallas Opera) 2001, Jenufa (Vienna State Opera) 2002, Turandot (Salzburg Festival) 2002, Wozzeck (ROH) 2002 (jt winner Olivier Award), Wilhelm Tell (Bastille Opera Paris) 2003, West Side Story (Bregenzer Festspiele) 2003, Boccaccio (Volksoper Vienna) 2003, The Dwarf, Seven Deadly Sins (Opera North, jt winner South Bank Show Award), The Ring Cycle (ROH) 2004–06, Maskarade (Bregenzer Festspiele and ROH) 2005 (Opernwelt Magazine nomination for Costume Designer of the Year), Peter Grimes (Opernhaus Zürich) 2005, Magic Flute (Volksoper Vienna) 2005, Moses and Aron (Bayerische Staatsoper) 2006, Die Soldaten (Ruhr Triennale) 2006–07, L'Étoile (Opernhaus Zürich) 2006, Khovanshchina (Welsh Nat Opera) 2007; winner Prague Quadriennale Golden Triga 2003 (jntly); *Television* The Big One 1991, Amahl and the Night Visitors 2001 (BAFTA nomination); *Recreations* photography, travel, gardening; *Style*— Mrs Marie-Jeanne Lecca; ✉ c/o PFD, Drury House, 34–43 Russell Street, London WC2B 5HA (tel 020 7344 1000, fax 020 7836 9543, e-mail lmamy@pfd.co.uk)

LECHLER, Prof Robert Ian; s of Dr Ian Sewell Lechler (d 1972), and Audrey Florence, *née* Wilson (d 1979); *b* 24 December 1951; *Educ* Monkton Combe Sch, Univ of Manchester (MB ChB), Univ of London (PhD); *m* Valerie Susan, da of Harold Ord Johnston (d 1988); 2 s (Alastair Robert b 4 Feb 1980, Toby Ian b 23 Dec 1982), 1 da (Suzannah Jane b 24 Feb 1988); *Career* sr renal registrar Professorial Med Unit Hammersmith Hosp 1983–84 (renal registrar 1982–83), Wellcome Tst travelling fell Lab of Immunology Bethesda Maryland USA 1984–86; Imperial Coll Sch of Med at Hammersmith Hosp (Royal Postgrad Med Sch until merger 1997): sr lectr in immunology 1986–89, reader in immunology 1989–92, hon conslt in med 1989–94, prof of molecular immunology 1992–94, prof and dir of immunology 1994–2004, dean of campus 2001–04, head Div of Medicine 2003–04; Hammersmith Hosps Tst: consIt transplant physician 1986–2004, chief of immunology serv 1995–2004; KCL: prof of immunology 2004–, vice-princ for health 2005–, dean GKT Sch of Medicine 2004–05, dean Sch of Medicine and Dental Inst Guy's, King's Coll and St Thomas' Hosps 2005–; hon consIt Dept of Renal Medicine and Transplantation Guy's Hosp 2004–; dir Ruggero Cepellini Sch of Immunology Naples 2001–; chm: Scientific Advsy Bd Embryonic Stem Cell Int 2003–, Chairs and Prog Grants Ctte BHF 2003–; memb Scientific Ctee Inst de transplantation et de recherche en transplantation Nantes 2000–; int advsr to NIH Immune Tolerance Network 2000–, cncllr Int Xenotransplantation Assoc 2001–; memb Editorial Bd Transplantation Jl; memb: Renal Assoc 1980, Int Transplantation Soc 1987, Assoc of Physicians 1988; FRCP 1990 (MRCP 1978), FRCPath 1996, FMedSci 2000; *Recreations* classical music, theatre, family; *Style*— Prof Robert Lechler; ✉ School of Medicine, King's College London, Hodgkin Building, Guy's Campus, London SE1 9RT

LECHMERE, Sir Reginald Anthony Hungerford; 7 Bt (UK 1818), of The Rhydd, Worcestershire; s of Anthony Hungerford Lechmere (d 1954, 3 s of 3 Bt), and Cicely Mary, *née* Bridges (d 1964); suc kinsman, Sir Berwick Hungerford Lechmere, 6 Bt (d 2001); *b* 24 December 1920; *Educ* Charterhouse, Trinity Hall Cambridge; *m* 1956, Anne Jennifer, da of late A C Dind, of Orbe, Switzerland; 1 da (Jennifer Sarah b 1959), 3 s (Nicholas Anthony Hungerford b 1960, Adam Francis b 1962, Mark Edmund Dind b 1966); *Heir* s, Nicholas Lechmere; *Career* formerly Capt 5 Royal Inniskilling Dragoon Gds; publicity mangr Penguin Books, antiquarian bookseller; *Style*— Sir Reginald Lechmere, Bt; ✉ Primeswell, Evendine lane, Colwall, Malvern Worcestershire WR13 6DT (tel 01684 540340)

LECK, Prof Ian Maxwell; s of Rev Arthur Simpson Leck (d 1952), and Margaret Mortimer, *née* Jagger (d 1983); *b* 14 February 1931; *Educ* Kingswood Sch Bath, Univ of Birmingham (MB ChB, PhD, DSc); *m* 25 July 1959, Ann Patricia Sarson; 2 da (Susan Margaret b 1960, Patricia Mary b 1965), 2 s (Christopher James b 1962, Jonathan Peter b 1967); *Career* Lt 1955–56 and Capt 1956–57 RAMC; house offr Walsall Gen Hosp 1954–55, lectr in social med Univ of Birmingham 1959–66 (res fell 1957–59), sr lectr in community med UCH Med Sch London 1966–71; Univ of Manchester: reader in social and preventive med later community med 1971–78, prof of community med then prof of epidemiology 1979–91, prof emeritus 1991; author of papers and chapters on epidemiology of malformations and cancer; assoc ed Teratology: the Journal of Abnormal Development 1972–80; memb: Ctee Soc for Social Med 1974–77, Editorial Bd Journal of Epidemiology and Community Health 1978–92, Editorial Bd Jl of Medical Screening 2001–06; hon sec and treas Heads of Academic Depts Gp (social and community med) 1985–87, hon sec: Soc for Social Med 1993–95, Churches Together in Oxon 2000–05; Milroy lectr RCP 1993; MSc (ex officio) Manchester 1982; FFCM 1972, FRCP 1985, FFPHM 1989; *Books* Childhood Cancer in Britain: Incidence, Survival and Mortality (with G J Draper, 1982), God of Science, God of Faith (with D Bridge, 1988), Antenatal and Neonatal Screening (with N Wald, 2 edn 2000, winner Public Health Section BMA Med Book Competition 2001); *Recreations* cycling, walking; *Style*— Prof Ian Leck; ✉ Pembury, 18 Cadogan Park, Woodstock, Oxfordshire OX20 1UW (tel 01993 811528, e-mail iannleck@supanet.com)

LEDERER, Helen; da of Peter Lederer, and Jeanne Lederer; *b* 24 September 1954; *Educ* Blackheath HS, Hatfield Poly (now Hatfield Univ), Central Sch of Speech & Drama; *m* Dr Chris Browne; 1 da (Hannah Louise b 28 April 1990); *Career* comedienne and actress; early work at the Comedy Store and similar venues; *Theatre* incl: Bunny in House of Blue Leaves (Lilian Bayliss Theatre), Educating Rita (with Julian Glover, *qv*), Doreen in Having A Ball (Comedy Theatre), Vagina Mololugues (West End) 2002 (and V-Day Celebrations Albert Hall London), Full House (Palace Theatre Watford), The Hairless Diva (Palace Theatre Watford); *Television* appearances incl: The Young Ones, Girls on Top, The French and Saunders Show, Flossie in Happy Families (BBC 2), 5 series of Naked Video (writing and performing own material in between sketches, BBC 2), Wogan, Hysteria, The New Statesman, Bottom, Absolutely Fabulous (BBC), One Foot in the Grave (BBC), presented Butter Fingers (Taste CRN), occasional presenter Heaven and Earth Show (BBC 1), cmmd to write sitcom for BBC2 2001–02; *Radio* female actress in BBC Radio 4's In One Ear (Sony Award for Best Comedy); other radio work incl: writer and performer two series of Life With Lederer (Radio 4), short story readings (Radio 3 and 4), Comic Cuts (Radio 5), reg writer and performer of comic monologues Woman's Hour (Radio 4), wrote and featured in All Change (Radio 4, Pick of the Week) 2001; *Film* Solitaire for Two, Dance to your Daddy, Speak Like a Child (Screen Two); *Publications* Coping With Lederer, Single Minding (1995); contrib author in Girl's Night In/Big Night Out; author of numerous articles for New Woman, Options and She magazines, The Guardian; regular writer for Independent on Sunday LIFE and travel, Mail on Sunday travel, Woman and Home, EVE; *Recreations* cinema, reading, friends, pilates; *Style*—Ms Helen Lederer; ✉ c/o Elizabeth Ayto, Media Ambitions Ltd, Suite 2, Ground Floor, 127 Ladbroke Grove, London W11 1PN (tel 020 7229 6610, e-mail elizabeth@mediaambitions.com)

LEDERER, Peter J; CBE (2005, OBE 1994); s of Thomas Francis Lederer, and Phoebe, *née* Blackman; *b* 30 November 1950; *m* 10 Oct 1981, Marilyn Ruth MacPhail; *Career* Four Seasons Hotels Canada 1972–79, vice-pres Wood Wilkings Ltd Toronto 1979–81; gen mangr: Plaza Group of Hotels Toronto 1981–83, The Gleneagles Hotel 1983–; dir Guinness Enterprises 1987, md Gleneagles Hotels plc 1987–; dir Leading Hotels of the World; pres Inst of Hospitality, chm Scottish Tourist Bd (VisitScotland), dir VisitBritain, tstee Hospitality Industry Tst Scotland; tstee Springboard Charitable Tst; fndn patron Queen Margaret UC Edinburgh; Master Innholder; Freeman City of London, Liveryman Worshipful Co of Innholders; Hon DBA Queen Margaret UC Edinburgh; hon prof Univ of Dundee; CIMgt, FHCIMA, FSQA; *Recreations* Matthew and Mark; *Style*— Peter J Lederer, Esq, CBE; ✉ The Gleneagles Hotel, Auchterarder, Perthshire PH3 1NF (tel 01764 694401, fax 01764 664444, e-mail peter.lederer@gleneagles.com)

LEDERMAN, David; QC (1991); s of Dr E K Lederman, of London, and Marjorie, *née* Smith; *b* 8 February 1942; *Educ* Clayesmore Public Sch, Gonville & Caius Coll Cambridge (MA); *Children* 2 da (Samantha b 7 Sept 1970, Chloe b 28 April 1973), 1 s (Ben b 16 Oct 1977); *Career* called to the Bar Inner Temple 1966; recorder of the Crown Court 1990–; *Recreations* horses, skiing; *Style*— David Lederman, Esq, QC

LEDGER, Christopher John Walton; JP (1993); s of Peter Walton Ledger, of Poundsbury, Dorset, and Barbara Nancy, *née* Eve; *b* 5 February 1943; *Educ* The Nautical Coll Pangbourne; *m* 1, 21 April 1971 (m dis 1973); m 2, 19 Sept 1977, Gillian Penelope, da of Col Paul Heberden Rogers (d 1972); 1 da (Nicola Kate b 10 Aug 1978), 1 s (James Walton Herberden b 17 July 1981); *Career* cmmnd 2 Lt RM 1962, offr 43 Commando 1964, OC Recce Tp 45 Commando 1965–66, ATURM Poole 1966–67, OC HMS Bulwark 1967–69, Adj RM Poole 1969–72, ATT HQ CO Forces 1972–74; Shell UK Ltd: joined 1974, PA mangr Expro 1976–77, mangr Small Business Initiative Films and Educnl Serv 1978–81, dir of PA 1981–84, chief exec World Energy Business 1984–86; chief exec The Phoenix Initiative 1986–91; dir: Reportboard Ltd, Freetrack Marine Ltd; Liveryman Worshipful Co of Grocers 1972; Queens Commendation for Brave Conduct 1965; FEI, FRSA; *Recreations* sailing, shooting; *Clubs* Royal Cornwall Yacht, Special Forces, Tamesis, RMSC; *Style*— Christopher Ledger, Esq; ✉ 21 The Green, Langdon Park, Teddington, Middlesex TW11 9PR (tel 020 8977 3451, fax 020 8943 9116); PO Box 6414, Sturminster Newton, Dorset DT18 9AH (tel 020 8943 9116, e-mail christopher.ledger@freetrackmarine.com, website www.freetrackmarine.com)

LEDGER, Sir Philip Stevens; kt (1999), CBE (1985); s of Walter Stephen Ledger (d 1986), of Bexhill-on-Sea, and Winifred Kathleen, *née* Stevens; *b* 12 December 1937; *Educ* Bexhill GS, King's Coll Cambridge (MA, MusB); *m* 15 April 1963, Mary Erryl, *née* Wells; 1 s (Timothy b 1964), 1 da (Katharine b 1966); *Career* master of music Chelmsford Cathedral 1962–65, dir of music UEA 1965–73 (dean Sch of Fine Arts and Music 1968–71), conductor Univ of Cambridge Musical Soc 1973–82, dir of music and organist King's Coll Cambridge 1974–82, princ RSAMD 1982–2001; pres: Royal Coll of Organists 1992–94, Incorporated Soc of Musicians 1994–95; Hon LLD Univ of Strathclyde 1987, Hon DUniv Central England 1998, Hon DMus RSAMD Univ of Glasgow and Univ of St Andrews 2001; FRCM 1983, Hon RAM 1984, FRNCM 1989, Hon GSM 1989, FRCO; *Recreations* swimming, theatre-going; *Style*— Sir Philip Ledger, CBE; ✉ 2 Lancaster Drive, Upper Rissington, Gloucestershire GL54 2QZ (tel 01451 820009)

LEDINGHAM, Prof John Gerard Garvin; s of Dr John Ledingham (d 1970), of Ladbroke Square, London, and Dr Una Christina Ledingham, *née* Garvin (d 1965); *b* 19 October 1929; *Educ* Rugby, New Coll Oxford (MA, DM), Middx Hosp Med Sch Univ of London (BM BCh); *m* 3 March 1962, Elaine Mary, da of Richard Glyn Maliphant (d 1977), of Cardiff; 4 da (Joanna b 22 March 1963, Catherine b 19 May 1964, Clare b 10 Oct 1968, Sarah b 20 Nov 1971); *Career* Nat Serv 2 Lt RA 1949–50; registrar in med Middx Hosp London 1960–62 (house offr 1957–58), sr registrar Westminster Hosp London 1963–65, visiting fell Columbia Univ NY 1965–66, consIt physician United Oxford Hosps 1966–74; Univ of Oxford: May reader in med 1974–95, prof 1989–95, dir of clinical studies 1977–81 and 1991–95; fell New Coll Oxford 1974 (emeritus 1996–, hon fell 2000); contrib various med and science jls; tstee: Nuffield Tst 1978–2003, Beit Tst, Oxford Hospital Devpt Improvement Fund, Commonwealth Scholarships Cmmn 1992–98; chm Nuffield Oxford Hospitals Tst 1995–2005; examiner in med: Univs of Cambridge, Glasgow, Oxford, London, Southampton and Sheffield, Sultan Qaboos Univ, Royal Coll of Physicians, Royal Coll of Surgns of Ireland; former memb GMC; chm Med Research Soc 1988–91, memb Animal Procedures Ctee of Home Sec 1985–92, memb Supra-Regnl Servs Ctee Dept of Health 1983–86, censor RCP 1984–85, memb Nuffield Cncl on Bioethics 2000–03; former hon sec and hon treas Assoc of Physicians of GB and Ireland, former pres Br Hypertension Soc; William Osler Memorial Medal 2000; FRCP 1971; *Books* Oxford Textbook of Medicine (ed with D J Weatherall and D A Warrell, 1983, 1987 and 1995), Concise Oxford Textbook of Medicine (ed with D A Warrell, 2000); *Recreations* music, golf; *Clubs* Vincent's (Oxford); *Style*— Prof John Ledingham; ✉ 124 Oxford Road, Cumnor, Oxford OX2 9PQ (tel and fax 01865 865806, e-mail jeled@btopenworld.com)

LEE, (Edward) Adam Michael; s of His Hon Judge Michael Lee, DSC, DL (d 1983), of Winchester, Hants, and Valerie Burnett Georges, *née* Drake-Brockman (d 1995); *b* 29 June 1942; *Educ* Winchester, ChCh Oxford (MA); *m* 5 July 1975, Carola Jean, da of Capt Frederick Le Hunte Anderson (d 1989), of Hungerford, Berks; 2 s (Frederick Edward Maconchy b 1977, (James) Michael Maconchy b 1981); *Career* called to the Bar Middle Temple 1964; cadet Glyn, Mills & Co 1964; Williams & Glyn's Bank: sr planner 1969, dep dir City Div 1974; local dir: Child & Co 1977–87, Holts Branches 1978–87, Drummonds 1985–87; asst gen mangr Royal Bank of Scotland 1985–87, gp devpt dir Adam & Co 1988–90; dir: Duncan Lawrie Tst Corp 1990–92, Trustee Resources 1993–96, Minmet plc 1993–96, Crediton Minerals plc 1996–99; chm Unison International plc 1992–94; advsr Cncl Grange Park Opera 1998–; consIt to various cos; chm Explosion! The Museum of Naval Firepower Gosport 2000–03; sec and treas: Inverforth Charitable Tst 1990–2007, Matthews Wrightson Charity Tst 1990–2007; tstee Chelsea Opera Gp; chm Temple Bar Masters Assoc 2004–; memb Ct of Assts Worshipful Co of Dyers' 1998 (Liveryman 1984, Renter Warden 2002–03, Prime Warden 2003–04); FCIB 1981; *Recreations* opera, tennis, golf, fly fishing, food and wine, travel; *Clubs* Travellers, Rye Golf, Chatham Dining (chm); *Style*— Adam Lee, Esq; ✉ The Farm, Northington, Alresford, Hampshire SO24 9TH (tel and fax 01962 732205)

LEE, Alan Peter; s of Peter Alexander Lee, of Sidmouth, Devon, and Christina, *née* Carmichael; *b* 13 June 1954; *Educ* Cavendish GS Hemel Hempstead; *m* 18 Oct 1980, Patricia Rosemary Drury, da of James Chesshire; 1 da (Victoria Helen b 22 Oct 1984), 1 s (James Patrick b 19 Feb 1987); *Career* sports writer; Watford Observer 1970–74, Hayter's Agency 1974–78; cricket corr: Mail on Sunday 1982–87, The Times 1988–99; covered England home test matches 1977–98; covered England tours: India and Aust 1976–77, Aust 1978–79, 1982–83, 1986–87, 1990–91, 1994–95, and 1998–99, W Indies 1981, 1986, 1990, 1994 and 1998, Pakistan 1983, India 1984–85, NZ 1988, 1992 and 1997; covered World Cups 1979, 1983, 1987, 1992 and 1996; racing correspondent The Times 1999–; highly commended Sports Magazine Writer of the Year 1987, shortlisted Sports Reporter of the Year 1999, Racing Journalist of the Year 2001, Sports Journalist of the Year 2002, Specialist Sports Corr of the Year 2002; *Books* over 20 on cricket, racing and golf incl: A Pitch in Both Camps (1979), Jump Jockeys (1980), Lambourn (1982), Fred (biography of Fred Winter, 1991), To be a Champion (1992), Lord Ted (1995), Raising the Stakes (1996); *Recreations* National Hunt racing, tennis; *Clubs* Cricketers' Club of London, Cricket Writers'; *Style*— Alan Lee, Esq; ✉ 8 The Courtyard, Montpellier Street, Cheltenham, Gloucestershire GL50 1SR (tel and fax 01242 572637); The Times, 1 Virginia Street, London E1 9XN (tel 020 7782 5944, fax 020 7782 5211, mobile 078 8764 2255)

LEE, Anthony D M; *b* 15 August 1956, Singapore; *Educ* St Lawrence Coll Ramsgate, Chatham House Ramsgate, Thanet Tech Coll, Westminster Hotel and Catering Coll; *m*;

1 s; *Career* The Connaught London: receptionist 1979–80, chef de brigade 1980–82; receptionist The Crillon Hotel Paris 1982–84; The Connaught London: reception mangr 1985–88 (asst reception mangr 1984–85), house mangr 1988–2002 (incl takeover by Blackstone Gp), gen mangr 2002–; memb: HCIMA, Amicale Internationale des Sous-Directeurs et Chefs de Réception des Grands Hôtels (AICR), Craft Guild of Chefs and Cookery and Food Assoc (ACFA), West One Mangrs' Assoc; awards for the Connaught incl: voted Number One Hotel In London by Travel and Leisure 2003, RAC Gold Ribbon 2003, AA Top 200 2003; *Recreations* sports incl tennis, sailing, music, design, current affairs, IT, travel, theatre and dining; *Style—* Anthony Lee, Esq; ✉ The Connaught, Carlos Place, Mayfair, London W1K 2AL (tel 020 7499 7070, fax 020 7314 3538, mobile 07771 665170, e-mail alee@the-connaught.co.uk)

LEE, Prof Christine Ann; *b* 5 March 1943, Hampton, Middx; *Educ* Tiffin Girls' Sch Kingston upon Thames, Somerville Coll Oxford (MA, Kirkaldy prize in natural scis), Univ of Oxford Med Sch (clinical entrance scholar, Nuffield travelling scholar, BM BCh, MD, Radcliffe prize in pathology), Univ of London (DSc); *m* Prof Roy Pounder, *qv*; 2 s (Jeremy, Tom); *Career* laboratory technician Dept of Haematology Royal Postgrad Med Sch London 1962, student Somerville Coll Oxford 1962–66, res asst Inst for Haematology Univ Clinic Freiburg W Germany 1966, student Univ of Oxford Med Sch 1966–69; house physicial and surgn Radcliffe Infirmary Oxford 1969–70; SHO: renal med Hammersmith Hosp London 1970–71, neurology United Oxford Hosps 1971, chest med Brompton Hosp London 1971–72, renal med Royal Free Hosp London 1972; registrar (haematology) St Mary's Hosp London 1973–76, sr registrar (haematology) St George's Hosp Med Sch London 1976–82, res sr registrar and hon lectr Haemophilia Centre and Haemostasis Unit Royal Free Hosp 1982–83, sr lectr in haematology Charing Cross and Westminster Med Sch 1984–87; conslt haematologist Haemophilia Centre and Haemostasis Unit Royal Free Hosp 1987– (pt/t hon conslt 1986–87), dir Haemophilia Centre and Haemostasis Unit Royal Free Hampstead NHS Tst 1992– (actg dir 1991–92), prof of haemophilia Royal Free Hosp Sch of Med 1997– (hon sr lectr 1987–97), prof of haemophilia Univ of London 1997; Alfred visiting professorship Melbourne 1999; chm Int Haemophilia Trg Centres Ctee of World Fedn Haemophilia 1996–, fndr and co-ed Haemophilia 1994; Henri Chagneau prize French Haemophilia Soc 1992 (jtly), Alpha Award 2001; memb: Br Soc of Haematology (BSH), World Fedn of Haemophilia (WFH), Int Soc of Thrombosis and Haemostasis (ISTH), BHIVA, BASL; FRCP 1990, FRCPath 1994; *Publications* author of over 300 published papers, articles and reviews in learned jls, author/ed of various textbooks; *Style—* Prof Christine A Lee; ✉ Haemophilia Centre and Haemostasis Unit, Royal Free Hospital, Pond Street, London NW3 2QG (tel 020 7830 2238, fax 020 7830 2178)

LEE, Christopher Frank Carandini; CBE (2001); s of Lt-Col Geoffrey Trollope Lee (d 1941), and Contessa Estelle Marie Carandini (d 1981); m descends from one of the six oldest Italian families, created Count 1184 and granted Arms Emperor Charlemagne by Emperor Frederick Barbarossa; *b* 27 May 1922; *Educ* Wellington; *m* 1961, Birgit, da of Richard Emil Kroencke (d 1982); 1 da (Christina b 1963); *Career* actor (entered film industry 1947), author, singer; served WWII RAF 1941–46, Flt Lt, Intelligence and Special Forces, W Desert, Malta, Sicily, Italy and Central Europe (despatches 1944); Officier Arts Sciences et Lettres (France) 1974, CStJ 1997 (OStJ 1986), Officier dans l'Ordre des Arts et des Lettres (France) 2002; *Film* over 250 feature film appearances worldwide incl: Moulin Rouge, Tale of Two Cities, Dracula, Rasputin, The Devil Rides Out, Private Life of Sherlock Homes, The Wicker Man, The Three Musketeers, The Four Musketeers, Man With The Golden Gun, To the Devil a Daughter, Airport 77, The Far Pavilions, 1941, The Return of Captain Invincible, The Disputation (TV), Round the World in 80 Days (TV), The Return of Musketeers, Gremlins 2: The New Batch, The French Revolution (TV), Sherlock Holmes and the Leading Lady (TV), Sherlock Holmes and the Incident at Victoria Falls (TV), Death Train, A Feast at Midnight, Jinnah, Sleepy Hollow, Gormenghast (TV), The Lord of The Rings: The Fellowship of the Ring, The Lord of the Rings: The Two Towers, The Lord of The Rings: The Return of the King, Star Wars: Episode II, Star Wars: Episode III, Charlie and the Chocolate Factory, The Corpse Bride, Greyfriars Bobby; also theatre, opera and TV; *Awards* Lifetime Achievement Award London Film Critics 1994, Lifetime Achievement Award Germany 2001, Lifetime Achievement Award Empire Awards 2002, Lifetime Achievement Evening Standard Awards 2002, World Award for Lifetime Achievement 2002; *Books* Christopher Lee's X Certificate (1975), Archives of Evil (1975), Tall, Dark and Gruesome (1977, reprint 1997), Lord of Misrule (2003); *Recreations* golf, travel, languages, opera; *Clubs* Buck's, MCC, Hon Co of Edinburgh Golfers, Travellers (Paris); *Style—* Christopher Lee, Esq, CBE; ✉ c/o ICM, Oxford House, 76 Oxford Street, London W1D 1BS (tel 020 7636 6565, fax 020 7323 0101)

LEE, David; *b* 12 August 1929; *Educ* Reay Central Sch, Royal GS Newcastle upon Tyne, Johannesburg Conservatoire of Music; *m* Leila Sklair; 2 da (Laura (Mrs Spicer), Dr Abigail Lee Six); *Career* fndr Jazz FM Radio (first UK jazz radio station) 1990; formerly: pianist and mangr Dankworth Orchestra, musical dir TV progs (incl Here Today, That Was The Week That Was and Not So Much A Programme), musical dir and advsr to Ms Judy Garland, composer and conductor of various film scores and TV signature tunes, music composer various advtg campaigns (incl British Airways, Kelloggs and Persil), composer hit songs incl Goodness Gracious Me (Ivor Novello award 1960); BBC Jazz Musician of the Year 1983, Media Personality of the Year 1990; *Publications* Nothing Rhymes with Silver; *Recreations* cricket, swimming, crossword puzzles; *Style—* David Lee, Esq; ✉ (tel 020 8549 2105, fax 020 8549 4601, e-mail jazdeelee@supanet.com)

LEE, Dr Gloria Lulu; da of Alexander John Burton Edlin (d 1989), of Highcliffe-on-Sea, Dorset, and Louise Violet, *née* Theobald (d 1991); *b* 22 October 1931; *Educ* St Paul's Girls' Sch London, Univ of London (BSc(Econ)), Univ of Birmingham (MSocSc, PhD); *m* 2 June 1951, Norman Lee, s of Enoch Lee; 3 da (Amanda Lulu b 8 Feb 1953, Roberta Lulu b 1 Feb 1955, Fiona Lulu b 6 May 1958); *Career* Aston Univ: lectr Dept of Industrial Admin 1968–86, sr lectr 1986–97, dir postgrad studies Aston Business Sch then dean Faculty of Management, Languages and European Studies 1993–97; prof of change mgmnt Bucks Chilterns UC 1997–; memb: Acad of Mgmnt, Western Acad of Mgmnt, Br Acad of Mgmnt, Euro Operations Mgmnt Assoc; *Books* Who Gets to the Top? (1981), The Manufacture of Disadvantage (jtly, 1987), Engineers and Management (jtly, 1992); *Recreations* swimming, sailing, windsurfing, canoeing, cruising inland waterways, mountain biking; *Style—* Prof Gloria Lee; ✉ Bridge House, 17 Noddington Lane, Whittington, Lichfield, Staffordshire WS14 9PA (tel 01543 432030, fax 01543 432137); Buckinghamshire Chilterns University College, Buckingham Business School, Newland Park, Gorelands Lane, Chalfont St Giles, Buckinghamshire HP8 4AD (tel 01494 522141, fax 01494 874230)

LEE, Prof Hermione; CBE (2003); da of Dr Benjamin Lee, and Josephine Lee; *b* 29 February 1948; *Educ* Lycée de Londres, City of London Sch for Girls, The Queen's Coll and St Hilda's Coll Oxford (MA, MPhil); *m* 1991, Prof John Barnard, *qv*; *Career* instr William and Mary Coll Williamsburg USA 1970–71, lectr Univ of Liverpool 1971–77; Univ of York: lectr 1977–88, sr lectr 1988–90, reader 1990–93, prof of English 1993–98; Goldsmiths' prof of English literature Univ of Oxford 1998–, fell New Coll Oxford; judge: Faber Prize 1981, Booker Prize 1981 and 2006 (chm of judges), W H Smith Prize 1987–92, Cheltenham Prize 1987, David Cohen Prize 1998; presenter: Book Four (Channel 4) 1982–86, Booker Prize (LWT) 1984–87; memb: Mgmnt Ctee Lumb Bank Arvon Fndn 1988–92, Arts Cncl Literature Panel 1998–2002; Rose Mary Crawshay Prize British Acad 1997; FRSL, FBA 2001; Hon DLitt Univ of Liverpool 2002; hon fell St Cross Coll and St Hilda's Coll Oxford 1998, fell American Acad of Arts and Scis 2003; *Books* The Novels of Virginia Woolf (1977), Elizabeth Bowen (1981 and 1999), Philip Roth (1982), Willa Cather: A Life Saved Up (1989), Virginia Woolf (1996), Virginia Woolf's Nose: Essays on Biography (2005), Body Parts: Essays on Life-Writing (2005), Edith Wharton (2007); editions and anthologies of: Kipling, Trollope, Woolf, Bowen, Cather; The Secret Self (short stories by women writers); *Clubs* Athenaeum; *Style—* Prof Hermione Lee, CBE, FRSL, FBA; ✉ New College, Oxford OX1 3BN (tel 01865 279555)

LEE, Howard Andrew Gabriel; s of Jack Lee, of Sydney, Aust, and Nora, *née* Blackburne; *b* 26 February 1953; *Educ* St Edward's Sch Oxford, Jesus Coll Cambridge (MA); *m* 16 Dec 1983, Jessica Lena, da of Robert Benton Bottomley; 2 da (Harriet Aimee b 29 January 1986, Rebecca Elizabeth b 9 March 1989), 2 s (James Jonathan b 2 June 1987, Jack b 17 Oct 1995); *Career* with Charles Barker 1974–78, dep dir of info Nat Enterprise Bd 1978–80, public affairs exec British Telecom 1980–82; Valin Pollen: joined 1982, assoc dir 1983, dir 1984, int dir 1985, dir Investor Rels Div 1988, md Carter Valin Pollen Ltd 1988 (chief exec 1989), dir Valin International plc, dir Valin Pollen plc 1989 (chief exec 1990); Gavin Anderson & Company Ltd: chief exec 1991–97, head of Europe 1997–, chm London 2000–, exec vice-chm of gp 2000–; memb City & Financial Group IPR 1985, assoc memb Investor Rels Soc 1989; *Recreations* shooting, wine; *Clubs* Savile; *Style—* Howard Lee, Esq; ✉ Gavin Anderson & Company, New Liverpool House, 15–17 Eldon Street, London EC2M 7LD (tel 020 7457 2345, fax 020 7457 2330)

LEE, James Giles; s of John Lee, CBE, and Muriel, *née* Giles; *b* 23 December 1942; *Educ* Trinity Coll Glenalmond, Univ of Glasgow, Harvard Univ; *m* 1966, Linn, *née* MacDonald; 2 da (Maggie b 1968, Katie b 1971), 1 s (John b 1974); *Career* ptnr McKinsey & Co 1969–80; dir S Pearson & Son 1981–84, dep chm Yorkshire TV 1982–85, chm Goldcrest Films and TV 1981–86, dir Boston Consulting Group Ltd 1987–92, md Lee & Co 1992–, dir Phoenix Pictures Inc 1995–2005; non-exec dir: Pearson Television Ltd 1993–2001, Natom Media Gp Kenya 2002–; chm: Performing Arts Labs Tst 1990–98, Scottish Screen 1998–2002, Maidstone & Tunbridge Wells NHS Tst 2003–; dir Film Cncl 1999–2005; Hon DLitt Caledonian Univ; *Recreations* photography, travelling, sailing; *Clubs* Reform, Harvard (NY); *Style—* J G Lee, Esq; ✉ Meadow Wood, Penshurst, Kent TN11 8AD (tel 01892 870309, e-mail jas.lee@btinternet.com)

LEE, Jennifer Elizabeth; da of Ernest M B Lee, and Mary, *née* Fowlie; *b* 21 August 1956; *Educ* St Margaret's Sch for Girls Aberdeen, Edinburgh Coll of Art (DipAD), RCA (MA); *m* 29 March 1990, Jake Tilson, *qv*, s of Joe Tilson; 1 da (Hannah Lee Tilson b 26 May 1995); *Career* potter; *Solo Exhibitions* The Scottish Gallery Edinburgh 1981, Anatol Orient London 1984, Crafts Cncl Sideshow ICA London 1985, Rosenthal Studio-Haus London 1985, Craft Centre Royal Exchange Theatre Manchester 1986, Crafts Cncl Shop V & A 1987, Craft Centre and Design Gallery City Art Gallery Leeds 1987, Galerie Besson London 1990, 1992 and 1995, Graham Gallery NY 1991, Galleri Lejonet Stockholm 1993, Röhsska Museum of Arts and Crafts Göteborg 1993, Aberdeen Art Gallery 1994, Osiris Brussels 1994, Galerie Besson London 1995, James Graham and Sons NY 1996, Galerie Besson London 1997 and 2000, James Graham & Sons NY 1999, Frank Lloyd Gall LA 2002, Galerie Besson London 2003, Frank Lloyd Gallery Santa Monica 2005, Liverpool Street Gallery Sydney 2006; *Group Exhibitions* incl: Three Generations British Ceramics (Maya Behn Zürich) 1984, Jugend Gestaltet (Exempla Munich) 1985, Jugend Formt Keramik (Mathildenhöhe Darmstadt Germany) 1985, British Ceramic Art (Transform NY) 1985, Zeitgenössische Keramik Aus Grossbritannien (Keramik Studio Vienna) 1986, New British Design (Osaka and Tokyo) 1987, On a Plate (The Serpentine Gallery) 1987, British Ceramics (Marianne Heller Galerie Sandhausen Germany) 1987, The New Spirit (Crafts Cncl Gallery London and tour) 1987, Craft and Folk Museum (Los Angeles) 1988, Ton in Ton (Landesmuseum Germany) 1988, Christmas Exhibition (Galerie Besson London) 1988, Sotheby's Decorative Award Exhibition (Yorakucho Seibu Japan) 1988, Galleri Lejonet (Stockholm) 1989, L'Europe des Ceramistes (Auxerre France touring Spain, Austria, Hungary) 1989, The Royal Scottish Museum (Edinburgh) 1989, Lucie Rie, Hans Coper and their Pupils (Sainsbury Centre Norwich) 1990, Int Art Fair (Chicago) 1990, The Fitzwilliam Museum (Cambridge) 1991, British Ceramics (Int Art Fair Bologna Italy) 1991, British Ceramics (Graham Gallery NY) 1991, Contemporary British Ceramics (Graham Gallery NY) 1992, Int Ceramic Art (Nat Museum of History Taipei Taiwan) 1992, Keramik aus Grossbritannien und Japan (Galerie Hinteregger Austria) 1992, Handbuilt Ceramics (Scottish Gallery Edinburgh) 1993, Towards the Future (Marianne Heller Germany) 1993, Visions of Craft (Crafts Cncl London) 1993, 20th Century European Ceramics (Los Angeles) 1993, Gallery Koyanagi Tokyo 1994, Sculpture, Objects and Functional Art (Chicago) 1994), The David Collection NY 1994, Wim Vromans Amsterdam 1995, James Graham & Sons NY 1995, Design im Wandel (Übersee Museum Bremen Germany) 1996, European Ceramics (Yufuku Gallery Tokyo) 1997, English Crafts (The Works Gallery Philadelphia) 1997, Gestaltendes Handwerk (Munich) 1998, Spirit of the Times (Bowes Museum Co Durham) 1998, Women in Europe (Galerie Marianne Heller Germany) 1998, Clay into Art (Metropolitan Museum of Art, NY) 1998, Current Context - new ways of seeing (Royal Museum, Edinburgh) 1999, Crafts Cncl 25th Anniversary Exhibition (V & A) 1999, Millennium Mugs (Galerie Besson London) 1999, Br Ceramics.2000.dk (Keramikmuseet Grimmerhus Denmark) 2000, Color and Fire: Defining Moments in Studio Ceramics 1950–2000 (Los Angeles County Museum of Art) 2000, Ceramic Biennale (Ichen World Ceramic Centre Korea) 2001, Poetics of Clay - An International Perspective, Philadelphia Art Alliance Philadelphia 2001, Bengt Julin's Ceramics, Gustavsbergs Porslinmuseum Sweden 2001, Modern Pots Ceramics from the Lisa Sainsbury Coll (Sainsbury Centre for Visual Arts UEA Norwich) 2001, Ceramic Modernism, The Gardiner Museum of Ceramic Art Toronto 2002, Vasen aus 10 Ländern (Bayerischer Kunstgewerbe-Verein Munich) 2002, Sofa (Chicago) 2002, British Ceramics (James Graham & Sons New York), British Cramics: Five Artists (Frank Lloyd Gallery Santa Monica CA) 2003, Constructed Clay (Galerie Besson London) 2003, SOFA (Chicago) 2003 and 2004, European Ceramics - Westerwald Prize (Keramik Museum Westerwald) 2004, Celebrating 30 Years (Crafts Cncl Shop at V&A) 2005, A Homage to Ruth Duckworth (Garth Clark Gallery NY) 2005, Modern Pots (Dulwich Picture Gallery) 2005, European Ceramics Biennale (Musée de l'Outil et de la Pensee Ouvriere Troyes) 2005, One Piece - One Artist (Galerie Marianne Heller Germany) 2005, Contemporary Potters (Galerie Besson London) 2005, Puur Klei (Pottenbakkers Museum Holland) 2006, Collect (V&A Museum London) 2006, Classic and Contemporary Ceramics (Galerie Besson London) 2006 and 2007, SOFA (NY) 2007; *Collections* work in numerous public collections incl: V&A London, Royal Scottish Museum, Glasgow Museums and Art Galleries, Los Angeles Co Museum of Art, Leeds City Art Gallery, Contemporary Art Society, Crafts Cncl Collection, The Sainsbury Centre (Norwich), Fitzwilliam Museum Cambridge, Hawkes Bay Art Gallery NZ, Peters Fndn London, Buckinghamshire Co Museum, Cleveland Collection Middlesbrough, Thamesdown Collection Swindon, Hove Museum and Art Gallery, Norwich Castle Museum, Aberdeen Art Gallery, Nat Museum of Sweden Stockholm, Cellmark Göteborg Sweden, Trustees Savings Bank Collection, Europa Kunst Handwerk Landesgerwerbeamt Stuttgart, Röhsska Konstslöjdmuseet Göteborg, Scripps Coll Claremont Calif, Norwich Castle Museum, Hove Museum and Art Gallery, Bellerive Museum Zurich, Tochigi Prefectural Museum of Fine Arts Japan, Kunstsammlungen der Veste Coburg Germany, Museum für Kunst und Gewerbe Hamburg, Fitzwilliam Museum Cambridge, Long Beach Museum of Art Calif, Minneapolis Inst of Art, Philadelphia Museum of Art, Metropolitan Museum of Art NY; *Awards* David Gordon Meml Tst

Prize 1979, Andrew Grant Travelling Scholarship 1979, Allen Lane Penguin Book Award 1983, Mathildenhöhe Award Rosenthal Germany 1984, Jugend Gestaltet Prize Munich 1985, Crafts Cncl Grant 1987, Br Cncl Exhibitions Grant 1991, Bayerischer Staatspreis 1998, Crafts Cncl Outward Missions Grant 2002; *Style*— Ms Jennifer Lee; ✉ c/o Galerie Besson, 15 Royal Arcade, 28 Old Bond Street, London W1S 4SP (tel 020 7491 1706)

LEE, Jeremy Charles Roger Barnett; s of Lt Cdr Charles Alexander Barnett Lee, RNR (d 1982), of Phyllis Kathleen Mary, *née* Gunnell (d 1986); *b* 10 July 1944; *Educ* Bristol Cathedral Sch; *m* 4 April 1972 (m dis 1983), Patricia Margaret Drake, *née* Coleridge; 3 da (Veryan Georgina Coleridge b 1974, Isobel Mary b 1977, Caroline Sybella b 1978); *Career* RM: 2 Lt 1962, Troop Cdr 40 Commando serving in Malaya and Sabah 1964–65, Lt 1965, Co Cdr Sultan's Armed Forces Muscat and Oman 1967–69, Adj (later Co Cdr) 40 Commando 1972–74, serving in NI and Cyprus (during Turkish invasion), Capt 1973, invalided 1976; admitted slr 1978; sr ptnr Symes Robinson and Lee (Exeter, Crediton and Budleigh Salterton) 1983–; Cons Pty: area treas Crediton 1980–88, chm Coldridge Brushford and Nymet Rowland Branch 1981–; Br Red Cross: chm 125 Ctee 1995–, chm Invitation Events Ctee 1996–2001, dir Solicitors Benevolent Assoc; rugby: Capt RM 1971, RN 1971, Exeter FC 1965–67 and 1969–72; memb: Anglo Omani Soc, Law Soc; ASBAH's Conversationalist of the Year 1990; Sultan's Bravery Medal 1968, Br Red Cross Cert of Commendation, Br Red Cross Badge of Honour for Distinguished Service; *Recreations* tennis, foxhunting, walking, marathon running, gardening, conversation; *Clubs* Army and Navy, LTA; *Style*— Jeremy Lee, Esq; ✉ Frogbury, Coldridge, Crediton, Devon EX17 6BW (tel 01363 83484); Symes Robinson and Lee, Manor Office, North Street, Crediton, Devon EX17 2BR (tel 01363 775566)

LEE, Jeremy James; s of Norman Lee, and Eileen, *née* Neave; *Educ* HS of Dundee; *Career* chef and food writer; chef: Old Mansion House Hotel Auchterhouse Angus Scotland, Bibendum, Alastair Little, Euphorium, Blue Print Cafe; food writer Guardian Weekend, conslt ed Saveur; *Recreations* eating, reading, film, music; *Clubs* Groucho, Union; *Style*— Jeremy Lee, Esq; ✉ David Higham's Associates, Lower John Street, London W1

LEE, Prof John Anthony; s of Cecil John Lee (d 1977), of Southsea, Hants, and Phyllis Gwendoline, *née* Fry (d 2001); *b* 18 March 1942; *Educ* The Portsmouth GS, Univ of Sheffield (BSc, PhD); *m* 17 April 1965, Barbara Lee, da of Thomas Harold Wright (d 1996); 2 s (Richard b 1968, Peter b 1971); *Career* Univ of Manchester: asst lectr in botany 1967, lectr 1970, sr lectr 1979, prof of environmental biology 1988–94, head Dept of Environmental Biology 1986–93; Univ of Sheffield: prof of environmental biology 1994–2005 (emeritus 2005–), chm Dept of Animal and Plant Sciences 1995–2002, Dean Faculty of Science 2002–05; ed The Journal of Ecology 1983–90, author of many scientific papers; pres: Br Ecological Soc 1996–97, Int Ecology Soc 1998– (vice-pres 1989–95); memb: Br Ecological Soc, Soc for Experimental Biology, Nat Tst Cncl 1999–; *Recreations* theatre, Portsmouth FC, hill walking; *Style*— Prof John Lee; ✉ Department of Animal and Plant Sciences, PO Box 601, The University of Sheffield, Sheffield S10 2UQ (tel 0114 222 0089, e-mail j.a.lee@sheffield.ac.uk)

LEE, Marcus; *Educ* Mackintosh Sch of Architecture Glasgow (BArch, Dip Arch); *Career* architect; YRM 1977–78, Nicholas Lacey Associates 1980–82, Richard Rogers Partnership 1982– (assoc dir 1996–); visiting lectr: Mackintosh School of Architecture Glasgow, UC Dublin, Univ of Birmingham; *Projects* incl: Gatwick Airport South Terminal, Lloyds of London HQ, Reuters HQ, Heathrow Airport Terminals 1 and 5, Madrid Airport, Greenwich Pennisula Masterplan, Millennium Dome; *Style*— Marcus Lee, Esq; ✉ Richard Rogers Partnership, Thames Wharf, Rainville Road, London W6 9HA

LEE, Eur Ing Prof Mark Howard; s of Clifford Howard Lee, of Derby, and Peggy Alice, *née* Osborne; *b* 9 April 1944; *Educ* Univ of Wales (BSc, MSc), Univ of Nottingham (PhD); *m* 24 July 1971, Elizabeth Anne, da of Rev Frank Andrew Willmot (d 1976), of London, 2 s (Matthew Peter Howard b 13 Oct 1976, Joseph Jonathan b 28 March 1979), 1 da (Bethan Louisa b 3 Jan 1984); *Career* lectr City of Leicester Poly 1969–74, prof of intelligent systems Univ of Wales Aberystwyth 1987– (lectr 1974–85, sr lectr 1985–87), visiting prof Univ of Auckland NZ 1988; FRSA, FIEE, CEng; *Books* Intelligent Robotics (1989), Intelligent Assembly Systems (ed with J J Rowland, 1995); *Recreations* mountaineering; *Style*— Prof Mark Lee; ✉ Department of Computer Science, University of Wales, Aberystwyth, Ceredigion SY23 3DB

LEE, Dr Melanie G; da of William Brown, and Pamela Brown; *Educ* Univ of York (BSc), Nat Inst for Med Research (PhD); *m* 1981, Christopher David Lee; 2 s (Oliver, Max); *Career* postdoctoral research fell: Cancer Research Campaign Imperial Coll London 1982–85, ICRF 1985–88; sr biologist rising to section head Glaxo Gp Research 1988–93, with Glaxo R&D 1993–95, research unit head GlaxoWellcome 1995–98; Bd dir Celltech plc 1998–2004, exec vice-pres R&D UCB 2004–; chm Cancer Research Technology (CRT) 2003–; chm Mgmnt Ctee Applied Genomics LINK Scheme Prog 2000–; tstee Cancer Research UK 2004–; FMedSci 2003; *Recreations* gym, keeping fit, gardening in containers, flowers; *Style*— Dr Melanie Lee; ✉ UCB, 208 Bath Road, Slough, Berkshire SL1 3WE (tel 01753 777142, fax 01753 447590, e-mail melanie.lee@ucb-group.com)

LEE, Prof (John) Michael; s of John Ewart Lee (d 1975), of Castle Donington, and May, *née* Humber (d 1992); *b* 29 March 1932; *Educ* Henry Mellish GS Nottingham, ChCh Oxford (MA, BLitt); *m* 23 June 1962, Mary Joy, da of James Philip Sorby Bowman (d 1962), of Barnack; 1 s (Matthew b 1964), 1 da (Helen b 1966); *Career* lectr and sr lectr in govt Univ of Manchester 1958–67, princ (academic secondment) HM Treasy 1967–69, sr lectr Inst of Cwlth Studies 1969–72, reader in politics Birkbeck Coll 1972–81, dean Faculty of Social Sciences Univ of Bristol 1987–90 (prof of politics 1981–92, emeritus prof 1992); visiting fell Centre for Int Studies LSE 1993–95; jt ed Jl of RIPA 1974–86, ed Richmond History 2001–05; Romney Street Gp: prog sec 1994–99, vice-chm 2001–04, chm 2004–; chm Friends of Richmond Libraries 2001–07; FRHistS 1971; *Books* Social Leaders and Public Persons (1963), Colonial Development and Good Government (1967), African Armies and Civil Order (1969), The Churchill Coalition (1980), At the Centre of Whitehall (1998) with GW Jones and June Burnham, The Making of Modern Twickenham (2005); *Style*— Prof Michael Lee; ✉ The Courtyard Cottage, 1 Cross Deep, Twickenham TW1 4QJ (tel 020 8744 2106)

LEE, Michael James Arthur; s of Brian Arthur Frederick Lee (d 1983), of Newton Abbot, Devon, and Rachel Dorothy Strange, *née* Wickham (d 1992); *b* 22 June 1942; *Educ* Blundell's, Univ of Durham (LLB); *m* 1, 4 March 1974 (m dis 1984), Judith Mary, da of Humphrey David Oliver of Alresford Hants; 1 da (Henrietta Victoria b 4 Oct 1976); m 2, 18 March 1993, Caroline Mary, da of Duncan Hamilton (d 1994), of Marston Magna, Somerset; 1 da (Olivia Grace b 28 Feb 1994); *Career* admitted slr 1966; articled clerk Lovell White and King 1963–66 (asst slr 1966–67); legal asst New Scotland Yard 1967–69; Norton Rose: asst slr 1970–73, ptnr 1973–, sr litigation ptnr 1993–, managing ptnr Paris Office 1997–; memb Worshipful Co of City of London Slrs; memb: Law Soc, Int Bar Assoc, dir City Disputes Panel; FCIArb; *Recreations* sailing, skiing; *Clubs* RAC; *Style*— Michael Lee, Esq; ✉ Norton Rose, Kempson House, Camomile Street, London EC3A 7AN (tel 020 7283 6000, fax 020 7283 6500, telex 883652)

LEE, Paul Anthony; s of Wilfred Lee (d 1970), of Manchester, and Anne, *née* Molyneux; *b* 26 January 1946; *Educ* Central GS Manchester, Clare Coll Cambridge (MA, LLB); *m* 16 Sept 1977, Elisabeth Lindsay, da of Maj Geoffrey Robert Taylor, of Manchester; 2 s (Jonathan b 1980, William b 1985), 1 da (Antonia b 1983); *Career* admitted slr 1970; Addleshaw Goddard (formerly Addleshaw Booth & Co): ptnr 1973–, managing ptnr 1991–, sr ptnr 1997–; dir: Leaf Properties 1986–, Barlows plc 1997–, Northern Ballet Theatre Ltd 1997–2005, Yorkshire Building Society 1998– (vice-chm 2005–), j4b plc 2000–05, Aberdeen Growth VCT I plc 2001–04, Hopkins and Jones Ltd 2001–; chm: Patrons and Associations Manchester City Art Gallery 1981–97, Bd of Govrs Chethams Sch of Music 1990–, NW Region CBI 1998–2000 (vice-chm 1997–98 and 2000–01, chm 1998–2000) NW Expansion Ctee The Prince's Tst 2001–, memb Bd CBI 2004–; govr Royal Northern Coll of Music 1991–; feoffee Chethams Hosp and Library 1990 (chm of Feoffees 2005–); *Recreations* the arts, travel, tennis, wine; *Clubs* Savile, Garrick, Real Tennis and Racquets (Manchester); *Style*— Paul A Lee, Esq; ✉ Riverbank Cottage, 2 Stanton Avenue, W Didsbury, Manchester M20 2PG; Addleshaw Goddard, 150 Aldersgate Street, London EC1A 4EJ (tel 020 7788 5511, fax 020 7606 4390, e-mail paul.lee@addleshawgoddard.com)

LEE, Richard Alan; s of late Air Chief Marshal Sir David Lee, GBE, CB, and Denise, *née* Hartoch; *b* 31 August 1943; *Educ* Bedford Sch, Fitzwilliam Coll Cambridge (MA, DipArch); *m* Elizabeth Daphne Lee; 1 s, 1 da; *Career* architect; currently: conslt to Alec French Partnership, RIBA client design advsr, memb Architecture and Planning Advsy Panel UWE, tstee St George's Bristol; previous positions incl: pres Canynges Soc, chm Avon Branch RIBA, pres Bristol Soc of Architects, chm Wessex Assoc of Conslt Architects, visiting tutor Sch of Architecture Univ of Bristol, external examiner Dept of Architecture Univ of Bath; major works incl Claire Palley Building St Anne's Coll Oxford (RIBA Award 1993); High Sheriff City of Bristol 2006–07; RIBA, FFB; *Recreations* music, sailing; *Clubs* Hawks' (Cambridge); *Style*— Richard Lee, Esq; ✉ Alec French Partnership, 27 Trenchard Street, Bristol BS1 5AN (tel 0117 929 3011, fax 0117 922 1121, e-mail richardlee@alecfrench.co.uk)

LEE, Robin John; s of John Johnson Lee, of Dublin, and Adelaide Elizabeth, *née* Hayes; *b* 23 October 1952; *Educ* Wesley Coll Dublin, Trinity Coll Dublin (BA, MB BCh, MA, MD); *m* 23 Sept 1978, (Sylvia) Jane Lucette, da of Ernest Herbert Bodell, of Dublin; 2 da (Sarah b 31 Jan 1981, Victoria b 10 Feb 1992), 2 s (Charles, Christopher (twins) b 25 Dec 1982); *Career* sr registrar in otolaryngology: Royal Victoria Eye and Ear Hosp Dublin 1985, Federated Dublin Vol Hops 1986, Beaumont Hosp Dublin 1988; res fell Dept of Otolaryngology Head and Neck Surgery Univ of Iowa 1987, conslt ENT surgn Kettering Gen Hosp 1988–; memb Ctee Young Consultants in Otolaryngology Head and Neck Survery 1989–94; memb: BMA 1988, RSM 1988, Br Assoc of Otolaryngologists 1988, Irish Otolaryngological Soc 1983; FRCSI 1984, FRCS (ad eundem) 1999; *Style*— Robin Lee, Esq; ✉ Kettering General Hospital, Rothwell Road, Kettering, Northamptonshire NN16 8UZ (tel 01536 492000 ext 2274, e-mail rblee3@aol.com)

LEE, Rosa; da of William W Y Lee, and Joyce Ying Lee (d 1987); *b* 1 February 1957; *Educ* Univ of Sussex (BA), Brighton Poly Faculty of Art and Design, St Martin's Sch of Art (BA), RCA (MA); *m* 7 May 1993, Mark A S Graham; 1 s (Nathan Graham b 1993); *Career* artist; pt/t fine art lectr, visiting fell in painting Winchester Sch of Art 1988–89; work in public collections; FRSA 2001; *Solo Exhibitions* Artist of the Day (Flowers East Gallery) 1989, Ellipsis (Winchester Gallery) 1989 (touring 1990), Interface (Todd Gallery London) 1990, New Work 1990–1992 (Todd Gallery) 1992, Conceits (La Centrale Galerie Powerhouse Montreal) 1995, New Work 1994–1996 (Todd Gallery) 1996, New Work 1996–1999 (Todd Gallery) 1999, Small Works (Great Eastern Hotel London) 2002, New Paintings (Ohos Gallery Reading) 2003, Rosa Lee Paintings (GlaxoSmithKline) 2006; *Group Exhibitions* incl: Whitechapel Open (Whitechapel Gallery) 1989, John Moores 16 (Walker Art Gallery Liverpool) 1989–90, 3 Ways (RCA/Br Cncl touring exhbn) 1990, Works on Paper (Todd Gallery) 1990, Broadgate Art Week 1990, Group Show (Todd Gallery) 1991, (dis)parities (Mappin Art Gallery Sheffield) 1992 and (Herbert Art Gallery and Museum Coventry) 1993, The Discerning Eye (Mall Galleries) 1992, John Moores 18 (Walker Art Gallery Liverpool) 1993–94, Lead and Follow, The Continuity of Abstraction (Bede Gallery Jarrow and Atlantis) 1994, British Abstract Art (Flowers East) 1994, Export-Import (Galerie Rähnitzgasse Dresden) 1994, Contemporary Art Society - Recent Purchases (Butler Gallery Kilkenny) 1995, A Question of Scale (Winchester Gallery) 1995, Pretexts: Heteronyms, Rear Window (Clink Street Studios Soho Wharf) 1995, Permission to Speak (Worcs City Museum and Gallery and tour to Derby and Peterborough) 1996, Shelf Life (Eagle Gallery) 1996, Br Abstract Art Part 3 - Works on Paper (Flowers East) 1996, Yellow (Todd Gallery) 1997, Craft (Richard Salmon Gallery, Kettle's Yard and Aberystwyth Arts Centre) 1997–98, Eliminate the Negative (Gasworks Gallery) 1998, Small is Beautiful Part XVI (Flowers East Gallery) 1998, Fabrications (Norwich Gallery) 1999, Warped: Painting and the Feminine (Angel Row Gallery and tour to Middlesbrough Art Gallery, Rugby Art Gallery and museum, Inside Space London) 2001–02, British Abstract Art 2001 (Flowers East Gallery) 2001, Art 2001 (Eagle Gallery), Business Design Centre London, Home collection (Home London) 2002, Temps Fantômal (Galerie Optica Montreal) 2002, Unframed (Standpoint Gall London) 2004, The Spiral of Time (OHOS Gallery Reading) 2005–06 and (APT Gallery London) 2006, Artsway Open Sway 2006, Celeste Open London 2006, Works on Paper (Eagle Gall) 2007; *Awards* ABTA Award 1986, Cwlth Festival prizewinner 1986, Mario Dubsky Travel Award 1988, John Moores 16 prizewinner 1989, Gtr London Arts Award 1989, Br Cncl Award 1995 and 2002, London Arts Award 2002, Arts Cncl Award 2006; *Style*— Ms Rosa Lee; ✉ e-mail rosa.lee@blueyonder.co.uk

LEE, Simon Philip Guy; s of Philip Lee (d 2003), and Janet, *née* Laverty; *b* 4 March 1961, Reading, Berks; *Educ* Tonbridge Sch, Univ of Leeds (BA); *m* 1 Aug 1987, Fiona, *née* Andrews; 3 da (Rebecca b 2 Nov 1992, Alice b 23 Feb 1995, Beatrice b 12 Dec 1996); *Career* md NatWest Home Mortgage Corp USA 1993–95, md NatWest US Retail Banking 1995–96, chief exec NatWest Offshore 1996–98, dir of wholesale markets NatWest Gp 1998–2000, chief exec Affinitas Ltd 2001–03, chief exec int businesses Royal & Sun Alliance plc 2003– (exec dir 2007–); non-exec dir Conister Tst plc 2002–06; dir Hilden Oaks Sch Tst Ltd 2001–; *Recreations* cricket, golf, skiing, reading; *Clubs* Yellowhammer CC, Dragons CC, Chessmen CC, Royal Ashdown Forest Golf; *Style*— Simon Lee, Esq; ✉ Barnes Street House, 3 Elm Lane, Golden Green, Tonbridge, Kent TN11 0LB (tel 01732 851493); Royal & Sun Alliance Insurance Group plc, Plantation Place, 30 Fenchurch Street, London EC3M 3BD (tel 020 7111 7000, e-mail simon.lee@gcc.royalsun.com)

LEE, Stewart; s of Graham Lee (d 2005), and Maureen Kemp, *née* Davis; *b* 5 April 1968, Wellington; *Educ* Solihull Sch, St Edmund Hall Oxford (BA); *m* 30 Nov 2006, Bridget, *née* Christie; 1 s (Luke Stagger b 24 April 2007); *Career* comedian, writer and dir; stand-up comedian 1987–, perfs incl Edinburgh Fringe (Tap Water Award 2004) and Montreal, Adelaide, Melbourne (Wood of Joy Award 2000) and Auckland festivals; contrib Culture Section Sunday Times 1995–; dir and co-writer Jerry Springer: The Opera (successively Battersea Arts Centre, Edinburgh Festival, RNT, Cambridge Theatre London and BBC2) 2001–05 (awards incl: Best Musical Evening Standard Theatre Awards 2003, Best Musical Olivier Awards 2004); Chortle Outstanding Contribution to Comedy Award 2006; memb: Nat Secular Soc, Br Humanist Assoc, Friends of Arthur Machen; *Books* The Perfect Fool (novel, 2001); contrib: Sit Down Comedy (2003), That Which Is Not Said (2006), Perverted by Language (2007), The Flash (2007); *Recreations* walking; *Style*— Stewart Lee, Esq; ✉ c/o Debi Allen, RDF Management, 3–6 Kenrick Place, London W1U 6HD (tel 020 7013 4102, e-mail debi.allen@rdfmedia.com); website www.stewartlee.co.uk

LEE, Prof Tak Hong; s of Ming Lee (d 1991), and Maria, *née* Tseng; *b* 26 January 1951; *Educ* Marlborough, Clare Coll Cambridge (MA, MB BChir, MD, ScD, Eton Fives half blue), Guy's Hosp Med Sch; *m* 25 Aug 1980, Andrée, *née* Ma; 1 s (Adrian b 11 Aug 1984), 1 da (Jacqueline b 23 Feb 1987); *Career* clinical lectr Nat Heart and Lung Inst

Brompton Hosp London 1980–82, research fell Harvard Med Sch 1982–84; UMDS Guy's Hosp London: lectr and hon sr registrar 1984–85, sr lectr and hon conslt physician 1985–88; currently UK Asthma prof of allergy and respiratory medicine KCL and hon conslt physician Dept of Asthma, Allergy and Respiratory Science Guy's Hosp London, dir MRC-Asthma UK Centre in Allergic Mechanisms of Asthma; visiting prof: Univ of Calif San Diego 1989, Lion's Club of Tai Ping Shan Dept of Med Univ of Hong Kong 1990, RSM Fndn 1991; Pfizer visiting prof: Nat Jewish Hosp Denver 1997, Harvard Med Sch 2002 and 2006; hon sec Clinical Immunology and Allergy Section RSM 1988–91; chm Jt Ctee on Immunology and Allergy RCP/RCPath 2000–04; memb: Nat Task Force on Asthma 1990– (chm Therapy Working Sub-Ctee 1991–96, chm Therapy Sub-Ctee 1996), Int Scientific Bd Pharmacia Allergy Research Fndn 1992–94, Ctee in Respiratory Med RCP 1993–96, Specialist Register of Referees Hong Kong Univ and Polys Grants Ctee 1993–, Cncl Collegium Internationale Allergologicum 1994–97, JCHMT SAC for Clinical Immunology and Allergy RCP 1996–2000, Specialist Trg Ctee in Immunology (S Thames) 1996–, Med Sub-Ctee Univ Grants Ctee Hong Kong 1997–2003, Panel of Referees NHS R&D Health Technol Assessment 2000–, Working Pty on Allergy RCP 2001–03; MRC: memb Physiological Med and Infections Bd 1995–99, memb Realising our Potential Award (ROPA) Ctee 1995–97, memb Health Services and Public Health Research Bd 1996–99, head Co-operative Research Gp in Asthma and Allergy 2000–, memb Scientific Strategy Ctee Gen Practice Research Framework 2001–; Nat Asthma Campaign: memb Research Ctee 1988–91 (chm 1990–91), memb Cncl 1990–91, tstee 1996, vice-pres 1999–, chm Consultation on Basic Research Strategy 2001, memb Research Advsy Gp to Tstees 2002–; advsr for allergic disorders Jt Formulary Ctee BMA and Pharmaceutical Soc of GB 1988–, advsr in allergy SE Thames Regn RCPath 1997– (advsr for SW Thames Regn 1998–); section ed European Respiratory Jl, article contrib and scientific referee for numerous jls; memb Editorial Bd: Clinical Immunotherapeutics 1993–96, Clinical and Experimental Allergy, Jl of Allergy and Clinical Immunology, Immunology, Allergology Int; Fogarty Int Research Fellowship Nat Insts of Health USA 1982, MRC Travelling Fellowship 1982, Saltwell Research Fellowship RCP 1983, T V James Fellowship BMA 1986; runner-up European UCB Research Award 1987, Doctor of the Year Research Award BUPA Med Fndn 1989, Pharmacia Int Scientific Research Award 1990; pres Br Soc for Allergy and Clinical Immunology 1996–99; fndr memb Transpacific Allergy and Immunology Soc; memb: Assoc of Physicians of GB and I, Assoc of Clinical Professors, BSACI (pres 1996–99, memb Cncl 1988–2003), Br Thoracic Soc (memb Cncl 1994–98, memb Research Ctee 1995–98), Br Soc for Immunology, BMA, Med Research Soc, American Thoracic Soc, Ammerican Assoc of Immunologists, American Acad of Allergy and Immunology, Collegium Internationale Allergologicum, Harveian Soc of London; FRCP 1989, FRCPath 1997, FMedSci 2000, FKC 2007; *Recreations* photography, tennis, swimming, skiing, golf, travel; *Clubs* RAC, Athenaeum, Wentworth; *Style*— Prof Tak Lee; ✉ Department of Asthma, Allergy and Respiratory Science, King's College London, 5th Floor, Thomas Guy House, Guy's Hospital, London SE1 9RT (tel 020 7188 1943, fax 020 7403 8640, e-mail tak.lee@kcl.ac.uk)

LEE, Prof Thomas Alexander (Tom); s of Thomas Henderson Lee (d 1970), of Edinburgh, and Dorothy Jane Paton, *née* Norman (d 1990); *b* 18 May 1941; *Educ* Melville Coll Edinburgh, ICAS, Univ of Edinburgh, Inst of Taxation, Univ of Strathclyde (MSc, D Litt); *m* 14 Sept 1963, Ann Margaret, da of John Brown (d 1971), of Edinburgh; 1 s (Richard Thomas b 19 July 1968), 1 da (Sarah Ann (Mrs Birchall) b 17 August 1965); *Career* auditor J Douglas Henderson & Co and Peat Marwick Mitchell 1959–66, lectr Univ of Strathclyde 1966–69, lectr Univ of Edinburgh 1969–73, prof Univ of Liverpool 1973–76, prof of accountancy and finance Univ of Edinburgh 1976–90, Culverhouse endowed chair in accountancy Univ of Alabama 1991–2001 (now emeritus prof), hon prof of accounting Deakin Univ 1994–2001, hon prof of accounting Univ of Dundee 1995–, visiting prof of accounting Univ of Newcastle-upon-Tyne 2003–, hon prof of accounting and corporate governance Univ of St Andrews 2006– (lectr in accounting and corporate governance 2007–); memb Exec Ctee AUTA (BAA) 1971–84, ed AUTA News Review 1971–75; ICAS: dir accounting and auditing res 1983–84, memb Cncl 1989–90, memb several ctees; memb Cncl Br Fin and Accounting Assoc 1973–77; ed Int Jl of Auditing 1995–2006, assoc ed Br Accounting Review 1993–97; memb Editorial Bd: Jl of Business Fin and Accounting 1976–82, Accounting Review 1977–80, Accounting and Business Research 1981–, Accounting, Auditing and Accountability Jl 1994–, Accounting Historians Jl 1995–, Accounting in the Public Interest 2000–; tstee Acad of Accounting Historians 1993–96 (vice-pres 1996–98, pres 1998–99); Burnum Distinguished Faculty Award Univ of Alabama 1997, Lifetime Achievement Award Br Accounting Assoc 2005, Accounting Hall of Fame Br Accounting Assoc 2005; elder: Church of Scotland 1984–, Presbyterian Church USA 1992–; memb Academic Advsy Ctee ASC 1987–90; memb: ICAS 1964, IT 1966, AAA 1969, AAH 1974; *Books* incl: Company Auditing (1972), Income and Value (1974), Company Financial Reporting (1976), Cash Flow Accounting (1984), Towards a Theory and Practice of Cash Flow Accounting (1986), The Closure of the Accounting Profession (1989), Corporate Audit Theory (1992), Shaping the Accountancy Profession (1995), Seekers of Truth: The Founders of Modern Public Accountancy (2006), Scottish Chartered Accountants and the American Public Accountancy Profession (2006), Financial Reporting and Corporate Governance (2006); *Recreations* road running, cricket, history; *Style*— Prof Tom Lee

LEE-JONES, Christine; DL (Gtr Manchester); da of George Pickup (d 1991), of Bolton; *b* 13 June 1948, Leeds; *Educ* Lawnswood HS Leeds, Univ of Wales (BEd), Univ of London (MA, Advanced Dip), Open Univ (Advanced Dip); *m* Aug 1972, Denys Lee-Jones, s of Robert Lee-Jones; 1 da (Amy b 31 Oct 1981); *Career* teacher tutor Inst of Educn Univ of London 1978–79, primary sch teacher Bethnal Green 1970–71, head of religious studies Archbishop Temple Sch Lambeth 1971–74, head of religious studies Archbishop Michael Ramsey Sch Camberwell 1974–82, sr lectr Woolwich Coll 1983–86, vice-princ Leyton Sixth Form Coll 1986–91, princ Eccles Sixth Form Coll Salford 1991–98, headmistress Manchester HS for Girls 1998–; memb Cncl GSA, jt chair GSA/HMC Professional Devpt Ctee; memb Gen Assembly Univ of Manchester (formerly memb Ct Victoria Univ of Manchester); friend Royal Acad of Arts, memb RSC; FRSA 1999; *Recreations* theatre, travel, wine, tennis; *Clubs* Univ Women's (assoc); *Style*— Mrs Christine Lee-Jones, DL; ✉ Manchester High School for Girls, Grangethorpe Road, Manchester M14 6HS (tel 0161 224 0447, fax 0161 224 6192, e-mail admin@mhsg.manchester.sch.uk)

LEE OF TRAFFORD, Baron (Life Peer UK 2006), of Bowdon in the County of Cheshire; John Robert Louis Lee; DL (Gtr Manchester 1995); s of Basil Lee (d 1983), and Miriam Lee (d 1982); *b* 21 June 1942, Trafford, Gtr Manchester; *Educ* William Hulme GS Manchester; *m* 1975, (Anne) Monique, *née* Bakirgian; 2 da (Elspeth, Deborah); *Career* CA 1964, Henry Cooke Lumsden & Co Manchester stockbrokers 1964–66, founding dir Chancery Consolidated Ltd investment bankers 1974; MP (Cons): Nelson and Colne 1979–83, Pendle 1983–92 (Parly candidate (Cons): Manchester Moss Side Oct 1974, Pendle 1992); jt sec Cons Backbench Industry Ctee 1979–81, PPS to Min of State for Industry 1981–83, PPS to Sec of State for Trade and Industry 1983, Parly under sec of state MOD 1983–86, Parly under sec of state Dept of Employment 1986–86, min for tourism 1987–89, memb Select Ctee on Defence 1990–92; Lib Dem spokesman on trade and industry, culture, media, sport and tourism and asst whip House of Lords 2006–; non-exec chm: Country Holidays Ltd 1989, Wellington Market plc 2006–; non-exec dir: Paterson Zochonis (UK) Ltd 1975–76, Paterson Zochonis plc 1990–99, Emerson Devpts (Hldgs) 2000–; chm Assoc of Leading Visitor Attractions (AVLA) 1990–, chair Museum of Science and Industry Manchester 1992–99, memb English Tourist Bd 1992–99; chair Christie Hosp NHS Tst 1992–98; vice-chm NW Conciliation Ctee Race Relations Bd 1976–77, chm Nat Youth Bureau 1980–83, vice-chair Lighter Evenings Experiment Gp 2006–; High Sheriff Gtr Manchester 1998–99; FCA; *Publications* Portfolio Man (2005); *Recreations* golf, stock market, salmon fishing, antiques; *Clubs* Hale Golf; *Style*— The Rt Hon the Lord Lee of Trafford, DL; ✉ House of Lords, London SW1A 0PW (tel 020 7219 3949, fax 020 7219 8640, e-mail leej@parliament.uk)

LEE-POTTER, Dr Jeremy Patrick; s of Air Marshal Sir Patrick Lee Potter, KBE, MD (d 1983), of Wittersham, Kent, and Audrey Mary, *née* Pollock (d 2007); *b* 30 August 1934; *Educ* Epsom Coll, Guy's Hosp Univ of London (MB BS, DCP); *m* 26 Oct 1957, Lynda (d 2004), da of Norman Higginson, of Culcheth, Lancs; 1 s, 2 da; *Career* Med Branch RAF 1960–68: sr specialist in pathology RAF Inst of Pathology and Tropical Med 1965–68, i/c Dept of Haematology 1966–68 (Sqdn Ldr); lectr in haematology St George's Hosp Med Sch Univ of London 1968–69, conslt haematologist Poole Hosp NHS Tst 1969–95; BMA: dep chm Central Conslts and Specialists Ctee 1988–90, chm Cncl 1990–93, vice-pres 1998–, chm Audit Ctee 1999–2002; memb: Standing Med Advsy Ctee 1990–93, GMC 1994–99 (dep chm Professional Conduct Ctee 1996–99), King's Fund Organisational Audit 1993–95, Clinical Disputes Forum 1998–99, Advsy Gp Cncl for Registration of Forensic Practitioners 1998–99; Engrg Cncl: memb Senate 2000–02, memb Bd for Engrs' Regulation 2001–02; pres Old Epsomian Club 2004–05; MRCS, LRCP 1958, DTM&H (Eng) 1964, FRCPath 1979; *Books* A Damn Bad Business: The NHS Deformed (1997); *Recreations* printing, print-making, visual arts, golf; *Clubs* Athenaeum, Parkstone Golf; *Style*— Dr Jeremy Lee-Potter; ✉ Icen House, Stoborough, Wareham, Dorset BH20 5AN (tel 01929 556307)

LEECH, Prof Geoffrey Neil; s of Charles Richard Leech (d 1973), of Bredon, Worcs, and Dorothy Eileen Leech (d 1967); *b* 16 January 1936; *Educ* Tewkesbury GS, UCL (BA, MA, PhD); *m* 29 July 1961, Frances Anne, da of George Berman, MBE (d 1985), of Lancaster; 1 s (Thomas b 1964), 1 da (Camilla b 1967); *Career* Nat Serv SAC RAF 1954–56; Harkness fell MIT 1964–65, lectr English UCL 1965–69 (asst lectr 1962–64), visiting prof Brown Univ RI 1972, emeritus prof Lancaster Univ 2001– (reader in English language 1969–74, prof of linguistics and modern English language 1974–2001); memb: Cncl The Philological Soc 1979–83 and 1996–99, English Teaching Advsy Ctee The Br Cncl 1983–91, Academia Europaea 1990–, Norwegian Acad of Science and Letters 1993–; hon prof Beijing Univ of Foreign Studies China 1994; Fil Dr Lund Univ Sweden 1987, DLitt Univ of Wolverhampton, DLitt Lancaster Univ; FBA 1987; *Books* English in Advertising (1966), A Linguistic Guide to English Poetry (1969), A Grammar of Contemporary English (with Randolph Quirk Sidney Greenbaum and Jan Svartvik, 1972), Semantics (1974), Studies in English Linguistics: For Randolph Quirk (ed with Sidney Greenbaum and Jan Svartvik, 1980), Style in Fiction: A Linguistic Introduction to English Fictional Prose (with Michael H Short, 1981), A Comprehensive Grammar of the English Language (with Randolph Quirk Sidney Greenbaum and Jan Svartvik, 1985), An A-Z of English Grammar and Usage (1989), Spoken English on Computer (ed with Greg Myers and Jenny Thomas, 1995), Corpus Annotation (ed with Roger Garside and Anthony McEnery, 1997), Longman Grammar of Spoken and Written English (with Douglas Biber, Stig Johansson, Susan Conrad and Edward Finegan, 1999), An A-Z of English Grammar and Usage (with Benita Cruickshank and Roz Ivanič, 2001), Longman Student Grammar of Spoken and Written English (with Douglas Biber and Susan Conrad, 2002), Word Frequencies in Written and Spoken English (with Paul Rayson and Andrew Wilson, 2001), A Glossary of English Grammar (2006); *Recreations* chamber music, playing the piano and the church organ; *Style*— Prof Geoffrey Leech, FBA; ✉ Department of Linguistics and English Language, Lancaster University, Bailrigg, Lancaster LA1 4YT (tel 01524 593036, fax 01524 843085)

LEECH, John; MP; *Educ* Manchester GS, Loreto Coll, Brunel Univ; *Career* cncllr (Lib Dem) Manchester City Cncl 1998–, MP (Lib Dem) Manchester Withington 2005–; *Style*— John Leech, Esq, MP; ✉ House of Commons, London SW1A 0AA

LEEDS, Bishop of (RC) 2004–; Rt Rev Arthur Roche; s of Arthur Francis Roche, and Frances, *née* Day; *b* 6 March 1950; *Educ* Christleton Hall Chester, English Coll Valladolid Spain, Pontifical Gregorian Univ Rome (STL); *Career* ordained priest 1975, asst priest Holy Rood Barnsley 1975–77, sec to Bishop William Gordon Wheeler 1977–82, vice-chllr Dio of Leeds 1979–89, co-ordinator of Papal visit to York 1982, asst priest Leeds Cathedral 1982–89, fin admin Dio of Leeds 1986–90, parish priest St Wilfrid's Leeds 1989–91, spiritual dir Ven English Coll Rome 1992–96, gen sec Catholic Bishops' Conf of England and Wales 1996–2001, aux bishop (RC) of Westminster 2001–02, coadjutor bishop of Leeds 2002–04; chm Int Cmmn for English in the Liturgy, chm Dept of Christian Life and Worship and memb Standing Ctee Catholic Bishops' Conf of England and Wales; *Recreations* gardening, walking, travel; *Style*— The Rt Rev the Bishop of Leeds; ✉ Bishop's House, 13 North Grange Road, Leeds LS6 2BR (tel 0113 230 4533, fax 0113 278 9890)

LEEDS, Sir Christopher Anthony; 8 Bt (UK 1812), of Croxton Park, Cambridgeshire; s of Maj Geoffrey Hugh Anthony Leeds (d 1962, yr bro of 6 Bt) by his w Yolande Therese Barre, *née* Mitchell (d 1944); suc cous, Sir Graham Mortimer Leeds, 7 Bt, 1983; *b* 31 August 1935; *Educ* King's Sch Bruton, LSE (BSc(Econ)), Univ of Southern Calif (MA); *m* 1974 (m dis 1981), Elaine Joyce, da of late Sqdn Ldr Cornelius Harold Albert Mullins; *Heir* kinsman, John Leeds; *Career* author; asst master: Merchant Taylors' Sch 1966–68, Christ's Hosp 1972–75, Stowe 1978–81; Univ of Nancy II: sr lectr 1982, assoc prof 1988–2000, researcher 2002–; visiting lectr Univ of Strasbourg I 1983–87, visiting research fell Univ of Kent at Canterbury 2000–2001; *Publications* incl: Political Studies (1968, 3 edn 1981), European History 1789–1914 (1971, 2 edn 1980), Management and Business Studies (with R S Stainton and C Jones, 1974, 3 edn 1983), Peace and War (1987), English Humour (1989); jl pubns incl Culture, Mediation and Peacekeeping in Peacekeeping Vol 8 (I) (2001); *Recreations* tennis, modern art, travel; *Style*— Sir Christopher Leeds, Bt; ✉ 6 Hurlingham, 14 Manor Road, Bournemouth, Dorset BH1 3EY; 7 Rue de Turique, 54000 Nancy, France (tel 00 33 3 83 96 43 83)

LEEK, Anthony Thomas (Tony); s of Thomas Henry Howard Leek (d 1987), and Mary, *née* Curtis (d 2003); *b* 15 February 1947; *Educ* Forest Sch, Univ of Southampton (LLB); *Career* admitted slr 1975; ptnr: Austin Ryder & Co 1977–86, DLA Piper UK LLP (formerly DLA) 1987–; memb Law Soc; *Recreations* cricket, theatre, music; *Style*— Tony Leek, Esq; ✉ DLA Piper UK LLP, 3 Noble Street, London EC2V 7EE (tel 020 7796 6216, fax 020 7796 6666)

LEEMING, Charles Gerard James; s of Gerard Pascal de Pfyffer Leeming (d 1998), and Joan Helen Mary (d 1954), da of Edmund Trappes-Lomax (d 1927); *b* 4 May 1936; *Educ* Ampleforth; *Career* admitted slr 1959, sr ptnr Wilde Sapte London 1987–96 (ptnr 1963–96), ret 1996; memb Lloyd's; memb Worshipful Co of Watermen and Lightermen of the River Thames, Liveryman Worshipful Co of Slrs; *Recreations* sailing, music, art, books, bee-keeping, collecting electronic gadgets; *Clubs* Little Ship, Cruising Assoc; *Style*— Charles Leeming, Esq; ✉ Picton House, 45 Strand-on-the-Green, Chiswick, London W4 3PB (tel 020 8994 0450, fax 020 8747 3062, e-mail charles.leeming@blueyonder.co.uk)

LEEMING, His Hon Judge Ian; QC (1988); s of Flt Lt Thomas Leeming (d 1981), of Preston, Lancs, and Lilian, *née* Male (d 1993); *b* 10 April 1948; *Educ* Catholic Coll Preston, Univ of Manchester (LLB); *m* 26 May 1973, Linda Barbara, da of Harold Cook, of Walton-le-Dale, Lancs; 2 da (Lucinda b 1976, Angela b 1981), 1 s (Charles b 1985); *Career* called to the Bar Gray's Inn 1970, Lincoln's Inn (ad eundem); in practice at the Chancery and Commercial Bars Northern Circuit 1971–2006, recorder 1989–2006 (asst recorder 1986–89), circuit judge (Western Circuit) 2006–; actg deemster IOM 1998; legal advsr to GMC 2002; fndr memb Northern Soc of Cons Lawyers (vice-chm 1985–89), chm Heaton Cons Assoc 1986–88, lectr in law Univ of Manchester 1972–76; co dir; fell Soc for Advanced Legal Studies 1999; chartered arbitrator; FCIArb; *Publications* ed Equity and Trust chapters of Butterworths Law of Limitation; *Recreations* squash and sports cars; *Style*— His Hon Judge Leeming, QC; ✉ Plymouth Combined Court, The Law Courts, 10 Armada Way, Plymouth, Devon PL1 2ER

LEES, Prof Andrew John; s of late Lewis Lees, of Harrogate, N Yorks, and Muriel, *née* Wadsworth; *b* 27 September 1947; *Educ* Roundhay Sch, Royal London Hosp Med Coll (MD); *m* 21 July 1973, Juana Luisa Pulin Perez-Lopez, da of late Juan Luis Pulin, of Geneva, Switzerland; 1 s (George Luis b 9 April 1975), 1 da (Nathalie Jasmine b 23 June 1976); *Career* prof of neurology Nat Hosp for Neurology and Neurosurgery and UCL Hosp; dir: Reta Lila Weston Inst of Neurological Studies, Sara Koe PSP Centre; visiting prof UF Ceara Fortaleza Brazil; pres Int Movement Disorder Soc, former co-ed-in-chief Movement Disorders; steward Br Boxing Bd of Control; FRSM, FRCP; *Books* Parkinson's Disease - The Facts (1982), Tics and Related Disorders (1985), Ray of Hope - The Ray Kennedy Story (1993); *Recreations* Hispanic and Latin American studies, memb and hon med advsr to Liverpool FC; *Style*— Prof Andrew Lees; ✉ The National Hospital for Neurology and Neurosurgery, Queen Square, London WC1N 3BG (tel 020 7837 3611, fax 020 7829 8748, e-mail alees@ion.ucl.ac.uk)

LEES, Sir (William) Antony Clare; 3 Bt (UK 1937), of Longdendale, Co Chester; s of Sir William Hereward Clare Lees, 2 Bt (d 1976), and Dorothy Gertrude, *née* Lauder; *b* 14 June 1935; *Educ* Eton, Magdalene Coll Cambridge (MA); *m* 1986, Joanna Olive Crane; *Heir* none; *Style*— Sir Antony Lees, Bt

LEES, Col Brian Musson; LVO (1979), OBE (1978); s of John Lees (d 1978), and Margaret, *née* Musson (d 1942), of Tamworth; *b* 9 October 1931; *Educ* Queen Elizabeth GS Tamworth, Univ of Leeds (BA); *m* 1963, (Diana) Caroline, da of John Harold Everall; 2 da (Diana (Mrs Richard Howorth) b 1964, Alexia (Mrs Guy Fetherstonhaugh) b 1966); *Career* cmmnd KOYLI 1954; served: Kenya (Mau Mau campaign), Cyprus (EOKA campaign), Arabian Peninsula (S Yemen emergency); CO 5 Bn LI 1971–73, def attaché Jedda and Sana'a 1975–79, Def Intelligence Staff MOD 1979–82, head Br Def Intelligence Liaison Staff Washington 1982–84, def attaché Muscat 1984–86, ret 1987; ME conslt; sr advsr: The Carlyle Gp Washington DC 1994–2002, The Capital Advsy Gp, LGT Bank in Liechtenstein; memb Cncl RSAA; cdr St John Ambulance Shropshire 1994–99; FRGS 1989; OStJ; *Books* The Al Sa'ud, Ruling Family of Saudi Arabia (1980); *Recreations* music, travel, reading; *Clubs* Army and Navy, MCC; *Style*— Col B M Lees, LVO, OBE, OStJ; ✉ 14 Ringmer Avenue, London SW6 5LW (tel 020 7731 7709, fax 020 7731 7811, e-mail brian_lees@talk21.com)

LEES, Sir David Bryan; kt (1991); s of Rear Adm Dennis Marescaux Lees, CB, DSO (d 1973), and Daphne May, *née* Burnett (d 1990); *b* 23 November 1936; *Educ* Charterhouse; *m* 1961, Edith Mary, da of Brig Ronald Playfair St Vincent Bernard, MC, DSO (d 1943); 2 s, 1 da; *Career* Nat Serv 2 Lt RA 1955–57; articled clerk with Binder Hamlyn & Co (chartered accountants) 1957–62, sr audit clerk 1962–63, chief accountant Handley Page Ltd 1964–68, fin dir Handley Page Aircraft Ltd 1969; GKN Sankey Ltd: chief accountant 1970–72, dep controller 1972–73, dir sec and controller 1973–76; GKN plc: gp fin exec 1976–77, gen mangr (fin) 1977–82, main bd dir 1982–2004, fin dir 1982–87, gp md 1987–88, chm and chief exec 1988–96, non-exec chm 1997–2004; non-exec chm: Courtaulds plc 1996–98 (non-exec dir 1991–98), Tate & Lyle plc 1998–; non-exec dep chm: Brambles Industries Ltd plc 2001–07, QinetiQ Gp plc 2005–; non-exec dir Bank of England 1991–99; dir Royal Opera House 1998–; memb Panel on Takeovers and Mergers 2001–; cmmr Audit Cmmn 1983–90; Engrg Employers' Fedn: memb Commercial and Economic Ctee 1985–87, ex-officio memb Mgmnt Bd and Gen Cncl 1987–, memb Policy Ctee 1988–94, vice-pres 1988, sr dep pres 1989, pres 1990–92; CBI: chm Econ and Financial Policy Ctee (now Economic Affrs Ctee) 1988–94, memb President's Ctee 1988–96; pres Soc of Business Economists 1994–99; memb: Listed Companies Advsy Ctee 1990–98, Midlands Industrial Cncl 1988–95, Euro Round Table 1995–2001, Nat Defence Industries Cncl 1995–2004; tstee Ironbridge Gorge Museum Devpt Tst 1989–2000; chm of govrs Shrewsbury Sch; govr Suttons Hosp Charterhouse; hon fell Univ of Wolverhampton (formerly Wolverhampton Poly) 1990, Award for Outstanding Achievement ICAEW 1999; awarded Offr's Cross of the Order of Merit FRG 1996; FCA, FRSA 1988; *Recreations* golf, music; *Clubs* MCC, Carlton; *Style*— Sir David Lees; ✉ Tate & Lyle plc, Sugar Quay, Lower Thames Street, London EC3R 6DQ (tel 020 7977 6132, fax 020 7977 6534)

LEES, Prof Peter; CBE (1994); s of Harold Edward Lees (d 1943), of Farnworth, Lancs, and Gladys, *née* Miller (d 2003); *b* 15 July 1940; *Educ* Canon Slade GS, Chelsea Coll of Sci and Technol (BPharm), RVC London (PhD, DSc); *m* 3 Aug 1968, Mary Hogg, da of John Moffat; 1 s (Matthew Peter b 9 June 1975), 1 da (Katherine Mary b 30 March 1978); *Career* Royal Veterinary Coll: asst lectr in pharmacology Dept of Physiology 1964–66, lectr in vet pharmacology Dept of Physiology 1966–76, reader in vet pharmacology 1976–88, prof of vet pharmacology 1988–2005, head Dept of Vet Basic Scis 1991–96, dep princ and vice-princ for teaching 1997–2001, emeritus prof of vet pharmacology 2005–; ed Jl of Vet Pharmacology and Therapeutics 1983–93 and 2003–06; memb: Vet Products Ctee 1978–98, Mgmnt Ctee Home of Rest for Horses 1988–98, Panel Research Assessment Exercise (Agric, Food Sci and Vet Sci) 2001–05 and 2005–08; Peter Wilson Bequest Lecture Univ of Edinburgh 1989, Bogan Meml Lecture Univ of Cambridge 1990, Sir Frederick Smith Meml Lecture Br Equine Vet Assoc 1993; Ciba-Geigy Prize for res in animal health 1985, Open Award Equine Vet Jl 1985 and 1998, Victory Medal Central Vet Soc 1987, George Fleming Prize Br Vet Jl 1987, Amoroso Award Br Small Animal Vet Assoc 1988, Jl of Vet Pharmacology and Therapeutics Prize 1999, Fifth Schering Plough Animal Health and World Equine Vetinary Assoc Award for Applied Res 2001, Selbourne Award Assoc of Vet Teachers and Research Workers 2004, Centenary Prize Central Vet Soc 2006; Dr (hc) Univ of Gent 1992; memb: Br Pharmacological Soc 1965–2007, Assoc for Vet Clinical Pharmacology and Therapeutics 1976–2007, European Assoc of Vet Pharmacology and Toxicology 1978–2007 (hon memb 1991, pres 1997–2000, sr vice-pres 2000–06); hon assoc RCVS 1987, hon fell European Coll of Vet Pharmacology and Toxicology 2000; FIBiol 1989; *Books* Pharmacological Basis of Large Animal Medicine (jtly, 1983), Veterinary Pharmacology, Toxicology and Therapy in Food Producing Species (jtly, 1988), Proceedings of the 6th International Congress of the European Association for Veterinary Pharmacology and Toxicology (co-ed, 1994); *Recreations* the works of Charles Dickens, Victorian and Edwardian history and literature, gardening; *Style*— Prof Peter Lees, CBE; ✉ Department of Veterinary Basic Sciences, The Royal Veterinary College, Hawkshead Campus, North Mymms, Hatfield, Hertfordshire AL9 7TA (tel 01707 666294, fax 01707 666371, e-mail plees@rvc.ac.uk)

LEES, Sir Thomas Edward; 4 Bt (UK 1897), of South Lytchett Manor, Lytchett Minster, Dorset, JP (Dorset 1951); s of Col Sir John Victor Elliott Lees, 3 Bt, DSO, MC (d 1955); *b* 1925; *Educ* Eton, Magdalene Coll Cambridge; *m* 1949, Faith Justin, JP (d 1996), o da of George Gaston Jessiman, OBE, of Great Durnford, Wilts; 3 da (Sarah Margaret (Mrs John M Omond) b 1951, Bridget Selina (Mrs Martin C Green) b 1954, Elizabeth Jane (Mrs Colin Bierton) b 1957), 1 s (Christopher James b 1952); m 2, 1998, Ann Christine, da of Cyril Thomas Kellaway, of Hamilton, NZ; *Heir* s, Christopher Lees; *Career* serv RAF 1943–45; High Sheriff of Dorset 1960; memb: Dorset CC 1951–72, Gen Synod C of E 1970–90; *Recreations* sailing; *Clubs* Royal Cruising; *Style*— Sir Thomas Lees, Bt; ✉ Little Chimney, Post Green Road, Lytchett Minster, Dorset BH16 6AP (tel 01202 622048)

LEESON, Helen Victoria; da of Michael John Leeson (d 1988), and Lesley Case, *née* Tyler; *b* 8 February 1961; *Educ* Oakham Sch, Univ of Manchester (BSc), CIM (Dip); *m* 14 June 1996, John Sandom, s of Eric Sandom; 1 da (Emily b 24 Oct 1995), 1 s (James b 29 June 1998); *Career* grad trainee rising to sales exec Jefferson Smurfitt Gp plc 1982–86, account mngr, account dir then gp account dir Graphics Div Holmes & Marchant plc 1986–92, co-fndr The Sandom Partnership Ltd and LLS Holdings Ltd 1992–93 (estab Impackt Ltd and Distillery Ltd as gp subsidiaries); MCIM 1986; *Recreations* sport, tennis, riding, social activities, reading; *Style*— Ms Helen Leeson; ✉ Sandom Group, Old Brewery, 22 Russell Street, Windsor, Berkshire SL4 1HQ (tel 01753 852488, fax 01753 857971, mobile 07850 776511, e-mail helen.leeson@sandomgroup.com)

LEESON, Air Vice-Marshal Kevin James; CBE (2003); s of A V Leeson, and I J Leeson, *née* Teal; *b* 11 June 1956; *Educ* Alcester GS, UMIST (BSc); *Career* joined RAF 1977, Dep ACOS HQ Strike Cmd 1996–98, RCDS 1999, dir Air Resources and Plans MOD 2000–04, ACDS (Logistic Ops) MOD 2004–07, ACDS (Resources and Plans) MOD 2007–; pres Combined Servs Winter Sports, vice-pres Royal Int Air Tattoo; CEng 1982, FIEE 1997; *Recreations* snow skiing, waterskiing, squash, tennis; *Clubs* RAF, Royal Cwlth; *Style*— Air Vice-Marshal Kevin Leeson, CBE; ✉ 3rd Floor, Zone B, Ministry of Defence, Main Building, Whitehall, London SW1A 2HB (tel 020 7218 2391, e-mail kevin.leeson383@mod.uk)

LEFANU, Prof Nicola Frances; da of William Richard LeFanu (d 1995), and Elizabeth Violet Maconchy, DBE (d 1994); *b* 28 April 1947; *Educ* St Mary's Sch Calne, St Hilda's Coll Oxford (MA), Harvard Univ (Harkness fellowship), Royal Coll of Music, Univ of London (DMus); *m* 16 March 1979, David Newton Lumsdaine; 1 s (Peter LeFanu b 13 Nov 1982); *Career* composer (sixty musical compositions); prof of music Univ of York 1994–; Hon DMus Univ of Durham, Hon DUniv Open 2004, Hon DMus Univ of Aberdeen 2006; FRCM, FTCL; *Recreations* conservation, natural history, feminism; *Clubs* Athenaeum; *Style*— Prof Nicola LeFanu; ✉ 5 Holly Terrace, York YO10 4DS (tel 01904 651759)

LEFÈVRE, Robin Charles; s of Jack Lefèvre, and Jean, *née* Syme; *b* 5 May 1947; *Educ* Irvine Royal Acad, The Royal Scottish Acad of Music and Dramatic Art; *m* 2 Oct 1970, Maureen, da of George Webster; 1 da (Laura b 15 Aug 1971); *Career* director; assoc dir Hampstead Theatre, prodns incl: Then and Now, Threads, Writer's Cramp, On the Edge, Fall, Bodies (transferred Ambassadors), Aristocrats (Evening Standard Best Play Award 1988, NY Drama Critics' Award for Best Foreign Play), Valued Friends (Long Wharf CT, Evening Standard Award), Give Me Your Answer Do, Disposing of the Body, Peggy for You, Peggy For You (also Comedy Theatre), Losing Louis; for Abbey Theatre Dublin incl: Someone Who'll Watch Over Me (also Hampstead, Vaudeville, and Broadway), The Cavalcaders (also Royal Court and Tricycle Theatre), The Bird Sanctuary, Translations, Observe the Sons of Ulster; for Gate Theatre Dublin: Private Lives, A Street Car Named Desire, Afterplay (also Gielgud Theatre), Pygmalion, Betrayal; for Donmar Warehouse: Three Days of Rain, Helpless, The Hotel in Amsterdam; other credits incl: Outside Edge (Queens), Rocket to the Moon (Apollo), Are You Lonesome Tonight? (Evening Standard Best Musical Award), Rowan Atkinson's New Review (Shaftesbury), The Entertainer (Shaftesbury), The Country Girl (Apollo), When We Are Married (NT), The Wexford Trilogy (Bush), Katherine Howard (Chichester Festival Theatre), Krapp's Last Tape (Pit and Ambassadors), The Homecoming (Comedy Theatre), Heartbreak House (Roundabout Theatre NY); television and film: Jake's Progress (by Alan Bleasdale), Self-Catering, A Piece of Monologue (by Samuel Beckett); *Style*— Robin Lefèvre, Esq

LEFF, Prof Julian Paul; s of Dr Samuel Leff (d 1962), of London, and Vera Miriam, *née* Levy (d 1980); *b* 4 July 1938; *Educ* Haberdashers' Aske's, UCL (BSc, MD); *m* 31 Jan 1975, Prof Joan Lilian Raphael-Leff, da of Jacob Raphael (d 1970), of Tel Aviv, Israel; 4 s (Michael b 1964, Alex b 1967, Jonty b 1976, Adriel b 1980), 1 da (Jessa b 1975); *Career* career scientist MRC 1972–2002, hon conslt physician Maudsley Hosp 1973–2002, clinical sub-dean Inst of Psychiatry 1974–79, hon sr lectr London Sch of Hygiene 1974–89, asst dir MRC Social Psychiatry Unit 1974–89, dir Team For Assessment of Psychiatric Servs (TAPS) 1985–2006, dir MRC Social and Community Psychiatric Unit 1989–95, prof of social and cultural psychiatry Inst of Psychiatry 1987–2002 (emeritus prof 2002–); Burghölzli Award 1999; MRCP, FRCPsych; *Books* Psychiatric Examination in Clinical Practice (1978), Expressed Emotion in Families (1985), Psychiatry Around the Globe (1988), Family Work for Schizophrenia (1992), Principles of Social Psychiatry (1993), Care in the Community: Illusion or Reality? (1997), The Unbalanced Mind (2001), Advanced Family Work for Schizophrenia (2005), Social Inclusion of People with Mental Illness (2006); *Recreations* squash, swimming, croquet, piano, silversmithing; *Style*— Prof Julian Leff; ✉ 1 South Hill Park Gardens, London NW3 2TD (e-mail j.leff@medsch.ucl.ac.uk)

LEGARD, Jonathan Antony; s of late Peter Herbert Legard, of Chester, and Brenda Valerie, *née* Kidd; *b* 17 July 1961; *Educ* Shrewsbury, Univ of Leeds (BA), Peterhouse Cambridge (Postgrad Cert in Educn); *m* 1996, Kate, *née* Chacksfield; 2s (Piers b 1999, Crispin b 2002), 1 da (Arabella b 2001); *Career* Cambridge Tutors Hong Kong 1984–85, Viper TV Chester 1986, BBC Radio Merseyside 1986–90 (reporter rising to prodr and presenter), reporter BBC Radio Sport 1990–; Radio 5 Live: sports news corr 1995–96, motor racing corr 1997–2004, football corr 2004–; *Recreations* golf, cricket, Chester City FC; *Clubs* Delamere Forest Golf; *Style*— Jonathan Legard, Esq

LEGG, Prof Brian James; s of late Walter Legg, and Mary, *née* Bunting; *b* 20 July 1945; *Educ* Wellingborough GS, Balliol Coll Oxford (BA), Imperial Coll London (PhD); *m* 1972, Philippa, da of John Kenneth Whitehead; 1 s, 1 da; *Career* voluntary work The Gambia VSO 1966–67, res scientist Rothamsted Experimental Station 1967–83; Silsoe Research Inst: head Res Div 1983–90, dir 1990–99; dir NIAB 1999–; visiting scientist Environmental Mechanics Div CSIRO 1980–82, visiting prof Silsoe Coll Cranfield Univ 1990–; pres Inst of Agricultural Engineers 1998–2000; contrib to numerous agric and environmental engrg jls; FREng 1994, FIAgrE, FIBiol; *Recreations* golf, music; *Style*— Prof Brian Legg, FREng; ✉ NIAB, Huntingdon Road, Cambridgeshire CB3 0LE (tel 01223 276381, fax 01223 342221)

LEGG, Dr Nigel John; s of John Burrow Legg, MBE (d 1958), of Harrow, Middx, and Constance Violet, *née* Boatwright (d 1984); *b* 5 February 1936; *Educ* UCS, St Mary's Med Sch London (MB BS); *m* 10 Sept 1960, Margaret Lilian, da of Frank Donald Charles (d 1958), of Harrow, Middx; 2 da (Kina b 1962, Fiona b 1964), 1 s (Benedick b 1967); *Career* conslt neurologist Hammersmith Hosp, sr lectr in neurology Imperial Coll Sch of Med at Hammersmith Hosp (Royal Postgrad Med Sch until merger 1997) and Inst of Neurology 1975–; author of pubns on Parkinson's disease, multiple sclerosis and other neurological diseases, specialises in migraine and other headaches; memb: Assoc Br Neurologists, Brain Research Assoc; Freeman City of London 1981, Liveryman Worshipful Soc of Apothecaries; *Books* Neurotransmitter Systems and their Clinical Disorders (ed, 1978); *Recreations* Dr Johnson, Bentleys, chamber music; *Clubs* Athenaeum, RSM; *Style*— Dr Nigel Legg; ✉ Salisbury House, Bullens Yard, Highgate Village, London N6 5JT (tel 020 8347 9137); 152 Harley Street, London W1G 7LH (tel 020 7935 8868, fax 020 7486 7557)

LEGG, Sir Thomas Stuart; KCB (1993, CB 1985), QC (1990); s of Francis Stuart Legg (d 1988), and Margaret Bonté Sheldon, *née* Amos (d 2002); *b* 13 August 1935; *Educ* Horace-Mann Lincoln Sch NY, Frensham Heights Sch Surrey, St John's Coll Cambridge

(MA, LLM); *m* 1, Aug 1961 (m dis 1983), Patricia Irene, da of late David Lincoln Dowie; 2 da (Lucy b 1969, Isobel b 1972); m 2, July 1983, Marie-Louise Clarke, da of late Humphrey Jennings; *Career* 2 Lt Royal Marines 1953–55 (45 Commando); called to the Bar Inner Temple 1960, Master of Bench 1984; Lord Chllr's Dept: joined 1962, private sec to Lord Chllr 1965–68, asst slr 1975, under sec 1977–82, SE circuit admin 1980–82, dep sec 1982–89, dep Clerk of Crown 1986, sec cmmns 1988, perm sec to Lord Chllr and Clerk of Crown in Chancery 1989–98, conducted Sierra Leone Arms Investigation 1998; conslt Clifford Chance 1998–; chm: Civil Service Benevolent Fund 1993–98 (tstee 1998–2000), Hammersmith Hosp NHS Tst 2000–, London Library 2004– (tstee 2000–); external memb House of Commons Audit Ctee 2000–, bd memb Audit Cmmn 2005–; visitor Brunel Univ 2001–06 (memb Cncl 1993–2000); Hon LLD Brunel Univ 2006; *Clubs* Garrick, Hurlingham; *Style*— Sir Thomas Legg, KCB, QC; ✉ 93 Rivermead Court, London SW6 3SA

LEGGAT, (John) Brian; s of James Leggat (d 1985), and Margaret Robertson Matthew, of Edinburgh; *b* 29 July 1948; *Educ* Edinburgh Acad, Univ of Edinburgh (LLB); *m* 29 April 1972, Iona Laird, da of Wallace Aitken; 1 s ((James) Douglas b 11 April 1982), 1 da (Joanna Rachel b 20 Nov 1983); *Career* apprentice Lindsay Duncan & Black WS 1969–71; Dundas & Wilson: asst slr 1971–73, ptnr 1973–, head Commercial Property Gp 1983–93, chm 1993–96, head Educn Gp 1996–; memb: Law Soc of Scotland 1971, Soc of Writers to HM Signet 1972; *Recreations* rugby, golf, sailing, curling, horseriding, music; *Clubs* New (Edinburgh), Hon Co of Edinburgh Golfers, Golf House (Elie); *Style*— Brian Leggat, Esq; ✉ Dundas & Wilson, Saltire Court, 20 Castle Terrace, Edinburgh EH1 2EN (tel 0131 228 8000, fax 0131 228 8888)

LEGGATE, Philippa Margaret Curzon (Pippa); da of Thomas Frederick Ellis, OBE, and Rozanne Mary Laura Curzon, *née* Woods; *b* 15 August 1950; *Educ* Royal Sch Bath, Univ of York (BA), Univ of Bristol (PGCE), Univ of Bath (MEd); *m* 1980, David Ian Leggate; 1 da (Emily Laura Ellis b 28 Sept 1983); *Career* teacher VSO Br W Indies, history teacher Churchill Comp Sch Avon 1973–75; Bahrain Sch: history and social studies teacher 1975–76, co-ordinator British Curriculum and history teacher 1976–81, dep head 1981–83, pt/t conslt (set up and prepared introduction of Int Bacc prog) 1983–86, Int Bacc co-ordinator and history teacher 1986; head of history Muscat English Speaking Sch 1986–87, founding princ American-British Acad Oman 1987–91, regnl dir Africa and ME Int Bacc Orgn 1991–93 (Int Bacc UK dir), head Overseas Sch of Colombo Sri Lanka 1993–97, head Malvern Girls Coll 1997–2006, educational conslt CfBT Educn Tst 2006–; chm Boarding Schs Assoc (BSA) 2005–06; memb: MacMillan Nursing Assoc, Euro Women of Achievement, Assoc of Friends of Sri Lanka; govr: The Elms, Terra Nova Prep Sch, Tockington Manor Prep Sch, Westonbirt Girls' Sch; memb: ASCL 1997–, ECIS 1980–; assoc memb GSA 1997– (Int Bacc Exec Ctee 1993–97); *Recreations* reading, tennis, riding, walking, gardening, travel, sailing; *Clubs* Royal Over-Seas League; *Style*— Mrs Pippa Leggate; ✉ Church Farm House, Stinchcombe, Gloucestershire GL11 6BQ (tel 01453 543039, fax 01453 544411, e-mail pleggate@aol.com)

LEGGATT, Rt Hon Sir Andrew Peter; kt (1982), PC (1990); s of Capt W R C (Peter) Leggatt, DSO, RN (d 1983), of Odiham, Hants, and (Dorothea) Joy, *née* Dreyer (d 1992); *b* 8 November 1930; *Educ* Eton, King's Coll Cambridge (MA); *m* 17 July 1953, Gillian Barbara (Jill), da of Cdr C P Newton, RN (d 1970), of Petersfield, Hants; 1 s (George Leggatt, QC, *qv*, b 1957), 1 da (Alice (Mrs Alistair McLuskie) b 1960); *Career* served Rifle Bde 1949–50 and TA 1950–59; called to the Bar Inner Temple 1954 (bencher 1976); QC 1972, recorder of the Crown Court 1974–82, judge of the High Court of Justice (Queen's Bench Div) 1982–90, a Lord Justice of Appeal 1990–97; Chief Surveillance Cmmr 1998–2006; conducted Review of Tribunals 2000–01; chm Appeal Ctee Takeover Panel 2001–06; memb: Bar Cncl 1971–82 (chm 1981–82), Top Salaries Review Body 1979–82; pres Cncl of the Inns of Court 1995–97; hon fell American Coll of Trial Lawyers 1996; *Recreations* listening to music, personal computers; *Clubs* MCC; *Style*— The Rt Hon Sir Andrew Leggatt; ✉ e-mail andrewleggatt@ntlworld.com

LEGGATT, George Andrew Midsomer; QC (1997); s of Rt Hon Sir Andrew Leggatt, *qv*, and Gillian Barbara, *née* Newton; *b* 12 November 1957; *Educ* Eton, King's Coll Cambridge (MA), Harvard Univ (Harkness fell), City Univ (Dip Law); *m* 1987, Dr Stavia Blunt, *qv*; 1 s (Peter b 1990), 1 da (Elly b 1993); *Career* Bigelow teaching fell Law Sch Univ of Chicago 1982–83, called to the Bar Middle Temple 1983, assoc Sullivan & Cromwell NY 1983–84, in practice Brick Court Chambers 1985–, recorder 2002–; vice-chair Bar Standards Bd 2006–; *Recreations* wine, philosophy, walking; *Style*— George Leggatt, QC; ✉ Brick Court Chambers, 7–8 Essex Street, London WC2R 3LD (tel 020 7379 3550, fax 020 7379 3558)

LEGGE, (John) Michael; CB (2001), CMG (1994); s of late Dr Alfred John Legge, of Guildford, Surrey, and late Marion Frances, *née* James; *b* 14 March 1944; *Educ* Royal GS Guildford, ChCh Oxford (MA); *m* 24 July 1971, Linda, da of late John Wallace Bagley, of Haywards Heath, W Sussex; 2 s (Christopher b 18 March 1975, Richard b 12 Nov 1978); *Career* MOD 1966–2001: asst private sec to Def Sec 1970, princ 1971, first sec UK Delgn to NATO 1974, asst sec 1978; Rand Corpn Santa Monica California 1982, asst under-sec of state for policy 1987, asst sec-gen for def planning and policy NATO 1988–93; dep under-sec of state: NI Office 1993–96, MOD 1996–2001; sec and dir of admin Royal Hosp Chelsea 2001–07; chm Civil Service Healthcare 2001–; *Books* Theatre Nuclear Weapons and the Nato Strategy of Flexible Response (1983); *Recreations* golf, gardening, travel; *Style*— Michael Legge, Esq, CB, CMG; ✉ 53 St Mary's Road, Leatherhead, Surrey KT22 8HB

LEGGE-BOURKE, Hon Mrs (Elizabeth) Shân (Josephine); *née* Bailey; LVO; o child of 3 Baron Glanusk, DSO (d 1948), and Margaret (d 2002) (who later m 1 Viscount De L'Isle); *b* 10 September 1943; *m* 2 June 1964, William Nigel Henry Legge-Bourke, *qv*; 1 s, 2 da; *Career* lady-in-waiting to HRH The Princess Royal 1978–; pres Welsh Cncl of Save the Children Fund 1989–; chief pres for Wales St John Ambulance Bde 1990–94, pres Royal Welsh Agric Soc 1997; memb Brecon Beacons Nat Park Authy 1989–98, pres Nat Fedn of Young Farmers Clubs England and Wales 1998–2000; High Sheriff Powys 1991–92, HM Lord-Lt Powys 1998–; *Style*— The Hon Mrs Legge-Bourke, LVO; ✉ Penmyarth, Glanusk Park, Crickhowell, Powys NP8 1LP (tel 01873 810230, e-mail glanuskestate@btinternet.com)

LEGGE-BOURKE, Victoria Lindsay; LVO (1986); da of Maj Sir Harry Legge-Bourke, KBE, DL, MP (d 1973), and Lady Legge-Bourke; *b* 12 February 1950; *Educ* Benenden, St Hilda's Coll Oxford; *Career* social attaché British Embassy Washington DC 1971–73, dir Junior Tourism Ltd 1974–81, lady-in-waiting to HRH The Princess Royal 1974–; special asst American Embassy London 1983–89, Price Investments Kansas City MO 1989–91, head of protocol American Embassy London 1991–94, exec dir Goldman Sachs International 1995–98, dir Lehman Brothers Ltd 1998–99, exec dir Goldman Sachs International 1999–2007; memb: Cncl The American Museum in Britain 1995–2007, Exec Bd LAMDA 2004–; govr ESU 1996–99; tstee St Bride's Tom Olsen Tst 2003–; *Recreations* cooking, crosswords, music, reading, theatre; *Clubs* Grillions, The Pilgrims; *Style*— Miss Victoria Legge-Bourke, LVO; ✉ Bolfer Cottage, 14 Swanton Road, Gunthorpe, Norfolk NR24 2NS (tel 01263 860937); 704 Keyes House, Dolphin Square, London SW1V 3NB (e-mail victoria@legge-bourke.com)

LEGGE-BOURKE, William Nigel Henry; DL (Powys 1997); er s of Sir Harry Legge-Bourke, KBE, DL, MP (d 1973), and (Catherine) Jean, *née* Grant of Monymusk; *b* 12 July 1939; *Educ* Eton, Magdalene Coll Cambridge (MA); *m* 2 June 1964, Hon (Elizabeth) Shân (Josephine) Bailey, LVO, da of 3 Baron Glanusk, DSO (d 1948) (Hon Mrs Legge-Bourke, LVO, *qv*); 2 da (Alexandra Shân (Mrs Charles Pettifer, MVO) b 1965, Zara Victoria (Mrs Angus Gordon Lennox) b 1966), 1 s (Harry Russell b 1972); *Career* cmmnd Royal Horse Guards (The Blues) 1958, Capt and Adj, ret 1968; ptnr Grieveson, Grant & Co 1973–86; dir: Kleinwort Benson Securities Ltd 1986–97, Kleinwort Benson Ltd 1993–97; memb Cncl and Bd Stock Exchange 1988–92 (chm Equities Rules Ctee 1991–97); dir Welsh Devpt Agency 1996–98; chm: Finance Wales Investments Ltd, Wales Innovation Fund Ltd 1999–2003, Swansea and Brecon Diocesan Bd of Finance Ltd 2002–; memb Representative Body of the Church in Wales 1987– (dep chm 2005–); pres: Welsh Scout Cncl 1992–, Brecknockshire Agric Soc 2005; High Sheriff Powys 2000–01, Hon Col Powys ACF 2001–06; FRSA; *Recreations* country sports, growing oaks; *Clubs* White's, Pratt's, Cardiff and County; *Style*— William Legge-Bourke, Esq, DL; ✉ Penmyarth, Glanusk Park, Crickhowell, Powys NP8 1LP (tel 01873 810230, e-mail glanuskestate@btinternet.com)

LEGH, Hon David Piers Carlis; DL (Derbys 2002); yr s of 4 Baron Newton (d 1992); *b* 21 November 1951; *Educ* Eton, RAC Cirencester; *m* 1974, Jane Mary, da of John Roy Wynter Bee, of West End, Surrey; 2 da (Charlotte Mary b 1976, Katherine Anna b 1991), 2 s (Hugo Peter David b 1979, Thomas John Rowland b 1984); *Career* chartered surveyor; John German: ptnr 1984–99, managing ptnr 1991–95, sr ptnr 1995–99; sr ptnr Germans 1999–2000, chm Fisher German 2000–; CLA: memb Cncl 1989–2005, chm Taxation Ctee 1993–97, pres Derbys Branch 2002– (chm 1992–94), chm E Midlands Region 2002–05 (vice-chm 2000–02); RASE: memb Cncl, rep Derbys 1986–91, nominated memb 1991–94; High Sheriff Derbys 2006–07; FRICS, MRAC; *Clubs* Farmers'; *Style*— The Hon David Legh, DL; ✉ Cubley Lodge, Ashbourne, Derbyshire DE6 2FB (tel 01335 330297, fax 01335 330159); Fisher German, 2 Rutherford Court, Staffordshire Technology Park, Stafford ST18 0AR (tel 01785 220044, fax 01785 220944, e-mail david.legh@fishergerman.co.uk)

LEGON, Prof Anthony Charles; s of George Charles Legon, and Emily Louisa Florence, *née* Conner (d 1993); *b* 28 September 1941; *Educ* Coopers' Company Sch, UCL (BSc, PhD, DSc); *m* 20 July 1963, Deirdre Anne, da of Edgar Albert Rivers (d 1944); 1 da (Victoria May b 11 March 1977), 2 s (Anthony Daniel Charles b 14 Nov 1979, Edward James b 14 July 1989); *Career* Turner and Newall fell Univ of London 1968–70, lectr in chemistry UCL 1970–83 (reader 1983–84), prof of physical chemistry Univ of Exeter 1984–89, Thomas Graham prof of chemistry UCL 1989–90, prof of physical chemistry Univ of Exeter 1990–2005, prof of physical chemistry Univ of Bristol 2005–; sr fell EPSRC 1997–2002; Tilden lectr and medallist RSC 1989–90, Hassel lectr Univ of Oslo 1997, Spectroscopy Award Royal Soc of Chemistry 1998; in excess of 300 papers published; memb Physical Chemistry Sub-Ctee Chemistry Ctee SERC 1984–87, vice-pres Faraday Div RSC 2001–; FRSC 1977, FRS 2000; *Recreations* watching soccer and cricket; *Style*— Prof Anthony Legon; ✉ School of Chemistry, University of Bristol, Cantock's Close, Bristol BS8 1TS (tel 0117 331 7708, fax 0117 925 0612, e-mail a.c.legon@bristol.ac.uk)

LEGRAIN, Gérard Marie François; s of Jean Legrain (d 1985), and Marie Hélène, *née* Merica (d 1962); *b* 16 April 1937; *Educ* Ecole St Louis de Gonzague, Sorbonne, Faculté de Droit, Inst d' Etudes Politiques, Ecole Nationale d'Administration Paris; *m* 1969, Katrin Ines, da of Harald Tombach, of Altadena, CA; 2 s (Philippe, *qv*, b 1973, Pierre b 1980), 1 da (Milli b 1976); *Career* Sub Lt 27 and 15 Bataillons de Chasseurs Alpins 1962; Citibank: Paris 1965, NY 1967, Mexico City 1969; vice-pres Citicorp International Bank Ltd London 1972–74, md Int Mexican Bank Ltd London 1974–93; dir: Foreign Banks & Securities Houses Assoc 1991–93, Govett High Income Investment Tst 1993–2001, Govett Emerging Markets Investment Tst 1993–2001; memb Advsy Bd Centre for Global Fin Lubin Sch of Business Pace Univ NY; hon treas: The French Benevolent Soc 1992, The French Clinic 1992–2002; *Recreations* skiing, swimming, tennis; *Clubs* Hurlingham; *Style*— Gérard Legrain, Esq; ✉ Hamilton House, 1 Temple Avenue, London EC4Y 0HA (tel 020 7353 4212, fax 020 7936 3735, e-mail legrain@btinternet.com)

LEGRAIN, Philippe (Phil); s of Gerard Legrain, *qv*, and Katrin Legrain; *b* 29 October 1973; *Educ* Westminster (scholar), LSE (BSc, ESRC scholar, MSc); *Career* economics corr then trade and economics corr The Economist 1997–2000, special advsr to the DG WTO 2000–01, ed World Link (World Economic Forum magazine) 2002; Britain in Europe: chief economist 2002–05, dir of policy 2004–05; contributing ed Prospect 2006–; writer: FT, The Guardian, The Times, New Statesman, Prospect, Wall St Jl Europe, New Republic, Foreign Policy; media commentator on globalisation, migration and European issues for BBC TV and radio; Highly Commended Young Financial Journalist of the Year Harold Wincott Press Awards 1999; journalism fell German Marshall Fund of the US 2007–, visiting fell European Inst LSE 2007–; *Publications* Open World: The Truth about Globalisation (2002), Immigrants: Your Country Needs Them (2007); *Style*— Phil Legrain; ✉ e-mail mail@philippelegrain.com, website www.philippelegrain.com

LEHANE, Brendan; s of Christopher Lehane (d 1968), and Honor Lehane (d 1996); *b* 17 May 1936, London; *Educ* Queen Elizabeth's GS Barnet, Eton, King's Coll Cambridge (MA); *m* 1968 (m dis), Judith, *née* Urquhart; *Career* freelance writer; contrib: Daily Telegraph, Weekend Section Daily Telegraph, Sunday Times, Country Life, Irish Times, Harpers, Cornhill; FRSL 1999; *Books* Quest of Three Abbots (1968), The Compleat Flea (1969), Companion Guide to Ireland (1973), Power of Plants (1977), Dublin (1978), North-West Passage (1981), Witches and Wizards (1984), Heroes of Valour (1985), Book of Christmas (1987), Ireland (1989), Wild Ireland (1995), Dorset's Best Churches (2006); *Style*— Brendan Lehane; ✉ 19 Frome Terrace, Dorchester, Dorset DT1 1JQ

LEHANE, Maureen Theresa (Mrs Peter Wishart); da of Christopher Lehane (d 1970), of London, and Honor, *née* Millar (d 1996); *Educ* Queen Elizabeth's Girls' GS Barnet, Guildhall Sch of Music and Drama; *m* 26 May 1966, Peter Wishart (d 1984); *Career* concert and opera singer specialising in Handel; debut Glyndebourne 1967; title and leading roles in thirteen Handel operas: with Handel Opera Socs of England and America, in Poland, Sweden, Germany, Holland; numerous master classes on the interpretation of Handel's vocal music; title roles in: Handel's Ariodante Sadlers Wells 1974, Peter Wishart's Clytemnestra London 1974, Purcell's Dido and Aeneas Netherlands Opera 1976, castrato lead JC Bach's Adriano London 1982; female lead Hugo Cole's The Falcon Somerset 1983, Peter Wishart's The Lady of the Inn Reading Univ 1983; festival appearances incl: Glyndebourne, Stravinsky Festival Cologne, City of London, Aldeburgh, Cheltenham, Three Choirs, Bath, Oxford Bach, Göttingen Handel Festival; tours incl: N America, Australia, Far East, Middle East; visits incl: Holland, Belgium, Germany, Lisbon, Poland, Rome, Warsaw; has sung with: Boulez, Boult, David, Leppard, Marriner, Eliot Gardiner, Mackerras, Pritchard, Sargent; recordings incl: Bach, Haydn, Mozart, Handel (Cyrus in first complete recording Belshazzar); TV appearances incl: BBC, ABC Australia, Belgian TV; regular appearances promenade concerts; memb Jury: Int Singing Comp Hertogenbosch Festival Holland 1982–, Llangollen Int Eisteddfod; teacher: Guildhall Sch of Music, Univ of Reading, Welsh Coll of Music and Drama; currently teaches privately; examiner Royal Acad of Music; fndr Great Elm Music Festival 1987–98, fndr and artistic dir Jackdaws Educnl Tst (founded 1993); *Books* Songs of Purcell (co ed Peter Wishart); *Recreations* cooking, gardening, reading; *Style*— Miss Maureen Lehane; ✉ Ironstone Cottage, Great Elm, Frome, Somerset BA11 3NY (tel 01373 812383, e-mail music@jackdaws.org, website www.jackdaws.org)

LEHMAN, Prof Meir M (Manny); s of Benno Lehman (d 1935), and Theresa, *née* Wallerstein (d 1988); *b* 24 January 1925; *Educ* Letchworth GS, Imperial Coll (BSc, ARCS, PhD, DIC, DSc); *m* 26 Aug 1953, Chava, da of Moses Robinson (d 1948); 3 s (Benjamin Moses, Jonathan David, Raphael Dan), 2 da (Machla Lea, Esther Dvora); *Career* apprentice

Murphy Radio Ltd 1942–50, jr logic designer Ferranti Ltd 1956–57, head digital computers Sci Dept Israel Miny of Defense 1957–64; IBM Res Div 1964–72: res staff memb, mangr Project IMP, computing service support gp; Imperial Coll of Sci and Technol: prof of computing sci 1972–84, head of computing sci section 1972–79, head Dept of Computing 1979–84, emeritus prof Dept of Computing 1984–2002, sr res fell 1989–2001; fndr and dir IST Ltd 1982–88 (chm 1982–84), fndr and md Lehman Software Technol Assocs Ltd 1984–, dir Eureka ESF ICST Project 1991–94, princ investigator Project FEAST/1 1996–98 and FEAST/2 1999–2001; author of numerous papers; FREng 1989, FIEE, FBCS, FIEEE, FACM; *Books* Program Evolution - Processes of Software Change (1985); *Recreations* Talmudic studies, DIY, fund raising for charity; *Style*— Prof Manny Lehman, FREng; ✉ School of Computer Science, Middlesex University, Ravensfield House, The Burrough, London NW4 4BT (tel 020 8411 4225, fax 020 8411 4397 or 020 8411 6411, e-mail mml@mdx.ac.uk, website www.cs.mdx.ac.uk/staffpages/mml)

LEHMANN, Peter; CBE (2003); s of Henry Lehmann (d 1989), and Lore, *née* Borg (d 1992); *b* 17 October 1944; *Educ* Manchester Grammar, CCC Oxford (BA), Univ of Sussex (MA, PhD), London C of C, Inst of Linguists; *m* 11 July 1970, Tara, da of Satnarine Samoondar; 1 da (Nina b 28 Nov 1973), 1 s (Ken b 19 Oct 1976); *Career* conslt Dept of Energy and lectr in economics Univ of Sussex 1969–71; British Gas: various depts 1971–82, mangr Gas Supplies 1982–87, business devpt mangr then dir of ops (global gas) 1987–93, memb Supervisory Bd VNG 1991–96, dir of competition and regulatory policy 1994, md Europe 1995–97; commercial dir and memb Bd Centrica plc 1997–98, chm Energy Saving Tst 1998–2005; chm HM Govt's Fuel Poverty Advsy Gp 2002–; non-exec dir and chm Audit Ctees Disability and Carers Agency Dept of Work and Pensions 2002–; non-exec dir Gaz de France 2004– (chm Strategy ctee); chm: Greenworks 2001–, Accuread 2003–05; memb: Plant Cmmn on Taxation and Citizenship 1998–2001, NI Energy Regulatory Authy 2003–06; tstee: Project Fullemploy 1999–2004, Nat Language Centre 1999–; mentor of headteacher in an inner city sch for Business in the Community Prog 1997–; *Recreations* cycling, walking, squash, travel; *Style*— Peter Lehmann, Esq; ✉ Energy Saving Trust, 21 Dartmouth Street, London SW1H 9BP

LEICESTER, 7 Earl of (UK 1837); Edward Douglas Coke; CBE (2005), DL (2005); also Viscount Coke (UK 1837); s of 6 Earl of Leicester (d 1994), and his 1 w, Moyra, *née* Crossley (d 1987); *b* 6 May 1936; *Educ* St Andrew's Coll Grahamstown South Africa; *m* 1, 28 April 1962 (m dis 1985), Valeria Phyllis, eld da of Leonard A Potter, of Berkhamsted, Herts; 2 s (Thomas Edward, Viscount Coke b 1965, Hon Rupert Henry John b 1975), 1 da (Lady Laura-Jane Elizabeth b 1968); m 2, 1986, Mrs Sarah de Chair, da of Noel Henry Boys Forde, of Wells-next-the-Sea, Norfolk, and formerly wife of Colin Graham Ramsey de Chair; *Heir* s, Viscount Coke; *Career* ldr BC of King's Lynn & West Norfolk 1980–85; elected pres Historic Houses Assoc 1998–2003, cmmr English Heritage 2002–; Hon Dr Laws De Montfort Univ 1996; *Clubs* Brooks's, White's, Farmers'; *Style*— The Rt Hon the Earl of Leicester, CBE, DL; ✉ Holkham Hall, Wells, Norfolk NR23 1AB (tel 01328 710227, fax 01328 711707, e-mail leicester@holkham.co.uk)

LEICESTER, Bishop of 1999–; Rt Rev Timothy John Stevens; s of Ralph Stevens, and Jean Ursula Stevens; *Educ* Chigwell Sch, Selwyn Coll Cambridge, Ealing Business Sch (Dip Mgmnt Studies), Ripon Coll Cuddesdon (DipTh, CertTheol); *Career* grad mgmnt trainee BOAC 1968–72, second sec S Asian Dep FCO 1972–73; curate East Ham Team Miny 1976–79, team vicar St Albans Upton Park 1979–80, team rector Canvey Island 1980–88, urban offr to Bishop of Chelmsford 1988–91, archdeacon of West Ham 1991–95, bishop of Dunwich 1995–99; memb Crown Appts Cmmn for See of Canterbury 2002, memb Archbishop's Cncl 2006–, memb Standing Ctee House of Bishops 2006–; pres Leicester Cncl of Faiths 2001–, chair Cncl The Children's Soc 2003; chair Community and Voluntary Forum for Eastern Religion 1997–99; memb House of Lords 2003–; govr De Montfort Univ 2005–, chair Cncl Westcott House 2006–; Hon LLD De Montfort Univ 2002, Hon DLitt Leicester Univ 2003; *Recreations* cricket, golf, swimming, North Yorkshire Moors; *Clubs* Royal Cwlth Soc; *Style*— The Rt Rev the Lord Bishop of Leicester; ✉ Bishop's Lodge Annexe, 12 Springfield Road, Leicester LE2 3BD (tel 0116 270 8985, fax 0116 270 3288, mobile 07860 692258, e-mail bptim@leicester.anglican.org)

LEIFERKUS, Sergei; *b* 4 April 1946; *Career* baritone; appeared at many international venues incl: Royal Opera House Covent Garden, Opera Bastille and Theatre Musical Paris, San Francisco Opera, Metropolitan Opera NY, Chicago Lyric Opera, Dallas Opera, Opera de Montreal, Liceu Barcelona, La Scala Milan, Royal Danish Opera Copenhagen, Netherlands Opera Amsterdam, Cologne Opera, Berlin State Opera, Vienna Staatsoper, Bolshoi Theatre Moscow, Mariinsky Theatre St Petersburg, Teatro Colon Buenos Aires, Concertgebouw Amsterdam, Salzburg Easter Festival, Glyndebourne Festival, Bregenz Festival, Edinburgh Festival, Wexford Festival; performed with numerous major orchs incl: London Symphony, Royal Philharmonic, BBC Symphony Orch, Berlin Philharmonic, Boston Symphony, New York Philharmonic, Philadelphia Orch, San Francisco Symphony, Royal Concertgebouw Orch, Montreal Symphony Orch, Chamber Orch of Europe, Bavarian Radio Symphony Orch; worked with leading conductors incl: Claudio Abbado, Riccardo Chailly, Sir Colin Davis, Valery Gergiev, Bernard Haitink, Nikolaus Harnoncourt, James Levine, Kurt Masur, Zubin Mehta, Riccardo Muti, Seiji Ozawa, Mstislav Rostropovich, Gennadi Rozhdestvensky, Sir Georg Solti; operatic roles incl: Pizarro in Fidelio, Mephistopheles in La Damnation de Faust, Escamillo in Carmen, Zurga in The Pearl Fishers, title role in Prince Igor, Enrico in Lucia di Lammermoor, Gérard in Andrea Chénier, Scarpia in Tosca, title role in Eugene Onegin, Nabucco and Don Giovanni, Albert in Werther, Count Almaviva in The Marriage of Figaro, Rangoni in Boris Godunov, Prince Andrei Bolkonsky in War and Peace, Ruprecht in The Fiery Angel, Marcello in La Bohème, Sharpless in Madama Butterfly, Veglasnyi in Mlada, Gryaznoi in The Tsar's Bride, title role in Aleko, Figaro in The Barber of Seville, title role in Mazeppa, Tomsky and Eletsky in The Queen of Spades, Robert and Ibn Hakir in Iolanta, Amonasro in Aida, Renato in Un Ballo in Maschera, Rodrigo in Don Carlos, Don Carlo in La Forza del Destino, title role in Macbeth, Giacomo in Giovanna d'Arco, Iago in Otello, Giorgio Germont in La Traviata, Conte di Luna in Il Trovatore, Telramund in Lohengrin; concert repertoire incl: Bach St Matthew Passion and various cantatas, Beethoven 9th Symphony, Mahler 8th Symphony and Lieder eines fahrenden Gesellen, Mozart Requiem, Brahms Requiem, Mussorgsky Song and Dances of Death, Orff Carmina Burana, Prokofiev Ivan the Terrible, Rachmaninov The Bells and Spring Cantata, Puccini Messa di Gloria, Shostakovich 13th and 14th Symphonies; numerous recitals incl: Royal Opera House Covent Garden, Wigmore Hall, Queen Elizabeth Hall, Purcell Room and St John's Smith Square London, Minterne Abbey Dorset, La Scale, Theatre Royal Glasgow, Theatre Royal Wexford, Musikverein Vienna, Philharmonie Cologne, Frick Collection and Alice Tully Hall NY, William Jewell Coll Kansas, Sunset Center Carmel, Radio France Paris, Concertgebouw Amsterdam, Hessischer Rundfunk Frankfurt; recordings: various for BMG/RCA, Decca, Philips, Sony, Deutsche Grammophon, Chandos and Teldec, currently recording complete songs of Mussorgsky and Tchaikovsky for BMG/Conifer and Shostakovich for Koch-schwann; *Style*— Sergei Leiferkus, Esq; ✉ c/o Askonas Holt, Lonsdale Chambers, 27 Chancery Lane, London WC2A 1PF (tel 020 7400 1732, fax 020 7400 1799)

LEIGH, Adam Michael; s of (Harvey) Roy Leigh, of Manchester, and Susan, *née* Kelner; *b* 24 January 1967; *Educ* Stockport GS, Univ of Manchester (LLB); *m* 2 Sept 2000, Charlotte Kate Watson-Smyth; 2 s (Isaac Edward b 3 March 2001, Noah James b 25 August 2003); *Career* reporter Burton Herald & Post 1989–90, reporter Burton Mail 1990–92, copytaster and dep news ed Birmingham Post 1992–95; The Independent: sub-ed 1995, copytaster 1996, chief features sub-ed 1997–98; news ed Independent on Sunday 1998–99; The Independent: dep foreign ed 1999–2000, home ed 2000–03, exec ed (features) 2003–; involved with: Nat Youth Theatre of GB 1981–87, Manchester Student TV 1985–89; *Clubs* Reform; *Style*— Adam Leigh, Esq; ✉ The Independent, 191 Marsh Wall, London E14 9RS (tel 020 7005 2000, fax 020 7005 2051, e-mail a.leigh@independent.co.uk)

LEIGH, Andrew; s of Walter Leigh (ka 1942), of London, and Marion, *née* Blandford; *b* 17 February 1941; *Educ* Bryanston, Christ's Coll Cambridge (MA, Henley Ladies' Plate 1960); *m* 1966, Margaret Anne, da of Robert Lyons; 2 s (Jacob b 1967, Benjamin b 1970), 1 da (Rebecca b 1969); *Career* mangr Palace Theatre Morecambe 1963, gen mangr Citizens' Theatre Glasgow 1965–68 (house mangr 1963–65), prodr Arturo Ui (Edinburgh Festival) and A Day in the Death of Joe Egg (WE and Euro tour) 1968–69, admin The Traverse Theatre Edinburgh 1969–70, gen mangr The Duke's Playhouse Lancaster 1970–73, admin dir The Haymarket and Phoenix Theatres Leicester 1973–79, dir and gen mangr The Old Vic 1979–98, exec prodr Into The Woods (Phoenix) 1990–91, chief exec Theatre of Comedy Co 1998–2000, admin dir Palace Theatre Watford 2000–01, chief exec Chichester Festival Theatre 2001–02, theatre conslt 2003–; dir: Paines Plough Theatre Co, Edinburgh Festival Fringe, Theater Impresariaat Internationaal BV; memb Arts Cncl Drama Panel and Touring Ctees until 1981, co-ordinator Theatre Def Fund 1982–, pres Theatrical Mgmnt Assoc 1985–91, chm Barclays Theatre Awards, vice-chm Theatres' Nat Ctee 1991–99; *Books* The Future of the Old Vic (1982), See the Actors Well Bestowed (Hong Kong, 1982); 6 theatre feasibility studies 1977–92; *Recreations* books, photography, food, travel; *Clubs* Garrick; *Style*— Andrew Leigh, Esq; ✉ 48 Pearman Street, London SE1 7RB (tel 020 7620 2402, fax 020 7787 6724, e-mail mirvprods@zoom.co.uk)

LEIGH, Bernard Malcolm; s of Lionel Leigh, of London, and Cecilia, *née* Ruderman; *b* 7 February 1950; *Educ* William Ellis GS, London Hosp Dental Inst Univ of London (BDS), Eastman Hosp Inst of Dental Surgery; *m* 25 Nov 1973, Yvonne Pamela, da of Leslie Wolfe; 2 da (Sara (Mrs Arieh Wagner) b 20 Nov 1974, Talia (Mrs Avi Smith) b 18 Oct 1980), 4 s (Daniel b 6 Nov 1976, Jeremy b 24 March 1979, Joshua b 25 July 1984, Avram b 27 July 1989); *Career* house offr London Hosp 1973; practised: City of London 1974–75, Hemel Hempstead 1976–82, London NW11 1976–84, Harley St 1982–; specialist in endodontics; hon clinical asst Dept of Cons Dentistry Inst of Dental Surgery Eastman Dental Hosp 1979–94; memb: Alpha Omega (Ctee 1984–88, chm 1999–2000), Br Endodontic Soc (Ctee 1981–82), Br Dental Assoc; *Recreations* music, computers, photography, writing; *Style*— Bernard Leigh, Esq; ✉ 82 Harley Street, London W1G 7HN (tel 020 7637 2200, fax 020 7637 9800, e-mail bmleigh@tiscali.co.uk)

LEIGH, 6 Baron (UK 1839) Christopher Dudley Piers Leigh; er s (but only one by 1 w) of 5 Baron Leigh (d 2003); *b* 20 October 1960; *Educ* Eton, RAC Cirencester; *m* 15 Aug 1990, Sophy-Ann, da of Richard Burrows, MBE, of The Old Hall, Groby, Leics; 1 s (Hon Rupert Dudley b 21 Feb 1994), 1 da (Hon Lucy Alexandra b 2 Nov 1995); *Heir* s, Hon Rupert Leigh; *Career* memb: British Field Sports Soc, Royal Agric Soc of England; *Recreations* racing, tennis; *Clubs* Turf; *Style*— The Rt Hon the Lord Leigh; ✉ Fern Farm, Adlestrop, Moreton-in-Marsh, Gloucestershire GL56 OYL (tel 01608 658203, fax 01608 658323)

LEIGH, His Hon Judge Christopher Humphrey de Verd; QC (1989); s of Wing Cdr Humphrey de Verd Leigh, OBE, DFC, AFC (d 1981), and Johanna Emily, *née* Whitfield Hayes (d 1999); *b* 12 July 1943; *Educ* Harrow; *m* 18 July 1970, Frances Raymonde, da of Col Raymond Henry Albert Powell, OBE, MC; *Career* called to the Bar Lincoln's Inn 1967 (bencher 1999); recorder of the Crown Court 1985, circuit judge 2001–; *Recreations* travel, photography; *Style*— His Hon Judge Leigh, QC; ✉ Southampton Combined Court Centre, London Road, Southampton SO15 2XQ (tel 023 8021 3200)

LEIGH, David Irvine; s of Frederick Leigh (d 1980), of Glasgow, and Mary, *née* David; *b* 16 April 1944; *Educ* Mackintosh Sch, Edinburgh Coll of Art Heriot-Watt Univ (DA); *m* 30 Aug 1975, Lynda, da of Frank Thomas Taylor (d 1970), of Hawkhurst, Kent; 1 da (Claire Francesca b 1971), 1 s (Elliot b 1983); *Career* architect; ptnr R J Wood Chapman and Hanson 1974, chm and md Chapman and Hanson 1989–91 (dir 1981–91), chm and md Leigh Blundell Thompson chartered architects and interior designers 1991–94, princ architect E Sussex CC 1995–98, princ David I Leigh Chartered Architects 1999–; designed HQ bldgs for: Charrington & Co London 1978, R S Components Corby 1984, Electrocomponents Knightsbridge 1987, W M Lighting Northampton 1989; memb Business Network Int; RIBA 1969; *Recreations* Arsenal FC, horse racing, travel, petanque, computing; *Style*— David Leigh, Esq; ✉ 7 Markwick Terrace, St Leonards-on-Sea, East Sussex TN38 0RE (tel and fax 01424 446604, e-mail davidileigh@architect1066.freeserve.co.uk)

LEIGH, Edward Julian Egerton; MP; s of Sir Neville Egerton Leigh, KCVO (d 1994), and Denise Yvonne, *née* Branch; *b* 20 July 1950; *Educ* The Oratory, Lycée Français de Londres, Univ of Durham; *m* 25 Sept 1984, Mary, eldest da of Philip Henry Russell Goodman, of London, and Sophie (Sonia), o da of late Count Vladimir Petrovitch Kleinmichel, CVO; 3 s, 3 da; *Career* barr; memb Inner Temple; former: pres Durham Union Soc, chm Durham Univ Cons Assoc; Parly candidate (Cons) Middlesbrough 1974; MP (Cons): Gainsborough and Horncastle 1983–97, Gainsborough 1997–; hon dir Coalition for Peace through Security, chm Nat Cncl for Civil Defence 1980–83, memb House of Commons Select Ctee for Defence 1983–87, vice-chm and sec for Backbench Ctees on Agric Employment and Defence 1983–90, PPS to Min of State Home Office 1990–92, under-sec of state for Industry and Consumer Affairs DTI 1990–93, chm Public Accounts Ctee 2001– (memb 2000–01); memb: House of Commons Agric Select Ctee 1995–97, House of Commons Social Security Select Ctee 1995–; memb: Richmond Borough Cncl 1977–81, GLC 1977–81; veteran memb HAC 2003–; memb Cncl Lincoln Cathedral 2003–; Knight of Honour and Devotion SMOM 1994; *Publications* Right Thinking (1976); *Style*— Edward Leigh, Esq, MP; ✉ House of Commons, London SW1A 0AA

LEIGH, Sir Geoffrey Norman; kt (1990); s of Morris Leigh, and late Rose Leigh; *b* 23 March 1933; *Educ* Haberdashers' Aske's Hampstead Sch, Univ of Michigan; *m* 1, 1955 (m dis 1975), Valerie Lennard (d 1976); 1 s, 2 da; m 2, 1976, Sylvia Pell; 1 s, 1 da; *Career* chm Sterling Homes 1980– (md 1965), chm Allied London Properties plc 1987–98 (md 1970–87); dir Arrow Property Investments 2000–06; fndr and first pres Westminster Jr C of C 1959–63; underwriting memb Lloyd's 1973–97; special advsr Land Agency Bd Cmmn for New Towns 1994–96; memb: Ctee Good Design in Housing 1978–79 (memb Ctee Good Design in Housing for Disabled 1977), British ORT Cncl 1979–80, Int Advsy Bd American Univ Washington 1983–97, Advsy Cncl Prince's Youth Business Tst 1985–, Main Fin Bd NSPCC 1985–2003 (hon memb Cncl 1995–), Governing Cncl Business in the Community 1987–2000, London Historic House Museums Tst 1987–98, Somerville Coll (Oxford) Appeal 1987–, Royal Fine Art Cmmn Art and Architecture Educn Tst 1988–2000, Per Cent Club 1988–2000, City Appeal Ctee Royal Marsden Hosp 1990–93, Review Body on Doctors' and Dentists' Remuneration 1990–93, Univ of Oxford Chllr's Ct of Benefactors 1991–, Emmanuel Coll Cambridge Devpt Campaign 1994–98, Wellbeing Cncl 1994–; chm St Mary's Hosp 150th Anniversary Appeal 1995–; cmmr and tstee Fulbright Cmmn 1991–99 (chm Int Advsy Bd 1995–); sponsor The Leigh City Technol Coll Dartford (chm of govrs 1988–2006, chm of tstees 2006–); fndr/sponsor Friends of the British Library 1987– (vice-pres 2000–); fndr Margaret Thatcher Centre Somerville Coll Oxford 1991; treas: Cwlth Jewish Cncl 1983–89, Cwlth Jewish Tst 1983–89; a treas

L

Cons Pty 1995–98; Hampstead and Highgate Cons Assoc: patron 1991–95, pres 1994–97, vice-pres 1997–; vice-pres Conservatives Abroad 1995–; tstee: Margaret Thatcher Fndn 1991–, Industry in Educn 1993–98, Philharmonia 1992–2000; treas and tstee Action on Addiction 1991–2003; govr: Royal Sch Hampstead 1991–2003, City Lit Inst 1991–98; hon memb Emmanuel Coll 1995–, fndn fell Somerville Coll Oxford 1998–; hon life memb The Conservative Med Soc 1998; Presidential Citation The American Univ 1987; Freeman City of London 1976; Liveryman: Worshipful Co of Furniture Makers 1987 (memb Ct of Assts 1992, honoris causa 2006), Worshipful Co of Haberdashers 1992; FRSA, FICPD; *Recreations* photography, reading, golf; *Clubs* Carlton, United and Cecil, Pilgrims, RAC, Wentworth, Palm Beach Country, Palm Beach Yacht; *Style*— Sir Geoffrey Leigh; ✉ 42 Berkeley Square, London W1J 5AW (tel 020 7409 5054)

LEIGH, Guy Ian Frederick; s of Arthur Benjamin Leigh, and Amelia, *née* Berger; *b* 22 November 1944; *Educ* Univ of Pennsylvania (BA), Law Sch Univ of Pennsylvania (JD), Trinity Hall Cambridge (DipIntLaw); *Career* admitted slr 1974; articled Clifford Turner 1972–74; Theodore Goddard (now Addleshaw Goddard): joined 1974, ptnr 1978–, competition/trade and regulatory law Mgmnt Ctee 1988–90; memb Jt Competition Working Pty of the Bars and Law Socs of UK, past pres and int and gen rapporteur Int League of Competition Law; ctee memb and former chm Competition Law Assoc; memb Law Soc of England and Wales, European Competition Lawyers Forum; *Books* The EEC and Intellectual Property (with Diana Guy, 1981), Outsourcing Practice Manual (contrib, 1998); various articles on EC competition law; *Recreations* languages (German, Italian, Spanish and French), boating, travel, photography; *Style*— Guy I F Leigh, Esq; ✉ Addleshaw Goddard, 150 Aldersgate Street, London EC1A 4EJ (tel 020 7606 8855, fax 020 7606 4390, telex 884678)

LEIGH, Howard D; s of Philip Mark Leigh (d 1987), of London, and Jacqueline, *née* Freeman; *b* 3 April 1959, London; *Educ* Clifton Coll Bristol, Univ of Southampton; *m* 14 Feb 1998, Jennifer, *née* Peach; 2 da (Olivia b 13 Jan 1999, Susannah b 28 Sept 2001); *Career* CA 1983; memb Bd Bolton Bldg Soc 1986–92, dir Cavendish Corporate Finance Ltd 1998–; memb Deregulation Taskforce DTI 1994–97; ICAEW: memb Cncl 1998–2004, chm Corporate Finance Faculty 1998–2004, memb (as alternate to ICAEW Pres) Takeover Panel Appeal Ctee 1998–; sr treas Cons Party 2005– (treas 2000–); chm Westminster Synagogue 2001–; tstee Jerusalem Fndn 1992–; memb Ct of Assts Worshipful Co of CAs 2003; memb Chartered Inst of Taxation 1985; *Clubs* Carlton; *Style*— Howard Leigh, Esq; ✉ Cavendish Corporate Finance Limited, 40 Portland Place, London W1B 1NB (tel 020 7908 6000, fax 020 7908 6006, e-mail hleigh@cavendish.com)

LEIGH, Prof Irene May; OBE (2006); da of Archibald Allen, of Liverpool, and May Lilian, *née* Whalley; *b* 25 April 1947; *Educ* Merchant Taylors', London Hosp Med Coll (BSc, MB BS, MD, DSc); *m* 1 (m dis); 1 s (Piers Daniel b 24 June 1973), 3 da (Andrea Yseult b 11 Oct 1975, Miranda Chloe b 17 June 1982, Rosalino Clio b 12 Jan 1988); m 2, 30 Sept 2000, Dr John E Kernthaler; 3 step c (Jeremy b 15 Feb 1974, Simon Charles 8 June 1975, Sophie Margaret 15 June 1980); *Career* conslt dermatologist London Hosp 1983, hon dir ICRF Skin Tumour Unit 1986, prof of dermatology London Med Coll 1992–2002 (sr lectr 1987–92); Bart's and Royal London Sch of Med and Dentistry: asst warden research 1997–2002, prof of cellular and molecular medicine 2000–06, research dir 2002–05; vice-princ and head of coll Univ of Dundee; Hon DSc (Med) 1999; FRCP 1989, FMedSci 1999; *Books* Keratinocyte Handbook (1994); *Style*— Prof Irene Leigh, OBE; ✉ College of Medicine, Dentistry and Nursing, University of Dundee, Level 10 Ninewells Hospital and Medical School, Dundee DD1 9SY (tel 01382 632763, fax 01382 644267)

LEIGH, John Roland; s of Adam Dale Leigh (d 1978), and Cecilia Winifred Leigh (d 1991); *b* 11 March 1933; *Educ* Winchester, King's Coll Cambridge; *m* 1957, Rosemary Renée, da of late Capt Gordon Furze, MC; 1 s, 3 da; *Career* merchant banker; ptnr Rathbone Bros & Co 1963–88; dir: Greenbank Trust Ltd 1969–81, Albany Investment Trust plc 1979–95, Rathbone Brothers plc 1988–93; chm: Blackburn Diocesan Bd of Fin Ltd 1976–98, Lancs CLA 1998–2000; memb: Gen Synod 1995–2005, Central Bd of Fin C of E 1995–98; ATII; *Clubs* Flyfishers', Athenaeum (Liverpool); *Style*— John Leigh, Esq; ✉ Robin Hood Cottage, Blue Stone Lane, Mawdesley, Ormskirk, Lancashire L40 2RG (tel 01704 822641, fax 01704 822691)

LEIGH, Prof Leonard Herschel; s of Leonard William Leigh (d 1976), of Edmonton, Canada, and Lillian Mavis, *née* Hayman (d 1965); *b* 19 September 1935; *Educ* Strathcona HS Edmonton Canada, Univ of Alberta (BA, LLB), Univ of London (PhD); *m* 17 Dec 1960, Jill Diane, da of George Gale (d 1986); 1 da (Alison Jane b 1965), 1 s (Matthew b 1967); *Career* cmmnd Royal Canadian Artillery 1955, transferred King's Own Calgary Regt 1959–62; called to the Bar: Alberta 1958, NW Territories 1960, Inner Temple 1993; in private practice Alberta 1958–60, advsy counsel Dept of Justice Canada 1960–62, in private practice England and Wales 1994–97; LSE: asst lectr 1964–65, lectr in law 1965–71, reader 1971–82, prof of criminal law 1982–97, convenor Law Dept 1987–91; visiting prof Queen's Univ Kingston Ontario 1973–74, Bowker visiting prof Univ of Alberta 1999; memb Criminal Cases Review Cmmn 1997–2005, memb Editorial Ctee European Jl of Crime and Criminal Justice 1992–; UK corr: La Revue de Science Criminelle (Paris), La Revue de Droit Penal et de Criminologie (Belgium), La Revue de Droit Africaine (Cameroun), La Revue Trimestrielle des Droits de l'Homme (Belgium); UK chm: Int Assoc of Penal Law 1986–, Université de l'Europe 1986–90; memb Cncl Int Penal and Penitentiary Fndn 1994–2006; pt/t conslt to govts of Canada, Quebec and Alberta; chm Awards Panel Canada Meml Fellowship 2001–; hon prof Faculty of Law Univ of Birmingham 2001–; *Books* The Criminal Liability of Corporations in English Law (1969), Northey & Leigh, Introduction to Company Law (1971, 4 edn 1987), Police Powers in England and Wales (1975, 2 edn 1985), Strict and Vicarious Liability (1982), Leigh and Edey, Companies Act 1981 (1982), A Guide to the Financial Services Act 1986 (jtly, 1986), Blackstone's Criminal Practice 1991– (contrib, 2004), English Public Law (contrib, 2004); *Recreations* music, walking; *Style*— Prof Leonard Leigh; ✉ 26 Gillhurst Road, Birmingham B17 8OS (tel 0121 428 2844); 2 Pump Court, Temple, London EC4Y 7AH (tel 020 7353 5597)

LEIGH, Mark Andrew Michael Stephen (Bertie); s of Robert Arthur Leigh, and Shelagh Elizabeth Leigh; *b* 30 August 1946, Stockport, Cheshire; *Educ* St Christopher Sch Letchworth, UEA (BA); *m* 1975, Helen Mary; 1 s (Tobias Timothy Edwin b 1976), 1 da (Harriet Celia Kathleen b 1980); *Career* admitted slr 1976; Hempsons: joined as trainee, ptnr 1977–, sr ptnr 1998–; tstee NCEPOD 2005–; govr City Lit Inst 2006–; Hon FRCPCH 1997, FRCOG ad eundem 2003; *Publications* Dewhursts' Obstetrics and Gynaecology (contrib, 1997 and 2007), Roberton's Neonatology (contrib, 1997 and 2005); *Clubs* Reform; *Style*— Bertie Leigh, Esq; ✉ Hempsons, Hempsons House, 40 Villiers Street, London WC2N 6NJ (tel 020 7839 0278, fax 020 7484 7566, e-mail mamsl@hempsons.co.uk)

LEIGH, Mike; OBE (1993); s of Alfred Abraham Leigh (d 1985), and Phyllis Pauline, *née* Cousin; *b* 20 February 1943; *Educ* Salford GS, RADA, Camberwell Sch of Arts and Crafts, Central Sch of Art and Design (Theatre Design Dept), London Film Sch; *m* 15 Aug 1973 (m dis 2001), Alison Steadman, the actress, da of George Percival Steadman; 2 s (Toby b 1978, Leo b 1981); *Career* dramatist, theatre/television and film director; assoc dir Midlands Arts Centre for Young People 1965–66, asst dir RSC 1967–68, lectr in drama Sedgley Park and De La Salle Colls Manchester 1968–69, lectr London Film Sch 1970–73; memb: Drama Panel Arts Cncl GB 1975–77, Dir's Working Pty and Specialist Allocations Bd 1976–84, Accreditation Panel Nat Cncl for Drama Trg 1978–91, Gen Advsy Cncl IBA 1980–82; chm of govrs London Film Sch 2001–; Hon MA Univ of Salford 1991, Hon MA Univ of Horthampton 2000, Hon DLitt Univ of Staffordshire 2000, Hon Dr Univ of Essex 2002; writer-dir: Nat Film Theatre Retrospectives 1979 and 1993, BBC TV Retrospective (incl Arena: Mike Leigh Making Plays) 1982, various US retrospectives incl MOMA NY 1992; writer-dir stage plays: The Box Play, My Parents Have Gone To Carlisle, The Last Crusade of the Five Little Nuns (Midlands Arts Centre) 1965–66, Nenaa (RSC Studio Stratford-upon-Avon) 1967, Individual Fruit Pies (E15 Acting Sch) 1968, Down Here And Up There (Royal Court Theatre Upstairs) 1968, Big Basil 1968, Glum Victoria And The Lad With Specs (Manchester Youth Theatre) 1969, Epilogue (Manchester) 1969, Bleak Moments (Open Space) 1970, A Rancid Pong (Basement) 1971, Wholesome Glory, Dick Whittington and his Cat (Royal Court Theatre Upstairs) 1973, The Jaws of Death (Traverse, Edinburgh Festival) 1973, Babies Grow Old (Other Place) 1974 (ICA) 1975, The Silent Majority (Bush) 1974, Abigail's Party (Hampstead) 1977, Ecstasy (Hampstead) 1979, Goose-Pimples (Hampstead, Garrick) 1981 (Standard Best Comedy Award), Smelling a Rat (Hampstead) 1988, Greek Tragedy (Belvoir St Theatre Sydney 1989, Edinburgh Festival and Theatre Royal Stratford East) 1990, It's A Great Big Shame! (Theatre Royal Stratford East) 1993; writer-dir BBC Radio play Too Much of A Good Thing 1979; writer-dir BBC TV plays and films: A Mug's Game 1972, Hard Labour 1973, The Permissive Society, Afternoon, A Light Snack, Probation, Old Chums, The Birth Of The 2001 FA Cup Final Goalie 1975, Nuts in May, Knock For Knock 1976, The Kiss of Death, Abigail's Party 1977, Who's Who 1978, Grown-Ups 1980, Home Sweet Home 1982, Four Days In July 1984; writer-dir Channel 4 films: Meantime 1983, The Short And Curlies 1987; writer-dir feature films: Bleak Moments 1971 (Golden Hugo, Chicago Film Festival 1972, Golden Leopard Locarno Film Festival 1972), High Hopes 1988 (Critics' Prize Venice Film Festival 1988, Evening Standard Peter Sellers Best Comedy Award 1990), Life Is Sweet 1990 (winner American Nat Soc of Film Critics' Award, Cariddi D'Oro & Maschera di Polifemo Taormina Film Festival 1991), Naked 1993 (winner Best Direction Cannes Film Festival, 1993), Secrets and Lies 1996 (winner Palme D'Or, Inter Critics' Prize, Ecumenical Prize Cannes Film Festival 1996, 5 Oscar nominations incl Best Dir and Best Screenplay 1997, BAFTA Award for Best Original Screen Play 1997), Career Girls 1997, Topsy-Turvy 1999 (Evening Standard Best Film 2000), All or Nothing 2002, Vera Drake 2005 (3 Oscar nominations incl Best Dir and Best Screenplay); *Books* Abigail's Party (1983), Goose-Pimples (1983), Smelling A Rat (1989), Ecstasy (1989), Naked and Other Screenplays (1995), Secrets and Lies (1997), Career Girls (1997), Topsy-Turvy (1999), All or Nothing (2002); *Style*— Mike Leigh, Esq, OBE; ✉ c/o PFD, Drury House, 34–43 Russell Street, London WC2B 5HA (tel 020 7344 1000, fax 020 7836 9543)

LEIGH, Peter William John; s of John Charles Leigh, JP (d 1961), of Harrow, Middx, and Dorothy Grace Jepps Leigh (d 1962); *b* 29 June 1929; *Educ* Harrow Weald Co GS, Coll of Estate Mgmnt; *m* 9 June 1956, Mary Frances, *née* Smith; 2 s (Simon b 1960, Howard b 1965), 1 da (Alison b 1961); *Career* Nat Serv RCS 1947–49; in private surveying practice 1949–53, valuation asst Middx CC 1953–60, commercial estates offr Bracknell Devpt Corp 1960–66; dir of valuation and estates GLC 1981–84 (previous sr appts 1966–81), dir of property servs Royal Co of Berks 1984–88, surveying and property conslt 1988–; memb: Exec Local Authy Valuers' Assoc 1981–88, Gen Cncl RICS 1984–86, GP Div Cncl RICS 1993–96, Govt Property Advsy Gp 1984–88; visiting lectr Reading Coll of Technol 1990–94; FRICS 1954; *Recreations* editing Old Wealden Assoc newsletter 1978–, drawing and painting, exploring Cornwall, gardening; *Style*— Peter Leigh, Esq; ✉ 41 Sandy Lane, Wokingham, Berkshire RG41 4SS (tel 0118 978 2732); Quinley, Bodinnick-by-Fowey, Cornwall PL23 1LX

LEIGH, Ray Hugh; MBE (2001); s of Dennis Leigh, OBE (d 1989), of Mickleton, Glos, and Amy Dorothy, *née* Symes (d 2001); *b* 6 June 1928; *Educ* Morecambe GS, AA Sch of Architecture (AADipl); *m* 1952, Jean, da of Col J Wykes, OBE; 1 da (Sarah Jane b 1953), 2 s (Simon Christopher b 1955 d 1996, David William b 1962); *Career* chartered architect and designer; architectural practice 1952–67; Gordon Russell Ltd (furniture makers): exec dir i/c design 1967–71, md 1971–82, chm 1982–86, re-appointed dir following takeover 1991–94; independent furniture designer and design mgmnt conslt 1986–, chm Luke Hughes & Co (furniture makers) 1990–94; pres: Design & Industries Assoc 1996–99, Furniture Trades Benevolent Assoc 1997–; dir: British Furniture Manufacturers Exports Ltd 1970–93 (past chm), Lygon Arms Hotel Broadway 1970–86, British Furniture Manufacturers Ltd 1994–99; fndr chm Contract Design Assoc 1978–82, chm British Furniture Cncl 1995, memb Crafts Cncl 1977–83; chm: Furniture Industry Research Assoc 1980–86, Edward Barnsley Educnl Tst Furniture Workshops 1980–90, Gordon Russell Tst; pres Glos Guild of Craftsmen 1980–90, memb Furniture Economic Devpt Ctee NEDC 1987–88; memb Ct of Assts Worshipful Co of Furniture Makers (Master 1994–95); RIBA, FCSD, FRSA, Hon FRCA; *Recreations* gardens, fell walking, photography, antiquarian books; *Style*— Ray Leigh, Esq, MBE; ✉ 5 The Green, Chipping Campden, Gloucestershire GL55 6DL (tel 01386 840208, fax 01386 840092, e-mail rayhleigh@aol.com)

LEIGH, Sir Richard Henry; 3 Bt (UK 1918), of Altrincham, Cheshire; s of Eric Leigh (d 1982), and his 1 w, Joan Fitzgerald Lane (d 1973), eldest da of Maurice Charles Lane Freer, of Kiambu, Kenya; suc unc Sir John Leigh, 2 Bt (d 1992); *b* 11 November 1936; *Educ* England and Switzerland; *m* 1, 1962 (m dis 1977), Barbro Anna Elizabeth, eldest da of late Stig Carl Sebastian Tham, of Sweden; m 2, 1977, Chérie Rosalind, eldest da of late Douglas Donald Dale, of La Blanchie, Cherval, France, and widow of Alan Reece, RMS; *Heir* half-bro, Christopher Leigh; *Style*— Sir Richard Leigh, Bt; ✉ PO Box 48621, London NW8 9WN

LEIGH, (Richard) Rowley; s of Robert Arthur Leigh, of Chulmleigh, and Shelagh Elizabeth, *née* Ruddin; *b* 23 April 1950; *Educ* Clifton, Tiffin Boys' Sch, Christ's Coll Cambridge (exhibitioner); *m* 1, 1982, Sara Patricia, da of Peter George, the author; 2 da (Ruth Bronwen b 22 Aug 1985, Daisy Dorothy b 2 Oct 1988); m 2, 2002, Katharine Sylvia, da of John Chancellor, author and bibliographer; 1 s (Sidney Robert Chancellor b 22 Feb 1998); *Career* chef tournant Joe Allen Restaurant 1978–79, commis chef Le Gavroche 1979–81, various posts in Roux Restaurants including patisserie, butchery, buying, etc 1981–83, head chef Le Poulbot 1984–87 (sous chef 1983–84), head chef/ptnr Kensington Place 1987–2006, fndr Le Cafe Anglais 2007–; contrib Guardian 1996–, food writer Sunday Telegraph 1998–2004, food writer FT 2004–; memb Académie Culinaire 1987; Glenfiddich Award for newspaper cookery writer of the year 1997, 2001 and 2006; *Recreations* reading, chess, music, golf; *Clubs* Groucho; *Style*— Rowley Leigh, Esq; ✉ 64 Wormholt Road, London W12 0LT (tel 020 8749 1452, e-mail rowleyleigh@hotmail.com); Le Cafe Anglais, 8 Porchester Gardens, London W2 (e-mail rowley@lecafeanglais.co.uk)

LEIGH FERMOR, Sir Patrick Michael; kt (2004), DSO (1944), OBE (Mil 1943); s of Sir Lewis Leigh Fermor, OBE, FRS (d 1954), and Muriel Eileen, da of Charles Taaffe Ambler (d 1972); *b* 11 February 1915; *Educ* King's Sch Canterbury; *m* 1968, Hon Joan Elizabeth (d 2003), da of 1 Viscount Monsell, GBE, PC; *Career* author; WWII: enlisted Irish Guards 1939, 2 Lt I Corps 1940, Lt Br mil mission to Greece, liaison offr Greek forces in Albania 1941, campaigns of Greece and Crete, Maj SOE German occupied Crete 1942–44, team Cdr Allied Airborne Reconnaissance Force N Germany; dep dir Br Inst Athens until 1946; hon citizen: Herakleion Crete 1947, Gytheion Laconia 1966, Kardamyli Messenia 1967; Gold Medal of Honour of the Municipality of Athens, Gold Medal City of Herakleion 1994; Hon DLitt: Univ of Kent 1991, Univ of Warwick 1996, American Coll of Greece; CLit 1991; visiting memb Acad of Athens; Officier dans l'Ordre des Arts et des Lettres (France) 1994, Cdr of the Order of the Phoenix (Greece) 2007; *Books* The Travellers Tree (1950, Heineman Fndn prize for literature 1950, Kemsley prize 1951), A Time to Keep

Silence (1953), The Violins of St Jacques (1953), Mani (1958, Duff Cooper meml prize, Book Soc's choice), Roumeli (1966), A Time of Gifts (1977, WH Smith & Son literary award 1978), Between the Woods and the Water (1986, Thomas Cook travel book award 1986, Int PEN/Time Life Silver Pen award 1986), Three Letters From The Andes (1991), Words of Mercury (2003); translated: Collete's Chance Acquaintances (1952), George Psychoundakis' The Cretan Runner (1955), Grand Prix Litteraire Jacques Audibertidi de la Ville d'Antibes (1992); *Recreations* travel, reading; *Clubs* Travellers, White's, Pratt's, Beefsteak, Special Forces, Puffins (Edinburgh); *Style*— Sir Patrick Leigh Fermor, DSO, OBE; ✉ c/o Messrs John Murray Ltd, 50 Albemarle Street, London W1S 4BD

LEIGH-HUNT, Barbara; da of Chandos Austin Leigh-Hunt (d 1970), of Bath, Somerset, and Elizabeth Jones (d 1993), latterly of Stratford-upon-Avon; *b* 14 December 1935; *Educ* Bath and Bristol Old Vic Theatre Sch (Bristol Evening Post Award for Most Promising Student 1953); *m* 1967, Richard Edward Pasco, *qv*, s of Cecil Pasco; 1 step s (William b 6 Nov 1961); *Career* actress; frequent broadcaster 1947–, has made many recordings incl a selection from the Psalms with Sir John Gielgud, Richard Pasco and Peter Orr, concert work incl performances with the Medici Quartet and at the Proms and numerous recitals at major UK arts festivals; assoc actor and govr RSC, patron Friends of the RSC, patron Assoc of Teacher of Speech and Drama; vice-pres: Royal Theatrical Fund, Theatrical Guild; pres Friends of the Other Places 1994–96; *Theatre* RSC incl: Winter's Tale, King Lear, Travesties, The Merry Wives of Windsor, That Good Between Us, Hamlet (Clarence Derwent Award for Best Supporting Actress 1982), Richard III; RNT incl: Cat on a Hot Tin Roof, Bartholomew Fair, The Voysey Inheritance, Racing Demon, An Inspector Calls (Olivier Award for Best Supporting Actress 1993), Absence of War; other roles incl: A Severed Head, Mrs Mouse, Are You Within? (all Bristol Old Vic and West End), Sherlock Holmes (Aldwych/Broadway), Every Good Boy Deserves Favour (Festival Hall), The Seagull (Old Vic/Bristol), Getting Married (tour), Pack of Lies (Lyric Theatre West End), One Thing More or Caedmon Construed (Chelmsford Cathedral), Barnaby and The Old Boys (Theatr Clwyd), A Woman of No Importance (Haymarket Theatre and nat tour), The Importance of Being Earnest (Birmingham Repertory and Old Vic); *Television* BBC incl: The Siegfried Idyll, Search for the Nile, Love Lies Bleeding, Games, Office Story, The Chief Mourner, The Voysey Inheritance, Mary's Wife, Paying Guests, Tumbledown, Pride and Prejudice, The Echo, Sunburn, Wives and Daughters; LWT incl: One Chance in Four, Cold Feet, A Perfect Hero (with Havahall Pictures), Anna Lee; other prodn incl: Wagner (Channel 4), All for Love (Granada), Inspector Morse (Zenith Prodns), The Best Man to Die (TVS), Kavanagh QC (Carlton), Longitude (Granada), Midsomer Murders (Bentley Prodns), Bertie & Elizabeth (Carlton and Whitehall Films); *Films* Frenzy, Henry VIII and His Six Wives, A Bequest to the Nation, Oh Heavenly Dog, Paper Mask, Keep The Aspidistra Flying 1997, Billy Elliott 1999, The Martins 2000, Elegy For Iris 2001, Vanity Fair 2003; *Clubs* Univ Women's; *Style*— Ms Barbara Leigh-Hunt; ✉ c/o Conway Van Gelder Ltd, 18–21 Jermyn Street, London SW1Y 6HP (tel 020 7287 0077, fax 020 7494 3324)

LEIGH PEMBERTON, Jeremy; CBE (1992), DL (2004); s of Capt Robert Douglas Leigh Pemberton, MBE, MC, JP (d 1964), and Helen Isobel, *née* Payne-Gallwey (d 1985); bro of Baron Kingsdown, KG, PC (Life Peer), *qv*; *b* 25 November 1933; *Educ* Eton, Magdalen Coll Oxford (MA), INSEAD Fontainebleau (MBA); *m* 1, 30 May 1968 (m dis 1980), Mary, da of John Ames, of Boston, MA; 1 s (Richard b 13 Dec 1971); m 2, 3 June 1982, Virginia Marion, da of Sir John Curle, KCVO, CMG (d 1997); *Career* Nat Serv Grenadier Gds 1952–54, cmmnd 2 Lt 1953; Brooke Bond Liebig 1957–69 (rising to gp mktg controller), md W & R Balston Group 1973–74 (gp mktg controller and corporate planner 1970–73), dep chm Whatman plc (formerly Whatman Reeve Angel plc) 1990–94 (md 1974–89); chm: Mid Kent Holdings plc until 1998, Morgan Grenfell Equity Income Trust plc (renamed Deutche Equity Income Trust plc) until 2003, JP Morgan Fleming US Discovery Investment Trust plc (formerly Fleming US Discovery Investment Trust plc) until 2004, Kent Co Crematorium plc; dir: London & Manchester Group plc until 1998, Bailey Products Ltd until 1998, Kent TEC Ltd until 1994, Understanding Industry Trust Ltd until 2002, Savoy Hotel plc until 1998, The Learning and Business Link Co 1999–2001, ADL Partner Ltd 2002–; chm: Tatem Ltd until 1999, Kent Economic Development Board until 1997, Business Link Kent Ltd until 1999 and 2003–, Claripoint Ltd 2000–07; CBI: former memb Nat Cncl, former memb Econ and Fin Policy Ctee, former memb Fin and Gen Purposes Ctee, fndr chm Kent Area Ctee (later chm SE Regnl Cncl); visiting prof in mktg INSEAD 1965–70; pres: INSEAD Int Alumni Assoc 1962–66, Kent branch Chartered Inst of Mktg 1988–92, Kent branch Inst of Mgmnt 1992–98; chm: The Haven Tst 1997–2006, D'Oyly Carte Charitable Tst 1998–; govr Kent Music Sch 1999–; tstee Lord Cornwallis Meml Fund; FCIM, FInstD; *Recreations* gardening, opera, fishing; *Style*— Jeremy Leigh Pemberton, Esq, CBE, DL; ✉ Hill House, Wormshill, Sittingbourne, Kent ME9 0TS (tel 01622 884472, fax 01622 884784, e-mail jeremy.lp@btinternet.com)

LEIGH-PEMBERTON, Robin (Robert); *see:* Kingsdown, The Rt Hon Lord

LEIGH-SMITH, District Judge (Alfred) Nicholas Hardstaff; s of Lt-Col Alfred Leigh Hardstaff Leigh-Smith, TD, DL (d 1978), of Stanwell Moor, Middx, and Marguerite Calvert, *née* Calvert-Harrison (d 1983); *b* 21 December 1953; *Educ* Epsom Coll, Univ of Leeds (LLB); *m* Samantha Sian, *née* Morgan; 2 s (Thomas David b 29 June 2002, Henry Nicholas b 17 Dec 2003); *Career* called to the Bar Lincoln's Inn 1976; dep clerk: Bromley Justices 1985, Brent Justices 1989; clerk to the justices Cambridge and E Cambridgeshire Justices 1995–2001, in private practice New Walk Chambers Leicester 2001–04; asst stipendiary magistrate 1999–2000, dep district judge (Magistrates' Court) 2000–04, dist judge (Magistrates' Court) 2004–; *Recreations* church bellringing, rugby union football, clay pigeon shooting, reading, walking; *Style*— District Judge Leigh-Smith; ✉ The Hermitage, 23 Earning Street, Godmanchester, Huntingdon, Cambridgeshire PE29 2JD (fax 01480 435906); 3 & 4 John Street, Penmachno, North Wales (e-mail a.leighsmith@btinternet.com); The Magistrates' Court, Stuart Street, Luton, Bedfordshire LU1 5BL (tel 01582 524200, fax 01582 524282)

LEIGHFIELD, John Percival; CBE (1998); s of late Henry Tom Dainton Leighfield, and late Patricia Zilpha Maud, *née* Baker; *b* 5 April 1938; *Educ* Magdalen Coll Sch Oxford, Exeter Coll Oxford (MA); *m* Margaret Ann, da of Charles Mealin; 1 s (Benjamin John b August 1968), 1 da (Rebecca Margaret b October 1970); *Career* with Ford Motor Co 1962–65, with Plessey Co 1965–72 (head of mgmnt info system 1970–72), with Br Leyland 1972–79 (IT dir Leyland Cars 1975–79), fndr and md ISTEL Ltd 1979–89, chm AT&T ISTEL (after AT&T acquired ISTEL) 1989–93, sr vice-pres and offr AT&T 1989–93; chm: RM plc 1993–, Birmingham Midshires Building Society 1996–99, Synstar plc 1998–2004; dir: TMA Ventures Ltd 1994–2002, IMPACT Programme Ltd 1998–2001, Halifax plc 1999–2001, KnowledgePool Ltd 2000–01, Getmapping plc 2005–; pro-chllr Univ of Warwick (chm Cncl), hon prof and memb Advsy Bd Warwick Business Sch; chm Alliance for Info Systems Skills; memb: Cncl of Computing Services and Software Assoc 1985–2002 (pres 1995–96), Bd of Intellect 2002–; chm of govrs Magdalen Coll Sch Oxford 1995–2002, chm Advsy Cncl Oxford Philomusica 2002–; Hon Dr: Univ of Central England, De Montfort Univ, Univ of Wolverhampton; fndr memb, Liveryman and Warden Worshipful Co of Info Technologists (Master 2005–06); FInstD 1989, fell Inst for the Mgmnt of Info Systems 1990 (pres 2000–), Hon FBCS 1991 (pres 1993–94), FRSA 1997; *Publications* author of several papers on IT; *Recreations* historical cartography, music, walking; *Clubs* RAC, Royal Fowey Yacht; *Style*— John Leighfield, Esq, CBE; ✉ 91 Victoria Road, Oxford OX2 7QG (e-mail john.leighfield@rmplc.co.uk)

LEIGHTON, Jane; *b* 17 March 1944; *Career* admin Br Pregnancy Advsy Service 1971–74, sec to Liverpool Community Health Cncl 1974–79, reporter and researcher World in Action Granada Television Ltd 1979–85; 1985–88: cr equal opportunities prog Littlewoods Orgn, prodr and dir Twenty Twenty Vision Channel 4, ed A Savage Enquiry; exec dir Mersey Television 1988–90, head of public affairs Granada Television Ltd 1990–92, HR and communications conslt Liverpool Housing Action Tst 1992–, chair Mental Health Servs Salford NHS Tst 1992–95, head of organisational devpt Tate Gallery 1995–97, chair Broadcasting Complaints Cmmn 1996–97 (cmmr 1993–96), dep chair Broadcasting Standards Cmmn 1997–, chair Camden and Islington Area Mental Health Ctee 1998–2002, non-exec dir Camden and Islington Communities Services NHS Tst 1998–2000, dir Virtuall 2000–04, chair Waveney Primary Care Tst 2003–06; non-exec dir: City of London Sinfonia 1992–97, Hallé Concerts Soc 1993–95, Royal Liverpool Philharmonic Orch; memb NW Arts Bd; govr Univ Coll Salford 1991–93; FRSA; *Awards* RTS Award for best int current affairs prog 1981, BMA Award for med progs 1983, Women in Mgmnt Award for best private sector equal opportunities prog 1987; *Style*— Ms Jane Leighton; ✉ 94 London Road, Halesworth, Suffolk IP19 8LS (tel 07718 538539, e-mail leightonjane@btinternet.com)

LEIGHTON, John; s of Edwin Leighton (d 1982), and Norah Schwab, *née* Winterheim; *b* 22 February 1959, Belfast; *Educ* Portora Royal Sch Enniskillen, Univ of Edinburgh, Edinburgh Coll of Art (MA), Courtauld Inst of Art London (MA); *Partner* Gillian Keay; 1 da (Alexandra b 12 Nov 1989), 1 s (Frederick b 28 Oct 1992); *Career* lectr and tutor Dept of Humanities Edinburgh Coll of Art 1983–86, curator of 19th-century paintings National Gallery London 1986–97, dir Van Gogh Museum Amsterdam 1997–2006, DG National Galleries of Scotland 2006–; memb Bd: De Pont Museum for Contemporary Art Tilburg 1998–, Stichting Nederlands Kunsthistorische Publicaties 1998–, Art Matters 2001–; editorial advsr Amsterdam Univ Press 1998–2001, memb Steering Bd Apeldoorn Conference 1999–2006, advsr Mondriaan Stichting 1999–2002, memb Advsy Bd Vereniging Rembrandt 1999–; Chevalier Ordre des Arts et des Lettres; *Exhibitions* Edinburgh-Dublin 1885–1985 (Edinburgh Coll of Art) 1985, Jacques-Louis David: Portrait of Jacobus Blauw (National Gallery London) 1987, French Paintings from the USSR: Watteau to Matisse (National Gallery London) 1988, Caspar David Friedrich: Winter Landscape (National Gallery London) 1990, Art in the Making: Impressionism (National Gallery London) 1990–91, Corot (Manchester City Art Gallery and Castle Museum Norwich) 1991, Van Gogh to Picasso: The Berggruen Collection at the National Gallery (National Gallery London) 1991, Manet: The Execution of Maximilian (National Gallery London) 1992, Friedrich to Hodler: German, Austrian and Swiss Paintings from the Oskar Reinhart Foundation, Winterthur (National Gallery London, Alte Nationalgalerie Berlin, Los Angeles County Museum of Art, Metropolitan Museum of Art NY, Musée Rath Geneva) 1994, Seurat's Bathers (Nat Gallery London) 1997, Signac 1863–1935 (Grand Palais Paris, Van Gogh Museum Amsterdam, Metropolitan Museum of Art NY) 2001, Manet and the Sea (Art Inst of Chicago, Philadelphia Museum of Art, Van Gogh Museum Amsterdam) 2003–04; *Publications* Vincent van Gogh: Wheatfield with Crows (1999), 100 Masterpieces in the Van Gogh Museum (2002), Manet: Impressions of the Sea (2004); also a number of exhibition catalogues; articles and reviews in various publications; *Style*— John Leighton, Esq; ✉ National Galleries of Scotland, The Mound, Edinburgh EH2 2EL

LEIGHTON, Sir Michael John Bryan; 11 Bt (E 1693), of Wattlesborough, Shropshire; s of Col Sir Richard Tihel Leighton, 10 Bt, TD (d 1957), and Kathleen Irene Linda, *née* Lees (d 1993); *b* 8 March 1935; *Educ* Stowe, RAC Cirencester, Tabley House Agric Sch; *m* 1, 1974 (m dis 1980), Mrs Amber Mary Ritchie; m 2, 1991, Mrs Diana Mary Gamble; 1 da (Eleanor Angharad Diana b 20 Jan 1992); *Heir* none; *Career* photographer of wildlife; ornithologist; *Recreations* panel 'A' gun dog judge, cricket, tennis, golf, writing poetry, cooking; *Clubs* MCC; *Style*— Sir Michael Leighton, Bt; ✉ Loton Park, Alderbury, Shrewsbury, Shropshire SY5 9AJ (tel 01743 884232)

LEIGHTON, Brig Richard; s of Robert Leighton (d 1996), and Margaret, *née* Walker; *b* 20 January 1948; *Educ* Creighton Sch Carlisle, City Univ (BSc), RMA Sandhurst; *m* 31 Dec 1993, Dianna, *née* Ring; 2 s from previous m (Christopher Richard b 2 Sept 1970, Martin Jonathan Robert b 19 Dec 1971); *Career* serv: 1 Bn Queen's Lancs Regt 1974–80, QOH 1981–84; Staff Offr Gen Staff 1987–93, Cdr SPS Eastern Dist 1994–95, dir Staff and Personnel Support (Army) 1998–2000, dir devpt Armed Forces Personnel Admin Agency (AFPAA) 2000–03; fell CIMA 1992; *Recreations* squash, gardening, Times crossword; *Clubs* Army and Navy; *Style*— Brig Richard Leighton

LEIGHTON, Tom James; s of Thomas James Leighton (d 1974), and Winifred Barclay, *née* Mearns; *b* 2 October 1944; *Educ* Cardinal Newman Coll Buenos Aires Argentina, Austin Friars Sch Carlisle, Derby Coll of Art (Dip Photography); *m* 1, 1964 (m dis 1969), Margaret Louise Lockhart Mure; 1 s (Lee Lockhart-Mure b 20 April 1967); m 2, 1970, Susan Gillian, da of Albert George Hollingsworth; *Career* fashion photographer for many magazines, advertising agencies and catalogues 1975–81, interiors photographer 1981–; assignments incl: American Vogue, World of Interiors, Sunday Times Magazine, Telegraph Magazine, Casa Vogue (Spain), La Casa de Marie Claire (Spain), Casa Vogue (Italy), Homes and Gardens, House and Garden, Laura Ashley, Elle Decoration, Architecktur and Wohnen (Germany), Harpers and Queen, Living Etc; *Photography Books* Junk Style (1997), Vital Colour (1998); *Style*— Tom Leighton, Esq; ✉ 17 Cedar Court, Sheen Lane, London SW14 8LY (tel 020 8876 8497)

LEIGHTON OF ST MELLONS, 3 Baron (UK 1962); Sir Robert William Henry Leighton Seager; 3 Bt (UK 1952); s of 2 Baron Leighton of St Mellons (d 1998); *b* 28 September 1955; *Style*— The Rt Hon the Lord Leighton of St Mellons

LEINSTER, 9 Duke of (I 1766); Maurice FitzGerald; Premier Duke, Marquess and Earl in the Peerage of Ireland, also Baron of Offaly (I *ante* 1203 restored 1554), Earl of Kildare (I 1316), Viscount Leinster of Taplow (GB 1747), Marquess of Kildare, Earl of Offaly (both I 1761), and Baron Kildare (UK 1870); s of 8 Duke of Leinster (d 2004), and Anne, *née* Eustace Smith; *b* 7 April 1948, Dublin; *Educ* Millfield; *m* 19 Feb 1972, Fiona Mary Francesca, *née* Hollick; 1 s (Thomas, Earl of Offaly b 12 Jan 1974 d 1997), 2 da (Lady Francesca Emily Purcell b 6 July 1976, Lady Pollyanna Louisa Clementine b 9 May 1982); *Heir* bro, Lord John FitzGerald; *Career* landscape gardener and designer Maxwell Communication Corporation plc 1984–92; pres Oxfordshire Dyslexia Assoc 1978–; chm Thomas Offaly Meml Fund 1999–; *Recreations* fishing, shooting, riding, sailing, diving, DIY; *Style*— His Grace the Duke of Leinster; ✉ Courtyard House, Oakley Park, Frilford Heath, Oxfordshire OX13 6QW

LEINSTER, Prof Samuel John; s of Victor Leinster, of Birmingham, and Jemina Eileen Eva, *née* McGeown; *b* 29 October 1946; *Educ* Boroughmuir Sr Secdy Sch Edinburgh, Univ of Edinburgh (BSc, MB ChB), Univ of Liverpool (MD); *m* 17 July 1971, Jennifer, da of James Woodward, of Wirral; 1 da (Angela b 1972), 3 s (Alistair b 1975, David b 1979, Benjamin b 1988); *Career* RAF Med Branch: PO 1969, Flying Offr 1971, Flt Lt 1972, MO 1972–77, Sqdn Ldr 1977, surgical specialist, ret 1977; lectr in surgery Welsh Nat Sch of Med 1978–81, sr lectr in surgery Univ of Liverpool and hon conslt surgn Liverpool HA 1982–90; Univ of Liverpool: reader in surgery 1990–93, prof of surgery 1993–2000, dir of med studies 1995–2000; dean of Sch of Med, Health Policy and Practice UEA 2001–; memb: BMA, Surgical Res Soc, Assoc of Surgns of GB and I, Assoc for the Study of Med Educn, Br Assoc of Surgical Oncology, Christian Med Fellowship, HE Acad, PLAB Bd GMC 2000–; FRCS, FRCSEd; *Books* Systemic Diseases for Dental Students (with T J Bailey, 1983), Mammary Development and Cancer (with P S Rudland, D G Ferning

L

and G G Lunt, 1997), Shared Care in Breast Cancer (with H Downey and T Gibbs, 2000); *Recreations* garedning, DIY, wood turning, active committed Christian; *Style—* Prof Samuel Leinster; ✉ University of East Anglia, Norwich NR4 7TJ (tel 01603 593939, fax 01603 593752, e-mail s.leinster@uea.ac.uk)

LEITÃO, Robert Mark; s of Eduardo Francisco Felipe Leitão, of Portugal, and Brenda Miriam, *née* Jarman; *b* 28 June 1963; *Educ* St Julian's Sch Carcavelos Portugal, Oratory Sch Woodcote, Imperial Coll London (BSc); *m* 8 July 1995, Lucy Claire, *née* Birkbeck; 2 s (Felix Edward Oliver b 2 July 1998, Tobias Alexander Robert b 26 July 1999), 1 da (Hermione Sophie Isabel b 19 July 2003); *Career* KPMG 1985–89, Morgan Grenfell & Co Ltd 1989–98, N M Rothschild & Sons 1998–; ARSM 1984, ACA 1987; *Style—* Robert Leitão, Esq; ✉ N M Rothschild & Sons, New Court, St Swithin's Lane, London EC4P 4DU (tel 020 7280 5000, e-mail robert.leitao@rothschild.co.uk)

LEITCH, Baron (Life Peer UK 2004), of Oakley in Fife; Alexander Park (Sandy) Leitch; s of Donald Leitch (d 1949), of Blairhall, Fife, and Agnes Smith, *née* Park (d 2006); *b* 20 October 1947; *Educ* Dunfermline HS; *m* 1 (m dis); 3 da (Hon Fiona b 1971, Hon Joanne b 1973, Hon Jacqueline b 1975); m 2, 29 Aug 2003, Noelle Dowd; *Career* chief systems designer National Mutual Life 1969, Hambro Life 1971 (bd dir 1981); Allied Dunbar plc: md 1988, dep chm 1990, chief exec 1993–96; chm Allied Dunbar Assurance plc 1996–98; chief exec: Br American Financial Services (UK and Int) Ltd 1996–98, Zurich Financial Services (UKISA) Ltd 1998–2001, Zurich Financial Services (UKISA/Asia Pacific) 2001–04; chm: Dunbar Bank 1994–2003, Eagle Star Holdings plc 1996–2004, Threadneedle Asset Management 1996–2004, ABI 1998–2000, Intrinsic Financial Servs 2005–, BUPA 2006– (dir 2005–); dir: BAT Industries plc 1997–98, United Business Media 2005–, Lloyds TSB 2005–, Paternoster 2006–; chm: SANE 1999–2000, Pensions Protection and Investment Accreditation Bd 2000–01, New Deal Task Force 2000–01, Nat Employment Panel 2001–, Balance Charitable Fndn for Unclaimed Assets 2004–05, Leitch Review of UK Skills 2005; dep chm Business in the Community 1997–2004, vice-chm Cwlth Educn Fund 2002–, vice-pres UK Cares 2004; tstee: Nat Galleries of Scotland 1999–2003, Philharmonia Orch 2000–04; Prince of Wales Ambassador's Award for Charitable Work 2001; Freeman City of London 2002, memb Worshipful Co of Insurers 2002; MBCS 1966; *Recreations* antiques, football, antiquarian books, poetry; *Style—* The Rt Hon the Lord Leitch

LEITCH, Maurice Henry; MBE (1999); s of Andrew Leitch (d 1983), of Templepatrick, Co Antrim, NI, and Jean, *née* Coid (d 1973); *b* 5 July 1933; *Educ* Methodist Coll Belfast, Stranmills Trg Coll Belfast (teaching dip); *m* 1, 23 July 1956, Isobel, da of James Scott; 1 da (Bronagh b 17 Sept 1965), 1 s (Paul b 17 Feb 1967); m 2, 18 Nov 1972, Sandra, da of Alfred Hill; 1 s (Daniel b 29 April 1974); *Career* teacher Antrim NI 1954–60; BBC Radio: features prodr Belfast 1960–70, drama prodr London 1970–77, prodr Book at Bedtime 1977–89; author of several novels, TV screenplays, radio dramas, features and short stories; Guardian Fiction Prize 1969, Whitbread Fiction Prize 1981, Pye award for Most Promising Writer New to TV 1980–1981; memb Soc of Authors 1989; *Style—* Maurice Leitch, Esq, MBE; ✉ 32 Windermere Avenue, London NW6 6LN

LEITH, Annie; *see:* Burgh, Anita, Lady; Anita Lorna

LEITH, Jake Quintin; s of Jack Leith, of Hove, E Sussex, and Louisa Teresa, *née* Quinn (d 2002); *b* 18 November 1958; *Educ* Bushey Meads Sch, Herts Coll of Art & Design, Loughborough Coll of Art & Design (BA), Birmingham Inst of Art & Design (MA); *Career* chartered designer; export designer Textile Dept Everest Fabrics Ghaziabad India 1983–84, interior designer/textile advsr Europa Shop Equipment Ltd 1984–85, self-employed interior designer Fantasy Finishes 1985–86, sr ptnr The Jake Leith Partnership interior designers specialising in furnishing fabrics and wall-coverings 1986–; private and commercial cmmns; CSD: memb assessor Textiles/Fashion 1996–, tstee and memb Cncl 1998–, chair Textiles/Fashion Bd 2001–03, memb Ethics and Professional Practice Ctee 2004– vice-pres 2004–; memb: Continual Professional Devpt Ctee 1995–97, Professional Standards Ctee 1995–98; external examiner, validator and advsr CHEAD 1997–, practicing assoc Acad of Experts 1998–2000; external examiner (Printed Textiles/Surface Decoration) Univ of E London 1998–2003; Loughborough Univ: ind assessor Multi-Media Textiles 1999–2000, internal examiner Furniture Design 2000–2002, co-ordinator and internal examiner Professional Business Studies 1999–2003; external advsr Utrecht Sch of Arts 2002–, external advsr Open Univ 2002–; Univ of Brighton: internal examiner 2002–, visiting lectr 2002–03, area ldr business studies fashion and textiles 2003–, academic prog ldr fashion and textiles 2004–06, course validator 2005–; external advsr Univ of Sussex 2005–; memb Assoc of Degree Courses in Fashion and textile Design 2004–, memb Colls Forum Steering Ctee British Fashion Cncl 2005–; visual arts advsr Dacorum Borough Arts 1996–2004, judge Healey & Baker Fashion Awards 2002–; FCSD 1995 (MCSD 1983), FRSA 1996; *Recreations* classical guitar, printmaking, catamaran sailing, gardening, songwriting, good food; *Clubs* Sopwell House Country; *Style—* Jake Leith, Esq; ✉ The Jake Leith Partnership, 12 Midland Road, Hemel Hempstead, Hertfordshire HP2 5BH (tel 01442 247010, fax 01442 245495, e-mai jake@jlp.uk.com, website www.jlp.uk.com)

LEITH, Prudence Margaret (Prue); OBE (1989), DL (Gtr London 1998); da of Stewart Leith (d 1961), of Johannesburg, South Africa, and Margaret, *née* Inglis; *b* 18 February 1940; *Educ* St Mary's Sch Johannesburg, Univ of Cape Town, Sorbonne Paris (Cours de la Civilisation Francaise); *m* 1974, (Charles) Rayne Kruger (author); 1 s (Daniel b 1974), 1 da (Li-Da b 1974); *Career* restaurateur, caterer, author, journalist; fndr: Leith's Good Food 1961, Leith's Restaurant 1969, Prudence Leith Ltd 1972, Leith's Sch of Food and Wine 1975, Leith's Farm 1976; dir: Leith's Restaurant Ltd 1969–95, Prudence Leith Ltd 1972–94 (md), Br Transport Hotels Ltd 1977–83, BR Bd 1980–85 (pt/t), Safeway plc 1989–96 (formerly Argyll Group plc, joined gp as conslt to Safeway stores 1988), Halifax plc (formerly Leeds Permanent Building Society and Halifax Building Society until 1997) 1992–99, UK Skills Ltd 1993–, Leith's Ltd 1994–96 (chm), 3E's Enterprises Ltd 1994–2007 (chm), Whitbread plc 1995–2005, Triven VCT 2000–03, Forum for the Future 2000–03 (chm), Woolworths plc 2001–06, Omega plc 2004–, Nations Healthcare 2006–07, Orient-Express Hotels 2006–; chair School Food Tst 2007–; memb Cncl Food From Britain 1983–87; chm: Restaurateurs' Assoc of GB 1990–94, Br Food Tst; vice-pres Royal Soc for the Encouragement of Arts, Manufactures and Commerce; team memb Opportunity 2000 Target; govr Ashridge Mgmnt Coll 1992– (chm 2002–07); appeared in: 26–part TV cookery series on Tyne-Tees TV, Best of Br BBC TV, The Good Food Show, Take 6 Cooks, Tricks of the Trade, Great British Menu; memb: Nat Trg Task Force Dept of Employment 1989–91, Centre for Tomorrow's Co 1990–, PO Stamp Advsy Ctee 1997–; master Univ of North London 1997; Hon Dr: Univ of Greenwich 1996, Univ of Manchester 1996, Open Univ 1997, City Univ 2005; FRSA (chm RSA 1995–97), Hon FCGI; *Books* written 12 cookery books between 1972 and 1991; Leaving Patrick (1999), Sisters (2001), A Lovesome Thing (2004); *Recreations* tennis, gardening, walking; *Style—* Ms Prue Leith, OBE, DL; ✉ The Office, Chastleton Glebe, Moreton-in-Marsh, Gloucestershire GL56 0SZ (tel 01608 674908, e-mail pmleith@dsl.pipex.com)

LEIVERS, Julie; *Educ* Univ of Newcastle upon Tyne (BA); *Career* product mangr and nat account mangr The Angelini Corp Swaddlers Ltd 1985–88, product mangr The Boots Co plc Farley's Baby Foods Crookes Healthcare Ltd 1988–91, gp product mangr and trade mktg Walkers Crisps Ltd 1991–93, mktg controller Coca Cola & Schweppes Beverages Ltd 1993–96, mktg dir McCain Foods (GB) Ltd 1996–2003, vice-pres (mktg and innovation) GlaxoSmithKline Nutritional Healthcare UK 2003–04, gp mktg dir Silentnight Group Ltd 2004–; former vol mktg dir Stephen Joseph Theatre; *Recreations* tennis, skiing, travel, mountain biking, landscape design; *Style—* Ms Julie Leivers; ✉ Silentnight Group Ltd, Silentnight House, Salterforth, Barnoldswick, Lancashire BB18 5UE

LEMAN, Adrianne; da of Frank George Jarratt (d 1978), and Frances Hannah, *née* King (d 1975); *b* 19 February 1938; *Educ* Edgehill Coll Bideford N Devon, Camberwell Sch of Arts and Crafts (NDD), Royal Coll of Art (ARCA); *m* 1, 1960 (m dis 1969), Martin LeMan, s of Arthur LeMan; m 2, 1979 (m dis 1992), Ian Stirling, s of Col William Stirling; *Career* art dir The Illustrated London News 1970–80, dir Addison Design Company Ltd 1982–87, md Holmes & Marchant Corporate Design 1987–92, chm C&FD 2002–04 (fndr md 1992–2001), chm 85Four (formerly C&FD) 2004–; dir DBA 1992–95; CSD: hon treas 1994–96, pres-elect 1996–97, pres 1997–98 (resigned); FRSA, MIRS; *Recreations* opera, cinema, books, art (seeing and collecting), spending time with friends; *Style—* Ms Adrianne LeMan; ✉ c/o 85Four, 85 Clerkenwell Road, London EC1R 5AR (tel 020 7400 4700, fax 020 7242 3848, mobile 07836 610577, e-mail adrianne.leman@85four.com)

LEMMON, Mark Benjamin; s of Edmund Lemmon (d 1984), of Great Bookham, Surrey, and Mary Patricia, *née* Bryan (d 2005); *b* 15 April 1952; *Educ* Wimbledon Coll, UCL (BA), LSE (MSc), Coll of Estate Mgmnt (Dip Prop Investment (RICS)); *m* 8 Aug 1980, Anna, da of Prof Tamas Szekely, of Budapest, Hungary; 3 da (Esther b 1981, Patricia b 1985, Bernadette b 1990); *Career* formerly with: Touche Ross, Grindlays Bank, Guinness Mahon, Hongkong and Shanghai Banking Corporation (sr corp mangr); dir ECGD; currently dep chief exec Project and Export Fin HSBC Bank plc; memb: Billingsgate Ward Club, Company of World Traders, Hungarian Soc, English Speaking Union; Freeman City of London; FCA 1978, ATII 1979, ACIB 1982, FRSA; *Recreations* squash, opera; *Clubs* Wimbledon Squash and Badminton, Old Wimbledonians, Wayfoong, Felpham Sailing, Star Gun, India, Royal Over-Seas League; *Style—* Mark Lemmon, Esq; ✉ HSBC Bank plc, 8 Canada Square, London E14 5HQ (e-mail mark.lemmon@hsbcib.com)

LEMMY, *see:* Kilmister, Lemmy

LENDRUM, Christopher John (Chris); CBE (2005); s of Herbert Colin Lendrum, of St Neots, Cambs, and Anne Margaret, *née* Macdonell; *b* 15 January 1947; *Educ* Felsted Sch, Univ of Durham; *m* 1 Aug 1970, Margaret Patricia, da of Joseph Ridley Parker; 1 s (Oliver David Ridley b 23 Sept 1976), 1 da (Victoria Alice b 11 Sept 1980); *Career* Barclays Bank plc: joined 1969, chief exec Corporate Banking 1996–2003, exec dir 1998–2004, chm Barclays Africa 2000–04, gp vice-chm 2004, chm Barclays Pension Fund Tstees Ltd 2005–; govr Kent Coll 2000–; memb Advsy Bd Nat Assoc of Citizens Advice Bureaux (NACAB) 2001–04, tstee CAB 2005–06; tstee: Aston Martin Heritage Tst 2003– (chm 2006–), City of London Endowment Tst for St Paul's Cathedral 2007–; govr Motability 2005– (tstee 10th Anniversary Tst 2003–); Freeman City of London 1999, Liveryman Worshipful Co of Woolmen 1999; FCIB 1992, CIMgt 2001; *Recreations* restoring neglected motor cars, travel, gardening; *Clubs* RAC; *Style—* Chris Lendrum, Esq, CBE

LENEY, Simon David; s of Colin Frank Leney, of E Sussex, and Patricia, *née* Easton; *b* 10 September 1952, Brighton; *Educ* Sherborne; *m* 6 Nov 1976, Jane, *née* Crouch; 2 s (George David b 16 Feb 1985, William James 6 Dec 1987); *Career* ptnr: Donne Mileham & Haddock 1980–94, Cripps Harries Hall LLP 1994–; memb: Law Soc 1977, Soc of Notaries Public 1989, Soc of Trust and Estate Practitioners 1991; MSI 1986; *Recreations* Porsche cars, rugby, house and garden; *Style—* Simon Leney, Esq; ✉ Cripps Harries Hall LLP, Wallside House, 12 Mount Ephraim Road, Tunbridge Wells TN1 1EG (tel 01892 506005, e-mail sdl@crippslaw.com)

LENG, James William (Jim); *b* 19 November 1945; *Career* ceo: Low & Bonar plc 1992–95, Laporte plc 1995–2001; non-exec dir: Pilkington plc 1998–2006, Corus Gp plc 2001– (chm 2003–), IMI 2002–05, JPMorganFleming Mid Cap Investment Tst plc 2003–04, Hanson 2004–; sr ind dir Alstom SA 2003– (chm Renumerations and Nominations Ctee), dep chm Tata Steel India 2007–; *Style—* J W Leng, Esq; ✉ 2nd Floor, 30 Millbank, London SW1P 4WY (tel 020 7717 4554, fax 020 7717 4654)

LENG, Gen Sir Peter John Hall; KCB (1978, CB 1975), MBE (1962), MC (1945); s of J Leng; *b* 9 May 1925; *Educ* Bradfield Coll; *m* 1 (m dis), Virginia Rosemary Pearson; 3 s, 2 da; m 2, 1981, Mrs Flavia Tower, da of Lt-Gen Sir Frederick Browning, KCVO, DSO (d 1965), and Dame Daphne du Maurier, DBE (d 1989); *Career* cmmnd 1944, served WWII, Cdr Land Forces NI 1973–75, Dir Mil Operations MOD 1975–78, Cdr 1 (Br) Corps 1978–80, Master-Gen of the Ordnance 1981–83, ret; Col Cmdt RAVC and RMP 1976–89; chm Racecourse Assoc 1985–89, patron Natural Therapeutic and Osteopathic Soc 1987–93; *Style—* Gen Sir Peter Leng, KCB, MBE, MC

LENIHAN, Conor Patrick; TD; s of Brian Lenihan (d 1995), and Ann, *née* Devine; *b* 3 March 1963, Dublin, Ireland; *Educ* Belvedere Coll, UC Dublin (BA), Dublin City Univ (Dip), INSEAD; *m* 10 Sept 1994, Denise, *née* Russell; 2 s (Brian, Jack) 1 da (Alex); *Career* political corr Irish News Westminster 1988, broadcast journalist Ind Radio News and 98FM 1990, mangr Radio Bohemia Prague 1992, sr exec Esat Digifone 1996, TD (Fianna Fáil) Dublin SW 1997–, min of state Dept of Foreign Affrs 2004–; *Recreations* football, swimming, tennis, hill walking; *Clubs* Tallaght Athletic, Templeogue Tennis; *Style—* Conor Lenihan, Esq, TD; ✉ 515 Main Street, Tallaght Village, Tallaght, Dublin 24, Ireland (tel 00 353 1 408 2031, fax 00 353 1 408 2024, e-mail conor.lenihan@dfa.ie)

LENMAN, Prof Bruce Philip; s of Jacob Philip Lenman (d 1986), of Aberdeen, and May, *née* Wishart (d 1976); *b* 9 April 1938; *Educ* Aberdeen GS, Univ of Aberdeen (MA, Forbes Gold Medal), St John's Coll Cambridge (MLitt, LittD); *Career* asst prof of history Victoria Univ 1963, lectr in Imperial and Commonwealth history Univ of St Andrews 1963–67, lectr Dept of Modern History Univ of Dundee 1967–72, reader in modern history Univ of St Andrews 1983–88 (lectr 1972–78, sr lectr 1978–83), James Pinckney Harrison prof Coll of William and Mary Virginia 1988–89, prof of modern history Univ of St Andrews 1992–2003 (reader 1989–92); Bird visiting prof Emory Univ Atlanta 1998; Br Acad fell Newberry Library Chicago 1982, John Carter Brown Library fell Rhode Island 1984, Cncl of Europe res fell 1984, Folger fell Folger Library Washington DC 1988–89 and 1997, Hill fell Huntington Library San Marino 2004; Weddell lectr Virginia Historical Soc 1991 (Mellon fell 1990); past pres Abertay Historical Soc; Scottish Arts Cncl Literary Award 1977 and 1980; FRHistS 1977, FRSE 2004; *Books* Dundee and its Textile Industry (1969), From Esk to Tweed (1975), An Economic History of Modern Scotland (1977), The Jacobite Risings in Britain (1980), Crime and the Law (ed, 1980), Integration and Enlightenment: Scotland 1746–1832 (1981), Jacobite Clans of the Great Glen (1984), The Jacobite Cause (1986), The Jacobite Threat: A Source Book (with John S Gibson, 1990), The Eclipse of Parliament (1992), Chambers Dictionary of World History (ed, 1993, 3 edn 2005), Colonial Wars 1550–1783 (2 vols, 2001); *Recreations* golf, curling, swimming, Scottish country dancing, badminton; *Clubs* Royal Commonwealth; *Style—* Emeritus Prof Bruce P Lenman; ✉ Apartment 4, 55 Victoria Place, Stirling FK8 2QT (tel 01786 446090, e-mail bruceplenman@yahoo.co.uk)

LENNARD, Thomas William Jay; s of late Thomas Jay Lennard, MBE, of Falkirk, and Elizabeth Jemima Mary Patricia, *née* Poole; *b* 25 October 1953; *Educ* Clifton, Univ of Newcastle upon Tyne (MB BS, MD); *m* 8 July 1978, Anne Lesley, da of Cyril Barber, of Ossett, W Yorks; 3 s (James Matthew Thomas b 1984, Jonathan Alexander Thomas b 1987, Oliver Thomas Jay b 1993); *Career* lectr in surgery Univ of Newcastle upon Tyne 1982–88, reader and conslt surgn Univ of Newcastle upon Tyne and Royal Victoria Infirmary Newcastle upon Tyne 1988–2002, prof of breast and endocrine surgery and head Sch of Surgical and Reproductive Scis Univ of Newcastle upon Tyne 2002–; pres Br Assoc of Thyroid and Endocrine Surgns 2007–09, memb N of England Surgical Soc;

FRCS 1980; *Books* Going into Hospital (1988); *Recreations* fly fishing, gardening; *Style*— Thomas Lennard, Esq; ✉ Ward 46, Royal Victoria Infirmary, Queen Victoria Road, Newcastle upon Tyne NE1 4LP (tel 0191 282 4661)

LENNARD-JONES, Prof John Edward; s of Sir John Lennard-Jones, KBE (d 1954), of Keele, Staffs, and Kathleen Mary, *née* Lennard; *b* 29 January 1927; *Educ* King's Coll Choir Sch Cambridge, Gresham's, CCC Cambridge (MA, MD), UCH Med Sch London; *m* 19 Feb 1955, Verna Margaret, da of Ebenezer Albert Down (d 1960); 4 s (David b 1956, Peter b 1958, Andrew b 1960, Timothy b 1964); *Career* med trg posts: UCH, Manchester Royal Infirmary, Central Middx Hosp 1953–65; memb Med Res Cncl Industrial Med and Burns Unit Birmingham Accident Hosp 1947–48, memb MRC Gastroenterology Res Unit Central Middx Hosp 1963–65, conslt gastroenterologist St Mark's Hosp London 1965–92, conslt physician UCH London 1965–74, prof of gastroentology London Hosp Med Coll 1974–87 (emeritus prof 1987–), hon sr research fell Div of Medical and Molecular Genetics UMDS Guy's and St Thomas's Hosps London 1996–2000; currently: hon consulting gastroenterologist Royal London Hosp, emeritus conslt gastroenterologist St Mark's Hosp London; author of scientific papers on gen med, gastroenterology and nutrition; Sir Arthur Hurst lecture Br Soc of Gastroenterology 1973, Humphrey Davy Rolleston lecture RCP 1977, Schorstein lecture London Hosp Med Coll 1987, Bryan Brooke lecture and medal Ileostomy Assoc 1991, Robert Annetts lecture Nat Assoc for Colitis and Crohn's Disease 1992, Louis Mirvish meml lectr South African Gastroenterological Assoc 1995; chm Med Ctee St Mark's Hosp 1985–90; Br Soc of Gastroenterology: hon sec 1965–70, memb Cncl 1965–90, pres 1983, chm Clinical Services Ctee 1986–90; pres Assoc of Gastrointestinal Physiologists 2002–03; memb Cncl RCP 1986–89 (chm Gastroenterology Ctee 1985–89), vice-chm Nat Assoc for Colitis and Crohn's Disease 1987–89 (chm Med Advsy Ctee 1979–90, hon life pres 1992), chm British Assoc for Parenteral and Enteral Nutrition 1991–95, pres Digestive Disorders Fndn 1992–2000, chm of tstees Sir Halley Stewart Tst 1997–2007; fell UCH Sch of Med London 1995; hon memb: Br Soc of Gastroenterology, Swedish Soc of Gastroenterology, Netherlands Soc of Gastroenterology, Ileostomy Assoc, South African Gastroenterology Soc; membre d'honneur: Swiss Soc of Gastroenterology, French Soc of Coloproctology; corresponding memb: Polish Soc of Internal Med, Italian Soc of Gastroenterology; Hon DSc Univ of Kingston 1999; FRCP 1968, FRCS 1992, Hon FRSM; *Books* Clinical Gastroenterology (jtly, 1968), Intestinal Transit (ed, 1991), Inflammatory Bowel Disease (jtly, 1992), Constipation (jtly, 1994); author of numerous scientific papers on general medicine, gastroenterology and clinical nutrition; *Recreations* ornithology, golf, gardening; *Style*— Prof John Lennard-Jones; ✉ 72 Cumberland Street, Woodbridge, Suffolk IP12 4AD (tel 01394 387717)

LENNON, Aaron Justin; *b* 16 April 1987, Leeds, Yorkshire; *Career* professional footballer; clubs: Leeds United 2003–05, Tottenham Hotspur 2005–; England: 2 caps, debut v Jamaica 2006, memb squad World Cup 2006; *Style*— Aaron Lennon, Esq; ✉ c/o Tottenham Hotspur Football Club, White Hart Lane, 748 High Road, London N17 0AP

LENNOX, *see also:* Gordon Lennox

LENNOX, Michael James Madill; s of Rev James Lennox; *b* 11 September 1943; *Educ* St John's Sch Leatherhead; *m* 4 May 1968, Ingrid Susan Elizabeth; 1 da (Rebecca b 6 Oct 1972), 1 s (Timothy b 6 Dec 1974); *Career* CA; Armitage & Norton Bradford 1961–68, Price Waterhouse (Montreal) 1968–70, Honeywell Ltd Toronto 1970–73, Honeywell Europe Brussels 1973–78, fin dir Cutler Hammer Europa Ltd (Bedford) 1978–85, gp fin dir C P Roberts & Co Ltd 1985–88, fin dir Central Trailer Rentco Ltd 1988–90, fin dir Charterhouse Development Capital Ltd 1990–92, fin dir Atisreal (formerly Weatherall Green & Smith) 1992–2006; FCA; *Recreations* tennis, golf, skiing; *Style*— Michael Lennox, Esq; ✉ Old Cottage Farm, Top End, Renhold, Bedford MK41 0LS (tel 01234 870370, e-mail lennox@renhold.freeserve.co.uk)

LENON, Barnaby John; s of Rev Philip John Fitzmaurice Lenon, of Dinton, Wilts, and Jane Alethea, *née* Brooke; *b* 10 May 1954; *Educ* Eltham Coll, Keble Coll Oxford (scholar, MA), St John's Coll Cambridge (univ prize for educn, coll prize, PGCE); *m* 27 August 1983, Penelope Anne, da of James Desmond Thain; 2 da (India Elizabeth Jane b 9 Nov 1989, Flora Catherine Dyne b 4 June 1992); *Career* teacher: Eton Coll 1976–77 and 1979–90 (latterly head of Geography Dept), Sherborne Sch 1978–79; dep headmaster Highgate Sch 1990–94; headmaster: Trinity Sch of John Whitgift 1995–99, Harrow Sch 1999–; govr: John Lyon Sch, Orley Farm Sch, Wellesley House Sch, Aysgarth Sch, The Beacon Sch, Francis Holland Schs, Papplewick Sch; FRGS 1987 (memb Cncl 1987–90 and 1998–2000), FRSA 1999; *Books* Techniques and Fieldwork in Geography (1982), London (1988), London in the 1990's (1993), Fieldwork Techniques and Projects in Geography (1994), Directory of University Geography Courses 1995 (jt ed, 1995, 2 edn 1996), The United Kingdom: Geographical Case Studies (1995); *Recreations* writing, oil painting, deserts, athletics; *Clubs* East India, Lansdowne; *Style*— Barnaby J Lenon, Esq; ✉ Harrow School, Harrow on the Hill, Middlesex HA1 3HT (tel 020 8872 8000, fax 020 8872 8012, e-mail hm@harrowschool.org.uk)

LENT, Penelope Ann (Penny); da of David Wilson (d 1984), of Stanmore, Middx, and Zipporah, *née* Jacobs; *b* 24 July 1947; *Educ* Whitegate Sch Harrow Weald, Middx Coll Wembley; *m* Nov 1968, Jeffrey Alan Lent; 1 da (Tiffany Dawn); *Career* secretary with advtg and music recording cos 1965–68; London Weekend Television: joined 1968, various location mgmnt positions, headed new business responsible for mktg The London Studios studio and prodn facilities 1988, dir London Studios for sales and mktg, currently dir of sales, mktg and devpt; *Style*— Ms Penny Lent; ✉ The London Studios, Upper Ground, London SE1 9LT (tel 020 7261 3683)

LENYGON, Bryan Norman; s of late Maj Frank Norman Lenygon, and Marjorie Winifred, *née* Healey; *b* 6 May 1932; *Educ* Univ of London (MA, LLB); *m* 15 Dec 2001, Victoria Annette, *née* Campbell, da of late Ronald William Campbell and Joyce Fleming Roberts; 2 da (Fiona b 1957, Sally b 1961); *Career* chartered accountant 1955; called to the Bar Gray's Inn 1976; dir several investment tst cos; gen cmmr City of London; Freeman City of London, Liveryman Worshipful Co of Loriners; FCA, FCIS, ATII; *Recreations* tennis; *Clubs* City of London, City Livery; *Style*— Bryan Lenygon, Esq; ✉ Highfield, Bells Yew Green, East Sussex TN3 9AP (tel 01892 750343, fax 01892 750609)

LEONARD, Anthony James; QC (1999); s of Hon Sir John Leonard (d 2002), and Lady Doreen Enid, *née* Parker (d 1996); *b* 21 April 1956; *Educ* Hurstpierpoint Coll, Inns of Court Sch of Law; *m* 4 June 1983, Shara Jane, da of John Macrae Cormack; 2 da (Olivia Mary b 13 Oct 1985, Stephanie Emma b 17 Jan 1989); *Career* short service ltd cmmn 1974–5, Maj 6/7 Queens Regt (TA) 1976–85; called to the Bar Inner Temple 1978 (bencher 2002); in practice SE Circuit, standing counsel to the Inland Revenue (SE Circuit) 1993–99, recorder 2000–; memb Criminal Bar Assoc 1979–; Liveryman Worshipful Co of Plaisterers; *Recreations* opera, wine; *Clubs* Garrick; *Style*— Anthony Leonard, Esq, QC; ✉ 6 King's Bench Walk, Ground Floor, Temple, London EC4Y 7DR (tel 020 7583 0410, fax 020 7353 8791)

LEONARD, Brian Henry; s of William Henry Leonard (d 1986), Bertha Florence, *née* Thomas (d 1977); *b* 6 January 1948; *Educ* Dr Challoner's GS, LSE; *m* 1975, Maggy, da of Charles Martin Meade-King; 2 s (Will Martin b 1 Jan 1977, James Henry b 20 July 1979); *Career* Heal & Son Ltd 1969–73, The Price Commission 1973–74; DOE: admin trainee 1974–77, HEO 1977–79, princ 1979–88, seconded to Circle 33 Housing Trust 1982–83, asst sec 1988–93, under sec and regnl dir of Northern Region 1993–94, regnl dir Govt Office for the South West 1994–97, dir Environmental Protection Strategy DETR 1997–98, head of regions Tourism, Millennium and International Gp DCMS 1998–2001, head Tourism, Lottery and Regions Directorate 2001–02, head Tourism, Libraries and Communities Directorate 2002–04, dir Industry 2004–; fell Hubert Humphrey Inst Minneapolis 1987–88; *Recreations* friends, games, pottering about; *Clubs* Marylebone Cricket; *Style*— Brian Leonard; ✉ 6th Floor, 2–4 Cockspur Street, London SW1Y 5DH (tel 020 7211 6384, fax 020 7211 6361, e-mail brian.leonard@culture.gsi.gov.uk)

LEONARD, Rt Rev Mgr and Rt Hon Graham Douglas; KCVO (1991), PC (1981); s of Rev Douglas Leonard; *b* 8 May 1921; *Educ* Monkton Combe Sch, Balliol Coll Oxford, Westcott House Cambridge; *m* 1943, (Vivien) Priscilla, da of late Dr Swann; 2 s; *Career* served WWII Oxford & Bucks LI as Capt; ordained Church of England 1947, archdeacon Hampstead 1962–64, bishop suffragan of Willesden 1964–73, bishop of Truro 1973–81, 130th Bishop of London 1981–91, received into RC Church and ordained priest *sub conditione* by HE Cardinal Basil Hume OSB 1994; pres Int Convention 'Path To Rome' 1997–2001; prelate of honour to HH The Pope 2000–; dean of HM's Chapels Royal 1981–91, prelate Order of the British Empire 1981–91; memb House of Lords 1977–91; delegate to fifth Assembly WCC Nairobi 1975, chm Gen Synod Bd for Social Responsibility 1976–83; Green lectr Westminster Coll Fulton Missouri 1987, Hensley Henson lectr Univ of Oxford 1991–92; chm: Churches Main Ctee 1981–91, Jerusalem and Middle East Church Assoc 1981–91, Bd of Educn and National Soc 1983–89; church cmmr 1973–91, episcopal canon St George's Cathedral Jerusalem 1981–91, prelate of the Imperial Soc of Knights Bachelor 1986–91; memb Polys and Colls Funding Cncl 1989–93, govr Pusey House Oxford 1990–95; superior gen Soc of Mary 1973–94 (vice-pres 1994–); hon guardian Shrine of Our Lady of Walsingham 1970–2000; hon master of the bench of Middle Temple 1981; Freeman City of London 1970; hon fell Balliol Coll Oxford 1986; Hon DD: Episcopal Theological Seminary Kentucky 1974, Westminster Coll Fulton Missouri 1987; Hon DCnL Nashotah House USA 1983, STD Siena Coll USA 1984, Hon LLD Simon Greenleaf Sch of Law USA 1987, Hon DLitt CNAA 1989; *Style*— The Rt Rev Mgr and Rt Hon Graham Leonard, KCVO; ✉ 25 Woodlands Road, Witney, Oxfordshire OX28 2DR

LEONARD, Jason; OBE (2004, MBE 2002); *b* 14 August 1968; *Career* rugby union player (loose-head prop); clubs: Barking, Saracens, Harlequins, ret 2004; England: 114 caps (world record for int appearances), B debut 1989 (2 caps v Fiji and France), full debut 1990, winners Five Nations Championship 1991, 1992, 1995, 1996 (Grand Slams 1991, 1992 and 1995), winners Six Nations Championship 2000, 2001 and 2003 (Grand Slam 2003), runners-up World Cup England 1991, 4th place World Cup South Africa 1995, unbeaten against South Africa, Australia and New Zealand autumn series 2002, ranked no 1 team in world 2003, unbeaten against New Zealand and Australia summer tour 2003, winners World Cup Australia 2003, ret 2004; British Lions: tour to NZ 1993 (2 tests), tour to South Africa 1997 (1 test), tour to Australia 2001 (2 tests); Special Merit Award Int Rugby Players Assoc 2002; *Style*— Jason Leonard, Esq, OBE

LEONARD, (Douglas) Michael; s of Maj Douglas Goodwin Russell Leonard, IXth Jat Regt India (d 1942), and Kathleen Mary Leonard, *née* Murphy; *b* 25 June 1933, Bangalore, India; *Educ* Hallet War Sch Nainital India, Stonyhurst Coll (sch cert), St Martin's Sch of Art (NDD); *Career* artist; freelance illustrator 1957–69, painter 1969–; cmmnd by Reader's Digest to paint portrait of HM The Queen to celebrate her 60th birthday 1984 (presented to Nat Portrait Gallery 1986); *Solo Exhibitions* Fischer Fine Art London 1974, 1977, 1980, 1983 and 1988, Harriet Griffin NYC 1977, Stiebel Modern NYC 1992, Thomas Gibson 1993, 1997 and 2004, Forum Gallery NYC 1999; *Retrospectives* Gemeentemuseum Arnhem 1977, Artsite Gallery Bath 1989, Michael Leonard: A Master of Ambiguity (Jonathan Edwards Coll Yale Univ) 2007; *Group Exhibitions* Fischer Fine Art London 1972, 1973, 1975, 1976, 1978, 1979, and 1981, Realismus und Realität (Darmstadt) 1975, John Moores Exhbns 10 and 11 Liverpool 1976 and 1978, Nudes (Angela Flowers Gallery London) 1980–81, Contemporary British Painters (Museo Municipal Madrid) 1983, The Self Portrait - A Modern View (touring) 1987–88, In Human Terms (Stiebel Modern NYC) 1991, Representing Representation (Arnot Art Museum Elmira NY) 1993, It's Still Life (Forum Gallery NYC) 1998, Still Life Painting Today (Jerald Melberg Gallery Inc Charlotte NC) 1998, The Nude in Contemporary Art (The Aldrich Museum of Contemporary Art Ridgefield CT) 1999, Still Lifes (William Baczek Fine Arts Northampton MA), The Male Form in Contemporary Art (Art and Culture Center Hollywood, Florida), Between Earth and Heaven (MOMA Oostende) 2001, Artists of the Ideal (Galleria d'Arte Moderna Verona) 2002, What is Realism? (Albemarle Gallery London) 2005; *Public Collections* Museum Boymans-van Beuningen Rotterdam, V&A, Nat Portrait Gallery London, Ferens Art Gallery Hull, New Orleans Museum of Art, Fitzwilliam Museum Cambridge, Arnot Art Museum Elmira NY; *Books* Changing - 50 Drawings (intro by Edward Lucie-Smith, 1983), Michael Leonard - Paintings (foreword by Lincoln Kirstein, interviewed by Edward Lucie-Smith, 1985); *Style*— Michael Leonard, Esq; ✉ 3 Kensington Hall Gardens, Beaumont Avenue, London W14 9LS; c/o Forum Gallery, 745 Fifth Avenue 5th Floor, New York, NY 10151, USA

LEONARD, Dr Robert Charles Frederick; s of André Lucien Maxime Leonard (d 1977), of Merthyr Tydfil, Wales, and Rosa Mary, *née* Taylor; *b* 11 May 1947; *Educ* Merthyr Tydfil Co GS, Charing Cross Hosp Med Sch (BSc, MB BS, MD); *m* 2 June 1973, Tania, da of Roland Charles Smith, and Keysoe, *née* North, of Louth, Lincs; 3 da (Victoria b 26 Sept 1974, Louisa b 26 Feb 1978, Emily b 18 Sept 1980); *Career* sr house offr: Charing Cross Hosp 1972, Hammersmith Hosp 1973; registrar Oxford Hosps 1974–76, res fell Leukaemia Res Fund 1976–79, lectr and sr registrar Newcastle Hosps 1979–82, fell Cancer Res Campaign 1981–82, res fell Dana Farber Cancer Inst Harvard Med Sch Boston 1982, conslt physician and hon sr lectr in clinical oncology Edinburgh 1983–2001, prof of cancer studies Univ of Wales Swansea 2001–, dir SW Wales Cancer Inst 2001–; memb: UKCCCR Breast Ctee, Br Breast Gp; memb Editorial Bd British Journal of Cancer; FRCPEd 1984, FRCP 1993, American Soc of Clinical Oncology; *Books* Understanding Cancer (1985), Serological Tumour Marks (1993), Breast Cancer: The Essential Facts (1995); author of over 300 scientific papers on cancer and related research; *Recreations* music, piano, soccer; *Style*— Robert Leonard; ✉ South-West Wales Cancer Institute, Singleton Hospital, Swansea SA2 8QA (tel 01792 285300, fax 01792 285301, e-mail r.c.f.leonard@swansea.ac.uk)

LEONARD, Dr Rosemary; MBE (2004); da of Gordon Harris Leonard (d 1996), and Edna Alice, *née* Read; *b* 22 July 1956, London; *Educ* Dr Challoners HS Little Chalfont, Newnham Coll Cambridge (entrance exhibitioner, coll scholar, Johnson & Florence Stoney scholar, MA, MB, BChir), St Thomas' Hosp Med Sch; *Children* 2 s (Thomas O'Reilly b 26 Sep 1989, William O'Reilly b 28 Oct 1991); *Career* GP; ptnr in gen practice 1988–, resident GP Breakfast News (BBC) 1998–; journalist Sun 1993–99, journalist Daily Mail 1999–2002, GP contrib and columnist Daily Express 2002–; GP rep Ctee of Safety of Medicines 2002–05, memb Human Genetics Cmmn 2006–; MRCGP 1988; *Publications* 7 Ages of Woman (2007); *Recreations* skiing, sailing, choral singing, arts and crafts movement, growing vegetables and delphiniums; *Style*— Dr Rosemary Leonard, MBE; ✉ c/o NCI Management Ltd, Second Floor, 51 Queen Anne Street, London W1G 9HS (tel 020 7224 3961)

LEOPARD, Peter James; s of Charles Henry Leopard (d 1974), of Dinas Powys, Glamorgan, and Dorothy Bertha, *née* Cole; *b* 1 September 1938; *Educ* Penarth GS, Guy's Hosp Dental and Med Schs London (MB BS, BDS); *m* 1; 1 da (Claire Angela (Mrs Sams) b 28 Sept 1963), 3 s (James Ashley b 11 June 1965 d 12 Oct 1988, Daniel Charles b 12 Aug 1985, Oliver Joseph b 17 June 1987); m 2, Diane Elizabeth; *Career* conslt maxillofacial surgn N Staffs 1972–2000; RCS: vice-dean Faculty of Dental Surgery 1992, memb Cncl

1995–2002, chm Intercollegiate Bd in Oral and Maxillofacial Surgery 1992–95, vice-chm then chm Euro Bd of Oral and Maxillofacial Surgery 1994–2002, chm Faculty Manpower Advsy Panel 1995–2002, memb Senate of Surgery 1996–2000; RCSEd: chm Speciality Advsy Bd 1991–95, chm Hosp Recognition Ctee Faculty of Dental Surgery 1992–95; pres Br Assoc of Oral and Maxillofacial Surgns 1997, pres Section of Oral and Maxillofacial Surgery UEMS (Euro Union of Med Specialists) 1997–2001; memb Specialist Workforce Advsy Gp (SWAG) Dept of Health 1995–2001 (chm W Midlands Med Workforce Advsy Gp 1997–2001), chm N Staffs Med Inst 1996–99; divnl surgn St John's Ambulance 1986–92; Down Surgical Prize Br Assoc of Oral and Maxillofacial Surgns 1994/95; memb: N Staffs Med Club, Oral Surgery Club of GB; LRCP, FDSRCS, FRCSEd, FRCS (without examination) 1987 (MRCS); *Recreations* skiing, gardening, narrow boating, music, formerly boxing (boxed for Univ of London) and rugby (schoolboy trialist for Wales); *Style*— Peter Leopard, Esq; ✉ Stone House, Basnetts Wood, Endon, Stoke-on-Trent ST9 9DQ (tel 01782 504095, fax 01782 504689, e-mail peter@leop38.freeserve.co.uk)

LEPPARD, David George; s of John C Leppard, and Elizabeth, *née* Hapgood (d 1968); *b* 6 August 1957; *Educ* Hampton GS, Univ of Leicester (BA, Wallace Henry Prize), Univ of Oxford (DPhil); *Career* journalist; reporter The Times 1986; Sunday Times: reporter, dep Insight ed 1990–93, home affairs corr 1993–95, home affairs ed and dep news ed (investigations) 1995–96, ed Insight team 1996–2001, asst ed (home affairs) 2001–; *Awards* Br Press Awards: nominated Reporter of the Year 1990 and 2007, nominated Scoop of the Year 2001 and 2004, winner Specialist Writer of the Year 2004; Freedom of the Media Award 1995, nominated Scoop of the Year London Press Club Awards 2004; *Publications* On the Trail of Terror (1991), Fire and Blood (1993); *Recreations* reading and relaxing; *Style*— David Leppard, Esq; ✉ Sunday Times, 1 Pennington Street, London E98 1ST (e-mail david.leppard@sunday-times.co.uk)

LEPPARD, Raymond John; CBE (1983); s of Albert Victor Leppard, and Bertha May, *née* Beck; *b* 11 August 1927; *Educ* Trinity Coll Cambridge; *Career* fell and lectr in music Trinity Coll Cambridge 1958–68, princ conductor BBC Northern Symphony Orch 1972–80, princ guest conductor St Louis Symphony Orch 1984–90, music dir Indianapolis Symphony Orch 1987–; Hon DUniv Bath 1972; Hon DMus: Indiana Univ 1991, Perdue Univ 1992; hon memb: RAM 1972, GSM 1984; Hon FRCM 1984; Commendatore al Merito Della Republica Italiana 1974; *Publications* Monteverdi: Il Ballo Delle Ingrate (1958), L'Incoronazione Di Poppea (1962), L'Orfeo (1965), Cavalli: Messa Concertata (1966), L'Ormindo (1967), La Calisto (1969), Il Ritorno D'Ulisse (1972), L'Eqisto (1974), L'Orione (1983), Authenticity in Music (1988), Raymond Leppard on Music: An Anthology of Critical and Autobiographical Writings (1993); *Recreations* theatre, books, friends, music; *Style*— Raymond Leppard, Esq, CBE

LEPPER, David; MP; s of Henry Lepper (d 1979), and Maggie, *née* Osborne (d 2000); *b* 15 September 1945; *Educ* Gainsborough Secdy Modern, Wimbledon Co Secdy Sch, Univ of Kent (BA), Univ of Sussex (PGCE, Dip Media Educn), Poly of Central London (Dip Film); *m* 1966, Jeane, *née* Stroud; 1 s (Joe b 1972), 1 da (Eve b 1975); *Career* English teacher: Westlain GS Brighton 1969–72, Falmer HS Brighton (latterly head of media studies) 1972–96; MP (Lab/Co-op) Brighton Pavilion 1997–; chair: All-Pty Gp on English Language Teaching, All-Pty Gp on Foyers, All-Pty Parly Gp on Town Centre Mgmnt Issues 1998–2004, House of Commons Broadcasting Select Ctee 2001–05; memb: Environment, Food and Rural Affairs Select Ctee 2001–, Administration Ctee 2005–; ldr Brighton BC 1986–87 (cncllr 1980–97), mayor of Brighton 1993–94; tstee ARDIS (Brighton), memb NUT; *Publications* John Wayne (BFI, 1987), also author of other articles on film; *Recreations* music, cinema, literature, the Arts, watching professional cycling; *Clubs* Brighton Trades and Labour; *Style*— David Lepper, MP; ✉ John Saunders House, 179 Preston Road, Brighton BN1 6AG

LEPSCHY, Prof Giulio Ciro; s of Emilio Lepschy (d 1994), and Sara, *née* Castelfranchi (d 1984); *b* 14 January 1935; *Educ* Liceo Marco Polo Venice, Univ of Pisa (Dott Lett), Scuola Normale Superiore (Dip & Perf Sc Norm Sup); *m* 20 Dec 1962, Prof (Anna) Laura Lepschy, *qv*, da of Arnaldo Momigliano, Hon KBE (d 1987); *Career* Univ of Reading: lectr 1964–67, reader 1967–75, prof 1975–98, emeritus 2000; hon prof UCL 1998–; pres MHRA 2001; Serena Medal Br Acad 2000; corresponding fell Accademia della Crusca 1991, laurea (hc) Univ of Turin 1998; FBA 1987; *Publications* A Survey of Structural Linguistics (1970), The Italian Language Today (with A L Lepschy, 1977), Saggi di Linguistica Italiana (1978), Intorno a Saussure (1979), Mutamenti di Prospettiva nella Linguistica (1981), Nuovi Saggi di Linguistica Italiana (1989), Sulla Linguistica Moderna (1989), Storia della Linguistica (1990), La Linguistica del Novecento (1992), History of Linguistics (1994), L'amanuense analfabeta e altri saggi (with A L Lepschy, 1999), Mother Tongues and Other Reflections on the Italian Language (2002); *Style*— Prof Giulio Lepschy, FBA; ✉ Department of Italian, University College, Gower Street, London WC1E 6BT (tel 020 7380 7784, fax 020 7209 0638, e-mail g.lepschy@ucl.ac.uk)

LEPSCHY, Prof (Anna) Laura; da of Arnaldo Dante Momigliano, Hon KBE (d 1987), of London, and Gemma Celestina, *née* Segre (d 2003); *b* 30 November 1933; *Educ* Headington Sch Oxford, Somerville Coll Oxford; *m* 20 Dec 1962, Prof Giulio Ciro Lepschy, FBA, *qv*, s of Emilio Lepschy, of Venice; *Career* jr fell Univ of Bristol 1957–59, lectr in Italian Univ of Reading 1962–68 (asst lectr 1959–62); UCL: lectr in Italian 1968–79, sr lectr 1979–84, reader 1984–87, prof 1987–; hon visiting fell Univ of Cambridge 2003–; vice-pres Associazione Internazionale Studi Lingua and Letteratura Italiana; memb: Soc for Italian Studies, Assoc for Study of Modern Italy, Pirandello Soc, Comparative Literature Assoc, Modern Humanities Research Assoc; hon fell Somerville Coll Oxford 2005; Commendatore della Repubblica Italiana 2004; *Books* Santo Brasca, Viaggio in Terrasanta 1480 (ed, 1967), The Italian Language Today (with G Lepschy, 1977), Tintoretto Observed (1983), Narrativa e Teatro fra Due Secoli (1984), Varietà linguistiche e pluralità di codici nel Rinascimento (1996), Davanti a Tintoretto (1998), L'amanuense analfabeta e altri saggi (with G Lepschy, 1999); *Recreations* swimming; *Style*— Prof Laura Lepschy; ✉ Department of Italian, University College, Gower Street, London WC1E 6BT (tel 020 7679 2144, fax 020 7209 0638, e-mail a.lepschy@ucl.ac.uk)

LEREGO, Michael John; QC (1995); s of Leslie Ivor Lerego (d 2001), and Gwendolen Frances, *née* Limbert (d 1990); *b* 6 May 1949; *Educ* Manchester Grammar, Haberdashers' Aske's, Keble Coll Oxford (open scholar, MA, BCL, Gibbs Prize in Law); *m* 24 June 1972, Susan, da of George Henry Northover (d 1969); 1 s (Colin Andrew b 8 Oct 1976 d 1977); 3 da (Louise Jane b 15 Feb 1979, Caroline Ruth, Victoria Ann (twins) b 26 Aug 1981); *Career* called to the Bar Inner Temple 1972 (bencher 2006); in practice 1972–, recorder 2002–, jt head of chambers Fountain Court 2003–07; weekender The Queen's Coll Oxford 1972–78; memb: Jt Working Party of Law Soc & Bar on Banking Law 1987–91, Sub-Ctee on Banking Law Law Soc 1991–96; arbitrator: Modified Arbitration Scheme Lloyd's 1988–92, Arbitration Scheme Lloyd's 1993–; tutor Coll of Law 2007– (visiting lectr 2006–07); govr Wroxham Sch Potters Bar 1995–2004; FCIArb 1997; *Publications* Commercial Court Procedure (contrib, 2000), The Law of Bank Payments (contrib, 3 edn 2004), Encyclopaedia of Insurance Law (regulatory ed, 2007), Blackstone's Criminal Practice (contrib, 2008); *Recreations* watching sport; *Style*— Michael Lerego, Esq, QC; ✉ Fountain Court, Temple, London EC4Y 9DH (tel 020 7583 3335, e-mail ml@fountaincourt.co.uk)

LERENIUS, Bo Ake; Hon CBE (2005); s of Ake Lerenius of Sweden, and Elisabeth Lerenius; *b* 11 December 1946; *Educ* Westchester HS LA, St Petri Sch Malmo Sweden, Univ of Lund (BA); *Family* 1 s (Jockum), 1 da (Sarah); m, 23 Dec 2002, Gunilla; *Career* divnl dir Tarkett Swedish Match 1983–85, gp pres and ceo Ernstromgruppen 1985–92, pres and ceo Stena Line 1992–98, vice-chm Stena Line and dir of new business investments Stena AB 1998–99, gp chief exec ABP Holdings plc 1999–2007 (non-exec dir 2007–); non-exec chm Momentum Sweden 1999–2004; non-exec dir: Inmarsat Ventures Ltd 2000–03, Group 4 Securicor plc 2004–, Land Securities 2004–; chm Cncl Swedish C of C London, memb BV Soc; Hon DBA; *Recreations* golf, shooting, downhill skiing; *Clubs* Royal Bachelors (Gothenburg), RAC, Falsterbo Golf (Sweden); *Style*— Bo Lerenius, CBE

LERNER, Prof David Nicholas; s of Laurence David Lerner, of Sussex, and Natalie Hope, *née* Winch; *b* 16 January 1950; *Educ* Hove GS for Boys, Univ of Cambridge (MA), Univ of London (MSc), Univ of Birmingham (PhD, DSc); *m* Fiona Roubaix, da of Patrick Gillmore; 3 c (Rose b 1984, Robin b 1986, Roubaix b 1987); *Career* various appointments: Anglian Water Authy 1972–77, Binnie & Partners 1977–84, Univ of Birmingham 1984–94, Univ of Bradford 1994–97; prof Univ of Sheffield 1998–; FGS 1990, FICE 1995, FREng 2001; *Recreations* family; *Style*— Prof David Lerner; ✉ Department of Civil and Structural Engineering, University of Sheffield, Mappin Street, Sheffield S1 3JD (tel 0114 222 5743, fax 0114 222 5701)

LERNER, (Prof) Laurence David; s of Israel Lerner (d 1967), and Mary, *née* Harrison (d 1955); *b* 12 December 1925, Cape Town, South Africa; *Educ* Univ of Cape Town (MA), Pembroke Coll Cambridge (BA); *m* 1948, Natalie, *née* Winch; 4 s (David b 16 Jan 1950, Edwin b 4 March 1953, Martin b 9 Nov 1954, Richard b 8 July 1959); *Career* lectr in English UC of the Gold Coast 1949–53, tutor then lectr in English Queen's Univ Belfast 1953–62, lectr then reader then prof of English Univ of Sussex 1962–84, prof of English Vanderbilt Univ Nashville TN 1985–95; former visiting prof: Munich 1968–69 and 1974–75, Paris 1982, Vienna 1994, Dijon, Ottawa, Illinois, Würzburg; Br Cncl and other lecture tours incl: Poland, Turkey, Spain, Israel, South America; former tutor Arvon Fndn; winner various literary prizes; FRSL; *Publications* poetry: Domestic Interior (1959, Poetry Book Soc recommendation), The Directions of Memory (1964), Selves (1969), ARTHUR: The Life & Opinions of a Digital Computer (1974), ARTHUR & MARTHA: The Loves of the Computers (1980), The Man I Killed (1980), Chapter & Verse: Bible Poems (1984), Selected Poems (1984, Poetry Book Soc recommendation), Rembrandt's Mirror (1987), Baudelaire: Selected Poems (trans, 1999); novels: The Englishmen (1959), A Free Man (1968), My Grandfather's Grandfather (1985), Wandering Professor (memoir, 1999); criticism incl: An Introduction to English Poetry (1975), Love and Marriage: Literature and its Social Context (1979, SE Arts Literature Prize), The Frontiers of Literature (1988), Angels & Absences: Child Deaths in the 19th Century (1997); other pubns incl: You Can't Say That: English Usage Today (2007); *Recreations* theatre, travel; *Style*— Laurence Lerner; ✉ Abinger, 1B Gundreda Road, Lewes, East Sussex BN7 1PT (tel 01273 472208, e-mail laurencelerner@tiscali.co.uk)

LERNER, Neil Joseph; *b* 31 May 1947; *Educ* Tiffin Sch, St John's Coll Cambridge (MA); *m* 27 June 1972, Susan Elizabeth, *née* Kempner; 2 s (Nicholas b 16 May 1979, Jonathan b 18 July 1981); *Career* KPMG: joined 1968, ptnr 1984–, head Corp Fin UK 1993–97, UK head Risk Mgmnt KPMG 1998– (head Transaction Servs 1997–98), global head Regulatory Affrs; chm Ethics Gp: ICAEW 2002–, CCAB; FCA 1971, MSI; *Clubs* Little Ship; *Style*— Neil Lerner, Esq; ✉ KPMG, 8 Salisbury Square, London EC4Y 8BB (tel 020 7311 8620 (direct), fax 020 7311 1623)

LERWILL, Robert Earl; s of Colin Roy F Lerwill, and Patricia (Luck) Lerwill; *b* 21 January 1952; *Educ* Barnstaple GS, Gosport GS, Univ of Nottingham (BA); *m* 1, 1980 (m dis 1994), Carol H G Ruddock; 1 s (Henry Robert b 1985), 1 da (Elizabeth Alice b 1991); m 2, 1994, Nicola Keddie; 2 da (Anna b 1995, Alice Margaret b 1997), 1 s (Edward b 2000); *Career* Arthur Andersen & Co: joined as articled clerk 1973, mangr 1978, sr mangr 1981–86; gp fin dir WPP Group plc 1986–96; Cable and Wireless plc: fin dir 1997–2002; dep gp chief exec 2000–03, chief exec Cable and Wireless Regnl 2000–03; chief exec Aegis Group plc 2005– (non-exec dir 2000–05); non-exec dir: Synergy Healthcare 2005–, British American Tobacco plc 2005–; memb Leadership Bd Univ of Nottingham 1995; dir Anthony Nolan Tst; MInstD 1987; FCA (ACA 1977), FSA 1995; *Recreations* travel; *Style*— Robert Lerwill, Esq; ✉ Aegis Group plc, 43–45 Portman Square, London W1H 6LY

LESLIE, Capt Alastair Pinckard; TD; s of Hon John Wayland Leslie (d 1991, s of 19 Earl of Rothes); *b* 29 December 1934; *Educ* Eton; *m* 1963, Rosemary, da of Cdr Hubert Wyndham Barry, RN; 2 da (Fiona (Mrs Richard de Klee) b 1965, Ann (Mrs Lorenzo Ali) b 1973), 1 s (David b 1967 d 1989); *Career* Capt Royal Scots Fusiliers (TA); md Willis Faber & Dumas (Agencies) Ltd 1976–85; dir: A P Leslie Underwriting Agency Ltd 1976–90, Wellington Members Agency Ltd 1990–95 and other Lloyds underwriting agencies 1976–95, United Goldfields NL until 1988, Hardy Underwriting Group plc 1996–2005, Paradigm Restaurants Ltd 2000–03; memb Queen's Body Guard for Scotland (Royal Co of Archers); Liveryman and memb Ct of Assts Worshipful Co of Clothworkers (Master 1998–99); *Recreations* fishing, stalking, shooting; *Clubs* Pratt's, New (Edinburgh); *Style*— Capt Alastair Leslie, TD; ✉ Seasyde House, by Errol, Perthshire PH2 7TA (tel 01821 642500, fax 01821 642883)

LESLIE, Dame Ann Elizabeth Mary; DBE (2007); da of late Norman Alexander Leslie, of Bourne End, Bucks, and late Theodora, *née* McDonald; *Educ* Convent of the Holy Child Mayfield, Lady Margaret Hall Oxford (BA); *m* 15 Feb 1969, Michael Fletcher, s of Arthur George Fletcher; 1 da (Katharine Cordelia b 8 Sept 1978); *Career* broadcaster and journalist; staff Daily Express 1961–67, freelance journalist 1967–; memb NUJ; *Awards* commendation Br Press Awards 1980, 1983, 1985, 1987, 1991, 1995, 1996 and 1999, Women of the Year Award for Journalism and Broadcasting Variety Club 1981, Feature Writer of the Year Br Press Awards 1981 and 1989, Feature Writer of the Year What the Papers Say (BBC2/Granada) 1991, Media Soc Lifetime Achievement Award 1997, James Cameron Meml Award for International Reporting 1999, Gerald Barry Lifetime Achievement Award What the Papers Say (BBC2/Granada) 2001, London Press Club Edgar Wallace Award for Outstanding Reporting 2002, Foreign Corr of the Year What the Papers Say (BBC2/Granada) 2004; *Recreations* family life; *Style*— Dame Ann Leslie, DBE; ✉ Daily Mail, Northcliffe House, 2 Derry Street, London W8 5TT (tel 020 7938 6000, e-mail ann.leslie@dailymail.co.uk)

LESLIE, Christopher Michael; s of Michael Leslie, and Dania Leslie; *b* 28 June 1972; *Educ* Bingley GS, Univ of Leeds (MA); *Career* research asst to Congressman Bernie Sanders US House of Representatives Washington DC 1992, research asst to Gordon Brown MP, *qv*, 1993, memb (Lab) Bingley City Bradford MDC 1994–98, researcher for Barry Seal, MEP, *qv*, 1996, MP (Lab) Shipley 1997–2005; PPS to Lord Falconer of Thornton, *qv* (as Min of State Cabinet Office), 1998–2001, Parly sec Cabinet Office 2001–02, Parly under sec of state ODPM 2002–03, Parly under sec DCA 2003–05; dir New Local Govt Network 2005–; *Recreations* travel, film, tennis, golf; *Style*— Christopher Leslie, Esq

LESLIE, Ian James; s of James Beattie Leslie (d 1973), of Brisbane, Aust, and Margaret Jean, *née* Ryan; *b* 23 January 1945; *Educ* Brisbane Boys' Coll, Univ of Queensland (MB BS), Univ of Liverpool (MChOrth); *m* 1 Sept 1975, Jane Ann, da of Col (Allan) Rex Waller, MBE, MC (d 1985), of Waddesdon Manor, Bucks; 1 da (Charlotte Ann b 1978), 1 s (James Henry Rex b 1982); *Career* RAAF 1968–72 (flying offr 1968, Flt Lt 1969, Sqdn Ldr 1971); resident MO Royal Brisbane Hosp Aust 1969, MO RAAF 1970–72 (sr MO Vietnam 1971), teaching surgical registrar Princess Alexandra Hosp Brisbane 1973, registrar then sr registrar Nuffield Orthopaedic Centre Oxford 1974–77, lectr then sr lectr Univ of Liverpool 1978–81, conslt orthopaedic surgn Bristol Royal Infirmary and Avon Orthopaedic Centre, clinical sr lectr Univ of Bristol 1981–; treas Br Orthopaedic Research Soc 1988–90, pres Br Soc Surgery Hand 2000 (memb Cncl 1986–88 and 1996–2001), pres

Br Orthopaedic Assoc 2005–06 (editorial sec 1990–92, hon sec 1994–95, memb Cncl 2003–05); UK delegate SICOT 1996–, Br delegate Fedn European Soc Surg Hand 2001–03; chm Interface Ctee Hand Surgery RCS 2001–02; chm Bd of Mgmnt Jl of Hand Surgery (Br and Euro vol) 1996–2000; memb Editorial Bd: Jl of Bone and Joint Surgery, Br Jl of Hand Surgery, Current Orthopaedics; former examiner: MChOrth Liverpool, RCS(Ed); memb: Aust Orthopaedic Assoc, Br Orthopaedic Assoc, Br Soc Surgery of the Hand, BMA, Aust Med Assoc, World Orthopaedic Concern; past memb Bd of Govrs Badminton Sch Bristol; FRCSEd 1974, FRCS (ad eundem) 1995; *Books* Fractures and Discolations (contrib), Arthroscopy in Operative Orthopaedics (1979), Operative Treatment of Fractures in Children and Surgery of Wrist in Operative Orthopaedics (1989); *Clubs* Army and Navy; *Style—* Ian Leslie, Esq; ✉ Collingwood, Easter Compton, Bristol BS35 5RE (tel 01454 632255, fax 01454 633602); Bristol Royal Infirmary, Marlborough Street, Bristol BS2 8HW (tel 0117 928 3899); 2 Clifton Park, Clifton Bristol BS8 3BS (tel 0117 906 4208)

LESLIE, Prof Ian Malcolm; s of Douglas Alexander Leslie, and Phyllis Margaret, *née* Duncan; *Educ* Univ of Toronto (BASc, MASc), Univ of Cambridge (PhD); *Career* Univ of Cambridge Computer Lab: lectr 1985–98 (asst lectr 1983–85), Robert Sansom prof of computer sci 1998–, head of dept 1999–2004; fell Christ's Coll Cambridge 1985–; pro-vice-chllr (research) Univ of Cambridge 2004–; contrib IEEE Jl on Selected Areas in Communications; MIEEE 1977, memb Assoc for Computing Machinery (ACM) 1983; *Recreations* house renovation, scuba diving; *Style—* Prof Ian Leslie; ✉ University of Cambridge Computer Laboratory, William Gates Building, JJ Thomson Avenue, Cambridge CB3 0FD (tel 01223 334607, e-mail ian.leslie@cl.cam.ac.uk)

LESLIE, Capt Sir John Norman Ide; 4 Bt (UK 1876), of Glaslough, Co Monaghan; presumed heir to the dormant Btcy of Leslie of Wardis; s of Sir (John Randolph) Shane Leslie, 3 Bt (d 1971), and Marjory Mary (d 1951), da of Henry Clay Ide, sometime govr of Philippine Is and American ambass to Spain; *b* 6 December 1916; *Educ* Downside, Magdalene Coll Cambridge (BA); *Heir* n, Shaun Leslie; *Career* cmmnd 2 Lt Irish Guards 1938, served WWII (POW 1940–45); artist, ecologist, restorer of old buildings; landowner (900 acres), previous to Irish Land Act 1910 forty nine thousand acres; Knight of Honour and Devotion SMOM, KCSG; *Recreations* ornithology, forestry; *Clubs* Travellers, Circolo della Caccia (Rome); *Style—* Capt Sir John Leslie, Bt; ✉ Glaslough, Co Monaghan, Ireland

LESLIE, Sir Peter Evelyn; kt (1991); s of Dr Patrick Holt Leslie (d 1972), of Oxford, and Evelyn de Berry; *b* 24 March 1931; *Educ* Dragon Sch Oxford, Stowe, New Coll Oxford; *m* 1975, Charlotte, da of Sir Edwin Arthur Chapman-Andrews, KCMG, OBE (d 1979); 2 step s (Francis, Mathew), 2 step da (Alice, Jessica); *Career* cmmnd Argyll and Sutherland Highlanders 1951, served 7 Bn (TA) 1952–56; Barclays Bank: gen mangr 1973–76, dir 1980, chief gen mangr and md 1985–88, dep chm 1987–91; dep chm Midland Bank 1991–92; chm NCM Credit Insurance Ltd 1995–98; chm: ODI 1988–95, Cwlth Devpt Corp 1989–95; memb: Bd of Banking Supervision Bank of England 1989–94, Supervisory Bd NCM Holding NV 1995–2000; chm: Exec Ctee Br Bankers' Assoc 1978–79, Exports Guarantee Advsy Cncl 1987–92 (memb 1978–81, dep chm 1986–87); govr Nat Inst of Social Work 1973–83; memb Cncl RIIA 1991–97; chm Cncl Queen's Coll London 1989–94, Audit Ctee Univ of Oxford 1992–2001, govr Stowe Sch 1983–2001 (chm 1994–2001); *Books* Chapman-Andrews and the Emperor (2005); *Recreations* natural history, historical research; *Style—* Sir Peter Leslie

LESLIE, Stephen Windsor; QC (1993); s of Leslie Leonard Leslie (d 1984), of Hove, E Sussex, and Celia, *née* Schulsinger (d 1991); *b* 21 April 1947; *Educ* Brighton Coll, KCL (LLB); *m* 1, 31 May 1974 (m dis 1989), Bridget Caroline, da of late Edwin George Oldham; 2 da (Lara Elizabeth b 27 Jan 1976, Ophelia Caroline b 19 Nov 1981); m 2, 29 July 1989 (m dis 2006), Amrit Kumari, da of George Ganesh Mangra; 1 s (Theodore Windsor b 18 July 1992); *Career* called to the Bar Lincoln's Inn 1971 (Sir Thomas More Bursary, bencher 2001); praticing barr at Furnival Chambers; Liveryman Worshipful Company of Feltmakers; *Recreations* travelling, Spain/Catalonia, gardening, the telephone and haggling for a bargain; *Clubs* Carlton, The Thunderers; *Style—* Stephen Leslie, Esq, QC; ✉ Furnival Chambers, 32 Furnival Street, London EC4A 1JQ (tel 020 7405 3232, fax 020 7405 3322, mobile 07850 654637)

LESLIE, Thomas Gerard; s of Thomas A Leslie, JP (d 1985), of Limestone, Muiravonside, Stirlingshire, and Ellen Slaven (d 1976), da of Hugh Francis McAllister; *b* 1 August 1938; *Educ* St Joseph's Coll Dumfries, Mons Offr Cadet Ssch Aldershot; *m* 12 June 1982, Sonya Anne (d 2000), da of Maj Leslie John Silburn (d 1980); 1 s (Thomas John Silburn b 1985); *Career* Nat Serv Scots Gds 1958, cmmnd Argyll and Sutherland Highlanders 1959, Lt HAC RARO; various exec posts: Canada Dry (UK) Ltd, Booker McConnell Ltd, Thos de la Rue; conslt The Corps of Commissionaires 1985–2001 (adj (capt) 1985–92); dir H&M Security Services Ltd 2001–02; chm London Caledonian Catholic Assoc 1983–87; fndr memb Clan Leslie Soc; file ldr The Company of Pikemen and Musketeers HAC; Freeman City of London 1974; FSA Scot 1980, MECI 1994; Knight SMOM 1998, KSG 2005; *Publications* The Leslie of Wardis and Findrassie Baronetcy; also author of various articles on Leslie families; *Recreations* heraldry, genealogy; *Clubs* HAC, British American Forces Dining; *Style—* Thomas Leslie, Esq, KSG, FSA (Scot); ✉ e-mail kincraigie@hotmail.co.uk

LESLIE MELVILLE, (Ian) Hamish; o s of Maj Michael Ian Leslie Melville, TD, DL (d 1997), s of Lt-Col Hon Ian Leslie Melville (4 s of 11 Earl of Leven and 10 Earl of Melville), and Cynthia, da of Sir Charles Hambro, KBE, MC; *b* 22 August 1944; *Educ* Eton, ChCh Oxford (MA); *m* 1968, Lady Elizabeth Compton, yr da of 6 Marquess of Northampton (d 1978); 2 s (James b 1969, Henry b 1975); *Career* dir Hambros Bank Ltd 1975–82, fndr and chief exec Enskilda Securities Ltd 1982–87, chm and chief exec Jamestown Investments Ltd 1987–92; chm: Capel-Cure Myers Capital Management Ltd 1988–91, Dunedin Fund Managers Ltd 1992–95; md Credit Suisse Securities (Europe) Ltd 1998–; chm: JPMorgan Fleming Mercantile Investment Tst plc, Mithras Investment Tst plc; dir Persimmon plc; *Clubs* New (Edinburgh); *Style—* Hamish Leslie Melville, Esq; ✉ Credit Suisse Securities (Europe) Ltd, One Cabot Square, London E14 9JS (tel 020 7888 8282, fax 020 7888 8284)

LESSER, Anton; s of late David Lesser, of Birmingham, and late Amelia Mavis, *née* Cohen; *b* 14 February 1952; *Educ* Moseley GS Birmingham, Univ of Liverpool (BA), RADA (Bancroft gold medal); *m* Madeleine Adams; *Career* actor; assoc artist RSC; *Theatre* for RSC incl: Richard in Henry VI, Dance of Death, Michael in Sons of Light, Romeo in Romeo and Juliet, Darkie in The Fool, Troilus in Troilus and Cressida (Stratford), Carlos Montezuma in Melons (The Pit), Bill Howell in Principia Scriptoriae (The Pit), Gloucester in Henry VI (Stratford and Barbican), title role in Richard III (Stratford and Barbican), Joe in Some Americans Abroad (Barbican), Bolingbroke in Richard II (Stratford), Forest in Two Shakespearian Actors (Stratford), Petruchio in The Taming of the Shrew, Ford in The Merry Wives of Windsor; other roles incl: Mark Antony in Julius Caesar (Tyne & Wear), Betty/Edward in Cloud Nine (Liverpool Everyman), Konstantin in The Seagull (Royal Court), Hamlet in Hamlet (Warehouse), Kissing God (Hampstead Theatre Club), Family Voices (Lyric Hammersmith), Feste in Twelfth Night (Riverside Studios), Stanley in The Birthday Party (RNT), Jack Rover in Wild Oats (RNT), Serge in Art (Wyndhams), William in Mutabilitie (RNT), Elyot Chase in Private Lives (RNT), Leo in The Lucky Ones (Hampstead Theatre Club); *Television* BBC incl: Orestes in The Oresteia, Philip in The Mill on the Floss, Abesey Ivanovich in The Gambler, Troilus in Troilus and Cressida, Trofimov in The Cherry Orchard, Edgar in King Lear, Wilheim Fliess in Freud, Willy Price in Anna of The Five Towns, Stanley in Stanley Spencer, Vincenzo Rocca in Airbase, Feste in Twelfth Night, Mungo Dawson in Downtown Lagos, Terell in Invasion Earth, Sir Pitt Crawley in Vanity Fair, Billy Blake in The Echo, Dr Andrew Ward in Pure Wickedness; Channel Four incl: Cox in Good and Bad At Games, Valerie Chaldize in Sakharov, Mark Hollister in the Politician's Wife, Robert Schumann in Schumann; other prodns incl: Ken in The Daughters of Albion (YTV), London Embassy (Thames), Wiesenthal (TVS/HBO), The Strauss Dynasty (mini-series), David Galilee in Sharman, Vladic Mesic in Bodyguards, Ezra Jennings in The Moonstone, Dunn in Always Be Closing, Picard in The Scarlet Pimpernel, Councillor in Lorna Doone, Paul Valley in Swallow, Charles Dickens in Dickens, Stephen in Perfect Strangers; *Film* incl: The Missionary, Monseigneur Quixote, Moses, Fairytale, Esther Kahn, Jack and the Beanstalk, Charlotte Gray, Imagining Argentina; *Style—* Anton Lesser, Esq; ✉ c/o Conway van Gelder Ltd, 18–21 Jermyn Street, London SW1Y 6HP (tel 020 7287 0077, fax 020 7287 1940)

LESSORE, John Viviand; s of Frederick Lessore (d 1951), of London, and Helen Lessore, OBE, RA, *née* Brook (d 1994); *b* 16 June 1939; *Educ* Merchant Taylors', Slade Sch of Fine Art London; *m* 1962, Paule Marie, da of Jean Achille Reveille (Officier de la Lègion d'honneur, d 1967), of Paris; 4 s (Remi b 1962, Vincent b 1967, Timothy b 1973, Samuel b 1977); *Career* artist; co-fndr Prince's Drawing Sch 2000; tstee Nat Gallery 2003–; Korn/Ferry Int Public Award 1st Prize 1991, Lynn Painter-Stainers 1st Prize and Gold Medal 2006; *Principal Exhibitions* incl: Beaux Arts Gallery 1965, New Art Centre 1971, Theo Waddington 1981, Stoppenbach & Delestre 1983 and 1985, Nigel Greenwood 1990, Theo Waddington and Robert Stoppenbach 1994, Solomon Gallery Dublin 1995, Theo Waddington Fine Art 1997, Miriam Shiell Fine Art Toronto 1997, Wolsey Art Gallery Christchurch Mansion Ipswich 1999, Ranger's House Blackheath 2000, Berkeley Square Gallery 2002, Annely Juda Fine Art 2004, Annandale Galleries Sydney 2005; *Works in Public Collections* incl: Leicester Educn Ctee, Arts Cncl Collection, Royal Acad of Arts, Tate Gallery, Swindon Museum and Art Gallery, CAS, Norwich Castle Museum, Br Cncl, Accenture (formerly Andersen Consulting), Nat Portrait Gallery, Br Museum; *Style—* John Lessore; ✉ c/o Annely Juda Fine Art, 23 Dering Street, London W1S 1AW (tel 020 7629 7578, fax 020 7491 2139); e-mail john.lessore@lineone.net, website www.johnlessore.com

LESTER, Adrian Anthony; *b* 14 August 1968; *Educ* RADA; *Career* actor; memb: Artistic Bd RNT, Bd RADA; memb: Amnesty Int, Greenpeace; patron Body & Soul; *Theatre* incl: Cory in Fences (Garrick) 1990, Paul Poitier in Six Degrees of Separation (Royal Court and Comedy Theatre) 1992 (Time Out Award), Anthony Hope in Sweeney Todd (RNT) 1994, Rosalind in As You Like It (Albery and Bouffes du Nord) 1995 (Time Out Award), Bobby in Company (Albery and Donmar) 1996 (Olivier Award), Hamlet in Hamlet (Bouffes du Nord, Young Vic and world tour) 2001, Henry in Henry V (RNT) 2003; *Television* incl: Hustle (BBC), Beyond (Fox); *Film* incl: Primary Colours, Love's Labour's Lost, The Day After Tomorrow, Storm Damage, Spiderman 3, As You Like It; *Recreations* street dance, martial arts, music; *Style—* Adrian Lester, Esq; ✉ c/o Sue Latimer, Artists' Rights Group, 4 Great Portland Street, London W1W 8PA (tel 020 7436 6400)

LESTER, Alexander Norman Charles Phillips (Alex); s of John Phillips Lester, of Walsall, W Midlands, and Rosemary Anne, *née* Edgely; *b* 11 May 1956; *Educ* Denstone Coll, Birmingham Poly (Dip Communication Studies); *Career* presenter/journalist: BBC local radio 1978–81, BBC Essex 1986–87; presenter: ind radio 1981–86, BBC Radio 2 and 4 1987– (incl Alex Lester Show); TV presenter The Boat Show (BBC 2) 1999; freelance announcer, voiceover artist and media trainer 1988–; memb Equity; patron: St Michaels Hospice St Leonards on Sea, Ambass Hosp Broadcasting Assoc, Hasting Winkle Club (fishermans charity); *Recreations* inland waterways, house restoration, travel, junk collecting, reading; *Style—* Alex Lester, Esq; ✉ MPC Entertainment, MPC House, 15/16 Maple Mews, Maida Vale, London NW6 5UZ (tel 020 7624 1184, fax 020 7624 4220, e-mail mpc@mpce.com)

LESTER, Anthony John; s of Donald James Lester, of Wallingford, Oxon, and Edith Helen Hemmings (d 1982); *b* 15 September 1945; *Educ* Gaveston Hall Nuthurst, St John's Coll Co Tipperary; *Career* ind fine art conslt, art critic, book reviewer and lectr; ed Watercolours, Drawings and Prints 1992–94; publisher and editorial dir Art Prices Review; fine art corr Antiques Trade Gazette and Antique Dealer and Collectors' Guide; contribs to numerous magazines incl: Woman, Antique Collecting, Artists' and Illustrators' Magazine, Art Business Today, Limited Edition, The World of Antiques, The Speculator, Antiques and Decoration, The Collector, The Big Issue, Galleries, Miller's Magazine, Art and Artefact; featured in Farmers' Weekly, Radio Times, Sunday Express Magazine, British Midland Voyager Magazine; regular broadcaster BBC TV: Antiques Roadshow 1986–89, Going for a Song 1999; judge: The Laing Art Exhbn 1997, Br Antiques and Collectables Awards 2002–, Watercolour C21 (RWS Open) 2003, GMAC Commercial Mortgage Europe Art Award 2004–; selector The Discerning Eye 2002; memb: Int Assoc of Art Critics, Glass Circle, Glass Assoc; Companion of the Pastel Soc; CRSBA, FRSA; *Books* The Exhibited Works of Helen Allingham (1979), The Stannards of Bedfordshire (1984), BBC Antiques Roadshow-Experts on Objects (contrib, 1987), The Pastel Society 1898–2000 (contrib, 2000); *Recreations* travel, entertaining friends, charity work; *Clubs* Chelsea Arts; *Style—* Anthony J Lester, Esq; ✉ Chine Lodge, 11 Eastcliff Road, Shanklin, Isle of Wight PO37 6AA (tel 01983 866970, mobile 07932 728671, e-mail anthonylester@fsmail.net)

LESTER, Charles Martin; s of Charles William Lester, of Banbury, Oxon, and Marjory Winnifred, *née* Pursail; *b* 20 March 1942; *Educ* N Oxfordshire Tech Sch, Oxford Coll of Technol, Gwent Coll of HE; *m* 16 March 1963, Patricia Caroline Lester, *qv*, da of Arthur Frederick Wake; 1 da (Georgina Caroline b 28 Oct 1964); *Career* research scientist ICI Fibres 1962–74, teacher of design craft and technol King Henry VIII Sch 1976–79, head Design Craft and Technol Dept Haberdashers' Monmouth Sch 1979–84, dir Charles & Patricia Lester Ltd (textile and fashion design co) 1984–; estab (with w) lifestyle shop incl fashion, textiles and interiors in Knightsbridge, London SW3, together developed unique method for finely hand pleating silk and decorating velvet and silks, developed original methods for structure of garments and interior pieces; estab couture house selling worldwide incl: Fortnum & Mason in London, Bergdorf Goodman, Neiman Marcus and Saks Fifth Avenue in US, other stockists in Germany, Italy, Hong Kong and Japan; additional products incl cushions, bedspreads, throws, unique silk tapestries, shawls and scarves; clients incl: HRH Princess Michael of Kent, Elizabeth Taylor, Barbra Streisand, Toni Braxton, Whitney Houston, Emma Kirkby; recreated Flaming June set for centenary of death of Lord Leighton (Leighton House) 1996; film work incl: costume designs for Wings of the Dove (Oscar nomination for costumes 1998), fabric for Hamlet, Greenfingers, Jack and the Beanstalk; theatre work incl all costumes for opera Iris (Holland Park Theatre 1997 and 1998, Teatro Grattacielo concert prodn Lincoln Centre NY 1998) and The Pearl Fishers (Opera Holland Park) 2002; featured in V&A Museum exhbn Cutting Edge 1997, solo exhbn Textile Experience (Leighton House) 1997; work featured in publications and collected in museums world-wide; Fit for Work Award (in recognition of commitment to the employment of disabled staff) 1985; *Recreations* Folly Fellowship, Steam Boat Association, rebuilding and restoring vintage boat, photography; *Style—* Charles Lester, Esq; ✉ Charles & Patricia Lester Ltd, The Workhouse, Hatherleigh Place, Union Road, Abergavenny, Monmouthshire NP7 7RL (e-mail cpl@charlespatricialester.com, website www.interior-design-world.com and www.charles-patricia-lester.co.uk)

L

LESTER, Michael; s of Jack Lester (d 1959), and Mary, *née* Sax (d 1987); *b* 10 March 1940; *Educ* Coopers' Company's Sch, New Coll Oxford (MA); *m* 17 Dec 1967, Pamela Frances Lester, da of Leopold Henry Gillis (d 1988); 1 da (Antonia b 1973), 1 s (James b 1976); *Career* Bigelow teaching fell Univ of Chicago Law Sch 1962–64, articled clerk and slr in private practice 1964–80; GEC plc: dir of legal affrs 1980–99, main bd dir 1983–99, vice-chm 1994–99; non-exec dir Premier Farnell plc 1998–; main bd dir BAE Systems plc 1999–; memb Law Soc, CCMI (CIMgt); *Style*— Michael Lester, Esq; ✉ 46 Sheldon Avenue, London N6 4JR (tel 020 8340 7868); BAE Systems plc, Stirling Square, 6 Carlton Gardens, London SW1Y 5DA (tel 01252 383904, fax 01252 383992)

LESTER, Patricia Caroline; MBE (1988); da of Arthur Frederick Wake, of NZ, and Dorothy Phyllis, *née* Flew; *b* 11 February 1943; *Educ* Thornton Coll, Oxford Coll of Technology; *m* 16 March 1963, Charles Martin Lester, *qv*, s of Charles William Lester; 1 da (Georgina Caroline b 28 Oct 1964); *Career* formerly employed as secretary St Anne's Coll Oxford then British steel Wales; textile, fashion and interior designer; fndr and currently dir Charles & Patricia Lester Ltd with husb, estab lifestyle shop incl fashion, textiles and interiors in Knightsbridge London; together developed unique method for finely hand pleating silk and decorating velvet and silks, developed original methods for structure of garments and interior pieces; estab couture house selling worldwide incl: Fortnum & Mason London, Bergdorf Goodman, Neiman Marcus and Saks Fifth Avenue US, other stockists in Germany, Italy, Hong Kong and Japan; additional products incl cushions, bedspreads, throws, unique silk tapestries, shawls and scarves; clients incl: HRH Princess Michael of Kent, Elizabeth Taylor, Barbra Streisand, Toni Braxton, Whitney Houston, Emma Kirkby; recreated Flaming June set for centenary of death of Lord Leighton (Leighton House) 1996; film work incl: costume designs for Wings of the Dove (Oscar nomination for costumes 1998), fabric for Hamlet, Greenfingers, Jack and the Beanstalk; theatre work incl all costumes for opera Iris (Holland Park Theatre 1997 and 1998, Teatro Grattacielo concert prodn Lincoln Centre NY 1998) and for The Pearl Fishers (Opera Holland Park 2002); featured in V&A Museum exhbn Cutting Edge 1997, solo exhbn Textile Experience (Leighton House) 1997; work featured in publications and collected in museums world-wide; Fit for Work Award (in recognition of commitment to the employment of disabled staff) 1985, Welsh Business Woman of the Year 1986 and 1987; *Recreations* gardening, painting, Folly Fellowship, Steam Boat Association; *Style*— Mrs Patricia Lester, MBE; ✉ Charles & Patricia Lester Ltd, The Workhouse, Hatherleigh Place, Union Road, Abergavenny, Monmouthshire (website www.interior-design-world.com and www.charles-patricia-lester.co.uk)

LESTER OF HERNE HILL, Baron (Life Peer UK 1993), of Herne Hill in the London Borough of Southwark; Anthony Paul Lester; QC (1975); s of Harry Lester (d 1984), of London, and Kate, *née* Cooper-Smith; *b* 3 July 1936; *Educ* City of London Sch, Trinity Coll Cambridge (BA), Harvard Law Sch (LLM); *m* 29 July 1971, Catherine Elizabeth Debora, da of Michael Morris Wassey (d 1969), of London; 1 s (Hon Gideon b 1972), 1 da (Hon Maya b 1974); *Career* 2 Lt RA 1956; called to the Bar Lincoln's Inn 1963 (bencher 1985), memb NI Bar and Irish Bar; former recorder S Eastern circuit 1987; special advsr to: Home Sec 1974–76, Standing Cmmn on Human Rights in NI 1975–77; memb: House of Lord's Select Ctee on Euro Communities Sub-Ctee (Law and Institutions) 1996–2003 and 2004–, Sub-Ctee on the 1996 Inter-Governmental Conf, Educn and Home Affairs, Parly Jt Human Rights Ctee 2001–; former memb Sub-Ctee on Social Affairs; pres Interights (Int Centre for Legal Protection of Human Rights) 1982–, chair Equal Rights Tst 2006–; chm Nat Ctee 50th Anniversary of UN Universal Declaration of Human rights 1998, memb Bd: Salzburg Seminar 1996–2000, Euro Roma Rights Center (co-chair 1999–2001); memb: Cncl JUSTICE 1977–, Advsy Bd Inst of European Public Law Univ of Hull, Advsy Ctee Centre for Public Law Univ of Cambridge 1999–, Int Advsy Bd Open Soc Inst 2000–, Ed Bd Public Law, Ed Bd Int Jl of Discrimination and the Law; ed-in-chief Butterworths Human Rights Cases, former chm and treas Fabian Soc, pres Lib Dem Lawyers' Assoc, co-fndr and former chm Runnymede Tst; hon visiting prof of law UCL; govr Br Inst of Human Rights, former chm and memb Bd of Govrs James Allen's Girls' Sch, former govr Westminster Sch; hon memb American Acad of Arts and Sciences 2002, memb American Philosophical Soc 2003; *Books* Justice in the American South (1964), Shawcross and Beaumont on Air Law (ed jtly, 3 edn 1964), Race and Law (jtly 1972); conslt ed and contrib Constitutional Law and Human Rights in Halsbury's Laws of England (4 edn, 1973, re-issued 1996); contrib: British Nationality, Immigration and Race Relations in Halsbury's Laws of England (4 edn, 1973, re-issued 1992), The Changing Constitution (ed Jowell and Oliver, 1985), Butterworths Human Rights Law and Practice (co-ed, 1999, 2nd edn 2004); *Recreations* walking, sailing, golf, water colours; *Style*— The Lord Lester of Herne Hill, QC; ✉ Blackstone Chambers, Blackstone House, Temple, London EC4Y 9BW (tel 020 7583 1770, sec 020 7404 4712, fax 020 7822 7350)

LETHBRIDGE, Prof Robert David; s of Albert Lethbridge (d 1988), and Muriel, *née* de Saram (d 2000); *b* 24 February 1947, New York; *Educ* Mill Hill Sch, Univ of Kent (BA), McMaster Univ (MA), St John's Coll Cambridge (MA, PhD); *m* 2 Jan 1970, Vera, *née* Laycock; 1 s (Jonathan b 23 Mar 1975), 1 da (Tamsin b 13 Jan 1979); *Career* Fitzwilliam Coll Cambridge: fell 1973–94 (Leathersellers' fell 1973–78), life fell 1994–, tutor 1975–92 (sr tutor 1982–92), master 2005–; lectr in French Univ of Cambridge 1985–94 (asst lectr 1980–85), prof of French language and lit Univ of London 1995–2005 (emeritus prof 2005–); Royal Holloway Univ of London: head Dept of French 1995–97, dean Grad Sch 1997–98, vice-princ (academic) 1997–2002, visiting prof 2003–05; dir Univ of London Inst in Paris (formerly Br Inst in Paris) 2003–05; visiting prof: Univ of California at Santa Barbara 1986, Univ of Melbourne 2003; hon prof Queen Mary Univ of London 2003–05; memb Society of Dix-neuviémistes (hon pres 2001–06), Chevalier dans l'Ordre des Palmes Académiques (France); *Publications* Maupassant: Pierre et Jean (1984), Zola and the Craft of Fiction (ed 1990), Artistic Relations, Literature and the Visual Arts in Nineteenth-Century France (ed 1994), editions of novels by Guy de Maupassant (2001) and by Emile Zola (1995, 2000, 2001), 50 essays in learned jls and collective works; *Recreations* watching rugby, contemplating the sea; *Clubs* Oxford and Cambridge; *Style*— Prof Robert Lethbridge; ✉ The Master's Lodge, Fitzwilliam College, Cambridge CB3 0DG (tel 01223 332029, fax 01223 332074, e-mail master@fitz.cam.ac.uk)

LETHBRIDGE, Sir Thomas Periam Hector Noel; 7 Bt (UK 1804), of Westaway House, and Winkley Court, Somerset; s of Sir Hector Wroth Lethbridge, 6 Bt (d 1978), and Evelyn Diana, *née* Noel (d 1996); *b* 17 July 1950; *Educ* Milton Abbey, RAC Cirencester; *m* 1, 1976 (m dis), Susan Elizabeth, eldest da of Lyle Rocke, of Maryland, USA; 4 s (John Francis Buckler Noel b 1977, Edward Christopher Wroth b 1978, Alexander Ralph Periam b 1982, Henry Charles Hesketh b 1984), 2 da (Georgina Rose Alianore b 1980, Rachael Elizabeth Mary b 1986); m 2, 28 Feb 2007, Mrs Ann Marie Fenwick; *Heir* s, John Lethbridge; *Career* art dealer in sporting subjects of 1700 to date, int agent for distinguished retail names; *Clubs* Voles; *Style*— Sir Thomas Lethbridge, Bt; ✉ c/o Drummonds, 49 Charing Cross Road, London SW1A 2DX

LETLEY, Peter Anthony; s of Sidney Charles Letley (d 1978), of Woodbridge, Suffolk, and Ruby, *née* Berry (d 1994); *b* 11 November 1945; *Educ* Woodbridge Sch, St John's Coll Oxford (BA); *m* 21 March 1970, (Alice) Emma Campbell, da of late Lt-Col Campbell K Finlay, of West Ardhu, Isle of Mull; 1 s (Alfred Thomas b 4 Sept 1988); *Career* joined HSBC Group 1974; Wardley Ltd: head of Lending Dept 1974–78, dir overseas ops and dir 1978–82, jt md Aust 1982–83, chief exec Hong Kong International Trade Finance Ltd (London) 1983–86; fin dir James Capel Bankers Ltd 1986–87 (md 1987–88), fin dir HSBC James Capel & Co 1988–93 (dep chm 1993–97), dep chm HSBC Investment Banking Group Ltd 1993–99; CIBC World Markets plc: chief admin offr and chief fin offr 1999–2004, head of Europe 2004–; alternate memb Takeover Panel; chm BFWG Charitable Fndn, non-exec dir Housing 21 (chm Audit Ctee and Performance Ctee); *Recreations* theatre, opera, reading; *Clubs* Hong Kong Jockey, Reform; *Style*— Peter Letley, Esq; ✉ 24 Princedale Road, London W11 4NJ; West Ardhu, Dervaig, Tobermory, Isle of Mull, Argyll PA75 6QR; CIBC World Markets plc, Cottons Centre, Cottons Lane, London SE1 2QL (tel 020 7234 6172, fax 020 7234 6088)

LETTE, Kathy; *Career* novelist; *Books* Puberty Blues (1979), Hit and Ms (1984), Girls' Night Out (1988), The Llama Parlour (1991), Foetal Attraction (1993), Mad Cows (1996), Altar Ego (1998), Nip'n Tuck (2001), Dead Sexy (2003), How to Kill Your Husband and Other Handy Household Hints (2006); *Style*— Ms Kathy Lette; ✉ c/o Ed Victor, 6 Bayley Street, Bedford Square, London WC1B 3HB

LETTS, Melinda Jane Frances; OBE (2003); da of Richard Francis Bonner Letts, of Cirencester, Glos, and Jocelyn Elizabeth, *née* Adami; *b* 6 April 1956; *Educ* Wycombe Abbey, Cheltenham Coll, St Anne's Coll Oxford (exhibitioner, BA); *m* 13 April 1991, Neil Scott Wishart McIntosh, s of William Henderson McIntosh; 1 s (Fergus George Christian b 15 Oct 1990), 1 da (Isobel Freya Johnstone b 15 Sept 1992); *Career* press and publicity offr Bubble Theatre Co 1980–81, research asst Sociology Dept Brunel Univ 1981–82, head orgn and admin CND 1982–84; VSO: head of admin 1985–86, prog funding mangr 1986–87, regnl mangr S Asia 1987–89; staffing mangr McKinsey & Co Inc 1989–91, chief exec Nat Asthma Campaign 1992–97 (dep dir 1991–92), chair Long-term Med Conditions Alliance (LMCA) 1998–2004 (tstee 1996–2004), chair Nat Strategic Partnersip Forum 2005–; currently strategic conslt and coach, assoc conslt Compass Partnership 1998–; dir Ask About Medicines Week 2003–; chair Ctee on Safety of Medicines Working Gp on Patient Information 2003–; memb: NHS Modernisation Bd 1999–2003, Cmmn for Health Improvement 1999–2004, Cmmn for Healthcare Audit and Inspection 2003–04; former memb Bd New Opportunities Fund; tstee Gen Practice Airways Gp; former tstee: Nat Cncl for Vol Orgns, Charity Projects Comic Relief; patron Men's Health Forum; MIMgt 1992, FRSA 1993; *Recreations* reading, swimming, crosswords; *Style*— Ms Melinda Letts, OBE

LETTS, Quentin Richard Stephen; s of R F B Letts, of Cirencester, Glos, and Jocelyn, *née* Adami; *b* 6 February 1963; *Educ* Haileybury, Bellarmine Coll Kentucky, Trinity Coll Dublin, Jesus Coll Cambridge; *m* 1996, Lois, *née* Rathbone; 1 s, 2 da; *Career* dustman and waiter 1981–84; ed: Oxon Magazine Oxford 1984–85, Mayday Magazine Dublin 1985–86, Filibuster Magazine Dublin 1986–87; journalist The Daily Telegraph 1988–95 (ed Peterborough Column), NY Bureau chief The Times 1995–97, freelance journalist 1997– (including parly sketch writer Daily Telegraph 1997–2000 and Daily Mail 2000–), theatre critic Daily Mail 2004–, writer Clement Crabbe column Daily Mail 2006–; winner Edgar Wallace Award London Press Club 2003; *Recreations* singing hymns, watching cricket; *Clubs* Savile; *Style*— Quentin Letts, Esq; ✉ The Old Mill, How Caple, Herefordshire HR1 4SR (tel 01989 740688)

LETTS CIARRAPICO, Dr Rosa Maria; *Educ* Univ of Rome (law degree), Brandeis Univ Massachusetts (MA, Fulbright scholar), Courtauld Inst London (BA), Warburg Inst London (MPhil); *Career* history of art and architecture teacher Extra Mural Dept Univ of London 1966–80, lectr on Italian European art (Renaissance and Baroque) and exhbns conslt Educn Dept V&A 1975–82; lectr: in Renaissance and Baroque art, Italian modern art design and architecture 1978–85, Sotheby's art courses, Italian contemporary design, architecture and fashion Phillip's courses on Contemporary Art 1985–86; fndr dir: Accademia Italiana delle Arti e delle Arti Applicate London 1988–, Euro Acad of the Arts 1994; memb Editorial Advsy Bd Apollo Magazine 1991, cultural cnsllr Italian Embassy London 1992–96; juror Euro Design Award RSA 1992–93, memb Panel of Judges Swiss Bank Competition for Euro Contemporary Art 1993–95; Cavaliere Ufficiale della Repubblica Italiana 1990, Judge Premio Strega; *Exhibitions* co curator The Splendours of the Gonzaga V&A 1981, curator Letts Keep a Diary The Mall Galleries 1987, co curator Manzu exhbn MOMA Rome, Scottish Nat Gallery of Modern Art, Walker Art Gallery Liverpool, MOMA Oxford 1987–88, curator Italy by Moonlight Museo de las Belas Artes, Rio De Janeiro, Ashmolean Oxford 1990, Accademia Italiana London 1991, Marino Marini retrospective exhbn 1999, Pompeii: Images from the Buried Cities Aberdeen Art Gall 2001; *Publications* La Pittura Fiorentina (1970, Eng trans 1982), Art Treasures of London (1972), Paola Malatesta Gonzaga 1392–1447 (MPhil, 1981), The Renaissance (1981, 3 edn 1991), Italy by Moonlight 1550–1850 (exhbn catalogue, 1990); numerous catalogue essays and articles; *Style*— Dr Rosa Maria Letts; ✉ Accademia Club, 59 Knightsbridge, London SW1X 7RA (tel 020 7235 6650, fax 020 7235 6659, e-mail info@accademia-club.com)

LETWIN, Rt Hon Dr Oliver; PC (2002), MP; s of Prof W Letwin, and Dr S R Letwin (d 1993); *b* 19 May 1956; *Educ* Eton, Trinity Coll Cambridge (MA, PhD); *m* 1984, Isabel Grace, da of Prof John Frank Davidson, FRS, *qv*; 1 s (Jeremy John Peter 5 July 1993), 1 da (Laura Shirley (twin) b 5 July 1993); *Career* visiting research fell Princeton Univ 1980–81, research fell Darwin Coll Cambridge 1981–82, special advsr Dept of Educn and Sci 1982–83, memb Prime Minister's Policy Unit 1983–86, md N M Rothschild and Sons Ltd 2003 (joined 1986, dir 1991–2003, non-exec dir 2005–); MP (Cons) Dorset W 1997–; oppn frontbench spokesman on constitutional affrs 1998–99, shadow fin sec to the Treasy 1999–2000, shadow chief sec to the Treasy 2000–01, shadow home sec 2001–03, shadow sec of state for economic affrs and shadow chllr of the Exchequer 2003–05, shadow sec of state for environment, food and rural affairs 2005, chm Cons Party Policy Review and Cons Research Dept 2005–; FRSA 1991; *Publications* Ethics, Emotion and the Unity of the Self (1984), Privatising the World (1987), Aims of Schooling (1988), Drift to Union (1990), The Purpose of Politics (1999); numerous articles in learned and popular jls; *Recreations* philosophy, walking, skiing, tennis; *Style*— The Rt Hon Dr Oliver Letwin, MP; ✉ House of Commons, London SW1A 0AA (tel 020 7219 3000)

LEVAGGI, Peter; *b* 24 December 1965; *Educ* Univ of York (BA); *Children* 2 da (Hazel, Molly); *Career* admitted slr 1992, slr advocate; slr: Rochman Landau 1992–96, Charles Russell Slrs 1996–; memb: Property Litigation Assoc, Insolvency Lawyers Assoc; *Style*— Peter Levaggi, Esq; ✉ Charles Russell, Buryfields House, Bury Fields, Guildford GU2 4AZ (tel 01483 252525, fax 01483 252552, e-mail peter.levaggi@charlesrussell.co.uk)

LEVEAUX, David Vyvyan; s of Dr Michael Leveaux, of Derby, and Eve, *née* Powell; *b* 13 December 1957; *Educ* Rugby, Univ of Manchester (BA); *Career* director; assoc dir Riverside Studios 1981–85; artistic dir Theatre Project Tokyo (TPT) 1993–; *Theatre* Almeida: Betrayal 1991, No Man's Land 1992, Moonlight 1993; A Moon for the Misbegotten (Riverside Studios), Easter (Leicester Haymarket), Therese Raquin (Chichester) 1990, 'Tis Pity She's a Whore (RSC), The Father (RNT), Nine (Donmar Warehouse and Buenos Aires) 1996, Electra (Chichester Festival, UK tour and Donmar) 1997, Electra (McCarter Theater, Princeton) 1998, The Real Thing (Donmar Warehouse/Albery); Berlin: The Dance of Death, Krapp's Last Tape; New York Broadway: A Moon for the Misbegotten (nominee Best Dir Tony Awards 1983/84), Anna Christie (nominee Best Dir and recipient Best Revival Tony Awards 1992/93); New York Off-Broadway: Messiah, Virginia; Tokyo: Les Liaisons Dangereuses, Madame de Sade 1990, Two Headed Eagle 1990, Lady from the Sea 1992; TPT: Therese Raquin 1993, Betrayal 1993, 'Tis a Pity She's a Whore 1993, Hedda Gabler 1994, Ellida 1994, The Two Headed Eagle 1994, The Ibsen Project 1994, The Changeling 1995, The Three Sisters 1995, two modern Noh plays 1995, Electra 1996, Macbeth 1996, Triumph of Love, Lulu; *Opera* The Turn of the Screw (Glasgow Tramway) 1996, The Marriage of Figaro (both Scottish Opera, 1995), Salome (ENO); *Style—* David Leveaux, Esq; ✉ c/o Simpson Fox Associates Ltd, 52 Shaftesbury Avenue, London W1V 7DE (tel 020 7434 9167, fax 020 7494 2887, e-mail cary@simpson-fox.demon.co.uk)

LEVEN AND MELVILLE, 14 Earl of Leven and 13 of Melville (S 1641); Alexander Robert Leslie Melville; also Lord Melville of Monymaill (S 1616), Lord Balgonie (S 1641), Viscount Kirkaldie, and Lord Raith, Monymaill and Balwearie (both S 1690); DL (Co of Nairn 1961); s of 13 Earl of Leven and (12 of) Melville, KT (d 1947), and Lady Rosamond Foljambe (da of 1 Earl of Liverpool); *b* 13 May 1924; *Educ* Eton; *m* 1953, Susan, da of late Lt-Col Ronald Steuart-Menzies of Culdares; 2 s, 1 da; *Heir* gs, Lord Balgonie; *Career* vice-pres Highland Dist TA, 2 Lt Coldstream Gds 1943, Capt 1947; ADC to Govr-Gen NZ 1951–52; pres Br Ski Fedn 1981–85; Lord Lt for Nairn 1969–99 (ret); convener Nairn Co Cncl 1970–74, chm Bd of Govrs Gordonstoun Sch 1971–89; *Recreations* shooting, skiing, fishing; *Clubs* New (Edinburgh); *Style—* The Rt Hon the Earl of Leven and Melville; ✉ Raith, Old Spey Bridge, Grantown on Spey, Moray PH26 3NQ (tel 01479 872908)

LEVENE, Ben; s of Mark Levene (d 1987), of London, and Charlotte, *née* Leapman (d 1987); *b* 23 December 1938; *Educ* St Clement Danes GS, Slade Sch of Fine Art (DFA); *m* 1; 2 da (Rachael Clare b 19 April 1959, Sophie Rebecca b 22 Sept 1962); m 2, 14 Feb 1978, Susan Margaret; 1 s (Jacob Daniel b 23 April 1979); *Career* artist; former pt/t lectr Camberwell Sch of Art, pt/t lectr RA Schs 1980–95, curator RA Schs 1995–98; works in various private collections in England and America RA 1986 (ARA 1975); *Solo exhibitions* Thackeray Gallery London 1973, 1975, 1978 and 1981, Browse and Darby London 1988, 1993 and 2001 (gallery artist); *Group exhibitions* incl regular exhibitor at RA Summer Exhbn, works shown in Jasper Galleries (Houston and NY); work featured in Oils Master Class (by Sally Bulgin) 1996; *Recreations* gardening under the supervision of my wife; *Style—* Ben Levene, Esq, RA; ✉ c/o Royal Academy of Arts, Piccadilly, London W1V 0DS (tel 020 7300 8000)

LEVENE, Prof Malcolm Irvin; s of Maurice Mordechai Levene, of Brighton, E Sussex, and Helen, *née* Kutner (d 1983); *b* 2 January 1951; *Educ* Guy's Hosp Med Sch (LRCP, MB BS, MD); *m* 1, 1972, Miriam Ann, *née* Bentley (d 1989); 3 da (Alysa b 20 Aug 1976, Katherine b 10 Jan 1979, Ilana b 13 Feb 1983); m 2, Susan Anne, da of Robert Cave; 1 da (Hannah Sophie b 2 Nov 1992), 1 s (David Jack b 18 May 1994); *Career* house surgn Royal Sussex Co Hosp Brighton March-Oct 1974, house physician Northampton Gen Hosp 1974, locum GP NSW Australia 1975–76, paediatric SHO Charing Cross Hosp 1976–77, registrar Derby Children's Hosp 1977–78, paediatric registrar Charing Cross Hosp 1978–79, hon sr registrar Hammersmith Hosp and Queen Charlotte's Hosp London 1979–82, research lectr in neonatal med Royal Postgrad Med Sch London 1979–82, hon conslt paediatrician Leicester Royal Infirmary and reader in child health Univ of Leicester Med Sch 1988 (sr lectr 1982–88); Univ of Leeds Med Sch: prof of paediatrics and child health, hon conslt paediatrician, dean of students 1989–; Scope (formerly The Spastics Soc): memb Med Advsy Ctee 1985–91, memb Combined Res Ctee 1986–91; memb Leicestershire Maternity Liaison Ctee 1984–88, chm Research Ctee Action Research 1993–96 (memb 1992–96), chm Centre for Reproduction, Growth and Devpt Research Sch of Med 1995–98; ed-in-chief Seminars in Neonatology; memb Editorial Bd: Developmental Med and Child Neurology 1985–93, Jl of Perinatal Med 1987–, Neuropaediatrics 1992–; hon sec Div of Child Health Leicestershire DHA; Handcock prize RCS 1974, British Cncl travelling fellowship 1980, Michael Blecklow Meml prize BPA 1982, Ronnie MacKeith prize BPNA 1984, Guthrie medal BPA 1986, BUPA Nat Research award 1988; memb: Neonatal Soc, RSM, Paediatric Research Soc, BPNA, British Assoc of Perinatal Med, Academic Bd Royal Coll of Paediatrics and Child Health 2002–; MRCS; FRCP, FMedSci 1999, fell Int Acad of Perinatal Medicine 2005; *Books* A Handbook for Examinations in Paediatrics (jtly, 1981), Ultrasound of the Infant Brain (jtly, 1985), Diseases of Children (jtly, 5 edn 1985), Current Reviews in Paediatrics (1987), Essentials of Neonatal Medicine (jtly, 1987, 2 edn 1993), Fetal and Neonatal Neurology and Neurosurgery (ed jtly, 1988, 3 edn 2001), Jolly's Diseases of Children (ed, 6 edn 1991); author of numerous chapters in books and articles in learned jls; *Publications* Paediatrics and Child Health (jtly, 1999); *Recreations* golf, gardening, music; *Style—* Prof Malcolm Levene; ✉ Acacia House, Acacia Park Drive, Apperley Bridge, West Yorkshire BD10 0PH (tel 0113 250 9959); Academic Unit of Paediatrics, University of Leeds, D Floor, Clarendon Wing, Leeds General Infirmary, Leeds LS2 9NS (tel 0113 292 3905, fax 0113 292 3902, e-mail medmil@leeds.ac.uk)

LEVENE OF PORTSOKEN, Baron (Life Peer UK 1997), of Portsoken in the City of London; Sir Peter Keith Levene; KBE (1989), JP (City of London 1984); s of Maurice Pierre Levene (d 1970), and Rose Levene (d 1991); *b* 8 December 1941; *Educ* City of London Sch, Univ of Manchester (BA); *m* 1966, Wendy Ann, da of Frederick Fraiman; 2 s, 1 da; *Career* chm United Scientific Holdings plc 1982–85 (md 1968–85), chm Defence Mfrs Assoc 1984–85, personal advsr to Sec of State for Defence 1984, chief of defence procurement MOD 1985–91, dir UK Nat Armaments 1988–91, chm European Nat Armaments Dirs 1989–90, personal advsr to Sec of State for the Environment 1991–92, personal advsr to Pres of the Bd of Trade 1992–95, efficiency advsr to the Prime Minister 1992–97; dep chm Wasserstein Perella & Co Ltd 1991–95, chm Docklands Light Railway 1991–94, chm and chief exec Canary Wharf Ltd 1993–96, sr advsr Morgan Stanley & Co Ltd 1996–98, dir Haymarket Group Ltd 1997–, chm Bankers Tst Int 1998–99, chm Investment Banking Europe Deutsche Bank 1999–2001, chm IFSL (formerly British Invisibles) 2000–, vice-chm Deutsche Bank 2001–02, non-exec dir J Sainsbury plc 2001–04, chm General Dynamics UK Ltd 2001–, chm Lloyd's 2002–, dir China Construction Bank 2006–; memb: Alcatel Chms Cncl 2000–03, Supervisory Bd Deutsche Börse AG 2004–05, Bd Total SA 2005–; govr: City of London Sch for Girls 1984–85, City of London Sch 1985–, Sir John Cass Primary Sch 1985–93 (dep chm); vice-pres City of London Red Cross, memb Ct HAC, chm London Homes for the Elderly 1990–93, Hon Col Cmdt RLC 1993– (RCT 1991–93); common cnclr Ward of Candlewick 1983–84, Alderman Ward of Portsoken 1984–95, Alderman Ward of Aldgate 2005–; Sheriff City of London 1995–96; Lord Mayor of London 1998–99; Master Worshipful Co of Carmen 1992–93, Liveryman Worshipful Co of Information Technologists, Hon Liveryman Worshipful Co of Management Conslts 2004–; fell QMC London 1995, Hon DSc City Univ 1998, Hon DSc Univ of London 2005; KStJ 1998 (OStJ 1996), Cdr Ordre Nationale du Mérite (France) 1996, Knight Cdr Order of Merit (Germany) 1998, Middle Cross Order of Merit (Hungary) 1999; *Recreations* skiing, swimming, watching association football, travel; *Clubs* Guildhall, City Livery, RAC; *Style—* The Lord Levene of Portsoken, KBE; ✉ One Lime Street, London EC3M 7HA (tel 020 7327 1000)

LEVENTHAL, Colin David; *b* 2 November 1946; *Educ* Univ of London (BA); *Career* slr 1971; head of copyright BBC until 1981, head of programme acquisition Channel Four TV 1981–86, dir of acquisition Channel Four TV 1987–97, md Channel Four International 1993–97, co-fndr of HAL Films 1998 (in partnership with Trea Hoving); *Recreations* film, television, theatre; *Style—* Colin Leventhal, Esq

LEVER, Prof Andrew Michael Lindsay; s of Ivor Lindsay Douglas Lever, and Sylvia Marion, *née* Tannock; *b* 23 June 1953; *Educ* Ripon GS, WNSM; *Career* various med posts 1978–82; MRC res fell 1983–84, Wellcome lectureship 1985–87, res fell Harvard Univ 1988–89, sr lectr St George's Hosp London 1989–1991; Univ of Cambridge: lectr and reader 1991–2000, fell Peterhouse 1993–, prof of infectious diseases 2000–; ed Jl of Infection 1996–2001, memb Gene Therapy Advsy Ctee; Croom lectr 1987 and 1992, Lennox K Black Prize 2001; Hon MD Univ of Cambridge 2001 (Hon MA 1998); FRCP 1993 (MRCP 1981), FRCPE 1993, FRCPath 1998 (MRCPath 1994), FMedSci 2000, FRSC 2006; *Publications* various scientific and clinical pubns on HIV and gene therapy; *Recreations* guitar, ornithology; *Style—* Prof Andrew Lever; ✉ University of Cambridge Department of Medicine, Addenbrooke's Hospital, Hills Road, Cambridge CB2 2QQ (tel 01233 330191, fax 01233 336486, e-mail tdb21@medschl.cam.ac.uk)

LEVER, His Hon Judge Bernard Lewis; s of Baron Lever (Life Peer, d 1977), by his w Ray; n of Baron Lever of Manchester (Life Peer, d 1995); *b* 1 February 1951; *Educ* Clifton, The Queen's Coll Oxford (Neale exhibitioner, MA); *m* 1985, Anne Helen, da of Patrick Chandler Gordon Ballingall, MBE, of Seaford, E Sussex; 2 da (Helen Jane b 28 Sept 1986, Isabel Elizabeth Rose b 2 March 1991); *Career* called to the Bar Middle Temple 1975, practised Northern Circuit 1975–2001, recorder of the Crown Court 1995–2001, circuit judge 2001–; standing counsel to Inland Revenue (Northern Circuit) 1997–2001; co-fndr of SDP in NW 1981, Parly candidate (SDP) Manchester Withington 1983; *Recreations* walking, music, fishing, picking up litter; *Clubs* Vincent's (Oxford); *Style—* His Hon Judge Lever; ✉ Manchester Crown Court, Minshull Street, Manchester M1 3FS (tel 0161 954 7500)

LEVER, Sir (Tresham) Christopher Arthur Lindsay; 3 Bt (UK 1911), of Hans Crescent, Chelsea; s of Sir Tresham Joseph Philip Lever, 2 Bt, FRSL (d 1975), and Frances Yowart Parker, *née* Goodwin (d 1959); step s of Pamela, Lady Lever (d 2003), da of Lt-Col the Hon Malcolm Bowes-Lyon, former w of Lord Malcolm Avondale Douglas-Hamilton; *b* 9 January 1932; *Educ* Eton, Trinity Coll Cambridge (MA); *m* 1, 1970 (m dis 1974), Susan Mary, da of late John Armytage Nicholson, of Crossmolina, Co Mayo, and Dunboyne, Co Meath; m 2, 1975, Linda Weightman McDowell, da of late James Jepson Goulden, of Tennessee, USA; *Heir* none; *Career* author; Lt 17/21 Lancers 1950; Peat Marwick Mitchell & Co 1954–55, Kitcat & Aitken 1955–56, dir: John Barran & Sons Ltd (later plc) 1956–64; conslt: Zoo Check Tst 1984–91, Born Free Fndn 1991–2003; memb: Cncl Soc for the Protection of Animals in N Africa 1986–88, Cncl Br Tst for Ornithology 1988–91, SOS Sahel Int (UK) 1995–; chm: African Fund for Endangered Wildlife (UK) 1987–90, Br Tst for Ornithology Nat Centre Appeal 1987–92, Ruaha Tst 1990–95, UK Elephant Gp 1991–92; Int Tst for Nature Conservation: tstee 1980–92, vice-pres 1986–91, pres 1991–92; dir: World Society for the Protection of Animals 1998–2003, Conservation, Educn and Research Tst (Earthwatch) 2003–04; IUCN: memb Species Survival Cmmn 1988–, memb UK Ctee 1989–; memb Cncl of Ambass World Wide Fund for Nature (UK) 1999–, fell WWF-UK 2005; memb Editorial Bd Jl of Applied Herpetology 2005–; patron: Rhino Rescue Tst 1985–2003 (tstee 1986–91), Lynx Educnl Tst for Animal Welfare 1991–, Respect for Animals 1995–; vice-patron Conservation Fndn 2005–06; hon life pres Tusk Tst 2004 (chm 1990–2004); hon life memb Brontë Soc 1988; FLS, FRGS; *Books* Goldsmiths and Silversmiths of England (1975), The Naturalized Animals of the British Isles (1977, paperback edn 1979), Wildlife' 80 - The World Conservation Yearbook (contrib 1980), Evolution of Domesticated Animals (contrib 1984), Naturalized Mammals of the World (1985), Beyond the Bars - The Zoo Dilemma (contrib 1987), Naturalized Birds of the World (1987), For the Love of Animals (contrib 1989), The Mandarin Duck (1990), They Dined on Eland - The Story of the Acclimatisation Societies (1992), The New Atlas of Breeding Birds in Britain and Ireland: 1988–91 (contrib, 1993), Naturalized Animals: The Ecology of Successfully Introduced Species (1994), The Introduction and Naturalisation of Birds (contrib, 1996), Naturalized Fishes of the World (1996), Stocking and Introduction of Fish (1997), The EBCC Atlas of European Breeding Birds: Their Distribution and Abundance (contrib, 1997), The Cane Toad: The History and Ecology of a Successful Colonist (2001), The Migration Atlas: Movements of the Birds of Britain and Ireland (contrib, 2002), Naturalized Reptiles and Amphibians of the World (2003), Biological Invasions: From Ecology to Control (contrib, 2005), Naturalised Birds of the World (2005); *Recreations* watching and photographing wildlife, ghillying, golf; *Clubs* Boodle's, Swinley Forest Golf; *Style—* Sir Christopher Lever, Bt; ✉ Newell House, Winkfield, Berkshire SL4 4SE (tel 01344 882604, fax 01344 891744)

L

LEVER, Colin David; s of Michael Lever (d 1991), of London, and Susan, *née* Cohen (d 1987); *b* 4 September 1938; *Educ* Hendon GS, Balliol Coll Oxford (MA); *m* 2 Sept 1962, Ruth, da of Rev Harry Bornstein (d 1943); 3 da (Claire b 1966, Joy b 1970, Naomi b 1973), 1 s (Alexander b 1968); *Career* ptnr Bacon & Woodrow 1966–99 (actuarial trainee 1960, sr ptnr 1982–93); dir: Pearl Group, AMP (UK) plc, AMP (UK) Holdings 1997–2003; chm Nat Assoc Pension Funds 1985–87 (memb Cncl 1981–83, vice-chm 1983–85); FIA 1965; *Books* Pension Fund Investment (with D P Hager, 1989); *Recreations* gardening, flying, narrow boating; *Style—* Colin Lever, Esq; ✉ 38 Oakleigh Park South, London N20 9JN (tel 020 8445 7880)

LEVER, Dr Eric G; s of Sam Lever (d 1978), and Freda, *née* Mann; *b* 5 April 1947; *Educ* Quintin Sch, Trinity Coll Cambridge (MA, MB BChir), Univ Coll Med Sch, Univ of Chicago (Endocrinology Diabetes fell); *m* 26 Aug 1985, Nicola, da of Bernard Langdon; 4 s (Elliott b 21 Jan 1988, Michael b 2 May 1989, Charles b 27 June 1994, Simon b 22 March 1996); *Career* jr hosp dr appts 1975–88: Univ Coll Hosp, Edgware Gen Hosp, Univ Hosp Nottingham, Royal Marsden Hosp, Hammersmith Hosp, King's Coll Hosp London, Billings Hosp Chicago; full-time private conslt in endocrinology diabetes and gen med 1988–: London Clinic, Wellington Hosp, Hosp of St John and St Elizabeth; MRCP 1978, FRSM 1988; author of many papers on endocrinology and diabetes; *Recreations* art, music and the philosophy of ideas; *Style—* Dr Eric G Lever; ✉ Wellington Hospital, London NW8 9LE (tel 020 8586 3213, fax 020 8371 8396)

LEVER, Sir Jeremy Frederick; KCMG (2002), QC (England and Wales 1972, N Ireland 1988); s of Arnold Lever (d 1980), and Elizabeth Cramer, *née* Nathan (d 1993); *b* 23 June 1933; *Educ* Bradfield Coll, UC Oxford, Nuffield Coll Oxford, All Souls Coll Oxford (MA); *Partner* (civil partnership 2006), Brian Collie; *Career* 2 Lt RA (E African Artillery) 1952–53; called to the Bar Gray's Inn 1957 (bencher 1985); head of chambers 1989–96; sr dean All Souls Coll Oxford 1988– (fell 1957–, sub warden 1982–84); visiting prof Wissenschaftszentrum Berlin für Sozialforschung 1999; memb: Arbitral Tbnl US/UK Arbitration concerning Heathrow Airport User Charges 1988–94, Ind Inquiry Univ of Portsmouth 1995; chm: Oftel Advsy Bd on Fair Trading in Telecommunications 1996–2000, Performing Right Soc Appeals Panel 1996–2002; non-exec dir: Dunlop Hldgs Ltd 1973–80, Wellcome Fndn Ltd 1983–94; memb Cncl and Ctee of Mgmnt Br Inst of Int and Comparative Law 1987–2004; pres Oxford Union Soc 1957 (tstee 1972–77 and 1988–); govr Berkhamsted Schs 1985–95; FRSA 1997; *Books* Chitty on Contracts (ed, 1961, 1968, 1972, 1977), Tort Law (co-author, 2000); *Recreations* music, ceramics; *Clubs* Garrick; *Style—* Sir Jeremy Lever, KCMG, QC; ✉ Monckton Chambers, 1 Raymond Buildings, Gray's Inn, London WC1R 5NR (tel 020 7405 7211, fax 020 7405 2084, e-mail chambers@monckton.com); All Souls College, Oxford OX1 4AL (tel 01865 279379, fax 01865 279299)

LEVER, John Darcy; s of Prof Jeffery Darcy Lever, of Ystrad Mynach, Mid Glamorgan, and Margaret Emily, *née* Eastwood; *b* 14 January 1952; *Educ* Westminster, Trinity Coll Cambridge (MA, Rowing blue), ChCh Oxford (PGCE); *m* 30 Dec 1981, Alisoun Margaret, da of Dr Alastair Pratt Yule; 2 da (Emily Clare b 10 Aug 1983, Rebecca Mary b 24 May 1988), 1 s (James Edward Darcy 21 Feb 1985); *Career* asst master St Edward's Oxford 1974–76; Winchester Coll: asst master 1976–84, housemaster 1984–92; headmaster Canford Sch 1992–; *Recreations* rowing, walking, solitude; *Style—* John Lever, Esq; ✉ Canford School, Wimborne, Dorset BH21 3AD (tel 01202 847434)

LEVER, (Keith) Mark; s of Keith Lever (d 2002), and Rosemary Anne, *née* Wakeley; *b* 20 September 1960, Luton, Beds; *Educ* Wakeman GS Shrewsbury, Royal Holloway Coll London (BSc), Cranfield Univ (MBA); *m* 11 Nov 1989, Amanda Jane Sackville, *née*

Davison; 4 s (William b 7 April 1994, Edward b 22 June 1997, Thomas b 4 Jan 1999, Joseph b 21 Feb 2002); *Career* ptnr and nat dir of HR and trg Kidsons Impey 1995; WRVS: dir of trg 1996, dir of strategic devpt 1999, chief exec 2002–; MICAEW 1986, MCIPD 1987, MCIM 2001; *Recreations* golf, music, Chelsea FC, family, charity discos; *Clubs* Harrow Golf; *Style*— Mark Lever, Esq; ✉ WRVS, Garden House, Milton Hill, Abingdon, Oxfordshire OX13 6AD (tel 01235 442900, fax 01235 861166, e-mail mark.lever@wrvs.org.uk)

LEVER, Sir Paul; KCMG (1998, CMG 1991); s of John Morrison Lever (d 1966), and Doris Grace, *née* Battey (d 1981); b 31 March 1944; *Educ* St Paul's, The Queen's Coll Oxford; m 1990, Patricia Anne, *née* Ramsey; *Career* HM Dip Serv 1966–2003: FCO 1966–67, third sec Helsinki 1967–71, second sec UK Delgn to NATO 1971–73, FCO 1973–81 (asst private sec to Foreign Sec 1978–81), chef de cabinet to Vice-Pres EC 1981–85, head UN Dept then Security Policy Dept FCO 1985–90, ambass and head UK Delgn to Conventional Forces in Europe Negotiations Vienna 1990–92, dep sec to Cabinet and chm Jt Intelligence Ctee 1994–96, economic dir FCO 1996–97, ambass to Germany 1998–2003; global devpt dir RWE Thames Water; chm RUSI; *Style*— Sir Paul Lever, KCMG; ✉ Royal United Services Institute, Whitehall, London SW1A 2ET

LEVER, Paul Ronald Scott; s of Thomas Denis Lever, of Sandy Gate, S Yorks, and Mary Barclay, *née* Scott; b 9 December 1946; m 23 Sept 1964, Elisabeth Barbara, da of Sir Richard Hughes, Bt (d 1970); 1 s (Christopher Mark b 17 July 1965), 2 da (Alison Clare b 25 Feb 1967, Catherine Elisabeth b 17 June 1969); *Career* md Tower Housewares (subsids of TI Gp) 1979–83, chm Darius Industrial Investments 1983–86, md Crown Paints Div (subsid of Reed International) 1986–88, md Crown Berger Europe Ltd 1988–89 (chm Ireland 1988–89); chm: Cuprinol Ltd 1988–89, Williams European Consumer Products Division (subsids of Williams Holdings plc) 1989, Alexander Drew & Sons Ltd 1990–92, BSM Group plc 1992–97, Dan Holdings Ltd 1994–97, Ashworth Hosp Authy 1996–99, Oxford Aviation Holdings Ltd 1997–2000, ATC Ltd, Bishop Gp Ltd, Intellexis plc, Lynwood Gp; exec chm Lionheart plc 1989–96, dir Crown Agents PSG 1998–2001 (special advsr 2001–04); Int Mgmnt Centre Europe: industrial fell mktg and business policy 1984, industrial prof of strategic mgmnt 1986, elected master teacher 1987, elected memb Cncl 1988, elected chm Cncl 1992; chm Service Authorities for the National Crime Squad (NCS) and the National Criminal Intelligence Service (NCIS) 2004– (memb 1998–, vice-chm 2003–04); memb Editorial Bd Management Digest 1987; FRSA; *Recreations* cooking, listening to classical music, watching cricket; *Clubs* Reform, MCC; *Style*— Paul Lever, Esq

LEVERETT, David; s of George Edgar Leverett, of Nottingham, and Doris, *née* Tebbit; b 12 January 1938; *Educ* John Player Sch Nottingham, Nottingham Sch of Art (NDD), Royal Acad Schs London (post grad dip, travelling scholar); m Sonia Loretta Wilhmena Holme; 2 s (Jason David b 2 June 1967, Simeon b 19 Jan 1970); *Career* artist; variously art teacher at instns incl: RCA, Dublin Coll of Art, Cooper Union NY; currently reg visiting lectr Slade Sch UCL; Sargant fell Br Sch at Rome 1990–91; poetry performance Running the Shadow (nat tour); *Solo Exhibitions* incl: Redfern Gallery London 1965, 1968, 1970, 1972, 1987 and 1990, Editions Alecto NY 1970, Studio La Citta Verona 1971, Galleria del Cavallino Venice 1972, Galerie Britta Herberle Frankfurt 1972, Ikon Gallery Birmingham 1973, ICA London 1974, Galleria G7 Bologna 1975, Gallery Desmos Athens 1975, Galerie Skulima Berlin 1975, Galleria Vinciana Milan 1976, Oliver Dowling Gallery Dublin 1977, Janus Suite Riverside Studios London 1979, Studio Gallery Palace of Culture Warsaw 1980, Gallery III Lisbon 1983, Bildornan Gallery Umea 1984, Curwen Gallery London 1985, Jersey Arts Centre St Helier 1986, Thumb Gallery London 1990 and 1992, Jill George Gallery London 1995, 1997 and 2001, Gallery In Collaboration Santa Monica 1996, Gallerie Maximillian Aspen 1998; *Group Exhibitions* incl: British Painting Monte Carlo 1966, British Painting and Sculpture (Whitechapel Gallery London) 1968, Play Orbit (ICA) 1969, British Drawing (Angela Flowers Gallery London) 1972, 6 Artists (Inglesi Galleria lo Spazio Berscia and Gallery Godel Rome) 1974, British Painting 1974 (Hayward Gallery) 1974, Empirica (Rimini City Museum) 1975, British Painting RA 1952–77 British Drawing from 1945 (Whitworth Art Gallery Manchester) 1979, Cralylus XV São Paulo 1979, Contemporary Choice 1979–81 (Contemporary Arts Soc and Serpentine Gallery London) 1982, One of a Kind (Maryland Inst Baltimore) 1983, Bradford Print Biennale Selection (V&A) 1986, Decade Exhbn Dublin 1986, Mediterranean Bienal graphic art Athens 1988, Ogle Fine Art 1989 and 1990, Thumb Gallery 1989, Int Art Fair Olympia 1990, Cabinet Paintings (Gillian Jason Gallery) 1991, Special Presentation (Merrill Chase Gallery Chicago) 1991, 1992 and 1995, Contraprint (Br Sch at Rome) 1991, Omphalos Series (Galleria Gianfranco Rosini Riccione) 1991, Cyril Gerber Gallery 1992, Cabinet Paintings (Hove Museum and Art Gallery and Glynn Vivian Art Gallery and Museum) 1992, Drawings 3 (Jill George Gallery London) 1995, Drawings (V&A) 1996, Small is Beautiful (Flowers East) 1998, Landmarks (Jill George Gallery) 1999, Mountain (Woverhampton Museum of Art) 1999, Galerie Maximillian Aspen 1999 Landscape (Flowers East) 1999, Scholar Fine Art London 2000, Editions Alecto 1960–1981 (Birmingham Museum and Art Gallery) 2000, A Fury for Prints (Whitworth Art Gallery Manchester) 2003, War and Peace (Flowers Central London) 2003; *Work in Public Collections* incl: Arts Cncl of GB, Br Cncl, V&A, Contemporary Arts Soc, Tate Gallery, Museum of Peace Hiroshima, Miny of Culture Athens, The State Collection Palace of Culture Warsaw, MOMA Sao Paulo, MOMA Campione, State Art Gallery NSW, Inst of Contemporary Graphics, MOMA Zagreb, Modern Art Gallery Koszalim, Umea Kommun, DOE, Reading Museum of Art, Nottingham City Museum, Univ of Liverpool, Univ of Warwick, British Rail Collection, London Press Exchange; *Publications* incl: A Possible Future - New Painting (1973), Colour in Painting - a European situation (1976), The Citadel (1994), The David Leverett Portfolio (1995), Dance Through the Labyrinth of Sand (1997), Between Night and Daylight (2001); *Style*— David Leverett, Esq; ✉ 132 Leighton Road, London NW5 2RG (tel 020 7485 3317, e-mail david@ecoart.demon.co.uk, website www.ecoart.demon.co.uk)

LEVESON, Rt Hon Lord Justice; Rt Hon Sir Brian Henry Leveson; kt (2000), PC (2006); s of Dr Ivan Leveson (d 1980), of Liverpool, and Elaine, *née* Rivlin (d 1983); b 22 June 1949; *Educ* Liverpool Coll, Merton Coll Oxford (MA); m 20 Dec 1981, Lynne Rose, da of Aubrey Fishel (d 1987), of Wallasey; 2 s (Andrew b 1983, James b 1989), 1 da (Claire b 1984); *Career* called to the Bar Middle Temple 1970 (bencher 1995), QC 1986; lectr in law Univ of Liverpool 1971–81, recorder of the Crown Court 1988–2000, dep High Court judge 1998–2000, judge of the High Court of Justice (Queen's Bench Div) 2000–, presiding judge Northern Circuit 2002–05, Lord Justice of Appeal 2006–, sr presiding judge for England and Wales 2007–; memb: Cncl Univ of Liverpool 1983–92, Parole Bd 1992–95, Cncl UCS Hampstead 1998–; fndn govr Liverpool Coll 2001; hon fell Merton Coll Oxford 2001; *Style*— The Rt Hon Lord Justice Leveson; ✉ Royal Courts of Justice, Strand, London WC2A 2LL

LEVETE, Amanda; da of Michael Levete (d 2003), and Gina, *née* Seagrim; b 17 November 1955, Bridgend; *Educ* AA Sch of Architecture; m 1991 (m dis), Jan Kaplicky, *qv*; 1 s (Josef); *Career* architect; in practice: Alsop & Lyall 1980–81, YRM Architects 1982–84, Richard Rogers & Partners 1984–89; ptnr Future Systems 1989– (projects incl Natwest Media Centre Lord's Cricket Ground and Selfridges Birmingham); *Style*— Ms Amanda Levete; ✉ Future Systems, The Warehouse, 20 Victoria Gardens, London W11 3PE (tel 020 7243 7670, fax 020 7243 7690, e-mail email@future-systems.com)

LEVETT, Michael; m 1966, Jill Aston; 2 s, 1 da; *Career* chm Old Mutual plc 1990–; non-exec dir: Barloworld Ltd 1985–, Nedcor Ltd 1987–, Old Mutual South Africa Tst plc 1994–,

South African Breweries plc 1999–; tstee Nelso Mandela Children's Fund, Coll of Medicine Fndn, WWF for Nature; founding patron The Children's Hospital Tst; fell Acturial Soc of SA, FIA, FFA; *Style*— Michael Levett, Esq

LEVEY, Sir Michael Vincent; kt (1980), LVO (1965); s of O L H Levey and Gladys Mary Milestone; b 8 June 1927; *Educ* The Oratory, Exeter Coll Oxford; m 1954, Brigid Antonia (the author Brigid Brophy; d 1995), o da of John Brophy (d 1965); 1 da; *Career* served Army 1945–48; Slade prof of fine art Univ of Cambridge 1963–64, dir Nat Gallery 1973–86 (asst keeper 1951–66); Slade prof of fine art Univ of Oxford 1994–95; hon fellow Exeter Coll Oxford 1973; Hon DLitt Univ of Manchester; FBA, FRSL; *Books* 14 vols non fiction, 3 vols fiction; *Style*— Sir Michael Levey, LVO, FBA, FRSL; ✉ 36 Little Lane, Louth, Lincolnshire LN11 9DU

LEVI, Renato (Sonny); s of Mario Levi (d 1972), and Eleonora, *née* Ciravegna; b 3 September 1926; *Educ* Coll de Cannes, St Paul's Sch Darjeeling, Bishop Cotton Sch Simla, Coll of Aeronautical Engrg London; m 12 June 1954, Ann Joan, da of John Douglas Watson (d 1969); 1 da (Gina b 1955), 2 s (Martin b 1958, Christopher b 1962); *Career* RAF: joined 1945, cmmnd 1946, demobbed 1948; designer high speed watercraft AFCO Ltd Bombay 1951–60, chief designer Navaltecnica Anzio 1960–65, freelance designer 1965–; work incl: Cowes-Torquay powerboat race winners, A Speranziella 1963, Surfury 1967, Virgin Atlantic Challenger II (1986 Blue Riband holder); originator of delta hull form and Levi surface propulsion; RDI 1987, FCSD 1989; *Books* Dhows to Deltas (1971), Milestones in My Designs (1992); *Recreations* power boating and travelling; *Clubs* Royal London Yacht; *Style*— Sonny Levi, Esq; ✉ c/o Faculty of Royal Designers for Industry, RSA, 8 John Adam Street, London WC2N 6EZ

LEVIEN, Robin Hugh; s of John Blomefield Levien, of Norwich, Norfolk, and Louis Beryl, *née* Squire; b 5 May 1952; *Educ* Bearwood Coll Wokingham, Central Sch of Art and Design (BA), Royal Coll of Art (MA); m 21 Aug 1978, Patricia Anne, da of Alan Newby Stainton; *Career* ceramics and glass designer; ptnr: Queensberry Hunt 1982–95 (joined 1977), Queensberry Hunt Levien (following name change) 1995–99, Studio Levien 1999–; mass market products for mfrs and retailers incl: Thomas China, Wedgwood, Ideal Standard, American Standard, Habitat, Dartington Crystal; major products incl: Trend dinnerware shape for Thomas China 1981 (Die Gute Industrieform Award Hanover 1982, Golden Flame Award Valencia 1983), Studio bathroom range for Ideal Standard 1986 (BT Prize BBC Design Awards 1987, runner-up DBA Design Effectiveness Awards 1989), Domi bathroom taps for Ideal Standard 1989 (runner-up Design Week Awards 1990), Symphony range of bathtubs for American Standard 1990 (Interior Design Product Award American Soc of Interior Designers 1991), Kyomi bathroom range for Ideal Standard 1996 (winner Design Week Award 1997), Home Elements kitchenware range for Villeroy and Boch 2003; lectr: RCA, Central St Martins Sch of Art and N Staffordshire Univ; visiting prof London Inst 1998; chm Product Design Panel Student Design Directions Awards RSA 1991–2000, memb Faculty of Royal Designers for Industry RSA; memb Friends of the Earth; fndr memb Brewcombe Woodland Tst, Cncl RCA 2001–; Hon Dr Staffordshire Univ 2006; FRSA, RDI 1995; *Recreations* 'Fulham Farmer' on 1952 Ferguson tractor, films, cooking; *Style*— Robin Levien, Esq, RDI; ✉ Studio Levien, 1 La Gare, 51 Surrey Row, London SE1 0BZ (tel 020 7928 2244, fax 020 7928 2255, e-mail robin@studiolevien.com)

LEVIN, David Roger; s of Jack Levin (d 1995), of Durban, South Africa, and Elizabeth Isobel, *née* Robinson (d 1976); b 2 October 1949; *Educ* Kearsney Coll, Univ of Natal, Univ of Sussex; m 1977, Jean Isobel, da of Maj John Paxton-Hall; *Career* mangr Cutty Sark Hotel Natal 1971–73, asst master Whitgift Sch 1974–75, slr Radcliffe & Co 1976–78, asst master Portsmouth GS 1978–80, head of economics Cheltenham Coll 1980–93 (second master 1987–93), headmaster Royal GS High Wycombe 1993–99, headmaster City of London Sch 1999–; chm Supporting Local Schools Initiative in Lambeth 1999–2002, memb City of London Acad Steering Gp 2001–03; govr Canford Sch 1996–; memb Secondary Heads Assoc 1993; Freeman City of London 2001; FRSA 1992; *Recreations* long distance swimming (organised and participated in second-ever cross-channel swimming relay race 1987), surfing, military history, theatre, opera; *Clubs* East India; *Style*— David Levin, Esq; ✉ City of London School, Queen Victoria Street, London EC4V 3AL (tel 020 7489 0291, fax 020 7329 6887, mobile 07947 429568, e-mail headmaster@clsb.org.uk)

LEVINE, Gemma Jennifer Ann; da of Ellis Josephs (d 1991), and Mae, *née* Phillips (d 2000); b 10 January 1939; *Educ* Hasmonean GS; m 5 March 1961 (m dis 1986), Eric A Levine, s of Jack D Levine; 2 s (James Andrew b 20 Nov 1963, Adam Edward b 17 June 1965); *Career* antique prints dealer 1961–, interior designer 1970–75, professional photographer 1975–, author 1978–; FRSA 1990; *Exhibitions* Four Seasons (photographs and watercolours, Casson Gallery London) 1977, With Henry Moore (photographs, Serpentine Gallery London (Arts Cncl of GB) and The Arts Club London) 1978, My Jerusalem (photographs and poetry, Jerusalem Theatre Gallery 1982 and The Royal Festival Hall 1983), Henry Moore (photographs, Tel-Aviv Univ) 1982, Henry Moore - Wood Sculpture (The Barbican London 1983, Leeds City Art Gallery 1984 and House of Commons 1985), Jerusalem (photographs, House of Commons) 1983, Tel-Aviv - Faces & Places (Tel-Aviv) 1984, Ethiopian Jews (Manor House London) 1985, Faces of the 80's (The Barbican London, opened by The Rt Hon Margaret Thatcher) 1987, Faces of British Theatre (The Royal Nat Theatre London, opened by HRH Prince Edward) 1990, Memories (The Berkeley Square Gallery) 1998, Gemma Levine 20 Years of Photography - Retrospective (Tom Blau Gallery for Camera Press) 1995, People of the 90's (Catto Gallery Hampstead, Cafe Royal, Barbican, Virgin Airways Terminal 3, Grosvenor House Gallery) 1995, Henry Moore (photographs, Berkeley Square Gallery) 1996–97, Gemma Levine 2000 (for the City of Westminster, Berkeley Square London), Celebration of Gemma Levine: Retrospective 25 Years (Scotts Restaurant Mayfair), Celebration of 25 Years Retrospective (Nat Portrait Gallery) 2001, Claridge's (Claridge's and Berkeley Square Gallery London) 2004, Israel Retrospective 1975–85 (Berkeley Square Gallery London) 2005; *Publications* 'Israel' Faces and Places (photographs, 1978), Living with The Bible (photographs and watercolours, 1978), With Henry Moore (photographs and taped text, 1978, 4 edn 1984), We live in Israel (photographs and text, 1981), Living in Jerusalem (1982), The Young Inheritors (photographs, 1982), Henry Moore - Wood Sculpture (photographs and taped text, 1983), Henry Moore (illustrated biography, 1985), Faces of the 80's (text by Jeffrey Archer, foreword by The Rt Hon Margaret Thatcher, 1987), Faces of British Theatre (text by Jonathan Miller, foreword by John Gielgud, 1990), People of the 90's (caption text by Sheridan Morley, foreword by HRH The Princess of Wales, 1995), Memories (foreword by Jonathan Miller, 1998), My Favourite Hymn (photographs, 1999), Claridge's: Within the Image (2004); *Recreations* the Arts, music; *Style*— Mrs Gemma Levine; ✉ Flat 19, Claridge House, 32 Davies Street, London W1K 4ND (fax 020 7491 4496)

LEVINGE, Sir Richard George Robin; 12 Bt (I 1704), of High Park, Westmeath; s of Maj Sir Richard Vere Henry Levinge, 11 Bt, MBE (d 1984), and his 1 w, Barbara Mary (d 1997), da of George Jardine Kidston, CMG (d 1954); b 18 December 1946; m 1, 1969 (m dis 1978), Hilary Jane, da of Dr Derek Mark, of Wingfield, Bray, Co Wicklow; 1 s (Richard Mark b 1970); m 2, 1978, Donna Maria Isabella d'Ardia Caracciolo, yr da of Don Ferdinando d'Ardia Caracciolo dei Principi di Cursi, of Haddington Road, Dublin 4; 1 s (Robin Edward b 1978), 1 da (Melissa Louise b 1980); *Heir* s, Richard Levinge; *Style*— Sir Richard Levinge, Bt; ✉ Clohamon House, Bunclody, Co Wexford

LEVINSON, Hugh Alexander; s of Clive John Levinson, and Doris Frieda Levinson; *Educ* Hove Co GS for Boys, Blatchington Mill Sch, Emmanuel Coll Cambridge; *Career* teacher

Kanto Gakuen Univ Japan 1985–87; trainee reporter BBC local radio 1987, reporter BBC Radio Merseyside 1987–90, sub ed The Japan Times Tokyo 1990–93, prodr The World at One (BBC Radio 4) 1993–97, prodr and reporter BBC Radio world current affairs 1997–; *Recreations* conjuring, playing guitar, running (slowly); *Clubs* Magic Circle; *Style*— Hugh Levinson, Esq; ✉ Room 1252, BBC, White City, 201 Wood Lane, London W12 7TS (tel 020 8752 6203)

LEVINSON, Jan Matthew; s of David Levinson, of Israel, and Pearl Shein, *née* Rose, of Edinburgh; *b* 8 May 1968, Bury; *Educ* Manchester Grammar, Univ of Newcastle upon Tyne (LLB), Coll of Law Chester; *m* 17 Aug 1997, Jayne, *née* Flacks; 1 s (Joshua *b* 2 Nov 1999), 2 da (Cate, Anya (twins) *b* 28 Dec 2001); *Career* slr; ptnr: Hammonds 1999–2003 (joined 1990), Beachcroft LLP 2003–; contrib: The Lawyer 2000, Law Soc Gazette 2005; memb: Law Soc 1990, Property Litigation Assoc (also memb Ctee), British Assoc for Sport and the Law; *Recreations* travel, sport, theatre, skiing, running; *Style*— Jan Levinson, Esq; ✉ Beachcroft LLP, St Ann's House, St Ann Street, Manchester M2 7LP (tel 0161 934 3000, fax 0161 934 3743, e-mail jlevinson@beachcroft.co.uk)

LEVINSON, Prof Stephen Curtis; *b* 6 December 1947; *Educ* King's Coll Cambridge (sr scholar, BA), Univ of Calif Berkeley (MA, Fulbright scholar, special career fell, PhD); *m* 18 Sept 1976, Penelope, *née* Brown; 1 s (*b* Oct 1980); *Career* teaching asst in linguistic anthropology Univ of Calif Berkeley 1972–73; Univ of Cambridge: asst lectr 1975–78, lectr in linguistics 1978–90, dir of studies archaeology and anthropology Emmanuel Coll 1978–80, Faculty Bd Archaeology and Anthropology Emmanuel Coll 1982–87, reader in linguistics 1991–94; prof Catholic Univ Nijmegen Netherlands 1995–, ldr Cognitive Anthropology Res Gp 1991–97 and dir Max-Planck-Inst for Psycholinguistics Nijmegen 1994–; Stanford Univ: visiting prof Linguistic Soc of America Linguistics Inst 1987, visiting assoc prof Dept of Linguistics 1987–88, convenor Research Seminar on Implicature Center for the Study of Language and Information 1987–88; memb editorial bd of numerous linguistics jls; memb High Table King's Coll Cambridge 1975–, Nijmegen lectr 1988, Stirling Prize American Anthropology Assoc 1992; memb: Scientific Ctee Fyssen Fndn Paris, Assoc of British Social Anthropologists, Linguistics Assoc of GB, American Anthropological Assoc, Linguistic Soc of America, European Assoc of Social Anthropologists, Academia Europaea; FBA; *Style*— Prof Stephen Levinson, FBA; ✉ Max Planck Institute, PB 310, NL 6500 AH Nijmegen, Netherlands (tel 00 31 24 352 1911, fax 00 31 24 352 1300)

LEVINSON, Stephen Michael (Steve); s of Alfred Levinson (d 1976), of London, and Golda Levinson (d 1992); *b* 19 January 1949; *Educ* Kilburn GS, Univ of Newcastle upon Tyne (BA); *m* 23 Dec 1973, Vivien Elaine, da of Col James Grant; 1 da (Jemma Debra *b* 3 Nov 1976), 1 s (Thomas Alex *b* 13 July 1979); *Career* grad trainee Westminster Press Ltd 1970–71, industrial corr South Shields Gazette 1972–73 (educn corr 1971–72); economics corr: Press Association Ltd 1976–86 (sub-ed/copy taster 1973–76), The Independent 1986–88, BBC TV 1988–92, Channel Four News ITN 1993–98, fndr dir HBL Media Ltd 1998–; editorial managing dir: World Finance Magazine 1999–, World Finance Television1999–, The Local Government Channel 2005–; Industrial Soc Broadcasting Award 1995–96, Winott Fndn Broadcast Award 1998–99; *Style*— Steve Levinson, Esq; ✉ HBL Media Ltd, Great Tichfield House, 14–18 Great Tichfield Street, London W1P 7AB (tel 020 7612 1830, e-mail steve@hblmedia.com)

LEVISON, Jeremy Ian; s of Eric Levison (d 2001), and Sarah Levison (d 2006); *b* 3 February 1952, Ryde, IOW; *Educ* Charterhouse, Univ of Kent at Canterbury (BA); *m* 1 Feb 2002, Norma; *Career* with Theodore Goddard 1974–80, ptnr Collyer Bristow 1980–98, founding ptnr Levison Meltzer Pigott 1998–; memb: Law Soc 1974, American Bar Assoc 1990, Resolution (formerly Slrs' Family Law Assoc); founding memb Int Acad of Matrimonial Lawyers (IAML) 1990; author of various articles in misc pubns; *Recreations* fine art, music, photography, cricket, fast cars, France, my wife!; *Clubs* Groucho; *Style*— Jeremy Levison, Esq; ✉ Levison Meltzer Pigott, 45 Ludgate Hill, London EC4M 7JU (tel 020 7556 2400, fax 020 7556 2401, e-mail jlevison@lmplaw.co.uk)

LEVITT, Tom; MP; s of John Levitt, and Joan, *née* Flood; *b* 10 April 1954; *Educ* Westwood HS Leek, Lancaster Univ (BSc), Univ of Oxford (PGCE); *m* 1983, Teresa, da of Waclaw and Halina Sledziewski; 1 da (Annie *b* 29 Nov 1983); *Career* science teacher: Wilts CC 1976–79, Glos CC 1980–91; supply teacher Staffs CC 1991–95, freelance research conslt sensory impairment and access to servs and info 1993–97, MP (Lab) High Peak 1997–; PPS to: Barbara Roche, MP 1999–2003, Baroness Amos 2003, Hilary Benn, MP 2003–; memb House of Commons Select Ctee on Standards and Privileges 1997–2003; sec Future of Europe Tst 1997–99, chm All-Pty Gp on Poland 1998–2000, co-chair All-Pty Minerals Gp 1998–2004, chm All-Pty Gp on the Voluntary Sector and Charities 2001– (jt vice-chm 1997–99), chair All-Pty Br-Swiss Parly Gp 2002–; cncllr: Cirencester PC 1983–87, Stroud DC 1990–92, Derbys CC 1993–97; chair Community Devpt Fndn 2004–; hon pres Buxton Arthritis Care; memb: Lab Pty 1977–, Br Deaf Assoc (life memb), Ct Univ of Derby 1997–, League Against Cruel Sports, Amnesty International; tstee RNID 1998–2003; *Publications* Sound Practice (for Local Govt Mgmnt Bd, 1995), Clear Access (for Local Govt Mgmnt Bd, 1997); *Recreations* cricket, theatre, walking; *Style*— Tom Levitt, Esq, MP; ✉ 20 Hardwick Street, Buxton, Derbyshire SK17 6DH (tel 01298 71111, fax 01298 71522)

LEVVY, George; *b* 30 November 1953; *Educ* Robert Gordon's Coll Aberdeen, Univ of Edinburgh (MB ChB); *m*; 1 da, 1 s; *Career* jr hosp doctor Edinburgh and London 1977–83, med dir Excerpta Medica Tokyo 1984–88, commercial mangr Countrywide Communications Group Ltd 1988–91, head mktg and communications British Red Cross 1991–94, chief exec Motor Neurone Disease Assoc 1995–2005, mgmnt conslt 2005–; FRSA; *Recreations* sailing, cricket, reading; *Style*— George Levvy, Esq; ✉ Beam Reach Consulting Ltd, 43 Kennett Road, Oxford OX3 7BH (tel 01865 766931, e-mail george@levvy.co.uk)

LEVY, Andrea; da of Winston Levy (d 1987), and Amy Levy; *b* 7 March 1956, London; *Educ* Highbury Hill HS, Middx Poly (BA); *m* Bill Mayblin; 2 step da (Maya *b* 11 June 1976, Hannah *b* 21 April 1978); *Career* novelist; judge: Saga Prize 1996, Orange Prize for Fiction 1997, Orange Futures 2001; memb Soc of Authors; FRSL; *Books* Every Light in the House Burnin' (1994), Never Far from Nowhere (1996), Fruit of the Lemon (1999, Arts Cncl Writers' Award), Small Island (2004, Whitbread Novel Award and Whitbread Book of the Year 2004, Orange Prize for Fiction 2004, Best Book Eurasia Region Cwlth Writers' Prize 2005, Best Overall Book Cwlth Writer's Prize 2005, Orange Best of the Best Prize 2005, shortlisted Literary Fiction Award British Book Awards, Romantic Novelists' Assoc Award and Decibel Writer of the Year British Book Awards all 2005); *Style*— Ms Andrea Levy; ✉ c/o David Grossman, David Grossman Literary Agency, 118B Holland Park Avenue, London W11 4UA (tel 020 7221 2770, fax 020 7221 1445, website www.andrealevy.co.uk)

LEVY, Andrew Paul; s of Isaac Oscar Levy (d 1976), and Ruby, *née* Ottolangui; *b* 17 June 1955; *Educ* Univ of Manchester (BA), Hertford Coll Oxford; *Career* grad trainee Ted Bates advtg, account mangr then planner Colman RSCG 1983–86, fndr ptnr and head of planning Madell Wilmot Pringle 1986–90, planner Lowe Howard-Spink 1990–92, planning dir Lowe Group 1992–93, fndr planning ptnr Mustoe Merriman Herring Levy 1993–; *Style*— Andrew Levy, Esq

LEVY, David Norman; s of Charles Levy, of Redbridge, Essex, and Mary, *née* Weisblatt; *b* 9 June 1948, London; *Educ* Wanstead Co HS, Hertford Coll Oxford (MA); *m* 20 Nov 1977, Ruth Marion, *née* Isenberg; 2 s (Jonathan Joseph *b* 6 Dec 1986, Simon Israel *b* 2 Jan 1991); *Career* admitted slr 1972; slr specialising in commercial real estate, especially

hotels and leisure; Paisner & Co: slr 1972–76, ptnr 1976–2001; ptnr Berwin Leighton Paisner 2001–; author of articles in various legal jls and the Estates Gazette; memb: Business in Sport and Leisure, Br Israel Law Assoc; former memb Bd of Mgmnt Finchley Synagogue; *Recreations* religious studies, watching football and other sport, family; *Style*— David Levy, Esq; ✉ Berwin Leighton Paisner, Adelaide House, London Bridge, London EC4R 9HA (tel 020 7760 1000, fax 020 7760 1111, e-mail david.levy@blplaw.com)

LEVY, His Hon Dennis Martyn; QC (1982); s of Conrad Levy, and late Tillie, *née* Swift; *b* 20 February 1936; *Educ* Clifton Coll, Gonville & Caius Coll Cambridge (MA); *m* 1967, Rachel Jonah; 1 s, 1 da; *Career* Granada Gp Ltd 1960–63, Time Products Ltd 1963–67; called to the Bar: Gray's Inn 1960, Hong Kong 1985, Turks and Caicos Is 1987; in practice 1967–91, recorder 1989–91 (asst recorder 1985–89), circuit judge (SE Circuit) 1991–2007; memb: Employment Appeal Tbnl 1994–2006, Lands Tbnl 1998; tstee Fair Trials Abroad; *Style*— His Hon Dennis Levy, QC; ✉ 25 Harley House, Marylebone Road, London NW1 5HE

LEVY, Baron (Life Peer UK 1997), of Mill Hill in the London Borough of Barnet; Michael Abraham Levy; s of Samuel levy (d 1975) of London, and Annie, *née* Berenbaum (d 1987); *b* 11 July 1944; *Educ* Hackney Downs GS; *m* 20 Aug 1967, Gilda, da of late Benjamin Altbach (d 1972), of London, and Emilie, *née* Kohn (d 2005); 1 s (Daniel Edward *b* 17 June 1968), 1 da (Juliet Bella *b* 18 May 1970); *Career* CA 1966–73, fndr and owner MAGNET (record and music publishing gp of cos) 1973–88, in music and entertainment industry 1992–97, conslt to various int cos 1998–; PM's personal envoy until 2007, advsr in Middle East; vice-chm: Phonographic Performance Ltd 1979–84, Br Phonographic Industry Ltd 1984–87; fndr and former chm Br Music Industry Awards Ctee (now Music Industry Tst), patron Br Music Industry Awards 1995–; pres Jewish Care 1998– (chm 1992–97), pres CSV 1998–; Jews Free Sch (JFS): govr 1990–95, pres 2001–; hon pres United Jt Israel Appeal 2000– (hon vice-pres 1994–2000, nat campaign chm Jt Israel Appeal (now UJIA) 1982–85); world chm Youth Aliyah Ctee Jewish Agency Bd of Govrs 1991–95; chm: Chief Rabbinate Awards for Excellence 1992–, Jewish Care Community Fndn 1995–, Fndn for Educn 1993–, Academies Sponsors Tst 2004–05; pres Specialist Schs and Acads Tst 2005–; vice-chm Central Cncl for Jewish Social Servs 1994–99; memb: Keren Hayesod World Bd of Govrs 1991–95, World Bd of Govrs Jewish Agency (GB rep) 1990–95, World Cmmn on Israeli-Diaspora Relations 1995–, Advsy Cncl Foreign Policy Centre 1997–, Int Bd of Govrs Peres Center for Peace 1997–, NCVO Advsy Ctee 1998–, Community Legal Service Champions Panel 1999–, Hon Ctee Israel Britain and Cwlth Assoc 2000–; chm Bd of Tstees New Policy Network Fndn 2000–; memb Exec Ctee Chai-Lifeline 2001–; tstee: Holocaust Educnl Tst 1998–; patron: Prostate Cancer Charitable Tst 1997–, Friends of Israel Educnl Tst 1998–, Save a Child's Heart Fndn 2000–, Simon Marks Jewish Primary School Tst 2002–; hon patron Cambridge Univ Jewish Soc 2002–; B'nai B'rith Award 1994, Friends of the Hebrew Univ of Jerusalem Scopus Award 1998, Israel Policy Forum (USA) Special Recognition Award 2003; Hon Dr Middlesex Univ 1999; FCA 1966; *Recreations* tennis, swimming; *Style*— The Rt Hon the Lord Levy; ✉ House of Lords, London SW1A 0PW (tel 020 7487 5174, fax 020 7486 7919, e-mail ml@lmalvy.demon.co.uk)

LEVY, Paul; s of Hyman Solomon Levy (d 1980), of Kentucky, USA, and Mrs Shirley Singer Meyers (d 1991); *b* 26 February 1941; *Educ* Univ of Chicago (AB, MA), UCL, Harvard Univ (PhD), Nuffield Coll Oxford; *m* 1977, Penelope, da of Clifford Marcus (d 1952); 2 da (Tatyana *b* 1981, Georgia *b* 1983); *Career* journalist and lapsed academic; food and wine ed The Observer 1980–92, wine and food columnist (as Amy DeVine) You magazine The Mail on Sunday 1992–, sr contrib Europe, Arts and Leisure page Wall Street Journal 1993–; regular contrib: The Independent, TLS, The Observer; frequent broadcaster on radio and TV; writer and presenter The Feast of Christmas (Channel 4) 1992 and 1993; national press specialist Writers' Commendations 1985 and 1987; tstee: Strachey Tst, Jane Grigson Tst; co-chair Oxford Symposium on Food and Cooking; memb Ct Oxford Brookes Univ; memb: Circle of Wine Writers, Critics Circle (music and theatre sections); FRSL; *Books* Lytton Strachey: The Really Interesting Question (ed, 1972), G E Moore and the Cambridge Apostles (1977, 3 edn 1989), The Shorter Strachey (ed with Michael Holroyd, 1980, 2 edn 1989), The Official Foodie Handbook (with Ann Barr, 1984), Out to Lunch (1986, new edn 2003), Finger-lickin' Good (1990), The Feast of Christmas (1992), The Penguin Book of Food and Drink (ed, 1996), Eminent Victorians, The Definitive Edition (ed, 2002), The Letters of Lytton Strachey (ed, 2005); *Recreations* being cooked for, drinking better wine, trying to remember; *Clubs* Groucho, Wednesday, Buckland; *Style*— Paul Levy, Esq; ✉ PO Box 35, Witney, Oxfordshire OX29 8YT (tel 01993 881312, fax 0871 715 3207, e-mail paullevy@paullevy.com, website www.paullevy.com)

LEVY, Peter Lawrence; OBE (1991); s of Joseph Levy, CBE, BEM (d 1990), and (Frances) Ninot, *née* Henwood; *b* 10 November 1939; *Educ* Charterhouse, Univ of London (BSc); *m* 29 June 1961, Colette, da of Harry Lynford; 2 da (Claudia Simone *b* 15 Nov 1962, Melanie Tamsin *b* 29 June 1965), 1 s (Jonathan David *b* 8 Aug 1967); *Career* ptnr DE & J Levy (surveyors) 1966–87, dir Stock Conversion plc 1985–86, chm Shaftesbury plc 1986–2004; chm: Inst for Jewish Policy Research, Jewish Chronicle Newspapers Ltd]; vice-pres: London Fedn of Clubs for Young People, Cystic Fibrosis Tst; Freeman City of London; FRICS; *Recreations* tennis, golf, walking, collecting old books and maps on London; *Clubs* RAC, Reform; *Style*— Peter Levy, Esq, OBE; ✉ 52 Springfield Road, London NW8 0QN (tel 020 7328 6109, fax 020 7372 7424, e-mail peterllevy@btinternet.com)

LEVY, Russell Anthony; s of David Baynes Levy, of Sydney, Aust, and Gabrielle, *née* Baumgarten; *Educ* Hyde Park HS Johannesburg, Univ of the Witwatersrand (BA), Univ of Warwick (LLB, Maxwell Law Prize), Coll of Law London; *m* 1985, Sarah Anne Rogers; 2 s (Samora Roger *b* 10 Feb 1989, Max Antony *b* 24 July 1992); *Career* articled clerk Farrer & Co 1982–84, admitted slr 1984; litigation slr Freehill, Hollingdale & Page Aust 1985, litigation slr Compton Carr 1985–90 (ptnr 1988–90), litigation ptnr Fisher Meredith 1990–91, ptnr Leigh, Day & Co 1991–; memb Dept of Constitutional Affairs working parties incl Civil Justice Cncl Clinical Negligence and Serious Injury Ctee; memb Steering Gp UK Cerebral Palsy Registers; worked with charities incl: Action Against Medical Accidents, Spinal Injuries Assoc, TB Network, Canon Collins Educnl Tst for Southern Africa; *Recreations* wildlife, snorkelling, memb Stroud Green Strollers; *Style*— Russell Levy, Esq; ✉ Leigh, Day & Co, 25 St John's Lane, London EC1M 4LB (tel 020 7650 1200, fax 020 7253 4433, e-mail russ@leighday.co.uk)

LEW, Dr Julian David Mathew; QC (2002); s of Rabbi Maurice Abram Lew (d 1989), of London, and Rachel Lew, JP, *née* Segalov (d 1998); *b* 3 February 1948, Johannesburg, South Africa; *Educ* Univ of London (LLB), Catholic Univ of Louvain (Doctorate Int Law); *m* 11 July 1978, Margot Gillian, da of Dr David Isaac Perk (d 1994), of Johannesburg, South Africa; 2 da (Ariella *b* 1981, Lauren *b* 1983); *Career* called to the Bar Middle Temple 1970; admitted slr 1981, attorney at law NY 1985; ptnr Herbert Smith 1995–2005, barr and arbitrator 2005–; dir and memb Court London Court of Int Arbitration; visiting prof and head Sch of Int Arbitration Queen Mary Univ of London; Freeman City of London 1985; FCIArb 1976; *Books* Selected Bibliography on East West Trade Law (1976), Applicable in International Commercial Arbitration (1978), Selected Bibliography on International Commercial Arbitration (1979), Contemporary Problems in International Commercial Arbitration (ed, 1986), International Trade: Law and Practice (ed jtly, 1985, 2 edn 1990), The Immunity of Arbitrators (ed, 1990), Enforcement of Foreign Judgements (ed jtly, 1994), Comparative International Commercial Arbitration (jtly, 2003), Parallel State and Arbitral Procedures in International Arbitration (jt ed, 2005), Pervasive Problems in International Arbitration (jt ed, 2006), Arbitration Insights: Twenty Years

L

of the Annual Lectures of the School of International Arbitration (jt ed, 2006); *Recreations* tennis, reading, religion; *Style*— Dr Julian D M Lew, QC; ✉ 20 Essex Street, London WC2R 3AL (tel 020 7842 1200, fax 020 7842 1270, e-mail jlew@20essexst.com)

LEWER, Michael Edward; CBE (2002), QC (1983); s of Lt-Col Stanley Gordon Lewer (d 1985), of Ashtead, Surrey, and Jeanie Mary, *née* Hay (d 1980); *b* 1 December 1933; *Educ* Tonbridge, Oriel Coll Oxford (MA); *m* 1965, Bridget Mary, da of Harry Anderson Clifford Gill (d 1980), of Buckland, Surrey; 2 s (William b 1966, Simon b 1969), 2 da (Natasha b 1967, Louise b 1977); *Career* called to the Bar Gray's Inn 1958 (bencher 1992); recorder of the Crown Court 1983–98, dep judge of the High Court 1989–98; memb Criminal Injuries Compensation Bd 1986–2000, memb Criminal Injuries Compensation Appeals Panel 1994– (chm 1994–2002), cmmr Parly Boundary Cmmn for England 1997–; *Style*— Michael Lewer, Esq, CBE, QC; ✉ 99 Queens Drive, London N4 2BE; Whitehouse Cottage, Horham, Suffolk; 76 Boulevard la Croisette, 06400 Cannes, France

LEWES, Bishop of 1997–; Rt Rev Wallace Parke Benn; s of William Benn (d 1956), and Lucinda Jane Benn (d 1985); *b* 6 August 1947; *Educ* St Andrew's Coll Dublin, UC Dublin (BA), Trinity Coll Bristol (DipTh awarded by Univ of London); *m* Lindsay Jane, da of Joseph Allan Develing; 1 da (Jessica Jane b 1983), 1 s (James William Thomas b 1987); *Career* ordained: deacon 1972, priest 1973; asst curate: St Mark's New Ferry Wirral Merseyside 1972–76, St Mary's Cheadle Cheshire 1976–82; vicar: St James the Great Audley Staffs 1982–87, St Peter's Harold Wood Essex 1987–97; pt/t hosp chaplain Harold Wood Hosp 1987–96; pres C of E Evangelical Cncl, pres Fellowship of Word and Spirit, memb Cncl REFORM, chm World Alive; *Publications* The Last Word (1996), Jesus Our Joy (2000); *Recreations* golf, reading, walking, keen rugby watcher and supporter; *Clubs* London Irish Rugby, National; *Style*— The Rt Rev the Bishop of Lewes; ✉ Bishop's Lodge, 16A Prideaux Road, Eastbourne, East Sussex BN21 2NB (tel 01323 648462, fax 01323 641514, e-mail lewes@clara.net)

LEWIN, Christopher George; s of George Farley Lewin, of Ascot, Berks, and Hilda Mary Emily, *née* Reynolds; *b* 15 December 1940; *Educ* Coopers' Cos Sch Bow London; *m* 1 Nov 1985, Robin Lynn, da of Robert Harry Stringham; 2 s (Andrew Christopher Philip b 3 July 1987, Peter Edward James b 19 Oct 1990); *Career* actuarial asst: Equity & Law Life Assurance Society 1956–63, London Transport Bd 1963–67; Br Railways Bd: actuarial asst 1967–70, controller corp pensions 1970–80, seconded memb Fin Insts Gp DOE 1981–82, co-ordinator private capital 1980–88; pensions dir Associated Newspapers Holdings Ltd 1989–92, head of gp pensions Guinness plc 1992–98, head of UK pensions Unilever plc 1998–2003, pensions mangr EDF Energy plc 2005; chm: Nat Fedn of Consumer Gps 1984–86, Jt Ctee on Corp Fin Inst and Faculty of Actuaries 1993–2001, working pty of actuaries and civil engrs (published RAMP (Risk Analysis and Management for Projects, 1998)) 1996–, Trading Standards Initiative (pensions industry) 2004–06; chm tstees Marconi plc pension scheme 2004–05; memb: Cncl Occupational Pensions Advsy Service 1983–97, Cncl Nat Assoc of Pension Funds 1983–87 and 1995–2003 (hon treas 1997–99), STRATrisk Steering Gp 2003–, Investment Ctee The Pensions Tst 2004–, Fin and Investment Bd of the Actuarial Profession; reviewer Deregulatory Review of Private Pensions Dept for Work and Pensions 2007; govr: NIESR, Pensions Policy Inst; Joseph Burn Prize Inst of Actuaries 1962, Messenger and Brown Prize Inst of Actuaries 1968, Inst of Actuaries Prize for paper Capital Projects (jt author) 1995, Finlaison Medal Inst of Actuaries; govr Central Fndn Sch for Girls 2001–04; FIA 1964, FSS, FPMI; *Publications* Pensions and Insurance before 1800: A Social History (2003), From Sumer to Spreadsheets: The History of Mathematical Table Making (contrib, 2004), Sarum Chronicle (contrib, 2005); author of numerous articles in various actuarial jls 1970–; *Recreations* family life, old books and manuscripts relating to British social history, old board games; *Clubs* Argonauts (chm 1997–98), Gallio (chm 2005–06), Actuaries; *Style*— Christopher Lewin, Esq; ✉ e-mail thirlestane1903@aol.com

LEWIN, Donald John (Don); OBE (1995); s of John Lewin (d 1997), of Chigwell, Essex, and Rose, *née* Hood (d 1951); *b* 11 June 1933; *m* 19 Dec 1953, Rose, da of James Palmer; 1 s (Clinton Stuart b 12 Aug 1961), 1 da (Deborah Michelle b 16 April 1968); *Career* founded Clinton Cards 1968 (chm 1988–); memb: Cons Pty, Royal Br Legion; patron Duke of Edinburgh Award; London Entrepreneur of the Year 2002; Freeman City of London 1995, Liveryman Worshipful Co of Poulters; MInstD 1982; *Recreations* swimming; *Style*— Don Lewin, OBE; ✉ Clinton Cards, The Crystal Building, Langston Road, Loughton, Essex IG10 3TH (tel 020 8502 3711, fax 020 8502 0295)

LEWIN, Prof John; s of Bernard Sidney Lewin (d 1987), of Newport, Dyfed, and Ruth, *née* French-Smith (d 1972); *b* 7 May 1940; *Educ* King Edward's Sch Bath, Univ of Southampton (BA, PhD); *m* 9 July 1966, Jane Elizabeth Sarah (d 2006), da of Capt Cecil Joy (d 1979), of Newport, Dyfed; 2 da (Jenny b 1967, Marianna b 1971); *Career* asst lectr Univ of Hull 1965–68; Univ of Wales Aberystwyth: prof of physical geography 1986–97 (prof emeritus 1997), dean Faculty of Science 1989–91, vice-princ 1993–97; FRGS 1963; *Books* Timescales in Geomorphology (ed, 1980), British Rivers (ed, 1981), Modern and Ancient Fluvial Systems (ed, 1983), Palaeohydrology in Practice (ed, 1987), Mediterranean Quarternary River Environments (ed, 1995); *Recreations* walking, reading; *Style*— Prof John Lewin; ✉ Institute of Geography and Earth Sciences, University of Wales, Aberystwyth, Ceredigion SY23 3DB (tel 01970 623111)

LEWIN, Lucille Patricia; da of Michael Witz (d 1969), of SA, and Elaine, *née* Hoffenberg (now Mrs Samuelson); *b* 27 July 1948; *Educ* Redhill Sch for Girls, Univ of Witwatersrand; *m* 1969, Richard Lewin, *qv*; 2 s (Joseph Michel b 1983, Jonathan Toby b 1988); *Career* fashion designer; design res Boston USA 1969–71, buyer Harvey Nichols 1973–76, fndr Whistles 1976–2001 (Br Design-led Retailer award Br Fashion Awards 1993 and 1995), creative dir Liberty 2002–03; *Style*— Ms Lucille Lewin

LEWIN, Richard David; s of Max Meyer Lewin (d 1987), of South Africa, and Evelyn Lilian Lewin (d 1964); *b* 17 February 1944; *Educ* Parktown Boys' HS Johannesburg, Univ of the Witwatersrand (BCom, Cert Theory of Accountancy), Harvard Univ (MBA); *m* 27 July 1969, Lucille Patricia, *qv*, da of Dr Michael Witz; 2 s (Joseph Michael b 23 July 1983, Jonathan Toby b 29 March 1988); *Career* Schwartz Fine Kane accountants 1966–68, Truworth Group retailers 1968–69, Burton Group fashion retailers 1972–74, Arthur Young consultancy 1975–78, md Whistles Ltd fashion retailers 1978–2001; CA (SA); *Recreations* skiing, squash; *Clubs* RAC, Harvard Club of London; *Style*— Richard Lewin, Esq

LEWIN, Russell Mark Ellerker; s of Robert Ellerker Lewin, of Canterbury, and Ann Margaret, *née* Bennett; *b* 21 March 1958; *Educ* Eltham Coll (Economics Prize, Drama Prize), St John's Coll Oxford (MA); *m* 1, 1983 (m dis), Emma Bridget, *née* Saunders; 2 s (Rowan b 1988, Kit b 1990); m 2, 2002, Sarah Hester Katriona, *née* Carter; 1 s (Jonah b 2003), 1 da (Pippa b 2005); *Career* Baker & McKenzie: trainee 1981–83, slr 1983–, seconded to Sydney office 1986–88, qualified slr NSW Aust 1987, ptnr 1990–, trainee recruitment ptnr 1994–96, qualified recruitment ptnr 1997–98, memb Mgmnt Ctee 1997–98, London managing ptnr 1998–2003, memb European Regnl Cncl and Global Policy Ctee 1998–2003, memb Global Exec Ctee 2003–06; author of various articles on intellectual property and commercial law issues; Managing Partner of the Year Legal Business Awards 2003; memb: Law Soc 1983, Acad for Chief Execs 1999–2003, Lib Dem Pty; tstee Social Mobility Fndn 2006–; supporter Action Aid, Centrepoint, NSPCC and other charities; *Recreations* swimming, bridge, cookery, football/rugby spectator, theatre, family; *Clubs* Old Elthamians Rugby; *Style*— Mr Russell Lewin; ✉ Baker & McKenzie, 100 New Bridge Street, London EC4V 6JA (tel 020 7919 1748, fax 020 7919 1999, e-mail russell.lewin@bakernet.com)

LEWINGTON, HE Richard; s of Ernest John (Jack) Lewington (d 1978), and Bertha Ann (d 1982); *b* 13 April 1948; *Educ* Orchard Secdy Modern Slough; *m* 25 March 1972, Sylviane, da of Armand Cholet; 1 s (Anthony b 13 May 1982), 1 da (Georgina b 7 Nov 1984); *Career* HM Dip Serv: joined 1967, f/t Russian language training 1971–72, third sec Ulaanbaatar 1972–75, second sec (Chancery/information) Lima 1976–80, second sec (commercial) Moscow 1982–83, first sec (commercial) Tel Aviv 1986–90; served FCO 1991–95, memb EC Monitoring Mission in Croatia and Bosnia 1991, dep high cmmr Valletta 1995–99, ambass to Kazakhstan 1999–2003 (concurrently non-resident ambass to Kyrgyzstan), ambass to Ecuador 2003–; memb Anglo-Kazakh Soc 2003–; hon sec Royal Soc for Asian Affrs 2004–; patron Dorset Expeditionary Soc 2004–, life memb Soc of Dorset Men 2005–; *Recreations* collecting old books and maps on Dorset, country walking, ipodding; *Style*— HE Mr Richard Lewington

LEWINTON, Sir Christopher; kt (1993); s of Joseph Lewinton, and Elizabeth Lewinton; *b* 6 January 1932; *Educ* Acton Tech Coll; *Career* Lt REME; pres Wilkinson Sword USA 1960–70, chief exec Wilkinson Sword Group (acquired by Allegheny International 1978) 1970–85, chm Int Ops Allegheny International 1978–85; TI Group plc: chief exec 1986–98, chm 1989–2000; chm (Europe) J F Lehman and Co 2001–, dir Messier-Dowty 1994–98; non-exec dir: Reed Elsevier 1993–99, WPP Group plc 1998–2003; memb Supervisory Bd of Mannesman AG 1995–99, memb Advsy Bd Morgan Stanley/Metalmark Capital 2001–, sr advsr Compass Ptnrs 2005–, dep chm Marina Mgmnt Int 2007–; Hon DTech Brunel Univ; Hon FRAeS, CEng, FREng, FIMechE; *Recreations* golf, shooting, reading; *Clubs* Boodle's, Sunningdale Golf, Royal Thames Yacht, MCC, Univ (NYC), Everglades (Palm Beach); *Style*— Sir Christopher Lewinton; ✉ C L Partners, 4 Grosvenor Place, 3rd Floor, London SW1X 7HJ (tel 020 7201 5490, fax 020 7201 5499)

LEWIS, Alan Frederick; s of Frederick Lewis, of Belfast, and Veronica Selina, *née* McCleery; *b* 3 February 1950; *Educ* Boys' Model Sch Belfast, Queen's Univ Belfast; *Career* Pacemaker Press (picture agency) Belfast: joined 1971, photographer 1971, chief photographer 1973–76; with Daily Mail 1976–93, fndr Photo Press Picture Agency Belfast 1993–; fndr memb Belfast Press Photographers' Assoc 1979, chm NI Press Photographers' Assoc 1990; *Awards* NI Press Photographer of the Year 1975, NI Press Photographer of the Year 1977, Rothmans NI Photographer of the Year 1980, Carrolls Press Photographers' Assoc of Ireland News Picture of the Year 1980 and 1984, Nikon UK Photographer of the Year 1984, Kodak UK Photographer of the Year 1984, Northern Bank News Picture of the Year 1984, Northern Bank People Picture of the Year 1987, NI Sports Cncl Colour Picture of the Year 1991, Guinness Sports Picture of the Year 1994, NI News Photographer of the Year 2001, Vodafone Sports Photographer of the Year 2007; *Books* A Day in the Life of Ireland (jtly, 1991), Out of the Darkness (jtly, 2007); *Recreations* fly fishing for trout and salmon; *Style*— Alan Lewis, Esq; ✉ 25 Queens Square, Belfast, Northern Ireland BT1 3F (e-mail alanlewis.pics@btinternet.com)

LEWIS, Andrew; *b* 1968; *Educ* Univ of N London, Mackintosh Sch of Architecture Glasgow; *Career* artist; work in Arts Cncl Collection; *Solo Exhibitions* Spatial Awareness Show (fig-1 London) 2000, Ark Royale with Cheese (Laurent Delaye Gallery London) 2001, Andrew Lewis: Systems (InIVA London) 2002, White Van Men (Galerie Serieuze Zaken Amsterdam) 2002, Photo Opportunities (The New Art Gallery Walsall) 2003–04; *Group Exhibitions* The Galleries Show (Royal Acad) 2002, Location UK (Gimpel Fils London) 2002; *Style*— Andrew Lewis, Esq; ✉ c/o Laurent Delaye Gallery, 11 Savile Row, London W1S 3PG (tel 020 7287 1546, fax 020 7287 1562, e-mail office@laurentdelaye.com); c/o Hans Ulricht Obrist, Musée d'Art Moderne de la Ville de Paris, 11 Avenue du Président-Wilson, 75116 Paris, France (tel 00 33 6 65 32 12 86)

LEWIS, Anthony Robert (Tony); CBE (2002), DL (Mid-Glamorgan); s of Wilfrid Llewellyn (d 1981), of Swansea, and Florence Majorie, *née* Flower; *b* 6 July 1938; *Educ* Neath GS, Christ's Coll Cambridge (MA, Rugby blue, Cricket blue and capt); *m* 22 Aug 1962, Joan, da of Owen Pritchard, of Neath; 2 da (Joanna Clare b 29 Nov 1967, Anabel Sophia b 28 July 1969); *Career* former cricketer; Glamorgan 1955–74: capt 1967–72, Eng capt tour to India, Ceylon and Pakistan 1972–73; sports presenter and commentator: HTV Wales 1971–82, BBC Radio and TV cricket progs 1974–98, Sport on Four (Radio 4) 1977–84; cricket corr The Sunday Telegraph 1974–92; memb: Sports Cncl for Wales 1972–75, Bd Br Tourist Authy 1992–99, Tourism Action Gp CBI 1995–99; chm: Glamorgan CCC 1987–93 (tstee 1993–, pres 1995–2003), Wales Tourist Bd 1992–2000, Sports Ambassador Programme Br Tourist Industry 2001–03; non-exec chm World Snooker Ltd 2003; MCC: memb Ctee 1992–94 and 1995–98, pres 1998–2000, tstee 2002–04, hon life memb, chm of cricket 2003–; Wales chm ABSA (Assoc of Business Sponsorship of the Arts) 1988–91; chm successful Wales Ryder Cup Bid for 2010; chm WNO 2003–06; marketing conslt Long Reach Int Insurance 2003–, conslt Univ of Wales Newport 2004–; hon fell: St David's Univ Coll Lampeter 1993, Univ of Glamorgan, Univ Coll of Wales Swansea, Cardiff Univ; *Books* Summer of Cricket (1975), Playing Days (1985), Double Century (1987), Cricket in Many Lands (1991), MCC Masterclass (1994), Taking Fresh Guard (2003); *Recreations* golf, classical music; *Clubs* MCC, Royal and Ancient Golf, Royal Porthcawl Golf, East India; *Style*— A R Lewis, Esq, CBE, DL

LEWIS, Charles William; s of Judge Peter Edwin Lewis (d 1976), of Seaford, and Mary Ruth, *née* Massey; *b* 25 June 1954; *Educ* Eastbourne Coll, UC Oxford (MA); *m* 20 Sept 1986, Grace Julia Patricia, da of Alphonsus McKenna, of Dublin; 2 da (Cliona Natasha b 14 July 1992, Helena Mary b 17 Feb 1994); *Career* called to the Bar Inner Temple 1977; *Recreations* skiing, bridge, golf, shooting; *Clubs* MCC, East India, Northamptonshire County Golf; *Style*— Charles Lewis, Esq; ✉ The Dower House, Church Walk, Great Billing, Northampton NN3 9ED (tel 01604 407189); 36 Bedford Row, London WC1R 4JH (tel 020 7421 8000, fax 020 7421 8080)

LEWIS, Very Rev Christopher Andrew; *b* 4 February 1944; *Educ* Marlborough, Univ of Bristol (BA), Corpus Christi Coll Cambridge (PhD), Westcott House Theol Coll; *m* 1970, Rhona Jane, *née* Martindale; 1 da (Andrea b 20 Aug 1973), 2 s (Aidan b 5 Feb 1979, Hugh b 27 Sept 1986); *Career* served RN 1961–66; curate Barnard Castle 1973–76, priest-in-charge Aston Rowant and Crowell 1978–81, vice-princ Ripon Coll Cuddesdon 1981–82 (tutor 1976–81), vicar of Spalding 1982–87, canon residentiary Canterbury Cathedral 1987–94, dir of Ministerial Trg Dio of Canterbury 1989–94, dean of St Albans 1994–2003, dean of Christ Church 2003–; *Recreations* bicycles, guinea fowl; *Style*— The Very Rev Christopher Lewis; ✉ The Deanery, Christ Church, Oxford OX1 1DP (tel 01865 276161)

LEWIS, Clive Hewitt; s of Sqdn Ldr Thomas Jonathen Lewis, OBE, AE (d 1990), of Sway, Hants, and Marguerita Eileen, *née* De Brule (d 1987); *b* 29 March 1936; *Educ* St Peter's Sch York; *m* 7 July 1961, Jane Penelope (Penny), da of Rowland Bolland White (d 1970), of Wakefield, W Yorks; 2 s (Simon Nicholas Hewitt b 1962, Mark Hewitt b 1966), 1 da (Victoria Jane b 1968); *Career* Pilot Officer RAF 1956–58, Lt 40/41 Royal Tank Regt (TA) 1958–62; sr ptnr Clive Lewis and Ptnrs 1963–93, jt chm Colliers Erdman Lewis Chartered Surveyors (formerly Edward Erdman) 1993–96; dir: St Modwen Properties plc 1985–2002, Town Centre Securities plc 1994–, Freeport Leisure plc 1997–2004; chm RICS Journals Ltd 1987–92, dir RICS Business Services Ltd 1987–92, pres gp div RICS 1989–90, pres RICS 1993–94 (vice-pres 1991–92, sr vice-pres 1992–93); dep chm Merseyside Devpt Corp 1989–98 (memb Bd 1986), pres Euro Cncl of Real Estate Professionals 1990–92; chm Propery Forum (Bank of England) 1994–2002; pres: Land Aid Charitable Tst 1989–2003, Worldwide FIABCI (Int Real Estate Fedn) 1983–84; Hon DLit South Bank Univ; Freeman: City of London 1983, Worshipful Co of Chartered Surveyors; FRICS 1961; *Sporting Achievements* Northern Counties sprint champion 1957, Cheshire county athlete;

Recreations golf, tennis; *Clubs* Totteridge CC, MCC, Forty, South Herts Golf; *Style*— Clive Lewis, Esq; ✉ 8 The Pastures, London N20 8AN (tel 020 8445 5109 or 020 8446 8334, fax 020 8446 8330)

LEWIS, (Peter) Daniel Nicolas David; s of Maj Robert Cholmeley Lewis, TD (d 1993), of Shere, Surrey, and (Miriam) Lorraine, *née* Birnage (d 2000); *b* 14 October 1957; *Educ* Westminster; *Career* dep warden day centre Age Concern Westminster 1976–79, mangr London Business Sch Bookshop 1979–82, ptnr London Town Staff Bureau 1982–88 (taken over by Burns Anderson Recruitment plc 1988), subsequently divnl md Burns Anderson Recruitment plc London Town Div 1988–1990, dir Smith & Manchester (clinical negligence specialists), currently divnl dir amLegal conslts; dir, vice-pres and fell Inst of Employment Conslts 1990–95, treas and govr Abinger Hammer Village Sch Tst 1995; fell Recruitment and Employment Confedn (FREC) 2000; *Recreations* driving, dogs, exploring Africa, flying; *Style*— Daniel Lewis, Esq; ✉ 6 Weston Yard, Albury, Surrey GU5 9AF (tel 01483 202922); amLegal, 37–38 Golden Square, London W1F 9LA (tel 020 7470 5500)

LEWIS, David Edward; s of Edward Arthur Lewis (d 1992), of Pontypridd, and Nancy, *née* Williams; *b* 26 March 1952; *Educ* Pontypridd Boys' GS, Univ of Exeter (LLB); *m* Susan Enid, da of James Eccleston; 2 s (Gareth Edward b 28 Feb 1986, Anthony David b 15 Jan 1990), 1 da (Alice Rebecca b 23 Nov 1987); *Career* Allen & Overy: articled clerk 1974–76, asst slr 1976–84, ptnr Tax Dept 1984–; memb Law Soc 1976; *Recreations* tennis, golf; *Clubs* RAC; *Style*— David Lewis, Esq; ✉ Allen & Overy, One New Change, London EC4M 9QQ (tel 020 7330 3000, fax 020 7330 9999)

LEWIS, David Gwynder; s of Gwynder Eudaf Lewis (d 1963), of Sketty, Swansea, and Gwyneth, *née* Jones (d 1979); *b* 31 August 1942; *Educ* Rugby; *m* 2 July 1966, Susan Joyce, da of Andrew Agnew, of Crowborough; 1 da (Alexandra b 1969), 1 s (George b 1972); *Career* Warrant Offr TA C Battery Hon Artillery Co; Hambros Bank Ltd: banker 1961–98, dir 1979–98, exec dir 1991–94, vice-chm 1994–98; chm Hambro Pacific Hldgs Ltd Hong Kong (md 1974–82), pres Hambro America NY 1982–85, dep chm Hambros Australia Ltd Sydney 1994–98, dir Hambros plc 1997; chm Hunters and Frankau Gp Ltd; dir Pelican Shipping Ltd; tstee Gwasg Gregynog; ACIB 1967; *Recreations* fishing, music, shooting, rare book collecting; *Clubs* Turf, RAC, Hong Kong, Royal Hong Kong Jockey, Shek O Country, MCC; *Style*— D G Lewis, Esq; ✉ 57 Victoria Road, London W8 5RH (tel 020 7937 2277, fax 020 7376 9542)

LEWIS, David John; *b* 17 May 1939; *Educ* Grocers' Sch, Univ of London (BSc); *m* 1961; 4 c; *Career* chartered surveyor; Town & City Properties 1959–62, Maybrook Properties 1962–64, sr ptnr David Lewis & Partners 1964–93; dir: Cavendish Land Co 1972–73, Hampton Trust 1983–87, Mount Martin Gold Mines 1985–92, TBI plc 1995–2001; chm Molyneux Estates plc 1989–95; chm Jewish Blind Soc 1979–89, sr vice-pres Jewish Care 1992– (chm 1991–92), pres European Cncl Jewish Communities 1992–99 (hon pres 1999–), govr Oxford Centre for Hebrew & Jewish Studies 1992– (chm Library 1974–), dir London Jewish Museum 2005–; fndr govr Harris City Technol Coll 1991–; FRICS 1969 (ARICS 1961); *Recreations* art, music; *Clubs* Savile; *Style*— D J Lewis, Esq; ✉ Catherine House, 76 Gloucester Place, London W1U 6HJ (tel 020 7487 3401, fax 020 7487 4211, e-mail david.lewis@catherinehouse.com)

LEWIS, Prof David Malcolm; s of Kenneth Stanley Lewis, and Kathleen Elsie, *née* Mann; *b* 24 May 1941; *Educ* Marling Sch Stroud, Univ of Leeds (BSc, PhD); *m* 14 Aug 1965, Barbara, da of Alfred Taylor (d 1965); 2 s (Stephen b 7 March 1967, Matthew b 15 April 1971), 1 da (Catherine b 5 May 1969); *Career* princ devpt offr Int Wool Secretariat 1965–78, sr res scientist CSIRO Geelong Aust 1978–79, princ devpt scientist IWS 1979–87; Univ of Leeds: prof and head of dept 1987–2004 (now emeritus prof), head Resource Centre Sch of Physical Sciences 1997–2003; chief scientific offr Perachem Ltd, research dir Inovink Ltd 2004–; hon visiting prof Xian Textile Inst PRC 1988, hon visiting prof Wuhan Inst of Science and Technology PRC 1999, hon visiting prof Heilangjiang Univ Harbin PRC; memb Br Nat Cttee for Chemistry, memb American Chemical Soc, memb and former chm WR Region Soc of Dyers and Colourists; pres Soc of Dyers and Colourists 1993–94; memb American Assoc of Textile Chemists and Colorists; author Wool Dyeing; Liveryman Worshipful Co of Dyers, Freeman City of London 1995; FRSC 1984, FRSA 1989; *Recreations* tennis, badminton, golf, walking; *Style*— Prof David Lewis; ✉ Department of Colour and Polymer Chemistry, University of Leeds, Leeds LS2 9JT (tel 0113 343 2931, fax 0113 343 2947, e-mail ccddml@leeds.ac.uk, telex 556473 UNILDS G)

LEWIS, David Thomas Rowell; JP (City of London 2002); s of Thomas Price Merfyn Lewis (d 1989); *b* 1 November 1947; *Educ* St Edward's Sch, Jesus Coll Oxford (MA); *m* 25 July 1970, Theresa Susan, *née* Poole; 1 da (Suzannah b 1974), 1 s (Tom b 1976); *Career* admitted slr 1972 (Hong Kong 1977); Norton Rose: articles 1969, ptnr 1977, managing ptnr Hong Kong Office 1979–82, head of corp fin 1989–94, head of professional resources 1994–99, sr ptnr and chm 1997–2003, conslt 2003–; former non-exec dir The Standard Life Assurance Co; memb: Co Law Ctee City Law Soc 1982–97, Legal Practice Course Bd Law Soc 1995–2000, Oxford Univ Law Devpt Cncl (chm 2003–06); tstee: Oxford Univ Law Fndn 1997–2007, Oxford Inst of Legal Practice 2001–03; pres: St Edward's Sch Soc 1995–96, Broad St Ward Club; govr: Oxford Brookes Univ 1995–2003 (memb Ct 2007–), Dragon Sch Oxford (chm 2003–), Christ's Hosp; churchwarden St Margaret Lothbury; alderman (Broad St Ward) City of London 2001– (sheriff 2006–07); Liveryman: Worshipful Co of Slrs (Jr Warden 2006–07), Worshipful Co of Fletchers, Welsh Livery Guild; hon fell Jesus Coll Oxford 1998; memb Law Soc; *Recreations* spoiling my dogs, keeping fit, collecting maps, travel; *Clubs* Achilles, Hong Kong, Soc of St George, Pilgrims; *Style*— David Lewis, Esq; ✉ Norton Rose, 3 More London Riverside, London SE1 2AQ (tel 020 7283 6000, fax 020 7283 6500, e-mail david.lewis@nortonrose.com)

LEWIS, David Whitfield; *b* 19 February 1939; *Educ* Central Sch of Art and Design London (BA), RSA bursary 1960; *Career* industrial designer, largely involved with Bang & Olufsen; freelance design conslt 1967–: with Jacob Jensen 1960–68, with Henning Moldenhawer 1968–80, first chief designer Bang & Olufsen from early 80s; design conslt 2000–: Elica, Indesit Company, Mizar Lighting; *Awards* ID Prize Denmark Design Awards 1982, 1986, 1990 and 1994, EC Design Prize 1988, G-Mark Grand Prix MITI Awards Japan 1991, Int Design Prize State of Badenwurttemberg 1993, Annual Prize Danish Design Co 2003; design work included in design collection of MOMA NY; hon fell RIBA 2007; RDI 1995; *Style*— David Lewis, Esq; ✉ David Lewis Designers, Blegdamsvej 28D, 2200 Copenhagen, Denmark (tel and fax 00 45 33 13 69 35)

LEWIS, Denise; OBE (2001, MBE 1999); *b* 27 August 1972; *Career* athlete (heptathlon); memb Birchfield Harriers; achievements at heptathlon: Gold medal Cwlth Games 1994, second place Grand Prix 1995, winner European Cup 1995, seventh place World Championships Gothenburg 1995, second place Grand Prix 1996, Bronze medal Olympic Games Atlanta 1996, Silver medal World Championships Athens 1997, Gold medal European Championships Budapest 1998, Gold medal Cwlth Games Kuala Lumpur 1998, Silver medal World Championships Seville 1999, Gold Medal Olympic Games Sydney 2000; achievements at long jump: second National Championships 1994 and 1995, winner National Championships 1996, fifth place European Cup 1996; ret 2005; awards incl: Sunday Times International Performance of the Year 1994, Sunday Times Sportswoman of the Year 1994, Royal Mail Female Athlete of the Year 1996, BAF Female Athlete of the Year 1996, Athletic Writers Assoc Sportswoman of the Year 1996, Variety Club Sportswoman of the Year 1997, Daily Express Sportswoman of the Year 1997, voted 2nd BBC Sports Personality of the Year 1998, British Athletic Writers' Assoc British

Athlete of the Year 2000; *Style*— Ms Denise Lewis, OBE; ✉ c/o MTC (UK) Ltd, 20 York Street, London W1U 6PU

LEWIS, Derek Compton; s of Kenneth Compton Lewis (d 1982), of Zeal Monachorum, Devon, and Marjorie, *née* Buick; *b* 9 July 1946; *Educ* Wrekin Coll, Queens' Coll Cambridge (MA), London Business Sch (MSc); *m* 26 April 1969, Louise, da of Dr D O Wharton (d 1986), of Colwyn Bay, North Wales; 2 da (Annabel b 1983, Julia b 1984); *Career* various appts with Ford Motor Co in Europe and USA 1968–82, chief exec Granada Group plc 1988–91 (joined 1984), chief exec UK Gold Television Ltd 1992–93 (non-exec chm 1993), DG HM Prison Service in England and Wales 1993–95; non-exec dir Courtaulds Textiles plc 1990–93; chm Sunsail International plc 1997–98; chm Patientline 1998–2006; *Clubs* Caledonian; *Style*— Derek Lewis, Esq

LEWIS, Derek William; s of Arthur George Lewis (d 1991), of Manor Barn, Snowshill, nr Broadway, Worcs, and Hilda, *née* Rushton (d 1999); *b* 23 October 1944; *Educ* Dean Close Sch Cheltenham; *m* 21 Oct 1972, Bridget Jennifer, da of Maj Bowes Bindon Greany, of Frant, E Sussex; 1 da (Sarah-Jane b 30 May 1974), 2 s (Christopher b 4 Feb 1977, James b 14 Feb 1980); *Career* admitted slr 1967; ptnr Addleshaw Goddard (formerly Theodore Goddard) 1977 (joined 1970, currently non-exec dir Governance Bd); non-exec dir PZ Cussons plc 2004–; memb: City of London Slrs' Co, Law Soc, Soc of Cons Lawyers; *Recreations* horse racing, golf, tennis; *Clubs* Royal Wimbledon Golf, Blackwell Golf, Broadway Golf, Roehampton and Cheltenham Steeplechase; *Style*— Derek Lewis, Esq

LEWIS, Derek William Richard; s of Percy William Lewis, of Worcs, and Edith, *née* Wisdom (d 1941); *b* 6 July 1936; *Educ* King's Sch Worcester; *m* 16 April 1963, Hedwig Albertine, da of Karl Kamps, of St Arnold, Rheine, W Germany; 2 s (Thomas b 1964, Ron b 1968), 1 da (Stephanie b 1967); *Career* RAEC 1957–59; The Hereford Times 1953–61, The Press Assoc 1961–62; BBC: seconded head of news Radio Zambia Lusaka 1966–68, TV news 1968, dep ed 1970–74 of The World at One, PM, The World This Weekend, ed 1974–76 of The World Tonight, Newsdesk and The Financial World Tonight, ed 1976–88 of The World at One (Radio Programme of the year 1976 and 1979), PM and The World this Weekend (Best Current Affrs Programme 1983); md Diplomatic News Services 1988–, media relations conslt Royal Botanic Gardens Kew 1991–2000; cncllr London Borough of Ealing 1989–94 (chm Planning and Regulatory Ctee 1990–94), memb Cncl The Royal Albert Hall; dir Malvern Museum; *Recreations* music, association football, exploring US National Parks; *Clubs* BBC, Ritz, St James's; *Style*— Derek Lewis; ✉ High View, Jubilee Drive, British Camp, Upper Colwall, Worcestershire WR13 6DW (tel 01684 540382)

LEWIS, Duncan; s of Geoffrey Lewis, and Jean, *née* Daragon; *b* 28 April 1951; *Educ* John Fisher Sch Purley, Ecole St Louis de Gonzague Paris, Queens' Coll Cambridge; *Career* Nat Economic Devpt Office 1979–82, STC plc 1981–85, British Telecom plc 1985–90, Hawker Siddeley plc 1990–91, Cable & Wireless plc 1991–95, Granada Media Gp 1996, Equant NV 1997–2000, GTS Inc 2001–02, advsr The Carlyle Gp 2003–; former dir Br Library, chm or dir various cos; *Recreations* travel, reading, theatre; *Style*— Duncan Lewis, Esq; ✉ The Carlyle Group, 57 Berkeley Square, London W1J 6ER (tel 020 7894 1645, fax 020 7894 1600, e-mail duncan.lewis@carlyle.com)

LEWIS, Edward Trevor Gwyn; s of Rev Gwyn Lewis (d 1984), and Annie Millicent, *née* Thomas; *b* 16 March 1948; *Educ* Ellesmere Coll, Lausanne Univ, KCL; *m* 6 April 1974, (Pamela) Gay, da of late Lt-Col Jimmy Wilson, DL, of Dorchester, Dorset; 3 da (Leone b 28 Feb 1975, Kim, Tamsin (twins) b 23 Jan 1979); *Career* called to the Bar Gray's Inn 1972, dep legal mangr Mirror Group Newspapers 1980–83, JP S Westminster Div 1981–84, prosecuting counsel Western Circuit DHSS 1985–, actg dist judge 1988–92, night lawyer: Daily Express, Sunday Express, The Sun; motoring corr: Penthouse Magazine, Country Magazine, The Sun; commissioned by FT, Mail on Sunday and Evening Standard; *Recreations* riding, opera, shooting, family, motor cars; *Clubs* Garrick; *Style*— Edward Lewis, Esq; ✉ 77 Lexham Gardens, London W8 6JN (tel 020 7370 3045); 4 Breams Buildings, Chancery Lane, London EC4A 1HP (tel 020 7092 1900)

LEWIS, Geraint; s of Melvyn Lewis (d 1992), and Mair Eluned, *née* Griffiths (d 1985); *b* 18 October 1954; *Educ* Bedwelty GS, Univ of Newcastle upon Tyne (BDS); *Career* photographer; graduated dental surgn Newcastle upon Tyne 1980, subsequently Dept of Oral Surgery London Hosp, in private practice until 1987; full time freelance photographer 1987–; worked with: Independent and Independent on Sunday, Royal Shakespeare Co, Daily and Sunday Telegraph, Evening Standard, RNT, Theatr Clwyd; dir photo gallery St Leonard's-on-Sea, former occasional lectr photojournalism course London Coll of Printing; exhbn of photographs: of Edinburgh Int Festival (Hampstead Theatre) 1993, of Israel (Lyric Theatre Hammersmith) 1993, of Poland (Polish Cultural Inst London) 1995 (also at Ty Llyen Gallery Swansea 1996), Polish Theatre (Moray House Edinburgh) 1996; highly commended Photography Award Br Arts Journalism Awards 1991 (nominated 1989); memb: Assoc of Photographers, Br Press Photography Assoc; *Recreations* cricket, football, cinema, photography; *Clubs* Archery Cricket, BFI, Photographers Gallery; *Style*— Geraint Lewis, Esq; ✉ mobile 07831 413452, e-mail geraint@geraintlewis.com, website www.geraintlewis.com

LEWIS, Gillian Margaret (Gill); da of Gwilym Thomas Lewis (d 1974), and Valerie, *née* Williams (d 1969); *b* 15 February 1944; *Educ* Howells Sch Llandaff (head girl), St Hilda's Coll Oxford (BA); *m* 1973, Anthony Joseph Lister (d 2000), s of late Walter Lister; 2 s (Timothy David b 1 Sept 1979, Adam Anthony b 30 Jan 1981); *Career* worked as advtg exec J Walter Thompson & Co and various sales and mktg appts in food industry 1967–74, gen mangr Europe Green Giant Co 1974–78, mgmnt conslt McKinsey & Co 1979–81, exec search conslt Fisher Dillistone & Associates 1981–86, dir of human resources and memb Gp Exec Ctee Courtaulds plc 1987–91, sr vice-pres human resources and corp affrs Nestlé SA Switzerland 1992–94; Heidrick & Struggles Exec Search Conslts: managing ptnr consumer practice 1995–98, managing ptnr HE/not-for-profit practice 2000–, sr ptnr English-speaking area 2001– (area managing ptnr 1998–2000); non-exec dir: Pearson plc 1992–2001, Zeneca Group plc 1993–96; memb Bd of Tstees NSPCC 1985–92 and 1997–2002; Veuve Clicquot UK Business Woman of the Year 1977; FIPD 1988, FRSA 1988; *Recreations* theatre, classical music, travel, good food; *Style*— Ms Gill Lewis; ✉ 3A Butler House, 16 Ormond Yard, London SW1Y 6JT (tel 020 7930 0793, fax 020 7075 4192, e-mail gmlewis@heidrick.com)

LEWIS, Hugh Wilson; s of Cdr Lewis, OBE, RN (d 1989); *b* 21 December 1946; *Educ* Clifton, Univ of Birmingham (LLB); *m* 2 Dec 1972, Philippa Jane, da of Lt-Col Terry (d 1988); 3 s (Edward b 1973, Thomas b 1975, Christopher b 1984), 1 da (Katharine b 1979); *Career* called to the Bar Middle Temple 1970; memb: Western Circuit, Family Law Bar Assoc; *Recreations* walking Dartmoor, archaeology, fly fishing, skiing; *Clubs* Naval and Military, Devon and Exeter Inst; *Style*— Hugh Lewis, Esq; ✉ DX 82506 Okehampton, Devon

LEWIS, Huw George; AM; s of David Lewis, and Marion, *née* Pierce, of Aberfan, Mid Glamorgan; *b* 17 January 1964; *Educ* Univ of Edinburgh (BSc), Open Univ (BA); *m* 1996, Lynne, *née* Neagle; 1 s (James b 25 June 2002); *Career* teacher 1988–89 and 1990–94; researcher to Nigel Griffiths MP 1989–90, head of organisation and asst gen sec Wales Lab Pty 1994–99, memb Nat Assembly for Wales (Lab Co-op) Merthyr Tydfil & Rhymney 1999–; *Style*— Huw Lewis, Esq, AM; ✉ National Assembly for Wales, Cardiff Bay, Cardiff CF99 1NA (tel 029 2089 8752)

LEWIS, Ivan; MP; s of Joel Lewis, and Gloria, *née* Goodwin; *Educ* William Hulme GS, Stand Coll, Bury Coll of FE; *m* 1990, Juliette, da of Lesley Fox; 2 s (Ben b 5 Nov 1994, Harry b 26 June 1996); *Career* co-ordinator Contact Community Care Gp 1986–89; Jewish Social Services: social worker 1989–91, community care mangr 1991–92, chief exec 1992–97; MP (Lab) Bury S 1997–; formerly PPS to Rt Hon Stephen Byers MP, *qv*, sec of state for

Trade and Industry; Parly under-sec of state DfES 2001–05, economic sec to HM Treasy 2005–06, Parly under sec of state Dept of Health 2006–; chair All Pty Parenting Gp, sec All Pty Cwlth Games Gp, vice-chair Labour Friends of Israel; memb Bury MBC 1990–98 (chm Soc Servs Ctee 1991–95); former chm Bury MENCAP, chm Bury S Lab Pty 1991–96; *Recreations* football (Manchester City FC); *Style*— Ivan Lewis, Esq, MP; ✉ House of Commons, London SW1A 0AA (tel 020 7219 6404)

LEWIS, His Hon Judge Jeffrey Allan; s of David Meyer Lewis (d 1969), and Esther Kirson (d 1995); *b* 25 May 1949; *Educ* Univ of the Witwatersrand (BA), UC Cardiff (PGCE), Univ of Leeds (LLB); *m* 18 May 1985, Elizabeth Ann, da of Geoffrey Threlfall Swarbrick; 1 da (Rachel Rose b 30 March 1986), 1 s (James David b 11 Aug 1988); *Career* teacher Hartridge HS Newport Gwent 1973–75; called to the Bar Middle Temple 1978, in practice NE Circuit 1978–2002, recorder 1997–2002 (asst recorder 1993–97), circuit judge (Northern Circuit) 2002–; pt/t chm Industrial Tbnls 1991–95; *Recreations* music, reading, skiing, gardening; *Style*— His Hon Judge Jeffrey Lewis; ✉ Manchester Crown Court, Minshull Street, Manchester M1 3FS (tel 0161 954 7500)

LEWIS, Jeremy Morley; s of late George Morley Lewis, FRCS, of Seaford, E Sussex, and Janet, *née* Iles; *b* 15 March 1942; *Educ* Malvern Coll, Trinity Coll Dublin (BA), Univ of Sussex (MA); *m* 1968, Jane Petra, da of Thomas Anthony Freston; 2 da (Jemima b 5 June 1971, Hattie b 23 Sept 1975); *Career* author; advtg trainee Foote Cone & Belding 1960–61, publicity asst William Collins 1967–68, publicity manager Geoffrey Bles Ltd 1968–69, ed André Deutsch Ltd 1969–70, literary agent A P Watt 1970–76, ed Oxford University Press 1977–79, dir Chatto & Windus Ltd 1979–89, freelance writer and ed 1989–, dep ed London Magazine 1991–94, ed conslt Peters, Fraser & Dunlop 1994–2002, commissioning ed The Oldie 1997–, ed-at-large Literary Review 2004–; memb Ctee and sec R S Surtees Soc 1990–; FRSL 1992; *Books* Playing For Time (1987), The Chatto/Vintage Book of Office Life, or Love Among the Filing Cabinets (ed, 1992), Kindred Spirits (1995), Cyril Connolly: A Life (1997), Tobias Smollett (2003), Penguin Special: The Life and Times of Allen Lane (2005); *Recreations* walking round Richmond Park, carousing with friends; *Clubs* Academy, Literary Soc; *Style*— Jeremy Lewis, Esq; ✉ 3 Percival Road, London SW14 7QE (tel 020 8876 2807, fax 020 8878 4801, e-mail jeremy.lewis5@btinternet.com); c/o Gillon Aitken Associates, 18–21 Cavaye Place, London SW10 9PT

LEWIS, John Henry James; OBE (2004); s of late Leonard Lewis, QC, of Newchapel, Surrey, and Rita Jeanette, *née* Stone (d 1994); *b* 12 July 1940; *Educ* Shrewsbury, UCL (LLB); *m* 30 Nov 1984, Susan Frances, da of Maj Robert Ralph Merton, of Burghfield, Berks; 2 da (Daisy Leonora Frances b 1 Jan 1985, Lily Charlotte Frances b 23 Feb 1986), 2 s (Barnaby Ralph James b 29 June 1989, Alfred Ralph James b 24 June 1992); *Career* admitted slr 1966; ptnr Lewis Lewis & Co 1966–82; conslt: Jaques & Lewis 1982–95, Eversheds 1995–; chm: Cliveden plc, Principal Hotels plc 1994–2001, Blakeney Holdings Ltd; vice-chm: John D Wood and Co plc 1989–98, Pubmaster Group Ltd 1996–2000; dir: GR (Holdings) plc, Grayshott Hall Ltd; BTA: memb Bd 1990–96, interim chm 1993; chm: The Wallace Collection, The Attingham Tst; memb Cncl Historic Houses Assoc; tstee The Watts Gallery, govr London Goodenough Tst for Overseas Graduates; Freeman City of London, memb Worshipful Co of Gunmakers; memb Law Soc; *Recreations* sculpture, architecture, tennis; *Clubs* Brooks's, Garrick; *Style*— John Lewis, Esq, OBE; ✉ Shute House, Donhead St Mary, Shaftesbury, Dorset SP7 9DG (tel 01747 828866, fax 01747 828821)

LEWIS, Maj John Henry Peter Sebastian Beale; s of Maj Peter Beale Lewis, MC (d 1961), and Mary Evelyn Louise Piers, *née* Dumas (d 1970); *b* 7 July 1936; *Educ* Eton; *m* 21 Dec 1971, Mary Virginia, da of Charles Barstow Hutchinson (d 1978); 2 s (Rupert Henry Alexander b 1974, Antony Rhydian b 1977); *Career* Maj 11 Hussars (PAO) 1955–69; dir: British Bloodstock Agency plc 1976–2001 (vice-chm 1992–2001), Lower Burytown Farm 1983–; rode over 25 winners under Jockey club rules; represented GB in Bobsleigh; *Clubs* Cavalry and Guards', MCC; *Style*— Maj J P Lewis; ✉ Antwick House, Letcombe Regis, Wantage, Oxfordshire OX12 9LH (tel 01235 763225, fax 01235 768850)

LEWIS, Jonathan; s of Henry Lewis, of London, and Jenny, *née* Cohen; *b* 2 November 1955; *Educ* St Paul's, Univ of Manchester (BA Econ); *m* 22 June 1980, Veronique; 3 da (Sara Giselle b 2 July 1983, Tanya Esther 4 May 1987, Gina Miriam Elisa 10 Sept 1999), 1 s (Joshua Prosper b 14 June 1985); *Career* D J Freeman: joined as trainee 1978, admitted slr 1980, ptnr 1982, memb Fin Ctee 1987–90, chief exec 1993–2001, head of property 2001–03; ptnr Olswang 2003–; govr Immanuel Coll; memb Bd UJS Hillel; Br under 20 sabre fencing champion 1973; memb Law Soc 1980; *Recreations* fundraising for charity, art, travel; *Style*— Jonathan Lewis, Esq

LEWIS, Jonathan Malcolm; s of Harold Lewis, of London, and Rene, *née* Goldser; *b* 27 March 1946; *Educ* Harrow County Sch, Downing Coll Cambridge (MA); *m* 4 July 1971, Rosemary, da of Lewis Mays (d 1971); 2 s; *Career* admitted slr 1971, asst slr 1971–74, ptnr and jt head of Co/Commercial Dept D J Freeman & Co 1974–92, ptnr and head of Insolvency Services Gp Theodore Goddard 1992–98, ptnr and head of Insolvency Gp Finers 1998–; dep district judge, Immigration special adjudicator, columnist (City Comment) Law Soc Gazette 1983–90, lectr and author on various legal topics; involved in the Scout movement; memb: Law Soc 1971, Int Bar Assoc 1981, Insolvency Lawyers Assoc 1987, Soc of Practitioners of Insolvency 1987; Freeman Worshipful Company of Basketmakers; Freeman Worshipful Co of Solicitors; Freeman of the City of London 1993; *Recreations* walking, theatre, family; *Style*— Jonathan M Lewis, Esq; ✉ Finers Stephens Innocent, 179 Great Portland Street, London W1N 6LS (tel 020 7344 5509, fax 020 7344 5602)

LEWIS, Dr Julian Murray; MP; s of Samuel Lewis, and Hilda, *née* Levitt (d 1987); *b* 26 September 1951; *Educ* Dynevor GS Swansea, Balliol Coll Oxford (MA), St Antony's Coll Oxford (DPhil); *Career* research in strategic studies 1975–77 and 1978–81, sec Campaign for Representative Democracy 1977–78, research dir and dir Coalition for Peace Through Security 1981–85, dir Policy Research Associates 1985–; MP (Cons) New Forest E 1997– (Parly candidate Swansea W 1983); oppn whip 2001–02, shadow def min 2002–04 and 2005–, shadow min for the Cabinet Office 2004–05; memb House of Commons: Select Ctee on Welsh Affairs 1998–2001, Select Ctee on Def 2000–01; dep dir Cons Research Dept 1990–96, sec Cons Parly Def Ctee 1997–2001, vice-chm Cons Parly Foreign Affrs Ctee & Euro Affrs Ctee 2000–01, Exec 1922 Ctee 2001; Parly chm First Defence 2004–; memb Armed Forces Parly Scheme: RAF 1998 and 2000, RN 2004, RCDS 2006; tstee Br Military Powerboat Tst 1998–2001 (hon vice-pres 2001–); vol seaman HM RNR 1979–82; Trench Gascoigne essay prize RUSI 2005, RCDS dissertation prize 2006; *Publications* Changing Direction: British Military Planning for Post-War Strategic Defence, 1942–1947 (1988, 2nd edn 2003), Labour's CND Cover-up (CCO, 1992), Who's Left? An Index of Labour MPs and Left-wing Causes, 1986–92 (CCO, 1992), What's Liberal? (CCO, 1996); author of articles and pamphlets; *Recreations* history, films, music, photography, living in the New Forest; *Clubs* Athenaeum, Totton Conservative (hon pres 2001–); *Style*— Dr Julian Lewis, MP; ✉ House of Commons, London SW1A 0AA (tel 020 7219 3000, website www.julianlewis.net)

LEWIS, Keith Allan; s of John William Lewis (d 1979), of London, and Violet, *née* Hill (d 2004); *b* 17 March 1946; *Educ* Henry Thornton GS; *m* 30 March 1968, Sandra Elaine, da of William Slade; 4 s (Clive Matthew b 20 March 1970, David Spencer b 29 Feb 1972, Andrew Christian b 29 June 1973, Jonathan Stuart b 10 June 1976); *Career* Financial Times 1962–78 (journalist, stock market reporter, co commentator, Lex contributor, head City Desk), dir fin PR Universal McCann 1978–81; dir: City & Commercial Communications 1981–82, Grandfield Rork Collins Financial 1982–85, Financial Strategy 1985 (merged with Streets); former md Streets Financial Marketing, chief exec Streets Communications 1987–92; chm: The Paternoster Partnership 1992–99, Luke-Collins 1993–99, The Albemarle Connection 1995–99, City Road Communications Ltd 2000–02; *Recreations* walking, photography, films; *Clubs* Le Beaujolais; *Style*— Keith Lewis, Esq; ✉ City Road Commmunications, 42–44 Carter Lane, London EC4V 5EA (tel 020 7248 8010, fax 020 7236 8320, mobile 07980 841061, e-mail keithlewis@cityroad.uk.com)

LEWIS, Kevin David; OBE (2003); s of Albert Ivor Lewis (d 1976), and Catherine Bradley, *née* Ryan; *b* 18 March 1951; *Educ* Wembley Co GS, Wadham Coll Oxford (BA), SOAS Univ of London (MA), City of London Poly (CDipAF); *m* 1975, Isabella (*née* Lee You Hsien), da of Lee Sow Fie; 2 s (Antony b 1982, Andrew b 1988); *Career* lectr Univ of North Sumatra 1972–75; Br Cncl: HE and Science Div 1976–78, Thailand 1978–83, Finance Div 1983–88, Portugal 1988–89, Finance Div 1989–95 (dep dir of finance 1992–95), Australia 1995, head of internal audit Finance Div 1995–97, dir Bulgaria 1997–2002, dir Israel 2002, currently dep dir global estates and head of overseas estates; tstee Lewin-Herzheimer Charitable Tst, memb Bd Church of Scotland Tabeetha Sch Jaffa Israel; author of various items of journalism; Golden Quill Award for contribution to the arts Bulgarian Classic FM Radio 2002; *Style*— Kevin Lewis, Esq, OBE; ✉ Greenmount, Ballydehob, Co Cork, Ireland (tel 00 353 28 37364, e-mail kevindlewis@hotmail.com); British Council, 10 Spring Gardens, London SW1A 2BN (tel 020 7930 8466)

LEWIS, Sir Leigh Warren; KCB (2007, CB 2000); s of Harold Lewis (d 1992), and Renée Lewis (d 1990); *b* 17 March 1951; *Educ* Harrow Co GS for Boys, Univ of Liverpool (BA); *m* 1973, Susan Evelyn, *née* Gold; 2 s (Richard Ian, Michael Adam); *Career* DfEE (formerly Employment Dept): joined 1973, private sec to parly under sec 1975–76, mangr Dept Personnel Unit 1976–78, princ and head of section Incomes Div 1978–79, team mangr Dept Efficiency Unit 1979–81, head of section Industrial Rels Policy Div, memb legislation teams (Employment Act 1982 and Trade Union Act 1984) 1981–84, princ private sec to Lord Young as min without portfolio and sec of state 1984–86, asst sec and head EC Branch 1986–87, dir of ops Unemployment Benefit Service 1987–88, seconded as gp personnel dir Cable and Wireless plc 1988–91, under sec 1991–, dir Int Div 1991–93, dir Fin and Resource Mgmnt Div 1994–95, dir of fin 1995–96; chief exec: Employment Serv 1997–2002, Jobcentre Plus 2002–03; perm sec Crime, Policing Counter Terrorism and Delivery Home Office 2003–05, perm sec Dept for Work and Pensions 2005–; MIPD 1989; *Recreations* tennis, phonecard collecting, Watford FC; *Style*— Sir Leigh Lewis, KCB; ✉ Department for Work and Pensions, Caxton House, Tothill Street, London SW1H 9DA

LEWIS, Linda Clare; da of Stephen Hood Lewis (d 1996), of Woodford Green, Essex, and Mary Monica, *née* Wood (d 2003); *b* 3 October 1954; *Educ* Ursuline HS Ilford, Woodford County HS, Lancaster Univ (BA); *m* 14 Sept 1991 (m dis Feb 2000), Peter Sergio Allegretti; 2 s (Aubrey Edward Lewis Allegretti b 24 March 1993, Elliott Fraser Lewis Allegretti b 24 Nov 1995); *Career* trainee Mirror Group Newspapers Plymouth 1975–77, news prodr BBC Radio Manchester 1977–79, BBC Parly journalist 1979–80, reporter Today prog BBC Radio 4 1980–83, reporter BBC TV News and Current Affrs 1983–88, corr European Business Channel TV Zürich 1989–90, presenter Financial Times TV London and NHK TV 1990–91, presenter BBC World Service News 1991–92, presenter/reporter business and magazine progs BBC Radio 4 1992–93, presenter PM BBC Radio 4 1993–96; currently mgmnt trainer and writer; *Recreations* children, skiing, music; *Style*— Ms Linda Lewis; ✉ e-mail llewis@homechoice.co.uk

LEWIS, Lynn Alexander Mackay; s of Victor Lewis (d 1982), journalist; *b* 23 August 1937; *Educ* Elizabeth Coll Guernsey, Trinity Kandy Sri Lanka; *m* 1959, Valerie Elaine, da of Harry Procter, journalist, of London; 1 da (Carol b 1959), 1 s (Lindon b 1961); *Career* reporter: Kentish Express 1954–57, Nottingham Evening Post 1959–61; fndr Corby News 1961, investigative reporter Sunday Mirror 1962–65 (subjects incl Profumo Affair, Kray Twins, Rachman Savundra), Rome bureau chief Sunday Mirror 1966–68, reporter LWT 1969, investigative reporter and presenter Nationwide (BBC TV) 1969–74 (subjects incl pyramid selling, Cottingley Fairies), fndr and md Nauticalia Gp (marine mktg, mail order and shops) 1974 (chm 1988–); publisher of Val Lewis's biography of Joanna Southcott 1998 and Ships' Cats in War and Peace 2001; chm: Marine Trades Assoc 1986–89, Shepperton C of C 2005–07; dir National Boat Shows Ltd 1988–94, dir Spelthorne C of C 1999–2000; Lord of the Manor of Shepperton-on-Thames; Queen's Award for Export 1998; *Recreations* Thames boating, cricket; *Clubs* Shepperton Cricket (chm 1992–94); *Style*— Lynn Lewis, Esq; ✉ The Tower House, Chertsey Road, Shepperton-on-Thames, Middlesex TW17 9NU (tel 01932 568385, fax 01932 566678); Nauticalia Ltd, The Ferry Point, Shepperton-on-Thames, Middlesex (tel 01932 244396, fax 01932 241679, mobile 07768 087601, e-mail lynn.lewis@nauticalia.com)

LEWIS, Prof Malcolm J; *Career* prof of cardiovascular pharmacology and head Dept of Pharmacology, Therapeutics and Toxicology Cardiff Univ, hon conslt in clinical pharmacology Cardiff and Vale NHS Tst; *Style*— Prof Malcolm J Lewis; ✉ Department of Pharmacology, Therapeutics and Toxicology, Wales College of Medicine, Cardiff University, Heath Hospital Campus, Cardiff CF14 4XN

LEWIS, Malcolm Neal; s of Neal Stanley Lewis, of Jersey, and Barbara Ann Lewis, *née* Able; *b* 20 August 1958; *Educ* Lancing, École Hoteliere de Lausanne (Dip); *m* 1, (m dis), Ragnhild Kjaernet; 1 s (David b 18 Aug 1984); m 2, Aug 1996, Florence Patricia Orr; 1 da (Sophie Louise b 2 March 2002), 1 s (James Malcolm b 10 Oct 2004); *Career* hotelier; receptionist Hotel Totem Flaine France 1977–78, École Hotelier de Lausanne 1978–81, chef Conaught Hotel London 1981–82, mangr and md Longueville Manor Hotel Jersey 1992–, chm Relais & Châteaux UK 2001–; pres Jersey Hospitality Assoc; *Recreations* tennis, boating, golf, reading; *Style*— Malcolm Lewis, Esq; ✉ Maison Catelain, La Route de la Francheville, Grouville, Jersey JE3 9UE; (tel 01534 619448); Longueville Manor, Longueville Road, St Saviour, Jersey JE2 7WF (tel 01534 725501, e-mail mlewis@longuevillemanor.com)

LEWIS, Martyn John Dudley; CBE (1997); s of Thomas John Dudley Lewis (d 1979), of Coleraine, NI, and Doris, *née* Jones; *b* 7 April 1945; *Educ* Dalriada GS Ballymoney, Trinity Coll Dublin (BA); *m* 20 May 1970, Elizabeth Anne, da of Duncan Carse, of Fittleworth, W Sussex; 2 da (Sylvie b 11 May 1975, Kate b 24 July 1978); *Career* TV journalist, presenter and newsreader; presenter BBC Belfast 1967–68, journalist and broadcaster HTV Wales 1968–70, joined ITN 1970, set up and ran ITN's Northern Bureau Manchester 1971–78; newsreader and foreign corr ITN: News at Ten, News at 5.45 1978–86; ITN reports 1970–86 incl: Cyprus War, Seychelles Independence, Fall of Shah of Iran, Soviet Invasion of Afghanistan, Vietnamese Boat People; co-presenter: ITV gen election programmes 1979 and 1983, ITV Budget programmes 1981–84, wrote and produced Battle for the Falklands video, wrote and presented The Secret Hunters documentary (TVS); joined BBC as presenter One O'Clock News 1986, presenter Nine O'Clock News 1987–94, presenter Six O'Clock News 1994–99; host Today's the Day (series, BBC2) 1993–99 (and BBC Radio 2 version 1996 and 1997); presenter: Crimebeat (series, BBC1) 1996, 1997 and 1998, Bethlehem Year Zero (ITV) 1999, Dateline Jerusalem (ITV) 2000, News '40 (ITV) 2000, Ultimate Questions (ITV) 2000–02; BBC documentaries: MacGregor's Verdict, Royal Tournament, Royal Mission Great Ormond Street - A Fighting Chance, Princess Anne - Save The Children, Help is There, Indian Summer, Fight Cancer, Living with Dying, The Giving Business, Health UK; presenter-in-chief The Medical Channel 2000; chm and fndr YouthNet UK (www.thesite.org and www.do-it.org) 1995–, chm and fndr Global Intercasting Ltd 1999–2007, chm and co-fndr Teliris Ltd 2001–, chm Nice TV Ltd 2005–; pres: United Response, The George Thomas

Centre for Hospice Care; vice-pres: Help the Hospices, Marie Curie Cancer Care, Macmillan Cancer Relief; tstee The Windsor Leadership Tst 2001–, chm The Beacon Fellowship Charitable Tst 2005–; patron: Cambridge Children's Hospice, Hope House Children's Hospice, South West Children's Hospice, Quidenham Children's Hospice, For Dementia, Volunteering England, Midmay Mission Hosp, The Tomorrow Project; advsr The Ogden Tst, memb Int Advsy Ctee RADA; Freeman City of London 1989, Liveryman Worshipful Co of Pattenmakers; Hon DLitt Univ of Ulster 1994; FRSA 1990; *Books* And Finally (1984), Tears and Smiles - The Hospice Handbook (1989), Cats in the News (1991), Dogs in the News (1992), Go For It (annual, 1993–98), Today's the Day (1995), Reflections on Success (1997), Seasons of Our Lives (1999); *Recreations* photography, tennis, good food, keeping fit; *Style—* Martyn Lewis, Esq, CBE; ✉ c/o Anita Land, Capel and Land Ltd, 29 Wardour Street, London W1V 3HB (tel 020 7734 2414, fax 020 7734 8101, e-mail anita@algrade.demon.co.uk)

LEWIS, (Patricia) Mary; da of late Donald Leslie Cornes, of Bayston Hill, Salop, and Eleanor Lillian, *née* Roberts; *Educ* Stonehurst Sch Shrewsbury, St Margaret's Yeaton Peverey, Shrewsbury Sch of Art, Camberwell Sch of Arts and Crafts (BA), Central Sch of Art Middx Poly (postgrad); *m* 2, 7 Jan 1992, Robert Moberly, *qv*, s of Sir Walter Moberly, GBE, KCB, DSO (d 1973); 1 da (Scarlett Rose b 28 May 1992); *Career* graphic designer; creative dir and founding ptnr Lewis Moberly 1984–; awards incl: British Design and Art Direction Gold Award for Outstanding Design and 3 Silver Awards, Design Business Assoc Grand Prix for Design Effectiveness, Br Design and Art Direction President's Award for Outstanding Achievement 2001; juror: BAFTA Graphic Design Awards, Millennium Products, BBC Design Awards, D&AD Awards, Communication Arts Awards USA; chm: BBC Graphic Design Awards 1996, Scottish Design Awards 2005; work exhibited: London (V&A), Los Angeles, Japan, NYC, Paris; pres Br Design and Art Direction 1995 (hon memb 1998); memb: Wedgwood Design Policy Gp 1998–99, Royal Mail Stamps Advsy Ctee 1998–2007, Br Food Heritage Tst 1999, Marks & Spencer Design Forum 1999–2007; participant Creative Britain Workshops 1997; contrib Radio 4 Food Prog 1997; hon masters degree Univ of Surrey 2002; FRSA; *Books* Understanding Brands (co-ed); *Recreations* daughter, horses, farm; *Style—* Ms Mary Lewis; ✉ Lewis Moberly, 33 Gresse Street, London W1T 1QU (tel 020 7580 9252, e-mail hello@lewismoberly.com)

LEWIS, Prof Mervyn Keith; s of Norman Malcolm Lewis (d 1982), of Adelaide, Aust, and Gladys May Valerie, *née* Way; *b* 20 June 1941; *Educ* Unley HS, Univ of Adelaide (BSc, PhD); *m* 24 Nov 1962, Kay Judith, da of Lt Royce Melvin Wiesner (d 1977), of Adelaide, Aust; 4 da (Stephanie b 1966, Miranda b 1967, Alexandra b 1969, Antonia b 1972); *Career* Elder Smith & Co Ltd 1957–58, Cwlth Bank of Aust 1959–64, assoc dean Univ of Adelaide 1981–83 (tutor and lectr 1965–84, sr lectr 1973–79, reader 1979–84), visiting scholar Bank of England 1979–80, conslt Aust Fin System Inquiry 1980–81, Midland Bank prof of money and banking Univ of Nottingham 1984–96, Nat Aust Bank prof in banking and finance Univ of S Aust 1996–; memb Multicultural Educn Ctee of S Aust 2000–02; series ed New Horizons in Money and Finance 2002–; visiting prof: of econs Flinders Univ of S Aust 1987–96, Wirtschaftsuniversität Wien 1987 and 1990–95, Int Teachers' Programme Bocconi Univ Milan 1988, Victoria Univ of Wellington 1991, Huazhong Univ of Science and Technol Wuhen 1998, Univ of Mauritius 2000–04, Univ of Goettingen 2001, Euro Med Marseille 2007; res assoc Center for Pacific Basin Monetary and Economic Studies Federal Reserve Bank of San Francisco 1991–; memb Australian Research Cncl Asia Pacific Futures Research Network Islam Node 2005–; pres Cncl Kingston Coll of Advanced Educn 1978–79; jt winner Blake Dawson Waldron Prize for Business Literature 2005; elected fell Acad of the Social Sciences in Aust 1986; *Books* Monetary Policy in Australia (1980), Australian Monetary Economics (1981), Monetary Control in the United Kingdom (1981), Australia's Financial Institutions and Markets (1985), Personal Financial Markets (1986), Domestic and International Banking (1987), Money in Britain: Monetary Policy, Innovation and Europe (1991), Current Issues in Financial and Monetary Economics (1992), The Australian Financial System (1993), Financial Intermediaries (1995, 2 edn 1996), Australian Financial System: evolution, policy and practice (1997), The Globalisation of Financial Services (1999), Monetary Economics (2000), Islamic Banking (2001), Public Private Partnerships: The Worldwide Revolution in Infrastructure Provision and Project Finance (2004), The Economics of Public Private Partnerships (2005), Reforming China's State-Owned Enterprises and Banks (2006), The Handbook of Islamic Banking (2007), Untangling the US Deficit: Evaluating Causes, Cures and Global Imbalances (2007), Islamic Finance (2007); *Recreations* rambling, tennis, music; *Clubs* East India; *Style—* Prof Mervyn Lewis; ✉ School of Commerce, University of South Australia, City West Campus, North Terrace, Adelaide, South Australia 5000 (e-mail mervyn.lewis@unisa.edu.au)

LEWIS, Rt Rev Michael; *see:* Cyprus and the Gulf, Bishop of

LEWIS, Michael ap Gwilym; QC (1975); s of Rev Thomas William Lewis (d 1946), of London, and Mary Jane May, *née* Selway (d 1975); *Educ* Mill Hill Sch, Jesus Coll Oxford (MA); *m*; 3 s (Meyric b 1962, Gareth b 1964, Evan b 1966), 3 da (Bronwen b 1960, Jennet b 1989, Harriet b 1992); *Career* cmmnd RTR 1952–53; called to the Bar Gray's Inn 1956, bencher 1986; recorder of the Crown Court 1976–97, memb Senate 1976–79, memb Criminal Injuries Compensation Bd 1993–2002; *Style—* Michael Lewis, Esq, QC; ✉ 2 Bedford Row, London WC1R 4BU

LEWIS, Michael David (Mike); s of David Lloyd Lewis, and Gwendoline Winifrid Frances, *née* Willard; *Educ* Erith GS; *m* Hilary, da of John East; 2 da (Gabrielle b 27 June 1990, Harriet b 10 Nov 1993); *Career* journalist Gravesend & Dartford Reporter, reporter Brighton Evening Argus, sports ed LBC/IRN; BBC Radio: head of sports and outside broadcasts 1990–93, dep controller BBC Radio 5 Live 1994–2000, controller Radio Sports Rights 1997–2007, head of boxing strategy 2000–07; sports rights and programming conslt 2007–; *Recreations* watching Arsenal, tennis, theatre, raising two daughters as well as possible; *Style—* Mike Lewis, Esq; ✉ tel and fax 020 8964 8865, mobile 07850 762259, e-mail mike-lewis@beeb.net

LEWIS, Neville Julian Spencer; s of Raymond Malcom Lewis (d 1980), of Llanishen, Cardiff, and Constance Margaret, *née* Jones; *b* 17 March 1945; *Educ* Radley, Pembroke Coll Oxford (MA); *m* 1, 14 July 1967 (m dis 1981), Caroline Joy, da of Robin Homes (d 1987), of Oare, Wiltshire; 1 s (David b 1978), 1 da (Miranda b 1974); m 2, 1994, Anna-Liisa, da of Aake Jarvinen, of Hyvinkää, Finland; 1 s (Kasperi b 1995); *Career* called to the Bar Inner Temple 1970, practises SE Circuit; Parly candidate (Lib) Paddington Feb and Oct 1974; *Books* Guide to Greece (1977), Delphi and the Sacred Way (1987); *Style—* Neville Spencer Lewis, Esq; ✉ 80 Upper Park Road, London NW3 2UX; 12 King's Bench Walk, Temple, London EC4Y 7EL (tel 020 7583 0811, e-mail spencer-lewis@12kbw.co.uk)

LEWIS, Paul; *Educ* Chetham's Sch of Music, Guildhall Sch of Music; *Career* pianist; reg performer of recital and chamber music, concerto soloist; Steinway & Sons 1000th registered Steinway Artist 1997, selected BBC's New Generation artist scheme1999, prof of piano Royal Acad of Music 2000–02; appeared at the Wigmore Hall 17 times 1999–2002, selected artist for Wigmore Hall in European Concert Halls Orgn's "Rising Stars" Scheme 2002; recitals incl: Aldeburgh, Bath, Brighton, Cheltenham, Chester, Edinburgh, Lichfield Festival, Perth Festival, Schubertiade Schwarzenberg, Luzern Piano Festival, Klavier Festival Ruhr, Vancouver Chamber Music Festival, Queen Elizabeth Hall, Purcell Room, Queen's Hall Edinburgh, Turner Sims Concert Hall Southampton, many concerts for music clubs and socs; performed concertos with the RPO, London Philharmonic, Royal Liverpool Philharmonic, Bournemouth Symphony, City of Birmingham Symphony Orch, City of London Sinfonia, BBC Scottish Symphony, Hallé Orch, Scottish Chamber Orch, BBC Symphony Orch, BBC Nat Orch of Wales, Wiener Kammerphilharmonie, Kölner Kammerorchester; perfomed with conductors incl: Mark Elder, *qv*, Marin Alsop, Ivor Bolton, *qv*, Richard Hickox, *qv*, Emmanuel Krivine, Alexander Polianichko, Joseph Swensen, *qv*, Vassily Sinaisky, Gerard Schwarz; appeared as chamber musician with: Yo-Yo Ma, Michael Collins, *qv*, Ernst Kovacic, Quatuor Sine Nomine, Leopold String Trio, Haffner Wind Ensemble, Katherine Gowers, Adrian Brendel; presented Schubert Piano Sonata Series at numerous venues in UK and abroad 2002 (South Bank Show Classical Music Award 2003); other performances incl: Carnegie Hall NY 2002, Musikverein Vienna 2002, Concertgebouw Amsterdam 2002, Palais des Beaux Arts Brussels 2002, Tonhalle Zurich 2002, Chan Center Vancouver 2002, Risor Chamber Music Festival 2002, La Coruna Mozart Festival 2002, with the Halli in UK and at Musikverein Vienna 2002, with the Seattle Symphony, BBC Proms (televised concert) with Bournemouth Symphony Orch 2002; *Recordings* incl: Schubert Sonatas D784 & D958 2002 (Diapason d'Or Choc de l'Annie France 2002), Schubert Sonatas D959 & D960 2003, Mozart: Piano Quartets 2003; *Style—* Paul Lewis, Esq; ✉ c/o Ingpen & Williams Ltd, 7 St George's Court, 131 Putney Bridge Road, London SW15 2PA (tel 020 8874 3222, fax 020 8877 3113)

LEWIS, Very Rev Richard; s of Rev Henry Lewis (d 1953), and Amy, *née* Poyner (d 1972); *b* 24 December 1935; *Educ* Royal Masonic Sch, Fitzwilliam House Cambridge (MA), Ripon Hall Oxford; *m* 1959, Jill Diane, da of Joseph Alfred Wilford; 2 s (Simon Wilford b 1966, Andrew Richard b 1969); *Career* curate: Hinckley 1960–63, Sanderstead (in charge of St Edmunds) 1963–66; vicar: All Saints South Merstham 1967–72, Holy Trinity and St Peter Wimbledon 1972–79, St Barnabas Dulwich 1979–90; fndn chaplain of Christ's Chapel Alleyn's Coll of God's Gift Dulwich 1979–90, dean of Wells 1990, currently dean emeritus of Wells; tutor in clinical theol 1964–68, gp psychotherapist St George's Hosp Tooting 1972–82, chaplain Worshipful Co of Barber Surgns 1987, occasional speaker's chaplain House of Commons 1988; currently: chm Bd of Govrs Wells Cathedral Sch, memb Bishop's Staff, warden of readers Dio of Bath and Wells, memb Gen Synod 1982–99, memb Archbishops' Cmmn on Cathedrals 1990–95, chm Conf of Deans and Provosts of England 1994–99, memb Crown Appointments Cmmn 1994–97; *Publications* Cathedrals Now (1996), Walking the Rainbow (CD, 1996); *Style—* The Very Rev Richard Lewis; ✉ Wells House, 152 Lower Howsell Road, Malvern Link, Worcestershire WR14 1DL (tel 01886 833820, e-mail dean.richard@wellshouse.co.uk)

LEWIS, Rt Rev (John Hubert) Richard; s of the Ven John Wilfred Lewis (d 1984), and Winifred Mary, *née* Griffin; *b* 10 December 1943; *Educ* Radley, King's Coll London (AKC); *m* 17 April 1968, Sara Patricia, da of Canon Gerald Murray Percival (Peter) Hamilton; 3 s (Peter John b 1970 d 1997, Michael James b 1972, Nicholas Richard b 1975); *Career* curate of Hexham 1967–70, industrial chaplain Diocese of Newcastle 1970–77, communications offr Diocese of Durham 1977–82, agric chaplain Diocese of Hereford 1982–87, archdeacon of Ludlow 1987–92, bishop suffragan of Taunton 1992–97, bishop of St Edmundsbury and Ipswich 1997–2007; memb House of Lords 2002–07; nat chm Small Farmers Assoc 1984–88; *Books* The People, The Land and The Church (jt ed, 1987); *Recreations* kit cars, bricklaying; *Style—* The Rt Rev Richard Lewis

LEWIS, Richard Alan; s of Wilfred Lewis (d 1988), and Marian, *née* Eveleigh (d 1991); *b* 6 December 1954, London; *Educ* Goffs GS; *m* 5 June 2005, Jan, *née* Carter; 2 s (Nicholas b 19 Aug 1983, Alexander b 4 Nov 1985); *Career* professional tennis player 1969–87, team memb Davies Cup 1977–83; LTA: dir of nat training 1987–98, dir of tennis 1998–2000; conslt Merryck & Co 2000–02, exec chm Rugby Football League 2002–, chair CCPR Major Spectator Sports Div 2007–; *Style—* Richard Lewis, Esq; ✉ RFL, Red Hall, Red Hall Lane, Leeds LS17 8NB (tel 0113 237 5012, e-mail richard.lewis@rfl.uk.com)

LEWIS, Prof Richard Alexander; s of Harold Charles Lewis, of Whitbourne, Herefords, and Olwyn, *née* Witcombe; *b* 4 November 1949; *Educ* Buckhurst Hill Co HS, St Thomas' Hosp Med Sch Univ of London (DM, BSc, MB BS); *m* 26 May 1973, Dr Anne Margaret Lewis, da of Cdr Donald Maclennan, of Tong, Isle of Lewis; 2 s (Christopher b 1977, Peter b 1986), 1 da (Elizabeth b 1982); *Career* house physician St Thomas' Hosp London 1975, rotational SHO in med Southampton Gen Hosp and Dist Hosp 1976–77, rotational registrar in gen med St Richard's Hosp Chichester and St Thomas' Hosp London 1977–79, res fell Dept of Respiratory Med Unit One Univ of Southampton 1979–82, sr registrar in gen and thoracic med Southampton and Portsmouth Dist Hosp 1982–86; conslt physician specialising in diseases of the chest: Worcester and Dist HA Worcester Royal Infirmary 1986–, Worcester Acute Hosps NHS Tst 1993–2000, Worcs Acute Hosps NHS Tst 2001–; hon sr research fell National Pollen Res Unit UCl Worcester 1999–, hon prof UC Worcester; vice-chm of govrs St Richard's Hospice Worcester, pres Malvern Asthma Soc; memb: Br Thoracic Soc, Euro Respiratory Soc, Christian Med Fellowship; MRCS, FRCP 1992 (LRCP, MRCP); *Books* contrib: Pharmacology of Asthma (1983), Drugs and the Lung (1984), Current Treatment of Ambulatory Asthma (1986), Difficult Asthma (1999); *Recreations* running, cycling, mountain walking, sailing, gardening, music, photography; *Style—* Prof Richard Lewis; ✉ Crews Court, Suckley, Worcester WR6 5DW (tel 01886 884552); Worcestershire Royal Hospital, Charles Hastings Way, Worcester WR5 1DD (tel 01905 760237, fax 01905 760549, e-mail Richard.Lewis@worcsacute.nhs.uk)

LEWIS, Hon Robin William; OBE (1988), DL (Dyfed 2002); 4 s of 3 Baron Merthyr, KBE, PC (d 1977), and Violet, *née* Meyrick (d 2003); *b* 7 February 1941; *Educ* Eton, Magdalen Coll Oxford (MA); *m* 28 April 1967, Judith Ann, o da of (Vincent Charles) Arthur Giardelli, MBE, of Pembroke; 1 s (Christopher b 1970), 1 da (Katharine b 1972); *Career* Cwlth Devpt Corp 1964–66, Alcan Aluminium 1967–68, National Westminster Bank Ltd 1968–72, Devpt Corp for Wales 1972–82, md Novametrix Medical Systems Ltd 1982–90 (chm 1989–90), chm The Magstim Co Ltd 1990–, chm JP Morgan US Discovery Investment Tst plc 2004– (dir 1995–); chm: Gen Advsy Cncl of Ind Broadcasting Authy 1989–90 (memb 1985–90), National Tst Ctee for Wales 1994–97 (memb 1983–97); chm of tstees Nat Botanic Garden of Wales 2006–, dep chm Welsh Devpt Agency 1995–98 (memb Bd 1994–2001); High Sheriff Dyfed 1987–88, Lord Lt Dyfed 2006–; *Recreations* sailing; *Clubs* Leander; *Style—* The Hon Robin Lewis, OBE, DL; ✉ The Cottage, Cresswell Quay, Kilgetty, Pembrokeshire SA68 0TE (e-mail robin.lewis@magstim.com)

LEWIS, Roger Charles; s of late Griffith Charles Job Lewis, and Dorothy, *née* Russ; *b* 24 August 1954; *Educ* Cynffig Comp Sch, Univ of Nottingham (BMus); *m* 5 July 1980, Dr Christine Lewis, da of Leslie Trollope; 2 s (Owen Rhys b 29 March 1985, Thomas Griffith b 16 Feb 1988); *Career* musician 1976–80, Avon Touring Theatre Co 1977–79, Birmingham Rep Theatre Studio 1978, Ludus Dance in Educn Co 1979, Scottish Ballet Workshop Co 1979, music offr Darlington Arts Centre 1980–82, presenter Radio Tees 1981–84, prodr Capital Radio 1984–85, head of music BBC Radio 1 1987–90 (prodr 1985–87), md Classical Div EMI Records 1995 (dir 1990–95), md EMI Premier 1995–97, pres Decca Records 1997–98, md and prog controller Classic FM 1998–2004, md ITV Wales 2004–; dir: Cleveland Arts 1982–84, The Radio Corp Ltd 1999–2001, Digital One 2003–04; non-exec dir Barchester Gp 2001–06, non-exec dep chm Boosey and Hawke's 2004–; chm: Classical Ctee BPI 1996–98, Tstees of the Ogmore Centre 1996–, Classic FM Charitable Tst 2000–04, Music and Dance Scheme Advsy Gp DFES 2000–04, Royal Liverpool Philharmonic 2003–; pres Bromley Youth Music Tst 2000–06 (vice-pres 2006–); vice-pres: London Welsh Male Voice Choir 2004–, Welsh Music Guild; memb: Bd GWR Gp plc 1998–2004, WNO Devpt Cicle 2001–06, Bd Liverpool European Capital of Culture 2003–, Bd Wales Millenium Centre 2004–, Wales Arts Review Panel 2006; tstee:

L

Masterprize (int composers competition) 1995–, Masterclass Charitable Tst 2000–04; hon fell Royal Welsh Coll of Music and Drama, hon memb Royal Coll of Music; *Awards* incl: Sony Award 1987–89, NY Grand Award Winner and Gold Medal 1987 (finalist 1989), finalist Monaco Radio Festival 1989, One World Broadcasting Tst award 1989, NTL Commercial Radio Programmer of the Year 2002; *Recreations* rugby football, walking, skiing; *Style—* Roger Lewis, Esq; ✉ ITV Wales, The Television Centre, Culverhouse Cross, Cardiff CF5 6XJ

LEWIS, Prof Roland Wynne; s of David Lewis (d 1958), and Mary Gladys, *née* Davies (d 1981); *b* 20 January 1940; *Educ* Amman Valley GS, UC Swansea (BSc, PhD, DSc); *m* 17 April 1965, Celia Elizabeth, da of Haydn Elgar Morris, of Ammanford, Dyfed; 2 da (Caroline b 16 June 1969, Angharad b 11 Feb 1973), 1 s ((David) Andrew b 4 March 1971); *Career* res engr ESSO Canada 1965–69, prof UC Swansea 1984– (lectr 1969–79, sr lectr 1979–82, reader 1982–84); chm Thermofluids Gp Nat Agency for Finite Element Methods and Standards; FICE 1991 (MICE 1973), FREng 1997; *Books* Civil Engineering Systems-Analysis and Design, Finite Elements in the Flow and Deformation of Porous Media, The Finite Element Method in the Static and Dynamic Deformation and Consolidation of Porous Media, The Finite Element Method in Heat Transfer Analysis; *Recreations* golf, photography, gardening; *Clubs* Clyne Golf (Swansea); *Style—* Prof Roland Lewis, FREng; ✉ Oakridge, 331 Gower Road, Killay, Swansea SA2 7AE (tel 01792 203166); Mechanical Engineering Department, University of Wales Swansea, Swansea SA2 8PP (tel 01792 295253, fax 01792 295705)

LEWIS, Dr S Mitchell; s of Coleman James Lewis (d 1966), and Fanny, *née* Zweiback (d 1959); *b* 3 April 1924; *Educ* Christian Brothers Coll Kimberley, Univ of Cape Town (BSc, MB ChB, MD); *m* 23 Oct 1959, Ethel Norma, da of Rachmiel Nochumowitz (d 1958); 1 s (Raymond b 1962); *Career* conslt haematologist Hammersmith Hosp 1961–93, organiser UKNEQAS in Haematology 1968–93, sr res fell Imperial Coll Sch of Med 1989–, emeritus reader Univ of London 1989– (reader in haematology 1970–89); dir WHO Collaborative Centre for Haematology 1987–2006, conslt WHO Prog on Health Technol 1995–2005; past chm Int Cncl for Standardization in Haematology, cnsllr-at-large Int Soc of Haematology; hon memb: Br Soc for Haematology (past pres), nat haematology socs of Germany, Italy, South Africa and Turkey; FRCPath, FIBMS; *Books* Practical Haematology (1963, 10 edn 2006), Modern Concepts in Haematology (1972), Postgraduate Haematology (1972, 4 edn 1999), Dyserythropoiesis (1977), The Spleen (1983), Thromboplastin Calibration (1984), Myelofibrosis (1985), Biopsy Pathology and Bone and Marrow (1985), Quality Assurance in Haematology (1988), Haematology Laboratory Management and Practice (1995); *Recreations* photography, reading, music; *Style—* Dr Mitchell Lewis; ✉ 6 Salisbury House, Somerset Road, Wimbledon, London SW19 5HY (tel 020 8946 2727, fax 020 8946 9146); Imperial College School of Medicine, Hammersmith Hospital, London W12 0NN (mobile 07855 553248)

LEWIS, (David) Simon; s of David Lewis, and Sally Elizabeth, *née* Valentine; *b* 8 May 1959; *Educ* Whitefield Sch, BNC Oxford, Univ of Calif Berkeley (Fulbright scholar, MA); *m* 1985, Claire Elizabeth, da of Eric Pendry, and late Jean Pendry; 2 s (Thomas Paul b 1989, Dominic William b 2000), 1 da (Olivia Rose b 1991); *Career* financial PR exec Shandwick Consultants 1983–86, seconded to S G Warburg in run-up to Big Bang 1986, political advsr SDP gen election 1987, head of PR S G Warburg Group 1987–92; dir of corporate affrs: NatWest Group 1992–96, Centrica plc (formerly British Gas plc) 1996–98; md Europe Centrica plc 2000–; communications sec Buckingham Palace (on secondment) 1998–2000; pres IPR 1997–98 (former chm City and Financial Group); tstee Treehouse Tst; UK Fulbright cmmr; hon prof Sch of Journalism, Media and Cultural Studies Univ of Cardiff; FRSA, FIPR; *Style—* Simon Lewis, Esq; ✉ Centrica plc, Millstream, Maidenhead Road, Windsor, Berkshire SL4 5GD

LEWIS, Simon James; *b* 14 February 1958; *Educ* Holland Park Secdy Sch, Poly of Central London (BA); *m* 1, 4 March 1983, Milka Javiera, *née* Valenzuela; m 2, 8 Aug 2003, Susan Hogg; *Career* prodr: Central TV 1989–91 and 1993–94, Yorkshire TV 1992–93 and 1994–95; controller of drama: United Film & TV Productions 1995–97, Granada TV 1997–2000; prodr BBC TV 2000–; prodns incl: Boon (Central TV, 1989–91), The Darling Buds of May (Yorkshire TV, 1992–93), Sharpe (BAFTA nominated Best Drama Series, Central TV, 1994), A Touch of Frost (Yorkshire TV, 1994–95), No Child of Mine (Best Single Drama BAFTA Award 1998), Touching Evil (nominated BAFTA and RTS Best Drama Series 1998), Where The Heart Is (nominated RTS Best Drama Series 1998), Grafters, The Last Train, Butterfly Collectors, A+E, Tough Love, Little Bird, Born and Bred, The Eustace Bros, Death in Holy Orders, The Murder Room, Cherished; *Style—* Simon Lewis

LEWIS, Stephen John; s of late Douglas John Lewis, of Codsall, Staffs, and late Dorothy Pauline, *née* Shaw; *b* 8 March 1948; *Educ* Wolverhampton GS, Balliol Coll Oxford (BA); *Career* ptnr Phillips & Drew 1980–85, dir Securities Ltd 1985–88, md Fifth Horseman Publications Ltd 1988–92, dir The London Bond Broking Co Ltd 1992–96 (also chief economist), chief economist Monument Securities Ltd (formerly Monument Derivatives Ltd) 1996–2006, chief economist Insinger de Beaufort 2006–; memb: Securities Inst, Soc of Business Economists; *Recreations* antiquities, European philosophy; *Clubs* Reform; *Style—* Stephen Lewis, Esq; ✉ Insinger de Beaufort, 131 Finsbury Pavement, London EC2A 1NT (tel 020 7190 7193, fax 020 7190 7220, e-mail sjlewis@insinger.com)

LEWIS, Stephen Michael; s of Harry Lewis, of Stanmore, Middx, and Celia, *née* Softness; *b* 23 August 1949; *Educ* Orange Hill Co GS for Boys, St Catherine's Coll Oxford (open exhibition, BA), Univ of London (LLB); *m* 3 March 1974, Erica, da of Jacob Pesate; 2 da (Ann Marie b 25 April 1976, Francesca Rose b 2 Sept 1986), 1 s (Adrian William b 9 April 1979); *Career* mgmnt trainee Reed International 1970–71, articled clerk Clintons slrs 1971–74, legal asst Law Cmmn 1975–80, ptnr Clifford Turner (now Clifford Chance) 1985– (asst slr 1980–85); memb: Law Soc, Sub-Ctee on Insurance Law City of London Law Soc; *Recreations* music, reading, running, swimming, politics; *Style—* Stephen Lewis, Esq; ✉ Clifford Chance, 10 Upper Bank Street, London E14 5JJ (tel 020 7006 1000, fax 020 7006 5555)

LEWIS, Stephen Richard; *b* 11 January 1959; *Educ* Deyes HS Maghull, Southport Coll of Art, Manchester Poly (BA), Jan Van Eyck Academie Maastricht; *Career* artist; visiting artist: Cyprus Sch of Art, Voss Sch Norway, Triangle Artists Workshop NY, Emma Lake Workshop Canada, Hardingham Sculpture Workshop UK; *Solo Exhibitions* incl: Francis Graham-Dixon Gallery 1988, 1990 and 1993, John Holden Gallery Manchester 1990, Christchurch Mansion Ipswich 1992, Galerie Schlassgoart Luxembourg 1996, Atrium Gallery London 1996; *Group Exhibitions* incl: New Contemporaries (ICA) 1979, Northern Young Contemporaries (Whitworth Gallery Manchester) 1979, The First Picture Show (Sainsbury Centre Norwich) 1980, Triangle Workshop Exhibition NY 1989, Kunst Europa (Kustverein Kirchzarten) 1991, Lancashire Contemporaries (Harris Museum Preston) 1992, Three Sculptors: Oleg Kudryashov, Stephen Lewis, Charles Quick (The Economist Building London) 1993, Three London Artists (Standoort Gallery Frankfurt) 1998, A Life Less Ordinary (Hammersons London) 2000; *Commissions* in London: Circumsphere River Thames Deptford 1999, Union Canal Project Southall 2001, Camden Plaques Camden Town 2002, Regent Quarter P&O Developments Sculpture Plaques Kings Cross 2003–04, Mumford Sculpture Greenwich 2004; *Work in Collections* incl: Simmons and Simmons London, Arbed Steel Co Luxembourg, Kunstlandschaft Germany; work in private collections in UK, Europe, USA and Canada; *Style—* Stephen Lewis, Esq

LEWIS, (John) Stuart; DL (Herts 2004); s of John Charles Lewis, OBE, JP (d 1999), and Kathleen Gertrude Clara, *née* Pennick (d 1973); *b* 9 March 1944; *Educ* Downer GS; *m* 19 July 1969, Bridget Margaret, da of Eric Billingham Nash (d 1987); 2 s (James b 1971, Edward b 1983), 1 da (Anna b 1973); *Career* ptnr Fielding Newson-Smith & Co 1975, first vice-pres Drexel Burnam Lambert Inc 1986, md Private Fund Managers Ltd 1988–95, md Close Portfolio Management Ltd 1996–98; chm Hertfordshire Community Fndn; chm Adenham Sch Elstree; Freeman City of London; FCIS 1974, MSI 1993; *Recreations* shooting, opera, reading, travel; *Style—* J Stuart Lewis, Esq, DL; ✉ Greenaway House, Rose Lane, Wheathampstead, Hertfordshire AL4 8RA (tel 01582 834611, e-mail stuart@greeanaway.demon.co.uk)

LEWIS, Susan; da of Kenneth Arthur Leslie Lewis (d 1986), and Elsie, *née* Woods (d 1955); *b* 7 November 1947; *Educ* Henry Smith Sch Hartlepool, Univ of Newcastle upon Tyne (BSc), Univ of Sheffield (DipEd); *Career* asst teacher Bradfield Sch Yorks 1970–74, head of dept and subsequently asst head of sixth form Shelley HS Kirklees 1974–80, dep head subsequently acting head Wisewood Sch Sheffield 1980–85; Estyn Her Majesty's Inspectorate for Educn and Training (Wales): joined 1986, staff inspr 1995–97, HM chief inspr of schs 1997–2000, HM chief inspr of Educn and Trg in Wales 2000–; certified mediator 2005, certified coach Sch of Psychotherapy and Counselling Regent's Coll London 2006; FRSA; *Recreations* gardening, photography, genealogy, painting and drawing; *Style—* Miss Susan Lewis; ✉ Estyn, Anchor Court, Keen Road, Cardiff CF24 5JW (tel 029 2044 6475, fax 029 2044 6448, e-mail chief-inspector@estyn.gsi.gov.uk, website www.estyn.gov.uk)

LEWIS, (Christopher) Terence; s of Dr C B Lewis (d 1980), and Rachel, *née* O'Connor (d 1956); *b* 24 May 1944; *Educ* UCL, Westminster Hosp Med Sch (MB BS, LRCP MRCS, FRCS); *m* 1975, Jill, da of Alan Weller; 2 da (Victoria b 1979, Abigail b 1981), 1 s (Freddie b 1985); *Career* conslt then sr const cardiothoracic surgn Royal London Hosp 1979–95, conslt cardiothoracic surgn St Bartholomew's Hosp London 1995–97, sr conslt cardiothoracic surgn SW Cardiothoracic Centre Derriford Hosp Plymouth 1997–, med dir Plymouth Hosp NHS Tst 2000–; dir: cardiac surgical research Royal London Hosp, Sir Henry Souttar Labs; UK rep European Initiative for the Devpt of Artificial Hearts 1985–92, memb Medical Engrg and Sensors Ctee Sci and Engrg Research Cncl 1992–96, regnl advsr Cardiothoracic Surgery for SW Region 2003– (for N Thames (E) 1992–95), med dir SW Advsy Ctee for Clinical Excellence Awards, memb Clinical Governance Steering Ctee Sperrin Lakeland Health and Social Servs Tst NI 2004–; pres: Soc of Perfusionists of GB 2003–07, Plymouth Heartbeat; vice-pres Heartswell SW; dir Heartswell House SW Carers Lodge; tstee Plymouth Marine Laboratories; memb and med dir Dean's Advsy Bd to SW Region; exec memb Soc of Cardiothoracic Surgeons of GB and I 1999–2003; memb: Br Cardiac Soc, Cardiac Surgical Res Club; *Recreations* fishing, sailing, shooting; *Clubs* Royal Fowey Yacht, Fowey Gallants Sailing, Army and Navy; *Style—* Terence Lewis, Esq; ✉ Medical Director, Plymouth Hospital NHS Trust Derriford Hospital, Plymouth PL6 8DH (tel 01752 792997, e-mail terence.lewis@phnt.swest.nhs.uk)

LEWIS, Thomas Warwick (Tom); s of Dr Edward Claude Lewis (d 2000), and Rosemary, *née* Batten (d 2004); *b* 5 April 1958, Reigate, Surrey; *Educ* Whitgift Sch, Westminster Coll (OND); *m* 13 June 1981, Rosemary Vivienne, *née* Hamley; 2 da (Anna Gwen b 28 May 1986, Ellen Rosemary b 19 Oct 1988); *Career* trainee mangr then asst food and beverage mangr The Dorchester London 1978–83, back of house mangr then food and beverage mangr Dukes Hotel London 1983–86, dep gen mangr The Lygon Arms Broadway 1986–88, dir and gen mangr The Feathers Hotel Woodstock 1988–97, gen mangr The Angel Hotel Midhurst 1997–99, hotel mangr Great Fosters Hotel Egham 1999–2002 and 2004–05, gen mangr Studley Priory Horton-cum-Studley 2002–04, gen mangr Le Manoir aux Quat'Saisons 2005–; Master Innholder 2007; MHCIMA 1978, FIH 2007; *Recreations* swimming, music; *Style—* Tom Lewis, FIH, MI; ✉ Le Manoir aux Quat'Saisons, Church Road, Great Milton, Oxfordshire OX44 7PD (tel 01844 277211, fax 01844 278383, e-mail tom.lewis@blanc.co.uk)

LEWIS, Prof Trevor; CBE (1992); s of Harold Lewis (d 1982), and Maggie, *née* Bakewell; *b* 8 July 1933; *Educ* Imperial Coll London (PhD, DIC), Univ of Cambridge (MA), Univ of Nottingham (BSc, DSc); *m* 21 March 1959, Margaret Edith, da of Frederick George Wells (d 1977); 1 da (Heather b 15 April 1961), 1 s (Roger b 1 Oct 1963); *Career* univ demonstrator in agric zoology Sch of Agric Univ of Cambridge 1958–61; Rothamsted Experimental Station: joined 1961, seconded ODA 1970, head Entomology Dept 1976–83, head Crop Protection Div and dep dir 1983–87, head Crop and Environment Protection Div 1987–89, head and dir Inst for Arable Crops Res 1989–93, Lawes Tst sr fell 1994–2003; sr res fell Univ of West Indies 1970–73, visiting prof of invertebrate zoology Univ of Nottingham 1977– (special lectr 1968–69 and 1973–75); AFRC assessor; memb: MAFF Advsy Ctee on Pesticides 1984–89, Cncl Br Crop Protection Cncl 1985–93, R&D Ctee Potato Mktg Bd 1985–89; dir British Crop Protection Enterprises Ltd 1994–; Hon FRES 2005 (memb 1956, pres 1985–87); *Publications* Introduction to Experimental Ecology (with L R Taylor, 1967), Thrips - Their Biology, Ecology and Economic Importance (1973), Insect Communication (ed, 1984), Thrips as Crop Pests (ed, 1997); numerous contribs to scientific jls on entomological and agricultural topics; *Recreations* gardening, music; *Style—* Prof Trevor Lewis, CBE; ✉ Rothamsted Research, West Common, Harpenden, Hertfordshire AL5 2JQ (tel 01582 763133, fax 01582 760981, telex 825726)

LEWIS, Trevor Oswin; CBE (1983), DL (Dyfed 1994); suc as 4 Baron Merthyr (UK 1911) in 1977, but disclaimed Peerage for life, and does not use his title of Bt (UK 1896); s of 3 Baron Merthyr, KBE, TD, PC (d 1977); *b* 29 November 1935; *Educ* Eton, Magdalen Coll Oxford; *m* 18 April 1964, Susan Jane, da of A J Birt-Llewellin; 3 da (Lucy (Mrs Lucy Harbinson) b 1967, Anne (Mrs Anne Fisher) b 1970, Jessamy (Mrs Marcus Elmhirst) b 1972), 1 s (David Trevor b 1977); *Heir* to Btcy and disclaimed Barony, s, David Lewis; *Career* memb: Dept of Transport Landscape Advsy Ctee 1968–92 (chm 1991–92), Countryside Cmmn 1973–83; JP Dyfed 1969–94; *Style—* Trevor Lewis, Esq, CBE, DL; ✉ Hean Castle, Saundersfoot, Pembrokeshire SA69 9AL (tel 01834 810347)

LEWIS-FRANCIS, Mark; MBE (2005); s of Shaun Lewis-Francis, and Hermine Francis; *b* 4 September 1982, Birmingham; *Career* athlete; memb Birchfield Harriers; achievements at 100m: World Youth Champion 1999, UK under 20 Champion 1999 and 2000, Silver medal European Jr Championships 1999, World Jr Champion 2000 (championship record), winner B race IAAF Grand Prix London 2000, winner Loughborough 2000 and 2002, semi-finalist IAAF World Championships 2001, European Jr Champion 2001, second place UK Championships 2001, winner European Cup Super League 2001, winner DVL Jr Gala Mannheim 2001, second place Penn Relays 2001, winner Talahassee 2001 and 2002, third place IAAF Grand Prix II Rieti 2002, fifth place IAAF Golden League Brussels 2002, UK Champion 2002, third place IAAF Golden League Paris 2002, second place IAAF Grand Prix II Sheffield 2002, second place Cwlth Games trials 2002, world ranking 8 Track and Field News 2002, second place IAAF Super Grand Prix Gateshead 2003, fourth place IAAF Golden League Paris 2003, winner IAAF Golden League Oslo 2003, winner European Cup 2003, winner IAAF Super Grand Prix Ostrava 2003; achievements at 60m: Bronze medal World Indoor Championships Lisbon (world jr record) 2001, second place Glasgow Indoor Match 2001, second place UK Indoor Championships 2002, second place Energizer Indoor Series Birmingham 2002, Silver medal European Indoor 2002, second place Glasgow Indoor Match 2003, third place Energizer Indoor Series Birmingham 2003, UK Indoor Champion 2003, fourth place World Indoor Championships Birmingham 2003, fifth place Birmingham Indoor Grand Prix 2004; achievements in 4x100m relay: World Jr Champion 2000 (European jr record),

European Jr Champion 2001, Gold medal Olympic Games Athens 2004; winner 200m Tallahassee 2002; Br Jr Male Athlete of the Year 2000 and 2001; *Style*— Mark Lewis-Francis, Esq, MBE; ✉ c/o Ricky Simms, PACE Sports Management, 6 The Causeway, Teddington, Middlesex TW11 0HE (tel 020 8943 1072, fax 020 8977 6582, e-mail r.simms@pacesportsmanagement.com, website www.pacesportsmanagement.com)

LEWIS-JONES, Dr (Margaret) Susan (Sue); da of Ian Robert Munro Campbell, and Jean Douglas, *née* Ramsay; *b* 12 April 1948; *Educ* Tudor Grange Girls' GS Solihull, Univ of Liverpool Med Sch (MB ChB); *Career* medical and surgical house offr 1972–73, demonstrator in anatomy Univ of Liverpool 1973–74, GP 1974–77, medical registrar 1982, conslt dermatologist 1987– (registrar 1982–85, sr registrar 1985–87), hon lectr in dermatology Univ of Liverpool and Univ of Wales 1987–99, hon sr lectr Univ of Dundee; chm Br Soc Paediatric Dermatology 2000–04 (sec 1999–2000), sec Scot Dermatological Soc 2001, convenor for dermatology RCPCH 2001–04; currently memb: BMA, Br Assoc of Dermatologists, American Acad of Dermatology, Liverpool Med Inst; FRCP 1994 (MRCP 1982), FRCPCH 2004; *Recreations* golf, skiing, gardening, music; *Style*— Dr Sue Lewis-Jones; ✉ Ninewells Hospital, Dundee DD1 9SY (tel 01382 660111, fax 01382 633916)

LEWIS OF NEWNHAM, Baron (Life Peer UK 1989), of Newnham in the County of Cambridgeshire; Sir Jack Lewis; kt (1982); *b* 13 February 1928; *Educ* Barrow GS, Univ of London (BSc, DSc), Univ of Nottingham (PhD), Univ of Manchester (MSc), Univ of Cambridge (MA, ScD); *m* 1951, Elfreida Mabel, *née* Lamb; 1 s, 1 da; *Career* sits as an Ind in the House of Lords; lectr Univ of Sheffield 1954–56, lectr Imperial Coll London 1956–57, lectr/reader UCL 1957–61; prof of chemistry: Univ of Manchester 1961–67, UCL 1967–70, Univ of Cambridge 1970–95; warden Robinson Coll Cambridge 1975–2001; visiting prof UCL 1996–; memb: Poly Ctee SRC 1973–79, Sci Ctee SRC1975–80, Univ Grants Ctee for Physical Scis 1973–80, Jt Ctee SERC/SSRC 1979–84, Cncl SERC 1979–84, Cncl Royal Soc 1982–84 and 1996–98 (vice-pres 1983–84), Sci Ctee NATO 1986–98, Select Ctee on Sci and Technol House of Lords; chm: DES Visiting Ctee to Cranfield Inst 1982–92, Royal Cmmn on Environmental Pollution 1986–92, Standing Ctee on Structural Safety 1998–2002, Research Tst Bd Environmental Servs Assoc 1998–, Veolia Environmental Tst, Veolia Advsy Bd; pres: Royal Soc of Chemistry 1986–88, Nat Soc for Clean Air and Environmental Protection 1993–95, Arthritis Research Campaign 1998–; Hon DUniv: Rennes 1980, Open Univ 1982, Kingston 1993; Hon DSc: UEA 1983, Univ of Nottingham 1983, Keele Univ 1984, Univ of Birmingham 1988, Univ of Leicester 1988, Univ of Waterloo (Canada) 1988, Univ of Manchester 1990, Univ of Wales 1990, Univ of Sheffield 1992, Cranfield Univ 1993, Univ of Edinburgh 1994, Univ of Bath 1995, Univ of Durham 1996, Univ of Hong Kong 1998, NUI 1999, Anglia Poly Univ 2004; hon fell: Aust Chemical Inst 1986, UCL 1990, UMIST 1990, Univ of Central Lancashire 1993, Soc of Chemical Industry 1999; FRS, FRIC, FRSA, Hon FRSC 1998; Chevalier dans l'Ordre des Palmes Académiques, Cdr Cross of the Order of Merit of the Republic of Poland; *Style*— The Rt Hon Lord Lewis of Newnham, FRS; ✉ 17 Champneys Walk, Cambridge CB3 9AW; Robinson College, Cambridge (tel 01223 339100)

LEWISHAM, Archdeacon of; *see:* Hardman, Ven Christine Elizabeth

LEWISOHN, Oscar Max; s of Max Lewisohn (d 1973), of Copenhagen, Denmark, and Jenny Lewisohn (d 1984); *b* 6 May 1938; *Educ* Sortedam Gymnasium Copenhagen; *m* 1, 4 Aug 1962, Louisa Madeleine (d 1985), da of Henry Grunfeld, of London; 3 s (Mark b 1963, Richard b 1965, James b 1970), 1 da (Anita b 1967); m 2, 24 Oct 1987, Margaret Ann, da of Don Paterson, of Wellington, NZ; 2 da (Jenny b 1989, Sophie b 1990); *Career* SG Warburg and Co Ltd 1962–95: exec dir 1969, dep chm 1987–94; dir SG Warburg Group plc 1985–95, dir HSBC Private Bank (Suisse) SA 1997–2006, dir Maxcor Fin Services Inc NY 2000–05; chm Soditic Ltd 1996–; vice-chm Euro Orgn for Res and Treatment of Cancer Fndn, chm Cncl Imperial Cancer Research Fund (constituent of Cancer Research UK); chm The Florestan Tst; dir Danish UK C of C; govr Yehudi Menuhin Sch 2006–; hon memb Christ's Coll Cambridge; FRSA 1992, FCIB 2002; Knight Order of the Dannebrog 1 (Denmark); *Recreations* music; *Style*— Oscar Lewisohn, Esq; ✉ Soditic Ltd, Wellington House, 125 Strand, London WC2R 0AP (tel 020 7872 7090, fax 020 7872 7104, e-mail oscar_lewisohn@soditic.co.uk)

LEWISON, Hon Mr Justice; Sir Kim Martin Jordan Lewison; kt (2003); s of Anthony Frederick Lewison (d 1993), and Dinora, *née* Pines (d 2002); *b* 1 May 1952; *Educ* St Paul's, Downing Coll Cambridge (MA, Betha Wolferstan Rylands Prize); *m* 1, 29 Sept 1979 (m dis 1998), Helen Mary, da of Josef Janecek (d 1980); 1 s (Joshua George b 1982), 1 da (Lydia Miriam b 1984); m 2, 15 Dec 2002, Sharon Moross; *Career* called to the Bar Lincoln's Inn 1975 (bencher 1998); QC 1991, recorder 1997–2003 (asst recorder 1993–97), dep judge of the High Court 2000–2003, judge of the High Court of Justice (Chancery Div) 2003–; memb Cncl: Lib Jewish Synagogue 1990–96, Leo Baeck Coll 1996–2001; govr Anglo-American Real Property Inst 1996– (chm 2002); tstee Centre for Jewish Educn 1999–2001; *Books* Development Land Tax (1977), Drafting Business Leases (2000), The Interpretation of Contracts (2003), Woodfall on Landlord and Tenant (gen ed); *Recreations* visiting France; *Style*— The Hon Mr Justice Lewison; ✉ Royal Courts of Justice, Strand, London WC2A 2LL

LEWITH, Dr George Thomas; s of Frank Lewith (d 1965), and Alice, *née* Schallinger; *b* 12 January 1950; *Educ* Queen's Coll Taunton, Trinity Coll Cambridge (MA), Westminster Hosp London (MB BChir), MD; *m* 7 May 1977, Nicola Rosemary, da of Bonham Ley Bazeley, DSC, of Stonehouse, Glos; 2 s (Thomas b 1981, Henry b 1986), 1 da (Emily b 1983); *Career* paediatric intern McMaster Univ Ontario 1974, jr positions Westminster Hosp and UCH 1974–78, GP Queensland Australia 1978, WHO studentship in acupuncture Nanjing Coll of Traditional Chinese Med 1978, lectr in general practice (initially trainee) Dept of Gen Practice Univ of Southampton 1979–82, co-dir Centre for the Study of Complementary Med 1982–, reader and conslt Dept of Med Univ of Southampton; visiting prof Univ of Westminster; formerly vice-chm Br Med Acupuncture Soc, memb numerous med orgns and ctees, author of numerous learned books and articles; MRCGP 1980, FRCP 1999; *Recreations* swimming, skiing, sailing, bee keeping, theatre; *Clubs* Royal Lymington Yacht, RSM; *Style*— Dr George Lewith; ✉ Swaywood House, Mead End Road, Sway, Lymington, Hampshire SO41 6EE (tel 01590 682129); Centre for Complementary and Integrated Medicine, 56 Bedford Place, Southampton, Hampshire SO15 2DT (tel 023 8033 4752, fax 023 8023 1835, e-mail gl3@soton.ac.uk)

LEWSEY, (Owen) Joshua (Josh); MBE (2004); s of David Glynne Lewsey, and Mair Elizabeth Lewsey; *Educ* Watford Boys GS, Univ of Bristol, RMA Sandhurst, Coll of Law London; *Career* rugby union player; clubs: Bristol RFC, London Wasps RFC (winners Tetley's Bitter Cup 1999 and 2000, Parker Pen Challenge Cup 2003, Zurich Premiership 2003, 2004 and 2005, Heineken Cup 2004 and 2007); England: 50 caps, debut v NZ 1998, winners World Cup Aust 2003, memb squad World Cup France 2007; memb squad Br & I Lions tour to NZ 2005; cmmnd Lt RA 2001; reg supporter Prince's Tst, Army Benevolent Fund, NSPCC and Sparks charities; vol teacher of special needs children; *Recreations* property development, surfing, expeditions, country sports, music, theatre and friends; *Style*— Josh Lewsey, Esq, MBE; ✉ c/o London Wasps RUFC, Twyford Avenue Sports Ground, Twyford Avenue, Acton, London W3 9QA

LEY, Philip Edward Francis; s of Francis James Ley, of Abingdon, Oxon, and Alexandrina, *née* Moonie (d 1993); *b* 16 July 1960; *Educ* Ampleforth, Univ of Oxford (MA); *m* Feb 1994, Anna Elizabeth, da of David Tate; *Career* Unilever 1982–86: UCMDS trainee Lipton Export Ltd, brand mangr Lipton Yellow Label Tea ME and Scandinavia; Marketing Solutions 1986–87, Trowbridge Ley Partnership specialising in interior design in USA and men's clothing shops in UK 1987–89; Virgin Mastertronic/Sega Europe 1989–94: mktg mangr Sega Products until 1991, mktg dir UK (when Sega bought Virgin Mastertronic) 1991–93, Euro mktg dir 1993–94; mktg dir BSkyB 1994–96, fndr md Branded Ltd (communications agency) 1996–; Mktg Soc Marketeer of the Year 1993; memb Mktg Soc 1994; *Recreations* swimming, football, drumming, Manchester United supporter; *Clubs* The Electric; *Style*— Philip Ley, Esq; ✉ Branded Ltd, Albert Bridge House, 127 Albert Bridge Road, London SW11 4PL (tel 020 7978 7780, fax 020 7801 9137, e-mail phil@branded.co.uk)

LEY, Prof Steven Victor; CBE (2002); *b* 10 December 1945; *Educ* Loughborough Univ (BSc, DIS, PhD), Univ of London (DSc); *m*; 1 c; *Career* post doctoral fell Ohio State Univ 1972–74; Imperial Coll London: post doctoral fell 1974–75, probationary lectr 1975–76, lectr 1976–83, prof of organic chemistry 1983–92, head of Dept 1989–92; BP (1702) prof of organic chemistry Univ of Cambridge 1992–, fell Trinity Coll Cambridge 1993–; chm Exec Ctee Ciba Fndn 1993–2004 (memb 1990–2004); memb: Newly Appointed Lectrs Grant Ctee Nuffield Fndn 1986–2004, Chemistry Leadership Cncl 2002–04; author of over 560 res papers and articles; Royal Soc of Chemistry: Corday Morgan medal and prize for 1980, Hickenbottom research fellowship 1981, Pfizer academic award 1983, Tilden lectr and medal 1988, award for organic synthesis 1989, Pedler lectr, medal and prize 1992, Simonsen lectr and medal 1993, 1992 natural products award 1994, pres Perkin Div Royal Soc of Chemistry 1993–96 (memb 1989–96), Flintoff medal 1995, Rhône-Poulenc lectr, medal and prize 1998, Haworth meml lectureship medal prize 2001, pres 2000–02; Pfizer academic award 1983, Dr Paul George Kenner prize and lectr Univ of Liverpool 1996, Janssen prize for creativity in organic synthesis Belgium 1996, Royal Soc Bakerian lectr 1997, Glaxo-Wellcome award for outstanding achievement in organic chemistry 1999, Royal Soc Davey medal 2000, Pfizer award for innovative science 2001, German Chemical Soc August-Wilhelm-von Hofman medal 2001, American Chemical Soc Ernest Guenther award 2003, Soc for Chemical Industry Messel medal 2004, Yamado Koga Prize (Japan) 2005; Hon DSc: Loughborough Univ, Univ of Huddersfield, Salamanca Univ, Univ of Cardiff; memb: American Chemical Soc, Chemical Soc of Japan, Soc of Chemical Industry (London), Swiss Chemical Soc, Royal Inst London, American Assoc for the Advancement of Science, Int Soc of Heterocyclic Chemistry; CChem 1980, FRSC 1980, FRS 1990, fell Japanese Soc for the Promotion of Science 1993, FMedSci 2005; *Style*— Prof Steven Ley, CBE, FRS

LEYSHON, Robert Lloyd; s of Sqdn Ldr Mervyn Leyshon, of Pencoed, Mid Glamorgan, and Joan Hilton, *née* Lloyd (d 1950); *b* 12 February 1948; *Educ* Ogmore Vale GS, St Mary's Hosp (BSc, MB BS); *m* 16 July 1977, Catherine (Kay), da of Luther Edwards (d 1984); 1 s (Aled Lloyd b 18 Nov 1978), 1 da ((Catherine) Nia b 23 Feb 1980); *Career* house surgn and casualty offr St Mary's Hosp 1972–74, rotating surgical registrar Cardiff Hosp 1974–77, sr orthopaedic registrar Cardiff and Swansea Hosp 1979–83, sr lectr in orthopaedic surgery Welsh Sch of Med 1983–84, conslt orthopaedic surgn Morriston Hosp Swansea 1984–; author of papers on the use of carbon fibre as ligament replacement, research into post menopausal osteoporosis and reviews of hip prostheses in fractures of femoral neck, on-going study into elbow replacement surgery in rheumatoid arthritis; pres Welsh Orthopaedic Soc, treas Rheumatoid Arthritis Surgical Soc 2000, fndr memb Expert Witness Inst 1997, hon orthopaedic surgn Llanelli Scarlets Rugby; FRCS 1977, FBOA 1983, memb Euro Rheumatoid Arthritis Surgical Soc 1997; *Recreations* skiing, golf; *Clubs* Clyne Golf; *Style*— Robert Leyshon, Esq; ✉ 19 Westport Avenue, Mayals, Swansea SA3 5EA (tel 01792 403003); St David's House, Sancta Maria Hospital, Ffynone Road, Uplands, Swansea SA1 6DF; Orthopaedic Department, Morriston Hospital, Swansea SA6 6NL (tel 01792 703450, fax 01792 703201)

LIANG, Prof (Wei) Yao; s of late Tien Fu Liang, of Hong Kong, and Po Seng Nio, *née* Lie; *b* 23 September 1940; *Educ* Pah Tsung Chinese HS Jakarta, Portsmouth Coll of Technol, Imperial Coll London (BSc, ARCS), Univ of Cambridge (PhD); *m* 17 Aug 1968, Lian Choo, da of late Choong Sam; 3 da (Yifan, Chiafan, Hweifan); *Career* Univ of Cambridge: demonstrator in physics 1971–75, lectr in physics 1975–92, reader in high temperature superconductivity 1992–93, prof of superconductivity 1994–, dir Interdisciplinary Research Centre 1989–98; Gonville & Caius Coll Cambridge: research fell 1968–71, official fell and lectr 1971–, dir of studies in natural sciences 1975–89, professorial fell 1994–, pres 2005–; visiting scientist Xerox Palo Alto Research Centre California 1975 and 1976; visiting prof: EPF Lausanne 1978, Acad Sinica Inst of Semiconductors Beijing 1983, Science Univ of Tokyo 2000, Univ of Tokyo 2001, Xiamen Univ 2001; fell American Physical Soc; CPhys, FInstP; *Books* Polarons and Bipolarons in High Temperature Superconductors and Related Compounds (ed with A S Alexandrov and E K H Salje, 1995), Fundamental Research in High Tc Superconductivity (jtly with W Zhou, 1999); *Recreations* music, conversation, photography; *Style*— Prof Yao Liang; ✉ Gonville and Caius College, Trinity Street, Cambridge CB2 1TA (tel 01223 332425, fax 01223 332456, e-mail wyl1@cam.ac.uk)

LIBOCK MBEI, HE Samuel; *b* 4 October 1940; *Educ* BA; *m* Hermine Libock; 4 c; *Career* Cameroonian diplomat; advsr Presidency of Cameroon 1970–80, gen mangr nat oil co and chm Bd of Dirs nat refinery Cameroon 1978–84, min and chief of cabinet of the Pres of Cameroon 1986–89, ambass to Nigeria 1989–94, high cmmr to UK 1995– (ambass April-Nov 1995); non-resident ambass to Denmark, Finland, Norway and Sweden; many nat and foreign decorations; memb Rotary Int London; *Recreations* golf, theatre, cinema; *Clubs* Highgate Golf, Yaoundé Golf (Cameroon); *Style*— HE Mr Samuel Libock Mbei; ✉ High Commission for the Republic of Cameroon, 84 Holland Park, London W11 3SB (tel 020 7727 0771, fax 020 7792 9353)

LICHFIELD, Bishop of 2003–; Rt Rev Jonathan Michael Gledhill; *b* 15 February 1949; *Educ* Strode's Sch Egham, Keele Univ (BA), Univ of Bristol (MA), Trinity Coll Bristol (BCTS); *m* 1971, Dr S Jane Gledhill; *Career* curate All Saints Marple 1975–78, priest i/c St George Folkestone 1978–83, vicar St Mary Bredin Canterbury 1983–96, rural dean Canterbury 1988–94, hon canon Canterbury Cathedral 1992–96, bishop of Southampton 1996–2003; tutor/lectr: Canterbury Sch of Ministry 1983–94, SE Inst for Theol Educn 1994–96; chm: Anglican Old Catholic Int Consultative Cncl 1998–, Nat Coll of Evangelists 1998–; memb Meissen Cmmn 1993–96; *Style*— The Rt Rev the Bishop of Lichfield; ✉ Bishop's House, 22 The Close, Lichfield, Staffordshire WS13 7LG

LICHFIELD, 6 Earl of (UK 1831); Thomas William Robert Hugh Anson; also Viscount Anson and Baron Soberton (both UK 1806); s of 5 Earl of Lichfield (d 2005), and Lady Leonora Mary, *née* Grosvenor, LVO, da of 5 Duke of Westminster, TD (d 1979); *b* 19 July 1978, London; *Educ* Harrow; *Heir* kinsman, Robert George Anson; *Career* property conslt; *Recreations* fishing, travelling, sculpture; *Style*— Viscount Anson; ✉ Shugborough Hall, Stafford ST17 0XA (tel 01889 881454)

LICHT, Leonard Samuel; s of Bernhard Licht (d 1982), and Hilde, *née* Müller; *b* 15 March 1945; *Educ* Christ's Coll Finchley; *m* 2 June 1973, Judith, da of Albert Grossman (d 1980); 1 s (Rupert b 27 July 1974), 1 da (Marina b 19 April 1976); *Career* investment banker; dir S G Warburg & Co Ltd 1982–85, vice-chm and founding dir Mercury Asset Mgmnt Gp plc 1986–92, chm Channel Islands and Int Investment Tst Ltd 1988–92, dep chm Jupiter Asset Mgmnt plc 1992–96, dir Falkland Islands Gp plc 1999–, chm HgCapital (HgInvestment Mangrs and HgPooled Mgmnt) 2001–; non-exec dir Royal Free Hampstead NHS Trust 1990–97, special tstee Royal Free Hosp 1991–99, tstee Conservative & Unionists Agents Superannuation Fund 1999–2001; *Recreations* philately, eating lunch, pug dog Bruno; *Clubs* Brooks's, MCC; *Style*— Leonard Licht, Esq;

L

✉ HgCapital, 2 More London Riverside, London SE1 2AP (tel 020 7089 7990, fax 020 7089 7997, e-mail leonard.licht@hgcapital.net)

LICKISS, Sir Michael Gillam; kt (1993), DL (Somerset 2003); s of Frank Gillam, and Elaine Rheta, *née* Lefeuvre; *b* 18 February 1934; *Educ* Bournemouth GS, LSE, Univ of London (BSc); *m* 1, 1959 (m dis 1979), Anita; 2 s, 2 da; m 2, 1987, Anne; 1 s; *Career* articled clerk Bournemouth 1955–58, cmmnd Army 1959–62, chartered accountant in practice Bournemouth 1962–68; Grant Thornton (formerly Thornton Baker): Bournemouth office 1968–73, London office 1973–94, exec ptnr 1975–85, nat managing ptnr 1985–89, sr ptnr 1989–94; chm Accountancy Television Ltd 1992–94; non-exec dir United News and Media plc 1996–98, chm/dir various smaller cos; DTI inspr (jtly with Hugh Carlisle, QC) 1986–88; fndr pres Assoc of Accounting Technicians 1980–82; ICAEW: memb Cncl 1971–81 and 1983–94, pres 1990–91; chm: Somerset Economic Partnership 1993–98, EDEXCEL Fndn (formerly BTEC) 1994–2000, W of England Devpt Agency 1994–97, SW England RDA 1998–2002, Visit Britain (BTA) 2003–04; memb: Cncl FEFC 1992–96, Ct of Govrs LSE 1993–, Senate Engrg Cncl 1995–98, Learning and Skills Nat Cncl 2001–03, Industrial Devpt Advsy Bd DTI 2000–02; lectr UK and overseas, author of numerous articles in learned jls; Liveryman Worshipful Co of Chartered Accountants; Hon DBA: UWE, Bournemouth Univ; Hon DEd Plymouth Univ 2006; FCA; *Recreations* walking in Lake District, sailing; *Clubs* RAC; *Style*— Sir Michael Lickiss, DL; ✉ Westerly, Little Falmouth, Flushing, Cornwall TR11 5UP

LICKORISH, Adrian Derick; s of Leonard John Lickorish, CBE (d 2002), and Maris, *née* Wright; *b* 29 October 1948; *Educ* Highgate Sch, Univ of London (LLB, LLM); *m* 16 May 1987, Vivien Mary, da of John Bernard Gould, of Wirswall Hall, Whitchurch, Shrops; *Career* slr 1974; ptnr: Durrant Piesse 1981, Lovells (formerly Lovell White Durrant) 1988–2006; conslt Lyons Davidson; ind memb Bd Dept for Regnl Devpt; memb Law Soc, Liveryman City of London Solicitors' Co; *Recreations* economic history, country activities, English literature, trout fishing; *Clubs* Farmers, Royal Over-Seas League, Travellers; *Style*— Adrian Lickorish, Esq; ✉ Woodhouse Farm, Avening, Gloucestershire GL8 8NH

LIDBETTER, Andrew William; s of William James Lidbetter (d 2005), and Margaret Ruth, *née* Smith; *b* 26 June 1965; *Educ* Eltham Coll, Worcester Coll Oxford (BCL, MA); *m* 7 Aug 1993, Elisabeth Jane, *née* Edser; 2 s (Michael William b 3 June 1996, Stephen Andrew b 11 March 2000); *Career* admitted slr 1990; Herbert Smith: articled clerk 1988–90, slr 1990–98, ptnr 1998–; memb: Administrative Law Bar Assoc, Assoc of Regulatory and Disciplinary Lawyers, Law Soc; *Books* Company Investigations and Public Law (1999), Blackstone's Civil Practice (contrib chapters on judicial review and human rights); *Style*— Andrew Lidbetter, Esq; ✉ Herbert Smith, Exchange House, Primrose Street, London EC2A 2HS (tel 020 7374 8000, fax 020 7374 0888, e-mail andrew.lidbetter@herbertsmith.com)

LIDDELL, Alasdair Donald MacDuff; CBE (1997); s of Ian Donald Macduff Liddell, WS (d 1976), and Barbara Macduff (d 2001); *b* 15 January 1949; *Educ* Fettes, Balliol Coll Oxford (BA), Thames Poly (DMS); *m* 20 Feb 1976, Jenny Abramsky, *qv*; 1 s (Rob b 22 Feb 1977), 1 da (Maia b 11 Dec 1979); *Career* admin (Planning and Policies) Tower Hamlets Dist 1977–79, area gen admin Kensington and Chelsea and Westminster AHA 1979–82, dist admin Hammersmith and Fulham HA 1982–84, dist gen mangr Bloomsbury HA 1985–88, regnl gen mangr E Anglian RHA 1988–94, dir of planning NHS Exec 1994–2000, ind conslt; dir UK eHealth Assoc 2003–; *Recreations* skiing, personal computers, buying wine; *Style*— Alasdair Liddell, Esq, CBE; ✉ 3 Brookfield Park, London NW5 1ES (tel 020 7813 1702, e-mail alasdair@aliddell.com)

LIDDELL, (Andrew) Colin MacDuff; WS (1980); s of Ian Donald MacDuff Liddell, WS (d 1976), and Barbara, *née* Dixon; descendent of MacDuffs of Strathbraan, Perthshire; *b* 21 June 1954; *Educ* Cargilfield Sch Edinburgh, Fettes, Balliol Coll Oxford (BA), Univ of Edinburgh (LLB); *Children* 2 da (Iona Michelle b 1983, Bryony Marsali b 1985); *Career* slr; sr ptnr J & H Mitchell WS Pitlochry and Aberfeldy; accredited specialist in charity law 2001–; sr pres Speculative Soc of Edinburgh 1983–84; chm: Pitlochry and District Tourism Mgmnt Prog 1994–99, Pitlochry Fringe Tst 2000–03, Pitlochry Civic Tst 2001–04, Aberfeldy Highland Ball 2004–, Pitlochry Area Initiative 2004–; sec: Millennium Forest for Scotland Tst 1995–, Scottish Tartans Authy 1995–, Highland Perthshire Communities Partnership 1996–, Highland Perthshire Communities Land Tst; dir Maritime Rescue Inst 2003–05; tstee: Clan Donnachaidh Museum 1992–, Scottish Community Fndn 2005–; patron Moulin & Pitlochry History Circle 1996–; govr: Cargilfield Sch Edinburgh 1985–93 (vice-chm 1987–93), Pitlochry Festival Theatre 2002– (vice-chm 2006–); commentator Pitlochry Highland Games; *Publications* Pitlochry - Heritage of a Highland District (1993, 2 edn 1994); *Recreations* skiing, windsurfing, sailing, writing, hill walking, curling; *Style*— Colin Liddell, Esq, WS; ✉ J & H Mitchell WS, 51 Atholl Road, Pitlochry PH16 5BU (tel 01796 472606, fax 01796 473198, e-mail j@hmitchell.co.uk)

LIDDELL, HE the Rt Hon Helen Lawrie; PC (1998); da of late Hugh Reilly, of Coatbridge, Lanarkshire, and late Bridget, *née* Lawrie; *b* 6 December 1950; *Educ* Univ of Strathclyde (BA); *m* 22 July 1972, Dr Alistair Henderson, s of Robert Liddell, of Airdrie, Lanarkshire; 1 s (Paul b 1979), 1 da (Clare b 1985); *Career* head Econ Dept Scot TUC 1971–75 (asst sec 1975–76), economics corr BBC Scotland 1976–77, Scottish sec Lab Pty 1977–88, dir of public and corp affrs Scottish Daily Record and Sunday Mail Ltd 1988–92, chief exec Business Venture Prog 1993–94; Parly candidate (Lab) E Fife 1974; MP (Lab): Monklands E 1994–97, Airdrie and Shotts 1997–2005; economic sec to the Treasy 1997–98, min of state Scottish Office 1998–99, min for tport DETR 1999, min for energy DTI 1999–2001, sec of state for Scotland 2001–03; high cmmr to Australia 2005–; non-exec dir: Scottish Prison Bd 1992–94, Central Scotland Broadcasting Ltd 1993–94; memb Nat Jt Cncl for Academic Salaries and Awards 1974–76, Cabinet rep Int Women's Year Ctee 1975, chair UN 50th Anniversary Ctee Scotland 1994–95; Hon LLD Univ of Strathclyde 2005; *Books* Elite (1990); *Recreations* writing, walking; *Style*— HE the Rt Hon Helen Liddell; ✉ c/o Foreign & Commonwealth Office (Canberra), King Charles Street, London SW1A 2AH

LIDDELL, (William) Ian; CBE (2000); s of Alexander Odell Crawford Liddell (d 1976), and Margaret Macmillan, *née* Fulton (d 1993); *b* 8 September 1938; *Educ* Fettes, St John's Coll Cambridge (MA), Imperial Coll London (DIC); *m* 1, Wendy Anne Kenny; 1 s (Dominic b 6 Dec 1962), 2 da (Zunetta b 19 June 1964, Siobhan b 1 Oct 1965); m 2, Susan Diane Ebrey, da of Samuel Herbert; 2 da (Arabel b 24 March 1978, Juliet b 25 Nov 1985); *Career* engr; grad engr Ove Arup & Ptnrs 1960–62, engr Holst & Co Ltd 1963–67, sr engr then assoc Ove Arup & Ptnrs 1967–76, founding ptnr Buro Happold 1976–2005 (managing ptnr 1993–96); visiting prof in the principles of engrg design Univ of Cambridge; memb: Ad Hoc Ctee IStructE 1975, Exec Ctee IABSE; tstee Smallpiece Tst; Hon DEng Univ of Bristol 2001; Hon FRIBA 2001; FIStructE 1967, MICE 1969, FREng 1996; *Awards* Henry Adams Award IStructE 1975, Oscar Faber Medal IStructE 1985, MacRobert Award Royal Acad of Engrg 1999, Gold Medal IStructE 1999, Curtin Medal ICE 2001, Int Award of Merit in Structural Engrg IABSE 2002; *Recreations* sailing; *Clubs* Aldeburgh Yacht; *Style*— Ian Liddell, Esq, CBE; ✉ The Old Vicarage, Church Street, Sudbury, Suffolk CO10 2BL (tel 01787 372400, e-mail ian.liddell@burohappold.com)

LIDDELL-GRAINGER, Ian Richard Peregrine; MP; s of David Liddell-Grainger of Ayton, and Anne, *née* Abel-Smith; *b* 23 February 1959; *m* 31 Oct 1985, Jill Nesbit; 1 s (Peter Richard b 6 May 1987), 2 da (Sophie Victoria b 27 Dec 1989, May Alexandra b 9 Sept 1993); *Career* MP (Cons) Bridgwater 2001–; *Style*— Ian Liddell-Grainger, Esq, MP; ✉ House of Commons, London SW1A 0AA (e-mail ianlg@parliament.uk); tel 01278 458383, fax 01278 433613

LIDDIARD, Michael Richard; s of Richard England Liddiard, CBE (d 1993) and Constance Lily, *née* Rook; *b* 15 November 1946; *Educ* Oundle, Univ of Exeter (BA), London Business Sch; *m* 14 March 1970, Judith Elizabeth Best, da of Wing Cdr Frederick John Edward Ison, DFC, RAF (d 1978); 1 s (James Stratton b 1973), 1 da (Amanda Brooke b 1975); *Career* C Czarnikow Ltd 1969–92: dir 1981, vice-chm 1983; dir C Czarnikow Sugar Ltd 1991–95, sr vice-pres C Czarnikow Sugar Inc NY 1995–99, currently conslt Kingsman Americas; dir Lion Mark Holdings 1983–90; memb: Cncl Assoc of Futures Brokers and Dealers 1986–90, London Clearing House Bd 1987–91, World Sugar Ctee NY 1996–; Freeman City of London 1970, memb Ct of Assts Worshipful Co Haberdashers 1987 (Liveryman 1971); *Recreations* tennis, shooting, squash; *Clubs* RAC, Union (NY); *Style*— Michael Liddiard, Esq

LIDINGTON, Dr David; MP; s of Roy Lidington, and Rosa Lidington; *b* 30 June 1956; *Educ* Haberdashers' Aske's, Sidney Sussex Coll Cambridge (MA, PhD); *m* 5 Aug 1989, Helen, da of late Lt-Col T F Parry; 4 s (Christopher David Parry b 4 June 1993, Thomas Stephen Anders b 21 March 1995, Edward Charles Panes, James Andrew Damant (twins) b 8 July 1997); *Career* with BP 1983–86, with RTZ Corporation 1986–87, special adviser to Rt Hon Douglas Hurd 1987–90, sr conslt Public Policy Unit 1991–92, MP (Cons) Aylesbury 1992– (Parly candidate (Cons) Vauxhall 1987); PPS to Home Sec 1994–97, PPS to ldr of HM's Oppn 1997–99; oppn spokesman on Home Affairs 1999–2001, oppn frontbench Treasy spokesman 2001–02, shadow min for Agric and Fisheries 2002, shadow sec of state for the Environment, Food and Rural Affrs 2002–03, shadow sec of state for NI 2003–07, shadow foreign office min 2007–; *Recreations* history, choral singing, reading; *Style*— David Lidington, Esq, MP; ✉ House of Commons, London SW1A 0AA

LIDSTONE, John Barrie Joseph; s of Arthur Richard Francis Lidstone (d 1930), and Lilian May, *née* Teppett (d 1973); *b* 21 July 1929; *Educ* Presentation Coll Reading, Univ of Manchester, RAF Educn Officers' Course; *m* 1957, Primrose Vivien, da of Vincent Russell (d 1947), of Derby, and Emily, *née* Macdonald (d 1995); 1 da (b 1960); *Career* Nat Serv RAF 1947–48; English master Repton Sch 1949–52; Shell-Mex and BP and Assoc cos 1952–62, dep md Vicon Agricultural Machinery Ltd 1962–63, dir and gen mangr Marketing Selections Ltd 1969–72; Marketing Improvements Gp plc: joined 1965, dir 1968–, dir and gen mangr 1972–74, dep md 1974–88, dep chm 1988–89, non-exec dir 1989–93; non-exec dir: Kalamazoo plc 1986–91, North Hampshire Tst Co Ltd 1986–93, St Nicholas' School Fleet Educational Trust Ltd 1982–90 and 1995–96; memb: Chemical & Allied Products Industry Trg Bd 1975–79, UK Mgmnt Consultancies Assoc 1978–88 (chm 1986–87), Nat Inter-Active Video Centre 1988–90; ed Lidstorian 1985–88, mktg ed Pharmaceutical Times 1994–; voted top speaker on mktg in Europe 1974, Dartnell lecture tours USA 1978–82, sr visiting lectr Univ of Surrey 1990–2003; memb: Nat Exec Ctee CIM 1985–90, Ct of Assts Guild of Mgmnt Consultants 1993–99, BAFTA, Soc of Authors; Freeman City of London, Liveryman Worshipful Co of Marketors; FCMC, FCMI, FInstD, FCIM; *Films and Video* tech advsr and script writer: The Persuaders (1975), Negotiating Profitable Sales (1979), Training Salesmen on the Job (1981, won highest award for creative excellence at US Industrial Film Festival 1982), Marketing for Managers (1985), Marketing Today (1985), Reaching Agreement and Interviewing (1987, 1988); *Publications* Training Salesmen on the Job (1975, 2 edn 1986), Recruiting and Selecting Successful Salesmen (1976, 2 edn 1983), Negotiating Profitable Sales (1977, made into two part film by Video Arts 1979), Motivating your Sales Force (1978, 2 edn 1995), Making Effective Presentations (1985), The Sales Presentation (jtly, 1985), Profitable Selling (1986), Marketing Planning for the Pharmaceutical Industry (1987, 2 edn 1999), Manual of Sales Negotiation (1991), Manual of Marketing (for Univ of Surrey, 1991), Beyond the Pay-Packet (1992), Face the Press (1992), Presentation and Media Relations Planning for the Pharmaceutical Industry (2003); contrib chapters to: The Best of Dilemma & Decision (1985), Marketing in the Service Industries (1985), Marketing Handbook (3 edn 1989), Gower Book of Management Skills (2 edn 1992), The Director's Manual (1992 and 1995), The Marketing Book (3 edn 1994), Ivanhoe Guide to Management Consultants (1994), International Encyclopedia of Business and Management (1996); author of the 1998 Churchill Soc Christmas Lecture 'The Reform of the Honours System'; expert evidence incl in House of Commons Public Administration Select Ctee 2004 report: 'A Matter of Honour: Reforming the Honours System'; articles contrib to: The Times and Sunday Times, Daily and Sunday Telegraph, FT, The Observer, Long Range Planning, International Management, Management Today, Marketing, Marketing Week; *Recreations* writing, cricket, golf (capt N Hants Golf Club 1992–93); *Clubs* Reform; *Style*— John B J Lidstone, Esq

LIEBERMAN, Prof (Alexander) Robert; *b* 7 July 1942; *Educ* UCL (BSc, PhD, DSc); *m* 1, (m dis 1975); 2 s (Gerald b 1963, Nicholas b 1967); m 2, 1976, Dr Margaret Mary Bird; 2 da (Elizabeth b 1977, Georgina b 1979); *Career* UCL: asst lectr Dept of Anatomy 1965–68, lectr 1968–74, sr lectr 1974–76, reader 1976–87, dean Faculty of Life Sciences (biological and med) 1990–2004, vice-dean UCL Med Sch 1990–98, vice-dean Royal Free and UC Med Sch 1998–99, fell 2001; prof of anatomy (neurobiology) Univ of Aarhus Denmark 1983–85, prof of anatomy Univ of London 1987–; ed-in-chief Jl of Neurocytology 1986–2005 (jt ed 1972–85), Euro ed Jl of Electron Microscopy 1996–2002; memb: Scientific Advsy Panel The Brain Research Tst 1991–97, Scientific Advsy Bd CNRS/INSERM Unité de Recherches Neurobiologique Marseille 1990–96, Sr Advsy Bd Int Jl of Diabetes 1992–, Scientific Ctee R&D Directorate UCL Hosps Tst 1996–, Ctee of Mgmnt Eastman Dental Inst 1995–99, Sci Ctee Int Spinal Research Tst 1997–2004, Prize Ctee Kemali Fndn for Neuroscience 2006–; govr Moorfields Eye Hosp NHS Tst 2004–; tstee: Alzheimer Research Tst 1997– (chm Scientific Advsy Ctee 2002–04), Alzheimer Brain Bank UK 2005–; memb: IBRO, BNA, ENA, RDA, Soc for Neuroscience, Physio Soc, Anatomical Soc; MD (hc) Charles Univ Prague 1998; FMedSci 1999; *Books* contrib: International Review of Neurobiology (1971), Essays On The Nervous System (1974), The Peripheral Nerve (1976), Neuron Concept Today (1976), Local Circuit Neurons (1976), Thalamic Networks for Relay and Modulation (1993), Progress in Neurobiology (1995), Progress in Brain Research (1998), Degeneration and Regeneration in the Nervous System (1999); *Recreations* cards, backgammon; *Style*— Prof Robert Lieberman; ✉ Department of Anatomy and Developmental Biology, University College London, Gower Street, London WC1E 6BT (tel 020 7679 3357, fax 020 7679 7349, e-mail ucgarol@ucl.ac.uk)

LIEBERMAN, Dr Stuart; s of Jerome Leon Lieberman, of Miami, Florida, USA, and Libby, *née* Mizus; *b* 4 October 1942; *m* 1, 1965 (m dis 1981), Susan Joan Lieberman; 3 s (Samuel, Steven, Simon); m 2, 30 Oct 1986, Sybil Margaret Battersby, da of Joseph Heath, of Wallheath, Wolverhampton; 3 da (Abigail, Gemma, Mel); *Career* Capt USAF 1965–70; sr lectr and conslt psychiatrist St George's Hosp Med Sch 1975–92, conslt psychiatrist in psychotherapy Heathlands Mental Health Tst 1992–99, med dir Priory Hosp Woking 2000–01, conslt Warby Hospital 2003–; fndr memb and treas Inst of Family Therapy London 1976–79, fndr memb and sec Assoc for Family Therapy 1975–78 (chm 1998–2000); FRCPsych 1983; *Books* Transgenerational Family Therapy (1979); *Style*— Dr Stuart Lieberman; ✉ 13 Barnby Road, Knaphill, Woking, Surrey GU21 2NL (tel 01483 481488)

LIEBERMANN, Frank Alec; s of Alfred H Liebermann (d 2001), and Ilse, *née* Weisz (d 1991); *b* 13 July 1939, Durban, SA; *Educ* Christian Brothers Coll Cape Town SA, The Neighborhood Playhouse NYC (BA); *m* 1, Jan 1961 (m dis 1965); m 2, 8 Sept 1973 (m dis), Linda Janice, *née* Marshall; 2 da (Alexis Claire b 15 Dec 1976, Danielle Laura b 11 Sept 1978); *Career* asst stage mangr/actor Hoffmeyer Theatre Cape Town SA 1956, student NYC 1958–60, emigrated to Toronto Canada with various engagements in TV, cinema and theatre 1960–62, emigrated to UK 1962, various employments in TV (starred in own TV series 1965), theatre and cinema, drama teacher The Arts Educnl Tst until 1972; prodr: James Garrett & Partners 1972–75, Brooks Fulford Cramer 1975–77; fndr Thorpe Lieberman Ltd prodn co 1977, prodr BSB Dorland Advertising 1987, dir and head of TV Abbott Mead Vickers BBDO Ltd 1987–2001, freelance advtg agency conslt 2001–04, exec head of TV McCann-Erickson 2004–06; recipient: Gold, Silver and Bronze Awards Cannes Film Festival, Clio Awards (NY), D&AD Awards, Br TV Awards, etc; memb: Equity 1962, ACTT 1974, IPA 1987, D&AD 1988; MIPA; *Recreations* theatre, cinema, music, reading, travel, food, cooking, grandchildren; *Style*— Frank Liebermann, Esq; ✉ McCann Erickson, 7–11 Herbrand Street, London WC1N 1EX (tel 020 7837 3737, e-mail frank.leibermann@europe.mccann.com)

LIEBMANN, Dr Stephen James; s of Dr Gehard Liebmann (d 1955), of Aldermaston, and Dora, *née* Badt (d 1989); *b* 4 September 1945; *Educ* Reading Sch, Univ of Sheffield (BEng, PhD); *m* 1972, Felicity Anne, da of Geoffrey A E Hodgkinson; 1 s (Nicholas b 11 Jan 1976), 1 da (Charlotte b 22 July 1979); *Career* BBC Radio Sheffield 1966–69 (freelance radio news and feature reporter, prog prodr and editor), journalist Electronics Weekly IPC Business Press 1969–72, Investors Chronicle Throgmorton Pubns 1972–77 (fin journalist, sr memb Editorial and Prodn Team); investment researcher: J M Finn & Co (stockbrokers) 1977–81, Seymour Pierce & Co (stockbrokers) 1981–83; ptnr i/c private catering business 1983–86, fin conslt 1983–86, gp chief press offr TSB Group plc 1986–87, dir Buchanan Communications Ltd 1987–2003, conslt Bankside Consultants Ltd 2003–; *Recreations* sailing; *Style*— Dr Steve Liebmann; ✉ Bankside Consultants Ltd, 1 Frederick's Place, London EC2R 8AE (tel 020 7367 8883, e-mail steve.liebmann@bankside.com)

LIFFORD, 9 Viscount (I 1781); (Edward) James Wingfield; DL (Hants 2004); also Baron Lifford (I 1768); s of 8 Viscount Lifford (d 1987), and (Alison) Mary Patricia, *née* Ashton; *b* 27 January 1949; *Educ* Aiglon Coll Switzerland; *m* 1976, Alison, da of Robert Law, of Withersfield, Suffolk; 2 da (Hon Annabel Louise b 1978, Hon Alice Mary b 1990), 1 s (Hon (James) Thomas Wingfield b 1979); *Heir* s, Hon Thomas Hewitt; *Career* dir Rathbone Bros plc 1996–2006, chm Rathbone Investment Mgmnt (CI) Ltd 2007–; non-exec dir McKay Securities plc 2006–; memb Securities Investment Inst; Liveryman Worshipful Co of Armourers and Brasiers; *Recreations* country sports; *Clubs* Boodle's, Pratt's, SMTC; *Style*— The Rt Hon Viscount Lifford, DL; ✉ Field House, Hursley, Winchester, Hampshire SO21 2LE

LIFFORD, William Lewis (Will); s of George Edward Lifford (d 1993), and Madge Elizabeth, *née* Lewis, of Tunbridge Wells, Kent; *b* 14 January 1951; *Educ* Sevenoaks Sch, Univ of Bristol (BSc); *m* 20 Aug 1977, Susanne, da of Stanley Woof (d 1998); 2 s (David b 18 May 1984, Michael b 24 March 1986); *Career* Deloitte & Co London 1972–79 (qualified CA 1975); Grant Thornton: London office 1979–82, ptnr Leeds 1982–98 and 2001–07, UK sr audit ptnr 2002–07; memb Urgent Issues Task Force (Accounting Standards Bd) 1994–97; chm Forum of Firms IFAC 2004–; *Recreations* hill walking, photography; *Style*— Will Lifford, Esq; ✉ 9 Rose Croft, East Keswick, Leeds LS17 9HR (tel 01937 572473)

LIGENZA-MILDENHALL, Gabriela Maria; da of Tadeusz Ligenza, of Gdynia, Poland, and Gertruda, *née* Szydlowska; *b* 14 May 1959; *Educ* Acad of Fine Arts in Warsaw (MA, UNESCO award); *m* 1, 1978 (m dis), Count Andrzej Borkowski; 1 da (Alicja b 13 Oct 1980); m 2, 1988, Richard Mildenhall; 1 s (Oscar b 8 Nov 1988); *Career* collaboration with Akademia Ruchu visual avant garde theatre in Warsaw and participation in many Euro theatre festivals 1976–83; fndr Gabriela Ligenza (high fashion hat design) 1985–; designed own collections and collaborated with others incl: Missoni, Jasper Conran, Paul Smith, Roland Klein, Laura Ashley, Myrene de Premonville; *Clubs* Chelsea Arts; *Style*— Mrs Gabriela Ligenza; ✉ c/o Gabriela Ligenza Hats, 5 Ellis Street, London SW1X 9AL (tel 020 7730 2200, e-mail ltc@gabrielaligenza.com, website www.gabrielaligenza.com)

LIGHT, John Vernon; s of Charles Vernon Light (d 1990), and Eva, *née* Blackburn (d 1994); *b* 25 April 1948; *Educ* Sedbergh, Clare Coll Cambridge (MA), Manchester Business Sch (Dip Business Admin); *m* 1974, Katy, *née* Donald; 1 s (Simon b 1974), 3 da (Jenny b 1975, Anna b 1978, Nicola b 1980); *Career* worked in industry 1969–75, teacher 1975–92, headmaster Oswestry Sch 1992–95, rector Edinburgh Acad 1995–; *Recreations* cricket, squash, golf, mountaineering, acting, choral singing; *Clubs* East India; *Style*— John Light, Esq; ✉ Edinburgh Academy, 42 Henderson Row, Edinburgh EH3 5BL (tel 0131 556 4603, fax 0131 556 9353, e-mail rector@edinburghacademy.org.uk)

LIGHTFOOT, Elizabeth (Liz); da of late John Richard Lightfoot, of Healing, nr Grimsby, NE Lincolnshire, and Ethne, *née* Stanton; *b* 27 September 1950; *Educ* Cleethorpes Girls' GS, Univ of Newcastle upon Tyne (BA), Univ of Durham (MA); *Children* 2 s (John Julian, Jamie Stanton (twins) b 6 Dec 1992); *Career* journalist; Hendon Times 1978–81, freelance 1981–83, Parly corr Press Assoc 1984–86, educn corr Mail on Sunday 1986–92, legal affairs corr Sunday Times 1992–96, educn corr The Daily Telegraph 1996–; *Style*— Ms Liz Lightfoot; ✉ The Daily Telegraph, 1 Canada Square, London E14 5DT (tel 020 7538 6113)

LIGHTFOOT, His Hon (George) Michael; s of Charles Herbert Lightfoot (d 1941), of Leeds, and Mary, *née* Potter (d 1974); *b* 9 March 1936; *Educ* St Michael's RC Coll Leeds, Exeter Coll Oxford (MA); *m* 20 July 1963, Dorothy, da of Thomas Miller (d 1977); 2 da (Catherine b 1968, Anne b 1973), 2 s (John b 1970, David b 1977); *Career* Nat Serv 1955–57, York and Lancaster Regt, Intelligence Corps; Exeter Coll Oxford 1957–60, schoolmaster 1962–66; called to the Bar Inner Temple 1966; practised NE circuit 1967–86, recorder of the Crown Court 1985–86, circuit judge (NE Circuit) 1986–2001 (dep circuit judge 2001–06); pres: Mencap Leeds 1987–2003, Leeds Friends of the Home Farm Tst; tstee Leeds Opportunity Tst for the Young; *Recreations* cricket and sport in general, reading; *Clubs* Catenian Assoc, City of Leeds Circle, Yorkshire CCC, Northern Cricket Soc; *Style*— His Hon Michael Lightfoot

LIGHTING, Jane; *b* 22 December 1956; *Career* fndr and md Minotar Int 1995–99, ceo Flextech 2002–03 (md Broadcast and Television 1999–2002), ceo Channel Five Broadcasting Ltd 2003–; chm Br Television Distributors Assoc 1995–96, chair RTS, dir Edinburgh Television Festival 1998–, govr Nat Film and Television Sch 2001–; FRSA; *Recreations* painting, escaping to the country; *Clubs* Groucho; *Style*— Ms Jane Lighting; ✉ Five, 22 Long Acre, London WC2E 9LY (tel 020 7550 5555, fax 020 7550 5512, e-mail jane.lighting@five.tv)

LIGHTMAN, Hon Mr Justice; Sir Gavin Anthony Lightman; kt (1994); *Educ* Univ of London (LLB), Univ of Michigan (LLM); *m* Dr Naomi Lightman; 1 s (Daniel), 2 da (Esther, Sarah); *Career* called to the Bar Lincoln's Inn 1963 (bencher 1987); QC 1980, judge of the High Court of Justice (Chancery Div) 1994–, assigned judge of the Crown Office 1995– (now Administrative Court), appointed judge of the Restrictive Practices Cncl 1997–2001; fell UCL 2002; *Style*— The Hon Mr Justice Lightman; ✉ Royal Courts of Justice, The Strand, London WC2A 2LL (tel 020 7936 6671)

LIGHTMAN, Prof Stafford Louis; s of Harold Lightman, QC (d 1998), and Gwendoline Joan, *née* Ostrer; *b* 7 September 1948; *m* 1977 (m dis), Susan Louise, da of John Stubbs, of London; 3 s (Sarne Louis b 1978, Joel David b 1979, Leon Alexander b 1982), 1 da (Elewys Gemma b 1987); *Career* prof of clinical neuroendocrinology Charing Cross Hosp London 1988–92, prof of medicine Univ of Bristol 1993–; ed Journal of Neuroendocrinology 1988–97; chm Pituitary Fndn 1996–2002; FRCP, FMedSci; *Books* Neuroendocrinology (ed with B J Everitt, 1986), The Functional Anatomy of the Neuroendocrine Hypothalamus (1992), The Management of Pituitary Tumours: A Handbook (ed with M Powell, 1996, 2 edn 2003), Horizons in Medicine: Vol 7 (ed, 1996), Endocrinology (with A Levy, 1997), Steroid Hormones and the T-Cell Cytokine Profile (with G Rook, 1997); *Style*— Prof Stafford Lightman; ✉ University of Bristol, Henry Wellcome Laboratories, Dorothy Hodgkin Building, Whitson Street, Bristol BS1 3NY (tel 0117 331 3167, fax 0117 331 3169, e-mail stafford.lightman@bristol.ac.uk)

LIGHTON, Sir Thomas Hamilton; 9 Bt (I 1791), of Merville, Dublin; o s of Sir Christopher Robert Lighton, 8 Bt, MBE (d 1993), and his 2 w, Horatia Edith, *née* Powlett (d 1981); *b* 4 November 1954; *Educ* Eton; *m* 1990, Belinda Jean, elder da of John Fergusson, of Castle Douglas, Kirkcudbrightshire; 1 da (Celina Hamilton b 26 May 1991), 3 s (James Christopher Hamilton, Harry John Hamilton (twins) b 20 Oct 1992, Christopher Nicholas Hamilton b 30 Aug 1994 d 1994); *Heir* s, James Lighton; *Career* dir Waddington Galleries Ltd, chm Soc of London Art Dealers 1993–95 and 1998–2000; *Style*— Sir Thomas Lighton, Bt

LIJN, Liliane; da of Herman Segall (d 1971), of Geneva, and Helena, *née* Kustanowitz; *b* 22 December 1939, NYC; *Educ* Sorbonne Paris, Ecole du Louvre Paris; *m* 1961 (m dis 1970), Takis Vassilakis, s of Athanasios Vassilakis; 1 s (Thanos Vassilakis b 17 April 1962); partner, Stephen Weiss; 1 s (Mischa Weiss-Lijn b 31 May 1975), 1 da (Sheba Weiss-Lijn b 24 Oct 1977); *Career* sculptor, poet and kinetic artist; experimented with fire and acids 1961–62, made and showed first kinetic poems Paris 1963–64, worked using natural forces Athens 1964–66, settled London 1966, numerous cmmns for large public sculptures 1971–; memb Cncl of Mgmnt Byam Shaw Art Sch 1983–90, memb Artslab and Operalab 1999; *Awards* Arts Cncl Award 1976, Alecto Award (Bradford Print Biennale) 1976, Arts Cncl Publishing Award for Crossing Map 1981, Arts Cncl Bursary for holography 1982, London Production Fund Award 1996; *Solo Exhibitions* incl: La Librairie Anglaise Paris 1963, Indica Gallery London 1967, Germain Gallery Paris 1972, Beyond Light (Serpentine Gallery London) 1976, toured Durham LI Museum Durham, Mappin Gallery Sheffield and Walker Art Gallery Liverpool 1977, Biting Through (Alecto Gallery London) 1977, Circle of Light (Eagle Walk Gallery Milton Keynes) 1980, Roundhouse Gallery London 1980, Aberdeen Art Gallery 1983, Paton Gallery London 1983, Heads (Galerie Peter Ludwig Cologne) 1985, Imagine the Goddess (Fischer Fine Art London) 1987, Poem Machines 1962–68 (Nat Arts Library, V&A) 1993, Her Mother's Voice (Eagle Gallery London) 1996, Koans (Galerie Lara Vincy Paris) 1997, Koans (Shirley Day Ltd) 2000, Iltempo G La Memoria (La Rocca Centro d'Arte Contemporanea Umbertide), Liliane Lijn: Light and Memory (La Rocca Centro d'Arte Contemporanea Umbertide and Studio Nardi Florence) 2002; *Group Exhibitions* incl: Light & Movement (Musée d'Art Modern Paris) 1967, Kinetic Art (Kunstnishus Oslo, Helsinki and Gothenburg) 1969 (also at Hayward Gallery London 1970), Agam-Bury-Lijn-Soto-Takis Delson-Richter Galleries Tel Aviv 1973, Art of the Sixties (Tate Gallery London) 1976, British Sculpture in the 20th Century (Whitechapel Art Gallery) 1981, Licht-Blicke (German Film Museum Frankfurt) 1984, 20th Century Drawings & Watercolours (V&A) 1984, Tecnologia e Informatica (Venice Biennale) 1986, The Artist's Notebook (Galerie Bernard Jordan Paris, Galerie Akiyama Tokyo, Atelier Nishinomiya Nishinomya and Art Works LA) 1987, Licht und Transparenz (Museum Bellerive Zurich) 1988, New Sculpture (Gillian Jason Gallery London) 1990, Chagall to Kitaj - Jewish Experience in 20th Century Art (Barbican Art Gallery London) 1990–, Le Livre Illustre (Bibliothèque Municipale Besançon) 1991, Les Artistes et La Lumière (Le Manege Reims) 1991, The Sixties Art Scene in London (Barbican Art Gallery London) 1993, Art Unlimited (South Bank Centre touring exhbn) 1994, British Abstract Art - Sculpture (Angela Flowers Gallery) 1995, Cabinet Art (Jason and Rhodes) 1995, Livres d'Artistes (Galerie Lara Vincy Paris) 1996, Rubies and Rebels (Barbican Gallery London) 1996, Chimériques Polymères (Musée d'Art Moderne et d'Art Contemporain Nice) 1996, Improvisations on a Line (Eagle Gallery London) 1999, Stelle Cadenti (Bassano Teverina) 1999, Forcefields (Barcelona and Hayward Gallery) 2000, Dream Machines (Arts Cncl touring exhbn) 2000, (S)cripturae (Galeria Civica Padova) 2001, Thinking Big Concepts for Twenty-First Century British Sculpture (Peggy Guggenheim Collection Venice) 2002, Editions Alecto: A Fury for Prints Artist's Multiples and Prints 1960–81 (Whitworth Art Gallery Univ of Manchester, Bankside Gallery London and City Art Gallery Edinburgh) 2003, Vaselle d'Autore per Il Vino Novello (La Vecchia Fornace Torgiano) 2003, Outside of a Dog (Baltic: The Centre for Contemporary Art Gateshead) 2003, Linea Umbra 02 - Artisti fuori dal Coro (Flashart Museum Trevi) 2004, Andata e Ritorno: Artiste Contemporanee Tra Europa e USA (Palazzo Bonacossi Ferrara) 2004, Daddy Pop: the Search for Art Parents (Anne Faggionato Gallery London) 2004, Art and the Sixties: This was Tomorrow (Tate Britain London and Birmingham Museum and Art Gallery) 2004; *Work in Public Collections* incl: New Hall Cambridge, NY Public Library, Tate Gallery, Arts Cncl of GB, V&A, Unilever plc, Arthur Andersen & Co, Br Cncl, Contemporary Art Soc London, Glasgow Museum Kelvingrove, Cleveland Educn Ctee, Castle Museum Nottingham, Musée de la Ville de Paris, Robert Mclaughlin Gallery Oshawa, MOMA NYC, Chicago Inst, Museum of NSW Sydney, Kunstmuseum Bern, Wellesley Coll MA; *Publications* incl: Six Throws of the Oracular Keys Paris (poems and drawings, 1982), Crossing Map (autobiographical sci fiction prose poem, 1983), A Symbolic Structure for the Turn of the Century (1988), Her Mother's Voice (artists' book/oral history, 1996), First Words (2000), Light and Memory (2002); author of numerous articles for magazines and jls; *Recreations* swimming and gardening; *Style*— Ms Liliane Lijn; ✉ 99 Camden Mews, London NW1 9BU (tel and fax 020 7485 8524, e-mail liliane@lilianelijn.com, website www.lilianelijn.com)

LIKIERMAN, Prof Sir (John) Andrew; kt (2001); s of Adolf Likierman (d 1988), and Olga, *née* Heldenbusch (d 1978); *b* 30 December 1943; *m* 1987, Dr Meira, da of Joshua Gruenspan; 1 step da (Ruth Thompson b 1976), 1 step s (James Thompson b 1979); *Career* divnl mgmnt accountant Tootal Ltd 1965–68, lectr Dept of Mgmnt Studies Univ of Leeds 1972–74 (asst lectr 1968–69), Qualitex Ltd 1969–72 (md Overseas Div 1971–72), visiting fell Oxford Centre for Mgmnt Studies 1972–74, non-exec chm Ex Libris Ltd 1973–74, non-exec chm Economist's Bookshop Ltd 1987–91 (non-exec dir 1981–91); London Business Sch 1974–76 and 1979–: dir Pt/t Masters Prog 1981–85, dir Inst of Public Sector Mgmnt 1983–88, chm Faculty Bd 1986–89, prof of accounting and fin control 1987–93, dean of external affairs 1989–92, ex-officio govr 1990–93 (elected govr 1986–89), dep princ 1990–93, visiting prof 1993–2001, prof of mgmnt practice 2001–, acting dean 2007; asst sec Cabinet Office and memb Central Policy Review Staff 1976–79 (advsr 1979–82); HM Treasy: head of Govt Accounting Serv and chief accountancy advsr 1993–2004, dir of fin mgmnt, reporting and audit 1994–2000, princ fin offr 1995–2000, md of fin mgmnt, reporting and audit 2000–04; advsr House of Commons Select Ctees on: Treasy and Civil Serv 1981–91, Employment 1985–90, Tport 1981 and 1987–90, Social Servs 1988, Social Security 1991; memb Govt Inquiries on: N Sea Cost Escalation 1975, Future of Power Plant Mfrg Indust 1976, Int Comparisons with PO and British Telecom 1981, Accounting for Econ Costs and Changing Prices 1986, Professional Liability (chm) 1989; memb Editorial Bd Public Money and Management 1988– (chm 1988–93); dir: Bank of England 2004–, MORI Ltd 2004–05 (chm 2005), Barclays plc 2004–; chm Applied Intellectual Capital plc 2006–; memb: Fin Ctee Oxfam 1974–84, Ctee on Med Costs Univ of London 1980–81, Current Affairs Advsy Gp Channel 4 1986–87, Audit Cmmn 1988–91, Ctee on Financial Aspects of Corp Governance 1991–95; memb Cncl: RIPA 1982–88, CIMA 1985–94 (pres 1991–92), Civil Serv Coll 1989–94, Defence Operational Analysis Centre 1992–93; observer: Accounting Standards Bd 1993–2004, Fin Reporting Cncl 1994–2004 (memb 1991–94), Tavistock and Portman NHS Tst Bd

2000–, Steering Ctee Corp Governance of UN 2006; Hon DBA: Southampton Business Sch, Oxford Brookes Univ; Hon DPhil London Met Univ; CIMA (Gold Medal), FCMA, FCCA; *Books* The Reports and Accounts of Nationalised Industries (1979), Cash Limits and External Financing Limits (1981), Public Sector Accounting and Financial Control (jtly, 1983, 4 edn 1992), Structure and Form of Government Expenditure Reports (jtly, 1984, 1985, 1990, 1991 and 1992), Public Expenditure (1988), Accounting for Brands (jtly, 1989), Ethics and Accountants in Industry and Commerce (1990); *Recreations* cycling, ideas, architecture, wine; *Clubs* Reform; *Style*— Prof Sir Andrew Likierman; ⊠ 5 Downshire Hill, London NW3 1NR (tel 020 7435 9888); London Business School, Sussex Place, Regents Park, London NW1 4SA

LILFORD, Prof Richard James; s of Maj Victor Lilford, and Eileen, *née* Gifford; *b* 22 April 1950; *Educ* St John's Coll Johannesburg, PhD; *m* 23 May 1981, Victoria Alice Lilford; 1 s (Peter), 2 da (Nicola, Philippa); *Career* formerly conslt obstetrician and gynaecologist Queen Charlotte's Hosp London, prof of obstetrics and gynaecology and chm Epidemiology Res Inst Univ of Leeds until 1995, dir of R&D NHS Exec W Midlands 1995–, prof of health servs research Univ of Birmingham 1995–; NHS clinical trials advsr, dir Central Programme on Methodology Research; MFPHM; FRCP, FRCOG; *Books* Basic Science for Obstetrics and Gynaecology (1984, 3 edn 1989), Prenatal Diagnosis and Prognosis (1990), Computing and Decision Suport in Obstetrics and Gynaecology (1991); *Recreations* flying, tennis; *Style*— Prof Richard Lilford; ⊠ University of Birmingham, Department of Public Health and Epidemiology, Edgbaston, Birmingham B15 2TT (tel 0121 414 6772, fax 0121 414 2752)

LILL, John Richard; CBE (2005, OBE 1978); s of G R Lill; *b* 17 March 1944; *Educ* Leyton County HS, Royal Coll of Music; *m* 2003, Jacqueline Clifton Smith; *Career* concert pianist; gave first recital aged nine, London debut playing Beethoven's Emperor (5th) Piano Concerto Royal Festival Hall 1962, first Br pianist to perform complete Beethoven Sonata Cycle (at the Queen Elizabeth Hall 1982, also at the Barbican Hall 1986 and Casals Hall Tokyo 1987); performed with orchs incl: LSO, LPO, CBSO, Royal Liverpool Philharmonic, BBC Welsh and Scottish Symphony Orchs, BBC Symphony, Hallé, Royal Philharmonic, Royal Scottish, Baltimore Symphony, Philadelphia, Cleveland, San Diego Symphony, Boston Symphony, NY Philharmonic, Leipzig Gewandhaus Orch, St Petersburg Philharmonic; worked with conductors incl: Sir Adrian Boult, Sir John Barbirolli, Seiji Ozawa, David Atherton, Eduardo Mata, Simon Rattle, Tadaaki Otaka, Rafael Frühbeck de Burgos, Andrew Davis, Walter Weller, James Loughran, Yuri Temirkanov, Kurt Masur; appeared at venues incl: Royal Festival Hall, Queen Elizabeth Hall, Konzerthaus Vienna, Hollywood Bowl, Le Châtelet Paris, Tanglewood, BBC Proms, Cardiff Festival, Swansea Festival; winner Moscow Int Tchaikovsky Competition 1970; *Recordings* incl: Beethoven Piano Concerto Cycle (with Scottish Nat Orch and Sir Alexander Gibson, and with CBSO and Walter Weller), Beethoven Sonata Cycle, Brahms Piano Concertos (with Hallé Orch and James Loughran), Tchaikovsky Piano Concerto No 1 (with LSO and James Judd), Prokofiev Sonatas, Rachmaninov complete works for piano (with BBC Nat Orch of Wales and Tadaaki Otaka); *Recreations* amateur radio, chess, computing; *Style*— John Lill, Esq, CBE; ⊠ c/o Askonas Holt, Lonsdale Chambers, 27 Chancery Lane, London WC2A 1PF

LILLEY, Prof David Malcolm James; s of Gerald Albert Thomas Lilley, of Colchester, Essex, and Betty Pamela, *née* Dickerson; *b* 28 May 1948; *Educ* Gilberd Sch Colchester, Univ of Durham (BSc, PhD), Univ of London (MSc, E Stickings Prize); *m* 1981, Patricia Mary, da of Ronald Biddle; 2 da (Katherine Suzannah b 1982, Sarah Anne b 1985); *Career* res fell Univ of Warwick 1973–75, ICI res fell Univ of Oxford 1975–76, sr res investigator Searle Res Laboratories 1976–81; Univ of Dundee: lectr in biochemistry 1981–84, reader 1984–89, prof of molecular biology 1989–, dir Cancer Res UK Nucleic Acid Structure Res Gp 1993–; res fell Royal Soc 1983–90; memb: Biochemical Soc 1974–, EMBO 1984–; memb Ctee: Br Soc for Cell Biology 1981–83, Tenovus Symposium 1981–88, Nucleic Acids and Molecular Biology Gp 1983–89, Biophysical Soc 1983–86; chair Nucleic Acid Gp 2005– (sec 1985–88); Colworth Medal 1982, G J Mendel Gold Medal Czech Acad of Sciences 1994, Prelog Medal for Stereochemistry ETH Zürich 1996, RSC Award in RNA and Ribozyme Chemistry 2001; FRSE 1988, FRS 2002; *Books* Nucleic Acids and Molecular Biology (jt ed); author of 290 scientific papers; *Recreations* foreign languages, running, skiing; *Style*— Prof David Lilley, FRS, FRSE; ⊠ Cancer Research UK Nucleic Acid Structure Research Group, MSI/WTB Complex, University of Dundee, Dundee DD1 5EH (tel 01382 384243, fax 01382 385893, e-mail d.m.j.lilley@dundee.ac.uk)

LILLEY, Rt Hon Peter Bruce; PC (1990), MP; s of Arnold Francis Lilley, and Lilian, *née* Elliott; *b* 23 August 1943; *Educ* Dulwich Coll, Clare Coll Cambridge; *m* 1979, Gail Ansell; *Career* energy industries investment advsr; Parly candidate (Cons) Haringey Tottenham Oct 1974; MP (Cons): St Albans 1983–97, Hitchen and Harpenden 1997–; chm Bow Gp 1973–75, sec Cons Backbench Energy Ctee 1983–84, memb Treasy Select Ctee 1983–84, PPS to Min of State for Local Govt 1984, PPS to Rt Hon Nigel Lawson as Chllr of Exchequer 1985–87, econ sec to the Treasy 1987–89, fin sec to the Treasy 1989–90; sec of state: for Trade and Industry 1990–92, for Social Security 1992–97; shadow chllr of the Exchequer 1997–98, dep ldr Cons Pty 1998–99; Cons Pty leadership challenger 1997; FInstPet 1978; *Books* Delusions of Incomes Policy (with Samuel Brittan), Do You Sincerely Want to Win - Defeating Terrorism in Ulster (1972), The End of the Keynesian Era (contrib, ed R Skidelsky, 1980), Thatcherism: The Next Generation (1989), Winning the Welfare Debate (1995), Patient Power (2000), Common Sense on Cannabis (2001), Taking Liberties (2002), Save Our Pensions (2003), ID Cards: Crisis of Identity (2004), Immigration: Too Much of a Good Thing? (2005); *Style*— The Rt Hon Peter Lilley, MP; ⊠ House of Commons, London SW1A 0AA

LILLEYMAN, Prof Sir John Stuart; kt (2002); s of Ernest Lilleyman (d 1992), of Sheffield, and Frances, *née* Johnson; *b* 9 July 1945; *Educ* Oundle, Bart's Med Coll (MB BS, MRCS); *Career* jr med posts Hemel Hempstead and Bart's 1968–70, registrar in haematology Sheffield 1970–72, research fell Cardiff 1972–74, sr registrar Sheffield 1974–75, conslt in haematology Children's Hosp Sheffield 1975–95, Mark Ridgwell chair of paediatric oncology Bart's / Royal London Med Sch 1995–2004, medical dir National Patient Safety Agency 2004–07, ret; first Distinguished Serv Medal RCPath (for establishing UK system of pathology lab accreditation) 1991, personal chair in paediatric haematology Univ of Sheffield (in recognition of research work on childhood leukaemia) 1993; DSc (med) Univ of London 1996; pres UK Assoc Clinical Pathologists 1998–99; pres: RCPath 1999–2002 (vice-pres 1993–96), RSM 2004–06; vice-chair: Acad of Med Royal Colls 2000–02, Jt Conslts Ctee 2001–02; Hon MD Univ of Sheffield 2003; FRCP 1986, hon fell Inst of Biomedical Science 1996, fndr FRCPCH 1997, FRCPEd 2000, Hon FFPathRCPI 2003, FMedSci 2007; *Books* Childhood Leukaemia - the Facts (1994, 2 edn 2000); *Style*— Prof Sir John Lilleyman; ⊠ Beehive Barn, Newton Lane, Sudborough, Northamptonshire NN14 3BX

LILLYCROP, David Peter; *b* 16 June 1956; *Educ* Univ of Exeter (LLB), Coll of Law London; *m* 1983, Dr Kaye Smith; 2 s (Jonathan b Oct 1985, Christopher b Aug 1988), 1 da (Catherine b Jan 1994); *Career* called to the Bar Middle Temple 1978; legal advsr Mabey & Johnson Ltd 1978–82, gp co sec and legal advsr Mabey Holdings Ltd 1982–85, co sec and legal dir Quaker Oats Ltd 1985–89; TI Group plc: joined 1989, gp co sec 1991–2000, gen counsel 1997–2000, main bd dir 1998–2000; gen counsel and main bd dir Smiths Gp plc (following merger of TI Gp and Smiths) 2000–; memb Int Bar Assoc; dist cncllr 1979–83; govr Abingdon Sch; former tstee Artificial Heart Fndn, former memb Cncl and Mgmnt Ctee Industry and Parliament Tst; FCMI; *Clubs* Mark's, Halton Village Lawn

Tennis; *Style*— David Lillycrop, Esq; ⊠ Smiths Group plc, 765 Finchley Road, London NW11 8DS (tel 020 8457 8291, fax 020 8457 8475)

LILLYWHITE, Lt-Gen Louis Patrick; MBE (1985), QHS (2002); s of Dr William Henry Lillywhite (d 2000), and Annie Kate, *née* Vesey; *b* 23 February 1948; *Educ* King Edward VI GS Lichfield, UC Cardiff (MB BCh), Welsh Nat Sch of Med, RMCS Shrivenham, Army Staff Coll, Univ of London (MSc, Soc of Occupational Med prize); *m* 2 August 1975, Jean Mary, da of late Bernard Daly; 1 s (William Bernard b 15 June 1977), 2 da (Felicity Rosemary b 23 April 1979, Anna Frances b 2 May 1981); *Career* Regtl MO 3 Bn Parachute Regt 1974–76, offr-in-charge Tech Div Army Med Serv Trg Centre 1977–81, CO 23 Parachute Field Ambulance 1984–89, Cdr Med 1 (UK) Armoured Div (incl Gulf War) 1990–92, head personnel branch Army Med Services 1992–94, dir Med Personnel, Trg and Policy 1999–2001, dir Br Forces Germany Health Servs 2001–03, DG Army Med Servs 2003–05, Surgn-Gen MOD 2006–; mentioned in dispatches 1991; graded conslt occupational physician 1990, memb BMA; cmmr Royal Hosp Chelsea 2003–06, govr Royal Star and Garter 2003–06; memb: Fell Runners Assoc, Br Army Orienteering Club, Long Distance Walkers Assoc, Br Army Mountaineering Assoc, Catenian Assoc; fell Med Soc of London 1984, MFOM RCP 1989, FRSM 1999, memb Inst of Healthcare Mgmnt 2008; OStJ 2007; *Publications* article on skin diseases in coal miners in Jl of Soc of Occupational Med 1990, articles on military parachuting in Jl of Royal Army Medical Corps, Gulf Logistics: Blackadders War (contrib, 1995); *Recreations* cross country, orienteering, fell running, hashing, long distance running, genealogy, computers, mountaineering; *Style*— Lt-Gen Louis Lillywhite, MBE, QHS, MFOM; ⊠ Level 7, Zone F, Main Building, Ministry of Defence, Whitehall, London SW1A 2HB (tel 020 7807 8807, e-mail louis@lillywhi.demon.co.uk)

LIM, Chwen Jeng; s of Ks Lim (d 2000), and Yk Leong; *b* 16 September 1963; *Educ* Lee Fndn Scholarship Singapore, Kuok Fndn Scholarship Malaysia; *Career* architect and academic; tutor: Architectural Assoc London 1989–90, lectr Bartlett Sch of Architecture UCL 1990–91, sr lectr Univ of East of London 1990–93, sr lectr Univ of North London 1991–99; Bartlett Sch of Architecture UCL: sr lectr 1993–, dir architecture research lab 1999–; visiting prof: Stadelschule Frankfurt, Curtin Univ Perth; int visiting critic and lectr; ast architect Eva Jiricna Architects and Cook & Hawley Architects 1983–91, fndr of studio with 8 architects 1994; *Selected Exhibitions* incl Kassel Documenta 87 1987, Nara/Toto World Architecture Triennale 1995, We'll Reconfigure the Space when you're Ready 1996; Archilab Orleans 99 1999; *Awards* winner Building Centre Tst Competition 1987, 3rd prize 6th Schinkenchiku/Takiron Int Competition 1994, winner UCL Cultural Centre Int Competition 1995, 2nd prize Concept House 2000 Ideal Home Exhbn 1999, 14th Membrane Design Int Competition 1999; RIBA: presidents medals 1997, 1998 and 1999; numerous articles on architecture for learned jls and catalogues; *Style*— Chwen Lim, Esq; ⊠ Bartlett School of Architecture UCL, Wates House, 22 Gordon Street, London WC1H 0QB (tel 020 7504 4842, mobile 07899 900 803)

LIM, Dr Frederick Thomas Keng Sim; s of late Khye Seng Lim, OBE, of Penang, Malaysia, and late Lian Hioh, *née* Goh; *b* 19 April 1947; *Educ* Radley, Middx Hosp London (MB BS); *m* July 1971, Catherine Mary; *Career* Middx Hosp: house surgn 1971, registrar 1974, sr registrar 1977–78; house physician QEII Hosp Welwyn Garden City 1972, sr house offr Lister Hosp 1973, sr registrar Charing Cross Hosp 1975; conslt physician in: genito-urinary med King's Coll Hosp 1979–86, med advsr Premier Model Agency, Campbell Hooper Solicitors, private practice 1986–; memb: Independent Doctors' Forum, London Conslts' Assoc, MSSVD; chm Bd of Dirs Tetronics Ltd; MRCP 1974; *Books* Textbook of Genito-Urinary Surgery (jtly, 1985); *Recreations* tennis, music, antiques, travel; *Style*— Dr Frederick Lim; ⊠ 26 Devonshire Place, London W1N 1PD (tel 020 7487 3529, fax 020 7224 1784)

LIMB, Sue; da of Lewis Wilfred Limb and Margaret Winifred, *née* Andrew; *b* 12 September 1946; *Educ* Pate's GS for Girls Cheltenham, Newnham Coll Cambridge (scholarship, BA); *m* 1, 1970 (m dis 1979), Roy Sydney Porter; *m* 2, 1984 (m dis 1991), Jan Vriend; 1 da (Elisabeth Susanna b 18 Feb 1985); *Career* researcher Cambridge 1968–70, clerk Halifax Building Soc 1970, kitchen asst Corpus Christi Cambridge 1971, teacher of English and drama 1971–75; writer and broadcaster 1976–; columnist: Good Housekeeping 1986–91, The Guardian (under name of Dulcie Domum) 1988–2001; author of numerous articles, children's books, etc; memb Green Party, Euro Parly candidate (Green) Cotswolds 1989; *Books* Captain Oates - Soldier and Explorer (biography, with Patrick Cordingley, 1982, reprinted 1995), Up the Garden Path (novel and radio and TV series, 1984), Love Forty (novel, 1986), The Wordsmiths at Gorsemere (book and radio series, 1987), Love's Labours (novel, 1989), Me Jane (teenage novel, 1989), Big Trouble (teenage novel, 1990), Bad Housekeeping (1990), Sheep's Eyes and Hogwash (1992), Come Back Grandma (1993), Dulcie Dishes the Dirt (1994), Passion Fruit (1995), Enlightenment (1997), Girl, 15, Charming but Insane (2004), Girl (Nearly) 16: Absolute Torture (2005), Girl 16: Pants on Fire (2006), Ruby Rogers Is a Waste of Space (2006), Ruby Rogers: Yeah Whatever... (2006), Girl, 15, Flirting for England (2007), Zoe and Chloe: On the Prowl (2007), Ruby Rogers is a Walking Legend (2007), Ruby Rogers: Get a Life! (2007); *Recreations* muck-raking, mostly literal; *Style*— Ms Sue Limb; ⊠ c/o PFD, Drury House, 34–43 Russell Street, London WC2B 5HA (tel 020 7344 1000, fax 020 7836 9539, e-mail postmaster@pfd.co.uk and suelimb@btinternet.com, website www.suelimb.com)

LIMEBEER, Prof David John Noel; s of Gerald John Limebeer (d 1988), and Joan Constance Limebeer (d 1997); *b* 31 July 1952; *Educ* Univ of the Witwatersrand (BSc), Univ of Natal (MSc, PhD), Univ of London (DSc); *Partner* Dr Suzanne Margaret Watt; *Career* asst engr Johannesburg City Cncl SA 1974–76, temp lectr Univ of Natal SA 1976–80, research assoc Univ of Cambridge 1980–84; Imperial Coll London: lectr 1984–89, reader 1989–93, prof of Control Engineering 1993–, head of Control Section 1996–99, head Electrical and Electronic Engrg Dept 1999–; sr motorcyclist instr IAM 1997; FREng 1997, FIEE 1994, FIEEE 1992; *Books* Linear Robust Control (co-ed 1995); *Recreations* motorcycling, antique lamp collecting, gym, table tennis; *Clubs* Middlesex Advanced Motorcyclists; *Style*— Prof David Limebeer, FREng; ⊠ 4 Hollingbourne Gardens, Ealing, London W13 8EN (tel 020 8998 5174, fax 020 8998 5174); Department of Electrical & Electronic Engineering, Exhibition Road, London SW7 2BT (tel 020 7594 6188, fax 020 7594 6328, e-mail d.limebeer@ic.ac.uk)

LIMERICK, 7 Earl of (I 1803); Edmund Christopher Pery; s of 6 Earl of Limerick, KBE, DL (d 2003); *b* 10 February 1963; *Educ* Eton, New Coll Oxford, Pushkin Inst Moscow, City Univ; *m* 1, 21 July 1990 (m dis 2000), Emily, o da of Michael Gavin Lynam Thomas, of Worcester; 2 s (Felix Edmund, Viscount Pery b 16 Nov 1991, Hon Ivo Patrick b 26 Oct 1993); *m* 2, 13 July 2002, Lydia Ann Johnson; *Heir* s, Viscount Pery; *Career* called to the Bar Middle Temple 1987; HM Dip Serv: FCO 1987–88, École Nationale d'Administration 1988–89, Quai d'Orsay 1990, second sec Dakar 1990–91, Amman 1991–92, resigned 1992; Clifford Chance slrs 1992–93, Freshfields slrs 1993–94, Milbank Tweed slrs Moscow 1994–96, dir Deutsche Bank AG Moscow, London and Dubai 1996–2004, Dubai International Capital 2004–05, ptnr Altima Partners LLP 2005–; *Recreations* tennis, skiing, kitesurfing; *Clubs* Sussex, Garrick; *Style*— The Earl of Limerick; ⊠ Chiddinglye, West Hoathly, East Grinstead, West Sussex RH19 4QT (e-mail eclimerick@hotmail.com)

LIMERICK AND KILLALOE, Bishop of 2000–; Rt Rev Michael Hugh Gunton Mayes; s of Thomas David Dougan Mayes (d 1983), and Hilary, *née* Gunton (d 1986); *b* 31 August 1941; *Educ* The Royal Sch Armagh, Trinity Coll Dublin (BA), Univ of London (BD); *m* 1966, Elizabeth Annie Eleanor, da of James Irwin; 1 s (Patrick Dougan James b 18 Nov 1967), 2 da (Soren Elizabeth Hilary b 15 June 1969, Natalya Vivienne Ann b 6 April

1974); *Career* ordained: deacon 1964, priest 1965; asst curate: St Mark's Portadown 1964–67, St Columba's Portadown 1967–68; USPG Missionary Japan 1968–74, USPG area sec Ireland 1974–75, incumbent St Michael's Union Cork 1975–86, archdeacon of Cork Cloyne and Ross 1986–93; incumbent: Moviddy Union Cork 1986–88, Rathcooney Union Cork 1988–93; warden of lay readers Cork Cloyne and Ross 1986–93; bishop of Kilmore, Elphin and Ardagh 1993–2000; *Recreations* music, photography, reading, golf, walking; *Style*— The Rt Rev the Bishop of Limerick and Killaloe; ✉ 12 Eden Terrace, North Circular Road, Limerick, Ireland (tel 00 353 61 451532, e-mail bishop@limerick.anglican.org)

LINACRE, Sir (John) Gordon Seymour; kt (1986), CBE (1979), AFC (1943), DFM (1941); s of John James Linacre (d 1957), of Norton Woodseats, S Yorks; *b* 23 September 1920; *Educ* Firth Park GS Sheffield; *m* 1943, Irene Amy, da of Alexander Gordon (d 1946); 2 da; *Career* WWII RAF; Yorkshire Post Newspapers Ltd: md 1965–83, chm 1983–90, pres 1990–; dep chm United Newspapers Ltd 1983–91 (chief exec 1981–88), dir Yorkshire TV 1968–90, chm Chameleon Television Ltd 1991–; pres Fédération Internationale des Editeurs de Journaux et Publications 1984–88, former pres Newspaper Soc, former chm and dir Press Assoc, chm Leeds TEC 1989–92; chm Univ of Leeds Fndn 1989–2000; pres Opera North 1998– (chm 1979–98); Hon LLD Univ of Leeds 1991; CIMI, FRSA; *Recreations* golf, fishing, country walking; *Clubs* Alwoodley Golf; *Style*— Sir Gordon Linacre, CBE, AFC, DFM

LINACRE, Nigel Guy Thornton; s of Vivian Thornton Linacre, of Edinburgh, and Joan Linacre; *b* 21 August 1957; *Educ* George Heriot's Sch, Imberhorne Sch, Univ of Reading (BA); *m* 1979, Sue, da of Ronald Farish; 2 da (Charlotte Lucy b 28 Nov 1982, Cordelia Mary b 4 Dec 1992), 2 s (Thomas Edward Benedict b 30 Sept 1986, George Henry Michael b 20 Feb 1989); *Career* account exec Charles Barker 1979–82, account mangr Collett Dickenson Pearce Financial 1982–85, advertising dir Boase Massimi Pollit Business 1985–87, exec dir Collett Dickenson Pearce Financial 1987–89, dir Charles Barker 1989–92, md Charles Barker Advertising 1989–92, dir Interactive Telephone Services 1992–95, dir ITS Group plc 1993–95, md Linacre Communications Ltd 1998–, chm SureTrack Monitoring plc 2007–, dir Linacre Land 2007–; exec coach Inside Out 2005–; Parly candidate (Cons): Ealing Southall 1983, N Cornwall 1997; Freeman of Chippenham; *Books* Advertising For Account Handlers (1987), The Successful Executive (1997), Recipes for Happiness (2007); also author of articles in European Jl among others; *Style*— Nigel Linacre, Esq; ✉ 51 St Mary Street, Chippenham, Wiltshire SN15 3JW (tel 01249 654615, e-mail nigelinacre@hotmail.com)

LINAKER, Dr Barry David; s of Allan Lawrence Linaker (d 1973), and Gwendoline, *née* Higgs; *b* 7 April 1947; *Educ* Wigan GS, KCH Med Sch Univ of London (MB BS, MD); *m* 14 April 1973, Carol Yvonne, da of Lt Cdr John Michael Ogden, of Sunningdale, nr Ascot; 2 da (Emma b 1975, Amanda b 1979); *Career* MRC res fell and sr registrar in gastroenterology Univ Dept of Med Hope Hosp Manchester 1978–80, sr registrar in med Liverpool 1980–81, conslt physician and gastroenterologist Warrington Hosp 1981, ret from NHS; currently private conslt gastroenterologist North Cheshire Hosp; author of papers in various jls especially on mechanisms of histamine stimulated secretion in rabbit ileal mucosa in gut; memb: Br Soc of Gastroenterology, Liverpool Med Inst, N Eng Gastro Soc, Merseyside and N Wales Physicians; memb BMA, FRCP 1989; *Recreations* sailing, clay pigeon shooting, golf, reading, travel; *Clubs* Port Dinorwic Sailing; *Style*— Dr Barry Linaker

LINAKER, Lawrence Edward (Paddy); s of late Lawrence Wignall Linaker, and Rose, *née* Harris; *b* 22 July 1934; *Educ* Malvern; *m* 1963, (Elizabeth) Susan, *née* Elam; 1 s (Sam), 1 da (decd); *Career* with Esso Petroleum 1957–63; M & G Group plc: joined 1963, dep chm and chief exec 1987–94, chm M & G Investment Management Ltd 1987–94; chm Marling Industries plc 1996–97, non-exec chm Fisons plc 1994–95; non-exec dir: Securities Inst 1992–94, Lloyds TSB Group plc 1994–2001, Fleming Mercantile Investment Trust plc 1994–, SAUL Trustee Company 1994–99, Wolverhampton and Dudley Breweries plc 1996–2002; chm: Institutional Fund Managers Assoc 1992–94, YMCA Nat Coll 1992–2000, Fleming Technol Investment Trust 1997–2001; dir Childline 1992–2000 (treas 1994–2000); memb Cncl RPMS 1977–89; memb Governing Body: SPCK 1976–94, Malvern Coll 1989–2003, Canterbury Christchurch Coll 1992–98; memb Ct Imperial Coll London 1998–; tstee: Lloyds TSB Fndn for England and Wales 1994–2001, Carnegie UK Tst 1995–; *Recreations* music and gardening; *Clubs* Athenaeum, Brooks's; *Style*— Paddy Linaker, Esq; ✉ Swyre Farm, Aldsworth, Cheltenham, Gloucestershire

LINCOLN, Archdeacon of; *see:* Hawes, Ven Arthur John

LINCOLN, Prof Dennis William; s of Ernest Edward Lincoln (d 1951), and Gertrude Emma, *née* Holmes (d 1987); *b* 21 July 1939; *Educ* Bracondale Sch, Essex Inst of Agric, Univ of Nottingham (BSc), CCC Cambridge (MA, PhD), Univ of Bristol (DSc); *m* 1, 1962, Rosemary Alice, *née* Barrell; 1 da (Karen Anne b 4 Oct 1965), 1 s (John Roderick b 13 Sept 1967); m 2, 1998, Beate, *née* Stiemer; *Career* res fell CCC Cambridge 1966–67, lectr, reader and subsequently prof Dept of Human Anatomy Univ of Bristol 1967–82, dir MRC Reproductive Biology Unit Centre for Reproductive Biology 1982–96, dep vice-chllr (research) Griffith Univ Aust 1996–2001, dean Faculty of Science Univ of NSW 2002–03; FRSE 1992; *Recreations* ornithology, travel, wildlife photography; *Style*— Prof Dennis Lincoln, FRSE

LINCOLN, Bishop of 2001–; Rt Rev Dr John Charles Saxbee; *b* 7 January 1946; *Educ* Cotham GS Bristol, Univ of Bristol, Univ of Durham, Cranmer Hall Durham; *m*; 1 da; *Career* curate Emmanuel with St Paul Plymouth 1972–76, vicar St Philip Weston Mill Plymouth 1976–81, team vicar Central Exeter Team Miny 1981–87, dir SW Miny Trg Course 1981–92, preb Exeter Cathedral 1988–92, archdeacon of Ludlow 1992–2001, bishop of Ludlow 1994–2001; *Style*— The Rt Rev the Bishop of Lincoln; ✉ Bishop's House, Eastgate, Lincoln LN2 1QQ (tel 01522 534701, fax 01522 511095, e-mail bishop.lincoln@lincoln.anglican.org)

LINCOLN, Paul; s of William Edward Lincoln, and Lucy Elizabeth Sillett; *b* 13 March 1955, Norwich, Norfolk; *Educ* Univ of Leicester (BSc), Univ of Birmingham (CertEd, Dip), Univ of Leeds (Dip); *Children* 2 s (Aaron b 16 Nov 1996, Jordan b 20 Aug 1998); *Career* scientific researcher MAFF 1976, teacher 1976–80, health promotion offr Wolverhampton HA 1980–84, dir of health promotion servs Birmingham HA 1984–89, dir Health Educ Authy 1989–2000, ceo National Heart Forum 2000–; Best Student Mgmnt Award DCMS; FFPH; *Recreations* art, antiques; *Style*— Paul Lincoln, Esq; ✉ National Heart Forum, Tavistock House South, Tavistock Square, London WC1H 9LG (tel 020 7383 7638, fax 020 7387 2799, e-mail paul.lincoln@heartforum.org.uk)

LINDLEY, Dr Bryan Charles; CBE (1982); s of Wing Cdr Alfred Webb Lindley (d 1988), of Lichfield, and Florence, *née* Pratten (d 1975); *b* 30 August 1932; *Educ* Reading Sch, UCL (BSc(Eng), PhD); *m* 2 May 1987, Dr Judith Anne Heyworth, da of Robert Heyworth, of Bramhall; 1 s ((John) Julian b 1960); *Career* Nat Gas Turbine Estab 1954–57, Hawker Siddeley Nuclear Power Co Ltd 1957–59, International Research and Development Company Ltd and CA Parsons Nuclear Res Centre 1959–65, mangr R&D Div CA Parsons & Co Ltd 1965–68, chief exec and md ERA Technology Ltd 1968–79 (concurrently chm ERA Patents Ltd and ERA Autotrack Systems Ltd), dir of technol Dunlop Holdings plc and dir Dunlop Ltd 1979–85, dir of technol and planning BICC Cables Ltd 1985–88, chief exec Nat Advanced Robotics Res Centre 1989–90, chm and chief exec Lord Lindley Associates 1990–; former chm: Dunlop Bioprocesses Ltd, Thermal Conversions (UK) Ltd, Soilless Cultivation Systems Ltd; dir: Thomas Bolton & Johnson Ltd 1985–88, RAPRA Technol Ltd 1985–97, Settle-Carlisle Railway Development Co 1991–93, J+B Imaging 1998–; chm N Lakeland Healthcare NHS Tst 1993–97; visiting prof Univ of Liverpool 1989–; memb: ACARD 1980–86, Materials Advsy Gp DTI 1984; fell UCL 1979; FIMechE 1968, FIEE 1968, FInstP 1969, FPRI 1980; *Recreations* music, photography, walking, skiing, sailing; *Style*— Dr Bryan Lindley, CBE; ✉ Lindenthwaite, Beacon Edge, Penrith, Cumbria CA11 8BN (tel 01768 890652)

LINDLEY, Dr David; OBE (1998); s of William Lindley (d 1980), and Millicent, *née* Caine; *b* 26 June 1939; *Educ* Manchester Central GS, Univ of Salford (Gen Sir William Platt prize, BSc), Univ of Wales (PhD), Univ of Cambridge (Cert Advanced Engrg Design); *m* 14 July 1962, Dorothy, da of John Turnock; 3 s (Simon David b 11 April 1963 d 1993, Nicolas Rhys b 17 Nov 1964, Jonathan Peter b 3 Oct 1969), 1 da (Sarah Jane Kirsty b 31 Dec 1974); *Career* mangr Pump Experimental Dept Mather & Platt Ltd Manchester 1962–63 (apprentice 1955–62), head Turbo Machinery Aero-thermodynamics Dept CEGB 1967–70, sr lectr in mech engrg Univ of Canterbury NZ 1970–75, res fell UKAEA 1975–, mangr Energy Systems Gp Jet Propulsion Laboratory Caltech 1975–76, sr lectr Univ of Canterbury NZ 1976–78; Taylor Woodrow plc: joined 1978, md Wind Energy Gp Ltd 1979–91, dir of Taywood Engineering Ltd 1984–90, vice-pres US WEG Inc 1986–91, divnl dir Taylor Woodrow Construction Ltd 1987–91, memb Severn Tidal Power Gp Mgmnt and Supervisory Bd 1987–91, dir Taylor Woodrow Management and Engineering Ltd 1988–91; md National Wind Power Ltd 1991–96, chm Ocean Power Delivery Ltd 2002–05 (non-exec dir 2005–), non-exec dir KP Renewables plc 2004–; dir: Euro Wind Energy Assoc 1980–96 (pres 1986–89), British Wind Energy Assoc 1980–96 (chm 1982 and 1994); memb: Advsy Cncl for R&D for Fuel and Power 1986–92, Renewable Energy Advsy Gp 1991–92, Electrical Engrg Coll of Peers EPSRC 1993–96, Professional Bodies Advsy Gp Design Cncl 1995–99, Exec Bd Royal Acad of Engrg Educn Prog 2001–, Advsy Cncl SAM Private Equity Sustainability Fund II Switzerland 2006–; visiting prof: Loughborough Univ of Technol, De Montfort Univ 1994–2003, Univ of Nottingham 1997–2003; academician Russian Int Higher Educn Acad of Science; MASME, memb American Inst of Aeronautics and Astronautics, FIMechE, FRMetS, FREng 1993, FRSA; *Awards* incl: James Watt medal ICE 1987, Stephenson medal Univ of Newcastle 1989, Melchett medal Inst of Energy 1990, Industry Award BWEA 1995, President's Award BWEA 1996; *Recreations* walking, skiing, collecting, sailing, photography, reading, music; *Style*— Dr David Lindley, OBE, FREng, FRSA; ✉ Lindley Asociates Ltd, Woodfield, Farm Lane, Jordans, Beaconsfield, Buckinghamshire HP9 2UP (tel 01494 676570, fax 01494 678917)

LINDLEY, Richard Howard Charles; s of Lt-Col (Herbert) Guy Lindley (d 1976), of Winchester, Hants, and Dorothea Helen Penelope Hatchell (d 1996); *b* 25 April 1936; *Educ* Bedford Sch, Queens' Coll Cambridge (exhibitioner, BA, chm Film Soc); *m* 1, 1976 (m dis 1986), Clare Fehrsen; 2 c (Thomas Paul Guy b 29 Dec 1977, Joanna Frances Eleanor b 12 April 1979); m 2, 1999, Carole, da of Harry Stone and Kathleen Stone; *Career* Nat Serv: 2 Lt Royal Hampshire Regt, served Malaya Emergency; prodr TV commercials Foote Cone and Belding 1960–62, reporter presenter and newscaster Southern TV Southampton 1963–64, reporter ITN (in Vietnam, Nigeria, Zimbabwe, Egypt and Israel) 1964–72, reporter and presenter Panorama and Saturday Briefing BBC Current Affairs Gp 1972–88, sr prog offr IBA 1988, reporter and presenter This Week (Thames TV) 1989–92; presenter: ITN World News 1992–94, Special Reports ITN News at Ten 1995–99; pres The Media Soc 2002–03; chm St Pancras Almshouses; dir Lindley Stone Ltd; *Books* Panorama - Fifty Years of Pride and Paranoia (2002), And Finally...? The News from ITN (2005); *Recreations* friends, food, familiar films; *Clubs* RTS; *Style*— Richard Lindley; ✉ 46 Oak Village, London NW5 4QL (tel 020 7267 5870, fax 020 7267 2668, e-mail linstone@btinternet.com)

LINDOP, Dr George Black McMeekin; s of George Lindop (d 1988); *b* 28 March 1945; *Educ* Hillhead HS Glasgow, Univ of Glasgow (BSc, MB ChB); *m* 22 Jan 1968, Sharon Ann, *née* Cornell; 2 s (Graeme Euan b 1975, Gavin Neil b 1978), 1 da (Amy Elizabeth b 1981); *Career* conslt in histopathology Ayrshire and Arran Health Bd 1976, reader and hon conslt in histopathology Univ of Glasgow and Gtr Glasgow Health Bd 2003, conslt pathologist N Glasgow Hosps Tst 2003; FRCPath 1987 (MRCPath 1975), FRCP 1996 (MRCP 1994); *Publications* author of papers, chapters and a book on the kidney, hypertension and cardiovascular diseases; *Recreations* sport, the outdoors, music, cinema; *Clubs* RSM; *Style*— Dr George Lindop; ✉ Sheikh Khalifa Medical City, PO Box 51900, Abu Dhabi, United Arab Emirates

LINDOP, Dr Michael John; s of Donald Frederick Lindop (d 2005), of Birmingham, and Phyllis Alice, *née* Burrows (d 1992); *b* 29 July 1942; *Educ* King Edward Sch Birmingham, Gonville & Caius Coll Cambridge (MA), Guy's Hosp (MB, BChir), FRCA 1971; *m* 16 Aug 1968, Kari, da of Per Brachel (d 1955), of Oslo, Norway; 3 da (Tanya b 1971, Michelle b 1973, Anne-Lise b 1978), 1 s (Tom b 1969); *Career* sr registrar Westminster Hosp 1969–74, instr Univ of Washington Seattle USA 1973, conslt in anaesthesia and intensive care 1974–, formerly dir anaesthesia servs Addenbrooke's Hosp; formerly examiner Royal Coll of Anaesthetists; pres Liver Intensive Care Gp of Europe 1996–2002; memb: Intensive Care Soc, Anaesthetic Res Soc; *Books* Anesthesia and Intensive Care for Organ Transplantation (ed with Dr J R Klinck, 1997); *Recreations* racquet control, weed control; *Style*— Dr Michael Lindop; ✉ Department of Anaesthesia, Box 93, Addenbrooke's Hospital, Cambridge CB2 2QQ (tel 01223 217433, fax 01223 217223, e-mail mikelindop@compuserve.com)

LINDRUP, Garth; s of Viggo H Lindrup (d 1957), and Betty, *née* Ashworth (d 1995); *b* 10 September 1948, S Africa; *Educ* Wrekin Coll, Manchester Poly (BA), St John's Coll Cambridge (LLM); *m* 1991, Julie, *née* Topham; 2 s (Oliver b 11 Oct 1991, James b 22 June 1994); *Career* admitted slr 1975; articled clerk then asst slr Leak Almond & Parkinson 1973–77, sole practitioner 1978–79; Addleshaw Goddard (formerly Addleshaw Sons & Latham then Addleshaw Booth & Co): asst slr 1979–84, ptnr 1984–2004, conslt 2004–; chm Law Soc European Gp 1994–95, hon lectr in law Univ of Manchester; memb: Competition Panel CBI, Competition Ctee ICC; memb: Law Soc 1975, Int Bar Assoc 1989, Ligue Internationale du Droit de la Concurrence 1985; FRSA; *Publications* Butterworths Competition Law Handbook (ed, 1987–), Butterworths Public Procurement & CCT Handbook (ed, 1997), Butterworths PFI Manual (jt gen ed, 1998–), Solicitors in the Single Market (ed), Butterworths Expert Guide to the European Union (contrib), author of numerous articles in jls and other pubns; *Recreations* gardening, theatre, reading, fell walking; *Clubs* Manchester Tennis & Rackets; *Style*— Garth Lindrup, Esq; ✉ Addleshaw Goddard, 100 Barbirolli Square, Manchester M2 3AB

LINDSAY, Andrew James Ronald; MBE (2001); s of Lt-Col S J Lindsay, of Acharacle, Argyll, and Ann, *née* Powell; *b* 25 March 1977; *Educ* Eton (scholar, capt of boats), BNC Oxford (scholar, BA, Rowing blue); *m* Lady Amy Jane, *née* Gordon; *Career* competitive career: jr int rower 1994 and 1995, pres OUBC 1998 (rowed in univ boat race 1997, 1998 and 1999), Gold medal men's eights Olympic Games Sydney 2000); memb Team of the Year BBC Sports Personality of the Year Awards 2000; currently commercial dir Telecom Plus plc; non-exec dir Ryness Electrical Supplies; tstee: Harry Mahon Cancer Research Tst, Dorney Rowing Lake; *Recreations* skiing, windsurfing, bagpipe playing; *Clubs* Vincent's (Oxford), Phoenix Soc (Oxford), Boodle's; *Style*— Andrew Lindsay, Esq, MBE; ✉ Invermoidart, Acharacle, Argyll PH36 4LR (tel 07900 087595, e-mail andrew@ryness.co.uk)

LINDSAY, His Hon Judge Crawford Callum Douglas; QC (1987); s of Douglas Marshall Lindsay, and Eileen Mary Lindsay; *b* 5 February 1939; *Educ* Whitgift Sch Croydon, St John's Coll Oxford (BA); *m* 1963, Rosemary Gough; 1 s, 1 da; *Career* called to the Bar

1961 (former head of chambers), recorder SE Circuit 1982–98, circuit judge (SE Circuit) 1998–; *Style*— His Hon Judge Lindsay, QC

LINDSAY, 16 Earl of (S 1633); James Randolph Lindesay-Bethune; also Lord Lindsay of the Byres (S 1445), Lord Parbroath (S 1633), Viscount Garnock, and Lord Kilbirnie, Kingsburn and Drumry (both S 1703); s of 15 Earl of Lindsay (d 1989), by his 1 w, Mary, *née* Douglas-Scott-Montagu; *b* 19 November 1955; *Educ* Eton, Univ of Edinburgh (MA), Univ of Calif Davis; *m* 2 March 1982, Diana Mary, er da of Nigel Chamberlayne-Macdonald, LVO, OBE, of Cranbury Park, Winchester; 3 da (Lady Frances Mary b 1986, Lady Alexandra Penelope b 1988, Lady Charlotte Diana b 1993), 2 s (William James, Viscount Garnock b 1990, Hon David Nigel (twin) b 1993); *Heir* s, Viscount Garnock; *Career* involved with the environment and the food industry; vice-chm Inter-Parly Union Ctee on Environment 1994–95 (memb 1993), Parly under sec of state Scottish Office 1995–97; chm: Landscape Fndn 1992–95, Assured British Meat Ltd 1997–2001, Scottish Quality Salmon (SQS) 1998–2006, RSPB Scotland 1998–2003, Elmwood Coll Bd of Mgmnt 2001–, UKAS (UK Accreditation Serv) 2002–; md MSCI (Marine Stewardship Cncl Int) 2001–04; non-exec dir: UA Gp plc 1998–2005, Mining (Scotland) Ltd 2001–, Scottish Agricultural College Ltd 2005– (dep chm 2006–), British Polythene Industries plc 2006–; advsr IndigoVision plc 2006–; pres: Int Tree Fndn 1995–2005 (vice-pres 1993–95 and 2005–), RSGS 2005– (vice-pres 2004–05); vice-pres: Royal Smithfield Club 1999–, RSPB 2004–; memb: Advsy Panel Railway Heritage Tst, Select Ctee on Sustainable Devpt 1994–95, World Resource Fndn 1994–98, Bd Cairngorms Partnership 1998–2003, UK Roundtable on Sustainable Devpt 1998–2000, Sec of State's Advsy Gp on Sustainable Devpt 1998–99, Better Regulation Cmmn 2006– (dep chair 2007–); oppn spokesman House of Lords 1997; associateship RAS 2000–; hon fell Inst of Waste Mgmnt 1998–; *Books* Garden Ornament (jtly), Trellis (1991); *Clubs* New (Edinburgh); *Style*— The Rt Hon the Earl of Lindsay; ✉ Lahill, Upper Largo, Fife KY8 6JE

LINDSAY, Hon Mr Justice; Sir John Edmund Fredric Lindsay; kt (1992); s of George Fredric Lindsay (ka 1944), and late Constance Mary, *née* Wright; *b* 16 October 1935; *Educ* Ellesmere Coll, Sidney Sussex Coll Cambridge (MA); *m* Patricia Anne, da of late William Bolton, of Cape Town; 3 da; *Career* called to the Bar Middle Temple 1961 (Astbury Pupillage prizeman and Harmsworth scholar, bencher 1987), jr treasy counsel in bona vacantia, QC 1981, judge of the High Court of Justice (Chancery Div) 1992–; judge Employment Appeal Tbnl 1996–99, pres Employment Appeal Tbnl 1999–2002, a judge of the Administrative Court 2002–; *Clubs* Athenaeum; *Style*— The Hon Mr Justice Lindsay; ✉ c/o Royal Courts of Justice, Strand, London WC2A 2LL

LINDSAY, Dr (John) Maurice; CBE (1979), TD (1946); s of Matthew Lindsay (d 1969), of Glasgow, and Eileen Frances, *née* Brock (1954); *b* 21 July 1918; *Educ* Glasgow Acad, Scottish Nat Acad of Music; *m* 3 Aug 1946, Aileen Joyce, da of Evan Ramsay Macintosh Gordon (d 1973); 3 da (Seona Morag Joyce b 1949 d 2006, Kirsteen Ann b 1951, Morven Morag Joyce b 1959), 1 s (Niall Gordon Brock b 1957); *Career* poet, author, broadcaster, music critic and environmentalist; drama critic Scottish Daily Mail 1946–47, music critic The Bulletin 1946–60, ed Scots Review 1949–50; Border TV: programme controller 1961–62, prodn controller 1962–64, features exec and chief interviewer 1964–67; dir The Scottish Civic Tst 1967–83 (conslt 1983–2002, hon tstee 2002–), hon sec gen Europa Nostra 1983–91, pres Assoc of Scottish Literary Studies 1988–90, hon vice-pres Scottish Environmental Educn Ctee 1990–96; Hon DLitt Glasgow 1982; Hon FRIAS 1990; *Poetry* The Advancing Day (1940), Perhaps Tomorrow (1941), Predicament (1942), No Crown for Laughter (1943), The Enemies of Love - Poems 1941–45 (1946), Selected Poems (1947), Hurlygush - Poems in Scots (1948), At the Wood's Edge (1950), Ode for St Andrew's Night and Other Poems (1951), The Exiled Heart - Poems 1941–56 (1957), Snow Warning and Other Poems (1962), One Later Day and Other Poems (1964), This Business of Living (1969), Comings and Goings (1971), Selected Poems 1942–72 (1973), The Run from Life (1975), Walking Without an Overcoat - Poems 1972–76 (1977), Collected Poems (1979), A Net to Catch the Winds and Other Poems (1981), The French Mosquitoes' Woman and Other Diversions and Poems (1985), Requiem For a Sexual Athlete (1988), Collected Poems 1940–90 (1990), On The Face of It - Collected Poems Vol 2 (1993), News of the World: Last Poems (1995), Speaking Likeness: A Postscript (1997), Worlds Apart (2000), A Book of Scottish Verse (4 edn 2002); *Prose* A Pocket Guide to Scottish Culture (1947), The Scottish Renaissance (1949), The Lowlands of Scotland - Glasgow and the North (3 edn 1979), Robert Burns, The Man, His Work, The Legend (3 edn 1980), Dunoon - The Gem of the Clyde Coast (1954), The Lowlands of Scotland - Edinburgh and the South (3 edn 1979), Clyde Waters - Variations and Diversions on a Theme of Pleasure (1958), The Burns Encyclopedia (4 paperback edn 1995), Killochan Castle (1960), By Yon Bonnie Banks - A Gallimaufry (1961), Environment - A Basic Human Right (1968), Portrait of Glasgow (second edn 1981), Robin Philipson (1977), History of Scottish Literature (1977, revd edn 1992), Lowland Scottish Villages (1980), Francis George Scott and the Scottish Renaissance (1980), The Buildings of Edinburgh (jt author, 1980, 2 edn 1987), Thank You for Having Me - A Personal Memoir (1983), Unknown Scotland (jt author, 1984), The Castles of Scotland (1986), Count All Men Mortal - A History of Scottish Provident 1837–1987 (1987), An Illustrated Guide to Glasgow 1837 (1989), Victorian and Edwardian Glasgow, Edinburgh Past and Present (1990), Glasgow (1989), The Scottish Dog (jtly, 1990); other work incl: A Pleasure of Gardens (jtly, 1990), The Scottish Quotation Book (jtly, 1991), The Music Quotation Book (jtly, 1992), The Theatre and Opera Lover's Quotation Book (jtly, 1993), The Burns Quotation Book (jtly, 1994), A Mini-Guide to Scottish Gardens (jtly, 1994), The Chambers Book of Good Scottish Gardens (jtly, 1995), Glasgow: Fabric of a City (2000), The Edinburgh Book of Twentieth Century Scottish Poetry (co-edited with Lesley Duncan, 2005); *Recreations* enjoying compact disc collection, walking, sailing on paddle-steamers; *Style*— Dr Maurice Lindsay, CBE, TD; ✉ Park House, 104 Dumbarton Road, Bowling G60 5BB (tel 01389 601662)

LINDSAY, Russell Grant (Russ); s of David Alexander Lindsay, of Catisfield, Hants, and Evelyn, *née* Birrell; *b* 12 July 1961; *Educ* Hardyes GS Dorchester, Prices GS Fareham, Southampton Coll of HE; *m* 15 June 1991, Caron Louisa Keating (d 2004); 2 s (Charlie b 1994, Gabriel Don b 1997); *Career* began career as DJ/Radio/TV broadcaster, co-prodr of TV progs, theatre and radio shows incl: Schofield's Quest, Dr Doolittle and the All Star Cup; currently md James Grant Media Group Ltd; dir: James Grant Management Ltd (fndr with Peter Powell, *qv* 1984), James Grant Productions Ltd, James Grant Music Publishing Ltd, James Grant Investments Ltd; fndr RIVA Digital Media Ltd; mgmnt for: Ant & Dec, Simon Cowell, Richard & Judy, Phillip Schofield; *Recreations* sport, art, leisure; *Clubs* East Horton Golf, Celtic Manor Golf, Pavillion Tennis; *Style*— Russ Lindsay, Esq; ✉ James Grant Media Group Ltd, 94 Strand on the Green, Chiswick, London W4 3NN (tel 020 8742 4950)

LINDSAY-FYNN, Nigel; s of Sir Basil Lindsay-Fynn (d 1988), and (Marion) Audrey Ellen, *née* Chapman (d 1991); *b* 4 May 1942; *Educ* Charterhouse, Oriel Coll Oxford (MA); *m* 12 May 1971, Heleen Vanda Mary, da of Bill Willson-Pemberton, of London; 2 s (Piers b 1975, Charles b 1989), 2 da (Miranda b 1978, Eleanor b 1981); *Career* fin dir: IRG plc 1991–2000, Stanley Davis Gp Ltd 2000–; chm The Crescent Tst Co (private equity portfolio mgmnt and trusteeship); treas Oriel Soc 1977–2002, pres Devon Co Agric Assoc 2007 (treas 1995–), tstee Exeter Cathedral Preservation Tst and other charities; Master Worshipful Co of Painter-Stainers 2005–06; *Recreations* playing the piano and composing, sailing, skiing; *Clubs* Garrick, Buck's, City Livery, Royal Yacht Squadron, Kildare St and Univ Dublin, Royal Irish Yacht, Irish Cruising, Kinsale Yacht; *Style*— Nigel Lindsay-Fynn, Esq; ✉ Lee Ford, Budleigh Salterton, Devon EX9 7AJ (tel 01395 445894, fax 01395 441100, e-mail crescent@leeford.co.uk); 74 Bedford Gardens, London W8 7EH (tel 020 7229 1684); Sea House, Kinsale, Co Cork, Ireland (tel 00 353 21 4777098)

LINDSAY OF BIRKER, 3 Baron (UK 1945); James Francis Lindsay; s of 2 Baron Lindsay of Birker (d 1994), and Hsiao Li, da of Col Li Wen Chi, Chinese Army; *b* 29 January 1945; *Educ* Canberra HS, Geelong GS Victoria, Bethesda-Chevy Chase HS, Keele Univ, Univ of Liverpool; *m* 1, 1966 (m dis 1985), Mary Rose, da of W G Thomas, of Cwmbran, Mon; m 2, 2000, Pamela Hutchison Collett, da of W Lon Hutchison, of Kansas City, MO; *Heir* cous, Alexander Lindsay; *Career* formerly lectr Dept of Physics Tunghai Univ Taichung Taiwan Repub of China; second sec Australian Embassy Santiago Chile 1973–76; first sec: Vientiane Laos 1979–80, Dhaka Bangladesh 1982–83, Caracas Venezuela 1986–90, Dept of Foreign Affrs and Trade Canberra 1991–93; dep high cmmr Australian High Cmmn: Islamabad Pakistan 1993–96, Nairobi Kenya 1996–2000; conslt Horn Relief Somalia 2000–05, lectr in Int Relations Beijing Foreign Studies Univ China 2003, conslt Uganda Rural Trg and Devpt Prog Kagadi Uganda 2004, co-fndr Sun Fire Cooking Somalia 2004; *Recreations* hiking, mountaineering, tennis; *Style*— The Rt Hon the Lord Lindsay of Birker; ✉ Apt 2E, 651 Oakland Avenue, Oakland, California 94611, USA (tel 001 510 595 7165, e-mail mukinduri@bigfoot.com)

LINDSELL, Charles Nicholas; s of Brig Robert Anthony Lindsell, MC, and Pamela Rosemary, *née* Cronk; *b* 31 December 1953; *Educ* Monkton Combe Sch; *m* 29 March 1980, Jill Penelope, da of Raymond Arthur Gransbury (d 1989); 3 s (David James b 1984, Philip Robert b 1993, Christopher Adam b 1995), 1 da (Nicola Jane b 1986); *Career* fund mangr Phillips & Drew 1972–82, dir Henderson Administration Ltd 1987–88 (joined 1982), dep md then md Midland Montagu Asset Management and chief investment offr James Capel Asset Management 1988–93, dir int equities Prudential Portfolio Managers Ltd 1993–96, chief investment offr Smith & Williamson Investment Mgmnt 1996–2004; FSI; *Recreations* shooting, fishing, tennis, wine soc; *Clubs* Army and Navy; *Style*— Charles Lindsell, Esq; ✉ tel 01923 855666

LINDSEY, Alan Michael; s of Philip Stanley Lindsey, of Stanmore, Middx, and Frederica Doris Lindsey; *b* 7 August 1938; *Educ* Harrow HS, Orange Hill Co GS, LSE (BScEcon); *m* 3 Dec 1967, Dr Caroline Rachel Lindsey, da of Eli Gustav Weinberg; 1 da (Rebecca Adina (Mrs Anthony Lindsey Asher) b 2 Aug 1975); *Career* chartered accountant; articled clerk Baker Sutton & Co (now part of Ernst & Young) 1960–63, exec Corp Fin Dept Hill Samuel and N M Rothschild & Sons 1963–66, mgmnt conslt and fin exec International Timber plc 1966–72, sr investigation mangr Thornton Baker 1972–79, in own practice Alan Lindsey & Co 1979–; author of numerous articles in professional accounting magazines 1967–; memb: Ctee London Dist Soc of CA's 1979–88 (fndr, memb Ctee and past chm North London Branch), Cncl ICAEW 1988–; memb Glyndebourne Festival Soc; assoc Inst of CPA (Israel) 1992–; FCA 1963; *Recreations* my three grandchildren, music (especially opera), theatre, cross country skiing, mountain walking, swimming; *Clubs* LSE; *Style*— Alan M Lindsey, Esq; ✉ Alan Lindsey & Co, 23 Gresham Gardens, London NW11 8NX (tel 020 8455 2882, fax 020 8455 1214, e-mail acclindsey@aol.com)

LINDSEY AND ABINGDON, 14 and 9 Earl of (E 1626 & 1682); Richard Henry Rupert Bertie; also Baron Norreys of Rycote (E 1572); s of Lt-Col Hon Arthur Michael Bertie, DSO, MC (d 1957), and Aline Rose, *née* Arbuthnot-Leslie (d 1948); suc cousin 13 Earl of Lindsey and (8 of) Abingdon 1963; *b* 28 June 1931; *Educ* Ampleforth; *m* 1957, Norah Elizabeth Farquhar-Oliver, 2 da of late Mark Oliver, OBE, and Norah (d 1980), da of Maj Francis Farquhar, DSO, 2 s of Sir Henry Farquhar, 4 Bt, JP, DL; 2 s (Henry Mark Willoughby, Lord Norreys b 6 June 1958, Hon Alexander Michael Richard b 8 April 1970), 1 da (Lady Annabel Frances Rose b 11 March 1969); *Heir* s, Lord Norreys; *Career* Cons Peer in House of Lords 1964–99; served with Scots Gds 1950 and Royal Norfolk Regt 1951–52, Lt; underwriting memb Lloyd's 1958–96; company dir 1965–92, chm Dawes & Henderson (Agencies) Ltd 1988–92; High Steward of Abingdon 1963–, pres Friends of Abingdon 1982–; chm Anglo-Ivorian Soc 1974–77; *Recreations* country pursuits; *Clubs* Pratt's, Turf; *Style*— The Rt Hon the Earl of Lindsey and Abingdon; ✉ Gilmilnscroft House, Sorn, Mauchline, Ayrshire KA5 6ND (tel 01290 551246, fax 01290 552906)

LINE, Matthew John Bardsley; s of John Line, of London, and Jill, *née* Rowland; *b* 22 April 1958; *Educ* Chiswick Sch, Univ of Exeter (BA); *m* 1987, Elinor, da of Ian Fairhurst; 2 da (Flora b 21 March 1992, Nancy b 17 July 1995); *Career* actor 1982; asst publisher Shepheard-Walwyn Publishers 1984–87, prodn dir Concertina Publications 1988, freelance journalist 1987–92, ed Up Country 1992–93, ed Dialogue 1993–95, launch ed Colour 1995, gp ed home interest titles Redwood Publishing 1996–97, ed Homes & Gardens 1997–2002, chief exec The Prince's Fndn 2002–04, ed-in-chief National Magazines 2004–, launch ed new She 2005–06, editorial conslt Rich magazine 2006, editorial dir Craft Publishing 2007–; launched Homes & Gardens V&A Classic Design Awards 1999; memb Ctee BSME 2001–02; *Books* Homes & Gardens Book of Design (2001); *Recreations* family, philosophy, gardening; *Style*— Matthew Line, Esq; ✉ Vallance House, 162 Peckham Rye, London SE22 9QH

LINEHAN, Stephen John; QC (1993); s of Maurice Gerald Linehan (d 1963), and Mary Joyce, *née* Norrish; *b* 12 March 1947; *Educ* Mt St Mary's Coll, King's Coll London; *m* 1976, Victoria Maria, da of Heiner Rössler; 1 s (Christopher b 1 Aug 1983); *Career* called to the Bar Lincoln's Inn (bencher 1999); recorder 1989–; *Style*— Stephen Linehan, Esq, QC

LINEKER, Gary Winston; OBE (1992); s of Barry Lineker, of Wigston, Leicester, and Margaret Patricia Morris, *née* Abbs; *b* 30 November 1960; *Educ* City of Leicester Boys' GS; *m* 5 July 1986, Michelle Denise, da of Roger Edwin Cockayne, of Leicester; 4 s (George b 2 Oct 1991, Harry b 25 July 1993, Tobias b 3 Feb 1996, Angus b 5 Aug 1997); *Career* former professional footballer, currently journalist and broadcaster; clubs: Leicester City 1978–85 (215 appearances, 100 goals), Everton 1985–86 (57 appearances, 40 goals), FC Barcelona 1986–89 (140 appearances, 54 goals), Tottenham Hotspur 1989–92 (139 appearances, 80 goals, FA Cup winners 1991), Grampus 8 Nagoya, Japan 1993–94, ret 1994; England: debut 1984, 80 caps, 48 goals, capt 1990–92, memb squad World Cup Mexico 1986 (leading goal scorer) and Italy 1990, memb squad European Championships W Germany 1988 and Sweden 1992, ret 1992; PFA Player of the Year 1986, Football Writers' Assoc Player of the Year 1986 and 1992; memb Sports Cncl 1995–; host Gary Lineker's Football Night (BBC Radio 5) 1992, team capt They Think It's All Over (BBC 1) 1995–2003, presenter Match of the Day (BBC 1) 1999–; columnist The Sunday Telegraph 1998–; Best Presenter RTS Sports Awards 2002 and 2004, Sports Presenter of the Year TRIC Awards 2003 and 2007; Hon MA: Univ of Leicester 1992, Loughborough Univ 1992; *Recreations* cricket, golf; *Clubs* MCC, Groucho; *Style*— Gary Lineker, Esq, OBE; ✉ c/o Jon Holmes Media Limited, 5th Floor, Holborn Gate, 26 Southampton Buildings, London WC2A 1PQ (tel 020 7861 2550, website www.jonholmesmedia.com)

LING, Prof Robin Sydney Mackwood; OBE (1992); s of William Harold Godfrey Mackwood Ling (d 1973), of Keighley, W Yorks, and Margaret Mona, *née* Price (d 1979); *b* 7 September 1927; *Educ* Shawnigan Lake Sch Vancouver Island, Univ of Oxford (MA, BM BCh), St Mary's Hosp London; *m* 18 Sept 1956, Mary, da of Capt W F Steedman, MC (d 1959); 2 da (Jennifer b 1959, Katherine b 1962); *Career* former conslt orthopaedic surgn: Royal Infirmary Edinburgh, Princess Margaret Orthopaedic Hosp Edinburgh; emeritus conslt orthopaedic surgn Princess Elizabeth Orthopaedic Hosp Exeter (formerly sr conslt); hon prof of bio-engrg Univ of Exeter; pres: Br Orthopaedic Res Soc 1979–80, Int

Hip Soc 1996–99; visiting prof: Louisiana State Univ 1983, Univ of Arizona 1985, Chinese Univ of Hong Kong 1985, Univ of Calif 1986, Baylor Univ TX 1986, Mayo Clinic 1992; memb SICOT; Lt Sir John Charnley meml lectr Univ of Liverpool 1986, Pridie meml lectr Univ of Bristol 1987, Robert Jones lectr RCS 1991, W S Baer lectr Johns Hopkins Hosp Baltimore 1991, Arthur Steindler lectr Orthopaedic Res Soc and American Acad of Orthopaedic Surgns 1992, Donald Julius Groen Prize IMechE 1993, Maurice E Muller Prize (jtly) 1999; contrib to leading med and scientific jls on hip surgery, implant fixation and properties of biomaterials; corresponding fell Aust Orthopaedic Assoc; FRCS, Hon FRCSEd, Hon FBOA (past pres); *Recreations* sailing; *Clubs* Royal Dartmouth Yacht, RSM; *Style*— Prof Robin Ling, OBE; ✉ 21 Anseres Place, Wells, Somerset BA5 2RT (tel 01749 672483, e-mail robin.ling@virgin.net); 2 The Quadrant, Wonford Road, Exeter, Devon EX2 4LE (tel 01392 437070)

LING, Timothy Andrew; s of Edward Andrew Ling (d 1973), of Maidstone, Kent, and Muriel Garnett, *née* Harford (d 1994); *b* 17 September 1948; *Educ* King's Sch Canterbury, The Queen's Coll Oxford (MA); *m* 9 May 1981, Sarah Elizabeth, da of David James; 2 s (Edward David b 30 July 1983, Richard James b 19 Jan 1985), 2 da (Emma Sarah b 8 May 1987, Sarah Rebecca b 7 March 1990); *Career* Freshfields: articled clerk 1971–73, asst slr 1973–77, ptnr 1977–2003, head Corp Tax Dept 1985–91, head Corp Fin Tax Gp 1991–2001; memb Law Soc (Revenue Law Ctee 1984–91); contrib various taxation pubns 1975–2003; *Recreations* music, sailing; *Clubs* Royal Dart Yacht; *Style*— Timothy Ling, Esq

LINGAM, Prof Sundara (Sam); s of Thambu Sabaratnam, of Sri Lanka, and Vijayalaxsmi; *b* 3 April 1946; *Educ* St John's Coll Jaffna, People's Friendship Univ Moscow (MD); *m* 12 June 1985, Susan Heather, da of Alex Reid, of Loughton, Essex; 1 da (Claire Anusha Laura b 1988), 1 s (Stephen Robert Surajah b 1991); *Career* registrar neurology Hosp for Sick Children Gt Ormond St 1980–83, hon sr registrar developmental paediatrics Wolfson Centre Inst of Child Health 1985–88, conslt paediatrician 1988–; hon sr lectr in community paediatrics 1991–, prof of medical educn and clinical dean for Europe Saba Univ Med Sch 1999–; assoc ed World Paediatrics and Child Care; exec med dir Assoc for the Prevention of Disabilities; hon sec and treas Int Coll of Paediatrics and Child Care (ICPCC) 1999–, hon asst ed Royal Coll of Paediatrics and Child Health (formerly Br Paediatric Assoc) 1994–, memb and tstee Autism London; FRCPCH, FRCP, DCH, DRCOG, LMSSA; *Books* Manual on Child Development (1988), It's Your Life (1982), Case Studies in Paediatric Radiology (1985), A - Z of Child Health (1995), Schedule of Growing Skills (SOGII) (1996); *Recreations* sports, writing, creating models; *Style*— Dr Sundara (Sam) Lingam; ✉ 42 Westland Drive, Brookmans Park, Hertfordshire AL9 2UQ (tel and fax 01707 662352); St Ann's Hospital, London N15 3TH (tel 020 8442 6331, fax 020 8442 9119)

LINGARD, Brian Hallwood; s of Capt Abel Keenan Lingard, MC (d 1955), of Wanstead, London, and Elsie May Lingard, BEM; *b* 2 November 1926; *Educ* Stockport GS, Manchester Coll of Art Sch of Architecture (DA); *m* 20 July 1949, Dorothy Gladys Lingard, da of Capt Herbert Clay (d 1978), of Bramhall, Cheshire; 2 s (Christopher b 1951, Timothy b 1953), 1 da (Rebecca b 1960); *Career* RN 1944–46; served: HMS Wolverine, Gibraltar 1944–45; architect; commenced private practice 1950; ptnr: Brian Lingard & Partners 1972–93, Lingard Styles Landscape (landscape architects) 1975–, Gallery Lingard (architectural historians) 1982–98; professional awards incl: RIBA Regnl Award (Wales), DOE and RIBA Housing Medal (7 awards), Civic Tst (21 awards), The Times/RICS Conservation Award (2 awards), Prince of Wales Conservation Award (3 awards); vice-pres Architects Benevolent Soc 2002– (chm 1988–92); FRIBA 1957 (ARIBA 1949); *Books* The Opportunities for the Conservation and Enhancement of our Historic Resorts (1983), Special Houses for Special People (2004), Thrifty Dwellings for Thrifty People (2008); *Recreations* swimming, writing, old buildings; *Clubs* Carlton, RAC; *Style*— Brian Lingard; ✉ Le Bouillon House, St George's Esplanade, St Peter Port, Guernsey (tel 01481 700244); Lingard Styles Landscape, 9 College Hill, Shrewsbury SY1 1LZ (tel 01743 233961)

LINGARD, Joan Amelia; MBE (1998); da of Henry James Lingard (d 1963), and Elizabeth Cunningham Beattie (d 1948); *Educ* Bloomfield Collegiate Sch Belfast, Moray House Coll of Educn Edinburgh; *m* 3 da; *Career* author; cncl memb Scottish Arts Cncl 1980–85 (memb Lit Ctee 1980–85); memb: PEN, Soc of Authors (chm Scotland 1982–86), Bd Edinburgh Book Festival 1994–; *Adult Novels* Liam's Daughter, The Prevailing Wind, The Tide Comes In, The Headmaster, A Sort of Freedom, The Lord on Our Side, The Second Flowering of Emily Mountjoy, Greenyards, Sisters By Rite, Reasonable Doubts, The Women's House, After Colette, Dreams of Love, Modest Glory, The Kiss, Encarnita's Journey; *Children's Novels* The Twelfth Day of July, Across The Barricades, Into Exile, A Proper Place, Hostages to Fortune, The Clearance, The Resettling, The Pilgrimage, The Reunion, Snake Among the Sunflowers, Frying As Usual, The Gooseberry, The File on Fraulein Berg, Strangers in the House, The Winter Visitor, The Freedom Machine, The Guilty Party, Rags and Riches, Tug of War, Glad Rags, Between Two Worlds, Hands Off Our School!, Night Fires, Lizzie's Leaving, Dark Shadows, A Secret Place, Tom and the Treehouse, The Egg Thieves, River Eyes, Natasha's Will, Me and My Shadow, Tortoise Trouble, The Sign of the Black Dagger; *Awards* Scottish Arts Cncl bursary 1967–68, Buxtehuder Bülle Award for children's lit Germany 1986, Scottish Arts Cncl Award 1994, Scottish Arts Cncl Book Award 1999; *Style*— Ms Joan Lingard, MBE; ✉ c/o David Higham Associates Ltd, 5–8 Lower John Street, Golden Square, London W1R 4HA (tel 020 7437 7888, fax 020 7437 1072)

LINGEN-STALLARD, Andrew Philip; s of Phillip Edward Stallard, and Maureen Louise, *née* Johnson; *b* 10 August 1962; *Educ* Dyson Perrins HS Malvern, Dorset Sch of Nursing, Dorset Sch of Midwifery, Chippenham Tech Coll, South Bank Univ, KCL (BSc, MSc); *m* 6 April 1985 (m dis 1996), Avril Clare Dove; 3 s (Adam David b 1986, Mark Daniel b 1988, Liam Andrew Alexander b 1991); civil partner 21 Dec 2005, Dr Lee Winter; *Career* charge nurse Chippenham Dist Hosp 1988–89, midwife Princess Margaret Hosp 1988–92, midwife Roehampton Hosp 1992–93, midwife KCH NHS Tst 1993–96, clinical midwifery mangr then sr nurse for surgery Lewisham NHS Tst 1996–2001; KCH NHS Tst: modern matron and sr midwife 2001–05, hon sr midwife 2005–; memb Midwifery Support Team and midwifery conslt Maternity Unit Northwick Park Hosp 2005, midwife advsr London Ambulance Serv 2006–, midwife advsr Nursing and Midwife Cncl 2006–; Royal Coll of Midwives: memb 1988–, elected memb Cncl 2003–, md and tstee 2003–, sec Southern Thames Branch 2003– (steward 1991–96), memb Employment Ctee 2003–05, memb Professional Policy Ctee 2003–, Benevolent Ctee 2006–; md: Lingen-Stallard & Winter Estates Ltd 2005–, Lingen-Stallard & MacDonald Entertainment Ltd 2006–; author of articles in jls; memb: Lab Pty, Amnesty Int, Genealogical Soc, White Lion Soc, Heraldic Soc, Nat Tst, RSPB, RHS; FRSA; *Recreations* women's health, politics, history, art, genealogy; *Style*— Andrew Lingen-Stallard, Esq; ✉ King's College Hospital NHS Trust, Denmark Hill, London SE5 9RS (tel 020 7737 4000, e-mail andrew.stallard@kch.nhs.uk)

LINGENS, Michael Robert; s of Dr Friedrich Otto Lingens, of Hamburg, Germany, and Karin Weber; *b* 15 May 1957; *Educ* St Edmund's Sch Canterbury, Trinity Coll Oxford (MA); *m* 9 May 1992, Rachel, da of Charles Fay (d 1998), and Patricia Fay, OBE; 1 s (Matthew b 20 Sept 1995); *Career* admitted slr 1982, ptnr Speechly Bircham (managing ptnr 1998–), chm Bow Group 1984–85; cncllr London Borough of Hammersmith and Fulham 1982–86; Parly candidate (Cons) Bolsover 1987; *Books* Beveridge and The Bow Group Generation, Winning on Welfare; *Recreations* real tennis, rackets, skiing; *Clubs* Queen's; *Style*— Michael Lingens, Esq; ✉ 34 Rylett Road, London W12 9SS (tel home 020 8743 1249, business 020 7427 6400, fax 020 7427 6600, e-mail michael.lingens@speechlys.com)

LINGWOOD, James Peter Boyce; s of Robert Lingwood (d 1980), and Patricia Lingwood; *b* 28 May 1959; *Educ* Univ of Oxford, (BA, MPhil); *Partner* Jane Hamlyn; 2 da (Scarlett b 25 Aug 1990, Evie b 18 Nov 1994), 1 s (Louis b 14 Jan 1992); *Career* exhbns curator ICA London 1986–90, ind curator 1991–; exhbns curated incl: Juan Muñoz (Tate Modern London) 2001, Douglas Gordon (Hayward Gallery London) 2002, Susan Hiller (Baltic Gateshead) 2004; co-dir Artangel 1991–, co-dir Artangel Media Ltd 2000–; Artangel projects incl: House (Rachel Whiteread), Breakdown (Michael Landy), The Cremaster Cycle (Matthew Barney), Carib's Leap/ Western Deep (Steve McQueen); memb Int Advsy Bd: Museu Serralves Porto, CAPC Musie d'Art Contemporain Bordeaux; tstee Paul Hamlyn Fndn 2003–; *Publications* Juan Muñoz: Double Bind at Tate Modern (2001), Robert Smithson, Bernd and Hilla Becher: Field Trips (2001), Off Limits - 40 Artangel Projects (2002), Susan Hiller: Recall (2004); *Style*— James Lingwood, Esq; ✉ Artangel, 31 Eyre Street Hill, London EC1R 5EW (tel 020 7713 1400, e-mail jl@artangel.org.uk)

LININGTON, Richard; s of Reginald Friend Linington (d 1981), of Birchington, Kent, and Gwendoline Florence Irene, *née* Amos (d 1986); *b* 31 March 1945; *Educ* Tonbridge, Birmingham Coll of Arts and Crafts (Dip Int Design); *m* 27 Sept 1969 (m dis 1994), (Hilary) Jane, da of Maj Ronald Jasper Lucas, of Chipping Campden, Glos; 2 s (Noel b 1971, Ben b 1975); *Career* designer; interior designer R Seifert and Ptnrs 1967–69, designer for architect Stephen Garrett 1969–72, assoc with Austin Smith Lord Architects 1972–79, princ Hurley Linington McGirr Design Ptnrshp 1979–87, ptnr Bloomer Tweedale Architects 1988–91, interior design mangr Austin-Smith Lord 1991–92, princ Linington - Architectural and Interior Design 1992–, design dir The Chadwick Group London 1994–96, ptnr PPML design practice 1996–; pres Int Fedn of Int Designers and Architects 1987–89 and 1991–93; memb Cncl New Kent Opera 2003–; FCSD 1987; *Recreations* music, gardening; *Clubs* East India; *Style*— Richard Linington, Esq; ✉ Medlicott Manor Farm, Wentnor, Bishop's Castle, Shropshire SY9 5EL (tel 01588 650185, e-mail chapel.farm@virgin.net)

LINKLATER, Alexander Ragnar (Alex); s of Magnus Linklater , *qv*, and Baroness Linklater of Butterstone (Life Peer), *qv*; *Educ* Glenalmond Coll Perthshire, Univ of Durham (BA), Univ of Glasgow; *Career* freelance journalist 1994–97; Glasgow Herald: feature writer 1997–98, architecture corr 1998–99, literary ed 1999–2000; dep arts ed Evening Standard 2000–01, assoc ed Prospect magazine, columnist The Guardian; judge Whitbread Novel of the Year Award 2000, fndr Nat Short Story Prize 2006; Scottish Arts Writer of the Year 2000, Bank of Scotland Press award; fell Nat Endowment for Science, Technol and the Arts 2005–06; *Clubs* The Union, Soho; *Style*— Alex Linklater, Esq; ✉ tel 020 7697 9166, e-mail alexlinklater@mac.com

LINKLATER, Prof Andrew; s of Andrew Linklater, and Isabella, *née* Forsyth; *b* 3 August 1949, Aberdeen; *Educ* Univ of Aberdeen (MA), Balliol Coll Oxford (BPhil), LSE (PhD); *m* Jane Christie, *née* Adam; *Career* lectr in political sci Univ of Tasmania 1976–81; Monash Univ: lectr in politics 1982–84, sr lectr in politics 1985–91, assoc prof 1992–93; prof of int rels Univ of Keele 1993–99, Woodrow Wilson prof of int politics Univ of Wales Aberystwyth 2000–; AcSS 2001, FBA 2005; *Publications* incl: Men and Citizens in the Theory of International Relations (1982, 2 edn 1990), Beyond Realism and Marxism: Critical Theory and International Relations (1990), The Transformation of Political Community: Ethical Foundations of the Post-Westphalian Era (1998), The English School of International Relations: A Contemporary Assessment (jtly, 2006); *Recreations* the Turf, Australian aboriginal art, woodland work, ECM recordings, guitar practice; *Style*— Prof Andrew Linklater; ✉ Department of International Politics, University of Wales, Aberystwyth, Ceredigion SY23 3FE (tel 01970 621596, fax 01970 622709, e-mail adl@aber.ac.uk)

LINKLATER, Magnus Duncan; s of Eric Robert Linklater, CBE, TD, and Marjorie MacIntyre (d 1997); *b* 21 February 1942; *Educ* Eton, Univ of Freiburg, Sorbonne, Trinity Hall Cambridge (BA); *m* 1967, Rt Hon Baroness Linklater of Butterstone (Life Peer), *qv*, da of Lt-Col Michael Lyle, OBE, JP, DL, of Riemore Lodge, Dunkeld; 2 s (Alexander, *qv*, b 1968, Saul b 1970), 1 da (Freya b 1975); *Career* journalist: Daily Express Manchester 1964–65, Evening Standard (ed Londoner's Diary) 1965–69, Sunday Times (ed Spectrum pages, ed Colour Magazine, asst ed News, exec ed Features) 1969–83; managing ed The Observer 1983–86; ed: London Daily News 1986–87, The Scotsman 1988–94; columnist: The Times 1994–, Scotland on Sunday 1998–; Scotland ed The Times 2007–; presenter BBC Radio Scotland 1994–97; chm: Scottish Daily Newspaper Soc 1991–93, Edinburgh Book Festival 1995–96, Scottish Arts Cncl 1996–2001; Scottish Daily Newspaper Soc Lifetime Achievement Award 2005, Hon Dr of Arts Napier Univ, Hon LLD Univ of Aberdeen, Hon DLitt Univ of Glasgow; FRSE; *Books* Hoax - The Howard Hughes Clifford Irving Affair (with Stephen Fay and Lewis Chester), Jeremy Thorpe - A Secret Life (with Lewis Chester and David May), The Falklands War (with the Sunday Times Insight team), Massacre - the story of Glencoe, The Fourth Reich - Klaus Barbie and the Neo-Fascist Connection (with Isabel Hilton and Neal Ascherson), Not with Honour - the inside story of the Westland Affair (with David Leigh), For King and Conscience - John Graham of Claverhouse, Viscount Dundee (with Christian Hesketh), Anatomy of Scotland (co-ed), Highland Wilderness (photographs by Colin Prior), People in a Landscape - The New Highlanders (photographs by Craig Mackay); *Recreations* opera, fishing, book collecting; *Clubs* MCC; *Style*— Magnus Linklater, Esq; ✉ 5 Drummond Place, Edinburgh EH3 6PH (tel 0131 557 5705, fax 0131 557 9757, e-mail magnus.linklater@blueyonder.co.uk)

LINKLATER OF BUTTERSTONE, Baroness (Life Peer UK 1997), of Riemore in Perth and Kinross Veronica Linklater; da of Lt-Col Michael Lyle, OBE, JP, DL, of Riemore Lodge, Dunkeld, Perthshire, and Hon Elizabeth Sinclair; *b* 15 April 1943; *Educ* Cranborne Chase Sch, Univ of Sussex, Univ of London (DipSocAdmin); *m* 1967, Magnus Duncan Linklater, *qv*, s of late Eric Robert Linklater; 2 s (Hon Alexander, *qv*, b 1968, Hon Saul b 1970), 1 da (Hon Freya b 1975); *Career* child care offr London Borough of Tower Hamlets 1967–68, co-fndr Visitors' Centre Pentonville Prison 1971–77, govr three Islington schs 1970–85, Prison Reform Tst project Winchester Prison 1981–82; The Butler Tst Prison Serv Annual Award Scheme: fndr, admin then conslt 1983–87, tstee 1987–2001, vice-pres 2001–; JP Inner London 1985–88; co-ordinator then tstee and vice-chm The Pushkin Prizes (Scotland) 1989–, pres Soc of Friends of Dunkeld Cathedral 1989–, fndr and chm The New Sch Butterstone 1991–2004 (pres 2004–); memb: Children's Panel Edinburgh South 1989–97, Ctee The Gulliver Award for the Performing Arts in Scotland 1990–96, Beattie Ctee (making recommendations on post sch provision for young people with special needs in Scotland) 1998–99, Advsy Bd Beacon Fellowship Charitable Tst 2003–, Scottish Assoc for the Study of Offending 2005–, Cncl Winston Churchill Meml Tst 2005–; dir Maggie Keswick Jencks Cancer Caring Ctee 1997–2004; assessor to the chllr Ct Napier Univ 2001–04; tstee: Esmée Fairbairn Charitable Tst 1991–, The Young Musicians Tst 1993–97, Univ of the Highlands & Islands 1999–2001; advsr Koestler Award Tst 2004–; patron: The Sutherland Tst 1993–2003, The Airborne Initiative 1998–2004, The Nat Schizophrenia Fell Scotland 2000–, Nat Family & Parenting Inst 2002–, The Calyx - Scotland's Garden Tst 2004–, Research Autism 2004–, Probation Bds Assoc 2005–, Action for Prisoners' Families 2005–; fndn patron Queen Margaret UC Edinburgh 1998, appeal patron Hopetoun House Preservation Tst 2001; chm: Rethinking Crime and Punishment 2001–, House of Lords All Pty Gp on Offender Learning Skills 2005–06; memb Scot Ctee Barnado's 2001–04; Parly candidate (Lib Dem) Perth and

L

Kinross (by-election) 1995; *Recreations* music, theatre, gardening, my family; *Style*— The Rt Hon Baroness Linklater of Butterstone; ✉ 5 Drummond Place, Edinburgh EH3 6PH (tel 0131 557 5705, fax 0131 557 9757, e-mail v.linklater@blueyonder.co.uk)

LINLEY, Viscount; *see: Royal Family section*

LINLITHGOW, 4 Marquess of (UK 1902); Sir Adrian John Charles Hope; 12 Bt (NS 1698); also Earl of Hopetoun, Viscount Aithrie, Lord Hope (all S 1703), Baron Hopetoun (UK 1809), and Baron Niddry (UK 1814); o son of 3 Marquess of Linlithgow, MC (d 1987), and his 1 w Vivien, *née* Kenyon-Slaney (d 1963); *b* 1 July 1946; *Educ* Eton; *m* 1, 9 Jan 1968 (m dis 1978), Anne Pamela, eld da of Arthur Edmund Leveson, of Hall Place, Ropley, Hants; 2 s (Andrew, Earl of Hopetoun b 22 May 1969, Lord Alexander b 3 Feb 1971); m 2, 1980 (m dis 1997), Peta Carol, da of Charles Victor Ormonde Binding, of Congresbury, Somerset; 1 da (Lady Louisa b 16 April 1981), 1 s (Lord Robert b 17 Jan 1984); m 3, 1997 (m dis 2004), Auriol Lady Ropner; *Heir* s, Earl of Hopetoun; *Style*— The Most Hon the Marquess of Linlithgow; ✉ Philpstoun House, Linlithgow, West Lothian EH49 7NB

LINNELL, Andrew John; s of Cyril Barrie Linnell, of Alsager, Cheshire, and Maureen, *née* Goodyear; *b* 28 June 1956; *Educ* Wolstanton GS, Univ of Salford (BSc), Keele Univ (PGCE), Mid Kent Coll of Further and Higher Educn (ACP); *m* 17 June 1989, Juliet, da of late Prof Oswald Hanfling; 1 da (Ruth Emily b 6 June 1990), 1 s (Simeon Jack b 14 July 1994); *Career* grad mgmnt trainee Royal Bank of Scotland plc 1977–78; geography teacher Howard Sch Gillingham 1979–84, youth tutor Rainham Sch for Girls and Howard Sch Rainham 1984–86, educn offr (community and youth) N Kent Area Educn Office 1986–89; Educn Dept Kent LEA: quality assurance conslt Mgmnt Review Team 1989–92, review mangr Local Mgmnt of Schs Scheme 1992; dep head teacher Sir Joseph Williamson's Mathematical Sch Rochester 1993–97, head master Reading Sch 1997–2005, headteacher Desborough Sch Maidenhead 2005–; memb Ct Univ of Reading 1998–; FRGS 1983 (memb Cncl 2005, vice-pres 2006), CGeog 2002, FCP 2005 (MCP 1989); *Recreations* running, travelling, local history; *Style*— Andrew Linnell, Esq; ✉ Desborough School, Shoppenhangers Road, Maidenhead, Berkshire SL6 2QB (tel 01628 634505, e-mail info@desborough.org.uk)

LINNELL, Stuart Swain Goodman; MBE (1994); s of Capt Eric Henry Goodman Linnell (d 1975), of Birmingham, and Dorothy Mary, *née* Swain (d 1974); *b* 22 January 1947, Birmingham; *Educ* King's Norton GS Birmingham; *m* 1981, Susan Marie, da of Desmond Reginald Cleobury, of Coventry; 2 s (Nicholas Charles Goodman b 15 Feb 1983, Matthew Stuart b 4 July 1985); *Career* radio and television presenter: BBC Radio Birmingham 1970–74, sports ed Radio Hallam (Sheffield) 1974–80, Mercia Sound (Coventry) 1980–94, Leicester Sound 1991–94, RAM FM (Derby) 1994, BBC Radio 5 Live 1995–96, BBC Radio WM (Birmingham and Coventry) 1995–2000, BBC TV 1995–2000, SkySports TV 2000–, ntl 2001–02, talkSPORT 2001–02, Today FM (Dublin) 2001–, Setanta TV 2006–; owner-trader First Principles Media Services 2000–; bid dir WBC 105.2 (Chrysalis Gp plc) 2003, ops dir Laser Broadcasting Ltd 2005–; corp hospitality host Coventry City FC 2000–; dep chm Coventry and Warks C of C (Coventry branch), memb Coventry Ambassador's Gp; patron: Jaguar (Coventry) Band, Circle Light Opera Co; Hon MA Coventry Univ 1999; *Awards* Gold Medal Int Radio Festival of NY 1990, Silver Medal Sony Radio Awards 1996, Gold Medal Sony Radio Awards 1997; *Recreations* the theatre, supporting Coventry City FC, walking my dogs; *Style*— Stuart Linnell, Esq, MBE; ✉ c/o Laser Broadcasting Limited, Barnet House, Dudley Court, Dudley Road, Darlington DL1 4GG (e-mail stuart.linnell@laserbroadcasting.com)

LINNETT, Simon John Lawrence; s of Prof John Wilfrid Linnett (d 1975), and Rae Ellen Fanny, *née* Libgott; *b* 14 February 1954; *Educ* The Leys Cambridge, Balliol Coll Oxford; *m* 28 Nov 1987, Penelope Jane, da of Sir Charles William Willink, Bt, of Highgate, London; 2 s (John Lawrence Humfrey b 1991, Henry Simon Albert b 1993); *Career* NM Rothschild & Sons Ltd: joined 1975, mangr 1982, asst dir 1984, dir 1987, dir Exec Ctee 1989, md investment banking 1998; memb Special Advsy Bd Nat Railway Museum 1997; *Recreations* environmental issues, walking; *Style*— Simon Linnett, Esq; ✉ c/o N M Rothschild & Sons Ltd, New Court, St Swithin's Lane, London EC4P 4DU (tel 020 7280 5062)

LINSCOTT, Gillian; da of Thomas Snow Linscott (d 1988), and Muriel Rosaline, *née* Fountain (d 1978); *b* 27 September 1944; *Educ* Maidenhead HS, Somerville Coll Oxford (MA); *m* 1988, Tony Geraghty; *Career* journalist: Liverpool Daily Post 1967–70, Birmingham Post 1970–72, The Guardian 1972–79, BBC 1979–90 (mainly as Parly journalist); freelance writer 1990–; author; memb Crime Writers' Assoc 1984; Crime Writers' Assoc Ellis Peters Historical Dagger 2000; *Books* A Healthy Body (1984), Murder Makes Tracks (1985), Knightfall (1986), A Whiff of Sulphur (1987), Unknown Hand (1988), Murder, I Presume (1990), Sister Beneath the Sheet (1991), Hanging on the Wire (1992), Stage Fright (1993), Widow's Peak (1994), Crown Witness (1995), Dead Man's Music (1996), Dance on Blood (1998), Absent Friends (1999), The Perfect Daughter (2000), Dead Man Riding (2002), The Garden (2002), Blood on the Wood (2003); *Recreations* horse riding, gardening, hill walking; *Style*— Ms Gillian Linscott; ✉ Wood View, Hope under Dinmore, Leominster, Herefordshire HR6 0PP

LINSELL, Richard Duncan; s of Dr William Duncan Linsell, of Ipswich, and Margaret Sybil, *née* Burns; *b* 21 June 1947; *Educ* Mill Hill Sch, Jesus Coll Cambridge (MA); *m* 25 Oct 1986, Briony Margaret, da of Dr James Wright Anderton Crabtree, OBE, TD (Col and former QHP), of Devon; 1 da (Katherine Jemima Cory b 14 Oct 1987); *Career* admitted slr 1973, ptnr Mayer, Brown, Rowe & Maw LLP (formerly Rowe & Maw) 1976–; non-exec dir DHL International (UK) Ltd 1977–97, non-exec chm Jas Bowman & Sons Ltd 1991–99, non-exec dir Sunseeker International (Boats) Ltd; numerous pubns on matters affecting the regulated professions, in particular the law relating to limited liability partnerships; memb: Law Soc, Int Bar Assoc; *Recreations* collecting and consuming wine, music, golf, walking; *Style*— Richard Linsell, Esq; ✉ 11 Pilgrim Street, London EC4V 6RD (tel 020 7248 4282, fax 020 7248 2009)

LINTHWAITE, Peter John Nicholas; *b* 3 December 1956; *Educ* New Coll Oxford (MA); *m* 18 Sept 1982, Gillian Deborah, *née* Oblitas; 2 da; *Career* md Murray Johnstone Asia Ltd 1995–2001, exec dir Royal London Private Equity Ltd 2001–05, ceo British Venture Capital Assoc (BVCA) 2005–; *Clubs* MCC; *Style*— Peter Linthwaite, Esq; ✉ British Venture Capital Association, 3 Clements Inn, London WC2A 2AZ (tel 020 7025 2950, fax 020 7025 2951)

LINTON, Martin; MP; *b* 1944; *Educ* Christ's Hosp, Pembroke Coll Oxford (MA), Univ of Lyon; *m* (wife decd); 2 da; *Career* journalist The Guardian 1981–97, MP (Lab) Battersea 1997–; PPS to: Min of State for the Arts 2001–03, Ldr of the House 2003–; pres Battersea Arts Centre, chm of govrs Somerset Nursery Sch Battersea; *Publications* Get Me Out of Here (1980), The Swedish Road to Socialism (1984), Labour Can Still Win (1988), The Guardian Guide to the House of Commons (ed, 1992), What's Wrong with First Past the Post? (1993), Money and Votes (1994), Was it the Sun Wot Won It? (1995), Guardian Election Guide (ed, 1997), Making Votes Count (1998); *Style*— Martin Linton, MP; ✉ House of Commons, London SW1A 0AA (tel 020 7219 4619)

LINTOTT, Prof Andrew William; s of Ernest Roworth Carl Lintott, and Edith Eileen, *née* Garland; *b* 9 December 1936; *Educ* Tonbridge, Exeter Coll Oxford (MA, Arnold Ancient History Prize), Univ of London (PhD), Univ of Oxford (DLitt); *Career* 2 Lt RA 1958–60; asst lectr then lectr in classics KCL 1960–67, lectr then sr lectr in ancient history Univ of Aberdeen 1967–81; Worcester Coll Oxford: fell and tutor in ancient history 1981–2004, reader 1996, prof 1999–; visiting memb Inst for Advanced Study Princeton 1990–, Hugh Last fell Brit Sch Rome 1994–, visiting prof Univ of Texas at Austin 2002–; *Books* Violence in Republican Rome (1968, 2 edn 1999), Violence, Civil Strife and Revolution in the Classical City (1982, reprinted 1987), Judicial Reform and Land Reform in the Roman Republic (1992), Imperium Romanum: Politics and Administration (1993), Cambridge Ancient History vol IX (ed with JA Crook and Elizabeth Rawson, 2 edn 1993), Cambridge Ancient History vol X (ed with Alan Bowman and Edward Champlin 1996), The Constitution of the Roman Republic (1999), The Roman Republic (2000); *Recreations* sailing, bridge; *Style*— Prof Andrew Lintott; ✉ Worcester College, Oxford OX1 2HB (tel 01865 278365, fax 01865 278303, e-mail andrew.lintott@worc.ox.ac.uk)

LINTOTT, Lesley Joan; da of John Desmond Hutson (d 1979), of Durham, and Marion Hush, *née* Mallabar (d 1977); *b* 28 June 1950; *Educ* Washington Grammar Tech Sch, St Hilda's Coll Oxford (MA); *m* 19 Aug 1972, Christopher John Lintott, s of John William Lintott (d 1972); *Career* Penningtons: articled clerk 1972–75, ptnr 1978, London admin ptnr 1990–96, head Private Client Dept 1995–, London managing ptnr 1996–97, nat managing ptnr 1997–; Freeman: City of London Slrs' Co 1992, City of London 1995; memb: City of London Law Soc, Soc of Tsts & Estates Practitioners (STEP); *Books* Butterworths Wills, Probate & Administration Service (revision ed, Wills Div); *Recreations* wine, art, music, cricket; *Clubs* Walbrook, Wine Soc Dining (vice-pres), Surrey CCC; *Style*— Ms Lesley Lintott; ✉ Penningtons, Bucklersbury House, 83 Cannon Street, London EC4N 8PE (tel 020 7457 3000, fax 020 7457 3240, e-mail lintottlj@penningtons.co.uk)

LIPKIN, Dr Malcolm Leyland; s of Dr Reuben Lipkin (d 1944), of Liverpool, and Evelyne, *née* Urding (d 1982); *b* 2 May 1932; *Educ* Liverpool Coll, Royal Coll of Music London, Univ of London (BMus, DMus); *m* 5 Aug 1968, Judith Eda, da of Jacob Frankel (d 1968), of Port Elizabeth, South Africa, and Eileen, *née* Orr (d 1995); 1 s (Jonathan b 21 Sept 1970); *Career* lectr in music Dept of External Studies Univ of Oxford 1967–75, lectr Sch of Continuing Educn Univ of Kent at Canterbury 1975–96, lectr Centre for Continuing Educn Univ of Sussex 1994–2000; composer; premieres incl: Piano Sonata no 3 (Gaudeamus Fndn Int Music Week Holland) 1951, Piano Sonata no 4 (Cheltenham Festival) 1955, Piano Concerto (Cheltenham Festival) 1959, Violin Concerto no 2 (Bournemouth Symphony Orch) 1963, Sinfonia di Roma Symphony no 1 (Royal Liverpool Philharmonic) 1966, Psalm 96 for Chorus and Orch (John Lewis Partnership cmmn) 1969, Clifford's Tower (Cheltenham Festival) 1980, Five Songs (BBC London) 1981, Harp Trio (Rye Festival) 1982, Naboth's Vineyard (Law Soc concerts) 1983, The Pursuit Symphony no 2 (BBC Philharmonic Manchester) 1983, Wind Quintet (BBC cmmn) 1986, Prelude and Dance in Memory of Jacqueline du Pré (City of London Festival) 1988, Piano Sonata no 5 (Gt Comp Festival) 1989, Piano Trio (Purcell Room London) 1989, Oboe Concerto (BBC cmmn) 1990, Variations on a Theme of Bartók for String Quartet (Newbury Spring Festival) 1992, Dance Fantasy for Solo Violin (Carl Flesch Int Violin Competition Cmmn London) 1992, Sun Symphony No 3 (BBC Philharmonic Manchester) 1993, Five Bagatelles (Wigmore Hall London) 1994, Second Violin Sonata (Green Room Cmmn Tunbridge Wells) 1998, From Across La Manche (Primavera Chamber Orch Cmmn Canterbury) 1998 (recorded by Royal Ballet Sinfonia 2006), Nocturne No 2 (Pianoworks Festival Blackheath) 1999; made numerous recordings, broadcasts and performances worldwide; memb Exec Ctee Composers' Guild of GB 1972–76; ARCM, LRAM; *Books* illustrated incl: Handel at Work (1963), A History of Western Music (1974), Casals and the Art of Interpretation (1976), The Nine Symphonies of Beethoven (1981), Tortelier - A Self-Portrait (1984), A Companion to the Concerto (1988); *Recreations* long country walks, travelling; *Style*— Dr Malcolm Lipkin; ✉ Penlan, Crowborough Hill, Crowborough, East Sussex TN6 2EA (tel 01892 652454, e-mail mail@malcolmlipkin.co.uk, website www.malcolmlipkin.co.uk)

LIPMAN, Maureen Diane; CBE (1999); da of late Maurice Julius Lipman of Hull, and late Zelma Lipman (d 2003); *b* 10 May 1946; *Educ* LAMDA; *m* 18 Feb 1973, Jack Rosenthal, CBE (d 2004), s of Samuel Rosenthal (d 1964); 1 da (Amy b 7 June 1974), 1 s (Adam b 3 Oct 1976); *Career* actress; columnist: She Magazine (PPA Columnist of the Year Award 1991), Good Housekeeping 1991–96; Hon DLitt Univ of Hull 1994, Hon MA Univ of Salford 1995; *Theatre* 3 years NT incl Kathleen in A Long Day's Journey into Night; other credits incl: The Knack (Palace Theatre Watford), Molly in The Front Page (Old Vic), Miss Richland in The Good Natured Man, Celia in As You Like It (RSC); West End incl: Outside Edge, Messiah (both SWET Award nomination for Best Actress), Chapter Two (Lyric Hammersmith), The Meg and Mog Show (Arts Theatre), Kitty McShane in On Your Way Riley (Theatre Royal), lead role in Night and Day (Greenwich), See How They Run (Olivier Award for Best Comedy Performance and Variety Club Award), musical debut Ruth in Wonderful Town (Queen's Theatre, Variety Club Award and Olivier Award nomination), devised and appeared in one-woman show Re: Joyce (life of Joyce Grenfell, three seasons, West End and Long Wharf Theatre Connecticut) 1988–91, The Cabinet Minister (Albery) 1991, Lost in Yonkers (Strand Theatre) 1992, The Sisters Rosensweig (Old Vic) 1994; Mrs Malaprop in The Rivals (Manchester Royal Exchange), Live and Kidding (solo performance, Chichester, Leeds, tour and Duchess Theatre London, also on video), Oklahoma! (RNT 1998, Lyceum Theatre 1999), Peggy Ramsay in Peggy for You (Hampstead Theatre Club 1999 and The Comedy Theatre and tour 2000), Nina in Sitting Pretty (by Amy Rosenthal, Hypothetical Theatre NY and English tour) 2001, Mrs Meers in Thoroughly Modern Millie (Shaftesbury Theatre) 2003–04 (Olivier Award nomination for Best Actress in a Musical), Dim Sum in Aladdin (Old Vic) 2004, Martha in Martha, Josie and the Chinese Elvis (tour) 2007; *Television* incl: The Evacuees, Jane Lucas in Agony (BAFTA Award nomination for Best Comedy Performance), Smiley's People, The Evacuees, The Knowledge, Rolling Home, Maggie in Outside Edge (both BAFTA Award nomination for Best Actress), The Princess of France in Love's Labour's Lost, Absent Friends, Shift Work, lead in All At No 20 (Thames, TV Times Best Comedy Actress Award), Miss Minchin in The Little Princess (2 series, LWT), About Face (2 series, Central) 1989 and 1990, Enid Blyton in Sunny Stories (BBC2, Bookmark), Agony Again 1995, Shani in Eskimo Day 1996, Cold Enough for Snow 1997, Coronation Street 2002, Jonathan Creek 2002, The Fugitives 2005, In Search of Style (presenter), Art Deco, Sensitive Skin (Channel 4), The Wire in Dr Who (BBC) 2006; numerous guest appearances incl Have I Got News for You (BBC) 1994; *Film* incl: Up the Junction (debut), Gumshoe, Educating Rita (BAFTA Award nomination for Best Supporting Actress), Water (with Michael Caine), Carry On Columbus 1992, Captain Jack 1997, Solomon & Gaenor 1998, The Discovery of Heaven 2001, The Pianist 2001; *Radio* incl: When Housewives Had The Choice (2 series), The Lipman Test 1994, Choice Grenfell 1997; *Books* How Was it for You? (1985), Something to Fall Back On (1987), You Got an 'Ology? (with Richard Phillips, 1989), Thank You For Having Me (1990), When's It Coming Out? (1992), You Can Read Me Like a Book (1995), Lip Reading (1999); *Style*— Ms Maureen Lipman, CBE; ✉ c/o Conway van Gelder Ltd, 18–21 Jermyn Street, London SW1Y 6HP (tel 020 7287 0077, fax 020 7287 1940)

LIPNER, Prof Julius Joseph; s of Vojtech Lipner, of Burlington, Canada, and Sylvia, *née* Coutts; *b* 11 August 1946, Patna, India; *Educ* St Xavier's Sch Calcutta, St Joseph's Coll Darjeeling, Bridgewater Sch Salford, Pontifical Athenaeum Pune, Jadavpur Univ Calcutta, KCL (PhD); *m* 20 Feb 1971, Anindita, *née* Neogy; 1 da (Tanya Maria b 24 March 1972), 1 s (Julius Alan b 10 July 1975); *Career* lectr in Indian religion Univ of Birmingham 1973–74; Univ of Cambridge: lectr in Indian religion and the comparative study of religion 1975–99, dir Dharam Hinduja Inst of Indic Res 1995–99, reader in Hinduism and the comparative study of religion 1999–2003, chm Faculty Bd of Divinity 2003–06, prof in Hinduism and the comparative study of religion 2003–; fell: St Edmund's

Coll Cambridge 1976–89, Clare Hall Cambridge 1990–; visiting fell Viswabharati Univ India 1984; visiting prof: Univ of Calgary 1987, 1989 and 1996 (chair of Christian thought), Vanderbilt Univ Nashville 1992, Liverpool Hope UC 2003–04; hon prof Kurukshetra Univ India 1995–97, hon res scholar Univ of Wales 2003–; memb Editorial Advsy Bd Jl of Hindu-Christian Studies, Editorial Advsy Bd Int Jl of Hindu Studies, Editorial Advsy Bd Religions of South Asia; numerous named lectures; tstee: Spalding Trusts, Woolf Inst Cambridge; memb: Br Assoc for the Study of Religions, Soc for the Study of Theology; Best Book in Hindu-Christian Studies 1997–1999 Soc for Hindu-Christian Studies (2000); MA by incorporation Univ of Cambridge 1975; *Books* The Face of Truth: A Study of Meaning and Metaphysics in the Vedantic Theology of Ramanuja (1986), Hindu Ethics: Purity, Abortion & Euthanasia (jtly, 1989), Hindus: Their Religious Beliefs and Practices (1994), Brahmabandhab Upadhyay: The Life and Thought of a Revolutionary (1999), The Writings of Brahmabandhab Upadhyay (jt ed, 1991, vol 2 2002), Anandamath, or The Sacred Brotherhood (translation and introduction, 2005), Truth, Religious Dialogue and Dynamic Orthodoxy: Essays in Honour of Brian Hebblethwaite (ed, 2005); *Recreations* reading, cricket, Indian and Western music, good food; *Style*— Prof Julius Lipner; ✉ Faculty of Divinity, University of Cambridge, West Road, Cambridge CB3 9BS (tel 01223 763002)

LIPPIETT, Rear Adm (Richard) John; CB (2004), MBE (1979); s of Vernon K Lippiett (d 1982), and Katherine F I S, *née* Langston Jones; *b* 7 July 1949; *Educ* Brighton Hove and Sussex GS, BRNC; *m* 1976, Jennifer, da of Richard B R Walker; 1 da (Louisa b 1977), 2 s (Marc b 1979, Oliver b 1982); *Career* RN 1967; jr offr with: HMS Eastbourne, HMS Eagle, HMS Yarmouth, HMS Appleton 1968–72; Flag Lt to C-in-C Fleet 1973–74; served in HMS Achilles subsequently CO HMS Shavington 1976–77, PWO HMS Fife 1978–79, course offr Rowallan Young Officers' Leadership Course HMS Raleigh 1980–81, RNSC Greenwich 1981, exec offr HMS Ambuscade Falklands 1982–83, 2 i/c Polaris HQ 1984–86, CO HMS Amazon 1986–87, JSDC 1987, naval asst to First Sea Lord 1988–90, Capt 9 Frigate Sqdn and CO HMS Norfolk 1991–92, RCDS 1993, COS Surface Flotilla 1993–95, Cdre Sch of Maritime Operations HMS Dryad 1995–97, Flag Offr Sea Trg (FOST) 1997–99, COS to Commander Allied Naval Forces Southern Europe and sr Br Offr Southern Region 1999–2002, Cmdt Jt Servs Command and Staff Coll 2002–03; chief exec Mary Rose Tst 2003–; tstee Naval Review 2001–, vice-pres (RN) Combined Cadet Force 2004–, patron Nautical Trg Corps 2007–; pres Ton Class Assoc 2007–; yr bro Trinity House; *Publications* Type 21 Frigate (1988), War & Peas: Intimate Letters from the Falklands War 1982 (2007); *Recreations* sailing, gardening, classical music; *Style*— Rear Adm John Lippiett, CB, MBE; ✉ c/o The Mary Rose Trust, HM Naval Base, Portsmouth PO1 3LX

LIPSCOMB, Rev (Edwin) Paul; s of Dr A George J Lipscomb (d 1975), and Kathleen A Lipscomb (d 1993); *b* 9 September 1933; *Educ* Blackfriars Sch Laxton; *m* 17 June 1961, Pauline Ann, da of Capt Henry John Farrell Palliser (d 1937); 1 s (Christopher John Farrell b 1962), 1 da (Catherine Ann Farrell (Mrs Tony Payton) b 1965); *Career* Nat Serv The Green Howards 1952–54, TA The Green Howards 1955–61, ret as Capt; CA George A Touche & Co (now Deloitte & Touche) 1955–62; fin dir: Biscuits Belin France (subsid of Nabisco) 1962–64, Levitt & Sons France 1964–65; Euro controller France Mead Corp 1965–68, mangr fin controls Belgium HQ ITT Europe 1968–72, divnl dir London HQ Rank Xerox 1972–75, exec vice-pres Amsterdam and London Cinema International Corp (now UIP) 1975–82, fin controller British Airways 1982–85, dir Borthwicks plc 1985–89, gp fin and prodn dir J W Spear & Sons plc 1989–96, chm Corgi Classics Ltd 1995–96; chm Standards Ctee and co-op memb Slough BC 1999–; tstee: Fortune Centre for Riding Therapy 1984–, Life Opportunities Tst 1991–; ordained permanent deacon 1999, chm Diocesan Ecumenical Cmmn 2002–; FCA, FCMI, AFST; *Recreations* travel, food and wine; *Clubs* Naval and Military, Savage; *Style*— The Rev Paul Lipscomb; ✉ c/o Naval and Military Club, 4 St James's Square, London SW1Y 4JU

LIPSEY, Baron (Life Peer UK 1999), of Tooting Bec in the London Borough of Wandsworth; David Lawrence; s of Lawrence Lipsey, and Penelope Lipsey; *b* 21 April 1948; *Educ* Bryanston, Magdalen Coll Oxford (BA); *m* 1982, Margaret Robson; 1 da; *Career* journalist; research asst GMWU 1970–72, special advsr to Anthony Crosland MP 1972–77 (DOE 1974–76, FCO 1976–77), PM's Staff 10 Downing St 1977–79, journalist New Society 1979–80, economic ed Sunday Times 1982–86 (political staff 1980–82), ed New Society 1986–88, fndr and jt dep ed Sunday Correspondent 1988–90, assoc ed The Times 1990–92, political ed The Economist 1994–1998 (joined 1992); chm Impower plc 2001–03, non-exec dir LWT 2004–06; non-exec dir Personal Investment Authy 1994–2000; chm Br Greyhound Racing Bd 1994–, non-exec dir Horserace Totalisator Bd 1998–2002, chm Shadow Racing Tst 2002–; memb: Exec Ctee Charter for Jobs 1984–86, Jenkins Ctee on the Electoral System 1998, Royal Cmmn on the Long-term Care of the Elderly 1998–99, Davies Panel on the BBC License Fee 1999, Cncl Advtg Standards Authy 1999–2005; sec Streatham Lab Pty 1970–72, chm Fabian Soc 1981–82, chair Make Votes Count 1999–, chm Social Market Fndn 2001–; *Books* Labour and Land (1974), The Socialist Agenda: Crosland's Legacy (co-ed Dick Leonard, 1981), Making Government Work (1982), The Name of the Rose (1992), The Secret Treasury (2001); *Recreations* horse racing, harness racing, greyhound racing, golf, opera; *Style*— The Rt Hon the Lord Lipsey; ✉ House of Lords, London SW1

LIPTON, Prof Michael; CMG (2003); s of Leslie Lipton (d 1977), and Helen, *née* Janssen (d 2001); *b* 13 February 1937; *Educ* Haberdashers' Aske's, Balliol Coll Oxford (MA), MIT, Univ of Sussex (DLitt); *m* 9 Dec 1966, Merle, da of Charles Babrow (d 1979); 1 s (Emanuel b 1 March 1974); *Career* res offr with G Myrdal on Asian Drama 1960–61, fell All Souls Coll Oxford 1961–68 and 1982–84; Univ of Sussex: asst lectr 1961–62, lectr 1962–66, reader 1966–71, fell Inst of Devpt Studies and professorial fell 1971–77, 1979–87 and 1990–, prof of devpt economics and dir Poverty Research Unit 1994–97, research prof 1997–; employment devpt advsr Govt of Botswana 1977–78, sr policy advsr World Bank 1981–82, prog dir consumption and nutrition prog Int Food Policy Res Inst Washington DC 1988–89, conslt UN Human Devpt Reports on Poverty 1997, Consumption 1998 and Technol 2001, sr advsr World Bank, World Devpt Reports on Poverty 1990 and 2000–01; extensive research and consultancy on agric research and technol, rural employment, econs of population change and nutrition, poverty reduction and land distribution especially in India, Bangladesh, Sri Lanka, Botswana, Sierra Leone, South Africa and Romania, follow-up of impact of GM on developing countries 2002–03; ed Jl of Devpt Studies 1968–80, chm Br Assoc for South Asian Studies 1985–87; memb: Devpt Studies Assoc, Int Assoc of Agric Economists, Nuffield Cncl for Bioethics Working Pty on Genetically Modified Plants 1999, Advsy Panel Int Development Enterprises 2002–, Programme Advsy Ctee HarvestPlus Biofortification Prog Consultative Gp for Int Agricultural Research 2003–; numerous papers and pubns in jls; pres British Chess Problem Soc 1999–2000; memb Governing Cncl Overseas Devpt Inst 2000–; FBA 2006; *Publications* Chess Problems: Introduction to an Art (with R Matthews and J Rice, 1962), Assessing Economic Performance (1968), The Crisis of Indian Planning (with P Streeten, 1968), The Erosion of a Relationship: India and Britain since 1960 (with J Firn, 1975), Migration from Rural Areas: The Evidence from Village Studies (with J Connell, 1976), Why Poor People Stay Poor: Urban Bias and World Development (1977), Botswana: Employment and Labour Use (1979), New Seeds and Poor People (1989), Does Aid Work in India? (with J Toye, 1990), Including the Poor (with J van der Gaag, 1993), How Third World Households Adapt to Dietary Energy Stress (with P Payne, 1994), Successes in Anti-poverty (2 edn 2001), 'Quality of Life' and 'Poverty' in Asian Devpt Bank (conslt and ed with Siddiqur Osmani and Arjan de Haan, 1997), Food and Nutrition Security: Why Food Production Still Matters in Food and Agric Organisation (2000), The Family Farm in a Globalizing World (2005); lead scholar Int Fund for Agric Devpt Report on Rural Poverty (2001); memb Editorial Bd: Jl of Devpt Studies, World Devpt; author of articles in learned jls; *Recreations* chess problems, music, play-going, poetry; *Clubs* Lansdowne; *Style*— Prof Michael Lipton, CMG, FBA; ✉ Poverty Research Unit, University of Sussex, Brighton BN1 9QN (direct tel 01273 678725, fax 01273 673563)

LIPTON, Prof Peter; *Educ* Wesleyan Univ (BA), Univ of Oxford (DPhil); *Career* teaching apprentice in physics and philosophy Wesleyan Univ 1974–76, tutor in philosophy of science Univ of Oxford 1979–82 (lectr Dept for External Studies 1979), asst research prof Clark Univ 1982–85, asst prof Williams Coll 1985–90; Univ of Cambridge: asst lectr 1991–94, lectr 1994–97, fell King's Coll 1994–, head Dept of History and Philosophy of Science 1996–, prof of the history and philosophy of science1997–; consulting ed Studies in the History and Philosophy of Science 1992–94 (advsy ed 1995–), memb Editorial Advsy Panel British Jl for the Philosophy of Science 1993–; memb Nuffield Cncl on Bioethics 2003–; *Books* Inference to the Best Explanation (1991, 2 edn 2004), Theory, Evidence and Explanation (1995); also author of numerous reviews and articles in learned jls; *Style*— Prof Peter Lipton; ✉ Department of History and Philosophy of Science, University of Cambridge, Free School Lane, Cambridge CB2 3RH (tel 01223 334540, fax 01223 334554, e-mail pl112@cam.ac.uk)

LIPTON, Sir Stuart Anthony; kt (2000); s of Bertram Green, of London, and Jeanette Lipton; *b* 9 November 1942; *Educ* Berkhamsted Sch; *m* 16 June 1966, Ruth Kathryn, da of Harry Marks (d 1986), of London; 2 s (Elliot Stephen b 17 March 1969, Grant Alexander b 20 Jan 1975), 1 da (Sarah Joanna b 15 June 1971); *Career* dir: Sterling Land Co 1971–73, First Palace Securities Ltd 1973–; jt md Greycoat plc 1976–83, chief exec Stanhope Properties plc 1983–95; Stanhope plc: chief exec 1996–2004, chm 2004–06; co-fndr and dep chm Chelsfield Ptnrs 2006–; chm Cmmn for Architecture and the Built Environment (CABE) 1999–2004; dir Nat Gallery Tst Fndn 1998–; dep chm Architecture Fndn 1992–99; advsr to: Hampton Site Co for Sainsbury Building Nat Gallery 1985–91, new Glyndebourne opera house 1988–94; property advsr DOE 1986–96; memb: Advsy Body Dept of Construction Mgmnt Univ of Reading 1983–91, Mil Bldgs Ctee MOD 1987–98, Cncl Br Property 1987–99, Governing Body Imperial Coll 1987 (FIC 1998), Bd Royal Nat Theatre 1988–98, Royal Fine Art Cmmn 1988–99, Barbican Centre Advsy Cncl 1997–, English Partnerships Millennium Housing Tst Jury 1998–99, Bd Royal Opera House 1998–2006, Jury RIBA Gold Medal Award 1998 and 1999; tstee: Whitechapel Art Gallery 1987–94, Urban Land Inst Washington 1996–, Millennium Bridge Tst 1998–2001; Edward Bass visiting fell Yale Sch of Architecture 2006; govr LSE 1999–2006; Hon LLD Univ of Bath 2005; hon bencher Inner Temple 2003–; memb Worshipful Co of Goldsmiths; Hon RIBA; *Recreations* architecture, crafts, art and technology, wine; *Style*— Sir Stuart Lipton

LIPWORTH, Sir (Maurice) Sydney; kt (1991), Hon QC (1993); s of Isidore Lipworth (d 1966), of Johannesburg, South Africa, and Rae, *née* Sindler (d 1983); *b* 13 May 1931; *Educ* King Edward VII Sch Johannesburg, Univ of the Witwatersrand (BCom, LLB); *m* 1957, Rosa, da of Bernard Liwarek (d 1943); 2 s (Bertrand, Frank); *Career* admitted slr SA 1955, called to the Bar SA 1956, called to Bar Inner Temple 1991 (hon bencher 1989); barr Johannesburg 1956–64, practising barr One Essex Court London 2002–; co dir 1965–67, dir Abbey Life Assurance Gp 1968–70; dir Allied Dunbar Assurance plc (formerly Hambro Life Assurance plc) 1971–88 (jt md 1980–84, dep chm 1984–87), chm Dunbar Bank 1983–88, chm Allied Dunbar Unit Tsts plc 1985–88 (md 1983–85); chm Zeneca Group plc 1995–99 (dir 1994), dep chm National Westminster Bank plc 1993–2000; dir: J Rothschild Holdings plc 1984–87, BAT Industries plc 1985–88, Carlton Communications plc 1993–2004, Centrica plc 1999–2002, Goldfish Bank Ltd 2001–04; chm: Monopolies and Mergers Cmmn 1988–93 (memb 1981–93), Financial Reporting Cncl 1994–2001; memb: Ctee on Financial Aspects of Corporate Governance 1994–95, Sr Salaries Review Body 1994–2002; chm Bar Assoc for Commerce, Finance and Industry 1991–92, memb Gen Cncl of the Bar 1991–94; chm of tstees: Philharmonia Orchestra 1993– (tstee 1982–, dep chm 1986–93), NatWest Gp Charitable Tst 1994–2001; tstee: Allied Dunbar Charitable Tst 1971–94, Royal Acad Tst 1988–2003, South Bank Fndn Ltd 1996–2003, Int Accounting Standards Ctee Fndn 2000–; chm Marie Curie Cancer Care 50th Anniversary Appeal 1997–2002; memb Advsy Panel Breakthrough Breast Cancer Research Tst 1991–; govr: Contemporary Dance Tst 1981–87, Sadler's Wells Fndn 1987–90; Hon LLD Univ of the Witwatersrand 2003; *Recreations* tennis, music, theatre; *Clubs* Queen's, Reform; *Style*— Sir Sydney Lipworth, QC

LISBURNE, 8 Earl of (I 1776); Capt John David Malet Vaughan; DL (Dyfed); also Viscount Lisburne and Baron Fethard (I 1695); the eld s and h appears to have been styled Lord Vaughan since 1776; s of 7 Earl of Lisburne (d 1965); *b* 1 September 1918; *Educ* Eton, Magdalen Coll Oxford; *m* 1943, Shelagh, da of late T A Macauley, of Montreal, Canada; 3 s; *Heir* s, Viscount Vaughan; *Career* 2 Lt Welsh Gds 1939, Capt 1943, served 1939–45; barr Inner Temple 1947–69; dir: British Home Stores plc 1961–87, S Wales Regnl Bd Lloyds Bank Ltd 1978–88, Nationwide Building Society (Welsh Bd); ret 1990; govr UCW; pres Wales Cncl for Voluntary Action, ret 1998 (chm 1976–93); memb Exec Ctee AA 1981–88; *Style*— The Rt Hon the Earl of Lisburne, DL; ✉ Bringewood, Burway Lane, Ludlow, Shropshire SY8 6EJ

LISHMAN, (Arthur) Gordon; CBE (2006, OBE 1993); s of Dr Arthur Birkett Lishman, and Florence May Lishman; *b* 29 November 1947; *Educ* Univ of Manchester (BA); *m* 1, 1968 (m dis 1972), Beverley Ann, *née* Witham; m 2, 1973 (m dis 1984), Stephanie Margaret, *née* Allison-Barr; 1 s, 1 da; m 3, 1988, Margaret Ann Brodie-Browne, *née* Long; 1 step da; *Career* Age Concern: field offr 1974–77, head of fieldwork 1977–87, ops dir 1987–2000, DG Age Concern England 2000–, dir Age Concern Hldgs Ltd 1995–; sec-gen Eurolink Age 2001–, int vice-pres Int Fedn on Ageing 2001–, memb Cncl AGE (European Older People's Platform) 2001– (sec 2001–07), memb Steering Gp Cmmn on Equalities and Human Rights 2004–06, memb Nat Stakeholder Forum Dept of Health 2006–; campaigner: age equality 1971–, homosexual law reform, homosexual equality; memb: Liberty, Fawcett Soc, Br Humanist Assoc, Friends of Ruskin's Brantwood, Lib Dem Pty 1963–; govr Pensions Policy Inst 2002–; hon fell Univ of Central Lancs 2002; MCMI, FRSA; *Style*— Gordon Lishman, Esq, CBE; ✉ Age Concern, Astral House, 1268 London Road, London SW16 4ER (tel 020 8765 7200)

LISLE, 9 Baron (I 1758); (John) Nicholas Geoffrey Lysaght; s of 8 Baron Lysaght (d 2003), and Mary Louise Blackwell, *née* Shaw; *b* 20 May 1960; *Educ* Lingfield Sch; *Heir* bro, Hon David Lysaght; *Career* charity vol; *Recreations* avid horticulturalist, collector of books and Christmas tree decorations of the Victorian era and later; *Style*— The Rt Hon the Lord Lisle; ✉ 50 The Fairstead, Scottow, Norwich, Norfolk NR10 5AQ (tel 01692 538409)

LISNEY, Prof Stephen John William; JP (N Somerset 1999); s of Raymond Laurence Lisney, and Jean Avril, *née* Ladell; *b* 30 April 1951; *Educ* Queen Elizabeth's GS Barnet, Univ of Bristol (BSc, BDS, MA, PhD, Bristol Teaching Hosp's Gold medal, Colgate prize for dental research); *m* 4 Jan 1975, Sandra Jane, da of Bertram Henry Mears; 2 s (Thomas James b 27 May 1977, Robert William b 22 Aug 1981); *Career* MRC travelling fell 1978–79; Univ of Bristol: lectr in physiology 1980–89, sr lectr 1989–2000, head Dept of Physiology 1995–97, chm of Med Scis 1997–2000, dean Faculty of Med 2000–03, prof 2000–; non-exec dir N Bristol NHS Tst 2003–06; author/co-author of articles in scientific jls and books; memb Physiological Soc 1980; *Recreations* gardening, outdoor pursuits, collecting; *Style*— Prof Stephen Lisney; ✉ Department of Physiology, School of Medical Sciences, University Walk, Bristol BS8 1TD (tel 0117 928 7814, e-mail s.j.w.lisney@bris.ac.uk)

LISSACK, Richard Antony; QC (1994); s of Victor Jack Lissack (d 1981), of London, and Antoinette Rosalind Lissack (d 2006); *b* 7 June 1956; *Educ* Univ Coll Sch Hampstead; *m* 31 May 1986, Carolyn Dare Arscott, da of Gp Capt R H Arscott, CBE; 3 da (Holly Victoria Dare, Lucy Barbara Dare (twins) b 25 July 1994, Emily Jessica Dare b 28 Sept 1998); *Career* called to the Bar Inner Temple 1978; asst recorder 1993–99, recorder 1999–, QC Eastern Caribbean 2002, foreign legal conslt NY 2007–; dir Kilmington Int Horse Trials 1997–, pres S & W Wilts Hunt 2002– (chm 1996–2002); *Recreations* breeding, competing and falling off thoroughbred horses, farming; *Clubs* Babbington House, Turf, Rock Sailing; *Style*— Richard Lissack, Esq, QC; ✉ Outer Temple Chambers, 222 Strand, London WC2R 1BA (tel 020 7353 6381, fax 020 7583 1786, e-mail law@rlqc.com)

LISSON, Kathryn (Kathy); *b* 11 March 1952, Montreal, Canada; *Educ* Carleton Univ Ottawa (BSc, univ medal); *m*; 2 c; *Career* sr analyst Finance Dept Canadian Govt and sr tech support Inorganic Chemistry Labs Yale Univ 1974–76, mangr and conslt Computer Servs Gp Price Waterhouse Toronto 1976–82, vice-pres info systems Barclays Bank of Canada 1982–86, ptnr financial instn consulting Price Waterhouse Toronto 1987–97 (dir 1986, memb Policy Bd 1996–97); Bank of Montreal: sr vice-pres mgmnt info 1997–98, exec vice-pres IT planning and strategy 1998–2000, exec vice-pres Emfisys gp of cos and e-business, technol strategy and delivery 2000–01, exec vice-pres consumer lending and pres Mortgage Corporation 2001–02, exec vice-pres special initiatives Investment Banking and Private Client Divs 2002; operational transformation dir Barclays Bank plc London 2002–05; Brit Insurance Hldgs plc: chief operating offr 2005–, exec dir and memb Bd 2006–; dir Ri3K Ltd; former dir: Intelligent Processing Solutions Ltd, Xceed Mortgage Co, Flinx Corp, MCAP Services Corp, dealerAccess, BMO Mortgage Corp; certified mgmnt conslt Inst of Mgmnt Conslts 1980; *Style*— Mrs Kathy Lisson; ✉ Brit Insurance Holdings plc, 55 Bishopsgate, London EC2N 3AS

LISTER, Anthony Charles Bramham; s of David Bramham Lister (d 1980), and Monica Joan, *née* Russell (d 1991); *b* 31 August 1939; *Educ* Sutton Valence, Coll of Estate Mgmnt London; *m* 1 June 1963, Susan Kitty, da of (Harold) Norman Funnell (d 1995); 3 s (Giles Anthony Bramham, Timothy Norman Bramham (twins) b 12 Jan 1966, Guy Bramham b 16 Oct 1968); *Career* equity ptnr Geering and Colyer Chartered Surveyors 1972–82, Black Horse Agencies 1982–90, dir Lister & Associates (commercial surveyors) 1991–2002, md Kentstone Properties Ltd 2002–; Freeman City of London 1961, Liveryman Worshipful Co of Leathersellers 1964 (Freeman 1961, memb Ct of Assts 1993, Master 2004–05); FRICS 1970; *Recreations* sheep farming, golf, sailing; *Clubs* Rye Golf; *Style*— Anthony Lister, Esq; ✉ Dean Court, Westwell, Ashford, Kent TN25 4NH (tel 01233 712924)

LISTER, John Thomas; s of Albert William Lister (d 1978), of Cardiff, and Joan Trenear, *née* Tarr; *b* 26 November 1941; *Educ* Cardiff HS; *m* 1988, Mary; 2 s (Stephen b 29 July 1967, Andrew b 17 Sept 1975), 1 da (Victoria b 13 Nov 1979); *Career* athletics administrator; former int athlete Wales 1959–70 and Cardiff Amateur Athletic Club; events competed at: 110m hurdles, decathlon, long jump, high jump (former Welsh record holder); hon treas: Cardiff Amateur Athletic Club 1968– (former pres and chm), AAA 1986–91, British Athletic Fedn 1991–96; memb Cncl European Athletic Assoc 1995–; qualified CA 1964, dir and shareholder Euro Investments Ltd; *Recreations* athletics; *Style*— John Lister, Esq

LISTER, Michael; s of William Mayes Lister, of Peebles, and Helen Tiernan, *née* Adams (d 2005); *b* 21 April 1962, Peebles; *Educ* Univ of Stirling (BA), Ecole Normale d'Ille-et-Vilaine France; *Partner* Iain Black; *Career* lectr Scottish Coll of Textiles 1988–96, ind campaigner and promoter of the arts in Scotland and fundraiser for various artistic projects 1996–; memb Saltire Soc; non-professional lay memb Royal Scottish Soc of Painters in Watercolour, lay memb Soc of Scottish Artists, life memb Scottish Artists' Benevolent Assoc, Memb Scottish PEN; *Publications* contrib to: History of Peebles (1990), The Paderewski Paradox (1991), Norman MacCaig: A Celebration (contrib, 1995), Spirits of the Age (2005), A Matter of Honours: Reforming the Honours System (2005); contrib to literary jls incl: Agenda, Chapman, Edinburgh Review, Scottish Book Collector, Textualities.net, TLS; *Recreations* book collecting, book reviewing, collecting contemporary Scottish art; *Style*— Michael Lister, Esq; ✉ 2/11 Port Hamilton, Edinburgh EH3 8JL (tel 0131 229 8354, e-mail mwwlister@hotmail.com)

LISTER, Paul Kenneth; s of Eric Lister, of Tewkesbury, Glos, and Mollie Ada Patience; *b* 7 August 1952; *Educ* Birmingham Sch of Architecture (DipArch), Aston Univ (BSc); *Career* ptnr Associated Architects Birmingham 1984–2006 (joined 1976); md: Associated Architects LLP 2003–06, 2B Clear Consultancy LLP; fndr memb Birmingham Young Architects' Gp, pres Birmingham Architectural Assoc 1994–96 (memb Ctee 1985–87 and 1988–96); RIBA 1979; *Style*— Paul Lister, Esq; ✉ 2B Clear Consultancy LLP, 44 Lee Crescent, Birmingham B15 2BJ (tel 07971 754769)

LISTER, Prof (Margot) Ruth Aline; CBE (1999); da of late Dr Werner Bernard Lister, of Manchester, and late Daphne, *née* Carter; *b* 3 May 1949; *Educ* Moreton Hall Sch, Univ of Essex (BA), Univ of Sussex (MA); *Career* dir Child Poverty Action Gp 1979–87 (legal res offr 1971–75, asst dir 1975–77, dep dir 1977–79), prof and head of Dept of Applied Social Studies Univ of Bradford 1987–93, prof of social policy Loughborough Univ 1994–; Donald Dewar visiting prof of social justice Univ of Glasgow 2005–06; tstee Friends of Citizens Advice Bureaux 1991–95, vice-chm NCVO 1991–93, chm Jt Univ Cncl Social Policy Ctee 1994–96, tstee Community Devpt Fndn 2000–; memb: Opsahl Cmmn NI 1992–93, Cmmn on Social Justice 1992–94, Cmmn on Poverty Participation and Power 1999–2000, Fabian Cmmn on Life Chances and Childhood Poverty 2004–06; founding Academician of Learned Societies for the Social Sciences 1999; Hon LLD Univ of Manchester 1987; *Books* Supplementary Benefit Rights (1974), Welfare Benefits (1981), The Exclusive Society (1990), Women's Economic Dependency and Social Security (1992), Citizenship: Feminist Perspectives (1997, 2 edn 2003), Poverty (2004), Gendering Citizenship in Western Europe (jtly, 2007); numerous articles, pamphlets and chapters in books; *Recreations* walking, tai chi, reading, music, films; *Style*— Prof Ruth Lister, CBE; ✉ Department of Social Sciences, Loughborough University, Loughborough, Leicestershire LE11 3TU (tel 01509 223350, fax 01509 223944, e-mail m.r.lister@lboro.ac.uk)

LISTER-KAYE, Sir John Philip Lister; 8 Bt (UK 1812), of Grange, Yorkshire; OBE (2003); s of Sir John Christopher Lister Lister-Kaye, 7 Bt (d 1982), and his 1 w, Audrey Helen (d 1979), da of Edwin James Carter, of Westbury-on-Trym, Glos; descended from Sir John Kaye, of Almondbury, W Yorks, Col of Horse, created Baronet in 1641 by Charles I, also Lord Mayor of York; this Baronetcy became extinct on the death of the 6 Bt in 1809, but Sir John Lister-Kaye, natural s of the 5 Bt, was cr a Bt 1812 for services to George III; Sir John Lister-Kaye, 3 Bt, was groom-in-waiting to Edward VII; *b* 8 May 1946; *Educ* Allhallows Sch; *m* 1, 1972 (m dis 1988), Lady Sorrel Deirdre Bentinck, da of 11 Earl of Portland; 1 s (John Warwick Noel Lister b 1974), 2 da (Amelia Helen, Melanie Jenifer (twins) b 1976); m 2, 17 Feb 1989, Lucinda Anne, eld da of Robin Law, of Withersfield, Suffolk, and formerly w of Hon Evan Baillie; 1 da (Hermione Anne Lucinda Lorne b 27 Sept 1990); *Heir* s, John Lister-Kaye; *Career* naturalist, author, lectr, farmer; dir of Aigas Field Centre Ltd 1977–; fndr dir Scottish Conservation Charity The Aigas Tst 1980–; chm Scottish Advsy Ctee RSPB 1986–92; memb: Int Ctee The World Wilderness Fndn 1983, Scottish Ctee of Nature Conservancy Cncl 1990–91; chm: NW Region Nature Conservancy Cncl for Scotland 1991–92, NW Region Scottish Natural Heritage 1992–96, Home Grown Timber Advsy Ctee Forestry Cmmn 1994–96; tstee Environmental Training Organisation 1995–98, memb Advsy Cncl of Millennium Forest for Scotland 1996–2000; pres Scottish Wildlife Tst 1996–2001 (hon memb 2003); vice-pres: Assoc of the Protection of Rural Scotland 1998–, RSPB 2006–; dir Aigas Quest Ltd 1997–; Wilderness Soc Gold Award for Conservation 1984; Hon DUniv Stirling 1995, Hon DUniv St Andrews 2005; *Books* The White Island (1972), Seal Cull (1979), The Seeing Eye (1980), Ill Fares the Land (1994), One for Sorrow (1994), Song of the Rolling Earth (2003), Nature's Child (2004); *Recreations* breeding horses and Highland cattle, beach-combing and digger driving; *Clubs* Farmers', Royal Scots; *Style*— Sir John Lister-Kaye, Bt, OBE; ✉ House of Aigas, Beauly, Inverness IV4 7AD (tel 01463 782729); Grange Estate Co Office (tel 01463 782443, fax 01463 782097, e-mail jik@aigas.co.uk)

LISTON, (Edward) Robin; s of David Joel Liston, OBE (d 1990), and Eva Carole, *née* Kauffmann (d 1987); *b* 30 October 1947; *Educ* Bryanston, Mercersburg Acad PA USA, Univ of Kent (BA); *m* 6 July 1969 (m dis 1987), Judith Margaret, da of Frederick Tye, CBE; 2 da (Rebecca b 1970, Victoria b 1974); *Career* dist ed Kent Messenger 1969–70, asst ed Benn Bros 1970–72; assoc dir: Forman House PR Ltd 1972–79, Welbeck PR Ltd 1981–84; dir: Carl Byoir Ltd 1984–86, Hill & Knowlton Ltd 1986–88; jt md Buckmans PR 1988–93, freelance conslt 1993–; *Books* Travels with My Heart (2007), Bradt Guide to St Helena (2007); *Recreations* music, films, railways, suburban architecture; *Style*— Robin Liston, Esq; ✉ Robin Communications Ltd, 26 Southern Road, London N2 9JG (tel 020 8883 7314, fax 020 8444 8834, e-mail robinliston@pobox.com)

LISTOWEL, 6 Earl of (I 1822); Francis Michael Hare; also Baron Ennismore (I 1800), Viscount Ennismore and Listowel (I 1816, usually shortened to Viscount Ennismore when used as a courtesy title for eldest s and h), and Baron Hare of Convamore (UK 1869, which sits as); s of 5 Earl of Listowel, GCMG, PC (d 1997), and his 3 w, Pamela Molly, *née* Day; *b* 28 June 1964; *Heir* bro, Hon Timothy Hare; *Clubs* Reform; *Style*— The Rt Hon the Earl of Listowel; ✉ House of Lords, London SW1A 0PW (e-mail listowelf@parliament.uk)

LITHGOW, Sir William James; 2 Bt (UK 1925), of Ormsary, Co Argyll, DL (Renfrewshire 1970); s of Sir James Lithgow, 1 Bt, GBE, CB, MC, TD, JP, DL (d 1952); *b* 10 May 1934; *Educ* Winchester; *m* 1, 1964, Valerie Helen (d 1964), da of Denis Herbert Scott, CBE (d 1958); m 2, 1967, Mary Claire, da of Col Frank Moutray Hill, CBE, of East Knoyle, Wilts; 1 da (Katrina Margaret b 5 Oct 1968), 2 s (James Frank b 13 June 1970, John Alexander b 8 Dec 1974); *Heir* s, James Lithgow; *Career* industrialist and farmer; Lithgows Ltd: dir 1954–, chm 1959–84 and 1988–99, vice-chm 1999–; chm: Hunterston Devpt Co Ltd 1987–, Scott-Lithgow Drydocks Ltd 1967–78, Western Ferries (Argyll) Ltd 1972–85; vice-chm Scott Lithgow Ltd 1968–78; dir: Bank of Scotland 1962–86, Landcatch Ltd 1981–96, Lithgows Pty Ltd 1972–; memb: Br Ctee Det Norske Veritas 1966–92, Exec Ctee Scottish Cncl Devpt and Indust 1969–85, Scottish Regnl Cncl of CBI 1969–76, Clyde Port Authy 1969–71, Bd Nat Ports Cncl 1971–78, W Central Scotland Plan Steering Ctee 1971–74, Gen Bd Nat Physical Lab 1963–66, Greenock Dist Hosp Bd 1961–66, Scottish Milk Mktg Bd 1979–83; chm Iona Cathedral Tstees Mgmnt Bd 1979–83, memb Cncl Winston Churchill Meml Tst 1979–83; hon pres: Students' Assoc, Mid Argyll Agric Soc 1976–99, West Renfrewshire Bn Boys Brigade 1962–2000, Inverclyde & District Bn Boys Brigade 1998–; memb Ct Univ of Strathclyde 1964–69; Hon LLD Strathclyde 1979, memb Queen's Body Guard for Scotland (Royal Co of Archers); *Recreations* rural life, invention, photography; *Clubs* Oriental, Western, Royal Scottish Automobile (Glasgow); *Style*— Sir William Lithgow, Bt, DL; ✉ Ormsary House, by Lochgilphead, Argyllshire (tel 01880 770252); Drums, Langbank, Renfrewshire (tel 01475 540606)

LITTLE, (Robert) Alastair; s of Robert Geoffrey Little, of Colne, Lancs, and Marion, *née* Irving; *b* 25 June 1950; *Educ* Kirkham GS, Downing Coll Cambridge (MA); *Family* 1 s ((Robert) George Tormod-Little), 1 da (Frederika Kirsten Tormod-Little); m, 2000, Sharon Jacob; 1 s (Alexander b 2004); *Career* self-taught chef; head chef Old Compton Wine Bar London 1974–76; chef/proprietor: Le Routier Wrentham Suffolk 1976–79, Simpsons Putney London 1979–81; chef: L'Escargot London 1981–82, 192 Kensington Park Road 1982–85; chef/proprietor Alastair Little: Frith Street 1985–2002, Lancaster Road 1996–2002; proprietor Tavola 2003–; Times Restaurant of Year 1993; memb Académie Culinaire; *Books* Keep It Simple (1993), Food of the Sun (1995), Italian Kitchen (1996), Soho Cooking (2000); *Recreations* reading, mycology, watching sport; *Style*— Alastair Little, Esq

LITTLE, (James) Allan Stuart; s of Robin Little, of Stranraer, and Elizabeth, *née* Clive; *b* 11 October 1959; *Educ* Stranraer Acad, Univ of Edinburgh (MA); *Partner* Sheena McDonald; *Career* broadcaster; with BBC Scotland 1983–85, reporter Today prog (Radio 4) 1988–90, reporter BBC News 1990–95, Africa corr BBC 1995–97 and 2000–01, Moscow corr BBC 1997–99, presenter Today prog (Radio 4) 1999–2002; Sony Radio Reporter of the Year 1992, Amnesty Int Reporter of the Year 1992, Bayeux War Corr of the Year 1994, Sony Documentary Gold Award 2000, Grierson Premier TV Documentary Award 2001; *Books* Death of Yugoslavia (1995); *Recreations* books, theatre, walking, talking, travel; *Style*— Allan Little, Esq; ✉ BBC News, Television Centre, Wood Lane, London W12 7RJ (tel 020 8743 8000, e-mail allan.little@bbc.co.uk)

LITTLE, Amanda Penelope Wyndham; da of Capt Alec Haines Little, CBE, of Hants, and Pamela, *née* Bolt; *b* 19 January 1948; *Educ* Winchester/London; *Career* asst PR offr Milk Mktg Bd 1972–79; literary agent Bolt & Watson Ltd 1981–83, md, owner and literary agent Watson Little Ltd 1983–; memb Assoc of Authors' Agents; *Recreations* singing, music, books; *Style*— Ms Amanda Little

LITTLE, Dr (Thomas William) Anthony (Tony); CBE; s of late Thomas Lowden Little, and late Marjorie Annie Little; *b* 27 June 1940; *Educ* Dame Allan's Sch Newcastle upon Tyne, Univ of Edinburgh (BVMS), Univ of London (DipBact, PhD); *m* 1, 1963 (m dis); 1 s, 1 da; m 2, 1985, Sally Anne Headlam; 2 s; *Career* gen vet practice March Cambs 1963–66; MAFF: Cental Vet Lab Weybridge 1966–82, sr res offr Weybridge 1973–82, dep regnl vet offr Tolworth 1982–85, vet head of section Tolworth 1985–86, dep dir CVL 1986–90, chief exec Central Vet Lab 1990–95, dir and chief exec Vet Labs Agency 1995–2000; vice-pres BVA 2000–02; chair of govrs Fullbrook Sch 2006–; MRCVS, FIBiol, FRSA; *Recreations* travel, food, wine, outdoor activities; *Style*— Dr Tony Little, CBE; ✉ 10 Fox Close, Pyrford, Woking, Surrey GU22 8LP (tel 01932 344858, e-mail tony.little2@ntlworld.com)

LITTLE, Anthony Richard Morrell (Tony); s of Edward Little (d 1990), and Rosemary Margaret, *née* Morrell; *b* 7 April 1954; *Educ* Eton, CCC Cambridge (choral exhibitioner, MA), Homerton Coll Cambridge (PGCE); *m* 29 July 1978, Jennifer Anne, da of Cdr Patrick Greenwood, RN; 1 da (Sophie b 15 Jan 1985); *Career* asst master Tonbridge Sch 1977–82, head of English and boarding housemaster Brentwood Sch 1982–89; headmaster: Chigwell Sch 1989–96, Oakham Sch 1996–2002, Eton Coll 2002–; govr: Northwood Coll 1990–97, St Albans Sch 1994–,Windsor Boys' Sch 2002–; FCP 1990, FRSA 1991; *Recreations* music, literature, film, theatre, Norfolk; *Clubs* East India; *Style*— Tony Little, Esq; ✉ Eton College, Eton, Windsor, Berkshire SL4 6DW (tel 01753 671231, fax 01753 671134)

LITTLE, Michael Robert; s of Robert William Little (d 1973), and Joan, *née* Brown; *b* 10 September 1949; *Educ* Blundell's; *m* 1, 16 June 1973 (m dis 1977), Susan Elizabeth, da of Desmond Richard Bowden (d 1972), of Ranby Hall, Lincoln; m 2, 18 July 1985 (m dis 1990), Ellen Louise, da of Winston Walker, of Welford-on-Avon, Warks; 1 s (Henry Robert William b 7 April 1986); m 3, 9 Aug 1991 (m dis 2004), Caroline Xania Garnham, *qv*; 1 s (Edward Charles Frank b 21 Nov 1992), 1 da (Georgia Elizabeth Medina b 10 Nov 1995); *Career* St Quintin Son and Stanley 1972–76; ptnr Molyneux Rose 1977–, chm

Molyneux Rose Ltd 1987–; Master N Cotswold Hunt 1985–88; MCIArb 1980, FRICS 1981; *Recreations* hunting, shooting, squash; *Clubs* RAC; *Style—* Michael Little, Esq; ✉ The Lydes, Toddington, Gloucestershire (tel 01242 621419); 104 Portsea Hall, Connaught Square, London W2; Molyneux Rose, 143 New Bond Street, London W1S 2TP (tel 020 7409 0130, fax 020 7499 7636, e-mail michael.little@molyrose.co.uk)

LITTLE, Dr Peter; s of Herbert Edwin Samuel Little, of Durham, and Emily Jewel, *née* Barr; *b* 9 July 1949; *Educ* Rendcomb Coll, Univ of Bristol (BSc, PhD, Rose Bracher Meml prize); *m* 1973, Helen Sheldon, da of Herbert Bruce Cowmeadow; 2 da (Anna Elizabeth b 30 Oct 1981, Abigail Claira b 6 March 1983), 2 s (Angus Stafford b 21 Nov 1984 d 1985, Andrew Samuel Barnabas b 9 May 1986); *Career* UKAEA Harwell: industrial res fell 1974–76, environmental res scientist 1976–79, commercial mangr 1980–87, head of nuclear mktg 1987; UKAEA Risley: head of mktg and sales 1987–90, commercial mangr AEA Reactor Services 1990–91; commercial and mktg dir Horticulture Research International 1991–96, commercial mangr HRI 1997–2003; author of 16 scientific papers; CBiol, MIBiol 1974; *Recreations* family, church, fell walking, travel, kayaking, music; *Style—* Dr Peter Little; ✉ The Old Manor, Little Bridge Road, Bloxham, Banbury, Oxfordshire OX15 4PU (tel 01295 721861, e-mail peter@littlehome.freeserve.co.uk)

LITTLE, Ralf; *Career* actor; *Theatre* Love on the Dole (RNT), Presence (Royal Court, nominated Most Promising Performer Olivier Awards 2002), Notes on falling Leaves (Royal Court), Billy Liar (tour); *Television* Sloggers (BBC, 2 series), Heartbeat (YTV), The Ward (Granada), Bostock's Cup (LWT), Flint Street Nativity (YTV), Always & Everyone (Granada), The Royle Family (BBC, 3 series), Two Pints of Lager and a Packet of Crisps (5 series, BBC), Aladdin (LWT), Paradise Heights (BBC, 2 series), Pear Shaped - North Face of the Eiger (BBC), Up Late With Ralf Little, Is Harry on the Boat?, The Ralf Little Show, The Eustace Bros; *Film* Al's Lads, 24 Hour Party People, Poison Arrows, Frozen, Fat Slags; *Style—* Ralf Little, Esq

LITTLE, Tasmin Elizabeth; da of George Villiers Little, the actor, of London, and Gillian, *née* Morris; *b* 13 May 1965; *Educ* Yehudi Menuhin Sch, Guildhall Sch of Music (Gold medal); *m* July 1993, Michael Hatch; 1 da (Chloe b 25 Nov 2000); *Career* violinist; debut Hallé Orchestra 1988; performed as soloist with orchs incl: LSO, NY Philharmonic, Cleveland, Philharmonia, Royal Philharmonic, Royal Liverpool Philharmonic, Hallé, BBC Symphony, Bournemouth Symphony, City of London Sinfonia, Gewandhaus, Berlin Symphony, Stavanger Symphony, Royal Danish; worked with conductors incl: Kurt Masur, Sir Simon Rattle, Vladimir Ashkenazy, Sir Charles Groves, Sir Charles Mackerras, Vernon Handley, James Loughran, Sir Edward Downes, Richard Hickox, Sian Edwards, Jan Pascal Tortelier, Jerzy Maksymiuk, Sir Yehudi Menuhin, Andrew Davis, Sir Peter Maxwell Davies; author of paper on Delius Violin Concerto for Delius Soc 1991; voted Woman of Tomorrow in the Arts Cosmopolitan Magazine 1990, Hon D Litt Univ of Bradford 1996, fell Guildhall Sch of Music and Drama 1998; plays a 1757 Guadagnini; *Performances* in UK incl: world premieres of concertos by Robert Saxton, David Earl, Dominic Muldowney, Paul Barker and Stuart MacRae, Vivaldi Four Seasons (Royal Festival Hall and Barbican) 1990, Janácek Violin Concerto with Welsh Nat Opera Orch (BBC Proms debut) 1990, Dvorák Violin Concerto (BBC Proms) 1991, Delius Double Concerto (BBC Proms) 1992, Walton Concerto (BBC Proms) 1993, Elgar Concerto (BBC Proms) 1994, soloist Last Night of the Proms 1995, Sibelius Violin Concerto (BBC Proms) 1996, Prokofiev 2nd Concerto (BBC Proms) 1997, Britten Double Concerto (London Premiere) BBC Proms 1998, Last Night of the Proms in Hyde Park 1998; charity performances incl: Sutton Place for Dr Barnardo's, St James's Palace for Nat Children's Home Appeal 1989, Wigmore Hall for Jacqueline Du Pré Meml Appeal 1990, Gala Concert with Royal Liverpool Philharmonic Orch before HM The Queen 1991; overseas performances incl: Brahms Violin Concerto (Malta Festival) 1990, tour with Piers Lane to S America 1991, concertos and recitals in Paris, Vienna, Prague, Germany, Israel, Spain, Cyprus, Canada, Greece, Zimbabwe, Hong Kong, China, Sultanate of Oman, Scandinavia, USA (debut Cleveland Blossom Festival) 1997, four performances of Liegti with Simon Rattle in London, Vienna, Birmingham, Cambridge 2000, Brahms Concerto with Simon Rattle (Aix-en-Provence Festival) 2000, debut in Japan concerts in Tokyo and Nagoya 2000, seven concerts with Simon Rattle and Berlin Philharmonic 2003; TV appearances incl: Highway (ITV), Little by Little (documentary with father, Yorkshire TV), recorded two movements of Mendelssohn Concerto (HTV), Royal Liverpool Philharmonic Gala Concert for HM the Queen (Granada TV), The Lost Child (presenter BBC documentary for The Works) 1997, World War II 60th Anniversary Festival of Commemoration Horse Guards Parade in presence of HM The Queen, HRH The Duke of Edinburgh, HRH The Prince of Wales and HRH The Duchess of Cornwall (BBC1) 2005; *Recordings* incl: Bruch and Dvorák Violin Concertos (with Royal Liverpool Philharmonic under Vernon Handley, EMI Classics for Pleasure) 1990, George Lloyd Sonatas for violin and piano (with Martin Roscoe, Albany) 1990, Vaughan Williams The Lark Ascending (with BBC Symphony Orch under Andrew Davis, WEA, Gramophone award nomination) 1990, Delius Double Concerto (with Raphael Wallfisch and Sir Charles Mackerras, EMI Eminence, Gramophone award nomination) 1991, Delius Violin Concerto 1991, Robert Saxton Violin Concerto (Collins Classics), Brahms and Sibelius Violin Concertos, Virtuoso Violin Disc (EMI Eminence), Arvo Part Disc (EMI Eminence) 1994, Rubbra Violin Concerto (Conifer, Gramophone award nomination) 1994, Walton Violin Concerto (Decca) 1995, French Violin Sonatas (EMI Eminence) 1995, Bruch Scottish Fantasy and Lalo Symphonie Espagnole (EMI Eminence) 1997, Delius Violin Sonatas (BMG Conifer) 1997, Diapason d'Or Prize 1998, Gramophone Award Nomination 1998, Dohnanyi Sonata and Serenade (ASV), Elgar and Bax Sonatas (GMN), Finzi Violin Concerto (Chandos), Karlowicz and Moskowski Concertos (Hyperion); *Recreations* theatre, languages, swimming, cooking; *Clubs* English Speaking Union; *Style—* Dr Tasmin Little; ✉ c/o Askonas Holt, Lonsdale Chambers, 27 Chancery Lane, London WC2A 1PF (tel 020 7400 1700, fax 020 7400 1799)

LITTLECHILD, Prof Stephen Charles; s of Sidney Littlechild, of Wisbech, Cambs, and Joyce, *née* Sharpe; *b* 27 August 1943; *Educ* Wisbech GS, Univ of Birmingham (BCom), Stanford Univ, Northwestern Univ, Univ of Texas at Austin (PhD), UCLA; *m* 1 Aug 1975, Kate (d 1982), da of Charles T Pritchard; 1 da (Elizabeth b 1976), 2 s (Harry b 1978, Richard b 1980); *Career* Harkness fell Stanford Univ 1965–67, sr res lectr Grad Centre for Mgmnt Studies Birmingham 1970–72, prof of applied econs Aston Univ 1973–75, prof of commerce and head Dept of Industrial Econs and Business Studies Univ of Birmingham 1975–94 (on leave 1989–94, hon prof 1994–2004, emeritus prof 2004–), dir-gen Office of Electricity Regulation (Offer) 1989–98; sr research assoc Judge Inst of Mgmnt Studies Univ of Cambridge 2004– (princ research fell 2000–04); visiting prof: NYU, Univ of Stanford, Univ of Chicago, Virginia Poly 1979–80; memb: Monopolies and Mergers Cmmn 1983–89, ACORD 1987–89, Postal Servs Cmmn (Postcomm) 2006–; advsr UK Govt on privatisation of BT, water and electricity, advsr NZ Govt Inquiry into electricity industry 2000; Hon DSc Univ of Birmingham 2001, Hon DCivLaw UEA 2004; *Books* Operational Research for Managers (1977), Fallacy of the Mixed Economy (1978), Elements of Telecommunications Economics (1979), Energy Strategies for the UK (with K G Vaidya, 1982), Regulation of British Telecoms Profitability (1983), Economic Regulation of Privatised Water Authorities (1986), Austrian Economics (3 vols, ed, 1990), Operations Research in Management (with M F Shutler, 1991); *Recreations* genealogy; *Style—* Prof Stephen Littlechild; fax 01564 742793, e-mail sclittlechild@tanworth.mercianet.co.uk

LITTLEFAIR, Henry George Peter (Harry); s of Bernard Littlefair (d 1975), of York, and Ellen Littlefair, *née* Houghton (d 1961); *b* 6 February 1931; *Educ* Ratcliffe Coll Leicester; *m* 9 Aug 1960, Mary Edith, da of Sydney Fryer Monkman, of York (d 1980); 2 s (Nicholas b 1962, Dominic b 1964); *Career* investment mangr; vice-chm Allied Dunbar Unit Tst 1986–88, md A D Unit Tst 1983–86 (dep md 1975–83); dir Metrotect Industries plc, former dir Persimmon plc; *Recreations* philately, music, chess, walking; *Style—* Harry Littlefair, Esq; ✉ 24 The Old Mill, Wetherby, West Yorkshire LS22 6NB (tel 01937 587863, fax 01937 587864)

LITTLEJOHN, Prof Gavin Stuart; *Educ* George Heriot's Sch Edinburgh, Univ of Edinburgh (BSc), Univ of Newcastle upon Tyne (PhD), Univ of Edinburgh (DSc); *m* 1966, Joan Margaret; 2 s (Iain, Andrew), 4 da (Joanna, Julie, Nicola, Alison); *Career* Cementation Co Ltd: sr geotechnical engr 1965–66, divnl liaison engr 1966–69, conslt Cementation Ground Engrg Ltd 1969–71; lectr Univ of Aberdeen 1971–76 (head Geotechnics Res Gp 1973–76); conslt Ground Anchors Ltd 1973–78; tech dir: The Cement Gun Co 1976–81, Losinger Systems (UK) Ltd 1979–84; dep md Colcrete Gp 1978–84 (tech dir 1976–84); conslt: Colcrete Ltd 1985–88, GKN Foundations Ltd 1988–90, Keller Colcrete Ltd 1990–92, Parsons Brinckerhoff & Morrison Knudsen 1992–94, AMEC Gp Ltd 1992–; dir COLROK Joint Venture Tarbela Dam Pakistan 1979–82; private conslt 1997–; Univ of Bradford: head Dept of Civil Engrg 1985–94, prof of civil engrg 1985–97, visiting prof 1998–2000, emeritus prof of civil engrg 2000–, memb Ct 2000–; visiting prof Univ of Newcastle upon Tyne 1980–83; external examiner: Portsmouth Poly 1981–84, Univ of Glasgow 1982–87, Univ of Newcastle upon Tyne 1983–86, Univ of Edinburgh 1987–89, UMIST 1989–91, Univ of Nottingham 1991–93, Univ of Salford 1993–96; govr: Bradford GS 1985–87, Harrogate GS 1997–2000; chm: Working Gp on Pre-stressed Ground Anchorages Fédération Internationale de la Précontrainte 1983–96, Steering Gp on Site Investigation 1991–94, Organising Ctee for Int Conference on Ground Anchorages ICE 1995–97, Environmental Civil Engrg Ctee SERC 1993–94, Res Panel ISE 1993–94, Civil Engrg Panel for 1996 Res Assessment Exercise 1995–96; senator Engrg Cncl 1999–2001 (memb Bd for Engineers Regulation, memb Educn Ctee); memb: Cmmn on Practical Construction Fédération Internationale de la Précontrainte 1983–96, Engrg Res Cmmn SERC 1993–94, Cmmn on Rock Grouting Int Soc of Rock Mechanics 1989–95, Res Panel ISE 1991–93, Anchor Ctee Post Tensioning Inst USA 1992–, Teaching Quality Assessment Panel Scottish Higher Educn Funding Cncl 1993, Shaft Isolation Method Review Task Force UKAEA 1997, Expert Review Panel Hydro Tasmania 2000–02, Int Review Panel South Deep Gold Mine South Africa 2000–06; memb Ctee: Ground Improvement, Int Soc of Soil Mechanics and Fndn Engrg 1990–97, British Standards Inst 1990–2000, Working Gp on High Pressure Bulkheads S African Nat Standard 2006–; memb Cncl: ISE 1991–94, ICE 1989–91 and 1992–95; assessor of mature candidates ICE 1988–97; FICE, FIStructE, FGS, FRSA, FREng 1993; *Style—* Prof G S Littlejohn, FREng; ✉ Almsford House, Fulwith Mill Lane, Harrogate, North Yorkshire HG2 8HJ (tel 01423 879430, fax 01423 872014, e-mail gslittlejohn@ntlworld.com)

LITTLEJOHN, Joan Anne; da of Thomas Littlejohn (d 1950), and Joan, *née* Wynn (Mrs Edward G Shepherd) (d 1999); *b* 20 April 1937; *Educ* Mary Datchelor Girls' Sch, Royal Coll of Music; *Career* freelance composer, poet, photographer and musicologist 1958–; postgrad study with Howells, Berkeley, Boulanger, Ruth Dyson and others; piano teacher Orpington GS 1958–59, admin staff Royal Coll of Music 1960–83, piano teacher Harrow 1972–73; asst to Br composers incl: Fricker, Howells, Hopkins, Poston; reassembled Howells Requiem 1980 and collated his MS sketches 1983; inducted memb Mozartgemeinde Vienna 1970s, memb Cncl Soc of Women Musicians 1970s, fndr memb Royal Coll of Music Staff Assoc 1976, chm Royal Coll of Music NALGO and London Music Colleges NALGO 1978–81, vice-chm Royal Coll of Music Local Jt Ctee 1978–81; creative works (music) incl: La Mascarade de Jean de la Fontaine, The Heights of Haworth, Poems from Palgrave, 4 Sea Songs (words by J M Ritchie), 4 Lieder von F Schnabl, London Street Cries (cmmnd by Beth Boyd), St Juliot Cornwall (words by Rachel Pearse), Dreams of Anubis, Settings of Blake, Burns, De La Mare, Shakespeare, Hardy, choral scena The Bonny Earl of Murray (cmmnd by Antony Hopkins), Chimborazo (tribute to Christopher Palmer), Cecilia, A Tune for All Musicians, Avalon's Lincoln and Lindsey; creative works (poetry) incl: Poems for Free, In The Furrowed Field, Towards Exmoor, Bingo's Totleigh Diary, The Hearth, Hymn of the Interviewers, Grandad's Dinner, Autun, Legend; recorded 90 tunes for The Queen Mother's 90th Year; MSS and music deposited in The American Music Res Center Calif, BIRS London, Nat Library Vienna, Clarence House, Buckingham Palace and private collections, contrib (by invitation) to permanent exhibitions at The Int Museum of Peace and Solidarity Samarkand; fndr dir The Joan Littlejohn Archive (collection of MSS, letters, diaries, genealogy, memorabilia of mainly 20th century artists and personalities (destined for the nation) to be housed at The Devon Record Office by arrangement with The Nat Heritage Meml Fund); memb: Br Fedn of Music Festivals, IBC Advsy Cncl, PRS, Women's Corona Soc, Brontë Soc, The Cinnamon Tst; UN Charter 50 patron 1994, fndr patron Dame Thora Hird Memorial Fund 2004–; in life fell American Biographical Inst Research Assoc 1983; recipient Howells' Composing Piano 1984, World Decoration of Excellence medallion American Biog Inst 1989, first recipient IBC Medal Collection 1989 (for most distinguished biographies), recipient Millenium Medal of Honour ABI 1998; GRSM, LRAM; *Publications* Howells Centenary (contrib), Poston Centenary (contrib); *Recreations* taming vandals, trying to avoid phone masts, animals especially dogs, psittacines and Dusty the cat; *Style—* Miss Joan Littlejohn; ✉ 49 Hamilton Lane, Exmouth, Devon EX8 2LW

LITTLEJOHN, William Hunter; s of William Littlejohn (d 1974), and Alice, *née* King (d 1984); *b* 16 April 1929; *Educ* Arbroath HS, Dundee Coll of Art (DA); *Career* artist; RSA 1973 (ARSA 1966), RSW, RGI; *Solo Exhibitions* The Scottish Gall 1963, 1967, 1972, 1977, 1984 and 1989, Univ of Aberdeen 1975, Univ of Leeds 1976, Peter Potter Gall 1978, The Loom Shop Gall 1980, 1983, 1985 and 1990, Kingfisher Gall 1993 and 1995; *Group Exhibitions* Contemporary Scottish Painting (Toronto) 1961, 20th Century Scottish Painting 1962, Contemporary Scottish Art (Reading Art Gall) 1963, Three Centuries of Scottish Painting (Nat Gall of Canada) 1968, Twelve Scottish Painters (tour USA and Canada) 1970, Art Spectrum (Aberdeen Art Gall) 1971, Painters In Parallel (Scottish Arts Cncl) 1978, Contemporary Art from Scotland (tour), Ten Scottish Painters (Royal Acad) 1986, The Scottish Collection (Fine Art Soc) 1989), Scottish Art (Hong Kong) 1994; *Work in Collections* Scottish National Gall of Modern Art, Scottish Arts Cncl, RSA, Edinburgh Civic Collection, Univ of Edinburgh, Univ of Aberdeen, Royal Bank of Scotland, Robert Fleming Holdings, Educational Inst of Scotland; *Awards* Guthrie Award RSA 1961, Cargill Prize RGI 1966 and 1990, Sir William Gillies Award RSW 1980, Alexander Graham Munro Award RSW 1993; *Style—* William Littlejohn, Esq, RSA; ✉ 43 Viewfield Road, Arbroath, Angus DD11 2DW (tel 01241 874402)

LITTLEJOHNS, Douglas George; CBE (1991, OBE 1984); s of Gordon Augustus Littlejohns (d 1994), and Margaret Goudie, *née* Smith (d 1997); *b* 10 May 1946; *Educ* Borden GS, RNC Dartmouth, Univ of Reading (BSc), Univ of Warwick Business Sch (MBA); *m* 1, 14 Nov 1970 (m dis 1987), Fiona, *née* Hilton; 1 s (Andrew b 1974), 2 da (Imogen b 1978, Diana b 1979); m 2, 4 June 1988, Deborah Anne, da of Captain Angus Andrew Nicol (d 1971); *Career* served RN until 1994; CO: HMS Osiris 1975–76, HMS Sceptre 1981–83, HMS London 1987–89; PSO to CDS 1989–91, Capt RNEC Manadon 1992–94; halls md Earls Court and Olympia Ltd 1994–96, dep chm Beeton Rumford Ltd 1995–96, pres and ceo Red Storm Entertainment Inc 1996–2000, business conslt 2001–; chm: Nice Tech Ltd

L

2005–, Marine Track Ltd 2006–; non-exec dir: Castle Granite Ltd 2005–, Drum Cussac Ltd 2007, DTM Ltd 2007; Freeman City of London 1988, Liveryman Worshipful Co of Fanmakers 2002; Younger Bro Trinity House 1989; CMath, FIMA 1995; *Recreations* golf, sailing, DIY, gardening; *Clubs* RN 1765 and 1785, IOD, MCC, Army and Navy; *Style—* Douglas Littlejohns, Esq, CBE; ✉ Hunters Ride, Brentor, Tavistock, Devon PL19 0NF (e-mail dandlittlejohns@aol.com)

LITTLEMORE, Christopher Paul; s of Frederick Percival Littlemore (d 2003), and (Edith) Marie, *née* Clarkson; *b* 8 March 1959; *Educ* Rugby, Univ of Manchester (BA, BArch), Univ of Bath (MSc); *m* 28 July 1984, Jane Evelyn, da of Derek Chalk (d 2007), of Broad Chalke, Wilts; 1 s (Andrew b 1987), 1 da (Katharine b 1989); *Career* architect Ellis Williams Partnership Manchester 1980–81, Pick Everard Leicester 1982; SMC Charter Architects (formerly The Charter Partnership): architect 1983–86, assoc dir 1987, dir 1989–2002, md 2002–; exhbns of paintings: Edwin Young Gallery Salisbury, Sadler Gallery Wells; RIBA 1984; *Recreations* mountaineering, flyfishing, watercolour painting, music; *Clubs* Midland Assoc of Mountaineers; *Style—* Christopher Littlemore, Esq; ✉ SMC Charter Architects, Tennyson House, 159–165 Gt Portland Street, London W1W 5BP (tel 020 7580 0400, fax 020 7580 6680, e-mail clittlemore@smccharterarchitects.com)

LITTLER, Brian Oswald; s of William Oswald Littler (d 1958), of London, and Mavis Pricilla, *née* Copping; *b* 22 November 1942; *Educ* St Dunstan's Coll, KCL (BDS, MB BS); *m* 19 Feb 1972, Susan Elizabeth, da of Arthur Stent, of Wonersh, Surrey; 1 s (Adam Oswald b 20 Oct 1975), 2 da (Elizabeth Ann b 30 May 1978, Bryony Susan Jayne b 24 Oct 1984); *Career* private conslt oral and maxillo-facial surgn to: The Thomas Rivers Med Centre, The London Ind Hosp, The Roding Hosp Redbridge; fell Br Assoc of Oral and Maxillo-Facial Surgns, FDS RCS 1969; *Recreations* sailing; *Style—* Brian Littler, Esq; ✉ Pentlow End, High Easter, Essex CM1 4RE (tel 01245 231626)

LITTLER MANNERS, Judy; da of Sir Emile Littler (d 1985), and Lady Cora Littler, *née* Goffin; *b* 16 October 1952; *Educ* St Mary's Hall Brighton, Charters Towers Sch Bexhill-on-Sea, St Anne's Coll Oxford (MA); *m* 12 June 1982 (m dis 1990), David Peter Manners; 1 s (Max b 27 March 1983), 1 da (Marina b 6 Sept 1986); *Career* floor asst and asst floor mangr BBC Studio Mgmnt Dept 1975–78, prodn asst Drama in Europe Ltd and Derek Glynne Assocs 1978–79, producer MMA Presentations Ltd 1979–83, prop and chief exec Mum's The Word 1984–92; dir: The Night Company Ltd 1985–96, GR Productions Ltd 1985–96, British Amalgamated Theatres Ltd 1985–; non-exec dir Stratagem Group plc (formerly London Entertainments plc) 1987–93; vice-pres The Actors' Charitable Trust 2006– (hon treas1988–96), tstee The Emile Littler Fndn, patron Theatre in Trust; memb Bd of Mgmnt Royal Hosp and Home Putney 1992–95 (chm Forget-me-not Ball 1988–92); *Recreations* theatre, tennis; *Clubs* Hurlingham, Harbour; *Style—* Mrs Judy Littler Manners; ✉ c/o Goodman Derrick & Co, 90 Fetter Lane, London EC4A 1EQ

LITTLEWOOD, Anthony George (Tony); s of George Kershaw Littlewood, of Ashton-under-Lyne, Lancs, and Sarah, *née* Rogers; *b* 3 October 1949; *Educ* Audenshaw GS, Univ of Nottingham (BPharm); *m* 11 Dec 1982 (m dis 1992), Nikola Ann, da of Lance James du Lys Mallalieu (d 1973); 3 s (Russell b 1984, Guy b 1986, Harry b 1988); *Career* pharmacist; chm and md George Hinchliffe Ltd 1973–; chm Northern (chemists) Ltd 1981–, md Amchem (UK) Ltd 1995–; chm Local Pharmaceutical Ctee 1989–; non-exec dir Tameside Family Health Servs Authy 1990–; chm Hulme GS PTA 1998–, treas Christ Church Friezland 1998–, tstee Age Concern 2002–, dir Centre Stage Concern 2003; fndr memb Aston Martin Heritage Tst; MRPharmS 1972, MIMgt 1980; *Recreations* tennis, golf, travel, (collecting) photographic, classic cars, gardening, restoring old buildings, endeavouring to solve sons' homework; *Clubs* Union (Ashton-under-Lyne), Henllys Hall Golf (Anglesey); *Style—* Tony Littlewood, Esq; ✉ Friezland Grange, Greenfield, Saddleworth OL3 7LQ

LITTLEWOOD, Graham; s of Ernest Charles Littlewood (d 1960), and Ivy Lilian, *née* Masters (d 1978); *b* 19 February 1944; *Educ* Royal Liberty Sch Romford; *m* 30 Aug 1971, Marianne; 2 da (Catherine Ann b 22 March 1973, Jane Elizabeth b 9 June 1975); *Career* accountant; Bristow Burrell & Co 1960–67, Coopers & Lybrand 1967–69, gp fin controller Gazocean France 1969–71, ptnr Keens Shay Keens & Co 1973; PKF: joined 1978, ptnr i/c Auditing Dept 1989–94, ptnr i/c London general practice 1995–2001, ret; hon treas Girlguiding UK 2004–; Freeman City of London 1983; FCA 1966; *Recreations* golf, reading; *Clubs* East India, Stapleford Abbotts Golf; *Style—* Graham Littlewood, Esq; ✉ Girlguiding UK, 17–19 Buckingham Palace Road, London SW1W 0PT (tel 020 7834 6242)

LITTLEWOOD, Prof Peter Brent; s of Horace Littlewood, and Edna May, *née* Cooper; *b* 18 May 1955; *Educ* St Olave's Sch Orpington, Trinity Coll Cambridge (BA), MIT (Kennedy Scholar), Cavendish Lab Univ of Cambridge (PhD); *m* Elizabeth, *née* Lamb; 1 s (Christopher), 1 da (Sophie b 2000); *Career* head Theoretical Physics Dept Bell Labs 1992–97 (joined 1980); Univ of Cambridge: fell Trinity Coll 1997–, prof of physics 1997–, head Dept of Physics 2005–; author of over 100 professional articles in the field of theoretical physics; fell American Physical Soc 1988; *Recreations* squash, music; *Style—* Prof Peter Littlewood; ✉ Department of Physics, University of Cambridge, Cavendish Laboratory, Madingley Road, Cambridge CB3 0HE (tel 01223 339991, fax 01223 337356, e-mail peter.littlewood@phy.cam.ac.uk)

LITTMAN, Jeffrey James; s of Louis Littman (d 1981), of Edmonton, Middx, and Sarah (Sadie), *née* Coberman (d 1974); *b* 19 February 1943; *Educ* Latymer Sch Edmonton, St Catharine's Coll Cambridge (MA); *m* 20 March 1975, Sandra Lynne, da of David Kallman (d 1975), of New York, USA; 2 da (Amanda, Léonie); *Career* called to the Bar Middle Temple 1974; in private practice specialising in commercial law, insolvency and the law of slrs and costs; ldr Mgmnt Gp Dept of Computing and Control Imperial Coll London 1990–92; writer, deviser and presenter of the course on civil procedure for TV Law 1993, presenter Seminars in Insolvency and Slr's Professional Negligence for Law Soc Continuing Professional Devpt (Wales) 2004; *Recreations* history, Jewish studies; *Style—* Jeffrey Littman, Esq; ✉ 9 Park Place Chambers, Cardiff CF10 3DP (tel 029 2038 2731, fax 029 2022 2542, mobile 07939 092741, e-mail jeffreylittman@aol.com)

LITTMAN, Mark; QC (1961); s of Jack Littman (d 1963), and Lilian, *née* Rose; *b* 4 September 1920; *Educ* Owens Sch, LSE (BSc), The Queen's Coll Oxford (MA); *m* 18 Sept 1965, Marguerite, da of Tyler Lamkin, of Monroe, Louisiana, USA; *Career* Lt RN 1941–46; called to the Bar Middle Temple 1947, in practice 1947–67 and 1979–, master of Bench 1971, master treas Middle Temple 1988, head of chambers; dep chm Br Steel Corp 1967–79; former dir: Burtons, Granada, Commercial Union (vice-chm), British Enkalon, Amerada Hess (US), RTZ; memb Royal Cmmn Legal Servs 1976–79; *Clubs* Reform, Garrick, Oxford and Cambridge, Century (New York); *Style—* Mark Littman, Esq, QC; ✉ 12 Gray's Inn Square, London WC1R 5JP (tel 020 7404 3072, fax 020 7404 4832, e-mail marklittman@compuserve.com)

LITTON, Andrew; *Educ* Juilliard Sch NY; *Career* conductor; assoc conductor to Mstislav Rostropovich NSO Washington (formerly asst), debut with BBC Symphony Orch 1982, debut with RPO 1983; princ conductor and artistic advsr Bournemouth Symphony Orch 1988–94 (conductor laureate 1994–), music dir Dallas Symphony Orch 1994–2006 (dir emeritus 2006–), music dir Bergen Philharmonic 2002–, artistic dir Minnesota Orch Sommerfest 2004; guest appearances with: all maj London orchs, English Chamber Orch, Scottish Chamber Orch, Royal Scottish National Orch, Oslo Philharmonic, Rotterdam Philharmonic, Stockholm Philharmonic, Orchestre Philharmonique de Monte Carlo, RAI Milan, RSO Berlin, l'Orchestre Suisse Romande, WDR Köln, Orchestre National de France, Czech Philharmonic, Chicago Symphony Orch, Los Angeles Philharmonic, Philadelphia Orch, Pittsburgh Symphony Orch and orchs of Minnesota, Montreal, Rochester, Toronto and Vancouver; opera debuts: Metropolitan Opera (Eugene Onegin, 1989), Royal Opera House (Trevor Nunn's Porgy and Bess, 1992), ENO (Falstaff, 1994); new prodn of Salome ENO 1996, new prodn of Britten's Bill Budd WNO 1998; *Recordings* incl: complete Tchaikovsky Symphonies (with Bournemouth Symphony Orchestra), all Rachmaninov Symphonies (with RPO), Mahler's Symphony No 1 and Songs of a Wayfarer, Elgar Enigma Variations, Walton symphonies and concertos, Bernstein The Age of Anxiety, Ravel and Gershwin piano concerti, Shostakovich Symphony No 10, Brahms Symphony No 1, recordings with Dallas Symphony Orch incl Shostakovich Symphony No 8, works by Schumann, Ives, Piston, complete cycle of Mahler Symphonies with the Dallas Symphony Orch, complete Rachmaninoff Concertos (Classical Brits/BBC Critics Award); *Style—* Andrew Litton, Esq

LITWIN-DAVIES, Stacey; da of D S Litwin (decd), and Mrs N Litwin, of Toronto, Canada; *b* 26 February 1955; *Educ* McGill Univ Montreal (BA), Ontario Coll of Art (BEd); *m* 7 May 1978, Dr P O Davies; 1 da (Isabel b 22 Feb 1991), 1 s (Matthew b 16 May 1994); *Career* jr designer/project co-ordinator Donald Ketcheson Ltd Toronto1979–86, project co-ordinator/project dir Rice Brydone Ltd Toronto 1986–88, dir Workplace Architecture Div/bd dir Fitch RS plc London 1988–90, ind conslt Wolff Olins London 1990–92, sabbatical in Paris 1992–94, ind conslt 1994–95, consultancy and design dir/bd dir Morgan Lovell London 1995–98, dir of strategic briefing DEGW London Ltd 1998–; *Recreations* art, music, theatre, avid reader, children; *Style—* Mrs Stacey Litwin-Davies; ✉ DEGW, 8 Crinan Street, London N1 9SQ (tel 020 7239 7734, fax 020 7278 3613)

LIU, David Tek-Yung; s of Pro Liu Tsu-Shya, of Sydney, Aust, and Mabel King, *née* Liang (d 1977); *b* 26 April 1941; *Educ* All Saints Bathurst NSW Australia, Univ of Sydney (MB BS), Univ of Sussex (MPhil); *m* 28 July 1976, Pamela Margaret, da of Arthur Heptinstall, of Surrey, England; 1 da (Natasha b 9 Sept 1981); *Career* res fell Univ of Sussex, lectr and res lectr UCL, sr lectr and hon conslt Univ of Nottingham 1989–, conslt Univ of Malaya 1989–91; City Hosp Nottingham: dir Fetal Care Unit 1981–, clinical dir Obstetric and Gynaecology Dept 1993–; co-fndr Embrace 1991; memb: Nottingham Charity Appeal for Pre-Natal Diagnosis, Birmingham and Midland Obstetric and Gynaecological Soc, jt MRC-RCOG Ctee Chorion Villus Sampling; FRCOG 1986, FRCOG (Aust) 1992, DM Univ of Nottingham 1992; *Books* Thinking, Feeling (1987), Labour Ward Manual (1985, 3 edn 2001), Chorion Villus Sampling (1987), Practical Gynaecology (1988); *Recreations* gardening, water sports, writing; *Clubs* Nottingham County Sailing; *Style—* David Liu, Esq; ✉ Department of Obstetrics & Gynaecology, City Hospital, Hucknall Road, Nottingham NG5 1PB (tel 0115 969 1169, fax 0115 962 7670, e-mail dliu@ncht.org.uk)

LIVELY, Penelope Margaret; CBE (2002, OBE 1989); da of Roger Vincent Low, and Vera Maud Greer, *née* Reckitt; *b* 17 March 1933; *Educ* St Anne's Coll Oxford (BA); *m* 1957, Prof Jack Lively (d 1998); 1 s (Adam), 1 da (Josephine); *Career* writer; book reviews and short stories in numerous magazines, various TV and radio scripts; former chm Soc of Authors (memb 1973–); memb: PEN 1985–, Arts Cncl Lit Panel 1990–92, Bd The British Library 1993–99, Bd Br Cncl 1997–; Hon DLitt; FRSL; *Children's Books* Astercote (1970), The Whispering Knights (1971), The Wild Hunt of Hagworthy (1971), The Driftway (1972), The Ghost of Thomas Kempe (Carnegie medal, 1974), The House in Norham Gardens (1974), Going Back (1975), Boy Without a Name (1975), A Stitch in Time (Whitbread award, 1976), The Stained Glass Window (1976), Fanny's Sister (1976), The Voyage of QV66 (1978), Fanny and The Monsters (1978), Fanny and The Battle of Potter's Piece (1980), The Revenge of Samuel Stokes (1981), Fanny and the Monsters (three stories, 1983), Uninvited Ghosts (1984), Dragon Trouble (1984), Debbie and the Little Devil (1987), A House Inside Out (1987); *Non-Fiction* The Presence of the Past (1976), Oleander, Jacaranda: A Childhood Perceived (1994), A House Unlocked (2001); *Fiction* The Road to Lichfield (1977), Nothing Missing but the Samovar (Southern Arts Literary prize, 1978), Treasures of Time (Arts Cncl Nat Book award, 1979), Judgement Day (1980), Next to Nature, Art (1982), Perfect Happiness (1983), Corruption (1984), According to Mark (1984), Pack of Cards, stories 1978–86 (1986), Moon Tiger (Booker prize, 1987), Passing On (1989), City of the Mind (1991), Cleopatra's Sister (1993), Heat Wave (1996), Beyond the Blue Mountains (1997), Spiderweb (1998), The Photograph (2003), Making it Up (2005), Consequences (2007); *Style—* Mrs Penelope Lively, CBE; ✉ c/o David Higham Associates, 5–8 Lower John Street, Golden Square W1R 4HA (tel 020 7437 7888)

LIVENS, Leslie John Phillip; s of Lt Leslie Francis Hugh Livens (d 1981), of London, and Betty Livens; *b* 13 December 1946; *Educ* Wimbledon County Secdy Sch; *m* 3 Aug 1968, Carole Ann, da of Henry William Todd, of London; 1 s (Stephen b 1970), 1 da (Clare b 1973); *Career* ed and conslt ed Taxation Practitioner (Jl of Inst of Taxation) 1974–84; former ed: Tax Planning International, Financial Times World Tax Report, Review of Parliament; managing ed Butterworths Tax Books 1977–81; Moores Rowland (formerly Nevill & Co): taxation conslt 1981–83, ptnr 1983–96, chm International Tax Group 1988–96; dir: Atlas Tst Co Ltd (Gibraltar) 1996–; CTA 1972, AITI 1983; memb Soc of Tst and Estate Practitioners 1995; *Publications* incl: Moores Rowland's Tax Guide (1982–87), Daily Telegraph Tax Guide (1987), Daily Telegraph Personal Tax Guide (1988), Debrett's International Offshore Finance (ed, 1992), Livens' Share and Business Valuation Handbook (1986–2005), Tolley's Tax Havens (2000); *Recreations* music, writing, walking, family; *Style—* Leslie Livens, Esq; ✉ 30 Ashley Court, Morpeth Terrace, London SW1P 1EN (tel 020 7834 0809, fax 020 7963 0808, e-mail leslie@atlastrustco.com)

LIVERMAN, Prof Diana Margaret; da of John Liverman, of Oxford, and Peggy, *née* Earl (d 2005); *b* 15 May 1954, Accra, Ghana; *Educ* UCL (BA), Univ of Toronto (MA), UCLA (PhD); *Career* asst prof Univ of Wisconsin 1984–90, assoc prof Penn State Univ 1990–96, prof and dir Centre for Latin American Studies Univ of Arizona 1996–2003, prof of environmental science and dir Environmental Change Inst Univ of Oxford 2003–; chair US Nat Acad Ctee on Human Dimensions of Global Environmental Change 1995–99, co-chair Scientific Advsy Ctee Int Inst for Global Change Research 1998–2002, chair Global Environmental Change and Food Security Prog of IHDP/IGBP/WCRP 2006–; Mitchell Prize for Sustainable Devpt 1991; life memb Assoc of American Geographers 1977, FRGS 2005; *Publications* People and Pixels (1998), World Regions in Global Context (co-author, 2005); *Style—* Prof Diana Liverman; ✉ Environmental Change Institute, Oxford University Centre for the Environment, South Parks Road, Oxford OX1 3QY (tel 01865 275848, e-mail diana.liverman@eci.ox.ac.uk)

LIVERMORE, Karen; da of Joseph Livermore (d 1982), and Glenys, *née* Howard; *Educ* Grays Sch, Thurrock Coll; *Career* freelance journalist and stylist various cos; Daily Star: fashion ed 1989–95, womans ed 1995–97; ed: Essentials magazine 1997–2004, Family Circle 2004–; *Style—* Miss Karen Livermore; ✉ c/o Essentials, King's Reach Tower, Stamford Street, London SE1 9LS

LIVERPOOL, Dean of; *see:* Hoare, Rt Rev Dr Rupert

LIVERPOOL, 5 Earl of (UK 1905); Edward Peter Bertram Savile Foljambe; also Baron Hawkesbury (UK 1893) and Viscount Hawkesbury (UK 1905); s of Capt Peter George William Savile Foljambe (ka Italy 1944), and Elizabeth Joan, *née* Flint (who m 2, Maj Andrew Gibbs, MBE, TD (d 2000), and d 1993); *Educ* Shrewsbury, Perugia Univ Italy; *m* 1, 29 Jan 1970 (m dis 1994), Lady Juliana Noel, da of 5 Earl of Gainsborough, *qv*; 2 s (Luke Marmaduke Peter Savile, Viscount Hawkesbury b 25 March 1972, Hon Ralph Edward Anthony Savile b 24 Sept 1974); m 2, 26 May 1995 (m dis 2001), Marie-Ange, eldest da of Comte Géraud Michel de Pierredon; m 3, 28 June 2002,

Georgina, yr da of Mrs Hilda Rubin; *Heir* s, Viscount Hawkesbury; *Clubs* Turf, Pratt's; *Style—* The Rt Hon the Earl of Liverpool; ✉ House of Lords, London SW1A 0PW

LIVERPOOL, Bishop of 1998–; Rt Rev James Stuart Jones; s of Maj James Stuart Anthony Jones (d 1990), and Helen Deans Dick Telfer, *née* McIntyre (d 2002); *b* 18 August 1948; *Educ* Duke of York's RMS Dover, Univ of Exeter (Kitchener scholar, BA), Keele Univ (PGCE); *m* 19 April 1980, Sarah Caroline Rosalind, da of Rev Canon Peter Marrow; 3 da (Harriet Emma b 26 May 1982, Jemima Charlotte b 13 Aug 1984, Tabitha Rose b 14 Feb 1987); *Career* asst master Sevenoaks Sch 1971–75, prodr Scripture Union 1975–81, assoc vicar Christ Church Clifton 1984–90 (asst curate 1982–84), vicar Emmanuel Church Croydon 1990–94, bishop of Hull 1994–98; memb House of Lords 2003–; author and broadcaster; chair Wycliffe Hall Univ of Oxford; Hon DD Univ of Hull 1998, Hon DLitt Univ of Lincolnshire and Humberside 2001; *Books* incl: Following Jesus (1984), Finding God (1987), Why do People Suffer? (1993), The Power and The Glory (1994), People of the Blessing (1998), The Moral Leader (2002), Jesus and the Earth (2003); *Recreations* swimming, opera and holidays in France; *Style—* The Rt Rev the Lord Bishop of Liverpool; ✉ Bishop's Lodge, Woolton Park, Woolton, Liverpool L25 6DT (tel 0151 421 0831, fax 0151 428 3055, e-mail bishopslodge@liverpool.anglican.org)

LIVERPOOL, Most Rev Archbishop of (RC) 1996–; Patrick Altham Kelly; s of John Kelly (d 1960), and Mary, *née* Altham (d 1989); *b* 23 November 1938; *Educ* Preston Catholic Coll, Venerable English Coll Rome, Pontifical Gregorian Univ Rome (PhL, STL); *Career* curate Lancaster Cathedral 1964–66, memb clery Archdiocese of Birmingham 1977, rector St Mary's Coll Oscott Birmingham 1979–84 (prof of dogmatic theology 1966–79), bishop of Salford 1984–96; sec Hierarchy Theology Cmmn 1967; prelate of honour to HH the Pope 1980–, consultor to the Pontificial Cmmn for Justice and Peace; *Recreations* reading, music, opera; *Style—* The Most Rev the Archbishop of Liverpool; ✉ Archbishop's House, Lowood, Carnatic Road, Liverpool L18 8BY (tel 0151 724 6398, fax 0151 724 6405, e-mail archbishop.liverpool@rcaolp.co.uk)

LIVERSEDGE, Richard Lorton; s of Lt-Col John Ridler Liversedge (d 1968), of Fawke House, Sevenoaks, Kent, and Grace Evelyn Liversedge (d 1982); *b* 31 August 1940; *Educ* Tonbridge, London Hosp Dental Sch (BDS), London Hosp Med Coll (MB BS); *m* 28 Oct 1972, Jennifer Jane, da of John Hurrel Robertson, of Johannesburg, South Africa; 1 s (Dominic b 1974), 2 da (Annabel b 1975, Belinda b 1979); *Career* registrar London Hosp 1970–72 (house surgn 1968–69), sr registrar Royal Dental Hosp and St George's Hosp 1972–77; conslt maxillo-facial surgn: Middx Hosp 1977–89, Barnet Gp of Hosps 1977–; responsible for various surgical instrument innovations; winter sportsman (luge); winner Br Luge Champs 1971; Winter Olympics: represented GB Grenoble 1968, capt Sapporo 1972, capt Innsbruck 1976; pres Br Racing Toboggan Assoc 1972–; chm Med Ctee Fedn Internationale de Luge de Course 1972–, memb Med Ctee Br Olympic Assoc 1976–; Freeman City of London 1968, Liveryman Worshipful Co of Skinners 1977; FDS RCSEd 1971, FDS RCS 1972; *Recreations* luge, Cresta run, moto polo; *Clubs* St Moritz Tobogganing; *Style—* Richard Liversedge, Esq; ✉ Oak Cottage, 117 Flaunden, Hertfordshire HP3 0PB (tel 01442 833 047); Flat 1, 43 Wimpole Street, London W1M 7AF (tel 020 7935 7909)

LIVERSIDGE, (Ann) Francesca; da of Henry Douglas Liversidge (d 2000), and Cosmina, *née* Pistola (d 1993); *b* 13 August 1958; *Educ* N London Collegiate Sch, Bedford Coll London (BA); *m* 3 Sept 1983, Ian Chignell, s of Stephen Chignell; *Career* editorial asst Bellew & Higton 1979–82, copy ed Hutchinson & Co 1982–84, managing ed Arrow Books 1984–87; Bantam Books: sr ed 1987–90, editorial dir 1990–95, publishing dir 1995–2002; sr publishing dir Transworld Publishers 2003–; *Recreations* countryside, cat breeding, music; *Style—* Ms Francesca Liversidge; ✉ Transworld Publishers, 61–63 Uxbridge Road, London W5 5SA (tel 020 8231 6627, fax 020 8231 6612, e-mail f.liversidge@transworld-publishers.co.uk)

LIVERSIDGE, Michael John Howard; s of William James Howard Liversidge (d 1993), and Mary Kathleen, *née* Heddon (d 1973); *b* 29 August 1947; *Educ* Prince of Wales Sch Nairobi, Abingdon Sch, Courtauld Inst of Art London (BA); *m* 1976, Stephanie Mary Leith, da of Prof Ross Macdonald; *Career* research asst Paul Mellon Fndn for Br Art London 1969–70; Univ of Bristol: lectr 1970–88, sr lectr in history of art 1988–, head History of Art Dept 1979–96, 2002–03 and 2005–06, dean Faculty of Arts 1996–2001 (dep dean 1983–85), emeritus dean of arts 2007–; visiting lectr Queens Univ Kingston Canada 1971, 1973 and 1977, visiting fell Yale Center for British Art Yale Univ 1978; dir SW Museums Cncl (formerly Area Museums Cncl for the SW) 1994–2002 (memb Bd of Mgmnt 1985–2002); govr Dauntsey's Sch 1995–; tstee Theatre Royal Bristol 2000–, memb Campaign Bd Children's Hospice SW 2004–; FSA 1982, FRSA 1983; *Books* Canaletto and England (1993), Imagining Rome. British Artists and Rome in the Nineteenth Century (1996); also author of numerous articles in publications such as The Burlington Magazine, Apollo, Antiquaries Journal and various exhibition catalogues; *Recreations* New York; *Style—* M J H Liversidge, Esq, FSA; ✉ History of Art Department, University of Bristol, 43 Woodland Road, Bristol BS8 1UU (tel 0117 954 6050, e-mail m.j.h.liversidge@bristol.ac.uk)

LIVERSIDGE, Pamela Edwards; OBE (1999), DL (1999); da of William H Humphries, of Bridgnorth, Salop, and Dorothy, *née* James; *b* 23 December 1949; *Educ* Bridgnorth GS, Aston Univ (BSc); *m* 1, 1971 (m dis 1981), Dr Dale S Edwards; m 2, 1991, Douglas B Liversidge; 2 step s (Mark b 28 Feb 1962, Andrew b 30 Nov 1963), 1 step da (Suzanne b 17 Dec 1968); *Career* GKN 1971–76: gp grad, prodn engr, special projects engr (Keeton Sons & Co Sheffield); G W Thornton (became Thornton Holdings plc) 1976–87: asst tech mangr, prodn control and customer liaison mangr, materials controller, precision forge and aerofoil products mangr, sales mangr, sales dir; East Midlands Electricity plc 1987–93: strategic planning mangr, divnl dir (responsible for corp planning); princ shareholder and md Scientific Metal Powders plc 1993–96; princ shareholder and md Quest Investments Ltd 1996–; chm Sheffield Business Link 1999–2001, dir Sheffield TEC 1999–2001; memb Women into Sci and Engrg (WISE) Nat Coordinating Ctee; senator Engrg Cncl 1997–99; govr Sheffield Hallam Univ 1994–2006; visiting prof in industrial mfrg Univ of Sheffield 1997–99, special prof Univ of Nottingham 1998–2000; finalist Young Business Personality 1982, UK Business Pioneer Global Summit of Women 1998; High Sheriff of Yorks 2004–05; Freeman Co of Cutlers in Hallamshire (Mistress 1998), Freeman City of London, Liveryman Worshipful Co of Engineers (Guardian Sheffield Assay Office 2005–); Hon DUniv Central England, Hon DSc Aston Univ, Hon DEng Univ of Bradford, Hon DEng Univ of Huddersfield, Hon DUniv Sheffield Hallam, Hon DEng Univ of Sheffield; CEng, FREng, FIMechE (pres 1997–98), FCGI, FRSA; *Recreations* golf, public speaking; *Clubs* Sicklehome, Hope Valley, Pelican Nest Golf, Naples (Florida); *Style—* Mrs Pam Liversidge, OBE, DL, FREng; ✉ Quest Investments Ltd, Nicholas Hall, Thornhill, Hope Valley S33 0BR (tel 01433 659 874, fax 01433 659 947, e-mail liversidge1@btconnect.com)

LIVESEY, Dr Anthony Edward; s of Joseph Livesey (d 1976), of Great Harwood, Lancs, and Dorothy, *née* Birtwhistle; *b* 16 January 1953; *Educ* St Mary's Coll Blackburn, Univ of Dundee (BMSc, MB BCh); *m* 17 Aug 1974, Apolonia Marie, da of Jan Wachala, of Blackburn, Lancs; 2 s (Joseph John b 18 Jan 1980, David Michael b 12 Feb 1983); *Career* registrar psychiatry Manchester 1981–84, sr registrar child psychiatry Sheffield 1984–86, conslt child and adolescent psychiatry N Derbys DHA 1986–2001, conslt adolescent psychiatrist Sheffield Children's NHS Tst 2001–; dir of med affrs Community Health Care Servs (N Derbys) NHS Trust 1994–99; MRCPsych 1983; *Recreations* cycling, walking, photography; *Style—* Dr Anthony Livesey; ✉ 32 Conalan Avenue, Bradway, Sheffield S17 4PG; Oakwood Young People's Centre, The Longley Centre, Northern General Hospital, Norwood Grange Drive, Sheffield S5 7JT (tel 0114 226 1577, e-mail anthony.livesey@sch.nhs.uk)

LIVESEY, Bernard Joseph Edward; QC (1990); s of Joseph Augustine Livesey (d 1965), of Hatch End, Middx, and Marie Gabrielle, *née* Caulfield (d 1999); *b* 21 February 1944; *Educ* Cardinal Vaughan Sch London, Peterhouse Cambridge (MA, LLB); *m* 25 Sept 1971, Penelope Jean, da of Samuel Walter Harper, of Fittleworth, W Sussex; 2 da (Sarah b 5 June 1973, Kate b 21 Aug 1977); *Career* called to the Bar Lincoln's Inn 1969 (bencher 1999); recorder 1987–, dep judge of the High Court 1998; fell Int Acad of Trial Lawyers 1993; chm Cncl of Friends of Peterhouse 2002–; *Style—* Bernard Livesey, Esq, QC; ✉ 4 New Square, Lincoln's Inn, London WC2A 3RJ (tel 020 7822 2000, fax 020 7822 2001, e-mail b.livesey@4newsquare.com)

LIVESEY, Dr David Anthony; s of Vincent Livesey (d 1963), of Derby, and Marie, *née* Parr (d 1983); *b* 30 May 1944; *Educ* Derby Sch, Imperial Coll London (BSc Eng), Christ's Coll Cambridge (PhD); *m* 30 Dec 1967, Sally Anne, da (Alfred) Noel Vanston; 1 s (Nathaniel James b 14 May 1970), 2 da (Ruth Laura b 6 April 1973, Harriet Sarah b 24 Oct 1980); *Career* Univ of Cambridge: res offr Dept of Applied Economics 1969–75, univ lectr Dept of Engrg 1975–91, sec gen of the Faculties 1992–2003; res fell Peterhouse Cambridge 1971–74; Emmanuel Coll Cambridge: official fell 1974–91, bursar 1983–91 professorial fell 1992–2003, life fell 2003–, vice-master 2006–; sec gen League of European Research Univs 2005–; dir Cambridge-MIT Inst Ltd 1999–2000; non-exec dir Addenbrooke's NHS Tst 1992–99; tstee: Bedford Charity 2004–, Citizens Advice 2005–; govr Henley Mgmnt Coll 2005–07; ACGI; *Recreations* swimming, learning Welsh; *Style—* Dr David Livesey; ✉ 33 St Barnabas Road, Cambridge CB1 2BX (tel 01223 364520); Emmanuel College, Cambridge CB2 3AP (tel 01223 334243, fax 01223 334426)

LIVESEY, Rodger Charles; JP; s of Roland Livesey; *b* 19 June 1944; *Educ* Downing Coll Cambridge (MA); *m* 29 May 1972, Pat; 2 s (Matthew b 1974, Graham b 1979), 1 da (Caroline b 1977); *Career* md Security Pacific Hoare Govett Ltd 1976–88, Tokai Bank Europe plc 1988–2002, chm W Hampton Ltd 1987–; dir: Securities and Futures Authy 1994–99, Beds and Herts NHS Tst 1994–2000, UFJI plc 2002–; gen cmmr of tax; dir Eastern Arts Bd 1998–2001; govr Univ of Luton 1999–; Freeman City of London, Liveryman Worshipful Co of Actuaries; FIA; *Style—* Rodger Livesey, Esq; ✉ 60 West Common, Harpenden, Hertfordshire AL5 2LD (tel 01582 767527)

LIVESEY, Tony; s of John Livesey, of Nelson, Lancs, and Jean, *née* Comber (d 1977); *b* 11 January 1964; *Educ* SS John Fisher and Thomas More HS Colne, Nelson and Colne Coll; *m* Barbara, *née* Maley; 1 da (Megan Maley b 23 Aug 1994), 1 s (Angus Maley b 23 May 1996); *Career* jr reporter Nelson Leader 1983–86, writer news and features Gulf News Dubai 1986–87, reporter Lancashire Evening Telegraph 1987–88; Sport Newspapers: successively sports reporter, sports ed, asst ed then dep ed Sunday Sport, launch ed News & Echo (since sold), managing ed Sunday and Daily Sport, ed Sunday Sport and gp managing ed 1993–95, gp ed-in-chief 1995–, md 1999–; columnist News of the World 1999–2002; NW Young Journalist of the Year 1988; presenter Traitor (quiz show, BBC2); *Books* 10 Years of Sunday Sport (1996), Babes, Booze, Orgies and Aliens (1998), Stan the Man - A Hard Life in Football; also author of a series of short children's stories (1986–87); *Recreations* reading, writing TV scripts, watching Burnley FC (often from behind the seat), after dinner speaking; *Style—* Tony Livesey, Esq; ✉ Sport Newspapers, 19 Great Ancoats Street, Manchester M60 4BT (tel 0161 236 4466, fax 0161 228 6847)

LIVESLEY, Prof Brian; s of Thomas Clement Livesley (d 1980), and Stella Livesley (d 1980); *b* 31 August 1936; *Educ* King George V GS Southport, Univ of Leeds Med Sch (MB ChB, DHMSA, MD (Lond)); *m* 1, 1963, Beryl, *née* Hulme (d 1966); 1 s; m 2, 1969, Valerie Anne, *née* Nuttall; 2 da; *Career* house appts: Leeds Gen Infirmary 1961–62, Dist and Univ Hosps in Leeds, Manchester and Liverpool 1963–68; Harvey res fell King's Coll Hosp London 1969–72, conslt physician in geriatric med Lambeth, Southwark and Lewisham Health Authy 1973–87, Univ of London's prof of med in the elderly Imperial Coll Sch of Med at Chelsea and Westminster Hosp (Charing Cross and Westminster Med Sch until merger 1997) 1988–2001, emeritus prof Univ of London 2003–; clinical examiner in med Univ of London 1980–95 (sr clinical examiner 1990–95), examiner in med Worshipful Soc of Apothecaries 1987–94, examiner for dip in geriatric med RCP 1987–93, external examiner in med Royal Free and UC Sch of Med 1998–2001, external assessor RCP 2000–01; NW Thames regnl advsr on med for the elderly 1990–96, invited expert on the care of elderly persons for several Police Constabularies and HM Coroners' Officers 1999–, conslt forensic physician 2001–; memb: Med Cmmn on Accident Prevention 1984–89 (chm Home and Family Safety Cmmn 1988–89), Br Acad Forensic Sciences 2002–, Assoc of Forensic Physicians 2004–06; govr: St Paul's Cray CE (controlled) Primary Sch Orpington 1986–87, Newstead Wood Sch for Girls Orpington 1987–92; Univ of London's Academic Cncl rep to Age Concern Bromley (chm 1992–93); DG St John Ambulance 1994–96 (asst DG 1993–94); JP 1983–96; fell Hunterian Soc 2003–05 (lectr 2003); Liveryman Worshipful Soc of Apothecaries (Yeoman 1975, memb Ct of Assts 1990, Master 2005–06, chm Futures Ctee 2000–03, chm Academic Ctee 2001–03, Osler Lectr 1975, Gideon de Laune Lectr 2001); memb BMA 1960, FRCP 1989 (MRCP), FRSM 1995; KStJ 1994 (OStJ 1992); *Publications* investigations into aspects of the history, pathophysiology, biochemistry, psychology, epidemiology, sociology and education in med and forensic med in our ageing society, book reviewer for professional jls; *Recreations* family, Christian culture study, encouraging people to think; *Style—* Prof Brian Livesley; ✉ PO Box 295, Oxford OX2 9GD (tel and fax 01865 793383, e-mail brian.livesley@doctors.org.uk)

LIVINGSTON, Dorothy Kirby; da of late Albert Paulus Livingston, and late Margaret Alice, *née* Kirby; *b* 6 January 1948; *Educ* Central Newcastle HS, St Hugh's Coll Oxford (MA); *m* 11 Sept 1971 (m dis 2002), Julian, s of late Alfred Millar; 2 da; *Career* Herbert Smith LLP: articled clerk 1970–72, slr 1972–80, ptnr 1980–, slr advocate (civil) 2005; memb: Law Soc 1979, City of London Slrs' Co 1979; chm Fin Law Ctee and memb Competition Law Ctee City of London Law Soc; *Publications* FT Law and Tax: Competition Law and Practice (1995), Euromoney: Leasing Finance (contrib, 3 edn 1997 and 4 edn 2003), Sweet & Maxwell: The Competition Act 1998: A Practical Guide (2001); *Recreations* gardening, photography, history; *Style—* Mrs Dorothy Livingston; ✉ Herbert Smith, Exchange House, Primrose Street, London EC2A 2HS (tel 020 7374 8000, fax 020 7496 0043, e-mail dorothy.livingston@herbertsmith.com)

LIVINGSTON, Ian Paul; s of Dr Vivian Livingston, of Glasgow, and Rhoda Livingston; *b* 28 July 1964; *Educ* Kelvinside Acad, Univ of Manchester (BA); *m* 1987, Deborah; 1 s, 1 da; *Career* former appts: Arthur Andersen 1984–87, Bank of America 1987–88, 3i plc 1988–91; Dixons Group plc: joined 1991, chief fin offr (US) 1992–94, gp fin controller 1994–95, fin/systems dir 1995–97, gp fin dir 1997–2002; gp fin dir BT Gp 2002–05, ceo BT Retail 2005–; non-exec dir Ladbrokes plc 2003–07; ACA 1987; *Style—* Ian Livingston, Esq; ✉ BT Group, 81 Newgate Street, London EC1A 7AJ (tel 020 7356 5000)

LIVINGSTON, Dr Martin Gerard; s of Arnold Louis Livingston, of Newton Mearns, Glasgow, and Joyce, *née* Levy; *b* 19 May 1953; *Educ* Hillhead HS Glasgow, Univ of Glasgow (MB ChB, MD); *m* 4 July 1974, Hilary Monica, da of Dr Basil Green, of Glasgow; 1 s (Richard Jack b 1983), 1 da (Judith Fiona b 1985); *Career* psychiatry rotation Southern Gen Hosp and Leverndale Hosp 1978–79; Univ of Glasgow: lectr Psychological Med Dept 1979–83, sr lectr and hon conslt psychiatrist 1983–98; conslt psychiatrist and hon clinical sr lectr Southern General Hosp Glasgow 1998–; regnl advsr on psychiatric rehabilitation

1987–, chm Glasgow Psychiatric Speciality Ctee 1989–92; chm: Mental Health Unit Audit Ctee, Mental Health and Community Servs Tst R&D Ctee; specialis advsr to GMC tribunals 2001–, pt/t cmmr Mental Welfare Cmmn 1994–97; memb: Collegium Internationale Neuropsychopharmacologicum (CINP), Euro Coll of Neuropsychopharmacology (ECNP), advocates discipline tribunal 2000–; FRCPsych 1994 (MRCPsych 1980); *Publications* Rehabilitation of Adults and Children with Severe Head Injury (contrib, 1989), CRAG/SCOTMEG Services for People Affected by Schizophrenia (1995); psychiatric advsr to Prescriber Jl; author of pubns on: rehabilitation in psychiatry, psychological impact of head injury and epilepsy on patients and their relatives, drug treatments in psychiatry; *Recreations* reading, photography, classical music; *Style—* Dr Martin Livingston; ✉ Department Psychiatry, Southern General Hospital, 1345 Govan Road, Glasgow G51 4TF (tel and fax 0141 201 1947, e-mail mgl2w@udcf.gla.ac.uk

LIVINGSTON, Roderick George; s of Hugh Livingston (d 1981), of Streetly, and Rhoda Margaret, *née* Mathieson (d 2001); *b* 10 December 1944; *Educ* Shrewsbury, Univ of Aberdeen (BSc, Rowing blue), Univ of Exeter (ADPA), Univ of Western Ontario; *m* 23 Sept 1974, Willma, da of William Watt (d 1977), of Edinburgh; 2 s (Alastair b 1976, Michael b 1981); *Career* admin asst UCW Aberystwyth 1970–72 (grad asst 1969–70), asst sec Univ of Dundee 1975–78 (sr admin asst 1972–75); Univ of Strathclyde: asst sec 1978–81, asst registrar 1981–85, sr asst registrar 1985–88, sr asst registrar and faculty offr 1988–2004, mangr Strathclyde Business Sch 2004–; UCCA: memb Cncl of Mgmnt 1982–93, memb Statistics Ctee 1986–93, dir of co 1982–95, memb Exec Ctee 1988–94; UCAS (following merger of UCCA and PCAS): memb Jt Advsy Bd 1992–93, memb Bd of Dirs 1993–99; memb CVCP Steering Gp for the Review of the Nat Applications/Admissions Procedures 1994–99; vice-chm Glasgow Area Bd Young Enterprise Scotland 1993–2004 (chm 1999–2000, memb Scottish Cncl 1993–2004, Gold Award 1998); sec and treas Glasgow Quality Forum 1995–99 (sec 1994–95); memb Scot Univs Cncl on Entrance 1987–90; memb Undergrad Steering Ctee Assoc of Business Schs 1997–2006; vice-chm Glasgow Coll of Nautical Studies 2004– (memb Bd of Mgmnt 2001–); memb Core Funding Ctee Scottish Further Educn Funding Cncl 2002–04, convenor Military Educn Ctee Univs of Glasgow and Strathclyde 2005– (vice-convenor 2004–05, memb 2000–), memb Lowland Reserve Forces' and Cadets' Assoc 2006–; pres Univ of Aberdeen Athletic Assoc 1967–68; sec Abertay Historical Soc 1975–78; FSA Scot 1963, FRSA 1996, FCIS 1998 (ACIS 1972), FInstD 2000; *Recreations* castles, coins, rowing, sailing; *Clubs* Lansdowne, Leander, Royal Northern and Clyde Yacht; *Style—* Roderick Livingston, Esq; ✉ 51 Strathblane Road, Milngavie, Glasgow G62 8HA (tel 0141 956 3851, e-mail r.livingston@debrett.net); University of Strathclyde, McCance Building, 16 Richmond Street, Glasgow G1 1XQ (tel 0141 548 2387, e-mail r.livingston@strath.ac.uk)

LIVINGSTONE, Prof David N; OBE (2002); *b* 15 March 1953, Banbridge, NI; *Educ* Queen's Univ Belfast (BA, DipEd, PhD); *m*; 1 s, 1 da; *Career* research fell ESRC 1982–84; Queen's Univ Belfast: curator of maps 1984–89, reader Sch of Geosciences 1991–93 (lectr 1989–91), prof of geography and intellectual history (initially prof of geography) 1993–; visiting prof of geography and history of science Calvin Coll MI 1989–90, visiting prof of history Univ of Notre Dame IN 1995, visiting prof Regent Coll Vancouver 1997, 2000 and 2003, distinguished visiting prof of history and science Baylor Univ TX 2003–, noted visiting scholar Univ of Br Columbia 1999; delivered numerous guest lectures at academic instns worldwide, organiser of confs; pres Geography Section BAAS 2005, vice-pres (research) RGS 2007–; chair History and Philosophy of Geography Research Gp RGS (with IBG) 1995–98, co-fndr and jt sec Working Party on the History and Philosophy of Geography IBG 1981–84; memb: Ctee Study Gp on the History and Philosophy of Geography IBG 1984–94, Cmmn on the History of Geographical Thought Int Union of the History and Philosophy of Science and Int Geographical Union 1988–96, Nat Ctee for the History and Philosophy of Science Royal Irish Acad 1988–96, Nat Ctee for Geography Royal Irish Acad 1996–2003, Structures Review Ctee Br Acad 1997–98, Steering Ctee John Templeton Fndn Seminars on Science and Religion Univ of Oxford 1998–2001 and 2001–, Strategic Plan Ctee Royal Irish Acad 2000–02, Co-ordinating Ctee European Science Fndn Workshops on Science and Human Values 2000–, Cncl Royal Irish Acad 2001–02; memb Editorial Bd: Annals of the Association of British Geographers 1990–93, Transactions of the Institute of British Geographers 1993–98, Ecumene 1993–99 (memb Advsy Bd 1999–), Isis 1995–97, The Cambridge History of Science CUP 1995–2002, Science and Christian Belief 1996–, Progress in Human Geography 1998–2002, History of Cartography Project Chicago Univ Press 2002–, Jl of Historical Geography 2003–; Charles Lyell lectr BAAS 1994–95, Admiral Black Award RGS 1997, Centenary Medal RSGS 1997, Templeton Fndn Lecture Series Award 1999, Br Acad Research Readership 1999–2001, Hettner Lectures Univ of Heidelberg 2001, Murrin Lectures Univ of Br Columbia 2002, Progress in Human Geography Lecture RGS-IBG Annual Conf 2005, Humboldt lectr UCLA 2007, Mawley lectr Royal Holloway Univ of London 2007; convocation speaker Gordon Coll MA 2000, memb Ct Univ of Ulster (Br Acad rep) 1996–; memb Academia Europaea 2002; FBA 1995, MRIA 1998, FRSA 2001, AcSS 2002; *Publications* Nathaniel Southgate Shaler and the Culture of American Science (1987), Darwin's Forgotten Defenders (1987), The Behavioural Environment: Essays in Reflection, Application and Re-evaluation (ed with F W Boal, 1989), The Preadamite Theory and The Marriage of Science and Religion (1992), The Geographical Tradition: Episodes in the History of a Contested Enterprise (1992), What is Darwinism? And Other Writings on Science and Religion by Charles Hodge (ed with Mark A Noll, 1994), Human Geography: An Essential Anthology (ed with John Agnew and Alistair Rodgers, 1996), Them and Us? Attitudinal Variation among Belfast Churchgoers (with F W Boal and M Keane, 1997), Ulster-American Religion: Episodes in the History of a Cultural Connection (with R A Wells, 1999), Evangelicals and Science in Historical Perspective (ed with D G Hart and Mark A Noll, 1999), Geography and Enlightenment (ed with Charles Withers, 1999), Evolution, Scripture, and Science: Selected Writings of B B Warfield (ed with Mark A Noll, 2000), Science, Space and Hermeneutics (2001), Putting Science in its Place: Geographies of Scientific Knowledge (2003), Adam's Ancestors: Race, Religion and the Politics of Human Origins (2008); numerous book chapters and articles; *Style—* Prof David Livingstone, OBE; ✉ School of Geography, The Queen's University of Belfast, Belfast BT7 1NN

LIVINGSTONE, Ian Lang; CBE (1998, OBE 1993); s of John Lang Livingstone (d 1998), of Motherwell, and Margaret Steele, *née* Barbour (d 1982); *b* 23 February 1938; *Educ* Hamilton Acad, Univ of Glasgow (BL); *m* 30 March 1967, Diane, da of Frank Hales (d 1989), of Lytham St Annes; 2 s (Andrew b 1968, Gordon b 1970); *Career* conslt slr, NP 1962; chm: Motherwell FC 1973–87, Lanarkshire Health Bd (now NHS Lanarkshire) 1993–2002 (memb 1988–), Lanarkshire Development Agency until 2000, Interchase Ltd, Bowmere Properties Ltd, New Lanarkshire Ltd, House Sales (Motherwell) Ltd, Langvale Ltd, Motherwell Coll Bd, UXL Ltd, Mansewood Investments Ltd, Mansewood Factors Ltd; dir: Motherwell Enterprise Development Co 1983, Scotland West Bd TSB plc 1985, Islay Developments Ltd, Clan F M Ltd, Fraser Tool Hire Ltd, Langvale Ltd, James Hepburn Ltd, Kingdom FM Ltd; chm Scottish Local Authorities Remuneration Ctee; hon pres: Motherwell United YMCA, Motherwell Branch St Andrew's Ambulance Assoc; hon slr Dalziel HS Meml Tst, memb Dalziel HS Bd 1990–, govr David Livingstone Meml Tst 1988–; *Recreations* golf, music; *Style—* Ian Livingstone, Esq, CBE; ✉ Roath Park, 223 Manse Road, Motherwell ML1 2PY (tel 01698 253750, fax 01698 276730)

LIVINGSTONE, Jack; s of Harry Livingstone, of Southport, and Ruth, *née* Kaye; *b* 27 April 1934; *Educ* Ackworth Sch, KCL; *m* 5 June 1963, Janice Vivienne, da of Lt Sidney Jeffrey Manson, of Salford, Manchester; 1 s (Terence b 1966), 2 da (Joanna b 1964 d 1978, Vanessa b 1970); *Career* sr aircraftsman 2 Tactical Force RAF, served Germany; hon life pres London Scottish Bank plc 2000–; chm Record Painting Ltd, vice-pres Manchester Balfour Tst, tstee Jerusalem Fndn, chm Marketing Ctee Christie Hosp Appeal; *Recreations* tennis, bridge; *Style—* Jack Livingstone, Esq

LIVINGSTONE, Ken; s of Robert Moffat Livingstone, and Ethel Ada Livingstone; *b* 17 June 1945; *Educ* Tulse Hill Comprehensive Sch, Philippa Fawcett Coll of Educn; *Career* cncllr (Lab) GLC: Norwood 1973–77, Hackney North 1977–81, Paddington 1981–86; leader GLC 1981–86; memb Lab NEC 1987–89 and 1997–98; MP Brent E: Lab 1987–2000, Ind 2000–01; Mayor of London: Ind 2000–04, Lab 2004–; memb Select Ctee on NI 1997–99; fell Zoological Soc of London (memb Cncl 1994–2000, vice-pres 1996–98); *Books* If Voting Changed Anything They'd Abolish It (1987), Livingstone's Labour (1989); *Recreations* thinking while gardening, cinema, science fiction; *Style—* Ken Livingstone; ✉ City Hall, The Queen's Walk, London SE1 2AA (tel 020 7983 4000)

LIVINGSTONE, Marco Eduardo; s of Leon Livingstone, of London, and Alicia, *née* Arce Fernández; *b* 17 March 1952; *Educ* Univ of Toronto (BA), Courtauld Inst of Art (MA); *Career* asst keeper of Br art Walker Art Gallery Liverpool 1976–82, dep dir MOMA Oxford 1982–86, area ed 20th century The Dictionary of Art 1986–91 (dep ed 19th and 20th centuries 1987–91), UK advsr to Art Life Ltd Tokyo 1989–98; freelance writer, ed and exhbn organiser; exhbns organised incl: Patrick Caulfield retrospective (Liverpool and London) 1981, Jim Dine retrospective (Japanese tour) 1990–91, Pop Art (Royal Acad of Arts, touring Cologne, Madrid and Montreal) 1991, Tom Wesselmann retrospective (Japanese tour) 1993, Hockney in California (Japanese tour) 1994, Duane Hanson retrospective (Montreal Museum of Fine Arts) 1994, Jim Dine: The Body and its Metaphors (Japanese tour) 1996, The Pop '60s: Transatlantic Crossing (Lisbon) 1997, George Segal retrospective (Montreal Museum of Fine Arts, touring Washington, New York, Miami) 1997–98, R B Kitaj retrospective (Oslo, Madrid, Vienna, Hanover) 1998, Duane Michals: Words and Images (Montreal Museum of Fine Arts and Nat Gallery of Canada) 1998–99, David Hockney: Egyptian Journeys (Cairo) 2002, Pop Art UK: British Pop Art 1956–1972 (Modena) 2004, R B Kitaj: Portrait of a Hispanist (Bilbao) 2004, British Pop (Bilbao) 2005–06; memb: Soc of Authors 1980, Association Internationale des Critiques d'Art (AICA) 1992; *Publications* Sheer Magic by Allen Jones (1979), David Hockney (1981, 3 edn 1996), Duane Michals (1985), R B Kitaj (1985, 2 edn 1992), David Hockney: Faces (1987), Pop Art (1990), Tim Head (1993), Jim Dine: Flowers and Plants (1994), Allen Jones Prints (1995), The Essential Duane Michals (1997), George Segal (1997), Jim Dine: The Alchemy of Images (1998), Patrick Caulfield (contrib, 1999), David Hockney: Space and Line (1999), Art: The Critics' Choice (contrib, 1999), Encounters: New Art from Old (contrib, 2000), D'Après L'Antigue (contrib, 2000), Enrico Baj (contrib, 2001), Kienholz Tableau Drawings (2001), Callum Innes: Exposed Paintings (2001), Langlands & Bell: Language of Places (2002), Maurice Cockrill (co-author, 2002), Clive Barker · Sculpture (co-author, 2002), Blast to Freeze · British Art in the 20th Century (contrib, 2002–03), Jim Dine: The Photographs So Far (contrib, 2003), David Hockney's Portraits and People (co-author, 2003), Red Grooms (co-author, 2004), Patrick Caulfield: Paintings (2005), David Hockney Portraits (contrib, 2006), Richard Woods (co-author, 2006), Tony Bevan (contrib, 2006), Gilbert & George: Major Exhibition (contrib, 2007); *Style—* Marco Livingstone, Esq; ✉ 36 St George's Avenue, London N7 0HD (tel 020 7607 0282, fax 020 7607 8694, e-mail marcolivingstone@aol.com)

LIVINGSTONE-LEARMONTH, John Christian; s of Lt-Col Lennox John Livingstone-Learmonth, DSO, MC (d 1988), and Nancy Winifred, *née* Wooler (d 1989); *b* 30 October 1950; *Educ* Eton, Univ of York (BA); *m* 13 Dec 1986, (Elizabeth) Fiona, da of Arthur Ivor Stewart-Liberty, MC (d 1990), of The Lee, Bucks; 1 s (Edward Miles Christian b 22 Sept 1988), 1 da (Marina Francesca b 4 May 1991); *Career* SA mktg offr James Buchanan and Co 1975–83, sr ptnr Livingstone Communication 1987–, dir City Decisions Ltd 1990–95; distinguished visitor to Miami; memb Circle of Wine Writers; Citoyen d'Honneur of Châteauneuf-du-Pape, Chevalier de l'Ordre du Mérite Agricole; *Books* The Wines of the Rhône (1978, 3 edn 1992), The Wines of the Northern Rhône (2005), Louis Roederer International Wine Book of the Year (2006); *Recreations* the turf, vegetables, fishing, wine tasting and writing; *Clubs* Turf, Irish; *Style—* John Livingstone-Learmonth, Esq; ✉ Livingstone Communication (tel 01424 844854, fax 01424 846970)

LIVSEY OF TALGARTH, Baron (Life Peer UK 2001), of Talgarth in the County of Powys; Richard Arthur Lloyd Livsey; CBE (1992), DL (2005); s of Arthur Norman Livsey, and Lilian Maisie, *née* James; *b* 2 May 1935; *Educ* Talgarth Sch, Bedales, Seale Hayne Agric Coll Newton Abbot (NDA), Univ of Reading (MSc); *m* 1964, Irene Martin Earsman; 2 s (Hon David, Hon Douglas), 1 da (Hon Jennifer); *Career* Nat Serv cmmnd RASC; ICI Ltd: asst Kirkcudbrightshire Dairy Farm 1961–62, commercial rep 1962–64, agric devpt offr Northumberland 1964–67; farm mangr Blair Drummond Estate Perthshire 1967–71, sr lectr in farm mgmnt Welsh Agric Coll Aberystwyth 1971–85, sheep farmer Llanon 1981–85; Parly candidate (Lib): Perth and E Perthshire 1970, Pembroke 1979, Brecon and Radnor 1983; MP (Lib then Lib Dem): Brecon and Radnor 1985–92, Brecon and Radnorshire 1997–2001; Lib agric spokesman 1985–87, Alliance countryside spokesman 1987, Lib Dem Water Bill spokesman 1988–90, Lib Dem Welsh affrs spokesman 1988–92 and 1997–2001, leader Welsh Lib Dems 1988–92 and 1997–2001; House of Lords: Lib Dem front bench rural affrs and agric spokesman 2001–06, Lib Dem front bench Welsh affrs spokesman 2002–, memb European Sub-Ctee D on Environment and Rural Affrs 2004–06; pres: Brecon and Dist Disabled Club 1987, Wales European Movement 2003–05, Brecknock Fedn of Young Farmers' Clubs 2003–05, Talgarth Cricket Club, Cor Meibion Ystradgynlais; chm Brecon Jazz Festival 1993–96, memb Talgarth Male Voice Choir 1993; assoc BVA; *Recreations* angling, cricket, drama, music, Welsh rugby; *Style—* Lord Livsey of Talgarth, CBE, DL

LLAMBIAS, Douglas Ernest John; s of Ernest Llambias (d 1943), and Hilda, *née* Peat (d 1984); *b* 13 November 1943; *Educ* De La Salle Sch London; *m* 24 June 1984, Renée; 1 s by previous m (Damian Heathcote Jotham b 1971); *Career* CA; Arthur Andersen 1968–70, chm The Business Exchange LLP 1984–, chm BEXBES plc; memb Cncl ICAEW 1981–2004; *Recreations* badminton, squash, wines; *Clubs* Reform, RAC; *Style—* Douglas Llambias, Esq; ✉ The Business Exchange LLP, 21 John Adam Street, London WC2N 6JG (tel 020 7930 8965, fax 020 7930 8437, e-mail info@business-exchange-plc.co.uk)

LLEWELLYN, Carl; s of Eryl D Llewellyn, of Hundleton, Pembroke, and Jean, *née* Harries; *b* 29 July 1965; *Educ* Pembroke Secdy Sch; *Career* national hunt jockey; turned professional 1986, winner Apprentice Championship setting record of 41 winners, rode Grand National winner Party Politics 1992, rode Grand National winner Earth Summit 1998; rep Br Jump Jockeys Team: Australia 1987 (series winners), Russia 1992; Pacemaker Jockey of the Year 1986–87; *Recreations* golf, water skiing, squash; *Style—* Carl Llewellyn, Esq; ✉ tel 01488 73311, mobile 07836 783223

LLEWELLYN, Sir David St Vincent (Dai); 4 Bt (UK 1922), of Bwllfa, Aberdare, Glamorgan; s of Sir Harry Llewellyn, 3 Bt (d 1999); *b* 2 April 1946; *Educ* Eton, Aix-en-Provence; *m* 15 March 1980 (m dis 1987), Vanessa Mary Theresa, da of Lt Cdr Theodore Bernard Peregrine Hubbard, and Lady Miriam Hubbard; 2 da (Olivia b 7 Oct 1980, Arabella b 1 Nov 1983); *Heir* bro, Roddy Llewellyn, Esq, *qv*; *Career* writer, broadcaster and impresario; Br Nat Export Cncl mission USA 1970, vice-pres Nat Dog Owners' Assoc 1982, ldr Yugoslavian relief convoy 1992, club dir Dorchester Park Lane 1994–95, presenter TV series The Lunch Club 1997; Chevalier de l'Ordre des Coteaux de

Champagne 1993, Knight of the Military and Hospitaller Order of St Lazarus of Jerusalem (KLJ) 2000 (CLJ 1995); *Recreations* equestrian sports and wildlife conversation; *Style—* Sir Dai Llewellyn, Bt; ✉ Studio Two, 2 Lansdowne Row, London W1J 6HL (tel 020 7413 9533, fax 020 7493 4935)

LLEWELLYN, Prof David Thomas; s of Alfred George Llewellyn (d 1990), of Gillingham, Dorset, and Elsie Elizabeth, *née* Frith; *b* 3 March 1943; *Educ* William Ellis GS, LSE (BSc); *m* 19 Sept 1970, Wendy Elizabeth, da of Henry Cecil James, MM (d 1973); 2 s (Mark b 15 Aug 1972, Rhys b 18 Dec 1978); *Career* economist: Unilever NV Rotterdam 1964–65, HM Treasy 1965–68; lectr Univ of Nottingham 1968–73, economist IMF Washington 1973–76, prof of money and banking Loughborough Univ 1976– (head Dept of Economics 1980–90); chm Loughborough Univ Banking Centre 1985–; visiting prof: London Business Sch 1997–98, Swiss Banking Sch Zurich 2003, Cass Business Sch London 2003–, IESE Business Sch Madrid, Swiss Finance Inst 2006–, Vienna Univ of Economics and Business; dir London Bd Halifax Building Soc 1986–93, memb Academic Bd Sundridge Park Mgmnt Centre 1990–95, public interest dir Personal Investment Authy 1994–2000; memb Bd PIA Ombudsman Bureau; SUERF (Société Universitaire Européene Recheches Financières): memb Cncl 1997–, pres 2000–; conslt economist: Harlow Butler Ueda 1989–99, Garban Intercapital 1999–; conslt Reserve Bank of South Africa 2000–04; memb: Exec Bd Euro Fin Mgmnt Assoc, Financial Services Panel DTI Technol Foresight Prog 1992–2000; Task Force on Competition in South African Banking Industry 2003–04, Expert Panel on Banking Bank Indonesia, Consultative Gp on Governance in Supervisory Authorities IMF Washington; former conslt The World Bank, OECD, regulatory authorities, building socs and banks; occasional memb Bank of England Panel of Academic Conslts; memb Int Advsy Bd: European Banking Report Italian Bankers' Assoc 1994–, Productivity Mgmnt Int 1995–2000, NCR Financial Solutions Gp 1996–2000; memb Editorial Bd: Banking World 1978–84, Jl of Retail Banking Int (NY), Jl of Fin Regulation and Compliance 2001–; Jl of Bank Regulation, Banking and Technol; managing ed Chartered Inst of Bankers Occasional Res Papers Series 1978–82; Bertil Danielsson Fndn visiting scholar Stockholm and Gothenburg Schs of Economics 1992; special advsr Jt Parly Ctee on the Fin Markets and Services Bill 1999; FCIB, FRSA; *Books* International Financial Integration (1980), Framework of UK Monetary Policy (1983), Regulation of Financial Institutions (1986), Evolution of British Financial System (1985), Reflections on Money (1990), Recent Developments in International Monetary Economics (1990), Surveys in Monetary Economics Vols 1 & 2 (with C Green, 1991), Competition or Credit Controls (Hobart Paper, 1991), The Economics of Mutuality and the Future of Building Societies (1997), Financial Regulation: Why, How and Where Now? (with Charles Goodhart, 1998), The New Economics of Banking (1999), Competitive Strategies in the New Economics of Retail Financial Services; *Recreations* boating, cooking, DIY, gardening, travel; *Style—* Prof David T Llewellyn; ✉ 8 Landmere Lane, Ruddington, Nottingham NG11 6ND (tel 0115 921 6071); Department of Economics, Loughborough University, Loughborough, Leicestershire LE11 3TU (tel 01509 222700, e-mail d.t.llewellyn@lboro.ac.uk); Villa 10, Les Pins, Les Hauts du Golf, 760 Chemin de la Tire, Mougins, France

LLEWELLYN, Dr (Graeme Ernest) John; s of Sir (Frederick) John Llewellyn (d 1988), and Joyce, *née* Barrett (d 2001); *b* 13 September 1944; *Educ* Christchurch Boys' HS NZ, Scots' Coll Wellington NZ, Victoria Univ of Wellington NZ (BA), Univ of Oxford (DPhil); *m* 8 Dec 1990, Ruth, *née* Doncaster; 2 da, 3 s; *Career* researcher First National Bank of Boston 1966–67, research offr Dept of Applied Economics Univ of Cambridge 1970–74, fell St John's Coll Cambridge 1972–77, asst dir of research Faculty of Economics Univ of Cambridge 1974–77; OECD: head Economic Prospects Div 1978–86, dep dir Directorate for Social Affrs Manpower and Educn 1986–89, head Sec-Gen's Private Office 1989–94; Lehman Brothers: chief economist Europe and md 1995–96, global chief economist and md 1996–2006, sr economic policy advsr and md 2006–; sec Degree Ctee Faculty of Economics Univ of Cambridge 1974–77, memb Bd of Graduate Studies Univ of Cambridge 1976–77, dir of studies St John's Coll Cambridge 1976–77; temp dir of research Centro de Investigacion y Docencia Economicas Mexico City 1976–77, lectr Univ of Southern California Sch of Int Rels London 1976–77; memb Editorial Bd: OECD Economic Studies 1983–89, Economic Modelling 1983–93; memb: Conseil Scientifique Fondation Nationale des Sciences Politiques Paris 1986–94 (pt/t lectr in contemporary economic policy 1990–94), Comité Consultatif Observatoire Français des Conjonctures Economiques 1987–94; currently memb: Pres of European Cmmn's Gp of Economic Policy Analysis, Cncl Soc of Business Economists, Cncl RIIA; tstee FIA Fndn for the Automobile and Soc; hon fell Univ of South Bank 1997; *Publications* Economic Forecasting and Policy - The International Dimension (with S J Potter and L W Samuelson, 1985), Economic Policies for the 1990s (ed with S J Potter, 1991), The Business of Change (2007); author of numerous articles in economic jls and the press; *Recreations* photography, music, writing; *Style—* Dr John Llewellyn; ✉ 25 Bank Street, London E14 5LE (tel 020 7102 2272, fax 020 7102 2603)

LLEWELLYN, Laurence Richard; s of Illtyd Raymond Llewellyn (d 1991), of Slough, Berks, and Marjorie Patricia, *née* Weaver (d 1991); *b* 9 February 1948, Slough, Berks; *Educ* Abingdon Sch, UMIST (BSc), Cranfield Sch of Mgmnt (MBA); *m* 30 March 1970 (m dis 2007), Margaret, *née* Henry; 1 s (Dr Christopher Ian Henry Llewellyn b 14 Oct 1975), 1 da (Clare Heidi Llewellyn b 29 Oct 1978); *Career* Ford Motor Co 1968–72; Citibank NA: various sr positions in UK, Europe and Asia 1973–98, head of wealth mgmnt business Western Europe 1998–2002; memb Bd F&C Mgmnt Ltd 2002–04, exec dir F&C Mgmnt plc 2004–05; vice-chm of govrs Hampton Sch; FCMA; *Recreations* cycling, swimming, theatre, playing the piano and guitar, composing; *Style—* Laurence Llewellyn, Esq; ✉ 52A Brook Green, London W6 7BJ (tel 020 7603 6245)

LLEWELLYN, Rev (Richard) Morgan; CB (1992), OBE (1979, MBE 1976), DL (Powys 2006); s of Griffith Robert Poynz Llewellyn (d 1972), of Baglan Hall, Abergavenny, Gwent, and Bridget Margaret Lester, *née* Karslake (d 1980); *b* 22 August 1937; *Educ* Haileybury, Salisbury and Wells Theological Coll (DipCThandM); *m* 24 Oct 1964, (Elizabeth) Polly Lamond, da of Lt-Col Francis Theodore Sobey, CBE, MC (d 1973), of Ilkley, W Yorks; 3 s (Huw b 1967, Glyn b 1971, Robert b 1979), 2 da (Sally b 1967 d 1977, Kitty b 1981); *Career* cmmnd Royal Welch Fusiliers 1956, active serv in Malaya 1957 and Cyprus 1958–59, instr Army Outward Bound Sch 1962–63, Staff Coll 1970, mil asst to Chief of Gen Staff 1971–72, Bde Maj 39 Inf Bde 1974–76, cmd 1 Bn Royal Welch Fusiliers 1976–79, jr directing staff RCDS 1979–81, cmd Gurkha Field Force Hong Kong 1981–84, Dir Army Staff Duties MOD 1985–87, GOC Wales 1987–90, Chief of Staff HQ UK Land Forces 1990–91, ret 1991 with rank of Maj Gen; Col: Gurkha Tport Regt 1984–92, Queen's Own Gurkha Tport Regt 1992–93, The Royal Welch Fusiliers 1990–97; ordained: deacon 1993, priest 1994; curate Brecon with Battle and Llanddew and minor canon of Brecon Cathedral 1993–95, chaplain Christ Coll Brecon 1995–2001, dir Christ Coll Brecon Fndn 2001–05; vice-pres Soldiers' and Airmen's Scripture Readers Assoc; chm Gurkha Welfare Tst in Wales; Welsh vice-patron War Memls Tst; hon chaplain Univ of Wales OTC; FCMI (FIMgt); *Recreations* reading, hill walking, painting; *Clubs* Army and Navy, Cardiff and County; *Style—* The Rev R M Llewellyn, CB, OBE, DL; ✉ Llangattock Court, Llangattock, Crickhowell, Powys NP8 1PH

LLEWELLYN, Roderic Victor (Roddy); 2 s of Sir Harry Llewellyn, 3 Bt, CBE (d 1999), and Hon Christine Saumarez (d 1998); bro, and hp of Sir David Llewellyn, 4 Bt, *qv*; *b* 9 October 1947; *Educ* Shrewsbury, Aix-en-Provence, Merrist Wood Agric Coll (Nat Cert of Horticulture, Surrey Co Cert in Landscape Construction); *m* 1981, Tatiana, da of Paul Soskin (d 1975), film producer; 3 da (Alexandra b 1982, Natasha b 1984, Rose-Anna b 1987); *Career* landscape designer, author, lectr, journalist and presenter; gardening corr: (Daily) Star 1981–86, Oracle 1982–83, Mail On Sunday 1987–99; gardening presenter TV-am 1984; co-presenter: The Gardening Roadshow (LWT) 1992 and 1993, Grass Roots (Meridian TV) 1993–; presenter Roddy Llewellyn's Garden Guide (Granada Sky Breeze) 1997–99, gardening presenter This Morning (ITV) 1998–2000, Gardens of Wales (HTV) 2001 and 2002, co-presenter Turf Wars (Channel 4) 2004, co-presenter Best of Britain (Channel 4) 2004; regular contrib: Country Life; patron Southport Flower Show 1997–; assoc memb Inst of Horticulture (AIHort) 1995; *Books* Town Gardens (1981), Beautiful Backyards (1985), Water Gardens (1987), Elegance and Eccentricity (1989), Growing Gifts (1992), I Grew It Myself (1993), Roddy Llewellyn's Gardening Year (1997); *Recreations* walking, jig-saw puzzles; *Style—* Roderic Llewellyn, Esq; ✉ Asterleigh Farm, Kiddington, Woodstock OX20 1BQ (tel 01608 644915, e-mail roddy.llewellyn@virgin.net, website www.roddyllewellyn.com)

LLEWELLYN, Samson Evan (Sam); s of Bishop William Somers Llewellyn, and Innis Mary, *née* Dorrien Smith; *b* 2 August 1948; *Educ* Eton, St Catherine's Coll Oxford (MA); *m* 1975, Karen Margaret Wallace; 2 s (William David b 1978, Martin Stephen b 1980); *Career* author; bass guitarist Spread Eagle 1971–72, ed Pan/Picador 1973–76, sr ed McClelland & Stewart Toronto Canada 1976–79; columnist Broad Sheep Practical Boat Owner; *Books* Hell Bay (1980), The Worst Journey in the Midlands (1983), Dead Reckoning (1987), Great Circle (1987), Blood Orange (1988), Death Roll (1989), Pig in the Middle (1989), Deadeye (1990), Blood Knot (1991), Riptide (1992), Clawhammer (1993), Maelstrom (1994), The Rope School (1994), The Magic Boathouse (1994), The Iron Hotel (1996), Storm Force from Navarone (1996), The Polecat Café (1997), The Shadow in the Sands (1998), Thunderbolt from Navarone (1998), Wonderdog (1999), The Sea Garden (2000), The Malpas Legacy (2001), Nelson (2004), Little Darlings (2004), The Beaufort Scale (2004), Emperor Smith: The man who built Scilly (2005), Bad, Bad Darlings (2005), The Return of Death Eric (2005), Desperado Darlings (2006), The Haunting of Death Eric (2006), Eye of the Cannon (2007); *Recreations* sailing, gardening, accompanying Mrs Llewellyn on the guitar and banjo; *Clubs* Cruising Assoc, Hebridean Open Boat Cruising, The Acad; *Style—* Sam Llewellyn, Esq; ✉ c/o Araminta Whitley, 14 Vernon Street, London W14 0RJ (tel 020 7471 7900); website www.samllewellyn.com

LLEWELLYN, Timothy Charles David (Tim); s of Charles Gordon Llewellyn (d 1940), of Cardiff, and Betty Ella, *née* Field; *b* 6 June 1940; *Educ* XIV Sch Bristol, Monkton Combe Sch; *m* Feb 1964 (m dis 1972), Geraldine, *née* McCallan; 1 s (Alun Brendan b 2 April 1965); 1 step da (Maccabee Szalwinska b 1978); *Career* reporter: Western Daily Press Bristol 1958–59, Barrie Examiner Barrie 1959–60, Toronto Telegram 1960–61; sub-ed: South Wales Echo Cardiff and Western Daily Press Bristol 1961, Press Assoc 1962–64, Globe and Mail 1964–66, Daily Sketch 1966; asst prodn team (Business Section) Sunday Times 1966, on staff prodn Times Business News 1967–71; BBC: chief sub/prodr 1971–73, newsroom 1973–76, corr Middle East 1976–80 and 1987–92 (East Africa 1980–82, foreign corr 1982–87); freelance 1992–; memb: RUSI, SOAS; *Recreations* permanent sloth punctuated by travel and desultory reading when unavoidable, talking; *Clubs* Travellers; *Style—* Tim Llewellyn, Esq

LLEWELLYN, Timothy David; OBE (2007); s of late Graham David Llewellyn, and late Dorothy Mary Driver; *b* 30 May 1947; *Educ* St Dunstan's Coll, Magdalene Coll Cambridge; *m* 1, 8 Aug 1970, Irene Sigrid Mercy, da of Sigurd Henriksen, of Copenhagen, Denmark; 1 s (Kristian b 1975); m 2, 9 Sept 1978, Elizabeth, da of late Prof Mason Hammond, of Cambridge, Mass, USA; *Career* Sotheby's: dir 1974–94, md 1984–91, chief exec 1991–92, dep chm Sotheby's Europe 1992–94; dir The Henry Moore Fndn 1994–2007; chm: The Friends of the Courtauld Inst 1986–2002, The Henry Moore Sculpture Tst 1994–99; memb: incl Villa I Tatti The Harvard Univ Center for Italian Renaissance Studies 1990–2005, Bd The Courtauld Inst 1991–2001, Visual Art Advsy Ctee British Cncl 1995–2007, Cncl The Walpole Soc 1995–99, Cncl The Br Sch at Rome 2000–; Miny of Culture and Fine Arts of the People's Republic of Poland Order of Cultural Merit 1986; tstee: Elgar Fndn 1991–99, Gilbert Collection Tst 1998–2001, Metropole Arts Tst 2004–, The Burlington Magazine 2006– (also dir); fell the Ateneo Veneto Venice; Hon DLitt Southampton Solent Univ; *Recreations* music, travel; *Clubs* Brooks's; *Style—* Timothy D Llewellyn, Esq, OBE; ✉ 3 Cranley Mansion, 160 Gloucester Road, London SW7 4QF (tel 020 7373 2333, fax 020 7244 0126)

LLEWELLYN SMITH, Prof Sir Christopher Hubert (Chris); kt (2001); s of John Clare Llewellyn Smith (d 1990), and Margaret Emily Frances, *née* Crawford; *b* 19 November 1942; *Educ* Wellington, New Coll Oxford (BA, DPhil); *m* 10 Sept 1966, Virginia, *née* Grey; 1 da (Julia Clare b 2 Nov 1968), 1 s (Caspar Michael b 24 Jan 1971); *Career* Royal Soc exchange fell Lebedev Inst Moscow 1967–68, fell Theoretical Studies Div CERN Geneva 1968–70, res assoc Stanford Linear Accelerator Centre (SLAC) Stanford 1970–72, staff memb Theoretical Studies Div CERN Geneva 1972–74; Univ of Oxford: fell St John's Coll 1974–98, lectr 1974–80, reader 1980–87, prof 1987–98, chm of physics 1987–92, hon fell 2000–; DG CERN Geneva (on leave of absence from Oxford) 1994–98, provost and pres UCL 1999–2002; dir UKAEA Culham Div 2003–; FRS 1984; *Style—* Prof Sir Chris Llewellyn Smith, FRS; ✉ UKAEA Culham Division, Culham Science Centre, Abingdon, Oxfordshire OX14 3DB (tel 01235 466531, fax 01235 466209, e-mail chris.llewellyn-smith@ukaea.org.uk)

LLEWELLYN-SMITH, Elizabeth Marion; CB (1986); da of John Clare Llewellyn Smith (d 1990), and Margaret Emily Frances, *née* Crawford; *b* 17 August 1934; *Educ* Christ's Hosp, Girton Coll Cambridge (BA, MA); *Career* govt serv Bd of Trade 1956, dep DG of Fair Trading 1982–87, dep sec DTI 1987–90; UK dir European Investment Bank 1987–90; princ St Hilda's Coll Oxford 1990–2001; memb: Cncl Consumers Assoc, Accountancy Investigation and Discipline Bd; hon fell: Girton Coll Cambridge, St Mary's Coll Durham, St Hilda's Coll Oxford; *Clubs* Univ Women's; *Style—* Miss Elizabeth Llewellyn-Smith, CB; ✉ Brook Cottage, Taston, near Chipping Norton, Oxfordshire OX7 3JL (tel 01608 811874, e-mail e.llewellynsmith@btopenworld.com)

LLEWELLYN SMITH, Sir Michael John; KCVO (1996), CMG (1989); s of John Clare Llewellyn Smith (d 1990), and Margaret Emily Frances, *née* Crawford; *b* 25 April 1939; *Educ* Wellington, New Coll Oxford (MA), St Antony's Coll Oxford (DPhil); *m* 8 April 1967, Colette, da of Georges Gaulier (d 1979), of France; 1 s (Stefan Gregory b 1970), 1 da (Sophie Alexandra b 1971); *Career* cultural attaché Moscow 1973–75, first sec Br Embassy Paris 1976–77, cnsllr Athens 1980–83, head of Soviet Dept FCO 1985–87, min Paris Embassy 1988–91; ambass: Poland 1991–96, Greece 1996–99; vice-pres Br Sch of Athens; memb Cncl London Univ 2000–; non-exec dir CCHBC SA 2000–; memb Cncl Anglo-Hellenic League; author; *Books* The Great Island - A Study of Crete (1965), Ionian Vision - Greece in Asia Minor 1919–22 (1983), Olympics in Athens 1896 - The invention of the Modern Olympic Games (2004), Athens - A Cultural and Literary History (2004); *Clubs* Oxford and Cambridge; *Style—* Sir Michael Llewellyn Smith, KCVO, CMG; ✉ c/o Oxford and Cambridge Club, 71 Pall Mall, London SW1Y 5HD (e-mail michael@mjls.demon.co.uk)

LLEWELYN, *see:* Venables-Llewelyn

LLEWELYN-EVANS, Adrian; s of Henry Llewelyn-Evans, and Beryl, *née* Morris; *b* 5 August 1953, Wales; *Educ* Glyn Sch Epsom, UC Durham (BA); *m* 1979, Catherine, *née* Forster; 3 s (Edward b 1986, Thomas b 1988, Hugh b 1988); *Career* slr Linklaters 1979–82, ptnr Burges Salmon 1984–; ADR conslt 2006–; memb: Law Soc, Int Bar Assoc, CEDR; *Recreations* fly fishing, gardening, hill walking; *Style—* Adrian Llewelyn-Evans, Esq;

✉ Burges Salmon LLP, Narrow Quay House, Narrow Quay, Bristol BS1 4AH (tel 0117 939 2272, fax 0117 902 4400, e-mail adrian.llewelyn-evans@burges-salmon.com)

LLOPIS RIVAS, Dr Ana María; da of Dr Álvaro Llopis, and Prof Regina Rivas; *b* 5 August 1950, Cumaná, Venezuala; *Educ* Univ Central de Venezuela, Univ of Maryland (Creole Fndn scholar), Princeton Univ, Univ of Calif at Berkeley (CONICIT scholar, MS, PhD); *m* Prof Félix Ynduráin Muñoz; 1 s (Jaime Yndurain b 27 Sept 1983); *Career* asst rising to sr brand mangr Procter & Gamble 1978–83, sales, distribution and mktg mangr Playtex Int and Spain 1983–87, assoc gen mangr Banesto 1988–91, assoc gen mangr Schweppes 1992–93, chm Baitol SA 1993–95, ceo OpenBank Banco Santander 1995–2000, exec chm and ceo Viaplus 2000–01, ceo then exec chm Razona 2001–03, exec vice-pres financial and insur markets Indra 2002–05, exec dep chm José Félix Llopis Fndn 2005– (fndr and vice-chm 2003–); non-exec dir: Reckitt Benckiser plc 1998–2005, Net TV 2000–01, British American Tobacco plc 2003–; memb: Advsy Bd Watson Wyatt 2000–03, Editorial Advsy Bd Expansion 2004–05, Working Gp Spanish New Corp Governance Code 2005–06; former exec vice-pres Financial Execs Spanish Assoc; *Recreations* art, writing short stories, printmaking; *Style*— Dr Ana Maria Llopis Rivas

LLOYD, Prof Alan Brian; s of Howard Brinley Lloyd (d 1989), of Tredegar, Gwent, and Doris Marian, *née* Walsh; *b* 24 September 1941; *Educ* Tredegar GS, UC Swansea (BA), The Queen's Coll Oxford (MA, DPhil); *m* 1, 14 Aug 1965, Caroline Barclay (d 1984), da of Hon Julius McDonald Greenfield, CMG, of Rondebosh, South Africa; 2 s (Julian b 14 Aug 1966, Duncan b 19 Nov 1967), 1 da (Katherine b 28 Feb 1970); *m* 2, 30 Nov 1985, Patricia Elizabeth, da of Patrick Cyril Ward, of Llandaff, Cardiff; *Career* Univ of Wales Swansea: asst lectr 1967, sr lectr 1977, reader 1983, prof 1988–, dean of arts 1991–93, pro-vice-chllr 1993–97; chm Ctee of Egypt Exploration Soc, sometime memb Cncl Hellenic Soc; FSA 1987; *Books* Herodotus Book II (1975–88); The Tomb of Hetepka (with G T Martin, 1978), Ancient Egypt (with B Trigger et al, 1983), Erodoto Le Storie Libro II (1989), Saqqara Tombs I and II (with W V Davies et al, 1984 and 1990); *Style*— Prof Alan Lloyd; ✉ Department of Classics, University of Wales Swansea, Singleton Park, Swansea SA2 8PP (tel 01792 295188, fax 01792 295739, e-mail a.b.lloyd@swansea.ac.uk)

LLOYD, Angus Selwyn; s of Selwyn Lloyd (d 1935), and Elaine Mary, *née* Beck (d 1992); *b* 12 July 1935; *Educ* Charterhouse; *m* 12 Jan 1961, Wanda Marian, da of Raymond Davidson, of Melrose, Scotland; 3 s (James, Christopher, Richard), 2 da (Virginia, Philippa); *Career* Nat Serv 1954–55, 2 Lt 15/19 King's Royal Hussars (serv Malaya 1955); dir: Nathaniel Lloyd & Co (printers) 1956–63, Oscar & Peter Johnson Ltd (fine art dealers) 1963–81, Sealproof Ltd (textile proofing) 1973–99; chm: Henri-Lloyd Ltd (textile mfrs) 1963–85, Craig-Lloyd Ltd (property) 1971–, Burlington Paintings Ltd (fine art/picture dealers) 1984–; tstee: Albany Piccadilly 1967–, Charterhouse in Southwark 1962–2003 (chm of tstees 1979–82); Freeman: City of London, Worshipful Co of Stationers and Newspaper Makers; *Recreations* golf; *Clubs* Royal St George's Golf (capt 1985), The Berkshire (capt 1978), Royal West Norfolk, Royal & Ancient, Swinley Forest, Walton Heath, PGA Nat (USA), Old Marsh Golf (USA), Hon Co of Edinburgh Golfers; *Style*— Angus Lloyd, Esq; ✉ East Court, Beech Avenue, Effingham, Surrey (tel 01372 458111); Burlington Paintings Ltd, 12 Burlington Gardens, London W1S 3EY (tel 020 7734 9984, fax 020 7494 3770, e-mail pictures@burlington.co.uk)

LLOYD, Anthony Joseph (Tony); MP; *b* 25 February 1950; *Educ* Univ of Nottingham, Manchester Business Sch; *m* Judith Lloyd; 1 s, 3 da; *Career* former university lectr; MP (Lab): Stretford 1983–97, Manchester C 1997–; oppn spokesman on: tport 1988–89, employment 1988–92, training (employment and educn) 1992–94, the environment and London 1994–97; min of state FCO 1997–99; cncllr Trafford Metropolitan Borough Cncl DC 1979–84; *Clubs* West Indian Sports & SocialStanley Street Working Men's Social Higher Openshaw; *Style*— Tony Lloyd, MP; ✉ House of Commons, London SW1A 0AA (tel 020 7219 3000)

LLOYD, Barbara Christine; da of Francis Kenneth Lloyd, of the Bahamas, and Herta Erica, *née* Menzler (d 1984); *b* 17 August 1946; *Educ* Putney HS for Girls, École Le Grand Verger Lausanne Switzerland, École Lemania Lausanne Switzerland, French Lycée London, Le Fleuron Florence Italy, Oskar Kokoschka Summer Acad Salzburg Austria; *Career* Marlborough Galleries 1967–90: shorthand typist and switchboard operator rising to registrar Marlborough Gallery NY, dir Marlborough Graphics 1979, subsequently dir Marlborough Fine Art London Ltd until 1990; responsible for exhibitions incl: all FIAC exhibitions Grand Palais Paris, Bill Brandt - A Retrospective, Brassai Secret Paris of the 30s, Irving Penn, Still Lives, Avigdor Arikha, Raymond Mason, Therese Oulton, Travelling Mason Retrospective; full time photographer 1990–; tstee: The Photographers Gallery London 1988– (chm 1994–97), Barry & Martins Tst London 1997–, Save A Child Tst Divyachaya, Bombay and Calcutta, Children of India 1995, Yorkshire Sculpture Park 1998–; memb Patrons of New Art Acquisitions Sub-Ctee Tate Gallery 1996–97; judge Kraszna-Krausz Fndn Photography Book Awards 1999 and 2000, advsr and judge Art in Prisons Koestler Award Tst; *Books* The Colours of India (1988), Reflections of Spain (1992), The Colours of Thailand (1997), Colours of Southern India (1999), Zent (2000), China: Travels Between the Yangtze and Yellow Rivers (2006); *Recreations* looking at and collecting art, opera, music, photography, reading, tennis, enjoying life; *Style*— Miss Barbara Lloyd; ✉ 23 Chepstow Villas, London W11 3DZ

LLOYD, Christopher; CVO; s of Rev Hamilton Lloyd, of Litchfield, Hants, and Suzanne, *née* Moon; *b* 30 June 1945; *Educ* Marlborough, ChCh Oxford (MA, MLitt); *m* 7 Oct 1967, (Christine Joan) Frances, da of George Henry Reginald Newth (d 1978), of Whitchurch, Hants; 4 s (Alexander b 1970, Benedict b 1972, Oliver b 1973, Rupert b 1980); *Career* asst curator pictures ChCh Oxford 1967–68; Dept of Western Art Ashmolean Museum Oxford: print room asst 1968, departmental asst 1969, asst keeper 1972–88; surveyor of the Queen's pictures 1988–2005; pres Nat Assoc of Decorative and Fine Arts Socs (NADFAS) 2007–; tstee: The Art Fund 2005–, Living Paintings Tst 2005–; govr Gainsborough's House 2005–; fell Villa I Tatti Florence (Harvard Univ) 1972–73, visiting res curator early Italian painting Art Inst Chicago 1980–81; FRSA; *Books* Art and Its Images (1975), A Catalogue of the Earlier Italian Paintings in the Ashmolean Museum (1977), Camille Pissarro (1980), A Catalogue of the Drawings by Camille Pissarro in the Ashmolean Museum (1980), The Journal of Maria Lady Callcott 1827–28 (1981), Camille Pissarro (1981), Dürer to Cézanne: Northern European Drawings from the Ashmolean Museum (1982), Impressionist Drawings from British Collections (1986), Catalogue of Old Master Drawings at Holkham Hall (1986), Studies on Camille Pissarro (ed and contrib, 1986), Woodner Collection Master Drawings (contrib, 1990), Henry VIII Images of A Tudor King (1990), The Queen's Pictures: Royal Collectors through the Centuries (1991), The Royal Collection. A Thematic Exploration of the Paintings in the Collection of Her Majesty The Queen (1992, revised paperback edn The Paintings in the Royal Collection (1999)), Italian Paintings before 1600 in the Art Institute of Chicago (1993), Gainsborough and Reynolds: Contrasts in Royal Patronage (1994), The Queen's Pictures. Old Masters from the Royal Collection (1994), Masterpieces in Little: Portrait Minitures from the Collection of Her Majesty Queen Elizabeth II (1996), The Quest for Albion: Monarchy and the Patronage of British Painting (1998), Arturo di Stefano (2001), Royal Treasures: A Golden Jubilee Celebration (contrib, 2002), Ceremony and Celebration: Coronation Day 1953 (2003), George III and Queen Charlotte: Patronage, Collecting and Court Taste (contrib, 2004), Enchanting the Eye: Dutch Paintings of the Golden Age (2004), Philip Morsberger: A Passion for Painting (2007); *Recreations* real tennis, theatre, music; *Clubs* Garrick; *Style*— Christopher Lloyd, Esq, CVO; ✉ Linstead Hall, Linstead Magna, Halesworth, Suffolk IP19 0QN (tel 01986 785519)

LLOYD, Prof David; s of Frederick Lewis Lloyd (d 1961), of Rhondda, Glam, and Annie Mary, *née* Wrentmore (d 1995); *b* 26 November 1940; *Educ* Porth Co GS for Boys, Univ of Sheffield (BSc, DSc), Univ of Wales Cardiff (PhD); *m* 5 April 1969, Margaret, da of Thomas John Jones, of Criccieth, Gwynedd; 2 s (Alun Lewis b 4 Aug 1970, Siôn Huw b 19 Sept 1973); *Career* MRC res fell Univ Coll of S Wales and Monmouth 1967–69 (ICI res fell 1964–67); Univ Coll Cardiff (now Cardiff Univ): lectr in microbiology 1969–76, sr lectr 1976, reader 1976–78, personal chair 1978–, head Dept of Microbiology 1982–87, established chair holder 1982–; memb: Biochemical Soc 1961, Ctee S Wales Cancer Res Campaign, Ctee of Welsh Scheme for Med and Social Sci Res, Soc of Gen Microbiology 1980; *Books* The Mitochondria of Micro-organisms (1974), The Cell Division Cycle: Temporal Organization and Control of Cellular Growth and Reproduction (1982), Ultradian Rhythms in Living Systems: A Fundamental Inquiry into Chronobiology and Psychobiology (1992), Flow Cytometry in Microbiology (1993), Microbiology Past, Present and Future (1994), Cellular and Metabolic Engineering (2002); author of more than 500 papers; *Recreations* music (especially opera); *Style*— Prof David Lloyd; ✉ Microbiology (BIOSI), Main Building, PO Box 915, Cardiff University, Cardiff CF10 3TL (tel 029 2087 4772, fax 029 2087 4305, e-mail lloydd@cf.ac.uk)

LLOYD, (William) David; s of Hywel Lloyd, and Jean, *née* Davies; *b* 7 August 1955, Oswestry, Shropshire; *Educ* Shrewsbury; *m* 12 May 1979, Jennifer, *née* Tait; 2 s (James, Allan), 1 da (Zoë); *Career* ceo and chm Lloyd's (Animal) Feeds Ltd; treas Inst of Orthopaedics; involved with Oswestry Hospital; FCA 1976; *Recreations* bibliophilia, music; *Style*— David Lloyd, Esq; ✉ Lloyd's (Animal) Feeds Limited, Morton, Oswestry, Shropshire SY10 8BH (tel 01691 830741, fax 01691 831582)

LLOYD, David Alan; s of Dennis Herbert Lloyd, of Leigh-on-Sea, Essex, and Doris, *née* Renshaw; *b* 3 January 1948; *Educ* Southend HS; *m* 14 Dec 1972, Veronica Jardine, da of Maj Cochran Kirkwood MacLennan, MBE (d 1984); 1 s (Scott b 1975), 2 da (Camilla b 1979, Laura b 1981); *Career* former tennis player; memb Br Davis Cup Team 1973–82 (former capt), men's doubles semi-finalist Wimbledon (with J Paish) 1973; capt Br Davis Cup Team 1995–2000; chm David Lloyd Leisure plc 1982–96 (national chain of 16 health and fitness clubs, stock market flotation 1993, sold to Whitbread plc 1995), md Next Generation Clubs 1998–; non-exec dir: Clubhaus 1996–98, M V Sports & Leisure (formerly Snakeboard) 1996–2002, GV Incentives; tennis commentator ITV, Sky TV and BBC Radio; launched Slater Tennis Fndn (sponsorship and coaching scheme for young players) with J Slater 1986; owner and chm Hull City FC 1997–2002; former Entrepreneur of the Year; Freeman City of London 1985; *Recreations* golf; *Clubs* National Hunt Racing, Queenwood Golf, Loch Lomond Golf; *Style*— David Lloyd, Esq

LLOYD, David Antony Thomas; s of Arthur Thomas Lloyd, of West Bridgford, Notts, and Betty Jean, *née* Newcombe; *b* 26 February 1961; *Educ* Rushcliffe Comp Sch Nottingham; *Career* with Lloyd's Bank 1979–80, various on- and off-air appts rising to presentation co-ordinator Radio Trent 1980–87, gen mangr Leicester Sound 1989–91 (dep prog controller 1987–89), prog controller Lincs FM 1991–95, head of programming and advtg Radio Authy 1995–98, md and gp programme dir Century Radio 106 1998–2000, md Galaxy Yorkshire 2000, regnl md Galaxy Yorkshire and Manchester 2002–06, md LBC Radio 2006–; presenter Saga 106.6 2003–; Sony Radio Award 1988; *Recreations* collie dogs, DIY; *Style*— David Lloyd, Esq

LLOYD, Dr David Rees (Dai); AM; s of Aneurin Rees Lloyd, and Dorothy Grace, *née* Jones, of Lampeter, Ceredigion; *b* 2 December 1956; *Educ* Lampeter Comp Sch, Welsh Nat Sch of Med Cardiff (MB BCh, MRCGP, DipTher); *m* 12 April 1982, Dr Catherine Jones, da of David Jones; 2 s (Aled b 19 July 1987, Gareth b 7 March 1991), 1 da (Anwen b 16 May 1989); *Career* jr hosp doctor 1980–84, NHS GP Swansea 1984–99; memb Nat Assembly for Wales (Plaid Cymru) South West Wales 1999–, shadow health sec for Wales 1999, shadow finance min for Wales 2003–; hon vice-pres Alzheimer's Disease Soc Swansea and Lliw Valley, hon vice-chair Swansea Neath Port Talbot Crossroads - Caring for Carers; lay preacher; FRCGP 2001; *Recreations* preaching, sport, music; *Style*— Dr Dai Lloyd, AM; ✉ National Assembly for Wales, Cardiff Bay, Cardiff CF99 1NA (tel 029 20898283); 39 St James Crescent, Uplands, Swansea SA1 6DR (tel 01792 646430)

LLOYD, Emily; da of Roger Lloyd Pack, *qv*, and Sheila Hughs, *née* Laden; *b* 29 September 1970; *Career* actress; *Theatre* Bella Kooling in Max Klapper - A Life In Pictures (Gate Theatre); *Films* credits incl: Wish You Were Here, Cookie, In Country, Chicago Joe and the Showgirl, Scorchers, A River Runs Through It, Under The Hula Moon, When Saturday Comes, Livers Ain't Cheap, Welcome to Sarajevo, Boogie Boy; *Awards* Nat Soc of Film Critics' Award, London Evening Standard Award, BAFTA nomination; *Recreations* singing, walking; *Clubs* Soho House, Groucho, Cobton; *Style*— Ms Emily Lloyd

LLOYD, Geoff; s of Geoff Lloyd Sr, and Rita Lloyd; *Educ* Ryles Park Co HS Macclesfield; *Career* writer and broadcaster; presenter Signal Radio Stockport 1992–96, prodn asst The Mrs Merton Show (Granada TV for BBC) 1995–96; presenter: Piccadilly Radio/Key 103 Manchester 1996–99, Virgin Radio 1999–, VH1/MTV Networks Europe 2001; columnist Manchester Evening News 1998–2001, head writer TFI Friday (Ginger Television for Channel 4) 2000, writer Comic Relief Red Nose Day 2001; EMAP Radio Award Best Daytime Show 1997 and 1998, Silver Award Best Daytime Music Programme Sony Radio Acad 1998, Gold Winner Music Programming Award Sony Radio Acad 2002; *Recreations* travel, gastronomy, all types of music including piano playing; *Clubs* Arts Theatre; *Style*— Geoff Lloyd, Esq; ✉ c/o Alex Armitage, Noel Gay Artists, 19 Denmark Street, London WC2 (tel 020 7836 3941)

LLOYD, Prof Sir Geoffrey Ernest Richard; kt (1997); s of William Ernest Lloyd (d 1975), of London, and Olive Irene Neville, *née* Solomon (d 1993); *b* 25 January 1933; *Educ* Charterhouse, King's Coll Cambridge (MA, PhD); *m* 14 Sept 1956, Janet Elizabeth, da of Edward Archibald Lloyd (d 1978), of Paris, France; 3 s (Adam b 1957, Matthew b 1962, Gwilym b 1963); *Career* Nat Serv Intelligence Corps 2 Lt/Actg Capt; Univ of Cambridge: fell King's Coll 1957–89, univ asst lectr in classics 1965–67, univ lectr 1967–74, sr reader 1974–83, prof of ancient philosophy and sci 1983–2000, master Darwin Coll 1989–2000; Bonsall prof Stanford Univ 1981, Sather prof of classics Univ of Calif Berkeley 1984; chm E Asian History of Sci Tst 1992–2002; hon fell: King's Coll Cambridge 1990, Darwin Coll Cambridge 2000; Hon LittD Univ of Athens 2003; hon foreign memb American Acad of Arts and Sciences 1995, memb Int Acad of the History of Sci 1997; fell Royal Anthropological Soc 1970; FBA 1983; *Books* Polarity and Analogy (1966), Aristotle The Growth and Structure of his Thought (1968), Early Greek Science (1970), Greek Science After Aristotle (1973), Hippocratic Writings (ed, 1978), Aristotle on Mind and the Senses (ed, 1978), Magic Reason and Experience (1979), Science Folklore and Ideology (1983), Science and Morality in Greco-Roman Antiquity (1985), The Revolutions of Wisdom (1987), Demystifying Mentalities (1990), Methods and Problems in Greek Science (1991), Adversaries & Authorities (1996), Aristotelian Explorations (1996), Greek Thought (ed, 2000), The Way and the Word (with N Sivin, 2002), The Ambitions of Curiosity (2002), In the Grip of Disease: Studies in the Greek Imagination (2003), Ancient Worlds, Modern Reflections (2004), The Delusions of Invulnerability (2005), Principles and Practices in Ancient Greek and Chinese Science (2006), Cognitive Variations: Reflections on the Unity and Diversity of the Human Mind (2007); *Recreations* travel; *Style*— Prof Sir Geoffrey Lloyd, FBA; ✉ 2 Prospect Row, Cambridge CB1 1DU (tel 01223 355970, e-mail gel20@hermes.cam.ac.uk)

LLOYD, Dr Geoffrey Gower; s of William Thomas Lloyd (d 1979), and Anne, *née* Davies (d 1993); *b* 7 June 1942; *Educ* Queen Elizabeth GS Carmarthen, Emmanuel Coll Cambridge

(MA, MB BChir, MD), Westminster Med Sch London, Inst of Psychiatry London (MPhil); *m* 19 Dec 1970, Prof Margaret Hazel Lloyd, da of Henry Doble Rose; 1 s, 2 da; *Career* sr registrar Maudsley Hosp London 1974–76 (registrar 1970–73), lectr Inst of Psychiatry and KCH Med Sch London 1976–79; conslt psychiatrist: Royal Infirmary Edinburgh 1979–85, Royal Free Hosp London 1985–2005 (chm Med Advsy Ctee 1996–98); med dir Grovelands Priory Hosp London 1997–2000; currently in private practice, visiting conslt psychiatrist Priory Hosp N London; ed Jl of Psychosomatic Res 1986–93; pres Section of Psychiatry RSM 1995–96; Freeman City of London, Liveryman Worshipful Soc of Apothecaries; FRCPEd 1981, FRCPsych 1984 (chm Liaison Psychiatry Faculty and memb Cncl 2000–), FRCP 1988; *Books* Textbook of General Hospital Psychiatry (1991), Handbook of Liaison Psychiatry (co-ed, 2007); *Recreations* golf, skiing, bridge, watching rugby football; *Clubs* Athenaeum, Hadley Wood Golf, Pennard Golf; *Style*— Dr Geoffrey Lloyd; ✉ 148 Harley Street, London W1N 1AH (tel 020 7935 1207); home: fax 020 8346 5090, e-mail g.glloyd@btinternet.com

LLOYD, Prof Howell Arnold; OBE (2004); s of John Lewis Lloyd (d 1971), of Llanelli, S Wales, and Elizabeth Mary, *née* Arnold (d 1986); *b* 15 November 1937; *Educ* Queen Elizabeth GS Carmarthen, UC Wales (BA), Jesus Coll Oxford (DPhil); *m* Sept 1962, Gaynor Ilid, da of Moses John Jones, of Mold, N Wales; 3 s (Jonathan, Timothy, Christian), 2 da (Susanna, Rebecca); *Career* fell Univ of Wales 1961–62; Univ of Hull: asst lectr in history 1962–64, lectr 1964–73, sr lectr 1973–82, reader 1982–85, prof 1985–, dean Sch of Humanities 1993–94, pro-vice-chllr then dep vice-chllr 1994–2003; fell commoner Churchill Coll Cambridge 1993 FRHistS 1975; *Books* The Gentry of South-West Wales, 1540–1640 (1968), The Relevance of History (with Gordon Connell-Smith, 1972), The Rouen Campaign, 1590–92 (1973), The State, France and the Sixteenth Century (1983), Charles Loyseau: A Treatise of Orders and Plain Dignities (ed, 1994), European Political Thought 1450–1700: Religion, Law and Philosophy (co-ed, 2007); *Recreations* walking, swimming; *Style*— Prof Howell A Lloyd, OBE; ✉ 23 Strathmore Avenue, Hull HU6 7HJ (tel 01482 851146); Department of History, The University of Hull, Hull HU6 7RX (tel 01482 465608)

LLOYD, His Hon Humphrey John; QC (1979); *Educ* Westminster, Trinity Coll Dublin (MA, LLB); *Career* called to the Bar Inner Temple 1963 (bencher 1985), recorder 1990–93, judge of Technology and Construction Ct (formerly official referee of the High Ct) 1993–2005; ed-in-chief: Building Law Reports 1977–93 (conslt ed 1993–98), The International Construction Law Review 1984–; conslt ed: Emden's Construction Law 1993–, Technol and Construction Law Reports 1999–; visiting prof Leeds Metropolitan Univ 2002–; chm ARB 2003–07 (memb 2001–07); hon professorial fell Queen Mary Coll 1987–, hon fell American Coll of Construction Lawyers 1997–, hon fell Canadian Coll of Construction Lawyers 2002–; *Style*— His Hon Humphrey LLoyd, QC; ✉ Atkin Chambers, 1 Atkin Building, Gray's Inn, London WC1R 5AT (tel 020 7404 0102, fax 020 7405 7456)

LLOYD, Dr (David) Huw Owen; s of Dr David Owen Lloyd (d 1984), of Denbigh, Clwyd, and Dilys Lloyd; *b* 14 April 1950; *Educ* Westminster, Gonville & Caius Coll Cambridge (MA, MB BChir), Guy's Hosp Med Sch London (DRCOG); *m* 1973, Dr Mary Eileen Pike, da of William Arthur George Pike; 3 da (Amy b 28 Dec 1976, Ceridwen b 4 April 1979, Bethan b 30 May 1986), 1 s (Dafydd b 17 July 1981); *Career* house surgn in orthopaedics Guy's Hosp 1974–75, house physician Beckenham Hosp 1975, SHO in psychiatry Joyce Green Hosp Dartford 1975, trainee GP Taunton 1976–79, princ GP Cadwgan Surgery Old Colwyn 1979–; chm Mental Health Task Gp RCGP, head Core Gp Wales Mental Health in Primary Care Network; memb N Wales Local Med Ctee; Faculty rep Welsh Cncl RCGP (former chm); memb PCC and churchwarden St Cynbryd's Llanddulas; memb BMA; FRCGP 1991 (MRCGP 1979); *Recreations* music, gardening, cooking, walking; *Style*— Dr Huw Lloyd; ✉ Cadwgan Surgery, 11 Bodelwyddan Avenue, Old Colwyn LL29 9NP (tel 01492 515787, fax 01492 513270, e-mail huw.lloyd@gp.w91007.wales.nhs.uk)

LLOYD, Illtyd Rhys; s of John Lloyd (d 1971), of Cwmafan, W Glamorgan, and Melvina Joyce, *née* Rees (d 1973); *b* 13 August 1929; *Educ* Port Talbot (Glan Afan) Co GS, UC Swansea (BSc, MSc, DipEd, DipStat); *m* 1955, Julia, da of David John Lewis (d 1951), of Pontyberem, Dyfed; 1 s (Steffan), 1 da (Catrin); *Career* RAF (Educn Branch) 1951–54, Flt Lt; second maths master Howard Sch for Boys Cardiff 1954–57, head Maths Dept Pembroke GS 1958–59, dep headmaster Howardian HS 1959–63; Her Majesty's Inspectorate: HM inspr 1964–71, staff inspr 1972–82, chief inspr (Wales) 1982–90; memb: Family Health Servs Authy S Glamorgan 1990–96 (vice-chm 1992–96), Ind Schs Tbnl 1990–, Cncl Baptist Union of Wales 1990– (hon treas 1992–2003, vice-pres 1995–96, pres 1996–97), Cncl Cardiff Baptist Theol Coll 1990–2003 (chm 1995–2003), Cncl CEWC (Cymru) 1990–2004 (treas 1962–63, chm 1997–2004), Churches Educn Network (England and Wales) 1990–93, Governing Body Swansea Inst of HE 1991–95, Cncl Univ of Wales Lampeter 1999–2004, Cncl FCC Wales 1992–2003, Churches Jt Educn Policy Ctee (England and Wales) 1993–2003, Educn Ctee FCC 1994–2001; Cytun (Churches Together in Wales): memb Fin Ctee 1991–2003, memb Cncl 1992–2003, vice-chm Fin Ctee 1995–99, chm Fin Ctee 1999–2003; sec Capel Gomer Welsh Baptist Church Swansea 1968–82, treas Tabernacl Welsh Baptist Church Cardiff 1990–; memb Fin Ctee CTBI 1994–2003; tstee: Churches Counselling Serv 1994–2000, Churches Tourism Network Wales 2001–05; chm: Governing Body Educn Resources Centre Univ of Aberystwyth 1992–2001, Mgmt Ctee Glyn Nest Residential Home 1992–2003, Mgmnt Ctee Bryn Llifon Residential Home 1999–2003; hon memb Gorsedd of Bards; hon fell Univ of Wales; *Publications* Geirfa Mathemateg (1956), Secondary Education in Wales 1965–85 (1991), Gwyr Y Gair (1993), Yr Hyn A Ymddiriedwyd I'n Gofal (1996); *Recreations* walking; *Style*— Illtyd Lloyd, Esq; ✉ 134 Lake Road East, Roath Park, Cardiff CF23 5NQ

LLOYD, Jeremy William; s of late Maj-Gen Richard Eyre Lloyd, CB, CBE, DSO, of Lymington, Hants, and Gillian, *née* Patterson; *b* 19 December 1942; *Educ* Eton, Pembroke Coll Cambridge (MA), Harvard Business Sch (MBA); *m* 2 Sept 1966, Britta Adrienne, da of Alfred de Schulthess, of Geneva, Switzerland; 3 da (Tara b 1971, Bettina b 1975, Antonia b 1985), 1 s (Adrian b 1979); *Career* called to the Bar Middle Temple; formerly with Hill Samuel & Co, subsid dir London & Co Securities Bank 1971–72, dir Manufacturers Hanover Property Services Ltd 1973–81, dir James Capel Bankers Ltd 1982–87, sr mangr HSBC Property Finance 1982–98, currently with JWL Property Finance Ltd; *Recreations* tennis, skiing; *Style*— Jeremy Lloyd, Esq; ✉ JWL Property Finance, 78 Ladbroke Road, London W11 3NU (tel 020 7727 8944, fax 020 7221 7788, e-mail jwl@lloydfamily.com)

LLOYD, Dr Jill Patricia; da of Peter Brown (d 1984), of Dublin, and Patricia Irene, *née* Tucker (d 2002); *b* 2 August 1955; *Educ* Courtauld Inst of Art (BA, PhD); *m* 1989, Michael Henry Peppiatt, *qv*, s of Edward George Peppiatt; 1 da (Clio Patricia b 16 Feb 1991), 1 s (Alexander Michael b 23 April 1994); *Career* lectr in art history UCL 1981–88, ed-in-chief Art International (Paris) 1990–94, freelance writer and curator 1994–; regular contrib to: The Burlington Magazine, the TLS; articles on early 20th century and contemporary art; essays in exhibitions catalogues incl: Lovis Corinth (Tate Gallery) 1997, Per Kirkeby (Tate Gallery) 1998, L'École de Londres (Musée Maillol Paris) 1998, Austrian Expressionism (Musée Maillol Paris) 2001, Max Beckman (Tate Modern) 2003; awarded Paul Getty postdoctoral scholarship 1989; memb Int Art Critics' Assoc, memb Soc of Authors; FRSA; awarded Order of Merit Germany; *Books* German Expressionism, Primitivism and Modernity (1991, Nat Art Book Prize 1992), Christian Schad and the Neue Sachlichkeit (2003), Kirchner the Dresden and Berlin Years (2003), Vincent van Gogh and Expressionism (2007), The Undiscovered Expressionist: A Life of Marie-Louise von Motesiczky (2007); *Clubs* RAC, Philadelphia Racquet; *Style*— Dr Jill Lloyd; ✉ 56 St James's Gardens, London W11 4RA (tel 020 7603 6249, e-mail j.lloyd@zen.co.uk)

LLOYD, John David; s of John Alfred Lloyd (d 1981), and Lilian Mary, *née* Griffiths; *b* 1 September 1944; *Educ* SW Essex Sch of Art, London Coll of Printing (DipAD); *m* 24 May 1975, Julia Patricia, da of Geoffrey Earnest Maughan; 1 s (Adam John b 17 June 1978), 2 da (Elinor Jane b 27 May 1980, Anna Carol b 20 Dec 1981); *Career* apprentice lithographic artist Edwin Jones & Sons (printers) 1960–64; Allied International Designers: graphic designer 1968–75, jt head of graphic design 1972–75, corp identity projects incl ABN Bank, Delta Group, Nicholas International and Meneba (Netherlands); Lloyd Northover (merged with Citigate Design 1993, Bass Yager LA 1997 and Marketplace Design 2006): fndr 1975, currently conslt, major corp identity projects incl Airport Express (Hong Kong), BAA, BNFL, British Biotech, Courtaulds, John Lewis, Land Tport Authy (Singapore), National Savings and Investments, Ordnance Survey, Partek (Finland), Taylor Woodrow, Tractebel (Belgium); visiting lectr in typographic design London Coll of Printing 1970–72, chm Br Design Export Gp 1983–85; external assessor and course advsr: Information Graphics Trent Poly 1984–89, Media Design and Production London Coll of Printing 1989–97, Graphic and Media Design London Coll of Communication 2005–; exhibitions of Lloyd Northover work: The Design Centre 1980–81, D&AD Assoc 1981–83, Art Directors' Club of NY 1988, London Coll of Communication 2005; frequent speaker on design and identity mgmnt at confs and seminars; Grand Prix in DBA/Mktg Design Effectiveness Awards for Courtaulds corp identity 1989, Int Gold Award for packaging design NY Art Dirs Club 1989; other design effectiveness awards: Amtico commercial interiors 1992, Partek corp identity 1998, JMC digital media 2001, National Savings and Investments digital media 2005; finalist: BRS corp identity 1994, AEA Technology corp identity 1995, Banner (HMSO) corp identity 1996; FCSD 1978, memb D&AD Assoc 1980, FRSA 2005; *Style*— John Lloyd, Esq; ✉ Mitre Farm House, Fordcombe Road, Fordcombe TN3 0RT (e-mail john@foggywells.f9.co.uk)

LLOYD, Jonathan Salusbury; *Career* md Grafton Books 1986–91, md Trade Div HarperCollins 1991–93, gp md Curtis Brown 1995– (dir 1994–95); pres Assoc of Authors' Agents 2000–02 (vice-pres 1997–99); *Clubs* Garrick, RAC, MCC; *Style*— Jonathan Lloyd, Esq; ✉ Curtis Brown Group Ltd, Haymarket House, 28/29 Haymarket, London SW1Y 4SP (tel 020 7393 4400, fax 020 7393 4401, e-mail jlloyd@curtisbrown.co.uk)

LLOYD, Mark William; s of Keneth Charles Lloyd, of Pontycymmer, Mid Glam, and Ivy, *née* Jones; *b* 5 February 1963; *Educ* Ynysawdre Comp Sch, Swansea Coll of Art, North Essex Sch of Art; *m* Joanna Caroline, da of Daniel James Peter Ryan; 1 da (Emily Elizabeth b 22 Oct 1989), 1 s (William Henry b 15 Nov 1993); *Career* designer Michael Peters & Partners 1984–87, designer rising to asst creative dir Coley Porter Bell and Partners 1987–91, design dir Smith & Milton Ltd 1991–2002, creative dir Lloyd Ferguson Hawkins 1992–2005, currently creative dir Webb Scarlett deVlam; *Style*— Mark Lloyd, Esq; ✉ Webb Scarlett deVlam, 12 Junction Mews, London W2 1PN (website www.webbscarlett.com)

LLOYD, Michael Raymond; *b* 20 August 1927; *Educ* Architectural Assoc Sch of Architecture (AADipl); *Career* chartered architect; dean and prof of architecture Faculty of Architecture Planning and Building Technol Kumasi Univ of Sci and Technol Ghana 1963–66; princ: Architectural Assoc Sch of Architecture 1966–71, Land Use Consultants London 1971–72; sr ptnr Sinar Associates Tunbridge Wells 1973–80; conslt head Hull Sch of Architecture UK 1974–77, sr lectr Development Planning Unit UCL 1976–79 (pt/t 1974–76), rector Bergen Sch of Architecture 1985–88; visiting prof and critic: Sch of Architecture Nat Univ of Costa Rica 1979–81, Sch of Architecture Univ of Baja Calif 1980, ITESO Guadalajara Mexico 1980; responsible for workshop Columbian Assoc of Schs of Architecture Bogotá 1980; tech offr ODA Br Govt (advsr on higher educn to Univs of Central America) 1979–81; Norconsult International AS Oslo Norway 1981–93: co-ordinating architect and planner Al Dora Township Baghdad for State Organization of Housing Government of Iraq 1981–83, exec conslt for physical planning Buildings Div 1981–86, project mangr Al Qassim Comprehensive Regnl Development Plan for Miny of Municipal and Rural Affrs Kingdom of Saudi Arabia 1983–86, sr conslt Development Gp on Third World Housing 1987–93; chm Habitat Norway 1993–94, prof of int studies Oslo Sch of Architecture 1993–96; extensive overseas work; author of: 14 papers on architectural and planning educn, 5 papers on housing, 7 reports for national govts, 2 books; external examiner Univs of: Edinburgh, Kuala Lumpur, Kumasi, Lund, Newcastle upon Tyne, Trondheim, Zaria, Oslo; external examiner Polytechnics of Central London and Hull; visiting lectr: Baghdad, Bogotá, Canterbury, Edinburgh, Enugu, Guadalajara, Guanajuato, Helsinki, Jyvaskyla, Kingston, Kuala Lumpur, Lund, Mexico City, Mexicali, Newcastle, Oslo, Oxford, Santiago, Trondheim, Valparaiso, Zaria, Zurich; extensive involvement with: International Union of Architects, UNESCO, Br Cncl; memb numerous professional ctees 1966–; memb Ct RCA 1968–80; RIBA; memb: Norwegian Architects' Assoc, AA; *Style*— Michael Lloyd, Esq

LLOYD, Sir Nicholas Markley; kt (1990); *b* 9 June 1942; *Educ* Bedford Modern Sch, St Edmund Hall Oxford (MA), Harvard Univ; *m* 1; 2 s, 1 da; m 2, 23 May 1979, Eve Pollard, *qv*; 1 s (Oliver b 6 Aug 1980); *Career* dep ed Sunday Mirror 1980–82; ed Sunday People 1982–84, dir Mirror Gp 1982–84, ed News of the World Jan 1984–85, dir News Gp Newspapers 1985–96, ed Daily Express 1986–96, presenter The Anne and Nick Show (with Anne Diamond) LBC 1996–99, chm Brown Lloyd James PR consultancy 1997–; *Style*— Sir Nicholas Lloyd; ✉ Brown Lloyd James, 25 Lower Belgrave Street, London SW1W 0NR (tel 020 7591 9610, fax 020 7591 9611)

LLOYD, Prof Noel Glynne; s of Joseph John Lloyd (d 1988), of Llanelli, and Gwenllian, *née* Davies; *b* 26 December 1946, Llanelli; *Educ* Llanelli GS, Queen's Coll Cambridge (MA, PhD); *m* 4 Aug 1970, Dilys June, *née* Edwards; 1 s (Hywel Glynne b 1976), 1 da (Carys Eleri b 1980); *Career* res fell St John's Coll Cambridge 1972–74; Univ of Wales Aberystwyth: lectr 1974–77, sr lectr 1977–81, reader 1981–88, prof 1988–, head Mathematics Dept 1991–97, dean of science 1994–97, pro-vice-chllr 1997–99, registrar and sec 1999–2004, vice-chllr and princ 2004–; memb Bd: Mid Wales TEC 1999–2001, QAA 2005–, Univs and Colls Employers' Assoc (UCEA) 2005–; memb Mid Wales Regnl Cttee ELW 2001–04; memb Governing Body Inst of Grassland and Environmental Research 2004–; chair Church and Soc Bd Presbyterian Church of Wales until 2004, sec Capel y Morfa Aberystwyth 1989–2004; ed London Mathematical Soc jl 1983–88, memb Editorial Bd Mathematical Proceedings, Cambridge Philosophical Soc; *Publications* Degree Theory (1978); numerous articles on nonlinear differential equations; *Recreations* music especially organ and piano; *Clubs* Oxford and Cambridge; *Style*— Prof Noel G Lloyd; ✉ Vice-Chancellor's Office, University of Wales Aberystwyth, King Street, Aberystwyth, Ceredigion SY23 2AX (tel 01970 622002, fax 01970 611446, e-mail ngl@aber.ac.uk)

LLOYD, Rt Hon Sir Peter Robert Cable; kt (1995), PC (1994); s of David Lloyd (d 1991), and his 1 w, late Stella Lloyd; *b* 12 November 1937; *Educ* Tonbridge, Pembroke Coll Cambridge (MA); *m* 1967, Hilary Creighton; 1 s, 1 da; *Career* former mktg mangr United Biscuits; chm Bow Gp 1972–73, ed Crossbow 1974–76; MP (Cons) Fareham 1979–2001 (Parly candidate (Cons) Nottingham W Feb and Oct 1974); House of Commons: sec Cons Parly Employment Ctee 1979–81, vice-chm Euro Affrs Ctee 1980–81, PPS to Adam Butler as min of state NI 1981–82, memb Select Ctee on Employment 1982, PPS to Sir Keith Joseph as sec of state for Educn and Sci 1983–84, asst govt whip 1984–86, a Lord Cmmr of the Treasy (Govt whip) 1986–88, Parly under sec DSS 1988–89, Parly under sec Home

Office 1989–92, min of state Home Office 1992–94, memb Select Ctee on Public Affrs 1996–97, vice-chm All-Pty Human Rights Gp 1996–2001, chm All-Pty Penal Affrs Gp 1997–2001, Parly advsr to the Police Fedn 1997–2001, memb House of Commons Cmmn 1998–2000, memb Treasy Select Ctee 1998–2000, chm Home Office Prisons Bds of Visitors Review Ctee 2000–01; vice-chm Br Section IPU 1994–99; chm NACRO Juvenile Remand Review Gp 1995–97, jt chm CAABU 1997–2001, pres Nat Cncl of Ind Monitoring Bds for Prisons 2003–; chm: New Bridge 1994–, Arab-Br Centre 2001–03, London English Sch 2007–; *Style*— The Rt Hon Sir Peter Lloyd; ✉ 32 Burgh Street, London N1 8HG (tel 020 7359 2871)

LLOYD, Phyllida Christian; da of Patrick John Lloyd, of West Anstey, Devon, and Margaret, *née* Douglas-Pennant; *b* 17 June 1957; *Educ* Lawnside Sch Malvern, Univ of Birmingham; *Career* theatre director; Arts Cncl trainee dir Wolsey Theatre Ipswich 1985 (prodns: Glengarry Glen Ross, Hard Times, Educating Rita), assoc dir Everyman Theatre Cheltenham 1986–87 (prodns incl Much Ado About Nothing, A Midsummer Night's Dream, Earth, Every Black Day, Woyzeck, Accidental Death of An Anarchist, Just Between Ourselves, and What the Butler Saw), assoc dir Bristol Old Vic 1989 (prodns: The Comedy of Errors, Dona Rosita The Spinster, A Streetcar Named Desire, Oliver Twist), Manchester Royal Exchange 1990–91 (prodns: The Winter's Tale, The School for Scandal, Death and the King's Horseman, Medea); RSC prodns: The Virtuoso 1991, Artists and Admirers 1992; Royal Court prodns incl: Six Degrees of Separation 1992, Hysteria 1993; RNT prodns: Pericles 1994, What the Butler Saw 1994, The Way of the World 1995, The Prime of Miss Jean Brodie 1998, The Duchess of Malfi 2003; Donmar Warehouse prodns: The Threepenny Opera 1994, Boston Marriage 2001, Mary Stuart 2005 (also Apollo Theatre); other credits incl: Dona Rosita (Almeida) 1997, Mamma Mia (worldwide), The Taming of the Shrew (Shakespeare's Globe), Wild East (Royal Court) 2005, The Fall of the House of Usher (Bregenz) 2006; operas: L'Étoile, La Bohème, Gloriana (ROH), Medea, Carmen, Albert Herring (Opera North), Macbeth (Opera National de Paris) 1999 (also ROH 2002), The Carmelites (ENO and WNO) 1999, The Handmaid's Tale (Royal Opera Copenhagen) 2000 and (also ENO 2003 and Canadian Opera Co Toronto 2004), Verdi's Requiem (ENO) 2000, The Rhinegold, The Valkyrie, Siegfried and Twilight of the Gods (ENO) 2004, Peter Grimes (Opera North) 2006; Gloriana - A Film 2000; Cameron Mackintosh visiting prof Univ of Oxford 2006; *Style*— Ms Phyllida Lloyd

LLOYD, Richard; *b* 6 June 1970, Cardiff; *Educ* Aberdare Boys' Comp Sch, Univ of Aberystwyth, Coll of Law Chester; *m* Aug 1997, Rosemary; 2 s, 1 da; *Career* slr specialising in planning law, regeneration and compulsory purchase; slr then sr slr Edwards Geldard 1994–98 (articled clerk 1992–94), ptnr Eversheds 2003– (slr then assoc 1998–2003); legal assoc RTPI; memb: Law Soc 1992 (memb Specialist Planning Panel), Compulsory Purchase Assoc; *Recreations* listening to and playing music, reading (historical, political, biographical), family life; *Style*— Richard Lloyd, Esq; ✉ Eversheds LLP, Eversheds House, 70 Great Bridgewater Street, Manchester (tel 07775 757827, e-mail richardlloyd@eversheds.com)

LLOYD, Sir Richard Ernest Butler; 2 Bt (UK 1960), of Rhu, Co Dunbarton; o s of Maj Sir (Ernest) Guy Richard Lloyd, 1 Bt, DSO, DL (d 1987), and Helen Kynaston, *née* Greg (d 1984); *b* 6 December 1928; *Educ* Wellington, Hertford Coll Oxford (MA); *m* 9 June 1955, Jennifer Susan Margaret, er da of Brig Ereld Boteler Wingfield Cardiff, CB, CBE (d 1988), of Easton Court, nr Ludlow, Shropshire; 3 s ((Richard) Timothy Butler b 12 April 1956, Simon Wingfield Butler b 26 July 1958, Henry Butler b 22 Feb 1965); *Heir* s, Timothy Lloyd; *Career* former Capt Black Watch, Nat Serv Malaya 1947–49; banker; exec then dir Glyn, Mills & Co 1952–70, chief exec Williams & Glyn's Bank 1970–78; Hill Samuel Bank Ltd: dep chm 1978–80 and 1991–95, dep chm and chief exec 1980–87, chm 1987–91; chm: Argos plc 1995–98, Vickers plc 1992–97; chm Business and Industry Advsy Ctee to OECD Paris 1998–99; former memb: Industrial Devpt Advsy Bd and Overseas Projects Bd of DTI, NEDC, Wilson Ctee on Financial Instns, Cncl CBI 1978–96, Advsy Bd RCDS 1987–95; pres British Heart Foundations 1996–2004 (former hon treas); govr Ditchley Fndn 1975–2005 (former hon treas); Freeman City of London 1964, Liveryman Worshipful Co of Mercers 1965, memb Guild of Freemen of Shrewsbury 1978; CIMgt, FCIB; *Recreations* fly fishing, gardening, walking; *Clubs* Boodle's; *Style*— Sir Richard Lloyd, Bt; ✉ Garden House, Easton Court, Little Hereford, Ludlow, Shropshire SY8 4LN (tel 01584 819377)

LLOYD, Robert Andrew; CBE (1991); s of Inspr William Edward Lloyd (d 1963), and May, *née* Waples; *b* 2 March 1940; *Educ* Southend HS, Keble Coll Oxford (MA), London Opera Centre; *m* 1, 1964 (m dis 1989), Sandra Dorothy, da of Douglas Watkins; 1 s (Marcus b 1965), 3 da (Anna b 1966, Candida b 1969, Alice b 1973); m 2, 1992, Lynda Anne Hazell, *née* Powell; *Career* freelance opera and concert singer (bass), writer and broadcaster; Instr Lt RN 1962–65, civilian tutor Bramshill Police Staff Coll 1966–68; princ bass: Sadler's Wells Opera 1969–72, Royal Opera 1972–83; performed at numerous int venues incl: Royal Opera House Covent Garden, La Scala Milan, Metropolitan Opera NY, Paris Opera, Munich, Vienna Staatsoper, San Francisco Opera; performances incl: title role in André Tarkovsky prodn of Boris Godunov (Kirov Opera Leningrad), Simon Boccanegra (Metropolitan Opera), Magic Flute (Bastille Opera), Pelleas and Melisande (Metropolitan Opera), L'Icoronazione di Poppea (San Francisco), Faust (Dallas), created role of Tyrone in Hoddinot's Opera Tower 1999; sr artist Royal Opera House Covent Garden 2004–; frequent broadcaster on radio and TV; memb: Exec Ctee Musicians' Benevolent Fund 1988–94, Conservatoires Advsy Gp HE Funding Cncl; pres Br Youth Opera 1989–94, pres Inc Soc of Musicians 2005–06, visiting prof RCM 1998–; Charles Santley Award 1998, Foreign Singer of the Year Buenos Aires 1997, Chaliapin Memorial Medal 1998, hon fell Keble Coll Oxford 1990, hon fell Royal Welsh Coll of Music and Drama 2005; Hon RAM 1999; *Recordings* various audio and video incl: Parsifal, Don Carlos, Entführung aus dem Serail, Magic Flute, Handel's Messiah, Dream of Gerontius, Fidelio, The Damnation of Faust, Verdi Requiem, The Coronation of Poppea, Samson and Dalilah 1999, Winterreise 1999; *Film* Parsifal (Artificial Eye), 6 Foot Cinderella (BBC), Bluebeard's Castle (BBC, Prix Italia 1989); *Recreations* sailing, hill walking; *Clubs* Garrick; *Style*— Robert Lloyd, Esq, CBE; ✉ c/o Askonas Holt, Lonsdale Chambers, 27 Chancery Lane, London WC2A 1PF

LLOYD, Simon Roderick; s of Desmond C F Lloyd (d 1978), and Amber, *née* Wallace-Barr; *b* 25 March 1947; *Educ* Wellington; *m* April 1972, Susan Margaret, *née* Cuthbert; 1 da (Rebecca Catherine b 1976), 1 s (Andrew James Wallace b 1978); *Career* media planner/buyer Garland Compton Advertising 1966–74; Foote Cone & Belding Advertising: joined 1974, bd/media dir 1978–80, vice-chm 1980–84, md 1984–86, dir of media Euro Region 1986–88; vice-pres media Publicis FCB Europe (alliance of FCB and Publicis) 1989–2002, chm Optimedia Worldwide (network of media planning/buying specialist cos owned by Publicis Group), chm International Media and Communications 2002–; MIPA, MIAA; *Recreations* sailing, cricket, walking, dogs, travel, almost any new experience!; *Clubs* MCC, Royal London Yacht, Seaview Yacht (Isle of Wight); *Style*— Simon Lloyd, Esq; ✉ tel 020 8946 9083

LLOYD, Stephen; s of Kenneth Lloyd (d 1978), and Elsie, *née* Smith (1996); *b* 15 March 1949, Sheffield; *Educ* Bournemouth Sch, Leicester Coll of Educn (CertEd), Univ of Leicester (BEd), Univ of Bristol (CertEd); *m* 1 June 1991, Diane, *née* Lolley; 4 da (Bethan, Sarah, Rebecca, Amy); *Career* early career in special educn, opened own private special sch 1975, fndr and chm Hesley Gp, charitable work via The Lloyd Fndn (previously The Hesley Fndn); MInstD; *Recreations* rugby, shooting, sailing, skiing; *Style*— Stephen Lloyd, Esq

LLOYD, His Hon Stephen Harris; s of Thomas Richard Lloyd (d 1951), and Amy Irene, *née* Harris (d 1971); *b* 16 September 1938; *Educ* Ashville Coll Harrogate, Univ of Leeds (LLB); *m* 2 June 1972, Joyce Eileen, da of Frederick Allen (d 1946); 2 step da (Caroline Anne (Mrs Freuler) b 27 May 1958, Elizabeth Mary (Mrs Harrison) b 18 Feb 1962); *Career* Dale & Newbery Slrs: joined 1961, admitted slr 1965, ptnr 1968–85, sr ptnr 1985–95; recorder of the Crown Court 1993–95 (asst recorder 1989–93), circuit judge (SE Circuit) 1995–2007; slr SW London Probation Service 1985–95; chm Nat Cncl for One Parent Families 1975–83, chm Mediation in Divorce 1986–90, chm Bd of Govrs Manor House Sch 1987–95; chm St Faith's Tst 2001–, vice-chm Bd St Peter's Nat Health Tst 1991–95; pres Ashvillian Soc 1993–94; memb Law Soc 1965–95; *Recreations* two 1930's motor vehicles, cottages in Yorkshire Dales, charity work, walking, music, entertaining; *Style*— His Hon Stephen Lloyd

LLOYD, Thomas Owen Saunders; OBE (2004), DL (Dyfed 2001); s of Maj John Audley Lloyd, MC (d 1999), of Court Henry, Carmarthen, and (Mary Ivy) Anna, *née* Owen; *b* 26 February 1955; *Educ* Radley, Downing Coll Cambridge (MA); *m* 7 Nov 1987, (Christabel) Juliet Anne (d 1996), da of Maj David Harrison-Allen (d 1976), of Cresselly, nr Pembroke; *Career* slr, author; chm: Historic Bldgs Cncl for Wales 1992–2004 (memb 1985–2004), Br Historic Bldgs Tst 1987–92, Pembrokeshire Historical Soc 1991–94, Buildings at Risk Tst 1992–, Carmarthenshire Antiquarian Soc 1999–2002, Wales region HHA 2004–, Picton Castle Tst 2006–; memb Cadw - Welsh Historic Monuments Advsy Ctee 1992–2004; tstee Architectural Heritage Fund 2006–; non-exec dir: Dyfed Family Health Servs Authy 1990–95 (chm Med and Dental Servs Ctees 1992–96), Wales Tourist Bd 1995–99; conslt Sotheby's (Wales) 1999–; hon memb Royal Soc of Architects in Wales 1993; FSA 1991; *Books* The Lost Houses of Wales (1986, 2 edn 1989); The Buildings of Wales series: Pembrokeshire (co-author, 2004), Carmarthenshire & Ceredigion (co-author, 2006); *Style*— Thomas Lloyd, Esq, OBE, DL, FSA; ✉ Freestone Hall, Cresselly, Kilgetty, Pembrokeshire SA68 0SY (tel and fax 01646 651493)

LLOYD, Rt Hon Lord Justice; Rt Hon Sir Timothy Andrew Wigram; kt (1996), PC (2005); s of Dr Thomas Wigram Lloyd (d 1984), and Margo Adela, *née* Beasley (d 2007); *b* 30 November 1946; *Educ* Winchester, Lincoln Coll Oxford (exhibitioner, BA, MA); *m* 1978, Theresa Sybil Margaret, da of late Ralph Kenneth Holloway; *Career* called to the Bar Middle Temple 1970, bencher 1994, QC 1986, Attorney Gen of the Duchy and Attorney and Serjeant within the Co Palatine of Lancaster 1993–96, judge of the High Court of Justice (Chancery Div) 1996–2005, vice-chllr Co Palatine of Lancaster 2002–05, Lord Justice of Appeal 2005–; hon fell Lincoln Coll Oxford 2006; *Books* Wurtzburg & Mills, Building Society Law (15 edn, 1989); *Recreations* music, travel; *Style*— The Rt Hon Lord Justice Lloyd; ✉ c/o Royal Courts of Justice, Strand, London WC2A 2LL

LLOYD, Tom; s of Sam Lloyd, of London, and Jane, *née* Watkins; *b* 18 September 1966, London; *Educ* Nottingham Trent Univ (BA), RCA (MA); *m* 19 Sept 1998, Polly Richards; 2 da (Molly Florence Gwendolen b 19 June 2001, Delilah Jocelyn Vera b 16 Jan 2004); *Career* early career as sr designer Pentagram London; co-fndr (with Luke Pearson, *qv*) PearsonLloyd 1997–; projects incl first class seat for Virgin Atlantic Airways 2001–03 and Westminster street light for Artemide 2001–04, other projects for clients incl Knoll International, Ettinger, Body Shop, Magis, Modus, Fritz Hansen and Ideal Standard; architectural design: Duffer of St George 1997–2002, Levis/Dockers UK 2000, Carhartt 2000, Cashmere by Design 2000–01, TSE Cashmere 2000–02; exhbns: Architecture Fndn London 1999, Crafts Cncl London 2001, Stuttgart Design Centre 2001, MOMA NY 2001, Design Museum London 2001 and 2002, V&A 2002, Br Cncl China 2003, Br Embassy Tokyo 2004, ICFF NY 2005; visiting lectr: Ecole Cantonale d'Art de Lausanne, RCA; numerous awards incl FX Designers of the Year 2002, other awards from D&AD, Red Dot, IDEA, Baden-Württemberg, IF and Design Week; *Style*— Tom Lloyd, Esq; ✉ Pearson Lloyd, 117 Drysdale Street, London N1 6ND (tel 020 7033 4440, fax 020 7033 4441)

LLOYD, Ursula Elizabeth; da of late Dr Joseph D B Mountrose, of London, and Maria, *née* Robinson; *b* 10 July 1943; *Educ* Francis Holland C of E Sch Clarence Gate London, Middx Hosp Med Sch (MB BS, LRCS); *m* William Lloyd, s of Roderick Lloyd; 2 da (Wendy b 28 Feb 1978, Anne b 6 Sept 1981); *Career* various trg posts Royal Marsden Hosp, Chelsea Hosp for Women and Queen Charlotte's Hosps; conslt obstetrician and gynaecologist: S London Hosp for Women 1982–87, St James' Hosp Balham 1987–89, St George's Hosp Tooting 1987–91, in private practice 1991–; Freeman City of London, Liveryman Worshipful Soc of Apothecaries; memb RSM, MRCP, FRCOG; *Style*— Mrs Ursula Lloyd; ✉ Portland Hospital for Women, 209 Great Portland Street, London W1W 5AH (tel 020 7935 3732 and 020 7390 8094, fax 020 7935 3732)

LLOYD, Wendy Anne; da of Geoffrey Hugh Lloyd, of Cambridge, and Irene Sylvia Lloyd; *b* 23 May 1969; *Career* film critic, writer, comedian, television and radio presenter, singer, songwriter, voice over artist, travel journalist; *Radio* credits incl: BBC Cambridge 1986–88, BBC GLR (Pop Life) 1988–91, BT's Music Service (Live Wire) 1988–89, BBC World Service, Radio Luxembourg 1992–93, Virgin Radio 1993–95, BBC Radio One (Clingfilm) 1995, Talk Radio 1996–98, LBC Radio 1998–; *Television* credits incl: Dial Midnight (LWT) 1993, The Little Picture Show (ITV) 1995, Top of the Pops 1995, Channel 1 Movie Show 1996–97, Empire Film Awards (ITV) 1997, Screentime (Meridian) 2000–04, Brainwaves (Meridian) 2001, Travel Bug Crete/Sri Lanka/Maldives/Tunisia (Travel Channel) 2000–03; contrib: Sky News, This Morning, Newsnight, GMTV; memb London Film Critics Circle; *Theatre* co-writer and co-performer Asteroid Haemorrhoid Edinburgh Fringe Festival 1999; *Recreations* yoga, skiing, gym, cycling, music; *Style*— Ms Wendy Lloyd; ✉ website www.wendylloyd.com; c/o Vocal Point (tel 020 7419 0700, website www.vocalpoint.net)

LLOYD-DAVIES, (Reginald) Wyndham; s of Dr Allan Wyndham Lloyd-Davies (d 1974), of Branksome Park, Dorset, and Muriel Constance, *née* Martin (d 1993); *b* 24 June 1934; *Educ* Rugby, Univ of London (MB, MS); *m* 1, 31 May 1958 (m dis 1981), Elizabeth Ann, da of Arthur Wesley Harding (d 1978); 2 da ((Susan) Vanessa Lloyd-Davies, MBE (Mil) b 1960 d 2005, Fiona Caroline b 1964); m 2, 20 Aug 1983, Jill Black, da of Austin Hemingsley (d 1969); *Career* res urologist San Francisco Med Center Univ of Calif 1969–70, conslt surgn Queen Victoria Hosp East Grinstead 1971–77, dep CMO Met Police 1983–98 (conslt surgn 1978–2003), sr conslt urologist St Thomas' Hosp London 1986–98 (MRC res fell Dept of Surgery 1965, sr surgical registrar in urology 1966–69, conslt urologist 1970–86), clinical dir urology and lithotripsy Guy's and St Thomas' Hosp Tst 1993–98 (urologist emeritus 1998–2004), surgn King Edward VII Hosp for Offrs London 1994–2004; memb Cncl RSM 1991–92; Urology Section RSM: memb Cncl 1975–87, treas 1983–87, pres elect 1990, pres 1991–92; author of numerous pubns on urological topics; late memb Bd Mgmnt London Mozart Players; Freeman City of London 1979, Liveryman Worshipful Soc of Apothecaries 1974; memb Br Assoc of Urological Surgns (memb Cncl 1980–83 and 1991–92); FRCS, FEBU, FRSM; *Recreations* shooting, fishing, stalking, music; *Clubs* Garrick; *Style*— Wyndham Lloyd-Davies, Esq; ✉ Church Cottage, Cold Aston, Cheltenham, Gloucestershire GL54 3BN (tel and fax 01451 810158)

LLOYD-DAVIS, Glynne Christian; s of Col G St G Lloyd-Davis (d 1956), and Daphne Mary, *née* Barnes (d 1995); *b* 9 March 1941; *Educ* St Paul's, Ealing Tech Coll, Royal Sch of Mines Univ of London, London Business Sch; *m* 20 April 1963, Dorothy Helen (d 2005), da of Michael O'Shea (d 1991), of Aust; 1 da (Sarah b 1964), 1 s (Simon b 1966); *Career* chartered sec; asst sec Rio Tinto plc 1976–98 (and dir of subsid companies); sec: The Mining Assoc of the UK 1987–98, The Mineral Industries Educn Tst 1987–98 (tstee 1999–); memb Ctee Royal Sch of Mines Assoc 1994–; hon sec Royal Sch of Mines Assoc

Tst 2000–; FCIS; *Recreations* reading, walking, sketching; *Clubs* Royal Over-Seas League; *Style—* Glynne Lloyd-Davis, Esq; ✉ Braemar, The Butts, Kenninghall, Norfolk NR16 2EQ

LLOYD-EDWARDS, Capt Norman; RD (1971, and Bar 1980); s of Evan Stanley Edwards (d 1986), of Cardiff, and Mary Leah, *née* Lloyd (d 1977); *b* 13 June 1933; *Educ* Monmouth, Quakers Yard GS, Univ of Bristol (LLB); *Career* Capt RNR, CO HMS Cambria, S Wales Div RNR 1981–84; slr; ptnr Cartwright Adams & Black 1960–93 (conslt 1993–98); memb Cardiff City Cncl 1963–87 (dep Lord Mayor 1973–74, Lord Mayor 1985–86); chapter clerk Llandaff Cathedral 1975–90, Prior for Wales 1989–2005; pres: Friends of Llandaff Cathedral 1990–, Friends of St John Parish Church Cardiff 1994–, South Wales Art Soc 2004–; memb Cncl BBC Wales 1987–90; chm: Wales Ctee Duke of Edinburgh Award 1980–96 (pres 1996–), Cardiff Festival of Music 1981–89, Nat Res Trg Cncl 1984–95, Glamorgan TA & VRA 1987–90; pres: S Glamorgan Scouts 1989–, Cardiff Branch Nat Tst, Wales Festival of Remembrance 1990–, Morgannwg Branch Br Red Cross 1994–, RFCA Wales 1999–2005; govr ESU 2005–; dep Lord Prior Order of St John 2005–; HM Lord-Lt S Glamorgan 1990– (Vice Lord Lt 1986); ADC to HM The Queen 1984; fndr Master Welsh Livery Guild 1992–95; Hon Col: 2 Bn Royal Regiment of Wales 1996–99, Royal Welsh Regiment 1999–2003; fell Royal Welsh Coll of Music and Drama (vice-pres 1995–); GCStJ 1996 (KStJ 1988, OStJ 1983); *Recreations* music, gardening, table talk; *Clubs* Army and Navy, Cardiff and Co, United Services Mess; *Style—* Capt Norman Lloyd-Edwards, RD; ✉ Hafan Wen, Llantrisant Road, Llandaff, Cardiff CF5 2PU (tel 029 2057 8278)

LLOYD GEORGE OF DWYFOR, 3 Earl (UK 1945); Owen Lloyd George; DL (Dyfed); also Viscount Gwynedd (UK 1945); s of 2 Earl Lloyd George of Dwyfor (d 1968, s of the PM 1916–22) and his 1 w, Roberta, da of Sir Robert McAlpine, 1 Bt; *b* 28 April 1924; *Educ* Oundle; *m* 1, 1949 (m dis 1982), Ruth Margaret (d 2003), da of Richard Coit (d 1960); 2 s, 1 da; m 2, 1982, (Cecily) Josephine (who m 1, 1957, as his 2 w, 2 Earl of Woolton, who d 1969; m 2, 1969 (m dis 1974), as his 2 w, 3 Baron Forres, who d 1978), er da of Sir Alexander Gordon Cumming, 5 Bt, MC (d 1939); *Heir* s, Viscount Gwynedd; *Career* Capt Welsh Gds 1942, serv 1944–45 in Italy; carried the sword at investiture of HRH The Prince of Wales, Caernarvon Castle 1969; memb Historic Buildings Cncl for Wales 1971–94; *Publications* A Tale of Two Grandfathers (1999); *Clubs* White's, Pratt's; *Style—* The Rt Hon the Earl Lloyd George of Dwyfor, DL; ✉ Ffynone, Boncath, Pembrokeshire SA37 0HQ; 47 Burton Court, Chelsea, London SW3 4SZ

LLOYD JONES, (Richard) David; s of Richard Francis Lloyd Jones (d 1976), and Hester, *née* Ritchie (d 1985); *b* 10 May 1942; *Educ* Edgeborough Sch, Bradfield Coll, AA Sch of Architecture (AADipl); *m* 1971, Linda Barbara, da of Duncan John Stewart; *Career* Stillman and Eastwick-Field Architects 1964, National Building Agency 1966–72, RMJM Ltd (previously Robert Matthew Johnson-Marshall & Partners) 1972–91 (dir 1986, chm Design Group 1987); projects incl: NFU Mutual and Avon Insurance Group HQ, Solar Offices Doxford International, Grange Park Opera House, Renewable Energy Systems Head Office and Visitor's Centre; dir Studio E Architects Ltd 1994–; UK rep Int Energy Agency Task 1995–2001; RIBA 1968 (memb London Regnl Cncl 1991–2001, memb Sustainable Futures Ctee 2004–), FRSA 1990; *Publications* Architecture and the Environment, Lawrence King (1999), BIPV Projects, DTI (2000); *Recreations* sculpture, painting, tennis, travelling; *Clubs* Architectural Assoc; *Style—* David Lloyd Jones, Esq; ✉ 24 Liston Road, London SW4 0DF; 28 Triqette Pupulyu, Ghammar, Gozo, Malta; Studio E Architects, Palace Wharf, Rainville Road, London W6 9HN (tel 020 7385 7126, fax 020 7381 4995, e-mail david@studioe.co.uk)

LLOYD-JONES, David Mathias; s of Harry Vincent Lloyd-Jones, and Margaret Alwyna, *née* Mathias; *b* 19 November 1934; *Educ* Westminster, Magdalen Coll Oxford (BA); *m* 23 May 1964, Anne Carolyn, da of Brig Victor Whitehead, of Montreal; 2 s (Gareth b 1966, Simon b 1968), 1 da (Vanessa b 1964); *Career* conductor; repetiteur with Royal Opera House Covent Garden 1959–60, chorus master and conductor New Opera Co 1961–64; freelance conductor engagements with: BBC, WNO, Scottish Opera; asst music dir Sadler's Wells and ENO 1972–78, artistic dir Opera North 1978–90; many opera and concert engagements abroad, numerous recordings of Br and Russian music; ed original version of Mussorgsky's Boris Godunov 1974; full score: Gilbert and Sullivan's The Gondoliers 1983, Walton's First Symphony 1998, Berlioz's The Childhood of Christ 1999; trans: Eugene Onegin, Boris Godunov, The Queen of Spades, The Love of Three Oranges; Hon DMus Univ of Leeds; *Style—* David Lloyd-Jones, Esq; ✉ 94 Whitelands House, Cheltenham Terrace, London SW3 4RA (tel and fax 020 7730 8695)

LLOYD-JONES, Jonathan; s of Peter Lloyd-Jones (d 1990), and Margaret, *née* Marshall; *b* 23 November 1954, Guildford, Surrey; *Educ* Sevenoaks Sch, Univ of Southampton (LLB); *m* 14 April 1984, Sarah Williams; 3 s (Thomas b 10 Feb 1986, Olly b 30 June 1987, Jamie b 25 Feb 1990); *Career* Stephenson Harwood 1977–80, Claude Hornby and Cox 1980–88, Blake Lapthorn Linnell 1988– (sr ptnr 2005–); vice-chm ADR Net Ltd, memb Law Soc 1979 (memb ADR Ctee); *Recreations* walking, family; *Clubs* QI, Scotch Malt Whisky Soc; *Style—* Jonathan Lloyd-Jones, Esq; ✉ Blake Lapthorn Linnell, Seacourt Tower, Westway, Oxford OX2 0FB (tel 01865 254204, fax 01865 244983, e-mail jonathan.lloyd-jones@bllaw.co.uk)

LLOYD-JONES, (Glyn) Robin; s of William Rice Lloyd-Jones (d 1980), and Esme Frances, *née* Ellis (d 2001); *b* 5 October 1934; *Educ* Blundell's, Selwyn Coll Cambridge (MA), Jordanhill Coll of Educn; *m* 30 July 1959, Sallie, da of Cdr John Hollocombe, RN (d 1981) and Kathleen, *née* Gregory (d 1964); 1 s (Glyn b 1962), 2 da (Kally b 1965, Léonie b 1969); *Career* educn advsr 1972–89; writer; pres Scot Assoc of Writers 1981–86, pres (Scot) PEN Int 1997–2000 (vice-pres 1991–97), co-ordinator Scottish Forum for Devpt Educn in Schools 1996–98; *Books* fiction incl: Where the Forest and the Garden Meet (1980), Lord of the Dance (winner BBC-Arrow First Novel competition, 1983), The Dreamhouse (1985), Fallen Angels (1992); other: Assessment from Principles to Action (with Elizabeth Bray, 1985), Better Worksheets (1986), Argonauts of the Western Isles (1989), Fallen Pieces of the Moon (2006), Red Fox Running (2007); *Radio Drama* Ice in Wonderland (Radio Times New Drama Script Award, 1992), Rainmaker (1995); *Recreations* mountaineering, sea-kayaking, chess, photography; *Style—* Robin Lloyd-Jones, Esq; ✉ 26 East Clyde Street, Helensburgh G84 7PG (tel 01436 672010, e-mail robinlloydjones@aol.com)

LLOYD MOSTYN, *see also:* Mostyn

LLOYD OF BERWICK, Baron (Life Peer UK 1993), of Ludlay in the County of East Sussex; Sir Anthony John Leslie Lloyd; kt (1978), PC (1984), DL (E Sussex 1983); s of Edward John Boydell Lloyd, of Little Bucksteep, Dallington, E Sussex; *b* 9 May 1929; *Educ* Eton, Trinity Coll Cambridge; *m* 1960, Jane Helen Violet, da of C W Shelford, of Chailey Place, Lewes, E Sussex; *Career* Nat Serv 1 Bn Coldstream Gds 1948; called to the Bar Inner Temple 1955 (treas 1999), QC 1967, attorney-gen to HRH The Prince of Wales 1969–77dge of the High Court of Justice (Queen's Bench Div) 1978–84, Lord Justice of Appeal 1984–93, Lord of Appeal in Ordinary 1993–98; former memb Top Salaries Review Body; chm Security Cmmn 1992–99; memb Parole Bd 1983–84; vice-pres Corporation of the Sons of the Clergy 1996–2004; chm Glyndebourne Arts Tst 1975–94, dir Royal Acad of Music 1979–98; chm Chichester Diocesan Bd of Fin 1972–76; Master Worshipful Co of Salters 2000; hon fell Peterhouse Cambridge 1981 (fell 1953); Hon LLD: Queen's Univ Belfast 2005, Univ of Sussex 2006; *Clubs* Brooks's; *Style—* The Rt Hon Lord Lloyd of Berwick, PC, DL; ✉ Ludlay, Berwick, East Sussex (tel 01323 870204); 68 Strand-on-the-Green, London W4 3PF (tel 020 8994 7790)

LLOYD PACK, Roger Anthony; s of Charles Lloyd Pack (d 1983), and Uli, *née* Pulay (d 2000), of London; *b* 8 February 1944; *Educ* Bedales, RADA; *m* Jehane, da of David Markham; 1 da (Emily Lloyd, *qv*, b 29 Sept 1970), 3 s (Spencer b 4 Feb 1981, Hartley b 16 Nov 1984, Louis b 29 May 1988); *Career* actor; *Theatre* rep at Northampton, Coventry, Bromley, Leatherhead and season RSC; roles incl: Tartuffe in Tartuffe (Royal Exchange Manchester), Rocco in Snow Orchid (Gate Theatre), Etienne Plucheux in Flea in Her Ear (Old Vic), Kafka in Kafka's Dick (Royal Court), Waldemar in Deliberate Death of a Polish Priest (Almeida), Tim in Noises Off (Lyric, Savoy), Joey in The Homecoming (Garrick), Aston in the Caretaker (Shaw), Victor in One for the Road (Lyric); RNT: Chrysaldus in School for Wives, Juan in Yerma, Rosmer in Rosmersholm, The Garden of England, Osip Mandelstam in Futurists, Osip in Wild Honey, Will in Caritas; other prodns incl: Fred in Party Time (Almeida), Oberon in A Midsummer Night's Dream (Haymarket Leicester), Albert Parker in When We Are Married (Savoy), Davies in The Caretaker, Aunt Augusta in Travels With My Aunt (Far East Tour), Prospero in the Tempest (Edinburgh Festival), Yvan in Art (Wyndham's Theatre, nat tour), Konik in Light (Theatre de Complicité), Dr Miller in The Deep Blue Sea (nat tour), Brian in The Dark (Donmar Warehouse), Robert in Blue/Orange (Sheffield Crucible), Draycott in The Winterling (Royal Court), Dame in Dick Whittington (Barbican), Censor in The Last Laugh (nat tour); *Television* incl: Newitt in Vicar of Dibley (ITV), Trigger in Only Fools and Horses (10 series, BBC), Phillips in Dandelion Dead (LWT), Fred in Party Time (Channel Four), Derek in Clothes in the Wardrobe (BBC), Quentin in Archer's Goon (6 episodes, BBC), Plitplov in The Gravy Train (2 series, Channel Four/Portman), David Irving in Selling Hitler (Euston Films), Mr Bean (Thames), Frankie in The Object of Beauty (BBC), Glendenning in The Contractor (BBC), Liz in The Naked Civil Servant (Thames), Sydney Bagley in Brassneck (BBC), Kavanagh QC, Mr Sowerberry in Oliver Twist (ITV), Captain Mann in Longitude (Granada), Murder Rooms (BBC), Norman Pendleton in Born and Bred (BBC), Dalziel and Pasco, Mick Mortimer in The Bill (ITV), Detective in Marjorie and Gladys, Inspector Caux in Poirot (Carlton), Lumic in Dr Who (BBC), Jim in What we did on our Holidays (Granada), Mr Johnson in The History of Mr Polly (ITV); *Films* incl: Fred in Young Poisoner's Handbook, piano teacher in Interview with a Vampire, Judge Haythorn in Princess Caraboo, Dr Butler in American Friends, Dr Pitman in Wilt, Geoff in The Cook, The Thief, His Wife & Her Lover, Charles in The Go-Between, The Virgin Soldiers, Young Anthony Quinn in The Magus, Barty Crouch in Harry Potter and the Goblet of Fire, Lord Brocklebank in The Living in the Land of the Dead; *Awards* British Theatre Assoc Drama Awards Best Supporting Actor (for Wild Honey and One for the Road) 1984; *Recreations* tennis, chess, gardening, travelling, reading, music; *Clubs* Garrick, Soho House; *Style—* Roger Lloyd Pack, Esq; ✉ Lucy Brazier, PFD, Drury House, 34–43 Russell Street, London WC2B 5HA (tel 020 7344 1010, fax 020 7836 9544, e-mail lbrazier@pfd.co.uk)

LLOYD PARRY, Eryl; s of Capt Robert Parry (d 1974), of Caernarfon, and Megan, *née* Lloyd (d 1962); *b* 28 April 1939; *Educ* Caernarfon GS, St Peter's Coll Oxford (BA, Dip Public and Social Admin, MA); *m* 5 Aug 1967, Nancy Kathleen, da of Lt-Col Sir Richard Kenneth Denby (d 1986), of Ilkley; 3 s (Richard b 14 Jan 1969, Robert b 15 Dec 1970, Roland b 16 Jan 1979), 1 da (Helen b 16 May 1974); *Career* called to the Bar Lincoln's Inn 1966; in practice Northern Circuit 1966–92, pt/t chm Industrial Tbnls 1977–92, vice-pres Merseyside and Cheshire Rent Assessment Panel 1985–92, full-time chm Employment Tbnls (Manchester Region) 1992–; lay reader C of E; book reviewer for various pubns, one-act plays variously performed, poems variously published; memb Amnesty Int; *Recreations* acting, playwriting, reading; *Clubs* Liverpool Bar Cricket (hon life memb), Southport Dramatic, Sussex Playwrights, Sefton Theatre Company, Formby Theatre, Equity; *Style—* Eryl Lloyd Parry, Esq; ✉ Employment Tribunals Regional Office, 1st Floor, Cunard Building, Pier Head, Liverpool L3 1TS (tel 0151 236 9397)

LLOYD-ROBERTS, George Edward; s of George Charles Lloyd-Roberts (d 1986), of Cheyne Place, London, and Catherine Ann, *née* Wright; *b* 21 March 1948; *Educ* Gordonstoun, Univ of London (MSc); *m* 2 Aug 1969, Elizabeth Anne, da of Horace Edward Kenworthy, of Cork, Eire; 1 s (Henry b 1977), 1 da (Sophie b 1975); *Career* underwriter GE Lloyd-Roberts Syndicate 55 at Lloyd's, Lloyd's non-marine assoc 1986–92 (chm 1992), Lloyd's Solvency and Security 1987–89; Lloyd's Regulatory Bd 1993–96; *Recreations* running, riding, reading; *Style—* George Lloyd-Roberts, Esq; ✉ Lloyd's, Lime Street, London (tel 020 7623 7100)

LLOYD WEBBER, Baron (Life Peer UK 1997), of Sydmonton in the County of Hampshire; Sir Andrew Lloyd Webber; kt (1992); s of late William Southcombe Lloyd Webber, CBE, DMus, FRCM, FRCO, and late Jean Hermione, *née* Johnstone; *b* 22 March 1948; *Educ* Westminster, Magdalen Coll Oxford, Royal Coll of Music; *m* 1, 1971 (m dis 1983), Sarah Jane Tudor, *née* Hugill; 1 s, 1 da; m 2, 1984 (m dis 1990), Sarah Brightman; m 3, 1991, Madeleine Astrid, *née* Gurdon; 2 s, 1 da; *Career* composer; FRCM 1988; *Musicals* The Likes of Us 1965, Joseph and the Amazing Technicolor Dreamcoat 1968 (revived 1973 and 1991), Jesus Christ Superstar 1970 (revived 1996), Evita 1976 (with lyrics by Tim Rice; stage version 1978); Jeeves (with lyrics by Alan Ayckbourn) 1975, Tell Me On a Sunday (with lyrics by Don Black) 1980, Cats (based on poems by T S Eliot) 1981, Song and Dance (with lyrics by Don Black) 1982, Starlight Express (with lyrics by Richard Stilgoe and Charles Hart) 1984, The Phantom of The Opera (with lyrics by Richard Stilgoe and Charles Hart) 1986, Aspects of Love (with lyrics by Don Black and Charles Hart) 1989, Sunset Boulevard (with lyrics by Christopher Hampton and Don Black) 1993, By Jeeves (book and lyrics by Alan Ayckbourn) 1996, Whistle Down the Wind (with lyrics by Jim Steinman; premiere Washington DC Dec 1996, West End 1998), The Beautiful Game (book and lyrics by Ben Elton) 2000, The Woman in White (book by Charlotte Jones, lyrics by David Zippel) 2004; prodr of many ventures incl: Joseph and the Amazing Technicolor Dreamcoat 1973 (also 1974, 1978, 1980 and 1991), Cats 1981, Song and Dance 1982, Daisy Pulls It Off 1983, On Your Toes 1984, Starlight Express 1984, The Hired Man 1984, The Phantom of the Opera 1986, Café Puccini 1986, Lend me a Tenor 1988, Shirley Valentine 1989, Aspects of Love 1989, La Bête 1992, Sunset Boulevard 1993, By Jeeves 1996, Jesus Christ Superstar 1996 and 1998, Whistle Down the Wind 1996 and 1998, The Beautiful Game 2000, Bombay Dreams 2002, The Sound of Music 2006 (appeared in How Do You Solve a Problem Like Maria? (BBC TV) 2006); *Film Scores* Gumshoe 1971, The Odessa File 1974; *Compositions* Variations 1978, Requiem Mass 1985, Amigos Para Siempre (Friends for Life) - official Olympic theme for 1992; *Awards* incl: 6 Tony Awards, 3 Grammy Awards, 5 Olivier Awards, a Golden Globe, an Oscar, the Praemium Imperiale, Richard Rodgers Award, Critics' Circle Award for Best Musical 2000; *Publications* Evita (with Tim Rice, 1978), Cats - the book of the Musical (1981), Joseph and the Amazing Technicolor Dreamcoat (with Tim Rice, 1982), The Complete Phantom of the Opera (1987), The Complete Aspects of Love (1989), Sunset Boulevard - from movie to musical (1993); *Recreations* architecture, food, art; *Style—* The Lord Lloyd Webber; ✉ c/o The Really Useful Group Limited, 22 Tower Street, London WC2H 9NS

LLOYD WEBBER, Julian; s of William Southcombe Lloyd Webber, CBE (d 1982), and Jean Hermione, *née* Johnstone (d 1993); bro of Baron Lloyd Webber (Life Peer), *qv*; *b* 14 April 1951; *Educ* Univ Coll Sch, Royal Coll of Music (ARCM), studied with Pierre Fournier (Geneva); *m* 1, 1974 (m dis 1989), Celia Mary, *née* Ballantyne; m 2, 1989 (m dis 1999), Zohra, *née* Mahmoud Ghazi; 1 s (David b 25 Feb 1992); m 3, 2001, Kheira, *née* Bourahla; *Career* musician; UK debut Queen Elizabeth Hall London 1972, US debut Lincoln Centre NY 1980, debut with Berlin Philharmonic Orch 1984; has performed with orchestras

L

worldwide and toured the USA, Canada, Germany, Holland, Africa, Bulgaria, Czechoslovakia, S America, Spain, Belgium, France, Scandinavia, Switzerland, Portugal, Australia, NZ, Singapore, Japan, Korea, Hong Kong and Taiwan; first recordings of works by: Malcolm Arnold, Benjamin Britten, Frank Bridge, Gavin Bryars, Frederick Delius, Gustav Holst, Michael Nyman, Joaquin Rodrigo, Dimitri Shostakovich, Ralph Vaughan Williams, Philip Glass; artistic dir Cellothon '88 South Bank Centre London; Best British Classical Recording (for Elgar Cello Concerto) 1987; FRCM 1994; *Books* incl: The Classical Cello (1980), The Romantic Cello (1981), The French Cello (1981), 6 pieces by Frank Bridge (1982), The Young Cellist's Repertoire Books 1, 2 & 3 (1984), Holst Invocation (1984), Vaughan Williams Fantasia on Sussex Folk Tunes (1984), Travels with My Cello (1984), Song of the Birds (1985), Recital Repertoire for Cellists (1986), Short Sharp Shocks (ed, 1990), The Great Cello Solos (1991), Cello Song (1993), The Essential Cello (1997), Cello Moods (1999), Married to Music (biography, 2001), Made In England (2003), Unexpected Songs (2007); *Recreations* countryside (especially British), soccer (Leyton Orient); *Style—* Julian Lloyd Webber, Esq, FRCM; ✉ c/o IMG Artists Europe, Lovell House, 616 Chiswick High Road, London W4 5RX (tel 020 7957 5800, fax 020 7957 5801, e-mail labrahams@imgartists.com)

LLWYD, Elfyn; MP; s of late Huw Meirion Hughes, and Hefina Hughes; *b* 26 September 1951; *Educ* Llanrwst GS, Ysgol Dyffryn Conwy, UCW Aberystwyth, Coll of Law Chester; *m* 27 July 1974, Eleri, da of Huw and Jane Lloyd Edwards; 1 s, 1 da; *Career* admitted slr 1977, pres Gwynedd Law Soc 1990–91; MP (Plaid Cymru) Meirionnydd Nant Conwy 1992–; Parly ambass NSPCC; Parly friend of UNICEF; pres: Club memb Parly Select Ctee on Welsh Affrs 1992–95 and 1998–, Parly whip (Plaid Cymru) 1995–99, Parly leader (Plaid Cymru) 1998; called to the Bar Gray's Inn 1997; govr Wesminster Fndn for Democracy 2001–; vice-chair All-Pty Organophosphates Gp; memb Ct of Govrs Univ of Wales (Sch of Medicine); memb British-Irish Parly Body; memb Gorsedd of Bards; *Recreations* pigeon breeding, choral singing, rugby, fishing; *Clubs* Clwb Rygbi Bala Rugby (pres), Clwb Rygbi Dolgellau Rugby (pres), Estimaner Fishing (pres), Peldroed Llanuwchllyn Football (pres), Peldroed Betws-y-Coed Football (pres); *Style—* Elfyn Llwyd, Esq, MP; ✉ House of Commons, London SW1A 0AA (tel 020 7219 5021/3555, fax 020 7219 2633, website www.sheila.williams@plaidcymru.fsnet.co.uk)

LOACH, Kenneth Charles (Ken); s of John Loach (d 1973), of Nuneaton, Warks, and Vivien Nora, *née* Hamlin; *b* 17 June 1936; *Educ* King Edward VI Sch Nuneaton, St Peter's Coll Oxford (BA); *m* 17 July 1962, Lesley, da of William Leslie Ashton (d 1967); 3 s (Stephen b 1963, Nicholas b 1965 d 1971, James b 1969), 2 da (Hannah b 1967, Emma b 1972); *Career* film director; Golden Lion Award for Lifetime Achievement, Special Award for Contribution to British Film Evening Standard British Film Awards 1999; Hon DLitt Univ of St Andrews; ACTT; *Film* incl: Up The Junction 1965, Cathy Come Home 1966, Poor Cow 1967, Kes 1969, Family Life 1971, Days of Hope 1975, The Price of Coal 1977, The Gamekeeper 1979, Black Jack 1979, Looks and Smiles 1981, Which Side Are You On? 1984, Fatherland 1986, The View from the Woodpile 1988, Hidden Agenda 1990, Riff-Raff 1991, Raining Stones 1993 (Jury Prize Cannes Film Festival 1993, Best Film Prize Evening Standard Film Awards 1994), Ladybird Ladybird 1994 (Best Actress Award for Crissy Rock, Critics' Award for Best Film Berlin Film Festival 1994), Land and Freedom 1995, Felix 1995 (European Film of the Year Award 1995), Carla's Song 1996, The Flickering Flame (documentary) 1996, My Name is Joe 1998, Bread and Roses 2000, The Navigators 2001, Sweet Sixteen 2002, 11'09"01 2002, Ae Fond Kiss 2003; *Recreations* watching football; *Style—* Ken Loach, Esq; ✉ c/o Sixteen Films, 187 Wardour Street (2nd Floor), London W1F 8ZB

LOADER, Adrian; *b* 3 June 1948, Thessaloniki, Greece; *Educ* Univ of Cambridge; *m* 1975, Isa; 3 da; *Career* human resources Shell UK 1970–72, Shell Venezuela 1973–74, Shell Malaysia 1975–76, gp planning Shell Int 1977–78, Shell Honduras 1979–81, gen mangr Shell Uruguay 1982–84, admin mangr Shell Exploration and Prodn Aberdeen 1984–87, head Central Recruitment Shell Int 1987–89, chief exec Shell cos Philippines 1989–93, div head Central/East Europe and former Soviet Union 1993–95; Shell Oil Products: dir South Zone (Africa and Latin America) 1996–97, dir East Zone (Middle East and Far East) 1997–99, pres Shell Europe Oil Products 1999–2003; dir Strategic Planning, Sustainable Devpt and External Affrs Shell Int 2003–; non-exec dir: Alliance Unichem, Shell Canada Ltd; FCIPD; *Recreations* skiing, scuba diving, wine, music; *Style—* Adrian Loader, Esq; ✉ Shell International, Shell Centre, York Road, London SE1 7NA

LOADER, Air Chief Marshal Sir Clive Robert; KCB (2006), OBE (1996); *Educ* Judd Sch Tonbridge, Univ of Southampton; *Career* univ cadet RAF 1972, offr trg 1973–74, flying trg (Jet Provost, Gnat, Hunter) 1974–76; joined Harrier force 1976; served tours on all front-line Harrier sqdns incl: cmd 3 (Fighter) Sqdn 1993–95, OC RAF Laarbruch Germany 1996–99; flown on ops Belize, Falkland Islands, Iraq, Bosnia; personal staff offr to C-in-C Strike Command 1991–93, head major review of admin support in RAF 1999–2000, Air Cdre Harrier RAF High Wycombe 2000–01, ACOS J3 UK Perm Jt HQ 2001–02, ACDS (Ops) MOD UK 2002–04, Dep C-in-C Strike Cmd 2004–07, C-in-C Air Cmd 2007–; ADC 2007; pres RAF Cricket; FRAeS; *Recreations* rowing; *Clubs* RAF; *Style—* Air Chief Marshal Sir Clive Loader, KCB, OBE, ADC, FRAeS; ✉ Headquarters Air Command, RAF High Wycombe, Buckinghamshire HP14 4UE (tel 01494 497602, fax 01494 497112)

LOADER, Prof Ian Spencer; *b* 2 April 1965, Harrow, Middx; *Educ* Univ of Sheffield (LLB), Univ of Edinburgh (MSc, PhD); *Career* lectr in law Liverpool Poly 1986–87; Centre for Criminology and the Social and Philosophical Study of Law Univ of Edinburgh: res asst 1988 and 1989, lectr in criminology and jurisprudence 1990–92; Univ of Keele: lectr 1992–99, sr lectr 1999–2002, reader 2002–04, prof of criminology 2004–05; prof of criminology and dir Centre for Criminology Univ of Oxford 2005–, professorial fell All Souls Coll Oxford 2005–; Jean Monnet fell Dept of Law European Univ Inst Florence 2004, visiting scholar Centre of Criminology Univ of Toronto 2003; ed Br Jl of Criminology 2006– (memb Editorial Bd 2001–), assoc ed Theoretical Criminology 1999–2002 and 2005– (book review ed 2002–05); memb Editorial Bd: Policing and Society 1998–, Int Political Sociology 2005–, Clarendon Studies in Criminology series 2005–; interviews and guest appearances on radio and TV; Radzinowicz Prize 2001; *Publications* Cautionary Tales: Young People, Crime and Policing in Edinburgh (jtly, 1994), Youth, Policing and Democracy (1996, shortlisted Philip Abrams Meml Prize Br Sociological Assoc 1996), Crime and Social Change in Middle England: Questions of Order in an English Town (jtly, 2000), Policing and the Condition of England: Memory, Politics and Culture (jtly, 2003), Civilizing Security (jtly, 2007), Emotions, Crime and Justice (co-ed, 2007); contribs to edited books, jl articles, conf and res papers, res reports; *Style—* Prof Ian Loader; ✉ Centre for Criminology, University of Oxford, Manor Road Building, Manor Road, Oxford OX1 3UQ (tel 01865 274440, e-mail ian.loader@crim.ox.ac.uk)

LOADES, Prof David Michael; s of Reginald Ernest Loades, and Gladys Mary, *née* Smith; *b* 19 January 1934; *Educ* Perse Sch Cambridge, Emmanuel Coll Cambridge (MA, PhD, LittD); *m* 1, 18 Dec 1965 (m dis 1984), Ann Lomas, *née* Glover; m 2, 11 April 1987, Judith Ann, formerly Atkins; *Career* Nat Serv PO RAF 1953–55; lectr in political science Univ of St Andrews 1961–63, reader Univ of Durham 1977–80 (lectr in history 1963–70, sr lectr 1970–77), prof of history UCNW Bangor 1980–96; hon research prof Univ of Sheffield 1996–; dir Br Acad John Foxe Project 1993–2004; FRHistS 1967, FSA 1984; *Books* Two Tudor Conspiracies (1965), The Oxford Martyrs (1970), Politics and the Nation 1450–1660 (1974), The Reign of Mary Tudor (1979), The Tudor Court (1986), Mary Tudor - A Life (1989), Politics, Censorship and the English Reformation (1991), Revolution in Religion - The English Reformation 1530–1570 (1992), The Mid-Tudor Crisis 1545–1565 (1992), The Tudor Navy - An Administrative, Military and Political History (1992), Essays in European History 1453–1648 (1993), The Politics of Marriage; Henry VIII and his queens (1994), Essays on the Reign of Edward VI (1994), John Dudley: Duke of Northumberland (1996), Power in Tudor England (1996), Tudor Government (1997), England's Maritime Empire 1400–1600 (2000), Chronicles of the Tudor Queens (2002), Elizabeth I (2003), Intrigue and Treason: The Tudor Court 1547–1558 (2004), The Church of Mary Tudor (2006), Mary Tudor: A Tragical History (2006), Henry VIII: Court, Church and Conflict (2007); *Style—* Prof David Loades, FSA; ✉ The Cottage, Priory Lane, Burford, Oxfordshire OX18 4SG (tel 01993 822625, e-mail david@history.u-net.com)

LOBBENBERG, (John) Peter; s of Hans Lobbenberg (d 1955), and Annemarie, *née* Rabl (d 1971); *b* 12 September 1939; *Educ* Leighton Park Sch Reading, Oriel Coll Oxford (MA); *m* 14 Dec 1969, Naomi, da of Ronald Green (d 1985); 1 s (David b 1971), 1 da (Anna b 1974); *Career* chartered accountant; sole practitioner, ptnr Clark Whitehill 1977–90; dir British Uralite plc 1984–88, chm Electronic Machine Co plc 1986–89; govr The Purcell Sch 1981–89; FAE; *Style—* Peter Lobbenberg, Esq; ✉ Peter Lobbenberg & Co, 74 Chancery Lane, London WC2A 1AD (tel 020 7430 9300, fax 020 7430 9315)

LOCATELLI, Giorgio; *m* 7 Aug 1995, Plaxy, da of Clive Exton; 1 s (Jack Exton b 18 June 1988), 1 da (Margherita b 27 Jan 1996); *Career* chef and restaurateur; early work in N Italy and Switzerland, The Savoy (with Anton Edelmann, *qv*) 1986–90, Restaurant Laurent and La Tour D'Argent Paris 1990–92, head chef Olivo London 1992–95; prop: Zafferano London 1995, Spighetta London 1997, Spiga 1998, Locanda Locatelli 2002–; conslt: Refettorio at Crowne Plaza City Hotel, Cecconi's; *Television* Pure Italian (UK Food) 2002, Tony and Giorgio (BBC 2) 2003; *Awards* for Zafferano: Best Italian Restaurant Carlton London Restaurant Awards 1997 and 1998, Restaurateur's Italian Restaurant of the Year Hotel and Restaurant Magazine 1998, 1999 and 2000, Michelin Star 1999; for Locanda Locatelli: Best New Restaurnat BMX/Squaremeal Award 2002, Best New Restaurant London Region Theme Bar and Restaurant Awards 2002, Best Italian Restaurant Restaurateur's Restaurant of the Year Awards 2002, 2003 and 2004, Best Italian Restaurant Carlton London Restaurant Awards 2003, Great Hotel Restaurants of the World Award Hotels Magazine 2003, 3 AA Rosettes 2003, Michelin Star 2003 and 2004; Best London Restaurant Theme Magazine Bar and Restaurant Awards (Cecconi's) 2001, voted Outstanding London Chef Moët & Chandon London Restaurant Awards 2001, Diploma di Buona Cucina Accademia Italiana della Cucina 2002, Premio Italia nel Mondo Fondazione Italia 2003, Int Five Star Diamond Award American Acad of Hospitality Sciences 2003; *Publications* Tony and Giorgio (2003); *Style—* Giorgio Locatelli, Esq; ✉ Locanda Locatelli, 8 Seymour Street, London W1H 7JZ (tel 020 7935 9088, fax 020 7935 1149, e-mail info@locandalocatelli.com, website www.locandalocatelli.com)

LOCHHEAD, Richard Neilson; MSP; s of Robert William Lochhead, and Agnes Robertson, *née* Neilson; *b* 24 May 1969; *Educ* Williamwood HS Glasgow, Univ of Stirling (BA); *m* 13 July 2002, Fiona Hepburn; *Career* fin trainee South of Scotland Electricity Bd 1987–89, office mangr for Alex Salmond MP, *qv*, 1994–98, economic devpt offr Dundee City Cncl 1998–99; MSP (SNP): Scotland North East (regnl list) 1999–2006, Moray 2006–; sec for rural affrs and the environment; *Recreations* reading fiction and history non-fiction, travel, cinema, squash and five-a-side football, listening to music; *Style—* Richard Lochhead, Esq, MSP; ✉ The Scottish Parliament, Edinburgh EH99 1SP (tel 0131 348 5713, fax 0131 348 5737, e-mail richard.lochhead.msp@scottish.parliament.uk)

LOCK, Barry David Stuart; s of John Albert Putnam Lock (d 1967), and Doris Nellie, *née* Amos (d 1975); *b* 28 July 1934; *Educ* King's Sch Canterbury, Magdalen Coll Oxford (Mackinnon scholar, MA, BCL); *Career* admitted slr 1961; ptnr: Coward Chance 1964–87, Clifford Chance 1987–92; conslt: Alsop Wilkinson 1992–97, Lawrence Graham 1997–2003; City of London Slrs' Co prize, Travers Smith scholar, Clements Inn prize; *Recreations* music, the fine arts, collecting Chelsea-Derby porcelain and 18th century enamel boxes of historical interest; *Clubs* Athenaeum; *Style—* Barry Lock, Esq; ✉ 16 Morpeth Mansions, Morpeth Terrace, London SW1P 1ER (tel 020 7233 5437); 19 Loader Street, De Waterkant, Cape Town 8000, South Africa (tel 00 27 21 425 3220)

LOCK, David Anthony; s of late John Kirby Lock, and Jeanette Lock; *b* 2 May 1960; *Educ* Esher GS, Woking Sixth Form Coll, Jesus Coll Cambridge (MA), Poly of Central London (DipL), Inns of Court Sch of Law (Wilson scholar Gray's Inn); *m* Bernadette, *née* Gregory; 1 s (Anthony), 2 da (Rebecca, Pippa); *Career* mgmnt trainee GEC Telecommunications 1982–83, barrister 1987–91,1992–97 and 2002–, MP (Lab) Wyre Forest 1997–2001; PPS: Lord Chancellor's Dept 1997–98, to Lord Chancellor and Parly sec at Lord Chancellor's Dept 1998–99; Parly sec Lord Chancellor's Dept 1999–2001; chm Serv Authorities for the Nat Criminal Intelligence Serv and Nat Crime Squad 2002–03; dir: Insolvency Management Ltd, Lawbook Consultancy Ltd, Property Flow Ltd; head Healthcare Practice Mills & Reeve slrs 2003–; Wychavon DC: memb 1995–97, chm Amenities and Econ Devpt Ctee, chm Wychavon Leisure Mgmnt Bd; memb: Br Student Debating Team 1985–86; *Recreations* family, paragliding, windsurfing, friends; *Style—* David Lock, Esq

LOCK, David Peter; CBE (2007); s of Arthur Lovering Lock, of Kent, and Kathleen Barbara, *née* Nash (d 1961); *b* 12 March 1948; *Educ* Sir Roger Manwood's GS, Nottingham Coll of Art and Design/Trent Poly (Dip Town and Country Planning); *m* 19 Sept 1970, Jeanette Anita, da of Frederick Charles Jones; 3 da; *Career* area planning offr Leicester City Cncl 1970–73 (asst branch sec Leicester City Branch NALGO 1971–73), planning aid offr Town & Country Planning Assoc 1973–78, planning mangr Milton Keynes Devpt Corp 1978–81, assoc dir Conran Roche Ltd 1981–88, chm David Lock Associates Ltd 1988–, chief planning advsr DOE 1994–97; memb Editorial Bd: Town & Country Planning Jl 1973–, Built Environment Quarterly 1975–, Urban Design Quarterly 1996–; chm: Milton Keynes Urban Studies Centre Ltd 1982–87, City Discovery Centre Ltd 1985–, David Lock Associates (Australia) Pty Ltd 1998–, DLA Architects Practice Ltd 2001–; dir: Rapid Tport Int plc 1997–2004, Integrated Tport Planning Ltd 1998–; visiting prof: town planning UCE Birmingham 1988–98, Centre of Planning Studies Sch of Business Univ of Reading 2002–; external examiner 1985–89: CNAA, Jt Centre for Urban Design, Oxford Poly; memb Cncl: RTPI 1975–80, Town & Country Planning Summer Sch 1974–79; chm Town & Country Planning Assoc 2002– (memb Cncl 1978–, vice-chm 1988–94 and 1998–2002); expert advsr Regnl Tport Strategy NI 2001–, expert advsr Nat Spatial Strategy Eire 2000–; tstee Lady Margaret Patterson Osborn Tst 2000–; memb Urban Design Advsy Panel London Docklands Devpt Corp 1990–94; memb: Town & Country Planning Assoc 1969, RTPI 1975, Land Use Soc 1980, Inst of Logistics 1993, Railways Task Force NI 2000; FRSA 1993; *Publications* incl: Control and Urban Planning (contrib, 1973), Planning Aid (jtly, 1974), Environmental Impact Assessment (contrib, 1975), People and their Settlements (contrib, 1976), Growth and Change in the Future City Region (contrib, 1976), Why the Poor Pay More (jtly, 1977), Planning and the Future (contrib, 1977), New Towns in National Development (contrib, 1980), The Office of the Future (contrib, 1981), Property and Technology: the needs of Modern Industry (jtly, 1983), Riding the Tiger: Planning the South of England (1989), Alternative Development Patterns: New Settlements (jtly, 1993), On Track (contrib, 1994), What Next after the Planning Green Paper? (2002), Ofplan (jtly, 2007), Best Practice in Sustainable Urban Extensions and New Settlements (jtly, 2007); *Recreations* history and geography, reading and research; *Style—* David Lock, CBE; ✉ David Lock Associates Ltd, 50 North Thirteenth Street, Central Milton Keynes, Buckinghamshire MK9 3BP (tel 01908 666276, fax 01908 605747, e-mail dlock@davidlock.com)

LOCK, Samuel; s of Sidney Avery (d 1972), of South Molton, Devon, and Edith May, *née* Lock (d 1972); *b* 24 April 1926, South Molton, Devon; *Educ* Barnstaple GS, St Paul's Coll

Cheltenham; *Career* painter, designer and writer; exhibited Gallery One London 1954 and 1956; theatre designer: several prodns Oxford Playhouse Co 1956, The Tiger and the Horse Queen's Theatre London 1960; collaborator documentary film (winner Mercurio d'Oro Prize Venice 1960); FRSL 2001; *Publications* novels: As Luck Would Have It (1995, Sagittarius Award Soc of Authors 1996), Nothing But the Truth (1998), The Whites of Gold (2001); When the World Was Young (memoir, completed 2007); also five plays; *Style*— Samuel Lock, Esq; ✉ c/o Gillon Aitken Associates, 18–22 Cavaye Place, London SW10 9PT (tel 020 7373 8672, fax 020 7373 6002, e-mail reception@aitkenassoc.demon.co.uk)

LOCK-NECREWS, John Ernest; JP (South Glamorgan); s of William Ernest Necrews (d 1982), and Mary Constance, *née* Lock (d 1987); *b* 30 August 1939; *Educ* Bridgend GS, Univ of Wales (DipArch); *m* 3 Jan 1978, Daphne, da of Maj Stanley Dickinson, of Cardiff; 1 s (Christian b 1979); *Career* chartered architect; formerly chief exec HLN Architects Ltd; ret; architectural awards: Prince of Wales, Civic Tst, Times and RICS, Cardiff 2000, Lord Mayor's Civic; guest speaker on architectural conservation UNESCO World Congress Basle 1983; chm Central Branch Soc of Architects Wales 1981–82 (memb Cncl 1974–82); ARIBA, ACIArb, FFB; *Recreations* golf, skiing, painting; *Clubs* Cardiff and Co, Royal Porthcawl Golf; *Style*— John E Lock-Necrews, Esq; ✉ Castle Edge, Llanblethian, Cowbridge, CF71 7JT (tel 01446 772511, fax 01446 775247, e-mail jln600@tiscali.co.uk)

LOCKE, Alasdair James Dougall; s of Donald Locke (d 2005), and Joan, *née* Foyster (d 2005); *b* 29 August 1953, Aldershot, Hants; *Educ* Uppingham, Wadham Coll Oxford; *m* 19 June 1993, Kathleen Anne, *née* Vincent; 2 s (Harry b 5 March 1995, George b 4 Aug 1997); *Career* Citibank 1974–78, Oceanic Finance Ltd 1979–81, dir Henry Ansbacher & Co 1982–87, dep chm and ceo Kelt Energy plc 1987–89, fndr and chm Abbot Gp plc 1990–; chm NI Energy Holdings plc, chm First Property Gp plc, dir MECOM Gp plc; Overall and Master Scot Entrepreneur of the Year 1999, Grampian Industrialist of the Year 2001, Entrepreneurial Exchange Hall of Fame 2003; *Recreations* shooting, skiing; *Clubs* Oxford and Cambridge; *Style*— Alasdair Locke, Esq; ✉ Abbot Group plc, Minto Drive, Altens, Aberdeen AB12 3LW (tel 01224 299600, fax 01224 230400, e-mail alasdair.locke@abbotgroup.com)

LOCKET, David Frank; s of late Frank Barton Locket, and Phyllis Jesie, *née* Lawson; *b* 29 June 1940; *Educ* Haileybury and ISC, Battersea Coll of Technol; *m* 1966, (Ingegerd) Christina, da of Ake Bontell, of Sweden; 1 s (Martin Frank b 1970), 1 da (Annicka Louise b 1972); *Career* Savoy Hotel (Strand Hotels) London 1972–78, catering mangr Anchor Hotels London 1978–83; md LMS (Consultants) Ltd 1983–97, Locket Enterprises 1997–2006; clerk emeritus Master Innholders; Freeman City of London 1973, Liveryman Worshipful Co of Innholders; FHCIMA; *Recreations* veteran cars, fishing, clocks; *Style*— David F Locket, Esq; ✉ Pinecrest, Northdown Road, Woldingham, Surrey CR3 7AA (tel 01883 653181)

LOCKETT, Andrew; s of Terence Anthony Lockett, and Isobel Lockett (d 1997); *Educ* Hazel Grove HS Stockport, Lincoln Coll Oxford (scholar, BA); *Career* ed (social sciences) Croom Helm and Routledge Publishers 1986–89, literature ed (academic) OUP 1989–97, head BFI Publishing 1997–2003, reference dir Rough Guides 2003–; literature advsr Southern Arts 1995; *Books* Television Studies (assoc ed, 2002); *Recreations* soccer, travel; *Style*— Andrew Lockett, Esq; ✉ Rough Guides, 80 Strand, London WC2R 0RL (tel 020 7010 3787, fax 020 7010 6787, e-mail andrew.lockett@roughguides.com)

LOCKHART, *see also:* Sinclair-Lockhart

LOCKHART, Sheriff Principal Brian Alexander; s of John Arthur Hay Lockhart, and Norah, *née* Macneil, of Glasgow; *b* 1 October 1942; *Educ* Glasgow Acad, Univ of Glasgow (BL); *m* 1967, Christine Ross, da of James B Clark, of Ayr; 2 s, 2 da; *Career* slr; ptnr Robertson Chalmers & Auld 1964–79; Sheriff: N Strathclyde 1979–81, Glasgow and Strathkelvin 1981–2005; Sheriff Principal S Strathclyde Dumfries and Galloway 2005–; memb Parole Bd for Scotland 1997–2003; pres Sheriffs' Assoc 2004–05; *Recreations* fishing, golf, family; *Style*— Sheriff Principal Brian Lockhart; ✉ 18 Hamilton Avenue, Glasgow (tel 0141 427 1921); Sheriff Court, Airdrie (tel 01236 639170)

LOCKHART, Brian Robert Watson; s of George Watson Lockhart, of Berwickshire, and Helen, *née* Rattray; *b* 19 July 1944; *Educ* George Heriot's Sch, Univ of Aberdeen (MA), Univ of Edinburgh (DipEd), Moray House Coll of Educn (CertEd); *m* 4 April 1970, Fiona Anne, da of James Barclay Sheddon; 2 da (Joanne b 2 July 1973, Catriona b 24 May 1976), 1 s (Ross b 6 Feb 1979); *Career* George Heriot's Sch: history teacher 1968–72, princ teacher 1972–81; dep rector Glasgow HS 1981–96, headmaster Robert Gordon's Coll 1996–2004; chm Scottish Standing Ctee UCAS 2001–02 (memb 1994–, co-chm 1998–99); memb: Cncl Headteachers' Assoc of Scotland 1998–2004 (asst sec 1988–93), HMC 1996– (sec Scottish Div 2003, chm Scottish Div 2004), Higher Still Implementation Gp 1997–2000, Business Ctee Univ of Aberdeen 2001– (vice-govr 2006–), Cncl St Margaret's Sch for Girls Aberdeen 2004–, Bd Hutchesons' GS Glasgow 2005–, Bd Voluntary Servs Aberdeen 2005–, Audit Ctee Univ of Aberdeen 2007–; *Publications* The History of the Architecture of George Heriot's Hospital and School, 1628–1978 (article, 1978), Jinglin' Geordie's Legacy (2003), Robert Gordon's Bequest (2007); *Recreations* reading biographies, sport, films, politics, architecture; *Style*— Brian Lockhart, Esq; ✉ 80 Gray Street, Aberdeen AB10 6JE (tel 01224 315776, e-mail brian.lockhard1@btinternet.com)

LOCKHART, His Hon Frank Roper; s of Clement Lockhart (d 1995), of Braithwell, S Yorks, and Betsy, *née* Roper (d 1981); *b* 8 December 1931; *Educ* King Edward VI GS Retford, Doncaster GS, Univ of Leeds (LLB); *m* 5 Aug 1957, Brenda Harriett, da of Cyril Johnson (d 1985), of Woodlands, S Yorks; 1 da (Jeanette Anne b 1959), 1 s (John Michael Roper b 1961); *Career* slr; ptnr Jefferies Slrs 1965–88; recorder 1985–88, circuit judge (SE Circuit) 1988–2004 (dep circuit judge 2004–); chm: Social Security Tbnls 1970–88, Industrial Tbnls 1983; *Recreations* golf; *Style*— His Hon Frank Lockhart; ✉ c/o South Eastern Circuit Office, New Cavendish House, 18 Maltravers Street, London WC2R 3EU (tel 020 7936 7235)

LOCKHART, Ian Stuart; s of Rev Prebendary Douglas Stuart Mullinger Lockhart (d 1983), and Hilda Mary, *née* Walker (d 2003); *b* 9 November 1940; *Educ* Rugby, Clare Coll Cambridge (MA); *m* 30 Nov 1974, Rosanna, da of Capt Edward Hugh Cartwright, RN (d 1998); *Career* admitted slr 1967; ptnr Peake & Co 1969–89, conslt Charles Russell 2001–06 (ptnr 1989–2001); dir Wynnstay Properties plc and assoc cos 1972–2006; govr: St Mary's Sch Wantage 1972–2006, Ludlow Coll 2004–06; memb: Ctee St Marylebone Almshouses 1990–2006, Cncl Corp of the Church House 2003–06; tstee Historic Churches Preservation Tst 1993–2006 (vice-pres 2006–); treas Ct of Assts Corp of The Sons of The Clergy 2000–06 (memb 1972–); Liveryman: Worshipful Co of Tylers & Bricklayers 1974, Worshipful Co of Merchant Taylors 2006; *Clubs* Athenaeum; *Style*— Ian S Lockhart, Esq; ✉ 44 Mill Street, Ludlow, Shropshire SY8 1BB (tel 01584 879987)

LOCKHART-BALL, Hugh Frederick; s of Lt Cdr Alfred Ernest Ball, RN (d 1965), and Margaret Daphne, *née* Lockhart (d 1993); *b* 18 April 1948; *Educ* Sedbergh, Birmingham Sch of Architecture; *m* 1 April 1972 (m dis), Godelieve Antoinette; 1 s (Simon Hugh b 1976), 1 da (Amelia b 1979); *Career* architect; princ Lockhart-Ball Assocs 1981–, chm London Energy & Environment Gp 1999– (chm 1983–95); chm S London Soc of Architects 1999–2001, chm Tooting Partnership Bd; former pres Rotary Club of Tooting 1986; *Recreations* conserving energy, sketching, reading, photography, building, jazz and blues, wine and food; *Style*— Hugh Lockhart-Ball, Esq; ✉ 934 Garratt Lane, London SW17 0ND (tel 020 8767 6955, office 020 8672 1056, fax 020 8767 9401, e-mail hughlb@btconnect.com)

LOCKHART-MUMMERY, Christopher John; QC (1986); s of Sir Hugh Evelyn Lockhart-Mummery, KCVO (d 1988), of Basingstoke, Hants, and Elizabeth Jean, *née* Crerar (d 1981); *b* 7 August 1947; *Educ* Stowe, Trinity Coll Cambridge; *m* 1, 4 Sept 1971 (m dis 1992), Hon Elizabeth Rosamund, da of Neil Patrick Moncrieff Elles, and Baroness Elles (Life Peer), *qv*, of London; 2 da (Clare b 1973, Alice b 1980), 1 s (Edward b 1975); m 2, 4 Feb 1993, Mrs Mary-Lou Putley; *Career* called to the Bar Inner Temple 1971 (bencher 1991); recorder of the Crown Court 1994–2004, dep judge of the High Court 1995–2004; former head of chambers; *Books* Hill and Redman's Law of Landlord and Tenant (specialist ed, 1973); *Recreations* fishing, opera; *Style*— Christopher J Lockhart-Mummery, Esq, QC; ✉ Hookeswood House, Farnham, Blandford Forum, Dorset DT11 8DQ (tel 01725 516259); 133 Abbotsbury Road, London W14 8EP (tel 020 7603 7200); Landmark Chambers, 180 Fleet Street, London EC4A 2HG (tel 020 7430 1221, fax 020 7430 1667)

LOCKHART OF THE LEE, Angus Hew; recognised as Chief of the Name Lockhart by The Lord Lyon 1957; s of late Maj Simon Foster Macdonald Lockhart of the Lee, and Ella Catriona Gordon (d 2000); *b* 17 August 1946; *Educ* Rannoch Sch, N of Scotland Coll of Agric; *m* 1970, Susan Elizabeth, da of Hon William Normand (d 1967), s of Baron Normand (Life Peer, d 1962), and Hon Mrs William Normand; 1 s, 1 da; *Career* landowner and land manager; memb Standing Cncl of Scottish Chiefs; *Recreations* shooting, skiing; *Clubs* New (Edinburgh); *Style*— Angus Lockhart of the Lee; ✉ Newholm, Dunsyre, Lanark ML11 8NQ (tel 01968 682254); Lee and Carnwath Estates, Estate Office, Carnwath, Lanark (tel 01555 840273, fax 01555 840044)

LOCKLEY, Andrew John Harold; s of (Archdeacon) Dr Harold Lockley (d 2004), of Market Harborough, Leics, and Ursula Margarete, *née* Wedell (d 1990); *b* 10 May 1951; *Educ* Marlborough, Oriel Coll Oxford (Nolloth scholar, BA, MA); *m* 1, 14 Sept 1974 (m dis 2005), Ruth Mary, da of (Laurence) John Vigor, of Bath; 2 s (Thomas Andrew b 1978, Philip Jonathan b 1981), 1 da (Naomi Jane Ursula b 1987); m 2, 16 April 2005, Caryl Jane Berry, da of Denis Seymour, of Sheffield; *Career* research scholar World Cncl of Churches 1973–75, trainee slr Messrs Kingsley Napley & Co London 1975–78; slr: Messrs Young & Solon London 1979–80, Messrs Meaby & Co London 1980–82; The Law Soc: sec Contentious Business Dept 1985–87 (asst sec 1982–85), dir of legal practice 1987–95, dir of corp and regnl affrs 1995–96; head of public law Irwin Mitchell 1996–, conslt Dept of Law Univ of Sheffield 1996–98, hon fell Univ of Sheffield 1999–; pt/t chm Special Educnl Needs and Disability Tbnl 1996–, pt/t chair Doctors and Dentists Disciplinary Procedures Appeal Panels 2007–; dir Solicitors Financial Services Ltd 1988–92, dir Solicitors' Property Centres Ltd 1997–2000 (chm 1998–2000); memb: Cmmn of Efficiency in Criminal Courts 1986–93, CITCOM Advsy Ctee 1988–90, IT and the Courts Ctee 1990–95; memb Editorial Advsy Bd Educn, Public Law and the Individual 2005–; govr William Austin Sch Luton 1992–96; memb Law Soc 1979; *Books* Christian Communes (1976), The Pursuit of Quality - a guide for lawyers (ed, 1993); *Recreations* growing fruit and vegetables, choral singing, swimming, travel, walking, reading; *Style*— Andrew Lockley, Esq; ✉ Irwin Mitchell, Riverside East, 2 Millsands, Sheffield S3 8DT (tel 0870 1500 100, fax 0114 275 3306, e-mail andrew.lockley@irwinmitchell.com)

LOCKLEY, Charles; s of John Edward Clare-Day, and Anne Francis, *née* Snell; *b* 22 February 1966; *Educ* Heathcote Sch Stevenage, Glasgow Poly; *m* 20 June 1998, Claire Eileen, da of William Grant; 2 s (Luke John b 4 May 2001, Josh William b 12 Feb 2003); *Career* chef; asst chef airport restaurant Baden Baden 1983–87, second chef Clifton House Hotel Nairn 1987–91, second chef rising to head chef Restaurant No 1 and later Café No 1 Inverness 1992–97, head chef Boath House Auldearn 1997– (4 AA Rosettes); work experience: Nico Ladenis 90 Park Lane London 1998, Foliage London 2005, Hibiscus Ludlow 2006; memb: Scottish Chefs Assoc 1996–, Master Chefs of GB 2001–; Scottish Chefs Assoc: Best Scottish Hotel Chef 2002, highly commended Scottish Chef of the Year 2006; *Style*— Charles Lockley, Esq; ✉ Boath House, Auldearn, Nairn IV3 5TE (tel 01667 454896, e-mail charlielockley@tiscali.co.uk)

LOCKS, Ian Roy; s of John Leonard Locks (d 1963), and Doreen Flower, *née* Bennett (d 1994); *b* 21 April 1941; *Educ* Felsted, SW Essex Poly (Dip Mgmnt Studies); *m* 10 Sept 1966, Valerie Jean, da of Edward George Surguy; 3 da (Katharine Elizabeth b 7 June 1968, Virginia Louise b 11 May 1970, Charlotte Claire b 22 May 1975); *Career* reporter and news ed W London and Essex 1958–64, sr editorial and mgmnt positions 1964–75 (incl editorial dir London, Middx and Essex Newspapers 1966–72), mangr regnl newspapers Printing and Publishing Trg Bd 1976–82, chief exec Assoc of Free Newspapers 1982–89, chief exec PPA 1989–; dir: Bd of Fin Advertising Standards Ctee 1989–, Audit Bureau of Circulation 1989–, Copyright Licensing Agency 1989–, Publishers Licensing Soc 1989–, Press Bd PCC 1991–, Publishing Nat Trg Orgn 2000–03; chm Trade Assoc Forum 2001–03; memb Cncl: Advertising Assoc 1982–, CBI Trade Assoc 2001–; tstee St Bride's Fleet Street 2001–; Freeman City of London, Ct Asst Worshipful Co of Stationers and Newspapermakers; MIMgt 1971, MInstD 1982; *Recreations* being a husband, father and grandfather, golf, tennis, walking, theatre, opera, travel; *Clubs* Theydon Bois Golf; *Style*— Ian Locks, Esq; ✉ Periodical Publishers Association, Queens House, 28 Kingsway, London WC2B 6JR (tel 020 7404 4166, fax 020 7404 4167, e-mail ian.locks@ppa.co.uk)

LOCKWOOD, Baroness (Life Peer UK 1978), of Dewsbury in the County of West Yorkshire; Betty Lockwood; DL (W Yorks); da of late Arthur Lockwood; *b* 22 January 1924; *Educ* Eastborough Girls' Sch Dewsbury, Ruskin Coll Oxford; *m* 1978, Lt-Col Cedric Hall (d 1988), s of late George Hall; *Career* sits as Lab Peer in House of Lords (dep speaker 1990–), memb Cncl of Europe and WEU 1992–94; Yorks regnl women's offr Lab Pty 1952–67, chief woman offr and asst nat agent Lab Pty 1967–75, chm Equal Opportunities Cmmn 1975–83, chm EEC Advsy Ctee on Equal Opportunities for Women and Men 1982–83; pres Birkbeck Coll London 1983–89; memb: Advtg Standards Authy Cncl 1983–92, Leeds Devpt Corp 1988–95; Univ of Bradford: memb Cncl 1983–, pro-chllr 1988–97, chm of Cncl 1992–97, chllr 1997–2005; memb Cncl Univ of Leeds 1985–91; chm Nat Coal Mining Museum for England 1995–2007 (pres 2007–); hon fell: UMIST (vice-pres 1992–95), Birkbeck Coll London; Hon DLitt Univ of Bradford, Hon LLD Univ of Strathclyde 1985, Hon DUniv Leeds Metropolitan Univ 1999, Hon Dr Univ of Edinburgh 2004; *Clubs* Soroptimist Int; *Style*— The Rt Hon the Lady Lockwood, DL; ✉ 6 Sycamore Drive, Addingham, Ilkley, West Yorkshire LS29 0NY (tel 01943 831098)

LOCKWOOD, David Stuart; s of Capt Ronald Arthur Lockwood, of Christchurch, Dorset, and Rachael, *née* Bamforth; *b* 15 May 1945; *Educ* Guthlaxton GS Leicester, Cambridge Sch of Art, Sch of Architecture Leicester, RIBA (DipArch); *m* 1, (m dis 1974); m 2, 25 May 1978 (m dis 2002), Marion Janice, da of Walter Glen Page (d 1974), of Sydney, Aust; *Career* Jr Leaders Regt RE 1960–63, RE 1963–66; architect; John Whisson and Ptnrs Newmarket 1966–67, Heaton and Swales Bury St Edmunds 1967–70, Gordon White and Hood Leicester 1973–74, Ivan P Jarvis and Assoc Leicester 1974–76; Cecil Denny Highton and Ptnrs London 1976–: assoc 1979, equity ptnr 1983, gp ptnr 1990, dir 1995; sr vice-pres and dir of commercial architecture HOK Int Ltd 1995–2000, dir HOK sports, venue and entertainment architects 2000–01; md: Ellerbe Becket Ltd, EBD Int Ltd 2001–03, DavidLockwood Consulting 2003–; RIBA, Comprehensive Design Architects (CDA), memb ARCUK 1974, assoc memb AIA 1994; Freeman: Worshpiful Co of Chartered Architects 2000, City of London 2001; *Recreations* sailing, skiing, architecture, ballet, cycling, squash; *Clubs* RAC, Corinthian Sailing, City Livery Yacht; *Style*— David S Lockwood, Esq; ✉ DavidLockwood Consulting, Studio 4, 9 Albert Embankment,

L

Salamanca Square, London SE1 7HD (tel 0870 443 8081, mobile 07787 853011, e-mail david@david-lockwood.com, website www.david-lockwood.com)

LOCKWOOD, John William; s of Arthur William Lockwood, of Spridlington, Lincs, and Heather, *née* Rogerson; *b* 24 August 1954; *Educ* Uppingham, UMIST (BSc); *m* 28 May 1982, Judith Ann, da of Patrick Henry Dickinson, of Gainsborough, Lincs; 2 s (George William b 5 March 1985, James Patrick Alexander b 21 Jan 1991), 1 da (Sarah Helen May b 2 Aug 1987); *Career* dir of various companies; MFH Burton Hunt 1981–; *Recreations* hunting; *Style*— John Lockwood, Esq; ✉ Cammeringham Manor, Cammeringham, Lincoln LN1 2SH (tel 01522 730342); Castle Square Developments Ltd, Scampton House, Scampton, Lincoln LN1 2SF (tel 01522 730730, fax 01522 731777)

LOCKWOOD, Rear Adm Roger Graham; CB (2005); s of Eric Garnett Lockwood (d 1985), and Nunda, *née* Doak; *b* 26 June 1950, Hitchin, Herts; *Educ* Kimbolton Sch, Univ of Warwick (BA); *m* 1 Sept 1984, Susan, *née* Cant; 3 s (William b 18 Oct 1985, Robb b 30 Jan 1988, Andrew b 10 Sept 1995), 2 da (Rosalyn b 10 May 1991, Jennie b 19 May 2001); *Career* RN 1971–2005: jr offr appts 1971–84, JSDC 1985, Base Supply Offr HMS Dolphin 1985–87, Cdr RN Supply Sch 1987–89, Supply Offr HMS Ark Royal 1989–91, Dep Dir Naval Serv Conditions (Pay) 1991–93, RCDS 1994, Sec to Second Sea Lord 1995–96, Sec to First Sea Lord 1996–98, Cdre HMS Raleigh 1998–2000, COS to Second Sea Lord 2000–02, Sr Directing Staff (Navy) RCDS 2002–05; chief exec Northern Lighthouse Bd 2006–; co sec Dunblane Devpt Tst 2005–, cmmr Queen Victoria Sch Dunblane 2006–, chm Perth Sea Cadet Unit 2006–; area vice-patron (Scotland) War Memls Tst; FCIPD 2001; *Recreations* family, studying the history of the SOE in France; *Clubs* New (Edinburgh); *Style*— Rear Adm Roger Lockwood, CB

LOCKYER, Bob; *b* 9 April 1942; *Career* dir, prodr and former exec prodr of dance progs for BBC TV; worked with choreographers incl: Sir Frederick Ashton, Sir Kenneth MacMillan, Sir Peter Wright, Birgit Culberg; chair Dance UK 1982–92; dir dance video courses in: Australia 1990, NZ 1990 and 1993, Canada 1992, 1994 and 1996, various in UK; winner Royal Philharmonic Soc Award 1993; *Director* with Robert Cohan and London Contemporary Dance Co: Stabat Mater 1979, Forest 1980, Cell 1983, Nymphaes 1983; with Rambert Dance Co: Pulcinella 1988, Soldat 1989; others incl: Les Noces (Royal Ballet) 1978, Dance Masterclasses with Sir Frederick Ashton and Sir Peter Wright (both 1987); *Executive producer* numerous ballet relays incl: Sleeping Beauty (Royal Ballet) 1994, Mayerling (Royal Ballet) 1995; also exec prodr: Points in Space (BBC cmmn, winner Dir's dip Prague Int TV Festival) 1988, Strange Fish (DV8, winner Grand Prix at Prix Italia) 1994, Outside In (Grand Prix Prague Int TV Festival) 1995, *Writer* various ballet scenarios incl Corporal Jan (choreographed and directed by Peter Wright); *Recreations* walking, collecting and cooking; *Style*— Bob Lockyer, Esq; ✉ 5 Walwers Lane, Lewes, East Sussex BN7 2JX

LODER, Sir Edmund Jeune; 4 Bt (UK 1887), of Whittlebury, Northamptonshire, and of Leonardslee, Horsham, Sussex; s of Sir Giles Rolls Loder, 3 Bt (d 1999); *b* 26 June 1941; *Educ* Eton; *m* 1, 1966 (m dis 1971), Penelope Jane, da of Ivo Forde; 1 da (Gillian Marie (Mrs James D P Morgan) b 1968); m 2, 1992, Susan Warren, da of V W Warren Pearl; *Heir* bro, Robert Loder; *Career* FCA; bloodstock breeder; *Style*— Sir Edmund Loder, Bt; ✉ Eyrefield Lodge, The Curragh, Co Kildare

LODER-SYMONDS, Roderick Francis (Roddy); s of Brig Robert Guy Loder-Symonds, DSO, MC (ka 1945), of Heytesbury, Wilts, and Mrs Merlin Audrey Houghton Brown, *née* Allen (d 1988); *b* 16 November 1938; *Educ* Radley, RAC Cirencester; *m* 20 July 1967, Caroline Anne, da of Cdr M F L Beebee (d 1988), of Womaston House, Presteigne, Radnorshire; 2 s (Robert b 31 Aug 1971, James b 28 May 1974), 1 da (Sacha (Mrs Michael Davies) b 19 Nov 1968); *Career* farmer Denne Hill Farms Womenswold Kent 1970–, ptnr Strutt & Parker 1976–99, ret; churchwarden Womenswold Church 1970–82; chm: Farmers' Club 1976 (tstee 1994–), Parish Cncl 1978–86, Canterbury Farmers' Club 1982; pres Kent Branch CLA 2004– (chm 1986–87); Bd memb Enterprise Agency E Kent 1985–98; tstee Huggens Coll Northfleet 1976–, KCA (UK) 2001–; govr Canterbury Christchurch Univ; High Sheriff Kent 2000–2001; Liveryman Worshipful Co of Farmers; FRICS 1976; *Recreations* shooting, golf; *Clubs* Farmers; *Style*— Roddy Loder-Symonds, Esq; ✉ Denne Hill Farm, Womenswold, Canterbury, Kent CT4 6HD (tel 01227 832202, fax 01227 830346)

LODGE, Anton James Corduff; QC (1989); *Educ* Univ of Cambridge (MA); *Career* called to the Bar Gray's Inn 1966 (bencher 1997), recorder; *Style*— Anton Lodge, Esq, QC

LODGE, Bryony; da of John Lodge, of Chester, and Elizabeth, *née* Cameron; *b* 22 October 1957; *Educ* Queen's Sch Chester, Univ of St Andrews (MA); *Career* civil servant; head Nat Lottery Distribution and Communities Div DCMS 2001–03, head Museums Policy Div DCMS 2003–; *Recreations* music; *Style*— Ms Bryony Lodge; ✉ Department for Culture, Media & Sport, 2–4 Cockspur Street, London SW1Y 5DH (tel 020 7211 6132)

LODGE, Prof David; s of Herbert Lodge, and Dorothy, *née* Moss; *b* 22 September 1941; *Educ* Weston Super Mare GS, Univ of Bristol (BVSc, PhD, DSc); *m* 1, 15 Feb 1964 (m dis), Susan, da of Sidney Hayling; 4 s (Marcus b 1964, Duncan b 1966, James b 1969, (Robert) Jolyon b 1971); m 2, 21 Oct 1995, Catherine Mary, da of Peter Sutton; 1 da (Josie Louise b 1993); *Career* jr fell and lectr Dept of Veterinary Surgery Univ of Bristol 1963–70, Wellcome Tst fell Dept of Physiology Animal Health Tst 1970–74; post doctoral res fell Aust Nat Univ 1974–79; Royal Veterinary Coll London: sr lectr 1979–84, prof of vet neuroscience 1984–91, prof of vet physiology and head of vet basic sciences 1989–91, research advsr CNS res Lilly Res Centre 1991–97; currently: visiting prof of vet physiology Univ of London, hon prof of physiology Univ of Cardiff, Benjamin Meaker visiting prof Univ of Bristol, dir of stroke research Eli Lilly & Co; ed Neuropharmacology 1992–; memb Ctee Physiological Soc 1983–87; MRCVS 1963, DVA 1969; *Books* Excitatory Amino Acid Transmission (1987), Excitatory Amino Acids in Health and Disease (1988), Ionotropic Glutanate Receptors as Therapeutic Targets (2002); *Recreations* rugby, running, skiing, coaching junior sport; *Style*— Prof David Lodge; ✉ Lilly Research Centre, Erlwood Manor, Windlesham, Surrey GU20 6PH (tel 01276 483900, fax 01276 483525)

LODGE, Prof David John; CBE (1998); s of William Frederick Lodge, and Rosalie Marie, *née* Murphy; *b* 28 January 1935; *Educ* St Joseph's Acad Blackheath, UCL (John Oliver Hobbes scholar, BA, MA, John Morley medal, Quain Essay prize), Univ of Birmingham (PhD); *m* 15 May 1959, Mary Frances, da of Francis Jacob (d 1969); 1 da (Julia Mary b 1960), 2 s (Stephen David b 1962, Christopher Adrian b 1966); *Career* Nat Serv RAC 1955–57; asst British Cncl Overseas Students Centre London 1959–60; Dept of English Univ of Birmingham: asst lectr 1960–62, lectr 1961–71, sr lectr 1971–73, reader in English literature 1973–76, prof of modern English literature 1976–87, hon prof of modern English literature 1987–2000, emeritus prof of English literature 2001–; visiting assoc prof Univ of Calif Berkeley 1969, Henfield fell in creative writing UEA 1977, Whitney J Oates short term visiting fell Princeton Univ 1981, E J Pratt lectr Meml Univ of St John's Newfoundland 1985, Lansdowne scholar Univ of Victoria BC 1986, Regents lectr Univ of Calif Riverside 1989; chm Booker Prize Judges 1989; hon fell: UCL 1982, Goldsmiths Coll London 1992; Hon DLitt Univ of Warwick 1997, Hon DLitt Univ of Birmingham 2001; FRSL 1976; Chevalier de l'Ordre des Arts et des Lettres (France) 1997; *Novels* The Picturegoers (1960), Ginger You're Barmy (1962), The British Museum is Falling Down (1965), Out of the Shelter (1970), Changing Places: a Tale of Two Campuses (1975), How Far Can You Go (1980), Small World: an academic romance (1984), Nice Work (1988), Paradise News (1991), Therapy (1995), Home Truths: a novella (1999), Thinks... (2001), Author, Author (2004); *Non-fiction* incl: Language of Fiction (1966), The Novelist at the Crossroads (1971), The Modes of Modern Writing (1977), Working With Structuralism (1981), Write On (1986), After Bakhtin (1990), The Art of Fiction (1992), The Practice of Writing (1996), Consciousness and the Novel (2002), The Year of Henry James (2006); *Stage and Screen* Between These Four Walls (with M Bradbury and J Duckett, 1963), Slap in the Middle (with M Bradbury, J Duckett and D Turner, 1965), Big Words - Small Worlds (Channel 4, 1987), Nice Work (BBC2, 1989, Silver Nymph Award), The Writing Game (Birmingham Rep 1990, adapted for Channel 4 1995), The Way of St James (BBC1, 1993), Martin Chuzzlewit (adapted from Charles Dickens' novel, BBC2, 1994), Home Truths (Birmingham Rep, 1998); *Style*— Prof David Lodge, CBE; ✉ Department of English, University of Birmingham, Birmingham B15 2TT

LODGE, Dr Denise Valerie; *b* 5 September 1951; *Educ* Bury GS, Royal Holloway Coll London (BSc, PhD), Chelsea Coll London (MSc); *m* Edward; 1 s (Duncan), 1 da (Alice); *Career* head of chemistry, head of sixth form and sr teacher (curriculum) Sir Roger Manwood's Sch Sandwich 1987–96, dep head (academic) Sheffield HS GDST 1996–99, headmistress Sydenham HS GDST 1999–2002, headmistress Putney HS GDST 2002–; treas and memb Educn Research Ctee GSA 2003–07; memb Ct Imperial Coll London 2007–; finalist Salters' Prize 1997, runner-up Tatler/HSBC Bank Best Headmistress of a Public Sch 2004; *Recreations* jazz, art, gym; *Style*— Dr Denise Lodge; ✉ Putney High School GDST, 35 Putney Hill, London SW15 6BH

LODGE, Jane Ann; da of John Humphrey Lodge (d 1984), of York, and Marian, *née* Smith; *b* 1 April 1955; *Educ* Mill Mount GS York, Univ of Birmingham (BSc); *m* 2 July 1983, Anthony (Tony) John Borton, s of Reginald Aubrey Borton (d 1980), of Rugby; 1 s (John Aubrey b 1988), 2 da (Emma Jane b 1990, Victoria Mary b 1992); *Career* Deloitte & Touche (formerly Touche Ross) Birmingham: trainee accountant 1973, qualified 1976, ptnr 1986–, ptnr i/c Allder Learning and Devpt 1999, office sr ptnr (Birmingham) 2000–02, practice sr ptnr (Midlands) 2002–05; UK mfrg industry ldr 2005–; memb: Ctee Birmingham and W Midlands Soc of Chartered Accountants 1987–96 (pres 1994–95), W Midlands Industrial Devpt Bd 1999–2004, W Midlands Regnl Cncl CBI 2001–, Bd Birmingham Forward 2001– (chm Business Growth Ctee 2002–04); memb Cncl Univ of Birmingham 1986–91 and 1993–2004 (pres Guild of Graduates 1987–88, memb Strategy Planning and Resources Ctee 1987–91, memb Audit Ctee 1997–), govr Arthur Terry Sch Sutton Coldfield Birmingham 1989–95; Midlands Businesswoman of the Year 2001, BWMSCA Lifetime Achievement Award 2003; FCA 1976; *Recreations* cookery, tapestry, golf; *Style*— Ms Jane Lodge; ✉ Deloitte & Touche LLP, Four Brindley Place, Birmingham B1 2HZ

LODGE, Prof Juliet; da of Arthur Robert Mayer, of Islington, and Lenore Mayer; *Educ* Coombe Co Girls' Sch, CNAA (BA), Univ of Reading (MA, MPhil, DLitt), Univ of Hull (PhD); *m*; 1 da (Keri-Michèle), 2 s (David, Christopher); *Career* lectr in European and int politics Univ of Auckland 1973–77, visiting fell Centre for Int Studies Dept of Int Relations LSE 1976–77; Univ of Hull: lectr in politics 1977–84, sr lectr in politics 1984–88, reader in EC politics 1988–91, prof of European politics 1991–96, Jean Monnet prof of European integration and co-dir EC Res Unit 1991–96; Univ of Leeds: dir Centre for Euro Studies 1996–, currently Jean Monnet prof of EU politics and public policy; freelance journalist and broadcaster; NATO res fell 1992; visiting prof: Université Libre de Bruxelles 1992–95, Vrije Universitet Brussel 1995, Institut fü Höhere Studien Vienna 1996; convenor UK Political Studies Assoc Study Gp on the EC 1980–, exec memb Univ Assoc for Contemporary European Studies 1988–94, dir Jean Monnet Gp of Experts on Enlargement and the 1966 Intergovernmental Conf; memb: Cncl for Europeanists NYC 1983–, Univs Assoc for Contemporary European Studies 1984–, Cncl European Consortium for Political Res (ECPR) 1985–96, Humberside TEC 1993–95, Team Europe, ESRC Postgrad Ctee, ESRC Research Bd, Nat Ctee of Women of Europe, Advsy Cncl Euro Movement, European Information Assoc; conslt to EU Cmmn on Ethical Implications of Biometrics e-IDs and liberty; awards: UK Woman of Europe 1991–92, European Woman of Europe 1992–93, European Woman of Achievement Award 1992; hon pres Assoc for Euro and Int Co-ordination in Schs; FRSA 1992; *Books* The European Policy of the SPD (1976), The New Zealand General Election of 1975 (co-author, 1978), The European Parliament and the European Community (co-author, 1978), The European Community and New Zealand (1982), Direct Elections to the European Parliament: A Community Perspective (co-author, 1982), Democratic Legitimacy and the EC (1991), The EU and the Challenge of the Future (1993), The 1994 Euro-Elections (1995), 1999 Euro-Elections (2001), Election of the European Parliament 2004 (2004), Biometrics: Are you who you say you are? (2007); Institutional Implications of EMU and the Euro at the European and National Levels; Euratom and the IGC's (report for the European Parl, 1999 and 2002), reports to the European Parl on civil liberties, Europol, biometrics and e-governance; ed numerous books and pubns on e-governance and e-justice; *Recreations* art, writing, laughing; *Style*— Professor Juliet Lodge; ✉ Jean Monnet Centre of Excellence, University of Leeds, Leeds LS2 9JT (tel 0113 343 4443, e-mail j.e.lodge@leeds.ac.uk)

LODHI, HE Dr Maleeha; *b* 15 November 1952, Lahore, Pakistan; *Educ* LSE (BSc, PhD); *Career* lectr in public admin Quaid-e-Azam Univ Islamabad 1977–78, lectr in politics and political sociology LSE 1980–85, ed The Muslim 1987–90, ed The News 1990–93, ambass to USA 1994–97, ed The News 1997–99, ambass to USA (with status of min of state) 1999–2002, distinguised visiting faculty Nat Defence Coll 2003, high cmmr to UK 2003–; memb UN Sec-Gen's Advsy Bd on Disarmament Affrs 2001–; awarded Hilal-e-Imtiaz for contrib to diplomacy and journalism; *Books* Pakistan's Encounter with Democracy (1994), The External Challenge (1994); *Style*— HE Dr Maleeha Lodhi; ✉ High Commission for Pakistan, 35–36 Lowndes Square, London SW1X 9JN (tel 020 7664 9232, fax 020 7664 9225, e-mail mlfs1@aol.com)

LOEFFLER, Frank; s of Ernst Loeffler (d 1967), and Bianka Klein, *née* Breitmann; *b* 21 January 1931; *Educ* Mill Hill Sch, Gonville & Caius Coll Cambridge, London Hosp Med Coll (MB BChir); *m* 10 Aug 1958, Eva Augusta, da of Sir Ludwig Guttmann (d 1981), of High Wycombe and Aylesbury; 2 da (Clare b 13 Dec 1959, Juliet b 26 June 1964), 1 s (Mark b 15 April 1961); *Career* in private practice Harley St; conslt: Central Middlesex Hosp 1967–68, St Mary's Hosp W2 1968–96, Queen Charlotte's Hosp 1983–96; ed Br Jl of Obstetrics & Gynaecology 1973–80; memb Ctee on Safety of Medicines 1987–92; memb Cncl RCOG 1987–90; FRCS 1959, FRCOG 1973; *Recreations* tennis, sailing, skiing; *Clubs* Aldeburgh Yacht, Aldeburgh Golf, Royal Soc of Med; *Style*— Frank Loeffler, Esq; ✉ 86 Harley Street, London W1G 7HP (tel 020 7486 2966, fax 020 7637 0994, e-mail frankloeffler@ukonline.co.uk)

LOEHNIS, Anthony David; CMG (1988); s of Cdr Sir Clive Loehnis, KCMG, RN (ret) (d 1992), and Rosemary (d 2006), da of Hon Robert Ryder (ka 1917, s of 2 Earl of Harrowby, KG, PC, and Lady Mary Cecil, da of 2 Marqess of Exeter); *b* 12 March 1936; *Educ* Eton, New Coll Oxford, Harvard Univ; *m* 7 Aug 1965, Jennifer, da of Sir Donald Anderson; 3 s; *Career* with FCO until 1966; Schroder Wagg 1967–80, exec dir Bank of England 1981–89 (assoc dir 1980–81), dir S G Warburg Gp plc and vice-chm S G Warburg & Co Ltd 1989–92; chm: Henderson Japanese Smaller Companies Tst plc (formerly HTR Japanese Smaller Companies Tst plc) 1993–2001, The Knox D'Arcy Tst plc 1996–2002; dir: UK-Japan 21st Century Gp 1990–2005, St James's Place Capital plc 1993–2005, Alpha Bank London Ltd 1994– (chm 2005–), Mitsubishi UFJ Securities International plc 1996–2003, AGCO Corp 1997–2005; chm Villiers Park Educnl Tst 2000–; memb: Cncl of Mgmnt Ditchley Fndn 1992–, Governing Bd Br Assoc for Central and Eastern Europe 1994–2003, Cncl Baring Fndn 1994–2005; chm Public Works Loan Commission

1997–2005 (cmmr 1994); *Style*— Anthony Loehnis, Esq, CMG; ✉ Haughton House, Churchill, Oxfordshire OX7 6NU

LOEWE, Prof Raphael James; MC (1943); s of Herbert Martin James Loewe (d 1940), of Cambridge, and Ethel Victoria, *née* Hyamson (d 1946); *b* 16 April 1919; *Educ* Dragon Sch Oxford, The Leys Sch Cambridge, St John's Coll Cambridge (MA); *m* 19 March 1952, Chloe, da of Mendel Klatzkin (d 1951), of London; 2 da (Elisabeth (Mrs Talbot) b 1953, Camilla (Mrs Verry) b 1957); *Career* served The Suffolk Regt, 142 Regt RAC N African and Italian Campaigns, wounded in action 1940–45; lectr in Hebrew Leeds 1949, Bye fell Caius Coll Cambridge 1954, visiting prof Brown Univ Providence RI USA 1963–64, Goldsmid prof of Hebrew UCL until 1984 (formerly lectr then reader); author of numerous articles in learned jls and presentation vols; Seatonian Prize (for poem on sacred subject) Cambridge 2000, recipient of presentation volume (Hebrew Scholarship and the Medieval World) 2001; former Elder Spanish and Portuguese Jews' Congregation London; past pres: Soc for Old Testament Study, Jewish Historical Soc of England, Br Assoc for Jewish Studies; FSA, fell Royal Asiatic Soc; *Books* The Position of Women in Judaism (1966), Encyclopaedia Judaica (contrib ed, 1971), Omar Khayyam (Hebrew version, 1982), The Rylands Haggadah (1988), Solomon ibn Gabirol (1989), The Barcelona Haggadah (contributing ed, 1992), History of Linguistics (contrib, 1994), North French Hebrew Miscellany (2003), Fables from a Distant Past, by Isaac Ibn Sahula (2004); *Recreations* travel, walking, translating English, Latin and Hebrew poetry; *Style*— Prof Raphael Loewe, MC, FSA; ✉ 50 Gurney Drive, London N2 0DE (tel and fax 020 8455 5379, e-mail layish@gotadsl.co.uk)

LOEWENSTEIN-WERTHEIM-FREUDENBERG, Prince Rupert Ludwig Ferdinand zu; also Count von Loewenstein-Scharffeneck; s of Prince Leopold zu Loewenstein-Wertheim-Freudenberg (d 1974; of the family of mediatised Princes, title of Bavarian Prince conferred 1812, stemming from the morganatic marriage of Elector Palatine Friedrich I (d 1476) to Klara Tott, of Augsburg; Counts of HRE 1494, recreated Loewenstein-Scharffeneck 1875), and Countess Bianca Fischler von Treuberg; *b* 24 August 1933; *Educ* St Christopher Sch Letchworth, Magdalen Coll Oxford (MA); *m* 1957, Josephine Clare, da of Capt Montague Lowry-Corry (d 1977, gggs of 2 Earl Belmore) by his 1 w, Hon Mary Biddulph, yr da of 2 Baron Biddulph; 2 s (Rev Father Rudolf Amadeus, OP b 1957, Rev Father Konrad Friedrich, FSSP b 1958), 1 da (Princess Maria Theodora Marjorie (Countess Manfredi della Gherardesca) b 1966); *Career* fin advsr, former merchant banker; CStJ; Knight of San Gennaro, Bailiff Grand Cross of Honour and Devotion SMO Malta (pres Br Assoc), Bailiff Grand Cross of Justice Constantinian Order of St George with collar (pres Br Assoc), Knight of Justice Order of St Stephen, Knight Cdr of St Gregory with Star; *Recreations* music; *Clubs* London: Beefsteak, Boodle's, Buck's, Portland, Pratt's, White's; NYC: The Brook, Regency; *Style*— Prince Rupert zu Loewenstein-Wertheim-Freudenberg; ✉ Rupert Loewenstein Ltd, 2 King Street, London SW1Y 6QL (tel 020 7839 6454, fax 020 7930 4032)

LOFTHOUSE, Marjorie Helen; MBE (1990); da of Ronald Douglas Minns (d 1968), of London, and Marjorie May, *née* Axford (d 1989); *b* 3 March 1943; *Educ* City of Bath Girls' Sch, Co of Stafford Trg Coll; *m* Ken Stephinson; 2 step da (Jacqueline, Joanne); *Career* broadcaster; formerly with HTV West; progs incl: Reports West, Here Today, Gallery; BBC: regular presenter of Pebble Mill at One (BBC 1), co-presenter Eating Out with Tovey (BBC 2), writer and narrator of many documentaries incl See for Yourself, presented The New Venturers series (BBC Scotland) 1990–91; radio: commenced broadcasting with Radio Metro Newcastle, presented Northern edn Woman's Hour (BBC Manchester and BBC Birmingham), developed Homing-In, created Vintage Cider (two part biography of Laurie Lee), presented Enterprise (BBC Radio 4), presented numerous features and documentaries, created Romantic Strings series (BBC Radio 2), own music prog Prelude (BBC Radio 4) 1989–95, presenter Business on the Move (BBC Radio 5); prodn work BBC Radio 4 incl: Feet First, Hair Today, The Long Sleep, Timpson's England, Norfolk Men, Free for All, This Stately Homes Business, The Big Day; presented Royal Show open air concert featuring Midland Concert Orch 1988, responsible for creating an annual competition to find Britain's most enterprising small businesses which were then featured on radio prog Enterprise 1984–91, voice-over artiste for corp and broadcast media trg; dir Stephinson Television; runner-up Sony Radio Awards for documentary Leslie 1986; pres Saddleworth Cancer Research Campaign, memb Bd Oldham Coliseum; *Books* The New Adventurers; *Style*— Ms Marjorie Lofthouse, MBE; ✉ Stephinson Television, Saddleworth Station, Dobcross, Lancashire OL3 5NS (tel 01457 820820, fax 01457 820111, e-mail mhl@stephinsontv.co.uk)

LOFTHOUSE, Simon Timothy; QC (2006); s of Adam Lofthouse, of Salop, and Angela, *née* Manning; *b* 25 August 1966; *Educ* Fernwood Sch Nottingham, Beckett Sch Nottingham, UCL (LLB); *m* 1 Oct 1994, Sophia, da of Stefan Gawlik; *Career* called to the Bar Gray's Inn 1988; tenant Atkin Chambers 1989– (specialising in construction, int arbitration, professional negligence and energy law); recorder 2003–; articles ed Current Law 1989–94; memb Bar Professional Conduct Ctee 2002–05, prosecutor for Bar Standards Ctee 2006–; memb: Technol and Construction Bar Assoc, Commercial Bar Assoc, Franco-British Lawyers Soc Ltd; accredited adjudicator, registed advocacy trainer; *Recreations* theatre, squash, travelling; *Style*— Simon Lofthouse, Esq, QC; ✉ Atkin Chambers, 1 Atkin Building, Gray's Inn, London WC1R 5AT (tel 020 7404 0102, fax 020 7405 7456, e-mail slofthouse@atkinchambers.com)

LOFTHOUSE, Stephen; s of Harry Lofthouse (d 1980), and (Janet) Mary Hume Scott, *née* Fraser (d 1996); *b* 23 March 1945; *Educ* Tauntons GS, Univ of Manchester (BA, MA); *Career* res assoc Univ of Manchester 1968, conslt United Textile Factory Workers Assoc 1968, lectr (later sr lectr) Manchester Poly 1969–72, lectr Manchester Business Sch 1972–75, visiting lectr Univ of Amsterdam 1974, dir Grade 10 Industries Assistance Cmmn Australia 1975, conslt Price Cmmn 1976–77, assoc Capel-Cure Myers 1977–83, conslt Br Sugar 1980–81, sr exec James Capel and Co 1983–85, dir (then chm) James Capel Fund Managers Ltd (formerly James Capel International Asset Management Limited) 1985–92, dir (then chm) James Capel Unit Trust Management Ltd 1988–92, dir James Capel & Co Limited 1990–91, md James Capel Asset Management Ltd 1991–92; dir: Wardley Investment Services Ltd 1988–92 (non-exec), Wardley Global Selection SICAV 1991–92, Wardley Investment Services (Luxembourg) SA 1991–92; writer 1993–; *Books* Equity Investment Management (1994), Readings In Investments (1994), How to Fix your Finances (1996), Investment Management (2001); numerous articles published in acad and professional jls; *Style*— Stephen Lofthouse, Esq; ✉ 4 North Several, Orchard Drive, London SE3 0QR (tel and fax 020 8318 7132, e-mail stephenlofthouse@aol.com)

LOFTHOUSE OF PONTEFRACT, Baron (Life Peer UK 1997), of Pontefract in the County of West Yorkshire; Sir Geoffrey Lofthouse; kt (1995), JP (Pontefract 1970); s of Ernest Lofthouse (d 1935), and Emma Lofthouse (d 1944); *b* 18 December 1925; *Educ* Featherstone Primary and Secondary Schs, Whitwood Tech Coll, Univ of Leeds; *m* 1946, Sarah (d 1985), da of Joesh Thomas Onions; 1 da; *Career* coal miner 1939–64, Manpower Office NCB 1964–70, personnel mangr NCB Fryston 1970–78; MP (Lab) Pontefract and Castleford Nov 1978–97, former memb Select Ctee on Energy, First Dep Chm of Ways and Means (dep speaker House of Commons) 1992–97, dep speaker House of Lords 1997–98; cncllr: Pontefract Borough DC 1962–74 (ldr 1969–74), Wakefield Metropolitan DC 1974–79 (first chm); chm: Wakefield HA 1998–2002, Mid-Yorkshire Hosps NHS Tst 2002–05; FIPM 1984; *Books* A Very Miner MP (autobiography, 1986), Coal Sack to Woolsack (autobiography, 1999); *Recreations* rugby league, cricket; *Style*— The Lord Lofthouse of Pontefract; ✉ 67 Carleton Crest, Pontefract, West Yorkshire (tel 01977 704 275); House of Lords, London SW1A 0PW (tel 020 7219 4050)

LOFTS, Joan; *Career* film librarian ITN 1964–69, researcher and assoc prodr Thames TV 1969–74; social worker Kent CC 1975–85; animation/acquisition exec TVS 1985–90, dep head of acquisitions and devpt Children's Dept BBC 1990–93; TCC: head of acquisition and devpt 1993–94, head of programming 1994–96, dir of programming 1996–97; conslt Polygram Visual Programming 1997–98, dir of progs and acquisitions Disney Channel UK 1998–99, currently head of TV Contender Entertainments Gp; chair Cardiff International Festival; memb Jr BAFTA Ctee; *Style*— Ms Joan Lofts

LOFTUS, Anthony Louis; s of Asher Loftus (d 1992), of London, and Rebecca, *née* Seder; *b* 26 November 1941, Hove; *Educ* Hasmonean GS Hendon; *m* 18 March 1979, Hannah, *née* Mandel; 2 da (Rachel, Melanie); *Career* dir Accurist; *Recreations* golf, skiing, poker; *Clubs* Brocket Hall Golf; *Style*— Anthony Loftus, Esq; ✉ Accurist, Asher House, Blackburn Road, London NW6 1AW (tel 020 7604 5900, fax 020 7625 5137)

LOGAN, Andrew David; s of William Harold Logan, of The Leys, Witney, Oxford, and Irene May, *née* Muddimer; *b* 11 October 1945; *Educ* Lord Williams's GS Thame, Burford GS, Oxford Sch of Architecture (DipArch); *Career* artist and sculptor; creator and artisitc dir The Alternative Miss World nos 1–11 1972–2004; opened Andrew Logan Museum of Sculpture Berriew 1991; designer: Wolfi (Ballet Rambert London) 1987, Bastet (Sadler's Wells Royal Ballet) 1988, jewelled sculptures for Magic Flute (San Diego OPera Co) 2001, designed and contrib spade for opening of Unicorn Children's Theatre 2004; *Exhibitions* incl: Biba's Sculpture Garden 1974, Goldfield (Whitechapel Art Gallery) 1976, Egypt Revisited Sand and Light Spectacular (Super Tent Clapham Common) 1978, Trigon-Graz (Austria) 1979, Goddesses (Cwlth Inst London) 1983, Henley Arts Festival 1984, The Book Show (Cylinder Gallery London) 1984, Galactic Forest (Functional Art Gallery, LA, Chicago and Limelight Club NYC) 1985, Daily Mail Ideal Home (Earls Court London) 1986, Winged Pegasus (Living Art Pavilion Arts Cncl) 1986, Glass Sculpture Singapore 1986, Monuments and Music (Botanical Gardens Rome) 1987, London Capital of New Ideas (Moscow)1989, Avant Garde (Russia tour) 1989, Wings Over Waves (Angela Flowers Ireland) 1990, Untamed Fashion Assembly (Riga) 1990, An Artistic Adventure (MOMA Oxford, Flowers East Gallery and The Old Library Cardiff) 1991, Jewels of Fantasy (V&A) 1992, Millfield British 20th Century Sculpture (Somerset) 1992, LA Art Fair 1992, Bonham's Knightsbridge 1992, Cracked Mirrors - Very Nice (Festival Hall Craft Gallery London) 1993, Olympian Arts (CentrePoint London) 1993, Monuments of Hope and Joy (display of Pegasus I and II Heathrow Airport) 1993, The Elements (Concord Lighting London) 1993, Andrew Logan Museum of Sculpture Berriew (solo exhbn) 1994, Northern Centre for Contemporary Art 1994, 101 Chairs (South Bank Centre) 1994, Fabulous Fakes and Flying Carpets (Bluecoat Display Centre Liverpool) 1994, Pegasus and Jewels (Roscarbery) 1994, Elvis and Marilyn: 2 x Immortal (Boston MA and US tour) 1994, Shining Through (Crafts Cncl Islington) 1995, The Happy Heart Show (Manchester City Art Galleries) 1995, Int Jewellery Conf (Univ of Northumbria) 1996, Fluid (Manchester Rochdale Canal) 1996, Carnival (Sainsbury Centre Norwich) 1996, Moscow Art Fair 1996, Wings Over Waves (De La Warr Pavilion Bexhill on Sea) 1996, Museo del Vidrio (perm exhbn of sculptures, Monterrey) 1996, New Times, New Thinking (Crafts Cncl London) 1996, Men on Women (Denbighshire) 1997, Eyeworks (Crafts Cncl, London and tour) 1997, Portraits show (National Portrait Gallery) 1997, London Open House 1997, L'Age d'Or (Air Gallery London) 1997, Reflections of the Heart (Museo del Vidrio Monterrey) 1997, Love: Divine & Profane (American Visionary Art Museum Baltimore) 1998, Magic Moments (Ruthin Craft Centre Wales) 1998, Brit Figurative Art (Flowers East London) 1998, Britain in Russia (Ekaterinburg) 1998, Baku Azerbaijan 1998, Decadence (Crafts Cncl London) 1999, China Chic - East Meets West (Museum at the Fashion Inst of Technol NY) 1999, Br Cncl Vilnius 1999, Rebels, Pretenders, Imposters (Br Museum) 1999, Fashion Assembly (Riga) 1999, Forever Fantasy, Fantasy Forever (Riverside Studios London and Univ of Exeter) 1999, Sweet Sounds (Bourdelle Museum Paris) 1999, Modern British and Contemporary Art (Redfern Gallery London) 2000, Universe of Smiles (Hanover) 2000, The Queen, Rose Man & the Elements (Anglo-Italian Celebration Royal Albert Museum Exeter and Ruskin Gallery Sheffield) 2000, Glittering Glass (Cheltenham Museum and Gallery) 2000, Genius of Rome (Royal Acad of Arts) 2001, Pegasus I (Harley Gallery Worksop) 2001, The Mountain (Royal Acad of Arts Summer Exhbn) 2001, Adorn & Equip (Oriel Gallery Leicester) 2001 and (Edinburgh) 2002, Newtown Art Festival 2002, Ludlow Art Festival 2002, St Petersburg Festival 2002, model cow for Cow Parade Charity Auction London 2002, A&D Gallery London 2002, Icarus (Guy's Hosp London), About Face Art Fair (Maggie Hambling Croydon) 2002, Home is Where the Heart Is (Nehru Centre London) 2002, Alternative Miss World Filmshow 1972–2002 (Norwich Gallery) 2002 and (Margaret Gallery Univ of Herts) 2003, Uniververse of Smiles (Flowers W Gallery LA) 2003, The Heart of the Matter (About Face Theatre Co Leominster) 2003, Portraits & Jewellery (Stratos Gallery, Moscow) 2003, Llanwrtydd Wells Festival 2005, Jewellery & Fashion Performance Lithuania 2005, Newton Art Festival 2005, Pegasus I & Universe of Smiles (Sadlers Wells Theatre London) 2005, Gloves & Hats (Leicester City Gallery) 2005, Cosmic Egg & Frolics in the Ocean (American Visionary Art Museum Baltimore) 2005, Big Draw Show (Trafalgar Square London) 2005, Series Music, Fashion, Visual Arts & Literature Festivals (Andrew Logan Museum of Sculpture) 2005, Sir George Solti's portrait (ROH) 2005, Jaipur Heritage Festival 2006, Moscow Fashion Week 2006, Icarus (American Visionary Art Museum Baltimore) 2006, International Festival of Glass (Ruskin Glass Centre West Midlands) 2006, Homage to the New Wave (Hayward Gallery London) 2006, Big Draw (Somerset House London) 2006, Yoga Art Show London 2006, All That Glitters (Scream Gallery London) 2006, Sparkling Surfaces (Diggi Palace Jaipur) 2007, An Artistic Adventure (Br High Cmmn Delhi) 2007, Swarovski's Runaway Rocks (ACE Gallery Beverley Hills) 2007, Being Beauteous (White Space Gallery London) 2007, Panic Attack - Art in the Punk Years (Barbican Art Gallery London) 2007; *Commissions* Millennium Pegasus (Dudley Sculpture Trail) 2001, Cosmic Egg (American Visionary Art Museum Baltimore) 2004, Two Cosmic Eggs (P&O super liner Arcadia) 2005, Cosmos Within (Grand Hyatt Hotel Mumbai) 2005, Wave (Guys and St Thomas Hosp Charitable Tst London) 2005, decorated a Vauxhall motor vehicle (Britain Int Motor Show) 2006, jewellery collection (Emmanuel Ungaro Paris) 2006, Teddy Noel Portrait (Jersey Museum) 2006, Bride of the Elements (Swarovski Crystals) 2007, Guitar (charity auction More London) 2007; *Style*— Andrew Logan; ✉ The Glasshouse, Melior Place, London SE1 3SZ (tel 020 7407 6575, fax 020 7403 6820, e-mail andrewdl@andrewlogan.com)

LOGAN, Sir David Brian Carleton; KCMG (2000, CMG 1991); s of Capt Brian Ewen Weldon Logan, RN (d 1995), of Linchmere, Surrey, and Mary, *née* Fass (d 1994); *b* 11 August 1943; *Educ* Charterhouse, UC Oxford (MA); *m* 4 March 1967, Judith Margaret, da of Walton Adamson Cole (d 1963); 1 da (Joanna b 1968), 2 s (Matthew b 1970 d 1988, James b 1976); *Career* HM Dip Serv: third sec then second sec Ankara 1965–69, private sec to Parly Under Sec of State for Foreign and Cwlth Affrs 1970–73, first sec UK Mission to the UN 1973–77, FCO 1977–82, cnsllr, head of Chancery and consul-gen Oslo 1982–85, head of Personnel Ops Dept FCO 1986–88, sr assoc memb St Antony's Coll Oxford 1988–89, min and dep head of mission Moscow 1989–92, asst under sec of state (central and eastern Europe) FCO 1992–93, asst under sec of state (int security) FCO 1994–95, min Washington 1995–97, ambass Turkey 1997–2001; dir Centre for Studies in Security and Diplomacy and hon prof Sch of Social Sciences Univ of Birmingham 2002–07, chm Br Inst at Ankara 2006–; memb Int Advsy Cncl Thames Water 2002–06, non-exec dir

L

European Nickel plc 2004–, memb Supervisory Bd Efes Breweries Int 2004–07, ind dir Magnitogorsk Iron and Steel Co 2007–; chm GAP Activity Projects 2002–; *Recreations* music, reading, sailing, tennis; *Clubs* Royal Ocean Racing; *Style—* Sir David Logan, KCMG; ✉ c/o European Nickel plc, Fortune House, 7 Stratton House, London W1J 8LE

LOGAN, Prof David Edwin; s of James Henry Logan and Mona Elizabeth Logan; *Educ* Sullivan Upper Sch Co Down, Trinity Coll Cambridge (MA, PhD); *m* 1981, Philippa Mary, *née* Walmsley; 2 da (Natasha, Georgina), 2 s (Crispin, Frederick); *Career* fell Christ's Coll Cambridge 1982–86, postdoctoral fell Univ of Illinois 1982–83; Univ of Oxford: lectr 1986–96, fell Balliol Coll 1986–2005 (emeritus fell 2005–), prof of chemistry 1996–2005, Coulson prof of theoretical chemistry 2005–, professorial fell Univ Coll 2005–; Marlow medal and prize RSC 1990, Corday-Morgan medal and prize RSC 1994, Tilden lectr and medal RSC 2007; MRSC 1989; *Publications* numerous articles on theoretical chemistry and physics in scientific res jls; *Recreations* music, poetry, politics, gardening; *Style—* Prof David Logan; ✉ Physical and Theoretical Chemistry Laboratory, South Parks Road, Oxford OX1 3QZ (tel 01865 275418, fa 01865 275410, e-mail david.logan@chem.ox.ac.uk)

LOGAN, Russell James Vincent Crickard; s of John Stuart Logan, of Kent, and Joan Ena, *née* Solly; *b* 5 October 1942; *m* 1978, Gillian Enid, da of Charles Redfern; *Career* studio mangr Forces Broadcasting Servs Cyprus 1960–62, freelance theatrical work 1963–67, systems analyst IBM 1967–70, sr project mangr Twinlock Computer Services 1970–71, memb Bd Book Club Associates 1977–79 (fulfillment mangr 1971), fndr and sr ptnr Business Aid 1979–2000; chm Database Mktg Ctee 1986–95, chm and organiser annual DMA Database Mktg Seminar 1986–95, speaker trade confs and educn courses, advsr Br companies and charities; chm Crime Writers' Assoc 2001–02; *Books* (all under pseudonym Russell James): Underground (1989), Daylight (1990), Payback (1991), Slaughter Music (1993), Count Me Out (1996), Oh No, Not My Baby (1999), Painting In The Dark (2000), The Annex (2002), Pick Any Title (2002), No One Gets Hurt (2003), Collected Stories (2007), The Great Detectives (2007), Great British Villains (2008); also We Never Shall Marry (film script, 1998), The Break (film script 1999); *Recreations* criminal research, travel to unlikely places; *Style—* Russell Logan, Esq; ✉ Penrose House, 30 Sydenham Road North, Cheltenham, Gloucestershire GL52 6EB

LOGAN, Rt Rev Vincent Paul; *see:* Dunkeld, Bishop of (RC)

LOGIE, Jamieson John; s of John Deas Logie, of St Andrews, and Jean Elizabeth, *née* Aitken; *b* 20 April 1961, Glasgow; *Educ* Univ of Glasgow (LLB), Univ of Dundee (DipLP); *m* 2 Aug 1986, Evelyn Mackenzie, *née* Brown; 2 s (Duncan Ross b 19 June 1988, James Cameron b 28 Dec 1989); *Career* slr; ptnr: Norton Rose 1992–99 (joined 1985), Sullivan & Cromwell LLP 2001– (joined 1999); memb: Law Soc Eng and Wales, Law Soc Scot, Int Bar Assoc; *Recreations* golf, skiing; *Clubs* Walbrook, New (St Andrews), Wisley Golf; *Style—* Jamieson Logie, Esq; ✉ Sullivan & Cromwell LLP, 1 New Fetter Lane, London EC4A 1AN (tel 020 7959 8900, fax 020 7959 8950, e-mail logiej@sullcrom.com)

LOGIE, John Robert Cunningham; s of Norman John Logie, TD (d 1972), and Kathleen Margaret Cameron, *née* Neill; *b* 9 September 1946; *Educ* Robert Gordon's Coll, Trinity Coll Glenalmond, Univ of Aberdeen (MB ChB, PhD); *m* 1, 1981, Sheila Catherine (d 2001), da of James Pratt Will (d 1957); 1 da (Joanna Catherine Neill b 1985), 1 s (David James Norman b 1989); m 2, 2004, Carol Joan, da of Gregor Macdonald; *Career* med trg Aberdeen Royal Infirmary 1970–81 (house offr, lectr, registrar, sr registrar), conslt gen surgn Raigmore Hosp Inverness 1981–; vice-pres RSC(Ed); FRCSEd 1974, FRCS 1975, FRCSGlas 1993; *Recreations* gardening, railway matters, ornamental waterfowl; *Style—* John R C Logie, Esq; ✉ The Darroch, Little Cantray, Culloden Moor, Inverness IV2 5EY (tel 01463 792090, fax 01463 798478); Raigmore Hospital, Inverness (tel 01463 704000)

LOGIE, Nicholas; *b* 12 May 1950; *Educ* Yehudi Menuhin Sch, Royal Coll of Music, Musikhochschule Detmold (German govt scholarship), Open Univ (BA, MA), Conservatorio Santa Cecilia Rome (Italian govt scholarship); *m*; 2 c; *Career* viola player; with Vienna Symphony Orch 1973–78, Chilingirian String Quartet 1978–81, freelance 1981–; princ viola Orch of the Age of Enlightenment; orch mangr: Kent Opera 1985–90, Glyndebourne Touring Opera 1990–; Royal Northern Coll of Music: sr lectr 1989–2000, dir of early music 1998–2000; numerous recordings; *Style—* Nicholas Logie; ✉ Lotts End, Highgate, Forest Row, East Sussex RH18 5BE (tel 01342 824 536, e-mail nick@nlogie.co.uk)

LOGUE, Christopher; CBE (2007); s of John Dominic Logue (d 1951), and Florence Mabel, *née* Chapman (d 1981); *b* 23 November 1926; *Educ* Portsmouth GS, Prior Park Coll Bath; *m* 1985, Rosemary Hill; *Career* writer, actor, Private Eye columnist; Wilfred Owen Award 1998, awarded Civil List pension for services to literature 2002; *Books* War Music: an Account of Books 16–19 of Homer's Iliad (1988), Kings: an Account of Books 1 and 2 of Homer's Iliad (1991), The Husbands: an Account of Books 3 and 4 of Homer's Iliad (1994), Selected Poems (ed Christopher Reid, 1996), Prince Charming a Memoir (1999), War Music (one vol edn of War Music, Kings and The Husbands, 2001), Audiologue (seven CD set of recordings 1958–98, 2001), All Day Permanent Red (2003), War Music (2003), Cold Calls: War Music Continued (2005, Whitbread Poetry Prize 2005); ed: The Children's Book of Comic Verse (1979), The Bumper Book of True Stories (1981), The Oxford Book of Pseuds (1983), Sweet and Sour: an Anthology of Comic Verse (1983), The Children's Book of Children's Rhymes (1986); Baal, The Seven Deadly Sins (by Bertold Brecht, translation, 1986); The Lily-White Boys (with Harry Cookson, a play with songs, music by Tony Kinsey and Bill le Sage, dir Lindsay Anderson, 1960); *Screenplays* Professor Tucholsky's Facts (poem used as screenplay of animated film by Richard Williams, 1963), The End of Arthur's Marriage (music by Stanley Myers, dir Ken Loach, 1965), Savage Messiah (dir Ken Russell, 1972), Crusoe (with Walon Green, dir Caleb Deschanel, 1988); performing versions of War Music and Kings (with Alan Howard, dir Liane Aukin 1984 and 1991); *Clubs* The Groucho, The Hotsy Totsy (Ghent); *Style—* Christopher Logue, CBE; ✉ 41 Camberwell Grove, London SE5 8JA (tel 020 7703 7853)

LOHN, Matthew Simon; s of Carl William Lohn (d 2005), and Ann Isobel, *née* Chattin; *b* 19 November 1965, Brentwood, Essex; *Educ* Brentwood Sch, London Hosp Med Coll (BSc, MB BS), Coll of Law (CPE); *m* 18 July 1992, Johanna Gabriella Miranda, *née* Cornwell; 1 da (Beatrix Gabrielle Rose b 7 Feb 1998); *Career* slr; jr house offr Epsom Hosp 1991–92; Field Fisher Waterhouse LLP: joined 1994, ptnr 1999–, main bd memb 2004–; memb Horseracing Regulatory Authy Disciplinary Panel 2005–; memb: GMC 1991, Law Soc 1994; *Recreations* gardening, tennis; *Clubs* RSM; *Style—* Matthew Lohn, Esq; ✉ Field Fisher Waterhouse LLP, 35 Vine Street, London EC3N 2AA (tel 020 7861 4000, fax 020 7488 0084, e-mail matthew.lohn@ffw.com)

LOKER, John Keith; s of Denis Loker, of Pudsey, W Yorks, and Irene May, *née* Threapleton (d 1968); *b* 15 September 1938; *Educ* Bradford Coll of Art and Design, RCA (Abbey minor travelling scholarship); *m* 1, 1961 (m dis 1970), Eva, da of Alfred Kalnins; 2 s (Daniel Valdis b 1962, Simon Andris b 1965); m 2, 13 Sept 1997, Emily Mayer (sculptor); *Career* artist; taught 1964–89: Manchester, Maidstone, Nottingham, Wolverhampton, Brighton, Portsmouth, Wimbledon, Chelsea, NE London, Middx; Nordstern Print Prize Royal Acad 1994; *Exhibitions* solo: studio exhbn London 1969, 1975, 1986 and 2001, Flowers Gallery 1970, 1973, 1975, 1978, 1980, 1982, 1983, 1985, 1988, 1990, 1992, 1993, 1994, 1995, 1998 and 2001, ICA 1970, Park Square Gallery Leeds 1975, 1978, Wetering Galerie Amsterdam 1978, 1980, 1982, 1986 and 1989, Arnolfini Gallery Bristol 1981, Newlyn Orion 1981, Cartwright Hall Bradford 1981, Newcastle Poly Gallery 1981, Galerie du Monde Hong Kong 1984, Watermans Arts Centre London 1992; numerous gp exhbns in UK and abroad; *Public Collections* Arts Cncl, Bradford City Art Gallery, British Cncl, Contemporary Art Soc, DOE, Dudley City Art Gallery, Ferens Art Gallery Hull, Hunterian Collection Glasgow, Leeds City Art Gallery, Manchester City Art Gallery, Power Inst of Fine Art Sydney, Rugby City Art Gallery, Tate Gallery, Van Reekumgalerie Apeldoorn, V&A, Wakefield City Art Gallery, Worcester City Art Gallery; *Commissions* Watmoughs Hldgs Bradford, Essex Gen Hosp, Stanhope Devpts for ITN Bldg (Norman Foster); *Publications* Thriding, Monogram - Arnolfini, Littered Ways; *Clubs* Chelsea Arts; *Style—* John Loker, Esq; ✉ Union Workhouse, Guilt Cross, Kenninghall, Norfolk NR16 2LJ (tel 01953 681730, e-mail john@flyingbear.co.uk);Flowers East, 82 Kingsland Road, London E2 8DP (tel 020 7920 7777, fax 020 7920 7770, e-mail gallery@flowerseast.com, website www.flowerseast.com)

LOMAS, Derek Frank; s of Derek Edward James Lomas, of 3 Whitewood Cottages, Eynsford, Kent, and Pauline Lomas, *née* Clements; *b* 10 October 1960; *Educ* Dartford West Kent Secdy Boys Sch, Medway Coll of Art and Design (DATEC Dip Photography); *m* Sarah Ellen Kipps; 2 s (Edward, Jacob); *Career* freelance photographer (editorial photography, mainly still life work for magazines incl: Vogue, Tatler, Elle, Marie Claire) 1989–; *Awards* AFAEP award for non-commissioned still-life 1989; memb Photographers Assoc 1989; *Recreations* walking, cinema, cooking, photography; *Style—* Derek Lomas, Esq; ✉ Derek Lomas Photography (tel 020 7622 0123)

LOMAS, Herbert; *b* 7 February 1924; *Educ* King George V Sch Southport, Univ of Liverpool (BA, MA); *Career* poet, translator and freelance writer; served WWII King's Liverpool Regt attached to Royal Garhwal Rifles (served Razmak Waziristan, Kohat NW Frontier Province) 1943–46; teacher of English Anargyrios Sch Spetsai Greece 1950–51, sr lectr Univ of Helsinki until 1965, princ lectr Borough Road Coll until 1982; poetry and articles published in: London Magazine, Encounter, The Spectator, The Hudson Review, Books From Finland, Ambit and other journals; trans Medicine in Metamorphosis by Dr Martti Siirala 1957; judge: Bennett Award 1987, Nat Poetry Competition 1989, Oxford Union Poetry Competition 1989, Aldeburgh Poetry Festival Prize 1990–94; pres Suffolk Poetry Soc 1999–; memb Finnish Acad, Knight (1st Class) Finnish Order of the White Rose 1991; *Awards* Guinness Poetry Competition 1961, runner up Arvon Fndn Poetry Competition 1980, Cholmondeley Award for Poetry 1982, Poetry Book Society Biennial Award for Translation 1991, Finnish State Prize for Translation 1991; *Books* A Handbook of Modern English for Finnish Students (jtly, 1957), Chimpanzees are Blameless Creatures (1969), Who Needs Money? (1972), Private and Confidential (1974), Public Footpath (1981), Fire in the Garden (1984), Letters in the Dark (1986), Trouble (1992), Selected Poems (1995), A Useless Passion (1998), The Vale of Todmorden (2003); trans and ed: Territorial Song (1981), Contemporary Finnish Poetry (1991); trans: Wings of Hope and Daring (1992), Fugue (1992), Black and Red (1993), The Eyes of the Fingertips are Opening (1993), Narcissus in Winter (1994), Two Sequences for Kuhmo (1994), The Year of the Hare (1995), In Wandering Hall (1995), Selected Poems of Eeva-Liisa Manner (1997), Three Finnish Poets (1999), A Tenant Here: Selected Poems of Pentti Holappa (1999), Not Before Sundown (2003); Crystal Mountain (film script, 2006); *Style—* Herbert Lomas, Esq; ✉ North Gable, 30 Crag Path, Aldeburgh, Suffolk IP15 5BS (e-mail herbert@hlomas.freeserve.co.uk, website www.hlomas.freeserve.co.uk)

LOMAX, (John) Kevin; *b* 8 December 1948; *Educ* Victoria Univ of Manchester (BSc); *m*; 3 c; *Career* various exec positions until 1985 (incl md British Furnaces, md Wellman Incandescent Ltd, dir Central Manufacturing and Trading Gp plc and electronic components div head STC), chief exec and fndr Misys until 2006; non-exec dir Marks & Spencer plc 2000–06; Hon DSc Univ of Birmingham 2003; *Recreations* golf, shooting, military history, opera; *Style—* Mr Kevin Lomax

LOMAX, Michael Acworth (Mike); s of Peter Francis George Lomax (d 1990), and Mary Rosamund Lomax (d 1993); *b* 9 January 1943; *Educ* Downside, Pembroke Coll Cambridge (BA); *m* 1, (m dis); 2 s; m 2, 1993, Margaret Ann Stone; *Career* account exec Sharps Advertising 1966–69, account mangr Foster Turner & Benson 1970–75 (dir 1972–75), dir Streets Financial 1975–84, jt md Charles Barker City 1984–87, chm First Financial Advertising/PR 1996–98 (md 1987–96); freelance mktg conslt 1998–; memb Nat Appeals Ctee Cancer Res Campaign 1974–90, nat chm Cancer Youth Action 1978–83, chm Mktg Ctee Cancer Res Campaign 1987–90; MIPA 1967; *Recreations* golf (capt Fin Advtg Golfing Soc 1989–90), cooking, hill walking, reading, opera; *Clubs* Roehampton; *Style—* Mike Lomax, Esq; ✉ First Finanical Advertising Ltd, One Red Lion Court, London EC4A 3EB

LOMAX, (Janis) Rachel; da of William Salmon, and Dilys Jenkins; *b* 15 July 1945; *Educ* Cheltenham Ladies' Coll, Girton Coll Cambridge (MA), LSE (MSc); *m* 1967 (m dis 1990), Michael Acworth Lomax; 2 s (Thomas b 1971, Daniel b 1973); *Career* HM Treasury: econ asst 1968–72, econ advsr 1972–78, sr econ advsr and asst sec 1978–86, princ private sec to Chancellor of the Exchequer 1985–86, under sec 1986–90, dep sec 1990–94; head Econ and Domestic Secretariat Cabinet Office 1994–95, vice-pres and COS World Bank Washington DC 1995–96; perm sec: Welsh Office 1996–99, DSS 1999–2001, DWP 2001–02, Dept for Tport 2002–03; dep govr (monetary policy) Bank of England 2003– (memb Monetary Policy Ctee 2003–); pres IFS; memb Royal Econ Soc 1989–94; memb and chm UK Selection Ctee Harkness Fellowships; memb Bd RNT; memb Bd of Govrs: De Montfort Univ, London Inst, Henley Coll of Mgmnt; hon fell: LSE, Cardiff, UCW Swansea, Girton Coll Cambridge; Hon Dr: Univ of Wales, Univ of Glamorgan, Cass Business Sch City Univ, Glasgow Univ; *Style—* Ms Rachel Lomax

LOMNICKA, Prof Eva Zofia; da of Adam Jan Lomnicki (d 2000), and Azdiz Josephine, *née* Szymanska; *b* 17 May 1951; *Educ* Girton Coll Cambridge (BA, MA, LLB, Chancellor's medal); *m* 1 Sept 1973, John Lewis Powell, QC, *qv*, s of Gwyn Powell; 2 da (Sophie Anna b 14 Feb 1980, Catrin Eva b 3 Jan 1982), 1 s (David John b 3 Feb 1985); *Career* called to the Bar Middle Temple 1974 (Harmsworth scholar); KCL: lectr 1975–90, reader 1990–94, prof of law 1994–; *Books* Encyclopedia of Consumer Credit (jt ed, 1976–), Encyclopedia of Financial Services Law (jtly, 1986–), Modern Banking Law (jtly, 2 edn 1995, 3 edn 2002, 4 edn 2006), The Financial Services and Markets Act 2000: An Annotated Guide (2002), The Law of Personal Security (jtly, 2007); *Recreations* family, hill walking, music; *Style—* Prof Eva Lomnicka; ✉ School of Law, King's College London, Strand, London WC2R 2LS (tel 020 7848 2278, fax 020 7848 2465, e-mail eva.lomnicka@kcl.ac.uk)

LOMONOSSOFF, Dr George Peter; s of George Lomonossoff (d 1954), of Montreal, and Gertrude Margaret, *née*, Winkworth; *b* 15 August 1954; *Educ* Cambs HS for Boys, St John's Coll Cambridge (Lister scholar, MA, PhD); *m* 11 July 1987, Kim Susan (d 2004), da of late Remington Charles Chesher and late Betty Chesher, *née* Read; 1 da (Katherine Elizabeth Sumi b 26 Jan 1990), 1 s (Michael George Remington b 8 Nov 1993); *Career* postdoctoral fell MRC Lab of Molecular Biology Cambridge 1979–80, memb of staff John Innes Inst 1981– (fell 1980–81); short term EMBO fell 1982 and 1990; Fulbright scholarship to Cornell Univ 1987–88; visiting scientist The Scripps Research Inst La Jolla 1998; achievements incl: determination of the genome structure of plant viruses, developing novel methods of producing virus resistant plants, and developing use of plant viruses as potential vaccines; numerous articles in scientific jls; memb: Soc for General Microbiology 1990, American Soc for Virology 1992; *Recreations* watching football, enjoying good food and drink; *Style—* Dr George Lomonossoff; ✉ Department of Biological Chemistry, John Innes Centre, Colney Lane, Norwich NR4 7UH (tel 01603 450351, fax 01603 450045, e-mail george.lomonossoff@bbsrc.ac.uk)

LONDESBOROUGH, 9 Baron (UK 1850); Richard John Denison; s of 8 Baron Londesborough, TD, AMICE (d 1968, gs of Lord Albert Denison, *née* Conyngham, 2 s of 1 Marquess Conyngham), by his 2 w (Elizabeth) Ann, *née* Sale (d 1994); *b* 2 July 1959; *Educ* Wellington, Univ of Exeter; *m* 26 Sept 1987, Rikki, da of J E Morris, of Bayswater; 1 s (Hon James Frederick (Jack) b 4 June 1990), 1 da (Hon Laura Rose b 29 June 1992); *Heir* s, Hon Jack Denison; *Style*— The Rt Hon the Lord Londesborough; ✉ Edw Cottage, Aberedw, Powys

LONDON, Archdeacon of; *see:* Delaney, Ven Peter Anthony

LONDON, Prof Nicholas John Milton (Nick); s of Dr J M London, and Mrs Christine Keats; *Educ* Solihull Sch, Univ of Birmingham; *Career* trained in med and gen surgery Leicester hosps 1983–94, prof of surgery Univ of Leicester 1997–; Hallet Prize RCS 1982, Hunterian prof RCS 1993, BUPA Fndn Res Dr of the Year 1994; FRCS 1986, FRCPEd 1999; *Publications* author of over 300 pubns in the areas of vascular surgery and related basic sci res; *Recreations* golf, snowboarding; *Style*— Prof Nick London; ✉ Department of Surgery, University of Leicester, RKCSB, Leicester Royal Infirmary, Leicester LE2 7LX (tel 0116 252 3252, fax 0116 252 3179, e-mail sms16@leicester.ac.uk)

LONDON, Bishop of 1995–; Rt Rev and Rt Hon Richard John Carew Chartres; PC (1995); s of late Richard Arthur Carew Chartres, and Charlotte Ethel, *née* Day; *b* 11 July 1947; *Educ* Hertford GS, Trinity Coll Cambridge (MA), Cuddesdon Theol Coll, Lincoln Theol Coll (BD); *m* 1982, Caroline Mary, da of Sir Alan McLintock; 2 s (Alexander b 1986, Louis b 1991), 2 da (Sophie b 1988, Clio b 1993); *Career* master int sch Seville 1971, ordained 1973, curate Bedford St Andrew 1973–75, chaplain to the Bishop of St Albans 1975–80, Archbishop's chaplain 1980–84, vicar of St Stephen Rochester Row London 1984–92, bishop of Stepney 1992–95; six preacher Canterbury Cathedral 1991–96; London area dir of ordinands 1985–92, Gresham prof of divinity 1986–92; Prelate: of the Most Excellent Order of the British Empire 1996–, of the Imperial Soc of Knights Bachelor 1996–; dean of HM's Chapels Royal 1996–; chm: C of E Heritage Forum; ecclesiastical patron Prayer Book Soc, tstee St Catherine's Sinai Fndn, fndr and tstee St Ethelburga's Centre for Reconciliation and Peace; church cmmr; memb House of Lords 1996–; memb Central Ctee of the Conference of European Churches; hon bencher Middle Temple 1997; Liveryman: Worshipful Co of Merchant Taylors, Worshipful Co of Vintners; Hon Freeman: Worshipful Co of Weavers, Worshipful Co of Woolman; Freeman: Leathersellers Co, Drapers Co; Hon DD: Queen Mary & Westfield Coll, City Univ, Brunel Univ; Hon DLitt London Guildhall Univ; Ehrendomprediger vom Berliner Dom; FSA; *Publications* The History of Gresham College 1597–1997; *Style*— The Rt Rev and Rt Hon Richard Chartres, Lord Bishop of London; ✉ The Old Deanery, Dean's Court, London EC4V 5AA (tel 020 7248 6233, fax 020 7248 9721, e-mail bishop@londin.clara.co.uk)

LONDON, Timothy James (Tim); s of Jonathan London, and Jeanne, *née* Roche; *b* 24 June 1968; *Educ* Wells Blue Sch, Cardiff Univ (LLB); *m* 2 Dec 2003, Jane, *née* Haynes; *Career* slr; Eversheds 1990– (assoc 2004–); memb: Law Soc, Wales Commercial Law Assoc; *Recreations* wine tasting, scuba diving; *Clubs* Jeroboam (Bristol); *Style*— Tim London, Esq; ✉ Eversheds LLP, 1 Callaghan Square, Cardiff CF10 5BT (tel 029 2047 7530, fax 029 2046 4347, e-mail timlondon@eversheds.com)

LONEY, Francis Greville; s of Greville Groves Loney (d 1981), of Durban, South Africa, and Marjory Grace, *née* Redman (d 1995); *b* 11 December 1936; *Educ* St Charles' Coll Pietermaritzburg, Regent St Poly London; *Career* freelance photographer 1966–; photographic career has covered all aspects of advtg and editorial photography incl fashion, beauty, interiors, still life, celebrities, CDs, books, magazine covers, theatre and corporate; *Recreations* theatre, ballet, cinema; *Style*— Francis Loney, Esq; ✉ e-mail francisloney@talktalk.net, website www.francisloney.co.uk

LONG, Prof Adrian Ernest; OBE (2006); s of Charles Long (d 1985), and Sylvia Evelyn Winifred, *née* Mills (d 1974); *b* 15 April 1941; *Educ* Royal Sch Dungannon, Queen's Univ of Belfast (BSc, PhD, DSc); *m* 18 March 1967, Elaine Margaret Long, da of James Thompson (d 1980); 1 s (Michael b 22 Feb 1971), 1 da (Alison b 18 Dec 1972); *Career* bridge design engr Toronto Canada 1967–68, asst prof Civil Engrg Dept Queen's Univ Kingston Canada 1968–71; Queen's Univ Belfast: lectr Civil Engrg Dept 1971–75, prof of civil engrg 1976–2006, prof and head Civil Engrg Dept 1977–89, dean Faculty of Engrg 1988–91 and 1998–2002, dir Sch of the Built Environment 1989–98, prof emeritus 2006–; visiting prof RMC Kingston Canada 1975–76, ed Jl of Engrg Structures 1985–94, visitor Tport and Road Research Lab 1989–92, co-ordinator of research PSAM Sub-Ctee EPSRC 1990–94, memb Civil Engrg Panel Research Assessment Exercise 1996, 2001 and (chm) 2008; fell Tport Research Fndn 2005; Royal Society/Esso Energy Award 1994; Hon DSc City Univ London 2007; FICE 1982 (chm NI Assoc 1985–86, memb Cncl 1989–92, vice-pres 1999–2002, pres 2002–03), FREng 1989, FIStructE 1989 (chm NI Branch 1993–94), FACI 1996, FIEI 1996, FICT 1997, FIAE 1998; *Recreations* walking, church activities, travel; *Style*— Prof Adrian Long, OBE, FREng; ✉ Civil Engineering Department, Queen's University, Belfast BT7 1NN (tel 028 9097 4005, fax 028 9066 3754, e-mail a.long@qub.ac.uk)

LONG, Brian; s of Harry Long (d 1955), and Doris Long (d 1977); *b* 30 August 1932; *Educ* Hanson GS; *m* 29 Dec 1956, Joan Iris, da of Charles Eric Hoggard (d 1994), of Huggate, Yorks; 2 s (Nigel b 10 Feb 1959, Gareth b 15 Jan 1962); *Career* qualified co sec 1953; International Computers and Tabulators Ltd 1955–65; joined Honeywell Ltd 1965, md Honeywell Information Systems Ltd 1978–86, memb Honeywell Advsy Cncl 1978–86, vice-pres Honeywell Inc 1981–86, chief exec Honeywell Ltd 1986 (vice-chm 1985), chm and chief exec Honeywell Bull Ltd (became Bull HN Information Systems Ltd) 1987, chm Bull Pension Trustees Ltd 1987–2003, dir Bull SA of France 1987–92, chm Bull HN Information Systems Ltd (became Bull Information Systems Ltd) 1990–98 (hon pres 1998), chm Zenith Data Systems 1990–97; memb Bd Nat Computing Centre (NCC) 1970–71, memb Industry Ctee Help the Aged 1988, tstee: ReAction Tst 1991–95, Third Age Challenge Tst 1995–2001; memb Cncl CBI 1992–98; Freeman City of London 1987, fndr memb Worshipful Co of Information Technologists 1987; FInstD 1970, CCMI (CIMgt 1987), FCIS 1988, FBCS 1989, CITP 2004; *Recreations* walking, music, theatre; *Clubs* RAC; *Style*— Brian Long, Esq; ✉ Grove Lodge, Long Grove, Seer Green, Buckinghamshire HP9 2QH

LONG, Colin; s of Gordon Long, of Brighton, Sussex (d 1982), and Doreen, *née* Collins (d 1990); *b* 1946, Carshalton, Surrey; *Educ* Epsom Coll, Univ of Bristol (LLB); *m* 1979, Sheila, *née* Hughes; 1 da (Emily b 1983), 1 s (Charles b 1986); *Career* admitted slr 1970; asst slr Clifford-Turner 1970–73 and 1974–78, slr ICI plc 1973–74; ptnr: Bird & Bird 1978–90, Coudert Brothers 1990–98, Olswang 1998–; memb: Law Soc 1970, Int Bar Assoc 1986; *Publications* Global Telecommunications Law and Practice (gen ed, 1988–); *Recreations* skiing, swimming, tennis; *Clubs* RAC, Hurlingham; *Style*— Colin Long, Esq; ✉ Olswang, 90 High Holborn, London WC1V 6XX (tel 020 7067 3179, fax 020 7067 3999, e-mail colin.long@olswang.com)

LONG, Prof Derek Albert; s of Albert Long (d 1981), of Gloucester, and Edith Mary, *née* Adams (d 1983); *b* 11 August 1925; *Educ* Sir Thomas Rich's Sch Gloucester, Jesus Coll Oxford (MA, DPhil), Univ of Minnesota; *m* 8 Aug 1951, Moira Hastings, da of William Gilmore (d 1978), of Sheffield; 3 s (David b 1954, Richard b 1959, Andrew b 1962); *Career* fell Univ of Minnesota 1949–50, res fell spectroscopy Univ of Oxford 1950–55; UC Swansea 1956–66: lectr, sr lectr, reader in chemistry; Univ of Bradford: prof of structural chemistry 1966–92, prof emeritus 1992–, chm Bd Physical Sciences 1976–79, dir Molecular Spectroscopy Unit 1982–88; OECD travelling fell Canada and USA 1964, Leverhulme res fell 1970–71; visiting prof: Reims, Lille, Bordeaux, Paris, Bologna, Florence, Keele; chm second int conf on Raman spectroscopy Oxford 1970, co-dir NATO Advanced Studies Inst Bad Windsheim 1982, memb Italian-UK mixed cmmn for implementation of cultural convention 1985, vice-chm Euro Laboratory for Non-Linear Spectroscopy Florence 1986–92; fndr ed and ed-in-chief Jl of Raman Spectroscopy 1973–99 (ed emeritus 2000–); Hon Docteur ès Sciences Reims 1979; FRCS, CChem; foreign memb Lincei Acad Rome 1979; *Books* Raman Spectroscopy (1977), Essays in Structural Chemistry (jt ed, 1971), Specialist Periodical Reports in Molecular Spectroscopy (jt ed vols 1–6, 1973–79), Non-Linear Raman Spectroscopy and its Chemical Applications (jt ed, 1982), Proceedings of the Eleventh International Conference on Raman Spectroscopy (jt ed, 1988), Sèvres Service des Arts Industriels in Tools and Trades Vol 9 (1997), The Raman Effect (2002), The Goodmanham Plane in Tool and Trades Vol 13 (2002), The Goodmanham Plane in Instrumentum No 18 (2003), chapter in RSC monograph on Raman Spectroscopy in Archaeology and Art History (2005), L'Effeto Raman in Rendiconti Serie IX Vol XIV (2005), More Early Woodworking Planes in Instrumentum No 25 (2006); around 200 sci papers in learned jls; *Recreations* collecting antique woodworking tools and their history, history of science, Pembrokeshire; *Clubs* Oxford and Cambridge; *Style*— Prof Derek A Long; ✉ 19 Hollingwood Rise, Ilkley, West Yorkshire LS29 9PW (tel and fax 01943 608472, e-mail dal@profdalong.demon.co.uk); Three Houses, Roch, Haverfordwest, Pembrokeshire SA62 6JX (tel 01437 710550); Structural Chemistry, University of Bradford, West Yorkshire BD7 1DP (tel 01274 232323, fax 01274 235350)

LONG, Martyn Howard; CBE (1991); s of Victor Frederick Long (d 1993), and Dorothy Maud, *née* Lawrence (d 1999); *b* 1933; *Educ* UCS London, Merrist Wood Agric Coll Surrey; *m* 4 Oct 1958, Veronica Mary Gascoigne, da of James Edward Bates (d 1952); 4 da (Helen b 1959, Maria b 1961, Samantha b 1965, Rosalind b 1969); *Career* Nat Serv RAF 1952–54; farmer 1949–85, dir of family firm; memb: W Sussex AHA 1973–77, SW Thames RHA 1980–81; chm: Mid-Downs HA W Sussex 1981–94, Nat Assoc of Health Authorities 1988–90; vice-chm Nat Assoc of Health Authorities and Tsts 1990–93 (chm HA Ctee 1990–93), chm Sussex Ambulance Service NHS Trust 1995–98; chm East Grinstead Cons Assoc 1972–75; W Sussex CC: cncllr (Cons) 1973–93, chm Policy and Resources Ctee 1985–89, chm 1989–93; cncllr: E Sussex CC 1970–74, Cuckfield RDC 1972–74, Mid Sussex DC 1973–79; memb Assoc of CCs 1979–89, chm ACC Social Servs 1987–89; chm Br Homoeopathic Assoc 1993–95, memb Cncl and Instn King Edward VII Hosp Midhurst 1992–2006 (chm 2000–03), tstee Mobility Tst 1993–97, former health policy advsr to Sussex Health Care; tstee Culfrey Land Tst 2005; memb St Andrew's Church Potterhanworth PCC 2005– (churchwarden 2007–); Lincoln Dio: memb Diocesan Cncl, chm Clegy Housing Ctee 2005–, memb Finance Exec 2005–; memb Magic Circle; DL Sussex until 2003; *Recreations* magic (assoc memb Inner Magic Circle with Silver Star); *Clubs* Farmers', Sussex; *Style*— Martyn Long, Esq, CBE; ✉ The Forge, Barff Road, Potterhanworth, Lincolnshire LN4 2DU (tel 01522 793408, martynlong@themagiccircle.co.uk)

LONG, Richard; *Educ* Bedminster Down Sch, W of Eng Coll of Art Bristol, St Martin's Sch of Art; *Career* artist; works in numerous public collections; has created works and walks in landscapes worldwide; Hon DLitt Univ of Bristol 1995; Chevalier de l'Ordre des Arts et des Lettres (France) 1990; *Solo Exhibitions* incl: Konrad Fischer Düsseldorf 1968, Whitechapel Art Gallery London 1971, MOMA NY 1972, Stedelijk Museum Amsterdam 1973, British Pavilion Venice Biennale 1976, Palacio de Cristal Madrid 1986, Solomon R Guggenheim Museum NY 1986, Tate Gallery London 1990, Hayward Gallery London 1991, Palazzo delle Esposizione Rome 1994, Setaguya Art Museum Tokyo 1996, Guggenheim Museum Bilbao 2000, Tate St Ives 2002; *Awards* Kunstpreis Aachen 1988, Turner Prize 1989, Wilhelm Lehmbruck-Pries Duisburg 1996; *Publications* incl: South America (1973), Richard Long (text by Rudi Fuchs, 1986), Old World New World (1988), Nile, Papers of River Muds (1990), Walking in Circles (1991), Mountains and Waters (1992), From Time to Time (1997), Mirage (1998), Every Grain of Sand (1999), Richard Long - A Moving World (2002), Walking the Line (2002), Walking and Sleeping (2004); *Style*— Richard Long; ✉ Haunch of Venison, 6 Haunch of Venison Yard, London W1K 5ES (tel 020 7495 5050, fax 020 7495 4050)

LONG, 4 Viscount (UK 1921); Richard Gerard Long; CBE (1993); s of 3 Viscount Long, TD, JP, DL (d 1967); *b* 30 January 1929; *Educ* Harrow; *m* 1, 2 March 1957 (m dis 1984), Margaret Frances, da of Ninian Frazer; 1 s, 1 da (and 1 decd); m 2, 1984 (m dis 1990), Catherine Patricia Elizabeth Mier Woolf, da of Charles Terrence Miles-Ede, of Leicester; m 3, 19 June 1990, Helen Millar Wright Fleming-Gibbons; *Heir* s, Hon James Long; *Career* The Wilts Regt 1947–49; vice-pres Wilts Royal Br Legion; oppn whip 1974–79, Lord in Waiting (Govt whip) 1979–97; Freeman City of London 1991; *Recreations* shooting, gardening; *Style*— The Rt Hon the Viscount Long, CBE; ✉ The Island, Newquay, Cornwall TR7 1EA

LONG, Dr Richard Glover; s of John Long (d 1978), of Higham, Kent, and Bridget, *née* Harrison (d 1999); *b* 13 August 1947; *Educ* Canford Royal Free Hosp Sch of Med (MB BS, MD); *m* 12 Feb 1983, Anita Rosemary, da of Kenneth Eaton Wilson, of Aldridge, West Midlands; 1 s (Charles Matthew b 1983 d 2000); *Career* hon sr registrar Hammersmith Hosp 1978–80, sr registrar St Thomas Hosp 1980–83, MRC travelling res fell San Francisco USA 1983, conslt gastroenterologist and clinical teacher Nottingham Hosp Med Sch 1983–; sr examiner RCP 2007– (censor 2006–08); memb: Assoc of Physicians of GB and Ireland, Br Soc of Gastroenterology, American Gastroenterology Assoc, Med Res Soc; FRCP 1989; *Books* Radioimmunoassay of Gut Regulatory Reptides (jt ed with S R Bloom, 1982), Textbook of Gastroenterology and Liver Disease (jt ed with B B Scott, 2005); *Recreations* fly fishing, gardening; *Style*— Dr Richard Long; ✉ Coach House, Old Hall Drive, Widmerpool, Nottingham NG12 5PZ (tel 0115 937 2467); City Hospital, Nottingham NG5 1PB (tel 0115 969 1169); Park Hospital, Sherwood Lodge Drive, Arnold, Nottingham NG5 8RX (tel 0115 967 0670)

LONG, Sarah; *see:* Clegg Littler, Hon Mrs (Sarah Victoria)

LONG, Dr Tracy Elisabeth; *b* 4 June 1962, London; *Educ* Univ of London (BA), Henley Mgmnt Coll (MBA, APDMC, DBA); *m* 27 Aug 1998, Andrew Tuckey; 2 da (Eleanor Charlotte Rosemary b 5 June 1999, Florence Cecily Rose b 23 July 2002); *Career* fndr Boardroom Review; non-exec dir: Lowland Investment Co plc, van Tulleken, Avalon Prdns 1987–90, Classic FM 1990–94, Baring Brothers 1994–96, CME 1996–97, Botts and Co 1997–2003, BSkyB 1999–2003; chm The King's Consort, memb Advsy Bd LSO; tstee NESTA; Keith McMillan Prize for Research 2005; fell Cass Business Sch; Hon ARAM; *Style*— Dr Tracy Long; ✉ Boardroom Review, 11 Horbury Mews, London W11 3NL (e-mail boardroomreview@aol.com)

LONG, William John; s of Maj Richard Samuel Long, d 1999, and Mary, *née* Charrington; *b* 11 November 1943; *Educ* Woodbridge Sch; *m* 15 Jan 1969, Sarah Jane, da of Philip Barton Lockwood (d 1992); 1 da (Jane (Mrs D Rolfe) b 6 Feb 1972), 2 s (Samuel b 18 April 1974, John b 8 April 1979); *Career* ptnr: Laing & Cruickshank 1973–79, Milton Mortimer & Co 1982–86; dir: Lockwoods Foods Ltd 1977–82, National Investment Group Ltd 1986–2000; exec dir Capel-Cure Myers Capital Management Ltd 1998–99 (dir 1990–99), business devpt dir Capel Cure Sharp Ltd 1999–2000; iimia plc: dir 2001–, chm 2001–04; chm iimia Investment Gp plc 2004–; underwriting memb Lloyd's 1989–2003; memb Earl Marshall's staff for state funeral of Sir Winston Churchill; FSI (memb Stock Exchange 1972); *Recreations* sailing, fishing, shooting and genealogy; *Style*— William Long, Esq; ✉ Coombe Fishacre House, Coombe Fishacre, Newton Abbot, Devon TQ12 5UQ (tel 01803 812242); iimia Investment Gp plc, 23 Cathedral Yard, Exeter EX1 1HB (tel 01392 475900, e-mail william.long@iimia.co.uk)

LONGAIR, Prof Malcolm Sim; CBE (2000); *b* 18 May 1941; *Educ* Morgan Acad Dundee, Queen's Coll Univ of St Andrews (James Caird travelling scholar), Univ of Cambridge (James Clerk Maxwell scholar, MA, PhD); *m* Deborah Janet; 1 s (Mark Howard b 13 Sept 1976), 1 da (Sarah Charlotte b 7 March 1979); *Career* lectr Dept of Physics and visiting asst prof of radio astronomy Calif Inst for Advanced Study Princeton 1978, exchange visitor to USSR Space Res Inst Moscow (on 6 occasions) 1975–79, regius prof of astronomy Univ of Edinburgh 1980–90, dir Royal Observatory Edinburgh 1980–90, Astronomer Royal for Scotland 1980–90; visiting lectr: Pennsylvania State Univ 1986 (in astronomy and astrophysics), Univ of Victoria Canada; Regents fellowship Smithsonian Instn at Smithsonian Astrophysical Observatory Harvard Univ 1990; Jacksonian prof of natural philosophy Univ of Cambridge 1991– (demonstrator Dept of Physics 1970–75, official fell and praelector Clare Hall 1971–80), head of Cavendish Laboratory 1997–; memb: IUE Observatory Ctee 1975–78, Working Gp Euro Space Agency 1975–78, Interdisciplinary Scientists for the Hubble Space Telescope 1977–, Anglo Aust Telescope Bd 1982–87, Space Science Programme Bd 1985–88; chm: Space Telescope Advsy Panel 1977–84, Astronomy II (AII) Ctee 1979–80 (memb 1977–78), Millimetre Telescope Users Ctee 1979–83, Space Telescope Science Inst 1982–84; author of numerous scientific papers, delivered numerous public lectures; Hon LLD Univ of Dundee 1982; FRAS, FRSE 1981, FRS 2004; *Books* Observational Cosmology (co-ed J E Gunn and M J Rees, 1978), High Energy Astrophysics (1981), Alice and the Space Telescope (1989), The Origins of Our Universe (1990), High Energy Astrophysics (Vol 1 1992, Vol 2 1994), Our Evolving Universe (1996), Galaxy Foundation (1998), Theoretical Concepts in Physics (2003); *Recreations* music, opera, art, architecture, mountain walking; *Style*— Prof Malcolm Longair, CBE; ✉ Cavendish Laboratory, University of Cambridge, Cambridge CB3 0HE (tel 01223 337429)

LONGDEN, Christopher John; s of John Stuart Longden (d 1994), of Sheffield, S Yorks, and Daisy, *née* Heath (d 2002); *b* 22 March 1955; *Educ* Granville Coll Sheffield, Blackpool Coll; *m* 31 March 1978, Carol, da of Bryan Pettinger; 2 s (Benjamin b 6 July 1981, James b 15 Feb 1984), 1 da (Jennifer b 31 March 1985); *Career* trainee mangr British Transport Hotels 1974–77, food and beverage mangr Hotel L'Horizon Jersey 1977–81, mangr Gleddoch House Hotel & Country Club Langbank 1981–85, md Gleddoch Hotels (incl Gleddoch House, Gleddoch Golf Club and Houstoun House Broxburn) 1985–91, exec gen mangr (pre-opening) Vermont Hotel Newcastle upon Tyne 1992–93, md Ballathie House Hotel Perthshire 2003– (gen mangr 1993–2003); Master Innholder 1986; Freeman City of London 1986; FHCIMA 1974; *Recreations* yacht racing; *Style*— Christopher Longden, Esq; ✉ Ballathie House Hotel, Kinclaven, by Stanley, Perthshire PH1 4QN (tel 01250 883268, fax 01250 883396, e-mail@ballathiehousehotel.com)

LONGDEN, John Charles Henry; s of Henry A Longden, FEng (d 1997), of Woldingham, Surrey, and Ruth, *née* Gilliat; *b* 10 May 1938; *Educ* Oundle, Royal Sch of Mines Imperial Coll London; *m* 1965, Marion Rose, da of W G S Maxwell; 1 da (Sarah b 1966), 2 s (Henry b 1969, Richard b 1971); *Career* British Coal Corporation (formerly National Coal Board): mining trainee 1960–63, various jr mgmnt posts 1963–67, mangr Welbeck Colliery Notts 1969–75 (dep mangr 1967–68), sr mining engr (planning and surveying) N Notts Area 1976–80, dep dir of mining S Midlands 1985 (chief mining engr 1980–85), dep dir of mining Notts 1986–88, dep operations dir HQ Eastwood 1988–89, actg area dir Notts and gp dir 1989–93, gp dir Midlands 1993–94; currently conslt specialising in safety mgmnt; MIOSH, FREng 1992, FIMM, FIMgt, FRSA; *Recreations* early motoring, sailing; *Clubs* Veteran Car Club of GB; *Style*— John Longden, Esq, FREng; ✉ Stonebank, Potter Lane, Wellow, Newark, Nottinghamshire NG22 0EB (tel 01623 861137, e-mail longdensmc@aol.com)

LONGE, Laurence Peter; s of Robert John Longe, of Hollywood, W Midlands, and Ellen, *née* Mullally; *b* 9 January 1955; *Educ* St Thomas Aquinas' GS King's Norton; *m* 6 Sept 1980, Allyson Daphne, da of William Daniel Roberts; 1 s (Simon Laurence b 26 Nov 1986), 1 da (Rachel Allyson b 8 May 1992); *Career* Inland Revenue 1974–78, tax sr Dearden Farrow 1979–80, tax mangr KPMG Peat Marwick 1981–87; Baker Tilly: tax dir 1987–88, managing ptnr London Tax Dept 1988–91, managing ptnr Watford office 1991–96, nat managing ptnr 1996–; ATII 1981, ACA 1986; *Recreations* scuba diving, reading, music, family; *Style*— Laurence Longe, Esq; ✉ Baker Tilly, 2 Bloomsbury Street, London WC1B 3ST (tel 020 7413 5100, fax 020 7413 5101, e-mail laurence.longe@bakertilly.co.uk)

LONGFORD, 8 Earl of (I 1785); Thomas Frank Dermot Pakenham; but does not use title; also Baron Longford (I 1756), Baron Silchester (UK 1821), Baron Pakenham (UK 1945); s of 7 Earl of Longford, KG, PC (d 2001), and Elizabeth, Countess of Longford, CBE (d 2002); *b* 14 August 1933; *Educ* Ampleforth, Magdalen Coll Oxford; *m* 1964, Valerie Susan, da of Maj Ronald Guthrie McNair Scott (d 1995); 2 s, 2 da; *Heir* s, Edward Pakenham; *Career* writer; freelance 1956–58; on editorial staff of: TES 1958–60, Sunday Telegraph 1961, The Observer 1961–64; fndr memb: Victorian Soc 1958 (memb Ctee 1958–64), Historic Irish Tourist Houses and Gardens Assoc (HITHA) (memb Ctee 1968–72); chm Br-Irish Assoc 2002– (treas 1972–2002), sec and co-fndr Christopher Ewart-Biggs Memorial Tst 1976, chm Ladbroke Assoc 1988–91, chm and fndr Irish Tree Soc 1990–; sr assoc memb St Antony's Coll Oxford 1979–81; *Publications* The Mountains of Rasselas: An Ethiopian Adventure (1959), The Year of Liberty: The Story of the Great Irish Rebellion of 1798 (1969), The Boer War (1979, Cheltenham Prize 1980), Dublin: A Traveller's Companion (selected and introduced with Valerie Pakenham,1988), The Scramble for Africa (1991, WH Smith Literary Award 1992, Alan Paton Award 1992), Meetings with Remarkable Trees (1996), Remarkable Trees of the World (2002); *Style*— Thomas Pakenham, Esq; ✉ Tullynally, Castlepollard, Co Westmeath (tel 00 353 44 61159)

LONGHURST, Andrew Henry; s of Henry Longhurst, and Connie Longhurst; *b* 23 August 1939; *Educ* Glyn GS, Univ of Nottingham (BSc); *m* 1962, Margaret; 2 da, 1 s; *Career* Cheltenham & Gloucester Building Soc: data processing mangr 1967–70, asst gen mangr (admin) 1970–77, dep gen mangr 1977–82, chief exec and dir 1982–95; Cheltenham & Gloucester plc: chief exec 1995–96, dir 1995–98, chm 1997–98; dir Lloyds Bank plc and TSB Bank plc 1995–98, gp dir Customer Fin Lloyds TSB Gp plc 1997–98, chm United Dominions Tst Ltd, Lloyds Bowmaker Ltd and Lloyds UDT Ltd 1997–98; chm United Assurance Gp 1998–2000; dir: Thames Water plc 1998–2000, Hermes Focus Asset Mgmnt 1998–, The Royal London Mutual Insurance Soc Ltd 2000–02 (dep chm), Abbey National plc 2005–; memb: Exec Ctee Cncl of Mortgage Lenders 1989–96 (chm 1994), DTI Deregulation Task Force on Financial Servs 1993; dir Nat Waterways Museum Tst 1989–99, pres Glos Operatic and Dramatic Soc 1990–98; memb Cncl Univ of Gloucestershire 2004–; CIMgt, FBCS, FCIB; *Recreations* golf; *Style*— Andrew Longhurst, Esq

LONGHURST, Scott Robert James; s of Robert Longhurst, and Joan, *née* Gaunt; *b* 6 June 1967, London; *Educ* Dartford GS, Univ of Birmingham (Coopers & Lybrand Accounting Prize, KPMG Accounting Prize, BCom), Harvard Business Sch; *m* 1 Nov 1991, Karen Patricia, *née* Lyons; 2 s (Max b 11 Feb 1993, Henry b 22 May 1995), 1 da (Madeline b 7 Dec 1997); *Career* asst mangr Ernst & Young 1988–91, gp accountant global reporting, planning and analysis Shell Int Petroleum Co 1991–93, audit mangr Shell Cos Gtr China 1993–95, dep controller Shell Chemicals Europe 1995–97, chief financial offr oil products jt ventures Shell Saudi Arabia 1997–2000, vice-pres finance TXU Europe 2000–01, vice-pres corp planning TXU Corp 2001–02, chief financial offr and sr vice-pres Oncor Gp 2002–04, gp controller and chief accounting offr TXU Corp 2004, gp finance dir AWG plc 2004–; FCA 2002 (ACA 1991); *Recreations* travel, tennis, golf; *Style*— Scott Longhurst, Esq; ✉ AWG plc, Anglian House, Ambury Road, Huntingdon, Cambridgeshire PE29 3NZ (tel 01480 323507, fax 01480 456018, e-mail scott.longhurst@awg.com)

LONGLEY, Adrian Reginald; OBE (1991); s of Evelyn Longley (d 1956), and Mary Anastasia, *née* Thompson (d 1962); *b* 27 September 1925; *Educ* Winchester, Trinity Coll Cambridge (MA); *m* 14 Dec 1957, Sylvia Margaret, da of Capt George Keith Homfray Hayter (d 1968); 3 da (Anne b 1959, Joanna b 1960, Melissa b 1963); *Career* Mil Serv Rifle Bde (A/Capt) served ME 1944–47; admitted slr 1959; Freshfields 1959–69, White Brooks and Gilman 1970–72; currently conslt Arlingtons Sharmas Slrs; also conslt to NCVO (legal advsr NCVO 1972–90), CPRE, Memorial Gates Tst, Slavery Meml Tst and other charities 1991–; memb NCVO Ctees: on Malpractice in Fundraising for Charity, Report 1986, on Effectiveness and the Voluntary Sector, Report 1990; hon legal advsr Ripon Int Festival 1997–; memb: Goodman Ctee on Charity Law and Voluntary Orgns 1974–76, Cncl L'Orchestre du Monde (Orchestra of the World) 1988, Standards Ctee Accrediting Bureau for Fundraising Orgns 1998; hon fell Inst of Fundraising (formerly Inst of Charity Fundraising Mangrs); tstee: Menerva Educnl Tst, Russian Euro Tst; UK contrib Les Associations et Fondations en Europe: Régime Juridique et Fiscal 1990 and 1994; *Publications* contrib: Charity Finance Handbook (1992–95 edns), Charity Law & Practice Review (1992), ICSA Charities Administration Manual (1992), Solicitors' Jl (1994 and 2000), Butterworths Encyclopaedia of Forms and Precedents Vol 6 (2) (Charities) (reissue, 1996), Charities: The Law & Practice (Sweet & Maxwell, formerly FT Law & Tax, Longmans, annually 1994–), CAF/ICFM Professional Fundraising Series: Trust Fundraising (1999); *Recreations* music, reading, foreign travel; *Clubs* Royal Commonwealth Soc, Cavalry and Guards', MCC; *Style*— Adrian R Longley, Esq, OBE; ✉ Arlingtons Sharmas Solicitors, 6 Arlington Street, St James's, London SW1A 1RE (tel 020 7299 8999, fax 020 7299 8900, e-mail law@arlingtons.co.uk); 10A Paveley Drive, London SW11 3TP (tel 020 7223 7515)

LONGLEY, Clifford; JP (Bromley 1999); s of Harold Anson Longley, of Purley, Surrey, and Gladys, *née* Gibbs; *b* 1940; *Educ* Trinity Sch Croydon, Univ of Southampton (BSc (Eng)); *m*; 3 c; *Career* journalist; reporter: Essex and Thurrock Gazette 1961–64, Portsmouth Evening News 1964–67; The Times: reporter 1967–69, asst news ed 1969–71, feature writer 1971–72, religious affairs corr and columnist 1972–87, ldr writer 1984–92, religious affairs ed and columnist 1987–92, asst ed (leaders) 1990–92; The Daily Telegraph: columnist 1992–2000, ldr writer 1992–95, religious affairs ed 1994–95; columnist and contributing ed The Tablet 1994– (actg ed 1996); conslt ed: The Common Good (Catholic Bishops Conf of Eng and Wales) 1996, Prosperity with a Purpose (Churches Together in Britain and Ireland) 2005; contrib: Thought for the Day (BBC Radio 4) 2002–, The Moral Maze (BBC Radio 4) 2004–; memb: Advsy Cncl Three Faiths Forum 1996–, Steering Ctee True Wealth of Nations project Univof Southern California 2006–, Dist Exec Royal Eltham Scout Dist 2006–; Univ of Oxford select preacher 1988, Hugh Kay meml lectr 1990; Br Press Awards Specialist Writer of the Year 1986, Gold medal Peace through Dialogue Int Cncl of Christians and Jews 2006; hon fell St Mary's Coll Univ of Surrey 1998; *Books* The Times Book of Clifford Longley (1991), The Worlock Archive (1999), Chosen People (2002); *Recreations* music; *Style*— Clifford Longley, Esq; ✉ 24 Broughton Road, Orpington, Kent BR6 8EQ (tel 01689 853189, fax 01689 811279, e-mail clifford.longley@ntlworld.com)

LONGLEY, James Timothy Chapman; s of Alan Timothy Chapman Longley, of York, and Avrill Ruth Nunn, *née* Midgley; *b* 21 May 1959; *Educ* Worksop Coll, Leeds Metropolitan Univ (BA); *m* 18 Sept 1999, Caroline Mary, da of Edmund Smith, and late Peggy Smith, of Dublin, Ireland; 1 s (Oliver b 13 Nov 2001); *Career* CA; Finnie and Co 1980–83, Arthur Andersen 1983–85, Creditanstalt-Bankverein 1985–88, Touche Ross and Co 1988–89, The Wilcox Group Ltd 1990, ptnr Dearden Chapman CAs; co-fndr: Bioprogress plc 1996–2002, Photobox Ltd 2000–06; dir: Bannaba Capital Investors Ltd, Chapman Longley Ltd; FCA 1983; *Recreations* skiing, racing, tennis; *Clubs* Groucho, Hurlingham; *Style*— James Longley, Esq; ✉ Dearden Chapman (tel 020 8816 8567, fax 020 8789 8253, e-mail jamestclongley@aol.com)

LONGLEY, Michael; *b* 1939, Belfast; *Educ* Royal Belfast Academical Instn, Trinity Coll Dublin; *m* Edna Longley, the critic; 3 c; *Career* poet and writer; sometime teacher Dublin, London and Belfast, combined arts dir Arts Cncl of NI until 1991; author of numerous scripts for BBC Schools Dept, regular broadcaster; work has been the subject of four films incl The Corner of the Eye (RTE, BBC and Channel 4); memb Aosdána, fndr memb Cultural Traditions Gp NI; FRSL; *Awards* Eric Gregory Award, British Airways Cwlth Poetry Prize, Whitbread Poetry Prize, T S Eliot Prize, Hawthornden Prize, Cholmondeley Award, Queen's Gold Medal for Poetry, Librex Montale Prize; other awards from Charitable Irish Soc of Boston, Irish American Cultural Inst and Ireland Funds of America; *Books* poetry collections: No Continuing City (1969), An Exploded View (1973), Man Lying on a Wall (1976), The Echo Gate (1979), Poems 1963–1983 (1985, re-issued 1991), Gorse Fires (1991), The Ghost Orchid (1995), Selected Poems (1998), The Weather in Japan (2000), Snow Water (2004), Collected Poems (2006); ed: Causeway (on the Arts in Ulster), Under the Moon, Over the Stars (children's verse), Selected Poems of Louis MacNeice, Poems of W R Rodgers; *Style*— Michael Longley, Esq, FRSL

LONGMAN, Dr (James Edward) Ford; s of George Lewis Ernest Longman (d 1989), and Alice Lizzie Mary (d 1954); *b* 8 December 1928; *Educ* Watford GS, Birkbeck Coll London (BSc), Univ of Leeds; *m* 22 May 1954, Dilys Menai, da of Reginald Wilfred Richard Hunt (d 1972); 2 s (Jonathan b 1955, Richard b 1962), 3 da (Sarah b 1957, Rachel b 1960, Margaret b 1965); *Career* RAF Radar/Wireless Sch and Educn Branch 1947–49; Miny of Health, Bd of Control and Office Min for Sci 1949–62; hon sec Watford Cncl of Churches 1950–62 (lay preacher); asst dir Joseph Rowntree Meml Tst 1962–70; dir Yorks (Regnl) Cncl Social Serv, sec seven other regnl bodies 1970–75; hon sec Yorks Arts Assoc and govr Harrogate Festival 1970–76, chm Yorks CSS 1967–70, sometime memb of ten Govt Ctees on Social Servs and Penal Matters (incl Ctee on Serv Overseas), memb Lord Chllr's Advsy Ctee on Crown Courts (NECCT), chm Bd HM Borstal Wetherby, conslt in social planning Govt of W Berlin and UNESCO, pioneered community devpt in Br, chm All-Pty United World Tst for Educn and Res, assoc Iona Community, exec memb Nat Peace Cncl, NCSS and YRCC, memb Yorks and Humberside Regnl Econ Planning Cncl 1965–72; jt fndr: Christian Industrial Leadership Schs, St Leonard's Housing Assoc, York Abbeyfield Soc, Regnl Studies Assoc, Community Devpt Tst 1968 (dir 1968–76); HM Inspr of Community Educn 1975–83; cncllr N Yorks CC 1985–97: dep ldr Lib Dem Gp 1989–93, memb Exec Ctee Assoc of CCs 1993–95, chm Soc Servs Ctee, chm Personnel Ctee, chm Appeals, dep chm Corp Policy Ctee; formerly: memb Yorks Provincial Cncl, memb N Yorks Police Authy, memb N Yorks Moors Nat Park Authy, govr UC Ripon and York St John; Parly candidate (Lib/SDP Alliance) Selby 1987; chm Ryedale Constituency Lib Dems 1994–99; currently memb: Soc of Friends (Quakers), Methodist Church (local preacher), Green Dems, Lib Dem Christian Forum; memb Ripon Diocesan Bd of Social Responsibility 1989–2001, N Yorks Valuation Court 1989–2001; tstee and govr Breckenbrough Sch, vice-chm and chaplain Ryedale Motor Neurone Disease Assoc; sometime govr fifteen colls and schs; life fell and hon prof of community devpt Univ of Victoria; Hon DD, Hon LLD, Hon DPhil; FRAI; Baron Ordre Royal de la Couronne de Bohème, Knight Order of Holy Grail, Knight Cdr Lofsensichen Ursinius-orden, Knight Templar Order of Jerusalem; *Recreations* painting, gliding, reading, renovating historic buildings (with wife, restored Healaugh Priory 1981–86), writing; *Style—* Dr Ford Longman; ✉ Toby's Cottage, Slingsby, York YO62 4AH (tel 01653 628402)

LONGMAN, Peter Martin; s of Denis Martin Longman (d 2003), of Somerset, and Mary Joy Longman (d 1977); *b* 2 March 1946; *Educ* Huish's Sch Taunton, Univ Coll Cardiff (BSc), Univ of Manchester (Dip Drama); *m* 22 May 1976, Sylvia June, da of John Lancaster Prentice (d 2006), of E Sussex; 2 da (Tania Louise b 1978, Natalie Therese b 1981); *Career* housing arts offr Arts Cncl GB 1969–78 (Fin Dept 1968–69), dep dir Crafts Cncl 1978–83, dir and sec Museums & Galleries Cmmn 1990–95 (dep sec 1983–84, sec 1984–90); dir: The Theatres Trust 1995–2006 (tstee 1991–95, conslt 2006–), Scarborough Theatre Tst 2005–, Charcoalblue Ltd 2006–; sec working pty reports on: Trg Arts Administrators Arts Cncl 1971, Area Museum Cncls and Servs HMSO 1984, Museums in Scot HMSO 1986, Act Now! Theatres Tst 2003; a dir The Walpole Fndn 1997–2005, a dir Orange Tree Theatre Ltd 2004–; chm Cncl and Exec Ctee Textile Conservation Centre Ltd 1998–2000 (memb Cncl 1983–); memb: Arts Centres Panel Gtr London Arts Assoc 1981–83, Bd of Caryl Jenner Prodns Ltd (Unicorn Theatre for Children) 1983–87, co-opted Bd Scot Museums Cncl 1986–95, British Tourist Authy Heritage Ctee 1991–95, Exec Ctee Cncl for Dance Educn and Trg 1996–97, Advsy Ctee Art in Churches 1996–98, Cncl Chichester Festival Theatre Tst 1998–2003, Restoration Ctee ENO 1999–2004; tstee Covent Garden Area Tst 2001–03; FRSA 1989, Hon FMA 1995; *Recreations* discovering Britain, listening to music, looking at buildings, studio ceramics; *Style—* Peter Longman, Esq; ✉ 8 Eastbourne Road, Chiswick, London W4 3EB (tel 020 8994 5958)

LONGMORE, Rt Hon Lord Justice; Rt Hon Sir Andrew Centlivres; PC (2001); s of Dr John Bell Longmore (d 1973), of Shrewsbury, and Virginia Albertina, *née* Centlivres; *b* 25 August 1944; *Educ* Winchester, Lincoln Coll Oxford (MA); *m* 17 Oct 1979, Margaret Murray, da of Dr James McNair (d 1980), of Milngavie, Glasgow; 1 s (James Centlivres b 1981); *Career* called to the Bar Middle Temple 1966, bencher 1990; QC 1983, recorder of the Crown Ct 1992–93, judge of the High Court of Justice (Queen's Bench Div) 1993–2001, Lord Justice of Appeal 2001–; memb Bar Cncl 1982–85, chm Law Reform Ctee 1987–90; *Books* MacGillivray and Parkington Law of Insurance (co-ed, 7 edn 1981, 8 edn 1988, 9 edn 1997); *Recreations* fell-walking; *Style—* The Rt Hon Lord Justice Longmore; ✉ Royal Courts of Justice, Strand, London WC2A 2LL

LONGMORE, Prof Donald Bernard; OBE (1999); s of Bernard George Longmore (d 1992), of Sandwich, Kent, and Beatrix Alice, *née* Payne (d 1993); *b* 20 February 1928; *Educ* Solihull Sch (head of sch), Guy's Hosp Med Sch (Sailing blue, MB BS, LRCP), Baylor Univ Texas, Univ of Texas, The London Hosp; *m* 2 April 1956, Patricia Christine Greig, da of Arthur Hardman Spindler (d 1984), of Bray on Thames, Berks; 3 da (Annabel (Mrs Anthony Armstrong) b 1958, Juliet (Mrs Stephen Harris) b 1959, Susan (Mrs Richard Venn-Smith) b 1962); *Career* Guy's Hosp: house appts 1953, jr lectr in anatomy 1954; surgical resident Baylor Univ TX 1956–58, surgical registrar London Hosp 1958–59, sr registrar Middx Hosp 1960–61, lectr in surgery St Thomas' Hosp 1962–63, conslt Nat Heart Hosp 1963–83, dir Magnetic Resonance Unit Royal Brompton Hosp and Nat Heart Hosp 1983–93 (ret), chm and chief exec MR 3000 1993–, cardiac surgn and memb Britain's first heart transplant team; co fndr: Coronary Artery Disease Res Assoc (CORDA), Preventing Heart Disease and Stroke (formerly Heart); hon citizen State of Alabama 1994; personal chair Univ of London; Freeman Co of Worldtraders 1993; memb Br Inst Radiology; MRCS, FRCSEd, FRCR; *Books* over 250 scientific pubns incl: Spare Part Surgery (1968), Machines in Medicine (1969), The Heart (1970), The Current Status of Cardiac Surgery (1975), Modern Cardiac Surgery (1978), Towards Safer Cardiac Surgery (1981); *Recreations* sailing, skiing; *Clubs* Royal Yacht Sqdn, United Hosps Sailing; *Style—* Prof Donald Longmore, OBE; ✉ Whitemayes, 97 Chertsey Lane, Egham, Surrey TW18 3LQ (tel 01784 452436); Slipway Cottage, The Parade, Cowes, Isle of Wight PO31 7QJ (tel 01983 292816)

LONGSDON, Col (Robert) Shaun; LVO (2006); s of late Wing Cdr Robert Cyril Longsdon, of Foxcote, Warwicks, and late Evadne Lloyd, *née* Flower; *b* 5 December 1936; *Educ* Eton; *m* 19 Dec 1968, Caroline Susan, da of late Col Michael Colvin Watson, OBE, MC, TD, of Barnsley, Glos; 3 s (James b 1971, Rupert b 1972, Charles b 1975), 1 da (Laura b 1983); *Career* reg Army Offr 1955–81; princ mil appts: Lt Col, mil asst (GSO1) to the Chief of Gen Staff 1975–77, CO 17/21 Lancers 1977–79, directing staff (GSO1 DS) NDC 1979–81; head of corp affairs Knight Frank & Rutley 1981–95, md Visual Insurance Protection Ltd 1995–97; The Queen's Body Gd of the Yeomen of the Guard 1985–2006, Clerk of the Cheque and Adjutant 1993–2002, Lt 2002–06; Col 17/21 Lancers 1988–93; RSC: govr 1982–99, memb Cncl 1988–99; Leonard Cheshire: chm Leonard Cheshire Home Gloucester 1995–99, tstee 2000–, chm Public Affairs 2000–04, chm Central Region 2001–; chm Glos branch SSAFA Forces Help 2004–; *Recreations* field sports; *Clubs* White's, Cavalry and Guards', Pratt's; *Style—* Col Shaun Longsdon, LVO; ✉ Southrop Lodge, Lechlade, Gloucestershire GL7 3NU (tel 01367 850284, fax 01367 850377)

LONGSON, Dr Geoffrey John; s of late Arthur Walter Longson, and late Mary Margaret, *née* Pratt; *b* 1 August 1935; *Educ* Tiffin Sch Kingston upon Thames, Guy's Hosp Dental Sch (open scholar, LDS RCS (Eng), Newland Pedley prize), Univ of London BDS; *m* 1, Dianne Frances Isaac; 1 s (Mark Frazer), 1 da (Tanya Clare Marie); m 2, Heather Jane Sutherland; 1 da (Olivia Jane Scott); *Career* dental surgn; in private practice Harley St; fell: Int Acad of Implantology, Int Coll of Dentists, American Coll of Dentists; memb: American Acad of Gnathology, European Acad of Gnathology (pres); FRSM; *Style—* Dr Geoffrey J Longson; ✉ 130 Harley Street, London W1N 1AH (tel 020 7636 6082, fax 020 7935 2385, car 07785 225075)

LÖNNGREN, Thomas; *Educ* Univ of Uppsala (MSc), Stockholm Sch of Econs, Mgmnt Sch of LOTS; *Career* lectr Inst of Social and Regulatory Sci Pharmaceutical Faculty Univ of Uppsala Sweden 1976–78; Nat Bd of Health and Welfare Dept of Drugs Sweden 1978–90 (sr pharmaceutical offr 1986–90); Med Prods Agency Sweden: dir of ops 1990–2000, dep DG 1998–2000; exec dir Euro Medicines Agency (EMEA) 2001–; expert governmental ctee on reforming Swedish reimbursement system for meds 1999; sr pharmaceutical conslt Swedish health co-operation prog Vietnam and advsr Vietnamese Miny of Health 1982–94; chm Pharmaceutical Evaluation Report Scheme (PER) Ctee (Int European Free Trade Assoc (EFTA) Convention) 1998; *Style—* Thomas Lönngren, Esq; ✉ European Medicines Agency (EMEA), 7 Westferry Circus, Canary Wharf, London E14 4HB (tel 020 7418 8406, fax 020 7418 8409, e-mail thomas.lonngren@emea.eu.int)

LONSDALE, Anne Mary; CBE (2004); da of late Dr Alexander Menzies, of Harrow, Middx, and Mabel, *née* Griffiths; *b* 16 February 1941; *Educ* St Anne's Coll Oxford (BA (2), MA); *m* 1, 1962, Geoffrey Griffin (d 1962); m 2, 1964 (m dis 1994), Prof Roger Harrison Lonsdale; 1 s (Charles John b 1965), 1 da (Katharine Georgina b 1966); *Career* Univ of Oxford: Davis sr scholar and lectr in Chinese St Anne's Coll 1971–74, univ administrator 1974–90, dir External Rels Office 1990–93; sec-gen Central Euro Univ Budapest, Prague and Warsaw 1993–96, pres New Hall Cambridge 1996–, dep vice-chllr Univ of Cambridge 2000– (pro-vice-chllr 1998–2003); tstee: Inter-Univ Fndn 1988–, Cambridge Overseas Tst 1996–2004, Cambridge Cwlth Tst 1997–2004, Cambridge Euro Tst 1998–2006, Newton Tst 1999–, Moscow Sch of Social and Economic Sciences 1999–, Lead UK 1999–, Camfed 2006–, CARA 2006–, BACEE 2007–; Cavaliere dell'Ordine al Merito della Repubblica Italiana 1988, Officier dans l'Ordre des Palmes Académiques France 2002; *Books* The Chinese Experience (contrib trans, 1978), University Administration in China (1983), The Government and Management of Indian Universities (1987); *Style—* Mrs Anne Lonsdale, CBE; ✉ New Hall, Cambridge CB3 0DF (tel 01223 762201, fax 01223 762217)

LONSDALE, Prof Roger Harrison; s of Arthur John Lonsdale (d 1977), of Hornsea, E Yorks, and Phebe, *née* Harrison (d 2004); *b* 6 August 1934; *Educ* Hymers Coll Hull, Lincoln Coll Oxford (BA, DPhil); *m* 1, 8 May 1964 (m dis 1994), Anne Mary, da of Alexander Charles Menzies, of Harrow, Middx; 1 s (Charles John b 5 July 1965), 1 da (Katherine Georgina b 16 Dec 1966); m 2, 20 Dec 1999, Nicoletta Momigliano, da of Massimo Momigliano, of Milan, Italy; *Career* Nat Serv navigator RAF 1952–54; English Dept Yale Univ 1958–60, fell and tutor in English literature Balliol Coll Oxford 1963–2000 (Andrew Bradley jr res fell 1960–63), prof of English literature Univ of Oxford 1992–2000 (reader in English literature 1990–92); FRSL 1990, FBA 1991; *Books* Dr Charles Burney: A Literary Biography (1965); ed: The Poems of Gray, Collins and Goldsmith (1969), Vathek (by William Beckford, 1970), Dryden to Johnson (1971), The New Oxford Book of Eighteenth Century Verse (1984), The Poems of John Bampfylde (1988), Eighteenth Century Women Poets (1989), Samuel Johnson's The Lives of the Poets (2006); *Recreations* music, book collecting; *Style—* Prof Roger Lonsdale, FRSL, FBA; ✉ Balliol College, Oxford OX1 3BJ

LOOKER, Roger Frank; *b* 20 October 1951; *Educ* Univ of Bristol (LLB); *Career* barr; dir Stafford Corp Consulting Ltd; *Recreations* rugby football; *Clubs* RAC, Carlton, Harlequin Football (Chairman); *Style—* Roger Looker, Esq

LOOMBA, Raj; s of Shri Jagiri Lal Loomba (d 1954), and Shrimati Pushpa Wati Loomba (d 1992); *b* 13 November 1943, Dhilwan, India; *Educ* DAV Coll Jalandhar, State Univ of Iowa; *m* 1966, Veena; 2 da (Reeta (Mrs Sarkar) b 5 Dec 1966, Roma b 10 May 1969), 1 s (Rinku b 1 Oct 1970); *Career* fndr and exec chm Rinku Gp plc, fndr chm and md India First plc; memb Cncl RIIA, memb Pres's Cncl London First 2004–06; fndr and chm of tstees Shrimati Pushpa Wati Loomba Meml Tst, fndr and chm of tstees British Indian Golden Jubilee Banquet Fund, fndr and chm tstee Dr L M Singhvi Fndn, tstee Maharajah Ranjit Singh Tst, vice-pres Barnardo's, vice-pres Safer London Fndn, chm Friends of the Three Faiths Forum, patron Children in Need Inst, fndr patron World Punjabi Orgn, vice-patron The Gates; Hind Rattan Award 1991, Int Excellence Award 1991, Asian of the Year UK 1997, Pride of India Gold Medal 1998, Into Leadership Award 2000, Beacon Prize 2004, Neville Shulman Charity Cup 2005; Freeman City of London 2000; MInstD, memb Rotary Int (Paul Harris fell 2005); FRSA; *Style—* Raj Loomba, Esq; ✉ Rinku Group plc, Loomba House, 622 Western Avenue, London W3 0TF (tel 020 8896 9922, fax 020 8993 2736, e-mail raj@loomba.com)

LOOSE, Helen Jane Elizabeth; da of Peter Loose, of London, and Barbara Loose; *b* 1966, Solihull; *Educ* C of E Coll for Girls Edgbaston, Univ of Manchester; *Career* slr; articled clerk Freshfields 1990–93, Cameron Markby Hewitt 1995–97, ptnr and head Environment Gp Ashurst 2000– (slr 1997–2000); former memb Cncl and treas UK Environmental Law Assoc, non-exec dir London First, memb Cncl Princes Tst London Region; MInstD; *Publications* A Practical Guide to Environmental Issues in Commercial Property Transactions (2006); author of numerous articles; *Recreations* opera, skiing, tennis; *Style—* Ms Helen Loose; ✉ Ashurst, Broadwalk House, 5 Appold Street, London EC2A 2HA (tel 020 7638 1111, fax 020 7638 1112, e-mail helen.loose@ashurst.com)

LOPEZ, Paul Anthony; s of Anthony William Lopez, of Wolverhampton, and Lillian, *née* Rowley; *b* 22 October 1959; *Educ* Pendeford HS Wolverhampton, Univ of Birmingham (LLB); *m* 3 Nov 1984, Diana Douglas, da of Douglas Black (d 1982); 2 da (Antonia Charlotte Elizabeth b 10 May 1991, Miranda Annabelle Lucy b 22 Nov 1993); *Career* called to the Bar Middle Temple 1982; tenant St Ives Chambers 1983– (ldr St Ives Chambers' Personal Injuries and Clinical Negligence Specialist Gp), treas St Ives Chambers 1996–; recorder of the Crown Court 2001–, family and civil recorder 2003–; memb: Midland Circuit, Family Law Bar Assoc, Birmingham Family Law Bar Assoc, Personal Injury Bar Assoc, Birmingham Medico-Legal Soc, Shropshire Child Care Gp; memb: Nelson Soc, 1805 Club; chm Bd St Dominic's Sch Brewood; *Recreations* horse riding, history, working, collecting Nelson memorabilia; *Style—* Paul Lopez, Esq; ✉ 5 Rectory Drive, Weston-under-Lizard, Shropshire TF11 8QQ (tel and fax 01952 850252, mobile 07850 898591); St Ive's Chambers, Whittall Street, Birmingham B4 6DH (tel 0121 236 0863, fax 0121 236 6961, e-mail stives.chambers@btinternet.com)

LOPEZ CABALLERO, HE Alfonso; s of Alfonso Lopez Michelsen, of Bogotá, Colombia, and Cecilia Caballero de Lopez; *b* 17 August 1944, Bogotá, Colombia; *Educ* Georgetown Univ Washington DC, INSEAD (MBA), Columbia Univ NY (MA, MPhil); *m* 22 Feb 1969, Josefina Andreu de Lopez; 1 da (Isabel b 25 Sept 1986); *Career* asst mangr First National City Bank of NY, business conslt Arthur Young & Co, congressman Colombia 1986–90, senator Colombia 1990–94, ambass to France 1990–92, min of agriculture Colombia 1992–93, ambass to Canada 1994–97, min of the interior Colombia 1997–98, Govt negotiator with the Farc guerrila during Colombian peace process 2000–02, ambass to the Ct of St James's 2002– (concurrently ambass to Ireland); lectr in macroeconomics and financial mgmnt Universidad de Bogotá Jorge Tadeo Lozano, lectr in Latin American economics Universidad de los Andes Bogotá; *Books* Un Nuevo Modelo de Desarrollo Para el Campo (1988); *Recreations* golf; *Clubs* Travellers, London Golf; *Style—* HE Mr Alfonso Lopez Caballero; ✉ Colombian Embassy, 3 Hans Crescent, London SW1X 0LN (tel 020 7589 9177, fax 020 7581 1829)

LOPPERT, Max Jeremy; *b* 24 August 1946; *Educ* Hyde Park Sch Johannesburg, Univ of the Witwatersrand (BA), Univ of York (BA); *m* Delayne, *née* Aarons; *Career* freelance music critic Venice and London 1972–76, teacher Oxford Sch Venice 1972, chief music and opera critic Financial Times 1980–96, assoc ed Opera Magazine 1986–97; visiting scholar Univ of Natal (Durban) 1998–99; memb Critics' Circle London 1974–99 (hon memb 2000–); *Recreations* cooking, cinema, swimming, walking in the Dolomites, pottery; *Style—* Max Loppert, Esq; ✉ Via Molinetto 12, 31020 Refrontolo (TV), Italy

LORD, Geoffrey; OBE (1989); s of Frank Lord (d 1978), of Rochdale, and Edith, *née* Sanderson; *b* 24 February 1928; *Educ* Rochdale GS, Univ of Bradford (MA); *m* 15 Sept 1955, Jean; 1 da (Karen Janet b 1959), 1 s (Andrew Nicholas b 1962); *Career* Midland Bank Ltd (AIB) 1944–58, Gtr Manchester Probation Serv 1958–77 (dep chief probation offr 1974–77); sec and treas Carnegie UK Tst 1977–93; fndr and vice-pres The Adapt Tst 1992–2007; chm of tstees Home Start UK 1995–97, chm Unemployed Voluntary Action Fund 1991–95, former chm Pollock Meml Missionary Tst, former vice-pres The Selcare Tst; tstee: Edinburgh Voluntary Orgns Tst 1997–, Nat Youth Orch of Scotland 1998–, The Playright Scotland Tst 1998–2007, Murrayfield Dementia Project 2006–, Faith in Older People Ltd 2007–; memb Ctee Scottish Arts Cncl Lottery Ctee 1994–98, former pres Centre for Environmental Interpretation; hon fell Manchester Metropolitan Univ 1987; FRSA 1985; *Books* The Arts and Disabilities (1981), Access for Disabled People to Arts Premises - The Journey Sequence (jtly, 2003); *Recreations* arts; *Clubs* New (Edinburgh); *Style—* Geoffrey Lord, Esq, OBE; ✉ 9 Craigleith View, Edinburgh EH4 3JZ

LORD, Graham John; s of Harold Reginald Lord, OBE (d 1969), of Beira, Mozambique, and Ida Frances, *née* McDowall (d 1966); *b* 16 February 1943; *Educ* Falcon Coll Essexvale Bulawayo, Churchill Coll Cambridge (BA); *m* 12 Sept 1962 (m dis 1990), Jane, *née* Carruthers (d 2000); 2 da (Mandy b 1963, Kate b 1966); partner, since 1988, Juliet, *née* Hayden; *Career* ed Varsity Cambridge 1964, reporter Cambridge Evening News 1964; Sunday Express: reporter 1965–69, literary ed 1969–92, launched Sunday Express Book of the Year Award 1987; Daily Telegraph columnist and arts corr 1993–94, The Times book reviewer and travel corr 1994–96; ed Raconteur (short story quarterly) 1994–95; Lambourn parish cncllr 1983–87, vice-chm Newbury Mencap 1982–88, chm Eastbury Poor's Furze Charity 1983–88, memb Sub-Ctee W Berks Cons Assoc Exec 1985–88, cncllr Newbury DC 1985–87; *Books* Marshmallow Pie (1970), A Roof Under Your Feet (1973),

L

The Spider and The Fly (1974), God and All His Angels (1976), The Nostradamus Horoscope (1981), Time Out Of Mind (1986), Ghosts of King Solomon's Mines (1991), Just the One: The Wives and Times of Jeffrey Bernard (1992), A Party To Die For (1997), James Herriot: The Life of a Country Vet (1997), Sorry, We're Going to Have to Let You Go (1999), Dick Francis: A Racing Life (1999), Arthur Lowe (2002), Niv: The Authorised Biography of David Niven (2003), John Mortimer: The Devil's Advocate (2005), Joan Collins: The Biography of an Icon (2007); *Recreations* walking, swimming, music, cinema, reading; *Clubs* Chelsea Arts, Garrick; *Style*— Graham Lord, Esq; ✉ Morning Glory, Matchman's Road, Gingerland, Nevis, West Indies (e-mail pelicans@caribsurf.com)

LORD, Sir Michael Nicholson; kt (2001), MP; s of John Lord, and Jessie, *née* Nicholson; *b* 17 October 1938; *Educ* Christ's Coll Cambridge (MA); *m* 1965, Jennifer Margaret, *née* Childs; 1 s, 1 da; *Career* formerly farmer, aboricultural conslt; Parly candidate Manchester Gorton 1979; MP (Cons): Suffolk Central 1983–97, Suffolk Central and Ipswich N 1997–; PPS to Rt Hon John MacGregor as Min of Agric, Fisheries and Food 1984–85 and as Chief Sec to the Treasy 1985–87; dep speaker 2001–; Parly delg to Cncl of Europe and WEU 1987–91; memb Select Ctee on Agric 1983–84, memb Select Ctee for the Parly Cmmr for Admin (Ombudsman), 2 dep chm Ways & Means 1997–; cncllr: N Beds BC 1974–77, Beds CC 1981–83; pres Arboricultural Assoc 1989–95; *Recreations* golf, sailing, trees; *Style*— Sir Michael Lord, MP; ✉ House of Commons, London SW1A 0AA (tel 020 7219 3000)

LORD, Terence Stuart; s of Eric Lord (d 1952), and Doris, *née* Mann (d 1954); *b* 12 February 1944; *Educ* Burnley GS, Manchester Poly; *m* 15 June 1964, Christine, da of Amos Bullock, and Mollie Rhodes; 3 s (John Antony b 29 March 1965, Bryan Andrew b 21 May 1968, Stuart Allan b 8 Oct 1975); *Career* chief accountant MOD Royal Ordnance Factories Birtley and Glascoed 1977–85; British Aerospace Royal Ordnance: fin controller Enfield 1985–88, divnl fin controller Nottingham 1988–89, commercial mangr Birtley 1989–93; fin controller Inland Revenue 1993–95, resources dir and dep chief exec Contributions Agency DSS 1995–99, chief exec Armed Forces Personnel Admin Agency MOD 1999–2003; patron Prince's Tst 1995–99; FCMA 1974; *Recreations* golf, walking, swimming, travel; *Style*— Terence S Lord, Esq, FCMA; ✉ Armed Forces Personnel Administration Agency, Building 182, RAF Innsworth, Gloucester GL3 1HW (tel 01452 712612 ext 7623, fax 01452 510874, e-mail ceafpaa@cix.compulink.co.uk)

LORENZ, Andrew Peter Morrice; s of Hans Viktor Lorenz (d 1985), and Catherine Jesse Cairns, *née* James; *b* 22 June 1955; *Educ* Stamford Sch, Worcester Coll Oxford (Open Exhibitioner, MA, sports and arts ed Cherwell); *m* 1 Sept 1988, Helen Marianne, da of Brig John Malcolm Alway; 2 s (James Andrew George b 13 Jan 1994, Harry Alexander Lewis b 8 June 1995); *Career* successively grad trainee, news reporter, labour reporter, educn corr then industrial corr The Journal Newcastle 1978–82, business corr The Scotsman 1982–86, dep city ed The Sunday Telegraph 1988–89 (City reporter 1986–88); Sunday Times: industrial ed 1989–91, assoc business ed 1991–94, dep business ed 1994–95, business ed 1995–; *Books* A Fighting Chance - The Revival and Future of British Manufacturing Industry (1989), BZW: The First Ten Years (1996); *Recreations* cricket, rugby, football, film; *Style*— Andrew Lorenz, Esq; ✉ The Sunday Times, 1 Pennington Street, London E1 9XN (tel 020 7782 5768, fax 020 7782 5765)

LORENZ, Anthony Michael; s of Andre Lorenz (d 1986), and Mitzi Lorenz (d 1999); *b* 7 December 1947; *Educ* Arnold House Sch, Charterhouse; *m* 1, 1 Feb 1986 (m dis), Suzanna Jane, da of Louis Solomon; 1 s (David Alexander b 5 June 1986), 1 da (Charlaine Alexandra b 15 Nov 1978); m 2, 30 Nov 1999, Jane Knights; *Career* former: sr ptnr Baker Lorenz Estate Agents, exec vice-chm Dunlop Heywood Lorenz; currently sr ptnr The Lorenz Consultancy; former chm Fundraising Ctee Multiple Sclerosis Soc; *Recreations* flying, polo, shooting, skiing; *Clubs* Hurlingham, Knepp Castle Polo; *Style*— Anthony Lorenz, Esq; ✉ The Lorenz Consultancy, 18 Hanover Square, London W1S 1HX

LORIMER, Prof (Andrew) Ross; CBE (2004); *b* 5 May 1937; *Educ* Uddingston GS, HS of Glasgow, Univ of Glasgow (MD); *m* 1963, Fiona, *née* Marshall; *Career* conslt physician and cardiologist Royal Infirmary Glasgow 1972–2001; memb: Assoc of Phyicians of the UK, Br Cardiac Soc; Hon DUniv Glasgow 2001; FRCP, FRCPI, FRACP, FACP, FCPS (Bangladesh), FRCPGlas (memb Cncl, pres 2000–03), FRCPEd, FMedSci, FRCS 2003, FRCSE 2003, fell Coll of Physicians of South Africa (FCP(SA)) 2004, FRCSI 2005; *Books* Cardiovascular Therapy (1980), Preventive Cardiology (1990); *Style*— Prof Ross Lorimer, CBE; ✉ Woodlands Cottage, 12 Uddingston Road, Bothwell G71 8PH (tel 01698 852156)

LORING, Anthony Francis; s of Brig Walter Watson Alexander Loring, CBE (d 1987), and Patricia Eileen, *née* Quirke; *b* 10 October 1954; *Educ* Ampleforth, Bedford Coll London (BA); *m* Elizabeth McClintock; 3 s, 1 da; *Career* admitted slr 1979; CMS Cameron McKenna (formerly McKenna & Co): resident ptnr in Bahrain 1988–90, ptnr London 1990–2003; memb Law Soc; *Recreations* tennis, bridge; *Clubs* Oriental; *Style*— Anthony Loring, Esq; ✉ Hall Farm, Cottesmore Road, Exton, Oakham LE15 8AN (e-mail afloring@ntlworld.com)

LORISTON-CLARKE, Anne Jennifer Frances (Jennie); MBE (1979); da of Lt Col John Fitzherbert Symes Bullen, RHA (d 1966), of Charmouth, Dorset, and Anne Harris St John (d 1963); *b* 22 January 1943; *Educ* privately; *m* 27 Feb 1965, Anthony Grahame Loriston-Clarke, s of Capt Geoffrey Neame Loriston-Clarke, CBE, RN; 2 da (Anne Frances b 19 Jan 1966, Elizabeth Jane b 27 July 1970); *Career* horse breeder, equestrian dressage; winner: City of London Cup for Best Rider 1953–56, Jr Jumping Championships Richmond Royal Horse Show 1955, Pony Club Horse Trials Championships; joined GB Dressage Team 1964; winner 6 World Cup qualifiers, Bronze medal World Dressage Championships (Goodwood) 1978; memb Br Olympic Team: Munich 1972, Montreal 1976, Los Angeles 1984, Seoul 1988; stud owner/mangr; developed The Catherston Stud, breeding competition Warmblood horses, pioneered the use of chilled and frozen semen in horses in the UK, international trainer and judge, author of 4 books and videos on dressage, longreining and training of young horses; chair Br Dressage 2007, vice-pres Br Horse Soc 2007; NPSDip, Duke of Edinburgh Gold Award, Animal Health Tst Special Award for Servs to the Equestrian Indust 2000; Queen's Award for Outstanding Services to Equestrianism 2006; Freeman Worshipful Co of Farriers 2001; FBHS; *Recreations* reading, writing, swimming, singing, walking the dog by bicycle; *Style*— Mrs Jennie Loriston-Clarke, MBE; ✉ Catherston Stud, Croft Farm, Over Wallop, Stockbridge, Hampshire SO20 8HX (tel 01264 782716, fax 01264 782717, e-mail catherston.stud@ukgateway.net, website www.catherstonstud.net)

LOTAY, Avtar; *Educ* Univ of Bristol (BA, Dip Arch); *Career* architect; project offr Royal Coll of Art; Richard Rogers Partnership: joined 1986, assoc dir 1996–; *Projects* incl: Billingsgate Market, European Ct of Human Rights Strasbourg, Channel 4 TV HQ, St Katharine's Dock, Farnborough Air Terminal and Masterplan, Grosvenor Road Redevelopment, Scientific Generics Cambridge, King's Dock Liverpool, Lloyd's Register of Shipping; *Style*— Avtar Lotay, Esq; ✉ Richard Rogers Partnership, Thames Wharf, Rainville Road, London W6 9HA

LOTEN, HE Graeme Neil; s of Richard Maurice, of Portsmouth, and Brenda Ivy Elizabeth, *née* Shaw, of Portsmouth; *b* 10 March 1959; *Educ* Portsmouth GS, Univ of Liverpool (BA); *Career* HM Dip Serv: FCO 1981–83, UK delg to NATO Brussels 1983–86, Br Embassy Khartoum 1986–87, Br Embassy The Hague 1988–92, dep head of mission Br Embassy Almaty 1993–97, ambass to Rwanda 1998–2001 (concurrently accredited to Burundi), ambass to Mali 2001–03, ambass to Tajikistan 2004–; *Recreations* tennis, travel, rabbit breeding, Portsmouth FC; *Clubs* Royal Commonwealth Soc, Royal Over-Seas League; *Style*— HE Mr Graeme Loten; ✉ c/o Foreign & Commonwealth Office (Dushanbe), King Charles Street, London SW1A 2AH (e-mail gnloten@compuserve.com)

LOTHIAN, 13 Marquess of (S 1701); Michael Andrew Foster Jude Kerr; PC (1996), QC (Scot 1996), DL (Roxburgh, Ettrick and Lauderdale, 1990), MP; also Lord Newbottle (S 1591), Lord Jedburgh (S 1622), Earl of Lothian, Lord Ker of Newbattle (*sic*) (both S 1631), Earl of Ancram (1633), Viscount of Briene, Lord Ker of Newbottle, Oxnam, Jedburgh, Dolphinstoun and Nisbet (all S 1701), and Baron Ker of Kersheugh (UK 1821); s of 12 Marquess of Lothian (d 2004), and Antonella Reuss (Marchioness of Lothian, OBE), *née* Newland; *b* 7 July 1945; *Educ* Ampleforth, ChCh Oxford (MA), Univ of Edinburgh (LLB); *m* 1975, Lady Jane Fitzalan-Howard, da of 16 Duke of Norfolk, KG, GCVO, GBE, TD, PC (d 1975), and Lavinia, Duchess of Norfolk, LG, CBE (d 1995); 2 da (Lady Clare b 1979, Lady Mary b 1981); *Heir* bro, Lord Ralph Kerr; *Career* advocate (Scot) 1970; MP (Cons): Berwickshire and E Lothian Feb-Sept 1974, Edinburgh S 1979–87 (also contested 1987), Devizes 1992–; chm Cons Party in Scotland 1980–83 (vice-chm 1975–80), Parly under-sec Scottish Office (Home Affairs and Environment) 1983–87, Parly under sec NI Office 1993–94, min of state NI Office 1994–97, shadow Cabinet oppn spokesman for constitutional affrs 1997–98, chm Cons Pty 1998–2001 (dep chm 1998), shadow sec of state for Foreign and Cwlth Affrs 2001–03, dep ldr Cons Pty 2001–05, shadow sec of state for Int Affrs and shadow foreign sec 2003–05, memb Cons Pty Policy Bd 2001–05; memb Public Accounts Ctee 1992–93, memb Select Ctee on Energy 1979–83, memb Intelligence & Security Ctee 2006–; chm Northern Corporate Communications Ltd 1989–91, memb Bd Scottish Homes 1988–90; chm Scottish Cncl of Ind Schs 1988–90; govr Napier Poly of Edinburgh 1989–90, pres Environmental Medicine Fndn 1988–92, chm Waverley Housing Tst 1988–90; *Recreations* photography, folksinging; *Clubs* New (Edinburgh), Pratt's, Beefsteak, White's; *Style*— The Most Hon the Marquess of Lothian, PC, QC, DL, MP; ✉ c/o House of Commons, London SW1A 0AA

LOTT, Dame Felicity Ann Emwhyla; DBE (1996, CBE 1990); da of John Albert Lott, and Iris Emwhyla, *née* Williams; *b* 8 May 1947; *Educ* Pate's Girls GS Cheltenham, RHC Univ of London (BA), RAM (LRAM); *m* 1, 22 Dec 1973 (m dis 1982), Robin Mavesyn Golding; m 2, 19 Jan 1984, Gabriel Leonard Woolf, s of Alec Woolf; 1 da (Emily b 19 June 1984); *Career* opera singer, debut in The Magic Flute (ENO) 1975; princ appearances: ENO, Glyndebourne, Covent Garden, WNO, Scottish Opera, Paris, Brussels, Hamburg, Chicago, Munich, NY, Vienna, Milan, San Francisco, Madrid; recordings for: EMI, Decca, Harmonia Mundi Chandos, Erato, Hyperion; Hon DMus Univ of Sussex 1989, hon fell Royal Holloway Univ of London 1994; Chevalier de l'Ordre des Arts et des Lettres (France) 1992, Officier dans l'Ordre des Arts et des Lettres 2000, Chevalier de la Légion d'Honneur 2001, Bayerische Kammersängerin 2003; Hon DLitt Loughborough Univ 1996, DMus (hc) Univ of London 1997, DMus RSAMD 1998, Hon DMus Univ of Leicester 2000, DMus (hc) Univ of Oxford 2001; FRAM 1986, FRCM 2006; *Recreations* reading, gardening; *Style*— Dame Felicity Lott, DBE; ✉ c/o Askonas Holt, Lonsdale Chambers, 27 Chancery Lane, London WC2E 8LA (tel 020 7400 1700, fax 020 7400 1799, website www.felicitylott.de)

LOUBET, Bruno Jean Roger; s of Clement Loubet, of Libourne Gironde, France, and Mauricette, *née* Lacroix (d 1989); *b* 8 October 1961; *m* 27 Dec 1983, Catherine, da of Jacques Mougeol; 3 da (Laeticia b 4 Aug 1985, Laura Claire b 8 April 1987, Chloé b 28 May 1998); *Career* lycée hotelier 1976–79; commis de cuisine: Hyatt Regency Brussels 1979–80, Restaurant Copenhague 1980–82; second maître Nat French Navy and chef to the Admiral TCD Ouragan 1982, commis chef Tante Claire London 1982; head chef: Gastronome One Fulham 1982–85, Le Manoir aux Quat'Saisons Great Milton 1985–86; chef mangr Petit Blanc Oxford 1986–88, chef Four Seasons Restaurant Inn On The Park 1988–93, chef/patron Bistro Bruno London 1993–96, opened L'Odeon London 1995, conslt Loubet Cuisine 1997–, devpt chef Gruppo Group 1998–, exec chef Isola 1999–2001, prop Bruno's Tables Toowong 2002–, exec chef Bugrette Restaurant 2007–; Young Chef of The Year Good Food Guide 1985, Acorn Award Caterer & Hotelkeeper 1988, Michelin Star 1990, Chef of the Year Courier Mail 2004 and 2005; memb Académie Culinaire de France GB 1990; *Publications* Bruno Loubet: Cuisine Courante (1991), Bistrot Bruno: Cooking from L'Odeon (1995); *Style*— Bruno Loubet, Esq; ✉ Loubet Cuisine, 45 Riverview Gardens, Barnes, London SW13 9QY; 9 Hakea Crescent, Chapel Hill, Queensland 4069, Australia (tel 0061 7 3878 3364, e-mail cloubet@iprimus.com.au)

LOUDON, Alasdair John; WS (1987); s of John Duncan Ott Loudon, of Edinburgh, and Nancy Beaton, *née* Mann; *b* 7 April 1956, Edinburgh; *Educ* Edinburgh Acad, Univ of Dundee (LLB); *Partner* Angela Elizabeth Entwistle; 1 da (Susannah Mary b 8 Dec 1984), 2 s (Malcolm John William b 17 March 1986, Paul Durward Mann b 16 Feb 1989); *Career* slr; legal apprenticeship Tods, Murray & Jamieson 1978–80, ptnr Warner & Co Slrs 1982–92 (asst slr 1980–82), fndr and ptnr Loudons WS 1992–2001, ptnr Turcan Connell Slrs 2001–; pres Edinburgh Bar Assoc 1996–98; memb: Law Soc of Scot 1980, WS Soc; *Recreations* food and wine, golf, watching football; *Clubs* Bruntsfield Links Golfing Soc, Luffness New Golf; *Style*— Alasdair Loudon, Esq, WS; ✉ Turcan Connell, Princes Exchange, 1 Earl Grey Street, Edinburgh EH3 9EE (tel 0131 228 8111, fax 0131 228 8118, e-mail ajl@turcanconnell.com)

LOUDON, George Ernest; *b* 19 November 1942; *Educ* Christlijk Lyceum Zeist Holland, Balliol Coll Oxford (BA), Johns Hopkins Univ Washington DC (MA); *m* Angela; 1 da (b 1970), 1 s (b 1972); *Career* fin analyst Lazard Frères & CIE Paris 1967–68, project mgmnt Ford Foundation NY and Jakarta 1968–71, project mgmnt McKinsey & Co Amsterdam 1971–76, memb Bd of MDs Amsterdam-Rotterdam Bank NV (Amro Bank) Amsterdam 1983–88 (gen mangr New Issue and Syndicate Dept 1976–83), dir Midland Bank plc 1988–92, chief exec Midland Montagu Ltd 1988–92 (chm 1991–92); chm: Altius Holdings Ltd 1999–, Pall Mall Capital Ltd 2001–, Helix Assocs Ltd until 2005; non-exec dir: Geveke NV (Netherlands) 1985–2001, Harrison/Parrott Ltd 1993–, Arjo Wiggins Appleton plc 1993–2000, M&G Group plc 1993–94, Global Asset Management Ltd 1994–99, CMG Ltd 1998–2002, LogicaCMG plc 2002–, Evolution (formerly Beeson Gregory Group plc) 2001–04; currently dir Viking River Cruises SA (Luxembourg); former vice-chm: Amsterdam Stock Exchange, Samuel Montagu & Co Ltd; former treas Stichting 1986–88; former chm and chief exec: Trinkaus und Burkhardt (Germany), Euromobiliare (Italy); memb Cncl of Japan Festival 1990; memb: Acquisitions Ctee MMOMA City of Amsterdam, Bd of Tstees Netherlands Royal Coll of Art, van den Berch van Heemstede Stichting; former tstee Tate Fndn, tstee South Bank Fndn, tstee and dir Galapagos Conservation Tst, tstee Royal Botanic Gardens Kew 2007–; *Style*— George Loudon, Esq; ✉ Pall Mall Capital Limited, 18A St James's Place, London SW1A 1NH

LOUDON, James Rushworth Hope; s of Francis William Hope Loudon (d 1985), and Lady Prudence Katharine Patton, *née* Jellicoe (d 2000); *b* 19 March 1943; *Educ* Eton, Magdalene Coll Cambridge (BA); *m* 17 May 1975, Jane Gavina, *née* Fryett; 1 da (Antonia Louise Cameron b 1977), 2 s (Hugo John Hope b 1978, Alexander Guy Rushworth b 1980); *Career* fin dir Blue Circle Industries plc 1987–2001 (joined 1977); non-exec dir: Lafarge Malayan Cement 1989–2004, Caledonia Investments plc 1995–, James Hardie Industries NV 2002–; govr: Univ of Greenwich 2001–, Royal Sch for Deaf Children 2002–05, Caldecott Fndn 2002–, Kent Air Ambulance Tst 2005–; High Sheriff Kent 2004–05; *Recreations* golf, cricket, opera; *Clubs* MCC, Rye Golf, Royal St George's Golf, Swinley Forest Golf; *Style*— James Loudon, Esq; ✉ Olantigh, Wye, Ashford, Kent TN25 5EW (tel 01233 812294)

LOUDON, Prof Rodney; s of Albert Loudon (d 1965), and Doris Helen, *née* Blane (d 1980); *b* 25 July 1934; *Educ* Bury GS, BNC Oxford (MA, DPhil); *m* 6 June 1960, Mary Anne, da of Eugene Philips; 1 da (Anne Elizabeth b 1961), 1 s (Peter Thomas b 1964); *Career* postdoctoral fell Univ of Calif Berkeley 1959–60, scientific civil servant RRE Malvern 1960–65, Bell Laboratories Murray Hill New Jersey 1965–66, prof of physics Univ of Essex 1967– (reader 1966–67), BT Laboratories 1984 and 1989–95; visiting prof: Yale Univ 1975, Univ of Calif Irvine 1980, École Polytechnique Lausanne 1985, Univ of Rome 1988 and 1996, Univ Libre de Bruxelles 1990, Univ of Strathclyde 1998–, Univ of Erlangen 1999–2002; chm Bd of Eds Optica Acta 1984–87; Thomas Young Medal and Prize Inst of Physics 1987, Max Born Award of the Optical Soc of America 1992, Alexander von Humboldt Research Award 1998; fell Optical Soc of America 1994; FRS 1987; *Books* The Quantum Theory of Light (1973, 3 edn 2000), Scattering of Light by Crystals (with W Hayes, 1978), Introduction to the Properties of Condensed Matter (with D J Barber, 1989); *Style*— Prof Rodney Loudon, FRS; ✉ 3 Gaston Street, East Bergholt, Colchester, Essex CO7 6SD (tel 01206 298550); Electronic Systems Engineering Department, Essex University, Colchester CO4 3SQ (tel 01206 872880, fax 01206 873598, e-mail loudr@essex.ac.uk)

LOUDOUN, 14 Earl of (S 1633); Michael Edward Abney-Hastings; assumed by deed poll 1946 surname of Abney-Hastings; s of Countess of Loudoun, and (first husb) Capt Walter Strickland Lord; *b* 22 July 1942; *Educ* Ampleforth; *m* 1969, Noelene Margaret (d 2002), da of W J McCormick; 3 da (Hon Amanda Louise b 1969, Hon Lisa Maree b 1971, Hon Rebecca Lee b 1974), 2 s (Simon Michael, Lord Mauchline (twin) b 1974, Marcus William b 1981); *Heir* s, Lord Mauchline; *Style*— The Rt Hon the Earl of Loudoun

LOUGHBOROUGH, Archdeacon of; *see:* Stanes, Ven Ian Thomas

LOUGHREY, (Stephen Victor) Patrick; s of Eddie Loughrey (d 1979), and Mary, *née* Griffin; *b* 29 December 1955; *Educ* Loreto Coll Milford Donegal, Univ of Ulster (BA), Queen's Univ Belfast (MA, PGCE); *m* 4 July 1978, Patricia, da of Thomas Kelly (d 1984); 1 s (Stephen b 26 Dec 1980), 2 da (Joanne b 26 Feb 1982, Christine b 10 June 1985); *Career* teacher St Colm's HS Draperstown 1978–84; BBC Northern Ireland: joined as prodr 1984, head of educnl broadcasting 1988–91, head of programmes 1991–, controller 1994–2000, dir Nations and Regions 2000–; former memb: NI Curriculum Cncl, Hist Monuments Cncl, Advsy Ctee NI Arts Cncl; tstee Ulster Local History Tst Fund; fell Radio Acad; *Books* Ordnance Survey of Ballinascreen (ed, 1981), The People of Ireland (ed, 1988); *Recreations* talking; *Style*— Patrick Loughrey, Esq; ✉ BMC4 A4, Media Centre, 201 Wood Lane, London W12 7TQ (tel 020 8008 1220)

LOUGHTON, David Clifford; s of Clifford Loughton (d 1973) of Harrow, Middx, and Hazel Loughton; *b* 28 January 1954; *Educ* Roxeth Manor Sch Harrow, Technical Colls in Harrow, Watford and Southall; *m* 1986, Deborah, da of George Wellington; 1 da (Georgina Anna b 12 July 1987), 1 s (Theodore David b 12 July 1990); *Career* asst hosp engr Hillingdon Area HA 1974–76, hosp engr Herts Area HA 1976–78, dir and gen mangr Ducost Ltd 1978–83, divnl mangr GEC Electrical Projects 1984–86, chief exec Walsgrave Hosp NHS Tst (now Univ Hosps Coventry and Warwickshire NHS Tst) 1986–2002, devpt dir InHealth Gp of Cos 2002–04, chief exec Royal Wolverhampton Hosps NHS Tst 2004–; memb: Nat Cncl NHS Confederation 2007–, Advsy Bd NHS Nat Inst for Health Research 2007–; chm Coventry and Warwickshire Educn & Trg Consortium (NHS) 1996–; memb: Inst of Health Services Mgmnt, Inst of Hosp Engrs, Inst of Plant Engrs; *Recreations* country pursuits; *Style*— David Loughton, Esq; ✉ Blacon Cottage, Norton Lindsey, Warwickshire CV35 8JN (tel 0192 684 2070); The Royal Wolverhampton Hospitals NHS Trust, Hollybush House, New Cross Hospital, Wolverhampton WV10 0QP (tel 01902 695951)

LOUGHTON, Timothy Paul (Tim); MP; s of Rev Michael Loughton, and Pamela, *née* Brandon; *b* 30 May 1962; *Educ* The Priory Sch Lewes, Univ of Warwick (BA), Clare Coll Cambridge; *m* Elizabeth Juliet, da of John B MacLachlan; 1 s (Hector b 14 Aug 1994), 2 da (Freya b 3 April 1996, Mathilda b 8 Dec 1997); *Career* dir Fleming Private Asset Management 1992–2000 (joined 1984), non-exec dir Netlink Internet Services 1995–99; MP (Cons) E Worthing and Shoreham 1997– (Parly candidate Sheffield Brightside 1992); oppn frontbench spokesman for the regions, urban regeneration, housing and poverty 2000–01, oppn frontbench spokesman on health 2001–; shadow min for Children 2003–; memb: Environmental Audit Select Ctee 1997–01, Fin Bill Standing Ctee 1997 and 1998, European Scrutiny C Standing Ctee 2000–01; vice-chm All-Pty Parly Gp on Autism; treas: Parly Maritime Gp, Parly Animal Welfare Gp, All-Pty Parly Gp Archaeology; chm Conservative Disability Gp 1998–2006, chm All Pty Gp on Wholesale Financial Services and Markets 2005– (vice-chm 2003–05); memb: Centre for Policy Studies, Inst of Econ Affrs, Tibet Action (UK), Jt Ctee on Financial Services and Markets 1999; pres: Shoreham Cons Club, Adur Athletic FC, Sussex Holiday Club; vice-pres Worthing MIND chm Ropetackle Centre Tst; jt chm APG Mental Health 2005–; patron: St Barnabas Hospice Worthing, League of Friends Worthing Hosp, League of Friends Southalnds Hosp, Worthing Churches Homeless Project, Worthing Hockey Club, TOAST (Obesity Awareness and Solutions Tst), West Grinstead and Dist Ploughing and Agric Soc; vice-patron Life Educn Centres W Sussex; memb Ct Univ of Sussex; MSI (Dip); *Recreations* archaeology, skiing, tennis, hockey, wine; *Style*— Tim Loughton, Esq, MP; ✉ House of Commons, London SW1A 0AA (tel 020 7219 4471, fax 020 7219 0461, e-mail loughtont@parliament.uk, website www.timloughton.com)

LOULOUDIS, Hon Mrs (Madeleine Mary); LVO (1997); 4 but 3 survg da (twin) of 20 Viscount Dillon (d 1979); *b* 29 October 1957; *m* 4 March 1989, Leonard Constantine Louloudis, o s of Constantine Louloudis; 1 s (Constantine Michael b 15 Sept 1991), 1 da (Theodora Catherine Lily b 6 July 1993); *Career* Lady in Waiting to HRH The Princess Royal 1997– (asst private sec 1988–97); *Style*— The Hon Mrs Louloudis, LVO; ✉ Flat 2, 66 Westbourne Terrace, London W2 3UJ (tel 020 7723 8816); The Malt House, Ditchley Park, Enstone, Oxfordshire OX7 4EP

LOUSADA, Charles Terence; s of Charles Rochford Lousada (d 1988), and Elizabeth, *née* Shaw (d 2006); *b* 21 September 1938, Farnborough, Hants; *Educ* Cokethorpe; *m* 1962 (m dis 1974); 1 s (Simon Charles b 1963), 1 da (Elizabeth Natasha (Mrs Pollard) b 1964); *Career* office boy January's estate agents Cambridge 1953, prop estate agency 1965–74, md Lousada plc 1969–; dir Imperial Bathroom 1990–, dir 20 other property cos; farms in SA; tstee of several local charities; chm SaBRE (Support for Britain's Reservists and Employers) for Beds, former chm Buy British campaign; High Sheriff Beds 1997–98; *Recreations* all country sports (still playing polo), helicopter pilot/owner; *Clubs* RAC, Kirtlington Polo; *Style*— Charles Lousada, Esq; ✉ Lousada plc, Crawley Park, Husborne Crawley, Bedford MK43 0UU (tel 01908 282860, fax 01908 282861, e-mail charles@lousada.com)

LOUSADA, Peter Allen; s of Air Cdre Charles Rochford Lousada, DL (d 1988), and Elizabeth, *née* Shaw; *b* 30 March 1937; *Educ* Epsom Coll; *m* 13 Oct 1962, Jane, da of Lt-Col Donald Gillmor (d 1972); 2 s (Toby b 1963, James b 1965), 1 da (Sarah b 1965); *Career* Nat Serv Flying Offr RAF, Canada & 61 Sqdn; vice-pres Cadbury Beverages Europe 1987–92; dir: Schweppes International Ltd, Cadbury Beverages Ltd 1990–92, chm Canadean Ltd 1997–2003; sr vice-pres Cadbury Beverages 1992–96; non-exec chm Hydrophane Ltd 1990–96; pres Union of Euro Soft Drinks Assocs 1991–95; cdr St John Ambulance Beds 2000–05; *Recreations* golf, fishing; *Clubs* RAF, Woburn Golf; *Style*— Peter A Lousada, Esq, DL; ✉ Well Cottage, Bow Brickhill, Buckinghamshire MK17 9JU (tel 01908 372186, fax 01908 372186)

LOUSADA, Sandra Reignier; da of Sir Anthony Baruh Lousada (d 1994), of London, and his 1 w, Jocelyn Herbert (d 2003), da of late Sir Alan Herbert, CH; *b* 29 June 1938; *Educ* St Paul's Girls' Sch, Regent St Poly, Central St Martin's; *m* 1 Jan 1965, Brian Richards (d 2004), son of Alexander Hodgson Richards; 1 s (Sam b 12 June 1966), 1 da (Polly b 17 May 1968); *Career* asst photographer Scaioni Studios 1956–59; freelance photographer 1959–63; work for magazines incl: Queen Magazine, Tatler, Nova, Brides, Vogue, Elle (Paris), Marie Claire (Paris), Vanity Fair, Mademoiselle and Glamour Magazines (NYC); work for English Stage Co incl: John Osborne's Luther and Wesker Trilogy; film work incl: The Loneliness of the Long Distance Runner, Tom Jones, The Charge of the Light Brigade; travelled and worked in USA, Japan, India and Russia; joined Whitecross Studios 1963–81; advtg work for agencies incl: J Walter Thompson, Ogilvy Benson & Mather, Collett Dickinson & Pearce; chm Assoc of Photographers (AOP) 1998–99; editorial work for most main magazines and some publishers in London and New York; Susan Griggs Agency 1981–94, frequent travel to Europe and India; current photographic work incl portraits, children, crafts, fashion, health and beauty for number of London magazines, book publishers, design gps and advtg agencies; work for charities: Wellbeing (formerly Birthright), Great Ormond Street Hosp for Sick Children, Tommy Campaign, Peper Harow Fndn; chm Assoc of Photographers 1999; Silver Award Assoc of Photographers 1988, Sainsbury Baby Book Award 2001, Features Photographer of the Year Award Garden Writers' Guild 2003; *Publications* London's Parks and Gardens (2003); *Style*— Ms Sandra Lousada; ✉ c/o Creative Talent Limited, 37 Radnor Mews, London W2 1PN (e-mail bo@creativetalent.co.uk); tel 020 7439 1877, fax 020 7434 1144, e-mail slousada@globalnet.co.uk

LOUTH, 16 Baron (I 1541); Otway Michael James Oliver Plunkett; s of 15 Baron (d 1950); *b* 19 August 1929; *Educ* Downside; *m* 1951, Angela Patricia, da of William Cullinane, of St Helier, Jersey; 3 s, 2 da; *Heir* s, Hon Jonathan Plunkett; *Style*— The Rt Hon the Lord Louth

LOUVEAUX, Bertrand Jean-Philippe Francois; s of Xavier Louveaux, of Belgium, and Evelyne, *née* Carbonnelle; *b* 28 April 1967, Brussels; *Educ* Rugby, LSE (MSc); *m* 3 Sept 1994 Sarah Jane, *née* Bowen; 1 s (Tristan b 17 Nov 1997), 1 da (Amelie b 22 April 1999); *Career* slr; ptnr Slaughter and May 2001– (joined 1992); *Style*— Bertrand Louveaux, Esq; ✉ Slaughter and May, 1 Bunhill Row, London EC1Y 8YY (tel 020 7090 4173, e-mail bertrand.louveaux@slaughterandmay.com)

LOVAT, 16 Lord (S 1458–64); Simon Fraser; 25 Chief of Clan Fraser; *de facto* 16 Lord, 18 but for the attainder; also Baron Lovat (UK 1837), of Lovat, Co Inverness; er s of Hon Simon Augustine Fraser, Master of Lovat (d 1994), and Virginia, *née* Grose; suc gf 15 Lord Lovat, DSO, MC, TD 1995; *b* 13 February 1977; *Educ* Harrow; *Heir* bro, Jack Fraser, Master of Lovat; *Style*— The Rt Hon the Lord Lovat; ✉ Beaufort Lodge, Beauly, Inverness-shire IV4 7BB

LOVE, Andrew; MP; s of James Love (d 1995), and Olive, *née* Mills (d 1997); *b* 21 March 1949; *Educ* Greenock HS, Univ of Strathclyde (BSc); *m* March 1983, Ruth Lesley, da of late Jack Rosenthal; *Career* sec CRS (London) Political Ctee 1985–92, parly offr Co-op Pty 1992–97; MP (Lab Co-op) Edmonton 1997– (Parly candidate 1992); PPS to min of state Dept of Health and DTI 2001–05; memb: Public Accounts Ctee 1997–2001, Deregulation Ctee 2000–01, Regulatory Reform Ctee 2001–05, treasy Select Ctee 2005–; chm All-Pty Parly Gp for Building Socs and Fin Mutuals 1997–2002, co-chair All-Pty Gp on Homelessness and Housing Need, sec All-Pty Solvent Abuse Gp 1997–2001, co-chair All-Pty Sri Lanka Gp 2004– (sec 2000–04), chm All-Pty Small Businesses Gp 2005– (sec 1999–2005); vice-chm Backbench ODPM Ctee; London Borough of Haringey: cncllr 1980–86, chm of fin 1984–85, chm of housing 1985–86; patron Beck House, patron HEAL Cancer Charity 2002–, vice-patron Helen Rollason Cancer Centre Appeal; memb: NE Thames RHA 1988–90, T&GWU, Fabian Soc, War on Want, Co-operative Gp; FCIS 2000; *Recreations* golf, opera, reading; *Style*— Andrew Love, Esq, MP; ✉ House of Commons, London SW1A 0AA (tel 020 7219 6377, fax 020 7219 6623, e-mail lovea@parliament.uk)

LOVE, Prof Philip Noel; CBE (1983), DL (Merseyside 1997); o s of Thomas Love (d 1992), of Aberdeen, and Ethel, *née* Philip (d 1995); *b* 25 December 1939; *Educ* Aberdeen GS, Univ of Aberdeen (MA, LLB); *m* 1, 21 Aug 1963, Isabel Leah (d 1993), da of Innes Mearns (d 1991), of Aberdeen; 3 s (Steven b 1965, Michael b 1967, Donald b 1969); m 2, 15 April 1995, Mrs Isobel Pardey; *Career* advocate in Aberdeen 1963; princ Campbell Connon Slrs Aberdeen 1963–74 (conslt 1974–2005); Univ of Aberdeen: prof of conveyancing and professional practice of law 1974–92, dean Faculty of Law 1979–82 and 1991–92, vice-princ 1986–90; vice-chllr Univ of Liverpool 1992–2002; memb Rules Cncl Court of Session 1968–92, vice-pres Scottish Law Agents' Soc 1970, chm Aberdeen Home for Widowers' Children 1971–92, local chm Rent Assessment Panel for Scotland 1972–92, Hon Sheriff Grampian Highlands and Islands 1978–; Law Soc of Scotland: memb 1963–, memb Cncl 1975–86, vice-pres 1980–81, pres 1981–82; chm: Grampian Med Ethical Ctee 1984–92, Registers of Scot Customer Advsy Gp 1990–92, Scot Conveyancing and Executry Servs Bd 1991–96; memb Butterworths Editorial Consultative Bd for Scot 1990–95, pt/t memb Scot Law Cmmn 1986–95; chm: Univs and Colls Employers Assoc 1995–2002, Knowledge Economy Key Priority Gp NW Regnl Assembly 2000–02, NW Univs Assoc 2001–02; memb: Scot Univs Cncl on Entrance 1989–92, Bd Univs UK 1996–2002, NW Sci Cncl 2001–02, Bd Rising Stars Growth Fund Ltd 2002–05; govr: Inst of Occupational Med Ltd 1990–, Liverpool Coll 2003–; pres Aberdeen GS Former Pupils' Club 1987–88, chm The Mersey Partnership 1995–98; tstee: Grampian and Islands Family Tst 1988–92, St George's Hall Tst 1996–, Merseyside Police and High Sheriff's Charitable Tst 1998–, Liverpool Charity and Voluntary Services 2003–, Liverpool Philharmonic Fndn 2005–; High Sheriff Merseyside 2007–08; Hon LLD: Univ of Abertay Dundee 1996, Univ of Aberdeen 1997, Univ of Liverpool 2002; fell Liverpool John Moores Univ 2002; FRSA 1995–2003, CIMgt 1996–2003, AcSS 2000; *Recreations* golf, watching sport, photography, music; *Clubs* New (Edinburgh), Artists (Liverpool), Formby Golf; *Style*— Prof Philip N Love, CBE, DL; ✉ 1 Mayfield Court, Victoria Road, Formby, Merseyside L37 7JL (tel 01704 832427, e-mail pnlmayco@aol.com)

LOVEDAY, Mark Antony; s of George Arthur Loveday (d 1981), and Sylvia Mary, *née* Gibbs (d 1967); *b* 22 September 1943; *Educ* Winchester, Magdalen Coll Oxford (MA); *m* 1981, Mary Elizabeth, da of John Tolmie; 1 s (Samuel George b 15 June 1982), 1 da (Lucy Sylvia Catherine b 9 Dec 1983); *Career* Cazenove & Co: joined 1966, corp fin ptnr 1974–94, sr ptnr 1994–2001; chm Foreign & Colonial Investment Tst plc 2002– (dir 2001–); tstee: Grosvenor Estate, Magdalen Coll Devpt Tst; memb Devpt Cncl Trinity Coll of Music; Freeman City of London, Liveryman Worshipful Co of Skinners; MSI (memb Stock Exchange 1974); *Recreations* golf; *Clubs* Boodle's, Hurlingham, City Univ, MCC, Royal St George's; *Style*— Mark Loveday, Esq; ✉ 4 Park Place, St James's, London SW1A 1LP (tel 020 7898 9109, e-mail loveday_mark@hotmail.com)

LOVEGROVE, Ross; s of Herbert William John Lovegrove, BEM, of Penarth, S Glamorgan, and Mary Eileen Lovegrove; *b* 16 August 1958; *Educ* St Cyres Comp Sch Penarth, Cardiff Coll of Art & Design, Manchester Poly (BA), RCA (MDes); *Partner* Miska Miller; 1 s (Roman S A Lovegrove); *Career* designer: Frogdesign Germany 1983–84 (projects incl: Apple Computers, Sony Walkman, AEG Telefunken and Louis Vuitton Luggage), Knoll International Paris 1984–86, Atelier De Nimes 1984, fndr ptnr Lovegrove & Brown 1986–90, fndr Lovegrove Studio X 1990– (clients incl: Knoll International, BA, Louis Vuitton, Hermes, Cappellini SPA, Connolly Leathers, London Underground, Apple Computers, Herman Miller, Luceplan, Driade Spa, Alessi Spa, Olympus Optical, Samsonite, Tag Heuer, Peugeot, Acco USA); winner: Oggetti Per Domus award for the pocket disc camera and film cassette system 1984, first prize (product design) Creative Review Pantone Colour awards, winner of ID of N America Award by the IDSA 1993, jt winner CSD Minerva Awards for FO8 chair 1994, shortlisted to final five of the BBC Design Awards 1994, winner of Grunen Point Award Stuttgart Design Centre 1994; work featured in various jls incl: Axis, Form, Intramuros, Design Week, Blueprint, L'Architecture d'Aujourd'hui, Domus, Architectural Review, Sunday Times, Financial Times, ID Magazine, New Scientist, The Independent, Design Report, Interni Magazine, Washington Post, New York Times, Architektur und Wohnen; exhibitions incl: Mondo Materials (California) 1989–90, Synthetic Visions (V&A London) 1990, 91 Objects by 91 Designers (Gallery 91 NY) 1991, Conran Fndn Collection, curator of first permanent collection London Design Museum 1993, Industrial Elegance (Guggenheim Museum NY) 1993, Mutant Materials (MOMA NY) 1995, FO8 (Stockholm) 1996, Ross Lovegrove Objects (Tokyo, Cologne) 1996, Design Highlights from Great Britain (Danish Museum of Decorative Art) 1997; visiting lectr at: RCA London, Ecole Cammondo Paris, ADI Milan, Univ of Aberdeen, Domus Acad; TV and radio: Late Show BBC 2, The Changing Domestic Landscape (LBC Design Week interview with Ken Grange), Ross Lovegrove Industrial Designer (BBC Wales interview); *Style*— Ross Lovegrove, Esq; ✉ Lovegrove Design Consultants, 21 Powis Mews, London W11 1JN (tel 020 7229 7104, fax 020 7229 7032)

LOVELACE, 5 Earl of (UK 1838); Peter Axel William Locke King; also Lord King, Baron of Ockham (GB 1725), and Viscount Ockham (UK 1838); s of 4 Earl of Lovelace (d 1964, seventh in descent from the sis of John Locke, the philosopher), and his 2 w, Manon Lis (d 1990), da of Axel Sigurd Transo, of Copenhagen, and widow of Baron Carl Frederik von Blixen Finecke; *b* 26 November 1951; *Educ* privately; *m* 1, 1980 (m dis 1989); m 2, 1994, Kathleen Anne Rose, da of Lem Smolders, of Milouka, Langwarrin, Australia; *Heir* none; *Style*— The Rt Hon the Earl of Lovelace; ✉ Torridon House, Torridon, Ross-shire IV22 2HA

LOVELL, Alan Charles; s of William George Lovell (d 1984), of Andover, Hants, and Mary Kerr, *née* Briant (d 1970); *b* 19 November 1953; *Educ* Winchester, Jesus Coll Oxford (MA, Lawn Tennis, Real Tennis and Rackets blues); *m* 10 July 1982, Hon Virginia, da of Baron Weatherill, PC, DL; 2 da (Emma b 19 March 1985, Lucinda b 3 Oct 1986); *Career* articled clerk then CA Price Waterhouse 1976–80, The Plessey Company plc 1980–89; chief exec: Conder Group plc 1991–92 (fin dir 1989–91), Costain Group plc 1995–97 (fin dir 1993–95), Dunlop Slazenger Group 2004 (fin dir 1997–2003), Jarvis 2004–06, Infinis Ltd 2006–; memb Cncl Lloyd's of London 2007–; non-exec memb Winchester Dist HA 1990–93, non-exec dir: Winchester and Eastleigh Healthcare Tst 1994–2001, Mid-Hampshire Primary Care Tst 2001–06; chm Mary Rose Appeal Ctee 2006–, memb Cncl Malvern Coll 1990–97; FCA 1989 (ACA 1979); *Recreations* real and lawn tennis (int real tennis player 1975–87), golf, gardening; *Clubs* All England Lawn Tennis, MCC, Queen's; *Style*— Alan Lovell, Esq; ✉ The Palace House, Bishop's Lane, Bishop's Waltham, Hampshire SO32 1DP (tel 01489 892838)

LOVELL, Dr Christopher Roland; s of Graham Ernest Lovell (d 1990), and Marion Gladys (d 1984); *b* 29 April 1950; *Educ* Bristol GS, Univ of Bristol (MD); *Career* sr registrar and tutor in dermatology Inst of Dermatology London 1978–84, conslt dermatologist Bath Health Dist 1985–; hon treas Dowling Club (formerly hon sec and hon pres); former hon sec Clinical Soc of Bath; FRCP, FRSM (former pres Section of Dermatology); *Books* Plants and the Skin (1993), The Skin in Rheumatic Disease (with PJ Maddison and GV Campion, 1990); *Recreations* cultivation and preservation of rare bulbs, music (medieval and renaissance recorder player), choral singing (especially church music); *Style*— Dr Christopher Lovell; ✉ Royal United Hospital, Combe Park, Bath BA1 3NG (tel and fax 01225 824524)

LOVELL, Margaret; *Educ* West of England Coll of Art Bristol, Slade Sch of Fine Art, Acad of Fine Art Florence; *m* with 2 da and 2 s; *Career Solo Exhibitions* Marjorie Parr Gall London, Park Square Gall Leeds, Fermoy Art Gall Kings Lynn, Mignon Gall Bath, Halesworth Gall Suffolk, City Art Gall Plymouth, Bruton Gall Somerset, The Arts of Living Bath, Armstrong Davis Gall Arundel, Minster Fine Art York; public commissions incl: sculpture at Grafham Water Hunts for Great Ouse Water Authy, sculpture for Barclays Bank Ltd Bristol, sculpture for City Museum & Art Gall Plymouth, sculpture Cadbury Heath Primary Sch Bristol, Unilever Growth Awards 2000 and 2003; work in public and private collections incl: Arts Cncl of Great Britain, Devon County Cncl, Leicestershire Educn Ctee, Univ of Southampton, Univ of London, Compton Acres Gardens Poole, Aldershot County HS, Godolphin & Latymer Sch; *Awards* Italian State Scholarship, Greek Govt Scholarship; memb RWA; FRBS; *Recreations* keeping sheep; *Style*— Ms Margaret Lovell; ✉ website www.margaretlovell.co.uk

LOVELL, Mary Sybilla; da of William George Shelton (d 1967), and Mary Catherine, *née* Wooley (d 2000); *b* 23 October 1941; *Educ* Notre Dame Collegiate Liverpool, UCLA; *m* 1, 22 Oct 1960 (m dis 1977), Clifford C Lovell; 1 s (Graeme Robert b 1961); m 2, 11 July 1992, Geoffrey Alan Howard Watts (d 1995); *Career* author; fin controller Baron Instruments Ltd 1969–76; dir and co sec: Yachting Provence 1976–78, Baron Computers & Security Ltd 1978–80; mangr Tech Writing Div Tabs Ltd 1982–86; MFH New Forest Hounds 1987–89; vice-pres R S Surtees Soc 1981–; FRGS 1994; *Books* A Hunting Pageant (1980), Cats as Pets (1981), Boys Book of Boats (1982), Straight on yill Morning (1986), The Splendid Outcast (ed, 1987), The Sound of Wings (1989), Cast No Shadow (1992), A Scandalous Life (1995), A Rage to Live (1998), The Mitford Girls: The Biography of an Extraordinary Family (2001), Bess of Hardwick: First Lady of Chatsworth (2005); *Recreations* foxhunting, flying, sailing, travel, reading; *Clubs* Lansdowne, New Forest Hunt; *Style*— Mrs Mary S Lovell; ✉ Stroat House, Stroat, Gloucestershire NP16 7LR

LOVELL-PANK, Dorian Christopher; QC (1993); s of Christopher Edwin Lovell-Pank (d 1966), of Madrid, and Jean Alston de Oliva Day, *née* McPherson (d 1979), of Buenos Aires and Cape Town; *b* 15 February 1946; *Educ* Downside, Colegio Sarmiento Buenos Aires, LSE, Inns of Court Sch of Law; *m* 1983, Diana, da of late Michael Cady Byford, and Sonia Byford, of Claret Hall, Clare, Suffolk; 1 da (Frederica Sonia b 2 May 1986), 1 s (Michael Christopher John b 20 June 1987); *Career* called to the Bar Inner Temple 1971 (bencher 1998); pupillage with Rt Hon Lord Brittan of Spennithorne, PC, QC, DL, *qv*, and Michael Worsley, QC, *qv*, criminal practitioner recorder 1989–2006; jr Middx Bar Mess 1977–80; memb Panel of Chm Police Discipline Appeal Tbnls 1991–; chm Bar Conf 1999; memb: Gen Cncl of the Bar 1989–92 and 1998–2005 (chm Int Rels Ctee 2001–05), Ctee Criminal Bar Assoc 1984–2006 (chm Int Rels Sub-Ctee 1993–2006), Int Bar Assoc 1993– (memb Cncl 2001–05), Human Rights Inst 1996– (memb Cncl 2000–04), American Bar Assoc (assoc) 1997–, Br Inst of Int and Comparative Law 2001–, Br Spanish Law Assoc 2001–, FCO Pro Bono Lawyers Panel 2002–; *Recreations* travel, reading, swimming, things latin; *Clubs* Garrick, Hurlingham, Riverside, Aldeburgh Yacht, RNVR Yacht; *Style*— Dorian Lovell-Pank, Esq, QC; ✉ 6 King's Bench Walk, Temple, London EC4Y 7DR (tel 020 7583 0410, fax 020 7353 8791, e-mail clerks@6kbw.com, telex DX 26 Chancery Lane)

LOVERING, John David; s of John George Lovering (d 1990), and Ruby Beatrice, *née* Edwards (d 1978); *b* 11 October 1949, London; *Educ* Dulwich Coll, Univ of Exeter (BA), Manchester Business Sch (MBA); *m* 18 Dec 1971, Brenda Joan, *née* Wotherspoon; 2 s (Nicholas John b 5 Dec 1974, Matthew William b 1 April 1977), 1 da (Kate Victoria b 21 March 1985); *Career* corp devpt exec Spillers Ltd 1975–78 (also commercial mangr Int Div), head of strategy planning Lex Service Gp plc 1978–82, finance dir Grand Metropolitan Retailing then commercial dir GM Foods 1982–85, head of financial planning and strategy Imperial Gp plc 1985–86, finance dir Sears plc 1986–92 (also md int ops and chm Sears Financial Services), chief operating offr and memb Bd Tarmac plc 1993–95, managing ptnr Lovering & Lovering 1995–; chm: Hoogenbosch Beheer BV 1996–97, Birthdays Gp Ltd 1996–2002 (ceo 1996–98), Peacock Gp plc 1997–2004, Fired Earth Ltd 1998–2001, Odeon Cinemas Ltd 2000–03, Homebase Ltd 2001–02, Laurel High Street Ltd 2002–05, Debenhams plc 2003–, Fitness First Ltd 2003–05, Somerfield Stores Ltd 2005–; vice-chm Barclays Capital 2007–; non-exec dir AGA Food Services Ltd 2003–05; tstee and dir Save the Children 1990–96; memb Chllr's Advsy Cncl Univ of Exeter 2003–; *Recreations* sport, farming, music; *Clubs* Alleyn, Hawkhurst Golf; *Style*— John Lovering, Esq; ✉ Debenhams, 1 Welbeck Street, London W1G 0AA (tel 020 7408 3065)

LOVETT, Ian Nicholas; s of Frederick Lovett, of Croydon, Surrey, and Dorothy Evelyn, *née* Stanley; *b* 7 September 1944; *Educ* Selhurst GS, Univ of Wales (BA); *m* 3 May 1969, Patricia Lesley; 2 da (Emma b 1977, Sophie b 1979); *Career* chm Dunbar Bank plc 2002– (ceo 1984–2004); FCIB 1982; *Recreations* cricket; *Clubs* MCC, Middlesex CCC; *Style*— Ian N Lovett, Esq; ✉ Dunbar Bank plc, 9 Sackville Street, London W1A 2JP (tel 020 7437 7844, e-mail ian.lovett@uk.zurich.com)

LOVICK, (Elizabeth) Sara; da of late Charles Trevor Lovick, of Cullompton, Devon, and Elizabeth Susan Hettie, *née* Phelps; *b* 3 February 1954; *Educ* North London Collegiate Sch Canons Edgware, Lady Margaret Hall Oxford (BA); *Career* admitted slr 1979; ptnr Cameron Markby Hewitt (now CMS Cameron McKenna) 1986–97; legal counsel: Amersham plc / Amersham Biosciences UK Ltd 1997–, IGE Healthcare 1997–; memb Law Soc; assoc memb: Chartered Inst of Patent Agents, The Inst of Trade Mark Attorneys; *Recreations* swimming, skiing, choral singing; *Style*— Miss Sara Lovick; ✉ Amersham Biosciences UK Limited, Legal Services, Pollards Wood, Chalfont St Giles, Buckinghamshire HP8 7SP

LOVILL, Sir John Roger; kt (1987), CBE (1983), DL (E Sussex 1983); s of Walter Thomas Lovill, and Elsie, *née* Page; *b* 26 September 1929; *Educ* Brighton Hove and Sussex GS; *m* 1958, Jacqueline, *née* Parker; 2 s, 1 da; *Career* SG Warburg 1951–55, dep gen mangr Securicor 1955–60; chm: Sloane Square Investments 1960–98, Municipal Mutual Insurance 1993– (dir 1984–), Prime Health Ltd 1993–94; memb E Sussex CC 1967–89 (leader 1973–77); Assoc of Co Cncls: memb 1973–89, leader 1981–83, chm 1983–86; pres Sussex Assoc of Local Cncls 1987–97; vice-pres: Lewes Cons Assoc 1986–94, Nat Assoc of Local Cncls 1991–94; chm: Brighton Pavilion Cons Assoc 1958–60, Sussex Police Authy 1976–79 (memb 1973–81), Local Authorities Conditions of Serv Advsy Bd 1978–83, Nationwide Small Business Property Tst 1989–95; *Recreations* opera, politics, marine paintings; *Style*— Sir John Lovill, CBE, DL; ✉ Hampden House, Glynde, Lewes, East Sussex BN8 6TA

LOW, *see also:* Morrison-Low

LOW, Alistair James; s of James Grey Low (d 1973), and Elsie Georgina, *née* Holden (d 1990); *b* 2 August 1942; *Educ* Dundee HS, Univ of St Andrews (BSc); *m* 30 Aug 1966, Shona Petricia, da of John Galloway Wallace, OBE, of Edinburgh; 2 s (John b 1970, Hamish b 1972), 1 da (Katharina b 1977); *Career* dir Cruden Investments; chm Scottish Golf Union; FFA 1967; *Recreations* golf, skiing; *Clubs* R&A (past chm), Hon Co of Edinburgh Golfers, Gullane Golf, New (Edinburgh); *Style*— Alistair Low, Esq; ✉ tel 07703 547853

LOW, Baron (Life Peer 2006), of Dalston in the London Borough of Hackney; Colin MacKenzie Low; CBE (2000); s of Arthur Eric Low, and Catherine, *née*Anderson; *Educ* Worcester Coll for the Blind, The Queen's Coll Oxford (MA), Churchill Coll Cambridge (Dip Criminology); *m* 1969, Jill Irene Coton; 1 s (Peter James), 1 da (Philippa Frances); *Career* lectr in law Univ of Leeds 1968–84, dir Disability Resource Team 1984–94, sr res fell City Univ 1994–2000 (visiting prof 2001–), chm RNIB 2000–, pres European Blind Union (EBU) 2003– (memb various cmmns 1996–2003); disability rights cmmr 2000–02; memb: Ctee Disability Alliance 1974– (chair 1991–97, vice-pres 1997–), Cncl Skill 1975–2003 (vice-pres 2003–), Special Educnl Needs Tbnl 1994–2007, Nat Disability Cncl 1996–2000, Disability Rights Task Force 1997–99; Snowdon Award 1984; memb Cncl St Dunstan's 2000–; *Recreations* music, wine appreciation; *Style*— The Rt Hon the Lord Low of Dalston, CBE; ✉ Graham Lodge, 19 Graham Road, London E8 1DA; Royal National Institute of the Blind, 105 Judd Street, London WC1H 9NE (tel 020 7391 2205, fax 020 7383 0508, e-mail colin.low@rnib.org.uk)

LOW, Gillian; da of William Edward Coysh, of Stanmore, Middx, and Elizabeth Joyce, *née* Legge; *b* 21 February 1955; *Educ* N London Collegiate Sch (Sophie Bryant leaving exhbn), Somerville Coll Oxford (Emma Clarke Beilby scholarship, MA), Trinity Coll Cambridge (tripos prize, PGCE); *Children* 1 s (Robin b 18 Oct 1985), 2 da (Alice b 1 June 1988, Corisande b 28 May 1991); *Career* mgmnt trainee Courtaulds Ltd 1977–79; teacher of English as a foreign language Italy 1979–80, English teacher then dep head of English Claverham Community Coll Battle 1981–88, head of English then dir of studies Bishop Ramsey Sch Ruislip 1989–94, dep headmistress Godolphin & Latymer Sch London 1994–98; head mistress: Francis Holland Sch Clarence Gate 1998–2004, Lady Eleanor Holles Sch Hampton 2004–; memb: SHA 1994, GSA 1998 (memb GSA/HMC Educn Ctee 2004–); govr: Sarum Hall Sch 2003–05, The Moat Sch 2003–06 (chm Educn Ctee 2004–06), Queen's Coll 2006–; *Recreations* travel, the arts; *Clubs* Lansdowne, Univ Women's; *Style*— Mrs Gillian Low; ✉ The Lady Eleanor Holles School, Hanworth Road, Hampton, Middlesex TW12 3HF (tel 020 8979 1601, fax 020 8941 8291)

LOW, Robert Nicholas; s of Leslie Walter Low (d 1983), of Bath, and Agnes, *née* Walsh; *b* 15 August 1948; *Educ* St George's Coll Weybridge, Fitzwilliam Coll Cambridge (BA); *m* 1983, Angela, da of Monte Levin; 1 s (Daniel Reuben b 1 Oct 1984); *Career* journalist; teacher Univ of Chile La Serena 1970–72, journalist Birmingham Post and Mail 1973–77, successively sub-ed, reporter, dep managing ed, sports ed, managing ed news then assoc ed features The Observer 1977–93, freelance journalist and author 1993–94, Euro Bureau chief Reader's Digest 1998– (sr ed then dep ed Reader's Digest Br edn 1994–98); *Books* The Kidnap Business (with Mark Bles, 1987), The Observer Book of Profiles (ed, 1991), La Pasionaria: The Spanish Firebrand (1992), W G: A Life of W G Grace (1997); *Recreations* watching cricket, playing tennis; *Clubs* Garrick, Groucho, Middlesex CCC, Paddington Lawn Tennis, RAC; *Style*— Robert Low, Esq; ✉ 33 Canfield Gardens, London NW6 3JP (tel 020 7624 9532, fax 020 7419 4042); Reader's Digest, 11 Westferry Circus, Canary Wharf, London E14 4HE (tel 020 7715 8025, e-mail bob.low@readersdigest.co.uk)

LOW, Roger L; s of Dr Niels L Low, of USA, and Mary Margaret Low; *b* 29 January 1944; *Educ* Columbia Coll, Columbia Univ (AB), Wharton Graduate Sch of Fin and Commerce, Univ of Pennsylvania (MBA); *m* 1967, Helen, da of Bates W Bryan, of Lookout Mountain TN; 1 s, 1 da; *Career* 1 Lt US Marine Corps, served Vietnam; Drexel Burnham & Co 1971–75, vice-pres Salomon Bros 1975–81, md Dean Witter Reynolds Overseas 1981–84, md Bear Stearns & Co 1984–; *Recreations* marathon running, skiing; *Clubs* St Anthony Hall (NYC), Wharton Alumni Club of the UK (chm); *Style*— Roger L Low, Esq; ✉ Bear Stearns International Ltd, 1 Canada Square, London E14 5AD (tel 020 7516 6114, e-mail debrett@rogerlow.com)

LOWBRIDGE, Roy Thomas; s of Thomas Eric Lowbridge, of Barnsley, S Yorks, and Anni Sophie, *née* Sievers (d 1990); *b* 17 October 1950; *Educ* Kirk Balk Comp Hoyland, Barnsley Coll of Technol; *m* 25 Aug 1984, Caroline, da of John Pinder; 1 da (Amy Marie b 15 Feb 1985), 2 s (Thomas James b 7 April 1987, Joshua Alexander b 20 Feb 1989); *Career* engr; tech apprentice Newton Chambers Engineering Sheffield 1967–71, production and product devpt engr F Parramore Tools Sheffield 1972–77, jig and tool designer Record Tools Sheffield 1977–80, devpt mangr Ernest H Hill Ltd Sheffield until 1991 (design engr 1981–88), design engr Caradon PCL Ltd (formerly Pneumatic Components Ltd) Sheffield

1991–96, trg conslt RTL Consultancy 1996–2001, dir RH Associates Total Business Solutions 2001–; winner Br Design award 1990; *Recreations* playing guitar and piano; *Clubs* Rotary (Newton Aycliffe); *Style*— Roy Lowbridge, Esq; ✉ RH Associates Total Business Solutions, Rosedale House, South View, Brafferton, Darlington DL1 3LB (tel 01325 320022, fax 01325 320088, e-mail info@rhassociates.co.uk, website www.rhassociates.co.uk)

LOWBURY, Dr Edward Joseph Lister; OBE (1980); s of Benjamin W Lowbury, and Alice S, *née* Halle; *b* 6 December 1913; *Educ* St Paul's, UC Oxford (BA, BM BCh), London Hosp Med Coll (MA), Univ of Oxford (DM); *m* 1954, Alison, *née* Young (d 2001); 3 da (Ruth b 1955, Pauline b 1957, Miriam b 1959); *Career* physician, poet and writer; bacteriologist MRC Burns Research Unit Birmingham Accident Hosp 1949–79, fndr hon dir Hosp Infection Research Lab Birmingham 1966–79; hon research fell Univ of Birmingham, hon prof of med microbiology Aston Univ 1979; writer on med, scientific and literary subjects; co-fndr Birmingham Chamber Music Soc; fndr memb and first pres Hosp Infection Soc; Hon DSc Aston Univ 1977, Hon LLD Univ of Birmingham 1980; FRCPath, FRSL, Hon FRCP, Hon FRCS; *Awards* literary: Newdigate Prize 1934, Matthew Arnold Meml Prize 1935, John Keats Meml Lectr Award 1973; medical/scientific: Everett Evans Meml Lectr Award 1977, A B Wallace Meml Lectr and Medal 1978; *Publications* poetry incl: Time For Sale (1961), Daylight Astronomy (1968), The Night Watchman (1974), Poetry and Paradox: Poems and an Essay (1976), Selected Poems (1978), Selected and New Poems (1990), Collected Poems (1993), Mystic Bridge (1997), Blind Man's Buff (2001); non-fiction incl: Thomas Campion: Poet, Composer and Physician (with Alison Young and Timothy Salter, 1970), Drug Resistance in Antimicrobial Therapy (with G A Ayliffe, 1974), The Poetical Works of Andrew Young (co-ed with Alison Young, 1985), Control of Hospital Infection: A Practical Handbook (co-ed, 1975, 3 edn 1992), Hallmarks of Poetry (essays, 1994), To Shirk No Idleness: A Critical Biography of the Poet Andrew Young (with Alison Young, 1998); author of numerous articles in reference works and learned jls; *Style*— Dr Edward Lowbury, Esq, OBE; ✉ 25 Churston Gardens, London N11 2NJ

LOWCOCK, His Hon Judge Andrew Charles; s of Eric Lowcock, and Elizabeth, *née* Kilner; *b* 22 November 1949; *Educ* Malvern, New Coll Oxford (MA); *m* 1, 14 Aug 1976 (m dis 1985), Patricia Anne, da of Emlyn Roberts; m 2, 7 Sept 1985, Sarah Elaine, da of Robert Edwards; 2 s (Robert Charles b 24 Feb 1988, Edward George b 23 Jan 1990); *Career* called to the Bar Middle Temple 1973, in practice Northern Circuit 1974–2001, recorder 1997–2001 (asst recorder 1993–97), circuit judge 2001–; govr The Ryleys Sch 1996–; *Recreations* music (princ timpanist Stockport Symphony Orchestra), cricket, theatre; *Clubs* Nefyn Golf, Stockport Garrick Theatre, Lancashire CCC, MCC; *Style*— His Hon Judge Lowcock; ✉ The Crown Court, Minshull Street, Manchester M1 3FS

LOWE, (John) Christopher (Chris); s of Sir Edgar Lowe, KBE, CB (d 1992), and Mary McIlwraith, *née* Lockhart; *b* 25 January 1949; *Educ* Dragon Sch Oxford, Haileybury, Brasenose Coll Oxford (MA, CertEd); *m* 1975 (m dis), Judith Anne Fielding; 1 s (Alexander b 3 Oct 1978), 1 da (Rebecca Anne b 11 Nov 1980); *Career* BBC: grad journalist trainee 1972–74, newsroom reporter 1974–76, political corr local radio and regnl TV 1976–81, news reporter network radio 1981–83, presenter Today (Radio 4) 1982–93, news reporter network TV 1983–86, presenter/reporter Newsnight (BBC2) 1986–89, presenter weekend TV news 1989–99, presenter PM (Radio 4) 1993–2000, currently presenter BBC News 24; other programmes presented incl: Talking Politics, Breakfast News, One O'Clock News, Six O'Clock News; vice-pres: Br Blind Sports, Middx Trust, Cricket Soc; chm Membership Middlesex CCC; former dir Ind Housing Ombudsman Service; *Recreations* sport (especially cricket, football and rugby), my children, a good book; *Clubs* Lord's Taverners, Middlesex CCC; *Style*— Chris Lowe, Esq; ✉ Room 2624, BBC TV Centre, Wood Lane, London W12 7RJ

LOWE, Prof Christopher Robin; s of Thomas Lowe (d 1971), of Maidenhead, Berks, and Hilda, *née* Moxham; *b* 15 October 1945; *Educ* Braywood C of E Sch, Windsor GS for Boys, Univ of Birmingham (BSc, PhD); *m* 14 Dec 1974, Patricia Margaret, da of late Albert Reed; 1 s (Alan Robert b 19 May 1979), 1 da (Andrea Elizabeth b 19 Oct 1981); *Career* postdoctoral res fell: Univ of Liverpool 1970–73, Univ of Lund Sweden 1973–74; sr lectr in biochemistry Univ of Southampton 1983–84 (lectr 1974–82), fell Trinity Coll Cambridge 1984, fndr dir Inst of Biotechnology Univ of Cambridge 1984–; prof of biotechnology Univ of Cambridge 1999–; dir: Affinity Chromatography Ltd 1988–99, Cambridge Sensors Ltd 1992–, Smart Holograms Ltd 2001–, Purely Proteins Ltd 2004–; 300 research publications, 60 patents, memb 17 editorial bds; Pierce Award (for outstanding contributions to the field of affinity chromatography) 1989, Jubilee Medal Chromatographic Soc 2002, Henry Dale Prize and Medal Royal Instn 2003; fell Int Inst of Biotechnology 1987; FREng 2005; *Books* Affinity Chromatography (1974), An Introduction to Affinity Chromatography (1979), Reactive Dyes in Protein and Enzyme Technology (1987), Biosensors (1987); *Recreations* travel, antiques; *Style*— Prof Christopher Lowe; ✉ The Limes, Hempstead, Saffron Walden, Essex CB10 2PW (tel 01799 599307); Institute of Biotechnology, University of Cambridge, Tennis Court Road, Cambridge CB2 1QT (tel 01223 334160, fax 01223 334162, e-mail crl1@biotech.cam.ac.uk)

LOWE, Sir Frank Budge; kt (2001); s of Stephen Lowe, and Marion Lowe; *b* 23 August 1941; *Educ* Westminster; *m* 2 s (Hamilton Alexander, Sebastian Christopher), 1 da (Emma Rose); *Career* fndr and chm Lowe and Partners Worldwide 1981–2003; dir ROH 2002–; *Style*— Sir Frank Lowe

LOWE, Ian Charles; *b* 7 July 1953; *Educ* Sidney Sussex Coll Cambridge (MA); *m* 19 April 1980, Elizabeth Anne, *née* Eyre; *Career* admitted slr 1978, ptnr Berwin Leighton (now Berwin Leighton Paisner) 1986– (currently ptnr Media and High-Tech Industries Gp); CEDR accredited mediator; memb City of London Slrs' Co; *Style*— Ian Lowe, Esq; ✉ Berwin Leighton Paisner, Adelaide House, London Bridge, London EC4R 9HA (tel 020 7760 1000, fax 020 7760 1111)

LOWE, Prof James Stephen; s of James Stephen Lowe, of Leeds, and Mary Eileen, *née* Middleton (d 1991); *b* 25 June 1955; *Educ* St Thomas Aquinas GS Leeds, Univ of Nottingham (BMedSci, BM BS, DM); *m* 18 July 1979, Pamela Lynne, da of Robert Urie (d 1998), of Garston, Herts; 2 s (Nicholas b 1985, William b 1987); *Career* prof of neuropathology Univ of Nottingham Med Sch and hon conslt neuropathology Queen's Medical Centre NHS Tst 1986–; ed-in-chief Neuropathology and Applied Neurobiology 1999–; memb Editorial Bd: Jl of Pathology 1990–2001, Acta Neuropathologica 1995–, Internet Medicine 1995–, PLOS Medicine 2005–; examiner RCPath 1993–; memb Cncl RCPath 1999–2002, vice-pres Neuropathological Soc 2006–; memb Int Acad of Pathologists; webmaster Pathological Soc of GB and Ireland 1998–; FRCPath 1996; *Books* Histopathology (1985, 4 edn 2004), Pathology (ed, 1987), Clinical Dermatopathology (1990), Histology (1991, 3 edn 2005), Picture Tests in Histology (1992), Pathology (1994, 2 edn 2000), Pathology Clinical Case Studies (1994), Neuropathology (1997); *CD-ROMs* Pathology (multimedia, 1995), Basic Histopathology (1996), Human Histology (1997 and 2005), Neuropathology (1998, 2 edn 2004), Functional Histology (5 edn 2006); *Recreations* guitar; *Style*— Prof James Lowe; ✉ Department of Pathology, Nottingham University Medical School, Queens Medical Centre, Nottingham NG7 2UH (tel 0115 970 9269, fax 0115 970 9759, e-mail james.lowe@nottingham.ac.uk, website www.int-r.net)

LOWE, John; s of Frederick Lowe (d 1987), of New Tupton, Chesterfield, and Phyllis, *née* Turner (d 1988); *b* 21 July 1945; *Educ* Clay Cross Secondary Sch; *m* 1, 1966 (m dis); 1 s (Adrian b 14 April 1973), 1 da (Karen b 8 Feb 1975); m 2, 12 Aug 1999, Karen, da of Kenneth Kirby; *Career* professional darts player; England Capt; winner: fourteen World Open Championships, Embassy World Championship (incl 1993), three times Embassy World Champion, World Masters, World Cup singles, News of the World, ten times Br pentathlon; played over one hundred times for England, first player to do a perfect game of 501 on TV 1984; chm World Professional Darts Players Assoc, memb Lord's Taverners; *Books* The Lowe Profile, The John Lowe Story, Darts The John Lowe Way, Old Stoneface: The Autobiography of Britain's Greatest Darts Player; *Recreations* golf, motor sport, gardening, darts; *Clubs* Chesterfield Golf, London Rugby; *Style*— John Lowe, Esq; ✉ 17 Greenways, Walton, Chesterfield, Derbyshire S40 3MF (tel 01246 229338, fax 01246 229 338, e-mail jloweprodart@aol.com, website www.legendsofdarts.com)

LOWE, John; *Educ* Chiswick Sch, Richmond upon Thames Coll, Oxford Brookes Univ (BA, Dip Arch); *Career* architect; Pascal & Watson 1983–86, Richard Rogers Partnership 1986–; *Projects* incl: American Airlines CIP lounge Gatwick Airport, refurbishment of Old Billingsgate Fish Market, Reuters Data Centre, Reuters Recreation, nine projects in Japan, Channel 4 TV HQ London, Heathrow Airport Terminal 1, Heathrow Airport Europier, VR Techno Centre Gifu Japan, Heathrow Airport Terminal 5, Skylight office Frankfurt Germany, Madrid Airport Spain, Nippon TV HQ Tokyo Japan; *Style*— John Lowe, Esq; ✉ Richard Rogers Partnership, Thames Wharf, Rainville Road, London W6 9HA (tel 020 7385 1235, 020 7385 8409, e-mail john.l@rrp.co.uk)

LOWE, (David) Mark; s of Capt Francis Armishaw Lowe, CBE, DSC, RN (d 1981), and Jean Christine, *née* Coates; *b* 17 June 1948; *Educ* Monkton Combe Sch, Univ of Kent (BA); *m* 15 Nov 1975, Christine Anne Elizabeth, da of Mostyn Thomas (d 1991); 2 da (Rebecca b 22 Aug 1978, Jessica b 5 Nov 1981); *Career* admitted slr 1974; asst slr Kidd Rapinet Badge 1974–75, ptnr Kingsley Napley 1976–80, ptnr and head of Litigation Dept Field Fisher Waterhouse 1980–; fndr memb Euro Cncl LCIA 1987; memb: Soc of Construction Law, Int Cultural Exchange; supporting memb The London Maritime Arbitrators' Assoc; memb: British Polish Legal Assoc, Cwlth Lawyers' Assoc; ACIArb 1988; *Publications* Pollution in the UK (jtly with Franklin and Hawke, 1995); *Recreations* flying, music, squash, tennis; *Style*— Mark Lowe, Esq; ✉ Field Fisher Waterhouse, 35 Vine Street, London EC3N 2AA (tel 020 7861 4000, fax 020 7488 0084)

LOWE, Mark Julian; s of Paul Lowe, of Bucks, and Jean, *née* Dolby; *b* 15 February 1950, Loughborough, Leics; *Educ* Balliol Coll Oxford (MA); *m* 20 Dec 1980, Zeinab, *née* Ibrahim Karam; 2 s (Omar, Khaled (twins) b 14 July 1982); *Career* dir Nomos Capital Ptnrs Ltd 1994–; *Style*— Mark Lowe, Esq; ✉ Nomos Capital Partners Limited, 103 Mount Street, Mayfair, London, W1K 2TJ

LOWE, Michael Allan; s of William Henry Herbert (d 1946), of Salisbury, Rhodesia, and Katherine Zita (d 1973); *b* 22 September 1940; *Educ* Prince Edward Secdy Sch Harare, Univ of Cape Town (BArch), Washington Univ St Louis (MArch and Urban Design); *m* 4 Feb 1995, Marian Catherine; 1 s (William Michael b 11 March 1996); *Career* architect and urban designer; architects Spencer & Anthony Parker 1957, project architect W S Atkins Architect and Engineers 1962–63, project architect F Lamond Sturrock Architect 1963–64, Victor Gruen Associates LA 1966–68, in private practice 1970–78, architect and urban design princ Arup Associates 1978–2005, conslt to Arup Urban Design 2005–; projects for Arup Associates incl: Zimbabwe Conf Centre Harare, IBM United Kingdom Ltd Havant, Eton Coll, Bedford HS, Clare Coll Cambridge, Stockley Park Heathrow, Closegate Newcastle upon Tyne, Great Common Farm Cambs, Olympia Quartier Berlin, Grande Porte des Alpes Lyon, Oxford Railway Station, Trawsfynydd Power Station competition, Stockley Business Park, Battersea Power Station, Stratford City, Spencer Dock Dublin, Bridge End Belfast, Canning Town, Lewisham Gateway; memb CABE Design Review Ctee 1999–2002; RIBA 1976, memb ARB 1980; *Publications* numerous papers and lectures on architecture and urban design; *Recreations* swimming, cycling, skiing; *Style*— Michael Lowe, Esq; ✉ Arup Urban Design, 38 Fitzroy Square, London W1T 6EY (tel 020 7755 2559, fax 020 7755 2561, e-mail michael.lowe@arup.com)

LOWE, Peter; s of George William Lowe, and Anne Elizabeth, *née* Tilyard; *Educ* Univ of Leicester (MA); *Career* broadcaster; BBC: prodr, exec prodr; Carlton Television: controller community programmes, controller digital programmes; currently md Screenchannel Ltd; winner of more than 50 nat and int programme awards as prodr or exec prodr incl two RTS awards; memb RTS; *Style*— Peter Lowe, Esq; ✉ Screenchannel Ltd, 29 Newman Street, London W1T 1PS (tel 020 7436 4808, e-mail peterlowe@screenchannel.co.uk)

LOWE, Prof Philip David; OBE (2003); *b* 29 March 1950, Hull; *Educ* Univ of Oxford (MA), Victoria Univ of Manchester (MSc), Univ of Sussex (MPhil); *m* 1 Jan 1972, Veronica, *née* Gibbins; 1 da (Sylvia b 13 July 1979), 1 s (Oliver b 13 Feb 1985); *Career* UCL: lectr in countryside planning 1974–89, reader in environmental planning 1989–92, co-dir Rural Studies Research Centre 1990–92; Univ of Newcastle upon Tyne: Duke of Northumberland chair of rural economy 1992–, fndr Centre for Rural Economy 1992, chm Research Ctee Faculty of Agric and Biological Sciences 1992–95, chm Small Grants Panel 1993–; research offr Union of Int Assocs Brussels 1973, visiting fell Science Centre Berlin 1983, research fell Woodrow Wilson Int Center for Scholars Washington DC 1985, visiting lectr Nat Agric Univ Wageningen Netherlands 1986; conslt and a founding ed ECOS (Jl of Br Assoc of Nature Conservationists) 1980–88, Br ed Sociologia Ruralis (Jl of European Soc for Rural Sociology) 1983–90, memb Editorial Bd Jl of Environmental Planning and Mgmnt 1992–, European ed Progress in Rural Policy and Planning 1993–96, memb Editorial Bd Jl of Environmental Planning and Policy 1998–; expert advsr: House of Commons Select Ctee on the Environment 1996, House of Commons Environment, Tport and Regnl Affrs Ctee 1997–99; chm: Northumberland Rural Devpt Ctee 1996–99, England Market Towns Advsy Forum 2001–; dir Rural Economy and Land Use (RELU); memb: Nat Policy Ctee CPRE 1992–, Socio-Economic Advsy Panel English Nature 1994–, HEFCE Research Assessment Panel for Agric 1996, Agric Sub-Gp UK Round Table on Sustainable Devpt 1997–98, Ind Advsy Gp to Min of Agric, Fisheries and Food 1997–98, Mgmnt Ctee European COST Network on Rural Innovation 1998–, Bd Countryside Agency 1999–, Foresight Panel for Food Chain Office of Science and Technol 1999–2001, Economists Panel MAFF 1999–, Science Advsy Cncl DEFRA 2003–; *Recreations* cycling, cinema; *Style*— Prof Philip Lowe, OBE; ✉ Room 317, Agriculture Building, Centre for Rural Economy, School of Agriculture, Food and Rural Development, University of Newcastle upon Tyne NE1 7RU (tel 0191 222 6887, fax 0191 222 5411, e-mail philip.lowe@ncl.ac.uk)

LOWE, Philip Martin; s of late Leonard Ernest Lowe, and late Marguerite Helen, *née* Childs; *b* 29 April 1947; *Educ* Reading Sch, St John's Coll Oxford (MA), London Business Sch (MSc); *m* 1, 1967 (m dis 1980), Gillian Baynton, *née* Forge; m 2, 1984, Nora Mai, *née* O'Connell; 2 s; *Career* Tube Investments Ltd 1968–73; EC Cmmn: joined 1973, asst to DG XVIII Credit and Investments 1979–82, memb Cabinet of EC Pres Thorn 1982–85, memb Cabinet of Cmmr Alois Pfeiffer 1985–86, asst to DG XXII Co-ordination of Structural Instruments 1986–87, head of unit for structural funds 1987–89, chef de cabinet to Cmmr Bruce Millan 1989–91, dir of rural devpt DG VI Agric 1991–93, dir Merger Task Force DG IV Competition 1993–95, chef de cabinet to Neil Kinnock, *qv* 1995–1997; DG for Devpt 1997–2000, chef de cabinet to vice-pres Neil Kinnock 2000–02, DG for Competition 2002–; *Recreations* music, theatre, running, hill walking; *Style*— Philip Lowe, Esq

LOWE, Rt Rev Stephen Richard; *see:* Hulme, Bishop of

LOWE, Dr Stuart Shepherd; s of Ian William Shepherd Lowe, of Chalfont St Giles, Bucks, and Margaret Isobella, *née* Reid; *b* 27 April 1954; *Educ* St Nicholas GS Northwood, St Mary's Hosp Med Sch London (MB BS, MRCS, LRCP); *m* 15 May 1976, Heather Donaldson, da of Thomas Oliver Donaldson Craig, of Surbiton, Surrey; 2 s (Matthew Shepherd, Simon Donaldson), 1 da (Emma Louise); *Career* SHO in anaesthetics Royal

L

Sussex County Hosp Brighton 1978–79; rotation registrar in anaesthetics 1979–82: Charing Cross Hosp London, Nat Hosp for Nervous Diseases, Brompton Hosp London, Royal Surrey County Hosp Guildford; sr registrar in anaesthesia and intensive care 1982–85: Addenbrooke's Hosp Cambridge, Papworth Hosp, W Suffolk Hosp; conslt in anaesthesia and intensive care W Suffolk Hosp 1985–; vice-chm W Suffolk Scanner Appeal, chm Div of Anaesthesia 1992–96 and 2000–05; memb: Intensive Care Soc, Assoc of Anaesthetists of GB and I; FRCA 1981; *Recreations* golf; *Style*— Dr Stuart Lowe; ✉ Intensive Care Unit, West Suffolk Hospital, Hardwick Lane, Bury St Edmunds, Suffolk IP33 2QZ (tel 01284 712819, fax 01284 713100)

LOWE, Sir Thomas William Gordon; 4 Bt (UK 1918), of Edgbaston, City of Birmingham; s of Sir Francis Reginald Gordon Lowe, 3 Bt (d 1986), and Franziska Cornelia Lanier, da of Siegfried Steinkopf, of Berlin; *b* 14 August 1963; *Educ* Stowe, LSE (LLB), Jesus Coll Cambridge (LLM); *m* Mozhgan, da of H Asilzadeh; 1 s; *Heir* s, Theodore Lowe; *Career* called to the Bar Inner Temple 1985, in practice at Wilberforce Chambers; memb: Commerical Bar Assoc, Chancery Bar Assoc; *Style*— Sir Thomas Lowe, Bt; ✉ 8 New Square, Lincoln's Inn, London WC2A 3QP (tel 020 7306 0102, fax 020 7306 0095)

LOWE, Prof (Alan) Vaughan; s of Alan Lowe, and Pamela; *b* 1952; *Educ* Univ of Wales (LLB, LLM, PhD), Univ of Cambridge (MA), Univ of Oxford (MA), Associé de l'Institut de Droit Int; *m* Sally Lowe; *Career* called to the Bar Gray's Inn; lectr and sr lectr: Univ of Cardiff 1973–78, Univ of Manchester 1978–88; reader in int law and fell CCC Cambridge 1988–99, Chichele prof of public int law and fell All Souls Coll Oxford 1999–; practising barr, memb Essex Court Chambers; arbitrator; sometime visiting prof: Univ of Thessaloniki, Univ of Helsinki, Tulane Univ New Orleans, Duke Univ NC; *Recreations* music, walking, thinking; *Clubs* Oxford and Cambridge; *Style*— Prof Vaughan Lowe; ✉ All Souls College, Oxford OX1 4AL (tel 01865 279379)

LOWE, Veronica Ann; da of late Arthur Ernest Bagley, and Agatha Amy Annie, *née* Blackham (d 1978); *b* 29 June 1951; *Educ* King Edward VI GS for Girls Handsworth Birmingham, St Hugh's Coll Oxford (MA), Oxford Poly (Inst of Linguist exams), City of Birmingham Poly (slrs qualifying exams); *m* 2 Dec 1977, Ian Stanley Lowe, s of late Arnold Lowe; 1 da (Rhiannon Sara Amy b 21 Dec 1983); *Career* articled clerk with Messrs Ryland Martineau & Co (now Martineau Johnson) Birmingham 1976–78, admitted slr 1979, lectr in labour law Aston Univ 1978–80, slr in private practice 1980–86, asst area dir Legal Aid Area No 8 1986–88, area dir Legal Aid Area No 6 1988–89, gp mangr (Midlands) Legal Aid Bd 1989–90, dir Slrs Complaints Bureau 1990–96, chief exec Valuation Office Agency Inland Revenue 1996–97; mgmnt conslt and author 1998–; slr Pinsent Curtis 1999–2000; sr legal counsel Faulding Pharmaceuticals plc 2000–03, European legal affrs conslt Mayne Pharma plc (formerly Faulding) 2003–; memb Bd European Generic Medicines Assoc 2002– (also memb Legal Affrs Ctee); pt/t immigration appeals adjudicator then immigration judge 2000–; memb Law Soc 1979; contrib to pubns on law for accountants and businessmen and articles on intellectual property law, generic medicines and European legislation; *Recreations* cooking, eating and drinking, travel, reading, talking, writing unfinished novels, home life; *Style*— Mrs Veronica Lowe

LOWENTHAL, Prof David; s of Max Lowenthal (d 1971), and Eleanor, *née* Mack (d 1965); *b* 26 April 1923; *Educ* Harvard Univ (BS), Univ of Calif Berkeley (MA), Univ of Wisconsin (PhD); *m* 1971, Mary Alice, da of Frederick Lamberty; 2 da (Eleanor b 1977, Catherine b 1979); *Career* served US Army 1943–45, with US State Dept 1945–46; asst prof of history and head Dept of Geography Vassar Coll 1952–56, conslt Inst of Social and Econ Studies Dept of History Univ of West Indies 1956–70, res fell and sec American Geographical Soc 1957–72, with Inst of Race Rels 1961–72, prof of geography UCL 1972–85 (prof emeritus 1985–, hon res fell 1986); Regents prof Univ of Calif Davis 1973, Katz distinguished prof of humanities Univ of Washington 1988; visiting prof: Univ of Calif Berkeley, Univ of Minnesota, Univ of Washington, Clark Univ, Harvard Univ, Columbia Univ, MIT, West Dean Coll, St Mary's Coll London; distinguished lectr Center of Humanities and the Arts Univ of Georgia 1998, A W Franks lectr Br Museum 1999, H Harvey distinguished lectr Univ of Newfoundland 1999, distinguished lectr Pinchot Conservation Inst 2001; chair Landscape Res Gp 1984–89; memb: Cncl AAAS 1964–71, Cncl Assoc of American Geographers 1968–71, US Nat Res Cncl 1968–71, Ethnic Rels Ctee SSRC 1972–77, Bd Inst of Latin American Studies Univ of London 1972–87, Bd Inst of Cwlth Studies Univ of London 1972–87; advsr to various orgns incl: US Peace Corps, UNESCO, Int Geographical Union, English Heritage, V&A, Science Museum, Br Museum, Int Cncl on Monuments and Sites (ICOMOS); memb various Editorial Bds incl: Environment and Behavior 1969–76, Geographical Review 1973–95, London Jl 1974–86, Progress in Geography 1976–90, Int Jl of Cultural Property 1989–; fellowships: Fulbright 1956–57, Guggenheim 1965, Res Inst for the Study of Man Landes 1992–93, Leverhulme 1992–94; Victoria Medal RGS 1997, Cullum Medal American Geographical Soc 1999, RSGS Medal 2004; FBA 2001; *Books* George Perkins Marsh: Versatile Vermonter (1958, Assoc of American Geographers Award), West Indies Federation (1961), West Indian Societies (1972), Geographies of the Mind (with M J Bowden, 1975), Our Past Before Us (with M Binney, 1981), The Past is a Foreign Country (1985, Historic Preservation (US) Book Prize), Landscape Meanings and Values (with E C Penning-Rowsell, 1986), Politics of the Past (with P Gathercole, 1989), Heritage Crusade and the Spoils of History (1997), George Perkins Marsh: Prophet of Conservation (2000, Assoc of American Geographers J B Jackson Book Prize, Br Acad Prize finalist); *Style*— Prof David Lowenthal; ✉ Department of Geography, University College London, Pearson Building, Gower Street, London WC1E 6BT (e-mail d.lowenthal@ucl.ac.uk)

LOWMAN, Ven David Walter; s of Cecil Walter Lowman, and Queenie Norah Lowman; *Educ* Crewkerne Sch, City of London Coll (Cert Civil Law), KCL (BD, AKC), St Augustine's Coll Canterbury; *Career* examiner Inland Revenue Estate Duty Office 1966–70; curate: St John Notting Hill 1975–78, St Augustine with St John Kilburn 1978–81; chaplain Church House Westminster 1981–86, selection sec, vocations advsr ACCM 1981–86, team rector Wickford and Runwell 1986–93, dir of ordinands Chelmsford Diocese 1993–2001, archdeacon of Southend 2001–; non-residentiary canon Chelmsford Cathedral 1993; memb Gen Synod C of E 1995–2005 (chair Vocations Advsy Panel); chair of Cncl N Thames Ministerial Trg Course, govr Brentwood Sch; *Recreations* travel, good food and wine, opera, cricket; *Clubs* Essex; *Style*— The Ven the Archdeacon of Southend; ✉ The Archdeacon's Lodge, 136 Broomfield Road, Chelmsford, Essex CM1 1RN (tel 01245 258257, fax 01245 250845, e-mail a.southend@chelmsford.anglican.org)

LOWNIE OF LARGO, Yr, Andrew James Hamilton; s of His Hon Ralph Hamilton Lownie of Largo, and Claudine, *née* Lecrocq; *b* 11 November 1961; *Educ* Fettes, Westminster, Magdalene Coll Cambridge (MA), Univ of Edinburgh (MSc), The Coll of Law Guildford; *m* 2 May 1998, Angela Caroline, da of Maj Peter Doyle; 1 s (Robert David Hamilton b 1999), 1 da (Alice Claudine Hamilton b 2001); *Career* dir: John Farquharson Ltd literary agents 1986–88, Andrew Lownie literary agency 1988–, Denniston and Lownie Ltd 1991–93, Thistle Publishing; journalist; contrib: Spectator, The Times, Scotland on Sunday; tstee Iain MacLeod Award, former pres Cambridge Union Soc; Parly candidate (Cons) Monklands West 1992, vice-chm Cons Gp for Europe 1992–95; *Books* The Edinburgh Literary Guide, North American Spies, John Buchan - The Presbyterian Cavalier, John Buchan's Poems (ed), John Buchan's Complete Short Stories (ed), The Scottish Shorter Fiction of John Buchan (ed), The Literary Companion to Edinburgh; *Recreations* music, outdoor pursuits; *Style*— Andrew Lownie, Esq; ✉ 36 Great Smith Street, London SW1P 3BU (tel 020 7222 7574, fax 020 7222 7576, e-mail lownie@globalnet.co.uk)

LOWRY, Peter; s of Frederick George Lowry (d 1971), of Carlisle, and Dora, *née* Corkhill (d 1984); *b* 25 April 1938; *Educ* Gregg Sch Carlisle; *Career* served RAF (despatches, GSM (Malaya) 1960) 1956–65, Photographic Branch 1960–65; prop photographic business covering portraiture, weddings, industrial and commercial photography 1975–; exhibited Epcot Center USA 1991; served Admissions and Qualifications Bd: BIPP 1990–99, Dutch Inst of Professional Photography 1998–2000; memb Distinctions Panel RPS 1989–2001; Nat Portrait Photographer of the Year 1983, 1984 and 1989, Kodak Gold Award 1985, 1986 and 1987; hon fell Dutch Inst of Professional Photography 1998; FRSA 1985, FRPS 1988, FBIPP 1989; *Recreations* angling, cycling, walking; *Clubs* Avon Tributaries Angling Assoc, Golden Scale, Veteran-Cycle; *Style*— Peter Lowry, Esq; ✉ Little Thatch, Tynts Hill, Mells, Frome, Somerset BA11 3PU (tel 01373 812716, mobile 07899 806115, e-mail email@peterlowry.com, website www.peterlowry.com); Church Hill House, 17 Bath Street, Frome, Somerset BA11 1DN (tel 01373 461779, fax 01373 461779)

LOWRY, Roger Clark; OBE (2001); s of Henry Lowry (d 1972), and Evelyn Wilson Blair (d 1970); *b* 20 September 1933; *Educ* Campbell Coll Belfast, Queen's Univ Belfast (BSc, MB BCh); *m* 3 April 1964, (Dorothy) Joan, da of David Smith (d 1976); 4 s (Kevin, Michael, Peter, Alan), 1 da (Julie); *Career* assoc prof of med Univ of Tennessee 1976–77, conslt physician Belfast City Hosp 1977–98; chm NI Chest Heart and Stroke Assoc 1980–; memb: Br Thoracic Soc, BMA; involvement in interprovincial squash; FRCP, FRCPI; *Recreations* golf, squash, tennis; *Clubs* Royal Co Down Golf, Royal Belfast Golf; *Style*— Roger Lowry, Esq, OBE; ✉ Milecross House, 49 Belfast Road, Newtownards, Co Down BT23 4TR (tel 028 9181 3284, e-mail rogerlowry@hotmail.com); Belfast City Hospital, Lisburn Road, Belfast BT9 7AB (tel 028 9026 3675)

LOWSON, Ven Christopher; s of George Frederick Lowson, of Lanchester, Durham, and Isabella Annie, *née* Spence; *b* 3 February 1953; *Educ* Newcastle Cathedral Sch, Consett GS, KCL (AKC), St Augustine's Coll Canterbury, Pacific Sch of Religion Berkeley CA (STM), Heythrop Coll London (MTh), Cardiff Law Sch (LLM); *m* 1976, Susan Mary, da of William James Osborne; 1 s (James b 1980), 1 da (Rebecca b 1982); *Career* ordained: deacon 1977, priest 1978; asst curate Richmond Surrey 1977–82, chaplain Avery Hill Coll of Educn 1982–85, vicar Holy Trinity Eltham 1983–91 (priest-in-charge 1982–83), chaplain to the Guild of St Bride Fleet Street 1983–, chaplain Thames Poly 1985–91, vicar Petersfield and rector Buriton Hants 1991–99, rural dean of Petersfield 1995–99, archdeacon of Portsdown 1999–; fndn tstee Gallipoli Meml Lecture Tst 1985–91, chm Portsmouth Diocesan Bd of Ministry, Bishop of Portsmouth's liaison offr for prisons 1999–2003, Bishop of Portsmouth's advsr to hosp chaplaincy 2003–06, archdeacon emeritus of Portsmouth 2006–, priest vicar Westminster Abbet 2007–; dir Portsmouth Educn Business Partnership 1999–2006, visiting lectr Univ of Portsmouth 199–2006, memb Ecclesiastical Law Soc 1999–2006, die of miny Archbishops' Cncl of the C of E 2006–; *Recreations* watching cricket, theatre; *Clubs* MCC, Athenaeum; *Style*— The Ven Christopher Lowson; ✉ Church House, Great Smith Street, London SW1P 4LB (tel 020 7898 1390, fax 020 7898 1421, e-mail christopher.lowson@c-of-e.org.uk)

LOWSON, Sir Ian Patrick; 2 Bt (UK 1951), of Westlaws, Co Perth; s of Sir Denys Colquhoun Flowerdew Lowson, 1 Bt (d 1975), and Hon Lady Lowson; *b* 4 September 1944; *Educ* Eton, Duke Univ USA; *m* 1979, Tanya Theresa, da of Raymond F A Judge; 1 s, 1 da (Katherine Louisa Patricia b 1983); *Heir* s, Henry Lowson; *Clubs* Boodle's, Pilgrims, Brook (New York); *Style*— Sir Ian Lowson, Bt; ✉ 23 Flood Street, London SW3 5ST

LOWSON, Prof Martin Vincent; s of Alfred Vincent Lowson (d 1961), of Wraysbury, Bucks, and Irene Gertrude, *née* Thorp (d 1982); *b* 5 January 1938; *Educ* King's Sch Worcester, Univ of Southampton (BSc, PhD); *m* 4 Nov 1961, (Roberta) Ann, da of Max Pennicutt, of Emsworth, Hants; 1 s (Jonathan b 1965), 1 da (Sarah b 1967); *Career* apprentice Vickers Armstrong 1955–60, res student and asst Univ of Southampton 1960–64, head of applied physics Wyle Laboratories Huntsville USA 1964–69, Rolls Royce reader Loughborough Univ 1969–73, chief scientist Westland Helicopters Ltd 1973–79, dir of corp devpt Westland plc 1979–86, prof of aerospace engrg Univ of Bristol 1986–2000, ceo Advanced Transport Systems Ltd 1995–; researcher and patentee in aerodynamics, acoustics, structures, and transport; FREng 1991, FRAeS, FASA, FAIAA, FCILT; *Recreations* research, squash, music; *Style*— Prof Martin Lowson, FREng; ✉ Alpenfels, North Road, Leigh Woods, Bristol BS8 3PJ (tel 0117 973 6497, e-mail martin@atsltd.co.uk)

LOWSON, Robert Campbell; s of George Campbell Lowson (d 1989), and Betty, *née* Parry (d 2006); *b* 7 March 1949; *Educ* Gravesend GS, BNC Oxford (BA); *m* 1973, Hilary May, da of Hubert Balsdon; 1 s (Andrew b 15 Nov 1980), 1 da (Judith b 18 Nov 1983); *Career* MAFF (now DEFRA): joined 1970, under sec Agricultural Inputs, Plant Protection and Emergencies Gp 1994–95, min (agric) UK Perm Representation to the EU 1995–99, dir of communications 1999–2001, dir Environment Strategy 2001–07, dir Regulation 2007 (seconded to European Environment Agency); *Style*— Robert Lowson, Esq

LOWTH, Simon Jonathan; s of Gerald Simon Lowth, of Ross-on-Wye, Herefords, and Ruth Elizabeth, *née* Carter; *b* 8 September 1961; *Educ* Gonville & Caius Coll Cambridge (MA), London Business Sch (MBA); *m* 1994, Helene, *née* Theodoly; 4 c (Manon b 29 Oct 2000, Faye, Grace (twins) b 10 Oct 2002, Marc b 20 Sept 2004); *Career* design engr Ove Arup & Ptnrs 1983–85, dir McKinsey and Co 1987–2003, exec dir corp strategy and devpt Scottish Power plc 2003–; *Style*— Simon Lowth, Esq; ✉ Scottish Power plc, 1 Atlantic Quay, Glasgow G2 8SP (tel 0141 248 8200, fax 0141 636 4580, e-mail simon.lowth@scottishpower.com)

LOWTHER, Col Sir Charles Douglas; 6 Bt (UK 1824), of Swillington, Yorks; s of Lt-Col Sir William Guy Lowther, 5 Bt, OBE, DL (d 1982), and Grania Suzanne, *née* Douglas-Campbell (d 2001); *b* 22 January 1946; *Educ* Winchester; *m* 1, 1969 (m dis 1975), Melanie Pensée FitzHerbert, da of late Roderick Christopher Musgrave; m 2, 1975, Florence Rose, da of late Col Alexander James Henry Cramsie, OBE, of O'Harabrook, Ballymoney, Co Antrim; 1 s (Patrick William b 1977), 1 da (Alice Rose b 1979); *Heir* s, Patrick Lowther; *Career* served HM Forces 1965–93, Col; businessman and farmer; dir Chester Race Co 1995–, chm Bangor-on-Dee Racecompany 2002–; memb HM Body Guard of the Hon Corps of Gentlemen at Arms 1997, High Sheriff Clwyd 1997; *Recreations* field sports, racing, travel; *Clubs* Cavalry and Guards', Jockey (racing memb 1999); *Style*— Col Sir Charles Douglas Lowther, Bt; ✉ Erbistock Hall, Wrexham LL13 0DE

LOWTHER, James; s of George Hugh Lowther, of Holdenby House, Northampton, and Sheila Rachel Isabel, *née* Foster; *b* 27 January 1947; *Educ* Eton, Keble Coll Oxford (MA History); *m* Karen Healey, da of James Wallace; 3 da (Natasha Jane b 26 Nov 1988, Mamie Grace b 6 Aug 1994, Oona Aphrodite 6 March 2001), 1 s (James William Dolfin b 29 Dec 1991); *Career* Saatchi & Saatchi 1977–95 (creative dir and dep chm 1991–95), chm M&C Saatchi 2000– (fndr creative dir 1995–2000); dir Children in Crisis; dir British Television Advtg Awards; memb: Historic Houses Assoc, Cncl for the Preservation of Rural England, Nat Tst, D&AD; *Awards* ITV Award for Best Cinema Commercial 1979 and for Best Commercial of the Year 1992, 3 times Best Black & White Press Advertisement Campaign Press Awards, 2 times Best Poster of the Year Campaign Poster Awards, 3 D&AD Silver Awards, 3 Silver and a Gold Cannes Int Advtg Festival, Ivor Novello Award (for composing advtg music for Schweppes), work incl in 100 Best Advertisements; *Books* The Copy Book (D&AD, contrib); *Recreations* listening to, playing and writing music; *Style*— James Lowther, Esq; ✉ M&C Saatchi Ltd, 34–36 Golden Square, London W1R 4EE (tel 020 7543 4500, fax 020 7543 4535, e-mail jamesl@mcsaatchi.com)

LOWTHER, Maurice James; s of James Lowther (d 1983), of Carnforth, Lancs, and Margaret Agnes Hind (d 1986); *b* 14 September 1926; *Educ* Lancaster Royal GS, Queen's Univ

Belfast (BSc); *m* 1, 1 Nov 1947 (m dis 1976), Audrey Margaret, da of George Holmes (d 1979), of Belfast; 3 da (Anne, Valerie, Pamela); m 2, 1977, Dr Rachel Shirley Lloyd (d 1997), da of Lt Cdr William F Hood (d 1980), of Handcross, W Sussex; m 3, 1999, Valerie Adèle Homer, da of C E Love, of Gillingham, Kent (d 1982); *Career* Capt RE 1944–48; md Newcastle and Gateshead Water Co 1971–86 (non-exec dir 1986–90), non-exec dir Stanley Miller plc 1983–90; nat pres Inst of Water Engrs and Scientists 1980–81, nat chm Water Cos Assoc 1984–87 (vice-pres 1987–), vice-pres Water Aid 1991– (fndr dir 1981–91), chm Br Inst of Mgmnt Tyne & Wear 1973–75; govr Lancaster Royal GS 1982–2004; Int Medal American Waterworks Assoc; Freeman City of London, Liveryman Worshipful Co of Plumbers; FICE 1962, FIWES 1967, CIMgt 1986; *Recreations* fell walking, angling, beekeeping; *Clubs* National, Northern Counties (Newcastle upon Tyne); *Style*— Maurice Lowther, Esq; ✉ The Old Schoolhouse, Wall Village, Hexham, Northumberland (tel 01434 681660)

LOWTHER, Merlyn Vivienne; da of Norman Edward Douglas Humphrey, and Joan Margaret, *née* Hewitt; *b* 3 March 1954; *Educ* Manchester HS for Girls, Victoria Univ of Manchester (BSc), London Business Sch (MSc); *m* 1 Nov 1975, David John Lowther; 1 s, 1 da; *Career* Bank of England: head Banking Div and dep chief cashier 1991–96, personnel dir 1996–98, chief cashier 1999–2004; non-exec dir Schroders plc 2004–; tstee: Henry Smith Charity, Winston Churchill Meml Tst; Hon LLD Victoria Univ of Manchester 1999; FRSA 1996, FCIB 1999, CCMI 1999; *Recreations* theatre, singing, reading, family; *Style*— Ms Merlyn Lowther; ✉ Schroders plc, 31 Gresham Street, London EC2V 7QA (tel 020 7658 3646)

LOYD, Jeremy Charles Haig; s of Geoffry Haig Loyd, of Herefords, and Patricia, *née* Maclean; *b* 4 July 1954; *Educ* Pangbourne Coll; *m* 6 Oct 1983, Sally, da of Duncan Robertson, TD, JP (d 1988), of Beadlam, N Yorks; *Career* account exec Michael Rice and Co Ltd 1974–79; dir: RTI Productions Ltd 1976–80, Project Art Ltd 1978–, Carlton Television 1991–95, Carlton Music 1993–96; ceo Pickwick Group 1993–95, formerly md Capital Radio; dir: First Oxfordshire Radio Co 1988–2002, Channel KTV 1995–97, Enterprise Radio Holdings 1995–96, ITFC Ltd 1995–, Capital Radio Investments Ltd and Capital Enterprises Ltd 1989–91, Wren Orchestra of London Ltd 1989–91, Devonair Ltd 1989–91; chm Direct Home Entertainment Ltd 1993–95; formerly dep chm Blackwell Ltd; tstee Help A London Child 1987–91; *Recreations* fishing, sailing; *Clubs* RNC, RAYC; *Style*— Jeremy Loyd, Esq

LOYN, David George; s of William George Grenville Loyn, and Elizabeth Margery, *née* Gent; *b* 1 March 1954; *Educ* Oundle, Worcester Coll Oxford (BA), Coll of Law London; *m* 1981, Estelle, da of Philip Daniel; 3 s (Thomas Jack b 18 Sept 1988, Christopher Mark b 19 Dec 1992, James Philip b 30 May 1995); *Career* reporter IRN/LBC 1979–87; BBC: joined 1987, S Asia corr 1993–97, foreign affrs corr 1997–; Sony Award for Radio Reporter of the Year 1985; RTS Awards: Journalist of the Year 1999, International News Reporter of the Year 1999; *Style*— David Loyn, Esq; ✉ Room 2505, BBC TV Centre, London W12 7RS (tel 020 8624 8548)

LUBA, Jan; QC (2000); *Educ* LSE (LLB), Univ of Leicester (LLM); *Career* called to the Bar 1980; practising barr specialising in housing and social welfare law, currently memb of Garden Court chambers; recorder 2000–, judge of the Employment Appeal Tbnl 2002–; memb: Bar Pro Bono Unit, Administrative Law Bar Assoc, Social Security Law Practitioners' Assoc, Legal Action Gp, Haldane Soc; patron Croydon Housing Aid Soc; *Publications* The Disabled Persons Handbook (1989), The Owner Occupier Handbook (1990), Rights Guide for Home Owners (co-author, 1990), Repairs: Tenants' Rights (co-author, 3 edn 1999), Housing and the Human Rights Act (2000), The Homelessness Act 2002 (co-author, 2002), Defending Possession Proceedings (co-author, 6 edn 2006), Housing Allocation and Homelessness (co-author, 2006); *Style*— Jan Luba, Esq, QC; ✉ Garden Court Chambers, 57–60 Lincoln's Inn Fields, London WC2A 3LS

LUBBOCK, John David Peter; s of Michael Ronald Lubbock, MBE (d 1989), and Diana Beatrix, *née* Crawley (d 1976); *b* 18 March 1945; *Educ* Radley, Royal Acad of Music (GRSM); *m* 12 Feb 1977 (m dis), Eleanor, *née* Sloan; 2 s (Daniel, Patrick); m 2, 13 July 1991, Christine Cairns, *qv*; 2 s (Adam Thomas b 28 Nov 1991, Alexander Michael b 30 June 1993); *Career* fndr and conductor Orchestra of St John's Smith Square; FRAM; *Recreations* tennis, racquets, Royal tennis; *Style*— John Lubbock, Esq; ✉ 7 Warborough Road, Warborough, Oxfordshire (tel 01865 858210)

LUBRAN, Jonathan Frank; s of Prof Michael Lubran, of LA, Calif, and Avril Roslyn, *née* Lavigne; *b* 27 April 1948; *Educ* Bedales, Univ of Chicago (BA), Univ of Cambridge (Dip, PhD); *m* 2003, Clare, *née* Berry; *Career* investment advsr Crown Agents for Overseas Govts 1979–80; md: Royal Bank of Canada Investment Management International 1980–88, Bankers Trust Investment Management Ltd 1988–94, Foreign & Colonial Institutional 1994–2000; exec dir Schroder Investment Management 2000–03, dir Mellon Global Investments 2003–; former treas Crisis at Christmas, memb London Project Ctee Nat Art Collections Fund 1977–88, dep warden Guild of Benefactors CCC Cambridge 1996–; *Recreations* opera, theatre, antiques, swimming, photography; *Clubs* Brooks's, Hurlingham; *Style*— Jonathan Lubran, Esq; ✉ c/o Brooks's, St James's Street, London SW1A 1LN

LUCAS, Prof Alan; s of Dr Saul H Lucas (decd), and Dr Sophia Lucas; *b* 30 June 1946; *Educ* Bedales, Clare Coll Cambridge (fndn scholar, BA), Oxford Med Sch (scholar, MB BChir), Univ of Cambridge (MD); *m* 1, 1967 (m dis), Sally, *née* Wedeles; m 2, 1978, Penny, *née* Hodgson; 1 s, 2 da; *Career* house physician, house surgn, SHO and registrar 1971–77; Wellcome research fell and Int Cncl of the Infant Food Industry (ICIFI) research fell Dept of Paediatrics Univ of Oxford 1977–79, registrar in gen paediatrics John Radcliffe Hosp Oxford 1979–80; Dept of Paediatrics Univ of Cambridge: clinical lectr in paediatrics 1980–82, hon conslt 1982–95; head of infant and child nutrition MRC Dunn Nutrition Unit Cambridge 1982–96, MRC clinical prof and dir Childhood Nutrition Centre Inst of Child Health London 1996–, hon conslt in paediatric nutrition Gt Ormond St Hosp for Children London 1996–, chair in paediatric nutrition UCL 2001–; Univ of Cambridge: lectr Trinity Coll 1972–76, coll supervisor Gonville & Caius Coll 1980–82, dir of med studies Peterhouse 1982–86, lectr in med sci 1982–90, fell Clare Coll 1982– (dir of studies in med 1982–97); coll lectr St Edmund Hall Oxford 1977–80; chm MRC Working Gp on Fluoride and Osteoporosis 1994; memb: DHSS Panel on Child Nutrition 1988–96, BPA Standing Ctee on Nutrition 1988–94, Working Gp on EEC Directive on Infant Formulae and Follow-up Milk 1988–, Academic Bd BPA 1989–94, Scientific Advsy Ctee Fndn for the Study of Infant Death 1992–94, MRC Physiological Med and Infections Bd 1992–96, MRC Steering Ctee Initiative in Fetal and Maternal Origins of Adult Disease 1993–, Central Research and Devpt Ctee Advsy Gp on Mother and Child Health 1994–95, MRC Physiological Med and Infection Bd (PMIB) 1995–96, Jt MRC/CCMRC (Cwealth Caribbean Medical Research Cncl) Working Gp (UK and Caribbean) 1995–, RCP Child Health Ctee on Nutrition 1996–2000; rep Health Services and Public Health Research Bd (HSPHRB) 1995–96, European rep Inst of Paediatric Nutrition USA 1995–, UK rep Int Inst of Paediatric Nutrition 2003–; delivered over 300 nat and int lectures 1980–, author of numerous articles and papers in professional jls; Wellcome visiting prof in basic med sciences USA 1993–94, BPA Guthrie Medal 1982; hon citizen Georgia 1994; FRCP 1991 (MRCP 1976), FMed Sci 2000; *Style*— Prof Alan Lucas; ✉ Institute of Child Health, 30 Guilford Street, London WC1N 1EH (tel 020 7905 2389, fax 020 7404 7109, e-mail a.lucas@ich.ucl.ac.uk)

LUCAS, Prof Arthur Maurice; AO (2005), CBE (2002); s of Joseph Alfred Percival Lucas (d 1985), of Colac, Victoria, and May Queen, *née* Griffin; *b* 26 October 1941; *Educ* Univ of Melbourne (BSc, BEd), Ohio State Univ (PhD); *m* 1970, Paula Jean, da of Geoffrey Ross Williams (d 1991); 1 da (Elizabeth Karen b 1974), 1 s (Arthur David b 1975); *Career* science/biology teacher Educn Dept of Victoria 1964–66, sr demonstrator in biology Flinders Univ of S Australia 1969–70 (demonstrator 1967–68), pt/t res assoc ERIC Analysis Center Ohio State Univ 1970–72, fndn lectr Educn Unit Warrnambool Inst of Advanced Educn 1973; Flinders Univ of S Australia: lectr in science educn 1974–75, sr lectr 1976–80, chm Sch of Educn 1977–79; KCL: prof of science curriculum studies 1980–2003 (emeritus prof 2003–), asst princ 1988–90, chm Res Strategy Ctee 1991–93, vice-princ (academic affairs) 1991–93, actg princ 1992–93, princ 1993–2003; dep vice-chllr Univ of London 1997–2002; pres Soc for the History of Natural History 2006–, vice-pres Cncl Zoological Soc of London 1993 (memb 1992–93); chm Med and Soc Panel Wellcome Fndn 1998–2002; memb: Exec Ctee Field Studies Cncl 1987–93, 1994–2000 and 2001–07, SE Thames RHA 1993–94, Ctee for Public Understanding of Sci (COPUS) 1993–96, Cncl Royal Instn of GB 1998–2004, Cncl Br Soc of History for Sci 1999–2002, Bd Quality Assurance Agency for HE 2001–, Lord Chllr's Advsy Cncl on the Public Records and Archives 2006–; author and contrib to many pubns and jls; fell Australian Coll of Educn 1995 (memb 1973), FIBiol 1981, FKC 1992; *Clubs* Athenaeum; *Style*— Prof Arthur Lucas, AO, CBE; ✉ c/o The Athenaeum, Pall Mall, London SW1Y 5ER

LUCAS, Ven Brian Humphrey; CB (1993); s of Frederick George Humphrey Lucas (d 1977), of Port Talbot, W Glamorgan, and Edith Mary, *née* Owen (d 1975); *Educ* Port Talbot Secdy GS, St David's Coll Lampeter (BA), St Stephen's House Oxford; *m* 23 July 1966, Joy, da of Roy Penn (d 1997); 2 s (Mark Stephen b 19 March 1969, (Alan) Simon b 3 Dec 1971), 1 da (Helen Penelope b 30 April 1975); *Career* ordained: deacon 1964, priest 1965; asst curate: Llandaff Cathedral 1964–67, Parish of Neath 1967–70; RAF: cmmnd chaplain 1970, Halton 1970–71, St Mawgan 1971–72, Luqa Malta 1972–75, Honington 1975–77, Marham 1977–79, staff chaplain to Chaplain-in-Chief 1979–82, Akrotiri Cyprus 1982–85, sr chaplain RAF Coll Cranwell 1985–87, asst chaplain-in-chief Germany 1987–89 then RAF Support Cmd 1989–91, archdeacon and Chaplain-in-Chief RAF 1991–95, archdeacon emeritus 1996–; Hon Chaplain to HM The Queen 1989–95; QHC 1988–95; canon emeritus of Lincoln 1995– (preb and canon 1991–95); rector of Caythorpe Fulbeck and Carlton Scroop 1996–2003; hon chaplain Bomber Command Assoc 2004–, hon chaplain Coastal Command Assoc 2005–,chaplain to High Sheriff of Lincs 2005–06; pres 3 Welsh Wing ATC 2007–; memb Gen Synod C of E 1991–95, vice-pres Clergy Orphan Corp 1991–95; hon sec Savage Club 1998–; memb Cncl: RAF Benevolent Fund 1991–95, Bible Reading Fellowship 1991–95; memb British Museum Soc 1980–96; FRSA 1993; *Recreations* archaeology of Near and Middle East, watching rugby football, writing, travel (avoiding tourist areas); *Clubs* RAF, Savage, Civil Service; *Style*— The Ven Brian Lucas, CB; ✉ Savage Club, 1 Whitehall Place, London SW1A 2HD

LUCAS, Caroline; MEP (Green) South East England; *b* 9 December 1960; *Family* married with 2 c; *Career* Green Pty: joined 1986, nat press offr 1987–89, co-chair 1989–90, princ speaker (various occasions), co cncllr Oxfordshire CC 1993–97, MEP SE England 1999–; memb Euro Parly Ctees on: Trade Industry Energy and Environment, Public Health and Consumer Policy; memb Palestinian Delegation, vice-pres Animal Welfare Intergroup, memb Intergroups on Peace Issues and Consumer Affairs; memb Advsy Bd Protect the Local, Globally, memb CND; *Publications* incl: Writing for Women (1989), The Trade Trap (with Belinda Coote, 1994), Reforming World Trade: The Social and Environmental Priorities (1996), Watchful in Seattle: World Trade Organisation Threats to Public Services, Food and the Environment (1999), The Euro or a Sustainable Future for Britain? A Critique of the Single Currency (with Mike Woodin, 2000), From Seattle to Nice: Challenging the Free Trade Agenda at the Heart of Enlargement (2000), Stopping the Great Food Swap: Relocalising Europe's Food.Supply (with Colin Hines, 2001), Time to Replace Globalisation (2001), Which Way for the European Union: Radical Reform or Business as Usual? (2001), Local Food: Benefits and Opportunities (with Andy Jones, 2003), Towards a GM free Europe: Halting the Spread of GMOs in Europe (2003), Global Warming, Local Warming: A Study of the Likely Impacts of Climate Change upon South East England (2004), Green Alternatives to Globalisation: A Manifesto (with Mike Woodin, 2004); *Style*— Dr Caroline Lucas, MEP; ✉ The European Parliament, 8G103, Rue Wiertz 60, 1047 Brussels, Belgium (tel 00 32 2 284 5153, fax 00 32 2 284 9153, e-mail clucas@europarl.eu.int); Office of the UK Green MEPs, 58 The Hop Exchange, 24 Southwark Street, London SE1 1TY (tel 020 7407 6281, fax 020 7234 0183, website www.carolinelucasmep.org.uk)

LUCAS, Christine Frances; da of John Hennessy (d 1969), and Ellen Alice, *née* Jones (d 1994); *b* 26 May 1944; *Educ* Our Lady's Convent Sch Cardiff, Cardiff Coll of Art, Ravensbourne Coll of Art and Design, Leicester Coll of Art and Design (DipAD); *m* 24 April 1971, John Lucas, s of Victor Lucas; *Career* asst knitwear designer Jaeger Co London 1966–70, design conslt for various men's and women's knitwear, leisurewear, swimwear, and loungewear companies 1970–80; Windsmoor Group 1980–90: successively designer Windsmoor and Planet knitwear, design team ldr on new design collections, product mangr, design co-ordinator, fndr and merchandise dir Précis petite collection; design dir Viyella Retail Div 1990–2001, design dir Alexon and Alex & Co 2002–03, md Viyella 2004–; Award for Excellence Coats Viyella Fashion Retail Div 1993; FRSA 2004; *Recreations* art, theatre, reading, travel, gardens, interiors; *Style*— Mrs Christine Lucas; ✉ Larkrise, Coneygree Fold, Chipping Campden, Gloucestershire GL55 6JL (tel 01386 849272)

LUCAS, Christopher Tullis; CBE (1994); s of Philip Gaddesden Lucas, GM (d 1982), and Maise Hanson (d 1984); *b* 20 December 1937; *Educ* Winchester; *m* 14 July 1962, Tina, da of Dr E T Colville; 2 da (Katherine b 1964, Suzannah b 1966); *Career* Nat Serv 1956–58; CA (Scot) 1965, Thomson McLintock and Co 1958–66, chief exec ICEM Ltd 1966–72, IBA 1972–74, first md Radio Forth Edinburgh 1974–77, sec and dir RSA 1977–94, initiator and administrator RSA Project 2001 1994–98; dir ANIMARTS 1999–, prodr and dir Eastfeast 2004–; *Recreations* Suffolk, creating a mini nature reserve, arts, carpentry, golf, skiing; *Clubs* Aldeburgh Allotment and Garden Assoc; *Style*— Mr Christopher Lucas, CBE; ✉ 60 Lebanon Park, Twickenham, Middlesex TW1 3DQ (tel 020 8892 6584)

LUCAS, Sir Colin; kt (2002); s of Frank Renshaw Lucas, and Janine, *née* Charpentier; *b* 25 August 1940, Egypt; *Educ* Sherborne, Lincoln Coll Oxford (MA, DPhil); *m* 1, 1964, Christiane Berchon de Fontaine Goubert (m dis 1975); 1 s; m 2, 1990, Mary Louise Hume; *Career* lectr: Univ of Sheffield 1965–69, Univ of Manchester 1970–73; Univ of Oxford: fell Balliol Coll 1973–90, tutor for admissions 1978–81, tutor for graduates 1989–90, memb Governing Bd Assoc Examinations Bd 1982–90; Univ of Chicago: prof 1990–94, chm Dept of History 1992–93, dean Div of the Social Sciences 1993–94; Univ of Oxford: master Balliol Coll 1994–2001, fell All Souls Coll 2001–06, pro-vice-chllr 1995–97, vice-chllr 1997–2004; sec Rhodes Tst and warden Rhodes House Oxford 2004–; chm Br Library 2006–; visiting appts: asst prof Indiana Univ 1969–70, prof Univ of Western Ontario 1975, prof Univ of Lyon-II 1977–78, prof Smith Coll 1987, sr fell in Soc for the Humanities Cornell Univ 1989; Leverhulme Faculty fell 1977–78, Radcliffe Research fell 1984–86; govr: Ludlow Coll 1975–90, Bradfield Coll 1987–90 and 1994–, Sherborne Sch 2002–06; chm Voltaire Fndn Fund Ctee 1994–97; Hon DLitt: Univ of Sheffield 2000, Univ of Western Australia 2000, Peking Univ 2002, St Francis Xavier Univ 2003, Oxford Brookes Univ 2004; Hon Dr Univ of Lyon-II France 1989, Hon Dr jur Univ of Glasgow 2001, Hon LLD Univ of Princeton 2002, Hon DCL Univ of Oxford 2003, Hon LLD Univ of Warwick 2005; hon fell: Lincoln Coll Oxford, Balliol Coll Oxford; FRHistS 1973; Officier de l'Ordre des Arts et des Lettres (France) 1990, Chevalier Ordre du Mérite 1994, Légion

L

d'Honneur 1998 (Officier 2005); *Books* The Structure of the Terror (1973), Beyond the Terror (with Gwynne Lewis, 1983), The Political Culture of the French Revolution (ed, 1988), Rewriting the French Revolution (ed, 1991); *Publications* author of numerous learned articles on eighteenth-century France, principally the French Revolution; *Clubs* Reform, Vincent's (Oxford); *Style*— Sir Colin Lucas; ✉ Rhodes House, Oxford OX1 3RG (tel 01865 270902, fax 01865 270914, e-mail warden@rhodeshouse.ox.ac.uk)

LUCAS, (Henry) Cornel; s of John Lucas (d 1949), of London, and Mary Ann Elizabeth Lucas (d 1946); *b* 12 September 1923; *Educ* Regent St Poly, Northern Poly; *m* 30 Jan 1960, Jennifer Susan Lindem, da of Maj James Frederick Holman, CBE (d 1974), of Loraine, St Ives, Cornwall; 3 s (Jonathan b 3 May 1961, Frederick b 29 Sept 1965, Linus b 5 March 1979), 1 da (Charlotte Rosie Linden b 29 May 1976); *Career* RAF Photographic Sch Farnborough 1941–46; Denham/Pinewood Studios 1947–59, opened own film studio 1959; work in permanent collections of: Nat Portrait Gallery, Nat Museum of Photography, Museum of Photography Bradford, Royal Photographic Soc, Bath and Jersey Museum of Photography Jersey; memb BAFTA (hon memb 1998), FRPS, FBIPP; *Books* Heads and Tales (1988), Shooting Stars (2005); *Recreations* music, painting, gardening; *Style*— Cornel Lucas, Esq; ✉ 57 Addison Road, London W14 8JJ (tel and fax 020 7602 3219, e-mail lucas@suzyt.wanadoo.co.uk)

LUCAS, Prof (George) Gordon; s of George Derrick Lucas and Florence Annie, *née* Bell; *b* 10 October 1933; *Educ* Lincoln Sch, Lincoln Tech Coll (ONC, HNC, IMechE endorsement), Coll of Aeronautics Cranfield (DCAe, now MSc), Loughborough Univ of Technol (PhD); *m* 11 Aug 1956, Mary Elizabeth, da of Samual Musgrave Ella; 1 da (Carol Mary (Mrs Waterfield) b 14 Dec 1959), 2 s (Kevin John b 5 Nov 1961, Neal Edward George b 6 March 1965); *Career* design engr Ruston & Hornsby Lincoln 1955–57 (apprentice 1950–55), design engr Lucas Gas Turbine Equipment Birmingham 1959–62; Loughborough Univ: lectr 1962–73, sr lectr 1973–87, reader 1987–90, Ford prof of automotive engrg 1990–98, dir Centre for Tport Engrg Practice 1980–87, dir MSc course in advanced automotive engrg 1987–98, ret, emiritus prof 1999–; FIMechE 1982; *Books* The Testing of Internal Combustion Engines (with A B Greene, 1969), Road Vehicle Performance (1986); *Recreations* bridge; *Style*— Prof Gordon Lucas; ✉ Department of Aeronautical and Automotive Engineering and Transport Studies, Loughborough University, Loughborough, Leicestershire LE11 3TU (tel 01509 223430, fax 01509 223946)

LUCAS, Ian; MP; *b* 1960, Gateshead, Tyne & Wear; *Educ* Newcastle Royal GS, New Coll Oxford; *Career* qualified slr 1985, ran slrs office 1989–92, former ptnr Stevens Lucas Slrs; MP (Lab) Wrexham 2001–; memb Transport Select Ctee 2003–05, PPS to Bill Rammell, MP (as Min of State for Lifelong Learning, Further and Higher Educn) 2005–06; *Style*— Ian Lucas, Esq, MP; ✉ House of Commons, London SW1A 0AA

LUCAS, Jeremy Charles Belgrave; s of Percy Belgrave Lucas, CBE, DSO, DFC, of London, and Jill Doreen, *née* Addison; *b* 10 August 1952; *Educ* Stowe, Pembroke Coll Cambridge (MA); *m* 4 Sept 1976, Monica Dorothea, *née* Bell; 2 s (Christopher b 1981, Timothy b 1984); *Career* slr Denton Hall and Burgin 1974–78; merchant banker Morgan Grenfell & Co Ltd 1978– (dir 1986–); *Recreations* tennis, golf; *Clubs* Royal West Norfolk Golf; *Style*— Jeremy Lucas, Esq; ✉ Deutsche Bank AG London, Global Corporate Finance, Winchester House, 1 Great Winchester Street, London EC2N 2DB (tel 020 7545 6315)

LUCAS, Prof (William) John; s of Leonard Townsend Lucas, and Joan, *née* Kelly; *b* 26 June 1937; *Educ* Hampton GS, Univ of Reading (BA, PhD); *m* 30 Sept 1961, Pauline; 1 s (Ben b 28 June 1962), 1 da (Emma b 11 Dec 1964); *Career* asst lectr Univ of Reading 1961–64, visiting prof Univs of Maryland and Indiana 1967–68, reader in English studies Univ of Nottingham 1975–77 (lectr 1964–71, sr lectr 1971–75), dean Sch of Educn and Humanities Loughborough Univ 1979–82 and 1988–96 (prof of English and drama and head of dept 1977–88), currently research prof Dept of English and Media Studies Nottingham Trent Univ; Lord Byron visiting prof of English lit Univ of Athens 1984–85; advsy ed: Jl of European Studies, Victorian Studies, Critical Survey, Literature and History; gen and commissioning ed: Faber Critical Monographs, Merlin Press Radical Reprints; co-ed Byron Press 1965–82, publisher Shoestring Press 1994–; regular contribs incl: Times Literary Supplement, Times Higher Educational Supplement, London Review of Books, New Statesman, The Listener, Poetry Review, BBC (Radios 3 and 4), Essays in Criticism, Cahiers Victoriens & Edourdiens Stand; FRSA 1984; *Books* incl: Tradition and Tolerance in 19th Century Fiction (with David Howard and John Goode, 1966), The Melancholy Man: A Study of Dickens (1970 and 1980), Arnold Bennett: A Study of his Fiction (1974), The Literature of Change (1977), Moderns & Contemporaries (1985), Modern English Poetry: from Hardy to Hughes (1986), Modern English Poetry (1986), England & Englishness (1990), Dickens: The Major Novels (1992), John Clare (1994), Writing and Radicalism (1996), Starting To Explain - Essays on 20th Century British and Irish Poetry (2003), Robert Browning (2003); poetry: About Nottingham (1971), A Brief Bestiary (1972), Chinese Sequence (1972), The Days of the Week (1983), Studying Grosz on the Bus (1989), Flying to Romania: A Sequence in Verse and Prose (1992), One for the Piano: Poems (1997), The Radical Twenties (1997), On The Track (2000), The Good That We Do (2001), Ivor Gurney (2001), A World Perhaps - New and Selected Poems (2002), The Long and the Short of It: Poems (2004), Flute Music: Poems (2007), 92 Acharnon Street (2007); *Style*— Prof John Lucas; ✉ 19 Devonshire Avenue, Beeston, Nottingham NG9 1BS; Department of English and Media Studies, The Nottingham Trent University, Clifton Lane, Nottingham NG11 8NS (tel 0115 941 8418, fax 0115 948 4266)

LUCAS, John Randolph; s of Ven Egbert de Grey Lucas (Archdeacon of Durham, d 1958), and Joan Mary, *née* Randolph (d 1982); *b* 18 June 1929; *Educ* Dragon Sch Oxford, Winchester, Balliol Coll Oxford (scholar, BA, John Locke Prize); *m* 17 June 1961, Helen Morar, er da of Adm Sir Reginald Portal, KCB, DSO (d 1983), of Marlborough, Wilts; 2 s (Edward b 1962, Richard b 1966), 2 da (Helen b 1964, Deborah b 1967); *Career* fell: Corpus Christi Coll Cambridge 1956–59, Merton Coll Oxford 1953–56 and 1960–96; memb Archbishops' Cmmn on Christian Doctrine; chm Oxford Consumer Gp; pres Br Soc for the Philosophy of Sci 1991–93; FBA 1988; *Books* The Principles of Politics (1964), The Concept of Probability (1970), The Freedom of the Will (1970), A Treatise on Time and Space (1973), Democracy and Participation (1976), Freedom and Grace (1976), On Justice (1980), Space, Time and Causality (1985), The Future (1989), Spacetime and Electromagnetism (1990), Responsibility (1993), Ethical Economics (1997), The Conceptual Roots of Mathematics (1999), An Engagement with Plato's Republic (2003), Reason and Reality (2006); *Style*— J R Lucas, Esq, FBA; ✉ Lambrook House, East Lambrook, South Petherton, Somerset TA13 5HW (tel 01460 240413, e-mail john.lucas@merton.oxford.ac.uk, web http://users.ox.ac.uk/jrlucas)

LUCAS, Matt; *b* 5 March 1974, London; *Educ* Univ of Bristol; *Career* comedian, actor and writer; acted with Nat Youth Theatre collaborated with comedy ptnr David Walliams, *qv* 1995–; columnist for Guardian 1999–2001; *Theatre* incl: Sir Bernard Chumley and Friends (Edinburgh Festival) 1995, 1996 and 1997, Troilus and Cressida 2000, Taboo (as Leigh Bowery) 2002, Little Britain Tour 2005–07; *Television* incl: Shooting Stars 1993, It's Ulrika 1997, Bang, Bang, It's Reeves and Mortimer 1999, Rock Profile 1999, Sir Bernard's Stately Homes 1998, Da Ali G Show (writer) 2000, Little Britain 2003–07, Casanova 2004, Catterick (BBC 2) 2004, Wind in the Willows (BBC 1) 2007; *Radio* incl: Little Britain (BBC Radio 4) 2001 and 2002; *Films* incl: Plunkett & Macleane 1999, Shaun of the Dead 2004; *Awards* for Little Britain incl: Silver Sony Radio Acad Award 2003, Gold Best Comedy Spoken Word Publisher Awards 2004, Best Comedy Performance and Best Entertainment RTS Awards 2004, Best Comedy Nat TV Awards 2004; British Comedy Awards: People's Choice Award 2004, Best Comedy Actor (joint with David Walliams) 2004, Best British Comedy 2004, Best TV Comedy 2005, Ronnie Barker Writer's Award 2005; BAFTA Awards: Best Comedy Series 2004 and 2005, Best Comedy Performance 2005; Best Comedy South Bank Show Awards 2005, Best Comedy Broadcast Magazine Awards 2005, Best TV Show NME Awards 2005, Best Comedy TRIC Awards 2005; *Style*— Matt Lucas, Esq; ✉ c/o Troika Talent, 3rd Floor, 74 Clerkenwell Road, London EC1M 5QA (tel 020 7336 7868)

LUCAS, Peter William; s of William George Lucas (d 1993), of Bradford Abbas, Dorset, and Jose Mabel, *née* House (d 2002); *b* 12 April 1947; *Educ* Foster's Sch Sherborne, Harrow Coll (DipM); *m* 10 June 1972, Gail (d 2000), da of John Small (d 1983), of Camberley, Surrey; 2 da (Zoe b 1978, Joanna b 1984), 1 s (James Peter William b 1981); *Career* mktg dir Lyons Tetley Ltd 1978–84, md Foodcare Ltd 1984–85, princ The Marketing Department 1985–2000, managing ptnr Mappin Parry Lucas 1988–91; dir: Custom Management (UK) Ltd 1990–92, Kingsbourne Ltd 1990–95, Kingsbourne International Marketing Ltd 1995–97, Orange Learning Ltd 1997–, Orange Logic Ltd 1998–, The Orange Simulation Co Ltd 1998–; md: Orange Development Ltd 1995–99, Insight People Development Ltd 1997–, The Orange Group Ltd 1999–; dir Assoc of Cereal Food Mfrs 1981–84; chm: Bd Govrs Watlington CPS 1988–91, Watlington Primary Sch Tst 1990–99; memb Mktg Soc 1980, FCIM 1987 (chartered marketer 2002), FInstD 1989; *Recreations* shooting, fishing; *Style*— Peter Lucas, Esq; ✉ Sejant House, The Green, Burton, Christchurch BH23 7NZ; The Innovation Centre, 78 Heyford Park, Upper Heyford, Oxfordshire OX25 5HD (tel 01869 238066, fax 01869 238024, mobile 078 3628 8621, e-mail peter.lucas@theorangegroup.com)

LUCAS, Robert R; s of John R Lucas, and Rosalind J W Lucas; *b* 28 August 1962, Lincoln; *Educ* Lincoln Christs Hosp Sch, Imperial Coll London (BEng); *m* 15 Sept 1989, Sara J Lowthorpe; 1 da (Darcey b 12 Jan 1999), 1 s (Bruno b 1 Jan 2002); *Career* GEC Marconi plc 1985–87, 3i plc 1987–96, managing ptnr CVC Capital Ptnrs Ltd 1996–; non-exec dir: IG Group Holdings plc 2003–, AA Group 2004–; *Style*— Robert Lucas, Esq; ✉ CVC Capital Partners, 111 Strand, London WC2R 0AG

LUCAS, Sir Thomas Edward; 5 Bt (UK 1887), of Ashtead Park, Surrey, and of Lowestoft, Co Suffolk; s of Ralph John Scott Lucas (ka 1941), late Coldstream Gds, gs of 1 Bt, and Dorothy (d 1985), da of H T Timson; *b* 16 September 1930; *Educ* Wellington, Trinity Hall Cambridge (MA); *m* 1, 1958, Charmian Margaret (d 1970), da of late Col James Stanley Powell; 1 s (Stephen Ralph James b 1963); m 2, 1980, Mrs Ann J Graham Moore; *Heir* s, Stephen Lucas; *Career* engr, scientist, author, speaker and holistic practitioner, co dir 1958–; cnsllr The Hale Clinic London 1996–2002; dir Digital Health Research Ltd 2000–02; chm: Medical Devices & Instrumentation Ltd 1996–98, EmDI Ltd 1998–2002, Oldfield Technologies plc 2000–01; conslt and seminar leader to EEC 1976–, UN, World Bank, public and private cos; sr tstee Inlight and Truemark Tsts 1996–; memb Scientific and Med Network; *Recreations* motor sport, travel, cooking, wine, art and architecture; *Style*— Sir Thomas Lucas, Bt

LUCAS OF CHILWORTH, 3 Baron (UK 1946); Simon William Lucas; s of 2 Baron Lucas of Chilworth (d 2001); *b* 6 February 1957; *Educ* Univ of Leicester (BSc); *m* 21 Sept 1993, Fiona, yr da of Thomas Mackintosh, of Vancouver, BC, Canada; 2 s (Hon John Ronald Muir b 1995, Hon Duncan Michael William b 1998); *Heir* s, Hon John Lucas; *Career* served with RE 1976–84; computer systems engr, geophysicist; *Style*— The Rt Hon the Lord Lucas of Chilworth

LUCAS OF CRUDWELL, 11 Baron (E 1663) and 8 Lord Dingwall (S 1609); Ralph Matthew Palmer; s of Anne Rosemary, Baroness Lucas of Crudwell (10 holder of the title) and Lady Dingwall (7 holder of the title in her own right) (d 1991), and Maj Hon Robert Jocelyn Palmer, MC (d 1991); *b* 7 June 1951; *Educ* Eton, Balliol Coll Oxford; *m* 1, 1978 (m dis 1995), Clarissa Marie, da of George Vivian Lockett, TD, of Stratford St Mary, Suffolk; 1 da (Hon Hannah Rachel Elise b 1984), 1 s (Hon Lewis Edward b 1987); m 2, 1995, Amanda Atha (d 2000); m 3, 2001, Antonia Vera Kennedy, da of late Anthony Benno Stanley Rubinstein, of London; 1 da (Hon Freya Anne b 2002); *Heir* s, Hon Lewis Palmer; *Career* S G Warburg & Co Ltd 1976–88; Lord in Waiting (Govt Whip) 1994–97, shadow Lords min for Int Devpt 1997–98; publisher The Good Schools Guide 1998–; Liveryman Worshipful Co of Mercers; FCA 1976; *Style*— The Lord Lucas of Crudwell and Dingwall; ✉ House of Lords, London SW1A 0PW (e-mail lucasr@parliament.uk)

LUCAS-TOOTH, Sir (Hugh) John; 2 Bt (UK 1920); s of Sir Hugh Vere Huntly Duff Munro-Lucas-Tooth of Teananich, 1 Bt (d 1985), and Laetitia Florence, OBE (d 1978), er da of Sir John Ritchie Findlay, 1 Bt, KBE; *b* 20 August 1932; *Educ* Eton, Balliol Coll Oxford; *m* 1955, Hon Caroline Poole, er da of 1 Baron Poole, PC, CBE, TD (d 1993); 3 da; *Heir* cous, James Warrand; *Clubs* Brooks's, Beefsteak; *Style*— Sir John Lucas-Tooth, Bt; ✉ 41 Lancaster Road, London W11 1QJ; Parsonage Farm, East Hagbourne, Didcot, Oxfordshire OX11 9LN

LUCE, Baron (Life Peer UK 2000), of Adur in the County of West Sussex; Sir Richard Napier; kt (1991), GCVO (2000), PC (1986), DL; s of Sir William Luce, GBE, KCMG (d 1977), and Margaret (d 1989), da of Adm Sir Trevelyan Napier, KCB; *b* 14 October 1936; *Educ* Wellington, Christ's Coll Cambridge; *m* 5 April 1961, Rose Helen, eldest da of Sir Godfrey Nicholson, 1 Bt (d 1991); 2 s (Alexander Richard b 1964, Edward Godfrey b 1968); *Career* Nat Serv Cyprus; dist offr Kenya 1960–62, former mangr Gallaher and Spirella Co (GB); Parly candidate (Cons) Hitchin 1970; MP (Cons): Arundel and Shoreham 1971–74, Shoreham 1974–92; PPS to Min for Trade and Consumer Affrs 1972–74, oppn whip 1974–75, oppn spokesman on foreign and Cwlth affrs 1977–79; FCO: Parly under sec 1979–81, min of state 1981–82 (resigned over invasion of Falkland Islands), re-appointed min of state 1983; min for the Arts and min of state Privy Cncl Office responsible for The Civil Serv Sept 1985–90, ret from Parl 1992; vice-chllr Univ of Buckingham 1992–97; govr and C-in-C Gibraltar 1997–2000; Lord Chamberlain to HM The Queen's Household 2000–06; chm: Cwlth Fndn 1992–96, Atlantic Cncl of the UK 1992–97; pres: Voluntary Arts Network, King George V Fund for Actors and Actresses 2007–; non-exec dir Meridian Broadcasting Ltd 1992–97, former non-exec dir Booker Tate Ltd; tstee Geographers A-Z Map Co; *Style*— The Rt Hon the Lord Luce, GCVO, PC, DL; ✉ House of Lords, London SW1A 0PW

LUCIE-SMITH, (John) Edward McKenzie; s of John Dudley Lucie-Smith, MBE (d 1943), and Mary Frances Maud, *née* Lushington (d 1982); *b* 27 February 1933; *Educ* King's Sch Canterbury, Merton Coll Oxford (MA); *Career* Nat Serv RAF Flying Offr 1954–56; worked in advtg 1956–66, poet, art critic and freelance writer and photographer with contribs to The Times, Sunday Times, The Independent, The Mail on Sunday, The Listener, The Spectator, New Statesman, Evening Standard, Encounter, London Magazine, Illustrated London News, Art Review, La Vanguardia (Barcelona); membre de l'Académie de Poésie Européenne; FRSL; *Books* A Tropical Childhood and Other Poems (1961), A Group Anthology (ed with Philip Hobsbaum, 1963), Confessions and Histories (1964), Penguin Modern Poets 6 (with Jack Clemo and George MacBeth, 1964), Penguin Book of Elizabethan Verse (ed, 1965), What is a Painting? (1966), The Liverpool Scene (ed, 1967), A Choice of Browning's Verse (ed, 1967), Penguin Book of Satirical Verse (ed, 1967), Towards Silence (1968), Thinking About Art (1968), Movements in Art since 1945 (1969), British Poetry since 1945 (ed, 1970), Art in Britain 1969–70 (with P White, 1970), A Primer of Experimental Verse (ed, 1971), French Poetry: The Last Fifteen Years (ed with S W Taylor, 1971), A Concise History of French Painting (1971), Symbolist Art (1972), Eroticism in Western Art (1972), The First London Catalogue (1974), The Well Wishers (1974), The Burnt Child (1975), The Invented Eye (1975), World of the Makers (1975), How the Rich Lived (with C Dars, 1976), Joan of Arc (1976), Work and Struggle (with C Dars, 1977), Fantin-Latour (1977), The Dark Pageant (1977), Art Today (1977), A Concise History of Furniture (1979), Super Realism (1979), Cultural Calendar of the Twentieth Century (1979), Art in the Seventies (1980), The Story of Craft (1981), The Body (1981), A History of Industrial Design (1983), Art Terms: An Illustrated Dictionary (1984), Art in the Thirties (1985), American Art Now (1985), The Male Nude: A Modern View (with François de Louville, 1985), Lives of the Great Twentieth Century Artists (1986), Sculpture Since 1945 (1987), The Self Portrait: A Modern View (with Sean Kelly, 1987), Art in the 1980's (1990), Art Deco Painting (1990), Fletcher Benton (1990), Latin American Art of the Twentieth Century (1993), Art and Civilization (1993), Wendy Taylor (1993), Race, Sex and Gender: issues in contemporary art (1994), Frink: a portrait (with Elizabeth Frink, 1994), John Kirby (1994), American Realism (1994), Art Today (completely new version, 1995), Visual Art in the 20th Century (1996), Albert Paley (1996), Ars Erotica (1997), Lynn Chadwick (1997), Adam (1998), Zoo (1998), Women and Art (with Judy Chicago, 1999), Judy Chicago (2000), Flesh and Stone (photographs, 2000), Changing Shape (2001), Roberto Marquez (2001), Art Tomorrow (2002), Carlo Bertocci (2002), Stefano di Stasio (2002), Paola Gandolfi (2003), Alberto Abate (2003), Philip Pearlstein (2004), Carlos Ferus Barela (2004), Ricardo Cinalli (2005), Elias Rivora (2006), Harry Holland (2006); *Recreations* computers; *Style—* Edward Lucie-Smith, Esq; ✉ c/o Rogers Coleridge & White, 20 Powis Mews, London W11 1JN

LUCK, Victor Leonard (Vic); *b* 31 May 1947; *Educ* Bromley GS, Univ of Salford (BSc); *m* Jan 1970, Susan Lesley, *née* Jones; 2 da (Dominie Cara b 20 June 1974, Victoria Marie b 4 June 1976); *Career* Philips Industries 1967–69, Chrysler Corporation 1970–73, Ford of Europe 1973–74, Chrysler Corporation 1974–77; PricewaterhouseCoopers (formerly Coopers & Lybrand before merger): joined 1977, managing ptnr UK Mgmnt Consultancy Servs 1994–98, managing ptnr Mgmnt Consultancy Servs EMEA 1998; formerly gen mangr IBM; currently ptnr Langsdale Crook; non-exec dir Professional Rugby Players Assoc, memb Analysis Bd The Captain's Club; FCMA 1973, FIMC 1981; *Recreations* playing and watching soccer, modern history, travel; *Style—* Vic Luck, Esq

LUCKETT, Nigel Frederick; s of George Ward Luckett (d 1958), of Wolverhampton, and Marjorie Phyllis, *née* Jeffery (d 1974); *b* 27 August 1942; *m* 18 Sept 1965, Janet Mary, da of late Albert Edward Sadler; 2 s (Richard Stephen b 18 Nov 1971, David Nigel b 6 Feb 1981); *Career* articled clerk Ridsdale Cozens & Purslow Accountants Walsall, Birmingham Office Peat Marwick Mitchell & Co 1964–66; ptnr Thomson McLintock & Co 1970–87 (joined 1966), ptnr KPMG Peat Marwick (following merger) 1987–95; non-exec dir Birmingham Stopper Ltd; memb: Ctee Birmingham and W Midlands Soc of Chartered Accountants 1975–83; FCA 1975 (ACA 1964); *Recreations* golf, classical music, antiques, sailing, walking, the technical analysis of securities; *Style—* Nigel Luckett, Esq; ✉ Englefield House, 108 White Hill, Kinver, Stourbridge, West Midlands DY7 6AU (tel 01384 872923)

LUCKHURST, Prof Geoffrey Roger; s of William Thomas Victor Luckhurst (d 1970), and Hilda Mary, *née* Flood (d 2001); *b* 21 January 1939; *Educ* Sir Joseph Williamson's Mathematical Sch Rochester, Univ of Hull, Univ of Cambridge; *m* 3 July 1965, Janice Rita, da of Colin Jack Flanagan (d 1995), of Romsey, Hants; 2 da (Nicola Jane b 25 Jan 1970, Caroline b 15 July 1972); *Career* Univ of Southampton: lectr 1967–70, reader 1970–77, prof of chemistry 1977–2004 (emeritus prof 2004–), dep-dean of sci 2000–03, sr library curator 1996–, chm Advsy Bd Sch of Chemistry 2004–07; pres Int Liquid Crystal Soc 1992–96 (honoured memb), chm Br Liquid Crystal Soc 1994–2000; coordinator of EC TMR Network 1999–2002, co-ordinator INTAS Project 2000–02; Leverhulme emeritus fell 2004–07; G W Gray Medal Br Liquid Crystal Soc 2002; FRSC 1982; *Style—* Prof Geoffrey Luckhurst; ✉ School of Chemistry, University of Southampton SO17 1BJ (tel 023 8059 3795, fax 023 8059 3781, e-mail gl@soton.ac.uk)

LUCKIN, (Peter) Samuel; s of Geoffrey Grimston Luckin (d 1986), of High Easter, nr Chelmsford, Essex, and Muriel Bessie, *née* Need (d 1962); *b* 9 March 1938; *Educ* Felsted; *Career* Nat Serv cmmnd Essex Regt 1956–58, platoon cdr BAOR; press aide for Rt Hon Edward Heath CCO 1960's, dep head of PR for Brewers' Soc 1970's, owner Sam Luckin Associates 1980–; freelance journalist; memb: Bd of Mgmnt Ashridge Mgmnt Coll Assoc 1982–85, Cncl IPR 1989–91 and 1992–95 (chm Membership Ctee 1991, memb Bd of Mgmnt 1991); FCIPR (FIPR 1990); *Recreations* swimming, management development, watching first class cricket; *Clubs* Farmers', MCC; *Style—* Samuel Luckin, Esq; ✉ 4 Huggens College, College Road, Northfleet, Kent DA11 9DL (tel and fax 01474 364440, e-mail samluckin@hotmail.com)

LUCY, *see:* Fairfax-Lucy

LUDDINGTON, Gary Anthony Cluer; s of Anthony William Davey Luddington (d 1998), of Peterborough, and Mae Luddington; *b* 20 February 1946; *Educ* Brockenhurst GS, Fitzwilliam Coll Cambridge (MA); *m* 1, 1968; 1 da (Victoria Louise b 31 July 1970), 1 s (Thomas James b 11 Jan 1972); m 2, 1978, Diana Elizabeth Parkinson, *née* Turnbull; 1 step da (Clair Elizabeth b 1966), 1 step s (Rufus Joseph b 1972); *Career* brand mangr: Beecham 1968–70, Warner Lambert 1970–72; mktg mangr Mars Confectionery 1972–77, md ATV Licensing 1977–79, mktg dir Carlsberg UK 1979–82, md Letraset UK 1982–83, mktg dir Guinness Brewing 1983–87, world wide gp mktg dir United Distillers Group 1987–89, chm Norman Broadbent International 1998–2000 (md 1989–98), ptnr Odgers Ray & Berndtson 2000–02, chm Milud Ltd 2004–; *Recreations* shooting, sailing, golf; *Clubs* Phyllis Court, Leander; *Style—* G Luddington, Esq; ✉ Foxhill Meadow, Bix, Henley-on-Thames, Oxfordshire RG9 6DE

LUDER, Ian David; JP (City of London, 2002); s of Mark Luder, of Eastbourne, and Frances, *née* Stillerman; *b* 13 April 1951; *Educ* Haberdashers' Aske's, UCL (BSc); *m* 21 Aug 1999, Lin Jane née Surkitt; *Career* Arthur Andersen 1971–78: joined as articled clerk, subsequently tax sr then tax mangr 1975; ptnr: MacIntyre Hudson CA's 1980–88, Arthur Andersen 1989–2002, Grant Thornton 2002–; cncllr Bedford BC 1976–1999; chm: Policy Ctee 1988–93, Planning & Transport Ctee 1995–1998; memb Ct of Common Cncl City of London 1998– (chm Fin Ctee 2003–06), Alderman Castle Baynard Ward 2005–, sheriff City of London 2007–08; non-exec dir Homerton Univ Hosp NHS Fndn Tst 2002–; Liveryman: Worshipful Co fo Coopers, Worshipful Co of Tax Advsrs; FCA 1974, FTII 1974 (pres 1994–95), FRSA 1993; *Books* Tolleys Personal Tax and Investment Planning (ed), Simon's Taxes (contrib), Butterworths Tax and Remuneration Strategies; *Recreations* cricket, local politics, music; *Clubs* MCC, Bedford RUFC; *Style—* Ian D Luder, Esq; ✉ Timbers, 110 High Street, Riseley, Bedfordshire MK44 1DF (tel 01234 709240, fax 01234 708281, e-mail theluders@aol.com); 25 Andrewes House, Barbican, London EC2Y 8AX

LUDER, (Harold) Owen; CBE (1986); s of Edward Charles Luder (d 1981), and Ellen Clara, *née* Mason (d 1986); *b* 7 August 1928; *Educ* Sch of Architecture Regent St Poly, Sch of Architecture Brixton Sch of Bldg; *m* 1, 29 Jan 1951 (m dis 1989), Rose Dorothy (Doris), *née* Broadstock; 4 da (Jacqueline Kim b 3 May 1953, Kathryn Joy b 8 July 1954, Sara Jayne b 16 Oct 1966, Judith Amanda b 29 Jan 1968), 1 s (Peter Jonathan Owen b 6 Oct 1965 d 8 Dec 1965); m 2, 10 May 1989, Jacqueline Ollerton; *Career* Nat Serv RA 1946–48; qualified architect 1954, started own practice Owen Luder Partnership 1957, withdrew 1987 to develop new consultancy Communication In Construction; designed many bldgs UK and abroad 1954–87, environmental conslt NCB - Belvoir coal mines 1975–87; non-exec dir Jarvis plc 1995–2003; various awards incl RIBA Bronze medallist 1963, Arkansas traveller USA 1971; columnist Building Magazine (Business Columnist of the Year 1985), contrib nat and tech press, radio and TV broadcaster; pres Norwood Soc 1981–92, pres RIBA 1981–83 and 1995–97 (hon treas 1975–78); chm ARB 2002–03 (vice-chm 1997–2002); vice-pres Membership Communications 1989–90; ARIBA 1954, FRIBA 1967, FRSA 1984, MBAE 1992; *Publications* Sports Stadia After Hillsborough (1991), Architects Guide to Keeping out of Trouble (1999, 3 edn 2005); *Recreations* writing, theatre, Arsenal FC; *Clubs* RAC; *Style—* Owen Luder, Esq, CBE, PPRIBA; ✉ Owen Luder Consultancy, 702, Romney House, 47 Marsham Street, London SW1P 3DS (tel 020 7222 0198, e-mail owen.luder@dsl.pipex.com)

LUDFORD, Baroness (Life Peer UK 1997), of Clerkenwell in the London Borough of Islington; Sarah Ludford; MEP (Lib Dem) London; da of Joseph Campbell Ludford, and Valerie Kathleen, *née* Skinner; *b* 14 March 1951; *Educ* Portsmouth HS for Girls, LSE (BSc, MSc), Inns of Court Sch of Law; *m* Steve Hitchins; *Career* barrister; called to the Bar Gray's Inn 1979; official Secretariat Gen and DG Competition EC 1979–85; Euro and UK policy advsr Lloyd's of London 1985–87, vice-pres corp external affrs American Express Euro 1987–90, Euro conslt 1990–99; MEP (Lib Dem) London 1999– (contested Euro Parly constituency seat: Wight and Hampshire E 1984, London Central 1989 and 1994; contested UK Parly constituency seat: Islington N 1992, Islington S and Finsbury 1997); memb Cncl Euro Lib Dem and Reform Pty; memb Ctee on Citizen's Freedoms and Rights, Justice and Home Affrs, memb Ctee on Foreign Affrs, Human Rights, Common Security and Def Policy; memb inter-Parly delgn: Cyprus, SE Euro; ELDR spokeswoman on Justice and Home Affrs, rapporteur on Anti-Racism Euro Parl 2000, vice-pres Euro Parl Anti-Rascism Inter-Gp, co-ordinator Euro Parl Kurdish Network; memb Lib Dem Pty; cncllr Islington BC 1991–99, vice-chair Lib Dem Fed Policy Ctee 1991–98, vice-pres Gay and Lesbian Lib Dems (DELGA); memb Cncl Federal Tst; memb: RIIA, Euro Movement; *Publications* The EU: From Economic Community to Human Rights Community (article contrib to To the Power of Ten (G Watson & H Hazelwood (eds), 2000)); *Recreations* theatre, ballet, gardening; *Style—* The Baroness Ludford, MEP; ✉ European Parliament, Office 10G-165, Rue Wiertz, B-1047, Brussels, Belgium (tel 00 32 2284 7104, fax 00 32 2284 9104, e-mail sludford@europarl.eu.int); European Parliament Office T-11-086, 6700, Strasbourg, France (tel 00 33 3 88 17 71 04, fax 00 33 3 88 17 91 04, e-mail sludford@europarl.eu.int); Constituency Office, 36 St Peter's Street, London N1 8JT (tel and fax 020 7288 2526, e-mail sludfordmep@cix.co.uk, website www.sarahludfordmep.org.uk)

LUDLAM, Prof Christopher Armstrong; *b* 6 June 1946; *Educ* Univ of Edinburgh (BSc, MB ChB, PhD); *Career* research fell MRC Univ of Edinburgh 1972–75, sr registrar Univ Hosp of Wales Cardiff 1975–78, lectr in haematology Univ of Wales 1979; Dept of Med Univ of Edinburgh 1980–: conslt haematologist, dir Edinburgh Haemophilia Centre, prof of haematology and coagulation med; numerous publications on blood coagulation; FRCPE, FRCPath; *Style—* Prof Christopher Ludlam; ✉ Department of Haematology, Royal Infirmary, Edinburgh (tel 0131 242 6811, fax 0131 242 6812, e-mail christopher.ludlam@ed.ac.uk)

LUDLOW, Her Hon Judge Caroline Mary; da of William George Woodward (d 1991), and Mary Josephine, *née* Atcheson (d 1980); *b* 25 September 1947; *Educ* Hillingdon Court, St Mary's GS, QMC London (LLM); *m* 2, 12 June 1987, John Warwick Everitt; 1 c (Merryn b 1 June 1988); *Career* called to the Bar Inner Temple 1970; in practice SE Circuit 1979–97, recorder 1995–97, circuit judge (SE Circuit) 1997–, designated family judge Chelmsford 2000–04, designated family judge Ipswich 2003–; bar co-ordinator Law In Action 1992–97, chair Children's Legal Centre Ltd 2002–, memb Advsy Ctee Law Sch Univ of Essex 1992– (memb Ct) 1997; tstee: Safeguardng Children Partnership Ltd 2005–, PACT 2006–; Guardian of the Foyer Ipswich 2004; *Recreations* reading, gardening; *Style—* Her Hon Judge Ludlow; ✉ Ipswich County Court, Arcade Street, Ipswich, Suffolk IP1 1EJ (tel 01473 214256)

LUDLOW, Christopher; s of Sydney Ludlow (d 1983), and Margaret Eleanor, *née* Barlee; *b* 7 September 1946; *Educ* King Edward VI Sch Macclesfield, London Coll of Printing (DipAD); *m* 1, 7 Sept 1969 (m dis 1980), Louise Frances Heather, da of Claude Duchesne Janitsch; 1 s (Edward b 1972); m 2, 27 May 2000, Françoise Ellery Lamaud, *née* Blaha-Sobieski; *Career* graphic designer; assoc Stevenson Ward Macclesfield 1971–, ptnr Gray Design Associates 1974–, princ Henrion Ludlow Schmidt 1981–; responsible for major corporate identities incl: Coopers & Lybrand, Amersham International, British Midland, London Electricity, Halcrow; responsible for orientation systems for: London Underground, BAA, Canary Wharf, Channel Tunnel Terminal Waterloo, Bluewater Park, Millennium Dome, Nat Gallery of Ireland; conslt to various companies/instns incl: British Airports Authy, British Rail, KLM Royal Dutch Airlines, London Underground, Solvay, Univ of Leeds; author of articles in various design pubns; memb and int liaison offr American Soc of Environmental Graphic Designers, chm Sign Design Soc 1993–95; FCSD 1981, FRSA 1994; *Recreations* music, antique models; *Style—* Christopher Ludlow, Esq; ✉ Henrion Ludlow Schmidt, 12 Hobart Place, London SW1W 0HH (tel 020 7245 4604, fax 020 7245 4601)

LUDLOW, Michael Richard; s of Sir Richard Ludlow (d 1956), and Katharine, *née* Wood (d 1975); *b* 30 March 1933; *Educ* Rugby, Trinity Coll Oxford (MA); *m* 1, 1962 (m dis 1969), Prunella, *née* Truscott; 1s, 1 da; m 2, 1969, Diane, *née* Wright (d 1995); 2 da; m 3, 1996, Sheila, *née* Holmes, wid of Russell Pratt; *Career* Nat Serv 1951–52, jr under offr (Eaton Hall) Royal Welsh Fus, cmmnd 2 Lt Queen's Regt 1952, seconded to Sierra Leone Regt 1952 (trg offr), Lt N Staffs Regt TA 1952–54; admitted slr 1959, sr ptnr Beale & Co Slrs 1982–93 (ptnr 1965–93), ret; chm London Branch Chartered Inst of Arbitrators 1993–95; Master Worshipful Co of Arbitrators 2000–01; memb Law Soc 1959–96; chm and hon sec Construction Contracts Mediators Gp (CCMG) 2000–01; FCIArb 1983; *Books* Fair Charges? (1982); *Recreations* golf; *Clubs* Reform, Vincent's (Oxford), I Zingari, Grannies Cricket, Roehampton; *Style—* Michael Ludlow, Esq; ✉ 2 Sarn Hill Grange, Bushley Green, Tewkesbury, Gloucestershire GL20 6AD (tel and fax 01684 296212)

LUDLOW, Bishop of 2002–; Rt Rev Michael Wrenford Hooper; s of Wrenford Arthur Hooper (d 1976), of Upton-St-Leonards, Gloucester, and Phyllis Edith Mary, *née* Little; *b* 2 May 1941; *Educ* Crypt Sch Gloucester, St David's Coll Lampeter (BA), St Stephen's House Oxford; *m* 1968, Rosemary Anne, da of Albert Edwards; 2 s (Wrenford James b 1970, Dominic Michael 1978), 2 da (Lucy Olivia b 1973, Annabel Laura b 1982); *Career* ordained: deacon 1965, priest 1966; asst curate St Mary Magdalene Bridgnorth Shropshire 1965–70, vicar of Minsterley and rector of Habberley 1970–81, rural dean of Pontesbury 1976–81, rector and rural dean of Leominster 1981–97, prebendary of Hereford Cathedral 1981–, archdeacon of Hereford 1997–2002; involved with Red Cross 1955–65; *Recreations* walking, cycling, dogs, reading, music, rugby, cricket; *Style—* The Rt Rev the Bishop of Ludlow; ✉ The Bishop's House, Covedale Road, Craven Arms, Shropshire SY7 9BT

LUETCHFORD, Robert Sellick; s of William Luetchford (d 1984), and Roma, *née* Lawrence; *b* 29 March 1949; *Educ* Harrow Co GS, Pembroke Coll Oxford (MA); *m* 7 Nov 1990, Nicola Christine, da of Michael Gilbert; *Career* International Computers Ltd 1971–74, Sperry Univac (UK) Ltd 1974–77; Plessey Co Ltd: Plessey Microsystems Ltd 1977–79, Plessey Corp Staff 1979–81, dir of planning and business devpt Plessey Office Systems Ltd 1981–84; Prudential Bache Securities: head of electronics res 1984–86, vice-pres 1986, sr vice-pres Corp Fin 1986; ceo Marshall Securities Ltd 1990– (dep chief exec 1986–90); fndr and non-exec dir Progressive Asset Management Ltd; *Recreations* opera, classical music, fly fishing; *Style—* Robert Luetchford, Esq; ✉ Marshall Securities Ltd, Crusader House, 145 St John Street, London EC1V 4QJ (tel 020 7490 3788, fax 020 7490 3787)

LUFF, Nicholas (Nick); *b* 11 March 1967; *Children* 1 da; *Career* articled with KPMG 1987–91, Peninsular & Oriental Steam Navigation Co 1991–2000 (gp treasurer 1994, head of corp finance 1996, finance dir 1999–2000), chief financial offr P&O Princess Cruises 2000–03, chief financial offr Peninsular & Oriental Steam Navigation Co 2003–07, gp finance dir Centrica plc 2007–; non-exec dir QinetiQ Group plc; ACA, MCT; *Clubs* Oxford and Cambridge; *Style*— Nick Luff, Esq; ✉ Centrica plc, Millstream, Maidenhead Road, Windsor SL4 5GD

LUFF, Peter James; MP; s of Thomas Luff (d 1963), and Joyce, *née* Mills (d 1985); *b* 18 February 1955; *Educ* Licensed Victuallers' Sch Slough, Windsor GS, CCC Cambridge (exhibitioner, MA); *m* May 1982, Julia Dorothy, da of Lt Cdr P D Jenks, RN; 1 da (Rosanna Amy b 29 Aug 1985), 1 s (Oliver Charles Henry b 10 Jan 1988); *Career* res asst to Rt Hon Peter Walker 1977–80, head of Private Office of Rt Hon Edward Heath 1980–82, asst md then md Good Relations Public Affairs Ltd 1980–87, special advsr to sec of state for Trade and Industry 1987–89, sr conslt Bell Pottinger Communications (formerly Lowe Bell Communications) 1989–90, co sec Luff and Sons Ltd Windsor 1980–87, asst md Good Relations Ltd 1990–92; MP (Cons): Worcester 1992–97, Worcestershire Mid 1997– (Parly candidate (Cons) Holborn and St Pancras 1987); PPS to: min for Energy 1993–96, Lord Chllr 1996–97, min for Prisons 1996–97; oppn whip 2000–02, asst chief whip 2002–05; memb Commons Select Ctee on: Welsh Affrs 1992–97, Tport 1993, Agric 1997–2000 (chm 1997–2000), Information 2001–05, Admin 2003–05; jt sec Cons Backbench Ctee on Transport 1992–93, patron Cons Students 1994–98, chm Cons Parly Friends of India 2001–05; FIPR; *Recreations* going to musicals and theatre, being with my family, scuba diving, shooting; *Clubs* Worcestershire CCC; *Style*— Peter Luff, Esq, MP; ✉ House of Commons, London SW1A 0AA; tel 01905 763952

LUFT, His Hon Arthur Christian; CBE (1988); s of Ernest Christian Luft (d 1962), and Phoebe Luft (d 1977); *b* 21 July 1915; *Educ* Bradbury Cheshire; *m* 1950, Dorothy, da of Francis Manley (d 1936); 2 s (Peter, Timothy); *Career* served RA and REME 1940–46; advocate Manx Bar 1940, HM Attorney Gen IOM 1973, HM Second Deemster (High Court judge) 1974, HM First Deemster, Clerk of the Rolls and dep govr IOM 1980–88; memb: Legislative Cncl of IOM 1988–98, Dept of Local Govt and Environment 1988–93, IOM Public Accounts Ctee 1988–98, Ecclesiastical Ctee of Tynwald 1992–98, Dept of Agric Fisheries and Forestry 1993–98; chm: Criminal Injuries Compensation Tbnl 1975–80, Prevention of Fraud Investment Act Tbnl 1975–80, Licensing Appeal Court 1975–80, Tynwald Ceremony Arrangements Ctee 1980–88, IOM Income Tax Cmmrs 1980–88, IOM Arts Cncl 1992–98; chm Diocesan Legislative Ctee 1983–98; pres: Manx Deaf Soc 1975–, IOM Cricket Club 1980–98, IOM Branch Betjeman Soc 2002–; hon memb IOM Law Soc; *Recreations* theatre, watching cricket, reading, gardening; *Style*— His Hon Arthur C Luft, CBE; ✉ Leyton, Victoria Road, Douglas, Isle of Man IM2 6AQ (tel 01624 621048)

LUGTON, (Charles) Michael Arber; s of Charles Ronald Hay Lugton (d 1984), and Elaine Susan, *née* Arber; *b* 5 April 1951; *Educ* St John's Coll Johannesburg, The Edinburgh Acad, Univ of Edinburgh (MA); *m* 1975, (Elizabeth) Joyce, da of late James and Anna Graham; 2 s (Charles b 1980, James b 1984); *Career* Scottish Office: joined 1973, private sec to Perm Under-Sec of State 1976–78, Police Division SHHD 1978–83, Town and Country Planning Division SDD 1983–87, head Public Health Division SHHD 1988–90, head Criminal Justice and Licensing Division SHHD 1990–95, princ private sec to Sec of State for Scotland 1995–97, dir of corp devpt 1998–99; Scottish Exec: head Constitution and Parly Secretariat 1999–2004, head Constitution and Legal Servs Gp 2004–05, chief exec Scottish Law Cmmn 2005–; memb Bd Civil Serv Healthcare 1998–; govr Merchiston Castle Sch 1998–; *Recreations* lawn tennis, contract bridge; *Style*— Michael Lugton, Esq; ✉ Scottish Law Commission, 140 Causewayside, Edinburgh EH9 1PR (tel 0131 668 2131, e-mail michael.lugton@scotlawcom.gov.uk)

LUKE, 3 Baron (UK 1929); Arthur Charles St John Lawson Johnston; s of 2 Baron Luke, KCVO, TD (d 1996), and Barbara, da of Sir Fitzroy Hamilton Anstruther-Gough-Calthorpe, 1 Bt; *b* 13 January 1933; *Educ* Eton, Trinity Coll Cambridge (BA); *m* 1, 6 Aug 1959 (m dis 1971), Silvia Maria, da of Don Honorio Roigt, former Argentine ambass at The Hague; 2 da (Hon Rachel Honoria (Hon Mrs Parrack) b 1960, Hon Sophia Charlotte (Hon Mrs Kirk) b 1966), 1 s (Hon (Ian) James St John Lawson Johnston b 4 Oct 1963); m 2, 1971, Sarah Louise, da of Richard Hearne, OBE; 1 s (Hon Rupert Arthur b 1972); *Heir* s, Hon James Lawson Johnston; *Career* art dealer; co cncllr Beds 1966–70 (chm of Staffing Ctee 1967–70), High Sheriff Beds 1969–70, DL Beds 1989–2005; cdr St John Ambulance Bde Beds 1985–90 (cmmr 1972–85); pres Nat Assoc of Warehouse-Keepers 1960–78; memb Ct: The Drapers Co 1993– (jr warden 1993, 2nd master warden 1999–2000, master 2001–02), Corp of the Sons of the Clergy 1980–2005; sits as Cons House of Lords, oppn whip and spokesman Culture Media and Sport 1997–, for Wales and for defence; *Recreations* shooting, fishing; *Style*— The Lord Luke; ✉ Camross Leys, 46 Main Street, Middleton, Leicestershire LE16 8YU (tel 01536 772129, fax 01536 771198); London: tel 020 7219 3703, fax 020 7219 6069, e-mail lukea@parliament.uk

LUKE, Colin Rochfort; s of Donald Alfred Rochfort Luke, of Jersey, CI, and Mary Blanche, *née* Bennett; *b* 24 January 1946; *Educ* Bristol GS, Exeter Coll Oxford (MA, memb Univ fencing team, pres OU Film Soc, films ed Isis magazine); *m* 1, 1971 (m dis 1976), Sarah Moffat Hellings; m 2, 1978, Hon Felicity Margaret, da of Baron Crowther (Life Peer, d 1972); 2 s (Theodore Rochfort b 1979, Harley Rochfort b 1981), 1 da (Claudia Mary b 1983); *Career* director and producer; BBC: joined as trainee film ed 1967, film and studio dirs course 1969, prodr/dir 1969–79; formed own co Wobbly Pictures Ltd 1977 (renamed Mosaic Pictures Ltd 1989), freelance film dir 1979–, dir Document Films Ltd 1982, formed Document Television Ltd 1987, md Mosaic Films 1996–, formed Mosaic Films LLP 2007; Freeman City of Louisville Kentucky 1963; fndr memb: BAFTA (dep vice-chm TV 1998–99), Dirs Guild of GB; memb: PACT, RTS; *Television* progs for BBC 1969–79: The World About Us, The Romance of the Indian Railways (with James Cameron), A Desert Voyage (with Dame Freya Stark), Albion in the Orient (with Julian Pettifer), Black Safari, Take Six Girls-Israel, Taste for Adventure, Half Million Pound Magic Carpet, Diamonds in the Sky; as freelance dir/prodr: Nature Watch (ATV/TV) 1980, Towards an Unknown Land (with Dame Freya Stark) 1981, The Arabs (Channel 4) 1981, Britain at the Pictures (BBC) 1983, Duneriders (Channel 4) 1985, Heart of the Kremlin (Central/ITV Network) 1991, Will They Ring Tonight (BBC) 1993, A Change of Heart (BBC) 1993, Frontline Vietnam (Channel 4) 1993, The Making of Them (BBC) 1994, Apocalypse Then (BBC) 1994; exec prodr: Assignment Adventure (Channel 4) 1984–85 (winner numerous Adventure Film Awards), A Russia of One's Own (Channel 4) 1987, Frontline Doctors (BBC) 1991, Nomads (Channel 4) 1992, Captain Pedro and the Three Wishes (Channel 4), Ivanov Goes to Moscow (Channel 4) 1997, The Long Weekend (Channel 4) 1998, Return to Wonderland (BBC) 1999, Pakistan Daily (BBC) 2002, The Tube (Carlton) 2003; dir: The Golden Road (TBS) 1986–87, The Baltic Style (TBS) 1987, An Affair in Mind (BBC) 1987–88, The Princess's People (BBC) 1998; series ed: Voyager (Central/ITV Network) 1988–89, The World of National Geographic (Central) 1988–89, Classic Adventure (BBC) 1991–92; series dir Russian Wonderland (BBC) 1995, United Kingdom! (BBC) 1997, Unholy Land (Channel 4) 1998, EUtopia (BBC/Arte, winner Adolf Grimme Special Prize Germany) 2000; as prodr Quality Time (BBC) 1996 (winner of Best Documentary Award Broadcasting Press Guild Awards 1996), Birth of a Salesman (Channel 4) 1996, Think of England (BBC) 1999, The Tube Series 2 (ITV) 2004, The Tube Series 3 (ITV/Sky) 2005, Games in Athens (BBC) 2005; *Recreations* family, travel, cinema, politics; *Clubs* BAFTA; *Style*— Colin Luke, Esq; ✉ Mosaic Films Ltd, 1A Flaxman Court, London W1A 0AU (tel 020 7734 7224, fax 020 7287 4810, e-mail colin@mosaicfilms.com)

LUKE, (William) Ross; s of Maj Hamish Galbraith Russell Luke TD, JP (d 1970), and Ellen Robertson Boyd, *née* Mitchell; *b* 8 October 1943; *Educ* Stowe; *m* 16 May 1970, Deborah Jacqueline, da of Derek John Gordon; 3 da (Alison b 1973 d 1998, Kirstene b 1974, Victoria b 1978); *Career* CA 1968; sr ptnr Luke, Gordon & Co CAs; vice-pres London Scottish RFC 1995– (hon sec 1988–92, hon treas 2006–); Met Police Commendation 1983; *Recreations* rugby football, subaqua diving; *Clubs* Caledonian Soc of London; *Style*— Ross Luke, Esq; ✉ Luke, Gordon & Co (Chartered Accountants), 105 Palewell Park, London SW14 8JJ (tel 020 8876 9228, fax 020 8878 3129)

LUMB, David John; s of George Spencer Lumb (d 1988), and Margaret Minnie, *née* Spencer (d 1995); *b* 25 July 1950; *Educ* Abbeydale GS, Leeds Sch of Architecture (Dip Arch); *m* Judith Margaret, da of James Sewell (m dis 2000); 1 s (Daniel James b 1978), 2 da (Amy Elizabeth b 1980, Rachel Lucy b 1984); *Career* project architect Property Services Agency NE Region 1975–77; Fletcher Ross & Hickling: joined as architect 1977, assoc 1980–86, sr assoc 1986–88; md: Trevor Wilkinson Associates 1989–95 (joined as dir 1988), D Y Davies (York) 1995–96, ML Design Group (Northern) Ltd 1996–2006, Design Group Three Ltd 2003–; dir: ML Design Group Ltd 1996–2003, Modular Architectural Solutions Ltd 2004–; vice-chm RIBA Companies Ltd 1995–97, fell West Yorkshire Soc of Architects 1991– (pres 1997–99); RIBA 1980; *Awards* for Wistow Shaft site: Festival of Architecture Award 1984, Concrete Soc Commendation 1984, Civic Tst Award 1986; White Rose Award (for Riccall and Stillingfleet Shaft sites) 1986, Concrete Soc Commendation (for Doncaster Crown Court) 1990, Craftmanship Award and Commendations (for York Crown Court) 1991; *Recreations* reading newspapers; *Style*— David Lumb, Esq; ✉ Design Group 3 Architects, Studio 12, 46 The Calls, Leeds LS2 7EY (e-mail d.lumb@dg3a.co.uk)

LUMLEY, Henry Robert Lane; s of Edward Lumley (d 1960), and Kathleen Agnew, *née* Wills (d 1978); *b* 29 December 1930; *Educ* Eton, Magdalene Coll Cambridge (MA); *m* 7 Oct 1959, Sheena Ann, da of Air Vice-Marshal Somerled Douglas MacDonald, CB, CBE, DFC (d 1979); 2 s (Peter b 1960, Robert b 1965); 1 da (Julia (Mrs Scott McKay) b 1962); *Career* insurance broker; dir Edward Lumley Holdings Ltd 1974–2003 (chm 1986–99); dir: Edward Lumley & Sons Ltd Lloyd's Brokers 1956–88, Lumley Corporation Ltd Aust 1974–89; chm Lumley Holdings Ltd 2003–07; hon vice-pres Br Insurance Brokers' Assoc 1992– (chm 1990–92), memb Cncl Insurance Brokers' Registration Cncl 1988–95; chm and md Windlesham Golf Management Ltd 1992–; hon fell Magdalene Coll Cambridge 1998; *Clubs* East India, Windlesham Golf; *Style*— Henry Lumley, Esq; ✉ Milton House, Windlesham, Surrey GU20 6PB (tel 01276 472273, fax 01276 451180, e-mail hlumley@tinyonline.co.uk)

LUMLEY, Joanna Lamond (Mrs Stephen Barlow); OBE (1995); da of Maj James Rutherford Lumley, 2/6 Gurkha Rifles, of Cranbrook, Kent and Thyra Beatrice Rose Weir, FRGS; *b* 1 May 1946, Srinagar, India; *Educ* Army Sch Kuala Lumpur, St Mary's Baldslow Sussex; *m* 1, 1970 (m dis 1971), John Jeremy Lloyd; m 2, 23 Oct 1986, Stephen William, s of George William Barlow, of Witham, Essex; 1 s (James b 16 Oct 1967); *Career* actress and comedienne; early career as model, sometime house model Jean Muir; FRGS 1982; *Theatre* incl: Don't Just Lie There Say Something 1971, Private Lives 1981, Noel and Gertie 1983, Hedda Gabler 1984, The Cherry Orchard (Dundee Rep) 1987, Blithe Spirit 1986, An Ideal Husband 1987, The Letter 1995, The Cherry Orchard 2007; *Television* incl: Coronation Street 1960, The New Avengers 1976, Sapphire and Steel 1979, The Glory Boys 1984, Mistral's Daughter 1984, Cluedo 1990, Absolutely Fabulous 1992–2001, Girl Friday 1994, The Tale of Sweeney Todd 1998, Mirrorball 2000, Marple: The Body in the Library 2004, Up in Town 2004, Sensitive Skin 2005 and 2007, Final Chance to Save Orangutans 2005; *Films* incl: On Her Majesty's Secret Service 1968, The Breaking of Bumbo 1970, The Satanic Rites of Dracula 1973, Trail of the Pink Panther 1982, Curse of the Pink Panther 1982, Shirley Valentine 1989, Cold Comfort Farm 1995, James and the Giant Peach 1996, Mad Cows 1999, Maybe Baby 2000, The Cat's Meow 2001, Ella Enchanted 2004, The Magic Roundabout 2005, The Corpse Bride; *Books* Peacocks and Commas (1983), Stare Back and Smile (memoirs, 1989), In the Kingdom of the Thunder Dragon (1992), Forces Sweethearts: Wartime Romance from the First World War to the Gulf (1993), Girl Friday (1994), No Room for Secrets (2004); *Recreations* reading, painting, travelling, collecting junk; *Style*— Miss Joanna Lumley, OBE; ✉ c/o International Creative Management, Oxford House, 76 Oxford Street, London W1N 0AX (tel 020 7636 6565, fax 020 7323 0101)

LUMLEY, John Adrian; s of Thomas Lumley (d 1983), and Patience, *née* Henn Collins (d 1987); *b* 29 May 1942; *Educ* Eton, Magdalene Coll Cambridge (MA); *m* 14 June 1969, Catita, da of Hans Lieb (d 1959), of Algeciras, Spain; 1 s (Joshua b 1970), 2 da (Eliza b 1973, Olivia b 1981); *Career* Christie's (Christie, Manson & Woods Ltd); joined 1964, dir 1969–, jt dep chm 1993–96, jt vice-chm 1996–2004, hon dep chm 2004–; dir Christie's Fine Art Ltd 1998–; memb Kent and E Sussex Regnl Ctee Nat Tst 1981–87; Liveryman Worshipful Co of Goldsmiths 1984; *Clubs* Brooks's; *Style*— John Lumley, Esq; ✉ Stonebridge Barn, Egerton, Ashford, Kent TN27 9AN (tel 01233 756249); Christie's, 8 King Street, London SW1Y 6QT (tel 020 7839 9060)

LUMSDEN, Prof Andrew Gino Sita; s of Edward Gilbert Sita-Lumsden (d 1974), and Stella Pirie Lumsden (d 1980); *b* 22 January 1947; *Educ* Kingswood Sch Bath, St Catherine's Coll Cambridge (scholar, Frank Smart Prize for zoology, BA), Yale Univ (Fulbright scholar), Univ of London (PhD); *m* 21 Nov 1970 (m dis), Anne Farrington, da of Paul Donald Roberg (d 1996); 2 da (Ailsa b 6 Oct 1979, Isobel b 24 Aug 1981); m 2, 2 Feb 2002, Kathleen Marie, da of Roger Wets; *Career* Guy's Hosp Med Sch: jr lectr in anatomy 1970–73, lectr 1973–79, sr lectr 1979–87; prof of developmental neurobiology Univ of London 1989– (reader in craniofacial anatomy 1987–89); int research scholar Howard Hughes Med Inst 1993–98, visiting prof Miller Inst Univ of Calif Berkeley 1994; FRS 1994; *Recreations* natural history, mechanical engineering; *Style*— Prof Andrew Lumsden, FRS; ✉ 16 Elephant Lane, London SE16 4JD; MRC Centre for Developmental Neurobiology, Kings College London, Guy's Hospital, London Bridge, London SE1 1UL (e-mail andrew.lumsden@kcl.ac.uk)

LUMSDEN, Andrew Michael; s of Sir David Lumsden, *qv*, of Soham, Cambs, and Sheila, *née* Daniels; *b* 10 November 1962; *Educ* Winchester (music scholar), RSAMD, St John's Coll Cambridge (organ scholar, MA); *Career* organist; chorister New Coll Oxford, asst to Dr George Guest St John's Coll Cambridge; asst organist Southwark Cathedral 1985–88, sub-organist Westminster Abbey 1988–92 (played for memorial services for Lord Olivier and Dame Peggy Ashcroft and 50th anniversary of Battle of Britain), organist and master of the choristers Lichfield Cathedral 1992–2002, organist and dir of music Winchester Cathedral 2002–; reg broadcaster on BBC radio and television; performances incl: LPO, English Chamber Orch, Busoni's Doktor Faust ENO 1990, recitals at Sydney, San Francisco, Budapest and Harare; recordings labels incl: Argo, Hyperion, Chandos, Virgin Classics, Nimbus; Nat Young Organist of the Year 1985, winner Manchester Int Competition 1986; ARCO 1979; *Recreations* travel, wine, flying; *Style*— Andrew Lumsden, Esq; ✉ Cathedral Office, 1 The Close, Winchester SO23 9LS (tel 01962 857200, fax 01962 857201)

LUMSDEN, Sir David James; kt (1985); s of Albert Lumsden (d 1985), and Vera, *née* Tate (d 1980); *b* 19 March 1928; *Educ* Dame Allan's Sch Newcastle upon Tyne, Selwyn Coll Cambridge (organ scholar, MA, MusB, PhD); *m* 1951, Sheila Gladys, da of George and Gladys Daniels; 2 s (Stephen, Andrew, *qv*), 2 da (Jennifer, Jane); *Career* asst organist St John's Coll Cambridge 1951–53, organist and choirmaster St Mary's Nottingham 1954–56, rector chori Southwell Minster 1956–59, fell and organist New Coll Oxford 1959–76, princ

Royal Scottish Acad of Music and Drama Glasgow 1976–82, Royal Acad of Music London 1982–93 (prof of harmony 1959–61); fndr and conductor Nottingham Bach Soc 1954–59, conductor Oxford Harmonic Soc 1961–63, conductor Oxford Sinfonia 1967–70, choragus Oxford Univ 1968–72, organist Sheldonian Theatre Oxford 1964–76; Hugh Porter lectr Union Theological Seminary NY 1967, visiting prof Yale Univ 1974–75; pres: Incorporated Assoc of Organists 1966–68, Incorporated Soc of Musicians 1984–85, Royal Coll of Organists 1986–88; chm Nat Youth Orchestra 1985–93; hon fell: Selwyn Coll Cambridge 1986, KCL 1990, New Coll Oxford 1996; Hon DLitt Univ of Reading 1991; Liveryman Worshipful Co of Musicians; Hon FRCO 1976, Hon RAM 1978, FRCM 1980, FRNCM 1981, FRSAMD 1982, Hon GSM 1984, FLCM 1985, FRSA 1985, FRSCM 1987, Hon FTCL 1988; *Publications* An Anthology of English Lute Music (1954), Thomas Robinson's Schoole of Musicke, 1603 (1971); *Recreations* hill walking, reading, friends; *Style*— Sir David Lumsden; ✉ 26 Wyke Mark, Dean Lane, Winchester SO22 5DJ (tel 01962 877807, fax 01962 877891, e-mail lumsdendj@aol.com)

LUMSDEN, Edward Gabriel Marr; s of Edward Gabriel Lumsden, of Ferndown, Dorset, and Isobel, *née* Dyker; *b* 4 July 1946; *Educ* Hampton GS, Westminster Hotel Sch (Nat Dip Hotelkeeping and Catering); *m* 2 Sept 2000, Linda Mary Bachari; *Career* area mangr Truman Taverns 1980–81, dir and gen mangr Arden Taverns 1981–83, tied trade dir Drybroughs of Scotland 1983–86, innkeeper dir Truman Ltd 1986, innkeeper ops dir Watney Co Reid & Truman 1986–88, innkeeper dir Watney Truman 1989–91, md TW Guest Trust Ltd 1991–95, conslt to hospitality industry 1995–96 and 2003–; SFI Group plc: dir of ops 1996–98, dir of property 1998–2003; conslt to hospitality industry 2003–; memb Mensa; FHCIMA, FCFA, FRSH, FCMI, FBII, FInstD; *Recreations* travel, gastronomy, vintage motor cars, bridge; *Clubs* Caledonian, Rugby Club of London; *Style*— Edward Lumsden, Esq; ✉ The Drill House, 46 Acreman Street, Sherborne, Dorset DT9 3NX (tel 01935 389140)

LUMSDEN, Ian George; s of James Alexander Lumsden, MBE, of Bannachra, by Helensburgh, Dunbartonshire, and Sheila, *née* Cross; *b* 19 March 1951; *Educ* Rugby, Corpus Christi Coll Cambridge (BA), Univ of Edinburgh (LLB); *m* 22 April 1978, Mary Ann, da of Maj Dr John William Stewart Welbon, of Cornwall; 1 s (Richard b 1984), 2 da (Sarah b 1986, Louise b 1989); *Career* ptnr Maclay Murray and Spens 1980– (trainee and asst slr 1974–78), asst slr Slaughter and May London 1978–80; memb: Law Soc of Scotland, Royal Faculty of Procurators; *Recreations* golf, shooting; *Clubs* New (Edinburgh), Prestwick Golf; *Style*— Ian Lumsden, Esq; ✉ The Myretoun, Menstrie, Clackmannanshire FK11 7EB (tel 01259 761453); Maclay Murray and Spens, 3 Glenfinlas Street, Edinburgh EH3 6AQ (tel 0131 226 5196, fax 0131 226 3174, e-mail ian.lumsden@mms.co.uk)

LUMSDEN, Prof Keith Grant; s of Robert Sclater Lumsden (d 1964), of Bathgate, and Elizabeth, *née* Brow (d 1990); *b* 7 January 1935; *Educ* The Acad Bathgate, Univ of Edinburgh (MA), Stanford Univ (PhD); *m* 21 July 1961, Jean Baillie, da of Capt Kenneth Macdonald, MC (d 1962), of Armadale; 1 s (Robert Alistair Macdonald b 1964); *Career* Stanford Univ: instr Dept of Econs 1960–63, assoc prof Graduate Sch of Business 1968–75 (asst prof 1964–67), prof of econs Advanced Mgmnt Coll 1971–90; currently affiliate prof of econs INSEAD France and dir Edinburgh Business Sch; res assoc Stanford Res Inst 1965–71, visiting prof of econs Heriot-Watt Univ 1969, academic dir Sea Tport Exec Programme 1984–96; dir: Stanford Univ Conf RREE 1968, Econ Educn Project 1969–74, Behavioral Res Laboratories 1970–72, Capital Preservation Fund Inc 1971–75, Nielsen Engineering Research Inc 1972–75, Hewlett-Packard Ltd 1981–92; memb: American Econ Assoc Ctee on Econ Educn 1978–81, Advsy Cncl David Hume Inst 1984–99; numerous articles in professional jls, creator of various software systems; Henry Villard Award 1994; FRSE 1992; *Books* The Free Enterprise System (1963), The Gross National Product (1964), International Trade (1965), New Developments in the Teaching of Economics, 1967), Microeconomics - A Programmed Book (with R E Attiyeh and G L Bach, new edn 1981), Economics - A Distance Learning Study Programme (1991); *Recreations* tennis, deep sea sports fishing; *Clubs* New (Edinburgh), Waverley Lawn Tennis, Squash, and Sports, Tantallon Golf; *Style*— Prof Keith Lumsden, FRSE; ✉ 40 Lauder Road, Edinburgh EH9 1UE (tel 0131 667 1612); Edinburgh Business School, Heriot-Watt University, Riccarton, Edinburgh EH14 4AS (tel 0131 451 3090, fax 0131 451 3002)

LUMSDEN OF CUSHNIE, David Gordon Allen d'Aldecamb; Representer of the Feudal Baronial House of Lumsden of Cushnie (Co of Aberdeen); s of Maj Henry Gordon Strange Lumsden, The Royal Scots (d 1969), of Nocton Hall, Lincs, and Sydney Mary Elliott (d 1985), of Tertain, Co Carlow; *b* 25 May 1933; *Educ* Seafield Park, Allhallows, Bedford Sch, Jesus Coll Cambridge (MA); *Career* London Scottish TA; exec Br American Tobacco 1959–82 (served Africa, India, E Europe and Far East); Garioch Pursuivant of Arms 1986; dir: Heritage Porcelain Ltd, Heritage Recordings Ltd; co fndr: Castles of Scotland Preservation Tst 1985, Scot Historic Organs Tst 1991; pres 1745 Assoc and Scot Military History Soc 1991, memb Cncl The Royal Stuart Soc; convenor Monarchist League of Scotland 1993, chllr Order of the Crown of Stuart 1989–; patron Aboyne Highland Games 1998–; memb Lloyd's 1985–2001; Freeman City of London 2006, Liveryman Worshipful Co of Spectacle Makers 2006; FSA Scot 1984; Knight of Justice Sacred Military Constantinian Order of St George 1978, Knight of Honour and Devotion SMOM 1980, Knight Mozarabe of Toledo 1980, Knight Order of St Maurice and St Lazarus 1999; *Books* The Muster Roll of Prince Charles Edward's Army 1745–46 (contrib, 1984); *Recreations* polo, rowing, sailing, architectural history, Scottish history, heraldry; *Clubs* Royal Northern & Univ (Aberdeen), Beefsteak (Sublime Society), Pitt (Cambridge), Hawks' (Cambridge), Leander, Hidalgos (Madrid), Puffin's (Edinburgh), Scottish Arts (Edinburgh); *Style*— David Lumsden of Cushnie, Garioch Pursuivant of Arms; ✉ Hamilton House, West Loan, Prestonpans, East Lothian EH32 9JY (tel and fax 01875 813681, e-mail lumcush@hotmail.com)

LUMSDEN OF THAT ILK AND BLANERNE, Patrick Gillem Sandys; s of Colin Cren Sandys-Lumsdaine (d 1967), of Scotland, and Joyce Dorothy, *née* Leeson (d 2000); formerly Patrick Gillem Sandys Lumsdaine of Innergellie but recognised as Chief of the Name and Arms of Lumsden by Interlocutor of the Lord Lyon King of Arms 27 March 1985; *b* 15 October 1938; *Educ* Charterhouse; *m* 1966, Beverley June, da of Capt Ralph Ernest Shorter (d 1982); 2 s (Cren Lumsden Yr of that Ilk b 1968, James Ralph, now Sandys Lumsdaine of Innergellie b 1976), 1 da (Amy Patricia b 1969); *Career* East India merchant; dir: George Williamson & Co Ltd 1977–98, George Williamson (Assam) Ltd 1978–98, Williamson Magor & Co Ltd 1982–98, Williamson Tea Holdings plc 1989–98; *Recreations* golf; *Clubs* Oriental, Tollygunge; *Style*— Lumsden of that Ilk and Blanerne; ✉ Stapeley House, Hoe Benham, Newbury, Berkshire RG20 8PX (tel 01488 608700)

LUNA, HE Ricardo V; s of Ricardo Luna, and Victoria Mendoza; *b* 19 November 1940; *Educ* Princeton Univ (BA, Dip), Columbia Univ NY (MA), Peruvian Diplomatic Acad; *m* 1969, Margarita Proaño; 1 da (Margarita); *Career* diplomat; third sec rising to ambass London, Tel-Aviv, Geneva, Washington DC, Paris, Quito and NY 1966–86, undersec of multi-lateral affrs Lima and coordinator Contadora-Apoyo and Rio gps 1987–89; ambass to: UN NY 1989–92, USA 1992–99, Ct of St James's 2006– (concurrently ambass to Repub of Ireland); advsr to Peruvian Finance Min for Int Affrs 2004; fell Centre for Int Affairs Harvard Univ 1980–81, Weinberg visiting prof of foreign affrs Princeton Univ 2000–01, Tinker visiting prof of foreign affrs Columbia Univ 2002, prof of int affrs Govt Inst San Martín de Porres Univ 2003, Cogut visiting prof of int affrs Brown Univ 2005, visiting prof of int affrs and coordinator of Latin American area Tufts Univ 2005–06, fell Inst of Politics Harvard Univ 2006; Order de Mayo (Argentina), Order Rio Branco (Brazil), Pan American Order (Panamerican Fndn); *Clubs* Colonial (Princeton), Phoenix (Lima), Univ (Washington DC), Cosmos (Washington DC), Harvard Club of NYC, Athenaeum, Travellers, Naval and Military, Sloane; *Style*— HE Mr Ricardo V Luna; ✉ The Embassy of Peru, 52 Sloane Street, London SW1X 9SP (tel 020 7235 1917 and 020 7235 2545, fax 020 7235 4463)

LUNAN, Dr (Charles) Burnett; s of Andrew Burnett Lunan (d 1999), and Jean Clarke, *née* Orr (d 2002); *b* 28 September 1941; *Educ* Glasgow HS, Univ of Glasgow (MB ChB, MD); *m* 6 March 1973, Helen Russell, da of John Ferrie (d 1963); 1 da (Kirsteen Burnett b 1974), 2 s (Robert Ferrie b 1977, Donald John b 1979); *Career* lectr in obstetrics and gynaecology Univ of Aberdeen 1973–75, sr lectr in obstetrics and gynaecology Univ of Nairobi Kenya 1975–77, conslt in obstetrics and gynaecology Royal Infirmary and Royal Maternity Hosp Glasgow 1977–, WHO conslt in maternal and child health Bangladesh 1984–85 and 1988–89; pres Royal Medico-Chirurgical Soc of Glasgow 1991–92 (treas 1982–90, vice-pres 1990–91), pres Glasgow Obstetrical and Gynaecological Soc 2002–04 (sec 1978–82, vice-pres 1998–2002); FRCOG 1983 (MRCOG 1970), FRCS 1985; *Recreations* gardening, photography, hill walking; *Style*— Dr Burnett Lunan; ✉ 1 Moncrieff Avenue, Lenzie, Glasgow (tel 0141 776 3227); Princess Royal Maternity Hospital, Alexandra Parade, Glasgow (tel 0141 211 5400)

LUND, Bryan; s of Capt Clifford Lund (d 1989), and Vera, *née* Miller (d 1975); *b* 15 April 1938; *Educ* Royal Liberty GS Havering; *m* 18 April 1964, Diana, da of Ernest Wilshaw (d 1986); 2 s (Mark b 1965, Paul b 1968), 1 da (Deborah b 1975); *Career* articled chartered accountant Hill Vellacott and Co 1954–59, Peat Marwick Cassleton Elliott 1960–62, gp audit mangr Touche Ross 1963–67, fin dir Norcros plc subsidiaries 1967–73, Euro fin dir Morton Thiokol Incorporated Chicago 1973–82; gp fin dir: Borthwicks plc 1982–87, Wonderworld plc 1987–98; mgmnt conslt; independent memb Herts Police Authy 1995–2003, chm Watford Police Community Partnership 1997–2003, non-exec dir Mount Vernon and Watford NHS Tst 1998–2000, chm 3 Rivers Community Safety Forum 1999–2003, chm Herts Home Safety and Secuirty Serv 2002–; Freeman: City of London 1982, Worshipful Co of CAs 1982, Worshipful Co of Butchers 1984; FCA 1960; *Recreations* golf, motoring; *Clubs* Northwood Golf, High Performance; *Style*— Bryan Lund, Esq; ✉ Maddox, Nightingale Road, Rickmansworth, Hertfordshire WD3 7DA (e-mail bryanlund@supanet.com)

LUND, Dr Charles Ames; s of (Henry) Charles Lund (d 1980), of Bebington, Cheshire, and (Sophia) Violet Iris, *née* Ames (d 1976); *b* 18 August 1942; *Educ* Birkenhead Sch, Univ of Liverpool (MB ChB), Univ of Aberdeen (Dip Psychotherapy); *m* 14 Feb 1968, Pauline, da of Arthur Morris Hunter, of Ponteland, Newcastle upon Tyne; 2 da (Sonia b 1969, Kathryn b 1974); *Career* SHO and registrar in psychiatry Sefton Gen Hosp Liverpool 1968–71 (house offr 1967–68), sr registrar in psychiatry Royal Southern Hosp Liverpool 1971–72; Univ of Aberdeen: Rowntree fell in psychotherapy 1972–73, lectr Mental Health Dept 1973–78; conslt psychotherapist Newcastle upon Tyne 1978–2000, dir of Newcastle Psychotherapy Course 1984–89, examiner for Membership Examination of RCPsych 1990–95; author of pubns in psychotherapy trg, gp therapy and visual representation; memb BMA; FRCPsych 1987 (MRCPsych 1972); *Recreations* walking, gardening; *Style*— Dr Charles Lund; ✉ 92 Errington Road, Darras Hall, Ponteland, Newcastle upon Tyne NE20 9LA (tel 01661 872018, e-mail charles@cplund.freeserve.co.uk)

L

LUND, Nicky; da of John Peter Lund, and Olive Kathleen, *née* Miles; *Educ* Bournemouth Sch for Girls, UEA (BA); *Career* TV prodr, head of devpt and script ed Mark Forstater Productions Ltd 1984–94 (credits incl Grushko (BBC) and Shalom Joan Collins (Channel 4)), film and TV agent David Higham Associates 1994– (dir 2003–); LWT/Broadcast First Timers Award 1990; *Recreations* travel, Latin American dancing, Italy; *Style*— Ms Nicky Lund; ✉ David Higham Associates Ltd, 5–8 Lower John Street, London W1F 9HA (tel 020 7434 5900, fax 020 7437 1072)

LUND, Prof Raymond Douglas; s of Henry Douglas Lund, and Rose, *née* Morgan; *b* 10 February 1940; *Educ* Bablake Sch Coventry, UCL (Bucknill scholar, BSc, PhD); *m* 1963, Jennifer Sylvia, da of Meredith W Hawes; 2 s (Benjamin Isambard b 3 Jan 1971, Simon Meredith b 26 July 1974); *Career* asst lectr then lectr Dept of Anatomy UCL 1963–66, res asst anatomy Univ of Pennsylvania 1966–67, asst prof of anatomy Stanford Univ Calif 1967–68, asst prof then prof of anatomy and neurosurgery Univ of Washington 1968–79, prof and head Dept of Anatomy Med Univ of S Carolina 1979–83, prof and head Dept of Neurobiology, Anatomy and Cell Science Univ of Pittsburgh 1983–91, prof and head Dept of Anatomy Univ of Cambridge 1992–95, Duke-Elder prof of ophthalmology Inst of Ophthalmology 1995–2000, prof and dir of research Department of Ophthalmology and Visual Sciences University of Utah Health Sciences Center 2000–; memb Scientific Advsy Bd Fndn Fighting Blindness; memb: Soc for Neuroscience 1970–, Assoc for Res in Vision and Ophthalmology 1983–; Herrick award American Assoc of Anatomists, MERIT award NIH; fell Clare Coll Cambridge 1992–95; FRS, FMedSci 1998; *Books* Development and Plasticity of the Brain (1978); author/co-author of more than 400 papers, books, book chapters, and abstracts; *Recreations* chamber music (LRAM); *Style*— Prof Raymond Lund, FRS; ✉ Department of Ophthalmology and Visual Sciences, Moran Eye Center, University of Utah Health Sciences Center, 75 North Medical Drive, Salt Lake City, UT 84132, USA

LUND, Prof Valerie Joan; da of George Andrew Lund, and Joan, *née* Henry (d 1984); *b* 9 May 1953; *Educ* Charing Cross Hosp Med Sch London (MB BS, MRCS LRCP), Univ of London (MS); *Career* hon conslt: Royal Nat Throat Nose and Ear Hosp 1987–, Moorfields Eye Hosp 1990–, Univ Coll Hosp 2004–; Inst of Laryngology and Otology: lectr in rhinology 1986–87, sr lectr 1987–93, reader 1993–95, prof 1995–; memb working parties: Int Consensus in Sinusitis 1993, Int Consensus in Rhinitis 1993–94, RCSEd Guidelines in Endoscopic Nasal Surgery 1993, RCS Working Pty on Minimal Access Therapy 1993, WHO - Mgmnt of Rhinitis 2000, EAACI Taskforce on Rhinosinusitis; co-chm EPOS 2005 and 2007; asst ed Jl of Laryngology and Otology, ed Rhinology; memb Editorial Bd: American Jl of Rhinology, Laryngoscope; Downs surgical travelling fell RSM 1985; European Rhinologic Soc: Special Prize 1986, Award of Merit 1996, Award of Excellence 1998; Lionel Colledge fell RCS 1986, Br Academic Conf in Otolaryngology Scientific Exhbn Award 1987, George Davey Howell Meml Prize 1990; McBride lectr Edinburgh 1993, Sir Arthur Sims travelling prof 2002, Guthrie lectr 2006, Leegaard lectr 2006, Bradshaw lectr 2006; memb: BMA, RSM, European Rhinologic Soc (treas 1992, UK rep 2000), Head and Neck Oncologists of GB, Euro Acad of Facial and Plastic Surgery (vice-pres UK 1993), Otorhinolaryngological Research Soc, Br Assoc of Otolaryngologists, Collegium ORLAS 1990, American Rhinologic Soc 1992, American Triologic Soc 1993; fell German ORL (Otorhinolaryngology) / HNS (Head and Neck Surgery) Soc 1999; FRCS 1982 (memb Cncl 1994, chm Educn Bd 1999 and 2002), FRCSEd 1993; *Books* Clinical Rhinology (with A Maran, 1990), Tumours of the Upper Jaw (with D F N Harrison, 1993), Nasal Polyps (with G Settipane 1997), Minimally Invasive Endonasal Sinus Surgery (with W G Hoseman, R K Weber and Keerl Rainer, 1999), Investigative Rhinology (with G Scadding, 2004); *Recreations* cooking and eating; *Style*— Prof Valerie Lund; ✉ Institute of Laryngology and Otology, 330 Gray's Inn Road, London WC1X 8DA (tel 020 7915 1497, fax 020 7833 9480, e-mail v.lund@ucl.ac.uk)

LUNGHI, Cherie Mary; da of Allessandro Lunghi (d 1989), of London, and Gladys Corbett Lee (d 1996); *b* 4 April 1952; *Educ* Arts Educn Trust London, Central Sch of Speech and Drama; former partner, Roland Joffé, *qv*; 1 da (Nathalie-Kathleen Lunghi-Joffé b 26 Aug 1986); *Career* actress; *Theatre* Irena in The Three Sisters and Lisa in Owners (Newcastle)

1973–74, Kate Hardcastle in She Stoops to Conquer (Nottingham Playhouse) 1974, Laura in Teeth'n'Smiles (Royal Court) 1975, Holiday (Old Vic) 1987, Ruth in The Homecoming (Comedy Theatre) 1991; RSC 1976–80: Hero in Much Ado About Nothing, Perdita in The Winter's Tale, Cordelia in King Lear, Destiny, Bandits, Celia in As You Like It, Saratoga, Viola in Twelfth Night; National Theatre London: Arcadia, Uncle Vanya; Piscasso's Women (Ambassadors Theatre Gp) 2002; *Television* incl: The Misanthrope (BBC) 1978, 'Tis Pity She's a Whore (BBC) 1979, The Manhood of Edward Robinson (Thames) 1981, The Praying Mantis (Channel 4) 1982, Desert of Lies (BBC) 1983, Huis Clos (BBC) 1984, Much Ado About Nothing (BBC) 1984, Letters From an Unknown Lover (Channel 4) 1985, The Monocled Mutineer (BBC) 1985, The Lady's Not For Burning (Thames) 1987, The Manageress (Channel 4) 1988 and 1989, Put on by Cunning (TVS) 1990, Covington Cross (Reeves Entertainment and ABC TV), The Buccaneers (BBC), Hornblower 1999, David Copperfield 1999, A Likeness in Stone 1999, The Brief 2004; TV mini series: Master of the Game (US) 1983, Ellis Island (US) 1984, The Man Who Lived at The Ritz (US) 1988, The Strauss Dynasty (Austria) 1990, Little White Lies (BBC), Maloney (CBS TV), Guests of the Emperor (ABC TV), The Canterville Ghost (NBC TV), Master of the Game (CBS TV), Oliver Twist (CBS TV); *Radio* Alice in Alice in Wonderland (BBC) 1965, Hedvig in The Wild Duck (BBC) 1965; *Films* Excalibur 1980, King David 1984, The Mission 1985, To Kill A Priest 1987, Jack and Sarah 1995, Frankenstein 1995; *Recreations* drawing and painting, going to the cinema and theatre, reading, walking, mothering; *Style*— Miss Cherie Lunghi

LUNN, (George) Michael; s of John Lunn (d 1969), of Edinburgh, and May, *née* Hope (d 1971); *b* 22 July 1942; *Educ* Kelvinside Acad Glasgow, Univ of Glasgow (BSc), Heriot-Watt Univ (Dip Brewing); *m* 27 Aug 1971, Jennifer, da of John Burgoyne, of Glasgow; 3 s (Stuart b 17 Jan 1974, Jamie b 27 July 1978, Alexander b 18 March 1981); 1 da (Victoria b 11 Jan 1976); *Career* Lt RNR 1956–66; chm and chief exec The Whyte & Mackay Gp plc until 1995, dir Gallaher Ltd until 1995; dir Montrose Estates (1993) Ltd; chm: Wm Muir Ltd until 1995, Invergordon Distillers until 1995, Michael Lunn Assocs Ltd 1995–, The Unwins Wine Gp Ltd until 2005; former dir Cncl Scotch Whisky Assoc; former chm Glasgow Devpt Agency; memb: Inst of Brewing, Lord's Taverners, Keepers of the Quaich, Assoc of Business Recovery Professionals; fell Soc of Turnaround Professionals; *Recreations* golf; *Clubs* IOD, R&A Golf, Glasgow Golf, New (Edinburgh), Buchanan Castle Golf; *Style*— Michael Lunn, Esq; ✉ Michael Lunn Associates Ltd, Fairmount, 17 Ledcameroch Road, Bearsden, Glasgow G61 4AB (tel 0141 931 5566, fax/data coms 0141 931 5577, e-mail me@michaellunnassociates.com)

LUNN-ROCKLIFFE, Victor Paul; s of Col W P Lunn-Rockliffe, DSO, MC (d 1994), and J A, *née* Jequier; *b* 5 December 1948; *Educ* Keele Univ (BA); *m* 1971, Felicity Ann, *née* O'Neill; 2 da (Katherine, Sophie); *Career* ECGD: joined 1973, dir Project Underwriting Middle East and North Africa 1987, dir Risk Mgmnt Dept 1989–94, dir Claims Dept 1994–95, gp dir Asset Mgmnt 1995–; *Recreations* drawing, painting, walking, ballet; *Style*— Victor Paul Lunn-Rockliffe, Esq; ✉ ECGD, PO Box 2200, 2 Exchange Tower, Harbour Exchange Square, London E14 9GS (tel 020 7512 7008, fax 020 7512 7400)

LUNT, Her Hon Judge Beverly Anne; da of Thomas Gordon Lunt (d 2007), of Huxley, Chester, and Mary, *née* Duff; *b* 8 March 1954, Rochester; *Educ* Oxford Poly (BA); *Career* called to the Bar Gray's Inn 1977; recorder 2000–04, circuit judge 2004– (currently sitting at Burnley and Preston Crown Courts); *Recreations* reading, theatre, cinema, entertaining, walking, supporting animal charities (RSPCA, WSPA, Battersea Dogs Home, Dogs Trust); *Style*— Her Hon Judge Lunt; ✉ Burnley Crown Court, Hammerton Street, Burnley BB11 1XD (tel 01282 416899)

LUNT, Prof Ingrid Cecilia; da of Canon Ronald Lunt (d 1994), and Veslemøy, *née* Sopp Foss; *b* 16 May 1947; *Educ* King Edward VI HS for Girls, St Hugh's Coll Oxford (scholar, MA), UCL (MSc), Inst of Educn Univ of London (PhD); *m* 11 March 1989, His Hon Judge Julian Hall, *qv*; *Career* teacher Wanstead HS London 1973–78, professional educnl psychologist Inner London Schs' Psychological Serv 1979–85; Inst of Educn Univ of London: lectr 1981–91, sr lectr 1991–96, reader in educnl psychology 1996–2000, asst dean of research 1998–2002, appointed prof of educnl psychology 2001, dean of doctoral sch 2002–05; sr research fell and prof Univ of Oxford 2005–; affiliate: American Psychological Assoc, American Educnl Research Assoc; vice-pres Int Union of Psych Science 2004– (memb Exec Ctee 2000–); memb Editorial Bds: Psychology Teaching Review, Euro Psychologist; memb: Assoc of Child Psychology and Psychiatry, Int Assoc of Applied Psychology (memb Exec Ctee), BERA, Euro Educnl Research Assoc, Euro Fedn of Professional Psychologists' Assocs (memb Exec Cncl 1990–99, pres 1993–97 and 1997–99); hon life memb Psychological Soc of South Africa; CPsychol, FBPsS (memb and chair Cncl, pres 1998–99), FRSA, AcSS; *Books* incl: Child Development: a first course (with K Sylva, 1982), Cognitive Development (contrib, 1983), Charting the Agenda: educational activity after Vygotsky (contrib, 1993), Working Together: inter-school collaboration for special needs (jtly, 1994), Professional Psychology in Europe: the state of the art (contrib, 1995), Psychology and Education for Special Needs: current developments and future directions (jt ed, 1995), Values in Special Education (contrib, 1997), A Century of Psychology. progress, paradigms and prospects for the new millennium (contrib, 1997); *Recreations* playing music (viola, piano, flute), walking and cross-country skiing, opera, gardening; *Style*— Prof Ingrid Lunt; ✉ Department of Educational Studies, University of Oxford, 15 Norham Gardens, Oxford OX2 6PY (tel 01865 274024, fax 01865 274027)

LUPTON, James Roger Crompton; s of Alec William Lupton (d 1999), and Margaret Crompton Lupton; *b* 15 June 1955; *Educ* Sedbergh, Lincoln Coll Oxford (MA); *m* 23 July 1983, Béatrice Marie-Françoise, *née* Delaunay; 3 da (Annabelle, Victoria, Camilla), 1 s (Sam); *Career* admitted slr 1979; Lovell White & King 1977–79, S G Warburg & Co 1979–80; Baring Brothers & Co Ltd: joined 1980, dir 1986–98, dep chm Baring Brothers Int Ltd 1996–98; md Greenhill & Co Int 1998–; chm Dulwich Picture Gallery; memb Law Soc; *Recreations* opera, visual arts, shooting, skiing; *Clubs* Brooks's; *Style*— James Lupton, Esq; ✉ Greenhill & Co International, Lansdowne House, 57 Berkeley Square, London W1J 6ER (tel 020 7198 7400, fax 020 7198 7501, e-mail jlupton@greenhill.com)

LUPU, Radu; s of Meyer Lupu, and Ana, *née* Gabor; *b* 30 November 1945; *Educ* High Sch Brasov Romania, Moscow Conservatoire; *Career* concert pianist; London debut 1969, Berlin debut 1971, USA debut NY 1972; first prize: Van Cliburn Competition 1966, Enescu Competition 1967, Leeds Competition 1969; Abbiati Prize 1989, Premio Internazionale Arturo Benedetti Michalangeli 2006; *Recordings* incl: Beethoven Piano Concertos (with Zubin Mehta and the Israel Philharmonic Orch), Mozart Sonatas for Violin and Piano (with Szymon Goldberg), Brahms Piano Concerto No 1 (with Edo de Waart and the London Philharmonic Orch), Mozart Piano Concerto K467 (with Uri Segal and the Eng Chamber Orch), various Beethoven and Schubert Sonatas (incl B Flat Sonata D960, Grammy Award 1995), Mozart and Beethoven Wind Quintets in E Flat, Mozart Concerto for 2 Pianos and Concerto for 3 Pianos transcribed for 2 pianos (with Murray Perahia and the Eng Chamber Orch), Schubert Fantasie in F Minor and Mozart Sonata in D for 2 Pianos (with Murray Perahia), Schubert Piano Duets (with Daniel Barenboim), two disks of Schubert Lieder (with Barbara Hendricks), Schumann Kinderszenen, Kreisleriana and Humoresque (Edison Award 1996); *Recreations* chess, bridge, history; *Style*— Radu Lupu, Esq; ✉ c/o Terry Harrison Artists Management, The Orchard, Market Street, Charlbury, Oxfordshire OX7 3PJ (tel 01608 810330, fax 01608 811331, e-mail artists@harrisonturner.co.uk, website www.harrisonturner.co.uk)

LUQMAN, Shaid; s of Mohammed Luqman, of Hale, Cheshire, and Sharifan Bibi; *b* 15 November 1968, Pakistan; *m* 9 June 2002, Sofia; 1 da (Imaan Isha b 26 June 2003); *Career* Citibank 1991–94, Parkfield Properties 1994–97, KG Properties 1997–2000, Pearl Holdings Europe Ltd (now Lexi Holdings plc) 2000–; Ernst & Young Entrepreneur of the Year 2004; *Recreations* golf, badminton, flying; *Style*— Shaid Luqman, Esq; ✉ Apartment 2, 3 Belgrave Place, Belgravia, London SW1X 8BU (tel 020 7493 1777, fax 020 7493 6777); Lexi Holdings plc, 43 Grosvenor Street, Mayfair, London W1K 3HL (e-mail shaid.l@lexiholdings.co.uk)

LUSBY, John Martin; s of William Henry Lusby (d 1990), of Hull, and Florence Mary, *née* Wharam; *b* 27 April 1943; *Educ* Marist Coll Hull, Ushaw Coll Durham, Maryvale Inst Birmingham (DipTheol), Open Univ (MA); *m* 1966, (Mary) Clare, da of John Gargan (d 1957), of York; 1 s (James b 3 Sept 1969), 1 da (Sophie b 30 July 1973); *Career* entered NHS 1961; jr appointments: De la Pole Hosp Hull 1961–66, County Hosp York 1966–67, Kettering Gen Hosp 1967–68; admin asst United Sheffield Hosps 1968–70, dep hosp sec E Birmingham Hosp 1970–72, hosp sec Pontefract Gen Infirmary and Headlands Hosp Pontefract 1972–74, area gen admin Kirklees AHA 1974–76; Merton, Sutton and Wandsworth AHA(T): asst dist admin (Patient Servs) 1976–79, dist admin Wandsworth and E Merton Dist 1979–81; area admin Doncaster AHA 1981; Doncaster HA: dist admin 1981–84, dist gen mangr 1984–90, exec dir 1990; Lothian Health Bd: gen mangr 1990–95, exec dir 1991–95 (memb 1990–91); chm Independent Review Panel NHS Complaints Procedure Northern and Yorkshire Region NHS Exec 1996–97; adjudicator (panel memb) Tbnls Serv Criminal Injuries Compensation Appeals Panel 1997–; tstee: Dementia Servs Devpt Centre Univ of Stirling 1991–95, The Scottish Dementia Appeal Tst 1994–95; memb: Scottish Cncl for Postgrad Med and Dental Educn 1992–95, Health Servs and Public Health Res Ctee (Scottish Office Home and Health Dept Chief Scientist Orgn) 1993–94, Scottish Implementation Gp Jr Doctors and Dentists' Hours of Work 1993–95, Jt Working Gp on Information Services NHS Scotland 1993–95, Catholic Theological Assoc of GB 1997–, Catholic Biblical Assoc of Great Britain 1998–, Catholic Inst for Int Relations 1999–2004, Soc for the Study of Theology 2000–, European Soc for Catholic Theology 2004–; DipHSM 1972, MHSM (AHA 1972); *Recreations* music, reading, travel, the study of theology; *Clubs* Middlesex CC; *Style*— John Lusby, Esq; ✉ Flat A, Copper Beech, 31 North Grove, London N6 4SJ (tel 020 8341 3426, mobile 07941 678056, e-mail john.lusby@btinternet.com)

LUSCOMBE, Prof David Edward; s of Edward Dominic Luscombe (d 1987), of London, and Nora, *née* Cowell (d 1995); *b* 22 July 1938; *Educ* Finchley Catholic GS, King's Coll Cambridge (MA, PhD, LittD); *m* 20 Aug 1960, Megan, da of John Richard Phillips (d 1967); 3 s (Nicholas b 1962, Mark b 1964, Philip b 1968), 1 da (Amanda b 1970); *Career* fell King's Coll Cambridge 1962–64, fell, lectr and dir of studies in history Churchill Coll Cambridge 1964–72; Univ of Sheffield: prof of medieval history 1972–95, Leverhulme personal research prof of medieval history 1995–2000, res prof of medieval history 2000–03, head Dept of History 1973–76 and 1979–84, dean of Faculty of Arts 1985–87, pro-vice-chllr 1990–94, chm Humanities Research Inst 1992–2003, dir of research Humanities Div 1994–2003; visiting prof: Royal Soc of Canada 1991, Univ of Connecticut at Storrs 1993, Japan Acad 1996; Leverhulme visiting European fell 1973, visiting fell All Souls Coll Oxford 1994; auditor Div of Quality Audit HE Quality Cncl 1994–95; pres Société Int L'Etude de la Philosophie Médiévale 1997–2002 (vice-pres 1987–97); hon sec Cambridge Univ Catholic Assoc 1968–70; memb: Governing Body St Edmund's House Cambridge 1971–84, Ctee Ecclesiastical History Soc 1976–79, Cncl Royal Historical Soc 1981–85, Ctee Soc for the Study of Medieval Languages and Literature 1991–96, Jt Supervisory Ctee of Br Acad and OUP for New Dictionary of Nat Biography 1992–99, Cwlth Scholarship Cmmn 1994–2000, Cncl Worksop Coll and Ranby House 1996–; British Acad: Raleigh lectr 1988, memb Cncl 1989–97, pubns sec 1990–97, chm Medieval Texts Editorial Ctee British Acad 1991–2004, memb Humanities Research Bd 1994–96; gen ed Cambridge Studies in Medieval Life and Thought 1988–2004 (advsy ed 1983–88); FRHistS 1970, FSA 1984, FBA 1986; *Books* The School of Peter Abelard (1969), Peter Abelard's Ethics (1971), David Knowles Remembered (jtly, 1991), Medieval Thought (1997, Portuguese translation 2000), The Twelfth Century Renaissance: Monks, Scholars and the Shaping of the European Mind (in Japanese, 2000); co-ed: Church and Government in the Middle Ages (1976), Petrus Abaelardus 1079–1142 (1980), D Knowles, The Evolution of Medieval Thought (1988), Anselm: Aosta, Bec and Canterbury (1996), The New Cambridge Medieval History Vol IV c1024–c1198 pt 1 and 2 (2004), Expositio in Hexameron (2004), Sententie Magistri Petri Abaelardi (2006); author of various articles and chapters in learned jls and books; *Recreations* grandchildren, using libraries, walking; *Style*— Prof David Luscombe, FBA; ✉ Department of History, The University, Sheffield S10 2TN (tel 0114 222 2559)

LUSH, David Michael; OBE (1992); s of Hyman Lush (d 1979), of London, and Bessie, *née* Tabor (d 1989); *b* 6 February 1931; *Educ* Poly Secdy Sch (Quintin Sch), Univ of London (BSc); *m* 29 March 1962, Brenda Straus, da of Bernard Pappe (d 1946); 1 s (Dean Anthony b 18 Sept 1964); *Career* conslt electrical engr; Nat Serv RAOC 1950–51; grad trainee Micanite and Insulators Co Ltd 1956–58, sr project engr Heating Investments Ltd 1958–60, sr sales engr then asst branch mangr (London and SE Regnl Office) Satchwell Control Systems Ltd 1961–69; Arup Associates/Ove Arup and Partners: specialist engr on M & E design problems 1970–79, tech dir Arup R&D 1979–93, dir Ove Arup and Partners 1993–94, conslt 1994–; external examiner BSc (Building Servs Engrg Degree) UMIST 1986–89, specialist advsr to House of Commons Environment Ctee (Indoor Pollution Enquiry) 1990–91; CIBSE: memb Cncl and Exec Bd, chm Technol Bd 1984–90, memb Chm's Ctee 1993, pres 1993–94; chm: Four Professions' (comprising CIBSE, CIOB, RIBA, RICS) Energy Gp (now CIC Sustainability Ctee) 1987–90, CIC Task Gp on Environmental Issues 1991–92, CIRIA Environmental Forum Steering Gp (for Environmental Issues in Construction Study) 1991–92, BS7750 (Environmental Mgmnt Systems) Pilot Task Gp for Construction Industry 1992–93, CIC Regulations Advsy Panel 1995–, CIC Approved Inspectors Registration Mgmnt Bd 2000–; memb Advsy Ctee UKAS 1996–; memb Cncl: BSRIA 1990–99, ERA 1990–96; memb Senate Engrg Cncl 1996–2000; author of numerous articles in learned jls, contrib various pubns and speaker at confs worldwide; CEng, MIEE 1969, Hon FCIBSE 2000 (FCIBSE 1985); *Recreations* bowls, bridge, family history, gardening, reading and travelling; *Style*— David Lush, Esq, OBE; ✉ 2 Snaresbrook Drive, Stanmore, Middlesex HA7 4QW (tel and fax 020 8238 2915)

LUSH, Denzil Anton; s of Dennis John Lush, MBE, and Hazel June, *née* Fishenden (d 1979); *b* 18 July 1951; *Educ* Devonport HS Plymouth, UCL (BA, MA), Coll of Law Guildford, CCC Cambridge (LLM); *Career* admitted slr England and Wales 1978, slr and NP Scotland 1993; ptnr Anstey Sargent & Probert Slrs Exeter 1985–95; Court of Protection: master 1996–2007, sr judge 2007–; memb Master of the Rolls' Working Pty on Structured Settlements 2002; former memb: Mental Health and Disability Ctee Law Soc, Steering Gp on Advance Directives BMA; pt/t chm Social Security Appeals Tbnls 1994–96; patron Slrs for the Elderly 2002–; tstee Pan-European Orgn of Personal Injury Lawyers (PEOPIL) Fndn 2004–06; FRSM 2001; *Books* Cohabitation and Co-Ownership Precedents (1993), Elderly Clients - A Precedent Manual (1996), Enduring Powers of Attorney (5 edn, 2001); contrib: Encyclopaedia of Forms and Precedents Vols 26 (Minors) and 31 (Powers of Attorney), Atkin's Court Forms Vol 26 (Mental Health), Butterworths Older Client Law Service, Butterworths Costs Service, Litigation Practice, Heywood and Massey Court of Protection Practice (gen ed); *Recreations* supporting Plymouth Argyle

FC, collecting commemorative pottery; *Clubs* Athenaeum; *Style*— Senior Judge Lush; ✉ Court of Protection, Archway Tower, 2 Junction Road, London N19 5SZ (tel 020 7664 7300, fax 020 7664 7705, e-mail denzil.lush@guardianship.gsi.gov.uk)

LUSH, Jane; *b* 10 August 1952; *Educ* Camden Sch for Girls; *m* 17 November 1974, Peter Tenenbaum; 1 da (Nancy b 28 August 1981), 1 s (Alex b 21 July 1987); *Career* BBC: dir Film...(with Barry Norman) 1979–81, prodr and dir 1981–90, head of devpt Features Dept 1990–95, head of TV devpt Features and Events Dept 1995–98, dep head of Features and Events 1995–98, head of Daytime TV 1998–2001, controller of entertainment commissioning 2001–05; co-fndr Splash 2005– prodr and dir: Hitchcock 1981, Barbara Streisand A Film is Born 1982; prodr Show Business 1983; series prodr: Film...(with Barry Norman) 1984–88, Friday People 1985, Head Over Heels 1989; ed Holiday 1990–95; exec prodr: Redundant 1991, Sean's Shorts 1992, GOSH 1993, Your Place or Mine 1995, Money for Old Rope 1995, Big Kevin Little Kevin 1995, VetsWorld 1995, Martin Clunes Born to be Wild 1997–98; chair Caring for Kids; fundraiser Inst of Child Health Great Ormond Street Hosp; *Style*— Ms Jane Lush

LUSHINGTON, Sir John Richard Castleman; 8 Bt (GB 1791), of South Hill Park, Berkshire; s of Sir Henry Edmund Castleman Lushington, 7 Bt (d 1988), and Pamela Elizabeth Daphne, *née* Hunter (d 2001); *b* 28 August 1938; *Educ* Oundle; *m* 21 May 1966, Bridget Gillian Margaret, o da of late Col John Foster Longfield, of Knockbeg, Saunton, N Devon; 3 s (Richard Douglas Longfield b 1968, Greville Edmund Longfield b 1969, Thomas Robert Longfield b 1975); *Heir* s, Wing Cdr Richard Lushington; *Style*— Sir John Lushington, Bt; ✉ Kent House, Barrington, Ilminster, Somerset TA19 0JP

LUSK, (Ormond) Felicity Stewart; da of Harold Stewart Lusk QC, of Waikanae, NZ, and Janet Kiwi, *née* Miller; *b* 25 November 1955; *Educ* Marsden Collegiate Sch Wellington, Victoria Univ (BMus), Christchurch Teachers' Coll (Dip Teaching), Massey Univ (DipEd); *m* 1976 (m dis 1996); 2 s; *Career* head Music Dept: Wellington East Girls' Coll 1978–85, Aotea Coll 1986–89; Hasmonean HS London: head Music Dept 1990–92, dep head teacher 1993–96; headmistress Oxford HS GDST 1997–; govr Guildhall Sch of Music and Drama 2000–; Woolf Fisher fell (NZ) 1985; cncllr London Borough of Enfield 1990–94; memb: SHA 1994, GSA 1997; *Recreations* swimming, reading, theatre, travel; *Style*— Miss Felicity Lusk; ✉ Oxford High School GDST, Belbroughton Road, Oxford OX2 6XA (tel 01865 559888, fax 01865 552343, e-mail f.lusk@oxf.gdst.net)

LUSTIG, Lawrence Barry; s of Ralph Lustig, of London, and Shelia Jeanette, *née* Bloom; *b* 17 September 1956; *Educ* Chingford HS; *m* 29 June 1984, Carol Ann, da of Ronald William Corless; 1 da (Laura Elizebeth b 20 March 1986), 3 s (Joe Lawrence b 2 June 1988, Jack Ryan b 8 June 1992, Matt Daniel b 6 Sept 1997); *Career* trainee photographer SKR Photos Int 1972–74, photographer Sporting Pictures UK 1974–79, freelance photographer 1980–86, staff photographer Daily Star 1986–; major sporting events covered incl World Cup football and World title boxing contests; Colour Sports Photographer of the Year 1990, Sports Picture of the Year from Royal Photographic Soc and Sports Cncl 1990; sports photographic awards from: Kodak, Ilford, BT, Fuji; memb: NUJ, Assoc of Int Press Sportees, Sports Writers' Assoc; fndr memb Fleet Street Sports Photographers' Assoc, hon life vice-pres World Boxing Union; *Recreations* football and boxing (non-participating); *Style*— Lawrence Lustig, Esq; ✉ The Daily Star, Express Newspapers, 245 Blackfriars Bridge Road, London SE1 (tel 020 7928 8000, car 078 3123 7035)

LUSTIG, Robin Francis; s of Fritz Lustig, and Susan, *née* Cohn; *b* 30 August 1948; *Educ* Stoneham Sch Reading, Univ of Sussex (BA); *m* 24 Feb 1980, Ruth, da of Dr W B Kelsey (d 1986), of London; 1 s (Joshua b 1982), 1 da (Hannah b 1985); *Career* journalist; Reuters: Madrid 1971–72, Paris 1972–73, Rome 1973–77; The Observer: news ed 1981–83, Middle East corr 1985–87, asst ed 1988–89; journalist and broadcaster 1989–, presenter The World Tonight (BBC Radio 4); *Books* Siege: Six Days at the Iranian Embassy (jtly, 1980); *Style*— Robin Lustig, Esq; ✉ The World Tonight, Room G690, BBC News Centre, Wood Lane, London W12 7RJ (tel 020 8624 9777)

LUSTY, Prof James Richard; s of Frank James Lusty (d 1985), and Myrtle Gladys, *née* Baldwin (d 1990); *b* 27 March 1951, Singapore; *Educ* Queen Elizabeth Coll London (BSc, PhD); *m* 1974, Jacqueline Ann, *née* Currell; 1 s (Matthew Richard b 14 Dec 1977), 2 da (Nicola Jayne b 7 Jan 1980, Helen Rachel b 4 April 1983); *Career* asst prof in inorganic chemistry Nat Univ of Petroleum and Minerals Saudi Arabia 1978–81, lectr in inorganic chemistry Nat Univ of Singapore 1981–83, sr lectr Nat Univ of Singapore 1983–84, temp lectr in inorganic chemistry Keele Univ 1984–85, lectr in bioinorganic chemistry Robert Gordon's Inst of Technol Aberdeen 1985–86, head Dept of Chemistry Lancs Poly 1987–90, dir of progs Lancs Poly 1990–93; Univ of Central Lancs: dean of inter faculty studies 1993–95, pro-vice-chllr 1995–2000, sr pro-vice-chllr 2000–01; vice-chllr and princ Univ of Wales Newport 2002–07 (emeritus prof 2007); author of articles published in a range of scientific jls; *Recreations* football, running, swimming, walking; *Style*— Prof James Lusty; ✉ c/o Vice-Chancellor's Office, University of Wales Newport, Caerleon Campus, Newport NP18 3YG (tel 01633 432111, fax 01633 432002)

LUTOSTAŃSKI, Matthew; s of Tadeusz Lutostanski (d 1986), and Maria Zuromska; *b* 22 July 1945, Tel Aviv, Israel; *Educ* Cardinal Vaughan Sch Kensington, City Univ (BA); *m* 1, 1969 (m dis 1979), Pamela Allport; 2 da (Alexandra Eleonora b 1973, Laura Maria b 1976); m 2, 1985 (m dis 2003), Carol Denley; 2 s (Sam Jonathan Tadeusz b 1988, Max Oliver George b 1989); *Career* advtg mangr Barclaycard 1967–73 (launched Britain's first credit card), head of advtg Barclays Bank (UK) 1986–93, fndr Generator Partnership 1993, subsequently jt chief exec Butler Lutos Sutton Wilkinson (following merger with Connell May Steavenson) until 1997, jt chief exec RPM3 (following merger with Cowan Kemsley Taylor) 1997–2000; chief exec Blu Orbit Int (London and NY) 2000, currently prop Ignite Retail Design Int; involved with: Tusk Force Charity (memb Advtg Ctee), Whale-Dolphin Preservation Soc (advtg fundraising campaigns), Elefriends Charity (advtg for new members), Rocks Lane Tennis Centre for Children, Anti Slavery International (advtg fundraising campaign); FInstM; *Recreations* tennis, skiing, football, squash, bridge; *Clubs* Queen's Tennis, Roehampton Tennis; *Style*— Matthew Lutostański, Esq

LUTYENS, Sarah Louise; da of Clive Bremner Cameron (d 1996), and Rosalind Louise, *née* Paget; *b* 12 February 1959, London; *Educ* Univ of Exeter (BA); *m* 1 Jan 1986, C Mark P Lutyens; 1 s (Arthur Eadred b 24 March 1997); *Career* literary agent Lutyens and Rubinstein 1993–; memb Assoc of Authors' Agents; *Style*— Ms Sarah Lutyens; ✉ Lutyens and Rubinstein, 231 Westbourne Park Road, London W11 1EB

LUX, Jonathan Sidney; s of Martin Lux (d 1995), of Highgate, London, and Ruth, *née* Swager (d 1983); *b* 30 October 1951; *Educ* Abbotsholme Sch Rocester, Univ of Nottingham (LLB), Université d' Aix-Marseille; *m* 3 Sept 1979, Simone, da of Shalom Itah, of Israel; 2 da (Ruth b 24 April 1981, Danielle b 24 Sept 1983), 1 s (Adam b 14 Jan 1986); *Career* admitted slr 1977, admitted slr Hong Kong 1986; Ince & Co: asst slr 1977–83, ptnr 1983–, mangr Hamburg branch office 2001–03 (also estab office); speaker at various maritime law confs and author of various articles 1983–; supporting memb London Maritime Arbitrators' Assoc; memb Int Bar Assoc (former chm Ctee A - Maritime and Tport Law), chm Ctee Corporate Social Responsibility; Freeman of City of London, Liveryman of Worshipful Co of Solicitors; memb Law Soc 1977, FCIArb, accredited mediator; *Books* The Law on Tug, Tow and Pilotage (jtly, 1982), The Law and Practice of Marine Insurance and Average (jtly, 1987), Classification Societies (1993), Alternative Dispute Resolution (2002), Bunkers (jtly, 2004), Corporate Social Responsibility (2005); *Recreations* single seater motor racing (holder of RAC nat racing licence), participated in 16,000 km Beijing to Paris rally 1997 (first in class and gold medal); *Clubs* Athenaeum, Royal Over-Seas League; *Style*— Jonathan Lux, Esq; ✉ Ince & Co, International House, 1 St Katherine's Way, London E1W 1UN (tel 020 7481 0010, fax 020 7481 4568, e-mail jonathan.lux@incelaw.com)

LYALL, Eric; CBE; s of late Alfred John Lyall, and Alice Amelia, *née* Jackson (d 1982); *b* 12 May 1924; *Educ* Chigwell Sch, King's Coll Cambridge; *m* 1952, Joyce, da of late Sydney Edward Smith; 1 s (Alexander); *Career* RAF 1943–47; ptnr Slaughter and May 1955–61, dir Guinness Mahon and Co 1961–75; chm: London Bd Commercial Banking Co of Sydney 1964–80, E Herts Cons Assoc 1964–68, UK Branch Australian Mutual Provident Soc 1965–94, Clarke Nickolls & Coombs plc 1968–96, Frewell Educational Tst 1972–91, E of England Provincial Area 1974–78, Letchworth Garden City Corp (now Letchworth Garden City Heritage Fndn) 1983–99, Pearl Group plc 1989–94, AMP Asset Management plc 1991–94, Rocla GB Ltd, AMP (UK) plc; dir Lockton Developments plc 1985–95; gen cmmr of income tax 1961–99; memb NW Thames Regnl HA 1985–88, charitable tstee Univ of Hertford; memb Royal Philatelic Soc; *Recreations* reading, stamp collecting, medieval history; *Clubs* Oriental, City of London, MCC; *Style*— Eric Lyall, Esq, CBE; ✉ Riders Grove, Old Hall Green, Ware, Hertfordshire SG11 1DN (tel 01920 821370)

LYALL, Dr Fiona Jane; MBE (1995), DL (Kincardine 1983); da of James Fraser (d 1984), and Christina Forbes (d 1983); *b* 13 April 1931; *Educ* Univ of Aberdeen (MB ChB, DPH); *m* 20 July 1957, Alan Richards Lyall, s of Alexander Lyall (d 1974); 1 da (Elizabeth Grace Hermione b 18 Oct 1958), 1 s (Peter James Fraser b 9 Oct 1961); *Career* GP Laurencekirk 1959–, dir Grampian TV plc 1980–; borough cncllr Laurencekirk, co cncllr Kincardineshire, regnl cnclr Grampian; *Recreations* skiing, provincial silver; *Style*— Dr Fiona Lyall, MBE, DL; ✉ Melrose Bank, Laurencekirk, Kincardineshire AB30 1FJ (tel 01561 377220)

LYALL, John Adrian; s of Keith Lyall (d 1990), of Hadleigh, Essex, and Phyllis, *née* Sharps (d 1999); *b* 12 December 1949; *Educ* Southend HS for Boys, AA Sch of Architecture; *m* 25 May 1991, Sallie Jean, da of Frank and Noelleen Davies; 1 s (Adam John b 27 June 1997), 1 da (Madeleine Rose b 14 April 2000); *Career* architect and urban designer; architectural appts: Cedric Price 1969–70, Gerard Brigden 1970–71, Piano & Rogers 1973–74, Raymond J Cecil 1974–75, Page & Broughton/Planarc 1975–77, Bahr Vermeer & Haecker 1977–78, Rock Townsend 1978–79; in private practice Alsop Lyall and Störmer 1980–91, md John Lyall Architects 1991–; numerous arts-related and urban renewal projects incl: Dance East and Cranfields Mill Ipswich, Riverside Studios Hammersmith, Gallery 2000 Inverness, Perran Foundry Cornwall, St Anne's Wharf Devpt Norwich (incl costume museum), BR and underground station Tottenham Hale, The Corn Exchange and White Cloth Hall Leeds, The Crown Court Kirkgate, architect Crystal Palace Park regeneration 2000–01, New World Square, Liverpool Waterfront, Perth City Hall, Hammersmith Pumping Station, various other urban design work and transport projects incl North Greenwich Jubilee Line Station; memb Design Panel: Cardiff Bay Devpt Corp 1989–2000, English Partnerships 1998–; memb Nat Design Review Panel CABE 2007–; vice-pres (Future Studies) RIBA 1997–2000; external examiner: Oxford Brookes Univ and Bartlett Sch of Architecture, Univ of Strathclyde; formerly: unit tutor AA and Greenwich Univ, visiting prof Ball State Univ Indiana, visiting lectr at other schs in UK, Ireland, USA, Bratislava and Moscow; chm RIBA Validation Task Force 2001, vice-chair RIBA Tst 2003–; conslt: CABE 2001–, Br Library 2003–05; memb Cncl Architectural Assoc 2005–; awards incl: William van Allen Medal for Architecure NY 1971, Leeds Award for Architecture 1990 and 1992, The Ironbridge Award (Br Archaeological Soc) 1990 and 1992, Design Week Award 1991, RIBA White Rose Award and Nat Award 1991, Europa Nostra Award 1991, RICS Urban Renewal Award 1995, Category and Regnl RIBA Award for N Greenwich Station 1999, Architectural Review/MIPIM Future Projects Award 2005; memb AA, RIBA, FRSA; *Publications* subject of: Architecture, Projects and Drawings of Will Alsop, Cliff Barnett and John Lyall (1984), New Buildings in Historic Settings (1998), John Lyall. Urban Regeneration: Context and Catalysts (1999); instigated and ed RIBA pubns: The Value of Design (2000), Tomorrow's Architect (2003); *Recreations* choral singing (memb Univ of Essex choir), fruit tree cultivation, supporting Tottenham Hotspur; *Clubs* Chelsea Arts; *Style*— John Lyall, Esq; ✉ John Lyall Architects, 13–19 Curtain Road, Shoreditch, London EC2A 3LT (tel 020 7375 3324, fax 020 7375 3325, e-mail john.lyall@johnlyallarchitects.com, website www.johnlyallarchitects.com)

LYALL, Michael Hodge; s of Alexander Burt Lyall, of Glenrothes, and Isabella Campbell, *née* Paterson; *b* 5 December 1941; *Educ* Buckhaven HS, Univ of St Andrews (MB ChB), Univ of Dundee (ChM); *m* 25 Dec 1965, Catherine Barnett, da of James Thomson Jarvie (d 1986), of Leven; 3 s (Grant Alexander b 18 Oct 1966, Stuart James Jarvie b 24 Jan 1968, Ewan Mark Stephen b 28 July 1969); *Career* conslt surgn NHS Tayside 1975–2006, med dir Tayside Univ Hosp Tst 2001–06; hon sr lectr Univ of Dundee 1975–2006; former fell Assoc of Surgns of GB and I; FRCS 1970; *Recreations* reading, rotary; *Clubs* Rotary of North Fife, Moynihan Chirurgical; *Style*— Michael Lyall, Esq; ✉ 1 Vernonholme, Riverside Drive, Dundee DD2 1QJ (tel 01382 630031, fax 01382 630076)

LYALL GRANT, Maj-Gen Ian Hallam; MC (1944); s of Col Henry Frederick Lyall Grant, DSO (d 1958), of Aberdeen, and Ellinor Lucy Hardy (d 1951), of Cork; *b* 4 June 1915; *Educ* Cheltenham, RMA Woolwich, Gonville & Caius Coll Cambridge (MA); *m* 1951, Mary Jennifer, da of Norman Moore (d 1980); 1 s (Mark, *qv*), 2 da (Sarah, Charlotte); *Career* cmmnd RE 1935, seconded Bengal Sappers and Miners 1938–46, served WWII 17 Indian Div Burma 1942–44, cmd 9 Para Sqdn 1951–52, cmd 131 AB Engr Regt 1955–56, DS JSSC 1957–58, Brig A/Q Aden 1962–64, Cmdt RSME 1965–67, Maj-Gen 1967, DQMG MOD 1967–70, ret 1970; Civil Serv DG Supply Co-ordination 1970–75; Col Cmdt RE 1972–77; pres Burma Campaign Fellowship Gp 1996–2002 (chm 1991–96); MICE 1968, FGA 1978; *Books* Burma: The Turning Point (1993), Burma 1942: The Japanese Invasion (jtly, 1998); *Recreations* author-publisher, fly fishing, gemmology, travel, bridge; *Clubs* Naval and Military; *Style*— Maj-Gen Ian Lyall Grant, MC; ✉ 6 St Martin's Square, Chichester PO19 1NT

LYALL GRANT, Sir Mark Justin; KCMG (2006, CMG 2003); s of Maj-Gen Ian Lyall Grant, MC, *qv*, of Chichester, W Sussex, and Mary Jennifer, *née* Moore; *b* 29 May 1956, London; *Educ* Eton (Newcastle scholar), Univ of Cambridge (scholar, MA), Université Libre de Bruxelles (Wiener-Anspach scholar, Licencié Speciale en Droit Européen); *m* July 1986, Sheila Jean, *née* Tresise; 1 s (Hallam b 3 Nov 1989), 1 da (Lucy b 28 Aug 1991); *Career* called to the Bar Middle Temple 1980; entered FCO 1980; posted: Islamabad 1982–85, Paris 1990–93, Pretoria 1996–98; dir for Africa FCO 2000–02, high cmmr to Pakistan 2003–06, political dir FCO 2007–; *Recreations* golf, bridge, sailing, quizzes; *Clubs* RAC, Royal Dart Yacht; *Style*— Sir Mark Lyall Grant, KCMG; ✉ c/o Foreign & Commonwealth Office, King Charles Street, London SW1A 2AH (tel 020 7008 2167, e-mail mark.lyall-grant@fco.gov.uk)

LYBURN, Andrew Usherwood (Drew); OBE (1995); s of Andrew Lyburn (d 1969), of Edinburgh, and Margaret Scott Glass (d 1988); *b* 16 August 1928; *Educ* Melville Coll, Univ of Edinburgh (MA); *m* 1, 1958, Joan Ann (d 1994), da of Eric Stevenson (d 1975), of Edinburgh; 3 s (Andrew b 1960, Colin b 1962, Iain b 1967), 1 da (Fiona b 1974); m 2, 1999, Evelyn Alison, da of John J S Knox, of Edinburgh; *Career* RAF Flying Offr Cyprus 1954–56; actuary; Scottish Widows Fund 1949–54 and 1956–57, Confed Life Toronto 1957–59; Standard Life: Montreal 1959–65, Edinburgh 1965–91; consulting actuary to Scottish Transport Group 1970–97; chm Cairn Petroleum Oil and Gas Ltd 1987–88, dir Dreamstar Properties Ltd 1989–94, conslt The Melrose Partnerships 1992–98; chm

Melville Coll Tst 1983–86; dir: Edinburgh Telford Coll 1992–95, The Royal Blind Asylum 1992–2007 (vice-chm 2003–07); convenor Scottish Nat Inst for the War Blinded 1993–2007; vice-pres Faculty of Actuaries 1987–91; memb: Occupational Pensions Bd 1982–97, Cncl of St Dunstan's 1994–2007; FFA 1957, FCIA (Canada) 1965, FPMI 1976; *Recreations* bridge, golf, gardening, rugby, squash, hill walking; *Clubs* RAF, Bruntsfield Links Golfing Soc (Edinburgh); *Style*— Drew Lyburn, Esq, OBE; ✉ 4 Cumlodden Avenue, Edinburgh EH12 6DR (tel 0131 337 7580, e-mail aul@sky.com)

LYCETT, Andrew Michael Duncan; s of Peter Norman Lycett (d 1979), and Joanna Mary, *née* Day (d 2005); *b* 5 December 1948; *Educ* Charterhouse, ChCh Oxford (MA); *m* 1981 (m dis 1989), Rita Diana Robinson; *Career* journalist and author; FRGS; *Books* Gaddafi and The Libyan Revolution (with David Blundy, 1987), Ian Fleming (1995), From Diamond Sculls to Golden Handcuffs (1998), Rudyard Kipling (1999), Dylan Thomas - A New Life (2003), Conan Doyle: The Man Who Created Sherlock Holmes (2007); *Recreations* travel, reading, cricket; *Clubs* RAC; *Style*— Andrew Lycett, Esq; ✉ 34 Torbay Road, London NW6 7DY; (home tel and fax 020 7328 4552, e-mail alycett@btinternet.com)

LYCETT, Christopher Ronald (Chris); s of Eric Laybourn Lycett, MBE (d 1974), of the IOM, and Thelma, *née* George (d 1987); *b* 3 December 1946; *Educ* Archbishop Tenison's GS Croydon, Ramsey GS IOM; *m* 6 June 1970, Anne, da of Richard Charles Frank Geary; 2 s (Daniel Christopher Laybourn b 15 March 1971, Nicholas Richard Charles Geary (Charlie) b 23 Dec 1981), 1 da (Sarah Anne Marie b 30 April 1974); *Career* BBC Radio 1: studio engr responsible for sight and sound simulcasts, prodr 1975–87, ed mainstream progs 1987–2000, head of music 1990–94, exec prodr live music 1995–99, co-ordinator Special Event for Music Live 2000; fndr Broadcast Event Productions 2000–; work as prodr incl: Live Aid 1986 (Sony Award), Nelson Mandela Concert 1988, Walters Weekly arts prog (Broadcasting Press Guild Award), Prince of Wales 40th Birthday Party, Prince's Tst Anniversary Concert Wembley, Oasis at Knebworth (Sony Award), U2 live from Sarajevo, BBC Music Live Golden Jubilee events in Hyde Park, HDTV Relay of Live8 2005; *Recreations* golf, walking, reading, theatre, music, cinema; *Style*— Chris Lycett, Esq; ✉ tel 020 7435 3326, mobile 07980 845655, e-mail chrislycett1@aol.com, website www.chrislycett.com

LYCETT, Maj Michael Hildesley Lycett; CBE (1987); s of Rev Norman Lycett (d 1963), of East Dean, W Sussex, and Ruth Edith, *née* Burns-Lindow (d 1965), of Irton Hall, Cumberland; *b* 11 December 1915; *Educ* Radley, Merton Coll Oxford; *m* 1, 4 Feb 1944, Moira Patricia Margaret (d 1958), da of Maj Norman Martin, CBE; 1 da (Anthea Theresa b 6 June 1954); m 2, 12 Oct 1959, Lady June Wendy Pelham, da of 5 Earl of Yarborough, MC (d 1948); *Career* Maj Royal Scots Greys 1935–47, served Palestine, Greece, Western Desert, Italy and Germany; md: Rhodesian Insurances Ltd 1949–61, Wright Deen Lycett Ltd Newcastle upon Tyne 1961–73, Lycett Browne-Swinburne & Douglas's Ltd (chm 1973–76); chm L B S and D (underwriting agents) 1976, dir L B S and D (Cumbria) Ltd, life pres L B S and D Ltd 1998–; chm Morpeth Div Cons Assoc 1966–72; Parly candidate (Cons) Consett Co Durham 1981 and 1983; chm Cons Northern Area 1985–87; pres Northumbria Euro Constituency, former memb Cons Nat Exec and GP Ctees; govr and first chm exec Bernard Mizeki Schs 1959–61; MFH Tynedale Hunt 1975–77; *Recreations* field sports, looking things up, writing rhymes, regretting; *Clubs* Cavalry and Guards', Pratt's, Boodle's, Northern Counties; *Style*— Maj Michael Lycett, CBE; ✉ West Grange, Scots Gap, Morpeth, Northumberland NE61 4EQ (tel 01670 774662)

LYDIARD, Andrew John; QC (2003); s of George Lydiard, of Leominster, Herefords, and Beryl, *née* Taylor; *b* 25 August 1957, Birmingham; *Educ* King's Sch Chester, UC Oxford (BA), Harvard Law Sch (LLM); *m* 10 Dec 1983, Mary Adair; 2 s (Robert George b 18 Jan 1992, Stephen John b 1 March 1995); *Career* called to the Bar 1980; *Style*— Andrew Lydiard, Esq, QC; ✉ Brick Court Chambers, 7–8 Essex Street, London WC2R 3LD (tel 020 7379 3550, fax 020 7379 3558, e-mail andrew.lydiard@brickcourt.co.uk)

LYE, Geoffrey Brian; s of James Douglas Lye, and Ruby Alma, *née* Cox; *b* 14 October 1949; *Educ* King Edward VI Sch Southampton, Gonville & Caius Coll Cambridge; *m* Linda May (m dis), da of George Arthur Muirhead; 2 da (Mary Elizabeth b 4 Sept 1975, Katherine Louise b 16 Nov 1978), 2 s (Charles Julian b 20 April 1982, Jonathan James b 29 Jan 1988); *Career* J Walter Thompson advtg agency 1972–74, General Foods 1974–80, gp dep chm Countrywide Porter Novelli Ltd 1980–97, chm BMP Countrywide 1997–99; dir SustainAbility Ltd 1995– (vice-chm 2004–); FRSA; *Style*— Geoffrey Lye, Esq

LYELL, 3 Baron (UK 1914); Sir Charles Lyell; 3 Bt (UK 1894), DL (Angus); s of Capt 2 Baron Lyell, VC, Scots Guards (ka 1943, VC awarded posthumously), and Sophie, *née* Trafford (whose family, of Wroxham Hall, Norfolk were a cadet branch of the Traffords now represented by the de Trafford Bts), whose mother was Lady Elizabeth Bertie, OBE, yst da of 7 Earl of Abingdon; *b* 27 March 1939; *Educ* Eton, ChCh Oxford; *Heir* none; *Career* 2 Lt Scots Gds 1957–59; chartered accountant; oppn whip House of Lords 1974–79, a Lord in Waiting (Govt Whip) 1979–84, Parly under sec of state NI Office 1984–89; memb Queen's Body Guard for Scotland (Royal Co of Archers); *Clubs* White's, Pratt's, Turf; *Style*— The Rt Hon the Lord Lyell, DL; ✉ Kinnordy House, Kirriemuir, Angus DD8 5ER (tel 01575 572848, estate office tel 01575 572665); 20 Petersham Mews, Elvaston Place, London SW7 5NR (tel 020 7584 9419)

LYELL OF MARKYATE, Baron (Life Peer UK 2005), of Markyate in the County of Hertfordshire; Sir Nicholas Walter Lyell; kt (1987), PC (1990), QC (1980); s of Hon Mr Justice Maurice Legat Lyell (d 1975), and his 1 w, Veronica Mary, *née* Luard (d 1950); step s of Hon Lady (Katharine) Lyell (d 1998); *b* 6 December 1938; *Educ* Stowe, ChCh Oxford (MA), Coll of Law; *m* 2 Sept 1967, Susanna Mary, da of Prof Charles Montague Fletcher, CBE (d 1995); 2 da (Hon Veronica b 8 May 1970, Hon Mary-Kate b 5 March 1979), 2 s (Hon Oliver b 1 July 1971, Hon Alexander b 8 Dec 1981); *Career* Nat Serv with RA 1957–59, 2 Lt 1957; with Walter Runciman & Co 1962–64; called to the Bar Inner Temple 1965 (bencher 1986); in private practice London 1965–86 and 1997–, recorder of the Crown Ct 1985; MP (Cons): Hemel Hempstead 1979–83, Beds Mid 1983–97, Beds NE 1997–2001; jt sec Constitutional Ctee 1979, PPS to Attorney Gen 1979–86, Parly under sec of state for Social Security DHSS 1986–87, Slr Gen 1987–92, Attorney Gen 1992–97, Shadow Attorney Gen 1997–99; chm Soc of Cons Lawyers 2001–, vice-chm BFSS 1983–86; govr Stowe Sch 1991– (chm of govrs 2001–); Freeman City of London 1964, memb Ct of Assts Worshipful Co of Salters (Master 2002); *Recreations* gardening, drawing, shooting; *Clubs* Brooks's, Pratt's, Beefsteak; *Style*— The Rt Hon the Lord Lyell of Markyate, PC, QC

LYES, Jeffrey Paul; s of late Joseph Leslie Lyes, of Daventry, Northants, and Rose Mary Anne, *née* Harris; *b* 19 April 1946; *m* 5 Oct 1968, Jan, da of late John Armstrong, of Oxford; 2 da (Sarah b 1974, Julia b 1977); *Career* journalist United Newspapers 1963–69, exec Hertford PR 1969–71, news ed Heart of Eng Newspapers 1971–73, press and PR offr Thames Valley Police 1973–78; dir: Lexington International PR (J Walter Thompson) 1978–81, Granard Communications 1981–84 (dep md 1984), Good Relations Group plc 1985–86; md: Good Relations Technology 1985–86, Good Relations Corporate Communications 1986–87; md Good Relations Ltd 1987–89; chm: Good Relations Ltd 1989–95, Bell Pottinger Good Relations (formerly Lowe Bell Good Relations Ltd) 1995–2000, Good Relations Gp 1998–2000; sr conslt Good Relations Gp 2001–; FIMgt 1985, FInstD 1988, FIPR 1998 (MIPR 1977); *Recreations* motor yacht cruising; *Clubs* Reform; *Style*— Jeffrey Lyes, Esq; ✉ Good Relations, 26 Southampton Buildings, Holborn Gate, London WC2A 1PQ (tel 020 7861 3030, fax 020 7861 3131)

LYGO, Kevin; s of Adm Sir Raymond Lygo, KCB, *qv*, and Pepper, *née* Van Osten (d 2004); *b* 19 September 1957; *Educ* Univ of Durham (BSc); *Career* comedy scriptwriter (Not the Nine O'clock News, Two Ronnies, Three of a Kind) 1982, trainee (prodr Omnibus) BBC 1983–85; art dealer 1986–91; BBC: comedy prodr 1991–96, head of independent prodn 1996–97; head of entertainment Channel 4 1997–2001, dir of programmes Five 2001–03, dir of TV Channel 4 2003–; *Recreations* tennis, Islamic art; *Style*— Kevin Lygo, Esq; ✉ Channel 4, 124 Horseferry Road, London SW1P 2TX

LYGO, Adm Sir Raymond Derek; KCB (1977); s of Edwin Lygo; *b* 15 March 1924; *Educ* Ilford Co HS, Clarke Coll Bromley; *m* 1950, Pepper Van Osten (d 2004), of USA; 2 s (1 of whom Kevin Lygo, *qv*), 1 da; *Career* on staff The Times 1940; served RN 1942–78 (vice-chief and chief of Naval Staff 1975–78); British Aerospace: md Hatfield/Lostock Div 1978–79, chief exec and chm Dynamics Gp 1980–82, memb Main Bd 1980, md 1983–86, chief exec 1986–89; chm Royal Ordnance 1987–88; aerospace def and industrial conslt 1990–; dir James Capel Corporate Finance 1990–92, non-exec dir LET plc 1990–92, non-exec chm Rutland Trust 1991–99; chm TNT (Express) UK Ltd 1992–97, TNT (Europe) Ltd 1992–97, chm Liontrust First UK Investment Tst 1997–; patron Nat Fleet Air Arm Assoc 1990–, pres Fleet Arm Offrs' Assoc 1990–; conducted review on mgmnt of HM Prisons 1991; pres City Livery Club 1996–97; memb: Cncl Industrial Soc 1980–, Cncl for Mgmnt and Educn 1989–; Liveryman: Worshipful Co of Coachmakers and Coach Harness Makers, Worshipful Co of Shipwrights; hon fell Univ of Westminster; Hon FRAeS, CIMgt, FRSA; *Clubs* Royal Naval & RAYC, IOD, City Livery, Les Ambassadeurs; *Style*— Adm Sir Raymond Lygo, KCB; ✉ Liontrust First UK Investment Trust plc, 2 Savoy Court, Strand, London WC2R 0EZ

LYLE, (Philip) Dominic; s of Robert Lyle, of Malveira, Portugal, and Helena, *née* Perks; *b* 6 March 1949; *Educ* Stonyhurst, Alliance Française, Université de Lausanne; *m* 5 Sept 1992, Vyvyan Lynne, *née* Mackeson; *Career* sales and mktg mangr Europe Tate & Lyle Refineries 1976–79; Cameron Choat & Partners: joined 1979, dir 1985–90, md 1990–91; dir Countrywide Communications (London) Ltd 1992–94, md Countrywide Porter Novelli (Brussels) 1994–2000, chm European technol practice Porter Novelli (Paris) 2000–02, DG European Assoc of Communications Agencies (EACA) 2002–; memb Mktg Soc, MIPR; *Recreations* opera, cooking; *Style*— Dominic Lyle, Esq; ✉ European Association of Communications Agencies, 152 Boulevard Brand Whitlock, B-1200 Brussels, Belgium

LYLE, Sir Gavin Archibald; 3 Bt (UK 1929), of Glendelvine, Co Perth; s of Capt Ian Archibald de Hoghton Lyle (ka 1942), and Hon Lydia, *née* Yarde-Buller, da of 3 Baron Churston; suc gf, Col Sir Archibald Moir Park Lyle, 2 Bt, MC, TD, 1946; *b* 14 October 1941; *Educ* Eton; *m* 1967 (m dis 1985), Susan, o da of John Vaughan Cooper; 5 s (Ian Abram b 1968, Jake Archibald b 1969, Matthew Alexander b 1974, Joshua b 1979, Samuel b 1981), 1 da (Rachel b 1971); *Heir* s, Ian Lyle; *Career* estate mangr; farmer; co dir; *Style*— Sir Gavin Lyle, Bt; ✉ Glendelvine, Caputh, Perthshire PH1 4JN

LYLE, Robert Arthur Wyatt; s of Maj Robert David Lyle (d 1989), and Irene Joyce, *née* Penn-Francis (d 1984); n of Lord Wyatt of Weeford (Life Peer, d 1997); *b* 5 May 1952; *Educ* Eton, Oriel Coll Oxford (MA); *m* 1, 9 March 1991 (m dis 2002), Hon Teresa (Tessa) Ruth, da of Baron Mayhew (Life Peer, d 1997); 1 s (Christopher Robert David Wyatt b 12 Feb 1992); m 2, 25 Aug 2005, Lysanne Amanda Koetser, da of Brian Leonard Koester, of Nutbourne, West Sussex; *Career* dir: Commonwealth Disaster Mgmnt Agency Ltd, Pall Mall Initiatives Ltd, NMG (Cornwall) Ltd, BPL Hldgs Ltd; Cornwall Light and Power Co Ltd (first wholly private commercial wind farm in UK): fndr 1989, sold 2005; advsr Global Trade Insurance PTE Singapore; worldwide corr to China International Economic Consultants 1983–87, EC advsr to Russian Govt on investment insurance 1991–93; advsr to World Energy Cncl on trade and political risk insurance 2002–, advsr to African Trade Insurance (COMESA) 2003–; BRCS: pres Cornwall Branch 1996–2001, vice-chm SW Regnl Cncl 1997–2001, vice-pres overseas territories 2002–, hon vice-pres Cornwall Branch 2002–; memb advsy ctee to the UK Natural Disaster Reduction Ctee 2000–, tstee and memb Cncl Int Social Service UK 2004–, tstee China Oxford Scholarship Fund 2004–, memb Advsy Bd Ashmolean Museum Oxford 2005–, tstee Elgar Soc Edition 2005–07; treas PCC St Keverne 1995–99, memb Upper Basildon PCC 1999–2002; Church Warden Aston Tirrold and Aston Upthorpe 2002–04; one of four Lords of the Lizard; Liveryman Worshipful Co of Glass Sellers; FRSA, FRGS; *Recreations* art, architecture, music, travel, fishing, sailing; *Clubs* White's, MCC, Lansdowne; *Style*— Robert Lyle, Esq; ✉ 93 Nottingham Terrace, Regent's Park, London NW1 4QE

LYLES, John; CVO (2004), CBE (1987), JP (Dewsbury 1968); s of Percy George Lyles (d 1958), and Alice Maud Mary, *née* Robinson (d 1968); *b* 8 May 1929; *Educ* Giggleswick Sch, Univ of Leeds (BSc); *m* 1953, Yvonne, da of G F Johnson (d 1954), of Waddesdon; 2 s (Jonathan, Christopher), 2 da (Jane, Anne); *Career* chm S Lyles plc until 1996; High Sheriff W Yorks 1985–86; chm: Yorks and Humberside CBI 1983–85, Yorks and Humberside Region Industry Year 1986; pres Calderdale Community Fndn 1994–2004, W Yorks Police Community Tst 1996–2004; memb Ct Univ of Leeds 1996–; chm Shrievalty Assoc 1993–95 (pres 1999–); Hon Col King's Own Yorkshire Yeo LI 1996–99; HM Lord-Lt W Yorks 1992–2004 (DL 1987); Hon DUniv Bradford 1995; *Recreations* gardening, photography, music, opera; *Style*— John Lyles, Esq, CVO, CBE; ✉ Thimbleby House, Hampsthwaite, Harrogate, North Yorkshire HG3 2HB

LYMBERY, Brian John; OBE (2007); s of Dr John Graham Lymbery (d 1974), and Joyce Winifred, *née* Keen; *b* 1 March 1947; *Educ* Alun GS Mold Clwyd, Keble Coll Oxford (BA); *m* 1975 (m dis 1996), Susan Joan, da of Percy Sherratt (d 1992); 1 s (Matthew b 1976), 1 da (Jessica b 1979); *Career* lectr and librarian Mid-Western Tech Coll Auchi Nigeria 1969–70, exec sec The Prince of Wales Ctee Bangor 1971–76, dir The Prince of Wales Ctee Cardiff 1976–83, dep dir Civic Tst London 1983–87, exec dir UK 2000 1987–90, dir CSD 1990; memb Industry Lead Body for Design 1990–97, treas Bureau Euro Designers' Assoc 1992–94; memb Nat Cncl VSO 1979–90, tstee Tst for Urban Ecology 1981–92, memb Gen Advsy Cncl IBA 1983–88 (memb Ctee for Wales 1977–83), chm Soc for the Interpretation of Britain's Heritage 1984–85, fndr chm Cncl for Occupational Standards and Qualifications in Environmental Conservation (COSQUEC) 1988–96, memb bd Environmental Training Organisation (ETO) 1995–98; currently chair Lewisham Primary Care Trust; govr: Gordonbrock Primary Sch London 1989– (chm 1989–97), Lucas Vale Primary Sch 1997– (chm 1998–99); tstee Lantra 1998–; FRSA 1981; *Recreations* enjoying opera, music, theatre and film, gardening, watching people; *Clubs* London Central YMCA; *Style*— Brian Lymbery, Esq, OBE

LYNAM, Desmond Michael; s of Edward Lynam, and Gertrude Veronica, *née* Malone; *b* 17 September 1942; *Educ* Varndean GS Brighton, Brighton Business Coll (ACII); *m* 1965 (m dis 1974), Susan Eleanor, *née* Skinner; 1 s (Patrick); *Career* in insurance and freelance journalism until 1967; local radio reporter 1967–69, reporter, presenter and commentator BBC Radio 1969–78, presenter and commentator BBC TV Sport 1978–99 (incl Grandstand, Match of the Day, Cwlth and Olympic Games, World Cup and Wimbledon); presenter: Holiday (BBC TV) 1988–89, How Do They Do That? (BBC TV) 1994–96, The Des Lynam Show (BBC Radio 2) 1998–99, ITV Sport 1999–2004, Des Meets... (BBC Radio Five Live) 2004–05, We'll Meet Again (BBC TV) 2005, The World's Greatest Sporting Legend (Sky One) 2005, Des at Wimbledon (BBC Radio Five Live) 2005, Are You Younger Than You Think? (BBC TV) 2005, Countdown (Channel 4) 2005–; TV Sports Presenter of the Year (TV and Radio Industries Club) 1985, 1987, 1988, 1993 and 1997, Male TV Personality (Radio Times/Open Air) 1989, Sports Presenter of the Year (RTS Awards) 1994 and 1998, Richard Dimbleby Award (BAFTA) 1994, Broadcasting Press Guild Award for best performer (non-acting) 1996, BBC Viewers' Top Television

Presenter on Auntie's All Time Greats a 60th Anniversary of the BBC 1996, Variety Club of Great Britain Media Award 1997, RTS Lifetime Achievement Award 2003; *Publications* Guide to Commonwealth Games (1986), The 1988 Olympics (1988), The Barcelona Olympics 1992 (with Caroline Searle, 1992), I Should Have Been at Work! (2005); *Recreations* golf, tennis, Brighton and Hove Albion FC, reading, theatre; *Style*— Desmond Lynam, Esq; ✉ c/o Jane Morgan Management, Thames Wharf Studios, Rainville Road, London W6 9HA (tel 020 7386 5345, fax 020 7386 0338, e-mail enquiries@janemorganmgt.com)

LYNCH, His Hon David; s of Henry and Edith Lynch; *b* 23 August 1939; *Educ* Liverpool Collegiate GS, Univ of London (external LLB); *m* 1974, Ann Knights; 2 s; *Career* served RAF 1958–61; teacher 1966–69; called to the Bar Middle Temple 1968, recorder 1988–90, circuit judge (Northern Circuit) 1990–2005; pres Mental Health Review Tbnls (restricted patients) 1991–2001; liaison judge: St Helens Justices 1991–2005, Liverpool John Moores Univ 1994–2005; hon fell Liverpool John Moores Univ 2003; *Recreations* classical guitar music, golf; *Style*— His Hon David Lynch; ✉ The Queen Elizabeth II Law Courts, Derby Square, Liverpool L2 1XA (tel 0151 473 7373)

LYNCH, James; s of Ronald F T Lynch, and Joy Ann, *née* Berry, of Seend, Wiltshire; *b* 12 July 1956; *Educ* Devizes Sch, Swindon Coll (Dip Graphic Design); *m* 1977, Kate Mary, da of John Argent Armstrong; 2 s (Thomas Albert b 1978, Arthur James b 1982), 1 da (Alice Mary b 1980); *Career* artist; *Solo Exhibitions* incl: Linfield Galleries Bradford-on-Avon 1982 and 1983, Odette Gilbert London 1988, Maas Gallery London 1991, 1993, 1995, 1997, 1999, 2001, 2003 and 2006; *Group Exhibitions* incl: RA Summer Shows annually 1984–89, Royal Soc of Painters in Watercolour 1986, Agnews London 1989 and 1990, Discerning Eye Mall Gallery 1991, Galerie Michael Beverley Hills 2002; *Commissions* incl Nat Tst and Folio Soc (illustrations for Wind in the Willows 1994); *Public Collections* Chatsworth Collection, Nat Tst Fndn for Art, Wessex Collection; *Awards* Elizabeth Greenshields Fndn Award 1983, RA Pimms Prize 1986, winner Adams/Spectator Painting Award 1993; *Recreations* cycling, motorcycling, paragliding; *Style*— James Lynch, Esq; ✉ Four Chimneys, High Ham, Langport, Somerset TA10 9BB (tel 01458 250367, website www.james-lynch.co.uk)

LYNCH, Jerome; QC (2000); s of Clifford James Lynch (d 1995), and Loretta Rosa, *née* Mazzolini (d 2004); *b* 31 July 1955; *Educ* Univ of Lancashire (BA); *m* 25 March 1983, Jacqueline Theresa, da of Daniel Alexander O'Sullivan; 1 s (Oliver Jerome b 25 Oct 1986); *Career* called to the Bar Lincoln's Inn 1983; co-presenter Nothing But The Truth (Channel 4) 1998–99, presenter Crime Team (Channel 4) 2002, presenter People's Court (ITV1) 2005; *Recreations* bad golfer, good skier, love wine; *Clubs* RAC; *Style*— Jerome Lynch, Esq, QC; ✉ Charter Chambers, 33 John Street, London WC1N 2AT

LYNCH, John Stewart; *Educ* Univ of London (BA); *Career* researcher BBC Science 1976–80, prodr 1981–83, ed Horizon (BBC) 1994–98, dep head BBC Science 1998–2000, creative dir BBC Science 2000–05, head BBC Science and History 2006–; *Awards* Prix Italia, Banff Rockie, Paris Int Sci TV Festival Grand Prix, Quebec Int Scientific Film Festival Grand Prix, Glaxo Sci Writers Award, BAFTA and RTS (for Horizon and Walking With Dinosaurs), Primetime Emmy (for Walking with Dinosaurs); *Publications* Wild Weather (2002), Walking with Cavemen (2003); *Recreations* rest; *Style*— John Lynch, Esq; ✉ c/o BBC, White City, 201 Wood Lane, London W12 7TS

LYNCH, Michael; AM (2001); *Career* joined Australia Cncl for the Arts 1973; former: mangr Nimrod Theatre, admin Australian Nat Playwrights Conf, casting dir Forecast (performing arts, film and TV agency), prodr Raw Nerve (feature film) 1988; gen mangr: Sydney Theatre 1989–94, Australia Cncl 1994–98; chief exec: Sydney Opera House 1998–2002, South Bank Centre 2002–; Bd memb Visit London 2004–, memb Performing Arts Centres Consortium N America, former chm Australia Asia Pacific Performing Arts Centres; *Style*— Michael Lynch, Esq, AM; ✉ South Bank Centre, Royal Festival Hall, Belvedere Road, London SE1 8XX

LYNCH, Prudence; da of Derek Renny (d 1970), and Hon Nicola, *née* Moncreiff (d 2003); *b* 21 February 1952, Dundee; *Educ* Blanchelande Coll Guernsey, Univ of St Andrews (MA), Goldsmiths Coll London (PGCE); *m* 22 Oct 1977, Paul Lynch; 2 s (James b 3 June 1980, Harry b 12 July 1983); *Career* teacher Heathfield Sch Pinner 1977–80, head of maths and IT Notting Hill & Ealing HS 1987–90, head of special needs Colet Court St Paul's Boys Prep Sch London 1990–98, head Notting Hill & Ealing Jr Sch 1998–2003, head Kensington Prep Sch 2003–; chair of govrs Grove Road Sch Hounslow; Best Headmistress of a Prep Sch Tatler 2006; memb: Psychological Soc 1976, ACT 1987, IAPS 2003, NAHT 2003; *Recreations* Arabic, singing, the sea; *Style*— Mrs Prudence Lynch; ✉ Kensington Preparatory School, 596 Fulham Road, London SW6 5BA (tel 020 7731 9300, fax 020 7731 9301, e-mail p.lynch@kenprep.gdst.net)

LYNCH, Roderick Robertson (Rod); s of late Nanson Lynch, and Catherine, *née* Robertson; *b* 22 May 1949; *Educ* Perth Acad, Univ of Dundee (MA); *m* 1972, Christina, da of William Williams; 2 s (James b 1975, Alexander b 1980); *Career* served RAC 1966–67; various positions British Airways 1971–89, md Air Europe 1989–91, dir Forte Hotels 1991–93, chief exec BBC Resources Directorate 1993–99, chief exec Olympic Airways Greece 1999–2000, chm and ceo GSS Ltd 2001–; memb Bd: CAA 1993–99, Nat Air Traffic Servs 1996–99; *Recreations* rugby, military history, music, aviation; *Clubs* Travellers; *Style*— Rod Lynch, Esq

LYNCH-BLOSSE, Sir Richard Hely; 17 Bt (I 1622), of Castle Carra, Galway; s of Sir David Edward Lynch-Blosse, 16 Bt (d 1971), and Elizabeth, *née* Payne; *b* 26 August 1953; *Educ* Welwyn Garden City, Royal Free Hosp Sch of Med London (MB BS); *m* 1 (m dis), Cara Lynne, o da of George Longmore Sutherland, of St Ives, Cambs; 2 da (Katherine Helen (Katy) b 1983, Hannah Victoria b 1985); m 2, Jacqueline Hall, *née* Francis, o da of late Gordon Francis; *Career* med practitioner, short serv cmmn with RAMC 1975–85; MO Oxfordshire Army Cadet Force, med offr to European Sch Culham; memb: BMA, Medical Defence Union, Soc of Ornamental Turner; LRCP, MRCS, DRCOG, MRCGP; *Recreations* archery, ornamental turning, precision engineering; *Style*— Sir Richard Lynch-Blosse, Bt; ✉ The Surgery, Clifton Hampden, Oxfordshire OX14 3EL

LYNCH-ROBINSON, Sir Dominick Christopher; 4 Bt (UK 1920), of Foxrock, Co Dublin; s of Sir Niall Bryan Lynch-Robinson, 3 Bt, DSC (d 1996), and Rosemary Seaton, *née* Eller (d 2001); *b* 30 July 1948; *m* 1973, Victoria, da of Kenneth Weir, of Sale, Manchester; 1 da (Anna Elizabeth Seaton b 19 July 1973), 1 s (Christopher Henry Jake b 1 Oct 1977), 1 step da (Joselyn Cleare b 12 July 1969); *Heir* s, Christopher Lynch-Robinson; *Career* global creative dir J Walter Thompson; *Style*— Sir Dominick Lynch-Robinson, Bt; ✉ Flat 3, 34 Montagu Square, London W1H 2LJ (tel 020 7724 1460); J Walter Thompson, 1 Knightsbridge Green, London SW1X 7NW

LYNDEN-BELL, Prof Donald; CBE (2000); s of Lt-Col Lachlan Arthur Lynden-Bell, MC (d 1984), and Monica Rose, *née* Thring; *b* 5 April 1935; *Educ* Marlborough, Clare Coll Cambridge; *m* 1 July 1961, Ruth Marion, da of Dr D N Truscott, of Ely; 1 da (Marion Katharine b 10 April 1965), 1 s (Edward Lachlan b 16 Dec 1968); *Career* res fell Clare Coll Cambridge and fell Cwlth (Harkness) Fund Caltech and Mt Wilson and Palomar Observatories 1960–62, dir of maths studies Clare Coll Cambridge and asst lectr Univ of Cambridge 1962–65, SPSO Royal Greenwich Observatory Herstmonceux 1965–72, visiting prof Univ of Sussex 1970–72, dir Inst of Astronomy Cambridge 1972–77, 1982–87 and 1992–95, prof of astrophysics Univ of Cambridge 1972–2001, prof fell Clare Coll Cambridge 1972–; Russell lectr American Astronomical Soc 2000; pres: Cambridge Philosophical Soc 1982–84, RAS 1985–87 (Eddington Medal 1984, Gold Medal 1993); Brower Prize American Astronomical Soc 1990; Bruce Gold Medal of the Astronomical Soc of the Pacific 1998, J J Carty Medal and Award of the US Nat Acad of Sciences 2000; Hon DSc Univ of Sussex 1987; hon memb American Astronomical Soc 2002–; hon fell Inter-Univ Centre for Astronomy and Astrophysics (IUCAA) Pune India 2004–; foreign assoc: US Nat Acad of Sci 1990, Royal Soc of SA 1994; FRS 1978; *Recreations* hill walking; *Style*— Prof Donald Lynden-Bell, CBE, FRS; ✉ 9 Storey's Way, Cambridge CB3 0DP (tel 01223 359557); Institute of Astronomy (Cambridge University), The Observatories, Madingley Road, Cambridge CB3 0DP (tel 01223 337525, fax 01223 337523, e-mail dlb@ast.cam.ac.uk)

LYNDHURST, Nicholas; *Career* actor 1971–; *Theatre* incl: Harding's Luck (Greenwich), Trial Run (Oxford Playhouse), Black Comedy (tour), The Private Ear (tour), The Foreigner (Albery), Straight and Narrow (Wyndhams) 1992, The Dresser (Duke of York's) 2005; also appeared in Royal Variety Performance (Theatre Royal Drury Lane) 1986; *Television* incl: Davy in Anne of Avonlea, Peter in Heidi, Tom Canty and Prince Edward in The Prince and the Pauper, Tootles in Peter Pan, Raymond in Going Straight (BBC), Adam in Butterflies (BBC), Philip in Father's Day (Granada), Tim in Fairies (BBC), Philip in Losing Her, Dobson in To Serve Them All My Days (BBC), Wilson in Spearhead, Rodney in Only Fools and Horses (BBC, 10 series), The Two of Us (LWT, 5 series), The Piglet Files (LWT, 3 series), Goodnight Sweetheart (BBC, 6 series) 1994, Gulliver's Travels (Channel 4) 1996, Uriah Heap in David Copperfield 1999, Butterflies Reunion Special 2000, Thin Ice (BBC) 2000, Murder in Mind (BBC) 2003, After You've Gone (BBC) 2007; *Awards* Best Television Ad Award 1997 and 2000 (for WHSmith campaign), Most Popular Comedy Performer National Television Awards 1998 and 2000; *Recreations* surfing, flying, diving; *Style*— Nicholas Lyndhurst, Esq; ✉ c/o Chatto & Linnit Ltd, 123A Kings Road, London SW3 4PL (tel 020 7352 7722)

LYNDON-SKEGGS, Andrew Neville; s of Dr Peter Lyndon-Skeggs (d 2002), of Preston Candover, Hants, and June Angela, *née* Reid; *b* 10 January 1949; *Educ* Rugby, Magdalene Coll Cambridge (MA); *m* 8 April 1972 (m dis); 2 da (Vanessa b 1975, Tessa b 1979); *Career* master and tstee Univ of Cambridge Drag Hunt 1968–71; chm Westbrook Property Developments Ltd 1981–, md and chief exec Town Pages Ltd and TownPagesNet.com.plc 1995–99, chm and chief exec TheGardenLine.com Ltd 2000–01, dir Enfranchisement and Leasehold Solutions Ltd (ELS) 2003–; FRICS; *Recreations* stalking, hunting, fishing, skiing, gardening, travelling; *Clubs* Mardens, Kandahar; *Style*— Andrew Lyndon-Skeggs, Esq; ✉ Westbrook House, Holybourne, Alton, Hampshire GU34 4HH (tel 01420 566900, fax 01420 594556, e-mail anls@btconnect.com); 18 Sloane Gardens, London SW1W 8DL

LYNE, HE Richard John; s of John Arthur Lyne (d 1991), and Sylvia Mary Raven, *née* Knott (d 1964); *b* 20 November 1948, Peterborough; *Educ* Kimbolton Sch; *m* 1977, (Jennifer) Anne, *née* Whitworth; 1 da (Alexandra Clare b 1982), 1 s (Christopher Richard John b 1985); *Career* diplomat; entered HM Dip Serv 1970, South Pacific Dept FCO 1970–71, East European Dept FCO 1971–72, registry offr Belgrade 1972–74, accountant Algiers 1974–77, admin offr Damascus 1977–80, Policy Planning FCO 1980–81, on loan to DTI 1982–84, second sec (commercial) New Delhi 1984–87, second sec then first sec (Chancery/info) Stockholm 1988–91, Western European Dept FCO 1992–94, Personnel Mgmnt Dept 1995–96, dep high cmmr Port of Spain 1996–2000, Conf and Visits Gp FCO Servs 2000–02, Personnel Servs then Human Resources Pay and Benefits Policy Team FCO 2002–04, high cmmr to Solomon Islands 2004–; *Recreations* family, watching sport, genealogy; *Clubs* Royal Over-Seas League; *Style*— HE Mr Richard Lyne; ✉ c/o Foreign & Commonwealth Office (Honiara), King Charles Street, London SW1A 2AH

LYNE, Sir Roderic Michael John; KBE (1999), CMG (1992); s of late Air Vice-Marshal Michael Lyne, CB, AFC, DL, and Avril Joy, *née* Buckley; *b* 31 March 1948; *Educ* Highfield Sch Liphook, Eton, Univ of Leeds (BA); *m* 13 Dec 1969, Amanda Mary, da of Sir Howard Frank Trayton Smith, GCMG; 2 s (Jethro b 10 Nov 1971, Andrei b 31 May 1974), 1 da (Sasha b 7 Jan 1981); *Career* entered HM Dip Serv 1970, Br Embassy Moscow 1972–74, Br Embassy Senegal 1974–76; FCO: Eastern Europe and Soviet Dept 1976–78, Rhodesia Dept 1979, asst private sec to Foreign and Cwlth Sec 1979–82; UK mission to UN NY 1982–86, visiting res fell RIIA 1986–87, head of Chancery and head of Political Section Br Embassy Moscow 1987–90, head of Soviet Dept FCO 1990–91, head of Eastern Dept FCO 1992–93; private sec to PM 1993–96, dir Policy Devpt for CIS, Middle East and Africa British Gas plc 1996, UK permanent rep to UN and other int organisations in Geneva 1997–2000, HM ambass to Russia 2000–04; business conslt and lectr; special advsr: BP plc, HSBC Gp; non-exec dir: Accor 2006–, Aricom plc 2006–; special rep ITE Gp plc 2005–, memb Strategic Advsy Gp QucomHaps Hldgs Ltd 2005–, chm Int Advsy Bd Altimo 2006–; visiting prof Faculty of Business and Law Kingston Univ 2005–; memb: Trilateral Cmmn Task Force on Russia 2005–06 (co-author report Engaging with Russia: The Next Phase 2006), Bd Russo-Br C of C 2006–, Exec Ctee UK/Russia Round Table 2006–; hon vice-pres GB-Russia Soc; memb Oxford Univ Task Force on Energy, the Environment and Devpt 2006–07, chm Advsy Ctee Centre for East European Language Based Area Studies 2007–; tstee World Race Tst, govr Ditchley Fndn 2005–, memb Bd Int Early Music Tst St Petersburg 2007–, patron Amur; Hon LLD Univ of Leeds 2002, Hon DBA Kingston Univ 2004, Hon DLit Heriot-Watt Univ 2004; *Recreations* sport, grandchildren; *Clubs* Travellers; *Style*— Sir Roderic Lyne, KBE, CMG; ✉ 39 Richmond Park Road, London SW14 8JU (e-mail roderic.lyne@btinternet.com)

LYNER, Peter Edward; OBE (1991); s of Alfred Lyner (d 1997), of Belfast, and Doreen Mary, *née* Devenney (d 1994); *b* 13 October 1942; *Educ* Royal Belfast Academical Inst, Univ of London (DPA); *m* 1964, Anne, da of Frederick Rogers (d 1974); 1 da (Anna Elizabeth b 1967), 1 s (Patrick Edward b 1970); *Career* librarian Belfast Public Library 1960–70, freelance journalist Irish Times until 1970; British Council: librarian Sudan 1970–73, librarian Yugoslavia 1973–76, inspr Mgmnt Servs Dept 1976–79, asst dir of educn Nigeria 1979–82, Russian language trg Univ of Strathclyde 1982–83, asst cultural attaché Moscow 1983–87, Bulgarian language trg SSEES 1987, cultural attaché Bulgaria 1987–90, dir Br Cncl N Ireland 1990–, admin Encounter 1998–; ALA 1966, DPA 1967, MIMgt 1981; *Books* Consignment of Ore (under pseudonym Peter Warden, 1983); *Recreations* music, writing, reading; *Style*— Peter Lyner, Esq, OBE; ✉ The British Council, Norwich Union Building, 7 Fountain Street, Belfast, BT1 5EG (tel 028 9023 3440 ext 224, fax 028 9024 0341)

LYNN, Bishop of 2004–; Rt Rev James Henry Langstaff; s of late Harry Langstaff, and Jillian Harper, *née* Brooks; *b* 27 June 1956, Hostert, Germany; *Educ* Cheltenham Coll, St Catherine's Coll Oxford (MA), Univ of Nottingham (BA), St John's Theological Coll Nottingham (Dip); *m* 28 Aug 1977, Bridget, *née* Streatfeild; 1 s (Alasdair b 28 Oct 1983), 1 da (Helen b 23 Jan 1986); *Career* ordained: deacon 1981, priest 1982; asst curate St Peter Farnborough 1981–86, vicar St Matthew Duddeston and St Clement Nechells 1986–96, area dean of Birmingham City 1995–96, chaplain to Bishop of Birmingham 1996–2000, rector Holy Trinity Sutton Coldfield 2000–04, area dean of Sutton Coldfield 2002–04; memb Bd FCH Housing and Care 1988–2002, non-exec dir Good Hope Hosp NHS Tst 2003–04, chair Flagship Housing Gp 2006–; memb E of Eng Regnl Assembly 2006–; *Recreations* golf, skiing, theatre, choral singing, contemporary fiction; *Style*— The Rt Rev the Bishop of Lynn; ✉ The Old Vicarage, Castle Acre, King's Lynn, Norfolk PE32 2AA (tel 01760 755553, e-mail bishoplynn@norwich.anglican.org)

LYNN, Jonathan Adam; s of Dr Robin Lynn, of London, and Ruth Helen, *née* Eban; *b* 3 April 1943; *Educ* Kingswood Sch Bath, Pembroke Coll Cambridge (MA); *m* 1 Aug 1967, Rita Eleonora Merkelis; 1 s (Edward b 19 Oct 1973); *Career* director, writer and actor; Hon MA Univ of Sheffield, Hon PsyD American Behavioral Studies Inst; *Theatre* actor in repertory: Leicester, Edinburgh, Bristol Old Vic; West End (incl Fiddler on the Roof, 1967); artistic dir Cambridge Theatre Co 1977–81 (produced 42 prodns and directed over 20); London dir incl: The Glass Menagerie 1977, The Gingerbread Man 1977, The Unvarnished Truth 1978, Songbook 1979 (SWET and Evening Standard Awards for Best Musical, re-titled The Moony Shapiro Songbook for Broadway Prodn 1981), Anna Christie (RSC) 1979, Arms and the Man 1981, Pass The Butler 1981, A Little Hotel On The Side (NT) 1984, Jacobowsky and the Colonel (NT) 1986, Three Men on a Horse (NT, Olivier Award for Best Comedy) 1987, Budgie 1988; company dir at NT 1986–87; *Television* as actor incl: Doctor in the House (series) 1970, The Liver Birds (series) 1972, My Brothers Keeper 1973 and 1974 (series, co-writer with George Layton), Barmitzvah Boy 1975, The Knowledge 1979, Outside Edge 1982, Diana 1984, as writer incl: Yes Minister 1980–82, Yes Prime Minister 1986–88 (with co-author Anthony Jay, BAFTA Writers' Award, Broadcasting Press Guild Award (twice), Pye Television Writers' Award (twice), Ace Award - best comedy writing on US cable TV, Special Award from The Campaign For Freedom of Information); TV dir: Smart Guys, Ferris Bueller (NBC TV pilots); *Film* as actor incl: Into The Night 1985, Three Men and A Little Lady 1990, Greedy 1993; screenplay The Internecine Project 1974; film as dir: Micks People (also wrote) 1982, Clue (also wrote) 1986, Nuns On The Run (also wrote, Golden Cane Award at Festival de Comedie in Vevey) 1989, My Cousin Vinny 1991, The Distinguished Gentleman 1991 (Environmental Media Award, Political Film Soc Special Award), Greedy 1993, Sgt Bilko 1995, Trial and Error 1997, The Whole Nine Yards 2000, The Fighting Temptations 2003 (NAACP Image Award); *Books* A Proper Man (1976), The Complete Yes Minister (1984), Yes Prime Minister vol 1 (1986), vol 2 (with Antony Jay, 1987), Mayday (1993); *Recreations* changing weight; *Style*— Jonathan Lynn; ✉ c/o Anthony Jones, Peters Fraser and Dunlop, DruryHouse, 34–43 Russell Street, London WC2B 5HA (tel 020 7734 1000)

LYNN, Prof Richard; s of Richard Lynn, and Ann Lynn; *b* 20 February 1930; *Educ* Bristol GS, King's Coll Cambridge (Passingham prize); *m* 1956 (m dis 1978), Susan Maher; 1 s, 2 da; m 2, 1989, Susan Lesley Hampson (decd); m 3, 2004, Joyce Walters; *Career* lectr in psychology Univ of Exeter 1956–67; prof of psychology: Dublin Economic and Social Research Inst 1967–72, Univ of Ulster 1972–96 (prof emeritus 1996–); currently head Ulster Inst for Social Research; awarded US Mensa award for Excellence (for work on intelligence) 1985, 1988 and 1993; *Books* Attention Arousal and the Orientation Reaction (1966), The Irish Braindrain (1969), The Universities and the Business Community (1969), Personality and National Character (1971), An Introduction to the Study of Personality (1972), The Entrepreneur (ed, 1974), Dimensions of Personality (ed, 1981), Educational Achievement in Japan (1987), The Secret of the Miracle Economy (1991), Dysgenics (1997), Eugenics: A Reassessment (2001), The Science of Human Diversity (2001), IQ and the Wealth of Nations (2002), Race Differences in Intelligence (2005), IQ and Global Inequality (jtly, 2006), The Global Bell Curve (2007); author of various articles on personality, intelligence and social psychology; *Recreations* DIY, woodcutting; *Clubs* Oxford and Cambridge; *Style*— Prof Richard Lynn

LYNN, Dame Vera Margaret; DBE (1975, OBE 1969); da of Bertram Welch, and Annie, *née* Martin; *b* 20 March 1917, East Ham; *Educ* Brampton Rd Sch East Ham; *m* 1941, Harry Lewis; 1 da (Virginia Penelope Ann); *Career* singer; with Ambrose Orch 1937–40, subsequently went solo, starred Applesauce (London Palladium) 1941, own radio show Sincerely Yours 1941–47; voted most popular singer Daily Express competition 1939, Forces' sweetheart WWII, toured Egypt, India, Burma 1944 (Burma Star 1985); subsequently: Tallulah Bankhead's Big Show (USA), London Laughs (Adelphi London), cabaret in Las Vegas, own TV show Vera Lynn Sings (BBC); numerous appearances over Europe, SA, Aust, NZ and Canada, 8 Command Performances, records incl Auf Wiedersehen (over 12 million copies sold), first British artist to top American Charts; pres: Aust Variety Ladies' Assoc, RAFA, Y-Care Int Fund for Africa, London Taxi Drivers' Benevolent Fund, Young Concert Artists' Assoc, Local Women's Br Legion; first woman pres Printers' Charitable Corp; vice-pres: Song Writers' Guild, Age Concern (memb Fund Raising Ctee); chm: Breast Cancer Tst Fund, Gilbert & Sullivan Tst Fund; vice-chm Stars Orgn for Spastics, life govr ICRF; Ivor Novello Award 1973, Show Business Personality Award Grand Order of Water Rats 1973, Music Publishers' Award and Songwriters of GB Award 1974 and 1975, Woman of the World Award 1987, int ambass Variety Club Int 1987 (Humanitarian Award 1985), Spirit of the 20th Century Award 2000; fndr Dame Vera Lynn Sch for Parents and Handicapped Children 1992, Master of Music City of London Univ 1992–; Freeman Cities of: London, Winnipeg, Melbourne, Cornerbrook, Nashville; Hon LLD Meml Univ Newfoundland; fell Univ of E London 1990; Cdr of Orange Nassau (Holland) 1976, OStJ 1998; *Books* Vocal Refrain (autobiography, 1975), We'll Meet Again (jtly, 1989), Unsung Heroines (1990); *Recreations* gardening, painting, needlework, knitting; *Style*— Dame Vera Lynn, DBE, LLD, MMUS

LYNNE, Elizabeth (Liz); MEP (Lib Dem) West Midlands; *b* 22 January 1948; *Educ* Dorking County GS; *Career* actress 1966–89, freelance speech and voice conslt 1989–92; Parly candidate (Lib Alliance) Harwich 1987; MP (Lib Dem) Rochdale 1992–97, MEP (Lib Dem) W Midlands 1999–; Lib Dem Shadow Sec of State social Security and Disability 1994–97; vice-pres Employment and Social Affrs Ctee, memb Human Rights SubCtee, memb delgn for relations with S Asia, S Asia Assoc for Regional Cooperation, vice-pres All-Pty Disability Intergroup, co-pres Parly Intergroup on Aging, co-chair MEPs Against Cancer, pres Lib Dem Friends of Kashmir; shadow rapporteur Working Time Directive, rapporteur for European Year of Disabled People 2003, rapporteur EU Action Plan for Disabled People 2006–07, rapporteur Social Reality Stocktaking 2007; chair Indonesian coordination gp Amnesty Int 1972–79, vice-pres: Campaign to Protect Rural England (Staffordshire), Droitwich Canal Tst; patron: Jennifer Tst for Spinal Muscular Atrophy, Blue Eyed Soul Dance Co, Friends of the Montgomery Canal, George Coller Meml Fund, Tourism For All UK, Fedn of European Motorcyclists' Assocs, Worcestershire Lifestyles, Shropshire and Wrekin ME Support, Grown Up Congenital Heart Patient Assoc, Parkside Centre Tst; *Recreations* tennis, motorbiking; *Style*— Liz Lynne, MEP; ✉ Constituency Office, 55 Ely Street, Stratford-upon-Avon CV37 6LN (tel 01789 266354, fax 01789 268848, e-mail lizlynne@cix.co.uk); Brussels Office, 10G262, 60, rue Wiertz, B-1047, Bruxelles, Belgium (tel 00 32 2 284 7521, fax 00 32 2 284 9521, e-mail elynne@europarl.eu.int, website www.lizlynne.org.uk)

LYNNE, Jeff; s of Philip Porter Lynne (d 1985), and Nancy, *née* Osborne (d 1988), of Birmingham; *b* 30 December 1947; *Educ* Alderlea Boys Sch Shard End Birmingham; *Career* producer, songwriter, singer and guitarist; band memb: Idle Race 1966–70, The Move 1970–72; formed: Electric Light Orchestra 1972–85 (toured America and Europe 1973–78, toured world 1978–82), The Traveling Wilbury's (with Roy Orbison, Bob Dylan, George Harrison and Tom Petty) 1988; writer, prodr, singer and guitarist of all ELO's records; albums incl: Eldorado (gold 1974), Face the Music (gold 1975), A New World Record (platinum 1976), Out of the Blue (quadruple platinum 1977, Nationwide Music Award/Album of the Year 1978), Discovery (double platinum 1979), ELO's Greatest Hits (platinum 1980, 4 million copies sold 2001), Xanadu (film score, platinum 1980), Time (gold 1982); singles incl: Evil Woman (gold 1975, BMI Songwriters Award for 1 million broadcasts in USA 1992), Livin' Thing (gold 1976, BMI Songwriters Award for 1 million broadcasts in USA), Telephone Line (gold 1977, BMI Songwriters Award for 1 million broadcasts in USA 2001), Don't Bring Me Down (gold 1980, BMI Songwriters Award for 1 million broadcasts in USA 1999), Xanadu (gold 1980, Ivor Novello Award for Best Film Theme Song 1981), Hold on Tight (gold 1982), Strange Magic (BMI Songwriters Award for 1 million broadcasts in USA 1999); co-prodr and co-writer Traveling Wilbury's: Vol 1 (triple platinum 1988, Grammy Award 1989), Vol 3 (platinum 1991); solo album Armchair Theatre 1990; as prodr of other artists: co-prodr Cloud Nine (George Harrison, platinum 1987), prodr and co-writer Full Moon Fever (album, Tom Petty, triple platinum 1988), prodr and co-writer You Got It (Roy Orbison, platinum 1988), prodr and co-writer Into the Great Wide Open (Tom Petty, platinum 1991), co-prodr Free As a Bird (The Beatles, 1994), co-prodr Real Love (The Beatles, 1995), co-prodr (with Sir Paul McCartney) Flaming Pie (album, gold 1997); other major awards incl: Ivor Novello Award for contrib to British music 1979, Best Producer Rolling Stone Magazine 1989, Ivor Novello Award for outstanding contrib to British music 1996; memb: ASCAP, BASCA, BAFTA; *Recreations* computers, tennis; *Style*— Jeff Lynne, Esq

LYON, Prof Christina Margaret; da of late Edward Arthur Harrison, of Liverpool, and Kathleen Joan, *née* Smith; *b* 12 November 1952; *Educ* Wallasey HS for Girls, UCL (LLB, Maxwell Law prize); *m* 29 May 1976, His Hon Judge Adrian P Lyon, s of Alexander Ward Lyon, of London; 1 da (Alexandra Sophie Louise b 5 Jan 1984), 1 s (David Edward Arandall b 8 July 1985); *Career* tutor and sometime lectr in law Faculty of Law UCL 1974–75; slr Bell & Joynson Liscard Wallasey Merseyside 1975–77; lectr in Law Faculty: Univ of Liverpool 1977–80, Univ of Manchester 1980–86 (sub-dean 1986); prof of law and head Sch of Law Keele Univ 1986–93; Univ of Liverpool: prof of common law and head Dept of Law 1993–97, dean Faculty of Law 1994–97, Queen Victoria prof of law 1998–; asst recorder of the Crown Court 1998–2000, recorder in HM Courts (crime and family) 2000–; dir Centre for the Study of the Child, the Family and the Law 1994–; ind chair Liverpool Early Years Devpt and Childcare Partnership 2001–; Dr Barnardos Res Fellowship 1987–91; chm and tstee Nat Youth Advocacy Serv 1998–2002; ed Journal of Social Welfare and Family Law 1984–, advsy ed Representing Children 1995–, ed Web Journal of Legal Issues 1995–, legal theory ed Amicus Curiae: The Journal of the Inst of Advanced Legal Studies 1998–, pres N Staffs RELATE (marriage guidance) 1987–93 (memb Nat Exec Ctee 1991–94), ind memb Merseyside Children's Secure Accommodation Panel 1988–93; memb ESRC Grants Bd 1988–91, memb Child Policy Review Gp NCB 1988–91, tstee, dir and chm IRCHIN 1988–98, tstee and dir Schs Cncls (UK) 1994–2003, vice-chair Merseyside Guardians ad Libem Ctee 1993–97; memb: Law Soc 1977, Soc of Public Teachers of Law 1977, Ctee of Heads of Univ Law Schs (memb Exec Ctee 1989–96); FRSA 1991; *Books* Matrimonial Jurisdiction of Magistrates Courts (1980), Cohabitation Without Marriage (1983), The Law of Residential Homes and Day Care Establishments (1984), Child Abuse (1990, 3 edn 2003), Atkins on Minors (1990), Butterworths Family Law Handbook (1991), Living Away From Home (1991), The Implications of the Children Act 1989 for Children with Disabilities (1991), Butterworths Law and Practice relating to Children (1992), Atkins on Infants (vols 1 and 2, 1992), The Law relating to Children (1993), Legal Issues Arising from the Care, Control and Safety of Children with Learning Disabilities who also Present Challenging Behaviour - Research Report and A Guide for Parents and Carers (1994), The Impact of the Law on Youth - The Years of Decision (1996), Butterworths Family Law Encyclopaedia (2005, also quarterly updates); contrib: The Impact of the Law on the Prevention of Child Abuse and Neglect in The National Commission of Inquiry Report into the Prevention of Child Abuse and Neglect 'Childhood Matters' (1996), Children Abused within the Care System in 'Child Protection and Family Support' (ed Parton, Routledge, 1997), Don't Forget Us (report for Mental Health Fndn, 1997), Children and the Law - Towards 2000 and Beyond. An Essay in Human Rights, Social Policy and the Law (1997), Effective Support Services for Children when Parental Relationships Break Down (1998), Loving Smack - Lawful Assault? (2000), A Trajectory of Hope (2000), Physical Interventions and the Law (2004), Breaking Down Walls (2004), A Parents' and Carers' Guide to Physical Intervention and the Law (2005); *Recreations* tennis, opera, theatre, foreign travel, writing; *Style*— Prof Christina Lyon; ✉ The Liverpool Law School, University of Liverpool, Chatham Street, Liverpool L69 7ZS (tel 0151 794 2818, fax 0151 794 2829, telex 627095 UNILPL G, e-mail c.m.lyon@liv.ac.uk)

LYON, George; s of Alister Lyon (d 1993), of Rothesay, Isle of Bute, and Mary, *née* McAlister (d 1998); *b* 16 July 1956; *Educ* Rothesay Acad, Nuffield Scholar 1987; *m* (sep 2002); 3 da (Lorna b 11 Oct 1984, Samantha b 20 Feb 1986, Amanda b 26 July 1990); *Career* farmer of family farms; dir Scottish Quality Beef and Lamb Assoc 1996–97; MSP (Lib Dem) Argyll & Bute 1999–2007; memb Nat Farmers Union of Scotland (held every office incl pres), assoc BVA; past chm Port Bannatyne Sch Bd; FRAgS; *Recreations* swimming, football, skiing, reading; *Clubs* Farmers; *Style*— George Lyon, Esq

LYON, John Macdonald; CB (2003); *b* 12 April 1948; *Educ* Univ of Cambridge (MA); *m*; 2 c; *Career* Home Office: joined 1969, asst sec Ctee on the Future of Broadcasting 1974–77, sec Inquiry into Prison Disturbances 1990–91, dir sentencing and correctional policy 1998–99, dir police policy 1999; DG Policing and Crime Reduction Group 2000–03, DG Legal and Judicial Servs Gp Miny of Justice (formerly Dept for Constitutional Affrs) 2003–; *Style*— John Lyon, Esq, CB

LYON, Thomas Stephen; s of Clifford Alexander Lyon (d 1962), and Felicia Maria Maximiliana, *née* Rosenfeld; *b* 26 November 1941; *Educ* Univ Coll Sch, Wadham Coll Oxford (MA), LSE (LLM); *m* 1971, Judith Elizabeth Jervis, da of Joseph Globe, of Toronto, Canada; 3 s (Edmund b 1971, Charles b 1973, Roger b 1974); *Career* slr; Woodham Smith Borradaile and Martin 1962–68, Berwin & Co 1968–70, Berwin Leighton 1970–2001, Berwin Leighton Paisner 2001–; memb City of London Slrs' Co; *Recreations* books, music; *Clubs* Reform; *Style*— Thomas Lyon, Esq; ✉ 24 Denewood Road, Highgate, London N6 4AJ (tel 020 8340 0846); Fernlea, Redmire, Leyburn, North Yorkshire (tel 01969 622776)

LYON, Victor Lawrence; QC (2002); s of Dr Jacqueline Beverley Lyon; *b* 10 February 1956; *Educ* Marlborough, Trinity Coll Cambridge (BA); *Career* called to the Bar Gray's Inn 1980; asst recorder Western Circuit 1999, recorder 2000; *Books* The Practice and Procedure of the Commercial Court (5 edn, with Sir Anthony Coleman, 2000); *Recreations* tennis, golf, swimming; *Clubs* Hurlingham; *Style*— Victor Lyon, Esq, QC; ✉ Essex Court Chambers, 24 Lincoln's Inn Fields, London WC2A 3EG (tel 020 7813 8000, fax 020 7813 8080)

LYON-DALBERG-ACTON, *see:* Acton

LYON-MARIS, Paul J; s of Peter David Lyon-Maris, of W Sussex, and Sheila Margaret Ageless Wake; *b* 7 June 1962; *Educ* Lancing; *Career* agent ICM; *Style*— Paul Lyon-Maris, Esq; ✉ ICM, Oxford House, 76 Oxford Street, London W1D 1BS

LYONS, Alastair David; CBE (2001); *b* 18 October 1953; *Educ* Whitgift Sch Croydon, Trinity Coll Cambridge (MA); *m* Shauneen, *née* Rhodes; 1 s (Edward Alexander Rhodes b 1982), 2 da (Lucy Jane b 1984, Tabitha Sallyanne b 1993); *Career* articled clerk rising to asst audit mangr Price Waterhouse & Co CAs 1974–79, corp finance mangr N M Rothschild & Sons Ltd 1979; H P Bulmer Holdings plc: gp treas 1979–82, gp financial controller 1983–88, fin dir H P Bulmer Drinks Ltd and actg gp fin dir 1988–89; divnl dir corp fin Asda Group plc 1989–90, fin dir Asda Stores Ltd 1990–91; National and Provincial Building Society: fin dir 1991–94, chief exec 1994–96, chm N&P Life Assurance Ltd and N&P Unit Trust Management Ltd; md Insurance Div Abbey National plc 1996–97; dir: Scottish Mutual Assurance plc 1996–97, Abbey National Life plc 1996–97, Commercial Union Underwriting Ltd 1996–; chief exec National Provident Institution 1997–99; dir of corporate projects Natwest Gp 1999–2000, exec chm Partners for Finance Ltd 2001–; non-exec chm: Admiral Gp Ltd 2000–, In Retirement Services Ltd 2002–, Legal Marketing Services Ltd 2002–, Health and Case Management Ltd 2003–, Buy-as-you-View Ltd 2004–, Highamgroup plc 2005–; non-exec dir: Benefits Agency 1994–97, DSS 1997–2001,

Dept for Work and Pensions 2001–02, Wishstream Ltd 2001–02, Dept for Tport 2002–05, Sesame Gp Ltd 2003–04; ATII, MCT; FCA; *Recreations* cycling, riding, hill walking, gardening, antiques; *Style*— Alastair Lyons, Esq, CBE; ✉ e-mail alastair_lyons@jaset.demon.co.uk

LYONS, Anthony; s of Alan Lyons, and Angela, *née* Collins; *b* 7 June 1967, London; *Educ* Mill Hill Sch; *m* 2 Sept 2001, Lucy, *née* Johnson; 1 da (Grace Ida Rose b 29 Aug 2003), 1 s (Edward Jack b 24 Oct 2005); *Career* Richman Conway Surveyors 1983–85, Davis Coffer Lyons 1985–2004, ceo Earls Court and Olympia 2004–; *Recreations* shooting, tennis, boating; *Clubs* Georges, Harry's Bar, Tramp, Annabel's; *Style*— Anthony Lyons Esq; ✉ Earls Court and Olympia Ltd, Earls Court Exhibition Centre, Warwick Road, London SW5 9TA (tel 020 7370 8007, fax 020 7370 8041, e-mail anthony.lyons@eco.co.uk)

LYONS, Isidor Jack; s of Samuel Henry Lyons (d 1960), of Leeds, and Sophia, *née* Niman; *b* 1 February 1916; *Educ* Leeds GS; *m* 21 Dec 1943, Roslyn Marion, da of Prof Dr Jacob Rosenbaum; 2 s (David Stephen, Jonathon Edward Lyons, *qv*), 2 da (Patricia Gail, Joanna Gaye); *Career* jt md: Alexandre Ltd 1953–73, Prices Tst Ltd 1955–80; dir: UDS Group 1955–80, Bain Capital Boston MA 1981–87 (dir Advsr Bd 1984–87); chm: J Lyons, Chamberlayne & Co 1985–2004, J E London Properties Ltd 1987–2004, Natural Nutrition Co Ltd 1989–90; fin advsr Chamberlayne Macdonald Tst 1981–88, advsr for Bain & Co to Guinness Gp plc 1985–87; chm: Leeds Triennial Musical Festival 1956–65, LSO Tst 1961–88, Shakespeare Quad-Centenary Exhbn 1963–66, USA Bicentennial (cultural FO appt) 1974–76; jt fndr and jt chm Leeds Int Piano Competition 1964–65, dep chm Fanfare for Europe 1971–73, fndr and chm of tstees Sir Jack Lyons Charitable Tst; fndr Sir Jack Lyons Hall Univ of York Music Dept 1964, co-fndr Sir Jack Lyons Theatre Royal Acad of Music 1971, tstee The Heslington Fndn Univ of York 1996–, jt chm Henry Wood Rehearsal Hall London; life tstee Shakespeare Birthplace Tst 1967; memb: Ct Univ of York 1965, The Pilgrims 1967–; govr Ort Braude Int Coll of Technology Karmiel Israel 1998; fndr memb World Wild Life 1001 Club 1970–, hon vice-pres United Jewish Israel Appeal (UIJA) 1986–, patron Tate Gallery 1997; hon memb LSO 1970–, hon vice-pres World Ort Geneva 2003–; Freeman City of London; Hon DUniv York 1975, Hon FRAM 1973; *Recreations* swimming; *Style*— Isidor Jack Lyons; ✉ 303 Le Mirador, Mont Pelèrin, CH 1801, Switzerland

LYONS, Sir John; kt (1987); *b* 23 May 1932; *Educ* St Bede's Coll Manchester, Christ's Coll Cambridge (BA, Dip Ed, PhD, LittD); *m* 1959, Danielle Jacqueline Simonet; *Career* lectr in comparative linguistics SOAS Univ of London 1957–61, lectr in gen linguistics Univ of Cambridge and fell Christ's Coll 1961–64, prof of gen linguistics Univ of Edinburgh 1964–76, prof of linguistics Univ of Sussex 1976–84 (pro-vice-chllr 1981–84), master Trinity Hall Cambridge 1984–2000; hon fell Christ's Coll Cambridge 1985; hon memb Linguistic Soc of America 1978; DèsL (hc) Univ Cath de Louvain 1980; Hon DLitt: Univ of Reading 1986, Univ of Edinburgh 1988, Univ of Sussex 1990, Univ of Antwerp 1992; FBA 1973; *Books* Structural Semantics (1963), Psycholinguistics Papers (ed with R J Wales, 1966), Introduction to Theoretical Linguistics (1968), Chomsky (1970), New Horizons in Linguistics (1970), Semantics 1 and 2 (1977), Language and Linguistics (1980), Language, Meaning and Context (1980), Natural Language and Universal Grammar (1991), Linguistic Semantics (1995); *Style*— Sir John Lyons, LittD, FBA

LYONS, John Trevor; s of Sir Rudolph Lyons, and Jeanette, *née* Dante; *b* 1 November 1943; *Educ* Leeds GS, Univ of Leeds (LLB); *m* 7 Sept 1969, Dianne Lucille, da of Geoffrey Saffer; 3 s (Alan b 1971, James b 1973, Benjamin b 1974); *Career* slr; conslt John Howe & Co; *Style*— John T Lyons, Esq; ✉ High Gable, Adel Mill, Eccup Lane, Leeds LS16 8BF (tel 0113 267 4575); John Howe & Co, 10 Park Place, Leeds LS1 2RU (tel 0113 243 3381, fax 0113 245 0559)

LYONS, Jonathon Edward; s of Isidor Jack Lyons, *qv*, and Roslyn M Lyons, *née* Rosenbaum, of Canada; *b* 1 May 1951; *Educ* Carmel Coll; *m* 30 Dec 1975, Miriam, da of Simon Djanogly (d 1980), of Switzerland; 2 s (Jacob b 1976, Simon b 1980), 1 da (Deborah b 1982); *Career* exec sales Alexandra Ltd Leeds 1968–71, chief exec John David Mansworld Ltd 1971–89, ptnr International Investments Ltd 1978–, chief exec H Alan Smith Ltd 1983–85, dir JLC Ltd London 1986, chm JE London Properties Ltd 1988–, private investment conslt Jonathon E Lyons & Co 1988–; dir: Britimpex Ltd Canada, Art Leasing Inc Canada, Johnson Fry plc (Jt Venture Property Div) 1994–96; memb Ctee: Cons Industrial Fund 1985–91, RMC, RAM; jt chm Hyde Park Ctee Central Br Fund 1975–80, tstee The Sir Jack Lyons Charitable Tst 1986; rotarian Int Rotary Club 1995–, vice-pres Int Rotary Club of Westminster 1997– (past elect 1999–2000), jt exec chm Jewish Music Heritage Tst 1998, hon jt vice-chm Jewish Music Inst at Sch of Oriental Arts & Studies; chm and prodr: The Jewel that is Jordan Ltd, The Jewel that is Europe Event Ltd; int advsr Ronson plc 1999–; patron Royal Acad of Arts; memb Renaissance Forum 2001; FInstD, memb FIMBRA; *Clubs* Carlton, IOD; *Style*— Jonathon E Lyons, Esq; ✉ Chalet Emeraude, 1660 Chateau d'Oex, Switzerland; 8 Ledbury Mews North, Kensington, London W11 2AF (tel 020 7229 9481, mobile 07785 330033, e-mail bentley3uk@aol.com)

LYONS, (Andrew) Maximilian; s of Dennis John Lyons, CB, of Fleet, Hants, and Elizabeth Dora Maria, *née* Müller Haefliger; *b* 16 January 1946; *Educ* Queen Mary's GS Basingstoke, Brixton Sch of Bldg (DipArch); *m* 18 June 1983, Katherine Jane (Kate), da of late Brig John Joseph Regan; 1 s (Shaun b 1984), 2 da (Rosalie b 1986, Charlotte b 1989); *Career* sr ptnr Lyons + Sleeman + Hoare architects 1977–; winner of numerous architectural design and environmental awards; tstee Lord Mayor Treloar Sch and Coll; chm Farnham Soc; RIBA 1974, FRSA 1993; *Style*— Maximilian Lyons, Esq; ✉ The Grange, 6 Old Park Lane, Farnham, Surrey GU9 0AH (tel 01252 820082); Lyons + Sleeman + Hoare, Nero Brewery, Cricket Green, Hartley Wintney, Hook, Hampshire RG27 8QA (tel 01252 844144, fax 01252 844800, e-mail maxlyons@lsharch.co.uk, website www.lsharch.co.uk)

LYONS, Roger Alan; s of Morris Lyons (d 1990), of Hove, and Phyllis, *née* Lebof (d 1989); *b* 14 September 1942; *Educ* Christ's Coll Finchley, UCL (BSc(Econ)); *m* Kitty, *née* Horvath; 2 da (Sarah b 1973, Hannah b 1982), 2 s (Gideon b 1975, Joshua b 1986); *Career* ASTMS: regnl offr (North West) 1966–70, nat offr 1970–86, asst gen sec 1986–88 (until merger with TASS to form MSF); MSF: asst gen sec 1988–92, gen sec 1992–, jt gen sec amicus 2002–04; pres TUC 2003–04; conslt; advsr Business Services Assoc; former memb: TUC Gen Cncl, Confedn of Shipbuilding and Engrg Unions (pres 1999–2001), Design Cncl; UCL: fell 1996, former memb Cncl; memb: Central Arbitration Ctee 2002–, Employment Appeals Tbnl 2003–; *Recreations* supporting Arsenal; *Style*— Roger Lyons, Esq; ✉ 22 Park Crescent, London N3 2NJ (tel 020 8346 6843, e-mail rogerlyons22@hotmail.com)

LYONS, His Hon Judge Shaun; CBE (2004); s of Jeremiah Lyons (d 1978), and Winifred Ruth, *née* Doble (d 2001); *b* 20 December 1942; *Educ* Portsmouth GS, Inns of Court Sch of Law; *m* 19 Dec 1970, Nicola Rosemary, da of Capt D F Chilton, DSC, RN; 1 s (Francis Daniel b 4 Jan 1972), 1 da (Victoria Clare b 26 Feb 1974); *Career* with RN 1961–92; Lt 1966, Lt Cdr 1974, called to the Bar Middle Temple 1975, Capt RN 1988 (Cdr 1981), chief naval judge advocate 1990–92, recorder of the Crown Court 1991–92 (asst recorder 1988–91), circuit judge (SE Circuit) 1992– (sr circuit judge 2002–), resident judge Wood Green Crown Court 1995–, chm Lord Chllr's Advsy Ctee on JPs for NW London 2004– (dep chm 1996–2004); *Recreations* reading, gardening, walking, boating; *Clubs* Army and Navy, Royal Yacht Squadron; *Style*— His Hon Judge Lyons, CBE; ✉ Wood Green Crown Court, Woodall House, Lordship Lane, London N22 4LF (tel 020 8881 1400)

LYONS, Prof Terence John; s of Peter John Lyons (d 2003), and Christobel Valerie, *née* Hardie, of Puddle, nr Lanlivery, Bodmin, Cornwall; *b* 4 May 1953; *Educ* Univ of Cambridge (BA), Univ of Oxford (DPhil); *m* 30 Aug 1975, (Christina) Barbara, da of late Joseph Epsom; 1 s (Barnaby b 1981), 1 da (Josephine b 1983); *Career* jr res fell Jesus Coll Oxford 1979–81, Hedrick visiting asst prof UCLA 1981–82, lectr in mathematics Imperial Coll of Sci and Technol London 1981–85; Univ of Edinburgh: Colin MacLaurin prof of mathematics 1985–93, head Dept of Mathematics 1988–91; prof of mathematics Imperial Coll of Sci Technol and Med 1993–2000; Wallis prof of mathematics Univ of Oxford 2000–; sr fell EPSRC 1993–98; Polya Prize London Mathematical Soc 2000; FRSE 1987, FRSA 1990, FIMA 1991, FRS 2002, FIMS 2004; *Recreations* cycling, writing software, family life; *Style*— Prof Terence Lyons, FRS, FRSE; ✉ University of Oxford, Mathematical Institute, 24–29 St Giles', Oxford OX1 3LB (e-mail tlyons@maths.ox.ac.uk)

LYONS, Tony; s of Michael Lyons, of London, and Edith, *née* Morris; *b* 12 April 1947; *Educ* Tottenham GS, Univ of London (BA), Univ of Kent; *m* 30 July 1969, Alison, da of Simon MacLeod; 2 s (Matthew Michael Simon b 30 Nov 1973, Frazer Alexander David b 3 Nov 1981), 1 da (Jessica Jane b 23 May 1976); *Career* dep ed Planned Savings 1969–71, journalist Sunday Telegraph 1971–78, dep city ed The Observer 1978–81, owner public houses 1982–85, asst city ed Birmingham Post 1985–86, dir Buchanan Communications 1986–93, dir Tavistock Communications 1993–97, currently freelance contrib to nat newspapers and the Evening Standard; *Recreations* good food, fishing, walking, films, relaxing; *Style*— Tony Lyons, Esq; ✉ City Desk, Evening Standard (tel 020 7938 6000)

LYSTER, Guy Lumley; DL (Essex 1975); s of Ronald Guy Lyster, OBE, Croix de Guerre avec Palm (d 1972), of Lances, Kelvedon, Essex, and Ada Erica, *née* Neal (d 1977); *b* 4 April 1925; *Educ* Winchester, Trinity Coll Cambridge (MA); *m* 10 May 1958, Gillian Rosemary, da of Michael Spencer Gosling (d 1979), of Little Maplestead, Essex; 1 s (Anthony b 1960), 1 da (Sarah (Mrs Michael Retallack) b 1961); *Career* Grenadier Gds 1943–47: served NW Europe 1945, Capt 1946; Strutt & Parker Coval Hall Chelmsford: chartered surveyor 1952, assoc ptnr 1958, ptnr 1969, dep sr ptnr 1979, ret 1992; farmer and breeder of pedigree Charolais cattle 1967–97; Master East Essex Foxhounds 1983–93, judge HIS (Hunter Improvement Soc) and Ponies UK Panels 1960–2000; Freeman City of London, Liveryman Worshipful Co of Salters 1955; FRICS 1961, FCAAV 1961; *Recreations* hunting, shooting, cricket; *Clubs* Cavalry and Guards'; *Style*— Guy Lyster, Esq, DL; ✉ Rayne Hatch House, Stisted, Braintree, Essex CM77 8BY (tel 01787 472087, fax 01787 476071)

LYSTER, Dr Simon; s of John Neal Lyster, and Marjorie Aird, *née* Everard; *b* 29 April 1952; *Educ* Radley, Magdalene Coll Cambridge (MA, PhD); *m* 1990, Sandra Elizabeth Charity; 2 c; *Career* admitted slr England and Wales 1978, qualified New York attorney-at-law 1979; slr Slaughter and May 1976–78, prog offr Defenders of Wildlife (USA) 1979–81, sec Falkland Islands Fndn 1982–86, criteria offr WWF International and head of conservation policy WWF UK 1986–95, DG The Wildlife Trusts 1995–2003; LEAD International (Leadership in Environment and Devpt): dir of devpt and progs 2003–05, ceo 2005–; non-exec dir Northumbrian Water Ltd 2006–; tstee: World Land Tst, Conservation Int Europe, Kilverstone Wildlife Charitable Tst; *Books* International Wildlife Law (1985); *Recreations* tennis, cricket, bird watching; *Style*— Dr Simon Lyster; ✉ LEAD International, Sundial House, 114 Kensington High Street, London W8 4NP (tel 0870 220 2918, fax 0870 220 2910, e-mail simon@lead.org)

LYTTELTON, Hon Christopher Charles; s of 10 Viscount Cobham, KG, GCMG, GCVO, TD, PC (d 1977), and Elizabeth Alison, *née* Makeig-Jones; *b* 23 October 1947; *Educ* Eton; *m* 1973, Tessa Mary, da of Col Alexander George Jeremy Readman, DSO (d 1973); 1 s (Oliver b 1976), 1 da (Sophie b 1978); *Career* dep chm Smith & Williamson Hldgs Ltd 2002–; *Recreations* gliding, golf, cricket; *Clubs* New Zealand Golf, MCC, Lasham Gliding Soc; *Style*— The Hon Christopher Lyttelton; ✉ 28 Abbey Gardens, London NW8 9AT; Smith & Williamson, 25 Moorgate, London EC2R 6AY

LYTTELTON, Humphrey Richard Adeane; descended from Humphrey Lyttelton who was executed for collaborating with Guy Fawkes in the Gunpowder Plot; *b* 23 May 1921; *Educ* Eton, Camberwell Art Sch; *Career* served WWII Grenadier Gds; former cartoonist London Daily Mail; jazz musician (trumpet, clarinet, tenor horn), bandleader, author, broadcaster and after-dinner speaker; trumpeter George Webb's Dixielanders 1947, formed The Humphrey Lyttelton Band (with Wally Fawkes on clarinet) 1948, solo visit to first Int Jazz Festival Nice 1948, early recordings made on own London Jazz label, signed recording contract with EMI and accompanied Sidney Bechet for Melodisc 1949, subsequent recordings for Parlophone Super Rhythm Style series incl Bad Penny Blues 1956, played series of London concerts alongside Louis Armstrong All Stars 1956, extended band to incl Joe Temperley, Tony Coe and Jimmy Skidmore (toured USA 1959), subsequent collaborations in Britain with Buck Clayton, Buddy Tate and singers Jimmy Rushing and Joe Turner, fndr Calligraph record label 1984; host The Best of Jazz (BBC Radio 2) for over 30 years, chm I'm Sorry I Haven't a Clue (BBC Radio 4) 1972–; Gold award Sony Radio Awards 1993; former regular contributor to Punch, The Field and BA Highlife magazines; pres Soc for Italic Handwriting 1991; Hon DLitt: Univ of Warwick 1987, Loughborough Univ 1988, Univ of Hertfordshire 1996; Hon DMus: Univ of Durham 1989, Keele Univ 1992; Hon Dr of Art De Montfort Univ 1996; *Books* incl: I Play As I Please (autobiography, 1954); *Recreations* birdwatching, calligraphy; *Style*— Humphrey Lyttelton, Esq; ✉ The Best of Jazz, BBC Radio 2, Pebble Mill, Birmingham B5 7QQ

LYTTELTON, Hon Richard Cavendish; s of 10 Viscount Cobham, KG, GCMG, GCVO, TD, PC (d 1977); *b* 1949; *Educ* Eton; *m* 1971, Romilly, da of Michael Barker; 1 s (Thomas), 1 da (May); *Career* md EMI Finland 1977–80, dir int ops EMI Records (UK) Ltd 1980–83, gp md EMI South Africa 1984–86, pres Capital Records-EMI of Canada 1986–88, pres EMI Classics 1988–2006; chm English Touring Opera 2003; *Recreations* music, shooting; *Style*— The Hon Richard Lyttelton; ✉ 5 Queen's Gate Place Mews, London SW7 5BG

LYTTON, 5 Earl of (UK 1880); Sir John Peter Michael Scawen Lytton; also Viscount Knebworth (UK 1880), 18 Baron Wentworth (E 1529), and 6 Bt (UK 1838); s of 4 Earl of Lytton; *b* 7 June 1950; *Educ* Downside, Univ of Reading; *m* 1980, Ursula, da of Anton Komoly, of Vienna; 1 da (Lady Katrina b 1985), 2 s (Philip Anthony Scawen, Viscount Knebworth b 7 March 1989, Hon Wilfrid Thomas Scawen b 8 Jan 1992); *Heir* s, Viscount Knebworth; *Career* Inland Revenue Valuation Office 1975–81, Permutt Brown & Co 1982–86, Cubitt & West 1986–87, sole principal John Lytton & Co (chartered surveyors) 1988–; chm Leasehold Advsy Serv (LEASE) 1997–2000; pres: Horsham C of C 1995–2001 (chm 1983–85), Sussex Assoc of Local Cncls 1997–, Nat Assoc of Local Cncls 1999–, Newstead Abbey Byron Soc; CLA: former memb Cncl and Exec, chm Sussex Branch 2003–05, regnl chm South East 2005–; tstee and memb Bd Action in Rural Sussex (Sussex Rural Community Cncl) 2001–; memb: RICS Countryside Policies Panel 1996–2000, RICS Boundaries and Party Walls Panel 1997–, RICS Public Affrs Ctee 2000–04; co dir, hill farmer; jt pres Int Byron Soc 2002–; hon memb Pyramus & Thisbe Club (party wall surveyors), hon fell Assoc of Bldg Engrs 1997; FRICS, MCIArb, IRRV; *Recreations* estate maintenance and management, DIY repairs, forestry, shooting, family history; *Style*— The Rt Hon the Earl of Lytton; ✉ Estate Office, Newbuildings Place, Shipley, Horsham, West Sussex RH13 8GQ (tel 01403 741650, fax 01403 741744)

LYVEDEN, 7 Baron (UK 1859) Jack Leslie Vernon; s of 6 Baron Lyveden (d 1999); *b* 10 November 1938; *m* 1961, Lynette June, da of William Herbert Lilley; 1 s, 2 da; *Style*— The Rt Hon the Lord Lyveden; ✉ 17 Carlton Street, Te Aroha, New Zealand

LYWOOD, Jeremy Hugh Gifford; s of Gp Capt Geoffrey Edwin Gifford Lywood (d 1969), of Fittleworth, W Sussex, and Joan Edith, *née* Hordern (d 1994); *b* 8 June 1934; *Educ* Charterhouse; *m* 1, 3 Dec 1955 (m dis 2000), Elizabeth Anne, da of Col David Evans; 4 da (Sarah Gay Gifford b 20 Feb 1957, Amanda Clare Gifford b 16 Dec 1961, Joanna

L

Elizabeth Gifford b 24 Dec 1963, Lucy Christian Gifford b 14 Aug 1975), 3 s (Rupert Charles Gifford b 14 May 1958, Simon James Gifford b 8 Feb 1960, Hugo Geoffrey Gifford b 14 Dec 1969); m 2, 12 Sept 2000, Jennifer, *née* Webb, wid of Jeremy Eadie; *Career* cmmnd 1 Bn King's Royal Rifle Corps 1952–54; progress chaser/buyer and PA to Sir Leonard Crossland Ford Motor Co 1954–60 (mgmnt trainee 1954–55), project mangr and

local dir John Thompson Gp 1960–66, md Econheat 1966–68; Filtermist International plc (formerly Hoccom Developments): fndr md 1968, plc 1990, Queen's Award for Export 1990, pres 1993–97; tax cmmr 1989–95 and 1996–98, High Sheriff for Co of Shropshire 1994–95; *Recreations* sailing, hunting, shooting, fishing; *Style*— Jeremy Lywood, Esq; ✉ Hunton Farm, Lyonshall, Kington, Herefordshire HR5 3JH (tel 01544 340522)

M

MAAS, Robert William; s of Richard Felix Maas (d 1948), of London, and Hilda Rose, *née* Gietzen (d 2002); *b* 13 February 1943; *Educ* Gunnersbury GS; *Career* articled clerk Godwin & Taylor 1959–65, tax ptnr Stoy Hayward 1970–77 (tax sr 1965–70), proprietor Robert Maas & Co 1977–83; tax ptnr: Casson Beckman 1983–87, Blackstone Franks 1987–; memb Editorial Bd Taxation; contrib of articles to various magazines and jls, lectr on a wide variety of tax topics; ICAEW: former chm Tech Ctee Tax Faculty, memb Tax Faculty Ctee; memb Cncl and chm Tech Ctee IIT; chm Small Practitioners Gp of Central London LSCA; FCA 1965, FTII 1965, FIIT 1997; *Publications* Tax Minimisation Techniques (4 edn, 1984), Taxation of Non-Resident Entertainers & Sportsmen (1987), Fringe Benefits (1987), Tax Planning for Entertainers (2 edn, 1987), Tax Planning for the Smaller Business (1990), Expat Investors Working and Retiring Abroad (1993), Taxation of Sportsmen and Entertainers (1993), Tottel's Property Taxes (18 edn, 2006), Tottel's Taxation of Employments (12 edn, 2006), Tottel's Anti-Avoidance Provisions; *Recreations* reading, walking, pubs; *Clubs* Reform, St James's (Manchester); *Style—* Robert Maas, Esq; ✉ 76 Thirlmere Gardens, Wembley, Middlesex HA9 8RE (tel 020 8904 0432); Blackstone Franks LLP, Barbican House, 26–34 Old Street, London EC1V 9QR (tel 020 7250 3300, fax 020 7250 1402, e-mail rmaas@blackstones.co.uk)

MABEY, Richard Thomas; s of Thomas Gustavus Mabey (d 1963), and Edna Nellie, *née* Moore (d 1993); *b* 20 February 1941; *Educ* Berkhamsted Sch, St Catherine's Coll Oxford (MA); *Career* lectr in social studies Dacorum Coll of FE 1963–65, sr ed Penguin Books (Educn Div) 1966–73, freelance writer and broadcaster 1973–; columnist BBC Wildlife; reg contrib: Countryside Voice, The Independent, Modern Painters, The Times, The Guardian; Leverhulme res fell 1983–84 and 1993–94; memb: Cncl Botanical Soc of the British Isles 1981–83, Nature Conservancy Cncl 1982–86, Cncl Plantlife 1989–; vice-pres Open Spaces Soc 2002– (memb Advsy Cncl 1994–), pres Norfolk Naturalists Tst 2005–06; pres London Wildlife Tst 1982–92; dir: Common Ground 1988–, Learning Through Landscapes Tst 1990–; patron John Clare Soc; *Awards* Times Educnl Supplement Information Books Award 1977, New York Acad of Sciences Children's Book Award 1984, Whitbread Biography Award 1986, British Book Awards 1996, Hon DSc Univ of St Andrews 1997; *Television* wrote and presented: The Unofficial Countryside (World About Us, BBC2) 1975, The Flowering of Britain (BBC2) 1980, A Prospect of Kew (BBC2) 1981, Back to the Roots (C4) 1983, White Rock, Black Water (BBC2) 1986, Postcards from the Country (BBC2) 1996; *Books* incl: Class (ed, 1967), Behind the Scene (1968), The Pop Process (1969), Food for Free (1972), Children in Primary School (1972), The Unofficial Countryside (1973), The Pollution Handbook (1973), The Roadside Wildlife Book (1974), Street Flowers (1976), Plants with a Purpose (1977), The Common Ground (1980), The Flowering of Britain (with Tony Evans, 1980), In a Green Shade (1983), Cold Comforts (1983), Oak and Company (1983), Second Nature (ed, 1984), The Frampton Flora (1985), Gilbert White (1986), The Gardener's Labyrinth (ed, 1987), The Flowering of Kew (1988), Home Country (1990), Whistling in the Dark (1993), The Wild Wood (with Gareth Lovett Jones, 1993), Landlocked (1994), The Oxford Book of Nature Writing (ed, 1995), Flora Britannica (1996), Selected Writings (1999), Nature Cure (2005, shortlisted Whitbread Biography Prize and Ondaatje Prize), Fencing Paradise (2005), Bird, Brittania (jtly, 2005); *Recreations* walking, birdwatching, food; *Style—* Richard Mabey, Esq; ✉ c/o Sheil Land Associates, 52 Doughty Street, London WC1N 2LS

MABEY, Simon John; *b* 29 September 1952; *Educ* City of London Sch, Clare Coll Cambridge (scholar, MA); *m* 9 May 1981, Carolyn Ann, *née* Crossman; 2 s (James b 1984, Richard b 1986), 2 da (Elizabeth b 1991, Victoria b 1993); *Career* CA Dixon Wilson & Co 1973–80; Smith & Williamson: joined 1980, ptnr 1981, currently sr tax dir and chm Banking Ctee; dir Smith & Williamson Trust Corporation Ltd 1986–; Westminster CC: memb 1982–90, chm Housing (private sector) Sub-Ctee and vice-chm Housing Ctee 1983–85, chm Social Servs Ctee 1985–89, Lord Mayor of Westminster (chm London Mayors' Assoc) 1989–90, dep high steward of Westminster 1989–90; Parly candidate (Cons) Knowsley North 1992, memb Cncl Assoc of Conservative Clubs Ltd 1993–2001; chm Bd of Tstees Charitable Tst City of Westminster 1989–90, govr Sherborne Sch for Girls 1994–; Freeman City of London 1981, Liveryman Worshipful Co of Bakers 1981, hon memb Worshipful Co of Master Mariners 1989–90; ATII 1976, FCA 1981 (ACA 1976); *Clubs* Carlton (currently vice-pres Political Ctee); *Style—* Simon Mabey, Esq; ✉ Smith & Williamson, 25 Moorgate, London EC2R 6AY (tel 020 7131 4000, fax 020 7131 4033)

MABUZA, HE Lindiwe; *b* Newcastle, Kwa-Zulu Natal; *Career* South African diplomat; teacher of English and Zulu literature Manzini Central Sch Swaziland 1962, lectr Dept of Sociology Univ of Minnesota, asst prof of literature and history Ohio Univ 1969–79, radio journalist African Nat Congress (ANC) Radio Freedo Zambia, ANC rep to Scandinavia 1979–87 (opened offices in Denmark, Norway and Finland), ANC chief rep to USA 1989–94 (opened American office), MP South Africa 1994, subsequently ambass to Philippines and Germany and high cmmr to Brunei Darussalam and Malaysia, high cmmr to UK 2001–; former chairperson ANC Cultural Ctee Zambia, former ed Voice of Women (ANC jl); Yari Yari Award for Human Rights and Literature NY; *Books* Malibongwe, One Never Knows, From ANC to Sweden, Letter to Letta, African to Me, Voices that Lead; *Style—* HE Ms Lindiwe Mabuza; ✉ High Commission for the Republic of South Africa, South Africa House, Trafalgar Square, London WC2N 5DP

MAC-FALL, Nigel James; s of Thomas Coulson Mac-Fall (d 1970), and Sylvia Dorothy, *née* Harriss (d 1987); *b* 27 April 1948; *Educ* Sch of Three Dimensional Design Ravensbourne Coll of Art and Design (BA), Sch of Furniture Design RCA (MA); *m* 1, 11 May 1974, Shirley Anne (d 1996), da of Ernest Chubb; 2 s (Julian James Chubb b 9 Jan 1976, Oscar Alexander James b 18 May 1981), 1 da (Rosina Sylvia Anne b 7 July 1977), 1 adopted da (Elaine Anne b 16 Aug 1968); m 2, 25 Sept 1997, Andrea Gudrun, da of Brian Fenwick-Smith; 2 s (Ambrose Brian James b 19 Oct 1998, Lucian Thomas James b 7 July 2001); *Career* furniture and product designer Planning Unit Ltd 1972–75, sr designer Supplies Div Property Services Agency 1975–78, ptnr, dir and head Dept of Three Dimensional Design Minale Tattersfield & Partners Ltd 1978–97, fndr ptnr and chm Red Studio Ltd 1997– (i/c architecture, interiors, exhgn, product, furniture, signage, packaging, jewellery and corporate); clients incl: Thompson Publishing USA (Frankfurt Book Fair), Glazer Associates UK (interior design), American Airfield Corporation (corp design), Mineral Holdings Luxembourg (corp design), Gondwana Luxembourg (corp design), Laurasia UK (interior/corp design), various private clients in Monaco (interior and aircraft design), British Library (exhibition design), Help the Hospices (interior design), Carter Wong (interior design), Texas Treasure Fields USA (largest private house in Texas), Post Office (interior design); *Recreations* family, swimming, cycling, sculpture, music, foreign travel; *Style—* Nigel James Mac-Fall, Esq; ✉ Red Studio Ltd, 6 Bedford House, The Avenue, Chiswick, London W4 1UD (tel 020 8994 7770, fax 020 8994 7779, e-mail info@red-studio.co.uk)

MAC NEICE, Rory John James; s of John Mac Neice, of Suffolk, and Pamela, *née* White (d 1968); *b* 28 March 1968, Reading; *Educ* Kings Coll Taunton, Oxford Brookes Univ (LLB), Univ of Exeter; *m* 24 Aug 1999, Martha, *née* Maher; 1 s (Charlie b 1 Oct 2000), 1 da (Lily Anna b 20 Feb 2006); *Career* slr specialising in sports and bloodstock law; professional Nat Hunt jockey 1988–91, slr Burges Salmon 1998–2004, ptnr Ashfords 2004–; memb Law Soc; *Recreations* horse racing; *Style—* Rory Mac Neice, Esq; ✉ Ashfords, Ashford House, Grenadier Road, Exeter EX1 3LH (tel 0870 427 3988, fax 0870 427 7194, e-mail r.macneice@ashfords.co.uk)

McADAM, Dr Elspeth Katharine; da of Prof Sir Ian McAdam decd, and Hrothgarde, *née* Gibson; *b* 16 October 1947; *Educ* Kenya HS, Newnham Coll Cambridge (MA), Middx Med Sch; *m* 1970 (m dis 1981), Prof (John) David Seddon, s of Eric Seddon (d 1950); 2 s (Michael David Indra b 10 May 1974, James Alexander b 28 April 1976); *Career* conslt child and adolescent psychiatrist 1987–, systemic social constructionist conslt 1991–; conslt Swedish Mental Health Services 1991–, dir Informetrics-Systemic Organisational Consultancy; FRCPsych 1997 (MRCPsych 1982); *Publications* Working Systemicly with Violence and Child Sexual Abuse (1992), Narrative Therapy in Asthma (1999); author of pubns in Cognitive and Systemic Therapies; *Recreations* tennis, golf, ecology, bird watching, gardening; *Style—* Dr Elspeth McAdam; ✉ 49 Elm Quay Court, 30 Nine Elms Lane, London SW8 5DF (e-mail Elspeth_McAdam@compuserve.com)

McADAM, James; CBE (1995); s of John Robert McAdam (d 1975), and Helen, *née* Cormack (d 1981); *b* 10 December 1930; *Educ* Lenzie Acad; *m* 4 Oct 1955, Maisie Una, da of Ernest James Holmes (d 1947); 2 da (Catherine Tryphena b 1956, Fiona Jane b 1961); *Career* J & P Coats Ltd: joined 1945, various overseas assignments 1953–70; fin dir Coats Patons (UK) 1972–75; Coats Patons plc: dir 1975, chief exec 1985, chm 1986, dep chm and chief ops offr Coats Viyella plc (following merger) 1986–91; chm Signet Group plc 1992–2006 (ceo 1992–2000); non-exec dir: London PO 1985–87, Scotia Holdings plc (formerly Efamol Holdings plc) 1991–97; non-exec chm: F C Brown (Steel Equipment) Ltd 1991–, Bisley Office Equipment 1991–; chm: Br Clothing Industry Assoc 1991–, Br Knitting and Clothing Confedn 1991–, Apparel, Knitting and Textiles Alliance 1992–, Br Apparel and Textile Confedn 1993–; memb: Exec Ctee The Scottish Cncl Devpt and Industry 1989–99; FRSA, CIMgt, FInstD; *Recreations* theatre, travel; *Style—* James McAdam, Esq, CBE; ✉ 43 Whitehall Court, London SW1A 2EP

McADAM, John David Gibson; s of John and Sarah McAdam, of Bowness-on-Windermere; *b* 30 April 1948; *Educ* Kelsick GS Ambleside, Lakes Sch Windermere, Univ of Manchester (BSc, PhD); *m* 20 Jan 1979, Louise Mary; 1 da (Laura Sarah Louise b 2 June 1981), 1 s (David John James b 27 April 1984); *Career* Unilever plc: joined 1974, various mgmnt positions with Birds Eye Foods, gen mangr Birds Eye Wall's 1984–86, tech dir PPF Int 1986–87, sr vice-pres Quest 1987–90, memb bd Birds Eye Wall's 1990–93, chm and ceo Unichema Int 1993–97; ICI plc: chm and ceo Quest Int 1997–98, memb Exec Mgmnt Ctee 1997, chm and ceo ICI Paints 1998–99, exec dir (memb plc bd) 1999–, ceo 2003–; non-exec dir Severn Trent plc 2000–05, sr non-exec dir J Sainsbury plc 2005–; memb Univ of Cambridge Chemistry Advsy Bd; *Recreations* watching cricket, rugby and football, walking; *Style—* Dr John McAdam; ✉ ICI plc, 20 Manchester Square, London W1U 3AN (tel 020 7834 4444, fax 020 7798 5876)

McADAM, Prof Keith Paul William James; s of Sir Ian William James McAdam, OBE, KB and (Lettice Margaret) Hrothgaarde, *née* Gibson (now Mrs Bennett); *b* 13 August 1945; *Educ* Prince of Wales Sch Nairobi, Millfield, Clare Coll Cambridge (MA, MB BChir), Middx Hosp Med Sch; *m* 27 July 1968, Penelope Ann, da of Rev Gordon Charles Craig Spencer; 3 da (Karen, Ruth, Cheryl); *Career* house physician and house surgn Middx Hosp London 1969–70; SHO appts London: Royal Northern Hosp 1970–71, Brompton Hosp 1971–72, Royal Nat Hosp for Nervous Diseases 1972–73; lectr Inst of Med Res PNG 1973–75, Med Res Cncl travelling fellowship Nat Cancer Inst 1975–76, visiting scientist Nat Inst of Health Bethesda 1976–77, asst prof Tufts Univ Sch of Med 1977–81, assoc prof New England Med Centre Boston 1982–84, Wellcome prof of tropical medicine LSHTM 1984–2004 (emeritus prof 2004–), physician Hosp for Tropical Diseases Camden & Islington HA 1984–95, dir Medical Research Cncl Unit Fajara The Gambia 1995–2003, dir Infectious Diseases Inst and prof of med Faculty of Medicine Makerere Univ Uganda 2004–; memb Med Advsy Bds: Br Leprosy Relief Assoc 1986–95, MRC 1988–93, Br Cncl 1988–93, Wellcome Trust 1985–90, Beit Trust 1990–95, The Leprosy Mission 1990–97; chief med offr conslt advsr 1989–95, expert advsr to House of Commons Soc Servs Ctee enquiry into AIDS 1987; FRSTM&H 1973, FRCP 1985, FWACP 1998; *Publications* original articles in medical and scientific jls on tropical medicine topics incl leprosy, tuberculosis, malaria, AIDS, inflammation and amyloidosis; ed books on travel medicine, parasitology, tuberculosis and infectious diseases; *Recreations* cricket, tennis, skiing; *Clubs* MCC; *Style—* Prof Keith McAdam; ✉ Oakmead, 70 Luton Lane, Redbourn, Hertfordshire AL3 7PY (tel and fax 01582 792833); Infectious Diseases Institute, Faculty of Medicine, Makerere University, PO Box 22418, Kampala, Uganda (tel 00 256 782 614 474, e-mail kmcadam@idi.co.ug)

MACALDOWIE, Dr (John) Kenneth; s of John Macaldowie (d 1984), and Mary Donald, *née* Main (d 2002); *b* 24 June 1944; *Educ* Robert Gordon's Coll Aberdeen, Hillhead HS Glasgow; *m* 1, 15 Oct 1968, Sheila (d 2002), da of Dr George Leslie (d 1991); 2 s (Colin Neil b 12 Feb 1970, Keith Gary b 24 April 1973); m 2, 11 Oct 2005, Jean Kelly; *Career* accountant (latterly audit mangr) Cooper Brothers & Co until 1972 (apprentice 1962–67); BDO Stoy Hayward (formerly BDO Binder Hamlyn and Wyllie Guild & McIntyre): ptnr 1972–2004, managing ptnr Edinburgh 1992–95, sr forensic accounting ptnr Scotland 1994–2004, chm Nat Partnership Ctee 1992–94; chm: Williamson & Wolfe 1980–2000, Salvation Army Housing Association (Scotland) Ltd 1992–2002; YMCA Glasgow: hon treas 1996–99, chm Exec Ctee 1999–2005, vice-pres 2005–06, pres 2006–; memb: Ct Glasgow Caledonian Univ 1985–98 (vice-chm 1995–98, chm Finance of the Ct 1988–98), Bd of Govrs Kelvinside Acad 1987–95, Bd of Mgmnt Anniesland Coll 2005– (chm 2006–); elder Church of Scotland (Merrylea Parish Church) 1982–, tstee and chm Audit Ctee Church of Scotland Gen Tstees 2005–; Deacon Incorporation of Coopers of Trades House of Glasgow 1984–85; Hon LLD Glasgow Caledonian Univ 1997; Freeman: City of Glasgow 1977, City of London 1986; Liveryman Worshipful Co of Coopers 1985; MICAS 1968 (memb Examination Bd 1982–90); *Recreations* tennis, gardening, reading, hill walking, travel, watching rugby and cricket; *Clubs* Western (Glasgow), Newlands Lawn Tennis, Hillhead Jordanhill Rugby (pres 2005–07); *Style*— Dr Kenneth Macaldowie; ⊠ 16 Letham Drive, Newlands, Glasgow G43 2SL (tel 0141 637 5456, e-mail john.macaldowie@ntlworld.com)

McALEESE, Pres Mary Patricia; *née* Leneghan; *b* 27 June 1951; *Educ* St Dominic's HS Belfast, Queen's Univ Belfast (LLB), TCD (MA), Chartered Inst of Linguistics (Dip Spanish); *m* 1976, Martin McAleese; 2 da (Emma b 21 Sept 1982, Sara-mai b 6 April 1985), 1 s (Justin (twin) b 6 April 1985); *Career* barrister-at-law: Inn of Court NI 1974 (practising barrister 1974–75), Hon Soc of King's Inns Dublin 1978; Reid prof of criminal law, criminology and penology TCD 1975–79 and 1981–87, TV presenter/journalist RTE 1979–85, pt/t presenter EUROPA (monthly current affairs prog) RTE 1981–85; Queen's Univ Belfast: dir Inst of Professional Legal Studies 1987–97, pro-vice-chllr 1994–97; pres of Ireland 1997–; former non-exec dir: Viridian plc (formerly Northern Ireland Electricity plc), Channel 4 Television, Royal Gp of Hospitals Tst; fndr memb Campaign for Homosexual Law Reform (Dublin); former fndr memb: Belfast Women's Aid, Irish Cmmn for Prisoners Overseas; former memb: Cncl of Social Welfare (Dublin), BBC Broadcasting Council for NI, Exec Ctee Focus Point for Homeless Young People (Dublin), Cmmn for Justice and Peace, Inst of Advanced Legal Studies, Irish Centre for European Law, Faculty of the Nat Inst of Trial Advocacy; hon pres NI Housing Rights Assoc; memb: Int Bar Assoc, European Bar Assoc, Inns of Court Northern Ireland, King's Inns (Dublin); Silver Jubilee Commemoration Medal Charles Univ Prague, Great Gold Medal Comenius Univ Bratislava, American Ireland Fund Humanitarian Award; hon bencher: King's Inns, Inns of Court NI; hon fell: TCD, Liverpool John Moores Univ; Hon LLD: NUI, Univ of Nottingham, Victoria Univ of Technol Aust, St Mary's Univ Halifax, Queen's Univ Belfast, Loyola Law Sch LA, Univ of Aberdeen, Univ of Surrey, TCD, Manchester Met Univ, Univ of Delaware, Univ of Bristol, Univ of Qld Brisbane, Harbin Inst of Technol, Shenzhen Univ, Univ of Chile, EHWA Univ Seoul, Villanova Univ Philadelphia, Notre Dame Univ, Univ of Edinburgh, St John's Univ NY; Hon Dr of Humane Letters Rochester Inst of Technol NY; Hon DLitt Univ of Ulster; MIL 1994, MRIA, Hon FIEI, Hon FRCS, Hon FRCA, FRSA, Hon FRCPS; *Publications* Reconciled Being: Love in Chaos (1997); author (and co-author) of various books, articles, conference papers and dicussion documents; *Style*— President Mary McAleese; ⊠ Office of the President, Áras An Uachtaráin, Phoenix Park, Dublin 8, Ireland (tel 00 353 1 617 1000, fax 00 353 1 617 1001, e-mail webmaster@president.ie)

McALISTER, Michael Ian; s of S McAlister, CBE (d 1972), of Walton-on-Thames, Surrey, and Jessie Anne, *née* Smith (d 1991); *b* 23 August 1930; *Educ* St John's Coll Oxford (MA); *m* 1, 4 July 1953 (m dis 1984), Patricia Evans, of São Paulo, Brazil; 4 s (Richard, Peter, Sam, James), 3 da (Maureen, Carolyn, Emma); *m* 2, 2 June 1984, Elizabeth Anne, da of Louis Hehn, and Marianne Hehn, of Hatfield Peverel, Essex; *Career* Nat Serv Army 1949–51, Acting-Capt Intelligence Corps 1951, (MI8) Austria (BTA 3); articled clerk Price Waterhouse & Co 1954–58, private and fin sec to HRH Duke of Windsor KG 1959–61, md Ionian Bank Tstee Co 1961–69, chm Slater Walker Securities (Australia) 1969–72, pres Australian Stock Exchanges 1972–75, Knight Int Inc Chicago and London 1975–78, corporate planning dir Cluff Resources plc 1979–89, chm Int Dynamics Ltd 1989–91, dir Ionian Corporate Finance Ltd 1991–99, md Tam Prog EBRD London 1993–2001; chm Woking Cons Assoc 1967–68, vice-chm Braintree Cons Assoc 1990–93; FCA 1969 (ACA 1959); *Recreations* carpentry and DIY; *Style*— Mr Michael McAlister; ⊠ tel 01483 577258, e-mail mielmcalister@aol.com

MacALISTER, Rev Randal George Leslie; s of Canon James Daniel Beaton MacAlister (d 1978), of Cushendall, Co Antrim, and Doreen, *née* Thompson (d 1990); *b* 31 December 1941; *Educ* Royal Sch Armagh, Trinity Coll Dublin (BA, MA); *m* 18 Sept 1964, Valerie Jane Letitia, da of late Samuel Nelson; 3 s (Paul Randal Neil b 27 April 1966, Mark Samuel Beaton b 25 April 1967, Nicolas Terence Bernard b 27 Aug 1969); *Career* ordained: deacon 1964, priest 1966; curate St Mark's Portadown Armagh Dio 1964–67, rector St Matthew's Keady with Armaghbreague Armagh Dio 1967–74, rector St Mary's Kirriemuir Dio of St Andrews 1974–81, rector St John's Greenock Dio of Glasgow 1981–87, rector St John's Forfar Dio of St Andrews 1987–95, canon of St Ninian's Cathedral Perth 1993–95, chaplain St Mark's Sophia Antipolis France Dio of Europe 1995–98, rector St Kessog's Auchterarder with St James Muthill Dio of St Andrews 1998–2006, dean of St Andrews 1998–2006, ret; memb: Rotary Int, An Commun Gaidhealach (The Gaelic Soc), Glens of Antrim Historical Soc; *Recreations* hill walking, languages, music, traditional fiddle playing, study of gaelic language and culture; *Style*— The Rev Randal MacAlister

McALISTER, William Harle Nelson (Bill); s of Flying Offr William Nelson (d 1940), and Marjorie Isobel, *née* McIntyre; *b* 30 August 1940; *Educ* St Edward's Sch Oxford, UCL (BA); *m* 1968 (m dis 1985), Sarah Elizabeth; 3 s (Daniel b 1969, Benjamin b 1977, Ned b 1985), 2 da (Leila b 1970, Alix b 1972); *Career* ind arts prodr; dir Almost Free Theatre 1968–72, dep dir Inter-Action Tst 1968–72, fndr dir Islington Bus Co 1972–77; dir: Battersea Arts Centre 1976–77, Sense of Ireland Festival 1980–; Bd dir London Int Theatre Festival 1983; chm for the Arts IT 82 Ctee 1982; co fndr Fair Play for Children 1974–75, advsr Task Force Tst 1972–74; tstee: Circle 33 Housing Tst 1972–75, Moving Picture Mime Tst 1978–80, Shape (Arts for the Disadvantaged) 1979–81; govr Holloway Adult Educn Inst 1974–76; dir: Inst of Contemporary Arts 1977–90, Creative Res Ltd 1988–91, Int House 1988–2004, Beaconsfield Gallery 1999–2003; cultural policy advsr Soros Fndns 1992–97; memb Cncl Africa Centre 1992–2000; memb: Ct RCA 1980–90, Bd World Circuit Arts 1995–2001, Hidden Art 2000–, Anglo-Polish Fndn 2004–; *Publications* Community Psychology (1975), EEC and the Arts (1978); also author of articles on arts policy; *Recreations* angling, tennis, travel; *Style*— Bill McAlister, Esq; ⊠ 151C Grosvenor Avenue, London N5 2NH (tel 07956 229796, e-mail bill.mcalister@gmail.com)

McALLISTER, Ian Gerald; CBE (1996); s of Ian Thomas McAllister, and Margaret Mary, *née* McNally; *b* 17 August 1943; *Educ* Thornleigh Coll Bolton, UCL (BSc); *m* 7 Sept 1968, Susan Margaret Frances, da of Allan Alexander Gordon Mitchell; 3 s (Robert Ian Thomas b 1971, Douglas Peter b 1974, James Alexander b 1977), 1 da (Catherine Jessica b 1983); *Career* Ford Motor Co: graduate trainee finance 1964, fin analyst 1965–66, sr analyst Ford Europe 1966–68, supervisor Market Price Analysis Parts Ops 1968–70, P&A market planning mangr Parts Ops 1970–71, mangr market planning Parts Ops 1971–77, mangr Car Mktg Plans Sales and Mktg 1977–79, gen field mangr Eastern Dist Sales 1979–80, dir Parts Sales 1980–81, dir prodn and mktg Parts Ops 1981–83, dir Car Sales Ops 1983–84, dir Mktg Plans and Programs 1984–87, dir sales Ford Germany 1987–89, gen mktg mangr Lincoln Mercury Div USA 1989–91, chm and md Ford of Britain 1992–2002 (md only 1991–92); chm Networkrail 2002–; non-exec dir Scottish & Newcastle plc 1996–; dir Business in the Community 1992–2002 (memb Cncl 1991–), vice-pres Inst of Motor Industry 1992–, pres SMMT 1996–98 (memb Exec 1991–); co chair Cleaner Vehicles Taskforce 1998–2000, chm The Carbon Tst 2001–; memb: New Deal Taskforce 1997–2001, Qualifications and Curriculum Authy 1997– (dep chm 2000–03), Advsy Cncl Imperial Coll Business Sch, Bd and Exec American Chamber of Commerce 1992–2000, Advsy Bd Victim Support, Bd Anglia Poly Univ 1996–2002; *Recreations* gardening, golf, computer studies, running; *Style*— Ian McAllister, Esq, CBE

McALLISTER, John Brian; s of Thomas McAllister (d 1979), and Jane, *née* McCloughan; *b* 11 June 1941; *Educ* Royal Belfast Academical Instn, Queen's Univ Belfast (BA); *m* 1966, Margaret Lindsay, da of William Walker (d 1964), of Belfast; 2 da (Lynne b 1970, Barbara b 1972); *Career* civil servant 1964–88; princ: Dept of Educn (NI) 1971 (asst princ 1968, dep princ 1969), NI Info Serv 1973; dep sec: Dept of Educn (NI) 1980 (asst sec 1976, sr asst sec 1978), Dept of Fin (NI) 1983; under sec DOE (NI) 1985; chief exec: Industrial Devpt Bd NI 1986 (dep chief exec 1985), Sapphire House Ltd 1999–; gp md CrestaCare Ltd 1988–90 (chief exec 1990–93), self-employed conslt 1993–94; chm: Dromona Quality Foods 1993–95, James Anderson Ltd 1994–97, Craegmoor Healthcare Ltd 1996–99 (chief exec 1994–96); *Recreations* family holidays, watching sport; *Clubs* Wolverhampton Wanderers; *Style*— John McAllister, Esq; ⊠ Sapphire House Ltd, Ragnall House, 18 Peel Road, Douglas, Isle of Man IM1 4LZ

McALLISTER, Victor Lionel; s of late Victor Lionel McAllister, and late Ethel Caroline McAllister; *b* 9 October 1941; *Educ* Sydney GS Aust, UCH (MB BS); *m* 22 April 1965, Pamela, da of Dr Denis Joel Johnson, MBE, TD (d 1982); 1 s (Peter Victor Lionel b 1970), 1 da (Karen Ann b 1967); *Career* conslt in admin charge neuroradiology Regnl Neurological Centre Newcastle Gen Hosp 1974– (clinical dir of neurosciences); invited lectr: Europe, India, Singapore, Aust; sec and treas Br Soc of Neuroradiologists 1982–86 (pres 1996–98), memb Euro Soc of Neuroradiology, UK delegate (Br Soc of Neuroradiologists) to Euro Soc of Neuroradiologists 1992–96; LRCP, MRCS, DMRD, FRCR; *Books* Subarachnoid Haemorrhage (1986), Pyogenic Neurosurgical Infections (1991); author of over 60 pubns on all aspects neuroradiology; *Recreations* travel, badminton; *Clubs* Ponteland Lions, '62 (radiological); *Style*— Victor McAllister, Esq

McALPINE, Angharad; *see:* Rees, Angharad Mary

McALPINE, Kenneth; OBE (1997), DL (Kent 1976); s of Sir Thomas Malcolm McAlpine, KBE (d 1967), and Maud Dees (d 1969); *b* 21 September 1920; *Educ* Charterhouse; *m* 1955, Patricia Mary, da of Capt Francis William Hugh Jeans, CVO, RN (d 1968); 2 s; *Career* WWII Flying Offr RAFVR; dir Sir Robert McAlpine & Sons Ltd 1941–91, chm McAlpine Helicopters Ltd 1969–; memb Construction Industry Trg Bd 1967–73, tstee Inst of Economic Affrs 1968–89; prop Lamberhurst Vineyards 1972–95; govr and dep chm Eastbourne Coll 1968–84, govr Royal Hosp of St Bartholomew 1972–74 (special tstee 1980–94); High Sheriff Kent 1973–74; FRAeS; *Clubs* Royal Yacht Sqdn, Air Sqdn, Br Racing Drivers; *Style*— Kenneth McAlpine, Esq, OBE, DL; ⊠ The Priory, Lamberhurst, Kent TN3 8DS

McALPINE, Stewart; *b* 2 January 1937; *Career* dep md Barham Group plc 1984–88; chm: SMA Group Ltd 1989–91, Smedley McAlpine Ltd 1960–91, IRB Group Ltd 1989–91, Cornwallis International Ltd 1992–93, Eagle Systems International Ltd 1993–95, Response Publishing Group plc 1993–98; dir: Airship Industries Ltd 1984–91, International Business Communications (Holdings) plc 1987–88, City of London PR Group plc 1988–91, FCB Advertising Ltd 1991–92, SMcA Ltd 1991–, World Trade Magazines Ltd 1996–98, freecom.net GB plc 2000–01, Systems Union plc 2001, Strategic Investments Ltd 2002–06, New Day Energy Ltd 2002–07, Lesotho Diamond Corp plc 2003–06, World Gold Corporation plc 2003–06, Madagascar Oil Ltd 2005–06; *Style*— Stewart McAlpine, Esq; ⊠ SMcA Ltd, 7 Mansion Gardens, London NW3 7NG (tel 020 7794 2120, fax 020 7794 4878, e-mail formax@btinternet.com)

McALPINE, Hon Sir William Hepburn; 6 Bt (UK 1918), of Knott Park, Co Surrey; eld s of Baron McAlpine of Moffat (Life Peer and 5 Bt, d 1990), and his 1 w, Ella Mary Gardner, *née* Garnett (d 1987); *b* 12 January 1936; *Educ* Charterhouse; *m* 1, 1959, Jill Benton (d 2004), o da of Lt-Col Sir Peter Fawcett Benton Jones, 3 Bt, OBE (d 1972); 1 s (Andrew William b 1960), 1 da (Lucinda Mary Jane b 1964); *m* 2, 2004, Judith Mary, da of William H Sanderson (d 2004), and wid of Graham Nicholls (d 1991); *Heir* s, Andrew McAlpine; *Career* Life Guards 1954–56; dir: Sir Robert McAlpine Ltd 1952–, Newarthill plc 1977–, Turner & Newall plc 1983–91; chm Railway Heritage Tst 1985–; High Sheriff Bucks 1999–2000; Liveryman Worshipful Co of Carmen; FRSE 1978, FCILT; *Recreations* railways and transport preservation; *Clubs* Buck's, Garrick, Caledonian; *Style*— The Hon Sir William McAlpine, Bt, FRSE; ⊠ Fawley Hill, Fawley Green, Henley-on-Thames, Oxfordshire RG9 6JA (tel 01491 637869, fax 01491 579674, e-mail office@sirwmcalpine.com)

McALPINE OF WEST GREEN, Baron (Life Peer UK 1984), of West Green in the County of Hampshire; (Robert) Alistair McAlpine; 2 s of Baron McAlpine of Moffat (Life Peer and 5 Bt, d 1990); *b* 14 May 1942; *Educ* Stowe; *m* 1, 1964 (m dis 1979), Sarah Alexandra, da of late Paul Hillman Baron, of London W1; 2 da (Hon Mary Jane b 1965, Hon Victoria Alice b 1967); *m* 2, 1980 (m dis 2000), Romilly Thompson, o da of Alfred Thompson Hobbs, of Cranleigh, Surrey; 1 da (Hon Skye b 1984); *m* 3, 2002, Athena Malpas; *Career* dir: Newarthill plc, George Weidenfeld Holdings Ltd 1975–83; vice-pres Euro League of Econ Cooperation 1975– (treas 1974–75); hon treas: Euro Democratic Union 1978–88, Cons and Unionist Pty 1975–90 (dep chm 1979–83); dir: ICA 1972–73, T I Finance Ltd 1981–90 (chm 1985–90); vice-chm Contemporary Arts Soc 1973–80; memb: Arts Cncl of GB 1981–82, Friends of V&A Museum 1976–91, Cncl British Stage Co 1973–75; tstee Royal Opera House Tst 1974–80; govr: Polytechnic of the South Bank 1981–82, Stowe Sch 1981–84; pres Br Waterfowl Assoc 1978–81 (patron 1981–); vice-pres: Friends of Ashmolean Museum 1969–, Gtr London Arts Assoc 1971–77; pres The Medical Coll of St Bartholomew's Hosp 1993–96; Liveryman Worshipful Co of Gunmakers; *Books* The Servant (1992), Journal of a Collector (1994), Letters to a Young Politician (1995), Once A Jolly Bagman (1997), The New Machiavelli (1997), Collecting and Display (1998), From Bagman to Swagman (1999), Essential Guide to Collectibles (2002); *Recreations* the arts, horticulture, aviculture, agriculture; *Clubs* Garrick, Pratt's; *Style*— The Rt Hon the Lord McAlpine of West Green; ⊠ House of Lords, London SW1A 0PW

McANALLY, Vice-Admiral John Henry Stuart; CB (2000), LVO (1982); s of Arthur Patrick McAnally (d 1983), and Mrs B H S McAnally (d 1999); bro of Mary McAnally, *qv*, *b* 9 April 1945; *Educ* Westminster, BRNC Dartmouth; *Career* with RN; Lt 1967, navigating and ops offr 6 warships incl US destroyer and Australian aircraft carrier 1968–78 (CO HMS Iveston 1973–75), navigation subspecialisation course HMS Dryad 1971, Lt Cdr 1975, RN Staff Coll (Director's Prize) 1978, 2 i/c HMS Birmingham 1978–79, Cdr 1979, navigating commander HM Yacht Britannia 1980 and 1981, desk offr (size and shape of future RN) DN Plans MOD 1982–83, CO HMS Torquay and HMS Alacrity 1984–86, Capt 1987, Sixth Frigate Sqdn (CO HMS Ariadne and HMS Hermione) 1987–89, asst dir (role of future RN) DN Plans MOD 1989–91, RCDS 1992, Higher Command and Staff Course 1993, Cdre 1993, dir Naval Logistic Policy 1993, dir Naval Staff 1994–95, Rear Adm 1996, Flag Offr Training and Recruiting 1996–98, Vice-Adm 1998, Cmdt RCDS 1998–2000; pres Royal Naval Assoc 2001–, govr Portsmouth GS 1996–98, naval advsr Flagship Trg Ltd 2001–05, sr military advsr 2006–; ind chm RO Selection Bds 2001–03; memb: Naval Review 1964, US Naval Inst (prize memb) 1978, RUSI 1978, Hon Co of Master Mariners 2002–; Younger Brother Trinity House 1987–; MInstD 1995, FNI, FRIN; *Recreations* golf, reading; *Clubs* Naval and Military, National Liberal, Leckford, Hayling & Royal Mid Surrey Golf, Royal Naval & Royal Albert Yacht (Portsmouth); *Style*— Vice-Admiral John McAnally, CB, LVO; ⊠ tel 023 9233 9000

McANALLY, Mary Basil Hamilton; da of Patrick McAnally (d 1983), of Old Portsmouth, Hants, and Basil, *née* Knight (d 1999); sis of Vice-Adm John Henry Stuart McAnally, CB, LVO, *qv*; *b* 9 April 1945; *Educ* Tiffin Girls' Sch, Wimbledon Sch of Art; *m* 1979, Hugh Macpherson; *Career* researcher Man Alive BBC TV 1969; Thames Television: researcher and writer This Is Your Life 1970–71, prodr Money-Go-Round 1973–82, prodr

Could Do Better 1977, prodr and dir What About the Workers? 1978, prodr and dir The John Smith Show 1979, ed 4 What it's Worth (for Channel 4) 1982–90, creator and exec network prodr The Time - The Place 1987–92, head of features 1989–92; Meridian Broadcasting: controller of regnl progs and community affrs 1992–94, dir of progs 1994–95, dir of progs and prodn 1995–96, md and dir of progs 1996–97, md 1997–2002; media conslt 2002–; dir: Southern Crimestoppers 1994–97, Southern Screen Cmmn 1998–2000, Skillstrain 1999–2001, Screen South 2002–03; memb: Nat Consumer Cncl 1987–97 (dir Nat Consumer Cncl Services Ltd 1995–97), Forum UK 1990, Advsy Ctee on Advtg 1999–2002, Bd SEEDA 2000–06 (memb Media and Creative Industries Task Force 1999–2003), SE England Cultural Consortium 2000–03, Exec Bd DTI 2002–04, SE Regnl Assembly 2007–; chm SE England Regnl Sports Bd 2003–, memb Mgmnt Ctee The Championships Wimbledon 2003–, non-exec dir Sport England 2004–06, SE rep 2012 Nations and Regions Gp 2005–; govr Univ of Portsmouth 1998–2000; awards incl: Freedom of Information Media Award 1989, San Francisco Gold Award, Santander Jury Prize, Glenfiddich Food Writer's Award, BMA Gold Award, Berlin Consumer Award, Monergy Award, NY Festival 1994; FRTS 1997, FRSA 1989; int tennis player 1963–67 (rep England and Surrey, competed Wimbledon Lawn Tennis Championships, former GB jr indoor champion (beating Virginia Wade in final)); *Books* Buy Right (jtly, 1978); *Recreations* tennis, golf, painting; *Clubs* All England Lawn Tennis, Cumberland Tennis, Winchester Tennis, Highgate Golf, Arts; *Style*— Ms Mary McAnally

MacANDREW, 3 Baron (UK 1959); Christopher Anthony Colin MacAndrew; er s of 2 Baron MacAndrew (d 1989); *b* 16 February 1945; *Educ* Malvern; *m* 1975 (m dis 2005), Sarah Helen, o da of Lt-Col Peter Hendy Brazier, of Nash Court Farmhouse, Marnhull, Dorset; 2 da (Hon Diana Sarah b 24 June 1978, Hon Tessa Deborah b 2 Aug 1980), 1 s (Hon Oliver Charles Julian b 3 Sept 1983); *Heir* s, Hon Oliver MacAndrew; *Career* farmer; tax cmmr 1996; *Recreations* golf, tennis; *Style*— The Rt Hon Lord MacAndrew; ✉ Hall Farm, Archdeacon Newton, Darlington, Co Durham DL2 2YB

McANDREW, Ian Christopher; *b* 20 February 1953; *Educ* Univ of Cambridge (MA); *m* 26 Aug 1978, Geraldine Baker; 2 da (Cathryn b 12 Jan 1985, Madeleine b 12 March 1989); *Career* Coopers & Lybrand 1975–88, fin and ops dir, co sec and compliance offr British and Commonwealth Merchant Bank plc 1988–92, fin dir Lawrence Graham 1992–2000, fin dir Clyde & Co 2001–; FCA (ACA 1978); *Style*— Ian McAndrew, Esq; ✉ 3 Frank Dixon Close, London SE21 7BD (tel 020 8693 3592, e-mail ian.mcandrew@clyde.co.uk)

MacANDREW, Hon Nicholas Rupert (Nick); yr s of 2 Baron MacAndrew (d 1989); *b* 12 February 1947; *Educ* Eton; *m* 1, 1975 (m dis 1994), Victoria Rose, da of George Patrick Renton, of Alton, Hants; 1 s, 2 da; m 2, 1998, Joy Elizabeth Meadows; *Career* Deloittes 1966–71, Schroders plc 1971–2002 (finance dir 1991–2002); non-exec dir: Fuller Smith & Turner plc 2001–, Wates Gp Ltd 2003–, Jardine Lloyd Thompson Group plc 2005–, F&C Asset Mgmnt plc 2007–; chair of tstees Save the Children 2003–; FCA 1971; *Style*— The Hon Nicholas MacAndrew; ✉ The Old Chapel, Greywell, Hook, Hampshire RG29 1BS (tel 01256 702390); Save the Children, 1 St John's Lane, London EC1M 4AR

McANDREW, Nicolas; s of Robert Louis McAndrew (d 1981), and Anita Marian, *née* Huband (d 1996, aged 100); *b* 9 December 1934; *Educ* Winchester; *m* 20 Sept 1960, Diana Leonie Wood; 2 s (Charles Gavin b 14 Jan 1962, Mark James b 16 Feb 1964), 1 da (Fiona Catherine Mary b 16 June 1968); *Career* Nat Serv 1 Bn The Black Watch 1953–55 (active serv Kenya); articled clerk Peat Marwick Mitchell & Co 1955–61, qualified CA 1961; S G Warburg & Co Ltd: investment mangr 1962–69, chm Warburg Investment Management 1975–78 (md 1969–75); md: NM Rothschild & Sons Ltd 1979–88, Rothschild Asset Management Ltd 1979–88, Murray Johnstone Ltd 1988–99 (chm 1992–99); chm: Investec Extra Income Tst Ltd 1995–2002, Derby Tst 1999–2003, Martin Currie Enhanced Income Tst plc 1999–2005; dep chm Burn Stewart Distillers plc 1990–99; memb: Bd Highlands and Islands Enterprise 1993–97, North of Scotland Water Authy 1995–2002, Liverpool Victoria Friendly Soc 1995–2005; memb Ct of Assts Worshipful Co of Grocers (Master 1978–79); *Recreations* fishing, shooting, gardening; *Clubs* White's; *Style*— Nicolas McAndrew, Esq; ✉ Kilcoy Castle, Muir of Ord, Ross-shire IV6 7RX (tel 01463 871393, fax 01463 871394, e-mail kilcoy@btinternet.com)

MACARA, Dr Sir Alexander Wiseman (Sandy); kt (1998); s of Rev Alexander Macara (d 1992), and Marion Wiseman, *née* Mackay (d 1972); *b* 4 May 1932; *Educ* Irvine Royal Acad, Univ of Glasgow (Carnegie bursar, MB ChB), LSHTM (DPH (Lond), Hecht prize, Sir Wilson Jameson travelling scholar); *m* 2 April 1964, Sylvia May, da of Edward Brodbeck Williams; 1 da (Alexandra Sarah b 1973), 1 s (James William b 1976); *Career* various hosp appts Glasgow Teaching Hosps 1958–60, GP experience Glasgow and London 1959–60, departmental med offr and sch med offr City and Co of Bristol 1960–63, hon community physician Bristol 1963–74; Univ of Bristol: lectr in public health 1963–73, sr lectr in community med and actg head of dept 1973–76, conslt sr lectr in public health med 1976–97; hon regnl specialist in public health med: South and Western RHA 1976–96, Avon HA 1996–97; hon visiting conslt Bristol Royal Infirmary 1976–97; hon visiting prof in health studies Univ of York 1998–2002; conslt/temp advsr WHO 1970–, dir WHO Collaborating Centre in Environmental Health Promotion and Ecology 1989–97; memb GMC 1979–2002; BMA: chm Jr Membs 1967, chm Public Health Conf 1979–84, chm Med Ethics Ctee 1982–89, chm Representative Body 1989–92, chm Cncl 1993–98, awarded Gold medal 1999; chm: Public Health Med Consultative Ctee 1998–2004, National Heart Forum 1998–; sec-gen: Assoc of Schs of Public Health in Europe 1976–89, World Fedn for Teaching and Res in Public Health 1988–97; treas Faculty of Public Health Med 1979–84; memb: Coronary Heart Disease (CHD) Task Force Dept of Health 2000–, Prevention and Inequalities Task Force Dept of Health 2001–; memb Ct of Govrs LSHTM 1995–; hon memb Hungarian Acad of Med Scis 1989, hon memb and Gold medallist Italian Soc of Hygiene, Preventative Med and Public Health 1991, hon life fell Soc of Public Health 1991; Dr of Public Health (hc) and Gerasimos Alizivatos Prize Athens Sch of Public Health 1992, James Preston Meml Award 1993, Public Health Award Soc of Public Health 1994, John Kershaw Award 1995, Médaille d'Or de l'Ordre de Médicin Français 1998, Stampar Medal Aspher Assoc of Schools of Public Health in Europe 2002; Harben lectr 1996; govr Redland High Sch for Girls Bristol 1999–; Hon DSc 1998, Hon FFOM 2000; FFCM 1973, FRIPHH 1973, fell BMA 1978, FRCGP (ad eundem) 1983, FFPHM 1989, FRCP 1991, FRSA 1995, FRCPEd 1998, fndr FMedSci 1998; *Publications* Personal Data Protection in Health and Social Services (jtly, 1988), chapters in books and papers on epidemiology, public health, environmental health and medical ethics; *Recreations* reading, writing, music, gardening, church and human rights activities; *Clubs* Athenaeum, RSM; *Style*— Dr Sir Sandy Macara; ✉ Elgon, 10 Cheyne Road, Stoke Bishop, Bristol BS9 2DH (tel 0117 968 2838, tel and fax 0117 968 4602, e-mail alexandermacara@yahoo.co.uk)

McARDELL, John David; s of Patrick John McArdell (d 1988), and Elizabeth Frances, *née* Powling; *b* 25 December 1931; *Educ* Haberdashers' Aske's; *m* 22 Aug 1959, Margaret Sylvia, da of George Lewis Cawley (d 1981); 2 da (Nicola Susan b 26 June 1964, Paula Frances b 19 Sept 1968); *Career* Nat Serv RAF Egypt 1950–52; former dep md Ecclesiastical Insurance Group (mangr mktg and planning 1975–81, gen mangr 1985–88); former dir: Aldwych Management Services Ltd, Blaisdon Properties Ltd, REI Investment Ltd Ireland, Allchurches Mortgage Company Ltd, Allchurches Life Assurance Ltd, EIO Trustees Ltd, CPS Ltd; currently dir Croftdeep Ltd; currently chm: Great Gate Management Company Ltd, Heathfield Management Ltd, Hithe Trust; tstee: Cncl for the Care of Churches, All Churches Trust Ltd; chm and memb Insurance Inst of London, Insurance Golfing Soc of London; former pres Insurance Inst of Gloucester, dep chm and dir Westonbirt Sch; Freeman City of London 1981; Liveryman: Worshipful Co of Insurers, Worshipful Co of Marketors; ACII 1957, FInstD 1980, FIM 1984, FCIM 1989, chartered insurer 1989; *Recreations* golf, bridge, rambling; *Clubs* IOD, City Livery; *Style*— John McArdell, Esq

McARDLE, Colin Stewart; *b* 10 October 1939; *Educ* Jordanhill Coll Sch Glasgow, Univ of Glasgow (MB ChB, MD); *m* June Margaret Campbell, *née* Merchant; 2 s (Peter Alexander b 1975, Alan Douglas b 1982), 1 da (Kirsten Anne b 1977); *Career* sr registrar in surgery Western Infirmary Glasgow 1972–75 (Nuffield res fell 1971–72); conslt surgn: Victoria Infirmary Glasgow 1975–78, Dept of Surgery Royal Infirmary Glasgow 1978–96 (hon prof of surgery 1991); currently prof of surgery Univ of Edinburgh; visiting prof Univ of Glasgow 1999; author of over 200 papers on: breast, colon and stomach cancer, liver tumours, pain and postoperative pulmonary complications, shock, surgical sepsis and intensive care; FRCSEd 1968, FRCS 1969, FRCS Glasgow 1980, FRSM 1986; *Books* Surgical Oncology (1990), Hepatic Metastases (1996), Regional Chemotheraphy (2000), Colorectal Cancer (2000) Imaging for Surgeons (2001); *Style*— Colin McArdle, Esq; ✉ 6 Collylinn Road, Bearsden, Glasgow G61 4PN; University Department of Surgery, Royal Infirmary, Edinburgh

McARDLE, John; s of John Joseph McArdle (d 1966), and Edeth, *née* Webster, of Liverpool; *b* 16 August 1949; *Educ* St Bede's Secdy Modern Sch, E15 Acting Sch Laughton; *Career* actor; various credits BBC Radio Manchester; also appeared in Horses for Courses (Br Film Sch); patron: Burnly and Rendle NSPCC, Bolton Octogon Theatre, Unity Theatre Liverpool, Liverpool Everyman Youth Theatre; hon memb NSPCC Cncl 1994; Best Actor Award RTS 2002; subject of This is Your Life 2003; *Theatre* began with various fringe cos in England and Wales; repertory: Liverpool Playhouse, Liverpool Everyman, Manchester Library Theatre, Contact Theatre, Forum Theatre, Oldham Coliseum, Bolton Octogan, Sheffield Crucible, Chester Gateway, Edinburgh Festival, Young Vic Theatre; The Arbour (RNT Studio) 1997, Snow White (pantomime, Theatre Royal Nottingham), Our Country's Good (Liverpool Playhouse); *Television* for BBC incl: Thacker, Underbelly, Gallowglass (Barbara Vine series), Spender, Bambino Mio (Screen One) 1994, Skallergrig (Screen One) 1994, Seaforth 1994, Rich Deceiver 1994, Throwaways (Sch TV) 1996, Born to Run 1996, Casualty 1997, City Central, Holby City, Out of Hours 1998, The Cazelet Chronicles 2001, Rough Aunty 2001, Silver Command (working title) 2001, The Bingo Club 2003, Casualty 2004, Holby City 2004, Merseybeat series II, III and IV, Dalziel and Pascoe, Busby Babes Story, The Muncih Disaster; for Granada incl: Coronation Street, Strangers, Kavanagh QC 1995, Prime Suspect V 1996, Metropolis 2000, My Fragile Heart 2000, Always and Everyone 2001, presenter Case Unsolved; other credits incl: Billy Corkhill in Brookside (Channel Four) 1986–91, Firm Friends (ITV), The Chief (police series, Anglia) 1994, Firm Friends II (Tyne Tees) 1994, Finney (ITV) 1994, Cracker (ITV) 1994, Wycliffe (HTV) 1995, Heartbeat (Yorkshire) 1995, Its Not Unusual (Short and Curlies, Channel Four) 1995, In the Place of the Dead (LWT) 1995, And the Beat Goes On (Mersey) 1996, Family Ties (Channel Four) 1997, Lloyd's Bank Film Challenge 1997, Playing the Field (ITV) 1998, Where the Heart Is (ITV), Peak Practice (ITV) 2000–01, Active Defence (ITV) 2001, My Fragile Heart (Tiger Aspect) 2001, Through her Eyes (Channel 7 Australia) 2004, Foyles War (Bently Productions) 2004, prodr Demolition Dave (ITV) 2004–05, Heartbeat (ITV) 2005, The Bill (Talkback Thames) 2005, Mobile (ITV); *Radio* The Circle (Radio 4), Stock "So Good They Named it Once" (Radio 4); *Film* The Duke (writer and dir) 1999, There's Only One Jimmy Grimble 2000, Revengers Tragedy 2002, Function at the Junction (short film), Killing Joke; *Recreations* windsurfing, fell walking; *Style*— John McArdle, Esq; ✉ c/o Denis Lyne Agency, 108 Leonard Street, London EC2A 4RH (tel 020 7739 6200, fax 020 7739 4101)

MacARTHUR, Brian Roger; s of S H MacArthur (d 1971), of Ellesmere Port, Cheshire, and Marjorie MacArthur (d 1993); *b* 5 February 1940; *Educ* Brentwood Sch, Helsby GS, Univ of Leeds (BA); *m* 1, (m dis 1971), Peta Deschampsneufs; m 2, 22 Aug 1975 (m dis 1997), Bridget da of Nicholas Rosevear Trahair, of South Milton, Devon; 2 da (Tessa b 1976, Georgina b 1979); m 3, 4 Feb 2000, Maureen da of John Waller, of Cooden Beach, E Sussex; *Career* educn corr The Times 1967–70, fndr ed The Times Higher Educnl Supplement 1971–76, exec ed The Times 1981–82, dep ed The Sunday Times 1982–84; ed: The Western Morning News 1984–85, Today 1985–86; exec ed The Sunday Times 1987–92, assoc ed The Times 1992–2006; Hon MA Open Univ 1976; *Recreations* reading, France; *Clubs* Garrick; *Style*— Brian MacArthur, Esq; ✉ Church Farm House, The Street, Little Barningham, Norwich NR11 7AG

McARTHUR, (Allan Robin) Dayrell; s of Alan John Dennis McArthur (d 1988), of Combe Hay, Bath, and Pamela Mary, *née* Henderson; *b* 28 June 1946; *Educ* Winchester; *m* 30 April 1977, Susan Diana, da of Christopher Cheshire, of Spain; 3 s (Alastair b 1979, Sam b 1981, Robert b 1985); *Career* Price Waterhouse 1965–69, McArthur Group Ltd 1969– (md 1971, chm 1987); pres Nat Assoc of Steel Stockholders 1986–88, pres Fédération Européenne du Négoce d'Acier (European Steel Trades Fedn) 1992–94; govr UWE 1990–2004; chm Clifton Suspension Bridge Tst 2001; Master Soc of Merchant Venturers of Bristol 1989–90; *Recreations* tennis, golf, cricket, rackets, music, theatre, skiing; *Clubs* MCC, Tennis & Rackets Assoc, Bristol and Clifton Golf, Leatherjackets Golf; *Style*— Dayrell McArthur, Esq; ✉ Moorledge Farm, Chew Magna, Bristol BS40 8TL (tel 01275 332357); McArthur Group Ltd, Foundry Lane, Fishponds Trading Estate, Bristol BS5 7UE (tel 0117 965 6242, fax 0117 958 3536, e-mail dayrell.mcarthur@mcarthur-group.com)

McARTHUR, Douglas B; OBE (2001); *b* 17 March 1951; *Educ* Univ of Glasgow (BSc); *Children* 3 da (Vicki b 1977, Kate b 1980, Jill b 1984); *Career* mktg mgmnt positions 1973–83: Procter & Gamble, Scottish & Newcastle, Campbell Soups; dir Hall Advertising 1978–79, commercial dir Town Art & Design 1979–82, sales and mktg dir Radio Clyde 1983–84; dir 1985–92: Balgray Gp, Baillie Marshall Advertising; md and chief exec Radio Advertising Bureau 1992–2006; dir: IMD plc, Empathy Marketing Ltd; memb: Inst of Mktg 1979, MRS 1986, Mktg Soc 1992; fell: CAM 1997, Radio Acad 1997; *Recreations* theatre, music, literature, swimming; *Style*— Douglas McArthur, Esq, OBE; ✉ Planning for Results, 30 Nightingale Lane, London SW12 8TD (tel 020 8772 0225, e-mail douglas@planningforresults.com)

MacARTHUR, Dame Ellen Patricia; DBE (2005, MBE); da of Kenneth John MacArthur, and Avril Patricia MacArthur; *b* 8 July 1976; *Educ* Anthony Gell Sch Wirksworth; *Career* professional offshore sailor; dir OC Group (formerly Offshore Challenges); winner Class 2 Route du Rhum solo trans-atlantic race on 50' Kingfisher 1998, winner Open 60 Class Europe/New Man Star solo trans-atlantic race on 60' Kingfisher 2000, second overall Vendée Globe non-stop round the world race on 60' Kingfisher 2001, winner Class 1 (Open 60) Route du Rhum race on 70' Kingfisher 2002, attempted to set new Jules Verne non-stop round the world record 2003 (attempt aborted after losing mast of Kingfisher 2 in Southern Ocean), single-handed circumnavigation of the world on 60' B&Q 2005 (set world record time 71 days, 14 hours, 18 minutes); fndr Ellen MacArthur Tst; *Awards* YJA Young Sailor of the Year 1995, YJA Yachtsman of the Year 1999, Forum Int de la Course Océanique (FICO) World Champion 2001, Int Sailing Fedn (ISAF) World Champion Woman Sailor 2001; *Publications* Taking on the World (autobiography, 2002); *Recreations* sailing, walking; *Style*— Dame Ellen MacArthur, DBE; ✉ c/o Natasha Fairweather, AP Watt, 20 John Street, London WC2N 2DR (tel 020 7405 6774)

McARTHUR, Dr Thomas Burns (Tom); s of Archibald McArthur (d 1967), of Glasgow, and Margaret Dymock Dow, *née* Burns (d 1986); *b* 23 August 1938; *Educ* Woodside Secdy Sch Glasgow, Univ of Glasgow (MA), Univ of Edinburgh (MLitt, PhD); *m* 1, 30 March

1963, Fereshteh (d 1993), da of Habib Mottahedin, of Teheran, Iran; 2 da (Meher b 11 Nov 1966, Roshan b 16 Nov 1968), 1 s (Alan b 30 April 1970); m 2, 7 July 2001, Jacqueline LAM Kam-mei, of Hong Kong; *Career* 2 Lt offr instr RAEC 1959–62; educn offr: Depot the Royal Warks Regt, Depot the Mercian Bde; asst teacher Riland-Bedford Boys HS Sutton Coldfield 1962–64, head of Eng Dept Cathedral and John Connon Sch Bombay 1965–67, visiting prof Bharatiya Vidya Bhavan Univ of Bombay 1965–67, dir of studies Extra Mural Eng Language Courses Univ of Edinburgh 1972–79, assoc prof of Eng Université du Québec à Trois-Rivières Quebec Canada 1979–83; hon res fell Univ of Exeter 1992–2001; distinguished visiting prof: Chinese Univ of Hong Kong 2000, Xiamen Univ 2001–03; hon fell Chartered Inst of Linguistics 2002–; editor: English Today: The International Review of the English Language 1984–2007, The Oxford Companion to the English Language 1987–; memb Editorial Bd: International Journal of Lexicography 1988–98, World Englishes Jl 1993–, LOGOS: The Professional Jl of the Book World 1994–96; editorial advsr The Good Book Guide 1992–99, The Hong Kong Linguist 1998–2006; conslt to: BBC, Bloomsbury, Collins, Longman, Chambers, Cambridge Univ Press, Good Book Guide, WHO, Henson International TV (creators of The Muppets), Govt of Quebec, Century Hutchinson (now Helicon), Macmillan, OUP, Time-Life Books; fndr memb and tutor Birmingham Yoga Club 1963, chm Scot Yoga Assoc 1977–79, co-chm Scots Language Planning Ctee 1978, memb Tech and Educnl Ctees Soc of Authors 1992–98; numerous broadcasts BBC Eng by Radio (World Serv); hon Dr Univ of Uppsala 1999; *Books* Building English Words (1972), Using English Prefixes and Suffixes (1972), Using Compound Words (1972), A Rapid Course in English for Students of Economics (1973), Using Phrasal Verbs (1973), Collins Dictionary of English Phrasal Verbs and Their Idioms (with Beryl T Atkins, 1974), Learning Rhythm and Stress (with Mohamed Heliel, 1974), Using Modal Verbs (with Richard Wakely, 1974), Times, Tenses and Conditions (with John Hughes, 1974), Languages of Scotland (ed with A J Aitken, 1979), Longman Lexicon of Contemporary English (1981), A Foundation Course for Language Teachers (1983), The Written Word: A Course in Controlled Composition (books 1 and 2, 1984), Worlds of Reference: Lexicography, Learning and Language from the Clay Tablet to the Computer (1986), Understanding Yoga: A Thematic Companion to Yoga and Indian Philosophy (1986), Yoga and the Bhagavad-Gita (1986), Unitive Thinking: A Guide to Developing a More Integrated and Effective Mind (1988), The English Language as Used in Quebec: A Survey (1989), The Oxford Companion to the English Language (ed, 1992, abridged edn 1996, concise edn 1998), The English Languages (1998), Lexicography in Asia (ed jtly, 1998), Living Words: Languages, Lexicography and the Knowledge Revolution (1998), The Oxford Guide to World English (2002); *Recreations* reading, television, walking, travel; *Style*— Dr Tom McArthur; ✉ 22–23 Ventress Farm Court, Cherry Hinton Road, Cambridge CB1 8HD (tel 01223 245934, e-mail scotsway@aol.com)

MacARTHUR CLARK, Judy Anne; CBE (2004); da of Archibald Alastair Cameron MacArthur (d 1990), of Manchester, and Elinore Muriel, *née* Warde Sandwich (d 2003); *b* 18 November 1950; *Educ* Orton GS Peterborough, Univ of Glasgow Coll of Vet Med (BVMS), RCVS (Dip, election to specialist register), European Coll of Lab Animal Medicine (Dip); *m* 16 Feb 1991, David Wayne Clark, s of Robert Clark (d 1982), of Tell City, Indiana; 1 da (Sophie Katherine b 28 Aug 1991); *Career* gen vet practice Sussex 1973–74, vet advsr Univs Fedn for Animal Welfare 1974–76, pt/t hon lectr RVC London 1974–87, sr scientific offr 1976–82, head of lab animal science Searle R&D High Wycombe 1983–86, dir of lab animal science Pfizer Central Research UK 1986–91, vet conslt JMC Consultancy 1991, vet dir BioZone Ltd Margate 1992–2005, vice-pres worldwide comparative medicine Pfizer Global R&D 2005–; memb: Cncl Section of Comparative Med RSM 1979–87, Cncl Br Lab Animals Vet Assoc (BLAVA) 1979–89 (vice-pres and pres 1983–89), RCVS 1982– (vice-pres 1991–92, pres 1992–93, chm various ctees), Animal Procedures Ctee (APC) 1994–99, BBSRC 1996–99, Farm Animal Welfare Cncl (FAWC) 1993– (chm 1999–2004, chm R&D Ctee 1994–98); memb: Technology Liaison Ctee Inst for Animal Health Compton 1994–, Animal Production and Welfare Strategy Gp Silsoe Research Inst 1994– (chm 1996–); chm Bill Hiddleston Award Fund Tstees 1985–92, vice-pres Inst of Animal Technol (IAT) 1991–; Winston Churchill travelling fell USA and Canada 1982, Victory Medal Central Vet Soc BVA 1992, Pres's Award Vet Mktg Assoc 1993; author of approx 100 scientific pubns and invited presentations; hon memb Assoc of Vet Teachers and Research Workers; memb: BVA, BLAVA, Fedn of Euro Lab Animal Science Assocs, Lab Animal Science Assoc, Research Defence Soc, Univs Fedn for Animal Welfare, Vet Benevolent Fund; DVMS (hc) Univ of Glasgow 2001; MCVRS 1973, FRSM 1978, FIBiol 1997, ARAgS 2002; *Recreations* company of family and friends; *Clubs* Farmers', RSM; *Style*— Dr Judy MacArthur Clark, CBE

MACARTNEY, Sir John Ralph; 7 Bt (I 1799), of Lish, Armagh; s of Sir John Barrington Macartney, 6 Bt; *b* 24 July 1945; *m* 1966, Suzanne Marie Fowler, of Nowra, NSW; 4 da (Donna Maree b 1968, Karina Lee b 1971, Katherine Anne b 1974, Anita Louise b 1979); *Career* Petty Officer RAN (ret); teacher (head of dept) ACT Inst of TAFE; successively: facilities mangr Mackay TAFE Qld Aust, coal communications offr Mount ISA Mines; *Style*— Sir John Macartney, Bt

MACASKILL, Ewen; s of John Angus MacAskill, of Erskine, Renfrewshire, and Catherine, *née* MacDonald; *b* 29 October 1951; *Educ* Woodside Sch Glasgow, Univ of Glasgow (MA); *m* Anne, da of John Hutchison; 3 s (Robbie b 19 Nov 1981, Andrew b 27 July 1984, Jamie b 29 Aug 1988); *Career* reporter Glasgow Herald 1974–77; journalist: Nat Broadcasting Cmmn of Papua New Guinea 1978–79, Reuters 1980, Scotsman 1981–83, China Daily Beijing 1984, Scotsman 1985, Washington Post (reporter) 1986; political ed Scotsman 1989–96 (journalist 1987), chief political corr The Guardian 1996–2000, diplomatic ed The Guardian 2000–; Scotland's Young Journalist of the Year 1974, What The Papers Say Scoop of the Year (Guardian Team) 1999; *Books* Always A Little Further (1983); *Recreations* mountaineering, theatre; *Clubs* Junior Mountaineering Club of Scotland; *Style*— Ewen MacAskill, Esq; ✉ 11 Norman Avenue, St Margarets, Twickenham, Middlesex TW1 2LY (tel 020 8891 0795); The Guardian, 119 Farringdon Road, London EC1R 3ER (tel 020 7239 9579)

MACAULAY, Anthony Dennis; s of Dennis Macaulay, of Wakefield, W Yorks, and Frances, *née* Frain; *b* 15 November 1948; *Educ* Queen Elizabeth GS Wakefield, Keble Coll Oxford; *m* 7 Oct 1978, Dominica Francisca, da of Dr Henri Compernolle, of Bruges, Belgium; 1 s (Thomas b 29 March 1985), 2 da (Laura b 20 April 1983, Rosemary b 4 Oct 1987); *Career* admitted slr 1974; articled clerk/slr Biddle & Co 1971–75, asst slr Wilkinson Kimbers & Staddon 1975–77, ptnr Herbert Smith 1983– (asst slr 1977–83), sec to Panel on Take-overs and Mergers 1983–85; memb Law Soc; memb Worshipful Co of Slrs 1987; *Books* Butterworths Handbook of UK Corporate Finance (contrib, 1988), Palmer's Company Law (memb Ed Bd, 1998); *Recreations* tennis, skiing, music, cooking, family; *Style*— Anthony Macaulay, Esq; ✉ Exchange House, Primrose Street, London EC2A 2HS (tel 020 7374 8000, fax 020 7374 0888, telex 886633)

McAULIFFE, Prof Charles Andrew; *b* 29 November 1941; *Educ* Victoria Univ of Manchester (BSc, DSc), Florida State Univ (MS), Univ of Oxford (DPhil); *m* 1 April 1967, Margaret Mary; 1 s ((Charles) Andrew b 30 Nov 1977), 2 da (Amy Noelle b 15 Oct 1972, Juliette Hilda b 12 Dec 1975); *Career* currently head Dept of Chemistry Univ of Manchester (formerly UMIST); memb Dalton Div Cncl RSC 1990–; FRSC; *Books* Transition Metal Complexes of Phosphine, Arsine and Antimony Ligands (with W Levason, 1978); *Style*— Prof Charles McAuliffe; ✉ The Coach House, 1 Pinewood, Bowdon, Cheshire WA14 3JG; Department of Chemistry, University of Manchester, Manchester M60 1QD (tel 0161 236 3311)

MacAUSLAN, Harry Hume; s of John Mechan MacAuslan, and Helen Constance Howden, *née* Hume; *b* 2 October 1956; *Educ* Charterhouse, Univ of Manchester (BA); *m* 1981, Fiona Caroline, da of Brian Martin Boag; 1 da (Clare Emily b 5 Jan 1985), 2 s (Samuel Alexander b 9 Aug 1987, James Hume b 8 April 1989); *Career* advertising exec; mktg trainee De La Rue 1979–80; J Walter Thompson: joined as graduate trainee 1980, bd dir 1989–, head of account mgmnt 1993–96, dep chm 1996–2005; Leo Burnett: global dir 2005–06, vice-chm EMEA 2005–; non-exec dir Sadler's Wells Trust Ltd 1995–, chm Sadler's Wells Devpt Cncl 2003–, govr Sadler's Wells 2005–; FRSA 2005; *Style*— Harry MacAuslan, Esq; ✉ Leo Burnett, Warwick Building, Kensington Village, Avonmore Road, London W14 8HQ (tel 020 7071 1307, e-mail harry.macauslan@leoburnett.co.uk)

McAVAN, Linda; MEP (Lab) Yorks and the Humber; da of Thomas McAvan, of Bradford, W Yorks, and Jean, *née* Cole (d 1995); *b* 2 December 1962; *Educ* St Joseph's RC Coll Bradford, Heriot-Watt Univ (BA), Université Libre de Bruxelles (MA); *m* 7 July 2000, Paul Blomfield; *Career* Lab Pty activist 1980–: former pres Lab Students Heriot-Watt Univ, former vice-chair Sheffield District Lab Pty; Euro policy expert Brussels 1984–91, Euro offr Coalfield Community Campaign 1991–95, princ strategy offr Barnsley Cncl 1995–98; MEP (Lab): Yorks S 1998–99 (by-election), Yorks and the Humber 1999–; dep ldr EPLP 1999–; Euro Parl Ctee memb: Foreign Affrs, Human Rights, Common Security and Defence Policy, Regnl Policy Transport and Tourism (subst memb); chair S Yorks Forum, tstee Support Dogs Charity, memb Advsy Ctee: Northern Coll, Nat Coalmining Museum; *Style*— Ms Linda McAvan, MEP; ✉ Labour Constituency Office, 79 High Street, Wath upon Dearne, South Yorkshire S63 7QB (tel 01709 875665, fax 01709 874207, e-mail lindamcavan@lindamcavanmep.org.uk)

McAVOY, James; *b* 1979, Glasgow; *Educ* Royal Scottish Acad of Music and Drama; *m* Anne-Marie Duff, the actress; *Career* actor; *Theatre* incl: Breathing Corpses (Royal Court Theatre) 2005; *Television* incl: Regeneration 1997, Lorna Doone 2000, Band of Brothers 2001, White Teeth 2002, State of Play 2003, Early Doors 2003, Shameless 2004–05, Macbeth 2005; *Films* incl: Swimming Pool 2001, Bright Young Things 2003, Wimbledon 2004, Inside I'm Dancing 2004, The Chronicles of Narnia: The Lion, the Witch and the Wardrobe 2005, Last King of Scotland 2006, Starter for Ten 2006, Penelope 2006, Becoming Jane 2006, Atonement 2007; *Style*—James McAvoy; ✉ c/o Peters Fraser & Dunlop, Drury House, 34–43 Russell Street, London WC2B 5HA (tel 020 7344 1000, fax 020 7836 9539)

McAVOY, Michael Anthony; s of Lt-Col John McAvoy, and Gertrude, *née* Gradidge (d 1962); *b* 31 July 1934; *Educ* Beaumont Coll, Lincoln Coll Oxford; *m* 1963, June Anne, da of Robert Harper; 1 da (Annabel Jane b 1966); *Career* Young & Rubicam Ltd: joined 1957, md Planned Public Relations Ltd 1965, chm Planned Public Relations 1970, chm GLH Marketing Ltd 1970, dir Young & Rubicam Holdings 1970, vice-pres Young & Rubicam International 1971, vice-chm Burson Marsteller Ltd 1979–81; fndr and ptnr McAvoy Wreford & Associates 1981–84, vice-chm McAvoy Wreford Bayley Ltd 1986–90 (dir 1984), vice-chm McAvoy Bayley Ltd 1990–92, chm GCI Europe 1992–94, conslt 1995–; fndr chm PRCA 1969–72; memb Cncl IPRA, FIPR; *Recreations* golf, gardening, travel; *Clubs* RAC; *Style*— Michael McAvoy, Esq; ✉ Middleton House, Milton Abbas, Blandford, Dorset DT11 0BS (tel 01258 880333)

McAVOY, Rt Hon Thomas McLaughlin; PC (2003), MP; s of Edward McAvoy (d 1985), and Frances McLaughlin McAvoy (d 1982); *b* 14 December 1943; *Educ* St Columbkilles Jr Secdy Sch; *m* 1968, Eleanor Kerr, da of William Kerr, of Rutherglen, Glasgow; 4 s (Thomas b 1969, Michael b 1971, Steven b 1974, Brian b 1981); *Career* regnl cncllr Strathclyde 1982–87; MP (Lab/Co-op): Glasgow Rutherglen 1987–2005, Rutherglen and Hamilton West 2005–; oppn whip 1991–93 and 1996–97, comptroller of HM Household (Govt whip) 1997–; *Style*— The Rt Hon Thomas McAvoy, MP; ✉ 9 Douglas Avenue, Rutherglen, Lanarkshire G73 4RA; House of Commons, London SW1A 0AA (tel 020 7219 3000)

McBAIN OF McBAIN, James Hughston; 22 Chief of Clan McBain (McBean); s of Hughston Maynard McBain of McBain (matriculated as Chief 1959, d 1977); *b* 1928; *Educ* Culver Mil Acad, Western Washington Coll, Univ of Arizona; *m* Margaret, *née* Stephenson; *Heir* s, Richard McBain; *Career* pres Scot Photo Shops AZ 1962–; *Recreations* golf, Scottish history, Scottish country dancing; *Clubs* Royal Scottish Country Dance Soc; *Style*—James McBain of McBain

MACBETH, Dr Fergus Robert; s of Dr Ronald Graeme Macbeth (d 1992), and Margaret, *née* Macdonald (d 1983); *b* 5 January 1948; *Educ* Eton, Merton Coll Oxford, KCH Med Sch London (MA, BM BCh, DM), Univ of Stirling (MBA); *Career* conslt in radiotherapy and oncology Beatson Oncology Centre Glasgow 1988–96, dir Clinical Effectiveness Support Unit for Wales 1996–2001, conslt oncologist 1996–, dir Nat Collaborating Centre for Cancer 2003–; FRCR 1987, FRCPGlas 1989, FRCP 1997; *Style*— Dr Fergus Macbeth; ✉ Velindre Hospital, Whitchurch, Cardiff CF14 2TL (tel 02920 615888)

McBRIDE, Brian; *Educ* Univ of Glasgow (MA); *m* Linda; 2 da (Susan, Jennifer); *Career* joined Xerox 1977, subsequent positions with IBM, Crosfield Electronics, Madge Networks, Lucent and Dell Computers, chm Virgin Mobile 2003, md T-Mobile UK 2003–05, md Amazon.co.uk Ltd 2006–; non-exec dir: SThree plc 2001–, Celtic plc 2005–; *Style*— Mr Brian McBride

McBRIEN, Michael Patrick; s of Leo Patrick McBrien (d 1969), and Elizabeth Rosemary, *née* Phillips (d 2005); *b* 4 July 1935; *Educ* Stonyhurst, St Thomas' Hosp Univ of London (MB BS); *m* 11 July 1964, Tessa Ann Freeland, da of Col Richard Bayfield Freeland (d 1980), of Beccles, Suffolk; 1 da (Emma b 12 March 1966), 2 s (James b 2 May 1968, Rowan b 6 May 1972); *Career* registrar in surgery: Southampton Hosp 1967–69, St Thomas' Hosp London 1969–70; sr registrar and lectr in surgery St Thomas' Hosp London 1970–73; sr consIt surgn: W Suffolk Gp of Hosps, St Edmund's Nuffield Hosp 1973–99, ret; Hunterian prof RCS 1974, clinical teacher and examiner in surgery Univ of Cambridge, lectr UEA; external examiner in surgery: RCS(Ed), St Thomas' Hosp and KCH Univ of London, Royal Coll of Surgns of Sri Lanka, Royal Coll of Surgns in Cairo; RCS: sec Ct of Examiners 1992–99, memb Hospital Recognition Ctee 1992–2003; GMC assoc; med memb Pensions Appeal Tbnls 1996–; memb Panel Professional Linguistics Assesment Bd (PLAB) GMC 2000–04, examiner PLAB OSCE (Objective Structured Clinical Examination) GMC 2001–06; nat dir Mannatech Inc; MS 1973; memb: BMA 1960–, RSM 1960; FRCS 1968; *Books* Postgraduate Surgery (1986); *Recreations* tennis, golf, cricket, shooting, bridge, skiing, travel; *Clubs* RSM, MCC; *Style*— Michael McBrien, Esq; ✉ Stanton House, Norton, Bury St Edmunds, Suffolk IP31 3LQ (tel 01359 230832, fax 01359 231266, e-mail mandtmcb@hotmail.com)

McBRYDE, Prof William Wilson (Bill); s of William McBryde (d 1964), of Burntisland, Fife, and Marjory Wilson, *née* Husband (d 1991); *b* 6 July 1945; *Educ* Perth Acad, Univ of Edinburgh (LLB, LLD), Univ of Glasgow (PhD); *m* 1, 4 Nov 1972 (m dis 1982), Elspeth Jean Stormont Glover; 1 da (Eileen b 23 Feb 1974), 1 s (Donald b 5 March 1976); m 2, 12 April 1986 (m dis 1999), Joyce Margaret, da of Rev James Marcus Gossip (d 1985), of Edinburgh; 1 da (Helen b 23 June 1988 d 2007); *Career* apprentice with Morton Smart Macdonald & Milligan WS 1967–70; admitted slr 1969; court procurator Biggart Lumsden & Co Glasgow 1970–72, lectr in private law Univ of Glasgow 1972–76, sr lectr in private law Univ of Aberdeen 1976–87, prof of Scots law Univ of Dundee 1987–99 (dean Faculty of Law 1989–90, dep princ Univ 1991–92, vice-princ 1992–94), prof of commercial law Univ of Edinburgh 1999–2005, Van der Grinten prof of commercial law

Univ of Nijmegen 2002–; visiting prof L'Université de Paris V René Descartes 2000–05; dir Scot Univ Law Inst 1989–95; specialist Parly advsr to House of Lords Select Ctee on European Communities 1980–83; memb: Scot Consumer Cncl 1984–87, Scot Advsy Ctee on Arbitration 1986–, Insolvency Permit Ctee ICAS 1990–95, Advsy Panel on Security over Moveable Property DTI 1994–, consultant to Scottish Law Cmmn 1997–98; Hon Sheriff Tayside, Central and Fife Dundee 1991–; FRSE 1994; *Books* Bankruptcy (Scotland) Act 1985 (1986), The Law of Contract in Scotland (1987, 2 edn 2001), Petition Procedure in the Court of Session (2 edn, with N Dowie, 1988), Bankruptcy (1989, 2 edn 1995), Bankruptcy (Scotland) Act 1993 (1993), Principles of European Insolvency Law (jt ed, 2003); *Recreations* walking, photography; *Style*— Prof Bill McBryde, FRSE; ✉ Faculty of Law, The University of Edinburgh, Old College, South Bridge, Edinburgh EH8 9YL (tel 0131 650 2038, fax 0131 650 6317)

McCABE, Bernice Alda; da of Alan Collis Wood, and Eileen May Wood; *Educ* Clifton HS Bristol, Univ of Bristol (BA, PGCE), Leeds Metropolitan Univ (MBA); *Career* teacher Filton HS Bristol 1974–81, head English Dept Cotham GS Bristol 1981–83, head English Faculty Collingwood Sch Camberley 1984–86, dep head Heathland Sch Hounslow 1986–90; headmistress: Chelmsford Co HS 1990–97, N London Collegiate Sch 1997–; dir HRH Prince of Wales Educn Summer Sch 2002–, co-dir The Prince's Teaching Inst and The Prince's Cambridge Prog for Teaching 2006–; exec Nat Grammar Schs Assoc 1995–97, memb Univs Sub-Ctee GSA/HMC 2001–; govr Orley Farm Sch 1997–2001; FRSA; *Recreations* family, reading, restoration of period home, gardening, entertaining, travel, swimming, running, gym, walking; *Clubs* Univ Women's; *Style*— Mrs Bernice McCabe; ✉ North London Collegiate School, Canons, Edgware, Middlesex HA8 7RJ (tel 020 8951 6401)

MacCABE, Prof Colin Myles Joseph; s of Myles Joseph MacCabe, and Ruth Ward MacCabe; *b* 9 February 1949; *Educ* St Benedict's Sch Ealing, Univ of Cambridge (MA, PhD), Ecole Normale Supérieure; *m*; 2 s, 1 da; *Career* research fell Emmanuel Coll Cambridge 1974–76, univ asst lectr in English Univ of Cambridge and coll lectr and fell King's Coll Cambridge 1976–81; Univ of Strathclyde: prof of English Univ of Strathclyde 1981–85, chm Dept of English Studies 1982–84, chm John Logie Baird Centre for Research in TV and Film 1985–91 (founding dir 1983–85), visiting prof in Prog for Literacy Linguistics 1985–91; prof of English Univ of Pittsburgh 1986– (distinguished prof of English and film 2002), prof of English Univ of Exeter 1998–; visiting fell Griffith Univ Brisbane 1981 and 1984, Mellon visiting prof Univ of Pittsburgh 1985, visiting prof Birkbeck Coll London 1992–; memb English Teaching Advsy Ctee Br Cncl 1983–85 (Br Cncl lectr Shanghai Foreign Language Inst 1984); Br Film Inst (BFI): head of prodn 1985–89, head of research 1989–98; ed Critical Quarterly 1987–; *Books* James Joyce and the Revolution of The World (1979), Godard: Images, Sounds, Politics (1980), The Talking Cure: Essays in Psychoanalysis and Language (ed, 1981), James Joyce: New Perspectives (ed 1982), Theoretical Essays: film, linguistics, literature (1985), The BBC and Public Sector Broadcasting (jt ed, 1986), High Theory Low Culture: Analysing Popular Television and Film (ed, 1986), Futures for English (ed, 1987), The Linguistics of Writing (jt ed, 1988), Who is Andy Warhol (jt ed, 1997), Performance (1998), The Eloquence of the Vulgar (1999), Godard: A Portrait of the Artist at 70 (2003); *Recreations* eating, drinking, talking; *Style*— Prof Colin MacCabe; ✉ Department of English, University of Exeter, Queen's Building, The Queen's Drive, Exeter EX4 4QH (tel 01392 263 262)

McCABE, John; CBE (1985); s of Frank McCabe (d 1983), and Elisabeth Carmen, née Herlitzius (d 1993); *b* 21 April 1939; *Educ* Liverpool Inst, Univ of Manchester (BMus), Royal Manchester Coll of Music (FRMCM), Hochschule für Musik Munich; *m* 1, (m dis 1973), Hilary Tann; *m* 2, 31 July 1974, Monica Christine, da of Jack Smith (d 1974); *Career* composer and pianist; res pianist Univ Coll Cardiff 1965–68, freelance music critic 1966–71, dir London Coll Music 1983–90; writer of operas, ballets, symphonies, concertos, choral and keyboard works, TV and film music; cmmnd works incl: Symphony No 4 Of Time and the River (BBC Symphony Orch and Melbourne Symphony Orch) 1995, Edward II (Stuttgart Ballet) 1995, Arthur Pendragon and Le Morte d'Arthur (Birmingham Royal Ballet) 2000–2001; numerous recordings incl 12 CD set complete piano works of Haydn; pres: Inc Soc Musicians 1982–83, Br Music Soc; memb Hon Cncl of Mgmnt RPS 1983–86, chm Assoc Professional Composers 1985–86, memb Gen Cncl and Donations Ctee Performing Rights Soc 1985–88; vice-pres: Malvern Music Club, Luton Music Club; memb: Wigmore Hall Board 1987–90, Mechanical Copyright Protection Soc; Hon DPhil Thames Valley Univ, Hon DMus Univ of Liverpool 2006; FLCM, FRCM, Hon RAM, FRNCM 1986, FTCL 1989; *Books* BBC Music Guide: Bartok's Orchestral Music (1974), Haydn's Piano Sonatas (1986), Gollancz Musical Companion (contrib, 1973), Novello Short Biography: Rachmaninov (1974), Alan Rawsthorne: Portrait of a Composer (1998); *Recreations* cinema, books, cricket, golf, (watching) snooker, bonfires (playing); *Style*— John McCabe, Esq, CBE; ✉ c/o Novello & Co Ltd (Music Publishers), 14–15 Berners Street, London W1T 3LJ (tel 020 7612 7400, fax 020 7612 7545)

McCABE, Stephen James (Steve); MP; s of James McCabe, and Margaret, née McCrorie; *b* 4 August 1955; *Educ* Port Glasgow HS, Moray House Coll Edinburgh (qualification in social work, Dip Social Studies), Univ of Bradford (MA); *m* 1991 (m dis), Lorraine Lea, née Clendon; 1 da (Rhianna Charlotte b 15 July 1993), 1 s (Keiron James b 5 Sept 1996); *Career* generic social worker Wolverhampton 1977–79, social worker with young offenders Wolverhampton 1979–83, mangr The Priory Centre for Adolescents Newbury 1983–85, lectr in social work N Worcestershire Coll 1986–89, pt/t social worker child care team Solihull 1989–91, pt/t social policy researcher Br Assoc of Social Workers (BASW) 1989–91, social work educn advsr Central Cncl for Educn and Trg in Social Work (CCETSW) 1991–97, MP (Lab) Birmingham Hall Green 1997–; asst Govt whip 2006–; *Recreations* reading, cooking, hill walking, football; *Style*— Steve McCabe, Esq, MP; ✉ House of Commons, London SW1A 0AA (tel 020 7219 4842/3509); Birmingham (tel 0121 622 6761)

McCABE, Thomas; MSP; *b* 28 April 1954; *Educ* St Martin's Secdy Sch, Hamilton Bell Coll of Technol (Dip Public Sector Mgmnt); *Career* 20 years industrial experience; welfare rights offr; elected to represent Larkhall West 1988–99, chair of Housing Hamilton District Cncl 1990–92; leader: Hamilton DC 1992–96, South Lanarkshire Cncl 1995–99; MSP (Lab) Hamilton South 1999–; min for Parl 1999–2001, dep min for Health and Community Care 2003–04, min for Fin and Public Serv Reform 2004–; former memb Bd: Lanarkshire Devpt Agency, Lanarkshire Civic Pride Campaign; vice-convenor Strathclyde Joint Police Bd 1996–99; *Recreations* sport, reading, golf, walking; *Style*— Tom McCabe, Esq, MSP; ✉ The Scottish Parliament, Edinburgh EH99 1SP (tel 0131 348 5830, fax 0131 348 5125, e-mail tom.mccabe.msp@scottish.parliament.uk)

McCAFFER, Eur Ing Prof Ronald; s of John Gegg McCaffer (d 1984), and Catherine Turner, née Gourlay (d 1979); *b* 8 December 1943; *Educ* Univ of Strathclyde (BSc, DSc), Loughborough Univ (PhD); *m* 13 Aug 1966, Margaret Elizabeth, da of Cyril Warner; 1 s (Andrew b 29 April 1977); *Career* design engr Babtie Shaw and Morton 1965–67; site engr: The Nuclear Power Gp 1967–69, Taylor Woodrow Construction 1969–70; Dept of Civil Engrg Loughborough Univ of Technol: lectr 1970–78, sr lectr 1978–83, reader 1983–86, prof of construction mgmnt 1986–, head of dept 1987–93, dean Sch of Engrg 1992–97, dep vice-chllr 1997–2002, dir Strategic Business Partnerships, Innovation and Knowledge Transfer 2002–06; ed Engineering, Construction & Architectural Management 1994–, memb Engrg Construction Industry Trg Bd 1994–2003, memb Technical Opportunities Panel EPSRC 2000–04; chm: Loughborough University

Enterprises Ltd 2002–06, Loughborough Innovation Centre Ltd 2002–06; dir Imago Ltd 2003–06; memb Cncl Innovation East Midlands 2005–; memb Bd of Tstees and advsr to Br Univ in Egypt 2005–; FREng 1991, Eur Ing, FICE, FCIOB, MCMI, MASCE; *Books* Worked Examples in Construction Management (1986), Managing Construction Equipment (1991), Estimating and Tendering for Civil Engineering (1991), Modern Construction Management (1995, 5 edn 2000), International Bid Preparation (1995), International Bidding Case Study (1995), Management of Off-Highway Plant and Equipment (2002); *Style*— Eur Ing Prof Ronald McCaffer, FREng; ✉ Department of Civil Engineering, Loughborough University of Technology, Loughborough, Leicestershire LE11 3TU (tel 01509 222600, fax 01509 223890, e-mail r.mccaffer@lboro.ac.uk, website www.mccaffer.com)

McCAFFERTY, Christine; MP; *b* 14 October 1945; *Career* MP (Lab) Calder Valley 1997–; chair: All Pty Population Devpt and Reproductive Health Gp 1999, All Pty Gp guides; elected Parly memb Cncl of Europe 1999; memb: Social Health and Family Ctee, Sub-Ctee for Children, Int Devpt Select Ctee 2001–05, Migration, Demography and Refugees Ctee 2001–05, Sub-Ctee on Refugees 2001–04; Political Advsy Ctee Environmental Industries Cmmn; memb North Region Assoc for the Blind 1993–96, chm APPG - Friends of Islam; founder memb/chm: Calder Valley Cancer Support Gp 1987–92, Calderdale Domestic Violence Forum 1989–97; dir Royd Regeneration Ltd; memb West Yorks Police Authy 1994–97, memb West Yorks Police Complaints Ctee 1994–97, chm Brighouse Police Community Forum 1994–97, chm Sowerby Bridge Police Community Forum 1994–97, lay prison visitor West Yorks 1994–97; tstee Trades Club Building Hebden Bridge; *Style*— Ms Christine McCafferty, MP; ✉ House of Commons, London SW1A 0AA (tel 020 7219 3000, e-mail chrismccaffertymp@btinternet.com)

McCAFFERTY, Ian Alexander; s of William John Edward McCafferty, and Mary, née Cutts; *b* 1 July 1956; *Educ* Dulwich Coll, Univ of Durham (BA), Univ of Amsterdam Europa Instituut (Nuffic scholar, MA); *m* 27 Feb 1982, Susan Jean, née Craig; 2 s (Andrew b 3 May 1988, Alexander b 17 May 1991); *Career* economist Int C of C Paris 1979–83, head of statistics The Economist newspaper 1983–85, head of economic trends CBI 1985–88, chief int economist Baring Securities 1988–92, chief int economist NatWest Markets 1992–98, head of macroeconomics BP plc 1998–2001, chief economic advsr CBI 2001–; memb Advsy Bd Centre for Business Research Judge Inst Univ of Cambridge; memb Soc of Business Economists 1985– (memb Cncl 2002–); FRSA 2007; *Recreations* cooking, rugby, golf, France; *Style*— Ian McCafferty, Esq; ✉ CBI, Centre Point, 103 New Oxford Street, London WC1A 1DU (tel 020 7395 8103, fax 020 7836 5856, e-mail ian.mccafferty@cbi.org.uk)

McCAHILL, His Hon Judge Patrick Gerard; QC (1996); s of John McCahill (d 1995), and Josephine, née Conaghan (d 2001); *Educ* Corby GS, St Catharine's Coll Cambridge (scholar, MA), Univ of London (LLM), BSc (Open Univ); *m* 8 Sept 1979, Liselotte Gabrielle Steiner; 2 da (Gabrielle Marie b 29 Nov 1980, Claire Elizabeth b 17 Aug 1984); *Career* supervisor St Catharine's Coll Cambridge; called to the Bar: Gray's Inn 1975 (Bacon scholar, Atkin scholar), King's Inns Dublin 1990; lectr St John's Coll Oxford 1975–78, asst dep coroner Birmingham and Solihull 1984–99, recorder of the Crown Court 1997–2001 (asst recorder 1993–97), circuit judge (Midland Circuit) 2001–, specialist chancery circuit judge 2007–; memb: Mental Health Review Tbnl 2000–, Parole Bd 2004–; FCIArb 1992; *Style*— His Hon Judge McCahill, QC; ✉ Birmingham Civil Justice Centre, 33 Bull Street, Birmingham B4 6DS

McCAIL, Chad; *b* 1961; *Educ* Univ of Kent (BA), Goldsmiths Coll London (BA); *Career* artist; *Solo Exhibitions* Collective Gallery Edinburgh 1998, Laurent Delaye Gallery London 1998 and 2000, Attitudes Geneva 1999, Snake (Laurent Delaye Gallery London) 2002; *Group Exhibitions* Performance collaboration (CCA Glasgow) 1992, Installation (Cracker Factory Edinburgh) 1992, Billboard and Performance (Aerial, Edinburgh) 1994, Paintings (Out of the Blue Edinburgh) 1994, Drawings (The Virtuous Space Edinburgh) 1995, Drawings (The Bongo Club Edinburgh) 1996, Collective Gallery Edinburgh 1997, Insulator (Gasworks London) 1997, Out of the Blue (New Street Exhbn Space Edinburgh) 1997, Afternoon in the Park (Laurent Delaye Gallery London) 1997, Connected (Northern Gallery for Contemporary Art Sunderland) 1997, Canny (Archway London) 1998, Family Credit (Edinburgh Festival Exhbn Collective Gallery Edinburgh) 1998, Eurocentral (Transmission Gallery Edinburgh) 1998, Social Security, Seguridad Social (RCA and Ex-Teresa Arte Actual Mexico City) 1998, Surfacing: Contemporary Drawing (ICA London) 1998, Accelerated Learning (Duncan of Jordanstone Coll Dundee) 1999, Locale (City Art Centre Edinburgh) 1999, Evolution is not over yet (Fruitmarket Gallery Edinburgh) 1999, Sampling (Ronald Feldman Fine Arts NY) 1999, Melbourne Biennial 1999, Protest and Survive (Whitechapel Art Gallery London) 2000, Because a fire was in my head (S London Gallery) 2000, Becks Futures (ICA London and tour) 2000, Give and Take (Harris Museum and Art Gallery) 2000, Landscape (Br Cncl touring show) 2000, 2001 and 2002, British Art Show 5 (tour) 2000–01, Utopia Now! (Oliver Art Centre CCAC Inst San Francisco) 2001, Here + Now: Scottish Art 1990–2001 (Dundee Contemporary Arts, Generator Projects and McManus Galleries Dundee, Aberdeen Art Gallery and Peacock Visual Arts Aberdeen) 2001, Invitation á...Laurent Delaye Gallery invitée par la galerie Anton Weller (Galerie Anton Weller Paris) 2001, The Other Britannia (Tecla Sala Barcelona and tour) 2001, Utopia Now! (and Then) (Sonoma Co Museum Santa Rosa Calif) 2002, The Gallery Show (Royal Acad) 2002; *Work in Public Collections* Br Cncl Collection, Cake Fndn Zurich, Fonds Municipal d'Art contemporain de Genève, Mamco Geneva, Middlesbrough Art Gallery, Scottish Nat Gallery of Modern Art, City Art Centre Edinburgh, Musée d'Art Moderne Grand-Duc Jean Luxembourg; *Style*— Chad McCail, Esq; ✉ Laurent Delaye Gallery, 11 Savile Row, London W1S 3PG (tel 020 7287 1546, fax 020 7287 1562, e-mail office@laurentdelaye.com)

McCALL, Carolyn; *b* 13 September 1961; *Educ* Univ of Kent (BA), Univ of London (MA); *Career* risk analyst Costain Gp plc 1984–86; The Guardian: planner 1986–88, advtg exec 1988–89, advtg mangr 1989–91, product devpt mangr 1991–92, display advtg mangr 1992, advtg dir Wired UK 1992–94, dep advtg dir 1994–95, advtg dir 1995–97, commercial dir 1997–98, dep md 1998–2000, ceo Guardian Newspapers Ltd 2000–06, ceo Guardian Media Gp plc 2006–; non-exec dir: New Look Gp plc 1999–2004, Tesco plc 2005–; chair Opportunity Now 2005–, tstee Tools for Schools (educnl charity) 2000–05; *Style*— Ms Carolyn McCall; ✉ Guardian Media Group plc, 60 Farringdon Road, London EC1R 3ER (tel 020 7239 9711, website www.gmgplc.co.uk)

McCALL, Christopher Hugh; QC (1987); yr s of late Robin Home McCall, CBE, and late Joan Elizabeth, née Kingdon; *b* 3 March 1944; *Educ* Winchester, Magdalen Coll Oxford (BA); *m* 20 June 1981, Henrietta Francesca, 2 da of late Adrian Lesley Sharpe, of Trebetherick, Cornwall; *Career* called to the Bar Lincoln's Inn 1966 (bencher 1993); second jr counsel to Inland Revenue in chancery matters 1977–87, jr counsel to HM Attorney-Gen in charity matters 1981–87; tstee Br Museum 1999–2004; *Recreations* mountains, music, travel, Egyptomania; *Clubs* Leander, Alpine; *Style*— C H McCall, Esq, QC; ✉ Sphinx Hill, Moulsford on Thames, Oxfordshire OX10 9JF (tel 01491 652162); Maitland Chambers, 7 Stone Buildings, Lincoln's Inn, London WC2A 3SZ (tel 020 7406 1200)

McCALL, David Slesser; CBE (1988), DL (Norfolk 1992); s of Patrick McCall (d 1987), of Norwich, and Florence Kate Mary, née Walker (d 2002); *b* 3 December 1934; *Educ* Robert Gordon's Coll Aberdeen, Univ of Aberdeen; *m* 6 July 1968, (Lois) Patricia, da of Ernest Lonsdale Elder (d 1985), of Glasgow; *Career* Nat Serv RAF 1959–60; accountant Grampian TV Ltd 1961–68; Anglia Television: co sec 1968–76, dir 1970–2001, chief exec 1976–94, chm 1994–2001; chm: TSMS Ltd (airtime sales co) 1994–96, Greene King plc

M

1995–2005, 99.9 Radio Norwich (formerly Crown FM) 2005–; fndr dir Channel 4 Television Co Ltd 1981–85; dir: British Satellite Broadcasting Ltd 1987–90, Independent Television News Ltd 1991–96, Hodder & Stoughton 1992–93, Cosgrove Hall Films Ltd 1993–96, Village Roadshow Ltd (Australia) 1994–96, Satellite Information Services 1994–96, United Broadcasting and Entertainment (formerly MAI Media UK Ltd) 1994–96, MAI plc 1994–96, Bernard Matthews plc 1996–2000, Anglo-Welsh Gp plc 1996–2000, Bakers Dozen Inns Ltd 1996–, Bernard Matthews Holdings Ltd 2002–; chm: ITV Assoc 1986–88, United Tstees Ltd 1997–, United Executive Tstees Ltd 1998–; hon vice-pres Norwich City FC 1988–93, dir Eastern Advsy Bd National Westminster Bank 1988–91, pres Norfolk and Norwich C of C 1988–90 (vice-pres 1984, dep pres 1986); chm: Norwich Playhouse 1992–98, The Forum Tst Ltd (formerly Norfolk and Norwich Millennium Bid Ltd) 1996–2005; UEA: treas 1995–97, chm Cncl 1997–2006; tstee CTBF 1995 (pres 1998); RTS: fell 1988, vice-pres 1992–99, hon pres E Anglia Centre 1993; MICAS 1958, CIMgt 1988, FRSA 1993; *Recreations* golf, tennis, skiing, soccer, travel; *Style*— David McCall, Esq, CBE, DL, DCL; ✉ Woodland Hall, Redenhall, Harleston, Norfolk IP20 9QW (tel 01379 854442)

McCALL, Davina; *b* 16 October 1967; *m* Matthew Robertson; 2 da, 1 s; *Career* TV personality, presenter and actress; formerly singer, booker Models One, restaurant mangr and singing waitress Paris; *Television* credits incl: Don't Try This At Home (3 series, ITV), Street Mate (Channel 4), Brit Awards 2000 (LWT), The British Fashion Awards (BBC), Big Brother (8 series, Channel 4), Oblivious (ITV), Closure (BBC), Comic Relief (BBC), The Vault (ITV), Popstars: The Rivals (ITV), Sam's Game (ITV), Brit Awards (ITV1), Reborn in the USA (ITV1), Love on a Saturday Night (ITV1), Davina (BBC), The BAFTAs (ITV1), Sports Relief (BBC1), Let's Talk Sex (Channel 4); *Style*— Ms Davina McCall; ✉ c/o John Noel Management, 10A Belmont Street, London NW1 8HH

McCALL SMITH, Prof Alexander; CBE (2007); *b* 24 August 1948; *Career* emeritus prof of med law Univ of Edinburgh and author; former vice-chm Human Genetics Cmmn; Author of the Year British Book Awards 2004, Author of the Year Booksellers Assoc 2004; *Legal Books* Law and Medical Ethics (1984), Butterworths Medico Legal Encyclopaedia (1987), The Criminal Law of Botswana (1992), Scots Criminal Law (1992), The Duty to Rescue (1994), Introduzione allo Studio del Diritto Penale Scozzese (1995), Forensic Aspects of Sleep (1996), Justice and the Prosecution of Old Crimes (2001), Errors, Medicine and the Law (2001); *Adult Fiction* Children of Wax (1989), Heavenly Date (1995), Lions and Anthropologists (1996), Portuguese Irregular Verbs (1997), The No 1 Ladies' Detective Agency (1998), Tears of the Giraffe (2000), Morality for Beautiful Girls (2001), The Kalahari Typing School for Men (2002), The Full Cupboard of Life (2003), The Sunday Philosophy Club (2004), In the Company of Cheerful Ladies (2004), 44, Scotland Street (2004), Espresso Tales (2005), Friends, Lovers, Chocolate (2005) Blue Shoes & Happiness (2006), Dream Angus (2006), The Right Attitude to Rain (2006), Love over Scotland (2006), The Good Husband of Zebra Drive (2006), The World According to Bertie (2006), The Careful Use of Compliments (2006); *Books for Children* incl: The Bubblegum Tree (2005), The Popcorn Pirates (2005), The Doughnut Ring (2005), The Spaghetti Tangle (2005), The Muscle Machine (2006), Teacher Trouble (2006), The Chocolate Money Mystery (2006), The Bursting Balloons Mystery (2006), The Joke Machine (2006), The Banana Machine (2006), Calculator Annie (2006), The Five Lost Aunts of Harriet Bean (2006); *Clubs* Scottish Arts, New; *Style*— Prof Alexander McCall Smith, CBE; ✉ c/o David Higham Associates, 5–8 Lower John Street, Golden Square, London W1F 9HA (tel 020 7434 5900)

McCALLIN, Tanya Carel Pitcairn; da of Clement McCallin (d 1978), and Philippa, *née* Gurney; *b* 4 December 1949; *Educ* Univ HS Melbourne Aust, Central St Martins Sch of Art and Design; *m* 1986, Michael Blakemore, *qv*, s of Conrad Blakemore; 2 da (Beatie b 20 Aug 1981, Clemmie b 25 Nov 1984); *Career* designer; lectr and examiner in stage design, exhibitions in Manchester, London and Prague; memb: Equity, Soc of Brit Theatre Designers *Theatre* Hampstead Theatre London: Ancient Lights, Dusa, Fish, Stars and Vi (also West End, Paris and NY), Abigail's Party (also BBC); West End: Bodies, Exchange, Uncle Vanya, Ride Down Mount Morgan; NT: The Elephant Man, Who's Afraid of Virginia Woolf?, After the Fall; My Mother Said (Royal Court), Regent's Park Theatre London: Hamlet, Richard II; other credits incl: Fool for Love (Donmar Warehouse London), The Recruiting Officer (Chichester Festival Theatre); *Opera* ENO: The Barber of Seville (also Barcelona), Manon (also Dallas USA and NZ); Macbeth (Mariinski-Kirov Co, St Petersburg, Met and London), Rigoletto (ROH), Der Rosenkvalier (Scot Opera), Les Contes d'Hoffmann (Salzburg Festival Opera), Cosi fan Tutte (Opera Nat du Rhin), Le Nozze di Figaro (ROH), Semele (Theatre des Champs Elysees), Carmen (ROH, Astralian Opera), Manon (Liceu Barcelona), The Turn of the Screw (St Petersburg); *Recreations* fine arts, theatre, film, opera, travel; *Style*— Ms Tanya McCallin; ✉ Richard Haigh, Performing Arts, 6 Windmill Street, London W1P 1HF (tel 020 7255 1362, fax 020 7631 4631, e-mail richard@performing-arts.co.uk)

McCALLION, John; s of Robert Bernard McCallion, of London, and Patricia, *née* Furnston-Evans; *b* 4 November 1957; *Educ* Stanway Sch Colchester, Colchester Inst of Technol (HND Business Admin), Poly of Central London (Postgrad Dip Mktg); *m* Kerry Jane; 1 s (James Elliot), 1 da (Harriet Laura); *Career* product mangr/buyer Marks & Spencer plc (Head Office) 1984–88 (joined as grad trainee 1981), commercial mangr Texas Homecare plc 1989–90 (gp product mangr 1988–89), sr mktg mangr Pizza Hut (UK) Ltd 1990–91, mktg dir Red Star 1991–93, mktg dir Great Western Trains Co 1993–98, chief exec Merlin Investments Ltd 1998–; exec chm Groundscope, chm Travel Assetts Gp Ltd; memb: IOD (dip in co direction), Mktg Soc, London Business Sch Entrepreneurs Club, Pi Capital; MCIM, MIDM; *Recreations* skiing, travel, private equity, golf; *Style*— John McCallion, Esq; ✉ Waterside House, 27 Wethered Park, Pound Lane, Marlow, Buckinghamshire SL7 2BH (tel 01628 478430, fax 01628 478746, e-mail john.mccallion@btinternet.com); Merlin Investments Ltd (tel 01628 472734, mobile 07970 164859)

MacCALLUM, Prof Charles Hugh Alexander; s of Alister Hugh McCallum (*sic*), of Pitlochry, and Jessie MacLean, *née* Forsyth; *b* 24 June 1935; *Educ* Hutchesons' GS Glasgow, Glasgow Sch of Architecture (BArch), MIT (MCP); *m* 27 Aug 1963, Andrée Simone; 2 da; *Career* architect; Gillespie Kidd and Coia Glasgow 1957–67; Univ Coll Dublin Sch of Architecture: lectr 1970–73, exec dir 1973–74; own practice 1974–, prof of architectural design Univ of Wales 1985–94, prof of architecture Univ of Glasgow and head of Mackintosh Sch of Architecture 1994–2000, emeritus prof of architecture Univ of Glasgow 2000–; memb Ctee Franco-British Union of Architects 2000–; conslt to Scots Kirk Paris 2000–04; commissaire of the bicentenary exhibition on Louis Visconti (Paris) 1991; Silver Medal Académie d'Architecture 2003; RIBA 1961, ARIAS 1986, FRSA 1993–2000; *Publications* Visconti (1791–1853) (1991), misc articles on C18 and C19 architecture and engineering in France and Russia, and on computer aided teaching of structures; *Recreations* gardening, watercolours; *Style*— Prof Charles MacCallum; ✉ 11A Charlbury Road, Oxford OX2 6UT

McCANDLESS, Air Vice Marshal Brian Campbell; CB (1999), CBE (1990); s of Norman Samuel McCandless, and Rebecca, *née* Campbell; *b* 14 May 1944; *Educ* Methodist Coll Belfast, RAF Tech Coll Henlow (BSc), Univ of Birmingham (MSc Quality and Reliability), RAF Staff Coll; *m* 19 April 1967, Yvonne; 1 s (Robin); *Career* RAF 1962–; sr lectr in operational research and reliability engrg RAF Coll Cranwell 1972–76, OC Engrg Sqdn RAF Gibraltar 1976–78, electrical engr (Communications) No 11 Gp 1978–80, OC Engr Liaison Team 1980–81, Wing Cdr Communications RAF Support Cmd Signals HQ 1981–85, OC No 26 Signals Unit 1985–87, Gp Capt 1987, OC RAF Henlow 1987–89, dep chief Architecture and Plans Div NATO CIS Agency Brussels 1989–92, Air Cdre 1992, dir Cmd and Control Mgmnt Info Systems (RAF) 1992–93, dir Communications and Info Systems (RAF) 1993–95, Air Vice Marshal 1996, Air Offr Communications, Info Systems and Support Systems and Air Offr Cmdg Support Units 1996–99, e-govt dir Oracle Corp 1999–2002, dir Govt Consltancy Services 2003–; CEng 1974, FIEE 1995, FRAeS 1997; *Recreations* bridge, music, sailing, hill walking; *Clubs* RAF; *Style*— Air Vice Marshal Brian McCandless, CB, CBE, RAF

McCANN, Christopher Conor; s of Noel McCann, and Katharine Joan, *née* Sultzberger; *b* 26 June 1947; *Educ* Downside, Clare Coll Cambridge (MA); *m* 1 June 1974, Merlyn Clare Winbolt, da of Dr Francis Lewis, of Bristol; 1 s (Edward), 2 da (Kate, Eleanor); *Career* Price Waterhouse and Co 1969–73, Barclays Merchant Bank 1973–82, sr vice-pres Barclays Bank plc NY 1983–87, vice-chm Bridgepoint Capital Ltd 1987–2002; chm: Numerica Gp plc 2001–05, Photobiochem BV 2002–; non-exec dir: Opus Holdings Ltd 1999–2005, Bright Talk Ltd 2004–; govr St Mary's Sch Shaftesbury; FCA 1972, ACIB 1978; *Recreations* skiing, sailing, travel, country pursuits; *Style*— Christopher McCann, Esq; ✉ 10 Lonsdale Square, London N1 1EN (e-mail christopher.mccann@btinternet.com)

McCANN, Prof Hugh; s of Daniel McCann (d 1989), and Helen, *née* Mathieson; *b* 5 August 1954; *Educ* St Joseph's Acad Kilmarnock, Univ of Glasgow (BSc, PhD); *m* 23 July 1977, Margaret Frances, *née* McCulloch; 1 da (Louise b 27 July 1979), 2 s (Michael b 9 March 1982, Paul b 20 March 1987); *Career* researcher HEP Physics Deutsches Elektronen Synchrotron Hamburg 1979–83 and Victoria Univ of Manchester 1984–86, sr scientist Royal Dutch/Shell Gp, Thornton Res Centre 1986–96, prof of industrial tomography Univ of Manchester (formerly UMIST) 1996– (head Dept of Electrical Engrg and Electronics 1999–2002); chm Virtual Centre for Industrial Process Tomography 2005–; chm Ctee of UK Profs and Heads of Electrical Engrg 2003–05 (memb Ctee 2002–07); memb Ctee: Engrg Professors' Cncl 2003–05, EPSRC Peer Review Coll 2003–; Arch T Colwell Merit Award Soc of Automotive Engrs 1994, Special Prize Euro Physical Soc 1995; parishoner St Vincent de Paul RC Church Bramhall; memb Lab Pty; MInstP 1987, CPhys 1987, FIEE 2000, CEng 2001, SMIEEE 2006; *Publications* 91 jl pubns in sci and engrg, and many conf papers; *Recreations* theatre, listening to a range of music, golf; *Clubs* Bramhall Golf; *Style*— Prof Hugh McCann

McCANNY, Prof John Vincent; CBE (2002); s of Patrick Joseph McCanny, of Ballymoney, Co Antrim, and Kathleen Brigid, *née* Kerr; *b* 25 June 1952; *Educ* Dalriada GS Ballymoney, Univ of Manchester (BSc), New Univ of Ulster (PhD), Queen's Univ Belfast (DSc); *m* 7 July 1979, Mary Bernadette (Maureen); 1 s (Damian Patrick b 28 June 1983), 1 da (Kathryn Louise b 4 Feb 1986); *Career* lectr in physics Univ of Ulster 1977–78 (postdoctoral research fell Physics Dept 1978–79); Royal Signals and Radar Estab (RSRE): higher scientific offr 1979–82, sr scientific offr 1982–84, princ scientific offr 1984; Queen's Univ Belfast: IT research lectr Dept of Electrical & Electronic Engrg 1984–87, reader 1987–88, prof of microelectronics engrg 1988–, dir Inst of Electronics, Communications and IT 2000–, head Sch of Electronics, Electrical Engrg and Computer Science 2005–; dir Inst of Advanced Microelectronics in Ireland 1989–92, co-fndr and dir Audio Processing Technology Ltd 1989–96, co-fndr and tech dir Amplicon Semiconductor Ltd 1990– (NI e-commerce exporters of the year 1999, Millennium Product Status 1999), non-exec dir Investment Belfast Ltd 1997–2002; chm IEEE Signal Processing Soc Technical Ctee on the design and implementation of Signal Processing Systems 1999–; memb: IEEE Signal Processing Tech Directions Ctee 1999–2001, Royal Acad of Engrg Standing Ctee for Engrg 2001–, Royal Soc Ctee on the future of HE in the UK 2003–, Royal Soc Research Fellowships Panel A(ii) Chemistry and Engrg 2003–, Royal Soc Sectional Ctee 4 2004– (chair 2004–06), EPSRC ICT Strategic Advsy Team 2006–; NI Info Technol Award 1987/88, DTI Smart Award for Enterprise 1988, 1990 and 1995, Royal Acad of Engrg Silver Medal (for outstanding and demonstrated personal contrib to Br Engrg leading to market exploitation) 1996, IEEE Millennium Medal for valued services and outstanding contributions 2000, Royal Dublin Soc/Irish Times Boyle Medal 2003, Br Computer Soc (Belfast Branch) IT Professional of the Year 2004, Faraday Medal Instn of Engrg and Technol 2006; memb European Acad of Sciences 2004; CPhys 1982, CEng 1985, FIEE 1992 (MIEE 1985), FInstP 1992 (MInstP 1982), FREng 1995, FRSA 1996, FIEEE 1999 (MIEEE 1988, Sr MIEEE 1995), MRIA 2000, FRS 2002, FIAcadE 2006, FIEI 2006, FIAE, MRIA; *Publications* VLSI Technology and Design (jtly, 1987), Systolic Array Processors (jtly, 1989), VLSI Systems for DSP (jtly, 1991), Signal Processing Systems - Design and Implementation (jtly, 1997), System-on-Chip Architectures and Implementation for Private Key Data Encryption (jtly, 2003); 320 published tech papers in books, int jls and conf proceedings; 20 patents; *Recreations* golf, swimming, tennis, supporting Manchester United FC, watching sports (soccer, golf, rugby, cricket), listening to music, photography, fine wine and good food; *Clubs* Clandeboye Golf; *Style*— Prof John McCanny, CBE, FRS, FREng, FIEEE; ✉ The Institute of Electronics, Communications and Information Technology, Queen's University Belfast, Nothern Ireland Science Park, Queen's Road, Queen's Island, Belfast BT3 9DT (tel 028 9097 1800, fax 028 9097 1802, e-mail j.mccanny@ecit.qub.ac.uk)

McCARTAN, Prof Eamonn Gerard; s of John McCartan (d 1978), of Belfast, and Margaret, *née* Barrett; *b* 23 January 1953; *Educ* St Joseph's Teacher Trg Coll Belfast (BEd), Queen's Univ Belfast (Dip Advanced Study in Educn) Univ of Ulster (Dip Mgmnt Studies), MBA; *m* 27 Dec 1976, Marian Francis, da of Patrick McFadden; 1 s (Kieran); *Career* PE teacher: St Mary's GS Belfast 1976–78, Sydney 1978–79, Christian Bros Secdy Sch Belfast 1979–80, St Mary's GS Belfast 1980–81; asst mangr Andersonstown Leisure Centre Belfast 1981–83, PA to asst dir of Leisure Servs Belfast CC 1983–84, asst dir of PE Queen's Univ Belfast 1984–94, chief exec Sports Cncl for NI 1994–; visiting prof Sch of Leisure and Tourism Univ of Ulster; dir: Chest Heart and Stroke Assoc, Odyssey Tst Co; chair Community Relations Cncl; memb Bd: Co-Operation Ireland, Odyssey Co; MCIM 1991, MIPD 1991; *Recreations* golf, basketball, gardening, current/political affairs; *Clubs* Malone Golf; *Style*— Prof Eamonn McCartan; ✉ Sport Northern Ireland, House of Sport, Upper Malone Road, Belfast BT9 5LA (tel 028 9038 1222, fax 028 9068 2757, mobile 07860 331475)

McCARTER, Keith Ian; s of Maj Peter McCarter (d 1971), of Edinburgh, and Hilda Mary, *née* Gates (d 1996); *b* 15 March 1936; *Educ* The Royal HS of Edinburgh, Edinburgh Coll of Art (DA); *m* 5 Jan 1963, Brenda Maude Edith, da of James A Schofield (d 1974), of Langley, Bucks; 1 da (Alix-Jane b 1966), 1 s (Andrew Keith b 1968); *Career* Nat Serv RA 1954–56; sculptor; primarily involved in architectural and landscaped situations; numerous cmmns incl: Ordnance Survey HQ Southampton 1967, Lagos Nigeria 1974, Wingate Centre City of London 1980, Goodmans Yard City of London 1982, 1020 19th Street Washington DC 1983, American Express Bank City of London 1984, Guy's Hosp NCC London 1986, Royal Exec Park NY 1986, Evelyn Gardens London 1987, London Docklands 1988, Midland Bank London 1989, Vogans Mill London 1989, Moody Gardens Galveston Texas USA (with Sir Geoffrey Jellicoe), Abbey Rd London 1991, Monks Cross York 1992, John Menzies HQ Edinburgh 1995, Aldermanbury Bradford 1998, F I Gp Edinburgh 1999, Monks Cross York 2001, Univ Hosp Norwich 2001, Forth Quarter Devpt Edinburgh 2004; works in private collections world-wide; Sir Otto Beit medal RBS 1993; FRSA 1970, ARBS 1991; *Recreations* music, literature, beachcombing; *Clubs* Farmers', Melrose RFC; *Style*— Keith McCarter, Esq; ✉ 10 Coopersknowe Crescent, Galashiels,

Selkirkshire TD1 2DS (tel 01896 751112, fax 01896 759010, website www.keith-mccarter.com)

McCARTHY, Arlene; MEP (Lab) North West England; da of John Joseph McCarthy, of Belfast, and June Florence McCarthy; *b* 10 October 1960; *Educ* The Friends' GS Lisburn, South Bank Poly (BA), Stuttgart Univ, Université de Clermont Ferrand, UMIST; *m* 1997, Prof David Farrell; *Career* researcher and press offr to ldr European Parly Lab Pty 1990–91; Freie Universität Berlin: lectr, DAAD scholar, guest res fell 1991–92; head of European affairs Kirklees MBC 1992–94; MEP (Lab): Peak District 1994–99, NW England 1999–; chair Internal Market and Consumer Protection Ctee 2006–; *Publications* Changing States (jt ed, 1996); *Recreations* swimming, dancing, travel, foreign languages and music; *Style*— Ms Arlene McCarthy, MEP; ✉ Express Networks, 1 George Leigh Street, Manchester M4 5DL (tel 0161 906 0801, fax 0161 906 0802, e-mail arlene.mccarthy@easynet.co.uk)

McCARTHY, Sir Callum; kt (2005); s of Ralph McCarthy (d 1974), and Agnes, *née* Graham (d 1966); *b* 29 February 1944; *Educ* Univ of Oxford, Univ of Stirling (PhD), Grad Sch of Business Stanford Univ (MS); *m* 30 July 1966, Penelope Ann, *née* Gee; 2 s (Tom b 1969, Christopher b 1972), 1 da (Melissa b 1975); *Career* economist and ops researcher ICI 1965–72; DTI 1972–85: princ private sec to Roy Hattersley, princ private sec to Norman Tebbit, under sec; dir of corp finance Kleinwort Benson 1985–89, md and dep head of corp finance BZW 1989–93, ceo Japan and N America Barclay's Bank 1993–98, DG Ofgas 1998–99, DG Ofgem 1999–2003, chm FSA 2003–; *Publications* Introduction to Technological Economics (with D S Davies, 1967); *Recreations* walking, reading; *Style*— Sir Callum McCarthy

McCARTHY, Dr Daniel Peter Justin; TD (1978, bar 1984 and 1990); s of Thomas Joseph McCarthy, GM (d 1988), and Margaret Mary Josephine, *née* Bowden; *b* 4 July 1939; *Educ* St Mary's Coll Crosby, Univ of Aberdeen (MB ChB), Coll of Law London, Heythrop Coll London; *m* 1977 (m dis 2000), Dr Bronwen Elizabeth Knight Teresa, da of Richard Knight Evans, of Wimbledon; 5 s (Oliver, Richard (twins), Simon, Philip, Nicholas); *Career* cmmnd 3 Bn The Gordon Highlanders 1964, MO 4 (V) Bn Royal Green Jackets 1982–, Maj RAMC (TA); called to the Bar Inner Temple 1978; med practitioner; HM dep coroner: City of London 1979–88, Inner W London 1980–97; divnl surgn St John Ambulance, med offr Royal Home and Hosp at Putney 1986–91, medicolegal advsr to MOD (Navy) 1996–97; Freeman City of London 1975; Liveryman: Worshipful Soc of Apothecaries 1974, Worshipful Co of Scriveners 1996; Knight Sovereign Military Order of Malta 1985, Donat of Justice (Malta) 1995, Knight of Magistral Grace in Obedience 1998; FSA Scot; Cross of Merit with Swords (pro merito melitensi) 1988, Knight Sacred Military Constantinian Order of St George 1994; FRSM; *Recreations* beagling, music; *Clubs* Athenaeum, Hurlingham; *Style*— Dr D P J McCarthy, TD; ✉ 328 Clapham Road, London SW9 9AE (tel 020 7622 2006, fax 020 7622 6256)

McCARTHY, David; s of late John Francis McCarthy, and late Ivy Eileen, *née* Davies; *b* 27 January 1942; *Educ* Ratcliffe Coll, Univ of Birmingham (LLB); *m* 1, Rosemary Ruth, *née* Norman; 2 s (Gavin Stephen b 19 Feb 1972, Nicholas James b 17 May 1974); m 2, Judith Spencer, *née* Chester; *Career* slr; articled with Wragge & Co Birmingham, ptnr Clifford Chance (formerly Coward Chance) 1978–94 (joined 1976); conslt: Banco Ambrosiano Veneto SpA, Clifford Chance, Chiomenti Studio Legale, Banca Intesa SpA, Banca Nazionale del Lavoro, Banca di Roma SpA, Banca Popolare di Milano, Caboto Holding SIM SpA and other instns; *Recreations* fly fishing, cricket, history; *Clubs* Richmond Cricket, Loch Achonachie Angling, Ferrari Owners'; *Style*— David McCarthy, Esq; ✉ Inishbeg, Cavendish Road, St George's Hill, Weybridge, Surrey KT13 0JX

McCARTHY, His Hon Judge David Laurence; s of Laurence Alphonsus McCarthy (d 1979), of Solihull, and Vera May, *née* Protheroe (d 1982); *b* 7 April 1947; *Educ* St Philip's GS Birmingham, ChCh Oxford (MA); *m* 2 May 1981, Rosalind Marguerite, da of Reginald Arthur Stevenson; 2 s (Charles Augustus Alexander Seraphim b 9 Aug 1983, Dominic Ambrose Emmanuel b 19 May 1986); *Career* called to the Bar Middle Temple 1970, recorder of the Crown Court 1992–95, circuit judge (Midland & Oxford Circuit) 1995–; *Recreations* science fiction, playing the organ; *Style*— His Hon Judge McCarthy; ✉ c/o The Regional Director, Midland Region, PO Box 11772, 6th Floor, Temple Court, Bull Street, Birmingham B4 6WF

McCARTHY, Declan James John; s of Christopher Noel McCarthy, and Catherine Bernadette Temple, *née* Kinsella; *b* 11 February 1969, Oxford; *Educ* Wheatley Park Sch, Oxford Coll of FE (HND); *m* 3 Sept 2005, Jeanette, *née* Nunn; 1 da (Georgia b 11 Dec 2003); *Career* Ashmolean Museum: publishing asst 1989–97, mktg mangr 1997–2002, publishing mangr 2002–06, commercial mangr 2007–; sec, ed and memb Ctee Assoc for Cultural Enterprise, memb Museums Assoc 1991, memb Assoc for Cultural Enterprise (ACE) 2001; *Style*— Declan McCarthy, Esq; ✉ Publishing Department, Ashmolean Museum, Beaumont Street, Oxford OX1 2PH (tel 01865 288070, fax 01865 278106, e-mail dec.mccarthy@ashmus.ox.ac.uk)

MacCARTHY, Fiona; da of Lt-Col Gerald MacCarthy (d 1943), and Yolande, *née* de Belabre; *b* 23 January 1940; *Educ* Wycombe Abbey, Univ of Oxford (MA); *m* 19 Aug 1966, David Mellor, CBE, *qv*, s of Colin Mellor (d 1970); 1 s (Corin b 1966), 1 da (Clare b 1970); *Career* design corr The Guardian 1961–69, women's ed Evening Standard 1969–71, critic The Times 1981–92, The Observer 1992–99; RSA Bicentenary Medal 1987, Wolfson History Prize 1994; Hon DLitt Univ of Sheffield 1996, Hon Dr Sheffield Hallam Univ 2001; sr fell RCA 1997 (hon fell 1989); hon fell Lady Margaret Hall Oxford 2007; FRSL 1997; *Books* All Things Bright and Beautiful (1972), The Simple Life: C R Ashbee in the Cotswolds (1981), British Design since 1880 (1982), Eric Gill (1989), William Morris: a Life for our Time (1994), Stanley Spencer, An English Vision (1997), Byron: Life and Legend (2002), Last Curtsey: The Death of the English Debutante (2006); *Style*— Ms Fiona MacCarthy, FRSL; ✉ The Round Building, Hathersage, Sheffield S32 1BA (tel 01433 650220, fax 01433 650944)

McCARTHY, Kerry; MP; *b* 26 March 1965; *Educ* Univ of Liverpool, City of London Poly, Goldsmiths Coll London; *Career* slr, political conslt; former Luton cncllr, legal advisor to Lab during 2001 election campaign; MP (Lab) Bristol E 2005–; vice-chair Lab E of England Regnl Bd; memb: Lab Nat Policy Forum, Lab Economic Policy Cmmn, TGWU, Howard League for Penal Reform, World Devpt Movement; *Style*— Ms Kerry McCarthy, MP; ✉ House of Commons, London SW1A 0AA

McCARTHY, Rosalind Judith; da of Rev Cyril James Wilson, and Helen Frances, *née* Horton; *Educ* Folkestone Girls' GS, Univ of Leeds (BA); *Family* 1 s, 1 da; *Career* short term teaching posts: Priory Girls' Sch London 1965–66, Beaufoy Boys' Comp Sch London 1966–67, Lanfranc Secdy Sch Surrey 1966–67; teacher rising to head of dept Mungwi Secdy Sch for Boys Kasama Zambia 1967–69, supply and pt/t teaching 1972–75, head of religious educn St Leonard's Girls' Sch Hythe 1975–78, head of humanities Brockhill and St Leonard's Sch Hythe 1978–83, head of religious studies and head of house Ashford Sch 1983–89, head Cobham Hall 1989–2003; memb Govt Advsy Gp on State/Ind Sch Partnerships 1997–98; Boarding Schs Assoc: memb NEC and Jt Trg Ctee 1992–95, area co-ordinator 1992–94, vice-chm 1995–96 and 1997–98, chm 1996–97; GSA: co-opted rep Nat Cncl 1993, boarding rep Nat Cncl 1993–96, memb Boarding Ctee 1994–96; memb: SE Region Ctee ISIS 1991–94, Exec Ctee Kent Branch representing Ind Schs SHA 1992–94, Int Cncl Round Square Schs 1992–94; govr St Mary's Westbrook Sch Folkestone 2003–06, cmmr Duke of York's Royal Mil Sch 2004–; managing tstee Leney Tst 1995–2002; friend: Stour Music Festival, Metropole Galleries, Folkestone and the Primavera Chamber Orch, Folkestone Literary Festival, Cobham Hall Heritage Tst; *Recreations* travel, music, theatre, the Arts, family and friends; *Style*— Mrs Rosalind McCarthy; ✉ Ullyett Cottage, Old School Mews, Sandgate Hill, Folkestone, Kent CT20 3ST (tel 01303 246122)

McCARTHY, Suzanne Joyce; da of Leo Rudnick (d 1966), and Lillian Thal (d 1998); *b* 21 November 1948, Utica, NY; *Educ* NYU (BA), Univ of Cambridge (LLM); *m* 25 Aug 1990, Brendan McCarthy; *Career* slr in private practice 1977–85, lectr in law Univ of Manchester 1986–89, various sr Civil Service appts 1989–; chief exec: Human Fertilisation and Embryology Authy 1996–2000, Financial Services Compensation Scheme 2000–04; Immigration Servs Cmmr 2005–; memb: Determinations Panel Pensions Regulator 2005–, Conduct Ctee CIMA 2006–, Public Guardian Bd 2007–; non-exec dir: Royal Brompton and Harefield NHS Tst until 2006, RIBA; memb Cncl Univ of London (dep chm); memb Soc of West End Theatres 2002 Dance Awards Panel (Lawrence Olivier Awards); Freeman City of London 2006, Yeoman Worshipful Co of Ironmongers 2006; *Recreations* ballet; *Clubs* Athenaeum; *Style*— Mrs Suzanne McCarthy; ✉ Office of the Immigration Services Commissioner, 5th Floor, Counting House, 53 Tooley Street, London SE1 2QN (tel 020 7211 1525, e-mail suzanne.mccarthy@oisc.gov.uk)

McCARTHY, Baron (Life Peer UK 1975), of Headington in the City of Oxford; William Edward John McCarthy; s of Edward McCarthy; *b* 30 July 1925; *Educ* Holloway Court Sch, Ruskin Coll, Merton Coll and Nuffield Coll Oxford (MA, DPhil); *m* 1957, Margaret, da of Percival Godfrey; *Career* formerly worker in men's outfitters and clerk; lectr in industrial rels Univ of Oxford, res dir Royal Cmmn on Trade Unions and Employers Assocs 1965–68, fell Nuffield Coll Oxford and Templeton Coll Oxford 1969–, chm Railway Staff Nat Tribunal 1974–86; dir Harland & Wolff Ltd 1976–86, special cmmr Equal Opportunities Cmmn 1977–79; oppn spokesman (Lords) Employment 1983–97; memb Civil Service Arbitration Tbnl; *Recreations* theatre, ballet, gardening; *Clubs* Reform; *Style*— The Rt Hon the Lord McCarthy; ✉ 4 William Orchard Close, Old Headington, Oxford (tel and fax 01865 762016)

McCARTHY-FRY, Sarah Louise; MP; da of Sidney Macaree (d 1984), and Constance, *née* Foster (d 1983); *b* 4 February 1955, Portsmouth, Hants; *Educ* Portsmouth HS; *m* 1, 1973, Roger Fry; 1 s (Barnaby b 1975), 1 da (Victoria b 1977); m 2, 1997, Tony McCarthy; *Career* GKN Aerospace Services Ltd: fin accountant 1988–2000, fin analyst (Europe) 2000–03, fin controller 2003–05; cncllr Portsmouth City Cncl 1994–2002, dep ldr Portsmouth City Cncl 1995–2000; MP (Lab Co-op) Portsmouth N 2005–; memb: Amicus, Co-op Pty; memb CIMA 2004; *Recreations* tap dancing, dog walking; *Style*— Ms Sarah McCarthy-Fry, MP; ✉ House of Commons, London SW1A 0AA (tel 020 7219 6517, fax 020 7219 0889, e-mail mccarthyfrys@parliament.uk)

McCARTNEY, Gordon Arthur; s of Arthur McCartney (d 1987), and Hannah, *née* Seel; *b* 29 April 1937; *Educ* Grove Park GS Wrexham; *m* 1, 23 July 1960 (m dis 1987), Ceris Isobel Davies; 2 da (Heather Jane b 11 April 1963, Alison b 6 Dec 1965); m 2, 26 March 1988, Wendy Ann Vyvyan, da of Sidney Titman; *Career* admitted slr 1959, chief exec Delyn Borough Cncl Clwyd 1974–81, sec Assoc of DCs 1981–91, co sec Local Govt Int Bureau 1988–91; dir National Transport Tokens Ltd 1984–91, md Gordon McCartney Associates 1991–, dir Leisure England Ltd 1993–; memb: Cmmn on the Legislative Process Hansard, Soc for Parly Govt 1991–93, Britain in Europe Cncl 2000–; chm Local Govt Gp for Europe 1997–; hon fell Inst of Local Govt Studies Univ of Birmingham; *Recreations* music, gardening, cricket; *Clubs* MCC; *Style*— Gordon McCartney, Esq; ✉ 33 Duck Street, Elton, Peterborough, Cambridgeshire PE8 6RQ (tel 01832 280659, fax 01832 280002)

McCARTNEY, Rt Hon Ian; PC (1999), MP; *b* 25 April 1951; *Career* Lab Pty organiser 1973–87, sec to Roger Scott, MP 1979–87; MP (Lab) Makerfield 1987–; memb Personal Social Servs Ctee and Select Ctee on Social Security 1988–92, oppn front bench spokesman on the NHS 1992–94, shadow min of state for employment 1994–97; min of state DTI 1997–2001, min of state for pensions 2001–03, min without portfolio 2003–06, chm Lab Pty 2003–06, min of state for trade, investment and foreign affrs DTI/FCO 2006–07; cncllr Wigan BC 1982–87; former chm All Pty Gps on: Home Safety, Child Abduction, Rugby League, Solvent Abuse; pres Wheelchair Fund; chm TGWU Parly GP 1989–91; memb: Wigan Family Practitioner Ctee 1984–86, Greater Manchester Fire and Civil Defence Authy 1986–87; *Style*— The Rt Hon Ian McCartney, MP; ✉ House of Commons, London SW1A 0AA (tel 020 7219 3000)

McCARTNEY, Joanne; AM; da of Donald McCartney, and Patricia Marilyn McCartney; *b* 12 December 1966, Kendal, Westmorland; *Educ* Univ of Warwick (LLB), Univ of Leicester (LLM); *Career* called to the Bar Inner Temple 1990; cncllr London Borough Enfield 1998–2006; GLA: memb London Assembly (Lab) Enfield and Haringey 2004–, chair Health and Public Services Ctee; memb London Bd Campaign for Racial Equality, memb Met Police Authy; subst memb Congress of Local and Regnl Authys of Europe; *Style*— Ms Joanne McCartney, AM; ✉ GLA, City Hall, The Queen's Walk, London SE1 2AA (tel 020 7983 4402, e-mail joanne.mccartney@london.gov.uk)

McCARTNEY, Sir (James) Paul; kt (1997), MBE (1965); s of late James McCartney, of Allerton, Liverpool, and late Mary Patricia, *née* Mohin; *b* 18 June 1942; *Educ* Liverpool Inst; *m* 1, 1969, Linda Louise (d 1998), da of late Lee Eastman, of New York City; 3 da (Heather b 1962, Mary b 1969, Stella b 1971), 1 s (James b 1977); m 2, 2002, Heather Mills; 1 da (Beatrice Milly b 2003); *Career* musician and composer; first group The Quarry Men 1957–59, Beatles formed 1960, first maj appearance Litherland Town Hall 1960, Please Please Me first Br No 1 1961, She Loves You cemented their success 1963, I Want to Hold Your Hand became the biggest selling Br single ever with worldwide sales of 15,000,000; 1963 appearances: UK, Sweden, Royal Variety Performance London; 1964 toured: UK, France, Sweden, Netherlands, Denmark, Hong Kong, NZ, Aust, Canada, USA; 1965 toured: UK, France, Spain, Italy, USA, Canada; other songs (with John Lennon) incl: Love Me Do, Can't Buy Me Love, I Saw Her Standing There, Eight Days A Week, All My Loving, Help!, Ticket To Ride, I Feel Fine, I'm A Loser, A Hard Day's Night, No Reply, I'll Follow The Sun, Yesterday, Eleanor Rigby, Yellow Submarine, All You Need Is Love, Lady Madonna, Hey Jude, We Can Work It Out, Day Tripper, From Me To You, Get Back, Paperback Writer, Hello Goodbye, Let It Be, The Long And Winding Road; Beatles albums: Please Please Me 1963, With The Beatles 1963, A Hard Day's Night 1964, Beatles For Sale 1964, Help! 1965, Rubber Soul 1965, Revolver 1966, Sgt Pepper's Lonely Hearts Club Band 1967, Magical Mystery Tour 1967, The Beatles (White Album) 1968, Yellow Submarine 1969, Abbey Road 1969, Let It Be 1970; Beatles films: A Hard Day's Night 1964, Help! 1965, Yellow Submarine 1968, Let It Be 1970; played live for last time together on roof of the Apple building London 1969; Beatles disbanded 1970; formed MPL group of cos, formed Wings 1971, returned to live work 1972, own TV special James Paul McCartney 1973, honoured by the Guinness Book of Records (Triple Superlative Award for sales of 100,000,000 albums 100,000,000 singles and as holder of 60 gold discs) making him the most successful popular music composer ever 1979, Wings disbanded 1981, performed at Bob Geldof's Live Aid concert 1985 and for The Prince's Trust concert 1986; tours incl: UK and Europe 1972–73, UK and Aust 1975, Europe and USA 1976, UK 1979, Europe, UK, Canada, USA and Brazil 1989–90, World tour 1993; albums incl: McCartney 1970, Ram 1971, Wildlife 1971, Red Rose Speedway 1973, Band On The Run 1973, Venus And Mars 1975, Wings At The Speed Of Sound 1976, Wings Over America 1976, McCartney II 1980, Tug Of War 1982, Pipes Of Peace 1983, Give My Regards To Broad Street 1984, Press To Play 1986, All The Best! 1987, CHOBA B CCCP 1988, Flowers In The Dirt 1989, Unplugged 1990, Tripping the Light 1992, Off the Ground 1993, Paul is Live 1993, Flaming Pie 1997, Driving Rain 2001, Back in the World (Live) 2003; Wings films: Rockshow 1981, Give My Regards To Broad

M

Street 1984, Rupert And The Frog Song 1984 (won Best Animated Film BAFTA); film scores: The Family Way 1967, Live And Let Die (title song, Oscar nomination for Best Song) 1973, Twice In A Lifetime (title song) 1984, Vanilla Sky (title song, Oscar nomination for Best Song) 2001; singles with Ringo Starr and George Harrison: Free as a Bird 1995, Real Love 1996; winner numerous Grammy awards incl Lifetime Achievement award 1990; Ivor Novello awards: best ever selling UK single (Mull Of Kintyre) 1977, Int Achievement 1980, Int Hit of the Year (Ebony And Ivory) 1982, Outstanding Contrib to Music 1989; PRS special award for unique achievement in popular music; Freeman City of Liverpool 1984; Hon DUniv Sussex 1988; *Books* Paintings (2000), Blackbird Singing: Poems and Lyrics 1965–1999 (2001), Wingspan (2002), High in the Clouds (2005); *Style*— Sir Paul McCartney, MBE; ✉ c/o MPL Communications Ltd, 1 Soho Square, London W1V 6BQ

McCARTNEY, Robert Law; QC (NI 1975); s of William Martin McCartney, and Elizabeth Jane, *née* McCartney; *b* 24 April 1936; *Educ* Grosvenor GS Belfast, Queen's Univ Belfast (LLB); *m* 1960, Maureen Ann, *née* Bingham; 1 s, 3 da; *Career* admitted slr Supreme Ct of Judicature NI 1962, called to the Bar NI 1968; memb NI Assembly 1983–87; MP (UK Unionist) North Down 1995–2001, MLA (UK Unionist) NI 1999–2007; memb NI Talks/Forum 1996–; ldr UK Unionist Party; contested N Down as Ulster Unionist 1983 and as Real Unionist 1987; pres Campaign for Equal Citizenship 1986–88; *Publications* Liberty and Authority in Ireland (1985), McCartney Report on Consent; *Recreations* reading (biography and military history), walking, sport (rugby and squash); *Style*— Robert McCartney, Esq, QC

McCAUGHAN, Prof Daniel Vincent; OBE (1993); s of Daniel Vincent McCaughan (d 1984), of Belfast, and Elizabeth Gabriel (d 1974); *b* 1942; *Educ* St Mary's GS Belfast, Queen's Univ Belfast (Sullivan and Lappin scholar, BSc, PhD, DSc); *m* 21 Aug 1968, Anne Patricia, da of John Kinsella, and Mary Kinsella; 1 s (Gareth John b 1970); *Career* memb Tech Staff Bell Laboratories Inc NJ 1968–74, sr princ scientific offr RSRE Malvern 1974–81, asst dir GEC Hirst Res Centre Wembley 1981–86; tech dir: Marconi Electronic Devices Ltd and Electro-Optic Div EEV Ltd 1986–87, GEC Electronic Devices Ltd 1987–88; dir: NI Telecommunications Engrg Centre Northern Telecom (NI) Ltd 1988–93, External Affrs Nortel (NI) Ltd 1993–2000; chief scientist: Bell Northern Research 1995–96, Nortel Technology 1996, Nortel Satellite Networks 1996–2000; pres and chief operating offr CDT Ltd 2000–01, managing ptnr McCaughan Associates 2001–, chief technol offr Trireme Systems NY 2002–, memb Tech Advsy Bd Kernel Capital Ptnrs Cork 2003–, dir Cratlon Ltd 2007–; visiting prof and professorial fell Queen's Univ Belfast 1982–, visiting prof UMIST 2002–; chm: Technol Bd for NI 1986–92, Bd Industrial Res and Technol Unit of Dept of Econ Devpt 1992–93, Tech Foresight Panel DTI 2001–02; memb Cncl Royal Acad of Engrg 1994–97, external bd memb DHSSPS(NI) 2006–; FInstP 1975, CPhys 1975, SMIEEE 1990, FIEE 1990, FInstD 1990, FREng 1992, FRAeS 1998, FIEI 1998, FIAcadE 2000; *Publications* tech chapters in numerous texts incl Handbook of Semiconductors; over 100 tech articles incl 20 patents; *Recreations* antique glass, photography, fungi, hiking; *Clubs* Physical Society, Royal NI Yacht; *Style*— Prof Daniel V McCaughan, OBE, FREng; ✉ McCaughan Associates, 20 Circular Road East, Cultra, Holywood, Co Down BT18 0HA (tel 02890 428366, fax 02890 428367, e-mail dvmcd@picatec.co.uk)

McCAUGHREAN, Geraldine Margaret; da of Leslie Arthur Jones (d 1980), and Ethel, *née* Thomas (d 2002); *b* 6 June 1951; *Educ* Enfield Co Sch for Girls, Christ Church Coll of Educn Canterbury (BEd); *m* 23 Nov 1988, John, s of William McCaughrean (d 1964), of Aughton, Lancs; 1 da (Ailsa b 12 Dec 1989); *Career* Thames Television Ltd 1970–77, Marshall Cavendish Partworks Ltd 1977–89 (sec, sub ed, staff writer); freelance writer 1989–; Br candidate Hans Christian Anderson Award 2004; hon fell Canterbury Christ Church Univ; memb Soc of Authors; *Books* incl: 1001 Arabian Nights (1982), The Canterbury Tales (1984), A Little Lower than the Angels (1987, Whitbread Children's Book of the Year, Katholischer Kindersbuchpreis Germany), A Pack of Lies (1988, Carnegie Medal, Guardian Children's Fiction Award), The Maypole (1989), St George and the Dragon (1989), El Cid (1989), Fires' Astonishment (1990), Vainglory (1991), Greek Myths (1992), The Odyssey (1993), Gold Dust (1993, Beefeater/Whitbread Children's Book of the Year), Stories from the Ballet (1994), Stories from Shakespeare (1994), The Golden Hoard, Silver Treasure, Bronze Cauldron, Crystal Pool (1995–98), Plundering Paradise (1996, Smarties Bronze Award), Lovesong (1996), Moby Dick (1996), God's People (1997), The Ideal Wife (1997), Forever X (1997), Unicorns! Unicorns! (1997), Greek Gods and Goddesses (1997), Starry Tales (1998), Never Let Go! (1998), God's Kingdom (1999), The Stones are Hatching (1999), A Pilgrim's Progress (1999 Blue Peter Book of the Year), Roman Myths (1999), Britannia - 100 Stories from British History (1999), Beauty and the Beast (1999), Love and Friendship (2000), The Kite Rider (2001, Smarties Bronze Award, Blue Peter Book to Keep Forever), Stop the Train (2001, Smarties Bronze Award, Highly Commended Carnegie Medal), My Grandmother's Clock (2002), Six Storey House (2002), Bright Penny (2002), Gilgamesh (2002), Showstopper! (2003), The Jesse Tree (2003), Doctor Quack (2003), Dog Days (2003), Treasury of Fairy Tales (2003), Hercules, Perseus, Odysseus, Theseus (2003), Jalopy (2003), The Questing Knights of the Faerie Queen (2004), Smile (2004, Smarties Bronze Award 2004), Not the End of the World (2004, Whitbread Children's Book of the Year 2004), The White Darkness (2005, shortlisted Whitbread Children's Book of the Year 2005, shortlisted Carnegie Medal 2005), Peter Pan in Scarlet (2006), Cyrano (2006), Father and Son (2006), Mo (2006), The Nativity (2007), Tamburlaine's Elephants (2007), The Longest Story in the World (2008); *Plays* Britannia on Stage (2000), Greeks on Stage (2002), Dazzling Medusa (Polka Theatre, 2005), Doctor Faustus (2006); *Radio Play* Last Call (1991); *Style*— Ms Geraldine McCaughrean; ✉ c/o David Higham Associates, 5–8 Lower John Street, Golden Square, London W1R 4HA (tel 020 7437 7888, fax 020 7437 1072, website www.geraldinemccaughrean.co.uk)

McCAUSLAND, Martin Patrick; s of Jack Patrick McCausland, and Audrey May, *née* Pomeroy; *b* 27 March 1961; *Educ* Hardye's GS Dorchester, Univ of Sheffield (BA); *m* 4 Sept 1988, Christine Dawn, *née* Burrows; *Career* articled clerk Chantrey Wood King CAs 1982–85, accountant Ernst & Young 1986–89; Carlton Communications plc: head office 1989–91, fin controller Carlton Television Ltd 1991–94, fin dir Carlton Television Ltd 1994, fin dir Carlton Productions Ltd 1995–; ACA 1985; *Style*— Martin McCausland, Esq

McCAVE, Prof (Ian) Nicholas; s of T T McCave (d 1941), and G M Langlois (d 1996); *b* 3 February 1941; *Educ* Elizabeth Coll Guernsey, Hertford Coll Oxford (MA, DSc), Brown Univ Providence RI (PhD); *m* 3 April 1972, Susan Caroline Adams, da of G de P Bambridge; 3 s (Thomas b 1973, Robert b 1975, Geoffrey b 1978), 1 da (Elise b 1981); *Career* NATO res fell Netherlands Inst voor Onderzoek der Zee 1967–69, reader Sch of Environmental Sci UEA 1976–84 (lectr 1969–76), adjunct scientist Woods Hole Oceanographic Institution 1978–87, Woodwardian prof of geology Univ of Cambridge 1985–, head Earth Sciences Dept Univ of Cambridge 1988–98; fell St John's Coll Cambridge 1986–; pres Scientific Ctee on Oceanic Res of the Int Cncl of Science Unions 1992–96; Shepard Medal for Marine Geology US Soc for Sedimentary Geology 1995, Huntsman Medal for Oceanography Canada 1999; FGS 1963; *Books* The Benthic Boundary Layer (ed, 1976); *Style*— Prof Nicholas McCave; ✉ Department of Earth Sciences, University of Cambridge, Downing Street, Cambridge (tel 01223 333400)

McCAWLEY, Leon Francis; s of Bernard McCawley, and Marian, *née* Sherwood; *b* 12 July 1973; *Educ* Chetham's Sch of Music Manchester, Curtis Inst of Music Philadelphia; *m* 3 June 1996, Anna H Paik; *Career* pianist; appeared with: CBSO under Sir Simon Rattle, BBC Philharmonic, LPO, RPO, Philharmonia, RLPO, Royal Scottish Nat Orch, Ulster Orch, BBC National Orch of Wales, Hallé; int orchestra appearances incl: Cincinnati Symphony, Dallas Symphony, Minnesota Orch, Philadelphia Orch, Malaysian Philharmonic, Austrian Radio Orchestra, Vienna Symphony Orchestra, Adelaide Symphony, Vienna Chamber Orch, Prague Symphony Orch; festival appearances incl: Spoleto, Edinburgh Int Festival, Brighton Festival, Helsinki, Bath and Cheltenham; debut BBC Proms with Bournemouth Symphony Orch 1995; int recital appearances: Berlin Philharmonie, Zurich Tonhalle, Vienna Musikverein, Kennedy Center, Washington DC, Festival Radio France, Deutschland Radio Berlin; UK recitals at Wigmore Hall, Purcell Room and Queen Elizabeth Hall, London; *Recordings* Barber: Solo Piano Music 1997, Beethoven: Sonatas and Variations 2001, Schumann: Piano Music 2003, Hans Gál: Complete Piano Music 2005, Mozart: Complete Piano Sonatas 2006; *Awards* winner piano section BBC Young Musician of the Year 1990, young soloist of the year LPO/Pioneer 1990, first prize Ninth Int Beethoven Piano Competition (Vienna) 1993, second prize Leeds Int Piano Competition 1993; *Style*— Leon McCawley, Esq; ✉ c/o Clarion Seven Muses, 47 Whitehall Park, London N19 3TW (tel 020 7272 4413, e-mail caroline@c7m.co.uk, website www.c7m.co.uk and www.leonmccawley.com)

McCLAREN, Steve; *b* 3 May 1961; *Career* professional footballer and manager; player: Hull City 1979–85, Derby County 1985–88, Bristol City 1988–89, Oxford United 1989–92; youth and reserve team coach Oxford United 1992–95, first team coach Derby County 1995–99 (promoted to Premiership 1996), asst mangr Manchester United 1999–2001 (winners League Championship 1999, 2000 and 2001, FA Cup 1999, UEFA Champions League 1999), mangr Middlesbrough 2001–06 (winners League Cup 2004, finalists UEFA Cup 2006), mangr Eng nat team 2006– (asst mangr and head coach 2000–06); *Style*— Mr Steve McClaren; ✉ c/o The Football Association, 25 Soho Square, London W1D 4FA

McCLARTY, David; MLA; s of Douglas McClarty, and Helen, *née* Watts; *b* 23 February 1951; *Educ* Coleraine Academical Inst, Magee Coll Londonderry; *Career* fire insurance underwriter 1973–84, insurance conslt 1984–98; elected to Coleraine BC 1989, 1993, 1997 and 2001; mayor of Coleraine 1993–95; MLA (UUP) E Londonderry 1998–; chm Bd of Govrs Christie Memorial Sch, memb Bd of Govrs Coleraine Academical Inst; Freeman City of London 1994; *Recreations* sport, reading, music, amateur dramatics, theatre; *Clubs* Ballywillan Drama, Coleraine British Legion, Royal Artillery Assoc (hon life memb); *Style*— David McClarty, Esq, MLA; ✉ Northern Ireland Assembly, Parliament Buildings, Stormont Estate, Belfast BT4 3XX (tel 028 9052 0310, fax 028 9052 0309, e-mail david.mcclarty@niassembly.gov.uk); 22 Slievebanna, Coleraine, Co Londonderry BT51 3JG (mobile 07771 605617)

McCLEAN, Prof (John) David; CBE (1994), Hon QC (1995); s of Maj Harold McClean (d 1983), of Prestbury, Cheshire, and Mabel, *née* Callow (d 1981); *b* 4 July 1939; *Educ* Queen Elizabeth GS Blackburn, Magdalen Coll Oxford (MA, BCL, DCL); *m* 10 Dec 1966, Pamela Ann, da of Leslie Arthur Loader (d 1959), of Yeovil, Somerset; 1 s (Michael b 1969), 1 da (Lydia b 1972); *Career* Univ of Sheffield: lectr 1961–68, sr lectr 1968–73, prof 1973–2004, pro-vice-chllr 1991–96, emeritus prof 2004–; visiting lectr Monash Univ 1968 (visiting prof 1978); lay vice-pres Sheffield Diocesan Synod 1982–94; memb: Gen Synod 1970–2005, Crown Appts Cmmn 1977–87; vice-chm House of Laity 1979–85 (chm 1985–95); chllr: Dio of Sheffield 1992–, Dio of Newcastle 1998–; bencher Gray's Inn 2001; FBA 2003; *Books* Criminal Justice and the Treatment of Offenders (jtly, 1969), Legal Context of Social Work (1975, 2 edn 1980), Defendants in the Criminal Process (jtly, 1976), Shawcross and Beaumont on Air Law (jtly, 4 edn, 1977, gen ed 2001–), Dicey and Morris, the Conflict of Laws (jtly, 10 edn 1980, 11 edn 1987, 12 edn 1993, 13 edn 1999, 14 edn 2006), Recognition of Family Judgments in the Commonwealth (1983), International Judicial Assistance (1992), International Co-operation in Civil and Criminal Cases (2002), Transnational Organized Crime (2007); *Recreations* detective fiction; *Clubs* RCS; *Style*— Prof David McClean, CBE, QC; ✉ 6 Burnt Stones Close, Sheffield S10 5TS (tel 0114 230 5794); School of Law, The University, Sheffield S10 2TN (tel 0114 222 6754, fax 0114 222 6823, e-mail j.d.mcclean@sheffield.ac.uk)

McCLEAN, Richard Arthur Francis; s of Donald Stuart McClean (d 1959), and Marjory Kathleen, *née* Franks; *b* 5 December 1937; *Educ* Marlborough; *m* 29 Aug 1959, Janna, da of Eric Constantine Doresa; 2 da (Lucinda b 27 June 1961, Philippa b 23 July 1966), 1 s (Paul b 23 Sept 1962); *Career* Financial Times: joined Advertising Dept 1955, advertising dir 1974, appointed to the Bd 1977, mktg dir 1979, md Marketing, md Europe 1981, dep chief exec 1983–93; chief exec and publisher International Herald Tribune July 1993–98; dir: The Financial Times (Europe) Ltd 1978, St Clements Press Ltd 1981, Financial Times Group Ltd 1984, FT Business Information Ltd 1984, Westminster Press Ltd 1986, Mercury European Privatisation Tst plc 1998, Henderson Electrical and General Tst plc 1998; *Recreations* golf, tennis; *Clubs* Garrick, Royal St George's Golf, Sunningdale Golf, MCC; *Style*— Richard McClean, Esq

McCLEARY, HE (William) Boyd; CVO (2004); s of Robert McCleary (d 1983), and Eleanor Thomasina, *née* Weir (d 1985); *b* 30 March 1949, Belfast; *Educ* Royal Belfast Academical Instn (High Hyndman scholar), Queen's Univ Belfast (BA); *m* 1, 1977 (m dis 1999), Susan Elizabeth Williams; 2 da (Alice Elizabeth b 23 Jan 1983, Katherine Eleanor b 3 Sept 1985); m 2, 2000, Jeannette Ann, *née* Collier; 1 da (Emily Hong-Hoa b 25 July 2001); *Career* asst princ then dep princ Dept of Agriculture NI 1972–75, first sec Agriculture then Chancery Br Embassy Bonn 1975–80, Western European Dept FCO 1981–83, European Community Dept FCO 1983–85, first sec, head of Chancery and consul Br Embassy Seoul 1985–88, asst head Far Eastern Dept FCO 1988–89, dep head of mission and dir of trade Br Embassy Ankara, cnsllr economic and trade policy Br High Cmmn Ottawa 1993–97, head Estate Dept FCO 1997–2000, consul-general and DG for trade and investment Dusseldorf Germany, dir global rollout for Oracle ERP system FCO 2005–06, high cmmr to Malaysia 2006–; *Recreations* spending time with family, squash, walking, reading; *Clubs* Royal Over-Seas League; *Style*— HE Mr Boyd McCleary, CVO; ✉ c/o Foreign and Commonwealth Office, King Charles Street, London SE1A 2AH (tel 00 60 3 2170 2224, e-mail boyd.mccleary@fco.gov.uk)

McCLELLAND, Dr (William) Morris; s of James McClelland, of Co Armagh, and May, *née* Johnston; *b* 22 June 1945; *Educ* Portadown Coll, Queen's Univ Belfast (MB BCh, BAO); *m* 14 Aug 1969; Margaret Christine, da of David Joseph Robinson, of Co Down; 2 da (Joanna b 7 May 1972, Sarah b 15 Jan 1976), 1 s (Jamie b 8 April 1978); *Career* chief exec NI Blood Transfusion Serv 1980–, hon lectr in haematology Queen's Univ Belfast 2001–; FRCPath; *Style*— Dr Morris McClelland; ✉ Northern Ireland Blood Transfusion Service, Belfast City Hospital, Lisburn Road, Belfast BT9 7TS (tel 028 9032 1414, fax 028 9043 9017, e-mail chiefexec@nibts.n-i-.nhs.uk)

McCLEMENT, Vice Adm Sir Timothy Pentreath (Tim); KCB (2006), OBE (1991); *b* 1951; *Educ* BRNC Dartmouth (Queen's Telescope, Queen's Sword); *m* Lynne; 2 s (Alastair, Angus); *Career* cmmnd RN 1971, qualified submariner 1975, Submarine CO's Qualifying Course 1981, exec offr HMS Conqueror 1981–83 (incl Falklands conflict), cmd HMS Opportune 1983–85, staff Capt Submarine Sea Trg 1985–87, promoted Cdr 1987, CO Submarine CO's Qualifying Course 1987–89, cmd HMS Tireless 1989–91, JSDC 1991–92, Capt 1992, CO HMS London 1992–94, served Directorate of Naval Staff Duties MOD 1994–95, Higher Command and Staff Course 1996, estab Plans Div Perm Jt HQ 1996–97, Cdre 1997, Dep Flag Offr Submarines 1997–99, Capt 2 Frigate Sqdn and CO HMS Cornwall 1999–2001, Revolution in Business Practices US Navy Flag Offrs' Course US Navy Postgrad Sch Monterey CA 2001, Rear Adm 2001, ACNS 2001–03 (memb Admiralty Bd), COS (Warfare) to C-in-C Fleet 2003–, Vice Adm 2004, Dep C-in-C Fleet 2004–06;

vice-pres RN Rugby Union; younger bro Trinity House; Freeman City of London; MInstD; *Style*— Vice Adm Sir Tim McClement, OBE

MACCLESFIELD, Archdeacon of; *see:* Gillings, Ven Richard John

MACCLESFIELD, 9 Earl of (GB 1721); Richard Timothy George Mansfield Parker; also Viscount Parker of Ewelme, Co Oxford (GB 1721), Baron Parker of Macclesfield, Co Chester (GB 1716); s of 8 Earl of Macclesfield (d 1992), and Hon Valerie Mansfield (d 1994), da of 4 Baron Sandhurst, OBE; *b* 31 May 1943; *Educ* Stowe, Worcester Coll Oxford; *m* 1, 1967 (m dis 1985), (Tatiana) Cleone Anne, da of Maj Craig Wheaton-Smith, US Army, and his 1 w, *née* Princess Tatiana Wiasemsky; 3 da (Lady Tanya Susan b 1971, Lady Katharine Ann, Lady Marian Jane (twins) b 1973); m 2, 1986, Mrs Sandra Hope Mead, da of Sylvio Fiore, of Florida, USA; *Heir* bro, Hon David Parker; *Style*— The Rt Hon the Earl of Macclesfield; ✉ Rectory Farmhouse, Church Lane, North Stoke, Wallingford, Oxfordshire OX10 6BQ

McCLEVERTY, Prof Jon Armistice; s of John Frederick McCleverty (d 1948), and Agnes Elder, *née* Melrose (d 1973); *b* 11 November 1937; *Educ* Aberdeen GS, Fettes, Univ of Aberdeen (BSc), Imperial Coll London (PhD); *m* 29 June 1963, Dianne Margaret, da of Ian William Barrack (d 1955); 2 da (Ashley b 1967, Roslyn b 1971); *Career* postdoctoral fell (Fulbright scholar) MIT USA 1963–64, lectr and reader Dept of Chemistry Univ of Sheffield 1964–80; prof of inorganic chemistry: Univ of Birmingham 1980–90, Univ of Bristol 1990–; SERC: memb Chemistry Ctee 1988–93 (chm 1990–93), chm Inorganic Chemistry Sub-Ctee 1988–90, memb Sci Bd 1990–93; memb Technical Opportunities Panel EPSRC 1998–; chm Ctee of Heads of Univ Chemistry Depts 1989–91; Royal Soc of Chemistry: memb Int Ctee 1992–2001, chm 1993–98, memb Cncl 1993–2001, pres Dalton Division 1999–2001, chm Sci and Technol Bd 2001–; Euro Community: memb COST Tech Ctee for Chemistry 1991–95, chm Action D4 for Molecular Electronics 1991–95; chm Euro Research Cncl Chemistry Ctees (CERC 3) (memb 1990–93 and 1995–99); memb Physics Engrg Sci Technol Panel NATO 1999–2002; *Recreations* gardening, jazz, travel, food and wine, Scottish and Irish clan history; *Style*— Prof Jon McCleverty; ✉ School of Chemistry, University of Bristol, Cantocks Close, Bristol BS8 1TS (e-mail jon.mccleverty@bristol.ac.uk)

McCLOSKEY, Jane; da of Brian McCloskey, of Wolverhampton, W Midlands, and Hilda, *née* Blunn; *b* 10 March 1966; *Educ* Wolverhampton Girls' HS, Univ of Birmingham (BA); *Career* various media projects 1984–86 incl: author of Into the Labyrinth for HTV West 1982, features writer for Select Magazine and Wolverhampton Post & Mail 1984–85; BBC 1986–92: researcher Pebble Mill at One, Pamela Armstrong and Reaching for the Skies (BBC 1 Network) 1986–87, successively asst prodr, studio dir then prodr Daytime Live (BBC 1 Network) 1988–90, prodr/studio dir Scene Today (BBC 1 Network) 1990, prodr People Today (BBC North), prodr/dir The Travel Show Guides (BBC North) and prodr BBC Election Night Special (BBC 1) and The Travel Show (BBC 2) 1991–92; freelance prodr 1993–94: series prodr Holiday Snaps and author of Holiday Snaps Brochure (GMTV), prodr Good Getaways (Carlton); head of features and prog devpt GMTV 1995–96 (head of features and entertainment 1994–95), dir of progs Westcountry Television 1996–2002, dir of progs West and Westcountry and controller South ITV 2002–, ed ITV Regnl Prodn Fund 2005–; *Recreations* dog walking, cooking, gardening, good wine; *Style*— Miss Jane McCloskey; ✉ Controller, Regional Programmes South, ITV Westcountry, Western Wood Way, Langage Science Park, Plymouth, Devon PL7 5BG (tel 01752 333376, fax 01752 333059)

McCLOY, Dr Elizabeth Carol; da of Edward Bradley, of Guildford, Surrey, and Ada, *née* Entwisle; *b* 25 April 1945; *Educ* Guildford Co GS, Univ Coll Hosp UCL (BSc, MB BS); *m* 1969 (m dis 1989), Rory McCloy; 2 s (Liam James b 22 March 1972, Sean Michael b 22 Aug 1974); *Career* clinical asst (med) W Middx Univ Hosp 1972–83; Manchester Royal Infirmary: sr clinical med offr (occupational health) 1984–88, conslt in occupational med 1988–93; dir of occupational health and safety Central Manchester Healthcare Tst 1988–93, chief exec and dir Civil Service Occupational Health Service (now OHSA Ltd) 1993–96, chief med offr UNUM Ltd 1997–98; memb Soc of Occupational Med (pres 1993–94); Peter Taylor medal; FRSM 1985, FRSA 1993, FRCP, FFOM; *Books* Hunter's Diseases of Occupations (contrib, 1988), Practical Occupational Medicine (jt ed, 1994), Oxford Textbook of Medicine (contrib, 1994); *Style*— Dr Elizabeth McCloy

McCLUGGAGE, Dr John Robert (Jack); *b* 15 November 1940; *Educ* Queen's Univ Belfast (MB BCh, BAO); *m* (m dis); 1 c; *Career* princ GP Cherryvalley Belfast and pt/t clinical asst (dermatology) Ards Hosp Newtownards 1967–80, princ/sr lectr in gen practice Dept of Gen Practice Queen's Univ Belfast 1980–87, sec NI Cncl for Postgrad Med Educn 1987–93, chief exec/postgrad dean NI Cncl for Postgrad Med and Dental Educn 1993–2004; examiner for membership: RCGP 1984–90, Irish Coll of Gen Practitioners 1987–93; memb: Conf of Postgrad Deans 1987–2004, Hosp Servs Sub-Ctee DHSS NI 1987–2004; GMC: memb Cncl 1989–2003, memb Professional Conduct Ctee 1989–2003, memb Assessment Referral Ctee 1996–98, memb Review Bd for Overseas Doctors 2001–04, memb Interim Orders Ctee 2002–; author of various pubns in academic jls; memb BMA, fell Ulster Med Soc (vice-pres 1994–95); FRCGP 1984, FRCPEd 1994, FRCP(Dublin) 1995; *Recreations* gardening, reading, music; *Style*— Dr Jack McCluggage; ✉ Apartment 2, Woodlodge, Croft Road, Holywood, Co Down BT18 0QB (tel 028 9042 7032)

McCLURE, Prof John; OBE (2007); s of Richard Burns McClure (d 1949), of Omagh, Co Tyrone, and Isabella McClure (d 1983); *b* 2 May 1947; *Educ* Queen's Univ Belfast (BSc, MD, BCh, BAO); *m* 26 June 1970, Sheena Frances, da of Alfred Henry Tucker (d 1973), of Belfast; 3 da (Sarah b 26 Oct 1971, Katy 13 Dec 1975, Emma 30 Jan 1978); *Career* trg posts in pathology Queen's Univ Belfast 1972–78, clinical sr lectr (also specialist and sr specialist tissue pathology) Inst of Med and Veterinary Sci and Univ of Adelaide 1978–83; Univ of Manchester: sr lectr and hon conslt histopathology 1983–87, Procter prof of pathology 1987–2003, assoc dean of undergrad med studies 1995–99; clinical dir of laboratory med Central Manchester Healthcare Tst 1996–2001; Br Red Cross Soc: pres Gtr Manchester Branch Cncl 1994–99, chm Northern Regnl Cncl 1997–99, memb Nat Bd of Tstees 1997– (vice-chm 2000–01 chm 2001–); FRCPath 1989 (MRCPath 1977); *Style*— Prof John McClure, OBE; ✉ Directorate of Laboratory Medicine, Central Manchester Healthcare Trust, Oxford Road, Manchester M13 9WL (tel 0161 276 8945, fax 0161 276 8996, e-mail john.mcclure@man.ac.uk)

McCLURE, Ven Timothy Elston (Tim); s of Kenneth Elston McClure (d 1997), and Grace Helen, *née* Hoar; *Educ* Kingston GS, St John's Coll Durham (BA), Ridley Hall Cambridge; *m* 1 Aug 1969, Barbara Mary, da of Ven George John Charles Marchant; 1 s (Matthew Elston b 1 July 1970), 1 da (Naomi b 27 Nov 1973); *Career* curate Kirkheaton PC Huddersfield 1970–73, mktg mangr Agrofax Labour Intensive Products Ltd Harrow 1973–74, chaplain to Manchester Poly 1974–82, curate St Ambrose Chorlton-on-Medlock Manchester 1974–79, team rector Parish of Whitworth Manchester and presiding chaplain 1979–82, gen sec Student Christian Movement 1982–92, dir Churches' Cncl for Industry and Social Responsibility (ISR) Bristol 1992–99, hon canon Bristol Cathedral 1992–, bishop's social and industrial advsr 1992–99, Lord Mayor's chaplain 1996–99, archdeacon of Bristol 1999–; non-exec chm Traidcraft plc 1990–97 (non-exec dir 1983–97), chm Christian Conf Tst 1998–2003, chm Social Enterprise Works 2000–; memb: Industrial Mission Assoc 1992, Anglican Assoc for Social Responsibility 1994, Ecclesiastical Law Soc 2000; *Recreations* cooking, gardening, reading, boat restoration, sailing; *Style*— The Ven Tim McClure; ✉ e-mail tim.mcclure@bristoldiocese.org

McCLURE FISHER, David Anthony; s of Douglas McClure Fisher (d 1991), and Mary Margaret, *née* Haley (d 1996); *b* 4 March 1939; *Educ* Tonbridge; *m* 30 Dec 1961, Lesley Carol, da of William Henry Chester-Jones (d 1971); 1 s (Duncan b 1964), 1 da (Joanna b 1968); *Career* md: Hogg Automotive Insurance Services Ltd 1984–94, Greyfriars Administration Services Ltd 1984–94, Hogg Insurance Brokers Ltd; dir: Hogg Group plc 1990–94, Bain Hogg Ltd 1994–95, IMC Insurance Services Ltd 1995–96; chm Warranty Direct Ltd 1997–; FCII, FInstD, FCIS, FIMI; *Recreations* golf, bridge; *Clubs* Moor Park Golf, Phyllis Court; *Style*— D A McClure Fisher, Esq; ✉ 1 Wargrave Hall, High Street, Wargrave, Berkshire RG10 8DA (tel 0118 947 4200, e-mail david@mcclure-fisher.co.uk)

McCLUSKEY, Baron (Life Peer UK 1976), of Church Hill in District of City of Edinburgh; John Herbert McCluskey; QC (Scot 1967); s of Francis John McCluskey (d 1961), of Edinburgh; *b* 12 June 1929; *Educ* St Bede's GS Manchester, Holy Cross Acad Edinburgh, Univ of Edinburgh (Vans Dunlop scholar, Harry Dalgety bursar, MA, LLB); *m* 1956, Ruth, da of Aaron Friedland, of Manchester; 2 s (Hon (John) Mark b 1960, Hon David Francis b 1963), 1 da (Hon Catherine Margaret b 1962); *Career* advocate 1955, advocate-depute 1964, sheriff princ of Dumfries and Galloway 1973–1974, slr gen for Scotland 1974–79, senator of the Coll of Justice in Scotland 1984–2000; BBC Reith lectr 1986; chm: John Smith Memorial Tst 1997–2004, Age Concern Scotland 2000–01; Hon LLD Univ of Dundee 1989; *Books* Law, Justice and Democracy (1987), Criminal Appeals (1991, 2 edn 2000); *Style*— The Rt Hon the Lord McCluskey; ✉ House of Lords, Westminster, London SW1A 0PW

McCLUSKIE, John Cameron; CB (1999), QC (Scot 1989); s of Thomas McCluskie, and Marjorie McCluskie; *b* 1 February 1946; *Educ* Hyndland Sch Glasgow, Univ of Glasgow; *m* 1970, Janis Mary Helen McArthur; 1 da (b 1971), 1 s (b 1976); *Career* admitted slr Scot 1970; apprentice slr Boyds Glasgow 1967–69, asst town clerk Burgh of Cumbernauld 1969–70, legal asst Macdonald Jameson and Morris Glasgow 1970, S of Scotland Electricity Bd 1970–72, asst rising to parly draftsman Lord Advocate's Dept 1972–89, legal sec to Lord Advocate and first Scottish parly counsel 1989–2006; memb Law Soc of Scotland 1970–74, admitted Faculty of Advocates 1974; parish cncllr Tunstall PC, chm Friends of Tunstall Church; *Recreations* vegetable growing; *Style*— John McCluskie, Esq, CB, QC

McCOLL, Prof William Finlay; s of William McColl (d 1975), and Jeanie, *née* Lilley (d 1973); *b* 2 May 1952; *Educ* Univ of Strathclyde (BSc), Univ of Warwick (PhD); *m* Irene Ruth, *née* Houston; 2 s (Robert William b 23 July 1982, Iain Fraser b 29 June 1986), 1 da (Caroline Anna b 13 March 1985); *Career* SRC postdoctoral research fell 1976–77; lectr in computer science: Univ of Leeds 1977–80, Univ of Warwick 1980–85, Univ of Oxford 1985–96; prof of computing science Univ of Oxford 1996–; fell Wadham Coll Oxford 1985–, MA (by incorporation) Univ of Oxford 1985; *Recreations* skiing, scuba diving; *Style*— Prof William McColl; ✉ 24A Sunderland Avenue, Oxford OX2 8DX (tel 01865 428346); Oxford University Computing Laboratory, Parks Road, Oxford OX1 3QD (tel 01865 273829, e-mail wfm@comlab.ox.ac.uk)

McCOLL OF DULWICH, Baron (Life Peer UK 1989), of Bermondsey in the London Borough of Southwark; Ian McColl; CBE (1997); s of Frederick George McColl (d 1985), of Dulwich, and Winifred Edith, *née* Murphy (d 1984); *b* 6 January 1933; *Educ* Hutchesons' GS Glasgow, St Paul's, Univ of London (MB BS, MS); *m* 27 Aug 1960, Dr Jean Lennox, 2 da of Arthur James McNair, FRCS, FRCOG (d 1964), of London; 1 s (Dr the Hon Alastair James b 25 July 1961), 2 da (Dr the Hon Caroline Lennox b 19 Aug 1963, Hon Mary Alison b 9 Oct 1966); *Career* surgn to Bart's and sub dean Med Coll 1967–71, prof of surgery at Guy's Hosp 1971–99, dir surgery Guy's Hosp 1985–99, chm Dept of Surgery UMDS 1987–93; hon conslt surgn to British Army 1984–99; Parly private sec (Lords) to PM 1994–97, dep speaker House of Lords 1994–2002, oppn spokesman on health House of Lords 1997–, memb Select Ctee on Euthanasia 1994–95 and Select Ctee on Sci 2000–; vice-chm Disablement Services Authy 1987–91; pres: Soc of Minimally Invasive Surgery 1991–94, Limbless Assoc (formerly Nat Assoc of Limbless Disabled), Assoc of Endo Surgns of Great Br and Ireland 1994–97, Leprosy Mission 1996–, Royal Med Fndn of Epsom Coll 2001–; vice-pres John Grooms Soc for the Disabled; dir Mercy Ships Int 1998–, chm Mercy Ships UK 2000–, vice-chm Int Bd Mercy Ships; chm Bd of Govrs: Mildmay Mission Hosp 1994– (pres 1985–94), James Allen's Girls' Sch 1998–2004; govr St Paul's Sch 2001–; memb: Cncl RCS 1986–94, Bd of Patrons RCS 1995–; Great Scot Award 2002, Nat Maritime Historical Soc Award USA 2002; Freeman City of London, Liveryman of Worshipful Soc of Apothecaries 1979, Middle Warden Worshipful Co of Barber Surgeons 1997 (Master 1999–2000, Upper Warden 1998, Liveryman 1986, dep Master 2000–01); FKC 2001, FRCS, FACS, FRCSEd, hon FDSRCS 2007; Order of Mercy 2007; *Books* Intestinal Absorption in Man (jtly, 1975), NHS Data Book (jtly, 1983); *Recreations* forestry; *Style*— The Rt Hon the Lord McColl of Dulwich, CBE; ✉ House of Lords, London SW1A 0PW (tel 020 7219 5141, e-mail mccolli@parliament.uk)

McCOMB, Dr Janet Mary; da of Samuel Gerald McComb, of Belfast, and Mary Clarke; *b* 22 August 1951; *Educ* Queen's Univ of Belfast (MB BCh, BAO, MD); *Career* clinical and research fell Harvard Med Sch and Massachusetts Gen Hosp 1983–86, conslt cardiologist Univ of Newcastle upon Tyne 1986– (sr lectr 1986–90); memb: Br Cardiac Soc, Br Pacing and Electrophysiology Gp, Assoc of Physicians; FRCP; *Style*— Dr J M McComb

McCOMB, Leonard; *b* 1930; *Educ* Manchester Sch of Art, Slade Sch of Art; *Career* artist; taught at various art colls (incl Oxford Poly, Royal Acad, Slade, Goldsmiths Coll London and John Cass) 1960–89, fndr Sunningwell Sch of Art 1977, fndr Vincent Soc of Drawing 1990; destroyed most of work up to 1976; cmmnd through Art for Work to paint 3 oil paintings of Kennecott Utah copper mines for RTZ London offices 1995; keeper of the Royal Acad 1995–; Hon Dr Oxford Brookes Univ 2004; RA 1990 (ARA 1987), fell Royal Soc of Painter Printmakers 1994, RP 2003, Hon RWS; *Exhibitions* incl: Human Clay (Arts Cncl) 1976, British Painting 1952–77 (Royal Acad) 1977, British Art Show (Arts Cncl touring exhbn), Venice Biennale - Painters of the 80's 1980, British Sculpture in the Twentieth Century (Whitechapel Art Gallery London) 1981, British Drawing Hayward Annual (Hayward Gallery) 1983, Leonard McComb Drawings, Paintings and Sculpture (Arts Cncl touring exhbn orgnd by MOMA Oxford) 1983, Hard Won Image (Tate Gallery) 1984, Human Interest: 50 Years of British Art (Corner House Manchester) 1985, Representation Abroad (Hirschhorn Museum Washington DC) 1986, Flowers in the Twentieth Century (Stoke on Trent City Museum touring exhbn) 1986, Large Watercolours and Drawings (Raab Gallery Berlin) 1986, Viewpoint Selection of British Art (MOMA Brussels) 1987, It's a Still Life (Plymouth City Museum and Art Gallery and tour) 1989, RA - Portraits Friends Room Exhbn 1989, various exhbns Gillian Jason Gallery London 1989–, Images of Paradise (Christie's London) 1990, The Discerning Eye (Mall Galleries London) 1992, The Sussex Scene (Hove and Eastbourne) 1993, Singer and Friedlander/Sunday Times watercolour competition (Mall Galleries) 1993, Drawings and Paintings (Browse & Darby London) 1993, Drawing on these Shores (mixed travelling exhbn) 1993–94, Browse and Darby Gallery London 1994, Open House exhbn (Kettles Yard Cambridge) 1995, The Pursuit of Painting (Irish MOMA Dublin) 1997, Portrait of Doris Lessing (Nat Portrait Gallery Coll) 1999, Leonard McComb Portraits (curated by David Cohen, NY Studio Sch) 2000, Between Earth and Heaven (MOMA Ostend) 2001, The Upright Figure (Turbine Hall Tate Modern) 2002, Leonard McComb Drawings, Paintings and Sculpture (Talbot Rice Gallery Edinburgh) 2004 (also at Wolsey Art Gallery Ipswich 2005); *Public Collections* Arts Cncl, Birmingham City Art Gallery, British Cncl, Contemporary Arts Soc, Manchester Art Gallery, Swindon Art Gallery, Tate Gallery London, Univ of Cambridge, V&A, Worcester Museum and Art Gallery, Towner

Art Gallery Eastbourne; cmmnd to produce tapestry design (woven at Edinburgh Weavers) for Boots Chemists Nottingham; *Awards* Jubilee Prize Royal Acad 1977, Korn Ferry Prize Royal Acad 1988, second prize Singer and Friedlander/Sunday Times watercolour competition 1993, second prize Singer & Friedlander/Sunday Times watercolour prize 1994, Sir Hugh Casson Prize for Drawing Royal Acad of Arts Summer Exhbn 2005; *Style*— Dr Leonard McComb, RA, RWS, RP, RE; ✉ 4 Blenheim Studios, 29 Blenheim Gardens, London SW2 5EU (tel and fax 020 8675510)

McCOMBE, Hon Mr Justice; Sir Richard George Bramwell McCombe; kt (2001); s of Barbara Bramwell McCombe, *née* Bramwell (d 1969); *b* 23 September 1952; *Educ* Sedbergh, Downing Coll Cambridge (MA); *m* 1 (m dis 1986), m 2, 1986, Carolyn Sara, da of Robert Duncan Birrell, of Limpsfield, Surrey; 1 s (Duncan b 4 April 1987), 1 da (Tamara b 20 Nov 1989); *Career* called to the Bar Lincoln's Inn 1975 (bencher 1996); first jr counsel to Dir Gen of Fair Trading 1987–89 (second jr counsel 1982–87), DTI inspr into the affrs of Norton Group plc (with J K Heywood, FCA) 1991–92 (report published 1993), recorder of the Crown Ct 1996–2001 (asst recorder 1993–96), dep High Ct judge 1998–2001, QC 1989, judge of the High Ct of Justice (Queen's Bench Div) 2001–, presiding judge Northern Circuit; Attorney-Gen of the Duchy of Lancaster and Attorney and Serjeant within the County Palatine of Lancaster 1996–2001; memb: Senate Inns of Ct and Bar Cncl 1981–86, Bar Cncl Ctees 1986–89 (chm Young Barristers' Ctee 1983–84), Bar Representation Ctee Lincoln's Inn 1992–96, Bar Cncl 1995–97 (chm Int Rels Ctee 1997); head UK Delgn to the Cncl of the Bars and Law Socs of the EC 1996–98; pres-elect Assoc of Lancastrians in London 2008; govr Sedbergh Sch 2002–; *Recreations* various sporting interests, travel, flying aircraft; *Clubs* RAC, Garrick, MCC, Lancs CCC, Middx CCC, London Scottish FC; *Style*— The Hon Mr Justice McCombe; ✉ Royal Courts of Justice, Strand, London WC2A 2LL (tel 020 7947 6868)

McCONACHIE, Neil Alexander; s of John and Margaret McConachie, of Lossiemouth; *b* 23 May 1950; *Educ* Fettes, Robert Gordon's Univ Aberdeen (BSc), Univ of Strathclyde (MSc); *m* 1974, Judy, da of Jack McLennan; 1 s (Iain b 1981), 1 da (Catriona b 1984); *Career* pharmacist: NHS 1974–75 and 1976–78, Wellcome Fndn 1976–78, DuPont 1982–95 (various posts UK and overseas); gen mangr Argyll and Clyde Health Bd 1995–; memb Royal Pharmaceutical Soc of GB 1975; *Recreations* golf, travel; *Clubs* MCC, Moray Golf; *Style*— Neil McConachie, Esq; ✉ Argyll and Clyde Health Board, Ross House, Hawkhead Road, Paisley PA2 7BN (tel 0141 842 7200)

McCONNACHIE, (John Sneddon) Iain; s of John Meek McConnachie, of Sale, Greater Manchester, and Charlotte Sneddon, *née* Christie (d 1984); *b* 11 March 1956; *Educ* Sale GS, Lymm GS, Oxford Poly (HND), Huddersfield Poly (Dip Mktg Studies); *m* 9 June 1979 (m dis 1998), Shirley Diane, da of Norman George Burgess (d 1983); 1 da (Sara Anne b 2 Feb 1985); m 2, Hilary Diana Ohrstrand, da of Lewis Trevor Evans; *Career* mktg asst Zockoll Group 1977–78, asst advtg mangr Baxter Travenol 1978–79, American Express 1979–88 (mktg exec, mktg mangr, mktg dir), vice-pres sales and mktg Chase Manhattan Bank 1988–91, md Financial Marketing Consultancy Group 1991–92, head of direct distribution Legal and General plc 1992–93, md Financial Marketing Consultancy Group 1993–97, ptnr S2 Ltd 1997–99, managing ptnr Inst of Direct Marketing Consulting 1999–; md Europe Direct Entertainment 2005–, European direct mktg dir ACE INA Insurance; MInstM 1989; *Recreations* golf, photography, shooting; *Clubs* Castle Royle Golf; *Style*— Iain McConnachie, Esq; ✉ Somerford House, Somerford Place, Beaconsfield, Buckinghamshire HP9 1AZ (tel 01494 671219, e-mail iain.mcconnachie@ace-ina.com)

McCONNELL, Charlie Stephen; s of Charles Harold McConnell (d 1993), and Elsie Amelia, *née* Hogben; *b* 20 June 1951; *Educ* BA, MPhil; *m* 28 April 1995, Natasha, *née* Smirnova; 1 adopted s (Timor b 1978), 1 da (Holly Isadora b 1995); *Career* Dobroyd Community Sch Calderdale 1974–75, Scottish Local Govt Res Unit 1975–77, Clydebank Coll of Further Educn 1975–77, Dundee Coll of Educn 1977–84, Nat Consumer Cncl London 1984–87, Action Resource Centre London 1987–88, dir public affairs and Euro progs Community Devpt Fndn London 1988–93; chief exec: Scottish Community Educn Cncl 1993–99, Community Learning Scotland 1999–2002; vice-pres Euro Social Action Network 1991–93, chair UK NTO for Community Learning and Devpt 1999–2002, nat sec UK Consumers' Congress 1985–87, sec-gen International Assoc for Community Devpt 1998–; Parly candidate 1983; community devpt policy advsr Scottish Exec 2002–03; chief exec Carnegie Tst 2003–; FRSA 2000; *Publications* Community Worker as Politiciser of the Deprived (1977), Deprivation, Participation and Commmunity Action (et al, 1979), Community Education and Community Development (ed, 1982), Post 16: Continuing Education in Scotland (ed, 1984), Consumer Action and Community Development (ed, 1988), Towards a Citizen's Europe (ed, 1990), Community Development in Europe (ed, 1992), Community Development and Urban Regeneration (ed, 1993), Community Education in Scotland - The making of an empowering profession (ed 1995), Community Government and Active Citizenship (ed, 1998), Lifelong Learning in Scotland (ed, 1998), Community Learning and Development: The Making of an Empowering Profession (ed, 2002); *Recreations* fell walking, building dacha in Russia; *Style*— Charlie McConnell, Esq; ✉ Corrieway, Easter Balgedie, Kinross, Perthshire KY13 9HQ

McCONNELL, Rt Hon Jack Wilson; PC (2001), MSP; s of William Wilson McConnell, and Elizabeth, *née* Jack; *b* 30 June 1960; *Educ* Arran HS 1971–77, Univ of Stirling (BSc, DipEd) 1977–83; *m* 1990, Bridget; 1 s, 1 da; *Career* mathematics teacher 1983–92, gen sec Scottish Lab Pty 1992–98, chief exec Public Affairs Europe 1998; cncllr Stirling DC 1984–93 (ldr 1990–92); MSP (Lab) Motherwell & Wishaw 1999–; Scottish Exec: finance min 1999–2000, educn, Europe and external affairs min 2000–01, first min 2001–07; ldr Scottish Lab Pty 2001–; *Recreations* golf, swimming, music; *Style*— The Rt Hon Jack Wilson McConnell, MSP; ✉ e-mail jack.mcconnell.msp@scottish.parliament.uk

McCONNELL, John; s of Donald McConnell (d 1982), and Enid, *née* Dimberline (d 1967); *b* 14 May 1939; *Educ* Borough Green Secdy Modern Sch, Maidstone Coll of Art (Nat Dip); *m* 1 March 1963, Moira Rose, da of William Allan Macgregor; 1 s (Sam b 20 Feb 1966), 1 da (Kate b 1 Feb 1969); *Career* designer; own practice 1963–74, co-fndr Face Photosetting 1967; ptnr Pentagram 1974–2005, ed Pentagram Papers 1975–2006; memb: PO Stamp Advsy Ctee, CNAA; D&AD Assoc President's Award for outstanding contrib to design 1985, special commendation Prince Philip Designer's Prize 2002; RDI 1987; *Books* Living By Design (jtly, 1978), Ideas on Design (jtly, 1986), Pentagram Book V (jtly, 1999); *Recreations* cookery, building; *Style*— John McConnell, Esq; ✉ McConnell Design Limited, 11 Needham Road, London W11 2RP (tel 020 7229 3477, fax 020 7727 9932)

McCONNELL, (Robert) Nigel; *b* 14 May 1958, Belfast; *Educ* Queens Univ Belfast (BSc); *m* Antonella, *née* Carminati; *Career* venture capital Industrial Devpt Bd NI 1981–83, MBO fin advsr Coopers & Lybrand 1983–85, dir Prudential Venture Mangrs 1985–91, managing ptnr Cognetas LLP 1991– (also chm Advsy Investment Ctee); ACA; *Style*— Nigel McConnell, Esq; ✉ Cognetas LLP, Paternoster House, 65 St Paul's Churchyard, London EC4M 8AB (tel 020 7214 4800, fax 020 7214 4801, e-mail nmcc@cognetas.com)

McCONVILLE, Coline Lucille; *b* 21 July 1964; *Educ* Flensburg Gymnasium, Univ of NSW Law Sch (BJuris, LLB, Westgarth Middletons law scholar), Harvard Grad Sch of Business Admin (Harvard fell, Baker scholar, MBA); *m*; 1 da; *Career* sales mgmnt Australian Consolidated Press 1984–85, assoc conslt The L E K Partnership Munich 1989–92, sr assoc McKinsey & Co Ltd 1994–96, gp devpt dir More Gp plc 1996–98, chief exec (Europe) Clear Channel International Ltd 1998–; non-exec dir HBOS plc 2000–; memb Ctee Childline Fndn 2004–; *Recreations* cooking, entertaining, learning the piano, playing with my daughter; *Style*— Mrs Coline McConville; ✉ Clear Channel International, 1 Cluny Mews, London SW5 9EG

MacCORKINDALE, Simon Charles Pendered; s of Gp Capt Peter Bernard MacCorkindale, OBE, and Gilliver Mary, *née* Pendered; *b* 12 February 1952; *Educ* Haileybury; *m* 1, 10 July 1976 (m dis), Fiona Elizabeth Fullerton; m 2, 5 Oct 1984, Susan Melody George, da of Norman Alfred George; *Career* actor, producer, writer and director; dir Amy International Productions; memb: Dirs' Guilds of America, GB and Canada, Screen Actors' Guild, British Actors' Equity, American Equity, Acad of Motion Pictures Arts and Scis, The British Acad of Film & TV Arts, Writers' Guild of Canada, The Alliance of Canadian Cinema, TV and Radio Artists; Evening News Most Promising Newcomer 1978; *Television* series incl: Manimal 1983, Falcon Crest 1984–86, Counterstrike 1990–93 (also prodr), Casualty (BBC) 2002–; films for TV incl: Jesus of Nazareth 1975, Quatermass 1978, Visitor from the Other Side 1980, The Manions of America 1980–81, Falcon's Gold 1982, Obsessive Love 1984, Sincerely Violet 1986, The House That Mary Bought (prodr/writer/dir) 1994, The Way to Dusty Death 1994, At The Midnight Hour 1995, While My Pretty One Sleeps 1996, The Sands of Eden 1997, Running Wild 1997, The Girl Next Door 1997, Poltergeist 1998, Dinosaur Hunter 1999, The Power of Love (prodr) 1999, Dark Realm 2000, The Queen of Swords (prodr) 2000, Relic Hunter (prodr/dir) 2001, Adventure Inc (prodr) 2003; *Films* incl: Juggernaut 1974, Road to Mandalay 1977, Death on the Nile 1977, The Riddle of the Sands 1978, The Quatermass Conclusion 1978, Cabo Blanco 1979, The Sword and the Sorcerer 1982, Jaws 3D 1983, Stealing Heaven (prodr) 1987, That Summer of White Roses (prodr and writer) 1988 (Tokyo Grand Prix 1989), Such a Long Journey (prodr) 2000; *Theatre* incl: The Unexpected Guest (nat tour) 2007; *Recreations* tennis, skiing, music, writing, photography, Arab horse breeding; *Clubs* St James's; *Style*— Simon MacCorkindale, Esq; ✉ c/o Ken McReddie & Associates, 36–40 Glasshouse Street, London W1B 5DL (tel 020 7439 1456)

MacCORMAC, Sir Richard Cornelius; kt (2001), CBE (1994); s of late Henry MacCormac, CBE, MD, FRCP, and Marion Maud, *née* Broomhall; *b* 3 September 1938; *Educ* Westminster, Trinity Coll Cambridge (BA), UCL (MA); *m* 1964 (sep), Susan Karin, *née* Landen; 1 s and 1 s decd; *Career* served RN 1957–59; project architect London Borough of Merton 1967–69, estab private practice 1969, estab MacCormac Jamieson Prichard Ltd 1972 (Inc 2002); major works incl: Cable & Wireless Coll Coventry (Royal Fine Art Commission/Sunday Times Bldg of the Year Award 1994), Garden Quadrangle St John's Coll Oxford (Independent on Sunday Bldg of the Year Award 1994), Bowra Bldg Wadham Coll Oxford, Ruskin Library Lancaster Univ (Independent on Sunday Bldg of the Year Award 1996, Royal Fine Art Cmmn/BSkyB Bldg of the Year Univs Winner 1998, Millennium Products status awarded by the Design Cncl 1999), Burrell's Fields Trinity Coll Cambridge (RIBA Regnl Award 1997, Civic Tst Award 1997), Southwark Station Jubilee Line Extension (Royal Fine Art Cmmn Tst/BSkyB Millennium Bldg of the Year Award 2000), Wellcome Wing Science Museum London (Celebrating Construction Achievement Regnl Award for Greater London 2000), Phoenix Initiative Coventry (shortlisted RIBA Stirling Prize 2004); Univ of Cambridge: taught in Architecture Dept 1969–75 and 1979–81, univ lectr 1976–77; visiting prof: Univ of Edinburgh 1982–85, Univ of Hull 1998–99; studio tutor LSE 1998; chm Good Design in Housing Awards RIBA London region 1977, dir Spitalfields Workspace 1981–, memb Royal Fine Art Cmmn 1983–93; pres RIBA 1991–93, cmmr English Heritage 1995–98; Royal Acad: chm Architecture Ctee 1997–; advsr: Br Cncl 1993–2001, Urban Task Force 1998–; pres London Forum of Amenity and Civil Soc 1997–, tstee Greenwich Fndn for RNC 1998–2002; RIBA 1967 (PPRIBA), FRSA 1982, RA 1993; *Publications* author of articles in Architectural Review and Architects Jl; *Recreations* sailing, music, reading; *Style*— Sir Richard MacCormac, CBE, PPRIBA, RA; ✉ 9 Heneage Street, Spitalfields, London E1 5JL (tel 020 7377 9262, website www.mjparchitects.co.uk)

McCORMACK, Stephen John; s of Anthony McCormack, of Worthing, W Sussex, and Teresa, *née* Longworth; *b* 30 March 1957; *Educ* Worthing HS for Boys, Univ of Liverpool; *Career* reporter Worthing Gazette and Herald 1979–81; BBC: reporter BBC Radio Stoke 1981–84, reporter then corr Parliamentary and Political Unit 1984–89, reporter BBC Radio News 1989–91, sports corr 1991–94, Berlin corr 1994; currently freelance journalist and teacher; *Recreations* squash, tennis, cricket; *Style*— Steve McCormack; ✉ 57 Yale Court, Honeybourne Road, London NW6 1JQ (e-mail stevemccormack@blueyonder.co.uk)

McCORMICK, John; s of Joseph McCormick (d 1977), and Roseann, *née* McNamara (d 1976); *b* 24 June 1944; *Educ* St Michael's Acad Irvine, Univ of Glasgow (MA, MEd); *m* 4 Aug 1973, Jean Frances, da of William Gibbons, of Kirkintilloch, Glasgow; 1 da (Lesley Anne b 1978), 1 s (Stephen b 1980); *Career* teacher St Gregory's Secdy Sch Glasgow 1968–70, educn offr BBC Sch Broadcasting Cncl for Scotland 1970–75, sr educn offr Scotland 1975–82, sec and head of info BBC Scotland 1982–87, sec of the BBC 1987–92, controller BBC Scotland 1992–2004; chm: Edinburgh Film Festival 1996– (memb Bd 1994–96), Scottish Qualifications Authy 2004; memb Bd: Scottish Screen 1997, Skillset 2001–04, Scot Acad of Music and Drama 2003, Glasgow Sch of Art 2004, Scottish Opera 2005–; non-exec dir Lloyds TSB Scotland 2005–; vice-chm Youth-at-Risk Scotland 1985–92; memb: Glasgow Children's Panel 1972–77, Visiting Ctee Glenochil Young Offenders Instn 1979–85, Bd of Tstees Glasgow Science Centre 1999–2005; memb Ct Univ of Strathclyde 1996–2002; Hon DLitt Robert Gordon Univ 1997, Hon LLD Univ of Strathclyde 1999; Hon DUniv: Glasgow 1999, Paisley 2003; FRTS 1998, FRSE 2003; *Style*— John McCormick, Esq

McCORMICK, John St Clair; OBE (2002); *b* 20 September 1939; *Educ* St Paul's Cathedral Choir Sch, Sedbergh, Univ of Edinburgh Med Sch (MB ChB, FRCS); *m* 1964, Fiona Helen, *née* McLean; 2 s (Neil St Clair b 21 Oct 1967, Keith Graeme b 9 Feb 1972); *Career* conslt surgn: Dunfermline and W Fife Hosp 1974–79, Dumfries and Galloway Royal Infirmary 1979–99 (med dir 1994–2001); memb Cncl Royal Coll of Surgns of Edinburgh 1994– (dir of standards 1997–2000, vice-pres 2000–03), Clinical Standards Bd for Scotland 1999–2002; Liveryman Worshipful Co of Wax Chandlers and Tallow Makers (memb 1963); memb: BMA 1964, Vascular Soc of GB and I 1976, Assoc of Surgns 1990; *Style*— John McCormick, Esq, OBE; ✉ Ivy Cottage, Kirkpatrickdurham, Castle-Douglas DG7 3HG (tel 01556 650245)

MacCORMICK, Prof Sir (Donald) Neil; kt (2001), Hon QC (1999); s of John MacDonald MacCormick (d 1961), of Glasgow, and Margaret Isobel, *née* Miller; *b* 27 May 1941; *Educ* HS Glasgow, Univ of Glasgow (MA), Balliol Coll Oxford (MA), Univ of Edinburgh (LLD); *m* 6 Nov 1965 (m dis 1991), (Caroline) Karen Rona; 3 da (Janet b 1966, Morag b 1969, Sheena b 1971); m 2, 12 June 1992, Flora Margaret Milne; *Career* lectr in law Univ of St Andrews (Queen's Coll Dundee) 1965–67, fell Balliol Coll Oxford 1967–72; Univ of Edinburgh: regius prof of public law and law of nature and nations 1972–97, Leverhulme personal research prof 1997–2003, vice-princ 1997–2000; pres Soc of Public Teachers of Law 1983–84; memb: Broadcasting Cncl Scotland 1985–89, Nat Cncl SNP 1978–84, 1985–86 and 1989–94, ESRC 1995–; foreign memb Finnish Acad of Sciences and Letters 1994; memb Academia Europaea 1995; MEP (SNP) Scot 1999–2004; Hon LLD: Univ of Saarland 1995, Queen's Univ Kingston Ontario 1996, Univ of Macerata 1998, Univ of Glasgow 1999; Juris Dr (hc) Univ of Uppsala 1986; FRSE 1986, FBA 1986; *Books* The Scottish Debate (ed, 1970), Lawyers In Their Social Setting (ed, 1976), Legal Reasoning and Legal Theory (1978), HLA Hart (1981), Legal Right and Social Democracy (1982), An Institutional Theory of Law (with Ota Weinberger, 1986), The Legal Mind (ed with P Birks, 1986), Enlightenment, Rights and Revolution (ed with Z Bankowski, 1989), Interpreting Statutes (ed with R S Summers, 1991), Interpreting Precedents (ed with R

S Summers, 1997), Questioning Sovereignty: Law, State and Nation in the European Commonwealth (1999); *Recreations* piping, hill walking, sailing; *Clubs* SNP (Edinburgh); *Style*— Prof Sir Neil MacCormick, FRSE, FBA, QC; ✉ Old College, South Bridge, Edinburgh EH8 9YL (tel 0131 650 2029, e-mail n.maccormick@ed.ac.uk)

McCORMICK, Peter David Godfrey; OBE (2000); s of Ronald Godfrey McCormick (d 1994), of Leeds, and Paulina, *née* Salzman; *b* 27 June 1952, Leeds; *Educ* Ashville Coll Harrogate, KCL (LLB); *m* 16 May 1981, Kathryn, *née* Gill; 1 s (Guy James Godfrey b 16 Aug 1982), 1 da (Charlotte Alix b 25 Sept 1985); *Career* admitted slr 1976; ptnr Levi and Co 1978–83 (asst slr 1976–78), fndr and sr ptnr McCormicks Slrs 1983–; chairperson Sports Dispute Resolution Panel; memb Legal Working Party FA Premier League; memb Assoc of Regulatory and Disciplinary Lawyers; Yorkshire Lawyer of the Year 2000, Gen Practice and Niche Practice Lawyer of the Year 2000; chm Yorkshire Young Achievers Awards, vice-pres Outward Bound Tst; tstee: War Memls Tst, Helen Feather Meml Tst, Nat Museum of Photography, Film and Television; *Publications* Sports Business (2005); author of numerous articles for legal and business jls and newspapers; *Style*— Peter McCormick, Esq, OBE; ✉ McCormicks, Britannia Chambers, 4 Oxford Place, Leeds LS1 3AX (tel 0113 246 0622, fax 0113 246 7488)

MacCORMICK, Sarah Jane; da of Donald MacCormick, of Kingston upon Thames, Surrey, and Lis Forester, of Chiswick, London; *b* 21 March 1970, Aberdeen; *Educ* Somerville Coll Oxford (BA); *Career* agent Conway van Gelder 1998–2002 (joined 1992), agent Curtis Brown 2002–; *Style*— Ms Sarah MacCormick; ✉ Curtis Brown Group Ltd, Haymarket House, 28–29 Haymarket, London SW1Y 4SP

McCORMICK, Sean Robert; s of late Lt-Col Robert McCormick, of Arundel, W Sussex, and Letitia *née* Worsley; *b* 1 May 1950; *Educ* Alexandra GS Singapore, Chard Sch; *m* 22 Nov 1977, Zandra, da of Frederick William Hollick; 1 s (Liam b 1978), 1 da (Katy b 1984); *Career* Actg Pilot Offr RAF, aircrew trg RAF Henlow; assoc dir/broadcast Leo Burnett 1970–76, Kirkwood & Co advertising 1976–78, media dir and ptnr SJIP advertising 1978–84, dep md BBDO UK (formerly SJIP/BBDO), ptnr and bd account dir Horner Collis & Kirvan 1984, fndr ptnr Juler McCormick West 1987, communications devpt dir Geers Gross plc 1992, exec dir McCann Erickson 1993, dir Total Communications Partnerships Ltd; dir Creative Midfield Ltd; MInstD; *Recreations* motor racing, go karting, rugby, cricket, family life; *Style*— Sean McCormick, Esq; ✉ Windyridge, High Park Avenue, East Horsley, Surrey KT24 5DF

McCORQUODALE, Ian Hamilton; er s of Hugh McCorquodale, MC (d 1963), and Dame Barbara Cartland, DBE (d 2000); half-bro of Raine, Countess Spencer, *qv*; *b* 11 October 1937; *Educ* Harrow, Magdalene Coll Cambridge; *m* 1, 1970 (m dis 1993), Anna, *née* Chisholm; 2 da (Iona b 1971, Tara b 1973); m 2, 2000, Bryony Brind, da of Maj Roger Michael Atchley Brind; *Career* former commercial and export mangr British Printing Corporation; ptnr Cartland Promotions 1976–, chm Debrett's Peerage Ltd 1981–97; *Recreations* fishing, shooting, gardening; *Clubs* Boodle's, White's; *Style*— Ian McCorquodale, Esq; ✉ The Home Farm, Camfield Place, Hatfield, Hertfordshire AL9 6JE (tel 01707 642629, fax 01707 663041)

McCOSH, Prof Andrew Macdonald; s of Rev Andrew McCosh (d 1970), of Dunblane, and Margaret, *née* MacDonald (d 1968); *b* 16 September 1940; *Educ* Edinburgh Acad, Univ of Edinburgh (BSc), Univ of Manchester (MBA), Harvard Univ (DBA), Univ of Glasgow (MTh), Inst of Chartered Accountants (CA); *m* 1965, Anne, da of Nicholas Rogers; 3 da; *Career* assoc prof of accounting Univ of Michigan 1966–71; prof of mgmnt accounting Manchester Business Sch 1971–85, dean Faculty of Business Univ of Manchester 1979–83, prof of the orgn of industry and commerce Univ of Edinburgh 1986–95 (prof emeritus and univ fell in fin 1995–); Alvah Chapman prof of fin and ethics Florida Int Univ Miami 2000–, dir The Pilgrim Mutual Funds NY 1996–2002; MICAS 1963; *Books* Practical Controllership (1973), Management Decision Support Systems (1978), Developing Managerial Information Systems (1983), Organisational Decision Support Systems (1988), Financial Ethics (1999); *Recreations* fishing, climbing, golf; *Clubs* New (Edinburgh); *Style*— Prof Andrew McCosh; ✉ University of Edinburgh, 50 George Square, Edinburgh EH8 9JY (tel 0131 650 3801, fax 0131 668 3053, e-mail a.mccosh@ed.ac.uk)

McCOSS, Dr Angus Murray; s of Leslie Hunter McCoss, of Kingsbarns, Fife, and Alison Gray, *née* Murray; *b* 13 November 1961, Broughty Ferry, Dundee; *Educ* Dundee HS, Univ of Dundee (BSc), Univ of Belfast (PhD); *m* 22 Aug 1984, Karen Anne, *née* James; 1 da (Fiona Ellen b 6 Oct 1988), 2 s (Fergus James b 8 Oct 1990, Calum Angus b 12 May 1993); *Career* Shell: exploration geologist The Netherlands, Syria, China and Oman 1987–98, exploration and prodn mangr Argentina 1998–2000, Brazil regnl business advsr and Americas regnl exploration vice-pres 2000–03, Nigeria exploration gen mangr 2003–06; gen mangr global exploration and exploration dir Tullow Oil plc 2006–; author of articles in Jl of Structural Geology 1986, 1987 and 1988; MInstD 2007; *Recreations* sailing, skiing, sabre; *Clubs* Heraldry Soc of Scotland; *Style*— Dr Angus McCoss; ✉ Tullow Oil plc, 3rd Floor, Building 11, Chiswick Park, 566 Chiswick High Road, London W4 5YS

McCOWAN, Sir David William Cargill; 4 Bt (UK 1934), of Dalwhat, Co Dumfries; s of Sir David James Cargill McCowan, 2 Bt (d 1965); suc bro Sir Hew Cargill McCowan, 3 Bt (d 1998); *b* 28 February 1934; *m*; 1 da (Caroline Elizabeth b 1966), 1 s (David James Cargill b 1975); *Heir* s, David McCowan; *Style*— Sir David McCowan, Bt

McCOY, Anthony Peter (Tony); MBE (2003); s of Paedar McCoy, of NI, and Claire McCoy; *Career* nat hunt jockey; winner: Cheltenham Gold Cup, Champion Hurdle, Queen Mother Champion Chase; 12 times champion Nat Hunt Jockey, Jump Jockey of the Year 1995–2007; ridden over 2000 winners (a record for a Br jump jockey); Hon Dr Queen's Univ Belfast 2002; subject of documentary The Real McCoy 2002; *Publications* McCoy: The Autobiography (2002); *Recreations* football, golf; *Style*— A P McCoy, Esq, MBE; ✉ Lodge Down, Lambourn Woodlands, Hungerford, Berkshire RG17 7BJ (e-mail ap.mccoy@talk21.com)

McCOY, Hugh O'Neill; s of Hugh O'Neill McCoy, and Nora May, *née* Bradley; *b* 9 February 1939; *Educ* Dudley GS, Univ of London; *m* Margaret Daphne, da of Robert John Corfield; *Career* md Horace Clarkson plc, chm H Clarkson & Co Ltd until 1999, chm Baltic Exchange until 2001; dir Benor Tanker Ltd Hamilton Bermuda, past dir Cammel Laird Holding plc; non-exec dir The Hadley Shipping Co, former non-exec dir Gartmore Korea Fund plc; pres Inst of Chartered Shipbrokers 1992–94; specially elected memb Gen Cncl Lloyd's Register of Shipping; hon vice-pres Maritime Vol Serv; former memb: Cncl Mercy Ships, Mgmnt Ctee London Sea Cadets; govr Warley Sch; tstee/dir Brentwood CAB; Freeman City of London, Liveryman Worshipful Co of Shipwrights; FICS; *Clubs* City, Royal Burnham Yacht; *Style*— Hugh O'Neill McCoy, FICS; ✉ 5 Heron Way, Hutton, Brentwood, Essex CM13 2LX

McCRAE, Dr (William) Morrice; s of William Boyd McCrae (d 1982), of Kilmarnock, and Jean Alexandra, *née* Morrice; *b* 11 March 1932; *Educ* Kilmarnock Acad, Univ of Edinburgh (MSc, PhD), Univ of Glasgow (MB ChB); *m* 28 March 1987, Jennifer Jane, da of John Graham (d 1985), of Aberdour, Fife; *Career* Capt RAMC 1955–57; Hall fell in med Univ of Glasgow, lectr in child health Univ of Glasgow, conslt physician Royal Hosp for Sick Children Edinburgh 1965, hon sr lectr Univ of Edinburgh; ret; coll historian RCPEd 2002–; FRCPE, FRCPGlas, FRCPCH; *Publications* The National Health Service in Scotland: Origins and Ideals (2003); also works on genetics and gastroenterology; *Recreations* gardening, history; *Clubs* New (Edinburgh), Scottish Art; *Style*— Dr Morrice McCrae; ✉ Seabank House, Aberdour, Fife KY3 1TY (tel 01383 860452)

McCREA, Rev Dr (Robert Thomas) William; MP, MLA; s of Robert Thomas McCrea, and Sarah Jane, *née* Whann; *b* 6 August 1948; *Educ* Cookstown HS, Theological Hall Free Pres Church of Ulster; *m* 25 June 1971, Anne Shirley, da of George McKnight (d 1983), of Rathfriland, Co Down; 3 da (Sharon b 1973, Faith b 1979, Grace b 1980), 2 s (Ian b 1976, Stephen b 1978); *Career* dist cncllr 1973– (chm 1977–81, chm Cncl 2002–03), memb NI Assembly 1982–86 and 1998–; MP (DUP): Mid Ulster 1983–97, Antrim S 2000–01 and 2005–; dep whip DUP 2003– (whip 1987–), memb DUP Forum 1996–98, vice-chm Central Exec Ctee DUP 2003–; memb NI Assembly Ctee on Procedures 2002–03, chm NI Assembly Environment Ctee 1998–2003; spokesman on: educn 1987–88, health and social servs 1988–90, security 1990–, environment 1998–, rural affrs 2005–, review of pubic administration 2005–; gospel singer and recording artist (1 platinum, 3 gold and 1 silver discs), dir Daybreak Recordings Co; Hon DD 1989; *Recreations* riding; *Style*— The Rev Dr William McCrea, MP, MLA; ✉ DUP Constituency Office, 69 Church Street, Antrim BT41 4BE

McCREE, Andrew Charles Gambon; s of Cyril Gerard Winifred McCree (d 1997), and Sheila, *née* Guthrie (d 1997); *b* 20 August 1957; *Educ* Mount St Mary's Coll, Fort Augustus Abbey Sch, Inst of Technol Glasgow; *m* 16 May 1980, Lesley Margaret, da of Leslie Eric Bromfield; *Career* Army 1975–76; grad trainee BP Oil Glasgow 1976–78; BP Petroleum Devpt: PR asst 1978–83, info offr 1983–84, press and info offr 1984–89; external affrs co-ordinator BP Exploration 1989–90, head of press and public affrs UKAEA 1990–93; AEA Technology: mangr public affrs 1993–94, gen mangr corp communications gp 1994–96, dir corp affrs 1996–97, exec dir corp affrs and HR 2000–02, gp md 2002–, ceo 2005–; *Recreations* current affairs, conservation, sport; *Style*— Andrew McCree, Esq; ✉ AEA Technology plc, 329 Harwell, Didcot, Oxfordshire OX11 0QJ (tel 0870 190 8114, mobile 07968 888800, fax 0870 190 8109, e-mail andrew.mccree@aeat.co.uk)

McCREESH, Paul Dominic; s of Patrick Michael McCreesh, and Valerie Mary Bernadette Connors; *b* 24 May 1960; *Educ* Campion Sch Hornchurch, Univ of Manchester (BMus); *m* 1983, Susan Hemington Jones; 1 s (Samuel Adam b 19 Nov 1989), 1 da (Hannah Frances b 25 Jan 1994); *Career* conductor; fndr Gabrieli Consort & Players (choir and period instrument ensemble) 1982; *Performances* with Gabrieli Consort & Players: BBC Proms, Vienna Konzerthaus, Bergen Festival, Glasgow Mayfest, Lucerne Festival, Cité de la Musique Paris, Bremen Musikfest, Covent Garden Festival, Accademia Santa Cecilia Roma, South Bank Centre, Jerusalem Festival, Polish Radio, Styriate Graz, Palau de la Musica Barcelona, Flanders Festival, Utrecht Festival, Ludwigsbrugher Schlossfestspiele, Handelfestspiele Halle, BBC and City of London Festival, Lincoln Center NY, Concertgebouw Amsterdam, Symphony Hall Birmingham, Théâtre des Champs-Elysées, Théâtre du Châtelet Paris; others incl: Northern Sinfonia, Orch Regionale Toscana Florence, Netherlands Bach Soc, Netherlands Chamber Choir, opera and stage prodns in UK, France, Holland and USA, Handel & Haydn Soc Boston, WNO, Nat Symphony Orch Washington, San Francisco Symphony Orch, Norwegian Nat Opera, Minnesota Orch, Copenhagen Philharmonic, Deutsche Kammerphilharmonie, Orchestre Philharmonique de Radio France, KölnerRundfunk, Orquesta Ciudad de Granada; *Recordings* works by Gabrieli, Monteverdi, Purcell, Praetorius, Palestrina, Josquin, Victoria, Morales, Biber, Handel, Bach; exclusive contract with Deutsche Grammophon Archiv Produktion; *Awards* Edison Award 1991 and 1995, Gramophone Award 1990 and 1993, Deutschen Schallplatten Preis 1994, Diapason d'Or 1994, ABC Record of the Year 1990, Studio Prize Poland 1998, Danish Grammy 1998, John Owens Award Univ of Manchester 2002; *Recreations* children, walking, eating well; *Style*— Paul McCreesh, Esq; ✉ c/o Intermusica Artists Management Ltd, 16 Duncan Terrace, London N1 8BZ

McCRICKARD, Donald Cecil (Don); *b* 25 December 1936; *Career* fin, mktg and gen mgmnt appts until 1975; American Express Co 1975–83: chief exec American Express UK 1975–78, regnl vice-pres American Express N Europe, ME and Africa 1978–79, sr vice-pres American Express Corporate NY 1979–80, chief exec American Express Asia, Pacific and Australia 1980–83, dir American Express International Inc 1978–83; TSB Group plc 1983–92: chief exec UDT Holdings 1983–88, chm UDT Bank 1984–89, chief exec TSB Bank 1989–92, gp chief exec TSB Group 1990–92; chm: Hill Samuel 1991–92, Verdandi Ltd (formerly SGi Ltd) 1998–2006, London Town plc 1995–2003; vice-chm National Counties Building Soc 1995–; non-exec dir: Carlisle Group plc 1993–96, BRIT Holdings plc 1995–2006, Allied London Properties 1997–2000; non-exec chm TM Group Holdings plc 1996–98; chm Barnet Enterprise Tst 1985–88; tstee: Crimestoppers Tst 1991–2004, Indust in Educn 1993–2005; FCIB; *Clubs* RAC; *Style*— Don McCrickard, Esq

McCRONE, Prof (Robert) Gavin Loudon; CB (1982); s of Robert Osborne Orr McCrone (d 1985), and Laura Margaret McCrone (d 1991); *b* 2 February 1933; *Educ* Stowe, St Catharine's Coll Cambridge (MA), UCW Aberystwyth (MSc), Univ of Glasgow (PhD); *m* 1, 27 June 1959, Alexandra Bruce Waddell, MBE (d 1998); 2 s, 1 da; m 2, 7 June 2000, Olive Pettigrew Moon, *née* McNaught; 2 step da; *Career* lectr Univ of Glasgow 1960–65, fell BNC Oxford 1965–70; Scottish Office: joined 1970, sec Industry Dept for Scotland 1980–87, sec Environment Dept 1987–92, chief economic advsr 1972–92; prof Centre for Housing Research Univ of Glasgow 1992–94; Univ of Edinburgh: hon fell Europa Inst 1992–, visiting prof Mgmnt Sch 1994–2005, cmmr Parly Boundary Cmmn for Scotland 1999–2006; memb Advsy Ctee Nuffield/Rowntree Ind Inquiry into Constitutional Reform 1995–97, memb Nat Review of Resource Allocation in the NHS in Scotland 1997–99; chm Ctee of Inquiry into Professional Conditions of Service for Teachers in Scotland 1999–2000, dep chm Royal Soc of Edinburgh Inquiry into Foot and Mouth Disease 2001–02, dep chm Inquiry into the Future of the Scottish Fishing Industry 2003–04, chm Royal Soc Edinburgh Inquiry into the Future of Scotland's Hill and Island Areas 2007–; dep chm: Royal Infirmary of Edinburgh NHS Tst 1994–99, Lothian Univ Hosps NHS Tst 1999–2001; memb Cncl: Royal Economic Soc 1977–82, Scottish Economic Soc 1982–91, ESRC 1986–89; memb Bd: Scottish Opera 1992–98 (tstee Endowment Tst 1999–), Queen's Hall 1999–2002; Royal Soc of Edinburgh: memb Cncl 1986–89 and 1998–2001, vice-pres 2002–05, gen sec 2005–07; Hon LLD Univ of Glasgow 1986; FRSE 1982, Hon FRSGS 1993; *Books* The Economics of Subsidising Agriculture (1962), Scotland's Economic Progress 1951–60 (1965), Regional Policy in Britain (1969), Scotland's Future (1969), Housing Policy in Britain and Europe (with M Stephens, 1995), European Monetary Union and Regional Development (1997); *Recreations* walking, music; *Clubs* New (Edinburgh); *Style*— Prof Gavin McCrone, CB, FRSE; ✉ 11A Lauder Road, Edinburgh EH9 2EN (tel 0131 667 4766)

McCRUDDEN, Prof (John) Christopher; s of Gerard McCrudden, and Theodora McCrudden; *b* 29 January 1952; *Educ* Queen's Univ Belfast (LLB), Yale Univ (LLM), Univ of Oxford (MA, DPhil); *m* 1990, Caroline Mary, *née* Pannell; 1 s, 1 da; *Career* Univ of Oxford: lectr in law Balliol Coll 1976–77, jr res fell Balliol Coll 1976–80, fell Lincoln Coll 1980–, CUF lectr 1980–96, reader in law 1996–99, prof of human rights law 1999–; overseas affiliated prof of law Univ of Michigan Law Sch 1998–; visiting fell and lectr Yale Law Sch 1986, visiting sr fell PSI 1987–89; visiting prof: Queen's Univ Belfast 1994–98, Univ of Texas Sch of Law 1996, Univ of Michigan Law Sch 1996–97; Harkness fell 1974–76; jt ed Law in Context series 1978–; memb Editorial Bd: Oxford Jl of Legal Studies 1983–, Int Jl of Discrimination and the Law 1996–, Jl of Int Econ Law 1998–; expert Network on Application of Equality Directives EC 1986–, specialist advsr NI Affrs Select Ctee 1999; memb: Advsy Ctee ESRC Res Unit on Ethnic Rels 1982–85, Sec of State for NI's Standing Advsy Cmmn on Human Rights 1984–88, Public Procurement Implementation Gp NI Exec 2001, NI Public Procurement Bd 2002–; called to the Bar: Gray's Inn 1996, Inns of Court NI 2006; Hon LLD Queen's Univ Belfast 2006; *Books* Regulation and Public Law

M

(with R Baldwin, 1987), Women, Employment and European Community Law (ed, 1988), Fair Employment Handbook (ed, 1990, 3 edn 1995), Racial Justice at Work: the enforcement of the Race Relations Act 1976 in Employment (jtly, 1991), Equality in the Law between Men and Women in the European Community: United Kingdom (1994), Individual Rights and the Law in Britain (ed with G Chambers, 1994), Equality between Women and Men in Social Security (ed, 1994), Regulation and Deregulation (ed, 1998), Buying Social Justice (2007); *Recreations* my family; *Style—* Prof Christopher McCrudden; ✉ Lincoln College, Oxford OX1 3DR (tel 01865 279772, fax 01865 279802, e-mail christopher.mccrudden@law.ox.ac.uk)

McCRUM, (John) Robert; s of Michael William McCrum (d 2005), of Cambridge, and Christine Mary Kathleen, *née* fforde; *b* 7 July 1953; *Educ* Sherborne, CCC Cambridge (scholar, MA), Univ of Pennsylvania (Thouron fell); *m* 1, 1979 (m dis 1984), Olivia Timbs; m 2, 1995, Sarah Lyall; 2 da (Alice b 2 Feb 1997, Isobel b 5 May 1999); *Career* reader Chatto & Windus 1977–79, ed-in-chief Faber & Faber 1990–96 (editorial dir 1979–89), lit ed The Observer 1996–, lit conslt to the Millennium Dome 1999–2000; patron Different Strokes; bye-fell Churchill Coll Cambridge 2001–03; *Books* In The Secret State (1980), A Loss of Heart (1982), The Fabulous Englishman (1984), The Story of English (non fiction, 1986, Peabody Award 1986, Emmy 1987), The World is a Banana (for children, 1988), Mainland (1991), The Psychological Moment (1992), Suspicion (1996), My Year Off (1998), Wodehouse: A Life (2004); *Style—* Robert McCrum, Esq; ✉ The Observer, 119 Farringdon Road, London EC1R 3ER (tel 020 7713 4603)

McCUE, Ian Roderick; s of John McCue, and Frances Mary, *née* Quantrill; *b* 24 May 1937; *Educ* Gravesend Tech Sch, SE London Tech Coll; *m* 1 April 1961, Stella Kathleen, da of Henry Battle; 1 s (Sean (decd)), 2 da (Jane b 1964, Sara b 1965); *Career* electrical engr; student apprentice Siemen Brothers Ltd 1953–59, co-fndr md Sarasota Automation Ltd 1966; dir: Sarasota Automation Inc USA 1978–90 (also pres), ceo Sarasota Technology plc 1982–88, Peek plc 1987–90; chm McCue plc 1990–; *Recreations* sailing, flying, photography; *Clubs* The Field (Sarasota, Florida), Royal Southern Yacht; *Style—* Ian R McCue, Esq; ✉ Parsonage Barn, Compton, Hampshire SO21 2AS (tel 01962 713049, e-mail irm@mccueplc.com)

McCULLOCH, Dr Andrew; *b* 21 April 1956; *Educ* Eltham Coll, Peterhouse Cambridge (MA), Univ of Southampton (PhD); *Career* Dept of Health: princ Policy Secretariat 1987–89, princ Child, Maternity and Prevention Div 1989–92, asst sec Gen Election Briefing Unit 1992, asst sec Mental Health and Community Care Div 1992–96; princ Andrew McCulloch Assocs 1996–2001, dir of policy The Sainsbury Centre for Mental Health 1996–2002, chief exec Mental Health Fndn 2002–; Haringey Healthcare NHS Trust: memb Audit Ctee 1998–1999, non-exec dir 1998–2001, chair Mental Health Act Managers 1999–2001, chair R&D Ctee 1999–2001 (honorary non-exec 2002); Mental Health Media: memb Cncl (and tstee) 1997–2004, chair 1999–2002; memb: Sub-Gp on Employment NSF Standard 1 Taskforce 2001–2002, Workforce Numbers Advsy Gp 2002–04, Overarching Gp Women's Mental Health Task Force 2002–03, Ministerial Advsy Gp on Vulnerable Children 2004–05; memb: Br Psychological Soc 1980– (memb Comms Bd 1999–2002), MIND Millennium Awards Assessment Panel 1997–1999; winner Mental Health Achievement Awards 2002; govr Lea Valley HS Enfield 1992–95; life memb: Hawk and Owl Tst, Essex Naturalists' Tst; memb: Norfolk Naturalists' Tst, Shakespeare's Globe 1000 Club, Tate Galleries; fell RSPB; *Recreations* birdwatching, tennis, cinema, reading, bridge, travel, classical music, wine, writing; *Style—* Dr Andrew McCulloch; ✉ Mental Health Foundation, 20 Upper Ground, London SE1 9QB (tel 020 7803 1100, fax 020 7803 1111, e-mail amcculloch@mhf.org.uk)

MACCULLOCH, Prof Diarmaid Ninian John; s of Rev Nigel J H MacCulloch, and Jennie, *née* Chappell; *b* 31 October 1951; *Educ* Stowmarket GS, Churchill Coll Cambridge (MA), Univ of Liverpool (Dip Archive Admin), Univ of Cambridge (PhD), Univ of Oxford (DipTh, DD); *Career* jr res fell Churchill Coll Cambridge 1976–78, approved lectr Univ of Cambridge 1977–78; tutor in history, librarian and archivist Wesley Coll Bristol 1978–90, pt/t lectr Univ of Bristol 1978–95, assoc scholar UEA 1984–87, fell St Cross Coll Oxford 1995– (sr tutor 1996–99), prof of the history of the church Univ of Oxford 1997–; pres Historical Assoc Bristol Branch 1994–95, pres Church of England Record Soc 2001–; co-ed Jl of Ecclesiastical History 1995–; res fell Leverhulme Tst 1990–91, Wingate Scholar 1993–95, delivered Birkbeck Lectures Univ of Cambridge lent term 1998; FSA 1978, FRHistS 1982, FBA 2001; *Publications* The Chorography of Suffolk (ed vol 19, 1976), Suffolk and the Tudors: politics and religion in an English County 1500–1600 (1986, RHS Whitfield Prize 1987), The Reign of Henry VIII: Politics, Policy and Piety (ed, 1995), Thomas Cranmer: a Life (1996, Whitbread Biography Prize 1986, Duff Cooper Prize 1996, James Tait Black Meml Prize 1996), Tudor Church Militant: Edward VI and the Protestant Reformation (1999), Reformation: Europe's House Divided 1490–1700 (2003, Wolfson History Prize 2004, British Acad Prize 2004, Nat Book Critics Circle of the US Award for Non-Fiction 2005); author of numerous books, articles and textbooks on history, topography and archaeology, and theology and the Church; *Style—* Prof Diarmaid MacCulloch; ✉ Faculty of Theology, 41 St Giles, Oxford OX1 3LW (e-mail diarmaid.macculloch@stx.ox.ac.uk)

McCULLOCH, Ian; s of William Baxter McCulloch (d 1940), of Glasgow, and Elizabeth Harper (d 2001); *b* 4 March 1935; *Educ* Eastbank Acad Glasgow, Glasgow Sch of Art (DA); *m* 1959, Margery, da of James Palmer; 2 s (Neil b 1969, Euan b 1970); *Career* fine art fell Univ of Strathclyde 1994– (lectr in fine art 1967–94), artist in residence Univ of Sussex 1976; SSA 1964, RSA 2005 (ARSA 1989); *Solo Exhibitions* incl: Artspace Galleries Aberdeen 1984, Camden Arts Centre 1986, Richard Demarco Gallery Edinburgh and tour 1986, Odette Gilbert Gallery London and tour 1987, Glasgow Print Studio 1989, The Return of Agamemnon and Other Paintings Aberystwyth Arts Centre, UC Wales Aberystwyth 1991, Aberdeen Art Gallery 1991–92, Relief Prints Peacock Printmakers Aberdeen 1994 (also tour), Recycled Lives: Paintings, Prints, Ceramics and Constructions 1997–2007 (Royal Scottish Acad Edinburgh) 2007; *Group Exhibitions* incl: Twentieth Century Scottish Painting (Arts Cncl of GB tour) 1963–64, Scottish Painters (Scottish Nat Gallery of Modern Art) 1964, Three Centuries of Scottish Painting (Nat Gallery of Canada Ottawa) 1968–69, New Tendencies in Scottish Painting (Demarco Gallery Edinburgh) 1969, Art Spectrum (Scottish Arts Cncl) 1971, Painters in Parallel (Scottish Arts Cncl) 1978, Stirling Smith Biennial 1985, Warwick Arts Tst (London) 1985, Reed Stremmel Gallery (San Antonia Texas) 1986, Chicago, LA and London Art Fairs 1986–88, Graven Image: Art, Religion and Politics (Harris Art Gallery Preston) 1988, Glasgow Printmakers (Berlin) 1988, John Moores Liverpool Exhbn 1989–90, New North (Tate Gallery Liverpool then tour) 1990, Unique and Original (Glasgow Print Studio then tour) 1992, Alter Ego/Self Portrait (Glasgow Print Studio then tour) 1992, Scottish Painting (Flower East Gallery London) 1993, Calanais (An Lanntair Gallery Stornoway and tour) 1995, Scottish Printmaking (Galerie Beeldspraak Amsterdam) 1995, Peacock 21 (Aberdeen Art Gallery) 1996, Day of the Dead (Galeria Otra Vez LA) 1996, Small is Beautiful (Flowers East Gallery London) 1996, Brave Art (Smith Art Gallery Stirling) 1996, Modern Scottish Graphics (Galerija Loskega Muzeja, Skofja Loka, Slovenia and tour) 1997, Scottish Spirit (Arthur Ross Gallery Univ of Pennsylvania and tour) 1998, Celtic Connections (Yorozu Tetsugoro Museum Japan) 1998, Scottish Painting (Albermarle Gallery London) 1999, On a Plate (Glasgow Print Studio) 1999, Liberation and Tradition: Scottish Art 1963–74 (Aberdeen Art Gallery and McManus Galleries, Dundee) 1999, Silver (Peacock Printmakers, Aberdeen) 1999, Connections (Royal Scottish Acad Edinburgh) 1999, Expressions: Scottish Art 1975–1989 (Aberdeen Art Gallery and McManus Galleries, Dundee, Dundee Contemporary Arts) 2000, Connections 2000 (Royal Scottish Acad, Edinburgh) 2000, The Dark Figure (Docherty Gallery Univ of NSW Sydney) 2001, Leabhar Mòr Book Exhibition and Tour (Stornoway Isle of Lewis) 2002–2003, Sons and Mothers Exhibition (Collins Gallery Univ of Strathclyde) 2003, Pittenweem Festival Exhibition 2004; *Work in Public Collections* City Art Gallery Edinburgh, Univ of Glasgow, Univ of Liverpool, Univ of Strathclyde, Perth Town Cncl, Contemporary Arts Soc, Kelvingrove Art Gallery Glasgow, Dundee Art Gallery, Saatchi Collection London, Smith Art Gallery Stirling, Lillie Art Gallery Milngavie, Royal Scottish Acad Colls, Pallant House Gallery Chichester, murals cmmnd by Italian Centre Glasgow; *Awards* RSA travelling scholarship 1957–58, Scottish Arts Cncl Awards 1967 and 1972, first prize Stirling Smith Biennial 1985, winner Glasgow Int Concert Hall Mural Competition 1989–90, Gillies Award RSA 1999, Hope Scott Tst Award 2001; *Publications* The Artist In His World, Prints 1986–97, with Eight Descriptive Poems by Alasdair Gray (1998), Images to Poems by Derick Thomson (2005); *Style—* Ian McCulloch, Esq; ✉ School of Architecture, University of Strathclyde, 131 Rotten Row, Glasgow G4 0NG (tel 0141 548 3023, fax 0141 552 3997, e-mail imccstudio@waitrose.com, website www.s-s-a.org/ianmccullochportfolio)

McCULLOCH, James Russell; s of Dr John McCulloch (decd), of Newlands, Glasgow, and Laura Patricia, *née* Russell; *b* 19 November 1954; *Educ* Glasgow Acad, Univ of Stirling (BA); *m* 16 Oct 1980, Sally Lindsay, da of Benjamin Butters; 3 da (Lindsay Anne b 17 July 1984, Victoria Jayne b 6 June 1986, Caroline Fiona b 12 April 1989); *Career* CA; articled clerk Coopers & Lybrand Glasgow 1976–79, audit mangr Coopers & Lybrand Houston Texas USA 1979–82, ptnr Speirs & Jeffrey 1985– (joined 1982, managing ptnr 2001–03, exec chm 2003–); memb Stock Exchange 1985; memb Merchant House of Glasgow 1990; MICAS 1979, FSI; *Recreations* golf, tennis, skiing; *Clubs* Glasgow Academical, Pollok Golf, Prestwick Golf, Elie Golf; *Style—* James R McCulloch, Esq; ✉ 2 Cypress Grove, Bridge of Weir, Renfrewshire PA11 3NJ (tel 01505 610547, e-mail jrm@speirsjeffrey.co.uk)

McCULLOCH, Ken; s of Archie McCulloch, of Glasgow, and Kathleen McCulloch; *b* 7 November 1948; *Educ* Gresham's; *Career* hotelier; mgmnt trg British Transport Hotels 1965–69, mgmnt Stakis Hotels 1969–74, dir Chardon Hotels 1974–76; proprietor: Le Provencal Glasgow 1976–, Charlie Parker's Glasgow 1976– and Edinburgh 1979–, Buttery Glasgow 1983–, Rogano Glasgow 1984–, One Devonshire Gardens 1986–, Malmaison 1994–98, Columbus Hotels 2001–; visiting prof Univ of Strathclyde Business Sch; Mktg Award (British Airways) BBC Scotland 1991, Best Hotel in Scotland (Book of the Best) 1992, County Restaurant of the Year (Good Food Guide) 1992 and 1993, UK Hotelier of the Year 1993, Egon Ronay Hotel of the Year 1994, Michelin Star 1996, Good Food Guide County Hotel of the Year 1997 (for Malmaison), Outstanding Achievement Award European Hotel Design Awards 2002; *Recreations* connoisseur of Scotland, cooking, Glasgow Rangers, motor racing; *Style—* Ken McCulloch, Esq

MacCULLOCH, Prof Malcolm John; s of William MacCulloch (d 1976), of Macclesfield, Cheshire, and Constance Martha, *née* Clegg; *b* 10 July 1936; *Educ* Kings Sch Macclesfield, Univ of Manchester (MB ChB, DPM, MD); *m* 1, 14 July 1962 (m dis 1975), Mary Louise, da of Ernest Sutcliffe Beton (d 1987), of Norwich, Norfolk; 1 s (Thomas Alistair b 1965), 1 da (Louise Elizabeth Mary b 1968); m 2, 24 Sept 1975, Carolyn Mary, da of Sqdn Ldr (William) Alan Walker Reid, of London; 2 da (Sarah Caroline b 1976, Sophie Isabel 1978); *Career* conslt child psychiatrist Cheshire 1966–67, lectr in child psychiatry and subnormality Univ of Birmingham 1967–70, sr lectr in psychiatry Univ of Liverpool 1970–75, sr princ med offr DHSS London 1975–79, med dir Park Lane Hosp Liverpool 1979–89, conslt WHO 1977–79, visiting prof of forensic psychiatry Toronto 1987–89, advsr in forensic psychiatry Ontario Govt 1987–92, emeritus prof of forensic psychiatry Univ of Wales Coll of Med Cardiff 2001– (prof of forensic psychiatry 1997–2001); ed Jl of Forensic Psychiatry and Psychology 2007– (ed-in-chief 2002–07), author of numerous pubns in professional jls; FRCPsych 1976; *Books* Homosexual Behaviour: Therapy and Assessment (1971), Human Sexual Behaviour (1980); *Recreations* music, golf, horse riding, inventing; *Style—* Professor Malcolm MacCulloch; ✉ 14 Tall Trees, Baunton Lane, Cirencester GL7 2AF (tel 01285 642689)

McCULLOCH, Rt Rev Nigel Simeon; *see:* Manchester, Bishop of

McCULLOUGH, Sir (Iain) Charles Robert; kt (1981); *b* 1931; *m* 1965, Margaret Joyce Patey; 1 s, 1 da; *Career* called to the Bar 1956, QC 1971, dep chm Notts Quarter Sessions 1969–71, recorder of the Crown Court 1971–81, judge of the High Court of Justice (Queen's Bench Div) 1981–98, surveillance cmmr 1998–, treas Middle Temple 2000; memb: Criminal Law Revision Ctee 1973–, Parole Bd 1984–86; visitor Loughborough Univ 2003–; *Clubs* Garrick, Pilgrims; *Style—* Sir Charles McCullough; ✉ OSC, PO Box 29105, London SW1V 1ZU

McCULLOUGH, Dr John; s of Henry Christie McCullough (d 2007), and Jessie, *née* Niven (d 1978); *b* 23 March 1949; *Educ* Model Sch Belfast, Paisley Coll of Technol, Portsmouth Poly (MSc, PhD); *m* 25 March 1971, Geraldine Mabel, da of Gerald Thomas Gardner (d 2002); 2 da (Katherine b 1979, Eleanor b 1985), 1 s (Alexander b 1982); *Career* conslt engr (various appts in NI, England and Scot), expert witness in cases of litigation, arbitration and public inquiry in Scot, England and abroad, expert determination in Eastern Europe; ptnr Hancox & Partners 1982–88; dir: Rendel Hancox Ltd 1988–91, Rendel Palmer & Tritton (Scot) Ltd 1991–97; chm Cadogan Conslts 2000– (princ 1992–97, md 1997–2000), dir Cadogan Tietz 1999–2001 (conslt 2001–04); chm Scot Region Inst of Energy 1984–85; Freeman City of London, Liveryman Worshipful Co of Engrs; CEng 1980, FEI 1983, FIMechE 1986, Eur Ing 1988, MAE; *Recreations* music, cycling, reading, walking; *Clubs* Royal Over-Seas League; *Style—* Dr John McCullough; ✉ Southpark, Kilmacolm, Renfrewshire PA13 4NN (tel 01505 872895); Cadogan Consultants, 39 Cadogan Street, Glasgow G2 7AB (tel 0141 270 7060, fax 0141 270 7061, mobile 07712 199356, e-mail j.mccullough@cadoganconsultants.co.uk)

McCUTCHEON, Prof John Joseph; CBE (1994); s of James Thomson McCutcheon (d 1964), and Margaret, *née* Hutchison (d 1984); *b* 10 September 1940; *Educ* Glasgow Acad, St John's Coll Cambridge (scholar, MA, Wright's prize), Univ of Liverpool (PhD, DSc); *m* 1978, Jean Sylvia, *née* Constable; *Career* actuarial student Scottish Amicable Life Assurance Soc 1962–65, conslt actuary Duncan C Fraser & Co 1965–66, demonstrator/sr demonstrator Dept of Pure Mathematics Univ of Liverpool 1966–70, assoc prof Dept of Actuarial and Business Mathematics Univ of Manitoba 1970–72; Heriot-Watt Univ: sr lectr 1972–75, prof of actuarial studies 1975–2001 (emeritus 2001–), dean Faculty of Science 1995–98; FFA 1965 (pres 1992–94), FRSE 1993; *Publications* An Introduction to the Mathematics of Finance (with W F Scott, 1986); author of papers in mathematics, actuarial science and mortality studies; *Recreations* reading, opera, tennis, skiing, travel; *Clubs* Colinton Lawn Tennis, Woodcutters' Cricket; *Style—* Prof John McCutcheon, CBE, FRSE; ✉ 14 Oswald Court, Edinburgh EH9 2HY

McDERMID, Prof John Alexander; s of John Alexander McDermid (d 1997), and Joyce Winifred, *née* Whiteley (d 1969); *b* 5 October 1952; *Educ* High Heaton GS, Univ of Cambridge (MA), Univ of Birmingham (PhD); *m* 29 March 1980, Heather Mair, *née* Denly; 2 da (Ailsa Gaynor b 26 Nov 1985, Catriona Isabel b 14 May 1993); *Career* student engr and research scientist MOD 1971–82, conslt then divnl mangr Systems Designers (now EDS) 1982–87, prof of software engrg Univ of York 1987–; dir Origin Consulting 2003, non-exec dir: High Integrity Solutions 2002, York PRT 2004; author of six books and approximately 300 conf papers and jl articles; IEE Heaviside Premium 1982, BCS IT Award 1993; govr Pocklington Sch 1997–2004; Freeman City of London 2002, Liveryman

Worshipful Co of Engrs 2002; FIEE 1975, FBCS 1982, FRAeS 1997, FREng 2002; *Recreations* reading, music, badminton, walking; *Style*— Prof John McDermid; ✉ Department of Computer Science, University of York, Heslington, York YO10 5DD (tel 01904 432726, fax 01904 432708, mobile 07802 234814, e-mail john.mcdermid@cs.york.ac.uk)

MacDERMOT, Brian Hugh; s of Francis Charles MacDermot (d 1975), of Paris, and Elaine Orr MacDermot (d 1974); *b* 2 December 1930; *Educ* Downside, New Coll Oxford (MA); *m* 23 March 1985, Georgina Maria, da of Dayrell Gallwey (d 1996), of Tramore, Co Waterford; 1 s (Thomas Patrick b 16 March 1986), 1 da (Elaine Francesca b 19 Nov 1987); *Career* Lt Irish Guards 1952–55; memb Stock Exchange 1959–90, ptnr Panmure Gordon and Co 1964–76, currently registered rep NCL Smith & Williamson, chm Mathaf Gallery Ltd; numerous contribs to jls; formerly: chm and tstee St Gregory Charitable Tst, vice-pres RAI, memb Cncl RGS; Hon Asst Worshipful Company of Bowyers (Master 1984–86); FRGS, FRAI; *Books* Cult of the Sacred Spear (1972); *Recreations* squash, tennis; *Clubs* Brooks's; *Style*— Brian MacDermot, Esq; ✉ Clock House, Rutland Gate, London SW7 1PB; Mathaf Gallery Ltd, 24 Motcomb Street, London SW1X 8JU

MacDERMOTT, Alasdair Tormod; s of Norman MacDermott (d 1977), and Mary, *née* Robertson (d 2003); *b* 17 September 1945; *Educ* Univ Coll Sch Hampstead, SOAS Univ of London, Br Embassy Language Sch Kamakura, Heidelberg Univ, London Business Sch, Ashridge Mgmnt Coll; *m* 1994, Gudrun; 2 da from previous m (Lucy, Fabia); *Career* diplomat; FCO assignments Afghanistan, Ghana, Togoland, St Lucia and Vietnam, political offr Colombo 1983–86, press offr Tokyo 1986–91, first sec FCO 1992–95, commercial sec Ankara 1996–98, first sec and head of section Africa Dept (Southern) FCO 1998–2001, high cmmr to Namibia 2002–07; chieftain St Andrew Soc of Yokohama and Tokyo 1990; memb: Royal Soc for Asian Affrs, Royal African Soc; *Recreations* reading, travel, Constantinople, Maigret, wood carving; *Clubs* Royal Commonwealth Soc, Royal Over-Seas League, Hill (Sri Lanka), Ceylon Sea Anglers (Sri Lanka); *Style*— Mr Alasdair MacDermott; ✉ British High Commission, PO Box 22202, Windhoek, Namibia (tel 00 264 61 274800)

McDERMOTT, Christopher James; s of Michael McDermott, of Bodmin, Cornwall, and Christopha Veronica, *née* Birch; *b* 2 November 1959; *Educ* Royal GS High Wycombe, Christ's Coll Cambridge (open exhibitioner, MA); *m* 23 Aug 1995, Isobel Jane, da of David Hitchcock-Spencer, of London; *Career* exploration asst Amoco Europe & West Africa 1984–85, account exec ABS Communications 1986–87, gp head Reginald Watts Associates 1987–90; dir: Ruder Finn UK 1990–94, Shandwick Communications 1994–97, Shandwick Consultants 1997–99; mktg dir EMEA/UK KPMG Consulting 1999–2003, mktg dir Coller Capital 2003–; FCIM (2005, MCIM 1996); *Recreations* literature, travel, diving, skiing; *Clubs* Three Per Cent; *Style*— Christopher McDermott, Esq; ✉ 36 Lamb's Conduit Street, London WC1N 3LD (tel 020 7404 3915)

McDERMOTT, Gerard Francis; QC (1999); s of Joseph Herbert McDermott, of Ashton-under-Lyne, and Winifred Mary, *née* Limon; *b* 21 April 1956; *Educ* De La Salle Coll Salford, Univ of Manchester (LLB), Coll of Law; *m* July 1996, Fiona, *née* Johnson, da of David Johnson, and Kay Johnson; *Career* called to the Bar Middle Temple 1978 (bencher 2005); recorder 1999–; attorney-at-law (NY) 1990, dir American Counsel Assoc 1998– (pres 2003–04); chm Young Barristers Ctee 1987, memb Gen Cncl of the Bar 1983–88, 1990–96, 1998–99 and 2003– (chm Int Rels Ctee 1999–2000), ldr European Circuit of the Bar 2006–08 (dep ldr 2003–05); *Clubs* Athenaeum; *Style*— Gerard McDermott, QC; ✉ 8 King Street Chambers, 8 King Street, Manchester M2 6AQ (tel 0161 834 9560, fax 0161 834 2733, e-mail gerard.mcdermott@8ks.co.uk); Outer Temple Chambers, 222 Strand, London WC2R 1BA (tel 020 7353 6381, fax 020 7583 1786, gerard.mcdermottqc@outertemple.com)

McDERMOTT, Jennifer; da of S K Harding, and E Harding, *née* Donkin; *b* 11 January 1957, Sunderland; *Educ* UCL (LLB); *Children* 1 s (Patrick Benedict), 1 da (Helen Frances); *Career* slr; Lovells (formerly Lovell White & King): articled clerk 1979–81, litigation assoc 1981–89, litigation ptnr 1989–2004; contentious ptnr specialising in media and public law Addleshaw Goddard 2004–; chair Exec Bd JUSTICE; *Style*— Mrs Jennifer McDermott; ✉ Addleshaw Goddard, 150 Aldersgate Street, London EC1A 4EJ (tel 020 7880 5922, fax 020 7606 4390, e-mail jennifer.mcdermott@addleshawgoddard.com)

McDERMOTT, Phelim Joseph; s of Edward William McDermott, and Stella Donovan; *Educ* Manchester Grammar, Middlesex Poly (BA); *Career* theatre dir and actor; co-fndr (with Julia Bardsley) and artistic dir dereck, dereck Prodns, shows incl Cupboard Man (performer, Fringe First Award), Gaudete (co-dir and performer, Time Out Dir's Award), The Vinegar Works, The Glass Hill and The Sweet Shop Owner (all dir); co-fndr (with Julian Crouch and Lee Simpson) and co-artistic dir Improbable 1996–, shows incl 70 Hill Lane (Time Out Best Fringe Show, Obie Award), Animo, Spirit, Cinderella, The Hanging Man, Theatre of Blood (NT) and Satyagraha (ENO) (all dir) and Shockheaded Peter (co-dir, Olivier Award for Best Entertainment, TMA Best Dir Award, South Bank Show Theatre Award nomination); other shows directed incl: The Ghost Downstairs (Leicester Haymarket), Dr Faustus and Improbable Tales (both Nottingham Playhouse), A Midsummer Night's Dream (English Shakespeare Co, TMA Best Touring Show Award), The Servant of Two Masters, The Hunchback of Notre Dame and The Government Inspector (all West Yorkshire Playhouse), Satyagraha (Met Opera); currently developing The Addams Family for Broadway with Elephant Eye Prodns; memb: Bd Actors Centre, Faculty of the Michael Checkov Assoc, Bd Open Space Inst US; guest performer Comedy Store Players; involved with annual Devoted and Disgruntled event Open Space Facilitator; Hon Doctorate Univ of Middlesex 2007; NESTA fell (researching improvisation and conflict resolution) ACE Cultural Leadership Prog 2006; *Recreations* shamanism, newspaper animation, improvisation; *Clubs* Blacks, The Hospital; *Style*— Mr Phelim McDermott; ✉ Improbable, 4th Floor, 43 Aldwych, London WC2B 4DN (tel 020 7240 4556, e-mail phelim@improbable.co.uk)

McDEVITT, Caroline Mary Margaret; da of John Peter Paul McDevitt, of Dublin, and Elizabeth-Anne, *née* Maher; *b* 6 January 1955; *Educ* St Victoire's Convent, St Martin's Sch of Art; *m* 1975 (m dis 1981), Richard Charles Burn Lyall, s of Richard Burn Lyall; *Career* draughtswoman on trg manuals for nuclear power station engrs CEGB 1975–77, statistician's asst MOD 1977–78, sales asst Trident Television 1978–79, sales exec Westward Television 1979–81, sales exec rising to head of sales Grampian Television 1981–89 (joined at start of franchise), sales controller TVMM Saleshouse 1990–92, bd dir Westcountry Television 1992–97 (from start of franchise), chief exec Broadcasters Audience Research Bd (BARB) 1998–2003; memb various ITV Ctees 1991–; memb: Women's Advtg Club of London, RTS, Mktg Soc; *Recreations* golf, shooting, fishing, entertaining, theatre, ballet; *Clubs* Reform; *Style*— Ms Caroline McDevitt

MacDONAGH, Lesley Anne; da of Arthur George Payne, and Agnes Dowie, *née* Scott; *b* 19 April 1952; *Educ* Queen Elizabeth I Sch Wimborne, Coll of Law Guildford and London; *m* 1, 1975 (m dis 1985), John Belton; 1 da; *m* 2, 1987, Simon Michael Peter MacDonagh; 3 s; *Career* admitted slr 1976; ptnr Lovells (formerly Lovell White Durrant) 1981–2006 (managing ptnr 1995–2005); non-exec dir: Bovis Homes Gp 2003–, Slough Estates plc 2007–; Law Soc: memb Planning and Environmental Ctee 1988–95, memb Cncl 1992–2001, memb Policy Ctee 1996–99, memb Audit Ctee 1999–2001; memb: Consultative Ctee Lands Tbnl 1991–95, Property Advsy Gp 1993–96; tstee Citizenship Fndn 1991–98, vice-chm Environmental Ctee Knightsbridge Assoc 1991–98; govr LSE until 2007; Liveryman Worshipful Co of Solicitors (memb Ct of Assts 1996–2006); *Recreations* family life, painting and drawing; *Style*— Mrs Lesley MacDonagh

McDONAGH, Siobhain; MP; *b* 20 February 1960; *Educ* Univ of Essex (BA); *Career* former housing devpt mangr Battersea Churches Housing Trust, MP (Lab) Mitcham and Morden 1997–; memb Social Security Select Ctee 1997–; *Recreations* music, reading, cooking; *Style*— Ms Siobhain McDonagh, MP; ✉ House of Commons, London SW1A 0AA (tel 020 7219 4678)

MACDONALD, Angus David; s of Surgn Capt Iain Macdonald, CBE (d 1976), of Strathtay, Perthshire, and Molly, *née* Barber (d 1983); *b* 9 October 1950; *Educ* Portsmouth GS, Jesus Coll Cambridge (MA), Univ of Edinburgh (BEd); *m* 10 April 1976, Isabelle Marjory, da of Maj John Ross, of Connel; 2 da (Mairi Catriona b 1982, Eilidh Iona b 1984); *Career* asst teacher Alloa Acad 1972–73, asst teacher Edinburgh Acad 1973–82, asst teacher King's Sch Paramatta NSW 1978–79, dep princ George Watson's Coll 1982–86 (head of geography 1982), headmaster Lomond Sch 1986–; chm Clan Donald Lands Tst; *Recreations* outdoor recreation, piping, sport, gardening; *Style*— Angus Macdonald, Esq; ✉ Ashmount, 8 Millig Street, Helensburgh, Argyll & Bute (tel 01436 679204); Lomond School, 10 Stafford Street, Helensburgh, Argyll & Bute (tel 01436 672476, e-mail admin@lomond-school.demon.co.uk)

McDONALD, Antony Rycroft; s of Alexander McDonald, of Weston-super-Mare, and Cicely Elaine, *née* Hartley; *b* 11 September 1950; *Educ* Monkton Coombe Sch, Central Sch of Speech and Drama, Manchester Poly Sch of Theatre, Univ of Manchester; *Career* theatre designer and director; asst dir The Community and Schs; Co of The Welsh Nat Opera and Drama Co 1974–76; RDI 2004 *Theatre* incl: Let's Make an Opera (Welsh Nat Opera) 1978, Jessonda (Oxford Univ Opera Soc) 1980, War Crimes (ICA) 1981, Degas (Ian Spink Dance Group and Channel 4) 1981, Dances from the Kingdom of the Pagodas (Royal Danish Ballet) 1982, Secret Gardens (Mickery Theatre Amsterdam) 1982, Insignificance (Royal Court) 1982, Mrs Gauguin, Hedda Gabler (Almeida) 1984, Tom and Viv (Royal Court) 1984 (also at Public Theatre NY 1985), Orlando (Scottish Opera) 1985, Midsummer Marriage (Opera North), Bösendorfer Waltzes (Second Stride, Munich New Dance Festival) 1986, Dancelines (Channel 4) 1986, A Streetcar Named Desire (Crucible Sheffield) 1987, The Trojans (WNO, Opera North and Scottish Opera) 1987, Billy Budd (ENO) 1988, Hamlet (RSC) 1988, Mary Stuart (Greenwich) 1988, Heaven Ablaze in his Breast (Second Stride), As You Like It (Old Vic) 1989, Beatrice and Benedict (ENO) 1990, Berenice (RNT) 1990, Mad Forest (Royal Court and NT Bucharest) 1990, Richard II (RSC) 1990, Benvenuto Cellini (Netherlands Opera) 1991, Lives of the Great Poisoners (Second Stride) 1991, Hamlet (American Repertory Theatre Cambridge MA) 1991, Marriage of Figaro (Aust Opera) 1992, The Seagull (American Rep Theatre Cambridge MA) 1992, Touch Your Coolness to My Fevered Brow (Dutch Nat Ballet) 1992, Euridice (Musica Nel Chiostro Italy) 1992, Why Things Happen (Second Stride) 1992, Orlando (Aix-en-Provence Festival) 1993, Wallenstein (RSC) 1993, Escape at Sea (Second Stride) 1993, Cherubin (Royal Opera House) 1994, Fearful Symmetries (Royal Ballet) 1994, Francesca Da Rimini (Bregenz Festival) 1994, Pelleas and Melisande (Opera North) 1995, Nabucco (WNO) 1995, Ebony Concerto (Royal Ballet), Nabucco (ROH) 1996, Pelleas and Melisande (Minnesota Opera) 1996, Orlando (Brooklyn Acad of Music) 1996, Now Langorous - Now Wild (Royal Ballet) 1996, Ariadne auf Naxos (Bavarian State Opera) 1996, A Midsummer Night's Dream (Metropolitan Opera NY) 1996, The Country Wife (Glasgow Citizens) 1997, Cheating, Lying Stealing (Scottish Ballet) 2003, Private Lives (Glasgow Citizens) 2003, The Tragedy of Fashion (Ballet Rambert) 2004; dir/designer: The Birthday Party (Glasgow Citizen's), Black Snow (American Rep Theatre Cambridge MA) 1992, Samson and Dalila (Scottish Opera) 1997, Jenufa (Netherlands Opera) 1997, Snatched by the Gods/Broken Strings (Scottish Opera) 1998, Beatrice and Benedict (Santa Fe Opera) 1998, The Makropulos Case 1998, Cheating, Lying, Stealing (Royal Ballet) 1998, Der Zwerg and L'Enfant et Les Sortileges (Paris Opera) 1998, Endgame (Nottingham Playhouse) 1999, Aida (Scottish Opera) 1999, Ballo In Maschera (Bregentz Festival) 2000, Hidden Variables (Royal Ballet) 2000, The Merry Widow (Metropolitan Opera) 2000, Pélleas and Mélisande (ENO) 2000, Jenufa (Lyric Opera Chicago) 2000, Beatrice and Benedict (Netherlands Opera) 2001, La Bohème (Bregenz Festival) 2001, Dido and Aeneas/Acis and Galatea (Bavarian State Opera) 2001, Manouvre (ENB) 2002, Julietta (Paris Opera) 2002, King Priam (Nat Reisopera Holland) 2003, Nathan The Wise (Minerva Theatre Chichester) 2003, The Nut Cracker (Scottish Ballet) 2003, Aida (Scottish Opera) 2003, Private Lives (designer, Glasgow Citizen's Theatre) 2003, Wonderful Town (Grange Park Opera) 2004, Beatrice and Benedict (Santa Fe Opera) 2004, Pélleas and Mélisande (Bavarian State Opera) 2004, One Touch for Venus (set designer, Opera North) 2004, The Knot Garden (dir and designer, Scottish Opera) 2005, Manon Lescaut (designer, Vienna State Opera) 2005, Cinderella (designer, Scottish Ballet) 2005, The Cunning Little Vixen (designer, Netherlands Opera) 2006, Eugene Onegin (designer, ROH) 2006, Marion (dir and designer, Nat Reisopera Holland), Eugene Onegin (Finnish Opera); *Style*— Antony McDonald, Esq, RDI; ✉ Loesje Sanders, 1 North Hill, Pound Square, Woodbridge, Suffolk IP12 1HH (tel 01394 385260, fax 01394 388734, e-mail antnymcdon@aol.com)

MACDONALD, His Hon Judge Charles Adam; QC (1992); s of Alasdair Cameron Macdonald, of Glasgow, and Jessie Catherine, *née* McCrow; *b* 31 August 1949; *Educ* Glasgow Acad, New Coll Oxford (MA), Cncl of Legal Educn; *m* 17 June 1978, Dinah Jane, da of Ronald Manns, of Wargrave, Berks; 3 da (Kate, Anna, Elspeth); *Career* called to the Bar Lincoln's Inn 1972; practised in maritime and commercial law, recorder 1999–2005 (asst recorder 1996–99), circuit judge (SE Circuit) 2005–; Lloyd's salvage arbitrator 2000; *Recreations* owns and breeds sport horses; *Style*— His Hon Judge Macdonald, QC; ✉ Maidstone Combined Court, Barker Road, Maidstone, Kent ME16 8EQ

MACDONALD, Chris; s of John Macdonald, of Oxford, and Cynthia, *née* Batts; *b* 13 March 1967, Oxford; *Educ* St Edward's Sch Oxford, Instituto Britannico de Firenze (Dip), Univ of Kent at Canterbury (BA); *m* 6 May 1995, Sarah, *née* Whitmore; 2 da (Georgina b 14 June 1996, Isadora b 15 May 2003), 1 s (Max b 31 Dec 1998); *Career* grad trainee DMB&B 1990–93, account dir and dir Lowe Howard-Spink 1993–97, head of account mgmnt Publicis London 1997–2000, managing ptnr RKCR/Y&R 2000–04, md McCann Erickson 2005–; memb: IPA, Mktg Soc; various industry awards incl IPA Effectiveness, Campaign Press and Poster awards and Cannes Silver; *Recreations* tennis; *Style*— Chris Macdonald, Esq; ✉ McCann Erickson, 7–11 Herbrand Street, London WC1N 1EX (tel 020 7961 2115, e-mail chris.macdonald@europe.mccann.com)

MacDONALD, Dr (Isabelle Wilma) Claire; da of William Garland (d 1972), of Glasgow, and Barbara Sutherland, *née* MacDonald; *b* 6 February 1951; *Educ* Hutchesons Girls GS, Univ of Glasgow (BSc, MB ChB); *m* 28 April 1977, David John MacDonald, s of Alastair J MacDonald (d 1991), of Glasgow; 2 da (Jennifer b 21 Aug 1979, Elizabeth b 6 Dec 1982), 1 s (Alastair b 31 July 1991); *Career* Victoria Infirmary Glasgow: house offr in surgery 1975–76, registrar in pathology 1977–79, sr registrar 1979–81; house offr in medicine Stirling Royal Hosp 1976, sr house offr in pathology Western Infirmary Glasgow 1976–77, lectr in pathology Univ of Aberdeen 1981–84; Pontefract Gen Infirmary: conslt histopathologist 1984–, chm Div of Pathology 1989–92, dir Functional Unit of Pathology 1992–99, dir Clinical Service Unit & Pathology Pinderfields & Pontefract NHS Tst 1999–2005, dir Pathology Mid Yorks NHS Tst 2005–; FRCPath 1994 (MRCPath 1982); *Recreations* swimming, reading; *Clubs* Caledonian Soc, Con; *Style*— Dr Claire MacDonald; ✉ Pathology Department, Pontefract General Infirmary, Pontefract, West Yorkshire WF8 1PL (tel 01977 600600)

M

McDONALD, Desmond; s of Thomas McDonald, of Ilford, and Briget, *née* Hackett; *b* 5 September 1965; *Educ* Canon Parlmer Secy Mod, Westminster Coll; *m* 15 June 1991, Diane Hilary, da of John Selner; 1 da (Emily); *Career* chef; commis chef Sheraton Park Tower Hotel, chef de partie Ritz Hotel, head chef Mr Garraway's Fish House, head chef The Ivy; Caprice Holdings: exec chef, currently md (signature restaurants incl: The Ivy, Le Caprice, J Sheekey, Daphne's, Bamboo and Pasha); dir and owner Rivington Grill Bar Deli; conslt Tate Modern Restaurants Ltd; *Recreations* arts, cinema, theatre, sports, restaurants, travel; *Clubs* Groucho, David Lloyd; *Style*— Desmond McDonald, Esq; ✉ Caprice Holdings Limited, 28–30 Litchfield Street, London WC2H 9NL (tel 020 7557 6095, fax 020 7240 9333, mobile 07711 139702, e-mail dmcdonald@caprice-holdings.co.uk); 27 The Meadway, Buckhurst Hill, Essex IG9 5PG (tel 020 8504 6074, e-mail des.mcdonald@zoom.co.uk)

MACDONALD, Euan Ross; s of Ian Somerled Macdonald (d 1958), and Elisabeth Barbara, da of Sir Denham Warmington, 2 Bt (d 1935); *b* 8 April 1940; *Educ* Marlborough, Trinity Coll Cambridge (BA), Graduate Sch of Business Columbia Univ NY (MBA); *m* March 1965, (Jacqueline) Anne Gatacre Evelyn-Wright; 4 s (Iain Graham b 12 Oct 1966, Russell Ross, James Curtis (twins) b 19 May 1969, Dougal Evelyn b 7 May 1974); *Career* Lazard Brothers & Co Ltd 1963–74, first gen mangr International Financial Advisers Kuwait 1974–79, dir gen Ifabanque SA Paris 1979–82, vice-chm S G Warburg & Co Ltd 1994 (dir 1982), chm Warburg Dillon Read (India) Bombay 1995–99, exec vice-chm HSBC Securities and Capital Markets India Private Ltd 1999–2001; head Corp Fin Advsy Team HSBC Republic London 2001–02; non-exec dir: Acrastyle Ltd 2004–, Vedanta Resources plc 2005–; tstee Cumberland Lodge 1995–; memb Worshipful Co of Clothworkers; *Style*— Euan Macdonald, Esq; ✉ Suffolk House, Chiswick Mall, London W4 2PR

MACDONALD, 8 Baron (I 1776); Godfrey James Macdonald of Macdonald; JP (1976), DL (1986); Chief of the Name and Arms of Macdonald; s of 7 Baron Macdonald, MBE (d 1970); 3 Baron m 1803 Louisa Maria La Coast, natural da of HRH Duke of Gloucester (issue b before m succeeded to Bosville MacDonald btcy); *b* 28 November 1947; *Educ* Belhaven Hill Sch Dunbar, Eton; *m* 14 June 1969, Claire (Glenfiddich's 1982 Writer of the Year), eld da of Capt Thomas Noel Catlow, CBE, RN; 3 da (Hon Alexandra Louisa b 1973, Hon Isabella Claire b 1975, Hon Meriel Iona b 1978), 1 s (Hon Godfrey Evan Hugo Thomas b 24 Feb 1982); *Heir* s, Hon Godfrey Macdonald of Macdonald; *Career* pres Royal Scottish Country Dance Soc 1970–73, memb Inverness CC 1970–75, fndr Clan Donald Lands Tst 1970, vice-convener Standing Cncl of Scottish Chiefs 1974–, memb of Skye and Lochalsh Dist Cncl 1975–83 (chm Fin Ctee 1979–83), chm Skye and Lochalsh Local Health Cncl 1978–80; memb Highland Health Bd 1980–89; *Clubs* New (Edinburgh); *Style*— The Rt Hon Lord Macdonald; ✉ Kinloch Lodge, Isle of Skye IV43 8QY (tel 01471 833214)

MacDONALD, Prof (Donald) Gordon; RD (1976, and Bars 1986 and 1996); s of Donald MacDonald (d 1981), of Milngavie, and Thelma Gordon, *née* Campbell (d 1975); *b* 5 July 1942; *Educ* Kelvinside Acad Glasgow, Univ of Glasgow (BDS, PhD); *m* 21 May 1966, Emma Lindsay (Linda), da of William Lindsay Cordiner (d 1961), of Coatbridge; 1 da (Katharine b 1968 d 1989), 2 s (Lindsay b 1969, Alastair b 1972); *Career* visiting assoc prof of oral pathology Univ of Illinois Chicago 1969–70, expert in forensic dentistry 1971–, hon conslt in oral pathology Glasgow 1974–, prof of oral pathology Univ of Glasgow 1991– (sr lectr 1974–82, reader 1982–91); vice-pres Assoc of Head and Neck Oncologists of GB 1987–90 (sec 1983–87), speciality rep for oral pathology RCPath 1988–2002; pres: Br Soc for Oral Pathology 1988–91, Int Assoc of Oral Pathology 2002–04; RCPSGlas: dean Dental Faculty 2001–04, vice-pres (dental) 2003–04; RNR: joined 1959, CO HMS Graham 1982–86, Cdre 1995–97; Hon ADC 1996–97 (ADC 1991–93); FRCPath 1985 (MRCPath 1971), FDSRCPS 1986; *Books* Colour Atlas of Forensic Dentistry (1989); *Recreations* golf, curling; *Style*— Prof D Gordon MacDonald, RD**; ✉ Glasgow Dental Hospital and School, 378 Sauchiehall Street, Glasgow G2 3JZ (tel 0141 211 9745, fax 0141 353 1593, e-mail d.g.macdonald@dental.gla.ac.uk)

MacDONALD, Hannah; da of Robert MacDonald (d 2001), and Vivien Rothwell; *b* 1971, London; *Educ* Wimbledon HS, Univ of Manchester (BA); *m* 14 Sept 2002, Paul Butterworth; *Career* former non-fiction ed Virgin Publishing and André Deutsch, subsequently joined Random House, currently publishing dir Ebury Press; memb Advsy Bd Kingston Univ Publishing MA; *Books* The Sun Road (2003, Betty Trask First Novel Award), Julianna Kiss (2006); *Recreations* travel, cooking, cinema; *Style*— Ms Hannah MacDonald; ✉ Ebury Press, Random House, 20 Vauxhall Bridge Road, London SW1V 2SA (tel 020 7840 8400, e-mail hmacdonald@randomhouse.co.uk); c/o Victoria Hobbs, AM Heath & Co Ltd, 6 Warwick Court WC1R SDT

McDONALD, Dr Henry; *Educ* Univ of Glasgow (BSc, DSc); *Career* engr Aerodynamics Dept Br Aircraft Corp 1960–65; United Technologies Research Centre CT: supervisor Theoretical Gas Dynamics Gp 1968–72 (research engr 1965–68), chief Gas Dynamics Section 1972–76; fndr, pres and ceo Scientific Research Assocs CT 1976–92, co-fndr Advanced Pulmonary Technologies Inc CT 1988–92, center dir NASA Ames Research Centre CA 1996–2002; memb: NASA/Rocketdyne Review Panel on Blade Cracking in the SSME Turbine 1986–87, US Air Force/Martin Marietta Special Review of Titian IV Test Failure 1991; chair: Space Shuttle Ind Assessment Team 2000, Review of the Aerodynamics Issues on the V-22 Osprey 2001; sr res fell Univ of Glasgow 1975–76, prof of mech engrg in residence Univ of Connecticut 1985–89, prof of mech engrg and asst dir Computational Sciences Pennsylvania State Univ Applied Research Lab 1991–97, prof of computational engrg Mississippi State Univ MS 1997–2002, distinguished prof and chair of excellence in engrg Univ of Tennessee at Chattanooga 2002–; visiting faculty memb Dept of Mechanical Engrg: Hong Kong Poly, Imperial Coll London; memb Advsy Ctee: Dept for Aeronautical Engrg Stanford Univ, Faculty of Engrg Univ of Calif Davis; memb: Bd of Dirs Connecticut Innovations, Govr's Advsy Cncl for High Technol CT 1989–90, Engrg Research Advsy Bd Mississippi State Univ 1996–2000, Sr Mgmnt Cncl NASA 1996–2002, Peer Ctee Aerospace Engrg Nat Acad of Engrg 2003–; assoc tech ed American Inst of Aeronautics and Astronautics (AIAA) Jl 1981–84; Small Business of the Year Award for High Technol CT 1989, NASA Outstanding Leadership Medal 1997 and 2000, NASA Gp Achievement Award (for Shuttle Ind Assessment Team) 2001, NASA Distinguished Service Medal 2001; Hon Dr Engrg Univ of Glasgow 1997; memb US Nat Acad of Engrg 2000, hon memb American Soc of Mechanical Engrgs 2001, fell American Inst of Aeronautics and Astronautics (AIAA), FRAeS, FREng 2003; *Style*— Dr Henry McDonald

MACDONALD, Prof Hugh John; *b* 31 January 1940; *Educ* Univ of Cambridge (MA, PhD); *Career* lectr in music: Univ of Cambridge 1966–71, Univ of Oxford 1971–80; visiting prof of music Indiana Univ 1979, Gardiner prof of music Univ of Glasgow 1980–87, Avis Blewett prof of music Washington Univ St Louis 1987–; gen ed New Berlioz Edition 1967–; Szymanowski Medal (Poland); FRCM; *Books* Skryabin (1978), Berlioz (1982), Selected Letters of Berlioz (1995), Berlioz's Orchestration Treatise (2002); *Style*— Prof Hugh Macdonald; ✉ Department of Music, Washington University, St Louis, MO 63130, USA (tel 00 1 314 935 5519, fax 00 1 314 863 7231)

MACDONALD, Iain Lachlan; TD (1993); s of Angus Macdonald (d 2000), of North Uist, Scotland, and Elizabeth, *née* Reid; *b* 9 July 1955; *Educ* Allan Glen's Sch Glasgow, Coventry Univ (MA), Univ of Glasgow (BArch, DipArch), Domus Acad Milan (Master of Industrial Design); *m* 16 June 1984, Frances, *née* McKay; 2 s (Ruaridh b 1990, James b 1993); *Career* architect and planner; Lt-Col Parachute Regt (V) 1980–95 (Lt 2 Bn 1982–83); various architectural appts 1979–91, dir Arquitectura 1992–98, dir Aukett 1998–2004, dir YRM 2006–; work exhibited: Europe, Asia and USA; winner Euro Medi-Park Competition 1992; MRTPI, RIBA, SIA; *Publications* Il Oggetto Neoclectico (1993), Architects Communicating Architecture (1997), Aukett (2001); *Recreations* drawing, bagpiping, golf; *Clubs* Caledonian; *Style*— Iain Macdonald, Esq; ✉ YRM, 32 York Way, London N1 9AB (tel 020 7014 4300, e-mail imacdonald@yrm.co.uk)

MACDONALD, Ian Alexander; QC (1988); s of Ian Wilson Macdonald (d 1989), of Gullane, E Lothian, and Helen, *née* Nicholson (d 1990); *b* 12 January 1939; *Educ* Glasgow Acad, Cargilfield Sch Edinburgh, Rugby, Clare Coll Cambridge (MA, LLB); *m* 1, 20 Dec 1968 (m dis 1977), Judith Mary, da of William Demain Roberts of Stockport, Cheshire; 2 s (Ian b 3 July 1970, Jamie b 25 Sept 1972); m 2, 12 Oct 1978 (m dis 1990), Jennifer, da of Roy Hall, of Grimsby, S Humberside; 1 s (Kieran b 17 Oct 1979); m 3, 31 Aug 1991 (m dis 2006), Yasmin Shahida, da of Mohammed Sharif, of Manchester; *Career* called to the Bar Middle Temple 1963 (Astbury scholar 1962–65, bencher 2002); jt head of chambers 1975–2002, lectr in law Kingston Poly 1968–72, sr legal writer and res conslt Incomes Data Servs 1974–80, pres Immigration Law Practitioners' Assoc 1984–, special advocate to Special Immigration Appeals Cmmn 1998–2004, memb Editorial Advsy Bd Immigration and Nationality Law and Practice Jl; memb: SE Circuit, Euro Law Assoc, Criminal Bar Assoc, Admin Law Bar Assoc, Inquiry into Disappearance of Gen Humberto Delgado 1965; chm: Ind Inquiry into Racial Violence in Manchester Schs 1987–88, Inquiry into Funding of Caribbean House Hackney 1989–90, Inquiry into Recruitment Fraud in Hackney 1995–96; Grande Oficial Ordem Da Liberdade (Portugal) 1995; *Books* Race Relations and Immigration Law (1969), Race Relations - The New Law (1977), The New Nationality Act (with N J Blake 1982), Murder in the Playground (1990), Immigration Law and Practice (6 edn 2005); *Recreations* swimming, watching football, reading; *Clubs* Cumberland Lawn Tennis; *Style*— Ian Macdonald, Esq, QC; ✉ Garden Court Chambers, 57–60 Lincoln's Inn Fields, London WC2A 3LS (tel 020 7993 7600, fax 020 7993 7700, e-mail info@gclaw.co.uk)

McDONALD, Dr Ian Archie; s of John Archie McDonald, and Thelma, *née* Seheult; *b* 18 April 1933, St Augustine, Trinidad; *Educ* Queens Royal Coll Trinidad, Clare Coll Cambridge (MA, capt lawn tennis team, pres Cambridge W Indian Soc); *m* 14 Sept 1984, Mary Angela, *née* Callender; 2 s (Jamie b 5 Feb 1983, Darren b 16 Dec 1988); 1 s from previous m (Keith b 15 May 1962); *Career* various positions in Guyana sugar industry 1955–76, dir of mktg and admin Guyana Sugar Corp 1976–99, ceo Sugar Assoc of the Caribbean 2000–; ed Kyk-Over-Al magazine 1984–, Sunday columnist Stabroek News Guyana 1986–, editorial asst W Indian Cmmn 1991–92; dir: Hand-In-Hand Fire and Life Insurance Gp 1990–, St Joseph's Mercy Hosp Guyana, Inst of Private Enterprise Devpt Guyana; memb Mgmnt Ctee Nat Art Collection Guyana; capt West Indies Davis Cup Tennis Team 1950s and 1960s; Guyana Sportsman of the Year 1957, Golden Arrow of Achievement (Guyana) 1986, Guyana Prize for Literature (Poetry) 1992 and 2004; Hon DLitt Univ of West Indies 1997; FRSL 1970; *Publications* The Humming-Bird Tree (novel, 1969, BBC film 1992, new edn 2004), Tramping Man (play, 1980), Mercy Ward (poems, 1988), Essequibo (poems, 1992), Heinemann Book of Caribbean Poetry (ed, 1992), Jaffo The Calypsonian (poems, 1994), Collected Poems of A J Seymour (ed, 2000), Between Silence and Silence (poems, 2003), Cricket at Bourda (cricket history); *Recreations* playing tennis, watching cricket, reading, enjoying my wife's beautiful garden; *Clubs* Georgetown Cricket, Georgetown, Hawks' (Cambridge), Int Lawn Tennis Club of GB; *Style*— Dr Ian McDonald; ✉ 16 Bel Air Gardens, Georgetown, Guyana (tel 00 592 2268099); 37 Sail Crescent, Vaughn, Ontario L6A 2Z4, Canada (tel 00 1 905 303 0345); c/o The Sugar Association of the Caribbean, Demerera Sugar Terminal, River View, Ruimveldt, Georgetown, Guyana (tel 00 592 2272051, fax 00 592 2266104, e-mail dstgsc@guyana.net.gy)

MACDONALD, Prof Ian Robert; s of Robert Harold Macdonald (d 1972), of Sutton, Surrey, and Jannette Wilhelmina (d 2007), *née* Marang; *b* 4 May 1939; *Educ* Whitgift Sch, Univ of St Andrews (MA, Miller Prize), Univ of Aberdeen (PhD); *m* 21 April 1962, Frances Mary, da of James Ranald Alexander; 3 s (Bruce Ian b 10 May 1966, Andrew James b 14 April 1968, Graeme Alan b 6 Oct 1973); *Career* United Steel Cos Ltd 1961–64, postgraduate student 1964–65; Univ of Aberdeen: lectr in Spanish 1965–84, sr lectr 1984–90, prof in Spanish 1991–2001, convener Bd of Studies in Arts and Social Sciences 1989–92, dean Faculty of Arts and Divinity 1992–96, vice-princ 1995–97, sr vice-princ 1997–2001, research fell 2001–; memb AHRB 1999–2002, convenor Res Ctee 2000–02, memb Nominations Ctee 2002–04, memb Univ of the Highlands and Islands Project Academic Advsy Bd 1999–2001; convenor: Further Educn Professional Devpt Forum 1997–2001; tstee Aberdeen Int Youth Festival 1993–2001, govr Dick Bequest Tst 1991–96, govr Northern Coll of Educn 1999–2001; *Books* Gabriel Miró: His Private Library and His Literary Background (1975), Gabriel Miró, El Obispo Leproso (ed, 1993); *Recreations* walking, digging, literary research; *Style*— Prof Ian Macdonald; ✉ Chemin de Montplo, 34310 Montouliers, France (tel 00 33 467 89 54 73, e-mail ianmacdonald@wanadoo.fr); School of Modern Languages, King's College, University of Aberdeen, Aberdeen AB24 3FX

MACDONALD, Dr James Stewart; s of Kenneth Stewart Macdonald (d 1959), of Mauritius and Perthshire, and Mary Janet, *née* McRorie (d 1991); *b* 11 August 1925; *Educ* Sedbergh, Univ of Edinburgh (MB ChB, DMRD); *m* 19 Oct 1951, Dr Catherine Wilton Drysdale, da of John Drysdale, CBE (d 1979), of Kuala Lumpur, Malaya and Perthshire; 2 s (Kenneth John Stewart, Murdo James Stewart); *Career* RAMC Maj 2 i/c 23 Para Field Ambulance 1952; asst radiologist St Thomas' Hosp London 1959–62; Royal Marsden Hosp: conslt radiologist 1962–85, vice-chm Bd of Govrs 1975–82 (memb Bd 1967–82), dir Diagnostic X-ray Dept 1978–85; hon sr lectr Inst of Cancer Research 1966–85, teacher in radiology Univ of London 1966–85; contrib to numerous books and scientific jls on radiology of cancer; memb: Cncl RCR 1968–73, numerous working parties MRC 1968–85, Ctee of Mgmnt Inst of Cancer Research 1969–82, Exec Ctee South Met Cancer Registry 1971–82, London Ctee Ludwig Inst for Cancer Research 1971–85; sec gen Symposium Ossium (London) Euro Assoc of Radiology 1968 (memb numerous ctees 1968–85); UK delg for diagnostic radiology Union Européene des Medicins Specialistes 1972–81; appeals sec Duke of Edinburgh's Award Scheme (Perth and Kinross) 1986–88, chm Timber Growers UK (E of Scotland) 1988–91, dep chm Timber Growers UK (Scotland) 1991–94; memb: Exec Ctee Scottish Cncl Devpt and Industry 1991–94, Cncl Scottish Landowners' Fedn 1991–94, Cncl Rural Forum Scotland 1990–94; tstee Scottish Forestry Tst 1991–94; memb Br Inst of Radiology; FRSM, FRCPEd, FRCR, FRSA; *Recreations* field sports; *Clubs* Army and Navy; *Style*— Dr J S Macdonald; ✉ Darquhillan, Gleneagles, Auchterarder, Perthshire PH3 1NG (tel 01764 662476, fax 01764 661086)

McDONALD, Prof Janet Brown Inglis; da of Robert Inglis Caldwell (d 1987), and Janet Gilbert, *née* Lindsay (d 1987); *b* 28 July 1941; *Educ* Hutchesons' Girls' GS Glasgow, Royal Scottish Acad of Music and Drama (pt/t), Univ of Glasgow (MA); *m* 1 July 1964, Ian James McDonald, s of James Murray McDonald (d 1947); 1 da (Katharine Lindsay b 14 April 1977); *Career* Univ of Glasgow: asst lectr Dept of English Literature 1965–66 (res fell 1963–65), lectr Dept of Drama 1968–79 (asst lectr 1966–68), prof of drama 1979–2005, dean of faculties 2006–; chair: Drama Ctee Scottish Arts Cncl 1985–88 (also memb Cncl), Drama Theatre Bd CNAA 1982–85, Performing Arts Bd CNAA 1989–91, Standing Ctee of Univ Depts of Drama 1982–85, Citizens' Theatre Ltd 1991–2005, Music and Performing Arts Res Bd Arts and Humanities Res Bd (AHRB); memb Creative and Performing Arts Advsy Panel Scottish Qualifications Authy (SQA) 2000–02, memb Bd AHRB 2002–04; govr RSAMD 1982–94 (memb Academic Bd 1994–2003), memb Ct Univ of Glasgow

1991–94; govr Merchants House of Glasgow 2002; FRSAMD 1992, FRSE 1991 (memb Cncl 1992–96, vice-pres Arts and Humanities 2005–); *Books* The New Drama 1990–1914 (1985), The Citizens' Theatre 1990 (with Claude Schumacher, 1991), Harley Granville Barker, An Edinburgh Retrospective (with Leslie Hill, 1993); *Style—* Prof Janet McDonald, FRSE, FRSAMD; ✉ 61 Hamilton Drive, Glasgow G12 8DP (tel 0141 339 0013)

MacDONALD, Maj-Gen John Donald; CB, CBE (OBE 1980), DL (City of Edinburgh 1996); s of Col John MacDonald, OBE, of St Andrews, and Isabelle Brown Watt Brown; *b* 5 April 1938; *Educ* George Watson's Coll Edinburgh, RMA Sandhurst, RMCS Shrivenham, DSSC India, Nat Def Coll Latimer; *m* 31 March 1964, Mary, da of Dr Graeme Warrack, CBE, DSO, TD, DL; 2 da (Sarah b 1 Nov 1965, Caroline b 14 Feb 1967), 1 s (Neil Alisdair b 19 Sept 1968); *Career* cmmnd King's Own Scottish Borderers 1958, RASC 1963, Royal Corps of Tport 1965, cmd Armd Div Tport Regt BAOR 1978–80 (Lt-Col), exchange instructor Aust Army Cmd and Staff Coll 1980–82, head of personnel and logistics Armd Div BAOR 1983–86 (Col), head of personnel and offr for human resources MOD London 1987–88, distribution and tport dir 1 Br Corps BAOR 1988–91 (Brig), DG Tport and Movement (Distribution) Army 1991–93 (Maj-Gen), Col Cmdt Royal Logistics Corp; gen sec: jt secretariat Royal Br Legion Scotland 1994–95, The Earl Haig Fund Scotland (chief exec) 1994–2003, Officers Assoc Scotland; HM cmmr Queen Victoria Sch Dunblane; Hon Col Scottish Transport Regiment RLC 1996–2004; Freeman City of London 1991, Liveryman Worshipful Co of Carmen 1991; FCIT 1988, FILDM 1990; *Recreations* travel, music, art, rugby (internationalist), athletics (internationalist), golf, skiing; *Clubs* Army and Navy, Royal and Ancient, Hon Co of Edinburgh Golfers; *Style—* Maj-Gen John MacDonald, CB, CBE, DL; ✉ Ormiston Hill, Kirknewton, West Lothian EH27 8DQ (tel 01506 882180)

MACDONALD, John Reginald; QC (1976); s of Ranald Macdonald, MBE (d 1959), and Marion Olive, *née* Kirkby (d 1981); *b* 26 September 1931; *Educ* St Edward's Sch Oxford, Queens' Coll Cambridge (MA); *m* 1958, Erica Rosemary, da of Lt-Col Eric Stanton (d 1987); 1 da (Hettie b 1962), 1 s (Toby b 1964); *Career* called to the Bar Lincoln's Inn 1955, bencher Lincoln's Inn 1985, in practice Chancery Bar specializing in human rights and constitutional cases 1957–; Parly candidate (Lib) Wimbledon 1966 and 1970, Parly candidate (Lib/Alliance) Folkestone & Hythe 1983 and 1987; chm: Lib Dem Lawyers 1991–93, Kent Opera 1996–; *Publications* The Law of Freedom of Information (jtly, 2003); *Recreations* cricket, theatre; *Clubs* MCC; *Style—* John Macdonald, Esq, QC; ✉ 12 New Square, Lincoln's Inn, London WC2A 3SW (tel 020 7419 8000, fax 020 7419 8050)

MACDONALD, Julien; OBE (2006); *Educ* Brighton Univ (BA), RCA (MA); *Career* fashion designer; at coll worked for Koji Tatsuno, Alexander McQueen, *qv*, and Karl Lagerfeld; former head knitwear designer Chanel Couture, Chanel mainline and Karl Lagerfeld collections (designed Chanel's best-selling outfit 1997); women's artistic dir House of Givenchy Haute Couture 2001–; other projects incl: couture dresses for Harrods Christmas windows, tour outfits for the Spice Girls, outfits for Jennifer Lopez's Euro tour, uniforms for BA staff, outfits for Kylie Minogue's world tour, conslt and designer Marks & Spencer Autograph range, uniforms for staff at Bluewater shopping complex; Br Glamour Designer of the Year 2001; *Fashion Shows* Mermaids (launch of own label, Imagination Gallery London) 1997, Modernist (London Fashion Week) 1997, Alerairauh 1998, Metallurgical (restaged at NY Fashion Week) 1998, Snowbusiness 1999, Frock & Roll (Roundhouse) 1999, Modern Skins (London Fashion Week) 2000, Feeling Hot Hot Hot (Park Lane Hotel) 2000, ...I Haven't Stopped Dancing Yet (Grosvenor House Hotel) 2001, It's All in the Mix 2001, Rock Bitch (London Fashion Week tents) 2001, Super Paradise (Grosvenor House Hotel) 2002, Temptation (Roundhouse) 2003; *Style—* Julien Macdonald, Esq, OBE; ✉ 65 Goldborne Road, London W10 5NT (tel 020 8968 9988, fax 020 8968 9989, e-mail julienmacdonald@btconnect.com)

MACDONALD, Sir Kenneth Donald John (Ken); kt (2007), QC (1997); s of Dr Kenneth Macdonald (d 1997), of Salisbury, Wilts, and Maureen, *née* Sheridan (d 2001); *b* 4 January 1953; *Educ* St Edmund Hall Oxford (BA); *m* 1980, Linda, da of Dr David Zuck; 1 da (Anna Maureen b 18 Nov 1981), 2 s (Edward Jonathan Kenneth b 23 March 1984, Theo Lindsay b 30 Sept 1993); *Career* called to the Bar Inner Temple 1978 (bencher 2003); specialising in criminal law; recorder of the Crown Court 2000, DPP 2003–; chair Criminal Bar Assoc 2003 (memb Exec Ctee 1997–, chm Educn Ctee 1999–, vice-chair 2002–03), vice-chair Bar Public Affairs Gp 2001–02; memb: Bar Cncl 2000, Treasy Counsel Selection Ctee (CCC); *Recreations* twentieth century history, crime fiction, film noir, Arsenal FC; *Style—* Sir Ken Macdonald, QC

McDONALD, Most Rev Kevin John Patrick; *see:* Southwark, Archbishop of (RC)

MACDONALD, Dr Lewis; MSP; s of late Rev Roderick Macdonald, and Margaret, *née* Currie; *b* 1 January 1957; *Educ* Inverurie Acad, Univ of Aberdeen (MA, PhD); *m* Sandra, da of Sandy and Jo Inkster; 2 da (Sophie b 28 Dec 1991, Iona b 2 March 1998); *Career* Parly researcher to Frank Doran MP 1987–92 and 1997–99, shadow cabinet advsr to Tom Clarke MP 1993–97; Lab UK Parly candidate for Moray 1997, memb Exec Ctee Scot Lab Pty 1997–99; MSP (Lab) Aberdeen Central 1999–; dep min for tport and planning 2001, dep min for enterprise, tport and lifelong learning 2001–03, dep min for enterprise and lifelong learning 2003–04, dep min for environment and rural devpt 2004–05, dep min for health and community care 2005–07; memb Cross-Pty Gps 1999–2001: Crofting, Gaelic in the Scot Parl, Oil and Gas, Strategic Rail Services for Scot, Media, Int Devpt, Agriculture and Horticulture; convenor Holyrood Progress Gp 2000–01; memb Grampian Racial Equality Cncl, past memb Mgmnt Ctee Aberdeen CAB; tstee: Aberdeen Safer Community Tst, Aberdeen FC Supporters' Tst; *Recreations* walking, football, history; *Style—* Dr Lewis Macdonald, MSP; ✉ The Scottish Parliament, Edinburgh EH99 1SP (tel 0131 348 5915, e-mail lewis.macdonald.msp@scottish.parliament.uk, website www.lewismacdonaldmsp.com); Constituency Office, 70 Rosemount Place, Aberdeen AB25 2XJ (tel 01224 646333, fax 01224 645450)

McDONALD, Prof Michael; s of Douglas Frederick McDonald (d 1999), and Joyce Mary Kathleen, *née* Burke (d 1977); *b* 10 December 1944; *Educ* Univ of Newcastle upon Tyne (BSc, Inst of Structural Engineers Prize), Univ of Southampton (PhD); *m* 1970, Millicent Elizabeth, *née* Agnew; 3 s (Robert Douglas b 1971, Duncan James b 1974, Alastair Michael b 1978); *Career* Univ of Southampton: Rees Jeffreys lectr in highway and traffic engrg 1971–86, sr lectr 1986–88, reader in transportation 1988–92, prof of transportation 1992–, dir Transportation Res Gp 1986–, head Dept of Civil and Environmental Engrg 1996–99; exec dir Roughton & Partners 1985–; chm UK Universities Tport Studies Gp 1996–98, chair and fndr memb ITS UK, vice-chm European Road Tport Research Advsy Cncl, advsr to EU research progs, external advsr Road and Vehicle Safety Res DETR, visiting fell Tport Res Fndn, chair ILT Road Pricing Working Pty; memb: Land Tport LINK Panel EPSRC, Built Environment Review Panel EPSRC, Tport Panel of the Technol Foresight Prog, TRF Nat Res Strategy Gp for Tport 1997–98, ICE Tport Editorial Panel, RAC Tech Ctee, Foresight Vehicle Telematic Thematic Gp; author of over 100 publications; FICE, MIHT, FCIT; *Recreations* golf, sailing; *Style—* Professor Michael McDonald; ✉ University of Southampton, Highfield, Southampton SO17 1BJ (tel 02380 592192, fax 02380 593152, e-mail mm7@soton.ac.uk)

MACDONALD, Murdo James Stewart; *b* 25 January 1955; *Educ* Hammersmith Coll of Art, Univ of Edinburgh (class medal, Sinclair-McDonald scholar, univ bursary, Drever prize, MA, PhD); *Career* hon post-doctoral fell Univ of Edinburgh 1987–88, freelance art critic 1987–94, lectr Centre for Continuing Education Univ of Edinburgh 1990–97, prof history of Scottish art Univ of Dundee 1997; tstee Patrick Geddes Meml Tst 1996–; Edinburgh Review ed 1990–94; memb: Assoc of Art Historians, Scottish Soc for Art History; FRSA 1998, FSA Scot 1999; *Publications* Scottish Art (2000); numerous articles, papers and reviews in learned jls; *Style—* Prof Murdo Macdonald; ✉ School of Fine Art, University of Dundee, Dundee DD1 4HN (tel 01382 344516, fax 01382 344000, e-mail m.j.s.macdonald@dundee.ac.uk)

MACDONALD, Nigel Colin Lock; s of T W Macdonald, of Banstead, Surrey, and B E Macdonald, *née* Whitbourn; *b* 15 June 1945; *Educ* Cranleigh Sch; *m* Jennifer Margaret; 1 da (Genevieve Clare b 16 Dec 1985); *Career* articled clerk Thomson McLintock 1962–68, ptnr Ernst & Young (formerly Ernst & Whinney, previously Whinney Murray & Co) 1976–2003; chm James Lock & Co 1979–; dir British Standards Instn 1992–2004, accounting advsr Int Oil Pollution Compensation Fund 2002–, dir CocaCola HBC 2005–; memb: Industrial Devpt Advsy Bd 1995–2001, Review Panel Fin Reporting Cncl 1990–2006, Electricity and Water Panels MMC 1998, Competition Cmmn 1999–2006; pres Inst of Chartered Accountants of Scotland 1993–94; tstee Nat Maritime Museum 2003–; MICAS 1968, FRSA 1993; *Clubs* RAC, City of London; *Style—* Nigel Macdonald, Esq; ✉ 10 Lynwood Road, Epsom, Surrey KT17 4LD (tel 01372 720853 or 07793 823376, e-mail nigel.macdonald@ntlworld.com)

McDONALD, Dr Oonagh A; CBE (1998); da of Dr and Mrs H D McDonald; *Educ* Roan Sch for Girls Greenwich, E Barnet GS, KCL (PhD); *Career* former philosophy lectr Univ of Bristol; MP (Lab) Thurrock 1976–87 (Parly candidate (Lab) Glos S Feb and Oct 1974); PPS to the chief sec to the Treasy 1977–79; oppn front bench spokesman on: defence 1981–83, Treasy and Civil Serv 1983–87; Gwilym Gibbon res fell Nuffield Coll Oxford 1988–89; currently res and mgmnt conslt; dir: SAGA Group Ltd 1995–98, Scottish Provident 1999–, Skandia 2001–; memb Bd: Investors' Compensation Scheme 1991–, Securities and Investments Bd (now FSA) 1993–98, Fin Services Ombudsman Scheme 1999–, Gen Insurance Standards Cncl 1999–, Insurance Brokers Registration Cncl 1999; ed Jl of Financial Regulation and Compliance 1995–; memb: Cncl Consumers' Assoc 1988–93, Gibraltar Financial Services Cmmn 1999–; FRSA 1993; *Books* Parliament at Work (1989), The Future of Whitehall (1992); *Style—* Dr Oonagh McDonald, CBE

McDONALD, Patrick John; s of Patrick McDonald, of Hepscott Manor, Morpeth, Northumberland, and Margaret, *née* Price; *b* 26 September 1962; *Educ* Northumberland Co Coll (Int Schoolboys Rugby); *m* 4 Aug 1984, Claire Alison, da of Brian Kell; 2 s (Samuel Patrick Donovan b 29 June 1987, Nathanial John Ryan b 11 March 1991), 1 da (Lois Amelia Kelly b 15 May 1993); *Career* chef de partie Granby Hotel Northumberland 1980–83, chef de partie then sr sous chef Grosvenor House Hotel 1983–84, sous chef Dorchester Hotel 1984–85, head chef Manor House Hotel Castle Combe Wilts 1985–87; exec chef: Ettington Park Hotel Stratford upon Avon 1987–88, Charingworth Manor Hotel Glos 1988–89; dir Designer Dinner Parties Ltd 1990–, chef/patron Epicurean Restaurant (Stow on the Wold then Cheltenham) 1990–96, dir Epicurean Restaurants Ltd 1994–, chef conslt Harvey Nichols plc 1995–96, conslt chef/restaurant advsr to Sir Rocco Forte and chef dir/co-owner Les Saveurs Restaurant Mayfair 1996–98, chef/patron Epicurean Restaurant Pershore Worcs 1998–, gp exec chef City Inn Hotel Gp 1999–, md Epicurean Brasseries Ltd 2002– (incl Epic Bar Brasseries); chef/patron Paris Restaurant Patrick McDonald Birmingham 2003–, dir Ford McDonald Consultancy 2005–, owner Epicurean Restaurant 2006–, owner Liberty Restaurants 2007–, co-owner Obika Restaurant London, dir F&B UK Ltd; conslt chef: Newcastle United FC 1998–, Burj Al Arab Hotel 1999–, Worcester RFC 1999–, Pat McDonald Consultancy Ltd 1999–, Eden Project 2000–; conslt advsr to: Selfridges 2004–05, Park Plaza Hotels 2004–05, La Rinescente Milan 2005; food and beverage dir Birmingham Mailbox 2002–04; FRSA 2004; *Television* Recipe for Success 1999, If you can't stand the heat (Channel 4) 1999–, Carlton Food (Network TV) 2000; *Awards* AA Best Newcomer of the Year Award 1990, Master Chef 1990, Good Food Guide Restaurant of the Year 1990, two AA Rosettes 1991, Egon Ronay Star 1991, Ackerman Clover Award 1991, three AA Rosettes 1993, Egon Ronay Rgnl Dessert of the Year 1993, Courvoisier Guide one of finest restaurants in world (by Lord Lichfield) 1993, Michelin Star 1994, two Egon Ronay Stars 1994, Good Food Guide County Restaurant 1994, four AA Rosettes 1995, Michelin Red M 1995, Moet et Chandon Premier Crew Award (Harpers & Queen Front of House Award) 1999, Best Service Standards outside of London 1999, Michelin Bib Gourmand 2002, 2003, 2004 and 2005, 3 AA Rosettes 2004, 4 AA Rosettes 2005–06; *Books* Simply Good Food, Potato Dishes; *Recreations* shooting, fishing, rugby coaching; *Style—* Patrick McDonald, Esq; ✉ c/o Head Office, 18 High Street, Pershore, Worcestershire WR10 1BG (tel 01386 555576, fax 01386 555572, e-mail patrickmcdonald199@msn.com, website www.fordmcdonaldconsultancy.com)

MACDONALD, Peter Cameron; DL (W Lothian 1987); s of Sir Peter George Macdonald, WS, JP, DL (d 1983), of Edinburgh, and Rachel Irene, *née* Forgan (d 1990); *b* 14 December 1937; *Educ* Loretto, E of Scotland Coll of Agric (Dip Agric); *m* 2 Aug 1974, Barbara Helen, da of David Ballantyne (d 1997), of Peebles; 2 step s (David Drimmie b 1964, Patrick Drimmie b 1967); *Career* farmer 1961–96; chm J Dickson & Son Gunmakers 1997–99 (dir 1968–99); Scottish Landowners Fedn: memb Cncl 1976–2001, convener 1985–88, chm Countryside Review Gp 1988, vice-pres 1989–2001; Scottish Landowners Fedn rep: Standing Conf on Countryside Sports 1985–2004, Scottish Ctee Game Conservancy 1988–2001, Steering Ctee The Code of Good Shooting Practice 1990–2004, Ctee FACE (UK) 1991–2004; memb: Cncl Blackface Sheepbreeders Assoc 1970–74, Pentland Hills Rural Land Mgmnt Gp 1977–84, W Lothian Dist Countryside Ctee 1978–81, Forth River Purification Bd 1979–87, W Lothian Countryside Advsy Ctee; dir Royal Highland Agric Soc of Scotland 1985; vice-chm: Pentland Hills Regnl Park Consultative Ctee 1987–89, Pentland Hills Regnl Park Advsy Ctee 1989–95; *Recreations* fishing, shooting, golf; *Clubs* Hon Co of Edinburgh Golfers; *Style—* Peter Macdonald, Esq, DL; ✉ Waterheads Farmhouse, Eddleston, Peeblesshire EH45 8QX (tel and fax 01721 730229, e-mail pmacdonald63@hotmail.com)

MACDONALD, Roderick Francis; QC (Scot 1988); s of Finlay Macdonald (d 1991), and Catherine, *née* Maclean (d 1996); *b* 1 February 1951; *Educ* St Mungo's Acad Glasgow, Univ of Glasgow (LLB); *Career* admitted advocate 1975, advocate-depute (crown counsel) 1987–93, home advocate-depute (sr crown counsel) 1990–93; called to the Bar Inner Temple 1997; memb Criminal Injuries Compensation Bd 1995–, legal chm Pensions Appeal Tbnls for Scotland 1995–, memb Criminal Injuries Compensation Appeals Panel 1997–; *Style—* Roderick Macdonald, QC; ✉ 6A Lennox Street, Edinburgh EH4 1QA (tel and fax 0131 332 72400); Advocates' Library, Parliament House, Edinburgh EH1 1RF (tel 0131 226 5071, fax 0131 225 3642, e-mail rodmac@cwcom.net, telex 727856 FACADVG)

MacDONALD, Prof Ronald; s of Duncan MacDonald, and Effie, *née* MacRae (d 1982); *b* 23 April 1955; *Educ* Heriot-Watt Univ (BA), Univ of Manchester (MA, PhD); *m* 1 Nov 2002, Catriona, *née* Smith; *Career* teaching asst Univ of Manchester 1979–82, Midland Bank research fell in monetary economics Loughborough Univ 1982–84, lectr Economics Dept Univ of Aberdeen 1984–88 (sr lectr 1988–89), Robert Fleming prof of fin and investment Univ of Dundee 1989–91, prof of int fin Univ of Strathclyde 1992–2004, Bonar MacFie prof of economics Univ of Glasgow 2005–06, Adam Smith prof of political economy 2006–; research fell CESifo Research Network Munich 2000–, int fell Kiel Inst of Economics 2006–; visiting prof: Economics Dept Queen's Univ Kingston Canada 1988, visiting prof Economics Dept Univ of NSW Sydney 1989 (visiting fell 1987), European Univ Inst Florence 1998 and 2000, Univ of Cergy-Pontoise Paris 1999, Zentrum für Europaische Wirschaftsforschung Mannheim 1999, Centre for Economic Studies Univ of

M

Munich 1999; Bank of Valetta visiting prof of int fin Univ of Malta 1994 and 1995, visiting scholar Central Bank of Norway 2003, int fell Kiel Inst of World Economics; conslt and visiting scholar IMF Washington DC 1991–95 and 1997–2000, conslt Reserve Bank of NZ 2000, conslt European Central Bank 2001 and 2002, economist African Dept IMF 2003; assessor Cwlth Scholarship Cmmn 2002–; external examiner: Univ of Glasgow 1989–92, Univ of Liverpool 1990–92, Scottish Doctoral Prog 1990–, Dept of Banking and Fin City Univ Business Sch 1992–95, Birkbeck Coll London 1996–99, Loughborough Univ 1999, Maynooth Coll Ireland 2000–05, Univ of St Andrews 2007–; presented numerous papers at confs, univs, private sector fin instns and central banks in UK and overseas; assoc ed: Scottish Jl of Political Economy 1999–2000, Jl of Int Financial Markets, Institutions and Money 2001–, Economic Studies 2005–, Int Economic Jl 2005–, Economie Internationale 2005, Economics 2007–; regular referee of articles for learned jls; memb: Royal Economic Soc, Scottish Economic Soc, Money Macro Finance Study Gp, Int Economics Study Gp; FRSE 2002; *Publications* International Money: Theory, Evidence and Institutions (with P Hallwood, 1986), Floating Exchange Rates: Theories and Evidence (1988), Exchange Rates and Open Economy Macroeconomics (ed with M P Taylor, 1989), Recent Developments in Australian Monetary Economics (ed with C P Kearney, 1991), The Economics of Exchange Rates, Vols 1 and 2 (ed with M P Taylor, 1992), International Money and Finance (with Paul Hallwood, 2 edn 1994, 3 edn 2000), Equilibrium Exchange Rates (ed with J Stein, 1999), Exchange Rate Modelling (with I W Marsh, 1999), Exchange Rate Economics: Theories and Evidence (2000), The Economics of Exchange Rates (ed, 2000), Central Europe Towards European Monetary Union (ed with Rod Cross 2000), Exchange Rate Economics: Theories and Evidence (2007); also author of conference papers, articles in books, refereed jl articles, discussion papers, mimeographs and book reviews; *Recreations* music, painting, photography, cycling, windsurfing; *Style—* Prof Ronald MacDonald; ✉ tel 0141 548 3861, fax 0141 552 5587

McDONALD, Simon Gerard; CMG (2004); s of James B McDonald, of Ilkley, W Yorks, and Angela, *née* McDonald; *b* 9 March 1961, Salford; *Educ* De La Salle Coll GS Salford, Pembroke Coll Cambridge (MA); *m* 1989, Hon Olivia Wright, da of Baron Wright of Richmond, GCMG (Life Peer), *qv*; 2 s (Felix Dominic b 1990, Joachim James Patrick b 1994), 2 da (Matilda Dorothy b 1992, Adelaide Mary b 1996); *Career* diplomat; joined FCO 1982, Arabic language trg SOAS Univ of London 1984, third sec Jedda 1985, second sec Riyadh 1985–88, second sec Bonn 1988–90, first sec FCO 1990, private sec to perm under sec of state 1993–95, served Washington DC 1995–98, cnsllr, dep head of mission and consul-gen Riyadh 1998–2001, princ private sec to sec of state for Foreign and Cwlth Affairs 2001–03, ambass to Israel 2003–06, dir Iraq FCO 2006–07, head of foreign and defence policy Cabinet Office 2007–; *Style—* Simon McDonald, Esq, CMG; ✉ Cabinet Office, 70 Whitehall, London SW1A 2AS

MacDONALD, Dr Stuart Wyllie; OBE (2006); s of Douglas MacDonald (d 1995), of Dundee, and Agnes, *née* Wyllie; *b* 8 September 1948; *Educ* Gray's Sch of Art Aberdeen (Dip Art), Aberdeen Coll of Educn (PGCE), Open Univ (Dip Educnl Mgmnt), Univ of Liverpool (PhD); *m* 25 Aug 1972, Catherine Elizabeth; 2 s (Duncan b 1977, Jamie b 1978), 1 da (Jennifer b 1980); *Career* head of art Forres Acad 1979–87, nat devpt offr for art and design 1983–85, sr advsr in art and design Strathclyde Regn 1991–96 (advsr 1987–91); educn dir: Glasgow Int Festival of Design 1996, Glasgow UK City of Architecture and Design 1996–98; dir Lighthouse (Scotland's Centre for Architecture, Design and the City) 1998–; memb Design Cncl 2005–, tstee Scottish Architectural Educn Tst; fell Nat Soc for Educn in Art and Design 1991; FRSA 1996, Hon FRIBA 2004; *Recreations* painting; *Style—* Dr Stuart MacDonald, OBE; ✉ 13 Woodside Crescent, Glasgow G3 7UL (tel and fax 0141 332 0644); The Lighthouse,11 Mitchell Lane, Glasgow G1 3NU (tel 0141 225 8402, fax 0141 221 6395)

McDONALD, Sir Trevor; kt (1999), OBE (1992); *b* 16 August 1939; *m*; 2 s, 1 da; *Career* television broadcaster; formerly local reporter and prog mangr with various local newspapers and radio stations WI, news presenter and interviewer Trinidad 1962–69, with BBC World Service 1969–73; ITN: reporter 1973–78, sports corr 1978–80, diplomatic corr 1980–82 (Channel Four News 1982–87), diplomatic ed Channel Four News 1987–89, news presenter News at 5:40 ITV and Channel Four News 1989–90, co-presenter News at Ten ITV 1990–92, sole presenter News at Ten ITV 1992–99, presenter ITV Evening News 1999–2001, presenter ITV News at Ten Thirty 2001–, presenter ITV Tonight with Trevor McDonald 1999–; reported from: USA, India, Pakistan, Hong Kong, Lebanon, Egypt, Syria, Uganda, Mexico, Argentina, Aust, NZ, Russia, Philippines, South Africa, Iraq, Mozambique, Zimbabwe, Cyprus; interviewed several leading international political figures incl: President Saddam Hussein, President Clinton, General Colin Powell, President Nelson Mandela, Chief Buthelezi, Asil Nadir; awards incl: BAFTA Award for Coverage of Philippines Elections 1985, Newscaster of the Year TRIC Awards 1993, 1997 and 1999, Most Popular Newscaster National TV Awards 1996, Gold Medal for Outstanding Contribution to TV News RTS 1998, BAFTA Richard Dimbleby Award for Outstanding Contribution to Television 1999; appointed chm Steering Gp for Better Use of English in Schools and the Workplace 1995–97, chm Nuffield Language Inquiry (a study into the learning of foreign languages) 1998–2000; chllr South Bank Univ 1999–; Hon DLitt: South Bank Univ 1994, Univ of Plymouth 1995, Univ of Nottingham 1997, Southampton Inst 1997; Hon LLD Univ of the West Indies 1996; Hon Dr: Open Univ 1997, Univ of Surrey 1997; fell Liverpool John Moores Univ 1998; *Publications* author of biographies on Viv Richards and Clive Lloyd, Fortunate Circumstances (autobiography, 1993), Favourite Poems (ed, 1997), World of Poetry (1999); *Recreations* tennis, golf, cricket (memb Surrey CCC); *Style—* Sir Trevor McDonald, OBE; ✉ Independent Television News Ltd, 200 Gray's Inn Road, London WC1X 8XZ

MACDONALD-BUCHANAN, Capt John; MC (1945), DL (Northants 1978); s of Sir Reginald Macdonald-Buchanan, KCVO, MBE, MC, DL (d 1981), and Hon Catherine Buchanan (d 1987), da of 1 Baron Woolavington; *b* 15 March 1925; *Educ* Eton, RMC; *m* 1, 3 Nov 1950 (m dis 1969), Lady Rose Fane, o da of 14 Earl of Westmorland (d 1948); 2 da (Fiona b 1954, Serena b 1956), 1 s (Alastair b 1960); m 2, 1969, Jill Rosamonde, o da of Maj-Gen Cecil Benfield Fairbanks, CB, CBE (d 1980), and former w of Maj Jonathan Salusbury-Trelawney (ggs of Sir William S-T, 10 Bt); 2 da (Kate b 1970, Lucy b 1972); *Career* 2 Lt Scots Gds 1943, served 1944–45 NW Europe, Malaya 1948–50, Capt 1948, ret 1952; High Sheriff Northants 1963–64, Vice Lord Lt Northants 1991–; sr steward Jockey Club 1978–82 (steward 1969–72), memb Horserace Betting Levy Bd 1973–78; *Clubs* Turf, White's; *Style—* Capt John Macdonald-Buchanan, MC, DL; ✉ Cottesbrooke Hall, Northamptonshire NN6 8PQ (tel 0160 124 732); 22 Cadogan Place, London SW1 (tel 020 7235 8615)

MACDONALD LOCKHART OF THE LEE, Angus Hew; *see:* Lockhart of the Lee, Angus Hew

MACDONALD OF SLEAT, *see:* Bosville Macdonald of Sleat

MACDONALD OF TRADESTON, Baron (Life Peer UK 1998), of Tradeston in the City of Glasgow; Angus John (Gus) Macdonald; CBE (1997), PC (1999); s of Colin Macdonald (d 1966), and Jean Macdonald (d 1995); *b* 20 August 1940; *Educ* Allan Glen's Sch Glasgow; *m* 7 Sept 1963, Alice; 2 da (Jean b 1965, Rowan b 1967); *Career* marine engr 1953–63, journalist The Scotsman 1965–67, prodr, presenter and dir Granada TV 1967–85; Scottish Media Group plc (formerly Scottish Television plc): dir of progs 1986–89, md 1990–96, chm 1996–97, non-exec chm 1997–98; min for business and industry Scottish Office 1998–99, min for tport DETR 1999–2001, min for the Cabinet Office 2001–03, chllr of the Duchy of Lancaster 2001–03; chm: ITV Broadcast Bd 1992–94, TVMM 1992–93; non-exec chm Taylor & Francis 1997–98, memb Bd Bank of Scotland 1998, sr advsr Macquarie Bank Ltd 2004–; visiting prof of film and media studies Univ of Stirling 1985–98; fndr chm Edinburgh Int TV Festival 1976, chm Edinburgh Int Film Festival 1994–96, vice-pres RTS 1994–98, memb Bd BFI 1997–98, govr Nat Film and TV Sch 1988–97; chm Cairngorms Partnership 1997–98, memb Bd Scottish Enterprise 1997–98; Scottish Business Elite Award 1993 and 1998; author; Hon Dr: Univ of Stirling, Napier Univ, Robert Gordon Univ, Univ of Glasgow; *Books* Victorian Eyewitness, Early Photography; *Recreations* words, music, pictures, sports; *Clubs* RAC; *Style—* The Rt Hon Lord Macdonald of Tradeston, CBE

MacDONALD ROSS, George; s of John MacDonald Ross, CBE, of London, and Helen Margaret, *née* Wallace; *b* 11 November 1943; *Educ* Mill Hill Sch, St Catharine's Coll Cambridge (MA); *m* 24 June 1974, (Margaret) Lynne Ross, da of Elwyn Chubb, of Cardiff; *Career* asst lectr in philosophy Univ of Birmingham 1969–72; Univ of Leeds: res fell in history and philosophy of sci 1972–73, lectr in philosophy 1973–88, sr lectr 1988–, head of Dept of Philosophy 1990–93, dean Faculty of Arts 1991–93; vice-princ and academic dean Univ Coll Scarborough 1994–96 (hon fell 1996–); dir Philosophical and Religious Studies Subject Centre HE Acad 2000–; chm Nat Ctee for Philosophy 1985–94; memb: Ctee Br Soc for the History of Philosophy, Cncl Royal Inst of Philosophy, Ctee Leibniz-Gesellschaft; pres Leibniz Assoc; SAPERE; FHEA (nat teaching fell 2006); *Books* Leibniz (1984); *Recreations* conviviality, bricolage, walking; *Style—* George MacDonald Ross, Esq; ✉ 43 Grove Lane, Leeds LS6 4EQ (tel 0113 294 7379); Department of Philosophy, University of Leeds, Leeds LS2 9JT (tel 0113 343 3283, fax 0113 343 3265, e-mail g.m.ross@leeds.ac.uk)

McDONNELL, Dr Alasdair; MP, MLA; *b* 1 September 1949, Cushendall, Co Antrim; *Educ* St MacNissi's Coll Garron Tower, UC Dublin (MB BCh, BAO); *m* Olivia Nugent; 1 da (Dearbhla), 2 s (Ruairi, Oisin); *Career* doctor 1979–2001; cncllr Belfast City Cncl 1977–2001, dep mayor Belfast 1995–96; memb NI Assembly 1998–, MP (SDLP) Belfast S 2005–; SDLP: spokesman on enterprise, trade and investment 1998–2003, spokesman for employment and learning 2003–, dep ldr 2004–; memb NI Forum for Political Dialogue; memb BMA; *Recreations* Gaelic sports; *Style—* Dr Alasdair McDonnell, MP, MLA; ✉ 143 Ormeau Road, Belfast BT7 1DA (tel 028 9024 2474, fax 028 9043 9935); House of Commons, London SW1A 0AA

McDONNELL, David Croft; CBE (2005), DL (Merseyside 2002); *b* 9 July 1943; *m* 9 Nov 1967, Marieke; 3 da (Emma, Sarah-Jane, Sophia); *Career* Bryce Hanmer & Co (became Thornton Baker 1964 then Grant Thornton 1985): ptnr 1972, nat managing ptnr 1989–2001, ceo worldwide 2001–; chm Bd of Tstees National Museums Liverpool 1995–2005; vice-pres Univ of Liverpool; hon fell Liverpool John Moores Univ 2002; FCA (ACA 1965); *Recreations* sailing, motor racing (spectating), walking, mountaineering; *Style—* David McDonnell, Esq, CBE, DL; ✉ Grant Thornton, 338 Euston Road, London NW1 3BG (tel 020 7391 9505)

McDONNELL, Prof James Anthony Michael (Tony); s of Michael Francis McDonnell (d 2003), of Madeley, Cheshire, and Vera Phyllis, *née* Redding (d 1987); *b* 26 September 1938; *Educ* St Joseph's Coll Stoke on Trent, Univ of Manchester (BS, PhD); *m* 22 July 1961, Jean Mary, da of George Gordon (d 1976); 2 s ((Benedict) Michael b 27 Feb 1965, Roger James b 1 June 1971), 1 da (Louise Anne b 21 Aug 1962); *Career* res asst Nuffield Radio Astronomy Labs 1964–65, post-doctoral res assoc NASA Goddard Spaceflight Centre USA 1965–67; Univ of Kent: lectr in physical electronics 1967–72, sr lectr in electronics 1972–77, reader in space sciences 1977–85, prof of space physics and head of space sci 1985–; prof emeritus Open Univ 2007–; contrib to Planetary Science in Europe JAM McDonnell (Planetary and Interstellar Dust) 1980; various chapters of Advanced Space Res incl: Progress in Planetary Exploration 1981, Recent Researches into Solid Bodies and Magnetic Fields in the Solar System 1982, Cosmic Dust and Space Debris 1986; organiser and orater of welcome address Comet Nucleus Sample Return ESA Cornerstone Workshop Canterbury 1986; memb Ctee Space Astronomy and Radio Div SERC 1979–81; memb: UK Halley Watch Steering Ctee (later CHUKCC) 1983–87, Space Sci Prog Br Nat Space Centre 1988–; COSPAR: memb and sec Panel 3 C 1973–79, memb Sub-cmmn B1 ISC B 1982–86, exec memb ISC B 1984–88, chm ISC B 1988–, memb Organising Ctee IAU Cmmn 22 1979; memb: Meteoroid Shield Design Workshop ESA Comet Halley Mission 1981, ESA Lunar Polar Workshop 1981; govr Workshop on Planetology European Sci Fndn 1981, chm Organisation Ctee Symposium 6 COSPAR IAU IUTAM 1982, discipline specialist Int Halley Watch 1983, memb ESA NASA Primative Bodies Study Team 1984; conslt: space station design USRA 1985, Comet nucleus sample return CNSR 1985–87, CAESAR assessment study 1986, VESTA phase A 1987; memb: Solar System Working Gp 1988–90, Rosetta Mission Definition Team ESA 1988; minor planet Asteroid 9159 named in recognition of role in NASA Stardust mission detectors; FRAS, FBIS 1987; *Books* Cosmic Dust (ed and co-author with John Wiley, 1978); *Recreations* tennis, woodwork; *Style—* Prof Tony McDonnell; ✉ PSSRI, Open University, Milton Keynes MK7 6AA (e-mail tony@unispacekent.co.uk)

McDONNELL, John; MP; *Career* MP (Lab) Hayes and Harlington 1997–; *Style—* John McDonnell, Esq, MP; ✉ Constituency Office, Pump Lane, Hayes, Middlesex UB3 3NB (tel 020 8569 0010, fax 020 8569 0109, website www.john-mcdonnell.net)

McDONNELL, John Beresford William; QC (1984); s of Beresford Conrad McDonnell (d 1960), and Charlotte Mary, *née* Caldwell (d 1981); *b* 26 December 1940; *Educ* City of London Sch, Balliol Coll Oxford (MA), Harvard Law Sch (LLM); *m* 3 Feb 1968, Susan Virginia, da of Wing Cdr Hubert Mortimer Styles, DSO (d 1942), and Audrey Elizabeth (now Lady Richardson); 2 s (Conrad b 1971, William b 1973), 1 da (Constance b 1975); *Career* called to the Bar Inner Temple 1968, Harkness fell 1964–66, Congressional fell American Political Sci Assoc 1965–66, Cons Res Dept 1966–69, HM Dip Serv 1969–71 (first sec, asst private sec to Sec of State 1970–71), in practice Chancery Bar 1972–, bencher Lincoln's Inn 1993; cncllr Lambeth BC 1968–69; *Recreations* sculling; *Clubs* Athenaeum, London Rowing; *Style—* John McDonnell, Esq, QC; ✉ 17 Rutland Street, London SW7 1EJ (tel 020 7584 1498, fax 020 7584 1698); Mortham Tower, Rokeby, Co Durham DL12 9RZ (tel 01833 626900, fax 01833 626901); 9 Stone Building, Lincoln's Inn, London WC2A 3NN (tel 020 7404 5055, fax 020 7405 1551)

MacDONNELL, John Graham Randal; s of John Patrick Randal MacDonnell (d 1964), of Ilfracombe, and Vera Fuggle; *b* 15 November 1955; *Educ* Fortescue House Sch Twickenham (Shaftesbury Homes), Thames Valley GS, King Edward VI Sch Witley, Ealing GS, Newcastle upon Tyne Poly (BA); *m* Barbara Anne (m dis 2002), da of William McBride, of Glasgow; 1 s (Graham Patrick Randal), 1 da (Lara Anne Siobhan); *Career* film ed BBC Scotland 1983–90; credits incl: Campus 1983, The Smith Boys 1983, A Kick Up The 80s 1984, The Visit 1984–88, Laugh - I Nearly Paid My Licence Fee 1985, The Master of Dundreich 1985, Naked Video 1986, Tutti Frutti (1987 BAFTA nomination, Kodak award), Arena - Byrne About Byrne 1988, The Justice Game 1989, Your Cheatin' Heart 1990; freelance film ed 1990–; credits: The Black Velvet Gown 1990 (NY Film & TV Festival Grand Award 1991), Accentuate the Positive 1991, The Blackheath Poisonings 1991–92, Blue Black Permanent 1992, Body and Soul 1992–93, Boswell and Johnson's Tour of the Western Isles 1993, Class Act 1993–94, Billy Connolly's World Tour of Scotland 1994, She's Out 1994–95, Class Act 1995, Silent Witness 1995–96, Billy Connolly's World Tour of Australia 1996, The Slab Boys 1997, Amazing Grace 1997, All for Love 1997, The Hello Girls 1998, Jonathan Creek Christmas Special 1998 and 2001, Wonderful You 1999, Badger 1999, Jonathan Creek 1999–2000, 2002–04, Border

Cafe 2000, Score 2000, Star Street 2001, Helen West, Shadow Play 2001, Holby City 2002 and 2003, The Brief 2004, Ultimate Force 2004, The Playground 2004, Love Soup 2005, The Last Detective 2006, Kingdom 2007, Love Soup 2007; *Recreations* parenting, cinema, galleries, photography, television, reading, swimming, snooker, music; *Style*— John G R MacDonnell, Esq; ✉ e-mail macutd@aol.com

McDONNELL, Jonathan Robert; *b* 3 April 1957; *Educ* Oratory Sch Woodcote, Wadham Coll Oxford (MA); *Career* md I B Tauris & Co Ltd (publishers) 1991–; *Style*— Jonathan McDonnell, Esq; ✉ I B Tauris & Co Ltd, 6 Salem Road, London W2 4BU (tel 020 7243 1225, fax 020 7243 1226, e-mail jmcdonnell@ibtauris.com)

MacDONNELL OF THE GLENS, The Count Randal Christian Charles Augustus Somerled Patrick; s of The Count and 24 Chief Robert Jarlath Hartpole Hamilton MacDonnell of the Glens (d 1984), of 5 Longford Terr, Monkstown, Dublin, and his 2 w, The Countess MacDonnell of the Glens, *née* Úna Kathleen Dolan; descent from Iain Mhóir MacDonnell, 2 s of John I Lord of the Isles and Princess Margaret, da of King Robert II of Scotland; *see* Burke's Irish Family Records 1976 and Burke's Peerage, Earl of Antrim (who descends from the yst s of 5 Chief and in the female line); f suc kinsman the 23 Chief (ka 1941); 19 Chief cr Bt 1872, dsp 1875; *b* 19 August 1950; *Educ* Stonyhurst, Trinity Coll, Dublin and the King's Inns, Dublin; *Heir* bro, Count Peter MacDonnell; *Career* 25 chief Clan Donald S of Antrim; officially recognised Chief of the Name by the Chief Herald of Ireland (Gaelic patronymic "Mac Iain Mhóir") Lord of the Glens of Antrim; Count of the Holy Roman Empire (which title, created in the preceeding generation passed to the heirs male of the 1st Count in 1766); Kt of Honour and Devotion SMOM 1971; *Books* The Lost Houses of Ireland (2002); *Recreations* opera, ballet, rugby, polo, history, parties, genealogy, architecture; *Style*— The Count Randal MacDonnell of the Glens

McDONOUGH, David Fergus; OBE (1998); s of late Alan James McDonough, of Eastbourne, E Sussex, and Shirley Davis; *b* 7 June 1953; *Educ* Stowe, Merton Coll Oxford (MA); *m* 1, 1978, Caroline Eugénie, *née* Axford; m 2 (m dis), 28 May 1992, Mrs Vanessa E L Reeves, da of late Douglas Gent; *Career* special advsr to The Lord Feldman 1975–79, md McDonough Assocs Ltd 1979–90, dep chm Bell Pottinger Consultants (formerly Lowe Bell Consultants), chm Kiki McDonough Ltd, chm The McDonough Partnership 2003–; co-fndr The October Club (chm 1988–98 and 2000–05, life pres 2005–), memb Bd of Regents Harris Manchester Coll Oxford; tstee CancerBACUP; Freeman City of London, Liveryman Worshipful Co of Merchant Taylors; FRSA; OStJ 2002; *Recreations* politics, reading, music, theatre; *Clubs* White's, Boodle's, Garrick; *Style*— David McDonough, Esq, OBE; ✉ The McDonough Partnership, 12 Park Place, St James's, London SW1A 1LP (tel 020 7493 9609, fax 020 7493 2620)

McDOUGALL, Prof Bonnie S; da of William Morris McDougall (d 1990), and Ruth Constance, *née* Mather (d 1978); *b* 12 March 1941; *Educ* St George Girls' HS Sydney, Wollongong HS, Peking Univ, Univ of Sydney (MA, PhD, Univ medal); *m* Dec 1979, (Harry) Anders Hansson; 1 s ((Carl) Torkel b 30 April 1980); *Career* Univ of Sydney: Oriental librarian 1967–68, res fell 1970–71, lectr in Oriental studies 1972–76; Nuffield travelling scholar SOAS Univ of London 1975, assoc Harvard Univ 1979–80 (res fell 1976–79), ed and translator Foreign Languages Press 1980–83, English teacher Coll of Foreign Affairs Peking 1984–86; prof of modern Chinese: Univ of Oslo 1987–90 (sr lectr 1986–87), Univ of Edinburgh 1990–; visiting lectr Harvard Univ 1977, 1978 and 1979; advsr Assoc of Chinese Translators and Interpreters in Scotland 1993–; memb: Amnesty International 1987–, Edgar Wallace Soc 1988–94, PEN International 1989–92, Universities' China Ctee 1990– (memb Exec Cncl 1990–93), Cncl Br Assoc of Chinese Studies 1991– (pres 1995–97), Bd Euro Assoc of Chinese Studies 1992–, Exec Ctee Scots Australia Cncl 1994–95; *Books* The Introduction of Western Literary Theories into China 1919–25 (1971), Paths in Dream: Selected Prose and Poetry of Ho Ch'i-fang (ed, 1976), Mao Zedong's Talks at the Yan'an Conference on Literature and Art (ed, 1980 and 1992), Notes from the City of the Sun: Poems by Bei Dao (ed, 1983), Popular Chinese Literature and Performing Arts in the People's Republic of China 1949–79 (ed, 1984), Bodong (ed, 1985), Waves (ed, 1985), The August Sleepwalker (ed, 1988), The Yellow Earth: A Film by Chen Kaige (1991), The Literature of China in the 20th Century (with K Louie, 1997), Chinese Concepts of Privacy (co-ed, 2002), Love-Letters and Privacy in Modern China: The Intimate Lives of Lu Xua and Xu Guaugping (2002), Fictional Authors, Imaginary Audiences: Modern Chinese Literature in the Twentieth Century (2003); author of numerous papers in jls; *Recreations* travel, reading, walking; *Style*— Prof Bonnie S McDougall; ✉ School of Asian Studies, University of Edinburgh, 8 Buccleuch Place, Edinburgh EH8 9LW (tel 0131 650 4227, fax 0131 651 1258, e-mail bonnie.s.mcdougall@ed.ac.uk)

McDOUGALL, Douglas Christopher Patrick; OBE (2001); s of Patrick McDougall (d 1950), and Helen McDougall (d 1980); *b* 18 March 1944; *Educ* Edinburgh Acad, ChCh Oxford (MA); *m* 4 June 1986, Hon Carolyn Jane, da of Baron Griffiths, MC, PC (Life Peer), *qv*; 2 da (Fiona Maria b 1987, Mary Helen b 1990); *Career* sr ptnr Baillie Gifford & Co 1989–99 (investment mangr and ptnr 1969); chm IMRO 1997–2000 (non-exec dir 1987–); non-exec dir: Provincial Insurance plc 1989–94, Baillie Gifford Japan Tst plc 1989–99, Pacific Horizon Trust plc 1992–, Stramongate Assets plc 2003–; chm: Institutional Fund Mangrs Assoc 1994–96, Assoc of Investment Tst Companies 1995–98, Foreign and Colonial Eurotrust plc 1999–, The Law Debenture Corp plc 2000–, 3i Bioscience Investment Tst 2000– (dep chm 1999–2000), The Independent Investment Tst 2000–, The Scottish Investment Tst plc 2003– (non-exec dir 1998–); dep chm Sand Aire Ltd 1999–2003; non-exec dir: The Law Debenture Corp plc 1998–, Sand Aire Ltd 1999–, The Monks Investment Tst plc 1999–, Herald Investment Tst plc 2002–; memb Investment Bd Univ of Cambridge 2005–; *Clubs* Brooks's, New (Edinburgh), Hon Co of Edinburgh Golfers; *Style*— Douglas McDougall, Esq, OBE; ✉ Linplum House, Haddington, East Lothian EH41 4PE (tel 01620 810242)

MacDOUGALL, John; MP; s of William MacDougall (d 1967), and Barbara, *née* Lyons; *b* 8 December 1947; *m* 21 Sept 1968, Catherine, da of Ludwic Wojcik; 1 s (Scott b 31 May 1969), 1 da (Julia b 17 May 1971); *Career* MP (Lab) Glenrothes 2001–; *Style*— John MacDougall, Esq, MP; ✉ House of Commons, London SW1A 0AA

MACDOUGALL, Patrick Lorn; s of James Archibald Macdougall, WS (d 1982), and Valerie Jean, *née* Fraser; *b* 21 June 1939; *Educ* schs in Kenya, Millfield, UC Oxford; *m* 1, 24 June 1967 (m dis 1982), Alison Noel, da of Herbert Charles Offer, MC (d 1991), of Cheshire; 2 s (Alasdair William Lorn b 1970, Thomas Hugh James b 1972); m 2, 15 April 1983, Bridget Margaret, da of Peter Scott Young (d 1988); 3 da (Laura Margaret Valerie b 1984, Nicola Elizabeth Bridget b 1987, Vanessa Emily Hope b 1990); *Career* called to the Bar Inner Temple 1962; mangr NM Rothschild & Sons 1967–70, chief exec Amex Bank (formerly Rothschild Intercontinental Bank) 1977–78 (exec dir 1970–77), exec dir Jardine Matheson Holdings 1978–85, chm West Merchant Bank Ltd (formerly Standard Chartered Merchant Bank) 1989–98 (chief exec 1985–97); non-exec chm Arlington Securities plc 1999–2005; dir: Global Natural Resources Inc 1994–96, Nuclear Electric plc 1994–96, National Provident Institution 1997–99; tstee SANE 2001– (chm 2002–06); FCA 1967, FRSA 1988; *Recreations* skiing, golf, opera, bridge; *Clubs* Athenaeum, Hurlingham, Shek-O CC (Hong Kong); *Style*— Patrick Macdougall, Esq; ✉ 110 Rivermead Court, London SW6 3SB (tel 020 7736 3506, fax 020 7731 8912)

McDOWALL, His Hon Judge Andrew Gordon; s of William C McDowall (d 1998), and Margery, *née* Wilson (d 1996); *b* 2 September 1948; *Educ* Glasgow Acad, The Queen's Coll Oxford (MA, BCL); *m* 21 Aug 1976, Cecilia, da of Harold Clarke; 1 s (Peter James b 7 May 1982), 1 da (Eleanor Katherine Louisa b 1 May 1985); *Career* called to the Bar 1972; circuit judge (SE Circuit) 1998–; memb London Orpheus Choir; *Recreations* squash, reading, music, paranomasia; *Style*— His Hon Judge McDowall; ✉ c/o 1 King's Bench Walk, Temple, London EC4Y 7DB

McDOWALL, Christopher John Eric (Chris); s of Ian Derek McDowall, of North Curry, Somerset, and Jocelyn Florence Malet, *née* Tongue; *b* 3 September 1944; *Educ* Sherborne, US Marine Corps Cmd & Staff Coll, Nigerian Higher Cmd & Staff Coll (RM rep skiing, rugby, athletics, sailing and riding); *m* 1974, Pieternella Hendrika, da of Joseph Kentgens; 1 da (Nina b 5 Feb 1975), 1 s (Duncan b 17 Aug 1976); *Career* RM Offr 1962–94: 42 and 45 Commandos RM 1964–74, seconded as Br Sr Directing Staff memb Nigerian Higher Cmd & Staff Coll 1987–89, dep chief exec Multi Discipline Special Forces Base 1989–91, sr mangr Govt Strategic Mission (RM Lt-Col UK Arms Control Implementation Gp) 1991–94; asst sec-gen InterParly Union Palace of Westminster 1994–96, exec dir PRCA 1996–; MIPD 1989, FIMgt 1990, MInstD 1996; *Recreations* sailing, skiing, fine art; *Clubs* Special Forces; *Style*— Chris McDowall, Esq; ✉ Public Relations Consultants Association, Willow House, Willow Place, London SW1P 1JH (tel 020 7233 6026, fax 020 7828 4797, e-mail chris@prca.org.uk)

McDOWALL, David Buchanan; s of Angus David McDowall (d 1957), and Enid Margaret, *née* Crook; *b* 14 April 1945; *Educ* Monkton Combe Sch, RMA Sandhurst, St John's Coll Oxford (MA, MLitt); *m* 19 April 1975, Elizabeth Mary Risk, da of Dr John McClelland Laird; 2 s (Angus b 1977, William b 1979); *Career* Subaltern RA 1965–70; Br Cncl (Bombay, Baghdad & London) 1972–77, UNRWA 1977–79; writer (for adults and children); *Books* Lebanon - A Conflict of Minorities (1983), The Kurds (1985), The Palestinians (children's book, 1986), The Palestinians (1987), The Spanish Armada (1988), An Illustrated History of Britain (1989), Palestine and Israel: The Uprising and Beyond (1989), The Kurds: A Nation Denied (1992), Europe and the Arabs: Discord or Symbiosis? (1992), Britain in Close-up (1993), The Palestinians: The Road to Nationhood (1994), A Modern History of the Kurds (1995, revised edn 2000), Richmond Park: the Walker's Historical Guide (1996, revised edn (Richmond Park: the Walker's Guide) 2006), Hampstead Heath: The Walker's Guide (jtly, 1998, revised edn 2006), The Thames from Hampton to Richmond Bridge (2002), The Thames from Richmond to Putney Bridge (2005), Windsor Great Park: the Walker's Guide (2007); *Style*— David McDowall, Esq; ✉ 31 Cambrian Road, Richmond, Surrey TW10 6JQ (tel 020 8940 3911)

MacDOWELL, Prof Douglas Maurice; s of Maurice Alfred MacDowell (d 1973), and Dorothy Jean, *née* Allan (d 1980); *b* 8 March 1931; *Educ* Highgate Sch, Balliol Coll Oxford (MA, DLitt); *Career* classics master: Allhallows Sch 1954–56, Merchant Taylors' Sch 1956–58; reader in Greek and Latin Univ of Manchester 1970–71 (asst lectr 1958–61, lectr 1961–68, sr lectr 1968–70), visiting fell Merton Coll Oxford 1969, prof of Greek Univ of Glasgow 1971–2001, emeritus prof and hon res fell Univ of Glasgow 2001–; sec Cncl of Univ Classical Depts 1974–76; chm Cncl Classical Assoc of Scotland 1976–82; FRSE 1991, FBA 1993; *Books* Andokides: On the Mysteries (1962), Athenian Homicide Law (1963), Aristophanes: Wasps (1971), The Law in Classical Athens (1978), Spartan Law (1986), Demosthenes: Against Meidias (1990), Aristophanes and Athens (1995), Antiphon and Andocides (with M Gagarin, 1998), Demosthenes: On the False Embassy (2000), Demosthenes: Speeches 27–38 (2004); *Clubs* Oxford and Cambridge; *Style*— Prof Douglas MacDowell, FRSE, FBA; ✉ Department of Classics, University of Glasgow, Glasgow G12 8QQ (tel 0141 330 5256)

McDOWELL, Sir Eric Wallace; kt (1990), CBE (1982); s of Martin Wallace McDowell (d 1968), of Belfast, and Edith Florence, *née* Hillock (d 1974); *b* 7 June 1925; *Educ* Royal Belfast Academical Inst; *m* 24 June 1954, Helen Lilian, da of William Montgomery (d 1951), of Belfast; 2 da (Kathleen b 24 Jan 1958, Claire b 25 March 1964), 1 s (Martin b 11 Nov 1959); *Career* WWII serv 1943–46; qualified CA 1948; ptnr Wilson Hennessy & Crawford 1952–73, sr ptnr in Belfast Deloitte Haskins & Sells 1980–85 (ptnr 1973–80); dir: NI Transport Holding Co 1971–74, Spence Bryson Ltd 1986–89, TSB Bank Northern Ireland plc 1986–92, Capita Management Consultants Ltd 1991–98 (chm 1992–98), First Trust Bank 1992–96, Shepherd Ltd 1992–2004; memb: Advsy Ctee NI Central Investment Fund for Charities 1975–98 (chm 1980–98), NI Econ Cncl 1977–83, Industrial Devpt Bd for NI 1982–91 (chm 1986–91), Broadcasting Cncl for NI 1983–86; memb: Bd of Govrs Royal Belfast Academical Inst 1959– (chm 1977–86), Cncl Inst of CAs Ireland 1968–77 (pres 1974–75), Exec Ctee Relate NI Marriage Guidance 1981–2002 (chm 1992–96), Bd Abbeyfield Belfast Soc Ltd 1986–2006 (treas 1986–99), Financial Reporting Review Panel 1990–94, Bd Tstees National Relate 1992–2000, Senate Queen's Univ of Belfast 1993–2001, Presbyterian Church in Ireland (trustee 1983–); pres: Confedn of Ulster Socs 1989–98, Belfast Old Instonians Assoc 1993–94; Hon DSc Econ Queen's Univ of Belfast 1989; FCA 1957; *Recreations* current affairs, music and drama, foreign travel; *Clubs* Ulster Reform (Belfast), Royal Over-Seas League; *Style*— Sir Eric McDowell, CBE; ✉ 7 Newforge Manor, 11 Newforge Lane, Belfast BT9 5NT (tel 028 9066 8771)

M

MacDUFF, His Hon Judge Alistair Geoffrey; QC (1993); s of Alexander MacDonald MacDuff (d 1985), and Iris Emma, *née* Gardner (d 1997); *b* 26 May 1945; *Educ* Ecclesfield GS nr Sheffield, LSE (LLB), Univ of Sheffield (LLM); *m* 1, 27 Sept 1969, Susan Christine (d 1991), da of Ronald David Kitchener, of Salthouse, Norfolk; 2 da (Karen b 1971, Jennifer b 1972); m 2, 9 July 1993, Katherine Anne, da of late Dr John Buckley, of Frampton on Severn, Glos; 1 da (Rebecca b 1995), 1 s (George b 1997); *Career* called to the Bar Lincoln's Inn 1969, recorder of the Crown Ct 1987–97, circuit judge (Midland & Oxford Circuit) 1997–, designated civil judge Birmingham 2000–, sr circuit judge 2002–; former chm local ward Lib Party; *Recreations* opera, theatre, golf, association football, travel; *Clubs* Hendon GC, Economicals AFC, Painswick RFC; *Style*— His Hon Judge MacDuff, QC; ✉ Birmingham Civil Justice Centre, 33 Bull Street, Birmingham B4 6DS (tel 021 681 4441)

McEACHRAN, Colin Neil; QC (Scot 1981); s of Eric Robins McEachran (d 1974), and Norah Helen, *née* Bushe (d 1995); *b* 14 January 1940; *Educ* Glenalmond Coll, Merton Coll Oxford (MA), Univ of Glasgow (LLB), Univ of Chicago (JD); *m* 27 Sept 1967, Katherine Charlotte, da of K D D Henderson, CMG; 2 da (Katrina Emily b 24 Oct 1968, Juliet Helen b 27 Jan 1971); *Career* admitted advocate 1968, advocate depute 1974–77; pt/t pres Pension Appeal Tbnl of Scotland 1995–; memb Scottish Legal Aid Bd 1990–98; chm Cwlth Games Cncl for Scotland 1995–99; *Recreations* target shooting, hill walking; *Style*— Colin McEachran, Esq, QC; ✉ 13 Saxe Coburg Place, Edinburgh EH3 5BR (tel 0131 332 6820)

MacECHERN, Gavin MacAlister; s of Dugald MacAlister MacEchern, and Diana Mary, *née* Body (d 2002); *b* 7 March 1944; *Educ* Tonbridge; *m* 1, 1972 (m dis 2002), Sarah Alison, da of late Eric and Cecil Walker, *née* Eaton-Evans; 3 da (Georgina b 1976, Tatiana b 1978, Christina b 1981); m 2, 2007, Caroline Valentine, da of Maj William Riley, MC, and late Patricia, *née* Pioleau; *Career* admitted slr 1967; fndr shareholder and dir Arlington Securities plc 1980–94, chm Mansford Holdings plc 1995–, chm Renaissance LifeCare plc 2005–; *Recreations* racing, skiing, shooting, tennis, golf; *Clubs* Turf, Wisley; *Style*— Gavin MacEchern, Esq; ✉ Mansford Holdings plc, 15 Bury Walk, London SW3 6QD

McENTEE, John; s of Andrew Francis McEntee (d 1997), of Cavan, and Julia, *née* Cusack; *b* 10 August 1954; *Educ* Poor Clares Convent Sch Co Cavan, De La Salle Sch Co Cavan, St Patrick's Coll Co Cavan; *m* 1976 (m dis 2003), Colette, *née* Fitzpatrick; 1 da (Laura b 1979), 2 s (Paul b 1981, Jack b 1989); *Career* journalist; trainee reporter The Anglo Celt 1970–72, reporter Dublin Evening Press 1972–73, reporter The Irish Press Group 1973–75, London corr The Irish Press Group 1975–88, dep ed Londoners Diary Evening Standard 1988–89, dep ed diary The Times 1989–91, feature writer Daily Express 1991;

Sunday Express: royal corr 1992, media corr 1993, London section 1993, arts ed 1994; dep ed diary Express 1994–96; William Hickey: 1996–98, columnist 1998–2000; columnist Daily Mail 2002–; memb Useless Information Soc 1997; supporter Goal; *Recreations* talking, thinking, lighting candles in churches; *Clubs* Reform, Gerry's, Capital; *Style—* John McEntee, Esq; ✉ Daily Mail, Northcliffe House, 2 Derry Street, Kensington, London W8 5TT (tel 020 7938 6325, fax 020 7938 7671, e-mail john.mcentee@dailymail.co.uk)

McEVOY, His Hon Judge David Dand; QC (1983); s of David Dand McEvoy (d 1988), of Stevenston, Ayrshire, and Ann Elizabeth, *née* Breslin (d 1994); *b* 25 June 1938; *Educ* Mount St Mary's Coll, Lincoln Coll Oxford (BA); *m* 6 April 1974, Belinda Anne, da of Lt-Col Thomas Argyll Robertson, OBE, of Pershore, Worcs; 3 da (Alice b 1978, Louise b 1979, Isabella b 1984); *Career* 2 Lt The Black Watch (RHR) 1957–59, served Cyprus 1958; called to the Bar Inner Temple 1964; recorder of the Crown Court 1979–96 (asst recorder 1977–79), circuit judge (Midland & Oxford Circuit) 1996–; *Recreations* racing, golf, fishing; *Clubs* Garrick, Highland Brigade, Senior Golfers' Soc, Blackwell Golf; *Style—* His Hon Judge McEvoy, QC; ✉ Worcester Combined Courts Centre, Shirehall, Worcester (e-mail davidmcevoy@compuserve.com)

McEVOY, Peter Aloysius; OBE (2003); s of Daniel Martin McEvoy, and Gladys Isabella Amelia McEvoy; *b* 22 March 1953; *Educ* Tudor Grange GS, Birmingham Coll of Law, Chester Coll of Law; *Career* amateur golfer; major tournament victories: Br Univs Stroke Play 1973, Leicestershire Fox 1976, Euro amateur championship 1977 and 1983, amateur champion 1977–78 (runner up 1987), Lytham Trophy 1978, Silver medal Open Championships 1978 and 1979, Scrutton Jug 1978, 1980 and 1985, Duncan Putter 1978, 1980 and 1987, Selborne Salver 1979 and 1980, English Open Amateur Stroke Play 1980 (tied, runner up 1978), Lagonda Trophy 1980, County Champion of Champions 1984, Berkshire Trophy 1985, Berkhamsted Trophy 1986, Hampshire Hog 1989; youth int 1974, England int 1976– (capt 1982–97), with Br team 1977–, capt GB and Ireland 1998–2001; memb team: Walker Cup 1977, 1979, 1981, 1985, 1989 (winners), 1999 (winners), 2001 (winners, first GB and I capt to win successive Walker Cups), Eisenhower Trophy 1978, 1980, 1984, 1986 and 1988, Fiat Trophy 1980; most successful English golfer (153 appearances), only player from any country to win a world individual title, play in a world championship winning team and captain a world championship winning team, only Br amateur to complete 72 holes in US Masters 1978; chm of selectors Walker Cup 2003 and 2004; Golf Writers Trophy 1978, Gerald Micklem Trophy 1999; articled clerk Rees Edward Maddox & Co (Slrs) 1977–81, md Sporting Concepts Ltd 1981–; *Recreations* all sports; *Clubs* Royal & Ancient; hon memb: Copt Heath, Handsworth, City of Derry, St Annes, Chantilly (France), L'Ancresse (Guernsey), European, Nairn, Royal Troon, Filey, Tewkesbury Park; *Style—* Peter McEvoy, Esq, OBE; ✉ Sporting Concepts Ltd, Cider Mill House, Old Manor Lane, Tewkesbury, Gloucestershire GL20 7EA (tel 01684 291345, fax 01684 273812, e-mail sportingconcepts@btconnect.com)

McEWAN, Ian Russell; CBE (2000); s of Maj David McEwan (d 1996), of Ash, Hants, and Rose Violet Lilian Moore; *b* 21 June 1948; *Educ* Woolverstone Hall Sch, Univ of Sussex (BA), UEA (MA); *m* 1, 1982 (m dis), Penelope Ruth, da of Dennis Allen, of Lewes, E Sussex; 2 s (William b 1983, Gregory b 1986), 2 step da (Polly b 1970, Alice b 1972); m 2, 1997, Annalena McAfee; *Career* author; began writing 1970; Shakespeare Prize 1999; Hon DLitt: Univ of Sussex 1989, UEA 1993, Univ of London 1998; FRSL 1982; *Books* First Love, Last Rites (1975), In Between The Sheets (1978), The Cement Garden (1978), The Comfort of Strangers (1981), The Imitation Game (1981), Or Shall We Die? (1983), The Ploughman's Lunch (1985), The Child in Time (1987), The Innocent (1990), Black Dogs (shortlisted Booker Prize, 1992), The Daydreamer (1994), Enduring Love (1997, shortlisted Whitbread Novel of the Year Award 1997, shortlisted Booker Prize 1998), Amsterdam (1998, winner Booker Prize 1998), Atonement (2001), Saturday (2005); *Film* The Ploughman's Lunch (1983), Last Day of Summer (1984), Sour Sweet (1989), The Innocent (dir by John Schlesinger, 1993), The Good Son (1993); *Style—* Ian McEwan, Esq, CBE; ✉ c/o Jonathan Cape Ltd, 20 Vauxhall Bridge Road, London SW1V 2SA (tel 020 7973 9730)

McEWAN, Mhairi; da of Edward McEwan, of Scotland, and Rose Helen, *née* Betts; *b* 5 July 1961; *Educ* St Michael's Sch Billingham, St Mary's Sixth Form Coll Middlesbrough, Univ of Leicester (BSc, Faculty of Sci prize); *m* 25 June 1988, Phillip Keague (Phil) Bentley, *qv*, s of Alan William Bentley; 1 da (Naomi Frances b 22 Jan 1992), 1 s (Guy Edward Keague b 29 April 1994); *Career* Lever Brothers Ltd UK: brand mangr 1982–86, nat account exec (sales) 1986–88, Euro brand mangr 1988–89, market mangr Egypt Unilever Export Cairo 1989–92, Euro mktg mangr Lever Europe Paris 1992–94; vice-pres mktg (Europe) Pepsi-Cola International Ltd London 1995–96, vice-pres mktg Walkers Snacks Ltd (pt of Pepsi-Co) 1996–97; int mktg conslt 1998–; md The Brand Learning Partners Ltd 2000–; memb: Mktg Soc, IoD; Chartered Marketer; FCIM 1995, RSA 2001; *Recreations* horse riding, skiing, tennis, piano; *Style—* Ms Mhairi McEwan; ✉ Brand Learning Partners Limited, Burgoine Quay, 8 Lower Teddington Road, Hampton Wick, Kingston KT1 4ER (tel 020 8614 8150, fax 020 8255 9057, e-mail mhairi.mcewan@brandlearning.com)

MacEWAN, Nigel Savage; s of Nigel Savage, and Ellen, *née* Wharton; *b* 21 March 1933; *Educ* Yale Univ (BA), Harvard Univ (MBA); *m* 1; 1 s (Nigel), 3 da (Alison, Pamela, Elizabeth); m 2, 2 Sept 1995, Judith Sperry; *Career* served USN 1955–57; assoc: Morgan Stanley & Co NYC 1959–62, White Weld & Co NYC 1962–63; vice-pres R S Dickson and Co Charlotte NC 1963–68, chm Financial Consultants Int Ltd Brussels 1965–68, ptnr then pres and dir White Weld & Co NYC 1968–78, sr vice-pres and dir Merrill Lynch Pierce Fenner and Smith NYC 1978–87, chm Merrill Lynch Capital Partners Inc 1985–87, pres, ceo and dir Kleinwort Benson N America Inc NYC 1987–93, dir Kleinwort Benson Aust Income Fund Inc 1987–93; former pres and dir Kleinwort Benson Holdings Inc; former dir: Alex Brown Kleinwort Benson Reality Advisors Inc, Kleinwort Benson Ltd, Kleinwort Benson Gp plc, Sharps Pixley Inc, Va Trading Corp, Supermarkets General, Amstar, Cellu-Craft, Sun Hung Kai Int Ltd, Merrill Lynch Int Ltd, Credit Suisse White Weld; chm NY Gp Securities Industry Assoc 1975–76; adjunct prof of business admin Univ of NY 1973–75; pres Tokeneke Tax Dist Darien 1978–80 (latterly treas); memb: Islesboro Sailors Museum Ctee 1994–2000, Islesboro Health Bd 1995–2005, Bd of Tstees Island Inst 1998–2001; memb Advsy Bd: Islesboro Island Tst 1997–, Conservation Law Fndn 1998–2006; memb Securities Industry Assoc (chm NY Gp 1975–76); *Clubs* Yale, Harvard (Fairfield Co), Tokeneke, Wee Burn, NY Yacht, Tarratine (pres 2002–), Clyde Cruising (Scotland), Cruising Club of America; *Style—* Nigel S MacEwan, Esq

McEWAN, Robin Gilmour; QC (Scot 1981); s of Ian Gilmour McEwan (d 1976), and Mary McArthur Bowman McEwan; *b* 12 December 1943; *Educ* Paisley GS, Univ of Glasgow (LLB, PhD); *m* 1973, Sheena, da of Stewart Francis McIntyre (d 1974); 2 da (Stephanie b 1979, Louisa b 1983); *Career* Sheriff of Lanark 1982–88, Sheriff of Ayr 1988–; temp judge Court of Session and High Court of Justiciary 1991–2000, senator Coll of Justice 2000–; *Recreations* golf; *Clubs* New (Edinburgh), Hon Co of Edinburgh Golfers, Prestwick Golf; *Style—* The Hon Lord McEwan

McEWEN, Prof James; s of Daniel McEwen (d 1973), of Kinross, and Elizabeth Wells, *née* Dishington (d 1962); *b* 6 February 1940; *Educ* Dollar Acad, Univ of St Andrews (MB ChB); *m* 24 Oct 1964, Elizabeth May, da of late Andrew Archibald; 1 s (Daniel Mark b 6 May 1966), 1 da (Ruth Elizabeth b 24 Jan 1968); *Career* various trg posts in hosp and general practice Dundee 1963–65, asst med offr of health Dundee 1965–66, lectr Dept of Social and Occupational Med Univ of Dundee 1966–74, sr lectr Dept of Community Health Univ of Nottingham 1975–81, chief med offr Health Educn Cncl 1981–82, prof of community med KCL and dir of public health Camberwell Health Authy 1982–89; Univ of Glasgow: Henry Mechan prof 1989–2000, prof of public health 2000–02, emeritus prof of public health 2002–; pres Faculty of Public Health Medicine RCP 1998–2001; chair: UK Voluntary Bd for Public Health Specialists 2003–, Pharmacy Healthlink 2004–, Health Protection Advsy Gp Scotland 2005–; FMedSci, FFPH, Hon FFPHMI, FFOM, FRCP, FDS RCS; *Books* Coronary Heart Disease and Patterns of Living (jtly, 1979), Participation in Health (jtly, 1983), Measuring Health Status (jtly, 1986); *Style—* Prof James McEwen; ✉ Auchanachie, Ruthven, Huntly AB54 4SS (tel and fax 01466 760742, e-mail j.mcewen@tiscali.co.uk)

McEWEN, Sir John Roderick Hugh; 5 Bt (UK 1953), of Marchmont, Co Berwick, and Bardrochat, Co Ayr; yr s of Sir Robert Lindley McEwen, 3 Bt (d 1980), and Brigid Cecilia, *née* Laver; suc bro, Sir James Francis Lindley, 4 Bt, 1983; *b* 4 November 1965; *Educ* Ampleforth, UCL, Univ of Glasgow; *m* 2000, Rachel Elizabeth, *née* Soane; 2 da (Susanna Alice Islay b 18 Feb 2002, Georgia Catherine Mamie b 31 March 2004); *Heir* cous, Adam McEwen; *Style—* Sir John McEwen, Bt

McEWEN, Prof Keith Alistair; s of George Charles McEwen (d 1979), and Marjorie Anne, *née* Field (d 1991); *b* 11 December 1944; *Educ* Dr Challoner's GS Amersham, Pembroke Coll Cambridge (MA, PhD); *m* 1, 12 April 1969 (m dis 1982), Anne, da of Rupert Thompson (d 1980); 1 s, 1 da; m 2, 20 May 1986, Ursula, da of Maximilian Steigenberger (d 1983); *Career* lectr in physics: Univ of Copenhagen 1970–73, Univ of Salford 1973–81; seconded as sr lectr to Institut Laue-Langevin Grenoble 1981–86, prof of experimental physics Birkbeck Coll London 1986–97, prof of physics UCL 1997–; CPhys, FInstP 1989; *Publications* 200 papers in physics research jls; *Recreations* music, walking, skiing; *Style—* Prof Keith McEwen; ✉ Department of Physics and Astronomy, University College London, Gower Street, London WC1E 6BT (tel 020 7679 3492, fax 020 7679 0595, e-mail k.mcewen@ucl.ac.uk)

MACEY, Roger David Michael; s of late Eric Hamilton Macey, and Margaret Maria, *née* Newman; *b* 15 November 1942; *Educ* St Mary's Coll Ireland; *m* 1, 1970 (m dis 1995), Julie Elizabeth, da of John Everard Mellors, of Mount Eliza, Melbourne, Aust; 2 s (Jonathan b 20 April 1973, Giles b 25 May 1976); m 2, 1996, Barbara; *Career* dir: Wm Brandts Sons & Co (insur) Ltd 1972–76, P S Mossé & Ptnrs Ltd 1977–83, Macdonagh Boland Group 1989; non-exec dir: J Jackson & Partners Ltd 1975–76, P S Mossé Life & Pensions 1977–83, George Miller Underwriting Agencies Ltd 1977–86; md Macey Williams Ltd 1976–94; chm: Macey Williams Insurance Services Ltd 1976–94, Macey Clifton Walters Ltd 1991–94, Conquest Security Services plc, K S Conquest plc, Aon Mergers and Acquisitions Gp UK; dir: Rollins Hudig Hall Ltd (following takeover of Macey Williams companies) 1994–96, Aon Risk Services Ltd (following name change) 1996–; memb Lloyd's 1974–; *Recreations* shooting, golf, tennis, horse racing; *Clubs* Turf, City of London, Mill Reef (Antigua); *Style—* Roger Macey, Esq; ✉ 62 Howards Lane, Putney, London SW15 6QD; Aon Mergers & Acquisitions, 8 Devonshire Square, London EC2M 4PL

McFADDEN, Jean Alexandra; CBE, JP, DL (City of Glasgow 1982); *b* 26 November 1941; *Educ* Hyndland Sch, Univ of Glasgow (MA), Notre Dame Coll of Educn, Univ of Strathclyde (LLB); *Career* classics teacher various secdy schs Glasgow and Lanarkshire 1964–86, sr lectr in law Univ of Strathclyde 1992–; Glasgow City Cncl (formerly Glasgow Corp then Glasgow DC): cncllr Cowcaddens Ward 1971–84, cncllr Scotstoun Ward following boundary change 1984–, convener Manpower Ctee 1975–77, opposition ldr 1977–79, ldr of the Cncl 1979–86 and 1992–94 (dep ldr 1990–92), hon city treas and convener Fin Ctee 1986–92, convener Glasgow City Cncl 1995–96, convener Social Strategy Ctee 1996–99, convener Strathclyde Police Jt Bd 2003–07; convener Regeneration Strategy Sub-Ctee 1999–2003; memb: Scottish Economic Cncl 1993–96, Health Appointments Advsy Ctee 1994–2000, Scottish Police Servs Authy 2007–; pres Convention of Scottish Local Authorities 1990–92, chm Scottish Charity Law Cmmn 2000–04; convener Scottish Local Govt Info Unit 1984–2003; memb Ancient Monuments Bd for Scotland 2000–03; memb Bd Citizens Theatre 1972–2006; Vice Lord-Lt City of Glasgow 1981–92; *Recreations* golf, west highland terriers, theatre-going; *Style—* Ms Jean McFadden, CBE, DL; ✉ 16 Lansdowne Crescent, Glasgow G20 6NQ (tel 0141 334 3522); Glasgow City Council, City Chambers, George Square, Glasgow G2 1DU (tel 0141 287 4054, fax 0141 287 4173, e-mail jean.mcfadden@councillors.glasgow.gov.uk)

McFADDEN, Patrick (Pat); MP; *b* 26 March 1965, Paisley; *Educ* Holyrood Sch, Univ of Edinburgh; *Career* political sec PM's Office 2002–05, MP (Lab) Wolverhampton SE 2005–; Parly under-sec of state Cabinet Office 2006–; memb: Community Union, TGWU; *Style—* Pat McFadden, MP; ✉ House of Commons, London SW1A 0AA

MACFADYEN, Air Marshal Ian David; CB (1991), OBE (1984); s of Air Marshal Sir Douglas Macfadyen, KCB, CBE (d 1968), and Priscilla Alfreda, *née* Dafforn (now Mrs P A Rowan); *b* 19 February 1942; *Educ* Marlborough (capt shooting team), RAF Coll Cranwell (Sword of Honour); *m* 28 Jan 1967, Sally, da of Air Cdre Ernest Bruce Harvey; 1 s (Simon James Douglas b 19 Aug 1968), 1 da (Katherine Elizabeth (Mrs I F Comaish) b 28 April 1971); *Career* RAF Coll Cranwell 1960–63, 19 Sqdn 1965–68, ADC HQ RAF Strike Cmd 1969, flying instr Cranwell 1970–73, RAF Staff Coll 1973, 111 Sqdn 1974–75, Flt Cdr 43 Sqdn 1975–76, HQ 2 ATAF(PSO) 1976–79, cmd 29 Sqdn 1980–84, cmd 23 Sqdn 1984, MOD London 1984–85, cmd RAF Leuchars 1985–87, RCDS 1988, MOD 1988–90, COS then Cdr Br Forces Middle East Riyadh 1990–91, Asst Chief of Defence Staff Operational Requirements (Air Systems) 1991–94, DG Saudi Arabian Projects 1994–98, ret RAF 1999; nat pres Royal Br Legion 2006–; tstee: RAF Museum 1999–2005 (chm 1999–2001), Berkley Priory Battle of Britain Tst 2006–; Lt Govr IOM 2000–05, Hon Air Cdre 606 (Chiltern) Sqdn RAuxAF 2007–; chm: IOM Prince's Tst 2002–05, IOM Golden Jubilee Tst 2002–05, Geoffrey de Havilland Flying Fndn 2001–; Liveryman Guild of Air Pilots and Air Navigators; QCVSA 1974, FRAeS 1991 (MRAeS 1984); OStJ 2001; *Recreations* shooting, gliding, golf, photography, watercolour painting, sailing, aviation history; *Clubs* RAF, Royal & Ancient; *Style—* Air Marshal I D Macfadyen, CB, OBE; ✉ tel 01454 238544, e-mail poacher3@aol.com

McFADYEN, Jock; s of James Lachlan McFadyen, of Carnoustie, Angus, and Margaret, *née* Owen; *b* 18 September 1950; *Educ* Renfrew HS, Chelsea Sch of Art (BA, MA); *m* 1, 1971 (m dis 1989), Carol Ann, *née* Hambleton; 1 s (James b 29 July 1972); m 2, 1991, Susie, *née* Honeyman; 1 da (Annie b 6 Feb 1993), 1 s (George b 23 June 1995); *Career* pt/t lectr Slade Sch of Art 1980–2005; designer The Judas Tree (Royal Opera House Covent Garden); *Exhibitions:* 35 solo exhibitions since 1978 incl: Acme Gallery, Blond Fine Art, National Gallery, Scottish Gallery, Camden Arts Centre, Talbot Rice Gallery Edinburgh Festival 1998, Pier Arts Centre St Magnus Festival Orkney 1999, Agnews 2001; many mixed exhibitions in Europe and USA incl: A13 (Wapping Project), Hayward Annual, John Moore's, Royal Academy, British Art Show, New British Painting (USA), British Cncl touring shows; *Works in Public Museums* incl: Tate Gallery, National Gallery (residency), V&A, Imperial War Museum, Kunsthalle Hamburg, Manchester, Birmingham, Glasgow, Govt Art Coll, Br Museum; *Commissions* incl: Arts Cncl purchase, National Gallery residency, Imperial War Museum Eastern Europe project; *Publications* monograph written by David Cohen (2001); *Recreations* greyhounds, motorcycles; *Clubs* Vintage Japanese Motorcycle; *Style—* Jock McFadyen, Esq; ✉ 15 Victoria Park Square, London E2 9PB (tel 020 8983 3825)

McFADZEAN, Hon (Gordon) Barry; s of late Baron McFadzean, KT (Life Peer; d 1996), and late Eileen, *née* Gordon; *b* 14 February 1937; *Educ* Winchester, ChCh Oxford (MA); *m* 1, 1968 (m dis 1982), Julia Maxine, da of late Sir Max Dillon, of Sydney, Aust; 2 da; m 2, 1984, Diana Rosemary, yst da of late Sam Waters, of Norfolk; *Career* Nat Serv 2 Lt RA

1955–57; CA 1963; dir of various merchant banks 1964–85, exec dir S G Warburg & Co Ltd (Merchant Bankers) 1975–78, exec chm Corporate Advisory Partnership Ltd 1986–2003; *Recreations* music, theatre, the French, aviation (PPL holder), humour; *Clubs* Boodle's, Australian (Sydney); *Style*— The Hon Barry McFadzean; ✉ La Roseraie du Cap, 134 Boulevard Francis Meilland, 06160 Cap d'Antibes, France (tel 00 33 4 92 93 92 54, fax 00 33 4 93 67 42 48, e-mail barrymcf@wanadoo.fr)

McFALL, John; MP, PC (2004); *b* 4 October 1944; *Career* former sch teacher; MP (Lab) Dumbarton 1987–; former oppn whip (with responsibility for foreign affrs, defence and trade and indust) resigned post during Gulf War; a Lord Cmmr of HM Treasy (Govt whip) 1997–98, Parly under sec NI Office 1998–; chair Treasy Select Ctee 2001–; former memb Select Ctee: on defence, on Sittings of the House, on information; former dep shadow sec of state for Scotland (with responsibility for indust, Highlands and Islands, fisheries and forestry, economic affrs, employment and trg, home affrs, tport and roads); former memb: Parly & Scientific Ctee (hon sec), Exec Ctee Parly Gp for Energy Studies; vice-chm Br/Italian Gp; sec: Retail Indust Gp, Roads Study Gp; jt sec Br/Peru Gp; treas: Br/Hong Kong Gp, Scotch Whisky Gp; *Recreations* golf, running, reading; *Style*— The Rt Hon John McFall, MP; ✉ 125 College Street, Dumbarton G82 1NH; House of Commons, London SW1A 0AA (tel 020 7219 3521)

McFARLAND, Sir John Talbot; 3 Bt (UK 1914), of Aberfoyle, Co Londonderry, TD; s of Sir Basil Alexander Talbot McFarland, 2 Bt, CBE, ERD (d 1986), and Annie Kathleen, *née* Henderson (d 1952); *b* 3 October 1927; *Educ* Marlborough, Trinity Coll Oxford; *m* 5 March 1957, Mary, eldest da of Dr William Scott Watson (d 1956), of Carlisle Place, Londonderry; 2 da (Shauna Jane (Mrs Andrew L H Gailey) b 11 Dec 1957, Fiona Kathleen (Mrs William Orme) b 1 Feb 1964), 2 s (Anthony Basil Scott b 29 Nov 1959, Stephen Andrew John b 23 Dec 1968); *Heir* s, Anthony McFarland; *Career* Capt RA (TA), Capt (RCT) 1962; memb Londonderry Co Borough Cncl 1955–69, High Sheriff Co Londonderry 1958, DL Londonderry 1962–82 (resigned), High Sheriff City of The Co of Londonderry 1965–67; memb North West HMC 1960–73, jt chm Londonderry & Foyle Coll 1976; dir: Donegal Holdings Ltd 1970–86, Ramelton Fishery Ltd 1993–99; chm: Malvay Ltd, Londonderry & Lough Swilly Railway Co 1951–82, Londonderry Gaslight Co 1955–87, McFarland Farms (formerly McFarland Farms Ltd) 1975–2006, Lanes Gp Ltd 1977–84, J T McFarland Holdings (now J T M Holdings Ltd) 1999–2004; *Recreations* golf, shooting; *Clubs* Kildare and Univ; *Style*— Sir John McFarland Bt, TD; ✉ Dunmore House, Carrigans, Lifford, Co Donegal, Republic of Ireland (tel 00 353 74 91 40120)

MACFARLANE, Prof Alan Donald James; s of Maj Donald Kennedy Macfarlane (d 1976), and Iris, *née* Rhodes James; *b* 20 December 1941; *Educ* Sedbergh, Worcester Coll Oxford (MA, DPhil), LSE (MPhil), SOAS Univ of London (PhD); *m* 1, 1966 (m dis), Gillian Ions; 1 da (Katharine b 1970); m 2, 1981, Sarah, *née* Tarring; *Career* Univ of Cambridge: lectr in social anthropology 1975–81, reader in hist anthropology 1981–, prof of anthropological science 1991–; fell King's Coll Cambridge 1981– (sr res fell 1971–74); FRHistS 1967, FRAI 1970, FBA 1986; *Books* Witchcraft in Tudor and Stuart England (1970), The Family Life of Ralph Josselin (1970), Resources and Population (1976), The Diary of Ralph Josselin (ed, 1976), Reconstructing Historical Communities (1977), The Origins of English Individualism (1978), The Justice and the Mare's Ale (1981), A Guide to English Historical Records (1983), Marriage and Love in England (1986), The Culture of Capitalism (1987), Bernard Pignède, The Gurungs, A Himalayan Population of Nepal (ed and trans, 1993), The Savage Wars of Peace (1997), The Riddle of the Modern World (2000), The Making of the Modern World (2002), Glass: A World History (2002), Green Gold: The Empire of Tea (jtly, 2003), Letters to Lily: On How the World Works (2005), Japan Through the Looking Glass (2007); *Recreations* gardening, second-hand book hunting, filming; *Style*— Prof Alan Macfarlane; ✉ 25 Lode Road, Lode, Cambridge CB5 9ER (tel 01223 811976); King's College, Cambridge CB2 1ST (tel 01223 331100, e-mail am12@cam.ac.uk, website www.alanmacfarlane.com)

McFARLANE, Hon Mr Justice; Sir Andrew Ewart McFarlane; kt (2005); s of Gordon McFarlane (d 1970), and Olive McFarlane (d 1991); *b* 20 June 1954; *Educ* Shrewsbury, Univ of Durham (BA, pres Student Union), Univ of Wales Cardiff (LLM); *m* 1981, Susanna Jane, *née* Randolph; 4 da (Laura b 29 Nov 1983, Mary b 19 Aug 1985, Iona b 27 Sept 1987, Philippa b 5 Nov 1991); *Career* called to the Bar Gray's Inn 1977; barr: 2 Fountain Court Birmingham 1978–93, One Kings Bench Walk Temple 1993–2005; QC 1998, recorder 1999–2005 (asst recorder 1995–99), judge of the High Court of Justice (Family Div) 2005– (dep judge 2000–05), Midland Circuit Family Div liaison judge; chair Family Law Bar Assoc 2002–03; chllr Diocese of Exeter, dep chllr Diocese of Wakefield 2004–07; tstee Young Minds; *Publications* Children: Law and Practice (co-author 1991), Child Care and Adoption Law (co-author, 2006), Family Court Practice (contrib to annual edns); *Recreations* family life, vegetables, popular culture; *Clubs* Garrick; *Style*— The Hon Mr Justice McFarlane; ✉ Royal Courts of Justice, Strand, London WC2A 2LL

McFARLANE, Prof Angela; *Educ* Univ of Bristol (BSc, PhD); *Career* science teacher, dir Centre for Research in Educational ICT Homerton Coll Cambridge, dir for evidence and practice British Educnl Communications and Technol Agency (Becta), prof of educn and dir of learning technol Univ of Bristol 2000–; *Books* Information Technology and Authentic Learning: Realising the Potential of Computers in the Primary Classroom (ed, 1996), ILS: A Guide to Good Practice (1999), A Digitally Driven Curriculum? (with David Buckingham, 2001), El aprendizaje y las techologias de la informacion (2001); *Style*— Prof Angela McFarlane; ✉ The Graduate School of Education, University of Bristol, 35 Berkeley Square, Bristol BS8 1JA

McFARLANE, Dr James Sinclair; CBE (1986); s of John Mills McFarlane (d 1959), and Hannah, *née* Langtry (d 1969); *b* 8 November 1925; *Educ* Manchester Grammar, Emmanuel Coll Cambridge (MA, PhD); *m* 31 March 1951, Ruth May, da of William Wallace Harden (d 1974); 3 da (Mary b 1952, Lucy b 1954, Joanna b 1959); *Career* ICI Ltd 1949–53, tech mangr and sales dir Henry Wiggin & Co Ltd 1953–69, chm and md Smith-Clayton Forge Ltd (GKN) 1969–76, md Garringtons Ltd (GKN) 1976–77, main bd dir GKN plc 1979–82, DG Engrg Employers' Fedn 1982–89; CEng, FIM, CIMgt; *Recreations* music; *Clubs* Caledonian; *Style*— Dr James McFarlane, CBE; ✉ 24 Broad Street, Ludlow, Shropshire SY8 1NJ (tel 01584 872495)

McFARLANE, John; OBE (1995); s of John McFarlane (d 1992), of Dumfries, Scotland, and Christina Campbell (d 1976); *b* 14 June 1947; *Educ* Dumfries Acad, Univ of Edinburgh (MA), Cranfield Sch of Mgmnt (MBA); *m* 1970 (m dis 2005) Anne, da of Rev Fraser Ian MacDonald (d 1983), of Dumfries, Scotland; 3 da (Kirsty b 14 March 1976, Rebecca b 17 March 1979, Fiona b 18 March 1983); *Career* Ford Motor Co 1969–74, Citicorp 1975–93 (md Citibank NA (UK), gp exec dir Standard Chartered plc 1993–97, ceo Australia & NZ Banking Gp Ltd Melbourne 1997–2007; non-exec dir: London Stock Exchange 1989–91, Securities Assoc 1989–91, Auditing Practices Bd 1991–97, Fin Law Panel 1994–99, Capital Radio plc 1995–98; chm Australian Bankers' Assoc; Australian Centenary Medal 2003, Distinguished Alumni Award Cranfield Sch of Mgmnt 2003; *Recreations* business education, art and music; *Style*— John McFarlane, Esq, OBE

MACFARLANE, John Foster; s of Alexander Macfarlane, and Agnes, *née* Thompson; *b* 1948, Glasgow; *Educ* Hillhead HS Glasgow, Glasgow Sch of Art; *Career* stage designer; Leverhulme Travelling Scholarship 1970, RSA Bursary 1970, Sam Mavor Bequest Scholarship 1970, Arts Cncl of GB Trainee Theatre Design Bursary 1972; fell Welsh Coll of Music and Dance; Chevalier de l'Ordre des Arts et des Lettres (France) 2002; *Designs for the Stage* incl: Othello (Ludlow Festival) 1974, Heroes (Royal Court) 1974, Miraculous Mandarin (Köln Tanz Forum) 1980, Forgotten Land (Stuttgart Ballet) 1981, Stravinsky's Firebird (Royal Danish Ballet Copenhagen) 1981, Stravinsky's Les Noces (Metropolitan Opera NY) 1982, Ravel's L'Enfant et les Sortileges (Holland Festival) 1984, Giselle (Royal Ballet London) 1985, Britten's Midsummer Night's Dream (Oper der Stadt Köln) 1988, The Nutcracker (Birmingham Royal Ballet) 1990, Benvenuto Cellini (Grande Théatre de Genève) 1992, Peter Grimes (Opera National La Monnaie Brussels) 1994, Swan Lake (Bayerisches Staatsballett Munich) 1994, Otello (Opéra National La Monnaie Brussels) 1997, Hansel and Gretel (WNO) 1998, Falstaff (Théatre Comunale La Monnaie Brussels) 1998, War and Peace (Bastille Paris) 2000, Agrippina (La Monnaie Brussles) 2000, Queen of Spades (WNO) 2000, Euryanthe (Glyndebourne) 2002, The Magic Flute (ROH) 2003, Trojans at Carthage (ENO) 2003; *Selected Exhibitions and Commissions* New Prints, Drawings and Sculpture (Akademia Salzburg) 1979, New Prints, Drawings and Paintings (Oriel Gall Cardiff) 1979, New Prints and Drawings (Andrew Knight Cardiff) 1984, Set and Costume Designs (Marina Henderson London) 1988, Set and Costume Designs (Marina Henderson London) 1991, Recent Paintings, Set and Costume designs (Marina Henderson London) 1993, New Paintings, Prints and Theatre Designs (Martin Tinney Cardiff) 1995; works in selected collections incl: Albertina Vienna, Welsh Arts Cncl, Kunsthalle Nuremberg, Glyn Vivian Art Gall Swansea, Nat Museum Wales, Hunterial Museum Glasgow; *Awards* nominated Olivier dance award for Nutcracker 1996, winner Olivier best opera award for Hansel and Gretel 2000, nominated South Bank Show best opera for Queen of Spades 2001, winner Olivier best opera production award for Lady Macbeth of Mtsensk 2004; *Recreations* playing piano, gardening; *Style*— John Macfarlane, Esq; ✉ c/o Gilly Adams, 25 Ilton Road, Cardiff CF23 5DU (tel and fax 029 2049 4243)

MACFARLANE, Jonathan Stephen; s of William Keith Macfarlane (d 1987), and Pearl Hastings, *née* Impey; *b* 28 March 1956; *Educ* Charterhouse, Oriel Coll Oxford (MA); *Career* admitted slr 1980; ptnr Macfarlanes 1985 (specialising in corporate finance and M&A), currently dir Professional Career Partnership; *Clubs* Leander, MCC; *Style*— Jonathan Macfarlane, Esq; ✉ The Professional Career Partnership, 19 St Swithin's Lane, London EC4N 8AD

MACFARLANE, Sir (David) Neil; kt (1988); s of late Robert and Dulcie Macfarlane, of Yelverton, S Devon; *b* 7 May 1936; *Educ* Bancroft's Sch; *m* 1961, June Osmond, er da of John King, of Somerset; 2 s, 1 da; *Career* Lt 1 Bn Essex Regt 1955–58, Capt RA 265 LAA TA 1959–69; cricketer Essex CCC 1952–56, Capt YA XI; with Shell Mex & BP 1959–74; Parly candidate: East Ham North 1970, Sutton & Cheam (by-election) 1972; MP (Cons) Sutton and Cheam Feb 1974–1992; dep arts min 1979–81; Parly under sec of state: DES 1979–81, for Sport 1981–85, DOE 1981–85; sec: Cons Greater London Membs, Cons Sports Ctee, Cons Energy Ctee; memb All-Pty Select Ctee on Sci and Technol; chm: Securicor plc, Associated Nursing Services plc; dir: RMC plc 1988–, Bradford & Bingley Building Society; tstee England and Wales Cricket Fndn; capt Parly Golfing Soc, vice-pres PGA European Tour; govr Sports Aid Fndn 1985–90; *Books* Politics and Sport (1986); *Recreations* golf; *Clubs* MCC, Essex CCC, Huntercombe Golf, Wentworth Golf, Sunningdale Golf, Royal and Ancient Golf, Loch Lomond Golf; *Style*— Sir Neil Macfarlane; ✉ Sutton Park House, 15 Carshalton Road, Sutton SM1 4LD; c/o Bradford & Bingley Building Society, Crossflatts, Bingley, West Yorkshire BD16 2UA (tel 01274 555555)

MACFARLANE, Nicholas Russel; s of John Macfarlane, DL, and Pamela, *née* Laing; *b* 21 February 1952; *Educ* Radley, Lancaster Univ (BA); *m* 25 July 1987, Elisabeth Anne, da of W David Crane, of Hallaughton; 1 s (James William Archibald b 7 Sept 1989), 1 da (Flora Emily Octavia b 11 Oct 1991); *Career* admitted slr 1977; ptnr Faithfull Owen & Fraser 1980 (amalgamated with Durrant Piesse 1985), currently ptnr specialising in intellectual property law Lovells (amalgamated with Durrant Piesse 1988); Freeman Worshipful Co of Slrs; memb: Law Soc, Intellectual Property Lawyers Assoc; *Recreations* fishing, shooting; *Clubs* City of London; *Style*— Nicholas Macfarlane, Esq; ✉ Lovells, Atlantic House, London EC1A 2FG (tel 020 7296 2000, fax 020 7296 2001)

M

MACFARLANE, Prof Peter Wilson; s of Robert Barton Macfarlane (d 1965), of Glasgow, and Dinah, *née* Wilson (d 2003); *b* 8 November 1942; *Educ* Hyndland Secondary Sch Glasgow, Univ of Glasgow (BSc, PhD, DSc); *m* 8 Oct 1971, Irene Grace, da of James Muir (d 1975), of Kirkintilloch; 2 s (Alan b 1974, David b 1977); *Career* Univ of Glasgow: asst lectr in med cardiology 1967–70, lectr 1970–74, sr lectr 1974–80, reader 1980–91, prof 1991–95, prof of electrocardiology 1995–; author and ed of various books and proceedings, res interest computers in electrocardiography, princ author of electrocardiogram analysis programme marketed worldwide; pres Int Soc of Electrocardiology 2007–, chm Working Gp on Computers in Cardiology European Soc of Cardiology 2002–04, memb Br Cardiac Soc 1974; FBCS 1976, CEng 1990, FESC 1991, FRSE 1992, FRCP (Glasgow) 2001; *Books* An Introduction to Automated Electrocardiogram Interpretation (1974), Computer Techniques in Clinical Medicine (1985), Comprehensive Electrocardiology (1989), 12–Lead Vectorcardiography (1995); *Recreations* jogging, playing the violin; *Style*— Prof Peter Macfarlane, DSc, FRSE

MACFARLANE, Maj-Gen William Thomson (Bill); CB (1981); s of James Macfarlane (d 1966), and Agnes Boylan (d 1970); *b* 2 December 1925; *m* 16 July 1955, Dr Helen Dora Macfarlane, da of Rev Leonard Nelson Meredith (d 1976); 1 da (Christina b 22 July 1957); *Career* served Europe, Near, Middle and Far East theatres 1946–1981; Cdr 16 Parachute Bde Signal Sqdn 1961–63, mil asst to C-in-C Far East Land Forces 1964–66, Cdr 1 Div HQ and Signal Regt Germany 1967–70, Cabinet Office Secretariat 1970–72, Cdr Corps Royal Signals Germany 1972–73, dir PR (Army) 1973–75, COS UK Land Forces 1975–78, chief jt services liaison Organisation Br Forces Germany 1978–81, Col Cmdt Royal Signals 1980–85, ret; co dir, conslt, lectr; ops dir Hong Kong Resort Co Ltd 1981–84, admin Sion Coll 1984–93, chm and dir Citicare Co Ltd 1984–95, dir Compton Manor Estates Ltd 1990–; *Clubs* Naval and Military; *Style*— Maj-Gen William T Macfarlane, CB; ✉ Colts Paddock, 24 Aveley Lane, Farnham, Surrey GU9 8PR

MACFARLANE OF BEARSDEN, Baron (Life Peer UK 1991), of Bearsden in the District of Bearsden and Milngavie; Sir Norman Somerville Macfarlane; KT (1996), kt (1982), DL (Dunbartonshire 1993); s of Daniel Robertson Macfarlane, and Jessie Lindsay Somerville; *b* 5 March 1926; *Educ* High Sch of Glasgow; *m* 1953, Marguerite Mary Campbell; 1s, 4 da; *Career* cmmnd RA 1945, served Palestine 1945–47; fndr N S Macfarlane & Co Ltd 1949 (became Macfarlane Gp (Clansman) plc 1973, hon life pres 1999), hon life pres Macfarlane Gp plc (chm 1973–98, md 1973–90); United Distillers plc 1996 (chm 1987–96); underwriting memb Lloyd's 1978–97; chm: The Fine Art Soc plc 1976–98 (hon life pres 1998), American Tst plc 1984–97 (dir 1980–), Guinness plc 1987–89 (jt dep chm 1989–92); dir: Clydesdale Bank plc 1980–96 (dep chm 1993–96), Edinburgh Fund Managers plc 1980–98, General Accident Fire & Life Assurance Corp plc 1984–96; chm Glasgow Devpt Agency (formerly Glasgow Action) 1985–92, dir Glasgow C of C 1976–79, memb Cncl CBI Scotland 1975–81, memb Bd Scottish Devpt Agency 1979–87; pres Royal Glasgow Inst of the Fine Arts 1976–87; dir: Scottish Nat Orch 1977–82, Third Eye Centre 1978–81; memb Royal Fine Art Cmmn for Scotland 1980–82, Scottish patron Nat Art Collection Fund 1978–; tstee: Nat Heritage Meml Fund 1984–97, Nat Galls of Scotland 1986–97; memb Ct Univ of Glagow 1979–87, regent RCS(Ed); pres: Stationers' Assoc of GB and Ireland 1965, Co of Stationers of Glasgow 1968–70, Glasgow HS Club 1970–72; hon pres: Charles Rennie Mackintosh Soc 1988–, HS of Glasgow 1992– (chm of govrs 1979–92), Scottish Ballet 2001– (dir 1975–87, vice-chm 1983–87), Glasgow Sch of Art 2001 (govr 1978–87, hon fell 1993), Tenovus Scotland 2006; patron Scottish Licensed Trade Assoc 1992–; Lord High Cmmr Gen Assembly Church of Scotland 1992, 1993 and 1997;

vice-pres PGA, hon patron Queen's Park FC, hon life memb Scottish Football League 2006; Glasgow St Mungo Medal 2005; Hon LLD: Univ of Strathclyde 1986, Univ of Glasgow 1988, Glasgow Caledonian Univ 1993, Univ of Aberdeen 1995; Hon DUniv Stirling 1992, Dr (hc) Univ of Edinburgh 1992; CIMgt 1996, Hon RSA 1987, Hon RGI 1987, Hon FRIAS 1984, Hon FScotvec 1991, FRSE 1991, Hon FRCPGlas 1992; *Recreations* golf, cricket, theatre, art; *Clubs* Glasgow Art, Royal Scottish Automobile (Glasgow), Hon Co of Edinburgh Golfers, Glasgow Golf; *Style*— The Rt Hon the Lord Macfarlane of Bearsden, KT, DL, FRSE; ✉ 50 Manse Road, Bearsden, Glasgow G61 3PN; Macfarlane Group plc, Clansman House, 21 Newton Place, Glasgow G3 7PY

McFARLANE OF LLANDAFF, Baroness (Life Peer UK 1979), of Llandaff in the County of South Glamorgan; Jean Kennedy McFarlane; da of James McFarlane (d 1963), and Elvina Alice McFarlane (d 1990); *b* 1 April 1926; *Educ* Howell's Sch Llandaff, Bedford and Birkbeck Colls London (MA, BSc); *Career* dir of educn Inst of Advanced Nursing Educn London 1969–71, sr lectr in nursing Dept of Social and Preventive Medicine Manchester Univ 1971–73, sr lectr and head Dept of Nursing Manchester Univ 1973–74, chm English National Bd for Nursing, Midwifery and Health Visiting 1980–83, prof and head Dept of Nursing Manchester Univ 1974–88; former memb: War Graves Cmmn, Royal Cmmn on NHS; memb Gen Synod of C of E 1990–95; fell Birkbeck Coll London 1997; Hon DSc Ulster 1981, Hon DEd CNAA 1983, Hon FRCP 1990, Hon MD Liverpool 1990, Hon LLD Manchester 1998, Hon DLitt Univ of Glamorgan 1995; SRN, SCM, FRCN; *Books* The Proper Study of the Nurse (1970), The Practice of Nursing Using the Nursing Process (1982); *Recreations* photography, walking, music, travel; *Style*— The Rt Hon the Lady McFarlane of Llandaff; ✉ 5 Dovercourt Avenue, Heaton Mersey, Stockport, Cheshire SK4 3QB (tel and fax 0161 432 8367)

MacFARQUHAR, Prof Roderick Lemonde; s of late Sir Alexander MacFarquhar; *b* 2 December 1930, Lahore; *Educ* Fettes, Keble Coll Oxford (BA), Harvard Univ (AM), LSE (PhD); *m* 1964, Emily Jane (d 2001), da of Dr Paul W Cohen, of NY; 1 da (Larissa b 1968), 1 s (Rory b 1971); *Career* Nat Serv 2 Lt; China specialist Daily Telegraph 1955–61, ed The China Quarterly 1959–68, reporter BBC Panorama 1963–64, co presenter BBC World Serv 24 Hours 1972–74 and 1979–80; MP (Lab) Belper 1974–79; Harvard Univ: prof of govt 1984–, dir Fairbank Centre for E Asian Research 1986–92 and 2005–06, Leroy B Williams prof of history and political science 1990–, chair Govt Dept 1998–2004; visiting prof Lee Kuan Yew Sch of Public Policy Nat Univ of Singapore 2005; fell: Research Inst on Communist Affairs and E Asian Inst Columbia 1969, RIIA 1971–74, Woodrow Wilson Int Centre for Scholars Washington DC 1980–81, American Acad of Arts and Sciences 1986–, Leverhulme Research Grant, Ford Fndn Research Grant, Rockefeller Fndn Research Grant; *Recreations* reading, travel, listening to music; *Style*— Prof Roderick MacFarquhar

McFEE, Bruce James; MSP; s of James McFee, and Ellen Margaret McFee; *b* 18 May 1961; *Educ* Johnstone HS Renfrewshire; *m* 4 July 1997, Iris, *née* Lille; *Career* memb Renfrew DC 1988–96, Renfrewshire gp ldr SNP 1992–2003, cncllr Renfrewshire Unitary Authy 1995–2003, MSP (SNP) W of Scot 2003–; customer serv mangr until 2003; *Recreations* travel, DIY; *Style*— Mr Bruce McFee, MSP

McGAIRL, Stephen James; s of John Lloyd McGairl (d 1979), of Chichester, W Sussex, and Lucy Hudson; *b* 18 February 1951; *Educ* Chichester HS, Worcester Coll Oxford (MA); *m* 24 May 1975, Madeleine, da of Christopher William Talbot Cox (d 1964), of Sidlesham, W Sussex; 4 s (Sam b 1977, Thomas b 1978, Joe b 1983, George b 1986); *Career* admitted slr 1976, admitted Conseil Juridique 1988, avocat 1992; Legal and Parliamentary Dept GLC 1974–77; Freshfields (now Freshfields Bruckhaus Deringer): joined 1977, ptnr 1984, Paris office 1986–92, head Moscow office 1994–95; chm Legal Advsy Panel Aviation Working Gp, dir and tstee UK Fndn for Int Uniform Law; memb: Law Soc, City of London Slrs' Co, Société Française de Droit Aérien; *Publications* Aircraft Financing (co-ed and contrib 3 edn, 1998), Contract Practices under the Cape Town Connection (2004); contrib various professional jls relating to aviation, asset and project fin and business in CIS; *Recreations* sailing, opera; *Clubs* Cercle de l'Union Interalliée, RAC, Little Ship; *Style*— Stephen McGairl, Esq; ✉ 25 Ashley Gardens, London SW1P 1QD (tel 020 7828 5889, e-mail mcgairl@btinternet.com)

McGANN, Paul; *Educ* Cardinal Allen GS Liverpool, RADA; *Career* actor; *Theatre* incl: Cain (Nottingham Playhouse) 1981, Oi For England (Royal Court Upstairs) 1982, Yakety-Yak (Half Moon and Astoria) 1982, The Genius (Royal Court) 1983, Loot (Ambassadors) 1984, A Lie of the Mind (Royal Court) 1987, Much Ado About Nothing (Horseshoe Theatre Basingstoke) 1996, Loot (Ambassadors) 1997, The Seagull (Liverpool Playhouse) 1998, A Lie of the Mind (Royal Court) 1999, The Little Black Book (Riverside Studios) 2003, Mourning Becomes Electra (Nat Theatre) 2003; *Television* Gaskin 1982, Give us a Break 1983, The Monocled Mutineer 1986, The Importance of Being Earnest 1986, Drowning in the Shallow End 1989, The Hanging Gale 1995, Dr Who (TV film) 1996, Forgotten 1999, Nature Boy 2000, Fish 2000, Hornblower 2000 and 2003, Sweet Revenge 2001, Blood Strangers 2002, The Biographer 2002, Lie with Me 2004; *Films* Withnail and I 1986, Empire of the Sun 1987, Streets of Yesterday 1988, The Rainbow 1988, Dealers 1988, Paper Mask 1989, Afraid of the Dark 1990, Alien III 1991, Downtime 1996, Fairytale - A True Story 1997, Queen of the Damned 2000, My Kingdom 2000, Hotel 2000, The Biographer 2000, Listening 2003; *Recreations* music, sport, travel; *Clubs* Liverpool FC; *Style*— Paul McGann, Esq

McGAREL-GROVES, Anthony Robin; s of Brig Robin Jullian McGarel-Groves, RM, OBE, of Lymington, Hants, and Constance Morton, *née* Macmillan; *b* 7 September 1954; *Educ* Eton, Univ of Bath (BSc); *m* 16 Dec 1978, Ann Candace (d 2006), da of Jack Dawes, of Ross-on-Wye, Herefords; *Career* Deloitte Haskins and Sells 1976–81, Kuwait Investment Office 1981–94, assoc dir Hambro's Fund Management plc 1994–97, Guinness Flight Hambro Asset Management plc 1997–1999, ptnr Mark Capital LLP 2001–07; memb: Faculty of Fin and Mgmnt, ICAEW; ACA; *Recreations* gardening, theatre, bridge, politics, vintage cars, old houses, countryside pursuits; *Style*— Anthony R McGarel-Groves, Esq; ✉ Clapton Revel, Wooburn Moor, Buckinghamshire HP10 0NH

McGARRY, Ian Patrick; s of John McGarry (d 1957), and Jean Dearing (d 1973); *b* 27 February 1942; *Educ* Chichester HS for Boys, Lewes Co GS; *m* 1964 (m dis), Christine, *née* Smith; 1 s (Andrew b 15 Dec 1971); *Career* Lab Pty constituency agent Putney 1964–76, gen sec British Actors' Equity Assoc 1991– (asst gen sec 1976–91); jt sec London Theatre Cncl and Provincial Theatre Cncl 1991–, memb Br Screen Advsy Cncl 1991–, vice-pres Int Fedn of Actors 1992–, tstee Nat Music Day Tst, jt sec Jt Films Cncl; *Style*— Ian McGarry, Esq; ✉ Equity, Guild House, Upper St Martin's Lane, London W1 (tel 020 7379 6000)

McGARVEY, Alan; s of William Johnson McGarvey (d 1967), and Rosina, *née* Plane; *b* 22 June 1942; *Educ* Wallsend GS, Univ of Newcastle upon Tyne (BSc), Cranfield Sch of Mgmnt (MBA); *m* 1, 11 Sept 1967, Eileen (d 1992); *m* 2, 31 May 1997, Shirlee Ann Gleeson; *Career* CA; Parsons 1958–64, RTZ Ltd 1968–71, Decca Group 1972–76, MK Electric Ltd 1976–78, National Enterprise Bd 1978–82, Greater London Enterprise Bd 1982–86, Greater Manchester Economic Development Ltd 1987–90; ind specialist in industrial devpt and restructuring 1990–93; EU (Phare) 1993–96; ind specialist in regnl devpt, restructuring and change mgmnt 1996–; UK memb Advsy Cncl for Ctee for Industrial Co-operation (EEC-ACP) Brussels 1980–95; memb Bd Northern Chamber Orch 1988–93; *Style*— Alan McGarvey, Esq; ✉ Willowbank, 9 Anglesey Drive, Poynton, Cheshire SK12 1BT (tel 01625 873869, fax 01625 873698, e-mail mcgarvey01@aol.com)

McGARVEY, Seamus; s of Jimmy McGarvey (d 1981), and Peggy McGarvey; *Educ* Christian Brothers' GS Armagh, PCL (BA); *Career* photographer and cinematographer; memb: BSC 1999, IATSE 600 (USA cinematography union) 1999, BAFTA 2000, AMPAS 2002; solo exhibitions at City Centre Art Gallery Dublin: Armagh in a New Light 1984, Eternity Where? 1989; RPS Lumiere Award for contributions to the art of cinematography 2004; *Television and Short Films* incl: Marooned, The Take Out, Hello Hello Hello, Skin (nomination Best Photography RTS Awards), Magic Moments, Flying Saucer Rock and Roll (Best Short Film Cork Film Festival 1997), Stand and Deliver, The End, I Could Read The Sky; with Sam Taylor-Wood, *qv*: Sustaining the Crisis, Mute, Strings, Ascension, Pieta, Crying Men, Atlantic (nominated Turner Prize 1998), Breach, Third Party; with Willie Doherty: Re Run (nominated Turner Prize 2003), Drive; documentaries incl The Work of Angels; numerous pop promotions incl work for: U2, Elton John, Paul McCartney, Pet Shop Boys, P J Harvey, Coldplay, The Cure, Robbie Williams, Dave Stewart, Terry Hall, Orbital; *Film* Look Me in the Eye 1996, Butterfly Kiss 1997, The Slab Boys 1998, Harald 1999, Jump the Gun 1999, The Winter Guest 1999, The War Zone 2000, The Big Tease 2000, A Map of the World 2000, High Fidelity 2000, Enigma 2001, Wit 2001, The Hours 2002 (Evening Standard British Film Award for Technical Achievement 2004), The Actors 2002, Sahara 2004, Along Came Polly 2004, Destricted 2005, World Trade Center 2006, Charlotte's Web 2006, Atonement 2007, #1 Ladies Detective Agency 2007; *Style*— Seamus McGarvey; ✉ c/o Sara Pritchard, Casarotto Marsh Ltd, Waverley House, 7–12 Noel Street, London W1F 8FQ (tel 020 7287 4450, e-mail sara@casarotto.co.uk)

McGEE, Prof James O'Donnell; s of Michael McGee (d 1981), and Bridget Gavin (d 1982); *b* 27 July 1939; *Educ* Univ of Glasgow (MB ChB, PhD, MD), Univ of Oxford (MA); *m* 26 August 1961, Anne McCarron Lee, da of Patrick Lee, of Cardonald, Glasgow; 1 s (Damon-Joel b 1969), 2 da (Leeanne b 1962, Sharon b 1964); *Career* lectr then sr lectr in pathology Univ of Glasgow 1967–75, prof Univ of Oxford 1975– (former head Nuffield Dept of Pathology and Bacteriology), fell Linacre Coll Oxford 1975– (now emeritus), assoc fell Green Coll Oxford 1981–; dir UK Telepathology Co-ordinating Unit 1994–; distinguished visiting scientist Roche Inst of Molecular Biology Nutley NJ USA 1981 and 1989 (Med Res Cncl travelling fell 1969–70, visiting scientist 1970–71), Kattle Meml lectr Royal Coll of Pathologists 1981, guest lectr Royal Coll of Physicians of Ireland 1985, keynote lectr Med Res Inst SA 1994, special guest lectr Hellenic Pathology Congress Crete 1994; visiting prof: Univ of Baghdad 1976, Univ of Kuwait 1981 and 1983 (academic advsr 1984–), Univ of Witwatersrand SA 1994; academic advsr Hong Kong Medical Res Cncl 1990–; memb: Scientific and Grants Ctee Cancer Res Campaign UK 1978–93, Ctee on Safety of Meds Med Div UK 1984–90, Nat Cmmn (UK) Breast Screening Pathology 1989–; hon conslt Pathologist Oxford Health Authy 1975–; Bellahouston Gold Medal Univ of Glasgow 1973; FRCPath 1986 (MRCPath 1973), FRCP 1989; *Books* Biopsy Pathology of Liver (1980, 2 edn 1988), In Situ Hybridisation: Principles and Practice (1990, 2 edn 1999), Oxford Textbook of Pathology (vols 1, 2a and 2b, with P J Isaacson and N A Wright, 1992, Italian edn 1994 and 1996), Diagnostic Molecular Pathology (vols 1 and 2 with C S Herrington, 1992), The Macrophage (with C E Lewis, 1992), The NK Cell (with C E Lewis, 1992); *Recreations* talking with my family, swimming; *Style*— Prof James O'D McGee; ✉ John Radcliffe Hospital, Headington, Oxford OX3 9DU

McGEECHAN, Ian Robert; OBE; s of Robert Matthew McGeechan (d 1969), and Hilda, *née* Shearer (d 1994); *b* 30 October 1946; *Educ* Moor Grange HS, West Park HS, Allerton Grange Comp, Carnegie Coll of Physical Educn; *m* 9 Aug 1969, Judith Irene, da of Thomas Fish (d 1976); 1 s (Robert James b 5 Nov 1978), 1 da (Heather Jane b 17 Aug 1983); *Career* rugby union player (fly-half) and coach; head of games Moor Grange HS 1968–72, head of humanities and year gp ldr Fir Tree Middle Sch 1972–90, trg mangr Scottish Life Assurance Company 1990–94; Hon MA Univ of Nottingham 1998, Hon Dr Leeds Metropolitan Univ 2004; *As Player* clubs: Headingley FC 1965–82 (300 appearances, capt 1972–73), Barbarians RFC 1973–78, Yorks CCC 1963–68 (played for second XI); Scotland: 32 caps, debut v NZ 1972, tour NZ 1975 (1 test appearance), capt 1977 and 1979, ret as player 1979; British and Irish Lions: toured South Africa 1974 (4 tests, won series 3–0, 1 drawn), toured NZ 1977 (4 tests); *As Coach* asst coach Scotland 1985–88, nat coach Scotland 1988–93 (Grand Slam winners 1990, fourth place World Cup 1991); dir: National Coaching Fndn 1995–, Northampton RFC 1996–99, English Premiership Rugby 1996–99, English Rugby Partnership 1996–99; technical and coaching conslt Scotland RFU 1997–98, nat coach Scotland 1999–2003, dir of rugby Scottish Rugby Union 2004–05, dir of rugby Wasps RFC 2005– (winners Heineken Cup 2007); coach British and Irish Lions Aust 1989 (won series 2–1), NZ 1993 (lost series 1–2), South Africa 1997 (won series 2–1), and NZ 2005; coach World XV v NZ (for NZ rugby centenary) 1992; Rugby Writers Rubert Cherry trophy 1989, Coach of the Year Rugby World 1989 and 1990, Rugby Writers Pat Marshall trophy 1990, Coach of the Year Br Inst of Sports Coaches 1990 and 1993, inducted into Nat Coaching Fndn Hall of Fame 1999, Sport Scotland special millennium award for services to coaching 2000; *Books* Scotland's Grand Slam (with Ian Robertson and M Cleary), So Close to Glory (1993 (British Lions tour of NZ)), Heroes All (1997 (British Lions Tour to South Africa)); *Recreations* caravanning, hill walking, family life, sailing, cricket; *Style*— Ian McGeechan, Esq, OBE

McGEEHAN, Prof Joseph Peter (Joe); CBE (2004); s of Joseph Patrick James McGeehan, of Liverpool, and Rhoda Catherine, *née* Sleight (d 1989); *b* 15 February 1946; *Educ* Bootle GS for Boys, Univ of Liverpool (BEng, PhD); *m* 3 Oct 1970, Jean, da of Alan Lightfoot (d 1969); 2 da (Kathryn Anne b 13 July 1978, Sarah Jane b 12 Feb 1981); *Career* sr scientist Allan Clark Research Centre (Plessey Group Ltd) 1970–72, lectr then sr lectr Sch of Electrical Engrg Univ of Bath 1972–85; Univ of Bristol: first dir Centre for Communications Res 1988– (estab 1987), head Dept of Electrical and Electronic Engrg 1991–98 (chair in communications engrg 1985–), dean Faculty of Engrg 1998–; md Telecommunications Research Lab Toshiba Research Europe Ltd 1998–; non-exec dir Renishaw plc 2001–; over 25 years' res in spectrum efficient modulation techniques and systems; memb various nat and int ctees CCIR 1980–, memb ctee studying comparative modulation schemes for mobile radio Home Office 1980–82, advsr to first MOD/DTI Defence Spectrum Review Ctee, memb Accreditation Ctee and Pool of Assessors IEE 1985–2000, sometime memb various res ctees EPSRC and DTI/EPSRC Link Mgmnt Ctee in Personal Communication Systems; dir Science Research Fndn (formed by Univs of Bristol and Bath); memb Women's Academic Initiative Bristol, memb int tech advsy panel Singapore's Centre for Wireless Communications (CWC) 2000–; Wolfson Fndn rep Bd of Govrs John Cabot City Technol Coll Bristol 1995–98; former memb and treas Friends of Bath HS; FRSA 1989, FIEE 1992, FREng 1994 *Awards* Mountbatten Premium (IEE) 1989, Neal Shepherd Award (IEEE, USA) 1990, Prince of Wales Award for Innovation 1992; *Publications* Radio Receivers (contrib, 1986); *Recreations* walking, music, cricket, cycling, theatre, reading, church; *Style*— Prof Joe McGeehan, CBE, FREng; ✉ Centre for Communications Research, Merchant Venturers Building, Woodland Road, Bristol BS8 1UB

McGEOCH, Callum James Farquharson; s of Angus McGeoch, of Farnborough, Oxon, and Judy Ann Farquharson; *b* 6 September 1974, London; *Educ* Marlborough, Univ of Newcastle upon Tyne (BSc); *m* 2 April 2005, Sophia Fleur, *née* Parker; *Career* creative dir Livity; contrib ed: Dazed and Confused, Another Magazine, Another Man Magazine; publisher Live Magazine; contrib: The Independent, Rolling Stone, Friends of the Earth; awarded Best Feature Pages Total Publishing Magazine Awards; *Publications* The

Annual (2001), T (2004), T2 (2005); *Recreations* travel, music, cycling; *Style—* Callum McGeoch, Esq; ✉ Livity Ltd, 33–34 Tunstall Road, London SW9 8DA (tel 020 7326 5979)

McGEOUGH, Prof Joseph Anthony; s of Patrick Joseph McGeough (d 1982), of Stevenston, Ayrshire, and Gertrude, *née* Darroch (d 1975); *b* 29 May 1940; *Educ* St Michael's Coll Irvine, Univ of Glasgow (BSc, PhD), Univ of Aberdeen (DSc); *m* 12 Aug 1972, Brenda, da of Robert Nicholson, of Blyth, Northumberland; 2 s (Andrew b 1974, Simon b 1977), 1 da (Elizabeth b 1975); *Career* res demonstrator Univ of Leicester 1966, sr res fell Queensland Univ 1967, res metallurgist International R&D Ltd 1968–69, sr res fell Univ of Strathclyde 1969–72; Univ of Aberdeen: lectr 1972–77, sr lectr 1977–80, reader in engrg 1980–83; regius prof of engrg Univ of Edinburgh 1983–2005 (prof emeritus 2005–), hon prof Nanjing Aeronautical and Astronautical Univ 1992–; visiting prof: Univ of Naples Federico II 1994, Glasgow Caledonian Univ 1997–2003, Tokyo Univ of Agric and Technol 2004, Monash Univ 2005; industrial fell SERC Royal Soc 1987–89; chm Scottish Branch Inst of Mechanical Engrg 1993–95, chm Bd CIRP UK 2000–03, vice-pres IMechE 2006–07; chm Int Conferences on Computer-Aided Prodn Engrg (CAPE) 1986–; ed-in-chief Processing of Advanced Materials 1991–94, CIRP ed Jl of Materials Processing Technology 1990–; various Scot Co AAA and universities Athletic Championship awards; FRSE 1990, FIMechE (memb Cncl 2000–03, memb Tstee Bd 2004–), FIET; *Books* Principles of Electrochemical Machining (1974), Advanced Methods of Machining (1988), section on Nonconventional Machining: Encyclopaedia Britannica (1987), entry on Mechanical Engineering, Encarta 99 Encyclopaedia (1999), Micromachining of Engineering Materials (ed, 2001); *Recreations* hill walking, gardening; *Style—* Prof Joseph McGeough, FRSE; ✉ 39 Dreghorn Loan, Colinton, Edinburgh EH13 0DF (tel 0131 441 1302); School of Engineering and Electronics, University of Edinburgh, King's Buildings, Edinburgh EH9 3JL (tel 0131 650 5682, fax 0131 650 6554, e-mail j.a.mcgeough@ed.ac.uk)

McGETTIGAN, Frank; OBE (2000); *b* 1951; *m*; 4 c; *Career* Channel Four Television: dir and gen mangr (and main bd dir) 1988–2000, md subsid 124 Facilities Ltd, chief exec Intelfax Ltd 2000–; chm SKILLSET (broadcasting industry trg orgn); dep chm Nat Film and TV Sch (and chm subsid Ealing Studios Ltd); *Style—* Frank McGettigan, Esq, OBE; ✉ e-mail frankmcgettigan@msn.com

McGETTRICK, Prof Andrew David; s of Bartholomew McGettrick, of Glasgow, and Marion, *née* McLean; *b* 15 May 1944; *Educ* Univ of Glasgow (Jack Scholar, Thomas Russell Bursar, BSc), Univ of Cambridge (PhD, Dip Computer Science); *m* 27 Dec 1974, Sheila Margaret, da of Eugene Girot; 5 s (Peter b 3 Dec 1975, Robert b 27 June 1977, Andrew b 13 Oct 1981, Rory b 20 June 1984, Michael b 20 Aug 1987), 1 da (Kathryn b 26 Oct 1979); *Career* Univ of Strathclyde: reader Dept of Computer Sci 1982–84 (formerly lectr), personal prof 1984–86, prof 1986–, head Dept of Computer Sci 1984–90 and 1996–; chm Safety Critical Systems Ctee Inst of Electrical Engrs; ed-in-chief Jl of High Integrity Systems; govr Scottish Cncl for Educnl Technol 1990–96; CEng, FBCS 1987, FIEE 1989, FRSE 1996, FRSA 1998; *Publications* over 110 edited books incl: Algol 68 - A First and Second Course (1978, reprinted 1980), The Definition of Programming Languages (1980), Program Verification using Ada (1982), Graded Problems in Computer Science (with P D Smith, 1983), Discrete Mathematics and uses in Computing, The Oxford Dictionary of Computer Science (1983, 2 edn 1985), Software Specification Techniques (ed with N Gehani, 1988), Concurrent Programming (ed with N Gehani, 1988); *Recreations* running, golf, squash; *Style—* Prof Andrew McGettrick, FRSE; ✉ 11 Coylton Road, Glasgow G43 2TA; University of Strathclyde, 26 Richmond Street, Glasgow G1 1XH (tel 0141 552 4400 ext 3305, fax 0141 552 5330, e-mail adm@cs.strath.ac.uk)

McGHIE, Hon Lord; James Marshall; s of James Drummond McGhie (d 1970), and Jessie Eadie Bennie (d 1975); *b* 15 October 1944; *Educ* Perth Acad, Univ of Edinburgh; *m* 1968, Ann Manuel, da of Stanley Gray Cockburn (d 1982); 1 s (Angus b 1975), 1 da (Kathryn b 1983); *Career* admitted Faculty of Advocates 1969; QC (Scot) 1983, advocate-depute 1983–86, pt/t chm Med Appeal Tbnls 1987–92, memb Criminal Injuries Compensation Bd 1992–96, chm Scottish Land Court and pres Lands Tbnl for Scotland 1996–; *Style—* The Hon Lord McGhie; ✉ Scottish Land Court, George House, 126 George Street, Edinburgh EH2 4HH (tel 0131 225 3595)

McGIMPSEY, Michael; MLA; *b* 1 July 1948; *Educ* Regent House GS Newtownards, Trinity Coll Dublin (BA); *m*; 1 s, 1 da; *Career* businessman; elected Belfast CC (Langbank Ward) 1993; MLA (UUP) S Belfast 1998–; min for culture, arts and leisure 1999–2001; *Recreations* reading, walking, gardening; *Style—* Michael McGimpsey, MLA; ✉ Ulster Unionist Constituency Office, Unit 2, 127–145 Sandy Row, Belfast BT12 5ET (tel 028 9024 5801, e-mail michaelmcgimpseymla@southbelfast.wanadoo.co.uk)

McGINTY, Lawrence Stanley; s of Lawrence McGinty, and Hilda, *née* Hardman; *Educ* Stand GS Manchester, Univ of Liverpool (BSc), Univ of Sheffield; *Career* asst ed Chemistry in Britain 1970–71, successively technol ed, health and safety ed, news ed New Scientist 1971–82, sci corr Channel 4 News 1982–87, health and sci ed ITN 1987–; memb: Assoc of Br Sci Writers 1971–, NUJ 1971–, Med Journalists Assoc 1982–; guest lectr: Ecole Polytechnique Paris, Soc for Radiological Protection, various other bodies; memb: RSPB, Friends of Kew, English Heritage, Friends of the RA; *Recreations* walking, wine, football, supporting Manchester United FC, etchings; *Style—* Lawrence McGinty, Esq; ✉ ITN, 200 Gray's Inn Road, London WC1X 8XZ (tel 020 7430 4290, e-mail lawrence.mcginty@itn.co.uk)

McGLADE, Prof Jacqueline Myriam; *b* 30 May 1955; *Educ* UCNW (BSc), Univ of Guelph Canada (PhD), Univ of Cambridge (MA); *Children*; 2 da (Katie b 28 May 1982, Rhiannon b 1 April 1985); *Career* sr research scientist Fed Govt Canada 1981–87, research assoc Museum of Zoology Univ of Cambridge 1986–88, assoc prof Cranfield Inst of Technol 1987–88, Adrian fell Darwin Coll Cambridge 1987–90, dir and prof of Inst Theoretical Ecology FZ Jülich Germany 1988–92, prof of biological sciences Univ of Warwick 1992–98, dir NERC Centre for Coastal & Marine Sciences 1998–2000, NERC prof UCL 2000–03, prof of mathematical biology UCL 2003–; exec dir European Environment Agency 2003–; memb: Br Ecological Soc 1992–, External Advsy Gp Environment, Energy & Sustainable Devpt (EU) 1998–2001, Bd Environment Agency 1998–2003; author of numerous papers and publications in learned jls; tstee: Earth Centre 1990–2003, Natural History Museum 2002–; hon prof Univ of Warwick 1998, hon fell Univ of Wales 1999, Hon DSc Univ of Kent 2004; FRICS 1987, FRSA 1997, FLS 1998; *Publications* Advanced Ecological Theory (1999), The Gulf of Guinea Large Marine Ecosystem (2002); *Style—* Prof Jacqueline McGlade; ✉ European Environment Agency, Kongens Nytorv 6, 1050 Copenhagen K, Denmark (tel 45 33 36 71 25, fax 45 33 36 71 98, e-mail jacqueline.mcglade@eea.europa.eu)

McGLONE, Heather Margaret; da of Eric Vickers McGlone, of Brighton, E Sussex, and Margaret Gavin Lamond, *née* Russell; *b* 15 February 1957; *Educ* N London Collegiate Sch, SCEGGS Sydney, Univ of Sydney, Univ of Sussex (BA), Université de la Sorbonne, City Univ London (Dip Journalism); *m* 3 Dec 1983, Louis Albert Francis Kirby, s of William Kirby, and Anne Kirby; 2 da (Clementine Margaret Allegra b 10 April 1987, Iona Alice Eliza b 17 Feb 1990); *Career* Western Morning News and Evening Herald 1981–83, freelance journalist 1983–86; The Express: dep woman's ed 1986–88, woman's ed 1988–91, features ed 1991–93, asst ed features 1993–94, assoc ed 1994, ed This Week magazine 1994–95, exec ed 1995; Daily Mail: commissioning ed Femail 1996–99, ed Weekend magazine 1999–; *Recreations* theatre, ballet, art galleries, horse riding; *Style—* Miss Heather McGlone; ✉ Daily Mail, Northcliffe House, 2 Derry Street, Kensington, London W8 5TT (tel 020 7938 6000, fax 020 7938 6117)

McGONAGLE, Declan George; s of Stephen McGonagle, and Margaret, *née* White; *b* 15 November 1952; *Educ* St Columb's Coll Derry, Coll of Art Belfast (BA, Higher Dip Painting); *m* 28 July 1980, Mary Bernadette (Moira), da of Anthony Carlin; 2 s (Declan b 26 Sept 1984, Paul b 2 March 1987); *Career* lectr in fine art Regnl Tech Coll 1976–78, organiser Orchard Gallery Derry 1978–84, dir of exhibitions ICA London 1984–86, visual arts organiser Derry 1986–90, dir Irish MOMA Dublin 1990–2001, dir City Arts Centre Civil Arts Inquiry 2001–04, chair of art and design and dir INTERFACE Research Centre Univ of Ulster 2004–; contributing ed Art Forum Magazine NY; Sunday Tribune Visual Arts Award 1987; *Recreations* politics, reading, piano; *Style—* Declan McGonagle, Esq; ✉ INTERFACE, School of Art and Design, University of Ulster, York Street, Belfast BT15 1ED (tel 028 9026 7260, e-mail dg.mcgonagle@ulster.ac.uk)

McGONIGAL, His Hon Christopher Ian; s of Maj H A K McGonigal, MC (d 1963), of Beverley, E Yorks, and Cora, *née* Bentley (d 1946); *b* 10 November 1937; *Educ* Ampleforth, CCC Oxford (MA); *m* 28 Sept 1961, (Sara) Sally Ann, da of Louis David Mesnard Fearnley Sander (d 1975); 3 s (Dominic b 1962, Gregory b 1967, Fergus b 1969), 1 da (Alice b 1964); *Career* slr 1965; Coward Chance: asst slr 1965–68, ptnr 1969–87, sr litigation ptnr 1972–79, sr resident ptnr ME 1979–83, sr litigation ptnr 1983–87; slr Hong Kong 1981; Clifford Chance: jt sr litigation ptnr 1987–92, sr litigation ptnr 1992–95, sr ptnr Contentious Business 1995–97; recorder of the Crown Court 1995–97 (asst recorder 1989–95), circuit mercantile judge (NE Circuit) 1997–2003, dep circuit judge and dep judge of the High Court 2003–05; Freeman Worshipful Co of Slrs 1972; *Recreations* local history, gardening, walking; *Style—* His Hon Christopher McGonigal

McGOUGH, Roger Joseph; CBE (2004, OBE 1997); *b* 9 November 1937; *Educ* St Mary's Coll Liverpool, Univ of Hull (BA, CertEd); *Career* poet; fell of poetry Loughborough Univ 1973–75, writer in residence Western Aust Coll of Advanced Educn Perth 1986; vice-pres The Poetry Soc 1996 (memb Exec Cncl 1989–93); Signal Award 1984 and 1998; Cholmondeley Award 1998, Centre for Literacy in Primary Educn (CLPE) Poetry Award 2004 and 2005; hon prof Thames Valley Univ 1993, hon fell Liverpool John Moores Univ; Hon MA UC Northampton; Hon DLitt: Univ of Hull 2004, Univ of Roehampton 2006, Univ of Liverpool 2006; Freeman City of Liverpool 2001; FRSL; *Poetry* The Mersey Sound (with Adrian Henri and Brian Patten, 1967), In the Glassroom (1976), Holiday on Death Row (1979), Summer with Monika (1978), Waving at Trains (1982), Melting into the Foreground (1986), Selected Poems (1989), Blazing Fruit (1990), You At The Back (1991), Defying Gravity (1992), The Spotted Unicorn (1998), The Way Things Are (1999), Everyday Eclipses (2002), Wicked Poems (2002), Collected Poems (2003); wrote and appeared in Thames TV prog Kurt Mungo BP and Me (BAFTA Award, 1984), wrote poems for and presented Channel Four TV prog The Elements 1992 (Royal Television Award); for children: The Great Smile Robbery (1983), Sky in the Pie (1983), The Stowaways (1986), Noah's Ark (1986), Nailing the Shadow (1987), An Imaginary Menagerie (1988), Helen Highwater (1989), Counting by Numbers (1989), Pillow Talk (1990), The Lighthouse That Ran Away (1991), My Dad's a Fire-eater (1992), Another Custard Pie (1993), Lucky (1993), Stinkers Ahoy! (1995), The Magic Fountain (1995), Sporting Relations (1996), The Kite and Caitlin (1996), Bad, Bad Cats (1997), Until I Met Dudley (1997), Good Enough to Eat (2002), What on Earth (2002), Moonthief (2002), The Bees Knees (2003), All the Best (2003), Dotty Inventions (2004), Daniel and the Beast of Babylon (2004); Said and Done (autobiography, 2005); *Clubs* Chelsea Arts (chm 1984–86, tstee 1993–); *Style—* Roger McGough, Esq, CBE, FRSL; ✉ c/o PFD, Drury House, 34–43 Russell Street, London WC2B 5HA

McGOVERN, James (Jim); MP; s of Thomas McGovern, of Dundee, and Alice *née* MacDonald; *b* 17 November 1956, Glasgow; *Educ* Lawside RC Acad Dundee; *m* 28 June 1991, Norma; 1 s (Grant b 26 August 1975), 1 da (Jillian b 7 August 1978); *Career* memb Tayside Regional Cncl 1994–96; MP (Lab) Dundee W 2005–; memb GMB; *Style—* Jim McGovern, Esq, MP; ✉ 125B Kinghorne Road, Dundee DD3 6PW (tel 01382 220991, e-mail mcgovernj@parliament.uk); House of Commons, London SW1A 0AA (tel 020 7219 3000)

M

McGOVERN, Sean; s of Thomas McGovern, of Coventry, Warks, and Margaret McGovern; *b* 31 May 1970; *Educ* Princethorpe Coll, Univ of Manchester (LLB); *m* 10 April 1999, Anita; 1 s (Thomas b 1 Sept 2000), 2 da (Amber, Madeleine (twins) b 18 May 2003); *Career* slr Clifford Chance 1992–96; Lloyd's of London: slr 1996–2000, head of legal 2000–02, dir and gen counsel 2002–; memb Law Soc 1994; *Style—* Sean McGovern, Esq; ✉ Lloyd's of London, One Lime Street, London EC3M 7HA (tel 020 7327 6142, fax 020 7327 5414)

McGOWAN, Alistair Charles; s of George (Mac) McGowan, and Marion McGowan; *Educ* Evesham HS, Univ of Leeds (BA), Guildhall Sch of Music and Drama; *Career* comedian, impressionist and actor; *Theatre* Kafka's Dick 1998, Endgame (Nottingham Playhouse) 1999, Art (Wyndham's Theatre) 2000; *Radio* Weekending (BBC Radio 4) 1989–93, The Harpoon 1990–92, The Nick Revell Show 1991–93, The Game's Up 1995–97, Life, Death and Sex with Mike and Sue 1997–99; *Television* Spitting Image (ITV) 1992–96, Preston Front (BBC1) 1994–97, Alistair McGowan's Big Impression (BBC1) 1999–2003 (Best Comedy Entertainment Prog Comedy Awards 2000, Comedy Award Variety Club Awards 2002, Best Entertainment Performance RTS Awards 2002, BAFTA Award for Best Comedy Programme 2003); *Video* Alistair McGowan's Football Backchat 1997, The Second Leg 1998; *Recreations* tennis, scrabble, classical music, theatre; *Style—* Alistair McGowan, Esq; ✉ c/o Paul Duddridge, Paul Duddridge Management, 28 Rathbone Place, London W1T 1JD (tel 020 7580 3580)

McGOWAN, Prof David Alexander; s of George McGowan, MBE (d 1979), of Portadown, Co Armagh, and Annie Hall, *née* Macormac (d 1994); *b* 18 June 1939; *Educ* Portadown Coll, Queen's Univ Belfast (BDS, MDS), Univ of London (PhD); *m* 21 June 1968, (Vera) Margaret, da of James Macauley, of Closkelt, Co Down; 1 s (Andrew), 2 da (Anna, Marion); *Career* lectr in dental surgery Queen's Univ Belfast 1968, sr lectr in oral and maxillofacial surgery London Hosp Med Coll 1970–77; Univ of Glasgow: prof of oral surgery 1977–99, postgrad advsr in dentistry 1977–90, dean of dental educn 1990–95, memb Court 1995–99; dean Dental Faculty RCPSG 1989–92, chm Nat Dental Advsy Ctee (Scotland) 1995–99, memb and vice-chm exec GDC 1989–99, memb EC Advsy Ctee on the Training of Dental Practitioners 1993–2001; FDSRCS 1964, FFDRCSI 1966, FDSRCPSG 1978, FDSRCSE 1999; *Books* An Atlas of Minor Oral Surgery (1989, 2 edn 1999), The Maxillary Sinus (1993); *Recreations* sailing, photography, music, dog walking; *Style—* Prof David McGowan; ✉ Rhu Lodge, Rhu, Helensburgh G84 8NF (e-mail mcgrhu@talk21.com)

McGOWAN, Sheriff John; s of Arthur McGowan (d 1993), of Kilmarnock, and Bridget, *née* McCluskey (d 2000); *b* 15 January 1944; *Educ* St Joseph's Acad Kilmarnock, Univ of Glasgow (LLB); *m* 16 April 1966, Elise, da of Owen Peter Smith; 2 s (Kenneth Owen b 6 May 1967, Christopher John b 27 March 1970); *Career* legal apprenticeship 1965–67, qualified slr 1967, sheriff of Glasgow and Strathkelvin 1993–2000 (temp sheriff 1986–93), sheriff in Ayr 2000–; chm DHSS Appeal Tbnl 1980–86; memb Cncl Law Soc of Scot 1982–85; *Recreations* theatre, concerts, reading, playing golf and tennis, swimming and curling; *Style—* Sheriff John McGowan; ✉ 19 Auchentrae Crescent, Ayr KA7 4BD (tel 01292 260139, e-mail sheriff.jmcgowan@scotcourts.gov.uk); Sheriff Court House, Wellington Square, Ayr KA7 1EE (tel 01292 292200)

McGOWAN, Malcolm Russell; s of Bernard Earnest McGowan, and Gwendoline Blanche McGowan (decd); *b* 24 October 1955; *Educ* Emanuel Sch, Univ of Westminster (BA Arch, DipArch); *m* Katherine Antonia, *née* Murphy; 1 s (Alexander Jamieson b 15 Nov 1998),

1 da (Sophia Blanche b 24 Aug 2000); *Career* architect; Arhends Burton Koralek 1981–84, Richard Rogers 1985–89; Sheppard Robson (architects, planners and interior designers): joined 1989, assoc 1996–98, ptnr 1998–, managing ptnr 2005; ARB, RIBA; *Recreations* rowing; *Style—* Malcolm McGowan, Esq; ✉ Sheppard Robson, 77 Parkway, London NW1 7PU (tel 020 7504 1700, fax 020 7504 1701, e-mail malcolm.mcgowan@sheppardrobson.com)

McGOWAN, Prof Margaret Mary; CBE (1998); da of George McGowan, and Elizabeth, *née* McGrail; *b* 21 December 1931; *Educ* Stamford HS for Girls, Univ of Reading (BA, PhD); *m* Prof Sydney Anglo; *Career* lectr in French: Univ of Strasbourg 1955–57, Univ of Glasgow 1957–64; Univ of Sussex: lectr in French 1964–66, reader 1966–74, prof 1974– (research prof 1997–), dean Sch of European Studies 1977–80, sr pro-vice-chllr 1992–97 (pro-vice-chllr 1981–86 and 1989–92); Una lectr Univ of Calif Berkeley 1980; pres Assoc of Professors of French 1981–82; memb Soc of Renaissance Studies; Hon DLitt Univ of Sussex 1999; Freedom City of Tours 1988; FBA 1993 (vice-pres 1996–98); *Books* L'Art du Ballet de Cour (1963), Montaigne's Deceits (1974), Ideal Forms in the Age of Ronsard (1985), Moy qui me voy (1989), The Vision of Rome in Late Renaissance France (2000); *Recreations* sport, music; *Style—* Prof Margaret McGowan, CBE, FBA; ✉ University of Sussex, Falmer, Brighton BN1 9QN (tel 01273 678210, fax 01273 678335)

MacGOWAN, Walter John; s of James Thomas MacGowan, and Edith May MacGowan; *Educ* Burford GS, Forest GS; *Career* govr HMP Lincoln 1989–92, govr HMP Manchester 1992–95, dir HMP Buckley Hill 1996–97, dir HMP Wolds 1994–97, dir HMP Altcourse 1997, dir of ops Group 4 Prison Services 1997, md GEO Group UK Ltd 2003–; Butler Tst award 1991; tstee Lower Moss Wood Animal Hosp; patron Apex Tst; memb: Nat Tst, Eng Heritage; *Recreations* reading (major interests history and RN), wine, travel; *Clubs* Kingston Wine Soc; *Style—* Walter MacGowan, Esq; ✉ The GEO Group UK Ltd, 10 Suttons Business Park, Sutton Park Avenue, Reading RG6 1AZ

McGRADY, Edward Kevin; MP; s of late Michael McGrady, of Downpatrick, and Lillian, *née* Leatham; *b* 3 June 1935; *Educ* St Patrick's Downpatrick; *m* 6 Nov 1959, Patricia, da of William Swail; 2 s (Jerome, Conaill), 1 da (Paula); *Career* ptnr MB McGrady & Co CAs and insurance brokers; Downpatrick UDC: cncllr 1961–73, chm 1964–73; Down DC: cncllr 1973–89, chm 1974, 1976, 1978 and 1981; fndr memb and first chm SDLP 1970–71; memb Northern Ireland Assembly 1973–74 and 1982–86, NI Convention 1975, min for co-ordination NI Exec 1974, SDLP chief whip 1975–; MP (SDLP) Down S 1987– (also contested 1979, 1983 and 1986), MLA (SDLP) S Down 1998–2003; chm: Down Regnl Museum 1981–89, Jobspace NI Ltd 1985–93, Down/Chicago Link 1991–93; memb: NI Affairs Select Ctee, SDLP's team to Forum for Peace and Reconciliation, front bench SDLP's team at Multi-Party Talks, Bd of Dirs Down/Chicago Link Ltd (resigned), NI Forum for Political Dialogue 1996 (resigned), NI Affrs Ctee, NI Policing Bd until 2006; FCA (ACA); *Recreations* gardening, walking, ancient monuments, choral music; *Style—* Edward McGrady, Esq, MP; ✉ Constituency Office, 32 Saul Street, Downpatrick, Co Down BT30 6AQ (tel 028 4461 2882, fax 028 4461 9574, e-mail e.mcgrady@sdlp.ie)

McGRAIL, Prof Sean Francis; *b* 5 May 1928; *Educ* Univ of Bristol (Harry Crook scholar, BA), Inst of Archaeology Univ of London, Univ of London (PhD), Campion Hall Oxford (MA), Univ of Oxford (DSc); *m* 28 July 1955, (Ursula) Anne Yates; 3 da (Frances Joanna b 26 May 1956, Mary Ursula b 9 March 1960, Catherine Clare b 29 March 1963), 1 s (Hugh Fergus b 29 Jan 1958); *Career* RN: cadet to Lt Cdr (qualified as Master Mariner) 1946–68, pilot Fleet Air Arm 1952–68 (cmd 849 Sqdn 1962–63); Nat Maritime Museum: asst keeper (archaeology) Dept of Ships 1972, head Dept of Archaeology of Ships 1973–76, chief archaeologist and head Archaeological Research Centre 1976–86 (dep keeper 1976–80, keeper 1980–86); prof of maritime archaeology Inst of Archaeology Univ of Oxford 1986–93; visiting prof: Univ of Southampton 1991–, Danish Nat Museum's Centre for Maritime Archaeology Roskilde 1994, Centre for Maritime Studies Univ of Haifa Israel 1995; memb Cncl: Prehistoric Soc 1980–83, Soc of Antiques 1983–86; memb: Dept of Nat Heritage Advsy Ctee on Historic Wrecks 1975–98, Wardour Catholic Cemetery Ctee 1976– (treas 1999–), Exec Ctee Mary Rose Tst 1980–86, Egyptian Antiques Orgn's Ctee on Establishment of a Nat Maritime Museum in Alexandria 1985–86, Academic Advsy Ctee of States of Guernsey Ancient Monuments Ctee 1985–, Editorial Bd Mary Rose Tst 1998–2002 and 2004–; vice-chm Tst for Preservation of Oxford Coll Barges 1987–93; excavations on prehistoric and medieval sites (Norway, Denmark, Orkney, Ireland, Britain) 1974–, maritime ethnographic fieldwork Bangladesh and India 1994–2001; FSA 1981, MIFA 1983; *Books* Sources and Techniques in Boat Archaeology (ed, 1977), Logboats of England and Wales (1978), Medieval Ships and Harbours in Northern Europe (ed, 1979), Rafts, Boats and Ships (1981), Aspects of Maritime Archaeology and Ethnography (ed, 1984), Ancient Boats in North-West Europe (1987, 2 edn, 1998), Seacraft of Prehistory (ed 2 edn, 1988), Maritime Celts, Frisians and Saxons (ed, 1990), Medieval Boat and Ship Timbers from Dublin (1993), Studies in Maritime Archaeology (1997), Boats of the World (2001, 2 edn 2004), Boats of South Asia (2003), Barland's Farm Romano-Celtic Boat (with N Nayling, 2004), Ancient Boats and Ships (2006); National Maritime Museum Archaeological Series (ed, 1977–86); *Style—* Prof Sean McGrail, FSA; ✉ Institute of Archaeology, 36 Beaumont Street, Oxford OX1 2PG (tel 01865 278240)

McGRATH, Rev Prof Alister Edgar; s of Edgar Parkinson McGrath, of Co Down, and Annie Jane, *née* McBride; *b* 23 January 1953; *Educ* Wadham Coll Oxford (MA), Linacre Coll Oxford, Merton Coll Oxford (DPhil, BD, DD), St John's Coll Cambridge; *m* 1980, Joanna Ruth, da of John Stuart Collicutt; 1 s (Paul Alister b 1981), 1 da (Elizabeth Joanna b 1983); *Career* curate St Leonard's Wollaton 1980–83, research lectr Univ of Oxford 1993–99, research prof of theol Regent Coll Vancouver 1993–98, princ Wycliffe Hall Oxford 1995–2004 (lectr 1983–95), prof of historical theology Univ of Oxford 1999–; Hon DD Virginia Theological Seminary 1996; FRSA 2005; *Books* Intellectual Origins of The Reformation (1987), The Genesis of Doctrine (1990), Encyclopaedia of Modern Christian Thought (1993), Christian Theology (1994), Foundations of Dialogue in Science and Religion (1998), In the Beginning (2001), A Scientific Theology (2002), The Twilight of Atheism (2004), Dawkins' God (2004), The Order of Things (2006); *Recreations* walking, wines; *Style—* The Rev Prof Alister McGrath; ✉ Harris Manchester College, Oxford OX1 3TD (tel 01865 271026, fax 01865 271012, e-mail alister.mcgrath@hmc.ox.ac.uk)

McGRATH, Anthony Charles Ormond; s of Patrick Anthony Ormond McGrath, MC, TD (d 1988), of Southwater, W Sussex, and Eleanor Mary Howard, *née* Horsman (d 2000); *b* 10 November 1949; *Educ* Worth Abbey Sch, Univ of Surrey (BSc), Open Univ (BA); *m* 20 July 1974, Margaret Mary, da of Capt William Arthur Usher, RN (d 1959), of Painswick, Glos; 1 s (Thomas b 21 Aug 1978), 1 da (Philippa b 20 Nov 1980); *Career* Deloitte Haskins & Sells 1971–76, Baring Brothers & Co Limited 1976–95, Baring Brothers Int Ltd 1995–97, Robert Fleming & Co Ltd 1997–2000, treas and tstee The King's Fund 2001–; non-exec dir W & F C Bonham & Sons Ltd 1987–90; memb Nat Cncl CBI (memb Cos Ctee 1996–99), memb London Regnl Cncl CBI 1994–97; tstee English Nat Stadium Tst 1996–99; non-exec memb Br Standards Inst Quality Assurance Bd 1986–90; memb Ctee London HE Consortium 2001–03; FCA 1974; *Clubs* Flyfishers'; *Style—* Anthony McGrath, Esq; ✉ The King's Fund, 11–13 Cavendish Square, London W1G 0AN

McGRATH, Prof Elizabeth; da of Thomas McGrath, and Emilie, *née* Melvin; *b* 20 March 1945; *Educ* St Joseph's HS Kilmarnock, Univ of Glasgow (MA), Univ of London (PhD); *Career* curator Photographic Collection Warburg Inst London 1991– (joined 1970); Durning Lawrence lectr UCL 1989, Slade prof Univ of Oxford 1990; ed Jl of the Warburg and Courtauld Insts 1977–; Hans Reimer prize Univ of Hamburg 1996; Mitchell Prize in the History of Art 1998, Eugène Baie Prize of Province of Antwerp 1999; memb Royal Flemish Acad of Arts and Sciences 2003; FBA 1998; *Books* Rubens: Subjects from History (1997); also author of articles in learned jls; *Style—* Prof Elizabeth McGrath, FBA; ✉ Warburg Institute, University of London, Woburn Square, London WC1H 0AB (tel 020 7862 8949, fax 020 7862 8955, e-mail elizabeth.mcgrath@sas.ac.uk)

McGRATH, Prof (John Christie) Ian; s of John (Jack) Christie McGrath, of Barrhead, Strathclyde, and Margaret Gilmore Cochrane, *née* Murray (decd); *b* 8 March 1949; *Educ* John Neilson Instn, Univ of Glasgow (BSc, PhD); *m* 25 June 1970, Wilma, da of late John Nicol; 1 s (Nicolas John b 13 Aug 1974), 1 da (Katie Isabella b 8 Jan 1981); *Career* Wellcome interdisciplinary res fell Dept of Pharmacology and Univ Dept of Anaesthesia Glasgow Royal Infirmary Univ of Glasgow 1973–75; Inst of Physiology Univ of Glasgow: lectr 1975–83, sr lectr 1983–88, reader 1988–89, titular prof 1989–91, regius prof, head Dept of Physiology 1991–93, head of Biomedical Sci Gp 1991–93, co-dir Clinical Research Initiative in Heart Failure 1994–99, head Div of Neuroscience and Biomedical Systems 1997–; chm Standing Ctee of Heads of UK Physiology Dept 2000–; memb: SERC Case Panel 1981–82, Ctee Physiological Soc 1988– (vice-chair 2004–06, chair 2006–), Cncl Biosciences Fedn 2007–; memb Editorial Bd: Br Jl of Pharmacology 1984–91 and 2000– (sr ed 2001–), Pharmacological Reviews 1989–98, Jl of Cardiovascular Pharmacology 1988–94, Jl of Vascular Res 1991–; Pfizer Award for Biology 1983; memb: Br Pharmacological Soc 1975 (Sandoz Prize 1980), Physiological Soc 1978, American Soc for Pharmacology and Therapeutics 1990, American Physiological Soc 1993; *Publications* articles in academic jls; *Recreations* travel, cycling, running, eating and drinking, politics (memb Labour Party); *Style—* Prof Ian McGrath; ✉ West Medical Building, University of Glasgow, Glasgow G12 8QQ (tel 0141 330 4483, fax 0141 330 2923, mobile 078 5050 2553, e-mail i.mcgrath@bio.gla.ac.uk)

McGRATH, Jim; *b* 22 May 1955; *Career* with Timeform Organisation 1974– (currently md); racing corr TV-AM 1983–89, ITV Racing 1981–85, C4 Racing 1985–; ind dir BHB 2004–; Horserace Writers and Photographers Assoc (HWPA): nominee Broadcasting Award 2002, nominee Specialist Award 2004; numerous videos, voice-overs and articles on horse racing; *Publications* Willie Carson: The People's Champion (1986); *Recreations* squash, golf; *Clubs* Saints and Sinners; *Style—* Jim McGrath, Esq; ✉ Timeform, 25 Timeform House, Northgate, Halifax, West Yorkshire HX1 1XF (tel 01422 330330, e-mail jcm@timeform.com)

McGRATH, John Brian; *b* 20 June 1938; *Educ* Brunel Univ (BSc); *m* Sandy McGrath; 1 da (Lucy b 19 April 1969), 1 s (Paul b 17 Aug 1971); *Career* various appts with UKAEA, National Coal Board, Ford Motor Co, Jaguar Cars and Stone-Platt Ltd 1956–81, chief exec Compair Ltd 1984 (md Construction and Mining Div 1982–83); Grand Metropolitan group: gp dir Watney Mann & Truman Brewers Ltd 1985, chm and md Grand Metropolitan Brewing 1986, jt md responsible for GrandMet Brewing, International Distillers & Vintners Ltd, IDV UK and Heublein 1988–91, chm and chief exec International Distillers & Vintners Ltd 1992–95 (md and chief operating offr 1991–92), gp chief exec Grand Metropolitan plc 1996–97, gp chief exec Diageo plc (following merger with Guinness plc) 1997–2000; non-exec dir: Boots plc 1997–2003 (chm 2000–03), ITV plc (formerly Carlton Communications) 2003–; chm Cicely Saunders Int 2002–; first chm The Portman Group (promoting responsible use of alcohol), chm The Scotch Whisky Assoc 1994–2000; govr Brunel Univ; Freeman City of London; *Style—* John McGrath

McGRATH, Dr John Neilson; s of John McGrath (d 1977), of Aberdare, Mid Glamorganshire, and Agnes Louisa Jones (d 1989); *b* 16 May 1941; *Educ* St Benedict's Sch Ealing, Univ Coll Cardiff (BSc, PhD), RNC Greenwich (MSc); *m* 14 April 1970, Zena Gladys, da of Norman William Haysom, of Portsmouth, Hants; 2 s (James 1971, Paul 1973); *Career* Lt 1967, Lt Cdr 1971, Cdr 1979, Capt 1986, trg cdr Career Trg HMS Sultan 1979–82, head of materials technol RNEC 1982–86, head of manpower computer systems HMS Centurion 1987–89, dean RNEC Manadon Plymouth 1990–93, Welsh dir The Open Univ 1993–98; chm Inst of Materials Professional Devpt Ctee 2000–01, chm Inst of Materials Professional Policy Bd 2001–04; vice-chm Grange Gp of Schs 1979–82; memb: Technician Educn Cncl Maritime Studies Ctee 1979–82, Devon Sci and Technol Regnl Orgn 1984–86, Ct of Govrs Univ of Wales 1994–98, Rail Users Consultative Ctee (RUCC) for Southern England 1999–2001, Rail Passengers Ctee Southern England 2001–05; fencing: Welsh épée champion 1965, Welsh foil champion 1970; CEng, FIMMM 1991, FIMarEst 1988 (memb: Professional Affrs and Educn Ctee, Membership Ctee); *Books* Naval Cutlass Exercise (2002), Swords for Officers of the Royal Navy (2004), Fencing in the Royal Navy and Royal Marines 1733–1948 (2004); *Recreations* fencing, gardening; *Style—* Dr John McGrath; ✉ Beech Lawn, Bridgefoot Drive, Fareham, Hampshire PO16 0DB (tel 01329 221376)

MacGREGOR, Alastair Rankin; QC (1994); s of Alexander MacGregor, and Anne, *née* Neil; *b* 23 December 1951; *Educ* Glasgow Acad, Univ of Edinburgh, New Coll Oxford (MA); *m* 21 Feb 1982, Rosemary Alison, da of Ralph Trevor Kerslake; 1 s (James b 13 June 1984), 1 da (Martha b 5 Jan 1989); *Career* called to the Bar Lincoln's Inn 1974, in practice London until 2004; memb Criminal Cases Review Commission 2004– (dep chm 2006–); *Style—* Alastair R MacGregor, Esq, QC; ✉ Criminal Cases Review Commission, Alpha Tower, Suffolk Street, Queensway, Birmingham B1 1TT (tel 0121 633 1800, fax 0121 633 1804)

McGREGOR, Alistair John; QC (1997); s of Lord McGregor of Durris (Life Peer, d 1997), and Nellie, *née* Weate; *b* 11 March 1950; *Educ* Haberdashers' Aske's, Queen Mary Coll London (LLB); *m* 14 Sept 1985, Charlotte Ann, da of Michael George East; 1 da (Emily Ann b 20 Feb 1987), 1 s (Alasdair Hugh b 17 March 1989); *Career* called to the Bar Middle Temple 1974; author of various articles in professional jls; memb: Nat Youth Orchestra of GB 1967–68, Nat Youth Jazz Orchestra of GB 1968–69; dir Forest Philharmonic Soc 1978–96; *Recreations* music, sport; *Clubs* Garrick; *Style—* Alistair McGregor, Esq, QC; ✉ 11 King's Bench Walk, Temple, London EC4Y 7EQ

MACGREGOR, Elizabeth Ann; da of late Rt Rev Gregor Macgregor, and Elizabeth Jean Macgregor, of Inverness; *b* 16 April 1958; *Educ* Stromness Acad Orkney, Univ of Edinburgh (MA), Univ of Manchester (post grad museums studies dipl); *m* 30 July 1988, Peter Simon Jenkinson; *Career* curator Scottish Arts Cncl Travelling Gallery 1980–84, art offr Arts Cncl of GB 1984–89, dir Ikon Gallery Birmingham 1989–99, dir Museum of Contemporary Art Sydney Aust 1999–; judge Turner Prize 1995; memb: Visual Arts & Galleries Assoc 1985, The Lunar Soc 1991, Women in Business Assoc 1991; memb Bd Public Art Devpt Tst; chair BBC Midlands Advsy Bd 1997–99; tstee Pier Art Centre Orkney; FRSA; *Style—* Ms Elizabeth A Macgregor; ✉ Museum of Contemporary Art, PO Box R1286, Sydney NSW 2001, Australia (tel 00 612 9252 4033, fax 00 612 9252 4361)

McGREGOR, Ewan; s of James McGregor, and Carol McGregor; *b* 31 March 1971; *Educ* Morisson's Acad Perthshire, Guildhall Sch of Music and Drama; *m* Eve; 2 da (Clara Mathilde, Esther Rose); *Career* actor; supporter: Children's Hospice Assoc, Meningitis Tst; ambass UNICEF; Hon DLitt Univ of Ulster 2001; *Theatre* incl: What the Butler Saw (Salisbury Playhouse), Little Malcolm and His Struggle Against the Eunuchs, Guys and Dolls (Piccadilly Theatre) 2005; *Television* incl: Lipstick on Your Collar (Channel Four), Scarlet and Black (BBC), Family Style (Channel Four), Kavanagh QC, Doggin' Around (Screen One), Cold War - Tales from the Crypt (HBO), ER (nominated Outstanding Guest Actor in a Drama Series Emmy Awards 1997), Long Way Round (factual travel series); *Film* incl: Being Human, Shallow Grave (Best Film Dinard Film Festival 1994, BAFTA

Alexander Korda Award for Outstanding British Film of the Year 1995, BAFTA Jt Best Actor Award, BAFTA Scotland Award for Best Feature Film), Blue Juice, The Pillow Book, Trainspotting, Emma, Brassed Off, Nightwatch, The Serpent's Kiss, A Life Less Ordinary, Curt in Velvet Goldmine, Star Wars: Episode I - The Phantom Menace, Star Wars: Episode II - Attack of the Clones and Star Wars: Episode III - Revenge of the Sith, Little Voice, The Eye of the Beholder, Rogue Trader, Moulin Rouge (Best British Actor Empire Awards 2002), Black Hawk Down, Big Fish, Robots, Valiant, Miss Potter 2006, Stay 2006, The Island 2006, Cassandra's Dream 2007, The Tourist 2007; *Style—* Ewan McGregor, DLitt; ✉ c/o PFD, Drury House, 34–43 Russell Street, London WC2B 5HA (tel 020 7344 1010, fax 020 7836 9543)

MacGREGOR, Prof Graham A; s of Prof A B MacGregor (d 1964), and Sybil, *née* Hawkey (d 1974); *b* 1 April 1941; *Educ* Marlborough, Trinity Hall Cambridge (MA, MB BChir), Middx Hosp; *m* 2 Nov 1968, Christiane, da of Maurice Bourquin (d 1956), of Switzerland; 2 da (Annabelle b 16 Nov 1970, Vanessa b 6 April 1972), 1 s (Christopher b 5 Sept 1973); *Career* dir Blood Pressure Unit (former sr lectr) Charing Cross and Westminster Med Sch 1979–89, prof of cardiovascular med St George's Hosp Med Sch 1989–; chm: Blood Pressure Assoc 1999–, Consensus Action on Salt and Health 1999–, World Action on Salt 2005–; FRCP 1982; *Books* Salt Free Diet Book (1985, 2 edn 1991), Hypertension in Practice (1987, 3 edn 1999), Salt Diet and Health: Neptune's Poisoned Chalice (1998), Fast Facts Hypertension (2006); *Style—* Prof Graham MacGregor; ✉ Blood Pressure Unit, St George's Hospital, London SW17 0RE (tel 020 8725 2989, fax 020 8725 2959, e-mail g.macgregor@sgul.ac.uk)

McGREGOR, Harvey; QC (1978); s of William Guthrie Robertson McGregor, and Agnes, *née* Reid; *b* 25 February 1926; *Educ* Inverurie Acad, Scarborough Boys' HS, The Queen's Coll Oxford (MA, BCL, DCL), Harvard Univ (Dr of Juridical Sci); *Career* Nat Serv 1944–48, Flying Offr; called to the Bar Inner Temple 1955 (bencher 1985); head of chambers 1986–2000; Bigelow teaching fell Univ of Chicago 1950–51, visiting prof NYU and Rutgers Univ 1963–69, conslt to Law Cmmn 1966–73, warden New Coll Oxford 1985–96 (fell 1972–85, hon fell 1996–); memb Editorial Bd Modern Law Review 1986– (memb Editorial Ctee 1967–86); memb Faculty of Advocates 1995; assoc memb Soc of Writers to HM Signet 2002; ind chm London Theatre Cncl and The Theatre Cncl 1992– (dep ind chm 1971–92), tstee Oxford Union Soc 1977–2004 (chm 1994–2004), tstee Migraine Tst 1999–; pres Harvard Law Sch Assoc of UK 1981–2001; fell Winchester Coll 1985–96, privilegiate St Hilda's Coll Oxford 2001–; memb Acad European Private Lawyers 1994–; *Books* McGregor on Damages (1961, 17 edn 2003), International Encyclopaedia of Comparative Law (contrib, 1972), Contract Code (1993); articles in legal journals; *Recreations* music, theatre, travel; *Clubs* Garrick, New (Edinburgh); *Style—* Harvey McGregor, Esq, QC; ✉ Hailsham Chambers, 4 Paper Buildings, Temple, London EC4Y 7EX (tel 020 7643 5000, fax 020 7353 5778, e-mail harvey.mcgregor@hailshamchambers.com); 29 Howard Place, Edinburgh EH3 5JY (tel 0131 556 8680, fax 0131 556 8686); Gray's Inn Chambers, Gray's Inn, London WC1R 5JA

MacGREGOR, Joanna Clare; da of Alfred MacGregor, of North London, and Angela, *née* Hughes; *b* 16 July 1959; *Educ* South Hampstead Sch for Girls, New Hall Cambridge (BA), Royal Acad of Music (recital dip, Gold medallist), Van Cliburn Inst Texas (masterclasses with Jorge Bolet); *m* 19 Sept 1986, Richard Williams; 1 da (Miranda (decd)); *Career* pianist; appeared as soloist with RPO, LSO, Eng Chamber Orch (tours to Bermuda and USA incl Carnegie Hall), BBC Symphony Orch, BBC Orch Scot, City of London Sinfonia, Nat Youth Orch (Proms 1990), London Mozart Players, BBC Symphony Orch, Rotterdam Philharmonic, CBSO, Orch of St John's, Dutch Radio Orch, Berlin Symphony Orch, Chicago Symphony Orch, Sydney Symphony Orchestra; soloist Last Night of the Proms 1996; tours: Senegal, Sierra Leone, Zimbabwe, The Phillipines, Norway, New Zealand, South Africa, Sweden, Germany, Singapore, Australia; premiered works by Br composers incl: Michael Finnissy, Hugh Wood and Harrison Birtwistle; jazz collaborations incl: Django Bates, Iain Ballamy; recordings incl: American Piano Classics (1989), Satie Piano Music, Britten Piano Concerto (with Eng Chamber Orch and Steuart Bedford), Barber/Ives Sonatas, Scarlatti Sonatas, Bach Art of Fugue, Nancarrow Canons and pieces by Ravel, Bartók, Debussy and Messiaen; composer Br music for theatre and TV prodns incl: Cheek By Jowl, Oxford Stage Co, C4; organised Platform Festival of New Music ICA 1991–93; artistic dir SoundCircus Bridgewater Hall Manchester 1996; author of fantasy play based on Erik Satie's writings (BBC Entry Prix d'Italia 1990, Sony Awards entry 1991); prof of music Gresham Coll London 1998–2000; radio presenter BBC Radio 3; TV presenter: BBC Omnibus, BBC Masterclass, Young Musician of the Year, Strings Bow and Bellows (BBC series); fndr SoundCircus 1997 (record label, website www.soundcircus.com; recordings incl: John Cage Sonatas, Nikki Yeoh Piano Language, Lou Harrison Piano Concerto); South Bank Show award for classical music 2000; memb Arts Cncl of England 1998–; FRAM, FTCL, Hon FRAM; *Recreations* windsurfing; *Style—* Ms Joanna MacGregor; ✉ c/o David Sigall, Ingpen & Williams Ltd, 7 St George's Court, 131 Putney Bridge Road, London SW15 2PA (tel 020 8874 3222, fax 020 8877 3113)

McGREGOR, John Cummack; s of John Alexander McGregor, OBE, of Edinburgh, and Isobel Millar, *née* Cummack; *b* 21 April 1944; *Educ* Paisley GS, Univ of Glasgow (Rainey bursary, BSc, MB ChB, John Hunter medal, David Livingston prize); *m* 22 July 1972, Moira, da of Gordon Imray; 1 da (Trudy Isabel b 1 Aug 1973), 1 s (Alan John Alexander b 26 March 1975); *Career* jr hosp posts in med Royal Alexander Infirmary Paisley then in surgery Western Infirmary Hosp Glasgow 1969–70, Hall fell Professorial Dept of Surgery Western Infirmary Glasgow 1970–71, registrar in gen surgery Stobhill Hosp Glasgow and locum registrar in plastic surgery Canniesburn Glasgow 1971–76, SHO/registrar in plastic surgery Nottingham City Hosp 1975–77, registrar in plastic surgery Canniesburn Glasgow 1977–78, sr registrar in plastic surgery Bangour Hosp nr Edinburgh 1978–80, conslt plastic surgn Bangour Edinburgh and St John's Hosps W Lothian 1980–; memb cncl Br Assoc of Plastic Surgns 2004–, memb Br Assoc of Aesthetic Plastic Surgns; Sir Ernest Finch research prize Trent RHA 1977; FRCS 1974, FRCSEd 1983; *Books* contrib chapters: Advances and Technical Standards in Neurosurgery (Resconstructive Surgery of the Head) (1981), Essential Surgical Practice (1988); author of over 90 pubns in med jls on various topics incl burns, pressure sores, breast surgery, compound leg injuries, skin cancer, plastic surgery audit and sport injuries; *Recreations* golf, tennis, watching football and rugby, keeping budgerigars, collecting cacti, writing medical articles; *Clubs* Bruntsfield Golf (Edinburgh), Royal Burgess Golf (Edinburgh); *Style—* John McGregor, Esq; ✉ c/o BUPA Murrayfield Hospital, 122 Corstorphine Road, Edinburgh EH12 6UD (tel 0131 334 0363, fax 0131 334 7338); St John's Hospital at Howden, Howden, Livingston, W Lothian EH54 6PP (tel 01506 419666)

MACGREGOR, HE John Malcolm; CVO; *b* 3 October 1946; *Educ* Balliol Coll Oxford (exhibitioner, organ scholar, BA), Univ of Birmingham; *m* 1982, Judith Anne, *née* Brown; 3 s, 1 da; *Career* diplomat; former teacher and musician; entered HM Dip Serv 1973, second then first sec New Delhi 1975–79, desk offr European Communities Dept FCO 1979–81, private sec to Min of State 1981, speechwriter to Foreign Min 1982, asst head Soviet Dept FCO 1983–86, dep head of mission Prague 1986–90, head of Chancery Paris 1990–93, head External EU Dept FCO 1993–95, DG for trade promotion in Germany and consul-gen Düsseldorf 1995–98, ambass to Poland 1998–2000, dir wider Europe FCO 2000–03, ambass to Austria 2003–, UK perm rep to UN 2006–; *Recreations* cycling, walking, reading, studying languages, music (piano and cello), DIY; *Style—* HE Mr John Macgregor, CVO; ✉ c/o Foreign & Commonwealth Office (Vienna), King Charles Street, London SW1A 2AH

MACGREGOR, HE Judith Anne; *née* Brown; LVO; *b* 17 June 1952, London; *Educ* Univ of Oxford; *m* 1982, John Malcolm Macgregor; 3 s, 1 da; *Career* diplomat; entered HM Dip Serv 1976, first sec (Chancery and info) Belgrade 1978–81, desk offr FCO 1981–83, head of recruitment FCO 1983–84, memb Planning Staff FCO 1985–86, on leave 1986–88, first sec (political and info) Prague 1989, on leave 1990–91, first sec (Chancery) Paris 1992, dep head Western European Dept FCO 1993–95, on leave 1995–2000, cnsllr and head Security Strategy Unit FCO 2001–03, FCO chair Civil Serv Selection Bd 2003–04, ambass to Slovakia 2004–07, dir Migration FCO 2007–; *Recreations* walking, gardening, reading; *Style—* Mrs Judith Macgregor, LVO; ✉ c/o Foreign & Commonwealth Office, King Charles Street, London SW1A 2AH

MacGREGOR, (Robert) Neil; s of Alexander Rankin MacGregor, and Anna Neil; *b* 16 June 1946; *Educ* Glasgow Acad, New Coll Oxford, Ecole Normale Supérieure Paris, Univ of Edinburgh, Courtauld Inst of Art; *Career* memb Faculty of Advocates Edinburgh 1972, lectr in history of art and architecture Univ of Reading 1975–81, ed Burlington Magazine 1981–87, dir Nat Gallery 1987–2002, dir British Museum 2002–; memb RSA; Hon Doctorate: Univ of York, Univ of Edinburgh, Univ of Reading, Univ of Leicester, Univ of Glasgow, Univ of Strathclyde, Univ of Oxford, Univ of Exeter, Univ of London; hon fell New Coll Oxford; Hon FBA; *Style—* Neil MacGregor; ✉ The British Museum, Great Russell Street, London WC1B 3DG (tel 020 7323 8000)

MacGREGOR, Susan Katriona (Sue); CBE (2002, OBE 1992); da of late Dr James MacWilliam MacGregor, and Margaret MacGregor; *b* 30 August 1941; *Educ* Herschel Sch Cape Town; *Career* programme presenter South African Broadcasting Corp 1962–67, BBC radio reporter (World at One, PM, World this Weekend) 1967–72; presenter BBC Radio 4: Woman's Hour 1972–87, Today 1984–2002, A Good Read 2003–, The Reunion 2003– (Sony Gold Award 2007); memb Bd: John Ellerman Fndn, Young Concert Artists' Tst, UNICEF UK; Hon DLitt: Univ of Nottingham, Nottingham Trent Univ, Staffordshire Univ, London Metropolitan Univ; Hon LLD Univ of Dundee; Hon MRCP, FRSA; *Books* Woman of Today: An Autobiography (2002); *Recreations* theatre, cinema, skiing; *Style—* Ms Sue MacGregor; ✉ c/o Knight Ayton Management, 114 St Martin's Lane, London WC2N 4BE (tel 020 7836 5333)

McGREGOR, Wayne; *b* 1970, Stockport; *Educ* Bretton Hall Coll, Univ of Leeds (BA), Jose Limon Sch NY; *Career* choreographer; fndr Random Dance Co 1992– (resident co of Sadler's Wells 2001–), choreographer in residence Royal Ballet 2006–, choreographer in residence The Place Theatre London, represented GB in Bancs d'Essai Internationaux, SKITE Project Lisbon and European Choreographic Forum; prodns for Random Dance Co: Xeno 1 2 3 (The Place) 1993, Labrax (The Place) 1994, Sever (The Place) 1995, AnArkos (The Place) 1995, For Bruising Archangel (cmmned ELRDC/LDDC), Jacob's Membrane (cmmned Yorkshire Dance Centre), Cyborg (cmmned Dance Umbrella), 8 Legs of the Devil (cmmned Suffolk Dance), The Millennarium (cmmned RFH) 1997 (Prix d'Auteur du Council General de Seine-Saint-Denis at Bagnolet 1998, L'Adami Prize for Performance Paris 1998), Sulphur 16 (cmmned RFH) 1998 (winner Ballett Int Choreographer In Residence Best Choreography Collaboration), Aeon (cmmned RFH) 2000 (nominated Benoise de la Danse 2002) 2000, digit01 (cmmned The Place) 2001, Nemesis (co-cmmned South Hill Park, Swindon Dance, Sadler's Wells, DanceEast) 2002, Alpha 2003, Polar Sequences 2003, Amu 2005 (nominated Critics' Circle Nat Dance Award for Best Choreography, Modern 2006), AtaXia 2005, Ossein 2005; ind cmmns: GCSE Nat Set Study (Northern Examinations and Assessment Bd), Vulcan (Swindon Youth Dance Co), White Out (The Boy's Project), Cyberdream (The Boy's Project), Artificial Intelligence (Nat Youth Dance Co), 9.7 recurring 2%Black (Nat Youth Dance Co), The Skinned Prey (4D, London Contemporary Dance Sch), Esc...otherspace (Birmingham Hippodrome), Ventolin (W Yorkshire Playhouse), Bach Suite (Crusaid Gala RNT), Encoder (Shobana Jeyasingh's Away Game), Trial By Jury (Melbourne Int Festival), Dance of the Broadband (Le Groupe de la Place Royale Ottowa), Vulture (Reverse Effect), Medusa (Olympic Ballet Co Milan), Urban Savage (Ricochet Dance Co), Intertense (Shobana Jeyasingh Dance Co), net/work Narrative(s) (Seda/Brighton Int Festival) 2000, The Field (ELD/G&D Int Festival) 2000, Telenoia (Canary Wharf) 2000, Fleur de Peux (with Vivianna Durante, *qv*, Royal Ballet) 2000, Symbiont(s) (Royal Ballet Covent Garden) 2000 (nomination Best Choreography Critics' Circle Awards 2002), Velociraptor (Dance East/Bury Festival) 2001, Detritus (Rambert Dance Co) 2001, Castlescape (E London Dance) 2001, HIVE (Nat Youth Dance Wales (2001), Brainstate (Royal Ballet/Random Dance) 2001, Phase Space (Gothenberg Ballet/Random Dance) 2002, Game of Halves (Nat Youth Dance Wales) 2002, PreSentient (Rambert Dance Co) 2002, Binocular (Adam Cooper Dance Co) 2003, Xenathra (Dance Umbrella) 2003, Qualia (Royal Ballet) 2003, Nautilus (Stuttgart Ballet) 2003, 2 Human (English Nat Ballet) 2003,Eden/Eden (Stuttgart Ballet) 2005, Engram (Royal Ballet) 2005, Skindex (NDT1) 2006, Chroma (Royal Ballet) 2006 (nominated Olivier Award for Best New Dance Prodn 2007 and Outstanding Achievement in Dance 2007 (for choreography)), Eden/Eden (San Francisco Ballet) 2007, [memeri] (DANCE) 2007; site specific cmmns: CeBit Dances (Imagination/Ericsson Hanover), Dragonfly (Alternative Hair Show Drury Lane London), Slam (The Arches Glasgow), Match Half (Nottingham Forest Stadium), opening of World Disabled Games (Birmingham Int Stadium), Installation over 4 (Selfridges Gallery Window), Bio-logical (for Bodycraze at Selfridges London/Manchester), LOVE (Imagination Frankfurt), BodyScript (Connect at Sadler's Wells), Cybergeneration (Belfast Int Festival at Queens), Zero Hertz (Cork Opera House Ireland), Neurotransmission (Snape Maltings Concert Hall Aldeburgh), S.I.N (Shed O Docklands London), Dragonfly (Nat Glass Centre), Series (Houses of Parliament), Black on White (South Bank Centre Ballroom), Chameleon (Barbican), x2 (Royal Museum Edinburgh), Scottish Opera/Random Collaboration (GOMA Glasgow), Angel (Natural History Museum London), In:terplay (Bruce Nauman, Hayward Gall London), Pointe (Saatchi Gall London), Equation (Centre George Pompidu Paris), 11 Digital Mantras (The Roundhouse London), Sentient Net (The Gallert Sadler's Wells), Velociraptor (The Crypt Bury St Edmunds), Castlescape (Goresbrook Estate London), Amu@Durham (Durham Cathedral); *Theatre* A Little Night Music (RNT, Arts Fndn Fellowship 1994 and nomination Best Choreographer Olivier Awards 1996), Cleansed (Royal Court), Antony and Cleopatra (RNT), Woman in White (Palace Theatre) 2004–05, Cloaca (Old Vic) 2004, Alladin (Old Vic) 2004–05, You Can Never Tell (Peter Hall Co) 2005, Much Ado About Nothing (Peter Hall Co) 2006; *Opera* Rinaldo/The Mikado (Grange Park Opera), Salome (ENO), The Marriage of Figaro (Scottish Nat Opera), Orpheus et Eurydice (Scottish Nat Opera and Scottish Opera Go Round), Hansel and Gretel (Scottish Nat Opera), La Boheme (Scottish Nat Opera), The Midsummer Marriage (Chicago Lyric Opera), Did and Aeneas (La Scala); *Television and Film* Redoxon commercial, Eurostar commercial, Physical Dysfunctional (BBC Knowledge), Horizone (Dance for Camera, BBC and ACE), Medusa (RaiUno Int), Bent (Channel 4 Films), Tomorrows World Live (cmmnd NESTA), The Last Siren (cmmnd RaiUno Italy), The Dancer's Body (BBC 2), Nemesis (BBC4/MJW), Symbiont(s) (BBC 2), Chrysalis (Arte), Dice Life (Channel 4), Dance USA (BBC 4), Harry Potter and the Goblet of Fire, Tremor (Channel 4); *Awards* Art Fndn fellowship, Lisa Ullmann travel scholarship 1997, nomination Outstanding Contribution to Dance Critics' Circle Awards 2001, nomination Award for Dance South Bank Show 2001, Outstanding Achievement in Dance Award Time Out Live awards 2001, Outstanding Choreography Award Time Out Live Awards 2003, Screen Choreography Award Monaco Dance Screen 2003,

Laurence Olivier Award for Best New Dance Production, Laurence Olivier Outstanding Achievemtn in Dance for Choreography, Critics' Circle Award for Best Modern Choreography, South Bank Show Award; *Style*— Wayne McGregor, Esq; ✉ Random Dance Company, Sadler's Wells Theatre, Rosebery Avenue, London EC1R 4TN (tel 020 7278 6015, fax 7278 5469, e-mail info@randomdance.org)

McGREGOR-JOHNSON, His Hon Judge Richard John; s of Maxwell McGregor-Johnson (d 1987), and Pamela, *née* Moy (d 2004); *b* 11 July 1950; *Educ* Dean Close Sch Cheltenham, Univ of Bristol (LLB); *m* 1974, Elizabeth, da of Sidney Weston; 1 s (James b 11 July 1978), 1 da (Caroline b 10 August 1980); *Career* called to the Bar Inner Temple 1973 (bencher 2001); in practice (specialising in criminal law) 1973–98, circuit judge 1998–; *Recreations* choral singing, sailing; *Style*— His Hon Judge McGregor-Johnson; ✉ The Crown Court, 36 Ridgeway Road, Isleworth, Middlesex TW7 5LP (tel 020 8380 4500)

MacGREGOR OF MacGREGOR, Malcolm Gregor Charles; 7 Bt (GB 1795), of Lanrick, Co Perth; 24 Chief of Clan Gregor; s of Brig Sir Gregor MacGregor of MacGregor, 6 Bt (d 2003), and Fanny MacGregor of MacGregor, *née* Butler; *b* 23 March 1959; *Educ* Eton, Cranfield Univ (MBA); *m* 1 (m dis), Cecilia Margaret Lucy, eld da of Sir Ilay Campbell of Succoth, 7 Bt; m 2, 14 May 2005, Fiona Kathryn Armstrong, *qv*, da of Robert Armstrong, of Preston, Lancs; *Career* Maj Scots Gds (ret), chief of staff 51 Highland Bde, served Hong Kong, NI, BAOR and UK; landscape photographer; memb Queen's Body Guard for Scotland (Royal Co of Archers); FRGS, FRPS, ABIPP; *Books* Wilderness Oman, Rob Roy's Country, Light over Oman, The Outer Hebrides; *Recreations* travel, fly fishing, tennis; *Clubs* Royal Perth; *Style*— Sir Malcolm MacGregor of MacGregor, Bt; ✉ Bannatyne, Newtyle, Angus PH12 8TR (e-mail malcolm_macgregor@btinternet.com)

MacGREGOR OF PULHAM MARKET, Baron (Life Peer UK 2001), of Pulham Market in the County of Norfolk; John Roddick Russell MacGregor; OBE (1971), PC (1985); s of late Dr N S R MacGregor, of Shotts; *b* 14 February 1937; *Educ* Merchiston Castle Sch Edinburgh, Univ of St Andrews, King's Coll London; *m* 1962, Jean Dungey; 1 s, 2 da; *Career* univ admin 1961–62; former chm: Fedn of Univ Cons and Unionist Assocs, Bow Gp; first pres Cons and Christian Democratic Youth Community; editorial staff New Society 1962–63, special asst to PM 1963–64, Cons Res Dept 1964–65, head of Ldr of Oppn's Private Office 1965–68; with Hill Samuel 1968–79 (dir 1973–79); MP (Cons) Norfolk S Feb 1974–2001, oppn whip 1977–79, a Lord Cmmr of the Treasy (Govt whip) 1979–81, Parly Under Sec for Trade and Industry incl responsiblity for small businesses 1981–83, Min of State for Agric Fisheries and Food 1983–85, Chief Sec to the Treasy 1985–87, Min for Agric Fisheries and Food 1987–89, Sec of State for Educn 1989–90, Lord Pres of the Council and Leader of the Commons 1990–92, Sec of State for Transport 1992–94; non-exec dep chm Hill Samuel Bank 1994–96; non-exec dir: Associated British Foods plc 1994–, Slough Estates plc 1995–2006, Uniq plc (formerly Unigate plc) 1996–2005; Friends Provident 1998–2007, Supervisory Bd DAF Trucks NV 2000–; vice-pres: Assoc of County Cncls 1995–97, Local Govt Assoc 1997–99; memb: Cncl King's Coll London 1996–2002, Ctee for Standards in Public Life 1997–2003, Cncl Norwich Cathedral 2002–; dep chm: Governing Bodies Assoc 1998–2002, Assoc of Governing Bodies of Ind Schs 2002–06; Hon LLD Univ of Westminster 1995; MInstD (memb Cncl 1996–); *Recreations* opera, gardening, travel, conjuring; *Style*— The Rt Hon the Lord MacGregor of Pulham Market, OBE, PC

McGRIGOR, Sir Charles Edward; 5 Bt (UK 1831), of Campden Hill, Middx; DL (Argyll and Bute); s of Lt-Col Sir Charles Colquhoun McGrigor, 4 Bt, OBE (d 1946), and Amabel Caroline, *née* Somers-Cocks (d 1977); Sir James McGrigor, 1 Bt, KCB, was Dir-Gen of the Army Med Dept for thirty-six years and three times Lord Rector of Marischal Coll Aberdeen; *b* 5 October 1922; *Educ* Eton; *m* 7 June 1948, Mary Bettine, da of Sir Archibald Charles Edmonstone, 6 Bt (d 1954), of Duntreath Castle, Blanefield, Stirlingshire; 2 s (James Angus Rhoderick Neil b 19 Oct 1949, Charles Edward b 7 Aug 1959), 2 da (Lorna Gwendolyn b 18 Feb 1951, Kirstie Rowena Amabel (Mrs Rory John MacLaren) b 3 Feb 1953); *Heir* s, James McGrigor, MSP, *qv*; *Career* 2 Lt Rifle Bde 1942, Capt 1943, served in N Africa and Italy (despatches); ADC to HRH The Duke of Gloucester, KG 1945–47 (Australia and England); memb Queen's Body Guard for Scotland (Royal Co of Archers); Exon of the Queen's Body Guard of Yeomen of the Guard 1970–85; life vice-pres RNLI (former dep chm); former convenor Scottish Lifeboat Cncl; *Recreations* gardening; *Style*— Sir Charles McGrigor, Bt, DL; ✉ Upper Sonachan, by Dalmally, Argyll PA33 1BJ (tel 01866 833229)

McGRIGOR, James Angus Rhoderick Neil; MSP; s and h of Sir Charles Edward McGrigor, 5 Bt, *qv*; *b* 19 October 1949; *Educ* Eton; *m* 1 (m dis), Caroline F, da of late Jacques Roboh, of Paris; 2 da (Sibylla b 1988, Sarah b 1989); m 2 1997, Emma da of David L Fellowes of Cladich Argyll; 1 s (Alexander b 1998), 2 da (Violet b 2001, Rosanna b 2003); *Career* farmer; memb Royal Company of Archers (Queen's Body Guard for Scotland); MSP (Cons) Highlands and Islands 1999–; *Recreations* fishing, shooting, travel, music, cinema; *Clubs* Chelsea Arts, White's, New; *Style*— James McGrigor, Esq, MSP; ✉ Ardchonnel House, by Dalmally, Argyll PA33 1BW; 10 Sydney Street, London SW3

McGROUTHER, Prof (Duncan) Angus; *b* 3 March 1946; *Educ* Univ of Glasgow (MB ChB, MD), Univ of Strathclyde (MSc); *Career* Cruden med res fell Bioengineering Unit Univ of Strathclyde 1972–73, sr registrar in plastic surgery Canniesburn Hosp Glasgow 1976–78 (registrar 1975–76), assistentarzt Klinikum rechts der Isar Munich 1978, hon clinical lectr Univ of Newcastle upon Tyne 1978–80; conslt plastic surgn: Northern RHA Shotley Bridge Gen Hosp 1979–80, Canniesburn Hosp Glasgow 1981–89; chm Div of Plastic and Maxillofacial Surgery 1986–, chair plastic and reconstructive surgery UCL (newly created, funded by Phoenix Appeal) 1989–2001; Univ of Manchester: fndr dept specialising in plastic and reconstructive surgery res, chair in plastic and reconstructive surgery 2001–; hon conslt surgn S Manchester Univ Hosps; asst ed Journal of Hand Surgery 1987; examiner in anatomy Royal Coll of Physicians and Surgns of Glasgow; Br Assoc of Plastic Surgns: memb 1978, sec Sr Registrars Travelling Club 1978–79, memb Educn and Res Ctee 1982–84 (chm 1988–), memb Editorial Bd Br Journal of Plastic Surgery 1981–83, memb Cncl 1986–89; Br Soc for Surgery of the Hand: memb 1980, memb Cncl 1983–85, memb Editorial Bd 1983–85; Int Fedn of Socs for Surgery of the Hand: memb Flexor Tendon Injuries Ctee, memb Res Ctee, chm Dupuytren's Disease Ctee; Royal Soc Wolfson Personal Merit Award 2003; FRCS 1973, FRCSGlas 1973, Hon FRCSEd 1993, FMedSci 2005; *Publications* contrib: Cleft Lip and Palate, Oral Surgery (1986), Microanatomy of Dupuytren's Contracture, Dupuytren's Disease (1986), Dupuytren's Disease, Methods and Concepts in Hand Surgery (1986), Surgery of the Thumb (with D A C Reid, 1986), Principles of Hand Surgery (with F D Burke and P Smith, 1990), Dupuytren's Disease (1990), Current Surgical Practice (vol 6, 1992), Microvascular Surgery and Free Tissue Transfer (1993), Gray's Anatomy (38 edn, 1995), Bailey and Love's Short Practice of Surgery (22 edn, 1995), Green's Operative Surgery (5 edn, 2004); The Interactive Hand (teaching CD-ROM, BMA Award, Millennium Product); author of numerous papers on hand and limb reconstructive surgery and basic science of wound healing; *Recreations* skiing; *Style*— Prof D Angus McGrouther; ✉ The University of Manchester, Stopford Building, Oxford Road, Manchester M13 9PT (tel 0161 275 1591, fax 0161 275 1813)

McGUCKIAN, John Brendan; s of Brian McGuckian (d 1967), of Cloughmills, Ballymena, and Pauline, *née* McKenna; *b* 13 November 1939; *Educ* St McNissis Coll Garrontower, Queen's Univ Belfast (BSc); *m* 22 Aug 1970, Carmel, da of Daniel McGowan, of Pharis, Ballyveeley; 2 s (Brian b 1972, John b 1981), 2 da (Breige b 1977, Mary Pauline b 1989); *Career* chm: Cloughmills MFG Co 1967–, Ulster TV plc 1991–, Tedcastle Ltd 1996–2001; dir: Munster & Leinster Bank 1972–, Allied Irish Bank plc 1976–2007, Harbour GP Ltd 1978–, Aer Lingus plc 1979–84, Unidare plc 1987–, Irish Continental Group plc 1988– (chm 2004–), United Dairy Farmers 2001–; memb: Derry Devpt Cmmn 1968–71, Laganside Corp 1988–92; chm: Int Fund for Ireland 1990–93, Northern Ireland Devpt Bd 1991–99; pro-chllr Queen's Univ Belfast 1990–99; Hon LLD Queen's Univ Belfast 2000; *Style*— John B McGuckian, Esq; ✉ Ardverna, Cloughmills, Ballymena; Lisgoole Abbey, Culkey, Enniskillen; 1 Ballycregagh Road, Cloughmills, Ballymena (tel 028 2763 8121, fax 028 2763 8122, e-mail jmcguckian@utvlive.com)

McGUCKIAN, Maeve Thérèse Philomena (Medbh); da of Hugh Albert McCaughan, of Belfast, and Margaret, *née* Fergus; *b* 12 August 1950; *Educ* Fortwilliam Convent GS Belfast, Queen's Univ Belfast (open scholar, BA, MA, Dip Ed, TC); *m* June 1977, John McGuckian, s of John McGuckian; 3 s (John Liam b 23 April 1980, Hugh Oisin b 6 July 1982, Fergus Joseph Gregory b 20 March 1985), 1 da (Emer Mary Charlotte Rose b 23 Aug 1989); *Career* teacher of Eng Fortwilliam Convent Belfast and St Patrick's Coll Belfast, writer in residence Queen's Univ Belfast, lectr in Eng St Mary's Trg Coll Belfast, lectr Seamus Heaney Centre for Poetry Queen's Univ Belfast, visiting fell Univ of Calif Berkeley 1991, writer in residence New Univ of Ulster Coleraine 1995–98; Irish memb Aosdána, hon fell Inst of Irish Studies Queen's Univ Belfast; *Awards* winner Nat Poetry Competition, Alice Hunt Bartlett Award, Rooney Prize for Lit, Gregory Award 1980, winner Cheltenham Poetry Prize, Irish-American Prize for Literature 1998, Tolman Cunard Prize for Best Single Poem 2002; *Books* incl: Single Ladies (1980), Portrait of Joanna (1980), The Flower Master (1982), Venus and the Rain (1984), On Ballycastle Beach (1988), Two Women - Two Shores (1988), Marconi's Cottage (1991), Captain Lavender (1994), Selected Poems (1997), Shelmalier (1998), Drawing Ballerinas (2001), The Face of the Earth (2002), Had I a Thousand Lives (2003), The Book of the Angel (2004), The Currach Requires No Harbours (2006); *Style*— Mrs Medbh McGuckian; ✉ c/o Henry Raddie, Downview Avenue, Antrim Road, Belfast BT15 4EZ

McGUFFIN, Prof Peter; s of Capt William Brown McGuffin, RD (d 1994), of Seaview, IOW, and Melba Martha, *née* Burnison; *b* 4 February 1949; *Educ* Leeds Univ Med Sch (MB ChB), Univ of London (PhD); *m* 11 July 1972, Prof Anne Elizabeth Farmer, da of Alfred Lesly Farmer; 2 da (Catrina b 1975, Lucy b 1978), 1 s (Liam b 1976); *Career* house offr then registrar St James' Univ Hosp Leeds 1972–77, registrar then sr registrar Bethlem Royal and Maudsley Hosps London 1977–79, MRC fell and lectr Inst of Psychiatry London 1979–82, visiting fell Washington Univ of St Louis MO 1981–82, MRC sr clinical fell, hon conslt and sr lectr Inst of Psychiatry and KCH London 1982–86, prof and head of dept of psychological med Univ of Wales Coll of Med 1987–98; pres Int Soc of Psychiatric Genetics 1995–2000, dir and prof of psychiatric genetics MRC SGDP Centre Inst of Psychiatry London 1998–2006, dean Inst of Psychiatry KCL 2007–; chair UoA9 (psychiatry and neuroscience) RAE 2008; former memb Neurosciences Bd MRC, Advsy Bd MRC, Scientific Advsy Ctee AMRC; FRCP 1988 (MRCP 1976), FRCPsych 1990 (MRCPsych 1978), fndr FMedSci 1998; *Books* The Scientific Principles of Psychopathology (with Shanks and Hodgson, 1984), A Psychiatric Catechism (with Greer, 1987), Schizophrenia: The Major Issues (with Bebbington, 1988), The New Genetics of Mental Illness (with Murray, 1991), Seminars in Psychiatric Genetics (with Owen, O'Donovan, Thapar and Gottesman, 1994), Essentials of Postgraduate Psychiatry (with Hill and Murray, 3 edn 1997), Behavioral Genetics (with Plomin, McClearn and DeFries, 4 edn 2001), Measuring Psychopathology (with Farmer and Williams, 2002), Psychiatric Genetics and Genomics (with Owen and Gottesman, 2002); *Recreations* classical guitar, horse riding, sailing; *Style*— Prof Peter McGuffin; ✉ Institute of Psychiatry, De Crespigny Park, London SE5 8AF (tel 020 7848 0154, fax 020 7848 0866, e-mail p.mcguffin@iop.kcl.ac.uk)

McGUFFOG, John Lee; s of Capt Donald McGuffog (d 1998), and Ethel Mary, *née* Lee (d 2000); *b* 18 August 1945; *Educ* Wallington GS; *m* 1, 1971 (m dis 1976), Patricia Anne White; m 2, 6 March 1978, Penelope Jayne, da of Philip Gordon Lee (d 1995); 1 da (Charlotte b 21 Feb 1979); *Career* surveyor 1963–, qualified chartered auctioneer 1968, chief surveyor Leonard W Cotton & Ptnrs 1969; Mann & Co (estate agents): joined 1972, dir 1975, chm commercial div 1985; main bd dir: Countrywide Surveyors Ltd 1988–, Douglas Duff Chartered Surveyors (formerly BBG Commercial then Countrywide Commercial) 1994–; memb Cranleigh and Dist Round Table 1978–86, chm Cranleigh and Dist 41 Club 1991–92, tstee and dir Cranleigh Village Hosp Tst; govr Farlington Sch Horsham 1993– (dep chm 2000–04, chm 2004–); memb City Owls (promoted by Worshipful Co of Chartered Surveyors); IRRV 1969, FRICS 1976, MCIArb 1979; *Recreations* fishing; *Clubs* 41; *Style*— John McGuffog, Esq; ✉ Douglas Duff Chartered Surveyors, Tower House, 15 Church Path, Woking, Surrey GU21 6EJ (tel 01483 722256, fax 01483 756229, mobile 07836 690542)

McGUINNESS, Anne Marie; da of Roland McGuinness, of Belfast, and Eileen, *née* Fitzpatrick; *b* 29 October 1954; *Educ* St Dominic's HS Belfast, Queen's Univ Belfast (MB BCh, BAO); *m* 10 March 1984, James William Park, s of James Boyd Park (d 1989), of Braintree, Essex; 2 s (Oscar Boyd b 1988, Hugo Blair b 1991); *Career* surgn in NI 1979–84, conslt Royal Free Hosp 1987–96, clinical dir in A&E UCH London 1996–; memb: BMA 1979, Br Assoc for Accident and Emergency Med 1986, Br Trauma Soc 1989, Br Assoc of Clinical Anatomists 1995; FMS (London) 1986, FRCSEd 1983, FCEM 2006; ind medicolegal conslt; overseas surveyor to the Leonard Cheshire Chair in Conflict Recovery, surveyor HQS 1996–, assessor CHI 2003, medical assessor Royal Pharmaceutical Soc 2007; *Publications* author of chapters in books and numerous articles and papers in learned jls on the subjects of head injury coma scales, trauma scoring models, plastic surgery and microvascular anatomy, and emergency med; *Recreations* writing, music, art; *Style*— Ms Anne McGuinness; ✉ Accident & Emergency Department, University College Hospital, Gower Street, London WC1E 6AU (tel 020 7380 9768, fax 020 7380 9610, e-mail anne.mcguinness@uclh.nhs.uk)

McGUINNESS, Rt Rev James Joseph; s of Michael McGuinness, and Margaret, *née* McClean; *b* 2 October 1925; *Educ* St Columb's Coll Derry, St Patrick's Coll Carlow, Oscott Coll Birmingham; *Career* ordained 1950, curate St Mary's Derby 1950–53, sec to Bishop Ellis 1953–56, parish priest Corpus Christi Parish Clifton Nottingham 1956–72, vicar gen Nottingham Diocese 1969, coadjutor Bishop of Nottingham and titular Bishop of St German 1972, bishop (RC) of Nottingham 1974–2000, ret; *Recreations* meeting people, walking, reading, music; *Style*— The Rt Rev James McGuinness

McGUINNESS, Martin; MP, MLA; *Career* MP (SF) Ulster Mid 1997–; min for educn NI Assembly 1999–; *Style*— Martin McGuinness, Esq, MP, MLA; ✉ c/o Sinn Fein, 51–55 Bothar na bhFal, Beal Feirste, Belfast B12 4PD

McGUINNESS, (John) Rory; s of John William McGuinness, and Moira McGuinness; *Educ* Kirrawee HS Sydney; *Career* cinematographer specialising in adventure, natural history and social documentary; projects incl: The Nature of Australia 1985, Passage out of Paradise 1987, Brumby Horse Run Wild 1988, Islands in the Sky 1989, Lord Howe Island - Jewel of the Pacific 1990, Blue Wilderness 1990, Islands of Fire and Magic 1993, Flight of the Rhino 1994, The Big Wet, Tracker 1995, Land of the Tiger, Kakadu - Australia's Ancient Wilderness 1996–98, Jurassic Shark 2000; filmed Australian scenes for The Life of Mammals 2001 (presented by Sir David Attenborough, *qv*); cameraman and subject of They Shoot Crocodiles... Don't They? 1996–98; winner numerous awards incl: Aust Geographic Writer of the Year 1995, Golden Tripod Aust Cinematographers Soc 2000 (for Kakadu), Victorian/Tasmanian ACS Gold Award 2001 (for Jurassic Shark); memb Aust Cinematographers Soc 2000; *Recreations* skiing, surfing, diving, cycling; *Style*—

Rory McGuinness, Esq; ✉ c/o Arafura Films, PO Box 301 Bright, Victoria 3741, Australia (tel 00 61 357 592 550, fax 00 61 357 592 539)

McGUIRE, Anne; MP; *Educ* Our Lady & St Francis Secdy Sch, Univ of Glasgow (MA), Notre Dame Teacher Trg Coll; *m* 1972, Len McGuire; 2 c; *Career* former teacher, depute dir Scottish Cncl of Voluntary Orgns until 1997, nat offr CSV 1988–93; MP (Lab) Stirling 1997–; asst Govt whip 1998–2001, a Lord Cmmr to HM Treasy (Govt whip) 2001–02, Parly sec Scotland Office 2002–05, Parly sec Dept for Work and Pensions 2005–; *Recreations* cooking, Scottish ceilidh dancing; *Style*— Mrs Anne McGuire, MP; ✉ House of Commons, London SW1A 0AA (tel 020 7219 3000); Constituency Office, 22 Viewfield Street, Stirling FK8 1UA (tel 01786 446515, fax 01786 446513, e-mail mcguirea@parliament.uk)

McGUIRE, Prof William Joseph (Bill); s of John McMillan McGuire (d 1984), and Audrey, *née* Wade Owens; *b* 1 December 1954; *Educ* St Michael's Coll Hitchin, UCL (BSc), CNAA (PhD); *m* Anna; 1 s (Fraser Robert John b 26 Nov 2003); *Career* volcanologist; lectr in igneous petrology and geochemistry W London Inst of HE (now Brunel Univ) 1981–90; Cheltenham and Gloucester Coll of HE: lectr 1990–93, sr lectr 1993–95, reader in volcanology 1995–97; Benfield prof of geophysical hazards and dir Benfield Hazard Research Centre UCL 1997–; dir DisasterMan Ltd, conslt on natural hazards and climate change HSBC Gp 2006–; chair Volcanic Studies Gp Geological Soc of London 1993–96, UK nat corr Int Assoc of Volcanology and Chemistry of the Earth's Interior 1993–96, UK rep European Volcanology Project Ctee European Science Fndn, memb Cncl Geological Soc of London 1997–99, memb: UK panel Int Union of Geodesy and Geophysics 1993–95 (sec 1996–2000), UK Govt Natural Hazard Working Gp 2005, Science Media Panel Royal Instn 2002–; memb Editorial Bd: Acta Vulcanologica, Volcanology and Seismology, Disasters, BBC Focus Magazine; presenter: Disasters In Waiting (BBC Radio 4) 2000, Scientists Under Pressure (BBC Radio 4) 2001; conslt Supervolcano (BBC1) 2005; annual science lectr Naural History Museum 2005; memb: Assoc of Br Science Writers, American Geophysical Union, AAAS; FGS 1976, fell Royal Inst 2003; *Books* Monitoring Active Volcanoes: Strategies, Procedures, and Techniques (1995), Apocalypse: A Natural History of Global Disasters (1999), Italian Volcanoes (2001), Natural Hazards and Environmental Change (2002), Raging Planet (2002), A Guide to the End of the World: Everything You Never Wanted to Know (2002), Guide to Global Hazards (2003), World Atlas of Natural Hazards (2004), Surviving Armageddon: Solutions for a Threatened Planet (2005), Global Catastrophes: A Very Short Introduction (2005), What Everyone Should Know About the Future of our Planet (2008); *Recreations* mountain biking, skiing, walking, gardening, stroking cats Jetsam and Driftwood, playing with son Fraser, worrying about the future of the planet; *Style*— Prof Bill McGuire; ✉ Benfield Hazard Research Centre, Department of Earth Sciences, University College London, Gower Street, London WC1E 6BT (tel 020 7679 3449, fax 020 7679 2390, e-mail w.mcguire@ucl.ac.uk)

McGURK, John Callender; s of John B McGurk (d 2005), and Janet, *née* Callender (d 1992); *b* 12 December 1952; *Educ* Tynecastle Secdy Sch Edinburgh; *m* 1984 (m dis 2005), Karen, da of Capt Peter Ramsay; 1 da (Chloe b 19 Aug 1991), 1 s (Josh b 13 Aug 1995); *Career* trainee journalist Scottish County Press 1970–74; reporter: Nottingham Evening Post 1974–75, Scottish Daily News 1975, Radio Clyde 1975–78; Sunday Mail: reporter 1978–85, news ed 1985–88, dep ed 1988–89; ed Sunday Sun Newcastle 1989–91, dep ed Daily Record 1991–94; ed: Edinburgh Evening News 1995–97, Scotland on Sunday 1997–2001 (UK Sunday Newspaper of the Year 1997, 1998 and 2000); ed dir The Scotsman Publications Ltd 2001–04, ed The Scotsman 2004–06, gp managing ed The Daily and Sunday Telegraph 2006; chm: Eds' Ctee, Scottish Daily Newspaper Soc 2001; memb PCC 2000–02; *Recreations* family, cinema, reading, dining out; *Style*— John McGurk, Esq; ✉ e-mail jmcgurk@bluyonder.co.uk

MACH, David Stefan; s of Joseph Mach, of Methil, Fife, and Martha, *née* Cassidy; *b* 18 March 1956; *Educ* Buckhaven HS, Duncan of Jordanstone Coll of Art Dundee (Duncan of Drumfork travelling scholar, Dip Art, Post Dip Art, Pat Holmes meml prize, SED minor and major prizes), RCA (MA, Royal Coll drawing prize); *m* 25 Aug 1979, Lesley June, da of William Ronald White; *Career* professional sculptor 1982–; visiting prof of sculpture Edinburgh Coll of Art 1999–, prof of sculpture Royal Acad London 2000–; exhibitions incl: British Sculpture' 83 (Hayward Gallery London) 1983, Fuel for the Fire (Riverside Studio London) 1986, A Hundred and One Dalmatians (Tate Gallery London) 1988, Five Easy Pieces (Barbara Toll Fine Art NY) 1989, Here to Stay (The Tramway Glasgow) 1990, Out of Order (Kingston upon Thames) 1990, David Mach Sculpture (Ujazdowski Castle Center for Contemporary Art Warsaw) 1993, Fully Furnished (Museum of Contemporary Art San Diego) 1994, David Mach New Drawings (Jill George Gallery London) 1995, David Mach (Galerie Andata/Ritorno Geneva) 1995, Train (Britain's largest contemporary sculpture, Darlington) 1997, Big Heids (M8 Motorway North Lanark) 1999, A National Portrait (The Dome at Greenwich) 1999; video Clydeside Classic (Channel 4) 1990; one of two Br reps at Sąo Paolo Biennale 1987, one of three Scottish reps at Venice Biennale 1990; nominated for Turner prize 1988; cmmns incl Peter Gabriel's US project 1992; City of Glasgow Lord Provost Prize 1992; LLD (hc) Univ of Dundee 2002; RA 1998; *Recreations* television, film, music; *Clubs* Chelsea Arts; *Style*— David Mach, Esq; ✉ 64 Canonbie Road, Forest Hill, London SE23 3AG (tel 020 8699 1668, e-mail davidmach@davidmach.com, website www.davidmach.com)

MacHALE, Joseph Patrick; s of Seamus Joseph MacHale (d 2006), and Margaret Mary, *née* Byrne (d 1982); *b* 17 August 1951; *Educ* Ampleforth, The Queen's Coll Oxford (MA); *m* 28 Feb 1981, Mary Ann, da of Rear Adm David Dunbar-Nasmith, CB, DSO; 3 s (Henry b 1983, Martin b 1986, Thomas b 1990), 1 da (Laura b 1985); *Career* with Price Waterhouse 1973–78, qualified CA 1976; joined J P Morgan Inc 1979, sr vice-pres Morgan Guaranty Tst 1986–89, md J P Morgan & Co Inc NY 1989–98, chief exec J P Morgan EMEA 1998–2001; non-exec dir: Morgan Crucible plc 2003–, Royal Bank of Scotland Gp plc 2004, Brit Insurance Holdings plc 2005; chm Prytania 2003–; tstee and treas Macmillan Cancer Support 2002–; FCA 1978; *Clubs* Brooks's; *Style*— Joseph MacHale, Esq; ✉ The Old House, Wonston, Winchester, Hampshire SO21 3LS

McHARDY, David Keith; s of Charles Stuart McHardy (d 1956), and Mary Isabella, *née* Laverick; *b* 29 August 1950; *Educ* Lord Wandsworth Coll Long Sutton, PCL (now Univ of Westminster) (LLB); *m* Barbara Lillian, da of Donald Farley (d 1956); 2 s (Alexander b 27 Sept 1981, Nicholas b 31 July 1984), 1 da (Susannah b 6 June 1992); *Career* admitted slr 1978; ptnr: Hutchins & Co 1979–2000, Family Law Consortium 2000–03, Family Law Assoc LLP 2003–; Slrs Family Law Assoc: chm Legal Aid Working Pty 1987–89 (memb 1985–89), nat chm 1989–91, ed Review 1994–2003; memb Legal Aid Area Ctee Legal Aid Bd; memb: Law Soc, Justice; past chm Hackney and E London Family Mediation Serv; lectr; dep dist judge Princ Registry of the Family Div London; Lieutenant Baliff of the Royal Court of Guernsey 2003–; MCIA; *Recreations* tennis, golf, West Essex Golf (capt 1998–99, chm 1999–); *Clubs* West Essex Golf; *Style*— David McHardy, Esq; ✉ Family Law Associates LLP, 1 The Courtyard, Lynton Road, Crouch End, London N8 8SL (tel 020 8340 7760, fax 020 8347 4227, website www.familylawassociates.co.uk)

McHARDY-YOUNG, Dr Stuart; s of John McHardy-Young (d 1974), of Twickenham, Middx, and Violet Collin; *b* 20 February 1936; *Educ* St Paul's, Guy's Hosp Univ of London (MD, MB BS), Stanford Univ; *m* 9 Sept 1961, Margaret Elizabeth, da of William Alan Cash (d 1949), of Eaglescliffe, Co Durham; 1 da (Catherine b 19 April 1978); *Career* post doctoral fell Stanford Univ Med Sch California 1967–68, sr lectr and hon conslt physician Guy's Hosp Med Sch 1970–72; conslt physician and endocrinologist: Central Middx Hosp 1972–, Royal Nat Throat Nose and Ear Hosp 1973–, Royal Masonic Hosp London 1982–96; subdean St Mary's Hosp Med Sch London 1983–88; hon clinical sr lectr UCL 1973–93; memb Br Diabetic Assoc, chm NW Thames Regnl Med Manpower Cmmn (memb Central Ctee), former univ memb Brent Health Authy; memb: BMA, RSM; *Recreations* golf, travel; *Clubs* Royal Mid-Surrey Golf, Naval; *Style*— Dr Stuart McHardy-Young; ✉ 20 Belmont Road, Twickenham, Middlesex TW2 5DA; 2 Hillview, Uplopers, Bridport, Dorset; 106 Harley Street, London W1N 1AF (tel 020 7935 2797, e-mail drsmchy@aol.com); Central Middlesex Hospital, London NW10

McHENRY, Brian Edward; s of Alexander Edward McHenry (d 1995), and Winifred Alice, *née* Wainford; *b* 12 December 1950, London; *Educ* Dulwich Coll, New Coll Oxford (MA), SE Inst for Theological Educn; *m* 19 Jan 1979, Elizabeth Anne, *née* Bray; 2 s (Thomas Edward b 12 March 1979, Joseph William b 9 Nov 1981); *Career* called to the Bar Middle Temple 1976; Treasury Slr's Dept 1978–92, legal advsr Monopolies and Mergers Cmmn 1992–96, slr to N Wales Tbnl of Inquiry into Child Abuse 1996–97, slr to BSE Inquiry 1998–2000, Treasury Slr's Dept 2000, chief legal advsr Competition Cmmn 2000–04, slr to OFT 2004–06, gen counsel to OFT 2006–; memb Crown Appts Cmmn 1997–2002; memb Gen Synod C of E 1980–85 and 1987–2005, memb Archbishops' Cncl 1999–2005, vice-chm House of Laity 2000–05, hon lay canon Southwark Cathedral 2004–; *Recreations* swimming, walking, travel, history, Arsenal FC; *Style*— Brian McHenry, Esq; ✉ 21 Maude Road, London SE5 8NY (tel 020 7701 9350); Office of Fair Trading, Fleetbank House, 2–6 Salisbury Square, London EC4Y 8JX (tel 020 7211 8892, fax 020 7211 8830, e-mail brian.mchenry@oft.gsi.gov.uk)

MACHIN, Derek Grenville; s of Eric Machin (d 1982), of Liverpool, and Vera, *née* Adams (d 2004); *b* 3 December 1948, Liverpool; *Educ* Liverpool Inst HS for Boys, Univ of Liverpool (MB ChB); *m* 3 Feb 1973, Dr Pamela Lesley Machin, *née* Halliday; 2 s (David Mark Grenville b 27 March 1980, Nigel Oliver Grenville b 14 Oct 1981); *Career* urologist; house offr Royal Southern Hosp Liverpool 1972–73, sr demonstrator Dept of Anatomy Univ of Liverpool 1973–75, surgical registrar Liverpool rotation 1975–77, middle grade gen surgical registrar St Catherine Hosp Birkenhead, Victoria Central Hosp Wallasey and Broadgreen Hosp Liverpool 1977–79, urological registrar Broadgreen Hosp Liverpool 1980–82; Royal Liverpool Hosp: Merseyside Assoc for Kidney Research research fell 1982–84, urological registrar 1984–85, urological sr registrar 1985–88; Univ Hosp Aintree: conslt urological surgn 1988–, clinical dir of urology 1993–; BMA: memb Cncl 1995–, chm Private Practice and Professional Fees Ctee 1995–97, memb Jt Conslts Ctee 1996–2004, chm Private Practice Ctee 1997–; Central Conslts and Specialists Ctee: memb 1991–, dep chm 1998–2002, chm Surgical Specialities Sub-Ctee 1992–98; author of papers on various urological topics and pain syndromes; FRCS 1977; *Recreations* reading, gardening, scuba diving, fine wines, good food; *Style*— Derek Machin, Esq; ✉ Department of Urology, University Hospital Aintree, Lower Lane, Liverpool L9 7AL (tel 0151 529 3595, fax 0151 529 3772, e-mail derek.machin@aintree.nhs.uk)

MACHIN, His Hon Judge John Vessey; s of William Vessey Machin (d 1970), and Margaret Dona, *née* Pryce (d 1985); *b* 4 May 1941; *Educ* Westminster; *m* 25 Feb 1967, Susan Helen, da of Edgar Frank Emery; 1 da (Charlotte Susanna Vessey b 1972), 1 s (Hugo Vessey b 1975); *Career* called to the Bar Middle Temple 1965; recorder 1994–97 (asst recorder 1990–94), circuit judge 1997–; chm Agric Land Tbnl (Eastern Area) 1999– (dep chm 1986–99), judicial memb Lincs Probation Bd 2006–; ptnr Gateford Hall Farms (family farm); memb Cncl: Ranby House Sch, Worksop Coll; fell Woodard Corpn; fndn govr St Matthew's C of E Primary Sch Normanton-on-Trent; *Recreations* rural pursuits; *Clubs* Garrick, Farmers', Newark Rowing; *Style*— His Hon Judge John Machin

MACHIN, Stephen James; s of Maj John Machin, of Sheffield, S Yorks, and Edna, *née* Young; *b* 9 November 1954; *Educ* King Edward VII Sch Sheffield, Univ of Cambridge (MA, LLB); *m* W Joanna Claire, *née* Spurway; 3 s (Alexander Peter b 22 April 1980, James Edward Spurway b 29 Dec 1995, Benedict Joshua Spurway b 30 Nov 2001), 2 da (Susannah Helen b 22 April 1982, Isabella Claire b 20 June 1999); *Career* admitted slr 1980, ATII 1982; ptnr: Ashurst Morris Crisp 1987–98, KPMG 1998–; *Recreations* golf, music, military history, riding, visiting Southern Africa; *Clubs* Carlton, Stellenbosch Golf, Royal Mid-Surrey Golf, Minchampton Golf; *Style*— Stephen Machin, Esq; ✉ KPMG LLP, 8 Salisbury Square, London EC4Y 8BB (tel 020 7311 1000, fax 020 7311 8690, e-mail stephen.machin@kpmg.co.uk)

McHUGH, James; CBE (1989); s of Edward McHugh (d 1962), and Martha, *née* Smith (d 1948); *b* 4 May 1930; *Educ* Carlisle GS, various colls, Sheffield C of C Prize in Mgmnt Studies; *m* 1953, Sheila, da of James Cape; 2 da (Janet Elisabeth (Mrs Hoskin) b 21 April 1955, Kathlyn Joan (Mrs Kaiser) b 20 Sept 1958); *Career* Nat Serv Army; articled pupil in gas industry 1947, various tech and engrg appts in Northern and E Midlands Gas Bds (prodn engr 1967, dir of engrg W Midland Gas Bd 1971), dir of ops British Gas Corporation 1975 (memb Bd 1979), md prodn and supply and exec dir British Gas plc (now BG plc) 1986–91, chm British Pipe Coaters Ltd 1991–95, dir United Kingdom Accreditation Service 1995–2000; dir Lloyd's Register Quality Assurance 1985–98; memb: Meteorological Ctee MOD 1981–85, Engrg Cncl 1989–92; Gold Medal Inst of Gas Engrs (pres 1986–87); pres: Inst of Quality Assurance 1992–97, World Quality Cncl 1997–; Freeman City of London, Liveryman Worshipful Co of Engrs; foreign memb Engrg Acad of St Petersburg; Hon FIQA, FIMechE, FIGasE, FInstPet, CIMgt, FRSA, FREng 1986; *Recreations* mountaineering, dinghy sailing; *Clubs* Royal Anglo-Belgian; *Style*— James McHugh, Esq, CBE, FREng; ✉ tel 0121 705 0836

McHUGH, Patrick; s of Capt B McHugh (d 1982), and Majorie Ann, *née* Mahoney; *b* 2 June 1952; *Educ* Mount St Mary's Coll, KCL (BSc(Eng)), Rose Bruford Coll (BA), Cheltenham Poly (Dip Mgmnt Studies); *m* 31 Jan 1975, Henrietta Theresa Maria, da of Dr Hugh Francis Devlin; 1 s (Thomas Charles b 19 May 1981), 2 da (Alice Florence Henrietta Rose b 19 June 1984, Beatrice Lily Henrietta Rosamond b 8 Oct 1991); *Career* project engr (thermal, hydraulic and nuclear energy) CCM Sulzer (France) 1973–76, successively prodn control mangr, product gp mangr (diesel assembly and test), mktg mangr (Belgium) and prodn mangr (diesel assembly, test and press shop) R A Lister (Hawker Sideley Group) 1976–82; Coopers & Lybrand: conslt in mfrg and distribution mgmnt 1982–86, ptnr (engrg and technol industries) 1986–95; princ EDS 1995, vice-pres A T Kearney 1995–1999, dir Strategic Partnership London Ltd 1996–2002, dir Gp e-Commerce J Sainsbury plc 2000–01, dir GlobalNetXChange 2000–01, chm Taste Network Ltd 2000–01, chm The Destination Wine Company 2001, chief exec Trinity Gp 2002–, chm B4baby 2002, chief exec Rangegate Mobile Solutions Ltd 2004–, chm Parametric Optimization Solutions Ltd 2005–; chm Media Group Action for Engrg Task Force 1993–95; memb: Inst Ops Mgmnt 1983, Cncl Fndn for Sci and Technol 1991– (hon sec 2000–), Br Assoc for Sci and Technol 1992, Tomorrow's Company Enquiry; fndr memb Guild of Mgmnt Conslts 1993, hon moorings offr Treaddur Bay Sailing Club 1991–98; pres Seabird Assoc 2004–05; pres Soc of Environmental Engrs 2003–; chair City Centre for Charity Effectiveness Tst 2004–; Liveryman: Worshipful Co of Mgmnt Conslts 2004 (Master 2002–03), Worshipful Co of Engrs 2004; CEng 1976, MIMgt 1978, FIMechE 1993, ACA 1994, FRSA, FIMC 1997; *Books* Business Process Re-engineering (with H J Johansson, A J Pendlebury and W A Wheeler III, 1993), The Chain Imperative (with Paul Hannon, 1994), Beyond Business Process Reengineering (with Giorgio Merli and W A Wheeler III, 1995); *Clubs* Trearddur Bay Sailing, Arts; *Style*— Patrick McHugh, Esq; ✉ 189 Camberwell Grove, London SE5 8JU (tel 020 7274 4069, e-mail patrickmchugh1@aol.com); Lia Fail, Ravenspoint Road, Trearddur Bay, Anglesey LL65 2AX (tel 01407 861521)

M

McHUGH, Peter; s of Peter McHugh, and May, *née* Mannion (d 1997); *b* 25 October 1946; *Career* journalist; former newspapers incl: Hartlepool Daily Mail, Northern Echo, Newcastle Journal, Daily Mail, The Sun; ed TV-am 1982, head of current affairs Tyne Tees Television 1983, formerly ed The Time...The Place, dir of programmes GMTV 1993–; *Recreations* journalism; *Style*— Peter McHugh, Esq

McILHENEY, Barry Wilson; s of David Parker McIlheney (d 1979), of Belfast, and Muriel, *née* Wilson; *b* 13 May 1958; *Educ* Belfast Royal Acad, Trinity Coll Dublin (BA), City Univ (Dip Journalism); *m* 16 March 1991, Lola, da of Francis Borg (d 1999), and Jean, *née* Pukkey; 1 s (Francis Salvador David b 5 June 1992), 1 da (Mary Sophia b 9 March 1996); *Career* reporter London Newspaper Group 1984–85, reviews ed Melody Maker 1985–86, ed Smash Hits 1986–88; managing ed: Empire 1992–94 (ed 1989–91), Premiere 1992–94; md EMAP Metro 1995–98, dir Délégué EMAP France 1999–2000, chief exec Emap élan network 2000–02, ed-in-chief Emap Consumer Media 2002–; Feature Writer of the Year 1985, EMAP Ed of the Year 1987 and 1991, PPA Magazine of the Year 1991, PPA Consumer Magazine Ed of the Year 1993; memb BSME 1986; *Recreations* sport, cinema, travel, eating, drinking, history; *Clubs* Soho House; *Style*— Barry McIlheney, Esq; ✉ EMAP Consumer Media, Endeavour House, 189 Shaftesbury Avenue, London WC2H 8JH

McILLMURRAY, Prof Malcolm Barron; s of Joseph McIllmurray, and Margot, *née* Jordon; *b* 7 December 1945; *Educ* Taunton's Sch Southampton, London Hosp Med Coll (MB BS), Univ of Nottingham (DM); *m* 27 July 1968, Geraldine Mary, da of Dr Daniel Gerard O'Driscoll (d 1992); 2 da (Joanna Maria (Mrs Kelly) b 1969, Naomi Jane (Mrs Altham) b 1977), 2 s (Daniel Joseph Barron b 1971, Matthew James Barron b 1975); *Career* lectr in therapeutics Univ of Nottingham and hon sr registrar in gen med Nottingham City Hosp 1973–78, Macmillan conslt in med oncology and palliative care Royal Lancaster Infirmary and Westmorland Gen Hosp Kendal 1994– (consIt physician and med oncologist 1978–94); med dir St John's Hospice Lancaster 1985–2002; Nat Lederle Bronze awarded to Lancaster Cancer Servs 1991, Ernest Finch lectr Univ of Sheffield 1992, Paul Harris fell Rotary Club of GB 1993; hon prof of biological scis Lancaster Univ; fndr tstee N Lancs and Lakeland Continuing Care Tst 1981–, fndr chm CancerCare - N Lancs and S Lakeland 1984–; govr Bentham Sch; FRCP 1985 (MRCP); *Books* ABC of Medical Treatment (contrib, 1979), Essential Accident and Emergency Care (contrib, 1981); author of numerous articles in learned jls; *Style*— Prof Malcolm McIllmurray; ✉ Royal Lancaster Infirmary, Ashton Road, Lancaster LA1 4RP

McILRATH, Shaun Fulton; s of Dr Edwin Maynard McIlrath, and Ella Mary, *née* Fulton; *b* 30 January 1963; *Educ* Methodist Coll Belfast, Christ Church Coll, Univ of Kent at Canterbury (BA); *m* 2 Dec 1995, Lisa, da of Edward Snook; 1 s (Rufus Connor b 1997) 1 d (Lily Eve b 1999); *Career* script writer BBC, RTE and ITV 1984–87, account exec The Moorgate Group plc 1988–91, copywriter FCB London 1991–93; creative dir: FCA London 1993–99, HHCL 2000, Heresy 2001– (also fndr); recipient over 80 awards across all mktg disciplines since 1993 from bodies incl: D&AD, Campaign Poster, Clio, One Show, DMA, ISP, PR and Media Week; voted UK's Most Innovative Marketer 2002; memb D&AD; *Recreations* spending time with family, fitness, food; *Clubs* The Irish; *Style*— Mr Shaun McIlrath

McILROY, Ian; *b* 28 December 1947; *Educ* Glasgow Sch of Art (DA); *m* Diane Elizabeth, *née* Murray; 1 s (Sean b 30 June 1983); *Career* designer; worked for: J & P Coats and William Collins 1972–79, Tayburn Design Group 1979–81; formed: McIlroy Coates 1981, EH6 Design Consultants 1992, Nevis Design Consultants 2001; independent design consIt 2003–; clients incl: Standard Life, The Nat Galleries of Scotland, The Design Cncl, The Clydesdale Bank; awards incl: Design Annual Award of Excellence 1984, D&AD Awards 1980, 1982, 1983 and 1990, Br Letterhead Awards 1981 and 1985, Scottish Designer of the Year runner up 1984, Scottish Annual Report prize 1988 and 1989; external degree course assessor graphic design Duncan of Jordanstone Coll of Art Dundee; memb: D&AD Assoc 1980, RSA 1999; FCSD 1991; *Style*— Ian McIlroy, Esq; ✉ 26 Rintoul Place, Edinburgh EH3 5JF (tel 0131 343 2795, e-mail ian.mcilroy@macunlimited.net)

McILVANNEY, William Angus; s of William Angus McIlvanney (d 1955), of Kilmarnock, and Helen Crawford, *née* Montgomery; *b* 25 November 1936; *Educ* Kilmarnock Acad, Univ of Glasgow (MA); *m* 1961 (m dis 1982), Moira Watson; 1 da (Siobhan Janet b 17 June 1967), 1 s (Liam Angus b 8 April 1970); *Career* writer; Irvine Royal Acad: asst teacher of English 1960–65, special asst 1965–68, princ teacher of English 1970–72; housemaster Ravenspark Acad 1969–70, tutor to US students Grenoble 1970–71, asst headmaster Greenwood Acad 1973–78; writer in residence: Univ of Strathclyde 1972–73, Univ of Aberdeen 1981–82 and 1993–94; visiting prof Univ of Strathclyde 1997–2000; TV presenter BBC Scotland 1979–81 and 1993–, columnist The Herald 1998–2000; *Awards* Geoffrey Faber Meml Award 1966, Scottish Arts Cncl Publication Award 1968, Whitbread Prize 1975, Silver Dagger 1977 and 1983, Edgar Allan Poe Special Award 1977 and 1983, The People's Prize Glasgow Herald 1990 and 1992, Scottish Arts Cncl Award 1991, BAFTA Scottish Award 1991, Saltire Scottish Book of the Year 1996, Scottish Newspaper Columnist of the Year 1999; *Novels* Remedy is None (1966), A Gift From Nessus (1968), Docherty (1975), Laidlaw (1977), The Papers of Tony Veitch (1983), The Big Man (1985), Strange Loyalties (1991), The Kiln (1996), Weekend (2006); *Poetry* The Longships in Harbour (1970), Landscapes and Figures (1973), These Words - Weddings and After (1983), In Through the Head (1988); *Short Stories* Walking Wounded (1989); *Non-Fiction* Surviving the Shipwreck (1991); *Style*— William McIlvanney, Esq

MacILWAINE, David Robin; s of Robin MacIlwaine, and Anne MacIlwaine (d 1967); *b* 16 December 1947; *Educ* Rydens Sch Walton-on-Thames, Univ of Leicester (BA); *Partner*, Rose Gray; 1 s (Dante MacIlwaine Gray b 1973), 3 step c (Hester Gray b 1963, Lucy Gray b 1964, Ossie Gray b 1965); *Career* Christies Contemporary Art 1986–89, sculpture dir Berkeley Square Gallery 1989–96, ind art consIt 1996–, ptnr EXACT (exhbns in art and architecture) 1997–, creative dir Hubble Space Telescope Inc USA 1998–; *Recreations* sculpting; *Style*— David MacIlwaine, Esq; ✉ 7 Plympton Street, London NW8 8AB (tel and fax 020 7258 1780)

McILWRAITH, Dr George Robert; s of Alexander Herd McIlwraith (d 1971), of Ruislip, Middx, and Kathleen Joan, *née* Heaton (d 1996); *b* 15 July 1941; *Educ* Merchant Taylors', Univ of St Andrews (MB ChB); *m* 24 July 1982, Isabel Margaret, da of Harry Jack Manwaring (d 1988), of Marden, Kent; 1 s (Harry Alexander b 1987); *Career* various jr appts in UK hosps; asst prof of internal med Pulmonary Div Univ of Michigan Med Sch 1979–80, consIt physician Maidstone Dist Hosps (merged forming Maidstone and Tunbridge Wells NHS Tst 2000) 1981–; author of pubns, chapters, papers and articles on cardiological and respiratory med matters; memb: Br Thoracic Soc, Euro Respiratory Soc; FRCP 1988; *Style*— Dr George McIlwraith; ✉ Noah's Ark Farmhouse, East Sutton Road, Headcorn, Ashford, Kent TN27 9PS (tel 01622 891278, e-mail mcilwraithgr@aol.com); The Maidstone Hospital, Hermitage Lane, Maidstone, Kent ME16 9QQ (tel 01622 729000, fax 01622 720807)

McINNES, Prof Colin Robert; s of Ian McInnes, of Glasgow, and Marion, *née* McDonald; *b* 12 February 1968, Glasgow; *Educ* Univ of Glasgow (BSc, PhD, DSc); *m* 7 March 1992, Karen, *née* McLaughlin; 3 s (Callum b 16 July 1996, Gregor b 15 April 1999, Ruaridh b 17 August 2001); *Career* prof of space systems engrg Univ of Glasgow 1991–2004, prof of engrg science Univ of Strathclyde 2004–; Bruce-Preller Prize Lectureship RSE 1997, Pardoe Space Award RAeS 2000, Philip Leverhulme Prize Leverhulme Trust 2001, Ackroyd Stuart Prize RAeS 2004, Makdougall-Brisbane Prize RSE 2006; FRAeS 1998, FRSE 2001, FREng 2003; *Publications* Solar Sailing (1999); contrib to numerous jls on space systems engrg; *Recreations* photography, hill walking, books; *Style*— Prof Colin McInnes; ✉ Department of Mechanical Engineering, University of Strathclyde, Glasgow G1 1XJ (tel 0141 548 2049, fax 0141 552 5105, e-mail colin.mcinnes@strath.ac.uk)

MacINNES, Hamish; OBE (1980), BEM (1965); s of Duncan MacInnes (d 1987), of Gourock, Renfrewshire, and Catherine, *née* MacDonald (d 1967); *b* 7 July 1930; *Educ* Gatehouse of Fleet Public Sch; *Career* writer, mfr, film dir (Glencoe Productions Ltd); designer of mountain rescue equipment stretchers (used internationally), first all metal ice axe and terodactyl climbing tools; dep ldr Everest SW Face expedition 1975 (taken part in 20 other expeditions to various parts of the world), special advsr to BBC and feature films, author of 22 books; former pres Alpine Climbing Gp, fndr and former ldr Glencoe Mountain Rescue Team, hon memb Scottish Mountaineering Club, former hon dir Leishman Rescue Laboratory; fndr and hon pres Search and Rescue Dog Assoc, patron Guide Dogs for the Blind, co-fndr Snow and Avalanche Fndn of Scotland (SAFOS); Hon DSc: Univ of Aberdeen 1988, Heriot-Watt Univ 1992; Hon LLD: Univ of Glasgow, Univ of Dundee 2004; Hon DUniv Stirling 1997; *Style*— Hamish MacInnes, Esq, OBE, BEM; ✉ Tigh a'Voulin, Glencoe, Argyll PH49 4HX (tel 01855 811258)

McINNES, Sheriff Principal John Colin; QC (Scot 1989), DL (Fife 1998); s of Ian Whitton McInnes (d 1976), of Cupar, Fife, and Lucy Margaret, *née* Wilson; *b* 21 November 1938; *Educ* Cargilfield Sch Edinburgh, Merchiston Castle Sch Edinburgh, BNC Oxford (BA), Univ of Edinburgh (LLB); *m* 6 Aug 1966, Elisabeth Mabel, da of late Hugh Royden, and Anne Neilson, of Kelso, Roxburghshire; 1 s (Ian b 1969), 1 da (Iona b 1972); *Career* 2 Lt 8 RTR 1956–58, Lt Fife and Forfar Yeo Scottish Horse TA 1958–64; advocate in practice Scottish Bar 1963–72, dir R Mackness & Co Ltd 1963–70, tutor Univ of Edinburgh 1964–72, chm Fios Group Ltd (continental quilt manufacturers) 1970–72; Parly candidate (Cons) Aberdeen N 1964; memb Ct Univ of St Andrews 1983–91, chm Fife Family Conciliation Serv 1988–90; vice-pres: Security Serv Tbnl 1989–2001, Intelligence Serv Tbnl 1994–2001, Cmmr for Northern Lighthouses 2000–; chm Youth Ct Project Gp (Scot) 2002); memb: Information Technology Forum (Scotland) 1996–2000, Criminal Justice Forum (Scotland) 1996–2000, Judicial Studies Ctee (Scotland) 1997–2000, Efficiency Task Gp 1997–98, Investigatory Powers Tbnl 2000–; Sheriff: Lothians and Peebles 1973–74, Tayside Central and Fife 1974–2000; Sheriff Principal South Strathclyde, Dumfries and Galloway 2000–; chm ctee to reform summary criminal justice in Scotland 2001–04; pres The Sheriff's Assoc 1995–97; Hon LLD Univ of St Andrews 1994; *Books* Divorce Law and Practice in Scotland; *Recreations* fishing, shooting, skiing, photography; *Style*— Sheriff Principal John McInnes, QC, DL; ✉ Sheriff Principal's Chambers, Sheriff Court House, Graham Street, Airdrie ML6 6EE (tel 01236 751121, fax 01236 750980)

McINNES, Kenneth William; QPM (2002); s of William Lee McInnes (d 1980), of Alexandria, Dunbartonshire, and Jessie Harper, *née* Mathieson; *b* 15 January 1949; *Educ* Vale of Leven Acad, Univ of Glasgow (BSc); *m* 21 Nov 1970, Eileen, da of late William Lynch, of Clydebank, Dunbartonshire, and Mary Walls; 1 s (Kenneth b 1972), 1 da (Fiona b 1979); *Career* systems analyst Babcock & Wilcox 1970–73, City of Glasgow Police 1973–75, Strathclyde Police 1975–96 (divnl cdr Dumbarton 1992–96), HM Inspectorate of Constabulary 1997–98, Asst Chief Constable Lothian and Borders Police 1998–2000, Dep Chief Constable Fife Constabulary 2000–01, Asst Inspector of Constabulary 2002–; memb ACPOS 1998; former footballer: St Mirren FC, Scottish Police nat team; *Recreations* football; *Style*— Kenneth McInnes, Esq, QPM; ✉ HM Inspectorate of Constabulary, St Andrew's House, Regent Road, Edinburgh EH1 3DG (tel 0131 244 5606, fax 0131 244 4131)

MacINNES, Michael Richard; s of Ronald MacInnes (d 1993), and Eleanor, *née* MacCaw; *b* 13 July 1944, London; *Educ* Marlborough; *m* 19 April 1968, Donna Sue, *née* Roderick; 1 s (Rupert John b 9 March 1971), 1 da (Nicola Joy (Mrs Clegg) b 31 Jan 1973); *Career* trainee then accountant Touche Ross 1962–68, stockbroker Wm Morris & Whitehead 1968–74, ptnr Moore Stephens chartered accountants 1979–2005 (joined 1974), former chm Moore Stephens International 2000–05; ACA 1968; *Recreations* sailing, skiing, tennis; *Clubs* Hurlingham, Bembridge Sailing (former Cdre), Royal Yacht Sqdn; *Style*— Michael MacInnes, Esq; ✉ Moore Stephens International, St Paul's House, Warwick Lane, London EC4P 4BN (tel 020 7334 9191, fax 020 7334 7976)

McINTOSH, Anne Caroline Ballingall; MP; da of Dr A B McIntosh, and G L McIntosh, *née* Thomson; *b* 20 September 1954; *Educ* Harrogate Coll, Univ of Edinburgh (LLB); *m* 19 Sept 1992, John Harvey; *Career* postgraduate studies Univ of Aarhus Denmark 1977–78, trainee EC Competition Directorate Brussels 1978, legal advsr Didier & Assocs Brussels 1979–80, trained Scottish Bar 1980–82, admitted Faculty of Advocates Edinburgh 1982, advocate Euro Community Law Office Brussels 1982–83, political advsr Euro Democratic Gp (EDG) Euro Parliament 1983–89; MEP (Cons): Essex N E 1989–94, Essex N and Suffolk S 1994–99; Br Conservative spokesman Euro Parliament: Tport Ctee 1992–, Rules of Procedure Ctee 1992–94; memb Euro Parliament Delegation with: Norway 1989–94 (chm 1994–95), Poland 1994–97, Czech Rep 1997–99; memb: Social Affrs Ctee 1992–94, Women's Rights Ctee 1992–94, Euro Scrutiny Ctee, Euro Standing Ctee; substitute memb: Legal Affrs Ctee 1989–, Jt Parly Ctee with EEA 1995–; asst EDG whip 1989–92, elected to Bureau Br Section EPP 1994–; MP (Cons) Vale of York 1997– (Parly candidate (Cons) Workington 1987); oppn frontbench spokesperson on culture, media and sport 2001–02, shadow min for Culture Media and Broadcasting 2001–02, shadow min for Tport 2002–, shadow min for Environment and Tport 2003–; memb Select Ctee on Environment, Tport and the Regions (also Tport Sub-Ctee); memb Exec Cncl Br Conservative Assoc Belgium 1987–89; memb Yorks Agric Soc; memb Anglo-Danish Soc; exec 1922 Ctee; pres: Anglia Enterprise in Europe 1989–99, Yorkshire First Enterprise in Yorkshire 1998–; memb: Chllr's Cncl Anglia Poly Univ until 1999, Governing Bd Writtle Coll until 1999; *Recreations* swimming, reading, cinema; *Clubs* Royal Over-Seas League, RAC; *Style*— Miss Anne McIntosh, MP; ✉ House of Commons, London SW1A 0AA (tel 020 7219 3541 or 01845 523835)

McINTOSH, (Alastair) Bruce; s of Robert Ian Fanshawe McIntosh (d 1988), of Devon, and Jane, *née* Rought (d 2007); *b* 25 February 1958; *Educ* Winchester, Univ of Cambridge (MA); *m* 1991, Sophia Mary, da of Lt-Col Sir Blair Aubyn Stewart-Wilson, KCVO, of Somerset; 3 da (Lily b 5 Jan 1993, Kitty b 24 April 1994, Tarn b 21 Dec 1995), 1 s (Harry b 8 May 1999); *Career* SG Warburg Group plc 1984–89; dir: John Govett and Co Ltd 1989–90, Perpetual Portfolio Management Ltd 1990–2002, iimia Investment Group plc 2003–; *Style*— Bruce McIntosh, Esq; ✉ Higher Tripp Farm, Watchet, Somerset TA23 0LW (tel 01984 640459)

MACINTOSH, Catherine Ailsa (Kate); MBE 1987; d of Ronald Hugh Macintosh, OBE (d 1998), and Bertha, *née* Holt (d 1978); *b* 2 July 1937; *Educ* Rudolf Steiner Sch Edinburgh, Sch of Arch Edinburgh Sch of Art (DipArch), Warsaw Poly (Br Cncl scholarship); *Partner* since 1968, George Bernard Finch; 1 s (Sean Alisdair Finch Macintosh b 1971); *Career* architect; Lennart Bergstrom (Stockholm office) 1962–63, Klaus Bremmer (Copenhagen) 1963, Toivo Korhonen (Helsinki office) 1963–64, Denys Lasdun 1964–65 (working on Nat Theatre project), London Borough of Southwark 1964–68 (designed Dawsons Heights Dulwich), London Borough of Lambeth 1968–72 (designed Leigham Court Rd Sheltered Housing), Ahrends Burton & Koralek 1972–74 (designed holiday devpt St Raphael), East Sussex Co Architects 1974–86 (team ldr and project architect for Halton Fire Station Hastings, Maresfield Fire Brigade Trg HQ Maresfield, Thornwood Old Persons Home and Sheltered Housing Bexhill, Preston Rd Family Centre Brighton, Fire Brigade Communications Centre Lewes and Battle Langton Primary Sch), Hampshire Co Architects 1986–95 (sr architect designing Rushmoor Fire Station, Priory

Sch Sports Hall and Music Suite, Solent Infants Sch and Audleys Close Centre for severely handicapped adults), in private practice as Finch Macintosh Architects Winchester 1995–, Weston Adventure Playground Southampton (completed 2004, RIBA Award 2005); Civic Tst commendations for Maresfield Fire Brigade Trg HQ, Preston Road Family Centre Brighton and Lewes Fire Brigade Communications Centre; Rushmoor Civic Design Award for Rushmoor Fire Station; Portsmouth Soc Award: for best bldg and best landscaping 1993 (Priory Sch Sports Hall and Music Suite), for best bldg 1995 (Solent Infants Sch) and 2003 (Weston adventure playground); sometime tutor/visiting lectr/external examiner various Schs of Arch; fndr chair Architects for Peace 1981–91, vice-chair Scientists for Global Responsibility 2005–; sec Sussex Heritage Tst 1978–84; RIBA 1965 (memb Cncl, vice-pres 1971, subsequently first chair Women's Architect Gp, vice-pres for public affrs 1996–97); *Books* Sussex after the Bomb (jtly, 1984); *Recreations* yoga, painting, theatre, walking; *Style—* Ms Kate Macintosh, MBE; ✉ Finch Macintosh Architects, Osborne Place, 11 West End Terrace, Winchester, Hampshire SO22 5EN (tel 01962 855240, fax 01962 852227, e-mail gk@finmacin.demon.co.uk, website www.finchmacintosh.co.uk)

McINTOSH, David Angus; s of Robert Angus McIntosh, of Scotland, and Monica Joan Sherring, *née* Hillier; *b* 10 March 1944; *Educ* Selwood Co Sch Frome; *m* 14 Sept 1968, Jennifer Mary, da of Jack Dixon, of Mill Hill, London; 2 da (Sarah Alison b 1973, Louise b 1978); *Career* clerk Ames Kent & Rathwell Somerset, articled clerk Davies Arnold Cooper 1964, admitted slr 1968, sr ptnr Davies Arnold Cooper 1976–2006 (ptnr 1968, conslt 2006–); Int Bar Assoc: chm ctee on Consumer Affrs, Advtg, Unfair Competition and Product Liability, chm Disaster Litigation Worldwide Prog Strasbourg; Law Soc: memb various working parties on reform and admin of civil law, memb Jt Working Ctee of the Senate of the Bar and Law Soc (made recommendations to Lord Chllr on proposed US/UK Reciprocal Enforcements Convention and allied jurisdictional matters), memb Supreme Court Procedure Ctee 1994–, memb Cncl 1996–, chm Civil Litigation Ctee; US Int Assoc of Defense Counsel: memb Exec Ctee, memb Excess and Reinsurance Product Liability Litigation Ctee, memb Toxic and Hazardous Substances Litigation Ctee; memb Legal Servs Consultative Ctee Dept for Constitutional Affrs 2003–, chair Governance Bd Chartered Inst of Insurers 2006–; Freeman City of London, Liveryman Worshipful Co of Blacksmiths; pres Law Soc of England and Wales 2001–02, chm City of London Slrs' Co 2004–; memb: Int Bar Assoc, Law Soc, US Int Assoc of Defense Counsel, Def Res and Trial Lawyers Assoc of America, Professional Liability Underwriters Assoc, lay memb Cncl School of Pharmacy Univ of London 2003–04; CIArb, Notre Dame Law Sch accredited mediator; *Publications* regular contrib to legal, insurance, and pharmaceutical journals, memb Editorial Bd The Litigator; *Recreations* family, golf, fitness; *Clubs* Chigwell Golf, City Livery, Real Sotogrande Golf, Caledonian; *Style—* David McIntosh, Esq; ✉ Davies Arnold Cooper, 6–8 Bouverie Street, London EC4Y 8DD (tel 020 7936 2222, fax 020 7936 2020)

McINTOSH, John Charles; OBE (1996); s of Arthur McIntosh, and Betty, *née* Styche; *b* 6 February 1946; *Educ* Ebury Sch, Shoreditch Coll, Univ of Sussex (MA); *Career* London Oratory Sch: asst master 1967–71, dep headmaster 1971–77, headmaster 1977–2007; memb: Catholic Union of GB 1978–, Educn Gp Centre for Policy Studies 1982–, Health Educn Cncl 1985–88, HMC 1986–, Educn Unit Advsy Cncl Inst of Econ Affairs 1988–, Nat Curriculum Cncl 1990–93, Cncl Centre for Policy Studies 2005–; tstee English Schs Orch and Choir 2007–, dean Acad of St Cecilia 2007–; govr St Philip's Prep Sch London, memb Abbot of Ampleforth Advsy Bd; Hon FCP, FRSA, Hon FASC; *Recreations* playing the organ, ballet, opera; *Clubs* Athenaeum; *Style—* John McIntosh, Esq, OBE; ✉ 75 Alder Lodge, River Gardens, Stevenage Road, London SW6 6NR (tel 020 7610 0834, mobile 07718 910888, e-mail cantemus@mac.com)

MACINTOSH, Kenneth Donald; MSP; s of Farquhar and Margaret Macintosh, of Edinburgh; *b* 15 January 1962; *Educ* Royal HS Edinburgh, Univ of Edinburgh (MA); *m* Claire Kinloch, *née* Anderson; 2 s (Douglas b 1 May 1999, Lachlan b 23 March 2003), 2 da (Catriona b 30 May 2001, Annie b 2 Nov 2005); *Career* joined BBC 1987, sr broadcast news and current affairs journalist until 1999; MSP (Lab) Eastwood 1999–; *Recreations* sport (football, golf, tennis); *Style—* Ken Macintosh, MSP; ✉ Eastwood Parliamentary Office, 1st Floor, 238 Ayr Road, Newton Mearns, East Renfrewshire G77 6AA (tel 0141 577 0100)

McINTOSH, Sir Neil; kt (2000), CBE (1990), JP (1999), DL (Dumfriesshire 1998); *Educ* King's Park Sr Secdy Sch Glasgow; *m* Marie; 1 s (Neil), 2 da (Hazel, Lorna); *Career* early career in mgmnt servs and personnel: Honeywell Controls, Stewarts & Lloyds, Berks Oxford and Reading Jt Mgmnt Servs Unit, Lanark County Cncl, Inverness County Cncl; Highland Regnl Cncl: personnel offr 1975–81, dir of manpower servs 1981–85; chief exec: Dumfries & Galloway Regnl Cncl 1985–92, Strathclyde Cncl 1992–96; head Convention of Scottish Local Authorities Consultancy 1996–99, chief counting offr for Scotland Scottish Parl Referendum 1997, chm Cmmn on Local Govt and the Scottish Parl 1999, memb UK Electoral Cmmn; advsr NI Review of Public Administration 2002–05; chm Judicial Appts Bd for Scotland; convenor Scottish Cncl for Voluntary Orgns 1996–2001, chm Nat Companies Contact Gp 1996–98, advsr Joseph Rowntree Fndn 2000–05 (chm Governance Ctee); tstee: National Museums of Scotland, Dumfries Theatre Royal 2003–06; non-exec dir BT Scotland 1998–2002; Hon DHL Syracuse Univ 1993, Hon LLD Glasgow Caledonian Univ 1999; memb Chartered Inst of Secs, FIPD, FRSA; *Recreations* antique bottle collecting, dry-stane dyking, hill walking, curio collecting, local history; *Style—* Sir Neil McIntosh, CBE

McINTOSH, Dr Robert (Bob); s of Robert H McIntosh, of Ayr, and Kathleen, *née* Frew; *b* 6 October 1951; *Educ* Linlithgow Acad, Univ of Edinburgh (BSc, PhD); *Career* Foresty Cmmn: asst dist offr Thetford Forest Dist 1973–75, asst dist offr Galloway Forest Dist 1975–78, silviculturist Northern Research Station 1978–84, dist mangr Kielder Forest Dist 1984–94, dir (ops) Forest Enterprise 1994–97, chief exec Forest Enterprise 1997–2003, dir Scotland Forestry Cmmn 2003–; contrib various articles to jls; FICFor 1975; *Recreations* farming, shooting, stalking; *Clubs* Farmers'; *Style—* Dr Bob McIntosh; ✉ East Brackley Grange, by Kinross KY13 9LU (tel 01577 862057); Forestry Commission, 231 Corstorphine Road, Edinburgh EH12 7AT (tel 0131 314 6456, fax 0131 314 6152, e-mail carol.finlayson@forestry.gsi.gov.uk)

McINTOSH, Thomas Lee; s of John Christian McIntosh (d 1967), of Washington DC, and Mildred White (d 1953); *b* 3 December 1938; *Educ* Juilliard Sch of Music (BSc, MSc); *m* 30 Sept 1982, Miranda Harrison Vincent, da of Vincent Booth Reckitt (d 1975), of Otley, W Yorks; *Career* conductor and music dir London City Chamber Orch 1973–; artistic dir: E Anglian Summer Music Festival 1978–, Penang Malaysia Music Festival 1986 and 1987, Opera Anglia 1989–, Artsanglia Ltd 1988–; princ guest conductor Canton Symphony Orch 1994; contributing ed eighteenth century symphonic music for Garland Symphony Series; Arrangements for Orch of the following: Valentine Waltzes (George Antheil), Rag Suite (various composers), Flower Rag Suite (Scott Joplin), Variations on Seven Japanese Folk Songs for Piano and Orchestra, Concerto for Piano (4 hands) and Orchestra 2007; FRSA; *Recreations* gardening, theatre; *Clubs* Civil Service; *Style—* Thomas McIntosh, Esq

McINTOSH OF HARINGEY, Baron (Life Peer UK 1982), of Haringey in Greater London; Andrew Robert McIntosh; PC (2002); s of late Prof Albert William McIntosh, OBE, (d 1994), and Helena Agnes (Jenny), *née* Britton (d 1989); *b* 30 April 1933; *Educ* Haberdashers' Aske's Hampstead Sch, Royal GS High Wycombe, Jesus Coll Oxford (MA), Ohio State Univ; *m* 1962, Prof Naomi Ellen Sargant (d 2006), da of Thomas Sargant, OBE, JP (d 1988), and Marie, *née* Hlouskova; 2 s (Hon Francis Robert b 1962, Hon Philip Henry Sargant b 1964); *Career* memb Hornsey BC 1963–65, memb Haringey BC 1964–68; IFF Research Ltd: md 1965–81, chm 1981–88, dep chm 1988–95, dir 1995–97; chm: Market Res Soc 1972–73 (pres 1995–98), Assoc for Neighbourhood Cncls 1974–80; memb GLC for Tottenham 1973–83, ldr GLC oppn 1980–81; House of Lords: chm Computer Sub-Ctee 1984–92, princ Lab oppn spokesman on home affairs 1992–97 (on educn and sci 1985–87, on environment 1987–92), dep ldr of the opposition 1992–97, Capt of the Queen's Body Guard of the Yeomen of the Guard (dep chief Govt whip) 1997–2003, min for media and heritage DCMS 2003–05; chm Fabian Soc 1985–86; pres GamCare 2005–, memb Gambling Cmmn 2006–; *Style—* The Rt Hon the Lord McIntosh of Haringey, PC; ✉ 27 Hurst Avenue, London N6 5TX (tel 020 8340 1496, fax 020 8348 4641, e-mail mcintoshar@parliament.uk)

McINTOSH OF HUDNALL, Baroness (Life Peer UK 1999), of Hampstead in the London Borough of Camden; Genista Mary McIntosh; *b* 23 September 1946; *Educ* Hemel Hempstead GS, Univ of York (BA); *m* 30 Jan 1971 (m dis 1990), Neil Scott Wishart McIntosh; 1 s (Hon Alexander b 22 Dec 1975), 1 da (Hon Flora b 25 April 1979); *Career* dir Marmont Management Ltd 1984–86; Royal Shakespeare Company: casting dir 1972–77, planning controller 1977–84, sr admin 1986–90, assoc prodr 1990; chief exec Royal Opera House 1997, exec dir Royal National Theatre 1997–2002 (also 1990–96), princ Guildhall Sch of Music and Drama 2002–03; tstee: Theatres Tst, Southbank Sinfonia; bd memb: The Roundhouse Tst, Almeida Theatre, Welsh Nat Opera, Nat Opera Studio; Hon DUniv York 1998, Hon DUniv Middlesex 2002, Hon DUniv City 2002; FRSA; *Style—* The Rt Hon the Baroness McIntosh of Hudnall

MACINTYRE, Charles Edward Stuart; s of John Macintyre (d 1978), and Mary, *née* Agnew; *b* 13 February 1932; *Educ* Priory GS Shrewsbury; *m* 28 June 1956, Barbara Mary, da of William Abley (d 1959); 3 da (Sarah (Mrs Garratt) b 10 April 1957, Ruth b 30 March 1958, Jane b 23 May 1963); *Career* dir and gen mangr Heart of England Building Soc 1983–92, chm Jephson Housing Association Ltd 1993–; pres Coventry Centre Building Soc's Inst; FCBSI 1969, FCIB; *Recreations* sport; *Style—* Charles Macintyre, Esq; ✉ 20 Hazler Orchard, Church Stretton, Shropshire SY6 7AL (tel 01694 723246)

McINTYRE, Sir Donald Conroy; kt (1992), CBE (1985, OBE 1975); s of George McIntyre, and Hermyn, *née* Conroy; *b* 22 October 1934; *Educ* Mount Albert GS NZ, Auckland Teachers Trg Coll, Guildhall Sch of Music London; *m* 29 July 1961, Jill Redington, da of Norton Mitchell, DFC (d 1989), of Barnstaple, Devon; 3 da (Ruth Frances b 1965, Lynn Hazel b 1967, Jenny Jane b 1971); *Career* int opera singer, bass baritone; debut UK Welsh Nat Opera 1959; princ bass: Sadler's Wells Opera 1960–67, Royal Opera House Covent Garden 1967–, Bayreuth Festival 1967–84; frequent int guest appearances: Metropolitan (NY), Vienna, Munich, Hamburg, Paris, Buenos Aires, La Scala (Milan), Berlin, Sydney and more; princ roles incl: Wotan and Wanderer in The Ring, Dutchman in Flying Dutchman, Telramund in Lohengrin, Amfortas, Klingsor and Gurnemanz in Parsifal, Kurwenal in Tristan and Isolde, Hans Sachs in Die Meistersinger, Barak in Die Frau Ohne Schatten, Golaud in Pelleas and Melisande, Pizzaro and Rocco in Fidelio, Kasper in Der Freischütz, Scarpia in Tosca, title role in Macbeth, Nick Shadow in Rake's Progress, Count in The Marriage of Figaro, title role in Cardillac, Shakloviti in Khovanshchina; numerous concert appearances worldwide; appeared as: Hans Sachs in Die Meistersinger (first ever staged prodn of this opera in NZ) 1990, Balstrode in Peter Grimes (Munich) 1991–92, Boris in Lady Macbeth of Mtsensk 1993; video films incl: Der Fliegende Holländer 1975, Electra 1979, Bayreuth Centenary Ring 1981, Die Meistersinger 1984, Mandryka in Arabella (San Francisco), Baron Prus in The Makropulos Case (Toulouse and Brussels), Trulove in The Rake's Progress (Brussels); recording incl: Pelleas and Melisande, The Messiah, Beethoven's Ninth Symphony, Damnation of Faust, Il Trovotore, Oedipus Rex, The Ring, Parsifal; Fidelio Medal (Assoc of Int Dirs of Opera) 1989, NZ Commemoration Award 1990; life memb Auckland Choral Soc; *Recreations* swimming, tennis, farming, walking; *Style—* Sir Donald McIntyre, CBE; ✉ c/o Ingpen & Williams Ltd, 7 St George's Court, 131 Putney Bridge Road, London SW15 2PA (tel 020 8874 3222, fax 020 8877 3113)

MACINTYRE, Donald John; s of Kenneth MacKenzie Campbell Macintyre (d 1988), and Margaret Rachel, *née* Freeman; *b* 27 January 1947; *Educ* Bradfield Coll, ChCh Oxford (BA), Univ Coll Cardiff (Dip Journalism); *Children* 1 s (James b 18 August 1979); *Career* journalist The Sunday Mercury 1971–75, industrial corr The Daily Express 1975–77, labour corr The Times 1977–83; labour ed: The Sunday Times 1983–85, The Times 1985–86, The Independent 1986–87; political ed: The Sunday Telegraph 1987–89, The Sunday Correspondent 1989–90, The Independent on Sunday 1990–93; The Independent: political ed 1993–96, chief political commentator 1996–, asst ed 2003–; *Books* Talking About Trade Unions (1980), Strike (co-author, 1985), Mandelson and the Making of New Labour (1999); *Style—* Donald Macintyre, Esq

MacINTYRE, Prof Iain; s of John MacIntyre (d 1954), of Tobermory, Mull, and Margaret Fraser Shaw (d 1967), of Stratherick, Inverness; *b* 30 August 1924; *Educ* Jordanhill Coll Sch Glasgow, Univ of Glasgow (MB ChB), Univ of London (PhD, DSc); *m* 14 July 1947, Mabs Wilson (d 2003), da of George Jamieson (d 1951), of Huntly, Aberdeenshire, and J C K K Jamieson, *née* Bell; 1 da (Fiona Bell b 1953); *Career* Royal Postgraduate Med Sch: prof of endocrine chemistry 1967–82, dir Endocrine Unit 1967–89, chm Academic Bd 1986–89, dir Dept of Chemical Pathology 1982–89, emeritus prof 1989; research dir William Harvey Research Inst St Bartholomew's and the Royal London Sch of Med and Dentistry Queen Mary Coll London 1995– (assoc dir 1991–95), conslt chem pathologist Hammersmith and Queen Charlotte's Hosps; memb: Hammersmith and Queen Charlotte's HA 1982–90, Br Postgraduate Fedn Central Academic Cncl 1983–89; Gairdner Int Award Toronto 1967, Elsevier Award for Distinguished Res 1992, Paget Fndn Award 1995, Buchanan Medal of the Royal Soc 2006; Hon MD: Turin Univ 1985, Univ of Sheffield 2002; FRCPath 1971 (MCRPath (fndr memb) 1965), FRCP 1977 (MRCP 1969), FRS 1996, memb Assoc of American Physicians 1998, fndr FMedSci 1998; *Recreations* tennis, chess; *Clubs* Athenaeum, Queen's, Hurlingham; *Style—* Professor Iain MacIntyre, FRS; ✉ Great Broadhurst Farm, Broad Oak, Heathfield, East Sussex TN21 8UX (tel 01435 883515, fax 01435 883611, e-mail calc@broadoak.demon.co.uk); William Harvey Research Institute, Charterhouse Square, London EC1M 6BQ (tel 020 7882 6168, fax 020 7882 3408, e-mail i.macintyre@qmul.ac.uk)

MACINTYRE, Iain Melfort Campbell; s of late John Macintyre, of Edinburgh, and late Mary, *née* Campbell; *b* 23 June 1944; *Educ* Daniel Stewart's Coll Edinburgh, Univ of Edinburgh (MB ChB, MD); *m* 8 April 1969, Tessa Lorna Mary, da of Rev Basil E R Millar; 3 da (Carol Anne Mary b 13 Nov 1969, Alison Jane b 5 Jan 1972, Lucy Nicola b 13 Oct 1975); *Career* trained in surgery Edinburgh and Durban SA; lectr in surgery Univ of Edinburgh 1974–78, locum prof of surgery Univ of Natal SA 1978–79, conslt surgn with administrative responsibility Gen Surgical Unit Leith Hosp Edinburgh 1979–85, conslt surgn Gen Surgical and Gastro-Intestinal Unit Western Gen Hosp Edinburgh 1985–2002 (conslt with administrative responsibility Surgical Review Office); chm Lister Postgraduate Inst 1995–2000 (asst dir of studies 1991–95); memb Nat Med Advsy Ctee 1991–94; vice-pres RCSEd 2003–06 (examiner 1979–, examiner Intercollegiate Bd in Gen Surgery 1994–99, memb Educn and Sci Ctee 1987–91, memb Editorial Bd 1991–2000, memb Educn and Trg Bd 1994–95, memb Cncl 1990–2000, dir of Educn 1997–2000, hon sec 2001–03, vice-pres 2003–06); chm Surgeons Hall Tst 2004–07; Cncl of Europe fell 1990, Continuing Med Educn fell in minimally invasive surgery 1992; Surgn to HM The Queen in Scotland 1997–2004; FRCSEd 1973, FRCPEd 1997; *Books* Venous

M

Thrombo-Embolic Disease (ed with C V Ruckley, 1975), Endoscopic Surgery for General Surgeons (ed and contrib, 1995), Surgeons' Lives (ed with I F MacLaren, 2005); *Recreations* golf, sailing, reading, music; *Clubs* Moynihan Chirurgical, Aesculapians, Bruntsfield Links Golfing Soc; *Style—* Mr Iain Macintyre; ✉ 20 Lygon Road, Edinburgh EH16 5QB (tel 0131 466 0095)

McINTYRE, Air Vice-Marshal Ian Graeme; QHDS (1995); s of Arthur McIntyre (d 1989), and Eileen, *née* Patmore (d 1949); *b* 9 July 1943; *Educ* Royal Masonic Sch for Boys, Univ of Durham (BDS), Univ of London (MSc); *m* 1966, Joan; 2 s (Mark b 1969, Angus b 1971); *Career* RAF: joined 1961, Asst Dir Dental Servs RAF 1990, CO RAF Inst of Dental Health & Trg 1994, Dir Dental Servs RAF 1995, Chief Exec Defence Dental Agency 1997–2001 (Dir Clinical Servs 1996–97); pres BDA (memb 1963, chm Armed Forces Gp, treas Benevolent Fund), conslt Dental Public Health Solihull and Warks HAs; memb Br Soc for General Dental Surgery 1984 (pres 1996, Cottrell Award 1998), pres elect Anglo Asian Odontological Gp 1996; Lean Meml Award 1990; MIMgt 1995, FDSRCS (Ed) 1998; *Recreations* hill walking, gardening, watching rugby; *Clubs* RAF, Saracens RUFC; *Style—* Air Vice-Marshal Ian McIntyre, QHDS; ✉ HQ Defence Dental Agency, RAF Halton, Aylesbury, Buckinghamshire HP22 5PG (tel 01296 623535 extn 6851, e-mail imcintyre@hqdda.demon.co.uk)

McINTYRE, Ian James; s of Hector Harold McIntyre (d 1978), of Inverness, and Annie Mary Michie (d 1979); *b* 9 December 1931; *Educ* Prescot GS, St John's Coll Cambridge (MA, pres Cambridge Union), Coll of Europe Bruges; *m* 24 July 1954, Leik Sommerfelt, da of Benjamin Vogt (d 1970), of Kragerø, Norway; 2 s (Andrew James, Neil Forbes), 2 da (Anne Leik, Katharine Elspeth); *Career* Nat Serv cmmnd Intelligence Corps; writer and broadcaster; BBC: current affrs talks prodr 1957–59, ed At Home and Abroad 1959–60, mgmnt trg organiser 1960–61, broadcasting contract 1970–76; controller: Radio 4 1976–78, Radio 3 1978–87; assoc ed The Times 1989–90; prog servs offr ITA 1961–62, dir of info and res Scot Cons Central Office Edinburgh 1962–70; author of book reviews for The Times, The Spectator and The Independent; contrib Oxford DNB; Parly candidate (Cons) Roxburgh, Selkirk and Peebles gen election 1966; *Books* The Proud Doers: Israel after Twenty Years (1968), Words: Reflections on the Uses of Language (1975), Dogfight: the Transatlantic Battle over Airbus (1992), The Expense of Glory: A Life of John Reith (1993), Dirt & Deity: A Life of Robert Burns (1995), Garrick (1999, Annual Book Prize Soc for Theatre Research), Joshua Reynolds: The Life & Times of the First President of the Royal Academy (2003); *Recreations* walking, swimming, gardening; *Clubs* Cambridge Union; *Style—* Ian McIntyre, Esq; ✉ Spylaw House, Newlands Avenue, Radlett, Hertfordshire WD7 8EL (tel 01923 853532, e-mail ian.mcintyre@waitrose.com)

McINTYRE, Keith Thomas; s of Gordon Leslie McIntyre, of Edinburgh, and Sheila, *née* McDonald; *b* 22 December 1959; *Educ* Trinity Acad Secdy Sch Edinburgh, Dundee Coll of Art (Drumfolk travelling scholar, Farquar Reid travelling scholar), Barcelona Paper Workshop; *m* 30 Dec 1983, Sheenagh Margaret Patience; 2 s (Lewis Cathcart b 22 Oct 1987, Casey John b 4 Sept 1991); *Career* artist; course ldr Fine Art Univ of Northumbria at Newcastle 1999–, visiting artist-in-residence Ludwig Fndn Havana Art Tst 1999, Louie A Brown Int Fell Valdosta State Univ Georgia 1997–98; solo exhibitions: Shore Gallery Leith 1982, 369 Gallery Edinburgh 1984 and 1986, Compass Gallery Glasgow 1985, Pittenweem Arts Festival Fife 1985, Raab Galerie Berlin 1987, Raab Gallery London 1988, The Paintings for Jock Tamson's Bairns (Tramway Theatre Glasgow and Raab Gallery London) 1990, Pittencrieff House Museum Dunfermline 1995, Northern Print Gallery N Shields 1996, Galerie Christian Dam Copenhagen 1996, Boukamel Contemporary Art London 1997, Valdosta State Univ Georgia 1998, GSU Gallery Statesboro Georgia 1998, Belenkey Gallery NY 1998, Harmonia Galerie Jyvaskyla Finalnd 2000, Galerie Habana Havana Cuba 2001, Indiana State Univ 2004; group exhibitions incl: Saltire Soc Edinburgh 1982, Clare Hall Cambridge 1984 and 1986, Five Contemporary Scottish Artists (Leinster Fine Art London) 1985, Open Circle (Schweinfurt Exhibition Germany) 1986, De Brakke Gallery Amsterdam 1987, The Lion Rampant: New Scottish Painting and Photography (Artspace San Francisco) 1988, Scottish Myths (Scot Gallery Edinburgh) 1990, Galerie Bureaux & Magasins Ostend Belgium 1991, Divers Memories (Pitt Rivers Museum Oxford), Premio Marco (MOMA Monterrey Mexico) 1997, Hibrida (Bradford Art Gallery) 2002, Hibrida II (Brno Museum of Art Czech Repub) 2005; public collections incl: Aberdeen Art Gallery, BBC, Dundee Coll of Commerce, Scot Nat Gallery of Modern Art, W Sussex CC; arts projects incl: visual dir Jock Tamson's Bairns (Tramway Theatre Glasgow) 1989–90, jt film venture (with Timothy Neat and John Berger) 1990; pt/t teacher in fine art Glasgow Sch of Art 1984–89, New Constellations (Baltic Centre for Contemporary Art Gateshead) 2004, keynote essay for Baltic Yearbook 2004; sr lectr in painting (now reader in art and interdisciplinary practices) Univ of Northumbria at Newcastle 1993–; artistic dir Songs for the Falling Angel (requiem for Lockerbie air crash victims, Edinburgh Int Festival) 1991, exhibition of paintings for Songs for the Falling Angel (Kelvingrove Art Gallery Glasgow) 1991/92; visual art dir: Rites (with Scottish Chamber Orch, Briggait Glasgow) 1993, Legend of St Julian (with Communicado, Traverse Theatre, Edinburgh Int Festival) 1993, Games (with Vocem and the Edinburgh Contemporary Art Trust) 1996, Mfalme Juha (with Parapanda Arts Tanzania) 2003, Heid (with Sounds of Progress and Parapanda Arts) 2006, Life Stories and Dreams (with Sounds of Progress and Scottish Nat Theatre Co) 2006, The Unconquered (with Stellar Quines Theatre Co) 2007; Hospitalfield scholar Arbroath 1981, RSA Carnegie 1982, RSA William Gillies 1983, Elizabeth Greenshields 1983, first prize Scottish Drawing Competition 1993, Arts Cncl Award 2004; *Style—* Keith McIntyre, Esq; ✉ Department of Fine Art, Squires Building, University of Northumbria at Newcastle, Sandyford Road, Newcastle upon Tyne NE1 8ST (tel 0191 227 4935)

McINTYRE, Prof Michael Edgeworth; s of Archibald Keverall McIntyre, and Anne Hartwell McIntyre; *b* 28 July 1941; *Educ* King's HS Dunedin NZ, Univ of Otago NZ (sr sci scholar, BSc, Robert Jack prize, NZ Inst of Chemistry prize), Trinity Coll Cambridge (Cwlth scholar, PhD); *m* 1968, Ruth Hecht; 2 step s, 1 step da; *Career* asst lectr in mathematics Univ of Otago NZ 1963, postdoctoral fell Woods Hole Oceanographic Inst 1967, postdoctoral res assoc Dept of Meteorology MIT 1967–69, res fell St John's Coll Cambridge 1968–71; Dept of Applied Mathematics and Theoretical Physics Univ of Cambridge: asst dir of res in dynamical meteorology 1969–72, lectr 1972–87, reader in atmospheric dynamics 1987–93, prof of atmospheric dynamics 1993–; co-dir Cambridge Centre for Atmospheric Sci 1992–2003; EPSRC sr res fell 1992–97; sr visiting fell Japan Soc for the Promotion of Sci 1984; sr conslt: Science and Technology Corporation Hampton Virginia 1987–2002, Jet Propulsion Laboratory Pasadena Calif 1991–2002; project scientist UK Univs' Global Atmospheric Modelling Prog 1987–2002 (memb Sci Steering Gp 1990–2002); memb: Editorial Bd Jl of Fluid Mechanics 1969–80, Int Cmmn for Meteorology of the Upper Atmosphere 1979–89, Atmospheric Sci Ctee NERC 1989–94, Strateole Scientific Steering Ctee 1992–2002, World Climate Res Prog SPARC Gravity Wave Ctee 1994–; vice-pres Catgut Acoustical Soc 1978–83, memb New Violin Family Steering Ctee Royal Coll of Music 1976–80; Adams prize Univ of Cambridge 1981, Julius Bartels Medal of the Euro Geophysical Soc 1999; FRMetS 1969, memb Academia Europaea 1989, FRS 1990, fell American Meteorological Soc 1991 (Carl-Gustaf Rossby Res medal 1987), fell AAAS 1999; *Publications* author of numerous papers in professional jls incl Jl of Fluid Mechanics, Quarterly Jl RMetSoc, Jl of the Atmospheric Sciences, Nature, Interdisciplinary Science Reviews; *Recreations* music, gliding, lucidity principles; *Style—* Prof M E McIntyre, MAE, FRS; ✉ Department of Applied Mathematics and Theoretical Physics, Wilberforce Road, Cambridge CB3 0WA (tel 01223 337871, secretary's tel 01223 337870, fax 01223 765900, website www.atm.damtp.cam.ac.uk/mcintyre/)

McINTYRE, Patrick; s of Patrick Owen McIntyre (d 1986), of Winnipeg, Canada, and Elizabeth May, *née* Gair (d 1985); *b* 18 June 1936; *Educ* St Paul's Coll Winnipeg, Open Univ (BA); *m* 27 June 1957, Margaret Inger (d 1990), da of Robert Jarman (d 1954); 1 s (Patrick), 1 step s (David), 1 step da (Hilary Patricia); *Career* Royal Winnipeg Ballet 1946–56, American Ballet Theatre 1957–58, West End Theatre (West Side Story) 1958–60, ten West End prodns 1960–83, numerous feature films and TV series 1960–83, house mangr Old Vic Theatre 1983–96; direction and choreography: RSC Stratford, LA Light Opera, Gaiety Theatre Dublin, various Br provincial theatres; performance assessor Arts Cncl 1996–; sr assessor Trinity Coll London 2000–, inspr OFSTED 2002–; *Publications* Once a Dancer (2003); *Recreations* walking, reading, travel; *Style—* Patrick McIntyre, Esq; ✉ Flat 3, 39 Brunswick Terrace, Hove, East Sussex BN3 1HA (tel 01273 731539, e-mail p.mcintyre@sky.com)

MACINTYRE, William Ian; CB (1992); s of Robert Miller Macintyre, CBE (d 1991), of Uckfield, E Sussex, and Florence Mary, *née* Funnell (d 2004); *b* 20 July 1943; *Educ* Merchiston Castle Sch Edinburgh, Univ of St Andrews (MA); *m* 2 Sept 1967, Jennifer Mary, da of Sir David Bruce Pitblado, KCB, CVO (d 1997), and Edith Mary, *née* Evans (d 1978); 2 da (Emma b 22 March 1969, Victoria b 6 Dec 1971), 1 s (Jonathan b 13 Sept 1974); *Career* BP Co Ltd 1965–72, ECGD 1972–73; Dept of Energy (now part of DTI): Oil Div 1973–77, seconded ICFC 1977–79, asst sec Gas Div 1979–1983, DG Energy Efficiency Office 1983–87, under sec Electricity Div 1987–88, under sec Electricity Div B 1988–91, under sec Coal Div 1991–94, head of Telecommunications Div 1994–95, head of Communications and Information Industries Directorate 1996–2002; memb Radiocommunications Agency Steering Bd 1997–2002; exec vice-pres Chelgate Ltd, dir Templeton Estates; govr: Shene Sch 1982–86, East Sheen Primary Sch 1974–92, Froebel Coll, Ibstock Place Sch (chm of govrs 2002–04); currently chm Incorporated Froebel Educnl Inst (IFEI, dep chm 2001–03), pro-chllr Roehampton Univ 2006– (memb Cncl 2000–06); warden parish of Mortlake with East Sheen 1991–95; *Style—* William Macintyre, Esq, CB; ✉ 56 East Sheen Avenue, London SW14 8AU (tel 020 8876 4659)

McISAAC, Ian; s of Archibald Hendry McIsaac (d 1976), and Elsie May, *née* Sampson (d 1975); *b* 13 July 1945; *Educ* Charterhouse (scholar); *m* 1, 21 Nov 1970 (m dis), Joanna, *née* Copland; 1 da (Miranda Jane b 1972), 1 s (Angus James Forbes b 1975); m 2, 2 April 1983, Debrah, *née* Ball; 1 da (Catherine Bennett b 1984), 1 s (Robert George Hendry b 1989); *Career* chartered accountant; ptnr: Touche Ross (UK) 1979–88, Touche Ross (Canada) 1983–85; chief exec Richard Ellis Financial Servs 1988–91; Deloitte & Touche (formerly Touche Ross): ptnr 1991–2005, UK chm emerging markets 2000–04, managing ptnr global risk mgmnt 2003–05; registered treas and finance dir Cons Party 2005–; dir City Disputes Panel; chm Soc of Turnaround Professionals 2001–04, memb Policy Advsy Gp DFID 2004–05; chm Care International UK 1997–2004 (dir 1985–2004), chm Friends of Care International, govr Sutton's Hosp Charterhouse 2006–; Freeman: City of London, Worshipful Co of Chartered Accountants; FCA 1979 (ACA 1969); *Recreations* golf, sailing, skiing; *Clubs* Carlton, Hurlingham, Royal Mid-Surrey Golf, High Post Golf, OCYC; *Style—* Ian McIsaac, Esq

McISAAC, Shona; MP; da of Angus McIsaac, and Isa, *née* Nicol; *b* 3 April 1960; *Educ* SHAPE Sch Belgium, Barne Barton Secdy Modern Plymouth, Stoke Damerel HS Plymouth, Univ of Durham (BSc); *m* 1994, Peter Keith; *Career* sub ed various women's magazines incl: Chat, Bella, Woman; MP (Lab) Cleethorpes 1997–; PPS to Rt Hon Baroness Scotland of Asthal 2003–; *Recreations* cycling, football, food, archaeology of UK; *Style—* Shona McIsaac, MP; ✉ House of Commons, London SW1A 0AA (tel 020 7219 3000)

MACIVER, Archie Duncan; s of Iain Duncan Maciver, of Carloway, Isle of Lewis, and Christine, *née* Macarthur; *b* 13 December 1959, Glasgow; *Educ* Hutchesons GS Glasgow, Univ of Strathclyde (LLB, DipLP); *m* 15 July 1987, Pamela Anne, *née* Richardson; 2 da (Victoria Elizabeth b 18 Nov 1989, Alexandra Christine b 30 May 1992); *Career* slr; Levy and McRae: trainee 1981–83, asst 1983–84, ptnr 1984–88; ptnr Brunton Miller 1988–; tutor Central Law Scotland Ltd, Scottish legal advsr and memb Ctee Bar Entertainment and Dance Assoc, accredited specialist in licensing law Law Soc of Scotland; chm Gtr Glasgow Health Bd Dental Discipline Tbnl; memb: Law Soc of Scotland, Scottish Law Agents Soc, Glasgow Bar Assoc; *Recreations* golf, reading, quality family time; *Clubs* East Renfrewshire Golf; *Style—* Archie Maciver, Esq; ✉ Brunton Miller, 22 Herbert Street, Glasgow G20 6NB (tel 0141 337 1199, fax 0141 337 3300, e-mail archiemaciver@bruntonmiller.com)

McIVER, Malcolm; OBE (1999); s of late Donald John McIver, and Jean Begg, *née* Macdonald (d 1958); *b* 9 March 1935; *Educ* The Nicolson Inst Stornoway, Univ of Glasgow (MA, LLB); *m* 15 April 1960, Margaret, da of Alexander Wilson Fox Elliot; 1 s (Calum Alexander b 10 July 1967); *Career* apprentice slr Baird Smith Barclay & Muirhead and Maclay Murray & Spens 1955–58; slr: Crawford Herron & Cameron 1958–59, Peter Morris & McTaggart 1959–60; ptnr: Crawford Herron & Cameron 1960–73, Bird Semple & Crawford Herron 1973–87; Bird Semple: ptnr 1987–97, sr ptnr 1991–97, conslt 1997–99; chm Sportech plc (formerly Rodime plc) 1991–2001; tutor in jurisprudence Univ of Glasgow 1960–85; chm Royal Scottish Acad of Music and Drama 1993–98, dep chm Accounts Cmmn 1994–98 (memb 1988–98); memb Incorporation of Hammermen Glasgow; memb: Law Soc of Scotland 1958, Royal Faculty of Procurators in Glasgow 1960; SSC, FEI, FRSA, FRSAMD; *Recreations* sailing, music; *Clubs* Western (Glasgow), Royal Western Yacht, Glasgow Art; *Style—* Malcolm McIver, Esq, OBE; ✉ 29 Hughenden Lane, Glasgow G12 9XU (tel 0141 339 8551)

McIVOR, Ian Walker; s of William Walker McIvor (d 1986), of Worsley, Manchester, and Susannah, *née* Glover (d 1990); *b* 19 January 1944; *Educ* Worsley HS, Bolton Inst, Univ of London (LLB); *Children* 4 da (Helen b 1970, Rachel b 1971, Caroline b 1974, Joanne b 1984), 1 s (Andrew Walker b 1977); *Career* AVR 2 Kings Regt OTC 1966–68; called to the Bar Inner Temple 1973 (Marshall Hall Tst Award and Pupillage Scholarship), head of chambers 1977–; *Recreations* golf, swimming, walking, DIY; *Clubs* Didsbury Golf; *Style—* Ian W McIvor, Esq; ✉ 10 Knight Street, Didsbury, Manchester M20 6WG

MACK, Anthony George (Tony); s of Anthony Mack (d 1991), of Bognor Regis, West Sussex, and Joyce Agnes, *née* Smith (d 2004); *b* 10 December 1948; *Educ* Imberhorne Sch; *m* 17 Feb 1979, Sally Frances, da of Frank Frederick Legg, of Sussex; 2 s (Alastair b 1981, Freddy b 1986), 1 da (Holly b 1982); *Career* Air Partner plc (formerly Air London Ltd): dir 1970, md 1979, chm 1989–; FFA, AMRAeS; *Recreations* sailing, horse riding, skiing, golf; *Clubs* Hamble River Sailing, Royal London Yacht; *Style—* Tony Mack, Esq; ✉ Air Partner plc, Platinum House, Gatwick Road, Crawley, West Sussex RH10 2RP (tel 01293 844800, fax 01293 536810, telex 87671)

MACK, Hazel Mary; da of Peter Nevard Perkins (d 1992), and Betty, *née* Walker (d 1998); *b* 4 April 1952; *Educ* Loughborough HS for Girls, Univ of Exeter (BA); *m* 19 May 1977, Brian Mack, s of Frank Mack (d 1982); *Career* co sec Morgan Grenfell & Co Ltd 1987–90 (joined 1980), dir Mergers and Acquisitions Practice Willis Ltd 1990–; ACIS; *Recreations* cooking, gardening, walking; *Style—* Mrs Hazel Mack; ✉ Pounce Hall Cottage, Sewards End, Saffron Walden, Essex CB10 2LE (tel 01799 527740); Willis Ltd, Ten Trinity Square, London EC3P 3AX (tel 020 7975 2329, fax 020 7488 8562, e-mail mackh@willis.com)

MACK, Prof (Brian) John; s of late Harold Brian Mack, of Belfast, and Joan Alexandra, *née* Kelly; *b* 10 July 1949; *Educ* Campbell Coll Belfast, Univ of Sussex (BA, MA), Merton Coll

Oxford (DPhil); *m* 1976, Caroline Helen Claire, *qv*, da of Rev Dr Daniel T Jenkins; 1 da (Katy b 12 Oct 1985), 1 s (Samuel b 13 Feb 1989); *Career* Dept of Ethnography British Museum: research asst 1976–77, asst keeper 1977–91, keeper 1991–2004, sr keeper 1998–2002; prof of world art studies UEA 2004–; visiting prof UCL 1997–2003; pres Br Inst in Eastern Africa 2005; memb: British Museum Res Bd, Advsy Cncl NACF, Bd W African Museums Programme, Bd for Academy Sponsored Insts and Socs British Academy, Bd of Visitors Pitt-Rivers Museum Oxford; tstee Horniman Museum and Gardens; govr Powell-Cotton Museum Kent; winner NACF Award for Images of Africa exhibition 1991; FRAI 1976, FSA 1994, FRSA 2005; *Publications* African Textiles (with J Picton, 1979, 2 edn 1989, Craft Advsy Cncl Book of the Year), Zulus (1980), Culture History in the Southern Sudan (with P T Robertshaw, 1982), Ethnic Sculpture (with M D McLeod, 1984), Madagascar, Island of the Ancestors (1986), Ethnic Jewellery (1988), Malagasy Textiles (1989), Emil Torday and the Art of the Congo 1900–1909 (1990), African Textile Design (with C Spring, 1991), Masks, the Art of Expression (1994), Images of other Cultures (with K Yoshida, 1998), Africa, Arts and Cultures (2000), Museum of the Mind (2003), The Art of Small Things (2007); also author of articles and reviews in learned jls; *Recreations* museums, galleries, walking; *Clubs* Aberdovey Golf (Gwynedd); *Style*— Prof John Mack; ✉ School of World Art and Museology, University of East Anglia, Norwich NR4 7TJ (tel 01603 456161)

McKANE, Christopher Hugh; s of Leonard Cyril McKane, MBE (d 1997), and (Eleanor) Catharine, *née* Harris; *b* 13 July 1946; *Educ* Marlborough, New Coll Oxford (MA); *m* 31 Oct 1970, Anna Rosemary, da of George Paul Henshell (d 1984); 3 da (Camilla b 1977, Sophie b 1979, Felicity b 1981); *Career* journalist: The Oxford Times 1968–71, The Birmingham Post 1971–74; The Times 1974–86; The Independent: dep home ed 1986–88, picture ed 1988–92, night ed 1992–94; The Times: rejoined 1994, night ed 1995–99, exec ed 1999–; church warden St Bride's Fleet St 2002–; Freeman City of London, Liveryman Worshipful Co of Stationers and Newspaper Makers (memb Ct of Assts 2000–); *Recreations* bonsai, sweet wines, distance running, rambling; *Clubs* Saracens FC; *Style*— Christopher McKane, Esq; ✉ The Times, 1 Pennington Street, London E98 1TT (tel 020 7782 1666, e-mail christopher.mckane@thetimes.co.uk)

MACKANESS, James; DL (Northants 1984); s of John Howard Mackaness (d 2002), of Northampton, and Majorie, *née* Andrews (d 2001); *b* 6 February 1945; *Educ* Millfield, RAC Cirencester; *m* 7 Jan 1972, Susan, da of Harold Pike; 1 da (Louise b 1973), 1 s (Oliver James b 1975); *Career* md A J Mackaness Ltd (family firm); dir Mixconcrete Holdings plc 1981–83; High Sheriff Northants 1995–96; tstee: Mackaness Family Charitable Tst 1994–, Three Shires Hosp Tst 1995–2001 (chm 1997–2001), Queen's Inst Relief in Sickness Fund 1997–; memb St John Ambulance 1974–2001, chm St John Cncl for Northants 1982–2001; govr St Andrew's Hosp 1987–; KStJ 1998; *Recreations* hunting, shooting, skiing; *Style*— James Mackaness, Esq, DL; ✉ A J Mackaness Ltd, Billing House, The Causeway, Great Billing, Northampton NN3 9EX (tel 01604 409096, fax 01604 407222, e-mail jmackaness@lineone.net)

MACKARNESS, Simon Paul Richard; TD (1980); s of Peter John Coleridge Mackarness, TD, of Petersfield, Hants, and Torla Frances Wedd, *née* Tidman; *b* 10 September 1945; *Educ* Portsmouth GS, Univ of Bristol (BA); *m* 9 Dec 1978, Diana, da of Dr Lewis Macdonald Reid, MC (d 1978); 1 da (Louise b 1981), 1 s (Daniel b 1982); *Career* Capt Royal Signals TA; admitted slr 1970, sr ptnr Mackarness & Lunt; memb Law Soc; *Recreations* amateur dramatics, motorcycling; *Style*— Simon Mackarness, Esq, TD; ✉ 16 High Street, Petersfield, Hampshire GU32 3JJ (tel 01730 265111, fax 01730 267994, e-mail simon.mackarness@macklunt.co.uk)

MACKAY, Andrew James; PC (1998), MP; s of late Robert James MacKay, and late Olive Margaret MacKay; *b* 27 August 1949; *Educ* Solihull; *m* 1, 1975 (m dis 1996), Diana Joy Kinchin; 1 s, 1 d; m 2, 1997, Julie Kirkbride, MP, *qv*; 1 s; *Career* ptnr Jones MacKay & Croxford Estate Agents 1974–, dir Birmingham Housing Industries Ltd 1975–83; chm Solihull Young Cons 1971–74, vice-chm Solihull Cons Assoc 1971–74, chm Britain in Europe Meriden Branch 1975; MP (Cons): Birmingham Stechford March 1977–79, Berkshire E 1983–97, Bracknell 1997–; PPS to: sec of state for NI 1986–89, sec of state for Defence 1989–92; asst Govt whip 1992–93, a Lord Cmmr of the Treasury (Govt whip) 1993–95, Vice-Chamberlain of HM Household (Govt whip) 1996, Treasurer of HM Household (dep chief whip) 1996–97, shadow sec for NI 1997–2001, dep chm Cons Pty 2004–05, sr political and parly advsr to Ldr of Cons Pty 2005–; memb Standards and Privileges Ctee 2002–06; memb Cons Party Nat Exec 1979–82, sec Cons Back Bench Foreign Affrs Ctee 1984–86; memb Br-Irish Parly Body 2001– (chm European Ctee); *Recreations* golf, squash; *Clubs* Berkshire Golf, Aberdovey Golf, Royal & Ancient; *Style*— The Rt Hon Andrew MacKay, MP; ✉ House of Commons, London SW1A 0AA (tel 020 7219 4109)

MACKAY, Andrew John (Andy); OBE (2006); s of John Mackay (d 1999), and Margaret, *née* Ogilvie (d 1996); *b* 28 July 1960, Cheltenham, Glos; *Educ* Clifton, Univ of Exeter (BA), Univ of Reading (MA), Univ of Durham (MBA); *m* 6 Oct 1990, Margaret Allport; 1 da (Isabel Margaret b 11 Aug 1996); *Career* British Cncl: asst dir Teaching Centre Cairo 1983–87, evaluation advsr 1988–89, dep dir Peru 1989–92, dir Dubai 1992–96, dir Barcelona 1996–2001, dir USA 2001–06; head strategy and partnerships, public diplomacy FCO 2006–; FRSA 2002; *Recreations* cinema, literature, Hispanic cultures, walking; *Style*— Andy Mackay, Esq, OBE; ✉ c/o British Council, 10 Spring Gardens, London SW1A 2BN (tel 020 7008 6101, e-mail andy.mackay@britishcouncil.org)

MACKAY, Prof Angus Victor Peck; OBE (1997); s of Victor Mackay (d 1982), of Edinburgh, and Christine, *née* Peck (d 1985); *b* 4 March 1943; *Educ* George Heriot's Sch Edinburgh, Univ of Edinburgh (BSc, MB ChB), Univ of Cambridge (MA, PhD); *m* 1969, Elspeth Margaret Whitton, da of Thomas Norris; 2 s (Jason b 20 Nov 1970, Aidan b 31 March 1978), 2 da (Ashley b 20 June 1972, Zoe b 17 Jan 1983); *Career* undergraduate trg in pharmacology and med Univ of Edinburgh 1962–69, house offr Med/Surgical Professorial Unit Edinburgh Royal Infirmary 1969–70, graduate trg Univ of Cambridge 1970–73 (MRC jr res fell and supervisor in pharmacology Trinity Coll Cambridge and hon registrar Fulbourn Hosp Cambridge), MRC clinical res fell MRC Brain Metabolism Unit Edinburgh, hon registrar in psychiatry Royal Edinburgh Hosp and hon lectr Dept of Pharmacology Edinburgh 1973–76, hon sr registrar Edinburgh Royal Infirmary 1976, sr clinical scientific staff memb and latterly dep dir MRC Neurochemical Pharmacology Unit Cambridge and lectr in pharmacology Trinity Coll Cambridge, hon conslt Cambridge Area HA and hon lectr Dept of Psychiatry Cambridge 1976–80; currently: physician supt Argyll and Bute Hosp, conslt psychiatrist, dir of mental health services Argyll and Bute NHS Tst, chm Health Technol Board for Scotland, hon prof Dept of Psycological Med Univ of Glasgow 1980–; UK rep Conf on Psychiatric Hosp Orgn and Mgmnt WHO 1983; memb: Res Ctee Mental Health Fndn 1981–88, Working Gp on Guidelines for Clinical Drug Evaluation WHO 1984–89, Ctee on Safety of Meds Dept of Health 1983–, Faculty of Neuroscience Univ of Edinburgh 1999–; chm: Multidisciplinary Working Pty on Research into Care of the Dementing Elderly Chief Scientist Orgn 1986–87, Working Gp on Mental Illness Servs in Scotland CRAG/SCOTMEG 1992–96, External Reference Gp Scottish Health Dept 1996–, Working Gp on Scottish Health Technol Assessment 1999–2000; memb NHS Policy Bd Scotland 1996–97; author of over 70 pubns; Keith Medal and Meml Lecture RSA 1974; FRCPEd 1989 (MRCP 1986), FRCPsych 1993 (MRCPsych 1976), TPsych 1995; *Recreations* sailing, rowing, rhododendrons; *Clubs* Ardrishaig Boat, American Rhododendron Soc; *Style*— Prof Angus Mackay, OBE; ✉ Tigh An Rudha, Ardrishaig, Argyll (tel 01546 603272); Argyll and Bute Hospital, Lochgilphead, Argyll PA31 8LD (tel 01546 602323, fax 01546 602606); Health Technology Board for Scotland, Delta House, West Nile Street, Glasgow (tel 0141 249 6665)

McKAY, Barrie John; s of late Thomas John McKay, of Grimsby, and Margaret, *née* Piercy; *b* 24 March 1946; *Educ* Winteringham Boys GS Grimsby, Nottingham Law Sch (BA); *m* Susan, da of Rex Rendle; 1 s (James b 29 Jan 1973); *Career* HM Customs and Excise: offr of Customs and Excise 1966–71, investigation offr 1971–83, slr 1983–97, asst treasy slr 1997, gp ldr Personal Injury Gp, gp ldr Comercial Employment and Property Gp 2001; chm Neighbourhood Police Liaison, former vice-pres First Div Assoc of Civil Servants; hon fell Brunel Univ; memb Law Soc 1983; *Recreations* travel, cooking, bridge, music, theatre; *Clubs* RAC; *Style*— Barrie McKay, Esq; ✉ The Treasury Solicitor, Queen Anne's Chambers, 28 Broadway, London SW1H 9JS (tel 020 7210 3091, fax 020 7210 3066)

MACKAY, Charles Dorsey; s of Brig Kenneth Mackay, CBE, DSO (d 1974), and Evelyn Maud, *née* Ingram (d 1982); *b* 14 April 1940; *Educ* Cheltenham Coll, Queens' Coll Cambridge (MA), INSEAD (MBA); *m* 11 July 1964, Annmarie, da of Fritz Joder (d 1978); 2 s (Hugo b 1965 d 1981, Caspar b 1971), 1 da (Romola b 1966); *Career* The British Petroleum Co Ltd: commercial apprentice 1957–59, univ apprentice 1959–62, mktg asst 1962–63, sales supervisor Algeria 1963–65, commercial dir Burundi/Rwanda/Congo 1965–68, sponsored at INSEAD 1968–69; McKinsey & Co Inc London/Paris/Amsterdam/Dar es Salaam: conslt 1969–71, jr engagement mangr 1971–72, sr engagement mangr 1972–76; Pakhoed Holding NV Rotterdam: dir Paktrans Div 1976–77, chm 1977–81; Chloride Group plc: dir 1981–86, chm Chloride Overseas 1981–85, chm Chloride Power Electronics 1985–86; Inchcape plc: dir 1986–96, chm Inchcape (Hong Kong) Ltd 1986–87, chm and chief exec Inchcape Pacific Ltd (Hong Kong) 1987–91, gp chief exec 1991–96, dep chm 1995–96; non-exec chm: DSL Defence Systems Ltd 1996–97, TDG plc 2000–, Eurotunnel Gp 2001–2004 (non-exec dir 1997–2004, non-exec dep chm 1999–2001); non-exec dep chm Thistle Hotels plc 1996–2003; non-exec dir: Union Insurance Society of Canton Ltd (Hong Kong) 1986–91, The Hongkong and Shanghai Banking Corporation Ltd (Hong Kong) 1986–92, HSBC Holdings plc 1990–98, Midland Bank plc 1992–93, British Airways plc 1993–96, Johnson Matthey plc 1999–; memb Supervisory Bd Gucci Group NV 1997–2001; memb Bd INSEAD 2000–; second vice-chm Hong Kong Gen C of C 1989–91 (memb 1987–91); memb: Gen Ctee Br C of C in Hong Kong 1987–91, Cncl Hong Kong Trade Devpt Cncl 1989–91, Bd Hong Kong Community Chest 1990–91; *Recreations* travel, tennis, skiing, classical music, opera, chess; *Clubs* Hong Kong, Brooks', Piscatorial Soc; *Style*— Charles Mackay, Esq

MACKAY, His Hon Judge David Ian; *b* 11 November 1945; *Educ* Birkenhead Sch, Brasenose Coll Oxford; *m* 1974, Mary Elizabeth; 2 da (Emily Jane b 1980, Harriet Louise b 1984), 1 s (James Hugh b 1981); *Career* called to the Bar Inner Temple 1969, circuit judge 1992, Official Referee's Business 1993–98, provincial judge Technol and Construction Court 1998–; chm of govrs Birkenhead Sch 1991–2001, chm Birkenhead Sch Fndn Tst 1998–2004; fell Soc for Advanced Legal Studies 2002; *Recreations* history, transport, travelling in France; *Clubs* Athenaeum (Liverpool); *Style*— His Hon Judge Mackay; ✉ Queen Elizabeth II Law Courts, Derby Square, Liverpool L2 1XA (tel 0151 473 7373)

MacKAY, Prof Sir Donald Iain; kt (1996); s of William MacKay (d 1980), and Rhona, *née* Cooper; *b* 27 February 1937; *Educ* Dollar Acad, Univ of Aberdeen; *m* 31 July 1961, Diana Marjory, da of Maj George Raffan (d 1980); 2 da (Deborah Jane b 1964, Paula Clare b 1967), 1 s (Donald Gregor b 1969); *Career* prof of political economy Univ of Aberdeen 1971–76, professorial fell Heriot-Watt Univ 1982–91 (prof of econs 1976–81); chm: Pieda plc planning, economic and devpt conslts 1976–97, DTZ Pieda Consulting 1997–2002, Malcolm Gp plc 1998–2003, Scottish Mortgage Tst 2003–; dir Edinburgh Income and Value Tst 1999–; memb: Sea Fish Indust Authy 1981–87, S of Scot Electricity Bd 1985–88, Scot Econ Cncl 1985–; govr NIESR; FRSE 1987, FRSGS 1994; *Books* Geographical Mobility and the Brain Drain (1970), Local Labour Markets and Wage Structures (1970), Labour Markets Under Different Employment Conditions (1971), Men Leaving Steel (1971), The Political Economy of North Sea Oil (1975), British Employment Statistics (1977); *Recreations* tennis, golf, bridge, chess; *Style*— Prof Sir Donald MacKay, FRSE, FRSGS

MACKAY, Eileen Alison (Lady Russell); CB; da of Alexander William Mackay, OBE (d 1967), of Dingwall, Ross-shire, and Alison Jack, *née* Ross (d 1982); *b* 7 July 1943; *Educ* Dingwall Acad, Univ of Edinburgh (MA); *m* 19 Aug 1983, Sir Muir Russell, KCB, DL, FRSE, *qv*, s of Thomas Russell (d 1988), of Glasgow; *Career* res offr Dept of Employment 1965–72; princ: Scottish Office 1972–78, HM Treasy 1978–80; policy advsr Central Policy Review Staff Cabinet Office 1980–83; The Scottish Office: asst sec 1983–88, under sec Housing Gp Environment Dept 1988–92, chm Castlemilk Urban Partnership 1988–92, princ fin offr 1992–96; non-exec dir: Moray Firth Maltings plc 1988–99, Royal Bank of Scotland Group plc 1996–2005, Edinburgh Investment Trust 1996–2005, ESRC 1999–2003; chm Standing Advsy Ctee on Trunk Road Assessment 1996–99; memb: Margaret Blackwood Housing Assoc 1996–2001, David Hume Inst 1996– (chm 2002–), Scottish Screen 1997–99, Ct Univ of Edinburgh 1997–2003, Scottish Television (Regional) Ltd 1998–99, Cmmn on Local Govt and Scottish Parliament 1998–99, Accountancy Review Bd 2000–03, Carnegie Tst for the Univs of Scotland 2001–, British Library 2003–; FRSE; *Recreations* reading, gardening, holidays in France; *Clubs* New (Edinburgh), Royal Soc of Arts; *Style*— Miss Eileen Mackay, CB, FRSE; ✉ Principal's Lodging, University of Glasgow G12 8QG (tel 0141 330 5098)

MACKAY, Air Vice Marshal (Hector) Gavin; CB (2002), OBE (1987), AFC (1982); s of John Maclean Mackay (d 1988), and Isobel Margaret, *née* Mackay (d 1988); *b* 3 October 1947; *Educ* Dingwall Acad, Univ of Glasgow (BSc), RAF Coll Cranwell, RN Staff Coll Greenwich, RCDS; *m* 28 Aug 1971, Elizabeth Stark Bolton; 1 da (Aimi Elizabeth b 29 July 1973), 1 s (Graeme John b 26 Dec 1974); *Career* cmmnd RAF; instr Jet Provost RAF Linton-on-Ouse 1973–75, pilot (Hunter) 45/58 Sqdn, pilot (Harrier) 20 Sqdn RAF Wildenrath, served 3 (F) Sqdn RAF Gütersloh (promoted Sqdn Ldr), exec offr 1 (F) Sqdn RAF Wittering 1979–82, Harrier specialist Central Tactics and Trials Org, Wing Cdr 1984, Cdr Examining Wing Central Flying Sch RAF Scampton, served Concepts Studies and Operational Requirements MOD (promoted Gp Capt) 1987–90, Cdr RAF Gütersloh and RAF Germany Harrier Force 1991–93, dep dir Air Offensive MOD 1993–94, ACOS Ops NATO HQ Allied Air Forces Central Europe 1995–96, Cmdt Central Flying Sch Cranwell 1996–99, ldr Jt Force 2000 Implementation Team 1999–2000, AOC and Cmdt RAF Coll Cranwell 2000–02; sr mil advsr Def Export Servs Orgn (DESO) MOD 2003–; Hon Air Cdre 2503 (Co of Lincoln) Sqdn RAuxAF Regt 2005; GAPAN: Liveryman 2002, Master Air Pilot 1998; memb Gaelic Soc of Inverness; Freeman City of London 2002; FRAeS 1997; *Recreations* flying, golf, walking; *Clubs* RAF; *Style*— Air Vice Marshal Gavin Mackay, CB, OBE, AFC, FRAeS; ✉ Senior Military Advisor, Defence Export Services Organisation, Ministry of Defence, Room 3/16 St Georges Court, 2–12 Bloomsbury Way, London WC1A 2SH

MACKAY, (Ernest Arthur) Graham; s of James Gavin Mackay (d 1996), and Mary, *née* Batchelor; *b* 26 July 1949; *Educ* Univ of the Witwatersrand (BSc), Univ of SA (BCom); *m* 1, 9 Dec 1972; 3 s (Gavin b 16 Feb 1974, Bruce b 1 May 1978, Alistair b 18 April 1984); m 2, 5 Jan 2000, Beverley (Bev), *née* Sawyer; 3 s (Aedan b 6 June 2000, Oliver b 5 Sept 2001, Callum b 10 Dec 2004); *Career* SABMiller plc (formerly South African Breweries Ltd): joined as systems mangr 1978, various sr positions incl exec chm in SA, gp md 1997–99, chief exec 1999–; non-exec dir Reckitt Benckiser plc 2005–; tstee

M

Ashridge; *Recreations* squash, shooting, tennis, reading; *Clubs* Annabel's, Harry's Bar, George, Bath & Racquets, Red Rice Health & Fitness; *Style*— Mr Graham Mackay; ✉ SABMiller plc, One Stanhope Gate, London W1K 1AF (tel 020 7659 0101, fax 020 7659 0140)

McKAY, Hilary Jane; da of Ronald Damms, of Boston, Lincs, and Mary Edith, *née* Hampton; *b* 12 June 1959; *Educ* Boston Girls' HS, Univ of St Andrews (BSc); *m* 13 Aug 1982, Kevin Kerr McKay; 1 s (James Rufus (Jim) b 8 Jan 1993), 1 da (Isabella Claire b 21 Dec 1996); *Career* writer; *Books* The Exiles series (3, 1991–93, jt winner Guardian Children's Fiction Award 1992, overall winner Smarties Prize for Children's Literature), Dog Friday (1994), The Amber Cat (1995), The Zoo in the Attic (1995), Saffy's Angel (2002, winner Whitbread Children's Book Award), Indigo's Star (2003), Permanent Rose (2005, shortlisted Whitbread Children's Book of the Year 2005); *Recreations* reading, gardening; *Style*— Mrs Hilary McKay

MACKAY, (Douglas) Ian; QC (Scot 1993); s of Walter Douglas Mackay (d 1982), of Inverness, and Carla Marie Anna, *née* Fröhlich (d 1974); *b* 10 August 1948; *Educ* Inverness HS, Univ of Aberdeen (LLB); *m* Susan Anne, da of William Nicholson; 1 da (Julie Anne b 2 Aug 1970), 2 s (Garry Ian b 28 July 1973, Andrew William Nicholas b 20 Feb 1986); *Career* admitted Faculty of Advocates 1980, chm Advocates Personal Injury Law Gp; *Recreations* Scottish art and antiques, travel, shooting and gundogs, mountaineering; *Style*— Ian Mackay, Esq, QC; ✉ St Ann's House, Lasswade, Midlothian EH18 1ND (tel 0131 660 2634, fax 0131 654 1600, e-mail ian@mackayqc.com); Mount Pleasant Farm, by Fortrose, Ross-shire (tel 01381 620888); c/o Advocates' Library, Parliament House, Edinburgh EH1 1RF (tel 0131 226 5071)

MACKAY, Ian Stuart; s of Rev Gordon Ernest Mackay (d 1991), of Adelaide, Aust, and Sylvia Viola Dorothy, *née* Spencer (d 1975); *b* 16 June 1943; *Educ* Kearsney Coll Bothas Hill, Univ of London (MB BS); *m* 1, 11 May 1968 (m dis), Angela; 1 s (Angus b 1971), 1 da (Fiona b 1972); m 2, 4 Sept 1981, Madeleine Hargreaves, *née* Tull; 1 da (Antonia b 1982), 1 step da (Charlotte b 1971); *Career* conslt ENT surgn Charing Cross Hosp and Brompton Hosp, hon conslt King Edward VII Hospital for Officers, hon sr lectr in rhinology Inst of Laryngology and Otology, hon sr lectr Cardiothoracic Inst Univ of London; jt ed Rhinology Volume in Scott-Brown's Otolaryngology, contrib section on rhinoplasty to Smith's Operative Surgery; pres Br Assoc of Otolaryngologists 1999–2003, chm Fedn of Surgical Specialty Assocs 2001–03; memb RSM, FRCS; *Style*— Ian S Mackay, Esq; ✉ 55 Harley Street, London W1G 8QR (tel 020 7580 5070)

MACKAY, Dr James Alexander; s of William James Mackay (d 1981), and Minnie Somerville, *née* Matheson (d 1990); *b* 21 November 1936; *Educ* Hillhead HS Glasgow, Univ of Glasgow (MA, DLitt); *m* 1, 24 Sept 1960 (m dis 1972), Mary Patricia, *née* Jackson; 1 da (Fiona Elizabeth b 5 April 1963), 1 s (Alastair Andrew b 29 July 1967); m 2, 11 Dec 1992, Renate Friederike, *née* Finlay-Freundlich; *Career* Nat Serv Lt RA Guided Weapons Range Hebrides 1959–61; asst keeper i/c philatelic collections Dept of Printed Books British Museum 1961–71, full-time writer 1972–; philatelic columnist The New Daily 1962–67, columnist Collecting Wisely 1967–72, philatelic and numismatics columnist Financial Times 1972–85 (columnist 1967–72), ed-in-chief IPC Stamp Encyclopaedia 1968–72; ed: Burns Chronicle 1977–91, Postal History Annual 1978–90, Burnsian 1986–89, Coin and Medal Bulletin 1990–91, Antiques Today 1992–93, Coin Yearbook 1993–, Medal Yearbook 1994–, Stamp Yearbook 1996–, Banknote Yearbook 2001–; publisher of books on postal history 1976–90, contrib to over 100 periodicals worldwide on philately, numismatics and applied and decorative arts 1959–; tstee James Currie Meml Tst 1988–97, sec Burns-Gaelic Tst 1992–99; chm Advsy Bd International Burns Suppers Ltd 1992–; Spellman Fndn Silver-Gilt medal for philatelic lit 1982, 1986 and 1990, Thomas Field award for servs to Irish philately 1982; *Books* 200 incl: A Guide to the Uists (1961–67), Commonwealth Stamp Design (1965), Modern Coins (1969), Airmails 1870–1970 (1971), The World of Classic Stamps (1972), Turn of the Century Antiques (1974), Robert Bruce, King of Scots (1974), Rural Crafts in Scotland (1976), Encyclopaedia of World Stamps (1976), Dictionary of Western Sculptors in Bronze (1977), Stamp Collecting (1980), Numismatics (1982), The Burns Federation 1885–1985 (1985), The Complete Works of Robert Burns (ed, 1986, 2 edn 1991), The Complete Letters of Robert Burns (ed, 1987, 2 edn 1991), History of Dumfries (1990), Coin Collecting (1991), Making Money Made Simple (with Noel Whittaker, 1991), Burns (1992, Scottish Book of the Year 1993), Kilmarnock (1992), Coin Facts and Feats (1992), Vagabond of Verse: A Life of Robert W Service (1995), William Wallace: Brave Heart (1995), Allan Pinkerton: The Eye Who Never Slept (1996), Michael Collins (1996), Sounds out of Silence: A Life of Alexander Graham Bell (1997), Little Boss: A Life of Andrew Carnegie (1997), Under the Gum: Background to British Stamps 1840–1940 (1997, Rowland Hill Award and American Philatelic Soc gold medal 1998), The Man Who Invented Himself: A Life of Sir Thomas Lipton (1997), I Have Not Yet Begun to Fight: A Life of John Paul Jones (1998), In the End is my Beginning: a Life of Mary Queen of Scots (1999), Scottish History (1999), Fans (2000), Scotland's Posts (2001), Glasgow's Other River (2001), Clans and Tartans of Scotland (2001), Antiques at a Glance (2002), Soldering on St Kilda (2002), Tartans of Scotland and Ireland (2003), Collect British Coins (2004), Encyclopedia of Stamps (2006), St Kilda Steamers (2006), Encyclopedia of Coins (2007); *Recreations* travel, learning languages, playing the piano, photographing post offices; *Style*— Dr James Mackay; ✉ 67 Braidpark Drive, Giffnock, Glasgow G46 6LY (e-mail james.mackay2@ntlworld.com)

MACKAY, Kenneth Finlay; s of Alexander Mackay, and Moira, *née* Finlay; *b* 29 May 1959; *Educ* Ballyclare Secdy Sch and HS, Canterbury Coll of Art (BArch), RCA (MA); *Career* architect; architect Rick Mather Architects 1983, design/project architect Jeremy and Fenella Dixon Architects 1983–85, design team leader Jeremy Dixon/BPD 1985–87, dir Harper Mackay Ltd 1987–2003, dir MAK Architects Ltd 2003–04, sr ptnr Mackay & Ptnrs LLP 2004–; clients incl: Anglia Television, Br Cncl, Japan Airlines, Carlton Communications plc, London Tport, M&C Saatchi, Polygram UK, Sony Music Entertainment, Tonbridge Sch, Virgin Media Gp, Bee Bee Developments, BBC, British Petroleum, Channel 4, Deloitte Consulting, Groupe Chez Gerard, Hilton Hotels plc, Horizon Serono Geneva, Ian Schrager Hotels, M & C Saatchi, McCann Erickson, N M Rothschild & Sons Ltd, Prudential Portfolio Mangrs, Sony Music Entertainment UK Ltd, Valtech Ltd, Workspace Gp; work featured in exhbns incl: 40 under 40 (RIBA London) 1988, Art and Architecture of Gardens (RIBA Heinz Gall London) 1989, 12 Br Architects (Mackintosh Museum Sch of Art Glasgow) 1990, The Venice Biennale 1991, Summer Show (Royal Acad London) 1991, Wordsearch (MIPIM 98 Cannes) 1998, New Br Architecture (The Architecture Centre London) 1998; dir Workdesign Fndn NY; RIBA 1991, FCSD 1992; *Awards* incl: RIBA portfolio prize 1980, heritage award Clifton Nurseries 1985 and 1987, Design Week Awards 1991, 1994, 1997, 1998, and 1999, D&AD Awards 1994, Minerva Awards 1994 and 1995, Birmingham Design Initiative Awards 1994, Br Cncl for Office award 1998 and 1999, FX Awards 1999, Best Hotel Design (St Martin's Lane) FX Awards 2000, Best Medium Office (Valtech) FX Awards 2001; *Recreations* skiing, diving, eating; *Clubs* Groucho, Shoreditch House; *Style*— Kenneth Finlay, Esq

McKAY, Maura; da of Bernard Herron, and Tess, *née* Flynn; *b* 3 November 1962; *Educ* St Joseph's Convent GS Donaghmore Co Tyrone, Queen's Univ Belfast (LLB); *m* 31 Aug 1992, Trevor McKay; 2 da (Clare b 14 Oct 1993, Kiera b 9 April 1998); *Career* slr specialising in liquor licensing; slr then ptnr Shean Dickson Merrick 1986–; memb Law Soc of NI; *Recreations* traditional Irish dance and music; *Style*— Mrs Maura McKay; ✉ Shean Dickson Merrick, 14/16 High Street, Belfast BT1 2BS

McKAY, Dr Neil Stuart; CB (2001); s of Roy McKay (d 1989), and Alison Maud, *née* Dent; *b* 19 February 1952; *Educ* Dame Allan's Boys' Sch Newcastle upon Tyne; *m* 17 Aug 1978, Deirdre Mary, da of Patrick Francis McGinn; 2 s (Sean Francis b 6 Jan 1981, Joseph Anthony b 8 Oct 1983); *Career* clerical offr trainee Univ of Newcastle HMC 1970–72, asst hosp sec Dunston Hill Hosp Gateshead 1972–74, admin asst Gateshead AHA 1974–75, hosp admin Dryburn Hosp Durham 1975–76, commissioning offr St George's Hosp London 1978–80 (asst sector admin 1976–78), planning admin Wandsworth HA 1980–82, hosp admin Springfield Hosp London 1982–85, gen mangr Doncaster Royal Infirmary 1985–88, gen mangr Northern Gen Hosp Sheffield 1988–91, chief exec Northern Gen Hosp NHS Tst 1991–96, regnl dir Trent Regional Office NHS Exec 1996–2000, dep chief exec NHS Exec 2000, chief operating offr Dept of Health 2000–02, chief exec Leeds Teaching Hosps NHS Tst 2002–; DipHSM; Hon LLD Univ of Sheffield; *Recreations* family pursuits, reading, sport (including following Sunderland AFC); *Style*— Dr Neil McKay, CB; ✉ Leeds Teaching Hospitals NHS Trust, Trust Headquarters, St James University Hospital, Beckett Street, Leeds LS9 7TF (tel 0113 206 5835, fax 0113 206 7007, e-mail neil.mckay@leedsth.nhs.uk)

MACKAY, Prof Norman; CBE (1997); s of Donald Mackay (d 1937), of Glasgow, and Catherine, *née* Macleod (d 1957); *b* 15 September 1936; *Educ* Govan HS, Univ of Glasgow (MB ChB, MD); *m* 10 Feb 1961, (Grace) Violet, da of Charles McCaffer (d 1959), of Kilwinning; 2 da (Susan b 28 July 1962, Violet b 24 July 1964), 2 s (Ronald b 8 Sept 1967, Donald b 30 Dec 1970); *Career* hon conslt physician Victoria Infirmary Glasgow 1989–94 (conslt 1973–89), dean of postgrad med and prof of postgrad med educn Univ of Glasgow 1989–2001; Royal Coll of Physicians and Surgeons Glasgow: hon sec 1973–83, visitor 1992–94, pres 1994–97; hon sec Conf of Royal Med Colls and Faculties in Scotland 1982–91; pres Southern Med Soc 1989–90; memb GMC 1999–; Hon FACP, Hon FRACP, Hon FCPC, FRCP, FAMS, FRCPGlas, FRCPEd, FRCSEd, FRCGP, FCPSP, FCPS (Bangladesh), FRCS, FRCSI, FRCPI, FAMM; *Recreations* soccer, golf, gardening; *Style*— Prof Norman Mackay, CBE; ✉ 5 Edenhall Grove, Newton Mearns, Glasgow G77; Department of Postgraduate Medical Education, The University, Glasgow G12 8QQ (tel 0141 339 3786, fax 0141 330 4526)

MACKAY, Peter; CB (1993); s of John Swinton Mackay, FRCS (d 1993), of Kinnoir, Aberdeenshire, and Patricia May, *née* Atkinson (d 1976); *b* 6 July 1940; *Educ* Glasgow HS, Univ of St Andrews (MA); *m* 29 Aug 1964, Sarah White, da of Reginald White Holdich (d 1992), of Cherry Burton, E Yorks; 1 s (Andrew), 2 da (Elspeth, Sally); *Career* teacher Kyogle HS NSW 1962–63, asst princ Scottish Office 1963, princ private sec to Sec of State of Scotland Rt Hon Gordon Campbell, MC and Rt Hon William Ross, MBE 1973–75, Nuffield Travelling fell (Canada, Aust, NZ) 1978–79, seconded dir Scotland Manpower Servs Cmmn 1983–85; under sec: Dept of Employment 1985–86, Scottish Educn Dept 1987–89, ret as sec and chief exec Scottish Office Industry Dept 1995; exec dir Advanced Mgmnt Programme in Scotland 1995–97, non-exec dir British Linen Bank Group 1996–2000, dir Business Banking Div Bank of Scotland 1999–2001; chm: Pacific Horizon Investment Tst 2004– (dir 2001–04), Northern Lighthouse Bd 2005–07 (cmmr 1999–, vice-chm 2003–05); memb: Univ Ct Napier Univ Edinburgh 1995–2004, Competition Cmmn (formerly Monopolies and Mergers) 1996–2002, Main Bd Scottish Natural Heritage 1997–2003; tstee Scottish Forestry Alliance 1999–, vice-chm Scottish Rights of Way and Access Soc 2002–; Hon LLD Robert Gordon Univ 1996; *Recreations* high altitudes and latitudes, mountains, sea canoeing, sailing; *Clubs* Clyde Canoe, Scottish Arctic; *Style*— Peter Mackay, Esq, CB; ✉ 6 Henderland Road, Edinburgh EH12 6BB (tel and fax 0131 337 2830)

MacKAY, Prof Robert Sinclair; s of Donald Maccrimmon MacKay (d 1987), and Valerie, *née* Wood; *b* 4 July 1956; *Educ* Newcastle HS Newcastle-under-Lyme, Trinity Coll Cambridge (entrance and sr scholarships, Yeats Prize, Tyson Medal, MA), Plasma Physics Lab Princeton Univ (Fulbright Hayes Scholarship, PhD); *m* May 1992, Claude Noëlle, *née* Baesens; 1 s (Alexandre b 19 March 2002); *Career* research asst applied mathematics QMC 1982–83, prof invité Institut des Hautes Etudes Scientifiques France 1983–84; Univ of Warwick: successively lectr in mathematics, reader then prof 1984–95, dir of Mathematical Interdisciplinary Research 2000–; prof of nonlinear dynamics DAMTP Univ of Cambridge and fell Trinity Coll Cambridge 1995–2000; visiting prof Laboratoire de Topologie Univ de Bourgogne 1994–95; Nuffield Fndn Science Research fell 1992–93, Stephanos Pnevmatikos Int Award for research in nonlinear phenomena 1993, Junior Whitehead Prize London Mathematical Soc 1994; memb: London Mathematical Soc 1990, FRS 2000, FInstP 2000 (MInstP 1993), FIMA 2003; *Publications* Hamiltonian Dynamical Systems: a reprint selection (co-ed, 1987), Renormalisation in Area-preserving Maps (1993); and also author of over 100 learned papers in jls and 33 contribs to conf proceedings; *Style*— Prof Robert MacKay; ✉ Mathematics Institute, University of Warwick, Coventry CV4 7AL (tel 02476 522218, fax 02476 524182, e-mail r.s.mackay@warwick.ac.uk)

MACKAY, Shena; da of Benjamin Carr Mackey, and Morag, *née* Carmichael; *b* 6 June 1944; *Educ* Tonbridge Girls' GS, Kidbrooke Comp; *m* 1964 (m dis), Robin Francis Brown; 3 da (Sarah Frances b 11 March 1965, Rebecca Mary b 21 Aug 1966, Cecily Rose b 15 May 1969); *Career* author; awarded: Arts Cncl grants 1970s, travelling scholarship Soc of Authors 1986, Fawcett Prize 1987, Scottish Arts Cncl Book award 1992 and 1994; judge: The Whitbread Prize 1998, The Macmillan Silver Pen for Fiction 1999, The Booker Prize 1999, The Macallan/Scotland on Sunday Short Story Competition 1999, John Llewellyn Rhys Prize; visiting prof Dept of English Middlesex Univ 2001–03; memb: PEN, London Arts Bd 1993–97, Soc of Authors, ALCS; FRSL 1999; *Books* Dust Falls on Eugene Schlumburger (1964), Toddler on the Run (1964), Music Upstairs (1965), Old Crow (1967), An Advent Calendar (1971), Babies in Rhinestones (1983), A Bowl of Cherries (1984), Redhill Rococo (1986), Dreams of Dead Women's Handbags (1987), Dunedin (1992), The Laughing Academy (1993), Such Devoted Sisters (ed, 1993), Collected Stories (1994), The Orchard on Fire (1996, shortlisted for Booker Prize), Friendship (ed, 1997), The Artist's Widow (1998), The Worlds Smallest Unicorn (1999), Heligoland (2003, shortlisted for Orange Prize and Whitbread Prize); *Style*— Ms Shena Mackay, FRSL; ✉ Rogers Coleridge & White Ltd, 20 Powis Mews, London W11 1JN (tel 020 7221 3717, 020 7229 9084)

McKAY, Sir William Robert; KCB (2001, CB 1996); s of William Wallace McKay (d 1986), of Newhaven on Forth, and Margaret Halley Adamson, *née* Foster (d 2003); *b* 18 April 1939; *Educ* Trinity Acad Leith, Univ of Edinburgh (MA); *m* 28 Dec 1962, Rev Margaret Muriel McKay, da of Eric Millard Bellwood Fillmore, OBE (d 1994); 2 da (Catriona Margaret, Elspeth Mary (Mrs David Smith)(twins) b 4 March 1967); *Career* Dept of the Clerk of the House of Commons 1961–2002, clerk Scot Affrs Ctee 1979–81, sec House of Commons Cmmn 1981–84, princ clerk Fin Ctees 1985–87, sec Public Accounts Cmmn 1985–87; jt clerk Br-Irish Inter-Parly Body 1989–94, clerk of the Jls 1987–91, clerk of Public Bills 1991–94, clerk asst 1994–97, clerk of the House 1998–2002; observer Cncl Law Soc of Scotland 2006–; interim clerk designate Scot Assembly 1978; hon prof Sch of Law Univ of Aberdeen 2003–07; *Books* Erskine May's Private Journal 1883–86 (ed, 1984), Mr Speaker's Secretaries (1986), Clerks in the House of Commons 1363–1989 a Biographical List (1989, revised edn 2002), Observations, Rules and Orders (ed, 1989), Erskine May's Parliamentary Practice (jt ed, 1997; ed, 2004), Halsbury's Laws of England (contrib, 4 edn 1997), A United Parish (with M M McKay, 2001), Stair Memorial

Encyclopaedia of the Laws of Scotland (contrib, 2002); author of articles in historical and parly jls, contrib Oxford DNB; *Recreations* historical research; *Style*— Sir William McKay, KCB; ✉ The Smithy, Knowes of Elrick, Aberchirder, Huntly, Aberdeenshire AB54 7PN

MACKAY-DICK, Maj Gen Sir Iain; KCVO, MBE; *Educ* Sherborne, RMA Sandhurst; *m* 1971, Carolynn; 3 da (Alexandra b 1972, Georgina b 1975, Olivia b 1979); *Career* cmmnd Scots Gds 1965, served as Platoon Cdr 1 Bn Scots Gds Borneo, platoon instr Gds Depot Pirbright 1967–69, Mortar Platoon Cdr 2 Bn Münster 1969–70, served Windsor and N Ireland 1970–71, Jr Div Staff Coll 1971, Adj 1 Bn 1971 (served Windsor, N Ireland and Germany), Co Cdr 2 Bn until 1974 (served Pirbright and N Ireland), Adj New Coll Sandhurst 1974–76, Army Staff Coll course 1976–78, Co Cdr 2 Bn Scots Gds Münster 1978–79, Bde Maj (COS) 3 Infantry Bde 1979–81, 2 i/c 2 Bn Scots Gds 1981–82 (served Falklands War), memb Directing Staff Army Staff Coll 1982–84, CO 2 Bn 1984–86 (served Cyprus), Cmdt Jr Div Staff Coll 1986–88, Higher Cmd and Staff Course Staff Coll 1989, Cdr 11 Armd Bde Minden 1989–91, Dep Mil Sec (A) MOD London 1991–92, GOC 1 Armd Div Germany 1992–93, Cdr Br Forces Falkland Is 1993–94, GOC London Dist and Maj Gen cmdg Household Div 1994–97; clerk to the tstees and chief exec Morden Coll 1997–; Hon Col 256 City of London Field Hosp RAMC (v) 2000–07; tstee Falkland Islands Meml Chapel Pangbourne 2005; Freeman City of London 2000; MRUSI 1979–2006, FCMI (FIMgt); *Recreations* military history, walking, all forms of sport (Army squash champion 1971); *Clubs* Edinburgh Angus, Jesters, Guards Golfing Soc, Army Golfing Soc, Public Schools Old Boys LTA, Sherborne Pilgrims; *Style*— Maj Gen Sir Iain Mackay-Dick, KCVO, MBE; ✉ Morden College, 19 St Germans Place, Blackheath, London SE3 0PW (tel 020 8858 3365, fax 020 8293 4887)

MACKAY OF CLASHFERN, Baron (Life Peer UK 1979), of Eddracchillis in the District of Sutherland; James Peter Hymers Mackay; KT (1997), PC (1979); s of James Mackay (d 1958); *b* 2 July 1927; *Educ* George Heriot's Sch Edinburgh, Univ of Edinburgh, Trinity Coll Cambridge; *m* 1958, Elizabeth Gunn Hymers, da of D D Manson; 1 s (Hon James b 1958), 2 da (Hon Elizabeth Janet (Hon Mrs Campbell) b 1961, Hon Shona Ruth b 1968); *Career* advocate 1955, QC Scot 1965; sheriff principal Renfrew and Argyll 1972–74, dean Faculty of Advocates 1976–79 (vice-dean 1973–76); cmmr Northern Lighthouses 1975–84, pt/t memb Scottish Law Cmmn 1976–79, dir Stenhouse Holdings Ltd 1976–77, memb Insurance Brokers' Registration Cncl 1977–79; Lord Advocate of Scotland 1979–84, Lord of Session 1984–85, Lord of Appeal in Ordinary 1985–87, Lord Chllr 1987–97, Lord High Cmmr 2005–06, Lord Clerk Register 2007–; Elder Bros Trinity House 1990; chllr Heriot-Watt Univ 1991–2005; Hon LLD: Univ of Dundee 1983, Univ of Edinburgh 1983, Univ of Strathclyde 1985, Univ of Aberdeen 1987, Univ of St Andrews 1988, Univ of Cambridge 1989, Coll of William and Mary 1989, Univ of Birmingham 1990, Nat Law Sch of India 1994, Univ of Bath 1994, Univ of Glasgow 1999, De Montfort Univ 1999, Robert Gordon Univ 2000; Hon DCL: Univ of Newcastle upon Tyne 1990, Univ of Birmingham 1990, Univ of Leicester 1996, Univ of Oxford 1998; hon fell: Trinity Coll Cambridge 1979, Girton Coll Cambridge 1989, American Coll of Trial Lawyers 1990; Hon Freeman Worshipful Co of Woolmen; fell Int Acad of Trial Lawyers 1979, Hon FTII 1983, FRSE 1984, Hon FICE 1989, Hon FRCSEd 1989, Hon FRCPEd 1990, Hon FRCOG 1996; *Clubs* New (Edinburgh), Athenaeum, Caledonian; *Style*— The Rt Hon the Lord Mackay of Clashfern, KT, PC; ✉ House of Lords, London SW1A 0PW

MACKAY OF DRUMADOON, Baron (Life Peer UK 1995), of Blackwaterfoot in the District of Cunninghame; Donald Sage Mackay; PC (1996), QC (Scot 1987); s of Rev Donald George Mackintosh Mackay (d 1991), of Edinburgh, and Jean Margaret, *née* McCaskie, of Edinburgh (d 1994); *b* 30 January 1946; *Educ* George Watson's Boys Coll Edinburgh, Univ of Edinburgh (LLB, LLM), Univ of Virginia (LLM); *m* 5 April 1979, Lesley Ann, da of late Edward Waugh; 2 da (Hon Caroline b 7 Sept 1980, Hon Diana b 19 Aug 1982), 1 s (Hon Simon b 20 Jan 1984); *Career* apprentice slr Davidson & Syme CS Edinburgh 1969–71, slr Allan McDougall & Co SSC Edinburgh 1971–76, called to the Scottish Bar 1976, advocate depute 1982–85, memb Criminal Injuries Compensation Bd 1989–95, Slr Gen for Scotland 1995, Lord Advocate for Scotland 1995–97, oppn spokesman on constitutional affrs House of Lords 1997–2000, Senator Coll of Justice in Scotland 2000–; *Recreations* golf, Isle of Arran; *Clubs* Western (Glasgow); *Style*— The Rt Hon Lord Mackay of Drumadoon, PC, QC; ✉ 39 Hermitage Gardens, Edinburgh EH10 6AZ (tel 0131 447 1412); Parliament House, Edinburgh EH1 1RQ (tel 0131 225 2595, fax 0131 225 8213)

McKEAN, Prof Charles Alexander; s of John Laurie McKean, of Glasgow, and Nancy Burns, *née* Lendrum; *b* 16 July 1946; *Educ* Fettes, Univ of Bristol (BA); *m* 18 Oct 1975, Margaret Elizabeth, da of Mervyn Yeo, of Cardiff; 2 s (Andrew Laurie b 1978, David Alexander b 1981); *Career* ed London Architect 1970–75; architectural corr: The Times 1977–83, Scotland on Sunday 1988–90; RIBA: London regnl sec 1968–71, Eastern regnl sec 1971–79, projects offr Community Architecture and Industrial Regeneration 1977–79; sec and treas RIAS 1979–94; Duncan of Jordanstone Coll Univ of Dundee: prof of architecture 1994–97, head of sch 1994–97, prof of Scottish architectural history 1997– (Dept of History); dir Workshops and Artists Studios Ltd 1980–85; memb Exhibitions Panel Scottish Arts Cncl 1980–83, memb Advsy Cncl for the Arts in Scotland 1985–88, memb Cncl Architectural Heritage Soc of Scotland 1987–96, memb Cncl Historic Environment Advsy Cncl for Scotland 2003–07, memb Scottish Ctee Heritage Lottery Fund 2003, convenor Buildings Ctee Nat Tst for Scotland; sec to the RIAS Hill House Tst 1979–82, memb Environment and Town Planning Ctee The Saltire Soc 1984–85; chm Edinburgh World Heritage Tst 2006–; tstee: Thirlestane Castle Tst 1983–93, Dundee City Arts Centre Tst 1995–97, St Vincent Street Church Tst 1996–99; former vice-chm Charles Rennie Mackintosh Soc, former memb Advsy Ctee Edinburgh Common Purpose; Architectural Journalist of the Year 1979 and 1983, RIBA Gordon Ricketts Award 1980, Building Journalist of the Year 1983, RSA Bossom Lecture 1986, RIAS Thomas Ross Award 1993, Nigel Tranter Award 2004; hon memb The Saltire Soc 1990, hon pres St Andrews Preservation Tst 2005; Hon DLitt RGU 1994; FRSA 1978, FSA Scot 1983, Hon FRIBA 1990, Hon FRSGS 1992, Hon FRIAS 1994, FRSE 1999; *Books* London 1981 (1970), Modern Buildings in London 1965–75 (with Tom Jestico, 1975), Living over the Shop (1976), Battle of Styles (with David Atwell, 1976), Funding the Future (1977), Fight Blight (1977), An Outine of Western Architecture (jtly, 1980), Architectural Guide to Cambridge and East Anglia since 1920 (1980), Edinburgh - an Illustrated Architectural Guide (1982), Dundee - an Illustrated Introduction (with David Walker, 1984), Stirling and the Trossachs (1985), The Scottish Thirties (1987), The District of Moray (1987), Central Glasgow (with Prof David Walker and Prof Frank Walker), Banff and Buchan (1990), For a Wee Country (1990), Edinburgh - Portrait of a City (1991), Dundee (with Prof D Walker, 1993), West Lothian (with Richard Jacques, 1994), Value or Cost (1993), Claim (1998), The Making of the Museum of Scotland (2000), The Scottish Château (2001), Battle for the North (2006); *Clubs* Scottish Arts; *Style*— Prof Charles McKean; ✉ 10 Hillpark Road, Edinburgh EH4 7AW (tel 0131 336 2753); University of Dundee, Perth Road, Dundee DD1 4HN (tel 01382 345738, e-mail c.a.mckean@dundee.ac.uk)

McKEAN, Lorne; da of Lt Cdr J A H McKean, RN (d 1981), and Beatrice Blanche Mowbray *née* Bellairs (d 1991); *b* 16 April 1939; *Educ* Elmhurst Ballet Sch, Guildford Art Sch, Royal Acad Schs; *m* 7 Nov 1964, Edwin John Cumming Russell, s of Edwin Russell; 2 da (Rebecca b 21 Jan 1966, Tanya b 25 April 1968); *Career* sculptor; public and large works include: A A Milne memorial London Zoo Bear Club, Arctic Terns Chester Zoo, Girl and the Swan Reading, 10' Horsham Heritage Sundial, Osprey Fountain Greenwich Connecticut USA, Great Swan Great Swan Alley EC2, Swan Fountain Horsham, Flight (27ft bronze) Norwich Union Leeds; equestrian and horse sculptures: HRH Prince Philip on his polo pony, HM The Queen's personal Silver Wedding gift to her husband, HRH The Prince of Wales on polo pony Pans Folly, John Pinches International Dressage Trophy, Galoubet French show jumping stallion, pony series for Royal Worcester Porcelain, racehorses Troy and Snurge; portraits include: the late Lord Salisbury (Hatfield House), Sir Michael Redgrave, HRH the late Prince William of Gloucester, the Earl of Lichfield televised for portrait series, HM The Queen, Drapers' Hall and RHHT; FRBS 1968; *Recreations* animals; *Style*— Miss Lorne McKean; ✉ Lethendry, Polecat Valley, Hindhead, Surrey GU26 6BE (tel 01428 605655)

McKEAN, Roderick Hugh Ross (Roddy); *b* 13 March 1956; *Educ* The HS of Dundee, Univ of Edinburgh (LLB); *Career* articled clerk Burness, WS 1978–80; admitted slr 1980; asst slr: Maclay Murray and Spens 1980–83, Lovell White & King 1984–88; ptnr Lovells 1988– (managing ptnr Asia 1996–2001); memb: Law soc, Law Soc of Scotland, Law Soc of Hong Kong; *Recreations* skiing, tennis, yachting, riding, golf; *Clubs* Royal London Yacht, Royal Corinthian Yacht, Royal Hong Kong Yacht, Woking Golf; *Style*— Roddy McKean, Esq; ✉ Lovells, Atlantic House, 50 Holborn Viaduct, London EC1A 2FG (tel 020 7296 2000, fax 020 7296 2001)

MacKEAN, His Hon Thomas Neill; *b* 4 March 1934; *Educ* Sherborne, Trinity Hall Cambridge (BA); *m* 20 Oct 1962, Muriel Sutton, da of late Rev Gwynne Hodder; 4 da; *Career* articled to Messrs White & Leonard Slrs London 1954–57, ptnr Hepherd Winstanley & Pugh Slrs Southampton 1960–93 (sr ptnr 1988–93), recorder 1990–93, HM coroner Southampton & New Forest 1990–93, circuit judge (Western Circuit) 1993–2004 (dep circuit judge 2004–06); *Style*— His Hon Thomas MacKean

McKECHIN, Ann; MP; da of late William J McKechin, of Paisley, and Anne, *née* Coyle; *b* 22 April 1961; *Educ* Sacred Heart HS Paisley, Paisley GS, Univ of Strathclyde (LLB); *Career* slr; Kelvin Lab Pty: constituency sec Glasgow 1995–98, women's offr Glasgow 2000–01; MP (Lab): Glasgow Maryhill 2001–05, Glasgow North 2005–; vice-chair PLP Int Devpt Ctee; memb Cncl World Devpt Movement 1998–2004, dir Mercy Corps Scot 2002–; memb Law Soc of Scot; *Recreations* dancing, films, art history; *Style*— Ms Ann McKechin, MP; ✉ House of Commons, London SW1A 0AA (tel 020 7219 8239, e-mail mckechina@parliament.uk); Constituency Office, 154 Raeberry Street, Glasgow G20 6EA (tel 0141 946 1300, fax 0141 946 1412, website www.annmckechinmp.net)

MACKECHNIE, John Allan; s of Allan Mackechnie (d 1986), and Christina Johan, *née* Mackenzie (d 1985); *b* 19 August 1949; *Educ* Hyndland Sr Secdy Sch, Glasgow Sch of Art (DA), Faculty of Art & Design Brighton Poly; *m* 28 June 1975, Susan Shirley, da of William Ian Burnett; 1 da (Kirsty Joanne Louise b 25 Feb 1978); *Career* printmaker; printmaking asst: Faculty of Art & Design Brighton Poly 1972–73, Faculty of Art & Design Newcastle Poly 1973–76; Glasgow Print Studio: etching technician 1978–79, workshop mangr 1980–82, dir 1983–; visiting lectr to art colls throughout UK; memb Soc of Scottish Artists 1984– (memb Ctee 1989), memb Advsy Bd Bradford Int Print Biennale 1990–91, memb Steering Ctee Glasgow Art Fair, memb Ctee Glasgow Visual Art Forum 1995–96, memb Jury World Print Festival 1998; advsr on printmaking to Northern Regn 1983–93, major contrib to Glasgow's year as 1990 European City of Culture through exhbns and artists exchanges and projects; organiser exhibitions: Slovenia 1997–98, India 1998; *Exhibitions* incl: Young Generation (Norrkoping Museum Sweden) 1974, Epinal Biennale France 1975, Bradford Int Print Biennale 1976, 30 Contemporary Printmakers (Arnolfini Gall Bristol) 1976, World Print Competition (MOMA San Francisco) 1977, Impressions (Scottish Arts Cncl tour) 1978, Scottish Print Open (touring UK and Aust) 1980, solo exhbn Third Eye Centre Glasgow 1981, solo exhbn Richard Demarco Gall Edinburgh 1981, Northern Printmakers (Gall F15 Norway) 1982, Ljubljana Print Biennale Slovenia 1983, New Scottish Prints (touring Scotland, USA and Canada) 1983, Photography in Printmaking Glasgow Print Studio 1983, solo exhbn Edinburgh Printmakers Workshop 1983, Scottish Prints Open tour 1984, Society of Scottish Artists 1984 and 1985, The Clyde Exhibition Glasgow Print Exhbn 1986, Urban Myth solo exhbn (Glasgow Print Studio) 1999, solo exhbn Eye 2 Gall Edinburgh 2000, solo exhbn RIAS Gall Edinburgh 2000, Expressions in Dundee Contemporary Art 2000, solo exhbn Rebecca Hossack Gallery London 2001; *Awards* Glasgow Educnl Tst award 1971, Northern Arts major award 1976 and 1978, Scottish Arts Cncl travel award 1982, Arts Cncl Incentive Funding award for Glasgow Print Studio 1989; *Public Collections* incl: Scottish Arts Cncl, Hunterian Museum & Art Gall, MOMA San Francisco, Norrkoping Museum Sweden, Aberdeen Art Gall, Br Cncl, V&A, Kelvingrove Museum and Art Gall; *Recreations* the visual arts, golf; *Style*— John Mackechnie, Esq; ✉ Glasgow Print Studio, 22 King Street, Glasgow G1 5QP (tel 0141 552 0704, fax 0141 552 2919, e-mail john@mackechnie.demon.co.uk

McKEE, Dr Angus Hugh; s of William Bissett McKee, of Glasgow, and Alice, *née* Ingram (d 1995); *b* 12 February 1946; *Educ* Buckhaven HS, Univ of Edinburgh (BSc, MB ChB); *m* 18 Oct 1980, Ruth Fraser, da of Alec McBain (d 1978), of Douglas, Lanarkshire; *Career* sr registrar in anaesthetics (former sr house offr, registrar) W Infirmary Glasgow 1972–77, conslt anaesthetist Stobhill Hosp Glasgow 1977–; Sunday sch teacher W Glasgow New Church; FRCA 1974; *Recreations* hill walking, preaching; *Style*— Dr Angus McKee; ✉ 526 Anniesland Road, Glasgow G13 1YA (tel 0141 954 1992); Stobhill General Hospital, Balornock Road, Glasgow (tel 0141 201 3000)

McKEE, Prof (James Clark St Clair) Sean; s of James Roy Alexander McKee (d 1996), and Martha (Mattie) Beattie, *née* Chalmer; *b* 1 July 1945; *Educ* George Watson's Coll Edinburgh, Univ of St Andrews (class medal, Duncan medal, BSc), Univ of Dundee (PhD), Univ of Oxford (MA, DSc); *m* 2, 1996, Joyce Elizabeth, *née* Houston; *Career* National Cash Register fell Univ of Dundee 1970–72, lectr in numerical analysis Univ of Southampton 1972–75; Univ of Oxford: CEGB sr res fell 1975–79, co-ordinator univ consortium for industrial numerical analysis 1979–86; head of mathematics and statistics Unilever Research Colworth and prof of industrial mathematics Univ of Strathclyde 1986–88, prof of mathematics Univ of Strathclyde 1988–; fell Hertford Coll Oxford 1975–86; ed: Mathematical Engrg in Industry, Applied Mathematics and Computation, Applied Mathematical Modelling, Fasciculi Mathematici; Inst of Mathematics and its Application (IMA): fell, memb Cncl 1996–99, chm Scottish Branch 1997–99; fndr memb and memb Cncl Euro Consortium for Mathematics in Industry (ECMI), fndr memb Inst for Contemporary Scotland (fndr memb and memb Sci and Technol Cmmn); memb: US Soc for Industrial and Applied Mathematics, Edinburgh Mathematical Soc, Sociedade Brasilieira de Matemática Applicada e Computacional, American Mathematical Soc; homenagem Univ of Saŏ Paulo 2003; FRSE 1996; *Books* Industrial Numerical Analysis (1986), Vector and Parallel Computing (1989), Artificial Intelligence in Mathematics (1990); also author proceedings the Third European Conference on Mathematics in Industry (1990); *Recreations* golf, gardening, hill walking, squash; *Clubs* Bonnyton Golf; *Style*— Prof Sean McKee, FRSE; ✉ Department of Mathematics, University of Strathclyde, Glasgow G1 1XH (tel 0141 548 3671, fax 0141 551 8657)

McKEE, William Stewart; CBE (2006); *Educ* Bangor GS, Queen's Univ Belfast (BSc), Ulster Poly (Dip Mgmnt Studies, MBA); *m* Ursula Catherine; 1 da (Catherine b 1 April 1987), 1 s (William b 27 June 1990); *Career* VSO teacher W Africa 1970–71, student Queen's Univ Belfast 1971–75, summer vacational student Conservation Branch NI Dept of the Environment 1973, 1974, 1975 and 1976, clerical offr Belfast City Cncl 1975–76, nat admin trainee NI Staffs Cncl for the Health and Social Servs 1976–78, sr admin offr Lisburn Health Centre and Dist Offices Eastern Health & Social Servs Bd 1978–79, units admin

M

Daisy Hill Hosp Southern Health & Social Servs Bd 1979–82; Eastern Health & Social Servs Bd: units admin Ulster Hosp 1982–84, gp admin Musgrave Park Hosp 1984–88, gp admin Royal Gp of Hosps 1988–90, unit gen mangr Royal Gp of Hosps 1990–92, chief exec Royal Gp of Hosps and Dental Hosp NHS Tst 1992–; pres Inst of Healthcare Mgmnt; dir Belfast City Partnership Bd, dir NI Centre for Competitiveness; *Style*— William S McKee, Esq, CBE; ✉ Royal Group of Hospitals Trust, Royal Victoria Hospital, Grosvenor Road, Belfast BT12 6BA (tel 028 9089 4755, fax 028 9024 0899)

McKELL, Iain Spiers; s of Joseph Duncan McKell, and Gwendoline Helen McKell; *b* 18 April 1957; *Educ* Clifton, Exeter Coll of Art and Design (SIAD Dip); *Career* fashion, advertising and editorial photographer since 1981, commercials director since 1993; subsequent experience in record sleeve photography 1982; fashion and portrait cmmns for Italian and English Vogue (Most Promising Newcomer 1982), ID and The Face, portrait cmmns for The Sunday Times and Observer magazines; memb: AFAEP, NUJ; subjects incl Madonna (her first magazine cover), Gilbert & George, Bob Hoskins, Sinead O'Connor, Boy George, Jilly Cooper, Tom Sharp, Jeremy Irons, Sir John Gielgud, Brad Pitt and Robert Carlyle; photographic advtg campaigns incl: Red Stripe 1986, Holsten Export 1988, Vladivar Vodka and Corona 1990, Levis (UK and Europe) 1991, Philip Morris (Germany) and Dunhill 1992; direction of Post Modern links for MTV (USA, UK and Europe) 1990; *Solo and Group Exhibitions* incl: Skinheads (Camera Obscura, Germany) 1981, Iain McKell Live (Open Day Studio Show) 1984, Iain McKell Live and Five Years of The Face (Photographers' Gallery) 1985, Fashion and Surrealism (V&A Museum) 1987, Creative Future Awards (cmmnd by Direction magazine) 1988 and 2000, BA sponsored exhbn (touring NY, Chicago, Los Angeles, Hong Kong, Tokyo and Sydney) 1989, Magnificent Seven 1992, Then & Now (Gallery Story London) 2001; *Awards* Bronze Arrow Award by BTAA and Clio USA-Europe for Fisherman's Friend commercial, BTAC Award for Sony Playstation commercial 1998; *Recreations* skiing, photography, drawing, writing; *Clubs* Soho House; *Style*— Iain McKell, Esq; ✉ tel 020 8968 8668

McKELLEN, Sir Ian Murray; kt (1991), CBE (1979); s of Denis Murray McKellen (d 1964), of Bolton, Lancs, and Margery Lois, *née* Sutcliffe (d 1952); *b* 25 May 1939; *Educ* Wigan GS, Bolton Sch, St Catharine's Coll Cambridge (BA); *Career* actor and director since 1961; dir: Liverpool Playhouse 1969, Watford and Leicester 1972, A Private Matter (Vaudeville) 1973, The Clandestine Marriage (Savoy) 1975; assoc dir RNT; pres Marlowe Soc 1960–61, memb Cncl Equity 1971–72, Cameron Mackintosh prof of contemporary theatre Univ of Oxford 1991; Walpole Medal of Excellence 2003; Hon DLitt: Univ of Nottingham 1989, Univ of Aberdeen 1993; hon fell St Catharine's Coll Cambridge 1982; *Theatre* first stage appearance A Man for all Seasons (Belgrade Theatre Coventry) 1961, Arts Theatre Ipswich 1962–63, Nottingham Playhouse 1963–64, first London stage appearance A Scent of Flowers (Duke of York's) 1964 (Clarence Derwent Award); RNT incl: Much Ado About Nothing (also Old Vic) 1965, Venice Preserv'd 1984, Coriolanus 1984–85 (London Standard Award), Wild Honey (also Los Angeles & NY) 1986–87 (Olivier Award, Plays and Players Award), Kent in King Lear and title role in Richard III 1990 (Olivier Award (assoc prodr for world tour 1990–91)), Napoli Milionaria 1991, Uncle Vanya 1992, Richard III (also USA tour) 1992, An Enemy of the People 1997, Peter Pan 1997; RNT as assoc dir, prodr and performer: The Duchess of Malfi 1985, The Real Inspector Hound 1985, The Cherry Orchard (also Paris and Chicago) 1985, Bent (also Garrick) 1990; RSC incl: Dr Faustus (Edinburgh Festival and Aldwych) 1974, Marquis of Keith (Aldwych) 1974–75, King John (Aldwych) 1975, Too True to be Good (Aldwych and Globe) 1975, Romeo and Juliet 1976, The Winter's Tale 1976, Macbeth 1976–77 (Plays and Players Award 1976), Pillars of the Community 1977 (SWET Award), Days of the Commune 1977, The Alchemist 1978 (SWET Award), Iago in Othello (The Other Place, Stratford and Young Vic) 1989 (Evening Standard and London Critics' Award); prodr RSC tour 1978: Three Sisters, Twelfth Night, Is There Honey Still for Tea; Actors Company (fndr memb): Ruling The Roost 1972, 'Tis Pity She's a Whore (Edinburgh Festival) 1972, Wood-Demon (Edinburgh Festival) 1973, King Lear (Brooklyn Acad of Music, Wimbledon Theatre season) 1974; Acting Shakespeare 1977–90, tours incl: Israel, Norway, Denmark, Sweden, Spain, NYC (Drama Desk Award), San Francisco, Washington DC, Los Angeles, Olney, Cleveland, San Diego, Boston (Elliot Norton Award), Playhouse London; other roles incl: A Lily in Little India (St Martin's) 1965, Man of Destiny/O'Flaherty VC (Mermaid) 1966, Their Very Own and Golden City (Royal Court) 1966, The Promise (Fortune, also Broadway) 1967, The White Liars/Black Comedy (Lyric) 1968, Richard II (Prospect Theatre Co) 1968, The Recruiting Officer 1970, Chips with Everything (Cambridge Theatre Co) 1970, Hamlet (Cambridge, UK and Euro tours) 1971, Ashes (Young Vic) 1975, Words, Words, Words (solo recital, Edinburgh and Belfast Festivals) 1976, Acting Shakespeare (Edinburgh and Belfast Festivals) 1977, Bent (Royal Court, Criterion) 1979 (SWET Award), Amadeus (Broadhurst) 1980–81 (Drama Desk, NY Drama League, Outer Critics' Circle and Tony Awards), Short List (Hampstead) 1983, Cowardice (Ambassadors) 1983, Henceforward (Vaudeville) 1988, A Knight Out (Lyceum Theatre, NYC, South Africa and UK tour, Vancouver) 1994–2002, Orpheus Descending (Broadway) 2001, Aladdin (Old Vic) 2004 and 2005; for West Yorkshire Playhouse: The Seagull 1998, Present Laughter 1999, The Tempest 1999; *Television* since 1966 incl: Loving Walter 1982 (RTS Performance Award), Walter and June 1983, Countdown to War 1989, And the Band Played On 1993 (Emmy nomination), Cold Comfort Farm 1994; appearences in: The Simpsons 2003, Coronation Street 2005; *Film* since 1968 incl: A Touch of Love 1968, Alfred the Great 1968, The Promise 1969, Priest of Love 1979, Scarlet Pimpernel 1982, Zina 1985, Plenty 1986, The Ballad of Little Jo 1992, I'll Do Anything 1992, Last Action Hero 1993, Six Degrees of Separation 1993, The Shadow 1993, Jack and Sarah 1994, Restoration 1995, Richard III 1996 (Evening Standard Best Film Award), Rasputin 1996 (Emmy nomination, Golden Globe Award for Best Supporting Actor), Bent 1997, Swept From the Sea 1997, Apt Pupil 1998, Gods and Monsters 1998 (Oscar nomination for Best Actor), X-Men 2000, The Lord of the Rings: The Fellowship of the Ring 2001 (Oscar nomination for Best Supporting Actor), The Lord of the Rings: The Two Towers 2002, The Lord of the Rings: The Return of the King 2003, X2 2003, Emile 2004, Asylum 2005, Neverwas 2005; *Style*— Sir Ian McKellen, CBE; ✉ c/o ICM Ltd, Oxford House, 76 Oxford Street, London W1N 0AX (tel 020 7636 6565, fax 020 7323 0101); c/o ICM, 8942 Wilshire Boulevard, Beverly Hills, CA 90211–1934, USA (tel 001 310 550 4000, fax 001 310 550 4100, website: www.mckellen.com)

McKENDRICK, Emma Elizabeth Ann; da of Ian Cameron Black, and (Patricia) Ann Black; *Educ* Bedford HS, Univ of Liverpool (BA), Univ of Birmingham (PGCE); *m* 19 Dec 1987, Iain Alastair McKendrick; 2 s (Fergus b 2002, Hamish b 2004); *Career* Royal Sch Bath: teacher of German 1986–88, head of sixth form and careers 1988–90, sixth form housemistress 1989–90, dep head 1990–93, headmistress 1994–97; headmistress Downe House 1997–; govr: Godstowe Prep Sch, Sandroyd Sch Salisbury, Cheam Prep Sch, Kings Sch Canterbury; memb: GSA 1994, BSA 1994, Exec Ind Schs Examinations Bd (ISEB); FRSA 2004; *Recreations* travel, theatre, cinema; *Clubs* Lansdowne; *Style*— Mrs Emma McKendrick; ✉ Downe House, Cold Ash, Thatcham, Berkshire RG18 9JJ (tel 01635 200286, fax 01635 202026, e-mail headmistress@downehouse.net)

McKENDRICK, Melveena; *b* 23 March 1941; *Educ* Neath Girls' GS, Dyffryn GS Port Talbot, KCL, Girton Coll Cambridge; *m* Neil McKendrick , *qv*; 2 da (Olivia Sarah Katherine b 20 Nov 1970, Cornelia Alexandra b 6 Sept 1972); *Career* Girton Coll Cambridge: Jex-Blake research fell 1967, fell and lectr in Spanish 1970–99, tutor 1970–83, sr tutor 1974–81, dir of studies in modern languages 1984–95, professorial fell 1999–; Univ of Cambridge: lectr in Spanish Univ of Cambridge 1980–92, reader in Spanish literature and society 1992–99, prof of Spanish Golden Age literature, culture and society 1999–, pro-vice-chllr (educn) 2004–, memb numerous bds and ctees; Br Acad: research readership 1990–92, memb Humanities Research Bd and Research Ctee of Br Acad 1996–98, chair Research Panel 2 (Other Languages and Literatures) 1996–98, memb AHRB, chair Research Panel 5 (Modern Languages and Lit) 1998–99; Lansdowne visitor Univ of Victoria BC 1997; conslt hispanic ed Everyman 1993–99; memb Editorial Bd: Donaire (the Spanish Embassy's scholarly jl) 1994–, Bulletin of Hispanic Studies 1998–; memb Advsy Bd Revista Canadiense de Estudios Hispánicos; LittD Univ of Cambridge 2002; FBA 1999; *Publications* Ferdinand and Isabella (1968), A Concise History of Spain (1972), Woman and Society in the Spanish Drama of the Golden Age (1974), Cervantes (1980), Golden-Age Studies in Honour of Alexander A Parker (1984), Theatre in Spain 1490–1700 (1989), El mágico prodigioso (1992), Playing the King: Lope de Vega and the Limits of Conformity (2000), Identities in Crisis: Essays on Honour, Gender and Women in the 'Comedia'; also author of numerous articles, chapters and int conference papers; *Style*— Prof Melveena McKendrick, FBA; ✉ Vice-Chancellor's Office, The Old Schools, Trinity Lane, Cambridge CB2 1TN (e-mail mcm1000@cam.ac.uk)

McKENDRICK, Neil; s of Robert Alexander McKendrick (d 1944), and Sarah Elizabeth, *née* Irvine (d 1996); *b* 28 July 1935; *Educ* Alderman Newton's Sch Leicester, Christ's Coll Cambridge (entrance scholar, Robert Owen Bishop Studentship, BA, MA); *m* 18 March 1967, Prof Melveena McKendrick, FBA, *qv*; 2 da (Olivia Sarah Katherine b 20 Nov 1970, Cornelia Alexandra b 6 Sept 1972); *Career* research fell Christ's Coll Cambridge 1958; Univ of Cambridge: asst lectr in history 1961–64, lectr in history 1964–95, chm Faculty of History 1985–87, reader in social and economic history 1995–2002; Gonville & Caius Coll Cambridge: fell 1958–96, lectr in history 1958–96, dir of studies 1959–96, tutor 1961–69, master 1996–2005; hon fell Christ's Coll Cambridge 1996; FRHistS 1971; *Books* Historical Perspectives (1974), The Birth of a Consumer Society: the Commercialisation of Eighteenth Century England (1983), Business Life and Public Policy (1986), The Birth of Foreign and Colonial: the world's first investment trust (1993), F & C: A History of Foreign and Colonial Investment Trust (1999); *Recreations* gardening, antiques, claret; *Clubs* Athenaeum, Bordeaux; *Style*— Neil McKendrick, Esq, FRHistS

McKENNA, Catherine Maria Paulina; da of William Thomas McKenna, of Skipton, N Yorks, and Carol Patricia, *née* Butler; *b* 21 November 1964, Ruthin, Wales; *Educ* Skipton Girls' HS, Univ of Nottingham (LLB), Chester Coll of Law; *m* 17 June 1995, Graeme Paul Stonehouse; 2 da (Anna Camilla b 28 Jan 1998, Isabel Maria b 21 June 2000); *Career* admitted slr 1989; Thomson Snell and Passmore slrs 1987–89, slr Alsop Wilkinson 1989–94, ptnr and head of pensions Hammonds 1994–; memb: Assoc of Pension Lawyers, Nat Assoc of Pension Funds, Pensions Mgmnt Inst 1996; *Publications* Pensions: The New Law (1995), Pensions Act 2004: A Guide to the New Law (2005); numerous articles and press comment; *Recreations* sport, travel; *Style*— Ms Catherine McKenna; ✉ Hammonds, 2 Park Lane, Leeds LS3 1ES (tel 0870 839 7045, fax 0870 460 3137, e-mail catherine.mckenna@hammonds.com)

McKENNA, Charles; s of John George McKenna (d 1987), and Bernadette, *née* Conney; *b* 9 April 1954; *Educ* St Bede's GS Lanchester Co Durham, Univ of Durham (BA); *m* 30 May 1986, Alison Jane, da of John Fearn; *Career* admitted slr 1978; ptnr Allen & Overy 1985– (articled clerk, asst slr 1978–85), seconded as legal advsr in Quotations Dept The Stock Exchange 1981–82; *Recreations* sport, travel; *Style*— Charles McKenna, Esq

McKENNA, Geraldine Martina Maria; da of John McKenna (d 1988), and Mary McKenna (d 1995); *b* 9 August 1955, Omagh, NI; *Educ* Loreto Convent Omagh; *Career* British Airways NI 1976–81, Aer Lingus/Enterprise Travel FL 1981–84, Belfast City Airport 1984–87, InterContinental Hotel Corp London 1987–91, InterContinental Hotel Corp NY 1991–96; The Savoy Gp: dir of mktg 1996–2001, chief exec 2001–02; chief exec Maybourne Hotel Gp (formerly The Savoy Gp) 2002–06, non-exec dir GuestInvest; memb: Int Women's Forum, Women's Irish Network; Hon Dr Schiller Int Univ 2004; FRSA; *Recreations* sailing, horse riding, travel; *Style*— Ms Geraldine McKenna

McKENNA, His Hon Judge Martin Nicholas; s of Bernard Malcolm McKenna, of Lytham St Annes, Lancs, and Anne Rose *née* Orsman; *b* 19 November 1955; *Educ* Catholic Coll Preston, Univ of Birmingham (LLB), Lincoln Coll Oxford; *m* 1, 1979 (m dis 1995), Deborah Jane Scott; 2 da (Katherine Sophie (Katie), Charlotte Lucy (Charlie) (twins) b 13 Nov 1988); m 2, 1996, Sarah Louise, da of Alan Arthur Malden; 2 step da (Emma Louise b 15 July 1989, Annie Ruth b 12 June 1991); *Career* slr; Eversheds (formerly Evershed & Tomkinson): trainee 1978, slr 1980, assoc 1984–87, ptnr 1987–2000, head of litigation 1994–99; circuit judge (Midland Circuit) 2000–; memb: Law Soc, Birmingham Law Soc, IPA, Assoc of Business Recovery Professionals, CEDR; *Recreations* sailing, skiing, rugby, cricket; *Clubs* East India; *Style*— His Hon Judge McKenna; ✉ c/o Midland Circuit Secretariat, The Priory Courts, 33 Bull Street, Birmingham B4 6DW (tel 0121 681 3200, fax 0121 681 3202, e-mail mmckenna@lix.compulink.co.uk)

McKENNA, Prof Patrick Gerald (Gerry); DL (Co Londonderry 2002); s of Gerald Joseph McKenna (d 1989), of Benburb, Co Tyrone, and Mary Teresa, *née* Smyth (d 1989); *b* 10 December 1953; *Educ* St Patrick's Acad Dungannon, Univ of Ulster (BSc), Queen's Univ Belfast (PhD); *m* 10 Aug 1976, Phil, *née* McArdle; 2 s (Gerald John b 11 Sept 1980, James Philip b 23 March 1983); *Career* lectr in human biology and genetics New Univ of Ulster 1978–84; Univ of Ulster: sr lectr in biology 1984–88, dir Biomedical Sciences Research Centre 1985–88, prof and head Dept of Biological and Biomedical Sciences 1988–94, dean Faculty of Science 1994–97, pro-vice-chllr (research) 1997–99, vice-chllr and pres 1999–; visiting prof: Univ of Malaya 1991, Univ Kebangsaan 1993, Univ of Calif Berkeley 1995; author of over 200 scientific pubns; vice-chair Ulster Cancer Fndn; Freeman Borough of Coleraine 2001; Hon DSc Nat Univ of Ireland 2001, Hon LLD Queen's Univ Belfast 2002; FIBMS 1982, FIBiol 1989, MRIA 2002; *Recreations* reading, the turf; *Clubs* Reform; *Style*— Prof Gerry McKenna, DL; ✉ University of Ulster, Cromore Road, Coleraine, Co Londonderry BT52 1SA (tel 028 7032 4329, fax 028 7032 4901, e-mail pg.mckenna@ulster.ac.uk)

McKENNA, Paul William; s of William Joseph McKenna, of Enfield, Middx, and Joan Brenda, *née* Garner; *b* 8 November 1963; *Educ* St Ignatius Coll Enfield, PhD in clinical hypnosis; *Career* hypnotist, entertainer and television presenter; disc jockey: Radio Caroline 1984, breakfast show Chiltern Radio 1985–87, Capital Radio 1988–91, BBC Radio 1 1991–92; first hypnotic show 1986, appeared at numerous major venues incl Royal Albert Hall 1992, TV debut Paul McKenna's Hypnotic Show (special then series, Carlton) 1993, series The Hypnotic World of Paul McKenna (Celador Productions and Paul McKenna Productions for Carlton/ITV Network) 1994–, presenter Network First factual prog Paul McKenna's Hypnotic Secrets (Man Alive Group and Paul McKenna Productions for Carlton) 1995, series The Paranormal World of Paul McKenna (Man Alive Group and Paul McKenna Productions for Carlton) 1996, special The World's Funniest Hypnotist (ABC) 1996; also recorded set of audio and video hypnotherapy tapes; chm Br Cncl of Professional Stage Hypnotists 1990–92, memb Fedn of Ethical Stage Hypnotists (FESH); *Awards* TRIC Celebrity Award for New Talent of the Year 1994, Capital Radio Best London Show Award for Paul McKenna's Hypnotic Show 1994; *Books* The Hypnotic World of Paul McKenna (1993), Paul McKenna's Hypnotic Secrets (1996), The Paranormal World of Paul McKenna (1997), Change Your Life in Seven Days (2004), I Can Make You Thin (2005); *Style*— Paul McKenna, Esq; ✉ PO Box 5514, London W8 4ZY (website www.paulmckenna.com)

McKENNA, Rosemary; CBE (1995), MP; *Career* MP (Lab): Cumbernauld and Kilsyth 1997–2005, Cumbernauld, Kilsyth and Kirkintilloch East 2005–; *Style—* Ms Rosemary McKenna, CBE, MP; ✉ House of Commons, London SW1A 0AA (tel 020 7219 3000)

McKENNA, Virginia Anne; OBE (2004); da of Terence Morell McKenna (d 1948), and Anne-Marie (Anne de Nys, the music composer), *née* Dennis (who m (2) Jack Drummond Rudd and (3) Sir Charles Richard Andrew Oakeley, 6 Bt, and d 1993); *b* 7 June 1931; *Educ* Herschel Cape Town, Herons Ghyll Horsham, Central Sch of Speech and Drama; *m* 1 1954 (m dis 1957), Denholm Mitchell Elliot, CBE (d 1992), the actor; m 2, 19 Sept 1957, William Inglis Lindon (Bill) Travers, MBE (d 1994), the actor, s of William Halton Lindon Travers (d 1966); 3 s (William Morrell Lindon b 4 Nov 1958, Justin McKenna Lindon b 6 March 1963, Daniel Inglis Lindon b 27 Feb 1967), 1 da (Louise Annabella Linden b 6 July 1960); *Career* actress and writer; co-fndr The Born Free Fndn (formerly Zoo Check Charitable Tst) 1984; patron: Elizabeth Fitzroy Support, Slade Centre, Plan International UK (formerly World Family), Children of the Andes 1991, Wildlife Aid 1991, The Surrey Badger Protection Soc 1996, Tayside Cat Shelter, Wirral Swallows & Amazons Adventure Gp, Sue Ryder Care, Cinnamon Tst, Polka Theatre; *Theatre* incl: season Old Vic 1955–56, The Devils 1961, Beggars Opera 1963, A Little Night Music 1976, The King and I (SWET Award for Best Musical Actress) 1979, Hamlet (RSC) 1984; *Television* incl: Romeo and Juliet (Best Actress Award ITV) 1955, Passage to India 1965, The Deep Blue Sea 1974, Cheap in August, The Scold's Bridle 1998, The Whistle Blower 2001; *Films* incl: The Cruel Sea 1952, A Town Like Alice 1954 (Academy Award for Best Actress), Carve Her Name With Pride (Belgian Prix Femina) 1957, Born Free (Variety Club Award for Best Actress) 1964, Ring of Bright Water 1968, Sliding Doors 1998, What Do You See? 2005; *Books* On Playing with Lions (with Bill Travers), Some of my Friends have Tails, Beyond the Bars (jt ed and jt author), Headlines from the Jungle (anthology of verse, co-ed, 1990), Into the Blue (1992), Journey to Freedom (1997), Back To The Blue (1997); *Audio books*: The Butterfly Lion (by Michael Morpurgo), Why The Whales Came (by Michael Morpurgo); *Recreations* reading, travelling, gardening; *Style—* Miss Virginia McKenna, OBE; ✉ The Born Free Foundation, 3 Grove House, Foundry Lane, Horsham, West Sussex RH13 5PL (tel 01403 240170, fax 01403 327838, e-mail virginia@bornfree.org.uk)

MACKENZIE, *see also:* Muir Mackenzie

MACKENZIE, Prof Andrew Peter (Andy); s of Alexander Colin Mackenzie, of Dornoch, Sutherland, and Bridget Mary, *née* Gordon; *b* 7 March 1964, Elderslie, Strathclyde; *Educ* Univ of Edinburgh (BSc), Univ of Cambridge (PhD); *m* 17 May 1991, Olga Maria; 2 da (Lucia Cristina Maria b 8 Dec 1999, Katrina Maria b 25 March 2003), 1 s (Alexander Daniel (twin) b 25 March 2003); *Career* researcher CERN Geneva 1986–87; Univ of Cambridge: Katherine and Charles Darwin research fell Darwin Coll 1991–94, univ research fell 1991–93, Royal Soc univ research fell 1993–2001; reader Univ of Birmingham 1997–2001, currently prof and dir of research Sch of Physics and Astronomy Univ of St Andrews; visiting posts: Bariloche Univ 1995, Stanford Univ 2003, Kyoto Univ 2004, Cornell Univ 2006; Mott lectr Inst of Physics 1999, Daiwa-Adrian Prize 2004; FInstP 2002, FRSE 2004; *Recreations* golf, reading, mountain walking; *Style—* Prof Andy Mackenzie; ✉ School of Physics and Astronomy, The University of St Andrews, North Haugh, St Andrews KY16 9SS (tel 01334 463108, fax 01334 463104, e-mail apm9@st-and.ac.uk)

MACKENZIE, Colin; s of Hector Colin Beardmore Mackenzie (d 1998), and Frances Evelyn, *née* Purkis (d 1996); *b* 4 November 1945; *Educ* Eastbourne Coll; *m* 19 Oct 1968, Fiona Maureen, *née* Barr; 2 da (Rebecca Ann b 7 April 1975, Elizabeth Fiona b 21 Dec 1976); *Career* chartered surveyor; Hampton & Sons: Mayfield E Sussex 1974–80, Sevenoaks Kent 1980–85, dir Country and Estates Depts 1987–98; ptnr Knight Frank Private Clients Buying Service 1998–2003; dir Colin Mackenzie Ltd 1995–; FRICS; *Recreations* country sports, vintage sports cars; *Style—* Colin Mackenzie, Esq; ✉ Bonischerch, Old Heathfield, East Sussex TN21 9AG (tel 01435 866988, fax 01435 866662, e-mail cm@cmproperty.co.uk)

McKENZIE, Dr Dan Peter; CH (2003); s of William Stewart McKenzie, and Nancy Mary McKenzie; *b* 21 February 1942; *Educ* Westminster, King's Coll Cambridge (BA, MA, PhD); *m* 5 June 1971, Indira Margaret; 1 s (James Misra b 3 April 1976); *Career* Univ of Cambridge: sr asst in res 1969–75, asst dir of res 1975–79, reader in tectonics 1979–84, currently Royal Soc prof of earth sciences; Balzan Prize of Int Balzan Fndn (with F J Vine and D H Matthews, 1981), Japan Prize Sci and Technol Fndn of Japan (with W J Morgan and X Le Pichon, 1990), Royal Medal of the Royal Soc 1991, Crafoord Prize of the Swedish Acad 2002; Hon MA Univ of Cambridge 1966; memb Royal Soc 1976, foreign assoc US Nat Acad of Scis 1989; *Publications* author of various papers in learned journals; *Recreations* gardening; *Style—* Prof Dan McKenzie, CH; ✉ Bullard Laboratories, Madingley Road, Cambridge CB3 0EZ

MacKENZIE, Prof Donald; *Educ* Univ of Edinburgh (BSc, PhD); *Career* prof of sociology Univ of Edinburgh; ESRC professorial research fell; FBA 2004; *Books* incl: Knowing Machines (1996), The Social Shaping of Technology (ed with Judy Wajcman, 2 edn, 1999), Mechanizing Proof: Computing, Risk and Trust (2001), An Engine, Not a Camera: How Financial Models Shape Markets (2006); *Style—* Prof Donald MacKenzie; ✉ School of Social and Political Studies, The University of Edinburgh, Adam Ferguson Building, Edinburgh EH8 9LL

McKENZIE, Justice Donald Cameron Moffat; s of John McKenzie (d 1975), of Perth, and Jessie Cameron Creelman, *née* Moffat (d 1989); *b* 3 March 1934; *Educ* St Ninian's Cathedral Sch, Balhousie Boys' Sch, Perth Commercial Sch, Queen's Coll; *m* 29 June 1967, Patricia Janet, da of Ernest Russell Hendry (d 1974), of Dundee; 2 da (Alison b 1968, Evelyn b 1972); *Career* Nat Serv RAPC; accountant Trinity Coll Glenalmond 1966–70, bursar Corp of High Sch Dundee 1970–80; co-cncllr magistrate social work and health convener Perth 1971–75, co-cncllr Perth and Kinross 1971–75, justice Dist Court 1975; estate factor Pitlochry Estate Tst 1980, govr Dundee Coll of Educn, dir R Dundee Instn for the Blind; capt Soc of High Constables; memb: Justices Ctee, Prison Visiting Ctee; FFA 1976, FCMI (FIMgt 1980); OStJ 1978; *Recreations* cricket, music, memb Roll Royce enthusiasts Club, memb Perth Burns Club; *Style—* Justice Donald McKenzie; ✉ Balnacraig, Moulin, Pitlochry, Perthshire (tel 01796 472591, Pitlochry Estate Office tel 01796 472114)

MacKENZIE, George Paterson; s of James Sargent Porteous MacKenzie (d 2000), and Flora Black Paterson; *b* 22 September 1950, Lenzie, E Dunbartonshire; *Educ* George Watson's Coll Edinburgh, Leeds GS, Univ of Stirling (BA, MLitt), Moray House Coll of Educn; *m* 22 October 2005, Caroline Morgan; *Career* teacher of history Larbert HS 1974–75, research asst Scottish Record Office 1975–82, departmental records offr Gen Register Office for Scotland 1983–85, head Liaison Branch and Preservation Servs Branch Scottish Record Office 1986–94, dep sec-gen Int Cncl on Archives Paris 1995–96, head of external rels Nat Archives of Scotland 1997–2000, Keeper of the Records of Scotland (ceo Nat Archives of Scotland) 2001–; consultancy work on archives and records (particularly on preservation issues and the protection of archives in armed conflict) for UNESCO, World Bank and ICA; author of articles on archives and records in specialist pubns, numerous invited lectures and talks internationally; *Recreations* travel, cooking, reading; *Style—* George MacKenzie, Esq; ✉ The National Archives of Scotland, HM General Register House, 2 Princes Street, Edinburgh EH1 3YY (tel 0131 535 1312, e-mail george.mackenzie@nas.gov.uk)

MACKENZIE, Gen Sir (John) Jeremy George; GCB (1998, KCB 1992), OBE (1982); s of Lt-Col John William Elliot Mackenzie, DSO, QPM (d 1990), and Valerie Margaret, *née* Dawes; *b* 11 February 1941; *Educ* Duke of York Sch Nairobi; *m* 12 April 1969, Elizabeth Lyon (Liz), da of Col George Leftwich Wertenbaker, USAF (d 1986); 1 s (Edward John George b 17 May 1976), 1 da (Georgina Elizabeth b 8 July 1978); *Career* cmmnd 1 Bn Queen's Own Highlanders 1961, CO Queen's Own Highlanders 1979–82, Cmd 12 Armd Bde (as Brig) 1984–87, Maj-Gen 1989, Cmdt Staff Coll Camberley 1989, GOC 4 Armd Div 1989–91, Lt-Gen 1991, cmd 1 British Corps Bielefeld 1991–92, cmd ACE NATO Rapid Reaction Corps (ARRC) 1992–94, Dep Supreme Cdr Allied Powers Europe (DSACEUR) 1994–98; govr Royal Hosp Chelsea 1999–; Brig Queen's Body Guard for Scotland (Royal Co of Archers) 1986–; Col Cmdt AGC 1992–98, Col The Highlanders Regt 1994–2001, Col Cmdt Army Physical Trg Corps 1999–; ADC Gen 1992–98; pres: Servs Branch Br Deer Soc, Combined Servs Winter Sports Assoc (life vice-pres); dir: Sirva plc 2003, Selex Communications Ltd 2004; memb Advsy Bd Blue Hackle Security 2006; Cdr US Legion of Merit 1997 and 1999, Cross of Merit (Czech Rep) 1st Class 1998, Hungary Offrs Cross Order of Merit 1998, Order of the Madara Horsemen of Bulgaria 1st Class 1999, Gold Medal of the Slovenian Armed Forces 2002; *Recreations* shooting, fishing; *Clubs* Caledonian; *Style—* Gen Sir Jeremy Mackenzie, GCB, OBE; ✉ Royal Hospital Chelsea, London SW3 4SR

McKENZIE, John Cormack; s of William Joseph McKenzie and Elizabeth Frances Robinson; *b* 21 June 1927; *Educ* St Andrew's Coll, Trinity Coll Dublin (MA, MAI), Queen's Univ Belfast (MSc), Tadzhikistan Univ (DSc), Univ of Nottingham (DSc); *m* 1954, Olga Caroline Cleland; 3 s, 1 da; *Career* civil engr: McLaughlin & Harvey, Sir Alexander Gibb & Partners 1946–48; asst lectr Queen's Univ Belfast 1948–50; civil engr and md Edmund Nuttall Ltd 1950–82 (dir 1967–82), chm Nuttall Geotechnical Services Ltd 1967–82, dir British Wastewater Ltd 1978–82, md Thomas Telford Ltd 1982–90, dir H R Wallingford Ltd 1990–95; perm sec Inst of Civil Engrs 1982–90, vice-pres Register of Engrs for Disaster Relief 1985–, sec gen WFEO 1987–97 (treas 1998–2001, presidential advsr 2001–), foreign sec Royal Acad of Engrg 1988–92, dep chm UK Ctee Int Decade for Natural Disaster Reduction 1989–92; pres Beaconsfield Advsy Centre 1978–2007; FREng 1984, FICE, FIE (Aust), FIEI, FRSA, FIAcadE 2003; *Publications* Research into Some Aspects of Soil Cement (1952), Engineers: Administrators or Technologists? (1971), Construction of the Second Mersey Tunnel (1972), Civil Engineering Procedure (3 edn, 1979), Mitigation of Wind Induced Disasters (1994), The Contribution of Engineers to the UN International Decade of Natural Disaster Reduction (1994), Sustainable Development and the Maintenance of Economic Viability (1994), Developments in the Application of Environmental Engineering and Sustainable Development (1994), Europe - Continuing Wealth Creation and Sustainable Development for Future Generations (1995), International Application of Ethics for Engineers (1996), To Save the World as We Know It (1996), Accreditation (1996), Beyond the Bottom Line (1996), Quo Vadis? (1997), The Complete Engineer (1997), To Reason Why (1998); *Recreations* philately, collecting ancient pottery; *Clubs* Athenaeum; *Style—* John McKenzie, FREng; ✉ The Cottage (Annex), 20 Ledborough Lane, Beaconsfield, Buckinghamshire HP9 2PZ (tel 01494 675191, fax 01494 676064, e-mail john@dalga.demon.co.uk)

McKENZIE, Prof John Crawford; s of Donald Walter McKenzie (d 1978), and Emily Beatrice, *née* Stracey (d 1992); *b* 12 November 1937; *Educ* LSE (BSc), Bedford Coll London (MPhil), Inst of Educn Univ of London (PGCE); *m* 5 Aug 1960, Ann; 2 s (Simon Andrew b 28 Feb 1964, Andrew John b 10 March 1966); *Career* princ: Ilkley Coll 1978, Bolton Inst of HE 1981; rector Liverpool Poly 1984; Univ of the Arts London (formerly The London Inst): rector 1986–96, govr and dir of int devpt 1996–; advsr: Tokyo Inst of Inter-Cultural Communications 1997–, Shanghai Municipal Govts 2002–; visiting prof Univs of London and Newcastle upon Tyne; chm Leeds United FC 2003–04; dir various cos; Chevalier de l'Ordre des Arts et des Lettres (France) 1992; *Books* Changing Food Habits (ed, 1964), Our Changing Fare (ed, 1966), The Food Consumer (ed, 1987); *Recreations* collecting antiquarian books, bridge; *Clubs* Athenaeum, Chelsea Arts, RSM; *Style—* Prof John McKenzie; ✉ University of the Arts London, 65 Davies Street, London W1K 5DA (tel 020 7514 6189, fax 020 7514 6212, e-mail j.mckenzie@arts.ac.uk)

MACKENZIE, John Leonard Duncan; s of Duncan Mackenzie (d 1970), of Edinburgh, and Anne, *née* Christy (d 1978); *b* 22 May 1932; *Educ* Holy Cross Acad, Univ of Edinburgh (MA); *m* 1960, Wendy Ann, da of Stanley Marshall; 3 da (Colyn Anne, Kate, Rebecca); *Career* freelance drama dir BBC TV 1967–78, freelance film dir 1979–; memb: Directors' Guild of America 1989–, Acad of Motion Pictures, Arts and Sciences 1990–, Directors' Guild of GB 1991–; *Television* BBC: Just Another Saturday (Prix Italia 1975), Passage to England, Double Dare; other credits incl: Bangelstein's Boys (LWT), The Black Dog (Granada), A Sense of Freedom (Scottish Televison, BAFTA nomination 1978), Looking After Jo Jo (BBC Scotland/Andrea Calderwood); *Film* Unman Whittering & Zigo, Made, The Long Good Friday, The Honorary Consul (aka Beyond the Limit), Act of Vengeance (Cable Ace Award 1983), The Innocent, The Fourth Protocol, Last of the Finest (aka Blue Heat), Ruby, Voyage, The Infiltrator, Deadly Voyage (Cable Ace Award 1998), Aldrich Ames - America Betrayed (aka A Spy Within), When the Sky Falls, Quicksand, The Water Carrier; *Recreations* hill walking; *Clubs* Groucho; *Style—* John Mackenzie, Esq; ✉ c/o Anthony Jones, PFD, Drury House, 34 Russell Street, London WC2B 5HA (tel 020 7344 1040, fax 020 7836 9539, e-mail ajones@pfd.co.uk)

MacKENZIE, Prof John MacDonald; JP; s of Alexander MacKenzie (d 1987), and Hannah, *née* Whitby (d 1984); *b* 2 October 1943, Manchester; *Educ* Ndola Govt Sch Northern Rhodesia, Woodside Sch Glasgow, Univ of Glasgow (MA), Univ of Br Columbia (PhD); *Career* teaching asst and research fell Univ of Br Columbia 1964–68; Lancaster Univ: successively lectr, sr lectr and prof 1968–2002, princ County Coll 1976–81, dean of humanities and dean of educn 1989–97, prof emeritus 2002–; hon research prof: Research Centre for Irish and Scottish Studies Univ of Aberdeen 2001–, Research Centre for Environmental History Univs of St Andrews and Stirling 2001–; Leverhulme Tst emeritus fell 2005–; historical advsr exhbn on David Livingstone Nat Portrait Gallery 1995–96, conslt curator exhbn on the Victorian Vision V&A 1997–2001; tstee Ruskin Fndn 1994–99; ed: Studies in Imperialism series Manchester Univ Press 1985–, Environment and History 2000–; memb and chm Lancaster Bench 1990–2000; chm of govrs Morecambe HS 1981–85; hon fell Univ of Edinburgh 2006–; FRHistS 1984, FRSE 2003; *Books* The Partition of Africa (1983), Propaganda and Empire (1984), The Railway Station, a Social History (jtly, 1986), Imperialism and Popular Culture (ed, 1986), Imperialism and the Natural World (ed, 1990), Popular Imperialism and the Military (ed, 1992), Orientalism: History, Theory and the Arts (1995), David Livingstone and the Victorian Encounter with Africa (ed, 1996), The Victorian Vision (ed, 2001), Peoples, Nations and Cultures (ed, 2005), The Scots in South Africa (2007); *Recreations* music, opera, deltiology, walking, travel; *Clubs* New Cavendish; *Style—* Prof John MacKenzie; ✉ Old Bank House, Bank Street, Alyth, Perthshire PH11 8DB (tel 01828 633469, e-mail john@mackenzie.enta.net)

McKENZIE, Julia Kathleen (Mrs Jerry Harte); da of Albion James Jeffrey McKenzie (d 1970), of Enfield, Middx, and Kathleen, *née* Rowe; *b* 17 February 1942; *Educ* Tottenham Co Sch, Guildhall Sch of Music and Drama; *m* 1972, Jerry Harte, s of Carl Harte; *Career* actress and director; Hon DLitt South Bank Univ 1999, Hon Dr Royal Acad of Music; FGSM 1985; *Theatre* West End and New York performances incl: Cowardy Custard, Miriam in Outside Edge, Lily Garland in On the Twentieth Century, Hobson's Choice, Schweyk in the Second World War, Miss Adelaide in Guys and Dolls (NT, Best Actress

M

Variety Club Awards, Best Actress Soc of West End Theatre Awards, Olivier Award), Sally in Follies, The Witch in Into the Woods, Company, Promises Promises, Mame, Side by Side (by Sondheim); Alan Ayckbourn plays incl: Norman Conquests, Ten Times Table, Communicating Doors, Woman in Mind (Best Actress London Evening Standard Awards 1986); Mrs Lovett in Sweeney Todd (RNT, Olivier Award for Best Actress in a Musical) 1994, Royal Family 2001, Philadelphia Story 2005; theatre dir: Stepping Out (Duke of York's Theatre), Steel Magnolias (Lyric Theatre), Just So (Watermill Theatre Newbury), Merrily We Roll Along (staged concert, 1988), Putting it Together (NY and London), Little Night Music (Tokyo), Musical of the World (Denmark), Honk (NT, USA and Denmark, Best Musical Olivier Awards) 2000–01; *Television* incl: Fame is the Spur, Dear Box Number, Those Glory Glory Days, Blott on the Landscape, Absent Friends, Hotel du Lac, Adam Bede, Hester in Fresh Fields and French Fields (voted Favourite Comedy Performer TV Times Viewers' Poll 1985, 1986, 1987 and 1989), The Last Detective, Death in Holy Orders, Celebration 2006, You Can Choose Your Friends 2007, Cranford Chronicles 2007; *Film* incl: Shirley Valentine, Old Curiosity Shop, Bright Young Things, Notes on a Scandal 2006; *Style*— Ms Julia McKenzie; ✉ c/o Ken McReddie, 36–40 Glasshouse Street, London W1B 5DL (tel 020 7439 1456, e-mail ken@kenmcreddie.com)

MacKENZIE, Kenneth John; CB (1996); s of Capt John Donald MacKenzie (d 1967), of Milngavie, Dunbartonshire, and Elizabeth Pennant Johnston, *née* Sutherland (d 1985); *b* 1 May 1943; *Educ* Birkenhead Sch, Pembroke Coll Oxford (MA), Stanford Univ (AM); *m* 3 Sept 1975, Irene Mary, da of William Ewart Hogarth (d 1947), of Mayfield, Paisley, Renfrewshire; 1 s (John b 1977), 1 da (Mary b 1979); *Career* asst princ Scot Home & Health Dept 1965–70, private sec to Jt Parly Under Sec of State Scot Office 1969–70; princ: Regnl Devpt Div Scot Office 1970–73, Scot Educn Dept 1973–77; Civil Serv fell: Downing Coll Cambridge 1972, Dept of Politics Univ of Glasgow 1974–75; princ private sec to Sec of State for Scotland 1977–79; asst sec: Scot Econ Planning Dept 1979–83, Scot Office Fin Div 1983–85; princ fin offr Scot Office 1985–88, under sec Scot Home and Health Dept 1988–91, sec Scot Office Agriculture and Fisheries Dept 1992–95 (under sec 1991–92), dep sec Econ and Domestic Affairs Secretariat Cabinet Office 1995–97, head Constitution Secretariat Cabinet Office 1997–98, sec Devpt Dept Scot Office 1998–2001; memb Agriculture and Food Research Cncl 1992–94, memb Biotechnology and Biological Sciences Research Cncl 1994–95, quinuennial reviewer for Court Serv Lord Chllr's Dept 2001–02; chm Historic Scotland Fndn 2001–; assoc conslt Public Administration International Ltd 2002–; St Cuthbert's Parish Church Edinburgh: session clerk 1971–91, convenor Congregational Bd 1991–95; memb: Edinburgh Civil Serv Dramatic Soc 1966–2005 (hon pres 1989–95), Br Waterways Scotland Gp 2002–, Christian Aid Bd 2005–; hon prof Dept of Politics Univ of Aberdeen 2001–04; *Clubs* Farmers'; *Style*— Kenneth J MacKenzie, Esq, CB; ✉ 30 Regent Terrace, Edinburgh EH7 5BS (tel 0131 557 4530, fax 0131 556 3622, e-mail kjmackenzie@freeuk.com)

McKENZIE, Kenneth Stevenson; *b* 18 June 1953; *Educ* Trinity Sch Croydon, Univ of Exeter; *m* 1985, Jane Helen Bowden; 2 da (Jennifer 1985, Alice b 1989), 1 s (James b 1987); *Career* admitted slr 1978; Davies Arnold Cooper: joined 1984, litigation ptnr 1986–, head of dispute resolution 2001–; specialism incl insurance, reinsurance and professional indemnity; author of numerous articles; memb Law Soc 1978; *Style*— Kenneth McKenzie, Esq; ✉ Davies Arnold Cooper, 6–8 Bouverie Street, London EC4Y 8DD (tel 020 7936 2222, fax 020 7936 2020, e-mail kmckenzie@dac.co.uk)

MacKENZIE, Madeleine; elder da of William Gordon MacKenzie, of Inverness, and Veronica Dorothy Rachel MacKenzie; *b* 27 August 1963; *Educ* Inverness HS, Univ of Aberdeen (LLB, DipLP); *Career* trainee slr, slr then assoc Sutherland & Co Inverness 1986–90, Notary Public 1988, asst Scottish Parly Counsel Lord Advocate's Dept London 1990–99, depute then Scottish Parly Counsel Edinburgh 1999–; FRSA 2004; *Recreations* bridge, reading, music, walking; *Clubs* Athenaeum; *Style*— Miss Madeleine MacKenzie; ✉ Office of the Scottish Parliamentary Counsel, Victoria Quay, Edinburgh EH6 6QQ (tel 0131 244 1667, fax 0131 244 1661, e-mail madeleine.mackenzie@scotland.gsi.gov.uk)

McKENZIE, Master; Michael; CB (1999), QC (1991); s of Robert McKenzie (d 1992), of Brighton, E Sussex, and Kitty Elizabeth, *née* Regan (d 1985); *b* 25 May 1943; *Educ* Varndean GS Brighton; *m* 19 Sept 1964, Peggy Dorothy, da of Thomas Edward William Russell, of Heathfield, E Sussex; 3 s (Justin Grant b 31 May 1968, Gavin John b 28 April 1971, Jamie Stuart b 14 Jan 1977); *Career* called to the Bar Middle Temple 1970 (bencher 1993); dep clerk of the peace Middx QS 1970–72, dep courts admin Middx Crown Court 1972–73, courts admin NE Circuit (Newcastle) 1974–79, head of the Central Criminal Court 1979–84, dep circuit admin SE Circuit 1984–86, asst registrar Court of Appeal (Criminal Div) 1986–88, Queen's Coroner and Attorney and Master of the Crown Office, registrar of Criminal Appeals and of Courts Martial Appeal Court and Master of the High Court of Justice (Queen's Bench Div) 1988–2003; memb Ind Monitoring Bd Lewes Prison 2004–06, registrar Qatar Financial Centre Civic and Commercial Court and Regulatory Tbnl 2006–; prof of law Wake Forest Univ Sch of Law NC 2001; Freeman City of London 1979; hon fell Univ of Kent 1991; FRSA 1990, memb NY Acad of Sci 1992, hon memb State Bar of Calif 1996; *Books* Butterworths Rules of Court (ed), Criminal Court Practice, A Review of the Working Methods of the European Court of Human Rights (with Lord Woolf, 2005); *Recreations* Northumbrian stick dressing, fell walking, shooting; *Style*— Master McKenzie, CB, QC; ✉ Selwyns Wood House, Cross in Hand, East Sussex TN21 0QN (tel 01435 862357)

MACKENZIE, Robert Stephen; s of Brig (Frederick) Stephen Ronald Mackenzie, OBE (d 1981), and Daphne Margaret, *née* Jickling (d 1993); *b* 12 November 1947; *Educ* Radley, RMA Sandhurst; *m* 24 March 1973, Amanda Clare, da of Lt Cdr Richard John Beverley Sutton; 1 da (Emily b 1977), 1 s (Rupert b 1982); *Career* serv Queen's Royal Irish Hussars; Allied Lyons 1978; md: Badger Inns 1984–98 (dir 1983–), Woodhouse Inns 1998– (dir 1983–), Heavitree Inns 1991–; dir Hall and Woodhouse; *Recreations* riding; *Style*— Robert Mackenzie, Esq; ✉ Woodhouse Inns, The Brewery, Blandford, Dorset DT11 9LS (tel 01258 451462, fax 01258 452122, car 077 6814 5520)

MACKENZIE, Dr Sir Roderick McQuhae; 12 Bt (NS 1703), of Scatwell, Ross-shire; s of Capt Sir Roderick Edward François McQuhae Mackenzie, 11 Bt, CBE, DSC (d 1986), and Marie Evelyn Campbell, *née* Parkinson (d 1993); *b* 17 April 1942; *Educ* Sedbergh, KCL, St George's Hosp (MB BS, MRCP (UK), FRCP (C), DCH); *m* 1970, Nadezhda (Nadine), da of Georges Frederic Leon Schlatter, Baron von Rorbas, of Buchs-K-Zurich, Switzerland; 1 s (Gregory Roderick McQuhae b 1971), 1 da (Nina Adelaïda b 1973); *Heir* s, Gregory Mackenzie; *Recreations* classical music (violin, viola), riding (3–day eventing), skiing, windsurfing; *Style*— Dr Sir Roderick Mackenzie, Bt; ✉ 2431 Udell Road, Calgary NW, Alberta, Canada T2N 4H4

MACKENZIE, Ruth; OBE (1995); da of Kenneth Mackenzie, of Paris, and Myrna Blumberg, of London; *b* 24 July 1957; *Educ* South Hampstead HS, Sorbonne (dip), Newnham Coll Cambridge (MA); *Career* co fndr, dir and writer Moving Parts Theatre Co 1980–82, dir of Theatre in the Mill Univ of Bradford 1982–84, artistic dir Bradford Multicultural Festival Bradford Met Cncl 1983–84, drama offr with responsibility for theatre writing Arts Cncl of GB 1984–86, head of strategic planning South Bank Centre 1986–90, exec dir Nottingham Playhouse 1990–97, gen dir Scottish Opera 1997–99, special advsr to Sec of State of Culture, Media and Sport 1999–2002, dir Time/Room Prodns Ltd 2002–, artistic dir Chichester Festival Theatre 2002–; memb Bd New Millennium Experience Co 1997–99; memb Exec Ctee Common Purpose 1993–97; memb Bd Arts Cncl Touring Panel 1992–99; memb Panel 2000 FCO 1998–99; memb QCA Ctee on Creativity 2000–; memb Chancellor's Forum London Inst 2001–; govr Trinity Coll of Music 2002–; Hon DLitt: Nottingham Trent Univ, Univ of Nottingham; hon fell Univ of Nottingham; FRSA 1992; *Recreations* work; *Style*— Ms Ruth Mackenzie, OBE

MACKENZIE, Sheriff (Colin) Scott; DL (Western Isles 1975); s of Colin Scott Mackenzie (d 1971), of Stornoway, Isle of Lewis, and Margaret Sarah Tolmie (d 1993); *b* 7 July 1938; *Educ* Nicolson Inst Stornoway, Fettes, Univ of Edinburgh (BL); *m* 1966, Christeen Elizabeth Drysdale, da of William McLauchlan (d 1968), of Tong, Isle of Lewis; *Career* admitted slr 1960; procurator fiscal Stornoway 1969–92, sheriff Grampian Highland and Islands at Kirkwall and Lerwick 1992–2003, pt/t sheriff 2004–; memb Cncl Sheriffs' Assoc 2002–03; dir Harris Tweed Assoc Ltd 1979–95 clerk to the Western Isles Lieutenancy 1974–92, Vice Lord-Lt Western Isles 1984–92; memb Cncl Law Soc of Scotland 1985–92 (convenor Criminal Law Ctee 1991–92); kirk elder 1985, convener Church and Nation Ctee Presbytery of Lewis 1990–92, convenor Study Gp on Young People and the Media for General Assembly of the Church of Scotland 1991–93; FSA Scot 1995; *Publications* The Last Warrior Band: The Ross Mountain Battery at Gallipoli 1915 (2003); *Recreations* fishing, boating, travel, amateur radio (GM7 RD0), private flying; *Clubs* New (Edinburgh), Royal Northern and Univ (Aberdeen); *Style*— Sheriff C Scott Mackenzie, DL; ✉ Park House, Matheson Road, Stornoway, Isle of Lewis HS1 2NQ (tel 01851 702008, e-mail colinsmackenzie@btinternet.com)

McKENZIE, Dr Sheila Agnes; da of Capt Raymond K McKenzie (d 1980), of Dollar, Scotland, and Agnes Muirhead, *née* Steel (d 1978); *b* 5 June 1946; *Educ* Dollar Acad, Univ of Edinburgh; *Career* conslt paediatrician Queen Elizabeth Hosp for Children London E2; regnl paediatric advsr Br Paediatric Assoc (RCP) 1988–95, advsr to Tushinskya Children's Hosp Moscow, conslt paediatrician and hon sr lectr Royal London Hosp 1999–; MD, FRCP 1989, FRCPE; *Recreations* hill walking, cultivation of old roses, photography; *Style*— Dr Sheila McKenzie; ✉ 69 Gordon Road, London E18 1DT (tel 020 8505 7481); An Sithean, Bonar Bridge, Sutherland (tel 01863 766461); Royal London Hospital, Whitechapel, London E1 1BB (tel 020 7377 7000 ext 3931)

MACKENZIE, Ursula Ann; Ian Alexander Ross Mackenzie, of Great Massingham, Norfolk, and Phyllis, *née* Naismith; *b* 11 December 1951; *Educ* Malvern Girls' Coll, Westlake Sch for Girls LA (ESU exchange scholar), Univ of Nottingham (BA, PhD); *Children* 1 s (Matthew James Johnson b 18 Sept 1987); *Career* lectr in English and American literature Univ of Hong Kong 1976–79, International Scripts Literary Agency 1979–80, rights mangr Granada Publishing 1981–84; Transworld Publishers: editorial and rights mangr Bantam Press, editorial and rights dir 1985–88, publishing dir 1988–95, publisher of hardback books 1995–2000, publisher Time Warner Books UK 2000–; *Style*— Ms Ursula Mackenzie; ✉ Time Warner Books UK, Brettenham House, Lancaster Place, London WC2E 7EN (020 7911 8910, fax 020 7911 8905, e-mail ursula.mackenzie@timewarnerbooks.co.uk)

MacKENZIE OF CULKEIN, Baron (Life Peer UK 1999), of Assynt in Highland Hector Uisdean MacKenzie; s of George Campbell MacKenzie (d 1986), and Williamina Budge, *née* Sutherland (d 1957); *b* 25 February 1940; *Educ* Nicolson Inst Stornoway, Portree HS Isle of Skye, Leverndale Sch of Nursing, W Cumberland Sch of Nursing (Lindsay Robertson Gold Medal, RGN, RMN); *m* 1961 (m dis 1991), Anna Roberston Morrison, da of George Morrison; 3 da (Catriona b 20 Aug 1961, Ishbel Georgina, Morag Sutherland (twins) b 23 April 1963), 1 s (David Hector b 15 Jan 1973); *Career* student nurse Leverndale Hosp Glasgow 1958–61, asst lighthousekeeper Clyde Lighthouses Trust 1961–64, staff nurse W Cumberland Hosp Whitehaven 1966–69 (student nurse 1964–66); COHSE: regnl sec Yorks and E Midlands 1970–74 (asst regnl sec 1969–70), national offr 1974–83, asst gen sec 1983–87, gen sec 1987–93; associate gen sec UNISON 1993–2000 (following merger of COHSE, NUPE and NALGO); pres TUC 1998–99 (memb Gen Cncl 1987–2000); co sec UIA (Insurance) Ltd 1996–2000; memb: Administrative and Clerical Staff Cncl NHS 1972–87, Professional and Technical Staff A Cncl (NHS), Nurses and Midwives' Negotiating Cncl 1979–90 (chm 1983–87); *Recreations* reading, aviation, travel, celtic music; *Style*— Lord MacKenzie of Culkein; ✉ House of Lords, London SW1A 0PW

MACKENZIE OF FRAMWELLGATE, Baron (Life Peer UK 1998), of Durham in the County of Durham; Brian Mackenzie; OBE (1998); s of Frederick George Mackenzie (d 1963), and Lucy, *née* Ward (d 1973); *b* 21 March 1943; *Educ* Eastbourne Boys' Sch, Univ of London (LLB), FBI Nat Acad Quantico USA (graduated 1985); *m* 6 March 1965, Jean, da of late James Seed; 2 s (Hon Brian James b 21 March 1968, Hon Andrew Craig b 18 May 1971); *Career* career police offr rising to chief superintendent Durham Constabulary (sometime head Durham drug squad and crime computer project team, also former advsr Home Office, govr Police Staff Coll Bramshill and memb Police Trg Cncl), ret 1998; special police advsr to Home Sec 1998–2001; patron Joint Security Industry Cncl 1999–; former vice-pres then pres Police Superintendents' Assoc; pres Assoc of Police and Public Security Suppliers 2000–, vice-pres Br Airlines Assoc (BALPA); *Publications* Two Lives of Brian (autobiography, 2004); *Recreations* swimming, music, after dinner speaking; *Clubs* Dunelm (Durham); *Style*— The Rt Hon the Lord Mackenzie of Framwellgate, OBE; ✉ House of Lords, London SW1A 0PW (tel 020 7219 8632, fax 020 7219 1997, e-mail mackenzieb@parliament.uk)

MACKENZIE OF GAIRLOCH, John Alexander; DL (Ross, Cromarty, Skye and Lochalsh 1984); s of Brig William Alexander Mackenzie of Gairloch, DSO, OBE (d 1982), and Marjory Kythé, *née* Stirling (d 1988); *b* 27 May 1944, Muir of Ord, Ross-shire; *Educ* Gordonstoun; *m* 12 April 1969, Frances Marian, o da of Lt Col E S Williams, OBE (d 1963); 1 da (Kythé Caroline b 6 Feb 1974), 1 s (Duncan James b 10 April 1976); *Career* landowner; 2 Lt Queen's Own Highlanders 1962–65, James Buchanan & Co Ltd 1966–80, Gairloch and Conon estates 1980–, chm Black Isle Grain Ltd 1987–90; memb Red Deer Cmmn 1987–98, chm Highland Region Scottish Landowners Fedn 1990–95; *Style*— John Mackenzie of Gairloch, DL; ✉ Conan House, Conon Bridge, Ross-shire IV7 8AL (tel 01349 861101)

McKENZIE OF LUTON, Baron (Life Peer UK 2004), of Luton in the County of Bedfordshire; William David (Bill) McKenzie; s of late George McKenzie, and Elsie May, *née* Doust (d 1979); *b* 24 July 1946, Reading; *Educ* Reading Sch, Univ of Bristol (BA); *m* Aug 1972, Diane Joyce, *née* Angliss; *Career* Price Waterhouse: joined London office 1973, ptnr 1980–86, joined Hong Kong office 1992, ptnr 1993–98, ptnr i/c Vietnam 1996–98; Parly under-sec (Lords) Dept for Work and Pensions 2007–; memb Luton BC 1976–92 and 1999–2005 (ldr 1999–2003); Hon MBA Univ of Luton; FCA 1979; *Recreations* swimming, reading; *Style*— The Lord McKenzie of Luton; ✉ 6 Sunset Drive, Luton, Bedfordshire LU2 7TN (tel and fax 01582 455384); Department of Work and Pensions, Caxton House, Fourth Floor, Tothill Street, London SW1H 9DA (tel 020 3267 5038, e-mail psl@dwp.gsi.giv.uk)

McKENZIE SMITH, Ian; OBE (1992); s of James McKenzie Smith (d 1977), of Aberdeen, and Mary, *née* Benzie (d 1989); *b* 3 August 1935; *Educ* Robert Gordon's Coll Aberdeen, Gray's Sch of Art Aberdeen (DA), Hospitalfield Coll of Art Arbroath; *m* 3 April 1963, Mary Rodger, da of John Fotheringham (d 1990); 1 da (Sarah Jane b 5 Jan 1965), 2 s (Patrick John b 8 Aug 1966, Justin James b 4 Feb 1969); *Career* artist; educn offr Cncl of Industrial Design Scottish Ctee 1963–68, dir Aberdeen Art Gallery and Museums 1968–89, city arts and recreation offr City of Aberdeen 1989–96; pres Royal Scottish Acad 1998– (treas and dep pres 1990–91, sec 1991–98); memb: Scottish Arts Cncl 1970–77, Scottish Museums Cncl 1980–87, Nat Heritage Scottish Gp 1983–99, Nat Tst for Scotland Curatorial Ctee, Buildings Ctee Cncl Nat Tst for Scotland, Museums and Galleries Cmmn 1997–2001;

memb Advsy Bd: Robert Gordon Univ 1992–95; memb Bd: RSA Enterprises 1972–, Scottish Sculpture Workshop 1979–2000, Aberdeen Maritime Museum Appeal 1981–98, Friends of the RSA, Grampian Hospitals Art Tst 1987–2000; tstee Nat Galleries of Scotland 1999–; chm: Marguerite McBey Tst 2002–, Patrick Allan-Fraser of Hospital Field Tst 2004–; external assessor: Glasgow Sch of Art 1982–86, Duncan of Jordanstone Coll of Art 1982–86; assessor Ruth Davidson Meml Tst, Morrison Portrait Award, Salvesen Art Tst, Noble Grossart Award, Royal Overseas League Scholarships; govr: Edinburgh Coll of Art, Robert Gordon Univ Aberdeen; fell Salzburg Seminar 1981, Hon LLD Univ of Aberdeen 1991, Hon DA Robert Gordon Univ 2000; Hon RA 1999, Hon RHA 1999, Hon RWA 2000; RSW 1981 (pres 1988–98), RGI 1999, FRSA 1973, FSS 1984, FMA 1987, FSA Scot 1970, FRSE 2003; *Work in Permanent Collections* Scottish Nat Gallery of Modern Art, Scottish Arts Cncl, Arts Cncl of NI, Contemporary Art Soc, Aberdeen Art Gallery and Museums, Glasgow Art Gallery and Museums, City Arts Centre Edinburgh, McManus Gallery Dundee, Perth Art Gallery, Abbott Hall Art Gallery Kendal, Hunterian Museum Glasgow, Nuffield Foundation, Carnegie Tst, Strathclyde Educn Authy, Lothian Educn Authy, Edinburgh District Cncl, Royal Scottish Acad, DOE, Robert Fleming Holding, IBM, Deutsche Bank, Grampian Hospitals Art Tst; *Awards* Inst of Contemporary Prints Award 1969, RSA Guthrie Award 1971, RSA Gillies Award 1980, ESU Thyne scholarship 1980; *Clubs* Caledonian, Royal Over-Seas League, Scottish Arts (Edinburgh), Royal Northern (Aberdeen); *Style*— Dr Ian McKenzie Smith, OBE; ✉ e-mail ian.mckenziesmith@hotmail.com

McKEON, Andrew John; s of Kenneth McKeon, of Manchester, and Maurine, *née* Ilsley; *b* 22 September 1955; *Educ* William Hulme's GS Manchester, St Catharine's Coll Cambridge (scholar, BA); *m* 1989, Hilary, da of Rev G Neville; 1 s (Christopher b 26 Feb 1990), 1 da (Sarah b 28 Nov 1991); *Career* joined Dept of Health 1976, dir of policy 2003–; *Style*— Andrew McKeon, Esq; ✉ Department of Health, Room 428, Richmond House, 79 Whitehall, London SW1A 2NS (tel 020 7210 5881, fax 020 7210 5660)

McKEOWN, Allan John; s of Albert Victor McKeown (d 1977), and Edith Mabel Alice, *née* Humphries (d 1970); *b* 21 May 1946; *Educ* Beal GS for Boys; *m* 27 Dec 1983, Tracey Ullman, *qv*; 1 da (Mabel Ellen b 2 April 1986), 1 s (John Albert Victor b 6 Aug 1991); *Career* TV commercials prodr 1970, md James Garratt Ltd TV advtg prodn co 1971, md JGP Ltd London and NY 1972–73, fndr British Lion Productions Ltd and conslt Shepperton Studios 1973, chief exec Pembridge Productions 1974–76, in US 1976–79, fndr WitzEnd Productions Ltd (with Dick Clement and Ian La Frenais) 1979; SelecTV plc: chief exec (following reverse takeover by WitzEnd) 1988–95, exec chm 1995–96, fndr SelecTV subsids Alomo Productions (with Laurence Marks, *qv*, and Maurice Gran, *qv*) 1988; co-fndr, dir of comedy programming and main bd dir Meridian Broadcasting (now part of ITV) 1991; fndr Selected Cable Station (now Carlton Select) 1995; SelecTV group progs incl: Auf Wiedersehen Pet (BAFTA Award nominated), Tracey Ullman Takes On New York (exec prodr, Emmy nominated), Lovejoy (US Cable Acad Award nominated), Birds of a Feather, Love Hurts, Pie in the Sky; exec prodr: Tracey Takes On 1996–99 (Emmy 1997), Tracy Ullman's TV series, Trailer Tails, Tracey Ullman's Best Bits, Tracey Ullman in the Trailer Tales 2003, Tracey Ullman: Live and Exposed 2005; theatre prodr: Jerry Springer the Opera (NT) 2004 (Olivier Award, Evening Standard Award, Critics Circle Award, prodr TV version 2005), Lennon (Curran Theatre San Francisco, transfer to Broadway 2005); memb: Acad of TV Arts and Sciences, BAFTA; FRTS; *Recreations* golf, running, French food; *Clubs* Sunningdale Golf, Royal Dornoch Golf, Riviera Country; *Style*— Allan McKeown, Esq

McKEOWN, Dermot William; s of Ronald Hubert McKeown, of Dungannon, and Rosemary, *née* McMorran; *b* 16 August 1954; *Educ* Royal Sch Dungannon, Univ of Edinburgh (MB ChB); *m* 23 July 1976, (Margaret Janet) Laurie, da of Samuel Clinton, of Strathaven; 1 s, 2 da; *Career* SHO, registrar then sr registrar in anaesthetics Edinburgh 1978–84, sr registrar in anaesthesia and intensive care Flinders Med Centre SA 1985, conslt in anaesthesia and intensive care Royal Infirmary of Edinburgh 1986–; FFARCS 1981, FRCS(Ed) 2002, FCEM 2005; *Style*— Dermot McKeown, Esq; ✉ 3 Merchiston Gardens, Edinburgh EH10 5DD (tel 0131 337 5967, e-mail dermot.mckeown@ed.ac.uk)

McKEOWN, Dr John; s of Edward McKeown (d 1984), and Anne, *née* McGladrigan; *b* 10 March 1945; *Educ* St Augustine's Sch Glasgow, Univ of Glasgow (BSc, PhD), Harvard Business Sch (Int Sr Mgmnt Prog); *m* 1967, Maureen Susan, da of Peter Doherty; 1 da (Morag Anne b 1973), 1 s (Kenneth John b 1975); *Career* CEGB research fell 1971–73; South of Scotland Electricity Board: asst Forward Planning 1973–76, sr engr Control & Instrumentation 1976–79, princ engr C&I 1979–83, mangr Electrical Dept 1983–88, mangr Nuclear Safety 1988–90; Scottish Nuclear: dir Safety 1990–92, dir Projects 1992–95, dir Safety & Environment 1995–96; princ John McKeown & Associates 1996–97, chief exec UKAEA 1997–2003; dir: UK Nirex Ltd 1997–2003, British Nuclear Indust Forum 1998–2003, Oxford Economic Partnership 1999–, Henred Strategy Ltd 2003–; author of various scientific and tech papers 1966–72; MInstD, FRSA 1992; *Recreations* golf, travel, jazz; *Clubs* Frilford Heath Golf; *Style*— Dr John McKeown; ✉ 4 Croft Orchard, Church Street, East Hendred, Oxfordshire OX12 8LA (e-mail john@mckeown8097.fsnet.co.uk)

McKEOWN, Prof Patrick Arthur (Pat); OBE (1991); s of Robert Matthew McKeown (d 1978), and Bessie Augusta, *née* White (d 1993); *b* 16 August 1930; *Educ* Cambridge GS, Bristol GS, Cranfield Inst of Technol (MSc); *m* 1954, Mary Patricia, da of Donald S B Heath, of Bristol; 3 s (Alistair Jonathan b 1957, Jeremy Patrick b 1960, Nicholas William b 1963); *Career* student apprentice Bristol Aircraft Co 1951–54 (nat state scholar 1954), Coll of Aeronautics Cranfield 1954–56, works and tech dir Société Genevoise d'Instruments de Physique 1964–68 (joined 1956), dir Cranfield Unit for Precision Engrg 1968–95, prof of precision engrg Cranfield Inst of Technol (now Cranfield Univ) 1974–95 (emeritus prof 1995), chm Cranfield Precision Engineering Ltd 1992–95 (fndr chm and chief exec 1987–92), dir Pat McKeown and Associates (conslts in advanced mfrg, precision engrg and nanotechnology) 1995–2003; non-exec dir: Control Techniques plc 1989–94, Cranfield Aerospace Ltd 2001–03; hon visiting prof Nanjing Aeronautical Inst People's Republic of China 1985, visiting prof of mechanical engrg Univ of Calif Berkeley 1994; int advsr GINTIC Inst of Mfrg Technol Singapore 1991–98; memb: Evaluation Ctee Nat Bureau of Standards USA 1980–86, Advanced Mfrg Technol Ctee DTI 1982–86, RCA Visiting Ctee 1984–87, UK Nanotechnology Strategy Ctee DTI/SERC 1987–94; pres: CIRP (int acad for prodn engrg) 1989–90, European Soc for Precision Engrg and Nanotechnology 1998–2000 (founding pres); Fulbright prof of mechanical engrg Univ of Wisconsin Madison 1982, F W Taylor medal USA Soc of Mfrg Engrs 1983, Thomas Hawksley Gold Medal IMechE 1987, Life Achievement Award American Soc for Precision Engrg 1998, Faraday Medal IEE 1999, Life Achievement Award European Soc for Precision Engrg and Nanotechnology 2002, Int Prize Japan Soc for Precision Engrg 2003, Georg Schlesinger Preis State of Berlin 2006; Hon DSc: Univ of Connecticut 1996, Cranfield Univ 1996; Freeman City of London 2007, Liveryman Worshipful Co of Engrs 2007; FREng 1986, FIMechE, FIEE, chartered fell American Soc of Mfrg Engrs; *Recreations* music, theatre, walking; *Style*— Prof Pat McKeown, OBE, FREng; ✉ tel 01234 267678, e-mail patmckeown@kbnet.co.uk

MACKERRAS, Sir (Alan) Charles MacLaurin; CH (2003), kt (1979), AC (1997), CBE (1974); s of Alan Patrick Mackerras (d 1973), and Catherine Brearcliffe (d 1977); *b* 17 November 1925; *Educ* Sydney GS, NSW Conservatorium of Music, Acad of Music Prague; *m* 1947, Helena Judith, da of Frederick Bruce Wilkins (d 1961); 2 da; *Career* staff conductor Sadler's Wells Opera 1948–54, princ conductor BBC Concert Orch 1954–56, first conductor Hamburg State Opera 1966–69, musical dir Sadler's Wells Opera later ENO 1970–77, chief guest conductor BBC Symphony Orch 1976–79, chief conductor Sydney Symphony Orch 1982–85, princ guest conductor Royal Liverpool Philharmonic Orch 1986–88, musical dir Welsh Nat Opera 1987–92 (conductor emeritus 1992–), music dir Orch of St Luke's NY 1998–2001 (emeritus 2001–); pres Trinity Coll of Music London 2000; princ guest conductor: Scottish Chamber Orch 1992–95 (conductor laureate 1995–), San Francisco Opera 1993–96 (emeritus 1996–), Royal Philharmonic Orch 1993–96, Czech Philharmonic Orch 1997–2003, Philharmonia Orch 2002–; Hon DMus: Univ of Hull 1990, Univ of Nottingham 1991, Univ of York 1994, Masaryk Univ of Brno 1994, Griffith Univ Brisbane 1994, Univ of Oxford 1997, Acad of Music Prague 1999, Napier Univ Edinburgh 2000, Univ of Sydney 2003, Univ of Melbourne 2003, Janáček Acad of Music Brno 2004, Univ of London 2005; hon fell: St Peter's Coll Oxford 1999, Univ of Cardiff 2003, Royal Welsh Coll of Music and Drama 2005; Hon LRAM 1969, Hon FRCM 1987, Hon FRNCM 1999, Hon FTCL 1999; Medal of Merit Czech Republic 1996, Royal Philharmonic Soc Gold Medal 2005, BBC Radio 3 Listeners' Award for Artist of the Year 2005, Queen's Medal for Music (first recipient) 2005, Classic FM/Grampohone Lifetime Achievement Award 2006, Worshipful Co of Musicians Silver Medal 2006; *Publications* Ballet Arrangements of Pineapple Poll (Sullivan), The Lady and the Fool (Verdi), reconstruction of Arthur Sullivan's lost Cello Concerto; Charles Mackerras: a Musicians' Musician (contrib appendices, 1987); *Style*— Sir Charles Mackerras, CH, AC, CBE; ✉ 10 Hamilton Terrace, London NW8 9UG (tel 020 7286 4047, fax 020 7289 5893)

McKERRELL OF HILLHOUSE, Charles James Mure; s of Capt Robert James Mure McKerrell of Hillhouse (d 1964), and Winifred Scott, *née* Walkinshaw (d 1997); matric arms Ct of the Lord Lyon 1973, recognised by the Lord Lyon as McKerrell of Hillhouse and Head of the Name by Interlocutor of Lord Lyon, also recorded arms Genealogical Office Dublin Castle and recognised as 15th Head of the Name by Chief Herald of Ireland; McKerrell of Hillhouse tartan and McKerrell of Hillhouse Dress tartan recorded by deed Court of the Lord Lyon 1982 and 2002; *b* 23 January 1941; *Educ* Cranleigh Sch; *m* 2 Jan 1991, May Weston Cochrane, NFNN, DLJ, FSAScot, da of Matthew Cochrane White (d 1967); *Career* fndr memb Heraldry Soc of Ireland, memb Bd Soc of Scottish Armigers; memb: Royal Celtic Soc, Royal Stuart Soc, Heraldry Soc of Scotland, Corona Legitima, Saltire Soc; assoc memb Convention of the Baronage of Scotland; Freeman City of London 2000; FSA Scot; Guardian of the Nobiliary Fraternity of the Nia Naisc, OStJ, Knight Order of St Michael of the Wing, Knight Grand Cross of Justice of the Order of St Lazarus of Jerusalem, Hereditary Companion of The Companionate of the Royal House of O'Conor, Chevalier Grand Cross of the Patriarchal Order of St Ignace of Antioche, hon capt Canadian Bush Pilots Sqdn of Canada; *Style*— McKerrell of Hillhouse; ✉ Magdalene House, Lochmaben, Dumfries DG11 1PD (tel and fax 01387 810439, e-mail mckerrellofhillhouse@ukonline.co.uk)

McKERROW, Colin William; s of William Henry McKerrow, MC (d 1976), and Phyllis Mary Livingstone, *née* Robinson (d 1980); *b* 22 January 1934; *Educ* The Downs Sch Colwall, Eastbourne Coll; *Career* trainee Royal Insurance Co plc 1951–58, stockbroker 1958–91 (incl Laing & Cruickshank 1980–91), fund mangr Ely Fund Managers Ltd 1991–2002; dir Derby County FC plc 1983–94; fndr MCC Bridge Soc 1994; fndr memb Peace Parks Bd (Southern Africa); MSI (memb Stock Exchange 1966), FRMetS 1994; *Recreations* travel, oenology, ornithology, playing bridge, watching sport generally; *Clubs* MCC, Hurlingham, Caledonian; *Style*— Colin McKerrow, Esq; ✉ 6 Thornton Road, Wimbledon, London SW19 4NE (tel and fax 020 8946 6195, e-mail colin.mckerrow@btinternet.com)

McKERROW, June; da of late Alexander Donald McKerrow, and Lorna McKerrow; *b* 17 June 1950; *Educ* Brunel Univ (MPhil); 1 adopted da; *Career* local govt housing 1967–71, housing mangr Paddington Churches Housing Assoc 1971–76, dep dir Church Army Housing 1977–80, dir Stonham Housing Assoc 1980–92, dir Mental Health Fndn 1992–2000; charity advsr 2000–; memb Nat Cncl of Nat Fedn of Housing Assocs 1982–90, tstee and vice-chair Shelter 1985–93, fndr memb Homeless Int 1987–93; tstee: Charity Projects 1992–96, Cherwell Housing Tst Oxford 1992–97, Autism Cymru 2001–04; memb Ctee English Rural Housing Assoc 1997–99, tstee and chair Housing Assocs Charitable Tst 1998–2002, memb Bd Advance Housing and Support 2000–03; non-exec dir Oxfordshire Mental Healthcare NHS Tst 2000–, tstee Winston's Wish 2001–03, dir Soundabout 2003–; memb Ct Oxford Brookes Univ; *Style*— Ms June McKerrow; ✉ 22 Buckingham Street, Oxford OX1 4LH (e-mail june@junemckerrow.co.uk)

MACKERSIE, Andrew James; s of John Anthony Mackersie, and Krystyna Anna, *née* Bragiel; *b* 16 November 1974; *Educ* St Benedict's Sch Ealing, St Peter's Coll Oxford (exhibitioner, MA); *Career* Citibank NA 1996–97; House of Lords: clerk Parl Office 1997–, judicial clerk 1998–2001 and 2002–03, clerk Constitution Ctee 2001–02, clerk Legislation Office 2003–; sec Assoc of Lord-Lts 2002–; *Publications* contrib on judicial functions of House of Lords and peerages to various pubns incl: Halsbury's Laws of England, Atkin's Court Forms, Civil Procedure, Erskine May's Parliamentary Practice; *Recreations* riding and equestrian sports, agriculture; *Clubs* Brooks's; *Style*— Andrew Mackersie, Esq; ✉ 1AA Carlisle Place, London SW1P 1NP (tel 020 7931 9542); House of Lords, London SW1A 0PW (tel 020 7219 3000)

MACKESON, Sir Rupert; 2 Bt (UK 1954), of Hythe, Co Kent; s of Brig Sir Harry Ripley Mackeson, 1 Bt (d 1964); *b* 16 November 1941; *Educ* Harrow, Trinity Coll Dublin (MA); *m* 22 July 1968 (m dis 1972), Hon Camilla Margaret, da of Baron Keith of Castleacre (Life Peer); *Career* Capt RHG, ret 1968; author of numerous books as Rupert Mackeson and Rupert Collens; *Books* incl: Bet Like a Man, A Look at Cecil Aldin Dogs and Hounds, Snaffles Life and Works, 25 Legal Luminaries from Vanity Fair, 50 Cheltenham Gold Cups; *Style*— Capt Sir Rupert Mackeson, Bt; ✉ Flat 3, 51 South Road, Weston-super-Mare, Somerset BS23 2LU

MACKESON-SANDBACH, Ian Lawrie; s of Capt Lawrie Mackeson-Sandbach (d 1984), of Llangernyw, Clwyd, and Geraldine, *née* Sandbach (d 2001); *b* 14 June 1933; *Educ* Eton, Univ of New Brunswick; *m* 6 May 1967, Annie Marie, da of J M G Van Lanschot (d 1983), of S'Hertogenbosch, Netherlands; 4 da (Antoinette b 1969, Sara (Mrs Fabio Fabrizio) b 1970, Louise (Mrs James) b 1973, Megan (Mrs Dalton) b 1976); *Career* Lt Welsh Gds emergency reserve 1952–57; md France Fenwick Ltd 1969–75, dir Demerara Co Ltd 1969–76, chief exec Ernest Notcutt Group Ltd 1976–82; chm Crown Estate Paving Cmmn 1983–2004 (cmmr 1974); Provincial Grand Master N Wales 1990–2004; Liveryman Worshipful Co of Grocers; memb Inst of Fire Engrs 1960; *Recreations* shooting, fishing; *Clubs* Boodle's, Pratt's, Royal St George's (Sandwich); *Style*— Ian Mackeson-Sandbach, Esq; ✉ 20 Hanover Terrace, Regent's Park, London NW1 4RJ (tel 020 7402 6290); office: tel 020 7723 3112, fax 020 7402 6390, e-mail mackeson@accademia-trustees.fsnet.co.uk

McKIE, Alastair John; WS; s of John Jack McKie, of South Queensferry, Flintshire, and Avril, *née* Quinton; *b* 15 June 1962, Ipswich, Suffolk; *Educ* Lornshill Acad Alloa, Univ of Dundee; *m* 6 Aug 2004, Dr Margaret McKinnon Mitchell; 1 da (Ava Lynne); *Career* admitted slr 1987; legal trainee Glenrothes Devpt Corp, with Kirkcaldy DC and Fife Cncl 1991–98, ptnr and head of planning and environment Anderson Strathern 1998–; accredited specialist in planning law Law Soc of Scotland; legal assoc RTPI; *Recreations* hill walking, fishing, tennis, dogs; *Clubs* Drummond Tennis; *Style*— Alastair McKie, Esq, WS; ✉ 3A Royal Crescent, Edinburgh EH3 6PZ; Anderson Strathern, 1 Rutland Court, Edinburgh EH3 8EY (tel 0131 625 7257, fax 0131 625 8030, e-mail alastair.mckie@andersonstrathern.co.uk)

M

MACKIE, His Hon Judge David Lindsay; CBE (2004), QC (1998); s of Alastair Cavendish Lindsay Mackie, CBE, DFC, of London, and Rachel, *née* Goodson; *b* 15 February 1946; *Educ* St Edmund Hall Oxford (MA); *m* 1, 13 Feb 1971 (m dis 1986); 2 s (James b 1974, Edward b 1976), 1 da (Eleanor b 1978); m 2, 6 Dec 1989, Phyllis, da of Robert Gershon, of NYC; *Career* admitted slr 1971, ptnr Allen & Overy 1975–2004 (head of litigation 1988–2004), recorder of the Crown Court 1992, dep judge of the High Court 1998, mercantile judge 2004–; dep chair RCJ Advice Bureau, a chm Financial Services and Markets Tribunal 2001; FCIArb; *Recreations* climbing; *Style—* His Hon Judge Mackie, CBE, QC

MACKIE, John David; CBE (2007); *b* 30 April 1953; *Educ* St Mary's GS Middlesbrough, Univ of Glasgow (BAcc); *m* 1982, Elaine, *née* Jackson; 2 da; *Career* numerous positions incl dj, lab asst and advtg salesman 1968–71, trainee mangr rising to gen mangr Woolco Dept Stores 1971–79, trainee accountant Arthur Andersen & Co 1982–85, investment dir 3i Gp plc 1985–89, fndr dir Morgan Grenfell Development Capital Ltd 1990–98 (bd memb Morgan Grenfell & Co (then Deutsche Morgan Grenfell) 1995–98), chief exec Br Venture Capital Assoc (BVCA) 2000–05; cnslt Technomark Medical Ventures 2000–03, dir Parallel Private Equity 2003–, chm August Equity Tst plc 2006–; supporter: Guide Dogs for the Blind Assoc, Br Lung Fndn; MICAS, MSI; *Recreations* family, books, cinema, theatre, wine; *Style—* John Mackie, Esq; ✉ Parallel Private Equity Ltd, 49 St James's Street, London SW1A 1JT (tel 020 7600 9105)

MACKIE, Dr Karl Joseph; s of John Mackie, and Ethel, *née* Freeman; *b* 31 March 1947; *Educ* Buckhaven HS, Univ of Edinburgh (MA), Univ of London (LLB), Univ of Nottingham (PhD), Open Univ (MBA), Univ of Edinburgh (DipEd); *m* 1, 1968 (m dis), Ann Douglas; 1 s, 1 da; m 2, 2001, Eileen Carroll; 1 step da (Jennifer); *Career* called to the Bar Gray's Inn 1982; research assoc Univ of Edinburgh 1971–72, lectr then sr lectr in law and social psychology Univ of Nottingham 1973–90, ptnr Network Associates Strategy Conslts 1985–90, chief exec CEDR 1990–; accredited mediator CEDR; memb: Panel of Ind Mediators and Arbitrators ACAS 1980–, Panel of Distinguished Neutrals CPR Inst NY, Singapore Commercial Mediation Panel; vice-chm Civil Mediation Cncl 2003–; hon prof in alternative dispute resolution: Univ of Birmingham 1994–2001, Univ of Westminster 2004–; memb editorial ctees of various jls; memb: Educn Ctee Bar Assoc for Commerce, Finance and Industry 1987–90, Specialisation Ctee Law Soc 1989–92; chm Write Away 2003–06; CPsychol 1989; FCIArb 1992, FRSA 1993; *Publications* Learning Lawyers' Skills (jt ed, 1989), Lawyers in Business and the Law Business (1989), A Handbook of Dispute Resolution (ed, 1991), Commercial Dispute Resolution (jtly, 1995, 2 edn (as ADR Practice Guide) 2000), International Mediation: the art of business diplomacy (jtly, 2000, 2 edn 2006), The EU Mediation Atlas (co-ed, 2004); *Recreations* film, photography, writing; *Style—* Dr Karl Mackie; ✉ Centre for Effective Dispute Resolution, International Dispute Resolution Centre, 70 Fleet Street, London EC4Y 1EU (tel 020 7536 6000, fax 020 7536 6001, e-mail kjmackie@cedr.co.uk)

MACKIE, Prof Neil; CBE (1996); s of William Fraser Mackie (d 1979), of King's Gate, Aberdeen, and Sheila Roberta, *née* Taylor (d 1973); *b* 11 December 1946; *Educ* Aberdeen GS, Royal Scot Acad of Music and Drama (DipMusEdRSAMD, DipRSAMD), Royal Coll of Music (fndn scholar, ARCM); *m* 1973, Kathleen Mary, da of William Livingstone (d 1972); 2 da (Alison Kathleen b 1980, Elinor Sheila b 1983); *Career* international concert singer (tenor); Royal Coll of Music: prof of singing 1985–, head of vocal studies 1994–2006; prof Fine Arts Faculty Agner Univ Norway 2005–; artistic dir Mayfield Festival 2005–; Gulbenkian fell, Caird scholar, Munster scholar; London recital debut Wigmore Hall 1972, London concert debut with Eng Chamber Orch under Raymond Leppard 1973; world premières incl: Unpublished Songs by Britten, Hans Werner Henze's Three Auden Settings, several Kenneth Leighton works incl Symphony No 3, many cmmnd works by Scottish composers; works especially written for him by Peter Maxwell Davies: The Martyrdom of St Magnus (title role), The Lighthouse (role of Sandy), Into the Labyrinth (solo cantata for tenor and orch), A Solstice of Light; Hon DMus Univ of Aberdeen 1993; FRSA 1991, FRSAMD 1992, FRSE 1996, FRCM 1996; CStJ 1996 (OStJ 1987); *Recordings* numerous on EMI, Decca, Philips, Chandos, Deutsche Grammophon, Unicorn-Kanchana, Somm, Accent, Collins, Abbey Records; *Awards* runner up Gramophone Solo Voice Recording of the Year for Britten Tenor, Horn and Strings (with Scottish Chamber Orch) 1989, Grammy Award 1993; *Recreations* reading, charity work and occasional gardening; *Clubs* Athenaeum, Royal Over-Seas League; *Style—* Prof Neil Mackie, CBE, FRSE; ✉ 70 Broadwood Avenue, Ruislip, Middlesex HA4 7XR (tel 01895 632115, e-mail neilmackie@talktalk.net)

MACKIE, Dr Peter Howard; s of Dr Lawrence Percival Mackie (d 1988), of Wellesbourne, Warks, and Elizabeth Bates; *b* 13 October 1947; *Educ* Cheltenham Coll, Hertford Coll Oxford (MA, BM BCh); *m* 14 July 1973, Joanna Jane, da of John Henry McGhee, TD (d 1987), of Kineton, Warks; 4 da (Sarah b 1975, Julia b 1978, Diana b 1980, Rachel b 1986); *Career* house physician Harefield Hosp 1973, house surgn Cheltenham Gen Hosp 1973–74, SHO and registrar Bristol Royal Infirmary 1974–76, hon tutor Univ of Bristol 1974–76, res registrar Queen Elizabeth Hosp Birmingham 1976–77, lectr Dept of Immunology Univ of Birmingham 1977–79, sr registrar (haematology) John Radcliffe Hosp Oxford 1979–82, conslt haematologist E Berks Dist 1982–, chm Div of Med E Berks Dist 1989–93, dir Lab Servs Heatherwood and Wexham Park Hosps Tst 1992–98 (chm Med Staff Ctee 1993–95), chm Regnl Devpt Gp for Haematology 1998–2001, med dir Heatherwood and Wexham Park Hosps Tst 1999–2002; memb Br Soc for Haematology 1978– (regl rep 1991–94 and 1998–2001), examiner RCP 2002–; memb: Ancient Soc of Coll Youths 1970–, Windsor and Dist Organists' Assoc 1984–94; FRCPath 1993 (MRCPath 1981), FRCP 1995 (MRCP 1978); *Recreations* music, bellringing, gardening; *Style—* Dr Peter Mackie; ✉ The Princess Margaret Hospital, Osborne Road, Windsor SL4 3SJ (tel 01753 633418, fax 01753 633444, e-mail phm@btinternet.com)

MacKIE, Prof Rona McLeod; CBE (1999); da of Prof J Norman Davidson, FRS (d 1972), of Bearsden, Glasgow, and Morag, *née* McLeod; *b* 22 May 1940; *Educ* Laurel Bank Sch, Univ of Glasgow (MB ChB, MD, DSc); *m* 1, 1962 (m dis); 1 da (Alison b 1963), 1 s (Douglas b 1965); m 2, 1994, Prof Sir James Whyte Black, FRS, *qv*; *Career* hon conslt dermatologist Gtr Glasgow Health Bd 1978– (conslt dermatologist 1973–78), prof of dermatology Univ of Glasgow 1978–; pres Br Assoc of Dermatologists, vice-pres Nat Eczema Soc; FRCPGlas 1978, FRSE 1983, FRCPath 1984, FRCP 1985, FIBiol 1988; *Books* Clinical Dermatology - An Illustrated Textbook (1981, 5 edn 2003), Eczema and Dermatitis (1983), Malignant Melanoma (ed, 1983), Current Perspectives in Immunodermatology (ed, 1984), Milne's Dermatopathology (ed, 1984), Clinical Dermatology An Illustrated Textbook (1994), Skin Cancer (1995); *Recreations* skiing, music especially opera, gardening; *Style—* Prof Rona MacKie, CBE, FRSE; ✉ Department of Public Health, University of Glasgow, Glasgow G12 8RZ (tel 0141 330 5013, fax 0141 330 5018, e-mail r.m.mackie@clinmed.gla.ac.uk)

MACKIE OF BENSHIE, Baron (Life Peer UK 1974), of Kirriemuir in the County of Angus; George Yull Mackie; CBE (1971), DSO (1944), DFC (1944), LLD (1982); s of Maitland Mackie, OBE, LLD, and bro of Baron John-Mackie (d 1994) and Sir Maitland Mackie, CBE, JP (d 1996); *b* 10 July 1919; *Educ* Aberdeen GS, Aberdeen Univ; *m* 1, 1944, Lindsay Lyall (d 1985), da of Alexander Sharp, advocate, of Aberdeen, and Isabella Sharp, OBE; 3 da (Hon Lindsay Mary (Hon Mrs Rusbridger) b 1945, Hon Diana Lyall (Hon Mrs Hope) b 1946, Hon Jeannie Felicia (Hon Mrs Leigh) b 1953), and 1 s decd; m 2, 29 April 1988, Jacqueline, wid of Andrew Lane and da of Col Marcel Rauch, Legion d'Honneur and Croix de Guerre; *Career* serv WWII Bomber Cmd; farmer 1945–89; chm Mackie Yule & Co, Caithness Glass Ltd 1966–85, Caithness Pottery Co, Benshie Cattle Co; rector Univ of Dundee 1980–83; MP (Lib) Caithness & Sutherland 1964–66; Parly candidate (Lib) Angus S 1959, European Parly candidate Scotland NE 1979; chm Scot Lib Pty 1965–70; chm Land & Timber Services Ltd 1986–88; Lib spokesman House of Lords on: Devolution, Agriculture, Scotland until 1999; memb: Parly Assembly Cncl of Europe 1986–97, WEU 1986–97; pres Scottish Lib Pty until 1988 (became SLD); Hon LLD 1982; *Recreations* golf, reading, social life; *Clubs* Garrick, Farmers', RAF; *Style—* The Rt Hon Lord Mackie of Benshie, CBE, DSO, DFC; ✉ Benshie Cottage, Oathlaw, By Forfar, Angus DD8 3PQ (tel 01307 850376)

McKILLOP, Prof James Hugh (Jim); s of Dr Patrick McKillop (d 1979), of Coatbridge, Strathclyde, and Dr Helen Theresa McKillop, *née* Kilpatrick (d 1998); *b* 20 June 1948; *Educ* St Aloysius' Coll Glasgow, Univ of Glasgow (BSc, MB ChB, PhD); *m* 17 Aug 1973, Caroline Annis, da of Charles Allen Oakley, CBE (d 1993), of Glasgow; 2 da (Beth b 1977, Jenny b 1981); *Career* Harkness fellowship Stanford Univ 1979 and 1980; Univ of Glasgow: lectr 1977–82, sr lectr 1982–89, Muirhead prof of med 1989–, assoc dean for med educn 2000–03, head Undergraduate Med Sch 2003–06, dep dean of medicine 2007–; treas Scottish Soc of Experimental Med 1982–87; Br Nuclear Med Soc: memb Cncl 1985–94, hon sec 1988–90, pres 1990–92; Euro Assoc of Nuclear Med: memb Exec Ctee 1995–99, congress pres 1997, chm Educn Ctee 1998–2000, memb Strategy Ctee 2000–06, memb Constitution Cmmn 2002–06; chm: Intercollegiate Standing Ctee on Nuclear Med 1995–98, ARSAC Ctee Dept of Health 1996–2004 (memb 1988–, vice-chm 1989–95), Scottish Med and Scientific Advsy Ctee 2001– (memb 1998–), MRCP Validation, Audit and Res Gp, NHS Educn Scotland Med Advsy Gp 2004–, Scottish Dean's Med Curriculum Gp 2005–; team leader GMC Quality Assurance of Basic Med Educn 2003–; vice-pres UEMS section of nuclear med 1998–2000, ed Nuclear Med Communications 1991–98; memb: Exec Ctee Assoc of Physicians of GB and Ireland 1999–2003, MRCP Policy Cmmn 1998–2005, Scottish Bd for Academic Medicine 2006–; FRCPGlas 1985, FRCPEd 1990, FRCP 1992, FRCR 1994, FMedSci 1998; *Books* Atlas of Technetium Bone Scans (with D L Citrin, 1978), Imaging in Clinical Practice (with A G Chalmers and P J Robinson, 1988), Clinician's Guide to Nuclear Medicine: Benign and Malignant Bone Disease (with I Fogelman, 1991); *Recreations* football, cricket, opera, reading; *Style—* Prof Jim McKillop; ✉ 18 Beaumont Gate, Glasgow G12 9ED (tel 0141 339 7000); Wolfson Medical School Building, University of Glasgow, Glasgow G12 8QQ (tel 0141 330 8041, fax 0141 330 2776, e-mail j.h.mckillop@clinmed.gla.ac.uk)

McKILLOP, Sir Thomas Fulton Wilson (Tom); kt (2002); s of Hugh McKillop, and Annie, *née* Wilson; *b* 19 March 1943; *Educ* Irvine Royal Acad, Univ of Glasgow (BSc, PhD), Centre de Mecanique Ondulatoire Appliquée Paris; *m* 1966, Elizabeth, *née* Kettle; 2 da, 1 s; *Career* research scientist ICI Corporate Laboratory 1969–75; ICI Pharmaceuticals: head of natural products research 1975–78, research dir France 1978–80, chemistry mangr 1980–84, gen mangr of Research Dept 1984–85, gen mangr of Devpt Dept 1985–89, tech dir 1989–94; ceo Zeneca Pharmaceuticals 1994–99; exec dir Zeneca Gp plc 1996–99, chief exec AstraZeneca plc 1999–2005; chm Br Pharma Gp 1994–2005; non-exec dir: Amersham International 1992–97, Nycomed Amersham plc 1997–2000, Lloyds TSB plc 1998–2004, BP plc 2004–, Royal Bank of Scotland 2005–06 (chm 2006–); pro-chllr Univ of Leicester 1998– (memb Gen Cncl); tstee Darwin Tst of Edinburgh; world pres Soc of Chemical Industry 2004–, pres Science Cncl until 2007; memb: Royal Institution, RSC, ACS, Soc for Drug Research, Cncl for Industry and HE 2002–; Hon LLD: Victoria Univ of Manchester 1999, Dundee Univ 2003; Hon DSc: Univ of Glasgow 2000, Univ of Leicester 2000, Huddersfield Univ 2000, Nottingham Univ 2001, St Andrews Univ 2004, Univ of Salford 2004, Univ of Manchester 2005; Hon Dr Middlesex 2006, Hon Degree Univ of Paisley 2006, Hon Dr of Letters Heriot Watt Univ 2006; Hon Fell: Lancashire 2004, Icheme 2006, Manchester Interdisciplinary Biocentre 2006; FRS 2005; *Recreations* music, sport, reading, walking, carpentry; *Clubs* Wilmslow Golf; *Style—* Sir Tom McKillop

MACKINLAY, Andrew; MP; *b* 1949; *Educ* Salesian Coll Chertsey, DMA, ACIS; *m*; 3 c; *Career* MP (Lab) Thurrock 1992–; memb Foreign Affrs Select Ctee, memb Br-Irish Parly Body; memb All-Pty: Poland Gp, Manx Gp; memb TGWU; Backbencher of the Year Zurich/Spectator Parly Awards 2001; *Style—* Andrew Mackinlay, Esq, MP; ✉ House of Commons, London SW1A 0AA (tel 020 7219 3000)

MACKINLAY, Col Hamish Grant; LVO (1979); s of James Johnstone Mackinlay (d 1988), of Tillicoultry, Clackmannanshire, and Margaret Keir, *née* Grant (d 1998); *b* 11 March 1935; *Educ* Dollar Acad, RMA Sandhurst; *m* 25 Jan 1964, Elizabeth (Elspeth) Paul Gray, da of Rev Peter Bryce Gunn (d 1979), of Ancrum, Roxburghshire; 1 s (Jamie b 1966), 1 da (Diana b 1969); *Career* cmmnd RCS 1955, sr seconded offr State of Qatar 1976–79, SO Army Staff Duties MOD 1979–82, dep head Mil Mission to HRH The Crown Prince of Saudi Arabia 1982–86, def and mil attaché Cairo 1986–88, dep govr HM Tower of London 1989–95; sec The Friends of Norwich Cathedral 1995–99; pres Friends of Gressenhall Rural Life Museum 1999–; tstee Royal British Legion Attendants Co Tst 1995–; non-exec dir Legion Security plc 1998–; Freeman City of London; FCMI, FRSA; *Clubs* Royal Commonwealth Soc, Norfolk; *Style—* Col Hamish Mackinlay, LVO; ✉ The Horseshoes, Gressenhall, Dereham, Norfolk NR20 4DT (tel and fax 01362 860302, e-mail hamish@mackinlay.net)

MACKINLAY, (Jack) Lindsay; *b* 24 January 1936; *m* 30 Sept 1961, Catherine Elizabeth (Elise); 1 s (Graham b 1966), 1 da (Carolyn b 1968); *Career* dir Rowntree Mackintosh plc 1973–89; chm: RPC Group plc 1992–2000, Bradford & Bingley plc 1995–2002; FCA 1959, FCMA 1968, FIMgt; *Recreations* golf, sailing, music; *Style—* Lindsay Mackinlay, Esq; ✉ The Cottage, Skelton, York YO30 1XX

McKINLAY, Peter; CBE (1998); s of Peter McKinlay (d 1991), and Mary Clegg, *née* Hamill; *b* 29 December 1939; *Educ* Campbeltown GS, Univ of Glasgow (MA); *m* 28 Sept 1963, Anne, da of David and Jane Rogerson Thomson; 2 s (Alasdair Rogerson b 31 Jan 1966, Fraser b 3 Jan 1975), 1 da (Shelagh b 13 Oct 1967); *Career* asst postal controller GPO HQ Edinburgh 1963–67; SO: asst princ 1967–70, princ 1970–77 (incl private sec to the Min of State, Rt Hon Bruce Millan), asst sec 1977–88, dir Scottish Prison Serv 1988–91; chief exec Scottish Homes 1991–99, chm Wise Gp 1998–; Hon DBA Napier Univ 1999; FRSA; *Recreations* family, friends, garden, television, reading, food, drink; *Clubs* Machrihanish Golf; *Style—* Peter McKinlay, Esq, CBE, FRSA

McKINLAY, Rebecca Kate; da of Hugh Edward Impey (d 2002), and Rachel Rosemary, *née* Moody; *b* 6 February 1970; *Educ* Guildford HS, Univ of Hull (BA); *m* 18 Jan 1997, Jason McKinlay, s of John Walden McKinlay; 1 da (Charlotte Kate b 11 Feb 1999), 2 s (Thomas Edward Player b 28 July 2002, Maximilian Angus b 15 June 2004); *Career* account planner Hall Harrison Cowley 1992–93, head of mktg Club 18–30 1993–96, advtg and media mangr News Gp Newspapers News Int 1996–99, dir Haygarth Digital 2000–01 (account dir 1999–2000), gp mktg dir Haygarth 2001–05, fndr Ambition Communications 2005–; *Recreations* tennis, golf; *Style—* Mrs Rebecca McKinlay; ✉ Ambition, Woodcock House, Gibbard Mews, Wimbledon Village, London SW19 5BY (tel 020 8791 3377, e-mail rebecca@ambition-communications.co.uk)

McKINNEY, Paul Benedict; s of James P McKinney, of Dumbarton, and Marie; *b* 21 May 1964; *Educ* St Thomas of Aquin's HS, United World Coll of the Atlantic (Int Bacc), UC Oxford (BA), Moray House Coll of Educn Edinburgh (PGCE); *Career* researcher and press offr to Gordon Brown, MP 1988–92, civil servant Scottish Office 1993; Scottish Television: researcher/reporter 1994, asst prodr news & current affairs 1994–96, chief news prodr 1996–99, head of news 1999–2000, head of news and current affairs 2000–;

Recreations cinema, theatre, opera; *Style*— Paul McKinney, Esq; ✉ Scottish Television, 200 Renfield Street, Glasgow G2 3PR (tel 0141 300 3377/3309, fax 0141 332 9274)

McKINNON, Prof Alan; s of Alexander Campbell McKinnon (d 1993), and Janet, *née* McPheat; *b* 19 September 1953; *Educ* Perth Acad, Univ of Aberdeen (MA, winner Royal Scottish Geographical Society medal), Univ of Br Columbia (MA, Canadian Commonwealth Scholarship), UCL (PhD); *m* 15 July 1983, Sabine, da of Werner Rohde; 2 s (Philip Alexander b 4 Dec 1985, Christopher Alan b 24 Aug 1988); *Career* lectr in geography Univ of Leicester 1979–87; Heriot-Watt Univ: lectr Dept of Business Organisation 1987–92, sr lectr 1992–94, reader 1994–95, prof of logistics 1995–, dir Logistics Res Centre 1998–, dir of research in Sch of Mgmnt and languages 2005–; chm Scottish Tport Studies Gp 1989–92, chm Foresight Retail Logistics Taskforce 2000–01, Euro ed Int Jl of Physical Distribution and Logistics Mgmnt 1990–95, ed-in-chief Tport Logistics Jl 1996–98, specialist advsr: House of Commons Scottish Affairs Ctee study of Future of Scotland's Tport Links with Europe 1992–93, Scottish Parl Local Govt and Tport Ctee Inquiry into Freight Tport in Scotland 2006; memb: Scottish Office's Nat Tport Forum 1998–99, Foresight Panel on the Built Environment and Tport 1999–2001, Cmmn for Integrated Tport Working Gp on lorry weight limits 1999–2000, Dept for Tport Freight and Logistics Research Gp 2003–; Herbert Crow Meml Award Worshipful Co of Carmen 2002, Sir Robert Lawrence Award Inst of Logistics and Tport 2003; FILT 1997, CFILT 2003; *Publications* Physical Distribution Systems (1989), Transport Logistics (ed, 2002); also articles in academic jls; *Recreations* piano playing, hill walking and cycling; *Style*— Professor Alan McKinnon; ✉ School of Management and Languages, Heriot-Watt University, Edinburgh EH14 4AS (tel 0131 451 3850, fax 0131 451 3498, e-mail a.c.mckinnon@hw.ac.uk)

McKINNON, Rt Hon Donald Charles; PC (1992); s of late Maj-Gen W S McKinnon, and late Anna B, *née* Plimmer; *b* 27 February 1939; *Educ* Nelson Coll NZ, Woodrow Wilson High Sch Washington DC, Lincoln Univ NZ; *m* 1; 1 da (Margaret), 3 s (Peter, Stuart, Cameron); m 2, 1995, Clare de Lore; 1 s (James b 1998); *Career* farm mangr, then mangr of own real estate business and farm mgmnt conslt until 1978; elected to NZ Parl 1978: Min for Disarmament and Arms Control, Min for Veterans' Affrs, Assoc Min of Defence, Min in Charge of War Pensions, Min for Pacific Island Affrs, Min of Foreign Affrs and Trade 1990–99, Dep PM 1990–96, Ldr House of Representatives 1992–97; chm Parly Ctee on Expenditure and Control; chief whip 1981–87; memb Privy Cncl 1992; dep chm Cwlth Ministerial Action Gp (CMAG) 1995–99, chm Cwlth Small States Meeting 1995, memb Cwlth Ministerial Mission on Small States 1998, Sec-Gen Cwlth 2000–; *Recreations* playing tennis, jogging, riding; *Style*— The Rt Hon Donald McKinnon; ✉ Commonwealth Secretariat, Marlborough House, Pall Mall, London SW1Y 5HX (tel 020 7747 6103, fax 020 7930 2299)

McKINNON, His Hon Judge Warwick Nairn; s of His Hon Judge Neil Nairn McKinnon (d 1988), of Purley, Surrey, and Janetta Amelia, *née* Lilley (d 1989); bro of Sir Stuart Neil McKinnon (Hon Mr Justice McKinnon); *b* 11 November 1947; *Educ* KCS Wimbledon, Christ's Coll Cambridge (MA); *m* 29 July 1978, Nichola Juliet, da of David Alan Lloyd, of Limpsfield, Surrey; 1 s (Rory b 1981), 1 da (Kirsty b 1982); *Career* called to the Bar Lincoln's Inn 1970; ad eundum SE Circuit, recorder of the Crown Court 1995–98, circuit judge (SE Circuit) 1998–, resident judge Croydon Crown Court 2006–; chm Essex Criminal Justice Strategy Ctee 1999–2001, liaison judge and chm SE London region Area Judicial Forum 2006–; *Publications* WordPerfect 5.1 for the Criminal Lawyer; *Recreations* travel, golf, gardening, music and opera; *Style*— His Hon Judge Warwick McKinnon; ✉ South Eastern Circuit Office, New Cavendish House, 18 Maltravers Street, London WC2R 3EU (tel 020 7936 7235)

McKINSTRY, Dr Thomas Herbert (Tom); s of Ebenezer Herbert McKinstry (d 1977), and Margaret, *née* Eccles (d 2002); *b* 19 March 1943, Belfast; *Educ* Belfast Royal Acad, KCL, Queen's Univ Belfast (MB, BCh, BAO); *m* 19 March 1967, Anna, *née* Miskimmin; 1 s (Caleb Eccles b 10 Sept 1968), 1 da (Zahra Hannah b 26 Aug 1978); *Career* registrar in psychiatry 1981–86, GP 1986–; memb Cncl BMA 1992– (chm E Dorset Divn 2005–), former chm Wessex and NI Junior Doctors Ctee; fell Belfast Royal Acad; Freeman City of London, Liveryman Worshipful Co of Gold and Silver Wyre Drawers; *Recreations* motor sport, theatre, rugby, polo, food and drink; *Clubs* Queen's Univ of London Assoc, New Forest Polo; *Style*— Dr Tom McKinstry; ✉ The Village Medical Practice, Vernon House, 164 Station Road, Ferndown, Dorset BH22 0JB (tel 01202 871999, fax 01202 892080)

MACKINTOSH, Dr Alan Finlay; s of Dr Finlay George Mackintosh (d 1989), and Eileen Ormsby, *née* Johnson; *b* 14 January 1948; *Educ* Oundle, King's Coll Cambridge (BA), Westminster Med Sch (MD BChir); *m* 16 Feb 1974, Susan Patricia, da of Col Claude Hugo Macdonald Hull (d 1979); 1 da (Clare b 18 April 1979), 1 s (Nicholas b 14 April 1982); *Career* med registrar: Brighton 1975–76, KCH London 1976–77; sr cardiology registrar Cambridge 1978–81; conslt cardiologist: Killingbeck Hosp Leeds 1981–97, St James's Univ Hosp Leeds 1981–, Leeds Gen Infirmary 1997–; sr lectr Univ of Leeds 1991– (lectr 1981–91); treas Br Cardiovascular Intervention Soc 1987–93, chm Jt Royal Colls and Ambulance Services Liaison Ctee 1995–98; FRCP, FESC; *Books* The Heart Disease Reference Book (1984), Case Presentations in Heart Disease (1985, 2 edn 1992); *Recreations* skiing, tennis, opera; *Style*— Dr Alan Mackintosh; ✉ 15 Charville Gardens, Shadwell, Leeds LS17 8JL (tel 0113 273 7293); St James's University Hospital, Beckett Street, Leeds LS9 7TP (tel 0113 243 3144)

MACKINTOSH, Sir Cameron Anthony; kt (1996); *b* 17 October 1946; *Educ* Prior Park Coll Bath, Central Sch of Speech and Drama (1 year); *Career* theatre producer; began work as cleaner, stagehand and later asst stage mangr Theatre Royal Drury Lane, work with Emile Littler (dep stage mangr 110 In The Shade, Palace Theatre) 1966 and Robin Alexandar 1967; chm Cameron Mackintosh Ltd 1981–, dir Delfont Mackintosh 1991–; hon fell St Catherine's Coll Oxford 1990; *Theatre* London prodns incl: Little Women 1967, Anything Goes (Saville Theatre) 1969, Trelawny 1972, The Card (Queen's) 1973 (revived Watermill Theatre Newbury 1992), Winnie the Pooh 1974 and 1975, The Owl and the Pussycat Went to See 1975, Godspell 1975, 1977 and 1978, Side By Side By Sondheim 1976–77, Oliver! 1977–80, 1983 and 1994–98, My Fair Lady 1979–81, Gingerbread Man 1979 and 1980, Oklahoma! 1980–81, Tomfoolery (London and NY) 1980–82, Jeeves Takes Charge 1980–81, Cats (New London and worldwide) 1981–2002, Song & Dance (London and NY) 1982–86, Blondel 1983, Little Shop of Horrors 1983–85, Abbacadabra 1983, The Boyfriend 1984–85, Les Miserables (Barbican, Palace and worldwide) 1985–, The Phantom of the Opera (Her Majesty's and worldwide) 1986–, Café Puccini 1986, Follies (Shaftesbury) 1987–89, Miss Saigon (Theatre Royal Drury Lane and worldwide) 1989–99, Just So 1990, Five Guys Named Moe (Lyric, Albery and worldwide) 1991, Putting It Together (NY) 1993 and 1999, Moby Dick 1992, Carousel 1993, Martin Guerre 1996–98 (Olivier Award for Best New Musical 1997), The Fix 1997, Swan Lake (NY) 1998, Oklahoma (NT) 1999, The Witches of Eastwick 2000–01, My Fair Lady (NT) 2001–03, Mary Poppins (London and NY) 2004–, Avenue Q 2006–; *Style*— Sir Cameron Mackintosh; ✉ Cameron Mackintosh Ltd, 1 Bedford Square, London WC1B 3RB (tel 020 7637 8866, fax 020 7436 2683)

MACKINTOSH, Dr Colin Edward; s of Colin Mayne Mackintosh (d 1974), and Mary Victoria, *née* Pitcairn; *b* 10 January 1936; *Educ* Melville Coll Edinburgh, Univ of Edinburgh (MB ChB); *m* 1, 1965 (m dis 1984); 2 da (Sarah b 29 June 1969, Celia b 1 March 1973); m 2, 2006, Hilary, *née* Atherton; *Career* house surgical and physician appts Leith Hosp and Edinburgh Royal Infirmary 1959–62, surgical sr house offr and registrar Kirkcaldy Hosp and Edinburgh Royal Infirmary 1962–64, registrar then sr registrar in diagnostic radiology Nat Hosp for Nervous Diseases Royal Free Hosp 1964–70, visiting assoc prof of radiology Univ of Southern Calif 1970–71, conslt radiologist Royal Free Hospital 1971–2001; contrib to British Journal of Hospital Medicine 1976–82, fndr of London Imaging Centre (first computerised tomogram clinic in the W End 1980), first person to run a private mobile CT scanner 1982; Rohan Williams medal; FRCS, FRCR; *Recreations* writing, music; *Style*— Dr Colin Mackintosh; ✉ 50 Harley Street, London W1G 9PX (tel 020 7255 1889, fax 020 7436 3365, e-mail colinm713@aol.com); The Old Headmaster's House, 60 School Lane, Newton, Lancashire PR4 3RT

McKINTOSH, His Hon Ian Stanley; s of Herbert Stanley McKintosh (d 1975), of Chester; *b* 23 April 1938; *Educ* Leeds GS, Exeter Coll Oxford (MA); *m* 2 Sept 1967, (Alison) Rosemary, da of Kenneth Blayney Large, of Erlestoke, Wilts; 2 s (Edward b 1970, William b 1975), 1 da (Alexandra b 1972); *Career* serv RAF UK and Germany 1957–59; admitted slr 1966, Slr's Dept New Scotland Yard 1966–68, private practice 1969–88, dep circuit judge 1976–81, recorder of the Crown Ct 1981–88, circuit judge (Western Circuit) 1988–2007; chm Swindon Branch of Stonham Housing Assoc, memb of Stonham Housing Assoc, memb of SW Legal Aid Area Local Gen and Area Appeals Ctees 1970–89; *Recreations* family, cricket, sailing, rowing, talking; *Clubs* MCC, XL; *Style*— His Hon Ian McKintosh; ✉ c/o Exeter Crown and County Court, Southernhay Gardens, Exeter EX1 1UH

MACKINTOSH, Steven; s of Malcolm Mackintosh, and Dorothy, *née* Parris; *Career* actor; *Theatre* credits incl: The Number of the Beast, A Midsummer Night's Dream (Bush Theatre), Comus (Ludlow Festival), Multiple Choice (Yvonne Arnaud Theatre), Brighton Beach Memoirs (NT/Aldwych), Entertaining Strangers (NT), Cymbeline (NT and tour), The Winter's Tale (NT and tour), The Tempest (NT and tour), Look Look (Aldwych), Cops (Greenwich Theatre), The Woman in Black (Fortune Theatre), My Zinc Bed (Royal Court Theatre); *Television* credits incl: The Browning Version (BBC), The Luck Child (TVS), Newshounds (Working Title), Inspector Morse (Zenith), Six Characters in Search of an Author (BBC), The Buddha of Suburbia (BBC), Midnight Movie (BBC), Safe (BBC), A Dark Adapted Eye (BBC), Karaoke (Whistling Gypsy Prodns), Prime Suspect (BBC/Granada), Our Mutual Friend (BBC), Undercover Heart (BBC), Bad Blood (Carlton), Care (BBC, RTS Award Best Actor), The Other Boleyn Girl, England Expects; *Film* credits incl: Prick Up Your Ears, Memphis Belle, London Kills Me, Princess Caraboo, The Return of the Native, Blue Juice, The Grotesque, Different for Girls, Twelfth Night, House of America, It's Good to Talk, Land Girls, Lock, Stock and Two Smoking Barrels, The Criminal, Far from China, The Tulse Luper Suitcases, Part 1: The Moab Story 2003, The Tulse Luper Suitcases, Part 2: Vaux to the Sea 2004; *Style*— Steven Mackintosh, Esq

MACKINTOSH OF HALIFAX, 3 Viscount (UK 1957); Sir (John) Clive Mackintosh; 3 Bt (UK 1935); s of 2 Viscount Mackintosh of Halifax, OBE, BEM (d 1980, whose f was head of the Mackintosh confectionery manufacturers), by his 2 w, Gwynneth, Viscountess Mackintosh of Halifax; *b* 9 September 1958; *Educ* The Leys Sch Cambridge, Oriel Coll Oxford (MA); *m* 1, 1982 (m dis 1993), Elizabeth, *née* Lakin; 2 s (Hon Thomas Harold George b 8 Feb 1985, Hon George John Frank b 24 Oct 1988); m 2, 1995, Mrs Claire Jane Wishart, yr da of Stanislaw Nowak; 1 da (Hon Violet Krystyna Jane b 5 Oct 2000); *Heir* s, Hon Thomas Mackintosh; *Career* chartered accountant; ptnr PricewaterhouseCoopers; pres OUCA 1979; FCA; *Recreations* cricket, golf, bridge; *Clubs* MCC, RAC, Beefsteak; *Style*— The Rt Hon the Viscount Mackintosh of Halifax; ✉ PricewaterhouseCoopers, 1 Embankment Place, London WC2N 6RH

McKITTERICK, Prof Rosamond D; da of Claude Anthony Pierce, and Melissa, *née* Heaney; *b* 31 May 1949; *Educ* Univ of Western Australia (Cwlth Univ scholar, Amy Jane Best Prize, BA), Univ of Munich, Univ of Cambridge (MA, PhD, LittD); *m* 15 May 1976, David John McKitterick; 1 da (Lucy Rosamond b 23 May 1983); *Career* temp tutor Dept of History Univ of Western Australia 1971; Univ of Cambridge: asst lectr 1979–85, lectr 1985–91, reader in early medieval Euro history 1991–97, prof (personal chair) in early medieval Euro history 1997–99, prof of medieval history 1999–; Newnham Coll Cambridge: fell 1977–97, research fell 1974–77, professorial fell 1997–2006, vice-princ 1996–98; Lady Margaret preacher Univ of Cambridge 1999, professorial fell Sidney Sussex Coll Cambridge 2007–; Royal Historical Soc: memb Cncl 1990–98 and 2000–, memb Publications Ctee 1992–95, Gen Purposes Ctee 1993–95, memb Editorial Bd Studies in History 1994–98, vice-pres 1994–98 and 2000–03; corresponding ed Early Medieval Europe 1999– (ed 1991–98), series ed Palaeography and Codicology, series ed Cambridge Studies in Medieval Life and Thought; memb Editorial Bd: Gazette du livre mediéval, Library History, Jl of Ecclesiastical History, Utrecht Studies in Medieval Literacy, Millennium Max Planck Institut für Rechtsgeschichte; memb various learned socs incl: Ecclesiastical History Soc, Int Soc for Anglo Saxonists, Henry Bradshaw Soc (memb Cncl 1988–), French History Soc, Soc for Promotion of Byzantine Studies; Hugh Balsdon fell Br Sch at Rome 2001–02, fell-in-residence Netherlands Inst of Advanced Studies 2005–06; fell: Euro Medieval Acad, Correspondierendes Mitglied, Monumenta Germaniae Historica 1999–; corresponding fell Medieval Acad of America 2006–, korrespondierendes milied im Ausland (phil-hist) Austrian Acad of Sciences 2006–; FRHistS 1980, FRSA 2001; *Books* The Frankish Church and the Carolingian Reforms 789–895 (1977), The Frankish Kingdoms under the Carolingians 751–987 (1983), The Carolingians and the Written Word (1989), Books, Scribes and Learning in the Frankish Kingdoms, Sixth to Ninth centuries (1994), Frankish Kings and Culture in the Early Middle Ages (1995), The Uses of Literacy in early mediaeval Europe (1990), Carolingian Culture: emulation and innovation (1994), The New Cambridge Medieval History, c.700–c.900 (1995), Edward Gibbon & Empire (with R Quinault, 1996), History and its Audiences (2000), The Short Oxford History of Europe: The early middle ages 400–1000 (2001), The Times Atlas of the Medieval World (2003), History and Memory in the Carolingian World (2004), Perceptions of the Past in the Early Middle-Ages (2006); also author of numerous book chapters and articles in learned jls; *Recreations* music, fresh air; *Style*— Prof Rosamond McKitterick; ✉ Sidney Sussex College, Cambridge CB2 3HU

McKITTRICK, David; s of Frey McKittrick (d 1987), of Belfast, and Rita, *née* Hegarty; *b* 10 August 1949; *m* 1978, Patricia, da of P J Hackett, of Coalisland, Co Tyrone; 2 da (Kerry b 1979, Julie b 1981); *Career* reporter East Antrim Times 1971–73; Irish Times: reporter Belfast 1973–76, Northern ed 1976–81, London ed 1981–85; journalist BBC Belfast 1985–86, Ireland corr The Independent 1986–; sometime Ireland corr: Sunday Times, Economist, Le Monde; contrib: Fortnight, Listener, New Statesman, Hibernia, Boston Globe, San Francisco Examiner, New York Times; numerous TV broadcasts; co-recipient Christopher Ewart-Biggs meml prize 1989, Irish media award for reporting on Ireland for a pubn abroad 1987, runner-up Reporter of the Year Br Press Awards 1987; memb: NUJ 1971, Exec Br-Irish Assoc; *Books* Despatches from Belfast (1989), Endgame (1994), The Nervous Peace (1996), The Fight for Peace (with Eamonn Maille, 1996); *Style*— David McKittrick, Esq; ✉ Ireland Correspondent, The Independent, Independent House, 191 Marsh Wall, London E14 9RS (tel 020 7293 2000, fax 020 7293 2435)

McKITTRICK, His Hon Judge Neil Alastair; s of Ian James Arthur McKittrick, OBE (d 1987), and Mary Patricia McKittrick, JP, *née* Hobbs; *b* 1 January 1948; *Educ* King's Sch Ely, Univ of London (LLB), Coll of Law Guildford; *m* 31 May 1975, Jean, da of Mark Armstrong (d 1998); 1 s (Mark Alastair b 1976), 1 da (Lucinda Mary b 1980); *Career* articled clerk then asst slr Cecil Godfrey & Son Nottingham 1967–73, prosecuting slr Notts 1973–77; clerk to the Justices: Darlington 1977–81, E Herts 1981–86, N Cambs

M

1986–89; dist judge (Magistrates Court) 1989–2001; recorder of the Crown Court 1996–2001, circuit judge 2001–, resident judge Ipswich Crown Court 2006–, magistrates liaison judge Suffolk 2007–; memb: Advsy Gp Magistrates' Trg Courses Univ of Cambridge 1989–96, Brent Magistrates' Cts Ctee 1990–96, Middx Area Probation Ctee 1990–2001; special licensing ed Justice of the Peace Reports 1983–2003, ed Justice of the Peace 1985–89, ed Jl of Criminal Law 1990–2000; *Books* Wilkinson's Road Traffic Offences (ed jtly, 13–18 edns, 1987–97), Blackstone's Handbook for Magistrates (with Pauline Callow, 1997, 2 edn 2000); *Recreations* writing, walking, flat racing; *Style*— His Hon Judge McKittrick; ✉ Ipswich Crown Court, 1 Russell Road, Ipswich IP1 2AG (tel 01473 228585)

MACKLEY, Ian Warren; CMG (1989), CVO (1999); s of Harold William Mackley (d 1973), and Marjorie Rosa Sprawson, *née* Warren (d 2004); *b* 31 March 1942; *Educ* Ardingly; *m* 1, 9 Nov 1968 (m dis 1988), Jill Marion, da of Frank Saunders (d 1955); 3 s (Jonathan b 1970, Nicholas b 1973, Christopher b 1983); m 2, 21 Jan 1989, Sarah Anne, da of John Churchley; 1 da (Elizabeth b 1989), 1 s (Richard b 1991); *Career* FCO: entered 1960, third sec Saigon 1963, asst private sec Min of State 1967, second sec 1968, served Wellington 1969, first sec 1972, FCO 1973, served New Delhi 1976, FCO 1980, seconded to ICI 1982, cnsllr 1984, dep head UK Delgn to CDE Stockholm 1984, chargé d'affaires Kabul 1987, dep high cmmr Canberra 1989, head of training FCO 1993–96, high cmmr to Ghana (concurrently non-resident ambass to Republic of Togo) 1996–2000, ret 2001; ctee clerk House of Lords 2002–; pres and capt Kabul Golf and Country Club 1988–89; *Recreations* golf; *Style*— Ian W Mackley, Esq, CMG, CVO; ✉ Ridgecoombe, Penton Grafton, Andover, Hampshire SP11 0RR

MACKLEY, Prof Malcolm Robert; s of Harold Mackley (d 1992), and Helen Mackley (d 2000); *b* 27 February 1947; *Educ* Gravesend Tech HS, Bath Tech Coll, Univ of Leicester (BSc), Univ of Bristol (MSc, PhD); *m* 27 July 1970, Margaret, *née* Barsby; 2 da (Emily, Sophie); *Career* lectr in material science Univ of Sussex 1976–79; Univ of Cambridge: lectr 1979–, reader 1991–, prof of process innovation Dept of Chemical Engrg 1999–; author of numerous papers and articles in learned jls; Beilby Medal RSC 1987, Charles Vernon Boys Prize Inst of Physics, Annual Award Br Soc of Rheology 2002; FIChemE 1994, FInstP 2003 (MInstP 1972), FREng 2003; *Recreations* sailing; *Clubs* Royal Harwich Yacht, Salcombe Yacht, Cambridge Univ Cruising; *Style*— Prof Malcolm Mackley; ✉ Department of Chemical Engineering, University of Cambridge, Pembroke Street, Cambridge CB2 3RA (tel 01223 334784, fax 01223 334796, e-mail mrm5@cam.ac.uk)

MACKLIN, Peter Richard; s of Lt-Col P H Macklin, OBE (d 1976), and Joan Elizabeth, *née* Butcher (d 1997); *b* 1 April 1946; *Educ* Wellington, Univ of Durham (BA); *m* 21 Aug 1971, Pamela Adele, da of A F Plant Jr, of Washington DC, USA; 3 s (Andrew b 1974, Jonathan b 1977, Christopher b 1981); *Career* slr Clifford Turner 1971–76, ptnr Freshfields 1979– (departmental managing ptnr Property Dept 1986–91); memb Cncl Br Property Fedn; memb: Worshipful Co of Slrs, Law Soc; tstee The Passage; *Recreations* family, opera, exploration; *Clubs* Malden Golf; *Style*— Peter Macklin, Esq; ✉ Whitefriars, 65 Fleet Street, London EC4Y 1HS (tel 020 7832 7001, fax 020 7248 3487/8/9)

MACKNEY, Paul Leon John; s of Rev Leon E Mackney (d 1962), and Margaret *née* Dickinson (d 2004); *b* 25 March 1950; *m* 1, 20 Sept 1969 (m dis), Rosemary Angela Draper; 1 s (Sean Leon Mackney b 26 June 1972); m 2, 28 May 1982, Cherry Margot Sewell; 1 da (Ruby Yasmin Mackney Sewell b 21 April 1988); *Career* trainee probation offr 1971–73, gen studies lectr Poole Tech Coll 1974–75, English for Speakers of Other Languages (ESOL) organiser Hall Green Tech Coll 1975–79, trade union studies tutor Hall Green Coll 1980–85, head Birmingham Trade Union Studies Centre S Birmingham Coll 1986–92; NATFHE (univ and coll lectrs union): branch offr then Birmingham sec 1975–92, W Midlands regional official 1992–97, general sec 1997–2006; jt gen sec Univ and Coll Union (UCU) 2006–; memb Gen Cncl TUC 2002–07, life memb Birmingham TUC (pres 1980–84); fndr memb Birmingham Campaign Against Racism and Fascism; former govr: Handsworth Coll, Bournville Coll; *Publications* Birmingham and the Miners' Strike; *Recreations* music, guitar, singing; *Clubs* Birmingham Bread and Roses; *Style*— Paul Mackney; ✉ UCU, 27 Britannia Street, London WC1X 9JP (tel 020 7837 3636, fax 020 7278 3177)

McKNIGHT, Eur Ing Prof James; *b* 21 April 1938; *Educ* Ayr Acad, Kilmarnock Slough and Barking Colls of Technol, Thurrock Tech Coll (HNC Business Studies), Mid Essex Mgmnt Coll (Dip Mgmnt Studies); *Career* Scottish Stamping and Engineering Co Ltd (GKN) 1954–63 (engrg apprentice, engrg draughtsman, asst to Forge Supt); Ford Motor Co 1963–77: successively resident engr Langley Truck Plant, project engr, princ engr then supervisor, mangr Advanced Truck Engrg; Leyland Vehicles Ltd 1977–87: chief engr Vehicle Engrg 1977–81, chief engr Test Ops Prototype 1981–83, controller Product Devpt Leyland Trucks 1983–84, chief engr Product Control 1984–85, product devpt dir Leyland Bus 1985–87, product devpt dir (following MBO) Leyland Bus Group Ltd 1987–88, product devpt dir Volvo Bus Ltd (Leyland Bus Ltd until 1991) 1988–95, chm Leyland Product Developments Ltd (formerly Volvo Bus Product Development) 1995–2004 (also md 1995–2001); visiting prof in mechanical engrg Univ of Leeds 1996–2003 (chm Industrial Advsy Ctee 1994–2002); course assessor Nat Dip in Engrg Scottish TEC 1978–86, memb Organising Ctee Int Symposium for Automated Testing of Automobiles 1981–86, memb Industrial Advsy Ctee Univ of Glasgow and Glasgow Sch of Art 1992–94; Instn of Mechanical Engrs: memb Qualifications Bd 1989–92 and 1994–96, chm Mechanical Pubns (MEP) Ltd, memb Cncl 1992–, memb Exec Ctee 1993–2001, vice-pres 1995–97, dep pres 1997–99, pres 1999–2000; SMMT: chm Heavy Commercial Vehicle Tech Ctee 1989–94, memb Engrg Ctee 1989–94; FISITA: memb Cncl 1992–2004, vice-pres 1994–98, pres 1998–2000; Engrg Cncl: senator 2000–02, memb Bd for the Engrg Profession 2000–02; memb Membership Ctee Royal Acad of Engrg 1998–2001; author of numerous papers in various professional jls; Eur Ing, DMS, CEng, FIMechE (past pres 2000–), FISITA (past pres 2000–05), FCMI, FRSA, MSAE, FREng 1997; *Recreations* golf, rugby union; *Style*— Eur Ing Prof James McKnight, FREng; ✉ 14 Furlong Lane, Poulton-le-Fylde, Lancashire FY6 7HQ (tel 01253 894070, fax 01253 893339, mobile 07973 174777, e-mail jmcknight@fsmail.net)

MACKRELL, Judith Rosalind (Mrs S P Henson); da of Alexander George Mackrell, of Surrey, and Margaret Elizabeth, *née* Atkinson; *b* 26 October 1954; *Educ* Sutton HS, Univ of York (BA), Univ of Oxford (DPhil); *m* Simon Peter Henson, s of Peter Henson; 2 s (Frederick Juan b 12 Feb 1990, Oscar Henson b 17 Dec 1992); *Career* pt/t lectr in English literature: Oxford Poly, Lincoln Coll Oxford, St Anne's Coll Oxford, City Lit London 1981–85; freelance dance writer 1984– (work published in Vogue, Tatler, Dance Theatre Journal); dance corr: The Independent 1986–94, The Guardian 1994–; broadcasts incl: Dance International BBC TV, South Bank Show, Radio 3, Radio 4 and World Service; hon fell Laban Centre London 1996; *Books* British New Dance (1991), Reading Dance (1997) A Life in Dance (with Darcey Bussell, 1998), Oxford Dictionary of Dance (with Debra Craine, 2000); *Recreations* family, travel, reading, food, music; *Style*— Ms Judith Mackrell

MACKRELL, Keith Ashley Victor; s of Henry George Mackrell (d 1967), of Romsey, Hants, and Emily Winifred Jesse Mackrell (d 1972); *b* 20 October 1932; *Educ* Peter Symonds Sch Winchester, LSE (BSc Econ); *m* 20 Feb 1960, June Mendoza; 3 da (Elliet b 1956, Kim b 1958, Lee b 1961), 1 s (Ashley b 1961); *Career* RAF Flying Offr 1953–55; dir: Cope Allman International 1977–86, Shell International 1977–91, Private Investment Corp for Asia (PICA) 1980–84, Shell Pensions Tst Ltd 1983–94, Rexam plc (formerly Bowater plc) 1991–97, Regalian Properties plc 1991–2001, Standard Chartered plc 1991–2002, Fairey Gp plc 1993–99, BG Gp plc (formerly British Gas plc) 1994–2005, Dresdner RCM Emerging Markets Tst plc 1998–2002, Gartmore Asia Pacific Tst plc (formerly Asia Recovery Tst plc) 1998–, Duke Ltd 2003– (vice-chm); govr LSE 1991–, pres emeritus Enterprise LSE; memb: Int Advsy Cncl East-West Centre Honolulu 1985, Cook Soc; hon fell LSE; Hon LLD Nat Univ of Singapore; FInstD 1977, CIMgt; *Clubs* Hurlingham, Wimbledon; *Style*— Keith Mackrell, Esq; ✉ Duke CE Ltd, London School of Economics and Political Science, Houghton Street, London WC2A 2AE (tel 020 7107 5273)

MACKWORTH, Sir Digby John; 10 Bt (GB 1776), of The Gnoll, Glamorganshire; s of Cdr Sir David Arthur Geoffrey Mackworth, 9 Bt (d 1998), and his 1 w, Mary Alice (Molly), *née* Grylls (d 1993); *b* 2 November 1945; *Educ* Wellington; *m* 1971, Antoinette Francesca, da of Henry James McKenna (d 1992); 1 da (Octavia b 1977); *Heir* kinsman, Dr Norman Mackworth; *Career* former Lt Aust Army Aviation Corps in Malaysia and Vietnam; helicopter pilot: Bristow Helicopters Iran 1972–77, British Airways Helicopters North Sea, China and India 1977–89; airline pilot British Airways Heathrow 1989–2000, airline pilot easyJet Luton 2000–06; MRIN, MRAeS; *Style*— Sir Digby Mackworth, Bt; ✉ Blagrove Cottage, Fox Lane, Boars Hill, Oxfordshire OX1 5DS (tel and fax 01865 735543, e-mail mackworth@btinternet.com)

MACKWORTH, Rosalind; CBE (1994); da of Rev Albert Walters (d 1963), and Alma, *née* Richards (d 1985); *b* 10 August 1928; *Educ* Moorfields Sch, Saxenholme Sch Southport, Queen's Univ Belfast (BA), Girton Coll Cambridge (MA); *m* 2 July 1960, Richard Charles Audley Mackworth, s of late Air Vice Marshall Philip Mackworth, CB, CBE; 2 da (Julia Kathleen b 27 June 1968, Victoria Alma Louise b 17 Feb 1971); *Career* articled clerk, admitted slr 1955, asst then ptnr Gregory Rowliffe Slrs 1955–67; ptnr: Mackworth & Co 1968–82, Mackworth Rowland 1982–2005, Ashley Wilson incorporating Mackworth Rowland 2005–; cmmr Social Fund for GB and Social Fund for NI 1987–95; memb: Value Added Tax Tbnls, Law Soc; *Recreations* restoring an old house; *Style*— Mrs Rosalind Mackworth, CBE; ✉ Ashley Wilson incorporating Mackworth Rowland, 19–21 Grosvenor Gardens, Belgravia, London SW1W 0BD (tel 020 7802 4831, fax 020 7802 4836, e-mail rmackworth@ashleywilson.co.uk)

McLACHLAN, John James; s of William McLachlan (d 1980), and Helen McLachlan (d 2000); *b* 28 August 1942; *Educ* Rock Ferry High GS; *m* 24 Sept 1966, Heather Joan, da of George Smith (d 1975), of Heswall; 1 da (Deborah b 19 Feb 1972), 1 s (Alexander b 4 Jan 1975); *Career* mgmnt accountant Norwest Construction 1966–67, investment analyst Martins Bank Trust Co 1967–69, investment res mangr Barclays Bank Trust Co 1969–71, dep investment mangr 1971–74, investment mangr British Rail Pension Fund 1974–83, dir pensions investment 1983–84, investment mangr Reed International plc 1984–88, investment dir United Friendly Insurance plc and United Friendly Group plc 1988–99; dir: United Friendly Unit Trust Managers Ltd 1993, United Friendly Asset Management plc 1993; Gp Investment Dir United Assurance Group plc 1996–99; former chm Investment Ctee Nat Assoc of Pension Funds; former memb: Panel on Take Overs and Mergers, Institutional Shareholders Ctee; non-exec chm: Booker Pensions Ltd, INVESCO Income Growth Trust plc, House of Fraser Pension Scheme; non-exec dir Falcon Property Trust Ltd; FCA, FRSA; *Recreations* travel, watching cricket and soccer, reading; *Style*— John McLachlan, Esq; ✉ home tel 01732 762776, fax 01732 762355

McLACHLAN, Marjory Jane; da of Walter Alexander, and Kate, *née* Turnbull; *b* 15 February 1942, Falkirk; *Educ* St Leonard's Sch St Andrews; *m* 1 Sept 1962, Colin McLachlan; 2 da (Jane b 7 Aug 1966, Katy b 12 Aug 1968); *Career* DL Stirling and Falkirk 2000–05, Lord-Lt Stirling and Falkirk 2005–; supporter: Save the Children, Cancer Research, Barnardo's, Friends of Falkirk Hosps, Scottish Soc for Autism; *Recreations* curling, bridge, golf, travel, family; *Style*— Mrs Marjory McLachlan; ✉ 23 Majors Loan, Falkirk FK1 5QG (tel and fax 01324 622633, e-mail marjmcl@aol.com)

macLACHLAN, Simon; MBE (1983), DL (Kent 2002); s of Geoffrey Cheasty macLachlan (d 1965), of Ipswich, Suffolk, and Violet Edith Gasgoigne (d 1990); *b* 17 December 1934; *Educ* Downside; *m* 11 May 1963, Julie, da of John Mannering (d 1985), of River, Kent; 2 s (Justin b 1964, Luke b 1965), 2 da (Martha b 1967, Hannah b 1972); *Career* 2 Lt Queens Own Royal West Kent Regt 1953–55, seconded 5 Bn Kings African Rifles 1953–54 (served in Kenya, despatches), Lt 4/5 BN Queens Own Royal West Kent Regt (TA) 1955–62; admitted slr 1959, ptnr Clifford-Turner 1964, assigning ptnr Co Dept 1980–87, ptnr Clifford Chance 1987–93 (head of corp practice 1987–91); non-exec dir: Mid Kent Holdings plc 1991–2001, Nelson Hurst plc 1993–97, Hiscox Select Insurance Fund plc 1993–98; chm: Capital Markets Forum Int Bar Assoc 1991–93, Cranbrook and District CAB 1994–99, New Islington and Hackney Housing Assoc 1967–83, Kent Rural Community Cncl 1994–99, Action with Community in Rural England (ACRE) 1997–2001; ind memb Kent Police Authy 1995–2003; tstee Circle 33 Housing Tst 1978–93, tstee Kent Community Fndn 2001–; *Books* Life After Big Bang (1987); *Recreations* gardening, fishing, tennis; *Clubs* RAC; *Style*— Simon macLachlan, Esq, MBE; ✉ Sissinghurst Place, Sissinghurst, Cranbrook, Kent TN17 2JP (tel 01580 714387, e-mail smaclachlan@btinternet.com)

McLAREN, Dr (Dame) Anne; DBE (1993); *b* 26 April 1927; *Educ* Univ of Oxford (MA, DPhil); *m* 1952, Donald Michie; 2 da (Susan b 1955, Caroline b 1959), 1 s (Jonathan b 1957); *Career* memb Scientific Staff of Agric Res Cncl's Unit of Animal Genetics Edinburgh 1959–74, dir Mammalian Devpt Unit MRC 1974–92, memb scientific staff Wellcome Tst/Cancer Research UK Gurdon Inst of Cancer and Developmental Biology Cambridge 1992–; memb: Govt Ctee on Human Fertilisation and Embryology 1982–84, Voluntary (Interim) Licensing Authy for Human Fertilisation and Embryology 1985–90, Human Fertilisation and Embryology Authy 1990–2001; Royal Medal Royal Soc 1990, US Soc for Devpt Biology Award for Lifetime Scientific Achievement 2001, Japan Prize 2002, March of Dimes Prize 2007; FRS 1975 (foreign sec 1991–96, first woman offr), FRSE 1971, FRCOG 1987, FMedSci 1998; memb: Polish Acad of Sciences 1988, Slovenian Acad of Sciences 1995, Russian Acad of Sciences 1999; *Books* Mammalian Chimeras (1976), Germ Cells and Soma (1981); *Style*— Dr Anne McLaren, DBE, FRS, FRCOG, FRSE; ✉ Wellcome Trust/Cancer Research UK Gurdon Institute, Tennis Court Road, Cambridge CB2 1QR

McLAREN, Hon Christopher Melville; s of 2 Baron Aberconway, CBE (d 1953); *b* 15 April 1934; *Educ* Eton, King's Coll Cambridge (MA); *m* 1973, Jane Elizabeth, da of James Barrie; 1 s (Robert Melville b 1974), 1 da (Lara Jane Christabel b 1976); *Career* Nat Serv Army in Malaya; called to the Bar; formerly with Baker Perkins Engrs; currently vice-chm System C Healthcare plc (chm 1989–2004); memb Kensington & Chelsea BC 1974–86; South Bank Univ (formerly South Bank Poly): chm of govrs 1989–99, chllr 1992–99; dep chm Ctee of Univ Chairmen 1993–97; ESU: govr 1992–, hon treas 1996–2002, hon sec 2005–; chm Samuel Courtauld Tst 2005–; Hon Dr of Laws South Bank Univ 2000; *Recreations* travel, hill walking, skiing, gardening, music, tennis; *Clubs* Boodle's; *Style*— The Hon Christopher McLaren; ✉ 31 Upper Addison Gardens, London W14 8AJ (tel 020 7602 1983, e-mail cmmclaren@clara.co.uk)

MACLAREN, Deanna; *née* Bullimore; *b* 4 February 1944; *m* 1, 1965, Patrick Maclaren; m 2, 1974, Michael Godfrey; m 3, 1987, Nicholas Kent; *Career* author, journalist, broadcaster and public speaker; presenter The Single Life (Channel Four); *Books* Little Blue Room, The First of all Pleasures, Dagger in the Sleeve, Your Loving Mother, Le Gardien, Ménage à Trois; non-fiction: The Single File, How to Live Alone and Like It; *Recreations* opera, gardening, exploring London and the South of France; *Clubs* Chelsea Arts; *Style*— Ms Deanna Maclaren

McLAREN, Ian Alban Bryant; QC (1993); s of Alban McLaren (d 1972), and Doris Martha, *née* Hurst (d 2003); *b* 3 July 1940; *Educ* Sandbach Sch, Blackpool GS, Univ of Nottingham (LLB); *m* 7 Sept 1964, Margaret, da of Alfred George Middleton; 2 s (Andrew b 28 Feb 1967, Mark Ian b 29 Aug 1968), 1 da (Rachel Margaret b 28 Dec 1970); *Career* called to the Bar Gray's Inn 1962 (entrance scholar, Mackaskie scholar, bencher 2004); law tutor Univ of Nottingham 1962–64, in practice at the Bar in Nottingham 1962–, recorder of the Crown Court 1996–2006 (asst recorder 1992), head Ropewalk Chambers 2000–06; pres Notts Medico-Legal Soc 1997–98; fell Inst Advanced Legal Studies; Hon LLD Nottingham Trent Univ 2005; *Recreations* wine, photography, gardening; *Style*— Ian McLaren, Esq, QC; ✉ Ropewalk Chambers, 24 The Ropewalk, Nottingham NG1 5EF (tel 0115 947 2581, fax 0115 947 6532)

McLAREN, Sir Robin John Taylor; KCMG (1991, CMG 1982); s of Robert Taylor McLaren (d 1981), of Richmond, Surrey, and Marie Rose, *née* Simond; *b* 14 August 1934; *Educ* Ardingly, St John's Coll Cambridge (scholar, MA); *m* 5 Sept 1964, Susan Ellen (Sue), da of Wilfrid Byron Hatherly (d 1988), of Little Rissington, Glos; 2 da (Emma (Mrs Nigel Davies) b 1965, Jessica (Mrs Robert Ramsay) b 1966), 1 s (Duncan b 1973); *Career* Nat Serv Sub Lt RN 1953–55; joined FO 1958, Chinese language student Hong Kong 1959–60, third sec Peking 1960–61, FO 1962–64 (asst private sec to Lord Privy Seal 1963–64), second (later first sec) Rome 1964–68, asst political advsr Hong Kong 1968–69, FCO 1970–75 (dep head Western Orgns Dept 1974–75), cnsllr and head Chancery Copenhagen 1975–78; FCO: head Hong Kong and Gen Dept 1978–79, head Far Eastern Dept 1978–81; political advsr Hong Kong 1981–85, ambass to Philippines 1985–87, asst under sec of state Asia 1987–90, sr Br rep Sino-Br Jt Liaison Gp 1987–89, dep under sec of state Asia/Americas 1990–91, ambass to China 1991–94, ret; dir: INVESCO Asia Trust plc 1995–, Fidelity Asian Values plc 1997–, Govett Oriental Investment Tst plc 1994–98, Govett Asian Recovery Tst plc 1998–2003, Gartmore Asia Pacific Tst plc 2003–06, Aberdeen All Asia Investment Tst plc; chm Cncl: Royal Holloway Coll London 1999–2004, Ardingly Coll 1999–2005; hon fell Royal Holloway Univ of London 2006; *Recreations* music; *Clubs* Oxford and Cambridge, Hong Kong; *Style*— Sir Robin McLaren, KCMG; ✉ 11 Hillside, Wimbledon, London SW19 4NH

MacLAREN of MacLAREN, HE The; Donald MacLaren of MacLaren and Achleskine; s of late Donald MacLaren of MacLaren; suc his father 1966 as Chief of Clan Labhran; *m* 1978, Maida Jane, da of late Robert Paton Aitchison, of Markinch, Fife; 3 s, 2 da; *Heir* Donald MacLaren, yr of MacLaren; *Career* diplomat; entered HM Dip Serv 1978, SE Asian Dept FCO 1978–79, second sec (Chancery) Berlin 1980–83, first sec Moscow 1984–87, FCO 1987–91, dep head of mission Havana 1991–94, Environment Policy Dept FCO 1995–97, cnsllr and dep head of mission Caracas 1997–99, dep head of mission and consul-gen Kiev 2000–03, ambass to Georgia 2004–; *Style*— HE The MacLaren of MacLaren; ✉ c/o Foreign & Commonwealth Office (Tbilisi), King Charles Street, London SW1A 2AH

McLARTY, Stuart William; s of William Ross McLarty, of Pinjarra, Aust, and Evelyn May, *née* Parkhill; *b* 7 July 1960; *Educ* Hale Sch Perth, Curtin Univ Perth, South Bank Univ; *m* 7 April 1990, Christine, *née* Oborne; 3 s (Joshua William, Matthew David, Oliver Stuart); *Career* Aukett: joined 1985, associate 1990, asst dir 1995, dir 1997, marketing dir 2002, plc bd dir 2003, projects incl Doxford Int Business Park 1998 (BCO commendation) and MCI HQ 2001; founding dir De Novo Architecture Ltd 2004; govr St Luke's C of E Sch; RIBA 1990, ARB 1990; *Recreations* skiing, mountain biking, tennis, rugby, cricket; *Clubs* Holmes Place, Barnes Common CC, Wimbledon Minis RFC; *Style*— Stuart McLarty, Esq; ✉ De Novo Architecture, The Brewery, 18 Petersham Road, Richmond, Surrey TW10 6UW (tel 020 8439 8470, fax 020 8439 8471, e-mail stuart@dn-a.com)

McLATCHIE, Cameron; CBE (1996, OBE 1988); s of Cameron McLatchie (d 1997), of Largs, and Maggie, *née* Taylor (d 2001); *b* 18 February 1947; *Educ* Ardrossan Acad, Univ of Glasgow (LLB, memb Scottish & British Junior Bridge Team); *m* 26 April 1973, (Helen) Leslie, da of Dr William R Mackie, of Largs; 2 s (Stuart b 19 April 1976, Fraser 4 Dec 1979), 1 da (Julie b 16 May 1985); *Career* British Polythene Industries plc (formerly Scott & Robertson plc): md 1983–88, chm and chief exec 1988–2003, chm 2003–; md Anaplast Ltd 1975–83, various positions with Thomas Boag & Co Ltd 1971–74, apprentice CA Whinney Murray & Co 1968–70; non-exec chm Hiscox Select plc 1993–98, non-exec dep chm Scottish Enterprise 1997–2000 (memb Bd 1990–95); non-exec dir: Motherwell Bridge Holdings Ltd 1993–97, Royal Bank of Scotland 1998–2002; memb: Advsy Ctee for Business and the Environment (ACBE-I) 1991–93, sec of state for Scotland's Advsy Gp on Sustainable Devpt (AGSD) 1994–95, Bd Scottish Environmental Protection Agency 1995–97; CIMgt 1995; *Recreations* golf, bridge, gardening; *Clubs* West Kilbride Golf, Western Gailes Golf; *Style*— Cameron McLatchie, Esq, CBE; ✉ Ailsa, Summerlea Road, Seamill, Ayrshire KA23 9HP (tel 01294 823650, fax 01294 822 853); British Polythene Industries plc, 96 Port Glasgow Road, Greenock PA15 2RP (tel 01475 501000, fax 01475 743143, mobile 078 3670 1716, e-mail mclatchie@aol.com)

McLAUCHLAN, Prof Keith Alan; s of Frederick William McLauchlan (d 1972), and Nellie, *née* Summers (d 1996); *b* 8 January 1936; *Educ* Queen Elizabeth's Hosp Bristol, Univ of Bristol (BSc, PhD, W E Garner prize for chemistry), Univ of Oxford (MA); *m* 23 Aug 1958, Joan Sheila, da of Howard Dickenson; 1 s (Gavin Ian b 4 June 1962), 1 da (Christine Anne b 4 Aug 1964); *Career* post doctoral fell Nat Research Cncl Ottawa 1959–60, sr res fell then sr scientific offr Nat Physical Laboratory 1960–65; Univ of Oxford: lectr 1965–94, reader in physical chemistry 1994–96, prof of chemistry 1996–2002 (now emeritus); fell Hertford Coll Oxford 1965– (now emeritus), Erskine fell Univ of Canterbury Christchurch 1997; visiting prof: Tata Inst Bombay 1986, Univ of Konstanz 1990, École Normale Supèrieure Paris 1998, Univ of Padua 1998, Univ of Chicago 1998; eminent scientist Inst of Physics & Chemistry Research Tokyo 2000–01; memb: Editorial Bd Chemical Physics Letters 1991–95, Exec Editorial Ctee Molecular Physics 1993–2002, Gen Bd Oxford 1993–97, Hebdomodal Cncl Oxford 1998–2000; pres Int EPR Soc 1993–96 (Silver Medal 1994, Gold Medal 2002), winner of Bruker Prize RSC 1997, Zavoisky Prize for EPR Kazan 2001; FRS 1992, fell Int EPR Soc 2005; *Books* Magnetic Resonance (1972), Molecular Physical Chemistry (2004); author of 180 pubns and reviews in scientific jls; *Recreations* skiing, walking, reading, listening to music, gardening, golf; *Style*— Prof Keith McLauchlan, FRS; ✉ Physical and Theoretical Chemistry Laboratory, South Parks Road, Oxford OX1 3QZ (tel 01865 275400, fax 01865 275410, e-mail keith.mclauchlan@chemistry.ox.ac.uk); Hertford College, Catte Street, Oxford

McLAUGHLIN, Brian Finbar; s of Patrick William John McLaughlin, of Buncrana, Donegal, and Frances McLaughlin; *b* 21 August 1949, Portsmouth; *Educ* St Augustine's Abbey Sch Ramsgate; *m* 28 Sept 1968, Susan, *née* Middlemist; 2 da (Louisa Jane b 27 Aug 1969, Katherine Francesca b 21 July 1987), 1 s (James William b 9 Dec 1973); *Career* HMV Gp plc: joined as first asst Portsmouth branch 1968, mangr Portsmouth 1971, mangr Leeds 1974, northern area mangr 1976, gen mangr of ops May 1980, ops dir and memb Bd HMV UK Nov 1980, oversaw launch of Oxford St branch (world's largest record store at the time) 1986, md HMV UK Ltd 1987–1996, md HMV Europe 1996–2001, acting md Waterstone's 2001, 2003–04 and 2004–06, chief operating offr 2001–05, non-exec dir 2006, conslt 2006–; dir Pangbourne & Goring Properties Ltd 2006–; chm Br Assoc of Record Dealers 1992–94 and 1998–2000, dir Music Industry Tst 2005–; memb Music Industry Forum DCMS 1998; chm Fundraising Ctee Nordoff-Robbins Music Therapy Centre 2005–, govr Nordoff Robbins Music Therapy 2006–; govr BRIT Sch 2001; Strat Award Music Week Awards 1996, Man of the Year Music Industry Tsts 2001; *Recreations* music, movies, wine, Portsmouth FC, horse racing, books; *Style*— Brian McLaughlin, Esq

McLAUGHLIN, David; s of Terence McLaughlin, of Chesterfield, Derbys, and Margaret Lees, *née* Pears; *b* 2 April 1971, Shipston on Stour, Warks; *Educ* Lakes Sch Windermere, Kendal Coll; *m* 1 April 2000, Janette, *née* Hunt; 1 s (Callum b 6 Feb 2003), 1 da (Neve b 14 June 2006); *Career* chef Wordsworth Hotel Grasmere 1988–93, Michael's Nook Grasmere 1993–2000, head chef Holbeck Ghyll Country House Hotel Windermere 2000– (Michelin star 2001–, Egon Ronay star, 3 AA Rosettes, Restaurant of the Year (Cumbria) Good Food Guide 2007); *Publications* 100 Best Risottos of the World (2007); *Style*— David McLaughlin, Esq; ✉ Holbeck Ghyll Country House Hotel, Holbeck Lane, Windermere, Cumbria LA23 1LU (tel 01539 432375)

McLAUGHLIN, Kevin; s of Henry McLaughlin (d 2000), and Patricia, *née* McCann; *b* 3 October 1956; *Educ* St Paul's Secdy Sch Belfast, Coll of Business Studies Belfast, Univ of Ulster, Queen's Univ Belfast, Univ of Leeds; *Career* clerical offr rising to exec offr I Eastern Health & Social Services Bd 1974–87 (disability advsr 1995–), disability liaison mangr Carmen Tst 1990–91, studies and vol community work 1991–97, devpt worker Forum for Community Work Educn 1997–99, pt/t regnl devpt mangr Leonard Cheshire NI 1999–2002, disability conslt KM Associates 1999–; cmmr NI Human Rights Cmmn 2001–; chair and memb Ctee Disabled Drivers Assoc 1990–93, co-ordinator W Belfast Carers Gp 1991–92, advsr N & W Belfast Health & Social Services Tst 1991–93, chair W Belfast Access Gp 1991–98, memb Ctee Disability Action Access Ctee 1992–95, tstee and memb Bd ADAPT NI 1992–97, bd dir Open Arts 1993–97, chair and memb Ctee Arts & Disability Forum 1994–97, vice-chair and memb Ctee Rights Now NI 1994–97, memb Exec Ctee Disability Action 1995–97, disability advsr Arts Cncl NI 1998–, memb Bd Centre for Independent Living 1999–, memb Bd Mid-Ulster Local Health and Social Services Gp 2002–, NI rep Ofcom Consumer Panel 2004–; vol memb Civic Forum 2001–; Person of Millennium Award Andersonstown News 2000, William Keown Adult Achievement Award NI C of C Cup 2001; memb CAMRA; *Recreations* fishing (represented Ireland Int Fly Fishing Disabled Angling Competition 1996); *Clubs* Clady and District Angling; *Style*— Kevin McLaughlin, Esq; ✉ Northern Ireland Human Rights Commission, Temple Court, 39 North Street, Belfast BT1 1NA (tel 028 9024 3987, e-mail mclaughlin_k_m@hotmail.com)

MacLAURIN, Brian David; s of Peter and Yvonne MacLaurin, of Kilmacolm, Scotland; *b* 7 December 1949; *Educ* Rannoch Sch, Sighthill Coll Edinburgh; *m* 1, 1974 (m dis 1983); 1 s (Peter b 17 Sept 1975), 1 da (Katie b 22 Feb 1978); m 2, 20 March 1987, Gill Elizabeth, *née* Ormston; 1 s (James b 10 Feb 1990), 1 da (Kirsten b 25 Jan 1994); *Career* journalist and presenter: Scottish TV plc 1971–73, ATV Network Ltd 1973–77; presenter and industrial ed ATV Network Ltd 1977–79; Scottish TV plc: head Press and PR Dept 1979–84, controller Press & PR Dept 1984–88; dir Media Relations Crown Group plc 1988–92, md MacLaurin Communications Ltd 1992–96, chief exec MacLaurin Ltd 1996–; md hatch-group UK Ltd, dir hatch Int Ltd 2001–03, fndr Brian MacLaurin Associates Ltd (media consultancy) 2003; memb RTS 1995; MInstD, MIPR 1996; pres La Molazul community Puerto Andratx Mallorca 2007; *Recreations* family, skiing, clay pigeon shooting; *Style*— Brian MacLaurin, Esq; ✉ The Malt House, Home Farm Close, Esher, KT10 9HA (tel 07768 461450); Brian MacLaurin Associates Limited, 26–28 Hammersmith Grove, London W6 7BA (tel 020 8834 1034, fax 020 8834 1180, e-mail brian@brianmaclaurin.com, website www.brianmaclaurin.com)

MACLAURIN, Robert Allister Charles; s of (Allister) James Maclaurin, and Mary, *née* Boniface; *b* 12 June 1961; *Educ* Edinburgh Coll of Art; *Career* artist; *Solo Exhibitions* incl: Mercury Gallery Edinburgh 1987, 369 Gallery Edinburgh 1989, Berkeley Square Gallery London 1990, 1997, 1999, 2001 and 2003, The Fruitmarket Gallery Edinburgh 1991, Benjamin Rhodes Gallery London 1991 and 1993, Edinburgh Printmakers Gallery 1993, Kirkcaldy Art Gallery & Museum 1994, Durham Art Gallery 1994, Glasgow Print Studio 1995, Compass Gallery Glasgow 1997, Niagara Galleries Melbourne 1998, Talbot Rice Gallery, Edinburgh Int Festival 1999, Open Eye Gallery Edinburgh 2005, Osborne-Samuel Gallery London 2006 and 2008, Axia Modern Melbourne 2007, Castlemaine Art Gallery and Museum Australia 2008; *Group Exhibitions* incl: New Scottish Painting (Art in General NY) 1988, Chicago International Art Exposition 1988–91, Athena Awards Exhibition (Barbican Art Gallery London) 1988–89, International Weeks of Painting (Slovenia, touring exhibition of former Yugoslavia) 1989–90, Scottish Art Since 1900 (Scottish Nat Gallery of Modern Art Edinburgh, Barbican Art Gallery London) 1989–90, The Int FIAR Prize Exhibition (touring to Milan, Rome, Paris, London, LA, NY) 1991–92, Expressions: Scottish Art 1945–2000 (touring) 2000, Scottish Landscape (Scottish Gallery Edinburgh) 2001, En plein air (Geelong Gallery and Australian tour) 2003, Scottish Artists (Bohun Gallery Henley-on-Thames) 2005, 7 Artists (Uber Gallery St Kilda Melbourne) 2005, Scots Abroad (Open Eye Gallery Edinburgh) 2007; *Work in Collections* Edinburgh City Art Centre, Contemporary Art Soc, Scottish Nat Gallery of Modern Art, Flemings/Wyfold Fndn Collection, Coopers Lybrand Deloitte, Phillips Petroleum (London), The Standard Life Assurance Company, McKenna and Co, Scottish Arts Cncl, Kirkcaldy Art Gallery & Museum, Unilever, Pearl Assurance, Tetrapak, Paris Banque, Anglo-American (London), Scottish Nat Portrait Gallery, Pioneer International Australia, Castlemaine Art Gallery and Museum Australia; *Awards* Hospital Field House Painting Sch 1982, John Kinross scholar RSA Florence 1984, Turkish Govt scholar 1984–85, Br Cncl travel grant 1988, Scottish Arts Cncl bursary 1988, Durham Cathedral artist in residence 1993–94, Dunmoochin Fndn Studio 1995–96, Sir Robert Menzies fellowship 1995, First Prize Winner Noble Grossart Scot Painting Prize 1998, First Prize John Farrell Self Portrait Prize Castlemaine Art Gallery and Museum 2005; *Style*— Robert Maclaurin, Esq; ✉ c/o Osborne-Samuel Gallery, London (website www.osbornesamuel.com and www.robertmaclaurin.com)

M

MacLAURIN OF KNEBWORTH, Baron (Life Peer UK 1996), of Knebworth in the County of Hertfordshire; Sir Ian Charter MacLaurin; kt (1989), DL (Herts 1992); s of Arthur George MacLaurin (d 1989), and Evelina Florence, *née* Bott (d 1970); *b* 30 March 1937; *Educ* Malvern Coll; *m* 1, 1960, Ann Margaret (d 1999), da of Edgar Ralph Collar (d 1968); 2 da (Fiona Margaret (Mrs Mason) b 1962, Gillian (Mrs O'Gorman) b 1964), 1 s (Neil Ralph Charter b 1966); m 2, 2002, Paula, da of Herbert Morris; *Career* Nat Serv RAF Fighter Cmd 1956–58; Tesco plc: first co trainee 1959, memb Bd 1970, md 1973, dep chm 1983, chm 1985–97; non-exec dir: Enterprise Oil plc 1984–90, Guinness plc 1986–95, National Westminster Bank plc 1990–96, Gleneagles Hotels plc 1992–97, Vodafone Group plc 1997– (dep chm 1998–2000, chm 2000–06), Whitbread plc 1997–2000 (dep chm 1999–2000), Evolution Gp plc 2004–, Heineken NV 2006–; chm: Food Policy Gp of the Retail Consortium 1980–84, UK Sports Cncl until 1997, England and Wales Cricket Bd 1996–2002, Cavendish Grant Ltd 2006–; pres Inst of Grocery Distribution 1989–92; chm Cncl Malvern Coll 2002–; memb Save The Children Fund Commerce and Industry Ctee, Stock Exchange Advsy Ctee 1988–91; chllr Univ of Hertfordshire 1996–2005; Freedom City of London 1981, Liveryman Worshipful Co of Carmen 1982; hon fell Univ of Wales Cardiff; Hon DPhil Univ of Stirling 1987; FRSA 1986, FInstM 1987, Hon FCGI 1992; *Recreations* cricket, golf; *Clubs* MCC, Royal & Ancient; *Style*— The Rt Hon Lord MacLaurin of Knebworth, DL; ✉ 14 Great College Street, London SW1P 3RX

MACLAY, 3 Baron (UK 1922); Sir Joseph Paton Maclay; 3 Bt (UK 1914); DL (Renfrewshire 1986); s of 2 Baron Maclay, KBE (d 1969); *b* 11 April 1942; *Educ* Winchester; *m* 1976, Elizabeth, da of George Buchanan, of Pokataroo, NSW; 2 s, 1 da; *Heir* s, Hon Joseph Maclay; *Career* md: Denholm Maclay Ltd 1970–83, Triport Ferries Mgmnt 1975–83, Denholm Maclay Offshore Ltd 1976–83; dir: Milton Shipping 1970–83, Br Steamship Short Trades Assoc 1976–83, N of England Protection & Indemnity Assoc 1978–83,

Denholm Ship Management (Holdings) Ltd 1990–93, Altnamara Shipping plc 1994–2002; gp mktg exec Acomarit Group 1993–99; md Milton Timber Servs Ltd 1984–89, chm Scottish branch Br Sailors Soc 1979–81, vice-chm Glasgow Shipowners & Shipbrokers Benevolent Assoc 1982–83 and 1997–98 (pres 1998–99); chm: Scottish Maritime Museum 1998–2005, Northern Lighthouse Bd 2001–03 (cmmr 1996–2003, vice-chm 2000–01, chm 2001–03), Scottish Nautical Welfare Soc 2002–04; tstee: Cattanach Charitable Tst 1991–, Western Isles Fisheries Tst 2004–, Western Isles Salmon Fishing Bd 2004–; *Recreations* gardening, fishing; *Clubs* Western; *Style—* The Rt Hon Lord Maclay, DL; ✉ Duchal, Kilmacolm, Renfrewshire (tel 0150 587 2255)

MACLAY, Michael William; s of William Paton Maclay, and late Janette Kiddie Maclay; *b* 14 July 1953; *Educ* Churcher's Coll Petersfield, Trinity Coll Cambridge (sr scholar, MA), Univ of Freiburg; *m* Dec 1980, Elfi, da of Adam Lunkenheimer; 1 da (Catriona b 1983), 1 s (Christopher b 1986); *Career* FCO 1976, Br High Cmmn Lagos 1977–79, UK Mission to UN NY 1980–83, Southern Africa Dept FCO 1983–84, researcher, reporter and prodr Weekend World (LWT) 1984–88, policy ed The Sunday Correspondent 1988–90, prodr 'War in the Gulf' (LWT) 1991, asst ed The European 1991–93, special advsr to the Foreign Sec 1993–95, special advsr to Carl Bildt High Rep Bosnia 1995–97, dir Hakluyt and Company 1997–2002, exec chm Montrose Assocs 2003–; tstee Citizenship Fndn 1993– (chm 2000–); non-exec dir Open Broadcast Network (Bosnia) 1998–2000; sr advsr Club of Three 2006– (exec dir 2000–06), memb Advsy Bd Br America Project 2005–; *Publications* Multi-Speed Europe? (1992), Maastricht Made Simple (ed, 1993), Pocket History of EU (1998); *Clubs* Oxford and Cambridge, Garrick; *Style—* Michael Maclay, Esq; ✉ 10 Lammas Park Gardens, London W5 5HZ (tel 020 8579 2739)

McLEAN, Alison Mary; da of Leo McLean (d 1981), and Mollie, *née* Hackett (d 2003); *b* 16 December 1950; *Educ* Univ of Bristol (BA), LSE (DSA), Aston Univ (MSc); *m* 17 Jan 1976, Adrian While; 1 s (Benjamin b 24 June 1977), 2 da (Jennifer May b 11 April 1980, Eleanor Ruth b 20 July 1983); *Career* coordinator/team ldr Poole's Park Tenant Co-op 1975–78, recruitment prog coordinator Mozambique Info Centre 1978–80, community worker Islington Community Voluntary Serv Employment Unit 1981–83, rural devpt offr Leominster Marches Project 1987–89, community worker Hereford and Worcester Cncl 1989–92, rural devpt area project offr Malvern Hills DC 1992–95, project team mangr S Marches Partnership 1995–98, econ resources and policy mangr Herefordshire Cncl 1998–2001, policy and commissioning mangr Herefordshire Partnership 2001–03, dir rural regeneration zone Shropshire Co Cncl 2003–05, ind conslt 2005–; memb Bd: Countryside Agency 2002–, RegenWM 2002–05; vice-chm W Midlands Rural Affairs Forum 2005–; *Publications* Rural Issues and an Enabling Church (1989), Progress in the Rural New Committment to Regeneration Pathfinders (2000); *Recreations* theatre, sailing, gardening; *Style—* Ms Alison McLean

MACLEAN, Prof Allan B; s of Bruce H Maclean, of Auckland, NZ, and Marie F, *née* Mackie; *b* 8 February 1947; *Educ* Univ of Otago (BMedSc, MB ChB, DipObst, MD); *m* Mary R, *née* Callanan; 2 da (Nicola b 19 March 1975, Fiona b 4 Aug 1977), 2 s (Simon b 16 April 1981, Allan b 10 Dec 1986); *Career* sr lectr Christchurch Clinical Sch of Med NZ 1980–85, sr lectr Dept of Midwifery Univ of Glasgow and conslt obstetrician and gynaecologist Queen Mother's Hosp and Western Infirmary Glasgow 1985–92, prof of gynaecology and head of dept Royal Free and UC Medical Sch 1992–; pres Br Soc for the Study of Vulval Disease; vice-pres Int Soc for the Study of Vulvo-Vaginal Disease, memb Int Gynaecologic Cancer Soc; FRCOG 1990 (MRCOG 1978); *Books* Clinical Infection in Obstetrics and Gynaecology (1990), Hormones and Cancer (ed with PMS O'Brien, 1999), The Effective Management of Ovarian Cancer (ed with Martin Gore and Andrew Miles, 1999), Infection and Pregnancy (ed with L Regan and D Carrington, 2001), Disorders of the Menstrual Cycle (jt ed, 2000), Pain in Obstetrics and Gynaecology (jt ed, 2001), Incontinence in Women (co-ed, 2002), Maternal Morbidity and Mortality (jt ed, 2002), Rapid Obstetrics and Gynaecology (jt ed, 2003), Lower Genital Tract Neoplasia (jt ed, 2003); *Recreations* rowing and rugby, the life and works of Robert Burns; *Style—* Prof Allan Maclean; ✉ University Department of Obstetrics and Gynaecology, Royal Free and University College Medical School, Royal Free Campus, Rowland Hill Street, London NW3 2PF

McLEAN, Prof André Ernest Michael; s of Dr Fritz Fraenkel (d 1943), of Berlin, and Hildegard Maria, *née* Leo; *b* 5 January 1931; *Educ* Christ's Hosp, Univ of Oxford, UCL (BM BCh, PhD); *m* 1, Oct 1956 (m dis 1992), Dr Elizabeth Kathleen Hunter, da of Donald Hunter (d 1978); 2 s (Thomas b 1958, Adam b 1960), 2 da (Angela b 1961, Martha b 1965); m 2, Alison Lamb; 3 s (James, Andrew (twins) b 1992, Daniel b 1995); *Career* Colonial Med Serv 1960–63; assoc prof Chicago Med Sch 1964–65, memb scientific staff MRC Jamaica and Carshalton 1965–67, prof of toxicology Univ of London 1980–1996 (emeritus prof 1996–); author of papers on human malnutrition and relation between diet and toxicity of drugs and chemicals; chm Br Toxicology Soc 1987–88, former memb ctees on food additives, pesticides, and Ctee on Safety of Medicines for Dept of Health, currently conslt toxicologist on chemicals and pharmaceuticals; FRCPath; *Recreations* canoe, gardening; *Style—* Prof André McLean; ✉ tel and fax 020 7380 1530, e-mail andre.mclean@ucl.ac.uk

McLEAN, Bruce; *b* 1944; *Educ* Glasgow Sch of Art, St Martin's Sch of Art; *Career* artist; solo exhibitions incl: King for a Day (Nova Scotia Coll of Art Gallery 1970 and Tate Gallery 1972), The Object of Exercise? (The Kitchen NY Rosi McLean) 1978, Chantal Crousel Paris 1981, Modern Art Galerie Vienna 1982, DAAD Gallery Berlin 1983, Whitechapel 1983, Tate Gallery 1985, Arnolfini Gallery Bristol 1990; selected group exhibitions incl: Five Young Artists (ICA) 1965, The British Avant Garde (Cultural Centre NY) 1971, Lives and Annual Exhibition (Hayward) 1979, Performance Symposium (Centre Georges Pompidou) 1979, A New Spirit in Painting (Royal Acad) 1981, British Sculpture in the Twentieth Centre (Whitechapel) 1981, New Art (Tate) 1983, An International Survey of Recent Painting and Sculpture (MOMA NY) 1984, British Art in the Twentieth Century (Royal Acad) 1987, Twenty Years of British Sculpture (Lettovre) 1988, Great British Art Show (Glasgow) 1990; performance artist and memb Nice Style 1965–; performance work incl: Interview Sculpture (with Gilbert & George, London) 1969, Sorry! A Minimal Musical in Parts (with Rosi McLean, Hayward) 1979, Simple Manners and Physical Violence (Tate, Riverside Studios and Kunstmuseum Dusseldorf) 1985, A Ball is Not a Dancing School (Whitechapel) 1988, Vertical Balcony (Arnolfini Gallery Bristol, Henry Moore Sculpture Tst Studio Halifax and Tramway Glasgow) 1990; designer Soldat (Rambert Dance Co) 1989; work in the collections of: Arts Cncl of GB, Br Cncl, Contemporary Arts Soc, Saatchi Collection, Nat MOMA Osaka, South Bank Centre, Canary Wharf, BR, Tate, Van Abbemuseum Eindhoven, V&A, Nat Museum of Scotland, Scottish National Modern Art Museum Edinburgh; *Style—* Bruce McLean, Esq

MACLEAN, Colin William; OBE (2000); s of Percy Kenneth Maclean (d 1975), and Elsie Violet, *née* Middleton (d 1986); *b* 19 June 1938; *Educ* William Hulmes GS, Univ of Liverpool (MVSc, FRCVS, William Hunting awards); *m* 19 Sept 1959, Jacqueline Diana, da of Frederick Brindley; 2 da (Antonia Karen b 12 Feb 1962, Nicola Janine b 20 Dec 1963); *Career* vet surgn 1961–66; Unilever Ltd: chief vet advsr 1966–72, mangr pig breeding 1972–74, md Farm Mark Ltd and Masterbreeders Ltd 1974–80, gen mangr (South) BOCM Silcock Ltd 1980–83; dep md and dir product devpt Glaxo Animal Health Ltd 1983–88, DG Meat and Livestock Cmmn 1992–98 (tech dir 1988–92); chm Royal Berks and Battle Hosps NHS Tst 2000–; fndr memb and pres Pig Vet Soc (memb 1966), past pres Br Cattle Vet Assoc; memb: Royal Counties Vet Assoc 1975 (past chm), RASE 1988; *Recreations* squash, rugby, football; *Clubs* Farmers'; *Style—* Colin Maclean, Esq, OBE; ✉ Royal Berkshire and Battle Hospitals NHS Trust, London Road, Reading RG1 5AN (tel 0118 987 7230, fax 0118 987 8042)

MACLEAN, David John; PC (1995), MP; *b* 16 May 1953; *Career* MP (Cons) Penrith and the Border July 1983– (by-election); *Style—* The Rt Hon David Maclean, MP; ✉ House of Commons, London SW1A 0AA (tel 020 7219 6494)

MACLEAN, Sir Donald Og Grant; kt (1985); s of Maj Donald Og Maclean, OBE, MC (d 1974), of Dalnabo, Crieff, and Margaret, *née* Smith (d 1972); *b* 13 August 1930; *Educ* Morrison's Acad Crieff, Heriot-Watt Univ; *m* 1, 11 Jan 1958, Muriel (d 1984), da of Charles Giles (d 1972); 1 da (Fiona b 1960), 1 s (Donald b 1962); m 2, 15 March 2002, Mrs Margaret Ross, da of John Harper; *Career* Nat Serv RAMC 1952–54; ophthalmic optician (optometrist) in practice 1954–2001: Edinburgh, Newcastle upon Tyne, Perth, Ayr; chm: Ayr Constituency Assoc (Cons) 1971–75, W of Scotland Area Cncl SCUA 1977–79; pres SCUA 1983–85; chm: Ayrshire Medical Support Ltd 1995–, Bell Hollingworth Ltd 1996–99, Carrick Cumnock and Doon Valley Cons and Unionist Assoc 1998–2000; vice-chm Scottish Cons Pty 1989–91 (dep chm 1985–89); former: pres W Highland Steamer Club, chm SW Scotland AOP and Local Optical Ctee, memb Local Tport Users Consultative Ctee; elder Church of Scotland; Freeman City of London 1987, Liveryman Worshipful Co of Spectacle Makers 1989; Dean of Guildry of the Guildry of the Royal Burgh of Ayr 1993–95; FBOA, FCOptom; *Recreations* photography, reading, seeking suicidal trout; *Style—* Sir Donald Maclean; ✉ 31 Belmont Road, Ayr KA7 2PQ

McLEAN, Prof Iain; *b* 13 September 1946; *Educ* Royal HS Edinburgh, ChCh Oxford (exhibitioner, BA), Nuffield Coll Oxford (BPhil, DPhil); *Career* research fell Nuffield Coll Oxford 1969–71, lectr in politics Univ of Newcastle upon Tyne 1971–78, lectr (CUF) in politics Univ of Oxford 1978–91 (fell and praelector UC Oxford), prof of politics Univ of Warwick 1991–93, official fell in politics Nuffield Coll Oxford and prof of politics Univ of Oxford 1993–; dir of grad admissions Dept of Politics and Int Studies Univ of Warwick 1992–93, dir of grad studies in politics Univ of Oxford 1994–95, dir of research trg in politics Univ of Oxford 1996–99; visiting prof of politics: Washington & Lee Univ VA 1980, Univ of Warwick 1993–96, Univ of Newcastle upon Tyne 1996; visiting prof Dept of Political Science Stanford Univ 1990–91, academic visitor Dir's Section Research Sch of Social Sciences ANU 1996 and 2002, William H Orrick visiting prof Prog in Ethics, Politics and Economics Yale Univ 2001; jt ed Electoral Studies 1993–99; memb Editorial Bd: Electoral Studies, Br Jl of Political Science, Jl of Theoretical Politics; radio and TV commentator on UK politics; memb Tyne & Wear MCC 1973–79 (chm Economic Devpt Ctee 1976–78), memb Oxford City Cncl 1982–86 (ldr Alliance Gp); appeals dir Welshpool and Llanfair Light Railway Preservation Co Ltd (dir 1978–92 and 1999–); Religious Soc of Friends: elder Oxford Preparative Meeting (treas 1995–99), managing tstee Witney Monthly Meeting; *Publications* Keir Hardie (1975), Elections (1976), Why Electoral Reform? (pamphlet with P M Williams, 1981), Dealing in Votes (1982), The Legend of Red Clydesid (1983), Public Choice: an introduction (1987), Consumers' Guide to Tactical Voting (pamphlet, 1987), Democracy and New Technology (1989), Condorcet: foundations of social choice and political theory (trans and intro with F Hewitt, 1994), Classics of Social Choice (ed, trans and intro with A B Urken, 1995), Concise Oxford Dictionary of Politics (gen ed and contrib, 1996), A Mathematical Approach to Proportional Representation: Duncan Black on Lewis Carroll (with A McMillan and B Monroe, 1996), Fixing the Boundary: defining and redefining single-member electoral districts (ed with D Butler, 1996), The Theory of Committees and Elections by Duncan Black and Committee Decisions with Complementary Valuation by Duncan Black and R A Newing (ed with A McMillan and D Monroe, 1998), Aberfan: government and disasters (with M Johnes, 2000), Rational Choice & British Politics: an analysis of rhetoric and manipulation from Peel to Blair (2001), International Trade and Political Institutions Instituting Trade in the Long Nineteenth Century (with F McGillivray, R Pahre and C Schonhardt-Bailey, 2001); also author of book chapters, website contributions, working papers, policy briefings, book reviews and numerous papers in refereed jls; *Recreations* mountaineering, skiing, choral music, narrow-gauge railway preservation (qualified steam and diesel locomotive driver); *Style—* Iain McLean; ✉ Nuffield College, Oxford OX1 1NF

MacLEAN, Dr Ian Hamish; *b* 9 October 1947, Bishop's Stortford, Herts; *Educ* King's Coll Choir Sch Cambridge (chorister), Felsted, Mid-Essex Tech Coll Chelmsford, Univ of St Andrews, Univ of Dundee (MB ChB); *m* Anne; 2 c; *Career* RAF flying scholarship 1964; house offr (gen surgery then gen med) Cumberland Infirmary Carlisle 1972–73, SHO (accident and emergency) Hexham Gen Hosp Northumberland 1973, MO Support Ships MAFF (Iceland Support Op) 1973–74, SHO (A&E) Hexham Gen Hosp 1974, locum GP Longtown and Kirkoswald Cumbria 1974, sessional MO Nat Blood Transfusion Serv 1975, registrar in community med Durham and Gateshead AHAs 1975–77, sr registrar in community med N Tyneside and Northumberland AHAs 1977–80, conslt in public health med Borders Health Bd 1980–89, chief admin MO and dir of public health Dumfries and Galloway Health Bd 1989–98, hon sr clinical lectr in public health Univ of Glasgow; chief MO and dir of Public Health Isle of Man Govt (retd); formerly chm COPPISH Project Bd; formerly vice-chm Scottish Directors of Public Health; formerly memb: Health Servs and Public Health Res Ctee, CHI/UPI Project Bd, Scottish Public Health Forum; FFCM 1989 (MFCM 1982); *Publications* author of published papers in learned periodicals; *Recreations* music (especially modern jazz), photography, art, sailing and boatbuilding, gliding and powered flying (PPL), model making, fishing, shooting, gardening, practical engineering (mechanical and civil), restoration of a ruinous mansion house built by Thomas Rickman; *Style—* Dr Ian MacLean; ✉ 26 Birch Hill Grove, Onchan, Isle of Man IM3 4EN

McLEAN, Prof (William Henry) Irwin; s of Henry McLean, of Dervock, Ballymoney (d 1971), and Rosetta, *née* McAleese (d 1999); *b* 9 January 1963, Ballymoney, Co Antrim; *Educ* Queen's Univ Belfast (BSc, PhD, DSc); *Career* Dept of Medical Genetics Queen's Univ of Belfast: research asst 1985–88, postdoctoral research asst 1988–91; research dir Ångström Laboratories 1991–92, postdoctoral research fell CRC Cell Structure Research Gp Univ of Dundee 1992–96, assoc prof Dept of Dermatology and Cutaneous Biology Jefferson Med Coll Philadelphia 1996–98; Human Genetics Unit Ninewells Med Sch Univ of Dundee: Wellcome Tst sr research fell, sr lectr and head of human genetics research 1998–2002, head of human genetics research and prof of human genetics 2002–; hon NHS clinical scientist 2000–; visiting prof of biochemistry Univ Tor Vergata Rome 2001–02; section ed Br Jl of Dermatology 2000–03, memb Editorial Bd Jl of Dermatological Science 2003–, assoc ed Jl of Investigative Dermatology 2003–; memb Scientific Advsy Bd Br Skin Fndn 2001–, chm Scottish Skin Biology Club 2004–; fndr memb Med and Scientific Advsy Bd: Pachyonychia Project 2004–, Hidradenitis Suppurativa Fndn 2006–; regular reviewer for various learned jls, author of 116 peer-reviewed scientific papers in genetics, dermatology and ophthalmology, 2 patents, invited speaker at nat and int meetings and seminars; Br Soc for Investigative Dermatology: Best Abstract Award 1993, Best Poster Award 2006; Nature Publishing Gp Best Clinical Sci Presentation 2006; Wellcome Tst Travel Award 1996; FRSE 2005; *Recreations* composing electronic music, reading, hill walking, geology, photography, astronomy; *Style—* Prof Irwin McLean; ✉ Human Genetics Unit, Division of Pathology and Neuroscience, University of Dundee, Ninewalls Hospital and Medical School, Dundee DD1 9SY (tel 01382 425618, fax 01382 425619, e-mail w.h.i.mclean@dundee.ac.uk)

McLEAN, John Talbert; s of late Talbert McLean, of Arbroath, and Dorothy, *née* Gladhill; *b* 10 January 1939; *Educ* Reform Street Sch Kirriemuir, Arbroath HS, Univ of St Andrews, Courtauld Inst Univ of London (BA); *m* 1964, Janet Alison, da of Edward Backhouse

Norman; *Career* teacher of art history: pt/t Chelsea Sch of Art 1966–74, UCL 1974–78; teacher of painting Winchester Coll of Art 1978–82, visiting tutor in painting at many art schs in GB, Canada and USA; solo exhibitions incl: Talbot Rice Art Centre (Univ of Edinburgh) 1975, 1985 and 1994, House Gallery London 1978, Nicola Jacobs Gallery London 1980, Art Placement Saskatoon Canada 1981 and 2000, Art Space Galleries Aberdeen 1982, Byck Gallery Louisville Kentucky USA 1983, Martin Gerrard Gallery Edmonton Canada 1984, Dept of Architecture (Univ of Edinburgh) 1986, Kapil Jariwala Gallery London 1987, Jariwala-Smith Gallery NY USA 1988, Francis Graham-Dixon Gallery London 1988, 1989, 1991/92, 1994, 1996 and 1997, Edinburgh Coll of Art 1989, Bourne Fine Art Edinburgh 1998 and 2000, Crawford Art Centre St Andrews 1999, Flowers East 1999, 2000, 2001, 2004 and 2006, Richard Ingelby Gallery Edinburgh 2000, Flowers Central 2003, Cross St Gallery London 2006, Poussin Gallery London 2007, Broadbent London 2007; paintings in public collections incl: Tate Gallery, Scot Nat Gallery of Modern Art, Arts Cncl of GB, Scot Arts Cncl, Br Cncl, DOE, Federated Union of Black Artists South Africa, Fitzwilliam Museum, Glasgow Museums and Galleries, Hunterian Collection Univ of Glasgow, City Art Centre Edinburgh, Whitworth Art Gallery Manchester; paintings in corporate collections worldwide; maj work incl cmmn for three large paintings for Pollock Halls Univ of Edinburgh 1971, five large paintings for Scottish Equitable Edinburgh 1996 and one large painting for Chelsea and Westminster Hosp 2007; *Awards* Arts Cncl award 1974, Arts Cncl maj award 1980, Br Cncl travel award 1981, 1984, 1993 and 2000, Lorne award 1992/93, Critics award Edinburgh Festival 1994; *Style—* John McLean, Esq; ✉ 704 Mountjoy House, Barbican, London EC2Y 8BP (tel 020 7628 3073)

MACLEAN, Maj Hon Sir Lachlan Hector Charles; 12 Bt (NS 1631), of Dowart and Morvern, Argyllshire; 28 Chief of Clan Maclean; CVO (2000), DL (1993 Argyll and Bute); o s of Baron Maclean, KT, GCVO, KBE, PC (Life Peer and 11 Bt, d 1990), and (Joan) Elizabeth, *née* Mann; *b* 25 August 1942; *Educ* Eton; *m* 1966, Mary Helen, eldest da of William Gordon Gordon, of Lude, Blair Atholl, Perthshire; 2 da (Emma Mary (Mrs Giovanni Amati) b 1967, Alexandra Caroline b 1975), 2 s (Malcolm Lachlan Charles b 1972, Andrew Lachlan William b 1979), and 1 da decd; *Heir* s, Malcolm Maclean; *Career* Maj Scots Gds (ret); former Adj Royal Co of Archers; *Style—* Maj the Hon Sir Lachlan Maclean, Bt, CVO, DL; ✉ Arngask House, Glenfarg, Perthshire PH2 9QA

MACLEAN, Lowry Druce; s of Ian Albert Druce Maclean (d 1985), and Diana Futvoye, *née* Marsden-Smedley (d 1979); *b* 22 July 1939; *Educ* Eton, Pembroke Coll Cambridge (MA), MIT; *m* 1966, Frances Anne, da of Henry Crawford (d 1967), of USA; 2 s, 1 da; *Career* dir: Karastan Inc 1970–72, John Crossley & Sons Ltd 1972–79; chm: Tomkinsons plc 1991–2000 (gp chief exec 1979–91), John Smedley Ltd 1991–; The Wesleyan Assurance Soc: jt md 1991–92, md 1992–99, vice-chm 1993–99, chm 1999–; dir Gaskell plc 2000–01; dir British Cs of C 1999–2002, pres Cncl Birmingham C of C and Industry 2000–01 (sr vice-pres 1995–2000); chm Aston Reinvestment Tst 2004–; vice-pres County Air Ambulance Tst 1993–, chm Med Sickness Soc 1997–; dir Birmingham Contemporary Music Gp 1997–; *Clubs* Lansdowne, Athenaeum; *Style—* Lowry Maclean, Esq; ✉ The Pound, Old Colwall, Great Malvern, Worcestershire WR13 6HG (tel 01684 540426); The Wesleyan Assurance Society, Colmore Circus, Birmingham B4 6AR (tel 0121 200 9070)

MacLEAN, Rt Hon Lord; Ranald Norman Munro MacLean; PC (2001); s of John Alexander MacLean (d 1992), and Hilda Margaret Lind, *née* Munro (d 2003); *b* 18 December 1938; *Educ* Fettes, Univ of Cambridge (BA), Univ of Edinburgh (LLB), Yale Univ (LLM); *m* 21 Sept 1963 (m dis 1993), Pamela, da of Prof Allan Dawson Ross, of London (d 1982); 1 da (Catriona Joan b 1967), 3 s (Fergus Ranald b 1970, Donald Ross b 1972, 1 s decd); *Career* called to Scottish Bar 1964, QC 1977; advocate-depute 1972–75, home advocate-depute 1979–82, Senator of the Coll of Justice 1990–2005, chm Ctee on Serious Violent and Sexual Offenders 1999–2000, chm Sentencing Cmmn for Scotland 2003–05, chm Billy Wright Inquiry Belfast 2005–; memb: Cncl on Tbnls 1985–90 (chm Scottish Ctee), Scottish Legal Aid Bd 1986–90, Sec of State for Scotland's Criminal Justice Forum 1996–2000, Parole Bd for Scotland 1998–2000 and 2003, Judicial Appts Bd for Scotland 2002–05; chm of govrs Fettes Coll 1996–2006; Hon LLD Univ of Aberdeen 2003; FRSE, FSA Scot; *Recreations* hill walking, Munro collecting, swimming; *Clubs* New (Edinburgh), Scottish Arts (Edinburgh); *Style—* The Rt Hon Lord MacLean; ✉ 38 Royal Terrace, Edinburgh EH7 5AH; Court of Session, Parliament House, Parliament Square, Edinburgh EH1 1RQ

McLEAN, Vice Adm Rory Alistair Ian; CB, OBE; *b* 4 April 1950, Shoreham by Sea, West Sussex; *Educ* George Watson's Coll Edinburgh; *Career* joined RN 1968, pilot 1973, cmd HMS Lewiston, cmd HMS Upton, Exec Offr HMS Brazen, Cdr HMS Jupiter, Cdr HMS Charybdis, cmd HMS Fearless, cmd HMS Invincible, Dir of Navy Plans and Progs MOD 1997–2001, ACDS (Resources and Progs) 2001–04, DCDS (Health) 2004–; life memb United Servs Mess Cardiff, memb Capt Scott Soc; Freeman City of London; *Recreations* golf, bowls, rugby, squash; *Style—* Vice Adm Rory McLean, CB, OBE; ✉ Ministry of Defence, Main Building, Horseguards Avenue, London SW1A 2HB (tel 020 7807 8847)

McLEAN, Prof Sheila Ann Manson; da of William Black (d 2003), of Dunblane, and Bethia, *née* Manson; *b* 20 June 1951; *Educ* Glasgow HS for Girls, Univ of Glasgow (LLB, MLitt, PhD); *m* 1976 (m dis 1987), Alan McLean; *Career* Area Reporter to the Children's Panel Strathclyde Regl Cncl 1972–75; Univ of Glasgow: lectr Dept of Forensic Medicine 1975–89, sr lectr Sch of Law 1989–90, Int Bar Assoc prof of law and ethics in med 1990–; dir Inst of Law and Ethics in Med Univ of Glasgow 1985– (co-dir with Prof K C Calman, *qv* 1985–87); rapporteur générale XXth Colloquy on Euro Law Cncl of Europe 1990; visiting researcher Univ of Otago New Zealand 1983; Sec of State appointee to UK Central Cncl for Nursing, Midwifery and Health Visiting; cmmnd by Dept of Health to review the consent provisions of the Human Fertilisation and Embryology Act 1990, specialist advsr to Jt Parly Ctee on the Human Tissue and Embryos Bill, ethico-legal advsr Tenovus Scotland; currently memb: BMA Ethics Ctee, Audit Ctee World Assoc of Medical Law, Int Bioethics Ctee UNESCO, Advsy Ctee ESRC Genomics Policy and Research Forum, AHRC Peer Review Coll, Ethics Ctee Int Fedn Obstetrics and Gynaecology; former chair: Scottish Criminal Cases Review Cmmn, Scottish Office Steering Gp on Female Offenders, Scottish Exec Independent Ctee of Enquiry into Organ Removal and Rentention at Post-Mortem; former vice-chair Ctee Multi-Centre Research Ethics for Scotland; former memb: SHEFC, Advsy Gp to Data Protection Registrar on Biotechnology, Sectional Ctee Philosophy, Theology and Law Royal Soc of Edinburgh, UK Xeno Transplantation Interim Regulatory Authy, Policy Advsy Ctee Nuffield Cncl on Bioethics, Review Body on Doctors' and Dentists' Remuneration, MRC Genetics Advsy Ctee, Broadcasting Cncl for Scotland; memb Editorial Bd: Int Jl of Medical Practice and Law, Medical Law Int, Bulletin of Medical Ethics, Jl of Law and Medicine; tstee: Scottish Civil Liberties Tst, Joyce Watson Meml Fund Re-Solv; Lifetime Achievement Award Scottish Legal Awards 2005; Hon LLD: Univ of Abertay Dundee 2002, Univ of Edinburgh 2002; FRSA 1996, FRSE 1996, FRCP (Edin) 1997, FRCGP 2003, FMedSci 2006; *Books* Medicine, Morals and the Law (co-author, 1983, reprinted 1985), A Patient's Right to Know: Information Disclosure, the Doctor and the Law (1989), The Case for Physician Assisted Suicide (jtly, 1997), Old Law, New Medicine (1999); edited books: Legal Issues in Medicine (1981), Human Rights: From Rhetoric to Reality (co-editor, 1986), The Legal Relevance of Gender (jt ed, 1988), Legal Issues in Human Reproduction (1989), Law Reform and Human Reproduction (1992), Compensation for Personal Injury: An International Perspective (1993), Law Reform and Medical Injury Litigation (1995), Law and Ethics in Intensive Care (1996), Death, Dying and the Law (1996), Contemporary Issues in Law, Medicine and Ethics (1996), Legal and Ethical Aspects of Health Care (jtly, 2003), Xenotransplantation: Law and Ethics (jtly, 2005), Modern Dilemmas: Choosing Children (2006), Disability and Impairment: Law and Ethics and the Beginning and End of Life (jtly, 2006), Assisted Dying: Some reflections on the need for law reform (2007); also author of numerous book chapters and articles in learned jls; *Recreations* playing guitar, singing, music, literature; *Clubs* Lansdowne; *Style—* Prof Sheila McLean, FRSE; ✉ School of Law, The University, Glasgow G12 8QQ (tel 0141 330 5577, fax 0141 330 4698, e-mail prof.s.mclean@law.gla.ac.uk)

MACLEAN, William James; s of John Maclean (d 1962), Master Mariner, of Harbour House, Inverness, and Mary Isabella, *née* Reid (d 1978); *b* 12 October 1941; *Educ* Inverness Royal Acad, HMS Conway, Grays Sch of Art Aberdeen (DA); *m* 18 Aug 1968, Marian Forbes, da of David Leven, of Fife, Scotland; 1 da (Miriam b 1971), 2 s (John b 1973, David b 1981); *Career* schoolteacher (art) Fife County 1970–79; Univ of Dundee: prof of fine art Duncan of Jordanstone Coll 1981–, emeritus prof 2001; numerous exhibitions in UK and abroad, incl retrospective Talbot Rice Gall Edinburgh 1992; works in public collections incl: British Museum, Fitzwilliam Museum Cambridge, Scottish National Gallery of Modern Art Edinburgh, Kelvingrove Art Gallery Glasgow; memb: SSA, Royal Glasgow Inst of the Fine Arts; assoc Royal Scot Acad 1978; Scottish Educnl Tst award 1973, Scottish Art Cncl Visual Arts award 1979, Royal Scottish Acad Gillies award 1988; hon DLitt Univ of St Andrews 2001, FSA Scot 1981, RSA 1991, RGI 1996, RSW 1997; *Style—* William Maclean, Esq

MACLEAN-BRISTOL, Maj Nicholas Maclean Verity; OBE (1994), DL (Argyll and Bute 1996); s of Arnold Charles Verity Bristol (d 1984), of Wotton, Surrey, and Lillias Nina Maclean, *née* Francis-Hawkins; *b* 25 May 1935; *Educ* Wellington, RMA Sandhurst; *m* 2 April 1965, Hon Lavinia Mary Hawke, da of 9 Baron Hawke (d 1985); 3 s (Charles Bladen b 1967, Alexander Stanhope b 1970, Lauchlan Neil b 1974); *Career* 2 Lt KOSB 1955, Malaya 1955–58, Lt 1957, ADC GOC 52(L) Inf Div and Lowland Dist 1958–60, Berlin 1960–61, Capt 1961, Aden 1962–64, Radfan 1964, Borneo 1965, GSO3 19 Inf Bde, GSO3 MOD (AT2) 1966–68, Maj 1968, Trg Maj 1 51 Highland 1970–72; proprietor Breacachadh Builders and Contractors 1983–98; The Project Tst: fndr 1967, dir 1968–70 and 1972–95, vice-chm 1970–72, pres 1995–; jt fndr West Highland and Island Historical Research 1972; *Books* Hebridean Decade: Mull, Coll and Tiree 1761–1771 (1982), The Isle of Coll in 1716 (1989), Warriors and Priests: The Clan Maclean 1300–1570 (1995), Murder Under Trust (1999), From Clan to Regiment: 600 years in the Hebrides 1400–2000 (2007); *Recreations* farming, Hebridean history, wine; *Clubs* Army and Navy, New (Edinburgh), Puffins; *Style—* Major Nicholas Maclean-Bristol, OBE, DL; ✉ Breacachadh Castle, Isle of Coll, Argyll PA78 6TB (tel 01879 230353); c/o The Project Trust, Isle of Coll, Argyll (tel 01879 230444, fax 01879 230357, e-mail nmbcoll@aol.com, website www.projecttrust.org.uk)

McLEAN-DALEY, Niomi (Ms Dynamite); da of Eyon Daley, and Heather McLean; *b* 1981, London; *Children* 1 s (Shavaar b 2003); *Career* singer; former presenter Flava (Channel 4); supporter Disarm Tst; *Albums* A Little Deeper 2002, Judgement Days 2005; *Singles* Booo! 2001, It Takes More 2002 (UK no 7), Dy-Na-Mi-Tee 2002 (UK no 5), Put Him Out 2002; *Awards* Mercury Music Prize for Album of the Year 2002, Best Single, Best Newcomer and UK Act of the Year MOBO Awards 2002, Best British Female Artist and Best Urban Act Brit Awards 2003, Big Voice Award Women of the Year Awards 2003; *Style—* Ms Dynamite; ✉ www.msdynamite.co.uk

MACLEAN OF DUNCONNEL, Sir Charles Edward; 2 Bt (UK 1957), of Dunconnel, Co Argyll; 16 Hereditary Captain and Keeper of Dunconnel in the Isles of the Sea; s of Sir Fitzroy Hew Maclean of Dunconnel, 1 Bt, KT, CBE (d 1996); *b* 31 October 1946; *Educ* Eton, New Coll Oxford; *m* 1986, Deborah, da of Lawrence Young, of Chicago; 4 da (Margaret Augusta b 1986, Katharine Alexandra b 1988, Charlotte Olivia b 1991, Diana Mary Elektra b 1997); *Heir* bro, James Maclean; *Books* Island on the Edge of the World, The Wolf Children, The Watcher, Scottish Country, Romantic Scotland, The Silence; *Style—* Sir Charles Maclean of Dunconnel, Bt; ✉ Strachur House, Argyll

M

MACLEAN OF PENNYCROSS, Nicolas Wolfers Lorne; a Chieftain of the Clan Maclean; s of Marcel Wolfers (d 1979), of London, and Audrey, *née* Maclean of Pennycross (d 1985); *b* 3 January 1946; *Educ* Eton, Oriel Coll Oxford (exhibitioner, MA), Universidad de Santander, PCL; *m* 22 Aug 1978, Qamar Sultan, da of Abdul Aziz, of Vancouver, Canada; 2 s (Mark Salim yr of Pennycross b 19 July 1982, Alexander Karim b 26 Feb 1988); *Career* started European and Japanese investment section J Henry Schroder Wagg & Co Ltd 1967–71, mangr European investment project PN Kemp Gee & Co 1971–72, mangr London Continental Pension Unit Tst then asst dir Project & Export Fin Dept Samuel Montagu & Co Ltd, asst dir Public Fin Dept then gp advsr Midland Bank Gp 1972–93, sr advsr (China) Robert Fleming plc 1994–97, gp advsr (Asia) Prudential Corp plc and exec dir Prudential Corp Asia Ltd 1997–99, chief exec MWM Consultancy Services 1999–; sr fell IISS 2000– (memb 2001–); seconded as COS to Rt Hon William Whitelaw, CH, MC, MP during European Referendum Campaign 1975 (pt/t res asst until 1983), seconded as political asst to Rt Hon Margaret Thatcher, MP during 1979, 1983 and 1987 Gen Election campaigns; elected chm Accepting Houses' Export Fin Sub-Ctee 1982; chm Japan Festival Educn Tst 2002– (dep chm 1992–2002), pt/t dir Loomba Tst 2001–02; fndr memb UK-Japan 21st Century Gp; memb: Bd UK-Korea Forum for the Future, Exec Ctee The British-American Project, Intermediate Technol Devpt Gp, Chm's Ctee and Corp and Cultural Ctee Asia House London, Russia and Eurasia Advsy Bd Chatham House, Bd Int Photography Cncl, Bd Project Tst; former memb: Cncl London C of C and Industry (also chm for China, Japan and Mongolia), Br Overseas Trade Bd Area Advsy Gp for Japan and for China, Africa Private Enterprise Gp; formerly: official expert Econ and Social Ctee Task Force on India (Brussels), hon treas and memb Exec Ctee Asia House London, chm for Asia UNICE Brussels, UK rep Vienna Cncl Task Force on Financial Sector Reform in Central and Eastern Europe, econ rapporteur on Africa; initiator Br Eng Teaching Prog (now JET) 1978 (memb Selection Bd 1978–); formerly: vice-pres Japan Soc, vice-pres Royal Soc for Asian Affrs; co-organiser of exhbns incl: Great Japan Exhibition (Royal Acad) 1976–82, Treasures from Korea (Br Museum) 1984, Visions from Vietnam (RCA) 1998; hon pres William Adams Assoc, hon vice-pres Clan Maclean Assoc; former govr Sadler's Wells Fndn, former memb Int Ctee Leonard Cheshire Fndn; cncllr Royal Borough of Kensington and Chelsea 1979–90; voted one of Britain's top ten fund mangrs Euromoney 1974, Japan Soc Special Millennium Award 2000; memb RIIA 1967 (former memb Cncl and membership chm), MInstD 1999; Hon Key to City of Osaka; *Publications* co-author: Trading with China: a Practical Guide (1979), Journey into Japan 1600–1868 (1981), The Eurobond and Eurocurrency Markets (1984), Mongolia Today (1988); author of numerous articles on international and financial issues; *Recreations* history, etymology, performing and visual arts, rowing, broadcasting, international affairs; *Clubs* Beefsteak; *Style—* Nicolas Maclean of Pennycross; ✉ The International Institute for Strategic Studies, Arundel House, 13–15 Arundel Street, Temple Place, London WC2R 3DX (e-mail maclean@iiss.org)

MacLEARY, Alistair Ronald; s of Donald Herbert MacLeary (d 1984), of Inverness, and Jean Spiers, *née* Leslie (d 1973); *b* 12 January 1940; *Educ* Inverness Royal Acad, Coll of Estate Mgmnt, Edinburgh Coll of Art (DipTP), Univ of Strathclyde (MSc); *m* 6 May 1967, Mary-Claire Cecilia (Claire), da of James Leonard (d 1976), of Livingston; 1 s (Roderic b 1976), 1 da (Kate b 1984); *Career* asst Gerald Eve & Co chartered surveyors 1962–65, asst to dir Murrayfield Real Estate Co Ltd 1965–67, asst and ptnr Wright and Partners Surveyors 1967–76, MacRobert prof of land economy Univ of Aberdeen 1976–89; chm:

Bd of Educn Cwlth Assoc Surveying and Land Econ 1980–90, Watt Ctee on Energy Working Gp on Land Resources 1977–79; memb: Govt Ctee of Inquiry into the Acquisition and Occupancy of Agricultural Land (The Northfield Ctee) 1977–79, NERC 1988–91, Lands Tbnl Scotland 1989–2005, Cncl on Tbnls 2005– (chair Scottish Ctee); pres planning and devpt div RICS 1984–85; hon fell Cwlth Assoc of Surveying and Land Economy (CASLE) 1992, hon prof Univ of Heriot-Watt 2005; FRICS, FRTPI, FRSA; *Books* Property Investment Theory (with N Nanthakumeran, 1988), National Taxation for Property Management and Valuation (1990); *Recreations* shooting, golf, hill walking; *Clubs* Royal Northern & Univ (Aberdeen), The New Golf (St Andrews); *Style*— Alistair MacLeary, Esq; ✉ St Helens, St Andrews Road, Ceres, Fife KY15 5NQ (tel 01334 828862, fax 01334 828862, e-mail alistair_macleary@tiscali.co.uk)

MACLEHOSE, Christopher C; s of Alexander MacLehose, and Elizabeth, *née* Hope Bushell; *Educ* Shrewsbury, Univ of Oxford (MA); *Career* literary ed Scotsman Newspaper 1964–67; editorial dir Chatto & Windus 1973–79, ed-in-chief William Collins 1981–84, publisher Collins Harvill 1984–95, chm and publisher The Harvill Press 1995–2002 (publisher at large 2004–06), publisher MacLehose Press 2006–; *Recreations* gardening, wood, the sea, Vizslas; *Style*— Christopher MacLehose, Esq; ✉ Arundel House, 3 Westbourne Road, London N7 8AR (fax 020 7700 5106)

McLEISH, Alexander (Alex); s of Alexander N McLeish (d 1981), and Jane (Jean), *née* Wylie; *b* 21 January 1959; *Educ* Barrhead HS, John Neilson HS Paisley; *m* 8 Dec 1980, Jill Moira, da of Daniel Taylor, of Aberdeen; 2 s (Jon Alexander b 28 May 1981, Jamie Daniel b 6 Aug 1985), 1 da (Rebecca Lisa b 7 July 1989); *Career* professional footballer; Aberdeen FC: European Cup Winners' Cup medal, Super Cup medal, five Scottish Cup wins, two Scottish League Cup wins, three championship medals; transferred as player/mangr Motherwell FC 1994; mangr: Hibernian FC 1998–2001, Rangers FC 2001–06 (winners Scottish Premier League 2003 and 2005, winners Scottish FA Cup 2003, Scottish League Cup 2002); Scotland: 77 full caps as player, mangr Scotland nat team 2007–; involved in local charities; *Books* Don of an Era (1988); *Recreations* tennis, cinema, golf; *Style*— Alex McLeish, Esq

McLEISH, Rt Hon Henry Baird; PC (2000); s of Harry McLeish, of Kennoway, Fife, and Mary, *née* Baird (d 1985); *b* 15 June 1948; *Educ* Buckhaven HS, Heriot-Watt Univ (BSc); *m* 1, 16 March 1968, Margaret (d 1995), da of Walter Drysdale; 1 s (Niall b 1 March 1974), 1 da (Clare b 29 May 1976); *m* 2, 1 May 1998, Julie, *née* Fulton; 1 s (James), 1 da (Carly); *Career* research offr Dept of Social Work Edinburgh Corp 1973–74; planning offr: Fife CC 1974–75, Dunfermline DC 1975–87; MP (Lab) Fife Central 1987–2001, MSP (Lab) Fife Central 1999–2003; shadow Scottish front bench spokesman for educn and employment 1988–89, shadow front bench spokesman for employment and trg 1989–92, shadow Scottish min of state 1992–94; shadow min of: tport 1994–95, health 1995–96, social security 1996–97; min for home affrs and devolution Scottish Office 1997–99; Scottish Executive: min for enterprise and lifelong learning 1999–2000, first min 2000–01; former cncllr: Kirkcaldy DC, Fife Regional Cncl (ldr 1982–87); pt/t lectr/tutor Heriot-Watt Univ 1973–86, pt/t employment consultancy work 1984–87; *Style*— The Rt Hon Henry McLeish; ✉ e-mail h.b.mcleish@btinternet.com

McLELLAN, Prof David Thorburn; s of Robert Douglas McLellan (d 1973), and Olive May, *née* Bush; *b* 10 February 1940; *Educ* Merchant Taylors', St John's Coll Oxford (MA, DPhil); *m* 1 July 1967, Annie, da of André Brassart; 2 da (Gabrielle b 8 Nov 1968, Stephanie b 8 May 1970); *Career* Univ of Kent: lectr 1966–70, sr lectr in politics 1970–75, prof of political theory 1975–2002; prof of political theory Goldsmiths Coll London 2002–; visiting prof SUNY 1969, visiting fell Indian Inst of Advanced Study Simla 1970; *Books* The Young Hegelians and Karl Marx (1969), Marx before Marxism (1970), Karl Marx: The Early Texts (1971), Marx's Grundrisse (1971), The Thought of Karl Marx (1971), Marx (1971), Karl Marx: His Life and Thought (1973), Engels (1977), Karl Marx: Selected Writings (1977), Marxism after Marx (1980), Karl Marx: Interviews and Recollections (1983), Marx: The First Hundred Years (ed, 1983), Karl Marx: The Legacy (1983), Ideology (1985), Marxism: Selected Texts (ed, 1987), Marxism and Religion (1987), Simone Weil: Utopian Pessimist (1990), Unto Caesar: The Political Relevance of Christianity (1992), Religion in Public Life (ed, 1993), Politics and Christianity (1995), Political Christianity: A Reader (1997), Western Marxism (2004), Karl Marx: A Biography (2006), Marxism after Marx (2007); *Style*— Prof David McLellan; ✉ c/o Macmillan Press Ltd, Brunel Road, Houndmills, Basingstoke, Hampshire RG21 6XS (tel 01256 29242, fax 01256 479476)

MACLELLAN, Ian David; s of Maj Henry Crawford Maclellan, MBE, TD, of Walton-on-the-Hill, Surrey, and Daphne Loya, *née* Taverner; *b* 21 February 1948; *Educ* Sherborne, Cranfield Business Sch (MBA); *m* 28 Sept 1974, Maja Ursula, da of Dr Hans Schaschek, of Weinheim, Germany; 1 da (Kirstin b 1980), 1 s (Henry b 1983); *Career* gp chief exec: Ibstock plc 1991–96, Cape plc 1998–2002; chm: Bristan Ltd 1997–2002, R A H Holdings Ltd 1999–2002, Farecla Products Ltd 2002–, Swan Hill Gp plc 2003–04 (dir 1992–04), Celotex Gp Ltd 2005–; treas Br Horse Soc 2006–; FCA; *Recreations* horses; *Style*— Ian D Maclellan, Esq; ✉ Wormleighton Grange, Southam, Warwickshire CV47 2XJ (tel 01295 770334)

McLELLAN, John; s of John McLellan, and Margaret, *née* Haviland; *b* 8 February 1962; *Educ* Hutchesons' GS Glasgow, Univ of Stirling (BA), Preston Poly; *m* 1993, Patricia; 1 da (Catriona b 10 March 1996), 2 s (Jamie b 8 April 2000, Fraser b 21 Sept 2004); *Career* journalist; reporter Chester Observer 1984–86, freelance 1986–87, reporter New Evening Mail 1987, dep ed Barrow News 1987–88, sports ed New Evening Mail 1988–90, asst ed The Journal 1991–93 (asst news ed 1990–91), ed Edinburgh Evening News 1997–2002 and 2005– (dep ed 1993–97), ed Scotland on Sunday 2002–04; chm Editors' Ctee Scottish Daily Newspaper Soc 2001–03; *Awards* for Edinburgh Evening News: Scottish Daily Newspaper of the Year 1997, BT Scottish Daily Newspaper of the Year 1997 and 1998, Scottish Newspaper of the year 2001; *Recreations* rugby, music; *Style*— John McLellan, Esq

MacLENNAN, David Ross; *b* 12 February 1945; *m* Margaret, *née* Lytollis; 2 da; *Career* HM Dip Serv: joined FO 1963, MECAS 1966–69, third then second sec Aden 1969–71, FCO 1972–75, UK Delgn OECD Paris 1975–79, Abu Dhabi 1979–82, asst head N America Dept FCO 1983–84, seconded to EC Brussels 1984–85, cnsllr and dep head of mission Kuwait 1985–89, dep high cmmr Cyprus 1989–90, consul-gen Jerusalem 1990–93, head Africa Dept (Equatorial) FCO and cmmr Br Indian Ocean Territory 1994–96, ambass to Lebanon 1996–2000, ambass to Qatar 2002–05, ret; *Style*— David MacLennan, Esq; ✉ c/o Foreign & Commonwealth Office, King Charles Street, London SW1A 2AH

MACLENNAN, Prof Duncan; CBE (1997); s of James Dempster Maclennan (d 1968), of Mull, and Mary Mackechnie, *née* Campbell; *b* 12 March 1949; *Educ* Allan Glen's Secdy Sch Glasgow, Univ of Glasgow (MA, Silver Medal and univ essay prize Royal Geographical Soc, pres Geographical Soc, MPhil); *m* 1971 (m dis 1997); 1 s (John Campbell b 14 July 1975), 1 da (Marjory Kate b 21 Sept 1977); *Career* res fell Univ of Glasgow 1974–76, lectr in economics Univ of Aberdeen 1976–79; Univ of Glasgow: lectr in applied econ 1979–84, dir Centre for Housing Res 1984–96, prof of applied economics 1985–88, prof of urban studies 1988–90, Mactaggart prof of economics and finance 1991–2004, chief economist Govt of Victoria 2004–; Susman prof Wharton Business Sch Univ of Pennsylvania 1989, Regents prof Univ of Calif 1996, prof RMIT 2004–; dir ESRC Prog on Cities 1996–99, exec chm Joseph Rowntree Area Regeneration Steering Gp 1996–2000; chm Care and Repair (Scotland) 1989–93; memb: Bd Scottish Homes 1989–99, European Urban Inst 1992–98, Co-ordinating Ctee European Housing Res Network 1989–98, bd Glasgow Alliance 1992–2002, Treasy Panel of Advisers on Public Policies 1996–99, Evidence Based Policy Fund (treas 2000); tstee David Hume Inst 1998–; economic advsr: housing Joseph Rowntree Fndn 1991–95, Duke of Edinburgh's second inquiry into British Housing 1990–91; special advsr to First Minister of Scotland 1999–2003; FRSA 1995, FRSE 1999, MCIH(Hon) 2002, MRTPI (Hon) 2002; *Books* Regional Policy: Past Experiences and New Directions (ed, 1979), Housing Economics (1982), Neighbourhood Change (1986), The Housing Authority of the Future (ed, 1992), Housing Finance (ed, 1993), Housing Policies for a Competitive Economy (1995), Fixed Commitments, Uncertain Incomes (1997), Changing Places, Engaging People (2001); *Recreations* walking, watching rugby, enjoying Glasgow; *Style*— Prof Duncan Maclennan, CBE; ✉ Department of Urban Studies, University of Glasgow, 25 Bute Gardens, Glasgow G12 8RS (tel 0141 330 5048, mobile 00 614 2378 4717, e-mail d.maclennan@socsci.gla.ac.uk)

MacLENNAN, Moray Alexander Stewart; s of Brig Donald Ross MacLennan, of Edinburgh; *b* 29 August 1961; *Educ* Fettes, Christ's Coll Cambridge (scholar, MA); *Career* Saatchi & Saatchi Advertising: joined 1983, bd dir 1988, md 1994–95; M&C Saatchi Ltd: jt chief exec 1995, currently chm Europe; *Recreations* golf, rugby, cooking; *Style*— Moray MacLennan, Esq; ✉ M&C Saatchi, 36 Golden Square, London W1F 9EE

MacLENNAN OF MacLENNAN, Ruairidh Donald George; 35 Chief of Clan MacLennan; o s of Ronald George MacLennan of MacLennan (d 1989), 34 Chief of Clan MacLennan, and Margaret Ann, *née* MacLennan (d 1993); *b* 22 April 1977; *Educ* Fettes, Univ of Aberdeen (MA, Aberdeen OTC piper); *Career* rural surveyor CKD Galbraith Inverness; *Recreations* piping, canoeing, 51 Highland Regt TA; *Style*— The MacLennan of MacLennan; ✉ The Old Mill, Dores, Inverness IV2 6TR

MACLENNAN OF ROGART, Baron (Life Peer UK 2001), of Rogart in Sutherland; Robert Adam Ross Maclennan; PC; s of Sir Hector Maclennan (d 1978), by his 1 w, Isabel, *née* Adam; *b* 26 June 1936; *Educ* Glasgow Acad, Balliol Coll Oxford, Trinity Coll Cambridge, Columbia Univ NY; *m* 1968, Helen, wid of Paul Noyes, and da of Judge Ammi Cutter, of Cambridge, MA; 1 s, 1 da, 1 step s; *Career* called to the Bar 1962; MP (Lab until 1981, SDP 1981–88, then Lib Dem): Caithness and Sutherland 1966–97, Caithness, Sutherland and Easter Ross 1997–2001; PPS to Cwlth Affrs Sec 1967–69 and to Min without Portfolio 1969–70, oppn spokesman on Scottish Affrs 1970–71, on Def 1971–72, Parly under sec for prices and consumer protection 1974–79, memb Commons Public Accounts Ctee 1979–99, oppn spokesman on foreign affrs 1979–80, SDP spokesman on agric 1981–87, SDP spokesman on home and legal affrs 1983–87, ldr of the SDP 1987–88, Lib Dem spokesman on home affrs and nat heritage 1988–94, Lib Dem spokesman on constitutional affrs and culture 1994–2001, pres Lib Dems 1994–98, Lib Dem spokesman on Europe 2001–, alt memb representing UK Parly on Convention on Future of Europe 2002–03; *Recreations* theatre, music and visual arts; *Clubs* Brooks's; *Style*— The Rt Hon the Lord Maclennan of Rogart, PC

McLEOD, Dr Andrew Alasdair; s of late Andrew Frederick McLeod, OBE, of Bathford, Somerset, and Janet Mary, *née* Comline; *b* 21 January 1948; *Educ* King Edward's Sch Bath, St Catharine's Coll Cambridge (MA, MB BChir, MD); *m* 1, 3 Sept 1983 (m dis 1994), Sharon, da of Wallace Redpath, of Appleton Park, Cheshire; 2 da (Anna Louise b 26 May 1989, Katharine Sian b 2 Feb 1991); m 2, 2 May 1998, Lindsay, da of Norman Pipler, of Poole, Dorset; *Career* assoc Faculty of Med Duke Univ Med Center N Carolina 1983 (Br Heart Fndn and American Heart Assoc fell 1981–83), conslt cardiologist King's Coll and Dulwich Hosps 1984–88, conslt cardiologist and physician Poole Gen Hosp Dorset 1988–; memb: Cncl Action on Smoking and Health, Rehabilitation Ctee Coronary Prevention Gp, Cncl Br Cardiac Soc; FRCP, FESC; *Recreations* golf, sailing, classical guitar, music; *Clubs* Parkstone Yacht, Royal Motor Yacht, Parkstone Golf; *Style*— Dr Andrew McLeod; ✉ Poole General Hospital, Longfleet Road, Poole, Dorset BH15 2JB (tel 01202 665511 ext 2572, fax 01202 442754, e-mail aam.heartdoc@virgin.net)

MacLEOD, Dr Calum Alexander; CBE (1991); s of Rev Lachlan Macleod (d 1966), of Glenurquhart, and Jessie Mary Morrison (d 1970); *b* 25 July 1935; *Educ* Nicolson Inst Stornoway, Glenurquhart HS, Univ of Aberdeen (MA, LLB); *m* 21 July 1962, Elizabeth Margaret, da of David Davidson (d 1973), of Inverness; 2 s (Allan b 1966, David b 1968), 1 da (Edythe b 1972); *Career* Nat Serv 2 Lt RAEC; ptnr Paull & Williamsons (advocates) Aberdeen 1964–80; chm: Albyn Ltd 1973–, Aberdeen Devpt Capital plc 1986–2006, STV (North) (formerly Grampian TV) 1993– (dep chm 1982), Britannia Building Soc 1994–99 (dep chm 1993–94 and 1999–2000); dep chm: Scot Eastern Investment Tst plc 1988–99, SMG plc 1997–2005 (acting chm 1998–99), Martin Currie Portfolio Investment Tst plc 1999–2002; dir: North Bd Bank of Scot 1980–2000, Caledonian Res Fndn 1990–94, Bradstock Gp plc 1994–98, Macdonald Hotels plc 1995–2003; chllr's assessor Univ of Aberdeen 1979–90; memb: White Fish Authy 1973–80, North of Scot Hydro-Electric Bd 1976–84, Highlands and Islands Devpt Bd 1984–91; chm: Robert Gordon's Coll 1981–94, Harris Tweed Assoc 1984–93, Scot Cncl of Ind Schs 1991–97, Grampian Health Bd 1993–2000, IOD Scot 2000–02; tstee: Carnegie Tst for the Univs of Scot 1997–; govr UHI Millennium Inst 2000–; Hon LLD Univ of Aberdeen 1986; memb Law Soc of Scot 1958, FInstD 1982; *Recreations* golf, music, travel, reading; *Clubs* Royal Northern, Royal Aberdeen Golf, Nairn Golf; *Style*— Dr Calum MacLeod, CBE; ✉ STV (North), The Television Centre, Craigshaw Business Park, West Tullos, Aberdeen AB12 3QH (tel 01224 848819, fax 01224 848800)

McLEOD, Sir Charles Henry; 3 Bt (UK 1925), of The Fairfields, Cobham, Surrey; s of Sir Murdoch Campbell McLeod, 2 Bt (d 1950), and Susan, *née* Whitehead (d 1964); elder bro Roderick Campbell McLeod ka, Salerno, 1943; *b* 7 November 1924; *Educ* Winchester; *m* 5 Jan 1957, (Anne) Gillian (d 1978), 3 da of late Henry Russell Bowlby, of London; 2 da (Belinda Ann b 1957, Nicola (Mrs John Bampfylde) b 1958), 1 s (James Roderick Charles b 1960); *Heir* s, James McLeod; *Career* Dip Master Brewer, MSI; *Recreations* reading; *Clubs* MCC, I Zingari, Free Foresters, Jesters; *Style*— Sir Charles McLeod, Bt; ✉ Burnham House, Burnham Road, Malmesbury, Wiltshire SN16 0BQ

McLEOD, Prof David; s of Norman McLeod (d 1985), and Anne, *née* Heyworth (d 1994); *b* 16 January 1946; *Educ* The GS Burnley, Univ of Edinburgh (BSc, MB ChB); *m* 16 Dec 1967, Jeanette Allison; 1 s (Euan b 1972), 1 da (Seona b 1974); *Career* SHO and res fell Princess Alexandra Eye Pavilion Edinburgh 1970–72, conslt ophthalmic surgn Moorfields Eye Hosp 1978–88 (resident surgical offr 1972–75, fell in vitreoretinal surgery and ultrasound 1975–78), conslt advsr in ophthalmology to the RAF 1984–2003, prof of ophthalmology Univ of Manchester 1988–2006 (emeritus prof 2006–, head Dept of Ophthalmology 1988–98), hon conslt ophthalmic surgn Royal Eye Hosp Manchester 1988–; visiting prof UMIST 1996–2006; vice-pres Royal Coll of Ophthalmologists 1997–2001; FRCS 1974, FCOphth 1988; *Recreations* walking, golf; *Clubs* Bramall Park Golf (Cheshire), RAF; *Style*— Prof David McLeod

MACLEOD, Dr Donald MacRae; s of Allan Martin MacLeod, of Glen House, Carloway, Isle of Lewis, and Margaret MacLeod; *b* 19 October 1956; *Educ* Nicolson Inst Stornoway, Univ of Aberdeen (MB ChB); *m* 19 April 1986, Moira Catherine, da of Thomas Anderson, of Marykirk; 1 s (Allan b 1987), 2 da (Alice b 1989, Elizabeth b 1992); *Career* lectr London Hosp Med Coll 1986–88, visiting assoc Duke Univ Med Centre Durham N Carolina USA 1988–89, conslt in anaesthetics Aberdeen Royal Infirmary 1989–; hon sr lectr Univ of Aberdeen; FFARCSI 1986; *Recreations* sailing, golf; *Clubs* Banff Sailing, Royal Aberdeen Golf; *Style*— Dr Donald Macleod; ✉ Westwood House, Kinellar, Aberdeen; Aberdeen Royal Infirmary, Aberdeen (tel 01224 681818)

MacLEOD, Duncan James; CBE (1986); s of Alan Duncan MacLeod (ka Sicily 1943), of Skeabost, Isle of Skye, and Joan Nora Paton, *née* de Knoop (d 1991); *b* 1 November 1934;

Educ Eton; *m* 14 June 1958, Joanna, da of Samuel Leslie Bibby, CBE, DL, of Headley, Surrey (d 1985); 2 s (Alan Hamish b 1959, Charles Alasdair b 1961), 1 da (Davina b 1965); *Career* CA 1958; ptnr Brown Fleming & Murray (now Ernst & Young) 1960–89; dir: Bank of Scotland 1973–91, Scottish Provident Institution 1976–2001, The Weir Group plc 1976–97, Harry Ramsden's plc 1989–99, Motherwell Bridge Holdings Ltd 1990–2001, Gartmore SNT plc 1998–2005; chm Scot Industrial Devpt Advsy Bd 1989–97 (memb 1980), memb Scot Tertiary Educn Advsy Cncl 1985–87; Hon Dr Univ of Stirling 2001; *Recreations* golf, shooting, fishing; *Clubs* Western (Glasgow), Prestwick Golf, Royal and Ancient, MCC; *Style—* Duncan J MacLeod, Esq, CBE; ✉ Monkredding House, Kilwinning, Ayrshire KA13 7QN (tel 01294 552336, fax 01294 558465)

McLEOD, Fraser Neil; s of James McLeod, of Cuffley, Herts, and Mary, *née* Yuill; *b* 13 July 1951; *Educ* Hertford GS, St Bartholomew's Hosp Med Coll (MB BS); *m* 16 April 1983, Angela Mary, da of Thomas Campbell, of Purley, Surrey; 1 s (David Paul Christopher b 13 Feb 1989), 1 da (Madeleine Kate b 17 June 1994); *Career* lectr in obstetrics and gynaecology and pioneer in test tube baby devpt Royal Free Hosp 1981–83, sr registrar in obstetrics and gynaecology Southmead Hosp Bristol 1983–85, conslt obstetrician and gynaecologist Frenchay and Southmead Hosps Bristol 1985–; memb: British Menopause Soc, South West Obstetrical and Gynaecological Soc; founding memb Expert Witness Inst; local treas BMA, examiner RCOG, past sec Hey Groves Med Soc, fndr memb Br Soc for Gynaecological Endoscopy; MRCOG 1980, MRCS; *Recreations* golf; *Clubs* Berkshire Golf, Henbury Golf; *Style—* Fraser McLeod, Esq; ✉ BUPA Women's Health Centre, 116 Pembroke Road, Clifton, Bristol BS8 3BW (tel 0117 974 1396, fax 0117 973 3809, e-mail mcleodfraser@aol.com)

MACLEOD, Prof Iain Alasdair; s of Donald MacLeod (d 1976), of Achiltibuie, Ross-shire, and Barbara Mary, *née* Mackenzie (d 1977); *b* 4 May 1939; *Educ* Lenzie Acad, Univ of Glasgow (BSc, PhD); *m* 18 Nov 1967, Barbara Jean, da of Allen Daven Booth (d 1983), of Salmon Arm, Br Columbia, Canada; 1 da (Mairi b 1975), 1 s (Alastair b 1976); *Career* structural engr: Crouch and Hogg Glasgow 1960–62, H A Simons Vancouver Canada 1966–67; structural res engr Portland Cement Assoc USA 1967–69, lectr Dept of Civil Engrg Univ of Glasgow 1969–73 (asst lectr 1962–66), prof and head Dept of Civil Engrg Paisley Coll of Technol 1973–81, prof of structural engrg Univ of Strathclyde 1981–2004 (emeritus prof 2004–); vice-pres IStructE 1989–90, memb Standing Ctee on Structural Safety 1989–97; FIStructE, FICE, FRSA; *Books* Analytical Modelling of Structural Systems (1990), Modern Structural Analysis (2005); *Recreations* sailing, hill walking; *Style—* Prof Iain MacLeod; ✉ Department of Civil Engineering, University of Strathclyde, 107 Rottenrow, Glasgow G4 0NG

MacLEOD, James Summers; s of Charles MacLeod (d 1982), and Margaret, *née* Summers (d 1986); *b* 3 August 1941; *Educ* Dumfries Acad, Univ of Glasgow (LLM); *m* 1, Sheila, da of George Stromier (d 2000); 1 da (Fiona b 1968), 2 s (Niall b 1971, Roderick b 1976); m 2, Rosemary Grant; *Career* lectr Univ of Edinburgh 1965–68; lectr Heriot-Watt Univ 1968–71; Ernst & Young (formerly Arthur Young McClelland Moores & Co): joined 1971, ptnr 1973–98; Univ of Edinburgh: prof Dept of Accounting and Business Method 1986–, prof Faculty of Law 2000–; chm: Martin Currie High Income Tst plc, Collective Assets Tst plc; dir: British Assets Tst plc, Invesco Geared Opportunities Tst plc; insurance ed Simons Taxes; CA (Scotland) 1965; FInstT 1971; *Books* Taxation of Insurance Business (4 edn, 1999); *Recreations* bridge, piano, music, gardening, political biography; *Clubs* New; *Style—* James MacLeod, Esq

MACLEOD, Dr John Alasdair Johnston; MBE (2002), DL (Western Isles 1979); s of Dr Alexander John Macleod, OBE (d 1979), of Lochmaddy, Isle of North Uist, and Dr Julia Parker, *née* Johnston (d 1989); *b* 20 January 1935; *Educ* Lochmaddy Sch, Nicolson Inst Stornoway, Keil Sch Dumbarton, Univ of Glasgow (MB ChB); *m* 4 Nov 1972, Lorna, da of Dr Douglas Ian Ferguson (d 1994), of Winterbourne Down, Avon; 2 s (Alasdair Ian b 1974, Torquil John b 1979), 1 da (Elizabeth Jane b 1975); *Career* Temp Actg Sub Lt RNVR 1957–59; jr hosp posts Glasgow and London 1963–70, RMO and sr registrar Middx London 1970–72, GP Isle of North Uist 1973–2000, police surgn Isle of North Uist 1973–2000, examing offr DHSS 1973–2000, MO Lochmaddy Hosp 1974–2000, Admty surgn and agent 1974–91, local MO 1974–2000; non-exec dir Olscot Ltd 1969–93; visiting prof Dept of Family Med Univ of N Carolina, visiting lectr Middlebury Coll Vermont 1998, visiting prof Univ of Western Ontario 1998, visiting lectr James Cook Univ Aust 2002; memb: BMA, World Orgn of Nat Colls Acads of Family Practice (memb Ctee on Rural Practice); dir Taigh Chearsabhagh Tst 2000–; chm Comann Na Mara 2000–; vice-chm Western Isles Local Med Ctee 1991–93 (sec 1977–91); hon life memb World Orgn of Family Doctors (WONCA) 2001–; GPWA Writer of the Year 2000, Lifetime Award for Rural Practice European Rural and Isolated Practitioners Assoc (EURIPA)/WONCA 2003; author of various articles and papers on isolated gen practice within the NHS; memb: North Uist Highland Gathering, North Uist Angling Club, Scandinavian Village Assoc, Western Isles Advsy Ctee on JPs 1985–2000; FRCGP, FRSM, FRCPGlas 2000, FFCS 2000; *Recreations* promoting Western Isles, time-sharing, arboriculture, writing; *Clubs* Western; *Style—* Dr John A J Macleod, MBE, DL, FRCGP, FRCPGlas; ✉ Tigh-na-Hearradh, Lochmaddy, Isle of North Uist, Western Isles HS6 5AE (tel 01876 500224, e-mail johnajmacleod@debrett.net)

MACLEOD, Dr Malcolm Robert; s of Robin Macleod, of Inverness, and Mary, *née* Hossack; *b* 26 August 1965; *Educ* Loretto, Univ of Edinburgh (pres Students' Union, BSc, MB ChB, PhD); *m* 26 June 1992, Lindsay Dorothy Greig Thomson, da of James Thomson; 2 s (Calum Alexander Thomson b 10 Sept 1995, Magnus James Thomson b 27 Sept 2000); *Career* med house offr Eastern Gen Hosp Edinburgh; Western Gen Hosp Edinburgh: neurosurgical house offr, SHO in med 1992–94, hon clinical fell Dept of Clinical Neurosciences 1995–2000, specialist registrar Neurology 2001–; sr SHO Falkirk & District Royal Infirmary 1994–95, MRC clinical training fell Dept of Pharmacology Univ of Edinburgh 1995–98, research fell British Brain and Spine Fndn Dept of Molecular Endocrinology Univ of Edinburgh 1998–2000; rector and chm Univ Ct Univ of Edinburgh 1994–97; MRCP 1994; *Recreations* juggling, hill walking, political history; *Style—* Dr Malcolm Macleod; ✉ Molecular Endocrinology, Molecular Medicine Centre, Western General Hospital, Crewe Road, Edinburgh EH4 2XU (tel 0131 651 1029, e-mail malcolm@apoptosis.freeserve.co.uk)

MacLEOD, Mary; da of late James MacLeod, of Ullapool, Ross and Cromarty, and Effie, *née* Campbell; *b* 18 February 1948; *Educ* Ullapool Sch, Dingwall Acad, Univ of Edinburgh (MA, DSA, Dip Social Work); *m* 26 March 1979, Prof Dennis Walder; 1 da (Anna Ruth b 22 Sept 1984), 1 s (Rohan James b 19 June 1986); *Career* social worker Barnardo's Scotland 1972–75, sr social worker Lothian Region Social Work Dept 1975–78, lectr in social work Univ of Edinburgh 1978–79, lectr then sr lectr in social work Poly of N London 1979–91; ChildLine: dir of HQ counselling servs 1991–95, dir of policy, research and devpt 1995–99, dep chief exec 1999; chief exec Nat Family and Parenting Inst 1999–, interim chief exec Nat Acad for Parenting Practitioners; memb: Advsy Gp on Marriage and Relationship Support Lord Chllr's Dept 1999–2001, Advsy Gp on Work-Life Balance Dept of Educn 1999–2002, NHS Children's Task Force for London 2000–02, Advsy Gp Children and Young People's Unit Dept of Educn 2001–03, Ind Advsy Gp on Teenage Pregnancy Dept of Health 2002–04, Advsy Gp on Domestic Violence Lord Chllr's Dept 2002–04, Bd Occupational Pensions Regulatory Authy 2002–05, Family Justice Cncl 2005–, Parenting Research Panel Joseph Rowntree Fndn, Research Advsy Gp Centre for Safety and Well-Being Univ of Warwick, Advsy Bd Thomas Coram Research Unit; memb numerous univ research advsy ctees; author of articles on family policy and family servs; tstee Nat Children's Bureau; hon research fell Univ of Warwick 1998–; FRSA; *Clubs* Cwlth; *Style—* Mary MacLeod; ✉ National Family and Parenting Institute, 430 Highgate Studios, 53–79 Highgate Road, London NW5 1TL (tel 020 7424 3465, fax 020 7485 3590, e-mail macleod@nfpi.org)

MacLEOD, Hon Sir (John) Maxwell Norman; 5 Bt (UK 1924), of Fuinary, Morven, Co Argyll; er s of Very Rev Baron MacLeod of Fuinary, MC, DD (Life Peer and 4 Bt, d 1991), and Lorna Helen Janet, *née* MacLeod (d 1984); *b* 23 February 1952; *Educ* Gordonstoun; *Heir* bro, Hon Neil MacLeod; *Style—* The Hon Sir Maxwell MacLeod, Bt; ✉ Fuinary Manse, Loch Aline, Morven, Argyll

McLETCHIE, David William; MSP; s of James Watson McLetchie (d 1988), of Edinburgh, and Catherine Alexander, *née* Gray; *b* 6 August 1952; *m* 1, 26 Nov 1977, Barbara Gemmell (d 1995), da of Daniel Baillie; 1 s (James Douglas Baillie McLetchie b 20 May 1981); m 2, 4 July 1998, Sheila Elizabeth, da of Thomas Foster; *Career* trainee slr Shepherd & Wedderburn 1974–76, slr Tods Murray 1976–80, ptnr Tods Murray 1980–2005; MSP (Cons): Lothians 1999–2003, Edinburgh Pentlands 2003–; ldr Scottish Cons Parly Pty 1999–2005; memb Law Soc of Scotland; *Recreations* golf, watching football, rock and country music, reading crime fiction and political biographies; *Clubs* Bruntsfield Links Golfing Soc, New (Edinburgh); *Style—* David McLetchie, Esq, MSP; ✉ The Scottish Parliament, Edinburgh EH99 1SP (tel 0131 348 5659, fax 0131 348 5935, e-mail david.mcletchie.msp@scottish.parliament.uk)

McLINTOCK, Michael George Alexander; s of Sir Alan McLintock, and Sylvia Mary, *née* Foster Taylor; *b* 24 March 1961; *Educ* Malvern Coll, St John's Coll Oxford (scholar, BA); *m* 1996, Nicola Fairles Ogilvy Watson; 2 da, 1 s; *Career* Morgan Grenfell & Co Ltd 1983–87, Baring Brothers & Co Ltd 1987–92; M&G Gp plc (acquired by Prudential 1999): PA to gp md 1992, head institutional and international desks until 1997, chief exec 1997–99; Prudential plc: chief exec M&G (formerly Prudential M&G Asset Mgmnt) 1999–, dir 2000–; dir Close Brothers Gp plc 2001–; *Recreations* family, friends, good wine; *Clubs* Army & Navy, Boodle's, MCC; *Style—* Michael McLintock, Esq; ✉ Laurence Pountney Hill, London EC4R 0HH (tel 020 7626 4588)

McLINTOCK, Sir Michael William; 4 Bt (UK 1934), of Sanquhar, Co Dumfries; s of Sir William Traven McLintock, 3 Bt (d 1987), and his 1 w, Andrée, *née* Lonsdale-Hands; *b* 13 August 1958; *Heir* s, James McLintock; *Style—* Sir Michael McLintock, Bt

McLOUGHLIN, Kevin; *b* 17 July 1952; *Educ* Xaverian Coll, Univ of Sheffield (MA), Univ of Salford (MA); *m* 16 Dec 1978, Sheila Mary McLoughlin; 1 s (Daniel b 27 July 1980), 1 da (Jessica b 14 Sept 1984); *Career* admitted slr 1978, slr advocate 2003; ptnr: DLA 1982–2005, Eversheds LLP 2005–; memb Law Faculty Bd Univ of Sheffield; *Style—* Kevin McLoughlin, Esq; ✉ 98 Riverdale Road, Ranmoor, Sheffield S10 3FD (tel 0114 230 7350); Eversheds LLP, Cloth Hall Court, Infirmary Street, Leeds LS1 2JB (tel 0113 200 4493, fax 0113 245 6188, e-mail kevinmcloughlin@eversheds.com)

McLOUGHLIN, Patrick; PC (2005), MP; *Career* MP (Cons) Derbyshire W 1986–; Parly under-sec of state: Dept of Tport 1989–92, Dept of Employment 1992–93, DTI 1993–94; a Lord Cmmr HM Treasy (Govt whip) 1995–97; oppn pairing whip 1997–98, oppn dep chief whip 1998–2005, oppn chief whip 2005–; *Style—* The Rt Hon Patrick McLoughlin, MP; ✉ House of Commons, London SW1A 0AA (tel 020 7219 3000)

McLUCAS, William Philip; s of James McLucas, of South Queensferry, and Jean Violet, *née* Stobie (d 1986); *b* 12 February 1955; *Educ* Daniel Stewarts Coll Edinburgh, Scottish Coll of Textiles Galashiels; *m* 25 March 1976, Blyth Agnes, da of late Thomas Russell McLaren; 1 s (James Thomas William b 19 June 1982), 1 da (Camilla Charlotte Blyth b 28 July 1984); *Career* investment analyst Scottish Amicable Life Assurance Soc 1967–77, moneybroker UDISCO Brokers Ltd 1977–78; stockbroker: Laurence Prust & Co (London) 1978–80, Jackson Graham Moore & Ptnrs (Sydney) 1980–84; chief exec Waverley Asset Mgmnt Ltd 1984–95, ceo Waverley Mining Finance plc 1995–98, chm Perseverance Corp Ltd (Aust), pres and ceo Thistle Mining Inc (Canada) 1998–, chm President Steyn Gold Mines (Free State) (Pty) Ltd (S Africa) 2002–04, dir Republic Gold Ltd (Aust) 2005–, chm Luzan Minerals 2005–, dir Longview Investments 2006, dir Willowswater Capital 2006–, chm Terra Nova Gold Corp 2007–; memb: Assoc of Mining Analysts 1981, Scottish Ski Club 1993, DHO 1994; *Recreations* skiing, sailing, travel; *Style—* William McLucas, Esq; ✉ 5 Multrees Walk, Edinburgh EH1 3DQ (tel 0131 557 6676, fax 0131 558 1232, e-mail wpm@mclucasfamilyholdings.com)

M

MACLURE, Sir John Robert Spencer; 4 Bt (UK 1898), of The Home, Whalley Range, nr Manchester, Co Palatine of Lancaster; s of Lt-Col Sir John William Spencer Maclure, 3 Bt, OBE (d 1980), and Elspeth King, *née* Clark (d 1991); *b* 25 March 1934; *Educ* Winchester; *m* 26 Aug 1964, Jane Monica, da of late Rt Rev Thomas Joseph Savage, Bishop of Zululand and Swaziland; 4 s ((John) Mark b 1965, Thomas Stephen b 1967, Graham Spencer b 1970, Stephen Patrick Ian b 1974); *Heir* s, Mark Maclure; *Career* 2 Lt KRRC 2 Bn BAOR 1953–55, Lt Royal Hants Airborne Regt TA; asst master Horris Hill 1955–66 and 1974–78; teacher: NZ 1967–70, St Edmund's Hindhead 1971–74; headmaster Croftinloan Sch 1978–92 and 1997–98; *Clubs* MCC, Royal Green Jackets; *Style—* Sir John Maclure, Bt; ✉ Howleigh Cottage, Blagdon Hill, Taunton, Somerset TA3 7SP (e-mail maclurej@aol.com)

McLYNN, Francis James (Frank); *b* 29 August 1941; *Educ* John Fisher Sch Purley, Wadham Coll Oxford (open scholar, MA), UCL Inst of Latin American Studies (MA, PhD); *Career* author; asst dir Bogotá and Colombia Br Cncl 1969–71 (joined 1968), Parry fell Buenos Aires Argentina 1971–72, Alistair Horne res fell St Antony's Coll Oxford 1987–88, visiting prof Dept of Literature Univ of Strathclyde 1996–2001, professorial fell Goldsmiths Coll London 2000–02; Cheltenham Prize for Literature 1985; FRHistS 1987, FRGS 1987; *Books* France and The Jacobite Rising of 1745 (1981), The Jacobite Army in England (1983), The Jacobites (1985), Invasion: From The Armada To Hitler (1987), Charles Edward Stuart (1988), Crime and Punishment in Eighteenth Century England (1989), Stanley: The Making of An African Explorer (1989), Burton: Snow Upon The Desert (1990), Of No Country (1990), Stanley: Sorcerer's Apprentice (1991), From The Sierras To The Pampas (1991), Hearts of Darkness (1992), Fitzroy Maclean (1992), Robert Louis Stevenson (1993), Jung: A Biography (1995), Napoleon (1997), 1066: The Year of the Three Battles (1998), Villa and Zapata (2000), Wagons West (2002), 1759: The Year Britain Became Master of the World (2004), Lionheart and Lackland (2006); *Style—* Frank McLynn, Esq; ✉ c/o Random House, 20 Vauxhall Bridge Road, London SW1V 2SA

McMAHON, Prof April Mary Scott; da of Irene Dugan, *née* Grant (d 1985); *b* 30 April 1964, Edinburgh; *Educ* Univ of Edinburgh (MA, PhD); *m* 1984, Dr Robert McMahon; 2 s (Aidan b 15 Dec 1994, Fergus b 29 Aug 1996), 1 da (Flora b 21 Oct 1999); *Career* fell Selwyn Coll Cambridge 1988, lectr in phonology and historical linguistics Univ of Cambridge 1988–2000; Univ of Sheffield: chair of English language and linguistics 2000–04, head Sch of English 2002–04, head Dept of English Language and Linguistics; Forbes chair of English language Univ of Edinburgh 2005–; pres Linguistics Soc of GB 2000–05, memb Cncl Philological Soc; memb Cncl AHRC 2005–; FRSE 2003, FBA 2005; *Books* Understanding Language Change (1994), Lexical Phonology and the History of English (2000), Change, Chance, and Optimality (2000), Time Depth in Historical Linguistics (ed with Colin Renfrew and R L Trask, 2000), An Introduction to English Phonology (2002), Language Classification by Numbers (with Robert McMahon, 2005); *Recreations* walking, cooking, Scottish country dancing; *Style—* Prof April McMahon; ✉ School of Philosophy, Psychology and Language Sciences, The University of Edinburgh, 14 Buccleuch Place, Edinburgh EH8 9LN (tel 0131 651 1999, e-mail april.mcmahon@ed.ac.uk)

McMAHON, Sir Brian Patrick; 8 Bt (UK 1817); s of Sir (William) Patrick McMahon, 7 Bt (d 1977); *b* 9 June 1942; *Educ* Wellington, Wednesbury Tech Coll (BSc); *m* 1981 (m dis 1991), Kathleen Joan, da of late William Hopwood; *Heir* bro, Shaun McMahon; *Career* AIM; *Style*— Sir Brian McMahon, Bt; ✉ PO Box 136, Greyton 7233, Western Cape, South Africa

McMAHON, Sir Christopher William (Kit); kt (1986); *b* 10 July 1927; *Educ* Melbourne GS, Univ of Melbourne, Magdalen Coll Oxford; *m* 1, 1956, Marion Kelso; 2 s; m 2, 1982, Alison Braimbridge; *Career* fell and economics tutor Magdalen Coll Oxford 1960–64; Bank of England: advsr 1964, advsr to the govrs 1966–70, exec dir 1970–80, dep govr 1980–85; Midland Bank plc: gp chief exec 1986–91, dep chm 1986–87, chm 1987–91; chm: Coutts Consulting Group plc 1992–96, Pentos plc 1993–95 (dir 1991–95); dir: Hongkong and Shanghai Banking Corp 1987–91, Eurotunnel plc 1987–91, Taylor Woodrow plc 1991–2000 (dep chm 1997–2000), ROH 1991–97, Angela Flowers Gallery 1992–2006, Aegis plc 1992–99, Newspaper Publishing plc 1992–94, FI Group plc 1994–2001; hon fell UCNW 1988; FInstM, Chevalier Legion d'Honneur (France) 1990; *Style*— Sir Kit McMahon; ✉ The Old House, Burleigh, Stroud, Gloucestershire GL5 2PQ (tel 01453 886887)

McMAHON, Rt Rev Malcolm Patrick; *see:* Nottingham, Bishop of

McMAHON, Michael Joseph; MSP; s of Patrick Kane McMahon, of Newarthill, Lanarkshire, and Bridget McMahon, *née* Clarke; *b* 18 September 1961; *m* 16 April 1983, Margaret Mary, *née* McKeown; 2 da (Siobhan Marie, Mairead Ann), 1 s (Gerard Francis); *Career* welder Terex Equipment Ltd Motherwell 1977–92, freelance socio-political researcher 1996–99; MSP (Lab) Hamilton N & Bellshill 1999–, ministerial Parly aide to first min (Rt Hon Jack McConnell, MSP), convenor Public Petitions Ctee; memb: Scottish Lab Pty, GMB; *Recreations* supporting Celtic FC, reading biographies and social histories, listening to jazz and soul music; *Style*— Michael McMahon, Esq, MSP; ✉ 7 Forres Crescent, Bellshill, Lanarkshire ML4 1HL; Parliamentary Advice Office, 188 Main Street, Bellshill, Lanarkshire ML4 1AE (tel 01698 304501, fax 01698 300223, mobile 0771 501 2463); The Scottish Parliament, Edinburgh EH99 1SP (e-mail michael.mcmahon.msp@scottish.parliament.uk)

McMAHON, Rt Rev Thomas; *see:* Brentwood, Bishop of (RC)

McMANUS, Prof John; s of Eric Stanley McManus (d 1986), of Harwich, Essex, and Jessie Amelia, *née* Morley (d 1991); *b* 5 June 1938; *Educ* Harwich Co HS, Imperial Coll London (BSc, PhD, Watts Medal), Univ of Dundee (DSc); *m* 31 July 1965, (Jean) Barbara (d 2007), da of David Kenneth Beveridge; 2 s (Steven b 21 Dec 1968, Neil b 21 July 1972), 1 da (Kay b 6 Dec 1974); *Career* lectr Univ of St Andrews 1964–67 (asst 1963–64); Univ of Dundee: lectr 1967–72, sr lectr 1972–80, reader 1980–88; Univ of St Andrews: reader 1988–93, prof 1993–2001, emeritus prof 2001–; memb Senate Univ of St Andrews (memb Ct 1991–95), former memb Senate Univ of Dundee; pres Estuary and Coastal Scis Assoc 1995–98 (tstee 2000–); memb: Aquatic Atmospheric Physical Scis Ctee Natural Environment Research Cncl 1971–75, Bd SE Regn Nature Conservancy Cncl (Scotland) SE Region 1990–91, UNESCO Panel on Reservoir Sediment 1982–85, BSI Ctee on Sedimentation 1991–, Geological Conservation Review Panel Jt Nature Conservancy Cncl 1993–94; Scottish Natural Heritage: memb Bd SE Region 1991–97, memb Sci Advsy Bd 1992–97, memb Bd Eastern Areas 1997–99; chm Transactions Editorial Bd Royal Soc of Edinburgh 1996–99, memb E Area Bd Scottish Environment Protection Agency 2000–07; pres: Cupar Choral Assoc 1970–79, Cupar Amateur Opera 1979–91; memb: E Fife Male Voice Choir, Fife Mining Heritage; MInstEnvSci 1973–2001, MIGeol 1979, FRSE 1980, CGeol 1986, Hon FRSGS 2001; *Books* Developments in Estuary and Coastal Study Techniques (jt ed, 1989), Geomorphology and Sedimentology of Lakes and Reservoirs (jt ed, 1993); *Recreations* making music; *Style*— Prof John McManus, FRSE; ✉ Department of Geography and Geosciences, University of St Andrews, St Andrews, Fife KY16 9ST (tel 01334 463948, fax 01334 463949, e-mail jm@st-andrews.ac.uk)

McMANUS, HE John Andrew; s of Andrew McManus, and Winifred, *née* Hazzard; *b* 20 May 1955, Whitehaven, Cumbria; *Educ* Univ of Sussex (BA); *Career* diplomat; entered HM Dip Serv 1977, posted Paris 1980–82, vice-consul Algiers 1983–85, commercial attaché Moscow 1988–91, presidency co-ordinator UKREP Brussels 1992–93, first sec (info) Berne 1993–97, head Korea Section FCO 1997–2000, head Political Section Brussels 2000–04, ambass to Guinea 2004–; *Recreations* watching athletics, food, languages; *Style*— HE Mr John McManus; ✉ c/o Foreign & Commonwealth Office (Conakry), King Charles Street, London SW1A 2AH

McMANUS, Liz; TD (1992); da of Timothy O'Driscoll (d 1998), and Elizabeth, *née* McKay (d 2005); *b* 23 March 1947; *Educ* UC Dublin (BArch); *m* 26 Oct 1970, John McManus; 3 s (Luke b 9 Aug 1972, Ronan b 22 Dec 1973, Sam b 27 May 1976) 1 da (Emily b 2 Jan 1982); *Career* worked as architect in Derry NI, Galway, Dublin and Wicklow 1969–76, fiction writer and novelist 1981–92, newspaper columnist 1985–92, teacher of creative writing 1986–89; TD (Lab) Co Wicklow 1992–, min of state for housing and urban renewal 1994–97 (also chair Taskforce on Needs of Travelling People), dep ldr Irish Lab Party 2002; memb Irish Writers Union; Irish Pen, Henessy and Listowel Awards; author of short fiction in numerous anthologies; *Books* Acts of Subversion; *Recreations* walking, reading, writing; *Clubs* Bray Strollers Hill Walking; *Style*— Ms Liz McManus, TD; ✉ 1 Martello Terrace, Bray, Co Wicklow, Ireland (tel 00 353 1 276 0583, fax 00 353 1 276 0584); Dáil Éireann, Kildare Street, Dublin 2, Ireland (tel 00 353 1 618 3131, fax 00 353 1 618 4591, e-mail liz.mcmanus@oir.ie)

McMANUS, (Jonathan) Richard; QC (1999); s of Frank Rostron McManus, and Benita Ann, *née* Haughton; *b* 15 September 1958; *Educ* Neale-Wade Comp Sch, Downing Coll Cambridge (MA, Maxwell Law Prize 1979); *Career* called to the Bar 1982, jr counsel to the Crown (Common Law) 1992–99; *Books* Education and the Courts (1997, 2 edn 2004); *Recreations* travel, music, cricket, photography; *Style*— Richard McManus, Esq, QC; ✉ 4–5 Gray's Inn Square, Gray's Inn, London WC1R 5AY (tel 020 7670 1518, fax 020 7242 7803, e-mail dzongkas@aol.com)

McMASTER, Sir Brian; kt (2003), CBE (1987); *b* 1943; *Educ* Univ of Bristol (LLB), Strasbourg Univ, Arts Cncl of GB (Arts Admin); *Career* admitted slr; memb Int Classical Div EMI 1968–73, controller of opera planning ENO 1973–76, md WNO 1976–91, dir Edinburgh Int Festival 1991–2006; artistic dir Vancouver Opera 1984–89; chm Nat Opera Studio, memb Arts Cncl of England; judge Cardiff Singer of the World Competition; Hon Dr: Univ of Bristol 1989, Univ of Edinburgh 1995, Heriot-Watt Univ 2000, Univ of Glasgow 2001, Napier Univ 2002; *Style*— Sir Brian McMaster, CBE; ✉ 13/5 James Court, Lawnmarket, Edinburgh EH1 2PB (tel and fax 0131 226 5520)

McMASTER, Paul; s of Dr James McMaster (d 1987), of Liverpool, and Sarah Lynne McMaster; *b* 4 January 1943; *Educ* Liverpool Coll, Univ of Liverpool (MB ChB), Univ of Cambridge (MA); *m* Aug 1969, Helen Ruth, da of Derek Bryce; 2 s (Michael Robert b 1971, Richard Benjamin b 1978), 1 da (Amanda Helen b 1974); *Career* conslt surgn; sr lectr dept of surgery Cambridge 1976–80, tutor Trinity Hall Cambridge 1978–80, dir Liver Transplant Services Queen Elizabeth Hosp Univ of Birmingham 1980–; memb: Cncl Nat and Int Transplantation Soc 1991–, Euro Soc Organ Transplantation (pres 1992–93); FRCS 1970; *Style*— Paul McMaster, Esq; ✉ Lilac Cottage, High Park, Ombersley Road, Droitwich, Worcestershire WR9 0RG (tel 01905 776961, e-mail pl.mcmaster@virgin.net); The Liver Unit, The Queen Elizabeth Hospital, University of Birmingham, Edgbaston, Birmingham (tel 0121 627 2413, fax 0121 414 8133)

McMEIKAN, Elizabeth; da of Dr Thomas Charles Dann, of Cambridge, and Jean, *née* Blackburn; *b* 15 March 1962, London; *Educ* King's HS for Girls Warwick, Jesus Coll Cambridge (exhibitioner, MA); *Children* 2 s (Cameron Eliot b 7 Oct 1995, Rory Thomas b 1 June 1997), 1 da (Sophie Gabriella b 4 Feb 1999); *Career* Colgate Palmolive 1984–89; Tesco plc: joined 1989, trading dir bakery 1993–94, devpt dir Tesco France 1994–95, md Tesco Express 1995–97, HR and change mgmnt dir Stores Bd 1997–2000; non-exec dir: J D Wetherspoon plc 2005–, Direct Wines Ltd 2006–; civil serv cmmr 2005–; ind memb Insolvency Serv Steering Bd DTI 2004–06; *Recreations* walking, travel, skiing, classical music, food; *Style*— Ms Elizabeth McMeikan; ✉ J D Wetherspoon plc, Wetherspoon House, Central Park, Reeds Crescent, Watford WD24 4QL

McMICHAEL, Prof Andrew James; s of Sir John McMichael, FRS (d 1993), and Sybil Eleanor, *née* Blake (d 1965); *b* 8 November 1943; *Educ* St Paul's, Gonville & Caius Coll Cambridge (MA), St Mary's Hosp Medical Sch (MB BChir); *m* 12 Oct 1968, Kathryn Elizabeth, da of Capt Alexander Alfred Cross, MBE (d 1998), of Whittonditch, Wilts; 1 da (Fiona b 1971), 2 s (Hamish b 1973, Robert b 1982); *Career* Nuffield Dept of Med Univ of Oxford: Wellcome sr fell in clinical science 1977–79, lectr 1979–82, MRC clinical res prof of immunology 1982–98, dir MRC Human Immunology Unit 1998–2000, dir Weatherall Inst of Molecular Med 2000–; fell Trinity Coll Oxford 1982–2000, fell CCC Oxford 2000–; memb: Scientific Ctee Cancer Res Campaign 1986–88 and 1999–, Cell and Molecular Med Bd MRC 1994–99, Cncl Royal Soc 1997–98; FRCP 1985, FRS 1992; *Books* Monoclonal Antibodies in Clinical Medicine (ed, 1981), Leucocyte Typing III, White Cell Differentiation Antigens (ed, 1987); *Recreations* walking, reading; *Style*— Prof Andrew McMichael, FRS; ✉ Weatherall Institute of Molecular Medicine, John Radcliffe Hospital, Oxford OX3 9DS (tel 01865 222336, e-mail andrew.mcmichael@ndm.ox.ac.uk)

MACMILLAN, Prof (John) Duncan; s of Prof William Miller Macmillan (d 1974), and Mona Constance Mary, *née* Tweedie, of Dorchester-on-Thame, Oxon; *b* 7 March 1939; *Educ* Gordonstoun, Univ of St Andrews (MA), Univ of London (Academic Dip), Univ of Edinburgh (PhD); *m* 5 June 1971, Vivien Rosemary, da of Canon W T Hinkley, of Alnwick, Northumberland; 2 da (Christina Rachel b 1973, Annabel Kate b 1976); *Career* Dept of Fine Art Univ of Edinburgh: lectr 1974–83, sr lectr 1983–88, reader 1988–94, personal chair history of Scottish art 1994–2001 (prof emeritus 2002–); dir Talbot Rice Gallery 1979–2004, curator Univ of Edinburgh Galleries and Collections 1988–2002; art critic The Scotsman 1994–2000 and 2002–; hon keeper of portraits RCSEd; Hon LLD Univ of Dundee; Hon RSA, FRSA, FRSE; *Books* Gavin Scobie (1984), Painting in Scotland - The Golden Age (1986), Scottish Art 1460–1990 (1990, Scottish book of the year Saltire Soc), Symbols of Survival - The Art of Will MacLean (1992), The Paintings of Steven Campbell (1993), Scottish Art in the Twentieth Century (1994), Eugenio Carmi (jtly with Umberto Eco, 1996), Elizabeth Blackadder (1999); *Recreations* walking; *Style*— Prof Duncan Macmillan; ✉ 20 Nelson Street, Edinburgh EH3 6LJ (tel 0131 556 7100, e-mail duncan.macmillan@ed.ac.uk)

McMILLAN, Fraser James John; s of John Wright McMillan, of Barrhead, E Renfrewshire, and Mary Wishart, *née* Nisbet; *b* 26 December 1967, Barrhead, E Renfrewshire; *Educ* Univ of Strathclyde (LLB, DipLP); *m* 14 June 1996, Amanda, *née* Tennant; 1 da (Sophie Anne b 6 July 2004), 1 s (Rory Charles b 3 Feb 2007); *Career* admitted slr Scotland 1991; trainee slr TC Young 1989–91, asst slr Bird Semple 1991–96, asst slr than assoc ptnr Dundas & Wilson CS: asst slr 1996–98; Pinsent Masons: sr assoc 1998–2000, ptnr 2000–, head of Scottish practice 2007–; memb: Law Soc of Scotland 1991, Soc of Construction Law; *Recreations* travel, running; *Style*— Fraser McMillan, Esq; ✉ Pinsent Masons, 123 St Vincent Street, Glasgow G2 5EA (tel 0141 249 5403, fax 0141 248 6655, e-mail fraser.mcmillan@pinsentmasons.com)

McMILLAN, Prof James Francis; s of John McMillan (d 1995), and Hannah, *née* McManus; *b* 10 March 1948; *Educ* St Mirin's Acad Paisley (Sch Dux), Univ of Glasgow (MA), Balliol Coll Oxford (DPhil); *m* 8 April 1989, Donatella, da of Roberto Fischer; *Career* temp lectr Univ of Glasgow 1972–73, lectr then sr lectr Dept of History Univ of York 1973–92, prof of European history Univ of Strathclyde 1992–99, Richard Pares prof of history Univ of Edinburgh 1999– (head of sch 2002–05, currently dir Centre for Second World War Studies); exchange prof California State Univ Long Beach USA 1987–88; convenor Scottish Catholic Historical Assoc 1995; FRSE 1996; *Books* Housewife or Harlot: the Place of Women in French Society 1870–1940 (1981), Dreyfus to De Gaulle: Politics and Society in France 1898–1969 (1985), Napoleon III (1991), Twentieth Century France: Politics and Society 1898–1991 (1992), France and Women 1789–1914: Gender, Society and Politics (2000), Modern France 1880–2002 (ed, 2003); *Recreations* opera, theatre, concerts, cinema, walking, travel; *Style*— Prof James McMillan, FRSE; ✉ Centre for the Study of the Two World Wars, University of Edinburgh, 24 Buccleuch Place, Edinburgh EH8 9LN

McMILLAN, (Duncan) Lindsay; s of late Duncan Alexander McMillan, and Phyllis Enrica, *née* Spencer; *b* 9 May 1940, Pretoria, South Africa; *Educ* St Stithian's Coll Johannesburg, Univ of Stellenbosch, Univ of the Witwatersrand (BSc, MB BCh); *m* Ceinwen Mair, da of late Dr Idwal James Mathias; 1 s (Duncan Rhydian b 15 June 1977), 1 da (Katrin Alexandra b 23 July 1979); *Career* former geophysical geologist for the Hans Merensky Tst Northern Cape in the Kalahari Desert; registrar/hon lectr (obstetrics and gynaecology) Royal Free Hosp London 1974–77, sr registrar/hon lectr (obstetrics and gynaecology) Mill Road Maternity Hosp Liverpool, The Women's Hosp Liverpool and Liverpool Maternity Hosp 1977–81, conslt (obstetrics and gynaecology) Whipps Cross Hosp London 1981– (chm Dept of Obstetrics and Gynaecology 1989–91), hon sr lectr St Bartholomew's Hosp and Univ of London 1993–; special interest in minimal access surgery in gynaecology and in pre-malignant and malignant diseases and their medical and surgical treatment; treas Br Soc of Gynaecological Endoscopy; memb: Int Soc for Gynaecologic Endoscopy, Br Soc of Colposcopy and Cervical Pathology, Euro Soc of Gynaecological Hysteroscopy and Laparoscopy, RSM (memb Ctee Obstetric and Gynaecology Div); FRCOG; *Recreations* skiing, mountaineering, theatre, music; *Style*— Lindsay McMillan, Esq; ✉ 17 Wimpole Street, London W1M 7AD (tel 020 7631 0914, fax 020 7323 9126)

MacMILLAN, Dr Margaret Olwen; *b* 23 December 1943, Toronto; *Educ* Univ of Toronto (BA), St Hilda' Coll Oxford (BPhil), St Antony's Coll Oxford (DPhil); *Career* prof of history Ryerson Univ 1975–2002 (chair History Dept 1987–92); Univ of Toronto: prof of history 1999–, provost Trinity Coll 2002–07; co-ed Int Jl 1995–2003; speaker at numerous confs and lectures; pres Victorian Studies Assoc of Ontario 1991–93, memb Bd Ontario Heritage Fndn 1992–98 and 2003–05, nat bd memb Canadian Inst of Int Affrs 1995–2006, jury memb Lionel Gelber Book Prize in Int Relations 1995, attended Bilderberg meetings 1998, 1999, 2001 and 2003, govr Canadian Cncl of Christians and Jews 2003–, memb Bd Historica 2004–; memb: Orgn for the History of Canada, Soc for Historians of American Foreign Relations; hon fell St Antony's Coll Oxford 2003 (sr assoc memb 1993, alumni rep for Canada 1994–97); FRSL 2003; *Awards* Duff Cooper Prize for History or Biography 2002, Hessell-Tiltman Prize for History PEN UK 2002, Samuel Johnson Prize for Non-fiction 2002, shortlisted Westminster Prize for Military History 2002, Silver Medal Council on Foreign Relations Arthur Ross Book Award 2003, Canadian Booksellers Libris Award for Non-fiction Book of the Year 2003, Govr-Gen's Award for Non-fiction 2003, shortlisted Gelber Prize 2004, shortlisted Charles Taylor Prize 2004; Warden St Antony's Coll Oxford 2007–; *Publications* Women of the Raj (1988, new edn 1996), Canada and Nato: Uneasy Past, Uncertain Future (co-ed with Dr. David Sorenson, 1990), The Uneasy Century: International Relations 1900–1990 (co-ed with Arne Kislenko, 1996), Peacemakers: The Paris Conference of 1919 and Its Attempt to End War (2001, reissued as Paris, 1919: Six Months that Changed the World, 2002), Parties Long Estranged: Canadian-Australian Relations (co-ed with Francine Mckenzie and contrib, 2003), Seize the Hour: When Nixon Met Mao (2006); author of numerous articles and reviews in newspapers and learned jls; *Style—* Dr Margaret MacMillan

McMILLAN, Moira Teresa; da of Austin Damer, of Surrey, and Sheila, *née* Griffin; *b* 6 April 1949; *Educ* Holy Trinity GS Bromley, Univ of Southampton (BSc); *m* William (Bill) McMillan; 1 da (Hannah Katy b 30 Nov 1988); *Career* research and mfrg Duracell UK 1970–76; Chemical Industries Assoc 1976–90: co-author Directory of Chemicals/Tech Exec, UK rep on Euro and int ctees (WHO and FAO), head of int trade representing industry to EEC Cmmn and GATT 1982, ldr various trade missions overseas; dir Paintmakers Association of GB Ltd 1990–93, chief exec British Coatings Federation Ltd 1993– (incorporating Paintmakers Assoc, Soc of Br Printing Ink Mfrs and Wallcovering Mfrs Assoc); *Recreations* painting, music; *Style—* Mrs Moira McMillan; ✉ British Coatings Federation Ltd, James House, Bridge Street, Leatherhead, Surrey KT22 7EP (tel 01372 360660, fax 01372 376069, e-mail moira.mcmillan@bcf.co.uk)

McMILLAN, Neil Macleod; CMG (1997); s of John Howard McMillan, CBE (d 1991), and Ruby Hassell, *née* Meggs (d 1994); *b* 21 October 1953; *Educ* Westminster City Sch, Univ of Exeter (BA), Univ of Kiel Germany, Univ of Regensburg Germany; *m* 1, 1978 (m dis 1985), Karin, *née* Lauritzen; m 2, 1994, Lena Madvig, *née* Madsen; 1 s (Christian Alexander Madvig b 29 March 1994); *Career* admin trainee Dept of Prices & Consumer Protection 1978, Steel Policy Dept of Indust 1979–80, Textile Trade Policy Dept of Trade 1981, private sec to Min for Industry and IT DTI 1982–84, advsr on telecomms reform Fed Miny of Research Bonn 1985, first sec UK Permanent Rep Brussels 1987–91, dir Int Communications Policy DTI 1991–98, dir EU Internal Trade Policy DTI 1998–2000; min and dep perm representative UK Mission Geneva 2001–05, dir Europe DTI 2005–; chm: Euro Ctee on Telecomms Regulatory Affairs 1992–95, Euro Telecomms Office Copenhagen 1992–95, Basic Telecomms Negotiations World Trade Orgn Geneva 1994–97, chm ITU Telecoms Policy Forum 1998; *Recreations* walking, reading, Medieval churches, languages; *Clubs* Athenaeum; *Style—* Neil McMillan, Esq, CMG

McMILLAN, Dr Nigel Charles; s of Ian McInnes McMillan (d 1980), and Joan Muriel McMillan, *née* Winchester; *b* 13 May 1950; *Educ* Loretto, Univ of Glasgow (MB ChB); *m* 24 March 1976, Linda Jean Douglas, da of Sqdn Ldr Archibald McDougall (d 2004); 1 s (Christopher b 1978), 1 da (Lorna b 1981); *Career* GP S Glasgow 1976–78, conslt radiologist to Western Infirmary Glasgow 1983– (registrar then sr registrar in radiology 1978–83), clinical dir diagnostic radiology West Glasgow Hosps Univ NHS Tst 1993–96; FRCR 1982, FRCPGlas 1997 (MRCPGlas 1995); *Recreations* Scottish country dancing, golf, skiing; *Style—* Dr Nigel McMillan; ✉ 5 Woodburn Road, Glasgow G43 2TN (tel 0141 637 1441, e-mail nigel.mcmillan@nhs.net)

McMILLAN-SCOTT, Edward Hugh Christian; MEP (Cons) Yorks & Humber; s of late Walter Theodore Robin McMillan-Scott, and late Elizabeth Maud Derrington Hudson; *b* 15 August 1949; *Educ* Blackfriars Sch Llanarth Raglan Monmouthshire, Blackfriars Sch Laxton Corby, Exeter Tech Coll; *m* 1972, Henrietta Elizabeth Rumney, da of Richard Derrington Mogridge Hudson, of Doynton, Avon; 2 da (Lucinda b 1973, Arabella b 1976); *Career* tour dir in Europe, Africa, USSR 1968–75; private exec then Parly conslt 1976–84, political advsr Falkland Islands Govt London Office 1983–85, MEP (Cons): York 1984–94, Yorkshire North 1994–99, Yorks & Humber 1999–; chm Conservatives in European Parl 1997–2001, vice-pres European Parl 2004–; *Style—* Edward McMillan-Scott, MEP; ✉ Wick House Farm, Wick, Pershore, Worcestershire WR10 3NU (tel 01386 552366, fax 01386 556038); European Parliament, Rue Wiertz, Brussels 1047, Belgium

McMULLEN, His Hon Judge Jeremy John; QC (1994, NI 1996); s of John E McMullen, and Irene, *née* Gardner; *b* 14 September 1948; *Educ* William Hulme's GS Manchester, BNC Oxford, LSE, Inns of Court Sch of Law; *m* 1973, Debbie, *née* Cristman; 1 s (Ben b 1976), 1 da (Katy b 1979); *Career* called to the Bar Middle Temple 1971; assoc attorney NY 1972–73, General and Municipal Workers' Union 1973–84, barr 1985–2001, circuit judge 2001–, judge Employment Appeal Tbnl 2002, sr circuit judge 2006–; vice-pres: Industrial Law Soc, Employment Law Bar Assoc; pt/t chm Employment Tbnl 1994–2002, sports arbitrator; pres Brasenose Soc; *Books* Rights at Work, Employment Law, Employment Tribunal Procedure; *Clubs* Reform; *Style—* His Hon Judge McMullen, QC; ✉ Employment Appeal Tribunal, 58 Victoria Embankment, London EC4Y 0DS

McMURRAY, Dr Cecil Hugh; CBE (2002); s of late Cecil Edwin McMurray, and Margaret Napier, *née* Smyth; *b* 19 February 1942; *Educ* Royal Belfast Academical Inst, Greenmount Agric Coll, Queen's Univ Belfast (BSc, BAgr), Univ of Bristol (PhD); *m* 3 Jan 1967, (Isabel) Ann, da of C A Stuart, of Belfast; 2 s (Alan, Trevor), 1 da (Rebecca); *Career* res fell Harvard Univ 1970–72, head of biochemistry Vet Res Labs Dept of Agric for NI 1972–84; joint appt as prof of food and agric chemistry Queen's Univ Belfast and dep CSO Dept of Agric for NI 1985–88, CSO Dept of Agric for NI 1988–2002; conslt in food and agric for World Bank and others specialising in transition economies as well as scientific reviewer of Govt Res Progs 2002–; memb: Bd Agricultural Systems Directorate, BBSRC 1993–97, Bd Northern Ireland Public Sector Enterprises Ltd 1994–2002, Advsy Ctee on Microbiological Safety until 2002, Governing Body Food Chain Certification Ctee 2003–; hon prof Queen's Univ Belfast 1998–2003; Salzburg fell 1983; FRSC 1981, FIFST 1987; *Publications* contrib: CIBA Fndn Symposia number 79 copper also number 101 Biology of Vitamin E, Trace Elements of Man and Domestic Animals Vol 5, and 6 Int Conference on Production Disease of Farm Animals, Selenium in Biology and Medicine; Detection Methods for Irriated Food (ed with others, 1996); also author of over 100 other scientific communications; *Recreations* photography, walking; *Style—* Dr Cecil McMurray, CBE; ✉ 25 Sheridan Drive, Helens Bay BT19 1LB (tel 028 9185 3655, e-mail cecil.mcmurray@dial.pipex.com)

McMURTRIE, Simon Nicholas; s of Anthony William Stratton McMurtrie, and Sally, *née* Bateson; *b* 20 February 1966; *Educ* Radley, Univ of Birmingham (BA); *m* 8 Aug 1992, Virginia, *née* Jagger; 1 da (Anna Charlotte b 22 Dec 1994), 1 s (Hugh William b 6 April 1998); *Career* William Heinemann Ltd 1988, Mandarin Paperbacks 1989, Octopus Publishing 1990, publishing dir Mitchell Beazley and Miller's Publications 1991, publishing dir Reed Illustrated Books 1992–93, md De Agostini Editions 1993–95, chief exec De Agostini UK 1995–99, chief exec International Masters Publishers Ltd 1999–2005, exec conslt De Agostini Editore SpA 2005–, mgmnt conslt Samlerhuset BV 2006, md int Direct Wines Ltd 2007–; publishing conslt Harvard University Press 1989–2003; *Clubs* Garrick; *Style—* Simon McMurtrie, Esq; ✉ e-mail simon.mcmurtrie@btinternet.com

McMURTRY, Sir David Roberts; kt (2001), CBE (1994); *b* 5 March 1940, Ireland; *Career* chm and chief exec Renishaw plc 1973–; RDI 1989; *Style—* Sir David McMurtry, CBE, RDI; ✉ Renishaw plc, New Mills, Wotton-Under-Edge, Gloucestershire GL12 8JR

McNAB, Andy; *b* 28 December 1959; *Career* boy soldier Inf Jr Ldr's Bn 1976, Sgt 2 Bn Royal Green Jackets 1977–83, Staff Sgt 22 SAS 1983–93; lectr to UK and US security and intelligence agencies 1996–; Light Division Sword 1977; MM (1980), DCM (1991); *Film* scriptwriter: Bravo Two Zero 1996, Bomber 2003, A Simple Life 2005; tech advsr: Heat 1995, Bravo Two Zero 1996, Timewatch 1996, Ultimate Warrior 1997, Conduct Under Capture 2000, London 2005; *Books* Bravo Two Zero (1993), Immediate Action (1995), Remote Control (1997), Crisis Four (1999), Firewall (2000), Last Light (2001), Liberation Day (2002) Dark Winter (2003), Deep Black (2004), Boy Soldier (2005), Payback (2005), Aggressor (2005), Recoil (2006), Avenger (2006); *Style—* Andy McNab

McNAB, Janice; *b* 1964, Aberfeldy; *Educ* Edinburgh Coll of Art (BA, Dip Painting), Glasgow Sch of Art (MFA), Hunter Coll NY (MFA exchange student); *Career* artist; *Solo Exhibitions* incl: Collective Gallery Edinburgh 1999, Laurent Delaye Gallery London 2001, doggerfisher Edinburgh 2001, The Greenock factory project (Tramway Glasgow) 2002, Galerie Volker Diehl Berlin 2002, Talbot Rice Gallery Univ of Edinburgh 2004, Drumcastle NTS/Iain Irvine Projects 2004; *Group Exhibitions* incl: Sick Building (Globe Collective Copenhagen) 1996, The Social Life of Stuff (Fly Gallery Glasgow) 1998, Sick Vitalists (Intermedia Glasgow) 1999, Anxiety (Collective Gallery Edinburgh) 1999, Evolution Isn't Over Yet (Fruitmarket Gallery Edinburgh, Lugar Comun Lisbon and The Dick Inst Kilmarnock) 1999, John, I'm Only Dancing (UH Galleries St Albans and Collective Gallery Edinburgh) 2000, 45th Salon de Mont Rouge (Galleries Mont Rouge Paris and ICA Lisbon) 2000, Art in the Home (Edinburgh and Yamaguchi) 2001, Here + Now (Dundee Contemporary Arts) 2001, Le mois de le photo (Galerie La Centrale Montreal) 2001, Tabu: Mavericks und Heisse Eisen (Kunsthaus Baselland Muttenz) 2002, The Gap Show (Musuem am Ostwall Dortmund) 2002, Sanctuary Goma Glasgow 2003, Now What? Bak Utrecht 2003, East Int Norwich 2004; *Awards* Glasgow City of Culture studio residency Vienna 1990, Wurlitzer Fndn of New Mexico studio residency 1998, Oppenheim-Downes Tst Award 1998, Hope Scott Tst Artists Award 1998 and 2001, Scottish Arts Cncl studio residency Amsterdam 2000, Br Cncl Artists Grant 2001; *Style—* Ms Janice McNab; ✉ Doggerfish Gallery, 11 Gayfield Square, Edinburgh EH1 3NT (tel 0131 558 7110, e-mail enquiries@doggerfish.com)

McNAB, John Stanley; s of Robert Stanley McNab (d 1974), and Alice Mary, *née* Sayers (d 1965); *b* 23 September 1937; *m* 1 (m dis 1977), Carol; 2 da (Lesley Anne b 12 Oct 1965, Jacqueline Carol Davey b 19 July 1968); m 2 (m dis 1997), Jacqueline; m 3, 2001, Susan; *Career* Nat Serv RE 1956–58; Port of London Authy: joined as jr clerical offr 1954, various accountancy appts rising to docks accountant Upper Docks 1971, md PLA (Thames) Stevedoring Ltd (formerly Thames Stevedoring (1965) Ltd) 1973, dir Upper Docks 1974, memb Bd 1978–92, exec dir manpower (formerly jt dir) 1978–82, dir docks ops 1982–83, dir Tilbury 1983–87, dir 1987–92; chief exec Port of Tilbury London Ltd 1992–95; dir Airflights Direct Ltd 2001–; chm London Port Employers' Assoc 1978–89, memb Nat Dock Lab Bd 1978–89; former memb: Exec and Mgmnt Ctees Nat Assoc of Port Employers, Nat Jt Cncl for Port Tport Indust; govr Thurrock Tech Coll 1988–2005 (chm Fin and Gen Purposes Ctee); Freeman: City of London 1988, Worshipful Co of Watermen and Lightermen of the River Thames 1989; MIMgt, FCCA, FCIT, FRSA; *Recreations* golf, gardening, swimming, DIY; *Style—* John McNab, Esq; ✉ 48 Daines Way, Thorpe Bay, Essex SS1 3PQ (tel 01702 587060)

McNAIR, 3 Baron (UK 1955); Duncan James McNair; s of 2 Baron McNair (d 1989); *b* 26 June 1947; *Educ* Bryanston, Gloucester Coll of Arts & Technol; *m* 1; 1 s (Hon Thomas John b 1972), 1 da (Hon Victoria (twin) b 1972), 1 adopted da (Charlotte b 1968); m 2, Hannah Margaret Elizabeth; 1 step s (Sean b 1968); *Heir* bro, Hon William McNair; *Career* chm: Emission Control Systems Int, Unitax Assoc 1994–97, DMCK Consultants 1996–97; vice-chm Parly Waterways Gp (Canals) 1994–99, fndr memb and memb Exec Ctee Cncl for Human Rights and Religious Freedom 1996, memb Exec Ctee Euro Parly Intercultural Ctee 1996–98; memb Sub-Ctee for Environment House of Lords Select Ctee on EC 1990–92, convened Ad Hoc Ctee to investigate descrimination against ethnic and religious minorities in Germany; memb All-Pty Parly Gp: Race and Community 1994–95, Human Rights, Drugs Misuse, Alcohol, Mental Health (vice-chm), Population Devpt and Reproductive Health; memb panel Conf of Int Educators for World Peace at UNESCO Paris 1999; dir Br Anti-Trafficking Orgn; reports on: political situation in Sudan 1995, allegations of slavery in Sudan 1997, humanitarian situation in Khartoum State Sudan 1999; vice-pres patron Black Int Construction Organization (BICO), vice-patron Police Community Clubs of England; special interests: human rights, particularly religious liberty, education, drug rehabilitation, environment, alternative energy sources, alternative health approaches appropriate to less well developed countries; currently int human rights and educn conslt with focus on Africa; Order of Merit of the European Community Assoc for work on human rights in Europe; Hon DLaws Univ of Khartoum 1999; memb Royal African Soc; *Publications* author (as rapporteur) of first report of the Ad Hoc Committee to Investigate Discrimination Against Ethnic and Religious Minorities in Germany (1996); *Style—* The Rt Hon the Lord McNair; ✉ e-mail lordmcnair@email.com

McNAIR SCOTT, Simon Guthrie; s of Thomas Michael McNair Scott (d 2002), of St Peter, Jersey, and Susannah, *née* Hodges (d 1993); *b* 12 May 1960; *Educ* Eton, Univ of Exeter (BA); *m* 1, 1988 (m dis 1991), Hon Camilla Birgitta, *née* Davidson, da of 2 Viscount Davidson; m 2, 8 Sept 1995, Natasha Jane, da of Alexander Stevenson (d 1994); 1 da (Charlotte b 6 May 1997), 1 s (Alexander Guthrie b 22 June 1999); *Career* film and TV freelance location mangr 1982–; credits incl: Mission: Impossible 1995, Eyes Wide Shut 1996–98, The Mummy Returns 2000, Johnny English 2003; advsr London Film Cmmn 1996; *Recreations* golf, surfing; *Clubs* Hurlingham, Brooks's; *Style—* Simon McNair Scott, Esq; ✉ The Old Rectory, Lesnewth, Boscastle, Cornwall PL35 0HR (tel 01840 261730)

McNALLY, Kevin Robert; s of Robert Gerard McNally, of Somerset, and Margaret June, *née* Sperring; *b* 27 April 1956; *Educ* Central GS Birmingham, RADA (Ronson Award, Bancroft Award); *Partner* Phyllis Logan; 1 s (David b 10 June 1996); another 2 c: 1 step s (Peter), 1 da (Rachel b 7 Nov 1988); *Career* actor; also writes for TV (with Bernard Dempsey); *Theatre* NT 1979–80: Lark Rise, The Passion, Dispatches, The Iceman Cometh; Loose Ends (Hampstead), Pistols and Airbase (The Arts), Andromache (Old Vic), Scenes from an Execution and Naked (with Almeida Co); West End theatre incl: Extremities (Duchess), Glengarry Glen Ross (Mermaid), Hidden Laughter (Vaudeville), Not Quite Jerusalem and Prayer For My Daughter (Royal Court), Dead Funny (Savoy) 1996, Plunder (Savoy) 1997, Naked (Playhouse) 1998, Lady in the Van (Queen's Theatre) 1999–2000, World Music (Donmar Warehouse) 2003; *Television* for BBC incl: Commitments, Poldark, I Claudius, Duchess of Duke Street, Diana, The Common Pursuit, Dad, Life on Mars; The Contract (YTV), Act of Will (Tyne Tees), Jekyll and Hyde (LWT), Full Stretch (Meridian), Underworld (Channel 4), Conspiracy, Shackleton, Spooks; *Film* incl: The Spy Who Loved Me, The Long Good Friday, Inside Man, Enigma, The Antagonists, Not Quite Jerusalem, The Berlin Affair, Cry Froddy Allen's Scoop, Pirates of the Caribbean I, II and III; *Clubs* Groucho, High Road House; *Style—* Kevin R McNally; ✉ c/o Hatton McKewan Management, PO Box 37385, London N1 7XF (e-mail kevinmcnally111@hotmail.com)

McNALLY, Baron (Life Peer UK 1995), of Blackpool in the County of Lancashire; Thomas (Tom) McNally; PC (2005); s of John Patrick McNally (d 1982), and Elizabeth May McNally (d 1982); *b* 20 February 1943; *Educ* Coll of St Joseph Blackpool, UCL (BSc); *m* 1, 1970 (m dis 1990), Eileen Isobel, da of Thomas Powell, of Dumfries; m 2, 1990, Juliet, da of George Lamy Hutchinson, of Swansea; 2 s (Hon John b 15 June 1990, Hon James George b 7 Aug 1993), 1 da (Hon Imogen b 28 Oct 1995); *Career* asst gen sec the Fabian Soc 1966–67, vice-pres NUS 1966–67, int sec Lab Party HQ 1969–74 (researcher 1966–67); political advsr: to Foreign and Cwlth Sec 1974–76, to PM (head of Political Office 10 Downing St) 1976–79, to Paddy Ashdown 1988–99; MP (Lab until 1981, whereafter SDP) Stockport S 1979–83; memb House of Commons Trade and Industry Select Ctee 1979–83; Lib Dem spokesman on Home Affairs in House of Lords 1998–2001, dep ldr Lib Dem House of Lords 2001–04, ldr Lib Dem House of Lords 2004–; memb House of Lords Select Ctee on: the Public Service 1997–98, Freedom of Information Act 1999; memb Jt Select Ctee on the Communications Bill 2002; public affrs advsr, head of public affrs Hill and Knowlton (UK) Ltd PR conslts 1987–93, vice-chm WeberShandwick UK PR conslts 1996–2004 (dir of public affrs 1993–96); memb Fed Exec Lib Dems 1987–99; fell UCL 1995; FCIPR, FRSA; *Recreations* watching sport, reading political biographies; *Clubs* Nat

M

Liberal; *Style—* The Rt Hon Lord McNally, PC; ✉ House of Lords, London SW1A 0PW (tel 020 7219 5443)

McNAMARA, Dr John Francis; s of Francis McNamara (d 1978), of Bolton, Lancs, and Olivia, *née* Whittingham (d 1982); *b* 18 July 1945; *Educ* Worsley-Wardley GS, Univ of Leeds; *m* 19 Dec 1981, Olwen, da of Richard Fellows, of Altrincham, Cheshire; 1 s (James Declan b 23 Oct 1983), 1 da (Katherine Jane b 16 March 1985); *Career* sr MO Br Nuclear Fuels Risley Nuclear Power Centre 1979–83, occupational health physician City of Salford 1983–87, conslt physician in occupational med Cheshire and Wirral Partnership NHS Tst Chester 1986–, conslt occupational physician and dir of occupational med Univ Hosp of S Manchester 1992–; memb Med Appeals Tbnl; memb: BMA 1971, Soc of Occupational Med 1977, Chester and N Wales Med Soc 1986, Cncl Assoc of Nat Health Occupational Physicians 1986; hon clinical lectr in occupational med Univ of Manchester 1993–; LLM Univ of Wales 1994; MRCS 1970, MRCGP 1975, MRCP (collegiate memb London) 1979 (LRCP 1970), FRCPGlas 1994, FRCPEd 1997, FFOM (RCP) 2002, FFFP (RCOG) 2005; *Books* The Patient with Respiratory Problems (contrib, 1989); *Recreations* bridge, swimming, walking, history; *Style—* Dr John McNamara; ✉ Upway, Parkhill Road, Hale, Altrincham, Cheshire WA15 9JX (tel 0161 980 5054); Occupational Health Unit, Baguley House, Wythenshawe Hospital, South Manchester University Hospitals NHS Trust, Southmoor Road, Manchester M23 9LT (tel 0161 291 2674, fax 0161 291 2460)

McNAMARA, (Joseph) Kevin; s of Patrick McNamara, of Liverpool; *b* 5 September 1934; *Educ* St Mary's Coll Crosby, Hull Univ (LLB); *m* 1960, Nora, da of John Jones, of Warrington; 4 s, 1 da; *Career* former lectr in law Hull Coll of Commerce and head History Dept St Mary's GS Hull; MP (Lab): Hull N 1966–74 and 1983–2005, Kingston upon Hull Central 1974–83; PPS to: sec of state for econ affrs 1967–69, min without portfolio 1969–70; chm PLP NI Gp 1974–79, oppn front bench spokesman on defence and disarmament 1982–87, chief oppn spokesman on Northern Ireland 1987–94, shadow spokesperson for the Civil Serv 1994–95 (resigned); vice-chm PLP NI Ctee, memb Cncl of Europe and Western European Assembly; Br vice-chm Br Irish Inter-Parly Body; formerly: chm Select Ctee on Overseas Devpt, memb Select Ctee on Foreign Affairs, memb NATO Parly Assembly; sec TGWU Parly Gp, vice-pres League Against Cruel Sports; *Style—* Kevin McNamara, Esq; ✉ 145 Newland Park, Hull, East Yorkshire HU5 2DX (tel 01482 448170)

McNAMEE, Dr Terence; s of Donald McNamee, and Joan, *née* Crawford; *b* 18 July 1969, Victoria, Canada; *Educ* Univ of Br Columbia Vancouver (BA), McGill Univ Montreal (MA), LSE (PhD); *m* 5 Aug 2000, Emily, *née* Outred; *Career* ed RUSI Jl 2002–, dir of publications RUSI 2003–; *Style—* Dr Terence McNamee; ✉ RUSI, Whitehall, London SW1A 2ET (tel 020 7930 5854, e-mail terrym@rusi.org)

McNAUGHT, His Hon John Graeme; DL (Wilts 2006); s of Charles William McNaught (d 1955), and Isabella Mary McNaught (d 1969); *b* 21 February 1941; *Educ* King Edward VII Sch Sheffield, The Queen's Coll Oxford (MA); *m* 1966, Barbara Mary, da of George Rufus Smith (d 1961); 2 s, 1 da; *Career* called to the Bar Gray's Inn 1963; in practice Western Circuit, recorder 1981–87, circuit judge (Western Circuit) 1987–2006, hon recorder Devizes 1996–; pres Mental Health Review Tbnl 2001–05, memb Parole Bd 1998–2004; *Style—* His Hon John McNaught, DL

McNAUGHTON, Prof Peter Anthony; *b* 17 August 1949, Auckland, NZ; *Educ* Auckland GS, Univ of Auckland (BSc), Balliol Coll Oxford (Rhodes scholar, DPhil); *m*; 4 c; *Career* research fell Clare Coll Cambridge 1974–78; Physiological Lab Univ of Cambridge: Elmore med research student 1977–78, univ demonstrator 1978–83, univ lectr 1983–91; fell and dir of studies in physiology Christ's Coll Cambridge 1983–91 (dir of studies in med 1989–91), Halliburton prof of physiology and head Dept of Physiology KCL 1991–99 (dean of basic med sciences 1993–96), Sheild prof and head Dept of Pharmacology Univ of Cambridge 1999–, fell Christ's Coll Cambridge 1999–; Nuffield science research fell 1988–89; chm Bio-imaging Initiative Panel BBSRC 1998–2002; memb: Biochemistry and Cell Biology Panel BBSRC 1996–2000, Neuroscience Bd Wellcome Tst 1998–2001, Inst Assessment Panel BBSRC 2001, Neurone Initiative Panel BBSRC 2001–04, Advsy Bd MRC 2001–, Selection Panel for Ramon y Cajal fellowships Spanish Fndn for Science and Technol 2002, Performance Based Research Fund Panel NZ; Physiological Soc: memb 1979–, memb Ctee 1988–92, mangr Dale and Rushton Funds 1989–2002; memb Br Pharmacological Soc 1999–; chm PTA Mill Hill Co HS 1997–99; hon prof Dept of Optometry and Vision Sciences Univ of Wales Cardiff 1998; *Style—* Prof Peter McNaughton; ✉ Department of Pharmacology, University of Cambridge, Tennis Court Road, Cambridge CB2 1PD (tel 01223 334012, fax 01223 334100, e-mail pam42@cam.ac.uk)

McNEANY, Kevin Joseph; s of Bernard Joseph McNeany, of Keady, Co Armagh, and Mary Christina, *née* McDonnell; *b* 10 April 1943; *Educ* St Patrick's Coll Armagh, Queen's Univ Belfast (BA), Univ of London, Univ of Manchester; *m* 1 Aug 1968 (m dis 1985), Christine, da of Stephen McNulty; 2 s (Matthew Ciaron b 1971, Myles Anthony b 1986); *Career* teacher: St Paul's Sch Lurgan Co Armagh 1964–66, Corpus Christi Sch Leeds 1966–68; lectr: Kitson Coll Leeds 1968–70, Southport Tech Coll 1970–73, Wythenshawe Coll Manchester 1973–77; co-fndr (with Christine McNeany 1972), exec chm Nord Anglia Education plc (formerly Nord-Anglia International) 2003–05 (chm and ceo 1977–2003), exec chm Acorn Educn and Care Ltd 2005–; fndr: Br Sch of Warsaw Poland 1992, Br Int Sch of Moscow 1994, English Sch Prague 1995, Br Sch of Kiev Ukraine 1997, Br Sch of Bratislava Slovakia 1997, Br Int Sch Shanghai China 2002; *Recreations* walking, cycling; *Clubs* National Liberal; *Style—* Kevin McNeany, Esq; ✉ Ridge Park, 32 Bramhall Park Road, Bramhall, Cheshire SK7 3JN (tel 0161 439 2563); Eagle Court, Concord Business Park, Manchester M22 0RR (tel 0870 351 1819)

MACNEE, (Daniel) Patrick; s of Daniel Macnee (d 1952), of Lambourn, Berks, and Dorothea Mary Henry, BEM (d 1985, niece of 13 Earl of Huntingdon); *b* 6 February 1922; *Educ* Summerfields, Eton; *m* 1, Nov 1942 (m dis 1956), Barbara Douglas; 1 s (Rupert b 1947), 1 da (Jennifer b 1950); m 2, April 1965 (m dis 1968), Kate Woodville; m 3, Feb 1988, Baba Sekerley, *née* Majos de Nagyzsenye; *Career* actor; served WWII 1942–46: Sub Lt HMS Alfred (Offrs' Trg Sch nr Brighton) 1942, Royal Naval Coll Greenwich 1943, 1 MTB Flotilla 1943, 1 Lt 1944, demobbed 1946; Long Service Medal, Atlantic Medal; memb: Palm Springs Youth Centre, Palm Springs Opera Guild; Freedom of Filey Yorks 1962, Freedom of City of Macon Georgia 1985; *Theatre* over 150 stage appearances incl: Sleuth (Broadway) 1972–73, Killing Jessica (West End) 1986–87; *Television* incl: The Avengers 1960–69 (filmed introductions to restored and remastered prints for 1998–99 TV and video release worldwide), Alfred Hitchcock presents, Dial M For Murder, Thriller, Columbo, For The Term of his Natural Life, Murphy's Law, Dick Francis Stories, Ray Bradbury Theatre 1991, The Golden Years of Sherlock Holmes 1990, Superforce 1991, PS I Luv U 1991, The Hound of London 1991, Dream On and Murder She Wrote 1992, Coach 1993, Kung Fu 1993, Thunder in Paradise 1993, Mysteries, Magic and Miracles (series) 1994–95, Spy Game 1996–97, Ghost Stories 1997, Nightman 1997, Diagnosis Murder 1998, Nancherrow 1998, Family Law 2000, guest star Frasier 2001, narrator The Second World War in Colour (2002–03); *Film* incl: The Life and Death of Colonel Blimp 1942, Hamlet 1948, The Elusive Pimpernel 1950, Scrooge 1951, Battle of the River Plate 1956, Les Girls 1957, Incense for the Damned (US: Bloodsuckers) 1970, Mr Jericho 1970, Matt Helm 1975, King Solomon's Treasures 1976, Sherlock Holmes in New York 1976, Battlestar Galactica 1979, The Sea Wolves 1980, The Howling 1981, This is Spinal Tap 1983, A View to a Kill 1984, Shadey 1984, Waxworks 1988, The Chill Factor 1988, The Lobster Man From Mars 1988, The Masque of the Red Death 1989, Eye of the Widow 1989, Scared Silly 1990, Waxwork II 1991, The Avengers 1997; *Recordings* incl: reading Jack Higgins stories on audio cassette 1994; Kinky Boots recorded with Honor Blackman 1964 (reached no 5 in the Top 40 singles Dec 1990); reading The Winter's Tale for The Children's Shakespeare on audio cassette 1998; reading the Hornblower series on audio cassette 1999; personal introductions to The Avengers TV series on DVD 2000; personal introductions to James Bond films on DVD 2000 *Awards* incl: Variety Club of GB Jt TV Personality of the Year Award (with Honor Blackman) 1963, Straw Hat Award (NY) 1975, Golden Camera Award (Berlin), Air Safety Award From the Admin of the Federal Airway Administration (Washington DC), Lifetime Achievement Award from Mary Pickford Film Fndn 1998; *Books* Blind In One Ear (autobiography, 1988), The Avengers and Me (with Dave Rogers, 1997); *Recreations* reading, conversing with friends, family life, a love of nature and the sea, creating a website; *Style—* Patrick Macnee, Esq; ✉ c/o Michael Whitehall Associates, 10 Lower Common South, London SW15 1BP (tel 020 8785 3737, fax 020 8788 2340, website www.patrickmacnee.com)

McNEECE, John; s of Francis McNeece (d 1967), and Mary Frances, *née* Ferguson (d 1990); *b* 27 October 1939; *Educ* Glasgow Sch of Art (DA); *m* 1, 1964 (m dis); 2 s (Adrian b 1965, Mark b 1968); m 2, 1980, Norma Margaret Lewis Zunterstein; *Career* design conslt; Keppie Henderson & Ptnrs 1963–64, J L Gleave & Ptnrs 1964–65; chm & chief exec McNeece (ptnr and dir 1962–2002), md John McNeece Ltd, Maritime PR and Mktg Conslts 2002–; cruise ship projects: Sovereign of the Seas (Royal Caribbean Cruises) 1988, Crown Odyssey (Royal Cruise Line) 1988, Horizon (Celebrity Cruises) 1991, Cunard Princess and Cunard Countess (Cunard Line) 1991, Zenith (Celebrity Cruises) 1992, refit Queen Elizabeth 2 (Cunard Line) 1994, Oriana (P&O Cruises) 1995, Century (Celebrity Cruises) 1995, Galaxy (Celebrity Cruises) 1996, Mercury (Celebrity Cruises) 1997, R1 and R2 (Renaissance Cruises) 1998, R3 and R4 (Renaissance Cruises) 1999, R5 and R6 (Renaissance Cruises) 2000, R7 and R8 (Renaissance Cruises) 2001, The World of Residensea (Residensea) 2002, Project America (American Classic Voyages Co), Aurora (P&O Cruises) 2000; concepts for: Quadruple Satellite Ship 1995, Crusie Bowl 1996, Cool One 1997, RASCon Project for Maritime and Coastguard Agency Innovation Gp 2001; fndr memb Maritime and Coastguard Agency Innovation Gp 2000; Seatrade Innovation Award 2000; visiting fell Seatrade Cruise Acad 1999–; Freeman: City of London 1989, Worshipful Co of Gardeners 1989; Liveryman Worshipful Co of Shipwrights 1996; FCSD 1970 (memb Cncl 1993, hon sec 1994–96), FRINA 2001 (memb Cncl 2002), FIMarEst 2003; *Recreations* golf, shooting, music, walking, charity; *Clubs* Naval; *Style—* John McNeece, Esq; ✉ The McNeece Consultancy, Sycamore House, Coach Hill Lane, Burley, Ringwood, Hampshire BH24 4HN (tel 01425 402051, e-mail john.mcneece@jm-pr.com)

MacNEIL, Angus; MP; *b* 21 July 1970; *Educ* Univ of Strathclyde (BEng), Jordanhill Coll (PGCE); *Career* former reporter BBC, teacher Eoligarry Sch Barra; MP (SNP) Na H-Eileanan An Iar 2005– (Parly candidate (Cons) Inverness 2001); *Style—* Angus MacNeil, Esq, MP; ✉ House of Commons, London SW1A 0AA

McNEILL, James Walker; QC (Scot 1991); s of James McNeill, and Edith Anna Howie, *née* Wardlaw; *b* 16 February 1952; *Educ* Dunoon GS, Univ of Cambridge (MA), Univ of Edinburgh (LLB); *m* 1986, Katherine Lawrence, da of William Crocket McDowall; 2 s, 1 da; *Career* advocate 1978; standing jr counsel to: Dept of Tport in Scot 1984–88, Inland Revenue in Scot 1988–91; judge Courts of Appeal of Jersey and Guernsey 2006–; memb Bd of Scottish Int Piano Competition 2004–; *Recreations* music, hill walking, golf, sailing, travel; *Clubs* New (Edinburgh), Isle of Colonsay Golf, Hon Co of Edinburgh Golfers; *Style—* James McNeill, Esq, QC; ✉ 28 Kingsburgh Road, Edinburgh EH12 6DZ

McNEILL, Prof John; s of Thomas McNeill (d 1972), of Edinburgh, and Helen Lawrie, *née* Eagle (d 1984); *b* 15 September 1933; *Educ* George Heriot's Sch Edinburgh, Univ of Edinburgh (BSc, PhD); *m* 1, 29 July 1961 (m dis 1990), Bridget Mariel, da of Paul Winterton; 2 s (Andrew Thomas b 1964, Douglas Paul b 1966); m 2, 6 April 1990, Dr Marilyn Lois James; *Career* asst lectr then lectr Dept of Agric Botany Univ of Reading 1957–61, lectr Dept of Botany Univ of Liverpool 1961–69, sr res scientist Biosystematics Res Inst Canada Ottawa 1977–81 (res sci when formerly known as Plant Res Inst 1969–77), prof and chm Dept of Biology Univ of Ottawa Canada 1981–87, regius keeper Royal Botanic Garden Edinburgh 1987–89 (hon assoc 1998–), dir and pres Royal Ontario Museum Toronto Canada 1991–97 (assoc dir curatorial 1989–90, actg dir 1990–91, dir emeritus 1997–); concurrently dir George R Gardiner Museum of Ceramic Art Toronto and pres Royal Ontario Museum Fndn; prof Dept of Botany Univ of Toronto, adjunct prof Dept of Biology Univ of Ottawa 1991; nomenclature ed Taxon - Int Jl of Plant Taxonomy, Phylogeny and Evolution 2000–; pres: Biological Cncl of Canada 1986–87 (vice-pres 1984–86), Canadian Cncl of Univ Biology Chairmen 1984–85 (vice-pres 1983–84); chm: Int Organization for Plant Information 1997–2000 (vice-chm 1993–96), Flora North America Mgmnt Ctee 1998–2001; rapporteur-général Nomenclature Section XVII and XVIII Int Botanical Congress 1999–; treas Int Organization for Systematic and Evolutionary Biology 1996–2002; exec memb Int Union of Biological Sci 1985–88 and 1991–94, admin of fin Int Assoc of Plant Taxonomy 1987–93 (cncllr 1981–87 and 1993–2005); author of numerous scientific papers and reports; memb 15 scientific socs; *Books* Phenetic and Phylogenetic Classification (ed with V H Heywood, 1964), Grasses of Ontario (with W G Dore, 1980), The Genus Atriplex in Canada (with I J Bassett et al, 1983), International Code of Botanical Nomenclature (adopted 1981, jt ed, 1983), International Code of Botanical Nomenclature (adopted 1987, jt ed, 1988), Preliminary Inventory of Canadian Weeds (with C W Crompton, A E Stahevitch and W A Wojtas, 1988), Flora of North America (Vols 1 and 2I, jt ed, 1993, Vol 3, jt ed, 1997, Vol 22, jt ed, 2000, Vol 23, jt ed, 2003, Vol 26, jt ed, 2002), International Code of Botanical Nomenclature (adopted 1993, jt ed, 1994), International Code of Nomenclature for Cultivated Plants (jt ed, 1995 and 2004), International Code of Botanical Nomenclature (adopted 1999, jt ed, 2000), International Code of Botanical Nomenclature (adopted 2005, chair Editorial Ctee 2006); *Style—* Prof John McNeill; ✉ Royal Botanic Garden, 20A Inverleith Row, Edinburgh EH3 5LR

McNEILL, Pauline; MSP; da of John P McNeill, and Teresa, *née* Ward (d 1989); *b* 12 September 1962, Paisley, Renfrewshire; *Educ* Our Lady's HS Cumbernauld, Glasgow Coll of Building and Printing (Dip, C&G), Univ of Strathclyde (LLB); *m* 23 Jan 1999, Joseph Cahill; 2 step s (Niall, Iain); *Career* pres NUS (Scotland) 1986–88, regnl organiser GMB Scotland 1988–99; MSP (Lab) Glasgow Kelvin 1999–; convenor Cross-Pty Gps on: Palestine, Scottish Contemporary Music Industry; *Recreations* guitar playing, music, PC games, dance; *Style—* Ms Pauline McNeill, MSP; ✉ 1274 Argyle Street, Glasgow G3 8AA (tel 0141 589 7120, fax 0141 589 7122)

McNEISH, Prof Alexander Stewart; s of Dr Angus Stewart McNeish (d 1964), and Minnie Howieson, *née* Dickson (d 1992); *b* 13 April 1938; *Educ* Glasgow Acad, Univ of Glasgow (MB ChB, MPhil), Univ of Birmingham (MSc); *m* 4 March 1963, Joan Ralston, da of William Hamilton (d 1970); 2 s (Alistair Stewart b 1964, Iain Alexander b 1968), 1 da (Fiona Hamilton b 1966 d 2004); *Career* fndn prof of child health Univ of Leicester 1976–80, Leonard Parsons prof of paediatrics and child health and dir Inst of Child Health Univ of Birmingham 1980–95 (dean Faculty of Medicine and Dentistry 1987–92), dir MRC Clinical Sciences Centre Royal Postgrad Med Sch London 1995–96, warden Bart's and the Royal London Med and Dental Sch and vice-prin Queen Mary & Westfield Coll London 1997–2000, emeritus prof in clinical sci Univ of London 2001–, hon prof Univ of Birmingham 2003–, hon fell Queen Mary and Westfield Coll 2007; memb Central Birmingham HA 1987–91, non-exec dir S Birmingham HA 1991–92, dir R&D W Midlands RHA 1992–95; pres European Soc for Paediatric Gastroenterology and Nutrition 1984–87; memb GMC 1985–95; FRCP 1977, FRCPGlas 1985, FRCPCH 1996, FMedSci 1997; *Recreations* golf, music, gardening; *Clubs* Athenaeum, Blackwell Golf, Southerness Golf, Rye Golf; *Style*— Prof Alexander McNeish; ✉ 128 Westfield Road, Birmingham B15 3JQ (tel 0121 454 6081, fax 0121 456 5465, e-mail asmcneish@btinternet.com); Drumbuie, Kirkbean, Dumfries and Galloway

McNICHOLAS, Bernard; s of Michael McNicholas (d 1962), and Mary, *née* Harwood; *b* 9 March 1941, London; *Educ* St James RC Sch Burnt Oak; *m* m 1, Patricia (d 1998); 3 da (Siobhan b 15 Oct 1965, Fiona b 31 Jan 1969, Lucy b 12 April 1974), 1 s (Sean b 17 Nov 1967); m 2, 18 March 2004, Pauline, *née* Mitchel; *Career* exec chm McNicholas Hldgs plc; AIB Businessman of the Year 1994; Hon LLD Galway Univ 2005; KSG 1999; *Recreations* golf, fishing, reading; *Style*— Bernard McNicholas, Esq; ✉ McNicholas Holdings plc, McNicholas House, Kingsbury Road, London NW9 8XA

McNICHOLAS, Conor; s of Edward McNicholas (d 2000), of Knockfall, Co Mayo, and Jacquie Howard, *née* Wilson; *b* 27 June 1973; *Educ* Belle Vue Boys' Sch Bradford, Univ of Manchester (BA); *m* Susan, *née* Foulis; *Career* journalist; treas and co-ed Sub magazine 1992–94, news ed Escape magazine 1996–98, dep ed Ministry magazine 1998, account exec MacLaurin PR 1999, news ed Mixmag 1999–2001, ed Muzik magazine 2001–02, ed NME 2002–; memb BSME 2001; *Recreations* music, cars, travel, wine, Arsenal FC; *Style*— Conor McNicholas, Esq; ✉ NME, 25th Floor, King's Reach Tower, Stamford Street, London SE1 9LS (tel 020 7261 6472, e-mail editor@nme.com)

MacNICOL, Dr David Dewar; s of Malcolm MacNicol (d 1979), and Kathleen Jean, *née* Dewar (d 1999); *b* 25 December 1939; *Educ* Hutchesons' Boys' GS, Univ of Glasgow (BSc, PhD, DSc); *Career* postdoctoral DSIR research fell Univ of Oxford 1965–66; Univ of Glasgow: lectr in chemistry 1966–76, sr lectr 1976–82, reader 1982–; exec ed Comprehensive Supramolecular Chemistry (Vols 1–11) 1996; FRSE 1996; *Recreations* numismatics, photography, angling; *Style*— Dr David MacNicol, FRSE; ✉ Department of Chemistry, University of Glasgow, Glasgow G12 8QQ (tel 0141 330 5289, fax 0141 330 4888, e-mail d.macnicol@chem.gla.ac.uk)

McNICOL, Duncan; s of Alfred McNicol (d 1989), of Isle of Skye, and Joan, *née* Fox; *b* 18 March 1952; *Educ* Cranford Sch, London Coll of Printing (HND Creative Photography); *m* 21 June 1975, Margaret, da of Albert Frederick Bradberry; 2 s (Ross b 13 Nov 1979, Ewan b 27 June 1981); *Career* photographic asst 1973–76, own studio (advtg and design photography) 1976–; main advtg clients incl: Citroën, Rover, Barclays Bank, Nat Westminster, Kit Kat, Armitage Shanks, De Beers, Br Telecom, Royal Mail, Royal Insurance, Spanish Tourist Bd, Scottish Tourist Bd, Du Pont, Compuserve, Polaroid, BICC, Tarmac; pt/t photographic teacher London Coll of Printing 1976–79; memb Assoc of Photographers 1977, memb RPS; *Awards* Assoc of Photographers Awards 1987, 1989, 1995 and 1996, Assoc of Photographers Gold Award 1994, Communication Arts Award (USA) 1994, John Kobal Awards 1996; finalist: Epica Awards 1993, Cannes Ad Awards 1993; *Recreations* photography, walking, theatre, cycling, art galleries; *Style*— Duncan McNicol, Esq; ✉ The Studio, Treyford, Midhurst, West Sussex GU29 0LD (tel 01730 825100)

MACNICOL, Malcolm Fraser; s of Rev Robert (Roy) Simson Macnicol (d 1986), of Edinburgh, and Eona Kathleen (d 2002); *b* 18 March 1943; *Educ* Royal HS Edinburgh, Univ of Edinburgh (BSc, MBChB), Stanford Univ CA, Harvard Univ MA, Univ of Western Aust, Univ of Liverpool (MChOrth); *m* 30 Sept 1972, Anne Morag; 1 da (Sarah Anne Marie b 1977), 2 s (Sean Malcolm Fraser b 1979, Calum Alexander Ruaridh b 1983); *Career* conslt orthopaedic surgn, regnl advsr in orthopaedic surgery S E Scot 1995–2002; sr lectr Univ of Edinburgh 1979–2005 (lectr 1976–79); chm Orthopaedic Specialists' Soc, treas Special Advsy Ctee in Orthopaedic Surgery; treas and memb Fin Ctee RCSEd; memb: Shaw Report team, Br Orthopaedic Res Soc, Br Orthopaedic Assoc (pres 2001–02), Br Assoc for Surgery of the Knee, Br Soc for Children's Orthopaedic Surgery, Cncl of Mgmnt and Editorial Bd Jl of Bone and Joint Surgery 1997–2002, Sub-Ctee Provision of Paediatric Surgery in Scotland 1997–99, Cncl British Orthopaedic Assoc 1998–2000 (chm Medicolegal sub ctee 1998–2003); hon med advsr Scottish Rugby Union; FRCSEd, FRCP, FRCS; *Books* Basic Care of The Injured Hand (1984), Aids To Orthopaedics (1984), The Problem Knee (1986, 2 edn 1995), Children's Orthopaedics and Fractures (1994, 2 edn 2002), Colour Atlas and Text of Osteotomy of the Hip (1995); *Recreations* tennis, squash, painting; *Clubs* Scottish Arts, Robert Jones; *Style*— Malcolm Macnicol, Esq; ✉ Red House, 1 South Gillsland Road, Edinburgh EH10 5DE (tel 0131 447 9104, e-mail mmacnicol@aol.com); New Royal Infirmary, Old Dalkeith Road, Edinburgh EH16 (tel 0131 242 3494); Royal Hospital for Sick Children, Sciennes Road, Edinburgh EH9 (tel 0131 536 0831), Murrayfield Hospital, 122 Corstorphine Road, Edinburgh EH12 6UD (tel 0131 334 0363)

McNICOLL, Air Marshal Iain Walter; CB (2006), CBE (2000); s of Walter McNicoll, of Dundee, and Maida Cameron, *née* Readdie (d 1987); *b* 3 May 1953, Dundee; *Educ* Dundee HS, Univ of Edinburgh (BSc); *m* 5 Sept 1980, Wendelien Henriëtte Maria, *née* van den Biggelaar; 2 da (Stephanie Henriëtte b 26 June 1983, Alexandra Frances b 10 April 1986), 1 s (Roderick Walter b 8 April 1989); *Career* cmmnd: RAFVR 1973, RAF 1975; offr and pilot trg 1975–77, Buccaneer S2B-XV Sqdn 1978–81 (qualified weapons instr 1979), Tornado GR1/4–45 (R) Sqdn 1982–85, 17 (Fighter) Sqdn 1985–86, 16 Sqdn 1986–89, RAF Staff Coll 1990, PSO to Dep C-in-C Strike Cmd 1991–92, OC 17 (Fighter) Sqdn 1992–95, MOD 1995–98, Station Cdr RAF Brüggen 1998–2000, Dir Force Devpt 2000–02, DG Jt Doctrine and Concepts 2002–05, AOC 2 Gp 2005–07, Dep C-in-C Ops Air Cmd 2007–; Queen's Medal 1977, QCVSA 1989; FRAeS 2001; *Recreations* golf, sailing, skiing; *Clubs* RAF; *Style*— Air Marshal I W McNicoll; ✉ Headquarters Air Command, Royal Air Force High Wycombe, Buckinghamshire HP14 4UE

McNISH, Althea Marjorie; da of Joseph Claude McNish (d 1964), of Port of Spain, and Margaret Bourne (d 1977); *Educ* Port of Spain (by father and others), London Coll of Printing (NDD (Special), Illustration prize), Central Sch of Art and Crafts, Royal Coll of Art (DesRCA); *m* 20 Aug 1969, John Saul Weiss, s of Woolf Weiss (d 1994), of London; *Career* freelance designer 1957–; exhibitions incl: Inprint 1964–71, Design Cncl USA and Sweden 1969, London 1970 and 1975–80, USA 1972, Design-In (Amsterdam) 1972–74, The Way We Live Now (V&A London) 1978, Indigo Lille 1981–82, Cwlth Festival Art Exhibition (Brisbane) 1982, Textile hangings (Peoples Gallery London) 1982, Textile hangings (Magazine Workspace Leicester) 1983, Designs for British Dress and Furnishing Fabrics (V&A London) 1986, Make or Break (Henry Moore Gallery London) 1986, Surtex NY 1987, Ascher (V&A London) 1987, Caribbean Connection 2: Island Pulse, five Caribbean-born artists (Islington Arts Factory, London) 1996, Paintings and hangings (Hockney Gallery London) 1997, Transforming the Crown: African, Asian and Caribbean Artists in Britain 1966–1996 (Caribbean Cultural Center NY) 1997, Trinidad & Tobago Through the Eye of the Artist: from Cazabon to the Millennium (Commonwealth Inst London) 1997, Gp exhbn (Fine Arts Soc London) 1998, Gp exhbn (198 Gallery London) 1998, Six into One: Artists from the Caribbean (Morley Gallery London) 1998; commissioned by Ascher and Liberty's 1957, designs for mfrs worldwide; visiting lectr: Central Sch of Art and Crafts and other colls, polys and univs (UK, USA, Italy, Germany, Slovenia)1960–; advsy tutor furnishing and surface design London Coll of Furniture 1972–90, external assessor for educnl and professional bodies incl CSD and CNAA 1966–, memb jury for Leverhulme scholarships 1968; judge: Portuguese textile design competition Lisbon 1973, Living Design Awards 1974, Carnival Selection Panels Arts Cncl of GB 1982–83; designer: murals for passenger cruise liner Oriana 1960, murals for hospitals and colls in Trinidad 1960–61, for Govt of Trinidad and Tobago in NY, Washington and London 1962, special features Daily Mail Ideal Home Exhibition 1966–78, for sec gen of the Cwlth 1975, bedlinen collection Courtaulds 1978, for BR Bd 1978–81, for London Office of High Cmmr of Trinidad and Tobago 1981, for Fede Cheti Milan 1987–91, murals and hangings for passenger liners Nordic Empress 1990 and Monarch of The Seas 1991; advsr on exhibition design for Govt of Trinidad and Tobago Cwlth Inst 1982–84; memb: Bd Design Cncl 1974–81, Selection Panels for Design Awards and Design Index 1968–80, Selection Panel Jubilee Souvenir 1976 and Royal Wedding Souvenir 1981, CNAA Fashion and Textiles Design Bd 1975–78, Governing Body Portsmouth Coll of Art 1972–81, London Local Advsy Ctee IBA 1981–90, Formation Ctee ILEA London Inst 1985; CSD: assessor and examiner 1966–, vice-pres 1977–78, memb Cncl and Ctees 1958–; FCSD, FSIA 1968 (MSIA 1960); Chaconia Gold Medal of the Repub of Trinidad and Tobago 1976, Scarlet Ibis Award of the Office of the High Cmmr for the Repub of Trinidad and Tobago London 1993; *Publications* textile designs produced in many countries and published in many jls and books incl: Decorative Art, Studio Books (1960, 1961 and 1962), Designers in Britain (1972), Did Britain Make It, Design Council (1986), Fabrics and Wallpapers (Bell and Hyman, 1986), Ascher (1987), English and American Textile from 1790 to the Present (1989), Fabrics and Wallpapers: Design sources and Inspirations (Ebury Press, 1991), The House of Liberty (Thames and Hudson, 1992), The Caribbean Artists Movement 1966–72 (New Beacon Books, 1992); *Recreations* skiing, travelling, music, gardening; *Clubs* Soroptimist; *Style*— Ms Althea McNish; ✉ 142 West Green Road, London N15 5AD (tel 020 8800 1686, e-mail althea.mcnish@virgin.net)

MACNIVEN, Duncan; TD (1985); *b* 1 December 1950; *Educ* Melville Coll Edinburgh, Univ of Aberdeen (MA, MLitt); *m* 4 Oct 1976, Valerie; 2 da (Rona b 1981, Morag b 1985); *Career* Scottish Office: grad trainee 1973–78, princ 1978–86, asst sec 1986–90, dep dir Historic Scotland 1990–95, head Police Div 1995–97, head Police, Fire and Emergencies Gp 1997–99; cmmr and Head of Corp Services Forestry Cmmn 1999–; with RE (TA) 1969–85 (latterly maj); *Recreations* walking, skiing, cycling, exploring, Scottish history; *Style*— Duncan Macniven, Esq, TD; ✉ Forestry Commission, 231 Corstorphine Road, Edinburgh EH12 7AT (tel 0131 314 6252, fax 0131 314 6526)

McNULTY, Anthony James (Tony); MP; s of James Anthony McNulty, and Eileen Anne, *née* Dawson; *b* 3 November 1958; *Educ* Salvatorian Coll Harrow, Stanmore Sixth Form Coll, Univ of Liverpool (BA), Virginia Poly Inst and State Univ (MA); *Career* princ lectr The Business Sch Univ of North London 1983–97; London Borough of Harrow: cncllr 1986–97, dep ldr (Lab) 1990–96, ldr (Lab) 1996–97; MP (Lab) Harrow E 1997–; PPS at the DFEE 1997–99, asst Govt whip 1999–2001, a Lord Cmmr to HM Treasy (Govt whip) 2001–02; Parly under sec of state: Office of the Dep PM 2002–03, Dept for Tport 2003–05, min of state Home Office 2005–; memb: Fabian Soc, Socialist Educn Assoc; *Recreations* rugby, reading, theatre, films, food, current affrs, history; *Style*— Tony McNulty, Esq, MP; ✉ House of Commons, London SW1A 0AA (tel 020 7219 4108, fax 020 7219 2417, e-mail mcnultyt@parliament.uk)

MacNulty, Christine Avril; da of William Arthur Ralph (d 1975), of Egerton, Lancs, and Marjorie Holland, *née* Hale; *b* 22 April 1945; *Educ* Bolton Sch, Univ of London, George Washington Univ Washington DC; *m* 26 Aug 1972, (William) Kirk MacNulty Jr, s of Brig-Gen William K MacNulty; *Career* systems analyst Plessey Radar Ltd 1967–69, sr memb staff International Research & Technology Corporation 1969–72, ptnr Many Futures 1972–76, conslt Progs Analysis Unit 1976–78, program mangr Europe Strategic Environment Centre SRI International 1978–82, conslt Int Res Inst on Social Change 1982–84, md Taylor Nelson Applied Futures 1984–88, chief exec Applied Futures Ltd 1988–, pres Applied Futures Inc 1993–; lectr: Univ of Bradford, Admin Staff Coll, Ashridge Management Coll, Brunel Univ, The Industrial Soc, Nat Defense Univ, Naval War Coll, Air War Coll, Industrial Coll of the Armed Forces; memb Inst for Transitional Dynamics; FRSA 1989; *Books* Industrial Applications of Technological Forecasting (jtly, 1971), The Future of the UK 2010 (jtly); author of numerous articles on scenario devpt, social change and forecasting; *Recreations* sailing, cooking, philosophy, psychology, comparative mythology; *Style*— Mrs Christine MacNulty; ✉ 4008 North Richmond Street, Arlington, VA 22207, USA (website www.exploit-the-future.com)

M

McNULTY, Dermot Anthony; s of William J McNulty (d 1970), of River Forest, Illinois, USA, and Margaret, *née* Reigh (d 1998); *b* 11 March 1949; *Educ* Marquette Univ USA (BA); *m* 11 June 1977, Paula, *née* Gaber; *Career* PR account dir Burson-Marsteller London 1977–81, sr vice-pres and md Burson-Marsteller Hong Kong 1981–87, exec vice-pres Burson-Marsteller NY 1987–89; exec vice-pres Shandwick North America NY 1989–90; Shandwick International plc: dir of int mktg 1990–91, chief operating offr 1991–94, chief exec 1994–98; with Burson-Marsteller 1998–2001 (pres and chief exec (Europe) 1999–2001), chm McNulty Consulting 2001–; *Recreations* golf, tennis, travel, reading; *Clubs* Naval and Military, Stoke Park, Hurlingham; *Style*— Dermot McNulty, Esq; ✉ McNulty Consulting (fax 001 804 4385982, e-mail mcnulty@clmail.co.uk)

McNULTY, Des; MSP; *b* 28 July 1952; *Educ* St Bede's GS Manchester, Univ of York, Univ of Glasgow; *m*; 2 s; *Career* formerly subject ldr in sociology and head of strategic planning Glasgow Caledonian Univ; Strathclyde cncllr 1990–96, Glasgow City cncllr 1995–99; MSP (Lab) Clydebank and Milngavie 1999–, memb Scottish Parl Corp Body 1999–2001, memb Tport and Environment Ctee 1999–2003, convenor Fin Ctee 2001–02, dep min for Social Justice 2002–03, fin convenor 2003–, convenor Cross Pty Int Devpt Gp; non-exec dir Greater Glasgow Health Bd 1998–99; chair: Glasgow Healthy City Partnership 1996–99, CoSLA task force on Non-elected Public Bodies 1996–99, Glasgow Festival of Architecture and Design 1999; memb Bd Wise Gp; memb: Ct Univ of Glasgow 1994–99, Kemp Cmmn on the Future of the Voluntary Sector in Scotland 1995–97; *Style*— Des McNulty, Esq, MSP; ✉ The Scottish Parliament, Edinburgh EH99 1SP (tel 0131 348 5918); Constituency Office, Clydebank Central Library, Dumbarton Road, Clydebank G81 1XH (tel 0141 952 7711)

McPARTLIN, Ant; *b* 18 November 1975, Newcastle upon Tyne; *Career* actor and presenter; performed with Declan Donnelly, *qv*, as 'Ant & Dec' since 1993; jt winner (with Declan Donnelly): Best Double Act Carling Loaded Awards 2000, People's Choice Comedy Awards 2000, Entertainment Personality of the Year Nat TV Awards 2001, TV Personality of the Year Variety Club Awards 2002, TV Personality of the Year TRIC Awards 2002, Special Recognition Award Nat TV Awards 2002, Most Popular Entertainment Presenter TV Quick Awards 2003, TV Personality Award GQ 2003 and 2004, Best Comedy Duo Loaded Awards 2003; *Television* as actor incl: Byker Grove (as PJ) 1990–93, A Tribute to the Likely Lads 2002; as presenter incl: The Ant & Dec Show 1995 (BAFTA, RTS Award), Ant and Dec Unzipped 1997 (BAFTA), SM:TV Live 1998–2001 (Best Entertainment Prog Children's BAFTAs 2000, Best Children's Show TV Quick Awards 2000 and 2001, Best Children's Entertainment Prog RTS Awards 2000, Best Children's Prog Broadcast Awards 2001, Best Children's Prog Indie Awards 2001, Best Presenters RTS Awards 2001, Kids Award Disney Channel 2001, TV Presenters of the Year RTS Awards 2002), CD:UK 1998–2001 (Best Teen Show TV Hits Awards 2000), Ant and Dec's Secret Camera Show 2000, Friends Like These 2000 (Bronze Rose Montreux Awards 2000), Slap Bang with Ant and Dec 2001, Pop Idol 2001 (Entertainment Prog of the Year TRIC Awards 2002, Best Entertainment Prog BAFTA Awards 2002, Golden Rose Montreaux Awards 2002, Best Entertainment Prog Nat TV Awards 2002), Brit Awards 2001, Party in the Park 2001, Comic Relief: Say Pants to Poverty 2001, Record of the Year 2001 and 2002, Ant & Dec's Saturday Night Takeaway 2002 (Best Entertainment Presenter Nat TV Awards 2002, 2003 and 2004, Best

Entertainment Prog TV Quick Awards 2003 and 2004, Best Entertainment Prog Nat TV Awards 2003 and 2004, People's Choice and Best Comedy Entertainment Performance Comedy Awards 2003, Best Comedy Entertainment Performance and Best Comedy Entertainment Prog Comedy Awards 2004, Best Entertainment Presenter RTS Awards 2005, Best Entertainment Prog Broadcast Awards 2006), I'm a Celebrity, Get Me Out of Here! 2002– (Best Reality Prog TV Quick Awards 2003 and 2004, Lew Grade Award for Entertainment Prog or Series BAFTAs 2005), Pride of Britain Awards 2003, Comic Relief: The Big Hair Do 2003, World Idol 2003, British Comedy Awards 2003 and 2004, Comic Relief: Red Nose Night Live 2005; *Films* incl Love Actually 2003; *Albums* with Declan Donnelly: Psyche 1994, Top Katz 1995, The Cult of Ant & Dec 1997; *Style*— Ant McPartlin; ✉ c/o James Grant Management, Syon Lodge, 201 London Road, Isleworth TW7 5BH (tel 020 8232 4100, fax 020 8232 4101)

McPARTLIN, Sheriff Noel; s of Michael Joseph McPartlin (d 1955), of Galashiels, and Ann, *née* Dunn (d 1978); *b* 25 December 1939; *Educ* Galashiels Acad, Univ of Edinburgh (MA, LLB); *m* 10 July 1965, June Anderson, da of David Anderson Whitehead, of Stirling (d 1961); 3 da (Alison b 1966, Diana b 1967, Julia b 1979), 3 s (Simon b 1970, Guy b 1972, Donald b 1982); *Career* slr 1964–76, advocate 1976; Sheriff: Grampian Highland and Islands at Peterhead and Banff 1983–85, Elgin 1985–2002, Lothian and Borders at Edinburgh 2002; *Recreations* country life; *Style*— Sheriff Noel McPartlin; ✉ Sheriff Court, Edinburgh

McPHAIL, Angus William; s of Peter Bigham McPhail (d 1996), and Sylvia Bridget, *née* Campbell (d 2005); *b* 25 May 1956, Ipswich, Suffolk; *Educ* Abingdon Sch, UC Oxford; *m* 13 Sept 1980, Elizabeth, *née* Hirsch; 2 s (Thomas Lachlan b 20 Oct 1987, William Mungo b 29 May 1989), 1 da (Flora Alison b 30 June 1992); *Career* Overseas Dept Bank of Eng 1978–82, asst mangr Glenalmond Coll 1982–85, head of econs and house master Sedbergh Sch 1985–93, headmaster Strathallan Sch 1993–2000, warden Radley Coll 2000–; govr: Cheltenham Ladies' Coll, Caldicott Sch Slough, Ashdown House, Moulsford Prep Sch; memb HMC; *Recreations* cricket, golf, hill walking, music; *Clubs* Cryptics Cricket, Frilford Heath Golf, West Sussex Golf, East India, Lansdowne; *Style*— Angus McPhail, Esq; ✉ tel 01235 543127, fax 01235 543158, e-mail warden@radley.org.uk

MacPHAIL, Sir Bruce Dugald; kt (1992); s of Dugald Ronald MacPhail; *b* 1 May 1939; *Educ* Haileybury, Balliol Coll Oxford, Harvard Business Sch; *m* 1, 1963, Susan Mary (d 1975), da of late Col T Gregory, MC, TD; 3 s; m 2, 1983, Caroline Ruth Grimston, o da of Capt Tatlock Hubbard, MC, RA, and former w of David Dangar Henry Honywood Curtis-Bennett; *Career* articled Price Waterhouse 1961–65, with Hill Samuel & Co 1967–69; fin dir Sterling Guarantee Trust 1969–74; md: Town & City Properties Ltd 1974–76, Sterling Guarantee Trust 1976–85, P&OSNCo 1985–2003 (dir 1983–2003); govr Royal Ballet Sch 1982–98; Univ of Oxford: tstee Balliol Coll 1991–, chm Cncl of Mgmnt Templeton Coll 1992–95 (memb 1986–), chm Cncl Sch of Mgmnt Studies 1995–2001, Barclay fell Templeton Coll 1995–, chm Business Advsy Forum Saïd Business Sch 2001–; non-exec dir: Chelsfield plc 1999–2004, Intelligent Engineering Ltd 2005–, Chelsfield Ptnrs 2006–, Scarborough Minerals 2006–; life govr and memb Cncl Haileybury 1992–, tstee Sir Jules Thorn Charitable Trust 1994–; FCA; *Style*— Sir Bruce MacPhail; ✉ Thorpe Lubenham Hall, Market Harborough, Leicestershire LE16 9TR

MACPHAIL, Hon Lord Iain Duncan Macphail; s of Malcolm John Macphail (d 1988), of Edinburgh, and Mary Corbett, *née* Duncan (d 1973); *b* 24 January 1938; *Educ* George Watson's Coll, Univ of Edinburgh (MA), Univ of Glasgow (LLB); *m* 1970, Rosslyn Graham Lillias, da of Edward John Campbell Hewitt, TD, of Edinburgh; 1 s (David b 1973), 1 da (Melissa b 1977); *Career* admitted to Faculty of Advocates 1963, practising advocate Scotland 1963–73, extra advocate-depute 1973, QC (Scot) 1990; Sheriff of: Glasgow and Strathkelvin (formerly Lanarkshire) 1973–81, Tayside, Central and Fife at Dunfermline and Alloa 1981–82, Lothian and Borders at Linlithgow 1982–88, Edinburgh 1988–89 and 1995–2002; Sheriff Principal of Lothian and Borders and Sheriff of Chancery 2002–05, senator Coll of Justice 2005–; Faulds fell in law Univ of Glasgow 1963–65, lectr in evidence and procedure Univ of Strathclyde 1968–69 and Univ of Edinburgh 1969–72, Arthur Goodhart prof in legal sci Univ of Cambridge 2001–02; chm Scottish Assoc for the Study of Delinquency 1978–81, cmmr Scottish Law Cmmn 1990–94, chm Sheriff Court Rules Cncl 2003–05, memb Judicial Studies Ctee Scotland 2003–05; cmmr Northern Lighthouse Bd 2002–05; Hon LLD Univ of Edinburgh 1992; FRSE 2005; *Books* The Law of Evidence of Scotland (1979), Evidence (1987), Sheriff Court Practice (1988); *Clubs* New (Edinburgh); *Style*— The Hon Lord Macphail, FRSE; ✉ Parliament House, 11 Parliament Square, Edinburgh EH1 1RQ

MacPHAIL, Ian Angus Shaw; s of Robert Shaw MacPhail (d 1938), and Edith Hadden (d 1968); *b* 11 March 1922; *Educ* Grays Sch of Art Aberdeen (Dip Graphic Design); *m* 1, 1943 (m dis 1948), Armorel Davie; 1 da (Diana); m 2, 12 March 1951, Michal Hambourg, da of Mark Hambourg; 1 s (Robert); *Career* RAF 1940–43; asst music controller ENSA 1944–46, asst music dir Arts Cncl 1946–52, publicity dir Dexion Ltd 1952–58, dir Greenway Advsy Serv 1958–60, PR conslt Brewers' Soc 1960–61, DG World Wildlife Fund (UK) 1961–67, chief info offr Arthur Guinness Son & Co Ltd (conslt in communications) 1968–79; Euro co-ordinator Int Fund for Animal Welfare 1976–92, chm Young People's Tst for Nature Conservation 1990–96, govr Brathay Hall Tst; hon PR advsr: Fauna Preservation Soc, Nat Assoc for Gifted Children; former chm PR Ctee Royal Soc for the Prevention of Accidents; ed: You and the Theatre, You and the Opera, English Music 1200–1750, Dexion Angle, Good Company, World Wildlife News; lectr to: publicity and Rotary clubs, schs, tech colls, univs, HM prisons and borstals, women's socs; graphic designer (responsible for prodn supervision of publicity): eight coronation concerts at the Royal Festival Hall, third congress Int Assoc of Gerontology, jt metallurgical socs meeting in Europe, house style and literature World Wildlife Fund, first World Conf on Gifted Children; MSIA, FIPR 1970; Friend of Peru 1997; Orden den Sol Cdr (Order of the Sun Peru) 1985, Knight Order of the Gold Ark (Netherlands); *Books* You and the Orchestra (1948), Birdlife of Britain and Europe (1977); *Recreations* ornithology, music, poetry; *Clubs* Savile, Wig and Pen; *Style*— Ian MacPhail, Esq

McPHEE, George McBeth; MBE; s of late George Hugh McPhee, and of late Daisy, *née* Clyne; *b* 10 November 1937; *Educ* Woodside Sch, Royal Scot Acad of Music, Univ of Edinburgh (BMus); *m* 22 July 1961, Margaret Ann, da of Robert Scotland (d 1951); 1 s (Colin b 1964), 2 da (Catriona b 1966, Susan b 1969); *Career* asst organist St Giles' Cathedral Edinburgh 1959–63, dir of music Paisley Abbey 1963–, lectr in music Royal Scot Acad of Music and Drama 1963–2000, visiting prof of organ St Andrews Univ; numerous performances, recordings, broadcasts and appearances; special commissioner Royal Sch of Church Music, adjudicator/examiner Assoc Bd Royal Schs of Music, chm Paisley Int Organ Festival; pres Incorporated Society of Musicians 1999–2000, vice-pres RCO 2005–; Hon Doctorate Univ of Paisley 1997; memb ISM 1965, hon fell Royal Sch of Church Music 1991; *Recreations* golf; *Clubs* Royal Troon Golf; *Style*— George McPhee, Esq, MBE; ✉ 17 Main Road, Castlehead, Paisley PA2 6AJ (tel 0141 889 3528, e-mail profmcphee@aol.com)

MACPHERSON, Angus John; s of Lt Archibald Norman Macpherson, RN, of Itchen Abbas, Hants, and Joan Margaret, *née* Backhouse; *b* 17 March 1953; *Educ* Stowe, Pembroke Coll Cambridge (MA); *m* 14 Aug 1982, Anne Louise Felicity, da of Capt Edward Morton Barford, of Godalming, Surrey; 2 da (Eloise Isobel b 5 Jan 1985, Myrtle Maud b 30 Jan 1991), 1 s (William Archibald b 19 March 1988); *Career* called to the Bar Inner Temple 1977, in practice SE circuit; *Recreations* tennis, Scottish history, cooking; *Clubs* Lansdowne; *Style*— Angus Macpherson, Esq; ✉ Orchard House, Longwood, Owslebury, Winchester, Hampshire SO21 1LB; 1 Temple Gardens, Temple, London EC4Y 9BB (tel 020 7583 1315, e-mail angusmacpherson@1templegardens.co.uk)

MACPHERSON, Donald Charles; s of Donald Hugh Macpherson (d 1947), and Hilda Mary, *née* Pulley (d 1952); *b* 3 January 1932; *Educ* Winchester; *m* 3 May 1962, Hilary Claire, da of Lt-Col Norman Standish, MBE (d 1988), of Port Elizabeth, SA; *Career* Nat Serv 2 Lt Black Watch 1950–52; mangr Thomson & Balfour Ltd 1952–57, sr ptnr Fielding Newson Smith & Co 1985 (joined 1957, ptnr 1961), md County NatWest Ltd 1989– (exec dir 1986–89); *Recreations* collecting, ballet, opera; *Style*— Donald Macpherson, Esq; ✉ 28 Campden Hill Square, London W8 7JY; Audrey House, Ely Place, London EC1N 6SN (tel 020 7242 1140, fax 020 7242 3965, e-mail donald.macpherson@dsl.pipex.com)

MACPHERSON, Ewen Cameron Stewart; s of G P S Macpherson (d 1981), and Elizabeth Margaret Cameron, *née* Smail (d 2004); *b* 19 January 1942; *Educ* Fettes, Queens' Coll Cambridge (MA), London Business Sch (MSc, Alumni Achievement Award 1997); *m* 1982, Laura Anne, da of 5 Baron Northbrook (d 1991); 2 s (James b 25 Oct 1983, George b 27 Nov 1985); *Career* rep Massey-Ferguson (Export) Ltd 1964–68, various appointments ICFC (now 3i Group plc) from 1970; 3i Group plc: memb Exec Ctee 1985–97, fin dir 1990–92, chief exec 1992–97 (ret); chm Glynwed International plc 1998–2000, chm Merrill-Lynch New Energy Technology plc 2000–; non-exec dir: Scottish Power plc 1996–2003, M & G Group plc 1996–99, Foreign & Colonial Investment Trust plc 1997–, Booker plc 1997–2000, Law Debenture Corporation plc 1998–2000, Pantheon International Participations plc 1998–2004 (chm 2003–04), Sussex Place Investment Management Ltd 1999–2002, Wm Grant & Sons Ltd 2005–; tstee Glaxo Wellcome Pension Fund 1997–2005 (chm 2000–05); govr NIESR 1993–; tstee Natural History Museum Devpt Tst 1998–2000, memb Devpt Bd London Business Sch 1998–99; hon fell Queens' Coll Cambridge 1996; *Recreations* gardening, sailing, classic motor cars; *Clubs* City of London, Caledonian, Royal Lymington Yacht; *Style*— Ewen Macpherson, Esq; ✉ Aston Sandford, Buckinghamshire HP17 8LP (tel and fax 01844 292576)

McPHERSON, Ian Andrew; s of Ian Douglas McPherson (d 1976), of Preston, Lancs, and Mary Elizabeth, *née* Simpson; *b* 25 March 1961, Preston, Lancs; *Educ* Univ of Central Lancs (MBA), Fitzwilliam Coll Cambridge (Dip); *m* 1 April 1984, Wendy Jayne, *née* Spence; 1 s (Jack Alexander b 23 Aug 1992), 1 da (Olivia Jayne b 17 May 1995); *Career* Lancs Constabulary: joined 1979, various detective and uniform roles, chief supt in cmd of Pennine Div 1999–2001; asst chief constable Merseyside Police: Operational Policing 2001–05, Force Modernisation 2005; dep chief constable N Yorks Police 2005–06, chief constable Norfolk Constabulary 2006–; Queen's Jubilee Medal, Queen's Long Service and Good Conduct Medal 2001; memb ACPO 2001; *Recreations* walking, reading, rugby; *Style*— Ian McPherson, Esq; ✉ Chief Constable's Office, Norfolk Constabulary, Jubilee House, Falconers Chase, Wymondham, Norfolk NR18 0WW (tel 01953 424210, e-mail mcphersonia@norfolk.pnn.police.uk)

MACPHERSON, Prof Ian Richard; s of George Macpherson (d 1974), of Aberdeen, and Violet Alice, *née* Warwick (d 1974); *b* 4 January 1934; *Educ* Aberdeen GS, Univ of Aberdeen (MA), Univ of Manchester (PhD); *m* 7 Aug 1959, Sheila Constance, da of Capt John Turner (d 1949), of Heaton Mersey; 2 s (David John b 21 Feb 1962, Peter Jeremy b 24 Jan 1964); *Career* temp lectr Univ of Manchester 1959–60, lectr Univ of Wales at Aberystwyth 1960–64; Univ of Durham: lectr 1964–72, sr lectr 1972–75, reader 1975–80, prof of Spanish 1980–93, emeritus prof 1993–; Queen Mary Univ of London: hon res fell 1993–; visiting prof Univ of Wisconsin Madison 1970–71; pres: Assoc of Hispanists of GB and I 1986–88, Br-Spanish Mixed Cmmn 1986–90; hon fell The Hispanic Soc of America 2001–, Socio de honor Asociación Hispánica de Literatura Medieval 1995–; Comendador de la Orden de Isabel la Católica (Spain) 1986; *Books* Juan Manuel - Libro de los estados (with R B Tate, OUP 1974, Castalia 1991), Spanish Phonology: Descriptive and Historical (1975), Juan Manuel Studies (1975), The Manueline Succession: The Poetry of Don Juan Manuel II and Dom Joao Manuel (1979), Juan Manuel: A Selection (1980), Federico Garcia Lorca: Yerma (with Jacqueline Minett, 1987), The Age of the Catholic Monarchs 1474–1516: Literary Studies in Memory of Keith Whinnom (with Alan Deyermond, 1989), The Medieval Mind (with Ralph Penny, 1997), The invenciones y letras of the Cancionero General (1997), Love, Religion and Politics in Fifteenth-century Spain (with Angus MacKay, 1998), Motes y glosas in the Cancionero General (2004); *Recreations* books, tennis, Europe; *Style*— Prof Ian Macpherson; ✉ Department of Hispanic Studies, Queen Mary, University of London, London E1 4NS (tel 01280 847174, fax 0870 124 2262, e-mail ianmac2006@tiscali.co.uk)

MACPHERSON, Ishbel Jean Stewart; da of Sir Thomas Macpherson of Biallid, CBE, MC, TD, DL, *qv*, and Jean, *née* Butler Wilson; *b* 16 July 1960, London; *Educ* French Lycée, Wycombe Abbey, Fettes, Univ of Edinburgh (MA); *Career* grad trainee rising to dir of corp fin Barclays de Zoete Wedd 1983–94, head of smaller companies corp fin Hoare Govett Ltd 1994–99, head of UK mid market corp fin Dresdner Kleinwort Wasserstein 1999–2005; non-exec dir: MITIE Group plc 2005–, GAME Group plc 2005–, Hydrogen Gp plc; govr Univ of Westminster 2000–; *Recreations* riding, walking, having fun; *Style*— Miss Ishbel Macpherson; ✉ West Bradfield House, Bradfield, Devon EX15 2QY (tel 01884 839875, e-mail email@ishbelmacpherson.co.uk)

McPHERSON, James Alexander Strachan; CBE (1982), JP (Aberdeenshire); s of Peter John McPherson (d 1953), and Jeannie Geddie, *née* Strachan (d 1969); *Educ* Banff Acad, Univ of Aberdeen (MA, BL, LLB); *m* 4 Aug 1960, Helen Marjorie, da of Capt Jack Perks, CBE, DSC, DL, RN (d 1973), of Kibworth, Beauchamp, Leics; 1 s (Ewan John b 1961), 1 da (Lesley Anne b 1963); *Career* Nat Serv cmmnd Lt RA 1952–54; slr Alexander George & Co Macduff, Banff & Buckie 1954–99, memb Macduff Town Cncl and Banff CC 1958–75, convener Banff CC 1970–75, provost of Macduff 1972–75, chm Public Protection Ctee Grampian Regnl Cncl 1974–86 (memb Cncl 1974–90); Lord-Lt of Banffshire 1987–2002, Hon Sheriff Grampian Highland and Islands at Banff 1972–; pres Banffshire Soc of Slrs 1977–80, vice-pres Scottish Highland Reserve Forces and Cadet's Assoc TAVRA 1987–2002; govr Scottish Police Coll 1974–86; dir: Banffshire Partnership, NE Scotland Preservation Tst, Deveron Care Servs; chm: Banff and Buchan JP Advsy Ctee 1987–98, Aberdeenshire JP Advsy Ctee 1998–2002; vice-chm Banff Preservation & Heritage Soc; fndr pres Talking Banffie and Turra Talk (talking newspaper for blind in NE Scotland); memb: Grampian Health Bd 1974–82, Police Advsy Bd for S 1974–86, Post Office Users' Nat Cncl for Scot 1976–80, Scottish Slr's Discipline Tbnl 1990–95, Ct Univ of Aberdeen 1993–97; elder and FWO treas Macduff Parish Church; FSA Scot 1974; *Recreations* reading, local history, swimming; *Clubs* Town and County (Banff), Duff House Royal Golf, Royal Northern & Univ (Aberdeen); *Style*— James McPherson, Esq, CBE, FSA; ✉ Dunalastair, Macduff, Banffshire AB44 1XD (tel 01261 832377, fax 01261 832350)

McPHERSON, Prof Klim; s of Anthony Willcock (ka 1943), of Albrighton, Shropshire, and Barbara, *née* Robinson (d 1959); *b* 17 September 1941, St Helens, Lancs; *Educ* Univ of Cambridge (MA), LSHTM (PhD); *m* 17 May 1968, Ann, *née* Egelnick; 1 s (Sam b 16 Sept 1969), 2 da (Tess b 12 April 1972, Beth b 2 Nov 1975); *Career* researcher LSHTM 1966–69, MRC scientific staff Clinical Research Centre Northwick Park 1969–73 and 1974–76, instr Dept of Community Medicine Harvard Medical Sch 1973–74, lectr Dept of Community Medicine Univ of Oxford and fell Nuffield Coll Oxford 1976–90; LSHTM: prof of public health epidemiology and head Health Promotion Unit 1991–1996, Cancer and Public Health Unit 1997–2001; prof of public health epidemiology MRC Health Services Research Unit Univ of Bristol 2001–03, visiting prof of public health epidemiology Dept of Obstetrics and Gynaecology Univ of Oxford and fell New Coll Oxford 2003–06; pres European Public Health Assoc 1996; past chair: British Breast Gp,

European Public Health Assoc, Soc for Social Medicine; memb: Ctee Safety of Medicines, MHRA Ctee on Women's Health, Public Health Interventions Advsy Ctee; author of articles in over 400 pubns on epidemiology, public health and women's health; FMedSci 1997, FFPH 2001; *Recreations* tennis, walking; *Style*— Prof Klim McPherson; ✉ 25 Norham Road, Oxford OX2 6SF (tel 01865 558743); New College, Oxford OX1 3BN (e-mail klim.mcpherson@new.ox.ac.uk); John Radcliffe Hospital, Oxford OX3 9DU (tel 01865 740885, e-mail klim.mcpherson@obs-gyn.ox.ac.uk)

MACPHERSON, Nicholas Ian; s of Ewen Macpherson, of Attadale, Scotland, and Nicolette, *née* van der Bijl; *b* 14 July 1959; *Educ* Eton, Balliol Coll Oxford, UCL; *m* 1983, Suky, *née* Appleby; 2 s; *Career* econ CBI 1982–83, econ Peat Marwick Mitchell 1983–85; HM Treasury: joined 1985, princ private sec to Chllr of the Exchequer 1993–97, head Work Incentives Policy 1997–98, dir (welfare reform) Budget and Public Fin Directorate 1998–2001, md Public Services Directorate 2001–04, md Budget and Public Finance Directorate 2004–05, perm sec HM Treasy 2005–; memb Civil Service Mgmnt Bd 2001–04; non-exec dir HM Revenue and Customs 2005–; visiting fell Nuffield Coll Oxford 2006–; *Style*— Nicholas Macpherson, Esq; ✉ HM Treasury, 1 Parliament Street, London SW1P 3AG (tel 020 7270 5939, fax 020 7270 5148, e-mail nicholas.macpherson@hm-treasury.gov.uk)

MACPHERSON, (Philip) Strone Stewart; s of G P S Macpherson, CBE, TD (d 1981), and Elizabeth Cameron, *née* Smail; *b* 21 July 1948; *Educ* Summer Fields Oxford, Fettes, Oriel Coll Oxford (MA), INSEAD (MBA); *m* 1981, Alexandra Grace, da of 5 Baron Northbrook, JP, DL (d 1991); 1 s (Philip Strone Alexander Stewart b 18 April 1984), 2 da (Temora Anne Stewart b 24 Jan 1988, Clementina Grace Stewart b 24 Sept 1989); *Career* trainee Bankers Tsts Co 1970–71, L Messel & Co stockbrokers 1971–74; Robert Fleming & Co Ltd: joined 1975, dir 1978–89, pres Robert Fleming Inc New York 1982–84; non-exec dir: Research Machines plc 1990–94, River and Mercantile Investment Mgmnt 1993–96, River and Mercantile Tsts plc 1979–96, Fleming Smaller Cos Investment Tsts 1990–, AXA UK plc 1999–, Investment and Audit Ctee Kings Fund 1999–, British Empire Securities and General Tst plc 2002–, Close Brothers Group plc 2003–, Kleinwort Benson Private Bank 2003–; Misys plc: non-exec dir 1989–91, exec dep chm 1991–2002, chm Misys Charitable Fndn 1999–; chm Tribal Gp plc 2004–; tstee Oriel Coll: Devpt Tsts 1981–, Investment Ctee 2001–; *Recreations* country pursuits, Scottish art, restoration of early motor cars; *Clubs* Caledonian; *Style*— Strone Macpherson, Esq; ✉ Armsworth Park House, Old Alresford, Hampshire SO24 9RH (tel 01962 735562)

MACPHERSON, Tim John; s of Charles Jaffrey Macpherson, of Kingsbridge, S Devon, and Barbera, *née* Pratt; *b* 11 September 1962; *Educ* Kingsbridge Comp Sch, Kingsbridge Sixth Form Coll, S Devon Art Coll; *m* 29 May 1993, Lesley Ann, da of David Waters; 1 s (Isaac Jaffrey b 16 Nov 1996); *Career* asst photographer Prudence Cuming Associates fine art photographers Dover St London 1983–89, asst to Ben Rice people photographer London 1989–90, freelance asst photographer 1990–92 (worked with Jillian Edelstein, Dave Gamble, Frank Herholdt, Duncan McNicol, Bob Miller and Michael Joseph), photographer 1992–; editorial cmmns incl: Sunday Times, Observer, ES and GQ Magazines, Sunday Telegraph; other assignments for indust, design and advtg; memb Assoc of Photographers; *Exhibitions* Icons, Idols & Heroes 1992 and Portrait 1994 (Association Gallery), National Portrait Gallery; *Awards* Individual Image & Portfolio award Assoc of Photographers Assistants Awards 1991, Individual Image Silver medal RPS 135th Int Print Exhbn 1991, represented Britain at Kodak Euro Panorama of Young Photography Arles France 1992, winner Individual Image Assoc of Photographers Eleventh Awards 1993, American Communication Arts Award 1995 and 1997, winner of Individual Image Assoc of Photographers Fourteenth Awards 1997; *Recreations* travel, photography; *Style*— Tim MacPherson, Esq

MACPHERSON-FLETCHER OF BALAVIL, Allan William; s of Rev John Fletcher (d 1990), of Edinburgh, and Elizabeth, *née* Stoddart (d 1966); nephew of Mrs H E Brewster-Macpherson of Balavil (d 1990); assumed additional surname of Macpherson 1990; *b* 27 July 1950; *Educ* Trinity Coll Glenalmond, Univ of Aberdeen (BSc); *m* 30 Oct 1976, Marjorie, da of George Daniel (d 1984), of Aberdeen; 1 s (James b 1979), 1 da (Elizabeth-Anne b 1978), 3 step s (Antony Sherlock b 1965, Michael Sherlock b 1966, Nicholas Sherlock b 1973); *Career* mangr McLaren Marine Queensland Aust 1973–75, proprietor Balavil Estate 1975–, dir Badenoch Land Management Ltd 1975–, mangr Bell-Ingram Sporting Dept 1987–89, sporting estate conslt Hamptons 1989–95 (dir E Midlands, Northern and Scottish region), Highland conslt Strutt and Parker 1996–; dir and govr Butterstone School Holdings Ltd 1988–93, ed Scottish and African Sporting Gazettes 1996–98, chm Highland Vernacular Bldgs Tst, pres Kingussie Sheep Dog Trial Assoc; memb Brenchley Vineyards Carriage Driving Team World Championships Poland 1995, Br nat champions Windsor 1995; memb: Northern Meeting Soc, Scottish Landowners' Fedn, Game Conservancy, the Highland Soc of London; *Recreations* shooting, stalking, fishing, skiing, diving, travel, wine; *Clubs* The Highland; *Style*— Macpherson-Fletcher of Balavil; ✉ Balavil, Kingussie, Inverness-shire (tel 01540 661413, fax 01540 662021, e-mail balavil@aol.com); 13 Sandend, Portsoy, Banffshire

MACPHERSON OF BIALLID, Sir (Ronald) Thomas Stewart; kt (1992), CBE (1967), MC (1943, and 2 Bars 1944 and 1945), TD (1960), DL (Gtr London 1972); 5 s of Sir (Thomas) Stewart Macpherson, CIE (d 1949), of Newtonmore, Inverness-shire, and Helen (d 1976), er da of Rev Archibald Borland Cameron, of Edinburgh; bro of 1 Baron Drumalbyn; cous of 15 Earl of Kinnoull and 2 Baron Strathcarron; *b* 4 October 1920; *Educ* Cargilfield, Fettes, Trinity Coll Oxford (MA, Athletics blue); *m* 1953, Jean Henrietta, yst da of David Butler-Wilson, of Alderley Edge, Cheshire; 2 s, 1 da (Ishbel, *qv*); *Career* cmmnd Queen's Own Cameron Highlanders 1939; served WWII: Scot Commando, parachutist (POW 1941–43), Maj 1943 (despatches); dir: Boustead plc 1986– (chm), Annington Holdings plc 1996– (chm), Entuity Ltd 2000– (chm), Nexus Investments Ltd 2001– (chm), XchangePoint Ltd 2001–05 (chm), Deutsche Annington Immobilien GmbH 2001–; advsr Advsy Cncl Terra Firma Capital Partners 2001–, chm European Advsy Bd Kenbay Inc 2006–; former dir: Mallinson-Denny plc 1948–82 (chm and md), Transglobe Expedition Ltd 1976–83, Brooke Bond Gp 1981–82, Birmid Qualcast plc 1982–88 (chm), Scottish Mutual Assurance Soc 1982–91, National Coal Board 1983–86, C H Industrials plc 1983–91, Cosmopolitan Textile Co Ltd 1983–91 (chm), Employment Conditions Abroad Ltd 1983–93 (chm), Allstate Reinsurance Co Ltd 1983–96 (chm), Webb-Bowen International Ltd 1984–94 (chm), Karablue Ltd 1985–96 (chm), Kymmene UK Holdings plc 1985–96, English Architectural Glazing Ltd 1985–99 (chm), TSB Scotland 1986–91, New Scotland Insurance 1986–93, Caledonian Paper plc 1987–96, Owl Creek Investments plc 1989–91 (chm), Keller Gp plc 1990–99 (dep chm), Global Satellite Communications (Scotland) plc 1991–92, Truswal Timber UK Ltd 1991–93, Societe Generale Merchant Bank plc 1991–93, Internet Network Services Ltd 1995–99 (chm), Wineworld London plc 1995–2000 (chm), Architectural Glazing (Scotland) Ltd 1998–99; memb Advsy Bd Bain & Co Inc UK 1987–99, advsr Candover plc 1989–94; chm: London C of C 1980–82, Br C of C 1986–88; fndr chm Nat Employers Liaison Ctee for Vol Res Forces 1986–92; memb: Cncl CBI (past memb DG's City Advsy Gp, past chm London SE Region), Scottish Cncl Devpt and Industry (London), Bd Strathclyde Univ Business Sch 1980–85, Ctee Invisible Exports 1982–85; pres: Achilles Club 1991–, Friends of Scottish Rugby 2000–, Commando Assoc 2000–05, Highland Soc of London 2001–05, Royal Scottish Corp 2003–; hon pres Assoc Euro C of C (pres 1992–94), vice-patron Prince of Wales Reserve Forces Ulysses Tst, fndn tstee Acad of Euro Law Germany 1994–; govr Fettes Coll 1984–92; High Sheriff Gtr London 1983–84; memb: Queen's Body Guard for Scotland (Royal Co of Archers), Worshipful Co of Dyers (Prime Warden 1985–86), Ct of Assts Worshipful Co of Carpenters; FRSA, FIMgt; Chevalier de la Legion d'Honneur, Croix de Guerre (2 Palms and Star); *Recreations* fishing, shooting, outdoor sport (former Univ of Oxford and London Scot rugby player, Univ of Oxford and Mid-Surrey hockey player and Scot int athlete); *Clubs* New (Edinburgh), Hurlingham, MCC; *Style*— Sir Thomas Macpherson of Biallid, CBE, MC, TD, DL; ✉ 27 Archery Close, London W2 2BE (tel 020 7262 8487); Craigdhu, Newtonmore, Inverness-shire PH20 1BS (tel 01528 544200, fax 01528 544274)

MACPHERSON OF DRUMOCHTER, 2 Baron (UK 1951); (James) Gordon Macpherson; JP (Essex 1961); s of 1 Baron (d 1965), and Lucy (d 1984), da of Arthur Butcher; *b* 22 January 1924; *Educ* Wells House Malvern, Loretto; *m* 1, 1947, (Dorothy) Ruth (d 1974), da of late Rev Henry Coulter, of Bellahouston, Glasgow; 1 s (decd), 2 da; m 2, 1975, Catherine Bridget, only da of Dr Desmond MacCarthy (d 2001), of Brentwood, Essex; 1 s, 2 da; *Heir* s, Hon James Macpherson; *Career* served with RAF 1941–46; chm: Godron Macrobin (Insurance) Ltd, A J Macpherson & Co (Bankers); chm and md Macpherson Train & Co Ltd (Food & Produce Importers and Exporters); memb: Cncl of London C of C 1958, Exec Ctee of W India Ctee 1959 (dep chm 1971, chm 1973), Cncl E Euro Trade Cncl 1969–72; fndr chm and patron Br Importers Confedn 1972–; life managing govr Royal Scottish Corp; chief Scottish Clans Assoc London 1972–74; memb Essex Magistrates' Courts Ctee 1974–75, dep chm Brentwood Bench 1972; govr Brentwood Sch 1970–75; hon game warden for the Sudan 1974; Freeman: City of London 1969, Worshipful Co of Butchers 1969; landowner (grouse, deer and salmon, with farming); FRES, FZS, FRSA; *Recreations* shooting, fishing, gardening; *Clubs* Boodle's; *Style*— The Rt Hon the Lord Macpherson of Drumochter; ✉ Kyllachy, Tomatin, Inverness-shire IV13 7YA (tel 01808 511212, fax 01808 511469)

MACPHERSON OF PITMAIN, (Michael) Alastair Fox; 17 Sr Chieftain of the Clan Macpherson; s of Stephen Marriott Fox (d 1971), of Surrey, and Margaret Gertude Macpherson of Pitmain; *b* 17 December 1944; *Educ* Haileybury, Magdalene Coll Cambridge (MA); *m* 10 June 1972, Penelope Margaret, da of Frederick William Birkmyre Harper (d 1977), of Oxon; 1 da (Isabella b 3 July 1973), 2 s (Alexander b 5 Feb 1976, Charles b 8 May 1980); *Heir* s, Alexander Macpherson, yr of Pitmain; *Career* admitted slr 1971; ptnr Ashurst Morris Crisp slrs 1974–2003, managing ptnr Ashurst Morris Crisp NY 2000–02; chm Maelor plc 1998–2006; non-exec dir: Smith & Nephew plc 1986–97, Johnson Fry plc 1987–89, Thomas Jourdan plc 1987–97; memb: Cncl White Ensign Assoc 1995–, Transatlantic Cncl of BritishAmerican Business Inc 2001–02; chm Clan Macpherson Assoc 1997–2000, memb Ctee of Mgmnt Highland Soc of London 2005–; memb Cncl: Nat Tst for Scotland 2004– (also London rep 2004–), Nat Tst 2005–; *Recreations* golf, shooting, rhododendrons; *Clubs* Boodle's, Royal St George's, Hurlingham, MCC (memb Membership Ctee 2004–); *Style*— Alastair Macpherson of Pitmain, Esq; ✉ Manningford Bruce House, Pewsey, Wiltshire SN9 6JW (tel 01980 635482, e-mail mafmacpherson@aol.com); Achara House, Duror of Appin, Argyll PA38 4BW (tel 01631 740262)

McQUAID, Dr James; CB (1997); s of James McQuaid (d 1981), and Brigid, *née* McDonnell (d 1988); *b* 5 November 1939; *Educ* Christian Brothers' Sch Dundalk, Univ Coll Dublin (BEng), Jesus Coll Cambridge (PhD), Nat Univ of Ireland (DSc); *m* 17 Feb 1968, Catherine Anne, da of Dr James John Hargan (d 1988), of Rotherham; 2 s (James Benedict b 1968, Martin Hargan b 1971), 1 da (Fiona Catherine b 1969); *Career* graduate engr apprentice Br Nylon Spinners Ltd 1961–63; Safety in Mines Res Estab: sr res fell 1966–68, sr sci offr 1968–72, princ sci offr 1972–78; dir Safety Engrg Laboratory 1980–85 (dep dir 1978–80), res dir Health and Safety Exec 1985–92, dir Strategy and Gen Div and chief scientist 1992–96, dir Science and Technology and chief scientist 1996–99; visiting prof: Univ of Sheffield 1997–, Univ of Ulster 1999–; memb Bd of Govrs EC Jt Research Centre 2001–07; memb Environmental Security Panel NATO 2005–; Hon DEng Sheffield; CEng, MIMechE 1972, FIMinE 1986, FREng 1991, FRSA 2000, FIEI 2000, FIAcadE 2002; *Recreations* model engineering, ornamental turning, industrial archaeology; *Clubs* Athenaeum; *Style*— Dr James McQuaid, CB, FREng; ✉ 61 Pingle Road, Sheffield S7 2LL (tel 0114 236 5349)

McQUARRIE, Sir Albert; kt (1987); s of Algernon Stewart McQuarrie (d 1955), and Alice Maud Sharman (d 1961); *b* 1 January 1918; *Educ* Highlanders Acad Greenock, Greenock HS, Royal Coll of Sci and Technol Univ of Strathclyde (MSE, PEng 1945); *m* 1, 1945, Roseleen McCaffery (d 1986); 1 s (Dermot Hugh Hastings, vice-pres/exec prodr TV); m 2, 1989, Rhoda Annie Gall; *Career* served in HM Forces 1939–45, Offr RE; chm: A McQuarrie & Son (Great Britain) Ltd 1946–88, Sir Albert McQuarrie & Associates Ltd 1988–, St George Ltd 2007–; dir: Hunterston Development Co 1989–, British American Corporation 1991–; planning conslt in private and public sector; vice-chm Clan McQuarrie Assoc 1980–; former Dean of Guild Gourock Town Cncl, chm Fyvie/Rothienorman/Monquitter Community Cncl 1975–79; Parly candidate (Cons): Kilmarnock 1966, Caithness and Sutherland 1974, E Aberdeenshire 1979, Banff and Buchan 1983; Euro Parly candidate Highlands and Islands 1989; MP (Cons): Aberdeenshire E 1979–83, Banff and Buchan 1983–87; chm Br/Gibraltar All Pty Gp 1979–87, vice-chm Cons Fisheries Sub Ctee 1979–87; sec: Scottish Cons Back Bench Ctee 1985–87, Scotch Whisky All Pty Gp 1979–87; memb Speaker's Panel of Chairmen 1986–87; memb Select Ctees: on Scottish Affrs 1979–83, on Agriculture 1983–85, on Private Bill Procedure 1987; memb Cncl Soc of Engrs 1978–87; chm Cunningham South Cons Assoc 1991–92, vice-chm Ayr Cons Assoc 1992–96, vice-chm Mintlaw Community Cncl 1999–; hon memb Cwlth Parly Assoc, hon vice-pres Gibraltar Assoc of Euro Rights 1996–; hon pres: Banff and Buchan Cons and Unionist Assoc 1989–, Gourock Hort Soc 1993– (hon vice-pres 1954–93); patron Ardgowan Hospice Greenock; FRSH 1952; Freeman City of Gibraltar 1982; GCSJ 2000 (KSJ 1991), CMSJ 2000; Sovereign Order of St John of Jerusalem Knights Hospitaller: elected Prior of Scotland 1999, elected Grand Prior of UK and Eire 1999, Grand Prior of Europe and Conventual Bailiff 2002; Knight Companionate of Merit Military and Hospitaller Order of St Lazarus of Jerusalem 2007; *Recreations* golf, bridge, music, soccer, swimming, horticulture; *Clubs* Lansdowne, Queens San Francisco; *Style*— Sir Albert McQuarrie; ✉ Kintara House, Newton Road, Mintlaw, Aberdeenshire AB42 5EF (tel 01771 623955, fax 01771 623956)

McQUAY, Elizabeth; da of Thomas Alexander Ireland McQuay (d 1997), and Margaret Doreen, *née* Currie (d 1997); *b* 29 August 1953, Blackburn; *Educ* Harrogate Ladies Coll, LSE (BA), Coll of Law Chester; *m* 14 Sept 1979, Martin Kersh; 1 da (Georgia b 5 July 1990), 1 s (Freddie b 1 Oct 1994); *Career* admitted slr 1979; slr specialising in matrimonial law; trainee slr Forsyte Kerman 1977–79, registrar Attorney-Gen's Office Nairobi 1979–80, ptnr Gordon Dadds 1980–88, ptnr Winward Fearon 1988–93, sole practitioner 1993–; accredited mediator Family Mediators Assoc; memb: Law Soc, Slrs Family Law Assoc (memb Ctee 1988, memb London Regnl Ctee 1992); *Recreations* tennis; *Style*— Miss Elizabeth McQuay; ✉ The Old Rectory, Bletchingdon, Oxfordshire OX5 3DH (tel 01869 351229, fax 01869 350231, e-mail law@elizabethmcquay.co.uk)

McQUAY, Prof Henry; *b* 16 September 1948; *Educ* Sedbergh, Balliol Coll Oxford; *Career* prof of pain relief Univ of Oxford 1985–; fell Balliol Coll Oxford; FRCPEd 2002; *Publications* Bandolier (print and Internet jl), Bandolier's Little Book of Pain (jtly, 2003); *Style*— Prof Henry McQuay; ✉ Pain Relief Unit, Churchill Hospital, Old Road, Headington, Oxford OX3 7LE (tel 01865 226161)

McQUEEN, Alexander; CBE (2003); *b* London; *Educ* St Martin's Sch of Art (MA 1992); *Career* fashion designer; successive appts with: Anderson and Shepherd (Saville Row tailors), Gieves and Hawkes (Saville Row), Angels and Bermans (theatrical costumiers),

M

Koji Tatsuno (Japanese designer), Romeo Gigli Milan; estab own label 1992–; men's and ladies' collections retailed worldwide incl London, NY, Paris, Japan and Milan; chief designer Givenchy 1996–2001; numerous private clients; subject of documentary The Works (BBC) 1997; *Collections* incl: Taxi Driver 1993, Nihilism 1993, Banshee 1994, The Birds 1994, Highland Rape 1995, The Hunger 1995, Dante 1996, La Poupee 1996, It' a Jungle Out There 1997, Untitled 1997; *Art Galleries and Exhibitions* involved with incl: Met Museum of NY, Bath Museum (Dress of the Year), Florence Biennale, Nat Gallery of Victoria Melbourne, V&A, Barbican Art Gallery, Design Museum (Erotic Design exhibition), Contrasts Gallery Hong Kong (The Oriental Curiosity: 21st Century Chinoiserie exhibition); *Other Projects* incl: designing 'Outfit of the Future' for NY Times 100 year celebration, collaborations with Nick Knight, *qv* for 'Visionaire' The Face magazine; *Awards* finalist Designer of the Year (CSD) 1997, winner British Designer of the Year (British Fashion Awards) 1996 and 2000, and jtly (with John Galliano, *qv*) 1997, Int Designer of the Year Cncl of Fashion Design of America (CFDA) 2003; *Style*— Alexander McQueen, CBE

MacQUEEN, Prof Hector Lewis; s of John MacQueen, of Damnaglaur, and Winifred, *née* McWalter; *b* 13 June 1956; *Educ* George Heriot's Sch Edinburgh, Univ of Edinburgh (LLB, PhD); *m* 29 Sept 1979, Frances Mary, da of Robert Young, of Dalkeith; 1 da (Sarah b 1982), 2 s (Patrick b 1984, Jamie b 1987); *Career* Univ of Edinburgh: lectr in law 1979–91, assoc dean Faculty of Law 1987–90, sr lectr 1991–94, reader 1994, prof of private law 1994–, dean 1999–2003, dean of research Coll of Humanities and Social Science 2004–; exec dir The David Hume Inst Edinburgh 1992–99, dir AHRC Research Centre on Intellectual Property and Technol Law 2002–07; visiting prof: Cornell Univ 1991, Utrecht Univ 1997, Stetson Univ Coll of Law FL 2007–; literary dir Stair Soc 1999–; ed Edinburgh Law Review 1996–2001; chair Scottish Records Advsy Cncl 2001–; memb: DTI Intellectual Property Advsy Ctee 2003–05, DCA Advsy Panel on Crown Copyright 2004–; FRSE 1995, FBA 2006; *Books* New Perspectives in Scottish Legal History (ed, 1984), Centenary - Heriot's FP Cricket Club 1889–1989 (1989), Copyright, Competition and Industrial Design (1989, 2 edn 1995), The College of Justice and Other Essays by R K Hannay (ed, 1991), Studying Scots Law (1993, 3 edn 2004), Common Law and Feudal Society in Medieval Scotland (1993), Scots Law into the 21st Century (ed, 1996), Contract Law in Scotland (jtly, 2000, 2 edn 2007), Human Rights In Scots Law (jt ed, 2002), Unjustified Enrichment (2004), Sale of Goods (jtly, 11 edn, 2004), European Contract Law: Scots and South African Perspectives (jt ed, 2006), Contemporary Intellectual Property: Law and Policy (jtly, 2007); *Recreations* cricket, things Scottish, walking, golf; *Clubs* Heriots FP Cricket; *Style*— Prof Hector MacQueen, FBA; ✉ 47 Falcon Gardens, Edinburgh EH10 4AR (tel 0131 447 3043); University of Edinburgh, School of Law, Old College, South Bridge, Edinburgh EH8 9YL (tel 0131 650 2060, fax 0131 662 4902, telex 727442 UNIVED G, e-mail hector.macqueen@ed.ac.uk)

MacQUEEN, Prof John; s of William Lochhead MacQueen (d 1963), of Springboig, Glasgow, and Grace Palmer, *née* Galloway (d 1983); *b* 13 February 1929; *Educ* Hutchesons' GS, Univ of Glasgow (MA), Christ's Coll Cambridge (MA); *m* 22 June 1953, Winifred Wallace, da of Wallace McWalter (d 1979), of Calderwood, East Kilbride; 3 s (Hector b 1956, Angus b 1958, Donald b 1963); *Career* PO, Flying Offr RAF 1954–56; asst prof Washington Univ St Louis MO 1956–59; Univ of Edinburgh: lectr 1959–63, Masson prof 1963–71, dir Sch of Scottish Studies 1969–88, prof of Scottish lit 1971–88 (now emeritus), endowment fell 1988–92, hon fell Faculty of Arts 1992–95; Hon DLitt Nat Univ of Ireland 1985; FRSE 1992, FRAS 2004; *Books* St Nynia (1961, 2 revised edn 2005), Robert Henryson (1967), Ballattis of Luve (1970), Allegory (1970), Progress and Poetry (1982), Numerology (1985), The Rise of the Historical Novel (1989), Scotichronicon 3 and 4 (jtly, 1989), Humanism in Renaissance Scotland (ed, 1990), Scotichronicon 1 and 2 (jtly, 1993), Scotichronicon 5 and 6 (jtly, 1995), Place Names of the Rhinns of Galloway and Luce Valley (2002), Complete and Full with Numbers (2006), The Latin Poems of Archibald Pitcairne (jtly, 2008), Place-Names of the Moors and Machars (2008); *Recreations* walking, reading, music, casual archaeology, astronomy; *Style*— Prof John MacQueen, FRSE; ✉ Slewdonan, Damnaglaur, Drummore, Stranraer, Wigtownshire DG9 9QN (tel and fax 01776 840637, e-mail jackmacqueen@aol.com)

McQUEEN, John; s of late Dr Leonard George McQueen, and late Mira Milstead, *née* Birch; *b* 20 May 1942; *Educ* Rugby, Trinity Coll Cambridge, St Thomas' Hosp Med Sch (MA, MB BChir); *m* Dorothy, da of Gilbert Dyke; 5 da (Katy b 1968, Deborah b 1971, Philippa b 1977, Sarah b 1984, Laura b 1987); *Career* sr registrar Queen Charlotte's Hosp and Chelsea Hosp, currently conslt obstetrician gynaecologist Bromley Hosps NHS Trust; author of various papers on obstetrics, gynaecology and the menopause; memb Int Menopause Soc; Freeman City of London, Liveryman Worshipful Soc of Apothecaries; FRCS 1972, FRCOG 1985 (memb 1973); *Recreations* travel, golf; *Clubs* London Obstetric, Gynaecological Soc; *Style*— John McQueen, Esq; ✉ Downs View, Heritage Hill, Keston, Kent BR2 6AU (tel 01689 859058, fax 01689 860965, e-mail john@heritage-hill.demon.co.uk); Princess Royal University Hospital, Farnborough Common, Orpington, Kent BR6 8ND

MacQUITTY, (Joanna) Jane; da of William Baird MacQuitty (d 2004), of London, and Betty, *née* Bastin; *Educ* Benenden; *m* 12 Aug 1988, Philip Killingworth Hedges; 2 da (Alicia b 28 Dec 1990, Maya b 29 March 1994), 1 s (William b 11 June 1992); *Career* wine and food writer; with House & Garden 1975–82, ed Which? Wine Guide and Which? Wine Monthly 1982–84, wine ed Good Housekeeping 1984–2000; wine and drink corr The Times 1982–; wine lectr and judge 1982–; memb: Circle of Wine Writers 1977–, Soc of Authors 1982–; Glenfiddich Awards: Wine Writer of the Year 1981, Whisky Writer of the Year 1981, Special Award for Which? Wine Guide 1983; *Publications* Which? Wine Guide (1983 and 1984), Jane MacQuitty's Guide to Champagne and Sparkling Wines (1986, 3 edn 1993), Jane MacQuitty's Guide to Australian and New Zealand Wines (1988); *Recreations* family, eating, drinking, talking, sleep; *Style*— Ms Jane MacQuitty; ✉ The Times Magazine, 1 Pennington Street, London E98 1TT (tel 020 7782 5447)

McRAE, Frances Anne; CBE (2004); da of Sir Alexander Kirkland (Alec) Cairncross, KCMG, FBA (d 1998); *b* 30 August 1944; *Educ* Laurel Bank Sch Glasgow, St Anne's Coll Oxford (MA), Brown Univ RI (MA); *m* 10 Sept 1971, Hamish McRae, *qv*; 2 da (Isabella Frances b 28 July 1977, Alexandra Barbara Mary b 5 Dec 1979); *Career* staff memb: The Times 1967–69, The Banker 1969, The Observer 1970–73, The Guardian (economics corr 1973–81, ed women's page 1981–84); The Economist: Br ed 1984–89, environment ed 1989–94, media ed 1994–97, public policy ed 1997–98, mgmnt ed 1998–2004; rector Exeter Coll Oxford 2004–; non-exec dir Prolific Group 1988–89, memb Bd Alliance & Leicester Building Society (now Alliance & Leicester plc) 1990–2004; chair ESRC 2001–07; memb: Economics Ctee SSRC 1972–76, Newspaper Panel Monopolies Cmmn 1973–80, Cncl Royal Economic Soc 1980–85, Inquiry into Br Housing 1984–85, Cncl Inst for Fiscal Studies 1995–2001; pres BAAS 2005–06; hon treas Nat Cncl for One Parent Families 1980–83, tstee Kennedy Meml Tst 1974–89, memb Sch Teachers' Review Body 1992–93, govr NIESR 1995–2001; visiting fell Nuffield Coll Oxford 2001–04; High Sheriff Gtr London 2004–05; hon fell: St Anne's Coll Oxford, St Peter's Coll Oxford; FRSE, life fell RSA 2006, hon fell BAAS 2006; *Books* Capital City (with Hamish McRae, 1971), The Second Great Crash (with Hamish McRae, 1973), The Guardian Guide to the Economy (1981), Changing Perceptions of Economic Policy (1981), The Second Guardian Guide to the Economy (1983), Guide to the Economy (1987), Costing the Earth (1991), Green Inc (1995), The Death of Distance (1997, latest edn 2001), The Company of the Future (2002); *Recreations* home life; *Style*— Mrs Hamish McRae, CBE; ✉ Exeter College, Oxford OX1 3DP

McRAE, Hamish Malcolm Donald; s of Donald Barrington McRae (d 1980), and Barbara Ruth Louise (Jasmine), *née* Budd (d 2003); *b* 20 October 1943; *Educ* Fettes, Trinity Coll Dublin (MA); *m* 10 Sept 1971, Frances McRae, CBE, *qv*, da of late Sir Alexander Kirkland (Alec) Cairncross, KCMG, FBA; 2 da (Isabella Frances b 28 July 1977, Alexandra Barbara Mary b 5 Dec 1979); *Career* grad trainee Liverpool Post 1966–67, asst ed then dep ed The Banker 1967–72, ed Euromoney 1972–75, fin ed The Guardian 1975–89, business and city ed The Independent 1989–91 (assoc ed 1991–); Harold Wincott Young Fin Journalist of the Year 1971, Harold Wincott Fin Journalist of the Year 1979, David Walt Prize 2005, Business and Finance Journalist of the Year British Press Awards 2006, Best Communicator Business Journalist of the Year Awards 2007; *Books* Capital City: London as a Financial Centre (with Frances Cairncross, 1973, current edn 1991), The Second Great Crash: how the oil crisis could destroy the world economy (with Nihon Keisai Shimbun, 1975), Japan's Role in the Emerging Global Securities Market (1985), The World In 2020: Power, Culture and Property - a vision of the future (1994), Wake-up Japan! (with Tadashi Nakamae, 2000); *Recreations* skiing and walking; *Style*— Hamish McRae, Esq; ✉ The Independent, 191 Marsh Wall, London E14 9RS (tel 020 7005 2635, fax 020 7005 2399)

MacRAE, Stuart Campbell; s of Iain Maclean MacRae, and Ola Vean, *née* Sutherland; *b* 12 August 1976; *Educ* Charleston Acad Inverness, Univ of Durham (BA), Guildhall Sch of Music and Drama (MMus); *Career* composer in assoc BBC Scottish Symphony Orch (SSO) 1999–2003; concerts incl: Philharmonia Orch Music of Today 2000, Edinburgh Int Festival 2001, BBC SSO 2003; featured composer Spannungen Kammermusikfest 2003; compositions incl: Boreraig 1994 (revised 1995), The Witch's Kiss 1997, Landscape and the Mind: Distance, Refuge 1997, Piano Sonata 1998, Sinfonia 1998–99, Stirling Choruses 1999, Sleep at the Feet of Daphne 1999, Piano Quintet 1999, One Man In His Time 2000–01, Violin Concerto (premiered BBC Proms) 2000–01, Ancrene Wisse (premiered Huddersfield Contemporary Music Festival) 2002, 32 for Piano 2002, String Quartet 2002, Interact 2002–03, Motus 2003, Hamartia 2003–04; recordings incl: The City Inside, Salm 42, Piano Sonata; *Awards* BBC/Lloyds Bank Young Composer Award (for Boreraig) 1996, BBC Symphony Orch Composer's Forum 1997, citations Royal Philharmonic Soc Award for Large Scale Composition 2002 (Violin Concerto) and 2003 (Ancrene Wisse); *Recreations* walking, climbing, golf; *Style*— Stuart MacRae, Esq; ✉ c/o Novello & Co, 8/9 Frith Street, London W1D 3BJ (tel 020 7434 0066, e-mail fiona.southey@musicsales.co.uk)

MACREADY, Sir Nevil John Wilfrid; 3 Bt (UK 1923), of Cheltenham, Co Gloucester; CBE (1983); s of Lt-Gen Sir Gordon Nevil Macready, 2 Bt, KBE, CB, CMG, DSO, MC (d 1956); *b* 7 September 1921; *Educ* Cheltenham Coll, St John's Coll Oxford (MA); *m* 1949, Mary (Emma) (d 2007), o da of Sir (John) Donald Balfour Fergusson, GCB (d 1963); 3 da (Caroline Elisabeth (Mrs Clive F Tucker) b 1950, Sarah Diana Mary b 1953, Anna Louise b 1963), 1 s (Charles Nevil b 1955); *Heir* s, Charles Macready; *Career* served RA 1942–47, Staff Capt 1945; BBC Euro Serv 1947–50, Mobil Oil Co Ltd 1952–85 (md 1975); pres: Royal Warrant Holders' Assoc 1979–80, Inst of Petroleum 1980–82; chm: Crafts Cncl 1984–91, Horseracing Advsy Cncl 1986–93, Mental Health Fndn 1993–97; dep chm Br Horseracing Bd 1993–95; tstee V&A Museum 1985–95; *Clubs* Boodle's, Jockey (Paris); *Style*— Sir Nevil Macready, Bt, CBE; ✉ The White House, Odiham, Hampshire RG29 1LG (tel 01256 702976)

MacRITCHIE, Kenneth; s of Norman MacRitchie, of Glasgow, and Daveen, *née* MacMillan; *b* 3 September 1956, Glasgow; *Educ* Univ of Glasgow (LLB), Univ of Aberdeen (BD), Univ of Manchester (MA); *m* Brenda, *née* Sinclair; 2 da (Rowena, Arabella), 1 s (Cameron); *Career* slr; ptnr Clifford Chance 1991–93, managing ptnr London office Milbank Tweed Hadley and McCloy 1993–96, ptnr Shearman & Sterling 1996– (managing ptnr 2002–); memb: Law Soc, Law Soc of Scotland; *Style*— Kenneth MacRitchie, Esq; ✉ Shearman & Sterling LLP, Broadgate West, 9 Appold Street, London EC2A 2AP (tel 020 7655 5000, fax 020 7655 5500, e-mail kmacritchie@shearman.com)

MACRORY, Henry David; s of Sir Patrick Arthur Macrory (d 1993), of Walton-on-the-Hill, Surrey, and Marjorie Elizabeth, *née* Lewis; *b* 15 December 1947; *Educ* Westminster, Univ of Kent (BA); *m* 4 April 1972, Janet Carolyn, da of Henry James Potts; 2 da (Julia b 1978, Caroline b 1980), 1 s (David b 1985); *Career* reporter Kent Messenger 1969–72; Sunday Express 1972–: reporter 1972–79, political columnist 1979–83, asst ed 1983, exec ed 1990, acting ed 1991, dep ed 1993; Daily Star: political ed 1993, exec ed 1996–2000; conslt Cons Pty 2000–; *Style*— Henry Macrory, Esq; ✉ 134 Humber Road, Blackheath, London SE3 7LY (tel 020 8858 5058)

MACRORY, Prof Richard Brabazon; CBE (2000); s of Sir Patrick Arthur Macrory (d 1993), of Walton-on-the-Hill, Surrey, and Marjorie Elizabeth, *née* Lewis (d 1997); *b* 30 March 1950; *Educ* Westminster, ChCh Oxford (MA); *m* 6 Oct 1979, Sarah Margaret, da of Bernard Christian Briant, CVO, of Aldeburgh, Suffolk; 2 s (Sam b 1980, Robert b 1983); *Career* called to the Bar Gray's Inn 1974; legal advsr FOE Ltd 1975–78; Imperial Coll Centre for Environmental Technol 1980–94 and 1996–98; dir Environmental Change Unit Univ of Oxford 1994–95, supernumerary fell Linacre Coll Oxford 1996–, prof of environmental law UCL 1999–; ed Jl of Environmental Law 1988–2007; standing counsel Cncl for Protection of Rural England 1981–92, specialist advsr House of Commons Select Ctee on the Environment 1982–97, first chm UK Environmental Law Assoc 1986–88, specialist advsr House of Lords Select Ctee on the EC (Environment Sub Ctee) 1992 and 1996, specialist advsr House of Commons Select Ctee on the Environment, Transport and the Regions 1997–; chm Steering Ctee European Environmental Advsy Cncls 2001–02; ldr Cabinet Office Review on Regulatory Sanctions 2005–06; memb: UK Nat Advsy Ctee on Eco-labelling 1990–91, Royal Cmmn on Environmental Pollution 1991–2003, Expert Panel UK Inter-Agency Ctee on Global Environmental Change 1995–96, Bd Environment Agency 1999–2004; hon pres Nat Soc for Clean Air and Environmental Protection 2004–05; rapporteur UK Nat Biotechnology Conference 1997; chm Merchant-Ivory Film Prodns Ltd 1992–2005; *Books* Nuisance (1982), Water Law: Principles and Practice (1985), Water Act 1989 (1989), Bibliography of European Community Law (1995), Principles of European Environmental Law (ed, 2004), Reflections on 30 Years of EU Environmental Law (ed, 2005); author of articles in learned jls; *Recreations* reading, board games, films; *Clubs* Atheneum; *Style*— Prof Richard Macrory, CBE; ✉ Faculty of Laws, University College London, Bentham House, Endsleigh Gardens, London WC1H 0EY (tel 020 7679 1543, fax 020 7679 1440, e-mail r.macrory@ucl.ac.uk); Brick Court Chambers, 7–8 Essex Street, London WC2R 3LD (tel 020 7379 3550, fax 020 7379 3558)

MacSHANE, Denis; PC (2005), MP; *b* 1948; *Educ* Merton Coll Oxford, Univ of London (PhD); *m* Natalie Pham; 4 c; *Career* prodr BBC 1969–1977, pres NUJ 1978–79, sometime int trade union official, dir European Policy Inst 1992–94; MP (Lab) Rotherham 1994–; PPS to FCO mins 1997–2001, Parly under sec of state FCO 2001–02, min for Europe 2002–; sr memb Exec Fabian Soc; *Publications* author of several books on international politics; regular contrib to nat and foreign newspapers and political jls; *Recreations* skiing, walking, gardening; *Style*— The Rt Hon Dr Denis MacShane, MP; ✉ House of Commons, London SW1A 0AA (tel 020 7219 4060)

McSHANE, Ian David; s of Henry McShane, of Manchester, and Irene, *née* Cowley; *b* 29 September 1942; *Educ* Stretford GS Leeds, RADA; *m* 1 (m dis), Suzan Farmer; m 2 (m dis), Ruth Post; 1 da (Kate b 18 April 1970), 1 s (Morgan b 7 July 1974); m 3, 30 Aug 1980, Gwendolyn Marie, da of Claude Humble; *Career* actor; memb: BAFTA, Acad of Motion Picture Arts and Sciences, Screen Actors' Guild, Directors' Guild; *Theatre* West

End: The Glass Menagerie 1965, Loot 1966, The Promise 1967, The Witches Of Eastwick 2000; Los Angeles: As You Like It 1979, Betrayal 1983, Inadmissible Evidence 1985; *Television* incl: Jesus of Nazareth, Wuthering Heights, Whose Life Is It Anyway?, Evergreen, The Letter, Marco Polo, AD, War and Remembrance, Dallas, Lovejoy, Columbo, The Young Charlie Chaplin, Madson, Trust, Deadwood, Trust; *Films* incl: The Wild and the Willing 1962, The Battle of Britain 1968, If It's Tuesday This Must Be Belgium 1969, Villain 1971, Sitting Target 1972, Cheaper to Keep Her 1977, Exposed 1984, Torchlight 1986, Sexy Beast 2000, Nine Lives 2005; *Style*— Ian McShane, Esq; ✉ c/o ICM Ltd, Oxford House, 76 Oxford Street, London W1D 1BS (tel 020 7636 6565, fax 020 7323 0101)

McSHARRY, Brendan John; MBE (1994); s of Charles Patrick McSharry (d 1976), and Emily Annie, *née* Poundall (d 1983); *b* 25 July 1949; *Educ* St James RC HS, Univ of Wales (BA), Univ of Exeter (PGCE), Univ of Leeds (MA), Univ of Cambridge (DTEFL); *Career* exec offr staff trg Dept of Employment 1972–74, English teacher Folk Univ Örebro/Karlstadt 1975–77; British Council: English teacher Milan 1977–79, asst dir of studies Milan 1979–81, asst dir of teacher trg studies 1982–85, dir Chiang Mai Thailand 1985–87, dir of studies Baghdad 1987–89, mangr and ODA project mangr English teaching in secdy schs Quito 1989–92, dir Milan 1992–95, dir Yemen 1995–; speaker on educnl methodology at various int confs; memb Int Sonnenberg Assoc of GB 1973; *Recreations* reading, running (completed Singapore marathon 1984); *Style*— Brendan McSharry, Esq, MBE; ✉ The British Council, As-Sabain St No 7, PO Box 2157, Sana'a, Yemen

MACTAGGART, Fiona Margaret; MP; da of Sir Ian Mactaggart (d 1987), and Rosemary, *née* Williams (d 1992); *b* 12 September 1953; *Educ* KCL (BA), Goldsmiths Coll London (Postgrad Teaching Cert), Inst of Educn Univ of London (MA); *Career* vice-pres and nat sec NUS 1978–81, gen sec Jt Council for the Welfare of Immigrants 1982–86, primary sch teacher 1987–92, univ lectr 1992–97, MP (Lab) Slough 1997–; PPS to sec of state for Culture, Media and Sport 1997–2001, Parly under sec of state Home Office 2003–06; memb Wandsworth Cncl 1986–90 (ldr of opposition 1988–90); *Recreations* walking, talking, arts, watching TV; *Style*— Ms Fiona Mactaggart, MP; ✉ House of Commons, London SW1A 0AA (tel 020 7219 3416, fax 020 7219 0989, e-mail mactaggartf@parliament.uk)

MACTAGGART, Sir John Auld; 4 Bt (UK 1938), of King's Park, City of Glasgow; s of Sir Ian (John) Auld Mactaggart, 3 Bt (d 1987), and Rosemary, *née* Williams (d 1992); *b* 21 January 1951; *Educ* Shrewsbury, Trinity Coll Cambridge (MA); *m* 1, 1977 (m dis 1990), Patricia, yst da of late Maj Harry Alastair Gordon, MC; m 2, 18 May 1991, Caroline, yst da of Eric Charles Williams, of Esher, Surrey; 2 da (Kinvara May b 18 Feb 1992, Aphra Hope b 8 July 1999), 2 s (Jack Auld b 11 Sept 1993, Sholto Auld b 16 Dec 1996); *Heir* s, Jack Mactaggart; *Career* chm: Western Heritable Investment Company, Bruichladdich Distillery Company; *Clubs* Boodle's, Argyllshire Gathering; *Style*— Sir John Mactaggart, Bt; ✉ Ardmore House, Ardtalla Estate, Islay, Argyll; One Red Place, London W1K 6PL (tel 020 7491 2948, fax 020 7629 0414)

McTAGUE, (George) Peter; s of George McTague, and (Eileen) Norah, *née* McCarthy; *b* 22 February 1951; *Educ* St Michael's Coll Leeds, The GS Harrogate; *m* 19 April 1980, Hilary Anne, da of Bernard Cheshire; 3 s (Richard William b 7 May 1982, Nicholas Michael b 22 Aug 1984, Patrick George b 15 Jan 1988); *Career* chain store mgmnt and personnel appts (latterly trg offr) The Littlewoods Organisation Ltd 1970–77; Stylo plc: gen mangr then commercial dir Stylo Barratt Shoes Ltd 1977–83, md Pennywise Discount Stores 1983–85; ops and property dir Comet Group plc 1985–91, dir Merry Hill Centre Mountleigh Group plc 1991–92, md NORWEB Retail 1992–96, devpt dir Comet Group plc 2001– (sales and property dir 1996–2001); conslt and property developer McTague Assocs 2001–03, non-exec dir PRG Powerhouse Ltd 2003–04, retail conslt and property developer 2004–; *Style*— Peter McTague, Esq; ✉ 3 Kent Road North, Harrogate, North Yorkshire HG1 2EX

McTEER, Janet; da of Alan McTeer, and Jean McTeer; *b* 5 August 1961; *Educ* Queen Anne GS for Girls York, RADA (Bancroft Gold Medal); *Career* actress; *Theatre* incl: The Grace of Mary Traverse (Royal Court) 1986, As You Like It, The Three Sisters, Cymbeline (all Manchester Royal Exchange) 1988–90, Much Ado About Nothing (Queen's) 1995, Uncle Vanya (RNT) 1995, Simpatico (Royal Court) 1996, A Doll's House (London and Broadway) 1997 (Olivier, Evening Standard and Tony Awards for Best Actress), The Duchess of Malfi (RNT); *Television* incl: The Governor (series I & II), Portrait of a Marriage, Precious Bane; *Film* Tumbleweeds (Oscar nominated), King is Alive, Songcatcher, The Intended (also co-writer); *Recreations* gardens, writing, cooking, people, life, love; *Style*— Ms Janet McTeer

MacTHOMAS OF FINEGAND, Andrew Patrick Clayhills; o s of Capt Patrick Watt MacThomas of Finegand (d 1970), and Elizabeth Fenwick Cadogan, *née* Clayhills-Henderson (d 1995), of Invergowrie, Angus; suc f 1970 as 19 Chief of Clan MacThomas; *b* 28 August 1942; *Educ* St Edward's Sch Oxford; *m* 1985, Anneke Cornelia Susanna, o da of late Albert and Susanna Kruyning-van Hout; 1 s (Thomas David Alexander b 1987), 1 da (Amy Elizabeth Susanna b 1989); *Heir* s, Thomas MacThomas, yr of Finegand; *Career* estab Visa in Scotalnd 1975–82, dir Scotworld Servs 1982–85, PR South Africa 1985–90, politcal lobbyist 1990–97, public affrs dir Barclays plc 1997–2005, dir Industry and Parliament Tst 2005–07; memb Standing Cncl of Scottish Chiefs; pres Clan MacThomas Soc, vice-pres Clan Chattan Assoc; FSA Scot; *Recreations* the clan, politics, wine, wit; *Clubs* Hurlingham; *Style*— Andrew MacThomas of Finegand; ✉ c/o Barclays Bank, Hide Hill, Berwick-upon-Tweed TD1

McTIGHE, (Robert) Michael (Mike); s of late Glen McTighe, and Mary, *née* Saunders; *b* 17 October 1953, Stourbridge, West Midlands; *Educ* Stourbridge GS, UCL (BSc); *partner* Ms Terry Vega; 1 da (Stephanie Martha b 8 June 1984), 2 s (Henry Marcus b 3 April 1987, William Michael b 17 Sept 1992); *Career* GEC Machines Ltd 1975–76, Thorn EMI plc 1976–80; General Electric: UK manufacturing dir GE Medical Systems 1986–88, ultrasound and nuclear medicine business mangr GE-CGR 1988–90; European Cellular Subscriber Div Motorola Inc: gen mangr UK manufacturing ops 1990–91, dir European manufacturing ops 1991–92, gen mangr OEM markets 1992–93, gen mangr Area III 1993–94; dir of ops Asia Pacific Cellular Subscriber Div Motorola Inc 1994–95; Philips Electronics NV: md Philips Consumer Communications 1995–97, pres and chief exec Philips Consumer Communications LP 1997–98; self-employed conslt to cos incl Siemens AG 1998–99; Cable and Wireless plc: exec dir and chief exec global ops 1999–2001, exec dir strategy and business devpt 2001; chm and chief exec Carrier 1 International SA 2001–02; currently chm: Pace Micro Technology plc, Cambridge Semiconductors Ltd, Phyworks Ltd, Perpetuum Ltd, Corvil Ltd, Frontier Silicon Holdings Ltd, Nujira Ltd; non-exec dir Alliance and Leicester plc, invited dir London Metal Exchange Holdings Ltd, memb Bd Ofcom 2007–; tstee and dir Venture Partnership Fndn; *Recreations* skiing, scuba diving, gardening; *Clubs* Home House; *Style*— Mike McTighe, Esq; ✉ Flat 2, 53 Eaton Place, London SW1X 8DE (tel 020 7235 7223); Danesbury House, 4 Waverley Grove, Solihull, West Midlands B91 1NP (tel 0121 704 1971)

MACUR, Hon Mrs Justice; Dame Julia Wendy; DBE (2005); da of Boleslaw Macur, and Betsy May Macur; *b* 17 April 1957; *Educ* Univ of Sheffield (LLB); *m* 1981; 2 s (Ben b 31 Dec 1991, Nicholas b 25 Jan 1995); *Career* called to the Bar Lincoln's Inn 1979; practising barr on Midland & Oxford Circuit 1979–2005, QC 1998, recorder of the Crown Court 1999–2005, judge of the High Court of Justice (Family Div) 2005–; *Style*— The Hon Mrs Justice Macur, DBE; ✉ c/o Royal Courts of Justice, Strand, London WC2A 2LL

McVAY, John Charles; s of John McVay, of Edinburgh, and Ruth, *née* Thomson; *Educ* Firhill Secdy Sch; *Partner* Ruth Buckingham; 3 s (Aidan McVay b 7 July 1996, Jamie McVay b 9 Feb 1998, Callum McVay b 22 Jan 2001); *Career* ind prodr 1983–85 and 1994–95; training mangr Edinburgh Video Training Co (EVTC) 1986–93; dir: Scottish Training Tst 1993–97, training Scottish Screen 1997–98, Research Centre for TV 1998–2001; chief exec Pact 2001–; fndr Edinburgh Video Course 1985; dir: Skillset, Independent Production Training Fund (IPTF); govr Nat Film Sch; FRTS 2001; *Recreations* fishing, gardening, reading; *Style*— John McVay, Esq; ✉ Pact, 45 Mortimer Street, London W1W 8HS (tel 020 7331 6035, mobile 07775 708922, e-mail john@pact.co.uk)

MACVE, Prof Richard Henry; s of Alfred Derek Macve, and Betty Lilian, *née* Simmons; *b* 2 June 1946; *Educ* Chigwell Sch, New Coll Oxford (scholar, MA), LSE (MSc); *m* 28 July 1973, Jennifer Jill, da of Leslie Charles Wort; 1 da (Joanna Catherine b 16 Sept 1977), 2 s (Thomas Charles b 25 March 1980, Arthur James b 5 March 1985); *Career* Peat Marwick Mitchell London 1968–74 (articled clerk, sr accountant, asst mangr), internal auditor seconded to MOD 1973–74, lectr in accounting LSE 1974–78, Julian Hodge prof of accounting and head of Dept of Accounting and Fin Univ of Wales Aberystwyth 1978–96, prof of accounting LSE 1996–, convenor Dept of Accounting and Finance LSE 2002–03; visiting assoc prof of accounting Rice Univ Houston TX 1982–83, hon prof Sch of Mgmnt and Business, Aberystwyth 2000–; memb Cncl ICAEW 1986–93, chm Cncl of Profs of Accounting 1990–92, memb Bd UK CEED 1993–2001, academic advsr to Research Bd and Centre for Business Performance ICAEW 1994–; ICAEW (first place intermediate examination 1969, second place final pt one 1970, first place final pt two 1971); FCA 1979 (ACA 1972), Hon FIA 2000; *Publications* A Survey of Lloyd's Syndicate Accounts (1985, 2 edn 1993), Accounting for Marketable Securities in The Financial Services Industry (1991), Accounting Principles for Life Insurance (1995), A Conceptual Framework for Financial Accounting and Reporting (1997), UK Life Insurance: Accounting for Business Performance (1997); *Recreations* sailing, mountain walking; *Clubs* Aberystwyth Boat, Athenaeum; *Style*— Prof Richard Macve; ✉ Bronwydd, 3 Trefor Road, Aberystwyth, Ceredigion SY23 2EH (tel 01970 624586); Department of Accounting, London School of Economics and Political Science, London WC2A 2AE (tel 020 7955 6138, fax 020 7955 7420, e-mail r.macve@lse.ac.uk)

McVIE, Prof (John) Gordon; s of John McVie, of Haddington, Lothian, and Lindsaye, *née* Mair; *b* 13 January 1945, Glasgow; *Educ* Royal HS Edinburgh, Univ of Edinburgh (BSc, MB ChB, MD, Gunning Victoria Jubilee Prize in Pathology); *m* 1, 1967 (m dis 1996), Evelyn Strang; 3 s (Malcolm b 24 June 1971, Tammas b 7 Aug 1975, Douglas b 31 Jan 1978); m 2, 1998, Claudia Burke; *Career* house offr Royal Hosp for Sick Children and Royal Infirmary Edinburgh 1969–70; Univ of Edinburgh: MRC fell Depts of Pathology and Therapeutics 1970–71, temp lectr in Therapeutics 1971–73, lectr in Therapeutics 1973–76; hon sr registrar Lothian Health Bd 1971–76, CRC sr lectr in clinical oncology Univ of Glasgow 1976–80, hon conslt in med oncology Gtr Glasgow Health Bd 1976–80, clinical research dir The Netherlands Cancer Inst Amersterdam 1984–89 (head Clinical Research Unit, conslt physician and chm Div of Experimental Oncology 1980–84), DG Cancer Research Campaign London 1996–2002 (dir Scientific Dept 1989–96), DG Cancer Research UK 2002, dir Cancer Intelligence 2002–; hon conslt in Oncology Velindre Cancer Centre Cardiff; sr conslt European Inst of Oncology Milan; visiting prof: Univ of Sydney NSW Aust 1983, Br Postgrad Med Fedn Univ of London 1990–96, Univ of Glasgow 1996–, Univ of Wales 2004–; visiting fell: Dept of Med Oncology Univ of Paris 1978, Netherlands Cancer Inst 1979; conslt in carcinogenesis of cytostatic drugs Int Agency for Research in Cancer WHO Lyon 1980, chm Int Union Against Cancer (UICC) Fellowships Prog 1990–, pres Euro Orgn for Research and Treatment of Cancer 1994–97 (memb Exec Ctee and Bd 1992–); ed-in-chief Euro Cancer News 1987–96, first Euro ed Jl of the National Cancer Inst 1994–; author of numerous articles in scientific jls; Honeyman Gillespie lectr in oncology 1977; Hon DSc: Univ of Abertay Dundee 1996, Univ of Nottingham 1997, Univ of Portsmouth 1999; FRCPEd, FRCPGlas, FRCP, FMedSci, FRCSEd; *Books* Cancer Assessment and Monitoring (with T Symington, 1979), Evaluation or Carcinogenic Risk of Chemicals to Man - Vol 26: Antineoplastic and Immunosuppressive Drugs (1981), Autologous Bone Marrow Transplantation and Solid Tumours (with I E Smith, 1984), Microspheres and Drug Therapy (with S S Davis, 1984), Clinical and Experimental Pathology and Biology of Lung Cancer (with D Carney, 1985); also author of book chapters; *Recreations* opera, music in general, walking, rugby, wine, cooking; *Clubs* New (Edinburgh), IOD; *Style*— Prof Gordon McVie; ✉ Cancer Intelligence, 4 Stanley Road, Bristol BS6 6NW (tel 07785 3252558, fax 01179 232699, e-mail info@cancerintelligence.com)

McVITTIE, John Bousfield; s of Brig Arthur Bousfield McVittie, OBE (d 1976), and Valerie Florence, *née* Crichton (d 1994); *b* 9 April 1943; *Educ* Radley, Selwyn Coll Cambridge (MA), Stanford Business Sch (MBA); *m* 4 Sept 1971, Jane Elizabeth, *née* Hobson; 2 da (Clare, Amy); *Career* md Privatbanken Ltd 1984–87, sr vice-pres and gen mangr First Interstate Bank of California 1987–89, md John Charcol Commercial 1989–92, ptnr Royal Trust Bank 1992–96, dir and gen mangr Tengra Ltd 1996–; chm Inker; Freeman: City of London 1969, Worshipful Co of Clothworkers 1974; *Recreations* skiing, tennis; *Clubs* Queen's; *Style*— John McVittie; ✉ 72 Scarsdale Villas, London W8 6PP (tel 020 7937 8926); Tengra Ltd, 85 Chelsea Manor Street, London SW3 5QP (tel 020 7565 0984, e-mail tengra.limited@btinternet.com)

McWALTER, Tony; s of Joe McWalter (d 1984), and Anne, *née* Murray (d 1984); *b* 20 March 1945; *Educ* UCW Aberystwyth (BSc), McMaster Univ Canada (MA), UC Oxford (BPhil, MLitt); *Career* secdy sch teacher 1963–64, long distance lorry driver 1964, teaching fell McMaster Univ 1968–69, lectr Thames Poly 1972–74; Univ of Hertfordshire (formerly Hatfield Poly until 1992): sr lectr in philosophy 1974–90, campus dir of computing 1989–92, princ lectr in philosophy 1990–97; MP (Lab/Co-op) Hemel Hempstead 1997–2005; memb Select Ctee on: NI 1997–2000, Science and Technol 2001–05, Procedure 2003–05; educnl conslt (mathematics and philosophy): Univ of Leeds 2005–, Univ of Hertfordshire 2005–; memb Bd: Cncl for Economic and Social Aspects of Genomics 2003–05, Br Philosophical Assoc 2004–05 (memb Exec 2003–06); treas Nat Ctee of Philosophy 1984–97; memb: Greenpeace, Friends of the Earth, Oxfam, World Devpt Movement, Compassion in World Farming, League Against Cruel Sports, Amnesty Int, CND, Co-op Pty; hon vice-pres Herts Conservation Soc 1997–2005; *Books* Kant and his Influence (jt ed with George MacDonald Ross, 1990); *Recreations* club tennis, bridge, croquet, theatre and the Arts, philosophy; *Style*— Tony McWalter, Esq

McWHIRTER, Prof John Graham; s of Francis David McWhirter (d 1982), of Newry, Co Down, and Elizabeth, *née* Martin (d 1984); *b* 28 March 1949; *Educ* Newry HS, Queen's Univ Belfast (fndn scholar, BSc, Purser research student, PhD); *m* 17 Aug 1973, Avesia Vivianne Wolfe; 1 da (Lindsey Joy b 17 Jan 1977), 1 s (Colin Francis b 13 Nov 1979); *Career* Defence Evaluation and Research Agency (DERA) Malvern: higher scientific offr 1973–77, sr scientific offr 1977–80, princ scientific offr 1980–86, sr princ scientific offr 1986–96, sr fell Signal Processing Gp 1996–2001; with Qinetiq Ltd 2001–; visiting prof: Electrical Engrg Dept Queen's Univ Belfast 1986–, Sch of Engrg Univ of Wales Cardiff 1997–; chm and proceedings ed IMA Int Conf on Mathematics in Signal Processing 1988, 1992, 1996 and 2000; pres IMA 2002–03 (vice-pres 1998–99), fndr memb Signal Processing Sub Gp IEE 1987–92, Euro Program chm Int Conf on Systolic Arrays 1989, memb IT Panel UK Technol Foresight Programme 1994, Euro Program chm Int Symposium on Computer Arithmetic IEEE 1995, memb EPSRC Peer Review Coll for IT

M

(Communications) 1995–; author of over 140 research papers, inventor and co-inventor 30 UK, European, US and Canadian patents; Hon DSc: Queen's Univ Belfast 2000, Univ of Edinburgh 2002; CMath, FIMA 1988, FIEE 1994, FREng 1996, FRS 1999, FInstP 1999; *Awards* Northern Ireland Info Technol Award Br Computer Soc (jtly with J V McCanny) 1987, J J Thomson Premium IEE (jtly) 1990, J J Thomson Medal IEE (for research on systolic arrays) 1994; *Recreations* swimming for exercise, building and flying radio controlled model gliders; *Clubs* Malvern Soaring Association; *Style*— Prof John McWhirter, FRS, FREng; ✉ QinetiQ Ltd, Malvern Technology Centre, St Andrew's Road, Malvern, Worcestershire WR14 3PS (tel 01684 895384, fax 01684 896502, e-mail mcwhirter@qinetiq.com)

McWILLIAM, Sir Michael Douglas; KCMG (1996); s of Douglas McWilliam (d 1969), of Oakridge Lynch, Glos, and Margaret, *née* Leach (d 1992); *b* 21 June 1933; *Educ* Cheltenham Coll, Oriel Coll Oxford (MA), Nuffield Coll Oxford (BLitt); *m* 1960, Ruth, da of Dr Friedrich Arnstein; 2 s (Robert b 1962, Martin b 1964); *Career* Treasy Kenya 1958–62, Samuel Montagu & Co 1962–66; The Standard Bank (subseq Standard Chartered Bank): joined 1966, a gen mangr 1973, gp md 1983–88; dir Sch of Oriental and African Studies Univ of London 1989–96; chm: Centre for Study of African Economies Oxford 1997–, Br Empire and Cwlth Museum 2006– (dep chm 2003–06), Cheltenham Festivals 2007– (dep chm 2006); memb Bd Cwlth Devpt Corp 1990–97, hon vice-pres Royal African Soc 1996– (memb Cncl 1979–91, vice-chm 1991–96, chm 1996–2004), vice-pres Royal Cwlth Soc 2003– (dep chm 1982–91, chm 1996–2002); dir: Shanghai Fund 1992–99, Bangladesh Fund 1994–99, Simba Fund 1995–2000, Indocam Mosais 1999–2001; pres Cncl Cheltenham Coll 1988–92 (memb 1977–92); hon fell SOAS 1997; *Publications* The Development Business: A History of the Commonwealth Development Corporation (2001); *Clubs* Royal Commonwealth Soc; *Style*— Sir Michael McWilliam, KCMG; ✉ Yew Tree Farm, Brimpsfield, Gloucestershire GL4 8LD (tel 01452 862614)

MADDEN, Andrew John; s of Dennis Madden, and Jennifer, *née* Brown; *b* 29 October 1962, Birmingham; *Educ* Woodhouse Comp Sch Tamworth, Univ of Birmingham (LLB), Coll of Law Chester; *m* 15 Oct 1988, Vivienne, *née* Wakelam; 2 s (Scott b 8 July 1994, Richard b 14 March 2001); *Career* slr; trainee slr Duggan Lea & Co 1985–87, asst, assoc then ptnr Edge & Ellison 1987–96, ptnr HBJ Gateley Wareing 1996–; non-exec dir Good Hope Hosp NHS Tst 2004–07, chair Birmingham Fundraising Ctee Charis; memb Law Soc 1987; *Recreations* football (Birmingham City), cricket, ballet, golf; *Style*— Andrew Madden, Esq; ✉ HBJ Gateley Wareing LLP, One Eleven, Edmund Street, Birmingham B3 2HJ (tel 0121 234 0034)

MADDEN, Anne; *Educ* Chelsea Sch of Art; *m* Louis le Brocquy; 2 s; *Career* artist; solo exhibitions: Leicester Galleries London 1959, 1961 and 1967, Dawson Gallery Dublin 1960, 1964, 1968, 1970 and 1974, New Gallery Belfast 1964, Oxford Gallery Oxford 1970, Gimpel Weitzenhoffer Gallery NY 1970, New Art Centre 1970, 1972, 1974, 1978 and 1990, Demarco Gallery Edinburgh 1971, Ulster Museum Belfast 1974, Galerie Darthea Speyer Paris 1976 and 1979, Galerie Le Dessin Paris 1978 and 1980, The Arts Cncl of NI Belfast 1979, Taylor Galleries Dublin 1979, 1982 and 1987, Fondation Maeght Saint-Paul France 1983, The Bank of Ireland Dublin 1984, Wexford Arts Centre Ireland 1984, Galerie Maeght Barcelona 1985, Galerie Joachim Becker Cannes 1985, Armstrong Gallery NY 1986, Galerie Jeanne Bucher Paris 1989, New Art Centre London 1990, The Kerlin Gallery Dublin 1990 and 1992, R H A Gallagher Gallery Dublin 1991, Crawford Municipal Gallery Cork 1992, Galerie Sapone 1993, The Kerlin Gallery Dublin 1995, Galerie Maeght Paris 1996, Château de Tours Municipal Art Gallery France 1997, Hugh Lane Municipal Gallery of Modern Art Dublin 1997, Butler Gallery Kilkenny 1998, Centre International d'Art Contemporain Carros 1998, Museum of Contemporary Art Oaxaza 2000, Taylor Galleries Dublin 2002, Gallery One Kilkenny 2003, New Art Centre Roche Court 2005, Centre Culturel Irlandais Paris 2005, Irish Museum of Modern Art Retrospective 2007; name given to Salle d'Honneur at Int Contemporary Arts Centre Carros, vaulted ceiling painting Empyrius inaugurated following year; group exhibitions: The Mirror and the Square (Burlington Galleries London) 1951, The Irish Exhibition of Living Art (Dublin) 1952, Art '65 (American Express Pavilion NY World Fair) 1965, Quatrième Biennale de Paris (representing Ireland) 1965, Modern Irish Painters (CIE Ulster Museum Belfast) 1966, Modern Irish Painting (Helsinki, Gothenburg, Norrköping, Stockholm) 1969, An Oireachtas Dublin 1970 and 1988, Les Abstractions Autour des Années 1970–80, The 8th International Biennial Exhibition of Prints Tokyo 1973, Irish Directions (touring) 1974–75, ICA Boston 1974–75, Salon de Montrouge (Paris) 1982, ROSC 84 (Dublin) 1984, Centre National d'Art Contemporain (CNAC) Nice 1985, A Propos de Dessin (Galerie Adrian Maeght Paris) 1987, Fonds Regional d'Art Contemporain Provence 1989, Modern Masters (Musée Jacquemart André Paris) 1989, The National Self Portrait Collection (Crawford Municipal Art Gallery Cork and Nat Gallery Dublin) 1990, Musée d'Art Moderne et d'Art Contemporain (MAMAC) Nice 1990; public collections possessing work incl: Contemporary Arts Society London, The Gulbenkian Fndn Portugal, The Arts Council of Ireland, The Arts Council of NI, The Arts Council of GB, The Hugh Lane Municipal Gallery of Modern Art Dublin, The J H Hirshhorn Museum and Sculpture Garden Washington DC, Contemporary Irish Arts Society, Musée d'Art Moderne de la Ville de Paris, La Fondation Maeght France, Musée Picasso Antibes, Foundation Van Gogh Arles France, Musée d'Art Moderne et d'Art Contemporain, Neuberger Museum New York, Smurfitt Foundation Dublin, Ulster Museum Belfast, Irish MOMA Dublin; subject of 60 min documentary Anne Madden Artist and Muse 2005; Hon LLD UC Dublin 2005; *Books* Louis le Brocquy: Seeing His Way (1993); *Style*— Ms Anne Madden; ✉ e-mail info@anne-madden.com, website www.anne-madden.com

MADDEN, Deirdre; *b* 20 August 1960; *Educ* St Mary's GS Co Derry, Trinity Coll Dublin (BA), UEA (MA); *m* 1987, Harry Clifton; *Career* writer; fell Atelierhaus Worpswede 1993–94, writer in residence UC Cork 1994–95, writer fell Trinity Coll Dublin 1996–97; memb Aosdána 1997; *Awards* Hennessy Award for short fiction 1979, Arts Cncl of NI literature bursary 1987 and 1991, Rooney Prize for Irish Literature 1987, Somerset Maugham Award 1989, Soc of Authors Award 1992, Hawthornden fellowship 1993, Kerry Book of the Year Award 1997, shortlisted Orange Prize 1997, Ellis Dillon Award 2006; *Books* Hidden Symptoms (1988), The Birds of the Innocent Wood (1988), Remembering Light and Stone (1992), Nothing is Black (1994), One by One in the Darkness (1996), Authenticity (2002), Snakes' Elbows (2005), Thanks for Telling Me, Emily (2007); *Style*— Ms Deirdre Madden; ✉ c/o A P Watt, 20 John Street, London WC1N 2DR (tel 020 7405 6774, fax 020 7831 2154, e-mail apw@apwatt.co.uk)

MADDEN, John Philip; s of William John Raleigh Madden, and Jean Elizabeth Hunt Mills; *b* 8 April 1949; *Educ* Clifton, Sidney Sussex Coll Cambridge (MA); *m* 1975, Penelope Jane, *née* Abrahams; *Career* film dir; artistic dir Oxford and Cambridge Shakespeare Co 1970–73, assoc prof Yale Sch of Drama 1977–80; hon fell Sidney Sussex Coll Cambridge 2000; Hon DLitt Univ of Portsmouth 2006; *Theatre* Wings, The Bundle, Measure for Measure, The Suicide, Terry by Terry, Grownups, Beyond Therapy, Salonika, Cinders, Between East and West, An American Comedy, Ivanov, Mrs Warren's Profession, Caritas, Proof; *Television* Poppyland, A Wreath of Roses, Sherlock Holmes, After the War, Widowmaker, Inspector Morse (four films), Prime Suspect: The Lost Child, Meat, Truth or Dare (BAFTA Scotland Award Best Single Drama 1997); *Radio* US Nat Public Radio: Wings (Prix Italia 1978), Star Wars, The Empire Strikes Back, Return of the Jedi; *Film* Ethan Frome 1992, Golden Gate 1994, Mrs Brown 1997, Shakespeare in Love 1998, Captain Corelli's Mandolin 2001, Proof 2005, Killshot 2006; *Recreations* cooking, walking, sailing; *Style*— John Madden, Esq; ✉ c/o Jenne Casarotto, Casarotto Ramsay Ltd, 4th Floor, 60 Wardour Street, London W1V 4ND

MADDEN, Michael; s of John Joseph Madden (d 1978), and Mary Ann, *née* Donnelly (d 1993); *b* 14 January 1937; *Educ* St Illtyd's Coll Cardiff, London Sch of Economics (BSc); *m* 27 Feb 1960, Patricia Margaret, da of Charles Gaspa, of Cliftonville, Kent; 2 s (Simon Jude b 1960, Stephen Paul b 1964), 1 da (Alison Maria b 1962); *Career* asst gen mangr Moscow Narodny Bank Ltd 1966–68 (economic advsr 1959–66), gen mangr First National Finance Corporation Ltd 1968–70, md Exim Credit Management Consultants Ltd 1971–76, exec dir Standard Chartered Merchant Bank Ltd 1977–86, dir Standard Chartered Merchant Bank Holdings 1984–86, md Standard Chartered Merchant Bank Ltd 1986, chief exec Standard Chartered Export Finance Ltd 1987–88, gen mangr Standard Chartered Bank 1987–88; non-exec dep chm and consIt (Int Ops) Afribank Nigeria plc 1989–99; former non-resident consIt: IBRD (World Bank) Washington, FAO (Investment Centre) Rome, International Trade Centre, UNCTAD Geneva; chm Harrow Community Health Servs NHS Tst 1991–94; *Recreations* rugby football, gardening, writing; *Clubs* Reform; *Style*— Michael Madden, Esq; ✉ Holly Lodge, 127 Chestnut Lane, Chesham Bois, Buckinghamshire HP6 6DZ (tel 01494 728821)

MADDEN, Nicholas Paul; s of Dr (Cyril) Paul Madden (d 1958), of Romford, Essex, and Barbara Joan, *née* Sykes (d 2003); *b* 12 June 1950; *Educ* Haileybury, Brasenose Coll Oxford (MA, BM BCh); *m* 11 Sept 1982, Su-Anna Margaret Boddy, *qv*; 1 s (Christopher Paul b 6 Feb 1987), 1 da (Katherine Anna b 15 Sept 1988); *Career* temporary lectr in anatomy Bart's Med Coll 1977–78, registrar in gen surgery and urology Luton and Dunstable Hosp 1980–82, registrar in paediatric surgery and urology Alder Hey Children's Hosp Liverpool 1982–85, res fell in paediatric surgery Inst of Child Health 1985–87, sr registrar paediatric surgn Leeds General Infirmary and St James's Univ Hosp Leeds 1987–91; consIt paediatric surgn: Chelsea and Westminster Hosp 1991–, St Mary's Hosp 1992–; memb: RSM 1991, British Assoc of Paediatric Surgns 1992 (prize 1987), European Soc for Paediatric Urology (ESPU) 1997, Br Assoc of Paediatric Urologists (BAPU) 1997; FRCS 1980; *Publications* author of numerous pubns in med jls; *Recreations* skiing, swimming, watching cricket; *Style*— Nicholas Madden; ✉ 15 Bridgefield Road, Cheam, Surrey SM1 2DG (tel 020 8661 7528); Department of Paediatric Surgery, Chelsea and Westminster Hospital, Fulham Road, London SW10 9NH (tel 020 8746 8696, fax 020 8746 8644, e-mail n.madden@imperial.ac.uk)

MADDEN, HE Paul Damian; s of Antony Angus Thomas Madden, of Devon, and Doris May, *née* Brewer; *b* 25 April 1959, Honiton, Devon; *Educ* Marist Convent Sch Ottery St Mary, King's Sch Ottery St Mary, Gonville & Caius Coll Cambridge (MA), Univ of Durham Business Sch (MBA); *m* 30 Sept 1989, Sarah Pauline, *née* Thomas; 2 s (Sebastian Xavier Francis b 2 Oct 1991, Rupert Christian St John b 27 Dec 1992), 1 da (Francesca Imogen Zara b 7 June 1996); *Career* diplomat; DTI: joined 1980, private sec to Rt Hon David Trippier, MP (as Min for Small Business) 1984–85, private sec to Rt Hon Michael Howard, MP (as Min for Corporate Affrs) 1985–86, head of Japan desk 1986–87; joined FCO 1987, Japanese language trg SOAS Univ of London 1987–88, first sec Tokyo 1989–92, Environment, Science and Energy Dept FCO 1992–94, EU Dept (external) FCO 1994–96, first sec Washington DC 1996–2000, dep high cmmr Singapore 2000–03, head Public Diplomacy Policy Dept FCO 2003–04, md UK Trade and Investment 2004–06, high cmmr to Singapore 2007–; FRGS; *Publications* Raffles: Lessons in Business Leadership (2003); *Recreations* travel, family; *Clubs* Tanglin (Singapore), Singapore Cricket; *Style*— HE Mr Paul Madden; ✉ British High Commission, 100 Tanglin Road, Singapore (tel 00 65 6424 4200, e-mail paul.madden@fco.gov.uk)

MADDICOTT, Dr John Robert Lewendon; s of Robert Maddicott (d 1990), and Barbara, *née* Lewendon (d 1996); *b* 22 July 1943; *Educ* Cheltenham GS, King Edward's Sch Bath, Worcester Coll Oxford (MA, DPhil); *m* 1965, Hilary, da of Thomas Owen; 2 da (Philippa b 1968, Sarah b 1972); *Career* asst lectr Univ of Manchester 1967–69, fell and tutor in modern history Exeter Coll Oxford 1969–2006 (sub-rector 1988–90, emeritus fell 2006–); visiting prof Univ of South Carolina 1983, Raleigh lectr Br Acad 2001, Ford lectr British History Univ of Oxford 2004; jt ed English Historical Review 1990–2000; FRHistS, FSA, FBA 1996; *Books* Thomas of Lancaster, 1307–1322 (1972), The English Peasantry and the Demands of the Crown, 1294–1341 (1975), Law and Lordship: Royal Justices as Retainers in Thirteenth and Fourteenth Century England (1978), Simon de Montfort (1994); *Recreations* hill walking, book collecting, poetry; *Style*— Dr John Maddicott, FSA, FBA; ✉ Exeter College, Oxford OX1 3DP (fax 01865 279630)

MADDICOTT, HE (David) Sydney (Syd); s of Patrick McCagh (d 2004), and Eileen, *née* Hannigan; adopted s of Sydney Walter Maddicott (d 1984), and Catherine, *née* O'Brien (d 1982); *b* 27 March 1953, Plymouth; *Educ* Becket Sch Nottingham, UCL (BA), UC Dublin, Univ of Exeter; *m* 1980, Elizabeth (Liz), *née* Wynne; 4 s (Edmund b 1980, Edgar b 1984, Edwin b 1990, Alfred b 1993), 1 da (Frances b 1982); *Career* diplomat; sales and mktg mangr Rank Xerox (UK) Ltd 1976–89, gen sales and mktg mangr Pitney Bowes (Ireland) Ltd 1989–90, consIt 1992–94; entered HM Dip Serv 1994, head of section Economic Rels Dept and UN Dept FCO 1994–96, on secondment to Canadian Dept of Foreign Affrs and Int Trade 1996–97, head of political, media and public affrs Ottawa 1997–2000, dep head Latin American and Caribbean Dept FCO 2000–03 (also head Caribbean Team), sr duty mangr Response Centre FCO 2003–05, high cmmr to Repub of Cameroon 2006– (concurrently non-resident ambass to Central African Repub, Chad and Gabon); *Recreations* singing, reading, speedway, cricket; *Clubs* Deddington CC, New Edinburgh CC (Ottawa), English Folk Dance and Song Soc (EFDSS); *Style*— HE Mr Syd Maddicott; ✉ c/o British High Commission, BP 547, Avenue Winston Churchill, Yaoundé, Cameroon (tel 00 237 22 22 0545, fax 00 237 22 22 0148, e-mail syd.maddicott@fco.gov.uk); c/o Foreign & Commonwealth Office (Yaoundé), King Charles Street, London SW1A 2AH

MADDISON, Peter Fenwick; QPM (2005); *Educ* Univ of Salford; *m*; 1 s; *Career* Durham Constabulary: joined 1975, Chief Inspr (Ops) 1989, seconded as Supt to Home Office District Policing Trg Centre 1990–92, head of force trg 1992–93, Divnl Cdr Darlington 1993–95, Supt (Force Ops) 1995–97; Hertfordshire Constabulary: Asst Chief Constable 1997–2000, Dep Chief Constable 2000–03; Chief Constable Northamptonshire Police 2003–; memb: Cabinet ACPO (also chair Performance Mgmnt Business Area), Milton Keynes/S Midlands Inter-Regnl Bd; *Recreations* family activities, running, reading, music, radio, current affairs, travel; *Style*— Peter F Maddison, Esq, QPM; ✉ Northamptonshire Police, Wootton Hall, Northampton NN4 0JQ

MADDISON, Prof Peter John; s of John Maddison, of London, and Renée, *née* Le Mesurier; *b* 12 December 1945; *Educ* St Albans Sch, Pembroke Coll Cambridge, St Bartholomew's Med Sch (MA, MB BChir, MD); *m* 17 Feb 1968, Merle Chadburn, da of late Denby Bamford, CBE, of Little Barrow, Cheshire; 1 s (Christopher); *Career* fell in rheumatology and immunology SUNY Buffalo 1974–77, asst prof of med 1977–79, consIt rheumatologist Royal Nat Hosp for Rheumatic Diseases Bath 1979–88; Univ of Bath: prof of bone and joint med 1988–96, dean Sch of Postgraduate Med 1989–95; chm and res dir Bath Inst of Rheumatic Diseases until 1996, res and educn dir Royal Nat Hosp for Rheumatic Diseases 1991–92; consIt rheumatologist NW Wales NHS Tst 1996–; prof of joint and muscle disorders Univ of Wales 1999–; Greenberg scholar Oklahoma Med Res Fndn 1992–93, Heberden Roundsman British Soc for Rheumatology 1994; author of over 250 scientific articles, reviews and chapters; med sec Arthritis and Rheumatism Cncl 1990–93, chm Wessex R&D Grants Ctee 1993–96, memb Scientific Bd Nat Osteoporosis Soc, memb Cncl British Soc of Rheumatology 2003–06 (also chair Heberden

Ctee), memb Educn Cmmn Arthritus Research Campaign 1999–2002; FRCP 1986; *Books* Rheumatological Medicine (with P A Dieppe, M Doherty and D G Macfarlane, 1985), The Skin In Rheumatic Diseases (with C L Lovell and G Campion, 1989), Rheumatology Examination and Injection Techniques (with M Doherty, J D Perry, C W Hutton and B L Hazelman, 1992), Oxford Textbook of Rheumatology (ed with D A Isenberg, P Woo and D N Glass, 1993, 3 edn 2005); *Recreations* cooking, music, golf; *Style*— Prof Peter Maddison; ✉ Bryn Selar, Glan Conwy, Colwyn Bay LL28 5SL (tel 01492 572126); Ysbyty Gwynedd, Bangor, Gwynedd LL57 2PW (tel 01248 385097)

MADDOCK, Baroness (Life Peer UK 1997), of Christchurch in the County of Dorset; Diana Maddock; *b* 19 May 1945; *Educ* Brockenhurst GS, Shenstone Teacher Trg Coll; *m* 1, 1966, Robert Frank Maddock; m 2, 2001, Rt Hon Alan Beith, MP , *qv*; *Career* teacher Southampton 1966–69 and 1972–73, ESL teacher Extra Mural Dept Stockholm Univ 1969–72, Bournemouth Anglo Continental Sch of English 1973–76, city cncllr Southampton 1984–93; MP (Lib Dem) Christchurch 1993–97; former Lib Dem spokesperson on: housing, the family and women's issues; vice-chair All-Pty Gp Electoral Reform; former vice-chm All-Pty Parly: Warm Houses Gp, Homelessness and Housing Need Gp (currently sec), Building Socs Gp; housing spokesperson Lib Dems in House of Lords 1997–2004, pres Lib Dems 1998–2000, CCncllr Northumberland 2005–, cncllr Berwick-upon-Tweed Borough Cncl 2007–; memb Ctee on Standards in Public Life 2003–; pres Nat Housing Forum, vice-pres Nat Housing Fedn, vice-pres Nat Home Improvement Cncl, vice-pres Neighbourhood Energy Action, pres The Micropower Cncl, tstee Richard Newitt Tst; pres Anglo Swedish Soc; *Recreations* travel, music and reading; *Clubs* National Liberal; *Style*— The Rt Hon Baroness Maddock; ✉ House of Lords, London SW1A 0PW

MADDOCKS, His Hon Bertram Catterall; s of His Hon George Maddocks (d 1980), of Southport, Lancs, and (Harriet) Mary Louisa, *née* Day; *b* 7 July 1932; *Educ* Rugby, Trinty Hall Cambridge (scholar, MA); *m* 13 June 1964, Angela Vergette, da of Michael Leetham Forster, of Aughton, Lancs; 2 s (Jeremy Christopher Catterall b 8 Dec 1985, Jolyon Simon Napoleon (Jo) b 4 Jan 1989), 1 da (Lucinda Jane Vergette (Cindy) b 8 Aug 1987); *Career* Nat Serv 2 Lt RA 1951; called to the Bar Middle Temple 1956 (Harmsworth scholar); recorder 1983–90, circuit judge (Northern Circuit) 1990–2005; pt/t chm VAT Tbnls 1977–90; memb Lincoln's Inn; Capt Duke of Lancaster's Own Yeo (TA) 1958–67; *Recreations* real tennis, lawn tennis, skiing, bridge; *Clubs* Cavalry and Guards', Manchester Tennis and Racquet; *Style*— His Hon Bertram Maddocks; ✉ Moor Hall Farm, Prescot Road, Aughton, Lancashire L39 6RT

MADDOCKS, Fiona Hamilton; *Educ* Blackheath HS London, Royal Coll of Music, Newnham Coll Cambridge (MA); *m* 1, 1989 (m dis), R Cooper; 2 da; m 2, 1995, Tom Phillips, CBE, RA, *qv*; *Career* teacher of English literature Istituto Orsoline Cortina D'Ampezzo Italy 1978, art publisher Medici Soc 1979, news trainee rising to sr prodr LBC 1980–82, launch ed Comment (Channel 4) 1982, regular contrib The Times 1983–86, asst commissioning ed Music (Channel 4) 1985, journalist, music ed and feature writer Independent 1986–91, fndr ed BBC Music Magazine 1992–97 (advsy ed 1997–98), chief music critic The Observer 1997–2002, ed BBC Proms Guide 1997–99, exec ed LSO Living Music magazine 1997–2003, memb Bd Opera magazine 1997–, chief arts feature writer and chief opera critic Evening Standard 2002–; memb Advsy Bd: BBC Fndn 2006–, Norbert Brainin Fndn 2006–; winner BP Arts Journalism Press Award 1990, various awards for BBC Music Magazine; govr Sherborne Sch 2002–; assoc Newnham Coll 1985–97; FRSA 2006; *Publications* Hildegard of Bingen (2001); *Style*— Miss Fiona Maddocks; ✉ c/o Evening Standard, Northcliffe House, 2 Derry Street, Kensington, London W8 5EE

MADDOX, Brenda Power Murphy (Lady Maddox); da of Dr Brendan W Murphy, and Edith Giamperoli; *b* 24 February 1932; *Educ* Bridgewater HS MA, Radcliffe Coll (cum laude); *m* 1960, Sir John Maddox; 1 s, 1 da, 1 step s, 1 step da; *Career* author and journalist; Patriot Ledger Quincy MA 1957–59, Reuters Ltd 1959–1960, The Economist 1962–72 and 1975–85 (latterly as Br ed then home affrs ed), media columnist Daily Telegraph 1987–1994, media columnist The Times 1994–97; vice-pres The Hay Festival; memb: Br Assoc of Science Writers (chm 1983–4), Broadcasting Press Guild (chm 1993–4); former non-exec dir London Broadcasting Co; former memb: UK Nat Cmmn for UNESCO, Mgmnt Ctee Soc of Authors, Royal Soc, Science in Society Ctee; Hon Phi Beta Kappa Harvard Univ 1978, Hon Dr Finch Univ 2004, Hon Dr Univ of Glamorgan 2005; FRSL 1994; *Publications* Beyond Babel: New Directions in Communications (1972), The Half-Parent (1975), Who's Afraid of Elizabeth Taylor? (biography, 1977), The Marrying Kind (1981), Nora: the Life of Mrs James Joyce (1988, LA Times Biography Prize 1988, Br Silver PEN Award 1989, Prix du Meilleur Livre Etranger 1990, adapted as film Nora 2000), D H Lawrence: The Married Man (1994, Whitbread Biography Award 1994), George's Ghosts: The Secret Life of W B Yeats (biography, 1999), Rosalind Franklin: the Dark Lady of DNA (2001, Marsh Biography Prize 2001, LA Times Science Prize 2002), Maggie: The First Lady (2003), Freud's Wizard: The Enigma of Ernest Jones (2006); author of reviews and articles for newspapers and magazines in GB and USA; *Recreations* gardening, cooking, exploring mid-Wales; *Clubs* Athenaeaum; *Style*— Brenda Maddox; ✉ c/o A P Watt, 20 John Street, London WC1N 2DR

MADDOX, Bronwen Maria; da of John R Maddox, and Brenda, *née* Murphy; *b* 7 May 1963; *Educ* St Paul's Girls' Sch London, Westminster, St John's Coll Oxford (BA); *Children* 1 da (Laura); *Career* venture capital analyst Charterhouse Bank 1985–86, Bd dir Kleinwort Benson Securities and head Media Res Team 1986–91; Financial Times: reporter 1991–94, leader writer 1994–96; The Times: US ed 1996–, foreign ed 1999–2006, chief foreign commentator 2006–; Br Press Award for Maxwell teams investigation; *Style*— Ms Bronwen Maddox; ✉ c/o The Times, 1 Pennington Street, London E1 9XN

MADDOX, Air Vice Marshal Nigel; CBE; s of Albert Maddox, of Hockley, Essex, and Beverley, *née* Brown (d 1997); *b* 1 April 1954, London; *Educ* Clark's Coll Southend-on-Sea, Westcliff HS, Open Univ (MBA); *m* 1 Sept 1979, Susan Armitage-Maddox, *née* Armitage; 1 da (Nicola Alexandra Beatrix b 16 June 1997); *Career* OC Ops Wing RAF Mount Pleasant Falkland Is, OC 12 Sqdn RAF Lossiemouth 1991–93, AD(W) Defence Commitments MOD 1993–95, sr RAF offr Germany and station cdr RAF Brüggen 1996–98, Air Cdre Maritime RAF Northwood 1999–2002, AOC No 2 Gp RAF High Wycombe 2002–; Freeman City of London, Freeman Worshipful Co of Carmen; *Recreations* squash, golf; *Clubs* RAF; *Style*— Air Vice Marshal Nigel Maddox, CBE; ✉ Air Officer Commanding, No 2 Group, Group Headquarters, RAF High Wycombe, Buckinghamshire HP14 4UE (tel 01494 496331)

MADDOX, Ronald Arthur; s of Harold George Maddox, and Winifred Maddox; *b* 5 October 1930; *Educ* Herts Coll of Art and Design, London Coll of Printing and Graphic Art; *m* 1, 1958, Camilla Farrin (d 1995); 2 s; m 2, 1997, Diana Goodwin; *Career* Nat Serv Air Miny Design Unit RAF 1949–51; graphic artist and art dir various advtg agencies London 1951–61, in private practice as artist, illustrator and conslt designer 1962– (cmmnd by nat and multinational cos, govt depts, local authys, TV and publishers); designer Br postage stamps and philatelic material 1972–; stamp issues designed incl: Village Churches, Historic Buildings, Urban Renewal, Industrial Archaeology; designer Landscape of Britain series Royal Mail aerogrammes, work widely reproduced as illustrations for books, calendars, prints and cards; exhibitions incl: Mall Galleries, Royal Acad, Bankside Galleries; works in the collections of: HM Queen Elizabeth the Queen Mother, 10 Downing St, Sultanate of Oman, Nat Tst, PO, DOE, Barclays Bank, BP, Shell, John Laing, Mobil Oil; winner Prix de l'Art Philatelique 1987, Winsor and Newton RI awards 1981 and 1991, Rowland Hilder RI Award 1996 and 2000 (for outstanding landscape painting); memb Mgmnt Bd Fedn of Br Artists, memb Cncl Artists' Gen Benevolent Inst (AGBI) 2000 (hon sec 2002); Royal Inst of Painters in Water Colours: memb 1959, vice-pres 1979, pres 1989– (re-elected 1999 and 2004); assessor: Royal Acad Summer exhbn, Turner Watercolour Award; patron: Danesbury/QVM Hospital Welwyn, Isabel Hospice Welwyn Garden City; tstee: Welwyn Scouts and Guides Assoc, Digswell Arts Tst; hon memb: Pastel Soc, Soc of Architect Artists, Fedn of Canadian Artists, United Soc of Artists, Soc of Graphic Artists, Campine Assoc of Watercolours Belgium; Freeman City of London 2000, Hon Freeman Worshipful Co of Painter-Stainers 2000; Hon RWS 1990, Hon RBA 2002, FCSD, FSAI, FRSA, Hon Memb The Arts Club; *Recreations* compulsive drawing, walking, cycling, gardening; *Style*— Ronald Maddox, Esq; ✉ Herons, 21 New Road, Digswell, Welwyn, Hertfordshire AL6 0AQ (tel 01438 714884)

MADDRELL, Geoffrey Keggen; s of Capt Geoffrey Douglas Maddrell (d 1975), of Port Erin, IOM, and Barbara Marie Maddrell (d 2000); *b* 18 July 1936; *Educ* King William's Coll IOM, CCC Cambridge (MA), Columbia Univ NY (MBA); *m* 12 Oct 1964, Winifred Mary Daniel, da of Frank Dowell Jones (d 1984), of St Asaph, Clwyd; 2 s (Paul b 1965, Michael b 1971), 1 da (Siân b 1966); *Career* Lt Parachute Regiment 1955–57; Shell Int Petroleum 1960–69; dir Bowater Corp 1978–86, chief exec Tootal Gp plc 1986–91; chm: Glenmorangie plc 1994–2002, ProShare 1994–2003 (chief exec 1991–94), Unite Gp 1999–, LDV Ltd, Westbury plc, Ivory and Sime ISIS Tst plc, Buildstore Ltd; dir: Transport Development Gp plc 1992–97, Goldcrest Homes Ltd; pt/t Civil Service cmmr 1992–96 and 2001–05; chm: Manchester TEC 1989–91, Airborne Forces Charities 1996–2005, Research Autism Tst; memb Bd of Govrs UMIST 1987–92; tstee Help the Aged 1983–86; *Recreations* running, golf; *Clubs* Serpentine Running, Rowany Golf; *Style*— Geoffrey Maddrell, Esq; ✉ 28 Sussex Street, London SW1V 4RL (e-mail geoffrey.maddrell@unite-group.co.uk)

MADDRELL, Prof Simon Hugh Piper; s of Hugh Edmund Fisher Maddrell (d 1969), farmer, and Barbara Agnes Mary, *née* Chamberlin (d 1996), photographer; *b* 11 December 1937; *Educ* Peter Symonds' Sch Winchester, St Catharine's Coll Cambridge (scholar, MA, PhD, ScD); *m* 1, Anna, *née* Myers; 1 da (Penelope Jane b 21 Feb 1962), 3 s (Robin Charles Fisher b 17 Jan 1965, Joseph Timothy b 19 June 1968, Samuel James b 2 Jan 1971); m 2, Katherine Mona, *née* Mapes; *Career* Nat Research Cncl of Canada postdoctoral research fell Dalhousie Univ Halifax Canada; Univ of Cambridge: SRC/NATO postdoctorate research fell Dept of Zoology 1964–65, fell and coll lectr Gonville & Caius Coll 1968–2006 (life fell 2006–), (open (prize) research fell 1964–68, also research assoc Univ of Massachusetts Amherst 1967), princ scientific offr ARC Unit of Invertebrate Chemistry & Physiology Dept of Zoology 1972–78 (sr scientific offr 1972, also research assoc Dept of Zoology Univ of Br Columbia 1974 and 1975), sr princ scientific offr (individual merit promotion) AFRC Unit of Insect Neurophysiology and Pharmacology Dept of Zoology 1978–90, hon reader in comparative physiology 1990–2003, hon prof of integrative physiology 2003–; currently investments mangr The Company of Biologists Ltd (fin sec 1965–); Centenary Year Scientific Medal Zoological Soc of London 1976; FRS 1981; *Recreations* swimming, gardening, art and architecture, wine, travel, photography; *Style*— Prof Simon Maddrell, FRS; ✉ The Company of Biologists Ltd, Department of Zoology, Downing Street, Cambridge CB2 3ED (e-mail shpm100@hermes.cam.ac.uk)

MADELEY, Richard; s of Christopher Madeley (d 1977), and Mary Claire, *née* McEwan; *b* 13 May 1956; *m* 21 Nov 1986; Judith Finnigan, *qv*; 1 s (Jack b 19 May 1986), 1 da (Chloe b 13 July 1987); 2 step s (Thomas, Daniel (twins) b 2 March 1977); *Career* television presenter; reporter Brentwood Argus Newspaper 1972–74, news ed/asst ed East London Advertiser 1975–76, reporter/presenter/news prodr BBC Radio Carlisle 1976–78, reporter/presenter Border TV 1978–80, reporter/presenter YTV 1980–82; presenter: Granada TV 1982–2001, Cactus TV 2001– (Richard and Judy (Channel 4), Br Book Awards (Channel 4) 2004–), Fortune (ITV); *Awards* RTS Team Award for This Morning 1994, Most Popular Daytime Programme National Television Awards 1998, 1999, 2000 and 2001; *Style*— Richard Madeley, Esq; ✉ c/o James Grant Management, 94 Strand on the Green, Chiswick, London W4 3NN (tel 020 8742 4950, fax 020 8742 4951)

MADHVANI, Manubhai; s of late Muijibhai Madhvani, and late Parvatiben Madhvani; *b* Uganda; *Educ* Uganda and India; *m* Shardaben, *née* Sharda; 2 c (Kamlesh, Shrai); *Career* jt md Kakira Sugar Works (1985) Ltd (part of Madhvani Gp of Cos); *Style*— Manubhai Madhvani, Esq; ✉ Kakira Sugar Works (1985) Ltd, PO Box 121, Jinja, Uganda

MADI, HE Gehad Refaat; s of Refaat Madi, and Fatma Madi; *b* 13 November 1951, Cairo, Egypt; *Educ* Ain Shams Univ (BA (Faculty of Languages), BA (Faculty of Law)); *m* Oct 1997, Mona, *née* El Shafei; 1 da (Salma b 30 May 1998); *Career* Egyptian diplomat; Embassy of Egypt Bonn 1978–82, memb Cabinet of the Min of Foreign Affrs 1982–84, press cnsllr to Min of Foreign Affrs 1984–86, cnsllr and legal advsr Perm Mission to UN in NY 1986–90, cnsllr i/c int orgns and legal affrs Cabinet of Foreign Min 1991–92, cnsllr and later min plenipotentiary Embassy of Egypt in London 1992–96, dep asst foreign min for int confs and then for legal affrs 1996–98, ambass to India 1998–2002, dep asst foreign min for human rights 2002–03, asst min of foreign affrs and dir Diplomatic and Consular Corps 2003–04, ambass to the Ct of St James's 2004–; fourth degree Order of the Arab Republic of Egypt, fourth degree Order of Merit (Egypt), Order of Merit (Germany); *Recreations* walking, reading, theatre, classical music; *Clubs* RAC, Travellers, Athenaeum; *Style*— HE Mr Gehad Madi; ✉ 75 South Audley Street, London W1K 1JF (tel 020 7499 2401); Embassy of the Arab Republic of Egypt, 26 South Street, London W1K 1DW (tel 020 7499 2567, fax 020 7355 3568)

MAGAN, George Morgan; s of Brig William Morgan Tilson Magan, CBE; *b* 14 November 1945; *Educ* Winchester; *m* 1972, Wendy Anne, da of Maj Patrick Chilton, MC; 2 s (Edward b 1975, Patrick b 1984), 1 da (Henrietta b 1977); *Career* merchant banker; pty treas Cons and Unionist Pty 2003–; chm: eMuse Dublin, Lion Capital Ptnrs, Mallett plc, Morgan Shipley Ltd Dubai, Rhône Gp Ltd; dir: Bank of Ireland, Edmiston & Co; tstee: Cons Pty Fndn, ROH Covent Garden 1995–2001, London Philharmonic Orch (chm), Br Museum Devpt Tst 1999–2003; FCA; *Clubs* Royal Yacht Sqdn, Turf, Boodle's, The Brook (NY), Kildare St and Univ (Dublin); *Style*— George Magan, Esq; ✉ 5 Princes Gate, Knightsbridge, London SW7 1QJ (tel 020 7761 1051)

MAGEE, Bryan; s of Frederick Magee; *b* 12 April 1930; *Educ* Christ's Hosp, Lycée Hôche Versailles, Keble Coll Oxford (MA), Yale Univ; *m* 1954 (m dis), Ingrid Söderlund; 1 da; *Career* writer, critic and broadcaster; formerly: columnist The Times, drama critic The Listener; music critic for numerous pubns 1959–; Parly candidate (Lab) Mid Beds 1959 and 1960, MP Leyton (Lab until 1982, Ind Lab 1982, SDP 1982–83); lectr in philosophy Balliol Coll Oxford 1970–71, visiting fell All Souls Coll Oxford 1973–74, hon sr fell in the history of ideas KCL 1984–94, visiting prof KCL 1994–2000, academic visitor LSE 1994–97; visiting fell: Wolfson Coll Oxford 1993–94 (visiting scholar 1991–93), New Coll Oxford 1995, Merton Coll Oxford 1998, St Catherine's Coll Oxford 2000, Peterhouse Cambridge 2001, Clare Hall Cambridge 2004 (life memb); visiting prof Univ of Otago NZ 2006; memb Arts Cncl (chm Music Advsy Panel) 1993–94; memb Cncl: Critics' Circle 1975– (pres 1983–84), Ditchley Fndn 1982– (govr 1979–); judge: Evening Standard Opera Award 1973–84, Laurence Olivier Opera Award 1990–91 and 1993–95, Royal Philharmonic Soc Annual Opera Award 1991–2000; pres Edinburgh Univ Philosophy Soc 1987–88; Silver Medal RTS 1978; fell: Queen Mary & Westfield Coll London 1989 (QMC 1988), Royal Philharmonic Soc 1990; hon fell Keble Coll Oxford 1994; Hon DLitt Univ of Leicester 2005; *Books* Crucifixion and Other Poems (1951), Go West Young Man

M

(1958), To Live in Danger (1960), The New Radicalism (1962), The Democratic Revolution (1964), Towards 2000 (1965), One in Twenty (1966), The Television Interviewer (1966), Aspects of Wagner (1968, revised edn 1988), Modern British Philosophy (1971), Popper (1973), Facing Death (1977), Men of Ideas (1978, re-issued as Talking Philosophy 2001), The Philosophy of Schopenhauer (1983, revised edn 1997), The Great Philosophers (1987), On Blindness (1995, re-issued as Sight Unseen 1998), Confessions of a Philosopher (1997), The Story of Philosophy (1998), Wagner and Philosophy (2000), Clouds of Glory: A Hoxton Childhood (2003, J R Ackerley Prize for Autobiography 2004), Growing Up in a War (2007); *Recreations* music, theatre; *Clubs* Garrick, Savile; *Style*— Bryan Magee, Esq; ✉ Wolfson College, Oxford OX2 6UD

MAGEE, Christopher Douglas; s of late Douglas David Magee, of Farnham, Surrey, and late Eva Mary, *née* Pope; *b* 3 November 1945; *Educ* George Abbott Sch Guildford, Guildford Coll of Technol, Univ of Reading (OND, HND, MSc); *m* 4 May 1985, Carol Elizabeth, da of Alan Boocock, of Bispham, Blackpool, Lancs; 2 da (Laura Victoria b 27 May 1986, Sarah Eve b 7 April 1988); *Career* mangr Jeddah W S Try International Ltd 1979, commercial exec W S Try Ltd 1984, gen mangr Barlow Turnkey Contracts Ltd 1986, dir George Kemp Stroud & Co Ltd 1988, md Knowles & Son (Oxford) Ltd 2003– (dir 1999); Liveryman Worshipful Co of Constructors 2007 (Freeman 2006); FCIOB 1981, FCMI (FIMgt 1982), MCIArb 2005; *Recreations* society secretary, photography, touring, gardening; *Style*— Chris D Magee, Esq; ✉ 45 Abbots Ride, Farnham, Surrey GU9 8HZ (tel 01252 723743, e-mail cdmagee172@aol.com); Knowles & Son (Oxford) Ltd, Holywell House, Osney Mead, Oxford OX2 0EX (tel 01865 249681, fax 01865 790601, mobile 078 3159 5915, e-mail cdm@knowlesandson.co.uk)

MAGEE, Sir Ian Bernard Vaughan; kt (2006), CB (2002); *b* 9 July 1946; *Educ* St Michael's Coll Leeds, Univ of Leeds (BA); *Career* private sec to Min for Social Security 1976–78, seconded to Enterprise Unit Cabinet Office 1984–86, dep to Dir of Personnel DSS 1986–89, dir Southern Territory Benefits Agency 1990–93; chief exec Information Technology Services Agency 1993–98, chief exec Court Service Agency 1998–2003, chief exec (second permanent sec) ops DCA 2003–05, dir St Albans Consulting Ltd 2006–, sr advsr Booz Allen Hamilton 2006–; *Recreations* sport, family, reading; *Clubs* MCC, RAC; *Style*— Sir Ian Magee, CB

MAGINNESS, Alban; MLA; s of Alphonsus Maginness (d 1999), of Belfast, and Patricia *née* O'Hara (d 2001); *b* 9 July 1950; *Educ* St Malachy's Coll, Univ of Ulster (BA), Queen's Univ Belfast; *m* 1 Aug 1978, Carmel, da of late Patrick McWilliams; 5 da, 3 s; *Career* barr-at-law Bar of NI 1976; Belfast CC 1985 (re-elected 1989, 1993 and 1997), Lord Mayor 1997–98; Parly candidate Westminster General Election N Belfast 1997 and 2001; MLA (SDLP) N Belfast 1998–, chair SDLP, chair Regnl Devpt Ctee; memb Ctee of the Regions EU 2002–; govr Linenhall Library; *Recreations* walking, reading, theatre, Donegal; *Style*— Alban Maginness, Esq, MLA; ✉ 228 Antrim Road, Belfast BT15 4AN; Northern Ireland Assembly, Parliament Buildings, Stormont Estate, Belfast (tel 028 9022 0520, fax 028 9022 0522)

MAGINNIS OF DRUMGLASS, Baron (Life Peer UK 2001), of Carnteel in the County of Tyrone; Kenneth Wiggins (Ken) Maginnis; s of Gilbert Maginnis (d 1974), of Dungannon, and Margaret Elizabeth Wiggins (d 1984); *b* 21 January 1938; *Educ* Royal Sch Dungannon, Stranmillis Teacher Trg Coll Belfast; *m* 1961, Joy Stewart, da of Herbert Moneymore (d 1976), and Jeannie Moneymore (d 2000); 2 s (Hon Stewart b 1963, Hon Steven b 1971), 2 da (Hon Gail b 1964, Hon Grainne b 1969); *Career* Ulster Special Constabulary 1958–65, UDR 1970–81 (RMA Sandhurst, Co Cdrs Course Warminster, Maj 1972); teacher: Cookstown Secdy Sch 1959–60, Drumglass Primary Sch Dungannon 1960–66; princ Pomeroy Primary Sch 1966–82; MP (UUP) Fermanagh and S Tyrone 1983–2001; memb: House of Commons Select Ctee on Def 1984–85, Southern Health and Social Servs Bd 1989–91, Armed Forces Bill 1990–91, Southern Health and Social Servs Cncl 1991–93, NI Affairs 1994–97; elected to NI Forum 1996–98; memb: Dungannon DC 1981–93 and 2001–, NI Assembly 1982–86; memb Assembly's: Fin and Personnel Ctee (dep chm 1982–86), Security and Home Affairs Ctee (chm 1982–86); vice-pres UU Cncl, memb Exec UU Party (spokesman on defence, and home affrs); fndr Police Rehabilitation and Retraining Tst; fndr memb Prison Offrs Tst NI; chm Moygashel Community Devpt Assoc; *Publications* McGimpsey & McGimpsey v Ireland (1989), Witness for the Prosecution (1993), Disarmament - Pathway to Peace (1999); author of various articles in national newspapers; *Style*— The Rt Hon the Lord Maginnis of Drumglass

MAGNUS, Sir Laurence Henry Philip; 3 Bt (UK 1917), of Tangley Hill, Wonersh, Co Surrey; s of Hilary Barrow Magnus, TD, QC (d 1987), and Rosemary Vera Anne, *née* Masefield; suc unc, Sir Philip Magnus-Allcroft, 2 Bt (d 1988); *b* 24 September 1955; *Educ* Eton, ChCh Oxford (MA); *m* 1983, Jocelyn Mary, eldest da of Robert Henry Foster Stanton; 2 s (Thomas Henry Philip b 1985, Edmund Robert Hilary b 1991), 1 da (Iona Alexandra b 1988); *Heir* s, Thomas Magnus; *Career* Samuel Montagu & Co Ltd: gen mangr Singapore branch 1984–88, exec dir and dep head UK Corp Fin 1988–95; exec dir Phoenix Securities Ltd 1995–97, exec md investment banking Donaldson, Lufkin and Jenrette Inc 1997–2000, md investment banking Credit Suisse First Boston Inc 2000–01, vice-chm Lexicon Partners 2001–; non-exec dir: FIM Services Ltd 1997–, TT Electronics plc 2001–, JP Morgan Income and Capital Investment Tst plc 2001–, Climate Exchange plc 2006–, The Cayenne Tst plc 2006–; non-exec chm: xchanging Ins-Sure Services Ltd 2001–; chm Eating Disorders Assoc (BEAT) 2005–, dep chm Nat Tst 2005– (chm Fin Ctee 2002–05 (memb 1997–2005), memb Cncl 2003–), tstee Windsor Leadership Tst 2006–; *Recreations* fishing, reading, hill walking; *Clubs* Millennium, Brooks's, City of London; *Style*— Sir Laurence Magnus, Bt; ✉ Flat 8, 44 Lower Sloane Street, London SW1W 8BP; Lexicon Partners Ltd, 1 Paternoster Square, London EC4M 3DX (e-mail lmagnus@lexiconpartners.com)

MAGONET, Rabbi Prof Jonathan David; s of Capt Alexander Philip Magonet (d 1978), and Esther, *née* Slonims (d 1972); *b* 2 August 1942; *Educ* Westminster, Middlesex Hosp Med Sch Univ of London (MB BS), Leo Baeck Coll (Rabbinic ordination), Univ of Heidelberg (PhD); *m* 10 May 1974, Dorothea Elsa Martha, da of Gerhardt Foth; 1 s (Gavriel b 4 May 1978), 1 da (Avigail b 28 April 1981); *Career* Leo Baeck Coll: lectr and head Dept of Bible Studies 1974–85, princ 1985–2005, prof of Hebrew and Biblical studies 1996–2005, emeritus prof of Bible 2005–; scholar in residence Dept of Jewish Educn Univ of Tel Aviv 1990–91; visiting prof: Kirchliche Hochschule Wuppertal 1992, 1993, 1995 and 2004, Carl von Ossietsky Univ Oldenburg 1999 and 2004, Universität Luzern 2003; vice-pres World Union for Progressive Judaism 1985–2005; ed European Judaism 2004– (memb Editorial Bd 1978–, co-ed 1992–2004); Hon Dr: Kirchliche Hochschule Wuppertal 2005, Open Univ 2006, Hebrew Union Coll Jewish Inst of Religion 2007; FRSA; Cross of the Order of Merit of the Federal Rep of Germany 1999; *Books* Form and Meaning: Studies in Literary Techniques in the Book of Jonah (1976), Forms of Prayer: Vol 1 Daily and Sabbath Prayerbook (co-ed with Lionel Blue, 1977), Forms of Prayer: Vol III Days of Awe Prayerbook (co-ed with Lionel Blue, 1985), The Guide to the Here and the Hereafter (co-ed with Lionel Blue, 1988), A Rabbi's Bible (1991 and 2004 (as A Rabbi Reads the Bible)), How To Get Up When Life Gets You Down: A Companion and Guide (co-ed with Lionel Blue, 1992), Bible Lives (1992), The Little Blue Book of Prayer (co-ed with Lionel Blue, 1993), A Rabbi Reads the Psalms (1994 and 2004), Forms of Prayer: Vol II Pilgrim Festivals (co-ed with Lionel Blue, 1995), Kindred Spirits: A Year of Readings (co-ed with Lionel Blue, 1995), Jewish Explorations of Sexuality (ed, 1995), The Subversive Bible (1997), Mit Der Bibel Durch Das Jüdische Jahr (1998), The Explorer's Guide to Judaism (1998), Sun, Sand and Soul (co-ed Lionel Blue, 1999),

Abraham-Jesus-Mohammed: Interreligiöser Dialog aus jüdischer Perspektive (2000), From Autumn to Summer: A Biblical Journey Through the Jewish Year (2000), Talking to the Other: Jewish Interfaith Dialogue with Christians and Muslims (2003); *Style*— Rabbi Prof Jonathan Magonet; ✉ Leo Baeck College, 80 East End Road, London N3 2SY (tel 020 8349 5600, fax 020 8343 2558, e-mail jonathan.magonet@lbc.ac.uk)

MAGORIAN, Michelle Jane; da of William Magorian, and Gladys Freda Evans (d 1975); *b* 6 November 1947; *Educ* Kilbreda Coll, Convent of the Cross, Rose Bruford Coll of Speech and Drama, L'Ecole Internationale de Mime Paris; *m* 18 Aug 1987 (m dis 1998), Peter Keith Venner, s of Albert Keith Venner; 2 s (Tom b 5 March 1989, George b 23 Sept 1993); *Career* writer, entertainer; in rep since 1970, one woman shows: touring Italy and UK 1980, The Pact 1993–, Food and Love - Play On! 1999, Life, Love and Second Helpings 2002; memb: Soc of Authors, PEN; *Books* Goodnight Mister Tom (1981, lyrics for stage musical 1992, audio book 1997, broadcast Radio 5, TV film 1998, book and lyrics 2001), Back Home (1985, made into TV films 1989 and 2001, dramatised for Radio 4 1995, audiobook 2001), Waiting For My Shorts To Dry (1989), Who's Going to Take Care of Me? (1990), Orange Paw Marks (1991), A Little Love Song (1991), In Deep Water (a collection of short stories, 1992, 3 dramatised for Radio 4 1999), Cuckoo in the Nest (1994), A Spoonful of Jam (1998), Hello Life! (book (jtly) and lyrics, 2001), Canapes for Company (book and lyrics, 2001, retitled Tinsel), Jump! (2002), Be Yourself (2003); short stories incl six anthologies; *Style*— Ms Michelle Magorian; ✉ c/o Patricia White, Rogers, Coleridge and White Literacy Agency, 20 Powis Mews, London W11 1JN (tel 020 7221 3717, website www.michellemagorian.com)

MAGOS, Adam László; s of László Aurel Pal Magos, of London, and Eva Maria, *née* Banjamin; *b* 26 September 1953, Budapest; *Educ* Whitgift Sch Haling Park S Croydon Surrey, King's Coll London (BSc), King's Coll Hosp Sch of Med London (MB BS, MD, MRCOG); *m* Anne Cyprienne, *née* Coburn; 3 s (Tiarnan Adam b 5 Aug 1985, Siadhal László b 16 March 1987, Abban Zoltan b 24 April 1990); *Career* clinical lectr and hon sr registrar Nuffield Dept of Obstetrics and Gynaecology John Radcliffe Hosp Oxford 1986–90, sr lectr and hon conslt Academic Dept of Obstetrics and Gynaecology Royal Free Hosp Sch of Med 1990–91, conslt obstetrician and gynaecologist and hon sr lectr Univ Dept of Obstetrics and Gynaecology Royal Free Hosp 1991–, conslt gynaecologist King Edward VII's Hosp for Offrs London 1992–; treas Br Soc for Gynaecological Endoscopy 1989–92; memb: Advsy Bd Euro Soc for Hysteroscopy 1990–96, Working Gp on New Technol in Endoscopic Gynaecological Surgery RCOG 1993–94, Editorial Bd Gynaecological Endoscopy 1993– (ed 1990–93), MAS Training Sub-Ctee RCOG 1998–2001; author of over 150 pubns in peer review jls and chapters in books; Syntex Award (Int Soc of Reproduction Med) 1988; hon memb: Aust Soc of Gynaecological Endoscopy 1994, Egyptian Soc of Gynaecological Endoscopy 1996; memb: Blair Bell Research Soc 1982, Euro Soc of Hysteroscopy 1988, European Soc for Gynaecological Endoscopy 1995–; fndr memb: Br Soc for Gynaecological Endoscopy 1989, Soc of Minimally Invasive Therapy 1990; Cannell lectr Soc of Obstetricians and Gynaecologists of Canada 1999; awarded: the Dr Bhaneuben M Nanavati Golden Jubilee Oration Award in Bombay 1994, Veress Memorial Medal from the Hungarian Soc for Gynaecological Endoscopy 1997; FRCOG 1998, hon fell Br Soc for Gynaecoloigical Endoscopy 2004; *Recreations* music, saxophone, jazz, computing, cooking; *Style*— Adam Magos, Esq; ✉ University Department of Obstetrics and Gynaecology, The Royal Free Hospital, Pond Street, Hampstead, London NW3 2QG (tel 020 7431 1321, fax 020 7431 1321, e-mail a.magos@medsch.ucl.ac.uk); King Edward VII's Hospital Sister Agnes, 10 Beaumont Street, London W1G 2AA (tel 020 7486 4411, fax 020 7224 4417)

MAGUIRE, Adrian Edward; s of Joseph Maguire, of Kilmessan, Co Meath, and Philomena Maguire (d 1995); *b* 29 April 1971; *Educ* Kilmessan Nat Sch, Trim Vocational Sch; *m* 1995, Sabrina; 1 da (Shannon b 1996), 1 s (Finian b 1998); *Career* racehorse jockey; achievements incl: champion pony race rider 1986, champion point-to-point rider 1990–91, champion conditional jockey 1991–92, ridden over 1000 winners; major races won: Cheltenham Gold Cup, Irish Grand Nat (youngest ever winning jockey), Galway Plate, Imperial Cup, Greenalls Gold Cup, Queen Mother Champion Chase (Cheltenham), King George VI Chase (Kempton Park), Triumph Hurdle and Cathcort Chase (both Cheltenham); records: most point-to-point winners in a season, most winners in a season for a conditional jockey (71) 1991–92; *Recreations* squash, watching TV; *Style*— Adrian Maguire, Esq; ✉ c/o The Jockey Club (Jockey Section), 42 Portman Square, London W1H 0EM

MAGUIRE, Dr Anne; da of Richard Patrick Maguire (d 1972), and Ruth Alice Maguire (d 1963); *Educ* Royal Free Hosp Sch of Med London (MB BS), CG Jung Inst Zurich (dip); *Career* dermatological trg St John's Hosp for Diseases of the Skin Guy's Hosp and Univ Coll Hosp 1956–64, in private practice Harley St; author of numerous papers in medicine and psychotherapy; Ratclyffe Crocker travelling fellowship Hosp Saint-Louis Paris; memb: Br Assoc of Dermatologists, Int Assoc of Analytical Psychologists; FRCP 1974 (MRCP 1956); *Books* Hauterkrankungen als Botschaften der Seele (1991, re-published in English as Skin Disease: A Message from the Soul, 2004), Vom Sinn der kranken Sinne (1993), The Seven Deadly Sins (published in German, 1996, re-published in English as Seven Deadly Sins: The Dark Companions of the Soul, 2004); *Style*— Dr Anne Maguire; ✉ 17 Wellington Street, St John's, Blackburn BB1 8AF (tel 01254 59910); 10 Harley Street, London W1G 9PF (tel 020 7467 8300)

MAGUIRE, Sheriff Principal John Joseph; QC (Scot 1990); s of Robert Maguire (d 1954), solicitor, of Glasgow, and Julia, *née* Long (d 1986); *b* 30 November 1934; *Educ* St Ninian's HS Kirkintilloch, St Mary's Coll Blairs, Pontifical Gregorian Univ (PhL), Univ of Edinburgh (LLB); *m* 23 April 1962, Eva, da of Thomas O'Hara, of Tralee; 2 s (Andrew Sean b 22 Jan 1964, Gordon Patrick b 3 Jan 1968), 2 da (Julia Mary b 8 June 1965, Aisling Elizabeth b 9 Sept 1969); *Career* called to the Bar 1958, standing jr to Miny of Public Bldgs & Works 1962–68, sheriff at Airdrie 1968–73, sheriff at Glasgow 1973–90, sheriff principal of Tayside, Central and Fife 1990–98; pres Sheriffs Assoc 1988–90 (sec 1982–87), memb Departmental Ctee on Alternatives to Prosecution 1977–82, Scottish rep Int Union of Judges 1984–87; chairman Northern Light Houseboard 1995–97; chm: St Philip's List D Sch 1969–77, Caldervale Dist Scouts 1975–85; chm and co-fndr PHEW charity for the mentally handicapped 1984–90, memb Parole Bd for Scotland 2000–; *Recreations* reading, travel (by train, if possible); *Clubs* County and City (Perth); *Style*— Sheriff Principal John Maguire, QC; ✉ Spring Lodge, Hatton Way, Perth PH2 7DP (e-mail johnjmaguire@blueyonder.co.uk)

MAGUIRE, Máiread Corrigan; da of Andrew and Margaret Corrigan; *b* 27 January 1944; *Educ* St Vincent's Primary Sch Falls Road Belfast, Miss Gordon's Commercial Coll Belfast; *m* 1981, Jackie Maguire; 2 s (John Francis b 1982, Luke b 1984), 3 step c (Mark, Joanne, Marie Louise); *Career* initiator of Peace Movement in NI, jt fndr Community of the Peace People, chm Peace People 1980–81, hon life pres Peace People; winner numerous honours and awards; jt recipient Nobel Peace Prize 1976; winner: Norwegian People's prize, Carl-Von-Ossietzky medaille for Courage Berlin 1976; special honouree: UN Women of Achievement programme 1978, American Acad of Achievement; winner Pacem in Terris (Peace and Freedom award) Davenport Iowa 1990, Hon Dr Yale Univ; co fndr Ctee for the Administration of Justice, former volunteer Legion of Mary (work with prisons and prisoners); previously employed as confidential sec to md A Guinness Son & Co (Belfast) Ltd; *Recreations* swimming, music; *Style*— Mrs Máiread Corrigan Maguire; ✉ 224 Lisburn Road, Belfast BT9 6GE (office tel 028 9066 3465, fax 028 9068 3947, e-mail info@peacepeople.com, website www.peacepeople.com.)

MAGUIRE, Robert Alfred; OBE (1983); s of Arthur Maguire (d 1950), of London, and Rose Lilian, *née* Fountain (d 1986); *b* 6 June 1931; *Educ* Bancroft's Sch, AA Sch of Architecture (AA Dipl); *m* 1, 6 Aug 1955 (m dis 1978), Robina Helen, da of Robert Finlayson; 4 da (Susan b 1956, Rebecca b 1958, Joanna b 1960, Martha b 1963); m 2, 26 Oct 1982, Alison Margaret, da of George Marshall Mason, of Henley-on-Thames; *Career* bldgs ed Architects' Jl 1954–59, private architectural practice 1956–2003, ptnr Robert Maguire and Keith Murray 1959–89; chm: Maguire & Co International 1990–2002, Maguire Glynn Miller Ltd 1991–95; consIt Maguire & Co 2003– (chm 1989–2003); most important works incl: St Paul's Church Bow Common London 1959 (listed Grade II Star), St Matthew's Church Perry Beeches Birmingham 1960 (listed Grade II), St Mary's Abbey West Malling extensions 1962 (listed Grade II) and new church 1964 (listed Grade II Star), Trinity Coll Oxford extensions 1965, student village Stag Hill Ct Univ of Surrey 1969, bldgs in Cathedral Precinct for King's Sch Canterbury 1975–86, Kindertagesstatte Berlin-Kreuzberg 1983, extensions Pembroke Coll Oxford 1986, extensions Magdalen Coll Oxford 1987, masterplan for Abha campus King Saud Univ Saudi Arabia 1993, Oxford Univ Club 2003; Surveyor of the Fabric to St George's Chapel Windsor Castle 1975–87; head Oxford Sch of Architecture 1976–85; tstee Stowe House Preservation Tst 1998–2006; RIBA 1953–2003, FRSA 1984; *Books* Modern Churches of the World (1963); *Recreations* growing sub-tropical fruits, writing, sculpture; *Clubs* Oxford Univ; *Style*— Robert Maguire, Esq, OBE; ✉ Hopewater House, Ettrickbridge, Selkirk TD7 5JN (tel 01750 52369, e-mail thebobmaguire@googlemail.com); Apartment P06, Waterspring Court, 108 Regency Street, London SW1P 4AW; Cortijo Pepe Pedro, Pago de Sarja, Cómpeta, Málaga, Spain

MAGURRAN, Prof Anne; *Career* prof of ecology and evolution Univ of St Andrews; assoc ed Proceedings at the Royal Society: Biological Sciences 1998–2003, British Antarctic Survey Integrated Prog Review Ctee 2001–2006, Royal Soc Working Pty on Biodiversity Measurement 2002–2003, Awards Ctee Zoological Soc of London; Royal Society/Leverhulme Trust sr research fell 2002–2003; FRSE 2004; *Books* Measuring Biological Diversity (jt ed, 2004), Evaluating Ecology (2005); *Style*— Prof Anne Magurran; ✉ University of St Andrews Gatty Marine Laboratory, East Sands, St Andrews KY16 8LB

MAHAFFY, Sarah Georgiana; da of Rupert Mahaffy (d 2003), of London, and Victoria, *née* Ponsonby (d 1995); *b* 21 July 1952; *Educ* Francis Holland Sch, St Hugh's Coll Oxford (BA); *m* W H Baker; 1 s (Charles), 1 da (Sophia); *Career* editorial asst Methuen Educational 1974–75, Macmillan Publishers 1975–84, fndr md Boxtree 1986–96, md Pan Macmillan 1996–97, fndr dir The Good Web Guide Ltd (www.thegoodwebguide.co.uk), dir Maharani Trading Ltd; memb Cncl Francis Holland Schs Trust 1998–; *Recreations* theatre, India, reading, family; *Clubs* The Academy; *Style*— Miss Sarah Mahaffy; ✉ 27 Canning Cross, London SE5 8BH; The Old Rectory, Scremby, Spilsby, Lincolnshire (e-mail sarah.mahaffy@zen.co.uk)

MAHAPATRA, Dr Sasi Bhusan; s of late Nila Kantha Mahapatra, and late Moti Mahapatra; *b* 2 November 1935; *Educ* BC HS Ranpur Orissa India, Ravenshaw Coll Cuttack Orissa India, SCB Med Coll and Utkal Univ Orissa India (MB BS, DPM); *m* 1 Oct 1963, Maureen Rose, da of late William Henry Piggott; 1 s (Timothy Martin, *qv*), 2 da (Sonjeeta Krishna, Rachelle Elizabeth); *Career* house offr and house surgn SCB Med Coll Cuttack Orissa 1958–59, med offr Manmunda Health Centre Orissa India 1959–61; sr registrar in psychiatry 1964–66: Runwell Hosp Wickford Essex (sr house offr and registrar 1961–64), St Clements Hosp, The London Hosp; consIt psychiatrist Univ of Leeds 1976– (lectr 1966–70, sr lectr and hon consIt 1970–76), consIt psychiatrist and sr clinical lectr St James's Hosp Univ Hosp 1976–94, dir of psychiatry servs Leeds Eastern HA 1986–90, med dir Harrogate Clinic 1990–2002, hon consIt psychiatrist Leeds Community and Mental Health Serv Tst Leeds 1994–, Lord Chllr's Medical Visitor 1995–; memb N Yorks Area HA 1971–76, sub dean RCPsych 1977–82; chm: NE Div RCPsych 1984–88, Sub Ctee of Overseas Psychiatry Trainees 1976–84; FRCP 1982, FRCPsych; *Books* Antidepressive Drugs - Side-Effects of Drugs (1972), Deafness and Mental Health (1972), Psychosomatic Aspects of Coronary Artery Disease - Psychosomatic Medicine (1973), Problems of Language in Examinations for Foreign Psychiatrists (1974), Short Term Effects of Antidepressive Drugs and Placebo (1975), Schizophrenic Language (ed, 1976), Handbook for Psychiatric Inceptors and Trainees (ed, 1980); *Recreations* cricket, gardening, sailing, music, skiing, photography; *Style*— Dr Sasi Mahapatra; ✉ Woodlands Grange, Woodlands Drive, Apperley Bridge, Bradford BD10 0NX; BUPA Hospital, Jackson Avenue, Rounday, Leeds LS8 1NT (tel 0113 269 3939); Cygnet Hospital, 23 Ripon Road, Harrogate HG1 2JL (tel 01423 500599)

MAHAPATRA, Timothy Martin; s of Dr Sasi Bhusan Mahapatra, *qv*, and Maureen Rose, *née* Piggott; *b* 16 March 1964; *Educ* Leeds GS, Univ of Birmingham (BComm), Manchester Business Sch (MBA); *Children* 1 da (Isabella Priya); *Career* ptnr Arthur Andersen until 2002, currently head of private equity transaction servs Deloitte; FCA 1990; *Recreations* skiing, travel, motor cars, boats; *Style*— Timothy Mahapatra, Esq; ✉ Deloitte & Touche LLP, Athene Place, 66 Shoe Lane, London EC4A 3BQ

MAHER, Paul; s of Francis John Maher (d 2003), and Bridget Rita, *née* Dillon; *b* 30 July 1959, Harlesden, London; *Educ* Harrow HS, John Lyon Sch Harrow, Univ of Bristol (LLB); *m* 16 Feb 1990, Amanda; 1 s (Jamie b 17 March 1992), 2 da (Charlotte b 5 April 1994, Lara b 7 Oct 2003); *Career* Boodle Hatfield 1982–84, ICI 1984–90, Rowe & Maw 1990–2002, Mayer, Brown, Rowe & Maw LLP 2002–; memb Law Soc; *Recreations* football, running, squash, tennis, current affairs, music, reading, wine, politics; *Clubs* Mosimann's; *Style*— Paul Maher, Esq; ✉ Mayer, Brown, Rowe & Maw LLP, 11 Pilgrim Street, London EC4V 6RW (tel 020 7782 8815, fax 020 7782 8760, e-mail pmaher@mayerbrownrowe.com)

MAHER, Stephen Francis; s of Francis John Maher, of Harrow, Middx, and Bridget Rita, *née* Dillon; *b* 19 February 1961; *Educ* The John Lyon Sch Middx, Balliol Coll Oxford (exhibitioner, MA, Coolidge Pathfinder award); *m* 23 Sept 1989, Sarah Jane, da of Adrian George Beckett; 2 da (Sophie Elizabeth b 10 March 1992, Beatrice Anna b 10 Feb 2001), 2 s (Edward Archie Francis b 3 Dec 1994, Frederick George b 7 Jan 1999); *Career* advtg grad account trainee Allen Brady & Marsh Ltd 1983; account mangr: ABM 1984–86, Abbott Mead Vickers SMS Ltd 1986–88; account dir AMV 1988–89; Simons Palmer Denton Clemmow & Johnson Ltd: account dir 1989–90, bd account dir 1990–93, head of account mgmnt 1993; ceo Maher Bird Associates Ltd 1994–; memb: IPA, Mktg Soc, Mktg Cncl; *Recreations* music, guitar, skiing, football; *Style*— Stephen Maher, Esq; ✉ Maher Bird Associates Ltd, 82 Charing Cross Road, London WC2H 0BA (tel 020 7309 7200, fax 020 7309 7201, e-mail stephen.maher@mba.co.uk)

MAHER, His Hon Terence; s of John Maher, and Bessie Maher; *b* 20 December 1941; *Educ* Burnley GS, Univ of Manchester (LLB); *m* 4 Sept 1965 (m dis 1983); 2 da (Catherine Helen b 1971, Elizabeth Jane b 1972); *Career* admitted slr 1966; formerly ptnr Cole and Cole 1973–83; met stipendiary magistrate 1983–95, chm Inner London Youth Court and Family Proceedings Court, recorder of the Crown Court until 1995, circuit judge (SE Circuit) 1995–2006; *Recreations* reading, walking, travel; *Clubs* Frewen (Oxford); *Style*— His Hon Terence Maher; ✉ Luton Crown Court, 7 George Street, Luton LU1 2AA

MAHER, Terence Anthony (Terry); s of Herbert Maher (d 1978); *b* 5 December 1935; *Educ* Xaverian Coll Manchester; *m* 1960, Barbara, da of Dr Franz Greenbaum (d 1961); 3 s (Nicholas b 1960, Anthony b 1962, Jeremy b 1964); *Career* with: Carborundum Co Ltd 1961–69, First Nat Fin Corp 1969–72; fndr, chm and chief exec Pentos plc 1972–93; chm: Dillons Bookstores 1977–93, Athena International 1980–93, Ryman 1987–93, Tempus Publishing Co Ltd 1994–98; fndr and chm: Maher Booksellers Ltd 1995–, Race Dynamics Ltd 1998–; fndr tstee Lib Dems 1988–2001, tstee Photographers' Gallery 1994–97, memb Advsy Cncl on Libraries 1996–98, led successful campaign to abolish price control on books; FCCA 1970 (ACCA 1960), FRSA 1988; *Books* Counterblast (co-author, 1965), Effective Politics (co-author, 1966), Against My Better Judgement (memoir, 1994), Unfinished Business (fiction, 2003), Grumpy Old Liberal: a political rant (2005); *Recreations* skiing, reading, walking, tennis, bridge; *Clubs* Savile, Portland; *Style*— Terry Maher, Esq; ✉ 33 Montagu Square, London W1H 2LJ (tel 020 7723 4254)

MAHLOUDJI, Alidad; *see:* Alidad

MAHMOOD, Khalid; MP; *Career* MP (Lab) Birmingham Perry Barr 2001–; PPS to Tony McNulty MP 2004–; memb Broadcasting Select Ctee, chm Race Rels Ctee 1990–93; memb: AMICUS, Socialist Health Assoc, Socialist Educn Assoc; Lab Finance and Industry Gp: memb, exec memb Midlands branch; former advsr to: Pres Olympic Cncl Asia, Danish Int Trade Union; *Style*— Khalid Mahmood, Esq, MP; ✉ House of Commons, London SW1A 0AA

MAHON, Alice; *Career* MP (Lab) Halifax 1987–2005; *Style*— Mrs Alice Mahon; ✉ 2 West Parade, Halifax, West Yorkshire HX1 2TA (tel 01422 251800, fax 01422 251888)

MAHON, His Hon Charles Joseph; *b* 16 August 1939; *Career* called to the Bar Gray's Inn 1962; recorder 1985–89, circuit judge (Northern Circuit) 1989–2005; *Style*— His Hon Charles Mahon

MAHON, Sir (John) Denis; CH (2003), kt (1986), CBE (1967); s of John FitzGerald Mahon (d 1942), 4 s of Sir W Mahon, 4 Bt, and Lady Alice Evelyn Browne (d 1970), da of 5th Marquess of Sligo; *b* 8 November 1910; *Educ* Eton, ChCh Oxford (MA); *Career* art historian; tstee Nat Gallery 1957–64 and 1966–73, memb Advsy Panel Nat Art Collections Fund 1975; specialist on 17th century painting in Italy and has notable collection (exhibited Nat Gallery Feb-May 1997); has long campaigned for fiscal measures to encourage support from private individuals for art galleries and museums; memb Ctee of the Biennial Exhibitions at Bologna Italy; awarded: medal for Benemeriti della Cultura 1957, Archiginnasio d'Oro City of Bologna 1968, Serena medal for Italian studies Br Acad 1972; elected Academico d'Onore Clementine Acad Bologna 1964; corresponding fell Accademia Raffaello Urbino 1968, Deputazione di Storia Patria per le provincie di Romagna 1969, Ateneo Veneto 1987; Hon Citizen Cento 1982, Hon Student ChCh Oxford 1996; Hon DLitt: Newcastle 1969, Oxford 1994, Rome (La Sapienza) 1998, Bologna 2002; FBA 1964, sr FRCA 1988, hon fell Royal Acad of Arts 2002, FRSA; *Publications* Studies in Seicento Art and Theory (1947), Mostra dei Carracci, Catalogo critico dei Disegni (1956, 1963), Poussiniana (1962), Catalogues of the Mostra del Guercino (Dipinti 1968, Disegni 1969), The Drawings of Guercino in the Collection of HM The Queen at Windsor Castle (with N Turner, 1989), Catalogues of exhibitions in 1991–92 in celebration of 4 centenary of Guercino's birth: Bologna/Cento (paintings), Bologna (drawings), Frankfurt (Schirn Kunsthalle, paintings), Washington (Nat Gallery of Art, paintings); contrib: Actes of Colloque Poussin (1960), Friedlaender Festschrift (1965), Problemi Guardeschi (1967), I Dipinti del Guercino (consIt to Luigi Salerno, 1988); author of numerous articles, especially on Caravaggio and Poussin, in art historical periodicals incl: Apollo, The Art Bulletin, The Burlington Magazine, Gazette des Beaux Arts, Art de France, Commentari, Paragone, Zeitschrift für Kunstwissenschaft; collaborated in compilation of catalogues raisonnés of many exhibitions incl: Artists in 17th Century Rome (London 1955), Italian Art in Britain (Royal Academy 1960), L'Ideale Classico del Seicento in Italia (Bologna 1962), Omaggio al Guercino (Cento 1967); *Style*— Sir Denis Mahon, CH, CBE, FBA; ✉ 33 Cadogan Square, London SW1X 0HU (tel 020 7235 7311, 020 7235 2530)

MAHON, Seán Patrick Lauritson; s of John Patrick Mahon (d 1983), of Sheffield, and Peggy Lauritson, *née* Bines (d 1978); *b* 16 April 1946; *Educ* Ratcliffe Coll Leics; *m* 14 Sept 1968, Pauline Kathleen, da of Eric Reginald Starling; 1 s (Sean Ciaran b 15 June 1971), 3 da (Victoria Amanda b 4 Oct 1972, Siobhan Katherine b 3 April 1975, Anne Marie b 3 Nov 1983 d 1986); *Career* CA 1969; articled clerk Smith Holloway and Clarke Sheffield 1964–69; PricewaterhouseCoopers (formerly Coopers & Lybrand before merger): joined 1969, ptnr Sheffield 1976, ptnr i/c Sheffield 1989, latterly sr ptnr Northern region and memb Managing Bd; chief exec Cattles plc 2001–07 (memb Bd 2000–07); chm Sheffield CAs Students Soc 1979–84, chm Sheffield CAs Tech Advsy Ctee 1982–87, memb Accreditation Bd ICAEW 1982–88, memb Tech Advsy Ctee ICAEW 1984–87, pres Sheffield & Dist Soc of CAs 1990–91; memb Univ of Sheffield Careers Advsy Bd 1982–88, pres Irish Soc of Sheffield & District 1982–87, chm Fin Ctee Boys' Clubs of S Yorks 1984–, dir S Yorks Met Ambulance and Paramedics Trust 1991–; capt: Sheffield RFC Colts, Yorkshire Rugby Colts; England U21 trialist; FCA (ACA 1969); *Recreations* fishing trout, salmon and pike, shooting; *Clubs* Sheffield, Abbeydale RFC, Abbeydale Golf; *Style*— Seán Mahon, Esq

MAHON, Col Sir William Walter; 7 Bt (UK 1819), of Castlegar, Co Galway; s of Sir George Edward John Mahon, 6 Bt (d 1987), and his 1 w, Audrey Evelyn (d 1957), da of Dr Walter Jagger; *b* 4 December 1940; *Educ* Eton; *m* 20 April 1968, Rosemary Jane, yr da of late Lt-Col Michael Ernest Melvill, OBE, of The Old Manse, Symington, Lanarkshire; 2 da (Annabel Jane (Mrs Richard Amphlett) b 1970, Lucy Caroline (Mrs Alexander Stroud) b 1972), 1 s (James William b 1976); *Heir* s, James Mahon; *Career* Irish Gds 1959–92, served Germany, Malaysia, Aden, Hong Kong, Pakistan, Spain; memb HM Bodyguard of the Hon Corps of Gentlemen at Arms 1993–; fundraiser for Macmillan Cancer Relief 1993–2002; chm Nat Army Museum Devpt Tst 2003–; *Recreations* travel, history, collecting; *Clubs* Army and Navy; *Style*— Col Sir William W Mahon, Bt

MAHONY, Stephen Dominic Patrick; s of Dermot Cecil Mahony, of Cork, Ireland, and late Kate, *née* O'Neill; *b* 3 March 1956; *Educ* Ampleforth, Keble Coll Oxford (scholar, MA); *m* 15 July 1983, Lucinda Margaret Ann, da of late Maj Donald Struan Robertson; 1 da (Caroline b 3 May 1987), 1 s (Dermot b 16 Nov 1988); *Career* Citibank NA 1977–82, Swiss Bank Corp International Ltd 1982–88 (exec dir 1986–88), head of eurosecurities and swaps Istituto Bancario San Paolo di Torino London 1989–91; dir: A Boursot & Co Ltd wine merchants 1992–98, Church House Tst plc (formerly Dryfield Tst plc) 1997–; *Books* The Muskerry Book of Hunting Fiction (ed, 1992), Borrower Briefings (1993), International Guide to Government Securities and Derivatives (1994), Understanding Options (1996), Using Options (1996), Eurobonds (1996), Mastering Government Securities (1996), The A-Z of International Finance (1997); *Clubs* Chelsea Arts; *Style*— Stephen Mahony, Esq; ✉ Broadclose House, Babcary, Somerton, Somerset TA11 7ED (tel 01458 223318, fax 01458 223999, e-mail stephen@mahony.co.uk)

MAHY, Dr Brian Wilfred John; s of Wilfred John Mahy (d 1966), of Guernsey, and Norah Lilian, *née* Dillingham (d 1968); *b* 7 May 1937; *Educ* Elizabeth Coll Guernsey, Univ of Southampton (BSc, PhD), Univ of Cambridge (ScD, MA); *m* 1, 27 Aug 1959 (m dis 1986), Valerie Elaine, da of John Victor Pouteaux (d 2006), of Guernsey; 2 s (Alex b 1964, Tim b 1966), 1 da (Penny b 1970); m 2, 29 Oct 1988, Penny Mary, da of Robert William Cunningham (d 1987), of Swansea; *Career* Univ of Cambridge: asst dir of research in virology 1965–80, Huddersfield lectr in special pathology 1980–84, fell Wolfson Coll 1966–84; dir: Animal Virus Research Inst 1984–89, Div of Viral and Rickettsial Diseases Centers for Disease Control and Prevention Atlanta GA 1989–2000; sr scientist Co-ordinating Center for Infectious Diseases Centers for Disease Control and Prevention Atlanta GA 2000–; past pres Int Union of Microbiological Socs 2002–05 (pres 2000–02, past chm Virology Div); fell American Acad of Microbiology Infectious Diseases Soc of America; memb: American Soc of Virology, American Soc for Microbiology, Soc for General Microbiology, American Acad of Microbiology; DSc (hc) Univ of Southampton;

M

Recreations violin, gardening; *Style*— Dr Brian W J Mahy; ✉ Steele Cobb House, 2632 Fox Hills Drive, Decatur, GA 30033, USA (tel 00 1 404 728 0564, fax 00 1 404 728 0032, e-mail virology@bellsouth.net); Centers for Disease Control and Prevention, 1600 Clifton Road, Atlanta, GA 30333, USA (tel 00 1 404 639 2915, fax 00 1 404 639 3039, e-mail bxm1@cdc.gov)

MAHY, Helen Margaret; da of Donald Gregory Mahy, of Guernsey, and Mary Margaret, *née* Chapman; *b* 4 March 1961, Guernsey; *Educ* Guernsey Ladies' Coll, Univ of Manchester (R G Lawson scholar and prize, LLB), Inns of Court Sch of Law; *m* 17 Dec 1993, Mark Roy Hughes; *Career* called to the Bar Middle Temple 1982; insurance advsr Hogg Robinson 1982–87, dep head Commercial and Legal Dept Crown Agents 1987–93, Babcock King-Wilkinson Ltd 1993–97 (latterly commercial and legal dir), Babcock Int Gp plc 1997–2002 (latterly gen counsel and co sec), co sec Lattice Gp plc and National Grid Transco plc 2002–03, gp co sec and gen counsel National Grid plc 2003–; non-exec dir AGA Food Service Gp plc 2003–; chair GC100 Gp 2007– (vice-chair 2005–07); memb Bar Cncl 2005– (memb Gen Mgmnt Ctee 2005–06, co-chair Employed Barrs' Ctee 2006–); chartered insurance practitioner 1996; ACII 1985 (Arthur J Watson Award 1985); *Recreations* husband, my spaniel, sleeping, writing children's stories, collecting dolls, movies, opera, trying to finish writing my novel, travelling to weird places; *Style*— Ms Helen Mahy; ✉ Jincox Farm, Popes Lane, Oxted, Surrey RH8 9PL (tel 01883 722711, fax 01883 722216, e-mail hughes.mahy@tinyworld.co.uk); National Grid plc, 1–3 Strand, London WC2N 5EH (tel 020 7004 3219, fax 020 7004 3221, e-mail helen.mahy@ngrid.com)

MAHY, Peter Julian; s of Rodney Mahy (d 2006), and Karen, *née* Gillingham, of Guernsey; *b* 16 April 1971, Guernsey; *Educ* Guernsey GS, Univ of Sheffield (LLB), Darwin Coll Cambridge (MPhil), Univ of Northumbria (LPC); *m* 18 May 2006, Dr Nicola Jordan-Mahy; *Career* admitted slr; Howells Slrs 1996– (ptnr 2002–, currently head Civil Liberties Dept); memb Law Soc 1998; *Clubs* cycling, sailing; *Style*— Peter Mahy, Esq; ✉ Howells Solicitors, 15–17 Bridge Street, Sheffield S3 8NL

MAIDEN, Prof Martin David; s of Kenneth Henry Maiden, and Betty, *née* Liddiard; *b* 20 May 1957; *Educ* King Edward VI Sch Southampton, Trinity Hall Cambridge (MA, MPhil, PhD); *Career* lectr in Italian Univ of Bath 1982–89, lectr in Romance philology Univ of Cambridge and fell Downing Coll Cambridge 1989–96, prof of Romance languages Univ of Oxford and fell Trinity Coll Oxford 1996–; conseiller to the Bureau de la Société Internationale de Linguistique et de Philologie Romanes 2001–; conslt ed Revue Romane 2001–; memb editorial bd: Bollettino Linguistico Campano 2001–, Legenda Publications 2002–; editorial advsr Troubador Pubns 2002–; memb Philological Soc 1981–; *Books* Interactive Morphonology. Metaphony in Italy (1991), A Linguistic History of Italian (1995), The Dialects of Italy (co-ed with M Parry, 1997), Storia linguistica dell'italiano (1998). Reference Grammar of Modern Italian (with C Robustelli, 2000); *Recreations* travel, bicycling, Romanian culture and history; *Style*— Prof Martin Maiden; ✉ Taylor Institution, University of Oxford, 41 Wellington Square, Oxford OX1 2JF (tel 01865 270488, fax 01865 270575, e-mail martin.maiden@mod-langs.ox.ac.uk)

MAIDMENT, Dr Susan Rachel; da of Peter Elman, of Jerusalem, Israel, and Frances, *née* Tuckman; *b* 15 February 1944; *Educ* South Hampstead HS for Girls, LSE (LLB, LLM), Keele Univ (LLD); *Children* 2 da (Alice b 1971, Eleanor b 1980), 1 s (Adam b 1973); *Career* called to the Bar Lincoln's Inn 1968, lectr in law Univ of Bristol 1967–70, sr lectr in law Keele Univ 1970–84, practising barr 1984–; visiting prof of law Inst of Law and Business Admin Israel 1996–; *Books* Child Custody and Divorce (1984); *Style*— Dr Susan Maidment; ✉ 1 King's Bench Walk, Temple, London EC4 7DB (tel 020 7936 1500)

MAIDSTONE, Bishop of 2001–; Rt Rev Graham Alan Cray; s of Alan Cray (d 1997), and Doris Mary Kathleen, *née* Hann (d 1963); *b* 21 April 1947; *Educ* Trinity Sch of John Whitgift Croydon, Univ of Leeds (BA), St John's Coll Nottingham; *m* 14 July 1973, Jaqueline, *née* Webster; 2 da (Catherine Ann b 29 Sept 1979, Sarah Emma b 29 Dec 1982); *Career* curate St Mark's Gillingham 1971–75, Northern co-ordinator Youth Dept Church Pastoral Aid Soc 1975–78, vicar St Michael-le-Belfrey York 1978–92, princ Ridley Hall Cambridge 1992–2001, six-preacher Canterbury Cathedral 1997–2002; chm Soul Survivor Tst; *Publications* David Watson - A Portrait by his Friends (contrib, 1985), By My Spirit (contrib, 1988), In Spirit and Truth (contrib, 1989), The Gospel and Tomorrow's Culture (1994), To Proclaim Afresh (contrib, 1995), Building a Relational Society (contrib, 1996), The Post-Evangelical Debate (contrib, 1997), John Wimber - His Influence and Legacy (contrib, 1998), Postmodern Culture and Youth Discipleship (1998), Mass Culture (contrib, 1999), Christ and Consumerism (contrib, 2000), Being Culturally Relevant (2000), Youth Congregations and the Emerging Church (2002), Mission-Shaped Church (report, 2004), Scriptural Truth in a Postmodern Age (contrib, 2006), Making Sense of Generation Y (contrib, 2006), The Future of the Parish System (contrib, 2006), Mission Shaped Youth (contrib, 2007), Disciples and Citizens (2007); *Recreations* listening to rock music, reading theology, following sport; *Style*— The Rt Rev the Bishop of Maidstone; ✉ Bishop's House, Pett Lane, Charing, Kent TN27 0DL (tel 01233 712950, fax 01233 713543, e-mail bishop@bishmaid.org)

MAILE, Nigel Kingsley; s of David G Maile, of Rowland's Castle, Hants, and Suzanne Mary, *née* Derham; *b* 4 September 1955; *Educ* Mill Hill Sch, Hatfield Poly; *m* 19 Oct 1985, Julia Eileen, da of Cdr John E Hommert, of Rowland's Castle, Hants; 1 da (Caroline Beatrice b 21 Feb 1993); *Career* chartered accountant Spicer & Oppenheim 1977–82, chief fin offr Bartle Bogle Hegarty (advtg agency) 1982–; ACA 1982; *Recreations* golf, walking, motorcycling; *Style*— Nigel Maile, Esq; ✉ Rowland's Castle, Hampshire PO9 6AF (tel 023 9241 2483); Bartle Bogle Hegarty Ltd, 60 Kingly Street, London W1B 5DS (tel 020 7734 1677, fax 020 7437 3666, e-mail nigel.maile@bbh.co.uk)

MAIN, Anne; MP; da of George Wiseman (d 1996), and Rita *née* Osborne; *b* Cardiff; *Educ* Univ of Swansea, Univ of Sheffield (PGCE); *m* 1, Stephen Tonks (decd); 1 s (Nick), 2 da (Claire, Jennifer); m 2, Andrew Main; 1 s (Alexander); *Career* MP (Cons) St Albans 2005–; cncllr (Cons) Beaconsfield Town Cncl 1999–2001, cncllr (Cons) S Bucks DC 2001–; *Style*— Mrs Anne Main, MP; ✉ House of Commons, London SW1A 0AA (e-mail maina@parliament.uk); Constituency Office tel 01727 825100, website www.annemain.com

MAIN, Prof Brian George McArthur; s of George McArthur Main, of Buckhaven, Fife, and Margaret Welsh, *née* Currie; *b* 24 August 1947; *Educ* Univ of St Andrews (BSc), Univ of Calif Berkeley (MBA, MA, PhD); *m* 4 July 1980, June Marks Lambert, da of James S Lambert; 2 s (Christopher b 23 June 1985, Simon b 4 July 1988), 1 da (Alice b 11 March 1992); *Career* prodn planning assoc and mangr Eli Lilly 1971–72, reader in economics Univ of Edinburgh 1983–87 (lectr 1976–83); prof of economics: Univ of St Andrews 1987–91, Univ of Edinburgh 1991–; memb Cncl Scottish Economic Soc 1982–91; FRSE 1998; *Recreations* running, fishing; *Style*— Prof Brian Main, FRSE; ✉ University of Edinburgh, Management School, Edinburgh EH8 9JY (tel 0131 650 8360, fax 0131 668 3053, e-mail brian.main@ed.ac.uk)

MAIN, Dr Monica Maitland; da of Kenneth Morrison (d 2006), and Gwynneth, *née* Austin; *b* 9 August 1952, Dingwall, Ross-shire; *Educ* Dingwall Acad, Univ of Aberdeen (MB ChB); *m* 12 July 1975, William George Main; 1 s (Robert Andrew Kenneth b 22 April 1980), 1 da (Jennifer Austin b 25 March 1983); *Career* med practitioner: Kingsmild Practice Inverness 1982–86, Brora 1992–; HM Lord-Lt Sutherland 2005–; DRCOG 1978, MRCGP 1979; *Recreations* curling, gardening; *Style*— Dr Monica Main; ✉ Col Bheinn, Victoria Road, Brora, Sutherland KW9 6QN (tel 01408 621234, fax 01408 621230); c/o The Highland Council, Main Street, Golspie KW10 6RB

MAINDS, Allan Gilfillan; s of Capt George Gordon Gilfillan Mainds, and Helen Northgate, *née* Woodhouse; *b* 15 December 1945; *Educ* Berkhamsted Sch; *m* 1, 17 July 1982 (m dis 1987), Hon Veronica Mary Addington, da of Viscount Sidmouth; m 2, 11 April 1992, Lavinia Marion, da of Christopher and Celia Prideaux; 2 da (Polly b 1994, Harriet b 1996); *Career* admitted slr 1972; called to the Bar Inner Temple 1977, recorder of the Crown Ct 1996–; *Recreations* flying light aircraft and gliding, rowing and sculling; *Clubs* London Rowing; *Style*— Allan Mainds, Esq; ✉ Chambers of Francis Oldham, QC, 36 Bedford Row, London WC1R 4JH (tel 020 7421 8000)

MAINELLI, Prof Michael R; s of Michael R Mainelli, and Katherine E, *née* Smith; *b* 19 December 1958; *Educ* Harvard Univ (Martin Marietta scholar, BA), Trinity Coll Dublin, LSE (PhD); *Family* 1 s (Nicholas b 7 Oct 1989); m, 1996, Elisabeth, *née* Reuss; 2 da (Xenia b 2 Feb 1998, Maxine b 12 Sept 2000); *Career* researcher Harvard Laboratory for Computer Graphics and Spatial Analysis 1977–81; Petroconsultants Group: Geodat project dir Petroconsultants Ltd 1979–82, general mangr Petroconsultants (CES) Ltd 1982–85; pres ISF Inc 1985–86, sr mangr Arthur Andersen & Co Management Consultants 1986–87, ptnr (BDO Consulting) BDO Binder Hamlyn 1988–94, ptnr Arthur Andersen & Co 1994–95; dir: Whale Conservation Inst 1994–97, Z/Yen Gp 1995–, Comax Secure Business Services Ltd 1997–99, Eyebright plc 2002–2004; corp devpt dir Defence Evaluation & Research Agency (DERA) MOD 1995–97; chief scientist The Financial Laboratory 1995–98; chm: Jaffe Associates 1999–2003, CityAxis 2001–; non-exec dir: Sirius Expoloration 2005–, UK Accreditation Serv 2005–; Mercers Sch meml prof of commerce Gresham Coll; memb: Strategic Planning Soc 1990–99 (dir 1995–98), Editorial Bd Jl of Strategic Change 1990–, Ed Bd Jl of Business Strategy, Advsy Bd City Univ Sch of Informatics 1999–2003; author of numerous pubns in learned jls; Br Computer Soc IT Dir of the Year 2004/05; chm Broad Street Ward Club 2004–05, Worshipful Co of World Traders; MInstPet 1986, MInstD 1988, MBCS 1989, FIMC 1990, FCCA 1996, FSI 1999; *Publications* Clean Business Cuisine: Now and Z/Yen (2000), Information Technology for the Not for Profit Sector (2001); *Recreations* sailing, bagpipes; *Clubs* Royal Corinthian Yacht, Harvard; *Style*— Prof Michael Mainelli; ✉ Z/Yen Group, 5–7 St Helen's Place, London EC3A 6AU (tel 020 7562 9562, fax 020 7628 5751, e-mail michael_mainelli@zyen.com); website www.lady-daphne.co.uk and www.zyen.com

MAINGARD DE LA VILLE-ÈS-OFFRANS, Sir (Louis Pierre) René; kt (1982), CBE (1961); s of Joseph René Maingard de la Ville-ès-Offrans (d 1956), and Véronique, *née* Hugnin (d 1969); *b* 9 July 1917; *Educ* St Joseph's Coll, Royal Coll of Mauritius, Business Trg Corp London; *m* 1946, Marie Hélène Françoise, da of Sir Philippe Raffray, CBE, QC (d 1975); 3 da (Catherine, Anne, Sophie); *Career* served WWII RAF Fighter Cmd 131 and 165 Sqdn 1939–45; chm De Chazal du Mée Assocs Ltd, chm and md Rogers & Co Ltd 1948–82; chm: Mauritius Steam Navigation Co Ltd 1964, Mauritius Portland Cement Co Ltd 1960–, Mauritius Molasses Co Ltd 1968–, United Docks Ltd 1960–; dir: Mauritius Commercial Bank Ltd 1956–, The Anglo-Mauritius Assurance Co; consul for Finland in Mauritius 1957–83; Order of the White Rose (Finland) 1973; *Recreations* golf, fishing, boating; *Clubs* Dodo, Mauritius Turf; *Style*— Sir René Maingard de la Ville-ès-Offrans, CBE; ✉ De Chazal Du Mée Associates Ltd, PO Box 799, Port Louis, Mauritius (tel 2638549)

MAINI, Prof Philip Kumar; s of Panna Lal Maini (d 1972), and Satya Wati, *née* Bhandari; *b* 16 October 1959, Magherafelt, NI; *Educ* Balliol Coll Oxford (open exhibitioner, Mouat-Jones scholar, Prosser Prize, MA, DPhil); *Career* lectr in applied mathematics CCC Oxford 1984, SERC postdoctoral research asst Centre for Mathematical Biology Mathematical Inst Univ of Oxford 1985 and 1986–87, asst master Eton Coll 1986, lectr in applied mathematics Balliol Coll Oxford and jr research fell Wolfson Coll Oxford 1987–88, asst prof Dept of Mathematics Univ of Utah Salt Lake City 1988–90 (research visitor 1985), tutorial fell BNC Oxford 1990–2005, prof of mathematical biology and dir Centre for Mathematical Biology Univ of Oxford 1998– (lectr in mathematical biology 1990–2005), professorial fell St John's Coll Oxford 2005–; visiting scientist Los Alamos Nat Lab 1985, visiting conslt Dept of Applied Mathematics Univ of Washington Seattle 1993, visiting scholar Centre in Statistical Science and Industrial Mathematics Queensland Univ of Technol 1994, visiting scholar Sch of Mathematics and Statistics Univ of Sydney 1994 and 1995, visiting prof Williams Coll MA 1995, visiting prof IMA Univ of Minnesota 1998, Royal Soc-Mexican Acad of Sciences exchange visitor Univ Nacional Autónoma de Mexico 1998, mathematician-in-residence New Coll Univ of S Florida 1999, visiting fell Clare Hall Cambridge 2001, visiting fell Queensland Univ of Technol 2001 and 2003, prof Université Pierre et Marie Curie Paris VI 2002, foreign visiting fell Research Inst for Electronic Science Hokkaido Univ Sapporo 2002, visiting prof Nat Center for Theoretical Sciences Nat Tsing Hua Univ 2002, visiting prof Univ Degli Studi di Modena e Reggio Emilia and Univ Degli Studi di Ancona 2003, affiliated researcher Biocomplexity Inst Indiana Univ Bloomington 2005, hon guest prof Univ of Electronic Science and Technol Chengdu China 2005, visiting prof Dept of Mathematics Chinese Univ of Hong Kong 2005, adjunct prof Sch of Mathematical Sci Queensland Univ of Technol 2006–; memb: Co-ordination Ctee European Network on Dynamics of Complex Systems in Biosciences 1991–94, Mathematics Coll EPSRC 1994–2006, Advsy Bd Interdisciplinary Center for the Study of Biocomplexity Univ of Notre Dame 2003–, Cncl IMA 2004– (founding memb Ctee Forum on Mathematics in Med and Biology 1991– (sec 1991–96)), Scientific Advsy Bd Centre for Mathematical Medicine Fields Inst Toronto 2005–, Bd of Govrs Mathematical Biosciences Inst Ohio State Univ 2006–; managing ed Bulletin of Mathematical Biology 2002–07, ed-in-chief Jl of Nonlinear Science 2004–; memb Editorial Bd: FORMA 1994–, Mathematical Applied Med and Biology 1995–, Jl of Theoretical Med 1996–2005, Wiley Series in Mathematical and Computational Biology 1998, Chapman and Hall Mathematical Biology and Med Series 2001, Discrete and Continuous Dynamical Systems Series B 2001–04, World Scientific Lecture Notes in Complex Systems 2001–, Jl of Mathematical Biology 2002–05, Springer Lecture Notes in Mathematics 2004, Applied Mathematics Research Express 2004–06, Mathematical Biosciences and Engrg 2004–, Mathematical Models and Methods in Applied Sciences 2005; memb: Br Soc for Developmental Biology 1988–, Soc for Mathematical Biology 1988– (memb Bd 1996–2000), Soc for Industrial and Applied Mathematics 1988– (memb Activity Gp on Life Sciences 2000–), European Soc for Mathematical and Theoretical Biology 1992– (memb Bd 1994–99), London Mathematical Soc 1992–, Physiological Soc 2004–; Bellman Prize 1997, Royal Soc Leverhulme Tst sr research fell 2001–02; life memb Clare Hall Cambridge 2002; FIMA 2003; *Publications* Experimental and Theoretical Advances in Biological Pattern Formation (ed, 1993), Morphogenesis and Pattern Formation in Biological Systems: Experiments and Models, Proceedings of Chubu 2002 Conference (ed, 2003); author of over 200 research articles; *Recreations* travel, football; *Style*— Prof Philip Maini; ✉ Centre for Mathmatical Biology, Mathematical Institute, 24–29 St Giles', Oxford OX1 3LB (tel 01865 283889, fax 01865 270515, e-mail maini@maths.ox.ac.uk)

MAIR, Alexander Stirling Fraser (Alistair); MBE (1987), DL (Perth and Kinross 1993); *b* 1935, Aberdeenshire; *Educ* Robert Gordon's Coll Aberdeen, Univ of Aberdeen (BSc), Open Univ (BA); *m*; 4 s, 1 da; *Career* short serv cmmn RAF 1960–62, tech offr Central Work Study Unit Air Miny; grad apprentice rising to shop control mangr and product centre mangr Rolls Royce Ltd Glasgow 1957–71, md Caithness Glass Ltd Wick 1971–75, mktg dir Worcester Royal Porcelain Co 1975–77; Caithness Glass plc: md 1977–91, cmmnd new factory Perth 1979, led MBO 1984, chm 1991–98, led second MBO 1993; non-exec dir: Grampian Television 1986–2001, Crieff Hydro Ltd 1994–2003 (chm 1996–2003), Murray

VCT 3 plc 1998–2006; CBI: memb Scot Cncl 1981–92, memb Cncl 1985–97, chm Scot 1989–91, memb Pres's Ctee 1990–91, chm Regnl Chairmen's Ctee 1990–91; pres Br Glass Manufacturers Confedn 1997–98 (dep pres 1995–96); govr Morrison's Acad Crieff 1985–2006 (chm 1996–2006), cmmr Queen Victoria Sch Dunblane 1992–97, memb Ct Univ of Aberdeen 1993– (convenor FE Ctee 1998–, chllr's assessor and vice-chm 2000–); chm: Crieff and Dist Aux Assoc (Richmond House) 1993–98, Perth (subsequently Ochil and S Perthshire) Cons & Unionist Assoc 1999–, Scot Ctee of Chairmen Higher Education Insts 2001–07; vice-chm Cons and Unionist Party Scotland 1992–93 (memb Scot Business Gp 1989–93); hon pres D of E Award Perth & Kinross Assoc 1993–; LLD Univ of Aberdeen 2004; FRSA 1986; *Clubs* Royal Northern and University (Aberdeen); *Style*— Dr Alistair Mair, MBE, DL; ✉ Woodend, Madderty, Crieff, Perthshire PH7 3PA (tel and fax 01764 683210)

MAIR, Avril; da of William Robert Mair, and Irene, *née* Nicol; *Educ* Buckie HS, Univ of Edinburgh (MA); *Career* journalist; clubs ed The List 1990–92, features ed Edinburgh Festival Times 1990–91; freelance contrib: Self Service, Raygun, Mixmag, The Herald On Sunday, Scotland On Sunday; i-D magazine: asst ed 1992–95, dep ed 1994–95, ed 1995–; *Books* Smilei-D: Fashion and Style, The Best From 20 Years of i-D (2001); *Style*— Ms Avril Mair; ✉ i-D Magazine, 124 Tabernacle Street, London EC2A 4SA (tel 020 7490 9710, fax 020 7251 2225, mobile 07787 500 235, e-mail editor@i-dmagazine.co.uk)

MAIR, Prof Robert James; s of Prof (William) Austyn Mair, CBE, FREng, of Cambridge, and Mary Woodhouse, *née* Crofts; *b* 20 April 1950; *Educ* Leys Sch Cambridge, Clare Coll Cambridge (MA, PhD); *m* 19 Sept 1981, Margaret Mary Plowden, da of Rt Hon Sir Patrick O'Connor (d 2001); 1 da (Julia b 29 May 1984), 1 s (Patrick b 13 May 1986); *Career* asst engr (later sr engr) Scott Wilson Kirkpatrick & Partners London & Hong Kong 1971–82 (seconded to Univ of Cambridge researching tunnelling in soft ground 1976–79); dir Geotechnical Consulting Group (specialising in geotechnical engrg) 1983–; Royal Acad of Engrg visiting prof Univ of Cambridge 1997–; prof of engrg Univ of Cambridge 1998–; master Jesus Coll Cambridge 2001–; Br Geotechnical Soc Prize 1981, ICE Unwin meml lectr 1992, Bishop Medal 1994, Sir Harold Harding meml lectr 1998, Gold medal ICE 2004; fell St John's Coll Cambridge 1998–2001; FICE 1990, FREng 1992, FRS 2007; *Publications* Pressuremeters : Methods and Interpretation (with D Muir Wood, *qv*, 1987); papers in jls on geotechnical engineering, particularly related to tunnelling; *Recreations* supporting QPR, sailing, tennis, golf, long walks; *Clubs* Hurlingham; *Style*— Prof Robert J Mair, FRS, FREng; ✉ Master's Lodge, Jesus College, Cambridge CB5 8BL (tel 01223 339442, fax 01223 339304, e-mail master@jesus.cam.ac.uk); Department of Engineering, Trumpington Street, Cambridge CB2 1PZ (tel 01223 332631, fax 01223 339713, e-mail rjm50@eng.cam.ac.uk)

MAIRS, Raymond John; s of David Mairs (d 1991), of Co Antrim, and Susan Elizabeth, *née* Colvin (d 1978); *b* 15 August 1951; *Educ* Ballyclare HS, Queen's Univ Belfast (BSc, DipArch); *m* 6 Aug 1976, Carol Jean Ruth, da of Neville Arthur Ginn, of Co Antrim; 3 da (Rachel Ruth b 1981, Rebecca Ann b 1985, Jessica Elizabeth b 1989); *Career* architect, fish farmer; private practice 1978, ptnr Mairs & Wray 1979–92, Raymond J Mairs Chartered Architects 1992–; memb RSUA Housing Ctee 1985–86; chm: Br Trout Assoc 1988–90, Euro Gp of Fédération Européenne de la Salmoniculture 1988–93, Southern Trout Co-op Ltd 1993–95, Northern Ireland Seafoods Ltd 1997– (dir 1993–); dir NI Food and Drink Assoc 1996–2000; rapporteur Aqua-Culture Working Gp of Fisheries Advsy Ctee to Euro Cmmn 1989–92, vice-chm Health Promotion Agency N Ireland 1997–2000 (memb 1990–2000), memb BBC NI Agric Advsy Ctee 1994–; *Style*— Raymond J Mairs, Esq; ✉ Glen Oak House, Crumlin BT29 4BW (tel 028 9442 3172, e-mail rjm@glenoak.co.uk); Raymond J Mairs Chartered Architects, Glen Oak Mills, Crumlin BT29 4XL (tel 028 9445 2975, fax 028 9442 2636)

MAISEY, Prof Michael Norman; *b* 10 June 1939; *Educ* Caterham Sch, Guy's Hosp Med Sch London (BSc, MB BS, MD); *m*; 2 c; *Career* Guy's Hosp: house physician, casualty offr, house surgeon 1964–65; SHO in med New Cross Hosp 1965; house physician in: chest diseases Brompton Hosp, rheumatology Hammersmith Hosp; registrar: in neurology Brook Gen Hosp 1965–67, registrar gen med Guy's Hosp 1969–70 (endocrinology and radioisotopes 1967–69); fell Nuclear Medicine Johns Hopkins Hosp Baltimore 1970–72; sr registrar gen med 1970–72; former appts conslt physician in nuclear med and endocrinology Guy's Hosp 1973–83, chm Guy's Hosp Unit Mgmnt Bd 1991–93, med dir Guy's Hosp 1991–93, jt med dir Guy's and St Thomas' Hosp Tst 1993–96; currently: honconslt physician in nuclear med Guy's & St Thomas' Hosp, emeritus prof of radiological sciences GKT, hon conslt in nuclear med to the Army; examiner Soc of Radiographers Dip in Nuclear Med 1976, pres British Nuclear Med Soc 1978–80 (sec 1976–78), pres BIR 2000–01; chm SAC (Nuclear Med) of JCHMT 1982–84; visiting prof of nuclear med Toronto 1976, visiting exchange prof Johns Hopkins Hosp Baltimore 1985, visiting lectr Forces Inst of Cardiology Pakistan 1987, visiting prof Shanghai Univ Hosp 1988, visiting prof Stanford Univ 1999; memb: Scientific Ctee on Euro Nuclear Med Congress 1989, Editorial Bd Nuclear Med Communications and Euro Jl of Nuclear Med; memb: British Nuclear Med Soc, Euro Nuclear Med Soc, American Soc of Nuclear Med, Thyroid Club; FRCR, FRCP; *Books* Nuclear Medicine - A Clinical Introduction (1980), An Altas of Normal Skeletal Scintigraphy (with J J Flannagan, 1985), An Altas of Nuclear Medicine (with I Fogelman, 1988, 2 edn 1994), Clinical Nuclear Medicine (ed with K E Britton, D L Gilday, 1983, 3 ed 1998), Atlas of Clinical Positron Emision Tomography (1999), Positron Emission Tomography (with P Valk, D Bailey and D Townsend, 2003); numerous articles in various learned jls; *Style*— Prof Michael Maisey; ✉ Guy's Hospital, St Thomas Street, London SE1 9RT (tel 020 7955 4531, fax 020 7955 4532)

MAITLAND, Colin Neil; s of Col Otis Edward Maitland, MBE (d 1977), of Surrey, and Margaret Joan, *née* Haslehurst (d 1955); *b* 7 July 1940; *Educ* Old Buckenham Hall, Embley Park Romsey; *m* 30 Sept 1967, Judy, da of Col Howard Watson Wright; 2 s (Mark Otis b 1976, Sam Ragen b 1980), 1 da (Kate Margaret b 1978); *Career* offr RM 1958–69; NOP 1969–70, Louis Harris 1970–71, res mangr Leo Burnett LPE 1971–73; md: Eyescan 1973–83, ISIS Research plc 1984–; chm Embley Park Sch 1969–90; *Books* New Product Launch Planner (1988), Colins Guides (China, Taiwan, Vietnam, Philippines) (1994), Positioning Research (1996); *Style*— Colin Maitland

MAITLAND, Viscount; Ian Maitland; The Master of Lauderdale; s and h of 17 Earl of Lauderdale, *qv*; *b* 4 November 1937; *Educ* Radley, BNC Oxford (MA); *m* 27 April 1963, Ann Paule, da of Geoffrey B Clark, of London; 1 s, 1 da; *Heir* s, Master of Maitland, *qv*; *Career* Lt RNR 1963–73; has held various appts in mfrg industry; National Westminster Bank plc: joined 1974, asst regnl mangr N Africa 1985, regnl mangr N Africa 1986, regnl mangr Middle East 1989, sr regnl mangr Africa and ME 1991–95; dir Maitland Consultancy Services Ltd 1995–; marketing advsr LSE 1995–2001; lectr: British Cncl Anglo-Egyptian Banking Seminar Alexandria 1994, Euromoney Pubns and NY Inst of Finance Central Europe, Africa, Asia and ME 1996–, LSE British Chevening Gurukul Scholarship Prog 1999; chm Tachbrook St Residents' Assoc, dir Pimlico Fedn of Residents' Assocs; memb Queen's Body Guard for Scotland (Royal Co of Archers); Liveryman Worshipful Co of Fan Makers; *Recreations* sailing, photography; *Clubs* Royal Ocean Racing, New (Edinburgh), Puffins; *Style*— Viscount Maitland; ✉ 150 Tachbrook Street, London SW1V 2NE (website www.clanmaitland.org.uk)

MAITLAND, The Master of; Hon John Douglas Peter Maitland; s and h of Viscount Maitland, *qv*; *b* 29 May 1965; *Educ* Emanuel Sch, Radley, Univ of Durham (BSc); *m* 21 April 2001, Rosamund, da of Mr and Mrs Nigel Bennett; *Style*— The Master of Maitland

MAITLAND, Lady (Helen) Olga; elder da of 17 Earl of Lauderdale, *qv*; *b* 23 May 1944; *Educ* Sch of St Mary and St Anne Abbots Bromley, Lycée Français de Londres; *m* 19 April 1969, Robin William Patrick Hamilton Hay, *qv*, s of William Reginald Hay, of Mapperley, Nottingham; 2 s (Alastair b 1972, Fergus b 1981), 1 da (Camilla b 1975); *Career* former trainee reporter: Fleet St News Agency, Blackheath and District Reporter; reporter and columnist Sunday Express 1967–91, freelance journalist 1991–, with Daily Mail 1998–2001; pres Defence & Security Forum 1992–; fndr and chm: Families for Defence 1983–; Parly candidate (Cons): Bethnal Green & Stepney 1987, Sutton and Cheam 2001; MP (Cons) Sutton and Cheam 1992–97; PPS to Rt Hon Sir John Wheeler as Min of State for NI 1996–97; former memb Select Ctees for: Educn, Health and Procedures; private membs bills: Prisoner's Return to Custody 1995, Offensive Weapons 1996; former sec to Cons Backbench: NI, Defence and Foreign Affrs Ctees, Yugoslav Parly Gp; public affrs conslt 2001–, ceo Int Assoc of Money Transfer Networks 2006; pres Algerian Br Business Cncl 2005; *Publications* Margaret Thatcher: The First Ten Years (1989), Faith in the Family (1997); contrib: Peace Studies in our Schools, Political Indoctrination in our Schools; *Recreations* theatre, travel; *Style*— The Lady Olga Maitland; ✉ 21 Cloudesley Street, London N1 0HX (tel 020 7837 9212)

MAITLAND SMITH, Geoffrey; s of Philip John Maitland Smith (d 1989) and Kathleen, *née* Goff (d 2000), of Ramsden Heath, Essex; *b* 27 February 1933; *Educ* UCS London; *m* 1, 1956 (m dis 1967) Winifred Patricia Lane; 3 s, 1 da; m 2, 1967 (m dis 1981), Gabriella Armandi; 1 s, 1 da; m 3, 1986, Lucinda Enid, da of Lt-Col Gerald Owen Whyte (d 1994); *Career* chm: Selfridges 1985–93, Sears plc 1985–95 (dir 1971–95, chief exec 1978–88), Mallett plc 1986–89, Hammerson plc 1993–99 (dir 1990–99), W & F C Bonham and Sons Ltd 1996–2000, Fiske plc 2000–04; dir: Asprey plc 1980–93, Central Independent Television plc 1983–85, Courtaulds plc 1983–90, Imperial Group plc 1984–86, Midland Bank plc 1986–96 (dep chm 1992–96), HSBC Holdings plc 1993–96; chm: Cncl UCS London 1987–96, Britain's 1996 Olympic Appeal; memb Fin Reporting Cncl 1990–98; FCA, FCIM; *Recreations* opera; *Clubs* Boodle's; *Style*— Geoffrey Maitland Smith, Esq

MAITLAND-TITTERTON, Col David Henry Sandford Leslie; s of Maj David Maitland-Titterton, TD, Herald Marchmont (d 1989), of Moberty, Airlie, and Mary Etheldritha Audrey Leslie (d 1988); *b* 4 January 1933; *Educ* Campbell Coll Belfast, Mons OCS, RMA Sandhurst, JSSC; *m* 23 April 1963, Rinalda Malvina, da of Sqdn Ldr the Hon Greville Baird (ka 1941); 1 s (Rupert Seymour Aulin Leslie b 1965), 1 da (Shân Gelda Jane (Mrs Redpath) b 1968); *Career* 2 Lt NIH (TA) 1952, 2 Lt 12 L 1954, GSOI US Army Armour Sch Fort Knox 1968, CO 9/12 Royal Lancers 1972, GSOI Br Army Trg Team Sudan 1974, GSOI (PE) 1977, Cmd Kuwait Liaison Team 1978, Col M3 (MOD) 1981, Defence Naval Military and Air Attaché Damascus and Beirut 1985–86, Dep COS (Army) HQ 1 Gp 1986, ROI Chief Inspr Range Safety Inspection Team (Army) 1989–98; chm English Branch N Irish Horse Old Comrades Assoc 2001, vice-chm Combined Irish Regts Assoc 2002; memb CPRE 1989; Order of Two Niles Sudan 1980; *Recreations* country pursuits, history, engineering; *Clubs* Civil Service; *Style*— Col David Maitland-Titterton; ✉ Rimes Gigot, Baughurst, Hampshire RG26 5LW (tel 0118 981 5098)

MAITLIS, Emily; da of Prof Peter Michael Maitlis, FRS, *qv*, and Marion, *née* Basco; *b* 6 September 1970; *Educ* King Edward VII Sch Sheffield, Queens' Coll Cambridge (MA); *m* 21 Dec 2000, Mark Gwynne; *Career* documentary maker TVB Hong Kong 1992–96, hand-over prodn team Channel 4 1997, business corr NBC Asia 1997–98, business corr Sky News 1998–2000, presenter Sky News 2000–01, anchor BBC London News 2001–06, presenter Newsnight (BBC 2) 2006–; *Recreations* menus and shoes; *Clubs* Marlowe Soc, Noble Rot, Foreign Correspondents, Hong Kong; *Style*— Ms Emily Maitlis; ✉ c/o The Roseman Organisation, 51 Queen Anne Street, London W1G 9HS

MAITLIS, Prof Peter Michael; s of Jacob J Maitlis (d 1984), and Judith, *née* Ebel (d 1985); *b* 15 January 1933; *Educ* Hendon Co GS, Univ of Birmingham (BSc), Univ of London (PhD, DSc); *m* 19 July 1959, Marion da of Herbert Basco (d 1977); 3 da (Niccola b 1963, Sally b 1965, Emily, *qv* b 1970); *Career* asst lectr Univ of London 1956–60, Fulbright fell Cornell Univ 1960–61, res fell Harvard Univ 1961–62, prof McMaster Univ Hamilton Canada 1967–72 (asst prof 1962–64, assoc prof 1964–67), prof of inorganic chem Univ of Sheffield 1972–94 (research prof 1994–2002, now emeritus); fell Alfred P Sloan Fndn (USA) 1968–70, EWR Steacie Prize (Canada) 1971, RSC medallist (UK) 1981, Tilden lectr 1979, Sir Edward Frankland lectr (UK) 1984, RSC Mond lectr (UK) 1996–97, Gordon Stone lectr Univ of Bristol 2001, Paolo Chini lectr Italian Chem Soc 2001, Glenn T Seaborg meml lectr Univ of Calif at Berkeley 2004–05; Kurnakov Medal (Russian Acad of Sci) 1998; various offices in RSC (pres Dalton Div 1984–86), chm SERC Chemistry Ctee 1985–88, memb BBC Sci Consultative Gp 1988–93, foreign memb Accademia Lincei (Italy) 1999; FRS 1984 (memb Cncl 1991–93), FRSC; *Books* The Organic Chemistry of Palladium (Vols 1 & 2 1971), Metal Catalysis in Industrial Organic Processes (jtly, 2006); res papers in various chemistry jls; *Recreations* travel, music, walking, dining; *Style*— Prof Peter Maitlis, FRS; ✉ Department of Chemistry, University of Sheffield, Sheffield S3 7HF

MAJEED, Ali Waqar; s of Haji Abdul Majeed, and Arshad Majeed; *b* 17 July 1959; *Educ* Cadet Coll Hasanabdal, King Edward Med Coll Lahore, Univ of Punjab (BSc, MB BS), Univ of Sheffield (MD); *m* Julia, da of Jonathan Hugh Dicks and Jennifer Lyn; 3 s (Adam Ali, Noah Ali, Jacob Ali); *Career* house offr Mayo Hosp Lahore 1984, demonstrator King Edward Med Coll Lahore 1985; SHO: Killingbeck Hosp Leeds 1986, St James's Univ Hosp Leeds 1986–87, Leicester Gen Hosp 1987–88, Leicester Royal Infirmary 1987–88; Peri-fellowship registrar Lincoln County Hosp 1988–89, res fell Univ Surgical Unit Royal Hallamshire Hosp Sheffield 1989–91, lectr in surgery and hon surgical registrar Chesterfield and N Derbys Royal Hosp 1993–94; Univ Surgical Unit Royal Hallamshire Hosp: lectr in surgery and hon sr registrar 1994–96, sr lectr in surgery and hon conslt surgn 1997–203, hon prof of surgery 2005–; Ronald Raven Travelling Fellowship Br Assoc of Surgical Oncology 1996, Dinwoody Travelling Fellowship Assoc of Surgns 2001, Sir Ernest Finch Travelling Fellowship 2001; Cutlers Prize 1992, Young Scientist Prize Euro Digestive Diseases Week Oslo 1994; FRCS 1989, FRCS(Gen) 1997; *Publications* author of numerous published book chapters, articles, papers and abstracts, mostly concerning the treatment of gallstones and colorectal liver metastases; *Recreations* photography, walking, gourmet food; *Style*— Ali Majeed, Esq; ✉ Department of Surgery, K Floor, Royal Hallamshire Hospital, Sheffield S10 2JF (tel and fax 01142 712208)

MAJOR, Christopher Ian; s of Edward Richard Major, of Friar's Cliff, Dorset and Audrey Yvonne, *née* Beardmore; *b* 14 June 1948; *Educ* Kingston GS, Wadham Coll Oxford (MA); *m* 19 Aug 1972, Susan Fenella, da of Harry Morrison Kirton (d 1984); *Career* slr 1973; ptnr: Lovell, White & King 1979–88, Lovells (formerly Lovell White Durrant) 1988–; memb: Worshipful Co Slrs 1974, Law Soc of England & Wales 1973, Int Bar Assoc 1979, American Bar Assoc 1981, American Arbitration Assoc 1981; *Recreations* tennis; *Style*— Christopher Major, Esq; ✉ Lovell White Durrant, 65 Holborn Viaduct, London EC1A 2DY (tel 020 7236 0066, fax 020 7236 0084)

MAJOR, Dr Edward; s of Morgan Major, of Llangynwyd, Bridgend, Mid Glamorgan, and late Nancy, *née* Jenkins; *b* 26 November 1948; *Educ* Maesteg GS, London Hosp Med Coll (MB BS); *m* 9 March 1974, Heather Gillian, da of Christopher Bevil Spiller, of Ipswich; 2 s (Euan Thomas, Huw Edward), 1 da (Sarah Ann); *Career* sr registrar Hosp for Sick Children Gt Ormond St 1979, sr lectr and conslt in anaesthetics London Hosp 1979–84 (sr registrar 1978–79), conslt in anaesthesia and intensive therapy Morriston Hosp Swansea 1984–; memb: elsh Intensive Care Soc, Intensive Care Soc (memb Cncl 1984–91, meetings sec 1987–89, chm 1989–91), Med Protetion Soc; *Books* Hazards and Complications of Anaesthesia (2 ed with T H Taylor, 1993); *Recreations* sailing; *Clubs* Swansea Yacht and Sub Aqua; *Style*— Dr Edward Major; ✉ Heddfan, 23 Tavistock Road, Sketty, Swansea SA2 0SL; Intensive Therapy Unit, Morriston Hospital, Swansea SA6 6NL (tel 01792 703470, e-mail e.major@ntlworld.com)

MAJOR, Rt Hon Sir John; KG (2005), CH (1999), PC (1987); s of Thomas Major (d 1963), and his 2 w, Gwendolyn Minnie, *née* Coates (d 1970); *b* 29 March 1943; *Educ* Rutlish Sch; *m* 1970, Dame Norma Christina Elizabeth, DBE, da of Norman Wagstaff (ka 1945); 1 da (Elizabeth b 1972), 1 s (James b 1975); *Career* AIB banker and various exec posts in UK and overseas Standard Chartered Bank plc 1965–79; memb Lambeth Borough Cncl 1968–71 (chm Housing Ctee 1970–71), Parly candidate (Cons) St Pancras N (Camden) 1974 (both elections); memb Bd Warden Housing Assoc 1975–83; MP (Cons): Huntingdonshire 1979–83, Huntingdon 1983–2001; jt sec Cons Party Parly Environment Ctee 1979–81, pres Eastern Area Young Conservatives 1983–85; PPS to Mins of State Home Office 1981–83, asst Govt whip 1983–84, a Lord Cmmr of the Treasury (Govt whip) 1984–85, parly under-sec of state for social security 1985–86, min of state for social security DHSS 1986–87, chief sec to HM Treasury June 1987–July 1989, sec of state for foreign and Cwlth affrs July-Oct 1989, Chancellor of the Exchequer Oct 1989–Nov 1990, leader of the Cons Party, Prime Minister and First Lord of the Treasury 28 Nov 1990–97 (resigned as leader of Cons Pty June 1995, re-elected July); chm: European Advsy Cncl Emerson Electric Co 1999–, European Bd Carlyle Gp 2001–05 (memb 1998–2005); sr advsr Credit Suisse First Boston 2001–, memb European Bd Siebel Systems Inc 2001–03, non-exec dir Mayflower Corp plc 2000–03; chm Ditchley Cncl 2000–; memb: Int Bd of Governors Peres Center for Peace Israel 1997–, Bd of Advisers Baker Inst Houston 1998–2005, InterAction Cncl Tokyo 1998–; hon pres Sight Savers Appeal 2001–; pres: Asthma UK 1998–, Br and Cwlth Cricket Charitable Tst 2002–; vice-pres: Macmillan Cancer Relief 2001–, Inst of Sports Sponsorship 2001–; patron: Mercy Ships, Prostate Cancer Charity, Support for Africa 2000, Atlantic Partnership 2001–, FCO Assoc 2001–, Professional Cricketers Assoc 2001–, Deafblind UK 2002–, Consortium for Street Children 2002–, 21st Century Tst 2002–, Goodman Fund Chicago 2002–, Norfolk Cricket Umpires and Scorers Assoc 2002–, Dickie Bird Fndn 2004–, Tim Parry and Johnathan Ball Tst; vice-patron The Atlantic Cncl of the UK; hon bencher Middle Temple 1997; hon Freeman Merchant Taylor's Co 2002; *Publications* The Autobiography (1999), More Than a Game (2007); *Recreations* music, theatre, opera, reading, travel, cricket and other sports; *Clubs* Athenaeum, Carlton, Farmers', Buck's, Pratt's, Surrey CCC (pres 2000–02, hon life vice-pres), MCC (memb Ctee 2001–04 and 2005–); *Style*— The Rt Hon Sir John Major, KG, CH; ✉ PO Box 38506, London SW1P 1ZW

MAJUMDAR, Bish; s of Pran Kumar Majumdar (d 1949), of Calcutta, and Sudha, *née* Sengupta; *b* 20 January 1944; *Educ* Univ of Calcutta (MB, BS), Univ of London (DLO); *m* 19 Jan 1979, Sutapa Majumdar, da of Kalyan Sengupta (d 1954); 2 da (Selina b 26 Jan 1983, Mita b 27 Nov 1985); *Career* registrar Dept of ENT Surgery: Univ Hosp of Wales 1974–76, W Infirmary Glasgow 1976–78; sr registrar: Sheffield Hosps 1978–80, Univ Hosps Nottingham 1980–82; conslt ENT surgn Derbys Royal Infirmary 1982–; clinical teacher otolaryngology Univ of Nottingham; memb: Portmann Fndn (Bordeaux), Res Soc, Br Assoc of Otolaryngology, Midland Inst of Otology; FRCSEd, FRCS, FRSM, FICS (USA); *Recreations* swimming, golf, travel; *Style*— Bish Majumdar, Esq; ✉ Beltoli, Malkin Lane, Mugginton, Ashbourne, Derbyshire DE6 4PL (tel 01335 361123); Derbyshire Royal Infirmary, Department of Otolaryngology, London Road, Derby (tel 01332 254659)

MAKAROVA, Natalia; *b* 1940, Leningrad; *Educ* Vaganova Sch Leningrad; *m* 1976, Edward Karkar; 1 s (Andrusha b 1 Feb 1978); *Career* ballet dancer and choreographer, also actress; with Kirov Ballet 1959–70, defected in London and joined American Ballet Theater (ABT) 1970 (but invited to dance with Kirov in Leningrad again in 1989, first ever Russian artistic exile so invited); guest artist with numerous int ballet cos incl: Royal Ballet, Paris Opera Ballet, National Ballet of Canada, Stuttgart Ballet, Royal Danish Ballet, English National Ballet (formerly London Festival Ballet), Béjart's Ballet of the 20th Century, Roland Petit's Ballet de Marseille; *Roles* with American Ballet Theater incl: debut in Giselle 1970, Tudor's Dark Elegies, Lilac Garden, Pillar of Fire and Romeo and Juliet, various by Balanchine, Robbins and Tetley; with Royal Ballet incl: Swan Lake, Giselle, Sleeping Beauty, Les Sylphides, Manon, Song of the Earth, Concerto, Cinderella, A Month in the Country, Voluntaries, Dances at a Gathering, Serenade, Elite Syncopations, Rituals, Checkmate, Les Biches and Romeo and Juliet; works created for her incl: Robbins' Other Dances, Ashton's Rossignol, Tetley's Sacre du Printemps and Contradance, a MacMillan Pas de Deux with Donald MacLeary, Neumeier's Epilogue, Petit's Blue Angel, Bejart's Mephisto; others incl: Onegin (Evening Standard Award 1985), La Bayadère, The Firebird, Don Quixote, Coppélia, La Fille Mal Gardée, Notre Dame de Paris, Carmen, Cranko's Romeo and Juliet, La Sylphide, Jullitta Messina in Fellini (première, Rome Opera House) 1995; *Productions staged* The Kingdom of the Shades from La Bayadère (for American Ballet Theater) 1974; full length prodn of La Bayadère with reconstructed last act: ABT 1980, Royal Swedish Ballet and Royal Ballet 1989, Teatro Colon Buenos Aires 1992, La Scala Milan 1992, Ballet Santiago 1997, Finnish Nat Ballet 1997, Australian Ballet 1998, Teatro Municipal Brazil 2000, Neumeiers Hamburg Ballet 2002, Teatr Week Warsaw 2004; Swan Lake: London Festival Ballet 1988, Teatro Municipal Brazil 2001, Perm Ballet Russia 2005; Giselle (Royal Swedish Ballet) 2000, Sleeping Beauty (Royal Ballet) 2003, Shades: London Festival Ballet, Nat Ballet of Canada, San Francisco Ballet; Paquita: American Ballet Theatre, Korean Ballet, San Francisco Ballet; *Television* ballet prodns incl: Swan Lake, Giselle, Romeo and Juliet, La Bayadère, The Leningrad Legend, excerpt from Swan Lake in reunion with Kirov Ballet 1988; other dances, other progs and series: Ballerina (BBC) 1987, In a Class of Her Own (Channel 4), Assoluta (BBC), Natasha (BBC), Makarova Returns (documentary on return to the Kirov Ballet) 1989, Great Railway Journeys St Petersburg to Tashkent (documentary on the Bolshoi Express for BBC) 1994; *Theatre* On Your Toes (musical comedy, Broadway, winner Tony award for best actress in a musical and seven other awards, later in West End, winner Olivier Award) 1983–84, Tovarich (Chichester Festival Theatre then West End) 1991, Two for the Seesaw (Moscow and St Petersburg) 1992, Misalliance (Chichester) 1997, Blithe Spirit (Palace Theatre Watford) 2000; *Books* A Dance Autobiography (1979); chapter St Petersburg to Tashkent (in Great Railway Journeys, 1994); *Style*— Ms Natalia Makarova; ✉ c/o Mrs ane Herman, JPH Consultants LLC, 91 Park Central West, 10D New York, NY 10023 (tel and fax 00 1 212 496 7202)

MAKEHAM, Peter Derek James; CB (2003); s of Derek James Stark Makeham, and Margaret Hélene Wilmott, *née* Carter; *b* 15 March 1948; *Educ* Chichester HS, Univ of Nottingham (BA), Univ of Leeds (MA); *m* 1972 (m dis 2003), Carolyne Rosemary, *née* Dawe; 1 s (William b 6 June 1979), 3 da (Sophie b 12 Nov 1980, Isabelle b 11 Oct 1982, Abigail b 5 Dec 1984); *Career* economist Dept of Employment 1971–82, seconded as economist Unilever 1982–83, speechwriter to Chllr and Chief Sec HM Treasy 1983–84, as economist Enterprise Unit Cabinet Office 1984–85, head Employment Policy Dept of Employment 1985–87, DTI 1987–90; Dept for Education and Employment (formerly Dept of Employment): head Fin Servs 1990–91, head Business Servs 1991–92, dir Strategy and Employment Strategy 1992–95; dir Employment and Adult Trg DfEE 1995–97; DfES: dir Sch Orgn and Funding 1997–99, dir Teachers Gp 1999–2000, DG Fin and Analytical Serv 2000–06, DG Strategy and Reform 2006–; *Style*— Peter Makeham, Esq, CB; ✉ Department for Education and Skills, Sanctuary Buildings, Great Smith Street, London SW1P 3BT (tel 020 7925 5486, fax 020 7925 6059)

MAKEPEACE, John; OBE (1988); s of Harold Alfred Smith (d 1957), of Fenny Compton, Warks, and Gladys Marjorie, *née* Wright (d 1996); *b* 6 July 1939; *Educ* Denstone Coll; *m* 1 (m dis); m 2, 3 Dec 1984, Jennifer Moores, da of Harry Brinsden; *Career* furniture designer and maker; dir John Makepeace Ltd 1963–; fndr and dir: The Parnham Tst (charitable educnl tst) 1977–2000; memb Crafts Cncl 1972–77; tstee V&A 1988–90; Award of Excellence The Furniture Soc USA 2002; govr Rycotewood Coll 1970–76; hon fell Arts Inst at Bournemouth 2007; Liveryman Worshipful Co of Furniture Makers 1977; FCSD 1975, FRSA; *Publications* Makepeace: A Spirit of Adventure in Craft and Design by Prof Jeremy Myerson (1995); *Recreations* travel, contemporary art and trees; *Clubs* Athenaeum; *Style*— John Makepeace, OBE; ✉ Farrs, Beaminster, Dorset DT8 3NB (tel 01308 862204, fax 01308 863806, e-mail info@johnmakepeacefurniture.com)

MAKEPEACE, HE Richard Edward; s of Edward Dugard Makepeace, and Patricia Muriel, *née* Malpas; *Educ* St Paul's, Keble Coll Oxford; *Career* served FCO 1976–77, 1985–89 and 1992–94; MECAS 1977–78; posted: Muscat 1979–80, Prague 1980–84, UKREP Brussels 1989–92, Cairo 1995–98; ambass to Sudan 1999–2002, ambass to United Arab Emirates 2003–06, consul-gen Jerusalem (Palestinian Territories) 2006–; *Recreations* travel; *Style*— HE Mr Richard Makepeace; ✉ c/o Foreign & Commonwealth Office (Jerusalem), King Charles Street, London SW1A 2AH

MAKGILL, Hon Diana Mary Robina; CVO (1990, LVO 1983, MVO 1971); da of 12 Viscount of Oxfuird, and Esther, *née* Bromley (d 1996); *b* 4 January 1930; *Educ* Strathcona Lodge Sch Vancouver Island; *Career* ceremonial offr Protocol Dept FCO 1961–90, protocol conslt 1990–; former pres Women of the Year Luncheon; memb Int Ctee Action on Addiction 1990–; conslt to Princess Helena Coll, govr St John and St Mary Primary Sch Hindon; hon steward of Westminster Abbey 1977–2002; memb Chalke Deanery Synod 1992–2002; Freedom of the City of London 1989; Jubilee Medal 1977; Order of Al Kawkab of Jordan 1966, Order of the White Rose of Finland 1969, Order of Star of Afghanistan 1971, Order of the Sacred Treasure of Japan 1971, Order of Independence of the UAE 1989; *Recreations* riding, reading, gardening; *Style*— The Hon Diana Makgill, CVO; ✉ Clouds Lodge, East Knoyle, Wiltshire SP3 6BE (tel and fax 01747 830260)

MAKIN, Prof Brian; s of Clifford Makin (d 1985), of Sheffield, and Edith Ivy, *née* Rogers; *b* 28 December 1935; *Educ* High Storrs GS Sheffield, Univ of Southampton (BSc, PhD); *m* 12 Dec 1959, Hazel, da of Major Jack Phillips; 3 s (Paul Brian b 12 May 1964, Andrew Philip b 15 May 1966, Darren Keith b 3 Feb 1970); *Career* project engr W G Pye and Co Ltd Cambridge 1964–66, lectr Dept of Electrical Engrg Univ of Southampton 1966–74; Univ of Dundee: Watson-Watt prof of electrical engrg and head Dept of Electrical Engrg 1974–87, prof Dept of Applied Physics and Electrical and Mechanical Engrg 1987–; FIEE 1980, FInstP 1985, FRSE 1993; *Recreations* gardening, fishing, walking; *Clubs* Rotary Claverhouse Dundee; *Style*— Prof Brian Makin, FRSE; ✉ Department of Electronic Engineering and Physics, University of Dundee, Dundee DD1 4JB (tel 01382 344394, fax 01382 345415, e-mail b.makin@dundee.ac.uk)

MAKIN, (Norman) Christopher; s of Windsor Makin, of Huddersfield, W Yorks, and Kathleen Mary, *née* Dyson; *b* 7 July 1943; *Educ* King James GS Huddersfield; *m* 9 Aug 1969, Gillian, da of late Eric Reginald Mitton; 1 da (Rebecca Jane b 3 May 1977); *Career* chartered accountant; ptnr: Charles F Beer & Co 1971–87, Revell Ward Chartered Accountants 1987–97, Mazars Neville Russell Chartered Accountants (formerly Neville Russell) 1997–98, conslt in litigation support and mediation Bentley Jennison Chartered Accountants 1998–2006, Chris Makin mediator 2006–; princ double bass: Leeds Symphony Orch, West Riding Opera; FCA 1969, FCMI 1978, FAE 1994, QDR 1998, MCIArb 2006; *Style*— N Christopher Makin, Esq; ✉ Well Cottage, 39 Water Royd Lane, Mirfield, West Yorkshire WF14 9SF; 3 Gray's Inn Square, London WC1R 5AH (tel 020 7430 0333, fax 01924 494421, e-mail chris@chrismakin.co.uk, website www.chrismakin.co.uk)

MAKINSON, John Crowther; CBE (2001); s of Kenneth Crowther Makinson (d 1974), and Phyllis Georgina, *née* Miller; *b* 10 October 1954; *Educ* Repton, Christ's Coll Cambridge (exhibitioner, MA); *m* Virginia Clare, da of Dr John Macbeth; 2 da (Emma Violet b 13 April 1990, Lucy India b 3 Dec 1991); *Career* journalist Reuters (London, Paris and Frankfurt) 1976–79, ed Lex Column and head of companies section Financial Times 1979–86, vice-chm Saatchi & Saatchi (US) Holdings 1986–89, fndr ptnr Makinson Cowell investor relations conslts 1989–94, md The Financial Times Ltd 1994–96, fin dir Pearson plc 1996–2002, chm and ceo Penguin Gp 2002–; *Recreations* music, theatre, travel; *Clubs* Groucho; *Style*— John Makinson, Esq, CBE; ✉ Pearson plc, 80 Strand, London WC2R 0RL (tel 020 7010 3030, fax 020 7010 6689, e-mail john.makinson@penguingroup.com)

MAKOWER, Andrew; s of Peter Makower, and Katharine, *née* Chadburn; *b* 5 October 1961; *Educ* St Paul's, Trinity Coll Cambridge (MA); *m*; 3 c; *Career* clerk House of Lords 1984–; *Style*— Andrew Makower, Esq

MAKSYMIUK, Jerzy; *b* 1936; *Educ* Warsaw Conservatory (studied violin, piano and conducting); *Career* conductor; winner Paderewski Piano Competition 1964; fndr Polish Chamber Orch, princ conductor Polish National Radio Orch 1975–77, conductor laureate BBC Scottish Symphony Orch 1993– (chief conductor 1984–93); has also worked with numerous other orchs incl: BBC Welsh, BBC Philharmonic, CBSO, Bournemouth Sinfonietta, LSO, LPO, The Philharmonia, Orchestre National de France, Ensemble Orchestral de Paris, Ensemble de Grenoble, Tokyo Metropolitan Symphony, Israel Chamber Orch, English National Opera (debut conducting Don Giovanni 1990, then Die Fledermaus 1993), Cracow Philharmonic Orch, Hallé Orch, Orchestre de Toulouse, Royal Liverpool Philharmonic, Prague Symphony Orch, New Zealand Symphony Orch, Winterthur Orchestra, Iceland Symphony Orchestra; conducted various world premières incl: Macmillan's The Confession of Isobel Gowdie (later recorded, Gramophone Contemporary Music Award 1993), Robin Holloway Violin Concerto (with BBC Philharmonic); Hon DLitt Univ of Strathclyde 1990; *Recordings* incl Medtner Piano Concerti Nos 2 and 3 (with BBC Scottish Symphony Orch, Gramophone Best Concerto Award 1992), works by Grieg (with BBC Scottish Symphony Orch), works by Rachmaninov (with Nat Symphony Orch of Ireland); *Style*— Jerzy Maksymiuk, Esq

MALAHIDE, Patrick; *b* 24 March 1945; *Educ* Douai Sch, Univ of Edinburgh; *Career* actor; patron Byre Theatre St Andrews Appeal Fund; *Theatre* Bristol Old Vic incl: The Tempest, The Cherry Orchard, King Lear, Accidental Death of an Anarchist, Clandestine Marriage, Uncle Vanya; Birmingham Rep incl: The Crucible, The Wedding Feast; Traverse incl: The Android Circuit, Every Good Boy Deserves Favour; Royal Court incl: Operation Bad Apple, In the Ruins; other credits incl: Judgement (Liverpool), Cockups (Manchester Exchange), Map of the Heart (Globe), Mutabilitie (RNT), Hinterland (RNT), Embers (Duke of York's); *Television* incl: The Standard, Love Lies Bleeding, Dying Day, Minder, Black Adder, Pickwick Papers, The Russian Soldier, The December Rose, The Singing Detective, After the War, The Franchise Affair, Inspector Morse, Lovejoy, A Doll's House, The Blackheath Poisonings, The Secret Agent, Force of Duty, The Inspector Alleyn Mysteries, Middlemarch, Deacon Brodie, Longitude, All the King's Men, Victoria and Albert, Goodbye Mister Chips, In Search of the Brontës, Amnesia, Friends and Crocodiles, Elizabeth I, Five Days; *Films* incl: The Killing Fields, Comfort and Joy, A Month in the Country, December Bride, A Man of No Importance, Two Deaths, Cutthroat Island, The Long Kiss Goodnight, US Marshals, Ordinary Decent Criminal, The World is not Enough, Billy Elliot, Quills, Captain Corelli's Mandolin, Sahara, Brideshead Revisited; *Screenplays* writer The Writing on the Wall (BBC) 1996; *Recreations* sailing, walking; *Clubs* Royal Fowey Yacht; *Style*— Patrick Malahide, Esq; ✉ c/o ICM Ltd,

Oxford House, 76 Oxford Street, London W1D 1BS (tel 020 7636 6565, fax 020 7323 0101)

MALCIC, Lawrence Michael; s of Lawrence Andrew Malcic, of St Louis, MO, and Marie Sprenger Malcic; *b* 22 September 1955; *Educ* Univ of Pennsylvania (BA, MArch); *m* 11 March 1995, Felicity Quevatre-Malcic, da of Leonard Quevatre; 2 s (Lawrence Justin b 13 Aug 1997, Luke Thomas b 12 Sept 1999); *Career* architect; architectural designer Robert L Boland Architects Inc St Louis 1978–79; Washington Univ St Louis: staff architect Urban Research and Design Center 1979–80, professional advsr for architecture and planning 1980–82, affiliate asst prof Sch of Architecture 1981–82, asst dean for planning and devpt Olin Sch of Business 1982–85; princ for design Gilmore, Malcic and Cannon Inc St Louis 1985–88, dir of design and sr vice-pres HOK Int Ltd London 1989–; visiting lectr in architecture Sch of Architecture and Environmental Design Univ of Texas 1987–88; architectural projects incl: Barclays Bank World HQ Canary Wharf, Cisco European HQ Amsterdam, Dexia Bank Tower Amsterdam, Forty Grosvenor Place London, Nortel Matra Campus Paris, NCR Netherlands HQ Amsterdam, Bow Bells House London, Darwin Centre Natural History Museum London, Washington Univ Plant Growth Lab St Louis, Ethyl Petroleum Research Lab St Louis, Passenger Terminal Amsterdam, VSM High Speed Rail Terminal St Petersburg, West India Quay Tower London, Metropole Hilton Hotel London, Taiz Hotel Yemen, St Barnabas Church Dulwich, Our Lady of Providence Church St Louis; planning project master plans incl: Oostelijke Handelskade (Eastern Docks) Amsterdam, Churchill Place Canary Wharf, Hof van Zuid (S Court), October Railway St Petersburg, Medun (Renault) Paris, Secheron Geneva, Washington Univ St Louis; AIA 1982; *Awards* incl: Medal of Honour Europa Nostra Awards 1997 and Special Commendation Obata Awards 1999 (both for FCO London), finalist Best Medium Sized Office FX Design Int Awards 1999 (for 216 Oxford St), Best Large Mixed-Use Scheme UK 1999 and Design Award Building Magazine 1999 (both for 02 Centre London), Commendation for Conversion/Restoration Environmental Awards Scheme 2000 (for Natural History Museum), Special Commendation Interior Design Times Gestetner Awards 2001 (for Goldings House Dept of Health London), finalist Best Large Office FX Design Awards 2001 and Special Commendation Times Gestener Awards 2001 (both for Cisco Bedfont Lakes Middx), Best Large Office Workplace FX Design Awards 2000 and Best Commercial Building SE Eng, Best Commercial Building Nat Award and Best of the Best all Categories and Regions Br Cncl for Offices Awards 2001 (all for Forty Grosvenor Place), Commendation Innovation in Real Estate Corenet Global Awards 2003 (for both Darwin Centre Natural History Museum and Cisco European HQ Amsterdam); *Publications* author of various articles for jls incl Architects' Jl; *Recreations* travel; *Clubs* University (St Louis), Penn (NY); *Style*— Lawrence Malcic, Esq; ✉ HOK International Ltd, 216 Oxford Street, London W1C 1DB (tel 020 7636 2006, fax 020 7636 1987, e-mail larry.malcic@hok.com); La Folie, Folie Lane, Vale, Guernsey GY3 5SE (tel 01481 246444)

MALCOLM, Derek Elliston Michael; s of J Douglas Malcolm (d 1967), and Dorothy Vera, *née* Elliston-Taylor (d 1964); *b* 12 May 1932; *Educ* Eton, Merton Coll Oxford (BA); *m* 1, 1962 (m dis 1966), Barbara, *née* Ibbott; 1 da (Jacqueline b 1962); m 2, 1994, Sarah, *née* Gristwood; *Career* amateur rider Nat Hunt 1951–53, actor 1953–56, drama critic Gloucestershire Echo Cheltenham 1956–62; The Guardian: features sub ed and writer 1962–69, racing corr 1969–71, film critic 1971–98; film critic Cosmopolitan 1974–96, film critic London Evening Standard 2004–; dir London Int Film Festival 1984–86, govr BFI 1989–92; pres: Critics Circle UK 1980, Int Film Critics 1991–2001 (chm UK Section 1982–), British Fedn of Film Socs 1993–; Int Publishing Co's Critic of the Year 1972; *Books* Robert Mitchum (1984), Derek Malcolm's Personal Best: A Century of Films (2000), Family Secrets (2003); *Recreations* cricket, tennis, squash, music; *Style*— Derek Malcolm, Esq; ✉ 28 Avenue Road, Highgate, London N6 5DW (tel and fax 020 8348 2013); The Dower House, Hull Place, Sholden, Kent CT14 0AQ (tel and fax 01304 364614, mobile 07710 989500, e-mail derekmalcolm@aol.com)

MALCOLM, Col Sir James William Thomas Alexander; 12 Bt (NS) 1665, of Balbedie and Innertiel, Co Fife; DL (Surrey 1991); s of Lt-Col Arthur William Alexander Malcolm, CVO (d 1989), and Hester Mary, *née* Mann (d 1992); suc kinsman, Sir David Peter Michael Malcolm, 11 Bt (d 1995); *b* 15 May 1930; *Educ* Eton, RMA Sandhurst; *m* 1955, Gillian Heather, only c of Elton Henry Humpherus, of Kennards, Leigh, Kent; 2 s (Alexander James Elton b 1956, Robin William b 1958), 2 da (Julia Mary (Mrs Julian Spurling) b 1960, Annabel Heather (Mrs Patrick Toyne Sewell) b 1967); *Heir* s, Col Alexander Malcolm, OBE; *Career* cmd 1 Bn Welsh Gds 1970–72, cmd Welsh Regt of Foot Gds 1972–76; appeals dir Br Heart Fndn 1976–89, High Sheriff Surrey 1991–92; *Recreations* golf; *Clubs* MCC, Royal St George's Golf, Berkshire Golf; *Style*— Col Sir James Malcolm, Bt, DL; ✉ Grove House, Wrecclesham Hill, Wrecclesham, Farnham, Surrey GU10 4JN (tel 01252 712167)

MALCOLM, Dr Noel Robert; *b* 26 December 1956; *Educ* Eton, Peterhouse Cambridge (BA), Trinity Coll Cambridge (MA, PhD); *Career* fell Gonville & Caius Coll Cambridge 1981–88; The Spectator: political columnist 1987–91, foreign ed 1991–92; political columnist Daily Telegraph 1992–95; visiting fell St Antony's Coll Oxford 1995–96, fell All Souls Coll Oxford 2002–; jt winner T E Utley Meml Prize for Political Journalism 1991; Liveryman Fishmongers' Co; FRSL 1997, FBA 2001; *Books* De Dominis 1560–1624 (1984), George Enescu: His Life and Music (1990), Bosnia: A Short History (1994), The Correspondence of Thomas Hobbes (1994), The Origins of English Nonsense (1997), Kosovo: A Short History (1998), Books on Bosnia: A Critical Bibliography (1999), Aspects of Hobbes (2002), JohnPell (1611–1685) (2004); *Style*— Dr Noel Malcolm, FBA, FRSL

MALCOMSON, James Martin; s of Edwin Watlock Malcomson, and Dorothy Madeline, *née* Stuart; *b* 23 June 1946; *Educ* Bootham Sch York, Gonville & Caius Coll Cambridge (exhbn, MA), Harvard Univ (graduate prize fellowship, MA, PhD); *m* 24 Aug 1979, Sally Claire, *née* Richards; 1 da (Emily Ruth b 26 Oct 1980 d 1988); *Career* teaching fell Harvard Univ 1969–71; Univ of York: Ellis Hunter Meml Fell 1971–72, lectr 1972–83, sr lectr 1983–85; visiting fell Université Catholique de Louvain 1983–84, prof of economics Univ of Southampton 1985–99, prof of economics Univ of Oxford 1999–, fell All Souls Coll Oxford 1999–; FBA 2000, fell Econometric Soc 2005; *Publications* author of numerous book contributions and research articles published in learned jls; *Recreations* walking, music, film, theatre; *Style*— Prof James Malcomson; ✉ All Souls College, Oxford OX1 4AL (tel 01865 279379, fax 01865 279299); Department of Economics, Manor Road Building, Oxford OX1 3UQ (tel 01865 271073, fax 01865 271094, e-mail james.malcomson@economics.ox.ac.uk)

MALE, David Ronald; CBE (1991); s of Ronald Male (d 1963), of Worthing, W Sussex, and Gertrude, *née* Simpson (d 1946); *b* 12 December 1929; *Educ* Aldenham; *m* 6 June 1959, Mary Louise, da of Rex Powis Evans, of St Albans, Herts; 2 da (Sarah b 1962, Charlotte b 1966), 1 s (James b 1964); *Career* Nat Serv 2 Lt RA 1948–49; Gardiner & Theobald: ptnr 1960–79, sr ptnr 1979–91, conslt 1992–; RICS: memb Gen Cncl 1976–93, pres Quantity Surveyors Divnl Cncl 1977–78, pres 1989–90; memb: Bd of Dirs Building Centre 1970–80, Govt Construction Panel 1973–74; memb Econ Devpt Cncl for Bldg 1982–86, chm Commercial Buildings Steering Group 1984–88; MCC: memb Ctee 1984–95 and 1996–99, chm Estates Sub-Ctee 1984–94; govr: Aldenham Sch 1974–93, Downe House Sch 2000–; pres Old Aldenhamian Soc 1986–89, non-exec dir London & Bristol Developments plc 1985–91; memb Bd of Mgmnt Macmillan Cancer Relief 1992–2000, memb Bd of Govrs The Wilson Centre Cambridge 1993–97; church cmmr 1989–93; Freeman City of London 1961, Liveryman Worshipful Co Painter-Stainers 1961–93, Past Master Worshipful Co of Chartered Surveyors (memb Ct of Assts 1977–90, Master 1984–85); ARICS 1954, FRICS 1964; *Recreations* opera, ballet, golf; *Clubs* Boodle's, Garrick; *Style*— David Male, Esq, CBE; ✉ Manor Farmhouse, Benham Park, Marsh Benham, Newbury, Berkshire RG20 8LX (tel 01635 522362, fax 01635 529046); 6 Bowland Yard, Kinnerton Street, London SW1X 8EE

MALEK, Ali; QC (1996); s of Ali Akbar Malek, and Irene, *née* Johnson; *b* 19 January 1956; *Educ* Bedford Sch, Keble Coll Oxford (MA, BCL); *m* Sept 1989, Francesca Shoucair; 2 da (Rokhsan Nesa b 18 July 1991, Mithra b 25 May 1993); *Career* called to the Bar Gray's Inn 1980 (Cynthia Terry Entrance Award, Malcolm Hilberry Award), specialist in commercial law; recorder 1998–; memb Commercial Bar Assoc; *Publications* Jack, Malek and Quest: Documentary Credits; *Recreations* running, skiing, golf, music; *Clubs* Vincent's (Oxford); *Style*— Ali Malek, Esq, QC; ✉ 3 Verulam Buildings, Gray's Inn, London WC1R 5NT (tel 020 7831 8441, fax 020 7831 8479, e-mail amalek@3vb.com)

MALEK, Hodge Mehdi; QC (1999); s of late Ali Akbar Malek, and late Irene Elizabeth, *née* Johnson; *b* 11 July 1959; *Educ* Bedford Sch, Sorbonne, Keble Coll Oxford (MA, BCL); *m* 1986, Inez Dies Louise, *née* Vegelin Van Claerbergen; 3 c; *Career* called to the Bar Gray's Inn 1983 (scholarships: Atkin 1983, Birkenhead 1983, Band 1984; bencher 2004); in practice 1983–, recorder of the Crown Court 2004–; lectr regulation and civil procedure; memb: Customs and Excise Prosecution List (European) 1992–, Supp Treasy Panel (common law) 1995–99, Commercial Bar Assoc (COMBAR), Admin Law Bar Assoc, Franco-British Lawyers Soc, Bar Sports Gp, Bar Disciplinary Tbnl 2001–; memb Governing Cncl Royal Numismatic Soc 1991–94; Shamma Prize 1997; *Publications* Discovery (with Paul Matthews, 1992), Disclosure (with Paul Matthews, 2001), Atkins Court Forms (jtly, 2003), Information Rights (contrib, 2004), The Dabuyid Ispahbads and Early 'Abbasid Governors of Tabaristan (2004), Phipson on Evidence (ed, 16 edn 2005); articles in various jls; *Recreations* singing, skiing, swimming, history; *Style*— Hodge Malek, Esq, QC; ✉ 4/5 Gray's Inn Square, Gray's Inn, London WC1R 5AH (tel 020 7404 5252, fax 020 7242 7803)

MALEM, Keir David; s of David Malem, of Greatstone, Kent, and Angela, *née* Wells; *b* 15 May 1965; *Educ* Southlands Comp Sch; *Career* fashion designer; fndr ptnr (with Patrick Whitaker, *qv*) Whitaker Malem 1988–; cmmns for: Givenchy Haute Couture 1997, Valentino Haute Couture 1997, Tommy Hilfiger Red Label 1998, Tommy Hilfiger 1999–2000; launched new line of male and female leather torsos (with Adel Roostein) 1995; lectr in fashion various colls of art and design incl visiting lectr RCA 1999–2000; memb Br Cncl and Br Embassy mission to promote Br fashion, lecture and set Acad project Vilnius Lithuania; special assignments incl: body sculptures for re-opening of Bauhaus Dessau, outfit for Naomi Campbell in Vauxhall advertising campaign 1993, collaboration with sculptor Allen Jones 1999–, piece for permanent collection Museum of Leather Craft Northampton 2000, collection for Alma Home launch 2000, R&D for Gucci collection 2000, cmmn by Allen Jones for new sculpture Waiting on Table (exhibited Royal Acad Summer Exhbn); private cmmns for: Mick Jagger, Cher, Pamela Anderson, Gloria Estefan, Janet Jackson, Jerry Hall, Bono, George Michael, Madonna, Jon Bon Jovi, Spice Girls, Steven Tyler; film cmmns incl: Mortal Kombat 1995, The Changeling 1995, Die Another Day 2002, Tomb Raider 2 2003, Troy 2004, Aeon Flux 2005, Harry Potter and the Goblet of Fire 2005, Eragon 2006, Casino Royale 2006, Harry Potter and the Order of the Phoenix 2007, Batman: The Dark Knight 2008, Speed Racer 2008; exhibitions: Unlaced Grace (Banbury Museum and nat tour) 1994–95, Inside Out (Design Museum London) 2000, Personal Space Br Cncl Show (and commn, NY, Milan, London) 2000, Art 2001 (with Jibby Beane, exhibited Chair sculpture) 2001, Tokyo Designers Weeks (Br Cncl exhibit Living Britain) 2001; *Recreations* film and soundtrack collecting, swimming, cooking, gardening; *Style*— Keir Malem, Esq; ✉ Whitaker Malem, The Garden Studio, 27 Buckingham Road, London N14 DG (tel and fax 020 7923 7887, website www.whitakermalem.co.uk)

MALET, Sir Harry Douglas St Lo; 9 Bt (GB 1791), of Wilbury, Wilts; JP; s of Sir Edward William St Lo Malet, 8 Bt, OBE (d 1990), and (Maria Johana) Benedicta (d 1979), da of Baron Wilhelm von Maasburg, of Vienna; *b* 26 October 1936; *Educ* Downside, Trinity Coll Oxford (BA); *m* 28 Aug 1967, Julia Gresley, da of Charles Harper, of Perth, W Australia; 1 s (Charles Edward St Lo); *Heir* s, Charles Malet; *Career* late Queen's Royal Irish Hussars; *Style*— Sir Harry Malet, Bt; ✉ Wrestwood, RMB 184, Boyup Brook, W Aust 6244, Australia

MALIK, Shahid; MP; *Career* chair Urban Forum 1998–2001, memb Cmmn for Racial Equality 1998–2000, memb Equality Cmmn for NI 1999–2000, vice-chair UNESCO UK 2000–03, MP (Lab) Dewsbury 2005–; memb Select Committee on Home Affrs 2005–, vice-chair All-Party Kashmir Gp 2005–; memb Lab Pty NEC 2000–05; govr Sheffield Hallam Univ 1995–2001; *Style*— Shahid Malik, Esq, MP; ✉ House of Commons, London SW1A 0AA

MALIK, Zubeida; da of Khurshid Ahmed, and Khalida Kurshid; *Educ* Univ of Southampton (BA, MA); *Career* reporter BBC Radio Oxford 1995, reporter BBC Thames Valley 1996, special corr Today prog BBC Radio 4 2000– (output ed 1997–2000), reporter Newsnight BBC; News Journalist of the Year BT Press and Broadcast Awards Radio 1997, Young Journalist of the Year Foreign Press Assoc Awards 2000, Radio News Journalist of the Year EMMA Awards 2001, Radio News Journalist of the Year EMMA Awards 2002, Media Personality Asian Women of Achievement 2002, Carlton TV Multicultural Award for TV and Radio 2003; *Recreations* photography, reading, films; *Style*— Ms Zubeida Malik; ✉ c/o Today Programme, BBC Radio 4, Room G630, Stage Six, Television Centre, Wood Lane, London W12 7RJ (tel 020 8624 9644, fax 020 8624 9633, e-mail zubeida.malik@bbc.co.uk)

MALIN, Prof Stuart Robert Charles; s of Cecil Henry Malin (d 1968), and Eleanor Mary, *née* Howe (d 1998); *b* 28 September 1936; *Educ* Royal GS High Wycombe, KCL (BSc), Univ of London (PhD, DSc); *m* 1, 30 March 1963, Irene (d 1997), da of Frederick Alfred Saunders (d 1989), of Polegate, E Sussex; 2 da (Jane b 1966, Rachel b 1969); m 2, 23 Feb 2001, Lindsey Jean, da of Peter Weetman Macfarlane (d 1991), of Hendon, London; *Career* Royal Greenwich Observatory Herstmonceux: asst experimental offr 1958–61, scientific offr 1961–65, sr scientific offr 1965–70, princ scientific offr 1970–76; Cape observer Radcliffe Observatory South Africa 1963–65, visiting scientist Nat Center for Atmospheric Res USA 1969; Inst of Geological Scis Herstmonceux and Edinburgh: sr princ scientific offr (individual merit) 1976–81, head Geomagnetism Unit 1981–82; Green scholar Scripps Inst Oceanography USA 1981, visiting prof Dept of Physics and Astronomy UCL 1983–2002; head: Dept of Astronomy and Navigation Nat Maritime Museum 1982–88, Mathematics Dept Dulwich Coll 1988–91 and 1992–94, Haberdashers' Aske's Hatcham Coll 1991–92; prof of geophysics Bosphorus Univ Turkey 1994–2001, conslt Rahmi M Koç Museum Turkey 1995–2001, visiting prof Cairo Univ 1996–; assoc ed Quarterly Jl of The Royal Astronomical Soc 1988–91, ed Geophysical Jl Int 1996–2004; Freeman: City of London 2003, Worshipful Co of Clockmakers 2003 (Liveryman (2006); FRAS 1961, FInstP 1971, CPhys 1985; *Books* The Greenwich Meridian (with C Stott, 1984), Spaceworks (with C Stott, 1985), The Planets (1987), Stars Galaxies and Nebulae (1989), The Story of the Earth (1991), The Rahmi M Koç Museum (with Rahmi M Koç, 1997), The Farnol Companion (2006); *Recreations* the novels of Jeffery Farnol, clocks; *Clubs* RAS; *Style*— Prof Stuart Malin; ✉ 30 Wemyss Road, Blackheath, London SE3 0TG (tel 020 8318 3712, e-mail stuart.malin7@ntlworld.com)

MALINOWSKI, Antoni Pawel; s of Wojciech Janusz Malinowski (d 1981), of Warsaw, and Krystyna Gąssowska (d 2004); *b* 13 June 1955, Warsaw; *Educ* Acad of Fine Art Warsaw,

Chelsea Coll of Art; *Career* artist; *Solo Exhibitions* Künstlerhaus Hamburg 1985, The Drawing Room installation London 1986, Galerie Wilma Tolksdorf Hamburg 1987 and 1988, Life Drawing installation and performance Chisenhale Gallery London 1987, Provisional Statements on the Rights of the Citizen installation Angel Studios London 1988, Mario Flecha Gallery London 1989, The Showroom London 1990, Galeria Dziekanka Warsaw 1991, Galerie Marie-Louise Wirth Zürich 1993, Gimpel Fils Gallery London 1993 and 1995, Newlyn Art Gallery Penzance 1997, Camden Arts Centre London 1997, Angel Row Gallery Nottingham 1997, Oriel Mosyn Wales 1997, Royal Court Theatre: Related Work Gimpel Fils London 1999, De La Warr Pavilion Bexhill-on-Sea 2001, Echoing The Pavilion (The Architectural Assoc London) 2001, THRESHOLDscape (Gimpel Fils London) 2002, New Paintings (Gimpel Fils London) 2004, Bridging Lines (Studio Visconti and Assab One Milan) 2005, Prism of Time (In Situ Warsaw) 2006, Gimpel Fils London 2007; *Group Exhibitions* Open Futures (Ikon Gallery Birmingham) 1988, Syzygy (Mario Flecha Gallery London) 1988, Whitechapel Open London 1989, 1990 and 1992, What is a Gallery (Kettles Yard Cambridge) 1990, Drawing Show (Mario Flecha Gallery London) 1990, Jestešmy (Zachęta Warsaw) 1991, New Voices (Br Cncl show Brussels) 1992, EC Young Painters (Seoul Korea), Moving into View - Recent British Painting (Royal Festival Hall and tour) 1993, Recent CAS Aquisitions (MOMA Oxford) 1994, Recent Contemporary Art Soc Purchases (Butler Gallery Kilkenny Castle) 1995, London Stories (GE Gallery, Winterthur Switzerland) 1995, The Subject of Art (NatWest Gp Art Collection London) 1997, What is a Photograph (Five Years London) 1998, The Difference Between You and Us (Five Years London) 2001, Tracing the Land (Gimpel Fils London) 2004, Dis/Continuity of Line (Assab One Milan), Summer Exhbn Royal Acad London; *Work in Public Collections* Arts Cncl, Br Cncl, Tate Gallery, CAS, MOMA (Oxford); *Commissions* private cmmn for Palazzo Venice 1998, wall drawing Royal Court Theatre London 1998–2000, floor Canary Square London 1999–2000, painting installation Luxor Theatre Rotterdam 2002, artist/colourist to the redevelopment of BBC Broadcasting House 2003–05; *Style*— Antoni Malinowski, Esq; ✉ c/o Gimpel Fils, 30 Davies Street, London W1K 4NB (tel 020 7493 2488, fax 020 7629 5732, e-mail info@gimpelfils.com)

MALINS, Humfrey Jonathan; CBE (1997), MP; s of Rev Peter Malins and late Lilian Joan Malins; *b* 31 July 1945; *Educ* St John's Sch Leatherhead, BNC Oxford (MA); *m* 1979, Lynda Anne; 1 da (Katherine b 1982), 1 s (Harry b 1985); *Career* former slr; MP (Cons): Croydon NW 1983–92, Woking 1997–; PPS: to min of state Home Office 1987–1989, to min of state Dept of Health 1989–92; shadow min Home Office 2001–03; fndr Immigration Advsy Serv 1993; *Recreations* rugby football, golf, gardening; *Clubs* Vincent's (Oxford); *Style*— Humfrey Malins, Esq, CBE, MP; ✉ House of Commons, London SW1A 0AA (tel 020 7219 3000)

MALINS, Julian Henry; QC (1991); s of Rev Peter Malins, and Joan, *née* Dingley; *b* 1 May 1950; *Educ* Greenways Sch Codford St Mary, St John's Sch Leatherhead, BNC Oxford (MA, Boxing blue); *m* 1 July 1972, (Catherine) Joanna Wilson, da of John Henry Pearce; 3 da (Annabel b 1977, Cressida b 1979, Miranda b 1984); *Career* called to the Bar Middle Temple 1972 (bencher 1996); memb: Ct Common Cncl, Gen Cncl of the Bar; govr Museum of London, govr Guildhall Sch of Music and Drama; Freeman City of London 1979; *Style*— Julian Malins, Esq, QC; ✉ 115 Temple Chambers, Temple Avenue, London EC4Y 0DA (tel 020 7583 5275, fax 020 7353 8869, e-mail malins@btinternet.com)

MALIPHANT, Russell Scott; s of Ralph Geoffrey Maliphant, and Patricia Anne, *née* Russell; *b* 18 November 1961; *Educ* Royal Ballet Sch, Rolf Inst of Structural Integration USA; *m* 12 Feb 2001, Dana, da of Theodore Fouras; 1 s (Jude Gabriel b 10 August 2000), 1 da (Aysa b 17 March 2003); *Career* choreographer and performer; with Sadlers Wells Royal Ballet 1982–88, freelance performer with DV8 Physical Theatre, Michael Clark & Co and Laurie Booth 1988–95, estab Russell Maliphant Co 1996; works created incl: Shift 1996, Unspoken 1996, Critical Mass 1998, Two 1998, Sheer 2001, Torsion 2002, One Part Two 2002, Broken Fall 2003, Choice 2003; toured worldwide incl Europe, India, Australia, Canada, Colombia and USA; maintains private practice of Rolfing Method of Structural Integration; represented GB The Int Bancs d'Essai 1995, fellowship Arts Cncl of England 2000–02; *Awards* Dance Umbrella Dance and Performance Award 1991, Time Out Award 1991, People's Choice Award Int Festival de Nouvelle Danse Montreal 2001, Time Out Live Award for Outstanding Collaboration 2002, South Bank Show Award for Dance 2003, Laurence Olivier Award for Best New Dance Publication (for Broken Fall) 2003; *Recreations* outdoor pursuits, parenting!; *Style*— Russell Maliphant, Esq; ✉ PO Box 43188, London E17 4XL (e-mail gwen@cueperformance.com, website www.russellmaliphantcompany.co.uk)

MALLABER, Judy; MP; *Career* MP (Lab) Amber Valley 1997–; *Style*— Ms Judy Mallaber, MP; ✉ c/o Louis Eustace, House of Commons, London SW1A 2LW

MALLABY, Sir Christopher Leslie George; GCMG (1996, KCMG 1988), GCVO (1992); s of Brig A W S Mallaby, CIE, OBE (ka 1945), and Margaret Catherine, *née* Jones; *b* 7 July 1936; *Educ* Eton, King's Coll Cambridge (BA); *m* 1961, Pascale, da of Francois Thierry-Mieg, of Paris; 1 s (Sebastian b 1964), 3 da (Emily b 1967, Julia b 1971, Charlotte b 1972); *Career* HM Dip Serv 1959–96: Moscow Embassy 1961–63 and 1975–77, first sec Berlin 1966–69, dep dir Br Trade Devpt Office (NY) 1971–74, head of Arms Control & Disarmament Dept 1977–79, then E Euro and Soviet Dept 1979–80, then Planning Staff FCO 1980–82, min Bonn 1982–85, dep sec Cabinet Office 1985–87, ambass Bonn 1988–92, ambass Paris 1993–96, ret; advsr then md UBS Investment Bank 1996–2006; dir: Sun Life & Provincial Holdings 1996–2000, Charter Pan-European Investment Tst 1996–2007, EDF Trading 1998–2003, Vodafone AG Germany 2000–; advsr: RMC 1996–2000, BAe 1997–98, Herbert Smith 1997–2001; vice-chm Reuters Founders Share Co 1998–; chm: Primary Immuno-Deficiency Assoc 1996–2002 and 2005–06, Grossbritannien Institut of the Humboldt Univ Berlin 1997–2005, Cncl German Studies Inst Univ of Birmingham 1998–2005, Charitable Tst of European Orgn for Research and Treatment of Cancer 2000–, Somerset House Tst 2002–06; tstee Tate Gallery 1996–2002; Hon LLD Univ of Birmingham 2004; Chllr Order of St Michael and St George 2005–; Grand Cross of the Order of Merit (Germany) 1992, Grand Officier of the Legion d'Honneur (France) 1996, Commandeur de l'Ordre des palmes Académiques (France) 2004; *Recreations* grandchildren; *Clubs* Brooks's, Beefsteak, Grillion's; *Style*— Sir Christopher Mallaby, GCMG, GCVO

MALLALIEU, Baroness (Life Peer UK 1991), of Studdridge in the County of Buckinghamshire; Ann Mallalieu; QC (1988); da of Sir (Joseph Percival) William Mallalieu (d 1980), and Harriet Rita Riddle, *née* Tinn; *b* 27 November 1945; *Educ* Holton Park Girls' GS, Newnham Coll Cambridge (MA, LLM); *m* 1979, as his 2 w, Sir Timothy Felix Harold Cassel, 4 Bt, QC, *qv*, eldest s of His Honour Sir Harold Felix Cassel, 3 Bt, TD, QC (d 2001); 2 da (Hon Bathsheba Anna b 1981, Hon Cosima Ione Harriet b 1984); *Career* called to the Bar Inner Temple 1970, bencher 1992; recorder 1985–94; oppn spokesman on home affrs and legal affrs House of Lords 1991–97; chm: Independent Cncl of the Ombudsman for Corp Estate Agents 1993–2000, Suzy Lamplugh Tst 1996–2000; first woman pres Cambridge Union Soc 1967, hon fell Newnham Coll Cambridge 1991, pres Countryside Alliance 1998–; memb Br Horseracing Bd 2004–; *Recreations* hunting, sheep, reading poetry, horse racing; *Style*— The Baroness Mallalieu, QC; ✉ House of Lords, London SW1A 0PW

MALLALIEU, Huon Lancelot; s of Sir (Edward) Lancelot Mallalieu, QC, MP (d 1979), and Betty Margaret Oxley, *née* Pride (d 1993); *b* 11 August 1946; *Educ* Harrow, Trinity Coll Oxford (MA); *m* 11 Dec 1982, Fenella Jane, *née* Rowse; 1 da (Ilaira b 4 June 1988), 1 s (Joshua b 25 Sept 1990); *Career* cataloguer for Christie's 1969–73; writer and journalist 1973–; contrib: The Times, Country Life, Sunday Telegraph, Financial Times, Antiques Trade Gazette, The Oldie; ed Watercolours and Drawings Magazine 1986–91, property ed Country Life 1989–90, saleroom writer Country Life 1990–; Residential Property Journalist of the Year 1998; assoc ed Oxford DNB; memb: Cncl for the Care of Churches 1992–2001, Ctee London Library 1994–98, Advsy Ctee Lambeth Palace Chapel 1996–2001, Lambeth Palace Refurbishment Gp 2001–; visiting lectr City Univ 2006; FSA 2005; *Books* incl: Crome, Cotman and The Norwich School (1974), The Dictionary of British Watercolour Artists (3 vols 1976, 1979, 1990, new edn 2002), How To Buy Pictures (1984), Understanding Watercolours (1985), The Illustrated History of Antiques (gen ed, 1991), Antiques Roadshow A-Z of Antiques Hunting (ed, 1995), Moving to the Country (2000); *Recreations* helicopters, writing novels, cartoons; *Style*— Huon Mallalieu, Esq, FSA; ✉ 100 Mortimer Road, London N1 4LA

MALLALIEU, Robin; *Educ* Univ of Manchester (BA, BArch), RIBA; *m* Angela Brady , *qv*; 2 c; *Career* architect; ptnr Brady Mallalieu Architects 11P 1987–; quinquennial inspr to C of E; *Awards* RIAI Award for house renovation in Islington London 1991, RIAI Award for office fitout for Groundwork Hackney London 1995, RIAI Award for Sch of Architecture Univ of North London 1997, RIAI Award for Barra plc Open Air Theatre 2005, RIAI Award for house in Knightsbridge London; *Books* Dublin: a guide to contemporary architecture (with Angela Brady, 1997); *Style*— Robin Mallalieu, Esq; ✉ Brady Mallalieu Architects, 90 Queens Drive, London N4 2HW (tel 020 8880 1544, fax 020 8880 2687, e-mail bma@bradymallalieu.com. website www.bradymallalieu.com)

MALLARD, Prof John Rowland; OBE (1992); s of John Edward Mallard (d 1947), of Northampton, and Margaret Gwendoline, *née* Huckle (d 1958); *b* 14 January 1927; *Educ* Northampton Town and County Sch, Univ Coll Nottingham (BSc), Univ of Nottingham (PhD, DSc); *m* 6 June 1958, Fiona MacKenzie Murdoch Lawrance, da of Robert Murdoch Lawrance (d 1934), of Aberdeen; 1 s (John b 1959), 1 da (Katriona b 1964); *Career* asst physicist Liverpool Radium Inst 1951–53, head Dept of Physics Hammersmith Hosp 1958–63 (physicist 1953–58), reader in bio-physics Postgrad Med Sch and St Thomas' Hosp Med Sch London 1963–65, dir of med physics Grampian Health Bd and prof of med physics Univ of Aberdeen 1965–92 (now emeritus); Julio Palacios lectr Lisbon 1974, Silvanus Thompson medal Br Inst of Radiolgy 1981 (Barclay prize 1976), Otto Glasser lectr Cleveland USA 1982, Royal Soc Wellcome Fndn prize and Gold medal 1984, Free Enterprise special award Aims for Industry 1984, George Van Hevesy medal Euro Soc for Nuclear Med 1985, Euro Workshop of Nuclear Magnetic Resonance in Med award 1987, Commemoration lectr Univ of Osaka Japan 1987, Sr Scientist Merit award Int Union of Physical and Engrg Sci in Med 1988 (fndr pres 1980–85), Royal Soc Mullard prize and medal 1990, Barclay medal Br Inst of Radiology 1991, Norman Veall Prize Br Nuclear Medicine Soc 1995, Dunottar Medal Royal Scottish Soc of Arts 1996, Royal Medal Royal Soc of Edinburgh 2002, Gold Medal Royal Coll of Radiologists 2004, European Fedn of Organisations of Medical Physics Medal (EFMOP) 2004; memb: Equipment Res Ctee Sec of State for Scotland 1973–77 (Bio-Engrg Study Gp 1969–72, Bio-Med Res Ctee 1973–77), Bds MRC 1975–86, UK Nat Ctee for Bio-Physics 1977–85, Admin Radioactive Substances Advsy Ctee DHSS 1982–85; chm UK Nat Ctee for Med Physics 1975–88 (sec 1965–75), cmmr Int Cmmn of Radiation Units and Measurements 1985–94; Freeman City of Aberdeen 2004; Hon DSc: Univ of Hull 1994, Univ of Nottingham 1996, Univ of Aberdeen 1997; hon fell Australian Coll of Physical Scis applied to Med 1978; hon memb: RCR 1966, Br Nuclear Med Soc, Br Inst of Radiology 2000; FIPEM 1951 (pres 1970–73, hon fell 1993), FInstP (CPhys) 1960, FIEE (CEng) 1962, FRSE 1972, FRCPath 1974, BES 1975 (pres 1975–76), FREng 1993; *Books* contrib: Radioisotopes in Medical Diagnosis (1971), Progress in Nuclear Medicine (1972), NMR Imaging (1983), Modern Microscopies (1989), Scientific Europe (1990), Twentieth Century Physics (1995); 240 scientific publications in medical imaging (Nuclear Medicine and MRI) 1951–97; *Recreations* handicrafts including jewellery making; *Style*— Prof John Mallard, OBE, FRSE, FREng; ✉ 121 Anderson Drive, Aberdeen AB15 6BG (tel 01224 316204); Department of Bio-Medical Physics & Bio-Engineering, University of Aberdeen and Grampian Health Board, Foresterhill, Aberdeen AB25 2ZD (tel 01224 681818 ext 52499, fax 01224 685645, telex 73458 UNIABN G)

MALLET, Victor John; s of Philip Louis Victor Mallet, and Mary Moyle Grenfell, *née* Borlase; *b* 14 May 1960; *Educ* Winchester, Merton Coll Oxford (BA); *Career* journalist and author; with Reuters in London, Paris, Johannesburg and Cape Town 1981–86; Financial Times: Africa corr 1986–88, Middle East corr 1988–91, SE Asia corr 1992–94, dep features ed 1995–96, Southern Africa corr 1998–2001, Paris corr 2001–03, chief Asia corr 2003–06, Asia ed 2007–; *Books* The Trouble With Tigers: the Rise and Fall of South East Asia (1999); *Style*— Victor Mallet, Esq; ✉ The Financial Times, 1 Southwark Bridge, London SE1 9HL (tel 020 7873 3000, e-mail victor.mallet@ft.com)

MALLICK, Prof Sir Netar P; kt (1998), DL (Gtr Manchester 1999); s of Dr Bhawani Mallick (d 1964), of Blackburn, Lancs, and Shanti Devi, *née* Talwar (d 1986); *Educ* Queen Elizabeth Sch Blackburn, Univ of Manchester (BSc, MB ChB); *m* 11 July 1960, Mary, da of Albert Wilcockson (d 1977), of Brough, E Yorks; 3 da (Andrea b 1964, Naomi b 1966, Paula b 1968); *Career* conslt physician Dept of Renal Med Manchester Royal Infirmary 1973 (sr lectr med 1972–73); vice-chm Blackburn Hyndburn Ribble Valley Health Authy 1985–90; prof of renal med Univ of Manchester 1994–2000, med dir Central Manchester Healthcare NHS Tst 1997–2000; med dir: Advsy Ctee on Distinction Awards 1999–2003, Advsy Ctee Clinical Excellence Awards 2003–06; pres: Manchester Lit and Philosophical Soc 1985–87, Renal Assoc of GB and I 1989–92, Manchester Medical Soc 2005–06; chm Registry Ctee Euro Renal Assoc 1991–94; High Sheriff Gtr Manchester 2002–03; FRCP 1976, FRCPEd 1992, FRCPI 1999, FRCSEd 2006; *Books* Renal Disease in General Practice (1979), Case Presentations in Renal Medicine (1983); *Clubs* Athenaeum; *Style*— Prof Sir Netar Mallick, DL; ✉ Department of Renal Medicine, Manchester Royal Infirmary, Oxford Road, Manchester M13 9WL (tel 0161 276 4111, fax 0161 276 8022)

MALLIN, Anthony Granville; s of Frederick Granville Mallin (d 1986), and Phyllis May Mallin; *b* 26 May 1955; *m* 1989, Marie-Louise; 2 da (Josephine Louise b 4 Dec 1990, Annabelle Marie b 18 Oct 1995), 1 s (Frederick Harry b 15 April 1993); *Career* former vice-chm Hambros Bank Ltd, dir Hambros plc 1995–; chief exec MRBS Capital Partners Ltd; chm: Leaseurope 1998–99, Equipment Leasing Assoc 1992–, Finance & Leasing Assoc 1993–; dir East London Youth & Minorities Activities Ltd (charity); *Recreations* rowing, golf, opera; *Clubs* Lea Rowing (pres), Leander, Highgate Golf; *Style*— Tony Mallin

MALLINCKRODT, George Wilhelm; *see:* Von Mallinckrodt, Georg Wilhelm

MALLINSON, Dr Christopher Niels; s of Lawrence Mallinson (d 1960), and Thea Ruth, *née* Bergmann (d 1990); *b* 29 October 1935; *Educ* Cheltenham, King's Coll Cambridge (VIII Henley), Guy's Hosp; *m* 1966, Helen Gillian, da of J Noel Bowen; 2 da (Polly Jane b 1973, Sarah b and d 1976), 1 s (William (twin) b and d 1976); *Career* house physician Guy's Hosp, registrar then sr registrar Guy's Hosp, res fell Pennsylvania USA; conslt physician and clinical tutor Greenwich Dist Hosp, lectr in physiology Guy's Hosp Med Sch 1969–79, conslt physican gastroenterologist Lewisham Hosp 1979–96, conslt physician in med communications Univ Hosp Lewisham; fndr memb and memb Ctee Pancreatic Soc of GB and Ireland (pres 1987–88), pres Gastroenterology Sub Ctee European Union of Med Specialists, dir Communications Research Gp, chm steering gp Med Communications Forum RSM, memb Br Soc of Gastroenterology 1965, fndr bd memb Euro Assoc for Communication in Health Care; FRCP 1973; *Publications* AA Glucagonoma Syndrome (article, 1974), Report of Royal College of Physicians Working Party on Communications in Medicine, Psychiatric Complications of Organic Disease (ed, RCP), Standards of Training in Gastroenterology in Countries in the European Union (1990), A Pilot Study for Developing Communications in Acute General Hospitals (1997), Communication in Health Care (in Clinical Medicine, 6 edn 2004); *Recreations* garden design, painting, opera, conversation, sailing; *Clubs* Garrick; *Style—* Dr Christopher Mallinson; ✉ 134 Harley Street, London W1G 7JY (tel 020 7935 4849)

MALLON, Seamus; s of Francis Patrick Mallon (d 1969), of Markethill, Armagh, and Jane, *née* O'Flaherty (d 1965); *b* 17 August 1936; *Educ* Abbey GS Newry, St Mary's Coll of Educn Belfast; *m* 22 June 1964, Gertrude Cora, da of Edward Cush, of Armagh; 1 da (Orla b June 1969); *Career* headmaster St James's PS Markethill 1960–73; memb: Armagh DC 1973–86, NI Assembly 1973–74, NI Convention 1975–76, Irish Senate 1982, New Ireland Forum 1983–84; MP (SDLP) Newry and Armagh 1986–2005; memb House of Commons Select Ctee on Agric 1986–92, memb Br-Irish Inter-Parly Body 1990–; MLA (SDLP) Newry and Armagh 1998–2003, dep first minister Northern Ireland Assembly 1998–2001; dep ldr SDLP until 2001; Humbert Summer Sch Peace Prize 1988; *Recreations* golf, angling, landscape painting; *Style—* Seamus Mallon, Esq; ✉ 5 Castleview, Markethill, Armagh

MALMESBURY, Archdeacon of; *see:* Hawker, Ven Alan Fort

MALMESBURY, 7 Earl of (GB 1800); James Carleton Harris; DL (Hants 1997); also Baron Malmesbury (GB 1788) and Viscount FitzHarris (GB 1800); s of 6 Earl of Malmesbury, TD, JP, DL (d 2000); *b* 19 June 1946; *Educ* Eton, Queen's Coll Univ of St Andrews (MA); *m* 14 June 1969, Sally Ann, da of Sir Richard Newton Rycroft, 7 Bt; 3 s (James, Viscount FitzHarris b 1970, Hon Edward b 1972, Hon Guy b 1975), 2 da (Lady Frances b 1979, Lady Daisy b 1981); *Heir* s, Viscount FitzHarris; *Style—* The Rt Hon the Earl of Malmesbury, DL; ✉ Greywell Hill, Greywell, Hook, Hampshire RG29 1DG (tel 01256 703565, e-mail eofmalm@btconnect.com)

MALONE, Dr Beverly; *b* 25 August 1948, Elizabethtown, KY; *Educ* Univ of Cincinnati (BSN, PhD), Rutgers State Univ (MS); *Career* private practice as clinical nurse 1973–96, clinical nursing and administrator positions Univ of Cincinnati Hosp Med Center 1973–86, dean Sch of Nursing North Carolina Agric and Tech State Univ 1986–2000 (interim vice-chllr 1994), dep asst sec for health Dept of Health and Human Servs USA 1999–2001, gen sec RCN 2001–; pres American Nurses Assoc (ANA) 1996–2000; sometime US rep World Health Assembly; numerous appts to public bodies incl former memb Advsy Cmmn on Consumer Protection and Quality in the Health Care Industry and Health Care Quality Measurement and Reporting Ctee (both USA); memb: NHS Modernisation Bd 2001–, HEFCE, Forum UK, Cncl Inst for Employment Studies; author of numerous articles on nursing, diversity and health care; Hon DSc: Indiana Univ, Ohio Univ, York Univ, NY State Univ; other hon degrees: Queen's Univ Belfast, Middlesex Univ, City Univ; fell American Acad of Nursing; *Style—* Dr Beverly Malone; ✉ Royal College of Nursing, 20 Cavendish Square, London W1G 0RN

MALONE, Jo; *Career* early career: Pulbrook and Gould (florist), pt/t gardener; chairwoman and creative dir Jo Malone, opened first store London 1994, opened flagship store 1999, other stores incl Sydney and NY, over 300 concessions worldwide; *Style—* Ms Jo Malone; ✉ Jo Malone, The Old Imperial Laundry, Warrinier Gardens, London SW11 4XW

MALONE-LEE, Michael Charles; CB (1995), DL; s of Dr Gerard Brendan Malone-Lee, and Theresa Marie Germaine Malone-Lee; *b* 4 March 1941; *Educ* Stonyhurst, Campion Hall Oxford (MA); *m* Claire Frances, da of Canon C M Cockin; 2 s (John b 1975, Francis b 1980); *Career* Civil Serv: joined 1968, princ private sec to Sec of State for Social Servs 1976–79, area admin City & East London AHA 1979–81, dist admin Bloomsbury HA 1982–84, under sec and dir of personnel DHSS HQ 1984–87, princ fin offr Home Office 1987–89, dep sec and dir of corp affrs NHS Mgmnt Exec Dept of Health 1990–93, head Policy Gp Lord Chllr's Dept 1993–95; vice-chllr Anglia Poly Univ 1995–2004; *Recreations* running, natural history, anything French; *Style—* Michael Malone-Lee, Esq, CB, DL

MALONEY, Michael Anthony Gerard; s of Gp Capt Gerard Maloney, of London, and Pamela Maloney; *b* 19 June 1957; *Educ* Ampleforth, LAMDA; *Career* actor; jt winner Alec Clunes Award LAMDA; *Theatre* RSC incl: Prince Hal in Henry IV Parts 1 and 2, Romeo in Romeo and Juliet, title role in Derek, Edgar in King Lear; other credits incl: Taking Steps (Lyric Theatre), William Blake in In Lambeth (Donmar Warehouse), Benjamin Britten in Once in a While the Odd Thing Happens (NT), title role in Peer Gynt (Cambridge), Two Planks and a Passion (Greenwich), Alice's Adventures Underground (RNT), Mouth to Mouth (Royal Court and Albery), title role in Hamlet (Greenwich, W Yorks Playhouse and nat tour); *Television* for BBC: Starlings (first prize Monte Carlo), Telford's Change, The Bell, Falkland in The Rivals, Relatively Speaking, Love On A Branch Line; other credits incl: Dominic in What if it's Raining, William Boot in Scoop, Prosper Proford in The Forsyte Saga, The Archbishop of Canterbury in The Six Wives of Henry VIII, Malvolio in Twelfth Night, Indiana Jones Chronicles, Sex & Chocolate, Macbeth, Children of the New Forest, Painted Lady, A Christmas Carol, The Swap, The Jury, Me and Mrs Jones, Believe Nothing; *Radio* Orsino in Twelfth Night, Brutus in Julius Caesar, title role in Alexander the Great, Konstantin in The Seagull, title role in Hitler, Lysander in A Midsummer Night's Dream, The Winslow Boy, Frankenstein, The Old Law, The Devil is an Ass, The Ambridge Chronicles, The Brothers Karamaov; *Film* incl: Dauphin in Henry V, Rosencrantz in Hamlet, Leonardo in La Maschera, Laertes in Hamlet, Michel in Bienvenue au Gite, Truly Madly Deeply, Ordeal By Innocence, Sharma and Beyond, In the Bleak Midwinter, Othello, American Reel, Sans Plomb, Hysteria; *Style—* Michael Maloney, Esq; ✉ c/o Markham & Froggatt Ltd, Julian House, 4 Windmill Street, London W1T 2HZ (tel 020 7636 4412, fax 020 7637 5233)

MALPAS, Prof James Spencer; s of Tom Spencer Malpas (d 1972); *b* 15 September 1931; *Educ* Sutton Co GS, Bart's Univ of London, Univ of Oxford; *m* 1957, Joyce May, da of Albert Edward Cathcart (d 1962); 2 s; *Career* St Bartholomew's Hosp Univ of London: dean Med Coll 1969–72, conslt physician 1973–95, sr physician 1993–95, former dir Imperial Cancer Res Fund Unit of Med Oncology and prof of med oncology, currently emeritus prof of med oncology; academic registrar RCP 1975–80, pres Assoc of Cancer Physicians 1994–99; Master London Charterhouse 1996–2001; special tstee Barts and the London Charitable Fndn 1999–2007; tstee: Med Coll of St Bartholomew's Tst 1999–, Mason le Page Charitable Tst 2001–; memb: Central Institutional Review Bd of Cancer Research Campaign 2001–04, Ctee Retired Fellows Soc RSM 2007–; Freeman City of London 1988; FRCP, FRCR,FRCPCH, FRI; *Recreations* sailing, history, painting, travel; *Clubs* Little Ship; *Style—* Prof James Malpas; ✉ 253 Lauderdale Tower, Barbican, London EC2Y 8BY (tel 020 7920 9337, e-mail jmalpas@aol.com)

MALPAS, (John) Peter Ramsden; s of A H Malpas (d 1942), and E N E D Malpas, *née* Gledhill (d 1992); *b* 14 December 1927; *Educ* Winchester, New Coll Oxford (MA); *m* 10 May 1958, Rosamond Margaret, da of R J Burn, RA (d 1984), of Chiswick, London; 3 s (Simon b 1959, David b 1962, Johnny b 1965); *Career* Lt RB served India and UK 1946–48; commercial asst Imperial Chemical Industries 1951–55, Chase Henderson & Tennant Stockbrokers 1956–58; Paribas Quilter Securities (formerly Quilter Goodison, previously Quilter & Co): joined 1959, dep sr ptnr and chm 1983–87; dir: Penny & Giles International 1988–92, West Wittering Estates plc 1995–2003; hon treas Royal Hosp for Neuro-Disability 1988–97, chm The Neuro-Disability Research Tst; memb Stock Exchange 1961–88; *Recreations* skiing, walking, sailing, the arts; *Clubs* Itchenor Sailing, Ski Club of GB; *Style—* Peter Malpas, Esq; ✉ 48 Berwyn Road, Richmond, Surrey TW10 5BS (tel 020 8878 2623, e-mail peter.malpas@ukgateway.net)

MALSBURY, Angela Mary; da of late Reginald Malsbury, and Madge Meagan, *née* Stenson; *b* 5 May 1945; *Educ* Loughborough HS for Girls, Kibworth Beauchamp GS, Royal Coll of Music; *m* 1965, David Robin Pettit; 1 s (Timothy Nicholas David b 1967); *Career* clarinettist; Wigmore Hall debut 1968, Royal Festival Hall debut with London Mozart Players 1976; princ clarinettist London Mozart Players, prof of clarinet Royal Acad of Music; memb: Albion Ensemble, Primavera Ensemble, De Saram Clarinet Trio, London Winds, Musicians of the Royal Exchange; also plays with: Acad of St Martin in the Fields, London Sinfonietta, Nash Ensemble; Mozart Meml Prize, Hon RAM; *Recordings* incl: Mozart's 13 Wind Serenade (variously with London Mozart Players, Acad of St Martin's and Albion Ensemble), Mozart's Clarinet Quintet (with Coull Quartet), Mozart's Clarinet Concerto (with London Mozart Players), Prokovieff's Overture on Yiddish Themes, Mississippi 5 (with Albion Ensemble), A Trio of French Styles (with De Saram Trio), The Classical Harmonie (with Albion Ensemble); *Recreations* swimming, walking, cooking, art; *Style—* Ms Angela Malsbury; ✉ c/o Stephannie Williams Artists, 16 Swanfold, Wilmcote, Stratford-upon-Avon CV37 9XH (tel 01789 266272, fax 01789 266467)

MALTBY, Colin Charles; s of George Frederick Maltby, MC (decd), and late Dorothy Maltby; *b* 8 February 1951; *Educ* George Heriot's Sch Edinburgh, King Edward's Sch Birmingham, ChCh Oxford (MA, MSc), Stanford Business Sch; *m* 1983, Victoria Angela Valerie, da of late Paul Guido Stephen Elton; 2 da (Lorna b 1976, Katherine b 1986), 1 s (Matthew b 1989); *Career* merchant banker; pres Oxford Union 1973, chm Fedn of Cons Students 1974–75; dir: Kleinwort Benson (ME) EC 1983–84, Kleinwort Benson Investment Mgmnt Ltd 1984–95, Banque Kleinwort Benson SA 1985–95 (chm 1993), Kleinwort Benson Group plc 1989–95; chief exec Kleinwort Benson Investment Mgmnt Ltd 1988–95, chm Kleinwort Overseas Investment Trust plc 1992–96; dir Fuji Investment Trust Mgmnt KK 1993–95, chief investment offr Equitas Reinsurance Ltd 1996–2000; non-exec dir: RM plc 1997–2000, H Young Holdings plc 1997–2001, CCLA Investment Mgmnt Ltd 1997–2003 (chm 1999–2003); chief exec BP Investment Mgmnt Ltd 2000–; investment advsr Br Coal Staff Superannuation Scheme 2001–, investment advsr British Airways Pension Schemes 2003–; memb: Tomorrow's Company Inquiry Team 1993–95, Funding Agency for Schools Finance Ctee 1996–99; fell Wolfson Coll Oxford 2002; FRSA, FRI, MSI; *Recreations* music, theatre, curiosity; *Style—* Colin Maltby, Esq; ✉ 51 Addison Avenue, London W11 4QU

MALTMAN, Christopher John (Chris); s of Robert John Maltman (d 2002), of Louth, Lincs, and Christine, *née* Lincoln; *b* 7 February 1970; *Educ* King Edward VI Sch Louth, Univ of Warwick (BSc), Royal Acad of Music (Dip RAM, LRAM, ARAM); *m* Leigh Woolf; 1 s (Maximus); *Career* opera singer; baritone; trained at Royal Acad of Music under Mark Wildman; princ operatic roles with: Met Opera NY, Royal Opera House, Glyndebourne Opera, Deutsche Staatsoper Berlin, Vienna Staatsoper, ENO, WNO, La Monnaie Brussels, Bayerisches Staatsoper Munich; worked under conductors incl: Sir Simon Rattle, Sir Colin Davis, Leonard Slatkin, Sir David Willcocks, Lord Menuhin; performed recitals at numerous venues incl: Wigmore Hall, Edinburgh Festival, Hohenems Schubertiade, Salzburg Festival, Lincoln Center NY, Carnegie Hall NY, Concertgebouw Amsterdam; *Recordings* with: BMG wth Placido Domingo, Decca, Deutsche Grammaphon, Erato, Colins Classics, Naxos, Hyperion; *Awards* winnner of Lieder Prize Cardiff Singer of the World 1997, Royal Philharmonic Soc Young Artist Award 1999 HM The Queen's Commendation for Excellence Royal Acad of Music; *Recreations* golf, fitness (gymnasium) cooking/food, watching sport of any kind; *Style—* Chris Maltman, Esq; ✉ c/o Askonas Holt, Lonsdale Chambers, 27 Chancery Lane, London WC2A 1PF

MALTZ, Dr Milton Beer; s of Prof Jayme Maltz, of Porto Alegre, Brazil, and Matilde, *née* Beer; *b* 2 October 1954; *Educ* Porto Alegre HS Brazil, Shawnee Mission S HS Kansas City (grad dip), Univ of Med Porto Alegre Rio Grande Do Sul Brazil (MD), Bart's Hosp Univ of London (Br Cncl scholar, dip gen med, MPhil), Univ of London and St Bartholomew's Med Coll; *Career* formerly casualty student offr Accident and Emergency Hosp Porto Alegre Brazil; Bart's London: sr house offr in gen med 1983–84, hon cardiac registrar Dept of Cardiology 1984–91, clinical asst in cardiology 1991–93; currently clinical asst in cardiology Royal Free Hosp and in private practice Harley St, chm Medical Centre Cardiac Research Ltd; med and nursing staff teacher for MB and GP trg on specialised courses, author of numerous med articles for learned jls, invited speaker at numerous int cardiac meetings; offr surgn St John Ambulance Prince of Wales District London; fell in gen med Univ of Med Porto Alegre Brazil 1984; *Books* The Clinical Evaluation on Angina Pectoris of a Calcium Antagonist - Tiapamil (thesis); *Recreations* tennis; *Clubs* Angela Bexton Tennis; *Style—* Dr Milton Maltz; ✉ 48 Harley Street, London W1N 1AD (tel 020 7323 9292 and 020 7580 3145, fax 020 7323 4484)

MALVERN, 3 Viscount (UK 1955); Ashley Kevin Godfrey Huggins; s of 2 Viscount Malvern (d 1978), and Patricia Margery, *née* Renwick-Bower; *b* 26 October 1949; *Heir* unc, Hon James Huggins; *Style—* The Rt Hon the Viscount Malvern

MALVERN, John; s of Harry Ladyman Malvern, CBE (d 1982), of Cookham, Berks, and Doreen, *née* Peters (d 2005); *b* 3 October 1937; *Educ* Fettes, Univ of London (BSc), London Hosp (MB BS); *m* 10 July 1965, Katharine Mary Monica, da of Hugh Guillebaud (d 1958), of Marlborough, Wilts; 2 da (Susan (Lady Wilmot) b 1966, Joanna b 1969), 1 s (James (Jack) b 1977); *Career* conslt obstetrician Queen Charlotte's Hosp 1973, conslt gynaecologist Chelsea Hosp for Women and hon sr lectr Inst of Obstetrics and Gynaecology 1973–2001, hon conslt gynaecologist King Edward VII's Hosp for Offrs; chm Academic Gp Inst of Obstetrics and Gynaecology 1986–88, pres Obstetrics and Gynaecology Section RSM 1990, hon treas and offr RCOG 1991–98 (memb Cncl 1977–83 and 1987–90), chm Investment Panel 2001–06; hon cellarer 2004–; examiner: RCOG, Central Midwives Bd, Univs of London, Edinburgh, Liverpool, Manchester, Benghazi, Colombo, Khartoum and Hong Kong, Coll of Physicians and Surgns Pakistan; Ninian Falkiner lectr Rotunda Hosp Dublin 1980; memb: Central Manpower Ctee 1981–84, PPP Healthcare Trust Ltd 1998–2002; pres: Queen Charlotte's Hosp Dining Club, Fothergill Club 1991; memb: Gynaecological Visiting Soc, Int Continence Soc (fndr memb), Med Soc of London, Blair Bell Res Soc; Advanced Certificate in Wines and Spirits (WSET) 2002; Liveryman Worshipful Soc of Apothecaries; hon memb New England Obstetrical and Gynaecological Soc 2000; FRCSEd, FRCOG, FRSM, FRGS; *Books* The Unstable Bladder (ed jtly, 1989), Turnbull's Obstetrics (contrib, 1995), Gynaecology by Ten Teachers (contrib, 1995), Lecture Notes on Gynaecology (ed jtly, 1996); various pubns on urogynaecology and obstetrics; *Recreations* wine tasting, golf, croquet, theatre, travel; *Clubs* RSM, Hurlingham; *Style—* John Malvern, Esq; ✉ 30 Roedean Crescent, Roehampton, London SW15 5JU (tel 020 8876 4943)

MAMDANI, Prof Ebrahim; s of Hassanali Mamdani (d 1965), of Tanzania, and Fatmabai Mamdani; *b* 1 June 1942; *Educ* Karimjee Government Sch Tanga Tanzania, Coll of Engrg Poona (BE), QMC London (MSc, PhD); *m* Oct 1968, Virginia Anne, da of V Edward Perkins; 1 s (Geoffrey Asif b 18 March 1976), 1 da (Caroline Sahira b 30 Oct 1978); *Career* Dept of Electrical Engrg QMC London: joined as lectr 1968, reader 1976, personal chair in electronics 1984–95; Nortel/Royal Acad of Engrg chair in Telecommunications Strategy and Services Imperial Coll London 1995–2001 (subsequently emeritus), ret 2005; visiting prof Tokyo Inst of Technol 1977 (summer); seconded to British Telecom Research Laboratories 1988–89; FIEE 1982, FIEEE (USA) 1993, FREng 1994; *Books* Fuzzy Reasoning and its Applications (co-ed, 1981), Non-Standard Logics for Automated

M

Reasoning (co-ed, 1988); *Recreations* computing, photography, cooking, conversation; *Style*— Prof Ebrahim Mamdani, FREng; ✉ 31 Roding Drive, Kelvedon Hatch, Brentwood, Essex CM15 0XA (tel 01277 374772); Intelligent and Interactive Systems Group, Department of Electrical and Electronic Engineering, Imperial College, Exhibition Road, London SW7 2BT (tel 020 7594 6316, fax 020 7594 6274, e-mail e.mamdani@imperial.ac.uk)

MAMUJEE, Dr Abdullah; s of Mulla Mamujee Nurbhai (d 1947), and Khatijabai, *née* Alibhai (d 1942); *b* 10 October 1934; *Educ* Univ of Poona (MB, BS); *m* 15 Dec 1966, Dr Nalini Mamujee, da of Vaikunth Gopal Shanbhag (d 1980); 1 da (Anila b 10 June 1968), 1 s (Salil b 5 Nov 1969); *Career* surgical registrar Ashford Hosp Middx, surgical registrar Poplar Hosp London, conslt and sr lectr in surgery Univ of Dar es Salaam Tanzania, conslt and head of Accident and Emergency Dept Ipswich Hosp 1978, conslt Suffolk Nuffield Hosp, chm Cncl of Racial Equality, chm Bd of Visitors Hollesley Bay Young Offenders Inst; RSM, BMA; FRCSEd; FFAEM; *Recreations* reading, writing; *Style*— Dr Abdullah Mamujee; ✉ Springfields, 151 The Street, Rushmere St Andrew, Ipswich, Suffolk IP5 7DG (tel 01473 272269, fax 01473 272269); Accident and Emergency Department, Ipswich Hospital, Heath Road, Ipswich, Suffolk (tel 01473 712233); Suffolk Nuffield Hospital, Foxhall Road, Foxhall, Ipswich (tel 01473 279111)

MANASSEH, Leonard Sulla; OBE (1982); *Educ* Cheltenham Coll, AA Sch of Architecture; *Career* pilot Fleet Air Arm 1943–46; asst architect CRE N London then Guy Morgan & Partners 1941, on teaching staff AA and Kingston Sch of Art 1941, asst architect Architects Dept Herts CC 1943–48, sr architect Stevenage Development Corporation 1948–50, winner Festival of Britain Competition 1950, fndr Leonard Manasseh & Partners 1950 (subsequently became Leonard Manasseh Partnership then, from 1994, LMP Architects Ltd); AA: on teaching staff Sch of Architecture 1951–59, memb Cncl 1955–66, pres 1964–65; memb Royal West of England Acad 1972– (pres 1989–94); memb Cncl: Industrial Design 1965–68, RIBA 1968–70 and 1976–82 (hon sec 1979–81), British Sch at Rome 1976–83, National Trust 1977–91; pres Franco-British Union of Architects 1978–79; chm Ctee Dulwich Picture Gallery 1988–93 (surveyor 1987–93), dep chm Chatham Historic Dockyard Tst 1991 (tstee 1984); RA nominee Bd of Govrs Dulwich Schools Fndn 1987–94; RA 1979 (ARA 1976), FRIBA 1964 (ARIBA 1941), FCSD 1965, FRSA 1967; membre de l'Academie d'Architecture de France; *Style*— Leonard Manasseh, Esq, OBE, RA, PPRWA, AADipl, FRIBA, FCSD; ✉ 6 Bacon's Lane, Highgate Village, London N6 6BL

MANCE, Baron (Life Peer UK 2005), of Frognal in the London Borough of Camden; Sir Jonathan Hugh Mance; kt (1993), PC (1999); s of Sir Henry Stenhouse Mance (d 1981), and Joan Erica Robertson, *née* Baker (d 2005); *b* 6 June 1943; *Educ* Charterhouse, UC Oxford (MA); *m* 26 May 1973, Dame Mary Howarth Arden, DBE (Rt Hon Lady Justice Arden), *qv*, da of Lt-Col Eric Cuthbert Arden (d 1973); 2 da (Hon Abigail b 1976, Hon Jessica b 1978), 1 s (Hon Henry b 1982); *Career* called to the Bar Middle Temple 1965, QC 1982, judge of the High Court of Justice (Queen's Bench Div) 1993–99, a Lord Justice of Appeal 1999–2005, a Lord of Appeal in Ordinary 2005–; dir Bar Mutual Indemnity Fund Ltd 1988–94; pres British Insurance Law Assoc 2000–02 (dep pres 1998–2000), chm various Banking Appeal Tbnls 1992–93; chm: Consultative Cncl of European Judges 2000–03, Bar Lawn Tennis Soc 2000–; tstee European Law Acad 2003–; hon fell UC Oxford 2006; *Recreations* tennis, music, languages; *Clubs* Cumberland Lawn Tennis; *Style*— The Rt Hon Lord Mance, PC; ✉ House of Lords, London SW1A 0PW

MANCHESTER, 13 Duke of (GB 1719); Alexander Charles David Drogo Montagu; also Baron Kimbolton (E 1620) and Earl of Manchester (E 1626, cr three days after Charles I's coronation); s of 12 Duke of Manchester (d 2002); *b* 11 December 1962; *m* 1992 (m dis 2006), Wendy Dawn, da of Michael Buford, of Yorba Linda, CA; 1 s (Alexander, Viscount Mandeville b 13 May 1993), 1 da (Lady Ashley Faith Maxine Nell Beatrix b 16 June 1999); *Heir* s, Viscount Mandeville; *Career* pres Global Atlantic Investments and Summit Investments Turks and Caicos Is BWI; *Style*— His Grace the Duke of Manchester; ✉ British Consulate, 11766 Wiltshire Boulevard, Suit 4000, West Los Angeles, California 90025, USA (e-mail lmontymont@aol.com or globalatlantic@aol.com)

MANCHESTER, Bishop of 2002–; Rt Rev Nigel Simeon McCulloch; s of Pilot Offr Kenneth McCulloch, RAFVR (ka 1943), and Audrey Muriel, *née* Ball; *b* 17 January 1942; *Educ* Liverpool Coll, Selwyn Coll Cambridge (MA), Cuddesdon Theol Coll; *m* 15 April 1974, Celia Hume, da of Rev Canon Horace Lyle Hume Townshend, of Norwich, Norfolk (*see* Burke's Irish Family Records, 1976); 2 da (Kathleen b 1975, Elizabeth b 1977); *Career* ordained 1966, curate of Ellesmere Port Merseyside 1966–70, Christ's Coll Cambridge: chaplain 1970–73, dir of theol studies 1970–75; diocesan missioner Norwich Diocese 1973–78, chaplain Young Friends of Norwich Cathedral 1974–78, rector St Thomas's and St Edmund's Salisbury 1978–86, archdeacon of Sarum 1979–86, hon canon Salisbury Cathedral and prebendary of Ogbourne 1979–86, prebendary of Wanstrow in Wells Cathedral 1986–91, bishop of Taunton 1986–92, chaplain Cncl of St John Somerset 1987–92, bishop of Wakefield 1992–2002; took seat House of Lords 1997, memb House of Lords Select Ctee on BBC Charter Renewal 2005–06, memb House of Lords Select Ctee on Communications 2007–; Credo columnist The Times 1996–2001; chm Cambridge War on Want 1971–73, chm C of E Decade of Evangelism Steering Gp 1989–96, chm Sandford St Martin Tst 1999–; memb: Br Cncl of Churches USA Exchange (Church Growth) 1972–75, Archbishops Cncl for Evangelism Res and Trg Gp 1974–79; govr: Westwood St Thomas, St Edmund & St Mark's Salisbury 1979–86, Salisbury-Wells Theol Coll 1981–82, Royal Sch of Church Music 1984–, Marlborough Coll 1985–91, Kings Bruton 1987–92, Somerset Coll of Art and Technol 1987–89, Huddersfield Univ 1996–2002; pres Somerset Rural Music Sch 1986–92; chaplain Royal Bath and West Show 1991–92, chm Somerset County Scout Assoc 1987–92; memb: Gen Synod Working Gp Organists & Choirmasters 1984–85, Bath and Wells Zambia Link Programme 1987–92; chm Fin Ctee ABM 1987–92, pres Central Yorkshire Scout Assoc 1992–2002; chm: C of E Communication Unit 1993–98, BOM Mission Renewal & Evangelism Ctee 1996–99, Gen Synod Legislation Gp on Women Bishops 2006; nat chm Cncl of Christians and Jews 2006–; memb: C of E Gen Synod 1990–, House of Bishops 1990–; Lord High Almoner to HM The Queen 1997–, nat chaplain Royal Br Legion 2002–, chaplain Cncl of St John S and W Yorks 1992–2002; Hon DCL Univ of Huddersfield 2003; *Books* A Gospel to Proclaim (1992), Barriers to Belief (1994); *Recreations* music, walking in the Lake District, broadcasting, gardening, brass bands; *Style*— The Rt Rev the Lord Bishop of Manchester; ✉ Bishopscourt, Bury New Road, Manchester M7 4LE (tel 0161 792 2096, e-mail bishop@bishopscourt.manchester.anglican.org)

MANCROFT, 3 Baron (UK 1937); Sir Benjamin Lloyd Stormont Mancroft; 3 Bt (UK 1932); s of 2 Baron Mancroft, KBE, TD (d 1987); *b* 16 May 1957; *Educ* Eton; *m* 20 Sept 1990, Emma L, eldest da of Tom Peart, of Kensington; 1 da (Hon Georgia Esme b 25 April 1993), 2 s (Hon Arthur Louis Stormont b 3 May 1995, Hon Maximillian Michael b 3 Aug 1998); *Heir* s, Hon Arthur Mancroft; *Career* chm Inter Lotto (UK) Ltd 1995–, dep chm ROK Corp 2003–; dep chm Phoenix House Housing Assoc 1990–96; patron: Patsy Handy Tst 1991–, Sick Dentists' Tst 1991–; chm: Addiction Recovery Fndn 1989–, Drug and Alcohol Fndn 1995–; vice-chm: Br Field Sports Soc 1992–98, Parly All-Pty Misuse of Drugs Gp 1992–; 1992–; exec: Assoc of Cons Peers 1989–94 and 1999–, Nat Union of Cons Assocs 1989–94; elected to sit in the House of Lords 1999–; hon sec Parly All-Pty Bloodstock and Racing Industries Ctee 1992–97; dir Countryside Alliance 1998–; jt master Vale of White Horse Hunt 1987–89; memb Bd Mentor Fndn (Geneva); patron Osteopathic Centre for Children 1997–; *Style*— The Rt Hon the Lord Mancroft

MANDELSON, Rt Hon Peter Benjamin; PC (1998); s of George Norman Mandelson (d 1989), and Hon Mary Joyce Mandelson, *née* Morrison (d 2006); *b* 21 October 1953; *Educ* Hendon Sr HS, St Catherine's Coll Oxford (BA); *Career* chm Br Youth Cncl 1977–80, cncllr Lambeth BC 1979–82, prodr Weekend World London Weekend TV 1982–85, dir of campaigns and communications Lab Pty 1985–90; MP (Lab) Hartlepool 1992–2004, oppn whip 1994–95, shadow Civil Service spokesman 1995–96, Lab Pty election campaign mangr 1996–97, min without portfolio Cabinet Office 1997–98, sec of state for trade and industry 1998–99, sec of state for NI 1999–2001; EU cmmr for external trade 2004–; chm The Policy Network 2001–; *Publications* The Blair Revolution: Can New Labour Deliver (co-author, 1996), The Blair Revolution Revisited (2002); *Recreations* countryside, swimming, walking, travel and reading; *Style*— The Rt Hon Peter Mandelson

MANDER, David Charles; s of Alan Mander (d 1998), of Warks, and Muriel Betty, *née* Whiteman (d 1975); *b* 16 April 1938; *Educ* Wrekin Coll, Univ of Birmingham (LLB); *m* Elizabeth Ann, da of late F W Thorn, of Warks; 2 s (Philip James b 1964, Nicholas David b 1967), 1 da (Charlotte Louise b 1972); *Career* slr; sr ptnr Mander Hadley & Co - incorporating Browetts Solicitors; dir Warks Law Soc Ltd 1969–99; memb: Warks Law Soc (sec 1969–72, vice-pres 1997–98, pres 1998–99), Birmingham Law Soc 1972–80; memb Cncl Law Soc for constituency of: W Midlands W Mercia and Welsh Marches 1980–89, Coventry and Warks 1989–96; chm: Coventry Diocesan Tstees 1985–2007, Law Soc Indemnity Insurance Ctee 1986–87, Law Soc Trg Review Ctee 1994–96; dir Solicitors Indemnity Fund Ltd 1987–2007 (chm 1987–89); former memb Ct Univ of Warwick, former tstee Spencers Charity (chm 1997–99); Freeman City of Coventry; *Recreations* golf, music; *Style*— David C Mander, Esq; ✉ Whitestitch House, Great Packington, Meriden, Warwickshire CV7 7JE (tel 01676 522362); Mander Hadley & Co, 1 The Quadrant, Coventry CV1 2DW (tel 024 76631212, fax 024 7663 3131, e-mail enquiries@manderhadley.co.uk)

MANDER, Michael Stuart; s of James Charles Stuart Mander (d 1974), and Alice Patricia Mander (d 1964); *b* 5 October 1935; *Educ* Tonbridge, Hackley NY; *Career* dir: Times Newspapers Ltd 1971–80, Int Thomson Orgn plc 1983–86; chm Thomson Directories 1983–86, chm and chief exec Thomson Info Services Ltd 1985–86; dir: Hill Samuel & Co Ltd 1987–96, Close Brothers Corporate Finance Ltd 1996–99; chm: MAID plc 1988–97, Nat Readership Surveys Ltd 1990–93, The Dialog Corp plc 1997–99, Book Data Ltd 1997–2002, HS Publishing Gp 2000–01; dir: Southnews plc 1989–2000, BLCMP (Library Services) Ltd 1993–99, TEMPUS Gp plc 1997–2000; vice-pres: Periodical Publishers' Assoc, Inst of Directors 1997–2004 (memb Cncl 1974–, chm 1993–97); memb Nat Employers Advsy Bd for the Reserve Forces 1997–2005, memb Disciplinary Ctee ICA; tstee St Bride's Church Appeal; Liveryman Worshipful Co of Marketors; FCIM, FRSA, FCAM; *Recreations* sailing; *Clubs* Royal Southern Yacht, Buck's; *Style*— Michael Mander, Esq; ✉ 41 Rivermill, Grosvenor Road, London SW1V 3JN (tel 020 7821 9651, fax 020 7976 6507)

MANDL, Dr Anita Maria; da of Dr Bohumir Mandl (d 1941), and Hanna, *née* Ascher (d 1944 in Auschwitz); *b* 17 May 1926; *Educ* Dudley Girls HS, Birkbeck Coll London (BSc), Univ of Birmingham (PhD, DSc), Birmingham Coll of Art (pt/t); *m* April 1965, Dr Denys Arthur Jennings (d 1995); *Career* sculptor; research asst London Hosp 1946–47, asst lectr, lectr and sr lectr Univ of Birmingham 1948–62, reader in reproductive physiology 1962–65; set up sculpture workshop 1965, specialises in animal carvings and bronzes; fndr Otter Valley Assoc; RSMA 1971 (resigned 1994), RWA 1978, FRBS 1980; *Exhibitions* Royal Acad, John Davies Gall Stow, Wildlife Art Gall Lavenham, Sinfield Gall Burford, Bruton Street Gall London, Llewellyn-Alexander Gall London, F T Sabin Gallery London, Martin's Gall Cheltenham, Red Rag Gall Stow, Embankment Gall London 1982, Spring Exhibition RWA Bristol 1982, Guildford House Gall Guildford 1983, Czechoslovak Embassy London 1992, New Acad Gall London 1996, 2001, 2004 and 2005, Alresford Gall Hants 1996, 2000 and 2004, Falle Fine Arts Jersey 1997 and 2002, Pangolin Gall Chalford 2001, Sinfield Gall Burford 2002, New Gall RWA Bristol 2004; *Group Exhibitions* Zoological Gardens Jersey, Albermarle Gall London, McHardy Gall London, Bow House Gall Barnet, Wykeham Gall Stockbridge, Alpha House Gall Sherborne, Bella Contemporary Art Gall Tetbury, Royal West of England Acad Bristol; *Publications* numerous papers in scientific journals, asst ed The Ovary (1962); *Recreations* gardening, swimming, walking, photography; *Style*— Dr Anita Mandl; ✉ 21 Northview Road, Budleigh Salterton, Devon EX9 6BZ (tel and fax 01395 443227, e-mail anitama@onetel.com)

MANDUCA, Charles Victor Sant; s of Victor John Sant Manduca (d 1989), and Ethel Florence, *née* Johnson (d 1960); *b* 21 November 1954; *Educ* Harrow, UCL (LLB); *Career* admitted slr 1979; ptnr Lovells (formerly Durrant Piesse) 1983–2003; gen counsel The ECU Gp 2006–; conslt: Jema Fund Management Ltd 2003–, Titanium Capital 2006–; Freeman Worshipful Co of Slrs 1988; memb: Law Soc, London Slrs' Litigation Assoc; *Recreations* golf, antique clocks; *Clubs* Wentworth Golf, IOD; *Style*— Charles Manduca, Esq

MANDUCA, Paul Victor Sant; s of Victor Sant Manduca (d 1989), and Elisabeth, *née* Johnson (d 1960); *b* 15 November 1951; *Educ* Harrow, Hertford Coll Oxford (MA); *m* 1982, Dr Ursula, da of Edmund Vogt, of Jollenbeck, W Germany; 2 s (Mark b 1983, Nicholas b 1988); *Career* md TR Industrial and General plc 1986–88, chm TR High Income plc 1989–94, chm Touche Remnant Hldgs 1989–92 (vice-chm 1987–89), dep gp md Henderson Administration plc (following takeover of Touche Remnant) 1992–94, chm Gresham Trust 1994–99; ceo: Threadneedle Asset Management 1994–99, Rothschild Asset Mgmnt 1999–2002, Deutsche Asset Mgmnt (Europe) 2002–05; chm: Uniq Tstees Ltd 2005–, Bridgewell Gp 2006–; dir: Clydesdale Investment Trust 1987–88, Henderson Smaller Companies Investment Trust plc 1987–2006, Allied Dunbar Assurance plc 1994–99, Eagle Star Holdings 1994–99, MEPC plc 1999–2000 (taken over by GE Capital), Wolverhampton Wanderers FC Ltd 1999–2006, Development Securities plc 2001–, Wm Morrison 2005–, JP Morgan Fleming European Fledgling Investment Tst plc 2005–, Aon UK Ltd 2006–, Kazmunaigaz plc, Intrinsic Ltd; chm Assoc of Investment Trust Cos 1991–93 (Takeover Panel 1991–93); memb: Investment Ctee Univs Superannuation Scheme 1993–2002, London Stock Exchange Institutional Investors Advsy Ctee 1998–2001; Freeman City of London 1988, Liveryman Worshipful Co of Bakers 1989; *Recreations* golf, squash, shooting; *Clubs* Wentworth, White's, Lansdowne; *Style*— Paul Manduca, Esq; ✉ 22 Rutland Gate, London SW7 1BB (tel 020 7584 3987)

MANFORD, Bruce Robert James; s of late John Julian Manford, and Ruth, *née* Heldmann; *b* 21 March 1957; *Educ* Haberdashers' Aske's, Keele Univ (BA); *m* 1992, Frances, *née* Turay; *Career* admitted slr 1981; ptnr Lawrence Graham 1988–96, DG Cncl Oilinvest (Netherlands) Gp 1996–; memb Law Soc 1981; *Clubs* RAC; *Style*— Bruce Manford, Esq; ✉ Tamoil Services S.A.M., 17 Avenue des Spélugues, Complexe Métropole, MC 98000, Monaco (tel 00 377 93 15 69 00, fax 00 377 93 15 69 05)

MANGNALL, Richard Anthony; JP (S Westminster 1986–2004, City of Westminster 2005, SW Surrey 2006–); s of late Col (Anthony) Derek Swift Mangnall, OBE, TD, of Chieveley, Berks, and (Cynthia) Mary, *née* Foster (later Lady FitzGerald); *b* 27 November 1942; *Educ* Douai Abbey; *m* 25 March 1975, Maureen Patricia, da of Lawrence Donnelly (d 1965), of Delhi, India; *Career* Sant & Co Loss Adjusters 1962–74, dir Tyler & Co (Adjusters) Ltd 1989–2000 (ptnr 1974–), conslt Marsh Private Client Services 2002–04, chm Proteus Open Space Mgmnt Ltd 1993–; pres: The Insurance Adjusters Assoc 1987–89 (assoc 1967, fell 1972), Chartered Inst of Loss Adjusters 1996–97; memb Ctee of Magistrates Inner London 1994–96; chm: S Westminster Bench 2002–04, City of Westminster Bench 2005; tstee

Inner London Poor Box Tst 1994–; Freeman: City of London 1989, Worshipful Co of Fletchers 1989, Worshipful Co of Insurers 1997; FCILA 1992, FInstD, FRSA; *Recreations* shooting, sailing; *Clubs* Boodle's, Royal Southern Yacht; *Style—* Richard Mangnall, Esq; ✉ Peper Harow House, Peper Harow Park, Surrey GU8 6BG (e-mail richard@mangnalls.com)

MANISTY, Edward Alexander; s of Henry Earle Manisty (d 1959), and Charlotte Evelyn Stephens, *née* Baird-Smith; *b* 12 May 1941, Staplefield, W Sussex; *Educ* Wellington Coll, New Coll Oxford (MA); *m* 8 Nov 1967, Dr Dinah Lake Manisty, *née* Watson; 2 s (Alexander b 7 Dec 1968, Mark Edward b 6 Feb 1974), 1 da (Louisa (Mrs Trandafilovska) b 29 Sept 1971); *Career* admitted slr 1968, ptnr Stephenson Harwood 1971–92; Christie's (Christie, Manson & Woods Ltd): dir i/c Heritage and Taxation Dept 1992–2006, vice-chm 1999–2006, conslt 2006–; conslt Farrer & Co 2006–; dir Samuel Courtauld Tst 1995–2006; Liveryman Worshipful Co of Merchant Taylors 1974; *Publications* contrib to tech jls on taxation of chattels and heritage property 1993–, contrib to Tolley's Administration of Estates 1997–2005; *Recreations* classical music, reading; *Style—* Edward Manisty, Esq; ✉ Christie's, 8 King Street, St James's, London SW1Y 6QT (tel 020 7829 9060, fax 020 7389 2300); Farrer & Co, 66 Lincoln's Inn Fields, London WC2A 3LH (tel 020 7242 2022, fax 020 7917 7109)

MANKTELOW, Rt Rev Michael Richard John; s of Sir (Arthur) Richard Manktelow, KBE, CB (d 1977), of Dorking, and (Edith) Helen Saxby (d 1965); *b* 23 September 1927; *Educ* Whitgift Sch Croydon, Christ's Coll Cambridge (MA), Chichester Theol Coll; *m* 1966, Rosamund, da of Alfred and Marjorie Mann, of Penrith; 3 da (Helen (Mrs Alistair Pearson) b 1967, Elizabeth b 1969, Katharine (Mrs Marcus Banks) b 1971); *Career* served RN 1948–51; ordained: deacon 1953, priest 1954; curate Boston Lincs 1953–57, chaplain Christ's Coll Cambridge 1957–61, chaplain and sub warden Lincoln Theol Coll 1961–66; vicar: Knaresborough 1966–73, St Wilfrid's Harrogate 1973–77; rural dean Harrogate 1972–77; bishop of Basingstoke 1977–93, canon residentiary of Winchester Cathedral 1977–91 (vice-dean 1987–91); asst bishop: of Chichester 1994–, in Europe 1994–; bursalis prebendary Chichester Cathedral 1997–2002; pres: Anglican and Eastern Churches Assoc 1980–97, Assoc for Promoting Retreats 1982–87; *Books* Forbes Robinson: Disciple of Love (ed, 1961), John Moorman: Anglican, Franciscan, Independent (1999); *Recreations* walking, reading, music; *Style—* The Rt Rev Michael Manktelow; ✉ 14 Little London, Chichester, West Sussex PO19 1NZ (tel 01243 531096)

MANLEY, Dr Brian William; CBE (1994); s of Gerald William Manley (d 1950), of Eltham, London, and Ellen Mary, *née* Scudder (d 1965); *b* 30 June 1929; *Educ* Shooter's Hill GS, Univ of London, Woolwich Poly (BSc), Imperial Coll London (DIC); *m* 1 May 1954, Doris Winifred, da of Alfred Dane (d 1966), of Eltham, London; 1 da (Susan b 1955), 1 s (Gerald b 1958); *Career* RAF 1947–49; Mullard Res Laboratories 1954–68, commercial gen mangr Mullard Ltd 1971–75; md: Pye Business Communications Ltd 1975–77, TMC Ltd 1977–82, Philips Data Systems Ltd 1979–82; gp md Philips Business Systems 1980–83, chm and md MEL Defence Systems 1983–86, dir for telecommunications def electronics and res Philips Electronic & Associated Industries Ltd 1983–87; chm: AT&T Network Systems (UK) Ltd 1986–89, Pye Telecommunications Ltd 1984–87, BYPS Communications Ltd 1989–91; managing ptnr Manley Moon Associates 1988–2000, chm Moondisks Ltd 1994–2001; pres: Telecommunications Engrg & Mfrg Assoc 1985–86, IEE 1991–92, Inst of Physics 1996–98; memb: Cncl Inst of Employment Studies 1986–97, Exec Ctee Nat Electronics Cncl 1986–88, NEDO Ctee on IT 1982–85, Police Scientific Devpt Ctee Home Office 1972–74, Cncl Engrg Trg Authy 1990–91, Bd Teaching Company Scheme 1996–98; Univ of Sussex: memb Cncl 1990–2001, dep chm 1992–94, chm of Cncl 1995–2001, sr pro-chllr 1995–2001; sr vice-pres Royal Acad of Engrg 1994–96 (vice-pres 1992–94), memb Senate Engrg Cncl 1995–96; govr Univ of Greenwich 1993–95 (chm Industrial Liaison Bd 1990–96); memb Cncl Loughborough Univ 1988–96; tstee: Daphne Jackson Meml Fellowship Tst 1998–, RC Dio of Arundel and Brighton 1999–; author of numerous published papers on electronics and communications; represented England in swimming 1947–50; Centenary fell Thames Poly (now Univ of Greenwich) 1991; Hon DSc: Loughborough Univ 1995, City Univ 1998, Univ of Sussex 2002; FInstP 1967, Hon FIET (FIEE 1974, Hon FIEE 1999), FREng 1984, FIProdE 1990, FCGI 1990; *Recreations* swimming, walking, gardening, second-hand books; *Clubs* Athenaeum; *Style—* Dr Brian Manley, CBE, FREng; ✉ Hopkins Crank, Ditchling Common, East Sussex BN6 8TP (tel 01444 233734, e-mail brianwmanley@aol.com)

MANLEY, Charlotte Elizabeth; LVO (2003), OBE (1996); da of (John) Patrick Manley, MVO (d 2000), and (Ann) Priscilla, *née* Bunting; *b* 15 March 1957; *Career* RN 1976–96, joined Royal Household 1996, chapter clerk Coll of St George Windsor Castle 2003–, also extra equerry to HRH The Duke of York; *Style—* Miss Charlotte Manley, LVO, OBE; ✉ Chapter Office, Windsor Castle, Berkshire SL4 1NJ

MANN, David William; s of William James Mann (d 1966), of Trimley Saint Mary, Suffolk, and Mary Ann, *née* Bloomfield (d 1987); *b* 14 June 1944; *Educ* Felixstowe Co GS, Jesus Coll Cambridge (MA); *m* 29 June 1968, Gillian Mary, da of Rev David Emlyn Edwards (d 1978), of Felixstowe, Suffolk; 2 s (Richard b 1972, Edward b 1975); *Career* computing systems conslt; CEIR (UK) Ltd (now EDS) 1966–69; Logica plc: joined on its formation 1969, mangr conslt 1971, mangr Advanced Systems Div 1972, dir Advanced Systems Gp 1976, md UK ops 1979, dep gp md 1982, md and chief exec 1987–93, dep chm 1993–94; chm Charteris plc 1996–; non-exec dir: Industrial Control Services Gp plc 1994–2000, Druid Gp plc 1996–2000, Room Solutions Ltd 1996–2006, Eurolink Managed Services plc 1999–2000, Aveva Gp plc 1999–, Ansbacher Holdings Ltd 2000–04; non-exec chm: Cambridge Display Technology Ltd 1995–97, Flomerics Gp plc 1995–, Velti Gp plc 2006–; pres Br Computer Soc 1994–95; memb Engrg Cncl 1993–95; chm Epping Forest Wine Soc 2005–; Master Worshipful Co of Info Technologists 1997–98 (chm of tstees 2002–07, tstee 2007–); CITP (Chartered IT Professional), CEng, CCMI, FInstD, FBCS; *Recreations* gardening, walking; *Clubs* Athenaeum; *Style—* David Mann, Esq; ✉ Theydon Copt, Forest Side, Epping, Essex CM16 4ED (tel 01992 575842, fax 01992 576593, e-mail david.mann@charteris.com)

MANN, Dr Felix Bernard; s of Leo William Mann (d 1956), and Caroline Lola Mann (d 1985); *b* 10 April 1931; *Educ* Shrewsbury, Malvern, Christ's Coll Cambridge, Westminster Hosp; *m* 1986, Ruth Csorba von Borsai; *Career* fndr Medical Acupuncture Soc (pres 1959–80), first pres Br Medical Acupuncture Soc 1980; awarded Deutscher Schmerzpreis 1995; *Books* (published in up to 8 languages): Acupuncture - The Ancient Chinese Art of Healing (3 edn, 1998), The Treatment of Disease by Acupuncture (3 edn, 1974), The Meridians of Acupuncture (1964), Atlas of Acupuncture (1966), Acupuncture - Cure of Many Diseases (2 edn, 1992), Scientific Aspects of Acupuncture (2 edn, 1983), Textbook of Acupuncture (1987), Reinventing Acupuncture (1992, 2 edn 2000); *Recreations* walking in the countryside; *Clubs* RSM; *Style—* Dr Felix Mann; ✉ 15 Devonshire Place, London W1G 6HF (tel 020 7935 7575)

MANN, Fred; s of Andrew Lonsdale, of London, and Rosemary, *née* Stones; *b* 11 March 1972; *Educ* Camberwell Coll of Art, Univ of Brighton (BA); *Career* curator of exhibitions at Milch with Lisa Panting incl: New Installations Steve Farrer 1996, Behalter, Till Exit, Come, Kate Davis (touring) 1997, Wish You Were Here!, New Swiss Painting 1998, The New Contemporaries99; offsite curation: Retrospective: Jean Mark Proveur, Drawings: Kate Davis, Works: Keith Milow; teaching: Ruskin Coll of Art 1998–99, Univ of Brighton 1998–99, Goldsmiths Coll 1999; lectr at Serpentine Gall for exhibitions by Louise Bourgeois, William Kentridge, Jane and Louise Wilson 1998, Felix Gonzales Torres 1999; exhibitions: Take My Life (Milch) 1996, Furniture (Richard Salmon Gall London) 1999; various art direction and prodn for video and films incl work for: Guns 'n' Roses, Rage Against the Machine, Roger Corman, MTV and Derek Jarman; Metronome 1 in magazine format with Tracey Emin, *qv*, Gary Hume, Langlands and Bell and Susan Hiller; Rhodes & Mann Gall (representing 18 artists): launch of artists at Art2000 London Jan 2000, opened April 2000, 1st gp exhbn May 2000; memb The Furniture History Soc; *Publications* Behalter (1996), Kate Davis (1996), New Swiss Painting (1998), ashowabouttime (intro, 1999); *Style—* Fred Mann, Esq; ✉ FRED, 45 Vyner Street, London E2 9DQ

MANN, Geoffrey Horton; s of Stanley Victor Mann (d 1986), of Coventry, and Dorothy, *née* Horton (d 1964); *b* 12 May 1938; *Educ* Warwick Sch, Univ of Liverpool (BArch), RIBA (MCD); *m* 28 Dec 1963, Meg, da of Francis Richard Evans, of Denton, Manchester; 4 da (Katherine b 1964, Clare b 1966, Rachel b 1968, Shelley b 1972); *Career* architect; W S Hattrell & Ptnrs Manchester 1963–70, sr ptnr RHWL (Renton Howard Wood Levin Partnership) 1980– (joined 1970); responsible for: Arena 2001 Coventry, Dublin National Arena, St Katharine's Dock, County Hall, Ludgate, Commercial Union Tower, Orion House, Queensbury House, several new buildings in Moscow; memb: children's charities, Bodmin & Wenford Railway; ARCUK 1965, ARIBA 1965; *Recreations* Coventry City FC, railways; *Clubs* Coventry City; *Style—* Geoffrey Mann, Esq; ✉ 41 Charles Street, Berkhamsted, Hertfordshire HP4 3DQ (tel 01442 864707); Saughtree Railway Station, Roxburghshire; RHWL, 77 Endell Street, London WC2H 9AJ (tel 020 7379 7900, fax 020 7836 4881, telex 896691 TLXIR G Renhow, car 078 0145 8153)

MANN, Jane Robertshaw; da of Jack Mann (d 1990), of Southport, and Jean, *née* Dixon; *b* 20 May 1955; *Educ* Nottingham HS for Girls, Univ of Manchester (BA); *m* 24 April 1982, Robert Klevenhagen, s of Dr Stan Klevenhagen; *Career* Leo Burnett Ltd 1976–86, Michael Peters Group 1986–90, fndr ptnr Dragon International (mktg and design co) 1991–; *Style—* Ms Jane Mann; ✉ Dragon International Consulting Ltd, 1 Craven Hill, London W2 3EN (tel 020 7262 4488, fax 020 7262 6406, e-mail jane.mann@dragonbrands.com)

MANN, Jessica D E (Jessica D E Thomas); da of Dr F A Mann, CBE (d 1991), of London, and Eleonore, *née* Ehrlich (d 1980); *b* 13 September 1937; *Educ* St Paul's, Newnham Coll Cambridge (MA), Univ of Leicester (LLB); *m* 1 July 1959, Prof A Charles Thomas, CBE, s of D W Thomas (d 1959), of Cornwall; 2 s (Richard b 1961, Martin b 1963), 2 da (Susanna b 1966, Lavinia b 1971); *Career* writer and journalist; memb: Carrick DC 1972–78, Cornwall AHA 1976–78, Employment Tbnls 1977–, SW RHA 1979–84, Med Practices Ctee 1982–87, Cornwall FPC 1985–88; DOE planning inspector 1991–93; chair: Ofwat (SW) 1993–2001, Network 200 SW Ltd 1995–99; memb: Advsy Ctee England Ofcom, SW Arts Board, Detection Club, ForumUK, PEN; *Books* A Charitable End (1971), Mrs Knox's Profession (1972), The Only Security (1973), The Sticking Place (1974), Captive Audience (1975), The Eighth Deadly Sin (1976), The Sting of Death (1978), Deadlier than the Male (1981), Funeral Sites (1982), No Man's Island (1983), Grave Goods (1985), A Kind of Healthy Grave (1986), Death Beyond The Nile (1988), Faith Hope and Homicide (1991), Telling Only Lies (1992), A Private Inquiry (1996), Hanging Fire (1997), The Survivor's Revenge (1998), Under a Dark Sun (2000), The Voice from the Grave (2002), Out of Harm's Way (2005), The Mystery Writer (2006); *Style—* Ms Jessica Mann; ✉ Lambessow, St Clement, Cornwall TR1 1TB (tel 01872 272980)

MANN, John; MP; s of James Mann, and Brenda Cleavin; *Educ* Univ of Manchester (BA); *Career* TUC Nat Trg Offr 1990–95, Nat Trade Union and Lab Pty liaison offr 1995–2000, head of research and educn AEU; MP (Lab) Bassetlaw 2001–; dir Abraxas Communications Ltd; MIPD 1992; *Recreations* football, cricket, hill walking; *Clubs* Manton Miners; *Style—* John Mann, Esq, MP; ✉ House of Commons, London SW1A 0AA (tel 020 7219 8130)

M

MANN, Martin Edward; QC (1983); s of late S E and M F L Mann; *b* 12 September 1943; *Educ* Cranleigh Sch; *m* 1966, Jacqueline Harriette, *née* Le Maitre; 2 da; *Career* called to the Bar: Gray's Inn 1968 (Lord Justice Holker sr exhibitioner), Lincoln's Inn (ad eundum) 1973 (bencher 1991); recorder 1991–, dep judge of the High Court (Chancery Div) 1992–; memb Senate of the Inns of Court and the Bar 1979–82, chm Bar Cncl Fees Collection Ctee 1993–95; memb: Chancery Bar Assoc, Commercial Bar Assoc, Insolvency Lawyers Assoc, Pension Lawyers Assoc, European Circuit, Bar of the Eastern Caribbean Supreme Court; *Publications* What Kind of Common Agricultural Policy for Europe (jtly, 1975), Tolley's Insolvency Law (contrib), Palmer's Company Law Manual (conslt ed); *Recreations* many and various interests incl farming; *Clubs* Garrick; *Style—* Martin Mann, Esq, QC; ✉ 24 Old Buildings, Lincoln's Inn, London WC2A 3UP (e-mail martin.mann@xxiv.co.uk, website www.xxiv.co.uk)

MANN, Rt Rev Michael Ashley; KCVO (1989); s of late Herbert George Mann, and Florence Mary *née* Kelsey, MBE (d 1950); *b* 25 May 1924; *Educ* Harrow, RMC Sandhurst, Wells Theol Coll, Harvard Business Sch (AMP); *m* 1, 25 June 1949, Jill Joan (d 1990), da of Maj Alfred Jacques (d 1960), of Thanet, Kent; 1 s (Capt Philip Ashley Mann, 1 Queen's Dragoon Gds b 1 Aug 1950 ka 1975), 1 da (Dr Elizabeth Mann b 22 Aug 1950); m 2, 25 May 1991, Elizabeth Margaret, da of Maj-Gen Roger Gillies Ekin, CIE, and wid of Rt Rev (George) Christopher Cutts Pepys, Bishop of Buckingham; *Career* 1 King's Dragoon Gds, served Italy 1943–44, Greece 1944–45, ME 1945, Palestine 1945–46, Capt 1945, Maj 1945; Colonial Admin Serv Nigeria 1946–55; ordained 1957, curate Newton Abbot 1957–59; vicar: Sparkwell 1959–62, Christ Church Port Harcourt 1962–67; dean Port Harcourt Social and Industrial Project 1963–67, home sec Missions to Seamen 1967–69, canon Norwich Cathedral 1969–73 (vice-dean 1971–73), Bishop of Dudley 1973–76; Dean of Windsor, Domestic Chaplain to HM The Queen, Register of the Order of the Garter 1976–89; Prelate of the Ven Order of St John of Jerusalem 1990–2000; nat chaplain Royal British Legion 1985–2001; dep chm of tstees: Imperial War Museum 1980–96, Army Museums Ogilby Tst 1984–95; tstee: Br Library 1990–93, Army Records Soc 1991–2000, Nat Army Museum; cmmr Royal Hosp Chelsea 1983–90, pres Friends Nat Army Museum, govr Harrow Sch 1976–91 (chm 1980–88); CIMgt; GCStJ (OStJ); *Books* A Particular Duty, A Windsor Correspondence, And They Rode On, China 1860, Some Windsor Sermons, Survival or Extinction, History of The Queen's Dragoon Guards, History of the Trucial Oman Scouts, The Veterans, Sermons for Soldiers; *Recreations* military history; *Clubs* Cavalry and Guards'; *Style—* The Rt Rev Michael Mann, KCVO; ✉ Lower End Farm Cottage, Eastington, Northleach, Gloucestershire GL54 3PN (tel and fax 01451 860767, e-mail michaelmann@onetel.com)

MANN, Prof (Colin) Nicholas Jocelyn; CBE (1999); s of Colin Henry Mann (d 1987), of Mere, Wilts, and Marie-Elise, *née* Gosling (d 2001); *b* 24 October 1942; *Educ* Eton, King's Coll Cambridge (MA, PhD); *m* 27 June 1964 (m dis 2003), Joelle, da of Pierre Emile Bourcart (d 1982), of Geneva; 1 da (Olivia Sophie b 1965), 1 s (Benedict Julian b 1968); m 2, 24 May 2003, Helen Margaret, da of Michael Anthony Stevenson, of Doncaster; 2 da (Clara Elizabeth b 2001, Verity Isabel b 2004); *Career* res fell Clare Coll Cambridge 1965–67, lectr Univ of Warwick 1967–72, visiting fell All Souls Coll Oxford 1972, fell and tutor Pembroke Coll Oxford 1973–90 (emeritus fell 1991, hon fell 2006), dir Warburg Inst and prof of the history of the classical tradition Univ of London 1990–2001, dean Sch of Advanced Study Univ of London 2002–07, pro-vice-chllr Univ of London 2003–07; memb Cncl: MOMA Oxford 1984–92 (chm 1988–90), Contemporary Applied Arts 1994–2006 (chm 1996–99), Br Acad 1995–98 and 1999–2006 (vice-pres and foreign sec 1999–2006), Royal Holloway Coll London 1996–98, RCA 2001–07; vice-pres ALLEA 2006–; tstee Cubitt Artists 1996–99; Hon DLitt Univ of Warwick 2006; FBA 1992, fell Euro Medieval Acad 1993–2007, fell Fondazione Lorenzo Valla 2007; *Books* Petrarch

Manuscripts in the British Isles (1975), Petrarch (1984), A Concordance to Petrarch's Bucolicum Carmen (1984), Lorenzo the Magnificent: Culture and Politics (jtly, 1996), Medieval and Renaissance Scholarship (jtly, 1996), Giordano Bruno, 1583–1585: The English Experience (jtly, 1997), The Image of the Individual: Portraits in the Renaissance (jtly, 1998), Photographs at the Frontier. Aby Warburg in America, 1895–1896 (jtly, 1998), Carnets de Voyage (2003), Pétrarque: les voyages de l'esprit (2004), Britannia Latina: Latin in the Culture of Great Britain from the Middle Ages to the Twentieth Century (jtly, 2005); *Recreations* yoga, poetry, sculpture; *Style*— Prof Nicholas Mann, CBE, FBA; ✉ Rue du Tourneur, 46160 Ca Jarc, France (tel +33 5 6534 9121, e-mail nicholas.mann@free.fr)

MANN, Sir Rupert Edward; 3 Bt (UK 1905), of Thelveton Hall, Thelveton, Norfolk; s of Edward Charles Mann, DSO, MC (d 1959), and great nephew of Sir (Edward) John Mann, 2 Bt (d 1971); *b* 11 November 1946; *Educ* Malvern Coll; *m* 1974, Mary Rose, da of Geoffrey Butler, of Stetchworth, Suffolk; 2 s (Alexander Rupert b 1978, William Edward b 1980); *Heir* s, Alexander Mann; *Career* farmer; *Clubs* Norfolk, MCC; *Style*— Sir Rupert Mann, Bt; ✉ Billingford Hall, Diss, Norfolk (tel 01379 740314)

MANNERS, Crispin Luke; s of Norman Donald Manners (d 2001), and Noeline Mary, *née* Blake (d 1994); *b* 2 August 1957; *Educ* Ranelagh GS Bracknell, Bedford Coll London (BSc); *m* 18 Aug 1979, Judith Ann, da of Peter Simpson; 2 s (Matthew b 1 July 1981, Philip b 12 May 1985); *Career* salesman CPC UK Limited 1978–80; The Argyll Consultancies plc: exec asst to chm 1980, account dir 1984, md 1987, chief exec 1989–; chm PR Conslts Assoc 2004–06; FIPR, FInstD; *Clubs* Surbiton Golf, Two Brydges; *Style*— Crispin Manners, Esq; ✉ The Argyll Consultancies plc, Central COurt, 25 Southampton Buildings, London WC2A 1AL (tel 020 3043 4151, e-mail crispin.manners@argyll.co.uk)

MANNERS, Prof Gerald; OBE (2005); s of George William Wilson Manners (d 1964), and Louisa Hannah, *née* Plumpton (d 1979); *b* 7 August 1932; *Educ* Wallington Co GS, St Catharine's Coll Cambridge (MA); *m* 1, 11 July 1958 (m dis 1982), Anne, *née* Sawyer; 2 da (Carolyn Jarvis b 16 Jan 1961, Katharine b 26 April 1967), 1 s (Christopher Winslow b 24 Oct 1962); m 2, 11 Dec 1982, Joy Edith Roberta, *née* Turner; 1 s (Nicholas Robert b 12 May 1985); *Career* Nat Serv Flying Offr RAF 1955–57; lectr in geography UC Swansea 1957–67; UCL: reader in geography 1967–80, prof of geography 1980–97, emeritus prof of geography 1997–; visiting scholar Resources for the Future inc Washington DC 1964–65; visiting fell: Harvard-MIT Jt Center for Urban Studies 1972–73, Aust Nat Univ 1991; memb: Location of Offices Bureau 1970–80, SE Econ Planning Cncl 1971–79; specialist advsr to: House of Commons Select Ctee on Energy 1980–92, House of Lords Select Ctee on Sustainable Devpt 1994–95, House of Commons Environmental Audit Ctee 1999–2000; tstee EAGA Partnership Charitable Tst 1992–, vice-pres Sadler's Wells Fndn 1995–99 (govr 1978–95, chm of govrs 1986–95), tstee City Parochial Fndn and Tst for London 1977–2007 (chm 1996–2004), chm Assoc of Charitable Fndns 2003–; FRGS; *Books* Geography of Energy (1964), South Wales in the Sixties (1964), Changing World Market for Iron Ore (1971), Spatial Policy Problems of the British Economy (1971), Minerals and Man (1974), Regional Development in Britain (1974), Coal in Britain (1981), Office Policy in Britain (1986); *Recreations* music, dance, theatre, walking; *Style*— Prof Gerald Manners, OBE; ✉ 338 Liverpool Road, London N7 8PZ (tel 020 7607 7920, fax 020 7609 2306, e-mail g.manners@ucl.ac.uk)

MANNERS, Hon John Hugh Robert (Willie); s and h of 5 Baron Manners, *qv*; *b* 5 May 1956; *Educ* Eton; *m* 1, 8 Oct 1983 (m dis 2005), Lanya Mary Patrica (Lala), da of late Dr H E Heitz, and Mrs Ian Jackson, and step da of late Ian Jackson; 2 da (Harriet Frances Mary b 29 July 1988, Catherine Mary Patricia b 18 Sept 1992); m 2, 24 Feb 2007, Juliet Elizabeth Anthea, da of David McMyn; *Career* admitted slr 1980; ptnr Macfarlanes 1987– (currently head of litigation); *Recreations* riding, shooting; *Clubs* Pratt's, Boodle's; *Style*— The Hon Willie Manners; ✉ North Ripley House, Avon, Christchurch, Dorset BH23 8EP (tel 01425 672249); 10 Norwich Street, London EC4A 1BD (tel 020 7831 9222, fax 020 7831 9607, e-mail willie.manners@macfarlanes.com)

MANNERS, 5 Baron (UK 1807); John Robert Cecil Manners; s of 4 Baron Manners, MC, JP, DL (d 1972, himself ggs of 1 Baron, who was in his turn 5 s of Lord George Manners-Sutton, 3 s of 3 Duke of Rutland, KG), by his w Mary Edith (d 1994), twin da of Rt Rev Lord William Gascoyne-Cecil, DD, 65 Bishop of Exeter and 2 s of 3 Marquess of Salisbury, the Cons PM; *b* 13 February 1923; *Educ* Eton, Trinity Coll Oxford; *m* 1949, Jennifer Selena (d 1996), da of Stephen Fairbairn (whose w Cynthia was gggda of Sir William Arbuthnot, 1 Bt); 1 s, 2 da; *Heir* s, Hon John Manners; *Career* joined RAFVR, Flying offr 1942, Fl Lt 1944; slr of the Supreme Ct 1949; Official Verderer of the New Forest 1983–93; *Clubs* Brooks's; *Style*— The Rt Hon the Lord Manners; ✉ Sabines Avon, Christchurch, Dorset BH23 7BQ (tel 01425 672317)

MANNERS, (Arthur Edward) Robin; DL; s of Arthur Geoffrey Manners (d 1989), and Betty Ursula Joan, *née* Rutter (d 1972); *b* 10 March 1938; *Educ* Winchester, Trinity Hall Cambridge; *m* 22 Oct 1966, Judith Mary, da of Lt-Col Francis William Johnston, MBE (d 1999); 2 s (George b 1968, Richard b 1970); *Career* 2 Lt 10 Royal Hussars 1956–58, Maj Staffordshire Yeo 1958–68; dir Bass plc 1983–93 (joined 1961), various non-exec appts 1993–2001, memb Employment Appeal Tribunal 1995–; High Sheriff of Staffordshire 1998–99; *Recreations* golf, shooting, fishing, gardening, skiing; *Style*— Robin Manners, Esq, DL; ✉ The Old Croft, Bradley, Stafford ST18 9DF (tel 01785 780286, fax 01785 780750)

MANNING, HE Sir David Geoffrey; KCMG (2001, CMG (1992)), CVO (2007); s of John Robert Manning, and Joan Barbara Manning; *b* 5 December 1949; *Educ* Ardingly, Oriel Coll Oxford (open history scholar, BA), Johns Hopkins Sch of Advanced Int Studies Bologna (postgrad scholar); *m* 1973, Dr Catherine Manning, da of Dr W Parkinson; *Career* HM Dip Serv: joined FCO 1972, third later second sec Warsaw 1974–76, second later first sec New Delhi 1977–80, E Euro and Soviet Dept FCO 1980–82, Policy Planning Staff FCO 1982–84, first sec (political internal) Paris 1984–88, cnsllr on loan to Cabinet Office 1988–90, cnsllr and head of Political Section Moscow 1990–93, head of Eastern (formerly Soviet) Dept FCO 1993–94, head of Policy Planning Staff FCO 1994–95 (concurrently Br rep on ICFY Contact Gp on Bosnia April-Oct 1994), ambass to Israel 1995–98, dep under sec of state FCO 1998–2000, UK perm rep UK Delgn NATO 2001, foreign policy advsr to PM (on loan to Cabinet Office) 2001–03, ambass to USA 2003–; *Style*— HE Sir David Manning, KCMG

MANNING, (Everard Alexander) Dermot Niall; s of Col Frederick Everard Beresford Manning, Indian Med Serv (d 1987), and Elizabeth Robina, *née* Webber (d 1999); *b* 20 February 1949; *Educ* Rossall Sch, The Middx Hosp Med Sch London (MB BS); *m* 1 Aug 1981, Ann Ming Choo, da of Pak Shoon Wong (d 1998), of Kuala Lumpur, Malaysia; 1 s (Edward b 1985), 1 da (Catherine b 1988); *Career* registrar in obstetrics and gynaecology: St Helier Hosp Carshalton 1981–83, The Middx Hosp London 1983–85; sr registrar in obstetrics and gynaecology Middx Hosp and Central Middx Hosp London 1985–87, conslt obstetrics and gynaecology Central Middx Hosp and hon clinical sr lectr St Mary's Hosp Med Sch 1987–; Br Soc for Colposcopy and Cervical Pathology FBI; FRCOG 1995 (MRCOG 1982), forum memb RSM 1985; *Recreations* photography, gemmology and jewellery; *Clubs* Wine Soc; *Style*— Dermot Manning, Esq; ✉ North West London Hospitals NHS Trust, Central Middlesex Hospital, Park Royal, London NW10 7NS (tel 020 8453 2410/2309, fax 020 8453 2408)

MANNING, Dr Jane Marian; OBE (1990); da of Gerald Manville Manning (d 1987), and Lily, *née* Thompson (d 1989); *b* 20 September 1938; *Educ* Norwich HS, Royal Acad of Music (GRSM, LRAM, ARCM), Scuola Di Canto Cureglia Switzerland; *m* 24 Sept 1966, Anthony Edward Payne, s of Edward Alexander Payne (d 1958), of London; *Career* int career as soprano concert singer; London debut 1964, more than 300 world premieres, regular appearances in leading halls and festivals, Brussels Opera 1980, Scottish Opera 1978, numerous tours of Aust, NY debut 1981, first BBC broadcast 1965 (over 300 since), numerous recordings incl Messiaen Song Cycles; visiting prof: Mills Coll Oakland Calif 1981, 1983 and 1986, Royal Coll of Music 1995–; hon prof Keele Univ 1996–2002; AHRC Creative Arts Research Fell Kingston Univ 2004–07; visiting lectr: Harvard Univ, Stanford Univ, Princeton Univ, Yale Univ, Cornell Univ, Columbia Univ, Pennsylvania Univ, Univ of York, Univ of Cambridge, Univ of Durham; vice-pres Soc for the Promotion of New Music, chm Eye Music Tst, fndr and artistic dir Jane's Minstrels Ensemble 1988; memb: Exec Ctee Musicians Benevolent Fund; received special award composers Guild of GB 1973; Hon DUniv York 1988, Hon DMus Keele Univ 2004, Hon DMus Univ of Durham 2007; memb RPS; FRAM 1984, FRCM 1998, ISM; *Books* New Vocal Repertory (1986, reissued 1993, Vol II 1998), A Messiaen Companion (contrib, 1995); *Recreations* cinema, theatre, swimming, ornithology, reading; *Style*— Dr Jane Manning, OBE; ✉ 2 Wilton Square, London N1 3DL (tel 020 7359 1593, e-mail janetone@gmail.com); 7 Park Terrace, Upperton Road, Tillington, Petworth, West Sussex GU28 9AE

MANNING, Patrick John Mannes (Paddy); s of late Col Francis James Manning, TD, of Wiveliscombe, Somerset, and late Sarah Margaret, *née* Jenkins; *b* 16 July 1940; *Educ* Downside, RMA Sandhurst; *m* 19 April 1986, Sally Gail, da of Maj Jeremy Green, of Bideford on Avon, Warks; 1 da (Charlotte b 1987), 2 s (Francis James Daniel b 5 March 1990, Jeremy Patrick Augustus b 31 March 1992); *Career* Lt 4/7 Royal Dragoon Gds 1961–64, Royal Yeo 1965–72; stockbroker Laurence Keen & Gardner 1965–70; dir: Charles Barker City Ltd 1970–80, St James Public Relations Ltd 1984–98; chm The Paddy Manning Co 1998–; hon PR advsr Br Cwlth Ex-Servs League 1984–2004; *Recreations* country sports, opera, ballet, travel, book collecting; *Clubs* Cavalry and Guards'; *Style*— Paddy Manning, Esq; ✉ Eastwood Dairy Farm, Alverdiscot Road, Bideford, North Devon EX39 4PN; The Paddy Manning Co, 12 Suffolk Street, London SW1Y 4HQ (tel mobile 07803 183622, e-mail paddy@pmanning.demon.co.uk)

MANNING, Peter; s of Harry Manning (d 2002), and Breda, *née* Carroll (d 1992); *b* 17 July 1956; *Educ* Chethams Hosp Sch of Music Manchester, Royal Northern Coll of Music (GRNCM, PPRNCM), Indiana Univ; *m* 1992, Marion, *née* Cookson; 3 s (Edward b 1983, Frederick b 1995, Orlando b 1997), 1 da (Isabelle b 1986); *Career* ldr LPO 1983–86, ldr Britten String Quartet 1986–96, ldr RPO 1997–99, concertmaster ROH 1999–; dir Soloists of Covent Garden; artistic dir and conductor The Manning Camerata; int tours as soloist, dir and conductor; Hon RCM, FRNCM, FRSA; *Recreations* sailing, fishing, mushroom hunting; *Style*— Peter Manning, Esq; ✉ 52 Stockwell Park Road, London SW9 0DA (tel 020 7733 5251, e-mail peter@manningcamerata.com)

MANNING-COX, Andrew Richard; s of Frederick Cox, of Kinver, Staffs, and Beatrice Maud, *née* Brown; *b* 23 April 1956; *Educ* Peter Symonds' Coll Winchester, Univ of Cambridge (MA); *m* 31 Oct 1987, Janet Elaine, da of Eric Binns, of Bramhall, Cheshire; 2 da (Octavia Freya, Verity Beatrice); *Career* admitted slr 1980; ptnr Wragge & Co 1985–, NP 1992, slr advocate 2002; memb Law Soc 1980; *Recreations* riding, walking, country pursuits; *Style*— Andrew Manning-Cox, Esq; ✉ Wragge & Co LLP, 55 Colmore Row, Birmingham B3 2AS (tel 0121 233 1000, fax 0121 214 1099, e-mail andrew_manning_cox@wragge.com)

MANOR, Prof James Gilmore; s of James Gilmore Manor, of Lakeland, Florida, and Ann Jones Manor; *b* 21 April 1945; *Educ* Yale Univ (BA), Univ of Sussex (DPhil); *m* July 1974, Brenda, da of Sydney Cohen; 1 s (Hugh Benjamin b 16 March 1989); *Career* asst lectr Chinese Univ of Hong Kong 1967–69, tutor SOAS London 1973–75, asst prof Yale Univ 1975–76, lectr Univ of Leicester 1976–85, prof of government Harvard Univ 1985–87, fell Inst of Devpt Studies Univ of Sussex 1987–, dir and prof of Cwlth politics Inst of Cwlth Studies Univ of London 1994–97; research fell: Australian Nat Univ 1974, MIT 1982; memb Senate Univ of Leicester 1980–84; memb Bd: Inst of Latin American Studies, British Documents on the End of Empire Project, Amsterdam Sch of Social Science Research, Centre for the Advanced Study of India Univ of Pennsylvania; conslt to: Ford Fndn, World Bank, OECD, UN Capital Devpt Fund, British, Dutch and Swedish govts; *Books* Political Change in an Indian State (1977), Transfer and Transformation: Political Institutions in the New Commonwealth (co-ed, 1983), Sri Lanka in Change and Crisis (ed, 1984), The Expedient Utopian: Bandaranaike and Ceylon (1989), States or Markets (co-ed, 1992), Rethinking Third World Politics (ed, 1992), Power, Poverty and Poison: Disaster and Response in an Indian City (1993), Nehru to the Nineties: The Changing Office of Prime Minister in India (ed, 1994); *Recreations* reading, theatre; *Style*— Prof James Manor

MANS, Keith Douglas Rowland; s of Maj Gen Rowland Spencer Noel Mans, CBE (d 2002), of Milford on Sea, Hants, and Violet, *née* Sutton; *b* 10 February 1946; *Educ* Berkhamsted Sch, RAF Coll Cranwell, Open Univ (BA); *m* 19 Aug 1972, Rosalie Mary, da of J McCann (d 1977), of Liverpool; 2 da (Louise b 5 Nov 1980, Emma b 6 May 1986), 1 s (David b 9 Sept 1982); *Career* former Flt Lt RAF, served UK, Malta, Cyprus and Malaya; formerly central buyer for electronics John Lewis Partnership; MP (Cons) Wyre 1987–97, memb House of Commons Select Ctee on the Environment 1987–91, sec Cons Aviation Ctee 1987–90, memb Select Ctee on Defence 1995–97; PPS to: Min of State for Health 1990–92, Sec of State for Health 1992–95, Sec of State for Nat Heritage 1995; chm: Parly Environment Group 1993–97, Parly Aerospace Group 1994–97; cncllr New Forest DC 1983–87 (sometime dep ldr); chief exec The Royal Aeronautical Soc 1998, vice-chm The Air League 1997–, chm Air Travel Greener By Design Gp 2003–; memb Ct: Cranfield Univ 2002–, Southampton Univ 2005–; sch govr 1984–87; Freeman City of London 2005, Liveryman Guild of Air Pilots and Navigators 2005; MRUSI 1965, FRAeS 1997, FRSA 2005; *Recreations* flying; *Clubs* Carlton, RAF; *Style*— Keith D R Mans, Esq

MANSEL, Sir Philip; 15 Bt (E 1622), of Muddlescombe, Carmarthenshire; s of Sir John Philip Ferdinand Mansel, 14 Bt (d 1947), and Hannah, *née* Rees; *b* 3 March 1943; *Educ* Grosvenor Coll Carlisle, Carlisle GS; *m* 24 Aug 1968, Margaret, o da of Arthur Docker, of Moorhouse, Carlisle; 1 da (Nicol b 1978), 2 s (John Philip b 1982, Richard James b 31 July 1990); *Heir* s, John Mansel; *Career* former chm and md Eden-Vale Engineering Co Ltd, ret; FInstSMM; *Style*— Sir Philip Mansel, Bt; ✉ 2 Deyncourt Close, Darras Hall, Ponteland, Northumberland NE20 9JY (e-mail manselphilip@hotmail.com)

MANSEL, Prof Robert Edward; CBE (2006); s of Regnier Ranulf Dabridgecourt Mansel, and Mary Germaine, *née* Littlewood; *b* 1 February 1948; *Educ* Llandovery Coll, Charing Cross Hosp Med Sch (Morgan Evanson scholar, MB BS), Univ of London (MS); *m* 1987, Elizabeth Clare, da of Dr John Skone; 6 c; *Career* house surgn Charing Cross Gp London 1971, house physician St Mary's Hosp IOW 1972, SHO Charing Cross Hosp London 1972–74, sr registrar in surgery Princess Margaret Hosp Swindon 1974–76, sr registrar in surgery E Glamorgan Dist Gen Hosp 1978–79, prof of surgery Univ Hosp of S Manchester 1989–92; Univ of Wales Coll of Med: MRC res fell 1976–78, clinical lectr in surgery 1979–82, sr lectr in gen surgery and hon conslt 1983–89, head Univ Dept of Surgery 1992–, prof of surgery 1992–, chm (by election) Div of Hospital Based Specialities 2001–; lead cancer clinician for Wales 2006–; prog dir Welsh Higher Surgical Trg Ctee 1992–2000, non-exec dir Morgannwg HA 1996–2001; pres Br Assoc of Surgical Oncology 2004–05, sec Surgical Res Soc 1995–98 (chm Breast Surgns Gp, memb Screening Ctee), All Wales Breast Gp, surgical rep Welsh Nat Advsy Gp on Breast Screening; memb: Scientific Ctee Cancer Res Campaign, Br Breast Gp, Med Faculty Res Ctee and Res and Devpt Ctee Univ of Manchester, Moore Working Pty (reviewing Manchester Med Sch),

Speciality Review Panels London Cancer Services, Standing Ctee for Cancer RCS, UKCCR Breast Cancer Gp; memb Editorial Bd Clinical Breast Cancer, memb Editorial Ctee Br Jl of Surgery; delivered numerous invited lectrs incl: Ivor Lewis Meml Lecture Rhyl 1990, Oscar Schuberth Annual Lecture Swedish Med Soc 1998, Welsh Livery Guild Annual Lecture 1998, Mary Breve Lecture Finnish Med Soc 1999, Turner Grey Meml Lecture Univ of Newcastle upon Tyne 2001; 30th Anniversary NHS Travelling Scholarship 1978, Hamilton Bailey Travelling Fellowship 1981, Churchill Meml Fellowship 1982, Surgical Res Soc/Br Jl of Surgery Travelling Fellowship 1982, UICC (Union International Contre le Cancer (Geneva)) and CRC (Cancer Research Campaign, now Cancer Research UK), UICC Int Fellowship 1982–83 (held at Univ of Texas), James IV Int Fellowship 1989 (memb 2000), Hunterian prof RCS 1989; Surgical Res Soc Patey Prize 1987, Br Assoc of Surgical Oncology Raven Prize 1988, Welsh Surgical Soc Registrar's Prize 1988 (jtly), Charles Gros Prize 1990; tstee Llandovery Coll 1996–; LRCP 1971, FRCS 1975 (MRCS 1971), FICS, Hon FRCSEd 2001; *Publications* author of 7 books and 200 papers; *Recreations* watching rugby, fishing, travel; *Style*— Prof Robert Mansel, CBE; ✉ Cardiff University College of Medicine, Heath Park, Cardiff CF14 4XN (tel 029 2074 2749, fax 029 2076 1623, e-mail manselre@cf.ac.uk)

MANSEL LEWIS, Sir David Courtenay; KCVO (1995), JP (1969); s of Charlie Ronald Mansel Lewis (d 1960), and Lillian Georgina (d 1982), da of Sir Courtenay Warner, 1 Bt; *b* 25 October 1927; *Educ* Eton, Keble Coll Oxford (MA); *m* 1953, Lady Mary, da of 3 Earl of Wharncliffe; 1 s, 2 da; *Career* Welsh Gds 1946–49, Lt 1948, RARO; High Sheriff Carmarthenshire 1965, DL 1971, HM Lt Carmarthenshire 1973–74, HM Lt Dyfed 1974–79, HM Lord-Lt Dyfed 1979–2003; pres: W Wales TAVRA 1979–90, Dyfed SSAFA - Forces Help 1986–2002, Mid and W Wales TAVRA 1990–95, Wales TAVRA 1995–99, Wales ACF 1995–99; fndr pres Llanelli Branch Welsh Guards Assoc 1974–, patron Carmarthenshire Royal Br Legion 1974; sub prior St John Priory for Wales 1998–2003; patron: Dyfed Branch Br Red Cross Soc, Cwlth Games Cncl for Wales 1998–; pres: Dyfed Branch Magistrates' Assoc 1979–2002, Carmarthen/Cardigan Branch CLA 1979–91, Dyfed Wildlife Tst 1987–2003, Dyfed Branch CLA 1991–, Welsh Assoc of Male Voice Choirs 1998–, St John Cncl for Dyfed, Carmarthenshire Assoc of Boy Scouts; chm: SW Wales Div Royal Forestry Soc 1963–93, S Wales Woodlands 1969–85; patron: Carmarthenshire Wildfowlers Assoc 1976–, Carmarthenshire Fedn of Young Farmers' Clubs; memb: Ct of Govrs UCW Aberystwyth 1974–2003, Cncl Nat Museum of Wales 1987–91 (memb Ct 1974–76); former memb: Music Ctee Wales Arts Cncl, Bd Welsh Nat Opera; former pres Swansea Philharmonic Choir; pres: Burry Port Operatic Soc, Llanelli Art Soc 1956–, Burry Port RNLI 1982–, Heart of Wales Line Travellers Assoc 1993–, W Wales Maritime Heritage Soc 2000–; vice-pres Welsh Music Guild 2005–; fndr chm Carmarthen-Cardigan Ctee Sail Trg Assoc 1968–, regnl chm Sail Trg Assoc S Wales 1985–, chm Llanelli Millennium Coastal Park Tst 1999–; fndr Cdre and pres Burry Port Yacht Club 1966–, patron Tall Ships Cncl of Wales 1991; Llandovery Coll: tstee 1985–2001, chm of tstees 2001–06, pres 2006–; hon fell Trinity Coll Carmarthen 1997; KStJ; *Recreations* sailing (yacht 'Wendy Woo'), music; *Clubs* RYS, Cruising Assoc, Cavalry and Guards', Army and Navy, Lansdowne; *Style*— Sir David Mansel Lewis, KCVO; ✉ Stradey Castle, Llanelli, Dyfed SA15 4PL (tel 01554 774626); 53 New Road, Llanelli, Dyfed SA15 3DD (tel 01554 773059)

MANSELL, Mark; *Educ* KCL (LLB); *Career* admitted slr 1985; specialises in employment law; articled clerk Rowe & Maw until 1985, legal advsr Employment Affrs Directorate CBI 1985–87, ptnr Allen & Overy 1992– (asst slr 1987–91); memb: City of London Slrs' Co, Employment Lawyers Assoc, European Employment Lawyers Assoc; *Style*— Mark Mansell, Esq; ✉ Allen & Overy LLP, One Bishops Square, London E1 6AO (tel 020 30 88 3663, e-mail mark.mansell@allenovery.com)

MANSELL-JONES, Richard Mansell; s of Arnaud Milward Jones (d 1964), of Carmarthen, and Winifred Mabel, *née* Foot (d 1978); *b* 4 April 1940; *Educ* Queen Elizabeth's Carmarthen, Worcester Coll Oxford (MA); *m* 30 June 1971, Penelope Marion, yr da of Maj Sir David Henry Hawley, 7 Bt (d 1988); *Career* articled clerk and investigation sr Price Waterhouse & Co 1963–68, mangr corp fin N M Rothschild & Sons Ltd 1968–72; Brown, Shipley & Co Ltd: dir 1972–88, dep chm 1984–88, chm 1992–2003; dir Brown Shipley Holdings plc 1984–93; Barloworld plc (formerly J Bibby & Sons plc then Barlow International plc): dir 1978–2003, dep chm 1987–88, chm 1988–2000; also chm: Finanzauto SA, Sociedade Tecnica de Equipmentos e Tractores SA 1992–2000; dir (exec) Barlow Ltd (formerly Barlow Rand) 1988–2001; non-exec dir: Fitzmaurice Management Ltd 1977–2002, Barr & Wallace Arnold Trust plc 1984–93, Standard Bank plc 1992–2005; chm Millfield Gp plc 2001–; patron Shaw Tst 1996– (tstee 1990–96), treas Royal Hospital for Neuro-Disability 2005– (tstee 2003–); FCA, MSI; *Clubs* Beefsteak, Boodle's, City of London; *Style*— Richard Mansell-Jones, Esq; ✉ c/o Brown, Shipley & Co Ltd, Founders Court, Lothbury, London EC2R 7HE (tel 020 7606 9833)

MANSER, (Peter) John; CBE (1992), DL (1999); s of Lt-Col Peter Robert Courtney Manser (d 1944), and Florence Delaplaine, *née* Ismay (d 1983); *b* 7 December 1939; *Educ* Marlborough; *m* 31 May 1969, Sarah Theresa Stuart (Tessa), *née* Todd; 2 da; *Career* CA; Robert Fleming group: with Brown Fleming & Murray 1959–66, dir Robert Fleming & Co Ltd 1967–75, md Jardine Fleming & Co Ltd 1975–79, chief exec Save & Prosper Group Ltd 1979–88, gp chief exec Robert Fleming Holdings Ltd 1990–97, chm Robert Fleming Holdings Ltd 1997–2000; chm: Delancey Estates 1997–2001, Shaftesbury plc 2004–, Intermediate Capital Gp plc, Hiscox Investment Mgmnt 2005–, London Asia Chinese Private Equity Fund Ltd; dep chm Colliers CRE 2000–; dir: Keppel Capital Holdings Ltd 1999–2001, SABMiller plc 2001–; dir Securities and Investments Bd 1986–93, chm London Investment Banking Assoc 1994–98; chm Wilts Community Fndn 1997–2002; Freeman City of London, Liveryman Worshipful Co of Grocers; FCA 1976; *Recreations* gardening, shooting, walking; *Clubs* Boodle's, MCC; *Style*— John Manser, Esq, CBE; ✉ 37–43 Sackville Street, London W1S 3DL (tel 020 7333 8118, fax 020 7333 0660, e-mail john.manser@shaftesbury.co.uk)

MANSER, Jonathan; s of Michael John Manser, of Chiswick, London, and Dolores Josephine, *née* Bernini; *b* 15 January 1955; *Educ* Westminster, Univ of Cambridge (MA, memb Boat Race crew 1976 and 1977), South Bank Poly (Dip Arch); *m* 1983, Sarah Christiane, da of Air Vice Marshal W V C Crawford-Compton, DSO, DFC; 2 da (Olivia Bianca Imogen b 1986, Claudia Augusta Marie-Claire b 1989); *Career* architect; Foster Associates 1974, Hulme Chadwick & Partners 1977–78, Renton Howard Wood Levine 1980–82, Chapman Taylor Partners 1982–83, self-employed sole practitioner 1983–85, dir The Manser Practice (formerly Manser Associates) 1986–; RIBA Award for Hilton Hotel Heathrow Airport, RIBA and Steel Award for Southampton Airport; also former int yachtsman; memb Br team: Onion Patch Cup 1978, Admiral's Cup 1979, Southern Cross Cup 1979; second place 6 metre class Euro Cup 1985, winner 6 metre class World Championships 1986; *Clubs* Hawks' (Cambridge), Groucho, Archetypals; *Style*—Jonathan Manser, Esq; ✉ The Manser Practice, Bridge Studios, Hammersmith Bridge, London W6 9DA (tel 020 8741 4381, fax 020 8741 2773, e-mail jonathanmanser@manser.demon.co.uk)

MANSER, Michael John; CBE (1993); s of Edmund George Manser (d 1971), and Augusta Madge, *née* Bonell (d 1987); *b* 23 March 1929; *m* 1953, Dolores Josephine, da of Isadore Bernini; 1 s (Jonathan), 1 da (Victoria); *Career* chartered architect; Nat Serv RE, Staff Capt; chm The Manser Practice (founded as Michael Manser Associates 1961); memb Cncl: AA 1971–72, RIBA 1979–81 (pres 1983–85), RSA 1985–91; memb Design Policy Ctee London Transport 1990–96; awards incl: two Civic Tst Awards, Euro Heritage Year Award, DOE Commendation for Good Design in Housing, Steel Award and Steel Award Commendation, Harrow Heritage Tst Award, two RIBA Awards and two RIBA Regnl Awards, RCFA/Sunday Times Building of the Year Award, British Construction Industry Award; architectural corr The Observer 1961–65; fndr chm DOE/RSA Art in Architecture Awards 1989–91; chm: Art in Workplace Awards 1995–2001, RIBA Awards Gp 1999–, Nat Home Builder Design Awards 1999, Stirling Prize Award 2000, National Homebuilder Design Award 1999–, Annual RIBA Manser Medal Award for Best One off House in UK 2001–; memb: Cncl RSA 1986–91, Cncl Nat Tst 1992–95, Royal West of England Acad, RIBA Communications Ctee 1999, City of Westminster Public Art Panel 1999; Hon FRAIC; RA 1995 (Cncl 1997, Audit Ctee 1998, Architecture Ctee 1999, Building Ctee 1999, Renumeration Ctee 2000); *Recreations* home, garden, books, music, walks, boats (Amadeus); *Clubs* Brooks's, Arts, Farmers; *Style*— Michael Manser, Esq, CBE, RA; ✉ 76 Whitehall Court, London SW1A 2EL; The Manser Practice, Bridge Studios, Hammersmith Bridge, London W6 9DA (tel 020 8741 4381)

MANSER, Paul Robert; s of Bob Manser, and Margaret, *née* Rubinstein; *b* 27 March 1950; *Educ* Eltham Coll, Univ of Warwick (BA); *m* 28 July 1972, Lindy, da of Harry Myers; 2 s (Nicolas b 19 June 1981, Edward b 18 Feb 1983); *Career* admitted slr 1977: currently ptnr Taylor Wessing; memb Law Soc; *Recreations* tennis, photography, music; *Style*— Paul Manser, Esq; ✉ Taylor Wessing, Carmelite, 50 Victoria Embankment, London EC4Y 0DX (tel 020 7300 7000)

MANSFIELD, Prof Averil O; CBE (1999); *b* 21 June 1937; *Educ* Blackpool Collegiate Sch, Univ of Liverpool (MB ChB, ChM); *m* Jack Bradley FRCS; *Career* formerly: lectr in surgery Univ of Liverpool, conslt surgn and hon sr lectr in surgery United Liverpool Hosps, conslt surgn Hillingdon and Hammersmith Hosps and St Mary's Hosp London, prof of vascular surgery Imperial Coll Sch of Med at St Mary's Hosp London, sr lectr in vascular surgery Royal Postgraduate Med Sch (Hammersmith Hosp), hon conslt in paediatric surgery/vascular surgery Hosp for Sick Children Great Ormond Street; postgraduate sub-dean St Mary's Hosp Med Sch 1987–91; currently emeritus prof; RCS: memb Cncl 1990–, Ct of Examiners (chm 1990–92), vice-pres 1998–2000; pres Section of Surgery RSM 1997–98; currently chm Stroke Assoc; chm: Intercollegiate Bd in Gen Surgery 1992–95, Fedn of Surgical Speciality Assocs 1993–95; memb: Audit Ctee Euro Carotid Stroke Surgery Trial, Steering Ctee Asymptomatic Carotid Surgery Trial; Moynihan fell Assoc of Surgns of Great Britain and I, Hunterian prof, Arnott demonstrator, Bradshaw lectr and Kinmonth lectr RCS, Hon FRACS and Syme orator RACS 1996; memb: Assoc of Surgns of GB and I (pres 1992–93), Vascular Surgery Soc (pres 1996–97), Surgical Res Soc, Euro Soc of Vascular Surgery; Hon MD Univ of Liverpool 1994; FRCSEd 1966, FRCS 1967, FRCPS 1998, Hon FACS 1998, FDSRCS 2003, FRCP 2005; *Style*— Prof Averil O Mansfield, CBE; ✉ The Stroke Association, 240 City Road, London EC1V 2PR (e-mail a.mansfield@imperial.ac.uk)

MANSFIELD, David James; s of Wilfred Victor Leonard Mansfield (d 1972), and Helen, *née* Preston; *b* 12 January 1954; *m* 15 Sept 1979, Alison Patricia, da of Gerald Frederick Hedley Pullin; 2 s (James William Robert b 1983, Edward Nicholas Jack (Ned) b 1994), 1 da (Clare Amy Frances b 1986); *Career* sales and sr mktg exec Scottish and Grampian TV 1977–80, mktg gp head and gen sales mangr Scottish TV 1981–84; Thames TV: mktg controller 1985–87, sales and mktg controller 1987–90, dep sales dir 1990–92; Capital Radio plc: gp commercial dir 1993–97, chief exec 1997–2005; dir Carphone Warehouse 2005–, exec dir Ingenious Media plc 2006–, advsr JCPR Ltd 2006–; former chief exec GCap (following merger with GWR), former dir Bd Radio Advertising Bureau; *Recreations* fly fishing, contemporary music; *Style*— David Mansfield, Esq

MANSFIELD, Guy Rhys John; QC (1994); 6 Baron Sandhurst (UK 1871); s of 5 Baron Sandhurst (d 2002), and Janet Mary, *née* Lloyd; *b* 3 March 1949; *Educ* Harrow, Oriel Coll Oxford (MA); *m* 1976, Philippa St Clair, da of late Digby Everard Verdon-Roe, of Le Cannet, France; 1 da (Hon Alice Georgina b 4 Feb 1980), 1 s (Hon Edward James b 12 April 1982); *Career* called to the Bar Middle Temple 1972 (Harmsworth exhibitioner, Winston Churchill pupillage award, bencher 2000), recorder of the Crown Court 1993–; chm Gen Cncl of the Bar 2005– (vice-chm 2004, chm Remuneration and Terms of Work Ctee 1998–99, memb Gen Mgmnt Ctee 1998–2005, chm Legal Services Ctee 2000–03); *Publications* Financial Provision in Family Matters (contrib), Human Rights and the Common Law (contrib), Personal Injury Handbook (contrib); *Recreations* cricket; *Clubs* Leander, MCC, Reform; *Style*— Guy Mansfield, QC; ✉ 1 Crown Office Row, London EC4Y 7HH (tel 020 7797 7500, fax 020 7797 7550, e-mail guy.mansfield@1cor.com)

M

MANSFIELD, Michael; QC; s of Frank Le Voir Mansfield (d 1960), of London, and Marjorie, *née* Sayer (d 1977); *b* 12 October 1941; *Educ* Highgate Sch, Keele Univ (BA); *m* 1, 28 Sept 1965 (m dis 1992), Melian, da of Lt Cdr Bordes; 3 s (Jonathan, Leo, Keiran), 2 da (Anna, Louise); m 2, 31 Dec 1992, Yvette Vanson; 1 s (Frederic); *Career* called to the Bar Gray's Inn 1967, estab chambers Tooks Court 1984; prof of law Univ of Westminster 1997; Hon LLD: South Bank Univ 1994, Keele Univ 1995, Univ of Hertfordshire 1995, Univ of Middx 1999; pres: Nat Civil Rights Movement (NCRM), Haldane Soc; hon fell Univ of Kent; memb TGWU, hon memb NUM; FRSA; *Style*— Michael Mansfield, Esq, QC; ✉ 14 Tooks Court, Cursitor Street, London EC4A 1JY (tel 020 7405 8828)

MANSFIELD, Sir Peter; kt (1993); s of Sidney George Mansfield (d 1966), of Lambeth, London, and Rose Lilian, *née* Turner (d 1985); *b* 9 October 1933; *Educ* William Penn Sch Peckham, QMC London (BSc, PhD); *m* 1 Sept 1962, Jean Margaret, da of Edward Francis Kibble (d 1972), of Peckham, London; 2 da (Sarah Jane b 1967, Gillian Samantha b 1970); *Career* Nat Serv RASC 1952–54; res assoc Univ of Illinois USA 1962–64; Univ of Nottingham: lectr, sr lectr then reader 1964–79, prof of physics 1979–94, prof emeritus 1994; sr res visitor Max Planck Inst for Med Res Heidelberg Germany 1971–72, pres Soc of Magnetic Resonance in Med 1987–88; Gold Medal Soc of Magnetic Resonance in Med 1982, Gold Medal and Prize Royal Soc Wellcome Fndn 1984, Duddell Medal and Prize Inst of Physics 1988, Sylvanus Thompson Medal Br Inst of Radiology 1988, Euro Workshop Trophy Euro Soc of Magnetic Resonance in Med and Biology 1988, Antoine Béclère Medal for Radiology 1989, Royal Soc Mullard Medal 1990, ISMAR Prize Int Soc of Magnetic Resonance 1992, Barclay Medal Br Inst of Radiology 1993, first Silver Plaque Euro Soc of Magnetic Resonance in Med and Biology 1993, Gold Medal Euro Assoc of Radiology 1995, Garmisch-Partenkirschen Prize for Magnetic Resonance Imaging 1995, Rank Prize 1997, Nobel Prize in Physiology or Medicine 2003, Nuffield lectr and Gold Medal RSM 2006, Euromar Medal Groupement Ampère 2006, Galen Medal Soc of Apothecaries 2006, Gold Medal Medicas Magnus Univ of Warsaw 2007, Mike Hogg Award Univ of Texas 2007; Dr (hc): Univ of Strasbourg 1995, Jagellonian Univ of Krakow 2000, Univ of Leicester 2006, Leipzig Univ 2006, Warsaw Univ 2007; DSc (hc): Univ of Kent 1996, Univ of Nottingham 2004; fell QMC London 1987; hon fell: Royal Coll of Radiology 1992, Inst of Physics 1996, RCP 2004, Hughes Hall Cambridge 2004; hon memb: Br Inst of Radiology 1993, Soc of Magnetic Resonance Imaging 1994; fell Soc of Magnetic Resonance 1994, European Soc Magnetic Resonance in Medicine & Biology 2002; memb Polish Acad of Medicine 2007; fndr FMedSci 1998; FRS 1987; *Books* NMR Imaging in Biomedicine (with P G Morris, 1982), NMR Imaging (ed with E L Hahn, 1990), MRI in Medicine (ed, 1995); *Recreations* languages, walking, flying (PPL and PPL(H)); *Style*— Sir Peter Mansfield, FRS; ✉ Magnetic Resonance Centre, Department of Physics and Astronomy, University of Nottingham, University Park, Nottingham NG7 2RD (tel 0115 951 4740, fax 0115 951 5166)

MANSFIELD, Prof Roger; s of Arthur George Mansfield (d 1985), and Edith, *née* Leggett (d 1985); *b* 18 January 1942; *Educ* Kingston GS, Gonville & Caius Coll Cambridge (BA),

Wolfson Coll Cambridge (MA, PhD); *m* 24 July 1969, Hélène Marie Louise, da of René Rica, of Quimper, France; 2 da (Marie-Anne (Mrs Ian Mackie) b 1972, Stephanie b 1977); *Career* student apprentice and res engr Stewarts and Lloyds Ltd Corby 1960–66; FME teaching fell Dept of Engrg Univ of Cambridge 1966–68, visiting lectr Yale Univ 1968–69, sr res offr London Business Sch 1969–73, lectr in industrial sociology Imperial Coll London 1973–76, prof of business admin Univ of Wales Cardiff Business Sch 1976–; head of dept: Business Admin and Accountancy UWIST 1977–85, Business and Economics UWIST 1985–87; dir Cardiff Business Sch 1987–, dep princ UWIST 1985–88, pro-vice-chllr Univ of Wales Cardiff 1996–2002; chm Br Acad of Mgmnt 1993–96, vice-chm Cncl of Univ Mgmnt Schs 1988–92; dir S Glamorgan Trg and Enterprise Cncl 1989–94; FRSA, CCMI; *Books* Managers in Focus: the British Manager in the Early 1980s (with M J F Poole, 1981), Organizational Structures and National Contingencies (1983), Frontiers of Management Research and Practice (1989); *Recreations* gardening, opera; *Style*— Prof Roger Mansfield; ✉ Crowhurst, 64 Bishops Road, Whitchurch, Cardiff CF14 1LW (tel 029 2061 7381); Cardiff Business School, Cardiff University, Aberconway Building, Colum Drive, Cardiff CF1 3EU (tel 029 2087 4417, fax 029 2087 4419, e-mail mansfield@cardiff.ac.uk)

MANSFIELD, Prof Terence Arthur (Terry); s of Sidney Walter Mansfield (d 1976), of Blackfordby, Leics, and Rose, *née* Sinfield (d 1979); *b* 18 January 1937; *Educ* Ashby-de-la-Zouch GS, Univ of Nottingham (BSc), Univ of Reading (PhD); *m* 1963, Margaret Mary, da of Henri Gerard James; 2 s (Timothy James b 1966, Michael Peter b 1968); *Career* research asst Univ of Reading 1961–65; Lancaster Univ: lectr 1965–71, reader 1971–77, prof 1977–, provost of science and engrg 1993–96; ed and chm Trustees of the New Phytologist 1979–2002; pres Shireshead and Forton Cricket Club 1993–2003; former govr Scottish Crops Research Inst; memb Soc for Experimental Biology 1962–, memb British Ecological Soc 1990; fell Inst of Biology 1984, FRS (memb Cncl 1990–92); *Books* Physiology of Stomata (1968), Effects of Air Pollution on Plants (1976), Plant Adaptation to Environmental Stress (1993); author of over 200 scientific papers; *Recreations* hill walking, music, cricket; *Clubs* Shireshead and Forton Cricket; *Style*— Prof Terry Mansfield, FRS; ✉ Department of Biological Sciences, Lancaster University, Lancaster LA1 4YQ (tel 01524 593779, e-mail mm-mansfield@beeb.net)

MANSFIELD, Terence Gordon (Terry); CBE (2002); s of Archer James Mansfield (d 1990), and Elizabeth Sally, *née* Cox (d 1994); *b* 3 November 1938; *Educ* South West Essex Tech Coll; *m* 31 July 1965, Helen, da of Peter Maurice Russell; 2 da (Anna Helen b 18 September 1966, Victoria Sally b 12 October 1970); *Career* Nat Serv RAF 1959–61; Condé Nast 1961–66: asst advertisement mangr Photography Magazine, sales rep for several magazines incl House & Gardens, Wine & Food, Men in Vogue and Vogue; sr sales rep Queen Magazine 1966–69 (latterly advertisement mangr); National Magazine Co: joined 1969, advertisement mangr Harpers Bazaar 1969–70, assoc publisher Harpers & Queen 1973–74, advertisement dir Harpers & Queen 1974–75, publisher Harpers & Queen 1975–80, dep md 1980–82, md 1982–2002, pres and ceo 2002, ret 2003; chm: COMAG 1984–2002, Mobo Orgn; bd dir and vice-pres Hearst Corp until 2003 (conslt to Hearst Corp 2002–); tstee: NewstrAid Benevolent Soc, United World Coll (St Donat's Castle); chair of tstees Victim Support 2003–05; PPA Marcus Morris Award 2001; Freedom City of London 1989, Liveryman Worshipful Co of Stationers & Newspaper Makers; *Clubs* Mark's, Harry's Bar, IOD, Hanbury Manor; *Style*— Terry Mansfield, Esq, CBE; ✉ 5 Grosvenor Gardens Mews North, Ebury Street, London SW1 0JP (tel and fax 020 7730 7740); The Hearst Corporation, 136 Sloane Street, London SW1X 9AY (tel 020 7565 6666, fax 020 7565 6675)

MANSFIELD AND MANSFIELD, 8 Earl of (GB 1776 and 1792); William David Mungo James Murray; JP (Perth and Kinross 1975), DL (1980); also Lord Scone (S 1605), Viscount Stormont (S 1621), Lord Balvaird (S 1641); hereditary keeper of Bruce's Castle of Lochmaben; s of 7 Earl of Mansfield, JP, LL (d 1971, whose family were long the owners of Robert Adam's neo-classical Kenwood; Lord Mansfield is sixth in descent from the bro of the celebrated Lord Chief Justice and 1 Earl who was Alexander Pope's 'silver-tongued Murray'), and Dorothea (d 1985), da of Hon Sir Lancelot Carnegie, GCVO, KCMG, 2 s of 9 Earl of Southesk; *b* 7 July 1930; *Educ* Wellesley House, Eton, ChCh Oxford; *m* 19 Dec 1955, Pamela Joan, da of Wilfred Neill Foster, CBE; 2 s (Alexander David Mungo, Viscount Stormont b 17 Oct 1956, Hon James b 7 June 1969), 1 da (Lady Georgina b 10 March 1967); *Heir* s, Viscount Stormont; *Career* Nat Serv Lt Scots Gds 1949–50 (Malaya); called to the Bar 1958; practising barrister until 1971; dir General Accident Fire & Life Assurance Corp and numerous cos 1972–79 and 1985–98; memb Br Delgn to Euro Parliament 1973–75; oppn front bench spokesman in the House of Lords 1975–79; min of state: Scottish Office 1979–83, NI Office 1983–84; first cmmr and chm The Crown Estate 1985–95; chm Historic Houses Assoc Scotland 1976–79; vice-pres Wildfowl & Wetlands Tst; pres: Scottish Assoc of Boys' Clubs 1976–79, Fédération des Associations de Chasse de l' Europe 1977–79, Royal Scottish Country Dance Soc 1977–, Scottish Orchid Soc 1997–; Hon Sheriff Perth 1974; Hon MRICS 1993; *Clubs* Turf, White's, Pratt's, Beefsteak; *Style*— The Rt Hon the Earl of Mansfield and Mansfield, DL; ✉ Scone Palace, Perthshire PH2 6BE (tel 01738 551115, fax 01738 552588)

MANSON, Scott James; s of James Manson, and Anne, *née* Colston; *b* 27 February 1970; *Educ* Newcastle Coll, Univ of Leeds (BA); *Career* journalist; clubs ed Venue 1994, gp ed Square One Publishing 1995; ed: Velocity 1997, Ministry 1998–2001, Loaded 2002–03 (dep ed 2001); memb BSME 2003; memb Ctee Nordoff-Robbins Music Therapy; *Clubs* Soho House; *Style*— Scott Manson, Esq; ✉ Loaded, IPC Media, Kings Reach Tower, Stamford Street, London SE1 9LS (tel 020 7261 5562)

MANTEL, Hilary Mary (Mrs Gerald McEwen); CBE (2006); da of Henry Thompson (took name of step f, Jack Mantel), and Margaret Mary, *née* Foster; *b* 6 July 1952; *Educ* Harrytown Convent Romiley Cheshire, LSE, Univ of Sheffield (BJur); *m* 1972, Gerald McEwen, s of Henry McEwen; *Career* author; film critic The Spectator 1987–90, writer of columns and criticism in a wide range of newspapers and magazines 1987–; memb Public Lending Right Advsy Ctee 1997–2003; Shiva Naipaul meml prize 1987, Winifred Holtby prize 1990, Cheltenham Festival lit prize 1990, Southern Arts lit prize 1991, Sunday Express Book of the Year award 1992, Hawthornden Prize 1996, Mind Book of the Year prize 2004, Yorkshire Post Fiction Prize 2006; Hon DLitt Univ of Sheffield 2005; FRSL 1990; *Novels* Every Day is Mother's Day (1985), Vacant Possession (1986), Eight Months on Ghazzah Street (1988), Fludd (1989), A Place of Greater Safety (1992), A Change of Climate (1994), An Experiment in Love (1995), The Giant, O'Brien (1998), Giving Up The Ghost (memoir, 2003), Learning To Talk (short stories, 2003), Beyond Black (2005); *Recreations* watching cricket; *Style*— Hilary Mantel, CBE, FRSL; ✉ c/o Bill Hamilton, 6 Warwick Court, Holborn, London WC1R 5DJ (tel 020 7242 2811, fax 020 7242 2711)

MANTELL, Rt Hon Sir Charles Barrie Knight; kt (1990), PC (1997); s of Francis Christopher Knight Mantell, and Elsie Mantell; *b* 30 January 1937; *Educ* Manchester Grammar, Univ of Manchester (LLM); *m* 1960, Anne Shirley; 2 da; *Career* flying offr RAF 1958–61; called to the Bar Gray's Inn 1960, in practice Manchester and London 1961–82, recorder of the Crown Ct 1978–82, QC 1979, judge of the Supreme Ct Hong Kong 1982–85, circuit judge 1985–90, bencher Gray's Inn 1990, judge of the High Ct of Justice (Queen's Bench Div) 1990–97, a Lord Justice of Appeal 1997–2004, judge Cts of Appeal of Jersey and Guernsey 2004–; sr presiding judge Western Circuit 1995–96 (presiding judge 1993–96); *Recreations* reading, watching cricket; *Style*— The Rt Hon Sir Charles Mantell

MANTLE, Richard John; *b* 21 January 1947, London; *Educ* Tiffin GS, Ealing Coll; *m* 1970, Carol June *née* Mountain; *Career* personnel and industrial rels mangr Beecham Gp UK (now GlaxoSmithKline) 1968–72, assoc dir and personnel mangr J Walter Thompson & Co 1972–79, dep md ENO 1979–85, md Scottish Opera 1985–91, gen dir Edmonton Opera Canada 1992–94, gen dir Opera North 1994–; artistic dir Music for Life Southbank Fest 1992; chm: Negotiating Ctee UK Nat Opera 1982–91, Glasgow Cultural Forum 1990–91, Opera Ctee Theatre Mangrs Assoc 1996–; negotiating chair Professional Opera Cos of Canada 1992–94, sec Eurolyrica 1996–; tstee: Nat Opera Studio London 1985–91 and 1994–, Audiences Yorkshire 1996–2006; memb: Arts Cncl of GB Touring Ctee 1986–91, Mayor's Ctee for the Arts in Edmonton Canada 1993–94, Advsy Cncl Royal Sch of Church Music 2000–; chm Bd of Trustees Abbotts Bromley Sch Fndn 1998–, guardian Shrine of Our Lady of Walsingham Norfolk 1997–; *Recreations* travel, churches, food, wine (not making!), listening to and playing music; *Clubs* Athenaeum; *Style*— Richard Mantle, Esq; ✉ Opera North, Grand Theatre, 46 New Briggate, Leeds LS1 6NU (tel 0113 243 9999, fax 0113 244 0418)

MANTON, 4 Baron (UK 1922) Miles Ronald Marcus Watson; s of 3 Baron Manton (d 2003); triplet with Hon Thomas and Hon Victoria; *b* 7 May 1958; *Educ* Eton; *m* 17 Oct 1984, Elizabeth A, eldest da of J R Story, of Westcott, Surrey; 2 s (Hon Thomas b 19 April 1985, Hon Ludovic Waldo Rupert b 31 March 1989); *Heir* s, Hon Thomas Watson; *Style*— The Rt Hon the Lord Manton

MAPLE, Graham John; s of Sydney George Maple (decd), of Croydon, and Thelma Olive, *née* Winter; *b* 18 December 1947; *Educ* Shirley Secdy Modern Sch Croydon, John Ruskin GS Croydon, Bedford Coll London (LLB); *m* 30 March 1974, Heather Maple, JP, da of James Anderson; 2 s (Andrew John b 30 March 1978, Christopher James b 18 March 1980); *Career* Lord Chancellor's Dept 1968, chief clerk Divorce Registry 1981–86, establishment offr 1986–89, sec Family Div 1989–91, district judge Principal Registry of the Family Div High Court of Justice 1991–2005; memb: Outer London Family Court Servs Ctee 1991–95, Outer London Family Forum 1995–2005; churchwarden St Mildred's Parish Church Tenterden 1992–98; *Books* Practioner's Probate Manual (jt ed 21 edn, 1979), Holloway's Probate Handbook (ed 8 edn, 1987), Rayden and Jackson on Divorce and Family Maters (co ed 13–17 edn, 1975–98, conslt ed 1998–2006); *Recreations* steam and model railways, Roman Britain, archaeology; *Style*— Graham Maple, Esq

MAPLES, John; MP; *b* 22 April 1943; *Educ* Marlborough, Univ of Cambridge (MA), Harvard Business Sch; *m* Jane; 1 s (Tom), 1 da (Rose); *Career* called to the Bar 1965; self-employed lawyer and businessman 1965–83 (USA and WI 1967–78); MP (Cons): Lewisham W 1983–92, Stratford-on-Avon 1997–; PPS to Chief Sec to the Treasy 1987–90, economic sec to Treasy 1990–92, jt dep chm Cons Pty 1994–95, shadow health sec 1997–98, shadow defence sec 1998–99, shadow foreign sec 1999–2000, memb Foreign Affrs Select Ctee; chm and chief exec Saatchi & Saatchi Government Communications Worldwide 1992–96, chm Rowland Sallingbury Casey 1992–96, chm Visual Technology 2000–; memb Cncl RIIA; Liveryman Worshipful Co of Vintners; *Style*— John Maples, Esq, MP; ✉ House of Commons, London SW1A 0AA (tel 020 7219 3000)

MAPLES, (Charles James) Julian; s of Charles John Maples (d 1973), and Renee Lolita Elisabeth Gordon, *née* Clark (d 1996); *b* 26 January 1949; *Educ* St Peter's Sch Seaford, Harrow, Univ of Liverpool (LLB); *m* 1972, Anne-Francoise, da of B B W Bromley (d 1996); 2 s (Charles James b 30 Sept 1978, John Henry b 10 June 1984); *Career* Theodore Goddard: articled clerk 1971, ptnr 1980–, head Banking Gp 1985–99, head Corporate Recovery Gp 1998–; memb: Worshipful Co of Fletchers, Worshipful Co of Weavers, Law Soc; *Recreations* shooting, sailing; *Style*— Julian Maples, Esq; ✉ Lower Parrock House, Hartfield, East Sussex (tel 01342 822666, fax 01342 825601); Theodore Goddard, 150 Aldersgate Street, London EC1A 4EJ (tel 020 7606 8855, fax 020 7606 4390, e-mail julianmaples@theodoregoddard.co.uk)

MAPLESON, Prof William Wellesley; s of Francis Mapleson (d 1959), of Amersham, Bucks, and Amy Kathleen, *née* Parsons (d 1968); *b* 2 August 1926; *Educ* Dr Challoner's GS Amersham, UC Durham (BSc, PhD, DSc); *m* 10 July 1954, Gwladys Doreen, da of William Horatio Wood (d 1981), of Cardiff; 1 da (Jenny b 1955), 1 s (Roger b 1963); *Career* Nat Serv instr in radar Flying Offr RAF 1947–49; Coll of Med Univ of Wales: lectr 1952–65, sr lectr 1965–69, reader 1969–73, prof of physics of anaesthesia 1973–91, emeritus prof and conslt Dept of Anaesthetics 1991–; Pask Certificate of Honour AAGBI 1972, Faculty Medal Royal Coll of Anaesthetists 1981, Dudley Buxton Medal Royal Coll of Anaesthetists 1992, Henry Hill Hickman Medal RSM Section of Anaesthesia 1999, Sir Ivan Magill Medal AAGBI 2002, Mushin Medal 2003; hon memb: Brazilian Soc of Anaesthesiology 1983, Assoc of Anaesthetists of GB and I 1991, Hon FRCA 1996; FInstP, fell Inst of Physics and Engrg in Med (FIPEM); *Books* Automatic Ventilation of the Lungs (jtly, 3 edn, 1980); author of more than 100 papers in learned scientific journals; *Recreations* theatre-going, walking; *Style*— Prof William Mapleson; ✉ Department of Anaesthetics, Wales College of Medicine, Cardiff University, University Hospital of Wales, Cardiff CF14 4XN (tel 029 2074 3110, fax 029 2074 7203)

MAR, Countess of (31 holder of S Earldom *ab initio*, before 1114); Margaret; *née* of Mar; also Lady Garioch (an honour originally held together with the ancient territorial Earldom of Mar; holder of Premier Earldom of Scotland by date (the oldest peerage in the Br Isles); the predecessors of the original Earls of Mar were Mormaers of Mar in pre-feudal Scotland, long before the term 'Earl' came to be used; maintains private offr-of-arms (Garioch Pursuivant); da of 30 Earl of Mar (d 1975), and Millicent Mary Lane, *née* Salton (d 1993); *b* 19 September 1940; *Educ* Lewes County GS for Girls; *m* 1, 1959 (m dis 1976), Edwin Noel of Mar (recognised in surname 'of Mar' by Warrant of the Lord Lyon 1969), s of Edwin Artiss; 1 da (Lady Susan Helen, Mistress of Mar b 31 May 1963); m 2, 1976, John (also recognised in the surname 'of Mar' by Warrant of Lord Lyon 1976), s of Norman Salton; m 3, 1982, John Henry Jenkin, MA(Cantab), LRAM, FRCO, ARCM, s of William Jenkin, of Hayle, Cornwall; *Heir* da, Mistress of Mar; *Career* British Telecom sales superintendent until 1982; goats' cheese maker (memb Specialist Cheese Makers Assoc); patron Gulf Veterans' Assoc and several ME charities; lay memb Immigration Appeals Tbnl; pres: Three Counties Agric Soc 2003, Elderly Accommodation Counsel; chm HonestFood; BBC Wildlife Magazine Green Ribbon Award 1997, Spectator Peer of the Year 1997, Laurent Perrier/Country Life Parliamentarian of the Year 1996; hon assoc RCVS 2006; *Recreations* gardening, painting, interior decoration; *Style*— The Rt Hon the Countess of Mar; ✉ St Michael's Farm, Great Witley, Worcester WR6 6JB (e-mail marm@parliament.uk)

MAR AND KELLIE, 14 and 16 Earl of (S 1565, 1619); James Thorne Erskine (Jamie); DL (Clackmannan, 1991); also Lord Erskine (S 1426), Baron Erskine of Dirletowne (*sic* as stated by The Complete Peerage, S 1604), and Viscount of Fentoun (S 1606), and Lord Dirletoun (S 1603); sits as Baron Erskine of Alloa Tower (Life Peer UK 2000), of Alloa, Clackmannanshire; also Hereditary Keeper of Stirling Castle; s of Maj the 13 Earl of Mar (and 15 of) Kellie, JP (d 1993), and Pansy Constance, OBE, JP, *née* Thorne (d 1996); *b* 10 March 1949; *Educ* Eton, Moray House Coll of Educn Edinburgh (Dip Social Work, Dip Youth and Co Work), Inverness Coll (Certificate in Bldg); *m* 1974, Mary Irene (Vice Lord-Lt Clackmannanshire 2007), yr da of Dougal McDougal Kirk (d 1992), of Edinburgh; 5 step c (1 decd); *Heir* bro, Hon Alexander Erskine; *Career* estate mangr; sits as a Scottish Lib Dem life peer in the House of Lords (hereditary 1994–99); Pilot Offr RAuxAF Regt 1979–82, Flying Offr 1982–86 (2622 Highland Sqdn), memb RNXS 1985–89; page of honour to HM The Queen 1962–63; community serv volunteer York 1967–68, youth and community worker Craigmillar 1971–73; social worker: Sheffield 1973–76, Elgin 1976–77,

Forres 1977–78, Aviemore 1979, HM Prison Inverness 1979–81, Inverness West 1981, Merkinch 1982; supervisor Community Serv by Offenders Inverness 1983–87, memb Visiting Ctee HM Young Offenders Inst Glenochil; bldg technician 1989–91; project worker SACRO Central Intensive Probation Project Falkirk 1991–93; canoe and small boat builder 1993–94; chm Strathclyde Tram Inquiry 1996; cmmr Burrell Collection (lending) Inquiry 1997; contested Ochil Scottish Parly elections 1999, Mid-Scotland and Fife regnl list (Lib Dem); appointed to House of Lords Select Ctee on the Constitution 2001–05, memb Religious Offences Select Ctee 2002–03, asst whip 2003–07, memb House of Lords Admin and Works Ctee 2004–, asst tport spokesman 2005–; memb Independence Convention 2004–; *Recreations* open canoeing, Alloa Tower, hill walking, gardening, Church of Scotland, railways; *Clubs* Farmers'; *Style*— The Earl of Mar and Kellie; ✉ Hilton Farm, Alloa, Clackmannanshire FK10 3PS (tel 01259 212438, fax 01259 212020)

MARAN, Prof Arnold George Dominic; s of John Maran (d 1969), of Edinburgh, and Hilda, *née* Mancini (d 1984); *b* 16 June 1936; *Educ* Daniel Stewart's Coll Edinburgh, Univ of Edinburgh (MB ChB, MD); *m* 25 April 1962, Anna Marie Terese; 1 da (Nicola Jane b 1963), 1 s (Charles Mark Damien b 1965); *Career* prof of otolaryngology Univ of Edinburgh; author of over 160 scientific papers; pres RCSEd, past pres Laryngology Section RSM; FRCSEd 1963, FACS 1974, FRCP 1988, FRCS 1991, Hon FDSRCS 1994, Hon FCS (S Africa), Hon FCS (Hong Kong) 1997, Hon FAM (Sing) (fell Acad of Med of Singapore); *Books* Clinical Otolaryngology (1964, 2 edn 1972), Head and Neck Surgery (1969, 4 edn 2000), Clinical Rhinology (1990); *Recreations* music, golf, travel; *Clubs* New (Edinburgh), Royal & Ancient Golf (St Andrews); *Style*— Prof Arnold Maran; ✉ 27 Learmonth Terrace, Edinburgh (tel 0131 332 0055); 2 Double Dykes Road, St Andrews (tel 013347 2939); 14 Moray Place, Edinburgh (tel 0131 225 8025); Royal College of Surgeons of Edinburgh, Nicolson Street, Edinburgh EH8 (DW (tel 0131 527 1635, fax 0131 557 9771)

MARANZANO, Alexander Mario (Alex); s of Michele Luciano Maranzano, and Iole, *née* Iannamico; *b* 27 November 1943; *Educ* RCA (MDes), Camberwell Coll of Art (NDD); *m* 14 Sept 1968, Rosemary Jean, da of Dennis Norman Licence; 3 s (Damian Paul b 27 Sept 1970 d 1989, Michael Anthony b 15 May 1976, James William b 25 May 1979), 1 da (Sonia Elisa b 13 May 1972); *Career* designer; Minale Tattersfield & Partners Ltd: joined 1968, ptnr and dep md 1983, md 1988–2001, chm 2001–; Gold award for Fox corp identify design NY 1976, Silver award Designers and Arts Dirs Club London for Heathrow subways 1978, designed Central TV symbol 1982, Most Outstanding Graphics Silver award for PO applied design 1984, designed concept for Br Airports Exhbn in MOMA NY; memb Exec Ctee D&AD 1985–87; FCSD; *Style*— Alex Maranzano, Esq, FCSD, FRSA; ✉ Minale Tattersfield & Partners Ltd, The Poppy Factory, 20 Petersham Road, Richmond, Surrey TW10 6UB (tel 020 8948 7999, fax 020 8948 2435, telex 8953130, e-mail alex@mintat.co.uk)

MARBER, Patrick; *b* 19 September 1964; *Educ* Wadham Coll, Univ of Oxford; *Career* writer, actor and director; FRSL; *Theatre* as dir and/or writer: '1953' (Almeida), Dealer's Choice (RNT and Vaudeville, Evening Standard Award for Best Comedy 1995, Writer's Guild Award for Best West End Play 1995), Blue Remembered Hills (RNT), Closer (RNT, Lyric and Broadway, Evening Standard Best Comedy Award 1997, Critics' Circle Best Play Award 1997, Olivier Award for Best New Play 1998, NY Drama Critics' Circle Award for Best Foreign Play), The Old Neighborhood (Royal Court at the Duke of Yorks), The Caretaker (Comedy), Howard Katz (RNT), Don Juan in Soho (Donmar Warehouse); *Television* as writer and actor for BBC2 incl: The Day Today, Paul Calf Video Diary, Knowing Me Knowing You, 3 Fights 2 Weddings and a Funeral (BAFTA Award); as writer and dir for BBC2 incl: The Curator, After Miss Julie; *Film* Closer (adaptation) 2004, Asylum 2005, Notes on a Scandal (adaptation) 2006; *Publications* Dealer's Choice (1995), After Miss Julie (1996), Closer (1997), Howard Katz (2001); *Style*— Patrick Marber, Esq

MARCELL, Philip Michael; s of Stanley Marcell (d 1972), and Mabel Isobel Thomas, *née* Coe; *b* 21 August 1936; *Educ* Wimbledon Coll, BRNC Dartmouth, RNC Greenwich, Univ of London (LLB), Cambridge (postgrad res); *m* 22 Dec 1962, Lucina Mary, da of Capt Ernest May (d 1988); 3 da (Susannah b 1964, Virginia b 1965, Harriet b 1973), 1 s (Andrew b 1967); *Career* RN cadet BRNC Dartmouth 1952–54, Midshipman 1955, Sub Lt 1956, Lt 1958, Lt Cdr 1966, Cdr 1972; dir Jardines Insurance Brokers 1980 (co sec 1978), chief exec American Reinsurance Co (UK) Ltd 1983; chm: Continental Reinsurance London, Continental Reinsurance Corp (UK) Ltd 1986–93, Unionamerica Insurance Co Ltd 1986–97; dir London Underwriting Centre Ltd 1994–98; non-exec chm Apollo Underwriting Ltd 1997–99; non-exec dir: Aegis Managing Agency Ltd 2000–06, TAWA (UK) Ltd 2002–05, CX Re 2005–; memb: Exec Ctee Reinsurance Offices Assoc 1985–90, Cncl London Insurance and Reinsurance Market Assoc (successor body to ROA) 1991–99 (chm 1995–97); Freeman Worshipful Co of Chartered Secs and Admins (Master 2001–02); FIFA 1977, MIMgt 1978, FCIS 1987; *Recreations* skiing, golf, sailing; *Clubs* Oxford and Cambridge; *Style*— Philip Marcell, Esq; ✉ Weavers End, Church Lane, Haslemere, Surrey GU27 2BJ (tel 01428 651421, fax 01428 641307)

MARCH, Lionel John; o s of Leonard March, and Rose March; *b* 26 January 1934; *Educ* Hove GS for Boys, Magdalene Coll Cambridge (state scholar, DipArch, MA, ScD); *m* 1 (m dis); 2 da (Candida b 1961, Talitha b 1966), 1 s (Ben b 1964); m 2, 23 July 1984, Maureen Mary Vidler; 1 step s (Ben b 1964), 2 step da (Anna b 1968, Sarah b 1969); *Career* Nat Serv Sub Lt RN 1953–55; Harkness fell (Cwlth Fund) Jt Centre for Urban Studies Harvard Univ and MIT 1962–64; Univ of Cambridge: res offr Estate Mgmnt Advsy Serv 1961–62, asst lectr Dept of Architecture 1966–67, dir Centre for Land Use and Built Form Studies 1969–73, lectr Dept of Architecture 1968–69 and 1973–76; prof Dept of Systems Design Faculty of Engrg Univ of Waterloo Ontario 1974–76, prof of design and head of design discipline Faculty of Technol Open Univ 1976–81, rector and vice-provost RCA London 1981–84, prof Grad Sch of Architecture and Urban Planning UCLA 1984–94 (vice-chm and head Architectural Prog 1985–90), prof emeritus of design and computation Sch of the Arts and Architecture UCLA 1994–2004; chm Bd of Dirs Applied Research of Cambridge Ltd 1969–73, vice-pres Applied Research of Cambridge (Canada) Ltd Toronto 1975–77, govr Imperial Coll of Science and Technol London 1981–84, memb Center for Medieval and Renaissance Studies UCLA 1992–; gen ed (with Sir Leslie Martin) Cambridge Urban and Architectural Studies 1970–, fndr ed Environment and Planning Series B Int Jl of Architectural and Design Science 1974–; FIMA 1979, FRSA 1979, FRCA 1981; *Books* Whitehall: A Plan for the Government and National Centre (with Sir Leslie Martin, 1965), The Geometry of Environment (with Philip Steadman, 1971), Urban Space and Structures (ed with Sir Leslie Martin, 1972), The Architecture of Form (ed, 1976), R M Schindler - Composition and Construction (ed with Judith Sheine, 1993), Architectonics of Humanism: Essays on Number in Architecture (1998); *Style*— Mr Lionel March; ✉ Spring Cottage, 20 High Street, Stretham, Cambridgeshire CB6 3JQ (tel 01353 649880, e-mail lmarch@ucla.edu)

MARCH, Prof Norman Henry; s of William Henry March, and Elsie May, *née* Brown; *b* 9 July 1927; *Educ* King Edward VII GS Coalville Leicester, KCL (BSc, PhD); *m* 23 April 1949, (Margaret) Joan (d 1994), da of George Hoyle; 2 s (Peter Henry b 1 May 1951, Anthony John b 29 March 1953); *Career* prof of physics Univ of Sheffield 1961–72, prof of theoretical solid-state physics Imperial Coll London 1972–77, Coulson prof and head Dept of Theoretical Chemistry Univ of Oxford 1977–94, professorial fell UC Oxford 1977–94, prof emeritus 1994–; former chm: Condensed Matter Physics Ctee Inst of Physics London, Advsy Ctee on Condensed Matter Int Centre for Theoretical Physics Trieste; Hon DTech Chalmers Univ Gothenburg 1980, Hon DPhys Catania Univ 2003; *Books* The Many-Body Problem in Quantum Mechanics (with W H Young and S Sampanthar, 1967), Liquid Metals (1968), Theoretical Solid State Physics (with W Jones, 1973), Self-Consistent Fields in Atoms (1974), Orbital Theories of Molecules and Solids (1974), Atomic Dynamics in Liquids (with M P Tosi, 1976), Collective Effects in Solids and Liquids (with M Parrinello, 1983), The Theory of the Inhomogeneous Electron Gas (with S Lundqvist, 1983), Coulomb Liquids (with M P Tosi, 1984), Amorphous Solids and the Liquid State (with M P Tosi, 1985), Chemical Bonds Outside Metal Surfaces (1986), Crystalline Semiconducting Materials and Devices (with P N Butcher and M P Tosi, 1986), The Single Particle Density in Physics and Chemistry (with B M Deb, 1987), Order and Chaos in Nonlinear Physical Systems (with S Lundqvist and M P Tosi, 1988), Electrons in Metals and Alloys (with J A Alonso, 1989), Liquid Metals - Concepts and Theory (1990), Chemical Physics of Liquids (1990), Electron Density Theory of Atoms and Molecules (1991), Chemical Physics of Free Molecules (with J F Mucci, 1993), Atoms and Molecules in Intense External Fields (with L S Cederbaum and K C Kulander, 1996), Electron Correlation in Molecules and Condensed Phases (1997), Mechanical Properties of Metals (with C W Lung, 1999), Electron Correlation in the Solid State (1999), An Introduction to Liquid State Physics (with M P Tosi, 2002); *Recreations* music, chess; *Style*— Prof Norman March; ✉ 66A Lancaster Road, Carnforth, Lancashire LA5 9LE

MARCH, Peter Reginald; s of Edwin Charles March (d 1987), of Bristol, and Alice Gladys, *née* Cave (d 1988); *b* 23 March 1940; *Educ* Bristol GS, Redland Coll, Univ of Bristol (ACE, DipEd); *m* 25 Aug 1962, Christine Ann, da of Ernest William Clark (d 1973), of Poole, Dorset; 2 s (Andrew b 1965, Daniel b 1972), 2 da (Alison b 1967, Rachel b 1974); *Career* contrib ed Aircraft Illustrated 1968–; Careers Res and Advsy Centre 1972, princ careers advsr Co of Avon 1974–87, managing ed RAF Benevolent Fund Publishing 1987–; freelance aviation broadcaster; aviation correspondent ITV West 1989–; chm Air Display Assoc UK 1994; ed: RAF Yearbook 1986–, Air Display International 1987–92, USAF Yearbook 1988–2004; contrib ed Air World International 1995–96, contrib ed Pilot Magazine 1998–; dir PRM Aviation Photo Library; *Books* 17+ Decisions - Your Choice Beyond School, Military Aircraft Markings (1978–2007), Preserved Aircraft (1980), Confederate Air Force (1991), Civil Airliner Recognition (1991, 1993, 1995, 1997 and 1999), Desert Warpaint (1991), Combat Aircraft Recognition (1991, 1998), Light Aircraft Recognition (1992, 1995 and 1997), Brace by Wire to Fly by Wire (1993 and 1998), International Air Tattoo 93 (1993), Royal Air Force Almanac (1994), International Air Tattoo 94 (1994), The Real Aviation Enthusiast II (1995), Hawk Comes of Age (1995), International Air Tattoo Silver Jubilee (1996), Sabre to Stealth (1997), abc Biz Jets (1997), Confederate Air Force - celebrating 40 Years (1997), Sabre to Stealth (1998), Eagles (1998), Freedom of the Skies (1999), Warplanes (2000), Directory of Military Aircraft of the World (2001), Wright to Fly (2002), The Concorde Story (2005), The Spitfire Story (2006), The Vulcan Story (2006), The Red Arrows Story (2006), Top Trumps Fighter Aircraft (2006), Top Trumps Airliners (2007), The Harrier Story (2007), The Hurricane Story (2007); *Recreations* private flying, photography; *Style*— Peter March, Esq; ✉ 25 Sabrina Way, Stoke Bishop, Bristol BS9 1ST (tel 0117 968 5193, e-mail peter.march@blueyonder.co.uk)

MARCHANT, Ian; s of Derek William Marchant, of Crawley, W Sussex, and Rosemary, *née* Bode; *b* 9 February 1961; *Educ* Trinity Sch Croydon, Univ of Durham (BA); *m* Elizabeth Helen; 1 da (Sarah Elizabeth b 4 Dec 1990), 1 s (James Richard b 18 Aug 1994); *Career* with Coopers & Lybrand 1983–92 (seconded Dept of Energy 1989–90); Scottish and Southern Energy plc (formerly Southern Electric plc): head of corp fin planning 1992–95, chief exec SE Power Generation 1995–96, gp fin dir 1996–2002, chief exec 2002–; non-exec dir John Wood Gp plc 2006–; chm UK Business Cncl for Sustainable Energy, memb Environmental Advsy Gp Ofgem, memb Energy Research Partnership; ACA 1983; *Recreations* golf, watching sport, travelling, reading; *Style*— Ian Marchant, Esq

MARCHANT, Peter James; s of Clifford James Marchant, of Bexhill, E Sussex, and Vivian Breta, *née* Sargent; *b* 7 September 1943; *Educ* Bexhill GS for Boys, Portsmouth Poly (HND); *m* 4 Oct 1969, Angela May, da of Walter Sydney Foster; 1 s (Christopher James b 28 Aug 1970), 1 da (Helen Elizabeth b 10 July 1973); *Career* engr BBC Engrg 1962–69, asst chief engr Centre for Educnl Television Overseas 1969; ITN: maintenance engr with special responsibility for intro of colour 1969–74, supervisory engr responsible for Television Standards conversion 1974–76, engrg mangr 1976–89, dep dir of engrg 1986–89; chief engr BBC Television 1989–94, chief engr (television) National Transcommunications Ltd (NTL) 1994–96, chief engr Channel Four Television Corporation 1996–2000, broadcast engrg conslt 2000–; CEng, FIET, FRTS; *Recreations* flying (PPL), languages, organ and piano; *Clubs* RAF Henlow Flying; *Style*— Peter Marchant; ✉ tel 01462 459465, e-mail peter@pmarchant.co.uk

MARCHANT, Ronald John; CB (2007); s of Arthur Ronald Marchant, of Brightlingsea, Essex, and late Bridget, *née* Dockery; *b* 6 November 1945, Glasgow; *Educ* West Ham Coll of Technol (BSc); *m* Aug 1969, Helen, *née* Walker; 3 da (Emma b 18 Jan 1971, Kate b 8 Sept 1977, Anna b 6 June 1980), 1 s (Karl b 28 Sept 1973); *Career* Patent Office: joined as examiner 1969, princ examiner i/c automation and examiner HR 1990, asst comptroller Patents 1992, ceo and comptroller gen 2003; Best Achievement in Nat and Int Affrs The European IP Awards 2006, World Leaders The European IP Awards 2006; FRSA; *Recreations* hill walking, reading, music, grandchildren; *Style*— Ronald Marchant, CB, FRSA; ✉ Ty Heol, The Landing, Pentwyn, Pontipool, Torfaen NP4 7TL

MARCHINGTON, Dr Anthony Frank (Tony); *b* 2 December 1955; *Educ* New Mills Sch, BNC Oxford (Hulme open exhbn, Brasenose Fndn travel scholar, MA, DPhil); *m* 1995, Caroline, *née* Purseglove; 1 s David (b 1996); 2 s from previous m (Robert b 1983, Joseph b 1985); *Career* product mangr ICI Plant Protection Div 1983–86 (technical offr 1979–83), mktg mangr ICI Agrochemicals S America 1986–87; md: Buxworth Steam Co Ltd 1987–89, Oxford Molecular Ltd 1989–94; ceo Oxford Molecular plc 1994; memb: Health & Life Sciences Panel Technology Foresight, Competitiveness Ctee DTI 1997–; co-scriptwriter and asst dir Through Joy and Beyond (documentary life of C S Lewis) 1978, subject of documentary film A Gambol on Steam (BBC 1) 1985; fndr Flying Scotsman Railways Ltd (now non-exec dir); Freeman City of London 1997, Liveryman Worshipful Co of Painter Stainers 1997; FRSA, FRSC; *Books* Bibliography of Ab-initio Molecular Wave Functions (1978); author of numerous papers, patents and monographs; *Recreations* Industrial Revolution, steam engines, English traditional fairgrounds, farming, English countryside, history, literature, sport; *Clubs* Oxford and Cambridge, IOD; *Style*— Dr Tony Marchington

MARCHWOOD, 3 Viscount (UK 1945); Sir David George Staveley Penny; 3 Bt (UK 1933); also Baron Marchwood (UK 1937); s of 2 Viscount Marchwood, MBE (d 1979), and Pamela, *née* Colton Fox; *b* 22 May 1936; *Educ* Winchester; *m* 1, 1964, Tessa Jane (d 1997), da of Wilfred Francis Norris, of Lurgashall, W Sussex; 3 s (Hon Peter b 1965, Hon Nicholas b 1967, Hon Edward b 1970); m 2, 2001, Sylva, wid of Peter Willis Fleming; *Heir* s, Hon Peter Penny, *qv*; *Career* 2 Lt, Royal Horse Gds (The Blues) in UK and Cyprus 1955–57; former dir of various cos in Cadbury Schweppes Group; former chm Moët Hennessy (UK) Ltd and former dir other cos in Moët Hennessy Group; pres Royal Warrant Holders Assoc 2002–03; *Recreations* real tennis, shooting, racing, golf; *Clubs* White's, Twelve, MCC; *Style*— The Rt Hon the Viscount Marchwood; ✉ Woodcock Farm, Chedington, Beaminster DT8 3JA (tel 01935 891444)

M

MARCUS, Marshall; s of Hyman Marcus, and Betty, *née* Gaunt; *b* 29 January 1955; *Educ* Leeds GS, Royal Coll of Music (ARCM), The Queen's Coll Oxford (MA), Trinity Coll Cambridge (CertEd); *m* 1984, Annia Casagrande; 2 da (Gaia b 2 Dec 1986, Elena b 29 March 1989); *Career* memb BBC Symphony Orch 1977–79, concert master Orquesta Philarmonica de Caracas 1979–81, prof Orquesta Juvenil de Venezuela, ldr Orch of St John's Smith Square 1988–94, chief exec Orch of the Age of Enlightenment (OAE) 2003–06 (chm 1994–2003), head of music Southbank Centre 2006–; memb Endymion Ensemble 1982–2002; performed in over 50 countries, appeared as a soloist in UK, Holland, Italy, Venezuela, Austria, Canada and USA; recordings with various London gps; teacher period instrument techniques: Royal Coll of Music, Royal Acad of Music, Nat Youth Orch of GB, Univ of Bristol, Universidad de Valparaiso de Chile, Camerata de Caracas Venezuela, Britten Pears Sch; designer and ldr of creative music projects at primary schs, secdy schs and univs; *Recreations* mountains, reading, jazz, skiing, the arts; *Style—* Marshall Marcus, Esq; ✉ Southbank Centre, Belvedere Road, London SE1 8XX (tel 020 7921 0835, e-mail marshall.marcus@southbankcentre.co.uk)

MARCUS, Steven David; s of Gerald Marcus, of Bushey, Herts, and Joan Kasmir; *b* 5 October 1951; *Educ* Merchant Taylors', Univ of Nottingham (BSc); *m* 5 Sept 1979, Madeleine, da of Godfrey Lee; *Career* Grant and Partners 1973–76 (jr negotiator, sr negotiator), Jones Lang Wootton 1976–78, assoc Allsop & Co 1978–84, ptnr then exec dir Druce & Co 1984–92 sr ptnr Marcus & Co 1992–; FRICS (prof assoc 1979); *Style—* Steven Marcus, Esq; ✉ Marcus & Co, Canons House, 7 Handel Close, Canons Drive, Edgware, Middlesex HA8 7QZ (tel 020 8952 3636, fax 020 8952 6633)

MAREK, Dr John; *b* 24 December 1940; *Educ* KCL (BSc, PhD); *m* 1964, Anne (d 2006), da of R H Pritchard; *Career* lectr in applied mathematics UCW Aberystwyth 1966–83; MP (Lab) Wrexham 1983–2001, oppn front bench spokesman: on health 1985–87, on Civil Service and Treasy matters 1987–92; memb Nat Assembly for Wales: (Lab) Wrexham 1999–2003, (Ind) Wrexham 2003–07; dep presiding offr Nat Assembly for Wales 2001–07; treas Cwlth Parly Assoc 2000–03; memb Int Astronomical Union; *Style—* Dr John Marek

MARENBON, Dr John Alexander; s of Arthur Marenbon (d 1984), of London, and Zena, *née* Jacobs; *b* 26 August 1955; *Educ* Westminster, Trinity Coll Cambridge (MA, PhD), Univ of Cambridge (LittD); *m* 1981, Sheila Margaret Mary, da of Arthur C Lawlor; 1 s (Maximus John Arthur b 10 Dec 1989); *Career* Trinity Coll Cambridge: research fell 1978–79, fell and dir of studies in English 1979–97, British Acad research reader 1991–93, fell in history of philosophy 1997–2004, sr research fell 2005–; memb Schs Examination and Assessment Cncl (SEAC) 1992–93; *Books* From the Circle of Alcuin to the School of Auxerre (1981), Early Medieval Philosophy (1983), Later Medieval Philosophy (1987), Aristotle in Britain during the Middle Ages (1996), The Philosophy of Peter Abelard (1997), Routledge History of Philosophy III: Medieval Philosophy (1998), Aristotelian Logic, Platonism and the Context of Early Medieval Philosophy in the West (2000), Poetry and Philosophy in the Middle Ages (ed, 2001), Peter Abelard: Collationes (ed with G Orlandi, 2001), Boethius (2003), Le Temps, la Prescience et les Futurs Contingents, de Boèce à Thomas d'Aquin (2005), Medieval Philosophy: An historical and philosophical introduction (2007); *Style—* Dr John Marenbon; ✉ Trinity College, Cambridge CB2 1TQ (tel 01223 338524, e-mail jm258@cam.ac.uk)

MARGADALE, 3 Baron (UK 1964); Alastair John Morrison; s of 2 Baron Margadale (d 2003), and Clare, *née* Barclay; *b* 4 April 1958; *Educ* Harrow, RAC Cirencester; *m* 1 (m dis); 1 s (Hon Declan James b 1993), 1 da (Hon Nancy Lorna b 1995); m 2, 2 Sept 1999, Amanda, *née* Fuller; *Heir* s, Hon Declan Morrison; *Career* ran film catering and hotel business, upkeep of estates in Wilts and Islay; pres Salisbury Cons Assoc, involved with various charities; *Recreations* racing and breeding, shooting, hunting, fishing; *Clubs* White's, Turf, Pratt's, Caledonian; *Style—* The Rt Hon the Lord Margadale; ✉ Fonthill Estate Office, Fonthill Bishop, Salisbury, Wiltshire SP2 5SH (tel 01747 820246)

MARGESSON, 2 Viscount (UK 1942); Francis Vere Hampden Margesson; s of 1 Viscount, PC, MC (d 1965, whose mother was Lady Isabel Hobart-Hampden, JP, 3 da of 7 Earl of Buckinghamshire); *b* 17 April 1922; *Educ* Eton, Trinity Coll Oxford; *m* 1958, Helena, da of late Heikki Backstrom, of Oulu, Finland; 1 s, 3 da; *Heir* s, Maj the Hon Richard Margesson; *Career* late ADC to Govr Bahamas, dir Thames & Hudson Publications Inc of N Y; Sub-Lt RNVR 1942–45; info offr Br Consulate-Gen N Y 1964–70; *Style—* The Rt Hon the Viscount Margesson; ✉ 63 The Hills, Port Ewen, NY 12466, USA

MARGETTS, Sir Robert John (Rob); kt (2006), CBE (1996); s of John William (decd) and Ellen Mary Margetts (decd); *b* 10 November 1946; *Educ* Highgate Sch, Univ of Cambridge (BA); *m* Joan Sandra; 3 s, 1 da; *Career* ICI plc: joined as process design engr 1969, dir Agricultural Div 1982–85, dir Petrochemicals & Plastics Div 1985, dir Research & Operations Chemicals & Polymers Gp 1987, dir ICI Engrg 1987–89, gen mangr personnel 1989–90, chm and chief exec Tioxide Gp 1991–92, exec dir 1992–97, vice-chm 1998–2000, chm ICI Pension Fund Tstee Ltd 1994–2000; chm Europe Huntsman Corp 2000–; non-exec dir: English China Clays plc 1992–99, Legal and General Gp plc 1996– (vice-chm 1998–2000, chm 2000–), Anglo American plc 1999– (sr ind dir 2003–), BOC Group plc 2001– (dep chm 2001–02, chm 2002–); govr memb Fin Ctee ICSTM 1991–2004; vice-pres Royal Acad Engrg 1994–97; chm: Action for Engrg 1995–97, NERC 2001–06, Govt Industry Forum Non-Food Uses of Crops 2001–04; dir Fndn for Science and Technology; tstee: Cncl for Industry and HE 2001– (memb 1992–), Brain Research Tst 2002–; memb: CIA Cncl 1992–96 and 2001–, Bd CEFIC 1993–95 and 1998–2000, Cncl for Sci and Technol 1998–, Advsy Ctee on Business and the Environment 1999–2001, Technol Foresight Steering Gp, Economy and Science & Technol Honours Ctees 2005–, Advsy Bd Teijin Ltd Japan 2004–06; Hon Freeman Salters' Co, Freeman City of London 2004; memb Ct Univ of Surrey; Hon DEng Univ of Sheffield 1997, Hon DSc Cranfield Univ 2003; hon fell Imperial Coll London 1999; fell City and London Guilds 2001, FREng, FIChemE; *Recreations* sailing, skiing, tennis, watersports; *Style—* Sir Rob Margetts, CBE, FREng; ✉ Huntsman Corporation, c/o Matlin Patterson, 7th Floor, Buchanan House, 3 St James's Square, London SW1Y 4JU

MARGO, David Philip; s of Gerald Margo, of Bexleyheath, Kent, and Rene, *née* Goldstein; *b* 14 May 1951; *Educ* Chislehurst and Sidcup GS for Boys; *m* 14 Nov 1976, Lezley Susan (d 1991), da of Maurice and Helen Kaye, of Bournemouth, Dorset; 2 da (Jodi Rochelle b 1980, Kerri Miriam b 1984), 1 s (Alexi Nicholas b 1981); *Career* admitted slr 1975; ptnr: Forsythe Saunders Kerman (formerly Saunders Sobell Leigh & Dobin) 1975–98, Lawrence Graham LLP 1998–2007; memb Law Soc; *Publications* A Practical Legal Approach to Problems in the Petrol Filling Station Letting Market (in Jl of Rent Review and Lease Renewal); *Recreations* bridge, running; *Style—* David Margo, Esq

MARGOLYES, Miriam; OBE (2002); *b* 1941, Oxford; *Educ* Newnham Coll Cambridge; *Career* actress; BBC Drama Co; *Theatre* credits incl: The Threepenny Opera, 84 Charing Cross Road, The White Devil, Orpheus Descending (with Vanessa Redgrave, *qv*), She Stoops to Conquer (for Sir Peter Hall, *qv*), Gertrude Stein & Companion (fringe first Award 1986), Little Dorrit, The Killing of Sister George, Dickens' Women; *Television* numerous comedy & drama credits incl: The Girls of Slender Means, Blackadder, Old Flames, Cold Comfort Farm, The History of Man, Oliver Twist, The Lost Tribe, Life & Loves of a She-Devil, Frannie's Turn (USA), Vanity Fair, Supply and Demand, The Phoenix and the Carpet; numerous guest appearances incl: Johnny Carson, Jay Leno, Terry Wogan, Michael Aspel; *Radio* and recordings incl: The Queen & I, Oliver Twist (Gramaphone Magazine's Best Audio Book 1994), Great Expectations (with Martin Jarvis, *qv*), A Christmas Carol; *Film* The Age of Innocence, Pacific Heights, Dead Again, I Love You to Death, As You Like It, The Fool, Ed & His Dead Mother, Stalin, Immortal Beloved, The Simon Wiesenthal Story, Balto, James and the Giant Peach, Romeo & Juliet, Different for Girls, The Nutcracker, Left Luggage, Fly's voice in Babe and Babe in the City, House, End of Days, Sunshine, Cats & Dogs, Harry Potter and the Chamber of Secrets, Life and Death of Peter Sellers, Being Julia, Chasing Liberty, Modigliani, Ladies in Lavender; *Awards* LA Critics' Best Supporting Actress for Little Dorrit 1989, Sony Best Actress Award for The Queen & I 1993, BAFTA Best Supporting Actress for The Age of Innocence 1994, Talkies Best Performer 1998; *Style—* Ms Miriam Margolyes, OBE; ✉ c/o PFD, Drury House, 34–43 Russell Street, London WC2B 5HA (tel 020 7344 1010, fax 020 7836 9539)

MARGRETT, David Basil; s of Basil Stanley Margrett, of Yelverton, Devon, and Kathleen Hilda Nellie, *née* Hayter; *b* 25 October 1953; *Educ* Plymouth Poly; *m* 15 March 1985, Pauline Annette, da of Donald Lowe; 2 s (Charles, Richard); *Career* chief exec Heath Lambert Gp 1996–2004 (joined predecessor co 1973); Willis Gp Holdings Ltd: md global markets 2004–05, ceo global specialities 2005–, memb Ptnrs Gp 2005–; *Style—* David Margrett, Esq; ✉ Willis Limited, Ten Trinity Square, London EC3P 3AX

MARGRIE, Prof Victor Robert; CBE (1984); s of Robert Margrie, of London, and Emily Miriam, *née* Corbett; *b* 29 December 1929; *Educ* Southgate Co GS, Hornsey Sch of Art (NDD, ATD); *m* 1, 1955 (m dis), Janet, *née* Smithers; 3 da (Joanna b 19 Oct 1959, Kate b 26 Dec 1961, Miriam b 10 Sept 1963); m 2, 2005, Rosemary, *née* Ash; *Career* own workshop 1952–71, pt/t teaching London Colls of Art and Design 1952–56, head of ceramics and sculpture Harrow Sch of Art 1956–71 (fndr studio pottery course 1963), sec Crafts Advsy Ctee 1971–77, dir Crafts Cncl 1977–84, prof RCA 1984–85, studio potter, critic and teacher 1985–, prof Univ of Westminster 1992–96; solo exhibitions Crafts Centre of GB (now Contemporary Applied Arts) 1964, 1966 and 1969, currently represented in Ashmolean Museum, V&A and other collections; external advsr: UWE Dept of Ceramics 1987–, Goldsmiths Coll London 1989–93, Sch of Fine Art Cardiff Inst of HE 1991–93, Nat Video and Electronic Archive of the Crafts 1993–; memb: Advsy Cncl Victoria and Albert Museum 1979–84, Ctee for Art and Design CNAA 1981–84, Fine Art Advsy Ctee Br Cncl 1983–86, UK Nat Cmmn UNESCO 1984–85, Faculty of Visual Arts Banff Centre for the Arts Alberta 1988–, Bd Studies in Fine Art Univ of London 1989–94, Founding Ctee National Centre of Ceramic Art 1996–98; govr Loughborough Coll of Art and Design 1984–92, memb Craft Initiative Gulbenkian Fndn 1985–89; memb: Craftsmen Potters Assoc 1960–89, Int Acad of Ceramics 1971, FCSD 1975; *Books* contrib: Europaische Keramik Seit 1950–79 (1979), Oxford Dictionary of Decorative Arts (1975), Lucie Rie (1981); assoc ed Studio Pottery 1993–2000, Ceramics in Society 2000–05; *Recreations* contemporary music and cooking; *Style—* Prof Victor Margrie, CBE; ✉ Bowlders, Doccombe, Moretonhampstead, Devon TQ13 8SS (tel 01647 440264)

MARKESINIS, Prof Sir Basil Spyridonos; kt (2005), QC; s of Spyros Markesinis, former PM of Greece, and Ieta Markesinis; *b* 10 July 1944; *Educ* Univ of Athens (LLB, DIur), Univ of Cambridge (Yorke prize, MA, PhD, LLD), Univ of Oxford (DCL); *m* 5 Sept 1970, Eugenie, da of late George Trypanis; 1 da (Julietta b 6 July 1971), 1 s (Spyros George b 30 Jan 1976); *Career* asst prof Law Faculty Univ of Athens 1965–68; Univ of Cambridge: res fell Churchill Coll 1970–73, fell Trinity Coll and dir of studies in law 1974–86, univ lectr 1974–86; Denning prof of comparative law Univ of London 1986–93 (dep dir Centre for Commercial Law Studies Queen Mary & Westfield Coll), prof of European private law UCL 1993–95; Univ of Oxford: prof of European law 1995–99, fndr and dir Inst of European Law and Comparative Law 1995–2000, prof of comparative law 1999–2000, fell BNC 1999–2000; prof of common law and civil law UCL 2001 (fndr and chm Inst of Global Law UCL); prof of Anglo-American private law Univ of Leiden 1986–2000 (fndr and dir Leiden Inst of Anglo-American Law), Jamail Regents chair in law Univ of Texas at Austin 1998–; Francqui visiting prof Univ of Ghent 1989–90 and 2004–06; professore a contratto: Univ of Siena 1985–86, Univ of Rome 1996; visiting prof: Cornell Law Sch (fall terms) 1981–84, Univ of Paris I & II 1982–83, Univ of Michigan Ann Arbor (fall term) 1986, Univ of Texas at Austin (fall terms) 1985, 1987–94 and 1996; Conseiller Scientifique du Premier Président de la Cour de Cassation France 2002–; special advsr for European affrs Clifford Chance 1999–2002; called to the Bar Gray's Inn 1973 (bencher 1991), advocate to the Supreme Court Athens 1976–86; Leverhulme fell 1981; Atkin lectr Reform Club 1989, Shimizhu lectr LSE 1991, Cohen lectr Hebrew Univ of Jerusalem 1993, Wilberforce lectr 1998, John Maurice Kelly meml lectr 2003, Eason-Weinmann lectr Tulane Law Sch 2005, Peter Taylor meml lectr Inner Temple 2006, Denning lectr Lincoln's Inn 2007; Humboldt Forschungspreise 1995, Silver Medal Univ of Leiden 1996; DIur (hc): Univ of Ghent 1992, Univ of Paris I (Panthéon-Sorbonne) 1998, Univ of Munich 1999, Univ of Athens 2007; memb: Int Acad of Comparative Law 1987–98, American Law Inst 1989, Institut Canadien d'Études Juridiques Supérieures 1990, Académie Internationale de Droit Comparé 2004; membre actif Cour d'Arbitrage et de Conciliation Paris 1991; corresponding memb: Unidroit 1992, Institut de France (Académie Sciences Morales et Politiques) 2004; foreign fell: Royal Belgian Acad 1990, Royal Netherlands Acad of Arts and Sciences 1995, Academia dei Lincei Rome 2005; fell Acad of Athens 1994; hon fell: Soc for Advanced Legal Studies 2000, Greek Archaeological Soc 2004; FBA 1997; Offr Ordre Nationale des Palmes Académiques (France) 1992, Cdr Order of Honour (Greece) 2000, Knight Grand Cross del Ordine al Merito (Republic of Italy) 2002 (Offr 1995, Knight Cdr 1999), Knight Cdr Order of Merit (Federal Repub of Germany) 2003 (Offr 1992, Cdr 1999), Commandeur dans l'Ordre National de la Légion d'Honneur 1995 (Chevalier 1995, Officier 2000), Knight Grand Cross Order of Merit (France); *Books* The Mother's Right to Guardianship According to the Greek Civil Code (1968), The Theory and Practice of Dissolution of Parliament (1972), The English Law of Torts - A Comparative Introduction (1976), An Outline of the Law of Agency (co-author, 1979, 4 edn 1998), Richterliche Rechtspolitik im Haftungsrecht (co-author, 1981), Tortious Liability for Unintentional Harm in the Common Law and the Civil Law Vol I and II (co-author, 1982), Tort Law (co-author, 1984, 6 edn 2007), La Réparation du Préjudice Corporel (co-author, 1985), The German Law of Torts - A Comparative Introduction (1986, 4 edn jtly with subtitle A Comparative Treatise, 2002), The Gradual Covergence - Foreign Ideas, Foreign Influences on English Law on the Eve of the 21st Century (ed and contrib, 1994), Bridging the Channel (ed and contrib, 1996), The German Law of Contract and Restitution (co-author, 1997), Foreign Law and Comparative Methodology: A Subject and a Thesis (1997), Law Making, Law Finding, and Law Shaping. The Diverse Influences (ed and contrib, 1997), The Impact of the Human Rights Bill on English Law (ed and contrib, 1998), Protecting Privacy (ed and contrib, 1998), The Coming Together of the Common Law and the Civil Law (ed and contrib, 2000), Tortious Liability of Statutory Bodies (co-author, 2000), Always on the Same Path: Essays on Foreign Law and Comparative Methodology (2001), The British Contribution to the Europe of the Twenty-First Century: The British Academy Centenary Lectures (ed and contrib, 2002), Comparative Law in the Courtroom and the Classroom: The Story of the Last Thirty-Five Years (2003), Compensation for Personal Injury in English, German and Italian Law: A Comparative Overview (co-author 2004), The German Law of Contract. A Comparative Treatise (co-author, 2006), Judicial Recourse to Foreign Law: A New Source of Inspiration? (co-author, 2006), Good and Evil in Art and Law (2007); author of numerous articles in US, Australian, Belgian, British, Canadian, French, German, Greek, Israel and Italian law jls; *Recreations* painting, music, archaeological digging, fund-raising; *Style—* Prof Sir Basil Markesinis, QC, DCL, FBA; ✉ Middleton Stoney House, Oxford Road, Middleton Stoney, Bicester, Oxfordshire OX25 4TE (tel 01869 343560, fax 01869 343562)

MARKEY, Air Vice Marshal Peter Desmond; s of Althorpe Hazel Christopher Markey, and Marjorie Joyce, *née* Thomas; *b* 28 March 1943; *Educ* RAF Coll Cranwell, Open Univ (BA), Cranfield Univ (MSc); *m* 1966, Judith Mary Widdowson; 1 s, 1 da; *Career* cmmnd supply offr RAF 1964, served Singapore, France and UK until 1981, Nat Def Coll 1981–82, HQ Strike Cmd 1982–83, HQ AFCENT The Netherlands 1983–85, MoD Carlisle 1986–88, station cdr Carlisle 1988–89, RCDS 1990, Central Staff MoD 1991, Dept of AMSO 1991, HQ Logistics Cmd 1994, dir gen of Support Mgmnt RAF 1995–97, dir of Resources NATO Maintenance & Supply Agency Luxembourg 1997–99, gen mangr NAMSA Luxembourg 1999–2004; author of various papers and contribs to learned jls; *Recreations* running, mountain walking, languages; *Clubs* RAF; *Style—* Air Vice Marshal Peter Markey, OBE

MARKHAM, Prof Alexander Fred (Alex); *Career* hon conslt physician NHS Yorks, dir Molecular Medicine Unit St James's Univ Hosp, prof of medicine Univ of Leeds 1993–, chm Nat Cancer Research Inst, chief exec Cancer Research UK 2003–07; advsr: Dept of Health, MRC, Wellcome Tst; FMedSci; *Style—* Prof Alex Markham; ✉ Cancer Research UK, PO Box 123, Lincoln's Inn Fields, London WC2A 3PX (tel 020 7242 0200, fax 020 7269 3100)

MARKHAM, (Arthur) Geoffrey; s of Col Frank Stanley Markham (d 1978), of Huddersfield, and Emma Woodhouse, *née* Spurr (d 1983); *b* 27 September 1927; *Educ* Giggleswick Sch, Univ of Leeds (LLB); *m* 26 Sept 1959, Patricia, da of John James Holliday (d 1935), of Barnsley, S Yorks; 1 s (Jonathan b 1962), 1 da (Sarah b 1966); *Career* admitted slr 1949, sr ptnr Raley and Pratt Barnsley 1967–89, conslt Raleys Barnsley 1990–99; chm Soc Security Appeal Tribunal 1981–95; historian; memb Law Soc 1949–; *Books* Woolley Hall, The Historical Development of a Country House (1979); *Recreations* reading, writing, music, freemasonry, gardening; *Style—* Geoffrey Markham, Esq; ✉ Petwood House, Woolley, Wakefield WF4 2JJ (tel 01226 382495)

MARKHAM, Dr Gillian Christine; da of late Harry Markham, of Plympton St Maurice, and late Irene Mary, *née* Aspinwall; *b* 22 December 1948; *Educ* Plympton GS, Univ of Liverpool Med Sch (MB ChB, DObstRCG, DMRD, FRCR); *m* 1 (m dis); 1 da (Katharine Sarah Markham b 2 Oct 1987), 1 s (Charles Henry North b 15 Jan 1990); m 2, 21 Feb 2003, John Davie; *Career* house offr Clatterbridge Hosp Wirral, obstetrics and gynaecology house offr Broadgreen 1971–72, paediatrics house offr Myrtle Street Children's Hosp 1972, radiological trg course Univ of Liverpool and on Mersey rotation 1972–77, conslt radiologist Whiston and St Helens Hosps 1977–2000, clinical lectr Dept of Radio-Diagnosis Univ of Liverpool 1978–2000, currently conslt breast radiologist N London Hospitals Tst and N London Breast Screening Prog; memb: Liverpool Med Instn 1970 (hon sec 1984–87, vice-pres 1988), Med Women's Fedn Exec 1978–94 (treas 1983–89, pres 1993–94), GMC 1994–99 (dep chm Assessment Referral Ctee 1996–98, memb Educn Ctee 1997–99, medical screener 1998–99); regnl educnl advsr RCR 1990–94; ed Medical Woman 2001–05 (memb Editorial Bd 1986–91); BMA: hon sec Mersey Conslts and Specialists Ctee 1995–2000, memb Central Conslt Specialists Ctee 1989–2000 and 2003–05, memb CCSC Gen Purposes Sub-Ctee 1998–2000, memb Career Progress of Doctors Ctee 1993–96, memb Radiological Sub-Ctee 1993–, chm Radiology Sub-Ctee 2003–05; dean and vice-pres Royal Coll of Radiologists 2005–; *Recreations* listening to music (particularly opera), choral singing, travel, sports, family activities; *Style—* Dr Gill Markham; ✉ 7 Meon Road, London W3 8AN

MARKHAM, Richard; s of Charles Roberts Markham, of Grimsby, Lincs, and Marion Edna, *née* Willows; *b* 23 June 1952; *Educ* Wintringham GS Grimsby, Royal Acad of Music, privately with Shirley Kemp and Max Pirani; *Career* concert pianist; London debut as soloist with Eng Chamber Orch under Raymond Leppard (Queen Elizabeth Hall) 1974, has toured internationally with David Nettle, *qv*, (Nettle-Markham Piano Duo), also with Raphael Wallfisch (cello) and Burlington Piano Trio; solo and piano duo performances at: Royal Festival Hall, Royal Albert Hall, Barbican Hall and at various major festivals incl BBC Proms; ARAM 1983; *Recordings* incl: works by Kabalevsky, Stravinsky and Rachmaninov (with Raphael Wallfisch, cello) 1976, Stravinsky's Rite of Spring and Petrushka (with David Nettle) 1984, Holst's The Planets 1985, Dyson's The Blacksmiths (with RCM Chamber Choir and RPO, 1987), Elgar's From the Bavarian Highlands 1987, Holst's Folksongs and works by Delius and Grainger 1988, Scenes from (Bernstein's) West Side Story (arranged and performed with David Nettle), Grainger's Fantasy on (Gershwin's) Porgy and Bess and Bennett's Four Piece Suite 1988, Rossini's Petite Messe Solennelle (with soloists Field, Owens, Barham and Tomlinson and CBSO chorus) 1990, South of The Border - Latin American Songs with Jill Gomez (with two pianos and NPO) 1990, Nettle and Markham in England 1993, Arnold's Concerto for Piano Duet 1993, Concerto for Two Pianos 1994, Nettle and Markham in France 1995, Brahms' Two-Piano Works 2006, Saint-Saens' Carnival of Animals and Poulenc's Babar the Elephant (with Jeremy Nicholas); *Awards* Nora Naismith Scholarship 1969–72, prizewinner Geneva Int Competition 1972, Countess of Munster Musical Tst Awards 1973 and 1974, Frederick Shinn Fellowship 1975, Gulbenkian Fndn Fellowship 1976–78, Music Retailers Assoc Award for Best Chamber Music Record 1985; *Recreations* travelling, theatre, playing cards, dining out; *Clubs* ISM, RAM; *Style—* Richard Markham, Esq; ✉ The Old Power House, Atherton Street, London SW11 2JE (tel 020 7738 1480, e-mail richardpiano@aol.com, website www.nettleandmarkham.com)

MARKHAM, Sarah Anne Judith; da of Leonard Markham, of Tithe Farm, Renhold, Beds, and Margaret Elizabeth, *née* Joyce; *b* 25 July 1957; *Educ* Bedford HS, Oxford and County; *Career* Shuttleworth Coll staff 1981–88, Christie's Old Master Picture Dept 1988–93, Sotheby's Old Master Paintings Dept 1993–95, art dealer 1995–2001, Cheffins Fine Art 2001–; *Recreations* riding, travelling, wildlife conservation; *Style—* Mrs Nicholas Flynn; ✉ Cheffins Fine Art, Clifton House, Clifton Road, Cambridge CB1 7EA (tel 01223 271937, e-mail sarah.flynn@cheffins.co.uk); Tithe Farm, Renhold, Bedfordshire MK41 0LX (tel 01234 771364, fax 01234 772337)

MARKING, Giles; s of Frank I Marking, of Wareham, Dorset, and Anne, *née* Percival; *b* 26 December 1947; *Educ* Duncan Hall Norfolk, Architectural Assoc Sch of Architecture (AADipl), Univ of Washington (MArch); *m* 11 Sept 1971, (Margaret Judith) Stacy, da of Canon R Patteson Stacy-Waddy, of Hindhead, Surrey; 1 da (Havana b 6 March 1972); *Career* designer Francisco and Jacobus NY 1967–68, film designer Maizin Wycoff NY 1968–70, graphic designer Inst of Contemporary Arts 1971–74, lectr in architecture Univ of Washington 1975–76, md Fitch London 1976–2002, md Marking Design Ltd 2002–; visiting prof Univ Metropolitana Mexico City 1980; FCSD; *Books* Emergency Housing in Peru - Architectural Design; *Recreations* travel, sheep farming, India and cricket; *Style—* Giles Marking, Esq; ✉ 17 Great Ormond Street, London WC1N 3RA; The Manor, Toller Whelme, Beaminster, Dorset DT8 3NU (tel 01308 862339, mobile 07074 333507, e-mail giles@markingdesign.com)

MARKS, David Joseph; MBE (2000); s of Melville Marks (d 1998), and Gunilla Marta, *née* Löven; *b* 15 December 1952; *Educ* Int Sch of Geneva, Kingston Poly Sch of Architecture, AA Sch of Architecture; *m* 17 July 1981, Julia Barbara Barfield, MBE, RIBA, *qv*, da of Arnold Robert Barfield; 1 s (Benjamin Jesse), 2 da (Maya Rosa Ray, Sarah Victoria Anna); *Career* architect; md: Marks Barfield Architects 1989–, London Eye Co (formerly Millennium Wheel Co) 1995–98; dir: David Marks Julia Barfield Architects, London Eye Co, World Sea Centre; project architect Richard Roger Partnership; Spiral Cafe Lightbox Brighton i360; subject of and contrib to TV and radio progs incl The Biggest Wheel in the World (BBC2) 1999 and Wheel (Channel 4) 2000 and 2001; RIBA, memb ARCUK; Freeman City of London; *Exhibitions* Tower Power Architecture Fndn, Royal Acad of Arts (annually) 1997–2001 and 2006, RIBA, Materials Gallery Science Museum (permanent exhbn), UKwithNY exhbn 2001, Sustainable London; *Awards* Special Commendation Prince Philip Designers Prize 2000, American Inst of Architects Design Award 2000, Corus Construction Award 2000, Dupont Benedictus Award for Innovation 2000, London First Millennium Award 2000, People's Choice Award London Tourism Awards 2000, Tourism for Tomorrow Award 2000, Leisure Property Forum Award 2000, RIBA Award 2000, 2004 and 2006, RICS Award 2000, Walpole Award 2001, Euro Award for Steel Structures 2001, Silver and Gold D&AD Awards 2001, Design Week Special Award 2001, Blueprint Award 2001, Pride of Britain Award for Innovation 2001, Barbara Miller Trophy Faculty of Bldg 2001, Architectural Practice of the Year 2001, Queen's Award for Enterprise 2003, CoolBrands (annually) 2003–06, Places and Genius overall winner BDI Awards 2005, Civic Tst Award 2006; *Recreations* family, walking, skiing; *Style—* David Marks, Esq, MBE, RIBA; ✉ Marks Barfield Architects, 50 Bromells Road, London SW4 0BG (tel 020 7501 0180, e-mail dmarks@marksbarfield.com)

MARKS, David Norman; s of Alex Marks, of London, and Edna, *née* Dufman; *b* 13 February 1953; *Educ* Orange Hill GS Edgware, LSE (BSc); *m* 22 June 1975, Selina Rachael, da of Michael Sharpe, of London; 2 s (Daniel b 1980, James b 1982); *Career* accountant; Arthur Andersen 1974–2002 (tax ptnr 1984), Deloitte & Touche 2002–05 (tax ptnr 2002), Apax Ptnrs 2005–; FCA 1978, ATII 1979; *Books* Practical Tax Saving (jtly, 1984), Tax Digest on Share Incentive Schemes for Institute of Chartered Accountants in England and Wales (1994), Profit-Related Pay (jtly, 1995); *Recreations* theatre, music; *Style—* David Marks, Esq; ✉ Apax Partners, 15 Portland Place, London W1B 1PT (tel 020 7872 6362, fax 020 7872 6366, e-mail david.marks@apax.com)

MARKS, Jonathan Clive; QC (1995); s of Geoffrey Jack Marks (d 2000), and Patricia Pauline, *née* Bowman (d 1995); *b* 19 October 1952; *Educ* Harrow, UC Oxford (BA); *m* 1, 18 Dec 1982 (m dis 1991), Sarah Ann Russell; 1 s (David b 1986), 1 da (Freya b 1988); m 2, 30 Oct 1993, Clementine Medina Cafopoulos, da of Panayiotes and Catherine Cafopoulos, of Athens; 2 da (Lara b 1996, Katya b 1998), 3 s (Alexander b 1999, Nicholas b 2001, Peter b 2006); *Career* called to the Bar Inner Temple 1975; in practice Western Circuit; visiting lectr in advocacy: Univ of Malaya Kuala Lumpur 1985 and 1989–91, Univ of Mauritius 1988, Sri Lanka Law Coll 1992; fndr memb SDP 1981, Euro Parly candidate for Cornwall and Plymouth 1984; Parly candidate: Weston-super-Mare 1983, Falmouth and Camborne 1987; memb Lib Dem Ctee for England 1988–89, chair Buckingham Constituency Lib Dems 2000–02, chm Lib Dem Lawyers Assoc 2001–, memb Lib Dem Federal Policy Ctee 2004–; Freeman: City of London 1975, Worshipful Co of Pattenmakers (memb Ct of Assts 1998–2004); *Recreations* skiing, tennis, theatre, food, wine, travel; *Clubs* RAC; *Style—* Jonathan Marks, Esq, QC; ✉ 4 Pump Court, Temple, London EC4Y 7AN (tel 020 7842 5555, fax 020 7583 2036, e-mail jmarks@4pumpcourt.com)

MARKS, Laurence; s of Bernard Marks (d 1975), and Lily, *née* Goldberg (d 1969); *b* 8 December 1948; *Educ* Holloway County Sch London, Guildhall Sch of Music; *m* 1 June 1988, Brigitte Luise, da of Friedrich Ludwig Ernst Kirchheim; 1 step s (Daniel Joel Kahn b 28 Feb 1968); *Career* trainee journalist Thomson Regional Newspapers, reporter N London Weekly Herald, Sunday Times and current affrs prog This Week (Thames TV) until 1980, television scriptwriter 1980–; creator and writer (with Maurice Gran, *qv*): Holding the Fort 1979–82, Roots, Shine on Harvey Moon 1982–85 and 1995–, Roll Over Beethoven, Relative Strangers, The New Statesman 1987–91, Birds of a Feather 1989–, Snakes and Ladders, So You Think You've Got Troubles, Get Back, Love Hurts 1991–93, Wall of Silence (film) 1993, Goodnight Sweetheart 1994–, Mosley 1997, Unfinished Business 1997, Starting Out 1999, Dirty Work 1999, Believe Nothing 2002, Playing God (stageplay) 2005, The New Statesman (stage play) 2006, My Blue Heaven (radio play) 2006, Me, My Dad and Moorgate (TV documentary) 2006, Dr Freud Will See You Now, Mrs Hitler (radio play) 2007, Mumbai Calling (TV comedy) 2007; fndr (with Maurice Gran and Allan McKeown *qv*) Alomo Productions 1988 (now part of Freemantle Television plc); pres Pipesmoking Cncl of Great Britain, Pipesmoker of the Year 1990; Freeman City of London 1992, Liveryman Worshipful Co of Tobacco Blenders and Briar Pipe Makers 1994; *Awards* Silver Medal Int Film and TV Festival NY for Relative Strangers 1985, Int Emmy for The New Statesman 1988, BAFTA Best Comedy Award for The New Statesman 1990, Mitsubishi TV Sitcom of the Year for Birds of a Feather 1991, Mitsubishi TV Drama of the Year for Love Hurts 1991, BAFTA Writer's Award (jtly with Maurice Gran) 1992, Berlin Film and TV Award 2007; *Books* Moorgate - The Anatomy of a Disaster (1976), Ruth Ellis - A Case of Diminished Responsibility (1977), Holding the Fort (with Maurice Gran, 1981), The New Statesman Scripts (with Maurice Gran, 1992), Dorien's Diary (with Maurice Gran, 1993), A Fan for all Seasons (1999); *Recreations* music (saxophone player), reading, English churches, tennis, medieval German, 18th and 19th century French literature, Chinese literature, the study of Freud, Jung and Breuer, British politics, The Peloponnesian War, mechanics of particles and molecular structures, the Chinese chemists and Oriental chemistry; *Clubs* Reform, Crescit, Arsenal Supporters'; *Style—* Laurence Marks, Esq; ✉ Lindaseifert Management, 22 Poland Street, London W1F 8QQ (tel 020 7292 7390)

MARKS, Prof Richard Charles; s of Maj William Henry Marks (d 1982), and Jeannie Eileen, *née* Piggott (d 1979); *b* 2 July 1945; *Educ* Berkhamsted Sch, QMC London (BA), Courtauld Inst of Art Univ of London (MA, PhD); *m* 19 July 1970, Rita, da of Charlie Spratley; *Career* researcher Corpus Vitrearum Ctee Br Acad 1970–73 (currently memb Ctee), asst keeper Dept of Medieval and Later Antiquities Br Museum 1973–79, keeper Burrell Collection and asst dir Glasgow Museums and Art Galleries 1979–85, dir Royal Pavilion Art Gallery and Museums Brighton 1985–92; prof of history of art and Centre for Medieval Studies Univ of York 1992–; pres Int Bd Corpus Vitrearum 1995–2004, vice-pres Soc of Antiquaries 1991–94; tstee River and Rowing Museum; FSA 1977; *Books* British Heraldry (jtly, 1978), The Golden Age of English Manuscript Painting (jtly, 1980), The Burrell Collection (jtly, 1983), Burrell: Portrait of a Collector (1983 and 1988), The Glazing of the Collegiate Church of the Holy Trinity Tattershall (1984), The Souvenir Guide to the Burrell Collection (1985), Sussex Churches and Chapels (jtly, 1989), Stained Glass in England during the Middle Ages (1993), The Medieval Stained Glass of Northamptonshire (1998), Gothic Art for England 1400–1547 (jtly, 2003), Image and Devotion in Late Medieval England (2004); *Recreations* opera, parish churches, travelling in the Levant, cricket, equestrianism; *Clubs* MCC, Clydesdale Rowing; *Style—* Prof Richard Marks; ✉ Hillcroft, 11 Stewkley Road, Soulbury, Bedfordshire LU7 0DH; Centre for Medieval Studies, The King's Manor, University of York, York YO1 2EP (tel 01904 433919, fax 01909 433918, e-mail rcml@york.ac.uk)

MARKS, Richard Leon; QC (1999); s of Harry Marks, and Denise, *née* Hilton; *b* 20 November 1953; *Educ* Clifton, Univ of Manchester (LLB); *m* 28 May 1987, Jane Elizabeth Tordoff; 1 da (Nicole Rebecca Tordoff b 15 Oct 1988), 1 s (Jacob Daniel Tordoff b 9 July 1999); *Career* called to the Bar Gray's Inn 1975, asst recorder (Northern Circuit) 1991, recorder (Northern Circuit) 1994; pres Mental Health (Restriced Patients) Review Tbnl 2000–; memb Criminal Bar Assoc; *Style—* Richard Marks, Esq, QC; ✉ Peel Court Chambers, 45 Hardman Street, Manchester M3 3PL (tel 0161 832 3791, fax 0161 834 3054)

MARKS, Prof Ronald; s of Isadore Marks (d 1966), and Jessie Marks (d 1991); *b* 25 March 1935; *Educ* St Marylebone GS, Guy's Hospital Med Sch (BSc, MB BS); *m* 1 (m dis 1978); 2 da (Louise Anne b 17 March 1962, Naomi Suzanne b 1 Jan 1965); m 2, 11 Nov 1978, Hilary, *née* Venmore; *Career* MO short service cmmn 1960, med div Queen Alexander Mil Hosp 1961–63, specialist in dermatology Br Mil Hosp Munster W Germany 1963–65; sr lectr Inst of Dermatology and conslt dermatologist St John's Hosp for Diseases of the

Skin London 1971–73; Univ of Wales Coll of Med Cardiff: sr lectr in dermatology Dept of Med 1973, reader 1977, personal chair in dermatology 1980, established chair in dermatology 1990–98 (prof emeritus 1998–); hon conslt in dermatology Univ Hosp of Wales 1973–98; clinical prof Dept of Dermatology and Cutaneous Surgery Univ of Miami Sch of Med 1995; author, ed, jt ed or contrib numerous papers in scientific jls, co-ed The Jl of Dermatological Treatment; lit award Soc of Cosmetic Chemists NY USA 1985; pres Br Cosmetic Dermatology Gp 1994,hon pres Int Soc for Bioengineering and the Skin; Freeman City of Besançon 1983; FRCP 1977 (memb 1964), FRCPath 1985; *Publications* jt ed and/or contrib to numerous books incl: Common Facial Dermatoses (1976), Investigative Techniques in Dermatology (ed, contrib, 1979), Psoriasis (1981), Practical Problems in Dermatology (1983, 2 edn 1996), Acne (1984), Roxburgh's Common Skin Diseases (1986, 16 edn 1993), Skin Diseases in Old Age (1987, 2 edn 1998), The Sun and Your Skin (1988), Acne and Related Disorders (jt ed, contrib, 1989), Retinoids In Cutaneous Malignancy (1991), Eczema (1992), Sun Damaged Skin (1992), The Environmental Threat to the Skin (1992), Clinical Signs and Procedures in Dermatology (1993), Skin Therapy (1994), Retinoids: a Clinicians Guide (1995), Emollients (1996), Photodamaged Skin: Clinical Signs, Causes and Management (1999), Facial Skin Disorders (2007); *Recreations* visual art of the 19th and 20th centuries; *Style*— Prof Ronald Marks; ✉ Cutest Medical Department, 214 Whitchurch Road, Heath, Cardiff CF14 3ND (tel 029 204 5080, fax 029 2061 4688, e-mail skincarecardiff@aol.com)

MARKS, Prof Shula Eta; OBE (1996); da of Chaim Winokur (d 1957), of Cape Town, South Africa, and Frieda, *née* Sack (d 2000); *b* 14 October 1938; *Educ* Univ of Cape Town (BA), Univ of London (PhD); *m* 31 March 1957, Prof Isaac Meyer Marks, s of Moshe Nahman Marks (d 1979), of Cape Town, South Africa; 1 da (Lara b 22 Jan 1963), 1 s (Rafi b 26 Jan 1965); *Career* Univ of London: lectr in history of Africa Inst of Cwlth Studies and SOAS (jtly) 1963–76, reader in history of Southern Africa 1976–84, dir Inst of Cwlth Studies 1983–93, prof of Cwlth history 1984–93, prof of history of Southern Africa SOAS 1993–2001 (prof emeritus 2001–, hon fell 2005), Douglas Southall Freeman prof Univ of Richmond VA 2005; conslt WHO 1977–80, chair World Univ Southern African Scholarships Ctee 1981–92, govr Inst of Devpt Studies Univ of Sussex 1988–91, chair Int Records Mgmnt Tst 1989–2004; vice-pres Royal African Soc 1999–; memb: Advsy Cncl on Public Records 1989–94, Cncl Soc for Protection of Sci and Learning (now Cncl for Assisting Refugee Academics (CARA)) 1983– (chair 1993–2004), Governing Body Queen Elizabeth House Oxford 1991–94, Cwlth Scholarships Cmmn 1992–98, Humanities Research Bd 1997–98, AHRB 1998–2000; Distinguished Africanist Award 2002; Hon DLitt Univ of Cape Town 1994, Hon DSocSci Univ of Natal 1996; distinguished sr fell Sch of Advanced Study Univ of London 2002, hon prof Univ of Cape Town 2005; FBA 1995; *Books* Reluctant Rebellion: An Assessment of the 1906–08 Disturbance in Natal (1970), Economy and Society in Preindustrial South Africa (ed jtly, 1980), Industrialisation and Social Change in South Africa (ed jtly, 1982), Ambiguities of Dependence in South Africa: Class, Nationalism and the State in Twentieth Century Natal (1986), The Politics of Race, Class and Nationalism in Twentieth Century South Africa (ed jtly, 1987), Not Either an Experimental Doll: The Separate Worlds of Three South African Women (1987), Divided Sisterhood: Race Class and Nationalism in the South African Nursing Profession (1994); *Recreations* theatre, cinema; *Style*— Prof Shula Marks, OBE, FBA; ✉ School of Oriental and African Studies, Thornhaugh Street, London WC1H 0XG (tel 020 7898 4612, fax 020 7898 4639, e-mail shulamarks@yahoo.co.uk)

MARKS, Susan Elizabeth; da of Edward George Howel Jones, of Wilmslow, Cheshire, and Anne, *née* Sutcliffe; *b* 14 October 1956; *Educ* Wilmslow GS for Girls, Jesus Coll Oxford (MA, Rowing blue, Athletics half blue), Univ of Leicester (Advanced Cert Educnl Mgmnt); *Family* 3 da (Stephanie Jane b 8 Dec 1984 d 2002, Victoria Claire b 24 March 1986, Charlotte Anne b 11 July 1991), 1 s (Andrew Edward Gordon b 10 July 1993); *Career* corporate lending offr Chemical Bank 1978–81, real estate lending offr Bank of America 1981–88, property team mangr Kleinwort Benson 1988–89, vice-pres and head EMEA Airline Lending Div Bank of America 1990–91, full time mother 1991–95, head of economics and politics St George's Coll Weybridge 1995–2000, headmistress Tormead Sch Guildford 2001– (head of sixth form 2000–01); memb: Ind Schs Inspectorate 1998–, GSA 2001– (hon treas 2007–); memb Ctee Stephanie Marks Appeal 2003–; *Recreations* reading, painting, golf; *Clubs* Univ Women's; *Style*— Mrs Susan Marks; ✉ Tormead School, Cranley Road, Guildford, Surrey GU1 2JD (tel 01483 575101, fax 01483 450592, e-mail head@tormeadschool.org.uk)

MARKS, Victor James (Vic); s of Harold George Marks (d 1989), and Phyllis Joan, *née* Farthing; *b* 25 June 1955; *Educ* Blundell's, St John's Coll Oxford (BA, Cricket blue, Rugby Fives half blue); *m* 9 Sept 1978, Annabelle Margaret, *née* Stewart; 2 da (Amy Tamsin b 27 Nov 1979, Rosie b 8 Nov 1987); *Career* cricket correspondent; professional cricketer: Somerset CCC 1974–89 (capt 1988–89), 6 test matches England 1982–84 (35 one day ints 1980–88); teacher Blundell's 1978–80, cricket corr The Observer 1990–, contrib BBC's Test Match Special 1990–, assoc ed The Wisden Cricketer magazine (formerly The Cricketer, dir 1990–); cricket chm Somerset 1999–; *Books* Somerset CCC Scrapbook (1984), Marks out of XI (1985), TCCB Guide to Better Cricket (1987), Ultimate One Day Cricket Match (1988), Wisden Illustrated History of Cricket (1989), My Greatest Game - Cricket (with Bob Holmes, 1994); *Recreations* golf; *Style*— Vic Marks, Esq

MARKUS, Prof Hugh Stephen; s of Dr Andrew Markus, and Dr Patricia Markus; *b* 9 March 1960; *Educ* Clare Coll Cambridge (BA), Univ of Oxford (BM BCh); *m* 1994, Philippa, *née* Hird; 1 da (Helen b 2000), 1 s (Jonathan b 2003); *Career* reader in neurology GKT 1997–2000 (sr lectr in neurology 1994–97), fndn prof of neurology St George's Univ of London 2000–; FRCP 1999; *Publications* Stroke Genetics (ed, 2003), Stroke Medicine (2006); over 100 papers on stroke research in scientific jls; *Style*— Prof Hugh Markus; ✉ Clinical Neuroscience, St George's, University of London, Cranmer Terrace, London SW17 0RE (tel 020 8725 2735, fax 020 8725 2950)

MARLAND, Baron (Life Peer 2006), of Odstock in the County of Wiltshire; Jonathan Peter Marland; s of Peter Marland, and Audrey, *née* Brierley; *Educ* Shrewsbury; *m* 1983, Penelope Mary, *née* Lamb; 2 s (Marcus, Hugo), 2 da (Allegra, Domenica); *Career* formerly dir Jardine Lloyd Thompson plc (formerly Lloyd Thompson plc); chm: Herriot Ltd, Janspeed Ltd, Harnham Water Meadows Tst, Clareville Capital Partners LLP; non-exec dir Jubilee Ltd; dir CChange; treas Cons Party; tstee and treas Atlantic Partnership; memb: Advsy Ctee Airey Neave Refugee Tst, Advsy Bd Peggy Guggenheim Museum Venice; tstee: Grainfarmers Pension Fund (chm), JP Marland Tst; *Recreations* tennis, skiing, shooting, wine, works of art, gardening, sport; *Clubs* MCC, Brooks's; *Style*— The Rt Hon the Lord Marland; ✉ 6 Wilton Place, London W1X 8RH (tel 020 7259 5092, fax 020 7245 0778)

MARLAND, (Peter) Michael; CBE (1977); s of Albert Marland (d 1977), of London; *b* 28 December 1934; *Educ* Christ's Hosp, Sidney Sussex Coll Cambridge (MA); *m* 1, 1955, Eileen (d 1968); 4 s (Edgell b 1956 d 1990, Oliver b 1959, Timothy b 1962, Benjamin Peter b 1967), 1 da (Folly b 1956); m 2, 1972 (m dis 1977), Rose; m 3, 1989, Linda; 1 s (Matthew b 1990); *Career* teacher: Der Halephagen Oberschule Hamburg 1957–58, Simon Langton GS Canterbury 1958–61; head of English Abbey Wood Sch London 1961–64, head of English then dir of studies Crown Woods Sch London 1964–71; headteacher Woodberry Down Sch London 1971–80, fndr headteacher North Westminster Community Sch (London's first multi-campus sch) 1980–99; hon prof of educn Univ of Warwick 1980–92, DfEE accredited Threshold Assessor of teachers' salary applications; chm City of Westminster Arts Cncl 1990–2005, vice-pres School Book Alliance Nat Working Pty, chm Westminster Race Equality Cncl Staying on Track Ctee; memb: Westminster Race Equality Cncl Exec Ctee, Birkbeck Coll Masculinities Res Advsy Gp, British Bd of Film Classification Consultative Cncl, British Inst of Biography, Cwlth Inst Educnl Advsy Ctee, DIVERT Nat Advsy Forum and Project Devpt Sub-Ctee, Educnl Writers Ctee Soc of Authors, ESU Educn Ctee, HM Prison Service Working Gp on Bds of Visitors, ICE Careers Ctee, Reading is Fundamental UK, Young Person's Concert Fndn, Br Educnl Mgmnt and Admin Soc, Educn Ctee Memorial Gates Tst; memb Nat Cncl and assoc ed Journal; London student teacher supervisor Texas Christian Univ; memb Editorial Bd Nat Assoc for Pastoral Care in Educn Journal; patron Tagore Fndn, tstee Miss Hawkins Woodfield Fndn; Kidscape Children's Champion 2000; Hon DEd Kingston Univ 2000, Hon DUniv Surrey Roehampton 2001, hon fell Inst of Educn Univ of London 2002; fell Coll of Teachers 2001, fell Br Educnl Leadership, Admin and Mgmnt Soc (BELMAS) 2005; FRSA 1991, FCP 1999; *Books* Pastoral Care (1974), Language Across the Curriculum (1977), Education for the Inner City (1980), Departmental Management (1981), Sex Differentiation and Schooling (1983), Meetings and Partings (1984), Short Stories for Today (1984), School Management Tasks (1985), New Directions in Pastoral Care (1985), The Tutor and the Tutor Group (1990), Marketing the School (1991), Craft of the Classroom (1993, revised edn 2002), Headship Matters, conversations with seven secondary school headteachers (1994), Scenes from Plays (1996), The Art of the Tutor (1997), Managing Arts in the Curriculum (2002), How to Be a Successful Form Tutor (2004), Ideas, Insights and Arguments (2007); numerous other editions and papers; gen ed: Longman Imprint Books, Heinemann Sch Management Series; *Recreations* reading, music; *Style*— Michael Marland, Esq, CBE, FRSA, FCP, Hon DEd, Hon DUniv; ✉ 22 Compton Terrace, Islington, London N1 2UN (tel 020 7226 0648, fax 020 7226 6373); The Green Farmhouse, Cranmer Green Walsham-le-Willows, Bury St Edmunds, Suffolk IP31 3BJ (tel 01359 259483, fax 01359 258371)

MARLAND, Paul; s of Alexander Marland, and Elsa May, *née* Lindsey; *b* 19 March 1940; *Educ* Gordonstoun, Trinity Coll Dublin; *m* 1, 1965 (m dis 1983), Penelope Anne Barlow; 1 s, 2 da; m 2, 1984, Caroline Anne Rushton; *Career* farmer; worked with Hopes Meal Windows 1964, London Press Exchange 1965–66; MP (Cons) Glos W 1979–97, jt PPS to Hon Nicholas Ridley as fin sec to the Treasy and Jock Bruce-Gardyne as econ sec to the Treasy 1981–83, PPS to Rt Hon Michael Jopling as min of Agric 1983–86, memb Agric Select Ctee 1986–97, chm Cons Backbench Agric Ctee 1989–97, pres Cons Pty Nat Convention 2005– (vice-pres 2002–05), memb Bd Cons Pty 2002–; *Style*— Paul Marland, Esq; ✉ Ford Hill Farm, Temple Guiting, Cheltenham, Gloucestershire GL54 3XU

MARLAND, Ross Crispian; s of John Marland (d 1988), and Sylvia, *née* Norris (d 2005); *b* 17 August 1940; *Educ* Stamford Sch, BRNC Dartmouth, UCL (LLM, Dip Air and Space Law); *m* 23 Oct 1965, (Daphne Mary) Virginia, da of Brig William Hugh Denning Wakely (d 1979); 1 s (Timothy b 27 July 1970), 1 da (Lavinia b 22 Sept 1974); *Career* graduated RNC Actg Sub Lt 1961, RAF 1963–79; called to the Bar Inner Temple 1975, in practice 1979–81; dir: International Insurance Services Ltd 1981–87, Airclaims Insurance Services Ltd 1987–91; mangr Tech Servs Div British Aviation Insurance Group 1991–97, ptnr Maxwell, Marland & Associates 1997–, conslt Clyde & Co 1997–2002, conslt LAD (Aviation) Ltd 2000–01; memb: Br Insurance Law Assoc, Air Law Gp Royal Aeronautical Soc, Bar Assoc Commerce Finance and Indust, Racehorse Owners' Assoc; Upper Freeman Guild of Air Pilots and Air Navigators 1999; MRIN 1973, MRAeS 1982, MCIArb 1999; *Recreations* salmon and trout fishing, equestrian sports; *Clubs* RAF; *Style*— Ross Marland, Esq; ✉ 84 East Hill, Wandsworth, London SW18 2HG (tel 020 8874 5964, fax 020 8488 7487, e-mail mma2@dircon.co.uk); Place de l'Église, 64390 Laàs, Pyrénées-Atlantiques, France (tel +33 559 385387, fax +33 559 385438, e-mail ross.marland@orange.fr)

MARLBOROUGH, 11 Duke of (E 1702); John George Vanderbilt Henry Spencer-Churchill; JP (Oxon 1962), DL (1974); also Baron Spencer (E 1603), Earl of Sunderland (E 1643), Baron Churchill of Sandridge (E 1685), Earl of Marlborough (E 1689), Marquess of Blandford (E 1702), Prince of the Holy Roman Empire (1704), and Prince of Mindelheim (1705, cr of the Emperor Joseph); s of 10 Duke of Marlborough (d 1972), by his 1 w, Hon Alexandra Cadogan, CBE, da of Viscount Chelsea and gda of 5 Earl Cadogan, KG; *b* 13 April 1926; *Educ* Eton; *m* 1, 1951 (m dis 1960), Susan Mary, da of Michael Charles St John Hornby (d 1987), of Pusey House, Berks, by his w Nicolette (d 1988), da of Capt Hon Cyril Ward, MVO, RN, 5 s of 1 Earl of Dudley; 1 s, 1 da (and 1 s decd); m 2, 1961 (m dis 1971), Mrs Tina (Athina) Livanos (d 1974), da of Stavros G Livanos, of Paris, and formerly w of Aristotle Onassis (d 1975); m 3, 1972, (Dagmar) Rosita (Astri Libertas), da of Count Carl Ludvig Douglas (d 1961); 1 s (Lord Edward b 1974), 1 da (Lady Alexandra b 1977) (and 1 s decd); *Heir* s, Marquess of Blandford, *qv*; *Career* proprietor of Blenheim Palace, said to be England's largest domestic bldg and one of the masterpieces of Sir John Vanbrugh; formerly Capt Life Gds to 1953; chm: Martini & Rossi Ltd 1979–96, London Paperweights Ltd; pres: Thames and Chilterns Tourist Bd 1974–, Oxon Assoc for Young People, Oxon CLA 1978–; former Oxon ccllr; memb House of Lords Bridge Team in match against Commons 1982; pres: Oxfordshire Branch SSAFA - Forces Help 1977, Oxford United Football Club 1975–2003, Sports Aid Fndn (Southern Area) 1981; hon vice-pres Football Assoc 1959, dep pres Nat Assoc Boys' Clubs; memb Cncl Winston Churchill Meml Tst 1966–2006; memb Trust House Charitable Tst 1993–; patron: Oxford Branch Red Cross, Heart UK; *Clubs* White's, Portland; *Style*— His Grace the Duke of Marlborough, DL; ✉ Blenheim Palace, Woodstock, Oxfordshire OX20 1PX (tel 01993 811666, fax 01993 813107); 1 Shepherd's Place, Upper Brook Street, London W1 (tel 020 7629 7971)

MARLESFORD, Baron (Life Peer UK 1991), of Marlesford in the County of Suffolk; Mark Shuldham Schreiber; DL (Suffolk 1991); s of John Shuldham Schreiber, AE, DL (d 1968), of Marlesford Hall, Woodbridge, Suffolk, and Constance Maureen, *née* Dent (d 1980); *b* 11 September 1931; *Educ* Eton, Trinity Coll Cambridge (MA); *m* 1969, Gabriella Federica, da of Conte Teodoro Veglio di Castelletto d'Uzzone; 2 da (Hon Nicola Charlotte (Hon Mrs Stacey) b 8 Aug 1971, Hon Sophie Louisa (Hon Mrs Franklin) b 8 Sept 1973); *Career* Nat Serv Coldstream Gds, 2 Lt; Fisons Ltd 1957–63, Conservative Res Dept 1963–67, dir Conservative Party Public Sector Research Unit 1967–70, special advsr HM Govt 1970–74, special advsr to leader of the Opposition 1974–75, editorial conslt The Economist 1974–91 (Parly lobby correspondent); memb: EU Select Ctee 2003–, Economic and Financial Affrs Sub-Ctee 2000–05, Home Affrs Sub-Ctee 2005–; dir: Eastern Group plc 1989–95, Times Newspapers Holdings Ltd (ind nat dir) 1991–, Baring New Russia Fund 1997–2007; advsr: Mitsubishi Corporation International NV 1990–2003, John Swire & Sons 1992–; pres Suffolk Preservation Soc 1998–; memb: Countryside Cmmn 1980–92, Rural Devpt Cmmn 1985–93; chm CPRE 1993–98; *Clubs* Pratt's; *Style*— The Rt Hon Lord Marlesford, DL; ✉ Marlesford Hall, Woodbridge, Suffolk IP13 0AU; 5 Kersley Street, London SW11 4PR (e-mail marlesford@parliament.uk)

MARLING, Sir Charles William Somerset; 5 Bt (UK 1882), of Stanley Park and Sedbury Park, Co Gloucester; s of Lt-Col Sir John Stanley Vincent Marling, 4 Bt, OBE (d 1977); *b* 2 June 1951; *Educ* Harrow; *m* 1979, Judi; 3 da (Georgina Katharine b 1982, Aimy Frances b 1984, Laura Beatrice b 1990); *Heir* none; *Clubs* White's; *Style*— Sir Charles Marling, Bt

MARLOW-THOMAS, Piers John Derrick; s of Michael John Marlow-Thomas (d 1983), of Leics, and Angela Claire, *née* Hignett (d 2002); *b* 11 October 1957; *Educ* Pangbourne Coll, RMA Sandhurst; *m* 1984, Julia Mary, da of Maj B H Heaton, MC, OBE, of Clwyd; 2 s (Oliver John Basil b 23 April 1987, Charles Michael Adrian b 4 May 1993), 1 da (Amelia

Daisy Bronwyn b 20 April 1993); *Career* served The Life Gds 1977–85; Bass plc 1985–88, Charles Barker plc 1989–92, mktg dir Hill & Knowlton UK 1992–95, dir business devpt Richards Butler 1995–97, mktg dir Shandwick Consultants 1997–98; ptnr Agency Insight, dir H2Glenfern Ltd; *Recreations* sailing, shooting, fishing, skiing; *Clubs* Buck's, City, Household Div Yacht; *Style—* Piers Marlow-Thomas, Esq; ✉ The Mill, West Hendred, Wantage, Oxfordshire OX12 8RJ; H2Glenfern Consulting Ltd, 161 New Bond Street, London W1S 2UF

MARMOT, Prof Sir Michael Gideon; kt (2000); s of Nathan Marmot, of Sydney, Aust, and Alice, *née* Weiner; *b* 26 January 1945; *Educ* Univ of Sydney (BSc, MB BS), Univ of Calif Berkeley (MPH, PhD); *m* 8 Sept 1971, Alexi, da of Bernard Ferster; 2 s (Andre b 1982, Daniel b 1986), 1 da (Deborah b 1992); *Career* Univ of Sydney: student fell in cardiovascular pharmacology 1965–66, res med offr Royal Prince Alfred Hosp 1969, fell in thoracic med 1970, travelling fell Postgrad Med Fndn 1971–72; lectr Dept of Biomedical and Environmental Health Sciences Univ of Calif Berkeley 1975–76, sr lectr (formerly lectr) in epidemiology LSHTM 1976–85, prof UCH and Middx Sch of Med 1985–; hon conslt Med Div UCH 1980–84; LSHTM: prof of epidemiology 1990–92, dir Int Centre for Health and Society 1994–, MRC research prof 1995–; adjunct prof of health and social behaviour Harvard Sch of Public Health; memb: Ctee on Med Aspects of Food Policy, CMO's Working Gp on Health of the Nation Dept of Health, Royal Cmmn on Environmental Pollution 1995–2002, HM Treasy Inter-Departmental Gp on Cross Cutting Spending Review 2001, NHS Task Force on Inequalities; foreign assoc memb Inst of Med NAS 2002–vice-pres Behavioural Scis Section Academia Europea 1996–, chair R&D Ctee Nat Inst for Clinical Excellence 2003, memb Bd of Advsrs RAND; FFPHM 1989 (MFPHM 1984), FRCP 1996, FMedSci 1998; *Books* Mortality of Immigrants to England and Wales (1984), Coronary Heart Disease Epidemiology (1992), Stress and the Heart (with S Stansfeld, 2002), Social Determinants of Health (with R Wilkinson, 1999); *Style—* Prof Sir Michael Marmot; ✉ Department of Epidemiology and Public Health, University College London, 1–19 Torrington Place, London WC1E 6BT (tel 020 7679 1680, fax 020 7813 0242, e-mail m.marmot@ucl.ac.uk)

MARNHAM, Patrick; *b* 1943, Jerusalem, Israel; *Educ* Downside, CCC Oxford (memb Univ of Oxford ski team); *Career* called to the Bar Gray's Inn 1966; reporter Private Eye 1966–76, asst features ed Daily Telegraph Magazine 1968–70, scriptwriter and presenter BBC TV and Granada TV 1968–71, literary ed The Spectator 1981–82, Paris corr The Independent 1986–92, Paris corr Evening Standard 1994–98; Thomas Cook Travel Book Prize 1985, Marsh Biography Award 1991–92; FRSL 1988; *Books* Road to Katmandu (1971), Nomads of the Sahel (1977), Fantastic Invasion: Dispatches from Africa (1980), Lourdes: A Modern Pilgrimage (1980), The Private Eye Story (1982), So Far From God: A Journey to Central America (1985), Trail of Havoc (1987), The Man Who Wasn't Maigret: A Biography of Georges Simenon (1992), Crime and the Académie Française (1993), Dreaming with His Eyes Open: The Life of Diego Rivera (1998), The Death of Jean Moulin: Biography of a Ghost (2000), Wild Mary: A Life of Mary Wesley (2006); *Clubs* Athenaeum, Academy; *Style—* Patrick Marnham, Esq; ✉ c/o Toby Eady Associates, 9 Orme Court, London W2 4RL (tel 020 7792 0092)

MAROT, Marc Etienne; s of Col Pierre Etienne Marot, MBE, of Shennington, Nr Banbury, and Gwendolin May, *née* Handley; *b* 5 May 1959; *m* 2 Sept 1989, Jacqueline; 2 s (Luc Etienne b 7 Nov 1990, Christian Roland b 17 June 1995); *Career* sometime A&R and talent scout; md: Blue Mountain Music Publishing (copyrights incl U2 and Bob Marley) 1984–86, Island Music Publishing 1986–90, Island Records Ltd (bought by Polygram Records 1990) 1990–2000; ceo music3w.com; dir: clickmusic.com, icrunch.com; *Recreations* music, gardening, computers and computing; *Style—* Marc Marot, Esq; ✉ Music3w.com, 4 Albion Court, Albion Place, Galena Road, London W6 0QT (tel 020 8735 6154, fax 020 8735 6151)

MARPER, (William) John; s of Ronald Marshall Marper, of Saltburn, and Caroline, *née* Jarville; *b* 9 December 1946; *Educ* Sir William Turners Sch; *m* 12 Dec 1976, Maureen Ann, da of Henry Pullen, of Eastbourne; *Career* CA; Charles Barker Group 1972–77, vice-pres Citicorp 1977–85, dir ANZ Merchant Bank 1985–89, exec dir The Co-operative Bank plc 1989–; FCA, MSI; *Recreations* tennis, English literature; *Style—* John Marper, Esq; ✉ 1 Balloon Street, Manchester M60 4EP (tel 0161 832 3456)

MARPLES, Graham; s of Ronald Marples (d 1992), of Derby, and Catherine (b 1999); *Educ* Long Eaton GS, Univ of Durham Business Sch (MBA); *m* 1986, Christine, *née* Lane; 2 da (Alice b 1988, Charlotte b 2000), 1 s (James b 1990); *Career* journalist; reporter: Long Eaton Advertiser, Raymond's News Agency Derby, Teesside Evening Gazette; chief reporter Northern Echo Darlington, news ed Teesside Evening Gazette; Tyne Tees Television: newsroom journalist, news ed, prodr, sr prodr, managing ed news; *Awards* New York Television Festival Awards 1996 and 1998 for documentaries Climbing K2 and Back to K2, RTS Best Regnl News Magazine 1997 for North East Tonight (shortlisted 1998 and 1999); Soc of Editors 2000; *Recreations* rugby, running, real ale, travel, theatre; *Style—* Graham Marples, Esq; ✉ News, Tyne Tees Television, City Road, Newcastle upon Tyne NE1 2AL (tel 0191 269 3700, fax 0191 232 4085, mobile 0973 925395, e-mail graham.marples@itv.com)

MARQUAND, Prof David Ian; s of Rt Hon Hilary Marquand (d 1972), and Rachel Eluned, *née* Rees (d 1996); *b* 20 September 1934; *Educ* Emanuel Sch, Magdalen Coll Oxford, St Antony's Coll Oxford, Univ of Calif Berkeley; *m* 12 Dec 1959, Judith Mary, da of Dr Morris Reed, of London; 1 s (Charles b 1962), 1 da (Ruth b 1964); *Career* Nat Serv RAF 1952–54; leader writer The Guardian 1959–62, res fell St Antony's Coll Oxford 1962–64, lectr in sch of social studies Univ of Sussex 1964–66; MP (Lab) Ashfield 1966–77; PPS to: Min of Works 1966–67, Min of Overseas Devpt 1967–69; Br delegate to Cncl of Europe and WEU Assemblies 1970–73, chief advsr European Cmmn Brussels 1977–78; prof of contemporary history and politics Univ of Salford 1978–91; Univ of Sheffield: prof of politics 1991–96, dir of Political Economy Research Centre 1993–96, hon prof 1996–; princ Mansfield Coll Oxford 1996–2002; jt ed The Political Quarterly 1987–97; chm High Peak SDP 1981–82 and 1987–88, pres High Peak SLD 1988–91; memb: Nat Ctee SDP 1981–88, Policy Ctee SLD 1988–90; Political Studies Assoc Sir Isaiah Berlin Prize for lifetime contribution to political studies 2001; FRHistS 1986, FRSA 1992, FBA 1998; *Books* Ramsay MacDonald (1977), Parliament for Europe (1979), European Elections and British Politics (with David Butler, 1981), John Mackintosh on Parliament and Social Democracy (ed, 1982), The Unprincipled Society (1988), The Progressive Dilemma (1991), The New Reckoning (1997), Decline of the Public (2004); *Recreations* walking, listening to music; *Style—* Prof David Marquand, FBA; ✉ 37 St Andrew's Road, Headington, Oxford OX3 9DL

MARQUIS, Simon John; s of Henry Derek Marquis, of Harpenden, Herts, and Margaret, *née* Parish; *b* 3 May 1953; *Educ* Lancing, Peterhouse Cambridge (MA); *m* 1 May 1993, Nicola Jane Horner, da of Capt Richard Bates, RN; 1 s (Edward James Richard b 7 July 1994), 2 step da (Sophie, Clio); *Career* Benton & Bowles advtg 1975–80, Allen Brady Marsh advtg 1980–83, md Burkitt Weinreich Bryant Clients & Co Ltd 1990–92 (media dir 1983–90), editorial dir Marketing magazine 1993–98, chm ZenithOptimedia until 2006; chm Nat Readership Survey 2005–, chm Media Circle, non-exec dir St Ives; FIPA; *Recreations* golf, skiing, birds, drawing; *Style—* Simon Marquis, Esq

MARR, Andrew William Stevenson; s of William Donald Marr, and Valerie, *née* Stevenson, of Longforgan, Perthshire; *b* 31 July 1959, Glasgow; *Educ* Dundee HS, Craigflower Sch, Loretto, Trinity Hall Cambridge (MA, exhibitioner); *m* Aug 1987, Jackie Ashley, *qv*, da of Baron Ashley of Stoke, CH, PC (Life Peer), *qv*; 1 s (Harry Cameron b 5 July 1989), 2 da (Isabel Claire b 4 Oct 1991, Emily Catherine b 3 Nov 1994); *Career* trained TRN Newcastle upon Tyne 1981; The Scotsman: trainee 1982, gen reporter then business reporter 1983–85, Parly corr 1985–86; political corr and Whitehall corr The Independent 1986–87, political ed The Scotsman 1988, political ed The Economist 1989–92; The Independent: chief political commentator 1992–96, ed 1996–98, ed-in-chief 1998; columnist The Express and The Observer 1998–2000, political ed BBC 2000–05, presenter Sunday AM (BBC1) 2005–; Columnist of the Year Br Press Awards 1995, Creative Freedom Award 2000, RTS Specialist Journalist 2001, Hansard/Channel 4 Political Journalist 2000 and 2001, Voice of Listener and Viewer TV Journalist 2001, Broadcasting Press Guild TV Performer 2001, Richard Dimbleby Award Bafta TV Awards 2004; *Books* The Battle for Scotland (1992), Ruling Britannia (1995), The Day Britain Died (2000); *Recreations* whining and dining; *Clubs* Buffers, St James's, Pinks, The Reaction; *Style—* Andrew Marr, Esq; ✉ BBC Westminster, 4 Millbank, Westminster, London SW1A

MARR, Lindsay Grigor David; s of Grigor Wilson Marr (d 1986), and Linda Grace, *née* Sergeant; *b* 14 September 1955; *Educ* The Perse Sch Cambridge, Gonville & Caius Coll Cambridge (MA); *m* 23 Feb 1991, Susan Ann, *née* Scott; 1 s (Andrew b 1992); *Career* admitted slr 1981; Freshfields Bruckhaus Deringer: articled clerk 1979–81, asst slr 1981–87, ptnr 1987–2006, princ conslt 2006–; Freeman City of London Slrs' Co 1988; memb Law Soc; *Recreations* reading, music, golf, sailing; *Style—* Lindsay Marr, Esq; ✉ 39 Broad Lane, Hampton, Middlesex TW12 3AL; 65 Fleet Street, London EC4Y 1HS (tel 020 7936 4000, fax 020 7832 7001, e-mail lindsay.marr@freshfields.com)

MARR-JOHNSON, His Hon Frederick James Maugham; s of Kenneth Marr-Johnson (d 1986), and Hon Diana Julia, *née* Maugham, da of 1 Viscount Maugham; *b* 17 September 1936; *Educ* Winchester, Trinity Hall Cambridge (MA); *m* 26 March 1966, Susan, da of Maj R P H Eyre, OBE (d 1982); 1 s (Thomas b 30 Sept 1966), 1 da (Rachel b 27 May 1969); *Career* Nat Serv RN 1955–56, midshipman RNVR; called to the Bar Lincoln's Inn 1962 (bencher 1999); recorder of the Crown Court 1986–91, circuit judge (SE Circuit) 1991–2006; Liveryman Worshipful Co of Merchant Taylors; *Recreations* sailing; *Clubs* Royal Yacht Sqdn, Bar Yacht (Rear Cdre 1999–2000); *Style—* His Hon Frederick Marr-Johnson; ✉ 33 Hestercombe Avenue, London SW6 5LL (tel 020 7731 0412, e-mail fmarrjohnson@rya-online.net)

MARRINER, Andrew Stephen; s of Sir Neville Marriner, the conductor; *b* 25 February 1954; *Educ* King's Coll Cambridge (chorister), King's Sch Canterbury, New Coll Oxford, Hochschule für Musik Hannover; *m* 1988, Elisabeth Anne, *née* Sparke; 1 s (Douglas Lawrence b 11 Oct 1989); *Career* solo chamber and orchestral clarinettist; freelance 1977–84, princ clarinet LSO 1985–, princ clarinet Acad of St Martin-in-the-Fields 1986–; solo and concert appearances at venues incl Royal Festival Hall, Barbican Hall, various in Paris, Berlin, Vienna, USA, Far East and Australia; concerto work with conductors incl Sir Neville Marriner, Sir Colin Davis, Leonard Bernstein, Mstislav Rostropovich, Michael Tilson Thomas and Richard Hickox; Hon RAM 1994; *Recordings* with Acad of St Martin-in-the-Fields incl: Schubert Octet (Chandos), Beethoven Octet (Philips), Spohr Octet and Nonet (Philips), Mozart Divertimenti (Philips), Weber Concerti (Philips); others incl: Mozart Clarinet Quintet (Classics for Pleasure), Mozart Clarinet Concerto (CFP), Schubert Octet (with Chilingirian, EMI); *Recreations* family, cricket; *Clubs* Lord's Taverners; *Style—* Andrew Marriner, Esq; ✉ 67 Cornwall Gardens, London SW7 4BA; c/o Ingpen & Williams Ltd, 7 St George's Court, 131 Putney Bridge Road, London SW15 2PA (tel 020 8874 3222, fax 020 8877 3113)

MARRIOTT, *see also:* Smith-Marriott

MARRIOTT, Martin Marriott; s of Rt Rev Philip Selwyn Abraham, Bishop of Newfoundland, Canada (d 1956), and Elizabeth Dorothy Cicely, *née* Marriott (d 1975); *b* 28 February 1932; *Educ* Lancing, New Coll Oxford (MA); *m* 10 Nov 1956, Judith Caroline Gurney, da of Lt-Col Michael Ronald Lubbock, MBE (d 1989), of Toronto, Canada; 1 s (Charles), 2 da (Virginia (Mrs O'Conor), Rebecca); *Career* educn officer RAF 1956–59; teacher: Heversham GS 1959–66, Haileybury Coll 1966–76; headmaster Canford Sch 1976–92; chm HMC 1989, chm of tstees The Bloxham Project 1996–2000 (memb Steering Ctee 1985–91), sr warden Kings Sch Bruton 1998–2004; lay canon Salisbury Cathedral 1993–2000; *Recreations* grandchildren, golf, gardening; *Clubs* East India; *Style—* Martin Marriott, Esq; ✉ Morris' Farm House, Baverstock, Dinton, Salisbury, Wiltshire SP3 5EL (tel 01722 716034, e-mail marriott@waitrose.com)

MARRIOTT, Michael; *Educ* RCA; *Career* product designer; clients incl: 20/21, Arts Cncl of England, DIM, Möve, SCP, Topolski, Trico; exhibited worldwide; design installations incl: Mies Meets Marx/MMM (Geffrye Museum), Bring Me Sunshine (Tokyo Design Week), Economy of Means (Camden Art Centre); winner Jerwood Furniture Prize 1999; tutor of design products RCA; *Style—* Michael Marriott, Esq; ✉ Unit F2, 2–4 Southgate Road, London N1 3JJ

MARRIS, Robert; MP; s of Dr Charles Marris (d 1989), of Wolverhampton, and Margaret Marris, JP, *née* Crawley; *b* 8 April 1955; *Educ* Univ of British Columbia (BA, MA), Birmingham Poly (CPE, Law Soc Finals); *partner* Julia Pursehouse; *Career* truck driver Vancouver 1977–79, bus driver Vancouver 1979–82; articled clerk Wolverhampton 1985–87, slr Wolverhampton 1987–88, trade union slr Birmingham and Stoke-on-Trent 1988–2001; MP (Lab) Wolverhampton SW 2001–; memb Law Soc; *Recreations* talking, Wolves, Canadiana; *Style—* Rob Marris, MP; ✉ House of Commons, London SW1A 0AA (tel 020 7219 8342)

MARRON, Peter Austin; s of Austin Marron, and Catherine, *née* Cassidy (d 2000); *b* 3 June 1944, Sunderland; *Educ* St Cuthbert's GS Newcastle upon Tyne, Univ of Liverpool (LLB), Coll of Law Guildford; *m* 17 March 1967, Christine, *née* Collins; 2 da (Kirsty b 6 March 1972, Sophie b 26 Feb 1975), 1 s (James b 11 Aug 1979); *Career* slr: IOW CC 1967–70, Leicester City Cncl 1970–72; slr and ptnr Gardiner & Millhouse 1972–78, fndr Marron Townsend (subsequently Marron Dodds, then Marrons, Slrs) 1978 (currently sr ptnr); memb: Law Soc 1970, CIArb 1991, RSA 1995, Soc of Advanced Legal Studies 1998, Int Bar Assoc 1996; legal assoc RTPI 1997; *Recreations* offshore sailing (RYA Ocean Yachtmaster 1994); *Clubs* Royal Yachting Assoc; *Style—* Peter Marron, Esq; ✉ The Hermitage, Church Lane, Lyddington, Oakham LE15 9LN (tel 01572 822338, fax 01572 821984); Marrons, Solicitors, 1 Meridian South, Meridian Business Park, Leicester LE19 1WY (tel 0116 289 2200, fax 0116 289 3973, e-mail petermarron@marrons.net)

MARSDEN, Edmund Murray; s of Christopher Alexander Marsden (d 1989), and Ruth, *née* Kershaw (d 1971); *b* 22 September 1946; *Educ* Winchester, Trinity Coll Cambridge; *m* 1982, Megan Catherine, *née* McIntyre; 1 s (Patrick William b 1984); *Career* publisher and ed Nuffield Fndn 1968–71; Br Cncl: assignments in Ghana, Belgium and Algeria 1971–77, mgmnt accountant 1977–80, dir Syria 1980–82, dir educnl contracts 1982–87, dir Turkey 1987–90, dir corp affrs 1990–93, asst DG 1993–99, dir India and regnl dir S Asia 2000–05; chair Intermediate Technol Devpt Gp 1995–98 and 1998–99; *Style—* Edmund Marsden, Esq; ✉ 21755 Ocean Vista Drive, Laguna Beach CA 92651, USA (e-mail emarsden01@aol.com)

MARSDEN, Gordon; MP; s of late George Henry Marsden, of Stockport, and late Joyce, *née* Young; *b* 28 November 1953; *Educ* Stockport GS, New Coll Oxford (scholar, MA, Gibbs prize in history), Warburg Inst Univ of London, Kennedy Sch of Govt Harvard Univ (Kennedy scholar in politics/int rels); *Career* tutor and lectr Open Univ 1977–97, public affrs/PR conslt 1980–85 (public affrs advsr Eng Heritage 1984–85), conslt ed New Socialist 1989–90, ed History Today 1985–97; MP (Lab) Blackpool S 1997– (Parly candidate (Lab) Blackpool S 1992); memb Commons Select Ctee Education and Employment 1998–2001 and 2005–, PPS to Sec of State for Culture, Media and Sport

M

2003–05; chair All-Pty Future of Europe Tst 2001–, convenor Lab MPs Seaside and Coastal Towns Gp; chm Young Fabians 1979–80, chair Fabian Soc 2000–01; pres British Resorts Assoc 1998–; tstee: Dartmouth Street Tst 1997–, History Today Ltd 1997–, History of Parliament 1999–; memb Bd Inst of Historical Res 1994–; nat vice-chair Early Educn 2000–; visiting Parly fell St Antony's Coll Oxford 2003, Historical Assoc centenary fell 2006–; *Books* The History Debate (contrib, 1990), Holland's War Against Hitler (contrib, 1991), Victorian Values? Personalities and Perspectives in Nineteenth-Century Society (2 edn, 1998), The English Question (contrib, 2000), Censorship: A World Encyclopedia (contrib, 2002); *Recreations* swimming, choral and early music, theatre, medieval culture and travel; *Style—* Gordon Marsden, Esq, MP; ✉ House of Commons, London SW1A 0AA (tel 020 7219 1262)

MARSDEN, Philip John; s of Christopher Marsden-Smedley, of Bristol, and Susan Penelope, *née* King; *b* 11 May 1961, Bristol; *m* 19 June 1999, Charlotte, da of Anthony Hobson; 1 da (Clio Tatyana b 4 Feb 2003), 1 s (Arthur James Anthony b 16 April 2005); *Career* author; Somerset Maugham Award 1994, Daily Telegraph/Thomas Cook Travel Book Award 1999; FRSL 1996; *Books* A Far Country: Travels in Ethiopia (1990), The Crossing Place: A Journey Among the Armenians (1993), The Bronski House (1995), The Spirit-Wrestlers (1998), The Main Cages (2002), The Chains of Heaven (2005); *Style—* Philip Marsden, Esq, FRSL; ✉ Downholm, St Mawes, Cornwall TR2 5AN (tel 01326 270073, e-mail philip@marsden.abel.co.uk); c/o Gillon Aitken Associates, 18–21 Cavaye Place, London SW10 9PT (tel 020 7373 8672)

MARSDEN, Sir Simon Neville Llewelyn; 4 Bt (UK 1924), of Grimsby, Co Lincoln; yr s of Sir John Denton Marsden, 2 Bt (d 1985); suc bro Sir Nigel John Denton Marsden, 3 Bt (d 1997); *b* 1 December 1948; *Educ* Ampleforth, Sorbonne; *m* 1, 1970 (m dis 1978), Catherine Thérèsa, yr da of late Brig James Charles Windsor-Lewis, DSO; m 2, 1984, Caroline, yst da of John Stanton, of Houghton St Giles, Walsingham, Norfolk; 1 da (Skye Atalanta b 24 Feb 1988), 1 s (Tadgh Orlando Denton b 25 Dec 1990); *Heir* s, Tadgh Marsden; *Career* author and photographer; collections in: V&A, Getty Museum Calif; *Books* In Ruins (The Once Great Houses of Ireland) (1980), The Haunted Realm (Ghosts, Witches and other Strange Tales) (1986), Visions of Poe (1988), Phantoms of the Isles (1990), The Journal of a Ghosthunter (1994), Beyond the Wall - The Lost World of East Germany (1999), Venice, City of Haunting Dreams (2001), The Twilight Hour (2003), This Spectred Isle (2005), Ghosthunter: A Journey Through Haunted France (2006); *Recreations* travel, fine wine; *Clubs* Chelsea Arts; *Style—* Sir Simon Marsden, Bt; ✉ The Presbytery, Hainton, Market Rasen, Lincolnshire LN8 6LR (tel and fax 01507 313646, e-mail info@marsdenarchive.com, website www.simonmarsden.co.uk)

MARSH, (Graham) Barrie; s of Ernest Heaps Marsh (d 1983), of Birkdale, Southport, and Laura Greenhalgh, *née* Baucher; *b* 18 July 1935; *Educ* Loughborough GS, Univ of Liverpool (LLB); *m* 5 April 1961, Nancy, da of Leslie Herbert Smith (d 1984), of Anstey, Leices; 1 s (Peter James b 1962), 2 da (Susan Nancy b 1964, Caroline Judith b 1966); *Career* Nat Serv with RASC 1957–59; admitted slr 1957; chm: Merseyside Chamber of Commerce and Industry 1984–86, Radio City plc 1988–94; dir Liverpool HA 1994–2000; nat chm Young Slr Gp Law Soc 1975; pres: Liverpool Law Soc 1978–79, Liverpool Publicity Assoc 1980, Slrs' Disciplinary Tbnl 1988–2001; chm Appeals Service 1989–; tstee Nat Museums and Galleries on Merseyside 1997–2006; former Belgian consul in Liverpool; FRIA; *Books* Employer and Employee (3 edn, 1989); *Recreations* hill walking, golf, birdwatching; *Clubs* Army and Navy; *Style—* Barrie Marsh, Esq; ✉ Calmer Hey, Benty Heath Lane, Willaston, Neston CH64 1SA (tel 0151 327 4863, mobile 07803 589532, e-mail g.barriemarsh@tiscali.co.uk)

MARSH, David John; s of Harry Cheetham Marsh (d 1979), of Solihull, Warks, and Florence, *née* Bold (d 1990); *b* 2 November 1936; *Educ* Leeds GS, Merton Coll Oxford (MA); *m* 26 May 1962, Hilary Joy, da of Edwin Leslie Pitt (d 1993), of Tetbury, Glos; 2 da (Carole b 1963, Rowena b 1965), 1 s (Nigel b 1966); *Career* admitted slr 1961, ptnr Wragge & Co Slrs 1963–92, ptnr Lenchwick Management Services 1992–; dir: Marla Tube Fittings Ltd 1965–, Pacs Services Ltd 2006–; chm Bd of Tstees: United Industries plc gp pension schemes 1992–2002, Neepsend plc gp pension scheme 1998–2004; memb Law Soc 1961; *Recreations* sport, travel, wine; *Style—* David Marsh, Esq; ✉ Lenchwick House, Lenchwick, Evesham, Worcestershire WR11 4TG (tel and fax 01386 442451)

MARSH, Eric Morice; s of Frederick Morice Marsh (d 1970), of Carnforth, Lancs, and Anne, *née* Leigh (d 2003); *b* 25 July 1943; *Educ* The Abbey Sch Fort Augustus, Courtfield Catering Coll Blackpool (Nat Dip Hotelkeeping & Catering); *m* 2 Sept 1968, Elizabeth Margaret, da of John (Jack) Lowes, of Macclesfield, Cheshire; 2 s (Andrew Paul b 4 Aug 1969, Christopher Simon b 5 July 1974), 2 da (Erika Louise b 26 Oct 1971, Lucy Anne b 4 Aug 1982); *Career* student Hotel Sch 1960–63, stagiaire George V Hotel Paris 1964–65, trainee The Dorchester 1965–68, asst mangr Royal Lancaster 1969–73, dir and gen mangr Newling Ward Hotels Ltd 1973–75, tenant Cavendish Hotel Chatsworth Estate 1975–; md: Paludis Ltd (trading as Cavendish Hotel) 1975–, Cavendish Aviation Ltd, Eudaemonic Leisure Ltd (trading as George Hotel Hathersage) 1996–; occasional contribs to professional pubns; dep chm Br Aerobatics Assoc; memb: Co-ordinator Ctee Neighbourhood Watch, Ctee Br Hospitality Assoc, Inst of Advanced Motorists; MInstM; *Recreations* collection of fine art, aviation (aerobatics), distance running; *Style—* Eric Marsh, Esq; ✉ Cavendish Hotel, Baslow, Derbyshire DE45 1SP (tel 01246 582311, fax 01246 582312, mobile 07770 860670, e-mail info@cavendish-hotel.net, website www.cavendish-hotel.net)

MARSH, Dr Francis Patrick (Frank); s of Horatio Septimus Marsh, of Leeds, W Yorks, and Violet Mabel Constance, *née* Murphy; *b* 15 April 1936; *Educ* Gonville & Caius Coll Cambridge (MA, MB BChir), London Hosp Med Coll Univ of London; *m* 31 Aug 1963, Pamela Anne Campbell, da of Richard Campbell Bradbury (d 1963), of London; 2 da (Penelope b 1964, Alexandra b 1971), 1 s (Nicholas b 1966); *Career* The Royal London Hosp: house offr 1960–61, registrar in med 1963–65, res fell Med Unit Med Coll 1965–67, lectr Med Coll 1967–70, sr lectr in med 1970–, conslt physician 1971–2001, sr clinical tutor 1972–85, dean of med studies Med Coll 1990–95 (memb Cncl of Govrs and Standing Ctee Med Coll 1990–95, memb Academic Bd Med Coll 1990–95, chm Bd of Examiners 1995); conslt physician London Ind Hosp 1985–2006 (emeritus conslt 2006–); SHO Kent and Canterbury Hosp 1961–62, registrar in med Royal Free Hosp 1962–63; memb Cncl Section Med RSM 1975–80 (sec 1975–77), sec NE Thames Conslts and Specialist Ctee 1984–87, chm NE Thames Regnl Med Advsy Ctee 1986–90, memb Tower Hamlets Dist Mgmnt Team 1988–89, memb Tower Hamlets Dist Exec Ctee 1990–91; emeritus conslt nephrologist Barts and the London NHS Tst 2001–; memb: Standing Ctee Bd of Studies in Med Univ of London 1976–79, Exec Ctee Renal Assoc 1983–87, Central Ctee for Hosp Med Servs 1984–87, Jt Formulary Ctee Br Nat Formulary 1986–, Jt Ctee on Higher Med Trg 1986–90, Bd of Faculty of Basic Med Sciences Queen Mary & Westfield Coll London 1990–95, Jt Academic Ctee City of E London Confedn for Med and Dentistry 1991–95, Bd of Dirs American Univ of the Caribbean 2000– (sec 2004–07, chm 2007–), Special Advsy Ctee on Renal Disease; referee/expert assessor for various medical jls and prizes and Bd of Science and Education BMA; memb: European Renal Assoc, RSM; patron: Hanbury Assoc of Renal Patients 1993–2002, Royal London Hosp Kidney Patients' Assoc 2002–; memb Mgmnt Ctee and social sec Bart's and The London Alumni Assoc 2000–03; Freeman City of London, Liveryman Worshipful Soc of Apothecaries; FRCP; *Books* incl: Hutchisons Clinical Methods (contrib, 1975, 1980, 1984, 1989 and 1996), Urology (contrib, 1976), Price's Textbook of Medicine (contrib, 1978), Oxford Textbook of Medicine (contrib, 1982, 1987), Postgraduate Nephrology (ed, 1985), Drugs and the Kidney (contrib, 1990); author of numerous original papers on renal diseases; *Recreations* music, violin playing; *Clubs* The Kennels, Goodwood Country; *Style—* Dr Frank Marsh; ✉ Butcher's End, 20 Butcher's Lane, East Dean, Chichester, West Sussex PO18 0JF (tel and fax 01243 811239, e-mail frank.marsh@virgin.net)

MARSH, Jeremy; s of Edward Marsh (decd), and Margaret, *née* Drysdale; *b* 11 May 1960; *Educ* Marlborough, West London Business Sch (BA), Harvard Business Sch (AMP); *m* Emma; 2 da (Georgina b 16 July 1990, Miranda b 13 Nov 1992); *Career* sales RCA Records 1983–84, product mgmnt Polygram records (artists incl: Brian Ferry, Roxy Music, Killing Joke, Level 42, Lloyd Cole) 1984–87, md AVL Virgin Label Div (artists incl: Neneh Cherry, Soul II Soul, Lenny Kravitz, T'Pau, Maxi Priest) 1987–90, md WEA Records (artists incl: Seal, Enya, Everything But the Girl, Madonna, REM, Prince) 1990–92, md RCA (artists incl: Robson and Jerome, M People, Take That, Annie Lennox) 1992–95, pres of music div BMG (UK) (artists incl: Natalie Imbruglia, Five, Whitney Houston, TLC) 1995–99, md Telstar Records (artists incl: Craig David, Mis-Teeq, The Hives, BBMak) 1999–2004, chm U-myx Ltd 2005–, dir Players Top 20 Ltd 2005–, md JML Ltd 2005–; co-chm Nordoff-Robbins Music Therapy Fund Raising Ctee; memb The Brits Ctee; *Clubs* Groucho, Hurlingham, Royal Lymington Yacht; *Style—* Jeremy Marsh, Esq; ✉ JML, Redloh House, 2 Michael Road, London, SW6 2AD (tel 020 7736 3377, fax 020 7731 0567, mobile 07785 317999, e-mail tash@jjdm.net)

MARSH, Prof Sir John Stanley; kt (1999), CBE (1993); s of Stanley Albert Marsh (d 1973), and Elsie Gertrude, *née* Powell (d 1969); *b* 5 October 1931; *Educ* George Dixon GS Birmingham, St John's Coll Oxford (MA); *m* 20 Sept 1958, Kathleen Edith, da of Eric Arthur Casey (d 1982); 1 s (Peter b 1967), 1 da (Christine b 1969); *Career* Nat Serv RAF 1950–52; Univ of Reading 1956–77: res economist, lectr, sr lectr, reader; prof of agric economics Univ of Aberdeen 1977–84; Univ of Reading 1984–97: prof of agric economics 1984–97, dean agric 1986–89 dir Centre for Agric Strategy 1990–97 (now emeritus); author of numerous articles and pubns on agric related topics; pres Br Inst of Agricultural Consits (BIAC); sec Agric Economics Soc 1969–84; chm: Agric Wages Bd 1990–99, Responsible Use of Resources in Agriculture and on the Land (RURAL) 1997–, Task Force on Pricing of Animal Medicines 2000–01, Task Force on Pricing of Inputs 2001, Centre for Dairy Information 2005; vice-chm Science Advsy Ctee Defra 2004–07; memb: Potato Mktg Bd 1979–84, SWP Food and Drink Mfrg 1990–92, Ctee Hunting with Dogs 2000; FRSA 1978, FRASE 1991, FRAgS 1993, CBiol, FIBiol; *Books* A Preliminary Study of the Small Dairy Farm and the Small Farm Scheme (1960), The National Association of Corn and Agricultural Merchants and the Merchant's Future (1967), A Future for European Agriculture (jtly, 1971), CAP: UK Priorities, European Opinion (1976), L'Ordre Alimentaire Mondial (contrib, 1982), The Human Food Chain (contrib, 1989), The Changing Role of the Common Agricultural Policy (jtly, 1991), GM Crops: The Scientists Speak (contrib, 2003); *Recreations* photography, caravanning; *Clubs* Farmers'; *Style—* Prof Sir John Marsh, CBE; ✉ 15 Adams Way, Earley, Reading, Berkshire RG6 5UT (tel and fax 0118 986 8434, e-mail john.marsh27@ntlworld.com)

MARSH, June Margaret; da of Frederick John Palmer (d 1981), of Cheshunt, Hertfordshire, and Ivy Margaret, *née* Tate; *b* 3 July 1948; *Educ* King Harold Sch Waltham Abbey Essex, London Coll of Fashion; *m* Graham John Marsh, s of late Frederick John Marsh; *Career* fashion ed: Woman's Own 1974–78, Evening News 1979–80, TV Times 1980–81; ed Browns magazine 1980–81, fashion and beauty ed Options 1981–86, tutor St Martin's Sch of Art 1986–; contrib ed: Sunday Times, Times, Evening Standard, Vogue, Observer, Sunday Express Magazine, New Woman, Company Magazine, The Daily Telegraph; fashion ed: Country Life 1986–95, Daily Mail 1995–97; freelance ed and writer 1997–memb NUJ; *Recreations* reading, writing, painting; *Style—* Mrs June Marsh; ✉ 12 King George Street, Greenwich, London SE10 8QJ (tel 020 8691 0568, fax 020 8961 5445, e-mail jmmarsh@ukonline.co.uk)

MARSH, Kevin John; s of John Marsh (d 1986), and Elizabeth Jill, *née* Linggard; *b* 14 November 1954; *Educ* Doncaster GS, ChCh Oxford (MA, chorister Exeter Coll), Salzburg Seminar; *m* 1 Dec 1979, Melissa Sue, *née* Fletcher; 1 s (John Frederick Alexander (Jack) b 1987), 1 da (Ellen Beatrice b 1990); *Career* joined BBC 1978; BBC Radio 4: ed PM 1989, ed World at One 1992, launched Broadcasting House 1998, ed Today 2002–06; ed BBC Coll of Jounalism 2006–; visiting fell: Bournemouth Univ 2006–, World Economic Forum Davos 2004, 2005 and 2006; Silver Sony Radio Award 1989, 1990 and 1991, Amnesty Int Radio Award 2000; alumnus Prince of Wales Business and the Environemtn Prog; memb Chatham House; FRSA; *Recreations* rugby, opera, lute music, theology, living in France; *Clubs* Wasps RFC; *Style—* Kevin Marsh, Esq; ✉ BBC College of Journalism, London W12 7TQ (website www.storycurve.blogspot.com)

MARSH, Dame Mary Elizabeth; DBE (2007); da of George Donald Falconer (d 1992), and Lesley Mary, *née* Wilson (d 1998); *b* 17 August 1946; *Educ* Birkenhead HS GPDST, Univ of Nottingham (BSc), Hatfield Poly (DipEd), London Business Sch (MBA); *m* 1968, Juan Enrique Marsh (d 1999); 4 s (Alexander b 18 April 1972, Tristan b 3 Dec 1973, George b 21 Aug 1976, Oliver b 29 Sept 1978); *Career* asst teacher Icknield HS Luton 1968–69, head of geography St Christopher Sch Letchworth 1969–71, full time mother 1972–80, dep head St Christopher Sch Letchworth 1980–90, head Queens' Sch Bushey 1990–95, head Holland Park Sch 1995–2000, dir and chief exec NSPCC 2000–; nat memb Learning and Skills Cncl 2005–; tstee: NCVCCO, Young Enterprise; memb Demos, govr Shooters Hill Post 16 Campus; hon pres Students' Union Univ of Nottingham; Hon LLD: Univ of Luton 2003, Univ of Nottingham 2005; FRSA; *Recreations* walking, swimming, music, reading; *Clubs* Reform, Reebok Sports (London); *Style—* Dame Mary Marsh, DBE; ✉ NSPCC, Weston House, 42 Curtain Road, London EC2A 3NH (tel 020 7825 2586, fax 020 7285 2587, e-mail mmarsh@nspcc.org.uk)

MARSH, Prof Paul Rodney; s of Harold Marsh, of Bournemouth, and Constance, *née* Miller; *b* 19 August 1947; *Educ* Poole GS, LSE (BSc Econ), London Business Sch (PhD); *m* 13 Sept 1971, Stephanie, da of Mark Simonow, of London; *Career* systems analyst: Esso Petroleum 1968–69, Scicon 1970–71; Bank of England res fell London Business Sch 1974–85; Centre for Mgmnt Devpt London Business Sch: non-exec dir 1984–91, prof of fin 1985–2006 (emeritus prof 2006–), memb Governing Body 1986–90, faculty dean 1987–90, dep princ 1989–90, assoc dean Fin Programmes 1993–2004; non-exec dir: M&G Investment Mgmnt 1989–97, M&G Gp plc 1998–99, Hoare Govett Indices Ltd 1991–, Majedie Investments plc 1999–2006, Aberforth Smaller Companies Tst 2004–; govr Examinations Bd Securities Inst 1994–2002; author of numerous pubns on corporate fin and investment mgmnt in: Jl of Finance, Jl of Business, Jl of Financial Economics, Harvard Business Review, Jl of the Institute of Actuaries, Research in Marketing, Long Range Planning, Financial Analysts Jl, Jl of Applied Corp Finance; memb CBI task force on city-industry relationships 1986–88; memb Exec Ctee Br Acad of Mgmnt 1986–89; memb: Euro Fin Assoc, American Fin Assoc; *Books* Cases in Corporate Finance (1988), Managing Strategic Investment Decisions (1988), Accounting for Brands (1989), Short-Termism on Trial (1990), The Millennium Book: A Century of Investment Returns (2000), Triumph of the Optimists (2002), Global Investment Returns Yearbook (annually, 2001–07), The HGSC Smaller Companies Index (annually, 1987–2007); *Recreations* gardening; *Style—* Prof Paul Marsh; ✉ London Business School, Regents Park, London NW1 4SA (tel 020 7000 7000, fax 020 7000 7001, e-mail pmarsh@london.edu)

MARSH, Baron (Life Peer UK 1981), of Mannington in the County of Wiltshire; Richard William Marsh; kt (1976), PC (1966); s of William Marsh, of Belvedere, Kent; *b* 14 March 1928; *Educ* Jennings Sch Swindon, Woolwich Poly, Ruskin Coll Oxford; *m* 1, 1950 (m dis 1973), Evelyn Mary, da of Frederick Andrews, of Southampton; 2 s (Hon Andrew b 1950,

Hon Christopher b 1960); m 2, 1973, Caroline Dutton (d 1975); m 3, 1979, Hon Felicity Carmen Francesca, o da of Baron McFadzean of Kelvinside (Life Peer, d 1992); *Career* health servs offr Nat Union of Public Employees 1951–59; memb Clerical and Admin Whitley Cncl for Health Serv 1953–59; MP (Lab) Greenwich 1959–71; memb Nat Exec Fabian Soc; Parly sec Miny of Labour 1964–65, jt Parly sec Miny of Technol 1965–66, Min of Power 1966–68, Min of Tport 1968–70; chm: Br Railways Bd 1971–76, Newspaper Publishers' Assoc 1976–90, Br Iron and Steel Consumers' Cncl 1977–83, Lee Cooper plc 1982–88, TV-AM (pt/t) 1983–84, China and Eastern Investment Trust (Hong Kong) 1987–99, Mannington Management Services Ltd 1989–, Laurentian Financial Group plc 1989–, Lopex plc 1990–97, Gartmore British Income & Growth Tst 1994–; dir Imperial Life of Canada (Toronto) 1984–97; chm Special Tstees Guy's Hosp 1983–97; Fell Inst of Mktg, FCIT, Fell IOD, FIMgt; *Style*— The Rt Hon the Lord Marsh, PC; ⊠ House of Lords, London SW1A 0PW

MARSH, Thérèse Virginia (Terry); da of late Rear Adm John Anthony Bell, CB, of Taunton, and Eileen Joan, *née* Woodman, of Esher; *b* 3 December 1946; *Educ* St Joseph's Convent London, Norfolk Catholic HS Virginia, Gumley House Isleworth, Univ of Liverpool (BEd), Univ of Surrey (MSc); *m* 1968 (m dis 1980), Michael Frederick Marsh, s of late Francis Joseph Marsh; 2 da (Suzanna Joan (Mrs Ian Fry) b 14 Nov 1970, Caroline Margaret b 7 Jan 1972); *Career* mathematics teacher Trinity HS Trinidad 1970, princ Ifold Nursery Centre Sussex 1972–76, financial controller Marsh Developments Guildford 1976–77, assoc lectr in statistics Univ of Surrey 1977–78; BBC: researcher BBC Educn 1979–80, dir Playschool 1980–83, prodr BBC Omputer Literacy Project BBC Continuing Educn 1984–89, exec prodr BBC School TV 1989–90, head of BBC School TV 1990–92, head bi-media BBC School Progs 1992–95; vice-pres programming Sci-Fi Europe 1995–97, conslt digital media strategy for various cos incl Granada, BBC Technol, Pearson and News Int, chief exec London Gifted and Talented 2004–05, currently dir WISE (Women into Sci, Engrg and Construction); memb: Steering Ctee TVYP Edinburgh Int TV Festival 1991–2004, Cncl RTS 2002–07; winner Times Technology Programme Award for Micro Live, City of Basle Award for Sex Education; memb RTS 1988; *Recreations* community theatre, dancing; *Style*— Ms Terry Marsh; ⊠ e-mail tv.marsh@virgin.net

MARSH, William Renold Arthur; s of Patrick Marsh, of London, and Ann, *née* Shell; *b* 12 March 1962, London; *Educ* Monkton Combe Sch Bath, Univ of Durham (BA), Coll of Law Guildford; *m* 20 June 1992, Dr Belinda Marsh, *née* Dawes; 3 s (Nicholas b 9 Dec 1992, James, Charles (twins) b 22 May 1996); *Career* slr; Osborne Clarke 1985–87 and 1988–90, Linklaters 1987–88; dir: CEDR 1990–2002, Conflict Mgmnt Int 2002–; memb Advsy Bd Int Centre for Reconciliation Coventry Cathedral; memb Law Soc 1987, accredited mediator CEDR 1992; *Publications* The ADR Practice Guide: Commercial Dispute Resolution (jtly, 1995), Mediators on Mediation (2005); *Recreations* music, fishing, family; *Style*— William Marsh, Esq; ⊠ Hurstwood Place, Hurstwood Lane, nr Haywards Heath, West Sussex RH17 7QY (tel 01444 443848, fax 01444 443847, e-mail wm@billmarsh.co.uk); Conflict Management International, 212 Piccadilly, London W1J 9HG (tel 020 7917 6040, fax 020 7917 6041, e-mail wm@cmi-consulting.com)

MARSHAL, Lyndsey; da of Abdul Baluch, and Sheila Handley; *Educ* Lostock HS, Shena Simon Coll, Welsh Coll of Music and Drama (BA); *Career* actress; *Theatre* Our Country's Good (Manchester Library Theatre) 1997, The Maids (Edinburgh Festival Theatre) 2000, Miss Julie (Hungarian tour) 2000, Top Girls (New Vic Theatre) 2000, Fire Face (Royal Court) 2000, Boston Marriage (Donmar Warehouse and New Ambassadors) 2001 and 2002 (nomination Best Supporting Actress Olivier Awards 2002), Redundant (Royal Court) 2001, Bright (Soho Theatre) 2002, A Midsummer Night's Dream (Bristol Old Vic) 2003 (TMA Award), The Crucible (Crucible Theatre Sheffield) 2004; nomination Best Newcomer Evening Standard Theatre Awards 2001, Best Newcomer Critics Circle Theatre Awards 2002; *Television* That's Not Me 1998, Peak Practice 2000, Midsomer Murders 2001, Sons and Lovers 2002, The Young Visitors 2003, Rome 2006, Green 2007; *Radio* Tess of the D'Urbervilles (BBC Radio 4) 2001, Holiday (BBC Radio 4) 2002, Bunn Eco (BBC Radio 4) 2002, Night Class (BBC Radio 4) 2002, Clear Water (BBC Radio 3) 2002, Before the Flood (BBC Radio 4) 2002, Heredity (BBC Radio 4) 2003, Lessons in Psychic Awareness (BBC Radio 4) 2004; *Film* The Hours 2001, Standing Room Only (short film) 2002, A Gathering Storm 2002, The Calcium Kid 2002, A Lonely War 2002, Frozen 2003, Festival 2004, Snuff Movie 2005; *Recreations* cinema, spending time with friends; *Style*— Miss Lyndsey Marshal

MARSHALL, Andrew Paul; s of Michael David Marshall, of Lowestoft, Suffolk, and Doris Constance, *née* Greaves; *b* 27 August 1954; *Educ* Lowestoft Co GS, Borough Rd Coll Isleworth, Inst of Educn London (BEd); *Partner* Mark Laidler; *Career* freelance screenwriter; contrib Week Ending (BBC Radio) during mid-1970's; work with David Renwick, *qv*: 47 episodes of The Burkiss Way (Radio 4); for LWT: End of Part One (Harlequin Award), Whoops Apocalypse (NY International Film and TV Festival Award, RTS Award 1981), Hot Metal (Emmy nomination); for BBC TV: Alexei Sayle's Stuff (3 series) 1989–91 (International Emmy, Broadcasting Press Guild Award, Writers' Guild Award), If You See God, Tell Him; others incl: The Steam Video Company (Thames), Whoops Apocalypse (film, ITC), Wilt (film, Rank/LWT); stage play Angry Old Men 1995; as solo writer: Sob Sisters (CTV) 1989, several episodes Poirot (LWT) 1991, 2point4 children (BBC, 8 series) 1990–99, Health & Efficiency (BBC) 1993–94, DAD (BBC) 1997–2000, Strange 2002–03 (BBC); *Books* The Burkiss Way, Whoops Apocalypse; *Recreations* feature animation, architecture, modern art, classic television; *Style*— Andrew Marshall, Esq; ⊠ c/o Nick Marston, Curtis Brown, 4th Floor, Haymarket House, 28–29 Haymarket, London SW1Y 4SP (tel 020 7396 6600)

MARSHALL, David; MP; *b* 7 May 1941; *Educ* Larbert, Denny and Falkirk High Schs, Woodside Sr Secondary Sch; *m* 1968, Christina; 2 s, 1 da; *Career* joined Lab Pty 1962, memb TGWU, former Lab Pty organiser for Glasgow, cncllr Glasgow Corp 1972–75, vice-chm Gtr Glasgow Passenger Tport Authy, regnl cncllr Strathclyde 1974–79 (chief whip, chm Manpower Ctee), former chm Manpower Ctee of the Convention of Scottish Local Authorities (COSLA), former memb LACSAB; MP (Lab) Glasgow Shettleston 1979–; chair Select Ctee on Scottish Affairs 1997–2001 (memb 1981–83), memb Select Ctee on Tport 1985–96 (chm 1987–92), memb Liaison Ctee 1987–92; sec Scottish Labour MPs 1981–2001, chm PLP Tport Ctee 1987–97, co-chm Parly Advsy Cncl for Tport Safety (PACTS) 1991–93; sponsored Solvent Abuse (Scotland) Act 1983; *Recreations* music, gardening; *Style*— David Marshall, Esq, MP; ⊠ 32 Enterkin Street, Glasgow G32 7BA (tel 0141 778 8125); House of Commons, London SW1A 0AA (tel 020 7219 5134, e-mail davidmarshallmp@parliament.uk)

MARSHALL, Dr Enid Ann; da of Rev John Marshall (d 1945), of Whitehills, Banff, and Lizzie, *née* Gilchrist (d 1975); *b* 10 July 1932; *Educ* Whitehills Jr Secdy, Banff Acad, Bell-Baxter Sch Cupar, Univ of St Andrews (MA, LLB, PhD); *Career* apprentice slr Pagan & Osborne WS Cupar 1956–59, lectr in law Dundee Coll of Technol 1959–72; Univ of Stirling: lectr in business law 1972–74, sr lectr in business law 1974–77, reader in business law 1977–94, reader in Scots Law Research Unit 1994–99; ed: Arbitration Section The Journal of Business Law 1976–, Scottish Law Gazette 1983–2001; chm Social Security Appeal Tbnl Stirling and Falkirk 1984–; memb: Law Soc of Scot 1959, Scot Law Agents Soc 1960; FRSA 1984, Hon ARICS 1986, ACIArb 1988; *Books* incl: General Principles of Scots Law (1971, 7 edn 1999), The Companies (Floating Charges and Receivers) (Scotland) Act 1972 (1972), Scottish Cases on Contract (1978, 2 edn 1993), Scottish Cases on Agency (1980), Scottish Cases on Partnerships and Companies (1980), Scots Mercantile Law (1983, 3 edn 1997), Oliver and Marshall's Company Law (12 edn

1994), Gill: The Law of Arbitration (4 edn, 2001); *Recreations* animal welfare, veganism; *Style*— Dr Enid A Marshall; ⊠ 3 Ballater Drive, Stirling FK9 5JH (tel 01786 472125)

MARSHALL, Ernest Harold; OBE (1999); s of Ernest Marshall (d 1931), of Chadwell Heath, London, and Annie Beatrice, *née* Lefever (d 1967); *b* 29 November 1924; *Educ* Rayleigh Sr Sch, Shrewsbury, Univ of Bonn, Univ of Tehran; *m* 21 July 1954, Christine Louise Harrad, of Thundersley, Essex; 2 s (Ian b 22 July 1960, Nicholas b 16 Dec 1964); *Career* RAF Polish Sqdn 1942–47, Pilsudski Medal (Poland) 1944; dir Sedgwick Group 1964–81, conslt 1981–; underwriter Lloyd's 1969–2001, vice-pres Insurance Inst London 1978–, chm Redcar Underwriting Ltd 2001–; St John Ambulance: pres Rayleigh Div 1984–91, dep pres Essex 1993–94, chm Cncl Essex 1994–99 and 2002–04 (memb 1986–), dir SE Essex Tech Coll 1989–91; pres Rochford Constituency Cons Assoc 1986–89; hon prof Tehran Univ 1976; Freeman City of London 1980, Liveryman Worshipful Co of Insurers 1981; memb: CIB 1974–81, IRIB 2000 (IBRC 1981), CStJ 1997 (OStJ 1988); *Books* Construction and Erection Insurance (1978, 1985 and 1999), Directors' and Officers' Liability (1986); *Recreations* travel, fine arts; *Style*— Ernest Marshall, Esq, OBE; ⊠ Beverley Lodge, Great Wheatley Road, Rayleigh, Essex SS6 7AP (tel 01268 775156, fax 01268 776919, e-mail 32marsh@waitrose.com)

MARSHALL, Prof Gordon; CBE (2003); *b* 20 June 1952; *Educ* Univ of Stirling (BA), Univ of Oxford (DPhil); *Career* research fell in sociology Nuffield Coll Oxford 1977–78, lectr in sociology Univ of Essex 1978–88 (sr lectr 1988–90), prof of sociology Univ of Bath 1990–93, official fell Nuffield Coll Oxford 1993–2000, chief exec ESRC 2000–02, vice-chllr Univ of Reading 2003–; visiting prof: Univ of Uppsala 1989, Central European Univ Prague 1993, Univ of Stockholm 1996; Morris Ginsberg Fellowship in Sociology LSE 1985, Sir Norman Chester Visiting Fellowship Nuffield Coll Oxford 1991, Br Acad/Leverhulme Tst Sr Research Fellowship 1992; Hon DUniv Stirling; memb: Acad of Social Sciences 2000, Euro Acad of Sociology 2001, Royal Norwegian Soc for Sciences and Letters 2001; FBA 2000; *Publications* Presbyteries and Profits: Calvinism and the Development of Capitalism in Scotland, 1560–1707 (1980), In Search of the Spirit of Capitalism (1982), Social Class in Modern Britain (1988), In Praise of Sociology (1990), The Oxford Dictionary of Sociology (1994), Against the Odds? Social Class and Social Justice in Industrial Societies (1997), Repositioning Class: Social Inequality in Industrial Societies (1997); numerous book chapters and articles in jls; *Style*— Prof Gordon Marshall, CBE; ⊠ The University of Reading, Whiteknights, PO Box 217, Reading RG6 6AH (tel 0118 378 6226, fax 0118 987 4062, e-mail g.marshall@reading.ac.uk)

MARSHALL, Her Hon Judge Hazel Eleanor; QC (1988); da of Geoffrey Briddon, of Barton on Sea, Hants, and late Nancy Briddon, *née* Nicholson; *b* 14 January 1947; *Educ* Wimbledon HS for Girls GPDST, St Hilda's Coll Oxford (MA); *m* 1, 24 June 1969, R Williamson; *m* 2, 16 Sept 1983, H Marshall, FRICS; *Career* called to the Bar Gray's Inn 1972 (Atkin scholar, bencher 1996); practised as barr as Miss Hazel Williamson, QC; dep High Ct judge 1994–, recorder 1996–2006, sr Chancery circuit judge Central London Civil Justice Centre 2006–; actg deemster IOM 1999–, chm Chancery Bar Assoc 1994–97; memb: Property Advsy Gp DOE/ODPM 1994–2003, Legal Advsy Bd Estates Gazette 2002–, Public Guardian Bd 2007–; jt ed and contrib Law and Valuation of Leisure Property; nat vice-pres Fedn of Townswomen's Guilds 2001–06; Lady Mayoress City of Wesminster 2001–02; hon memb: ESU, Royal Soc of St George; accredited mediator ADR Chambers (UIC) 2000; FCIArb 1992; *Recreations* gardening, opera, occasional offshore sailing; *Clubs* Royal Over-Seas League (hon memb); *Style*— Her Hon Judge Hazel Marshall, QC; ⊠ Central London Civil Justice Centre, 26 Park Crescent, London W1B 1HT (tel 020 7917 7893)

MARSHALL, Prof (Ian) Howard; s of Ernest Ewart Marshall (d 1977), and Ethel, *née* Curran; *b* 12 January 1934; *Educ* Dumfries Acad, Aberdeen GS, Univ of Aberdeen (MA, BD, PhD), Univ of Cambridge (BA), Univ of Göttingen; *m* 25 March 1961, Joyce Elizabeth (d 1996), da of Frederick John Proudfoot (d 1971); 1 s (Neil), 3 da (Morag, Aileen, Alison); *Career* asst tutor Didsbury Coll Bristol 1960–62, methodist min Darlington 1962–64; Univ of Aberdeen: lectr 1964–70, sr lectr 1970–77, reader 1977–79, prof 1979–99, dean Faculty of Divinity 1981–84, head Dept of Divinity with Religious Studies 1996–98, hon res prof of New Testament 1999–; Hon DD Asbury 1996; *Books* Eschatology and the Parables (1963, 1978), Pocket Guide to Christian Beliefs (1963, 1978, 1989), The Work of Christ (1969, 1994), Kept by the Power of God (1969, 1975, 1995), Luke: Historian and Theologian (1970, 1989), The Origins of New Testament Christology (1976), New Testament Interpretation (ed 1977, 1979), The Gospel of Luke (New International Greek Testament Commentary, 1978), I Believe in the Historical Jesus (1977, 2002), The Epistles of John (New International Commentary on the New Testament, 1978), Acts (Tyndale NT Commentaries, 1980), Last Supper and Lord's Supper (1980), Biblical Inspiration (1982, 1995), 1 and 2 Thessalonians (New Century Bible, 1983), Christian Experience in Theology and Life (ed, 1988), Jesus The Saviour (1990), I Peter (IVP New Testament Commentary Series, 1991), The Theology of the Shorter Pauline Letters (with K P Donfried, 1992), The Acts of the Apostles (New Testament Guides, 1992), The Epistle to the Philippians (1993), Witness to the Gospel (ed with D Peterson, 1998), The Pastoral Epistles (1999), Moulton and Geden: Concordance to the Greek New Testament (ed, 2002), Exploring the New Testament, Volume 2: The Letters and Revelation (with S Travis and I Paul, 2002), Beyond the Bible (2004), New Testament Theology (2004); *Recreations* reading, walking, gardening, music; *Style*— Prof I Howard Marshall; ⊠ School of Divinity, History and Philosophy, University of Aberdeen, Aberdeen AB24 3UB (tel 01224 272388, fax 01224 273750)

MARSHALL, Dr James Charles; OBE (2004); s of James Charles Marshall (d 1964), of London, and Beatrice Fanny, *née* Wingrove (d 1984); *b* 29 July 1923; *m* 1, 1942 (m dis 1971), Violet Elizabeth, da of Samuel Wheeler Dover; 1 s (Terry b 15 March 1944); *m* 2, 1975 (m dis 1982), Irene, *née* Philips; 1 da (Victoria b 18 Aug 1971); *Career* professional musician and singer, then drummer, dance, band leader and drum teacher 1949–60; md: Jim Marshall & Son 1960–63, J & T Marshall Ltd 1963–66, Marshall Amplification plc 1962–, Marshall Music 1966–80; mfr of Marshall Amplification and winner Queen's Award for Export Achievement 1984 and 1992; handprints in: Rock Wall of Fame Sunset Boulevard Hollywood, Mexican Walk of Fame; vice-pres: London Fedn of Boys' Clubs, Bucks Assoc of Youth Clubs; former pres Bedfordshire Youth Assoc, memb ctee MacIntyre Homes Milton Keynes; companion Grand Order of Water Rats (awarded badge of merit 2003); Freeman City of London; *Style*— Dr James Marshall, OBE; ⊠ Marshall Amplification plc, Denbigh Road, Bletchley, Milton Keynes MK1 1DQ (tel 01908 375411, fax 01908 376118)

MARSHALL, (John) Jeremy Seymour; s of Edward Pope Marshall (d 1983), of Truro, Cornwall, and Nita Helen, *née* Seymour; *b* 18 April 1938; *Educ* Sherborne, New Coll Oxford (MA); *m* 20 July 1962, Juliette Anne, da of (Archibald) Donald Butterley (d 1957), of Leicester; 2 da (Sarah b 1964, Anna b 1971), 1 s (Simon b 1965); *Career* Nat Serv Lt Royal Signals 1956–58; Wiggins Teape 1962–64, Riker Laboratories 1964–67, CIBA Agrochems 1967–71, Hanson plc 1971–87; md: Dufaylite Developments Ltd 1971–76, SLD Olding Ltd 1976–79; chief exec: Lindustries Ltd 1979–86, Imperial Foods Ltd 1986–87, BAA plc 1987–89, De La Rue plc 1989–98; non-exec dir: John Mowlem & Co plc 1991–97, Camelot Group plc 1993–98, BTR plc 1995–99; chm: Hillsdown Holdings plc 1998–99, Nexus plc 1998–2000, Trans Siberian Gold plc 2001–06; memb Cncl Sch of Mgmnt Studies Univ of Oxford 1995–2002, non-exec dir Fleet Exec Bd RN 2001–05; tstee Design Museum 1996–2006 (hon treas), chm Varrier Jones Fndn, chm St John's Ambulance Cambs; High Sheriff Cambs 2006–07 CIMgt, FCILT; *Recreations* tennis, squash, skiing, shooting, golf; *Clubs* RAC; *Style*— Jeremy Marshall, Esq; ✉ Willow House, Bourn, Cambridge CB3 7SQ (tel 01954 719435, fax 01954 718447, e-mail jmarshall@clara.net)

MARSHALL, Margaret Anne (Mrs Graeme Davidson); OBE (1999); *b* 4 January 1949; *Educ* Stirling HS, Royal Scottish Acad of Music and Drama; *m* 25 March 1970, Graeme Griffiths King Davidson; 2 da (Nicola b 19 Nov 1974, Julia b 29 Dec 1977); *Career* soprano; first prize Munich Int Festival 1974; concert and opera appearances at numerous international venues incl: Royal Opera House Covent Garden, La Scala Milan, Vienna Staatsoper, Frankfurt Opera, Salzburg Festival, Florence, Hamburg, Cologne; winner Gulliver Award for Performing Arts in Scotland 1992; has made numerous recordings incl: Cosi fan Tutte (Mozart, with Riccardo Muti, live from Salzburg Festival), Stagat Mater (Pergolesi, with Claudio Abbaddo), Orfeo (Mozart, with Great Mozart Singers), All Sacred Vocal Music (Vivaldi); *Recreations* skiing, squash, tennis, cooking; *Clubs* Gleneagle Country; *Style*— Miss Margaret Marshall, OBE

MARSHALL, Prof Mary Tara; OBE (1997); da of Percy Johnson Marshall, and April Johnson Marshall (d 1999); *b* 13 June 1945, Darjeeling, India; *Educ* Univ of Edinburgh (MA), LSE (Dip Social Admin), Univ of Liverpool (Dip Applied Social Studies); *Partner* Ronald Scott Smith; *Career* child care offr London Borough of Lambeth 1967–69, social worker Liverpool Personal Service Soc 1970–74, research project organiser Age Concern Liverpool 1974–75, lectr in applied social studies Univ of Liverpool 1975–83, dir Age Concern Scotland 1983–89, dir Dementia Services Devpt Centre Univ of Stirling 1989–2006, now emeritus prof; currently sessional inspr Scottish Social Work Inspection Agency; memb: Editorial Advsy Bd Health & Social Care in the Community, Editorial Bd Alzheimer's Care Quarterly (ACQ), 21st Century Social Work Ctee 2004–06; former chair: Liverpool Housing Tst, Liverpool Cncl for Voluntary Services Welfare Orgns Ctee, Assoc of Chief Offrs of Scottish Voluntary Orgns, Exec Ctee Br Soc of Gerontology; former memb: Advsy Panel Centre for Policy on Ageing (also former govr), Royal Cmmn on Long Term Care of the Elderly, Modernisation Bd NHS in Scotland, Nat Care Standards Ctee, Bd Edinvar Housing Assoc; Hon DEd Queen Margaret UC Edinburgh, Hon DSc Univ of Edinburgh 2004, DUniv Stirling 2006; memb Br Assoc of Social Workers (BASW) 1971 (sometime memb Health and Handicap Advsy Panel); AcSS 2002, FRSE 2003, FRSA 2003; *Publications* Social Work in Action (jt ed, 1979), Teamwork: For and Against (jt ed, 1979), Loss (jt ed, 1983), Social Work with Old People (1983, 4 edn 2006), New Services for Old People (jtly, 1983), Social Work in the Eighties (jt ed, 1984), Guidelines for Social Workers Working with People with Dementia and their Carers (ed, 1988), Working with Dementia. Guidelines for Professionals (ed, 1990), Effective Management (jt ed, 1991), Dementia: New Skills for Social Workers (jt ed, 1993), Dementia Care (jtly, 1994), Social Work with Old People (jt ed, 1996), "I Can't Place This Place At All": Working with People with Dementia and their Carers (1996), The State of Art in Dementia Care (ed, 1997), Past Trauma in Late Life: European Perspectives on Therapeutic Work with Older People (jt ed, 1997), Dementia and Technology (1997), Design for Dementia (jt ed, 1998), Facing our Futures: Discrimination in Later Life (jtly, 1998), Keeping in Touch: Ethical Dimensions (1998), A Guide to Using Technology within Dementia Care (ed, 2000), Food, Glorious Food, Perspectives on Food and Dementia (ed, 2003), Perspectives on Rehabilitation and Dementia (ed, 2005), Dementia: walking nor wandering (jtly, 2006); author of numerous book chapters, articles, reports and published papers; *Recreations* bird watching, photography; *Clubs* Drumsheugh Baths; *Style*— Prof Mary Marshall, OBE; ✉ 24 Buckingham Terrace, Edinburgh EH4 3AE (tel 0131 343 1732, e-mail mary@marymarshall7.wanadoo.co.uk)

MARSHALL, Michael John; CBE (1999), DL (Cambs 1989); s of Sir Arthur Gregory George Marshall, OBE, DL (d 2007), and Rosemary Wynford, *née* Dimsdale (d 1988); *b* 27 January 1932; *Educ* Eton, Jesus Coll Cambridge (MA, Rowing blue, rep GB in European Championships 1955); *m* 1, 1960 (m dis 1977), Bridget Wykham Pollock; 2 s, 2 da; m 2, 1979, Sibyl Mary Walkinshaw, *née* Hutton; 2 step s; *Career* RAF pilot 1950–52; Marshall of Cambridge (Engineering) Ltd: joined 1955, dep chm and md 1964–90; chm and chief exec Marshall of Cambridge (Holdings) Ltd 1990–; dir Eastern Electricity Bd 1971–77; chm BL Cars Distributor Cncl 1977 and 1983 (memb 1975–84); vice-pres: IMI 1980–, Engrg Employers Fedn 1993–; chm Cambs Manpower Ctee 1980–83, chm Cambridge Olympic Appeal 1984, vice-chm Cambs Youth Involvement Ctee Silver Jubilee Fund 1977–78, memb Ely Cathedral Restoration Appeal Co Ctee 1978–, pres Cambridge Soc for the Blind 1989–92, chm Prince's Tsts' Cambs Appeal Ctee 1991–92, pres Cambridge 99 Rowing Club 1996–2002, pres Fund for Addenbrooke's 2000–, memb Bd Great Cambridge Partnership 2002–; chm: Civilian Ctee 104 (City of Cambridge) Sqdn ATC 1975–, Beds and Cambs Wing ATC 1987–93; memb: Air Cadet Cncl 1994–2006, Cncl Air League 1995– (chm 1998–2003, pres 2003–); hon vice-patron Royal Int Air Tattoo 2003–; Hon Air Cdre No 2623 (East Anglian) Sqdn RAuxAF 2003–; High Sheriff Cambs 1988, Vice Lord-Lt Cambs 1992–2006; Freeman City of London, Liveryman Guild of Air Pilots and Air Navigators; Hon DUniv Anglia Ruskin 2001; IEng, Licentiate Automobile Engr (LAE), FRAeS, FRSA, FIMI, CIMgt, FInstD; *Recreations* flying, friends, countryside; *Clubs* RAF, Hawks' (Cambridge); *Style*— Michael Marshall, Esq, CBE, DL; ✉ Marshall of Cambridge (Holdings) Ltd, The Airport, Cambridge CB5 8RX (tel 01223 373245/373825, fax 01223 324224)

MARSHALL, Nigel Bernard Dickenson; s of Norman Dickenson Marshall (d 1958), of Lea, Lincs, and (Gertrude) Olga, *née* Pumfrey (d 1991); *b* 9 April 1935; *Educ* Rugby, Queens' Coll Cambridge (MA, LLM); *Career* slr Herbert Smith & Co London 1961–63; ptnr: Underwood and Co London 1964–90, Miller and Co Cambridge 1969–88; sole practitioner 1990–2006; clerk: St Edward's Parochial Charity Cambridge 1967–90, The Great St Mary's Charity Cambridge 1967–71, The Wray Jackenett Merrill & Elie Charity Cambridge 1971–72; sec Cambridge and Dist Trade Protection Assoc 1967–86; *Recreations* gardening, collecting; *Clubs* Boodle's, East India, Oxford and Cambridge, Pitt (Cambridge), City Univ, Oriental, Lansdowne; *Style*— Nigel Marshall, Esq; ✉ The Old Rectory, Lea, Gainsborough, Lincolnshire DN21 5JA; 50 Rawlings Street, London SW3 2LS

MARSHALL, Paul Roderick Clucas; s of Alan Marshall, of London, and Mary Sylvia Clucas Hanlin; *b* 2 August 1959; *Educ* Merchant Taylors', St John's Coll Oxford (BA), INSEAD (Louis Frank scholar, MBA); *m* 1986, Sabina Perrini de Balkany, da of Giorgio Perrini; 1 s (Winston Aubrey Aladar b 20 Dec 1987), 1 da (Giovanna Mary Ilus b 2 Oct 1990); *Career* int trainee Germany and Switzerland then foreign exchange dealer London Lloyds Bank International 1981–84; Mercury Asset Management Group plc: joined 1985, dir i/c Continental European equity investenmt Warburg Asset Management 1989, dir Mercury Asset Management plc 1995; currently co-fndr Marshall Wace Asset Management; research asst to Charles Kennedy MP 1984, Parly candidate (SDP/Lib Alliance) Fulham 1987, chm City Lib Dems 1994, memb Exec Ctee Lib Dem Business Liaison Gp 1995; *Recreations* family, history, soccer (Manchester United), tennis, music; *Style*— Paul Marshall, Esq

MARSHALL, Peter Joseph; s of Steve Marshall (d 1977), and Vera Marshall (d 2004); *b* 28 July 1952; *Educ* De La Salle Coll Jersey, Birmingham Poly; *m* 3 Nov 1973, Carole, *née* McWhinney; 1 da, 1 s; *Career* political ed Radio City 1975–78, reporter World at One and The World This Weekend (BBC Radio 4) 1979–85, reporter BBC TV current affairs 1985–87, corr Newsnight (BBC 2) 1987–; radio and TV documentaries; reported from Europe, Asia, Africa, N and S America; covered 10 US presidential and congressional elections; *Recreations* football (Liverpool FC), music (Beatles, Bob Dylan, Super Furry Animals); *Clubs* Somali (Liverpool), Cadillac (Washington DC); *Style*— Peter Marshall, Esq

MARSHALL, Prof Robin; s of Robert Marshall (d 1944), and Grace Eileen, *née* Ryder (d 1999); *b* 5 January 1940; *Educ* Ermysted's GS Skipton, Univ of Manchester (BSc, PhD); *m* (m dis); 2 s, 1 da; *Career* DSIR fellowship 1965–67, research fellowship German Elektron Synchrotron DESY 1967–68, research scientist MIT 1968–70, research fellowship and princ scientific offr Daresbury 1970–78, princ scientific offr rising to sr princ Rutherford Appleton Lab 1978–1992, prof of physics Univ of Manchester 1992–; author of many scientific papers and books; dir and co sec Frontiers Science and Television Ltd; Max Born Medal and Prize German Physical Soc 1997; FRS 1995; *Recreations* looking after ducks on inner-city canals, authoring DVDs, writing novels and historical science books; *Style*— Prof Robin Marshall; ✉ Department of Physics and Astronomy, University of Manchester, Manchester M13 9PL

MARSHALL, Dr Rosalind Kay; da of Arthur Frederick Kay Robertson Marshall (d 1982), and Nan, *née* Duncan (d 1997); *b* 23 March 1939, Dysart, Fife; *Educ* Kirkcaldy HS, Univ of Edinburgh (MA, PhD); *Career* asst ed Dictionary of the Older Scottish Tongue 1970–71, freelance archivist 1971–73, head of archive Scottish Nat Portrait Gallery 1973–99, writer of historical books and articles 1973–; research assoc Oxford DNB 1998–; memb Cncl Scottish Record Soc 1996–, memb Int Ctee Saltire Soc 1997–2004, vice-chm Virtual Hamilton Palace Tst 2004–; FRSL 1974, FSA Scot 1983, FRSA 2000; *Awards* Sr Dobson Morpeth Prize in Scottish History 1966, Hume Brown Prize in Scottish History 1970, Jeremiah Dalziel Prize 1970, New Writing Award Scottish Arts Cncl 1974, R B K Stevenson Award Soc of Antiquaries of Scotland 1997; *Publications* The Days of Duchess Anne: Life in the Household of the Duchess of Hamilton, 1656–1716 (1973, new edn 2000), Mary of Guise (1977), Virgins and Viragos: A History of Women in Scotland 1080–1980 (1983), Queen of Scots (1986), Bonnie Prince Charlie (1988), Henrietta Maria: The Intrepid Queen (1990), Elizabeth I (1991), Mary I (1993), The Winter Queen (1998), John Knox (2000), Ruin and Restoration: St Mary's Church, Haddington (2001), Mary of Guise (2001), Scottish Queens 1034–1714 (2003), Queen Mary's Women (2006); author of exhbn catalogues, numerous scholarly articles and reviews, incl more than 50 articles in Oxford Dictionary of National Biography (2004); *Recreations* needlepoint, gardening, reading, listening to music, travelling, cats; *Style*— Dr Rosalind K Marshall

MARSHALL, Sally Christine; da of Maj John Trevor Marshall (d 1985), of Broadstone, Dorset, and Marjorie Kathleen, *née* Cooke; *b* 19 October 1949; *Educ* Mountford House West Hallam, Clifton Hall Nottingham, UCW Aberystwyth (BScEcon); *Career* investment mangr Hill Samuel 1972–80, Henderson Administration Group 1980–94, institutional mktg dir Hill Samuel Investment Management Ltd 1994–97, sr vice-pres and head of UK mktg Lombard Odier 1997–2001, exec dir UK business devpt Goldman Sachs Asset Management 2001–07, corporate conslt Gerrard Seel Wine Merchants 2007–; Freeman City of London; *Recreations* wine, skiing, travel, golf; *Clubs* Broadstone Golf; *Style*— Miss Sally Marshall; ✉ 4 Putney Common, London SW15 1HL (e-mail sally.marshall@yahoo.co.uk)

MARSHALL, Steven; s of Victor Marshall (d 1992), and Kathleen Sarah, *née* Higginson; *b* 11 February 1957, Isleworth, Middx; *Educ* Isleworth GS; *Career* BOC Gp plc 1977–82, Black & Decker Ltd 1982–84, Burton Gp plc 1984–87, dep finance dir and co sec Parkdale Holdings plc 1987–89, successively head of worldwide planning and analysis, gp investor rels dir and finance dir European Wines and Spirits Div Grand Metropolitan plc 1989–95, gp finance dir then gp chief exec Thorn plc 1995–99, gp finance dir then gp chief exec Railtrack Gp plc 1999–2002, exec chm Queens' Moat Houses plc 2003–04, non-exec chm Delta plc 2005– (non-exec dir 2004–); non-exec dir: Southern Water plc 2005–, Balfour Beatty plc 2005–; non-exec chm Torex Retail plc 2007–; FCMA; *Style*— Steven Marshall, Esq; ✉ Delta plc, Bridewell Gate, 9 Bridewell Place, London EC4V 6PW (tel 020 7842 6050, fax 020 7842 6078)

MARSHALL, Dr William Jasper; s of Edward Alwin Marshall (d 1986), of Tenterden, Kent, and Lorna Alice, *née* Jeffery (d 1988), of Bromley, Kent; *b* 1 April 1944; *Educ* St Dunstan's Coll, St Catherine's Coll Oxford (MA), Univ of London (PhD, MB BS, MSc); *m* 1 (m dis 1991), Anne Katharine Stewart; 2 da (Eleanor Ruth b 24 Nov 1970, Harriet Lorna Mary b 13 Aug 1973); m 2, Wendy Rowena French, *née* Morgan-Jones; *Career* sr lectr King's Coll Sch of Med and Dentistry 1980–98, reader and hon conslt in clinical biochemistry Guy's King's and St Thomas' Sch of Med 1998–2004 (chm MB BS Bd 1998–2004, sub-dean examinations), emeritus reader in clinical biochemistry KCL 2004–, currently conslt clinical biochemist and clinical dir of pathology The London Clinic; RCPath: asst registrar 1996–98, dir of pubns 1997–2001, treas 1998–2003; hon sec Inst of Biology 2007–; hon memb Assoc of Clinical Biochemists 2005 (chm Publications Ctee 1996–99); memb: BMA, Soc of Authors (chm Med Writers' Gp 1994–95); Coll Medal RCPath 2004, IFCC/Beckman Coulter Award for distinguished contribution in educn 2005; FRCP 1993 (MRCP 1979), FRCPath 1992 (MRCPath 1980), FRCPEd 1996, FIBiol 1999; *Books* Clinical Chemistry (1988, 5 edn jtly, 2004), Clinical Chemistry, an Illustrated Outline (1991), Intensive Care and Clinical Biochemistry (jtly, 1994), Clinical Biochemistry: Metabolic and Clinical Aspects (jtly, 1995, 2 edn 2007), Primary Care and Laboratory Medicine (jtly, 1996), Nutrition and Laboratory Medicine (jtly, 2007); *Recreations* being outside, writing, gardening, visiting war graves; *Style*— Dr William Marshall; ✉ Department of Pathology, The London Clinic, London W1G 6BW (tel 020 7935 4444, e-mail 1wjmarshall@doctors.net.uk)

MARSHALL-ANDREWS, Robert Graham; QC (1987), MP; s of Robin Marshall-Andrews (d 1986), and Eileen Norah Marshall-Andrews (d 1996); *b* 10 April 1944; *Educ* Mill Hill Sch, Univ of Bristol (LLB); *m* Gillian Diana; 1 da (Laura b 1971), 1 s (Tom b 1973); *Career* called to the Bar Gray's Inn 1967 (bencher 1996); MP (Lab) Medway 1997– (Parly candidate (Lab) Medway 1992); dep chair Theatre Cncl; tstee: George Adamson Wildlife Tst, Geffrye Museum; former chm Grey Court Sch; fndr Old Testament Profits; winner Observer Mace Nat Debating Competition; *Books* Palace of Wisdom (novel, 1989), A Man Without Guilt (novel, 2002); *Clubs* Druidston (Pembrokeshire), Garrick; *Style*— Robert Marshall-Andrews, Esq, QC, MP; ✉ Carmelite Chambers, 9 Carmelite Street, London EC4Y 0DR (tel 020 7936 6300, fax 020 7936 6301); House of Commons, London SW1A 0AA (tel 020 7219 5188/6920)

MARSHALL OF KNIGHTSBRIDGE, Baron (Life Peer UK 1998), of Knightsbridge in the City of Westminster; Sir Colin Marsh Marshall; kt (1987); s of Marsh Edward Leslie Marshall, and Florence Mary Marshall; *b* 16 November 1933; *Educ* Univ Coll Sch Hampstead; *m* 1958, Janet Winifred, da of John Cracknell; 1 da (Anna (Hon Mrs Birkett)); *Career* Orient Steam Navigation Co 1951–58; Hertz Corporation: joined as mgmnt trainee (Chicago and Toronto) 1958, gen mangr (Mexico) 1959–60, asst to pres (NY) 1960, gen mangr (UK) 1961–62, gen mangr (UK, Netherlands and Belgium) London 1962–64; Avis Inc: regnl mangr and vice-pres (Europe 1964–66, Europe and ME 1966–69, worldwide 1969–71), exec vice-pres and chief operating offr (NY), pres 1975, chief exec 1976, co chm 1979 (following takeover by Norton Simon Inc NY of which he became exec vice-pres 1979–81); dir and dep chief exec Sears Holdings plc 1981–83; British Airways plc: chief exec 1983–95, dep chm 1989–93, chm 1993–2004; chm: Inchcape plc 1995–2000, Invensys plc (formerly Siebe and BTR/Siebe plc) 1999–2003, Pirelli UK Ltd 2003–, Nomura International plc 2004–; dep chm British Telecommunications plc 1996–2001 (dir 1995–2001); dir: Grand Metropolitan plc 1988–95, Midland Bank Group 1989–1994, IBM UK Holdings Ltd 1990–1995, HSBC Holdings plc 1993–2004, US Air 1993–96, Qantas Airways 1993–96 and 2000–01, NY Stock Exchange 1994–2000, RAC Holdings Ltd

1998–99, Nomura Europe Holdings plc 2004–; CBI: pres 1996–98, chair Int Advsy Bd 2002–; chm: London First Centre (formerly London Inward) 1993–98, London Devpt Partnership 1998–2000; memb Int Advsy Bd British-American Business Cncl 1989– (chm 1994–96), dep chm Fin Reporting Cncl 1996–2000; dir Women's Econ Devpt Team Business in the Community (BIC) 1990–99; pres CIM 1991–96, vice-pres Advtg Assoc, co-fndr and chm The Mktg Cncl 1995–96, chm RIIA 1999–2003, chm Bd of Tstees The Conference Bd 2000–03, chm VisitBritain 2005–06; memb: Cncl IOD, Exec Ctee IATA 1983–96, Hong Kong Assoc 1996–2000; pres Cwlth Youth Exchange Cncl (CYEC) 1998–; tstee: Duke of Edinburgh Cwlth Study Conf (now UK Leadership Forum) 1990–, RAF Museum 1991–2000; vice-chm World Travel and Tourism Cncl 1990–99; chm of govrs Birkbeck Coll London 2003–; Liveryman Guild of Air Pilots and Air Navigators, Liveryman Worshipful Co of Information Technologists; Hon Dr: Suffolk Univ Boston USA 1984, Univ of Durham 1997; Hon DSc: Univ of Buckingham 1990, Cranfield Univ 1997, Middlesex Univ; Hon LLD: Univ of Bath 1989, Richmond Coll American Univ in London 1993, Lancaster Univ 1997, Univ of Nottingham 1999; Hon LittD Univ of Westminster 1999, Hon Dr of Business London Guildhall Univ 2000; *Recreations* tennis; *Clubs* Queen's, RAC, All England Lawn Tennis and Croquet; *Style*— The Lord Marshall of Knightsbridge; ✉ Pirelli UK Ltd, 15 Grosvenor Street, London W1K 4QZ (tel 020 7355 0701, fax 020 7355 0727, e-mail c/o sec anne.hensman@pirelli.com)

MARSLAND, Prof David; s of Ernest Marsland (d 1991), of Leavesden Green, Herts, and Fay, *née* Savoury (d 1993); *b* 3 February 1939; *Educ* Watford GS, Christ's Coll Cambridge (scholar, BA, MA), LSE, Brunel Univ (PhD); *m* Dr Athena Leoussi-Marsland; 4 da; *Career* Dept of Sociology Brunel Univ 1964–88 (lectr, sr lectr, dir postgrad studies, prof assoc), prof of social res West London Inst of Higher Educn 1989–95, prof of social scis Brunel Univ 1995–2004, prof of sociology Univ of Buckingham 2004–; asst dir The Social Affairs Unit London 1981–89; dir Centre for Evaluation Research (CER) 1989–2004; special advsr to Parly Social Security Ctee 1993–95; memb: Social Scis Bd UNESCO 1983–86, Social Scis Ctee CNAA 1987–92; formerly memb EC Social Res Assoc and hon gen sec Br Sociological Assoc; first Thatcher Award winner for contribs to analysis of freedom 1991; memb: BSA 1964, SRA 1985; MIMgt 1987, FRSH 1990; *Books* Seeds of Bankruptcy (1988), Cradle to Grave (1989), Understanding Youth (1993), Work and Employment (1994), Self-Reliance (1995), Welfare or Welfare State? (1996); *Recreations* reading and writing poetry, music, theatre; *Style*— Prof David Marsland; ✉ University of Buckingham, Buckingham MK18 1EG (tel 020 8572 7398)

MARSLEN-WILSON, Prof William David; s of David William Marslen-Wilson (d 1983), and Pera, *née* Funk (d 2005); *b* 5 June 1945; *Educ* St John's Coll Oxford (BA), MIT (PhD); *m* 1982, Lorraine Komisarjevsky Tyler; 2 da (Eliza and Lydia), 1 s (Jack); *Career* asst prof Dept of Behavioural Sciences Univ of Chicago 1973–78, scientific assoc Max-Planck-Institut für Psycholinguistik Nijmegen 1977–82, univ lectr Dept of Experimental Psychology Univ of Cambridge 1982–84, co-dir Max-Plank-Institut für Psycholinguistik Nijmegen 1985–87, sr scientist MRC Applied Psychology Unit Cambridge 1987–90, prof of psychology Birkbeck Coll London 1990–97, dir MRC Cognition and Brain Sciences Unit Cambridge 1997–, hon prof of language and cognition Univ of Cambridge 2002–; Sloan fell MIT 1980–81, visiting prof Univ of Southern Calif LA 1989–90, visiting prof Univ of Arizona 1994–95, hon dir Beijing Normal Univ 1995–, fell Birkbeck Coll London 2000–, fell Wolfson Coll Cambridge 2000–, Wei Lan visiting prof Chinese Univ of Hong Kong 2000; fell Academia Europaea 1996, FBA 1996; *Publications* author of numerous articles in learned jls, conference proceedings and book chapters; *Style*— Prof William Marslen-Wilson, FBA; ✉ Medical Research Council, 15 Chaucer Road, Cambridge CB2 7EF (tel 01223 355294, fax 01223 500250, e-mail william.marslen-wilson@mrc-cbu.cam.ac.uk)

MARSTON, (Jeffery) Adrian Priestley; s of Maj J E Marston, DSO, MC (d 1945), and Doreen, *née* Norris (d 1980); *b* 15 December 1927; *Educ* Marlborough, Magdalen Coll Oxford (MA, DM, MCh), St Thomas' Hosp Med Sch London; *m* 17 July 1951, Sylvie Colin; 1 da (Joanna b 24 Sept 1954), 2 s (John b 24 Feb 1960, Nicholas, *qv*, b 4 Jan 1963); *Career* Nat Serv Lt RAMC, then Capt 1954–57; surgical registrar and sr registrar St Thomas' Hosp 1960–65, sr lectr in surgery Middx Hosp Medical Sch (later Faculty of Clinical Science UCL) 1965–92; conslt surgn: The Middx Hosp 1968–92, Royal Northern Hosp 1970–85, UCH 1985–92; vice-pres RCS 1991–92, chm Senate of RCS Euro Ctee, memb Jt Conslts Ctee 1993–96; RSM: hon treas 1993–95, dean 1995–98, vice-pres 1998–2000; pres: Vascular Surgical Soc of GB and I 1985, Assoc of Surgns of GB and I 1986; memb d'honneur Association Française de Chirurgie 1986, socio de honor Asociación Espanola de Cirujanos 1987; Hon MD Nice 1986; FRCS 1958; Chevalier de l'Ordre National du Mérite de France; *Publications* Intestinal Ischaemia (1976), Contemporary Operative Surgery (1979), Visceral Artery Reconstruction (1986), Splanchnic Ischemia and Multiple Organ Failure (1989), Hamilton Bailey, a Surgeon's Life (1999), London Surprises (jtly, 2006); author of numerous papers on vascular surgery and gastroenterology; *Recreations* literature, languages, travel, music; *Clubs* Hurlingham; *Style*— Adrian Marston, Esq, FRCS; ✉ 4 Hereford Square, London SW7 4TT (tel 020 7373 7678, fax 020 7373 3753, e-mail adrimar@btinternet.com)

MARSTON, David Charles; s of Reginald Charles Moor Marston (d 1991), and Catherine Ann, *née* Romanes; *b* 22 March 1955; *Educ* Shrewsbury, Univ of Newcastle upon Tyne (BA); *Career* Deloittes (now part of PricewaterhouseCoopers) 1976–80 (student then staff accountant), under sec Auditing Practices Ctee 1980–82, audit mangr Grant Thornton 1982–84, Citibank Gp 1984–98 (fin controller of various subsids, then group compliance offr); project dir Auditing Practices Bd (now part of Fin Reporting Cncl) 1998–; memb profession's Fin Reporting Ctee 1990–98 and Investment Business and Pensions Ctees 1999–; hon treas London Gardens Soc; Liveryman Worshipful Co of Gardeners; FCA 1989 (ACA 1979); *Recreations* tenor in church choir, asst scout leader; *Style*— David Marston, Esq; ✉ 65 Turle Road, Norbury, London SW16 5QW

MARSTON, John James; s of John Wilfred Marston (d 1984), and Elsie, *née* Shepherd (d 1978); *b* 19 February 1935, London; *Educ* Rugby, UMIST (BSc, Rugby maroon); *m* 29 Feb 1964, Mette; 1 da (Nicola Jane b 19 May 1968), 1 s (Andrew John b 26 March 1970); *Career* Costain: site engr 1957, runway engr Maldive Is 1958–59, special projects design engr 1960–61, site mangr 1961; W J Marston & Sons Ltd (family firm): joined as contracts mangr 1961, dir 1971, md 1978; chm: W J Marston Holdings Ltd 1980–2000, Marston Properties Holdings Ltd 2000–, Marston Hotel Holdings Ltd 2000–06; memb Cncl Nat Fedn of Building Trade Employees (chm Central and City of London 1976); memb Governing Body and Corporation Hammersmith & W London Coll of FE 1970–, chm of govrs Granard Primary Sch 2003– (govr 1996–); MICE 1968, CEng 1990; *Recreations* sailing (skippered own yacht to Russia and back 1996, yacht deliveries UK to Majorca and France to Turkey, Atlantic ARC 2003), swimming; *Clubs* Shirley Wanderers RFC (tstee, chm 1976–86, pres 1996–99), Royal Harwich Yacht; *Style*— John Marston, Esq; ✉ Marston Properties Holdings Limited, Mills Yard, Rear 2 Hugon Road, Fulham, London SW6 3EN (tel 020 7736 7133, fax 020 7731 8412, e-mail nicky@marstonproperties.co.uk)

MARSTON, Nicholas (Nick); s of (Jeffrey) Adrian Priestley Marston, *qv*, and Sylvie, *née* Colin; *b* 4 January 1963; *Educ* Westminster, Univ of Durham; *Career* literary and film agent A P Watt Ltd 1988–97, md Media Div Curtis Brown Gp Ltd 1997– (owning ptnr 2001–), exec prodr MOJO 1997, dir Touchpaper Television Ltd 2001–, md Cuba Pictures Ltd 2003–, exec prodr Boya (Channel 4) 2007; course tutor ARISTA story ed workshop 1999–; judge RTS Awards 1996 and 2000; memb BAFTA 1999–, Euro Film Acad 1999–; winner Vogue talent contest 1988; *Recreations* theatre, film, football, France, tennis; *Clubs* Soho House; *Style*— Nick Marston, Esq; ✉ 57 Bromfelde Road, London SW4 6PP (tel 020 7622 8851); Curtis Brown Group Ltd, Haymarket House, 28/29 Haymarket, London SW1Y 4SP (tel 020 7393 4450, mobile 07768 356970, fax 020 7396 0110, e-mail nick@curtisbrown.co.uk)

MARTEN, (Richard) Hedley Westwood; s of Capt Lewis Westwood Marten (ka 1944), and Kathleen, *née* Ogston (d 1988); n of Rt Hon Sir Neil Marten, MP, Min for Overseas Devpt 1979–83, gn of Sir Henry Marten, KCVO, Provost of Eton and personal tutor to HM The Queen, and descendant of Sir Henry Marten, republican statesman and signatory to the death warrant of Charles I; *b* 24 January 1943; *Educ* Winchester, Magdalene Coll Cambridge (MA); *m* 1971 (m dis 1983), Fiona Mary, da of George William Carter Sinclair, and sis of Sir Clive Sinclair, *qv*; 1 da (Laura b 19 April 1973), 2 s (Benedict b 9 Sept 1976, Alexander b 24 July 1978); *Career* called to the Bar Lincoln's Inn 1966 (bencher 2000); in practice Chancery Bar 1968–, Chancery Bar rep Bar Cncl 1990–95, memb Inst 1995–, head of chambers 1995–, pres Inst 2006; *Publications* Contentious Probate Claims (co-author, 2003); *Recreations* playing tennis and Bach, alpine walking, romanesque architecture, playing with Kitty; *Clubs* Brooks's, Butterflies Cricket, Academy; *Style*— Hedley Marten, Esq; ✉ Radcliffe Chambers, 11 New Square, Lincoln's Inn, London WC2A 3QB (tel 020 7831 0081, fax 020 7405 2560)

MARTEN, Hon Mrs (Mary Anna Sibell Elizabeth); OBE (1980), DL (Dorset 1989); da of 3 Baron Alington (ka 1940), and Lady Mary Ashley Cooper (d 1936), da of 9 Earl of Shaftesbury; *m* 25 Nov 1949, Lt Cdr George Gosselin Marten, LVO, DSC (d 1997); 1 s, 5 da; *Career* tstee: Br Museum 1985–98, Roman Research Tst 1999–2001, Royal Collection Tst 1999–2005; High Sheriff Dorset 1989; *Style*— The Hon Mrs Marten, OBE, DL; ✉ Crichel, Wimborne, Dorset BH21 5DT

MARTIN, Prof Alan Douglas; s of Frederick Charles Martin, MICE (d 1979), and Emily May, *née* Berkley (d 1990); *b* 4 December 1937; *Educ* Eltham Coll, UCL (BSc, PhD); *m* 4 April 1964 (m dis 1999), Canon Penny Elizabeth Martin, da of William Eric Leggett Johnson, BEM (d 1985); 2 da (Rebecca b 30 March 1966, Rachel b 23 March 1974), 1 s (Robert b 4 April 1967); m 2, 19 February 2000, Robin Louise, da of Dr Edward Sydney Thodey; *Career* res assoc: Univ of Illinois 1962–63, Rutherford Laboratory 1963–64; successively lectr, sr lectr, reader then prof Univ of Durham 1964–2003; Leverhulme Emeritus Fellowship 2004–06, Max Born Medal and Prize Inst Physics and German Physics Soc 2007; CPhys, FInstP, FRS; *Books* Elementary Particle Theory (with T D Spearman, 1970), Quarks and Leptons (with F Halzen, 1984), Hadron Interactions (with P D B Collins, 1984), Particle Physics and Cosmology (jtly, 1989); *Recreations* tennis, skiing, walking, music; *Style*— Prof Alan Martin; ✉ 8 Quarry Heads Lane, Durham City DH1 3DY (tel 0191 386 0217); Institute for Particle Physics Phenomenology and Department of Physics, University of Durham, Durham City DH1 3LE (tel 0191 334 3672, fax 0191 334 3658, e-mail a.d.martin@durham.ac.uk)

MARTIN, Barry Robert; *b* 18 July 1950; *Educ* Kingston GS, St Catharine's Coll Cambridge (MA, Hockey blue), Univ of London (PGCE), Loughborough Univ of Technol (MBA); *m* Fiona; 2 c; *Career* asst master Kingston GS 1973–75; with Overseas Dept (EEC affrs) Bank of England 1975–78; head of economics/business studies and housemaster Caterham Sch 1978–83, head of economics ReptonSch 1983–85, successively dir of economics/business studies, housemaster and dir of studies Mill Hill Sch 1985–92, princ Liverpool Coll 1992–97, headmaster Hampton Sch 1997–; chief examiner A Level Business Studies 1987–2002; memb HMC 1992– (hon treas 2007–), MCIB 1975, FCMI 1983, FRSA 1994; *Publications* The Complete A to Z Business Studies Handbook (co-author), Business Studies (co-author), and also author of numerous learned articles in Business Review; *Recreations* watching sport, spending time with family, theatre and music, walking, learning information technology, Cornwall; *Style*— Barry Martin, Esq; ✉ Hampton School, Hanworth Road, Hampton TW12 3HD (tel 020 8979 5526, fax 020 8941 7368)

M

MARTIN, Prof Benjamin Raymond (Ben); s of Adrian Sidney Martin, MBE, of Budleigh Salterton, Devon, and Joan Dorothy, *née* Mingo; *b* 9 August 1952; *Educ* Blundell's, Churchill Coll Cambridge (Kitchener scholar, MA), Univ of Manchester (MSc, Rowing maroon); *m* 7 July 1973, Valerie Ann Martin, *qv*, da of William Herbert Bennett; 2 s (Paul Frederick b 3 June 1980, David Christopher b 10 Sept 1985), 1 da (Sarah Ann b 5 Dec 1982); *Career* VSO sci teacher Nigeria 1973–75; SPRU - Sci and Technology Policy Research: res fell 1978, lectr 1983, sr fell 1986, sr lectr 1990, prof 1996, dir 1997–2004; visiting lectr Imperial Coll London 1983–84; visiting fell Max-Planck-Inst Für Gesellschaftsforschung Cologne 1987; memb: Steering Gp UK Technology Foresight Prog 1993–2000, Senate Univ of Sussex 1997–2004 (memb Cncl 1997–2002), Tech Opportunities Panel (TOP) EPSRC 2001–04; Derek de Solla Price medal for sci studies 1997; *Publications* Foresight in Science (with J Irvine, 1984), Research Foresight (with J Irvine, 1989), Investing in the Future (with J Irvine and P A Isard, 1990), Equipping Science for the 21st Century (with J Irvine et al, 1997), The Political Economy of Science, Technology and Innovation (with A Nightingale, 2000), Creative Knowledge Environments (with S Hemlin and C M Allwood, 2004); *Recreations* indoor rowing (tenth place World Indoor Rowing Championships Boston 1998), skiing, reading, DIY, gardening, family - balancing demands of two professional careers and three children!; *Style*— Prof Ben Martin; ✉ Linden Lea, 4 Foxglove Gardens, Purley, Surrey CR8 3LQ (tel 020 8660 0329); SPRU - Science and Technology Policy Research, University of Sussex, Falmer, Brighton BN1 9RF (tel 01273 678174, fax 01273 685865, e-mail b.martin@sussex.ac.uk)

MARTIN, Bonita Elizabeth (Bonnie); da of James William Martin, of London, and Barbara Margaret, *née* Walker; *b* 18 February 1959, Chiswick, London; *Educ* Lady Eleanor Holles Sch for Girls, Univ of Reading (BA), Univ of Nottingham, Coll of Law Guildford; *partner* John Grist-Taylor; 2 s (George Zachery, Oscar William); *Career* admitted slr 1985; articled clerk then asst slr Lewis Silkin 1983–87, asst slr Crossman Block & Keith 1987–90, ptnr Masons (latterly Pinsent Masons) 1992–2005 (asst slr 1990–92), ptnr Clarke Willmott 2005–; lectures to RICS, ARBRIX and Univ of Bristol; memb: ARBRIX, Town and Country Planning Assoc, Property Litigation Assoc, Bristol Property Agents Assoc, Nat Tst, WWF, RHS; memb Law Soc 1985; *Recreations* wine, walking, riding, films, skiing; *Style*— Miss Bonnie Martin; ✉ Clarke Willmott, 1 Georges Square, Bath Street, Bristol BS1 6BA (tel 0117 916 9650, fax 0117 917 5594, e-mail bmartin@clarkewillmott.com)

MARTIN, Charles David Zelenka; s of John Martin, and Joy Martin; *b* 2 February 1961, London; *Educ* Merchant Taylors', Univ of Bristol (LLB); *m* 1 Oct 1988, Sarah, *née* Wilson; 3 s (Ben b 22 Dec 1990, Harry b 13 Jan 1993, Alex b 1 Oct 1997); *Career* ptnr Macfarlanes 1990– (joined 1983); *Recreations* food, skiing, running; *Style*— Charles Martin, Esq; ✉ Macfarlanes, 10 Norwich Street, London EC4A 1BD

MARTIN, David; s of Edward Sydney Morris Martin, of Exeter, and Dorothy Mary, *née* Cooper; *b* 11 February 1952; *Educ* Worthing HS for Boys, St John's Coll Cambridge; *m* 24 Aug 1991, Ruth Kathryn, da of Terence Colin Howells; 2 da (Abigail Ruth b 10 May 1994, Naomi Hope b 22 Feb 1997); *Career* ptnr Herbert Smith 1986– (asst slr 1979–86, tax slr 1979–); memb Religious Soc of Friends; *Recreations* reading, walking; *Style*— David Martin, Esq; ✉ Herbert Smith, Exchange House, Primrose Street, London EC2A 2HS (tel 020 7374 8000, fax 020 7374 0888)

MARTIN, David Clifford; s of Rev John Bernard Martin (d 1986), and (Elizabeth) Alma, *née* Jones; *b* 20 December 1956; *Educ* Chigwell Sch, UC Durham (BSc, PGCE); *m* 17 Dec 1988, Sally Elizabeth, *née* Bennett; 1 da (Elizabeth b 11 Feb 1990), 2 s (Andrew b 28 March

1992, Peter b 28 Sept 1993); *Career* teacher: Kenya 1978–79, Dronfield Derbys 1980–84; Microelectronics Educn Prog and TVEI 1984–87, European Educnl Software 1987–88; Br Cncl: educn advsr 1988–94, dep dir Nigeria 1994–98, dir Palestinian Territories 1998–2002, dir Central Africa 2002–06, dir Hungary 2007–; memb Church Missionary Soc, memb World Devpt Movement; *Recreations* music, gardening; *Style*— David Martin, Esq; ✉ British Council, Benczúr u 26, 1068 Budapest, Hungary (e-mail david.martin@britishcouncil.hu)

MARTIN, David John Pattison; s of John Besley Martin, CBE (d 1982), and Muriel, *née* Pattison (d 2002); *b* 5 February 1945; *Educ* Kelly Coll Tavistock, Fitzwilliam Coll Cambridge (BA); *m* 8 Jan 1977, Basia Constance, da of Tadeusz Dowmunt (d 2003); 4 da (Naomi b 1978, Melissa b and d 1980, Francesca 1981, Charis b 1983), 1 s (Henry b 1985); *Career* called to the Bar Inner Temple, in practice 1969–76 and 1998–; MP (Cons) Portsmouth S 1987–97, PPS to Rt Hon Alan Clark as min of state for defence procurement 1990, PPS to Rt Hon Douglas Hurd as sec of state for foreign and Cwlth affrs 1990–94, served on De-Regulation and Parly Procedure Select Ctees 1995–97; Parly candidate (Cons) Rugby and Kenilworth 2001, Parly candidate (Cons) Bristol West 2005–; dir Martins Caravan Co and assoc cos until 1990; *Recreations* music, golf; *Clubs* Hawks' (Cambridge); *Style*— David Martin, Esq

MARTIN, David MacLeod; s of Allan MacLeod Martin (d 1976), and Jessie McCurdie, *née* Harris (d 1974); *b* 30 December 1922; *Educ* Govan HS, Glasgow Sch of Art (Dip Art); *m* 30 July 1951, Isobel Agnes Fowlie (d 2000), da of George Frances Fowlie Smith (d 1972); 4 s (Brian b 4 Aug 1954, Allan b 26 Sept 1956, Kenneth b 21 July 1960, Derek b 30 Sept 1966); *Career* served WWII Sgt RAF 1943–46; teacher and princ teacher Hamilton GS 1973–83; painter 1983–; annual exhibitions: RSA, RSW, RGI (RA 1984); numerous group shows incl: Lynn Stern Assoc London, London 20th Century Art Fair, Miami Art Fair, Mall Galleries London 2000, RSA Gallery Edinburgh 2000, Richmond Hill Gallery 2001, 2003, 2004 and 2005, Affordable Art Fair London 2003; one man shows: Glasgow, Edinburgh, Perth, Greenock & Stone Gallery Newcastle, Thackery Gallery London 1992 and 1994, Ferguson Fine Art Islington Art Fair 1994, Fosse Gallery Stow on the Wold 1995, John Martin of London 1995, 1997, 2000, 2002 and 2006, Richmond Hill Gallery 1997, Wren Gallery Burford 1997, Art International NY 1998, Perth Festival Exhibition Perth Museum 1999, Roger Bilcliffe Gallery 2001, 2003, 2005 and 2007, Open Eye Gallery Edinburgh 2002, Edgar Modern Gallery Bath 2005, Lemon St Gallery Truro 2007; work in numerous private and public collections incl: The Fleming Collection London, Credit Lyonnaise London, The Earl of Moray, late Lord Goold, Lord MacFarlane, Lady MacKay, Scottish Arts Cncl, Royal Bank of Scotland Collection; work cmmnd by Lord Bute for Bute Fabrics, featured artist in Perth Festival of the Arts 1999, special award of merit Robert Colquhoun Meml Art Prize Kilmarnock 1974, prizewinner Friends of the Smith Gallery Stirling 1981, May Marshall Brown Award RSW 1984, EIS Purchase Prize 1986, prizewinner Hamilton museum exhibition 1988, £1,000 prizewinner The Laing Collection Art Competition 1990 and 1993, David Cargill Award RGI 1995, RSW Cncl Award 2003; memb Cncl: RGI, RSW (past vice-pres); memb: SSA 1949 (hon memb 1992), RSW 1961, RGI 1981, Visual Arts Scotland (formerly SAAC) 1992; *Recreations* gardening, period ship modelling, music; *Style*— David M Martin, Esq; ✉ The Old Schoolhouse, 53 Gilmour Street, Eaglesham, Glasgow G76 0LG (tel 01355 303308)

MARTIN, David Weir; MEP (Lab) Scotland; s of William Martin and Marion Weir; *b* 26 August 1954; *Educ* Liberton HS, Heriot-Watt Univ (BA, MA), Univ of Leicester (MA); *Career* former stockbroker's asst and animal welfare campaigner; memb Lab Pty 1975–, Lothian regnl cncllr Inch/Gilmerton 1982; MEP (Lab): Lothian 1984–99, Scotland 1999–; ldr Br Lab Gp European Parl 1987–89, vice-pres European Parl 1989–2004, memb International Trade Ctee; memb: TGWU, GMB, Fabian Soc; vice-pres Advocates for Animals; *Books* Traditional Industrial Regions of the European Community (report), Bringing Common Sense to the Common Market - A Left Agenda for Europe (pamphlet, 1988), The Democratic Deficit (chapter in A Claim of Right for Scotland, ed by Owen Dudley Edwards), European Union and the Democratic Deficit (pamphlet, 1990), Europe - An Ever Closer Union (1991), Refreshing the Parts (contrib), The Intergovernmental Conferences in the Context of Parliament's Strategy for European Union (4 reports on Maastricht), Towards a Wider, Deeper, Federal Europe (pamphlet, 1992), European Union - The Shattered Dream? (pamphlet, 1993), To be Efficient, the Commission Needs Major Reform (chapter in What Future for the European Commission, ed Giles Merritt, 1995), Power to the People (chapter in Changing States - A Labour Agenda for Europe, ed Glyn Ford, Glenys Kinnock, Arlene McCarthy, 1996), A Partnership Democracy for Europe (pamphlet, 1996); *Recreations* reading, sport; *Style*— David Martin, Esq, MEP; ✉ PO Box 27030, Edinburgh EH10 7YP (tel 0131 654 1606, fax 0131 654 1607, e-mail david@martinmep.com)

MARTIN, (Thomas) Geoffrey; OBE (2002); s of Thomas Martin (d 1973), Belfast, NI, and Sadie Adelaide, *née* Day (d 1991); *b* 26 July 1940; *Educ* Newry GS, Queen's Univ Belfast (BSc); *m* 6 July 1968, Gay Madeleine Annesley, da of Herbert Annesley Brownrigg, of Bognor Regis; 1 s (Thomas), 3 da (Bluebell, Poppy, Gabriella); *Career* pres NUS 1966–68, dir Shelter 1972–73, dip staff Cwlth Secretariat 1973–79, head Euro Cmmn Office NI 1979–85, head of Press and Info Serv EC SE Asia 1985–87, head of external relations Euro Cmmn Office London 1987–94, head Euro Cmmn Representation in the UK 1994–2002, Office of the Cwlth Sec Gen 2002–; hon doctorate Univ of Plymouth; *Recreations* running; *Clubs* Travellers; *Style*— Geoffrey Martin, Esq, OBE; ✉ Commonwealth Secretariat, Pall Mall, London SW1Y 5HX (tel 020 7747 6500, fax 020 7925 1024, e-mail g.martin@commonwealth.int)

MARTIN, Prof Geoffrey Almeric Thorndike; s of Albert Thorndike Martin (d 1947), and Lily, *née* Jackson (d 1964); *b* 28 May 1934; *Educ* Palmer's Sch Grays Thurrock, UCL (BA), CCC Cambridge, Christ's Coll Cambridge (MA, PhD, LittD); *Career* Lady Wallis Budge research fell in Egyptology Christ's Coll Cambridge 1966–70; UCL: lectr in Egyptology 1970–78, reader in Egyptian archaeology 1978–87, prof of Egyptology (ad hominem) 1987, Edwards prof of Egyptology 1988–93 (prof emeritus 1993); field dir jt Egypt Exploration Soc and Leiden Museum expdn in Egypt 1975–98, field dir jt Leiden Museum and Leiden Univ expdn in Egypt 1998 (hon dir 2001), Amarna Royal Tombs Project Valley of the Kings 1998–2003, Cambridge expdn to Valley of the Kings 2005; Christ's Coll Cambridge: hon keeper of the Muniment Rm 1997, fell commoner 1998, hon keeper of the Plate 2000, hon keeper of the Archives 2004; corresponding memb German Archaeological Inst 1982; FSA 1975; *Books* Egyptian Administrative and Private-Name Seals (1971), The Royal Tomb at El-Amarna (vol 1 1974, vol 2 1989), The Tomb of Hetepka (1979), The Sacred Animal Necropolis at North Saqqara (1981), Canopic Equipment in the Petrie Collection (with V Raisman, 1984), Scarabs, Cylinders and other Ancient Egyptian Seals (1985), The Tomb Chapels of Paser and Raia (1985), Corpus of Reliefs of the New Kingdom (vol 1 1987), Excavations in the Royal Necropolis at El-Amarna (with A El-Khouly, 1987), The Memphite Tomb of Horemheb (1989), The Hidden Tombs of Memphis (1991, German edn: Auf der Suche nach dem verlorenen Grab, 1994), A Bibliography of the Amarna Period (1991), The Tomb of Tia and Tia (1997), The Tombs of Three Memphite Officials (2001), Stelae from Egypt and Nubia in the Fitzwilliam Museum Cambridge (2005); *Recreations* travel, English history, bibliography; *Style*— Prof Geoffrey Martin; ✉ Christ's College Cambridge, Cambridge CB2 3BU (fax 01223 339557)

MARTIN, Geoffrey Haward; CBE (1986); s of Ernest Leslie Martin (d 1967), of Colchester, and Mary Hilda, *née* Haward (d 1987); *b* 27 September 1928; *Educ* Colchester Royal GS, Merton Coll Oxford (MA, DPhil), Univ of Manchester; *m* 12 Sept 1953, Janet Douglas, da of Douglas Hamer, MC (d 1981), of Sheffield, and Enid Hope, *née* Porter (d 1986); 3 s (Christopher b 1957, Patrick b 1963, Matthew b 1963), 1 da (Sophia b 1961); *Career* prof of history Univ of Leicester (formerly UC Leicester) 1973–82 (lectr 1952–66, reader 1966–73), keeper of Public Records 1982–88, visiting prof Carleton Univ Ottawa 1958–59 and 1967–68, sr visiting fell Loughborough Univ of Technol 1987–95, visiting research fell Sch of Library Archive and Info Studies UCL 1988–, distinguished visiting prof of history Univ of Toronto 1989, Leverhulme emeritus research fell 1989–91, sr research fell Merton Coll Oxford 1990–93, research prof Univ of Essex 1990–, research assoc Oxford DNB 1997–; chm: Br Records Assoc 1981–92, Cwlth Archivists Assoc 1984–88; memb Royal Cmmn on Historical Monuments (England) 1987–94, govr Museum of London 1989–95; pres Cumberland and Westmorland Antiquarian and Archaeological Soc 1999–2002; vice-pres: Br Records Assoc, Essex Archaeological Soc, Assoc of Genealogists and Record Agents; chm Humanities Arts and Design Res Degrees Sub-Ctee Cncl for Nat Acad Awards 1987–92; hon memb Int Cmmn for the History of Towns 1988–; miembro Distinguido del Sistema Nacional de Archivos Mexico 1988; Besterman Medal Library Assoc 1972; Hon DUniv Essex 1989; FSA 1975, FRHistS 1958 (vice-pres 1984–88); *Books* The Story of Colchester (1959), The Town: A Visual History (1961), The Royal Charters of Grantham (1963), Bibliography of British and Irish Municipal History (with Sylvia McIntyre, 1972), Ipswich Recognizance Rolls (1973), The Dublin Merchant Guild Roll (with Philomena Connolly, 1992), Portsmouth Royal Charters 1194–1974 (1995), Knighton's Chronicle 1337–96 (1995), A History of Merton College, Oxford (with J R L Highfield, 1997); *Recreations* bibliophily, conversation; *Clubs* Oxford and Cambridge; *Style*— Prof G H Martin, CBE, FSA; ✉ Church View Cottage, Finsthwaite, Ulverston, Cumbria LA12 8BJ (tel 01539 531054)

MARTIN, Judge Geoffrey William; OBE (1992); s of late Bertie Philip Martin, of Suffolk, and Marion, *née* Bonney (d 1968); *b* 9 November 1935; *Educ* Framlingham Coll, St John's Coll Cambridge (MA); *m* 1, Patricia, *née* Jones; 2 da (Jane Elizabeth b 7 Dec 1960, Jill Marion b 9 June 1962); m 2, Marie Turner; *Career* dist offr and magistrate Tanganyika 1959–62, admitted slr 1966, private practice (litigation) 1966–77, registrar Co Court and dist 1977–86, puisne judge Tonga 1986–88, chief justice Tonga 1988–91, pt/t judge Vanuatu Court of Appeal 1988–95, pt/t judge Western Samoa Court of Appeal 1990, dist judge 1992–2003 (dep dist judge 2003–), pt/t chief justice St Helena 1992–2006, pt/t judge of appeal Tonga 1994, pt/t judge Falkland Islands 1996, chief justice Turks and Caicos Islands 2004–05 (p/t judge 2005–); memb: Law Soc, Cwlth Magistrates and Judges' Assoc; *Recreations* books, music, travel; *Clubs* Royal Over-Seas League; *Style*— Judge Geoffrey Martin, OBE; ✉ e-mail geoffrey.martin@tiscali.co.uk

MARTIN, Sir George Henry; kt (1996), CBE (1988); s of Henry Martin (d 1967), and Bertha Beatrice, *née* Simpson (d 1948); *b* 3 January 1926; *Educ* St Ignatius Coll, Bromley County Sch, Guildhall Sch of Music; *m* 1, 3 Jan 1948 (m dis 1966), Sheena Rose, *née* Chisholm; 1 da (Alexis Jane b 1953), 1 s (Gregory Paul b 1957); m 2, 24 June 1966, Judy, da of late Kenneth Lockhart Smith; 1 da (Lucie Annabel b 1967), 1 s (Giles Henry Blake b 1969); *Career* Fleet Air Arm 1944–46; BBC (6 months) 1950, EMI 1950–65, record prodr and head Parlophone Records, fndr and chm Air Studios (merged with Chrysalis 1974) 1965–, fndr Air Studios Montserrat W Indies 1979, main bd dir Chrysalis plc 1985–2005, chm Heart 106.2FM (subsid of Chrysalis) 1995–; original sponsor British Sch for Performing Arts, professional patron Salford Coll for Performing Arts; Rock and Roll Hall of Fame 1999; Hon DMus Berklee Coll of Music Boston MA1989, Hon MA Salford UC 1992; FGSM 1998, Hon RAM 1999; *Books* All You Need Is Ears (1979), Making Music (1983), Summer of Love - The Making of Sgt Pepper (1993), Playback (2002); *Recreations* music, design, boats, snooker; *Clubs* Oriental; *Style*— Sir George Martin, CBE; ✉ Air Studios, Lyndhurst Hall, Lyndhurst Road, Hampstead, London NW3 5NG (tel 020 7794 0660, fax 020 7794 0623)

MARTIN, Glenn Philip; s of Walter Philip, and Eileen Denton, *née* Savage; *b* 11 February 1949; *Educ* KCS Wimbledon, Wadham Coll Oxford (BA); *m* 4 July 1970, Beryl, da of Albert Darby, of Sale; 3 s (Christopher, Alastair, Nicholas), 1 da (Sarah); *Career* dir of ops Swiss Bank Corporation 1995–96 (dir of banking ops 1990), chief info offr Salomon Smith Barney Europe 1996–2000, chief info offr Schroder Salomon Smith Barney 2000–01, chief technol offr Cazenove 2001–05, chief info offr JP Morgan Cazenove 2005, chief exec ShareMaestro Ltd 2007–; *Recreations* tennis, drumming; *Style*— Glenn Martin, Esq; ✉ Hatchetts, Westerham Road, Limpsfield, Surrey RH8 0SW (tel 01883 723685, e-mail glennpmartin@sharemaestro.co.uk)

MARTIN, Iain James; s of John H Martin, of Paisley, Scotland, and Margaret, *née* Davison; *b* 2 October 1971; *Educ* Castlehead HS, Univ of Glasgow; *m* 2 April 2001, Fiona, da of James McJannet; *Career* journalist; reporter Sunday Times Scotland 1993–97, political ed Scotland on Sunday 1997–2000, political ed The Scotsman 2000–01, dep ed Scotland on Sunday 2001, ed The Scotsman 2001–04, ed Scotland on Sunday 2004–06, dep ed The Sunday Telegraph 2006–; fell Br American Project; *Style*— Iain Martin, Esq; ✉ The Sunday Telegraph, 111 Buckingham Palace Road, London SW1W 0DT (tel 020 7538 5000, e-mail iain.martin@telegraph.co.uk)

MARTIN, Ian Alexander; *b* 1935; *Educ* Univ of St Andrews (MA), ICA Scotland (CA); *Career* Grand Metropolitan plc: chm and chief exec Watney Mann & Truman Brewers 1982 (joined 1979), GrandMet main bd dir 1985–94, chief exec Pillsbury Co, chm Burger King world-wide 1989–92, gp md and chief operating offr 1991–93, dep chm 1993–94; chm and chief exec Glenisla Group Ltd 1994–97, exec chm Heath Lambert Fenchurch Insurance Holdings Ltd 1999–; non-exec chm: Uniq plc (formerly Unigate plc) 1995–2001, Baxi Group Ltd (building materials gp, formerly Newmond plc) 1997–, 365 plc 1999–2002, SSL International plc 2001–05; non-exec dir: Granada Group plc 1992–98, House of Fraser plc 1994–2000; int cnsllr Centre for Strategic and Int Studies; Freeman City of London, Liveryman Worshipful Co of Brewers; MICAS; *Clubs* Buck's; *Style*— Ian Martin, Esq; ✉ Heath Lambert Holdings Ltd, Friary Court, 65 Crutched Friars, London EC3N 2NP (tel 020 7560 3573, fax 020 7560 3551)

MARTIN, Ian Robert; s of William Otway Martin (d 1985), of Wallington, and Marion Weir, *née* Gillespie (d 1976); *b* 29 December 1935; *Educ* Wallington Co Sch, ChCh Oxford (MA); *m* 1 Aug 1964, Susan, da of Neville Joseph Mountfort (d 1992), of Olton, Solihull; 1 da (Sally), 3 s (Andrew, Roger, Alan); *Career* Nat Serv RN 1954–56; current affrs and feature progs incl Face to Face BBC TV 1959–68; Thames TV: exec prodr documentaries 1968–70, ed This Week 1971, exec prodr features 1972–75, controller features educn and religion 1976–85, head of documentaries 1986–87, head of music and theatre 1988–92; chief exec HD Thames and The Electronic Theatre Company 1992–2005; exec prodr many major documentaries and specials incl: St Nicolas 1977, The Gospel According to St Mark 1979, Swan Lake 1980, first Br fund-raising Telethon 1980, Rigoletto 1982, The Mikado 1987, Jessye Norman's Christmas Symphony 1987, Martin Luther King - The Legacy 1988, In From the Cold? Richard Burton 1988, Twelfth Night 1988, Xerxes 1989, The Midsummer Marriage 1989, The Tailor of Gloucester 1989, Una Stravaganza dei Medici 1990, La Bayadère 1991, Mozart at Buckingham Palace 1991, The Return of Columbus (in high definition television HDTV) 1992, D W Griffith: Father of Film 1993, Winter Olympics Lillehammer (HDTV) 1994, World Figure Skating Championships (HDTV) 1995, Les Miserables (HDTV) 1995, Who Could Ask for Anything More? (Ira Gershwin) 1996, Hey Mr Producer 1998, Bernadette Peters in Concert 1998, Audra McDonald at the Donmar 1999, The Complete Works of William Shakespeare: Abridged 2000; initial trials Electronic Theatre 2002–04, dir Coiledspring Games 2004–; chm Cncl

Vision 1250, pres HIPA 1250; govr Isleworth and Syon Sch; memb: BAFTA (former chm TV and Awards Ctees), Exec Ctee Br Shakespeare Assoc; *Books* From Workhouse to Welfare (1969); *Recreations* collecting puzzles and quotations; *Style—* Ian Martin, Esq; ✉ c/o BAFTA, 195 Piccadilly, London W1J 9LN (e-mail ian@coiledspring.co.uk)

MARTIN, Jessica Cecelia Anna Maria Thérèse; da of Placido Martin, of London, and Mary Bernadette, *née* Maguire; *b* 25 August 1962; *Educ* St Michael's Convent GS London, Westfield Coll London (exhibitioner, BA); *m* June 1997, Nigel Wolfin; 1 s (Benjamin b 27 Oct 1998), 1 da (Francesca b 20 Nov 2001); *Career* actress; awarded scholarship UCLA; *Pantomime* Cinderella (De Montfort Hall Leicester 1985, The Palace Manchester 1987), Aladdin (The Grand Wolverhampton) 1986, The Wizard of Oz (Theatre Royal Plymouth) 1988, Peter Pan (Swan Theatre Wycombe) 1996–97, Mother Goose (Cambridge Arts) 1999; *Theatre* nat tour with Rory Bremner 1987, Babes in Arms (Regents Park) 1988, Me and My Girl (Adelphi Strand (nat tour 1993)) 1989–91, The Case of the Dead Flamingo Dancer (Thorndike Theatre Leatherhead) 1991, Curtain Up (Edinburgh Festival) 1992, Shakers (Nottingham Playhouse) 1994, The Card (Regents Park) 1994, Lonely Hearts (Oxford Fire Station) 1995, Something for the Boys and Leave it to Me (Barbican lost musicals season) 1995, Swingtime Canteen (King's Head) 1995, Mack and Mabel (Piccadilly) 1996, Blame It On My Youth (Jermyn Street) 1996, I Can Get It For You Wholesale (Barbican lost musicals season), The Surprise Party (Nuffield Theatre Southampton and nat tour) 1997, South Pacific (Churchill Theatre Bromley and nat tour) 1997, Candida (New End Theatre) 1998, Hey Mr Producer (Lyceum Theatre) 1998, On a Clear Day You Can See Forever (Barbican Last Musicals Season) 1998, Vivian Ellis Awards (Theatre Royal Drury Lane) 1998, A Saint She Ain't (King's Head Theatre) 1999, Blame it on My Youth (New End Theatre) 1999, Finian's Rainbow (Fortune Theatre: Lost Musicals Season) 1999, Sweeney Todd (Bridewell Theatre) 2000, Veronique - A Lifelong Cult (Edinburgh Festival) 2001, Let's Kick Arts (Bridewell Theatre) 2002, Fifty Million Frenchmen (Linbury Studio, Lost Musicals Season) 2002, Larkin With Women (Belgrade Theatre Coventry) 2003, Me, Myself and I (Orange Tree Theatre Richmond) 2003–04, Taste the Love (Jermyn Street Theatre) 2004, Tracy Beaker Gets Real (Nottingham Playhouse and nat tour) 2006; *Television* Spitting Image 1985, Copycats 1985, And There's More 1985, Bobby Davro on the Box 1985, Bobby Davro's TV Weekly 1986, Summertime Special 1986, Tarby and Friends 1986, Royal Variety Show 1987, Bobby Davro's Christmas Annual 1987, Dr Who 1988, A Night of a Hundred Stars 1990, Tonight at 8.30 1991, Gibberish 1992; *Radio* The Big Broadcast of 1991 (Radio 2) 1991, Where Are You (Radio 5) 1992, Full Steam A-Hudd (Radio 2) 1995, Ned Sherrin's Review of Revues (Radio 2) 1996, Glossies (Radio 4) 1996, I Can Do That (Radio 4) 1999, Stage Mother, Sequinned Daughter (Radio 4) 2002, Jack Rosenthal's Last Act (Radio 4) 2006; *Style—* Miss Jessica Martin; ✉ c/o Jeffrey, White and Silvey Associates Limited, 9–15 Neal Street, London WC2H 9PW

MARTIN, Dr Joan Eleanor; da of Herbert Martin (d 1995), of Belfast, and Sarah, *née* Neagle; *b* 25 March 1950, Belfast; *Educ* Univ of Warwick (MA), Univ of Ulster (DPhil); *m* 3 Jan 1987, Paul Lawson Hunt; 1 s (Timothy); *Career* occupational therapist KCL 1972–73, head of occupational therapy Atkinson Morleys Hosp London 1973–77, lectr and course dir in occupational therapy Univ of Ulster 1977–2000; memb GMC 2003– (memb Fitness to Practice, Educn, and Diversity and Equality Ctees); memb: Appeals Serv NI 1994–, ARB 1999–2004, Architects' Liaison Gp Queen's Univ Belfast, Ct Univ of Nottingham, Health Professions Cncl; fell Coll of Occupational Therapists 1981 (memb 1972); *Publications* Eating Disorders, Food and Occupational Therapy (1998); *Recreations* travelling, cooking, craftwork, fair-weather gardening; *Style—* Dr Joan Martin; ✉ General Medical Council, 350 Euston Road, London NW1 3JN (tel 0845 357 8001)

MARTIN, (Leonard) John; CBE; s of Leonard A Martin (d 1983), and Anne Elizabeth, *née* Scudamore (d 1975); *b* 20 April 1929; *Educ* Ardingly; *m* 3 March 1956, Elisabeth Veronica, da of David Samuel Jones, MBE (d 1968); 1 s (Christopher John b 15 July 1958), 1 da (Rosemary Elisabeth Scudamore b 12 May 1960); *Career* Nat Serv Navy 1949–50, Sub Lt RNVR, ret Lt Cdr RNR 1975; R Watson & Sons: joined 1952, qualified actuary 1954, ptnr 1957, sr ptnr 1983–93; pres Inst of Actuaries 1992–94; chm: Assoc of Conslt Actuaries 1985–87, Occupational Pensions Jt Working Gp 1986–87, Consultative Gp of Actuaries in EEC 1988–91; dep chm Occupational Pensions Bd 1988–92, non-exec dir NPI (formerly National Provident Institution) 1993–99; Liveryman: Guild of Air Pilots and Air Navigators, Worshipful Co of Actuaries; FIA 1954, FPMI 1958, FSS 1958; *Recreations* singing, sailing and flying; *Clubs* Naval; *Style—* John Martin, Esq, CBE

MARTIN, His Hon Judge John Alfred Holmes; QC (1989); s of Very Rev Dr Alfred Martin (d 1986), of Belfast, and Doris Muriel, *née* McRitchie (d 2000); *b* 31 May 1946; *Educ* Royal Belfast Academical Instn, Queen's Univ Belfast (LLB, Dip Law, capt Univ Boat Club 1966–67); *m* 30 Aug 1983, Barbara Elizabeth Margaret, da of Rev Thomas Kyle (d 1995); 1 da (Amanda b 1986), 1 s (Peter b 1991); *Career* called to the Bar: NI 1970 (bencher 2000), Gray's Inn 1974, Ireland 1975; in practice 1970–88, called to the Inner Bar of NI (QC) 1989, County Court judge 1990– (dep County Court judge 1983–88), Crown Court judge 1990–97, recorder of Londonderry 1993–94, additional judge for County Court Belfast 1994–97; chief social security cmmr and chief child support cmmr NI 1997–, chief pensions appeal cmmr NI 2005–, dep social security cmmr GB 2005–; hon sec Cncl of HM County Court Judges in NI 1995–97 (memb Cncl 1990–); pt/t lectr in matrimonial practice and procedure NI Inn of Court 1977–80, asst dist electoral area cmmr 1984, chm of Industrial Tbnls 1988–89 (pt/t chm 1981–88), vice-pres Industrial Tbnls and Fair Employment Tbnl 1990, chm and pres Pensions Appeal Tbnls for NI 2001–, memb Cncl of HM Social Security and Child Support Cmmrs of the UK; pres Irish Legal History Soc 2004–06 (vice-pres 2000–03); memb NI Bar Cncl 1983; fell Soc for Advanced Legal Studies 2000–; govr Presbyterian Orphan and Children's Soc 1991–; vice-pres Irish Amateur Rowing Union 1978–79 (also chm Ulster Branch), int rowing umpire 1977–86, jury memb and umpire rowing events of Olympic Games 1980 and Cwlth Games 1986; *Recreations* rowing, hill walking, gardening, reading; *Clubs* Ulster Reform, Leander; *Style—* His Hon Judge Martin, QC; ✉ Office of the Social Security Commissioners and Child Support Commissioners, Headline Building, 10–14 Victoria Street, Belfast, BT1 3GG (tel 02890 728731, fax 02890 313510)

MARTIN, John Joseph Charles; s of Benjamin Martin (d 1987), and Lucille, *née* Miranda (d 1976); *b* 25 November 1940; *Educ* Latymer Upper Sch; *m* 1978, Frances, *née* Oster; 1 da (Lucy b 1980), 1 s (James b 1982); *Career* Illustrated Newspapers 1960–63, Planned Public Relations 1963–68, Martin Dignum Assocs 1969; Welbeck Golin/Harris Communications Ltd: joined 1969, dir 1972, chief exec 1984, chm 1988–97 (clients incl: Lever Brothers, McDonald's, ICI Dulux, Rowntrees, Govt of Bermuda, Brittany Ferries; devised Bottle Bank scheme for Glass Mfrs Fed); fndr John Martin Communications 1997– (clients incl Nestle UK); memb Advsy Cncl London Mozart Players; FCIPR 1994 (MIPR 1968); *Recreations* painting, tennis; *Style—* John Martin, Esq; ✉ 53 Hampstead Way, Hampstead Garden Suburb, London NW11 7DP (tel 020 8458 8281)

MARTIN, John Vandeleur; QC (1991); s of Col Graham Vandeleur Martin, MC, of Salisbury, Wilts, and Margaret Helen, *née* Sherwood; *b* 17 January 1948; *Educ* Malvern, Pembroke Coll Cambridge (MA); *m* 24 Dec 1974, Stephanie Johnstone, da of Maj Michael Johnstone Smith, MC, of Bedford; 2 s (Timothy b 1979, Nicholas b 1985), 1 da (Josephine b 1983); *Career* called to the Bar Lincoln's Inn 1972 (bencher 1999); in practice Chancery Bar: Northern Circuit 1973–81, London 1981–; dep judge of the High Court 1993–; Freeman City of London 1969, Liveryman Worshipful Co of Drapers 1973; *Recreations* opera, walking; *Style—* John Martin, Esq, QC; ✉ Wilberforce Chambers, 8 New Square, Lincoln's Inn, London WC2A 3QP (tel 020 7306 0102, fax 020 7306 0095)

MARTIN, Kevin Joseph; s of James Arthur Martin (d 1961), of Coventry, and Ivy Lilian, *née* Reeson (d 1986); *b* 15 June 1947; *Educ* Cotton Coll; *m* 7 Oct 1971, Maureen Dympna, da of Kevin James McCormack; 2 s (James Roland b 21 Oct 1975, Richard Thomas b 3 Oct 1977); *Career* admitted slr 1970, ptnr Mackintosh & Co Birmingham 1972–79 (joined 1970), fndr and sr ptnr K J Martin & Co 1979–2001, conslt Lodders (following merger) 2001–; Law Soc: memb Young Slrs' Gp 1978–82, memb Cncl 1996–, chm Compliance Bd 2001–03, memb Main Bd 2001–06, dep vice-pres 2003–04, vice-pres 2004–05, pres 2005–06; co-proprietor (with wife) Davenport Lodge Sch Coventry 1986–2007; Freeman City of Coventry 1970; memb Law Soc 1970; *Recreations* golf, skiing, watching cricket, rugby, classical music, literature; *Clubs* Ladbrook Park Golf, Coventry and North Warwickshire Cricket, Drapers' (Coventry); *Style—* Kevin Martin, Esq; ✉ The Law Society, 113 Chancery Lane, London WC2A 1PL (tel 020 7320 5602, fax 020 7320 5759, e-mail kevinj_martin@btinternet.com)

MARTIN, Kit; s of Prof Sir John Leslie Martin, and Sadie, *née* Speight; *b* 6 May 1947; *Educ* Eton, Jesus Coll Cambridge (MA, DipArch); *m* 1, 24 Oct 1970 (m dis 1978), Julia Margaret, da of Dr Peter Dennis Mitchell, of Bodmin, Cornwall; m 2, 15 Sept 1980, Sally Martha, da of Sqdn Ldr Edwin Hector Gordon Brookes, AFC (d 1947), of Laxton, Northants; 1 da (Amy Victoria b 17 Sept 1992); *Career* ptnr Martin & Weighton 1969–76, chm Kit Martin Historic Houses Rescue Ltd 1974–; responsible for rescue, restoration and conversion of various important listed bldgs incl: Dingley Hall, The Hazells, Gunton Park, Cullen House, Keith Hall, Callaly Castle, Tyninghame House, Burley; memb Historic Bldgs Cncl for Scotland 1987–99; projects conslt The Phoenix Trust (The UK Historic Building Preservation Tst) 2001– (dir 1997–2001); tstee Save Europe's Heritage 1994–; Hon FRIBA; *Publications* The Country House - To Be or Not To Be, Jamaica's Heritage: An Untapped Resource; *Recreations* skiing, squash, private flying, landscape gardening; *Style—* Kit Martin, Esq; ✉ Park Farm, Gunton Park, Hanworth, Norfolk NR11 7HL (tel 01263 761270)

MARTIN, Prof Sir Laurence Woodward; kt (1994), DL (Tyne & Wear 1987); s of Leonard Martin (d 1983), and Florence Mary, *née* Woodward (d 1987); *b* 30 July 1928; *Educ* St Austell GS, Christ's Coll Cambridge (MA), Yale Univ (MA, PhD); *m* 18 Aug 1951, Betty (d 2005), da of William Parnall (d 1958); 1 da (Jane Martin b 1959), 1 s (William Martin b 1962); *Career* Flying Offr RAF 1948–50; instr political sci Yale Univ 1955–56, asst prof of political sci MIT 1956–61, assoc prof of European diplomacy Sch of Advanced Int Studies Johns Hopkins Univ 1961–64, Woodrow Wilson prof of int politics Univ of Wales 1964–68 (dean Faculty of Social Sci 1966–68), prof of war studies KCL 1968–77, vice-chllr Univ of Newcastle upon Tyne 1978–90 (emeritus prof 1991); chief exec RIIA 1991–97; Center for Strategic and Int Studies (CSIS, formerly Georgetown Center of Strategic Studies) Washington DC: Arleigh Burke prof of strategy 1998–2000, sr advsr 2000–, memb Int Research Cncl 1969–77 and 1979– (co-chm 1998–); memb: SSRC 1969–76, Cncl IISS 1975–83; Lees-Knowles lectr Univ of Cambridge 1981, BBC Reith lectr 1981; Hon DCL Univ of Newcastle upon Tyne 1991; FKC 1984; *Books* The Anglo-American Tradition in Foreign Affairs (with Arnold Wolfers, 1956), Peace without Victory: Woodrow Wilson and British Liberalism (1958), Neutralism and Non-Alignment (1963), The Sea in Modern Strategy (1966), America and The World (jtly 1970), Arms and Strategy (1973), Retreat from Empire (jtly 1973), Strategic Thought in the Nuclear Age (ed 1979), The Two-Edged Sword: Armed Force in the Modern World (1982), Before The Day After (1985), The Changing Face of Nuclear Warfare (1987), British Foreign Policy: Choices and Challenges (with J Garnett, 1997); *Style—* Prof Sir Laurence Martin, DL; ✉ 35 Witley Court, London WC1N 1HD

MARTIN, Lionel; s of Max Rosenthal, and Renée, *née* Marks; *b* 9 August 1950; *Educ* Quintin Sch; *m* 20 July 1975, Carole, da of Michael Packer; 3 da (Carly b 1978, Joanna b 1981, Lily b 1987); *Career* CA; ptnr Martin Greene Ravden; ACA 1973, FCA 1983, FCCA 1983; *Recreations* tennis, music (incl professional writing); *Clubs* David Lloyd Slazenger Racquet; *Style—* Lionel Martin, Esq; ✉ 55 Loudoun Road, St John's Wood, London NW8 0DL

MARTIN, Rt Hon Michael John; PC (2000), MP; s of Michael Martin, and Mary Martin; *b* 3 July 1945; *Educ* St Patrick's Boys' Sch Glasgow; *m* 1966, Mary McLay; 1 s, 1 da; *Career* Rolls Royce (Hillington) AUEW shop steward 1970–74, trade union organiser 1976–79; MP: (Lab) Glasgow Springburn 1979–2000, (Speaker) Glasgow Springburn 2000–05, (Speaker) Glasgow NE 2005–; PPS to Rt Hon Denis Healey MP 1980–83, chm Scottish Grand Ctee 1987–97, memb Speaker's Panel of Chairmen 1987–97, chm Administration Ctee 1992–97, memb Select Ctee on House of Commons Servs, dep speaker and first dep chm Way & Means 1997–2000, speaker House of Commons 2000–; memb Coll of Piping; *Recreations* playing and listening to the Scottish pipes, hill walking, folk music, local history; *Style—* The Rt Hon Michael J Martin, MP; ✉ Speakers House, House of Commons, London SW1A 0AA

MARTIN, Paul; MSP; Michael John Martin and Mary Martin; *b* 17 March 1967; *Career* researcher, cncllr Glasgow City Cncl 1993–99; MSP (Lab) Glasgow Springburn 1999–; memb: Audit Ctee, Justice 1 Ctee, Cross-Pty Gp on Children and Young People, Cross-Pty Gp on Chronic Pain, Cross-Pty Gp on Tobacco Control; memb AEEU; *Recreations* football, golf, reading, walking; *Style—* Paul Martin, Esq, MSP; ✉ The Scottish Parliament, Edinburgh EH99 1SP (tel 0131 348 5844, e-mail paul.martin.msp@scottish.parliament.uk, website www.paulmartinmsp.org.uk)

MARTIN, Dr Paul; *Educ* Christ's Coll Cambridge (MA, PhD); *Career* Harkness fell and postdoctoral scholar Dept of Psychiatry and Behavioral Sciences Stanford Univ 1982–84, jr lectr Univ of Cambridge 1984–86, fell Wolfson Coll Cambridge 1984–86 and 2001–; civil servant MOD 1986–2000, dir of communication Cabinet Office 2000–01; science writer and conslt 2001–; *Books* Measuring Behaviour (with Patrick Bateson, 1993), The Sickening Mind (1998), Design for a Life (with Patrick Bateson, 1999), Counting Sheep (2002), What Worries Parents (with Kristina Murrin, 2004), Making People Happy (2005); *Style—* Dr Paul Martin

MARTIN, Robert Logan (Roy); QC (Scot 1988); s of late Robert Martin, MC, of Crosbie Wood, Paisley, and late Janet Johnstone, *née* Logan; *b* 31 July 1950; *Educ* Paisley GS, Univ of Glasgow (LLB); *m* 9 Nov 1984, Fiona Frances, da of John Roxburgh Bingham Neil, of St Ives, NSW; 1 s (Robert John Neil b 12 Aug 1987), 2 da (Camilla Nancy Neil b 25 Sept 1988, Phoebe Logan Neil b 2 Sept 1991); *Career* slr 1973–76, admitted to Faculty of Advocates 1976, memb Sheriff Courts Rules Cncl 1981–84, standing jr counsel to Dept of Employment (Scotland) 1983–84, advocate-depute 1984–87, admitted to Bar of NSW 1987, called to the Bar Lincoln's Inn 1990; dean Faculty of Advocates 2004– (vice-dean 2001–04); temporary sheriff 1988–90; pt/t chm Industrial Tbnls 1991–96, chm Scottish Planning, Local Govt and Environmental Bar Gp 1991–96, chm Police Appeals Tbnl 1997–, co-chair Forum for Barristers and Advocates 2002–, co-chair Int Cncl of Advocates and Barristers 2004–; hon sec Wagering Club 1982–91; govr Loretto 2002–, hon prof Univ of Glasgow 2006–; affiliate RIAS 1995; *Recreations* shooting, skiing, modern architecture, vintage motoring; *Clubs* New (Edinburgh); *Style—* Roy Martin, Esq, QC; ✉ Advocates' Library, Parliament House, Edinburgh (tel 0131 226 5071); Landmark Chambers, 180 Fleet Street, London EC4A LHG (tel 020 7430 1221)

MARTIN, Stanley William Frederick; CVO (1992, LVO 1981), JP (Inner London 1993–2000); s of Stanley Martin (d 1976), of Walmer, Kent, and Winifred Rose Kilburn (d 1976); *b* 9 December 1934; *Educ* Bromley GS, UC Oxford (MA, pres OU Law Soc 1957); *m* 3 Sept

1960, Hanni Aud, da of Aage Valdemar Johannes Hansen (d 1957), of Copenhagen, Denmark, and Oda Maja Valborg Nielsen (d 1989); 1 s (Nicholas b 1962), 1 da (Birgit b 1964); *Career* mil serv 2 Lieut RASC 1953–55; entered CRO 1958, asst private sec to Sec of State 1959–62; first sec: Canberra 1962–64, Kuala Lumpur 1964–67; Planning Staff and Personnel Dept FCO 1967–70, seconded to CSD (CSSB) 1970–71, asst marshal Dip Corps 1972–81, first asst marshal Dip Corps 1981–92, assoc head Protocol Dept FCO 1986–92, ret Dip Serv 1992, protocol advsr FCO 1993–; Extra Gentleman Usher to HM The Queen 1993–; visiting prof Univ of Westminster 1987– (hon fell 1998); freelance lectr 1993–; diplomatic conslt: Hyde Park Hotel 1993–99, Grosvenor House 1999–2002; advsr: The Consular Corps of London 1993–, London Mayors' Assoc 2004– (hon memb 2006); memb: Ctee London Diplomatic Assoc 1972–, Cncl The Oxford Univ Soc 1993–2002, Advsy Cncl Spanish Inst of Protocol Studies 1997–, Cwlth Observer Gp Guyana Elections 1997, Ctee European Atlantic Gp 2002–; tstee: The Attlee Fndn 1993–99, Toynbee Hall 1996–99, Jt Commonwealth Socs Tst 2005–; patron Apex Tst 2002– (vice-patron 1995–2002); govr Goodenough Coll for Overseas Graduates 2005–; Freeman City of London 1988; FRSA 1985; Companion Order of Distinguished Serv (Brunei) 1992; *Publications* Diplomatic Handbook (contrib, 2 edn 1977, 8 edn 2004), Royal Service: History of Royal Victorian Order, Medal and Chain (jtly, Vol I 1996, Vol II 2001), The Order of Merit: One Hundred Years of Matchless Honour (2006); also contrib to Jl of Orders and Medals Res Soc, Jl of Royal Over-Seas League, Diplomat Magazine; *Recreations* collecting books, manuscripts and obituaries, historical research and writing, walking, siestas, watching old films in the afternoon; *Clubs* Royal Over-Seas League (memb Central Cncl 1982–, memb Exec Ctee 1993–, vice-chm 2002–05, chm 2005–), Oxford and Cambridge, Danish; *Style*— Stanley Martin, Esq, CVO; ✉ 14 Great Spilmans, London SE22 8SZ (tel 020 8693 8181)

MARTIN, Stephen Alexander; MBE (1994); s of James Alexander Martin, of Bangor, Co Down, and Mamie, *née* Weir; *b* 13 April 1959; *Educ* Bangor GS, Univ of Ulster (BA); *m* 13 April 1987, Dorothy Esther Elizabeth, da of William Edwin Armstrong, of Belmont, Belfast; 1 s (Patrick Armstrong b 14 Nov 1991), 1 da (Hannah Rebecca b 18 Jan 1996); *Career* former hockey player; Bronze medal World Champions Trophy 1984 (vice-capt), Bronze medal Olympic Games LA 1984, Silver medal World Champions Trophy 1985, Gold medal Olympic Games Seoul 1988, sixth place Olympic Games Barcelona 1992 (capt); 94 caps GB 1983–92, 135 caps Ireland 1980–91 (capt 1984–85, European Cup 1983, 1987 and 1991, World Cup 1990, total 229 most capped player in GB and Ireland), World Champions Trophy 1984–92; played Ulster 1980–91; sports broadcaster; chief exec Olympic Cncl Ireland 2006–; dep chef de mission Team GB Olympic Games Salt Lake City 2002 and Olympic Games Athens 2004; ambass London 2012 Olympic Games bid; memb Bd Irish Sports Inst; memb: Br Assoc of Sports Med/Sci, Br Olympians Club, Br Inst of Sports Coaches; Hon DUniv Ulster 2001; *Recreations* hockey, golf; *Clubs* Bangor, Belfast YMCA, Holywood 87, Newry Olympic, Annadale Hockey, Donaghadee Golf; *Style*— Dr Stephen Martin, MBE; ✉ 5 The Coaches, Brown's Brae, Holywood, Co Down BT18 0LE (tel 028 9042 1338, e-mail stephen@olympicsport.ie)

MARTIN, Stephen Graham Balfour; s of Graham Hunter Martin (d 1985), and Ragna, *née* Balch-Barth; *b* 21 October 1939; *Educ* Tonbridge; *m* 1, 1966 (m dis 1969), Angela Wood; 1 s (Diccon Carl Henry b 1967); m 2, 1976, Elizabeth Mary, da of Dennis John Ward, of Chatteris, Cambs; 2 da (Charlotte Louise Elizabeth b 1978, Olivia Rose Ragna b 1993); *Career* chm and md: Intermail plc, Home Shopping Club Ltd; dir: Strategic Marketing Databases Ltd, Union Pen Co Inc; Past Master Worshipful Co of Armourers and Brasiers; FIDM, DipDM; *Recreations* fishing, shooting, gardening; *Clubs* Flyfishers', Norske; *Style*— Stephen Martin, Esq; ✉ Manor Farm House, Chilton Foliat, Hungerford, Berkshire RG17 0TJ; Intermail plc, Horizon West Canal View Road, Newbury, Berkshire RG14 5XF (fax 01635 41678, e-mail stephen.martin@intermail.co.uk)

MARTIN, Timothy Charles (Tim); s of Godfrey Martin (d 1975), of Findon, W Sussex, and Nancy Cordelia, *née* Orrom (d 1996); *b* 17 May 1951; *Educ* King's Coll Cambridge (MA); *m* 31 March 1984, Sarah, da of Arthur James Moffett, FRCS, of Cooksey Green, Worcs; 2 s (Alexander Dods b 19 Aug 1985, Charles Murray b 15 Jan 1988); *Career* admitted slr 1977, Allen and Overy 1975–79; dir (corp fin) Hill Samuel and Co 1986–87, dir Barclays de Zoete Wedd Ltd 1988–97, dir Euro Utilities Credit Suisse First Boston 1997–99, head Euro Utilities Flemings 1999–2000, dir JP Morgan Chase 2000–01; chief economist and dir of infrastructure and economic regulation Office of Rail Regulation 2001–; *Recreations* tennis, gardening, opera, collecting modern British pictures; *Clubs* Lansdowne; *Style*— Tim Martin, Esq; ✉ Office of Rail Regulation, 1 Waterhouse Square, 138–142 Holborn, London EC1N 2TQ (tel 020 7282 2139, fax 020 7282 2042, e-mail tim.martin@orr.gsi.gov.uk)

MARTIN, Valerie Ann (Val); da of William Herbert Bennett (d 1996), of Purley, Surrey, and Ann Georgina, *née* Hon (d 1977); *b* 15 October 1951; *Educ* King George V Sch Hong Kong, Girton Coll Cambridge (MA); *m* July 1973, Prof Benjamin Raymond Martin; 2 s (Paul b 3 June 1980, David b 10 Sept 1985), 1 da (Sarah b 5 Dec 1982); *Career* teacher VSO W Africa 1973–75, NHS nat mgmnt trainee Manchester 1975–77, asst sector administrator Univ Hosp S Manchester 1977–78, unit administrator New Cross Hosp London 1978–82, project mangr for reorganisation and merger of Guy's and Lewisham Health Dist 1982–83, dep unit general mangr Guy's Hosp London 1983–85, mangr Dist Industrial Servs Lewisham and N Southwark HA 1988–89, head Business Planning Unit Guy's Hosp 1989–90, project mangr for NHS Tst status application for Guy's and Lewisham NHS Tst 1990–91, gen mangr Lewisham and Hither Green Hosps 1991–93, chief exec Lewisham Hosp NHS Tst 1993–99, fell Leadership Devpt King's Fund 2000–; MHSM, FRSA; *Recreations* reading, swimming, trekking, enjoying life; *Style*— Mrs Val Martin; ✉ King's Fund, 11–13 Cavendish Square, London W1M 0AN (tel 020 7307 2599, fax 020 7307 2600)

MARTIN, Dr Vivian Max; s of Martin Martin, of Melbourne, Aust, and Rachel, *née* Godfrey; *b* 9 October 1941; *Educ* Monash Univ Aust (MB BS), RCP; *m* Dec 1967, Penelope Georgina, da of Leon Samuels; 2 s (Simon James b 22 Nov 1971, Nicholas Giles b 23 Dec 1973); *Career* jr RMO Launceston Gen Hosp Tasmania 1968, sr RMO Sutherland Dist Hosp Sydney 1969–70, sr RMO Queen Victoria Meml Hosp Melbourne 1970–71; SHO Royal Free Hosp 1972–73, registrar Whittington Hosp 1973–76; sr registrar UCH 1976–81; conslt rheumatologist: Cromwell Hosp 1982–, Manor House Hosp 1991–99; conslt physician PPP Med Centre 1985–94; memb: BMA, RSM, Br Soc for Rheumatology; MRCP; *Publications* author of articles in various learned journals; *Style*— Dr Vivian Martin; ✉ 121 Harley Street, London W1G 6AX (tel 020 7486 2365, fax 020 7224 0034); Cromwell Hospital, Cromwell Road, London SW5 0TU (tel 020 7460 2000, fax 020 7460 5555); Albert House, 47 Nottingham Place, London W1U 5LZ (tel 020 7034 5041, fax 020 7034 5042)

MARTIN, William Edward (Bill); s of Joseph Edward Martin (d 1987), of Upminster, Essex, and Pamela Maud, *née* Ruse (d 2001); *b* 10 March 1951; *Educ* Beal Essex, Univ of Exeter (BA), Univ of Wales (MSc); *m* 28 Aug 1976, Yvette Mary, da of James Geard McBrearty (d 1976); 1 s (Samuel b June 1978), 1 da (Anna b May 1980); *Career* economist DTI 1973–81, advsr Central Policy Review Staff Cabinet Office 1981–83; UBS Ltd: joined UBS Phillips & Drew 1983, chief UK economist UBS until 1996, md of economic research 1996–98; chief economist Phillips & Drew (later UBS Global Asset Mgmnt) 1998–2004, economic conslt 2004–; advsr Treasy and Civil Serv Select Ctee 1986–97; visiting lectr Faculty of Economics Univ of Cambridge; *Books* The Economics of the Profits Crisis (ed 1981); *Recreations* theatre, art; *Style*— Bill Martin, Esq

MARTIN, William Wylie Macpherson (Bill); s of Ian Alistair Macpherson (d 1985), of Glasgow, and Lettia, *née* Wylie; *b* 9 November 1938; *Educ* Glasgow; *m* Janet Mary, da of Maj Bruce Anthony Olley (d 1981), and Jeanne, *née* Blackburn; 1 s (Angus), 3 da (Meran, Alison, Melanie); *Career* songwriter: Puppet on a String (first Br songwriter to win Eurovision Song Contest), Congratulations, My Boy, The Water Babies, Shanga-lang and 50 other top ten songs; music publisher: Sky, Van Morrison, Bay City Rollers, BA Robertson, Billy Connolly; record producer: Billy Connolly, Bay City Rollers, Elkie Brooks; Variety Club Silver Heart award for servs to charity; Freeman: City of London 1981, City of Glasgow 1987; Liveryman Worshipful Co of Distillers; *Recreations* golf; *Clubs* RAC (past capt Golf Club), Annabel's, St George's Hill, MCC; *Style*— Bill Martin, Esq; ✉ 14 Graham Terrace, Belgravia, London SW1W 8JH (fax 020 7730 3368, mobile 07850 845280, e-mail bill.puppetmartin@virgin.net, website www.billmartinsongwriter.com)

MARTIN ALEGI, Lynda Margaret; da of George Watt (d 1990), and Dorothy May, *née* Humphreys; *b* 7 March 1952; *Educ* Woodford Co HS, Newnham Coll Cambridge (MA), Université Libre de Bruxelles - Institut D'Etudes Européenes (License Spécial en Droit Européen); *m* 6 Jan 1989, Peter Alegi; *Career* Baker & McKenzie: articled clerk 1975–77, asst slr 1977–81, ptnr 1981–, ptnr i/c EC, Competition and Trade Dept 1989–, memb Professional Devpt Ctee 1989–93; memb: Competition Panel CBI 1990–, Law Ctee IOD 1993–95, Competition Ctee Int C of C UK 1995–; ed Competition Law chapter Encyclopaedia of Information Technology Law (Sweet & Maxwell) 1989–; numerous articles and speeches on Euro and competition law issues; memb: Law Soc 1977, Slrs' Euro Gp 1977; *Recreations* Italian hill towns, wine and gardens; *Style*— Ms Lynda Martin Alegi; ✉ Baker & McKenzie, 100 New Bridge Street, London EC4V 7JA (tel 020 7919 1000, fax 020 7919 1999, mobile 07968 612556)

MARTIN-JENKINS, Christopher Dennis Alexander; 2 s of Lt-Col Dennis Frederick Martin-Jenkins, TD (d 1991), of Cranleigh, Surrey, and Dr Rosemary Clare Martin-Jenkins, *née* Walker (d 2000); *b* 20 January 1945; *Educ* Marlborough, Univ of Cambridge (MA); *m* 1971, Judith Oswald, da of Charles Henry Telford Hayman (d 1950), of Brackley, Northants; 2 s (James b 1973, Robin b 1975), 1 da (Lucy b 1979); *Career* BBC: sports broadcaster 1970–, cricket corr 1973–80 and 1984–91; ed The Cricketer 1981–91 (dep ed 1967–70), cricket corr Daily Telegraph 1991–99, cricket corr The Times 1999–; pres Cricket Soc 1998–, chm Brian Johnston Meml Tst 1998–2000; played cricket for Surrey second XI and MCC; pres Rugby Fives Assoc 1993–95; Sports Reporter of the Year 1996, Wisden Cricket Writer of the Year 1997–2006; *Books* author of various books on cricket; *Recreations* cricket, golf, tennis; *Clubs* MCC and many other CCs, W Sussex Golf, Royal St George's Golf, East India; *Style*— Christopher Martin-Jenkins, Esq; ✉ The Times, 1 Pennington Street, London E1 9XN (e-mail christopher.martin-jenkins@thetimes.co.uk)

MARTIN-JENKINS, David Dennis; eldest s of Lt-Col Dennis Frederick Martin-Jenkins, TD (d 1991), of Cranleigh, Surrey, and Dr Rosemary Clare Martin-Jenkins, *née* Walker (d 2000); *b* 7 May 1941; *Educ* Kingsmead, Meols, St Bede's Eastbourne, Marlborough; *m* 24 June 1967, Anthea, da of Arthur Milton de Vinny (d 1983); *Career* dir: JW Cameron and Co Ltd 1972–82, Ellerman Lines plc 1974–82, Tollemache and Cobbold Breweries Ltd 1976–82; chm MN Offrs Pension Fund Investment Ctee 1976–82; dir: Primesight plc 1984–99, National Home Loans Holdings plc 1985–95, Capital and Regnl Properties plc 1986–95; chm: Paragon Gp plc Pension Fund 1991–2006, Electoral Reform Services Ltd 2001–06; tstee John Ellerman Fndn 1991–; treas Shipwrecked Mariners' Soc 1995–2006; FCA 1965; *Recreations* sport (Tranmere Rovers and Liverpool FCs), politics (Lib Dem), hill walking (climbed Mera Peak (21,200ft) Nepal 1986, Aconcagua (22,835ft) Argentina 1993, Pisco (18,867ft) Peru 1996), the countryside; *Clubs* Lancashire CCC; *Style*— David Martin-Jenkins, Esq; ✉ Jobson's Cottage, Jobson's Lane, Haslemere, Surrey GU27 3BY (tel 01428 707294, fax 01428 708097)

MARTINDALE, Richard John; s of Eric Martindale (d 1970), of Hindley, Lancs, and Margaret Joyce, *née* Whiteside (d 1993); *b* 25 October 1950; *Educ* Bolton Sch, Univ of Sheffield (LLB); *m* 1, 5 Aug 1971 (m dis 1992), Jackie Avril, da of Philip Watkin Edwards; 4 s (Nicholas Jolyon b 16 April 1977, Timothy George b 8 Aug 1978, Alastair James b 16 July 1982, Justin Matthew b 31 Aug 1984); m 2, 18 June 1994, Carole Mary, da of George Harold Ellicock; *Career* Hill Dickinson Liverpool: articles until 1974, ptnr 1979, specialist in commercial law; chief examiner in shipping law RSA 1980–84; memb Law Soc 1974–; supporting memb London Maritime Arbitrators Assoc; *Recreations* music, reading, walking, travel, ancient Egypt; *Style*— Richard Martindale, Esq; ✉ Banhadlen Ganol, Llanarmon-yn-Ial, Mold, Denbighshire CH7 4QD (tel 01824 780431); Hill Dickinson, Pearl Assurance House, Derby Square, Liverpool L2 9XL (tel 0151 236 5400, fax 0151 236 2175, e-mail richard.martindale@hilldickinson.com)

MARTINEAU, His Hon Judge David Nicholas Nettlefold; s of Frederick Alan Martineau (d 1990) of Chobham, Surrey, and Vera Ruth, *née* Naylor; *b* 27 March 1941; *Educ* Eton, Trinity Coll Cambridge (MA, LLB); *m* 20 Jan 1968, Elizabeth Mary, da of Maurice James Carrick Allom (d 1995), of Ightham, Kent; 1 s (Luke b 27 March 1970), 1 da (Alice b 8 June 1972 d 2003); *Career* called to the Bar Inner Temple 1964; recorder 1986–94 (asst recorder 1982), circuit judge (SE Circuit) 1994–; memb Nat Exec Ctee Cystic Fibrosis Res Tst 1989–2004; *Recreations* skiing, water-skiing, windsurfing, music, wine and food; *Clubs* Hawks' (Cambridge), MCC; *Style*— His Hon Judge David Martineau; ✉ Blackfriars Crown Court, Pocock Street, London SE1 0BJ (tel 020 7922 5800)

MARTLEW, Eric Anthony; MP; *b* 3 January 1949; *Educ* Harraby Sch, Carlisle Technical Coll; *m* Elsie, *née* Duggan; *Career* formerly lab technician then personnel mangr Nestlé; MP (Lab) Carlisle 1987–; shadow defence spokesman (RAF) 1992–95, oppn whip 1995–97; PPS to: Chllr Duchy of Lancaster 1997–98, Leader of House of Lords 1998–; chm TGWU Parly Gp; memb Carlisle City Cncl 1972–74, memb Cumbria CC 1973–88 (chm 1983–85), memb Cumbria HA then East Cumbria HA 1975–88 (chm 1977–79); *Recreations* photography, fell walking, local history; *Style*— Eric Martlew, Esq, MP; ✉ House of Commons, London SW1A 0AA (tel 020 7219 3000)

MARTONMERE, 2 Baron (UK 1964) John Stephen Robinson; s of Hon Richard Anthony Gasque Robinson (d 1979), and Hon Mrs (Wendy Patricia) Robinson; gs of 1 Baron Martonmere, GBE, KCMG, PC (d 1989); *b* 10 July 1963; *Educ* Lakefield Coll Sch, Seneca Coll; *m* 12 Dec 2001, Marion Elizabeth, da of Ian Wills, of Toronto, Canada; 2 s (Hon James Ian b 26 Feb 2003, Hon Andrew Roland b 10 May 2005); *Heir* s, Hon James Robinson; *Style*— The Rt Hon Lord Martonmere; ✉ 67 Denwoods Drive, Toronto, Ontario, Canada M4N 2G6 (tel 00 1 416 322 3692)

MARTYN, John Reid; s of Ernest John Martyn (d 1970), of Ealing, London, and Evelyn Isobel, *née* Reid (d 1973); *b* 16 June 1944; *Educ* Ealing GS for Boys, Univ of Exeter (BA); *m* 4 Aug 1967, Frances Howell, da of Cyril Howell Williams; 1 s (Gareth John b 4 Sept 1974), 1 da (Charis Jane b 15 Sept 1977); *Career* with Ford Motor Co 1965–80, with BICC plc 1980–84 (gp fin dir 1983–84), gp fin dir The Littlewoods Organisation plc 1984–87, gp fin dir Dalgety plc 1987–97, estates bursar Trinity Coll Oxford 1997–2002, investment bursar Trinity Coll Oxford 2002–06; non-exec dir Lloyds Abbey Life plc 1993–97, non-exec (link) dir The Littlewoods Organisation 1996–2002; vol for various charities; FICMA; *Recreations* gardening, golf; *Style*— John Martyn, Esq; ✉ Redcroft, Stanville Road, Cumnor Hill, Oxford (tel 01865 862740, e-mail frances.martyn@virgin.net)

MARTYN-HEMPHILL, Hon Charles Andrew Martyn; s of 5 Baron Hemphill, *qv*; *b* 8 October 1954; *Educ* Downside, St Benet's Hall Oxford; *m* 1985, Sarah J F, eld da of Richard Edward Walter Lumley, of Windlesham, Surrey; 3 da (Clarissa Mary b 31 May 1986, Amelia Rose b 31 March 1988, Marina Olivia Astrid b 22 Oct 1992), 2 s (Richard Patrick

Lumley b 17 May 1990, Oliver Francis Robert b 10 Dec 1998); *Career* md Deutsche Asset Mgmnt Deutsche Bank 1994–; *Recreations* sailing, skiing, shooting, hunting; *Clubs* White's; *Style*— The Hon Charles Martyn-Hemphill; ✉ Deutsche Asset Management, 1 Appold Street, London EC2A 2UU (tel 020 7545 6000); 66 Manville Road, London SW17 8JL (tel 020 8672 2536)

MARTYR, Peter McCallum; s of John Walton Martyr, and Jean Wallace Robertson, *née* McCallum; *b* 31 March 1954; *Educ* Clifton, Univ of Wales (LLB); *m* 27 May 1978, Carol Frances, da of Donald Edgar Busby; 1 s (Luke b 26 Dec 1985), 1 da (Laura b 7 Nov 1988); *Career* admitted slr 1979, chief exec Norton Rose 2002– (ptnr 1985–, specialising in insurance, shipping and energy disputes); Freeman Worshipful Co of Solicitors 1979; *Recreations* skiing, collector's motor cars, music; *Style*— Peter Martyr, Esq; ✉ Norton Rose, 3 More London Riverside, London SE1 2AQ (tel 020 7283 6000, fax 020 7283 6500)

MARUNCHAK, Alexander (Alex); s of Ivan Marunchak, of Westminster, and Paraskewia, *née* Korpesio; *b* 31 May 1951; *Educ* St Marylebone GS London, Kilburn Poly; *m* 1, 1976 (m dis 1978), Susan Tatarczuk; m 2, 1982, Jennifer Hickman; 2 s; *Career* journalist; Slough Observer 1977–79, Middlesex Chronicle 1979–80, Evening Echo 1980–81; News of the World: joined 1981, crime reporter 1983–85, chief crime reporter 1985–87, dep news ed 1987–91, news ed 1992–95, asst ed (news) 1995–97, assoc ed 1997–98, sr exec ed 1998–; appointed special advsr Embassy of Ukraine 1999; chm: N Westminster Young Libs 1979–81, Ukrainian Soc 1981–82; contested (Lib) Westminster City Cncl 1981; *Recreations* politics, reading, languages (speaks Ukrainian and Russian); *Clubs* National Liberal; *Style*— Alex Marunchak, Esq; ✉ News of the World, 1 Virginia Street, London E1 9XR (tel 020 7782 4000, fax 020 7583 9504)

MARVEN, Gary; s of Robert and Margaret Marven; *Educ* Bolton GS, Univ of Leeds; *Career* broadcaster; Granada plc 1996–98: commercial dir, business technol, sr fin exec; BBC 1998–: fin dir of prodn 1999–, chief operating offr factual and learning div 2000–; ICA; *Recreations* squash, running, reading; *Style*— Gary Marven, Esq; ✉ BBC, Room 3220, 201 Wood Lane, London W12 7TS (tel 020 8752 6604, mobile 0771 4667891, e-mail gary.marven@bbc.co.uk)

MARWICK, George Robert; CVO (2007), JP (1970); *b* 27 February 1932; *Educ* Bryanston, Edinburgh Sch of Agriculture (Scot Dip); *Career* chm and md Swannay Farms Ltd 1972–, chm Campbeltown Creamery Ltd 1974–90; chm North of Scotland Water Board 1970–73; dir: North Eastern Farmers Ltd 1968–98, Orkney Islands Shipping Co 1972–87; memb: Countryside Commission for Scotland 1978–86, Scottish Agricultural Consultative Panel 1972–98, Cncl National Trust for Scotland 1979–84; vice chm Orkney Co Cncl 1970–74, convenor Orkney Islands Cncl 1974–78; HM Lord-Lt for Orkney 1997–2007 (DL 1976, Vice Lord-Lt 1995); Hon Sheriff of Grampian Highlands and Islands 2000; *Recreations* shooting, motor sport; *Clubs* Farmers', New (Edinburgh); *Style*— George Marwick, Esq, CVO; ✉ Swannay House, by Evie, Orkney (tel 01856 721263, fax 01856 721227)

MARWICK, Tricia; MSP; da of John (d 1995), and Mary, *née* Lynch (d 1994); *b* 5 November 1953; *m* 19 July 1975, Frank Marwick; 1 s, 1 da; *Career* public affairs offr Shelter Scotland 1992–99; elected memb SNP Nat Exec 1997–, MSP (SNP) Scotland Mid & Fife 1999–; *Recreations* reading (anything), sport (watching); *Style*— Mrs Tricia Marwick, MSP; ✉ The Scottish Parliament, Edinburgh EH99 1SP (tel 0131 348 5680, e-mail tricia.marwick.msp@scottish.parliament.uk)

MARWOOD, Roger Paul; s of Kenneth Ian Marwood (d 1988) and Blanche Greenberg (d 1980); *b* 23 July 1947; *Educ* Cheltenham GS, Univ of London (MB BS, MSc, Water Polo double purple); *m* 21 Feb 1976, Suzanne Christine, da of Francis Brown; 1 s (Joseph Roger George b 31 Oct 1984), 2 da (Rebecca Alice Georgina b 25 March 1978, Sophie Christine Blanche b 30 Dec 1979); *Career* sr registrar in obstetrics and gynaecology St Mary's Hosp 1980–82 (registrar 1975–80); conslt in obstetrics and gynaecology Chelsea & Westminster Hosp 1982–, conslt gynaecologist to King Edward VII Hosp 1985–; contrib to numerous jls on clinical obstetrics and gynaecology; pres Section of Obstetrics and Gynaecology RSM 2000–01, memb Cncl for London RCOG, memb Hosp Recognition Ctee RCOG; memb Worshipful Soc of Apothecaries 1985; FRCOG 1989 (MRCOG 1977); *Recreations* opera, skiing, sailing, swimming; *Clubs* Garrick; *Style*— Roger Marwood, Esq; ✉ 96 Harley Street, London W1G 7JY (tel 020 7637 7977, fax 020 7486 2022); Chelsea & Westminster Hospital, Fulham Road, London SW10 5NH (tel 020 8746 8218, fax 020 8846 7998)

MARYON-DAVIS, Prof Alan Roger; s of Cyril Edward Maryon-Davis (d 1994), of Osterley, Middx, and Hilda May, *née* Thompson (d 1995); *b* 21 January 1943; *Educ* St Paul's, St John's Coll Cambridge (MA, MB BChir), St Thomas' Hosp Med Sch London, LSHTM (MSc); *m* 14 March 1981, (Glynis) Anne, da of Dr Philip Trefor Davies (d 1970) of Hartlepool, Cleveland; 2 da (Jessica b 1983, Elizabeth b 1985); *Career* med conslt, public health specialist, writer and broadcaster; clinical med 1969–74, community and preventive med 1974–, chief MO Health Educn Cncl 1984–87, hon sr lectr in community med St Mary's Hosp Med Sch London 1985–89, hon specialist in community med Paddington and N Kensington HA 1985–88, conslt in public health med W Lambeth HA (later Lambeth, Southwark and Lewisham HA) 1988–2002, dir of public health for Southwark 2002–07; KCL: sr lectr in public health med 1988–2007, prof of public health 2007–; vice-chair Nat Heart Forum 2005–, chair Royal Inst of Public Health 2006– (vice-chair 2002–06), pres UK Faculty of Public Health 2007–; regular med advice columnist Woman magazine 1988–2005, regular columnist Public Health News 2003–06; MRCP 1972, FFCM 1986, FRIPHH 1989, FRCP 2005, FRSH 2005; *Radio* BBC Radio 4 series: Action Makes the Heart Grow Stronger 1983, Back in 25 Minutes 1984, Not Another Diet Programme 1985, Cancercheck 1988; *Television* BBC series: Your Mind in Their Hands 1982, Save a Life 1986, Bodymatters 1985–89; *Books* Family Health & Fitness (1981), Bodyfacts (1984), Diet 2000 (with J Thomas, 1984), How to Save a Life (with J Rogers, 1987), Pssst a Really Useful Guide to Alcohol (1989), Cholesterol Check (1991), The Good Health Guide (1994), Ruby's Health Quest (1995), The Body-Clock Diet (1996), Feeling Good (2007); *Recreations* relaxing in the Yorkshire Dales, singing in the group 'Instant Sunshine'; *Style*— Prof Alan Maryon-Davis

MASCHLER, Thomas Michael; s of Kurt Leo Maschler; *b* 16 August 1933; *Educ* Leighton Park Sch Reading; *m* 1970, Fay Goldie (the writer on restaurants Fay Maschler) (m dis), da of Arthur Coventry (d 1969); 1 s (Benjamin Joseph b 1974), 2 da (Hannah Kate b 1970, Alice Mary b 1972); m 2 1987, Regina Kaliniez; *Career* publisher; chm Jonathan Cape 1970– (editorial dir 1960, md 1966); prodn asst André Deutsch 1955, ed MacGibbon & Kee 1956–58, fiction ed Penguin Books 1958–60; *Recreations* tennis, skiing; *Style*— Thomas Maschler Esq; ✉ Jonathan Cape Ltd, Random House, 20 Vauxhall Bridge Road, London SW1V 2SA

MASDIN, Dr (Edward) Guy; s of Frank Masdin (d 1986), and Marjorie Mary, *née* Clark (d 1980); *b* 9 May 1936; *Educ* Ecclesfield GS, Univ of Sheffield (BSc, PhD, univ first XI cricket); *m* 21 June 1958, Beryl Monica, da of George Barnes; 2 s (Robert Howard b 1962, Philip Carl b 1970), 2 da (Kay Judith b 1964, Linda Ruth b 1966); *Career* div head Shell Research Ltd 1966–73, tech mktg mangr Shell Coal International 1973–81, head Res Planning and Co-ordination Shell International Petroleum Co 1981–91; dir: Shell Research Ltd 1981–91, Shell Recherches 1981–91; res mgmnt conslt 1991–; past pres Inst of Energy; FInstE, FIChemE, FREng 1986; *Recreations* golf, gardening, bowls; *Clubs* Berks CCC, North Hants Golf; *Style*— Dr Guy Masdin, FREng; ✉ 2 Martins Drive, Wokingham, Berkshire RG41 1NY (tel 0118 978 5880, fax 0118 962 9752, e-mail guy.masdin@ntlworld.com)

MASEFIELD, Sir Charles; kt (1997); s of Sir Peter Masefield, of Reigate, Surrey, and Lady Patricia Masefield; *b* 7 January 1940; *Educ* Eastbourne Coll, Jesus Coll Cambridge (MA); *m* 1970, Fiona Anne; 2 s (Ashley Charles b 1971, Fraser Graham b 1975); *Career* test pilot and sales exec Beagle Aircraft Ltd 1964–70, test pilot Hawker Siddeley Aviation (flying Nimrods, Victors, Vulcans) 1970–76; British Aerospace: dep chief test pilot Manchester 1976–78, chief test pilot Manchester 1978–80, project dir 1980–81, prodn dir Chadderton 1981–84, gen mangr Manchester 1984–86, pres BAe Commercial Aircraft Ltd 1990–93 (md 1986–90), sr vice-pres (commercial) Airbus Industries 1993–94, head Defence Export Services Orgn MoD 1994–98, vice-chm GEC plc 1998–1999, pres BAE Systems 2003– (gp mktg dir 2000–01, vice-chm 2002), chm Microsulis Medical Ltd 2003–, chm Helvetica Wealth Mgmnt 2004–; memb Bd: Bank Piguet Geneva 2003–05, Qatar Fndn 2003–; flying achievements: holder of existing London-NY record for bi-planes flying a 1935 DH90 dragonfly 1964, winner King's Cup Air Race flying P51–D Mustang 1967, Br Air Racing Champion 1968; pres RAeS 1994–95; memb Cncl: Air League, RAeS; Liveryman Guild of Air Pilots and Navigators; CEng 1986, FRAeS 1985, FIMechE 1986, (Hon FIMechE 2005); *Recreations* occasional golf; *Style*— Sir Charles Masefield; ✉ Old Hall, Markyate, Hertfordshire AL3 8AR (tel 01582 849132, fax 01582 849134); BAE Systems, 6 Carlton Gardens, London SW1Y 5DA (e-mail sir-charles.masefield@baesystems.com)

MASHAM OF ILTON, Baroness (Life Peer UK 1970), of Masham in the North Riding of Yorkshire; Susan Lilian Primrose Cunliffe-Lister (Susan, Countess of Swinton); DL (N Yorks 1991); da of Maj Sir Ronald Norman Sinclair, 8 Bt, and Reba Inglis, later Mrs R H Hildreth (d 1985); *b* 14 April 1935; *Educ* Heathfield Sch Ascot, London Poly; *m* 8 Dec 1959, 2 Earl of Swinton (d 2006); 1 s, 1 da (both adopted); *Career* sits as Independent peer in House of Lords; memb: Parly All-Pty Disablement Gp Drug Misuse Ctee (vice-chm), Parly Gps on Children, Alcohol Misuse, Breast Cancer, Food and Health, Skin and Epilepsy, Penal Affairs, Primary Care and Public Health; vice-chm Parly AIDS Ctee; memb: Bd of Visitors for Wetherby Borstal (now Young Offenders Inst) 1963–94, Yorks RHA 1982–90, Family Health Services Authy N Yorks 1990–96, Gen Advsy Cncl of BBC until 1991; chm: Home Office Ctee on Young People Alcohol and Crime, Cncl London Lighthouse; dir Assoc for the Prevention of Addiction; pres: N Yorks Red Cross 1963–88 (patron 1989–), Yorks Assoc for Disabled 1963–98, Spinal Injuries Assoc 1982–, The Psoriasis Assoc, The Registration Cncl of Scientists in Health Care, League of Friends of Harrogate Hosps, Inst of Welfare Offrs; vice-pres: Coll of Occupational Therapists Action for Dysphasic, Hosp Saving Assoc; patron: Disablement Income Group, Adults (DIA), Int Spinal Res Tst; pres, vice-pres and patron of numerous other orgns; Freeman Borough of Harrogate 1989; hon fell Bradford & Ilkley Community Coll 1988; Hon MA: York 1985, Open Univ 1985; Hon LLD: Univ of Leeds 1988, Teesside Univ 1993, UEA 2001; Hon DSc Univ of Ulster 1990, Hon DLitt Keele Univ 1993; hon fell: Royal Coll of GPs 1981, Chartered Soc of Physiotherapy 1996; *Recreations* swimming, breeding Highland ponies, gardening; *Style*— Baroness Masham of Ilton, DL; ✉ Dykes Hill House, Masham, Ripon, North Yorkshire HG4 4NS (tel 01765 689241, fax 01765 688184, e-mail susan@masham1935.fsnet.co.uk); 46 Westminster Gardens, Marsham Street, London SW1P 4JG (tel 020 7834 0700)

MASKELL, John Michael; s of Horace Maclean Maskell (d 1985), and Kathleen Muriel, *née* Hatton (d 1990); *b* 26 March 1942; *Educ* Winchester, Peterhouse Cambridge (MA, LLB); *m* 1, 6 Aug 1966 (m dis 1982), Elisabeth Joan (d 1986), da of Montagu Ralph Threlkeld Edwards (d 1983); 1 da (Jane Elisabeth b 26 March 1971), 1 s (Paul Nicholas b 18 Oct 1973); m 2, 7 Jan 1992, Margaret Joy, da of Norman Leslie Upton (d 1982); *Career* admitted slr 1966; ptnr: Norton Rose 1971–93, Shaw and Croft 1993–95; marine arbitrator; chm London Maritime Arbitrators' Assoc Supporting Membs 1980–84, pres Aldgate Ward Club 1986–87, memb London Maritime Arbitrators' Assoc; *Recreations* bridge, war games, music; *Clubs* MCC; *Style*— John Maskell, Esq; ✉ Justice Wood, Wheelers Hill, Little Waltham, Chelmsford, Essex (tel 01245 362456)

MASKREY, Simeon Andrew; QC (1995); s of Norman Walter Maskrey, of Seaford, and Brenda, *née* Rose; *b* 17 May 1955; *Educ* King's Sch Grantham, Leicester Univ (LLB); *Family* 2 s, 1 da; *Career* pupil of Sir Igor Judge (Lord Justice of Appeal) and Sir John Goldring, recorder 1997– (asst recorder 1993–97), dep High Ct judge 2000–; *Style*— Simeon Maskrey, Esq, QC; ✉ 7 Bedford Row, London WC1R 4BU (tel 020 7242 3555, fax 020 7242 2511, e-mail clerks@7br.co.uk)

MASOJADA, Bronislaw Edmund (Bronek); s of Milek Edmund Masojada, and Shirley Mary, *née* Johnston; *b* 31 December 1961; *Educ* Durban HS, Univ of Natal (BSc), Trinity Coll Oxford (Rhodes scholar, MPhil); *m* 1986, Jane Elizabeth Ann Lamont; 3 s (Adam Lamont b 14 Aug 1987, Dominik Edmund b 19 Nov 1995, Marek Roderick b 13 Oct 1999), 2 da (Michaela Jane b 11 March 1991, Lara Eva b 19 Oct 1993); *Career* Nat Serv South African Army Engrg Corps 1983–84; with McKinsey & Co Sydney, London and Tokyo 1989–93, md Hiscox Hldgs 1993–95, md Hiscox plc 1996–99, ceo Hiscox plc 2000–06, ceo Hiscox Ltd 2007–; dep chm Cncl Lloyd's 2001–07, dir Xchanging Insure Services 2003–06; chm Lloyd's Underwriting Agents Assoc 2000 (memb Ctee 1993–98), memb Ctee Lloyd's Market Assoc; pres Insurance Inst of London 2004–05; pres Lloyd's Croquet Soc 2004–; tstee Lloyd's Tercentenary Fndn 2007–; *Recreations* windsurfing, kite surfing, skiing; *Style*— Mr Bronek Masojada; ✉ Hiscox plc, 1 Great St Helens, London EC3A 6HX (tel 020 7448 6012, fax 020 7448 6598, e-mail bronek.masojada@hiscox.com)

MASON, Anthony Denzil (Tony); s of Brian Duncan Mason, of Dorking, Surrey, and Doris Edna, *née* Patient (d 2007); *b* 17 June 1954, Kingston upon Thames, Surrey; *Educ* Chislehurst and Sidcup GS for Boys, Univ of Birmingham (BSocSc); *m* 10 Feb 1979, Vivien Susan, *née* Long; 2 da (Rowena Claire b 31 Aug 1984, Hilary Elaine b 5 April 1987); *Career* with Guardian Royal Exchange 1975–80; Lane Clark & Peacock 1980–2007 (ptnr 1985, managing ptnr 1997, md 2002, chm 2006), chief exec Medical Proection Soc 2007–; FIA 1985; *Recreations* tennis, bridge, table tennis; *Clubs* RAC; *Style*— Tony Mason, Esq; ✉ Medical Protection Society, 33 Cavendish Square, London W1G 0PS (tel 020 7399 1300)

MASON, Col Colin Rees; OBE (2003), TD, DL; s of Clifford Harold Mason (d 1969), and Ann, *née* Jones (d 1986); *b* 19 August 1943; *Educ* Gwent Coll, St Julian's HS Newport, Univ of Wales Aberystwyth (BA), Magdalene Coll Cambridge (MPhil), Harvard Grad Sch of Business (OPM); *m* 22 Aug 1968, (Grace) Angela, da of Ernest Alan St Helier Tweney (d 1979); 1 s (Richard Colin St Helier b 12 Oct 1970), 1 da (Penelope Jane St Helier b 19 March 1974); *Career* former broadcaster; began in USA while postgrad researcher Rice Univ TX in 1960s; formerly with: Ulster TV, BBC Local Radio; Natural History TV Unit BBC until 1974, prog dir Swansea Sound 1974–79, asst md Standard Broadcasting 1979, fndr md Chiltern Radio plc 1980–95, dep chm Choice FM Group 1995–2004, md Chiltern Broadcast Management 1997–; dir Network News (Radio) Ltd 1991–96; Lt-Col Royal Regt of Wales (TA), served Gulf War 1991, CO Pool of Public Info Offrs TA 1990–93, 15 (UK) Psychological Ops Gp 1998–2003; served: Kosovo 1999–2000, Sierra Leone 2001, Macedonia 2001, Afghanistan 2002, Iraq 2003; Co Commandant 2000–2004; Hon Col 15 (UK) Psychological Ops Gp 2004–; dir Milton Keynes C of C and Industry 1984–91; High Sheriff Beds 2002; *Recreations* travel, rowing; *Clubs* Army and Navy, Reform; *Style*— Col Colin Mason, OBE, TD, DL; ✉ Hall End House, Hall End, Bedfordshire MK43 9HJ (tel and fax 01234 766123, e-mail masonradio@aol.com)

MASON, David Gwyn; s of Gwyn Meirion Mason (d 2006), and Nansi Bronwen, *née* Roberts (d 1966); *b* 7 August 1949, Birkenhead, Cheshire; *Educ* Cheadle Hulme Sch, Univ

M

of Liverpool (LLB); *m* 3 May 1980, Patricia Mary, *née* Gerrard; 3 da (Jennifer Mary b 11 Oct 1984, Emily Ann, Alice Wendy (twins) b 22 Feb 1987); *Career* slr; ptnr Park & Co slrs 1975–81, ptnr Birch Cullimore slrs 1983– (joined 1981); under sheriff: City of Chester 1990–2003, Cheshire 2003–; tstee YMCA Chester; memb: Law Soc, Soc of Tst and Estate Practitioners, Agric Law Assoc; *Recreations* gardening, sport; *Clubs* Chester City, Deeside Ramblers Hockey; *Style*— David Mason, Esq; ✉ Birch Cullimore, Friars, White Friars, Chester CH1 1XS (tel 01244 321066, fax 01244 312582, e-mail david.mason@bclaw.co.uk)

MASON, David Paul; s of Charles Percy Mason, MBE (d 2001), and Barbara Joan, *née* Pafford (d 2002); *b* 16 October 1955; *Educ* Winchester, Oriel Coll Oxford (MA), City Univ (Dip Law); *m* 29 Dec 1999, Louise Deborah Caroline, da of Patrick Meagher; 1 s (Felix Paul b 23 March 1989), 1 da (Saskia Jane b 18 July 1990); *Career* called to the Bar 1984; admitted slr 1990; ptnr Capsticks 1990–, specialises in public law for NHS, cases incl Victoria Climbie and Clifford Ayling Inquiries; def slr Lord Woolf's Steering Gp for Medical Negligence 1995–96, def slr rep Clinical Disputes Forum 1996–2001; hon legal advsr Coll of Health 1994–2002; fell Soc for Advanced Legal Studies 1998; *Publications* Litigation: A Risk Management Guide to Midwives (co-author, 1993), Pre Action Protocol for the Resolution of Clinical Disputes (co-author, 1998), Service Reconfiguration, Consultation and Judicial Review (co-author, 2004); *Recreations* reading, sunbathing, collecting fossils; *Style*— David Mason, Esq; ✉ Capsticks, 77–83 Upper Richmond Road, London SW15 2TT (tel 020 8780 4702, fax 020 8780 4758, e-mail dmason@capsticks.co.uk)

MASON, David Peter; DL (Oxon); s of Michael Henry Mason (d 1982), and Dorothy Margaret, *née* Sturdee; *b* 13 August 1951; *Educ* Eton; *m* 1980, Monique Agnès, *née* Juranville; 3 da (Natalie b 1981, Catherine b 1984, Chantal b 1989), 1 s (Michael b 1991); *Career* offr 1 Bn Welsh Guards 1970–78, seconded to Desert Regt Sultan of Oman's Armed Forces 1974–76 (Sultan's Bravery Medal 1975), Transglobe expedition 1979–82, High Sheriff Oxon 1994–95; *Books* Shadow Over Babylon (1993), Little Brother (1996); *Recreations* travel, shooting, skiing; *Clubs* White's, Beefsteak, Turf, Shikar; *Style*— David Mason, Esq, DL; ✉ Eynsham Park, Witney, Oxfordshire OX29 6PP

MASON, Edward Geoffrey; s of Robin Mason (d 1995), and Elizabeth, *née* Eden; *b* 3 December 1961; *Educ* Oundle, Univ of Durham (BA, pres Union Soc); *m* (m dis 2006); 1 da (Georgina b 1991), 1 s (Hector b 1994); *Career* managing ptnr Jones Mason Barton Antenen 1998–99, ceo Claydon Heeley Jones Mason 1999–2000 (md 1997–98); chm City Championships Ltd 2003–; non-exec dir: Mango Event Mgmnt 2001–, Fortnum & Mason plc 2004–; FRSA 2003; *Recreations* sculpture, vintage car racing; *Style*— Edward Mason, Esq; ✉ City Championships Ltd, Trafalgar House, 11 Waterloo Place, London SW1Y 4AU (e-mail edward@citychampionships.com)

MASON, Eileen Janet Vicky (Mrs Johnson); da of Garnald Percy Mason (d 1972), of Walsall, and June Barbara, *née* Lawrence; *b* 13 October 1950; *Educ* Bluecoat Sch, Walsall Coll of Art, Sandwell Coll of Photography; *m* 1981, Bill Johnson; 2 da (Laura b 1979, Bobbie b 1985), 1 s (Martyn b 1983); *Career* trained as photographer Rubery Owen Co Ltd 1968–73, chief photographer Wolverhampton Educn Authy 1973–74, chief photographer Simon Livingstone Studio 1974–75, Eileen Mason Photography 1975–; memb Professional Photographers of America 1985, Craftsman with Distinction Guild of Wedding Photographers 1993; first woman to achieve fellowship of BIPP and MPA in wedding photography; *Awards* Guild Wedding Photographer of the Year (Nat Award) 1991, 1993 and 1995, British Inst Portrait Photographer of the Year (Midland region) 14 times in past 15 years, winner BIPP Midland Wedding Portfolio 1999, 2000 and 2001; FBIPP, FRPS, FMPA; *Recreations* theatre, music, comedy, movies (from old English black and white films to modern blockbusters), walking, French food and Indian curries; *Clubs* Walsall Rotary; *Style*— Eileen Mason; ✉ Eileen Mason Photography, 120 Lichfield Road, Rushall, Walsall, West Midlands WS4 1ED (tel 01922 625229, fax 01922 613937, e-mail info@eileenmason.co.uk, website www.eileenmason.co.uk)

MASON, Brig Harvey Christopher; *b* 22 December 1932; *Educ* Rothesay Acad, Univ of Glasgow (MB ChB), London (DTM & H); *m* 27 Dec 1957, Rosemary Elizabeth, *née* Fisher; 2 s (Christopher b 27 Feb 1960, Jon b 8 July 1962), 1 da (Ailie b 5 June 1965); *Career* serv in Korea, W Germany Cyprus; cmd advsr in GP BAOR 1977–80 and 1985–87, dir of Army GP 1988–91; Hon Surgn to HM The Queen 1989; memb BMA; Montefiore medal 1971; FMS London, FRCGP 1977 (MRCGP 1972); OStJ 1987; *Recreations* food, wine, opera, reading, cats; *Style*— Brig Harvey Mason; ✉ Mytilus House, 75 Brown Street, Salisbury, Wiltshire SP1 2BA (tel 01722 337705)

MASON, Prof Haydn Trevor; s of Herbert Thomas Mason (d 1973), and Margaret Ellen, *née* Jones (d 1973); *b* 12 January 1929; *Educ* Greenhill GS Tenby, Univ Coll of Wales Aberystwyth (BA), Middlebury Coll Vermont (AM), Jesus Coll Oxford (DPhil); *m* 1, 5 Feb 1955 (m dis 1982), Gretchen; 1 s (David b 24 March 1961), 1 da (Gwyneth b 8 April 1964); m 2, 14 Sept 1982, Adrienne Mary, da of Alfred Barnes, of Sutton Coldfield; 1 step da (Kate b 26 Nov 1968); *Career* Nat Serv 1951–53, 2 Lt RASC 1952; instr in French Princeton Univ USA 1954–57, lectr Univ of Newcastle 1960–63, reader Univ of Reading 1965–67 (lectr 1964–65), prof UEA 1967–79, prof Université de Paris-III (Sorbonne Nouvelle) 1979–81, prof Univ of Bristol 1981–94 (emeritus prof 1994–); pres: Assoc of Univ Profs of French 1981–82, Soc of French Studies 1982–84, Br Soc for Eighteenth Century Studies 1984–86 (hon fell 2006–), Int Soc for Eighteenth Century Studies 1991–95, Modern Humanities Research Assoc 1999; dir Voltaire Fndn Univ of Oxford 1977–97 (chm 1989–93); chm Clifton and Hotwells Improvement Soc 1994–98; gen ed Complete Works of Voltaire 1998–2001; Officier dans L'Ordre des Palmes Académiques 1985, Médaille d'Argent de la Ville de Paris 1989; *Books* Pierre Bayle and Voltaire (1963), Voltaire (1975), Voltaire: A Biography (1981), French Writers and their Society 1715–1800 (1982), Cyrano de Bergerac: L'Autre Monde (1984), Voltaire: Candide (1992); ed: Marivaux: Les Fausses Confidences (1964), Voltaire: Zadig and Other Tales (1971), Essays Presented in Honour of W H Barber (with R J Howells, A Mason and D Williams, 1985), Myth and its Making in the French Theatre: Studies Presented to W D Howarth (with E Freeman, M O'Regan and S W Taylor, 1988), The Impact of the French Revolution on European Consciousness (with W Doyle, 1989), Voltaire: Candide (1995), Voltaire: Micromégas and Other Short Fictions (2002); *Recreations* walking, crosswords, local history; *Style*— Prof Haydn Mason; ✉ 11 Goldney Avenue, Bristol BS8 4RA (tel 0117 973 5767)

MASON, John Muir; MBE (1987); s of James William Mason, Sheriff Clerk (d 1962), of Wigtown, and Tomima Watt, *née* Muir (d 1972); *b* 21 January 1940; *Educ* Kirkwall GS, Douglas Ewart HS Newton Stewart, Univ of Edinburgh (BL); *m* 25 Jan 1967, Jessica Hilary Miller, da of John Groat (d 1981) of Stronsay, Orkney Islands; 1 s (James Muir Angel b 1969), 2 step s (Peter John Chalmers b 1960, Rognvald Inkster Chalmers b 1963); *Career* slr; sr ptnr Waddell & Mackintosh Slrs Troon, md J D C Pubns Ltd, dir private cos, memb Soc of Tst and Estate Practitioners (TEP); princ conductor and musical dir The Strings of Scotland and The Scottish Fiddle Orch; chm The Rev James Currie Meml Tst, life govr ICRF, tstee Niel Gow Memorial Tst; former deacon Incorporation of Skinners and Glovers Trades House of Glasgow; FSA Scot; *Recreations* music, history; *Style*— John Mason, Esq, MBE; ✉ 36 West Portland Street, Troon, Ayrshire KA10 6AB (tel 01292 312222)

MASON, Prof (John) Kenyon French; CBE (1973); s of Air Cdre John Melbourne Mason, CBE, DSC, DFC (d 1955), and Alma Ada Mary, *née* French (d 1983); *b* 19 December 1919; *Educ* Downside, Univ of Cambridge (MA, MD), Univ of Edinburgh (LLD); *m* 14 Jan 1943, Elizabeth Hope (d 1977), da of Trevor Latham (d 1960); 2 s (Ian b 1944, Paul b 1947); *Career* RAF: Sqdn MO 1943–47, pathologist trg 1948, conslt in pathology and offr i/c Dept of Aviation and Forensic Pathology RAF Inst of Pathology 1955–73, ret Gp Capt 1973; Univ of Edinburgh: regius prof of forensic med 1973–85, hon fell Faculty of Law 1985–; pres Br Assoc in Forensic Med 1982–84; Hon LLD Univ of Edinburgh 2005; FRCPath, FRCPE, FRSE; King Haakon VII Freedom Medal (Norway) 1945; *Books* Forensic Medicine for Lawyers (1978, 4 edn 2001), Human Life and Medical Practice (1988), The Courts and the Doctor (co-author, 1990), Medico-legal Aspects of Reproduction and Parenthood (1990, 2 edn 1998), Forensic Medicine, An Illustrated Reference (1993), Law and Medical Ethics (co-author, 7 edn 2005), The Pathology of Trauma (ed, 3 edn 2000), Legal and Ethical Aspects of Healthcare (co-author, 2003), The Troubled Pregnancy (2007); *Clubs* RAF; *Style*— Prof Kenyon Mason, CBE, FRSE; ✉ 66 Craiglea Drive, Edinburgh EH10 5PF (tel 0131 447 2301, fax 0131 447 4137); Faculty of Law, Old College, South Bridge, Edinburgh EH8 9YL (tel 0131 650 2051, fax 0131 650 6317, e-mail ken.mason@ed.ac.uk)

MASON, Martin Derrick; s of Derrick William Mason, of Chichester, W Sussex, and Jean Margaret, *née* Pennicott (d 1999); *b* 22 February 1963, Sussex; *Educ* Chichester Sch for Boys; *m* 10 June 1994, Jacqueline, *née* Pratt; 1 da (Charlotte Isobel b 24 Nov 1996); *Career* sales dir John Smedley 1994–99, sales and mktg dir Pringle 1999–2003, mktg dir Mulberry 2003–06, chief exec Tanner Krolle 2006–; memb: Br Fashion Cncl, Br Menswear Guild; PR Week Campaign of the Year 2002 (Pringle: Faldo to Beckham) 2002; *Recreations* sailing, walking, travel, history; *Style*— Martin Mason, Esq; ✉ Tanner Krolle, 43 Berkeley Square, London W1J 5AX (tel 020 7529 5831, fax 020 7691 7898, e-mail martin.mason@tannerkrolle.co.uk)

MASON, Michael; s of Thomas and Janet Mason; *b* 1 June 1935; *Educ* Ashton-under-Lyne Sch of Art, Manchester Regnl Sch of Art, Br Sch at Rome; *m* Barbara; 1 s, 1 da; *Career* sculptor; princ lectr in sculpture Manchester Metropolitan Univ 1982–96; fndr memb Partnership Environmental Art Studio; sculpture fell Br Sch at Rome; FRBS; *Solo Exhibitions* Zaydler Gallery London 1969, 57 Gallery Edinburgh 1970, Heaton Park outdoor event Manchester 1972, West Park outdoor event Macclesfield 1972, The Anonymous Exhibition Oriel Gallery Univ of Wales 1974, Peterloo Gallery Manchester, Univ of Exeter, Royal Exchange Manchester 1977, Whitworth Art Gallery Univ of Manchester, Arts Centre Gallery Univ of Wales 1978, Serpentine London 1979, South Manchester Gallery 1985, Bury Metro Arts 1987, Galeria Bass Caracas, AVAF Caracas 1993, Mariners Gallery St Ives 1994, Scultpure Court Hanley Museum and Art Gallery Stoke-on-Trent 1997; *Group Exhibitions* G6 Salford City Art Gallery, Peterloo Gallery Manchester 1964, Here and Now Chester Cathedral 1965, Grosvenor Gallery Manchester 1968, V&A London 1970, Manchester City Art Gallery, Leeds City Art Gallery, Summer Show Piccadilly London 1971, Undercroft Gallery Manchester Poly 1973, Manchester Acad City Art Gallery 1974, 1991, 1992 and 1993, Br Sch at Rome 1976, Artists Market Gallery London 1979, Sculpture in the Botanic Gardens Edinburgh 1980, The British Art Show tour 1984, Red Rose Holden Gallery Manchester Poly 1985, Artizana Gallery Prestbury 1986, Hanover Gallery Liverpool 1987, Zagreb 3rd World Trienniale 1990, Fletcher Challenge Onehunga 1991, Zagreb 4th World Trienniale 1994, Warsaw Acad 1994, Galerie Vromans Amsterdam 1995, Sherborne Contemporary Arts 2002–03, Cultural Landscape Workshop Croatia, Mariner's Gallery St Ives 2004, Study Gallery Poole 2006, Bloomberg Arts 2006, Lighthouse Gallery Poole 2007; commissions incl: Cheshire County Cncl, Manchester City Cncl, St David's Church Hale, Severn Trent Water, Int Ring of Magicians, Hackney Empire, Shell UK, Royal Exchange Manchester, Prince of Wales Theatre Cardiff, Asociacion Venezolana de las Artes del Fuego; work in collections incl: Arts Cncl of GB, V&A, Aucklands Studios, Arte Feugo Caracas, Zagreb Gallery of Modern Art; *Awards* NW Arts ACGB, Royal Manchester Inst Haywards Prize, Titograd Prize Zagreb; *Recreations* T'ai chi chuan; *Style*— Michael Mason, Esq; ✉ e-mail mikem@madasafish.com

MASON, Michael Hugh; *b* 1 April 1934; *Educ* Wrekin Coll; *m* 5 Feb 1959, Barbara Ann, da of John Birtles; 2 s (1 decd), 2 da; *Career* memb Stock Exchange 1958, ptnr Charles W Jones & Co stockbrokers 1959–75, ptnr Tilney & Co (following merger with Charles W Jones) 1975, sr ptnr Tilney & Co 1984–86, chm Charterhouse Tilney 1986–96 (non-exec dep chm 1996–99); chm Merrill Lynch Asset Allocator plc 1999–; dir: Charterhouse plc 1986–93, The Greenalls Group Pension Trustees Ltd 1992–2000; tstee: Nuffield Medical Tst 1995–, Nuffield Dominions Tst 1995–, Nuffield Oxford Hospitals Fund 1997–; memb Cncl Int Stock Exchange 1982–86; *Recreations* skiing, golf; *Clubs* Formby Golf, Huntercombe Golf; *Style*— Michael H Mason, Esq

MASON, Monica Margaret; OBE (2002); da of Richard Mason, and Mrs E Fabian; *b* 6 September 1941; *Educ* Johannesburg, Royal Ballet Sch; *m* 1968 (m dis 1980), Austin Bennet; *Career* Royal Ballet Co: joined 1958, princ dancer 1968, asst to Sir Kenneth Macmillan 1980, asst to princ choreographer 1980–84, princ repetiteur 1985, asst to dir 1988–91, asst dir 1991–2002, dir 2002–; Hon Dr Univ of Surrey 1996; *Style*— Miss Monica Mason, OBE

MASON, Prof Paul James; CB (2003); s of Charles Ernest Edward Mason, and Phyllis Mary, *née* Swan; *b* 16 March 1946; *Educ* Univ of Nottingham (BSc), Univ of Reading (PhD); *m* 1968, Mary, *née* Slaney; 1 da, 1 s; *Career* The Met Office: scientific offr 1967–71, sr scientific offr 1971–74, princ scientific offr 1974–79, head Meteorological Res Unit 1979–85, asst dir Boundary Layer Branch 1985–89, dep dir Physical Res 1989–91, chief scientist 1991–2003; dir NCAS/Univs Weather Research Network 2003–06; prof emeritus Dept of Meteorology Univ of Reading; chm Global Climate Observing Steering Ctee 2001–06; pres RMS 1992–94, memb Ed Bd Boundary Layer Meteorology 1988–2001, memb Academia Europaea 1998; Buchan Prize RMS 1986, L G Groves Prize for Meteorology MoD 1980; FRS 1995; *Publications* scientific papers in meteorology and fluid dynamics jls; *Recreations* walking and exploring the countryside; *Style*— Prof Paul Mason, CB, FRS; ✉ Department of Meteorology, University of Reading, Earley Gate, PO Box 243, Reading RG6 6BB (tel 01183 788957, fax 01183 788791, e-mail p.j.mason@reading.ac.uk)

MASON, Air Vice Marshal Richard Anthony (Tony); CB (1988), CBE (1982), DL (Glos 2002); s of William Mason (d 1971), and Maud, *née* Jenkinson (d 1978); *b* 22 October 1932; *Educ* Bradford GS, Univ of St Andrews (MA), Univ of London (MA), Univ of Birmingham (DSc); *m* 17 Nov 1956, Margaret Sneddon, da of Alexander McNab Stewart, MBE, of Burntisland, Fife, and Jean Young; 2 da (Alice Lindsay b 21 Sept 1957, Pamela Anne b 17 Aug 1959 d 1985); *Career* RAF: cmmnd 1956, USAF War Coll 1971, RAF Staff Coll 1972; dir: Defence Studies 1976–82, Personnel (Ground) 1982–84; Air Sec 1986–89 (dep 1985–86); Leverhulme Airpower res dir Fndn for Int Security 1989–94, memb Bd Brassey UK Ltd 1989–97; Univ of Birmingham: visiting sr fell 1989–96, prof of aerospace security 1996–98, dir Centre for Studies in Security and Diplomacy 1998–2001, prof Sch of Social Scis 2002–; head SBAC Eurofighter Info Unit 1992–94; pres Cheltenham Branch RAF ASSOC 1987; memb: IISS 1966, RUSI 1966; Hon Freeman Borough of Cheltenham 2001; Hon FRAeS 2001; *Books* History of RAF Staff College (1972), Readings in Airpower (1978), Airpower in the Next Generation (1979), The Royal Air Force Today and Tomorrow (1982), Airpower in the Nuclear Age (1983/5), British Airpower in the 1980s (1984), War in the Third Dimension (1986), The Soviet Air Force (1986), Airpower: an Overview of Roles (1987), To Inherit the Skies (1990), Air Power: A Centennial Appraisal (1994), Aerospace Power: Revised Roles and Technology (1998); author of many articles in int jls on defence policy and strategy; *Recreations* music, travel; *Clubs* RAF; *Style*— Air Vice Marshal Tony Mason, CB, CBE, DL; ✉ c/o Lloyds Bank, Montpellier, Cheltenham GL50 1SH

MASON, Prof Roger Maxwell; *b* 24 October 1940; *Educ* Welsh Nat Sch of Med UC Cardiff (MB BCh, PhD), Univ of London (MD); *m*; *Career* house physician Professorial Med Unit Cardiff Royal Infirmary 1965–66, house surgn St David's Hosp Cardiff 1966, MRC jr research fell Biochemistry Dept UC Cardiff 1966–69, lectr in biochemistry Univ of Nottingham Med Sch 1969–73, visiting scientist NIH Bethesda MD 1978–79, sr lectr in biochemistry Charing Cross Hosp Med Sch 1973–83; Imperial Coll Faculty of Med (Charing Cross and Westminster Med Sch until merger 1997): reader in biochemistry 1983–88, prof of biochemistry 1988–2003 (emeritus prof of renal medicine 2003–), head Dept of Biochemistry 1992–97, vice-chm Bio-Medical Sciences Div 1997–2000, head Molecular Pathology Gp 1997–2000; visiting prof Dogliotti Coll of Med Univ of Liberia (sponsored by Inter-Univ Cncl) 1977, guest worker Dept of Biochemistry Monash Univ Melbourne (Wellcome-Ramaciotti research travel grant) 1981; chm Research Sub-Ctee Arthritis Research Campaign 1998–2001; author of numerous scientific pubns on connective tissues and their diseases; Lettsomian lectr Med Soc of London 1995; memb Br Soc Matrix Biology (chm 1992–96); FRSA, FRCP 2000; *Style*— Prof Roger Mason; ✉ Renal Section, Division of Medicine, Imperial College London, Hammersmith Hospital, Du Cane Road, London W12 0NN (tel 020 8383 3152, fax 020 8383 2062, e-mail roger.mason@imperial.ac.uk)

MASON, Stephen Maxwell; s of Harold Geoffrey Mason (d 1986), and Ursula, *née* Habermann; *b* 19 May 1949; *Educ* Bradford GS, Gonville & Caius Coll Cambridge (MA); *m* 27 March 1976, Judith Mary, da of Hebbert, of Ilkley; 2 da (Fiona b 1979, Nicola b 1985), 1 s (Alistair b 1981); *Career* slr; ptnr Mason Bond, Leeds, ed Travel Law Jl; memb Civil Litigation Ctee Law Soc 1997–; author of numerous articles on package holiday law including Don't Shoot the Tour Operator (1983), Holiday Law (jtly, 1995, 2 edn 1998); *Recreations* writing, travel by train; *Clubs* Law Soc; *Style*— Stephen Mason, Esq

MASON, Timothy Ian Godson; s of Ian Godson Mason (d 1992), and Marjorie Muriel Berkeley (d 2001), *née* Vaile, of Alverstoke, Hants; *b* 11 March 1945; *Educ* St Alban's Sch Washington DC, Bradfield Coll, ChCh Oxford (MA); *m* 1975, Marilyn Ailsa, da of Frederic George Williams (d 1969), of Wellington, NZ; 1 da (Grace b 1979), 1 s (Giles b 1982); *Career* asst admin Oxford Playhouse 1966–67, asst to Peter Daubeny World Theatre Season London 1967–69, administrator Ballet Rambert 1970–75, administrator Royal Exchange Theatre Manchester 1975–77, dir Western Aust Arts Cncl 1977–80, dir Scottish Arts Cncl 1980–90, conslt to Arts Cncl and Office of Arts and Libraries 1990–91, chief exec London Arts Bd 1991–95, dir Museums & Galleries Cmmn 1995–2000, arts and heritage conslt 2000–, govr KCH 2004–; memb: BBC Gen Advsy Cncl 1990–96, Gen Cncl Cwlth Assoc of Museums 2003–; *Publications* Shifting Sands (2003), Designed With Care (2006); *Recreations* arts, family; *Style*— Timothy Mason, Esq; ✉ 30 Chatsworth Way, London SE27 9HN (tel 020 8761 1414, e-mail tim.mason@bigfoot.com)

MASON, Timothy John Rollit (Tim); s of late John Milton Rollit Mason, and late Ailsa Mary, *née* Garland; *b* 23 July 1957; *Educ* Stowe, Univ of Warwick (BA); *Children* 4 da, 1 s; *Career* successively trainee Walls Meat Co, asst product mangr then product mangr Unilever 1979–82; Tesco Stores Ltd: joined 1982, successively product mangr, mktg mangr, controller product mktg, assoc dir (devpt and mgmnt Healthy Eating prog), trading dir, regnl md 1990–93, mktg ops dir Tesco Stores Ltd 1993–95, Main Bd mktg dir Tesco plc 1995–; dir Business in the Community 1998; non-exec dir Capital Radio plc 2000–; Marketer of the Year 1997; *Recreations* triathlon, skiing; *Style*— Tim Mason, Esq; ✉ Tesco plc, Tesco House, Delamare Road, Cheshunt, Hertfordshire EN8 9SL (direct tel 01992 644117, direct fax 01992 644553)

MASON, Tony; s of George Donald (d 1982), and Hattie, *née* Mockett (d 1986); *Educ* Lancaster Royal GS, MCAM, FIMI; *m* Susan; 1 da (Emma); *Career* early career training with various advtg and mktg agencies; former co-driver in Ford works team, winner numerous events incl RAC Rally (with Roger Clark) 1972, later appointed competition co-ordinator with Ford, export dir Mill Accessory Group 1975, fndr own accessory co 1979, contracted to commentate on Lombard RAC Rally and joined Top Gear as a presenter (both with BBC) 1987, also contracted as occasional presenter for Channel 9 TV Aust, Sky and Discovery TV, fndr Tony Mason Motorsport (distributing motor sport products), regular contrib to numerous other pubns, fndr Tony Mason Associates (PR, TV and Motorsport consultancy) 1992; after dinner speaker (with over 1000 appearances); *Books* author of 4 books incl Rallying (with Stuart Turner); *Style*— Tony Mason, Esq; ✉ Tony Mason Associates, Moreton Pinkney, nr Daventry, Northamptonshire NN11 3NL (tel 07811 387267)

MASON OF BARNSLEY, Baron (Life Peer UK 1987), of Barnsley in the County of South Yorkshire; Roy Mason; PC (1968), DL (1992); s of late Joseph Mason, of Carlton, nr Barnsley; *b* 18 April 1924; *Educ* Carlton and Royston Elementary Schs, LSE; *m* 1945, Marjorie, da of Ernest Sowden, of Royston, W Riding; 2 da (Hon Susan Ann (Hon Mrs Duke) b 1947, Hon Jill Diane (Hon Mrs Martin) b 1955); *Career* former coal miner 1938–53; MP (Lab) Barnsley 1953–83, Barnsley Central 1983–87; oppn spokesman Def and Post Office 1960–64; min of state BOT 1964–67; min Def Equipment 1967–68, postmaster-gen 1968, min Power 1968–69; pres BOT 1969–70; oppn spokesman Civil Aviation Shipping Tourism Films & Trade 1970–74; sec of state: Def 1974–76, NI 1976–79; oppn spokesman Agric Fish & Food 1979–; former NUM official; chm: Yorks Gp Labour MPs, Miners Gp of Labour MPs, Prince's Youth Business Tst of S Yorks 1985–, Barnsley Business and Innovation Centre; originator and convenor of Lords and Commons Fly Fishing Club 1983, originator and pres Lords and Commons Pipe and Cigar Club 1985; DUniv Hallam Univ Sheffield 1993, Hon DCL Univ of Northumbria 2005; *Books* Paying the Price (autobiog); *Style*— The Rt Hon Lord Mason of Barnsley, PC; ✉ 12 Victoria Avenue, Barnsley, South Yorkshire

MASON-WATTS, Christopher Nigel Stuart; s of Maj Ronald Henry Watts (d 1982), of Carlisle, Cumbria, and Eva Maria-Louise, *née* Gliese; *b* 6 March 1954; *Educ* Univ of Aberdeen (MA, LLM); *m* 24 Dec 1986, Nicola Clare, da of Wilfred Albert Mason, of Ashby-de-la-Zouch, Leics; 1 da (Poppy b 1988), 3 s (Billy b 1990, Joscelyn b 1991, Rollo b 1992); *Career* admitted slr 1980; with: Mason-Watts & Co Newcastle Emlyn, James Jones Son & Francis Llandysul; dir Mason-Watts Fine Art; former legal memb Mental Health Act Cmmn, pres Mental Health Review Tbnl; chm Mental Health Strategy and Review Ctee Warks HA 1993–96, memb Ceredigion Community Health Cncl 1996–2004, chm of govrs Sch Gp; *Recreations* music, opera, theatre; *Clubs* Lansdowne; *Style*— Christopher Watts, Esq; ✉ Noyadd Trefawr, Cardigan, West Wales SA43 2RF (tel 01239 682608); 14 McCleods Mews, London SW7

MASSAM, (Arthur) David Wright; s of Arthur Greenwood Massam (d 1989), of Southport, Lancs, and Emily, *née* Wright (d 1945); *b* 18 November 1934; *Educ* King George V Sch Southport, Univ of Manchester (MPS), Univ of London (LLB); *m* 1957 (m dis 1970), Angela, da of Joseph Smith (d 1986), of Southport, Lancs; 1 da (Melinda Jane b 1958), 1 s (Nigel Robin b 1961); *Career* Nat Serv RAMC 1956–58; C F Thackray Ltd 1958–70; Datapharm Publications Ltd: exec dir 1980–92, dir 1993–97; sec Assoc of the Br Pharmaceutical Industry 1982–92 (joined 1970), dir Prescription Medicines Code of Practice Authy 1993–97 (conslt 1997–); former memb: Advsy Cncl on Misuse of Drugs, Poisons Bd, Standing Pharmaceutical Advsy Ctee; memb Hon Soc of the Inner Temple 1968; Freeman: Worshipful Soc of Apothecaries 1993, City of London 1994; FRPharmS 1980 (MRPharmS 1956); *Recreations* history, reading; *Style*— David Massam, Esq; ✉ 80A Westbury Road, Finchley, London N12 7PD (tel 020 8922 3249)

MASSER, David William; s of William Stanley Masser (d 1991), and Rose, *née* Lewis (d 2004); *b* 8 November 1948, London; *Educ* Trinity Coll Cambridge (MA, PhD); *m* 1988, Hedda, *née* Freudenschuss; *Career* lectr Univ of Nottingham 1973–75, research fell Trinity Coll Cambridge 1975–76; Univ of Nottingham: lectr 1976–79, reader 1979–83; prof Univ of Michigan 1983–92, prof Univ of Basle 1992–; memb London Mathematical Soc 1974; FRS 2005; *Publications* Elliptic Functions and Transcendence (1975); author of 75 papers in mathematical jls; *Recreations* travelling to restaurants; *Style*— David Masser; ✉ Mathematisches Institut, Universität Basel, Rheinsprung 21, 4051 Basel, Switzerland (tel 0041 61 2672698, fax 0041 61 2672695, e-mail david.masser@unibas.ch); Nadelberg 17, 4051 Basel, Switzerland (tel 0041 61 2620873)

MASSEREENE AND FERRARD, 14 & 7 Viscount (I 1660 & 1797); John David Clotworthy Whyte-Melville Foster Skeffington; also Baron of Loughneagh (I 1660), Baron Oriel of Collon (I 1790), and Baron Oriel of Ferrard (UK 1821, which sits as); o s of 13 Viscount Massereene and Ferrard (d 1992), and Annabelle Kathleen, *née* Lewis; *b* 3 June 1940; *Educ* Millfield, Inst Monte Rosa; *m* 1970, Ann Denise, da of Norman Rowlandson (d 1967); 2 s (Hon Charles John Foster Clotworthy Whyte-Melville b 1973, Hon Henry William Norman Foster Clotworthy b 1980), 1 da (Hon Harriette Denise Margaretta Eileen b 1975); *Heir* s, Hon Charles Skeffington; *Career* served Grenadier Gds 1959–61; chm R M Walkden & Co Ltd; stockbroker M D Barnard & Co Ltd; pres Monday Club; *Recreations* shooting, vintage cars, history; *Clubs* Turf, Pratt's; *Style*— The Rt Hon the Viscount Massereene and Ferrard; ✉ M D Barnard & Co, 150 Minories, London EC3N 1LS

MASSEY, Ray John Thomas; s of Kenneth Edwin Massey (d 1988), of Taunton, Somerset, and Dorothy May, *née* Brooks (d 2000); *b* 26 September 1951; *Educ* Ladymead Secdy Sch Taunton, Somerset Coll of Art, Medway Coll of Art and Technol; *m* (sep), Annie, da of Maurice Geay, of Pessac, France; 3 s (Jethro b 6 Jan 1978, Jean-Michel b 24 Feb 1983, Joshua b 30 Sept 2006); *Career* asst photographer 1970–71, freelance photographer 1972–; numerous exhbns incl: Assoc of Photographers London, JIP Arles France, IIP Ireland; life memb Assoc of Photographers; *Recreations* travel, swimming, photography; *Clubs* BSAC, Porsche Owners'; *Style*— Ray Massey, Esq; ✉ Horton-Stephens, 157 Kennington Lane, London SE11 4EZ (tel 020 7582 0082, fax 020 7582 0001, e-mail ray@raymassey.com, website www.raymassey.com)

MASSEY, Raymond (Ray); s of David Massey, of Newcastle upon Tyne, and Elizabeth Irene, *née* Jeffrey (d 1987); *b* 7 June 1960; *Educ* Walbottle Grammar Northumberland, Univ of Warwick (Lord Rootes fndn scholar, Deutscher Akademischer Austauschdienst Stipendium, BA); *m* 1996, Elizabeth Kay, *née* Clinton; 2 s (Cameron b Oct 1997, Aidan b 22 July 2000); *Career* journalist and author; Coventry Evening Telegraph 1982–87 (reporter, industrial corr, feature writer and diarist, China corr); educn corr Press Assoc 1988–90 (news reporter 1987–); Daily Mail: educn corr 1990–95, motoring corr 1995–2000, tport ed 2000–; FRSA; *Books* Parent Power (1993); *Recreations* golf, travel; *Style*— Ray Massey, Esq; ✉ The Daily Mail, Northcliffe House, 2 Derry Street, London W8 5TT (tel 020 7938 6102/6000, fax 020 7937 5287)

MASSEY, Dr Roy Cyril; MBE (1997); s of Cyril Charles Massey (d 1966), of Birmingham, and Beatrice May, *née* Morgan (d 1987); *b* 9 May 1934; *Educ* Moseley GS Birmingham, Univ of Birmingham (BMus); *m* 22 Feb 1975, Ruth Carol Craddock, da of Frederick George Grove (d 1958), of Fron-y-Gog, Machynlleth, Montgomeryshire; *Career* organist: St Alban's Conybere St Birmingham 1953–60, St Augustine's Edgbaston Birmingham 1960–65, Croydon Parish Church 1965–68; warden Royal Sch of Church Music Addington Palace Croydon 1965–68, conductor Birmingham Bach Soc 1966–68, organist and master of the choristers Birmingham Cathedral 1968–74, dir of music King Edward's Sch Birmingham 1968–74, organist and master of the choristers Hereford Cathedral 1974–2001, conductor Three Choirs Festival and Hereford Choral Soc 1974–2001; chm Hereford Competitive Music Festival; memb Cncl: RCO, Royal Sch of Church Music 1976–98; fell St Michael's Coll Tenbury 1979–88; pres Incorporated Assoc of Organists 1991–93, pres RCO 2003–05; Hon DMus Canterbury 1991, ARCM 1954, FRCO 1956, FRSCM 1972; Hon FGCM 2000; *Recreations* the countryside, walking the dog on the Malvern hills, motoring; *Style*— Dr Roy Massey, MBE; ✉ 2 King John's Court, Tewkesbury, Gloucestershire GL20 6EG

M

MASSEY, Rupert John Candide; s of Zenke Stefan, of Warsaw, Poland, and Sonia Mary Massey (d 1978); *b* 21 November 1945; *Educ* Clayesmore Sch, Balliol Coll Oxford (BA); *m* 6 Jan 1984, Kate Miranda, da of Philip Rae-Scott, of Richmond, Surrey; 3 s (Thomas Jack b 14 Dec 1985, Jacob Jonathan, Joel Peter (twins) b 23 Aug 1988); *Career* warden youth and community centre S London 1968–72, called to the Bar Inner Temple 1972, barr-at-law; broadcasting journalist; contrib to: Granada TV, Capital Radio, BBC Radio 4, Thames ITV and nat press; performer and actor: Clockwise 1986, Intimate Contact (Zenith) 1987, Life Story (BBC TV) 1987, Battalion 1988, Moon & Son (BBC TV) 1991; guest speaker Cranworth Law Soc Downing Coll Cambridge 1991, guest speaker various univs and colls incl St Thomas' Hosp Postgrad Med Sch Dept of Psychiatry and Bournemouth Univ Dept of Media Production and Studies; specialist advsr in french law with recgnised right of audience at Cour d'Appel Rouen; hon legal and policy advsr Fedn of Small Businesses, pres Bd YMCA (Winton); memb: NUJ, Br Equity, BAFTA, BECTU, Hon Soc of Inner Temple London; *Recreations* deep sea sailing/cruising, all water sports, youth and community work, work with young offenders, psychology; *Clubs* Cruising Assoc; *Style*— Rupert Massey, Esq; ✉ 141 Sheen Road, Richmond upon Thames, Surrey TW9 1YJ (tel 020 8940 3672); Barristers' Chambers, Eaton House, 4 Eaton Road, Branksome Park, Poole, Dorset BH13 6DG (tel 01202 766301, fax 01202 766301)

MASSEY, William Greville Sale; QC (1996); s of Lt Col Patrick Massey, MC (d 2002), of Liss, Hants, and Bessie Lee, *née* Byrne (d 1978); *b* 31 August 1953; *Educ* Harrow, Hertford Coll Oxford (MA); *m* 2 Dec 1978, Cecilia D'Oyly, da of Daniel Edmund Awdry, TD, DL, of Beanacre, Wilts; 3 s (Patrick William Edmund b 31 July 1983, Richard Daniel Hugh b 8 May 1985, Edmund Greville Robert b 12 June 1990); *Career* called to the Bar Middle Temple 1977 (bencher 2004); memb: Chancery Bar Assoc, Revenue Bar Assoc; govr: Harrow Sch, Summer Fields Sch Oxford; *Books* Potter and Monroe's Tax Planning with Precedents (jtly, 9 edn), Encyclopaedia of Forms and Precedents (contrib); *Recreations* skiing, gardening, music, chess; *Style*— William Massey, Esq, QC; ✉ Pump Court Tax Chambers, 16 Bedford Row, London WC1R 4EF (tel 020 7414 8080, fax 020 7414 8099, e-mail clerks@pumptax.com)

MASSEY OF DARWEN, Baroness (Life Peer UK 1999), of Darwen in the County of Lancashire; Doreen Elizabeth; da of Jack Hall (d 1989), of Darwen, Lancs, and Mary Ann, *née* Sharrock (d 1973); *Educ* Darwen GS, Univ of Birmingham (BA, DipEd, vice-pres Student Union, Hockey and Cricket blues), Univ of London (MA); *m* Dr Leslie Massey, s of James York Massey, of Conisbrough, S Yorks; 3 c (Elizabeth Caitlin b 1969, Owen John b 1971, Benjamin James b 1973); *Career* family planner; grad serv overseas Gabon 1962–63, Springside Sch Philadelphia USA 1967–69, Pre-Sch Play Group Assoc 1973–77, Walsingham Sch 1977–83, advsr Inner London Educn Authy 1983–85, mangr Young People's Prog Health Educn Authy 1985–87, dir The Family Planning Assoc 1989–94 (dir of educn 1987–89); chair Nat Treatment Agency for Substance Abuse 2002–, chair All-Pty Parly Gp for Children 2001–; memb Bd: Teachers Advsy Cncl on Alcohol and Drugs Educn (TACADE), Tst for the Study of Adolescence; ind conslt in health skills and sexual health; memb numerous voluntary orgns, primary sch govr; FRSA; *Books* Sex Education: Why, What and How (1988), Sex Education Sourcebook (1994), Lovers' Guide Encyclopaedia (conslt ed, 1996); *Recreations* theatre, cinema, opera, reading, art and design, vegetarian cookery, travel, walking, yoga, sport; *Clubs* Lady Taverners; *Style*— Baroness Massey of Darwen

MASSIE, Allan Johnstone; s of Alexander Johnstone Massie, of Banchory, Aberdeenshire, and Evelyn Wilson, *née* Forbes; *b* 16 October 1938; *Educ* Drumtochty Castle, Glenalmond, Trinity Coll Cambridge (BA); *m* 22 June 1973, Alison Agnes Graham, da of Robert Scott Langlands, of Kelso, Roxburghshire; 2 s (Alexander, Louis), 1 da (Claudia); *Career* school master Drumtochty Castle 1960–71, TEFL Rome 1972–75; author, journalist and playwright; princ fiction reviewer The Scotsman 1975–, TV critic The Sunday Standard 1981–83; columnist: Glasgow Herald 1985–88, Sunday Times Scotland 1987–91 and 1997–, The Daily Telegraph 1991–, Daily Mail 1994–; winner: Frederick Niven Prize for the Last Peacock 1981, Fraser of Allander Award Critic of the Year 1982, Scottish Arts Cncl Book Awards 1982 and 1986, The Scotsman, Scottish Book of the Year 1990; tstee Nat Museum of Scotland 1995–98; memb Scottish Arts Cncl 1989; FRSL 1982, Hon FRIAS 1997; *Books* Change and Decay in All Around I See (1978), The Last Peacock (1980), The Death of Men (1981), The Caesars (1983), Portrait of Scottish Rugby (1984), One Night in Winter (1984), Augustus (1986), Byron's Travels (1987), A Question of Loyalties (1989), Glasgow (1989), The Hanging Tree (1990), Tiberius (1991), The Sins of the Father (1991), Caesar (1993), These Enchanted Woods (1993), The Ragged Lion (1994), King David (1995), Shadows of Empire (1997), Antony (1997), Nero's Heirs (1999), The Evening of the World (2001); *Plays* Quintet in October, The Minstrel and The Shirra (1989), First Class Passengers (1995); *Recreations* reading, watching rugby, cricket, walking the dogs; *Clubs* Academy, Selkirk RFC; *Style*— Allan Massie, Esq; ✉ Thirladean House, Selkirk TD7 5LU (tel 01750 20393)

MASSIE, Sir Herbert William (Bert); kt (2007), CBE (2000, OBE 1984); s of Herbert Douglas Massie, of Liverpool, and Joan Lucy, *née* Roberts; *b* 31 March 1949; *Educ* Sandfield Park Special Sch Liverpool, Portland Trg Coll for the Disabled Mansfield, Hereward Coll Coventry, Liverpool Poly (BA), Manchester Poly (CQSW); *m* 2007, Maureen Lilian Shaw; *Career* Wm Rainford Ltd 1968, West Cheshire Newspapers Ltd 1968–70, Liverpool Assoc for the Disabled 1970–72, Disabled Living Fndn 1977, dir The Royal Assoc for Disability and Rehabilitation (RADAR) 1990–99 (joined 1978), chm Disability Rights Cmmn 2000–, cmmr Cmmn for Equality and Human Rights 2006–; prop Bert Massie Ltd 2007–; memb: Mgmnt Ctee Disabled Drivers Assoc 1968–71, Careers Serv Advsy Cncl for Eng 1979–83, Exec Ctee OUTSET 1983–91, Access Ctee for Eng 1984–93, BR Advsy Gp on Disabled People 1986–94, Disabled Persons Tport Advsy Ctee 1986–2002, Nat Advsy Cncl on Employment of People with Disabilities 1991–98, Ind Cmmn on Social Justice 1993–94, DSS Panel of Experts on Review of Incapacity Benefit 1994, Cabinet Office Working Gp on Equal Opportunities in the Sr Civil Serv 1994–2000, Advsy Gp New Deal Taskforce 1997–2000, Bd Euro Disability Forum 1997–2000; vice-pres: Fndn for Assistive Technol 2000–, Disabled Living Fndn; vice-chm: Assoc of Disabled Professionals 1986–94 (memb Exec Ctee 1979–99), Vol Cncl for Handicapped Children 1985–93 (memb 1980–93), Tripscope 1989–2006 (memb 1986–2006); dep chm Nat Disability Cncl 1998–2000 (memb 1996–2000); tstee: BEAMA Fndn for Disabled People 1990–2000 (sec 1986–90), Ind Living Fund 1990–93, Habinteg Housing Assoc 1993–, Mobility Choice 1998–, Inst for Employment Studies 2000–07, CSV 2001, Merseyside Neurological Tst 2004–, United Tsts 2006–; govr: Pensions Policy Inst 2002–07, Motability 2002; patron Disabled Living Servs Manchester 1990–, patron Heswall Disabled Children's Holiday Fund 2003–, UK nat sec Rehabilitation Int 1993–2000 (dep vice-pres for Euro 1996–2000); Master Wheelwrights Award Worshipful Co of Wheelwrights 2002; hon fell Liverpool John Moores Univ 2002, Hon LLD Univ of Bristol 2005, Hon DUniv Staffs 2007; FRSA 1988, MInstD 2001; *Publications* Work and Disability 1977 (with M Greaves, 1979), Employers Guide to Disabilities (with M Kettle, 1982, 2 edn 1986), Aspects of the Employment of Disabled People in the Federal Republic of Germany (1982), Day Centres for Young Disabled People (jtly, 1984), Travelling with British Rail (1985), Wheelchairs and their Use (with J Weyers, 1986), Choosing a Wheelchair (with J Male, 1990), Seat Belts and Disabled People (with J Isaacs, 1990), Social Justice and Disabled People (1994), Getting Disabled People to Work (2000); *Style*— Sir Bert Massie, CBE; ✉ Bert Massie Limited, 2 North Sudley Road, Liverpool L17 0BG (tel 0151 727 3252, e-mail bert@massie.com); 3rd Floor, Fox Court, 14 Grays Inn Road, London WC1X 8HN (tel 020 7543 7100, fax 020 7543 7055, e-mail bert.massie@drc-gb.org, website www.drc-gb.org)

MASSINGBERD, Hugh John Montgomery-; s of John Michael Montgomery-Massingberd (d 2004), formerly of Gunby, Lincs, and Marsali Winlaw, *née* Seymour Seal (d 2004); *b* 30 December 1946; *Educ* Harrow, Law Soc's Coll of Law; *m* 1, 1972 (m dis 1979), Christine Martinoni; 1 da (Harriet b 1974), 1 s (Luke b 1977); m 2, 1983, Caroline, er da of Sir Hugh Ripley, 4 Bt (d 2003); *Career* author and journalist; gave up place reading history at Selwyn Coll Cambridge to join editorial staff of Burke's Peerage publications (asst ed 1968–71, ed 1971–83), contributing ed The Field 1984–86; Daily Telegraph: obituaries ed 1986–94, heritage columnist and feature writer 1987–96, television critic 1994–96; former pres now vice-pres Anthony Powell Soc; former memb: Cncl Assoc of Genealogists and Record Agents, Research Ctee Historic Houses Assoc; *Books* The Monarchy (1979), The British Aristocracy (with Mark Bence-Jones, 1979), The London Ritz (with David Watkin, 1980, revised 1989), The Country Life Book of Royal Palaces, Castles and Homes (with Patrick Montague-Smith, 1981), Diana - The Princess of Wales (1982), Heritage of Royal Britain (1983), Royal Palaces of Europe (1984), Blenheim Revisited (1985, revised edn: Blenheim and the Churchills 2004), Her Majesty The Queen (1986), Debrett's Great British Families (1987), The Field Book of Country Houses and their Owners: Family Seats of the British Isles (1988), Great Houses of England and Wales (with Christopher Simon Sykes, 1994, concise edn 2000), Great Houses of Scotland (with Christopher Simon Sykes, 1997, concise edn 2001), Great Houses of Ireland (with Christopher Simon Sykes, 1999), Queen Elizabeth The Queen Mother (1999, revised edn 2002), English Manor Houses (with Christopher Simon Sykes, 2001), Daydream Believer: Confessions of a Hero-Worshipper (2001); also edited: Burke's Landed Gentry (1972), Burke's Guide to The Royal Family (1973), Burke's Presidential Families of the USA (1975, 2 edn 1981), Burke's Irish Family Records (1976), Burke's Family Index (1976), Burke's Royal Families of the World (Vol I 1977, Vol II 1980), Burke's Guide to Country Houses (Vol I 1978, Vol II 1980, Vol III 1981), Lord of the Dance: A Moncreiffe Miscellany (1986), The Daily Telegraph Record of the Second World War (1989), A Guide to the Country Houses of the North West (1991), The Disintegration of a Heritage: Country Houses and their Collections 1979–1992 (1993), The Daily Telegraph Book of Obituaries: A Celebration of Eccentric Lives (1995), The Daily Telegraph Second Book of Obituaries: Heroes and Adventurers (1996), The Daily Telegraph Third Book of Obituaries: Entertainers (1997), The Daily Telegraph Fourth Book of Obituaries: Rogues (1998), The Daily Telegraph Fifth Book of Obituaries: 20th Century Lives (1999), The Very Best of The Daily Telegraph Books of Obituaries (2001); *Plays* Ancestral Voices (2002), Love & Art (2005); *Recreations* theatre, cinema, cricket, National Hunt racing; *Clubs* Travellers, Pratt's, Academy, Lansdowne, I Zingari, Butterflies Cricket, Harrow Wanderers, Surrey CCC, MCC (assoc); *Style*— Hugh Massingberd, Esq; ✉ Flat 1, 101 Hereford Road, London W2 5BB (tel 020 7727 1669)

MASSINGHAM, David Charles; s of Derek George Massingham (d 1976), and Margaret Catherine, *née* Callaghan; *b* 26 June 1959; *Educ* Dame Alice Owens GS, Laban Centre for Movement and Dance (BA, Advanced Performance Certificate); *Career* choreographer and creative prodr; fndr/dancer Geographical Duvet 1984–86, dancer Transitions 1986, fndr dir/choreographer/dancer Adventures in Motion Pictures 1986–88, choreographer int course for choreographers and composers 1988, fndr David Massingham Dance 1989, choreographer in res Northern Arts 1995, currently dir DanceXchange Birmingham and artistic dir Bare Bones Dance Co; major works incl: Companion Pieces 1989, The Immortals 1990, Cradle 1994, Hinterland 1996, Untold 1998, The Elbow Room 2001, With the Company We Keep 2006; theatre incl: The Tempest (RNT), The Red Balloon (Birmingham Rep), Cabaret (Newcastle Live Theatre); Bonnie Bird Award 1992; *Recreations* motorcycling; *Style*— David Massingham, Esq; ✉ DanceXchange, Birmingham Hippodrome, Thorp Street, Birmingham B5 4TB (tel 0121 689 3170, fax 0121 689 3179, e-mail david.massingham@dancexchange.org.uk)

MASSY, 10 Baron (I 1776); David Hamon Somerset; s of 9 Baron (d 1995); *b* 4 March 1947; *Educ* St George's Coll Weybridge; *Career* serving with Merchant Navy; *Style*— The Rt Hon the Lord Massy

MASTER, (Humphrey) Simon Harcourt; s of Humphrey Ronald Master, of Thetford, Norfolk, and Rachel Blanche, *née* Plumbly (d 1989); *b* 10 April 1944; *Educ* Ardingly, Univ de La Rochelle; *m* 3 May 1969, Georgina Mary, da of Sir Brian Caldwell Cook Batsford (d 1991), of Winchelsea, E Sussex; 2 s (Nicholas Harcourt b 1973, Matthew Harcourt b 1976); *Career* sr ed: Pan Books Ltd 1966–69, B T Batsford Ltd 1969–70; Pan Books Ltd: editorial dir 1970–73, publishing dir 1980–87; chief exec Random House UK Ltd 1987–89, exec vice-pres int Random House Inc 1989–91, dep chm Random House Group 1989–2004, exec chm Arrow Books 1990–92, exec chm Random House Gen Books Div 1992–2004 (non-exec dir 2004–); non-exec chm London Book Fair 2006–, memb Bd Br Book Acad 2006–; dir HMSO 1990–95; Publishers Assoc: memb Cncl 1989–95, vice-pres 1995–96, pres 1996–97 and 2001–02; *Recreations* reading, golf, classic cars, gardening; *Clubs* Groucho, Sherborne Golf; *Style*— Simon Master, Esq; ✉ Random House, 20 Vauxhall Bridge Road, London SW1V 2SA (tel 020 7840 8400)

MASTERMAN, His Hon Judge Crispin Grant; s of Osmond Janson Masterman (d 1988), of Gerrards Cross, Bucks, and Anne, *née* Bouwens (d 1999); *b* 1 June 1944; *Educ* St Edward's Sch Oxford, Univ of Southampton (BA); *m* 3 Jan 1976, Margaret Elizabeth Clare, da of Robert Fletcher (d 1967), of Cardiff; 2 da (Claudia b 21 Sept 1977, Laura b 9 Aug 1982), 1 s (Kerrin b 25 Oct 1979); *Career* cmmnd RAFVR 1967 PO; called to the Bar Middle Temple 1971, recorder of the Crown Court 1988–95, circuit judge (Wales & Chester Circuit) 1995–, designated family judge for Cardiff and Pontypridd 2006–; memb Cncl Cardiff Univ 1995–2004 (vice-chair 1998–2004); FCIArb 1991; *Recreations* family and friends; *Style*— Crispin Masterman, Esq; ✉ 28 South Rise, Llanishen, Cardiff, South Glamorgan CF14 0RH (tel 029 2075 4072)

MASTERS, Blythe Sally Jess; da of Gordon Robert Levett (d 2000), and Sally Elizabeth Ann, *née* Scott; *b* 22 March 1969, Oxford; *Educ* Ashford Sch for Girls, King's Sch Canterbury, Trinity Coll Cambridge (BA); *Partner* Gareth Evans; 1 da (Honour Radegund b 3 Aug 1993); *Career* JPMorgan: various roles in fixed income incl head of credit derivatives 1991–2000, global head of credit portfolio and credit policy and strategy 2000–03, investment bank chief financial offr 2003–06, global head of currencies and commodities 2006–; memb Bd: American Friends of Royal Court Theatre, Nat Dance Inst, Susan G Komen Fndn, Race for the Cure (NY Chapter); vice-chair Securities Industry and Financial Markets Assoc 2006; *Recreations* equestrian; *Style*— Mrs Blythe Masters; ✉ JPMorgan, 270 Park Avenue, New York City, NY 10017, USA (tel 00 1 212 834 5677, fax 00 1 212 834 6200, e-mail blythe.masters@jpmorgan.com)

MASTERS, Dr Christopher; CBE (2002); s of Wilfred Masters, and Mary Ann Masters; *b* 2 May 1947; *Educ* Richmond GS, KCL (BSc, AKC), Univ of Leeds (PhD); *m* 1971, Gillian Mary; 2 da; *Career* research chemist Shell Research BV Amsterdam 1971–77, PA to md Shell Chemicals UK 1977–78, corp planner Shell UK 1978–79; Christian Salvesen plc: business devpt mangr 1979–81, dir of planning Merchants Refrigerating Co USA (following takeover by Christian Salvesen) 1981–83, md Christian Salvesen Seafoods 1983–85, md Industrial Servs Div 1985–89, main bd dir 1987–97, chief exec 1989–97; exec chm Aggreko plc (demerged from Christian Salvesen) 1997–2002; non-exec chm: Babtic Gp Ltd 2002–04, SMG plc 2004–07, Sagentia Gp AG 2006–; non-exec dir: Wood Gp plc, British Assets Tst plc, Alliance Tst plc, The Crown Agents, Scottish Chamber Orch Tst; chm: Scottish Higher Educn Funding Cncl 1998–2005, Festival City Theatres Tst; Hon Dr: Strathclyde Univ 2006, Univ of St Andrews 2006; FRSE 1996; *Recreations* wines, music, opera; *Style*— Dr Christopher Masters, CBE, FRSE; ✉ Sagentia Group Limited, Harston Mill, Harston Cambridge CB22 7GG (tel 01223 875200)

MASTERS, Jeffrey (Jeff); s of John William Masters, of Barnsley, and Joan, *née* Fury; *b* 6 August 1940; *Educ* Barnsley and Dist Holgate GS, Univ Coll Swansea (BSc); *m* 1 Sept 1964, June, *née* Niland; 1 s (John James b 21 Dec 1972), 1 da (Anna Jane b 1 Jan 1979); *Career* HGV driver, mechanic of the mine; British Gas plc (now BG plc): joined 1965, specialised in energy utilisation in industry, commerce, transport and power generation, ret as prog ctllr 1996; vice-pres Energy Int Inc 1996–2003; William Dieterichs Memorial Award Inst of Gas Engrs Award 1974, Gold Medal Inst of Gas Engrs 1981, Royal Soc Esso Award 1983; chm Solihull Mencap, ed Ferncumbe News; FREng 1998, FIMechE; *Publications* author of several learned articles and jls; *Recreations* walking, reading; *Clubs* Stratford Oaks Golf (srs captain); *Style*— Jeff Masters, Esq, FREng; ✉ Kingswood Farm, Old Warwick Road, Lapworth, Solihull, West Midlands B94 6LX (tel 01564 7822489, fax 01564 785469, e-mail jeffmasters@tiscali.co.uk)

MASTERSON, David Napier; s of Philip Bursell Edwin Masterson (d 1985), of Upminster, Essex, and Pamela, *née* Napier; *b* 20 June 1959; *Educ* Brentwood Sch, City of London Poly; *Career* Kingston Smith LLP Chartered Accountants: trainee 1977–81, ptnr 1988–; memb Audit Registration Ctee ICAEW 1991–96; FCA 1991 (ACA 1981); *Recreations* golf, skiing; *Clubs* Greenford Rotary, Soc of Old Brentwoods; *Style*— David N Masterson, Esq; ✉ Kingston Smith LLP, Devonshire House, 60 Goswell Road, London EC1M 7AD (tel 020 7566 4000, e-mail dmasterson@kingstonsmith.co.uk)

MASTERSON, (Margaret) Valerie (Mrs Andrew March); CBE (1988); da of Edward Masterson, and Rita McGrath; *Educ* Holt Hill Convent, studied in London and Milan on scholarship with Edwardo Asquez; *m* 1965, Andrew John March; 1 s ((Edward) Jason b 13 May 1969), 1 da (Caroline Louisa b 13 Aug 1973); *Career* opera and concert singer; prof of singing Royal Acad of Music and Trinity Coll of Music 1992–; debut Landestheater Salzburg; appearances with D'Oyly Carte Opera, Glyndebourne Festival Opera, ENO, Royal Opera House Covent Garden; has appeared at numerous major opera houses incl: Paris, Aix en Provence, Toulouse, NY (Metropolitan and Carnegie Hall), Munich, Madrid, Geneva, Barcelona, Milan, San Francisco, Chicago, Chile, Brazil; leading roles in: La Traviata, Le Nozze di Figaro, Manon, Faust, Alcina, Die Entführung, Julius Caesar, Rigoletto, Romeo and Juliet, Carmen, Count Ory, Mireille, Louise, Idomeneo, Les Dialogues des Carmelites, The Merry Widow, Xerxes, Orlando; recordings incl: La Traviata, Elisabetta, Regina d' Inghliterra, Der Ring des Nibelungen, The Merry Widow, Kismet, Song of Norway, Julius Caesar Scipione, several Gilbert and Sullivan; broadcasts regularly on radio and TV; hon pres Rossini Soc Paris, vice-pres Br Youth Opera, patron Mousehole Male Voice Choir 2002–; Soc of West End Theatre Award 1983; Hon DLitt 1999; FRCM 1992, Hon RAM 1993; *Recreations* tennis, swimming; *Style*— Ms Valerie Masterson, CBE; ✉ c/o Music International, 13 Ardilaun Road, Highbury, London N5 2QR

MASTERTON, Gordon Grier Thomson; s of Alexander Bain Masterton (d 1973), and Mary Low Grier, *née* Thomson (d 2003); *b* 9 June 1954, Charlestown, Fife; *Educ* Dunfermline HS, Univ of Edinburgh (Trevelyan scholar, ICE Prize, Lindsay Prize, Innes Prize, BSc), Open Univ (BA), Imperial Coll London (MSc, DIC); *m* 17 July 1976, Lynda Christine, *née*

Jeffries; 1 s (Matthew Gordon Grier b 13 Sept 1983), 1 da (Natalie Elizabeth b 19 March 1986); *Career* Jacobs UK (formerly Babtie Gp): engr 1976–82, project engr 1982–91, dir responsible for bridge works 1991–95, estab Kuala Lumpur office 1995–96, dir i/c buildings and bridge works 1997–2001, md Facilities Business Centre 2001–02, md Environment Business Centre 2003–, vice-pres environment 2004–; many structural design projects incl: Buccleuch Street Bridge Dumfries (design commendation Saltire Awards 1986), A75 Annan Bypass (Annan River Bridge awarded design commendation Saltire Awards 1990) and Dumfries Bypass, A74 upgrade to D3 motorway; ICE: memb Cncl 1999–, vice-pres 2002–05, pres 2005–06, chm Glasgow & West of Scot Assoc 2000–01 (hon sec 1986–89), chm Structural and Buildings Bd 2000–02, memb Archive Panel 2001–, memb Investigating Panel 2001–04, chm Working Gp on Registers Approved Lists and Licensing of Engrs, fndr memb Panel for Conservation Accreditation Register for Engrs; chm Professional Bodies Coll of Scot Construction Industry Gp 2001–04, cmmr Royal Cmmn on the Ancient and Historic Monuments of Scotland; memb: Wolfson Bridge Research Unit Advsy Ctee Univ of Dundee 1994–97, Structural Engrg Research Advsy Gp Univ of Dundee 1997–2002, ICE/IStructE Working Gp on Codes and Standards 1999–2000, ICE/IStructE Study Gp Safety in Tall Buildings 2001–02, Advanced Concrete and Masonry Centre Mgmnt Gp Univ of Paisley 2001–03, Master of Research Panel Univ of Dundee 2002–07, Historic Scotland/English Heritage Working Gp on Accreditation of Professionals in Conservation Projects; pt/t tutor Open Univ 1984–88, hon lectr Univ of Strathclyde 1991–94, visiting prof Univ of Paisley 1998–2003; author and co-author numerous technical papers in engrg jls; dir Thomas Telford Ltd; tstee: Forth Bridges Visitor Centre Tst 1988–, Scottish Lime Centre Tst 1998–; reader The Royal Anniversary Tst; Jr Members' Prize IStructE Scot Branch 1977, Harding Prize Br Tunnelling Soc 1981, Philip Gooding travelling scholar Concrete Soc 1982; Hon DTech Glasgow Caledonian Univ 2007; CEng 1980, MIWEM 1981, FICE 1993 (MICE 1980), FIStructE 1994, fell Inst of Engrs and Shipbuilders in Scotland 2001, FREng 2006, FRSE 2007; *Recreations* sailing, cycling, books, opera, engineering history; *Clubs* Smeatonians, Western (Glasgow); *Style*— Gordon Masterton, Esq; ✉ Corrievreck, Montrose Terrace, Bridge of Weir, Renfrewshire PA11 3DH (tel 01505 613503, e-mail themastertons@btinternet.com); Jacobs UK, 95 Bothwell Street, Glasgow G2 7HX (tel 0141 566 8418, e-mail gordon.masterton@jacobs.com)

MATES, James Michael; s of Rt Hon Michael Mates, MP, *qv*, and Mary Rosamund, *née* Paton; *b* 11 August 1961; *Educ* King's Coll Sch, Marlborough, Farnham Coll, Univ of Leeds (BA); *m* Fiona Margaret, da of John Standish Bennett; 2 s (Leo James de Vars b 4 Nov 1991, Charles Michael John b 2 Nov 1997), 1 da (Flora Katherine b 3 March 1994); *Career* ITN: joined as grad trainee 1983, Tokyo corr 1989–91, N of England corr 1991–92, Moscow corr 1992–93, diplomatic ed 1993–97, Washington corr 1997–2001, sr news corr 2001–; *Recreations* water sports, bridge; *Style*— James Mates, Esq

MATES, Rt Hon Michael John; PC (2004), MP; s of Claude Mates; *b* 9 June 1934; *Educ* Salisbury Cathedral Sch, Blundell's, King's Coll Cambridge; *m* 1, 1959 (m dis 1980), Mary Rosamund Paton; 2 s (1 of whom James Michael Mates, *qv*), 2 da; *m* 2, 1982 (m dis 1995), Rosellen, da of W. T Bett, of W Wittering, W Sussex; 1 da; *m* 3, 1998, Christine, da of Count Moltke, of Copenhagen; *Career* army offr 1954–74 (Royal Ulster Rifles, Queen's Dragoon Gds RAC, Maj 1967, Lt-Col 1973); MP (Cons): Petersfield Oct 1974–1983, Hants E 1983–; min of state NI Office 1992–93 (resigned); chm: All-Pty Anglo-Irish Gp 1979–92, Select Ctee on Defence 1987–92 (memb 1979–92), Cons Home Affrs Ctee 1987–88 (vice-chm 1979–87), NI Select Ctee 2001–05; vice-chm Cons NI Ctee 1979–81 (sec 1974–79), sec 1922 Ctee 1987–88 and 1997–, memb Intelligence and Security Ctee 1994–, memb Butler Review of Intelligence on Weapons of Mass Destruction 2004; Liveryman Worshipful Co of Farriers 1975 (Master 1986); *Style*— The Rt Hon Michael Mates, MP; ✉ House of Commons, London SW1A 0AA

MATEV, HE Dr Lachezar Nikolov; s of Nikola Matev (d 1987), and Rosa Matev; *b* 5 August 1951, Sofia, Bulgaria; *Educ* Tech Univ Sofia (MSc), Sofia Univ (MSc), Moscow Diplomatic Acad (MA, PhD); *m* 16 July 1977, Bisserka; 1 s (Nikolay), 1 da (Emily); *Career* Bulgarian diplomat; memb Bd Higher Educn Cncl Miny of Educn 1977–82, Eastern European Countries Dept Miny of Foreign Affrs 1982, first sec Prague 1982–89, Foreign Economic Policy Directorate and Int Economic Orgns Directorate 1989–92, co-fndr and md Int Business Devpt magazine and md VECCO Ltd 1992–93, head UN Agencies Section Foreign Economic Policy Dept 1993–95, memb and head Delgn to UNDP Exec Bd NY 1994–95, cnsllr Madrid 1995–98, head of unit European Integration Directorate Miny of Foreign Affrs 1998–2002, min plenipotentiary and dep head of mission London 2002–05, ambass extraordinary and plenipotentiary to the Ct of St James's 2005–; Knight Commander of the Royal Order of Francis I (KCFO); *Recreations* art, classical music and opera, theatre, sport (tennis, swimming, karate, basketball, rowing and skiing), gardening, business and finance; *Style*— HE Dr Lachezar Matev; ✉ Embassy of the Republic of Bulgaria, 186–188 Queen's Gate, London SW7 5HL (tel 020 7591 0781, fax 020 7584 4948, e-mail ambass.office@bulgarianembassy.org.uk)

MATHER, Clive; s of Ronald Mather, and Ivy Mather; *b* 19 September 1947; *Educ* Warwick Sch, Lincoln Coll Oxford (MA); *m* 1976, Ann; 1 s, 2 da; *Career* Shell: joined 1969, early career UK, Brunei and Gabon, retail regnl mangr Shell UK 1984–86, dir of personnel and public affrs Shell South Africa 1986–91, dir of human resources and admin Shell UK and dir Shell Research Ltd 1991–95, chief information offr Shell Int 1995–97, dir (int) Shell 1997–99, chief exec Shell Services Int 1999–2002, chm Shell UK Ltd 2002–04, head of global learning 2002–, chm/ceo Shell Canada 2004–; chm Petroleum Employers' Cncl 1994, chm industry/govt Steering Gp on Corp Social Responsibility, cmmr Equal Opportunities Cmmn 1991–94; memb: Supervisory Bd Office of Govt and Commerce, Advsy Bd Relationships Fndn, President's Ctee CBI, memb UK Advsy Bd INSEAD; chm: IMD Business Cncl, Lensbury Ltd, Lambeth Educn Action Zone Forum 1998–; dep chm Windsor Leadership Tst, tstee Royal Anniversary Tst; *Recreations* sport, good food and wine; *Style*— Clive Mather, Esq

MATHER, Graham Christopher Spencer; er s of Thomas Mather, and Doreen Mather; *b* 23 October 1954; *Educ* Hutton GS, New Coll Oxford (Burnet law scholar, MA); *m* 1, 18 Sept 1981 (m dis 1995), Fiona Marion McMillan, er da of Sir Ronald Bell, QC, MP (d 1982); 2 s (Oliver James William b 20 June 1987, Alexander Richard Christopher b 30 March 1991); *m* 2, 17 July 1997, Geneviève Elizabeth, wid of James Seton Fairhurst; *Career* slr and subsequently conslt Cameron Markby 1978–80; IOD: asst to DG 1980–83, head of Policy Unit 1983–86; Inst of Econ Affrs: dep dir 1987, gen dir 1987–92; pres: European Policy Forum 1992–, European Media Forum 1997–, European Financial Forum 1999–; visiting fell Nuffield Coll Oxford 1992–2000; vice-pres: Strategic Planning Soc 1993–99, Assoc of Dist Cncls 1994–99; Parly candidate (Cons) Blackburn 1983; MEP (Cons) Hampshire N and Oxford 1994–99; conslt: Tudor Investment Corporation 1992–; radio and TV broadcaster, contributor to The Times and various jls; memb: Westminster City Cncl 1982–86, Cncl Small Business Research Tst, HM Treasy Working Pty on Freeports 1983, MMC 1989–94, Competition Appeal Tbnl 2000–, Ofcom Consumer Panel 2004–; *Clubs* Oxford and Cambridge; *Style*— Graham Mather, Esq; ✉ European Policy Forum, 125 Pall Mall, London SW1Y 5EA (tel 020 7839 7565, fax 020 7839 7339, e-mail graham.mather@epfltd.org)

MATHER, Jim; MSP; *b* 6 March 1947, Lochwinnoch, Renfrewshire; *Educ* Paisley GS, Greenock HS, Univ of Glasgow; *Career* apprentice CA Welsh Walker Ritchie & Co 1964–70, accountant Chivas Bros Ltd 1970–73, mktg mangr IBM UK Ltd 1973–83, dir Computers for Business Ltd Scotland 1983–96, dir Startech Ptnrs Ltd 1997–99, MSP (SNP) Highlands and Islands 2003–; SNP spokesperson on enterprise; chm Global Recycle Ltd, dir The Scotland Funds Ltd; *Style*— Jim Mather, Esq, MSP; ✉ Constituency Office, 31 Combie Street, Oban, Argyll PA34 4HS (tel 01631 571359, fax 01631 571360); The Scottish Parliament, Edinburgh EH99 1SP (tel 0131 348 5700, e-mail jim.mather.msp@scottish.parliament.uk)

MATHER, Richard Martin (Rick); s of Richard John Mather (d 1993), and Opal, *née* Martin (d 1995); *Educ* Dept of Urban Design Architectural Assoc London, Sch of Architecture and Allied Arts Univ of Oregon; *Career* architect; princ Rick Mather Architects 1973–; projects incl: Times Newspaper HQ Building London (RIBA Award 1992), Studio Drama Centre UEA, Constable Terrace UEA (Architectural Deisgn Award 1986, RIBA Gold Award 1994 and Civic Tst Award 1995), Nelson Ct UEA, ARCO Bldg Keble Coll Oxford (RIBA Award 1996 and Civic Tst Award 1997), All Glass Structure Hampstead (RIBA Award 1994), ISMA Centre Univ of Reading (RIBA Award and Civic Tst Award 1999), The Priory Hampstead (RIBA Nat Award 1998, Civic Tst Award 1998, AIA Award 1997), Nat Maritime Museum Greenwich 1999 (Civic Tst Award 2000), Wallace Collection London 2000, Dulwich Picture Gallery London 2000 (RIBA Conservation Award 2001, AIA Business Week/Architectural Record Award 2001, Civic Tst Award 2002), Masterplan Southbank Complex London 2000, RHS Lindley Library 2001, Univ of Lincoln Masterplan 2001 (Architectural Review Future Projects Award 2004, Cloane Robinson Civic Tst Award commendation 2005), Virginia Museum of Fine Arts USA 2001, Sloane Robinson Building Keble Coll Oxford 2002, Central Milton Keynes Residential Quarter 2002, Greenwich World Heritage Site Masterplan 2002, Lincoln School of Architecture 2003, Masterplan and Extension Ashmolean Museum Oxford 2002, Masterplan Nat History Museum 2004, Masterplan and Design Acad Liverpool John Moores Univ 2005, new library for Queen's Coll Oxford 2006, music room for CCC Oxford 2006, 1.7 acre redevpt of Acland Hosp sit for Keble Coll Oxford 2006, masterplan Barking Town Centre 2006; conslt architect: Architectural Assoc 1978–92, UEA 1988–94, Univ of Southampton 1996–, Jubilee Sports Centre Univ of Southampton 2004, Lyric Theatre Hammersmith 2004; teacher 1967–88: Bartlett Sch of Architecture UCL, Univ of Westminster, Architectural Assoc London, Harvard Grad Sch of Design; Thomas Jefferson prof Univ of Virginia 2003; RIBA external examiner 1986–: Univ of Cambridge, Bartlett Sch of Architecture Univ of London, Univ of Westminster, De Montfort Univ, Univ of Central England, Mackintosh Sch of Architecture Glasgow, Univ of Ulster, Univ of Newcastle; numerous exhbns and lectrs; memb Cncl: Architectural Assoc London 1992–96, RIBA 1998–2000; tstee:V&A 2000–, Br Architectural Library Tst 2004–; *Books* Zen Restaurants: Architecture in Detail (1992), Urban Approaches: A Blueprint Monograph (1993), Rick Mather Architects (2006); *Recreations* gardens, food, skiing; *Style*— Rick Mather; ✉ Rick Mather Architects, 123 Camden High Street, London NW1 7JR (tel 020 7284 1727, fax 020 7267 7826, e-mail info@rickmather.com)

MATHERS, James Irvine; s of James Cuthbert Mathers, of Glasgow, and Jean Benton, *née* Cobb; *b* 26 September 1947; *Educ* Lenzie Acad, Univ of Strathclyde (BSc, DMS); *m* 12 July 1970, Janis Chalmers, da of Douglas Bell (d 1959), of Glasgow; 1 s (Craig b 1973), 1 da (Lynne b 1975); *Career* analyst and programmer Singer Sewing Machines 1968–74, sr systems analyst Hepworth Tailoring 1974–79, sr systems analyst Consolidated Pneumatic Tool Co 1979–80; Hydro Electric: systems mangr 1980–89, computer ops mangr 1989–93, IT Services Manager 1993–; elder Church of Scot; MIMgt 1988; *Style*— James Mathers, Esq; ✉ Hydro Electric, Ashgrove Road West, Aberdeen AB9 2NY (tel 01224 287601)

MATHESON, Alexander (Sandy); OBE (1990), JP (Western Isles 1972); s of Dr Alexander Matheson (d 1978), of Stornoway, Isle of Lewis, and Catherine Agnes, *née* Smith (d 1986); *b* 16 November 1941; *Educ* Nicolson Inst Stornoway, Robert Gordon Tech Coll Aberdeen; *m* 29 March 1965, Irene Mary, da of Alex Davidson; 2 s (Alexander b 2 Sept 1966, Donald Roderick b 9 Nov 1972), 2 da (Isobel Mary b 27 Nov 1969, Irene Louise Catherine b 26 March 1975); *Career* apprentice pharmacist Davidson & Kay Ltd (qualified 1965); Roderick Smith Ltd: superintendent pharmacist 1965–98, md 1967–82, chm 1967–; memb: Stornoway Town Cncl 1967–75 (provost 1971–75), Stornoway Tst Estate 1967– (chm 1971–81), Stornoway Pier and Harbour Cmmn 1968– (chm 1970–72 and 1991–2001), Ross and Cromarty CC 1967–75; fndr chm Western Isles Devpt Fund 1972–; memb: Western Isles Health Bd 1974–2001 (chm 1993–2001), Western Isles Cncl 1974–94 (convener 1982–90); pres Islands Cmmn of Conf Peripheral Maritime Regions of Europe 1987–91; dir Western Isles Enterprise 1991–95; chm Harris Tweed Authy (formerly Harris Tweed Assoc) 2001– (dir 1991–94, memb 1995–); chm Highlands and Islands Airports Ltd 2001–07; memb Stornoway Branch RNLI 1974–2004 (chm 1974–79 and 1994–2004); Hon Sheriff of the Western Isles 1972, HM Lord-Lt of the Western Isles 2001 (DL 1994, Vice-Lt 1994–2001); memb: Royal Soc of Health 1965, Inst of Pharmacy Mgmnt Int 1968; FRPharmS 1993 (MRPharmS 1965); *Recreations* local history, genealogy, European and Islands travel; *Style*— Sandy Matheson, Esq, OBE; ✉ 33 Newton Street, Stornoway, Isle of Lewis HS1 2RW (tel 01851 702082, fax 01851 700415); Roderick Smith Ltd, 8–10 Cromwell Street, Stornoway, Isle of Lewis HS1 2DA (tel 01851 702082, fax 01851 700415, e-mail sandy.matheson@tinyworld.co.uk)

MATHESON, His Hon Judge Duncan; QC (1989); *Educ* Rugby, Trinity Coll Cambridge (MA, LLM); *Career* called to the Bar Inner Temple 1965 (bencher 1994); in practice SE Circuit, recorder of the Crown Court 1985–2000, circuit judge 2000–; standing jr counsel to the Law Soc in legal aid matters 1981–89; chm No 1 (London S) Legal Aid Area 1989–92, chm London Legal Aid Area 1993–96; *Style*— His Hon Judge Matheson, QC; ✉ Middlesex Guildhall Crown Court, Broad Sanctuary, London SW1P 3BB

MATHESON, Jamie Graham; s of James M Matheson (d 1985), and Marjorie Graham, *née* Todd; *b* 19 May 1954, Glasgow; *Educ* Loretto Sch Edinburgh; *m* 1 June 1990, Angela, *née* Thompson; *Career* Parsons & Co (latterly Allied Provincial Securities Ltd) 1972–96 (dir 1986–96); Brewin Dolphin Holdings plc: divnl dir Bell Lawrie 1996–2001, dir 2001–, exec chm 2005–; non-exec dir: AIM VCT2 plc, SMG plc 2007–; chm Glasgow Jr C of C 1984–85; deacon Incorporation of Bonnetmakers and Dyers of Glasgow 1986–87, precis Grand Antiquity Soc of Glasgow 1996–97; FSI 2000; OStJ; *Recreations* sailing, golf, field sports; *Clubs* Royal Thames Yacht, New (Edinburgh), Caldwell Golf, Clyde Cruising, W Kirkbride Golf; *Style*— Jamie Matheson, Esq; ✉ Brewin Dolphin Holdings plc, 12 Smithfield Street, London EC1A 9BD (tel 0141 314 8101, fax 0141 314 8296, e-mail jamie.matheson@brewin.co.uk)

MATHESON, Michael; MSP; s of Edward Matheson, and Elizabeth, *née* Coyle; *Educ* John Bosco Secdy Sch Glasgow, Queen Margaret Coll Edinburgh (BSc), Open Univ (BA, Dip Applied Social Sciences); *Career* state registered occupational therapist; community occupational therapist: Highland Regnl Cncl Social Work Dept 1991–93, Stirling Cncl Social Work Services 1993–99; MSP (SNP): Scotland Central 1999–2007, Falkirk W 2007–; dep shadow min for justice and land reform 1999–2004, shadow min for culture and sport 2004–06, memb Parly Enterprise and Culture Ctee, former memb Parly Justice Ctee, memb Glasgow Airport Rail Link Ctee 2006–07, co-convenor Cross-party Gp on Malawi, vice-convenor Cross-party Gp on Sport, memb Parly Health and Sport Ctee; state registered occupational therapist (Health Professions Cncl); memb Ochils mountain rescue team; *Recreations* mountaineering, travel; *Style*— Michael Matheson, Esq, MSP; ✉ The Scottish Parliament, Edinburgh EH99 1SP (tel 0131 348 5671, fax 0131 348 6474, e-mail michael.matheson.msp@scottish.parliament.uk); Constituency Office tel 01324 629271, fax 01324 635576

M

MATHESON OF MATHESON, Maj Sir Fergus John; 7 Bt (UK 1882), of Lochalsh, Co Ross; Chief of Clan Matheson; yr s of Gen Sir Torquhil George Matheson, 5 Bt, KCB, CMG (d 1963); suc bro, Maj Sir Torquhil Alexander Matheson of Matheson, 6 Bt, DL (d 1993); *b* 22 February 1927; *Educ* Eton; *m* 17 May 1952, Hon Jean Elizabeth Mary Willoughby, da of 11 Baron Middleton, KG, MC; 2 da (Elizabeth Angela Matilda (Mrs Martin C Thompson) b 1953, Fiona Jean Lucia (Mrs Andrew T Kendall) b 1962), 1 s (Lt Col Alexander Fergus Matheson of Matheson, yr b 1954); *Heir* s, Lt Col Alexander Matheson of Matheson, yr; *Career* serv 1 and 3 Bns Coldstream Gds 1944–64: Palestine, N Africa, Germany, Adjt Mons OCS 1952–55, memb HM Body Guard of Hon Corps of Gentlemen at Arms 1979–97, Standard Bearer 1993–97; *Clubs* Army and Navy; *Style*— Maj Sir Fergus Matheson of Matheson, Bt; ✉ The Old Rectory, Hedenham, Norfolk NR35 2LD (tel and fax 01508 482218)

MATHEW, Prof Christopher George Porter; s of Gother Donaldson Porter Mathew, QC (d 1984), of Port Elizabeth, South Africa, and Evelyn Mary, *née* O'Connor; *b* 7 September 1949; *Educ* St Andrew's Coll Grahamstown, Univ of Cape Town (BSc), Univ of London (PhD); *m* Denise, da of Charles Manning; *Career* sr biochemist Provincial Hosp Port Elizabeth 1972–77, PhD student Inst of Cancer Research London 1977–80, South African Med Research Cncl trg fell Dept of Biochemistry St Mary's Hosp London 1980, sr biochemist Univ of Cape Town 1981–82, specialist (med sci) Univ of Stellenbosch 1983–86, team ldr Section of Human Cancer Genetics Inst of Cancer Research Sutton Surrey 1986–89, dir South Thames (East) Regnl DNA Lab and hon sr lectr Div of Med and Molecular Genetics UMDS London 1989–98, prof of molecular genetics Guy's and St Thomas' Sch of Med London 1999–; Ranbaxy Sci Fndn visiting prof All-India Inst of Med Scis New Delhi 1995; memb: Ctee on Clinical Genetics RCP 1994–, Br Soc of Human Genetics Cncl 1996–, Euro Soc of Human Genetics, Human Genome Orgn; FRCPath (memb Cncl and chm Genetics Speciality Advsy Ctee 1993–96), FMedSci 2001; *Recreations* golf, cycling, theatre; *Style*— Prof Christopher Mathew; ✉ Division of Medical Molecular Genetics, Guy's Hospital, London SE1 9RT (tel 020 7955 4653, fax 020 7955 4644, e-mail christopher.mathew@kcl.ac.uk)

MATHEW, Robert Knox (Robin); QC (1992); s of Robert Mathew, TD, MP (d 1966), and Joan Leslie, *née* Bruce (d 1989); *b* 22 January 1945; *Educ* Eton, Trinity Coll Dublin (BA); *m* 13 Sept 1968, Anne Rosella, da of Brig Robert Elliott, RA; 1 da (Juliet Alexa Liberty); *Career* journalist 1967–75; called to the Bar 1974; *Recreations* country pursuits, racing; *Clubs* Boodle's; *Style*— Robin Mathew, Esq, QC; ✉ Church Farm, Little Barrington, Burford, Oxfordshire OX18 4TE (tel 01451 844311, fax 01451 944768); 12 New Square, Lincoln's Inn, London WC2A 3SW (tel 020 7419 8000, fax 020 7419 8050, e-mail robin.mathew@newsquarechambers.co.uk)

MATHEWS, Arthur; s of James Mathews, and Joan, *née* Fallon; *Educ* Castleknock Coll, Coll of Mktg and Design Dublin; *Career* writer; columnist: Irish Times, Big Issue; cartoonist: New Musical Express, Observer Sport magazine; *Television* credits with Graham Linehan incl: Paris, Father Ted (BAFTA 1996 and 1998, Writers Guild, RTS and Comedy awards), Big Train (Comedy Award), The Fast Show, Brass Eye, Jam, The All New Alexi Sayle Show; solo credits incl: Hippies, Big Train (series 2); *Theatre* I, Keano; *Radio* Luneen Live; *Books* Well Remembered Days (2001); *Recreations* history, football, TV documentaries, music, radio; *Style*— Arthur Mathews, Esq; ✉ c/o TV Writers, 74 The Drive, Fulham Road, London SW6 5JH

MATHEWS, Dr John Alan; s of Henry Alexander Mathews, and Dora, *née* Apley; *b* 19 June 1934; *Educ* Haberdashers' Aske's, Jesus Coll Cambridge, Guy's Hosp Med Sch (MA, MD); *m* 14 July 1957, Wendy, da of Jack Dewhurst, and Anita, *née* Cohen; 1 s (Colin David b 1960), 2 da (Gillian Anne b 1962, Catherine Jane b 1972); *Career* conslt physician emeritus and Hon conslt physician Dept of Rheumatology St Thomas' Hosp London (conslt 1970–2000); sometime memb Cncl Br Soc for Rheumatology; sec: Heberden Soc, Br Assoc for Rheumatology and Rehabilitation; physician i/c of Musicians' Clinic; past pres Rheumatology and Rehabilitation Section RSM; FRCP; *Style*— Dr John A Mathews; ✉ 67 Walpole House, 126 Westminster Bridge Road, London SE1 7UN (tel 020 7401 8187); Department of Rheumatology, St Thomas' Hospital, London SE1 7EH (tel 020 7188 5901, e-mail jamathews@doctors.org.uk)

MATHEWS, Simon; s of Denis Mathews (d 1986), and Simone, *née* Hayward; *b* 24 July 1961; *Educ* Radley, Univ of Manchester (BA); *m* 7 Sept 1991, Emma Claire, da of Rodney Gillett; 2 s (Gabriel b 3 April 1993, Donovan b 19 Dec 1995); *Career* Saatchi & Saatchi Garland Compton: media trainee 1981–82, media exec 1982–85, dep gp dir 1985–87; Young & Rubicam: asst media planning dir 1987–88, media planning dir 1988–89, jt media dir 1989–92, exec media dir 1993–94; chief exec Equinox Communications 1994–96, md Optimedia International (UK) 1996–2003, founding ptnr Rise Communications 2003–; *Style*— Simon Mathews, Esq; ✉ Rise Communications, Bramah House, 65–71 Bermondsey Street, London SE1 3XF

MATHEWSON, David Carr; s of H Douglas C Mathewson (d 1980), and Evelyn, *née* Carr; *b* 26 July 1947; *Educ* Daniel Stewarts Coll Edinburgh, Univ of St Andrews (BSc, capt athletics team), Wits Business Sch Johannesburg; *m* 23 Sept 1972, Janet, da of late James N McIntyre; 1 s (Ewan b 3 July 1981), 1 da (Emily b 4 Aug 1983); *Career* articled clerk Deloittes Edinburgh 1972, with Williams Glyn & Co London 1972–76, various sr appts Nedbank Group Johannesburg 1976–85; Noble Grossart Ltd merchant bankers: joined 1985, asst dir 1987–89, dir 1989–2000; also dir: Quicks Gp plc 1991–97, Martin Currie High Income Tst plc 1998–2005, Edinburgh UK Tracker Tst plc 1998–, Noble & Co Ltd 2003–, Murray VCT plc 2004–06, Robertson Gp Ltd 2006–, various private cos; chm: Geared Opportunities Income Tst plc 2000–06, Sportech plc 2002–06 (formerly Rodime plc, dir 1992–2002), Amazing Hldgs plc 2004–, Asian Growth Properties Ltd 2006–, Corsie Gp plc 2006–, CGTV Games (Ireland) Ltd 2006–; conslt Andersen Corp Fin 2000–02; memb Bd of Tstees Royal Botanic Gardens Edinburgh 2001–; memb Cncl St Leonards Sch 1999–2006, memb Bd New Park Sch St Andrews 2005–06; MICAS 1972; *Recreations* golf, shooting, gardening, family interests; *Clubs* Bruntsfield Links Golfing Soc, Dukes (St Andrews), New (Edinburgh), Desert Springs (Spain); *Style*— David Mathewson, Esq; ✉ Dalveen, 7 Barnton Park, Edinburgh EH4 6JF (tel 0131 336 3214, fax 0131 476 5780, e-mail dopey@blueyonder.co.uk)

MATHEWSON, Sir George Ross; kt (1999), CBE (1985); s of George Mathewson, of Perth, by his w Charlotte Gordon, *née* Ross; *b* 14 May 1940; *Educ* Perth Acad, Univ of St Andrews (BSc, PhD), Canisius Coll Buffalo NY (MBA); *m* 1966, Sheila Alexandra Graham, da of Eon Bennett (d 1975), of Bridge of Earn, Perth; 2 s; *Career* asst lectr Univ of St Andrews 1964–67; with Bell Aerospace (Buffalo, NY) in res and devpt and avionics engrg 1967–72, joined ICFC Edinburgh 1972 (area mangr Aberdeen 1974, asst gen mangr and dir 1979), chief exec and memb Scottish Devpt Agency 1981–87; The Royal Bank of Scotland Group plc: dir of strategic planning and development 1987–90, dep gp chief exec 1990–92, gp chief exec 1992–2000, exec dep chm 2000–01, chm 2001–06; chm Toscafund Ltd 2006–; dir: Scottish Investment Tst Ltd 1981–, IIF Inc 2001–06, Santander Central Hispano 2001–04; non-exec dir Stagecoach 2006–; pres Br Bankers Assoc 2002–04; Hon LLD Univ of Dundee 1983, Hon LLD Univ of St Andrews 2000, Hon DUniv Glasgow 2001, Dr (hc) Univ of Edinburgh 2002; FRSE 1988, FCIB (Scot) 1994, CEng, MIEE, CCMI (CIMgt); *Recreations* rugby, golf, business; *Clubs* New (Edinburgh); *Style*— Sir George Mathewson, CBE; ✉ The Royal Bank of Scotland Group plc, Gagarburn, Edinburgh EH12 1HQ

MATHEWSON, Dr Hew Byrne; s of Alexander Mackechnie Mathewson, of Elie, Fife, and Dorothy Wightman, *née* Reid; *b* 18 November 1949; *Educ* HS of Glasgow, Univ of Glasgow (BDS), Univ of Wales Cardiff (LLM); *m* 1971, Lorna Anne Marshall, da of George S McConnachie; 1 da (Elizabeth b 1977), 1 s (Andrew b 1980); *Career* assoc dental surgn: Glidden and Archibald Wishaw 1974, Atkins & Cox Canterbury 1975–77; sr ptnr Mathewson & Associates dental practice Edinburgh 1977–; regnl gen practice vocational trg advsr for SE Scotland 1988–96, dental postgrad advsr for SE Scotland 1987–98, asst dir of dental studies Univ of Edinburgh 1987–99; BDA: memb Scottish Gen Dental Servs Ctee 1981–85 and 1991–2003 (chm 1991–97), pres E of Scotland branch 1985–86, Scottish sec 1985–90, chm Sick Dentist Mgmnt Gp 1990–97, memb Gen Dental Servs Ctee 1991–2003, memb Exec 1991–2003, memb Scottish Dental Practice Exec 2000–03, vice-chm 2000–2003; pres GDC 2003– (memb 1996–, jt-chair Professional Conduct Ctee 2001–03, vice-chm Postgrad Sub-Ctee 2001–03); memb: Dental Ctee Scottish Cncl for Postgraduate Med and Dental Educn 1987–98 and 1999–2001, Cncl for the Regulation of Healthcare Professionals 2003– (vice-chair 2006–07); memb and chm various Scottish Dept of Health Working Parties; memb Editorial Bd British Dental Jl 1992–2003; pres Conference of Orders and Assimilated Bodies of Dental Practitioners in Europe (CODE) 2007; chm Peggy's Mill Assoc 1986–88; memb: BDA 1970, Royal Odonto Chirurgical Soc of Scotland 1986, DGDP (UK), FGDP RCS 1992, FDSRCSE 1995; *Recreations* carpentry, walking, theatre, cinema; *Clubs* Edinburgh Sports; *Style*— Dr Hew Mathewson; ✉ Mathewson & Associates, 176 St John's Road, Edinburgh EH12 8BE (tel 0131 334 2704, fax 0131 312 7007, e-mail hbm@blueyonder.co.uk)

MATHIAS, Prof Christopher Joseph; s of Lt Elias Mathias, and Hilda, *née* Pereira; *Educ* St Aloysius Sch Visakhapatnam, St Joseph's Euro HS Bangalore, St John Med Coll Bangalore Univ (MB BS), Worcester Coll and Wolfson Coll Oxford (Rhodes scholar, DPhil), Univ of London (DSc); *m* Rosalind (Lindy), *née* Jolleys; 2 s (James, Timothy), 1 da (Sarah); *Career* SHO (med) St Martha's Hosp Bangalore 1972 (med and surgical house offr 1971–72), res offr and hon registrar Dept of Neurology Churchill Hosp Oxford 1972–76, clinical asst and res fell Nat Spinal Injuries Centre Stoke Mandeville Hosp 1973–76, SHO Dept of Med Royal Postgrad Med Sch Hammersmith Hosp 1976–77, registrar in med St Mary's Hosp Portsmouth and Dept of Renal Med Univ of Southampton 1977–79, Wellcome Tst sr res fell in clinical sci St Mary's Hosp Med Sch London 1979–84, conslt physician St Mary's Hosp London 1982–, Wellcome Tst sr lectr in med sci St Mary's Hosp Med Sch London and Inst of Neurology UCL 1984–92, conslt physician Nat Hosp for Neurology and Neurosurgery London 1985–, dir Neurovascular Med (Pickering) Unit St Mary's Hosp London 1987–, dir Autonomic Unit Nat Hosp for Neurology and Neurosurgery London 1989–, prof of neurovascular med Univ of London 1991– (jtly with Imperial Coll London and Inst of Neurology/UCL); visiting prof Academic Med Centre Univ of Amsterdam 1988, Nimmo visiting prof Univ of Adelaide 1996, visiting prof Univ of Hawaii 1999, visiting prof Univ of Adelaide Aust 2007; chm: Clinical Autonomic Res Soc of GB 1987–98 (fndn sec 1982–86), Res Ctee on Autonomic Disorders World Fedn of Neurology 1993–97 (memb 1989–93); memb: NW Thames Regnl Res Ctee 1987–93, Scientific Ctee Int Spinal Res Tst 1996–, Bd of Dirs American Autonomic Soc 1996–2004, NW Thames Regnl Advsy Ctee for Distinction Awards 1999–2001, task force American Spinal Injuries Assoc 2004–06, task forces European Fedn of Neurological Socs 2004–, Sec of State for Transport Hon Med Advsy Panel on Driving and Disorders of the Nervous System 2004–; conslt European Space Agency 1997–2000 (memb Jt European Space Agency/NASA Neuroscience Review Panel 1997); delivered numerous invited lectures at confs and symposia worldwide; fndr ed-in-chief Clinical Autonomic Research 1991–; memb Editorial Bd: Hypertension 1990–93, Functional Neurology 1990–2002, Jl of Pharmaceutical Med 1991–95, High Blood Pressure and Cardiovascular Med 1992–, Jl of Hypertension 1994–97, Parkinsonism and Related Disorders 1995–2005; pres European Fedn of Autonomic Socs 1998–2004; memb: European Fedn of Neurological Societies 2004– (chm Scientific Panel on the Autonomic Nervous System 1994–99), European Brain Cncl 2005–; govr Nat Soc for Epilepsy 2004–; chm Dr P M Shankland (Pushpa Chopra) Charitable Tst Prize Fund 1998–2003; patron: Autonomic Disorders Assoc Sarah Matheson Tst 1997–, Syncope Tst (Stars) 2001–; Prof Ruitinga Fndn Award 1988; FRCP 1987 (LRCPE, LRCP Glasgow, MRCP 1978), FMedSci 2001; *Publications* Mild Hypertension: Current controversies and new approaches (jt ed, 1984), Concepts in Hypertension: a Festschrift for Professor Sir Stanley Peart (jt ed, 1989), Autonomic Failure: A textbook of clinical disorders of the autonomic nervous system (ed with Sir Roger Bannister, *qv*, 3 edn 1992, sr author 4 edn 1999, reprinted 2002); also author of book chapters and scientific papers; *Recreations* gardening, badminton, watching cricket and football, observing human and canine behaviour; *Clubs* Athenaeum, Vincent's (Oxford), Royal Soc of Med; *Style*— Prof Christopher Mathias; ✉ Meadowcroft, West End Lane, Stoke Poges, Buckinghamshire SL2 4NE (fax 01753 645566, e-mail cj.mathias@btinternet.com); Neurovascular Medicine (Pickering) Unit, Faculty of Medicine, Imperial College London at St Mary's Hospital, Praed Street, London W2 1NY (tel 020 7886 1468, fax 020 7886 1540, e-mail c.mathias@imperial.ac.uk)

MATHIAS, (Jonathan) Glyn; s of Roland Mathias, of Brecon, and Mary Annie, *née* Hawes; *b* 19 February 1945; *Educ* Llandovery Coll, Jesus Coll Oxford (MA), Univ of Southampton (MSc); *m* Ann, *née* Hughes; 1 s (Mathew b 1971), 2 da (Megan b 1975, Hannah b 2001); *Career* reporter South Wales Echo 1967–70, reporter BBC Southampton 1970–73; ITN: political corr 1973, home affrs corr 1979–81, political ed 1981–86, asst ed 1986–91, controller of public affrs 1991–93, chief political corr 1993–94; political ed BBC Wales 1994–99; electoral cmmr 2001–; chm Parly Lobby 1985; hon fell Univ of Wales Inst Cardiff (UWIC) 2004; *Books* Televising Democracies (contrib, ed Bob Franklin, 1992); *Recreations* walking; *Clubs* Reform; *Style*— Glyn Mathias, Esq

MATHIAS, Julian Robert; s of Anthony Robert Mathias (d 1973), and Cecily Mary Agnes, *née* Hughes (d 2005); *b* 7 September 1943; *Educ* Downside, UC Oxford (MA); *m* 1996, Frances Bone, *née* Bartley, wid of Douglas Bone; *Career* mangr Hill Samuel and Co Ltd 1964–71, ptnr Buckmaster and Moore 1971–81, dir Foreign and Colonial Management Ltd 1981–95; *Recreations* wine tasting, bridge, golf, shooting; *Clubs* Boodle's, Berkshire Golf; *Style*— Julian Mathias, Esq; ✉ 8 Grove Court, Drayton Gardens, London SW10 9QY (tel 020 7373 2725, and 01608 674868, e-mail jrm@julianmathias.co.uk)

MATHIAS, Prof Peter; CBE (1984); s of John Samuel Mathias (d 1960), and Marion Helen, *née* Love; *b* 10 January 1928; *Educ* Colston's Hosp, Jesus Coll Cambridge (MA), Harvard Univ, Univ of Oxford (LittD), Univ of Cambridge (DLitt); *m* 5 April 1958, (Elizabeth) Ann, da of Robert Blackmore (d 1979), of Bath; 2 s (Sam b 3 March 1959, Henry b 15 May 1961), 1 da (Sophie b 25 July 1964); *Career* Univ of Cambridge: res fell Jesus Coll 1952–55 (hon fell 1987), history lectr 1955–68, fell and dir of history studies Queens' Coll 1955–68 (tutor 1957–68, hon fell 1987), sr proctor 1965–66; Univ of Oxford: Chichele prof of econ history and fell All Souls Coll 1969–87, curator Bodleian Library 1972–87; master Downing Coll Cambridge 1987–95 (hon fell 1995); visiting prof: Toronto Univ 1961, Delhi Univ 1967, Univ of Calif Berkeley 1967, Pennsylvania Univ 1972, Columbia Univ (Virginia Gildersleeve prof) 1972, Johns Hopkins Univ 1979, Natal Univ 1980, ANU 1981, Geneva Univ 1986, Leuven Univ 1990, San Marino Univ 1990, Waseda 1996, Osaka Gakuin Univ 1998, Bolzano 1999, Kansai 2006; hon pres Int Econ History Assoc 1978– (pres 1974–78); vice-pres: Royal Historical Soc 1975–80 (hon vice-pres 2001), Business Archives Cncl 1980–84 and 1995– (chm 1967–72, pres 1984–95), Int Inst of Econ History Datini Prato Italy 1987–99, Econ History Soc 1992– (pres 1989–92); hon treas: Econ History Soc 1967–88, Br Acad 1979–89; chm: Int Advsy Ctee Univ of Buckingham 1979–84, Advsy Panel for History of Med Wellcome Tst 1980–88, Friends of Kettle's Yard 1990–95, Nat Advsy Cncl Br Library 1994–2000 (memb Humanities and Social Scis

Advsy Cncl 1990–94), Great Britain Sasakawa Fndn 1997– (pres 2005–), Advsy Bd of Central Euro Univ Press Budapest 2000–; memb: Advsy Bd for the Res Cncls 1983–89, Round Table Cncl of Indust and Higher Educn 1989–93, Beirat Wissenschaftskolleg Berlin 1992–98; memb Syndicate Fitzwilliam Museum Cambridge 1987–, chm Fitzwilliam Museum Enterprises Ltd 1990–99; Hon LittD: Univ of Buckingham 1985, Univ of Hull 1992, Univ of Warwick 1995, De Montfort Univ 1995; Hon DLitt: Univ of Birmingham 1988, UEA 1999; Hon Dr: Russian Acad of Sciences 2002–, Kansai Univ Japan 2006; memb: Econ History Soc 1951, Academia Europaea 1989; foreign memb: Royal Danish Acad 1982, Royal Belgian Acad 1988; FRHistS 1972, FBA 1977; Order of the Rising Sun (Japan) 2003; *Books* The Brewing Industry in England 1700–1830 (1959), English Trade Tokens (1962), Retailing Revolution (1967), The First Industrial Nation (1969, 1983), Science and Society (ed and contrib, 1972), The Transformation of England (1979), The First Industrial Revolutions (ed with J A Davis and contrib, 1989), Innovation and Technology in Europe (ed with J A Davis and contrib, 1991), L'Economia Britannica dal 1815–1914 (1994), Cinque lezioni di teoria e storia (2003); *Recreations* travel; *Style*— Prof Peter Mathias, CBE, FBA; ✉ 33 Church Street, Chesterton, Cambridge CB4 1DT (tel and fax 01223 329824)

MATHIAS, Sean Gerard; s of John Frederick Mathias (d 1983), of Swansea, and Anne Josephine Patricia, *née* Harding; *b* 14 March 1956; *Educ* Bishop Vaughan Comp Swansea; *Career* director and writer; as playwright: Cowardice 1983, Infidelities (Edinburgh Fringe Festival (Perrier Pick of the Fringe Award), transferred to Donmar Warehouse and Boulevard Theatre) 1985, Prayer for Wings (Edinburgh Fringe Festival (Fringe First Award), transfered to Bush Theatre) 1985, Poor Nanny (King's Head) 1989, adapted The Lost Language of Cranes by David Leavitt (BBC, WNET Playhouse series USA (Golden Gate Award Best Television Drama, nominated Radio Times Best Screenplay 1992)); as dir: Acting Shakespeare (Ian McKellen's one-man show on Broadway), A Prayer for Wings (Bush Theatre) 1985, Infidelities (Donmar Warehouse and Boulevard Theatre) 1986, Exceptions (New End Theatre), The Bed Before Yesterday (int tour), Talking Heads (Theatre Royal) 1991, Noel and Gertie (nat tour and season at Duke of York) 1991, Ghosts (Sherman Theatre) 1993, Design for Living (Donmar Warehouse and Gielgud) 1994 (Evening Standard Award for Best Dir 1994 and Critics' Circle Award for Best Dir 1995), Indiscretions 1995 (Les Parents Terribles in UK (Barrymore Theatre NY, 9 Tony Award nominations incl Best Dir 1995, Fany Award for Best Dir)), Marlene (Lyric Shaftesbury) 1996 (nominated for two Olivier Awards); RNT: Bent 1991 (City Limits Best Revival of the Year Award), Uncle Vanya (5 Olivier Award nominations incl Best Dir 1992), Les Parents Terribles (Evening Standard Drama Award for Best Dir 1994 and Critics' Circle Award for Best Dir 1995, 7 Olivier Award nominations incl Best Dir 1994), A Little Night Music (4 Olivier Award nominations) 1995, Antony and Cleopatra 1998; other credits incl: Marlene (Cort Theatre Broadway) 1999 (nominated for 2 Tony Awards), Suddenly Last Summer (Comedy Theatre) 1999, Servicemen (New Group at St Clements NYC) 2001, Dance of Death (Broadhurst Theatre Broadway) 2001 (nomination Tony Award), The Elephant Man (Royale Theatre Broadway, 2 Tony Award nominations) 2002, Company (Sondheim Celebration at the Kennedy Center) 2002, Dance of Death (Lyric Theatre) 2003 (also at Sydney Festival 2004), Antigone (Grahamstown Festival and Baxter Theatre Cape Town) 2004, Aladdin (Old Vic) 2004, Shoreditch Madonna (Soho Theatre) 2005, Aladdin (Old Vic) 2005, The Cherry Orchard (Mark Taper Forum LA) 2006, Triptych (Market Theatre Johannesburg); *Films* Bent 1997 (premiered Official Cannes Film Festival winning La Prix de la Jeunesse); *Books* Manhattan Mourning (1988); *Style*— Sean Mathias, Esq; ✉ c/o Judy Daish Associates Ltd, 2 St Charles Place, London W10 6EG (tel 020 8964 8811, fax 020 8964 8966)

MATHIESON, (John) George; CBE (1982), TD (1964), DL (1977); *b* 15 June 1932; *Educ* George Watson's Coll Edinburgh, Univ of Glasgow (LLB); *m* 1958, Shirley Bidder, *née* Clark; 1 s (John George b 30 Oct 1959), 1 da (Elspeth Catherine b 13 Feb 1962); *Career* Nat Serv Royal Artillery 1950–51; slr; articled McGrigor Donald and Maclay Murray & Spens, ptnr Clark Oliver Dewar & Webster Slrs 1959 (joined 1957), chm Thorntons WS (successor firm) 1990–97; Scottish dir Woolwich Building Society 1975–97; chm: Scottish Slrs' Discipline Tbnl 1982–90, Ind Tbnl Serv 1990–2002, Earl Haig Fund Arbroath 1980–97, Royal Br Legion Arbroath 1983–96, Scottish Wildlife Tst (Dundee & Angus Branch) 1970–75, Angus Jubilee Ctee 1975–77, Lloyds TSB Fndn for Scotland 1999–2002, Dundee Branch SSAFA 2002–07; TA: Cmdg Offr The Highland Regt RA 1964–66, Col Highlands 1972–76, ADC (TA) to HM The Queen 1975–80, chm Highland TAVRA 1976–82; elder Church of Scotland (Colliston PC) 1962–; Hon Col 105 (Scottish) Air Def Regt (RA) (V) 1986–91, hon pres Angus Bn Boys' Bde 1985–98; Hon Sheriff Arbroath 1994–; *Recreations* shooting, golf, gardening; *Clubs* New (Edinburgh); *Style*— George Mathieson, Esq, CBE, TD, DL; ✉ Willanyards, Colliston, Angus DD11 3RR (tel 01241 890286, e-mail jgeorgemat@aol.com)

MATHIESON, Ian Douglas; s of Robert James Mathieson (d 1958), of Harrow, Middx, and Violet Lilian, *née* Jones (d 1981); *b* 1 October 1942; *Educ* Harrow Weald GS, Coll of Estate Mgmnt Univ of London (BSc), UCL (DipTP); *m* 19 Aug 1967, Lesley, da of Jack Stanley Glass, of Pinner, Middx; 2 s (Mark James b 1973, John Robert b 1977); *Career* chartered surveyor in local govt and private practice until 1973, md Commercial Union Properties Ltd 1984–99 (property investment mangr 1974–80, dir 1980–2000), dep md Commercial Union Asset Management Ltd 1987–99, md Morley Properties Ltd 1999–2000, dir Morley Fund Management 1999–2000; dir South Bucks NHS Tst 1993–2000, memb Wycombe Dist HA 1983–93; memb Teesside Devpt Corp 1990–98; Freedom City of London 1986; FRICS 1975 (ARICS 1967); *Clubs* RAC; *Style*— Ian Mathieson, Esq; ✉ Alloway, Maplefield Lane, Chalfont St Giles, Buckinghamshire HP8 4TY (tel 01494 764820, fax 01494 762263, e-mail idmathieson@yahoo.co.uk)

MATHIESON, John; s of Col A A Mathieson, MC, and Shirley, *née* Peal; *Educ* Uppingham, Bucks Coll of HE; *Career* cinematographer; dir of photography on feature films, commercials and music videos (incl Madonna, Tina Turner and Rolling Stones); memb: BSC, BECTU, Int Cinematographers Guild (IATSE); patron Learning for Life, memb Thorney Is Soc; Chevalier de l'Ordre des Arts et des Lettres (France) 1996; *Film* Pigulle 1993, Bye-Bye 1994, Love is the Devil 1998, Plunkett & Macleane 1999, Gladiator 2000 (Best Cinematography BAFTA Awards, AFI Award, Broadcast Film Critics Assoc Award, nomination Best Cinematography Oscars), Hannibal 2000, K-Pax 2002, Matchstick Men 2003,The Phantom of The Opera 2004 (nomination Best Cinematography Oscars); *Recreations* skiing, diving, shooting; *Clubs* Royal Over-Seas League; *Style*— John Mathieson, Esq, BSC; ✉ 37 Talbot Road, London W2 5JH (tel 020 7221 0476, fax 020 7243 4926); c/o Chris Smith, ICM, Oxford House, 76 Oxford Street, London W1D 1BS (tel 020 7636 6565, fax 01844 261740); c/o Paul Hook, 8942 Wilshire Boulevard, Beverley Hills, CA 90211, USA (tel 00 1 310 550 4474)

MATSON, Malcolm John; s of Gp Capt Jack Norman Matson (d 1991), and Wynne Ruth, *née* Parker (d 2000); *b* 4 October 1943; *Educ* Strode's Sch Egham, Trinity Coll of Music, Univ of Nottingham (BA), Harvard Univ (MBA); *m* 1, 1969 (m dis 1988), Judith Helen Wellby, da of Arthur Kenneth Colley (d 1986); 2 s (Thomas Daniel Blandford b 5 Feb 1975, Henry Samuel Quarrington b 21 Dec 1977), 1 da (Cecilia Elspeth Adean b 26 Feb 1980); m 2, 6 Aug 1991, Alexandra Mary, da of William Alexander Noble, MRCVS (d 2002); *Career* J Walter Thompson 1966–69, Winston Churchill fell 1969, mgmnt conslt 1972–84, gen commercial mangr Westland Helicopters Ltd 1978–81, conslt MMG Patricof (venture capital) 1982–84, fndr and chm Nat Telecable Ltd 1984–; fndr and chm: Colt Telecom 1988–92, Telecable One Ltd 1994, DataTrust Corp Ltd 1999–; chm: Chester Square Ltd 1994, Trinity Square Ltd, InfinateFibre Ltd 2001–; co-founder and chm Centre for Marketplace Theology, chief exec European Internet Capital plc 2000, md Openplanet Ltd 2004–; fndr The OPLAN Fndn; Freeman City of London 1967, elected alderman Ward of Bread Street City of London 1995, Liveryman: Worshipful Co of Coopers (Upper Warden 1991, Renter Warden 2001), Worshipful Co of Glass Sellers 1988; FIMgt 1982; *Recreations* music, motor cycling, thinking, chocolate; *Clubs* National; *Style*— Malcolm Matson, Esq; ✉ 77 Andrewes House, London EC2Y 8AY (tel 020 7638 2344, e-mail cityman@city.co.uk); website www.oplan.org

MATTHEW, Christopher Charles Forrest; s of Leonard Douglas Matthew (d 1984), of Wells-next-the-Sea, Norfolk, and Doris Janet Matthew (d 1988); *b* 8 May 1939; *Educ* King's Sch Canterbury, St Peter's Coll Oxford (MA); *m* 19 Oct 1979, Wendy Mary, da of Kenneth Henry Whitaker (d 1987), of Tilford, Surrey; 2 s (Nicholas b 1980, William b 1982), 1 step da (Charlotte b 1970); *Career* writer and broadcaster; columns incl: Punch, Vogue, The Daily Telegraph, The Observer, The Daily Mail; *Radio* chm: Something to Declare, The Travelling Show; presenter: Points of Departure, Invaders, Plain Tales from the Rhododendrons, Cold Print, A Nest of Singing Birds; contrib: Fourth Column, Quote Unquote, Freedom Pass (with Alan Coren); writer: A Portrait of Richard Hillary 1980, Madonna's Plumber 2003, Original Shorts 2005 and 2006; *Television* scripts for The Good Guys (LWT/Havahall Pictures Ltd); *Theatre* Summoned by Betjeman; *Publications* The Times Travel Guide (ed 1972–74), A Different World: Stories of Great Hotels (1974), Diary of a Somebody (1978), Loosely Engaged (1980), The Long-Haired Boy (1980, adapted for TV as A Perfect Hero, 1991), The Crisp Report (1981), Three Men in a Boat (annotated edn with Benny Green, 1982), The Junket Man (1983), How to Survive Middle Age (1983), Family Matters (1987), The Amber Room (1995), A Nightingale Sang in Fernhurst Road (1998), Now We Are Sixty (1999), Knocking On (2001), Now We Are Sixty (and a Bit) (2003), Summoned by Balls (2005), When We Were Fifty (2007); *Recreations* sailing, golfing, walking in the country with a dog, lunching with friends; *Clubs* Aldeburgh Golf, Chelsea Arts; *Style*— Christopher Matthew, Esq; ✉ 35 Drayton Gardens, London SW10 9RY (tel 020 7373 5946, e-mail cmatt@onetel.com)

MATTHEW-WALKER, Robert; s of Samuel Walker (d 1964), of Eltham, and Mary Elizabeth Walker; *b* 23 July 1939; *Educ* St Olave's GS, Goldsmiths Coll, London Coll of Music, London Coll of Printing; *m* 27 Dec 1969, Lynn Sharon, da of Kenneth Herbert Alfred Andrews (d 1981), of Bromley, Kent; 1 s (Paul b 1971); *Career* Nat Serv RASC 1959–62; private composition study with W Darius Milhaud Paris 1962–63, co sec Thom and Cook Ltd 1963–70, head of Classical Dept CBS Records UK 1971–74, dir mktg CBS Records 1974, dir of masterworks Europe CBS 1974–75, head of Classical Dept RCA Records 1975–78, fndr Chandos Records Ltd 1979–80, fndr Phoenix Records 1982–87, ed Music and Musicians Int 1984–88; dir classical music: Filmtrax plc 1986–88, AVM Records (UK) 1988–90, Allied West Entertainments Ltd 1989–91; md: Grayways Ltd 1989–91, Alfred Lengnick & Co Ltd 1989–91; first performances of compositions incl: Sonata for String Orch Tehran Orch 1976, Piano Trio Cardiff Festival 1978, Sinfonia Solemnis RNCM 1981, Sinfonia Magna For Organ Cologne Cathedral 1984, Christ On The Road to Emmaus City of London Festival 1988; prodr of over 120 records, awarded Grand Prix Du Disque of Académie Charles Cros Paris (for Sonatas for String Quartet by Brian Ferneyhough) 1980; memb: PRS, Critics' Circle; chm E Lewisham Cons Assoc; *Books* Rachmaninoff - His Life and Times (1980), Muhammad Ali - His Fights In The Ring (1978), Elvis Presley - A Study in Music (1979), Simon and Garfunkel (1984), David Bowie - Theatre of Music (1985), Madonna (1989), The Keller Column (1990), The Symphonies of Robert Simpson (1990), A Composer and the Gramophone - Alun Hoddinott on Record (1993), The Recordings of Edvard Grieg (1993), Edvard Grieg (1993), New World Music (1994), Heartbreak Hotel - The Life and Music of Elvis Presley (1995), Havergal Brian (1995), Cincinnati Interludes (1995); *Recreations* history, politics; *Clubs* National Liberal; *Style*— Robert Matthew-Walker; ✉ 1 Exford Road, London SE12 9HD (tel 020 8857 1582)

MATTHEWMAN, His Hon Keith; QC (1979); s of Lt Frank Matthewman (d 1976), and Elizabeth, *née* Lang (d 1985); *b* 8 January 1936; *Educ* Long Eaton GS, UCL (LLB); *m* 1962, Jane, da of Thomas Maxwell (d 1957); 1 s (Adrian Keith b 1968); *Career* sch teacher Barking Essex then Heanor Derbys 1958–61; called to the Bar Middle Temple 1960; commercial asst (Int Div) Rolls Royce Ltd 1961–62; in practice at the Bar 1962–83 (Midland Circuit, later Midland & Oxford Circuit), recorder of the Crown Court 1979–83, circuit judge (Midland & Oxford Circuit) 1983–2001; memb: Ctee of the Cncl of Her Majesty's Circuit Judges 1984–89, Notts Probation Ctee 1986–2001, Mental Health Review Tbnl (Trent Region) 1993–99; judge appraiser Parole Bd 2002–04 (memb 1996–2002); inaugural pres Friends of the Galleries of Justice (Museum of Law) Nottingham 1998–2007; 12 weekly television appearances in Crimestalker (Central) 1993; external examiner Bar Vocational course Nottingham Law Sch 2000–03; memb (Lab) Heanor UDC 1960–63; newspaper columnist Beeston Express Notts 2004–06; patron: Criminal Justice Assoc, Nottingham Cartoon Festival; *Publications* subject of biography A Judge Too Far (Narvel Annable, 2001); *Recreations* gardening, reading; *Clubs* Victoria (Nottingham), Beeston Fields Golf; *Style*— His Hon Keith Matthewman, QC; ✉ Nottingham Crown Court, Nottingham NG1 7EL

MATTHEWS, Belinda Mary; da of Maj-Gen Richard Eyre Lloyd, CB, CBE, DSO (d 1991), and Gillian, *née* Patterson (d 2006); *b* 26 June 1946, Worksop, Notts; *Educ* Downe House Newbury; *m* 29 Oct 1977, Dr Colin Matthews; 2 da (Jessica Ruth b 22 March 1972, Lucy Imogen b 2 July 1980), 1 s (Daniel John b 29 Sept 1978); *Career* Faber Music Ltd 1966–78; Faber and Faber Ltd: joined 1988, music books ed 1997, editorial dir 2003, memb Bd 2005–; dir Wandsworth Children's Opera Gp 1987–90; ALCM; *Recreations* piano, cello, reading, gardening; *Style*— Mrs Belinda Matthews; ✉ Faber and Faber Ltd, 3 Queen Square, London WC1N 3AU

MATTHEWS, Christopher Wynne (Chris); s of Heilwynne James Matthews (d 1968), and Evelyn Christian, *née* Brodie; *b* 31 October 1955; *Educ* Royal HS Edinburgh, Univ of Newcastle upon Tyne (BA); *m* 11 Nov 2001, Sarah Fiona Watson-James; *Career* Arthur Andersen & Co 1977–82, fin dir Grass Roots Partnership 1982–85, Valin Pollen 1985–88, chief exec Shandwick Consultants 1993–97 (joined 1988), managing ptnr The Hogarth Partnership 1997–; *Recreations* high-level walking, skiing, motorcycling; *Style*— Chris Matthews, Esq; ✉ The Hogarth Partnership, No 1 London Bridge, London SE1 9BG (tel 020 7357 9477, e-mail cmatthews@hogarthpr.co.uk)

MATTHEWS, Dr Colin Herbert; s of Herbert Henry Matthews (d 1975), of London, and Elsie Lillian (d 2006); *b* 13 February 1946; *Educ* Univ of Nottingham (BA, MPhil), Univ of Sussex (DPhil); *m* 29 Oct 1977, Belinda Mary, da of Maj-Gen R E Lloyd, CB, CBE, DSO (d 1991), of Lymington; 2 da (Jessica b 1972, Lucy b 1980), 1 s (Daniel b 1978); *Career* composer; lectr Univ of Sussex 1971–72 and 1976–77; more than ninety compositions since 1968 incl: orchestral Fourth Sonata 1974, Night Music 1977, Landscape 1981, Cello Concerto 1984, Monody 1987, Cortège 1989, Broken Symmetry 1991, Memorial 1993, Cello Concerto No 2 1996, Renewal 1996, Unfolded Order 1999, Aftertones 2000, Pluto 2000, Continuum 2000, Horn Concerto 2001, Reflected Images 2003, Berceuse for Dresden (2005), Turning Point (2006), 24 Debussy Preludes (2006), Alphabicycle order (2007); assoc composer: London Symphony Orch 1991–99, Hallé Orch 2001–; Prince Consort prof of composition Royal Coll of Music 2001–; S Nat Orch Ian Whyte Award 1975, Park Lane Gp Composer Award 1983, Royal Philharmonic Soc Award 1996; dir Holst Estate and Fndn 1973–, memb Cncl and Exec Soc for Promotion of New Music 1981–93 and 1994–2002, tstee Britten Pears Fndn and exec dir Britten Estate 1983–99 (chm 2000–),

M

memb Exec Cncl Aldeburgh Fndn 1984–93, patron Musicians against Nuclear Arms 1986–, fnder NMC Recordings 1988–, dir Performing Right Soc 1992–95, govr RNCM 2000–; distinguished visiting fell Univ of Manchester 2001–; Hon DMus Univ of Nottingham 1998; FRNCM, FRCM; *Style*— Dr Colin Matthews; ✉ c/o Faber Music Ltd, 3 Queen Square, London WC1N 3AU (tel 020 7278 7436, fax 020 7837 8668, e-mail promotion@fabermusic.co.uk)

MATTHEWS, His Hon Judge (William) David; s of Edwin Kenneth William Matthews (d 1970), of Hereford, and Bessie, *née* Raiswell (d 1994); *b* 19 November 1940; *Educ* Wycliffe Coll; *m* 4 Sept 1965, Pauline Georgina May, da of Percival James Lewis; 2 s (Alastair Charles David b 14 Feb 1967, Duncan Kenneth Craig b 30 Jan 1970); *Career* admitted slr 1964, ptnr Messrs T A Matthews Slrs; recorder of the Crown Court 1990, circuit judge (Midland & Oxford Circuit) 1992–; memb Mental Health Review Tbnl 2001–; pres Herefordshire Breconshire and Radnorshire Incorporated Law Soc 1987–88, chm West Mercia Criminal Justice Strategy Ctee 2000–03; memb Law Soc 1964; *Recreations* National Hunt racing, cricket, boating; *Style*— His Hon Judge Matthews; ✉ Queen Elizabeth II Law Courts, Newton Street, Birmingham B4 7NA (tel 0121 681 3300)

MATTHEWS, Jeffery Edward; MBE (2004); s of Henry Edward Matthews (d 1960), and Sybil Frances, *née* Cooke (d 1951); *b* 3 April 1928; *Educ* Alleyn's Sch Dulwich, Brixton Sch of Building (NDD); *m* 12 Sept 1953, (Sylvia Lilian) Christine (d 1994), da of Cecil Herbert William Hoar (d 1974); 1 s (Rory b 1956), 1 da (Sarah Jane b 1958); *Career* graphic designer J Edward Sander 1949–52, pt/t tutor 1952–55, lettering and calligraphy assessor SIAD 1970–; designs for the PO: decimal 'To Pay' labels 1971, font of numerals for definitive stamps 1981, new range of colours for stamps 1987; stamps: United Nations 1965, British Bridges 1968, definitives for Scotland, Wales, NI and IOM 1971, Royal Silver Wedding 1972, 25th Anniversary of the Coronation 1978, London 1980, 80th Birthday of the Queen Mother 1980, Christmas 1980, Wedding of Prince Charles and Lady Diana Spencer 1981, Quincentenary of the College of Arms 1984, 60th Birthday of the Queen 1986, Wedding of Prince Andrew and Sarah Ferguson 1986, Order of the Thistle Tercentenary of Revival 1987, 150th Anniversary of The Penny Black 1990, self-adhesive definitives 1993, The Queen's Beasts 1998, Jeffery Matthews miniature sheet 2000, End of War miniature sheet 2005, Machin definitives 40th Anniversary miniature sheet 2007; also: first day covers, postmarks, presentation packs, souvenir books and posters; designer featured in film Picture to Post 1969; other work incl: title banner lettering and coat of arms Sunday Times 1968, cover design and lettering for official programme Royal Wedding 1981, The Royal Mint commemorative medal Order of the Thistle 1987, Millennium commemorative crown piece 1999/2000, End of War commemorative medal 2005, official heraldry and symbols HMSO, hand-drawn lettering COI, calligraphy, packaging, promotion and book binding designs, logotypes, brand images and hand-drawn lettering; work for various firms incl: Unicover Corp USA, Harrison & Sons Ltd, Metal Box Co, John Dickinson, Reader's Digest Association Ltd, Encyclopaedia Britannica International Ltd, ICI, H R Higgins (Coffee-Man) Ltd; designed stained glass window for Forest Hill Methodist Church (and accompanying film documenting the creative process) 2007; work exhibited in A History of Bookplates in Britain and at V&A Museum 1979; contrib Br Library's Oral History of the Post Office collection 2001; Royal Mail Rowland Hill Award for outstanding contribution 2004, Phillips Gold Medal for Stamp Design 2005; Citizen & Goldsmith of London (Freedom by patrimony) 1949; FCSD 1978, FRSA 1987; *Books* Designers In Britain (contrib 1964, 1971), 45 Wood-Engravers (contrib, 1982), Royal Mail Year Book (contrib, 1984, 1986, 1987, 1998), Queen Elizabeth II - A Jubilee Portrait in Stamps (contrib, 2002); *Recreations* furniture restoration, playing the guitar, gardening, DIY; *Style*— Jeffery Matthews, Esq, MBE

MATTHEWS, Prof John Burr Lumley (Jack); s of Dr John Lumley Matthews (d 1971), of Leamington Spa, and Susan Agnes, *née* Burr (d 1990); *b* 23 April 1935; *Educ* Warwick Sch, St John's Coll Oxford (MA, BSc, DPhil); *m* 28 July 1962, Jane Rosemary, da of Eric Goldsmith (d 1946); 1 s (Roderic John b 1964), 2 da (Susan Jane b 1966, Eleanor Mary b 1971); *Career* Nat Serv 15/19 King's Royal Hussars 1953–55 (served Germany and Malaya); sr scientific offr Oceanographic Laboratory Edinburgh 1964–67, visiting prof Univ of Br Columbia 1977–78, prof of marine biology Univ of Bergen 1978–84 (sr lectr 1967–78), hon prof Univ of Stirling 1988–; hon fell Scottish Assoc for Marine Science 1999– (dep dir 1984–88, dir 1988–96, sec 1988–99), dir Dunstaffnage Marine Laboratory NERC 1989–94; memb: Ctee for Scotland Nature Conservancy Cncl 1989–90, SW Region Bd Scottish Natural Heritage 1991–96 (dep chm 1994–96), Bd and Academic Cncl Univ Highlands Islands Project 1990–96, Sci Advsy Ctee Scottish Natural Heritage 1994–98; sec: Int Assoc of Biological Oceanography 1994–2000, MARS Network of Euro Marine Stations 1994–99; tstee: Int Sch Bergen 1980–84, Oban Hospice 1999–2005, Hebridean Whale and Dolphin Tst 2000– (chm 2001–), Nadair Tst 2003–07; pres Oban Rotary Club 1997–98; fndr fell Inst Contemporary Scotland; FRSE 1988, FRSA 1989; *Books* Freshwater on the Sea (jt ed), Aquatic Life Cycle Strategies (jt ed), Achievements of the Continuous Plankton Reorder Survey and a Vision for its Future (jt ed); author of numerous scientific articles in professional jls; *Recreations* gardening, hill-walking, pethau cymreig; *Style*— Prof Jack Matthews, FRSE; ✉ The Well, 18 Manse Road, Milnathort, Kinross KY13 9YQ (tel 01577 861066, e-mail matthews.oban@tiscali.co.uk)

MATTHEWS, John Waylett; s of Percy Victor Matthews (d 1970), and Phyllis Edith, *née* Waylett; *b* 22 September 1944; *Educ* Forest Sch; *m* 27 May 1972, Lesley Marjorie, da of Alastair Herbert Menzies Halliday; 2 s (Jonathan b 1975, Edward b 1977), 1 da (Anna b 1981); *Career* Dixon Wilson & Co 1962–69, NM Rothschild and Sons 1969–71, dir County NatWest Ltd 1971–88, dep ceo Beazer plc 1988–91 (dep chm 1982–91), ceo Indosuez Capital Ltd 1991–94; chm: Crest Nicholson plc 1996–2007, Mercury Holdings plc 1998–99, Media Systems Ltd 1999–, Regus Gp plc 2002–; dep chm Ludgate Group Ltd 1997– (chm 1991–97); non-exec dir: Ulster Investment Bank Ltd 1988–91, Mithras Investment Trust 1992–94, R W Baird 1995–2002, Perry Group plc 1997–2002, Rotork plc 1998–, SDL plc 2001–, Allied Healthcare Inc 2002–03, Diploma plc 2003–, Center Parcs (UK) Gp plc 2003–; chm Cncl Forest Sch; FCA; *Recreations* golf, tennis, shooting, bridge; *Clubs* City of London, RAC; *Style*— John Matthews, Esq

MATTHEWS, Michael Gough; s of late Cecil Gough Matthews, and Amelia Eleanor Mary Matthews; *b* 12 July 1931; *Educ* Chigwell Sch, Royal Coll of Music; *Career* pianist, teacher and adjudicator of int piano competitions; dip of honour and prize Chopin Int Piano Competition 1955, Italian Govt scholarship 1956, Chopin fellowship Warsaw 1959; Royal Coll of Music: dir Junior Dept and prof of piano 1972–75, registrar 1975, vice-dir 1978–84, dir 1985–93, vice-pres 1997–; dir Assoc Bd of the Royal Schs of Music; music conslt: Jaguar Cars 1995, HM The Sultan of Oman 1995; memb: Nat Youth Orchestra, Royal Philharmonic Soc, Mgmnt Bd London Int String Quartet Competition, Music Study Group EEC, Comité d'Honneur Presence de l'Art Paris, Cncl Purcell Tercentenary Tst; vice-pres: Royal College of Organists, Nat Youth Choir, Herbert Howells Soc; tstee: Ballantine's Music Fndn, Prince Consort Fndn 1993; hon vice-pres Governing Ctee Royal Choral Soc, hon dir The Royal Music Fndn Inc; chm of adjudicators: Awards Ctee Musicians' Benevolent Fund 1994, Royal Over-Seas League 2006–07; Hon FLCM 1976, Hon RAM 1979, ARCO, ARCM, FRCM 1972, FRSAMD 1986, Hon GSM 1987, FRNCM 1991; *Recordings* 3 CDs of piano music by Gabriel Fauré and Johannes Brahms; *Recreations* gardening; *Clubs* Athenaeum; *Style*— Michael Gough Matthews, Esq; ✉ 608 The Bridge, 334 Queenstown Road, London SW8 4NP

MATTHEWS, Paul Bernard; s of Leonard William Matthews, of London, and Noreen Elizabeth Matthews (d 1985); *b* 21 August 1955, Brentwood, Essex; *Educ* St Peter's Sch Bournemouth, UCL (Charlotte Ashby Prize, Andrews Prize, LLB), St Edmund Hall Oxford (BCL), Inns of Court Sch of Law, Univ of London (LLD); *m* 1986, Katie Bradford; *Career* called to the Bar Gray's Inn 1981 (Stuart Cunningham Mackaskie KC Award, Mould scholar); admitted slr: Eng and Wales 1987, Ireland 1997; slr-advocate Eng and Wales 2001; lectr in law UCL 1979–83 (pt/t tutor 1978–79), pt/t tutor St Edmund Hall Oxford 1979–80, barr in private practice 1982–84; Hopkins & Wood: legal asst 1984–87, ptnr 1987–92, conslt 1992–96; conslt slr Withers LLP 1996–; HM coroner City of London 2002– (dep coroner 1994–2002), dep coroner Royal Household 2002–06, dep coroner ad hoc N London 2004–07; visiting lectr: City Univ 1981–84, UCL 1985–86, Inst de Droits des Affaires Univ d'Aix-Marseille 1991–99; visiting prof KCL 1995– (visiting sr lectr 1991–94); memb Coroners Unit Resources Sub-Gp Home Office 2004–05, memb experts gp PRM III-IV EU 2005–, specialist advsr House of Commons Constitutional Affrs Ctee 2006–, coroner memb Review Bodies 2006–; dep chair Tst Law Ctee 2005– (memb Working Party on: Tstee Exoneration Clauses 1997–98, Tstee Indemnities 1998–99); vol N Islington Law Centre 1981–88; memb: Soc of Legal Slrs 1979–, Law Soc of Eng and Wales 1987– (memb Coroner's Courts and Inquests Working Party 2003–), Br Inst of Int and Comparative Law 1989–, Coroner's Soc of Eng and Wales 1994–, Soc of Tst and Estate Practitioners 1996–, Law Soc of Ireland 1997–, Assoc of Contentious Tst Probate Specialists, Slrs' Assoc of Higher Court Advocates 2001–, Seldon Soc 2002–, Stair Soc 2003–, Assoc Il Tst in Italia; tstee David Isaacs Fund 2003–; academician Int Acad of Estate and Tst Law 2004–; Liveryman City of London Slrs' Co 1992–; FRSA 1994, FRSM 2005; *Books* Jervis on Coroners (contrib, 10 edn 1986, 11 edn 1993, and 12 edn 2002), The Jersey Law of Trusts (jtly, 1988, 3 edn 1994), The Jersey Law of Property (jtly, 1991), Disclosure (jtly, 1992, 3 edn 2007), A Guide to the Leasehold Reform, Housing and Urban Development Act 1993 (jtly, 1993), A Practitioner's Guide to the Trusts of Land and Appointment of Trustees Act 1996 (jtly, 1996), Butterworths Business Landlord and Tenant Handbook (co-ed, 1996, 3 edn 2004), Trusts: Migration and Change of Proper Law (1997), Hill and Redman's Law of Landlord and Tenant (contrib, 18 edn 1999), Trust and Estate Disputes (1999), Halsbury's Laws of England (author Mistake, 4 edn reissue 1999 and 2005, and ed Cremation and Burial, 4 edn reissue 2002), Underhill & Hayton's Law of Trusts and Trustees (jt ed, 17 edn 2006); author, co-author, book reviewer and ed of numerous articles in learned jls and professional pubns incl Law Soc's Gazette and Law Quarterly Review; *Recreations* reading, music, local history, cinema, languages; *Clubs* Athenaeum; *Style*— Paul Matthews, Esq; ✉ School of Law, King's College, Strand, London WC2R 2LS (tel 020 7848 1176, e-mail paul.matthews@kcl.ac.uk); Withers LLP, 16 Old Bailey, London EC4M 7EG

MATTHEWS, Prof Paul McMahan; *Educ* St Edmund Hall Oxford (BA), Univ of Oxford (DPhil), Stanford Univ Sch of Med (MD); *Career* intern (med) Stanford Univ Med Center 1986–87; McGill Univ Montreal: asst prof of neurology and neurosurgery and human genetics 1993–96, adjunct prof of neurology 1996–; Univ of Oxford: fell St Edmund Hall 1997–, prof of neurology 1998– (reader 1995–98), head Dept of Clinical Neurology 2004–; dir Oxford Centre for Functional Magnetic Imaging of the Brain 1995–; memb Advsy/Editorial Bd: Brain, Nature, Clinical Neurology, Jl of Neuroimaging, Experimental Brain Research; memb GMC 1995; FRCP(C) 1990, FRCP 2000; *Awards* MRC (Canada) Clinician-Scientist Award 1990, Penfield-McNaughton Award 1990, Barbeau Prize for Neurosciences Research 1990, Baxter Award 1999; *Publications* Diagnostic Tests in Neurology (jtly, 1991), Metabolic Myopathies (jtly, 1995), Functional Magnetic Resonance Imaging: Methods for Neuroscience (jt ed, 2001), The Bard on the Brain (2003); author of numerous peer reviewed papers, invited reviews, chapters in books and letters; *Style*— Prof Paul Matthews; ✉ Neurology Department, The Radcliffe Infirmary, Woodstock Road, Oxford OX2 6HE (tel 01865 222493, fax 01865 222717, e-mail paul@fmrib.ox.ac.uk)

MATTHEWS, Peter John; s of William John Matthews (d 1990), of Norwich, and Pamela Mary, *née* Butt; *b* 6 January 1945; *Educ* Uppingham; *m* 1 Nov 1969, Diana Joan, da of John Randell; 2 s (John Paul b 22 Dec 1972, Michael Robert b 1 Nov 1975); *Career* Arthur Guinness Son & Co Ltd 1963–77: information offr Guinness 1975–77, dir Guinness Publishing 1989–96 (gen mangr 1977–80, editorial dir 1980–84), ed Guinness Book of Records 1991–95 (sports ed 1982–91); media info mangr for athletics Olympic Games Atlanta 1996; chief announcer Athletics Commonwealth Games 1970 and 2002, athletics commentator IAAF 1991– (ITV 1985–97, BBC Radio 1975–85), athletics commentator Sky 2001–; ed Int Athletics Annual 1985–, co-publisher Athletics Int 1993–; chm Nat Union of Track Statisticians; *Books* Guinness Book of Athletics Facts and Feats (1982), Official Book of the 1986 Commonwealth Games (1986), Guinness Encyclopaedia of Sports Records and Results (1987, 1990, 1993 and 1995), Cricket Firsts (with Robert Brooke, 1988), Who's Who in British Athletics (1990), Guinness International Who's Who of Sport (1993), All-Time Greats of British Sport (with Ian Buchanan, 1995), Whitaker's Almanack International Sports Records and Results (1998); *Style*— Peter Matthews, Esq; ✉ 10 Madgeways Close, Great Amwell, Ware, Hertfordshire SG12 9RU (tel 01920 870434, e-mail pmatthews@macunlimited.net)

MATTHEWS, Richard Burnell; s of Robert Matthews (d 2000), and Julia, *née* Watson (d 1993); *b* 10 December 1948, Romford, Essex; *Educ* Endsleigh Sch Colchester, North-East Essex Tech Coll Colchester; *m* 1, 1971, Charlotte Jeffery; 1 s (Merlin b 4 Feb 1973); *m* 2, 1979, Gay Hutchings; 1 s (Robert b 8 May 1984), 1 da (Candice b 30 Jul 1985); *m* 3, 1995, Louise Athron; partner, Denette Wilkinson; *Career* salesman E N Mason 1966–68, fndr Colchester Mktg (later Drinkmade Vending Co) 1968–79, fndr and chm Oyster Marine 1974–; chm: Oyster Properties Ltd, Fox's Marina Ipswich Ltd, Southampton Yacht Services Ltd; Queen's Award for Export Achievement 1991, Queen's Award for Int Trade 2000; former Br rep Offshore Racing Cncl; MInstD; *Recreations* yacht racing and cruising, golf, flying helicopters; *Clubs* West Mersea Yacht, Royal Ocean Racing (formerly Vice-Cdre), Royal Thames Yacht, Royal Corinthian Yacht, Royal NZ Yacht Sqdn, Storm Trysail; *Style*— Richard Matthews, Esq; ✉ The Oyster Group, Fox's Marina, Ipswich, Suffolk IP2 8SA (tel 01473 688888, fax 01473 686861, e-mail rm@oystermarine.com)

MATTHEWS, Suzan Patricia; QC (1993); *Career* called to the Bar Middle Temple 1974; in practice in chambers: Bradford 1974–79, Guildford 1979–2003; recorder of the Crown Court 1995–2003 (asst recorder 1991–95), asst boundary cmmr 1992–2003, dep High Ct judge 1999–; chm: Ctees of Investigation MAFF 1994–2003, Richard Neale Inquiry 2003–04; rep London & SE Regn Gas Consumers Cncl 1987–96; memb: Criminal Injuries Compensation Appeals Panel 1996–2003 (dep chair 2002–03), Criminal Injuries Compensation Bd 1999–2000, Lord Chllr's Advsy Bd on Family Law 1997–2002; chm The Valley Trust; FRSA; *Style*— Her Hon Judge Suzan Matthews, QC; ✉ Kingston Crown Court, 6–8 Penrhyn Road, Kingston upon Thames, Surrey KT1 2BB (tel 0208 240 2500)

MATTHEWS, Timothy John (Tim); s of Kenneth James Matthews, of Kingston, S Devon, and Vera Joan, *née* Fittall; *b* 24 June 1951; *Educ* Plymouth Coll, Peterhouse Cambridge (exhibitioner, BA); *m* Sally Vivien, da of William Tudor Davies; 2 s (Tom Alexander b 14 Sept 1984, James Osborn Louie b 5 Sept 1987); *Career* DHSS: admin trainee 1974, private sec to perm sec 1978–80, princ 1980–84; dist gen administrator Bloomsbury HA 1984–85, gen mangr The Middx Hosp Div Bloomsbury HA 1985–88, dist gen mangr Maidstone HA 1988–91, dist gen mangr W Lambeth HA and chief exec St Thomas' Hosp 1991–93, chief exec Guy's and St Thomas' Hosp NHS Trust 1993–2000, chief exec Highways Agency 2000–03; md Parsons Brinckerhoff Ltd 2003–; dir: Focus Central

London TEC 1997–2001, South Bank Careers 1997–2000, South Bank Employers Gp 1998–2000, John Laing plc 2004–07; memb Cmmn for Integrated Tport 2000–03; MHSM 1985, FIHT 2001; *Clubs* Surrey CCC; *Style—* Tim Matthews, Esq

MATTHIESEN, Patrick David Albert Francis Jonathan; s of Francis Matthiesen, and Olga, *née* Bode; *b* 1 March 1943; *Educ* Harrow, Oriel Coll Oxford (Briscoe Owen scholar, MA), Courtauld Inst of Art London; *m* 4 Oct 2002, Hiromi, da of Gen-Ichi Kaminishi, of Sendai Japan; 2 da (Alexandra, Takara-Julie (twins) b 17 April 2004); *Career* art dealer; supervisor of restoration sculpture project in Florence after floods 1966–67, supervisor in founding Conservation Inst for Sculpture in Venice in liaison with V&A 1968–69, ind art dealer 1970, asst Queensbury Investments Ltd property developers 1970–71; P & D Colnaghi Ltd: assoc ind conslt 1972, i/c Research Dept 1972–73, gen mangr 1973–75, dir Old Master Paintings Dept 1976–77; fndr, chm and md Matthiesen Fine Art Ltd 1978–; exhibitions mounted and publications by Matthiesen Fine Art incl: Important Italian Paintings 1600–1700 1981, Early Italian Paintings and Works of Art 1300–1480 1983, From Borso to Cesare d'Este: School of Ferrara 1450–1628 1984, Around 1610: The Onset of Baroque 1985, Varlin 1985, Baroque III 1986, Paintings from Emila 1500–1700 1987, The Settecento: Italian Rococo and Early Neoclassical Paintings 1700–1800 1987, A Selection of French Paintings 1700–1840 1989, Louis Léopold Boilly's 'L'Entrée du Jardin Turc' 1991, Fifty Paintings 1535–1825 1993, Paintings 1600–1912 1996, Gold Backs 1250–1480 1996, An Eye on Nature 1997, Collectanea: 1700–1800 1998, An Eye on Nature II - The Gallic Prospect 1999 and European Paintings 2001 (in association with Stair Sainty Matthiesen Inc), 2001: An Art Odyssey 2001, A Del Sarto Rediscovered 2002, Il Porto di Ripetta 2002, Chardin's Têtes d'Études au Pastel 2003, Virtuous Virgins 2004, Bertin's Ideal Landscapes 2004, Polidoro da Caravaggio 2005, Jacobello del Fiore 2007; chm and fndr The Matthiesen Fndn, hon sec Sparkman & Stephens Assoc 2002–07; *Recreations* gardening, music, travel, sailing, skiing, riding, good food and wine; *Clubs* RAC; *Style—* Patrick Matthiesen, Esq; ✉ Matthiesen Gallery, 7–8 Mason's Yard, Duke Street, London SW1 (tel 020 7930 2437, fax 020 7930 1387, e-mail gallery@matthiesengallery.com, website www.thematthiesenfoundation.org and www.matthiesengallery.com)

MATTINGLY, Prof David John; s of Harold Mattingly, of Cambridge, and Erica, *née* Stuart; *b* 18 May 1958, Nottingham; *Educ* Lawnswood Sch Leeds, Univ of Manchester (BA, PhD); *m* 30 May 1981, Jennifer, *née* Warrell-Bowring; 2 da (Rebecca Jane b 5 March 1987, Susanna Frances b 27 Nov 1989), 1 s (Douglas Robert b 5 Nov 1993); *Career* Br Acad postdoctoral fell Univ of Oxford 1986–89, asst prof Dept of Classical Studies Univ of Michigan 1989–91; Sch of Archaeology and Ancient History Univ of Leicester: lectr 1991–95, reader 1995–98, prof of Roman archaeology 1998–; chm Soc for Libyan Studies 1996–2001; James R Wiseman Book Award 2001; FSA 1993, FBA 2003; *Books* incl: Town and Country in Roman Tripolitania. Papers in Honour of Olwen Hackett (jt ed, 1985), Libya. Research in Archaeology, Environment, History and Society 1969–1989 (jt ed, 1989), An Atlas of Roman Britain (jtly, 1990, revised edn 1993), Leptiminus (Lamta): A Roman Port City in Tunisia, Report no 1 (jtly, 1992), Tripolitania (1995), Farming the Desert. The UNESCO Libyan Valleys Archaeological Survey. Volume I, Synthesis (jtly, 1996), Farming the Desert. The UNESCO Libyan Valleys Archaeological Survey. Volume II, Gazetteer and Pottery (princ ed, 1996), Dialogues in Roman Imperialism. Power, Discourse and Discrepant Experience in the Roman Empire (ed, 1997), Life, Death and Entertainment in Ancient Rome (jt ed, 1999), Geographical Information Systems and Landscape Archaeology (jt ed, 1999), Economies beyond Agriculture in the Classical World (jt ed, 2000), Leptiminus (Lamta): Report no 2, The East Baths, Cemeteries, Kilns, Venus Mosaic, Site Museum and Other Sites (jtly, 2001), The Archaeology of Fazzan. Volume I, Synthesis (jtly, 2003), An Imperial Possession: Britain and the Roman Empire (2006), The Libyan Desert: Natural Resources and Cultural Heritage (jt ed, 2006), The Cambridge Dictionary of Classical Civilization (jt ed, 2006), The Archaeology of Fazzan Vol 2: Site Gazetteer, Pottery and Other Finds (jtly, 2007); *Recreations* men's reading group, mediterranean cuisine, family; *Style—* Prof David Mattingly; ✉ School of Archaeology and Ancient History, University of Leicester, Leicester LE1 7RH (tel 0116 252 2610, fax 0116 252 5005, e-mail djm7@le.ac.uk)

MATTINSON, Deborah Susan; da of R R Mattinson, of Cheadle Hulme, Cheshire, and J M Mattinson; *b* 17 September 1956, Darlington, Co Durham; *Educ* Cheadle Hulme Sch, Univ of Bristol (LLB); *m* 1 July 1989, David Pelly; 1 da (Clara b 18 Sept 1990), 2 s (Theo b 10 Feb 1992, Francis b 19 April 1994); *Career* advtg account dir 1978–85, Gould Mattinson (political consultancy) 1985–89, GMA Monitor (research consultancy) 1989–92, jt ceo Opinion Leader Research 1992–; jt chair Chime Research Gp; cmmr Equal Opportunities Cmmn; tstee Green Alliance; MMRS; *Recreations* reading, walking, relaxing with family; *Style—* Ms Deborah Mattinson; ✉ Opinion Leader Research, 4th Floor, Holborn Gate, 330 High Holborn, London WC1V 7QG (tel 020 7861 3080, fax 020 7861 3081, e-mail dmattinson@opinionleader.co.uk)

MATTISON, John Eric; s of Alfred James Mattison (d 1973), of Lingwood, Norfolk, and Mildred Edith, *née* Temperley (d 1974); *b* 12 August 1940; *Educ* City of Norwich Sch, LSE (BSc); *m* March 1964, Margaret Jane, da of Patrick Malervy; 3 s (John Patrick b 17 March 1965, James Gerard b 24 July 1966, Nicholas Frank b 30 Nov 1970); 2 da (Sally Jane b 22 March 1968, Catherine Temperley b 5 Sept 1975); *Career* financial journalist Investors' Chronicle, Evening Standard and Sunday Times 1962–70; dir: McLeish Associates 1970–80, Lopex Public Relations 1980–85, Hill & Knowlton 1985–88; chief exec Burson-Marsteller Financial 1988–93, dir Shandwick Consultants 1993–95; chm Mattison Public Relations 1995–; former memb Cncl CIPR; *Books* Bluffer's Guide to Finance (1968); *Recreations* golf, sailing; *Style—* John Mattison, Esq

MATTOCK, John Clive; s of late Raymond Jack Mattock, of Sidmouth, Devon, and Eva Winifred Zoë, *née* Ward; *b* 21 January 1944; *Educ* Dartford GS; *m* 1985, Susan, da of Richard Clulow, of Harlow, Essex; 2 s (Anthony b 1986, Christopher b 1988); *Career* stockbroker; ptnr Fiske and Co 1975–88; dep chm: Carlisle Group plc 1985–90, Peak Tst Ltd 1988, Corporate Services Group plc 1989; dir: Stalwart Assurance Group plc 1986–89, Care First plc 1986–89, Seymour Pierce Gp plc 1991–2006, Ellis Stockbrokers 2006–; FCA 1967; *Recreations* tennis, swimming administration; *Clubs* Bexley Lawn Tennis (vice-pres), East Grinstead Swimming (dep chm); *Style—* J C Mattock, Esq; ✉ Seymour Pierce Ellis, Talisman House, Jubilee Walk, Three Bridges, Crawley, West Sussex RH10 1LQ (tel 01293 517744)

MAUD, Hon Sir Humphrey John Hamilton; KCMG (1993, CMG 1982); s of Baron Redcliffe-Maud (Life Peer; d 1982), and Jean, *née* Hamilton (d 1993); *b* 17 April 1934; *Educ* Eton, King's Coll Cambridge, Nuffield Coll Oxford; *m* 1963, Maria Eugenia Gazitua; 3 s; *Career* Nat Serv Coldstream Gds 1953–55; instr in classics Univ of Minnesota 1958–59; joined FO 1959, Madrid 1961–63, Havana 1963–65, FCO 1966–67, seconded to Cabinet Office 1968–69, Paris 1970–74, sabbatical at Nuffield Coll Oxford studying economics 1974–75, head of financial rels FCO 1975–79, min Madrid 1979–82, ambass to Luxembourg 1982–85, asst under-sec of state (int economic affairs and trade rels) FCO 1985–88, high cmmr to Cyprus 1988–90, ambass to Argentina 1990–93; Cwlth dep sec-gen (economic and social) 1993–99; chm: Emerging Markets Partnership-Financial Advisers 1999–2002, Cwlth Disaster Management Agency Ltd 1999–, Pall Mall Initiatives 2001–; advsr to DG VIII European Cmmn 1999–2000; memb S Atlantic Council 2004–; dir Orch of St John's 1994–2000, tstee Parkhouse Award 1995–, tstee Prince Consort Fndn 2002–07; memb Ctee Queen's Medal for Music 2005–; FRCM 2002 (memb Cncl 1993–2002); *Recreations* music ('cellist NYO 1949–52), golf, bird watching; *Clubs* Oxford and Cambridge, Garrick, Royal Mid-Surrey; *Style—* The Hon Sir Humphrey Maud, KCMG; ✉ 31 Queen Anne's Grove, Bedford Park, London W4 1HW (tel 020 8994 2808, e-mail hmaud@cdma.org.uk)

MAUDE, Rt Hon Francis Anthony Aylmer; PC (1992), MP; yr s of Baron Maude of Stratford-upon-Avon, TD, PC (Life Peer; d 1993) and Barbara Elizabeth Earnshaw, *née* Sutcliffe (d 1997); *b* 4 July 1953; *Educ* Abingdon Sch, Corpus Christi Coll Cambridge (BA); *m* 1984, Christina Jane, yr da of A Peter Hadfield, of Copthorne, Shrewsbury; 3 da (Julia Elizabeth Barbara b 26 Dec 1986, Cecily Mary Anne b 29 July 1988, Lydia Helen Grace b 28 Feb 1996), 2 s (Henry Peter Angus b 10 Sept 1990, Alastair Timothy Charles b 17 March 1994); *Career* called to the Bar Inner Temple 1977 (Law scholarship, Forster Boulton Prize), barr in chambers of Sir Michael Havers, QC, MP (later Lord Havers); memb Westminster City Cncl 1978–84; MP (Cons): Warwickshire N 1983–92, Horsham 1997–; PPS to Hon Peter Morrison as min of state for Employment 1984–85, a Govt whip 1985–87; Parly under sec of state: corporate and consumer affrs DTI 1987–88, corporate affrs 1988–89; min of state FCO 1989–90, financial sec to the Treasy 1990–92; shadow culture sec 1997–98, shadow chllr of the Exchequer 1998–2000, shadow foreign sec 2000–01, chm Cons Pty 2005–07, shadow min for the Cabinet Office and shadow chllr of the Duchy of Lancaster 2007–; chm HM Govt Deregulation Task Force 1994–97; advsr to Hongkong and Shanghai Banking Corp on bid for Midland Bank 1992, a dir of corporate finance (head of Privatisation Unit) Salomon Brothers International 1992–93, head of privatisation and an md Morgan Stanley 1993–97; non-exec chm: Prestbury Holdings plc 2002–, Incepta 2004–06; non-exec dir: Asda Group plc 1992–99, Brit Insurance 1994–99, Benfield Gp 1999– (dep chm 2003–); chm of govrs Abingdon Sch 1994–2003; *Recreations* skiing, cricket, music, opera; *Style—* The Rt Hon Francis Maude, MP; ✉ House of Commons, London SW1A 0AA (tel 020 7219 3000)

MAUDSLAY, Richard Henry; CBE (2006); s of Cecil Winton Maudslay (d 1969), and Charity Magdalen, *née* Johnston (d 1995); *b* 19 November 1946; *Educ* Christ's Hosp, Univ of Edinburgh (BSc); *m* 3 Aug 1968, Rosalind Elizabeth, da of James Slater Seville; 2 da (Diana Elizabeth b 29 Jan 1973, Helen Catherine b 4 Sept 1974); *Career* grad trainee Scottish Electrical Trg Scheme 1968–69, systems analyst Parsons Peebles Ltd 1969–71, systems mangr Reyrolle Belmos Ltd 1971–72, systems and programming mangr Parsons Peebles Ltd 1972–74, prodn mangr Parsons Peebles Power Transformers 1974–78, general mangr Transformadores Parsons Peebles de Mexico 1978–85; md: NEI Parsons Ltd 1985–92, Rolls-Royce Industrial Power Group 1992–97 (memb Bd Rolls-Royce plc 1994–97); dep chm Hardy & Greys Ltd 1999–; non-exec dir: Domnick Hunter Gp plc 2000–05, The NG Bailey Organisation Ltd 2001–; chm: NE Science and Industry Cncl 2004–, Dstl (Defence Science and Technol Lab) 2005–; FREng 1994, FIEE; *Recreations* music; *Clubs* Royal Over-Seas League; *Style—* Richard Maudslay, Esq, CBE, FREng; ✉ Hardy & Greys Ltd, Willowburn, Alnwick, Northumberland NE66 2PF (tel 01665 602771, fax 01665 602225)

MAULEVERER, (Peter) Bruce; QC (1985); s of Maj Algernon Arthur Mauleverer (d 1979), of Poole, Dorset, and Hazel Mary, *née* Flowers (d 1983); *b* 22 November 1946; *Educ* Sherborne, Univ of Durham (BA); *m* 7 Aug 1971, Sara, da of Dr Michael Hudson-Evans, of St Maughans, Gwent; 2 s (Edward b 1972, Barnaby b 1974), 2 da (Harriet b 1977, Clementine b 1982); *Career* called to the Bar Inner Temple 1969 (bencher 1993); recorder of the Crown Court 1985–2004, dep judge of the High Court 1992–2004, head of chambers 1992–2000; hon sec gen Int Law Assoc 1986–93 (vice-chm 1993–); vice-pres Int Social Science Cncl (UNESCO) 1998–2000, tstee UNICEF UK 2002; FCIArb 1997; *Recreations* sailing, skiing; *Clubs* Garrick, Royal Ocean Racing; *Style—* Bruce Mauleverer, Esq, QC; ✉ Eliot Vale House, 8 Eliot Vale, Blackheath, London SE3 0UW (tel 020 8852 2070, fax 020 8852 4614, e-mail bruce@mauleverer.com)

MAUNDERS, Prof Keith Terrence; s of Roy Keith Maunders, of Newport, Gwent, and Hilda Violet, *née* Brett; *b* 11 September 1939; *Educ* Newport High Sch, Univ of Hull (BSc); *m* 26 July 1969, Julie, da of James E Mantle, of Leeds; 2 da (Helen b 1976, Hannah b 1980); *Career* prof of business fin and accounting Univ of Leeds 1978–89, prof of accounting Univ of Hull 1989–2004, academic dir Central European Univ Business Sch 2004–06, head Sch of Accounting and Finance Univ of the South Pacific 2006–; visiting prof: Univ of Texas 1985, Univ of Sydney 1986, ANU 1989; pres Stuttgart Inst of Mgmnt and Technol 1998–2000; gen sec Br Accounting Assoc; FCCA; *Books* Accounting Information Disclosure and Collective Bargaining (1977), Corporate Social Reporting (1987); *Recreations* birdwatching; *Style—* Prof Keith Maunders; ✉ School of Accounting and Finance, University of the South Pacific, Suva, Fiji (tel 00 679 323 2240, fax 00 679 323 1506, e-mail maunders_k@usp.ac.fj)

MAUNDRELL, John William; s of Rev Canon Wolseley David Maundrell, of Chichester, W Sussex, and Barbara Katharine, *née* Simmons (d 1985); *b* 27 September 1955; *Educ* Winchester, Courtauld Inst of Art Univ of London (BA); *m* 31 Oct 1987 (m dis 2003), Hazel, da of Francis Walter Monck; 1 da (Alexandra Katharine b 30 Sept 1989), 1 s (William Frederick b 22 Nov 1991); m 2, 21 Feb 2004, Amanda, da of Christopher Horace Ireland; *Career* articled clerk Deloitte Haskins & Sells 1979–82, qualified chartered accountant 1982, asst dir County Bank Ltd/County NatWest 1986–87 (joined 1982), dir Gilbert Eliott Corporate Finance Ltd 1989–90 (asst dir 1987–89), dir Rea Brothers Limited 1991–93; co sec Hobson plc 1994–96, dir Utilitec plc (formerly Cruden Bay plc) 1996–97, dir Corporate Advsy Services 1998–, various public co directorships 1998–; ACA; *Recreations* mountaineering, swimming, tennis; *Style—* John Maundrell, Esq; ✉ Box Cottage, Hempstead, Saffron Walden, Essex CB10 2PD (tel 01799 599268, e-mail jwmbox@aol.com)

MAUNSELL, Michael Brooke; s of Capt Terence Augustus Ker Maunsell, RN (d 1972), of Weybridge, Surrey, and Elizabeth, *née* Brooke (d 1974); *b* 29 January 1942; *Educ* Monkton Combe Sch, Gonville & Caius Coll Cambridge (MA, LLB); *m* 1, 7 Aug 1965 (m dis 1986), Susan Pamela, da of George Cruickshank Smith (d 1969), of Attenborough, nr Nottingham; m 2, 8 Aug 1986, (Caroline) Harriet Maunsell, OBE, da of Prof Geoffrey Sharman Dawes, CBE, of Oxford; *Career* solicitor; ptnr: Lovell White & King 1971–88 (joined 1965), Lovell White Durrant 1988–97 (jt managing ptnr 1993–97); tstee Highgate Cemetery Charity 1988–95; sr fell Br Inst of Int and Comparative Law 1998–2000; memb Determinations Panel Pensions Regulator 2005–; administrator City Solicitor's Educnl Tst 2000–07; govr Bishopsgate Fndn 2002– (dep chm 2007); Liveryman Worshipful Co of Slrs 1980; memb Law Soc 1967; *Recreations* walking, watching birds, opera, travelling; *Style—* Michael Maunsell, Esq; ✉ 41 Colebrooke Row, London N1 8AF (tel 020 7226 7128, fax 020 7226 6532)

MAURICE, Clare Mary; da of Antony Colin Deans Rankin, of Manton, Wilts, and Barbara, *née* Vernon; *b* 25 February 1954; *Educ* Sherborne Sch for Girls, Univ of Birmingham (LLB); *m* 20 Dec 1980, Ian James Maurice, s of Douglas Creyke Maurice (d 1968); 2 da (Anna b 10 March 1987, Kate b 8 Oct 1989); *Career* admitted slr 1978; Allen & Overy: articled 1976, asst slr 1978, ptnr 1985–, head of private client dept 2002–; dir: English Touring Opera 1995–2001, United Response in Business Ltd 1999–2001; chm St Bartholomew's and the Royal London Charitable Fndn 2001–; memb Int Acad of Estate and Trust Law; *Recreations* theatre, racing, travel; *Clubs* Reform; *Style—* Mrs Clare Maurice; ✉ 33 Norland Square, London W11 4PU (tel 020 7221 0962)

MAURICE-WILLIAMS, Robert Stephen; s of Dr Hubert Cecil Maurice-Williams, OBE (d 1981), of Southampton, and Eileen Florence, *née* Lauder; *b* 14 June 1942; *Educ* Winchester, Pembroke Coll Cambridge (MA, MB BChir), St Thomas' Hosp Med Sch; *m* 9 Sept 1968, Elizabeth Anne, da of Dr Swithin Pinder Meadows, of London; 3 da (Francesca Clare

Louise b 1971, Harriet Elizabeth Anne b 1974, Vanessa Christina Alice b 1982), 1 s (Julian Robert Cecil b 1979); *Career* registrar in neurosurgery Guy's Maudsley Neurosurgical Unit 1971–73, sr registrar in neurosurgery Bart's 1973–77, conslt neurosurgn Brook Hosp 1977–80, sr conslt neurosurgn The Royal Free Hosp 1980–; papers on surgery and physiology of the central nervous system; ed Br Jl of Neurosurgery 1992–99, memb Ct of Examiners RCS 1992–99; fell Hunterian Soc 1980; FRCS 1971, FRCP 1990 (MRCP 1973); *Books* Spinal Degenerative Disease (1981), Subarachnoid Haemorrhage (1988); *Recreations* walking; *Clubs* Athenaeum, Pitt (Cambridge); *Style*— Robert Maurice-Williams, Esq; ✉ Royal Free Hospital, Regional Neurosurgical Unit, London NW3 2QG (tel 020 7794 0500 ext 3356/3357); Neurosurgical Unit, Wellington Hospital, London NW8 9LE (tel 020 7483 5102)

MAVER, Prof Thomas Watt; *b* 10 March 1938; *Educ* Univ of Glasgow (BSc, PhD); *Career* Univ of Strathclyde: personal prof 1974–80, chair of computer-aided design 1980–2003, dir of grad sch Dept of Architecture and Building Science 1992–2002, vice-dean Faculty of Engrg 1996–2001, emeritus prof 2003–; hon prof Glasgow Sch of Art 2006–; Royal Soc Esso Gold Medal; Hon FRIAS, hon fell Design Research Soc; *Style*— Prof Thomas Maver; ✉ 8 Kew Terrace, Glasgow G12 0TD (tel 0141 339 7185, e-mail t.w.maver@strath.ac.uk)

MAVOR, Michael Barclay; CVO (1983); s of William Ferrier Mavor (d 1997), and Sheena Watson, *née* Barclay (d 1995); *b* 29 January 1947; *Educ* Loretto, St John's Coll Cambridge (MA); *m* 20 Aug 1970, (Jane) Elizabeth, da of Albert Sucksmith (d 1959), of Lima, Peru; 1 da (Veronica b 5 Oct 1977), 1 s (Alexander b 31 Oct 1981); *Career* Woodrow Wilson fell Northwestern Univ Illinois 1969–72, asst master Tonbridge Sch 1972–78, course tutor Open Univ 1974–76; headmaster: Gordonstoun 1979–90, Rugby Sch 1990–2001, Loretto Sch 2001–; chm HMC 1997; memb Queen's Body Guard for Scotland (Royal Co of Archers); *Recreations* fishing, golf, painting, theatre; *Clubs* Hawks' (Cambridge); *Style*— Michael Mavor, Esq, CVO; ✉ Loretto School, Musselburgh, East Lothian EH21 7RE (tel 0131 653 4441, fax 0131 653 4445, e-mail mbmavor@loretto.com)

MAVROSKOUFIS, Dr Filippos; s of Simeon Mavroskoufis, of Thessaloniki, Greece, and Leontia, *née* Vassilakaki; *b* 15 August 1952; *Educ* Thessaloniki HS, Dental Sch Aristotelion Univ of Thessaloniki (DDS), UCL (MSc, PhD), Univ of Lund Malmö; *m* 25 May 1985, Janice Gibson, da of John Sailes Clark, and Margaret, *née* Fleming; 1 s (Simeon b 30 July 1985), 2 da (Antigoni b 15 July 1989, Elektra b 19 Aug 1991); *Career* UCH: registrar Prosthetics Dept Dental Sch 1977–78, registrar Community Med Dept 1978–79, involved in teaching of prosthetic dentistry and treating of patients Dental Sch 1977–83; in general practice: pt/t 1981–83, full-time 1983–; in Harley St 1988–; presented 3 scientific papers to dental confs of Euro Prosthodontic Assoc, published 6 scientific papers in dental jls of Europe and America; memb: Br Soc for Study of Prosthetic Dentistry 1977, Euro Prosthodontic Assoc 1977, Gen Dental Practitioners Assoc 1989, Hellenic Soc of Professional People and Scientists in GB, Hellenic Med Soc in GB, Macedonian Soc of GB (vice-pres 1996–99, pres 1999–2001), Int Coll of Prosthodontists 1998; *Recreations* basketball, opera, stamp collecting, cooking, debating, skiing; *Clubs* YMCA; *Style*— Dr Filippos Mavroskoufis; ✉ 22 Mercers Road, London N19 4PJ (tel 020 7272 5200); 44 Harley Street, London W1N 1AD (tel 020 7580 5828, fax 020 7255 1492, e-mail fm@harleystreetsmile.co.uk, website www.harleystreetsmile.co.uk)

MAW, (John) Nicholas; s of Clarence Frederick Maw (d 1967), and Helen, *née* Chambers (d 1950); *b* 5 November 1935, Grantham, Lincs; *Educ* Royal Acad of Music; *Partner* Maija-Leena, *née* Silvennoinen; 1 da (Natasha b 1963), 1 s (Adrian Lindsay (Louis) b 1964); *Career* composer; former tutor in composition: Royal Acad of Music, Univ of Cambridge, Univ of Exeter, Yale Sch of Music, Boston Univ, Milton Avery Grad Sch for the Arts Bard Coll NY; currently prof of composition Peabody Conservatory of Music Baltimore MD; former memb: Arts Panel Arts Cncl of GB, Cncl Performing Right Soc; fndr memb and first chm Assoc of Professional Composers; fell commoner Trinity Coll Cambridge 1966; FRAM 1973; *Compostions* orchestral works incl: Scenes and Arias 1962, Sinfonia 1966, Sonata for Strings and Two Horns 1967, Odyssey 1972–87, Life Studies 1973–76, Serenade 1973–77, Summer Dances 1981, Spring Music 1982–83, Sonata Notturna 1985, Little Concert 1987, The World in the Evening 1988, Shahnama 1992, Concerto for Violin 1993, Voices of Memory 1995, Dance Scenes 1995, Concerto for Cor Anglais 2004; chamber music and ensemble works incl: Chamber Music 1962, Flute Quartet 1981, Ghost Dances 1988, Roman Canticle 1989 and 1991, Piano Trio 1990–91, The Head of Orpheus 1992; string quartets incl: String Quartet No 1 1965, String Quartet No 2 1982, String Quartet No 3 1994, Intrada 2001; instrumental works incl: Essay 1961, Personae I-III 1974, Night Thoughts 1982, Little Suite 1984, Personae IV-VI 1985–86, Music of Memory 1989 and 1991, Cadenzas to Mozart's Piano Concerto K491 1991, Sonata for solo violin 1996–97, Stanza 1997, Narration 2001; choral works incl: Three Hymns 1989, One Foot In Eden, Still I Stand 1990, Swete Jesu 1992, Hymnus 1995–96; vocal works incl: Five American Folksongs 1989, Roman Canticle 1989 and 1991, The Head of Orpheus 1992; wind band works incl American Games 1991; stage works incl: The Rising of the Moon 1970, Sophie's Choice 2002; *Commissions* incl: BBC, ROH, Barbican, South Bank Summer Music Festival, Bath Festival, Lichfield Festival, King's Lynn Festival, Norwich Festival, Cheltenham Festival, LSO, Philharmonia Orch, London Sinfonietta, English Chamber Orch, Northern Sinfonietta, Nash Ensemble, Philadelphia Orch, St Luke's Orch of NY, Da Capo Ensemble, Chamber Music Soc of Lincoln Center; *Performances* in America incl: Philadelphia Orch, Chicago Symphony Orch, San Francisco Symphony Orch, Pittsburgh Symphony Orch, St Louis Orch, Nat Symphony Orch Washington DC, Indianapolis Symphony Orch, Baltimore Symphony Orch, Minnesota Orch, St Luke's Orch, American Symphony Chamber Orch, Seattle Symphony New Music Series, Twentieth Century Consort Washington DC, Boston Musica Viva, Da Capo Ensemble, Chamber Music Soc of Lincoln Center, Aspen Festival; in Europe incl: Deutsche Oper Berlin, Vienna Volksoper, BBC Symphony Orchestras, Royal Opera House Covent Garden, Philharmonia, London Philharmonic, London Symphony, the Nash, Acad of St Martin's in the Field, English Chamber Orchestra, Bath Festival, Aldeburgh Festival; *Recordings* incl: Odyssey, Violin Concerto, Dance Scenes, Shahnama, Little Concert, Sonata Notturna, Hymnus, Life Studies, Scenes & Arias, Sinfonia, Sonata for Strings and Two Horns, American Games, La Vita Nuova, The Voice of Love, String Quartet No 1, Chamber Music for Wind and Piano, Piano Trio, Flute Quartet, Ghost Dances, Roman Canticle, Night Thoughts, Sonata for Solo Violin, One Foot In Eden, Still I Stand, Third String Quartet; *Awards* Lili Boulanger Prize 1959, Midsummer Prize City of London 1980, Sudler Int Wind Band Prize (for American Games) 1991, Elise L Stoeger Prize for Composers of Chamber Music Chamber Music Soc of Lincoln Center 1993; *Style*— Nicholas Maw, Esq; ✉ c/o Sally Cavender, Faber Music, 3 Queen Square, London WC1N 3AU (tel 020 7833 7926, fax 020 7833 7939, e-mail sally.cavender@fabermusic.com)

MAWER, Sir Philip John Courtney; kt (2002); *b* 30 July 1947; *Educ* Hull GS, Univ of Edinburgh (MA), Univ of London (External Dip Public Admin); *m* 1972, Mary Ann, *née* Moxon; 1 s, 2 da; *Career* sr pres Student Representative Cncl Univ of Edinburgh 1969–70; Home Office: joined 1971, private sec to Min of State 1974–76, princ 1976–83 (Nuffield and Leverhulme travelling fell 1978–79), sec Lord Scarman's Inquiry into Brixton Disturbances 1981, asst sec/head of industrial rels Prison Dept 1984–87, princ private sec to Home Sec 1987–89, under sec Cabinet Office 1989–90; C of E: sec gen Gen Synod 1990–2002, sec gen Archbishops' Cncl 1999–2002; Parly Cmmr for Standards 2002–; hon lay canon St Albans Cathedral 2003–; Hon DLitt Univ of Hull 2006; FRSA 1991; *Recreations* family and friends; *Style*— Sir Philip Mawer; ✉ House of Commons, London SW1A 0AA (tel 020 7219 0311, fax 020 7219 0490, e-mail mawerp@parliament.uk)

MAWHINNEY, Baron (Life Peer UK 2005), of Peterborough in the County of Cambridgeshire; Sir Brian Stanley Mawhinney; kt (1997), PC (1994); s of Stanley Mawhinney; *b* 26 July 1940; *Educ* Royal Belfast Academical Inst, Queen's Univ Belfast (BSc), Univ of Michigan (MSc), Univ of London (PhD); *m* 1965, Betty Louise Oja; 2 s, 1 da; *Career* asst prof of radiation res Univ of Iowa 1968–70; lectr and sr lectr Royal Free Hosp Sch of Med 1970–84; memb: MRC 1980–83, Gen Synod 1985–90; pres Cons Trade Unionists 1987–90; Parly candidate (Cons) Stockton-on-Tees Oct 1974; MP (Cons): Peterborough 1979–97, Cambridgeshire NW 1997–2005; PPS to Barney Hayhoe (as Min of State Treasury) 1982–84, PPS to Rt Hon Tom King (as Sec of State for Employment then NI) 1984–86, Parly under sec of state NI Office 1986–90, min of state for NI 1990–92, min of state Dept of Health 1992–94, sec of state for tport 1994–95, chm Cons Pty 1995–97, Cabinet min without portfolio 1995–97, shadow home sec 1997–98; chm The Football League 2003–; *Publications* In the Firing Line, Conflict and Christianity in Northern Ireland (with Ron Wells); *Style*— The Rt Hon the Lord Mawhinney, PC; ✉ House of Lords, London SW1A 0PW

MAWREY, Richard Brooks; QC (1986); s of Philip Stephen Mawrey, of Benson, Oxon, and Alice Brooks, *née* Blezard; *b* 20 August 1942; *Educ* Rossall Sch, Magdalen Coll Oxford (Eldon law scholar, BA, MA), Gray's Inn (Albion Richardson scholar); *m* 18 Sept 1965, Gillian Margaret, da of Francis Butt (d 1985); 1 da (Eleanor Frances b 1977); *Career* barr; called to the Bar Gray's Inn 1964 (bencher 2004); lectr in law: Magdalen Coll Oxford 1964–65, Trinity Coll Oxford 1965–69; recorder of the Crown Court 1986– (asst recorder 1982–86), dep High Court judge 1994–; co-fndr and tstee Historic Gardens Fndn, chm Oxfordshire Gardens Tst; *Books* Computers and the Law (1988); *Recreations* opera, history, cooking; *Style*— Richard B Mawrey, Esq, QC; ✉ 2 Harcourt Buildings, Temple, London EC4Y 9DB (tel 020 7583 9020, fax 020 7583 2686)

MAWSON, Dr David Charles; s of Richard Mawson, and Alice Margaret, *née* Greenhalgh (d 1997); *b* 8 April 1947; *Educ* Aldenham, UCH London (MB BS, DPM); *m* 3 Oct 1970, Mina Mawson; 2 s (Benjy b 1971, Ben b 1977), 1 da (Laura b 1980); *Career* conslt forensic psychiatrist Broadmoor Hosp and sr lectr Inst of Psychiatry 1981–86; med dir: Moss Side Hosp 1986–89, AMI Stockton Hall 1989–91; ind practice in forensic psychiatry 1991–93; conslt forensic psychiatrist: Broadmoor Hosp 1993–98 (latterly dir of Med Servs), Maudsley Hosp 1998; memb Parole Bd of England and Wales 2001–; author of chapters and articles on general and forensic psychiatry; DPM 1976, FRCPsych 1989 (MRCPsych 1976); *Style*— Dr David Mawson

MAX, Robert Ian; s of Michael G Max, and Wendy, *née* Segal; *b* 7 February 1968; *Educ* St Paul's, Royal Acad of Music (GRSM, DipRam, LRAM), Royal Northern Coll of Music (postgrad dip), Julliard Sch NY; *m* 21 March 1993, Zoë Solomon; 1 da (Sophie b 23 Aug 1997), 2 s (Noah b 29 Nov 1998, Hugo b 1 May 2002); *Career* cellist; plays 'Saveuse' Stradivarius cello of 1726; winner: Euro Music for Youth Cello Competition Brussels 1984, Int Young Concert Artists Tst competition (strings section) 1989; solo concert performances in UK, USA, Germany, Austria, Belgium, Denmark, Romania, Russia and France; as cellist of Barbican Piano Trio: recording for ASV 1989, 1994 and 2000, Guildmusic 2000, Black Box 2004, Dutton 2005; toured Denmark, Germany, France, Belgium, Italy, Bulgaria, USA, Russia, S America, Far East, Uzbekistan and UK; princ cello London Chamber Orch, guest princ cello Royal Philharmonic Orch, Philharmonia, London Symphony Orch and Copenhagen Philharmonic Orch; broadcasts incl: BBC Radio 3, French TV and BBC World Service; chm Music Aid 1992–95; musical dir: Nonesuch Orch 1993–96, Zemel Choir 1994–98, Oxford Symphony Orch 2005–; conductor of symphony and string orchs Royal Holloway Univ of London 2001–; conductor: Arad Philharmonic Orch Romania, Covent Garden Chamber Orch; 2 recordings for Olympia, 1 recording for Chandos; musical dir Pro Corda 1998–2000; memb: Incorporated Soc of Musicians, European String Teachers Assoc; hon prof Rachmaninov Inst Tambov Russia; *Recreations* cooking Indian food, reading, walking, gardening, skiing; *Style*— Robert Max, Esq; ✉ 21 Middleway, London NW11 6SN (tel 020 8458 2839, e-mail robandzoe@aol.com)

MAXLOW-TOMLINSON, Paul Christian; s of John Maxlow-Tomlinson, and Marjorie Maude, *née* Muhlenkamp; *b* 24 October 1931; *Educ* Cranleigh Sch, Trinity Coll Dublin, Wadham Coll Oxford (MA); *m* 1, 1 Nov 1959 (m dis 1962), Jeanette McDonald; m 2, 28 June 1969 (m dis 1994), Anne, da of Charles Trench Stewart; 1 da (Claudia Lucy b 6 March 1972), 1 s (Charles Henry b 29 July 1974); m 3, 6 Feb 1994, Julia, *née* Pipe-Wolferstan; *Career* cmmnd Queen's Royal Regt 1950–52; Mercantile Credit Co: Zimbabwe 1956–62, London 1962–63, NI 1963–64; Grand Circle Travel Co 1965–69; admitted slr 1971, former sr ptnr Stones Slrs joined 1972 (conslt 1997–99), former conslt BNB plc; currently conslt: Stewarts Slrs, Lincoln's Inn Fields; arbitrator Int Court of Arbitration for Sport Lausanne 1995–, CAS arbitrator Commonwealth Games Manchester 2002; Br rep Legal Ctee Federation Internationale de Ski 1988–96, memb Sports Dispute Resolution Panel; chm Ski Club of GB 1982–87 (memb Cncl 1978–82), dir Br Ski Fedn 1982–87; memb: Devon Probation Ctee 1983–86, Exec Cncl Br Acad of Forensic Sciences 1987–90; fndr memb and chm Oakfields Project (ex-prisoners' hostel in Exeter), chm Prisoners Educn Tst 2001–06 (patron 2006–); dir Omnijuris (consortium of Euro lawyers) 1992–95; hon slr Lord's Taverners 2001–05; memb Law Soc (memb Childrens Panel 1987–97); author of various articles and lectr on international skiing law; *Recreations* skiing, shooting, fishing, painting; *Clubs* Garrick, Ski Club of GB; *Style*— Paul Maxlow-Tomlinson, Esq; ✉ c/o Stewarts, 63 Lincoln's Inn Field, London WC2A 3LW (tel 020 7242 6462)

MAXMIN, Dr (Hiram) James (Jim); s of Henry W Maxmin (d 1992), of USA, and Louise, *née* Strousse (d 1977); *b* 26 September 1942; *Educ* Cheltenham HS, Grinnell Coll Iowa (BA), Fitzwilliam Coll Cambridge, KCL (PhD); *m* 1987, Prof Shoshana Zuboff; 1 s (Jacob b 1995); 2 da (Kate b 1971, Chloe b 1992) and 3 s (Peter b 1972, Jonathan b 1977, Ben b 1983) from previous m; *Career* trainee Unilever Ltd 1968–69, Lever Bros 1969–71, dir Unilever Orgn 1971–73, mktg dir Volvo Concessionaires UK 1975–78, jt chm and md Volvo UK 1978–83, dir Thorn EMI plc 1983–92, chm and chief exec Thorn Home Electronics 1983–92, pres Thorn EMI Inc (USA) 1983–92, chief exec Laura Ashley plc 1991–94; chm: Informate Associates 1994–, Think Ahead Inc 1996–2002, Animated Images 1998–2001, Maine Farms Venison 1998–; chm and managing ptnr Global Brand Development Ltd; fndr and chm Netfaiday.com 1999; ptnr Mast Global Ltd 2000; non-exec dir: Geest plc 1993–97, BAA plc 1994–98, Streamline Inc 1995–98, Dawson International plc 1995–2000, ABM Ltd 1996–97, Scottish Provident 1998–2000; former offr SMMT; lectr at business coll, fundraiser Fitzwilliam Coll Cambridge, involved in local educn initiatives; FIMI 1983, CIMgt 1985; *Publications* The Support Economy - Why Corporations Are Failing Individuals and the Next Episode of Capitalism (2002); *Recreations* rugby, fishing, swimming; *Style*— Dr Jim Maxmin; ✉ Flat 14, 51 Iverna Gardens, London W8 6TP (tel 020 7937 2858); Lake Field Farm, Morang Cove Road, Nobelboro, Damiscrotta 04555, Maine, USA (tel 00 1 207 832 4781, e-mail maxmin@midcoast.com)

MAXTON, Baron (Life Peer UK 2004), of Blackwaterfoot in Ayrshire and Arran; John Alston Maxton; s of John Maxton, and Jenny Maxton; *b* 5 May 1936; *Educ* Lord Williams' GS Thames, Univ of Oxford; *m* Christine Maxton; 3 s; *Career* joined Lab Pty 1970, MP (Lab) Glasgow Cathcart 1979–2001; oppn spokesman on: health, local govt and housing in Scotland 1985–87, Scotland 1987–92; memb: Scottish Select Ctee 1981–83, Public

Accounts Ctee 1983–84, Nat Heritage Select Ctee 1992–97, Culture, Media and Sport Select Ctee 1997–2001; memb Speaker's Panel of Chairmen 1994–2001; *Style*— The Rt Hon the Lord Maxton

MAXTONE GRAHAM, Ysenda; *see:* Maxtone-Smith, Ysenda May

MAXTONE-SMITH, Ysenda May; da of Robert Mungo Maxtone Graham, of Sandwich, Kent; *b* 31 December 1962; *Educ* The King's Sch Canterbury, Girton Coll Cambridge (MA); *m* 14 Aug 1993, Michael James Smith (who upon marriage adopted by deed poll surname of Maxtone-Smith), s of David Smith, JP, of Keyworth, Notts; 3 s (Toby Robert b 2 July 1994, Charles Mungo b 8 Oct 1996, Francis James b 8 March 2002); *Career* as Ysenda Maxtone Graham: columnist for the Express on Sunday, freelance journalist writing for Sunday Telegraph, Evening Standard, Daily Mail, Church Times, Harpers and Queen, Tatler and others; *Books* The Church Hesitant, a Portrait of the Church of England Today (1993), Without a Guide (contrib, 1996), The Real Mrs Miniver (2001); *Style*— Mrs Ysenda Maxtone-Smith; ✉ 1 Avalon Road, London SW6 2EX (tel 020 7736 8710, e-mail ysenda@talk21.com)

MAXWELL, Donald; s of Kenneth M MacAlpine, of Perth, Scotland, and Margaret MacAlpine; *b* 12 December 1948; *Educ* Perth Acad, Univ of Edinburgh (MA); *m* Alison Norman; 1 da; *Career* baritone; Scottish Opera 1976–82: John Noble bursary, debut 1977, title role in Barbiere di Siviglia, Sharpless in Madama Butterfly, Enrico in Lucia di Lammermoor, Zurga in Les Pecheurs de Peries, Shiskov in From the House of the Dead; WNO 1982–85: Renato in Un Ballo in Maschera, Shishkov, Marcello in La Boheme, Don Carlos in Ernani, Rigoletto, Iago in Otello, The Count in Le Nozze di Figaro, title role in Falstaff, Golaud in Pelleas and Melisande; freelance 1985–; ROH debut 1987; performances at ROH incl: Bartolo Barbière di Siviglia, Faninal Rosenkavalier, Kothner in Die Meistersinger von Nurnberg, Gunther in Götterdämmerung; ENO: title role in Il Barbiere di Siviglia, Wozzeck; Opera North: Germont in La Traviata, Pizarro in Fidelio, title role in Der Fliegende Holländer, Scarpia in Tosca; other performances incl: Berg's Lulu (BBC Proms) 1996, Don Alhambra in The Gondoliers (BBC Proms) 1997, First Night BBC Proms 1998; artistic dir Buxton Festival 1999, dir Nat Opera Studio 2001, dir of Opera Studies Royal Welsh Coll of Music and Drama 2004; numerous appearances in UK festivals and in foreign operas incl Paris, Vienna, NY, Tokyo, Milan, Buenos Aires, Amsterdam and Salzburg; regular contribs to radio and TV operas; memb Music Box; recordings incl: Carmina Burana, Kismet, Amahl and The Night Visitors, Sir John in Love, Midsummer Night's Dream, Noye's Fludde, The Song of Norway; Hon DMus Univ of Abertay Dundee; fell Royal Welsh Coll of Music and Drama (FRWCMD); *Recreations* railways; *Style*— Donald Maxwell, Esq; ✉ Music International, 13 Ardilaun Road, Highbury, London N5 2QR (tel 020 7359 5183, fax 020 7226 9792)

MAXWELL, Prof (James) Douglas; s of Henry Alastair Maxwell (d 1996), of Inverness, and Sheila Margaret, *née* Stewart (d 1957); *b* 15 September 1940; *Educ* Aberdeen GS, The HS of Glasgow, Univ of Glasgow (BSc, MB ChB, MD, Hunter medal), Univ of Calif; *m* 1, 1965 (m dis 1973), Gisela, *née* Michler; 1 s (Nicholas b 1969); m 2, 1976, Jane Elisabeth, *née* Sherwood; 1 da (Katherine b 1977), 1 s (Edward b 1979); *Career* jr med posts and McIntyre research scholarship Glasgow Royal Infirmary 1964–69, hon lectr Liver Unit KCH London 1969–72, research fell Depts of Med and Pharmacology Univ of Calif San Francisco 1972–74, conslt physician and sr lectr in med St George's Hosp and Med Sch London 1975–87; St George's Hosp Med Sch London: reader in med and dean of clinical studies 1987–97, prof of med 2003–, chair Accelerated Graduate Entry Programme (AGEP); dep dir Refugee Doctors Course 2005–06; clinical examiner Univ of London, Soc of Apothecaries and United Examining Bd; memb: Br Soc of Gastroenterology, Br Assoc for Study of the Liver, Caledonian Soc, Royal Scottish Corp of London; Winston Churchill Travelling Fellowship 1998; FRCPGlas, FRCP; *Publications* Surgical Management of Obesity (co-ed, 1981), Substance Abuse and Dependence (1990); papers on gastroenterology, liver disease, vegetarian diet in relation to vitamin D deficiency and tuberculosis in immigrant Indian sub continent Asians; *Style*— Prof Douglas Maxwell; ✉ St George's University of London, Cranmer Terrace, Tooting, London SW17 0RE (tel 020 8725 1541, fax 020 8725 3520, e-mail maxwell@sgul.ac.uk)

MAXWELL, Glyn Meurig; s of Dr James Maxwell, and Mary Buddug, *née* Powell; *b* 7 November 1962; *Educ* Stanborough Sch Welwyn Garden City, Worcester Coll Oxford (exhibitioner, BA), Boston Univ Mass USA; *m* 1997, Hon Geraldine, *née* Harmsworth, da of 3 Viscount Rothermere (d 1998); 1 da (Alfreda b 1997); *Career* editorial asst W H Allen & Co plc 1989, poet and freelance ed/writer 1989–; writing fell Nanyang Technological Univ Singapore 1995, writer in residence Univ of Warwick 1997, visiting writer Amherst Coll Mass USA 1997–2000, adjunct prof: The New School NY 2002–, Columbia Univ NY 2002–, Princeton Univ NJ 2003–04; poetry ed The New Republic 2001–; contrib to various magazines and jls UK and USA incl: TLS, London Review of Books, Vogue, New Statesman, Spectator, The Independent, The Independent on Sunday, The Sunday Times, Poetry Review, The New Republic, The New Yorker, The New York Times, Atlantic Monthly, Manhattan Review, Massachusetts Review, Partisan Review; included on New Br Poets tour of UK 1990; third prize Nat Poetry Competition 1989, winner Eric Gregory Award 1991, Somerset Maugham Travel Prize 1992, shortlisted for Sunday Times Young Writer of the Year 1990 and 1992, winner E M Forster Prize American Acad of Arts and Letters 1997; FRSL; *Books* Tale of the Mayor's Son (Poetry Book Soc choice 1990, shortlisted for John Llewellyn Rhys Meml Prize 1990), Out of the Rain (Poetry Book Soc recommendation 1992, shortlisted Whitbread Poetry Prize 1992), Gnyss the Magnificent (1993), Blue Burneau (1994, shortlisted Whitbread First Novel Prize 1994), Rest for the Wicked (1995, shortlisted Whitbread Poetry Prize and T S Eliot Prize 1995), Moon Country (with Simon Armitage, 1996), The Breakage (1998, shortlisted for Forward Prize and T S Eliot Prize), The Boys at Twlilight: Poems 1990–95 (2000), Time's Fool (2001), The Nerve (2002); work incl in various anthologies incl: Poetry with an Edge (1988), Poetry Book Society Anthology (1988, 1990 and 1991), Soho Square (1991), New Writing (1991 and 1992), Penguin Modern Poets 3 (1995), British Poetry Since 1945 (1998), The Firebox (1998), Scanning the Century (1999), The Best of English Poetry (audio tape, 1999); *Plays* The Heart in Hiding (1995), Wolfpit (1996), Broken Journey (1999), Anyroad (2000), The Last Valentine (2000), The Only Girl In The World (2001), The Lifeblood (2001); *Style*— Glyn Maxwell, Esq, FRSL; ✉ c/o Micheline Steinberg Associates, 4th Floor, 104 Great Portland Street, London W1 (e-mail micheline@steinplays.com)

MAXWELL, James Rankin; s of John James Maxwell (d 1990), and Helen Morrison, *née* Tait; *b* 20 April 1941; *Educ* HS of Glasgow, Univ of Glasgow (BSc, PhD), Univ of Bristol (DSc); *m* 1964, Joy Millar, da of John Hunter; 1 da (Jane b 5 Dec 1966), 1 s (Keir b 28 Dec 1970, d 1977); *Career* research asst Univ of Glasgow 1967, postdoctoral research chemist Univ of Calif Berkeley 1967–68; Univ of Bristol: postdoctoral fell 1968–69, research assoc 1969–72, lectr 1972–78, reader 1978–90, prof 1990–, head Section of Environmental and Analytical Chemistry 1991–99, sr research fell 1999–; J Klarence Karcher Medal Univ of Oklahoma 1979, Treibs Medal Geochemical Soc USA 1989, Interdisciplinary Award in Chemistry RSC 1994, jt geochemistry fell Geochemical Soc USA and Euro Assoc of Geochemistry 1996; FRS 1997; *Publications* author of over 250 papers in learned jls; *Recreations* walking, gardening, cooking; *Style*— Prof James Maxwell, FRS; ✉ School of Chemistry, University of Bristol, Cantock's Close, Bristol BS8 1TS (tel 0117 928 7669, fax 0117 929 3746, e-mail j.r.maxwell@bristol.ac.uk)

MAXWELL, Dr John; s of Henry Maxwell (d 1985), of Doncaster, and Ada, *née* Rooth; *b* 15 May 1939; *Educ* Univ of London (BPharm), Univ of Bradford (PhD); *m* 9 August 1961, Elizabeth Sheila, da of Arthur William Wright; 6 c (Timothy Alexander b 11 May 1962 (decd), Donia Elizabeth b 4 Aug 1964 (decd), Helen Rebecca b 14 Nov 1965, Kathryn Fiona b 14 Nov 1966, Jonathan David b 14 Sept 1974, Simon Mark b 27 April 1979); *Career* quality assurance Pharmaceutical Industry 1962–66, lectr/sr lectr in pharmaceutical chemistry Sunderland Poly 1969–76, princ pharmacist Quality Assurance Trent Regnl Health Authy 1976–84, dir of pharmacy Rotherham Gen Hosp 1984–97, visiting sr lectr in clinical pharmacy Univ of Nottingham 1980–99; MRPharmS 1962; Church of Jesus Christ of Latter-day Saints: joined 1957, served at local, stake, national and international levels, currently memb Europe W Area Presidency; *Publications* author of over 20 scientific papers; *Recreations* walking, gardening, reading; *Style*— Dr John Maxwell; ✉ Church of Jesus Christ of Latter-day Saints, 751 Warwick Road, Solihull, West Midlands B91 3DQ (tel 0121 712 1200, fax 0121 712 1111)

MAXWELL, John Frederick Michael; s of late Lt Frederic Michael Maxwell (RIN), of Sidcup, Kent, and late Mabel Doreen, *née* Turner; *b* 20 May 1943; *Educ* Dover Coll, New Coll Oxford (MA); *m* 1, 1964 (m dis 1986), Jennifer Mary; 1 da (Alice b 1966), 1 s (Edward b 1967); m 2, 1986, Jayne Elizabeth, da of George Douglas Hunter (d 1984), of Birmingham; *Career* called to the Bar Inner Temple 1965; practised Midland Circuit, recorder of the Crown Court 1995–2005, standing counsel to HM Customs & Excise for the Midland Circuit 1995–2005, standing counsel ro Revenue & Customs Prosecutions Office 2005, circuit judge 2005–; chm Birmingham Karma Ling Buddhist Centre, tstee Rokpa Tst; *Recreations* music, yachting; *Clubs* Royal Yachting Assoc, Portishead Cruising, Old Gaffers Assoc; *Style*— His Hon Judge Maxwell; ✉ Stafford Crown and County Courts, Victoria Square, Stafford ST16 2QQ (e-mail jfmmaxwell@aol.com)

MAXWELL, John Hunter; s of late John Hunter Maxwell, OBE, and Susan Elizabeth Una Smith; *b* 25 September 1944; *Educ* Melville Coll Edinburgh, Dumfries Acad, Univ of Edinburgh; *m* 1967, Janet Margaret, *née* Frew; 3 s; *Career* articled clerk T Hunter Thompson & Co CA 1962–67, qualified CA 1967, regnl dir (Far East) Rank Xerox Ltd 1967–83, gp fin controller Grand Metropolitan plc 1983–86, chief exec Provincial Group 1986–92, chief exec BPB Industries plc 1992–93, corp devpt dir Prudential Corporation plc 1994–96, DG Automobile Association 1996–2000; non-exec dir: Alliance & Leicester Building Society 1993–94, Wellington Underwriting 1999–2003 (chm 2000–03), Provident Financial plc 2000–, The Big Food Gp plc 2001–05, Parity Gp plc 2002–, Royal Sun Alliance Gp plc 2003–, Homeserve plc 2004–; chm: IAM 2002– (memb Cncl 1997–), DX Services plc 2005–06; dir Motor Sports Assoc 2007–; tstee Friends of UCL 1995–2002, govr Royal Ballet Sch; Freeman City of London 1998, Liveryman Worshipful Co of Coachmakers and Coach Harness Makers 1998–; CCMI, FRSA, FIMI; *Recreations* sailing, classic cars, motoring, travel, arts; *Clubs* Royal Thames Yacht, RAC (dir 2000); *Style*— John H Maxwell, Esq

MAXWELL, Sir Michael Eustace George; 9 Bt (NS 1681), of Monreith; o s of Maj Eustace Maxwell (d 1971), and Dorothy Vivien (Dodo), *née* Bellville (d 2003); suc unc, Capt Sir Aymer Maxwell, 8 Bt, 1987; *b* 28 August 1943; *Educ* Eton, Univ of London; *Heir* unascertained; *Career* chartered surveyor; currently running Monreith Estate and holiday accommodation; ARICS; *Style*— Sir Michael Maxwell, Bt; ✉ Monreith House, Port William, Newton Stewart DG8 9LB (tel 01988 700248); 56 Queensmill Road, London SW6 (tel 020 7610 2270)

MAXWELL, Richard; QC (1988); s of Thomas Maxwell (d 1957), and Kathleen Marjorie, *née* Truswell (d 1979); *b* 21 December 1943; *Educ* Nottingham HS (scholar), Hertford Coll Oxford (state scholar and Baring scholar, MA); *m* 10 Sept 1966, Judith Ann, da of Hedley Vincent Iliffe, of Breaston, Derby; 2 da (Karen Laetitia b 1968, Catharine Antonia b 1969), 2 s (Richard Alexander b 1971, Thomas Daniel b 1973); *Career* called to the Bar Inner Temple 1968; recorder of the Crown Court 1992–, dep judge of the High Court 1998–; *Recreations* golf, squash, fly fishing, watercolours, walking, half-marathon, malt whisky, wine; *Clubs* Nottingham Services, Darley Dale Fly Fishing, Peak Forest Angling, Beeston Fields Golf, PIGS Golf, Nottingham Squash Rackets; *Style*— Richard Maxwell, Esq, QC; ✉ Ropewalk Chambers, 24 The Ropewalk, Nottingham NG1 5EF (tel 0115 947 2581); Doughty Street Chambers, 11 Doughty Street, London WC1N 2PG (tel 020 7404 1313)

MAXWELL, Dr Robert James; CVO (1998), CBE (1993); s of Dr George Barton Maxwell, MC (d 1972), and Cathleen Maxwell, *née* Blackburn; *b* 26 June 1934; *Educ* Leighton Park Sch Reading, New Coll Oxford (MA), Univ of Pennsylvania (MA), LSE (PhD); *m* 1960, Jane, da of Geoffrey FitzGibbon, JP, of Dursley Glos; 3 s (Patrick, Benedict, Geoffrey), 2 da (Catherine, Favell); *Career* Lt Cameronians (Scot Rifles) 1952–54; asst mangr Union Corp 1958–66, princ McKinsey and Co 1966–75, admin Special Tstees for St Thomas' Hosp London 1975–80, sec/chief exec King's Fund 1980–97; chm Glos Partnership NHS Tst 2002–; tstee Joseph Rowntree Fndn, Thrive; JP 1971; Hon DUniv Brunel, Hon DLitt UWE; hon memb Assoc of Anaesthetists, hon fell MDU, Hon MRCP (London), Hon FRCGP, FRCPEd; *Recreations* walking, poetry; *Clubs* Brooks's, Royal Soc of Arts, Royal Soc of Med; *Style*— Dr Robert Maxwell, CVO, CBE; ✉ Pitt Court Manor, North Nibley, Dursley, Gloucestershire GL11 6EL (tel 01453 542942)

MAXWELL, Simon Jeffrey; CBE (2007); s of Frederic Norman Maxwell (d 2001), and Ruth Salinsky; *b* 1 May 1948, Birmingham; *Educ* Univ of Oxford (BA), Univ of Sussex (MA); *m* 1 Sept 1973, Catherine Elisabeth, *née* Pelly; 3 s (Daniel Julius b 8 April 1976, Oliver Conran b 10 Nov 1977, Dominic Giles b 4 Jan 1981); *Career* jr professional offr UNDP Nairobi 1970–72, asst resident rep UNDP New Delhi 1973–77, temp research offr Inst of Devpt Studies Univ of Sussex 1977–78, agricultural economist (farm systems) Centro de Investigacion Agricola Tropical (CIAT) Santa Cruz Bolivia Br Tropical Agric Mission ODA 1978–1981, fell and head Food Security Unit Inst of Devpt Studies Univ of Sussex 1989–1997 (prog mangr Poverty Reduction, Sustainable Devpt and the Rural Sector 1991–1997) dir ODI 1997–; pres Devpt Studies Assoc UK & Ireland 2001–05 (memb Cncl 1998–2005); memb: Oxfam Field Ctee for Latin America 1981–84, Ind Gp on Br Aid 1982–, UN Advsy Gp on Nutrition 1990–96, Prog Advsy Panel Fndn for Devpt Cooperation 1997–; external examiner Wye Coll Univ of London 1995–98, govr Inst of Devpt Studies 1996–97, tstee Action for Conservation through Tourism (ACT) 1998–2002, patron One World Broadcasting Tst 1998–; hon fell Foreign Policy Assoc NY 2003–, forum fell World Economic Forum 2003–; *Publications* author, co-author or ed of numerous books, articles in books and jls, briefing papers, commissioned studies and reports; *Style*— Simon Maxwell, Esq, CBE; ✉ Overseas Development Institute, 111 Westminster Bridge Road, London SE1 7JD (tel 020 7922 0345, fax 020 7922 0399, e-mail s.maxwell@odi.org.uk)

MAXWELL, Prof Thomas Jefferson (Jeff); OBE (1998); *b* 7 October 1940; *Educ* Silcoates Sch, Univ of Edinburgh (BSc, PhD); *Career* animal husbandry advsy offr E of Scotland Coll of Agric 1967–70, princ scientific offr Hill Farming Research Orgn 1975–79 (sr scientific offr Animal Studies Dept 1971–75), livestock research offr Victorian Dept of Agric Australia (secondment) 1979–80, head Animal Production Dept Hill Farming Research Orgn 1981–87, dir Macaulay Land Use Research Inst 1987–2000; chief exec Macaulay Research and Consultancy Servs Ltd 1995–2000; vice-chm Research Bd Scientific Advsy Ctee Scottish Natural Heritage 1992–99; memb: Cncl Br Soc of Animal Production 1976–79, Sec of State's Hill Farming Advsy Ctee 1987–2000, Sci Research and Devpt Bd Nature Conservation Cncl (Scotland) 1990–92, Cncl Aberdeen Research Consortium 1992–2000 (chm Land Mgmnt and Environmental Scis Research Centre 1992–98), Steering Ctee for a Euro Environmental Inst 1994–96, Plant and Soil Dept Users Liaison Ctee Univ of Aberdeen 1995–2000, Bd Euro Environmental Mgmnt Inst Ltd Aberdeen 1996–98, Countryside and Nature Conservation Ctee Nat Tst for Scotland 1999–2006,

M

Cncl Nat Tsts Scotland 2000–03, Ctee Nat Tst Scotland (NE Region) 2001–, Agric and Environment Biotechnology Cmmn 2000–05, Scottish Exec Environment and Rural Affrs Dept (SEERAD) Agric Strategy Gp 2005–06, Agric Strategy Implementation Gp 2006–; conslt to Min of Agric Lesotho (ODA sponsored) 1991; tstee Macaulay Development Tst 1995–2000; chm: Tenant Farming Forum (Scotland) 2005–, Countryside and Nature Conservation Panel Nat Tst for Scotland 2007–; hon prof of land use systems Univ of Aberdeen, hon research fell Univ of Edinburgh; Scottish Cashmere Producers' Assoc: chm 1986–88, dir and memb Cncl 1988–93; CIBiol, FRSGS 1995, FRSE 1996, FIBiol 1997, FRAgS 2001; *Publications* numerous contribs to learned jls; *Style*— Prof Jeff Maxwell, OBE, FRSE; ✉ 12 Kingswood Crescent, Kingswells, Aberdeen AB15 8TE (tel 01224 743857, e-mail jeff.maxwell@btinternet.com)

MAXWELL DAVIES, Sir Peter; kt (1987), CBE (1981); s of Thomas Maxwell Davies, and Hilda Maxwell Davies; *b* 8 September 1934, Manchester; *Educ* Leigh GS Salford, Univ of Manchester (MusB), Royal Manchester Coll of Music; *Career* composer and conductor; studied with Goffredo Petrassi in Rome 1957, dir of music Cirencester GS 1959–62, Harkness fell Grad Sch Princeton Univ (studying with Roger Sessions, Milton Babbitt and Earl Kim) 1962–64; fndr and co-dir (with Harrison Birtwistle) The Pierrot Players 1967–71, fndr and artistic dir The Fires of London 1971–87, fndr and artistic dir St Magnus Festival Orkney Islands 1977–86 (pres 1986–), artistic dir Dartington Hall Summer Sch of Music 1979–84, assoc composer/conductor Scottish Chamber Orch 1985–94, conductor/composer BBC Philharmonic Orch Manchester 1992–2001; assoc composer/conductor Royal Philharmonic Orch 1992–2000, composer laureate Scottish Chamber Orch 1994–, master of the Queens' music 2004; visiting Fromm prof of composition Harvard Univ 1985; pres: Schools Music Assoc 1983–, North of England Educn Conf Chester 1985, Composers' Guild of GB 1986–, Nat Fedn of Music Socs 1989–, Cheltenham Arts Festivals 1994–96, Soc for Promotion of New Music 1995–; major retrospective festival (28 works) South Bank Centre London 1990, Max: Peter Maxwell Davies - A Musician of Our Time (two week festival) South Bank Centre, Royal Acad of Music and Westminster Cathedral 2005; memb: Accademica Filarmonia Romana 1979, Bayerische Akademie der Schönen Künste 1998; hon memb: Guildhall Sch of Music and Drama 1981, Royal Philharmonic Soc 1987; hon fell: Royal Incorporation of Architects in Scotland 1994, Univ of Highlands and Islands 2004; Hon DMus: Edinburgh 1979, Manchester 1981, Bristol 1984, Open Univ 1986, Glasgow 1993, Durham 1994, Hull 2001, Kingston 2005; Hon LLD: Aberdeen 1981, Warwick 1986; Hon DLitt Salford 1999; Hon Dr Heriot-Watt Univ 2002; Freeman City of Salford 2004; Officier de l'Ordre des Arts et des Lettres (France) 1988; memb Royal Swedish Acad of Music 1993; hon memb RSA 2001; FRNCM 1978, hon RAM 1978, FRSAMD 1994, FRCM 1994, fell Br Acad of Composers and Songwriters 2005; *Awards* Cobbett Medal for services to chamber music 1989, First Award Assoc of British Orchs (ABO) 1991, Gulliver Award for the Performing Arts in Scotland 1991, Nat Fedn of Music Socs Charles Groves Award for outstanding contrib to Br music 1995, Royal Philharmonic Soc Award for large-scale composition (for Symphony No 5) 1995, Distinguished Musicians Award Inc Soc of Musicians 2001; *Works* incl Sonata (for trumpet and piano) 1955, Alma redemptoris mater (for ensemble) 1957, Five Motets (for SATB Soli, SATB Chorus and ensemble) 1959, O Magnum Mysterium (for SATB chorus) 1960, First Fantasia on an In Nomine of John Taverner (for orch) 1962, Second Fantasia on John Taverner's In Nomine (for orch) 1964, Revelation and Fall (for soprano and ensemble) 1966, Antechrist (for ensemble) 1967, Missa super L'Homme Armé (for speaker and ensemble) 1968, St Thomas Wake-Foxtrot for Orch 1968, Worldes Blis (for orch) 1969, Eight Songs for a Mad King (music theatre work for ensemble) 1969, Vesalii Icones - music theatre work (for dancer and ensemble) 1969, Taverner (opera in two acts) 1970, From Stone to Thorn (for mezzo soprano and ensemble) 1971, Stone Litany (for mezzo soprano and ensemble) 1973, Miss Donnithorne's Maggot (music-theatre work for mezzo-soprano and ensemble) 1974, Ave Maris Stella (for ensemble) 1975, Symphony No 1 1976, The Martyrdom of Saint Magnus (chamber opera) 1976, The Two Fiddlers (opera for children to perform) 1978, Le Jongleur de Notre Dame (music theatre work for juggle, baritone and ensemble) 1978, Salome (ballet in two acts) 1978, Black Pentecost (for mezzo-soprano, baritone and orch) 1979, Solstice of Light (for tenor, SATB chorus and organ) 1979, Cinderella (pantomime opera for children to perform) 1979, Symphony No 2 (for orch) 1980, Piano Sonata 1981, Brass Quintet 1981, Image, Reflection, Shadow (for ensemble) 1982, Sinfonia Concertante (for tenor and orch) 1983, Into the Labyrinth (for tenor and orch) 1983, The No 11 Bus (music theatre work for mime, singers and dancers and ensemble) 1984, Symphony No 3 (formorch) 1985, An Orkney Wedding with Sunrise (for orch) 1985, Violin concerto (for violin and orch) 1985, Strathclyde Concerto No 1 for oboe and orch 1986, Resurrection (opera) 1987, Strathclyde Concerto No 2 for Cello and orch 1988, Concerto for Trumpet and orch 1988, The Great Bank Robbery (music theatre work for children to perform) 1989, Symphony No 4 1989, Strathclyde Concerto No 3 for Horn, Trumpet and Orchestra 1989, Strathclyde Concerto No 4 for Clarinet and Orchestra 1990, Caroline Mathilde (ballet in two acts) 1990, Ojai Festival Overture (for orch) 1991, Strathclyde Concerto No 5 (for violin, viola and string orch) 1991, Strathclyde Concerto No 6 (for flute and orch) 1991, Strathclyde Concerto No 7 (for double bass and orch) 1992, The Turn of the Tide (for orch) 1992, Strathclyde Concerto No 8 (for bassoon and orch) 1993, A Spell for Green Corn: The MacDonald Dances (for orch) 1993, Symphony No 5 1994, Cross Lane Fair (for orch) 1994, Strathclyde Concerto No 9 (for six woodwind instruments and string orch) 1994, The Beltane Fire (choreographic poem for orch) 1995, The Three Kings (for chorus, orch and soloists) 1995, The Doctor of Myddfai (cmmnd Welsh National Opera 50th Anniversary season), Symphony No 6 (London premiere BBC Proms with RPO 1996), Strathclyde Concerto No 10: Concerto for orch 1996, Concerto for Piccolo 1996, Job - Oratorio (for chorus, orch and soloists) 1997, Mavis in Las Vegas - Theme and Variations (for orch) 1997, Orkney Saga I: Fifteen Keels Laid in Norway for Jerusalem-farers (for orch) 1997, The Jacobite Rising (for chorus, orch and soloists) 1997, Concerto for Piano 1997, Orkney Saga II: In Kirkwall, the first red St Magnus stones (for orch) 1997, A Reel of Seven Fisherman (for orch) 1998, Sea Elegy (for chorus, orch and soloists) 1998, Rome Amor Labyrinthus (for orch) 1998, Orkney Saga III: An Orkney Wintering - Stone poems in Orkahowe: 'great treasure...' (for alto saxophone and orch) 1999, Trumpet Quintet (for string quartet and trumpet) 1999, Mr Emmet Takes a Walk (music theatre work for soprano, baritone, bass and instrument ensemble) 1999, Horn Concerto 1999, Orkney Saga V: Westerly Gale in Biscay, Salt in the Bread Broken (for SATB chorus and orchestra) 2000, Symphony No 7 (for orch) 2000, Antarctic Symphony (Symphony No 8) (for orch) 2000, Canticum Canticorum (cantata for chorus, orch and SATB soloists) 2001, De Assumtione Beatae Mariae Virginis (for ensemble) 2001, Crossing Kings Reach (for ensemble) 2001, Mass (SATB chorus and organ) 2002, Naxos Quartet No 1 (string quartet) 2002, Piano Trio 2002, Naxos Quartet No 2 (string quartet) 2003, Naxos Quartet No 3 (string quartet) 2003, Naxos Quartet No 4: Children's Games (string quartet) 2004, Magnificiat and Nun Dimitis (SATB and organ) 2004, Naxos Quartet No 5 (string quartet) 2004, Hymn to Artemis Locheia (for clarinet quintet) 2004, The Fall of the Leafe (string orch) 2004, Naxos Quartet No 6 (string quartet) 2005, Commemoration Sixty (children's chorus, military band, military trumpets and trombones and orch) 2005, Beacons of Hope (Military Wind Band) 2005; *Style*— Sir Peter Maxwell Davies, CBE; ✉ c/o Intermusica Artists' Management Limited, 16 Duncan Terrace, London N1 8BZ (tel 020 7278 5455, fax 020 7278 8434, e-mail mail@intermusica.co.uk, website www.maxopus.com)

MAXWELL-IRVING, Alastair Michael Tivey; s of Reginald Tivey (d 1977), of Warks, and Barbara Annie Bell Irving (d 1988); *b* 1 October 1935; *Educ* Lancing, Univ of London (BSc), Univ of Oxford, Univ of Stirling; *m* 21 Sept 1983, Esther Mary, da of Rev James Hamilton, formerly of Auchterhouse, Angus; *Career* chartered engr: English Electric Co 1960–64, Annandale Estates 1966–69, Weir Pumps Ltd 1970–91; quality conslt 1992–94; architectural and historical writer and archaeologist; sometime hon asst Royal Cmmn on Ancient and Historical Monuments Scotland; memb: Castle Studies Gp, Cncl for Scot Archaeology, Dumfries and Galloway Antiquarian Soc, Hawick Archaeological Soc, Stirling Field and Archaeological Soc, Clackmannan Field Soc, Friends of Alloa Tower, Friends of Sauchie Tower, Scottish Castles Assoc; fndr memb and sec BIM Central Scotland 1975–79, community cncllr Logie 1984–97; Nigel Tranter Meml Award 2003; FSA Scot 1967, AMICE 1970, MIEE 1972, CEng 1973, MIMgt 1974, FSA 2001; *Publications* incl: The Irvings of Bonshaw (1968), The Irvings of Dumfries (1968), Early Firearms and their Influence on the Military And Domestic Architecture of the Borders (1974), Cramalt Tower (1982), Borthwick Castle (1982), Hoddom Castle (1989), Lochwood Castle (1990), The Castles of Buittle (1991), Torthorwald Castle (1993), Scottish Yetts and Window-Grilles (1994), The Dating of the Tower-houses at Comlongon and Elphinstone (1996), The Tower-houses of Kirtleside (1997), Kenmure Castle (1997), The Border Towers of Scotland: Their History and Architecture - The West March (2000), Lordship and Architecture in Medieval and Rennaissance Scotland (contrib, 2005), Family Memoirs (2007); *Recreations* architecture and history of the Border towers of Scotland, archaeology, family history and genealogy, art and architecture of Tuscany, horology, heraldry, photography, gardening; *Style*— Alastair Maxwell-Irving, Esq, FSA; ✉ Telford House, Blairlogie, Stirling FK9 5PX (tel 01259 761721, e-mail a.maxwellirving@tesco.net)

MAXWELL SCOTT, Sir Dominic James; 14 Bt (E 1642), of Haggerston, Northumberland; er s of Sir Michael Fergus Constable Maxwell Scott, 13 Bt (d 1989), and Deirdre Moira, *née* McKechnie; *b* 22 July 1968; *Educ* Eton, Univ of Sussex; *m* 2004, Emma Jane, *née* Perry; 1 da (Flora Elizabeth b 30 Nov 2004); *Heir* bro, Matthew Maxwell Scott; *Style*— Sir Dominic Maxwell Scott, Bt

MAY, Rt Hon Lord Justice; Rt Hon Sir Anthony Tristram Kenneth May; kt (1991), PC (1998); s of Dr Kenneth Sibley May (d 1985), and Joan Marguérite, *née* Oldaker (d 1985); *b* 9 September 1940; *Educ* Bradfield Coll, Worcester Coll Oxford (MA); *m* 4 May 1968, Stella Gay, da of Rupert George Pattisson (d 1976); 2 da (Charmian b 1971, Lavinia b 1972), 1 s (Richard b 1974); *Career* called to the Bar Inner Temple 1967 (bencher 1985); QC 1979, recorder of the Crown Court 1985–91, cmmr Savings and Investment Bank Public Enquiry Isle of Man 1990, judge of the High Court of Justice (Queen's Bench Div) 1991–97, a Lord Justice of Appeal 1997–, dep head of civil justice 2000–03, vice-pres Queen's Bench Div 2002–; chm Guildford Choral Soc 1980–91 (vice-pres 1991–); hon fell Worcester Coll Oxford 1999; *Publications* Keating on Building Contracts (6 edn, 1995); *Recreations* gardening, music, books; *Clubs* Garrick; *Style*— The Rt Hon Lord Justice May; ✉ Royal Courts of Justice, Strand, London WC2A 2LL

MAY, Brian Harold; CBE (2005); s of Harold May, and Ruth May; *b* 19 July 1947; *Educ* Hampton GS, Imperial Coll London (BSc, PhD); *m*; 1 s (Jimmy), 2 da (Louisa, Emily); *Career* guitarist and songwriter; formed first band '1984' 1964; co-fndr: Smile 1968, Queen 1970– (with Freddie Mercury (d 1991), Roger Taylor, *qv* and John Deacon, *qv*); albums incl: Queen (1973, Gold), Queen II (1974, Gold), Sheer Heart Attack (1974, Gold), A Night at the Opera (1975, Platinum), A Day at the Races (1976, Gold), News of the World (1977, Gold), Jazz (1978, Gold), Live Killers (1979, Gold), The Game (1980, Gold), Flash Gordon Original Soundtrack (1980, Gold), Greatest Hits (1981, 9 times Platinum), Hot Space (1982, Gold), The Works (1984, Platinum), A Kind of Magic (1986, double Platinum), Live Magic (1986, Platinum), The Miracle (1989, Platinum), Queen at the Beeb (1989), Innuendo (1991, Platinum), Greatest Hits Two (1991), Made In Heaven (1995); other albums: Gettin' Smile (earlier recordings of Smile, 1982), Starfleet Project (Brian May & Friends, 1983), Back to the Light (solo, 1993), Another World (solo, 1998); number 1 singles: Bohemian Rhapsody 1975 and 1991, Under Pressure 1981, The Stonk 1988, Innuendo 1991; numerous tours worldwide, performed at Live Aid Concert Wembley Stadium 1985; opened HM The Queen's Golden Jubilee Party at the Palace by playing solo guitar on the roof of Buckingham Palace 2002; voted Best Band of the Eighties ITV/TV Times 1990, Br Phonographic Indust award for Outstanding Contribution to Br Music 1990, Ivor Novello Award for best song musically and lyrically (Too Much Love Will Kill You) 1997; Hon DSc Univ of Hertfordshire 2002; ARCS; *Clubs* Grand Order of Water Rats; *Style*— Dr Brian May, CBE; ✉ Duck Productions Ltd, PO Box 141, Windlesham, Surrey GU20 6YW (tel 01344 875448)

MAY, David Oliver; s of John Oliver May (d 1960), and Joan, *née* Harrison (d 1996); *b* 1 March 1935; *Educ* Wellington, Univ of Southampton; *m* March 1960, Baroness Catherine, da of Baron Van Den Branden De Reeth (d 1966); 2 s (Brian, Dominic), 1 da (Georgia); *Career* Nat Serv Sub Lt RN 1954–55; chm: Berthon Boat Co Ltd, Lymington Marina Ltd, Lymington Marine Garage, Nat Boat Shows 1986–88; tstee Br Marine Inds Fedn 1988; dir: Independent Energy plc, Westgolf (UK) Ltd; Liveryman Worshipful Co of Shipwrights; FRINA 1964, CEng; *Recreations* yacht racing, sailing, shooting; *Clubs* Royal Thames Yacht, Royal Ocean Racing, RN, Royal Lymington Yacht, Royal London Yacht, Island Sailing; *Style*— David Oliver May, Esq; ✉ Berthon Boat Co Ltd, The Shipyard, Lymington, Hampshire SO41 3YL

MAY, Derwent James; s of Herbert Alfred May (d 1982), and Nellie Eliza, *née* Newton (d 1959); *b* 29 April 1930; *Educ* Strode's Sch Egham, Lincoln Coll Oxford (MA); *m* 22 Sept 1967, Yolanta Izabella, da of Tadeusz Sypniewski, of Lodz, Poland (d 1970); 1 s (Orlando James b 1968), 1 da (Miranda Izabella b 1970); *Career* theatre and film critic Continental Daily Mail Paris 1952–53, lectr English Univ of Indonesia 1955–58, sr lectr in English lit Univs of Warsaw and Lódź Poland 1959–63, ldr writer TLS 1963–65, lit ed The Listener 1965–86, lit and arts ed The Sunday Telegraph 1986–90, ed Élan (the arts magazine of the European) 1990–91, feature writer The Times 1993– (contrib of nature notes 1981–, European arts ed 1992); memb Booker Prize Jury 1978, memb Hawthornden Prize Ctee 1987– (chm 1997 and 2004); FRSL 1996; *Books* The Professionals (1964), Dear Parson (1969), The Laughter in Djakarta (1973), A Revenger's Comedy (1979), Proust (1983), The Times Nature Diary (1983), Hannah Arendt (1986), The New Times Nature Diary (1993), Feather Reports (1996), Critical Times: The History of the Times Literary Supplement (2002), How to Attract Birds to Your Garden (2002), The Times: A Year in Nature Notes (2004); ed: Good Talk: An Anthology from BBC Radio (1968), Good Talk 2 (1969), The Music of What Happens: Poems from The Listener 1965–80 (1981); *Recreations* birdwatching, opera; *Clubs* Beefsteak, Garrick, Academy; *Style*— Derwent May, Esq, FRSL; ✉ 45 Burghley Road, London NW5 1UH (tel 020 7485 2788)

MAY, Douglas James; QC (Scot 1989); s of Thomas May (d 1977), of Edinburgh, and Violet Mary Brough Boyd or May (d 1995); *b* 7 May 1946; *Educ* George Heriot's Sch Edinburgh, Univ of Edinburgh (LLB); *Career* advocate 1971, temp sheriff 1990–99, dep social security cmmr 1992–93, social security cmmr Child Support Cmmn 1993–; Parly candidate (C): Edinburgh E Feb 1974, Glasgow Cathcart 1983; capt Scottish Univs Golfing Soc 1990, pres Edinburgh Photographic Soc 1996–99; memb Faculty of Advocates, FRPS 2002; *Recreations* golf, photography, travel, concert going; *Clubs* Bruntsfield Links Golfing Soc, Merchants of Edinburgh Golf (capt 1997–99), Luffness New Golf; *Style*— Douglas May, Esq, QC; ✉ Office of the Social Security Commissioners, George House, 126 George Street, Edinburgh EH3 7PW (tel 0131 271 4310)

MAY, Evelyn Jane; da of Henry May (d 1980), and Jane Bonner, *née* Brown; *b* 16 January 1955; *Educ* Glasgow HS for Girls, Univ of Glasgow (BDS), Univ of Wales (MScD), FDS RCPS (Glasgow), DOrthRCS (Eng); *Career* postgrad student in orthodontics Welsh Nat Sch of Med Cardiff 1981–83, registrar in orthodontics Raigmore Hosp Inverness 1983–84, sr registrar in orthodontics Glasgow Dental Hosp 1984–88 (house offr, sr house offr, then registrar 1977–81), conslt Middlesbrough Gen Hosp 1988, currently conslt and lead clinician in orthodontics James Cook Univ Hosp Middlesbrough; memb: Br Orthodontic Soc, Conslt Orthodontists Gp, BDA, Craniofacial Soc of GB; *Style*— Miss Evelyn May

MAY, Dr Geoffrey John; s of James Ebrey Clare May (d 1986), of London, and Eleanor Isobel, *née* Tate (d 1989); *b* 7 May 1948; *Educ* Eltham Coll London, Fitzwilliam Coll Cambridge (MA, PhD); *m* 5 Jan 1974, Sarah Elizabeth, da of Stanley George Felgate (d 1986), of Chislehurst; 2 s (Timothy b 1976, Daniel b 1980); *Career* Chloride Gp plc 1974–82, Hawker Siddeley Gp (BTR plc) 1982–90 and 1991–2000, dir Tungstone Batteries Ltd 1982–88, dir and gen mangr Hawker Fusegear Ltd 1988–90, dir Caparo Industries plc, md Barton Abrasives Ltd 1990–91, dir Hawker Batteries Gp 1991–2000, dir Invensys Power Systems 1998–2000, exec dir FIAMM SpA 2000–03, princ Focus Consulting 2003–; CEng 1978, FIM 1987; *Recreations* skiing, gardening, sailing; *Style*— Dr Geoffrey May; ✉ Troutbeck House, 126 Main Street, Swithland, Loughborough, Leicestershire LE12 8TJ (tel 01509 890547, fax 01509 891442, e-mail geoffrey.may@tiscali.co.uk)

MAY, James Nicholas Welby; s of Richard Percy, and Caroline Rosemary Welby, *née* Jack; *b* 21 February 1949; *Educ* Sherborne, Univ of Southampton (BSc), Coll of Law; *m* 19 May 1979, Diana Mary Tamplin; 2 s (George Thomas Welby b 18 Nov 1983, Henry James Otto b 4 May 1986); *Career* called to the Bar Lincoln's Inn 1974; prog officer UN Environmental Prog Nairobi 1976–77, res officer IUCN Bonn 1977–78, legal officer and co sec Friends of the Earth Ltd 1978–79, head of legal servs NFU 1980–89, DG British Retail Consortium 1989–97, DG UK Offshore Operators' Association 1997–2003, chm Land Command Audit Ctee MOD 2004–; memb: Cncl Nat Retail Trg Cncl 1989–94, Bd EuroCommerce 1992–97, Bd Distributive Occupational Standards Cncl 1994–97, CBI Cncl 1996–2003, Meteorological Ctee 1997–99, HSE Open Govt Complaints Panel 2003–05; non-exec dir The Met Office 2000–07, non-exec chm Common Data Acces Ltd 2000–03, non-exec memb Land Command Bd 2004–, non-exec memb Defence Audit Ctee 2005–07; tstee Sherborne Fndn 1999–2004; *Recreations* skiing, tennis, travel; *Clubs* Roehampton; *Style*— James May, Esq; ✉ e-mail jnwmay@blueyonder.co.uk

MAY, Jane Veronica; da of Reginald Sydney Miller (d 1975), and Enid Brunt (d 1990); *b* 10 June 1956, Orpington, Kent; *Educ* Orpington Girls GS, Kingston Univ (BA); *m* 18 Sept 1982, Michael James May, s of Leslie Arthur May; 1 da (Anna Louise b 22 Aug 1991), 1 s (James Christopher b 18 March 1993); *Career* Freemans Mail Order: joined 1978, Freemans Int 1978–88, mktg and business devpt 1988–91, customer servs dir 1991–93; customer servs dir Thames Water 1994–2000; currently non-exec dir: Office of Rail Regulation (ORR), Office of Water Regulation (Ofwat), SITA Tst, Public Guardianship Office; memb RHS; chair Berkshire Autistic Soc; *Recreations* gardening, travel, reading; *Style*— Mrs Jane May

MAY, Peter N J; *Career* md Charterhouse Securities Ltd 1993–2000 (joined Charterhouse Bank 1982), chm MacArthur & Co Ltd 2000–; *Style*— P N J May, Esq; ✉ MacArthur & Co Limited, 60 Lombard Street, London EC3V 9EA

MAY, Dr Simon Philip Walter; s of Walter May (d 1963), and Marianne Louise, *née* Liedtke; *b* 9 August 1956; *Educ* Westminster, ChCh Oxford (MA), Birkbeck Coll London (BA, PhD); *Career* Euro affrs advsr to Rt Hon Douglas Hurd MP 1977–79, foreign affrs advsr to Rt Hon Edward Heath 1979–83, memb Cabinet of Vice-Pres EEC Cmmn 1983–85, co fndr Action Ctee Europe 1985–86, dir Northern Telecom Europe 1986–88, chief exec Mondiale Ltd 1988–92, conslt in telecommunications 1992–; dir Whatman plc 1994– (dep chm 2001–); memb Int Investment Ctee Activ Investment Partners Tokyo 2001–; research fell Dept of Philosophy Birkbeck Coll London 1997–; visiting prof Tokyo Univ 2000–01; *Books* The European Armaments Market and Procurement Cooperation (1988), The Pocket Philosopher (1999), Nietzsche's Ethics (1999), From Behind the Akamon Gate: Snapshots of the fall and rise of Japan (2004), The Little Book of Big Thoughts (2005), Atomic Sushi (2006); *Recreations* music, wine, walking; *Clubs* George; *Style*— Dr Simon May; ✉ School of Philosophy, Birkbeck College, Malet Street, London WC1E 7HX (tel 07977 500946, e-mail s.may@philosophy.bbk.ac.uk)

MAY, Stephen Charles; s of Paul May, CBE (d 1996), and Dorothy Ida, *née* Makower (d 1961); *b* 5 September 1937; *Educ* Berkhamsted Sch, ChCh Oxford (MA); *m* 2 June 1977, Jeannette de Rothschild (d 1980), da of Frederick Ernest Bishop (d 1940); *Career* Nat Serv 2 Lt RA 1956–58; John Lewis Partnership: joined 1961, md Edinburgh 1973–75, md Peter Jones 1975–77, dir of personnel 1978–92, gen inspr 1992–97, ret; memb Mgmnt Ctee British Retail Consortium (chm Employment Ctee) 1995–97, memb Mgmnt Ctee Involvement and Participation Assoc 1991–97; chm of tstees Action Medical Research (formerly Action Research) 1999–2007, chm Advsy Bd The Relationships Fndn 1998–2006 (memb 1994–2006), dir Employee Ownership Assoc 1999–, tstee The Scott Bader Cwlth Ltd 2001–07; *Recreations* mountains, fishing, tennis, travel; *Style*— Stephen May, Esq; ✉ 10 Cheyne Gardens, London SW3 5QU (tel 020 7352 6463, fax 020 7565 2862)

MAY, Stephen Richard (Steve); s of Robert May, ISM, and Vera *née* Edwards; *Educ* Lincoln GS, Durham Johnston Sch, Wyggeston Boys' GS Leicester, Univ of Leicester (BA); *m* 1993, Carol *née* Style; 1 da (Camilla Jayne b 1993), 1 s (James William b 1996); *Career* broadcaster; sports reporter: BBC Radio Leicester 1978–82, BBC Sport 1982–; sports presenter Today BBC Radio 4 1989– (featured in 2000 progs), football reporter Grandstand BBC1 1989–, sports presenter BBC Newsroom South East 1992–95, presenter BBC World Sport 1995–2000; author of various articles; *Recreations* cricket, swimming, football, family; *Clubs* Belgrave St Peters CC (sec 1984–99); *Style*— Steve May, Esq; ✉ c/o BBC Television Centre, Wood Lane, London W12 (e-mail may.s@btinternet.com)

MAY, Rt Hon Theresa Mary; PC (2003), MP; da of Rev Hubert Brasier (d 1981), and Zaidee, *née* Barnes (d 1982); *b* 1 October 1956; *Educ* Wheatley Park Comp, St Hugh's Coll Oxford (MA); *m* 1980, Philip John May, s of John May (d 1999); *Career* with Bank of England 1977–83, Inter-Bank Research Organisation 1983–85, Association for Payment Clearing Services 1985–97 (head of Euro Affrs Unit 1989–96); cncllr London Borough of Merton 1986–94; Parly candidate: NW Durham 1992, Barking (by-election) 1994; MP (Cons) Maidenhead 1997–; oppn frontbench spokesman on educn and employment, disability issues and women 1998–99, shadow sec of state for educn and employment 1999–2001, shadow sec of state for educn and skills 2001, shadow sec of state for tport, local govt and the regions 2001–02, chm Cons Pty 2002–03, shadow sec of state for environment and transport 2003–04, shadow sec of state for the family 2004–05, shadow sec of state for culture, media and sport and the family 2005, shadow ldr of the House 2005–; *Recreations* walking, cooking; *Clubs* Maidenhead Conservative; *Style*— The Rt Hon Theresa May, MP; ✉ House of Commons, London SW1A 0AA (tel 020 7219 5206)

MAY OF OXFORD, Baron (Life Peer UK 2001), of Oxford in the County of Oxfordshire; Prof Sir Robert McCredie May; OM (2002), kt (1996), AC (1998); s of Henry Wilkinson May, of Sydney, Australia; *b* 8 January 1936; *Educ* Sydney Boys' Sch, Univ of Sydney (BSc, PhD); *m* 3 Aug 1962, Judith, da of Jerome Feiner, of New York, USA; 1 da (Hon Naomi Felicity b 25 March 1966); *Career* Gordon Mackey lectr in applied mathematics Harvard Univ 1959–61 and 1966, prof of physics Univ of Sydney 1962–72, prof of astrophysics Caltech 1967; prof of plasma physics: UKAEA Lab Culham 1971, Magdalen Coll Oxford 1971, Inst for Advanced Study Princeton 1972, King's Coll Res Centre Cambridge 1976; visiting prof Imperial Coll London 1975–88, Class of 1877 prof of zoology Princeton Univ 1973–88, Royal Soc res prof Univ of Oxford and Imperial Coll London 1988–95 (leave of absence 1995–2000); chief scientific advsr to UK Govt and head of Office of Sci and Technol 1995–2000; pres British Ecological Soc 1991–93, pres Royal Soc 2000–; memb: NRC, Sci-Advsy Cncl for WWF (US) 1978, Int Whaling Cmmn 1978–82, US Marine Animals Cmmn 1979–, Governing Bd Soc of Conservation Biologists 1985–88, Advsy Bd Inst for Sci Info 1986–; chm Bd of Tstees Natural History Museum 1994–99 (tstee 1989–94); tstee: WWF (UK) 1990–94, Nuffield Fndn 1993–, Royal Botanic Gardens Kew and Wakehurst Place 1991–94; contribto various scientific jls incl Nature and Science; Rockefeller scholar Italy 1986; Weldon Medal in Biometrics Univ of Oxford 1980, MacArthur Award American Ecological Soc 1984, Zoological Medal Linnean Soc 1991, Marsh Award for Conservation Science Zoological Soc 1992, Frink Medal Zoological Soc of London 1996, Crafoord Prize Royal Swedish Acad of Sciences 1996, Balzan Prize 1998, The Blue Planet Prize 2001; Hon Degrees: Univ of London 1989, Uppsala Univ 1990, Yale Univ 1993, Univ of Edinburgh 1994, Heriot-Watt Univ 1994, Univ of Sydney 1995, Princeton Univ 1996, Univ of Warwick 1997, Univ of Salford 1997, Univ of Kent 1997, ICL 1997, Brunel Univ 1999, Univ of Manchester 2001, Univ of Reading 2002, Univ of Nottingham 2002, Univ of Sussex 2003, ETH Zurich 2003; fell American Acad of Arts and Sciences 1977, fell Aust Acad of Sciences 1991, foreign memb US Nat Acad of Sciences; FRS 1979 (pres 2000–), Hon FREng 2005; *Books* Stability and Complexity in Model Ecosystems (1973, 2 edn 1974, re-issued 2000), Theoretical Ecology: Principles and Applications (ed 1976, 2 edn 1981), Population Biology of Infectious Diseases (ed with R M Anderson, 1982), Exploitation of Marine Ecosystems (ed, 1984), Perspectives in Ecological Theory (ed with J Roughgarden and S A Levin, 1988), Population Regulation and Dynamics (ed with M P Hassell, 1990), Infectious Diseases of Humans: Transmissions and Control (with R M Anderson, 1991), Large Scale Ecology and Conservation Biology (ed with P J Edwards and N R Webb, 1994), Extinction Rates (ed with J H Lawton, 1995), Evolution of Biological Diversity (ed with A Magurran, 1999), Virus Dynamics: Mathematical Principals of Immunology and Virology (with M A Nowak, 2000), SARS: A Case Study in Emerging Infections (ed with A McLean, J Pattison and R A Weiss, 2005); *Recreations* running, tennis; *Style*— The Rt Hon the Lord May of Oxford, PRS; ✉ Department of Zoology, University of Oxford, Oxford OX1 3PS (tel 01865 271276, fax 01865 281060)

MAYALL, David William; s of Arthur William Mayall, of Derby, and Pamela, *née* Bryant; *b* 19 July 1957; *Educ* Repton, Univ of Cambridge (MA); *m* 22 June 1985, Wendy Madeleine, da of Peter Black of Douglas, IOM; 1 s (James b 13 April 1988), 1 da (Sophie b 31 May 1990); *Career* called to the Bar Gray's Inn 1979, pt/t special adjudicator 1993–; *Recreations* bridge, tennis, golf; *Style*— David Mayall, Esq; ✉ Highstone House, 148 Totteridge Lane, Totteridge, London N20 8AJ; 4 King's Bench Walk, Temple, London EC4Y 7DL; Murray House, Hammers Lane, Mill Hill, London NW7 4DY

MAYALL, Prof James B L; *b* 14 April 1937; *Educ* Sidney Sussex Coll Cambridge (open scholar, BA); *Career* Nat Serv 2 Lt Queen's Own Nigeria Regt 1955–57; Sir John Dill fell Princeton Univ 1960–61, asst princ Board of Trade 1961–63, Treasy Centre for Admin Studies 1963–64, first sec (econ) Br High Cmmn New Delhi 1964–65, princ Bd of Trade 1965–66; LSE: lectr Int Relations Dept 1966–75, sr lectr 1975–83, reader 1983–91, rep Inter-Univ Ctee for Study on Africa 1984–, prof and convenor of Int Relations Dept 1991–94; visiting lectr: Univ of New Brunswick 1976–77, Univ of Cape Town 1977–78; visiting prof of govt Dartmouth Coll NH 1982, 1984, 1989, 1990, Centre for Political Studies Jawaharlal Nehru Univ New Delhi 1988; assoc ed Survey and Documents on Int Affairs RIIA 1968–72; convenor: South Africa Study Gp RIIA 1990–, research project on Int Soc after the Cold War (funded by Ford Foundation) 1993–95; chm Steering Ctee and Ed Bd LSE Centre for Int Studies 1991 (memb 1975); memb: Cncl RIIA 1992–, Exec Ctee Br Int Studies Assoc 1981–85 and 1987–88, Research Ctee Int Africa Inst 1986–88, Editorial Ctee Ethnic and Racial Studies 1989–94, Nations and Nationalism 1994–; *Books* Documents on International Affairs, 1962 (ed with D C Watt and Cornelia Navari, 1971), Current British Foreign Policy (3 vols ed with D C Watt, 1970, 1971, 1972), Africa: The Cold War and After (1971), A New International Commodity Regime (ed and contributor with Geoffrey Goodwin, 1979), The End of the Post War Era: Documents on Great Power Relations, 1968–75 (ed and introduced with Cornelia Navari, 1981), The Community of States (ed, 1982), Nationalism and International Society (1990); author of articles in various political jls; *Style*— Prof James Mayall; ✉ Centre for International Studies, London School of Economics and Political Science, Houghton Street, London WC2A 2AE (tel 020 7955 7400 (direct), 020 7405 7686, fax 020 7955 7556, telex 24655 LSELON G)

MAYALL, Richard Michael (Rik); s of John Mayall, and Gillian Mayall; *b* 7 March 1958; *Educ* Univ of Manchester; *m* Barbara, *née* Robbin; 2 da (Rosemary Elizabeth, Bonnie), 1 s (Sidney Richard); *Career* comedian, actor and writer; *Theatre* incl: Nick in The Common Pursuit (Phoenix) 1988, Vladimir in Waiting for Godot (Gielgud Theatre) 1991–92, Khelstakov in The Government Inspector, Sean Bourke in Cell Mates (Albery) 1995, A Family Affair (Theatre Royal Bath); *Television* incl: Rick in The Young Ones (originator and co-writer, 2 series, BBC) 1982 and 1984, The Comic Strip Presents (Channel Four) 1983–84 and 1992, George's Marvellous Medicine (5 episodes, Jackanory, BBC) 1985, Alan B'Stard in The New Statesman (4 series, YTV) 1987–88, 1990 and 1994 (Int Emmy Award 1989, BAFTA Best New Comedy 1990, Int Film & Festival and TV Festival of New York 1991, Special Craft Gold Medal Best Performer/Narrator), Grim Tales (2 series, Central) 1990, Bottom (3 series, BBC) 1990, 1992 and 1994 (Comedy Awards Best New Comedy 1992), Rik Mayall Presents (2 trilogies of films, Granada TV) 1992–94 (British Comedy Awards Best Comedy Actor 1993), Wham Bham Strawberry Jam! (BBC) 1995, The Alan B'Stard Interview with Brian Walden (BBC) 1995, J Creek Christmas Special (BBC) 1998, In the Red (BBC) 1998, The Bill (Thames TV) 1998, 4 Men In a Plane (Comic Strip) 1999, The Knock (LWT) 2000, Believe Nothing 2002; *Films* incl: Whoops Apocalypse 1982, Drop Dead Fred 1990, Horse Opera 1992, Remember Me 1996, Bring Me the Head of Mavis Davis 1996, The Canterville Ghost, Merlin -The Return 1998, Guest House Paradiso 1999, Kevin of the North 2000, Churchill: The Hollywood Years 2003; voices for animations incl: Tom Thumb in World of Peter Rabbit & Friends - Tale of Two Bad Mice 1994, Toad in Wind in the Willows and Willows in Winter 1995 (Emmy Award 1997), The Robber King in The Snow Queen 1995, Prince Froglip in The Princess & The Goblin, Hero Baby in How to be a Little Sod 1995, A Monkey's Tale 1995 Young William Tell in Oscar's Orchestra 1996, Tom and Vicky 1997 and 1998, Jellikins 1998, Watership Down 1999, Day of Sirens 2002, Alone in the Dark 2002; *Live Stand Up* incl: Comic Strip 1982, Kevin Turvey and Bastard Squad 1983, Rik Mayall Ben Elton Andy De La Tour (UK tour & Edinburgh Fringe) 1983, Rik Mayall and Ben Elton 1984–85, (Aust tour) 1986 and 1992, Rik Mayall and Andy De La Tour 1989–90, Rik Mayall and Adrian Edmondson (UK tours) 1993, 1995, 1997 and 2001; *Radio* for BBC Radio 4: The Story of Is, The Sound of Trumpets 1999, A Higher Education 2000; *Style*— Rik Mayall, Esq

MAYBURY, Neil Martin; s of Leonard Albert Maybury (d 1992), of Harborne, Birmingham, and Kathleen Margaret, *née* Howse (d 1982); *b* 25 August 1943; *Educ* King Edward's Sch Birmingham, Univ of Birmingham (LLB); *m* 10 May 1980, Sally Elizabeth, da of Kenneth Carroll, of Streetly, W Midlands; 3 s (Thomas Charles b 1983, Toby George b 1985, Henry Giles b 1992), 1 da (Natasha Poppy b 1987); *Career* admitted slr 1969; asst slr Clifford-Turner & Co London (now Clifford-Chance) 1969–72, ptnr Pinsent & Co (now Pinsent Masons) 1975–95, ptnr Dibb Lupton Alsop (now DLA) 1995–2000, ptnr

M

Hammond Suddards Edge 2001–03, ptnr Maybury & Co 2003–; dir: Vodart Ltd, Tantell Ltd, Tantell Construction Ltd, Au Pair Holdings Ltd; chm: Birmingham Rep Devpt Ctee 2000–02, Birmingham Business Focus 2002–; memb Cncl Soc for Computers and Law 1979–88, memb Law Soc, chm Hood Down Club 1986–; *Books* Guide to The Electronic Office (with Keith James, 1988); *Recreations* tennis, flying, gardening, classic cars, skiing, classical music; *Clubs* Edgbaston Priory, Edgbaston Golf, Halfpenny Green Flying; *Style*— Neil Maybury, Esq; ✉ Maybury & Co, One Victoria Square, Birmingham B1 1BD (tel 0121 632 2111, e-mail neil@sheinwood.com)

MAYER, Charlotte; da of Frederick Mayer (d 1996), and Helen, *née* Stutz (d 1974); *b* 4 January 1929; *Educ* Goldsmiths Coll London, RCA; *m* 1952, Geoffrey Salmon; 1 s (Julian b 1956 d 1989), 2 da (Antonia, Louise (twins) b 1959); *Career* sculptor; numerous public sculptures; work in public and corporate collections incl: Br Petroleum plc, JCDecaux, McDonald's Ltd, Wadham Coll Oxford, J Walter Thompson Ltd, BNP Paribas; work in private collections in Europe, Japan and USA; FRBS (winner silver medal 1991), ARCA; *Exhibitions* Amnesty Int London, 'Art in Action' Waterperry Oxon, 'Art in Steel' London, Ashbourne Gall Derbys, Bear Lane Gall Oxford, Belgrave Gall London, Berkeley Square Gall London, British Artists Show London, Bruton Gall Somerset, Cavalier Gall Stanford USA, Chelsea Harbour London, Crypt of St John's Hampstead London, Sculpture at Goowood Sussex, Richard Hagen Worcs, Foundation Helan-Arts Belgium, Gallery Pangolin Chalford, Gallery 108 London, Garden Gall Stockbridge, IOD London, Iveagh Bequest London, Marjorie Parr Gall London, Hannah Peschar Sculpture Garden Surrey, Royal Acad London, Royal West of England Acad Bristol, RBS London, Sladmore Gall London, 'Ten Sculptors/Two Cathedrals' Winchester and Salisbury, V&A London, Thompson's Gall London, New Academy & Curwen Gall London; *Recreations* friends; *Style*— Charlotte Mayer; ✉ 6 Bloomfield Road, Highgate, London N6 4ET (tel and fax 020 8340 6302, e-mail charlottemayer@talktalk.net)

MAYER, Dr Christopher Norman; s of George Emanuel Mayer, of Bath, Avon, and Margaret, *née* Jones; *b* 30 August 1954; *Educ* City of Bath Boys Sch Avon, Welsh Nat Sch of Med Cardiff (MB BCh); *m* 12 Sept 1981, Joanna Paget, da of Michael James Lock, of Arundel, W Sussex; 3 da (Alice b 25 July 1984, Annabel b 9 Feb 1986, Felicity b 30 July 1988), 1 s (Humphrey b 2 Sept 1991); *Career* sr registrar Dept of Psychiatry St George's Hosp London 1983–86, conslt psychiatrist W Suffolk Hosp Bury St Edmunds 1986–, med dir Alcohol Treatment Prog Dukes Priory Hosp Chelmsford 1992–; lead conslt in adult mental health for LHP Tst 1999–2000; pubns incl papers on anorexia nervosa; TV appearances incl: The Purchase and Importation of Camels from North Africa (BBC 2), The Crisis of British Public Conveniences (Channel 4); short-term WHO consultancy to UAE 1999; patron W Suffolk Relate; FRCPsych 1997; *Recreations* digging in the garden, 19th Century literature; *Style*— Dr Christopher Mayer; ✉ Cattishall Farmhouse, Great Barton, Bury St Edmunds, Suffolk IP31 2QT (tel 01284 787340); West Suffolk Hospital, Hardwick Lane, Bury St Edmunds, Suffolk IP33 2QZ (tel 01284 713592, e-mail cnmayer@bigfoot.com)

MAYER, Prof Colin Peter; s of late Harold Charles and late Anne Louise Mayer, of London; *b* 12 May 1953; *Educ* St Paul's, Oriel Coll Oxford (MA), Wolfson Coll Oxford (MPhil), Harvard Univ (Harkness fell), Univ of Oxford (DPhil); *m* Annette Patricia, da of late Annesley Haynes; 2 da (Ruth Sarah b 21 Oct 1984, Hannah Claire b 21 July 1987); *Career* HM Treasy 1976–79, fell in economics St Anne's Coll Oxford 1980–86, prof of corporate finance City Univ Business Sch 1987–92, prof of economics and finance Univ of Warwick 1992–94, prof of mgmnt studies Univ of Oxford 1994–, professorial fell Wadham Coll Oxford 1994–2006, dir Oxford Financial Research Centre 1998–2006, dean Saïd Business Sch Univ of Oxford 2006–, professorial fell St Edmund Hall Oxford 2006–; Houblon Norman fell Bank of England 1989–90; memb Exec Ctee Royal Economic Soc 2002–06; chm OXERA Holdings Ltd, delg OUP 1996–2006; fell European Corp Governance Inst; hon fell: St Anne's Coll Oxford, Oriel Coll Oxford; *Books* European Financial Integration (with A Giovannini, 1991), Capital Markets and Financial Intermediation (with X Vives, 1993), Hostile Takeovers: Defence, Attack and Corporate Governance (with T Jenkinson, 1994), Asset Management and Investor Protection (with J Franks and L Correia, 2002); *Recreations* piano playing, jogging, reading philosophy and science; *Style*— Prof Colin Mayer; ✉ Saïd Business School, University of Oxford, Park End Street, Oxford OX1 1HP (tel 01865 288811)

MAYES, Ian; QC (1993); *b* 11 September 1951; *Educ* Highgate Sch (Fndn Scholar), Trinity Coll Cambridge (Hooper Prizeman); *Children* 2 s (Oliver Tobias b 31 Oct 1988, Theo Alexander b 9 Feb 1992); *Career* called to the Bar Middle Temple 1974 (Harmsworth scholar, bencher); recorder; Dept of Trade Inspection London Capital Group Ltd 1975–77, standing counsel to Inland Revenue 1983–93; chm Disciplinary Tbnl Lloyd's of London, memb Justice Ctee on Fraud; chm Art First; *Recreations* photography; *Clubs* Garrick; *Style*— Ian Mayes, Esq, QC; ✉ 3 (North) King's Bench Walk, Temple, London EC4Y 7HR (tel 020 7797 8600, fax 020 7797 8699)

MAYES, Rt Rev Michael Hugh Gunton; *see:* Limerick and Killaloe, Bishop of

MAYES, Tessa; *Career* journalist; TV reporter and author: Panorama (BBC) 2000, Channel 4 2001; contrib: The Spectator, Sunday Times, spiked-online.com, British Journalism Review; shortlisted Race in the Media Awards Cmmn for Racial Equality 1994, special mention Women of Achievement Awards Cosmopolitan magazine 1999; Int Journalist Prog Bursary Award Die Welt Belrin 2005; memb NUJ; *Books* Disclosure: media freedom and the privacy debate after Diana (1998), Restraint or Revelation?: free speech and privacy in a confessional age (2002); *Style*— Ms Tessa Mayes; ✉ c/o Knight Ayton Management, 114 St Martin's Lane, London WC2N 4BE (tel 020 7836 5333)

MAYHEW, David; *b* 20 May 1940; *Career* with Panmure Gordon 1961–69; Cazenove & Co: joined 1969, ptnr 1971–, dealing ptnr 1972, ptnr i/c Capital Markets Dept 1986–2001, chm Cazenove Gp Ltd (formerly Cazenove Gp plc) 2001–, chm JPMorgan Cazenove 2005–; non-exec dir Rio Tinto plc and Rio Tinto Ltd 2000–; *Style*— Mr David Mayhew; ✉ Cazenove Group Limited, 20 Moorgate, London EC2R 6DA

MAYHEW, Jeremy Paul; s of Yon Richard Mayhew, and Cora Angela, *née* Lamboll; *b* 1 February 1959; *Educ* Clifton, Western Reserve Acad Ohio (ESU scholarship), Balliol Coll Oxford (scholar, sec and treas Oxford Union), Harvard Business Sch (MBA); *Career* BBC TV: trainee asst prodr 1980–82, asst prodr Current Affrs 1982–84; ind prodr/dir (making documentary and current affrs progs for Channel 4) 1984–87, mgmnt conslt Booz Allen & Hamilton 1989–90, special advsr to Rt Hon Peter Lilley MP (DTI and DSS) 1990–93; head of BBC Strategy Devpt 1993–95; BBC Worldwide Ltd: dir New Media 1995–99, dir New Ventures and Strategy 1999–2001, bd dir 1997–2001; dir and head of strategy practice Human Capital (media strategy and res consultancy) 2001–02, ptnr Spectrum Strategy Consultants 2003– (sr advsr 2002–03); non-exec bd memb: Learning and Skills Devpt Agency 1999–2002, Strategic Rail Authy 2000–06; memb Cncl London C of C and Industry 1998–; constituency offr Hammersmith Cons Assoc 1990–93; memb: Cncl Bow Gp 1990–93, Ct City Univ 1996–; tstee: Hammersmith United Charities 1991–96, Br Friends of Harvard Business Sch 1993–, City Arts Tst 2001–, Thames Festival Tst 2004–; pres Harvard Business Sch Club of London 1997 and 1998; govr: Sacred Heart Junior Sch 1990–96, City Literary Inst 1998–2002, London Guildhall Univ 2000–02, Clifton Coll 2000–, London Metropolitan Univ 2002–; donation govr Christ's Hosp 1998–; Common Councilman Corp of London (Aldersgate Ward) 1996– (chm Educn Ctee 2005–06, dep chm Finance & Barbican Centre Ctees 2007–); Freeman City of London, Liveryman Worshipful Co of Loriners; memb RTS 1990–; *Recreations* collecting political caricatures, theatre, cinema, arguing!; *Clubs* Reform; *Style*— Jeremy Mayhew, Esq; ✉ Spectrum Strategy Consultants, Greencoat House, Francis Street, London SW1P 1DH (tel 020 7808 6241); home (tel 020 7256 8224, e-mail jeremymayhew@btinternet.com)

MAYHEW, Kenneth (Ken); s of Albert Chadwick Mayhew (d 1967), and Alice, *née* Leigh (d 2000); *b* 1 September 1947; *Educ* Manchester Grammar, Worcester Coll Oxford (MA), LSE (MSc); *Children* 1 da (Rowena Kate b 1978 d 2004), 1 s (Alexander Chadwick b 1991); *Career* economist; economic asst HM Treasy 1970–72; res offr: Queen Elizabeth House Oxford 1972, Inst of Econs Oxford 1972–81; Pembroke Coll Oxford: fell 1976–, vicegerent 2000–03; econ dir NEDO 1989–90, dir ESRC Research Centre on Skills and Knowledge and Organisational Performance 1998–; assoc ed Oxford Review of Economic Policy and Oxford Economic Papers; *Books* Pay Policies for the Future (ed with D Robinson, 1983), Improving Incentives for the Low Paid (ed with A Bowen, 1990), Reducing Regional Inequalities (ed with A Bowen, 1991), Providing Health Care (ed with A McGuire and P Fenn, 1991), Britain's Training Deficit (ed with R Layard and G Owen, 1994), The Economics of Skills Obsolescence (jt ed, 2002); *Recreations* travel, literature; *Clubs* Reform; *Style*— Ken Mayhew, Esq; ✉ Pembroke College, Oxford OX1 1DW (tel 01865 276434, fax 01865 276418)

MAYHEW JONAS, Dame Judith; DBE (2002); *b* 18 October 1948; *Educ* Otago Girls' HS NZ, Univ of Otago; *Career* admitted: barr and slr NZ 1973, slr England and Wales 1993; lectr in law: Univ of Otago 1970–73, Univ of Southampton 1973–76 (also sub dean), KCL 1976–89 (also sub dean and dir Anglo French law degree Sorbonne); employment lawyer and dir of trg Titmuss Sainer Dechert 1989–94, employment lawyer and dir of educn and trg Wilde Sapte 1994–2000, special advsr Clifford Chance 2000–03, non-exec dir Merrill Lynch & Co Inc USA 2006– (advsr 2003–06); provost King's Coll Cambridge 2003–06; Corp of London: memb Ct of Common Cncl and various Ctees (Finance, Housing, Social Services, Police) 1986–2004, chm Educn Ctee 1989–94 (memb 1986–2004), chm Policy & Resources Ctee 1996–2003 (dep chm 1993–96 and 2003–04); memb Leaders' and Educn Ctees Assoc of London Govt 1995–2003, city and business advsr to Mayor of London 2000–04; chm ROH 2003–; memb Bd: London Devp Agency (chair Private Investment Cmmn), Int Fin Servs London 2000–04, 4Ps; tstee Nat History Museum 1998–2006, chm ROH Covent Garden 2003–; memb Bd Gresham Coll 1990–, chm of govrs Birkbeck Coll London 1993–2003, memb Ct and Cncl Imperial Coll London 2001–04; fell: Birkbeck Coll, London Business Sch; Hon LLD: Univ of Otago 1998, City Univ 1999, London Met Univ 2003; hon fell Inst of CPD 2004, fell City and Guilds 2004; *Recreations* opera, theatre, old English roses, tennis; *Clubs* Guildhall; *Style*— Dame Judith Mayhew Jonas, DBE; ✉ 25 Victoria Square, London SW1W 0RB

MAYHEW OF TWYSDEN, Baron (Life Peer UK 1997), of Kilndown in the County of Kent; Sir Patrick Barnabas Burke Mayhew; kt (1983), PC (1986), QC (1972), DL (Kent 2001); s of (Alfred) Geoffrey Horace Mayhew, MC (d 1985), of Sevenoaks Weald, Kent, and Sheila Margaret Burke, *née* Roche; *b* 11 September 1929; *Educ* Tonbridge, Balliol Coll Oxford (MA); *m* 15 April 1963, Rev Jean Elizabeth Mayhew, OBE, 2 da of John Gurney (d 2000), of Walsingham Abbey, Norfolk; 4 s (Hon James b 1964, Hon Henry b 1965, Hon Tristram b 1968, Hon Jerome b 1970); *Career* served 4/7 Royal Dragoon Gds, Capt (Nat Serv and AER); called to the Bar Middle Temple 1956, bencher 1982; Parly candidate (Cons) Camberwell and Dulwich 1970, MP (Cons) Tunbridge Wells Feb 1974–97; vice-chm Cons Home Affrs Ctee and memb Exec 1922 Ctee 1976–79, Parly under sec for employment 1979–81, min of state Home Office 1981–83, Slr-Gen 1983–87, Attorney-Gen 1987–92, sec of state for Northern Ireland 1992–97; chm PM's Advsy Ctee on Business Appointments 2000–; non-exec Western Provident Assoc 1998– (vice-chm 2000–); *Recreations* country pursuits; *Clubs* Pratt's, Beefsteak, Garrick, Tunbridge Wells Constitutional; *Style*— The Rt Hon Lord Mayhew of Twysden, PC, QC; ✉ House of Lords, London SW1A 0PW (tel 020 7219 3000)

MAYHEW-SANDERS, Sir John Reynolds; kt (1982); s of Jack Mayhew-Sanders (d 1982); *b* 25 October 1931; *Educ* Epsom Coll, RNC Dartmouth, Jesus Coll Cambridge (MA); *m* 1958, Sylvia Mary (d 1995), da of George S Colling (d 1959); 3 s, 1 da; *Career* RN 1949–54; formerly with Mayhew-Sanders Chartered Accountants and with PE Consulting Group Ltd; John Brown & Co Ltd: dir 1972–83, chief exec 1975–83, chm 1978–83; chm Heidrick & Struggles 1985–87; non-exec dir: Rover Group plc 1980–88, Dowty Group plc 1982–86; memb: Cncl of Engrg Employers' Fedn 1977–80, BOTB 1980–83, BBC Consultative Gp Industrial and Business Affrs 1981–83; chm Overseas Project Bd 1980–83, pres Br-Soviet C of C 1983–88; govr Sadler's Wells Fndn 1983–89, dir Sadler's Wells Tst, chm New Sadler's Wells Opera Co; FCA, CIMgt; FRSA; *Recreations* fishing, shooting, music, astronomy; *Style*— Sir John Mayhew-Sanders; ✉ Great Deptford House, High Bickington, Umberleigh, Devon EX37 9BP

MAYNARD, Prof Alan Maynard; s of late Edward Joseph Maynard, of W Kirby, Wirral, Merseyside, and late Hilda Marion, *née* McCausland; *b* 15 December 1944; *Educ* Calday Grange GS W Kirby Merseyside, Univ of Newcastle upon Tyne, Univ of York (BPhil); *m* 22 June 1968, Elizabeth Mary, da of Kevin Joseph Shanahan (decd), of Edinburgh; 2 s (Justin b 11 Feb 1970, John b 24 Oct 1971), 2 da (Jane b 31 July 1974, Samantha b 8 Nov 1976); *Career* asst lectr and lectr in economics Univ of Exeter 1968–71, prof of economics and founding dir Centre for Health Economics Univ of York 1983–95 (lectr in economics 1971–76, sr lectr and dir Graduate Prog in Health Economics 1976–83), sec Nuffield Provincial Hosps Tst 1995–96, prof of health economics Univ of York 1997–; visiting prof: LSE, Univ of Aberdeen; adjunct prof Univ of Technol Sydney Aust; visiting lectr: Italy, NZ, Sweden; memb York Health Authy 1983–91, non-exec dir York NHS Tst Hosp 1991–97, chm York NHS Tst 1997–; conslt: DfID, World Bank, WHO; memb: York Health Authy 1982–91, ESRC 1983–86 (memb Human Behaviour and Devpt Ctee 1988–89), MRC Health Servs Res Ctee 1986–92; chm Evaluation Panel for Fourth Med and Health Res Prog Euro Cmmn 1990; memb: Royal Commonwealth Soc, Royal Society of Medicine; over 250 articles in jls; Hon DSc Univ of Aberdeen 2003, Hon LLD Univ of Northumbria 2006; FMedSci 2000; *Books* Health Care in the European Community (1976), Public Private Mix for Health (ed with G McLachlan, 1982), Controlling Legal Addictions (ed with D Robinson and R Chester, 1989), Preventing Alcohol and Tobacco Problems (ed with P Tether, 1990), Competition in Health Care: Reforming the NHS (ed, with A J Culyer and J Posnett), Non Random Reflections on Health Services Research (ed, with I Chalmers, 1997), Being Reasonable about Health Economics (ed, with A J Culyer, 1997), Advances in Health Economics (ed, with A Scotland and R Elliott, 2003), The Public-Private Mix for Health (ed, 2005); *Recreations* reading, walking, current affairs and cricket; *Clubs* RSM, Royal Cwlth Soc; *Style*— Prof Alan Maynard; ✉ York Health Policy Group, Department of Health Sciences, University of York, Heslington, York YO10 5DD (tel 01904 321333, e-mail akm3@york.ac.uk)

MAYNARD, Alice Mary; da of Charles Rupert Gordon Maynard, of Wakefield, W Yorks, and Mary Ada Maynard; *b* 28 November 1957; *Educ* Univ of York (BA), Ashridge Business Sch (MBA); *m* 1994 (m dis 2000); *Career* software devpt IT industry 1980–90, mktg conslt GA Property Services 1991, dir Equal Ability 1992–96, sr conslt Churchill & Friend 1997–98, head of disability strategy Network Rail (Railtrack) 1998–2003, disability HR conslt London Underground (secondment) 2001, social inclusion advsr Transport for London (secondment) 2001–02, fndr and md Future Inclusion Ltd 2003–; memb Human Genetics Cmmn, assoc Employers' Forum on Disability, chair Milton Keynes Racial Equality Cncl 2006–07, memb Advsy Gp Milton Keynes Common Purpose, memb Eastern Area Ctee Jephson Housing Assoc, memb UK Disabled People's Cncl; *Publications* articles in various pubns incl: Counselling at Work, Therapy Weekly (1993–97); Adequate Technology (paper to Ecart III, 1995), The Way Forward: A development pack for organisations of disabled people (1996), COST 335 European Action Report (contrib, 1999), Breaking Down Bureaucratic Barriers (co-author, 2000), Transed (2007); *Style*— Ms Alice Maynard; ✉ Future Inclusion Ltd, PO Box 5672, Milton Keynes MK15 9WZ (tel 01908 665850, fax 07043 017425)

MAYNARD, (Henry) Charles Edward; s of Henry Maynard, of Coleshill, Bucks, and Diana Elizabeth, *née* Lee; *b* 10 February 1941; *Educ* Bryanston, Imperial Coll London (BSc); *m* 17 March 1984, Susan Marjorie, da of Edward George Hedges Barford; 2 da (Catherine Anna b 1 May 1986, Rebecca Jane b 28 April 1989); *Career* ptnr Moores Rowland CA's 1969 (ptnr i/c London Office 1979–85, vice-chm Moores Rowland Int 1987–91, chm 1991–97); ptnr BDO Stoy Hayward 1999–2001; FCA 1967; *Recreations* golf, tennis, sailing, English watercolours; *Clubs* Hurlingham, Royal West Norfolk Golf, Royal Wimbledon Golf; *Style*— Charles Maynard, Esq; ✉ 6 Favart Road, London SW6 4AZ (tel 020 7731 4795, fax 020 7736 4919, e-mail hcemaynard@hotmail.com)

MAYNARD, John David; s of Albert William Henry Maynard (d 1968), of Surrey, and Ellen Hughes-Jones (d 1970); *b* 14 May 1931; *Educ* Whitgift Sch, Charing Cross Hosp London (MB BS, Gold medal Clinical Medicine and Surgery), Univ of London (MS); *m* 1, 13 Aug 1955 (m dis 1971), Patricia Katharine, da of C W F Gray (d 1985), of Sutton, Surrey; 2 da (Sarah b 1956, Julia b 1962), 2 s (Andrew b 1959, Nicholas b 1962); m 2, 23 June 1972, Gillian Mary, da of H F Loveless, of Milford-on-Sea, Hants; 1 s (Timothy b 1976); *Career* Capt RAMC 1956; lectr in anatomy London Hosp 1958–59, sr conslt surgn Guy's Hosp London 1967–93, dir of the Pathology Museums of Guy's and St Thomas' Med Schs 1969–96, teacher Univ of London 1963–96, hon sr lectr in surgery Guy's Hosp 1992–96; hon conslt surgn St Luke's Hosp for the Clergy 1990–98; surgical tutor: RCS 1967–76, Guy's Hosp Med Sch 1967–76; sr examiner of surgery Univ of London 1962–85, examiner of surgery Soc of Apothecaries 1962–70; chm The Salivary Gland Tumour Panel England 1970–90, RCS advsr on surgical services to HM Prison Serv 1995–, memb Cncl RSM 1996–, surgical advsr to Dir of Museums Royal Coll of Surgns 1996–, vice-pres Grand Charity 2006– (memb Cncl and med advsr 1997–), memb Bd of Tstees Hunterian Collection at RCS 2006–; author of various papers on diseases of salivary glands; memb Soc of Expert Witnesses, memb Law Soc Directory of Expert Witnesses; Hunterian prof RCS 1963; Liveryman The Worshipful Soc of Apothecaries 1962; memb: BMA 1954, Med Soc of London 1961, The Chelsea Clinical Soc 1962; scientific FZS 1956; fell: Assoc of Surgeons 1967, Hunterian Soc 1985 (pres 2005); FRSM 1958, FRCS, fell Br Acad of Forensic Scientists 2006; *Books* Surgery (jtly, 1974), Surgery of Salivary Glands in Surgical Management (1984, 1988), Contemporary Operative Surgery (1979), Carcinoma of Salivary Glands in Head & Neck Oncology (1991), Text Book and Colour Atlas of Diseases of Salivary Glands (contrib chapters on Parotid Surgery, 1995); *Recreations* golf, hill walking, photography; *Clubs* Savage; *Style*— John D Maynard, MS, FRCS; ✉ 14 Blackheath Park, London SE3 9RP (tel 020 8852 6766); Mountsloe, Frogham, Fordingbridge, Hampshire SP6 2HP (tel 0142565 3009); Guy's Hospital, London SE1 9RT; 97 Harley Street, London W1N 1DF (tel 020 8852 6766, fax 020 8852 3581)

MAYNE, Prof David Quinn; s of Leslie Harper Mayne (d 1963), and Jane, *née* Quin (d 1998); *b* 23 April 1930; *Educ* Christian Brothers Coll Boksburg, Univ of the Witwatersrand (BSc, MSc), Univ of London (PhD, DSc); *m* 16 Dec 1954, Josephine Mary, da of Joseph Karl Hess (d 1968); 3 da (Susan Francine (Mrs Leung) b 9 March 1956, Maire Anne b 16 July 1957, Ruth Catherine b 18 April 1959); *Career* lectr Univ of the Witwatersrand 1950–54 and 1957–59, R&D engr Br Thomson Houston Co Rugby 1955–56; Imperial Coll London: lectr 1959–67, reader 1967–71, fell 2000; research fell Harvard 1971; Imperial Coll: prof of control theory 1971–91, head of Electrical Engrg Dept 1984–88; prof Dept of Electrical and Computer Engrg Univ of Calif Davis 1989–96 (prof emeritus 1996–); sr research fell Imperial Coll London 1996– (prof emeritus Dept of Electrical and Electronic Engrg); Hon DTech Univ of Lund 1995, hon fell Imperial Coll London 2000, hon prof Beihang Univ Beijing 2006; FIEE 1980, FIEEE 1981, FRS 1985, FREng 1987, fell Int Fedn of Automatic Control 2006; *Books* Differential Dynamic Programming (1970); *Recreations* walking, cross country skiing; *Style*— Prof David Mayne, FRS, FREng; ✉ Department of Electrical and Electronic Engineering, Imperial College of Science, Technology and Medicine, London SW7 2BT

MAYO, Benjamin John; s of Dr Frank Mayo, OBE, of Fawley, Hants, and Gladys Margaret, *née* Mason; *b* 8 November 1944; *Educ* Churcher's Coll Petersfield, Univ of Birmingham (BSc); *m* 1973, Hon Christine Mary Plumb, da of Baron Plumb, DL (Life Peer), *qv*; 3 da (Katharine Elizabeth b 28 Jan 1977, Sarah Louise b 14 Nov 1979, Stephanie Caroline b 9 April 1983); *Career* ICI: joined 1966, process engrg mangr Plastics Div 1980–81, prodn mangr Dumfries Works 1982–83, works mangr Oil Works Billingham 1984–85, chief engr (NE) Engrg Dept Billingham 1986–87, ops dir ICI Imagedata 1988–90, research and technol dir ICI Films Wilton 1993–98 (ops dir 1991–92); tech dir European Process Industries Competitiveness Centre (EPICC) 1998–2002, dir Ben Mayo & Assocs 2002–; memb EU Hydrogen and Fuel Cells Technol Platform 2003–; vice-pres Inst of Chemical Engrg 1998–2000 (memb Cncl 1990–93, chm Qualifications Bd); FIChemE 1990, FREng 1993; *Recreations* squash, lawn tennis, real tennis, piano; *Style*— Benjamin Mayo, Esq, FREng; ✉ The Garth, Kirby Lane, Great Broughton, North Yorkshire TS9 7HH (tel 01642 712214, e-mail ben.mayo@btinternet.com)

MAYOR, (Frederick) James; s of Fred Hoyland Mayor (d 1973), and Pamela Margaret, *née* Colledge (d 1994); *b* 20 March 1949; *Educ* Charterhouse; *m* 1978, Viviane Martha Cresswell, da of John Leigh Reed (d 1982); 2 da (Louisa Harriett Cresswell b 1981, Alice Marina Pamela b 1984 d 2002); *Career* asst: Galerie Louise Leiris Paris 1968, Perls Galleries NY 1968, Impressionist Painting Dept Sotheby's London 1969, i/c Contemporary Painting Dept Parke-Bernet Inc NY 1969–72; The Mayor Gallery Ltd London: md 1973–, chm 1980–; memb Exec Ctee Soc of London Art Dealers 1981–88; *Recreations* cooking, painting and gardening; *Clubs* Buck's, The Travellers (Paris), Chelsea Arts, Shrewsbury Hunt; *Style*— James Mayor, Esq; ✉ The Mayor Gallery Ltd, 22A Cork Street, London W1S 3NA (tel 020 7734 3558, fax 020 7494 1377)

MAYOR, Susan; da of Fred Hoyland Mayor (d 1973), and Pamela Margaret, *née* Colledge (d 1994); *b* 1 March 1945; *Educ* Lycée Français London; *m* 9 July 1975, Prof Joseph Mordaunt Crook, CBE, *qv*, s of Austin Mordaunt Crook (d 1967); *Career* Christie's: joined 1964, dir 1984–2002, conslt fans, costume and textiles 2002; memb Ctee: Costume Soc 1975, Fan Circle Int 1975–; tstee Fan Museum Greenwich 2003–; *Books* Collecting Fans (1980), Letts Guide to Collecting Fans (1991), The Collector's Guide to Fans (1995), Unfolding Pictures Fans in the Royal Collection (co-author, 2005); *Recreations* travelling; *Style*— Miss Susan Mayor; ✉ 55 Gloucester Avenue, London NW1 7BA (e-mail susan.mayor@zoom.co.uk)

MAYOU, Prof Richard; *b* 23 November 1940; *Educ* Univ of Oxford; *Career* various med posts Birmingham and London, trg in psychiatry Bethlem Royal Hosp and Maudsley Hosp; Univ of Oxford: appointed 1973, clinical reader in psychiatry and hon conslt psychiatrist 1976, fell Nuffield Coll 1976–, currently emeritus prof of psychiatry, memb univ and medical sch ctees 1989–; fndr and first chm Section for Liaison Psychiatry RCPsych, ed Jl of Psychosomatic Research 1994–99; FRCP, FRCPsych; *Books* Oxford Textbook of Psychiatry (jtly, 1983, 4 edn 2001), Medical Symptoms Not Explained by Organic Disease (jt ed, 1992), Treatment of Functional Somatic Symptoms (jt ed, 1995), Psychiatric Aspects of Physical Disease (jt ed, 1995), Psychiatry (jtly, 1999, 3 edn 2005), ABC of Psychological Medicine (jt ed, 2003); author of more than 200 papers in medical jls; *Style*— Prof Richard Mayou; ✉ Department of Psychiatry, University of Oxford, Warneford Hospital, Oxford OX3 7JX

MAYR-HARTING, Prof Henry Maria Robert Egmont; s of Herbert Mayr-Harting (d 1989), of Vienna, and Anna, *née* Münzer (d 1974); *b* 6 April 1936; *Educ* Douai Sch, Merton Coll Oxford (Amy Mary Preston Read scholar, MA, DPhil); *m* 1968, Caroline Mary Humphries, da of Dr Thomas H Henry; 1 s (Felix b 1969), 1 da (Ursula b 1972); *Career* asst lectr and lectr in medieval history Univ of Liverpool 1960–68; Univ of Oxford: fell and tutor in medieval history St Peter's Coll 1968–97 (emeritus fell 1997–), lectr in medieval history Merton Coll 1976–97, Slade prof of fine art 1987–88, reader in medieval history 1993–97, regius prof of ecclesiastical history 1997–2003, lay canon Christ Church 1997–2003; correspndong memb Austrian Acad of Sciences 2001; visiting fell Peterhouse Cambridge 1983, Brown Fndn fell Univ of the South Tennessee 1992; Hon Dr: Lawrence Univ Wisconsin 1998, Univ of the South Tennessee 1999; FBA 1992; *Books* The Acta of the Bishops of Chichester 1075–1207 (1965), The Coming of Christianity to Anglo-Saxon England (1972, 3 edn 1991), Ottonian Book Illumination: An Historical Study (2 vols, 1991, 2 edn 1999), Christianity: Two Thousand Years (ed with Richard Harries, 2001); *Recreations* music (especially playing keyboard instruments), watching cricket; *Clubs* Athenaeum; *Style*— Prof Henry Mayr-Harting, FBA; ✉ St Peter's College, Oxford OX1 2DL; 29 Portland Road, Oxford OX2 7EZ (tel 01865 515666)

MAYS, (Catherine) Jane; da of Michael Mays (d 1978), and Mary, *née* Poyntz Stewart (d 1995); *b* 30 May 1952; *Educ* Francis Holland Sch; *m* David John Bradbury, s of Vivian Bradbury; *Career* journalist; advtg account exec 1970–76, editorial asst Business Traveller 1976–80, freelance journalist Paris and NY 1980–85, sub ed arts page Daily Telegraph 1986–88, exec features ed Evening Standard 1988–92, literary ed Daily Mail 1992–; *Recreations* theatre, literature, food and wine, travel; *Style*— Ms Jane Mays; ✉ 21 Marsden Street, London NW5 3HE (tel 020 7428 0444, e-mail davidjane.bradbury@blueyonder.co.uk); Daily Mail, Northcliffe House, 2 Derry Street, London W8 4TT (tel 020 7938 6701, fax 020 7937 0332, mobile 07885 400928, e-mail jane.mays@dailymail.co.uk)

MEACHER, Rt Hon Michael Hugh; PC (1997), MP; s of George Hubert Meacher (d 1969), of Berkhamsted, Herts; *b* 4 November 1939; *Educ* Berkhamsted Sch, New Coll Oxford; *m* 1, 1962 (m dis 1987), Molly Christine, da of William Reid, of Grayshott, Surrey; 2 s, 2 da; m 2, 1988, Lucianne, da of William Craven, of Gerrards Cross, Bucks; *Career* joined Lab Pty 1962, sec Danilo Dolci Tst 1964, lectr in social admin Univ of York 1966–69 and LSE 1970; MP (Lab): Oldham W 1970–97, Oldham W and Royton 1997–; Parly under sec of state: Dept of Industry 1974–75, DHSS 1975–76, Dept of Trade 1976–79; memb Treasy Select Ctee 1980–83, chm Select Ctee on Lloyd's Bill 1982, contested Lab dep leadership election 1983, elected to Shadow Cabinet 1983, memb NEC Oct 1983–; chief oppn spokesman on: health and social security 1983–87, employment 1987–89, social security 1989–92, devpt and co-operation 1992–93, Citizen's Charter 1993–94, tport 1994–95, employment 1995–96, environmental protection 1996–97; min of state for the environment: DETR 1997–2001, DEFRA 2001–03; author; *Books* Taken for a Ride (1972), Socialism with a Human Face (1982), Diffusing Power: the Key to Socialist Revival (1992); *Style*— The Rt Hon Michael Meacher, MP; ✉ 34 Kingscliffe Gardens, London SW19 6NR; House of Commons, London SW1A 0AA (tel 020 7219 3000)

MEAD, Anthony John; RD (1986); s of James Reginald Mead, JP (d 1984), and Muriel Violet, *née* Johnston (d 1993); *b* 3 February 1942; *Educ* Wrekin Coll, Open Univ (Dip Religious Studies, BA, BA Hons); *m* 25 March 1988, June, da of Sydney Thomas Farrington, DFC (d 1981); *Career* RNR Lt 1971, Lt Cdr 1979; chartered accountant; articles Foster and Stephens Birmingham 1960–64, Touche Ross and Co Birmingham 1964–65, ptnr Daffern and Co Coventry 1965–75, princ Mead and Co Kenilworth and Kingswear 1975–2001; memb NEC 1995–96, vice-chm Nat Taxation Legal and Fin Ctee Engrg Industries Assoc 1995–96 (memb 1974–96); memb Cncl Univ of Warwick 1984–87, tstee 29th May 1961 Charitable Tst 1984–, clerk Kingswear Parish Cncl 1987–93, memb Kingswear Parish Cncl 1993–95 (vice-chm 1994–95), memb Totnes Town Cncl 2004– (dep mayor 2006–07); HM Coastguard Auxiliary Serv 1991–92, memb Port of Dartmouth Royal Regatta Ctee 1994; govr: Kingswear County Primary Sch 1993–96 (chm 1996), The Grove Sch Totnes 2005–; tstee Totnes Bounds Charity 2004–; FCA; *Recreations* reading, rugby union football, walking, gardening, photography; *Style*— Anthony J Mead, Esq, RD, FCA; ✉ 10 Castle Street, Totnes, Devon TQ9 5NU

MEAD, Richard Barwick; s of Thomas Gifford Mead, MBE (d 2004), and Joyce Mary, *née* Barwick (d 1990); *b* 18 August 1947; *Educ* Marlborough, Pembroke Coll Cambridge (MA); *m* 25 June 1971, Sheelagh Margaret, da of James Leslie Thom; 2 s (Timothy b 1973, Rupert b 1977), 1 da (Nicola b 1975 d 1976); *Career* audit supervisor Arthur Young 1969–73, corporate fin exec Brandts Ltd 1973–75, dir and head Corporate Fin Dept Antony Gibbs and Sons Ltd 1975–83, dir corporate fin Credit Suisse First Boston Ltd 1983–85, ptnr and nat dir corporate fin Ernst & Young 1985–94, independent fin advsr 1994–; non-exec chm Stonemartin plc 2001–; non-exec dir: IX Europe plc 1999–, Greythorn Gp Ltd 2006–; FCA 1972, MSI 1993; *Recreations* gardening, history, music, family; *Clubs* Oxford and Cambridge; *Style*— Richard Mead, Esq; ✉ Clayfurlong House, Kemble, Cirencester, Gloucestershire GL7 6BS (tel 01285 770762, fax 01285 770841)

MEADE, Stephen Thomas; s of P J Meade, and A E Meade, *née* Hughes, of Maidstone, Kent; *b* 15 October 1960; *Educ* Maidstone GS, St John's Coll Oxford (Heath Harrison scholar, gap year Vienna Univ, MA); *m* 16 Feb 1990, Donna Patricia Mary, *née* Ainsworth; 2 da (Gabriella Catherine, Chlöe Alice Elizabeth), 1 s (Ethan Alexander); *Career* advtg exec; McCormick-Publicis 1985–88, Publicis Conseil (Paris) 1988–89, Howell Henry Chaldicott Lury 1989–91; Publicis: bd dir 1994–2001, managing ptnr 1997–2001, client servs dir 1998–2001, head of brand devpt 2000–01; md Springpoint Brand Consultancy 2001–03; planning dir McCann-Erickson EMEA 2003–; *Style*— Stephen Meade, Esq; ✉ McCann-Erickson, 7–11 Herbrand Street, London WC1N 1EX (tel 020 7961 2570, e-mail stephen.meade@europe.mccann.com)

MEADEN, Deborah Sonia; da of Brian Douglas Meaden, and Sonia Irene, *née* Coneley (Sonia Meaden, OBE, *qv*); *b* 11 February 1959, Taunton, Somerset; *Educ* Godolphin Sch Salisbury, Trowbridge HS for Girls, Brighton Coll; *m* 13 Feb 1993, Paul Lawrence Farmer; *Career* ops dir Bryson Enterprises Leisure Ltd 1989–93, md Weststar Holidays Ltd 1995–99 (ops dir 1993–95), gp md TGGL Ltd 1999–2005; memb SW Tourism advsy panel; judge Dragons' Den (BBC TV); MInstD 2000, FRSA 2006; *Recreations* horse riding, travel, property devpt; *Style*— Mrs Deborah Meaden; ✉ Meadenspeak, The Granary, Bowdens Business Centre, Hambridge, Somerset TA10 0BP (tel 01458 259371)

MEADEN, Sonia Irene; OBE (2004); da of Marshal Coneley, of Brixham, Devon, and Irene, *née* Bowles; *b* 27 November 1936; *Educ* Oswestry Girls' HS, Kidderminster GS; *m* 1, 1954 (m dis 1960), Henry Charles; 2 da (Gail b 1956, Deborah, *qv*, b 1959); m 2, 1962 (m dis 1964), Raymond Peagram; m 3, 1966, Brian Meaden, s of Thomas Meaden (d 1982); 2 da (Emma b 1969, Cass b 1972); *Career* first lady: nat pres Br Amusement Catering Trades Assoc 1985–87 (chm 1983, vice-pres 1987–), chm Nat Amusement Cncl 1987–, dir and chm Amusement Trades Exhibition Co 1988–; memb George Thomas Fellowship; tstee: The Grand Order of Lady Ratlings, BACTA Charitable Tst 1989– (chm 1989–96), The Billy Butlin Charity Tst 1997–; dir Cornwall Tourist Bd 1992–94, vice-chm South West Tourism Bd 1996– (dir 1992–); *Recreations* boating, theatre, travel; *Style*— Mrs Sonia Meaden, OBE

MEADES, Jonathan Turner; s of John William Meades (d 1981), of Salisbury, Wilts, and Marjorie Agnes (Bunty), *née* Hogg (d 1993); *b* 21 January 1947; *Educ* King's Coll Taunton, Univ of Bordeaux, RADA; *m* 1, 15 Sept 1980 (m dis), Sally Dorothy Renée, da of Raymond Brown (d 1996); 2 da (Holly, Rose (twins) b 7 May 1981); m 2, 1 June 1988 (m

M

dis), Frances Anne, da of Sir William Bentley (d 1998); 2 da ((Eleanor) Lily b 31 Dec 1986, (Evelyn) Coral b 15 April 1993); m 3, 1 May 2003, Colette Claudine Elizabeth, da of Michael Forder; *Career* journalist, writer and TV performer 1971–; contrib to: Books and Bookman, Time Out, Curious, The Observer, Architects Jl, Sunday Times, Harpers & Queen, Literary Review, Tatler, A La Carte, The Times, The Independent, Sunday Correspondent, Evening Standard, magazines in Canada and USA; ed Event 1981–82, pt/t memb editorial staff Tatler 1982–87, restaurant critic The Times 1986–2001, columnist The Times 2002–05; TV series incl: The Victorian House 1987, Abroad in Britain 1990, Further Abroad 1994, Jerrybuilding 1994, Even Further Abroad 1997, Travels with Pevsner: Worcestershire 1998, Heart Bypass 1998, Victoria Died In 1901 and is Still Alive Today 2001, tvSSFBM 2001, Meades Eats 2003, Abroad Again in Britain 2005, Joebuilding 2006, Meades Abroad Again 2007, Herring and Schnapps 2008; *Awards* Glenfiddich Awards 1986, 1990, 1995 and 1999, Essay Prize Paris Int Art Film Festival 1994, Glenfiddich Trophy 1999; *Books* This is Their Life (1979), An Illustrated Atlas of The World's Buildings (1980), Filthy English (1984), Peter Knows What Dick Likes (1989), Pompey (1993), The Fowler Family Business (2002), Incest and Morris Dancing (2002), The Times Restaurant Guide (2002); *Scripts* L'Atlantide (dir Bob Swaim, 1993); *Recreations* buildings, mushrooms, woods, sloth; *Clubs* Groucho, Academy; *Style*— Jonathan Meades, Esq; ✉ c/o Anita Land, Capel & Land Ltd, 29 Wardour Street, London W1D 6PS (tel 020 7734 2414, e-mail jtm.juvarra@orange.fr)

MEADOWS, Prof (Arthur) Jack; s of Flt Sgt Arthur Harold Meadows (d 1971), and Alice, *née* Elson (d 1962); *b* 24 January 1934; *Educ* New Coll Oxford (MA, DPhil), UCL (MSc); *m* 6 Dec 1958, (Isobel) Jane Tanner, da of Stanley Charles Bryant (d 1937); 2 da (Alice b 1960, Sally b 1962), 1 s (Michael b 1962); *Career* Nat Serv Lt Intelligence Corps 1952–54; Univ of Leicester 1966–86: lectr, sr lectr, prof 1972–86, head Depts Astronomy and History of Sci; head Primary Communications Research Centre 1976–86, head Office Humanities Communication 1983–86, prof Dept of Info Sci Loughborough Univ 1986–2001 (dean Educn and Humanities 1991–94, pro-vice-chllr 1995–96); author of twenty books and approximately 300 research papers; hon vice-pres Library Assoc 1995; Hon DSc City Univ 1995; FInstP 1983, FLA 1989, FIInfSc 1987; *Recreations* sleeping; *Style*— Prof Jack Meadows; ✉ 47 Swan Street, Seagrave, Leicestershire LE12 7NL (tel 01509 812557); Department of Information Science, Loughborough University, Loughborough, Leicestershire LE11 3TU (tel 01509 223051, fax 01509 223053, e-mail a.j.meadows@lboro.ac.uk)

MEADOWS, Dr John Christopher; s of Dr Swithin Pinder Meadows (d 1993), and Doris Steward, *née* Noble; *b* 25 March 1940; *Educ* Westminster, Univ of Cambridge (BA, MB BChir, MD); *m* 9 July 1966, Patricia, da of late John Appleton Pierce, of IOM; 2 s; *Career* former conslt neurologist St George's Hosp, conslt neurologist King Edward VII Hosp, hon neurologist Newspaper Press Fund; FRCP; *Recreations* gardening, walking, travelling, reading; *Style*— Dr John C Meadows; ✉ c/o 143 Harley Street, London W1N 1DJ (tel 020 7935 1802)

MEADOWS, Pamela Catherine; da of late Sidney James Meadows, and Hilda Catherine Meadows; *b* 9 January 1949; *Educ* Kenya HS Nairobi, Univ of Durham (BA), Birkbeck Coll London (MSc); *m* 26 Aug 1975, Paul Andrew Ormerod; 1 s (Andrew Whitworth b 3 Sept 1982); *Career* research offr NIESR 1972–74 (research asst 1970–71); Home Office Economic Planning Unit: sr econ asst 1974–77, econ advsr 1977–78; Dept of Employment: econ advsr 1978–79, seconded to OECD 1979–80, econ advsr 1980–84, princ Manpower Policy Div I 1984–85, econ advsr Employment Market Research Unit 1985–87, head Economics Branch (sr econ advsr) 1988–90, head Educn and Skills Analysis Branch (sr econ advsr) 1990–91, head Labour Market Briefing and Labour Market Analysis Branch (sr econ advsr) 1991–92, chief econ advsr and dir Economics Research and Evaluation Div 1992–93; dir PSI 1993–98, chm Synergy Research Consulting Ltd 2004–; visiting fell NIESR 1998–, visiting prof Arbetslivsinstitutet Stockholm 1998–2000; memb: Editorial Bd Prospect, Guardian panel of economic advsrs, Cabinet Office Better Regulation Task Force 1997–2000; govr Birkbeck Coll London 1997–2000; *Publications* Work out - or work in (ed, 1996), The Working Families Tax Credit (1999), The Flexible Labour Market: Implications for Pension Provision (1999), Young Men on the Margins of Work (2001), Beyond Employment (with Alain Supiot and others, 2001), Access to Financial Services (2000), Poverty Among Pensioners (2001), Early Retirement and Income in Later Life (2002), Recruitment and Retention of Childcare, Early Years and Playworkers: Research Study (jtly, 2003), Retirement Ages inthe UK (2003), Sure Start Local Programmes: Improving the Employability of Parents (with C Carbers, 2004), Economic Contribution of Older People (with W Cook, 2004); numerous articles in other pubns; *Style*— Ms Pamela Meadows; ✉ NIESR, 2 Dean Trench Street, Smith Square, London SW1P 3HE (e-mail pmeadows@niesr.ac.uk)

MEAKIN, Henry Paul John; s of Wing Cdr Henry John Walter Meakin, DFC and bar, RAF (d 1989), of Harare, Zimbabwe, and Elizabeth Wilma, *née* Fairbairns; *b* 2 January 1944; *Educ* Plumtree Sch Rhodesia; *m* 2 Jan 1971, Vicki Lynn, da of Maurice James Bullus (d 1990), of Harrogate, N Yorks; 1 da (Katie b 1972), 2 s (Oliver b 1975, Harry b 1980); *Career* exec dir Pensord Press Ltd 1970–74; Aspen Communications plc: fndr dir, md 1975–91, chm 1991–97; fndr dir GWR Gp plc 1981–87; Classic FM plc: fndr chm 1991–93, dir 1993–; chm: GWR Gp plc 1988–2001, Aspen Gp Ltd 1999–, Value Initiatives Ltd 2003, Cardionetics Ltd 2005–; memb Wine Guild of the UK; FRSA; *Recreations* tennis, golf, music; *Style*— Henry Meakin, Esq; ✉ Swan Yard, 9–13 Market Place, Cirencester GL7 2NH (tel 01285 885884, fax 01285 641305, e-mail henry@hmeakin.com)

MEAKINS, Prof Jonathan Larmonth; OC (2000); s of Jonathan Fayette Meakins (d 2000), and Mildred Dawson, *née* Larmonth (d 1992); *b* 8 January 1941, Toronto, Canada; *Educ* McGill Univ Montreal (BSc), Univ of Western Ontario (MD), Univ of Cincinnati (DSc); *m* 17 June 1972, Dr Jacqueline McClaran, da of J Robert McClaran; *Career* surgical trg Royal Victoria Hosp and McGill Univ Montreal 1967–69 and 1972–74, research fell in surgical infections and immunobiology Univ of Cincinnati 1969–72; Royal Victoria Hosp Montreal: asst surgn 1974–79, assoc surgn 1979–87, sr surgn 1987–2002, chief Green Service 1982–94, surgn-in-chief 1988–98; conslt Montreal Children's Hosp 1974–2002, attending surgn Montreal Gen Hosp 1990–2002, consltg memb Dept of Surgery Queen Elizabeth Hosp Montreal 1991–92, head Surgical Services McGill Univ Health Centre Montreal 1998–2002, hon consit Oxford Radcliffe Tst 2003; McGill Univ Montreal: assoc prof of surgery and microbiology 1979–84 (asst prof 1974–79), prof of surgery and microbiology 1984–2002, assoc memb Centre for Studies in Age and Ageing 1987–2002, chm Dept of Surgery 1988–93 and 1998–2002, Edward W Archibald prof of surgery 1993–2002; Nuffield prof of surgery Univ of Oxford 2002–; professeur associé Université de Paris XII 1980–81, memb Groupe de recherche sur la chirurgie du foie et e l'hypertension portale Paris 1987–88; memb: Montreal Bd Ludwig Inst for Cancer Research 1986–91, Research Advsy Bd Shriner's of America 1986–96, Research Advsy Bd Toronto Hosp for Sick Children 1990–91, Scientfic Advsy Cncl Alberta Heritage Fndn for Med Research 1990–2003, Advsy Ctee Nat Plan for Controlling the Surgical Infections Spain 1997–; MRC of Canada: memb Fellowship Ctee 1984–87, memb Grants Ctee for Clinical Investigation 1990–93, chm Site Visit (Univ of Toronto) 1991, memb Standing Ctee on Science and Research 1997–98; co-ed Canadian Jl of Surgery 1992–2003, reviewer for numerous med and surgical jls; memb Editorial Bd: Réanimation: Soins Intensifs, Médecine d'Urgence 1984–, Jl of Critical Care 1985–91, Infection Control and Hosp Epidemiology 1986–, Current Practice in Surgery 1988–, Debates in Clinical Surgery 1989–, Critical Care Med 1990–96, HPB Surgery 1990–, (Complications) in Surgery 1990–, Annales de chirurgie 1992–, Med Intelligence Unit Reports 1992–, Videoscopic Surgery 1992–, Surgery 1993–98, Jl of the American Coll of Surgns 1994– (sr assoc ed 1997–), Br Jl of Surgery 1994–2000, Sepsis 1996–2002; memb: Assoc for Academic Surgery 1975–95, Reticuloendothelial Soc 1976–92, Transplantation Soc 1978–93, Canadian Infectious Diseases Soc 1978–2002, American Assoc for Surgery of Trauma 1979–94, Soc of Critical Care Med 1982–94, Canadian Critical Care Soc 1982–95, Soc of Surgical Chairmen (American and Canadian) 1988–93 and 1998–, Canadian Forces Health Services Cncl (CFHSC) 1997–2001, Assoc of Surgns of GB and Ireland 2003, American Coll of Surgns (memb Bd of Regent 1993–2002, vice-chm 2000–02), American Soc of Microbiology, American Surgical Assoc, Canadian Assoc of Clinical Surgns, Canadian Assoc of Gen Surgns, Canadian Inst of Academic Med, Canadian Soc for Clinical Investigation, Central Surgical Assoc, Infectious Diseases Soc of America, Int Fedn of Surgical Colls (pres 2000–03), Int Soc of Surgery, Int Surgical Gp, James IV Assoc of Surgns, Montreal Medico-Chirurgical Soc, Quebec Assoc of Gen Surgns, Quebec Med Assoc, Soc for Surgery of the Alimentary Tract (chair Research and Educn Ctee 1993–97), Soc for Univ Surgns, Surgical Biology Club III, Surgical Infection Soc (pres 1989), World Assoc of Hepato-Pancreato-Biliary Surgery; corresponding memb Brazilian Coll of Surgns; Ciba Prize in Med 1965, Swedish Soc of Med Sciences Medal 1980, Optimah/Merck Frosst Award for Med Leadership 1995; Fraser Scholarship McGill Univ Montreal 1975–79, Schering Scholarship Canadian Soc for Clinical Investigation 1980–81; Lister Fellowship RCPEd 1979, Detweiler Fellowship RCS 1980–81, Walter C MacKenzie Ethicon Travel Fellowship 1987–88, Fondation pour la Recherche Médicale Fellowship 1987–88; James IV Traveller for Canada 1985, Janes visiting prof Royal Coll of Physicians and Surgns of Canada 2000; vice-pres Acquisition Ctee Montreal Museum of Fine Arts 1998–2002 (tstee 1997–2002); ambass by appt Le Club des Ambassadors 2002; miembro de honor Asociación Española de Cirujanos 1998, fifth hon life memb CNIS 2002; memb Royal Coll of Physicians and Surgns of Canada, FRCSGlas (ad eundem) 1998, Hon FRCS 2002, Hon FCS S Africa; Knight Cdr of Merit SMOM; *Publications* ed of six books, also author of 77 book chapters and 202 articles; *Recreations* golf, tennis, art, music, travel, history; *Clubs* Frilford Heath Golf, Royal Montreal Golf, Univ; *Style*— Prof Jonathan Meakins, OC; ✉ Nuffield Department of Surgery, John Radcliffe Hospital, Headley Way, Headington, Oxford OX3 9DU (tel 01865 221297, e-mail jonathan.meakins@nds.ox.ac.uk)

MEALE, (Joseph) Alan; MP; s of Albert Henry Meale (d 1986), and Elizabeth, *née* Catchpole (d 1997); both parents trade union shop stewards; *b* 31 July 1949; *Educ* Univ of Durham, Ruskin Coll Oxford, Sheffield Hallam Univ; *m* 15 March 1983, Diana, da of Lt Cdr John Gillespy, RN (ret); *Career* nat employment devpt offr (Home Office funded) 1977–79, asst to Ray Buckton as Gen Sec ASLEF 1979–83, Parly and political advsr to Michael Meacher MP 1983–87; MP (Lab) Mansfield 1987–; oppn whip 1992–94, PPS to John Prescott: as Dep Ldr of Lab Pty 1994–97, as Dep PM 1997–98; under sec of state for the environment 1998–99; war graves cmmr 2003–; first vice-pres Cncl of Europe CTT Environment, Agriculture, Local and Regnl Democracy 2003–; memb Parly Select Ctees on: Euro Legislation 1988–90, Home Affrs 1990–92; Parly rep SSAFA 1989–95; chm PLP East Midlands and Central Groups 1988–95, chm Br Cyprus Ctee; former vice-chm Employment Ctee PLP; memb: War Pensions Bd 1990–95, SSAFA Bd 1990–94, Parly Ct of Referees 1997–, Parly Racing and Bloodstocks Gp, Cncl of Europe and Western European Union 2000–; former exec memb Inter Parly Union; exec memb Cwlth Parly Assoc; former sec All-Pty Parly Greyhound Gp; former treas: Cwlth Parly Assoc Cyprus Ctee (UK) Gp, Parly Football Ctee; founder, former chm and exec memb Parly Beer Industries Ctee; govt advsr on the racing indust and its needs 2002–; fell and postgrad Industry and Parly Tst; conslt and unpaid shareholder Mansfield Town FC; fomer company sec Sherwood TV; author; journalist of various publications; Hon Citizen of Morphou (Cyprus), Hon Citizen Mansfield Ohio (USA), Hon Senator Louisiana (USA); *Recreations* reading, writing, arts, politics, Cyprus, sports and Mansfield Town FC; *Clubs* Mansfield Labour, Bellamy Road and Mansfield Woodhouse Working Men's, Mansfield Town FC; *Style*— Alan Meale, Esq, MP; ✉ House of Commons, London SW1A 0AA (tel 020 7219 3000, e-mail enquiries@alanmeale.co.uk, website www.alanmeale.co.uk)

MEARS, Patrick Michael; s of Alex Benjamin Albert Mears, of Henley-on-Thames, Oxon, and Moira Denise, *née* Buzetti; *b* 19 January 1958; *Educ* Henley GS, LSE (LLB); *m* 1, 27 Aug 1983, Carol Lucia (d 1987), da of Carl William Anders (d 1965), of Rochester, NY; 1 da (Elizabeth Helen Carol b 8 Sept 1987); m 2, 7 Dec 1995, Rachel Elizabeth, da of Prof M S Anderson, of Highgate, London; 1 s (Matthew Patrick b 16 Aug 1999); *Career* admitted slr 1982; ptnr Allen & Overy 1988– (currently head Global Taxation Gp); memb Addington Soc; Freeman Worshipful Co of Slrs; memb Law Soc; *Recreations* parenting, theatre, tennis; *Clubs* Dulwich Sports; *Style*— Patrick Mears, Esq; ✉ Allen & Overy LLP, One New Change, London EC4M 9QQ (tel 020 7330 3000, fax 020 7330 9999)

MEARS, Roger Malcolm Loudon; s of Dr Kenneth Patrick Geddes Mears (d 2001), and Dr Eleanor Mears, *née* Loudon (d 1992); *b* 15 February 1944; *Educ* City of London Sch, CCC Cambridge (MA, DipArch); *m* 4 Nov 1978, Joan Adams Speers; 3 da (Emily b 1981, Rebecca b 1983, Jessica b 1986); *Career* princ Roger Mears Architects (specialising in historic bldgs and conservation); work incl: Tudor House Cheyne Walk, The Ham Wantage, South Eggardon House nr Bridport; memb Ctee SPAB 1996–; RIBA; *Recreations* chamber music (viola player), watermills, walking, sculling (gold medals Henley Veterans' Regatta); *Style*— Roger Mears, Esq; ✉ Roger Mears Architects, 2 Compton Terrace, London N1 2UN (tel 020 7359 8222, fax 020 7354 5208, e-mail rm@rmears.co.uk, website www.rmears.co.uk)

MEASEY, Dr Laurence George; s of George Measey, of Worthing, W Sussex, and Mary, *née* Tonge; *b* 12 February 1941; *Educ* Charing Cross Hosp Univ of London (MB BS, DPM); *m* 1963, Eileen; 2 s (Richard George b 8 Dec 1964, Gavin John b 6 Dec 1968), 1 da (Anita Jane b 27 June 1966); *Career* conslt psychiatrist Coventry NHS Healthcare Tst 1973–2002; hon civil conslt in psychiatry to the RN 1994–2004; chm W Midlands Psychiatric Trg Ctee 1997–2002; memb Cncl and chm Rehabilitation and Social Psychiatry Section RCPsych 1997–2001, memb Validation Gp for Incapacity Benefit DSS, hon conslt psychiatrist St Luke's Hosp; reader: Dio of Coventry, Dio of the Windward Islands W Indies; author of various papers on social and rehabilitation psychiatry; Freudenberg Lecture 1990; memb RSM, FRCPsych 1988 (MRCPsych 1972); *Recreations* theology, gardening, travel; *Style*— Dr Laurence Measey; ✉ e-mail lg@measey.com

MEATH, 15 Earl of (I 1627); John Anthony Brabazon; also Baron Ardee (I 1616), and Baron Chaworth (UK 1831), in which title he sits in the House of Lords; s of 14 Earl of Meath (d 1998); *b* 11 May 1941; *Educ* Harrow; *m* 1973, Xenia Goudime; 2 da (Lady Corinna Lettice b 9 Nov 1974, Lady Serena Alexandra b 23 Feb 1979), 1 s (Anthony Jacques, Lord Ardee b 30 Jan 1977); *Heir* s, Lord Ardee; *Career* page of hon to HM The Queen 1956–58, served Grenadier Gds 1960–63; *Style*— The Rt Hon the Earl of Meath; ✉ Killruddery, Bray, Co Wicklow, Ireland

MEATH, Bishop (RC) of 1990–; Most Rev Michael Smith; s of John Smith, and Bridget Fagan, of Liss, Oldcastle, Co Meath; *b* 6 June 1940; *Educ* St Finian's Coll Mullingar, Lateran Univ Rome; *Career* ordained 1963; *Style*— The Most Rev Bishop of Meath; ✉ Bishop's House, Dublin Road, Mullingar, Co Westmeath, Ireland (tel 00 353 44 934 2038, fax 00 353 44 934 3020, e-mail bishop@dioceseofmeath.ie)

MEATH AND KILDARE, Bishop of 1996–; Most Rev Dr Richard Lionel Clarke; *b* 25 June 1949; *Educ* Wesley Coll Dublin, TCD (MA, PhD), KCL (BD); *m* 1975, Linda; 1 s (Nicholas b 1977), 1 da (Lindsey b 1981); *Career* teacher Iran (Church Missionary Soc vol scheme) 1971–72; ordained: deacon 1975, priest 1976; curate: Holywood Co Down (Down Dio), St

Bartholomew's with Christ Church Leeson Park (Dublin Dio) 1977–79; dean of residence (chaplain) TCD 1979–84, rector Bandon Union of Parishes (Cork Dio) 1984–93, dean St Fin Barre's Cathedral Cork (incl chaplaincies of UC Cork and the Univ Hosp) 1993–96; *Publications* And Is It True? (2000), A Whisper of God (2006); *Recreations* walking, France, music (Mozart, jazz), cricket; *Style—* The Most Rev Dr Richard Clarke, Bishop of Meath and Kildare; ✉ Bishop's House, Moyglare, Maynooth, Co Kildare, Ireland (tel 00 353 1 628 9354)

MEDAWAR, Anthony Crosland (Tony); s of Nicholas Antoine Macbeth Medawar, QC, of London, and Joyce Catherine, *née* Crosland-Boyle; *b* 6 September 1962; *Educ* Univ of Kent; *m* 30 June 1990, Nicola, da of Alan Frank Seager; 1 s (Guy Richard Seager), 1 da (Lara Circe Seager); *Career* civil servant; private sec to Sir Peter Gregson, GCB 1990–91, head Departmental Deregulation Unit DTI 1991–93, nat expert Competition Directorate Gen Euro Cmmn 1993–96, head Policy Unit Export Control Org DTI 1996–2000, dep dir Central Secretariat Cabinet Office 2000–02, dir Regnl Policies and Enterprise Govt Office for the SW 2002, dir sponsorship and fin RDA DTI 2003–06, dir of strategy and policy London Devpt Agency 2006–; *Publications* contrib: Crime and Detective Stories (CADS), Bottle Street Gazette, Sherlock Holmes Jl, The Armchair Detective, Tune in to Yesterday, Old-Time Detection, Railway Cuttings; ed various books; *Recreations* detective stories, anomalous phenomena, amusing my wife; *Clubs* Noughts and Crosses; *Style—* Tony Medawar; ✉ Palestra, 197 Blackfriars Road, London SE1 8AA (tel 020 7593 8290, text phone 020 7593 8001, e-mail tonymedawar@lda.gov.uk)

MEDAWAR, His Hon Nicholas Antoine Macbeth; QC (1984); s of late Antoine Nicolas Medawar, and Annie Innes Logie Tulloch, *née* Macbeth; *b* 25 April 1933; *Educ* Keswick Sch, Trinity Coll Dublin (BA, LLB); *m* 1, 1962 (m dis 1977), Joyce Catherine, *née* Crosland-Boyle; 1 s (Anthony Crosland b 1962), 1 da (Zohara Dawn b 1966 (decd)); m 2, 1977, (Caroline) Mary, da of late Harry Samuel Collins; *Career* Nat Serv 1957–59, cmmnd RASC, served UK and Cyprus; called to the Bar Gray's Inn 1957; a legal assessor Gen Optical Cncl 1984–87, recorder 1985–87, circuit judge (SE Circuit) 1987–2006; memb Ethnic Minorities Advsy Ctee to Judicial Studies Bd 1993–96; *Recreations* divers; *Style—* His Hon Nicholas Medawar, QC

MEDLAM, Charles Samuel; s of Wilfrid Gaston Medlam, of Eastcombe, Glos, and Virginia Medlam; *b* 10 September 1949; *Educ* Winchester, Salzburg Mozarteum, Vienna Acad, Paris Conservatoire; *m* 1979, Ingrid, da of Günther Seifert; 1 s (Lukas b 31 Dec 1985), 1 da (Hannah b 8 July 1988); *Career* dir London Baroque 1978–; ensemble has appeared at numerous festivals and venues worldwide incl Salzburg, Bath, Stuttgart, Innsbruck, Vienna and Utrecht; regular tours to USA and Japan; *Recordings* over 40 CDs of baroque chamber music for EMI, Harmonia Mundi (France) and Bis (Sweden); *Recreations* literature, classics; *Style—* Charles Medlam; ✉ Brick Kiln Cottage, Hollington, Newbury, Berkshire RG20 9XX (tel 01635 254331, e-mail c.medlam@btinternet.com, e-mail www.londonbaroque.com)

MEDLAND, David Arthur; s of James William Medland (d 1986), and Merle Ermyntrude, *née* Rotchell (d 1994); *b* 23 September 1946; *Educ* St Paul's Sch Darjeeling India; *m* (m dis 1979), Patricia Ann, da of Timothy Wood (d 1971); 1 s (Christopher James b 25 Dec 1968); *Career* CA; RSM Robson Rhodes: joined 1965, asst mangr 1973, mangr 1974, sr mangr 1976, ptnr 1979–2007, memb Exec Ctee 1990–92, seconded as asst dir Serious Fraud Office 1993–96; ptnr Grant Thornton UK LLP (following merger) 2007–; FCA 1979 (ACA 1971); *Books* The Unlisted Securities Market - A Review; *Recreations* golf, music, theatre; *Style—* David A Medland, Esq; ✉ Grant Thornton UK LLP, 30 Finsbury Square, London EC2P 2YU (tel 020 7184 4300, fax 020 7250 0801, e-mail david.medland@gtuk.com)

MEDLICOTT, Michael Geoffrey; s of late Geoffrey Henry Medlicott, of Hythe, Kent, and late Beryl Ann, *née* Burchell; *b* 2 June 1943; *Educ* Downside (scholar), Lincoln Coll Oxford (scholar, MA); *m* 1, 8 Sept 1973 (m dis 1998), Diana Grace, da of Brian Fife Fallaw, of Gosforth, Northumberland; 1 s (Oliver), 3 da (Charlotte, Annabel, Flora); m 2, 6 March 1999, Susan Caroline, da of Desmond Stevens Whittall, of Hartley Wintney, Hants; *Career* P&O: joined as mgmnt trainee 1965, gen mangr fleet 1975–80, gen mangr Europe 1980–83, dir Europe 1983–86, md P&O Air Holidays 1980–86, dir P&O Travel 1980–84, md Swan Hellenic 1983–86; chief exec Br Tourist Authority 1986–93; vice-pres (Europe) Delta Air Lines Inc 1993–96 (also vice-pres Asia 1996–97), memb Bd Deltair Investments UK Ltd 1995–97, pres Delta Air Lines Moscow 1996–97; transaction dir Nomura International Principal Finance Gp 1997–2000, ceo Servus Holdings Ltd 1997–2002, chm Servus Facilities Mgmnt Ltd 1998–2002, chm Servus b2b Ltd 2000–02; non-exec dir: Heritage of London Tst Ltd 1986–, John Laing plc 2004–, Manchester Airport Group plc; chm DATE Inc (Moscow) 1996–97; memb: Cncl of Mgmnt Passenger Shipping Assoc 1983–86, Br Travel Educn Tst 1986–93, Tidy Britain Gp 1986–, Bd London Tourist Bd 1992–93, Advsy Panel Languages Lead Body 1990–93, Advsy Cncl Univ of Surrey Tourist Mgmnt Dept 1991–, Bd Gatwick Handling 1995–97, Lesteris Ltd 1995–97, Bd Br-American C of C 1996–97, Bd Grand Facilities Mgt Co Ltd 1998–2000; chm European Travel Cmmn 1992–93 (chm Planning Ctee 1990–92); LEA govr Ecchinswell and Sydmonton C of E Primary Sch; hon memb Univ Centre Hellenic and Euro Studies (Piraeus) 1996–97; Queen Mother's Birthday Awards for Environmental Improvement 1993 and 1995; FRSA; *Recreations* philately, gardening, bibliophily, music, travelling in perfect company; *Clubs* Royal Philatelic Soc, Oxford and Cambridge; *Style—* Michael Medlicott, Esq

MEDLYCOTT, Sir Mervyn Tregonwell; 9 Bt (UK 1808), of Ven House, Somerset; s of late Thomas Anthony Hutchings Medlycott (d 1970), 2 s of Sir Hubert Medlycott, 7 Bt, of Edmondsham House, Dorset, and Cecilia Mary Eden, da of late Maj Cecil Harold Eden, of Cranborne, Dorset; suc unc, Sir (James) Christopher Medlycott, 8 Bt (d 1986); *b* 20 February 1947; *Heir* none; *Career* genealogist; Somerset and Dorset Family History Soc: fndr 1975, hon sec 1975–77, chm 1977–84, pres 1986–; FSG; *Style—* Sir Mervyn Medlycott, Bt; ✉ The Manor House, Sandford Orcas, Sherborne, Dorset DT9 4SB (tel 01963 220206)

MEEHAN, Prof Anthony Edward (Tony); s of late Edward Joseph Meehan, of Glasgow, and late Mary, *née* Whelan; *b* 24 August 1943; *Educ* St George's Westminster London; *m* 24 Oct 1975, Linda Jane, da of John Alexander Portugal Stone, of Vancouver Island, BC; 1 s (Michael Anthony b 1980), 1 da (Claire Louise b 1982); *Career* chm: Tony Meehan and Assocs Ltd 1976–, TMA Communications 1985–, RAAM Mgmnt Ltd 2004–, Omnicom Ltd 2005–; chm: IPR Scottish Gp 1987–89 (chm Educn Ctee 1984–87, vice-chm 1985–87), SPRCA 1995–97; visiting prof Glasgow Caledonian Univ, fell Strathclyde Inst; chm Obesity Mgmnt Assoc 2002–; memb Scottish Soc of Epicureans 1994–; dir Nat Piping Centre of Scotland 1998–2006; Freeman City of Glasgow; FRSA, FIPRA, FCIPR; *Clubs* Scottish Soc of Epicureans; *Style—* Prof Tony Meehan; ✉ Foxcote, Main Road, Fairlie, Largs, Ayrshire KA29 0AA (tel 0141 357 1991, fax 0141 357 3322, e-mail tmeehan@tmac.co.uk)

MEEK, Alison Fiona; da of Prof Ronald L Meek (d 1978), and Dorothea L, *née* Schulz; *b* 31 October 1959, Glasgow; *Educ* Beauchamp Coll Oadby, UCL (BA), Coll of Law London; *m* 1, 22 March 1991 (m dis 2002), Christopher Gayford; 1 s (William Augustus b 13 Oct 1992), 1 da (Katherine Elizabeth Dorothea b 19 May 1995); m 2, 2007, Robert Francis, QC, *qv*; *Career* admitted slr 1986; asst slr: Herbert Smith (articled clerk 1984–86), Winckworth and Pemberton, Withers; ptnr: Boodle Hatfield 1997–2004, Speechly Bircham 2005–; memb Wills and Equity Ctee Law Soc, memb Ctee and treas Assoc of Contentious Tsts and Probate Specialists (ACTAPS); memb UCL History Alumni Assoc; memb Dinner Ctee St Christopher's Hospice; *Publications* A Practitioners' Guide to Contentious Trusts and Estates (jt author); contrib to professional jls; *Recreations* family, cooking, gardening, music; *Style—* Ms Alison Meek; ✉ Speechly Bircham, 6 St Andrew Street, London EC4A 3LX (tel 020 7427 6400, fax 020 7427 6600, e-mail alison.meek@speechlys.com)

MEEK, Marshall; CBE (1989); s of Marshall Meek (d 1955), of Auchtermuchty, Fife, and Grace Robertson, *née* Smith (d 1970); *b* 22 April 1925; *Educ* Bell Baxter HS Cupar, Univ of Glasgow (BScEng); *m* 2 March 1957, Elfrida Marjorie, da of William George Cox (d 1946), of Purley, Surrey; 3 da (Hazel Valerie b 1960, Ursula Katherine b 1962, Angela Judith b 1966); *Career* Caledon Shipbuilding 1942–49, Br Ship Research Assoc (BSRA) 1949–53, chief naval architect and dir Ocean Transport & Trading Ltd 1967–78 (joined 1953), head of ship technol British Shipbuilders 1979–84, dep chm British Maritime Technology 1984–86, conslt naval architect 1986–2000; visiting prof in naval architecture: Univ of Strathclyde 1972–83, UCL 1983–86; pres: NE Coast Inst of Engrs & Shipbuilders 1984–86, RINA 1990–93, master Faculty of Royal Designers for Industry 1997–99; dir: North of England Microelectronics Inst 1996–2002; vice-pres RSA 1997–99; memb: DSAC 1989–97, Marine Safety Agency Res Ctee 1992–98, Tech Ctee Lloyd's Register of Shipping 1979–2001; chm: NE Coast Engrg Tst 1994–96, NE Region RSA 1992–97, Argonautics Maritime Technologies Ltd 1995–2002; JP Liverpool 1977–78; chm Northumberland Branch Gideons Int UK 2000–03, tstee Northumberland and Newcastle Police Court Mission Fund 1990–; Hon DSc Univ of Strathclyde 2005; Hon RDI (RSA) 1986; FREng 1990, FRINA, FIMarEST, FRSA; *Publications* There Go the Ships (2003); contrib numerous tech papers to learned jls; *Recreations* garden, church; *Clubs* Caledonian; *Style—* Dr Marshall Meek, CBE, RDI, FREng; ✉ Coppers, Hillside Road, Rothbury, Northumberland NE65 7PT (tel 01669 621403, e-mail marshallmeek@rothbury.net)

MEEKE, (Robert) Martin James; QC (2000); s of James Alexander Meeke, and Mildred Alverta Meeke; *b* 25 December 1950; *Educ* Allhallows Sch, Univ of Bristol (LLB); *m* Beverley Ann, *née* Evans; 1 s, 1da; *Career* called to the Bar Gray's Inn 1973; recorder 1996–, currently head of chambers; *Style—* Martin Meeke, Esq, QC; ✉ Colleton Chambers, Colleton Crescent, Exeter EX2 4DG (tel 01392 274898, fax 01392 412368)

MEERS, Jeffrey (Jeff); s of James Meers, of London, and Marie Ellen, *née* Hugkulstone; *b* 10 February 1953; *Educ* Ashford Co GS, Univ of Nottingham (BSc); *m* 1, 2 s (James b 5 July 1982, David b 22 Oct 1983); m 2, Louise Michelle; *Career* psychologist RN (MOD) 1975; advtg exec: BMP and WCRS (award winning ads for Courage Best, John Smiths Yorkshire Bitter, Carling Black Label, BMW, Cadbury, Unisys, St Ivel, 3M, Nationwide); vice-chm Bozell Europe 1987–94, IPA Advtg Effectiveness Awards 1982 and 1994 Int Advtg Assoc (Global and Europe Awards); founding chm MAID (now DIALOG) 1985–93; worldwide pres IDG Global Solutions 1994–2000; ceo: SPARZA, Software Div Officeshopper.com, Bright Station e-Commerce; dir: Logistics Int plc 2000–05, Transaction Media 2003–; fndr Koodos.com 2004–06; fndr: SAMStax.co.uk 2006–, Shinymedia.com 2007–; chm Ashford Sports Club Ltd 1992–93; memb Mktg Soc, MIPA; *Books* Advertising Effectiveness (1982); *Recreations* golf (Team Faldo sport nutritionist), cricket and hockey (former Surrey Schs, Middx Colts Cricket Teams, Ashford Hockey Club and Surrey Youth Hockey, 1st XI Cricket and Hockey captain), skiing, opera; *Clubs* Burhill Golf; *Style—* Jeff Meers, Esq; ✉ Chamuel, 5 Thorne Close, Claygate, Esher, Surrey KT10 0HE (e-mail jeffmeers@brightstation.com)

MEERS, Dr John Laurence; s of Laurence Wilfred Victor Lord Meers, of Southend-on-Sea, Essex, and Elizabeth Audrey, *née* Hooker; *b* 4 February 1941; *Educ* Westcliff HS Essex, Univ of London (BSc, PhD); *m* 1, 1961 (m dis 1982), Pamela Mary, *née* Milsom; 1 s (Ian), 1 da (Jennifer); m 2, 1985; *Career* res and devpt dir John and E Sturge Ltd 1978–87; dir: Glumamates Ltd 1981–87, Sturge Chemicals Ltd 1981–87; md Sturge Enzymes 1982–84 (tech dir 1979); chief exec Enzymatix Ltd 1987–91 (co since demerged to form Chiroscience Ltd and Celsis International Ltd); chm and chief exec: Biognosis Ltd 1996–, Biognosis UK Ltd, Hebnosis Ltd 1996–, Bionet AG Dusseldorf 1999–, Biognosis GmbH Julich Germany 1999–; memb: Biotechnol Directorate Sci and Engrg Res Cncl, Fauna and Flora Preservation Soc, Rare Breeds Survival Tst; *Recreations* sailing, golf, singing; *Style—* Dr John Meers; ✉ Biognosis Ltd, PO Box 175, Frances House, Sir William Place, St Peter Port, Guernsey GY1 4HQ

M

MEERS, Nicholas Raymond Beaghen (Nick); s of Peter Rupert Neame Meers (d 2000), of Cheltenham, Glos, and Rachel Barbara, *née* Beaghen; *b* 16 May 1955; *Educ* Bryanston, W of England Sch of Art Bristol, Guildford Sch of Photography (Dip), W Surrey Coll of Art and Design; *m* 2001, Trudie Ballantyne; 1 da (Kirsty b 13 Nov 2004); *Career* photographer; numerous editorial and advtg cmmns (landscape, architectural, etc) 1978–; photographs have appeared on various book jackets, magazine front covers, calendars, postcards and in numerous magazines; memb: Assoc of Photographers, Int Assoc of Panoramic Photographers (IAPP); *Photographic Books* Amsterdam (1978), Paris (1978), California (1978), Los Angeles (1979), Orchids (Hawaii, 1979), Holland (1979), Wisconsin, USA (1979), Ohio, USA (1979), National Parks of California (1979), Israel the Promised Land (1980), Barbados (1980), Cayman Islands (1980), Bahamas (1980), Puerto Rico (1980), Parish Churches of England (1980), Senegal, West Africa (1981), Ivory Coast, West Africa (1981), Ireland and her People (1981), Ferrari (California, 1982), Porsche (California, 1982), The National Parks of Canada (1982), San Francisco (1983), Gardens of Britain (1985), New Shell Guide to South & Mid-Wales (with Wynford Vaughan-Thomas, 1986), New Shell Guide to the Channel Islands (1986), Christopher Wray's Guide to Decorative Lighting (with Barty Phillips, 1986), New Shell Guide to Oxfordshire & Berkshire (1987), The Spirit of the Cotswolds (with Susan Hill, 1987), New Shell Guide to Gloucestershire, Hereford & Worcester (1988), New Shell Guide to Sussex (1989), Enigmatic England (with Sue Seddon, 1989), Panoramas of English Gardens (with David Wheeler, 1990), Panoramas of England (with Adam Nicolson, 1991), Panoramas of English Villages (1992), Gardens of the National Trust (1996), A Year in the Garden (National Trust) 2001, Stretch, The World of Panoramic Photography (2003); *Recreations* panoramic photography, kite flying, astrocartography; *Style—* Nick Meers; ✉ mobile 07961 829829, e-mail nick@meersphoto.com, website www.nickmeers.com

MEHTA, Bharat; OBE (2000); s of Maganlal Jinabhai Mehta (d 1971), and Rattanben Mehta; *b* 5 March 1956; *Educ* Shenfield Sch, Plymouth Poly (BA), UCL (MSc); *m* 29 Sept 1990, Sally Ann, da of Reginald Chambers; 2 c (Kriyaa Uma b 30 Sept 1991, Puja Kavita b 10 Nov 1993); *Career* research asst MRC UCH Med Sch 1979–80; community worker Pensioners Link 1981–83, policy offr NCVO 1983–87, princ offr for vol orgns London Borough of Waltham Forest 1987–89, chief exec National Schizophrenia Fellowship 1994–98 (dir of devpt 1989–94), chief exec and clerk to the tstees City Parochial Fndn 1998–; memb Bd Rowntree Fndn 2003–; non-exec dir N Middx UH NHS Tst 2005–; patron Revolving Doors Agency; chm Bowes Primary Sch Governing Body 2000–05; fell Br American Project, Graduate of Common Purpose; FRSA 2003; *Recreations* hockey, squash, swimming; *Clubs* Southgate Adelaide Hockey (vice-pres 2002–); *Style—* Bharat Mehta, OBE; ✉ 18 Kelvin Avenue, Palmers Green, London N13 4TG (tel 020 8888 9873); City Parochial Foundation, 6 Middle Street, London EC1A 4PH (tel 020 7606 6145, fax 020 7600 1866, e-mail info@cityparochial.org.uk)

MEHTA, Bharat; s of Himatlal Mehta, of Mombasa, Kenya, and Rasika Vora Mehta (d 1998); *b* 20 November 1952, Bombay, India; *Educ* MBA; *m* 22 July 1979, Renu; 2 s (Harshil b 26 Nov 1980, Ishil b 9 Oct 1987); *Career* prop Necessity Supplies 1987–; *Clubs* Lions

(Acton branch); *Style*— Bharat Mehta, Esq; ✉ PO Box 509, Uxbridge, Middlesex UB10 9EP

MEHTA, Zubin; *Educ* Vienna Musikakademie (studied with Hans Swarawsky); *Career* conductor, debut Vienna 1958; asst conductor Royal Liverpool Philharmonic Orchestra, musical dir for life Israel Philharmonic Orchestra; musical dir: Montreal Symphony Orch 1960–64, Los Angeles Philharmonic Orch 1961–78, NY Philharmonic Orch 1978–91 (longest ever holder of post, over 1000 public concerts); work incl: Live from Lincoln Centre (for TV), Pension Fund Concert (with Daniel Barenboim), New Year's Eve Concert (with June Anderson), Mozart Bicentennial Celebration, Salute to Carnegie Hall (with Isaac Stern) 1990, Bartók's Piano Concerto No 2 (with Andras Schiff) 1993; tours with NY Philharmonic incl: Argentina and the Dominican Repub 1978, Europe 1980 and 1988, US and Mexico 1981, S America 1982, US 1983, Asia 1984 and 1989, Europe and Israel 1985, Latin America 1987, Soviet Union (incl jt concert in Gorky Park Moscow with State Symphony Orchestra of Soviet Miny of Culture) 1988; advsr to Maggio Musicale Fiorentino, frequent guest conductor for maj orchs and opera cos; numerous recordings with NY Philharmonic incl: Mahler's Symphony No 5, Holst's The Planets, Sibelius Symphony No 2 and Finlandia, Stravinsky's La Sacre du Printemps and Symphony in Three Movements, Gershwin Collection (incl Rhapsody in Blue, An American in Paris and excerpts from Porgy and Bess), Paine's Symphonies Nos 1 and 2, Overture to As You Like It, Dvořák's Violin Concerto (with Midori), Domingo at the Philharmonic; recordings with Berlin Philharmonic incl: Richard Strauss' Alpine Symphony, Bartók's Concerto for Orchestra, Miraculous Mandarin Suite and Violin Concertos Nos 1 and 2 (with Midori); recordings with Israel Philharmonic incl: Chopin's Piano Concertos Nos 1 and 2 (with Murray Parahia), Fauré Schoenberg and Sibelius settings of Pelléas et Mélisande; *Awards* first prize Int Conductors Competition Liverpool 1958, Padma Bhusham of Indian Govt (Order of the Lotus), Gold medal from Pope Paul VI, commendation from PM Golda Meir for contrib to the cultural life of Israel, Commendatore Repub of Italy 1976, Nikisch Ring (bequeathed by Karl Boehm), Vienna Philharmonic Ring of Honor; hon citizen of Tel Aviv; *Style*— Zubin Mehta, Esq; ✉ 27 Oakmont Drive, Los Angles, CA 90049, USA

MEIRION-JONES, Prof Gwyn Idris; s of Maelgwyn Meirion-Jones (d 1989), of Manchester, and Enid, *née* Roberts (d 1962); *b* 24 December 1933; *Educ* N Manchester GS, KCL (BSc, MPhil, PhD); *m* 1 April 1961, Monica (d 2003), da of George Havard, of Winchester (d 1961), and Marion, *née* Milson (d 1976); *Career* Nat Serv RAF 1954–56; schoolmaster 1959–68, lectr in geography Kingston Coll of Technol 1968; London Metropolitan Univ (formerly Sir John Cass Coll, then City of London Poly, then London Guildhall Univ): sr lectr in geography 1969, head of geography 1970–89, prof 1983–89, Leverhulme res fell 1985–87, emeritus prof 1989–; visiting prof of archaeology Univ of Reading 1995–2007; author and conslt on historic bldgs; author of papers on scientific, archaeological and ethnological jls; dir Soc of Antiquaries 2001–02; Ancient Monuments Soc: memb Cncl 1974–79 and 1983–94, hon sec 1976–79, vice-pres 1979–, ed 1985–94; Br Assoc for the Advancement of Science: sec 1973–78, memb Cncl 1977–80, memb Gen Ctee 1977–83, recorder 1978–83, pres Archaeology and Anthropology Section 1992–93; ed Medieval Village Res Gp 1978–86, memb Royal Cmmn on the Historical Monuments of England 1985–97, pres Surrey Domestic Bldgs Res Gp 1986–91 (hon vice-pres 1991–), memb Advsy Ctee on Buildings and Domestic Life Welsh Folk Museum 1991–95; hon corr memb Société Jersiaise 1980–, corr memb Compagnie des Architectes en Chef des Monuments Historiques 1989–, hon corr memb Soc d'Hist et d'Archéol Bretagne 1997–; FSA 1981; *Books* La Maison Traditionnelle (1978), The Vernacular Architecture of Brittany (1982), Aimer les Châteaux de Bretagne (with Prof Michael Jones, 1991, also English and German edns), Les Châteaux de Bretagne (with Prof Michael Jones, 1992), Manorial Domestic Buildings in England and Northern France (1993), La Ville de Cluny et ses Maisons (XIe-XVe siècles) (jtly, 1997), Historic Buildings and Dating by Dendrochronology (1999), The Seigneurial Residence in Western Europe AD c800–1600 (jtly, 2002); *Recreations* food, wine, music, walking, fly fishing; *Clubs* Athenaeum, Royal Scots (Edinburgh); *Style*— Prof Gwyn Meirion-Jones, FSA; ✉ 11 Avondale Road, Fleet, Hampshire GU51 3BH (tel and fax 01252 614300, mobile 077 7494 6075, e-mail gm-j@wanadoo.fr)

MELCHETT, 4 Baron (UK 1928); Sir Peter Robert Henry Mond; 4 Bt (UK 1910); s of 3 Baron Melchett (d 1973, gs of 1 Baron, better known as Sir Alfred Mond, first chm of ICI and min of Health 1921–22); *b* 24 February 1948; *Educ* Eton, Pembroke Coll Cambridge, Keele Univ; *Career* sat as Lab peer in House of Lords; at LSE and Addiction Res Unit 1973–74; a lord in waiting (govt whip) 1974–75, Parly under-sec of state DOI 1975–76, min of state NI Office 1976–79; chm: Working Pty on Pop Festivals 1975–76, Community Industry 1979–85, Greenpeace UK 1986–88 (exec dir 1988–2000), Greenpeace Japan 1995–2001; memb: Greenpeace Int Bd 1988 and 2001, Govt Organic Action Plan Gp 2002–, BBC Rural Affairs Ctee 2004–, DfES Sch Meals Panel 2005–; pres Ramblers' Assoc 1981–84; policy dir Soil Assoc 2002–; *Style*— The Rt Hon the Lord Melchett

MELDING, David Robert Michael; AM; s of David Graham Melding, of Neath, and Edwina Margaret, *née* King; *b* 28 August 1962; *Educ* Dwr-y-Felin Comp Sch Neath, Univ Coll Cardiff, Coll of William and Mary Va USA; *Career* memb Cons Research Dept 1986–89, dep dir Welsh Centre for Int Affairs 1994–96 (exec offr 1989–94), mangr Carers Nat Assoc in Wales 1996–99; memb Nat Assembly for Wales (Cons) South Wales Central 1999–, spokesperson on Health, Social Services and Equal Opportunities 1999–, chm Ctee on Standards of Conduct 2000–; chm Governing Body Meadowbank Special Sch Cardiff; *Recreations* swimming, golf; *Style*— David Melding, Esq, AM; ✉ National Assembly for Wales, Cardiff Bay, Cardiff CF99 1NA (tel 029 2089 8328, fax 029 2089 8329)

MELDRUM, Sir Graham; kt (2002), CBE (1994), QFSM (1988); s of George Meldrum, and Agnes, *née* Gordon; *b* 23 October 1945; *Educ* Inverurie Acad; *m* 1963, Catherine Mary Elizabeth, da of Peter Meier; 1 s (Clive b 12 March 1972), 1 da (Jill b 29 Oct 1979); *Career* fireman rising to station offr London Fire Bde 1963–73, instr (asst divnl offr) Fire Serv Coll 1973–74, divnl offr III Hants Fire Serv 1974–76; Tyne & Wear Fire Serv: divnl offr II 1976–79, divnl offr I 1979–80, sr divnl offr 1980–83; W Midlands Fire Serv: asst chief offr 1983–84, dep chief fire offr 1984–90, chief fire offr 1990–98; HM Chief Inspr of Fire Servs (Home Office) 1998–2007, chm W Midlands Ambulance Serv NHS Tst 2007–; pres Chief and Asst Chief Fire Offrs' Assoc 1994–95; pres Fire Servs Youth Trg Assoc, pres The Fire Service Princes Tst Assoc, vice-pres Fire Servs Nat Benevolent Fund; vice-pres The Healing Tst; Hon DUniv UCE 1997; FIFirE 1994, CIMgt 1995; OStJ 1998; *Recreations* classic cars, motor boats; *Clubs* Farmers; *Style*— Sir Graham Meldrum, CBE, QFSM; ✉ West Midlands Ambulance Service NHS Trust, Waterfront Business Park, Waterfront Way, Brierly Hill, West Midlands DY5 1LX

MELFORD, Dr David Austin; OBE (1990); s of Austin Melford (d 1971), of London, and Jessie, *née* Winter (d 1971); *b* 16 October 1927; *Educ* Hall Sch Hampstead, Charterhouse, Clare Coll Cambridge (MA, PhD, ScD); *m* 3 Sept 1955, Amanda Patricia, da of Leonard Farrar (Cdr RN, d 1959); 1 s (Mark Austin b 29 April 1969), 1 da (Clare Amanda b 14 June 1973); *Career* Army Serv 1946–48, cmmnd 2 Lt Royal Signals; TI fell Cavendish Laboratory Cambridge 1955–57; TI Group: research scientist TI Research Laboratories, design and devpt Scanning Electron Probe Microanalyser 1957–68, chief metallurgist and head of Metallurgy Div 1968–79, dir of research and dep gen mangr 1979–87; materials research conslt 1987–97, Royal Acad of Engrg visiting prof Dept of Materials Science and Metallurgy Univ of Cambridge 1994–96; former: memb Engrg Bd, memb Materials Cmmn SERC, chm Materials Advsy Ctee DTI, memb Cncl, memb Standing Ctee on Engrg and assessor SERC Cncl Royal Acad of Engrg; Hadfield medallist 1975, Pfeil medallist 1976, Platinum medallist Inst of Materials 1993; author of numerous contribs to learned jls especially jl of Inst of Metals; FIM 1975 (sometime vice-pres, memb Cncl and memb Exec Ctee), FREng 1984; *Recreations* writing, instrument making, gardening and historical research; *Clubs* MCC; *Style*— Dr David Melford, OBE, FREng; ✉ Ryders, Strethall, Saffron Walden, Essex CB11 4XJ

MELHAM, Prof Thomas Frederick; s of Frederick Elias Melham (d 1960), and Hildur Margaret Harms, *née* Lien; *b* 16 January 1960; *Educ* Univ of Calgary (BSc), Univ of Cambridge (PhD); *m* 16 Nov 2002, Karen Annette, *née* van der Meulen; *Career* research fell Gonville & Caius Coll Cambridge 1987–91; Univ of Glasgow: lectr 1993–97, sr lectr 1997–98, prof of computing science 1998–2002; Univ of Oxford: lectr in computer science 2002–04, tutorial fell in computation Balliol Coll Oxford 2002–, prof of computer science 2004–; memb EPSRC Peer Review Coll for IT/Computing 1997–; FRSE 2002; *Books Publications* incl: Introduction to HOL: A theorem proving environment for higher order logic (ed with M J C Gordon, 1993), Higher Order Logic and Hardware Verification (1993); also various refereed pubns, invited papers and other pubns; *Recreations* music, philosophy; *Style*— Prof Thomas Melham; ✉ Balliol College, Oxford OX1 3BJ; Oxford University Computing Laboratory, Wolfson Building, Parks Road, Oxford OX1 3QD (tel 01865 273824, fax 01865 273839, e-mail tom.melham@comlab.ox.ac.uk)

MELIA, Dr Terence Patrick; CBE (1993); s of John Melia (d 1975), and Kathleen, *née* Traynor (d 1984); *b* 17 December 1934; *Educ* Sir John Deane's GS Northwich, Univ of Leeds (PhD); *m* 21 May 1976, Madeline, da of Arthur Carney (d 1975); 1 da (Alexandra b 1980); *Career* tech offr ICI Ltd 1961–64, lectr and sr lectr Univ of Salford 1964–70, princ N Lindsey Coll of Technol 1970–74; HM inspr of schs 1974–92: regnl staff inspr NW 1982–84, chief inspr higher educn 1985–91, sr chief inspr 1991–92; chief inspr Further Educn Funding Cncl 1993–96; chm: Further Educn Staff Devpt Forum 1996–99, RSA Examinations Bd Educn Policy Ctee 1996–98, Further Educn Devpt Agency 1997–2000, OCR Examinations Bd Qualifications Ctee 1998–99, Further Educn National Trg Orgn 1999–2001, Learning and Skills Devpt Agency 2000–; visiting prof Leeds Metropolitan Univ 1993–; Hon DSc Univ of Salford 1998; FRSC, CChem; *Recreations* golf, gardening; *Clubs* Berkhamsted Golf; *Style*— Dr Terence Melia, CBE; ✉ Learning and Skills Development Agency, Regent Arcade House, 19–25 Argyll Street, London W1F 7LF (tel 020 7297 9005)

MELLAART, James; s of Jacob Herman Jan Mellaart (d 1972), of London, and Apollonia Dingena, *née* Van Der Beek (d 1934); *b* 14 November 1925; *Educ* Gymnasiums The Hague and Maastricht Holland, UCL (BA); *m* 23 April 1954, (Meryem) Arlette, da of Kadri Cenani, OBE (d 1984), of Istanbul; 1 s (Alan b 1955); *Career* archaeologist; asst dir Br Inst of Archaeology Ankara Turkey 1959–61 (scholar and fell 1951–58), specialist lectr Istanbul Univ 1961–63, lectr in Anatolian archaeology Inst of Archaeology Univ of London 1964–91; excavations: Beycesultan (with S Lloyd) 1954–59, Hacilar 1957–60, Çatal Hüyük 1961–63 and 1965; FSA 1964, FBA 1980; *Books* Beycesultan (excavation reports with Seton Lloyd, Vol I 1962, Vol II 1965), Earliest Civilisations of The Near East (1965), The Chalcolithic and Early Bronze Ages in The Near East and Anatolia (1966), Çatal Hüyük, A Neolithic Town in Anatolia (1967), Excavations at Hacilar (1970), The Neolithic of the Near East (1975), The Archaeology of Ancient Turkey (1978), The Goddess from Anatolia, II, Çatal Hüyük and Anatolian Kilims (1989), Beycesultan (vol III.2, with Ann Murray, 1995); *Recreations* music (Baroque and Gaelic), art (Celtic and Turkish), geology, ancient history; *Style*— James Mellaart, Esq, FBA; ✉ 12–13 Lichen Court, 79 Queen's Drive, London N4 2BH (tel 020 8802 6984)

MELLIS, Margaret; da of Rev David Barclay Mellis (d 1961), and Margaret Blaikie, *née* MacKenzie (d 1970); *b* 22 January 1914; *Educ* Queen Margaret's PNEU Sch Edinburgh, Edinburgh Coll of Art (DA, MacLaine Watters medal for colour, Andrew Grant postgrad award, travelling scholarship, 2 year fellowship); *m* 1, 1938, Adrian Stokes (the writer), s of Durham Stokes; 1 s (Telfer b 1940); *m* 2, Francis Davison (the collagist), s of George Davison; *Career* artist; studied in Paris, Spain and Italy, worked Euston Road Sch London, lived and worked St Ives Cornwall then Cap d'Antibes France, currently based Suffolk; *Solo Exhibitions* AIA Gallery London 1958, Scottish Gallery Edinburgh 6 1959, UEA 1967, Bear Lane Gallery Oxford 1968, Grabowski Gallery London 1969, Richard Demarco Gallery Edinburgh 1970, Univs of Stirling and Exeter 1970, Basil Jacobs Gallery London 1972, Compass Gallery Glasgow 1976, Pier Art Centre Orkney 1982, New '57 Gallery Edinburgh 1982, Redfern Gallery London 1987, 1990 and 1994, Aldeburgh artist in residence Aldeburgh Festival Exhibition 1991, Gainsborough House Museum 1992, A Retrospective (touring exhbn, City Arts Centre Edinburgh, Kapil Jarawala London and Pier Gallery Orkney) 1997, Austin/Desmond Fine Art and Newlyn Art Gallery Penzance 2001, Phoenix 369 Edinburgh 2004, Austin/Desmond Fine Art London 2005, Strand Gallery Aldeburgh 2005, Austin/Desmond Fine Art London 2008, Sainsbury Centre UEA 2008; *Group Exhibitions* incl: Waddington Galleries 1959–62, John Moores Liverpool Exhibition 4 and 5 1963 and 1965, Edinburgh Open 100 1967, Painting in Cornwall 1945–55 (New Art Centre London) 1977, The Women's Art Show 1550–1970 (Castle Museum Nottingham) 1982, Objects (recent acquisitions, V&A) 1978, Pier Gallery Collection Exhibition (Tate Gallery), St Ives 1939–64 (Tate Gallery) 1985, Art Since 1900 (Scottish Nat Gallery of Modern Art and Barbican London) 1989, Glasgow's Great British Art Exhibition (McLellan Galleries) 1990, New Gallery of Modern Art Glasgow 1996, Bede Gallery Jarrow (with Francis Davison) 1996, A Female Focus (Wolsey Gallery Ipswich) 1999; *Work in Collections* incl: Tate Gallery, V&A, Kelvin Grove Museum and Art Gallery Glasgow, Nuffield Fndn, Sztuki W Lodzi Museum Poland, Scottish Nat Gallery of Modern Art Edinburgh, Pier Collection Orkney, Scottish Arts Cncl, Arts Cncl of GB, Graves Collection Sheffield, Sainsbury Centre Norwich, Gallery of Modern Art Glasgow, Norwich Castle Museum 1996; major retrospective exhbn: City Art Centre Edinburgh 1997, Kapil Jariwala Gallery London 1997, Pier Gallery Orkney 1998, The King of Hearts Gallery Norwich Exhibition 1998, Austin/Desmond Fine Art 2001, Newlyn Art Gallery 2001; *Recreations* music, reading, dancing, walking, ballet, opera, cinema; *Style*— Margaret Mellis; ✉ Austin/Desmond Fine Art, 68–69 Great Russell Street, London WC1B 3BN (tel 020 7242 4443)

MELLIS, Patrick David Barclay Nairne; s of Capt David Mellis, DSC, RN, and Anne Patricia, *née* Wingate-Gray (d 1994); *b* 14 May 1943; *Educ* Loretto, Univ of Glasgow (BSc); *m* 26 Nov 1969, Elizabeth Jane Workman, *née* Carslaw; 2 da (Rosemary Anne Nairne b 14 Nov 1975, Catherine Fiona Nairne b 25 April 1977), 1 s (Robert Barclay Nairne b 13 May 1980); *Career* student apprentice Alex Stephens & Sons (shipbuilders) Glasgow 1961–66 (design draughtsman 1966–68); naval architect: Litton Industries Mississippi USA 1968–70, A Darden & Sons (conslts) New Orleans USA 1970–72, International Offshore Services London 1972–74; project mangr P&O Three Quays 1974–83, marine dir Seaforth Maritime Ltd Aberdeen 1983–89, project mangr Saudi Arabian Oil Co Saudi Arabia 1990–96, md P&O Three Quays 1996–, md Three Quays International 2001–; memb Br Maritime League; memb Instn of Engrs and Shipbuilders in Scotland 1962, MRINA 1962, memb Soc of Naval Architects and Marine Engrs USA 1972; *Recreations* squash, golf, sailing; *Style*— Patrick Mellis, Esq; ✉ Three Quays Marine Services Ltd, 12–20 Camomile Street, London EC3A 7AS (tel 020 7621 2936, fax 020 7929 1650)

MELLISS, Simon Richard; s of Laurence Melliss, of Sherborne, Dorset, and Joan, *née* Franklin; *b* 2 July 1952, London; *Educ* Christ's Hosp, Univ of York (BA); *m* 4 Sept 1976, Jennifer Susan, *née* Webberley; 2 s (Oliver Simon b 31 Jan 1981, Dominic James b 1 June 1983); *Career* Whinney Murray & Co (later Ernst & Young) 1974–78, Reed Int plc 1978–88, fin controller Sketchley plc 1989–91; Hammerson plc: fin controller 1991–95, gp fin dir 1995–; memb Ctee of Mgmnt Hermes Property Unit Tst, non-exec dir: Assoc British Ports Holdings plc 2006, Whitbread plc 2007–; FCA 1978; *Recreations* pottering around; *Style*— Simon Melliss, Esq; ✉ Hammerson plc, 10 Grosvenor Street, London W1K 4BJ (tel 020 7887 1000, fax 020 7887 1008, e-mail simon.melliss@hammerson.com)

MELLITT, Prof Brian; s of John Mellitt (d 1990), of Preston, and Nelly, *née* Heaney (d 2002); *b* 29 May 1940; *Educ* Preston GS, Loughborough Univ (BTech), Imperial Coll London (DIC); *m* 30 Dec 1961, Lyn, da of Edward Waring, of Preston; 1 s (John Edward b 1967), 1 da (Anna Jane b 1969); *Career* design engr (Electric Traction) English Electric 1956–66, sr lectr Huddersfield Poly 1966–68, sr princ scientific offr Res Div British Railways Bd 1968–71; Univ of Birmingham: lectr 1971, sr lectr 1981, prof 1983, head Undergraduate Sch 1983, head Electrical Engrg and Electronics Dept 1985, dean Faculty of Engrg 1987–88, hon prof 1989; head Power Electronics and Traction Gp 1971–88 (conslt engr to various railways incl LUL, Hong Kong MTRC, Singapore MRTC, CIE, Metro Madrid), engrg dir London Underground 1989–95, dir engrg and prodn Railtrack plc 1995–99 (ret), pt/t engrg advsr Railtrack (UK) plc 1999–2000; hon ed IEE Proceedings - Electric Power Applications 1978–; Leonardo da Vinci Award Italian Industrial Design Assoc 1989; chm Railway Forum 1998–2000; non-exec chm: Building Research Establishment 1998–, Metro Consulting 2000–02, SIRA Ltd 2001–06, Rail Personnel Int Hong Kong 2002–03; non-exec dir: Catalis Rail Trg Ltd 1998–2001, Jarvis plc 2002–; rail conslt to NM Rothschild 1999–; Hon DTech Loughborough Univ 1991, Hon DSc Univ of Huddersfield 1997, Hon DEng Univ of Birmingham 1999; pres Welding Instn 2000–01; FIEE 1978 (vice-pres 1996–99, dep pres 1999–2001, pres 2001–02), FIMechE 1986, FIRSE 1984, FREng 1990; *Books* Computers in Railway Operations (ed, 1987), Computer Applications in Railway Operations (ed, 1990); *Recreations* bridge; *Clubs* Athenaeum; *Style*— Prof Brian Mellitt, FREng; ✉ The Priory, 36 Church Street, Stilton, Cambridgeshire PE7 3RF (tel 01733 240573, fax 01733 240467, e-mail brianmellitt@msn.com)

MELLODEW, John; s of Eric Mellodew (d 1989), and Sybil, *née* Woods (d 1993); *b* 26 June 1941; *Educ* Reigate GS; *m* 13 Nov 1965, Jennifer; 2 da (Karen b 1966, Anita b 1970), 1 s (David b 1969); *Career* journalist; sports ed Surrey Mirror 1962–64, sub-ed Manchester Evening News 1964–66, sub-ed London Evening News 1966–69, chief sub-ed Southend Evening Echo 1969–73; News of the World: sub-ed 1973–77, chief sub-ed 1977–78, production ed 1978–87, asst ed 1987–2004, ret; memb NUJ; *Recreations* running, squash, gardening; *Clubs* Lansdown, Bath Squash; *Style*— John Mellodew, Esq; ✉ Minster Cottage, Hazelbury Hill, Box, Corsham, Wiltshire SN13 8LB (tel 01225 742700, mobile 07867 942259)

MELLON, Sir James; KCMG (1989, CMG 1979); *b* 25 January 1929; *Educ* Univ of Glasgow; *m* 1, 1956, Frances Murray (d 1976); 1 s, 3 da; *m* 2, 1979, Mrs Philippa Shuttleworth, *née* Hartley; *Career* joined FO 1963, commercial cnsllr E Berlin 1975–76, head of Trade Rels and Export Dept FCO 1976–78, high cmmr to Ghana and ambass to Togo 1978–83, ambass to Denmark 1983–86, consul-gen New York 1986–89; chm: Scottish Homes 1989–96, Regent Pacific Corporate Finance 1991–2000, Thamesmead Town 1993–96, RTM (Radio Thamesmead) 1993–96, Charlemagne Capital (UK) Ltd 2000–; *Style*— Sir James Mellon, KCMG; ✉ Charlemagne Capital, 39 St James's Street, London SW1A 1JD (tel 020 7518 2100, e-mail sirjames@charlemagnecapital.com)

MELLOR, David; CBE (2001, OBE 1981); s of Colin Mellor (d 1970), and Ivy Mellor (d 1975); *b* 5 October 1930; *Educ* Sheffield Coll of Art, Royal Coll of Art (hon fell 1966), Br Sch at Rome; *m* 1966, Fiona MacCarthy, *qv*, da of Col Gerald Heggart MacCarthy (d 1943); 1 s, 1 da; *Career* designer, manufacturer and retailer; conslt DOE 1963–70, chm Design Cncl Ctee of Inquiry into Standards of Design in Consumer Goods in Britain 1982–84, chm Crafts Cncl 1982–84, tstee V&A 1983–88; V&A/Homes & Gardens Lifetime Achievement Award 2006; RDI 1962; Hon DLitt Univ of Sheffield 1986, Hon DDes De Montfort Univ 1997, Hon Dr RCA 1999, Hon DTech Loughborough Univ 2006; *Style*— David Mellor, Esq, CBE; ✉ The Round Building, Hathersage, Sheffield S32 1BA (tel 01433 650220, fax 01433 650944)

MELLOR, Prof David Hugh; s of Sydney David Mellor, and Ethel Naomi, *née* Hughes; *b* 10 July 1938; *Educ* Pembroke Coll Cambridge (BA), Univ of Minnesota (MS), Univ of Cambridge (PhD, ScD, MEng); *Career* tech offr ICI Central Instruments Laboratories 1962–63; Univ of Cambridge: asst lectr in philosophy 1965–70, lectr in philosophy 1970–83, reader in metaphysics 1983–86, prof of philosophy 1986–99, pro-vice chllr 2000–01; Philosophy Faculty Univ of Cambridge: librarian 1970–76, chm Bd and Degree Ctee 1976–78 and 1991–93 (sec 1981–85), dir Graduate Studies 1988–90; pres Cambridge Assoc of Univ Teachers 1976–78; Univ of Cambridge: memb Cncl of the Senate 1976–78, memb Library Syndicate 1976–78, memb Bd of Graduate Studies 1989–93, memb General Bd of the Faculties 1995–98; official fell Pembroke Coll Cambridge 1966–70 (Draper's res fell 1964–66); dir Studies in Philosophy: Pembroke Coll 1964–83, Downing Coll 1966–83, Trinity Hall 1982–83; Darwin Coll: fell 1971–2005, vice-master 1983–87; external examiner in philosophy: Univ of Khartoum 1978–79, Univ of Warwick 1978–80, UCNW Bangor 1982–84; visiting fell in philosophy Aust Nat Univ Inst Advanced Study 1975, Radcliffe Tst Fell in Philosophy 1978–80, visiting prof of philosophy Univ of Auckland 1985; pres: Br Soc for Philosophy of Sci 1985–87, Aristotelian Soc 1992–93; tstee Analysis Tst 1987–; memb: Analysis Ctee Cncl Royal Inst of Philosophy 1987–, Exec Ctee Mind Assoc 1982–86; Hon PhD Univ of Lund 1997; FBA 1983; *Books* The British Journal for The Philosophy of Science (ed, 1968–70), Cambridge Studies in Philosophy (ed, 1978–82), Australasian Journal of Philosophy (memb Editorial Bd, 1977–89), The Matter of Chance (1971), Science, Belief and Behaviour (ed, 1980), Prospects for Pragmatism (ed, 1980), Real Time (1981), Matters of Metaphysics (1991), Ways of Communicating (ed, 1991), The Facts of Causation (1995), Properties (co-ed 1997), Real Time II (1998), Probability: A Philosophical Introduction (2005), Ramsey's Legacy (co-ed, 2005); *Recreations* theatre; *Style*— Prof D H Mellor; ✉ 25 Orchard Street, Cambridge CB1 1JS (tel and fax 01223 740017, e-mail dhm11@cam.ac.uk)

MELLOR, The Rt Hon David John; PC (1990), QC (1987); s of late Douglas H Mellor; *b* 12 March 1949; *Educ* Swanage GS, Christ's Coll Cambridge (LLB); *m* 1974 (m dis 1996), Judith Mary; 2 s (Anthony, Frederick); *Career* chm Univ of Cambridge Assoc 1970; called to the Bar Inner Temple 1972; Parly candidate (Cons) West Bromwich E Oct 1974, MP (Cons) Putney 1979–97; PPS to Francis Pym as Ldr of the House 1981; Parly under sec state: for energy 1981–83, Home Office 1983–86; min of state: Home Office 1986–87, FCO 1987–88, for Health 1988–89, Home Office 1989–90, Privy Cncl Office (min for the Arts) 1990; chief sec to the Treasury 1990–92, sec of state for Nat Heritage April-Sept 1992; advsr to major British and international cos 1992–; columnist: The Guardian 1992–95, Evening Standard (weekly football column), Sunday People (Man of the People column); arts and music critic Mail on Sunday 2000; contrib to various newspapers; host 6.06 phone-in show (Radio Five Live, BBC Radio Personality of the Year 1995 Variety Club Awards) 1992–; presenter: Vintage Years (BBC Radio 3), Across the Threshold (Classic FM), David Mellor Prog (BBC Radio 5), If You Liked That (Classic FM); judge: Sony Radio Awards 1993, Whitbread Literary Prize 1993, Sunday Express Award for Fiction; chm Panel of Judges Science Book Awards 1994; chm Sports Aid Fndn 1993–97, chm Football Task Force 1997–2000; pres Bournemouth Symphony Orch 2000–; govr Nat Youth Orchestra (memb cncl); tstee Fund for the Replacement of Animals in Medical Experiments (FRAME) 2004– (also co-patron); former dep chm London Philharmonic Tst, former memb Bd ENO; hon assoc BVA 1986; FZS; *Style*— The Rt Hon David Mellor, QC; ✉ DM Consultancy, 8th Floor, 7 Farm Street, Mayfair, London W1J 5RX (tel 020 7514 5522, fax 020 7499 1811, e-mail david@davidmellorconsultancy.co.uk)

MELLOR, Hugh Salusbury; s of Wing Cdr Harry Manners Mellor, MVO (ka 1940), and Diana Marion, *née* Wyld; *b* 16 March 1936; *Educ* Harrow, ChCh Oxford (MA); *m* 6 Feb 1966, Sally, da of Flt Lt Clive Newton Wawn, DFC, RAF, of Victoria, Australia; 2 s (Nicholas Hugh b 29 May 1967, Andrew Harry Clive b 3 Jan 1970), 1 da (Sari b 14 July 1972); *Career* Nat Serv 2 Lt Coldstream Gds 1954–56; asst dir Morgan Grenfell & Co Ltd 1968 (joined 1960), exec Dalgety plc (formerly Dalgety Ltd) 1970–90 (bd memb 1968); dir: Pearl Group plc (formerly Australian Mutual Provident Society) 1979–94, Bank of NZ (London) 1983–89, Burmah Castrol plc (previously Burmah Oil plc) 1984–97, Meghraj Bank Ltd 1987–, Elementis plc (formerly Harrisons & Crosfield plc) 1991–, Govett Oriental Investment Trust plc 1994–; fell RSPB, fell Br Tst for Ornithology; *Recreations* ornithology, entomology; *Style*— Hugh Mellor, Esq; ✉ Blackland Farm, Stewkley, Leighton Buzzard, Bedfordshire LU7 0EU

MELLOR, Ian; s of Dr Michael James Mellor, and Ruth Mary, *née* Alexander; *Educ* Bournemouth Sch (J J Dodds prize), Univ of Durham (BA); *Career* ICC Information Ltd 1989–91, asst ed Communicable Disease Report Public Health Lab Serv 1991–94; Martin Dunitz Ltd: ed 1994–97, jls mangr 1997–2001; special sales (jls) Informa plc 2001–06, business devpt Inst of Physics Publishing 2006–; *Recreations* oil painting, writing, badminton; *Clubs* Cheltenham Art Soc, Cheltenham Ladies' Coll Sports; *Style*— Ian Mellor, Esq; ✉ Institute of Physics, Dirac House, Temple Back, Bristol BS1 6BE (tel 0117 929 7481, fax 0117 920 0812, e-mail ian.mellor@iop.org)

MELLOR, Dame Julie Thérèse; DBE (2006); da of Gp Capt Edward Veron Mellor, of Oxford, and Patricia Ann, *née* Jenner-Baden (d 1994); *Educ* BNC Oxford (BA); *m* 23 Sept 1990, Nick Reed; 1 s, 1 da; *Career* teacher Inst for Educn and Research on Women and Work and Eleanor Emerson fell in labour educn Cornell Univ NY 1979–81, employee rels advsr Shell UK 1981–83, economic devpt offr London Borough of Islington 1983–84, dep head of contract compliance Equal Opportunities Unit and sr employment policy advsr GLC/ILEA 1984–89, HR mangr TSB Gp 1989–91, corp HR dir British Gas 1992–96, prop and princ conslt Julie Mellor Conslts 1996–99, chair Equal Opportunities Cmmn 1999–2005, ptnr PricewaterhouseCoopers 2005–; cmmr Cmmn for Racial Equality 1996–2003; memb Bd Nat Consumer Cncl 2001–07, chair Employer's Forum on Disability; chair Fathers Direct; Hon Dr Anglia Poly Univ 2003; hon fell BNC Oxford 2003; FCGI 2003; *Recreations* theatre, travel, food; *Style*— Dame Julie Mellor

MELLOR, Simon John; s of Raymond Mellor, and Phyllis, *née* Canter; *b* 10 September 1954; *Educ* Univ of Bristol (BSc); *m* 3 Feb 1990, (Carolyn) Mary, da of Ewen Langford; 2 da (Phoebe b 23 April 1991, Imogen b 12 July 1993), 2 step s (Dominic b 18 Nov 1975, Thomas b 23 June 1977); *Career* Saatchi & Saatchi Co plc: asst to chm 1976–78, corp devpt mangr 1978–84, assoc dir 1984–, dir Main Bd 1985, dep ceo Communications Div 1988, responsible for co's corp communication 1990, commercial dir Saatchi & Saatchi Advertising Worldwide 1991–94; gp commercial dir Blenheim Group plc 1994–96; managing ptnr: Mellor Watts 1996–2005, The Mellor Partnership 2005–; Freeman City of London, memb Worshipful Co of Clockmakers; *Recreations* theatre, cinema, soccer, cricket; *Style*— Simon Mellor, Esq; ✉ The Mellor Partnership, High Holborn House, 52/54 High Holborn, London WC1V 6RL (tel 020 7692 0505, fax 020 7692 0502, e-mail simon@mellorpartnership.com)

MELLORS, Prof Colin; s of George Mellors, and Phyllis, *née* Buxton; *b* 2 June 1949; *Educ* Firth Park GS Sheffield, Univ of Sheffield (BA, MA), Univ of Bradford (PhD); *Career* tutor Univ of Sheffield 1971–73, lectr in politics Univ of Southampton 1973–74; Univ of Bradford: lectr 1974–84, sr lectr 1984–94, dean Faculty of Social Sciences 1992–94, prof 1994–, pro-vice-chllr 1994–2001; former tutor Open Univ and educn advsr NALGO; pro vice-chllr Univ of York, dir of HE strategy Yorkshire Forward (RDA), non-exec dir Corp Mgmnt Bd Govt Office for Yorkshire and Humber; dep electoral cmmr and memb Boundary Ctee for England 2002–; dep chair of govrs Bradford GS; FHEA, FRSA; *Publications* British MP (1978), Promoting Local Authorities in the EC (1986), Local Government in the Community (jtly, 1987), Political Parties and Coalitions in European Local Government (jtly, 1988), EC Regional Policy (jtly, 1989), Training for Europe (ed, 1992), Language Training and Services for Business (ed, 1993), Managing without a Majority (1996), Dod's Constituency Guide (jtly, 2002, 2003 and 2005); also author of numerous reports and articles in learned jls; *Recreations* photography, fell walking; *Style*— Prof Colin Mellors; ✉ Innovation Centre, York Science Park, University of York, Heslington, York YO10 5DG

MELMOTH, Sir Graham John; kt (2002); *m* Jenny; 2 s; *Career* early career with BOC, Fisons and Letraset; Co-operative Group (CWS) Ltd: joined 1975, sec 1976, chief exec 1996–2002; chm Ringway Developments plc 1995–2002; chm NCVO 2004–; pres International Co-operative Alliance (ICA) 1995–97; *Recreations* co-operative history and ideas, opera, theatre; *Style*— Sir Graham Melmoth

MELROSE, Margaret Elstob; DL (Cheshire 1987); da of Samuel Chantler Jackson (d 1978), of Prestbury, Cheshire, and Annie Young, *née* Arnot (d 1978); *b* 2 May 1928; *Educ* Howell's Sch Denbigh, Girton Coll Cambridge (Drapers' Co scholarship); *m* 19 June 1948 (m dis), Kenneth Ramsay Watson, s of late Albert Watson; assumed surname of Melrose by deed poll; 1 da (Joanne b 1953); *Career* vice-consul for the Lebanon for N England, Scotland and NI 1963–; Cheshire CC: cncllr (Cons) 1967–2001, Cons chief whip 1977–83 and 1994–2000, chm 1984–85 and 1986–87, 'father' of Cheshire CC 1997–2001, hon alderman 2001–; cncllr: Macclesfield RDC 1968–74, Nether Alderley PC 1968–2004, Alderley Edge PC 2002–; memb Cheshire Police Authy 1985–97; gen cmmr of taxes Salford and N Manchester 1985–2003; chm: NW Regnl Children's Planning Ctee 1977–81, Bd of Govrs Crewe and Alsager Coll of Higher Educn 1978–92, Tatton Park Mgmnt Ctee 1985–98, Manchester Airport Consultative Ctee 1986–2002, Cheshire Rural Community Cncl 1988–96; vice-chm David Lewis Centre for Epilepsy 1993–98 (dir 1989–98), govr Manchester Met Univ 1993–99; vice-pres: Cheshire Agric Soc 1985– (lady patroness 1996–97), Ploughing and Hedgecutting Soc 1986–2004, Reaseheath Tst 1992–98, Tatton Constituency Cons Assoc 1999–2001 and 2004– (vice-chm 1995–99 and 2001–04); pres Macclesfield Constituency Cons Assoc 1988–95; memb: Runcorn New Town Devpt Corp 1975–81, Miny of Tport Sleep Research Steering Gp 1990–93, 1998–2001 and 2003–, ESU 1995–; N of England Woman of the Year 1985, Cheshire Woman of the Year 1986; *Recreations* sea and snow, horses, bridge, country life; *Style*— Mrs Margaret Melrose, DL; ✉ The Coach House, Stamford Road, Alderley Edge, Cheshire SK9 7NS (tel 01625 585629, fax 01625 590647, e-mail margaret@mmelrose.freeserve.co.uk)

MELUA, Katie; *b* 16 September 1984, Kutaisi, Georgia; *Educ* Brit Sch for Performing Arts; *Career* singer and songwriter 2003–; highest selling female artist in Britain 2004 and 2005; albums: Call off the Search 2003, Piece by Piece 2005; singles: The Closest Thing to Crazy 2003, Call Off the Search 2004, Crawling Up a Hill 2004, Nine Million Bicycles 2005, I Cried for You 2005, Spiders' Web 2006; Best Int Newcomer ECHO Awards (Germany) 2004, Biggest Selling Br Album World Music Awards, Best Female Artist Int Rock/Pop Echo Music Award 2007; *Style*— Ms Katie Melua; ✉ c/o Sue Harris, Republic Media, 202 Westbourne Studios, 242 Acklam Road, London W10 5JJ

MELVILLE, (Richard) David; QC (2002); s of Col Robert Kenneth Melville, of London, and Joan Emerton, *née* Hawkins (d 1996); *b* 22 April 1953; *Educ* Wellington, Pembroke Coll Cambridge (MA); *m* 31 Oct 1981, Catharine Mary, da of late Hon William Granville Wingate, QC, of Heathfield, E Sussex; 1 s (Thomas Wingate b 29 Aug 1985), 1 da (Emma

M

Rose b 21 July 1987); *Career* called to the Bar Inner Temple 1975; recorder; chm London Common Law and Commercial Bar Assoc; *Recreations* sailing; *Clubs* Royal Corinthian Yacht, Bar Yacht; *Style*— David Melville, Esq; ✉ 39 Essex Street, London WC2R 3AT (tel 020 7832 1111, fax 020 7353 3978)

MELVILLE, Prof Sir David; kt (2007), CBE (2001); s of Frederick George Melville (d 1981), and Mary, *née* Smith (d 2005); *b* 4 April 1944; *Educ* Clitheroe Royal GS, Univ of Sheffield (BSc, PhD), Columbia Univ NYC (NASA scholarship, Dip Space Physics); *Children* 2 da (Ruth Helen b 27 July 1971, Jane Cathryn b 17 Nov 1973), 1 s (Richard Sean b 20 Oct 1975); *Career* Univ of Southampton: ICI research fell 1968, lectr in physics 1968–78, sr lectr in physics 1978–84; Lancashire Poly: prof and head Sch of Physics and Astronomy 1985–86, asst dir 1986–89, vice-rector 1989–91, hon prof Univ of Central Lancs 1991–; dir Middlesex Poly 1991–92, vice-chllr Middlesex Univ 1992–96 (hon prof 1996–); chief exec Further Educn Funding Cncl 1996–2001; vice-chllr Univ of Kent 2001–07 (emeritus prof 2007–); visiting researcher: CNR Italy 1974 and 1976, ICI plc 1975; visiting prof: Univ of Parma Italy 1974–79, Oporto Univ Portugal 1984, Univ of Warwick 1997–2002; chm: HE Statistics Agency 2003–07 (memb Bd 2002–), Univ Vocational Awards Cncl 2003–, HE South East 2003–06, Health and Safety Ctee Univs and Colleges Employers Assoc 2003–07, HE Race Consultation Project 2003–04, Lifelong Learning Sector Skills Cncl 2006– (memb Bd 2004–); memb: Cncl for Industry and HE 1993–2007, Cncl Inst of Employment Studies 1998–2001, Educn and Libraries Task Gp DfEE/DCMS 1999–2000, Bd HE Prospects 2002–07, Bd The Place 2002–, Tomlinson Review of 14–19 Curriculum and Qualifications 2003–04, Fndn Degrees Task Force 2003–04, Qualifications and Skills Advsy Ctee QCA 2004–, Foster Review of FE Colls 2005–06, Bd Edexcel 2005–, Bd IFS Sch of Finance (formerly Inst of Financial Servs) 2005–, DfES External Advsy Gp on 14–19 Diplomas 2005–, HE Engagement Project Bd 2006–; bd memb British Non-Ferrous Metals Ltd 1987–92; chm Kent and Medway Learning and Skills Cncl 2006–07; vice-chm: CVCP 1995–96, Kent Public Serv Bd 2004–07, Kent Strategic Partnership 2003–07; memb: Kent Ambassadors 2002–, Kent Partnership Bd 2003–07, Bd Medway Renaissance Partnership 2005–07; vice-chm of tstees Marlowe and Folkestone Acads 2005–, tstee Learning from Experience Tst 1999–, patron 157 Gp of FE Colls 2006–; Hon DSc Univ of Sheffield 1997, Hon DUniv Derby 2000, Hon DSc Univ of Southampton 2001; FInstP 1978; *Recreations* sailing, hill walking, skiing, plumbing; *Clubs* IOD; *Style*— Prof Sir David Melville, CBE; ✉ 55A Chilbolton Avenue, Winchester, Hampshire SO22 5HJ

MELVILLE, Nigel Edward; s of Maj E K L Melville (d 1991), and P D Melville (d 1998); *b* 5 June 1945; *Educ* Sedbergh, Trinity Coll Oxford (MA), London Business Sch (MSc); *m* 15 Aug 1970, Maria Hadewij, *née* Van Oosten; 1 s (Christopher Patrick b 8 Dec 1978), 1 da (Sophie Olivia b 15 Dec 1980); *Career* with Baring Brothers rising to dir responsible for int corp fin 1974–95; currently: ptnr Melville Partners, chm Emtelle Holdings, chm JPMorgan Fleming Chinese Investment Tst; FCA; *Recreations* tennis, golf, skiing, flying, cycling, opera, ballet; *Clubs* Hurlingham, Oriental; *Style*— Nigel Melville, Esq; ✉ Melville Partners, 3rd Floor, Garfield House, 86–88 Edgware Road, London W2 2EA (tel 020 7240 8000)

MELVILLE, 9 Viscount (UK 1802); Robert David Ross Dundas; also Baron Duneira (UK 1802); only s of Hon Robert Maldred St John Melville Dundas (ka 1940, yr s of 7 Viscount); suc uncle 1971; the 2 Viscount was First Lord of the Admty (1812–27 and 1828–30) and an enthusiast for Arctic exploration; Melville Sound is named after him; *b* 28 May 1937; *Educ* Cargilfield Sch, Wellington; *m* 23 July 1982, Fiona Margaret, da of late Roger Kirkpatrick Stilgoe, of Derby House, Stogumber, Taunton; 2 s (Robert Henry Kirkpatrick b 23 April 1984, James David Brouncker b 19 Jan 1986); *Heir* s, Hon Robert Dundas; *Career* served in Scots Gds (Nat Serv), Reserve Capt Scots Gds, Lt Ayrshire Yeo (TA); cncllr and dist cncllr Midlothian; pres Lasswade Civic Soc, tstee Poltonhall Community Assoc; *Recreations* shooting, fishing, golf, chess; *Clubs* Cavalry and Guards'; *Style*— Capt the Rt Hon the Viscount Melville; ✉ Frith Wood, Far Oakridge, Stroud, Gloucestershire; Wey House, Norton Fitzwarren, Taunton, Somerset

MELVILLE, Toby; s of George Melville, and Margaret, *née* Swabey; *b* 2 July 1970, Haslemere, Surrey; *Educ* Midhurst Sch, Wadham Coll Oxford (BA), Stradbroke Coll Sheffield (NCTJ); *Career* staff photographer: Bristol Evening Post and Western Daily Press 1994–98, Press Assoc 1998–2003; sr photographer Reuters 2003–; extensive travel in 5 continents covering news and sport incl Olympic Games 2000 and 2004 and World Cup 2002 and 2006; memb: Sustrans, Cyclists Touring Club, BPPA 2004; various photographic awards incl: UK Press Gazette Sports Regnl Photographer of the Year 1996 and 1998, UK Press Gazette Regnl Photographer of the Year 1997 and 1998, Nikon Sports Photographer of the Year 1998, Picture Ed's Sports Photographer of the Year 1998 and 2004, Nikon Photographer of the Year 1999, UK Sports Photographer of the Year 2000; *Publications* contrib: Reuters: The Art of Seeing II (2004), Assignments (2006), Reuters: State of the World (2006); *Recreations* marathon running, cycling, swimming, surfing, travel, arts; *Clubs* Serpentine Runners; *Style*— Toby Melville, Esq; ✉ c/o Reuters UK Picture Desk, The Reuters Building, 30 South Colonnade, Canary Wharf, London E14 5EP (tel 020 7542 7949, fax 020 7542 6996, e-mail toby.melville@reuters.com)

MELVILLE-ROSS, Timothy David (Tim); CBE (2005); s of Lt Cdr Antony Stuart Melville-Ross, DSC, RN (ret) (d 1993), and Anne Barclay Fane, *née* Gamble; *b* 3 October 1944; *Educ* Uppingham, Portsmouth Coll of Technol (Dip); *m* 19 Aug 1967, Camilla Mary Harlackenden, da of Lt-Col Richard Harlackenden Carwardine Probert, of Bures, Suffolk; 2 s (Rupert b 1971, James b 1972), 1 da (Emma b 1975); *Career* chief exec Nationwide Building Society 1985–94, DG IOD 1994–99; chm: Investors in People UK 1999–2006, DTZ plc 2000–, Bank Insinger de Beaufort NV 2000–05, Manganese Bronze Holdings plc 2003– (dir 2000–03), Bovis Homes plc 2005– (non-exec dir 1997–), Royal London Mutual Insurance Society Ltd 2006– (dir 1999–, dep chm 2002–05); non-exec dir Monument Oil & Gas plc 1993–99 (dep chm 1997–99); memb Cncl Inst of Business Ethics 1994–, memb Greenbury Ctee on executive remuneration 1995; chm Cncl Univ of Essex 2001–07, chair HEFCE 2008–; *Recreations* reading, bridge, walking, the countryside, family; *Style*— Tim Melville-Ross, Esq, CBE; ✉ Little Bevills, Bures, Suffolk CO8 5JN (tel 01787 229188); DTZ Holdings plc, 1 Curzon Street, London W1A 5PZ (tel 020 7643 6039, fax 020 7643 6060, e-mail tim.melville-ross@dtz.com)

MELVIN, Peter Anthony Paul; s of Charles George Thomas Melvin (d 1959), and Elsie, *née* Paul (d 1983); *b* 19 September 1933; *Educ* St Marylebone GS, Poly Sch of Architecture (DipArch); *m* 23 April 1960, Muriel, da of Col James Cornelis Adriaan Faure (d 1984); 1 da (Joanna Claire b 1962), 2 s (Jeremy Paul b 1964, Stephen James b 1967); *Career* architect; fndr ptnr Melvin Lansley & Mark until 1995, ptnr Atelier MLM 1995–; awards: RIBA Bronze medal for offices, vicarage and parish hall Tring 1975, Civic Tst awards for Tankerfield Place and Old Garden Court St Albans and violin workshop for W Hill & Sons; projects incl: Civic Centres Hemel Hempstead and Amersham, Emmanuel Church Guildford, HQ for Sir William Halcrow & Partners Swindon; RIBA: chm Eastern Region 1974–76, memb Cncl 1977–83 and 1985–88, vice-pres 1982–83 and 1985–87; visiting fell Natal Sch of Architecture 1983; visiting tutor Dept of Architecture Univ of Dundee 1991–92; external examiner: Univ of Dundee 1993–96, South Bank Univ 1994–97; memb RIBA visiting bd: to South Africa validating the Schs of Architecture at Univs of Cape Town, Witwatersrand, Natal, the Orange Free State and Port Elizabeth 1995, 1996 and 2000, to Chile validating the Schs of Architecture at Univs of Catholica, Santiago, Concepcion, Talca, La Serena and Valparadiso 1996, 2000, 2002 and 2003; FRIBA 1971, FAE; *Recreations* music, walking, sketching, looking; *Clubs* Ronnie Scott's; *Style*— Peter Melvin, Esq; ✉ Atelier MLM, Woodlands, Beechwood Drive, Aldbury, Tring, Hertfordshire HP23 5SB (tel and fax 01442 851518, e-mail atelier.mlm@virgin.net)

MELZACK, Harold; s of Lewis Melzack (d 1938), and Celia Melzack (d 1987); *b* 6 February 1931; *Educ* Christ's Coll London, Coll of Estate Management; *m* 22 June 1954, June, da of Leonard Lesner, of London; 2 da (Gillian b 1957, Susan b 1960); *Career* chartered surveyor; jt founding sr ptnr Smith Melzack (now Smith Melzack Pepper Angliss (SMPA)) 1961 (currently sr conslt), former chm Br Numismatic Trade Assoc; Freeman City of London; Lamda Alpha: hon sec, int fell 2001; FCIArb; *Recreations* golf, history, historic documents, bridge; *Clubs* Hartsbourne Golf and Country, Bushey; *Style*— Harold Melzack, Esq; ✉ Smith Melzack Pepper Angliss, 7/10 Chandos Street, Cavendish Square, London W1G 9AJ (tel 020 7393 4000, fax 020 7393 4114, e-mail haroldmelzack@sm-pa.co.uk)

MENAUL, Christopher; s of Stewart William Blacker Menaul (d 1987), and Helene Mary, *née* Taylor; *b* 25 July 1944, Cambridge; *Educ* Hurstpierpoint Coll, St Catharine's Coll Cambridge; *m* 4 Feb 1989, Kathleen Elizabeth Mackie, 1 s (Maximillian Bennett, b 1997), 1 da (Lucinda Helene b 1999); *Career* film and television drama director; credits incl: Precious Bane (BBC) 1989 (Public Jury Prize Best Fiction Film Télévision Rencontres Européennes de Reims 1990, nominated Best Single Drama RTS Awards 1989), Nice Work (BBC) 1989 (Best Drama Serial RTS Awards 1989, nominated BFI TV Award 1990), Prime Suspect (Granada) 1991 (Best Drama Serial BAFTA 1991, Best Drama Broadcasting Press Guild Awards 1991, Best Drama Serial RTS Awards 1991, Best Drama and Best Mini Film Awards Banff Festival 1992, Golden Plaque Chicago Int Film Festival), A Dangerous Man - T E Lawrence After Arabia (Enigma Films) 1992 (Int Emmy Best Drama 1992), Homicide (Baltimore Pictures/NBC) 1993, Fatherland (HBO) 1994 (Golden Globe nomination for Best Film), Feast of July (Merchant Ivory prodn) 1995, Bright Hair (Monogram/BBC) 1997, The Passion of Ayn Rand (Showtime) 1998, One Kill (Showtime/CBS) 1999, The Forsyte Saga (Granada) 2001, State of Mind (Monogram/ITV) 2002, Wall of Silence (Granada) 2003 (nominated Prix Italia 2004), Web of Belonging (ITV) 2004 (Prix Special de la Mise en Scene Rheims 2006), Planespotting (ITV) 2005 (nominated Grierson Award 2005), Secret Smile (ITV) 2005, See No Evil (ITV) 2006 (Best Drama Award: RTS NW 2006, Broadcast 2007, South Bank Show 2007, BAFTA 2007); *Style*— Christopher Menaul, Esq; ✉ c/o Tim Corrie, PFD, Drury House, 34–43 Russell Street, London WC2B 5HA (tel 020 7344 1043); c/o Jeff Shumway, William Morris Agency (tel 00 1 310 859 4170)

MENDELOW, Prof (Alexander) David; s of Harry Mendelow, of Johannesburg, South Africa, and Ruby, *née* Palmer; *b* 19 May 1946; *Educ* Univ of the Witwatersrand (MB BCh, PhD); *m*; 1 da (Toni Andrea b 1969), 2 s (Trevor Neil b 1971, Robert Kevin b 1974); *Career* registrar in neurosurgery Univ of the Witwatersrand and Johannesburg Hosp 1970–76, sr registrar Univ of Edinburgh 1977–79, sr lectr Univ of Glasgow 1980–86, prof of neurosurgery Univ of Newcastle upon Tyne 1987–; author of articles in scientific journals and books on head injury and stroke; convenor Br Neurosurgery Res Group, pres Euroacademia Multidisciplinaria Neuotraumatologica (EMN); pres Int Soc for Brain Oedema; memb: RSM, Soc of Br Neurosurgeons, Surgical Res Soc; FRCSEd 1974; *Books* Pyogenic Neurosurgical Infections (1991), Fibre Systems of the Brain and Spinal Cord (1997); *Recreations* sailing, flying; *Style*— Prof A David Mendelow; ✉ Department of Neurosurgery, University of Newcastle upon Tyne, Regional Neurosciences Centre, Newcastle General Hospital, Westgate Road, Newcastle upon Tyne NE4 6BE (tel 0191 233 6161, fax 0191 256 3267)

MENDELSOHN, (Heather) Leigh; da of Maurice Raymond Mendelsohn (d 1989), and Hazel Francis, *née* Keable (d 1997); *b* 20 February 1946; *Educ* Fleetwood GS, Rothwell GS, Pudsey GS; *Career* trainee journalist R Ackrill Ltd Harrogate 1965–69, dep ed Action Desk Western Mail Cardiff 1969–71, dep Women's Page ed Daily Record Glasgow 1971–73, fashion ed Reveille London 1973–74, contract foreign corr The Sun Amsterdam 1975, freelance TV current affairs researcher 1976, fndr dir Phoenix PR 1978–, fndr RivieraPress (press agency) 2006–; Int Mass Media vice-chm of European Union of Women; media trainer for emerging democracies; memb: NUJ, Conservative European Candidates List; *Recreations* social history, swimming, the good life; *Style*— Ms Leigh Mendelsohn; ✉ Phoenix Public Relations, 13 Offas Lane, Winslow, Buckinghamshire MK18 3JS (mobile 07802 409956, e-mail phoenixpr07@gmail.com); RivieraPress, Golden Park, 14–16 rue Beaulieu, 06400, Cannes, France (tel 00 33 493 68 82 05)

MENDELSOHN, Dr Martin; s of Arthur Mendelsohn (d 1961), and Rebecca, *née* Caplin (d 1975); *b* 6 November 1935; *Educ* Hackney Downs Sch; *m* 20 Sept 1959, Phyllis Linda, da of late Abraham Sobell; 2 s (Paul Arthur b 1962, David Edward b 1964); *Career* admitted slr 1959; Adlers Solicitors: ptnr 1961–90, sr ptnr 1984–90, conslt 1990–92; ptnr MPM Consultancy 1990–92, ptnr Jaques & Lewis (now Eversheds) Slrs 1992–2000, conslt Eversheds 2000–; visiting prof of franchise mgmnt Middx Univ Business Sch, hon prof of Int Franchise Acad Beijing Normal Univ at Zuhai; warden Kenton Synagogue 1976–78, hon slr to various charitable instns; Freeman City of London 1964, Liveryman Worshipful Co of Slrs; memb: The Law Soc, Int Bar Assoc (fndr chm Int Franchising Ctee Section on Business Law, chm Membership Ctee 1988–92), American Bar Assoc; FCIArb; *Books* Obtaining A Franchise (for DTI, 1977), Comment Negocier une Franchise (jtly, 2 edn 1983), International Franchising - An Overview (ed, 1984), The Ethics of Franchising (1987, 3 edn 2004), How to Franchise your Business (1989, 6 edn 2005), How to Franchise Internationally (1989, 5 edn 2008), The International Journal of Franchising Law (ed), Franchising and the Block Exemption Regulation (jtly, 1991), Franchising in Europe (ed, 1992), Franchising and Business Development (A Study for the ILO Geneva) (1993), Franchising Law (jtly, 1995, 2 edn 2004), Franchisor's Manual (2 edn 1996), How to Evaluate a Franchise (6 edn 1996, 8 edn 2006), The International Encyclopaedia of Franchising Law (jt gen ed 1998–2003, gen ed 2003–), A Guide to Block Exemption Regulation for Vertical Restraints (jtly, 2001), How to Buy a Franchise (2002), Negotiating an International Master Franchise Agreement (jtly, 2002), The Guide to Franchising (7 edn 2004); contrib and lectr to pubns and audiences worldwide; books have been published in 15 languages (incl Chinese and Russian); *Recreations* cricket; *Clubs* MCC; *Style*— Dr Martin Mendelsohn; ✉ 9 Sandown Court, Marsh Lane, Stanmore, Middlesex HA7 4HZ (tel 020 8954 9384, mobile 077 6860 4367, e-mail romebrand@btclick.com); Eversheds, Senator House, 85 Queen Victoria Street, London EC4V 4JL (tel 0845 4974784, fax 0845 497 4919, e-mail mendelm@eversheds.com)

MENDELSON, Prof Maurice Harvey; QC (1992); s of William Maizel Mendelson (d 1959), of London, and Anne, *née* Aaronson; *b* 27 August 1943; *Educ* St Marylebone GS, New Coll Oxford (MA, DPhil); *m* 26 Dec 1968, Katherine Julia Olga, da of late Bertalan Kertesz, of London; 2 da (Charlotte b 1 Nov 1972, Rachel b 15 Sept 1974); *Career* called to the Bar Lincoln's Inn 1965 (bencher), in practice 1971–; lectr in law KCL 1968–74, fell and tutor in law St John's Coll Oxford 1975–86, prof of int law UCL 1987–2001 (now emeritus); memb: American Law Inst, Exec Cncl Br Branch Int Law Assoc; memb RIIA; FRGS; *Recreations* painting, the arts, riding, swimming, tennis (real and lawn); *Clubs* Athenaeum; *Style*— Prof Maurice Mendelson, QC; ✉ Blackstone Chambers, Blackstone House, Temple, London EC4Y 9BW (tel 020 7583 1770, fax 020 7822 7350, e-mail mauricemendelson@blackstonechambers.com)

MENDELSON, Paul Anthony; s of Monty Mendelson (d 1992), of Pinner, Middx, and Yetta, *née* Dresner; *b* 6 April 1951; *Educ* Royal GS Newcastle upon Tyne, Glasgow HS, Harrow Co GS, Emmanuel Coll Cambridge (MA); *m* 31 March 1974, Michal Zipora, da of Armand Safier; 2 da (Zoë Rachel b 17 April 1976, Tammy Polly b 3 Feb 1978); *Career* scriptwriter;

articled Gasquet Metcalf & Walton slrs 1973, trainee copywriter rising to creative gp head Ogilvy & Mather advtg agency 1973–80, dep creative dir Wasey Campbell Ewald 1980–82, creative gp head Dorland Advertising 1982–88, creative dir Capper Granger 1988–90, full-time freelance TV writer 1990–; creator and writer: May to December (BBC comedy series, nominated Best Comedy Series BAFTA 1990), So Haunt Me (BBC comedy series), Under the Moon (BBC), My Hero (BBC comedy series); writer: Pigsty (BBC Children's TV), Losing It (ITV, nominated Televisual Best Writing Award 2007), Snap (BBC Radio 4), Dover (BBC Radio 4), Bewitched (in devpt), Lost Souls/A Meeting in Seville (film projects in devpt); winner advtg awards incl: Cinema, TV and Best Radio Commercial and Best Radio Campaign (for Don't Drink and Drive), D&AD, Best Media Commercial Clio; judge on various panels incl London Int Advtg Awards, British Comedy Awards; memb Writers' Guild 1991; *Recreations* walking, theatre, collecting obscure Broadway musical recordings, carpentry, family; *Clubs* Groucho; *Style*— Paul A Mendelson, Esq; ✉ ABR, Fairgate House, 78 New Oxford Street, London WC1A 1HB (tel 020 7079 7990, fax 020 7079 7999)

MENDES, Samuel Alexander (Sam); CBE (2000); s of James Peter Mendes, of London, and Valerie Hélène, *née* Barnett; *b* 1 August 1965; *Educ* Magdalen Coll Sch Oxford, Peterhouse Cambridge (scholar, BA); *m* May 2003, Kate Winslet, *qv*; 1 s (Joe b 2003); *Career* artistic director; asst dir Chichester Festival Theatre 1987–88, artistic dir Chichester Festival Theatre Tent 1988, artistic dir Minerva Studio Theatre Chichester 1989 (prodns incl Summerfolk and Love's Labour's Lost), freelance dir, artistic dir Donmar Warehouse until 2002; *Theatre* prodns incl: London Assurance (Chichester and Haymarket) 1989, The Cherry Orchard (Aldwych) 1989, Troilus and Cressida (RSC, Swan) 1990, Kean (Old Vic and Toronto) 1990, Plough and the Stars (Young Vic) 1991, The Alchemist (RSC, Swan) 1991, The Sea (RNT) 1991, The Rise and Fall of Little Voice (RNT and Aldwych, Olivier and Evening Standard Awards) 1992, Richard III (RSC regnl and world tour) 1992, Assassins (Donmar Warehouse, Critics' Circle Award) 1992, Translations (Donmar Warehouse) 1993, The Tempest (RSC, RST) 1993, Cabaret (Donmar Warehouse and Carlton TV, Gold Camera Award US Int Film Festival) 1993, The Birthday Party (RNT) 1994, Glengarry Glen Ross (Donmar Warehouse) 1994, Oliver! (London Palladium) 1994, The Glass Menagerie (Donmar Warehouse and Comedy, Critic's Circle Award) 1995, Company (Donmar and Albery, Critics' Circle Award) 1996, Habeas Corpus (Donmar Warehouse) 1996, Othello (RNT, Salzburg Int tour) 1997, The Fix (Donmar Warehouse) 1997, The Front Page (Donmar Warehouse) 1997, Cabaret (Roundabout Theatre NY, Tony Award for Best Revival of a Musical) 1998, The Blue Room (Donmar Warehouse) 1998, To The Greenfields Beyond (Domar Warehouse) 2000, Uncle Vanya (Donmar Warehouse) 2002, Twelfth Night (Donmar Warehouse) 2002, Gypsy (Broadway NY) 2003; *Films* American Beauty 1999, Road to Perdition 2002; *Awards* Hamburg Shakespeare Scholarship 1989, London Critics' Circle Most Promising Newcomer Award 1989, Olivier Award for Best Director (Company and The Glass Menagerie) 1996, Acad Award for Best Director and Best Film (American Beauty) 1999, numerous other awards for American Beauty, Hamburg Shakespeare Prize 2000, Olivier Awards for Best Revival and for Best Director (Uncle Vanya and Twelfth Night) 2003; *Recreations* watching and playing cricket; *Style*— Sam Mendes, CBE; ✉ c/o Scamp Film and Theatre Ltd, 26–28 Neal Street, London WC2H 9QQ

MENDONÇA, Dennis Raymond; s of Walter Mendonça, and Adelaide, *née* De Souza; *b* 9 October 1939; *Educ* Med Coll Bombay (MB BS, MS), Univ of London, FRCS; *m* 1, 8 Dec 1966 (m dis 1993), Dr Lorna Maria Mendonca, da of late Joaquim Noguer; 2 s (Neil Dennis b 25 July 1967, Nolan Andrew b 2 Sept 1971), 1 da (Nicola Maria b 3 Dec 1969); m 2, 19 March 1994, Judith Mary (barr), da of late Dr Cyril Lynch; *Career* surgn in England 1967–; sr house surgn Farnborough Kent, registrar Ashford Folkstone and Dover, sr registrar for ENT Sheffield and Leicester, sr registrar Univ of Toronto (sabbatical year), conslt ENT surgn Queen Mary's Hosp London 1975–, private practice Queen Mary's Hosp Roehampton until 2004, ret; memb: Med Protection Soc, Br Assoc of Otolaryntology, GMC, BMA; FCPS (India) 1966; *Recreations* playing the piano, accordion, guitar and tennis; *Style*— Dennis R Mendonça, Esq; ✉ 2 Roedean Crescent, Roehampton, London SW15 5JU (tel and fax 020 8878 7271)

MENDOZA, June Yvonne; AO (1989), OBE (2004); da of John Morton, and Dot, *née* Mendoza; *Educ* Lauriston Girls' Sch Melbourne, St Martin's Sch of Art; *m* Keith Mackrell; 1 s (Ashley), 3 da (Elliet, Kim, Lee); *Career* portrait painter; work for governments, regiments, industry, med, academia, theatres, literature and sport; exhibited in public and private int collections; portraits incl: HM The Queen, HRH The Prince of Wales, HRH The Princess of Wales, HM Queen Elizabeth The Queen Mother, The Princess Royal, Margaret Thatcher, John Major, three successive Archbishops of Canterbury (Donald Coggan, Robert Runcie and George Carey), Corazón Aquino (former pres of the Philippines), Vigdis Finnbogadottir (former pres of Iceland), Ratu Sir Kamisese Mara (PM of Fiji), Sir John Gorton (former PM of Australia), Lee Kuan Yew (sr min Singapore); gp portraits incl: House of Commons in Session, Cncl Royal Coll of Surgns, Australian House of Representatives; continuing series of musicians incl: Yehudi Menuhin, Georg Solti, Joan Sutherland, Charles Mackerras, Colin Davis; memb: Royal Soc of Portrait Painters, Royal Inst of Oil Painters; hon memb Soc of Women Artists; Hon DLitt: Univ of Bath 1986, Loughborough Univ 1994; Hon Dr Open Univ 2003; Freeman City of London 1998; *Style*— Miss June Mendoza, AO, OBE; ✉ 34 Inner Park Road, London SW19 6DD (website www.junemendoza.co.uk)

MENEVIA, Bishop of (RC) 2001–; Rt Rev Mark Jabalé; OSB; *b* 16 October 1933, Alexandria, Egypt; *Educ* Belmont Abbey Sch, Fribourg Univ; *Career* ordained priest 1958; headmaster Belmont Abbey Sch 1969–83, supervised building of Tambogrande Monastery Peru 1983–86, abbot of Belmont 1993–2000 (prior 1986–93), coadjutor bishop of Menevia 2000–01; steward Henley Royal Regatta 1985–, former chm Nat Rowing Championships of GB; *Recreations* rowing, computers; *Style*— The Rt Rev the Bishop of Menevia; ✉ 79 Walter Road, Swansea SA1 4PS (tel 01792 650534); Curial Office, 27 Convent Street, Swansea SA1 2BX (tel 01792 644017, fax 01792 458641, e-mail bishopmenevia@aol.com)

MENHENNET, Dr David; CB (1991); s of Thomas William Menhennet (d 1970), of Redruth, Cornwall, and Everill Waters, *née* Nettle (d 1992); old Cornish families, both sides; *b* 4 December 1928; *Educ* Truro Sch, Oriel Coll Oxford (BA), The Queen's Coll Oxford (MA, DPhil); *m* 29 Dec 1954, Audrey, da of William Holmes (d 1958), of Accrington, Lancs; 2 s (Mark b 1956, Andrew b 1958); *Career* House of Commons Library: joined 1954, dep librarian 1967–76, librarian 1976–91; gen ed House of Commons Library Documents Series 1972–90; memb Bd of Mgmnt House of Commons 1979–91; chm Bibliographic Servs Advsy Ctee Br Library 1986–92, memb Exec Ctee Friends of the Nat Libraries 1991–96; visiting fell Goldsmiths Coll London 1990–2002; Freeman City of London 1990, Liveryman Worshipful Co of Stationers and Newspaper Makers 1990; FRSA 1966 (life fell 2001); *Books* Parliament in Perspective (with J Palmer, 1967), The Journal of the House of Commons: A Bibliographical and Historical Guide (1971), The House of Commons in the Twentieth Century (contrib, 1979), The House of Commons Library: A History (1991, 2 edn 2000), Essays and Articles on Bernardin de Saint-Pierre (printed privately, 1998); *Recreations* National Trust activities, family history, visiting Cornwall; *Clubs* Athenaeum; *Style*— Dr David Menhennet, CB; ✉ Meadow Leigh, 3 Westfield Close, Bishop's Stortford, Hertfordshire CM23 2RD (tel 01279 755815)

MENKES-SPANIER, Suzy Peta; OBE (2005); da of Edouard Gerald Lionel Menkes (d 1943), and Betty Curtis, *née* Lightfoot; *b* 24 December 1943; *Educ* Brighton & Hove HS, Newnham Coll Cambridge (MA); *m* 23 June 1969, David Graham Spanier (d 2000), s of Eric John Spanier (d 1973); 3 s (Gideon Eric Lionel b 26 Sept 1971, Joshua Edward Graham b 11 Nov 1973, Samson Curtis b 3 Oct 1978), 1 da (Jessica Leonie Salome b 24 May 1977 d 1977); *Career* jr reporter The Times London 1966–69, fashion ed The Evening Standard 1969–77, women's ed Daily Express 1977–80; fashion ed: The Times 1980–87, The Independent 1987–88, International Herald Tribune 1988–; Freeman of Milan 1987; Hon FRCA 1999; Chevalier de la Legion d'Honneur (France) 2005; *Books* The Knitwear Revolution (1983), The Royal Jewels (1985), The Windsor Style (1987), Queen and Country (1992); *Recreations* family life; *Style*— Mrs Suzy Menkes-Spanier, OBE; ✉ International Herald Tribune, 6 bis des Rue des Graviers, 92521 Neuilly, France (tel 00 33 1 4143 9341, fax 00 33 1 4143 9338, e-mail smenkes@iht.com)

MENON, Prof David Krishna; s of Parakat Govindan Kutti Menon (d 1982), of India, and Violet Rebecca Menon (d 1999); *b* 21 August 1956; *Educ* Univ of Madras India (MB BS, MD), Univ of London (PhD); *m* 23 July 1988, Wendy, *née* Rutter; 1 s (Stephen Gareth b 11 April 1994); *Career* residency (internal med) Jawaharlal Inst Pondicherry India 1978–83, registrar (med) Professorial Med Unit Leeds Gen Infirmary 1984–86, SHO (anaesthetics) Leeds Gen Infirmary 1986–87, registrar (anaesthetics) Royal Free Hosp London 1987–88, MRC research fell Robert Steiner MR Unit Hammersmith Hosp London 1989–91; Univ of Cambridge: clinical lectr 1992–93, lectr in anaesthesia 1993–2000, princ investigator Cambridge Brain Repair Centre 1995–, princ investigator and co-chair Acute Brain Injury Prog Wolfson Brain Imaging Centre 1997–, Clinical Sch Faculty Bd 2000–, prof of anaesthesia 2001–, professorial fell in med scis Queens' Coll 2001–; Addenbrooke's Hosp Cambridge: lead conslt and dir of neurocritical care 1993–2001, first dir of neurointensive care 1997–2001, hon conslt Neurosciences Critical Care Unit and hon conslt anaesthetist 1993–; Br Oxygen prof Royal Coll of Anaesthetists 2006–; visiting prof: Univ of Washington St Louis 1998, Stroke Prog Univ of Alberta 2000, Dept of Neurosurgery Univ of Southampton 2002, Critical Care Unit Univ of Alberta at Calgary 2003; Charles Sherrington prof Royal Coll of Anaesthetists 1999–2000; memb: Bd of Referees Health Technol Assessment Cmmn 1997–, Regnl Intensive Care Med Training Ctee 1998–, Strategic Regnl Intensive Care Review Gp 1999–, Regnl Anaesthetic Training Ctee, Bd of Referees Canada Fndn for Innovation 2000–, MRC Medical Advsy Bd 2000–, Nat Cncl Intensive Care Soc UK 2003– (memb Research Ctee 2002–); numerous invited lectrs, media appearances and public speeches; Royal Coll of Anaesthetists: Sir Robert Macintosh Medal 1988, Jubilee Fellowship Award 1998; Lewin lectr Univ of Cambridge 2000, Datex-Ohmeda lectr Assoc of Anaesthetists 2003; FRCA 1988, FMedSci 1998, FRCP 1999 (MRCP 1984); *Publications* author of textbooks, chapters and monographs, and numerous articles in jls; *Recreations* reading, basketball, cooking, lego; *Clubs* RSM; *Style*— Prof David Menon; ✉ Division of Anaesthesia, University of Cambridge, Box 93, Addenbrooke's Hospital, Cambridge CB2 2QQ (tel 01223 217889, fax 01223 217887)

MENTETH, *see:* Stuart-Menteth

MENZIES, Hon Lord Duncan Adam Young; s of Douglas William Livingstone Menzies (d 1977), of Edinburgh, and Margaret Adam, *née* Young (d 2000); *b* 28 August 1953; *Educ* The Edinburgh Acad, Cargilfield Sch, Glenalmond Coll (scholar), Wadham Coll Oxford (scholar, MA), Univ of Edinburgh (LLB); *m* 31 March 1979, Hilary Elizabeth McLauchlan, da of Col T R R Weston, OBE, TD; 2 s (Jamie Douglas Adam b 1985, Ruaraidh Duncan McLauchlan b 1988); *Career* admitted Faculty of Advocates 1978, standing jr counsel to Admiralty Bd 1984–91, QC (Scot) 1991, memb Faculty ADR Panel 1991–2000, temp sheriff 1996–97, advocate depute 1998–2000, home advocate depute 1998–2000, senator Coll of Justice (Lord of Session) 2001–; memb Faculty Cncl 1998–2000; chm Scottish Planning Local Govt and Environmental Bar Gp 1997–2001; Parly candidate (Cons): Midlothian 1983, Edinburgh Leith 1987; chm Ptarmigan Wines 1979–89; *Recreations* shooting, golf, wine, gardening; *Clubs* New (Edinburgh), Hon Co of Edinburgh Golfers; *Style*— The Hon Lord Menzies; ✉ Supreme Courts, Edinburgh EH1 1RQ

M

MENZIES, Dr John Barrie; s of late Henry John Menzies, of Sibsey, Lincs, and late Eva Ellen Menzies; *b* 7 November 1937; *Educ* Univ of Birmingham (BSc, PhD), City Univ (Dip CU); *m* 2 Sept 1961, Ann, da of late Frank Naylor; 1 da (Theresa Margaret b 4 Oct 1962), 2 s (Ian Anthony b 17 Nov 1963, Robert John b 4 Aug 1965); *Career* dir Geotechnics and Structures Gp Building Res Estab DOE 1982–1990 (joined 1962), ptnr Andrews Kent & Stone Consltg Engrs 1990–92; hon prof of engrg Univ of Warwick 1988–98, visiting prof in principles of engrg design Univ of Plymouth 1998–2004; vice-chm Construction and Building Standards Ctee BSI 1990–91; chm: EC Task Gp on Actions 1985–90, Eurocode for Actions Sub Ctee Euro Ctee for Standardisation 1990–2000; memb Standing Ctee on Structural Safety 1988–91 (sec 1991–2002); pres Br Masonry Soc 1989, vice-chm Br Gp Int Assoc for Bridge and Structural Engrg 1989–2004; IStructE: hon treas 1988–89, hon sec 1989–90; FIStructE 1977, FREng 1989; *Recreations* travel, good food and wine, swimming, walking; *Style*— Dr John Menzies, FREng; ✉ 20 Acresview Close, Allestree, Derby DE22 2AY (tel 01332 551749)

MENZIES, (Rowan) Robin; s of Capt George Cunningham Paton Menzies, DSO (d 1968), and Constance Rosabel, *née* Grice Hutchinson; *b* 30 October 1952; *Educ* Stowe, Trinity Coll Cambridge (BA); *Career* ptnr Baillie Gifford and Co (investment mangrs); *Style*— Robin Menzies, Esq; ✉ Baillie Gifford and Co, 1 Greenside Row, Edinburgh EH1 3AN (tel 0131 275 2000, fax 0131 275 3999, e-mail robin.menzies@bailliegifford.com)

MEON, Archdeacon of; *see:* Hancock, Ven Peter

MERCER, Dr (Robert) Giles Graham; s of Leonard Mercer (d 1961), of Langholm, Dumfriesshire, and Florence Elizabeth, *née* Graham (d 2002); *b* 30 May 1949; *Educ* Austin Friars Sch Carlisle, Churchill Coll Cambridge (MA), St John's Coll Oxford (DPhil); *m* 2 March 1974, Caroline Mary, da of Alfred Harold Brougham (d 1983), of Tackley, Oxon; 1 s (Edward b 1977); *Career* head of history Charterhouse Sch 1974–76, asst princ MOD 1976–78, dir of studies and head of history Sherborne Sch 1979–85; headmaster: Stonyhurst Coll 1985–96, Prior Park Coll Bath 1996–; vice-pres Catholic Ind Schools Conf 2005– (memb Ctee 1993–, chm 2000–04); govr: All Hallows Prep Sch 1998–, St Mary's Sch Shaftesbury 2005–; life memb Catholic Union of GB; FRSA 2005; Papal Knighthood Order of St Gregory 2004; *Books* The Teaching of Gasparino Barzizza (1979); *Recreations* swimming, art, music, reading; *Clubs* East India, Public Schools; *Style*— Dr Giles Mercer; ✉ Kent House, Prior Park College, Bath BA2 5AH (tel 01225 835353, fax 01225 835753, e-mail headmaster@priorpark.co.uk)

MERCER, Prof Ian Dews; CBE (1996); s of Eric Baden Royds Mercer (d 1955), of Herongate, Wombourn, Staffs, and Nellie Irene, *née* Dews (d 1999); *b* 25 January 1933; *Educ* King Edward's Sch Stourbridge, Univ of Birmingham (BA); *m* 1, 7 July 1957 (m dis 1976), Valerie Jean, da of late Eric Hodgson; 4 s (Jonathan b 1958, Benjamin b 1961 d 1997, Thomas b 1963, Daniel b 1966); m 2, 10 Dec 1976, Pamela Margaret Gillies, da of late Maj Thomas Waldy Clarkson; *Career* Nat Serv Sub-Lt RNR 1954–56; warden Slapton Ley Field Centre Kingsbridge 1959–68, lectr St Luke's Coll Exeter 1968–70, co conservation offr Devon CC 1970–73, chief offr Dartmoor Nat Park Authy 1973–90, chief exec Countryside Cncl for Wales 1990–96; sec gen Assoc of Nat Park Authorities 1996–2001; prof of rural conservation practice Univ of Wales 1991–; pres: Devonshire Assoc 1983, Assoc of Countryside Rangers 1986–93, Field Studies Cncl 1986–, Devon Wildlife Tst 1986–; vice-pres Cncl for Nat Parks 2001–; chm: Regnl Advsy Ctee W England Forestry Cmmn 1987–90, Devon FMD Inquiry 2001, Dartmoor Commoners Cncl 2004–, SW Forest Partnership 2002–, chm Devon Rural Network 2005–; memb: England Ctee Nature Conservancy Cncl 1977–87, Gen Advsy Ctee BBC 1981–86, Inland Waterways Amenity Advsy Cncl 1995–2001, Devon and Cornwall Ctee Nat Tst

1996–2005, Rural Affrs Advsy Ctee BBC 1998–2002, Br Ecological Soc; govr: Univ of Plymouth 1996–2005, Stover Sch 1996–2005 (chm of govrs 2003–04); Hon LLD Univ of Exeter 1994, Hon DSc Univ of Plymouth 1995; FRAgS 1996, fell Landscape Inst 1997; *Books* Nature Guide to South West England, Conservation in Practice (contrib, 1973), Environmental Education (contrib, 1974), National Parks in Britain (contrib, 1987); *Recreations* golf, painting, birdwatching, watching sons play cricket; *Clubs* Farmers', Symonds; *Style—* Prof Ian Mercer, CBE; ✉ Ponsford House, Moretonhampstead, Newton Abbot, Devon TQ13 8NL (tel 01647 440612, e-mail ian.mercer@freeuk.com)

MERCER, Patrick; OBE (1997, MBE 1992), MP; s of Rt Rev Eric Arthur John Mercer, Bishop of Exeter, and Rosemary, *née* Denby; *b* 26 June 1956; *Educ* King's Sch Chester, Exeter Coll Oxford (MA, Boxing blue), RMA Sandhurst; *m* 1990, Catriona Jane, *née* Beaton; 1 s; *Career* Army Serv: trg team in Uganda post civil war 1986, fndr memb Province Exec Ctee NI 1992, instr Army Staff Coll Camberley 1994–95, CO 1 Bn Worcs and Sherwood Foresters Bosnia and Canada 1995–97, head of strategy Army Trg and Recruiting Agency 1997–98, nine tours NI (mentioned despatches 1983, gallantry commendation 1990); journalist Today (BBC Radio 4) 1999, freelance journalist 2000–01; memb KCL Mission to East Timor 2000; MP (Cons) Newark 2001–, PPS to Hon Bernard Jenkin, MP, *qv*, as shadow sec of state for Defence 2003, shadow min for Homeland Security 2003–07; memb Defence Select Ctee 2001–03; *Recreations* history, watercolour painting, country sports, writing; *Style—* Patrick Mercer, Esq, OBE, MP; ✉ House of Commons, London SW1A 0AA (tel 020 7219 8225)

MERCER, (Andrew) Philip; s of Maj Laurence Walter Mercer (d 1951), of Huntingtower, Perthshire, and Josephine Madeline, *née* Moran (d 2001); *b* 24 August 1937; *Educ* Stonyhurst, Univ of Edinburgh (BArch); *m* 2 Oct 1965, Alexandra Margaret, da of Capt John Cyril Dawson, of Sussex (d 2001); 2 da (Claudia Alexandra, Portia Andrea (twins) b 1977); *Career* chartered architect; princ of architectural practice 1969– (specialising in planning and restoration in Central London and historic bldgs in Scotland); ARIBA; *Recreations* yachting, travelling, gardening; *Clubs* New (Edinburgh); *Style—* Philip Mercer, Esq, ARIBA; ✉ Hillslap Tower, Galashiels TD1 2PA; 25E Frognal, London NW3 6AR (e-mail philip@mercer.uk.com)

MERCER, Roger James; OBE (2005); s of Alan James Mercer, and Patricia, *née* Hicks; *b* 12 September 1944; *Educ* Harrow Co GS, Univ of Edinburgh (MA); *m* 28 March 1970, Susan Jane, da of (William) Stephen Fowlie; 1 da (Katherine Jane b 26 Aug 1975), 1 s (Andrew James b 3 Dec 1981); *Career* inspr of ancient monuments Dept of the Environment 1969–74; Dept of Prehistoric Archaeology Univ of Edinburgh: lectr in archaeology 1974–82, reader in archaeology 1982–90, actg head of dept 1983–87; sec Royal Cmmn on the Ancient and Historical Monuments of Scotland 1990–2004; Br Acad/Br Gas reader 1990; external examiner Univs of Durham, Birmingham, Cambridge, Newcastle, Bradford and York; visiting prof Univ of Durham 1995–, hon prof Univ of Edinburgh 1998–; vice-pres: Prehistoric Soc 1987–91 (treas 1972–76), Cncl for Br Archaeology 1991–94; FSA Scot 1969 (treas 1977–87, vice-pres 1988–92, pres 2005–08), FSA 1976, FRSE 1993, Hon MIFA 2004 (fndr memb 1982); *Books* Hambledon Hill - A Neolithic Landscape (1981), Grimes Graves Excavations 2 vols (1981), The Excavation of a Neolithic Enclosure Complex at Carn Brea, Illogan, Cornwall (1981), Causewayed Enclosures (1990); *Recreations* music, reading; *Style—* Roger Mercer, Esq, OBE, FSA, FSA Scot, FRSE, Hon MIFA; ✉ 4 Old Church Lane, Duddingston, Edinburgh EH15 3PX (e-mail rogerjmercer@aol.com)

MERCER, (Christine) Ruth; da of George Mercer, and Joan, *née* Stopforth; *Educ* Penwortham Girls' GS, Bedford Coll London (BA), Univ of Oxford (PGCE); *m* 1988, Colin Horsley; 2 c; *Career* teacher; successively head of years 8 and 9, head of years 10 and 11 and head of history and politics Notting Hill and Ealing HS 1986–98, dep headmistress Godolphin & Latymer Sch 1998–2002, headmistress Northwood Coll 2002–; *Recreations* fell walking, reading, genealogy; *Style—* Mrs Ruth Mercer; ✉ Northwood College, Maxwell Road, Northwood, Middlesex HA6 2YE (tel 01923 825446, fax 01923 836526)

MERCER, Dr Wendy Sara; da of Charles William Mercer (d 1976), of Castletown, Isle of Man, and Thelma Margaret Hawkins (formerly Mercer), *née* Higgins; *b* 23 December 1956; *Educ* Bedford Coll London (BA, MA), Univ of London (PhD), Sch of Educn Univ of Durham (PGCE), Heidelberg Univ; *Career* French teacher Greycoat Sch Westminster 1979–80, lectr Université de Paris X (Nanterre) 1981–83, visiting lectr in French Bedford Coll London 1983–84, visiting lectr Royal Holloway and Bedford New Coll London 1984–85 and 1988–91, pt/t visiting lectr in French Buckingham Univ 1984–85, lectr École Normale Supérieure Fontenay-aux-Roses 1985–87, pt/t chargée de cours Ecole Nationale de Statistique et d'Administration Economique 1985–87, pt/t res asst UCL 1987–88, British Acad Postdoctoral Res Fellowship RHBNC and UCL 1988–91, lectr Dept of French UCL 1991–; Medaille d'honneur Ville de Pontarlier 1992; *Books* Xavier Marmier (1808–1892) - Un Fils de Pontarlier Célèbre dans le Monde, Jane Osborn - Drama by Léonie d'Aunet (ed), Voyage d'une Femme au Spitzberg (ed, by Léonie D'Aunet); *Style—* Dr Wendy Mercer; ✉ Department of French, University College London, Gower Street, London WC1E 6BT

MERCER-NAIRNE, Lord Robert Harold; s of George John Charles Mercer-Nairne, 8 Marquess of Lansdowne, PC, JP (d 1999) and Barbara Dempsey Chase (d 1965) of Santa Barbara, CA; *b* 1947; *Educ* Gordonstoun, Univ of Kent at Canterbury (BA), Univ of Washington Grad Sch of Business Admin (MBA), PhD; *m* 1972, Jane Elizabeth, da of Lt-Col Lord Douglas Gordon; 2 s, 1 da; *Career* writer; md Blackman Martin Gp 1972–82, self-employed 1982–83, Univ of Washington 1983–89, managing tstee Meikleour Tst 1989–99; memb River Tay Flood Steering Gp 1990–94; elder Church of Scotland 1990–98; hon lectr Univ of Dundee 1992–97; Liveryman Worshipful Co of Fishmongers; FCMI; *Publications* In Malta (poetry, 2002), On Fire (poetry, 2004), The Letter Writer (fiction, 2004), Like No Other (fiction, 2005), Warlord (fiction, 2007); *Style—* Lord Robert Mercer-Nairne; ✉ Meikleour House, Meikleour, Perth PH2 6EA

MERCHANT, Piers Rolf Garfield; s of Garfield Frederick Merchant, of Nottingham, by his w Audrey Mary Rolfe-Martin; *b* 2 January 1951; *Educ* Nottingham HS, Univ of Durham (MA); *m* 1977, Helen Joan, da of James Frederick Albert Burrluck, of Colchester; 1 da (Alethea b 20 March 1984), 1 s (Rolf b 9 Oct 1991); *Career* news ed The Journal 1980–82 (joined as reporter 1973), ed Conservative Newsline 1982–84; Parly candidate Newcastle Central 1979; MP: Newcastle Central (after boundary change) 1983–87, Beckenham 1992–97 (resigned seat); PPS to Rt Hon Peter Lilley as sec of state for Social Security 1992–97; co-chm Freeflow of Info Ctee Int Parly Gp 1986–89, vice-chm All-Pty Parly Ctee on AIDS 1987; dir of corp publicity Northern Engineering Industries plc 1987–90, dir of public affrs The Advertising Association 1990–92, md The Cavendish Gp plc 1999–2000, exec dir Made in London 2000–04, non-exec dir London Asset Management Ltd 2000–04; dir of campaigns London C of C 2001–04; dir European Public Health Fndn 1995–2004; memb: London Business Bd 2001–02, London Sports Bd 2001–03, London Fund Mangrs Advsy Ctee 2002–04, Team London 2002–04, Economic Resarch Advsy Bd GLA 2003–04; UKIP: lead candidate NE region European Parl election 2004, temp chief exec 2004, political advsr to Roger Knapman (as Pty Ldr) 2005–; freelance political conslt 2005–; *Recreations* DIY, electronics, genealogy; *Clubs* SCR of UC Durham; *Style—* Piers Merchant, Esq

MEREDITH, Christopher; s of Roger Meredith, of Northwich, Cheshire, and Gill, *née* Riley; *b* 29 June 1974, Warrington; *m* 24 June 2000, Linsey, *née* Stockdale; *Career* chef; commis chef The Grosvenor Chester 1993–94, first commis chef Paul Heathcotes 1994–95 (2 Michelin Stars, 4 AA Rosettes), chef de partie Arkle Restaurant The Grosvenor Chester 1995–96 (1 Michelin Star, 3 AA Rosettes); sr chef de partie: The Dorchester 1996–98, Hostellerie de Levernois Beaune France 1998, Michael's Nook Grasmere 1998 (1 Michelin Star, 4 AA Rosettes); sous chef: Pool Court and Brasserie 44 Leeds 1998–99 (1 Michelin Star), The Great Eastern Hotel 1999–2000, The Aubergine 2000–02 (1 Michelin Star, 4 AA Rosettes); head chef The Samling 2003–04 (1 Michelin Star, 3 AA Rosettes), exec chef Gilpin Lodge 2004– (1 Michelin Star, 3 AA Rosettes); memb Acad of Culinary Arts, memb Lancs Educn Tst; *Publications* Flavours of the North East (2004), Chefs of Distinction (2004); *Recreations* motorbike racing, fishing; *Style—* Christopher Meredith, Esq; ✉ Gilpin Lodge Country House Hotel, Crook Road, Windermere, Cumbria LA23 3NE (tel 01539 488818)

MEREDITH, David Wynn; s of Rev John Ellis Meredith (d 1981), of Aberystwyth, Dyfed, and Elizabeth, *née* Jones; *b* 24 May 1941; *Educ* Ardwyn GS Aberystwyth, Normal Coll Bangor Gwynedd (Univ of Wales Teaching Dip); *m* 23 March 1968, Luned, da of Prof Emeritus Alun Llywelyn Williams, and Alis Llywelyn Williams; 3 c (Owain Llywelyn b 11 Feb 1969, Elin Wynn b 6 Jan 1971, Gruffydd Seimon Morgan b 7 Feb 1974); *Career* specialist teacher Welsh Cardiff Educn Authy 1961–65, mid-Wales mangr then advtg and sales exec Wales Tourist Bd 1965–68, head of press and PR HTV Cymru/Wales 1968–89, co-fndr dir STRATA (PR co) 1989–90, estab David Meredith PR 1990–95, head of press and PR S4C Television 1995–2001; reg contrib to radio and TV in Wales; presenter in Eng and Welsh HTV: Pwy Fase'n Meddwl (quiz series), Gair o Wlad y Sais (lit prog), Arlunwyr (art series); memb: Royal Welsh Show Publicity Ctee 1969–, Mktg Bd Nat Eisteddfod of Wales 1990–2001, Cncl Nat Library of Wales 2002–, Presbyterian Church of Wales Publicity Ctee, Welsh Academi; centenary offr Royal Welsh Agric Soc 2002–04; RTS Award for Best Contrib to Television 1997–98; fell PR Soc of Wales 1984 (former chm), first BAFTA Cymru/Wales fell 2001; *Books* Michelangelo (Life and Work), Rembrandt (Life and Work), Congrinero (for children), Anturiaethau Fôn Fawr a Bili Bach (with Owain Meredith, with design and visuals by SEI), Pwy Fase'n Meddwl (autobiography, 2002), Kyffin in Venice: An Illustrated Conversation (with artist Sir Kyffin Williams RA, 2006); *Recreations* pottering on the farm, visiting art galleries and growing trees; *Style—* David Meredith, Esq; ✉ Ty'n Fedw, Cynllwyd, Llanuwchllyn, Bala, Gwynedd LL23 7DF (tel 01678 540255, fax 01678 540530)

MEREDITH, George Hubbard; s of George Thomas Meredith (d 1959), of Birmingham, and Ivy Lilian, *née* Hubbard (d 1972); *b* 16 January 1943; *Educ* Marlborough; *m* 9 April 1983, Wendy, da of Frank David Gardiner (d 1999); 2 da (Claire b 1984, Jane b 1986), 1 s (John b 1991); *Career* called to the Bar Gray's Inn 1969; in practice: London 1970–72, Exeter 1972–2001 (head of chambers 1975–90), Plymouth 2001–; dep district judge 1991–95; former chm tstees Belmont Chapel; *Recreations* family life, reading, computers, hill walking; *Style—* George Meredith, Esq; ✉ Kings Bench Chambers, 115 North Hill, Plymouth PL4 8JY (tel 01752 221551)

MEREDITH-HARDY, Penelope Jane; OBE (1995); da of late Hon Bartholomew Pleydell-Bouverie, s of 6 Earl of Radnor and late Doreen Pleydell-Bouverie, da of 6 Earl of Donoughmore; *b* 4 November 1932; *m* 1955, Michael Francis Meredith-Hardy, s of late Howard Meredith-Hardy; 4 s; *Career* memb: Supplementary Benefits Tbnl 1972–89, Stevenage Drugsline 1975–82, Herts Link Scheme 1983–99, Herts Care Tst 1986–, Herts Probation Ctee 1978–2001 (chm 1987–93), Central Probation Cncl 1989–95 (chm Ct and Community Ctee 1990–95); chm: Herts branch Magistrates Assoc 1996–2002, Herts Alcohol Problems and Advice Serv 2002– (tstee 1996–); tstee Nat Forum of Care Tst 1993– (chm 1994–99); JP Herts 1973–2002 (memb Advsy Ctee 1998–2001); interviewer for Independent Tribunal Service 1999–2000; *Style—* Mrs Penelope Meredith-Hardy, OBE; ✉ Radwell Mill, Baldock, Hertfordshire SG7 5ET (tel 01462 730242, e-mail mmh@flymicro.com)

MEREDITH HARDY, Simon Patrick; s of Patrick Talbot Meredith Hardy (d 1986), of Bembridge, IOW, and Anne, *née* Johnson (d 1994); *b* 31 October 1943; *Educ* Eton; *m* 26 July 1969, Hon Joanna Mary, da of Baron Porritt, GCMG, GCVO, CBE (Life Peer); 2 s (Henry Patrick b 1975, George Peter b 1978); *Career* cmmnd LG 1964, ADC to HE The Govr-Gen of NZ 1967–68, left army 1969; stockbroker; formerly ptnr Wood Mackenzie & Co, dir NatWest Securities Ltd, dir Henderson Far East Income Tst plc, chm Framlington Income and Capital Trust plc; *Recreations* skiing, sailing; *Clubs* Household Division Yacht; *Style—* Simon P Meredith Hardy, Esq; ✉ 23 Baronsmead Road, London SW13 9RR (tel 020 8748 1476)

MEREDITH-WINDLE, Glynis Margaret; da of Donald Charles Frank Windle (d 1978), of London, and Gwynneth Maud, *née* Meredith (d 1988); *b* 14 August 1951; *Educ* Parliament Hill Sch for Girls (Hockey blue, hockey capt), Hendon Gp of Hosps Sch of Nursing (SRN), Central Sch of Counselling and Therapy (Cert Counselling); *Career* qualified SRN 1973, med ward sister (then yst in UK) 1974, sister various med and coronary care units NHS hosps 1974–80; Llewelyn-Davies Weeks: joined as nurse planning conslt 1980, pioneer of patient-focused healthcare in UK (in association with Booz Allen and Hamilton) 1989, assoc LDW 1992–95; independent conslt to Dept of Health and others as Meredith-Windle Associates Health Planning Consultancy 1996–; corp dir of healthcare planning HLM Architects 1998–2000; involved in devpt of evaluation tool for PFI hospital scheme for Dept of Health in assoc with DEGW 2001–02, launch of Archealth (consultancy for comprehension planning of health facilities) 2006; fundraiser Sir Robert Mond Meml Tst for research into mental illness; memb Ed Advsy Bd Dept of Health NHS Estates 1999–; memb E & N Herts Acute Tst Cmmn for Patient and Public Involvement in Health (CPPIH); ARCN 1970, MIHSM 1989, MInstD 1996; *Recreations* golf, cycling, badminton, theatre, opera, Cajun dancing; *Clubs* Champneys, Aldwickbury Golf; *Style—* Ms Glynis M Meredith-Windle; ✉ Meredith-Windle Associates, 8 Dell Close, Harpenden, Hertfordshire AL5 4HP (tel 01582 621539, e-mail glynis@archealth.com, website www.archealth.com)

MEREWORTH, 3 Baron (UK 1926) Dominick Geoffrey Thomas Browne; also 5 Baron Oranmore and Browne (I 1836); s of 4 Baron Oranmore and Browne (d 2002), and his 1 w Mildred Helen (d 1980), da of Hon Thomas Egerton, and gda of 3 Earl of Ellesmere; *b* 1 July 1929; *m* 25 Oct 1957 (m dis 1974), Sara Margaret, da of late Dr Herbert Wright; *Career* poet, playwright and author; *Style—* The Rt Hon The Lord Mereworth; ✉ e-mail brownedominick@hotmail.com

MERRICK, District Judge John Sebastian; *b* 13 June 1942; *Educ* St Albans Cathedral Sch, Law Soc Coll of Law; *Career* articled slr London 1959, admitted 1964; ptnr Berry and Berry Slrs 1970–92 (asst slr 1965–70), district judge (SE Circuit) 1992– (dep district judge 1981–92); trg co-ordinator SE Circuit; memb: Law Soc, Int Bar Assoc, Assoc of Hungarian Lawyers, Chartered Inst of Arbitrators; scout ldr 1965–85 (Wood badge, Long Serv Award, Chief Scouts Commendation); *Recreations* hill walking (Mountain Leadership Cert, instructor ten yrs), travel, theatre, art, cooking, literature, fitness training, music, mediation, after dinner speaking, Nat Tst, William Morris Soc; *Clubs* Rotary; *Style—* District Judge J S Merrick; ✉ The Law Courts, William Street, Brighton, East Sussex BN2 2LG (tel 01273 674421)

MERRICKS, Walter Hugh; CBE (2007); s of Dick Merricks (d 1999), of Icklesham, E Sussex, and Phoebe, *née* Woffenden (d 1985); *b* 4 June 1945; *Educ* Bradfield Coll, Trinity Coll Oxford (MA); *m* 27 Nov 1982, Olivia, da of late Dr Elio Montuschi; 1 s (William b 1983), 1 da (Susannah b 1986), 1 step s (Daniel b 1971); *Career* admitted slr 1970, Hubbard travelling scholar 1971, dir Camden Community Law Centre 1972–76, lectr in law Brunel Univ 1976–81, legal affrs writer New Law Jl 1982–85, dir of professional and legal policy Law Soc 1995–96 (head of communications 1985–95), Insurance Ombudsman 1996–99, chief ombudsmen Financial Ombudsmen Service 1999–; memb: Royal Cmmn on Criminal Procedure 1978–81, Ctee on Fraud Trials 1984–86, Human Fertilisation and Embryology Authy 2002–; chm British and Irish Ombudsman Assoc 2001–02 (memb Exec Ctee 1997–99); vice-pres British Insurance Law Assoc 2004–, memb Law Soc 1970; The Achievement Award British Insurance Awards 2004; memb Worshipful Co of Insurers 1999; Hon Dr of Laws London Guildhall Univ 2001; Hon FCII 2005; *Style—* Walter Merricks, Esq, CBE; ✉ Financial Ombudsman Service, South Quay Plaza, 183 Marsh Wall, London E14 9SR (tel 020 7964 1000, fax 020 7964 1001, e-mail enquiries@financial-ombudsman.org.uk)

MERRILL, Paul; s of Rupert Merrill, of Seale, Surrey, and Pauline Merrill; *b* 6 February 1968, Farnham, Surrey; *Educ* Woolmer Hill Secdy Sch, Godalming Coll, Loughborough Univ (BSc), Highbury Coll Cosham (NCTJ); *m* 4 July 2000, Ruth; 2 da (Eliza, Lois (twins) b and d 7 Dec 1997), 2 s (Joss b 12 May 1999, Louis b 25 Sept 2001); *Career* with Farnham Herald 1990–93; freelance journalist: The Sun, The Guardian, The Times; ed Chat 2001–03 (features ed 1997–98, asst ed 1998–2001), ed Zoo 2003–05, ed Zoo Aust 2005–; memb: BSME, PPA; *Style—* Paul Merrill, Esq; ✉ Emap, Level 6 187 Thomas Street, Haymarket, NSW 2000, Australia (tel 0061 2 8916 6632, e-mail paul.merrill@emap.com.au)

MERRIMAN, Dr Nicholas (Nick); s of Michael Merriman, of Sutton Coldfield, and Pamela, *née* Ford; *b* 6 June 1960, Sutton Coldfield; *Educ* King Edward's Sch Birmingham, St John's Coll Cambridge (Anglia Prize, BA), Univ of Leicester (Cert), Univ of Cambridge (PhD); *m* 22 Oct 1993 (sep), Caroline Beattie; 2 s (Robert b 22 Feb 1997, Lucas b 23 Oct 2000); *Career* hon curator Ely Museum 1984–86; Museum of London: curator of prehistory 1986–90, head Dept of Early London History and Collections 1990–97; Inst of Archaeology UCL: sr lectr in museum studies 1997–98, reader 1998–2005; UCL Museums and Collections: curator 1998–2004, dir 2004–05; dir Manchester Museum Univ of Manchester 2006–; chm Soc of Museum Archaeologists 1994–97, chm Int Cncl of Museums UK 2001–04, pres Cncl of Br Archaeology 2005–; fell Clore Leadership Prog 2004–06; AMA 1990, FSA 1994; *Publications* Beyond the Glass Case: The Past, the Heritage and the Public in Britain (1991), The Peopling of London: Overseas Settlement from Prehistoric Times to Present (1993), Making Early Histories in Museums (1996), Public Archaeology (2004); *Recreations* playing football with my children, running; *Clubs* West Bromwich Albion FC; *Style—* Dr Nick Merriman; ✉ Manchester Museum, Oxford Road, Manchester M13 9PL (tel 0161 275 2634, e-mail nicholas.merriman@manchester.ac.uk)

MERRIMAN, District Judge Richard John; *b* 30 April 1947; *Educ* Oakham Sch, Univ of Liverpool (LLB); 1 da (Alexandra Jane b 17 June 1975), 1 s (Daniel George b 30 Nov 1977); *Career* admitted slr 1971, dep registrar Midland & Oxford Circuit 1986–92, district judge Leicester 1992–; *Recreations* squash, swimming, walking; *Style—* District Judge Merriman; ✉ Leicester County Court, 90 Wellington Street, Leicester LE1 6ZZ

MERRISON, Lady; Maureen Michèle; da of John Michael Barry (d 1944), and Winifred Alice, *née* Raymond; *b* 29 October 1938; *Educ* Bedford Coll London (BA); *m* 23 May 1970, as his 2 w, Sir Alexander (Alec) Walter Merrison, DL, FRS (d 1989), s of Henry Walter Merrison (d 1965); 1 da (Andria b 1972), 1 s (Benedict b 1974); *Career* lectr in history Univ of Bristol 1964–90; dir: HTV Group plc 1982–97, Bristol and West plc 1997–2002 (Bristol and West Building Society 1990–97), Western Provident Assoc 1990–98, Greater Bristol Tst 1987–96, Universities' Superannuation Scheme Ltd 2003–; memb: Bristol Devpt Corp 1993–96, HTV West Advsy Bd 1997–99, Ct Univ of Bristol 1986–; vice-pres Bishop Bristol's Urban Fund 1989–90; chm: Govrs Colston's Girls' Sch 1992–96, Advsy Ctee on Historic Wreck Sites 1996–2002, HTV Pension Scheme 1994–, Bristol Cathedral Cncl 2002–05; tstee of various pension schemes and charitable tsts; FRSA 1993; *Style—* Lady Merrison; ✉ Universities' Superannuation Scheme Limited, Royal Liver Building, Liverpool L3 1PY

MERRIVALE, 3 Baron (UK 1925); Jack Henry Edmond Duke; s of 2 Baron, OBE (d 1951); *b* 27 January 1917; *Educ* Brightlands Sch, private tuition SW France, Ecole des Sciences Politiques Paris; *m* 1, 1939 (m dis 1974), Colette, da of John Douglas Wise; 1 s, 1 da; m 2, 1975, Betty (d 2002), wid of Paul Baron; *Heir* s, Hon Derek Duke; *Career* joined RAF 1940, Flt Lt 1944 (despatches); formerly chm Scotia Investments Ltd, past pres Anglo-Malagasy Soc; past pres: Inst of Traffic Admin, Railway Devpt Assoc; formerly chm Br Ctee for the Furthering of Rels with French-Speaking Africa; chm: Grecian Investments (Gibraltar) Ltd 1990–, GB-Senegal Friendship Assoc 1991; fndr memb Club of Dakar 1974; Freeman City of London 1979, Hon Freedom City of Gibraltar 2001; FRSA 1964; Chev Nat Order of Madagascar 1968, Cdr Nat Order of the Lion (Senegal) 1992; *Style—* The Rt Hon the Lord Merrivale; ✉ 16 Brompton Lodge, 9–11 Cromwell Road, London SW7 2JA (tel and fax 020 7581 5678)

MERRON, Gillian; MP; *Educ* Wanstead HS, Lancaster Univ (BSc); *Career* former: business devpt advsr, local govt offr, sr offr UNISON Lincolnshire 1995–97; MP (Lab) Lincoln 1997–; PPS to: Doug Henderson, MP, *qv*, 1998–99, The Rt Hon Baroness Symons of Vernham Dean, *qv*, 1999–2001, Rt Hon Dr John Reid, MP, *qv*, 2001–02; asst Govt whip 2002–04, a Lords cmmr to HM Treasy (Govt whip) 2004–06, Parly under sec of state for tport 2006–; memb Select Ctee on Trade and Industry 1997–98; chair E Midlands Gp of Lab MPs 1999–2002; vice-chm: regnl Labour Party Exec, Parly Labour Party Backbench Ctee on Foreign and Cwlth Affairs 1997–98, E Midlandsl Region Gp of Lab MPs 1997–, PLP Ctee on Foreign and Cwlth Affrs 1997–99; memb: Armed Forces Parly Scheme (RAF) 1997–98, Bd Westminster Fndn for Democracy 1988–2001, Labour Friends of Israel; assoc memb British-Irish Inter-Parly Body 2001–02; fell-elect Indust and Parl Tst; vice-chair Lincoln Co-operative Voluntary Party, pres Lincoln and District Branch Parkinson's Disease Assoc, pres Lincoln Mencap, pres Breathe Easy Lincoln; patron: Friends of the Mary Gordon, Friends of St Helen's Church, Boultham Ermine Community Gp; capt House of Commons Women's Tug-of-War team 2003–05; memb: Amnesty International, Cats Protection League, Lincoln Civic Tst, Co-operative Pty, Unison; *Recreations* swimming, walking, films, Lincoln City FC; *Style—* Ms Gillian Merron, MP; ✉ House of Commons, London SW1A 0AA (tel 020 7219 4031)

MERRY, David Byron; CMG (2000); s of Colin Merry (d 1951), and Audrey, *née* Handley (d 2006); *b* 16 September 1945, Frecheville, Derbys; *Educ* King Edward VII Sch Sheffield, Ecclesfield GS; *m* 4 March 1967, Patricia Ann, *née* Ellis; 2 da (Catherine Ann b 1969, Carolyn Jane b 1972), 1 s (Derek John b 1971); *Career* Miny of Aviation 1961–65; HM Dip Serv: joined 1965, served Bangkok 1969–73, served Budapest 1974–77, FCO 1977–81, first sec (economic) and civil air attaché Bonn 1981–85, head of Chancery E Berlin 1985–88, FCO 1989–93, dep head of mission Manila 1993–97, dep high cmmr Karachi 1997–2000, FCO 2000–01, high cmmr to Botswana 2001–05, ret; *Recreations* swimming, walking; *Style—* David Merry, Esq, CMG; ✉ 22 Orchard Close, Hawley, Camberley, Surrey GU17 9EX

MERRYLEES, Andrew; s of Andrew Merrylees (d 1984), and Mary McGowan, *née* Craig (d 1999); *b* 13 October 1933; *Educ* Wishaw HS, Univ of Strathclyde (sr design prize, life drawing prize, BArch, Dip Town Planning); *m* Mary Anne, da of James Dewar Crawford; 1 da (Fiona Jean b 28 June 1961), 2 s (Andrew Gary b 5 June 1963, James Scott b 30 Jan 1968); *Career* architect; Sir Basil Spence, Glover & Ferguson: joined as trainee 1957, assoc 1968, ptnr 1972–85; estab own practice Merrylees and Robertson (formerly Andrew Merrylees Associates) 1985 (merged with Hypostyle Architects 2001); conslt architect Standing Conf of Nat and Univ Libraries; memb: Advsy Cncl for the Arts in Scotland, Edinburgh Festival Soc, Cockburn Assoc (memb Cncl 1987–89), Cncl RIAS; RIBA 1958, FRIAS 1977, FCSD 1978, RSA 1991 (ARSA 1984), FRSA 1993 *Major Projects* incl: Univ buildings at Edinburgh, Heriot-Watt, Dublin, Liverpool and Aston, Scottish Headquarters AA, Post Office sorting office, National Library of Scotland, British Golf Museum, Motherwell Heritage Centre, Dundee Science Centre; hon prof of architecture Univ of Dundee; *Awards* RIBA Bronze Medal, Saltire Award, Civic Trust Award, Art in Architecture Award, RSA Gold Medal, Concrete Award, SCONUL Design Award, Sir William Gillies Award; *Recreations* architecture, cooking, walking; *Clubs* Scottish Arts'; *Style—* Prof Andrew Merrylees, RSA; ✉ 204 Bonkle Road, Newmains, Lanarkshire ML2 9AA (tel 01698 384914); Quadrant, 17 Bernard Street, Edinburgh EH6 6PW (tel 0131 555 0688, fax 0131 554 1850)

MERSEY, 5 Viscount (UK 1916); Edward John Hallam Bigham; also 14 Lord Nairne (S 1681); s of 4 Viscount Mersey (d 2006); *b* 23 May 1966; *Educ* Eton, Balliol Coll Oxford, Trinity Coll of Music London; *m* 2001, Caroline Clare, *née* Schaw Miller; 2 da (Hon Flora Diana Joan, Mistress of Nairne b 17 May 2003, Hon Polly Joanna Jean b 2006); *Heir* (to Viscountcy of Mersey) unc, Hon David Edward Hugh Bigham; (to Lordship of Nairne) da, Hon Flora Bigham, Mistress of Nairne; *Career* music composer; *Style—* The Viscount Mersey; ✉ e-mail ned@oceanbloem.com

MERTHYR, Barony of ; *see:* Lewis, Trevor

MERTON, William Ralph; s of Sir Thomas Ralph Merton, KBE, FRS (d 1969), of Berks, and Violet Marjory Sawyer (d 1976); *b* 25 November 1917; *Educ* Eton, Balliol Coll Oxford (MA); *m* 1, 6 July 1950, Anthea Caroline (d 1976), da of Henry F Lascelles (d 1936); 3 s (Michael b 1951, Rupert b 1953, Jeremy b 1961); m 2, 30 April 1977, Judy, da of Col Alexander John Buckley Rutherford, CVO, CBE (d 1979); *Career* WWII served: Operational Res Unit HQ Coastal Cmd RAF 1941–43, sci asst to Lord Cherwell War Cabinet 1943–45; called to the Bar Inner Temple; merchant banker; dir: Fulmer Res Inst 1946–80 (chm 1958–74), Erlangers Ltd 1950–60; chm: Alginate Industries Ltd 1952–79, Robert Fleming Holdings Ltd 1974–80; dir Robert Fleming and Co Ltd 1963–80; FInstP; *Recreations* gardening, woodworking; *Style—* William Merton, Esq; ✉ Kingsbrook House, Headley, Thatcham, Berkshire RG19 8AW (tel 01635 268458, e-mail wmerton80@aol.com)

MESSERVY-WHITING, Maj-Gen Graham G; CBE (2003, MBE 1980); *b* 20 October 1946; *Educ* Lycée Français de Londres, Army Staff Coll, RAF Staff Coll, JSDC, RCDS; *m* 1 Feb 1969, Shirley, *née* Hitchinson; 1 s (Charles b 8 Sept 1972); *Career* cmmnd Intelligence Corps 1967; regtl duty incl: 1 KOSB and service in Germany, Libya, Cyprus and Hong Kong, cmd Intelligence and Security Gp Germany 1986–88; staff duty incl: plans offr N Ireland 1978–80, Secretariat of Chiefs of Staff MOD 1984–86, briefing offr to NATO Supreme Allied Cmd Europe 1988–91; mil advsr to Lord Owen as co-chm Int Conf on Former Yugoslavia 1992–93, promoted Brig 1993, res fell Centre for Def Studies KCL 1993, Dir Def Commitments Overseas (Far E and W Hemisphere) MOD 1994–95, Dep Dir and COS then Dir Western European Union PC 1995–98, asst dir operations GCHQ 1998–2000, promoted Maj-Gen 2000, COS European Union Military Staff 2000–03, dep dir Centre for Studies in Security and Diplomacy Univ of Birmingham 2003–; memb Pensions Tbnl 2005–; assoc fell Chatham House 2003; memb Game Conservancy; MIL, MInstD, FCMI, fell RUSI; *Recreations* working gundogs, bridge; *Clubs* Army and Navy; *Style—* Major-General G G Messervy-Whiting, CBE; ✉ e-mail g.messervywhiting@bham.ac.uk

MESTEL, Prof Leon; s of Rabbi Solomon Mestel (d 1966), of London, and Rachel, *née* Brodetsky (d 1974); *b* 5 August 1927; *Educ* West Ham Secdy Sch London, Trinity Coll Cambridge (BA, PhD); *m* 15 Nov 1951, Sylvia Louise, da of Lt-Col Stanley James Cole, CMG, OBE (d 1949), of Cambridge; 2 da (Anne Leonora b 1953, Rosemary Judith b 1959), 2 s (Andrew Jonathan b 1957, Benjamin David b 1960); *Career* ICI res fell Univ of Leeds 1951–54, Cwlth Fund fell Princeton Univ Observatory 1954–55, fell St John's Coll Cambridge 1957–66, lectr in maths Univ of Cambridge 1958–66 (asst lectr 1955–58), visiting memb Inst of Advanced Studies Princeton 1961–62, JFK fell Weizmann Inst for Sci Israel 1966–67, prof of applied maths Univ of Manchester 1967–73, prof of astronomy Univ of Sussex 1973–92 (emeritus prof 1992); Eddington Medal Royal Astronomical Soc 1993, Gold Medal Royal Astronomical Soc 2002; FRAS 1952, FRS 1977; *Books* Magnetohydrodynamics (jtly, 1974), Stellar Magnetism (1999); *Recreations* reading, music; *Style—* Prof Leon Mestel, FRS; ✉ 13 Prince Edward's Road, Lewes, East Sussex BN7 1BJ (tel 01273 472731); Astronomy Centre, SCITECH, University of Sussex, Falmer, Brighton BN1 9QH (tel 01273 606755 ext 8110, fax 01273 873124, e-mail lmestel@sussex.ac.uk)

M

MESTON, His Hon Judge; 3 Baron (UK 1919); James; QC (1996); s of 2 Baron Meston (d 1984), and Diana, Baroness Meston; *b* 10 February 1950; *Educ* Wellington, St Catharine's Coll Cambridge, Univ of Leicester; *m* 1974, Jean Rebecca Anne, yr da of John Carder, of Chalvington, E Sussex; 1 s (Thomas b 1977), 2 da (Laura b 1980, Elspeth b 1988); *Heir* s, Hon Thomas Meston; *Career* called to the Bar Middle Temple 1973; jr counsel to the Queen's Proctor 1992–96, recorder 1997–99, circuit judge (Western Circuit) 1999–; *Clubs* Hawks' (Cambridge); *Style—* His Hon Judge the Lord Meston, QC; ✉ Queen Elizabeth Building, Temple, London EC4Y 9BS

MESTON, Prof Michael Charles; s of Alexander Morrison Meston (d 1980), of Aberdeen, and Isabel Helen, *née* Robertson (d 1968); *b* 13 December 1932; *Educ* Robert Gordon's Coll Aberdeen, Univ of Aberdeen (MA, LLB), Univ of Chicago (JD); *m* 5 Sept 1958, Dorothea, da of James Munro (d 1947), of Montrose; 2 s (Donald b 1960, John b 1963); *Career* lectr in private law Univ of Glasgow 1959–64; Univ of Aberdeen: sr lectr 1964–68, prof of jurisprudence 1968–71, prof of Scots law 1971–96, prof emeritus 1996–, vice-princ 1979–82, dean 1988–91; hon sheriff Grampian Highlands and Islands 1972–, temporary sheriff 1993–99; tstee Nat Museum of Antiquities of Scotland 1982–85, dir Aberdeen Royal Hosps NHS Tst 1992–98; memb Law Soc of Scotland 1957; *Books* The Succession (Scotland) Act 1964 (1964), The Matrimonial Homes (Family Protection) (Scotland) Act 1981 (1981), The Scottish Legal Tradition (1991), The Aberdeen Stylebook 1722 (2000), Meston's Succession Opinions (2000); *Recreations* golf, clock repairing; *Clubs* Royal Northern and Univ, Royal Aberdeen Golf; *Style—* Prof Michael Meston; ✉ 4 Hamilton Place, Aberdeen AB15 4BH (tel and fax 01224 641554, e-mail mcmeston@corgarff.demon.co.uk)

METCALF, Prof David; s of Geoffrey Metcalf (d 1983), and Dorothy Rosa, *née* Vecchia (d 2005); *b* 15 May 1942; *Educ* Univ of Manchester (MA), Univ of London (PhD); *m* 20 July 1968, Helen (d 2003), da of Percival Harnett; 1 s (Thomas b 25 Nov 1980); *Career* special advsr to Min for Social Security 1976–79; prof of economics Univ of Kent 1977–85, prof of industrial relations LSE 1985–; cmmr Low Pay Cmmn 1997–2007; memb: Royal Econ Soc, Br Univs' Industrial Relations Assoc; *Books* Minimum Wage Policy in Great Britain (1981), New Perspectives on Industrial Disputes (1993), Trade Unions: Resurgence or Decline? (2005); *Recreations* watching Tottenham Hotspur FC, horse racing (jockey club steward at Plumpton, Kempton Park and Folkestone); *Clubs* MCC; *Style—* Prof David Metcalf; ✉ London School of Economics and Political Science, Houghton Street, London WC2A 2AE (tel 020 7955 7027, fax 020 7955 6848, e-mail d.metcalf@lse.ac.uk)

METCALF, Prof (David) Michael; s of Rev Thomas Metcalf, and Gladys Metcalf; *b* 8 May 1933; *Educ* St John's Coll Cambridge (MA, DPhil, DLitt); *m* 1958, Dorothy Evelyn, *née* Uren; 2 s, 1 da; *Career* keeper Heberden Coin Room Ashmolean Museum Oxford 1982–98 (asst keeper 1963–82); Univ of Oxford: fell Wolfson Coll 1982–98, prof of numismatics 1996–98; Royal Numismatic Soc: sec 1974–84, ed Numismatic Chronicle 1974–84, pres 1994–99; pres UK Numismatic Tst 1994–99; FSA; *Books* Coinage in South-Eastern

Europe 820–1396 (1979), Coinage of the Crusades and the Latin East (1983, revised 1995), Sceattas in England and on the Continent (1984), Coinage in Ninth-century Northumbria (1987), Thrymsas and Sceattas in the Ashmolean Museum Oxford 3 Vols (1993–94), Suevic Coinage (1997), An Atlas of Anglo-Saxon Coin Finds (1998), Corpus of Lusignan Coinage 3 vols (1996–2000), Byzantine Lead Seals from Cyprus (2004), The Monetary Economy of the Netherlands (jtly, 2007); *Style*— Prof Michael Metcalf, FSA; ✉ c/o Ashmolean Museum, Oxford OX1 2PH (tel 01865 278062, fax 01865 278057)

METCALFE, George Ralph Anthony; s of Sir Ralph Ismay Metcalfe (d 1977), and Betty Penhorwood, *née* Pelling (d 1976); *b* 18 March 1936; *Educ* Lancing, Univ of Durham (BSc, BSc); *m* 11 Aug 1962, (Anne) Barbara, da of Anthony Watson, of Cumbria; 2 da (Elizabeth Anne (Mrs Smedley), Sarah Rosalind (Mrs Faulkner)); *Career* asst to MD Marine Div Richardsons Westgarth 1954–63, head of planning Polaris Project Vickers Armstrongs Engineers 1963–70, md Initial Services (chm and dir various subsids of BET and Initial Services) 1970–78, md Bath & Portland Group 1978–83, chm UMECO plc 1983–97; dep chm: Sailport plc 1994–, Science Systems plc 1997–2002; former memb: Smaller Firms Cncl CBI, Economic Affrs Ctee CBI, Greenbury Ctee, Corp Govrs Ctee City Gp for Smaller Cos (CISCO), Listing Particulars Ctee London Stock Exchange, HM Treasury Smaller Quoted Companies Working Gp; Freeman City of London, Liveryman Worshipful Co of Shipwrights; *Recreations* sailing, music, gardening; *Style*— George Metcalfe, Esq; ✉ 4 Tower Street, Cirencester, Gloucestershire GL7 1EF (tel 01285 885303, e-mail gmetcalfeesq@aol.com)

METCALFE, Julian; MBE (2000); s of David Metcalfe, and Alexa, *née* Boycun (d 1966); *b* 14 December 1959; *Educ* Harrow; *m* Melanie, da of John Michael Willson; 2 s (Billy, Misha), 1 da (Allegra); *Career* co fndr Pret A Manger; *Clubs* White's; *Style*— Julian Metcalfe, Esq, MBE; ✉ Pret A Manger, 1 Hudson's Place, London SW1V 1PZ (tel 020 7827 8000, fax 020 7827 8787)

METCALFE, Peter; s of Arthur Metcalfe, of Tottington, Lancs, and Marjorie, *née* Smith; *b* 1 October 1944; *Educ* Bury GS; *m* 26 July 1969, Patricia Jean, da of Frank Noel Brierley; 1 s (Nicholas Philip b 18 Jan 1975), 1 da (Jane Helen b 11 July 1976); *Career* Peat Marwick Mitchell 1961–70 (Manchester 1961–69, Leeds 1969–70); ptnr: J A Crawshaw & Co Bury 1970–87, KPMG Peat Marwick (following merger) 1987–92, Mitchell Charlesworth Chartered Accountants 1993–2007; FCA 1975 (ACA 1969); *Recreations* table tennis, soccer, travelling (especially France); *Style*— Peter Metcalfe, Esq; ✉ Plants Farm, Greenside, Ainsworth, Bolton, Lancashire BL2 5SF (tel 01204 528949, e-mail peter@solutionsforhr.co.uk)

METCALFE, Robin Hunt (Rob); s of R M B Metcalfe (d 1984), of Darlington, and Avis, *née* Hunt (d 2005); *b* 9 August 1956, Darlington, Co Durham; *Educ* Barnard Castle Sch, Univ of Nottingham (LLB); *Partner* Caroline Baird; *Career* slr specialising in corporate law and M&A; Browne Jacobson: joined 1980, ptnr 1985–, head Commercial Gp 1998–2001, head of business servs 2001–; listed as a leading corporate lawyer by Commercial Lawyer, Chambers & Partners and Legal 500; memb Law Soc 1980; *Recreations* sport (playing squash, keeping fit, watching soccer and cricket), food and drink, music, travel, the great outdoors; *Style*— Rob Metcalfe, Esq; ✉ Browne Jacobson LLP, 44 Castle Gate, Nottingham NG1 7BJ (tel 0115 976 6254, fax 0115 947 5246, e-mail rmetcalfe@brownejacobson.com)

METCALFE, Stanley Gordon; s of Stanley Hudson Metcalfe, and Jane Metcalfe (d 1975); *b* 20 June 1932; *Educ* Leeds GS, Pembroke Coll Oxford (MA); *m* 1968, Sarah, da of John F A Harter; 2 da; *Career* chm Ranks Hovis McDougall plc 1989–93 (chief exec 1982–89, dep chm 1987–89), chm Queens Moat Houses plc 1993–2001; *Recreations* golf, cricket; *Clubs* MCC, I Zingari, Royal & Ancient, Boodle's; *Style*— Stanley Metcalfe, Esq; ✉ The Oast House, Lower Froyle, Alton, Hampshire GU34 4LX (tel 01420 22310)

METHAM, Patricia; JP; da of John (Jack) Andrews, and Jane Starrett Andrews; *Educ* Upper Chine Sch IOW, Univ of Bristol (BA); *Career* teacher Wimbledon HS 1975–82, fell Merton Coll Oxford 1981, head of sixth form and English Francis Holland Sch London 1982–87, head Farlington Sch 1987–92, head Ashford Sch 1992–97, headmistress Roedean Sch 1997–; chair Boarding Ctee GSA 1999–2001; govr: St Andrews Prep Sch Eastbourne, Cumnor House Sch, Newton Prep Sch; Ind Schs Examination Bd (vice-chm 1999), Boarding Sch Assoc (memb Exec Ctee 1999–2001); *Publications* ed of critical play texts (student edns): The Birthday Party (Pinter), The Caretaker (Pinter), The Importance of Being Earnest (Wilde), Lady Windermere's Fan (Wilde), A Streetcar Named Desire (Williams), The Father (Strindberg), Lear (Bond); *Recreations* theatre, choral singing, travel to archaeological and cultural centres (mainly Europe), good food and good wine; *Clubs* Univ Women's, Lansdowne; *Style*— Mrs Patricia Metham; ✉ Roedean School, Roedean Way, Brighton BN2 5RQ (tel 01273 603181, fax 01273 680791)

METHERELL, Ian Patrick; s of Clarence George Metherell (d 1998), and Ethel Muriel, *née* Dyer; *b* 19 September 1943; *Educ* Bideford GS, Univ of Southampton (BA); *m* 7 April 1969, Louise Whitefield, da of James Edward Westwood (d 1986); 2 s (Andrew b 1977, Nicholas b 1981); *Career* PR conslt; chief exec MPR Leedex Group Ltd 1987–89, chm Proclaim Network Ltd 1991–98, chm EuroPR Ltd 1992–; dir: AS2 Ltd 1994–97, Communication Skills Europe Ltd 1997–2003, Aflame Ltd 2004–; non-exec dir Mosaic Management Consulting Group 1984–88; treas PR Conslts Assoc 1987–89; memb Aylesbury Vale DC 1995–2007; chm Buckingham Constituency Lib Dems 2004–06; FIPR 1988; *Style*— Ian Metherell, Esq; ✉ 2 Forge Close, Marsh Gibbon, Bicester, Oxfordshire OX27 0HZ (tel 01869 277620, e-mail imetherell@aol.com)

METHLEY, Peter Charles; s of Charles Harry Methley (d 1995), of Surrey, and Alice Elizabeth, *née* Stimpson (d 1984); *b* 2 April 1938; *Educ* King's Coll Sch; *m* 15 July 1961, Marianne, *née* Evans; 2 da (Lisette b 1963, Annie b 1970), 1 s (Michael Peter b 1965); *Career* insurance broker Lloyd's; chm: Stewart Wrightson Int Gp 1969–79, Leslie and Godwin Ltd 1979–85; chief exec C E Heath plc until 1986, chm and chief exec H J Symons Gp of Cos 1987–93; chm Unirisx Ltd 2004, currently chm Niche Insurance Mktg Ltd; played hockey for Guildford and Surrey 1956–70; memb Lloyd's; Freeman: City of London, Worshipful Co of Insurers (fndr memb); *Recreations* golf, tennis; *Clubs* Sunningdale Golf, R&A, City of London; *Style*— Peter Methley, Esq; ✉ Longreach, Pannells Ash, Ifold, West Sussex RH14 0UF (tel 01403 753036, e-mail pcmethley@btinternet.com)

METHUEN, Richard St Barbe; QC (1997); s of John Methuen (d 1990), and Rosemary Methuen; *b* 22 August 1950; *Educ* Marlborough; *m* 18 May 1974, Mary Catherine Methuen; 2 da (Harriet b 10 May 1977, Alice b 20 Feb 1980), 1 s (David b 4 March 1982); *Career* called to the Bar Lincoln's Inn 1972; head of chambers 2000–05, recorder 2002–; arbitrator Untraced Drivers' Agreement 2001–; mediator 2005–; *Style*— Richard Methuen, Esq, QC; ✉ 12 King's Bench Walk, Temple, London EC4Y 7EL (tel 020 7583 0811, fax 020 7583 7228, e-mail methuen@12kbw.co.uk)

METHUEN, 7 Baron (UK 1838); Robert Alexander Holt Methuen; s of 5 Baron Methuen (d 1975), and Grace Durning, *née* Holt (d 1972); suc bro, 6 Baron, 1994; *b* 22 July 1931; *Educ* Shrewsbury, Trinity Coll Cambridge; *m* 1, 1958 (m dis 1993), Mary Catherine Jane, da of Ven Charles German Hooper, Archdeacon of Ipswich; 2 da (Hon Charlotte Mary (The Rev and Hon Dr Charlotte Franke) b 1964, Hon Henrietta Christian (Hon Mrs Methuen-Jones) b 1965); m 2, 1994, Margrit Andrea, da of Friedrich Karl Ernst Hadwiger, of Vienna, Austria; *Heir* cous, James Methuen-Campbell; *Style*— The Lord Methuen; ✉ House of Lords, London SW1A 0PW

METLISS, Jonathan Alexander; s of Cyril Metliss, and Anita, *née* Lander; *b* 12 June 1949; *Educ* Haberdashers' Aske's, Univ of Southampton (LLB); *m* 15 Dec 1974, Vivienne Hilary, da of Samuel Woolf; 1 s (Joshua b 25 Nov 1980), 2 da (Miriam b 4 Nov 1983, Elizabeth b 4 July 1988); *Career* slr; asst slr Nabarro Nathanson 1973–76, merchant banker Capel Court Corp Sydney Aust 1976–78, asst slr Berwin Leighton 1978–82, sr corp fin ptnr, head of Sports Business Gp and fndr memb SJ Berwin 1982–, conslt Shore Capital Gp plc, conslt Structadene Ltd; dir: London Freeholds plc, Interlaw Ltd 1993–, The Weizmann Inst Fndn, Southern Africa Business Assoc; British-Israel Chamber of Commerce (also memb Exec); chm British Friends of Haifa Univ, vice-chm Friends of the Weizmann Inst (UK); memb Exec: The Weizmann Inst Fndn, Israel-Britain Business Cncl; vice-pres Cwlth Jewish Cncl; jt sec and exec memb Inter-Parly Cncl Against Anti-Semitism, Parly Cncl Against Anti-Semitism; memb: Cons Friends of Isreal Tikkun SA, Exec Br Israel Communications and Res Centre (BICOM), Parkes Centre Devpt Bd Univ of Southampton, Advsy Bd Tel Aviv Univ Business Sch, Bd of Govrs Haifa Univ, Ctee on South African Trade (COSAT, a Br overseas trade bd business advsy gp), Govt Working Gp on Football Disorder, Trade Partners UK, African and ME Advsy Gp, Royal African Soc, Law Soc, Holborn Law Soc, Advsy Gp Kick It Out (football anti-racism orgn); advsy memb Trade Partners UK 2001–, memb Hong Kong UK Business Forum; memb: RHS, RSPB, Guild of Freemen of the City of London, Advsy Gp Kick It Out (Kick Racism Out of Fooball); MInstD; *Recreations* squash, soccer, cricket, travel, work Israel and S Africa, RHS; *Clubs* MCC, Arundel CC, Middx CCC, Sussex CCC, Surrey CCC, RAC, Saracens RC, Alcester RC, Middx Co RFU, Rugby, Broadgate, Mark's, Queen's, Lord Taverner's Primary; *Style*— Jonathan Metliss, Esq; ✉ SJ Berwin, 222 Gray's Inn Road, London WC1X 8HB (tel 020 7533 2222, fax 020 7533 2000)

METTER, Veronica Ann; da of Louis William Metter, of South Africa, and Valerie Phyllis, *née* Harris; *b* 9 January 1954; *Educ* Univ of the Witwatersrand (BA), Univ of London (BA); *Career* slr; ptnr Berwin Leighton (now Berwin Leighton Paisner) 1987–; memb Law Soc; *Recreations* theatre, tennis; *Style*— Miss Veronica Metter; ✉ Berwin Leighton Paisner, Adelaide House, London Bridge, London EC4R 9HA (tel 020 7623 3144, telex 886420, fax 020 7623 4416)

MEWIES, Sandy; AM; da of Tom Oldland (d 1990), and Margaret Owens (d 2006); *b* 16 February 1950, Wrexham; *Educ* Grove Park Girls' GS Wrexham, Open Univ (BA); *m* 17 July 1976, Paul Mewies; 1 s; *Career* journalist 1966–83, advsr Clwyd Community Care 1991–93, lay schs inspr 1993–2003, memb Nat Assembly for Wales (Lab) Delyn 2003–; co cncllr Wrexham 1987–2004 (sometime mayor); former: dir Wales European Centre Brussels, former memb N Wales Probation Bd; hon fell NE Wales Inst; *Recreations* reading; *Style*— Mrs Sandy Mewies, AM; ✉ National Assembly for Wales, Cardiff Bay, Cardiff CF99 1NA (tel 029 2089 8280, fax 029 2089 8281, e-mail sandy.mewies@wales.gov.uk); Constituency Office, 64 Chester Street, Flint, Flintshire CH6 5DH (tel and fax 01352 763398)

MEXBOROUGH, 8 Earl of (I 1766); John Christopher George Savile; also Baron Pollington (I 1753) and Viscount Pollington (I 1766); s of 7 Earl (d 1980; himself gs of the 4 Earl who, as Lord Gaverstock, featured in a minor role in Disraeli's Coningsby, and who, for the last seven and a half months of his life, enjoyed the distinction of being the last living ex-member of the unreformed House of Commons), and Josephine Bertha Emily, *née* Fletcher (d 1992); *b* 16 May 1931; *Educ* Eton, Worcester Coll Oxford; *m* 1, 1958 (m dis 1972), Lady Elisabeth Hariot Grimston, da of 6 Earl of Verulam; 1 s (John Andrew Bruce, Viscount Pollington b 1959), 1 da (Lady Alethea Frances Clare b 1963 d 1994); m 2, 1972, Catherine Joyce, da of James Kenneth Hope, CBE, DL, and formerly wife of 6 Baron Vivian (d 2004); 1 da (Lady Lucinda b 1973), 1 s (Hon James b 1976); *Heir* s, Viscount Pollington; *Career* late 2 Lt Grenadier Gds; MIMI; *Recreations* travel, motor cars, American popular music; *Clubs* White's, All England Lawn Tennis, Air Sqdn, Mill Reef (Antigua); *Style*— The Rt Hon the Earl of Mexborough; ✉ Arden Hall, Hawnby, North Yorkshire YO62 5LS (tel 01439 798348, fax 01439 798336, e-mail jmexborough@hotmail.com); 14 Lennox Gardens Mews, London SW1X 0DP (tel 020 7589 3669, fax 020 7584 2836)

MEYER, Lady; Catherine Irene; da of Maurice Jean Damien Laylle, Légion d'Honeur, Croix de Guerre, and Olga, *née* Ilyina; *b* 26 January 1953, Baden-Baden, Germany; *Educ* French Lycée of London (Bacc), SSEES Univ of London (BA); *m* 1, 1984 (m dis); 2 s (Alexander Volkmann b 26 May 1985, Constantin Volkmann b 17 May 1987); m 2, 1997, Sir Christopher Meyer, KCMG, *qv*, s of Flt Lt Reginald Meyer (ka 1944); *Career* account exec: Merrill Lynch, Pierce, Fenner & Smith 1976–79, Dean Witter Reynolds Ltd 1979–80, E F Hutton Inc 1980–86; co-fndr Int Centre for Missing and Exploited Children (ICMEC) 1999, fndr PACT 2000; co-chair Vote 2004; non-exec dir Liffe 2003–; Adam Walsh Rainbow Award, Women's Center Leadership Award; *Publications* Mechanism of Commodity Options on the London Metal Exchange (1980), Two Children Behind a Wall (1997), They are My Children too (1999); *Recreations* tennis, skiing, politics; *Clubs* Sloane; *Style*— Lady Meyer; ✉ PACT, PO Box 31389, London SW11 4WY (website www.pact-online.org)

MEYER, Sir Christopher John Rome; KCMG (1998, CMG 1988); s of Flt Lt Reginald Henry Rome Meyer (ka 1944), and Evelyn Landells, *née* Campani (decd); *b* 22 February 1944; *Educ* Lancing, Lycée Henri IV Paris, Peterhouse Cambridge (MA), Sch of Advanced Int Studies Bologna; *m* 1, 11 Dec 1976 (m dis), Francoise Elizabeth, da of late Air Cdre Sir Archie Winskill, KCVO, CBE, DFC, AE; 2 s (James b 21 March 1978, William b 20 June 1984), 1 step s (Thomas (Hedges) b 28 Aug 1972); m 2, 30 Oct 1997, Catherine Irene Meyer, *qv*, da of Olga and Maurice Laylle; 2 step s (Alexander Volkmann b 26 May 1985, Constantin Volkmann b 17 May 1987); *Career* Dip Serv: third sec West and Central African Dept FO 1966–67, Russian language trg 1967–68, third (later second) sec Br Embassy Moscow 1968–70, second later first sec Madrid 1970–73, first sec E Euro and Soviet Dept FCO 1973–76, first sec planning staff 1976–78, first sec UK rep to Euro Community Brussels 1978–82, cnsllr and head of Chancery Moscow 1982–84, head News Dept and chief FCO spokesman 1984–88; visiting fell Center for Int Affrs Harvard Univ 1988–89; min (commercial) Washington 1989–92, min and dep head of Mission Washington 1992–93, chief press sec to the PM 1994–96, ambass to Germany 1997, ambass to USA 1997–2003; chm PCC 2003–; chm Ambo Consultancy Ltd, non-exec dir GKN plc; govr ESU; memb Exec Ctee Pilgrims Soc; hon fell Peterhouse Cambridge 2001; *Publications* DC Confidential (2005); *Recreations* tennis, reading, jazz; *Clubs* Garrick, Metropolitan (Washington DC); *Style*— Sir Christopher Meyer, KCMG

MEYER, Rev Canon Conrad John Eustace; s of late William Eustace Meyer; *b* 2 July 1922; *Educ* Clifton, Pembroke Coll Cambridge (MA), Westcott House Cambridge; *m* 1960, Mary, da of late Alec John Wiltshire; *Career* Lt (S) RNVR and later chaplain RNVR; vicar Devoran Truro 1954–64; diocesan: youth chaplain 1956–60, sec for educn 1960–69; hon canon of Truro 1960–79, archdeacon of Bodmin 1969–79, examining chaplain to Bishop of Truro 1973–79, area bishop of Dorchester 1979–87, hon asst bishop Truro Dio 1990–94, provost of Western Div of the Woodard Schs 1970–92; ordained Roman Catholic priest 1995; hon canon Plymouth RC Cathedral 2001–; vice-pres SPCK 1990– (vice-chm 1989–90, chm Appeal Ctee until 1990); chm Cornwall Civil Aid and co cmmr 1993–96; hon fell Woodard Corporation (Western Div) 1993–94, fell (hc) Inst of Civil Defence and Disaster Studies; *Recreations* civil defence, archaeology, swimming, walking; *Clubs* Royal Cwlth Tst; *Style*— The Rev Canon C J Meyer; ✉ Hawk's Cliff, 38 Praze Road, Newquay, Cornwall TR7 3AF (tel 01637 873003)

MEYERS, Dr Jeffrey; s of Rubin Meyers, of NYC, and Judith Meyers; *b* 1939; *Educ* Univ of Michigan (BA, jr year at Univ of Edinburgh), Univ of Calif Berkeley (MA, PhD); *Career* writer; asst prof UCLA 1963–65, lectr Far East Div Univ of Maryland 1965–66, asst prof

Tufts Univ Boston 1967–71, professional writer in London and Málaga 1971–75, prof Univ of Colorado 1978–92 (assoc prof 1975–78), Jemison prof Univ of Alabama 1992, professional writer 1992–; visiting prof: Univ of Kent Canterbury 1979–80, Univ of Massachusetts Amherst 1982–83; visiting scholar Univ of Calif Berkeley 1986–87 and 1992–94, Univ of Colorado research lectr 1988; Award in Lit American Acad of Arts and Letters 2005; FRSL 1983; *Biographies* A Fever at the Core: The Idealist in Politics (1976), Married to Genius (1977), Katherine Mansfield: A Biography (1978), The Enemy: A Biography of Wyndham Lewis (1980), Hemingway: A Biography (1985), Manic Power: Robert Lowell and His Circle (1987), D H Lawrence: A Biography (1990), Joseph Conrad: A Biography (1991), Edgar Allan Poe: His Life and Legacy (1992), Scott Fitzgerald: A Biography (1994), Edmund Wilson: A Biography (1995), Robert Frost: A Biography (1996), Bogart: A Life in Hollywood (1997), Gary Cooper: American Hero (1998), Privileged Moments: Encounters With Writers (2000), Orwell: Wintry Conscience of a Generation (2000), Inherited Risk: Errol and Sean Flynn in Hollywood and Vietnam (2002), Somerset Maugham: A Life (2004), Impressionist Quartet: The Intimate Genius of Manet and Morisot, Degas and Cassatt (2005), Modigliani: A Life (2006), Samuel Johnson: The Struggle (2008); *Literary Criticism* Fiction and the Colonial Experience (1973), The Wounded Spirit: A Study of 'Seven Pillars of Wisdom' (1973), A Reader's Guide to George Orwell (1975), Painting and the Novel (1975), Homosexuality and Literature 1890–1930 (1977), D H Lawrence and the Experience of Italy (1982), Disease and the Novel 1860–1960 (1985), The Spirit of Biography (1989), Hemingway: Life into Art (2000); *Bibliographies* T E Lawrence: A Bibliography (1974), Catalogue of the Library of the Late Siegfried Sassoon (1975), George Orwell: An Annotated Bibliography of Criticism (1977); *Collections Edited* George Orwell: The Critical Heritage (1975), Hemingway: The Critical Heritage (1982), Robert Lowell: Interviews and Memoirs (1988), The Sir Arthur Conan Doyle Reader (2002), The W Somerset Maugham Reader (2004); *Original Essays Edited* Wyndham Lewis: A Revaluation (1980), Wyndham Lewis by Roy Campbell (1985), D H Lawrence and Tradition (1985), The Craft of Literary Biography (1985), The Legacy of D H Lawrence (1987), The Biographer's Art (1989), T E Lawrence: Soldier, Writer, Legend (1989), Graham Greene: A Revaluation (1990); *Recreations* tennis, travel, avoiding boredom; *Style*— Dr Jeffrey Meyers; ✉ 84 Stratford Road, Kensington, CA 94707, USA (e-mail vjmeyers@sbcglobal.net)

MEYERS, Jonathan Rhys; *b* 27 July 1977, Dublin; *Career* actor; *Theatre* Darkblood (RNT); *Television* Samson & Delilah, Gormenghast, The Magnificent Ambersons (Best Upcoming Young Actor in a Lead Role Venice TV & Film Festival 2000); *Film* A Man of No Importance, The Disappearance of Finbar Flynn, Michael Collins (Best Young Irish Actor 1998), The Maker, Telling Lies in America, B Monkey, The Governess, Velvet Goldmine (Special Jury Prize Cannes Film Festival 1999), Ride with the Devil, The Loss of Sexual Innocence, Titus, Prozac Nation, Tangled, Happy Now, Bend It Like Beckham, Tesseract, Octane, I'll Sleep When I'm Dead, The Emperor's Wife, The Lion in Winter, Vanity Fair, Match Point; *Style*— Jonathan Rhys Meyers; ✉ c/o ICM, Oxford House, 76 Oxford Street, London W1D 1BS

MEYRIC HUGHES, Henry Andrew Carne; s of Reginald Richard Meyric Hughes (d 1961), and Jean Mary Carne Brooke, *née* Pratt; *b* 1 April 1942; *Educ* Shrewsbury, Univ of Rennes, Univ of Munich, UC Oxford (BA), Univ of Sussex (MA); *m* 3 Aug 1968, Alison Hamilton, da of David Bruce Faulds (d 1976), of Chester; 1 da (Henrietta b 1971), 1 s (Steffan b 1975); *Career* Br Cncl: asst regnl dir W Berlin 1968–71, asst rep (arts) France 1971–73, asst dir and curator of permanent collection Fine Arts Dept 1977–79, regnl dir N Italy Milan 1979–83, dir Visiting Arts Office GB and NI 1984–86, dir Fine Arts Dept 1986–92; dir (also i/c nat touring exhibitions and Arts Cncl Collection) Hayward Gallery London 1992–96; freelance curator/conslt 1996–; dir Riverside Tst 1986–94, memb Ct RCA 1986–92, hon memb SCR RCA 1988–, int pres Int Assoc of Art Critics (AICA) 2002– (pres 1988–91, vice-pres Br Section 1991–); pres Int Bd Manifesta Rotterdam 1996, Luxembourg 1998, Ljubljana 2000, Frankfurt 2002, Donostia-San Sebastian 2004, Nicosia 2006, Bolzano/Trento 2008; memb Bd: Watermans Arts Centre Brentford 1991–93, Academy Forum 1992–96, Inst for Int Visual Arts 1993–; The Br Sch at Rome: memb Faculty of Fine Arts 1988–92, memb Exhibitions Ctee 1996–98; memb: Bd Inst of Int Visual Arts (inIVA) 1986–, Slade Ctee Univ of London 1988–97, Advsy Gp Hayward Gallery London 1986–92, CIMAM (UNESCO), Internationale Kunstausstellungsleitertagung eV (IKT, memb Int Bd 1992–97), Mgmnt Ctee Matts Gallery London 1993–, Bd Göteborg Kunsthallen 1995–2000, Ctee E Europe Contemporary Art Network (SEECAN), Scientific Ctee Museum Moderner Kunst Stiftung Ludwig Wien 2000–01, Galleria d'Arte Moderna Bologna 2001–05, Scientific Ctee Archives de la Critique d'Art Château Giron 2002–, Bd Dox Prague 2004–, Bd Arnolfini Bristol 2006–, Gp of Conslts Cncl of Europe Exhbns 2006–; observer: Art Panel Scottish Arts Cncl, Visual Arts Panel Arts Cncl of GB 1986–92; adjudicator Claremorris Open Ireland 1987; jury memb: Turner Prize 1988, European Painting Prize Oostende 1990, ACC Euro Studios Prog Weimar 1998, Biennale de Cetinje 2002, V Caribbean Biennial 2003, Gwangju Biennale 2004 (chair), Premio Furla Bologna 2005, Dakar Biennial 2006; Br cmmr Venice Biennale 1986–92 (Auerbach 1986, Cragg 1988, Kapoor 1990, Contemporary British Architecture 1991, Hamilton 1993), co-selector and catalogue contrib The Vigorous Imagination Edinburgh Festival 1987, chm Selection Ctee for Eighty (touring exhibition) Strasbourg 1988, chm of jury Contemporary View competition RCA 1990, chm of jury for the diploma exams Ecole Nationale Supérieure des Beaux-Arts Paris 2004; co-curator The Romantic Spirit in German Art 1790–1990 Edinburgh, London and Munich 1994–95, assoc curator The Age of Modernism Berlin 1997, co-curator Blast to Freeze: British Art in the 20th Century (Wolfsburg and Toulouse) 2002–03; curator: Cypriot Pavilion Venice Biennale 2003, Grenseløs/Boundless Oslo 2005–06, Plus que vrai Paris 2005; numerous contributions to exhibition catalogues, translator of historical and art historical publications from French and German, author of articles on cultural policy and contemporary art; contributing ed Tema Celeste (Milan); contrib Times HE Supplement; Silver medal Czechoslovak Soc for Int Cultural Relations 1986; Officier de l'Ordre des Arts et des Lettres (France) 1997; Pour le mérite Federal Republic of Germany 2002; FRSA 1988; *Recreations* music, Europe; *Style*— Henry Meyric Hughes, Esq; ✉ 13 Ashchurch Grove, London W12 9BT (tel and fax 020 8749 4098, e-mail henry@h-meyrichughes.homechoice.co.uk)

MICHAEL, Rt Hon Alun; PC (1998), JP (Cardiff 1972), MP; *b* 22 August 1943; *Educ* Colwyn Bay GS, Keele Univ; *m* 23 July 1966; 2 s, 3 da; *Career* journalist 1966–71, youth and community worker 1971–87, magistrate 1972– (chm Cardiff Juvenile Bench until 1987), memb Cardiff City Cncl 1973–89 (sometime chm: Planning Ctee, Fin Ctee, Econ Devpt Ctee, Performance Review Ctee); MP (Lab and Co-op) Cardiff S and Penarth 1987–, AM (Lab) Wales Mid & W 1999–2000; oppn whip 1987–88, shadow min for Welsh affrs 1988–92, shadow min for home affrs and for voluntary sector 1992–97; min of state Home Office 1997–98, sec of state for Wales 1998–99, first min Nat Assembly for Wales 1999–2000, min of state Rural Affrs 2001–06; chm Co-op Parly Gp 1990–92 (memb Nat Exec Ctee 1999–); variously: chm All-Pty Gp on Somalia, sec All-Pty Gp for Colleges, vice-chm British-German Parly Gp, chm All-Pty Gp on Alcohol Misuse, sec All-Pty Gp on Personal Social Services; chair Parly Hearings for Int Year of Vols 2001; chm Parly Friends of the Welsh National Opera, dep chm Cardiff Bay Opera House; former vice-pres YHA, former vice-pres Building Societies Assoc; FRSA 2003; *Recreations* long-distance running, hill walking, opera, music and reading; *Style*— The Rt Hon Alun Michael, MP; ✉ House of Commons, London SW1A 0AA (tel 020 7219 5980, e-mail alunmichaelmp@parliament.uk); constituency office tel 029 2022 3533

MICHAEL, Anthony Colin; s of Edwin George Michael (d 1993), and Maureen Ellen, *née* McCabe; *b* 18 October 1958; *Educ* Erith GS, St Martins Sch of Art (BA); *Partner* Stephanie Joy Nash, *qv*; 2 s (Montgomery Louis Spencer b 6 May 1996, Nelson Bartholomew Edwin b 28 Nov 1998), 1 da (Astor Elizabeth Pearl b 8 Jan 2003); *Career* former gardener; self employed ptnr Michael Nash Associates 1984–; initially designers of record sleeves for artists incl Neneh Cherry, Fluke, Etienne Daho and Seal, subsequently cmmns for fashion designers Marc Jacobs, Jasper Conran, Issey Miyake, Jil Sander and Philip Treacy, etc, graphic designers for Harvey Nichols own brand food products 1992–, packaging designers for Egg (fashion retail outlet) 1994; *Awards* (for Harvey Nichols food packaging) Gold Award D&AD for the Most Outstanding Packaging Range 1993, Silver Award D&AD for the Most Oustanding Packaging - Individual Pack 1994, Art Dirs' Club of Europe Award 1994, CSD Minerva Award for Graphic Design 1994 and NY Festivals Gold Medal and Grand Award 1994, Silver Award D&AD for Compact Disk Packaging for Massive Attack 1995, Silver Award D&AD for Packaging UTH Retail Stores, D&AD Silver Award for John Galliano packaging; various others from music indust; memb AGI; *Style*— Anthony Michael, Esq; ✉ Michael Nash Associates, 44 Newman Street, London W1T 1QD (tel 020 7631 3370, fax 020 7637 9629, e-mail anthony@michaelnash.co.uk)

MICHAEL, Prof Christopher; s of David Parry Martin Michael, CBE (d 1986), of Newport, and Mary Horner, *née* Hayward; *b* 28 May 1942; *Educ* Jesus Coll Oxford (MA, DPhil); *m* 1964, Marilyn; 2 s (Nicholas b 1964, David b 1967); *Career* staff memb Theory Div CERN Geneva 1969–74, prof of theoretical physics Univ of Liverpool 1974–; FInstP 1976; *Publications* numerous res articles on theoretical high energy physics; *Recreations* underwater hockey, sub aqua diving; *Style*— Prof Christopher Michael; ✉ Division of Theoretical Physics, University of Liverpool, Liverpool L69 3BX (tel 0151 794 3771, fax 0151 794 3784, e-mail c.michael@liv.ac.uk)

MICHAEL, George, né Georgios Panayiotou; *b* 25 June 1963; *Educ* Bushey Meads Sch; *Career* singer and songwriter; memb Wham! 1981–86; released first single Wham Rap! (Enjoy What You Do?) 1982; albums with Wham!: Fantastic (UK no 1) 1983, Make It Big (UK no 1) 1984, The Final (compilation, UK no 2) 1986; solo albums: Faith (UK no 1) 1987, Listen Without Prejudice, Vol 1 (UK no 1) 1990, Older 1996 (first album since legal dispute with Sony Music), Ladies and Gentleman: The Best of George Michael 1998, Songs from the Last Century 1999, Patience 2004, Twenty-Five 2006; singles incl: Careless Whisper (UK no 1) 1984, A Different Corner 1986, I Knew You Were Waiting (with Aretha Franklin) 1987, I Want Your Sex 1987, Hard Day 1987, Faith 1987, Father Figure 1988, One More Try 1988, Monkey 1988, Kissing a Fool 1988, Praying For Time 1990, Waiting For That Day 1990, Mother's Pride 1990, Freedom! '90 1990, Heal The Pain 1991, Don't Let The Sun Go Down On Me (with Elton John) 1991, Too Funky 1992, Jesus to a Child 1995, Fastlove (UK no 1) 1996, Star People '97, Outside (UK no 2) 1998, As (with Mary J. Blige) 1999, If I Told You That (with Whitney Houston) 2000, Freeek! 2002, Amazing 2004, Flawless (Go to the City) 2004, Round Here 2004, John and Elvis Are Dead (digital single) 2005, An Easier Affair 2006, This is Not Real Love (with Mutya) 2006; awards incl: Songwriter of the Year Ivor Novello Awards 1985, 1990 and 1997, Best British Male Artist BRIT Award 1988, R&B Grammy Award 1988, Album of the Year (for Faith) 1989, two American Music Awards 1989, Video Vanguard Award MTV 1989, Best British Album of the Year Award BRIT Award 1991, Best Male Singer Rolling Stone Readers' Awards 1991; organised and headlined HRH The Princess of Wales's Concert of Hope 1993; *Books* Bare (autobiography, 1990); *Style*— George Michael, Esq

MICHAEL, Dr Sir Jonathan; kt (2005); s of Prof Ian Michael, CBE, of Bristol, and Molly, *née* Bayley; *b* 21 May 1945; *Educ* Bristol GS, St Thomas' Hosp Med Sch London (MB BS); *m* 1, 1975 (m dis 1991), Jacqueline, *née* Deluz; 3 da (Susannah b 1977, Charlotte b 1981, Philippa b 1985), 1 s (Stephen b 1978); m 2, Karen, *née* Richards; *Career* consl physician Queen Elizabeth Hosp Birmingham 1980–2000, chief exec Univ Hosp Birmingham NHS Tst 1996–2000, chief exec Guy's and St Thomas' Hosp NHS Tst 2000–07, dep md (healthcare) BT 2007–; FRCP 1985 (MRCP 1973); *Style*— Dr Sir Jonathan Michael; ✉ BT Health, Fleet Place House, 2 Fleet Place, Holborn Viaduct, London EC4M 7RF

MICHAEL, Peter Anthony; CBE (1998); s of Taxis Michael, of Athens, Greece, and Helen, *née* Kelly; *b* 2 July 1954; *Educ* Pierrepont Sch, City of London Poly (Dip); *m* 18 March 1989, Joanne Elizabeth, *née* Angel; 2 da (Marianne Louise b 21 July 1990, Natasha Alexis b 13 Nov 1992); *Career* early career DHSS, secondment HM Treasy industrial policy 1978–79, secondment Treasy Private Office 1981–82; Inland Revenue: princ (Grade 7) 1985–89, princ (Grade 7) Int Div 1989–90, asst dir EC Unit Int Div, dir EU Div and dir EU Co-ordination and Strategy Int 1990–2001, dir Tax Law Rewrite Project 2001–03, dir Revenue Policy Strategy and Co-ordination 2003–05; HM Revenue and Customs: dir Strategy and Co-ordination Central Policy 2005–06, dir Improvement and Professionalism Central Policy 2006–07, dep dir Central Policy 2007–; *Recreations* music, fishing, computers, bridge, snooker; *Style*— Peter Michael, Esq, CBE; ✉ Central Policy, HM Revenue and Customs, Room 73, First Floor, 100 Parliament Street, London SW1A 2BQ (tel 020 7147 2357, e-mail peter.michael@hmrc.gsi.gov.uk)

MICHAEL, Sam; s of David Michael, of Aust, and Marion Michael; *b* 29 April 1971, Geraldton, Aust; *Educ* Univ of NSW (BE); *m* 28 Feb 1998, Vanessa, *née* Fielding; 1 da (Toni b 16 Aug 1999), 1 s (Jacques b 18 June 2001); *Career* design engr Team Lotus 1993–94, race engr Jordan Grand Prix 1995–2000; Williams F1: chief engr 2001–04, tech dir 2004–; *Recreations* running, surfing; *Style*— Sam Michael, Esq

MICHAEL, Simon Laurence; s of Anthony Denis Michael, of London, and Regina, *née* Milstone; *b* 4 January 1955; *Educ* King's Coll London (LLB); *Family* 2 da (Kay b 1988, Roxanne b 2001), 1 s (Alastair b 1990); *Career* called to the Bar Middle Temple 1978; chm Road Victims Tst; memb: Personal Injury Bar Assoc, Professional Negligence Bar Assoc; *Books* The Usurper (jtly, 1988), The Cut Throat (1989), The Long Lie (1991); *Style*— Simon Michael, Esq; ✉ No 5 Chambers, Steelhouse Lane, Birmingham B4 6DR (tel 0121 606 0500, fax 0121 606 1501, e-mail slm@no5.com)

MICHAELS, Robert Stewart John; s of Alexander Michaels, of Stanmore, and Evelyn, *née* Susman; *Educ* Ravensfield Coll Orange Hill, St Martin's Sch of Art, Université d'Aix en Provence; *m* 19 June 1966, Marilyn, da of Edward Lee; 2 s (Mark John Louis b 4 Oct 1972, Daniel David b 19 Sept 1977); *Career* chm and md Robert Michaels Holdings plc 1974–; dir: Mardan Properties Ltd, John Crowther plc 1987, Robert Mark Ltd, Marongate plc, Twenty One Clothing Company Ltd, Independent Storage and Distribution Ltd, RMD Ltd; tstee Bryanston Tst, memb Permanent Panel Nat Econ Devpt Office; cncllr (Cons) Knightsbridge Ward Westminster City Cncl 1990–94 (chm Investments Ctee, vice-chm Financial Mgmnt and Personnel Ctee, whip 1991), dir Westminster Enterprise Agency 1990–, vice-pres and memb Policy Gp Small Business Bureau 1991–, memb House of Lords Rural Economy Gp 1991; chm: Bd of Govrs Sussex House Sch, Cncl for Devpt Westminster Sch; Freeman City of London 1979, life memb Guild of Freemen City of London; Liveryman Worshipful Companies of: Horners, Farriers, Pattenmakers; FInstD 1980; *Recreations* family, reading, martial arts (kickboxing 1st Dan), cricket, racing cars; *Clubs* Carlton, MCC (life memb), Ferrari Owners', Annabel's; *Style*— Robert Michaels, Esq; ✉ e-mail robertmichaels20@aol.com

MICHAELS-MOORE, Anthony; s of John Moore, of Grays, Essex, and Isabel, *née* Shephard; *b* 8 April 1957; *Educ* Gravesend Sch for Boys, Univ of Newcastle upon Tyne, St Mary's

M

Teacher Trg Coll, RSAMD; *m* 16 Feb 1980, Ewa Bozena Maria, da of Stanislaw Migocki; 1 da (Kathryn Ashley Maria b 7 Feb 1987); *Career* baritone; teacher St John's CE Sch Crowborough 1979–84, opera course RSAMD 1984–85, professional debut Opera-go-Round Scottish Opera 1985; first Br winner Luciano Pavarotti/Opera Co of Philadelphia competition 1986; sung with orchs incl: Toronto Symphony, Scot Nat, The Philharmonia, Royal Philharmonic, LSO, CBSO, Vienna Philharmonic, BBC Symphony Orch (under Bernard Haitink, BBC Proms) 1997; *Roles* incl: Marcello in La Bohème Bohème (Opera North, Royal Opera House Covent Garden, ENO), Belcore in L'Elisir d'Amore, Dr Malatesta in Don Pasquale, (Royal Opera House), Ping in Turandot (Covent Garden), Forester in The Cunning Little Vixen (Covent Garden), Zurga in the Pearl Fishers (ENO debut 1987), Count Almaviva in The Marriage of Figaro (ENO, Bavarian State Opera), Figaro in The Barber of Seville (WNO debut 1990, Barcelona 1991, Royal Opera House 1993, Vienna 1995), Guglielmo in Cosi fan Tutte (USA debut Philadelphia 1988, Canadian Debut Canadian Opera Co 1991), Giorgio Germont in La Traviata (Opera North 1991), Marquis of Posa in Don Carlos (Opera North 1993 and Pittsburgh 1997), Licinius in La Vestale (La Scala Milan debut 1993), Lescaut in Manon Lescaut (Vienna Staatsoper debut 1994, Naples debut 1994), Sharpless in Madama Butterfly (Opèra Bastille debut 1994), Don Giovanni (Tel Aviv 1994), Hamlet Opera North 1995, Orestes in Iphigene en Tauride (Opera Bastille) 1995, Onegin in Eugene Onegin (Opera Bastille) 1995, Baron Scarpia in Tosca (Royal Opera House) 1996, Marcello in La Boheme and Silvio in Pagliacci (Met NY debut, 1996), Gérard in Andrea Chénier (Teatro Colon Buenos Aires debut, 1996), title role in Macbeth (Royal Opera House 1997), Rigoletto (Brussels 1999, Vienna 2000), Montforte in Sicilian Vespers (Vienna 2000), Iago in Otello (Paris 2001, Glyndebourne 2001), Ezio in Attila (Chicago 2001, ROH 2002); *Recordings* La Vestale (with La Scala under Riccardo Muti), The Fairy Queen (under Harnoncourt), Mendelssohn Die Erste Walpurgisnacht (with The Philharmonia), Orff Carmina Burana (with Vienna Philharmonic under Andre Previn), Gilbert & Sullivan Yeomen of the Guard, Szymanowski Stabat Mater (with The Philharmonia under Claus Peter Flor), Mercadante Orazi i Curiazi (Opera Rara recording), Opera Spectacular (with the Royal Philharmonic Orch), Die Fledermaus (video, with Royal Opera Co), Puccini Favourites (with Royal Opera Co), Lucia di Lammermoor (under Charles Mackerras), Falstaff (with Sir John Eliot Gardiner), Aroldo (with Fabio Luisi), La Favorite (with Marcello Viotti); *Recreations* clay pigeon shooting, football, cricket, swimming, Indian food; *Style*— Anthony Michaels-Moore, Esq; ✉ c/o IMG Artists, Lovell House, 616 Chiswick High Road, London W4 5RX (tel 020 8233 5800, fax 020 8233 5801)

MICHEL, Keith; s of George Richard Michel (d 2005), and Winifred Eve Michel (d 1972); *b* 19 May 1948; *Educ* Bradfield Coll, Fitzwilliam Coll Cambridge (MA, Football blue, Oxbridge rep team Japan 1969, Univ Crusaders CC); *m* 16 Dec 1972, Rosemary Suzannah, da of Stanley Joseph Simons, of Southgate, London; 1 s (Edward b 30 April 1980); *Career* slr; articled clerk Coward Chance (now Clifford Chance) 1971–73, asst slr Clyde & Co 1973–75, ptnr Holman Fenwick & Willan 1978–2003 (joined as asst slr, conslt 2003–07); visiting prof of laws UCL 2006–; author of various pubns incl: Lloyd's List, Lloyd's Maritime Commercial Law Quarterly, Law Society's Gazette; memb: Grasshoppers CC, Free Foresters CC, Old Bradfieldion FC; tstee Univ of Cambridge FC; memb: Law Soc 1973, City of London Solicitors Co 1990; KM; *Books* Contraband (1988), Countdown (1991), Caracara (1995), Karakan (2000), War Terror and Carriage by Sea (2004); *Recreations* family life, football, cricket, windsurfing, history, archaeology, wildlife conservation, photography, calligraphy; *Clubs* Hawks' (Cambridge); *Style*— Keith Michel, Esq; ✉ Thatchdale, Pennymead Drive, East Horsley, Surrey KT24 5AH (tel 01483 283595, e-mail michelhaffie@zoom.co.uk)

MICHELL, Keith Joseph; s of Joseph Michell (d 1957), and Alice Maude Alsat (d 1957); *b* 1 December 1926; *Educ* Warnertown Sch, Port Pirie HS, SA Sch of Arts and Crafts, Adelaide Teachers Coll, Adelaide Univ, Old Vic Theatre Sch London; *m* 1957, Jeannette Laura, da of Frank Sterk (d 1985); 1 s (Paul b 1960), 1 da (Helena b 1961); *Career* artist and actor; memb original Young Vic Theatre Co, first appearance And so to Bed (London) 1951; leading actor Shakespeare Meml Theatre Co 1952–56, joined Old Vic Co 1956, artistic dir Chichester Festival Theatre 1974–77; *Theatre* with Shakespeare Meml Theatre Co: Orsino in Twelfth Night, Macduff in Macbeth, Hotspur in Henry IV, Orlando in As you like it, Petuchio in The Taming of the Shrew, Theseus in A Midsummer Night's Dream, Archilles in Troilus and Cressida, Master Ford in The Merry Wives of Windsor, Parolles in All's Well That Ends Well (Parolles); with Old Vic Co: Benedick in Two Gentlemen of Verona, Antony in Antony & Cleopatra, Aaron in Titus Andronicus; other London roles incl: Oscar/Nector in Irma la Douce (also NY) 1958–61, lead role in Robert and Elizabeth 1964, The King's Mare 1966, Don Quixote in Man of La Mancha (also NY) 1968–70, Abelard in Abelard & Heloise (also NY) 1971, title role in Hamlet (Bankside) 1972, Robert Browning in Dear Love 1973; other credits incl: The Director in Tonight We Improvise, Oedipus in Oedipus Tyrannus, Iago in Othello 1974, Cyrano in Cyrano De Bergerac 1975 (Othello and Cyrano presented at Hong Kong Arts Festival), Twelfth Night (dir and designer) 1976, Major Matthew in Monsieur Perrichons Travels 1976, In Order of Appearance (dir and designer) 1977, Magnus in The Apple Cart (toured Luxembourg, London, Brussels and Aust) 1977, Othello (tour to Aust), Sherlock Holmes in The Crucifer of Blood (London) 1979, Oscar in On the 20th Century (London) 1980, lead in Pete McGynty and the Dream Time (Melbourne Theatre Co) 1981, Captain Beaky Christmas Show London 1981–82, Sir Arthur in On the Rocks 1982, Prospero in The Tempest (Brisbane) 1982, One Man Show Port Pirie (Aust) 1982, Salieri in Amadeus 1983, La Cage aux Folles (San Francisco, NY, Sydney and Melbourne) 1985–86, Rochester in Jane Eyre (Chichester) 1986, Augustus John in Portraits (Malvern Festival and London) 1987, Gordon-Cumming in The Royal Baccarat Scandal (Chichester and London) 1988–89, Henry VIII 1991, George in Aspects of Love (Toronto 1991–92 and Chicago 1992), Scrooge Melbourne 1993–94, Caesar in Caesar and Cleopatra (Edmonton Canada) 1994, Brazilian Blue (Aust) 1995, Monsieur Amilcar (Chichester) 1995, Family Matters 1997, All The World's A Stage 1998–2002 (also Adelaide Festival Theatre and Keith Michell Theatre Port Pirie 2004), The Artisan's Angel (actor and dir, RSM London); *Television* in UK incl: Pygmalion, Act of Violence, Mayerling Affair, Wuthering Heights, The Bergonzi Hand, Ring Round the Moon, Spread of the Eagle (series of Roman plays), An Ideal Husband, The Shifting Heart, Loyalties, Kain, The Six Wives of Henry VIII, Keith Michell Special, Keith Michell Christmas Show, Keith Michell at the Shows, Dear Love, Keith Michell in Concert at Chichester, Captain Beaky and his Band, Captain Beaky (Vol II); US TV incl: The Story of the Marlboroughs, Jacob and Joseph, The Story of David, The Tenth Month, The Day Christ Died, The Miracle, Captain Cook, Murder She Wrote (series of 6), Prince and the Pauper; videos: Pirates of Penzance (Maj-Gen), The Gondoliers (Grand Inquisitor), Ruddigore (Robin Oakapple); *Film* appearances incl: Dangerous Exile, The Hell Fire Club, Seven Seas to Calais, The Executioner, House of Cards, Prudence and the Pill, Henry VIII and his Six Wives, Moments, The Deceivers; *Recordings* Ancient and Modern, At the Shows, Words Words Words, The Sonnet and the Prophet, Captain Beaky and his Band, Captain Beaky Vol II, Kent to Gielgud's Lear (BBC), Guys and Dolls (CD), King and I; *Exhibitions* one man painting shows: Jamaica 1960, New York 1962, Portugal 1963, Outback in Australia 1965, Don Quixote 1969, Abelard and Heloise 1972, Hamlet 1972, Self Portrait Henry VIII (screen print) 1972, Piktors Metamorphosis (lithograph) 1972, Shakespeare Sonnets (lithographs) 1974, Capt Beaky 1982, Alice In Wonderland 1982, Vincent Gall Adelaide 1989, Majorcan Paintings The Century Galleries 1991; *Awards* London Critics' Best Actor in a Musical (Man of La Mancha) 1968, Best Actor (Soc of Film and TV Arts) 1970, Show Business Personality of the Year (Grand Order of Water Rats) 1971, Top Actor (Sun TV Award) 1971, Special Award (Royal Variety Club of GB) 1971, Outstanding single performance by an actor (Royal Acad of TV Arts) 1971, British Film Award (Evening News) 1973, Logie Award (Aust) 1974; *Publications* illustrator Captain Beaky books of poems, author/illustrator of Practically Macrobiotic Cook Book (1 edn 1987, 3 edn 2000); *Recreations* gardening, reading; *Style*— Keith Michell, Esq; ✉ c/o Chatto and Linnit, 123A Kings Road, London SW3 4PL (tel 020 7352 7722)

MICHELL, Prof (Alastair) Robert; s of Dr Charles Francis Michell (d 1960), of London, and Eva, *née* Freyhan; *b* 28 December 1940; *Educ* Dulwich Coll, RVC London (BSc, BVetMed, PhD, DSc, MRCVS, pres RVC Students' Union); *m* 1963, Pauline, da of Frederick Arthur Mountford Selley (d 2007); 1 da (Tania Claire b 1968); *Career* Harkness fell (Cwlth Fund of NY) Rockefeller Univ, Nat Inst of Health and UCLA (Cedars Sinai Hosp) USA 1969–71, Beit meml research fell in med 1971–73, MRC research fell Nephrology Section Univ of Chicago Med Sch 1974–76; RVC London: lectr in physiology 1976–83, reader in med 1983–93, prof of applied physiology and comparative med 1993–; prof of comparative med Bart's 2001–; Evelyn Williams fell Univ of Sydney 2000; vice-chm Comparative Clinical Science Fndn 2001–; chm RCVS/BVA Jt Ctee on Continuing Professional Devpt 1988–92; pres: Euro Soc for Vet Nephrology 1985–88, Vet Research Club 1988–89, RVC Alumnus Assoc 1989–91, Assoc of Vet Teachers and Research Workers 1994–95; memb Cncl: BVA 1983–85, 1988–92, 1995–99, 2002–, RVC 1986–94 and 1995–96, RCVS 1992–2004 (elected memb, pres 1999–2000), Comparative Med Section RSM (vice-pres 1992–94), Technol Foresight (Health Sciences Panel) 1995–99; memb Advsy Cncl Campaign for Science and Engrg 2001–; runner-up first Perspectives in Biology and Medicine writing award for young scientists 1975, Blaine award (Br Small Animal Vet Assoc) for outstanding contribs to the advancement of small animal med 1990, Weipers commemorative lectr 1991, Centenary Lecture (Central Vet Soc) 1991 and 1997, George Fleming prize (Br Vet Jl) 1992 and 2005, BVA Dalrymple-Champneys Cup and Medal 2007; memb numerous professional bodies incl: Physiological Soc, Nutrition Soc, Assoc for Vet Clinical Pharmacology and Therapeutics, London Hypertension Soc, Renal Assoc, Consensus for Action on Salt and Hypertension, Central Vet Soc (pres 2002–03); tstee Hunterian Museum RCS; govr Addenbrooke's Hospital Fndn Tst 2004–; MRPharmS (memb Cncl, Privy Cncl rep), FRSM, FRSA; *Books* Renal Disease in Dogs and Cats: Comparative and Clinical Aspects (ed, 1988), An Introduction to Veterinary Anatomy and Physiology (jtly, 1989), Veterinary Fluid Therapy (jtly, 1989), The Advancement of Veterinary Science (ed, 4 vols, 1992), Clinical Biology of Sodium (1995), Veterinary Verse In Newer Veins (ed with E Boden, 1997); over 300 contributions to scientific and professional jls; *Recreations* music, theatre, tennis, travel, writing (including scientific journalism); *Style*— Prof Robert Michell; ✉ Department of Biochemical Pharmacology, St Bartholomew's & Royal London School of Medicine and Dentistry, Charterhouse Square, London EC1M 6BQ (tel 020 7882 6073, fax 01638 578605); tel 01638 577994

MICHELL, Prof Robert Hall (Bob); s of Rowland Charles Michell, and Elsie Lorna, *née* Hall; *b* 16 April 1941; *Educ* Crewkerne Sch, Univ of Birmingham (BSc, PhD, DSc); *m* 1, 13 Jan 1967 (m dis 1971), June Mary, *née* Evans; m 2, 28 July 1992, Esther Margaret Oppenheim; 2 s (Jo b 1974, Ben b 1991), 1 da (Naomi b 1986); *Career* Harvard Med Sch 1966–68; Univ of Birmingham: res fell 1965–66 and 1968–70, lectr 1970–81, sr lectr 1981–84, reader in biochemistry 1984–86, prof 1986–87, Royal Soc res prof 1987–2006, emeritus prof of biochemistry 2006–; memb Editorial Bd: Jl of Neurochemistry 1974–78, Cell Calcium 1979–89, Biochemical Jl 1982–88 (ed Advsy Panel 1981–82), Current Opinion in Cell Biology 1988–, Biological Sciences Review 1988–, Proceedings of The Royal Society of London 1989–97, Jl of Molecular Endocrinology 1991–99, Molecular Membrane Biology 1994–, Faculty of 1000 2004–; fndn lectr RCPath 1989, Bertram Lewis Abrahams lectr RCP 1990, Wellcome visiting prof Univ of Vermont 1987, Royal Soc UK-Canada Rutherford lectr 1994, Morton Lecturer Biochemical Soc 2002; memb: Biochemical Soc (CIBA medal 1988), Br Nat Ctee for Pharmacology 1982–87, Br Nat Ctee for Biochemistry 1988–89, Physiological Systems and Disorders Res Bd MRC 1985–90, Brain Res Assoc, Br Soc for Cell Biology, BAAS, Int Rels Ctee Royal Soc 1991–94, Med and Scientific Advsy Panel Leukaemia Res Fund 1989–92, Advsy Bd Beit Meml Tst 1993–2006, Biochemistry Panel for 1996 and Biological Sciences Panel for 2001 and 2008 Research Assessment Exercises HEFCE, Sci Advsy Bd Babraham Inst 1997–2000, Sci Advsy Bd Lister Inst for Preventive Med 1998–2004, Human Frontiers Sci Programme Fellowships and Workshops Panel 1999–2001, Sci Advsy Bd Electromagnetic Fields (EMF) Biological Research Tst 2000– (tstee 2004–); chm Systems Bd Grants Ctee MRC 1988–90; memb EMBO 1991; govr Cadbury Sixth Form Coll 1991–99 and 2003–; FRS 1986 (memb Cncl 1995–97), FMedSci 2002; *Books* Membranes And Their Cellular Functions (with J B Finean and R Coleman, 1974, 3 edn 1984), New Comprehensive Biochemistry (contrib ed with J B Finean, 1981), Cell Calcium (contrib ed, 1982), Inositol Lipids and Transmembrane Signalling (ed with M J Berridge, 1988), Inositol Lipids and Cellular Signalling (ed with A H Drummond and C P Downes, 1989); *Style*— Prof Robert Michell; ✉ School of Biosciences, University of Birmingham, Birmingham B15 2TT (tel 0121 414 5413, fax 0870 137 7947, e-mail r.h.michell@bham.ac.uk)

MICHELL, Roger; s of H D Michell, DFC, and J Michell, *née* Green; *b* 5 June 1956; *Educ* Clifton, Queens' Coll Cambridge (exhibitioner, BA); *m* Kate Buffery (m dis 2002); 2 c (Harry b 6 Dec 1991, Rosanna b 17 March 1996); *Career* director; Brighton Actors Workshop 1977, Thames TV training bursary Royal Court 1978–80, RSC 1985–91, Drama Director's Course BBC TV 1990; Judith E Wilson sr fell Trinity Coll Cambridge 1989; *Theatre* for RSC incl: Temptation, The Dead Monkey, Restoration, Some Americans Abroad, Two Shakespearean Actors, The Constant Couple, Hamlet, Merchant of Venice; others incl: The Catch (Royal Court), The Coup (RNT), The Key Tag (Royal Court), Private Dick (Edinburgh Festival and West End), Marya (Old Vic), Under Milk Wood (RNT), My Night with Reg (Royal Court and West End), Some Sunny Day (Hampstead), The Homecoming (RNT) 1997, Blue/Orange (RNT and West End) 2000, Honour (RNT) 2003, Old Times (Donmar Warehouse) 2004; *Films* Downtown Lagos 1991, Buddha of Suburbia 1993, Ready When You Are Mr Patel 1995, Persuasion 1995, My Night with Reg 1996, Michael Redgrave - My Father 1997, Titanic Town 1997, Notting Hill 1998, Changing Lanes 2001, The Mother 2002, Enduring Love 2003, Venus 2005; *Awards* Buzz Goodbody Award RSC 1977, Edinburgh Fringe First Award 1977, Drama Desk nomination NY 1990, BAFTA nomination for Buddha of Suburbia; for Persuasion incl: BAFTA, RTS nomination; Critics' Circle Award; for Titanic Town: Grand Prix Festival de Laon, Ecumenical Prize Locarno, Trades Union Award, Emden; for Notting Hill: Evening Standard Peter Sellers Award, BAFTA Audience Award, Empire Magazine Award; *Style*— Roger Michell

MICHELS, Sir David Michael Charles; kt (2006); *b* 8 December 1946; *m* 15 Sept 1970, Michelle Ann; *Career* various sales and mktg positions rising to worldwide mktg dir Grand Metropolitan 1966–81; Ladbroke Group plc: sales and mktg dir hotels 1981–83, md Leisure Div 1983–85, md Ladbroke Hotels 1985–87; sr vice-pres sales and mktg Hilton International 1987–89, dep chm Hilton UK and exec vice-pres Hilton Worldwide 1989–91; chief exec: Stakis plc 1991–99, Hilton Int 1999–2000, Hilton Gp plc 2000–05; non-exec dir: Arcadia Gp plc 2000–, British Land Co plc 2003–, EasyJet 2006–; Hon DLitt Glasgow Caledonian Univ; FHCIMA; *Recreations* tennis, reading; *Clubs* Vanderbilt; *Style*— Sir David Michels

MICHIE, Alastair John; s of John Michie (d 1966), of Alyth, Perthshire, and Margaret, *née* Heggie; *b* 21 March 1948; *Educ* Blairgowrie HS; *m* 28 July 1971, Dawn Elizabeth, da of James Edward Thomson Wittet (d 2000), of Alyth, Perthshire; 1 da (Caroline Jane b 1975), 1 s (Graham James b 1980); *Career* Clydesdale Bank plc 1964–74; co sec: Lloyds Bank International Ltd 1981–85 (joined 1974, asst sec 1978–80), Lloyds Bank plc 1985–95, Lloyds TSB Group plc 1995–; memb CIB (Scotland) 1969; ACIS 1973, FCIS 1981, FCIBS 1996; *Recreations* golf, swimming; *Style—* Alastair Michie, Esq; ✉ 14 Marlyns Close, Burpham, Guildford, Surrey GU4 7LR (tel 01483 826688); Lloyds TSB Group plc, 25 Gresham Street, London EC2V 7HN (tel 020 7626 1500, fax 020 356 1038, e-mail alastair.michie@lloydstsb.co.uk)

MICHIE, Prof David Alan Redpath; OBE (1997); s of James Beattie Michie (d 1960), and Anne Redpath, OBE (d 1965); *b* 30 November 1928; *Educ* Hawick HS, Edinburgh Coll of Art (DA); *m* 27 March 1951, Eileen Anderson (d 2003), da of James Temple Michie (d 1931); 2 da (Alison Jane b 1953, Lindsey Elizabeth b 1955); *Career* Nat Serv RA 1947–49; lectr in drawing and painting Grays Sch of Art Aberdeen 1957–61; Edinburgh Coll of Art: lectr 1961–74, vice-princ 1974–77, head Sch of Drawing and Painting 1982–90; prof of painting Heriot-Watt Univ 1988–91 (emeritus prof 1991–); visiting artist: Univ of the Arts Belgrade 1979, Univ of Calif Santa Barbara 1992; memb: Gen Teaching Cncl for Scotland 1975–80, Edinburgh Festival Soc 1977–, Convocation and Ct Heriot-Watt Univ 1979–82, Cncl Br Sch in Rome 1980–85, Museums and Galleries Cmmn 1991–96, Scottish Int Educn Tst 2004–, Nat Life Story Collection; memb SSA 1955, RSA 1972 (ARSA 1964), RGI 1983, FRSA 1990, FFCS 2000, RWA 1991–2000; *Solo Exhibitions* Mercury Gallery London 1966, 1969, 1971, 1974, 1980, 1983, 1992, 1996 and 1999, Mercury Gallery Edinburgh 1986, Lothian Region Chambers Edinburgh 1977, Scottish Gallery Edinburgh 1980,1994, 1998 and 2003, The Loomshop Gallery Lower Largo 1981 and 1987, Kasteel De Hooge Vuursche Baarn and Mia Joosten Gallery Amsterdam 1991; *Group Exhibitions* incl: Fourteen Scottish Painters (Cwlth Inst London) 1963, Edinburgh Ten 30 Wales 1975, Contemporary Scottish Painting (The Alamo Gallery London) 1978, Contemporary Art from Scotland (touring) 1981–82, Works on Paper (Faculty of Fine Art Gallery Belgrade) 1986, Artists' Self Portraits (Tate Gallery London) 1989, Artist Families (Fine Art Soc Edinburgh) 1989, Guthrie Award Prize Winners Exhibition (Fine Art Soc Edinburgh and Glasgow) 1990, Art Studio Faculty Exhibition Univ of Calif Santa Barbara 1991, Scottish Art in the 20th Century (Royal W of England Acad Bristol) 1991, The Scottish Gallery - The First 150 Years (Edinburgh) 1992, The Edinburgh School (The Scottish Gallery) 1993, Contemporary Scottish Painting Hong Kong 1994 and 1996, Scottish Painters (Solomon Gallery Dublin) 1999, RSA members (Albemarle Gallery London) 1999, Les Belles Etoiles d'Ecosse (Napier Gallery St Helier) 2001, The Scottish Show (Thompson's Gallery London) 2001, Scottish Painting (Chelsea Gallery Palo Alto CA) 2005, Divided Selves (Talbot Rice Gallery Edinburgh and Fleming Gallery London) 2006; *Collections* incl: HM The Queen, Aberdeen Art Gallery and Museum, Barings Dumbarton Educnl Tst, Perth Art Gallery, Allied Lyons, James Capel, Edinburgh Educn Authy, Robert Fleming Holdings, Kirkcaldy Art Gallery, Glasgow Art Gallery and Museum, Kleinwort, Heriot-Watt Univ, Liverpool Univ, Nuffield Fndn, Queen Elizabeth Coll London, Reading Art Gallery, NM Rothschild, RAC, Royal Scottish Acad, Royal W of Eng Acad, Scottish Life Assurance Co, Scottish Nat Gallery of Modern Art, Tate Gallery Archive; *Awards* Guthrie Award RSA 1964, David Cargill Prize RGI 1977, Lothian Region Award RSA 1977, Sir William Gillies scholarship RSA 1980, RGI Prize 1990, Cornelissen Prize RWA 1992; *Recreations* music, gardening; *Style—* Prof David Michie, OBE

MICHIE, Prof Donald; s of James Kilgour Michie (d 1967), and Marjorie Crain, *née* Pfeiffer (d 1986); *b* 11 November 1923; *Educ* Rugby, Balliol Coll Oxford (scholar, MA, DPhil, DSc); *m* 1, 1949 (m dis 1951), Zena Margaret, *née* Davies; 1 s (Christopher b 1950); m 2, 1952 (m dis 1958), Hon Anne Laura Dorinthea, *née* McLaren, da of 2 Baron Aberconway, CBE (d 1953); 2 da (Susan Fiona Dorinthea b 1955, Caroline Ruth b 1959), 1 s (Jonathan Mark b 1957); m 3, 1971, Jean Elizabeth *née* Crouch (d 2002); *Career* FO Bletchley 1942–45; res assoc Univ of London 1952–58; Univ of Edinburgh: sr lectr in surgical sci 1958–62, reader 1962–65, dir experimental programming unit 1963–73, personal chair of machine intelligence 1967–84, head of machine intelligence res unit 1974–84, prof emeritus 1985–; chief scientist Turing Inst 1986–92 (dir of res 1984–86); ed-in-chief Machine Intelligence 1967–2000; assoc memb Josef Stefan Inst Slovenia 1995, corresponding memb Slovenian Acad of Sciences and Arts 2005, foreign memb American Acad of Arts and Sciences; Pioneer Award (jtly with Dr Anne McLaren) of Int Embryo Transfer Soc 1988, Achievement Award of IEE 1995, Feigenbaum Medal Int Congress on Expert Systems 1996, Research Excellence Award Int Jt Congress on Artificial Intelligence 2001, Lifetime Achievement Award BCS 2004; Hon DSc: CNAA 1991, Salford Univ 1992, Univ of Aberdeen 1999; Hon DUniv: Stirling 1993, York 2000; FRSE 1969, FBCS 1971; *Books* Machine Intelligence and Related Topics (1982), The Creative Computer (with Rory Johnston, 1984), On Machine Intelligence (2 edn, 1986); *Recreations* travel; *Clubs* New (Edinburgh), Chelsea Arts; *Style—* Prof Donald Michie, FRSE; ✉ e-mail profdmichie@hotmail.co.uk

MICHIE OF GALLANACH, Baroness (Life Peer UK 2001), of Oban in Argyll and Bute; Janet Ray Michie; da of late Lord and Lady Bannerman of Kildonan; *b* 4 February 1934; *Educ* Aberdeen HS for Girls, Lansdowne House Sch Edinburgh, Edinburgh Coll of Speech Therapy; *m* 11 May 1957, Dr Iain Michie, FRCP, s of Malcolm and Margaret Michie; 2 da and 1 da decd; *Career* area speech therapist Argyll and Clyde Health Bd 1977–87; MP (Lib Dem) Argyll and Bute 1987–2001, dep ldr Scottish Lib Dems, memb: House of Commons Select Ctee on Scottish Affrs 1992–97, Chm's Panel 1997–2001; Lib spokesman on tport and rural devpt 1987–88; Lib Dem spokeswoman: on Scotland 1988–97, on Women's Issues 1988–94; jt vice-chm All-Pty Parly Gp on Whisky Industry 1990–2001; vice-chair Scottish Lib Pty 1976–78, chair Scottish Lib Dem Pty 1992–93; vice-pres Royal Coll of Speech and Language Therapists 1991–; memb: An Comunn Gaidhealach, Scottish National Farmers' Union (SNFU), Scottish Crofting Fndn (SCF); hon pres Clyde Fishermen's Assoc, hon assoc Nat Cncl for Women in GB; MCST; *Recreations* golf, swimming, gardening and watching rugby; *Clubs* National Liberal; *Style—* The Rt Hon the Baroness Michie of Gallanach; ✉ House of Lords, London SW1A 0PW

MICHNA-NOWAK, Krysia Danuta; da of Sqdn Ldr Wladyslaw Jan Nowak (d 1982), and Henrietta Nowak (d 1994); *b* 18 March 1948; *Educ* Notre Dame GS Sheffield, Henry Hartland GS Workshop, Ealing Coll London (BA), Garnett Coll London (PGCE); *Career* artist; Br Cncl lectr Poznan Univ Poland 1977 and 1978, lectr American Inst of Foreign Study in Paris, Florence, Rome, Amsterdam and Munich 1979–82; held pt/t positions at: The Drian Galleries London 1973, The Grabowski Gallery London 1973, Inst of Contemporary Art London 1973, 359 Gallery Nottingham 1974 (asst), Sheffield City Art Galleries 1975–87 (art educn offr); freelance interior designer for hospitals and clinics 1991–; arts advsr Northern Gen Hosp 1992–; Sheffield City Cncl: memb Cleansing Dept Keep Br Tidy 1985–87, Dept of Land and Planning A City Centre for People 1985–87, arts designer and advsr Arundel Gate Scheme 1985–87, public subway mural Hollywood Parade Sheffield; voluntary work: League of Friends N Gen Hosp 1979–82, sec Polish Med Aid Appeal Sheffield 1981, organiser charity fashion show for Ethiopia Graves Art Gallery Sheffield 1985, organiser designer fashion show Wentworth House 1987; pres Worksop Soc of Artists 1976, tstee York Arts Space Assoc 1986–87, fndr memb Anglo-Polish Soc Sheffield 1986–87, memb Open Learning Ctee BBC Radio Sheffield 1986–87, interior designer specialising in hosps and clinics 1990–96, arts advsr Northern Gen Hosp Sheffield 1991–93, memb Assoc of Polish Artists 1996, memb Printmakers Cncl; numerous paintings in public and private collections; *Solo Exhibitions* Drian Galleries, Waterloo Gallery, Stoke on Trent, Nottingham Playhouse, Crucible Theatre Sheffield, Philip Francis Gallery Sheffield, Worksop Library, Univ of Sheffield, New Work (Café des Arts Hampstead) 1997, Golfe de St Donat France 1999, Dragon International London 1999, Nice Airport 2000, Air Gallery London 2000, Letchworth Museum 2000, Seven Springs Gallery Ashwell 2000, Thomas Plunkett Fine Art St Albans 2000, St Raphael Gallery London 2001, Courtyard Arts Hertford 2001, The Old Laundry Gallery Wimpole Estate Cambs 2002, Hitchin Museum Herts 2002, Affordable Art Fair Battersea 2002, Boxfield Gallery Stevenage 2003, Letchworth Museum 2004, The Chapel Gallery Riseley 2005, Open Studios 2005, Letchworth Arts Centre Letchworth 2007; two person show Posk Gallery London 1997, two person show Hitchin Museum and Art Gallery 2007 (with Anne Songhurst); *Group Exhibitions* Seven Springs Gallery Ashwell 1999, Heiffer Gallery London 1999, Luton Museum 2000, Concourse Gallery Barbican 2000, The Place Arts Centre Letchworth 2000, Broughton House Gallery Cambridge 2000, Cambridge Contemporary Art Gallery 2000, McNeill Fine Art Gallery Radlett Herts 2000, Mayfest Exhibition Grosvenor Square London 2000, Thomas Plunkett Fine Art (with Richard Sorrel and Robin Hazlewood) 2002, Kaleidoscope Gallery London 2004, Marston Vale 2004, Sheridan Russell Gallery London 2005, Knowl Piece Gallery 2006 and 2007; *Public Collections* hertford County Public Collection, Hitchin Museum; *Awards* shortlisted for Woman of the Midlands 1987, winner Dulux 2nd Nat Prize for Community Arts Project 1987, John West Memorial Award 2000; *Publications* Poland (contrib), The Planet of the Towers (illustrator, 1982); contrib article The Artist magazine 2004; *Recreations* painting, cooking, travelling, design (interior design and graphics), mural painting; *Style—* Miss Krysia D Michna-Nowak; ✉ 12 Knowl Piece, Wilbury Way, Hitchin, Hertforshire; Mandelieu, 309 Wedon Way, Bygrave, Baldock, Hertfordshire SG7 5DX (tel 01462 893983, fax 01462 896836)

MICKLETHWAIT, (Richard) John; s of Richard Miles Micklethwait, DL, of Preston, and Jane Evelyn, *née* Codrington; *b* 11 August 1962; *Educ* Ampleforth, Magdalen Coll Oxford; *m* 1992, Fevronia Read; 3 s (Richard Thomas b 10 April 1997, Guy William, Edward Hugh (twins) b 6 Feb 1999); *Career* The Economist: finance writer 1987–89, media corr 1989–90, Los Angeles corr 1990–93, business ed 1993–97, New York bureau chief 1997–99, United States ed 2000–06, ed 2006–; *Publications* with Adrian Wooldridge: The Witch Doctors (1996), A Future Perfect (2000), The Company (2003), The Right Nation (2004); *Style—* John Micklethwait, Esq; ✉ The Economist, 25 St James' Street, London SW1A 1HG (tel 020 7830 7000)

MIDDLEBURGH, Rabbi Dr Charles Hadley; s of Hyman Middleburgh (d 1987), and Elizabeth Middleburgh; *b* 2 October 1956; *Educ* Brighton Coll, UCL (BA, PhD), Leo Baeck Coll (ordained 1986); *m* 11 May 1984, Gill, *née* Blyth; *Career* lay reader Brighton & Hove Progressive Synagogue 1975–77, min Kingston Lib Synagogue 1977–83, rabbi Harrow & Wembley Progressive Synagogue 1983–97, exec dir Union of Lib and Progressive Synagogues 1997–2002, rabbi Dublin Jewish Progressive Congregation 2002–, rabbi Progressive Jewish Forum Copenhagen 2003–05, rabbi Cardiff Reform Synagogue 2005–; lectr in bible, Aramaic and practical rabbinics Leo Baeck Coll 1985–2001, lectr in Jewish-Christian relations Irish Sch of Ecumenics TCD 2002–, lectr in Aramaic rabbinic literature and medieval bible commentaries Leo Baeck Coll 2003–; occasional broadcaster RTE, Radio Eireann, BBC Radio 4 and World Serv; FZS, FRSA; *Publications* Union of Liberal and Progressive Synagogues Daily, Sabbath and Festival Prayer Book (assoc ed, 1995), Union of Liberal and Progressive Synagogues High Holy Day Prayer Book (co-ed, 2003), Tefillot Ve-Tachanunim: Prayers in Times of Illness and Death (co-ed, 2006); *Recreations* photography, birdwatching, hill walking, cycling, theatre, ballet, needlepoint, studying animals, horse riding; *Style—* Rabbi Dr Charles H Middleburgh; ✉ c/o Leo Baeck College, 80 East End Road, London N3 2SY (tel 020 8349 5600, e-mail charles@middleburgh.co.uk)

MIDDLETON, Edward Bernard; s of Bernard Middleton (d 1987), and Bettie Mabel, *née* Knight (d 2005); *b* 5 July 1948; *Educ* Aldenham; *m* 22 May 1971, Rosemary Spence, da of Maj Denis Frederick Spence Brown, MC, TD (d 1995), of Lincoln; 3 s (Nicholas b 1976, Simon b 1978, Hugo b 1982); *Career* sr Pannell Fitzpatrick & Co London 1971–73, mangr Pannell Bellhouse Mwangi & Co Nairobi 1973–75, ptnr PKF 1979– (mangr 1975–79), dir PKF consultancy services 1996–; seconded to DTI as dir/under sec Industrial Devpt Unit 1984–86; memb Cncl The British Assoc of Hospitality Accountants 1997–; hon treas Hospitality Action 1992–; memb Worshipful Co of Spectaclemakers 2005; FCA 1972; *Recreations* sailing, photography; *Clubs* Reform; *Style—* Edward Middleton, Esq; ✉ Barrans, Bury Green, Little Hadham, Ware, Hertfordshire SG11 2ES (tel 01279 658684); PKF (UK) LLP, Farringdon Place, 20 Farringdon Road, London EC1M 3AP (tel 020 7065 0000, fax 020 7065 0650, e-mail edward.middleton@uk.pkf.com)

MIDDLETON, 12 Baron (GB 1711); Sir (Digby) Michael Godfrey John Willoughby; 13 Bt (E 1677), MC (1945), DL (N Yorks); s of 11 Baron Middleton, KG (d 1970); *b* 1 May 1921; *Educ* Eton, Trinity Coll Cambridge; *m* 14 Oct 1947, Janet Marshall-Cornwall, JP (fndr chm Lloyd's External Names Assoc), da of Gen Sir James Handyside Marshall-Cornwall, KCB, CBE, DSO, MC; 3 s; *Heir* s, Hon Michael Willoughby; *Career* 2 Lt Coldstream Gds 1940, Temp Maj served in NW Europe 1944–45 (despatches and Croix de Guerre); land agent 1951; JP E Riding Yorks 1958; cncllr: E Riding 1964–74, N Yorks 1974–77; memb Yorks and Humberside Econ Planning Cncl 1968–79; pres: Yorks Agric Soc 1976, CLA 1981–83; Hon Col 2 Bn Yorks (TAVR) Volunteers 1976–88; memb: Nature Conservancy Cncl 1986–89, House of Lords Select Ctee on Euro Community; chm Food and Agriculture Sub-Ctee 1989–96; *Clubs* Boodle's; *Style—* The Rt Hon the Lord Middleton, MC, DL; ✉ Birdsall House, Birdsall, Malton, North Yorkshire YO17 9NR (tel 01944 768202)

MIDDLETON, (David) Miles; CBE (1992); s of Harry Middleton (d 1990), of Corbridge, Northumberland, and Dorothy Hannah, *née* Nisbet; *b* 15 June 1938; *Educ* Sedbergh; *m* 1, 1962 (m dis 1979), Mary Elizabeth Gale; 1 da (Georgina Claire b 9 Sept 1964), 1 s (Nicholas Miles Heathcliffe b 9 March 1966); m 2, 1980, Elizabeth Mary (Bobbie) Lancaster; 2 step s (Charles Antony Lancaster, Benjamin Michael Lancaster), 2 step da (Victoria Mary Lancaster (Mrs Darrall), Katherine Elizabeth Lancaster (Mrs Oliver)); *Career* chartered accountant; Coopers & Lybrand: mangr Zurich 1964–93; in practice Middleton Associates 1993–; pres Northern Soc of CAs 1986–87 (vice-pres 1984, dep pres 1985–86); chm Northern Enterprise Limited; Teesside C of C: vice-pres 1982, pres 1984–85; pres Assoc of Br C of C 1990–92 (dep chm 1988–90), chm Rural Devpt Cmmn 1998–99 (cmmr 1993–99), dir North West Chambers of Commerce Assoc 1994–97; chm Hadrian Wall Tourism Partnership, chm Tees Valley Learning and Skills Cncl 2000–04; memb: Bd NE RDA 1999–2001, Countryside Agency 1999; chm: Tynedale Housing Assoc 2003–, Penny Plain Ltd 2004–; FCA 1972 (ACA 1962); *Recreations* sailing, golf, beekeeping, opera, ballet; *Clubs* Northern Counties (Newcastle upon Tyne), Hexham Golf, Bassenthwaite Sailing, Corbridge Leek; *Style—* Miles Middleton, Esq, CBE; ✉ Ingleboro, St Helen's Lane, Corbridge, Northumberland NE45 5JD (tel 01434 633545, fax 01434 632330)

MIDDLETON, Rear Adm (John) Patrick Windsor; CB (1992); s of Cdr John Henry Dudley Middleton (d 1989), of Wimbledon, and Norna Mary Tessimond, *née* Hitchings (d 1996); *b* 15 March 1938; *Educ* Cheltenham Coll, RNC Dartmouth, RN Engrg Coll Manadon Plymouth; *m* 31 March 1962, Jane Rodwell, da of Leslie Stephen Gibbs (d 1978), of Letchmore Heath, Herts; 1 s (Toby b 1963), 1 da (Isobel b 1965); *Career* entered RN 1954; served HMS: Lion 1962, Ambush 1965, Warspite 1969; Cdr 1973, NDC 1976, HMS Blake 1977, Capt 1981; CSO(E): Flag Officer Submarines 1981, Falklands 1983; Capt naval

M

drafting 1984, dir in serv submarines 1987, Rear Adm 1989, CSO(E) Fleet 1989, CSO (Support) Fleet 1991, ret 1992; chm Conservation Direct 1993–94, sec Royal Cmmn for the Exhibition of 1851 1995–2002; chm CARE 1998–2007 (govr 1993–2007); Liveryman Worshipful Co of Armourers and Brasiers 1971 (memb Ct of Assts 1995, Master 2001–02); MIMechE 1965, MIMarE 1965, FIMgt 1989; *Style*— Rear Adm Patrick Middleton, CB; ✉ Manora, Chilmark, Wiltshire SP3 5AH (tel 01722 716231, e-mail mimanora@aol.com)

MIDDLETON, Peter; *Educ* Friends Sch Great Ayton, Nottingham Coll of Art; *Career* cinematographer; with BBC Film Dept Ealing Studios 1965–67, freelance dir of photography 1967–; work on TV and film incl: Jubilee, The Tempest, Body and Soul, Devil's Advocate, Call Red, Holding On, Painted Lady, Wuthering Heights, Cold Feet, The Alchemist, Trust, Extremely Dangerous, Last Christmas, Other People's Children, The Hunt, Whistleblower, The Jury, Foyle's War, Promoted to Glory, Henry VIII; BAFTA nominations: South Bank Show, Holding On 1996, Cold Feet 1997; memb BSC 1994; *Recreations* photography; *Style*— Peter Middleton, Esq, BSC; ✉ c/o PFD, Drury House, 34–43 Russell Street, London WC2B 5HA (tel 020 7344 1000)

MIDDLETON, Sir Peter Edward; GCB (1989, KCB 1984); *b* 2 April 1934; *Educ* Sheffield City GS, Univ of Sheffield (BA), Univ of Bristol; *m* 1, 1964, Valerie Ann, *née* Lindup (d 1987); 1 s (d 1991), 1 da; m 2, 20 Jan 1990, Constance Jean Owen, *née* Close; 2 step s, 1 step da; *Career* served RAPC 1958–60; HM Treasy: sr info offr 1962, princ 1964, asst dir Centre for Admin Studies 1967–69, private sec to Chllr of the Exchequer 1969–72, press sec 1972–75, head Monetary Policy Div 1975, under sec 1976–80, dep sec 1980–83, perm sec 1983–91; Barclays Bank plc: dep chm 1991–98, chief exec 1998–99, chm 1999–2004; chm Barclays Capital (formerly BZW) 1991–98 (non-exec dir 1998–89); chm: Camelot Gp 2004–, Reyniers & Co 2004–, Marsh Ltd 2005–, Three Delta 2006–; UK chm Marsh & McLennan Cos 2007– (memb Advsy Bd 2004–); non-exec dir: Bass plc 1992–2001, CGU plc (following merger of General Accident and Commercial Union) 1992–98, United Utilities plc 1994– (dep-chm 1994–99 and 2002–, chm 1999–2001), Mobile TeleSystems OJSC; memb Advsy Bd Financial Dynamics 2004–, Fenchurch Advsy Ptnrs 2005–; chm CEDR 2004–; pres Br Bankers' Assoc 2004–06; visiting fell Nuffield Coll Oxford 1981–89; dir: English Chamber Orch and Music Soc 1992–2001, Inst of Contemporary Br History 2001–04 (chm 1992–2001), Int Monetary Conf 2001–02; chm: Sheffield Urban Regeneration Co Ltd 'Sheffield One' 2000–06, Creative Sheffield 2006–; govr: London Business Sch 1984–90, Ditchley Fndn 1985, NIESR 1991–2006; memb: Cncl Manchester Business Sch 1985–92, Cncl Sheffield Univ 1991– (chllr 1999–), Exec Ctee Centre for Economic Policy Research 1991–, UK Advsy Bd Nat Economic Research Assoc 1991–, Int Advsy Panel Monetary Authy of Singapore 2002–05; Cdre Civil Serv Sailing Assoc 1984–91; *Recreations* hill walking, music, outdoor sports; *Clubs* Reform; *Style*— Sir Peter Middleton, GCB

MIDDLETON, Stanley; s of Thomas Middleton (d 1936), and Elizabeth Ann, *née* Burdett; *b* 1 August 1919; *Educ* Bulwell St Mary's, Highbury Sch Bulwell, High Pavement Sch Nottingham, Univ of London (BA), Univ of Nottingham (MEd); *m* 22 Dec 1951, Margaret Shirley Charnley, da of Herbert Welch (d 1971), and Winifred Vera, *née* Loop, of Ewell, Surrey; 2 da (Penelope b 1956, Sarah b 1958); *Career* WWII RA and RAEC; head of English High Pavement Coll Nottingham 1958–81, Judith E Wilson visiting fell Emmanuel Coll Cambridge 1982–83; jt winner Booker Prize for Fiction (Holiday) 1974; Hon MA Univ of Nottingham 1975, Hon MUniv Open Univ 1995, Hon DLitt De Montfort Univ 1998, Hon DLitt Nottingham Trent Univ 1998; fell PEN, FRSL 2000; *Books* A Short Answer (1958), Harris's Requiem (1960), A Serious Woman (1961), The Just Exchange (1962), Two's Company (1963), Him They Compelled (1964), Terms of Reference (1966), The Golden Evening (1968), Wages of Virtue (1969), Apple of the Eye (1970), Brazen Prison (1971), Cold Gradations (1972), A Man Made of Smoke (1973), Holiday (1974), Distractions (1975), Still Waters (1976), Ends and Means (1977), Two Brothers (1978), In A Strange Land (1979), The Other Side (1980), Blind Understanding (1982), Entry into Jerusalem (1983), The Daysman (1984), Valley of Decision (1985), An After Dinner's Sleep (1986), After A Fashion (1987), Recovery (1988), Vacant Places (1989), Changes and Chances (1990), Beginning to End (1991), A Place to Stand (1992), Married Past Redemption (1993), Catalysts (1994), Toward the Sea (1995), Live and Learn (1996), Brief Hours (1997), Against the Dark (1998), Necessary Ends (1999), Small Change (2000), Love in the Provinces (2002), Brief Garlands (2004), Sterner Stuff (2005), Mother's Boy (2006); *Recreations* music, listening, painting; *Style*— Stanley Middleton, Esq; ✉ 42 Caledon Road, Sherwood, Nottingham NG5 2NG (tel 0115 962 3085)

MIDGLEY, (David) William (Bill); s of Norman Midgley (d 1995), of Huddersfield, and Margaret, *née* Alderson (d 1986); *b* 1 February 1942; *Educ* Huddersfield Coll; *m* 1, 19 Dec 1964, Anne Christine (d 1976), da of Charles Foreman, of Huddersfield; 1 s (Edward William b 1967), 1 da (Rachel Sarah b 1969); m 2, 10 June 1977, Ada Margaret, da of John Banks; 1 da (Louise Isobel b 1980); *Career* chief exec Newcastle Building Society 1986–98 (latterly exec vice-chm); pres Br C of C 2004–, past pres NE C of C (Trade & Industry); pres Northern Constitutional Club; chm: Century Radio Ltd, Norcare Ltd, Your Homes Newcastle Ltd; memb Lord Chllr's Advsy Ctee; vice-pres Marie Curie Cancer Care, chm Mgmnt Ctee Salvation Army; dir N Tyneside Coll; tstee Theatre Royal Tst; FCIB, FRSA; *Recreations* golf; *Style*— Bill Midgley, Esq; ✉ 17 Beaumont Drive, Whitley Bay, Tyne & Wear NE25 9UT (tel 0191 297 0401, fax 0191 251 1525); Office: Portland House, Portman Road, Newcastle upon Tyne, NE2 1AQ (tel 0191 261 2228, fax 0191 261 2260, e-mail dw@midgley1.fsnet.co.uk)

MIDHA, Dr Arun Daniel; JP (Cardiff 1994); s of Rajendra Nath Midha (d 1983), of Campbellpur, India, and Olive Marion, *née* Wroe; *b* 24 April 1964; *Educ* Gowerton Comp Sch, Univ of Wales Swansea (BSc Econ, PhD), Exeter Coll Oxford (Dip), Univ of Wales Cardiff (MBA); *m* Aug 1991, Susan Margaret, da of John Rees Williams, of Caeo; 1 da (Sara Gwenan b 9 June 1997), 1 s (Elis Daniel b 30 May 2000); *Career* grad recruit Lloyds Bank plc 1988–89, commerce and industry advsr Health Promotion Authy for Wales 1990–94, prog mangr Public Health Med Specialist Registrar Trg Scheme Wales 1994–2000, dir of strategy and research Sch of Postgrad Med and Dental Educn Cardiff Univ 2000–; non-exec dir Welsh Servs NHS Ambulance Tst 2000–02; GMC: lay memb 2000–, memb Educn Ctee 2001–, President's Advsy Ctee 2001–, tstee 2002–, treas 2003–, chair Resources Ctee 2003–; chair Renal Advsy Bd Wales 2006–; contrib to numerous jls; memb: Bd Welsh Language Bd 2000–, Broadcasting Cncl for Wales 2006–07, Audience Cncl for Wales 2007–; referee Welsh Rugby Union 1992–2003; Hon MFPHM 1998; *Recreations* rugby, music, theatre; *Style*— Dr Arun Midha; ✉ Nanmor, 92 Heol Isaf, Radyr, Cardiff CF15 8EA (tel 029 2084 4880, fax 029 2075 4966, e-mail midhaad@cardiff.ac.uk)

MIDLANE, Stephen Peter; s of Peter Alan Midlane (d 1986), of Pinner, Middx, and Muriel, *née* Young (d 2001); *b* 7 October 1951; *Educ* UCS London, Univ of Exeter, Univ of Birmingham; *Partner* Doris Settle; 1 s (Jonathan b 1980), 1 da (Becky b 1984); *Career* exec dir Polka Theatre for Children 1977–; memb Bd: Quicksilver Theatre for Children 1989–99, Yellow Earth Theatre 2004–; memb Action for Children's Arts; *Style*— Stephen Midlane, Esq; ✉ Polka Theatre for Children, 240 The Broadway, Wimbledon, London SW19 1SB (tel 020 8545 8323, fax 020 8545 8365, e-mail stephen@polkatheatre.com)

MIDLETON, 12 Viscount (I 1717); Alan Henry Brodrick; also Baron Brodrick of Midleton (I 1715) and Baron Brodrick of Peper Harow (GB 1796); the full designation of the Viscountcy is Midleton of Midleton; s of Alan Rupert Brodrick (d 1972), and Alice Elizabeth, *née* Roberts; suc uncle 11 Viscount 1988; *b* 4 August 1949; *Educ* St Edmund's Canterbury; *m* 1, 1978 (m dis 2002), Julia Helen, da of Michael Pitt, of Lias Cottage, Compton Dundon, Somerton, Somerset; 2 s (Hon Ashley Rupert b 1980, Hon William Michael b 1982), 1 da (Hon Charlotte Helen b 1983); m 2, Maureen Susan, da of Joseph Sime, of Bessacarr, Doncaster; *Heir* s, Hon Ashley Brodrick; *Career* horologist; Keeper of Horology Gershom Parkington Collection Bury St Edmunds 1986–2002; conslt Vost's Auctioneers 1997–2000; memb Cncl and chm Br Horological Inst Museum Tst 1993–; chm Br Horological Inst 1998–2001 (vice-chm 1997–98); curator and librarian Br Horological Inst 2001–; memb Museum Ctee Nat Assoc of Watch and Clock Collectors of America 1997; FBHI; *Recreations* bicycling, walking; *Clubs* Athenaeum; *Style*— The Rt Hon the Viscount Midleton

MIDWINTER, Dr Eric Clare; OBE (1992); *b* 11 February 1932; *Educ* St Catharine's Coll Cambridge (BA, MA), Univ of Liverpool (MEd), Univ of York (DPhil); *Career* social historian and writer; academic appts 1955–68, dir of priority educnl project Liverpool 1968–75, head of Public Affrs Unit Nat Consumer Cncl London 1975–80, dir Centre for Policy on Ageing London 1980–91; chm: Advsy Centre for Educn 1976–80, London Regnl Passenger Ctee 1977–96, Health and Social Welfare Bd Open Univ 1983–90, Community Educn Devpt Centre 1994–2001; memb: Prince of Wales' Advsy Ctee on Disability 1990–95, Advsy Ctee on Telecommunications for Disabled and Elderly People (DIEL) 1990–96; visiting prof of educn Univ of Exeter 1992–2001; pres Assoc of Cricket Statisticians and Historians 1997–2004, chm Centre for Policy on Ageing 2003–; Hon Dr Open Univ 1989; *Books* Victorian Social Reform (1968), Social Administration in Lancashire (1969), Old Liverpool (1971), Nineteenth Century Education (1970), Teaching in the Urban Community School (ed, 1972), Education for sale (1977), Make 'em Laugh: Famous Comedians and Their World (1979), W G Grace: His Life and Times (1981), The Wage of Retirement: the Case for a New Pensions Policy (1985), Caring for Cash: the Issue of Private Domiciliary Care (1986), Fair Game: Myth and Reality in Sport (1986), The Lost Seasons: Cricket in Wartime (1987), New Design for Old (1988), Red Roses Crest the Caps (1989), Creating Chances (1990), The Old Order (1990), Out of Focus (1991), Brylcreem Summer: the 1947 Cricket Season (1991), The British Gas Report on Attitudes to Ageing (1991), The Illustrated History of County Cricket (1992), Lifelines (1993), The History of Social Welfare in Britain (1994), First Knock; Cricket's Opening Pairs (1994), Surrey CCC: 150 Years - A Celebration (1995), Darling Old Oval: Surrey Cricket at the Oval (1995), State Educator: The Life and Enduring Influence of W E Forster (1995), Pensioned Off: Retirement and Income Examined (1997), The Billy Bunter Syndrome: Or Why Britain Failed to Create a Relevant Secondary School System (1998), Yesterdays: The Way We Were (1998), From Meadowland to Multinational: a Review of Cricket's Social History (2000), Yesterdays: Our Finest Hours (2001), Best-remembered: a Hundred Stars of Yesteryear (2001), Quill on Willow: Cricket in Literature (2001), As One Stage Door Closes - John Wade, Jobbing Magician (2002), Novel Approaches: a guide to the popular classic novel (2003), 500 Beacons: the USA Story (2004), Red Shirts and Roses: The Story of the Two Old Traffords (2006), Out on Pleasure Bent: Collective Leisure (2006), An Outline of Political Thought and Action (2006), The People's Jesters: Twentieth Century British Comedians (2006), Lord Salisbury (2007); *Recreations* writing, sport, theatre; *Clubs* MCC, Lancashire CCC, Savage; *Style*— Dr Eric Midwinter, OBE; ✉ Savage Club, 1 Whitehall Place, London SW14 2HD (tel 020 7930 8118)

MIERS, Richenda Francis Capel; da of Rear Adm Peter Douglas Herbert Raymond Pelly, CB, DSO (d 1980), of Alderney, CI, and Gwenllian Violet, *née* Edwardes (d 1987); *b* 27 January 1939; *Educ* Ipswich HS, Loreto Convent Gibraltar, Ipswich Tech Coll; *m* 3 April 1959, Col Douglas Alexander Nigel Capel Miers, s of Col Ronald Douglas Martin Capel Miers, DSO (d 1974), of Ross-Shire, Scotland; 3 da (Mary b 1961, Victoria b 1964, Henrietta b 1966), 1 s (Lucian b 1962); *Career* author; *Books* as Richenda Francis: Told From An Island (1979); as Frances Ramsay: Carve It In Doves (1984), Mine Is The Heart (1984), No Other Desire (1984); as Richenda Miers: Cumbria (1986), Cadogan Guide to Scotland's Highlands and Islands (1994, 1998, 2000, 2002 and 2006); contrib as Francis Capel: Cadogan Guide To Thailand, Burma (1988); as Richenda Francis: The Blood Is Strong (1989 and 1994); Cadogan Guide To Scotland (1987, 1989, 1991, 1994, 1998, 2000, 2002 and 2006); *Recreations* reading, writing, sailing, walking, gardening; *Style*— Mrs Douglas Miers; ✉ Lettoch, North Kessock, by Inverness IV1 3XB

MIFLIN, Dr Benjamin John (Ben); s of Stanley Benjamin Miflin (d 1971), of Lower Slaughter, Glos, and Kathleen Noel, *née* Davies (d 1999); *b* 7 January 1939; *Educ* Univ of Nottingham (BSc), Univ of Illinois (MS), Univ of London (PhD); *m* 3 Oct 1964, Hilary Frances, da of Wilfred Edward Newman; 3 da (Gail Kathryn b 12 Feb 1967, Clare Josephine b 2 Aug 1968, Johanna Frances b 8 May 1971); *Career* lectr in plant sciences Univ of Newcastle 1965–73, head Molecular Sciences Div Rothamsted Experimental Station 1983–85 (head Biochemistry Dept 1973–85), head of res devpt Ciba-Geigy Seeds 1985–93, dir Inst of Arable Crops Research 1994–99, chm Crop Evaluation Ltd 2000–; visiting prof of plant sciences Univ of Nottingham 1981–85 and 1994–99, Lawes Tst sr fell 1999–; corresponding memb American Soc of Plant Physiologists; ed of several scientific books and author of over 100 scientific papers; *Recreations* photography, theatre, gardening; *Style*— Dr Ben Miflin; ✉ The Studio, 4 Dean Court Road, Rottingdean, Sussex BN2 7DF (e-mail ben.milfin@bbsrc.ac.uk)

MIFSUD, Jean-Pierre; s of Ernest Xavier Mifsud (d 1954), of Port Fouad, Egypt, and Eugenie, *née* Grima; *b* 26 February 1944; *Educ* Coll des Frères St-Marie, Ealing GS; *m* 1, 1966, Carole, *née* Fearnhead (decd); 1 da (Amelia b 1 July 1974), 1 s (Dominic Xavier b 17 June 1977); m 2, 1983, Janet Elizabeth, da of Ernest Aubrey Dedman; 1 step da (Sarah Kathleen b 3 Jan 1970), 1 step s (Ross James b 21 Aug 1975); *Career* hotelier; hotel conslt and inspr hotels and restaurants AA until 1983 (joined 1970), prop: The Lake Country House and Spa Llangammarch Wells Powys 1983– (Johansens Restaurant of the Year 2005), Dinham Hall Hotel Ludlow 1994–, Northcote Manor Hotel Burrington Devon 2002–; Johansens Restaurant of the Year 1991–92, AA 3 Red Stars and 2 rosettes for food 1995, RAC Gold Ribbon, Good Hotel Guide Welsh Country House of the Year (Cêsar Award for Lake Country House Hotel) 1993, Pride of Britain Hotel; memb: Advsy Ctee Br Tourist Authy 1988–92; *Recreations* antique collecting, architectural renovation; *Style*— Jean-Pierre Mifsud, Esq; ✉ Lake Country House Hotel and Spa, Llangammarch Wells, Powys LD4 4BS (tel 01591 620202, fax 01591 620457, e-mail info@lakecountryhouse.co.uk, website www.lakecountryhouse.co.uk)

MIGDAL, Clive Stephen; s of Jack Migdal (d 1977), of East London, South Africa, and Anne, *née* Cohen (d 1999); *b* 19 February 1948; *Educ* Selborne Coll East London, Univ of Cape Town and Groote Schuur Hosp Cape Town (MB ChB, MD, DO); *Career* registrar in pathology Groote Schuur Hosp 1973 (house physician then house surgn 1972), SHO in ophthalmology Bart's 1974, registrar in ophthalmology Groote Schuur Hosp 1975–77, resident surgical offr (registrar and sr registrar) Moorfield Eye Hosp London 1977–80, sr registrar in ophthalmology Bart's 1980–89, clincial research fell Moorfields Eye Hosp 1981–94, conslt ophthalmic surgn The Western Eye Hosp and St Mary's Hosps 1989–; memb Examinations Ctee Royal Coll of Ophthalmologists; sec European Glaucoma Soc; Gold Medal for Best Scientific Paper Int Congress of Ophthalmology Singapore 1990, Lewis Rudin Prize for Glaucoma Research 1995, Trantos Medal 2005; memb: American Acad of Ophthalmology 1986, Euro Glaucoma Soc 1986, Assoc of Research and Vision in Ophthalmology 1992; BMA 1992; FRCS 1979, FRCOphth 1989 (memb Cncl); *Books* Duane's Clinical Ophthalmology (contrib chapter, 1992); *Recreations* swimming, schooling polo ponies, classical music; *Style*— Clive Migdal, Esq; ✉ The Western Eye Hospital, Marylebone Road, London NW1 5YE (tel 020 7886 3258, fax 020 7886 3259);

149 Harley Street, London W1N 2DE (tel 020 7935 4444, fax 020 7486 3782, e-mail cmigdal@compuserve.com)

MILANI, Roy; *Educ* Lycee Français de Londres, Univ of Swansea (BSc); *Career* cameraman Univ of London TV 1973–74, studio mangr BBC Radio 1974–76, vision mixer BBC Network TV 1978–82, sr prodr BBC Children's TV 1995–98 (asst prodr 1982–87, prodr 1986–95), head of factual progs and ed Newsround CBBC 1998–2001, head news and factual progs CBBC 2001–; *Awards* RTS Award 1994 and 1996, BAFTA Award 1994, 1996, 2000 and 2002, Prix Danube 1995, Prix Jeunesse (twice) 1996, Race in the Media Award 1996 and 2001, Broadcast Award 2002; *Style*— Roy Milani, Esq; ✉ Room E111, BBC Television Centre, Wood Lane, London W12 7RJ (tel 020 8576 3118)

MILAŠINOVIĆ, HE Dr Tanja; da of Rade Milašinović, and Radosava, *née* Ranilović; *b* 28 June 1962, Kozarska Dubica, Bosnia and Herzegovina; *Educ* Mining, Geology and Petroleum Faculty Zagreb Croatia (MSc), Faculty of Mechanical Engrg Ljubliana and Ludwig Maximilians Univ Munich (PhD); *Career* asst Mining Geology and Petroleum Faculty Zagreb 1986–87, researcher and asst Ludwig Maximilians Univ Munich 1987–91, asst then asst prof for thermodynamics and thermotechnique Faculties of Agric and Forestry Univ of Belgrade 1992–98, asst min Miny of Foreign Economic Affrs Repub of Srpska Govt Bosnia and Herzegovina 1998–2001, min-cnsllr and charge d'affaires Mission of Bosnia and Herzegovina to the EU 2001–05, ambass to Ct of St James's 2005–; numerous professional publications on energy and thermodynamics for sci jls; *Recreations* tennis; *Clubs* Athenaeum; *Style*— HE Dr Tanja Milasinovic; ✉ Embassy of Bosnia and Herzegovina, 5–7 Lexham Gardens, London W8 5JJ (tel 020 7373 0867, fax 020 7373 0871, e-mail tanja.milasinovic@mfa.gov.ba)

MILBANK, Sir Anthony Frederick; 5 Bt (UK 1882), of Well, Co York, and of Hart, Co Durham; s of Maj Sir Mark Vane Milbank, 4 Bt, KCVO, MC (d 1984), and his 2 w, Hon Verena Aileen Maxwell (d 1995), da of 11 Baron Farnham; *b* 16 August 1939; *Educ* Eton; *m* 1970, Belinda Beatrice, yr da of Brig Adrian Clements Gore, DSO, of Horton Priory, Sellinge, Kent; 1 da (Alexina Victoria b 1971), 2 s (Edward Mark Somerset b 1973, Toby Adrian Jameson b 1977); *Heir* s, Edward Milbank; *Career* farmer and landowner; chm: Northern Uplands Moorland Regeneration Project 1999–2002; pres Yorkshire Wildlife Tst 2000–03; former: chm Moorland Assoc 1987–2001, High Sheriff Co Durham, memb RSPB Cncl, memb CLA Executive Ctee, memb Nature Conservancy Cncl Ctee for England; *Recreations* all sports: field, individual and winter; *Style*— Sir Anthony Milbank, Bt; ✉ Barningham Park, Richmond, North Yorkshire DL11 7DW (tel 01833 621202, fax 01833 621298, e-mail milbank@teesdaleonline.co.uk)

MILBORNE-SWINNERTON-PILKINGTON, Sir Thomas Henry; 14 Bt (NS 1635); o s of Sir Arthur William Milborne-Swinnerton-Pilkington, 13 Bt (d 1952), and Elizabeth Mary (d 1997), er da of late Col John Fenwick Harrison, JP, DL, of King's Walden Bury, Hitchin; *b* 10 March 1934; *Educ* Eton; *m* 1961, Susan, eld da of Norman Stewart Rushton Adamson, of Durban, South Africa; 2 da (Sarah b 1962, Joanna b 1967), 1 s (Richard b 1964); *Heir* s, Richard Milborne-Swinnerton-Pilkington; *Career* chm: Charente Ltd 1977–2003, dep chm Cluff Mining Ltd 1996–2003; *Clubs* White's, City of London; *Style*— Sir Thomas Pilkington, Bt; ✉ King's Walden Bury, Hitchin, Hertfordshire

MILBORROW, Ruan Leslie; s of Robert Leslie Milborrow (d 1986), of Wanstead, London, and Elizabeth Edith, *née* Cook (d 2006); *b* 11 July 1958; *Educ* Forest Sch, RAC Cirencester (MRAC, DipFM); *Career* sr art dir Yellowhammer Advertising Ltd 1984–91, creative dir Harari Page Ltd 1992–98, art dir Travis Sully Harari Ltd 1998–2001, creative ptnr cdp-travissully Ltd 2001–07, creative ptnr mr.h Ltd 2007–; memb Devpt Bd Forest Sch 2005; Freeman City of London 1984; MIPA 1989; *Recreations* art, music, literature, theatre, association football; *Style*— Ruan Milborrow, Esq; ✉ 10 Edwards College, South Cerney, Cirencester, Gloucestershire GL7 5TR

MILBURN, Rt Hon Alan; PC (1998), MP; s of Evelyn Metcalfe; *b* 27 January 1958; *Educ* John Marlay Sch, Stokesley Comp Sch, Lancaster Univ (BA), Univ of Newcastle upon Tyne; *Partner* Ruth Briel; 2 s; *Career* co-ordinator Trade Union Studies Information Unit Newcastle upon Tyne 1984–90, sr business devpt offr N Tyneside Cncl 1990–92, MP (Lab) Darlington 1992–; shadow health spokesman 1995–96, shadow treasy spokesman 1996–97, min of state Dept of Health 1997–98, chief sec to Treasy 1998–99, sec of state for Health 1999–2003, Chllr of the Duchy of Lancaster (memb Cabinet) 2004–05; chm PLP Treasy Dept Ctee 1992–95, memb Public Accounts Ctee 1994–95; chm Newcastle Central Constituency Lab Pty 1988–90, memb Exec Northern Region Lab Party 1990–92; co-ordinator Sunderland Shipyards Campaign 1988–89, pres NE Regn MSF 1990–92; *Recreations* cricket, football, music, cinema; *Style*— The Rt Hon Alan Milburn, MP; ✉ House of Commons, London SW1A 0AA

MILBURN, Anthony; s of Lawrence Anderson Milburn (d 1958), of Halifax, and Constance, *née* Laskey (d 1985); *b* 3 August 1942; *Educ* Rastrick GS, Univ of Bradford (BTech), Univ of Birmingham (MSc); *m* 4 June 1983, Julia Margaret, da of Maj Charles Pierson Weeden (d 1996); 1 da (Catherine b 1986), 1 s (Richard b 1988); *Career* civil engr 1958–71, trg mangr National Water Cncl 1972–80, exec dir Int Assoc on Water Quality 1981–99, DG Int Water Assoc 1999–2002, chm and ceo Ambourne Environments 2002–, dir Dukeville Securities Ltd, fndr IWA Publishing Ltd; advsr to: UNESCO, World Water Assessment Prog; memb Int Water Acad 1999, hon memb Int Water Assoc 2002; prodr Kingston Talking Newspaper for the Blind; Freeman City of London, memb Ct of Assts Worshipful Co of Water Conservators; Hon DEng Tech Univ of Istanbul 2001; MInstD (Dip Co Direction); FICE, FCIWEM 1972, fell Euro Acad of Sci and Arts 2000; *Books* Water Pollution Research and Control (ed, 1985, 1987, 1989, 1991), Water Quality Management (jt ed, 1993, 1995, 1997 and 1999); *Publications* UN World Water Development Report (co-author, 2006); *Recreations* motor cycling, philosophy, amateur dramatics; *Style*— Dr Anthony Milburn; ✉ Ambourne Environments, 34 Church Meadow, Surbiton, Surrey KT6 5EW

MILBURN, Sir Anthony Rupert; 5 Bt (UK 1905), of Guyzance, Parish of Acklington, Northumberland; s of Maj Rupert Leonard Eversley Milburn (d 1974, yr s of 3 Bt), and Anne Mary, *née* Scott-Murray (d 1991); suc unc, Sir John Nigel Milburn, 4 Bt (d 1985); *b* 17 April 1947; *Educ* Eton, RAC Cirencester; *m* 1977, Olivia, yst da of Capt Thomas Noel Catlow, CBE, DL, RN (ret), of Tunstall, Lancs; 2 s (Patrick Thomas b 1980, Edward Jake b 1987), 1 da (Lucy Camilla Anne b 1982); *Heir* s, Patrick Milburn; *Career* landowner; ARICS, MRAC; *Clubs* New (Edinburgh); *Style*— Sir Anthony Milburn, Bt; ✉ Guyzance Hall, Acklington, Morpeth, Northumberland NE65 9AG (tel 01665 513047, fax 01665 513042)

MILDON, David Wallis; QC (2000); s of Arthur Mildon, and Iva, *née* Wallis; *b* 19 September 1955; *Educ* Emmanuel Coll Cambridge (MA, LLB); *m* 13 Aug 1983, Lesley Mary, *née* Richardson; 1 da (Anne b 16 Dec 1986), 1 s (Peter b 25 Feb 1990); *Career* called to the Bar: Middle Temple 1980, Antigua and Barbuda 1990; practising barr, currently memb Essex Court Chambers; memb Ctee London Common Law and Commercial Bar Assoc 1999–; tstee Father Thames Tst; *Publications* Agreements to Agree (2005), Property in Commingled Gas (2006); *Recreations* music, sailing; *Clubs* Royal Solent Yacht; *Style*— David Mildon, Esq, QC; ✉ Essex Court Chambers, 24 Lincoln's Inn Fields, London WC2A 3ED (tel 020 7813 8000, fax 020 7813 8080, e-mail dmildon@essexcourt.net)

MILDRED, Prof Mark; s of John Mildred (d 1996), of Usk, Gwent, and Eileen Smith (d 1969); *b* 16 September 1948; *Educ* Lancing, Clare Coll Cambridge (exhibitioner, MA); *m* 19 Oct 1974, Sarah Ruth, da of Harold Christopher Rackham; 2 s (Joe b 13 July 1976, Tom b 16 May 1979); *Career* articled clerk B M Birnberg & Co 1973–75; ptnr: Messrs Mildred and Beaumont 1978–86, Pannone & Partners and Pannone Napier 1986–93, Evans Butler Wade 1993–95; prof of litigation Nottingham Law Sch 1995–, conslt in complex litigation matters 1995–; memb Legal Advsy Panel Nat Consumer Cncl 1987–2000, pt/t legal memb Family Health Services Appeal Authy 2002–; gen ed Civil Procedure Reports 2000–; non-exec dir Wandsworth Primary Care Tst 2003– (vice-chair 2005–); memb: Law Soc 1975 (memb Consumer Law Ctee), Soc of Labour Lawyers 1975, Assoc of Personal Injury Lawyers 1990 (co-ordinator Multi-Party Actions Special Interest Gp); tstee Trinity Hospice 2001–, chair SW London Local Improvement Finance Tst 2005–; *Books* 1989 Group Actions - Learning From Opren (Nat Consumer Cncl, 1989), Butterworths Product Liability and Safety Encyclopaedia (1992), Butterworths Clinical Negligence (contrib chapter on Class Actions, 3 edns), Product Liability: Law and Insurance (gen ed, 1994), Responsibility for Drug Induced Injury (1998), Product Liability in Comparative Context (contrib, 2005); *Recreations* singing, cooking, walking, racquet games; *Clubs* Scorpions; *Style*— Prof Mark Mildred; ✉ 67 Sisters Avenue, London SW11 5SW (tel and fax 020 7228 1321, e-mail mild0000@aol.com)

MILES, Adrian Spencer; s of Herbert Beal Miles (d 1952), of London, and Marjorie Phyllis, *née* Harris; *b* 16 November 1947; *Educ* Rutlish Sch, QMC London (LLB); *m* 28 June 1975, Hilary, da of William Nelson (d 1980); 1 s (Jonathan Francis b 20 May 1968), 2 da (Julie Clare b 11 Oct 1978, Anna Kirsty b 7 July 1980); *Career* admitted slr 1972, Boodle Hatfield 1972–74, Norton Rose 1974–76, ptnr Denton Wilde Sapte (formerly Wilde Sapte) 1976– (head Banking Dept); memb Law Soc; *Recreations* chess, tennis, music; *Style*— Adrian Miles, Esq; ✉ Denton Wilde Sapte, 5 Chancery Lane, Clifford's Inn, London EC4A 1BU

MILES, Alastair Paul; s of John Charles Miles, of Harpenden, Herts, and Judith, *née* Baker; *b* 11 July 1961; *Educ* St Marylebone GS London, Guildhall Sch of Music and Drama (Performer's Dip Flute), Nat Opera Studio; *m* Alison Jane, *née* Parry; 2 s (Jonathan Henry Alastair b 31 Oct 1991, Gregory Charles Frederick b 27 July 1995), 1 da (Felicity Miranda Jane b 11 Dec 1997); *Career* int operatic bass; given concert performances with numerous major orchs incl: LSO, London Philharmonic, Philharmonia, BBC Symphony, BBC Scottish, RPO, CBSO, Bournemouth Symphony and Bournemouth Sinfonietta, Ensemble d'Orchestre de Paris, Baltimore Symphony, NY Philharmonic, Atlanta Symphony, English Baroque Soloists, Concentus Musicus, London Classical Players, English Concert, Israel Philharmonic, Royal Scottish Nat Orch, Vienna Philharmonic, Boston Symphony; over 60 recordings for numerous labels incl Operatic Arias for Chandos; *Performances* operatic roles incl: debut as Truelove in The Rake's Progress (with Opera 80) 1985, Pietro in Simon Boccanegra (Glyndebourne Touring Opera) 1986–87, Colline in La Bohème (Vancouver Opera 1986–87, WNO 1988, ENO 1989, Opera de Lyon 1991), Poacher in The Cunning Little Vixen (ENO) 1988, Raimondo in Lucia di Lammermoor (WNO) 1989, Speaker of the Temple in Die Zauberflöte (Glyndebourne Festival and Touring) 1990, Giorgio in I Puritani (Deutsche Oper Berlin) 1991, Da Silva in Ernani (WNO) 1992, Lord Sydney in Viaggio a Rheims (Covent Garden) 1992, Lorenzo in Capuleti e i Montecchi (Covent Garden) 1992, Don Fernando in Fidelio (Covent Garden) 1992, Giorgio in I Puritani (San Francisco) 1993, Figaro in Lenozze di Figaro (Netherlands Opera) 1993, Sparafucile in Rigoletto (Covent Garden) 1994, Alidoro in La Cenerentola (Covent Garden), Colline in La Bohème (Covent Garden) 1995, Fiesco in Simon Boccanegra (Verdi Festival Covent Garden) 1995, Giorgio in I Puritani (Vienna State Opera) 1995, Zaccaria in Nabucco (WNO), Mephistopheles in Faust (WNO) 1995–96, Basilio in Barber of Seville (San Francisco), Sparafucile in Rigoletto (Metropolitan NY), Fiesco in Simon Boccanegra (WNO), Giorgio in I Puritani (Metropolitan, NY) 1997, Il Prefetto in Linda di Chamounix (Vienna State Opera) 1997, Fiesco in Simon Boccanegra (Glyndebourne Festival) 1998, Philip II in Don Carlos (Opera North) 1998, Raimondo in Lucia di Lammermoor (Metropolitan, NY) 1998, title role in Mefistofele (ENO), Cardinal Brogni in La Juive (Vienna State Opera) 1999, Zaccaria in Nabucco (ENO) 2000, Philip II in Don Carlos (Madrid) 2001, Rodolfo in La Sonnambula (Covent Garden) 2002, Banquo in Macbeth (Covent Garden) 2002, Zaccania and Silva in Ernami (Vienna State Opera) 2002; *Awards* Decca/Kathleen Ferrier Prize 1986, Esso/Glyndebourne Touring Opera Award 1986, John Christie Award 1987; *Recreations* golf, cooking, flute playing, reading, decorative painting; *Clubs* Brocket Hall Golf, Old Philologians; *Style*— Alastair Miles, Esq; ✉ c/o Jenny Rose, AOR Management, Westwood, Lorraine Park, Harrow Weald, Middlesex HA3 6BX (tel 020 8954 7646, fax 020 8420 7499, e-mail aormanagementuk@compuserve.com, website www.alistairmiles.com)

MILES, Brian; CBE (1994), RD; s of Terence Clifford Miles (d 1945), and Muriel Irene, *née* Terry (d 1992); *b* 23 February 1937; *Educ* Reeds Sch, HMS Conway Cadet Sch; *m* 10 Oct 1964, (Elizabeth) Anne, *née* Scott; 1 s (Martin b 30 Aug 1966), 2 da (Amanda b 29 May 1968, Sara b 10 April 1970); *Career* P&O Shipping Co: cadet 1954–57, deck offr 1958–64, master mariner (FG) 1964; RNLI: inspr of lifeboats 1964–73, staff appts 1974–81, dep dir 1982–87, dir 1988–98; hon memb Parkstone Rotary Club; chm: Friends of Dolphin Tst 1989–, Poole Arts Tst 1996–2003; chm The Fishermen's Mission 2005– (memb Cncl 1999–2001, dep chm 2001–05); Freeman City of London 1993, Yr Bro Trinity House 1994, memb Hon Co of Master Mariners 1994; FNI, CIMgt 1994; Cross Cdr Order of the Lion of Finland 1997; *Recreations* country pursuits, walking, reading, music, theatre; *Style*— Brian Miles, Esq, CBE, RD; ✉ 8 Longfield Drive, West Parley, Ferndown, Dorset BH22 8TY (tel 01202 571739, e-mail brianandanne@lineone.net)

MILES, Prof David; *b* 1959; *Educ* Univ of Oxford (BA, MPhil), Univ of London (PhD); *Career* lectr in economics UC Oxford 1981–83, economist Bank of England 1983–89, research fell LSE 1988–89, reader in financial economics Univ of London 1989–93, economic advsr Bank of England 1993–94, chief UK economist Merrill Lynch 1994–96, prof of finance Imperial Coll London 1996–2004 (visiting prof of financial economics 2004–), md and chief UK economist Morgan Stanley 2004–; non-exec dir FSA 2004–; author The Miles Report on the UK mortgage market HM Treasy 2004; ed: Fiscal Studies, World Economics; *Books* Housing, Financial Markets and the Wider Economy, Macroeconomics: Understanding the Wealth of Nations (co-author); *Style*— Prof David Miles; ✉ Economic Research Department, Morgan Stanley, 25 Cabot Square, Canary Wharf, London E14 4QA

MILES, James Archibald Robertson; s of Hamish Alexander Drummond Miles, of Edinburgh, and Jean Marie, *née* Smits; *b* 8 September 1961; *Educ* King Edward's Sch Birmingham, New Coll Oxford (BA Chinese); *m* 1 Aug 1992, Catherine Ruth, da of Trenwith John Wallis Sampson; 1 s (Alistair John Robertson b 10 June 1996), 2 da (Rachel Pamela Winifred b 15 Jan 1998, Kirsten Lily Wallis b 6 Nov 2000); *Career* business reporter South China Morning Post Hong Kong 1984; United Press International (UPI): Hong Kong reporter 1984–85, S Asia corr 1985–86, Beijing corr 1986–87; Beijing corr BBC Radio and Television 1987–94, Burton R Benjamin fell in broadcast journalism Michigan Univ 1994–95, Hong Kong corr BBC World Service 1995–97, sr Chinese affrs analyst BBC News 1997–2000, ed Strategic Comments and res fell for Asia The Int Inst for Strategic Studies 2000–01, Beijing corr The Economist 2001–; Reporter of the Year Sony Radio Awards 1990, One World Broadcasting Award 1990; *Publications* The Legacy of Tiananmen, China in Disarray (Univ of Michigan Press, 1996); *Recreations* shooting, walking; *Style*— James Miles, Esq; ✉ The Economist, 25 St James's Street, London SW1A 1HG (tel 020 7830 7000, e-mail jarmiles@usa.net)

MILES, Jeremy Dylan; s of Hugh Miles (d 2005), and Pat Miles (d 2006); *b* 24 May 1955, Bromsgrove, Worcs; *Educ* Gordonstoun, Westminster; *m* 14 Feb 1981, Karina; 1 da (Tess b 7 Jan 1989); *Career* Abbott Mead Vickers BBDO: trainee account exec 1980–85, bd dir (Sainsbury's) 1985–84, bd dir (The Economist) 1985–99, bd dir (BT) 1994–99, bd dir (BT

M

Global) 1995–99, vice-chm 1998–99; co-fndr and chm Miles Calcraft Briginshaw Duffy 1999–; memb: Marketing Soc 1985, Marketing Gp of GB 2001, Thirty Club 2005; *Awards* 9 Gold Campaign Awards, 24 Silver Campaign Awards, 8 D&AD Silver Pencils, Gold British Television Award, Gold IPA Effectiveness Award; *Recreations* travel, reading, ballet, watching sport, theatre and film; *Clubs* MCC, Reform, Harry's Bar, Annabel's, George; *Style*— Jeremy Miles, Esq; ✉ Miles Calcraft Briginshaw Duffy, 15 Rathbone Street, London W1T 1NB (tel 020 7073 6900, e-mail milesj@mcbd.co.uk)

MILES, Prof John Richard; s of Thomas William Miles (d 1988), and Hilda Mary, *née* Davis (d 1994); *b* 22 June 1944; *m* (m dis); *Career* designer and tutor; colourist designer and conslt Fidelis Furnishing Fabrics (later amalgamated with Tootals) 1969–74, work shown in prototype Exhibition at Design Council 1970; designer of fashion furnishings and household textiles for worldwide market 1969–; clients incl: Courtaulds, Heal's, Liberty's, Christian Dior, Yves Saint Laurent; set up own studio: Calver & Pound Designs 1973–77, Peppermint Prints 1977–81; design dir of home furnishings and apparel fabrics Courtaulds plc 1986–87 (design dir of home furnishings 1985–86); Next Interior: design mangr 1987, design and buying mangr 1987–88; set up own studio Miles Whiston & Wright 1989–96, fndr John Miles Partnership 1996–2002; CNAA: chm Fashion and Textile Panel 1984–87 (memb 1978–81), memb Ctee for Art and Design 1984–87 and 1988–, specialist advsr to Ctee for Art and Design 1987; memb: Textile Ctee Design Centre Selection 1985–88 (memb Knitwear Ctee 1984–86), Selection Panel for Young Designers into Industry RSA 1987–89, Advsy Panel BFC 1994–97; sr lectr i/c of textiles St Martin's Sch of Art 1974–75, head of Fashion Dept and Textiles Course leader Brighton Poly 1979–85 prof of textiles and fashion RCA 1989–97, dir of product mktg Dollfus Mieg and Cie France 1997–2001, prof of design Univ of Southampton 2001–02, currently prof of fashion and textiles Bath Spa UC; co-fndr and conslt studio Claire and Lyn 1992; memb Industrial Lead Body for Art and Design 1990–96, memb Res Assessment Panel Univ Funding Cncl 1992–; pt/t and visiting lectr; memb numerous academic ctees Brighton Polytechnic and RCA; internal and external assessor; memb Assoc of Heads of Degree Courses for Fashion and Textiles 1979–85; Hon Dr Univ of Southampton 1998; *Recreations* gardening, cooking, theatre, films, reading, music; *Style*— Prof John Miles; ✉ 12 Penderyn Way, Carleton Road, London N7 0EW (tel 020 7609 0836)

MILES, Keith Charles; OBE (1999); s of Leslie Maurice Miles, and Doris Ellen Wyard Miles; *b* 28 November 1941; *Educ* Owens Sch, Ljubijana Univ; *m* 20 Dec 1969, Slava, da of Jože Blenkus (d 1977), and Alojzija Blenkus; 1 s (Andrew Karel Scott b 1973 d 2002), 1 da (Jane Helena Louise b 1977); *Career* chartered accountant; dir of fin and ops Cable Authy 1985–88, dir of fin and admin Inst of Econ Affrs 1988–90, special advsr Putnam Hayes & Barlett 1989–90, co sec and gp fin dir Etam plc 1990–95; dir: Slovenia Trade and Investment Corporation Ltd 1996–2002, Bay Trading (Epcoscan Ltd) 1996–99, Lexecon Ltd 2000–05; only English memb Economic Advsy Cncl of the Cabinet of Repub of Slovenia 1990, hon sec-gen UK Representative Office Repub of Slovenia 1991–92, econ advsr in London Bank of Slovenia 1992–, rep Ljubljana Stock Exchange in UK 1995–, memb Economic Devpt Cncl Repub of Slovenia 2005–; chm British-Slovene Soc 1993–; memb Review Body for Nursing Staff, Midwives, Health Visitors and Professions Allied to Nursing 1996–99; cncllr Chiltern DC 2003–06; Liveryman Worshipful Co of Glass Sellers; FRSA; *Publications* various articles on accountancy, free market economics and Central & Eastern Europe; reg contrib Finance (Slovene fin newspaper); *Recreations* skiing, reading, swimming; *Style*— Keith Miles, Esq, OBE; ✉ 19 Elmtree Green, Great Missenden, Buckinghamshire HP16 9AF (tel 0870 410 0088, e-mail kcmengland@gmail.com)

MILES, (Henry) Michael Pearson; OBE (1989); s of Brig H G P Miles (d 1966), of London, and Margaret, *née* Mounsey (d 1974); *b* 19 April 1936; *Educ* Wellington; *m* 25 Oct 1967, Carol Jane, da of Harold Berg (d 1955); 2 s (Henry James Pearson b 1969, Mark Edward Pearson b 1975), 1 da (Sasha Jane Pearson b 1971); *Career* Nat Serv cmmnd Duke of Wellington's Regt 1955–57; md John Swire and Sons (Japan) Ltd 1973–76; dir: Swire Pacific Ltd 1978–, Hongkong and Shanghai Banking Corporation 1984–88, John Swire & Sons Ltd 1988–; former chm: John Swire & Sons (Hong Kong) Ltd, Swire Pacific Ltd, Cathay Pacific Airways Ltd, Hong Kong Tourist Assoc; chm: Johnson Matthey plc 1998–2006 (dir 1990–2006), Schroders plc 2003–; dep chm Barings plc; also dir: BP plc 1994–2006, Portals plc, Thomas Cook Group, Fleming Far Eastern Investment Tst, Sedgwick Lloyd's Underwriting Agents, BICC 1996–2002; memb: Bd Navy Army and Air Force Inst, Int Advsy Bd Creditanstalt Vienna, Anglo-Taiwan Trade Ctee, China-Britain Trade Group (vice-pres 1996–); govr Wellington Coll 1990–2005; *Recreations* golf, tennis, shooting; *Clubs* Royal and Ancient, Berkshire Golf, Queen's, White's; *Style*— Michael Miles, Esq, OBE

MILES, Nicholas Charles James; s of Kenneth Norman Miles, and Audrey Mary, *née* Rhodes; *b* 23 October 1958; *Educ* Tonbridge, Corpus Christi Coll Cambridge (MA); *m* 12 May 1990, Suzanne Katharine, *née* Chauveau; 3 da (Lucy Florence b 1 Sept 1991, Katharine Rose b 8 April 1993, Sophy Arabella b 26 March 1996); *Career* dir: BMP Business Ltd 1985–87, Lowe Bell Financial Ltd 1987–92; chief exec Financial Dynamics Ltd 1992–2001, chm Business Communications Int Gp 2001–02, fndr M: Communications 2002; performed in Death in the Aisles, Nightcap Cambridge Footlights Revues 1979; *Recreations* gym, shooting, cigars; *Clubs* Annabel's, Hurlingham, RAC; *Style*— Nicholas Miles, Esq; ✉ e-mail miles@mcomgroup.com

MILES, Peter Thomas; s of Thomas Harry Miles (d 1968); *b* 1 August 1939; *Educ* Bromsgrove Sch; *m* 18 June 1971, Gail, da of Trevor Davies; 2 c (Juliet Elizabeth b 24 Sept 1972, Edward Thomas b 10 Feb 1975); *Career* chartered accountant; ptnr: Russell Durie Kerr Watson & Co 1968, Spicer & Pegler (following merger), Touche Ross 1990–96 (following merger, now Deloitte); dir: Delcam plc; FCA; *Recreations* fly fishing, golf, gardening; *Style*— Peter T Miles, Esq; ✉ The Old Barn, Cakebole, Chaddesley Corbett, Worcestershire DY10 4RF (e-mail peterthomasmiles@aol.com)

MILES, Robert; QC; s of David and Marion Miles; *b* 29 November 1962; *Educ* ChCh Oxford (MA, BCL); *m* 1999, Lisabel, *née* Macdonald; *Career* called to the Bar Lincoln's Inn; *Style*— Robert Miles, Esq, QC; ✉ 4 Stone Buildings, Lincoln's Inn, London WC2A 3XT (tel 020 7242 5524)

MILES, Roger Tremayne; s of Lt Cdr Peter Tremayne Miles, RN (d 1995), of Maidenhead, Berks, and Christine, *née* Perks; *b* 9 March 1962; *Educ* Tonbridge, Trinity Coll Oxford (exhibitioner, MA); *m* 28 May 1990, Deirdra Moynihan; 1 s, 2 da; *Career* bd dir OTG (Oxford Theatre Gp) Productions Ltd 1981–83, articled Price Waterhouse 1984, bd dir Charles Barker Ltd 1990–92, bd dir Georgeson and Company Ltd 1992–95, head of communications British Bankers' Assoc 1996–99, bd dir BBA Enterprises Ltd 1997–2000, bd dir The Entertainment Team Rides Ltd 1998–99, ptnr Regester Larkin - Reputation Risk Mgmnt 1999–2001, princ Repute 2002–04, risk communications advsr Civil Serv 2004–; visiting lectr: ICC Commercial Crime Bureau 1999–, Cabinet Office Emergency Planning Coll 2000–, Fin Servs Forum 2001–, Univ of London 2003–04; CMIPR 1991, MInstD 1994, FRSA 2001; *Recreations* fatherhood, music making, novels, new technologies; *Style*— Roger Miles, Esq; ✉ King's Centre for Risk Management, King's College, 138–142 Strand, London WC2R 1HH (e-mail r@carltonhouse.org)

MILES, Stephen Antony David; s of late Antony Richard Miles, of Chorleywood, Herts, and Marjorie, *née* Allwork; *b* 21 June 1947; *Educ* Marist Brothers Coll Inanda Johannesburg, Univ of the Witwatersrand (MB BCh); *Career* various trg posts in Johannesburg, sr registrar accident and emergency Bart's and UCH 1979–82, conslt Bart's and Homerton Hosp 1982–95, conslt Royal London and Homerton Hosps 1995–2005, assoc dean (specialities) The London Deanery 2001–04, conslt Homerton Univ Hosp 2005–, assoc dean N Central London 2005–; past pres A&E Section RSM; med advsr to Bd London Ambulance Serv 1990–97, hon sec Br Assoc for A&E Med 1990–96; memb Bd Intercollegiate Faculty of A&E Med 1993–97; Freeman City of London 1984; memb: BMA 1980, RSM 1987; FRCSEd 1975; *Recreations* music, ballet, theatre; *Style*— Stephen Miles, Esq; ✉ London Deanery, 20 Guilford Street, London WC1N 1DZ (tel 020 7692 3385)

MILES, Sir William Napier Maurice; 6 Bt (UK 1859), of Leigh Court, Somersetshire; s of Lt-Col Sir Charles William Miles, 5 Bt, OBE (d 1966); *b* 19 October 1913; *Educ* Stowe, Jesus Coll Cambridge; *m* 1946, Pamela, da of late Capt Michael Dillon; 2 da (Catherine Anne Elizabeth (Mrs Peter C Beloe) b 1947, Lorraine (Mrs Martin H Sessions-Hodge) b 1950), 1 s (Philip John b 1953); *Heir* s, Philip Miles; *Career* chartered architect (ret); ARIBA; *Style*— Sir William Miles, Bt; ✉ Old Rectory House, Walton-in-Gordano, Clevedon BS21 7AW (tel 01275 873365)

MILFORD, 4 Baron (UK 1939); Sir Guy Wogan Philipps; 4 Bt (UK 1919); QC (2002); s of 3 Baron Milford (d 1999), and Hon Mary (Mollie) Makins (now Viscountess Norwich), da of 1 Baron Sherfield; *b* 25 July 1961; *Educ* Eton (King's scholar), Magdalen Coll Oxford (Roberts-Gawen scholar, MA); *m* 1996, Alice Sherwood; 2 s (Hon Archie Sherwood b 12 March 1997, Hon Ben Aroya b 26 May 2000); *Heir* s, Hon Archie Philipps; *Career* called to the Bar Inner Temple 1986; *Style*— The Rt Hon the Lord Milford, QC; ✉ 68 Westbourne Park Road, London W2 5PJ (tel 020 7229 1844, e-mail lordmilford@hotmail.com)

MILFORD, His Hon Judge John Tillman; QC (1989); s of Dr Roy Douglas Milford (d 1982), of Strathtay, Perthshire, and Essie, *née* Rhind (d 1972); *b* 4 February 1946; *Educ* Hurstpierpoint Coll, Univ of Exeter (LLB); *m* 1975, Mary Alice, da of Dr Edmund Anthony Spriggs (d 1989), of Wylam, Northumberland; 3 da (Alice (Mrs Charles Bubear) b 1977, Sarah b 1979, Emily b 1981); *Career* called to the Bar Inner Temple 1969 (bencher 1998); practising Newcastle upon Tyne 1970–2002, recorder of the Crown Court 1985–2002, head of Trinity Chambers Newcastle upon Tyne 1986–99, dep judge of the High Court 1994–2002, circuit judge (NE Circuit) 2002–, liaison judge to Northumberland and N Tyneside justices 2003–; chm Northumbria Area Judicial Forum 2004–; co-chm for S Northumberland BFSS 1996–98, chm River Tyne Fishing Festival 1997, vice-chm Newcastle & District Beagles 1998–2005, regnl chm NE England Countryside Alliance 1999–2002 (co-chm S Northumberland 1998–99), chm Bywell Show 1999 and 2000, chm of tstees Get Hooked on Fishing Charitable Tst 2004–; *Recreations* fishing, shooting, stalking, gardening; *Clubs* Northern Counties (Newcastle upon Tyne, chm 2003–07), Durham County; *Style*— His Hon Judge Milford, QC; ✉ The Law Courts, The Quayside, Newcastle upon Tyne NE1 3LA

MILFORD HAVEN, 4 Marquess of (UK 1917); George Ivar Louis Mountbatten; also Earl of Medina and Viscount Alderney (both UK 1917); s of 3 Marquess of Milford Haven, OBE, DSC (d 1970, himself gs of HSH Prince Louis of Battenberg, who relinquished, at the King's request, the style and title of Serene Highness and Prince of Battenberg, instead assuming the surname of Mountbatten by Royal Licence 1917); gn of late Earl Mountbatten of Burma and, through his paternal grandmother (Nada), ggggs of Emperor Nicholas I of Russia; *b* 6 June 1961; *Educ* Gordonstoun; *m* 1, 8 March 1989 (m dis 1996), Sarah Georgina, er da of George Alfred Walker, fndr and former chief exec Brent Walker Group plc, and former w of Andreas L Antoniou; 1 da (Lady Tatiana Helen Georgia b 16 April 1990), 1 s (Harry David Louis, Earl of Medina b 19 Oct 1991); m 2, 20 Aug 1997, Mrs Clare Wentworth-Stanley, da of late Anthony N Steel; *Heir* s, Earl of Medina; *Style*— The Most Hon the Marquess of Milford Haven

MILIBAND, David; PC (2005), MP; s of Ralph Miliband (d 1994), and Marion *née* Kozak; bro of Edward Miliband, MP, *qv*; *b* 15 July 1965; *Educ* Haverstock Comp Sch, CCC Oxford (BA), MIT (MSc); *m* 1998, Louise Shackelton; *Career* Parly offr Nat Cncl for Voluntary Orgns 1987–88, research fell Inst of Public Policy Research 1989–94, head of policy Office of the Ldr of the Opposition 1994–97, head PM's Policy Unit 1997–2001; MP (Lab) South Shields 2001–; min for schools DfES 2002–04, min of state Cabinet Office 2004–05, minister of communities and local govt 2005–06, sec of state for environment, food and rural affrs 2006–07, sec of state FCO 2007–; sec Social Justice Cmmn 1992–94; *Publications* Reinventing the Left (ed, 1994), Paying for Inequality (co-ed, 1994); *Clubs* Whiteleas Social, Cleadon, South Shields Recreation, South Shields FC; *Style*— The Rt Hon David Miliband, MP; ✉ House of Commons, London SW1A 0AA

MILIBAND, Rt Hon Edward (Ed); PC (2007), MP; bro of Rt Hon David Miliband, MP, *qv*; *b* 24 December 1969, London; *Educ* Univ of Oxford, LSE; *Career* HM Treasy: special advsr to the Chllr 1997, took sabbatical to teach at Harvard Univ 2002–04, chm Cncl of Economic Advsrs 2004; MP (Lab) Doncaster N 2005–; min for the third sector Cabinet Office 2006–07, min for the Cabinet Office and for social exclusion and Chllr of the Duchy of Lancaster 2007–; memb TGWU; *Style*— The Rt Hon Ed Miliband, MP; ✉ House of Commons, London SW1A 0AA

MILL, Ian Alexander; QC (1999); s of Ronald MacLauchlan Mill (d 1984), and Thelma Anita, *née* Boliston; *b* 9 April 1958; *Educ* Epsom Coll, Univ of Cambridge (MA); *m* 13 June 1987, (Mary) Emma, da of Roger and Marian Clayden, of Los Gatos, CA; *Career* called to the Bar Middle Temple 1981; commercial barr specialising in entertainment and sports law 1982–; *Recreations* cricket, golf, good food and wine, travel; *Clubs* MCC; *Style*— Ian Mill, Esq, QC; ✉ Blackstone Chambers, Blackstone House, Temple, London EC4Y 9BW (tel 020 7583 1770, fax 020 7822 7350)

MILL, Peter Stuart; s of Donald Norman Mill (d 1981), of London, and Heather Mary, *née* Lavelle; *b* 21 June 1957; *Educ* Claremont HS Kenton, Watford Coll of Technol (DipAD); *m* 4 Oct 1987, Susan Ann, da of Dennis Austin Goode; 4 da (Helen Michelle b 23 Aug 1985, Hannah Catherine b 28 Dec 1988, Katie Heather b 15 June 1995, Rosie May Jennifer b 31 Oct 1998); *Career* jr copywriter BBDO Advertising London 1975–76; copywriter: Fletcher Shelton Delaney 1976–78, Hall Advertising 1978–84; fndr ptnr and exec creative dir The Leith Agency 1984–, sr ptnr new business 1995–, dir of new media 2000–2001; md Leith Interactive 2001–, founding ptnr and dir 60 Watt Ltd 2002–; Silver Campaign Press Award, Campaign Poster Award, EPICA Award, Cannes Advtg Film Festival Silver Lion, Br TV Advtg Silver Award, Scottish Advtg Awards annually 1988–93, Roses Awards annually 1988–94; memb D&AD 1983–; *Style*— Peter Mill, Esq; ✉ Beechmount, Kingscavil, Linlithgow, W Lothian EH49 6NA (tel 0131 220 8231, fax 0131 625 8268, e-mail pete@60w.co.uk)

MILLA, Prof Peter John; s of John Milla (d 1961), of Sandown, IOW, and Betty Violet, *née* Barton; *b* 4 August 1941; *Educ* Whitgift Sch, Bart's Med Coll London (MB BS), Chelsea Coll London (MSc); *m* Sept 1969, (Pamela) Jane, da of John Davis, of Bedhampton, Hants; 1 s (Richard b 1972), 1 da (Elizabeth b 1974); *Career* Inst of Child Health Univ of London: sr lectr in paediatric gastroenterology 1983–94, reader 1994–98, prof of paediatric gastroenterology and nutrition 1998–; Marvin L Dixon visiting prof Harvard Univ 1997–98, visiting prof Univ of Tampere and Univ of Leuven 1997–; consulting ed Pediatric Res; memb Editorial Bd: Gut, Archives of Disease of Childhood, Jl of Paediatric Gastroenterology and Nutrition, Jl of Neurogastroenterology and Motility; advsr Wellcome Tst, advsr National Inst Health USA; pres European Soc of Paediatric Gastroenterology and Nutrition 2001–04 (sec 1994–97); treas United European Gastroenterology Fedn (chm 2003–04), chm European Bd of Paediatrics; memb: British Soc of Gastroenterology, American Gastroenterology Assoc, British Soc of Paediatric Gastroenterology and Nutrition; FRCP 1985, FRCPCH 1996; *Books* Harries' Paediatric

Gastroenterology (ed with D R P Muller, 1988), Disorders of Gastrointestinal Motility (1988); *Recreations* sailing, motoring, gardening, model engineering; *Style*— Prof Peter J Milla; ✉ Gastroenterology Unit, Institute of Child Health, University of London, 30 Guilford Street, London WC1N 1EH (tel 020 7405 9200 ext 0347/5307, fax 020 7404 6181, e-mail p.milla@ich.ucl.ac.uk)

MILLAR, *see also:* Hoyer Millar

MILLAR, Anthony Bruce (Tony); s of James Desmond Millar (d 1965), and Josephine Georgina, *née* Brice; *b* 5 October 1941; *Educ* Haileybury and ISC; *m* 3 July 1964, Judith Anne, da of Capt John Edward Jester (d 1984), of Drayton, Hants; 2 da (Cassilda Anne b 1966, Katrina Mary b 1967); *Career* asst to gp mgmnt accountant and gp treas Viyella International Federation Ltd 1964–67; United Tport Overseas Ltd Nairobi 1967–70: chief accountant to subsidiary, gp internal auditor for E Africa, PA to chief agent, dep gp fin controller London 1970–72; conslt Fairfield Property Co 1975–77 (fin dir 1972–75), md Provincial Laundries Ltd 1977–81, dep chm Hawley Group Ltd 1981, hon pres The Albert Fisher Group plc 1992–2000 (chm 1982–92), chm Canadian Zinc Corporation 1994–2000; Freeman City of London, Liveryman Worshipful Company of Fruiterers 1993– (hon asst 2001–03); FCA 1974 (ACA 1964), CIMgt 1986–91; *Recreations* swimming, scuba diving, walking, bridge, travel; *Clubs* Mark's; *Style*— Tony Millar, Esq; ✉ Frensham Vale House, Lower Bourne, Farnham, Surrey GU10 3JB

MILLAR, David William; s of Brig William Semple Millar, of Camberley, Surrey, and Maureen Heather, *née* Jones; *b* 30 January 1951; *Educ* Morrison's Acad, Univ of Edinburgh (BSc); *m* 3 Sept 1977, Daniele Yolande Germaine, da of Maurice Robert Ferreyrol; 1 s (Hamish Robert b 10 June 1983), 1 da (Pascaline Myrto b 10 Aug 1988); *Career* joined J Walter Thompson 1973, dir J Walter Thompson 1985–94, md JWT Direct 1990–94, head of communications strategy British Gas plc (now BG Group plc) 1995–97, head of corp mktg BG Group plc 1997–2003; MIPA 1982, FRSA 2000; *Recreations* golf; *Clubs* Hampton Court Palace Golf; *Style*— David Millar, Esq; ✉ Transpectra, 7 Flanchford Road, London W12 9ND (tel 020 8749 2410)

MILLAR, Douglas George; CB (2007); s of George Sydie Gray Millar (d 1982), and Doris Mary, *née* Morris (d 1996); *b* 15 February 1946; *Educ* City of Norwich Sch, Univ of Bristol (BA), Univ of Reading (MA); *m* 1, 26 Aug 1967 (m dis 1986), Susan Mary, *née* Farrow; 1 da (Victoria Mary b 8 March 1972), 1 s (Timothy George b 8 Oct 1974); m 2, 23 May 1987, Jane Victoria, da of John Edgar Howard Smith; 1 s (George Oliver Howard b 20 April 1989), 1 da (Fleur Elizabeth b 26 July 1990); *Career* House of Commons: asst clerk 1968–73, sr clerk 1973–81, dep princ clerk 1981–89, clerk Def Ctee 1979–83, clerk i/c Private Membs Bills 1983–87, clerk Home Affairs Ctee 1987–89, concurrently princ clerk, clerk Fin Ctees, clerk Treasy and Civil Serv Ctee and sec Public Accounts Cmmn 1989–91, second clerk of Select Ctees 1991–94, clerk of Select Ctees 1994–97, departmental fin offr 1994–2003, princ clerk Table Office 1998–2001, clerk of Legislation 2001–02, clerk asst 2003–; jt sec Assoc of Secs Gen of Parls 1971–77, memb Study of Parl Gp (jt sec 1980–83); chm Teddington Soc 1976–78 and 1982–83; contrib to Parly jls; *Recreations* family, watching football (Norwich City), golf; *Clubs* Roehampton, Parl Golfing Soc (hon sec 1995–99); *Style*— Douglas Millar, Esq, CB; ✉ House of Commons, London SW1A 0AA

MILLAR, Prof Fergus; *b* 5 July 1935; *Educ* Edinburgh Acad, Loretto, Trinity Coll Oxford (BA), All Souls Coll Oxford (fell 1958–64, MA, DPhil, Conington Prize); *m* 1959, Susanna Friedmann; 2 s, 1 da; *Career* fell and tutor in ancient history The Queen's Coll Oxford 1964–76, prof of ancient history UCL 1976–84, fell Brasenose Coll Oxford 1984– (emeritus fell 2002–), prof of ancient history Univ of Oxford 1984–2002 (DLitt 1988), Sather prof of classical lit Univ of Calif Berkeley 2003; visiting appt Inst for Advanced Study Princeton 1968 and 1984; Br Sch at Rome: Balsdon sr fell 1983, memb Cncl 1989, vice-chm 1993, acting chm 1994–95, chm Cncl 1995–97, hon fell 2001; ed Jl of Roman Studies 1975–79; delg OUP 1989–95; pubns sec Br Acad 1997–2002; pres: Classical Assoc 1992–93, Soc for the Promotion of Roman Studies 1989–92 (chm Pubns Ctee 1980–89); foreign memb: German Archaeological Inst 1978, Bavarian Acad 1987, Finnish Acad of Science and Letters 1989, Russian Acad 1999, American Acad of Arts and Sciences 2003; sr assoc fell at Oxford Centre for Hebrew and Jewish Studies 1990; hon fell: Trinity Coll Oxford 1992, The Queen's Coll Oxford 1999; Hon DPhil Helsinki 1994, Hon DLitt Univ of St Andrews 2004; Prize Cultori di Roma 2005, Kenyon Medal for Classical Studies Br Acad 2005; FBA 1976, FSA 1978; *Books* A Study of Cassius Dio (1964), The Roman Empire and its Neighbours (1967), E Schürer, A History of the Jewish People in the Age of Jesus Christ (175 BC-AD 135) I-III (ed, 1973–87), The Emperor in the Roman World (31 BC-AD 337) (1977, 2 edn 1992), Caesar Augustus: Seven Aspects (ed with Erich Segal 1984), The Roman Near East (31 BC-AD 337) (1993), The Crowd in Rome in the Late Republic (1998), The Roman Republic in Political Thought (2002), The Roman Republic and the Augustan Revolution (jtly, 2002), Government, Society and Culture in the Roman Empire (jtly, 2004), Romans, Greeks and Jews in the Hellenistic and Roman Near East (jtly, 2006), A Greek Roman Empire: Power and Belief under Theodosius II, 408–450 (2006); *Style*— Prof Fergus Millar, FBA; ✉ e-mail fergus.millar@bnc.ox.ac.uk

MILLAR, Peter John; s of Norman Millar (d 1992), and Maureen Nelson, *née* McMaster (d 1998); *b* 22 February 1955; *Educ* Bangor GS Co Down, Magdalen Coll Oxford (MA); *m* 1981, Jacqueline Carol, *née* Freeman; 2 s (Patrick James Arthur b 1984, Oscar Alexander b 1987); *Career* Reuters corr: Brussels 1978–79, E Berlin 1981–83, Moscow 1983–85; journalist Daily Telegraph 1985–86, Euro corr Sunday Telegraph 1986–89, Central Euro corr Sunday Times 1989–90; The European: dep ed 1990–91, managing ed 1997–98; freelance columnist, broadcaster, literary translator and writer 1991–; contrib: Sunday Times, The Times, Daily Mail, The Guardian, The FT, BBC, Sky TV, German TV ARD and Westdeutsche Rundfunk; popular fiction critic The Times 1994–, beer columnist Sainsbury's Magazine 1994–; Foreign Corr of the Year Granada TV What the Papers Say Awards 1989, commended Int Reporter Category Br Press Awards 1989; *Books* Tomorrow Belongs To Me (1991), Stealing Thunder (1999), Bleak Midwinter (2001), Schwarzer Winter, Hallowe'en Geschichten (2003), Gottes Feuer (2004), Eiserne Mauer (2005), Schwarze Madonna (2007); trans: The White Masai (trans, 2005), Return to Barsaloi (2006), Deal with the Devil (2007); *Recreations* cooking, skiing, painting; *Clubs* Groucho; *Style*— Peter Millar, Esq; ✉ Staddle Cottage, Bell's Lane, Hook Norton OX15 5LJ

MILLAR, (John) Richard; s of William Hugh Millar (d 1967), and Eileen Phyllis May Millar (d 1996); *b* 16 February 1940; *Educ* Wellington; *m* 2 Dec 1978, Rosemary Margaret, da of Alfred Thomas Hanson (d 1998); *Career* admitted slr 1963, sr ptnr Bischoff & Co 1990–93 (ptnr 1968–93), jt chm Frere Cholmeley Bischoff 1993–97 (conslt 1997–98), conslt Eversheds 1998–2006; hon slr: Br Uruguayan Soc 1973–2006; memb Law Soc Company Law Ctee 1987–2003 (chm Collective Investment Scheme Sub-Ctee 1991–2006), memb Law Soc 1963–; tstee: Fidelity UK Fndn 2000–, St Ethelburga's Centre for Reconciliation and Peace 2002–; Freeman City of London, Liveryman City of London Solicitors' Co (additional asst 2006–); *Recreations* sailing, gardening; *Clubs* City of London, Offshore Yachts Class Owners Assoc, Little Ship; *Style*— Richard Millar, Esq; ✉ c/o St Ethelburga's Centre, 78 Bishopsgate, London EC2N 4AG

MILLAR, Syd; CBE (2005, MBE 1988); *b* 23 May 1934, Ballymena, Co Antrim; *Career* chm: Int Rugby Bd (memb 1992–), Rugby World Cup; as player: Ballymena RFC 1950–72, Ulster 1957–70, Ireland 1958–70 (37 caps), British and Irish Lions 1959, 1962 and 1968 (9 tests), Barbarians 1959–70; as coach: Ballymena RFC, Ireland 1973–75 (winners Five Nations Championship 1974), British and Irish Lions 1974 (only unbeaten Lions team); as mangr: Ireland World Cup 1987, British and Irish Lions 1980; pres Ulster Branch Irish RFU (memb 1962–), pres Irish RFU (memb 1985–2004), memb Six Nations Championship Ctee 1992–, chm British and Irish Lions Ctee 1998–2001 (memb 1996–2003), chm NI Sports Cncl, memb Sports Cncl Republic of Ireland; former co dir; Freeman Borough of Ballymena; Hon Dr Univ of Ulster; *Style*— Dr Syd Millar, CBE

MILLARD, Dennis Henry; s of Henry Edward Millard, of Durban, South Africa, and Edna Elizabeth, *née* Battale; *b* 28 February 1949; *Educ* Marist Brothers Coll, Univ of Natal (capt Natal under-20 rugby XV), Univ of Cape Town (MBA, Gold Medal); *m* 22 March 1972, Paula Teresa Felicity, da of late William Coulter; 1 da (Lisa Catherine b 1972), 2 s (Sean Patrick b 1975, James Henry b 1988); *Career* audit clerk then audit sr H E Mattinson & Partners Chartered Accountants Durban 1967–73, mgmnt accountant then fin dir Hultrans Ltd Durban 1973–77, MBA 1978, gp mangr corp planning Hulletts Corporation Durban 1979–80, gp mangr corp planning then fin dir Plate Glass Group Johannesburg 1980–93, fin dir Medeva plc London 1994–96, fin dir Cookson Group plc 1996–2005; non-exec dir: ARC Int plc 2000–, Debenhams plc 2006–, Xchanging Ltd; memb Economic Advsy Cncl CBI 1998–2002; memb South African Soc of Chartered Accountants 1973; MInstD 1991; *Recreations* golf, tennis, jogging, surfing; *Clubs* Wisley Golf; *Style*— Dennis Millard, Esq

MILLARD, Prof Peter Henry; s of Edward Joseph Millard (d 1968), and Thelma Fanny, *née* Burrows; *b* 18 July 1937; *Educ* MB BS, MD, PhD; *m* 27 Jan 1962, Alys Gillian, da of Hubert Morley Thomas, of Swansea, S Wales; 3 s (Paul William b 1963, Stephen b 1964, David b 1969); *Career* conslt in geriatric med St George's Hosp 1968–79, Eleanor Peel prof of geriatric med St George's Hosp Med Sch London 1979–99 (emeritus prof 1999–); visiting prof Univ of Westminster; author of articles on bed modelling, ageing, dementia and social policy; memb: Guild of Catholic Doctors, Br Geriatric Soc (past pres),Operational Research Soc; FRCP 1978, FRIPHH 1983; *Books* The Dwarfs and Their King, Modelling Hospital Resource Use; Go with the Flow (ed with Prof S I McClean); *Recreations* walking, reading obscure books; *Style*— Prof Peter Millard; ✉ 12 Cornwall Road, Cheam, Sutton, Surrey SM2 6DR (tel 020 8642 0040, e-mail phmillard@tiscali.co.uk)

MILLER, Ambrose Michael; s of Ambrose Miller, of Penzance, Cornwall, and Margaret Dorothy, *née* Dennett; *b* 15 April 1950; *Educ* Radley, Magdalene Coll Cambridge, King's Coll London (BMus); *m* 4 April 1981, Celia Frances Sophia, da of Sir Desmond Arthur Pond (d 1986); *Career* mangr Royal Ballet Orchestra 1974–81, gen mangr Scottish Baroque Ensemble 1981–83, fndr and artistic dir European Union Chamber Orchestra 1983 (currently DG), artistic dir King's Lynn Festival 1998–; Freeman City of London, Liveryman Worshipful Co of Musicians; *Recreations* cooking, reading; *Style*— Ambrose Miller, Esq; ✉ Hollick Farm, Yarnscombe, Devon EX31 3LQ (tel 01297 858249, e-mail eucorch1@aol.com)

MILLER, Prof Andrew; CBE (1999); s of William Hamilton Miller (d 1956), and Susan, *née* Auld (d 1978); *b* 15 February 1936; *Educ* Beath HS, Univ of Edinburgh (BSc, PhD), Univ of Oxford (MA); *m* 19 June 1962, Rosemary Singleton Hannah, da of Thomas Carlyle Fyvie (d 1962); 1 da (Lisa Rosemary b 7 Aug 1966), 1 s (Stephen Andrew Fyvie b 23 Oct 1968); *Career* res fell CSIRO Div of Protein Chemistry Melbourne Aust 1962–65, staff MRC Lab for Molecular Biology Cambridge 1965–66; Univ of Oxford: lectr in molecular biophysics 1966–83, fell Wolfson Coll 1967–83; head European Molecular Biology Lab Grenoble France 1975–80; Univ of Edinburgh: asst lectr in chemistry 1960–62, prof of biochemistry 1984–94, vice-dean of med 1991–93, vice-provost of med and veterinary med 1992–93, vice-princ 1993–94; princ and vice-chllr Univ of Stirling 1994–2001 (emeritus prof 2001–); dir Scottish Knowledge plc 1997–2002, dir of research (pt/t) European Synchrotron Radiation Facility Grenoble France 1986–91, chm Int Center for Mathematical Sciences Edinburgh 2001–05; scientific advsr on UK-Wellcome-French synchrotron Wellcome Tst 1999–2000; memb: Scientific Cncl Univ of Grenoble France 1990–91, Minister of Educn Action Gp on Standards in Scottish Schools 1997–99, Scottish Science Strategy Review Gp 1999–2000, Ct of Univ of Edinburgh 1991–92, various Ctees SERC 1970–86, Univ Grants Biological Sciences Ctee 1985–88, Biological Sciences Advsy Gp Univ Funding Cncl 1989, Cncl Open Univ 2001–05, Bd Food Standards Agency 2003–05; dep chm Scot Food Advsy Ctee 2003–05; interim chief exec Cancer Research UK 2001–02; sec and treas Carnegie Tst for the Univs of Scotland 2004–; Leverhulme emeritus fell 2001–03; hon fell Wolfson Coll Oxford 1995; DUniv: Stirling 2002, Open 2007; FRSE 1986 (memb Cncl 1997–2005, gen sec 2001–05 and 2007–); *Books* Minerals in Biology (co-ed, 1984); *Recreations* reading, music, walking; *Clubs* New; *Style*— Prof Andrew Miller, CBE, FRSE; ✉ 5 Blackford Hill Grove, Edinburgh EH9 3HA

M

MILLER, Andrew; MP; s of late Ernest Miller, and Daphne Miller; *b* 23 March 1949; *Educ* Hayling Island Secdy Sch, Highbury Tech Coll, LSE; *m*; 2 s, 1 da; *Career* technician Geology Dept Portsmouth Poly, student LSE 1976–77, regnl offr MSF 1977–92, MP (Lab) Ellesmere Port and Neston 1992–; Team PPS to DTI 2001–05; chair: Regulatory Reform Select Ctee 2005–, Parly IT Ctee (PITCOM) 2005–; *Style*— Andrew Miller, Esq, MP; ✉ House of Commons, London SW1A 0AA (tel 020 7219 3580, fax 020 7219 3796, tel 0151 357 3019, fax 0151 356 8226, e-mail millera@parliament.uk, website www.andrew-miller-mp.co.uk)

MILLER, Carolyn; da of Norman Miller, and Irene, *née* Hanger (d 2005); *b* 20 November 1951, London; *Educ* Univ of Southampton (BSc), City Univ London (DipTP); *Career* various local govt posts 1973–84, sr advsr Miny of Planning Nicaragua 1984–87; Save the Children: dir Mozambique/Angola 1987–89, head Southern Africa regnl office 1989–91, dir Asia, Latin American, Caribbean and Middle East 1991–96, dir of progs 1996–2001; dir Europe, Middle East and Americas DFID 2001–05, chief exec Merlin 2005–; *Recreations* walking, cinema, theatre; *Style*— Ms Carolyn Miller; ✉ Merlin, 12th Floor, 207 Old Street, London EC1V 9NR (tel 020 7014 1610, fax 020 7014 1601, e-mail carolyn.miller@merlin.org.uk)

MILLER, Sheriff Colin Brown; s of James Miller (d 1980), of Paisley, and Isabella Millar Nicol Brown (d 1995); *b* 4 October 1946; *Educ* Paisley GS, Univ of Glasgow (LLB); *m* 28 Jan 1972, Joan Elizabeth, da of Robert Marshall Blyth; 3 s (James Douglas b 24 May 1973, Alasdair Robert b 7 July 1975, Euan Colin b 19 Jan 1977); *Career* legal apprentice Mitchells Johnston & Co Glasgow 1967–69, asst slr D S & W Semple Paisley 1969–70 (ptnr 1971), ptnr McFadyen & Semple Paisley 1971–91 (sr ptnr 1987–91); sheriff: for S Strathclyde Dumfries & Galloway at Hamilton 1991–95, at Ayr 1995–; dean Faculty of Procurators Paisley 1991; Law Soc of Scot: memb Cncl 1983–91, convener Conveyancing Ctee 1986–89, convener Judicial Procedure Ctee 1989–91, convener Rights of Audience in Supreme Courts Working Party 1990–91; NP; *Recreations* family interests, walking, Clyde steamers, railways, motor vehicles and photography; *Style*— Sheriff Colin Miller; ✉ Sheriffs' Chambers, Sheriff Court, Wellington Square, Ayr KA7 1EE (tel 01292 268474, fax 01292 292249)

MILLER, (Peter) David; s of John Morton Miller, and June Rosalind, *née* MacLellan; *b* 4 February 1966, Edinburgh; *Educ* King's Sch Canterbury, Girton Coll Cambridge; *m* 4 Dec 1999, Kate, *née* Colquhoun; 2 s (Frederick David b 12 Dec 2000, William Arthur b 8 Aug 2003); *Career* literary agent; Rogers, Coleridge & White Ltd 1990– (dir 1997–); treas Assoc of Authors' Agents 1996–98; memb Joseph Conrad Soc of the UK, contrib of articles to The Conradian; *Recreations* family, cooking, Conrad, music and mischief; *Style*— David Miller, Esq; ✉ Rogers, Coleridge & White, 20 Powis Mews, London W11 1JN (tel 020 7221 3717, fax 020 7229 9084, e-mail davidm@rcwlitagency.co.uk)

MILLER, (James) David Frederick; CBE (1997); s of Sir John Wilson Edington Miller, KBE, CMG (d 1957), and Jessie Kathleen, *née* Reed (d 1966); *b* 5 January 1935; *Educ* Edinburgh

Acad, Emmanuel Coll Cambridge (MA), LSE (Dip IPM); *m* 27 Feb 1965, Saffrey Blackett, da of Fred Oxley (d 1963); 3 s (Andrew b 21 Dec 1965, Simon b 13 Sept 1967, Matthew b 10 Aug 1970 d 1991), 1 da (Katherine b 28 June 1973); *Career* dir: J & P Coats Ltd 1972–92, Coats Patons plc 1977–92, The Wolverhampton & Dudley Breweries plc 1984–2001 (chm 1992–2001), Royal Scottish National Orchestra 1985–93, Outward Bound Tst Ltd 1985–95, Coats Viyella plc 1986–92, Scottish Enterprise Forth Valley 1994–2004 (vice-chm 1996–), Scottish Life Assurance Co 1995–2001, J & J Denholm Ltd 1997–2005; vice-chm Inst of Mgmnt 1995; govr Scottish Coll of Textiles 1987–92; chm: Scottish Vocational Educn Cncl 1992–97, Ct Univ of Stirling 1992–99, Scottish Examination Bd 1995–97, Scottish Qualifications Authy 1996–2000, Fairbridge Scotland 1998–2006, Univ of Stirling Innovation Park 2004–05, Clackmannan Coll of FE 2004–2005; cmmr Queen Victoria Sch 1987–97; dir Edinburgh Military Tattoo 1990–2000; Freeman: City of London, Worshipful Co of Needlemakers 1983; Hon DUniv: Stirling 1984, Paisley 1997; FIPM, CIMgt; *Recreations* tennis, golf, gardening; *Style*— David Miller, Esq, CBE; ✉ Blairuskin Lodge, Kinlochard, Aberfoyle, by Stirling FK8 3TP (tel and fax 01877 387346)

MILLER, David James; s of James Samuel Miller, of Lymington, Hants, and Beryl Mary, *née* Jones; *b* 28 February 1952; *Educ* Stockport GS, Emmanuel Coll Cambridge (MA); *m* 17 Sept 1988, Sophie Kay Voss, da of Flemming Christian Rathsach, of Pindon Manor, Bucks; *Career* called to the Bar Middle Temple; dep chief exec Life Assurance & Unit Tst Regulatory Orgn 1986–89, dir legal & secretarial Royal & Sun Alliance Insurance Group plc 1989–99 (legal advsr and unit tst business mangr 1977–86); memb Ind Monitoring Bd Pentonville Prison; *Recreations* travel, history of art; *Clubs* Oxford and Cambridge; *Style*— David Miller, Esq; ✉ 100 Rosebery Avenue, London EC1R 4TL (tel 020 7833 3963)

MILLER, David John; OBE; s of Air Cdre John Douglas Miller, CBE (d 1998), of Guildford, Surrey, and Sybil Francis, *née* Powell; *b* 7 March 1947; *Educ* Dragon Sch Oxford, St Edward's Sch Oxford, Jesus Coll Cambridge (MA); *m* 24 Jan 1976, Maryrose, da of John Edgar Dulley; 3 s (Fergie b 8 June 1979, Bertie b 26 March 1981, Gregory b 28 Nov 1984); *Career* Joseph Sebag stockbrokers 1969–72; Robert Fleming Group: joined 1972, special advsr to Govt of Abu Dhabi 1975–78, Jardine Fleming Hong Kong 1979–81, Jardine Fleming Tokyo 1981–88, dir Robert Fleming Holdings until 1992; md State Street Global Advisors 1992–94, chief exec Wheelock NatWest Ltd Hong Kong 1994–97, md FBG Investment Ltd 1998–; chm Connect Mortgage Gp 2005–, dir Titus Int 2006–; *Recreations* golf, tennis, children; *Style*— David Miller, Esq, OBE

MILLER, Francis Edward; s of Alfred Lewis Miller (d 1971), and Emily Johannah, *née* Lark (d 1993); *b* 20 January 1940; *Educ* Brixton Sch of Building, Univ of Westminster; *m* 28 Nov 1964 (m dis 1987), Valerie, da of Sydney Victor Read (d 1985); 2 s (Richard Lewis b 7 Nov 1970, John Francis b 24 May 1976); *Career* jr quantity surveyor 1956, subsequently surveyor and mangr of bldg and civil engrg projects, commenced practice 1972 (specialising in resolution of disputes in bldg, civil engrg and process industries as conslt, conciliator, mediator, adjudicator and arbitrator); ed Arbitration - News and Views (CIArb) 1991–93; pres Law Alumni Assoc of Univ of Westminster 1997–99; memb Arbitration Panel: RICS 1975–94, CIArb; memb Worshipful Co of Arbitrators 1981 (memb Ct of Assts 1992–99); FRICS 1975–94, assoc Inst of Patentees and Inventors 1975–99, FCIArb 1975– (chartered arbitrator), FInstD 1979–91; *Books* Arbitration - Recommendations and Survey (1988), Building and Civil Engineering - Cost Value Comparison (1991), Arbitration - The Arbitrator and the Parties (1994), Civil Justice - Another Chance to Get it Right (1995), Disputes - The Avoidance and Resolution of Disputes (1995), Arbitration - The Arbitration Bill (1996), Arbitration - The Arbitration Act 1996 (trilogy of mock judgments) (1997), The Arbitration Act 1996 - The 46(1)(b) Brigade (1997), The Arbitration Act 1996 - Section 9 and Halki Shipping (1998), Disputes - the square root of disputes (1998), Wing-tip Philosophy (2000), The Japanese Language - Where have all the Pronouns Gone? (2001), The Japanese Language - We're a little muddled about mo (2002), The Japanese Language - Millers Kanji Workbook (2002), Alphabet (A-Z) (2007); *Recreations* writing, walking, talking; *Style*— Francis Miller, Esq; ✉ Candida, Harlequin Lane, Crowborough, East Sussex TN6 1HU (tel 01892 662957)

MILLER, Rt Rev Harold Creeth; *see:* Down and Dromore, Bishop of

MILLER, Sir Harry; 12 Bt (E 1705), of Chichester, Sussex; s of Sir Ernest Henry John Miller, 10 Bt (d 1960); suc bro, Sir John Holmes Miller, 11 Bt (d 1995); *b* 15 January 1927; *m* 1954, Gwynedd Margaret, da of R P Sherriff, of Paraparaumu, New Zealand; 1 s (Anthony Thomas b 1955), 2 da (Sara Margaret (Mrs Laing) b 1957, Judith Christine b 1960); *Heir* s, Anthony Miller; *Style*— Sir Harry Miller, Bt; ✉ 53 Koha Road, Taupo, New Zealand

MILLER, Hugh; s of James Weir Miller (d 1991), of Wishaw, Scotland, and Alice, *née* Waddell (d 1990); *b* 27 April 1937; *Educ* Wishaw Acad, Wishaw HS, Stow Coll, Univ of Glasgow; *m* 18 May 1981, Annette Elizabeth, da of Albert John Slater; 3 c (by previous marriages) (Lesley b 1960, James b 1967, Rachel b 1972); *Career* author; asst to Dr John Grierson 1959, princ photographer Scottish TV 1961–62, co-owner Unique Magic Co London 1963–70; memb: Magic Circle 1965, Mark Twain Soc USA 1976; *Books* The Open City (1973), Ambulance (1975), The Dissector (1976), The Saviour (1977), Casualty (1981), Silent Witnesses (1984), An Echo of Justice (1990), Skin Deep (1991), Indelible Evidence (1991), Scotland Yard (co-author, 1993), Seaforth (1994), Unquiet Minds (1994), Proclaimed in Blood (1995), Prime Target (1996), Borrowed Time (1997), Forensic Fingerprints (1998), Secrets of the Dead (2000), Charlie's Case Notes (2000), More Secrets of the Dead (2001), Crimewatch Solved (2001), What the Corpse Revealed (2002), Mindset (2003), Dereliction Day (screenplay, 2005), Penumbra (2006); *Recreations* travel, walking, reading; *Style*— Hugh Miller, Esq; ✉ 40 St John's Court, Warwick CV34 4NL (tel 01926 491809, e-mail hugh.miller@netmatters.co.uk); c/o Lucas Alexander Whitley Ltd, 14 Vernon Street, London W14 0RJ (tel 020 7471 7900, fax 020 7471 7910)

MILLER, Prof Hugh Graham; OBE (1996); s of Robert Graham Miller (d 2003), of Auckland, NZ, and Anne Farmer *née* Fleming (d 1968); *b* 22 November 1939; *Educ* Strathallan Sch, Univ of Aberdeen (BSc, PhD, DSc); *m* 1, 4 July 1966 (m dis 1993), Thelma; 1 s (Ewen b 1969), 1 da (Andrea b 1971); m 2, 27 July 1994, June; *Career* princ scientific offr Macaulay Inst for Soil Res 1976 (scientific offr 1963, sr scientific offr 1970), prof of forestry Univ of Aberdeen 1984–2004 (head of dept 1984–2000); chm Forestry Cmmn North of Scotland Regnl Advsy Ctee 1997–2004; chm Res Advsy Ctee Forestry Cmmn 1994–2003; pres Inst of Chartered Foresters 1994–96; FICFor 1979, FRSE 1985, FRSA 1986, FIBiol 1988; *Recreations* the outdoors; *Clubs* Royal Northern and Univ; *Style*— Prof Hugh Miller, OBE, FRSE; ✉ 102 Osborne Place, Aberdeen AB25 2DU (tel 01224 639872, e-mail hugh.miller3@btopenworld.com)

MILLER, James; CBE (1986); s of Sir James Miller, GBE (d 1977), of Belmont, Edinburgh, and Lady Ella Jane, *née* Stewart (d 1993); *b* 1 September 1934; *Educ* Edinburgh Acad, Harrow, Balliol Coll Oxford (MA); *m* 1, 27 July 1959, Kathleen (d 1966), da of James Dewar (d 1969), of Edinburgh; 2 da (Susan b 1960, Gail b 1962), 1 s (James b 1962); m 2, 11 Jan 1969, Iris, da of Thomas James Lloyd-Webb (d 1959), of Southampton; 1 da (Heather b 1970); *Career* RE 1956–58, cmmnd 2 Lt 1957; James Miller & Ptnrs (The Miller Gp Ltd 1986): joined 1958, dir 1960, md 1970–91, chm 1970–99, ret; non-exec dir: British Linen Bank Ltd 1983–99 (govr 1997–99), Bank of Scotland 1993–2000; memb Scottish Advsy Bd British Petroleum plc 1990–2001; FCEC: chm Scottish Section 1981–83, chm 1985, pres 1990–93; chm Scottish Branch CIArb 1985–87; pres Edinburgh C of C 1981–83, Master Merchant Co of Edinburgh 1992–94 (ct asst 1982–85, treas 1990–92); chm: Ct Heriot-Watt Univ Edinburgh 1990–96, Royal Scottish Nat Orch Soc 1997–2002 (dir 1996–2002); hon consul for the Repub of Austria 1993–2003; Freeman: City of London 1956, Worshipful Co of Horners 1956; Hon DUniv Heriot-Watt 1996; FCIOB 1974, FCIArb 1976, CIMgt 1983; *Recreations* shooting; *Clubs* City Livery; *Style*— James Miller, Esq, CBE; ✉ Alderwood, 49 Craigcrook Road, Edinburgh EH4 3PH (tel 0131 332 2222, fax 0131 332 1777)

MILLER, James Francis Xavier; s of Lt-Col J F Miller, of Camberley, Surrey, and B M Miller, *née* Cooke; *b* 3 March 1950; *Educ* Douai Sch, Merton Coll Oxford; *m* 1976, Ruth Ellen Rowland, da of Canon C R Macbeth; 2 s (Tom b 4 March 1979, Richard b 2 Oct 1980); *Career* Winchester Coll: asst master 1972–89, master i/c cricket 1976–87, head of economics 1978–82, housemaster 1982–89; headmaster Framlingham Coll 1989–94, headmaster Royal GS Newcastle upon Tyne 1994–; chm Amazing Grades Ltd; FRSA 1992; *Recreations* golf, cricket, motor sport, opera, malt whisky; *Clubs* Free Foresters, Morpeth GC; *Style*— James Miller, Esq; ✉ Royal Grammar School, Eskdale Terrace, Newcastle upon Tyne NE2 4DX (tel 0191 281 5711, fax 0191 212 0392, e-mail hm@rgs.newcastle.sch.uk)

MILLER, James Lawson; s of David Wardrop Miller (d 1966), and Helen Frew, *née* Baxter (d 1952); *b* 26 January 1931; *Educ* The John Lyon Sch Harrow, St John's Coll Cambridge (MA); *m* 29 June 1957, Margaret Ann (d 2007), da of Beverley Robinson (d 1984); 2 s (David b 1958, Jeremy b 1959), 1 da (Jane b 1962); *Career* chartered builder, construction co chief exec; chm and dir: James Lawson Holdings Ltd, James Lawson Property Ltd 1965–; chm R Harding (Cookham) Ltd 1985–; dir: Saxon Developments Ltd 1994–, The Shell Bay Holding Company Ltd 1996–, Roxylight Homes Ltd 1999–; pres The Builders' Conference 1985; fell Chartered Inst of Building; *Books* Computer Aided Estimating (1977); *Recreations* duplicate bridge, Church of England activities; *Clubs* Leander; *Style*— James L Miller, Esq; ✉ Clavering, North Park, Gerrards Cross, Buckinghamshire SL9 8JP

MILLER, James Young; s of James Young Miller (d 1960), and Alison Lyons, *née* Brown; *b* 23 January 1942; *Educ* Glasgow HS; *m* 3 April 1970, Gillian Mhairi, da of Alan G Millar; 2 da (Susan b 19 June 1972, Fiona b 5 July 1974), 1 s (Donald b 29 Sept 1976); *Career* KPMG (formerly Thomson McLintock & Co): trainee Glasgow 1959–65, qualified CA 1965, mangr 1969–74 (asst mangr 1966–69), specialist forensic accounting ptnr 1974–99, head of audit Galsgow 1980–92, head of audit Scotland 1992–99, conslt 1999–2000, memb UK Accounting and Audit Practice Ctees; memb Accountancy Investigation and Discipline Bd Financial Reporting Cncl 2005–; govr: RSAMD, HS of Glasgow, Bell Coll Lanarkshire 2005–; MICAS 1965; *Recreations* golf, choral singing, music, reading; *Clubs* Royal Scottish Automobile; *Style*— James Miller, Esq

MILLER, Prof (Christopher) John; s of late Stanley Miller, of Henley-on-Thames, Oxon, and late Joan Beryl Gill; *b* 4 November 1941; *Educ* Bishop Vesey's GS Sutton Coldfield, Univ of Nottingham (BA, LLM); *m* 4 Sept 1964, Michèle Marie Juliette, da of late Raymond Michel Guérault, of Paris; 1 s (Mark), 1 da (Anne Marie); *Career* barr; lectr in law Univ of Durham 1966–70, reader in common law Univ of Leeds (lectr in law 1970–77), prof of law Univ of Warwick 1980–89 (reader 1979); Univ of Birmingham: prof of English law 1989–2003 (emeritus prof of law 2003–), dean Faculty of Law 1994–97; pt/t chm Social Security Appeals Tbnls and Disability Appeals Tbnls 1986–95; *Books* Contempt of Court (1976, 3 edn 2000), Product Liability (jtly, 1977, 2 edn 2004), Product Liability and Safety Encyclopaedia (1979–2007), Comparative Product Liability (ed, 1986), Business Law (jtly, 1991), Benjamin's Sale of Goods (jt ed, 1992, 7 edn 2006), Consumer and Trading Law: Text Cases and Materials (jtly, 1998); *Recreations* classical music, gardening, walking, sport; *Style*— Prof John Miller; ✉ Faculty of Law, Chancellor's Court, University of Birmingham, PO Box 363, Birmingham B15 2TT (tel 0121 414 8113, fax 0121 414 3585, e-mail c.j.miller.law@bham.ac.uk)

MILLER, John Harmsworth; CBE (2006); s of Charles Henry Miller (d 1984), and Brenda Ellen, *née* Borrett; *b* 18 August 1930; *Educ* Charterhouse, Architectural Assoc (DipAA, AA Tropical Dip); *m* 1, 20 Feb 1957 (m dis 1975); 2 da; m 2, 15 Feb 1985, Susan Jane, da of Marcus Brumwell, CBE (d 1983); *Career* Nat Serv 13/18 Hussars RAC 1948–50; architect; with Lyons Israel & Ellis London 1956–59, asst to Sir Leslie Martin 1959–61, ptnr Colquhoun & Miller 1961–90, ptnr John Miller & Partners 1990–; tutor 1961–73: Interior & Environmental Design Sch RCA, Architectural Assoc; visiting critic Cornell Univ Sch of Architecture NY 1966, 1968 and 1971, tutor Cambridge Univ Sch of Architecture 1969–70; visiting critic: Princeton Univ Sch of Architecture NJ 1979, Dublin Univ Sch of Architecture 1972–73; prof Sch of Environmental Design RCA 1975–85, chm Academic Policy Ctee RCA 1983–84; visiting prof: Dublin Univ Sch of Architecture 1985–86, Univ of Manchester Sch of Architecture 1986–87; external examiner: Architectural Assoc 1975, Poly of Central London 1976–80, Thames Poly Sch of Architecture 1981–85, Univ of Bath Sch of Architecture 1982–85, Univ of London Bartlett Sch of Architecture 1986–88, Poly of South Bank Sch of Architecture 1986–89, Canterbury Sch of Architecture 1988–92; exhibitions of own work incl: Royal Coll of Art and Univ of Palermo 1974, Collegio Arquitectos Santiago Chile Biennale 1981, Paris Biennale 1983, Royal Academy Summer Exhbn 1984, National Gallery entries exhibition 9H Gallery 1986, Royal Academy Summer Exhibition 1988, 1989, 1991, 1999, 2000 and 2001, Univ of Valencia 1990, Stevens Building RCA 1992, Royal West of England Acad 1994, City of Valencia 1994, Frankfurt 1995, Barcelona 1995, Vienna 1995, Prince of Wales Fndn for Architecture and the Urban Environment 1999; guest ed Architectural Review 1964; assessor Civic Tst Awards 1978–86; memb: Cncl Architectural Assoc 1966, Awards Ctee Royal Inst of Architects 1967–68 and 1970, Cncl RCA 1980–83; ARIBA 1959, FRCA 1976, FRSA 1984; *Recreations* gardening; *Style*— John Miller, Esq, CBE; ✉ The Elephant House Brewery, 35 Hawley Crescent, London NW1 (tel 020 7482 4686, fax 020 7267 9907)

MILLER, Sir Jonathan Wolfe; kt (2002), CBE (1983); s of Emanuel Miller, DPM, FRCP; *b* 21 July 1934; *Educ* St Paul's, St John's Coll Cambridge (MB BCh); *m* 1956, Helen Rachel Collet; 2 s, 1 da; *Career* television, theatre and opera director; stage dir London and NY 1965–67, res fell in history of med UCL 1970–73, assoc dir Nat Theatre 1973–75, visiting prof in drama Westfield Coll London 1977–, assoc prodr ENO 1980–, res fell in neuro-psychology Univ of Sussex 1981–83, artistic dir Old Vic 1988–90; memb Arts Cncl 1975–76, Silver medal Royal TV Soc 1981, Albert medal RSA 1990; curate exhibition Nat Gallery London 1998; From the Look of Things (lectures) 1995, River's lectr King's Coll Cambridge 1997; fell UCL 1981, hon fell St John's Coll Cambridge 1982, hon fell RA 1991; Hon DLitt: Univ of Leicester 1981, Univ of Cambridge 1996; FRCP 1997, FRCPEd 1998; *Stage* Nottingham Playhouse: School for Scandal 1968, The Seagull 1969, The Malcontent 1973; Old Vic: King Lear 1970, The Merchant of Venice 1970, Andromache 1988, One Way Pendulum 1988, Bussy D'Ambois 1988, The Tempest 1988, Candide 1988, King Lear 1989, The Liar 1989; The Tempest (Mermaid) 1970, Hamlet (Arts Theatre Cambridge) 1970; NT: Danton's Death 1971, School for Scandal 1972, Measure for Measure 1974, Marriage of Figaro 1974, The Freeway 1974; Chichester: The Taming of the Shrew 1972, The Seagull 1973; Greenwich: Family Romances 1974, The Importance of Being Earnest 1975, All's Well 1975, She Would If She Could 1979; Long Day's Journey Into Night (Haymarket) 1986; The Taming of the Shrew: (RSC Stratford) 1987, (Barbican) 1988; jtly adapted and directed The Emperor (Royal Court, televised 1988) 1987; A Midsummer Night's Dream (Almeida) 1996, She Stoops to Conquer (Gate Theatre London), As You Like It (Gate Theatre London), King Lear (Stratford Festival) 2002, King Lear (Lincoln Centre Theatre) 2004, The Cherry Orchard (Crucible Theatre Sheffield) 2007; *Television* ed BBC Monitor 1965, directed films for BBC TV 1966, The

Body in Question (BBC series) 1978, exec prodr BBC Shakespeare series 1979–81; presenter: Madness series (ITV) 1991, Born Talking, Atheism: A brief history of disbelief (BBC) 2005; *Film* Take A Girl Like You 1970; *Opera* Arden Must Die (Sadler's Wells Theatre) 1974, The Cunning Little Vixen (Glyndebourne) 1975 and 1977; ENO: The Marriage of Figaro 1978 (directorial debut), The Turn of the Screw 1979, Arabella 1989, Otello 1981, Rigoletto 1982 and 1985, Don Giovanni 1985, The Magic Flute 1986, Tosca 1986 (transferred from Maggio Musicale Florence, subsequently revived Houston Grand Opera), The Mikado 1986, 1988, 1993 and 2001, The Barber of Seville 1987, The Turn of the Screw 1993, Rigoletto 1993, Rosenkavalier 1994 and 2003, Carmen 1995; Kent Opera: Cosi Fan Tutte 1975, Rigoletto 1975, Orfeo 1976, Eugene Onegin 1977, La Traviata 1979, Falstaff 1980 and 1981, Fidelio 1982, 1983 and 1988; Maggio Musicale Florence 1990–2001: Don Giovanni, Cosi Fan Tutte, The Marriage of Figaro, Idomeneo, Ariadne, La Boheme, Don Pasquale; Metropolitan Opera NY: Katya Kabanova, The Rake's Progress, Marriage of Figaro, Pelléas and Mélisande; Zurich Opera: Die Gezeichneten, Nabucco, Magic Flute, Die Sweigsamen Frau, Falstaff, Seraglio; other prodns incl: Fanciulla del West (La Scala), Figaro (Vienna State Opera), The Magic Flute (Israel Philharmonic prodn) and Roberto Devereux (Monte Carlo Opera) 1990–92, Manon Lescaut (La Scala) 1992, Maria Stuarda (Monte Carlo Opera), Capriccio and Falstaff (Deutsche Staatsoper Berlin) 1993, Bach's St Matthew Passion (Holy Trinity London) 1993, Anna Bolena (Monte Carlo Opera) 1994, Fedora (Bregenz Festival) 1993, L'incoronazione di Poppea (Glimmerglass Opera) 1994, Cosi fan Tutte (ROH, debut) 1995, Tamerlano (Glimmerglass Opera) 1996, Anna Bolena (Bayerische Staatsoper), I Puritani (Bayerische Staatsoper), Seraglio (Zurich Opera) 2003, Orfeo (Southbank Centre) 2003, L'Elisir d'Amore (Stockholm Opera) 2003, Falstaff (New Nat Theatre Tokyo) 2004, La Traviata (Lithuanian Opera) 2005, St Matthew's Passion (Brooklyn Acad of Music) 2006, L'Elisir d'Amore (NYC Opera) 2006, Don Giovanni (Palau des Arts Valencia) 2006, Rosenkavalier (New Theatre Tokyo) 2007; *Books* McLuhan (1971), Freud: The Man, His World, His Influence (ed, 1972), The Body in Question (1978), Subsequent Performances (1986), The Don Giovanni Book: Myths of Seduction and Betrayal (1990), Nowhere in Particular (1999); *Style*— Sir Jonathan Miller, CBE; ✉ c/o Cordelia Dyer, IMG Artists Europe, Lovell House, 616 Chiswick High Road, London W4 5RX (tel 020 8233 5800, fax 020 8233 5801, e-mail cdyer@imgworld.com)

MILLER, Prof Karl Fergus Connor; s of William Miller (d 1962), of London, and Marion Connor Miller (d 1980), of Edinburgh; *b* 2 August 1931; *Educ* Royal HS Edinburgh, Downing Coll Cambridge; *m* 4 Feb 1956, Jane Elisabeth, da of Robert Collet; 2 s (Daniel Collet b 6 July 1957, Samuel Robert b 13 Jan 1962), 1 da (Georgia Anna b 29 Jan 1964); *Career* various jobs HM Treasury, BBC Television, Lord Northcliffe prof of modern Eng lit UCL 1974–92 (prof emeritus 1992–); lit ed: Spectator, New Statesman; ed The Listener, ed then co-ed London Review of Books 1979–92; James Tait Black Prize 1975, Scottish Arts Cncl Award 1993; FRSL 1992; *Books* Memoirs of a Modern Scotland (ed), Cockburn's Millennium, Doubles, Authors, Rebecca's Vest, Dark Horses, Electric Shepherd; *Recreations* watching football; *Style*— Karl Miller; ✉ 26 Limerston Street, London SW10 0HH (tel and fax 020 7351 1994)

MILLER, Keith Manson; CBE (2005); s of John Manson Miller (d 1982), and Dolores, *née* McLauchlan (d 1970); *b* 19 March 1949, Edinburgh; *Educ* Loretto, Heriot-Watt Univ (BSc), Univ of Glasgow (Dip in Mgmnt Studies); *m* 10 Jan 1975, Lee, *née* Marshall; 3 da (Deborah b 19 April 1976, Lauren b 3 April 1978, Kathryn b 21 Oct 1980); *Career* The Miller Group Ltd (formerly James Miller & Partners Ltd): joined as dir Miller Mining 1975, gp bd dir 1976, md Miller Developments 1986, gp ceo 1994–; Scottish Business Achievement Award 2003, Ernst & Young Scottish Entrepreneur of the Year 2006; Hon DEng Napier Univ 2005; FCIOB 2003; *Recreations* sailing, ski-mountaineering, golf, shooting; *Clubs* RYS; *Style*— Keith Miller, Esq, CBE; ✉ The Miller Group Ltd, Miller House, 2 Lochside View, Edinburgh Park, Edinburgh EH12 9DH (tel 0870 336 5108, fax 0870 336 5110, e-mail keith.miller@miller.co.uk)

MILLER, Maria; MP; *b* 1964, Wolverhampton; *Educ* Brynteg Comp Bridgend, LSE; *m* Iain; 3 c; *Career* joined Cons Pty 1983; account mangr Grey 1985–90, mktg mangr Texaco Ltd 1990–95, dir Grey 1994–99, dir Rowland/Saatchi 1999–2003; Parly spokesman Basingstoke 2003–; Parly candidate (Cons) Wolverhampton NE 2001, MP (Cons) Basingstoke 2005–; shadow min for educn 2005–06, shadow min for family welfare 2006–; *Style*— Mrs Maria Miller, MP; ✉ House of Commons, London SW1A 0AA (e-mail millerm@parliament.uk)

MILLER, Michael Dawson; s of Cyril Gibson Risch Miller, CBE (d 1976), and Dorothy Alice, *née* North-Lewis (d 2002); *b* 12 March 1928; *Educ* Rugby; *m* 17 July 1954, Gillian Margaret, da of Dr Eric Gordon-Fleming (d 1948); 3 da (Caroline b 1957, Clare b 1961, Jane b 1961); *Career* Parachute Regt Regs 1946–48, TA 1949–55, HAC 1957–63; articled clerk 1949, in practice as slr 1954–55, ptnr Thos R Miller & Son 1962–90 (exec 1955–62, ptnr Bermuda 1969–90); dir: Shipowners Assurance Mgmnt Montreal 1973–84, AB Indemnitas Stockholm 1983–90, Thos Miller War Risks Services 1985–90; conslt Planning Bd for Ocean Shipping 1970–; Liveryman: Worshipful Co of Shipwrights 1977, Worshipful Co of Solicitors 1986; memb: Law Soc 1954, London Maritime Arbitrators' Assoc 1963; Silver medal Hellenic Merchant Marine Greece 1983; *Books* Marine War Risks (1, 2 and 3 edns, Br Insurance Law Assoc Prize 1991), Uncommon Lawyer, Wars of the Roses; *Recreations* going to sea on small ships, opera, history, reaching remote places, ancient civilisations, targeting intellectuals; *Clubs* Royal Ocean Racing, Royal Bermuda Yacht, Royal Thames Yacht, City, Hurlingham; *Style*— Michael Miller, Esq; ✉ 52 Scarsdale Villas, London W8 6PP (tel 020 7937 9935); Dairy Cottage, Donhead, St Andrews, Wiltshire; c/o Thos R Miller & Son, International House, 26 Creechurch Lane, London EC3A 5BA (tel 020 7283 4646, fax 020 7283 5614, telex 885271)

MILLER, Dr (John) Paul; s of John Frederick William Miller (d 1961), and Edith Mary Miller; *b* 10 July 1940; *Educ* Repton, Keble Coll Oxford (MA, DPhil, BM BCh), Univ of London (MSc), Guy's; *m* 19 Aug 1978, (Constance) Mary, da of Kenneth Anderson (d 1997); 1 da (Claire b 1981), 1 s (Christopher John Kenneth b 1984), 1 adopted s (Nicholas Francis Haynes b 1977), 1 adopted da (Jackie Marie Haynes b 1979); *Career* house physician Guy's 1968, house surgn Addenbrooke's Hosp Cambridge 1969, team leader Save the Children Fund Nigerian Civil War, sr house offr and registrar Hammersmith Hosp 1970–72, hon sr registrar St James's Hosp Leeds 1972–75, lectr med Univ of Leeds 1972–75, sr lectr med Univ of Manchester 1975–81, hon conslt physician Univ Hosp of S Manchester 1975–81, visiting prof med Baylor Coll Houston (MRC travelling fell) 1978–79, conslt gastroenterologist Univ Hosp of S Manchester 1981–2006 (clinical sub dean 1982–88); chm: Bd Faculty of Med, Dentistry, Nursing and Pharmacy Univ of Manchester 1997–2004, Cncl Med Protection Soc 1996–2003; pres Manchester Med Soc 2003–04 (chm Cncl 1997–2001), treas Br Atherosclerosis Soc 1997–2002; author of sci papers and reviews on: respiratory physiology, gastroenterology (especially peptic ulceration), disorders of lipoprotein metabolism; formerly: treas Br Hyperlipidaemia Assoc, regnl advsr N W Reg RCP; currently memb Manchester Literary and Philosophical Soc; memb: Br Soc Gastroenterology, Assoc Physicians GB and Ireland; FRCP 1982; *Recreations* walking, cycling; *Style*— Dr Paul Miller; ✉ 1 Ballbrook Avenue, Manchester M20 6AB (e-mail jpmiller@btinternet.com)

MILLER, Sir Peter North; kt (1988); s of Cyril Thomas Gibson Risch Miller, CBE (d 1976), and Dorothy Alice North Miller, JP; *b* 28 September 1930; *Educ* Rugby, Lincoln Coll Oxford (MA), City Univ (DSc); *m* 4 Feb 1991, Jane Suzanne; 1 s (2 s, 1 da by previous m); *Career* Nat Serv Intelligence Corps 1949–50; joined Lloyd's 1953, called to the Bar 1954; Thos R Miller & Son (Insurance): joined 1953, ptnr 1959, sr ptnr 1971; chm Thos R Miller & Son (Holdings) Ltd 1971–83 and 1988–96 (name changed to The Miller Insurance Gp Ltd 1991); Lloyd's Insurance Brokers' Assoc Ctee: memb 1973–77, dep chm 1974–75, chm 1976–77; chm: Lloyd's 1984–87, Br Ctee of Bureau Veritas 1980–2002, Lloyd's Tercentenary Fndn 1988–; memb: Ctee on Invisible Exports 1975–77, Insurance Brokers' Registration Cncl 1977–81, Ctee of Lloyd's 1977–80 and 1982–89; memb HM Cmmn of Lieutenancy for the City of London 1987–; Freeman City of London 1986, Liveryman Worshipful Co of Shipwrights 1987; Hon DSc City Univ 1987, hon fell Lincoln Coll Oxford 1992; Commendatore Ordine al Merito della Repubblica Italiana 1989; memb Chief Pleas Sark 1969–; *Recreations* all sport (except cricket), incl tennis, running and sailing, wine, music, gardening, old churches; *Clubs* City of London, Vincent's (Oxford), Thames Hare and Hounds, Travellers; *Style*— Sir Peter Miller; ✉ c/o The Miller Insurance Group, Dawson House, 5 Jewry Street, London EC3N 2PJ

MILLER, Richard Hugh; QC (1995); s of Sir Stephen James Hamilton Miller, KCVO (d 1996), and Lady Heather Miller; *b* 1 February 1953; *Educ* Charterhouse, Univ of Sussex (BSc); *Career* called to the Bar Middle Temple 1976 (specialising in patent matters); chm Intellectual Property Bar Assoc 2005– (vice-chm 2004–05), memb Bar Cncl 2006– (memb European Ctee 2005–), memb Cncl Int Assoc for the Protection of Intellectual Property (UK Gp) 2006–; *Books* Terrell on the Law of Patents (jt ed, 14, 15 and 16 edns); *Recreations* travel, films; *Style*— Richard Miller, Esq, QC; ✉ 3 New Square, Lincoln's Inn, London WC2A 3RS (tel 020 7405 1111, fax 020 7405 7800)

MILLER, (James Adrian) Rodney; s of Walter Miller, of Belfast, and Elizabeth Munnis; *b* 22 January 1949; *Educ* Dr Renshaw's Tutorial Coll Belfast, Univ of Ulster Coll of Art & Design (BA); *m* 25 Sept 1975, Patricia Woodburn, da of Frederick Wilmot, of Perth, Western Aust; 1 s (Jonathan Anthony Walter b 1977), 2 da (Victoria Beatrice b 1979, Emma Elizabeth b 1989); *Career* graphic designer: AFA Belfast 1972–73, N Ireland Housing Exec 1973–75; head Design Dept NIHE 1977–79 (sr graphic designer 1975–77), fndr Rodney Miller Associates 1979–; maj design projects: N Ireland Tourist Bd pubns, Zimbabwe Tourist Bd pubns, various public sector design projects; winner: Kodak award for Excellence (Br Business Calendar Awards) 1989, Three ICAD Bells Dublin 1994, ICAD Gold Bell 1996; past memb Nat Cncl CSD (chm NI Region 1990–92), design course advsr Univ of Ulster, memb HND Industrial Liaison Panel Univ of Ulster; memb Design Forum, assoc memb D&AD, memb Inst Designers in Ireland, MCSD 1977; *Recreations* bird watching, fishing, family; *Style*— Rodney Miller, Esq; ✉ 16 Circular Road, West, Cultra, Holywood, Co Down BT18 0AT (tel 028 9042 5468); Rodney Miller Associates, 83–85 Great Victoria Street, Belfast BT2 7AF (tel 028 9024 0785, fax 028 9023 2901, e-mail rodney@rodneymillerassoc.com)

MILLER, Ronald Alan; s of Eric Norman Miller (d 1978), of London, and Rosemary, *née* Winter; *b* 10 March 1951; *Educ* Westminster, St Bartholomew's Hosp Med Sch London (MB BS, MS); *m* 1, 1975 (m dis 1995), Sarah Jane, da of Richard Griffiths Lumley, of Ross on Wye, Glos; 1 s (Mark Rudolph b 1979), 1 da (Rosalind Margaret Louise b 1982); m 2, March 1996, Linda Katheryn, da of Michael James Stanley Berriman, of Petersfield, Hants; 1 da (Georgina Megan Mallory Miller b 4 March 1999); *Career* Hunterian prof of surgery RCS 1985, Simpson Smith lectr Charing Cross Hosp 1986; currently: dir Dept of Urology and Minimally Invasive Surgery Whittington, hon conslt Hosp of St John and Elizabeth; former postgrad dean Royal Northern Hosp; hon sr lectr: Inst of Urology, Royal Free Hosp, UCH; author of 200 papers on urological subjects; Cutler Prize RCS 1984; sec N E Thames Advsy Ctee on Urology; chm NE Thames Urological Tumour Bd; memb: Cncl Biological Engrg Soc, Instrument Ctee Br Assoc Urological Surgns, Steering Ctee Soc of Minimally Invasive Therapy (hon treas), Cncl Urological Section RSM; consulting ed: Endourology, Urology, Jl of Minimally Invasive Surgery, Jl of Day Surgery, Jl of Ambulatory Surgery; memb: BMA, RSM, Br Assoc Urological Surgns, American Urological Assoc, Endo Urology Soc, Minimally Invasive Soc; md Woolaston House Ltd 1999, chm Encyclomedia Ltd 2000; Order of Lenin; FRGS, MB BS 1974, MRCS LRCP 1974, FRCS England 1978, MS London 1986, MInstD; *Books* Percutaneous Renal Surgery (1983), Endoscopic Surgery (1986), Second Generation Lithotripsy (1987); *Recreations* riding, climbing, shooting, reading, military history; *Style*— Ronald Miller, Esq; ✉ Woolaston House, 25 Southwood Lane, London N6 5ED (tel 020 8341 3422, fax 020 8340 1376)

MILLER, Sir Ronald Andrew Baird; kt (1993), CBE (1985); *Educ* Daniel Stewarts Coll Edinburgh, Univ of Edinburgh (BSc); *Career* chm Dawson International plc 1982–1995; non-exec dir: Securities Trust of Scotland plc 1983–2001, Christian Salvesen plc 1987–97, Scottish Amicable 1987–97, Aggreko plc 1997–2002; vice-pres British Fashion Exports; dir Quality Assurance Agency for Higher Education 1997–2003; memb Scottish Higher Educn Funding Cncl 1992–95; chm Ct Napier Univ 1998–2001; Freeman: City of London, Worshipful Co of Woolmen; Hon DSc Heriot-Watt Univ 1992, Hon Dr Napier Univ 2001; MICAS; *Recreations* golf, skiing, travel, gardening, art, music; *Clubs* Caledonian; *Style*— Sir Ronald Miller, CBE

MILLER, Dr Roy Frank; s of Thomas Richard Miller (d 1978), and Margaret Ann, *née* Tattum; *b* 20 September 1935; *Educ* Wembley Co GS, Univ of Exeter (BSc), Univ of London (PhD); *m* 18 March 1961, Ruth Naomi, da of William Kenchington (d 1956); 1 s (Stephen b 1965); *Career* Royal Holloway Coll London: lectr in physics 1960, sr lectr 1972–81, vice-princ 1978, princ 1981–85; Royal Holloway and Bedford New Coll London (now Royal Holloway Univ of London): vice-princ 1985–98, hon research fell in physics 1998–, hon fell 2000–; res assoc Case Western Res Univ Cleveland Ohio 1968–69; chm Inst of Classical Studies Univ of London 1982–2001; tstee and govr Strode's Coll Egham 1981–; FInstP 1978, FRSA 1983–2004, CPhys 1986; *Recreations* music, climbing; *Clubs* Athenaeum; *Style*— Dr Roy Miller; ✉ Celyn, 3 Parsonage Road, Englefield Green, Egham, Surrey TW20 0JW (tel 01784 432753, fax 0870 133 9861)

MILLER, Sarah; da of John Harmsworth Miller, and Patricia, *née* Rhodes; *Educ* Camden Sch for Girls, Wadham Coll Oxford (BA); *Career* journalist; contributing ed Blueprint magazine and Wordsearch pubns (Eye magazine and Tate magazine) 1983–89, style ed Cosmopolitan 1984–85 (features asst 1983–84), co-ordinating ed Elle (Br launch) 1985–86, Look ed Sunday Times 1987–1989 (dep Look ed 1986–87), asst ed Sunday Times Magazine 1989–1992, assoc features ed Daily Telegraph 1992–94, arts ed Daily Telegraph 1994–95, features ed Saturday Telegraph Magazine 1995–97, ed Condé Nast Traveller 1997–; memb: Ctee BSME (chairwoman 2002), Educn and Parly Affrs Ctee, Press and Periodical Assoc, Cncl RCA; Ed of Year BSME 2000, 2001 and 2003, Consumer Lifestyle Magazine of the Year 2005; *Recreations* arts, films, architecture, design, travel, literature; *Style*— Ms Sarah Miller; ✉ Condé Nast Traveller, Vogue House, Hanover Square, London W1S 1JU (tel 020 7499 9080, fax 020 7493 3758, e-mail editorcntraveller@condenast.co.uk)

MILLER, Sienna; *Educ* Heathfield Sch Ascot, Lee Strasberg Inst NY; *Career* actress; *Theatre* Cigarettes and Chocolate (NY), The Striker (NY), A School for Scandal (NY), Independence (NY); *Television* Keen Eddie, Bedtime; *Film* South Kensington, Joyrider, High Speed, Layer Cake, Alfie, Casanova, Factory Girl; *Style*— Ms Sienna Miller; ✉ c/o PFD, Drury House, 34–43 Russell Street, London WC2B 5HA (tel 020 7344 1010, fax 020 7836 9544)

MILLER, Stephen Charles; s of Stanley Scott Miller (d 1996), and Madeline Ellice, *née* McGown; *b* 5 January 1965, Aberdeen; *Educ* Robert Gordon's Coll Aberdeen, Univ of Aberdeen (LLB, DipLP); *m* 1 Oct 1994, Paula Mary Nicola, *née* O'Reilly; 2 s (Matthew Whiteford b 24 March 1998, James Stanley b 4 July 1999), 1 da (Christina May b 21 Jan

M

2003); *Career* slr; ptnr: Harper Macleod 1994–2002, MacRoberts 2002–; ind legal chm Scottish Football Assoc; memb Law Soc of Scotland 1989; *Publications* Sport and the Law: The Scots Perspective (jt author, 2001); *Recreations* cycling, golf, books, DJing; *Style*— Stephen Miller, Esq; ✉ Rosslyn, 37 Drymen Road, Bearsden G61 2RA (tel 0141 942 2976, e-mail stephen.miller321@btinternet.com); MacRoberts, 152 Bath Street, Glasgow G2 4TB (tel 0141 332 9988, fax 0141 332 8886)

MILLER, Stewart; s of late Richard Miller, and late Margaret Miller; *b* 27 December 1952; *Educ* South Shields GS for Boys, Univ of Sheffield (BA); *m* 1994, Kathleen Ann, *née* Watson; 2 s (Neil Stewart Richard b 30 Aug 1976, Gary Paul Michael b 12 Aug 1978); *Career* roles in brand mgmnt, new product devpt and sales mgmnt Unilever; Whitbread plc: free trade sales policy and mktg dir Whitbread E Pennines and Scot 1983, dir and gen mangr Whitbread Westward Inns 1984, chief exec Pizza Hut UK 1988 (ops dir 1987), ops dir and property dir Beefeater 1991, sales and mktg dir Whitbread Inns 1994, md Whitbread Pub Partnerships 1996, md The Pub and Bar Co @ Whitbread 2000, main bd dir Whitbread plc 2000–05, md David Lloyd Leisure 2001–05; dir: Business in Sport and Leisure, Skills Active UK; memb Business Cncl Langholm Private Equity; various qualifications from short progs at business schs incl London Business School, Bradford Business Sch, INSEAD, Stanford Exec Prog; *Recreations* tennis, jogging, exercise, fell walking, sailing, gardening, holidays; *Style*— Stewart Miller, Esq

MILLER, Prof William Lockley; s of William Lockley Miller (d 1999), of Hamilton, and Florence, *née* Ratcliffe (d 1986); *b* 12 August 1943; *Educ* Univ of Edinburgh (MA), Univ of Newcastle upon Tyne (PhD); *m* 19 July 1967, Dr Nancy Fiona Miller, da of David Thomson, of Newport-on-Tay, Fife; 2 s (Iain b 3 July 1971, Andrew b 15 June 1977), 1 da (Shona b 9 Nov 1974); *Career* prof of politics Univ of Strathclyde 1985 (lectr 1968–83, sr lectr 1983–85), Edward Caird prof of politics Univ of Glasgow 1985–; FBA 1994, FRSA 1997, FRSE 1999; *Books* Electoral Dynamics (1977), The End of British Politics? (1981), The Survey Method (1983), Elections and Voters (1987), Irrelevant Elections? (1988), How Voters Change (1990), Media and Voters (1991), Alternatives to Freedom (1995), Political Culture in Contemporary Britain (1996), Values and Political Change in Postcommunist Europe (1998), Models of Local Governance (2000), A Culture of Corruption (2001), Anglo-Scottish Relations from 1900 to Devolution and Beyond (2005), Multicultural Nationalism: Islamophobia, Anglophobia and Devolution (2006), The Open Economy and its Enemies: Public Attitudes in East Asia and East Europe (2006); *Style*— Prof William Miller, FBA, FRSE; ✉ Department of Politics, Adam Smith Building, The University, Glasgow G12 8RT (tel 0141 330 5980, fax 0141 330 5071, e-mail w.l.miller@socsci.gla.ac.uk)

MILLER OF CHILTHORNE DOMER, Baroness (Life Peer UK 1998), of Chilthorne Domer in the County of Somerset; Susan Elizabeth Miller; da of Oliver Meddows Taylor (d 1984), and Norah, *née* Langham (d 1998); *b* 1 January 1954; *Educ* Sidcot Sch, Oxford Poly; *m* 1, 1980 (m dis 1998), John Christopher Miller; 2 da (Hon Charlotte Sarah b 24 May 1981 d 13 January 2001, Hon Madeleine Lucy b 3 Dec 1984); m 2, 1999, Humphrey Temperley; *Career* in publishing; formerly with David & Charles, Weidenfeld & Nicolson, Penguin Books; self employed bookseller Sherborne and Yeovil; ldr S Somerset DC 1996–98 (cncllr 1991–98), cncllr Somerset CC 1997–2005; Lib Dem spokesman in Lords Rural Affairs & Agriculture 1999– (now Environment, Agriculture and Rural Affairs), memb Euro Sub-Ctee 1998–2002 and 2005–; chm Somerset Food Links; vice-pres Cncl for National Parks, BTCV; memb: Lib Dems and Women Lib Dems, Devon and Somerset Wildlife Tst, Fawcett Soc, Marine Conservation Soc; *Recreations* walking, reading, sailing, friends; *Style*— The Rt Hon the Baroness Miller of Chilthorne Domer; ✉ House of Lords, London SW1A 0PW

MILLER OF GLENLEE, Sir Stephen William Macdonald; 8 Bt (GB 1788), of Glenlee, Kirkcudbrightshire; s of Sir (Frederick William) Macdonald Miller of Glenlee, 7 Bt (d 1991), and (Marion Jane) Audrey, *née* Pettit; *b* 20 June 1953; *Educ* Rugby, St Bartholomew's Hosp (MB BS); *m* 1, 1978, Mary Carolyn (d 1989), o da of G B Owens, of Huddersfield; 1 s (James Stephen Macdonald b 1981), 1 da (Katherine Helen b 1983); m 2, 1990, Caroline Mary, da of Leslie A E Chasemore, of Shebbear, Devon, and widow of Harold Frederick Clark; *Heir* s, James Miller of Glenlee; *Career* GP Shebbear; FRCS, FRCGP; *Style*— Sir Stephen Miller of Glenlee, Bt; ✉ The Lawn, Shebbear, Beaworthy, Devon EX21 5RU

MILLER OF HENDON, Baroness (Life Peer UK 1993), of Gore in the London Borough of Barnet; Doreen Miller; MBE (1989), JP (Brent 1971); da of Bernard Henry Feldman; *b* 13 June 1933; *Educ* LSE; *m* 1955, Henry Lewis Miller, s of Ben Miller; 3 s (Hon Michael Steven b 1956, Hon Paul Howard b 1959, Hon David Philip b 1962); *Career* co dir; chm: Barnet Family Health Services Authority 1990–94, Crown Agent 1990–94; memb Monopolies & Mergers Cmmn 1992–93; pres Greater London Area Conservative Assocs 1996–98 (treas 1990–93, chm 1993–96); House of Lords: oppn whip 1997–99, shadow min for trade and industry 1999–2006, oppn spokesman on educn and skills 1999–2001; chm Nat Assoc of Leagues of Hosp and Community Friends 1997–2003; Baroness in Waiting Queen's Household until 1997; *Clubs* Rotary (London), Soroptimist Int; *Style*— The Baroness Miller of Hendon, MBE; ✉ House of Lords, London SW1A 0PW

MILLER SMITH, Charles; s of William Smith, and Margaret Pettigrew Brownlie Wardrope; adopted gf's surname Miller Smith 1963; *b* 7 November 1939; *Educ* Glasgow Acad, St Andrews Univ (MA); *m* 1, 1964, Dorothy Agnes Wilson Adams (d 1999); 1 s, 2 da; m 2, 2004, Debjani Jash; *Career* Unilever plc: fin dir Vinyl Products 1970–73, head of planning 1974, fin dir Walls Meat Co 1976, vice-chm Hindustan Lever 1979–81, Speciality Chemicals Gp 1981, fin dir Bd 1989, exec Unilever Foods 1993–94; Imperial Chemical Industries: dir 1994–2001, chief exec 1995–99, chm 1999–2001; chief exec PPF Int 1983, chief exec Quest Int 1986, non-exec dir Midland Bank 1994–96, non-exec dir HSBC Hldgs plc 1996–2001; advsr Goldman Sachs 2002–05. sr advsr Warburg Puncus 2005–; chm: Scottish Power 2000–07 (chm Advsy Bd 2007–), Asia House 2007–; memb Mngmnt Bd MOD 2002–; Hon LLD St Andrews Univ 1995; ACCA; *Recreations* reading, walking; *Clubs* National; *Style*— Charles Miller Smith, Esq; ✉ Scottish Power plc, 5th Floor, 30 Cannon Street EC4M 6XH (tel 020 7651 2002)

MILLETT, Anthea Christine; CBE (2000); da of Rupert Millett, of Salisbury, Wilts, and Lucy, *née* Sutton; *b* 2 November 1941; *Educ* Erdington GS for Girls, Univ of London (BA); *Career* asst teacher: Channing Sch Highgate, Bournville Grammar-Tech Sch; head of dept Solihull HS, dep head Tile Hill Wood Sch Coventry; DFE 1978–92: successively HM inspr, staff inspr and chief inspr; dir of inspection OFSTED 1992–94, chief exec Teacher Training Agency 1995–2000; chm Wilts AHA 2000–02, chair Avon, Glos and Wilts HA 2002–; memb Cncl: Commonwealth Inst, Francis Holland Schools; memb Taylor Ctee on the Management and Governance of Schools; FRSA, FRGS; *Style*— Ms Anthea Millett, CBE; ✉ Avon, Gloucestershire and Wiltshire Health Authority, Jenner House, Langley Park, Chippenham, Wiltshire SN15 1GG (tel 01249 858672)

MILLETT, Prof Martin John; s of John Millett (d 2001), and Sybil Vera, *née* Paine (d 1987); *b* 30 September 1955; *Educ* Weydon Co Secdy Sch Farnham, Farnham Sixth Form Coll, Univ of London (BA), Merton Coll Oxford (DPhil); *m* Joanna Story; 1 da (Julia Maud b 31 Oct 2005); *Career* asst keeper of Archaeology Hants Co Museums 1980–81; Univ of Durham: lectr 1981–91, sr lectr 1991–95, prof of archaeology 1995–98; prof of classical archaeology Univ of Southampton 1999–2001, Laurence prof of classical archaeology Univ of Cambridge 2001–, fell Fitzwilliam Coll Cambridge 2001–; Royal Archaeological Inst: hon ed 1990–95, vice-pres 1998–2003; FSA 1984 (dir 2001–07, treas 2007–), FBA 2006; *Publications* The Romanization of Britain (1990), Roman Britain (1995); *Recreations* wine, travel, food, outdoors; *Style*— Prof Martin Millett; ✉ Faculty of Classics, University of Cambridge, Sidgwick Avenue, Cambridge CB3 9DA (tel 01223 335161, e-mail mjm62@cam.ac.uk)

MILLETT, Baron (Life Peer UK 1998), of St Marylebone in the City of Westminster; Peter Julian Millett; kt (1986), PC (1994); s of Denis Millett (d 1965), of London, and Adele Millett, *née* Weinberg (d 1997); *b* 23 June 1932; *Educ* Harrow, Trinity Hall Cambridge (MA); *m* 1959, Ann Mireille, da of David Harris (d 1980), of London; 3 s (Richard, Andrew, Robert d 1965); *Career* standing jr counsel to BOT and DTI 1967–73, QC 1973, bencher Lincoln's Inn 1980; memb Insolvency Law Review Ctee 1977–82, judge of the High Court of Justice (Chancery Div) 1986–94, a Lord Justice of Appeal 1994–98, a Lord of Appeal in Ordinary 1998–2004, non-permanent judge of the Court of Final Appeal Hong Kong 2000–; treas Lincoln's Inn 2004; hon fell Trinity Hall Cambridge 1994; Hon LLD Univ of London 2000; *Style*— The Rt Hon the Lord Millett, PC; ✉ 18 Portman Close, London W1H 9BR (tel 020 7935 1152, fax 020 7935 1103); 38 Kewhurst Avenue, Cooden, East Sussex TN39 6BH (tel 014243 2970)

MILLETT, Timothy Patrick; *b* 6 January 1951; *Educ* St Benedict's Sch Ealing, Wadham Coll Oxford (MA); *Career* called to the Bar Gray's Inn 1975; official of Court of Justice of the EC 1976–98; legal sec to advocate general: Sir Gordon Slynn 1984–88, Francis Jacobs 1988–89; head div legal service Euro Parl 1998–2000; currently legal sec to judge Cunha Rodrigues, Court of Justice of the EC, vice-pres Bd of Appeal Community Plant Variety Office; *Books* The Court of First Instance of the European Communities (1990), Judicial Control in the EU (2004); *Style*— Timothy Millett, Esq; ✉ Court of Justice of the EC, Luxembourg L-2925 (tel 00 352 4303 2358, fax 00 352 4303 3182, e-mail timothy.millett@curia.europa.eu)

MILLHAM, David Harry; s of Harry Sidney Millham (d 1982), and Emily Harriet Millham, *née* Edwards (d 1998); *b* 20 June 1938; *Educ* William Morris Country Tech Coll Walthamstow, IMEDE Lausanne Switzerland; *m* 27 March 1965, Frances, da of Francis William DuBarry; 1 s (Alexander Gareth David b 20 March 1970), 1 da (Lisa Jane b 14 March 1967); *Career* Financial Times 1959–69 (new issues ed, gen fin news writer), The Times 1969–71 (new issues ed, contrib Fin Ed's Column), PR conslt ICFC 1971–74, dir Shandwick PR Company 1974–79; Shandwick Consultants: dep chm 1979–91, md Fin PR Div 1990–91; exec dep chm Streets International Ltd 1992, chm Millham Communications Ltd 1992–2001, chm DHM Associates 2002–, non-exec dir and co sec Cyprus Aviation Services Ltd; Freeman City of London 1988; *Recreations* watching football, gardening, reading, music; *Style*— David Millham, Esq; ✉ DHM Associates (tel 020 7334 0244 and 01245 351276, e-mail DHMillham@aol.com)

MILLIGAN, Eric; JP (Edinburgh); *b* 27 January 1951; *Educ* Tynecastle HS, Napier Coll Edinburgh; *m* Janis; *Career* former printer; memb Edinburgh DC 1974–78, memb Lothian Regnl Cncl 1978–96 (chm Fin Ctee 1980–82 and 1986–90, convenor 1990–96), convenor City of Edinburgh Cncl 1995–96, Lord-Lt and Lord Provost City of Edinburgh 1996–2003, convenor Lothian Borders Police 2003–07; cncllr Stenhouse Div West Edinburgh; dir Edinburgh International Jazz and Blues Festival Ltd; Convention of Scottish Local Authorities 1980–82 and 1986–96; pres COSLA 1988–90; memb Lab Pty; Hon DBA Napier Univ 1999; Hon FRCSEd 2000; Hon Doc Heriot Watt Univ 2004; Chevalier dans l'Ordre National du Mérite France 1996; *Recreations* watching football and rugby as played by Heart of Midlothian FC and Boroughmuir RFC, listening to music; *Style*— Eric Milligan; ✉ The City of Edinburgh Council, City Chambers, High Street, Edinburgh EH1 1YJ (tel 0131 200 2000)

MILLIGAN, Dr George William Elliott; s of George Burn Milligan (d 1985), of Tullochard, Kingussie, and Kathleen Dorothea Milligan; *b* 2 April 1945; *Educ* Trinity Coll Glenalmond, UC Oxford (BA), Univ of Glasgow (MEng), Univ of Cambridge (PhD); *m* 18 July 1966 (m dis 1992), Baroness Barbara Wanda Borowska, da of Baron Tadeusz Borowski, and Countess Janina, step da of Herbert Charles Story, of Tunbridge Wells, Kent; 2 s (Robert George b 1968, Jan Charles b 1970); *Career* chartered civil engr; lectr Univ of Oxford and tutor and fell Magdalen Coll Oxford 1979–96, dir Geotechnical Consulting Group 1998–; author of tech papers on soil mechanics and geotechnical engineering, co-author of book on basic soil mechanics; FICE; *Recreations* golf, walking, fishing, music; *Style*— Dr George W E Milligan; ✉ Tullochard, West Terrace, Kingussie, Highland PH21 1HB (tel 01540 661243); Geotechnical Consulting Group, 57A Cromwell Road,, London SW7 5BE (tel 020 7581 8348, fax 020 7584 0157, e-mail g.w.e.milligan@gcg.co.uk)

MILLIGAN, Iain Anstruther; QC (1991); s of Maj Wyndham MacBeth Moir Milligan, MBE, TD (d 1999), of Stalbridge, Dorset, and Helen Penelope Eirene, *née* Cassavetti (d 2002); *b* 21 April 1950; *Educ* Eton, Magdalene Coll Cambridge (exhibitioner, scholar (hc), MA); *m* 19 May 1979, Zara Ann Louise, da of Sir Alexander Cadwallader Mainwaring Spearman (d 1982); 2 da (Diana Rose b 1981, Evelyn Louise b 1983), 1 s (Ivar Francis b 1984); *Career* called to the Bar Inner Temple 1973; head of chambers 1999–; *Recreations* forestry, walking; *Style*— Iain Milligan, Esq, QC; ✉ 38 Linden Gardens, London W2 4ER (tel 020 7229 3083); Dunesslin, Dunscore, Dumfries DG2 0UR (tel 01387 820345); 20 Essex Street, London WC2R 3AL (tel 020 7842 1200, fax 020 7842 1270)

MILLIGAN, His Hon Judge Timothy James (Tim); s of late Dr Peter James Wyatt Milligan, and late Rosemary Elizabeth Ann, *née* Dutton; *b* 16 March 1940; *Educ* Winchester, Grenoble Univ; *m* 31 Aug 1976, Sally Marcella, da of late Brig Robert T Priest, OBE, RA, and late Lady Marcella Florence Slessor; 2 step s (Jonathan Ivor Robert Price b 2 Feb 1969, Alexander David William Price b 20 March 1971); *Career* solicitor; articled clerk Taylor & Humbert 1960–64, asst slr Leeds Smith 1967–69, asst slr then ptnr Triggs Turner & Co Guildford 1969–74, ptnr Warner & Richardson Winchester 1974–91, dep registrar 1976–86, asst recorder 1986–89, recorder 1989–91, HM coroner Central Hants 1982–91, circuit judge (Western Circuit) 1991–; memb: Law Soc 1967 (now hon), Coroners' Soc of GB 1982 (now hon); *Recreations* cricket, football, rackets, music, reading, theatre, cinema; *Clubs* Tennis & Rackets Assoc, Jesters, Hants CCC, MCC; *Style*— His Hon Judge Tim Milligan

MILLIN, Peter Jack; s of Henry Millin (d 1977), of London, and Lily Millin, of USA; *b* 28 December 1930; *Educ* Farnham GS, Sch of Econ Science Univ of Liverpool, Adleman Soc (Psychology & Hypnotherapy); *m* 1969 (m dis); 1 s (David b 1960); *Career* psychologist, counsellor and hypnotherapist 1960–; princ Friendship/Marriage Bureau 1950–60, pres Professional Hypnotherapist Centre, princ Acad of Hypnotherapy, lectr various orgns and contrib to various jls; winner of various medals for ballroom dancing; memb Complementary Medicine Soc; *Recreations* philosophy, theatre, classical music, travel; *Clubs* Unique Social (fndr), Kaleidescape; *Style*— Peter Millin, Esq; ✉ 28 Lakeside Crescent, East Barnet, Hertfordshire EN4 8QJ (tel 020 8441 9685); Academy of Hypnotherapy (tel 020 8441 9685)

MILLINGTON, Andrew; s of Walter Millington (d 1985), and Margaret, *née* Burley; *b* 28 June 1960; *Educ* Adwick Sch, UEA (BA); *m* 1989, Tamara, da of John Ingram; 1 s (Maximillian Isidore b 4 April 1991), 1 da (Anya Eve b 31 Dec 1992); *Career* gallery asst, journalist and PR exec 1981–89, account mangr Biss Lancaster 1989–92; dir: Christow Consultants 1992–95, Shandwick International 1995–; MIPR 1997; *Recreations* art, opera, theatre, friends; *Style*— Andrew Millington, Esq

MILLINGTON, Caroline Sarah (Caro); da of Ernest Rogers Millington, of Couze, France, and Gwen, *née* Pickard (d 1979); *b* 4 August 1949; *Educ* Greycoat Hosp Sch Westminster, Univ of York (BA); *Career* trainee journalist BBC 1970–72; prodr: The World Tonight and Newsdesk (BBC Radio 4) 1973–77, Nationwide (BBC1) 1978–79, The Week in

Westminster, Talking Politics, In Business and documentaries (BBC Radio 4) 1980–84, Brass Tacks (BBC2) 1986; special asst to BBC's Asst DG 1985; BBC Radio: head of magazine progs 1988–93, controller of production 1993–96; controller of multimedia devpt BBC Production 1996–98, project dir BBC 1998–99; chm NW London Strategic HA 2004–06 (non-exec dir 2002), non-exec dir Ealing Hounslow and Hammersmith HA 1996–2002; chm The Moat Studios 1995–2005; memb NUJ; jt fndr, first chair and fell Radio Acad; art student 2006–; *Recreations* walking, music; *Style*— Ms Caro Millington; ✉ 6A Sterne Street, London W12 8AD (e-mail c_millington@yahoo.com)

MILLINGTON, Gordon Stopford; OBE (1996); s of Percival Richard Millington (d 1981), of Killinchy, and Irene Ellen, *née* Forster; *b* 29 June 1935; *Educ* Campbell Coll, Queen's Univ Belfast (BSc); *m* 1, 30 April 1960, Margaret Jean (d 1999), da of Leslie Pegler (d 1964), of Croydon; 2 s (Mark Stopford b 28 Feb 1962, Gavin Paul b 11 Dec 1965), 1 da (Kathryn Margaret b 26 Feb 1964); m 2, Sept 2000 Norma Joan, *née*, Jordan; *Career* asst engr Sir William Halcrow & Partners 1957–59, Kirk McClure & Morton (engr 1959–66, ptnr 1966–87, sr ptnr 1988–98); chm: Amelwood Ltd, Stanwood Estates Ltd, NI Assoc ICE 1979–80; pres Belfast Rotary Club 1980–81; chm: Bd of Govrs Grosvenor HS 1983–90, NI Branch Inst of Highways and Transportation 1989–90, Structures and Building Bd ICE 1992–94, NI 2000 1992–2000; external examiner Cork Regnl Tech Coll; memb Exec Inst of Engrs of Ireland 1994–2000; dir: Ulster Orchestra Soc 1997–2000, Irish Engineering Publications 1997–99, Ormeau Baths Gall 1999– (chm 2000–03); pres Irish Acad of Engrg 2000–02; memb CBI - IBEC Tport Logistics Gp, memb Gen Consumer Cncl Energy Tport Gp 1998–2004; hon sec Mundell Fund 1998–2003; DSc (hc) Queens Univ of Belfast 2001; Hon FICE (vice-pres 1994–96), FIStructE, FIEI (vice-pres 1995–97, pres 1997–98), FIHT, MASCE; *Recreations* yachting; *Clubs* Quoile Yacht; *Style*— Gordon Millington, Esq, OBE; ✉ One Malone View Road, Belfast BT9 5PH (tel 028 9061 1303, fax 028 9029 0282, e-mail gordon.millington@ntlworld.com)

MILLMAN, Stewart Ian; s of Sidney Woolf Millman (d 1984), of London, and Doris, *née* Gerstein (d 2000); *b* 21 November 1948; *Educ* City of London Sch, New Coll Oxford (MA); *Career* Lazard Securities Ltd 1971–81 (dir 1979–81), de Zoete & Bevan 1981 (ptnr 1984), dir Barclays de Zoete Wedd Securities Ltd 1986–93, jt md de Zoete & Bevan Ltd 1988–93; NatWest Markets: dep chm Equity Primary Markets 1993–95, head of Euro investment banking 1995–97; md Corp Fin and Advsy Div HSBC Investment Bank plc 1998–2002, chm Patsystems plc 2003–; non-exec dir: Intellisponse Inc USA 2002–, Decillion Ltd (SA) 2003–04, Leadcom Integrated Solutions Ltd (Israel) 2005–06 (chm 2006–), MTI Wireless Edge (Israel) 2006–; memb Cncl Soc of Investment Analysts 1979–89; tstee New Coll Oxford Devpt Fund 1992–; FSI, MRSC, AIIMR, FRSA; *Recreations* playing cricket, watching football, travel; *Style*— Stewart Millman, Esq; ✉ Quantum Corporate Finance Consultancy, 27 Hyde Park Gardens Mews, London W2 2NX (tel 020 7402 6202, fax 020 7402 1193)

MILLNER, Etienne Henry de la Fargue; s of Guy Millner, of Cumbria, and Frances *née* Johnston (d 2000); *b* 15 January 1954; *Educ* Stowe, Goldsmiths' Coll Sch of Art (BA), Royal Acad Sch (postgrad cert); *m* 1987, Mary Elizabeth, da of Jack Castle; 2 da (Daisy b 1989, Polly b 1998), 1 s (William b 1991); *Career* figurative sculptor in plaster and clay for bronze working mainly in small and monumental portraiture; exhibitions incl: RA Summer Shows 1979, 1982, 1984, 1985, 1986 and 1988, National Portrait Gall (NPG) New Faces 1987, Art for Sale Whiteleys 1992, Chelsea Harbour 1993, Cadogan Contemporary Summer Show 1993, one-man show Cadogan Contemporary 1994, NPG 1994, Soc of Portrait Sculptors 1995–2007, Rye Festival 1997, Piers Feetham Gall Aldeburgh 1998, People's Portrait (touring exhibition) 2000–2001, Alan Kluckow Gall Selected Portraits 2000; work in permanent collections incl: Wellington Coll 1993, NPG 1996, Harris Manchester Coll Oxford 1996, Arndean Gallery 1999–2002, Goodwood House, Longford Castle, Holdenby; Soc of Portrait Sculptors: memb Cncl 1996, vice-pres 2005; FRBS 1997 (ARBS 1992); *Recreations* walking, riding; *Clubs* Chelsea Arts; *Style*— Etienne Henry de la Fargue Millner, Esq; ✉ 5 Priory Grove, London SW8 2PD (tel 020 7720 6695)

MILLS, Andrew; s of Robin Gerald Mills, of Benington, Herts, and Alice Daphne Mills; *b* 28 July 1958; *Educ* Haileybury (scholar), City Univ (BSc), RMA Sandhurst, City Univ Business Sch (MBA); *m* 11 July 1987, Vanessa Anne, *née* Harford; 3 s (Charles b 6 Sept 1990, Thomas b 26 May 1993, Henry b 8 March 1995), 2 da (Alice b 27 Nov 1991, Lucinda b 5 Feb 1998); *Career* Capt 3 Bn Para Regt 1980–83; equity salesman Nat West Securities 1984–87, assoc dir of research BZW 1987–90, dir of corp affrs BET plc 1990–94; Kingfisher plc: dir of investor rels 1994–2001, seconded as retail ops controller Woolworths 1999–2000, dir of corp affrs 2001–03; gp communications dir Rexam plc 2004–; non-exec dir The 9th Floor plc 1996–2002; assoc Soc of Investment Professionals 1986–2003; fell Investor Rels Soc 1997 (non-exec dir 1994–97, chm 1997–99); memb RCO; Liveryman Worshipful Co of Merchant Taylors 1990; *Clubs* Naval and Military, Parachute Regt Assoc, Tadmarton Heath Golf; *Style*— Andrew Mills, Esq; ✉ Rexam plc, 4 Millbank, London SW1P 3XR (tel 020 7227 4100)

MILLS, Angela Margaret; da of Dr Ronald Hubert Bonfield Mills (d 1989), and Audrey Vera, *née* Mountjoy; *b* 24 January 1948; *Educ* Vaynor and Penderyn Sch, Somerville Coll Oxford (MA, BM BCh), St Thomas' Hosp Med Sch; *Career* conslt gynaecologist; nat MO Family Planning Assoc 1983–88, hon lectr Dept of Obstetrics and Gynaecology Univ Coll Hosps London 1983–2002 (now hon sr lectr), currently emeritus conslt gynaecologist and hon sr lectr Univ Coll Hosps NHS Tst; formerly conslt gynaecologist United Elizabeth Garrett Anderson Hosp and Hosp for Women Soho; author of various pubns in jls; memb: Sub-Ctee RCOG on problems associated with AIDS in relation to obstetrics and gynaecology, Bd Faculty of Community Health 1991–94, Continuing Educn Sub-Ctee of Faculty of Community Health 1990–94, Bd Faculty of Family Planning and Reproductive Health Care 1994–96 (chm Clinical and Scientific Ctee 1994–98, examiner 1998–2005, chm Educn Ctee 2004–06), Professional Conduct Ctee GMC 2001–06, Ethical Ctee RCOG 2006–; chm London Soc Family Planning Doctors 1985–88, vice-chm Nat Assoc of Family Planning Doctors 1989–93, chm Women's Visiting Gynaecological Club 2003–, tstee Women's Health Concern; memb: Cncl Nat Assoc of Family Planning Doctors 1993–94, American Soc of Fertility and Sterility, Soc of Advancement of Contraception, Br Soc of Clinical Colposcopists, BMA; FRCOG 1993, MFPHM 1996; *Recreations* travelling, music, gardening; *Clubs* Network, RSM, Reform; *Style*— Miss Angela Mills; ✉ 80 Harley Street, London W1G 7HL (tel 020 7637 0584, fax 020 7637 0242, website www.drangelamills.co.uk)

MILLS, Dame Barbara Jean Lyon; DBE (1997), QC (1986, NI 1991); da of John Lyon Warnock, and Nora Kitty Warnock; *b* 10 August 1940; *Educ* St Helen's Sch Northwood, Lady Margaret Hall Oxford (Gibbs scholar, MA); *m* 1962, John Angus Donald Mills, s of Kenneth McKenzie Mills; 3 da (Sarah b 1963, Caroline b 1965, Lizzie b 1969), 1 s (Peter b 1971); *Career* called to the Bar Middle Temple 1963 (bencher 1990); recorder of the Crown Court 1982–92; jr Treasury counsel Central Criminal Court 1981–86, legal assessor to GMC and GDC 1988–90, dir The Serious Fraud Office 1990–92, Dir of Public Prosecutions 1992–98, the Adjudicator 1999–; memb: Criminal Injuries Compensation Bd 1988–90, Parole Bd 1990, Gen Advsy Cncl BBC 1991–92; hon vice-pres Inst for the Study and Treatment of Delinquency 1996–; chm Forum UK 1999; memb Competition Cmmn 2001; govr London Guildhall Univ (now London Metropolitan Univ) 1999, tstee Victim Support 1999–2004; Hon LLD: Univ of Hull 1993, Nottingham Trent Univ 1993, London Guildhall Univ 1994; hon fell: Lady Margaret Hall Oxford 1991, Soc for Advanced Legal Studies 1997; CIMgt 1993; *Style*— Dame Barbara Mills, DBE, QC; ✉ The Adjudicator's Office, Haymarket House, 28 Haymarket, London SW1Y 4SP (tel 020 7930 2292, fax 020 7930 2298, e-mail adjudicators@gtnet.gov.uk)

MILLS, Bradford Alan (Brad); s of Bradford Mills, and Elizabeth Leisk Mills; *b* 12 September 1954, Washington DC, USA; *Educ* Stanford Univ (BS, MS); *m* 1994, Carol; 3 c (Taybrook b 8 Sept 1986, Bradford b 2 Feb 1995, Morgan b 1 Oct 1998); *Career* formerly with: Magma Copper Co, Echo Bay Mines, BHP (then BHP Billiton); pres and ceo (base metals) BHP Billiton Ltd 2001–04, ceo Lonmin plc 2004–; supporter Mills Fndn; memb: Soc of Economic Geologists, Minelogical Soc of USA, American Inst of Mining Engrs; *Recreations* flyfishing, tennis, skiing, reading; *Clubs* Leash (NYC); *Style*— Brad Mills, Esq; ✉ Lonmin plc, 4 Grosvenor Place, London SW1X 7YL

MILLS, Christopher Harwood Bernard; s of Cyril Bertram Mills (d 1991), and Marie Beatrice Louise Francoise, *née* Harwood (d 2002); *b* 5 November 1952; *Educ* Eton, Guildhall Univ; *m* 10 Oct 1987, Lynne Theresa, *née* Egan; 3 s (Charlie b 3 Sept 1988, Nicholas b 4 Aug 1990, Harry b 30 May 1994); *Career* Samuel Montagu Ltd 1970–85, ceo North Atlantic Smaller Companies Tst 1983–, dir Invesco MIM 1985–93, dir J O Hambro Capital Management Group Ltd 1993–; non-exec dir: SiRViS IT plc 2007–, Catalyst Media Group plc 2007–; awards incl Sunday Telegraph Investment Mangr of the Year 1993; *Recreations* shooting, diving; *Clubs* Whites, Annabel's, Harry's Bar; *Style*— Christopher Mills, Esq; ✉ 10 Cliveden Place, London SW1W 8LA; Bradley Court, Chieveley, Berkshire RG18 9XZ; J O Hambo Capital Management Group Limited, Ryder Court, 14 Ryder Street, London SW1Y 6QB (tel 020 7747 5600, 020 7747 5647, e-mail cmills@johcm.co.uk)

MILLS, 3 Viscount (UK 1962); Sir Christopher Philip Roger Mills; 3 Bt (UK 1953); also Baron Mills (UK 1957); o s of 2 Viscount Mills (d 1988); *b* 20 May 1956; *m* 29 March 1980, Lesley Alison, er da of Alan Bailey, of Lichfield, Staffs; *Career* area mangr fisheries, recreation and ecology NRA NW Region 1991–95, area mangr Thames Region NE Area Environment Agency 1995–2000, area mangr Thames Region SE Area Environment Agency 2000–; memb Cncl: Inst of Fisheries Mgmnt, RSPB; *Style*— The Rt Hon Viscount Mills

MILLS, Colin James Edmund; s of James Oliver Mills (d 1986), of Holcot, Northants, and Ada, *née* Cox (d 2001); *b* 28 November 1937; *Educ* Northampton GS, Leicester Sch of Architecture (DipArch); *m* 2 Sept 1961, Eileen Patricia, da of Charles Frederick Swain (d 1986); 1 s (James b 1965), 3 da (Kathryn b 1967, Rosalind b 1969, Clare b 1982); *Career* chartered architect; ptnr Morrison & Partners 1970–77, dir Morrison Design Partnership 1977–86, princ Colin J E Mills 1986–2002; fndr chm Friends of Brodick Castle and Country Park 1996–98; compiler The Nigel Tranter Bibliography 2003; ARIAS; *Recreations* painting, ornithology, reading, history; *Style*— Colin Mills, Esq; ✉ Roadend, Shiskine, Isle of Arran KA27 8EW (tel 01770 860448); studio (tel and fax 01770 860475, e-mail caileanmills.roadend@virgin.net)

MILLS, David John; s of John Mills (d 1958), and Violet, *née* Germaine (d 1970); *b* 9 February 1944; *Educ* Beal GS; *m* 27 March 1967, Lesley Jacqueline, *née* Wand; 1 s (Nigel John), 2 da (Penelope Jacqueline, Susan Jennifer); *Career* Midland Bank (now HSBC Bank plc): asst gen mangr mktg 1983–85, regnl dir 1985–87, IT dir 1987–89, direct banking dir 1990–93, chm First Direct 1990–93 and 2000–01, dir Midland General Ltd, Midland Unit Tst Mgmnt Ltd and Midland Bank Pension Tst Ltd 1993–94, gen mangr card services and mktg 1993–95, gen mangr business devpt and md personal fin services 1995–99, chm HSBC Life (UK) Ltd (formerly Midland Life Ltd) 1995–2001 (chief exec 1993–94), gen mangr personal banking 1999–2002, memb Asset & Liability Mgmnt and Exec Ctees 1995–2001, memb Chief Exec Ctee 2000–01; chief exec Post Office Ltd 2002–05, dir Royal Mail Holdings plc 2002–05, dir Royal Mail Gp plc 2002–05, chm Post Office Fin Services 2004–05; chm First Rate Travel Services Ltd 2002–04, dir First Rate Travel Services Holdings Ltd 2002–04; chm Mondex Int Ltd 1995–2001; dir: Mastercard/Europay UK Ltd 1990–94 (chm 1992–93), Euro Travellers' Cheque Int SC 1990–2001, Europay Int SA 1992–2001, European Payment Systems Services SA 1992–2001, Personal Investment Ombudsman Bureau Ltd 1995–2000, Personal Investment Authy Ltd 1995–2000, Maestro Int Inc 1995–2001, British Interactive Broadcasting (Market Contributions) Ltd 1995–2001, British Interactive Broadcasting Ltd 1995–2001, Camelot Gp plc 2003–05, Camelot Int Services Ltd 2003–05; Assoc of Payment and Clearing Services (APACS): dep chm Card Payment Gp 1992–93 (memb 1990–92), chm Cash Services Gp 1995–2000, memb Cncl 1995–2000 (memb Managing Ctee 1995–2000); sr ind dir Cardpoint plc 2007–; chm The Move Factory Ltd 2007–; chm Employers Forum on Disability Ltd 2004–06 (dir 1993–2003), memb Nat Disability Cncl 1995–2000; tstee Royal Assoc for Disability and Rehabilitation 2004–; distinguished Sloan Fell London Business Sch; memb Inst of Fin Servs, FBIC; *Recreations* family, wine, fishing, motorsport; *Clubs* RAC; *Style*— David Mills, Esq; ✉ e-mail david@davidjmills.com

MILLS, David John; s of Terence John Mills, and Geraldine Patricia, *née* Edwards; *b* 4 January 1963; *Educ* Wolverhampton GS, Gonville & Caius Coll Cambridge; *m* 27 July 1990, Janet Elizabeth, *née* Lazarus; 2 s (Frederick Lazarus b 26 April 1994, Albert Norman b 18 Nov 1995), 1 da (Matilda Rose Geraldine b 8 April 1998); *Career* ed The Artist's and Illustrator's Magazine 1986–89, managing ed Arts and Leisure The Sunday Times 1996– (dep arts ed 1989–90, arts ed 1990–96); *Recreations* cricket, music, squash, learning the violin; *Clubs* Groucho, Coolhurst Lawn Tennis and Squash Racquets; *Style*— David Mills, Esq; ✉ The Sunday Times, 1 Pennington Street, London E1 9XW (tel 020 7782 5000)

MILLS, Gloria; CBE (2005, MBE 1999); *Career* early career in law publishing, held various positions publishing unions Nat Soc of Operative Printers and Assts (NATSOPA) and SOGAT, sr nat offr and mangr Nat Union of Public Employees (NUPE) 1987–93, dir of equal opportunities UNISON 1993– (also memb Sr Mgmnt Gp); cmmr Cmmn for Racial Equality 2002–; memb: Gen Cncl and Exec TUC 1994– (also memb European Ctee, Women's Ctee, Employment Appeals Tbnl and Race Rels Ctee), Race Rels Forum Home Office 1998–2001, Lab Party Nat Policy Forum, Gen Cncl ITUC 2006; Public Servs Int: chair European Women's Ctee 2003–, vice-chair World Women's Ctee 2004–; Hon LLD Univ of Staffordshire 2006; MCIPD, FRSA; *Style*— Ms Gloria Mills, CBE; ✉ UNISON, 1 Mabledon Place, London WC1H 9AJ (tel 0845 355 0845)

MILLS, Dr Harold Hernshaw; CB (1995); s of Harold George Mills (d 1988), and Margaret Elliot Mills (d 2000); *b* 2 March 1938; *Educ* Greenock HS, Univ of Glasgow (BSc, PhD); *m* 1 Aug 1973, Marion Elizabeth, da of John Beattie (d 1999); *Career* cancer res scientist Roswell Park Meml Inst Buffalo NY 1962–64; lectr Univ of Glasgow 1964–69; princ Scot Home and Health Dept 1970–76, asst sec Scot Office 1976–81, Privy Cncl Office 1981–83, under sec Scot Devpt Dept 1984–88 (asst sec 1983–84), princ fin offr Scot Office 1988–92, sec Environment Dept Scot Office 1992–95, sec and head Devpt Dept Scot Office 1995–98; chm: Land Tst 1998–, Edinburgh World Heritage Tst 1999–2006, Caledonian MacBrayne Ltd 1999–2006, David MacBrayne Ltd 1999–2006, Caledonian MacBrayne Holdings Ltd 1999–2006, CalMac Ferries Ltd 2006–; dir: Northlink Orkney and Shetland Ferries Ltd 2000–, Northlink Ferries Ltd 2006–; memb: Home in Scotland 1998– (chm 2000–04), Home Gp Ltd 2000–04, Home Housing Tst 2000–04, Edinburgh City Centre Partnership 2002–05; memb Bd Queen Margaret UC Edinburgh 1998–2004; tstee: Scot Maritime Museum 1998–, Edinburgh Old Town and South Side Tst 2000–06; dir City of Adelaide Charitable Tst 2005–; *Style*— Dr Harold Mills, CB; ✉ 21 Hatton Place, Edinburgh EH9 1UB (tel 0131 667 7910, fax 0131 668 3027)

MILLS, Hayley Catherine Rose Vivien; da of Sir John Mills, CBE (d 2005), and Mary Hayley Bell, JP (d 2005); *b* 18 April 1946; *Educ* Elmhurst Ballet Sch, Institute Alpine Videmanette

M

Switzerland; *m* 20 June 1971 (m dis 1977), Roy Boulting (d 2001); 1 s (Crispian Boulting Mills b 18 Jan 1973); has son by Leigh Lawson; 1 s (Jason (Ace) Lawson b 30 July 1976); *Career* actress; patron: Mountview Theatre Sch, Jan de Vries Benevolent Tst, Only Make Believe NY, Shooting Star Children's Hospice, Gtr London Fund for the Blind, World Vision, Peta; fndr memb: VIVA, SOS; serving sis OStJ 1999; *Theatre* incl: Peter Pan 1969, The Wild Duck 1970, Trelawney of the Wells 1972, The Three Sisters 1973, A Touch of Spring 1975, Rebecca 1977, My Fat Friend 1978, Hush of Hide 1979, The Importance of Being Earnest 1979, The Summer Party 1980, Tallys Folly 1982, The Secretary Bird 1983, Dial M for Murder 1984, Toys in the Attic 1986, The Kidnap Game 1991, The King and I (Gordon Frost Prodns Australia) 1991–92, Fallen Angels 1993, The Card 1994, Dead Guilty 1995–96, Brief Encounter 1996, The King and I (USA tour) 1997–98, Suite in Two Keys (NY) 2000, Vagina Monologues (NY) 2001, Little Night Music (USA) 2001, Wait Until Dark (USA) 2003, Humble Boy (UK) 2003, The Bird Sanctuary (USA) 2005, Two Can Play (USA) 2005; *Television* incl: Deadly Strangers 1974, Only a Scream Away 1974, two Loveboat Specials 1978, The Flame Trees of Thika 1980, Illusion of Life 1981, Amazing Stories 1986, Murder She Wrote 1986, Tales of the Unexpected 1987, Good Morning Miss Bliss 1988, Back Home 1989, Walk of Life 1990, Wild at Heart 2006–07, US Variety TV, The Danny Kaye Show, The Andy Williams Show; *Films* incl: Tiger Bay 1959, Pollyanna 1960, Parent Trap 1961, The Castaways 1962, Whistle Down the Wind 1962, Summer Magic 1963, The Moonspinners 1964, The Chalk Garden 1964, That Darn Cat 1965, Sky West & Crooked 1965, The Truth About Spring 1965, The Family Way 1966, The Trouble with Angels 1966, Pretty Polly 1967, Twisted Nerve 1968, Take A Girl Like You 1970, Endless Night 1972, Mr Forbush and the Penquins 1972, What Changed Charlie Farthing 1975, The Diamond Hunters 1975, Parent Trap II 1986, Parent Trap III 1989, Parent Trap IV 1989, Appointment with Death 1988; *Books* My God (1988); *Recreations* reading, travel, walking; *Style—* Miss Hayley Mills; ✉ The Don Buchwald Agency, 10 East 44th Street, NY 10017, USA (tel 00 1 212 867 1200, fax 00 1 212 972 3209); Chatto & Linnit Ltd, 123a Kings Road, London SW3 (tel 020 7352 7722)

MILLS, Sir (George) Ian; kt (2001); s of George Haxton Mills, and Evelyn Mary, *née* Owen; *b* 19 November 1935; *Educ* Taunton's GS Southampton; *m* 1968, Margaret Elizabeth Dunstan; 1 s, 1 da (and 1 s decd); *Career* articled clerk Beal Young & Booth Chartered Accountants Southampton 1954–60; Price Waterhouse: joined London Office 1960, seconded to World Bank team assisting Govt of Pakistan Treasy 1962–63; chief accountant Univ of Ibadan Nigeria 1965–68; Price Waterhouse: rejoined London Office 1968–70, mangr i/c northern and Scot mgmnt consultancy ops Newcastle upon Tyne 1970–73, ptnr i/c Africa mgmnt consultancy ops London 1974–78, ptnr i/c UK mktg 1978–82, nat dir of Central Govt servs 1983–85; Mgmnt Bd NHS: dir of fin mgmnt 1985–88, dir of resource mgmnt 1988–89; Price Waterhouse 1989–92: rejoined as sr ptnr i/c business devpt Europe, memb Euro Mgmnt Bd and World Mgmnt Ctee; dir and chm IHSM Consultants 1992–96; chm: Lewisham and North Southwark Health Authy 1991–93, SE London Health Authy 1991–93, SE London Health Cmmn (later Authy) 1993–96, N Thames Regnl Office NHS Exec 1996–98, London Regnl Office NHS Exec 1999–2001; cmmr London Region NHS Exec Dept of Health 2001–03; memb Editorial Advsy Bd: Health Serv Jl 1992–95, Br Jl of Health Care Mgmnt 1996–2003; memb: NHS Policy Bd 1996–98, sec of state for Health's Regnl Chairs' Meeting 1999–2001, NHS Appointments Cmmn 2001–03; dir Blackheath Preservation Tst 1990–2004, dep chair rising to chair Cncl of Mgmnt St Christopher's Hospice 1993–2003, tstee SE London Community Fndn 1995–2000, chair Ind Remuneration Panel London Borough of Lewisham 2001–, chair Blackheath Historic Bldgs Tst 2003–; FCA 1960, FIMC 1964 (CMC), FHSM (MHSM 1985); *Clubs* Royal Commonwealth, Royal Soc of Arts; *Style—* Sir Ian Mills; ✉ 60 Belmont Hill, London SE13 5DN (tel 020 8852 2457); Blackheath Historic Buildings Trust, Chapman House, 10 Blackheath Village, London SE3 9LE (tel 020 8318 5692, fax 020 8463 0609)

MILLS, Prof Ian Mark; s of John Mills (d 1972), of Streatley, Berks, and Marguerita Alice Gertrude, *née* Gooding (d 1977); *b* 9 June 1930; *Educ* Leighton Park Sch Reading, Univ of Reading, Univ of Oxford; *m* 23 Aug 1957, Margaret Mary, da of Prof Julian Lewis Maynard (d 1954), of Univ of Minnesota; 1 s (William b 1960), 1 da (Jane b 1962); *Career* res fell: Univ of Minnesota 1954–56, Corpus Christi Coll Cambridge 1956–57; lectr, reader then prof Univ of Reading 1957–95 (prof emeritus 1995–), Leverhulme emeritus research fell; pres Consultative Ctee on Units of the Bureau International des Poids et Mésures; memb Faraday Div Royal Soc of Chem, fell Optical Soc of America, memb Cncl Royal Instn; FRS 1996; *Books* Quantities, Units & Symbols in Physical Chemistry (1988 and 1993), also author of research papers in Molecular Spectroscopy; *Recreations* walking, sailing; *Style—* Prof Ian Mills, FRS; ✉ Department of Chemistry, University of Reading, Berkshire RG6 2AD (tel 0118 378 8456, fax 0118 931 6331, e-mail i.m.mills@rdg.ac.uk)

MILLS, John Frederick; s of Henry Alfred Mills (d 1973), and Jean Margaret Aitchison; *b* 6 September 1950; *Educ* Highgate Sch, The Queen's Coll Oxford, Merton Coll Oxford (Domus sr scholar, BLitt, MA); *m* 1974, Jean Marie, da of Aloysius Theodore Correia (d 1999); 1 s (Theodore b 1978), 3 da (Julia b 1980, Cecily b 1983, Claudia b 1983); m 2, 2003, Imogen Stephanie Nicholls; *Career* DTI 1974–: private sec to Min of State for Industry 1976–78, princ 1978–81, seconded as princ asst sec Govt of Hong Kong 1981–85, asst sec and head of Int Telecommunications Policy Branch 1986–89, memb PM's Policy Unit 1989–92, under sec and dir of Consumer Affairs OFT 1992–95; memb Advsy Panel OFT 2001–03; chief exec: Cornwall CC 1995–99, Policy and Resources Dept States of Jersey 1999–2003; dir Cityshap plc 1991–; govr Highgate Sch 1993– (chm and treas 1999–); *Style—* John Mills, Esq; ✉ The Coach House, Chairvale Road, Jersey JE2 3YQ (tel 07970 781104)

MILLS, Jonathan Edward Harland; s of Frank Harland Mills, and Elayne Mary Mills; *b* 21 March 1963, Sydney, Australia; *Educ* Univ of Sydney (BMus), RMIT Univ Melbourne (MArch); *Career* artistic dir Blue Mountains Festival 1988–90; RMIT Univ: composer-in-residence and research fell in environmental acoustics 1992–97, adjunct prof in environmental acoustics 1998–03; artistic dir Melbourne Festival 2000–01 (incl dir: Melbourne Millennium Eve Celebrations 1999, Fedn Festival 2001), composer-in-residence Bundanon Tst 2002, adjunct prof La Trobe Univ 2004–07, Vice-Chllr's professorial fell Univ of Melbourne 2006, dir Edinburgh Int Festival 2007–; artistic advsr: Brisbane Biennial Int Music Festival 1995–97, Melbourne Recital Centre and Elisabeth Murdoch Hall 2005–; dir Alfred Deakin Innovation Lectures 2003–; cmmr Australian Heritage Cmmn 2002–04; chair: Review into the Australian Youth Orchestra & the Australian Nat Acad of Music Cwlth Govt 2004–05, Review of Opera Victorian Govt 2005; memb: Australian Int Cultural Cncl 1998–2003, Bd Synergy Percussion 2001–06, New Media Arts Bd Australia Cncl 2003–05, Bd Melbourne Recital Hall 2004–05, Australian Heritage Cncl 2004–06, Maj Performing Arts Bd Australia Cncl 2005–, Bd Arts Exhibitions Australia 2005–; artistic dir Seaborne Broughton & Walford Fndn 1988–; memb Jury: Pratt Prize for Musical Theatre 2002–, Ian Potter Fndn Music Cmmns 2003–05; patron Leigh Warren & Dancers 2001–; various works and performances for radio, film, theatre and concert incl: Ethereal Eye (electro-acoustic dance opera) 1996, The Ghost Wife (chamber opera) 1999–2002, Sandakan Threnody (for solo tenor, chorus and orchestra) 2001 (touring 2004–06, Prix Italia 2005), The Eternity Man (chamber opera) 2003; Genesis Prize Cmmn for Opera 2003; Centenary Medal Australia 2002; FRSA; *Style—* Jonathan Mills, Esq; ✉ Edinburgh International Festival, The Hub, Castlehill, Edinburgh EH1 2NE (tel 0131 473 2032, fax 0131 473 2002)

MILLS, Sir Keith Edward; kt; s of Edward James Mills (d 2002), of Brentwood, Essex, and Margaret Katherine, *née* Weber (d 1992); *b* 15 May 1950, Brentwood, Essex; *Educ* St Martins Sch Brentwood; *m* 31 Aug 1974, Maureen Elizabeth, *née* Simmons; 1 s (Alexander James Eaton b 5 May 1984), 1 da (Abigail Louisa Charlotte b 23 Nov 1988); *Career* ceo Mills Smith & Ptnrs Ltd 1984–89, ceo Air Miles UK Ltd 1988–92; chm and ceo: KEM Mgmnt Ltd 1994–, First Call plc 1999–2002; chm Loyalty Mgmnt Gp Ltd 2001–; int pres and ceo London 2012 Ltd 2003–06, dep chm London Organising Ctee 2012 Olympic Games 2006–; team princ Team Origin (Americas Cup team); dir: Breakthrough Breast Cancer Charity, AT Racing Ltd; non-exec dir Tottenham Hotspur Football Club plc; Master Entrepreneur of the Year 2005, Business Ldr of the Year London Business Awards 2005, Chief Exec Award for Mktg 2005, Sports Industry Personality of the Year 2005; Hon PhD Loughborough Univ 2006; fell Mktg Soc, life fell Inst of Direct Mktg; *Recreations* sailing, skiing, music, travelling; *Clubs* Royal Ocean Racing, Royal Southern Yacht, Royal Thames Yacht, Salcombe Sailing; *Style—* Sir Keith Mills; ✉ London 2012, 1 Churchill Place, London E14 5LN (tel 020 3201 2000, e-mail keith.mills@london2012.com)

MILLS, Leif Anthony; CBE (1995); s of Victor William Mills (d 1967), and Bergliot, *née* Ström-Olsen (d 1989); *b* 25 March 1936; *Educ* Kingston GS, Balliol Coll Oxford (MA); *m* 2 Aug 1958, Gillian Margaret (d 2003), da of William Henry Smith (d 1966); 2 s (Adam, Nathanial), 2 da (Susannah, Harriet); *Career* 2 Lt RMP 1957–59; Nat Union of Bank Employees (now Banking Insurance and Fin Union) 1960–96: res offr 1960–62, asst gen sec 1962–68, dep gen sec 1968–72, gen sec 1972–96; Parly candidate (Lab): Salisbury gen election 1964, Salisbury by-election 1965; TUC: memb Non Manual Workers Advsy Ctee 1967–72, memb Gen Cncl 1983–96, chm Fin Servs Ctee 1983–90, chm Educn and Trg Ctee 1989–96, pres TUC 1994–95; memb: Manpower Econs Advsy Ctee on Equal Pay 1971, Ctee to Review the Functioning of Fin Instns (Wilson Ctee) 1977–80, Civil Serv Pay Res Unit Bd 1978–81, BBC Consultative Gp on Social Effects of TV 1978–80, Armed Forces Pay Review Body 1980–87, Monopolies and Mergers Cmmn 1982–91, Ctees TUC, Int Ctees FIET, Fin Reporting Cncl 1990–96, Nat Cncl for Vocational Qualifications 1992–96, Investors in People UK 1993–96, PIA Ombudsman Cncl 1994–2000, Cncl Consumers Assoc 1996–2002, Bd of Employment Tbnls Serv 1996–2001; chm: Cncl for Admin (formerly Admin Standards Cncl) 1997–99, Covent Garden Market Authy 1998–2005; tstee Civic Tst 1989–96, govr London Business Sch 1989–92, hon sec St John the Baptist PCC West Byfleet 1990–94; *Books* Frank Wild: A Biography (1999); *Recreations* rowing, chess; *Clubs* Oxford and Cambridge, Weybridge Rowing; *Style—* Leif Mills, Esq, CBE; ✉ 31 Station Road, West Byfleet, Surrey (tel 019323 42829)

MILLS, Neil McLay; s of Leslie Hugh Mills (d 1980), and Gwladys Mills (d 1982); *b* 29 July 1923; *Educ* Epsom Coll, UCL; *m* 1950, Rosamond Mary, da of late Col and Hon Mrs A C W Kimpton, of Tisbury, Wilts; 2 s, 2 da; *Career* farmer; served WWII Lt RNVR Coastal Forces (despatches 1944); underwriting memb of Lloyd's 1955–91; chm: Bland Welch & Co 1965–74, Bland Payne Holdings 1974–79, Sedgwick Forbes Bland Payne 1979–80, Sedgwick Gp plc 1980–84; dir: Montagu Tst 1966–74, Midland Bank Ltd 1974–79, Wadlowgrosvenor International Ltd 1984–88, Thread-Needle Publishing Gp plc 1986–94; memb Ctee Lloyd's Insurance Brokers' Assoc 1974–77; vice-pres: Insurance Inst of London 1971–84, Br Insurance Brokers' Assoc 1978–84 (memb Int Insurance Brokers' Ctee); memb: Bd Church Army 1957–64 (vice-chm 1959–64), Cncl Oak Hill Theol Coll 1958–62; tstee and govr Lord Mayor Treloar Tst 1975–81; Freeman City of London 1980, Liveryman Worshipful Co of Insurers 1984–86; *Recreations* reading, cooking; *Clubs* Pilgrims; *Style—* Neil McLay Mills, Esq; ✉ The Old Post House, 23 Broad Street, Alresford, Hampshire SO24 9HR (tel 01962 732464)

MILLS, Nigel Gordon; *b* 14 April 1955; *Career* Hoare Govett Ltd: joined as food mfrg sector investment analyst 1978, dir 1985–2005, joined Corp Fin Dept 1986, ceo 1994–2005; chm UK corp broking Citigroup 2005–; *Style—* Nigel Mills, Esq

MILLS, Russell Thomas; s of Sqdn Ldr Harry Wyndham Mills, DFM, RAF, ret, of Llantwit Major, S Glamorgan, and Mary, *née* Jeyes; *b* 22 November 1952; *Educ* Royal Alexandra & Albert Sch Reigate, Canterbury Coll of Art, Maidstone Coll of Art (BA), Royal Coll of Art (MA, travelling scholarship Berlin, Berger award); *m* 17 Aug 1974, Ann Elizabeth, *née* Symes; 1 s (Samuel Asher b 4 Aug 1992); *Career* artist, musician and prodr; lectr at numerous colls, polys and schs of art throughout Britain and USA; visiting prof: UWE, RCA London; visiting lectr: Glasgow Sch of Art, Liverpool John Moores Univ, Manchester Metropolitan Univ, Salford Univ, Leeds Metropolitan Univ; TV and radio appearances incl: London Weekend Show (ITV) 1977, Arena - Double Vision (BBC2) 1980; involved with: Grizledale Arts Hawkshead 2000–, The Armitt Trust Ambleside 2001–; *Solo Exhibitions* Fine Lines (The Thumb Gallery) 1980, ...returns an echo (Curwen Gallery and tour) 1983, Ciphers (Curwen Gallery and Metropole Arts Centre Folkestone) 1986, Enter the Silences (Parco Space 5 Tokyo) 1987, Silent Systems (Curwen Gallery) 1989, Planet and Glow-Worm (Visual Arts Museum NY) 1989, Sixteen Shimmers (Parco Space 5 Tokyo and Kirin Plaza Osaka) 1990, Within Without (Huntington Gallery Boston) 1991, The Possible Slow Fuse (Pentagram Gallery London) 1995, RSC Works (RSC Stratford-upon-Avon and Barbican) 1995, Trace Elements (Base Gallery Tokyo) 1998, Moth (The Lighthouse Glasgow) 2001, Extended Wings (Kendal) 2002, Cleave/Soft Bullets (Kendal) 2002; *Two-Person Exhibitions* Ember Glance (with David Sylvian, Tokyo) 1990, Earth Murmurs (with Ian Walton, Curwen Gallery) 1992, Between Two Lights (installation with Ian Walton, Charlotte Mason Coll Ambleside as part of Ambleside Mountain Festival) 1994, MW Undark (exhbn with Ian Walton, Zeffirellis Ambleside) 1994, Measured in Shadows (installation with Ian Walton, Tullie House Museum Carlisle) 1996 (also at Guinness Hopstore Dublin 1997), Looming (with Ian Walton, Eagle Gallery London) 1996, Nature's Teeth (with Ian Walton, The Samling at Dovenest Windermere) 1997, Spirit (with Ian Walton, Grizedale Forest Hawkshead, 1997), Ex Libris (with Ian Walton, Sun Street Studios, Lancaster Literature Festival, 1997), Filters: Past Presents (with Ian Walton, Gallery Al Ajibe, Arrecife, Lanzarote, 1997), The Gradual Instant (with Ian Walton, Dean Clough Galleries Halifax) 1998, Words and Images (The Samling at Dovenest Windermere) 1998, Still Moves (installation with Ian Walton in the Forest of Bowland, also guest speaker at accompanying conference in Ambleside) 1999, Sonic Boom: The Art of Sound (Hayward Gallery) 2000, Republic of Thorns (with Ian Walton, The Wordsworth Tst Grasmere) 2001, Black Ice (with Ian Walton, Buddle Arts Centre Gateshead) 2001, The Space of a Door (with Ian Walton, Futuresonic04 Urbis Manchester) 2004, Hold (Palazzo delle Papesse Centre for Contemporary Art Siena) 2004–05, Blue Tears (with Ian Walton and Mike Fearon, Silo Espaco Cultural Oporto) 2005; *Group Exhibitions* Cyprus Summer School 1972, Geek Work (Air Gallery and Greenwich Theatre Art Gallery) 1977, Contemporary British Illustrators (Belgrave Gallery) 1978, Shoes (Neal St Gallery) 1979, Five English Artists (Galerie Mokum Amsterdam) 1979, Summer Reflections (Thumb Gallery) 1981, Hayward Annual (Hayward Gallery) 1982, Images for Today (Graves Art Gallery Sheffield) 1982, Britain Salutes New York (Brooklyn MOMA NY) 1983, Out of Line (ICA) 1985, Ambit (Royal Festival Hall) 1985, Interaction (Camden Arts Centre) 1986, Critical Lines (Talbot Rice Gallery Edinburgh and Watershed Bristol) 1986, Art Meets Science (Smith's Gallery) 1986, Faber Artists (Cartoon Gallery) 1986, New British Design (Japan) 1987, Sydney Biennale (Art Gallery of NSW and Nat Gallery of Victoria) 1987 and 1988, Doobraak (Berlage Amsterdam) 1989, Pictures of Rock (European tour) 1990–91, The Art of Selling Songs (V&A) 1991, Art and Science (Plymouth City Museum and Art Gallery) 1991, Ember Glance (installation with Ian Walton and David Sylvian, Architectural Assoc

London) 1993, Shelf Life (The Eagle Gallery London) 1994, Little Pieces from Big Stars (Flowers East Gallery London) 1994, Fuse (RCA) 1994, The Artists Bookfair Royal Festival Hall (with The Eagle Gallery London) 1995, Soundings: Sub Rosa (installation with Ian Walton and Hywel Davies, Green Park Station Bath as part of Bath Festival) 1995, Liquid Architecture (Brisbane and Melbourne) 2004; numerous RCA and Curwen Gallery exhibitions; *Work in Collections* Br Cncl, Br Museum, Kent CC, Reuters, V&A, Tate Gallery; *Commissions* Chatto & Windus Publishers, Decca Records, Polydor Records, Virgin Records, The Face, Harpers & Queen, The Sunday Times, Telegraph Magazine, Vogue, Nothing Records, BT, English Heritage, RSC, Fareham Town centre; *Awards* International Editorial Design Three Award of Excellence 1983, D&AD Silver Award 1984, Diamond Record Cover Award (with Dave Coppenhall) Diamond Awards Festival Antwerp Belgium 1989; *Albums* Undark (1996), Undark II: Pearl and Umbra (1999); many recordings with Dome, BC Gilbert and G Lewis, Bill Laswell, Nils Petler Molvaer, and for Unknown Public; *Publications* The Luftschifer Park Piece (1976), Evening Breakers (1977), More Dark than Shark (1986), Russell Mills/Ian Walton (1990), Ember Glance: The Permanence of Memory (1991), Looming (with Ian Walton, 1996), Trace Elements (1998), Sonic Boom (2000), Republic of Thorns (2001), Cleave/Soft Bullets (2002), Hold (2004), Blue Tears (2005); *Recreations* music, reading, contemplating natural phenomena; *Clubs* Bull Terrier, Labour Pty, Chelsea Arts; *Style—* Russell Mills

MILLWARD, Edwina Carole (Mrs David Bicker); da of Eric Millward, and Frances Morris, *née* Norton; *b* 20 September 1943; *Educ* Thornes House Sch Wakefield, Ilkley Coll of Housecraft, Univ of London (LLB); *m* 11 Nov 1972, David Charles Bicker, s of Arthur Charles Bicker; *Career* teacher 1965–67; admitted slr 1972; appointed by Lord Chllr to sit as dist judge in Co Court and Dist Registry High Court 1995; nat pres UK Fedn of Business and Professional Women 1985–87, pres Kent Law Soc 1994–95 (memb 1968–), sr vice-pres Assoc of District Judges 2007; FRSA; *Recreations* acting, swimming, needlework; *Style—* District Judge Edwina Millward; ✉ Maidstone County Court, The Law Courts, Barker Road, Maidstone, Kent ME16 8EQ (tel 01622 202000)

MILMAN, David Patrick; 10 Bt (GB 1800), of Levaton-in-Woodland, Devonshire; er s of Lt-Col Sir Derek Milman, 9 Bt, MC (d 1999); *b* 24 August 1945; *Educ* Univ of London (BEd, MA); *m* 1969, Christina, da of John William Hunt; 1 da (Katharine Jane b 1975), 1 s (Thomas Hart b 1976); *Heir* s, Thomas Milman; *Career* headteacher 1981, asst dir Sch Mgmnt South 1989, sr area advsr NW Kent 1993 (area advsr 1991); freelance educl conslt 2000; *Books* Take a Look (1974/75), What Do You Think (1977), Senior Managers Personal Profile: Management Portfolio (jtly, 1991); *Style—* Sir David Milman, Bt; ✉ 71 Camden Road, Sevenoaks, Kent (e-mail dpmilman.sevenoaks@virgin.net)

MILMO, His Hon Judge John Boyle; QC (1984); s of Dermod Hubert Francis Milmo (d 1973), and Eileen Clare, *née* White (d 1994); *b* 19 January 1943; *Educ* Downside, Univ of Dublin (MA, LLB); *Career* called to the Bar Lincoln's Inn 1966 (bencher 1992); recorder of the Crown Court 1982–2004 (dep circuit judge 1980–82), dep High Court judge 1993, circuit judge (Midland Circuit) 2004–; head of chambers 1 High Pavement Nottingham 1990–2004; memb Gen Cncl of the Bar 1992–2002; *Clubs* United Services (Nottingham); *Style—* His Hon Judge Milmo, QC

MILNE, Antony Michael (Mike); s of Anthony Kenneth Milne, and Barbara, *née* King Chidley; *Educ* Westminster; *Career* computer animator; dir of production Electric Image Ltd 1984–91, head of graphics The Bureau Ltd 1991–92, dir computer animation Framestore-CFC Ltd 1992–; animation dir: Walking with Dinosaurs (BBC TV series) 1999, Walking with Beasts (BBC TV series) 2001; D&AD Silver Award (Outstanding TV Graphics) 1984, BAFTA Innovation Award 2000; Emmy Awards: Best Visual Effects 2000, Best Animated Prog 2000 and 2001; Hon Dr of Arts Bournemouth Univ 2002; *Recreations* watching wildlife, reading evolutionary theory, visiting ancient ruins; *Style—* Dr Mike Milne; ✉ Framestore-CFC Ltd, 9 Noel Street, London W1V 4AL (tel 020 7208 2600, fax 020 7208 2626, e-mail mike.milne@framestore-cfc.com)

MILNE, David Calder; QC (1987); s of Ernest Ferguson Milne, OBE (d 1995), of Walton Heath, Surrey, and Helena Mary, *née* Harkness (d 2007); *b* 22 September 1945; *Educ* Harrow, Univ of Oxford (MA); *m* (m dis 1999); 1 da (Bryony b 1980), 1 s (George b 2004); *Career* CA 1969; articled to Whinney Murray & Co Chartered Accountants 1966–69, called to the Bar Lincoln's Inn 1970; recorder 1989–2006; FCA 1974; *Recreations* natural history, music, golf, rugby football; *Clubs* Garrick, Hurlingham, Gnomes, Walton Heath Golf; *Style—* David Milne, Esq, QC; ✉ Pump Court Tax Chambers, 16 Bedford Row, London WC1R 4EF (tel 020 7414 8080, fax 020 7414 8099, e-mail dmilne@pumptax.com)

MILNE, Prof Gordon Stewart; OBE (2002); s of Arthur Milne, OBE (d 1984), of Edinburgh, and Thomasina, *née* Gilroy (d 2002); *b* 1 October 1936; *Educ* Royal HS of Edinburgh, Leith Nautical Coll, Heriot-Watt Coll Edinburgh, Coll of Estate Mgmnt London; *m* 15 Oct 1961, Kathleen Mary; 2 s (Rhoderic Michael Stuart b 12 Feb 1965, Hector Arthur Stuart b 12 July 1966); *Career* local dir Guardian Royal Exchange Assurance 1979–92, md Scottish Metropolitan Property plc 1986–92 (dir 1969–92); memb Clyde Port Authy 1989–93; currently hon prof in land economy Univ of Aberdeen (visiting prof of land economy 1992–95); vice-pres Edinburgh Jr C of C 1968–69, DG Euro Conf of Jr C of C 1972; non-exec dir European Utilities Trust plc 1994–2006; memb NEDC Scot Strategy Planning Ctee 1974–76, former memb Exec Scot Devpt and Indust; chm: The European Urban Inst 1995–2001, Local Govt Property Cmmn (Scotland) 1995–98, Sec of State for Scot Valuation and Rating Cncl 1996–2001; memb: Livingston Devpt Corp 1992–97, Capital Advsy Ctee Scottish Higher Educn Funding Cncl 1993–95, Faculty of Advocates Disciplinary Tbn 1994–96, Gen Convocation Heriot-Watt Univ; FRICS 1964, Hon FRIAS 1997; *Recreations* ornithology, hill walking, swimming, music; *Clubs* New (Edinburgh); *Style—* Prof Gordon S Milne, OBE; ✉ 25 Dovecot Grove, Edinburgh EH14 2LU (tel 0131 466 6396)

MILNE, John Duff; s of Alexander Keen Milne, of Dundee, and Margaret Harrow, *née* Duff; *b* 13 May 1942; *Educ* Harris Acad Dundee; *m* 29 March 1967, Jennifer Frances, da of Robert Lewis Brown (d 1989), of Dundee; 2 s (Grigor b 1970, Jonathan b 1973); *Career* newspaper sub ed D C Thomson Dundee 1959–63, newspaper sub ed and feature writer The Scotsman Edinburgh 1963–67, news ed Swiss Broadcasting Corp Bern 1967–71, presenter and reporter BBC Scotland 1971–; *Recreations* sport, music; *Style—* John Milne, Esq; ✉ BBC Broadcasting House, Queen Margaret Drive, Glasgow G12 8DG (tel 0141 338 2159)

MILNE, Lisa; *Educ* Royal Scottish Acad of Music & Drama; *Career* soprano; Scottish Opera (contract princ) roles incl: Gianetta in L'Elisir d'Amore (debut), Dew Fairy in Hansel and Gretel, Coryphee in Alceste, Adele in Die Fledermaus, Adina in L'Elisir d'Amore, Zerlina in Don Giovanni, Susanna in Le Nozze di Figaro, Ilia in Idomeneo, Despina in Cosi Fan Tutte; other roles incl: Morgana in Alcina (ENO), Annchen in Der Freischütz (ENO), Servilia in La Clemenza di Tito (WNO), Gretel in Hansel and Gretel (Stuttgart Opera), Ilia in Idomeneo (Royal Danish Opera), Atalanta in Xerxes (Göttingen Handel Festival), title role in Theodora (Glyndebourne Festival Opera), title role in Rodelinda (Glyndebourne Festival Opera), Marzelline in Fidelio (Glyndebourne Festival Opera), Anna Trulove in The Rake's Progress (ENO), James McMillan's Parthenogenis (world premiere, The Cambridge Corn Exchange), Simon Holt's Sunrise, Yellow Noise (CBSO world premiere, under Sir Simon Rattle), Sophie in Der Rosenkavalier (Scottish Opera), title role in Alcina (ENO), Micaela in Carmen (Glyndebourne Festival Opera), Marzelline in Fidelio (Dallas Opera), Pamina in Die Zauberflöte (Glyndebourne Festival Opera); *Awards* Scottish Opera John Noble Bursary 1992, Maggie Teyte Prize 1993, Glyndebourne Festival Opera John Christie Award 1996, Royal Philharmonic Soc Young Artists Award 1998; Hon DMus: Univ of Aberdeen, Robert Gordon's Univ Aberdeen; *Recordings* incl: Ilia in Idomeneo (EMI), Handel and Vivaldi Cantatas with King's Consort, Vaughan Williams' Serenade to Music, Xerxes, Ireland songs, Quilter songs, Hebridean folk songs; *Style—* Miss Lisa Milne; ✉ c/o Askonas Holt, Lonsdale Chambers, 27 Chancery Lane, London WC2A 1PF (tel lisa.milne@btinternet.com)

MILNE, Nanette Lilian Margaret; OBE (1993), JP (Aberdeen), MSP; *Educ* Aberdeen HS for Girls, Univ of Aberdeen (MB ChB); *m*; 1 s, 1 da; *Career* various med appts rising to registrar 1965–73, pt/t researcher Genetics Dept Univ of Aberdeen 1978–80, MO (oncology) Aberdeen Hosps 1980–92; dir: Grampian Enterprise Ltd 1992–98, Aberdeen Countryside Project 1997–99; MSP (Cons) NE Scotland 2003–, Cons dep spokesman on health and community care, memb Equal Opportunities Ctee; Cons Pty: joined 1974, various positions at branch, constituency and area level 1981–2002, vice-chm Scottish Cons Pty 1988–92, cncllr Aberdeen City/District Cncl 1988–99, Scottish Parly candidate Aberdeen S 1999, UK Parly candidate Gordon 2001; memb: Aberdeen and Grampian Tourist Bd 1992–95, Ct Univ of Aberdeen 1996–; tstee: Gomel Tst 1995–99, Aberdeen Int Youth Festival 1995–99 and 2000–; FFARCS 1969; *Recreations* music, the countryside, hill walking, skiing, golf, gardening; *Clubs* Aberdeen Ladies Curling; *Style—* Mrs Nanette Milne, OBE, MSP; ✉ The Scottish Parliament, Edinburgh EH99 1SP

MILNE, Neil Morrison; s of Brig John Brebner Morrison Milne, OBE, and Marjory, *née* Duncan; *b* 24 June 1951; *Educ* Royal HS Edinburgh, Univ of Edinburgh (MA), Univ of Nottingham (MA); *Career* Butler Till Ltd 1975–78, Standard Life Assurance Co 1978–81, sr mangr Euro Banking Co Ltd, exec dir York Trust Group plc 1984–90, managing ptnr Copernicus Capital Partners 1994–, md Copernicus Ventures Ltd 1994–; non-exec dir: ICM Computer Gp plc, KP Koncorcjum Sp Z.0.0; *Recreations* tennis, skiing, reading; *Clubs* RAC; *Style—* Neil M Milne, Esq; ✉ York Trust Ltd, Smithfield House, 92 North Street, Leeds LS2 7PN (tel 0113 222 3555, fax 0113 222 3550, e-mail n.milne@copernicus-capital.com)

MILNE-WATSON, Sir Andrew Michael; 4 Bt (UK 1937), of Ashley, Longbredy, Co Dorset; s of Sir Michael Milne-Watson, 3 Bt, CBE (d 1999); *b* 10 November 1944; *Educ* Eton; *m* 1, 1970, Beverley Jane Gabrielle, er da of late Philip Cotton, of Majorca; 1 s (David b 1971), 1 da (Emma b 1974); m 2, 1983, Mrs Gisella Stafford, da of Hans Tisdall, of London; 1 s (Oliver b 1985); *Heir* s, David Milne-Watson; *Career* dir Ogilvy & Mather 1970–82; chm: Phoenix Advertising 1982–86, Lewis Broadbent Advertising 1986–88, Minerva Publications Ltd 1988–90, GMW Fabrics 1989–; md ADR Associates Ltd 1993–; Liveryman Worshipful Co of Grocers; *Clubs* Garrick; *Style—* Sir Andrew Milne-Watson, Bt; ✉ 22 Musgrave Crescent, London SW6 4QE (e-mail mwandrew@globalnet.co.uk)

MILNER, Prof (Arthur) David; s of Arthur Milner (d 1984), and Sarah-Ellen, *née* Gaunt (d 1965); *b* 16 July 1943; *Educ* Bradford GS, Lincoln Coll Oxford (open scholar, MA), Inst of Psychiatry London (Dip Psychology, PhD); *m* 24 July 1965, Christine, *née* Armitage; 2 s (Benedict Jon b 28 July 1966, Edward b 5 Oct 1969); *Career* res asst Univ of London 1966–70; Univ of St Andrews: lectr in psychology 1970–82, sr lectr 1982–85, chm Dept of Psychology 1983–88, reader 1985–90, prof 1990–2000, dean Faculty of Science 1992–94, head Sch of Psychology 1994–97; prof of cognitive neuroscience Univ of Durham 2000–; Chichele lectr and visiting fell All Souls Coll Oxford 2006; memb: Int Neuropsychological Symposium 1971, Experimental Psychology Soc 1972; tstee Dundee Science Centre 1998–2000; FRSE 1992; *Books* The Neuropsychology of Consciousness (with Rugg, 1992), The Visual Brain in Action (with Goodale, 1995, 2 edn 2006), Comparative Neuropsychology (1998), Cognitive and Neural Bases of Spatial Neglect (with Karnath and Vallar, 2002), The Roots of Visual Awareness (with Heywood and Blakemore, 2003), Sight Unseen: The Neuropsychology of Unconscious Vision (with Goodale, 2004); *Recreations* walking, reading, writing, films, jazz; *Style—* Prof A D Milner, FRSE; ✉ Wolfson Research Institute, University of Durham Queen's Campus, University Boulevard, Stockton-on-Tees TS17 6BH (tel 0191 334 0433, fax 0191 334 0452, e-mail a.d.milner@dur.ac.uk)

MILNER, Prof John; s of James William Milner, of Derby, and Iris May, *née* Young; *b* 11 June 1946; *Educ* Bemrose GS Derby, Courtauld Inst of Art Univ of London (BA, PhD); *m* 1970, Lesley, da of late Denis Hill Marlow; 3 s (Henry George Marlow b 18 March 1971, Edward John b 16 July 1975, Michael James Denis b 21 April 1980); *Career* lectr Bournemouth and Poole Coll of Art and Hornsey Coll of Art London 1968–69; Dept of Fine Art Univ of Newcastle upon Tyne: lectr 1969, sr lectr 1979, reader 1985, head of dept 1985–91, prof of art history 1992–2004, prof emeritus 2004–; ind art historian, exhbn organiser and painter 2005–; dir Hatton Gallery Univ of Newcastle upon Tyne until 1991; memb Assoc of Art Historians; Leverhulme fellowship 1985 and 1993; AHRB Award 1992, Br Acad Award 2004; *Books* Symbolists and Decadents (1971), Russian Revolutionary Art (1979), Vladimir Tatlin and the Russian Avant-Garde (1983), The Studios of Paris, the Capital of Art in the Late Nineteenth Century (1988), Mondrian (1992), Dictionary of Russian Artists (1994), Kazimir Malevich and the Art of Geometry (1996), Art, War and Revolution: France 1870–1871 (2000), Kenneth Rowntree (2002); *Recreations* painting; *Clubs* Chelsea Arts; *Style—* Prof John Milner; ✉ Department of Fine Art, School of Arts and Culture, University of Newcastle upon Tyne NE1 7RU (tel 0191 222 6047, e-mail john.milner@ncl.ac.uk)

MILNER, Prof (Arthur John) Robin Gorell; s of Lt-Col John Theodore Milner, OBE (d 1957), of Tisbury, Wilts, and Muriel Emily, *née* Barnes-Gorell (d 1971); *b* 13 January 1934; *Educ* Eton, King's Coll Cambridge (major scholar, BA); *m* 16 Nov 1963, Lucy Petronella, da of Frewen Moor (d 1984), of East Meon, Hants; 2 s (Gabriel John b 1965, Barnabas Mark b 1966), 1 da (Chloë June b 1968); *Career* Nat Serv 2 Lt RE 1952–54; mathematics teacher Marylebone GS 1959–60, computer programmer Ferranti Ltd 1960–63, mathematics lectr City Univ 1963–68; research assoc: in computing theory UC Swansea 1968–70, in artificial intelligence Stanford Univ 1970–72; Univ of Edinburgh: lectr in computer science 1973–78, reader 1978–84, prof 1984–95; prof Computer Laboratory Univ of Cambridge 1995– (head of laboratory 1996–99); fndr memb Academia Europaea 1988; A M Turing award ACM 1991, Royal medal RSE 2004; Hon DSc Chalmers Univ of Technol 1988; foreign memb French Acad of Sciences 2006; FRS, FBCS 1989, FRSE 1993; *Books* Edinburgh LCF (1978), A Calculus of Communicating Systems (1980), Communication and Concurrency (1989), Definition of Standard ML (1990, revised 1996), Commentary on Standard ML (1990), Communicating and Mobile Systems: the Pi Calculus (1999); *Recreations* music, carpentry, walking; *Style—* Prof Robin Milner, FRS, FRSE; ✉ 24 Lyndewode Road, Cambridge CB1 2HN (tel 01223 503159); University of Cambridge, The Computer Laboratory, William Gates Building, JJ Thomson Avenue, Cambridge CB0 3FD (tel 01223 334718)

MILNER, Sir Timothy William Lycett; 10 Bt (GB 1717), of Nun Appleton Hall, Yorkshire; s of Sir (George Edward) Mordaunt Milner, 9 Bt (d 1995), and his 1 w Barbara Audrey, *née* Belsham (d 1951); *b* 11 October 1936; *Heir* bro, Charles Milner; *Style—* Sir Timothy Milner, Bt; ✉ c/o Oude Natte Valleij, Box 4, Klapmuts 7625, Cape, South Africa

MILNER OF LEEDS, 3 Baron (UK 1951); Richard James Milner; s of 2 Baron Milner of Leeds, AE (d 2003), and Sheila Margaret, *née* Hartley (d 2000); *b* 16 May 1959, London; *Educ* Charterhouse, Univ of Surrey (BSc); *m* 25 June 1988, Margaret Christine, da of Gerald Francis Voisin, of Jersey; 2 da (Hon Charlotte Emma b 8 May 1990, Hon Nicola Louise Christine b 3 Feb 1992); *Style—* The Lord Milner of Leeds

MILNES COATES, Prof Sir Anthony Robert; 4 Bt (UK 1911), of Helperby Hall, Helperby, North Riding of Yorkshire; only s of Lt-Col Sir Robert Edward James Clive Milnes-Coates, 3 Bt, DSO, JP (d 1982), and Lady (Ethel) Patricia Hare, da of 4 Earl of Listowel; *b* 8

M

December 1948; *Educ* Eton, St Thomas' Hosp London (BSc, MB BS); *m* 1978, Harriet Ann, yr da of Raymond Burton, of Slingsby, N Yorks; 2 da (Sara b 1981, Sophie b 1984), 1 s (Thomas b 1986); *Heir* s, Thomas Milnes Coates; *Career* prof of med microbiology St George's Hosp Med Sch London; mayor Royal Borough of Kensington and Chelsea 2002–03; FRCPath, FRCP, MD; *Style*— Prof Sir Anthony Milnes Coates, Bt; ✉ Helperby Hall, Helperby, North Yorkshire YO61 2QP

MILNES-SMITH, Philippa; da of Trevor Owen Dyke, and Anita Eileen, *née* Smith (d 1981); *Educ* Bishop Fox GS Taunton, Westfield Coll London (BA); *m* 1986, Tom Milnes-Smith; 1 da (Eleanor Phoebe b 1992), 1 s (John James b 1996); *Career* md Puffin Books 1998–2001 (publisher 1995–98); dir Lucas Alexander Whitley Ltd; *Recreations* walking, music, arts in general; *Style*— Ms Philippa Milnes-Smith; ✉ 14 Salcott Road, London SW11 6DE

MILOW, Keith Arnold; s of Geoffrey Keith Milow, of Majorca, Spain, and Joan Ada, *née* Gear (d 1990); *b* 29 December 1945; *Educ* Baldock Secdy Modern Sch, Camberwell Sch of Art (DipAD), RCA; *Career* artist; *Solo Exhibitions* incl: Nigel Greenwood Inc 1970, 1973, 1974 and 1976, Gregory Fellows Exhibition (Leeds City Art Gallery) 1971, J Duffy & Sons NY 1973, Hester Van Royen Gallery London 1975, Kettles Yard Gallery Cambridge 1976, Gallerie Albert Baronian Belgium 1977, Park Square Gallery Leeds 1977, Just Crosses (Roundhouse Gallery) 1978, Galerie Loyse Openheim Geneva 1979, Annina Nosei Gallery NY 1981 and 1982, Nigel Greenwood Gallery 1986, Gouaches (Alexander Wood Gallery NY) 1987, John Davis Gallery NY 1988, 100 Drawings (Nigel Greenwood Gallery) 1989, 25 Drawings (Gallery 630B New Orleans and Nohra Haime Gallery NY) 1990; *Group Exhibitions* incl: Young Contemporaries (Tate Gallery London) 1967, Mostra Mercato d'Arte Contemporan (Florence) 1968, Six at the Haywood (Haywood Gallery) 1969, Works on Paper (MOMA NY) 1970, The Road Show (São Paulo Biennale & S American tour) 1971, The New Art (Hayward Gallery) 1972, Homers (MOMA) 1973, Xieme Biennale of Art (Menton France) 1974, The British Exhibition (Basel Art Fair) 1975, 25 Years of British Painting (RCA) 1976, Recent British Art (Br Cncl tour) 1977–78, The British Art Show (Sheffield) 1979, British Art Now (Solomon R Guggenheim Museum NY) 1980, Aspects of British Art Today (Tokyo Met Museum of Art) 1982, Pintura Británica Contemporánea (Museo Municipal Madrid) 1983, Chill Out (Kenkeleba Gallery NY) 1983, The Show Room (Michael Katz Gallery NY) 1985, Modern British Sculpture (Whitechapel Art Gallery) 1986, Emerging Artists 1978–1988: Selections from the Exxon Series (Solomon R Guggenheim Museum NY) 1987, Modern British Sculpture (Tate Gallery Liverpool) 1988, Works on Lead (Nohra Haime Gallery NY) 1989, Sixth Sense (Pence Gallery Santa Monica) 1990, Personal Portraits (Annina Nosel Gallery NY) 1991; *Public Collections* works in numerous incl: Guggenheim Museum NY, Imperial War Museum, MOMA NY, Tate Gallery London, V&A London, Nat Gallery of Australia; *Public Commissions* Glaxo Wellcome, Stevenage Boardroom, Canary Wharf Ltd, Lobby Sculpture; *Awards* Gregory Fellowship Univ of Leeds 1970–72, Harkness fellowship to USA 1972–74, Calouste Gulbenkian Fndn Visual Arts award 1976, major award Arts Cncl of GB 1979, first prize Tolly Cobbold/Eastern Arts Second Nat Exhibition 1979, Edward Albee Fndn award 1983; *Style*— Keith Milow, Esq; ✉ 32 W 20th Street, New York, NY 1001, USA (tel 00 1 212 929 0124)

MILTON, Anne; MP; *b* 1955; *Educ* Haywards Heath GS, St Bartholomew's Hosp; *m* Graham Henderson; 4 c; *Career* former nurse; MP (Cons) Guildford 2005–; former vice-chm Cons Medical Soc; *Style*— Mrs Anne Milton, MP; ✉ House of Commons, London SW1A 0AA (tel 020 7219 8392, e-mail miltona@parliament.uk)

MILTON, Prof Anthony Stuart; s of Ernest Thomas Milton (d 1964), of Beckenham, Kent, and Gladys Ethel Milton (d 1989); *b* 15 April 1934; *Educ* Cranleigh Sch, St Catherine's Coll Oxford (MA, DPhil, DSc); *m* 16 June 1962, Elizabeth Amaret, da of Russell Freeman, of Richmond, Virginia; 1 s (Nathaniel Gavin Nicolas b 6 Oct 1964), 2 da (Imogen Hillary b 7 Oct 1967, Kirstin Abigail b 8 Dec 1969); *Career* lectr Dartmouth Med Sch New Hampshire 1959–60, res fell Stanford Univ 1960–61, res fell and hon lectr Univ of Edinburgh 1961–63, sr lectr Sch of Pharmacy Univ of London 1967–73 (lectr 1966–67); Univ of Aberdeen: prof of pharmacology 1973–94, prof of immunopharmacology 1994–99, emeritus prof of pharmacology 1999–; Dept of Pharmacology Univ of Cambridge 1996– (visiting scientist 1996–), sr memb Robinson Coll Cambridge 1997–; Leverhulme emeritus fell 1996–98; md Univ of Aberdeen Trading Co (U-Travel) 1986–93; community cncllr 1982–85, parish cncllr Whaddon Cambs 2002–, memb Melbourn Cambridge County Cncl 2003–05; tstee Aberdeen Int Youth Festival of Music and Arts 1985–91; chm East Anglia Border Terrier Club 2005–; memb: Physiological Soc, Br Pharmacological Soc; FRSA; *Books* Pyretics and Antipyretics (1982); *Recreations* collecting the stamps of Newfoundland, breeding Border Terriers; *Style*— Prof Anthony Milton; ✉ Chestnut Tree Farm, Whaddon, Royston, Cambridgeshire SG8 5RS (tel 01223 207105); Department of Pharmacology, University of Cambridge, Tennis Court Road, Cambridge CB2 1PD (tel 01223 334000, fax 01223 334100, e-mail asm27@cam.ac.uk)

MILTON, Frank William; s of Capt Cyril Frank, of Worthing, W Sussex, and Mabel Laura, *née* Neal; *b* 29 November 1949; *Educ* Hove Co GS, UC Oxford (BA); *m* 29 Sept 1973, Lesley Pamela, da of Capt Dennis Arthur Jack Adams, RE, of Glossop, Derbys; 2 s (Andrew Paul Frank, Graham Alexander Neil); *Career* trainee Turner & Newall 1972–73, sales asst Shell Chemicals UK Ltd 1973–75 (sales rep 1975–78), planning mangr Shell International Chemical Co Ltd 1978–80; former ptnr PricewaterhouseCoopers (previously Coopers & Lybrand), currently ind mgmnt conslt; CDipAF, MInstM; *Recreations* hill walking, windsurfing, sailing, listening to jazz, running; *Style*— Frank Milton, Esq; ✉ Alligin, Norrels Drive, East Horsley, Surrey KT24 5DL (tel 01483 283832)

MILTON, Dr Marcus Peter; s of Peter Maurice Milton (d 1979), and Eileen, *née* Browne (d 2006); *b* 2 December 1951; *Educ* De La Salle Coll Hove, Univ of Newcastle upon Tyne (BA), Tuebingen Univ (PhD); *m* Monika, *née* Geyer; 1 s (Patrick Lee b 4 March 1984), 1 da (Philippa Maren b 19 March 1986); *Career* trainer IBM Deutschland 1976–82 and 1984, lectr Univ of Zimbabwe 1982–84; Br Cncl: joined 1985, asst dir Tanzania 1986–89, asst regnl dir Southern Germany 1989–92, dep dir Sri Lanka 1992–94 (concurrently dep cultural attaché Br High Cmmn Colombo), head science and public affrs Germany 1994–98, dir Zimbabwe 2000–02 (dep dir 1998–2000), dir Burma 2002– (concurrently cultural attaché Br Embassy Rangoon); *Publications* articles on classical subjects in learned jls; *Clubs* Royal Over-Seas League; *Style*— Dr Marcus Milton; ✉ British Council, 10 Spring Gardens, London SW1A 2AH (e-mail marcus.milton@britishcouncil.org.mm)

MILVERTON, 2 Baron (UK 1947); Rev Fraser Arthur Richard Richards; s of 1 Baron Milverton, GCMG (d 1978), and Noelle Benda, da of Charles Basil Whitehead, of Torquay; *b* 21 July 1930; *Educ* Ridley Coll, Ontario, Clifton, Egerton Agric Coll Njoro Kenya, Bishop's Coll Cheshunt; *m* 1957, Mary Dorothy, da of Leslie Aubrey Fly (d 1983; a composer of music, teacher and civil servant), of Bath; 2 da (Susan (Hon Mrs Cross) b 1962, Juliet (Hon Mrs Steuart-Corry) b 1964); *Heir* bro, Hon Michael Richards; *Career* sat as Cons peer in House of Lords; Royal Signals 1949–50, Kenya Police 1952–53; deacon 1957, ordained priest 1958; curate: St George's Beckenham Kent, St John the Baptist Sevenoaks Kent, St Nicholas Great Bookham Surrey; vicar Okewood Hill with Forest Green Surrey, rector Christian Malford with Sutton Benger and Tytherton Kellaways (Wilts) 1967–93, chaplain Wilts ACF until 1981; govr Clifton Coll 1990–; *Recreations* family, current affairs, reading, international rugby, cricket, tennis, swimming, music, theatre; *Style*— The Rev the Rt Hon the Lord Milverton

MILWARD, Prof Alan Steele; s of Joseph Thomas Milward (d 1965), and Dorothy, *née* Steele (d 1985); *b* 19 January 1935; *Educ* UCL (BA), LSE (PhD); *m* 1, 23 Nov 1963 (m dis 1994), Claudine Jeanne Amelie, *née* Lemaitre; 1 da (Colette Victoire Zoe b 22 Feb 1977); m 2, 28 March 1998 Frances Lynch; 1 da (Laura Katherine Milward-Lynch b 21 April 1992); 1 further da (Maya b 14 Aug 1972); *Career* lectr in econ history Univ of Edinburgh 1960–65, lectr Sch of Social Studies UEA 1965–68, assoc prof of economics Stanford Univ 1969–71, prof of Euro studies UMIST 1971–83, prof of contemporary history Euro Univ Inst 1983–86 and 1996–2002, prof of econ history LSE 1986–96 (prof emeritus 1996–); official historian Cabinet Office 1993–2007; visiting prof: Stanford Univ, Univ of Illinois, École des Hautes Études en Sciences Sociales, Univ of Siegen, Univ of Oslo, Univ of Aarhus, Univ of Trondheim; associate Univ of N London (now London Met Univ) 2001–04, visiting sr fell St John's Coll Oxford 2002–03; McArthur lectr Univ of Cambridge 1983, Schumpeter lectr Univ of Graz 2002; memb: Econ History Soc, The Econ History Assoc; Hon MA Univ of Manchester 1976; FBA 1987, fell Norwegian Acad of Arts and Scis 1994; *Books* The German Economy at War (1965), The New Order and The French Economy (1970), War, Economy and Society, 1939–45 (1979), The Reconstruction of Western Europe, 1945–51 (1984), The European Rescue of the Nation-State (1993), The Rise and Fall of a National Strategy 1945–1963 (Vol 1 of The United Kingdom and The European Community, 2002); *Recreations* theatre; *Style*— Prof Alan Milward, FBA

MILWARD, Timothy Michael; s of Francis John Milward (d 1997), and Rosemary Gwendoline, *née* Smedley-Aston (d 2005); *b* 24 March 1937; *Educ* Rugby, Clare Coll Cambridge (MA, MB BCh); *m* 17 Jan 1970, Susan Isabel, da of Maj Glover Iggulden (d 1983), of Herne Bay, Kent; 4 da (Jessica b 24 Dec 1971, Caroline (Mrs Adrian West) b 15 June 1973, Eleanor, Camilla (twins) b 21 Aug 1978); *Career* Nat Serv, midshipman RNR 1955–63, Lt in RNR; med trg St Thomas' Hosp London 1960–63, registrar in plastic surgery Canniesburn Hosp Glasgow 1971–72, sr registrar in plastic surgery QMH London 1972–76, Hand Surgery fell Louisville Kentucky 1975; conslt plastic surgn Leicester Royal Infirmary, Pilgrim Hosp Boston and Lincoln County Hosp 1976–2002 (emeritus 2002–); in private practice 2002–; assessor GMC 2004–; pres: Br Assoc of Aesthetic Plastic Surgns 1987–89, Br Assoc of Plastic Surgns 1996; memb Cncl Br Soc for Surgery of the Hand 1982–83; FRCS 1966; *Recreations* squash, walking, tennis, silver beating; *Style*— Timothy Milward, Esq; ✉ Pine House, Gaddesby, Leicester LE7 4XE (tel 01664 840213, fax 01664 840660)

MIMPRISS, Peter Hugh Trevor; CVO (2001); yr s of Hugh Trevor Baber Mimpriss (d 1990), and Gwyneth Mary, *née* Bartley (d 1982); *b* 22 August 1943; *Educ* Sherborne; *m* 1, 1971 (m dis 1992), Hilary Ann Reed; 2 da (Isobel b 19 Oct 1973, Victoria b 22 Feb 1979); m 2, 1992, Elisabeth Lesley Molle; *Career* admitted slr 1967; ptnr Allen & Overy 1972–2002, dir Edmond J Safra Philanthropic Fndn 2002–04, charities advsr to HRH The Prince of Wales 2004–06; chm Chariguard Group of Common Investment Funds 1994–2000; univ slr Univ of London 1995–2002; dir: Leeds Castle Fndn 1980–, Weston Park Fndn 1986–99, Chatham Historic Dockyard Tst 1988–2000, Prince's Youth Business Tst 1997–99, Lawcare Ltd 1997–2002, Prince's Tst 1998–2006, King George's Jubilee Tst 2000–06, The Queen's Silver Jubilee Tst 2000–, Prince's Regeneration Tst 2002–; chm Charity Law Assoc 1992–97; tstee: Inst of Philanthropy 2000–07, World Trade Center Disaster Fund 2001–07, Prince of Wales Arts and Kids Fndn 2004–, Prince's Sch of Traditional Arts 2005–, Autism Speaks 2005– (dep chm), Sir Edward Heath Charitable Fndn 2005–, Jewish Museum 2006–; Hon DCL Univ of Durham 2003; *Recreations* walking, maritime history, vintage cars, collecting books; *Clubs* Athenaeum, Garrick; *Style*— Peter Mimpriss, Esq, CVO

MINFORD, Prof (Anthony) Patrick Leslie; CBE (1996); s of Leslie Mackay Minford (d 1970), and Patricia Mary, *née* Sale; *b* 17 May 1943; *m* 10 Feb 1970, Rosemary Irene, da of Gordon Hedley Allcorn; 2 s (Paul, David), 1 da (Lucy); *Career* econ asst UK Miny of Overseas Devpt 1965–67, econ advsr Malawi Miny of Fin 1967–69, asst on econ matters of fin dir Courtauld Co 1970–71, econ advsr Balance of Payments Div UK Treasy 1971–73 (delgn to Br Embassy Washington 1973–74), Hallsworth res fell Univ of Manchester 1974–75, ed NIESR Economic Review 1975–76, Edward Gonner prof of applied economics Univ of Liverpool 1976–97, prof Cardiff Business Sch 1997– (visiting prof 1993–97); memb: Monopolies and Mergers Cmmn 1990–96, HM Treasy independent panel of economic forecasting advisers 1992–96; *Books* Substitution Effects, Speculation and Exchange Rate Stability (1978), Unemployment: Cause and Cure (with D H Davies, M J Peel and A Sprague, 1983, 2 edn also with P Ashton, 1985), Rational Expectations and the New Macroeconomics (with D A Peel, 1983, 2 edn, sole author, as Rational Expectations Macroeconomics, 1992), The Housing Morass (with M J Peel and P Ashton, 1987), The Supply Side Revolution in Britain (1991), The Cost of Europe (ed/contrib, 1992), Markets not Stakes (1998), Britain and Europe: Choices for Change (with W Jamieson, 1999), Advanced Macroeconomics - A Primer (with D A Peel, 2002), Money Matters - essays in honour of Alan Walters (ed, 2004), Should Britain Leave the EU? An Economic Analysis of a Troubled Relationship (with V Mahambare and E Nowell, 2005), An Agenda for Tax Reform (2006); *Style*— Prof Patrick Minford, CBE; ✉ Cardiff Business School, University of Cardiff, Aberconway Building, Colum Drive, Cardiff CF10 3EU (tel 029 2087 5728, fax 029 2087 4419, e-mail minfordp@cf.ac.uk)

MINGOS, Prof (David) Michael Patrick; s of Vasso Mingos (d 1962), of Athens, and Rose Enid Billie, *née* Griffiths; *b* 6 August 1944; *Educ* Harvey GS Folkestone, King Edward VII Sch Lytham, UMIST (Dept of Chemistry Prize, BSc), Univ of Sussex (DPhil); *m* 18 March 1967, Stacey Mary, da of Richard Joseph Fayrer Hosken; 1 da (Zoë Sarah b 14 Dec 1971), 1 s (Adam Toby Vasso b 2 Oct 1973); *Career* Fulbright fell Northwestern Univ 1968–70, ICI fell Univ of Sussex 1970–71, lectr QMC London 1971–76; Univ of Oxford: lectr in chemistry 1976–90, reader 1990–92, fell Keble Coll 1976–92, lectr Pembroke Coll 1977–92, univ assessor 1991–92; Sir Edward Frankland BP prof of inorganic chemistry Imperial Coll London 1992–99, dean Royal Coll of Science 1996–99, princ St Edmund Hall Oxford 1999–; memb: SERC, AFRC, ACOST, HEFCE, European Science Fndn Ctees; memb Editorial Bd: Transition Metal Chemistry, Advances in Inorganic Chemistry, Chemistry Soc Reviews, New Jl of Chemistry, Inorganic Chemistry; regnl ed Jl of Organometallic Chemistry, managing ed Structure and Bonding (also memb Editorial Bd); vice-pres Dalton Div RSC 1993–96; Corday Morgan Medal RSC 1980, Chemistries of Noble Metals Prize RSC 1983, Tilden lectr and Medal RSC 1988, Wilhelm Manchott Prize 1995, Michael Collins Award 1996, Lee Meml Lecture Univ of Chicago 1997, Alexander von Humbolt Stiftung Forschungs Preis 1999; govr Harrow Sch; fell by special election Keble Coll Oxford 1993 (hon fell 1999), distinguished prof Xi'an Petroleum Univ 1994, Univ of Auchland Fndn visitor 2000; Hon DSc UMIST 2000, Hon DSc Univ of Sussex 2001; memb American Chemical Soc 1988; CChem, FRSC 1984, FRS 1992; *Books* Introduction to Cluster Chemistry (1990), Essentials of Inorganic Chemistry (I 1995, II 1998), Essential Trends in Inorganic Chemistry (1997), Structural and Electronic Paradigms in Cluster Chemistry (ed, 1997), Comprehensive Organometallic Chemistry III (ed-in-chief, 2007); *Recreations* tennis, cricket, walking, travelling; *Style*— Prof Michael Mingos, FRS; ✉ St Edmund Hall, Oxford OX1 4AR (tel 01865 279003, fax 01865 279030, e-mail michael.mingos@seh.ox.ac.uk)

MINOGUE, Prof Kenneth Robert; s of Denis Francis Minogue (d 1988), and Eunice Pearl, *née* Porter (d 1949); *b* 11 September 1930; *Educ* Sydney Boys' HS, Univ of Sydney (BA), LSE (BScEcon); *m* 16 June 1954 (m dis 2000), Valerie Pearson, da of Frederick George Hallett (d 1974); 1 s (Nicholas Robert b 1955), 1 da (Eunice Karen Hallett b 1957); *Career* asst lectr Univ of Exeter 1955–56; LSE: asst lectr 1956, sr lectr 1964, reader 1971, prof of political science 1984–95; dir Govt and Opposition Centre for Policy Studies, chm Bruges Group 1991–93; tstee Inst for the Study of Civil Soc 2000–; Centenary Medal

(Australia) 2003; hon fell London Sch of Economics 2002; *Books* The Liberal Mind (1963), Nationalism (1967), The Concept of a University (1974), Alien Powers: The Pure Theory of Ideology (1985), Politics: A Very Short Introduction (1995), Conservative Realism: New Essays in Conservatism (ed, 1996), The Silencing of Society (1997), Waitangi Morality Reality (1998); *Recreations* wine, women and song; *Clubs* Garrick; *Style*— Prof Kenneth Minogue; ✉ 43 Perrymead Street, London SW6 (tel 020 7736 2380, fax 020 7371 9135); Department of Government, London School of Economics and Political Science, Houghton Street, London WC2A 2AE (fax 020 7371 9135, e-mail k.minogue@lse.ac.uk

MINOGUE, Martin Michael; s of Martin Bernard Minogue (d 1996), and Josephine Minogue (d 1985); *b* 23 December 1937; *Educ* King James's GS Knaresborough, Gonville & Caius Coll Cambridge (MA); *m* 17 Aug 1968 (m dis 1985), Elizabeth, da of Harold Worthy Wray, of Darley, N Yorks; 2 s (Nicholas b 7 March 1974, Ben b 6 Nov 1975); *Career* Nat Serv RAF 1957–59; second sec HM Dip Serv (formerly third sec) 1962–65, asst princ BOT 1965–66, lectr in social science Univ of Kent 1966–69; Univ of Manchester: lectr (later sr lectr) 1969–84, dir Int Devpt Centre 1984–96, dir of research Centre on Regulation and Competition Inst of Devpt Policy and Mgmnt 2000–06; conslt UN Devpt Prog 1990–, memb ESRC 1996–; *Books* African Aims and Attitudes (ed with J Molloy, 1974), Documents on Contemporary British Government (ed, 1977), A Consumer's Guide to Local Government (ed, 1977 and 1980), Perspectives on Development (ed with P Leeson, 1988), Beyond the New Public Management (ed with C Polidano and D Hulme, 1998), The Internationalisation of Public Management (ed with W McCourt, 2001), Development Theory and Practice: Challenging the Orthodoxies (ed with U Kothari, 2001), Leading Issues in Competition, Regulation and Development (ed with P Cook, 2004), Regulatory Governance in Developing Countries (ed with L Carino, 2006); *Recreations* reading, theatre, tennis, golf; *Clubs* Withington Golf, Northern Lawn Tennis; *Style*— Martin Minogue, Esq; ✉ 8 Bamford Road, Didsbury, Manchester M20 8GW (tel 0161 445 4669)

MINOPRIO, (Frank) Charles; 2 s of late (Charles) Anthony Minoprio, of London; *b* 9 August 1939; *Educ* Harrow, Grenoble Univ; *m* 1, Patricia Mary (d 1995), er da of late Brian W Dixon; 2 da (Victoria b 1966, Charlotte b 1972), 1 s (George b 1969); m 2, 1998, Mrs Colleen Thompson; *Career* served as Lt RA in Germany; wine conslt; dir Haulfryn Group Ltd (formerly Haulfryn Est Co Ltd), chm Inst of Masters of Wine 2002–03, chm Champagne Acad 1986; Master Worshipful Co of Distillers 1987 (memb Ct of Assts); *Recreations* tennis, squash, golf, gardening; *Style*— Charles Minoprio, Esq; ✉ Staughton Manor, Great Staughton, Cambridgeshire PE19 5BD (tel 01480 869035, fax 01480 861565)

MINTER, Graham Leslie; s of Norman Leslie Minter, of Edgware, and Beryl Winifred, *née* Damen; *b* 4 January 1950; *Educ* Orange Hill Co GS; *m* 1975, Peter Anne, da of Col Cyril Scott; 1 da (Monique b 1972), 1 s (Christopher b 1978); *Career* HM Dip Serv: FCO 1968–71, passport offr Anguilla 1971–72, Latin American floater 1973–75, third sec Asuncion 1975–78, FCO 1978–79, second later first sec Mexico City 1979–84, FCO 1984–89, first sec Canberra 1990–94, FCO 1994–98, ambass to Bolivia 1998–2001, FCO 2001–05; sr conslt responsble business solutions Int Business Ldrs Forum 2005–; *Recreations* travel, music, walking, tennis, table tennis, football; *Style*— Graham Minter, Esq, LVO

MINTER, Jonathan Charles; s of John Minter, CBE, DL, of Essex, and Barbara Geraldine MacDonald, *née* Stanford; *b* 22 July 1949; *Educ* Repton, Univ of Birmingham (BA); *m* 9 July 1983 (m dis 1997), Diana Claire, da of Austin Brown, of Sussex; 1 s (Benjamin b 1986), 1 da (Isabel b 1988); *Career* vice-chm: Julius Baer Investment Management Inc, Julius Baer Investments Ltd; ret 2001; Second Warden Worshipful Co of Skinners; *Recreations* shooting, sailing, farming; *Clubs* Royal Ocean Racing, MCC; *Style*—Jonathan C Minter, Esq; ✉ Rivers Hall, Boxted, Colchester, Essex CO4 5SN

MINTER, Trevor John; OBE (1997), DL (Kent, 2002); s of John Minter, and Kathleen Edith, *née* Lee; *b* 19 August 1953; *Educ* Harvey GS Folkestone, Christ's Coll Finchley, Lancaster Univ (BA), RMA Sandhurst, Army Staff Coll; *m* 8 May 1976, Elizabeth Ann, da of Allan Kerry, and Vivian Kerry; 1 da (Alexandra Louise b 1 Dec 1978), 1 s (Edward Patrick George b 23 Nov 1980); *Career* cmmnd Royal Regt of Fusiliers 1973 (mentioned despatches 1989); CO 1 Bn 1993–96, cmd tour incl Bosnia (UN and NATO), staff appt HQ Br Forces Hong Kong 1986–88, Mil Asst to Chief of Defence Staff 1990–93, chief Jt Ops Centre SHAPE 1996–98, Cdr 2 (SE) Bde and 207th Dep Constable Dover Castle 1998–2001; Dep Col (Northumberland) Royal Regt of Fusiliers 1996–2002 (ret), Dep Col Tyne Tees Regt (TA) 1998–2002 (ret); dir: Kent Partnership Kent CC, Creative Fndn Folkestone; chm Interim Exec Bd Minster Coll Isle of Sheppey; observer Ashford's Future Delivery Bd, memb Kent Economic Bd, memb Project Steering Gp Sheppey Acad; former: offr Confederation of the Cinque Ports, pres Fusiliers Assoc of Northumberland, chm Fifth Fusiliers Central Fund, chm Fusiliers of Northumberland Benevolent Fund; former tstee: Fusiliers Museum of Northumberland, Adml Ramsay Meml Appeal; patron: Dover Bells Appeal, Market Garden Veterans Assoc 1998–2001; lay memb Canterbury Diocesan Synod; Col Royal Regt of Fusiliers 2007; Freeman City of London 1994; MInstD; *Recreations* shooting, hill walking, history; *Style*— Trevor Minter, OBE, DL; ✉ c/o Sessions House, County Hall, Maidstone, Kent ME14 1XQ

MINTO, Anne Elizabeth; OBE (2000); da of Robert Mitchell (d 1980), and Elizabeth Ann Geddes, *née* Rennie; *b* 29 May 1953, Aberdeen; *Educ* Ellon Acad, Univ of Aberdeen (LLB), Robert Gordon Univ Aberdeen (Dip); *Career* admitted slr 1977; NP 1978; with Shell UK Exploration and Production 1979–92, dep DG EEF 1993–98, gp HR dir Smiths Gp plc 1998–2002, gp dir HR Centrica plc 2002– (also memb Exec Ctee and chm pensions schemes); chm Bd and vice-pres Inst of Employment Studies; FRSA 1988, FCMI (FIMgt 1998), FCIPD 2000; *Recreations* travelling, opera, watching rugby; *Style*— Ms Anne Minto, OBE; ✉ Centrica plc, Millstream, Maidenhead Road, Windsor, Berkshire SL4 5GD (tel 01753 494202, e-mail anne.minto@centrica.com)

MINTO, 7 Earl of (UK 1813); (Gilbert) Timothy George Lariston Elliot-Murray-Kynynmound; 10 Bt (S 1700); also Baron Minto (GB 1797) and Viscount Melgund (UK 1813); s of 6 Earl of Minto, OBE (d 2005); *b* 1 December 1953; *Educ* Eton, North East London Poly (BSc); *m* 30 July 1983, Diana Barbara, da of Brian S L Trafford, of Rudgwick, W Sussex; 3 s (Gilbert, Viscount Melgund b 1984, Lorne b and d 1986, Hon Michael b 1987), 1 da (Lady Clare Patricia b 1991); *Heir* s, Viscount Melgund; *Career* Lt Scots Gds 1972–76; worked in property devpt 1976–80, WH Smith 1983–95, chief exec Paperchase 1995–; memb Queen's Body Guard for Scotland (Royal Co of Archers); ARICS; *Clubs* White's; *Style*— The Rt Hon the Earl of Minto

MINTON, Yvonne Fay; CBE (1980); da of Robert Thomas Minton (d 1974), of Sydney, Aust, and Violet Alice, *née* Dean (d 1997); *b* 4 December 1938; *Educ* Sydney Conservatorium of Music; *m* 21 Aug 1965, William Barclay, s of William Barclay (d 1964), of Scotland; 1 s (Malcolm Alexander b 1971), 1 da (Alison Elizabeth b 1973); *Career* mezzo-soprano; memb Royal Opera Covent Garden 1964–, guest memb Cologne Opera 1969–; guest singer: Aust Opera, Met Opera NY, Lyric Opera Chicago, San Francisco, Paris, Vienna, Bayreuth, Salzburg; Hon RAM; *Recordings* incl: Der Rosenkavalier, Marriage of Figaro, Parsifal, Tristan and Isolde, various song cycles; *Recreations* reading, gardening; *Style*— Ms Yvonne Minton, CBE; ✉ c/o Ingpen & Williams Ltd, 7 St Georges Court, 131 Putney Bridge Road, London SW13 2PA (tel 020 8874 3222, fax 020 8877 3113)

MINTON-TAYLOR, Robert; s of late Richard Harold Minton-Taylor, MBE, of East Hagbourne, Oxon, and Joan, *née* Clarke; *b* 25 February 1948; *Educ* Clayesmore Sch, Wallingford GS, Bournemouth Tech Coll; *m* 13 Sept 1986, Caroline, da of late dr Peter Deller, OBE; 2 s (Jasper, Fabian); *Career* journalist Link House Publications Croydon 1967–71, press offr Townsend Thoresen Car Ferries 1973–77, head of promotions European Ferries Group 1977–79; Burson-Marsteller 1979–94: main bd dir 1987–94, dir leisure travel and transport 1988–94, sr PR cncllr 1989–94, dir media servs 1990–94; md Charles Walls Public Relations 1994–95, assoc sr lectr Faculty of Business and Law Leeds Business Sch Leeds Metropolitan Univ 2002– (tutor 1995–2002), managing conslt Minton-Taylor Consultancy 1995–; media relations mangr Global Corporate Affrs Wallenius Wilhelmsen Logistics 2007–; PR Week awards: nominated Best Design for Public Relations (for Atlantic Container Line) 1987, Best International Campaign (for Galileo) 1988, Best Non-Commercial Campaign (for Prince's Youth Business Tst) 1989, commended Solo Practitioner of the Year 2002; Chartered Inst of Public Relations Excellence Awards: Community Relations (for Business in the Community) 1990, Special Projects (for Seville World Expo '92) 1993, Outstanding Achievement by an Independent Consultant 2002 (finalist 2003), finalist Team Working in Educn and Trg at Leeds Metropolitan Univ 2004, finalist Small PR Team of the Year PRide Awards Yorks and Humber Region CIPR 2006; memb: Chartered Inst of Journalists 1971– (memb Cncl and Exec 1992–, pres 1992–93), Seahorse Club 1982– (chm 1990), Media Soc (memb Cncl 1992–, dir 1995–); MIPR 1980 (memb Cncl 1990–91 and 1993–96, chm Professional Practices Ctee 1995, vice-chm 1996, fell 1998), fell Inst of Travel and Tourism 1986 (memb 1981, chm London and SE England Region 1986–90), fell Motor Industry Public Affairs Assoc 1999; *Recreations* art, architecture, books, cars and Saab aficionado, classical ballet and modern dance, architecture and design, F1 motor racing, merchant ships, modern history, politics, rock and blues music and composers Bach, Beethoven, Copland, Elgar and Holst, French films, travel, Provence, Norway, Sweden, Yorkshire and especially the Yorkshire Dales, cool northern UK cities eg Leeds, Manchester and Newcastle; *Style*— Robert Minton-Taylor; ✉ The Coach House, Meadow Lane, Cononley, Keighley, West Yorkshire BD20 8NA (tel 01535 634634 (office) and 01535 630483 (home), fax 01535 634773 (office), mobile 07947 818816, e-mail robert@minton-taylor.com, website www.minton-taylor.com)

MIQUEL, Raymond Clive; CBE (1981); *b* 28 May 1931; *m*; c; *Career* Arthur Bell & Sons: joined 1956, md 1968–85, chm 1973–85; chm Wellington Importers Ltd USA 1984–85, Gleneagles Hotels plc 1984–85, chm and chief exec Belhaven plc 1986–88, dir Golf Fund plc 1989–94; chm and chief exec: Lees Foods plc 1992–, Lees of Scotland Ltd 1993–; visiting prof of business devpt Univ of Glasgow 1984–; chm Scottish Sports Cncl 1987–91, govr Sports Aid Fndn; memb: Central Cncl of Physical Recreation, Sports Cncl 1988–91; CCMI (CIMgt 1981); *Books* Business as Usual - The Miquel Way (biography, 2000); *Style*— Raymond Miquel, Esq, CBE; ✉ Whitedene, Caledonian Crescent, Gleneagles, Perthshire (tel 01764 662642)

MIRO, Victoria; da of Montagu Cooper, and Jane Cooper; *Educ* Slade Sch of Fine Art; *Career* prop Victoria Miro Gallery 1985–; artists represented incl: Chris Ofili, Peter Doig, Isaac Julien, Doug Aitken, Thomas Demand, Grayson Perry, Inka Essenhigh, Anne Chu, Ian Hamilton Finlay; tstee Little Sparta Tst; *Style*— Mrs Victoria Miro; ✉ Victoria Miro Gallery, 16 Wharf Road, London N1 7RW (tel 020 7336 8109, e-mail victoria@victoria-miro.com)

MIROŠIČ, HE Iztok; s of Drago Mirošič, and Suzanna Mirošič; *b* 21 March 1968, Postojna, Slovenia; *Educ* Ljubljana Univ (Prešeren Award, UN Assoc of Slovenia Award, BA); *m* 19 Aug 2005, Tina; *Career* Slovenian diplomat; joined Foreign Miny 1995, sr advsr for rels with Italy, the Vatican and cooperation in the Central European Initiative 1995–97, head Office of the State Sec and Dep Foreign Min 1997–2000, state under-sec Miny of Foreign Affrs 2000–03, state sec Miny of Foreign Affrs and dep foreign min 2003, state sec Office of the PM and chief foreign policy advsr to PM 2003–04, ambass to the Ct of St James's 2004– (also ministerial cncllr in int rels Office of the PM and chief foreign policy and EU advsr to PM); Repub of Slovenia perm rep to IMO 2006–; *Recreations* football, free diving, fly fishing; *Clubs* Athenaeum; *Style*— HE Mr Iztok Mirošič; ✉ Embassy of the Republic of Slovenia, 10 Little College Street, London SW1P 3SH

M

MIRRÉ, HE Federico; s of Emilio Juan Mirré (d 1994), and Maria Teresa, *née* Gavaldá-Lavin (d 1986); *b* 7 August 1938, Buenos Aires, Argentina; *Educ* Manuel Belgrano Sch of Marist Brothers, Univ of Buenos Aires; *m* Cecilia, *née* Duhau; 2 da (Constanza b 13 April 1970, Virginia b 30 July 1974); *Career* Argentine diplomat; asst prof of public int law Faculty of Law Univ of Buenos Aires 1977–79; cnsllr Argentine Delgn to Papal Mediation Vatican 1979–81, Southern Patagonia dip liaison offr Int Red Cross 1982 (during Malvinas War), memb Delgn to First Post-War Br-Argentine Negotiations on Malvinas Berne 1984, ambass to Côte d'Ivoire, Burkina Faso and Niger 1988–91, agent for Argentine Repub on Laguna del Desierto boundary case with Chile 1991–94, ambass to Norway and Iceland 1994–99, legal advsr Miny of Foreign Affrs 1999, head Dept of Western Europe Miny of Foreign Affrs 2002, ambass to the Ct of St James's 2003–; perm rep Int Maritime Orgn 2003–; dir Fundación Andina 1991, chm Tech Ctee Maritime Front of the River Plate Montevideo 1991–94; ed Perspectiva Monthly 1991–94; pres Professional Assoc of the Foreign Serv 1992–94; *Recreations* yachting, golf; *Clubs* White's, Canning, Caledonian; *Style*— HE Mr Federico Mirré; ✉ Embassy of the Argentine Republic, 65 Brook Street, London W1K 4AH (tel 020 7318 1321, fax 020 7318 1305)

MIRREN, Dame Helen; DBE (2003); *b* 26 July 1946; *Career* actress; *Theatre* RSC 1970–72 incl: Troilus and Cressida, Two Gentlemen of Verona, Hamlet, Miss Julie, The Man of Mode; other credits incl: International Centre of Theatre Research (with Peter Brook, Paris, Africa/America tour) 1972–73, Macbeth (RSC) 1974, Teeth 'n' Smiles (Royal Court/Wyndhams) 1974, The Seagull (Lindsay Anderson Co) 1976, The Bed Before Yesterday (Lyric) 1976, Henry VI parts 1, 2 and 3 (RSC) 1977–78, Measure For Measure (Riverside) 1979, The Duchess of Malfi (Royal Exchange Manchester 1980, Roundhouse 1981), Faith Healer (Royal Court) 1981, Antony and Cleopatra (RSC) 1982–83, The Roaring Girl (RSC) 1983, Extremities 1984, Madame Bovary (Watford Palace) 1987, Two Way Mirror (Young Vic) 1988, Sex Please, We're Italian (Young Vic) 1991, The Writing Game (New Haven, Conn) 1993, A Month in the Country (Albery 1994 and Roundabout NY 1995, nominated for Best Actress Tony Award), Antony and Cleopatra, Collected Stories (Theatre Royal) 1999, Orpheus Descending (Donmar Warehouse) 2000, Dance of Death (Broadway) 2001, Mourning Becomes Electra (RNT) 2003–04; *Television* for BBC incl: Cousin Bette (series) 1971, Miss Julie 1972, Jackanory 1973, Little Minister 1973, The Changeling (with Stanley Baker) 1974, The Apple Cart 1974, The Philanthropist 1975, Mussolini and Claretta Petacci 1975, The Country Wife 1976, Rosalind in As You Like It 1978, Blue Remembered Hills 1978, Oresteia in The Serpent Son 1978, A Midsummer Night's Dream 1981, Mrs Reinhart (with WNET/USA) 1981, After the Party 1982, Imogen in Cymbeline 1982; for ATV incl: Behind the Scenes 1971, Coffin for the Bride 1973, Quiz Kids 1978; for Granada The Collection 1976, DCI Jane Tennison in Prime Suspect I, II, III, IV and V 1990–96, VI 2003 and VII 2006 (BAFTA and BPG TV & Radio Best Actress Awards 1992, BAFTA Best TV Actress Award 1993, BAFTA Best TV Actress Award 1994, Emmy Award for Best Actress 1996); other credits incl: Bellamira (Thames) 1974, Coming Through (Central) 1985, Alma Rattenbury in Cause Celebre (Anglia) 1987, Red King, White King (HBO) 1988, Losing Chase 1996 (Golden Globe Award for Best Actress), Painted Lady 1998, dir Happy Birthday (US TV Film) 2000, Door to Door 2002, Georgetown 2002, Pride 2004, Elizabeth I 2005 (Best Actress in a Miniseries or TV Movie Golden Globe Awards 2007); *Films* Age of Consent 1969, Savage Messiah 1971, O Lucky Man 1972, Caligula 1976, Hussy 1979, The Long Good Friday 1979, Fu Man Chu 1980, Excalibur 1981, Cal 1983 (Best Actress Award Cannes

Film Festival 1984), 2010 1984, White Knights 1984, Heavenly Pursuits 1985, Mosquito Coast 1986, Pascali's Island 1987, When the Whales Came 1988, Bethune, Making of a Hero 1988, The Cook, The Thief, His Wife and Her Lover 1989, The Comfort of Strangers 1989, Where Angels Fear to Tread, The Gift 1991, The Hawk 1992, Prince of Jutland 1993, Queen Charlotte in The Madness of King George 1994, Some Mothers Son 1995, Critical Care 1996, The Passion of Ayn Rand 1998 (Emmy Award Best Actress), The Killing of Mrs Tingle, Last Orders 2001, Gosford Park 2001 (Oscar nomination for Best Supporting Actress 2002), Calendar Girls 2003, The Clearing 2004, Raising Helen 2004, The Queen 2006 (Best Actress in a Drama Golden Globe Awards 2007, Best Actress in a Leading Role BAFTA Awards 2007, Best Actress Oscar 2007); *Style*— Dame Helen Mirren, DBE; ✉ c/o Ken McReddie Ltd, 21 Barrett Street, London W1U 1BD

MIRRLEES, Prof Sir James Alexander; kt (1997); s of late Prof George B M Mirrlees; *b* 5 July 1936; *Educ* Trinity Coll Cambridge (BA, PhD), Univ of Edinburgh (MA); *m* m 1, 1961, Gillian Marjorie (d 1993); 2 da (Catriona, Fiona); m 2, 2001, Patricia; *Career* advsr MIT Center for Int Studies India Project New Delhi 1962–63, asst lectr rising to lectr in economics Univ of Cambridge 1963–68 (fell Trinity Coll Cambridge), advsr Pakistan Inst of Devpt Economics Karachi 1966–68, Edgeworth prof Univ of Oxford 1968–95 (fell Nuffield Coll Oxford), visiting prof Dept of Economics MIT 1968, 1970–71, 1976 and 1987; prof of political economy Univ of Cambridge 1995– (fell Trinity Coll); Ford visiting prof Dept of Economics Univ of Calif Berkeley 1986, visiting prof Dept of Economics Yale Univ 1989, asst editor Review of Econ Studies 1969–74 (memb Bd 1963–); Econometric Soc: fell 1970–, memb Cncl 1970–74 and 1976–, vice-pres 1980–82, pres 1983–84; memb Treasy Ctee on Policy Optimization 1976–78, co-editor Econometrica 1980–84; foreign hon memb: American Acad of Arts and Scis 1981, American Econ Assoc 1982; memb Cncl Royal Econ Soc 1982–, chm Assoc of Univ Teachers of Economics 1983–87, vice-pres Atlantic Econ Soc 1986–87, pres Royal Econ Soc 1989–92, pres European Econ Soc 2000, foreign assoc US Nat Acad of Sciences 1999; Nobel Prize for Economics (jtly) 1996; Hon DLitt: Univ of Warwick, Univ of Portsmouth, Brunel Univ, Univ of Edinburgh, Univ of Oxford, Univ of Liège; Hon FRSE 1998; FBA; *Publications* Manual of Industrial Project Analysis in Developing Countries Vol II (with I M D Little, 1969), An Exploration in the Theory of Income Taxation (Review of Eocnomic Studies, 1971), Optimal Taxation and Public Production (with P A Diamond, American Economic Review, 1971), On Producer Taxation (Review & Economics Studies, 1972), Notes on Welfare Economics, Information and Uncertainty (Essays in Equilibrium Behaviour under Uncertainty 1974), Arguments for Public Expenditure (Contemporary Economic Analysis 1979), The Economic Uses of Utilitarianism (Utilitarianism and Beyond 1982); *Recreations* reading detective stories, mathematics, playing the piano, travelling; *Style*— Prof Sir James Mirrlees, FBA; ✉ Trinity College, Cambridge CB2 1TQ (tel 01223 339516, e-mail j.mirrlees@econ.cam.ac.uk)

MIRZA, Shahana; da of Yaqub Mirza, of Edinburgh, and Asia, *née* Hussain; *b* 29 August 1973, Glasgow; *Educ* James Gillespie's HS Edinburgh, Heriot-Watt Univ (BEng, Conoco Achievement Award, BP Chemicals Prize); *Career* engr; Courtaulds Fibres Ltd: process devpt engr 1995–96, tech support engr AL 1996–97, process devpt, design and commissioning engr 1997–98, critical process engr and critical process engrg mangr Smith & Nephew Medical Ltd 1998–2000, site process safety advsr and comah project tech mangr BASF plc 2000–02, section head technical HSE compliance Engrg Safety Foster Wheeler Energy Ltd 2003– (princ ops safety engr 2002–03); Nat Gen Cert in Occupational Health and Safety 1999, Nat Dip in Occupational Safety and Health 2002 and 2004, Client/Contractor Nat Safety Gp (CCNSG) Safety Passport; memb Bd Engrg Cncl (EC(UK)); MIChemE 2000 (registered safety professional 2004), CEng 2000, MIOSH 2004, FRSA 2004; *Recreations* actively supporting the engineering profession; *Style*— Miss Shahana Mirza; ✉ Foster Wheeler Energy Limited, Shinfield Park, Reading, Berkshire RG2 9FW (tel 0118 913 2544, fax 0118 913 8438, e-mail shahana_mirza@fwuk.fwc.com)

MIRZOEFF, Edward; CVO (1993), CBE (1997); s of late Eliachar Mirzoeff, of Edgware, Middx, and Penina, *née* Asherov; *b* 11 April 1936; *Educ* Hasmonean GS, The Queen's Coll Oxford (open scholar, MA); *m* 4 June 1961, Judith, da of Harry Topper, of Finchley, London; 3 s (Nicholas b 1962, Daniel b 1965, Sacha b 1969); *Career* market researcher Social Surveys (Gallup Poll) Ltd 1959–60, asst ed Shoppers' Guide Magazine 1962–63; BBC TV 1963–2000, freelance television conslt, exec prodr, prodr and dir 2000–; prodr and dir of many documentaries incl: Elizabeth R, Metro-land, A Passion for Churches, The Queen's Realm, The Front Garden, The Englishwoman and the Horse, Police - Harrow Road, The Regiment, Target Tirpitz, The Ritz, Torvill and Dean: Facing the Music, Treasures in Trust, John Betjeman - The Last Laugh; series prodr: Choice, Bird's-Eye View, Year of the French, In at the Deep End, Just Another Day, The Richard Dimbleby Lecture, A J P Taylor Lectures; ed 40 Minutes 1985–89; exec prodr of many documentary series since 1982 incl: Pandora's Box, The Ark, True Brits, Situation Vacant, The House, Full Circle with Michael Palin, The 50 Years War: Israel and the Arabs, Children's Hospital, Michael Palin's Hemingway Adventure, Queen Elizabeth the Queen Mother, The Lords' Tale, A Very English Village; BAFTA Award for best documentary 1982, BAFTA Awards for best factual series 1986 and 1989, BFI TV Award 1988, Samuelson Award Birmingham Festival 1988, BAFTA Alan Clarke Award for outstanding contribution to television 1994, Int Emmy 1996, Broadcasting Press Guild Award 1996, Royal Philharmonic Soc Music Award 1996; BAFTA: memb Cncl 1988–99, vice-chm TV 1991–95, chm 1995–97, tstee 1999–; memb Bd Dirs and Prodrs Rights Soc 1999–; chm Grierson Tst 2002–06 (tstee 1999–); memb Cncl Salisbury Cathedral 2002–; vice-pres Betjeman Soc 2006–; *Recreations* opera, gossip; *Clubs* Garrick; *Style*— Edward Mirzoeff, Esq, CVO, CBE; ✉ 9 Westmoreland Road, London SW13 9RZ (tel 020 8748 9247)

MISCAMPBELL, Gillian Margaret Mary; OBE (1982), DL (Bucks 1993); da of Brig Francis William Gibb (d 1969), of Rosemount, Blairgowrie, Perthshire, and Agnes Winifred Gibb; *b* 31 December 1935; *Educ* St Leonard's Sch; *m* 5 April 1958, Alexander Malcolm Miscampbell, s of Alexander Miscampbell (d 1965), of Hoylake, Cheshire; 3 s (Andrew Ian Farquharson b 18 June 1959, Ian Alexander Francis b 27 Feb 1962, Alexander James b 19 Aug 1964); *Career* vice-chm Nat Women's Advsy Ctee Cons Pty 1979–80; chm: Aylesbury Cons Assoc 1975–78, Aylesbury Vale HA 1981–93, Bucks CC 1989–93 (memb 1977–93, chm Educn Ctee 1985–89), Stoke Mandeville NHS Tst 1995–2001, Cancer Care and Haematology Fund Stoke Mandeville Hospital 2004–; dir Buckinghamshire Fndn 1999–2006; memb: Area Manpower Bd 1985–88, Bd Milton Keynes Devpt Corp 1990–92, Bucks HA 1993–95; vice-chm Cncl Univ of Buckingham 1994–2005 (memb 1985–, chm Fin and Gen Purposes Ctee 1993–98), chm Aylesbury GS Fndn 2005–; Hon Dr Univ of Buckingham 1998; *Style*— Mrs Alec Miscampbell, OBE, DL; ✉ Rosemount, Upper Street, Quainton, Buckinghamshire HP22 4AY (tel and fax 01296 655318)

MISHCON, Hon Jane Malca (The Hon Mrs Landau); da of Baron Mishcon (Life Baron); *b* 1950; *Educ* Univ of Oxford (MA); *m* 1, 1971 (m dis), Anthony Jay; 1 s (Adam), 1 da (Lucy); m 2, 30 Oct 1990, Edward Landau; *Career* called to the Bar Gray's Inn 1979, practising barr specialising in clinical and slrs' negligence; chair 8 ind inquiries into homicides by mentally disordered patients; memb Professional Negligence Bar Assoc; *Style*— Miss Jane Mishcon; ✉ Hailsham Chambers, 4 Paper Buildings, Temple, London EC4Y 7EX (tel 020 7643 5000)

MISHCON, (Hon) Peter Arnold; er s of Baron Mishcon, QC, DL (Life Peer); *b* 1946; *Educ* City of London Sch, Birmingham Coll of Art, Poly of Central London (DipArch); *m* 1967,

Penny Green; 1 s (Oliver b 1968), 3 da (Anna b 1972, Kate b 1973, Eliza b 1977); *Career* chartered architect and designer; princ Mishcon Associates 1976–; Housing Centre Trust Jubilee Award for Outstanding Achievement in Housing, Royal Borough of Kensington and Chelsea Environment Award, Times/RICS Conservation Award, Arango Design Fndn (USA) Award; chm Keniston Housing Association Ltd 1984–2001; RIBA; *Recreations* Nelson boats, breakfast, fixing things; *Style*— Peter Mishcon; ✉ Pembridge Studios, 27A Pembridge Villas, London W11 3EP (tel 020 7229 9103, fax 020 7229 6744, e-mail peter@mish.com)

MISIEWICZ, Dr J J; *b* 28 March 1930, Lwow, Poland; *Educ* Lord Weymouth's GS, Univ of London (BSc, MB BS); *m* Marjorie Alice; *Career* hon conslt physician and jt dir Dept of Gastroenterology and Nutrition Central Middx Hosp London; pres Br Soc of Gastroenterology 1987–88; ed: Gut 1980–87, Euro Jl of Gastroenterology and Hepatology 1989–; hon conslt gastroenterologist RN until 1999; memb Governing Cncl European Assoc for Gastroenterology and Endoscopy 1990–; memb: BMA, Br Soc of Gastroenterology, American Gastroenterology Assoc, Euro Assoc for Gastroenterology and Endoscopy; FRCP, FRCPE; *Books* Diseases of the Gut and Pancreas (jt ed); also author of papers on peptic ulcer, Helicobacter pylori, irritable bowel syndrome and ulcerative colitis; *Recreations* friends, the arts, country, food; *Style*— Dr J J Misiewicz; ✉ e-mail misiewicz@dial.pipex.com

MISKIN, Charles James Monckton; QC (1998); s of Nigel Monckton Miskin, of London, and Hilda Meryl, *née* Knight (d 1962); *b* 29 November 1952; *Educ* Charterhouse (Sutton prize), Worcester Coll Oxford (open exhbn, MA); *m* 1982 (m dis), Kass, da of Ronald Booth; 1 s (Harry b 7 February 1983), 3 da (Cici b 11 May 1984, Julia b 19 November 1990, Flora b 10 November 1992); *Career* called to the Bar Gray's Inn 1975, standing counsel to the Inland Revenue 1993–98, recorder of the Crown Court 1998– (asst recorder 1992–98), head of chambers 23 Essex St 2003–; memb: SE Circuit, Criminal Bar Assoc 'Justice'; Liveryman: Worshipful Co of Armourers and Brasiers, Worshipful Co of Wax Chandlers; *Recreations* travel, history, opera, theatre (chm Bar Theatrical Soc 1986–), walking; *Clubs* Hurlingham, Travellers; *Style*— Charles Miskin, Esq, QC; ✉ 23 Essex Street, London WC2R 3AS (tel 020 7413 0353, fax 020 7413 0374, e-mail clerks@essexstreet23.demon)

MISRA, Prof Prem Chandra; JP (Glasgow 1985); s of Dr Man Mohan Lal Misra (d 1980), of Hardoi, India, and Bindeshawri (d 1970); *b* 24 July 1941; *Educ* KK Degree Coll Lucknow India (BSc), King George's Med Coll Lucknow India (MB BS), Royal Coll of Surgeons and Physicians Glasgow & Edinburgh (DPM); *m* 24 Jan 1970, Sandhya, da of Mr Manohar Lal Khanna, of Bombay, India; 2 da (Deepali b 1970, Nisha b 1980), 1 s (Vivek b 1975); *Career* demonstrator Dept of Human Physiology King George's Med Coll Lucknow India 1967, resident house surgn in gen surgery Royal Infirmary Wigan 1968–69, resident house physician in gen med Whelley Hosp Wigan 1969–70; Bolton Dist Gen Hosp Farnworth: resident sr house offr of gen psychiatry 1970–71, resident registrar of gen psychiatry 1971–73; Hollymoor Hosp Birmingham: sr psychiatric registrar 1973–76, conslt psychiatrist and sr clinical lectr Dept of Psychological Med Univ of Glasgow 1976–; memb Exec Ctee Strathclyde Community Relations Cncl 1981–87, pres Indian Assoc of Strathclyde, memb Bd of Dirs Scottish Refugee Cncl 1995–2001, govr Glasgow Caledonian Univ 1999–, lead conslt contact in Scotland Register of Psychiatrists with an Interest in Transcultural Issues RCP; American Gerontological Soc; fell: Indian Psychiatric Soc 1980–, RSM; memb American Psychiatric Assoc 1974–, chm Academic Ctee Br Soc of Med and Dental Hypnosis Scotland 1993– (hon sec Div of Psychiatry 1980–95, pres 1987–89), memb Ethical Ctee (Eastern Dist Glasgow) 1980–93, life memb Scottish Assoc for Mental Health, fndr memb Glasgow Assoc for Mental Health; memb: Exec Ctee European Soc of Hypnosis, Int Soc of Hypnosis, Int Sci Ctee of Sexuality and Handicap in Paris, Exec Ctee Br Soc of Res on Sex Educn; media spokesperson (hypnosis, sexual disorders and phobia) Univ of Glasgow 1986–; mentor for newly arrived overseas doctors in Scotland Scottish Cncl for Postgrad Med and Dental Educn; hon prof Glasgow Caledonian Univ 2003; Award for Dedicated and Exceptional Service to Patients: Greater Glasgow Health Cncl, Indian Writers Assoc of Scotland, Med Assoc of Krakow; Asian Fedn of Sexology Hon (for pioneering health care contribution in developing new methods of hypnotherapy for psychosexual disorders); FRCPsych (MRCPsych); *Books* Modern Trends in Hypnosis (ed with Waxman et al, 1985), author of 20 res papers on hypnosis and sexual disorders in med jls; *Recreations* classical music, walking in Scottish highlands, travelling to various countries in the world; *Style*— Prof Prem Misra; ✉ 21 Victoria Road, Lenzie, Glasgow G66 5AN (tel 07775 687849, fax 0141 5786549)

MISSELBROOK, Peter; s of Dr D B Misselbrook (d 2005), and Anne, *née* Goodman; *b* 4 March 1953; *Educ* Winchester, Univ of Dundee (LLB); *m* 2 June 1979, Fiona Jane; 1 da (Katie); *Career* admitted slr 1978; trainee Maclay Murray & Spens, ptnr J & A Hastie SSC 1981–96, ptnr Tods Murray LLP 1996– (chm 2002–04, exec ptnr 2004–); formerly: chm BASC, pres Fedn of Fieldsports Assocs of the EU (FACE), memb Firearms Consultative Ctee Home Office, memb Cncl and Exec RZS of Scotland; memb Law Soc of Scotland; memb High Constables and Guard of Hon Holyrood House; *Recreations* shooting, fishing, stalking, hill walking, gardening, tennis, reading; *Clubs* New (Edinburgh); *Style*— Peter Misselbrook, Esq; ✉ Southfield Farmhouse, Cousland, Dalkeith, Edinburgh EH22 2NX; Tods Murray LLP, Edinburgh Quay, 133 Fountainbridge, Edinburgh EH3 9AG (tel 0131 656 2000, fax 0131 656 2020, e-mail peter.misselbrook@todsmurray.com)

MITCHARD, Anthony Keith; s of Albert Ernest James Mitchard, and Florence, *née* West; *b* 26 December 1934; *Educ* King Edward's Sch Bath; *m* 31 March 1956, Kathleen Margaret, da of Albert Henry Smith; 3 da (Andrea Marie b 27 Feb 1958, Susan Elizabeth b 16 Aug 1959, Alison Judith b 16 Aug 1971), 2 s (Michael David b 25 Oct 1963, John Robert b 27 June 1967); *Career* dir Avon Rubber Co Ltd 1974, chief exec Avon Rubber plc 1986–94, ret; pres Community First, dir Wiltshire Strategic Economic Partnership, tstee King Edward's Sch Bath; FPRI; *Recreations* golf, cricket, rugby, reading; *Style*— Anthony Mitchard, Esq; ✉ e-mail tony.mitchard@lineone.net

MITCHARD, (Gerald Steven) Paul; s of Gerald Albert Mitchard, of Charlton, Wilts, and Janet Margaret, *née* Gregory; *b* 2 January 1952; *Educ* Taunton Sch, Univ of Oxford (MA); *m* 1, 28 June 1980 (m dis 1985), Shirley Anne Mitchard, *qv*, da of Dennis Robert Wilkins Chappell; m 2, 2 May 1987, Dorothy Neleitha, da of Leslie Grant, of Hornsey, London; 2 s (David Max Gregory b 10 Feb 1988, George Henry Steven b 2 Dec 1990); *Career* admitted slr England and Wales and slr-advocate (civil) 1974; asst slr Slaughter and May 1977–84; Simmons & Simmons: asst slr 1984–85, ptnr 1985–98, head of litigation 1994–98; ptnr Wilmer Cutler & Pickering 1999–2001, head of Euro litigation and arbitration Skadden, Arps, Slate, Meagher & Flom UK LLP 2001–; qualified slr Hong Kong 1984 and Br Virgin Islands 2006; CEDR accredited mediator 1993; Liveryman City of London Solicitors' Co; memb: Law Soc 1977, American Bar Assoc, Int Bar Assoc, CPR's Panel of Distinguished Neutrals 1994; FCIArb 1993; *Recreations* reading, walking; *Style*— Paul Mitchard, Esq; ✉ Skadden, Arps, Slate, Meagher & Flom UK LLP, 40 Bank Street, Canary Wharf, London E14 5DS (tel 020 7519 7050, fax 020 7519 7070, e-mail pmitchard@skadden.com)

MITCHARD, Shirley Anne; da of Dennis Robert Wilkins Chappell, and Joan Gladys, *née* Woolcott; *b* 15 February 1953; *Educ* Weirfield Sch Taunton, Portsmouth Univ (BA); *m* 28 June 1980 (m dis 1985), (Gerald Steven) Paul Mitchard, *qv*; *Career* KPMG Peat Marwick 1975–81 (Tax Dept 1979–81), Tax Div Arthur Andersen & Co 1981–84 (sr mangr 1983), corp tax ptnr Clark Whitehill 1987–97 (joined 1985); BDO Stoy Hayward: corp tax ptnr

1997–2001, conslt Private Client Gp 2001–; non-exec dir Cedar Int Ltd 2007; memb CISCO Tax Ctee 1999–2001; ACA 1978, MInstD; *Recreations* the arts, gardening, cricket; *Style*— Ms Shirley Mitchard; ✉ 27 Ashcombe Street, London SW6 3AW (tel 020 7371 0609); BDO Stoy Hayward, 8 Baker Street, London W1 (tel 020 7893 3465, e-mail shirley.mitchard@bdo.co.uk)

MITCHELL, Adrian; *b* 24 October 1932; *Career* poet and playwright; Nat Serv RAF 1951–52; reporter 1955–63 (Oxford Mail, Evening Standard); freelance journalist: Daily Mail, The Sun, Sunday Times; Granada fell in the arts Lancaster Univ 1967–69, fell Centre for the Humanities Wesleyan Univ USA 1972; resident writer: Sherman Theatre Cardiff 1974–75, Unicorn Theatre 1982–83; visiting fell Billericay Comp Sch 1978–80, Judith E Wilson fell Univ of Cambridge 1980–81, poetry ed New Statesman and Society 1994–96, Dylan Thomas fell UK Year of Lit Festival Swansea 1995–96; Hon Dr Univ of N London 1997; FRSL 1986; *Theatre* plays for the theatre: Tyger (NT), Man Friday (7:48 Theatre Co), Mind Your Head (Liverpool Everyman), A Seventh Man (Hampstead), White Suit Blues (Nottingham Playhouse), Uppendown Mooney (Welfare State International), The White Deer (Unicorn Theatre for Children), Hoagy Bix and Wolfgang Beethoven Bunkhaus (Tricycle Theatre), Mowgli's Jungle (Contact Theatre), C'mon Everybody (Tricycle Theatre), Satie Day/Night (Lyric Studio Hammersmith), Anna on Anna (Theatre Workshop Edinburgh), The Siege (Schs Nat Playwright Commissioning Gp); stage adaptations for NT: Animal Farm (lyrics), The Mayor of Zalamea, Fuente Ovejuna, The Government Inspector; stage adaptations for RSC: Marat/Sade, Life's a Dream (with John Barton); other stage adaptations: The Great Theatre of the World (Medieval Players), Peer Gynt (Oxford Playhouse), Mirandolina (Bristol Old Vic), Lost in a Mirror (Southwark Theatre), The Little Violin (Tricycle Theatre); other stage shows: The Wild Animal Song Contest (Unicorn Theatre), In the Unlikely Event of an Emergency (South West Music Theatre), King Real (Ongar Youth Theatre), The Last Wild Wood in Sector 88 (Derby Music Theatre), The Pied Piper (NT), The Blue (Walk the Plank), Unicorn Island (Dartington), The Snow Queen (ESIPA, Albany USA), A New World and The Tears of the Indians (Southampton Nuffield Theatre), Sir Fool's Quest (Puppetcraft), Tom Kitten and His Friends (Unicorn Theatre), Tyger Two (Emmanuel Univ Boston), Jemima Puddleduck and Her Friends (Unicorn Theatre), The Lion, The Witch and The Wardrobe (RSC), The Heroes (Kageboushi Tokyo), The Mammoth Sails Tonight (Dream Factory Warwick), Start Again (Morecambe), Alice in Wonderland (RSC), Peter Rabbit and His Friends (Unicorn Theatre), Nobody Rides the Unicorn (Puppetcraft), Aladdin (Doublejoint Belfast), King of Shadows (NYSTI), Perseus and the Gorgon's Head (Puppetcraft); *Television Plays* Daft as a Brush, Silver Giant, Wooden Dwarf, The Fine Art of Bubble Blowing, Something Down There is Crying (BBC), You Must Believe All This, Glad Day (Thames TV); *Opera* Houdini (with Peter Schat); *Films* Man Friday (1975), King Real and the Hoodlums (1985); *Novels* If You See Me Comin' (1962), The Bodyguard (1970), Wartime (1973); *Poetry* Poems (1964), Out Loud (1968), Ride the Nightmare (1971), The Apeman Cometh (1975), For Beauty Douglas (collected poems 1953–79) (1982), On the Beach at Cambridge (1984), Nothingmas Day (1984), All My Own Stuff (1991), Adrian Mitchell's Greatest Hits - the Top Forty (1992), Blue Coffee (1996), Heart On The Left (1997), All Shook Up (2000), Blackbird Singing: Poems and Lyrics of Paul McCartney (ed, 2001), The Shadow Knows (2004); *Literary Criticism* Who Killed Dylan Thomas? (illustrated by Ralph Steadman, 1998); *Children's Books* incl: The Baron Rides Out (1985), The Baron on the Island of Cheese (1986), Our Mammoth (1986), The Baron all at Sea (1987), Our Mammoth goes to School (1987), Our Mammoth in the Snow (1989), All My Own Stuff (1992), The Orchard Book of Poems (1993), The Thirteen Secrets of Poetry (1993), Maudie and the Green Children (1996), Gynormous! (1996), Balloon Lagoon (1997), My Cat Mrs Christmas (1998), Robin Hood and Marian (1998), Twice My Size (1998), Nobody Rides the Unicorn (1999), Dancing in the Street (1999), The Odyssey (2000), A Poem A Day (2001), Zoo of Dreams (2001), Daft as a Doughnut (2004); *Style*— Adrian Mitchell, Esq, FRSL; ✉ c/o Peters, Fraser and Dunlop, 34–43 Russell Street, London WC2B 5HA (tel 020 7344 1000)

MITCHELL, Andrew John Bower; MP; s of Sir David Bower Mitchell, DL, and Pamela Elaine, *née* Haward; *b* 23 March 1956; *Educ* Rugby, Jesus Coll Cambridge (MA); *m* 27 July 1985, Sharon Denise, da of David Benedict Bennett; 2 da (Hannah Katherine b 1987, Rosie Olivia Louise b 1990); *Career* 1 RTR (SSLC) 1975; pres Cambridge Union 1978, chm Cambridge Univ Cons Assoc 1977, chm The Coningsby Club (Cons Graduates) 1983–84; int and corp business Lazard Bros & Co Ltd 1979–87; Parly candidate (Cons) Sunderland S 1983; MP (Cons): Gedling 1987–97, Sutton Coldfield 2001–; sec One Nation Gp of Cons MPs 1989–92 and 2005–, a vice-chm Cons Pty 1992–93, asst Govt whip 1992–94, a Lord Cmmr and Govt whip 1994–95, Parly under-sec of state DSS 1995–97, shadow home affrs min 2004–05, shadow sec of state for int devpt 2005–; dir: Lazard Bros 1997–, Miller Insurance Group 1997–2001, Financial Dynamics 1998–2002, CM Group 1998–2002; sr strategy advsr at: Boots 1997–2000, sr strategy advsr Accenture 1997–; advsr to Bd Hakluyt & Co 1998–2001; vice-chm Alexandra Rose Charity 1998–; memb: Cncl SOS Sahel 1990–, ESU Int Debating Ctee 1999–; tstee GAP Activity Projects 2000–06; pres Norman Laud Assoc; Liveryman Worshipful Co of Vintners; *Recreations* skiing, sailing, reading; *Clubs* Cambridge Union Soc, Conservative Club Sutton Coldfield; *Style*— Andrew Mitchell, Esq, MP; ✉ 30 Gibson Square, Islington, London N1 0RD (tel 020 7226 5519); Manor House Farm, Screveton, Nottinghamshire; 8 Tudor Road, Sutton Coldfield (0121 355 5519)

MITCHELL, Andrew Robert; QC (1998); s of Malcolm Mitchell (d 1998), of Aldwick Bay, W Sussex, and Edna Audrey Cherry, of Boca Raton, Florida; *b* 6 August 1954; *Educ* Haberdashers' Aske's, Cncl of Legal Educn; *m* 1, 1982 (m dis 1990), Patricia Anne, *née* Fairburn; m 2, Carolyn Anne Blore; 1 s (Harry Aubrey b 8 March 1993), 1 da (Tiffany Rose b 26 Aug 1994); *Career* called to the Bar Gray's Inn 1976 (bencher 2005); memb Irish Bar, head of chambers 32 Furnival St 1991–, asst recorder of the Crown Ct 1995–99, recorder 1999–; memb: Criminal Bar Assoc, Justice; memb Cncl London Borough of Haringey 1984–94 (ldr oppn 1990 and 1991), Parly candidate (Cons) Islington S and Finsbury 1987; chm Bd of Govrs Highgate Primary Sch 1997–99; *Publications* Confiscation (looseleaf, 1992, 3 edn 2002); *Recreations* playing tennis, watching football and cricket; *Clubs* RAC, MCC; *Style*— Andrew Mitchell, Esq, QC; ✉ Chambers of Andrew Mitchell, QC, Furnival Chambers, 32 Furnival Street, London EC4A 1JQ (tel 020 7405 3232, fax 020 7405 3322, e-mail arm@furnivallaw.co.uk)

MITCHELL, Austin Vernon; MP; s of Richard Mitchell and Ethel Mary Mitchell; *b* 19 September 1934; *Educ* Woodbottom Cncl Sch, Bingley GS, Manchester Univ, Nuffield Coll Oxford (DPhil, fell 1967–69); *m* 1 (m dis), Patricia Jackson; 2 da (Kiri, Susan); m 2, Linda McDougall; 1 s (Jonathan), 1 da (Hannah); *Career* lectr in history Univ of Otago NZ 1959–62, sr lectr in politics Univ of Canterbury 1962–67, journalist with Yorkshire TV 1969–71 and 1973–77, presenter BBC Current Affrs 1972–73, presenter and interviewer Sky Television 1989–98; MP (Lab): Grimsby 1977–83, Great Grimsby 1983–; PPS to min of state for prices and consumer protection 1977–79, oppn whip 1980–85, opposition front bench spokesman on trade and industry 1988–89; former memb Treasy and Civil Service Select Ctee; memb: Agriculture Select Ctee 1997–2001, Environment and Food Ctee, Public Accounts Cmmn; chm: All Pty Fisheries Gp, All Pty Transpennine Gp, All Pty Icelandic Gp, All Pty Photographic Gp, Labour Economic Policy Gp, All Pty Media Gp, Hansard Soc, Labour Campaign for Electoral Reform, Labour Euro-Safeguards Campaign; former chm PLP Treasy Gp; fell of the Indust and Parly Tst, memb Exec Fabian Soc; *Books* incl: Westminster Man: A Tribal Anthology of the Commons People (1982), The Case for Labour (1983), Four Years in the Death of the Labour Party (1983), Yes Maggie, There is an Alternative (1983), Yorkshire Jokes, Teach Thissen Tyke, Britain: Beyond the Blue Horizon (1989), Competitive Socialism (1989), Accounting for Change (1993), Election 45 (1995), Corporate Governance Matters (1996), The Common Fisheries Policy: End or Mend? (1996), Last Time: Labour's Lessons from the Sixties (with David Wienir, 1997), Fishermen: The Rise and Fall of Deep Water Trawling (with Anne Tate, 1997), Parliament in Pictures (1999), Farewell My Lords (1999), Pavlova Paradise Revisited (2002), Austin Mitchell's Talking Yorkshire (2002); *Recreations* photography, comtemplating exercise; *Style*— Austin Mitchell, Esq, MP; ✉ House of Commons, London SW1A 0AA (tel 020 7219 4559, fax 020 7219 4843, e-mail mitchellav@parliament.uk)

MITCHELL, Dr Charles James; s of Col P C Mitchell, MC, FRCPE, of Insch, Aberdeenshire, and Josephine Selina, *née* White; *b* 11 November 1946; *Educ* Trinity Coll Glenalmond, Univ of Edinburgh (BSc, MB ChB); *m* 21 Oct 1972, Elisabeth Bullen, da of Frank George Meakin, of Southfleet, Kent; 1 da (Alice b 1975), 1 s (Alexander b 1977); *Career* house physician Royal Infirmary Edinburgh 1971, SHO and registrar KCH London 1972–74, registrar Academic Dept of Med Royal Free Hosp London 1974–76, conslt physician Scarborough Health Authy 1981–, hon conslt physician St James's Univ Hosp Leeds 1981–92 (lectr in med 1976–81); regnl advsr Royal Coll of Physicians 1994–97, sec Specialist Advsy Ctee General (Internal) Med 1999–2004; pres Pancreatic Soc of GB and Ireland 1992 (memb Ctee 1981–84), medical memb Appeals Panel PMETB 2005–, elected memb Cncl Royal Coll of Physicians of Edinburgh 2005–; memb: Br Soc of Gastroenterology (memb Ctee 1987–90 and 1999–2002), Euro Pancreatic Club; chm Derwent Hunt 1998–; FRCPEd 1987, FRCP 1988; *Books* Pancreatic Disease in Clinical Practice (ed jtly and contrib, 1981), Textbook of Gastroenterology (contrib, 1992); *Recreations* field sports, piping, gardening; *Clubs* Royal Scot Pipers Soc, New (Edinburgh); *Style*— Dr Charles Mitchell; ✉ The Old Rectory, Ebberston, Scarborough, North Yorkshire YO13 9PA; Leafield, Dalton, Dumfriesshire; Department of Gastroenterology, Scarborough Hospital, Scarborough, North Yorkshire YO12 6QL (tel 01723 368111, fax 01723 352471)

MITCHELL, His Hon Judge David Charles; s of Charles Mitchell (d 1982), and Eileen, *née* Aveyard (d 1990); *Educ* Batley Boys' GS, Queen Mary's Sch Basingstoke, Cavendish Sch Hemel Hempstead, St Catherine's Coll Oxford (MA); *m* 30 June 1973, Susan, *née* Cawthera; 1 da (Joanna b 4 Nov 1980), 1 s (Andrew b 31 July 1982); *Career* called to the Bar Inner Temple 1972 (scholar); barr: Bradford Chambers 1972–99, 6 Pump Court 1999–2001; recorder 1993–2001 (asst recorder 1989–93), circuit judge (SE Circuit) 2001–, designated civil judge Kent (Canterbury) 2003–; chm Mental Health Review Tbnl 2003–05; patron Salvation Army; *Recreations* hill walking, skiing, theatre, classical music, anything French; *Style*— His Hon Judge David Mitchell; ✉ Canterbury Combined Court Centre, Chaucer Road, Canterbury, Kent CT1 1ZA

MITCHELL, David Smith; TD (1972 and 2 Bars); s of Edward Mitchell (d 1975), and Kathleen Mitchell (d 1990); *b* 5 August 1937; *Educ* Chesterfield Sch, Pembroke Coll Oxford (MA); *m* 14 Sept 1963, Karin, da of William Embleton Hall (d 1978); 1 da (Anna-Marie b 1969), 1 s (Edward b 1972); *Career* served RAF 1956–58, TA; co sec: various cos within J Lyons & Co Ltd 1961–72, J Lyons & Co Ltd 1983–87 (asst sec 1972–83), Allied-Lyons plc 1987–94, Allied Domecq plc (following name change) 1994–2000; co sec Navy, Army and Air Force Insts 2002–; FCIS; *Recreations* Territorial Army; *Clubs* RAF; *Style*— David Mitchell, Esq, TD; ✉ c/o RAF Club, 128 Piccadilly, London W1V 0PY

MITCHELL, David Stephen; s of Stan Mitchell, of Malvern, Worcs, and Jenny, *née* Cox; *b* 12 January 1969; *Educ* Univ of Kent (BA, MA); *m* 6 Oct 2001, Keiko, *née* Yoshida; 1 da (Hana May b 4 May 2002), 1 s (Noah Sean b 29 Sept 2005); *Career* author; named in Granta 20 List 2003; *Publications* Ghostwritten (1999, John Llewelyn-Rhys Prize 1999), Number9Dream (2001, shortlisted Booker Prize 2001), Cloud Atlas (2004, Best Literary Fiction Br Book Awards, South Bank Show Literature Prize, Richard and Judy Best Read of the Year, shortlisted for six awards incl James Tait Black Award and Man Booker Prize), Black Swan Green (2006, longlisted Man Booker Prize); *Style*— David Mitchell, Esq; ✉ c/o Curtis Brown, Haymarket House, 28–29 Haymarket, London SW1Y 4SP (tel 020 7396 6600, fax 020 7396 0110, e-mail jonnyp@curtisbrown.co.uk)

M

MITCHELL, Dr David Sydney; CBE (1992); s of Ernest S Mitchell (d 1973), and Emma, *née* Carter (d 1967); *b* 3 April 1930; *Educ* QMC London (BSc, PhD); *m* July 1954, Winifred Mary, *née* Tollow; 1 s (Eric Charles b 1958), 1 da (Caroline Elisabeth b 1960); *Career* Nat Service RAF; Rolls Royce: joined 1956, with Naval Nuclear Propulsion Derby, consequently mangr and chief engr Admiralty Reactor Test Establishment Dounreay, md Rolls Royce and Associates 1968, md Small Engine Div, asst commercial dir, dir commercial services 1981; chm: Soc of Br Aerospace Cos Marketing Ctee, Australian and New Zealand Trade Advsy Gp; Master Worshipful Co of Engineers 1998–99; CEng, FIMechE; *Recreations* gardening, music, model engineering; *Clubs* Athenaeum; *Style*— Dr David Mitchell, CBE; ✉ 9 Old Town Farm, Great Missenden, Buckinghamshire HP16 9PA (tel and fax 01494 864324, e-mail dsmgm2003@yahoo.co.uk)

MITCHELL, David William; CBE (1983); s of William Baxter Mitchell (d 1983), and Betty Steel, *née* Allan (d 1959); *b* 4 January 1933; *Educ* Merchiston Castle Sch Edinburgh; *m* 1965, Lynda Katherine Marion, da of Herbert John Laurie Guy (d 1975); 1 da (Louisa-Jayne b 1972); *Career* cmmnd (NS) RSF 1950; memb Bd Western Regional Hosp 1965–72, pres Timber Trades Benevolent Soc of UK 1974, Scot Cncl CBI 1979–85, dir Mallinson-Denny (Scotland) 1977–90, Hunter Timber Scotland 1990–92, jt md M & N Norman (Timber) Ltd 1992–96 (non-exec 1996–98); pres: Scot Timber Trade Assoc 1980–82, Scot Cons and Unionist Assoc 1981–83; memb: Scot Cncl (Devpt and Industry) 1984–95, Bd Cumbernauld New Town 1985 (chm 1987–97), Bd of Mgmnt Craighalbert Centre for Children with Motor Impairment 1992–96; Scot Cons Pty: treas 1990–93 and 1998–2001, chm 2001–04, pres 2004–; *Recreations* fishing, shooting, golf; *Clubs* Western (Glasgow), Prestwick, Royal and Ancient (St Andrews), Queen's Park FC; *Style*— David W Mitchell, Esq, CBE

MITCHELL, His Hon Judge Fergus Fergus Irvine; s of Sir George Mitchell, CB, QC (d 1978), and Elizabeth, *née* Leigh Pemberton (d 1989); *b* 30 March 1947; *Educ* Tiffin Boys' Sch Kingston; *m* 1 July 1972, Sally, yr da of late Sir Derrick Capper, QPM; 1 da (Rebecca Elizabeth b 22 March 1977), 1 s (Ewen George William b 15 Feb 1980); *Career* called to the Bar Gray's Inn 1971, head of chambers 1994–96, circuit judge (SE Circuit) 1996–; memb Gen Cncl of the Bar 1993–96 (memb Professional Conduct and Race Rels Ctees); chm Lord Chllr's Advsy Ctee SW London 2001–; *Recreations* farm in Aveyron (France), opera, military history; *Style*— His Hon Judge Fergus Mitchell; ✉ Kingston Crown Court, 6–8 Penrhyn Road, Kingston upon Thames, Surrey KT1 2BB (tel 020 8240 2500)

MITCHELL, Gary George; s of Charles Henry Mitchell, and Alexandra, *née* Moreland; *Educ* Rathcoole Secdy Sch; *m* 10 Jan 2004, Alison, *née* Butler; *Career* writer and dir; writer in residence National Theatre of GB and NI 1998–; *Theatre* Independent Voice 1993, Suspicious Minds 1993, Alternative Future 1994, That Driving Ambition 1995, In a Little World of Our Own 1997 (Best Drama Belfast Arts Awards, Irish Times Theatre Awards: Best Dir, Best Actor, Best Play), Sinking 1997 (Best Drama Belfast Arts Awards), Tearing the Loom 1998, As the Beast Sleeps 1998, Trust 1999 (Pearson Prize Best Play), Energy 1999, Marching On 2000 (nominated Best Play Theatre Mgmnt Award UK, nominated Best Play Irish Times), The Force of Change 2000 (jt winner George Devine Award, winner Evening Standard Charles Wintour Award Most Promising Playwright, nominated South Bank Show Award), Remorse 2002, Deceptive Imperfections 2003,

Loyal Women 2003, Remnants of Fear 2006 (winner Outstanding Achievement in Culture and Arts Aisling Awards 2006); *Television* Made in Heaven (BBC2) 1996, Made in Heaven Unplugged (BBC2) 1996, Red, White and Blue (BBC1) 1998; *Radio* Radio 4: The World, the Flesh and the Devil 1991 (award winner Young Playwrights' Festival), A Tearful of Dreams 1993, Independent Voice 1993, Poison Hearts 1994, Mandarin Lime (with Jimmy Murphy) 1995; Dividing Force 1995: Useless Tools (episode one), Raising the Standard (episode two), Above the Law (episode three); Drumcree 1996, At the Base of the Pyramid 1997, The Force of Change 2001, Stranded (Radio 3) 1995, Loyal Women (BBC World) 2003; *Film* An Officer from France (RTE) 1998, As The Beast Sleeps (BBC2) 2001, Suffering (short film) 2002 (Best Short Film Belfast Film Festival 2003); *Publications* Tearing the Loom and In a Little World of Our Own (one vol, 1998), Trust (1999), The Force of Change (2000), As the Beast Sleeps (2001), Loyal Women (2003); *Recreations* soccer, swimming, listening to The Ramones; *Style*— Gary Mitchell, Esq; ✉ c/o PFD, Drury House, 34–43 Russell Street, London WC2B 5HA (tel 020 7344 1000, fax 020 7836 9543)

MITCHELL, Geoffrey Bentley; OBE (1999); s of Arthur Hale Mitchell (d 1990), and Eunice Bentley, *née* Wood (d 1989); *b* 20 June 1944; *Educ* Univ of Adelaide (BEcon); *m* 26 Jan 1967, Diedre Maria, *née* McKenna; 2 s (Mark James b 19 Oct 1971, Matthew Paul b 13 Oct 1973), 1 da (Melissa Kate b 22 Sept 1977); *Career* articled clerk Thomas Sara Macklin & Co Adelaide S Aust, lectr then sr lectr Univ of Adelaide 1966–77, reader The Flinders Univ S Aust 1977–81, sec gen International Accounting Standards Ctee 1981–85, tech dir ICAEW 1985–90; Barclays Bank plc: sr mangr 1991–93, head of accounting policies 1993–94, gp fin servs dir Chief Accountants Dept 1994–96, chief accountant 1996–2002, dir fin projects 2002–2006; non-exec dir Mizuho Int plc 2003– (chm Audit and Compliance Ctee 2006–); chm EU Standards Advice Review Gp 2007–; memb: Cncl ICAEW 2001–04 (memb Bd 2003–04), Audit Ctee RCA 2003–07 (chm Pension Tstees 2004–07), Audit Ctee The Law Soc 2004–07, Urgent Issues Task Force 2004–, Audit and Compliance Ctee CREST Co Ltd 2006–07, Pension Tstees MCC 2006–; Freeman City of London 1995; memb Inst of CAs in Aust 1967, FCA 1982; *Books* Principles of Accounting (Prentice Hall of Aust, 1981); *Recreations* tennis; *Clubs* Garrick, MCC; *Style*— Geoffrey Mitchell, Esq, OBE; ✉ Scriventon Oast, Stockland Green, Speldhurst, Tunbridge Wells TN3 0TU (e-mail gbmitchell101@aol.com); Mizuho International plc, Bracken House, One Friday Street, London EC4M 9JA (tel 020 7090 6971, e-mail geoffrey.mitchell@uk.mizuho-sc.com)

MITCHELL, Geoffrey Roger; s of Horace Stanley Mitchell (d 1974), of Fordingbridge, and Madge Amy, *née* Rogers (d 1984); *b* 6 June 1936; *Educ* Exeter Cathedral Choristers' Sch, Brentwood Sch; *Career* Nat Serv leading coder educnl RN 1954–56; counter-tenor lay-clerk: Ely Cathedral 1957–60, Westminster Cathedral 1960–61; counter-tenor vicar-choral St Paul's Cathedral 1961–66, gen mangr John Alldis Choir 1966–, prof Royal Acad of Music and conductor Chamber Choir 1972–92, conductor New London Singers 1972–87, dir Geoffrey Mitchell Choir 1975–, choral mangr BBC 1977–92; conductor Trinity Coll Music vocal ensemble 1977–89, conductor London Festival Singers 1987–, guest conductor Camerata Antiqua Curitiba Brazil 1989–; Nat Fedn Cathedral Old Chorister Assocs: vice-chm 1987–92, chm 1992–97, vice-pres 1997–; Hon ARAM 1981, Hon FTCL 1989; *Recreations* food, collecting antiques and prints, swimming; *Clubs* Athenaeum; *Style*— Geoffrey Mitchell, Esq; ✉ 49 Chelmsford Road, Woodford, London E18 2PW (tel 020 8491 0962, fax 020 8559 7477, e-mail geoffrey-mitchell@ntlhome.com)

MITCHELL, George Edward; CBE (2006); s of George Mitchell, and Wilhelmina, *née* Brookes; *b* 7 April 1950; *Educ* Forrester HS, Heriot-Watt Univ; *m* 12 June 1971, Agnes Barr Rutherford; 3 da (Alison b 28 Oct 1977, Kathryn b 27 Aug 1981, Jennifer b 5 Feb 1986); *Career* Bank of Scotland (now HBOS plc): joined 1966, gen mangr Centrebank Div 1994, dir Bank of Scotland 2000, treas and md Bank of Scotland 2001, chief exec Corp Banking HBOS plc 2001, govr Bank of Scotland 2003, ret 2005; FIBScot 1993 (AIBScot 1971); *Recreations* tennis, football; *Style*— George Mitchell, Esq, CBE

MITCHELL, (George) Grant; s of Prof George Archibald Grant Mitchell, OBE, TD, (d 1993), and Mary *née* Cumming (d 1977); *b* 22 September 1939; *Educ* William Hulme's GS Manchester, Univ of Manchester Med Sch (MB ChB); *m* 14 July 1962, Sandra Joan; 2 da (Caroline b 1963, Victoria b 1965), 1 s (Andrew b 1975); *Career* house surgn and physician Manchester Royal Infirmary, Oldham Royal Infirmary and St Mary's Hosp 1962–64, Geigy res fell Manchester Royal Infirmary 1964–65, princ in gen practice Altrincham Cheshire 1965–68, SHO and registrar Withington, St Mary's and Crumpsall Hosps 1968–73, sr registrar in obstetrics Withington and Oldham Hosps 1973–76, conslt gynaecologist Hope Hosp Salford 1976–2005, clinical dir Dept of Obstetrics and Gynaecology and Salford Royal IVF Unit Hope Hosp Salford 1994–99; FRCSEd 1974, FRCOG 1984 (MRCOG 1971); *Recreations* travel, music, photography; *Style*— Grant Mitchell, Esq; ✉ tel 0161 928 4586, e-mail g_g_mitchell@lycos.co.uk

MITCHELL, Gregory Charles Mathew; QC (1997); s of John Mathew Mitchell, of Surrey, and Eva Maria Mitchell; *b* 1954; *Educ* Bryanston, Univ of London (BA, PhD), City Univ (Dip Law), Cncl of Legal Educn; *Children* 3 s (Frederick b 11 July 1992, George b 24 Jan 1996, Edmund b 16 Oct 2006), 1 da (Alice Isabel Maria b 19 Oct 2003); *Career* called to the Bar Gray's Inn 1979 (bencher); recorder of the Crown Court 2000–; *Recreations* skiing, tennis, scuba diving; *Style*— Gregory Mitchell, Esq, QC; ✉ 3 Verulam Buildings, Gray's Inn, London WC1R 5NT (tel 020 7831 8441, fax 020 7831 8479)

MITCHELL, Iain Grant; QC (1992); s of John Grant Mitchell (d 1990), of Perth, and Isabella, *née* Gilhespie (d 1997); *b* 15 November 1951; *Educ* Perth Acad, Univ of Edinburgh (LLB); *Career* apprentice Steedman Ramage & Co WS 1973–75, admitted Faculty of Advocates 1976, pt/t tutor in mercantile law Univ of Edinburgh 1975–80, temporary sheriff 1992–97; local govt candidate (Cons) 1973–82; Parly candidate (Cons): Falkirk West 1983, Kirkcaldy 1987, Cumbernauld and Kilsyth 1992, Dunfermline East 1997, Edinburgh N and Leith 2001; Scottish Parly candidate: Dundee East 1999, Falkirk W 2003; Euro Parly candidate Scotland 1999; hon sec: Scottish Cons and Unionist Assoc 1993–98, Scottish Cons and Unionist Party 1998–2001; memb Strathclyde Cmmn 1997–98; chm: Fac of Advocates Information Technology Gp 1999–, Scottish Lawyers Euro Gp 2002–, Scottish Soc Computers & Law; jt ed E-Law Review 2001–05; memb: Exec Ctee Scottish Cncl Euro Movement 1992–, Central Advsy Ctee on Justices of the Peace 1999–2005, Ctee Perth Civic Tst 1999–2002; chm: Tst for Int Opera Theatre for Scotland 1984–, Scottish Baroque Ensemble Ltd 2001–03, N Queensferry Arts Tst 2004–; vice-chm: N Queensferry Community Cncl 2002–, Perthshire Public Arts Tst 2006–, N Queensberry Station Tst 2006–; reader Church of Scotland 2005–; FSA Scot 1974, FRSA 1988, FFCS 2002; *Recreations* music and the arts, photography, cinema, walking, travel, finding enough hours in the day; *Style*— Iain G Mitchell, Esq, QC; ✉ c/o Advocates' Library, Parliament House, High Street, Edinburgh EH1 1RF (tel 0131 226 5071, fax 0131 225 3642, mobile 078 3670 0556, e-mail igmitchell@easynet.co.uk)

MITCHELL, John David; s of Charles Mitchell (d 1955), of Warrington, and Ruth, *née* Tilston; *b* 7 March 1942; *Educ* The Craig Windermere, Sedbergh; *m* 7 July 1970, Sarah; 1 s (Mark b 15 Feb 1974); *Career* mgmnt trainee Thames Board Mills 1959, trainee Henry Cooke 1960; Tilney & Co asset mangrs: joined 1962, ptnr 1977, md 1986–93 (following takeover by Charterhouse plc), chief exec 1993–99 (following MBO), chm 1999–2001, ret; dir various other cos; dir SFA 1995– (memb Stock Exchange 1977); *Recreations* golf, walking, gardening, travel, eating and drinking; *Clubs* Warrington Golf; *Style*— John Mitchell, Esq; ✉ Ashfield Cottages, Dark Lane, Higher Whitley, Warrington, Cheshire WA4 4QG (tel 01925 730605); Tilney & Co, Royal Liver Buildings, Pier Head, Liverpool L3 1NY (tel 0151 236 6000, fax 0151 236 1252)

MITCHELL, Prof John Francis Brake; OBE (2001); s of Norman Brake Mitchell (d 1969) and Edith Alexandra Mitchell, *née* Reside (d 1997); *b* 7 October 1948, Belfast; *Educ* Down HS Downpatrick, Queens Univ Belfast (BSc, PhD); *m* 6 June 1973, Catriona; 1 s (Ewan Keith b 18 Nov 1976), 2 da (Mairi Ruth b 26 Nov 1978, Eileen Elizabeth b 27 Mar 1982); *Career* Met Office: research scientist 1973–77, forecaster 1977–78, head Climate Group 1978–88, head of modelling climate change 1988–2002, chief scientist 2002–; visiting prof Sch of Maths, Physics and Meteorology Univ of Reading 2004; chm World Climate Research Prog (WCRP) Jt Scientific Ctee-Climate Variability and Predictability Study (JSC-CLIVAR) Working Gp on Coupled Models 2001–, memb: World Meteorological Orgn (WMO) Steering Gp on Global Climate Models 1990–94, WCRP-Int Geosphere-Biosphere Prog (IGBP) Paleoclimate Modelling Intercomparison Project Scientific Steering Ctee 1994–2001, WCRP CLIVAR Numerical Experimentation Gp II 1995–97, Euro-CLIVAR Ctee 1995–98, WCRP CLIVAR Scientific Steering Gp 1996–2000, WCRP JSC-CLIVAR Working Gp on Couple Models 1997–2000, Intergovernmental Panel on Climate Change Task Gp on Climate Impact Assessment 1997–, WMO Cmmn for Climatology Gp on Climate Change Detection 1998–, IGBP Global Analysis Integration and Modelling Task Force 2001–04, UK Environmental Research Funders Forum 2002–, UK Global Environmental Change Ctee 2002–, NERC Nat Centre for Atmospheric Sciences Advsy Gp 2003, Scientific Advsy Panel UK Environment Agency 2003, Forum on Atmospheric Science and Technol NERC 2003, UK Inter-Agency Ctee on Marine Science and Technol 2003, Industrial Advsy Ctee Univ of Exeter 2003; memb Editorial Bd Climate Dynamics 1994–, author of numerous articles in peer-reviewed jls; Symons meml lectr RMS 2003; LG Grove Prize for Meteorology Met Office 1984, Norbert Gerbier MUMM Int Award WMO (jtly) 1997 and 1998, Outstanding Scientific Paper Award Environmental Research Labs (jtly) 1997, Hans Oeschger Medal European Geophysical Union 2004; hon prof of environmental sciences UEA 2003; chartered meteorologist 2004; memb Academia Europaea 1998, fell Inst of Maths and its Applications 2003, FRS 2004; *Recreations* sport, outdoor activities, photography; *Style*— Prof John Mitchell, OBE; ✉ Met Office, Fitzroy Road, Exeter, Devon EX1 3PB (tel 01392 884604, fax 01392 884400, e-mail john.f.mitchell@metoffice.gov.uk)

MITCHELL, Jonathan James; QC (Scot 1992); s of John Angus Macbeth Mitchell, of Edinburgh, and Ann Katharine, *née* Williamson; *b* 9 August 1951; *Educ* Edinburgh Acad, Marlborough, New Coll Oxford (BA), Univ of Edinburgh (LLB); *m* 28 Aug 1987, Melinda Jane, da of Michael McGarry; 1 da (Hannah Catriona McGarry b 1 March 1988), 1 s (Ewan Patrick Macbeth b 28 December 1992); *Career* apprentice Simpson & Marwick 1976–77, legal offr Citizens' Rights Office 1977, asst to Allan MacDougall 1977–78, admitted to Faculty of Advocates 1979, temp sheriff 1988–96, dep social security cmmr 1994–2002; *Books* Eviction and Rent Arrears (1994); *Clubs* Scotch Malt Whisky Soc; *Style*— Jonathan Mitchell, Esq, QC; ✉ 30 Warriston Crescent, Edinburgh EH3 5LB (tel 0131 557 0854, fax 0870 124 8222, e-mail jm@jonathanmitchell.info, website www.jonathanmitchell.info); c/o Advocates' Library, Parliament House, Edinburgh EH1 1RF

MITCHELL, Jonathan Stuart; s of Rev Ronald Frank Mitchell, and Margery Mabel, *née* Callaghan; *b* 29 January 1947; *Educ* Mill Hill Sch, Trinity Coll Dublin (BA, MA); *Partner* Ute Bierbaum; 1 s (Christian Stuart b 21 Nov 1980), 1 da (Emily Katharina b 4 April 1982); *Career* Mktg Div Courtaulds Textiles 1969–72, PR John Laing 1972–73; called to the Bar Middle Temple; in practice SE Circuit 1974–; memb Int Criminal Bar 2003, writer on legal/political issues 1998–2006; treas Euro Criminal Bar Assoc (fndr memb 1997); memb Exec Ctee SDP Southwark 1981–87; local govt candidate: SDP Dulwich 1982, 1984 and 1986, Lib Dem Dulwich 1994; Parly candidate (Lib Dem) Dulwich and W Norwood 2005; cncllr East Dulwich London Borough of Southwark 2006–; memb Ctee Lib Dem Lawyers Assoc 2003, Burma co-ordinator Lib Dem Human Rights Gp; memb Herne Hill Baptist Church; *Recreations* gardening, swimming, rowing, sailing; *Style*— Jonathan Stuart Mitchell, Esq; ✉ 35 Pickwick Road, Dulwich, London SE21 7JN (e-mail mitchbrief@hotmail.com); 25 Bedford Row, London WC1R 4HD (tel 020 7067 1500, fax 020 7067 1507, e-mail clerks@25bedfordrow.com); tel 07903 967911, e-mail jonathan.mitchell@southwark.gov.uk

MITCHELL, Julian; s of late William Moncur Mitchell, and Christine Mary, *née* Browne (d 1994); *b* 1 May 1935; *Educ* Winchester, Wadham Coll Oxford (BA), St Antony's Coll Oxford; *Career* Nat Serv Sub Lt RNVR 1953–55; Harkness fell USA 1959–61, freelance writer 1962–, regular critic on BBC arts progs; formerly: govr Chelsea Sch of Art, memb Lit Ctee English Arts Cncl, chm Drama Ctee Welsh Arts Cncl; curator Joshua Gosselin exhbn Chepstow 2003; Wolfson Lectr 2003; FRSL 1985; devised and narrated Adelina Patti - Queen of Song (1987); *Awards* incl John Llewelyn Rhys Prize 1965, Somerset Maugham Award 1966; *Books* Introduction (stories, 1960); novels: Imaginary Toys (1961), A Disturbing Influence (1962), As Far As You Can Go (1963), The White Father (1964), A Circle of Friends (1966), The Undiscovered Country (1968); Jennie, Lady Randolph Churchill (biography, with Peregrine Churchill, 1974); contrib: The Welsh History Review, The Monmouthshire Antiquary; *Stage Plays* incl: A Heritage and its History (1965), A Family and a Fortune (1975), Half-Life (1977), Another Country (1981, Play of the Year), Francis (1983), After Aida (1986), Falling Over England (1994); trans Pirandello's Henry IV (John Florio prize 1980), August (version of Chekhov's Uncle Vanya, 1994); *Television* incl: Elizabeth R (Emmy Award 1971), A Question of Degree, Rust, Jennie, Lady Randolph Churchill (series), Abide With Me (Int Critics Prize Monte Carlo and US Humanities Award 1977), The Mysterious Stranger (Golden Eagle Award 1983), Inspector Morse (RTS and Writers' Guild Awards 1991, 10 episodes), Survival of the Fittest, All the Waters of Wye (documentary); *Films* Arabesque (dir Stanley Donen, 1965), Another Country (dir Marek Kanievska, 1984), Vincent and Theo (dir Robert Altman, 1990), August (dir Anthony Hopkins, 1995), Wilde (dir Brian Gilbert, 1997); adaptations of books for screen incl: Persuasion, Staying On, The Good Soldier; *Other Publications* New Bats in Old Belfries (introduction, 2005), author of numerous reviews for magazines and newspapers; *Style*— Julian Mitchell, Esq

MITCHELL, Prof Juliet Constance Wyatt; *b* 4 October 1940, Christchurch, NZ; *Educ* King Alfred Sch London, St Anne's Coll Oxford (exhibitioner, MA, state studentship); *Career* asst lectr Univ of Leeds 1962–63, lectr in English Univ of Reading 1965–71, trainee psychotherapist Paddington Centre for Psychotherapy 1975–77, sr psychotherapist Camden Cncl for Social Services 1976–78, psychoanalyst in private practice 1978–96; Univ of Cambridge: lectr in gender and soc, social and political sciences 1996–, convenor Sec-Gen's Working Pty for the Estab of Gender Studies in Cambridge Univ 1998–, prof of psychoanalysis and gender studies 2000–, head Dept of Social and Political Sciences 2002–03; A D White prof-at-large (distinguished visiting professorship) Cornell Univ 1994–99 (also sometime visiting prof), visiting fell Social Science Res Unit Univ of London 1995–96, visiting prof Euro Univ Inst Florence 1996–97, visiting prof Central Euro Univ Budapest 1997–99, visiting prof Dept of Comparative Lit Yale Univ 1999, visiting Freud Archive prof Univ of Essex 2000– (visiting prof 1999); sometime visiting prof: SUNY, Washington Univ, Univ of Calif Santa Barbara, Univ of Calif Irvine, Stanford Univ, Austin Riggs Psychiatric and Psychoanalytical Trg Clinic, Intercollegiate Sch of Theory and Criticism Dartmouth Coll, Washington Inst of Psychiatry, Cornell Univ, Deakin Univ Aust; Henry Luce visiting scholar Yale Univ, Sigma Chi Fndn - William P Huffman scholar in residence Miami Univ; numerous named lectures; memb Bd of Gender Studies Central Euro Univ Budapest, hon memb Bd of Women's Studies Yale Univ; clincial work: Br Assoc of Psychotherapists, Lincoln Centre, London Centre for

Psychotherapy, Guild of Psychotherapists, Arbours Fndn, Philadelphia Assoc, Addenbrooke's Hosp Cambridge; conslt psychoanalyst: Lima 1984, Brisbane 1988; fndr memb and devisor of educnl prog S of England Soc of Psychotherapists, mentor New Directions Prog Washington Psychoanalytic Fndn 1996–; sometime broadcaster and critic on TV and radio; memb Editorial Bd: Winnicott Studies, Gradiva, Common Knowledge, Gender and Psychoanalysis, Liverpool Studies in Language and Discourse, PsychCritique, Int Advsy Bd of Signs USA, Psychoanalytic Studies, Humanities Inst Stonybrook, Jl of the Inst for Psychological Study of the Arts, New Directions, Studies in Gender and Sexuality, Jl of Classical Sociology, New Left Review; memb: Br Psychoanalytical Soc 1988– (assoc memb 1978), Int Psychoanalytical Assoc 1988– (assoc memb 1978), Br Confedn of Psychotherapists 1996–; *Publications* Women's Estate (1972, 2 edn 1986), Psychoanalysis and Feminism (1974, 2 edn 2000), The Rights and Wrongs of Women (jt ed, 1977), Daniel Defoe: Moll Flanders (ed, 1978), Feminine Sexuality: Jacques Lacan and the ecole freudienne (jt ed, 1984, reprinted 1996), Women: The Longest Revolution: essays on feminism, literature and psychoanalysis (1984), What is Feminism? (jt ed, 1986), The Selected Melanie Klein (ed, 1986, 2 edn 2000), Before I Was I: Psychoanalysis and the Imagination. The Work of Enid Balint (ed, 1992), Who's Afraid of Feminism? (jt ed and contrib, 1997), Mad Men and Medusas: Reclaiming Hysteria and the Effects of Sibling Relations on the Human Condition (2000), Siblings (2003); author of numerous chapters in books and articles in learned jls; *Recreations* swimming, seeing films, art galleries, reading; *Style*— Prof Juliet Mitchell; ✉ Jesus College, Cambridge CB5 8BL (tel 01223 339696, fax 01223 339696, e-mail jcwm2@cam.ac.uk)

MITCHELL, Kathryn; da of Dr W Mitchell, of Cleveland, and Margaret Mitchell; *b* 5 January 1964; *Educ* Teesside HS for Girls, Stockton Sixth Form Coll, Cleveland Coll of Art, Liverpool Poly (BA); *Career* with: Br Cncl 1987–89, Yorkshire Tyne Tees TV 1990–92, Sky TV 1992–96, Channel 5 Broadcasting Ltd 1997; head of programming UK Gold 1997–99; head of programming UKTV 1999–2000, controller UKTV channels 2000–01, sr vice-pres programming Comedy Central NY 2001–; memb: RTS, Women in Film and TV Advsy Ctee Edinburgh International TV Festival; *Style*— Miss Kathryn Mitchell

MITCHELL, Katie Jane; da of Michael J Mitchell, of Marlborough, Wilts, and Sally, *née* Powell; *b* 23 September 1964; *Educ* Godolphin Sch Salisbury, Oakham Sch, Magdalen Coll Oxford; *Career* theatre dir; began career as prodn asst Kings Head Theatre Club 1986–87; asst dir: Paines Plough 1987, The Writer's Company 1988, RSC 1988–89; fndr own co Classic on a Shoestring (COAS) 1990; assoc dir: RSC 1996–98, Royal Court 2000–03, RNT 2003–; *Theatre* Gate Theatre London/COAS prodns incl: Vassa Zheleznova 1990, Women of Troy 1991, The House of Bernarda Alba 1992; RSC prodns incl: Dybbuk 1992, Ghosts 1993, Henry IV (part III) 1994, Easter 1995, The Phoenician Women 1995, The Mysteries 1997, Beckett Shorts 1997, Uncle Vanya 1998; RNT prodns incl: Rutherford and Son 1994, Machine Wreckers 1995, Oresteia 1999, Ivanov 2002, Three Sisters 2003, Ilanoy 2004, Dream Play 2005, Seagull 2006, Waves 2006, Attempts on Her Life 2006, Women of Troy 2007; WNO prodns incl: Don Giovanni 1996, Jenufa 1998, Katya Kabanova 2001, Jephtha 2003; Royal Court prodns incl: The Country 2000, Ashes to Ashes/Mountain Language 2001, Nightsongs 2002, Forty Winks 2004; other prodns incl: Arden of Faversham (COAS/Old Red Lion) 1990, Live Like Pigs (COAS/Royal Court) 1993, The Last Ones (Abbey Theatre Dublin) 1993, Widowing of Mrs Holroyd (BBC 2) 1995, Iphigenia at Aulis (Abbey Theatre Dublin) 2001; Jephtha (ENO) 2005; *Television* The Turn of the Screw (BBC) 2004; *Awards* Winston Churchill Memorial Tst Travel Fellowship 1989, Time Out Theatre Award (for Arden of Faversham, Women of Troy and Vassa Zheleznova) 1991, Prudential/Arts Cncl of GB Nomination for Contribution to Theatre 1995, Olivier Award nomination for Best Dir 1995, Evening Standard Award for Best Director (for The Phoenician Women) 1996; *Style*— Ms Katie Mitchell; ✉ c/o Leah Schmidt, The Agency, 24 Pottery Lane, Holland Park, London W11 4LZ (tel 020 7727 1346, fax 020 7727 9037)

MITCHELL, Dr Leslie Arthur; s of John Thomas Cornes Mitchell (d 1994), of Malpas, Cheshire, and Hilda May, *née* Lievesley (d 1999); *b* 29 February 1940; *Educ* Sir John Talbots GS, Univ of Liverpool (BEng, PhD); *m* 16 March 1963, Janet Elsie, da of Charles William Bate (d 1973); 1 da (Kerry Janet b 9 June 1964), 2 s (Roderick Leslie b 5 Aug 1967, Alexander Leslie b 10 Dec 1977); *Career* CEGB: head of surface physics Berkeley Nuclear Laboratories 1971–76 (res offr 1964–71), laboratory mangr Marchwood Engrg Laboratories 1981–85 (branch mangr structural engrg 1976–81), dir of laboratories Technol Planning and Research 1987–89 (dir PWR 1985–87); head of business planning National Power 1989–90, dir of technol Nuclear Electric plc 1991–96 (head of business review and internal audit 1990–91), dir of technol and central engrg Magnox Electric plc 1996–2001; conslt LAM Consulting 2001–; memb Radioactive Waste Mgmnt Advsy Ctee (RWMAC) DOE 1991–2004; FREng 1994, FIMechE 1992; *Recreations* Cotswold stone building renovation, gardening, reading, occasional golf; *Style*— Dr Leslie Mitchell, FREng; ✉ LAM Consulting, Kearney House, Balls Green, Minchinhampton, Gloucestershire GL6 9AR (tel 01453 834746, e-mail leslieamitchell@btinternet.com)

MITCHELL, Margaret; JP (South Lanarkshire 1992), MSP; da of late John Aitken Fleming, and Margaret McRae, *née* Anderson; *b* 1952; *Educ* Coatbridge HS, Jordanhill Teacher Trg Coll (Cert), Hamilton Teacher Trg Coll (DipEd), Open Univ (BA), Univ of Strathclyde (DipLP, LLB); *m* 1978, Henry Thomson Mitchell; *Career* sch teacher primary and special educn N and S Lanarkshire 1974–91, co dir Fairfield Properties Ltd 1990–, special advsr to David McLetchie MSP and Lord James Douglas-Hamilton MSP 1999–2002, supply teacher N Lanarkshire 2002–03, MSP Central Scotland (Cons) 2003– (UK Parly candidate Hamilton 1992 and Cunningham North 1997, Scottish Parly candidate Hamilton South 1999 and 2003); memb Scot Parl Cross Party Gp on: Dyslexia, Survivors of Childhood Sexual Abuse, Scottish Economy; Scottish Cons Party: spokesman on women's issues 1997, chm Local Govt Advsy Ctee 1997–98, depute spokesman on educn 1999, justice spokesman 2003–07, convenor Equal Opportunities Ctee 2007–; cncllr and gp ldr Hamilton DC 1988–96; non-exec dir Stonehouse and Hairmyres NHS Hosp Tst 1992–95, memb Hamilton Crime Prevention Panel 1995–; *Recreations* photography, cycling, music; *Style*— Mrs Margaret Mitchell, JP, MSP; ✉ The Scottish Parliament, Edinburgh EH99 1SP (tel 0131 348 5639, fax 0131 348 6483, e-mail margaret.mitchell.msp@scottish.parliament.uk)

MITCHELL, Paul England; s of Ronald England Mitchell, of Fordingbridge, Hants, and Katia Patricia, *née* Hannay; *b* 2 November 1951; *Educ* Canford Sch, Univ of Bristol (LLB); 1 da (Charlotte Daniele b 24 Sept 1986), 1 s (Mark England b 11 May 1989); *Career* articled clerk Joynson-Hicks 1974–76, ptnr Joynson-Hicks (now Taylor Wessing) 1978–; chm Br Copyright Cncl; dir Ballet Rambert Ltd; memb Advsy Bd Roald Dahl Fndn; Freeman City of London, memb Worshipful Co of Fishmongers; memb Law Soc; FRSA; *Recreations* family, theatre, food and wine; *Clubs* Garrick; *Style*— Paul Mitchell, Esq; ✉ Taylor Wessing, Carmelite, 50 Victoria Embankment, London EC4Y 0DX (tel 020 7300 7000, fax 020 7300 7100, mobile 077 6776 1575, e-mail p.mitchell@taylorwessing.com)

MITCHELL, Peter John; s of John and Madeleine Mitchell; *Educ* Harrow, Ecole de Louvre Paris, Courtauld Inst of Art (BA); *Career* art dealer; joined John Mitchell and Son 1962; memb Concordia; memb Soc of London Art Dealers *Exhibitions* Early English Watercolours 1970, Alfred Stevens 1823–1906 1973, The Inspiration of Nature 1976, Antoine Guillemet 1841–1918 1981 and 1998, Pick of the Bunch (loan exhbn of flower paintings from Fitzwilliam Museum Cambridge) 1998; *Publications* European Flower Painters (1973); contrib: Dictionary of Art (1996), Dictionary of Natural Biography on

Jean Pillement 1728–1808; numerous exhbn catalogues; *Recreations* travel, golf, reading, family; *Clubs* Buck's, Royal West Norfolk Golf; *Style*— Peter Mitchell, Esq; ✉ John Mitchell Fine Paintings, 44 Old Bond Street, London W1S 4GB (tel 020 7493 7567, fax 020 7493 5537, e-mail enquiries@johnmitchell.net)

MITCHELL, Robert Henry (Robin); s of Henry Gordon Mitchell, of East Bergholt, Colchester, and Elizabeth Margaret Katherine, *née* Richards; *b* 17 August 1955; *Educ* Stowe, Peterhouse Cambridge (MA); *m* 16 June 1979, Helen Miranda, da of John Victor Akerman, of Brockenhurst, Hants; 1 s (Jonathan b 1988), 2 da (Philippa 1984, Claire b 1986); *Career* admitted slr 1980, ptnr Norton Rose 1986–; specialises in major commercial property devpt, investment and financing; *Recreations* hockey, skiing, tennis, swimming; *Style*— Robin Mitchell, Esq; ✉ Norton Rose, Kempson House, Camomile Street, London EC3A 7AN

MITCHELL, Robin Paul; s of late Frederick James Mitchell, of Enfield, Middx, and Maud Patricia, *née* Pawson; *b* 15 February 1955; *Educ* Latymer Sch; *m* Maria Ann, da of Sean Joseph Kealy, of Enfield, Middx; 2 s (John Paul b 26 April 1979, David Frederick b 2 Feb 1981), 1 da (Lucy Elizabeth b 9 April 1986); *Career* Charles Stanley & Co: unauthorised clerk 1973–75, authorised clerk 1975–81, sr dealer 1981–85, head dealer 1985–, dir of dealing 1998–; MSI; *Recreations* football, cricket, tennis, golf; *Clubs* Stock Exchange Veterans, Bush Hill Park Golf, Norsemen FC; *Style*— Robin Mitchell, Esq; ✉ Charles Stanley & Co Ltd, 25 Luke Street, London EC2A 4AR (tel 020 7739 8200)

MITCHELL, Prof Stephen; s of David Mitchell (d 1997), of Oxford, and Barbara Marion, *née* Davis; *b* 26 May 1948; *Educ* Magdalen Coll Sch Oxford, St John's Coll Oxford (MA, DPhil); *m* 1974, Matina Warren, *née* Weinstein; 3 s (Lawrence b 1982, Daniel b 1984, Samuel b 1985); *Career* temp lectr Univ of Bristol 1973–74, res lectr ChCh Oxford 1974–76; Univ of Wales Swansea: lectr 1976–83, sr lectr 1983–88, reader 1988–93, prof 1993–2001; Leverhulme prof of hellenistic culture Univ of Exeter 2002–; visiting fell Inst for Advanced Study Princeton Univ 1983–84, Br Acad research reader Univ of Göttingen Ger 1990–92; memb Cncl Br Inst of Archaeology at Ankara 1974–99 and 2005 (hon sec 1984–85 and 1995–99), memb Cncl Roman Soc 1986–89 and 1992–95, corresponding memb German Archaeological Inst 1996–, memb Cncl Arts and Humanities Research Bd (AHRB) 1999–2001 (chm Postgrad Panel 1 1999–2002), pres Br Epigraphy Soc 1999–2001, memb Panel 57 Res Assessment Exercise 2001, memb Standing Ctee Cncl of Univ Classical Depts 2002–04; DTh (hc) Humboldt Univ Berlin 2006; FBA 2002 (memb Cncl 2006); *Publications* Anatolia: Land, Men and Gods in Asia Minor (2 vols, 1993), A History of the Later Roman Empire AD 284–641 (2007); *Style*— Prof Stephen Mitchell; ✉ Department of Classics and Ancient History, University of Exeter, Exeter EX4 4QH (tel 01392 264201, fax 01392 264377, e-mail s.mitchell@ex.ac.uk)

MITCHELL, Stephen Graham; s of Derek Mitchell, of Loughborough, and Margaret, *née* Rigden; *b* 14 July 1949; *Educ* Loughborough GS, Univ of Manchester; *m* 27 Aug 1977, Barbara Vina, da of Robert Henry Gilder; 1 da (Francesca b 6 Oct 1988), 1 s (Struan b 15 Aug 1990); *Career* with Thomson Regional Newspapers until 1974; BBC Radio: journalist 1974–91, managing ed BBC Radio News 1991–93, ed radio news progs 1993–97, dep head of news progs 1997–99, acting head of news progs 1999–2000, head of radio news 2000–; *Recreations* spending time with my family; *Style*— Stephen Mitchell, Esq; ✉ BBC News, Room LG600, News Centre, Television Centre, Wood Lane, London W12 7RJ (tel 020 8624 9859, fax 020 8624 9874)

MITCHELL, Stuart Robert; s of Arthur Robert Mitchell, of Long Marston, York, and Margaret Patricia, *née* Marshall; *b* 22 December 1960; *Educ* Tadcaster GS, UMIST (BSc); *m* 27 July 1985, Tracey Victoria, *née* Webb; 1 da (Georgina Victoria b 31 Jan 1993), 1 s (Rory James b 2 Feb 1997); *Career* grad retail trainee J Sainsbury plc 1981–84, salesman Kalamazoo Business Systems 1984; Sainsbury's: trainee buyer 1984, sr mangr meat buyer 1989, vice-pres (store format) Shaw's Supermarkets USA 1993, dir of procurement, primary agric, strategy 1994, Bd trading dir 2000, md 2003– (asst md 2001–03); memb Business in the Community; MInstD 2000; Liveryman Worshipful Co of Butchers; *Recreations* rugby, sailing, golf, cookery; *Clubs* RAC, Dorking Rugby Football, Chichester Yacht; *Style*— Stuart Mitchell, Esq; ✉ Sainsbury's Supermarkets Ltd, 33 Holborn, London EC1N 2HT (tel 020 7695 7818, fax 020 7695 7818)

MITCHELL, Timothy James (Tim); s of Robert Sayers Mitchell, and Pamela, *née* Draisey; *b* 11 August 1965; *Educ* Westbourne Coll Penarth, Assoc of Br Theatre Technicians Paddington Coll; *Career* lighting designer and tech conslt, over 200 prodns worldwide; chief electrician Sherman Theatre Cardiff 1985–88 (electrician and projectionist 1982–83, dep chief electrician 1983–85), dep chief electrician and lighting designer Bristol Old Vic 1988–90; Birmingham Rep Theatre: head of lighting 1990–95, lighting conslt and designer 1995–2001, assoc artist; lighting conslt Sheffield Theatre 2001–; memb: Assoc of Lighting Designers, United Scenic Artists Local 829 (USA); fell Royal Welsh Coll of Music and Drama (FRWCMD); *Theatre* Birmingham Rep: The Free State (also tour), My Best Friend (also Hampstead Theatre London), Paddy Irishman, Paddy Englishman, Paddy... (also Tricycle Theatre London), The Wind in the Willows, Absurd Person Singular, St Joan, The Threepenny Opera, Macbeth, The Atheist's Tragedy (Gold medal Prague Quadrennial 1995), Of Mice and Men, A View from the Bridge, Hamlet, The Doll's House (also tour); RNT: The Red Balloon, The Alchemist; Donmar Warehouse: A Lie of the Mind, Merrily We Roll Along; RSC: A Midsummer Night's Dream, Comedy of Errors, Women be Aware of Women, Oroonoko, The Winter's Tale, Romeo and Juliet, Macbeth, The Lieutenant of Inishmore, Jubilee, King John, Henry IV Parts I and II (Olivier Award nomination for Best Lighting Design 2002), Antony and Cleopatra, Much Ado About Nothing, Measure for Measure, Richard III, Titus Andronicus, King Lear, Othello (also Japan tour), The Tamer Tamed (Kennedy Center Washington and West End), The Taming of the Shrew (also at Kennedy Center Washington and West End), Henry IV Parts I and II (Shakespeare Theater Washington, nominated Helen Hayes Award for Outstanding Lighting Design 2005); Crucible Theatre Sheffield: Edward II, High Society, Richard III, A Chorus Line, Sweet Charity, Lear, Ain't Misbehavin, Piaf; Derby Playhouse: Danny Bouncing, Speaking in Tongues, Ain't Misbehavin', Les Liaisons Dangereuses, Our Boys; other credits incl: Two Pianos Four Hands (Comedy Theatre London), A Raisin in the Sun (Young Vic London), Pajama Game (Toronto and New Victoria Palace Theatre London), Speaking in Tongues (Hampstead Theatre London), A Small Family Business (Chichester Theatre), Hand in Hand (Hampstead Theatre London), Hamlet (Elsinore Denmark), Mahler's Conversation (Aldwych London), Noises Off (RNT, Piccadilly Theatre London, Broadway and tour), The Snowman (Peacock Theatre London), Sweet Panic (Duke of York's Theatre London), The Play What I Wrote (UK tour and Broadway), Of Mice and Men (West End), Hamlet (Sadlers Wells), A Small Family Business (WYP), Benefactors (Albery Theatre London), Hamlet (WYP), Sleeping Beauty (Young Vic London), Winnie the Witch (nat tour), Anna Weiss (Whitehall Theatre London), Dames at Sea (Ambassadors Theatre London), Wodehouse on Broadway (BBC TV and Theatre Royal Plymouth), As You Like It (Wyndhams Theatre), Blood Wedding (Almeida), Brighton Rock (Almeida), Annie Get Your Gun (nat tour), Hamlet (Horripro, Japan and London), Dirty Dancing (London, Toronto and Hamburg), Enemies, (Almeida), Big White Fog (Almeida); *Opera and Dance* Covent Garden Festival: The King and I, The Gondoliers, A Midsummer Night's Dream; Kammeroper Vienna: The Marriage of Figaro, Requiem Ballet, Don Giovanni; Royal Coll of Music: Les Enfants Prodigues, Le Rossignol; other credits incl: On the Town (LSO, Barbican London, BBC TV), Prometheus (Berlin Philharmonic Orchestra), Carmen Negra (Icelandic Opera), Yeoman of the Guard (D'Oyly Carte), Die Fledermaus (WNO), Ariadne Auf Naxos (WNO), St Davids Day Gala

Concert (Channel 4/WNO), Hamlet (Northern Ballet), Lady and the Fool (Birmingham Royal Ballet), Elektra (Mariinsky Theatre St Petersburg); *Recreations* reading, music; *Style*— Tim Mitchell, Esq; ✉ 8 Brockwell Close, Fishburn TS21 4HF (tel 01740 620062, mobile 07976 273239, e-mail timmitchell@lightdesign.fsnet.co.uk); c/o Clare Vidal-Hall, 28 Perres Road, London W6 0EZ (tel 020 8741 7647, fax 020 8741 9459)

MITCHELL, Valerie Joy; OBE (2001); da of Henry Frederick Twidale, of São Paulo, Brazil, and Dorothy Mary, *née* Pierce, MBE; *b* 2 March 1941; *Educ* St Paul's Sch São Paulo, Beaufront Sch Camberley, McGill Univ Montreal (BA); *m* 1, 15 Aug 1962 (m dis 1970), Henri Pierre, s of Frederic Henri Eschauzier; 2 s (Marc William Frederick b 30 Aug 1965, James Henri b 2 Jan 1967); m 2, 1 Sept 1972, Graham Rangeley, s of Arthur Mitchell; 1 da (Samantha Anna b 13 Jan 1974); *Career* lectr in opera, PR conslt to Mayer-Lismann Opera Workshop and PA to asst Dean of Arts and Science McGill Univ Montreal 1962–80; English Speaking Union of the Commonwealth: asst Educn Dept 1980–83, dir of branches and cultural affrs 1983–94, dep DG 1989–94, DG and sec-gen Int Cncl 1994–; memb Exec Ctee European Atlantic Gp Cncl 2003–; tstee: Shakespeare's Globe Tst 2006– (memb Int Ctee Shakespeare Globe Centre 2000–05), Longborough Opera Festival Glos 2006–, Royal Acad of Dance 2007–; FRSA 1987; *Recreations* music, theatre, tennis, walking; *Style*— Mrs Valerie Mitchell, OBE; ✉ The English Speaking Union, Dartmouth House, 37 Charles Street, London W1J 5ED (tel 020 7529 1550, fax 020 7495 6108)

MITCHELL, William; s of William Mitchell (d 1959), and Eileen, *née* King (d 1996); *b* 8 August 1944; *Educ* Campbell Coll Belfast, Oriel Coll Oxford (MA, Dip Social Studies); *m* 1, 1969, Pratima, *née* Bhatia; 1 da (Priya b 21 Feb 1971); m 2, 1993, Natalina, *née* Bertoli; 2 s (Luca b 4 May 1994, Rafael b 25 August 1997); *Career* dir of int divs and gp bd dir Oxford University Press UK 1970–85, exec ed Reference Publishing Oxford University Press USA 1985–88, exec dir Children's Publishing Reed Publishing Group UK 1988–89, md Children's Publishing Div and md Reference Div HarperCollins Publishers UK 1990–92, md JM Dent Ltd and dep gp md Orion Publishing Group Ltd 1992–93, md Bertoli Mitchell Specialist Publishing Brokers 1993–; *Recreations* normal; *Clubs* Groucho; *Style*— William Mitchell, Esq; ✉ Bertoli Mitchell, Plaza 535, Kings Road, London SW10 0SZ (tel 020 7349 0424, e-mail wm@bertolimitchell.co.uk)

MITCHELL COTTS, Sir Richard Crichton; 4 Bt (UK 1921), of Coldharbour Wood, Rogate, Sussex; er s of Sir (Robert) Crichton Mitchell Cotts, 3 Bt (d 1995), and Barbara Mary Winefride, *née* Throckmorton (d 1982); *b* 26 July 1946; *Educ* Oratory Sch; *Heir* bro, Hamish Cotts; *Style*— Sir Richard Mitchell Cotts, Bt

MITCHELL-HEGGS, Dr Nita Ann; da of Maj (Dr) Lewis Posner (d 1975), and Olivia, *née* Jones (d 1999); *b* 6 June 1942; *Educ* N London Collegiate Sch, London Hosp Med Coll (MB BS, DCH); *m* 26 July 1967, Dr Peter Francis Mitchell-Heggs, s of Maj Francis Sansome Mitchell-Heggs (d 1986); 2 da (Emily b 2 July 1974, Sophie b 23 March 1977); *Career* formerly held posts in paediatrics, psychiatry, occupational med, student health; currently conslt occupational physician St George's Healthcare NHS Tst, sr lectr St George's Hosp Med Sch; memb SOM; FRCP, FFOM; *Publications* chapters and articles on mental health, occupational medical ethics etc; *Recreations* travel, skiing, theatre, opera; *Clubs* RAC; *Style*— Dr Nita Mitchell-Heggs; ✉ St George's Hospital, Blackshaw Road, Tooting, London SW17 0QT (tel 020 8725 1662, fax 020 8725 3087)

MITCHELL-INNES, Alistair Campbell; s of Peter Campbell Mitchell-Innes (d 1960), and Frances Jocelyn (d 1977); *b* 1 March 1934; *Educ* Charterhouse; *m* 1957, Penelope Ann, *née* Hill; 1 s, 2 da; *Career* Lt Queen's Own Royal W Kent Parachute Regt 1953–54; dir Macfisheries Ltd 1971–75, vice-chm Walls Meat Co Ltd 1975–77, dir Brooke Bond Group plc 1979–85, chief exec Nabisco Group Ltd 1985–88; chm: Sidney C Banks plc 1994–2000, Anglo and Overseas Trust plc 1996–2004; dep chm HP Bulmer (Holdings) plc 1984–2000, non-exec dir and dep chm Next plc 1989–2004; memb Cncl Br Heart Fndn; *Recreations* golf, gardening; *Clubs* Caledonian, MCC, The Berkshire Golf; *Style*— Alistair Mitchell-Innes, Esq; ✉ 9 Market Street, Rye, Kent TN31 7LA

MITCHINER, Dr John Edward; s of late Geoffrey Morford Mitchiner, and Ursula Angela, *née* Adolph; *b* 12 September 1951; *Educ* Beaumont Coll, Univ of Bristol (BA), SOAS Univ of London (MA, PhD); *m* 1983, Elizabeth Mary Ford; *Career* HM Dip Serv; Cwlth research fell Visva Bharati Univ Santiniketan 1977–78, Bipradas Palchaudhuri fell Calcutta Univ 1978–79, joined FCO 1980, third then second sec (info) Istanbul 1983–85, FCO 1985–87, second sec (devpt) New Delhi 1987–91, second then first sec (political) Berne 1991–95, head Japan Section FCO 1995–96, ambass to Republic of Armenia 1997–99, dep high cmmr Calcutta 2000–03, high cmmr to Sierra Leone and ambass to Liberia 2003–06, ret; *Publications* Studies in the Indus Valley Inscriptions (1978), Traditions of the Seven Rsis (1982, 2 edn 2000) The Yuga Purana (1986, 2 edn 2002), Guru: the search for enlightenment (1992); contribs to learned jls; *Recreations* sheep farming and breeding llamas, bridge, tennis, family history, karabash; *Clubs* Royal Cwlth Soc, Royal Asiatic; *Style*— Dr John Mitchiner; ✉ Bower Farm, Whitland SA34 0QX

MITCHINSON, David; s of Robert Stockdale Mitchinson (d 1988), of London, and Winifred May, *née* Earney (d 1975); *b* 8 December 1944; *Educ* Bath Acad of Art (Dip); *Career* designer; Kröller Muller Museum Otterlo 1967–68, Henry Moore 1968–77; The Henry Moore Fndn: joined 1977, keeper of graphics 1980–86, keeper of graphics and sculpture 1986–87, curator 1987– (organiser major exhbns 1982–95); dir: Raymond Spencer Co 1989–90, HMF Enterprises Ltd 1991–; tstee Hat Hill Sculpture Fndn Goodwood 1994–2001; *Publications* incl: Henry Moore Graphic Work 1973–86, Henry Moore: Unpublished Drawings (1972), With Henry Moore: The Artist at Work photographed by Gemma Levine (1978), Henry Moore Sculpture (1981), Life and Times, Henry Moore - A Short Biography (1984), Henry Moore: Life and Times (1995), Celebrating Moore (1998); *Style*— David Mitchinson, Esq; ✉ The Henry Moore Foundation, Dane Tree House, Perry Green, Much Hadham, Hertfordshire SG10 6EE (tel 01279 843333, fax 01279 843647, e-mail curator@henry-moore-fndn.co.uk)

MITHEN, Prof Steven John; s of William Mithen, of Petersfield, Hants, and Patricia, *née* Caporn; *b* 16 October 1960, Ashford, Kent; *Educ* Slade Sch of Fine Art, Univ of Sheffield (BA), Univ of York (MSc), St John's Coll Cambridge (PhD); *m* 25 May 1985, Susan; 2 da (Hannah b 28 Jan 1988, Heather b 8 Aug 1994), 1 s (Nicholas b 26 May 1990); *Career* research fell in archaeology Trinity Hall Cambridge 1987–89, lectr in archaeology Univ of Cambridge 1989–91, research assoc in archaeology McDonald Inst for Archaeological Research Univ of Cambridge 1991–92; Univ of Reading: lectr in archaeology 1992–96, sr lectr in archaeology 1996–98, reader in early prehistory 1998–2000, prof of prehistory 2000–, head Sch of Human and Environmental Sciences 2003–; British Acad Research Readership 2001–03; memb Cncl Prehistoric Soc of GB 1995–97; memb Editorial Bd: Cambridge Archaeological Jl 1994–, Jl of Social Archaeology 2000–, Jl of Cognition and Culture 2000–, Jl of Evolutionary Psychology 2000–; author of numerous articles and papers in learned jls; fell New England Inst for Cognitive Science 2001, fell Inst for Cultural Research 2003; FSA Scot 1993, FSA 1998, MRI 2003, FBA 2004; *Books* incl: Thoughtful Foragers: A Study of Prehistoric Decision Making (1990), The Prehistory of the Mind: A Search for the Origins of Art, Science and Religion (1996), After the Ice: A Global Human History, 20,000–5,000 BC (2003), The Singing Neanderthals: The Origins of Music, Language, Mind and Body (2005); *Style*— Prof Steven Mithen; ✉ School of Human and Environmental Sciences, University of Reading, PO Box 227, Whiteknights, Reading RG6 6AB (tel 0118 378 6102, fax 0118 931 0279, e-mail s.j.mithen@reading.ac.uk)

MITTLER, Prof Peter Joseph; CBE (1981); s of Dr Gustav Mittler (d 1962), of Leeds, and Gertrude Mittler (d 1987); *b* 2 April 1930; *Educ* Merchant Taylors', Pembroke Coll Cambridge (MA, PhD); *m* 1, 2 April 1955 (m dis 1997), Helle, da of Dr Ernst Katscher (d 1980), of Vienna; 3 s (Paul b 1955, Stephen b 1959, Martin b 1964); m 2, 19 August 1997, Penelope Anastasia Platt, da of Lt Cdr John Brooke Westcott, RNVR, BEM; *Career* Nat Serv Ordnance Corps 1949–50, RAMC 1950–80 (Capt Res); clinical psychologist 1954–63, lectr in psychology Birkbeck Coll London 1963–68, prof of special educn and dir Hester Adrian Res Centre 1968–82, dir Sch of Educn and dean Faculty of Educn Univ of Manchester 1991–94, emeritus prof of special educn 2000, fell Centre for Soc Policy Dartington 1995–, distinguished visiting prof Univ of Hong Kong 1997–98; former memb: Sch Examination and Assessment Cncl 1988–90, Prince of Wales Advsy Gp on Disability 1984–90; pres Int League of Socs for Persons with Mental Handicap 1982–86; tstee British Inst for Learning Disabilities 1995–2000 (chm 1995–97); hon fell Manchester Poly 1985; FBPsS 1966, CPsychol 1989; *Books* Psychological Assessment (1970), Study of Twins (1971), Advances in Mental Handicap Research (2 vols 1981, 1983), Parents, Professionals and Mentally Handicapped People (1983), Staff Training and Special Educational Needs (1988), Teacher Training for Special Needs in Europe (1995), Changing Policy and Practice for People with Learning Disabilities (1996), Working Towards Inclusive Education: Social Contexts (2000); *Recreations* travel, listening to music; *Style*— Prof Peter Mittler, CBE; ✉ tel and fax 0161 434 5625, e-mail peter.mittler@manchester.ac.uk

MOAT, Frank Robert; s of Frank Robert Moat (d 1976), of Tynemouth, and Grace, *née* Hibbert (d 1989); *b* 10 August 1948; *Educ* Giggleswick, The Coll of Law (LLB); *Career* called to the Bar Lincoln's Inn 1970; memb Western Circuit, in practice in London and on the Western Circuit, recorder 1995–2001; rep on the Bar Cncl Western Circuit 1989 and 1990; memb Wine Ctee of the Western Circuit 1988–92 and 1994–98, fndr memb Ctee Kensington and Chelsea Nat Tst Assoc; *Recreations* theatre, music, antiques, architecture; *Clubs* Garrick; *Style*— Frank Moat, Esq; ✉ 3 Pump Court, Temple, London EC4Y 7AJ (tel 020 7353 0711, fax 020 7353 3319)

MOAYEDI, Paris; s of Issa Moayedi (d 1977), of Iran, and Masoud, *née* Dastouri (d 1998); *b* 20 November 1938; *m* 9 June 1962, Jenny, *née* Paterson; 1 s (Paul b 6 Nov 1962), 1 da (Zara (Mrs Fearon) b 4 March 1971); *Career* AMEC Gp: site engr 1964–74, area mangr NE 1974–77, divnl dir NE 1977–79, md Midlands 1979–82, md civil engrg E Africa 1982–83; md Walter Lawrence Project Mgmnt Ltd 1983–88, estab Team Service plc (fndr) 1988, chm and chief exec Jarvis Projects plc 1994, chm Jarvis plc 2002– (gp chief exec 1994–2002); Construction Personality of Year 1998, Entrepreneur of Year 1999; MInstD, FRSA, FIMgt; *Recreations* skiing, scuba diving, deep sea fishing, riding, cooking, reading; *Style*— Paris Moayedi, Esq; ✉ Jarvis plc, Frogmore Park, Watton-at-Stone, Hertfordshire SG14 3RU (tel 01920 832800, fax 01920 832832, e-mail paris.moayedi@jarvis-uk.com)

MOBERLY, Robert William Gardner; s of Sir Walter Hamilton Moberly, GBE, KCB, DSO (d 1973), and Gwendolen, *née* Gardner (d 1975); *Educ* Winchester, Lincoln Coll Oxford (BA, Capt of Boats, Desborough Medal); *m* 7 Jan 1992, (Patricia) Mary Lewis, *qv*, da of late Donald Cornes; 1 da (Scarlett Rose b 28 May 1992); *Career* 2 Lt Oxford and Bucks LI 1951–53, seconded to Northern Rhodesia Regt 1952, ADC to GOC E Africa (Sir Alexander Cameron) 1953; Beecham Foods Ltd 1960–63, Foote Cone & Belding Ltd (advertising) 1964–83 (dir 1979–83), fndr ptnr Lewis Moberly Ltd (design conslts) 1983 (md until 1998, chm 1998–); fndr memb DBA, memb Mktg Soc 1966, FRSA 1996; *Recreations* golf; *Clubs* Leander; *Style*— Robert Moberly, Esq; ✉ 10 Furlong Road, London N7 8LS (tel 020 7607 4553, fax 020 7607 6909); Whalleybourne Farm, Wrentnall, Pulverbatch, Shropshire SY5 8EB (tel 01743 792878); Lewis Moberly Ltd, 33 Gresse Street, London W1T 1QU (tel 020 7580 9252, fax 020 7255 1671, e-mail hello@lewismoberly.com, website www.lewismoberly.com)

MOCHAN, Charles Francis; s of Charles Mochan (d 1974), and Margaret, *née* Love (d 1956); *b* 6 August 1948; *Educ* St Patrick's HS Dumbarton; *m* 27 June 1970, Ilse Sybilla, da of Anthony Burney Clement Carleon Cruttwell (d 1973), and Jane, *née* Regan (d 2001); 1 da (b 1971), 1 s (b 1974); *Career* MOD Navy 1966; HM Dip Serv: FCO 1967, vice-consul Port Elizabeth 1970–72, Kingston 1972–74, Seoul 1977–80, Helsinki 1981–84, dep high cmmr Mauritius 1988–91, asst head trg dept FCO 1993–95, consul-gen Casablanca 1995–98, ambass to Madagascar 1999–2002 (concurrently non-resident ambass to Federal Islamic Republic of the Comoros 2001–02), high cmmr to Fiji Islands 2002–06 (concurrently non-resident high cmmr to Nauru, Kiribati and Tuvalu), ret; *Recreations* walking, soccer, golf, ornithology, music; *Style*— Charles Mochan, Esq

MODELL, David; *b* 21 February 1969; *Educ* William Ellis Sch, Barnet Coll of HE; *Family* 2 s (Louis b 15 Feb 1997, Theo b 9 Sept 2000), 1 da (Martha b 17 June 2003); *Career* photojournalist and film maker; fndr memb Int Photographer's Gp (IPG) 1995–; worked with: Time Out, City Limits, Sunday Telegraph, various colour supplement magazines, Independent on Saturday Magazine; photography for ad campaigns for cos incl Hugo Boss, IBM-Lotus, Arthur Andersen, AT&T and Ford 1992–; TV work: short TV documentaries Channel 4 News 1999; other Channel 4 documentaries: Young, Nazi and Proud 2002 (winner three awards incl BAFTA for Best Current Affairs Prog of Year), Keep Them Out 2004, Being Pamela 2005, Mad About Animals 2006; *Publications* Tory Story (2001); *Recreations* family life, carpentry; *Style*— David Modell, Esq; ✉ c/o Bonakdar Cleary, 35 Charles Square, London N11 6HT (tel 020 7490 1133, fax 020 7490 1155, e-mail seamus@bonakdarcleary.com)

MODGILL, Vijay Kumar; s of Sansari Lal Modgill, of NZ, and Dwarka, *née* Devi (d 1978); *b* 1 September 1942; *Educ* Eastleigh Sch Nairobi, Leeds Univ Med Sch (MB ChB); *m* 14 Sept 1974, (Elizabeth) Margaret, da of John Harrop Lawton, CBE (d 1987), of Wakefield, W Yorks; 2 da (Victoria b 1977, Elizabeth b 1985), 1 s (Alexander b 1979); *Career* house physician Leeds Univ Med Sch 1967–68, registrar St James's Hosp Leeds 1968–70 (house surgn 1968), sr registrar Leeds and Bradford Hosps 1972, conslt in vascular and gen surgery Halifax Gen Hosp 1975– (clinical tutor 1975–83); chm of Med Staff Ctee 1986–89, currently chm of Med Ctee of Elland BUPA Hosp; memb Vascular Soc of GB; memb Assoc of Surgns of GB, FRCS 1972, FRCSEd 1972; *Publications* Renal Transplants; *Recreations* golf, cricket; *Clubs* Lightcliffe Golf (Halifax), Fixby Golf (Huddersfield), member of XL; *Style*— Vijay Modgill, Esq; ✉ Linden Lea, Cecil Avenue, Lightcliffe, Halifax, West Yorkshire (tel 01422 202182); Halifax General Hospital, Salterhebble, Halifax, West Yorkshire (tel 01422 357171); Elland BUPA Hospital, Elland Lane, Elland, Halifax, West Yorkshire (tel 01422 375577)

MODOOD, Prof Tariq; MBE (2001); s of Mirza Sabauddin Modood, and Nafeesa Modood; *b* 4 October 1952, Karachi, Pakistan; *Educ* Univ of Durham (BA, MA), Univ of Wales Swansea (PhD); *m* 6 April 1979, Glynthea Margaret, *née* Thompson; 2 da (Ghizala-Ruth, Yasmin-Cariad); *Career* equal opportunity offr London Borough of Hillingdon 1987–89, princ employment offr Cmmn of Racial Equality 1989–91, Gwilyn Gibbon res fell Nuffield Coll Oxford 1991–92, Hallsworth res fell Univ of Manchester 1992–93, sr res fell Policy Studies Inst 1993–97, prof of sociology Univ of Bristol 1997–; dir Centre for the Study of Ethnicity and Citizenship Univ of Bristol 1999–; advsr Cmmn on the Future of Multi-Ethnic Britain Runnymede Tst 1997–2000, memb Cmmn on National Security IPPR 2007–; tstee Inst of Community Studies 2001–; founding ed Ethnicities 1999–; AcSS 2004; *Books* Not Easy Being British (1992), Ethnic Minorities in Britain (co-author, 1997), Ethnicity, Social Mobility and Public Policy in the US and UK (co-ed, 2005), Multiculturalism (2007); *Style*— Prof Tariq Modood, MBE, AcSS; ✉ Department of Sociology, 12 Woodland Road, Bristol BS8 1UQ (e-mail t.modood@bristol.ac.uk, website www.bristol.ac.uk/sociology/ethnicitycitizenship)

MOFFAT, Alexander; OBE (2006); s of John Moffat (d 1956), of Cowdenbeath, Fife, and Agnes Hunter, *née* Lawson (d 1995); *b* 23 March 1943; *Educ* Daniel Stewart's Coll Edinburgh, Edinburgh Coll of Art (Andrew Grant scholar, Dip Art); *m* 1968 (m dis 1983), Susan Potten; 1 s (Colin b 1969); *Career* artist; photographer Scottish Central Library 1966–74, dir New 57 Gallery Edinburgh 1968–78; visiting lectr: Winchester Sch of Art 1973–74, Croydon Sch of Art 1974–75, RCA 1986–88; Glasgow Sch of Art: lectr in painting studios 1979–88, sr lectr in painting studios Glasgow Sch of Art 1988–92, head of painting and printmaking 1992–2005, chair Sch of Fine Art 1998–2000; external examiner: Canterbury Coll of Art (Kent Inst) 1988–91, N Staffs Poly Stoke 1989–92, Chelsea Coll of Art & Design (London Inst) 1997–2000, Gray's Sch of Art (RGU) Aberdeen 2002–, Univ of Brighton 2003–; sr external examiner Univ of the Highlands and Islands Project 2000–02; external expert Univ of London 1993–98; Scottish Arts Cncl 1982–84 (memb Cncl, memb Art Ctee, chm Awards Panel), memb Bd Fruitmarket Gallery Edinburgh 1986–92, chm Bd ALBA magazine 1988–92; writer of numerous catalogue texts; memb Edinburgh Festival Soc; hon research fell Univ of Glasgow 2006; RSA (elect) 2005; *Solo Exhibitions* incl: A View of the Portrait (Scottish National Portrait Gallery) 1973, Gallery of the Press Club Warsaw 1975, Seven Poets (Third Eye Centre Glasgow and tour) 1981–83, Portrait Drawings (N E of Scotland Library and Museums Service) 1984, Portraits of Painters (Scottish Nat Gallery of Modern Art) 1988, Glasgow Art Gallery & Museum 1990, Pittencrieff House Museum Dunfermline 1991; *Group Exhibitions* incl: Scottish Realism (Scottish Arts Cncl tour) 1971, The Human Clay (Hayward Gallery London and Scottish Nat Gallery of Modern Art) 1976, Three Painters (Midland Gp Gallery, Nottingham) 1978, Narrative Paintings (Arnolfini Bristol and ICA London) 1979, Private Views (Arts Cncl of GB and tour) 1982, In Their Circumstances (Lincoln Usher Gallery) 1985–86, Picturing People: Figurative Painting from Britain 1945–89 (Far East tour) 1989, Scottish Art since 1990 (Scottish Nat Gall of Modern Art) 1989–90, Turning the Century (Raab Gallery London & Berlin) 1990, The Discerning Eye (Mall Galleries London) 1990, The Line of Tradition (National Galleries of Scotland) 1993, The Scottish Renaissance (Hong Kong Land Co Hong Kong) 1996, Scotland's Art (City Art Centre, Edinburgh) 1999, Expressions (Aberdeen Art Gallery) 2000; *Work in public collections*: Scottish Nat Portrait Gallery, Scottish Nat Gallery of Modern Art, Arts Cncl of GB, Yale Center for British Art; *Portraits* Dr George Elder Davie 1999, Tom Fleming 2000, Robin Jenkins (Saltire Soc) 2002; *Clubs* The Glasgow Art; *Style*— Alexander Moffat, Esq, OBE; ✉ 20 Haddington Place, Edinburgh EH7 4AF (tel 0131 556 2731)

MOFFAT, Alistair Murray; *b* 16 June 1950; *Educ* Kelso HS, Univ of St Andrews (MA), Univ of Edinburgh (CertEd), Univ of London (MPhil); *m* Lindsay, *née* Thomas; 1 s, 2 da; *Career* organiser Edinburgh Festival Fringe 1976–81; Scottish Television: arts correspondent, prodr then controller of features 1981–90, dir of progs 1990–93, chief exec Scottish Television Enterprises 1993–99; *Books* The Edinburgh Fringe (1978), Kelsae: A History of Kelso from Earliest Times (1985), Remembering Charles Rennie Mackintosh (1989), Arthur and the Lost Kingdoms (1999), The Sea Kingdoms (2001), The Borders: A History of the Borders from Earliest Times (2002), Homing (2003), Heartland (2004), Before Scotland (2005), Tyneside (2005), East Lothian (2006); *Recreations* sleeping, supporting Kelso RFC; *Style*— Alistair Moffat; ✉ The Henhouse, Selkirk TD7 5EY (e-mail alistairmoffat@scottishborders.com)

MOFFAT, Anne; MP; *b* 30 March 1958; *Educ* Woodmill HS; *Career* former nurse Lynebank Hosp Dunfermline; MP (Lab) E Lothian 2001–; memb: Accommodation and Works Select Ctee 2001–, Commons Modernisation Select Ctee 2001–05, European Scrutiny Select Ctee 2004–05, Trade and Industry Select Ctee 2005–; memb Ashford BC 1994–98; memb: Unison 1975– (former nat pres), Lab Pty NEC 1990–, Lab Pty Nat Policy Forum; *Style*— Ms Anne Moffat, MP; ✉ House of Commons, London SW1A 0AA

MOFFAT, Sir Brian Scott; kt (1996), OBE (1982); s of Festus David Moffat (d 1995), and Agnes Scott Moffat (d 1991); *b* 6 January 1939; *Educ* Hulme GS Oldham; *m* 1964, Jacqueline Mary, *née* Cunliffe; 1 s (b 1969), 1 da (b 1974); *Career* chartered accountant Peat Marwick Mitchell 1961–68; British Steel Corp (subsequently British Steel plc): joined 1968, dir Assoc Products Gp 1973–76, dir Port Talbot Works 1976, md Finance 1986–91 (heavily involved in privatisation 1988), memb Bd 1987–, chief exec 1991–99, chm 1993–99; chm Corus Gp plc 1999–2003 (actg chief exec 2000–01); non-exec dir: Enterprise Oil plc 1995–2002, HSBC Holdings plc 1998– (dep chm), Bank of England 2000–06, Macsteel Global BV (formerly Nosmas Hldgs BV) 2003–; Hon DSc: Univ of Warwick 1998, Univ of Sheffield 2001; Inst of Materials Bessemer Gold Medal 1996; FCA 1961, FRSA; *Recreations* farming, fishing, shooting; *Clubs* Fly Fishers; *Style*— Sir Brian Moffat, OBE; ✉ Springfield Farm, Earlswood, Chepstow, Monmouthshire NP16 6AT (e-mail sirbmoffat@aol.com)

MOFFAT, David A; s of James Graham Moffat, of Cambridge, and Myra Constance, *née* Paul; *b* 27 June 1947; *Educ* St Nicholas' Sch Northwood, Univ of London (BSc, MB BS, LRCP, MRCS, FRCS, MA 1985); *m* 5 Dec 1970, Jane Elizabeth, da of Flt Lt David Dougherty Warwick, DFC, of Northwood Middx; 1 da (Claire b 29 Oct 1974), 2 s (Simon b 11 May 1976, Mark b 10 Oct 1979); *Career* sr registrar The London Hosp 1977–79, fell in otoneurosurgery Stanford Univ California 1979–80, conslt ENT surgn Westminster Hosp London 1980, conslt ENT surgn Addenbrooke's Hosp Cambridge and assoc lectr Univ of Cambridge 1981–, estab E Anglian and Supra Regnl Otoneurosurgical Serv base in Cambridge; author of papers and chapters on: otological surgery, otology, otoneurosurgery, skull base surgery, audiology, evoked response audiometry; past pres Otology Section RSM; memb: SAC, Med Defence Union, Politzer Soc; past chm Intercollegiate Faculty Bd; Br rep IFOS (chair Otol/Neurotol Ctee); *Recreations* theatre, golf; *Clubs* Gog Magog; *Style*— David Moffat, Esq; ✉ Department of Otolaryngological and Skull Base Surgery, Addenbrooke's Hospital, Hills Road, Cambridge CB2 2QQ (tel 01223 586638, fax 01223 217559)

MOFFAT, Dr Robin John Russell; s of A C Russell Moffat (d 1969), of London, and Gladys Leonora, *née* Taperell (d 1959); *b* 18 October 1927; *Educ* Whitgift, Guy's Hosp Med Sch, Univ of London (DObstRCOG), LRCP; *m* 1; 1 da (Pamela Jane (Mrs Blake, SRN) b 25 Aug 1951), 2 s (Jeremy Guy b 7 Dec 1954, Dr Timothy Julian Moffat b 3 Nov 1960); m 2, 18 Nov 1980, Beryl Gwendoline Longmoor, *née* Wild; *Career* Nat Serv RN 1946–48, ORA (SBA Branch) RN Hosp Haslar; house surgn Guy's Hosp 1954–55, house physician Croydon Hosp 1957, resident obstetrician Mayday Hosp 1957–58, in gen med practice Croydon 1958–88, met police surgn 1959–88, sr forensic med examiner 1988–99, conslt in forensic med 1999–; MO Whitgift Fndn 1960–90; memb Int Bd Jl of Clinical Forensic Med; chm Met Gp Assoc of Police Surgns 1986; fell/tstee MOs of Schs Assoc (pres 1979–81); memb: Croydon Med Soc 1963 (former pres), Br Acad Forensic Sciences 1972 (memb Cncl 2005), Medico-Legal Soc (memb Cncl 2006), Expert Witness Inst 1997, American Acad Forensic Sciences 1998; memb: Croydon Community Police Conslt Ctee 1999–, Cncl Police Rehab Tst 2002–; life memb BMA 2006 (memb 1958); life subscriber Entertainment Artists Benevolent Fund 1986, life memb Max Miller Appreciation Soc 2005; RSM: sr hon sec and fell 1993–99, former pres Section of Clinical Forensic Med 1989–91, hon memb 2001; Freeman City of London 2001, Liveryman Worshipful Soc of Apothecaries 1970; MRCS 1954, FRCGP 1991 (MRCGP 1962, life memb 2006), fell Faculty of Forensic and Legal Med RCP 2006; *Publications* numerous pubns in the medical press on medico-legal subjects; *Recreations* theatre, book collection; *Clubs* The Naval, RSM; *Style*— Dr Robin Moffat; ✉ 8A Bedford Towers, Cavendish Place, King's Road, Brighton, East Sussex BN1 2JG (tel and fax 01273 205601, mobile 07778 901935, e-mail pierview8a@ntlworld.com)

MOFFAT, Sheilagh; da of Alexander Findlay (d 1968), and Daphne Mary, *née* Ireland (d 1992); *b* 24 November 1948; *Educ* Bishops Coll Colombo Sri Lanka, Albyn Sch for Girls Aberdeen; *m* 11 Sept 1971, David Cunningham Moffat, s of James Cunningham Moffat; 1 da (Caroline Alexandra b 12 Jan 1981); *Career* chartered accountant; articled clerk Deloitte Plender Griffiths & Co London 1966–70, fndr own practice 1973; dir Mutual Accountants Professional Indemnity Co 1988–2005; memb Cncl ICAEW 1994–; pres: Warks Soc of chartered accountants 1990–91 and 2003–04; Birmingham & District Soc of chartered accountants 1999–2000 (GP bd rep 1992–97); practising assoc Acad of Experts 1996–; hon treas Warks Co Branch Br Red Cross Soc 1975–95; Freeman City of London 1999, Liveryman Worshipful Co of Chartered Accountants; FCA 1979 (ACA 1970); *Recreations* antiques, films, reading; *Style*— Mrs Sheilagh Moffat; ✉ Moffat Gilbert, 5 Clarendon Place, Leamington Spa, Warwickshire CV32 5QL (tel 01926 334373, fax 01926 881464, e-mail moffat@btinternet.com)

MOFFATT, Clive; s of Harold and Olive Moffatt; *b* 27 December 1948; *Educ* Thornes House Sch, LSE (BSc); *m* 1977, Kathleen, da of Robert Maguire; 1 s, 1 da; *Career* res economist to New Zealand Treasury 1972–75; conslt economist and writer Economist Intelligence Unit Ltd London 1975–76, chief sub-ed (fin unit and CEEFAX) BBC 1976–78, business ed Investors Chronicle 1978–79, corporate affrs conslt Guinness Peat Group plc 1979–81, chief exec Blackrod Ltd 1981–88, fndr and md Moffatt Associates (mgmnt and mktg consultancy) 1988–; memb Inst of Risk Mgmnt; *Publications* Trends in Commercial Due Diligence (1999), A Risk Manager on Every Desktop (2000), Trends in the UK Telecoms Consultancy Market (2001), The World of Business Services - Some Personal Reflections (2002); *Recreations* rugby, tennis, art, music; *Style*— Clive Moffatt, Esq; ✉ 3 Waldeck Road, London W13 8LY (tel 020 8997 2128, e-mail clivem@moffatt-associates.com)

MOFFATT, Prof (Henry) Keith; s of Frederick Henry Moffatt (d 1974), and Emmeline Marchant, *née* Fleming (d 1997); *b* 12 April 1935; *Educ* George Watson's Coll Edinburgh, Univ of Edinburgh (BSc), Trinity Coll Cambridge (scholar, Ferguson scholar, BA, PhD, ScD, Smith's prize); *m* 17 Dec 1960, Katharine (Linty), da of Rev David Syme Stiven, MC, DD (d 1986); 2 s (Fergus b 1961 d 1987, Peter b 1962), 2 da (Hester b 1966, Penelope b 1967); *Career* Univ of Cambridge: asst lectr 1961–64, lectr 1964–76, prof of mathematical physics 1980–2002 (prof emeritus 2002–), head Dept of Applied Mathematics and Theoretical Physics 1983–91, dir Isaac Newton Inst 1996–2001; Trinity Coll Cambridge: fell lectr and dir Studies in Mathematics 1961–76, tutor 1970–74, sr tutor 1975, professorial fell 1980–; prof of applied mathematics Univ of Bristol 1977–80; professeur (temps partiel) en Mécanique Ecole Polytechnique Palaiseau 1992–99; sec IUTAM Congress Ctee 1984–92 (memb 1980–), memb Gen Assembly of IUTAM 1980–, memb Bureau of IUTAM 1992– (pres 2000–04), Blaise Pascal Int Chair 2001–03; Panetti-Ferrari Int Prize and Gold Medal 2002, Euromech Fluid Mechanics Prize 2003, Sr Whitehead Prize of London Mathematical Soc 2005, Hughes Medal Royal Soc 2005; Docteur (hc): Inst Nat Poly Grenoble 1987, Tech Univ Eindhoven 2006; Hon DSc: SUNY 1990, Univ of Edinburgh 2001, Univ of Glasgow 2007; foreign memb: Royal Netherlands Acad of Arts and Sciences 1991, Academia Europaea 1994, Officier des Palmes Académiques 1998, associé étranger Académie des Sciences (Paris) 1998, Accademia dei Lincei (Rome) 2001, FRS 1986, FRSE 1988, fell APS 2003, Hon Fell IMA 2007; *Books* Magnetic Field Generation in Electrically Conducting Fluids (1978), Topological Fluid Mechanics (ed, 1990), Topological Aspects of the Dynamics of Fluids and Plasmas (ed, 1992), Perspectives in Fluid Dynamics (ed, 2000), Tubes, Sheets and Singularities in Fluid Dynamics (ed, 2003); *Recreations* breadmaking, French country cooking; *Style*— Prof Keith Moffatt, FRS, FRSE; ✉ Trinity College, Cambridge (e-mail hkm2@cam.ac.uk)

MOFFATT, Laura Jean; MP; *b* 9 April 1954; *Educ* Hazelwick Sch, Crawley Coll; *m* Colin; 3 s (Russell, Alistair, Edward); *Career* registered staff nurse isolation/haematology ward Crawley Hosp for 25 years until 1997; Crawley BC: cncllr 1984–96, chm Environmental Servs and vice-chm Planning Ctee 1987–96, mayor 1989–90; MP (Lab) Crawley 1997–, PPS to Rt Hon David Blunkett MP 2005–; memb: House of Commons Defence Ctee 1997–2001, PLP Health Ctee 1997–, All-Pty Parly Gp on AIDS, All-Pty Parly Gp on Drug Misuse; pres: Crawley Town Access Gp, N and SW Sussex Relate, Crawley Hospital League of Friends; hon vice-pres Port Health Authorities, hon pres Town Hall UNISON Branch; memb UNISON; *Style*— Mrs Laura Moffatt, MP; ✉ House of Commons, London SW1A 0AA (tel 020 7219 3619)

MOFFATT, Nigel; *b* 22 May 1954; *Career* playwright, singer/songwriter and poet; recorded Peace, Love and Harmony for Respond Records 1984, performed African Crisis and Poetry for Here and Now (Central TV) 1984, founded Writers' Gp Walsall 1984, runs Black Writers in Walsall project 2005, ed Multicultural magazine 2006, runs recording project in Walsall 2007; currently making ind film Angel; writer in residence: Nat Theatre Studio 1985, Haymarket Theatre Leicester 1988, Shrewsbury Prison 1996–98; Winston Churchill travel fellowship 1989; advsr to W Midlands Arts; plays: Rhapsody in Black 'n' White (Nat Theatre Studio) 1985, Tony (Nat Theatre Studio 1985, Oval House 1987), Celebration (Royal Ct Theatre) 1986, Mamma Decemba (Temba Theatre Co and Birmingham Reperatory Co) 1987, Keeping Walsall Boxed In (W Midlands Arts Cncl) 1987, Opportunity (cmmnd by Br Film Inst) 1987, Prime Time (Haymarket Leicester) 1989, Beau Monde (Br Film Inst) 1990, Stop the Carnival (Cannon Hill Puppet Theatre) 1991, Musical Youth (Birmingham Reperatory Theatre) 2001, Gun Crime (Arts Cncl of England Bursary) 2004; radio plays: Lifetime (BBC) 1988, Lame Ducks (BBC) 1989, Selling Out (BBC) 1989, Wishful Thinking (BBC) 1990, Mamma Decemba (BBC) 1994, Wasteland (BBC) 1997, Fish Ain't Bitin' (BBC) 1998; TV: When Love Dies (Channel 4) 1989, Opportunity (BBC) 1992, Strange Fruit (BBC) 1993; awards: Samuel Beckett Award for Mamma Decemba 1987, Giles Cooper Award for Lifetime 1987; Butler Tst Prison Service Annual Award; *Style*— Nigel Moffatt, Esq; ✉ 44 Harrowby Place, Shepwell Green, Willenhall, West Midlands WV13 2RA (tel 01902 632244, mobile 07919 515858, e-mail nigel@moffatt75.freeserve.co.uk)

MOFFITT, Prof Terrie E; *Educ* Univ of N Carolina Chapel Hill, Univ of Southern Calif (PhD); *Career* clinical trg UCLA Neuropsychiatric Inst, clinical psychologist, prof of social behaviour and devpt Inst of Psychiatry KCL; princ investigator MRC Environmetal-Risk Study (E-risk), assoc dir Dunedin Multidisciplinary Health and Devpt Research Unit Univ of Otago Med Sch; Distinguished Scientific Award for Early Career Contrib to Psychology American Psychological Assoc 1993, Wolfson Merit Award Royal Soc 2002, Stockholm Prize in Criminology 2007; FMedSci 1999, fell American Soc of Criminology 2003, FBA 2004; *Books* Sex Differences in Antisocial Behaviour: Conduct Disorder, Delinquency, and Violence in the Dunedin Longitudinal Study (jtly, 2001); *Style*— Prof Terrie E Moffitt; ✉ Box No P080, Social, Genetic and Developmental, Psychiatry Centre, Institute of Psychiatry, De Crespigny Park, London SE5 8AF

MOGER, Christopher Richard Derwent; QC (1992); s of the late Richard Vernon Derwent Moger, of Dartmouth, Devon, and late Cecile Eva Rosales, *née* Power; *b* 28 July 1949; *Educ* Sherborne, Univ of Bristol (LLB); *m* 1, 1974 (m dis 1991), Victoria, da of Arthur George Cecil Trollope, of Overton, Hants; 3 s (Robin b 1979, Sholto b 1981, Dominic b 1985); m 2, 1991, Prudence, da of Francis Anthony Leopold da Cunha, of Bowden, Cheshire; *Career* called to the Bar Inner Temple 1972 (bencher 2000); recorder of the Crown Court 1993–, dep judge of the High Court 1999–; *Recreations* fishing, tennis, walking; *Clubs* Garrick, Blue Coconut, Pulborough; *Style*— Christopher Moger, Esq, QC;

M

✉ 4 Pump Court, Temple, London EC4Y 7AN (tel 020 7842 5555, fax 020 7583 2036, e-mail chambers@4pumpcourt.com)

MOGG, Sir John Frederick; KCMG (2003); s of Thomas W Mogg, and Cora M Mogg; *b* 5 October 1943; *Educ* Bishop Vesey's GS, Univ of Birmingham (BA); *m* 1967, Anne, *née* Smith; 1 da, 1 s; *Career* Rediffusion Ltd 1965–74; princ: Office of Fair Trading 1974–76, Dept of Trade 1976–79; first sec UK Permanent Rep 1979–82; DTI: asst sec Minerals and Metals Div 1982–85, princ private sec to Sec of State 1985–86, under sec European Policy Div 1986–87, under sec Industrial Materials Market Div 1987–89; dep head European Secretariat Cabinet Office 1989–90; European Cmmn: dep DG Industry and Internal Market (DG III) 1990–93, DG Internal Market 1993–2002; memb Gas and Electricity Markets Authy 2003, non-exec chair Ofgem 2003–, memb EC's High level Gp on Competitiveness, Energy and the Environment; visiting prof Univ of Parma; chair of govrs Univ of Brighton, tstee Brighton Philharmonic Orchestra; *Style*— Sir John F Mogg, KCMG

MOGGACH, Deborah; da of Richard Alexander Hough, and Helen Charlotte, *née* Woodyatt; *b* 28 June 1948; *Educ* Camden Sch for Girls London, Univ of Bristol (BA), Univ of London (DipEd); *m* 1971 (m dis), Anthony Austin Moggach; 1 s (Alexander b 1 Sept 1975), 1 da (Charlotte Flora b 9 May 1977); *Career* OUP 1970–72, journalist and teacher Pakistan 1972–74, full-time writer (for newspapers, magazines and TV) and novelist 1975–; Young Journalist of the Year 1975, Best Adapted TV Series Award Writer's Guild 1993, nomination BAFTA 2006; Hon DLitt Univ of Bristol; FRSL; *Novels* incl: You Must Be Sisters (1978), Close to Home (1979), A Quiet Drink (1980), Hot Water Man (1982), Porky (1983), To Have and To Hold (1986), Smile and Other Stories (1988), Driving in the Dark (1989), Stolen (1990), The Stand-In (1991), The Ex-Wives (1993), Changing Babies and Other Stories (1995), Seesaw (1996), Close Relations (1997), Tulip Fever (1999), Final Demand (2001), These Foolish Things (2004); *Short stories* in various anthologies incl: Best Short Stories 1986, Best Short Stories 1988, The Best of Fiction Magazine (1986), The Woman's Hour Book of Short Stories (1990), Best Short Stories 1991; *Plays* Double-Take (produced 1990 and 1992); *Television* series: To Have and To Hold, Stolen, Goggle-Eyes (adaptation), Close Relations, Seesaw, Love in a Cold Climate (adaptation), Final Demand; *Film* Pride and Prejudice; *Recreations* walking around London looking into people's windows; *Style*— Ms Deborah Moggach; ✉ c/o Curtis Brown Group Ltd, 28–29 Haymarket, London SW1Y 4SP (tel 020 7396 6600, fax 020 7396 0110); c/o Rochelle Stevens & Co Ltd, 2 Terrett's Place, Upper Street, London N1 1QZ (tel 020 7359 3500, fax 020 7354 5729); website www.deborahmoggach.com

MOGGRIDGE, Harry Traherne (Hal); OBE, VMH; s of Lt-Col Harry Weston Moggridge, CMG, Chevalier de la Legion d'Honneur (d 1961), of Tonbridge, Kent, and Helen Mary Ferrier Taylor (artist, d 1989); *b* 2 February 1936; *Educ* Tonbridge, AA (Leverhulme scholar, AADipl); *m* 1 Dec 1962, Catherine (Cass) Greville Herbert; 1 da (Harriet b 23 Sept 1965), 2 s (Geoffrey b 8 Sept 1967, Lawrence b 19 Feb 1970); *Career* Nottinghamshire CC 1960, asst to Sir Geoffrey Jellicoe 1960–63, site architect Sir William Halcrow & Partners Tema Harbour Ghana 1964–65, landscape asst GLC 1966–67, own landscape design practice, ptnr Colvin and Moggridge Landscape Consultants 1969–97 (ptnr with late Brenda Colvin, CBE, to 1981, then continuing conslt with Christopher Carter, Mike Ibbotson, Mark Darwent 1997–), prof of landscape architecture Univ of Sheffield 1984–86; memb Cncl Landscape Inst 1970–83 (hon sec, vice-pres and pres 1979–81, chm Int Ctee and delg to Int Fedn of Landscape Architects 1981–93 and 2001–06), chm The Landscape Foundation 1995–99, chm Penllergare Tst 2000–; RHS Victoria Medal of Honour 1999, Landscape Inst President's Medal 2002; memb: Bd Landscape Res Gp 1983–88, Royal Fine Art Cmmn 1988–99, Nat Tst Architectural Panel 1990–; PPLI, FIHort, RIBA, FRSA; *Publications* author of numerous articles and chapters of books describing works or technical subjects; *Recreations* looking at pictures, gardens, buildings, towns, landscapes and people in these places, walking, theatre; *Clubs* Royal Soc of Arts, Farmers'; *Style*— Hal Moggridge, Esq, OBE, VMH; ✉ Colvin and Moggridge, Filkins, Lechlade, Gloucestershire GL7 3JQ (tel 01367 860225, fax 01367 860564, e-mail filkins@colmog.co.uk)

MOHAN, Thomas Vincent; s of James Bernard Mohan, and Anna, *née* Quinn; *b* 9 July 1959; *Educ* Royal GS Newcastle upon Tyne, CCC Oxford (MA), organ scholar Westminster Cathedral and Countess of Munster Tst scholar; *m* 1999, Johanna, *née* Heckmann; *Career* music master Westminster Sch 1983–86; clerk House of Lords 1986–, clerk Euro Communities/Union Ctee 1996–2001, secondment to the Parly Assembly of the Cncl of Europe 1997–98, clerk Private Bills 2001–02, clerk Public and Private Bills 2002–; FRCO 1983; *Recreations* music, gardening, travel; *Style*— Thomas Mohan, Esq; ✉ House of Lords, London SW1A 0PW (tel 020 7219 3152, fax 020 7219 5933, e-mail mohant@parliament.uk)

MOIGNARD, Prof Elizabeth Ann; da of Lionel Arthur Moignard (d 2000), and Joan Pudsey, *née* Dawson (d 1982); *b* 3 January 1951, Poole, Dorset; *Educ* King's HS Warwick, St Hugh's Coll and Hertford Coll Oxford (sr scholar, Charles Oldham scholar, Thomas Whitcombe Greene scholar, MA, DPhil, sr scholar); *m* 22 July 1985, Alec Ernest Yearling; 1 step s (Simon Nicholas b 3 March 1977), 1 step da (Rebecca Kate b 13 June 1979); *Career* temp lectr in classical archaeology Univ of Newcastle upon Tyne 1977–78; Univ of Glasgow: lectr in Greek 1978–96, sr lectr in classics 1996–2000, dir Inst for Art History 1998–2005, prof of classical art and archaeology 2000–, dean Faculty of Arts 2005– (vice-dean 1999–2005); memb Academic Cncl Glasgow Sch of Art 1998–; quality assurance assessor Welsh HE Funding Cncl 1997, subject reviewer Quality Assurance Agency (QAA) 2000–, memb Peer Review Coll AHRC 2004–; chair Cncl Classical Assoc of Scotland 2003–05 (pres Glasgow and West Centre 2000–02), memb Strategic Advsy Bd Inst of Classical Studies 2005–; memb Cncl Soc for the Promotion of Hellenic Studies 1987–90, Scottish Hellenic Soc (Glasgow) 1992– (chm 1994–97); memb: British Sch at Athens, Classical Assoc, Assoc for Contemporary Jewellery, Scottish Art Historians' Forum; James Knott Fellowship Univ of Newcastle upon Tyne 1978; FSA 2002, FRSE 2004; *Books* Corpus Vasorum Antiquorum: Great Britain - The National Museums of Scotland, Edinburgh (1989), Corpus Vasorum Antiquorum: Great Britain - The Glasgow Collections: The Hunterian Museum, The Glasgow Museum and Art Gallery, Kelvingrove, The Burrell Collection (1997), Greek Vases: An Introduction (2006), Corpus Vasoxum Antiquorum: Great Britain - Aberdeen University, Marischal Collection (2006); *Recreations* choral singing, walking, cooking, detective fiction; *Style*— Prof Elizabeth Moignard; ✉ Faculty of Arts, University of Glasgow, Glasgow G12 8QQ (tel 0141 330 5253, fax 0141 330 3874, e-mail e.moignard@classics.arts.gla.ac.uk)

MOIR, Dr (Alexander Thomas) Boyd; s of Dr William Dugald McKinlay Moir (d 1990), and Margaret, *née* Shepley (d 1997); *b* 1 August 1939; *Educ* George Heriot Sch Edinburgh, Univ of Edinburgh Med Sch (MB ChB, BSc, PhD); *m* 11 Aug 1962, Isabel May (d 1997), da of Richard Greig Sheehan (d 1993); 2 da (Alison May b 9 Dec 1964, Fiona Margaret b 23 April 1966), 1 s (William Greig b 6 March 1970); *Career* rotating internship NY 1964–65; Brain Metabolism Res Unit Univ of Edinburgh: joined Medical Res Cncl staff 1965–72, hon registrar and subsequently hon sr registrar Therapeutics and Clinical Toxicology 1967–72; SO Home and Health Dept: sr med offr 1972–77, princ med offr 1977–86, dir of Chief Scientist Office and dep chief scientist 1986–96, ret; consultancy and clinical practice 1996–; hon clinical sr lectr of public health Univ of Glasgow, hon fell of molecular and clinical med Univ of Edinburgh; numerous articles and papers on pharmacology, research, mgmnt and public health; MRCP (UK) 1972, FRSS 1974, FRCPEd 1979, FIBiol 1979, MFOM 1985, FRCPGlas 1986, FIFST 1987, FRCPath 1988, FFPHM 1993, MFPM 1996; *Recreations* playing games, listening to music, singing, reading, walking, cycling, folk history; *Style*— Dr Boyd Moir; ✉ 23 Murrayfield Gardens, Edinburgh EH12 6DG (tel 0131 337 3937, e-mail boyd_moir@msn.com)

MOIR, Sir Christopher Ernest; 4 Bt (UK 1916), of Whitehanger, Fernhurst, Co Sussex; s of Sir Ernest Ian Royds Moir, 3 Bt (d 1998); *b* 22 May 1955; *Educ* KCS Wimbledon; *m* 1983, Vanessa, yr da of Victor Alfred Crosby, of Merton Park, London; 2 s (Oliver Royds, Alexander Victor (twins) b 1984), 1 step da (Nina Louise b 1976); *Heir* s, Oliver Moir; *Career* CA; *Style*— Sir Christopher Moir, Bt; ✉ Three Gates, 174 Coombe Lane West, Kingston upon Thames, Surrey KT2 7DE

MOIR, Judy; da of Dr Leon Nussbaum (d 1985), and Becky, *née* Abraham; *b* 1 February 1957; *Educ* Townsend HS, Univ of Edinburgh (MA, Christie Bequest); *m* 6 Feb 1981, Neville Moir; 1 da (Helen Louise b 11 April 1986), 1 s (Stephen Leon William b 24 Dec 1988); *Career* freelance ed 1980–81, admin exec then dir Scottish Publishers Assoc 1981–86, freelance ed and book reviewer 1986–96 (worked for publishers incl: Mainstream, Canongate, Edinburgh Univ Press, Jonathan Cape, Transworld, Little Brown), pt/t lectr Napier Univ 1992–96, editorial and rights mangr Canongate Books 1996–99, editorial dir Canongate Books 2000–03, Scottish ed Penguin Books 2004–; dir Edinburgh Book Festival 2001–03, memb Bursary Panel Scottish Arts Cncl 1995–98, memb New Directions Lottery Ctee 1996–97; shortlisted Ed of the Year Br Book Awards 2003; *Recreations* music, reading, travel; *Style*— Ms Judy Moir; ✉ Penguin Scotland, 4 Keith Terrace, Edinburgh EH4 3NJ (tel 0131 343 6674, fax 0131 343 6674, e-mail judy.moir@penguin.co.uk)

MOIR, Dr Lance Stuart; *b* 26 January 1957; *Educ* Cranfield Univ (PhD); *Career* account mangr Corp Banking Dept Grindlays Bank plc 1980–85, treas Br Home Stores plc 1985–86, head of corp finance and planning Storehouse plc 1988–90 (gp treas 1986–88), dir of corp finance Bass plc 1991–94, sr conslt MTM Partnership Ltd 1995–97, ind conslt 1995–97, finance dir First Choice Holidays plc 1997–98, sr lectr finance and accounting Cranfield Sch of Mgmnt 1998–2007, finance dir WIN plc 2007–; non-exec dir: Johnshaven Precision Engineering Ltd 1998–2005, Raft International Ltd 2000–06, Gartmore Global Tst plc 2007–; memb Examination Review Bd Assoc of Corp Treasurers; ACIB 1983, FCT 1990, FRSA 2003; *Books* Introduction to Corporate Finance (memb Ed Panel), Managing Liquidity; *Recreations* singing, opera; *Style*— Dr Lance Moir; ✉ WIN plc, High Wycombe HP12 3YZ (tel 01494 750500)

MOIZER, Prof Peter; s of Albert Moizer, of Blackburn, Lancs, and Kathleen, *née* Burton; *b* 6 October 1951, Blackburn, Lancs; *Educ* Queen Elizabeth's GS Blackburn, Merton Coll Oxford (MA), Victoria Univ of Manchester (MA, PhD); *m* 9 June 1989, Susan, *née* Hatch; 2 s (Mark b 1980, Richard b 1983), 1 da (Helen b 1994); *Career* auditor and asst mangr Price Waterhouse & Co 1974–79, lectr then sr lectr Victoria Univ of Manchester 1979–89, prof of accounting Univ of Leeds 1989–; reporting memb Competition Cmmn; advsr Gtr Manchester Pension Fund 1987–; sr moderator PS exams ICAEW 2003–; FCA; *Publications* The Audit Expectations Gap in the United Kingdom (1992), Resignations and Dismissals of UK Auditors (2004), Governance and Auditing (2005); *Recreations* theatre, opera, viola; *Style*— Prof Peter Moizer; ✉ Leeds University Business School, Maurice Keyworth Building, The University of Leeds, Leeds LS2 9JT (tel 0113 343 4499, e-mail pm@lubs.leeds.ac.uk)

MOLDEN, Dr Nigel Charles; JP (Burnham 1991, Wycombe and Beaconsfield 1996); s of Percival Ernest Molden(d 2001), and Daisy Mary, *née* Currill; *b* 17 August 1948; *Educ* City of Oxford HS, Univ of London (BSc), Brunel Univ (MSc), Fairfax Univ Inst (PhD); *m* 14 Aug 1971, (Hilary) Julia, da of Frederick Withers Lichfield (d 1969); 3 s (Nicholas Stuart b 1974, Simon Charles b 1977, Alexander Giles b 1983); *Career* Warner Brothers Records: label mangr 1976–77, gen mangr 1977–78; WEA Records: field promotion mangr 1972–75, int gen mangr 1978–80; chm Magnum Music Group Ltd 1985–97, jt chief exec TKO Magnum Music Ltd 1997–2002, chief exec Synergie Logistics Ltd 2002–; Beaconsfield town cncllr 1989–91, Chiltern dist cncllr 1991–95; chm: Beaconsfield Town Cons Assoc 1991–93, Seer Green & Jordans Cons Assoc 1991–94; magistrate Burnham/Wycombe and Beaconsfield Bench 1991, dep chm Wycombe and Beaconsfield Bench 2004–, memb Thames Valley Magistrates Courts Ctee (TVMCC) 2000–05 (chm Trg Sub-Ctee), memb HM Courts Bd for the Thames Valley 2005–; govr Royal GS High Wycombe 1989–93, partnership govr Claremont HS Harrow 2000 (chm of govrs 2006); chm Oxford Sch Old Boys Soc 1989–92 (pres 1993–96); fndr and tstee The Magnum Tst, tstee Oxford Past and Present Tst; Freeman City of London 1990, Liveryman Worshipful Co of Marketors 1989–2000; FInstD 1982, FIMgt 1987, FCIM 1988, FRSA 1995, Chartered Marketer 2001; *Recreations* music, rugby football, motor sports; *Style*— Dr N C Molden; ✉ Ashcombe House, Deanwood Road, Jordans, Buckinghamshire HP9 2UU (tel 01494 678177, e-mail synergielogistics@btconnect.com)

MOLE, Chris; MP; *Career* ldr Suffolk CC 1993–2001, dep ldr East of England Devpt Agency (EEDA) 1998–2001, MP (Lab) Ipswich (by-election) 2001–; memb Select Ctee on Regulatory Reform 2002–05, memb Jt Ctee on Statutory Instruments 2002–05, memb Select Ctee on ODPM 2002–05 (memb Urban Affairs Sub-Committee 2003–), memb Select Ctee on Information 2004–, vice-chair Lab Pty Departmental Ctee for Educn and Skills 2002–, sec All-Pty Telecommunications Gp 2005–; *Style*— Chris Mole, Esq, MP; ✉ House of Commons, London SW1A 0AA

MOLE, His Hon Judge David Richard Penton; QC (1990); s of late Rev Arthur Penton Mole, and late Margaret Isobel, *née* Heggie; *b* 1 April 1943; *Educ* Trinity Coll Dublin (MA), LSE (LLM); *m* 29 March 1969, Anu-Reet, da of Alfred Nigol; 3 s (Matthew David Penton b 20 Nov 1971, Joseph Tobias b 9 April 1974, Thomas Alfred William b 24 Aug 1978), 1 da (Susannah Juliet Martha b 5 July 1984); *Career* lectr City of London Poly 1967–74; called to the Bar Inner Temple 1970 (ad eundem Gray's Inn 1973); standing jr counsel to the Inland Revenue (Rating and Valuation) 1984–90, recorder of the Crown Court 1995–2002, circuit judge (SE Circuit) 2002–, dep judge of the High Court 2004–; jt head of chambers 4–5 Gray's Inn Square 2000–02; memb Parole Bd 2003, legal memb Lands Tbnl 2006–; *Recreations* walking, drawing and painting; *Style*— His Hon Judge Mole, QC; ✉ c/o Harrow Crown Court, Hailsham Drive, Harrow, Middlesex HA1 4TU (tel 020 8424 2294)

MOLESWORTH, 12 Viscount (I 1716); Robert Bysse Kelham Molesworth; also Baron Philipstown (I 1716); s of 11 Viscount (d 1997), by his w, Anne, *née* Cohen (d 1983); 3 Viscount (Richard, d 1758), was ADC to Duke of Marlborough, whose life he saved at Battle of Ramillies by giving his horse to the unhorsed Duke (he later became C-in-C of HM Forces in Ireland); *b* 4 June 1959; *Educ* Cheltenham, Univ of Sussex (BA); *Heir* bro, Hon William Molesworth; *Style*— The Rt Hon the Viscount Molesworth

MOLESWORTH-ST AUBYN, Sir William; 16 Bt (E 1689), of Pencarrow, Cornwall; s of Lt-Col Sir (John) Arscott Molesworth-St Aubyn, Bt, MBE, DL (d 1998), and Iona Audrey Armatrude, *née* Tottenham; *b* 23 November 1958; *Educ* Harrow; *m* 13 Feb 1988, Carolyn, da of William Tozier; 1 da (Jemima b 28 Oct 1995), 2 s (Archie b 27 March 1997, Jake b 10 Sept 1999); *Heir* s, Archie Molesworth-St Aubyn; *Career* late Capt Royal Green Jackets; *Style*— Sir William Molesworth-St Aubyn, Bt

MOLL, Francis Raphael; s of Frederick Charles Moll (d 1994), of Sheffield, S Yorks, and Anita Lilian, *née* Francis (d 1998); *b* 15 August 1947; *Educ* Repton, Birkbeck Coll London; *Career* Royal Free Hosp/Royal Free and UC Med Sch: radiographer 1969–74, biomedical photographer, imaging tecnologist and virtual learning environment developer 1974–, radiation protection supervisor 1987–; radiation protection supervisor PolyMASC Pharmaceuticals 1995–2000; dir and tstee Braintree and Bocking Civic Soc Ltd 1991–;

memb: Anglian Water Customer Consultative Ctee (S Gp) 1984–89, Braintree and Bocking Civic Soc 1986– (chm 1988–94), Burma Action Gp UK 1996–, Racehorse Owners Assoc 2001–, Liberty 2003–, The GB-China Centre, Royal Cwlth Soc and Club, Scarborough CC; ptnr Yorkshire Racing Club; churchwarden SS Peter and Paul Black Notley 1985–87; campaigner Refugee Cncl 2000–; Freeman City of London, Liveryman Worshipful Soc of Apothecaries 1968; DSR 1969, AIMI 1986 (now MIMI), ARPS 1986; *Recreations* racehorse ownership (Quiet Times and Wahoo Sam), networking at Asia House and the Chopsticks Club, the Far East, its culture, economics and people, learning putonghua, empowering myself through knowledge and intelligent investing, photography, jazz, chess, cinema; *Style*— Francis Moll, Esq; ✉ 10 Brook Close, Braintree, Essex CM7 2PY (tel and fax 01376 325974, mobile 07941 138572); Pathology Learning Resource Centre, Department of Histopathology, Royal Free and University College Medical School, Hampstead Campus, Rowland Hill Street, Hampstead, London NW3 2PF (tel 020 7830 2227, e-mail f.moll@medsch.ucl.ac.uk)

MOLLAN, Prof Raymond Alexander Boyce; s of Alexander Mollan, of Belfast, and Margaret Emma Boyce (d 1984); *b* 10 August 1943; *Educ* Belfast Royal Acad, Queen's Univ (MB BCh, BAO, HD); *m* 1 Sept 1969, Patricia Ann Fairbanks, da of Alexander Scott (d 1961); 3 s (Ian Alexander b 1972, Andrew John b 1973, David William b 1975), 1 da (Susan Patricia b 1977); *Career* RNR 1968–84; trg grades: med 1964–69, obstetrics 1970–72, surgery 1972–74, orthopaedic surgery 1974–79; conslt orthopaedic surgn Ulster Hosp 1979–80; Queen's Univ Belfast: sr lectr in orthopaedic surgery 1980–84, prof of orthopaedic surgery 1984–95; currently orthopaedic surgn Green Park Trust Belfast; Br Orthopaedic Assoc: past chm Educn Ctee, past memb Cncl, past chm Info Technol Ctee; fndr memb and treas Br Hip Soc; memb: Irish, Edinburgh and English Coll of Surgns, BMA, Irish Orthopaedic Assoc; *Recreations* sailing, skiing; *Clubs* The Naval, Royal Ulster Yacht; *Style*— Prof Raymond Mollan; ✉ 167 Bangor Road, Holywood, Co Down BT18 0ET (tel 028 9042 3529); Department Orthopaedic Surgery, Musgrave Park Hospital, Belfast BT18 01ET (tel 028 9066 9501, fax 028 9066 1112, telex 74487)

MOLLISON, Prof Denis; s of Prof Patrick Loudon Mollison, and Margaret Doreen, *née* Peirce; *b* 28 June 1945; *Educ* Westminster, Trinity Coll Cambridge (ScD); *m* 1 June 1978, Jennifer, da of Dr John Hutton; 3 da (Clare b 1979, Hazel b 1980, Daisy b 1982), 1 s (Charles b 1986); *Career* res fell King's Coll Cambridge 1969–73; Heriot-Watt Univ: lectr 1973–79, reader 1979–86, prof of applied probability 1986–2003 (now emeritus); SERC visiting fell Isaac Newton Inst and visiting fell commoner Trinity Coll Cambridge 1993; author of various res papers on epidemics, ecology and wave energy; convener Scottish Green Lib Dems 2001–; chm Mountain Bothies Assoc 1978–94 (sec 1974–78); memb: Cncl Nat Tst Scotland 1979–84, 1999–2004 and 2005–, Bernoulli Soc 1975; John Muir Tst: co-fndr 1983, tstee 1986–2007; tstee Hebridean Whale and Dolphin Tst 1999–; FRSS 1977; *Recreations* hill walking and bothying, photography, music, real tennis; *Style*— Prof Denis Mollison; ✉ The Laigh House, Inveresk, Musselburgh EH21 7TD (tel 0131 665 2055); Department of Actuarial Maths & Statistics, Heriot-Watt University, Riccarton, Edinburgh EH14 4AS (tel 0131 451 3202, e-mail d.mollison@ma.hw.ac.uk, website www.ma.hw.ac.uk/-denis)

MOLLON, Prof John Dixon; s of Arthur Greenwood Mollon, of Scarborough, N Yorks, and Joyce, *née* Dixon; *b* 12 September 1944; *Educ* Univ of Oxford (BA, DPhil); *Career* Univ of Cambridge: lectr 1976–93, reader 1993–98, prof of visual neuroscience 1998–, fell Gonville & Caius Coll 1996–; chm Colour Gp of GB 1991–93; hon sec Experimental Psychology Soc 1974–78; Rank Prize Funds Award for Work on Genetics of Colour Vision 1988, Edridge-Green lectr 1988, Champness lectr 1998, Newton Medal 1999, Kenneth Craik Award 2000, Tillyer Medal 2000, Verriest Medal 2005; FRS 1999; *Books* The Senses (with H B Barlow, 1982), Colour Vision (with L T Sharpe, 1983), Normal and Defective Colour Vision (with J Pokorny and K Knoblauch, 2003); *Style*— Prof John Mollon, FRS; ✉ Gonville & Caius College, Cambridge CB2 1TA

MOLONY, Peter John; s of Sir Joseph Thomas Molony, KCVO, QC (d 1978), and Carmen Mary, *née* Dent (d 2003); hp to Btcy of kinsman (Sir) (Thomas) Desmond Molony (3 Bt, who does not use title); *b* 17 August 1937; *Educ* Downside, Trinity Coll Cambridge (MA); *m* 1964, Elizabeth Mary, eldest da of late Henry Clervaux Chaytor, of Cambridge; 4 s ((James) Sebastian b 1965 d 2001, (John) Benjamin b 1966, (Simon) Benedict b 1972, (Thomas) Francis b 1975), 1 da ((Carmen) Jane b 1967); *Career* sr vice-pres Sea Containers Inc 1968–73; dir: Post Office 1973–75, Scottish & Newcastle Breweries 1975–79, Rolls-Royce plc 1979–86; md: Chaytor King Ltd 1986–93, Addis Ltd 1993–94, Otford Group Ltd 1995–96; chief exec Chemring Group plc 1997–99; non-exec dir: Allied Leisure plc 1994–2000, Chemring Gp plc 1999–2005; FCA; *Recreations* music, gardening, reading, making lists; *Clubs* Oxford and Cambridge; *Style*— Peter J Molony, Esq; ✉ Mill House, Great Elm, Frome, Somerset BA11 3NY (tel 01373 812332)

MOLYNEAUX OF KILLEAD, Baron (Life Peer UK 1997), of Killead in the County of Antrim; Sir James Henry Molyneaux; PC (1983), KBE (1996); s of William Molyneaux (d 1953), of Seacash, Killead, Co Antrim; *b* 27 August 1920; *Educ* Aldergrove Sch Co Antrim; *Career* served RAF 1941–46; MP (UUP): Antrim South 1970–83, Lagan Valley 1983–97; vice-pres UUP Cncl 1974–79, ldr UUP Parly Pty 1974–95, ldr UUP 1979–95; memb Antrim CC 1964–1973, vice-chm Eastern Special Care Hosp Ctee 1966–73, chm Antrim Branch of NI Assoc for Mental Health 1967–1970; JP Co Antrim 1957–86; *Style*— The Rt Hon Lord Molyneaux of Killead, PC, KBE; ✉ Aldergrove, Crumlin, Co Antrim (tel 028 9442 2545); House of Lords, London SW1A 0PW

MOLYNEUX, Anne; da of late Robert Molyneux, and Audrey, *née* Young; *b* 12 January 1959; *Educ* Southport HS for Girls, Univ of Sheffield (LLB), Chester Coll of Law; *m* 1, 30 May 1987 (m dis 2006), Joseph Jeremy Ogden, s of late Robert David Ogden; 1 da (Joanna Frances b 19 April 1988), 1 s (Henry Robert b 23 Dec 1989); m 2, 2 Sept 2006, George Jonathan Morris, s of late George Russell Morris and Dorothy Elizabeth, *née* Robb, of NZ; *Career* articled clerk Jacobson Ridley 1981–84; assoc ptnr Lawrence Messer & Co 1984–87; Masons: joined 1987, ptnr 1989–, head of property litigation 1992–2003; ptnr Sprecher Grier Halberstam 2003–; recorder 2000–; memb Parole Bd for England and Wales 2003; shadow tstee Tomorrow's People; speaker various confs; memb Law Soc; *Recreations* family, literature; *Clubs* Ealing and Fulham Book; *Style*— Miss Anne Molyneux; ✉ Sprecher Grier Halberstam, 30 Farringdon Street, London EC4A 4HJ (tel 020 7544 5555, fax 020 7544 5565, e-mail annem@sghlaw.com)

MOLYNEUX, Prof David Hurst; s of Reginald Frank Molyneux (d 1974), of Northwich, and Monica Foden Stubbs; *b* 9 April 1943; *Educ* Denstone Coll, Emmanuel Coll Cambridge (MA, PhD), Univ of Salford (DSc); *m* 1969, Anita Elisabeth, da of George Edgar Bateson; 1 da (Elisabeth Camilla b 18 Dec 1974), 1 s (Oliver James b 7 Jan 1978); *Career* lectr in parasitology Liverpool Sch of Tropical Med 1968–77 (seconded to Nigeria 1970–72, seconded to Burkina Faso as project mangr UN Devpt Prog/WHO 1975–77); Univ of Salford: prof of biology 1977–91, dean Faculty of Sci 1984–88, chm Dept of Biological Scis 1988–91; dir Liverpool Sch of Tropical Med 1992–2000, dir Lymphatic Filariasis Support Centre 2000–; Chalmers medal Royal Soc of Tropical Med 1986, Wright medal British Soc for Parasitology 1988; pres British Soc for Parasitology 1992–94, pres-elect Royal Soc of Tropical Med and Hygiene (vice-pres 1995–97); memb Bd JRS Biodiversity Fndn 1998–, memb Governing Bd Inst of Animal Health 2001–, memb Int Task Force for Disease Eradication 2001–; tstee National Museum and Galleries on Merseyside 1997–2000; Hon FRCP 2006; *Books* Biology of Trypanosoma and Leishmania (with R W Ashford, 1983), Human Parasitic Disease Control (guest ed, 2006); *Recreations* golf, antiques, African art; *Clubs* Delamere Forest Golf (capt 2007–08); *Style*— Prof David Molyneux; ✉ School of Tropical Medicine, Pembroke Place, Liverpool L3 5QA (tel 0151 705 3291, fax 0151 709 0354, e-mail david.molyneux@liv.ac.uk)

MONBIOT, George; s of Raymond Monbiot, *qv*, of Burnham Market, Norfolk, and Rosalie Vivien Gresham Cooke, OBE, da of late R G Cooke, CBE, MP; *b* 27 January 1963; *Educ* Stowe, Brasenose Coll Oxford (open scholar, BA); *Career* investigative journalist, author and broadcaster; prodr natural history and environment progs BBC Radio 4 1985–87, prodr current affrs BBC World Service 1987, researching and writing book Poisoned Arrows: An Investigative Journey Through Indonesia 1987–89, researching and writing book Amazon Watershed (also series on Radio 4) 1989–91, fndr Forest Network (campaign to stop mahogany imports) 1989–91, researching and writing No Man's Land: An Investigative Journey Through Kenya and Tanzania (prodr and presenter No Man's Land series Radio 4) 1992–94, columnist The Guardian 1996–; presenter various programmes for BBC and C4; visiting fell Green Coll Oxford 1993–95, visiting prof of environmental sci Univ of E London 1995–99, hon prof of politics Keele Univ 1998–2000, visiting prof Dept of Philosophy Univ of Bristol 1999–2000, currently visiting prof Dept of Planning Oxford Brookes Univ; fndr The Land is Ours Campaign 1995; patron: African Initiatives, Mikron Theatre; tstee: Naturesave Tst, African Initiatives, Advsy Cncl Environmental Law Fndn; radio production award Sony Awards 1987, Lloyd's National Screenwriting Award (for The Norwegian) 1987, United Nations Global 500 Award for outstanding environmental achievement 1995, named by Evening Standard as one of 25 most influential people in Britain 1996, named by Independent on Sunday as one of the 40 int prophets of the 21st century 1997, One World Nat Press Award 1998; Hon Dr Univ of Essex 2007; hon fell Sch of Journalism Univ of Cardiff 2007; *Books* Poisoned Arrows: An Investigative Journey Through Indonesia (1989), Amazon Watershed (Sir Peter Kent Award, 1991), No Man's Land: An Investigative Journey Through Kenya and Tanzania (1994), Captive State: The Corporate Takeover of Britain (2000), The Age of Consent: A Manifesto for a New World Order (2003), Heat: How to Stop the Planet Burning (2006); *Recreations* natural history, palaeontology, reading, gardening, ultimate frisbee, kayaking; *Style*— George Monbiot; ✉ website www.monbiot.com

MONBIOT, Raymond Geoffrey; CBE (1994, MBE 1981); s of Maurice Ferdinand Monbiot (d 1976), and Ruth Monbiot (d 1995); *b* 1 September 1937; *Educ* Westminster, London Business Sch; *m* 1961, Rosalie Vivien Gresham, OBE (1992), da of R G Cooke, CBE, MP (d 1970); 3 c (incl George Monbiot, *qv*, Eleanor Monbiot, OBE, and one of whom d 1997); *Career* with J Lyons & Co Ltd 1956–78, md Associated Biscuits Ltd 1978–82; chm: Campbell's UK Ltd 1982–88, Campbell's Soups Ltd 1983–88; pres Campbell's Frozen Foods Europe 1987–88, chm and md Rotherfield Management Ltd 1988–, vice-chm R & B Provisions Ltd 1990–95; dir: Pets Choice Ltd 1991–97, Paterson Bronte Ltd 1993–95, Arran Provisions Ltd 1993–95, Paramount Foods plc (formerly Canadian Pizza plc) 1996–98; chm Creative Food Systems Ltd 1997–2000; dep chm Cons Pty 2003–06; pres: S Oxon Cons Assoc 1980–92 (chm 1974–78), Cons Voluntary Pty 2000–01 (vice-pres 1997–2000), NW Norfolk Cons Assoc 2002–05; chm: Upper Thames Euro Constituency 1982–84, Oxon and Bucks Euro Constituency 1984–89, Cons Pty Nat Trade and Industry Forum 1988–96, Wessex Area Cons Pty 1995–98, Cons Pty Conf 2000, Cons Pty Nat Convention 2003–06; memb: Cons Pty NEC 1987–98, Cons Pty Fin and Gen Purposes Ctee 1989–93 and 1995–98, Cons Pty Bd 1998–2001 and 2003–06; memb: Cncl BIM 1981–84 (chm Westminster Branch 1978–82), Business Liaison Ctee London Business Sch 1984–88; chm Duke of Edinburgh Award for Industrial Projects Northants then Berks 1976–87; Prince Philip Cert of Recognition 1987; Freeman City of London 1990, Liveryman Worshipful Co of Butchers; *Books* How to Manage Your Boss (1980), One Hundred Not Out (2000), The Burnhams Book of Characters and Memories (2002), Characters of North Norfolk (2003), More Characters of North Norfolk (2006); *Recreations* writing, charity work, cooking; *Clubs* Leander, Farmers'; *Style*— Raymond Monbiot, Esq, CBE; ✉ Eastgate House, Overy Road, Burnham Market, Norfolk PE31 8HH (tel 01328 730928, fax 01328 730368, e-mail rmonbiot@rotherfieldmgmnt.demon.co.uk)

MONCADA, Prof Salvador Enrique; s of Salvador Moncada, of Tegucigalpa, Honduras, and Jenny Seidner (d 1985); *b* 3 December 1944; *Educ* Univ of El Salvador (MD), Univ of London (PhD); *Family* 1 da (Claudia Regina b 15 Nov 1966), 1 s (Salvador Ernesto b 6 May 1972 d 1982); m 2, HRH The Princess Maria Esmeralda de Belgique; 1 da (Alexandra Leopoldine b 4 Aug 1998), 1 s (Leopoldo Daniel b 21 May 2001); *Career* The Wellcome Res Laboratories: dir of Theraputic Res Div 1984–86, dir of res 1986–95; prof and dir Wolfson Inst for Biomedical Res (formerly The Cruciform Project) UCL 1996–; editorial work: ed Gen Pharmacology Section Prostaglandins 1975–80, conslt ed Prostaglandins 1980; memb Ed Bd: British Jl of Pharmacology 1980–85, Atherosclerosis 1980, European Jl of Clinical Investigation 1986, Thrombosis Res 1989; scientific ed The British Medical Bulletin no 39 Part 3; recipient of numerous int med awards incl: Royal Medal, Prince of Asturias Prize, Amsterdam Prize; inventor of various patented pharmaceutical compositions; memb Br Pharmacological Soc 1974, hon memb Colombian Soc of Int Med 1982, hon memb Peruvian Pharmacological Soc 1983, memb Nat Acad of Scis 1994; FRS 1988, FRCP 1994; *Books* Nitric Oxide from L-arginine: a bioregulatory system (1990), Clinical Relevance of Nitric Oxide in the Cardiovascular System (1991), The Biology of Nitric Oxide (Parts 1–7, 1992–2000), Nitric Oxide and the Vascular Endothelium (ed jtly, 2006); *Recreations* music, theatre, literature; *Style*— Prof Salvador Moncada, FRCP, FRS; ✉ The Wolfson Institute for Biomedical Research, University College London, Gower Street, London WC1E 6BT (e-mail s.moncada@ucl.ac.uk)

MONCK, Sir Nicholas Jeremy (Nick); KCB (1994, CB 1988); s of Bosworth Monck (d 1961), and Stella Mary, *née* Cock (d 1997); *b* 9 March 1935; *Educ* Eton, King's Coll Cambridge, Univ of Pennsylvania, LSE; *m* 1960, Elizabeth Mary Kirwan; 3 s; *Career* asst princ MOP 1959–62, NEDO 1962–65, NBPI 1965–66, sr economist Miny of Agriculture Tanzania 1966–69; HM Treasy: joined 1969, asst sec 1971, princ private sec to Chllr of the Exchequer 1976–77, under sec 1977–84, dep sec 1984–90, second perm sec (public expenditure) 1990–92; perm sec Employment Dept Gp 1993–95, ret; conslt to Govts in Hungary, Bulgaria, Mexico, South Africa, Malawi and Tanzania; chm Oxford Policy Inst 2004–; dir Standard Life Assurance Co 1997–2005; chm British Dyslexia Assoc 1995–2000; memb: Fin Ctee Nat Tst 1990–2005, Bd IMRO 1995–2000, Advsy Cncl Transparency Int (UK) 1999–, Cncl of Mgmnt NIESR 2001–, UCL Hospitals NHS Fndn Tst 2005–; tstee Glyndebourne Art Tst 1996–2004; memb BSC 1978–80; *Style*— Sir Nick Monck, KCB; ✉ 31 Lady Margaret Road, London NW5 2NG (tel 020 7485 8474)

MONCKTON, Hon Anthony Leopold Colyer; yst s of 2 Viscount Monckton of Brenchley, CB, OBE, MC, DL, FSA; *b* 25 September 1960; *Educ* Harrow, Magdalene Coll Cambridge; *m* 1985, Philippa Susan, yr da of late Gervase Christopher Brinsmade Wingfield; 1 s (Edward Gervase Colyer b 1988), 1 da (Camilla Mary b 1989); *Career* cmmnd 9/12 Royal Lancers 1982, Capt 1984, ret 1987; HM Dip Serv: second sec FCO 1987, UK Disarmament Delgn Geneva 1990–92, first sec 1991, first sec FCO 1992, first sec (political) Zagreb 1996–98, head BR Embassy Office Banja Luka 1998–99, first sec FCO 1999, cnsllr Belgrade 2001, cnsllr FCO 2004; *Clubs* MCC; *Style*— The Hon Anthony Monckton; ✉ c/o Foreign & Commonwealth Office, King Charles Street, London SW1A 2AH

MONCKTON OF BRENCHLEY, Hon Christopher Walter Monckton; s and h of late 2 Viscount Monckton of Brenchley, CB, OBE, MC, DL, FSA by his w Marianna Laetitia, da of Cdr Robert Tatton Bower, RN; *b* 14 February 1952; *Educ* Harrow, Churchill Coll Cambridge (MA), Univ Coll Cardiff (Dip Journalism); *m* 19 May 1990, Juliet Mary Anne,

M

da of Jørgen Malherbe Jensen, of London; *Career* ldr writer Yorkshire Post 1975–77 (reporter 1974–75), press offr Cons Central Office 1977–78, ed The Universe 1979–81, managing ed Telegraph Sunday Magazine 1981–82, ldr writer The Standard 1982, special advsr to PM's Policy Unit (Home Affrs) 1982–86, asst ed Today 1986–87, consltg ed and chief ldr writer Evening Standard 1987–92, dir Christopher Monckton Ltd public affrs conslts 1987–2006; memb St John Ambulance Bd Wetherby Div 1976–77, sec CPS Health, Employment and Policy Study Gps 1981–82, tstee Hales Trophy for the Blue Riband of the Atlantic 1990–, govr London Oratory Sch 1991–96; Liveryman Worshipful Co of Broderers; student memb Middle Temple 1979–; DL 1987–96; OStJ 1973, Knight SMOM 1973; *Books* The Laker Story (with Ivan Fallon, 1982), Sudoku X series (2005–06); *Recreations* clocks and sundials, computers, hill walking, inventions, motor-cycling, number theory, politics, public speaking, recreational mathematics, romance, sailing, science fiction, Scotland, Yorkshire; *Clubs* Beefsteak, Brooks's, Pratt's; *Style*— The Viscount Monckton of Brenchley; ✉ Carie, Rannoch, Perthshire PH17 2QJ (tel 01882 632341, fax 01882 632776, e-mail monckton@mail.com)

MONCREIFF, 6 Baron (UK 1874) Rhoderick Harry Wellwood Moncreiff; s of 5 Baron Moncreiff (d 2002); *b* 22 March 1954; *Educ* E of Scotland Coll of Agric (HND); *m* 1982, Alison Elizabeth Anne, o da of late James Duncan Alastair Ross, of Dollar, Clackmannanshire; 2 s (Hon Harry James Wellwood b 12 Aug 1986, Hon James Gavin Francis b 29 July 1988); *Heir* s, Hon Harry Moncreiff; *Style*— The Rt Hon the Lord Moncreiff

MONCREIFFE OF THAT ILK, Lady; Hermione Patricia; o da of Lt-Col Walter Douglas Faulkner, MC (ka 1940), and Patricia Katharine (now Patricia, Countess of Dundee); *b* 14 January 1937; *m* 1 May 1966, Sir Rupert Iain Kay Moncreiffe of that Ilk, 11 Bt (d 1985); 2 step s (Earl of Erroll, Hon Peregrine Moncreiffe of that Ilk, *qqv*), 1 step da (Lady Alexandra Connell); *Style*— Lady Moncreiffe of that Ilk; ✉ 28 Ingelow House, Holland Street, London W8 4NF

MONCREIFFE OF THAT ILK, Hon Peregrine David Euan Malcolm; Baron of Moncreiffe and Easter Moncreiffe (both Scottish territorial baronies); 2 s of late Countess of Erroll (d 1978), and Sir Iain Moncreiffe of that I1k, 11 Bt (d 1985); *b* 16 February 1951; *Educ* Eton, ChCh Oxford (MA); *m* 27 July 1988, Miranda Mary, da of Capt Mervyn Fox-Pitt, of Grange Scrymgeour, Cupar, Fife; 2 s (Ossian b 3 Feb 1991, Euan b 12 Sept 2000), 4 da (Idina b 3 Nov 1992, Elisabeth b 2 Feb 1995, Alexandra b 19 Nov 1996, Lily b 6 Nov 1998); *Career* Lt Atholl Highlanders; Slains Pursuivant 1970–78; investment banker; Credit Suisse First Boston 1972–82, Lehman Bros Kuhn Loeb/Shearson Lehman 1982–86, E F Hutton & Co 1986–88, Buchanan Partners 1990–99, currently chm UA Gp plc; Royal Commissioner on the Ancient and Historical Monuments of Scotland 1989–94; memb Queen's Body Guard for Scotland (Royal Co of Archers); Freeman City of London, memb Worshipful Co of Fishmongers 1987; *Recreations* running, rowing, rustic pursuits, dance; *Clubs* Turf, White's, Pratt's, Puffins (Edinburgh), New (Edinburgh), Leander, Brook (NY); *Style*— The Hon Peregrine Moncreiffe of that Ilk; ✉ Easter Moncreiffe, Perthshire PH2 8QA (tel 01738 813833, fax 01738 813063, e-mail moncreiffe@bloomberg.net)

MOND, Gary Stephen; s of Ferdinand Mond, of London, and Frances, *née* Henry; *b* 11 May 1959; *Educ* UCS Hampstead, Trinity Coll Cambridge (MA, Swimming blue); *m* 3 Feb 2001, Robyn, *née* Feinman; 1 da; *Career* chartered accountant 1981–84, Guinness Mahon & Co Ltd 1984–86, assoc dir Chancery Corporate Services Ltd 1986–89, Greig Middleton & Co Ltd 1989–91, fin business and trg conslt 1992–, conslt City Univ Business Sch 1992–97, md Redcliffe Training Assoc Ltd 1995–; memb ICAEW Corp Fin Faculty Exec 2003–; Parly candidate (Cons) Hamilton Scot 1987, Parly candidate (Cons) Mansfield 1992, CPC chm Kensington and Chelsea Cons Assoc 1995–99, cncllr Royal Borough of Kensington & Chelsea 1996–2002, memb Cons Way Forward Exec 2004–; competitive butterfly swimmer: Nat Under 14 champion 1972, GB Int and Olympic trialist 1976, World Record holder long distance butterfly (six and a quarter miles) 1980; FCA 1995 (ACA 1985); *Recreations* swimming, theatre, chess; *Clubs* Coningsby, Renaissance Forum; *Style*— Gary Mond, Esq; ✉ Flat 10, Two Avenue Road, London NW8 7PU (tel 020 7586 5751, fax 020 7631 2060, e-mail garymond@redcliffetraining.co.uk)

MONDAL, Dr Bijoy Krishna; s of Jagneswar Mondal (d 1974), of Pirojpur, Barisal, and Madhu Bala Mondal (d 1983); *b* 28 September 1940; *Educ* Dacca Univ (MB BS), Univ of Liverpool (DTM&H); *m* 12 March 1971, Dolly, da of Dr Jagadish Chandra Mandal, of Calcutta; 2 da (Bipasha b 16 April 1975, Bidisha b 21 April 1980), 1 s (Krishnendu b 9 Oct 1981); *Career* house offr in gen surgery Dacca Med Coll Hosp 1964–65, house offr in gen med St Tydfil 1965–66; sr house offr in gen med: Warrington Gen Hosp 1966–67, Ashton Gen Hosp 1967–68; med registrar: in gen med The Grange Hosp Northwich 1968–70, in gen med/chest Ladywell Hosp Salford 1970–74; sr registrar in geriatric med Dudley Rd Hosp Birmingham 1974–75, conslt physician in geriatric med Rotherham Health Authy 1975–, clinical dir Badsley Moor Lane/Wathwood Hosps Unit 1990– (unit gen mangr 1985–); numerous articles in professional jls on: haematology, endocrinology, rheumatology, neurology; exec memb BMA (chm Rotherham div 1990), past cncl memb Br Geriatric Soc, pres Rotherham Parkinson's Disease Soc, chm Rotherham Stroke Club, memb Overseas Doctors' Assoc; FRCPG 1984, FRCPE 1986, FRCP 1987 (MRCP 1973); *Recreations* gardening, photography, travel; *Style*— Dr Bijoy Mondal

MONDAY, Christopher Harry; s of Clifford Walter Monday (d 1992), and Isobel Phyllis Grace, *née* Lear (d 1992); *b* 1 June 1943; *Educ* Thornbury GS, Swansea Coll of Technol (Inst of Marine Engrs prize, OND), Riversdale Tech Coll, Bristol Coll of Technol (HNC Mech Engrg); *m* 21 Oct 1967, Heather, da of William Bengree Burgess; 1 s (Richard Paul b 13 Oct 1976); *Career* Shell Oil Co: apprentice 1959–64, fifth engr offr 1964–65; sub assembly supervisor Automatic Handling Ltd 1965–68, sr tech engr (tech engr 1968–70) Rolls Royce Aero Engines Ltd 1970–76; NNC Ltd: res engr 1976–77, site rep 1977–81, section head (Electronics) 1981–87, sr section head 1987–90, gp head 1990–92, tech sales exec 1992–94; dir Community Integrated Care Ltd 1989–94, md CTSS Ltd 1990–99; CIC Ltd: former head of tech servs, former head of IT and communications, currently head of IT and compliance, asst dir 2003–; chm Inst of Tech Engrs 1983–85, memb Engrg Cncl 1988–94, memb Cncl Instn of Engrg and Technol 2006–; hon treas Instn of Incorporated Engrs 1999–2006; *Recreations* DIY (built my own house), travel, badminton, fanatic supporter of American football; *Style*— Christopher Monday, Esq; ✉ The Dairy, Bradley Hall, Bradley Lane, Frodsham, Cheshire WA6 7EP (tel 01928 733221); CIC Ltd, 2 Old Market Court, Miners Way, Widnes, Cheshire WA8 7SP (tel 0151 422 5301, fax 0151 495 3146, e-mail chris.monday@c-i-c.co.uk)

MONDS, Prof Fabian; CBE (1997); *b* 1 November 1940; *Educ* Christian Brothers GS Omagh, Queen's Univ Belfast (BSc, PhD); *m* 1967, Eileen Joan Graham; 2 da; *Career* formerly provost Magee Coll and pro-vice-chllr for planning Univ of Ulster, held positions at Purdue Univ and Queen's Univ Belfast; fndr ptnr: Medical and Scientific Computer Services Ltd, Western Connect Ltd; BBC: memb Bd of Govrs 1999–2006, nat govr for NI 1999–2006; chm: Invest NI 2000–05, Centre for Trauma and Transformation Omagh; CCMI; *Style*— Prof Fabian Monds, CBE, CCMI; ✉ Northern Ireland Centre for Trauma and Transformation, 2 Retreat Close, Omagh BT79 0HW

MONE, Rt Rev John; *see:* Paisley, Bishop of (RC)

MONEY, Julian David Kyrle; s of Robert Washborn Money (d 1986), of Truro, Cornwall, and Brenda, *née* Mitchell; *b* 28 July 1959; *Educ* Blundell's, St Austell Sixth Form Coll, Falmouth Art Sch, Kingston Poly (BA); *m* 1992, Katharine Pethick; 1 s (Freddy Bob b 29 April 1987), 1 da (Tabitha Lily b 27 March 1989); *Career* designer specialising in packaging systems; fndr (with w) Pethick & Money 1984 (design consultancy specialising in graphics for corp identities, packaging and multi-media clients); clients incl: Marks & Spencer, Tesco, Boots, J Sainsbury, Alfred Dunhill, Mont Blanc, Walt Disney, Jaeger, CBRE; created M-Pak packaging system and FFW flexible food wrap; founded RAP Ltd (Rapid Action Packaging) manufacturing packaging for quick service restaurant indust; clients incl: Pret, MacDonalds, Starbucks, Nero, Costa, Boots, Tesco, Asda, Wild Bean Café, KFC, Greggs, Abrakebabra Ireland; winner BBC Design Award and BBC Technol Award 1996; *Recreations* sailing, tennis, squash, fishing, golf, film, gardening; *Style*— Julian Money, Esq; ✉ 8 Sydney Road, Richmond, Surrey TW9 1UB (tel 020 8948 3184); RAP Ltd (tel 020 8392 8320, fax 020 8392 3821, e-mail julian.money@rapuk.com)

MONEY-COUTTS, Sir David Burdett; KCVO (1991); s of Lt-Col the Hon Alexander Burdett Money-Coutts, OBE (d 1994; 2 s of 6 Baron Latymer), and Mary Elspeth (d 1990; er da of Sir Reginald Arthur Hobhouse, 5 Bt); *b* 19 July 1931; *Educ* Eton, New Coll Oxford (MA); *m* 17 May 1958, (Helen) Penelope June Utten, da of Cdr Killingworth Richard Utten Todd, RIN; 2 da (Harriet b 1959, Laura (Mrs Jamie Corrie) b 1965), 1 s (Benjamin b 1961); *Career* served 1 Royal Dragoons 1950–51, Royal Glos Hussars (TA) 1951–67; Coutts & Co: joined 1954, dir 1958–96, md 1970–86, chm 1976–93; chm Coutts & Co Int Holding AG 1991–93; dir: National Discount Co 1964–69, United States & General Tst Corp 1964–73, Charities Investment Mangrs 1964–2000 (chm 1984–2000), Gerrard Gp plc (formerly Gerrard & National Holdings plc) 1969–99 (dep chm 1969–89), Dun & Bradstreet 1973–87, National Westminster Bank 1976–90 (dir SE Region 1969–88 (chm 1986–88), chm S Advsy Bd 1988–92), Phoenix Assurance 1978–85, Sun Alliance and London Insurance 1984–90, M & G Gp 1987–97 (chm 1990–97), Inst of Sports Med 1997–2006 (chm 1997–2006); hon treas Nat Assoc of Almshouses 1960–92; govr Middx Hosp 1962–74 (chm Med Sch 1974–88, special tstee 1974–2000, chm Special Tstees 1974–97); memb: Health Educn Cncl 1973–76, Kensington Chelsea and Westminster AHA(T) 1974–82 (vice-chm 1976–82), Bloomsbury HA 1982–90 (vice-chm 1982–88), Cncl UCL 1987–97; chm Old Etonian Tst 1976–2001 (hon fell Eton Coll 1996); tstee: Multiple Sclerosis Soc 1967–99, Mansfield Coll Oxford 1988–95, Scout Fndn 1992–2001 (chm 1994–2001); FCIB; *Clubs* Leander; *Style*— Sir David Money-Coutts, KCVO; ✉ Magpie House, Peppard Common, Henley-on-Thames, Oxfordshire RG9 5JG (tel 01491 628005, fax 01491 629241, e-mail dbmcoutts@aol.com)

MONK, Prof Anthony John (Tony); s of John Andrew Monk, and Dorothy Marjorie, *née* Pettifer; *b* 11 September 1936; *Educ* Windsor County Boys' Sch, UCL (Dip Arch, Alfred Bossom Atelier Prize), Yale Univ (Henry Fund fell, ESU scholar, MArch); *m* 1964, Ann Monk, JP; 1 s (Craig Antony b 1973), 1 da (Jane Elizabeth b 1977); *Career* jt winner Paisley Civic Centre architecture competition 1963; fndr ptnr Hutchison Locke & Monk (architects) 1964–88, fndr and non-exec dir Acton Housing Assoc 1969–74, md HLM Architects Ltd 1988–91, non-exec dir Building Centre London 1991–96, prof of architecture Univ of Luton 1994–2001 (Pr lectr 1994, head of architecture 1994–97), architectural advsr Lottery Awards Panel Sports Cncl 1995–98, chm BDA Awards Panel 2000; negotiator RIBA Part I exemption for BSc(Hons) Architecture 1993; RIBA 1961, ARIAS 1967, FFB 1968, MBAE 1994; *Awards* Paisley Civic Centre Civic Tst Award 1968, Civic Tst Commendation Darville House Windsor 1983, Civic Tst Award and Brick Devpt Assoc Award Chariott House Windsor 1985, Building Magazine Premier Practice Award (nationwide competition) HLM Architects 1991, DOE Housing Project Design Award Cromwell House Mortlake 1992, winner St Albans Ryder competition 1995; *Publications* The Art and Architecture of Paul Rudolph (1999), Hospital Builders (2004); author of numerous publications featuring architectural projects; *Recreations* cricket, golf; *Clubs* MCC, Wentworth; *Style*— Prof Tony Monk; ✉ Millrun, White Lilies Island, Mill Lane, Windsor, Berkshire SL4 5JH (tel 01753 861917, fax 01753 866874, website www.tonymonk.com); Edgington Spink and Hyne, Riding Court, Riding Court Road, Datchet, Windsor, Berkshire SL3 9LE (tel 01753 580033, fax 01753 580633)

MONK, Paul Nicholas; s of George Benbow Monk, of Godalming, Surrey, and Rosina Gwendoline, *née* Ross; *b* 3 December 1949; *Educ* Royal GS Guildford, Pembroke Coll Oxford (MA); *m* 14 Feb 1985, Roma Olivia Cannon, da of Hamilton Haigh; 2 da (Georgina, Lucinda), 1 s (Charles); *Career* slr: England & Wales 1974, Hong Kong 1995; articled to Durrant Cooper & Hambling 1972–74, ptnr Allen & Overy 1979 (joined 1975), currently legal counsel Capital Partnership Ltd; memb Worshipful Co of Slrs; memb: Law Soc 1972, Int Bar Assoc; *Recreations* sailing, cross-country skiing; *Clubs* Hurlingham, Royal Southern Yacht; *Style*— Paul Monk, Esq

MONK, Stuart John; s of John Monk (d 1989), and Margaret, *née* Holmes; *b* 7 August 1949, Epping, Essex; *Educ* Durham Johnson Grammar Tech; *m* 2 June 1979, Jennifer, *née* Spink; 1 da (Jane b 4 Nov 1980), 1 s (Stephen b 19 March 1983); *Career* articled clerk King Hope & Co 1969–71; self employed 1972–, currently md Jomast Property & Finance Co Ltd; *Recreations* tennis, golf; *Style*— Stuart Monk, Esq; ✉ Jomast Property & Finance Company Limited, Oriel House, Bishop Street, Stockton-on-Tees TS18 1SW (tel 01642 674203, fax 01642 618153, e-mail stuart@jomast.co.uk)

MONK BRETTON, 3 Baron (UK 1884); John Charles Dodson; DL (E Sussex 1983); s of 2 Baron, CB, JP, DL (d 1933), by his w Ruth (herself da of Hon Charles Brand and gda of 1 Viscount Hampden and 23 Baron Dacre); *b* 17 July 1924; *Educ* Westminster, New Coll Oxford; *m* 1958, Zoé Diana, da of Ian Douglas Murray Scott (d 1974); 2 s; *Heir* s, Hon Christopher Dodson; *Career* took Cons whip in House of Lords; retired farmer; *Style*— The Rt Hon the Lord Monk Bretton, DL; ✉ Chemin de La Becque 24, CH 1814, La Tour de Peilz, Switzerland

MONKMAN, Prof Andrew Paul; *b* 6 September 1963; *Educ* QMC London (BSc, PhD); *m* Sophia Carmen; 1 s (Maximilian Cirus), 1 da (Misha Cornelia); *Career* Sch of Engrg and Applied Science (now Dept of Physics) Univ of Durham: lectr Applied Physics Gp 1988–97, promoted to readership 1997, promoted prof 2002, dir Photonic Materials Inst 2004–; ESRC: memb Materials Coll, memb Photonics Panel (chm Oct 2001 meeting); Swedish Fndn for Int Co-operation in Research and HE (STINT) fell Swedish govt 1998 (held at Univ of Linkoping), Leverhulme fell 2002–03; guest lectr and speaker at confs and symposia; author of numouers books contribs and peer-reviewed papers; fndr memb Northern Dales Branch Int Wine and Food Soc; memb American Physical Soc; CPhys, FInstP; *Recreations* classical, jazz and rock music, hill walking, skiing, football, motor sport, rallying and driving (frightening passengers!), cooking, being a father; *Style*— Prof Andrew Monkman; ✉ Organic Elecroactive Materials Research Group, Department of Physics, University of Durham, Science Laboratories, South Road, Durham DH1 3LE (tel 0191 374 2406, fax 0191 374 3848, mobile 07714 066462, e-mail a.p.monkman@durham.ac.uk)

MONKS, John; *Educ* Univ of Nottingham (BA); *Career* jr mangr Plessey Co Ltd 1967–69; TUC: joined 1969, head Orgn and Industrial Rels Dept 1977, dep gen sec 1987–94, gen sec 1994–2003; gen sec European TUC 2003–; memb: ACAS 1979–95, ESRC 1988–91, Learning and Skills Cncl 2000–04; visiting prof Sch of Mgmnt Univ of Manchester; *Style*— John Monks, Esq; ✉ ETUC, ITU House, Boulevard du Roi Albert II 5, B-1210 Brussels, Belgium

MONKS, John Christopher; *Educ* Liverpool Poly, RCA (MA); *Career* artist; visiting artist Garner Tullis Workshop Santa Barbara California 1987, British Council artist in residence British Inst Madrid 1990; numerous solo exhibitions incl: Evidence 1989 and New Work 1990 (both Paton Gallery London), John Monks, Paintings 1990–93 (Manchester City Art Galleries) 1994, Beaux Arts 1996 and 1997, Peter Findlay Gallery

NYC 1999; work in group exhibitions incl: New Contemporaries (ICA London, prizewinner) 1976, Three College Show (RCA) 1979, Alternative Tate (Paton Gallery London) 1982, Artists for the 1990s (Paton Gallery) 1984, Monotypes (Paton Gallery) 1986, Birthday Offering (five years of Paton Gallery) 1986, Six Figurative Painters (Paton Gallery) 1987, 20 British Artists (London, Glasgow, NY) 1988, Metropolitan Museum of Art (NY) 1988, Recent Work (Paton Gallery) 1990, The New British Painting (Queen's Museum NY) 1990, Paton Gallery 1993, Beaux Arts London 1994, Artists of Fame and Promise (Beaux Arts) 1995; work in collections incl: Metropolitan Museum of Art (NY), Contemporary Art Society (London), Gulbenkian Foundation (Lisbon Portugal), Arts Council (GB), British Institute (Madrid), Manchester City Museum, Yale Center for British Art (Conn USA), Unilever plc, Ocean Trading and Transport plc; awarded British Council grant for working visit to NY 1990; solo show incl: Peter Findlay NY 2004 and 2006, Long & Nyle London 2005 and 2007; guest lecture tour of American Art Centres Spring 1992; guest speaker: Tate Gallery 1993, Sch of The Art Inst Chicago USA 1997, NY Studio Sch NY 1998; *Style—* John Monks, Esq; ✉ c/o Long & Ryle, 4 John Islip Street, London SW1P 4PX; c/o Peter Findlay Gallery, 41 East 57th Street, New York, NY 100200, USA

MONKS, Sandra Elizabeth; TD; da of George Jagger (d 1993), and Maisie Campbell, *née* Watson (d 1998); *b* 27 March 1945; *Educ* Grove Acad Broughty Ferry, Santa Ana Jr Coll UCLA; *m* 1965 (m dis 1970), Terence John Monks; *Career* civil servant Dept of Educn 1962–66, insurance exec International Group Plans Inc Washington DC 1966–68; D C Thomson & Co Ltd 1970–: sub-ed Romeo magazine, sub-ed Jackie magazine, chief sub-ed Jackie, ed Jackie, ed Annabel magazine, ed My Weekly magazine, fiction and rights ed; Maj RCS (TA) 39th (City of London) (V) (SC), ret; *Recreations* Territorial Army, horse riding, swimming, sailing; *Style—* Ms Sandra Monks, TD; ✉ My Weekly Magazine, Albert Square, Dundee DD1 9QJ (tel 01382 575888, fax 01382 322214, e-mail smonks@dcthomson.co.uk)

MONKSWELL, 5 Baron (UK 1885); Gerard Collier; s of William Adrian Larry Collier, MB (disclaimed Barony of Monkswell for life 1964; d 1984), and his 2 w, Helen, *née* Dunbar; *b* 28 January 1947; *Educ* George Heriot's Sch Edinburgh, Portsmouth Poly; *m* 1974, Ann Valerie, da of James Collins, of Liverpool; 1 da (Hon Laura Jennifer b 1975), 2 s (Hon James Adrian b 1977, Hon William Robert Gerard b 1979); *Heir* s, Hon James Collier; *Career* product quality engr Massey Ferguson Man Co Ltd 1972–84, service admin mangr MF Industrial 1984–89; memb Manchester City Cncl 1989–94; sat as memb of House of Lords 1994–99; self-employed 1999–; *Style—* The Rt Hon the Lord Monkswell

MONMOUTH, Dean of; *see:* Fenwick, Very Rev Dr Richard David

MONMOUTH, Bishop of 2003–; Rt Rev Dominic Edward William Murray Walker; *b* 28 June 1948; *Educ* Plymouth Coll, KCL (AKC), Heythrop Coll London (MA), Univ of Wales (LLM); *Career* ordained priest 1972, chaplain to the Bishop of Southwark 1973–76, rector of Newington 1976–85, rural dean of Southwark and Newington 1980–85, team rector and rural dean of Brighton 1985–97, canon and prebendary of Chichester Cathedral 1985–97, bishop of Reading 1997–2003; memb Oratory of the Good Shepherd (father supr 1990–96); vice-pres RSPCA 2001–; Hon DLitt Univ of Brighton; *Publications* The Ministry of Deliverance (1997); *Style—* The Rt Rev the Bishop of Monmouth; ✉ Bishopstow, Stow Hill, Newport NP20 4EA (tel 01633 263510, fax 01633 259946, e-mail bishop.monmouth@churchinwales.org.uk)

MONNOU, HE Edgar-Yves; s of Benjamin Monnou, and Jacqueline, *née* Zodehougan; *b* 9 February 1953, Abomey, Benin; *Educ* DEUG Université d'Orléans, Université de Paris II (Maîtrise en Droit, CAPA), Université de Paris I Sorbonne (Diplôme Hautes Etudes Judiciares, Doctorat Troisième Cycle Droit Privé); *m* 14 Sept 1996, Virginie Dopchie; 5 c; *Career* diplomat; advocate: Court of Appeal Paris 1979–83, Court of Appeal Cotonou 1983–; memb Order of Advocates of Benin; dep Nat Assembly 1991–95 and 1999–2003, min of Foreign Affrs and Co-operation 1995–96, perm rep of Benin to ACP/EU 1999–2003, ambass to the Court of St James's 2004–; Commandeur de l'Ordre National (Benin), Grand Officier de la Légion d'Honneur (France); *Style—* HE Mr Edgar-Yves Monnou; ✉ Benin Embassy, 87 Avenue Victor Hugo, 75116 Paris, France (tel 00 33 1 45 00 98 82, fax 00 33 1 45 01 82 02)

MONRO, (Andrew) Hugh; s of Andrew Killey Monro, MD, FRCS (d 1993), of Rye, E Sussex, and Diana Louise, *née* Rhys (d 2005); *b* 2 March 1950; *Educ* Rugby, Pembroke Coll Cambridge (MA, PGCE); *m* 27 July 1974, Elizabeth Clare, da of Lyndon Rust, of Mayhill, Glos; 1 da (Lucy b 1980), 1 s (James b 1983); *Career* production mangr Metal Box Co 1972–73; teacher Haileybury 1974–79 (Noble & Greenough Boston Mass 1977–78), head of history and housemaster Loretto Sch 1980–86; headmaster: Worksop Coll 1986–90, Clifton Coll 1990–2000; master Wellington Coll 2000–05; govr: Terrington Yorks, Mount House Tavistock, Brambletye East Grinstead; *Recreations* golf, American politics; *Clubs* Hawks' (Cambridge); *Style—* Hugh Monro, Esq

MONRO, Brig the Hon Hugh Brisbane Henry Ewart; CBE ((Mil) 2003, MBE (Mil) 1988); s of Baron Monro of Langholm (Life Peer) (d 2006), and Elizabeth Anne, *née* Welch; bro of Maj-Gen the Hon Seymour Monro, CBE , *qv*; *b* 1953; *Educ* Trinity Coll Glenalmond; *m* Catriona Elizabeth, da of Rev and Mrs Ronald Torrie; 3 da (Flora, Clare, Ailsa); *Career* cmmnd Queen's Own Highlanders 1972; last CO 1 Bn Queen's Own Highlanders 1993–94, first CO 1 Bn The Highlanders 1994–95, Col MOD 1995–98, Bde Cdr 52 Lowland Bde 1998–2001, Col The Highlanders 2001, Cmdt Sch of Infantry 2001–05; memb Queen's Body Guard for Scotland (Royal Co of Archers); *Recreations* golf, country sports; *Clubs* Northern Meeting, Army and Navy; *Style—* Brig the Hon Hugh Monro, CBE

MONRO, James Lawrence; s of John Kirkpatrick Monro, of Marlborough, Wilts, and Landon, *née* Reed; *b* 17 November 1939; *Educ* Sherborne, London Hosp Med Coll (MB BS); *m* 29 Sept 1973, Caroline Jane, da of Robert Dunlop, MBE, of Aldingbourne, W Sussex; 2 s (Charles b 13 Aug 1975, Andrew b 10 Aug 1981), 1 da (Rosanne b 20 Nov 1978); *Career* surgical registrar The London Hosp 1967–69, res surgical offr Brompton Hosp 1969–70; sr registrar Cardio Thoracic Unit: Green Lane Hosp Auckland NZ 1970–72, The London Hosp 1972–73; conslt cardiac surgn Dept Cardiac Surgery Gen Hosp Southampton 1973–2004, ret; memb: BMA 1964, Soc of Cardiothoracic Surgeons of GB and I 1974 (pres 2000–01), Br Cardiac Soc 1974, British Paediatric Cardiac Assoc 1978, Euro Assoc for Cardio Thoracic Surgery 1987 (vice-pres 2002–03, pres 2003–04), RSM 1996; FRCS 1969; *Books* A Colour Atlas of Cardiac Surgery - Acquired Heart Disease (1982), A Colour Atlas of Cardiac Surgery - Congenital Heart Disease (1984); *Recreations* skiing, riding, tennis; *Style—* James Monro, Esq; ✉ Rolle House, East Tytherley, Salisbury, Wiltshire SP5 1LQ (tel 01794 340266)

MONRO, Dr Jean Anne; *b* 31 May 1936; *Educ* St Helen's Sch Northwood, London Hosp Med Coll (MB BS); *m* 1 (widowed); 2 s (Alister, Neil); m 2, 1993 (widowed); *Career* house offr London Hosp 1960; W Herts Hosp Gp: SHO geriatric med 1962 (paediatrics 1961), registrar 1963, med asst 1967–79; hon clinical asst Nat Hosp for Nervous Diseases London 1974–84, assoc physician Edgware Gen Hosp 1979–82, clinical allergist Humana Hosp Wellington London 1982–84, Allergy and Environmental Med Clinic Hemel Hempstead 1984–88, Breakspear Hosp for Allergy and Environmental Med Abbots Langley 1988–93, Breakspear Hosp Hemel Hempstead 1993–, conslt physician in environmental med Fachkrankenhaus Nordfriesland Schleswig-Holstein 1994–; med dir Allergy and Environmental Med Dept (ltd co 1986–91) located at: Nightingale Hosp London 1984–86, Lister Hosp London 1986–89, Hosp of St John and St Elizabeth London 1989, Middlesex Hosp 1989–90, London Welbeck Hosp 1990–91; author of numerous pubns on allergy and nutrition related topics; formerly med journalist contributing to Hospital Doctor, Doctor and other jls; memb Bd Inst of Functional Med 1994–; former memb Sub-Ctee of Central Ctee for Hosp Med Servs; diplomate Int Bd of Environmental Med; memb: American Coll of Occupational and Environment Med, Soc of Occupational Med (GB), RSM, Hunterian Soc, Br Soc of Immunology; fell American Acad of Environmental Med; MRCS, LRCP, FAAEM, MACOEM; *Books* incl: Some Dietary Approaches to Disease Management (1974), Chemical Children (jtly, 1987), Handbook of Food Allergy (contrib, 1987), Food Allergy and Intolerance (contrib), Immunology of Myalgic Encephalomyelitis (contrib, 1988), Breakspear Guide to Allergies (contrib, 1991), Blanc Vite (contrib, 1998), Electromagnetic Environments in Buildings (contrib, 2004); *Style—* Dr Jean Monro; ✉ Breakspear Hospital, Hertfordshire House, Wood Lane, Hemel Hempstead, Hertfordshire HP2 4FD (tel 01442 261333, fax 01442 266388)

MONRO, Maj Gen the Hon Seymour Hector Russell Hale; CBE (1996); s of Baron Monro of Langholm, PC, AE (Life Peer) (d 2006), and Elizabeth Anne, *née* Welch; bro of Brig the Hon Hugh Monro, CBE, *qv*; *b* 7 May 1950; *Educ* Glenalmond Coll, RMA Sandhurst (Sword of Honour), Canadian Staff Coll Toronto, Army Staff Coll, Aust Coll of Defence and Strategic Studies (ACDSS) Canberra; *m* 16 April 1977, Angela, da of Wing Cdr Barney Sandeman; 3 s (Harry Seymour Edward b 29 Nov 1979, Alexander Hector Barney b 6 Sept 1981, Robert John Ewart b 15 Dec 1983); *Career* instr Army Staff Coll Camberley 1986–89, CO 1 Bn Queen's Own Highlanders (Germany, Belfast, the Gulf) 1989–91, Gen Staff MOD 1991–93, Cdr 39 Infantry Bde NI 1994–95, Pres Regular Commissions Bd Westbury 1996–97, Dep Chief Jt Ops Bosnia 1997, Dir of Infantry HQ Infantry 1998–2001, ADC 1998–2001, Dep Cdr NATO Rapid Reaction Corps (Italy) Milan 2001–03; dir Atlantic Salmon Tst 2004–; adjutant Queen's Body Guard for Scotland (Royal Co of Archers); vice-pres Royal Br Legion Scotland, chm Highlands and Islands Bd Prince's Tst Scotland 2004–07; *Recreations* stalking, shooting, fishing, golf, conservation, photography, reading, rugby, travel; *Clubs* New (Edinburgh); *Style—* Maj Gen the Hon Seymour Monro, CBE; ✉ Atlantic Salmon Trust, King James VI Business Centre, Friarton Road, Perth PH2 8DG (e-mail director@atlanticsalmontrust.org)

MONROE, Alexander John (Alex); s of William Stuart Monroe, of Suffolk, and Peggy-Ann, *née* Parish; *b* 27 June 1963; *Educ* Ipswich Sch for Boys, Ipswich Art Sch, Sir John Cass Sch of Art (BA); *m* m 25 July 1998, Denise Elizabeth, *née* Hill; 3 da (Verity Alice b 19 Oct 1997, Constance Bella b 3 April 1999, Liberty Grace b 28 June 2001); *Career* jewellery designer/mfr (estab 1987); exhibitions incl: Jablonex Int Jewellery Fair Czechoslovakia 1987, Br Designer Show London 1987 and 1990, Pret à Porter NY 1988, Fish and Foul (Hibiscus Gallery) 1989, A Beast of an Exhibition (Hollyhouse Gallery) 1989, London Works 1991, Sundials in the Study London 1991, London Works (Smiths Gallery London) 1991, The Who's Who Exhibition London 1992, London Designer Show 1992, Crafts in Performance (Crafts Cncl) 1993, Premier Classe 1993; work cmmnd by: Br Museum, BBC, World Gold Cncl, Browns (London), Barneys (NYC); work in the collections of: Sedgwick collection, Sainsbury private collection; Prince's Tst bursary 1987, Design Centre selection 1988, Gtr London Arts bursary (to make sundials) 1991; pt/t tutor Camden and Central London Insts and lectr Croydon Coll, London Enterprise Agency and Battersea Adult Educn 1988; memb Br Sundial Soc 1992–; *Publications* A Guide to Sundials with Special Reference to Portable Dial and Navigational Equipment (1990); *Recreations* sailing; *Style—* Alex Monroe, Esq; ✉ 9A Iliffe Yard, London SE17 3QA (tel 020 7703 8507)

MONSON, (John) Guy Elmhirst; s of Maj the Hon Jeremy Monson, and Patricia Mary Monson; *b* 11 September 1962; *Educ* Eton, Univ of Oxford (BA); *m* 17 March 1995, Lady (Olivia) Rose Mildred FitzRoy, da of 11 Duke of Grafton, KG, *qv*; 2 da (Olivia Effie Fortune b 8 Dec 1995, Leonora Grace b 19 Aug 1999); *Career* Sarasin Investment Management Ltd: joined 1984, dir 1989–, chief investment offr 1993–2007, ceo 2007–; chief investment offr Bank Sarasin Gp 1997–, ptnr Bank Sarasin & Co 2001; memb IMRO; *Recreations* flying, real tennis; *Clubs* White's, Pratt's; *Style—* Guy Monson, Esq; ✉ Sarasin Investment Management Ltd, Juxon House, 100 St Paul's Churchyard, London EC4M 8BU (tel 020 7038 7000, fax 020 7038 6850, e-mail guy.monson@sarasin.co.uk)

MONSON, 11 Baron (GB 1728); Sir John Monson; 15 Bt (E 1611); s of 10 Baron Monson (d 1958), and Bettie Northrup, da of late Lt-Col E Alexander Powell of Connecticut, USA (who m 2, 1962, Capt James Arnold Phillips d 1983); *b* 3 May 1932; *Educ* Eton, Trinity Coll Cambridge; *m* 1955, Emma, da of Anthony Devas (d 1958), and Mrs Rupert Shephard (d 1987); 3 s; *Heir* s, Hon Nicholas Monson; *Career* sits as Independent in House of Lords; pres Soc for Individual Freedom; *Style—* The Rt Hon the Lord Monson; ✉ The Manor House, South Carlton, Lincoln LN1 2RN (tel 01522 730263)

MONSON, Prof John Patrick; s of Joseph Patrick Monson (d 1973), and Margaret, *née* Connor (d 2004); *b* 11 July 1950; *Educ* Guy's Hosp Sch of Med (MB BS, MD), St George's Hosp, Royal London Hosp; *m* Eva Helena, *née* Lind; 2 s (Kevin b 8 Dec 1977, Andrew b 6 Jan 1981); *Career* reader in endocrinology London Hosp Med Coll 1994–95 (sr lectr 1982–94), reader in med Dept of Endocrinology Bart's 1995–99, prof and head clinical endocrinology Bart's and the Royal London Sch of Med and Dentistry 1999–2005, currently emeritus prof Queen Mary Univ of London and conslt physician and endocrinologist London Clinic Centre for Endocrinology; pres Ilford and Dist Diabetes Club; memb: MRS 1978, Soc for Endocrinology 1983, American Endocrine Soc 1995, Assoc of Physicians, Diabetes UK; FRCP, FRCPI; *Publications* Challenges in Growth Hormone Therapy (1999); author of numerous papers and articles on diabetes and endocrinology with particular reference to pituitary disease; *Recreations* theatre, film, music, skiing; *Clubs* Athenaeum; *Style—* Prof John Monson; ✉ London Clinic Centre for Endocrinology, 5 Devonshire Place, London W1G 6HL (tel 020 7616 7790, fax 020 7616 7791, e-mail johnmonson@aol.com)

MONTAGU, Sir Nicholas Lionel John; KCB (2001, CB 1993); s of John Eric Montagu (d 1990), and Barbara Joyce Montagu, OBE, *née* Gollin (d 1991); *b* 12 March 1944; *Educ* New Coll Oxford (MA); *m* 8 Aug 1974, Jennian, da of Ford Irvine Geddes, MBE; 2 da (Clare Barbara b 1976, Johanna Kythé b 1980); *Career* lectr in philosophy Univ of Reading 1969–74 (asst lectr 1966–69); DHSS (later DSS): princ 1974, seconded to Cabinet Office 1978–79, asst sec 1981, under sec 1986, dep sec 1990; dep sec (in charge public tport policy) Dept of Tport 1992–97, head Econ and Domestic Affairs Secretariat Cabinet Office 1997; chm Bd of Inland Revenue 1997–2004; memb Corp Finance Advsy Bd PricewaterhouseCoopers 2004–; Hon DUniv Middx 2001; *Publications* Brought to Account (Report of Scrutiny on National Insurance Records) 1981; *Recreations* cooking, wild flowers; *Style—* Sir Nicholas Montagu, KCB

MONTAGU OF BEAULIEU, 3 Baron (UK 1885); Edward John Barrington Douglas-Scott-Montagu; s of 2 Baron, KCIE, CSI, VD, JP, DL, pioneer motorist and sometime MP New Forest (d 1929, gs of 5 Duke of Buccleuch and Queensberry, KG, KT), by his 2 w, (Alice) Pearl, *née* Crake (d 1996, aged 101); *b* 20 October 1926; *Educ* St Peters Ct Broadstairs, Ridley Coll Ontario, Eton, New Coll Oxford; *m* 1, 1959 (m dis 1974), (Elizabeth) Belinda, o da of Capt Hon John de Bathe Crossley, JP (d 1935, yr bro of 2 Baron Somerleyton); 1 s (Hon Ralph b 1961), 1 da (Hon Mary Rachel b 1964); m 2, 1974, Fiona Margaret, da of R L D Herbert; 1 s (Hon Jonathan Deane b 1975); *Heir* s, Hon Ralph Douglas-Scott-Montagu; *Career* sits as Cons peer in House of Lords; proprietor of Beaulieu Estate and Abbey (originally a Cistercian Fndn of 1204); served with Grenadier Gds 1945–48; fndr: Montagu Motor Museum 1952 and Motor Cycle Museum 1956, Nat Motor Museum at Beaulieu 1972; fndr and ed Veteran and Vintage Magazine 1956–79; pres: Historic Houses Assoc 1973–78, Union of European Historic

M

Houses 1978–81, Fédération Internationale des Voitures Anciennes 1980–83, Museums Assoc 1982–84, Southern Tourist Bd 1977–2004, Assoc of Br Engrg Tport Museums; memb Devpt Cmmn 1980–84; chm: English Heritage (aka Historic Bldgs and Monuments Cmmn) 1983–92, British Vehicle Salvage Fed 1998–99; pres: Fedn Br Historic Vehicle Clubs 1989–, UK Vineyards Assoc, Tourism Soc, Inst of Journalists; chllr Wine Guild of the UK; author and lectr; hon DTech, hon memb RICS, FRSA, FIMI; *Publications* The Motoring Montagus (1959), Jaguar (1961), The Gordon Bennett Races (1963), The Gilt and the Gingerbread (1967), Lost Causes of Motoring: Europe (Vol I and II, 1969 and 1971), More Equal Than Others (1970), Early Days on the Road (1976), Royalty on the Road (1980), Home James (1982), The British Motorist (1987), English Heritage (1987), Daimler Century (1995), Wheels Within Wheels - An Unconventional Life (2000); *Recreations* shooting, water sports, sailing (yacht 'Cygnet of Beaulieu'), music, travel; *Clubs* House of Lords Yacht (Vice-Cdre), Beaulieu River Sailing (Cdre), Nelson Boat Owners' (Cdre), Historic Commercial Vehicle Soc (pres), Disabled Drivers' Motor (pres), Veteran Car (vice-pres), RAC, Beefsteak; *Style*— The Rt Hon the Lord Montagu of Beaulieu; ✉ Palace House, Beaulieu, Brockenhurst, Hampshire SO42 7ZN (tel 01590 614701, fax 01590 612623, e-mail lord.montagu@beaulieu.co.uk); Flat 11, Wyndham House, 24 Bryanston Square, London W1H 2DS (tel 020 7262 2603, fax 020 7724 3262)

MONTAGU-POLLOCK, Sir Giles Hampden; 5 Bt (UK 1872), of the Khyber Pass; s of Sir George Seymour Montagu-Pollock, 4 Bt (d 1985), and Karen-Sofie (d 1991), da of Hans Ludvig Dedekam, of Oslo, Norway; *b* 19 October 1928; *Educ* Eton, de Havilland Aeronautical Tech Sch; *m* 1963, Caroline Veronica, yr da of late Richard Francis Russell, of Wimbledon, London; 1 s (Guy Maximilian b 1966), 1 da (Sophie Amelia b 1969); *Heir* s, Guy Montagu-Pollock; *Career* with Airspeed Ltd 1949–51, G P Eliot at Lloyd's 1951–52, de Havilland Engine Co Ltd 1952–56; advtg mangr: Bristol Aeroplane Co Ltd 1956–59, Bristol Siddeley Engines Ltd 1959–61; assoc dir J Walter Thompson Co Ltd 1961–69; dir: C Vernon & Sons Ltd 1969–71, Acumen Marketing Gp 1971–74, 119 Pall Mall Ltd 1972–78; mgmnt conslt in mktg 1974–, assoc John Stork & Partners Ltd 1980–88, Korn/Ferry Int 1988–2002; *Recreations* water-skiing, sailing, photography, reading; *Style*— Sir Giles Montagu-Pollock, Bt; ✉ The White House, 7 Washington Road, London SW13 9BG (tel 020 8748 8491)

MONTAGUE, Sir Adrian Alastair; kt (2006), CBE (2001); s of Charles Edward Montague (d 1985), of Sevenoaks, Kent, and Olive, *née* Jones (d 1956); *b* 28 February 1948; *Educ* Mill Hill Sch, Trinity Hall Cambridge (MA); *m* 1, May 1970 (m dis 1982), Pamela Joyce (d 2000); 2 da (Emma b 1974, Olivia b 1980), 1 s (Edward b 1977); m 2, 8 Nov 1986, Penelope Jane Webb; 1 s (William b 1988); *Career* Linklaters & Paines: asst slr 1973–74, asst slr Paris 1974–77, asst slr London 1977–79, ptnr 1979–94; dir and head of project fin Kleinwort Benson Ltd 1994–97, co head global project fin Dresdner Kleinwort Benson 1997, chief exec Private Fin Initiative Taskforce HM Treasy 1997–2000, dep chm Partnerships UK plc 2000–01, sr int advsr Société Générale 2001–04, chair Michael Page International plc 2002– (dir 2001–), dep chm Network Rail 2002–04, chm British Energy 2002–, chm Cross London Rail Links 2004–; dir CellMark AB, chm Friends Provident 2005– (dir 2004–), chm Infrastructure Investors Ltd 2005–; memb Law Soc; *Books* Joint Ventures (ed with C G E Nightingale, 1989); *Style*— Sir Adrian Montague, CBE

MONTAGUE, Sarah Anne Louise; da of John Anthony Montague, and Mary Elizabeth, *née* O'Malley; *Educ* Blanchelande Coll, Univ of Bristol (BSc); *m* 2002, Richard Christopher Brooke; 3 da (Hope Mary, Florence Faith Harriet, Carola Irene Charity); *Career* broadcaster; stockbroker and eurobond dealer Natwest Capital Markets 1987–89; reporter Channel Television CI 1991–94, Reuters Television 1994–96, Sky News 1996–97, BBC radio and TV presenter 1997–, currently presenter Today Prog (Radio 4); also presented: Newsnight (BBC 2), news bulletins (BBC 1 and BBC News 24), Hardtalk (BBC World); *Style*— Ms Sarah Montague; ✉ BBC, Television Centre, Wood Lane, London W12 7RJ (tel 020 8624 9644, e-mail sarah.montague@bbc.co.uk)

MONTAGUE-JOHNSTONE, Roland Richard; s of Maj Roy Henry Montague-Johnstone, MBE (d 2004), of London, and Barbara Marjorie, *née* Warre (d 1990); gs of Maj F W Warre, OBE, MC, sometime chm of Sotheby's; ggs of Rev Edmond Warre, CB, CVO, DD, sometime headmaster and subsequently provost of Eton; *b* 22 January 1941; *Educ* Eton; *m* 24 Feb 1968, Sara Outram Boileau, da of Lt-Col John Garway Outram Whitehead, MC and Bar (d 1983), of Canterbury, Kent; 2 s (Andrew, William); *Career* KRRC served NI and Berlin 1958–62; admitted slr 1967; ptnr Slaughter and May 1973–91 (articled clerk 1962–67, asst slr 1967–73); warden St Mary the Virgin Powerstock 1994–2000; memb: Law Soc, CLA; *Recreations* reading, walking, gardening; *Clubs* Celer et Audax, Royal Green Jackets, ESU, Royal Over-Seas League; *Style*— Roland Montague-Johnstone, Esq; ✉ Poorton Hill, Powerstock, Bridport, Dorset DT6 3TJ

MONTAGUE-MASON, Perry; s of Arthur John Mason (d 1991), of Brighton, and Lily Beulah, *née* Montague; *b* 12 November 1956; *Educ* St Marylebone GS, Royal Acad of Music; *m* June 1979 (m dis 1981), Elizabeth, *née* Staples; m 2, May 1996, (Elizabeth) Anne Collis; 1 step da (Sally Elisabeth Sophia Lawrence-Archer b 1979); *Career* memb BBC Concert Orch 1976–80, guest princ London Philharmonic Orch; guest ldr: BBC Concert Orch, Ulster Orch, New Symphony Orch, New Sadler's Wells Opera Orch; co-ldr London Chamber Orch; ldr Mantovani Orch 1983–91, ldr and artistic dir Nat Symphony Orch 1992–; many major West End musicals incl Phantom of the Opera; session violinist with numerous musical acts incl Oasis, Bjork, Elton John, Spice Girls, Wet Wet Wet, Jamiroquai, Eric Clapton and Rod Stewart among many others 1994–; numerous performances on radio and TV; memb: Perry Montague-Mason Trio, Lochrian String Quartet, Quartet Caravaggio; memb Ctee Central London Branch Musicians' Union 1990–93; ARAM; *Recreations* ornithology, walking, riding, reading; *Style*— Perry Montague-Mason, Esq; ✉ 31 Roman Road, Birstall, Leicester LE4 4BB (tel 0116 267 2008)

MONTEAGLE OF BRANDON, 6 Baron (UK 1839); Gerald Spring Rice; s of 5 Baron (d 1946), and Emilie de Kosenko (d 1981), da of late Mrs Edward Brooks, of NY; *b* 5 July 1926; *Educ* Harrow; *m* 1949, Anne, da of Col Guy James Brownlow, DSO, DL (d 1960); 1 s, 3 da; *Heir* s, Hon Charles Spring Rice; *Career* Capt Irish Gds, ret 1955; memb: London Stock Exchange 1958–76, Lloyd's 1978–98, HM Body Guard of Hon Corps of Gentlemen-at-Arms 1978–96; *Clubs* Cavalry and Guards', Pratt's, Kildare St and University (Dublin); *Style*— The Rt Hon the Lord Monteagle of Brandon; ✉ Glenamara, Stradbally, Co Waterford, Ireland (tel 00 353 51 293136)

MONTEIRO DE CASTRO, Antonio; s of Antonio Monteiro de Castro, and Maria Jose Moreira; *b* 25 May 1945, São Paulo, Brazil; *Educ* Getulio Vargas Fndn São Paulo, Babson Coll Boston (MBA); *m* 3 March 1970, Reina; 3 da (Gabriela, Fernanda, Claudia); *Career* Gillette do Brasil 1968–79 (latterly finance dir), finance dir Alcoa 1979–89; British American Tobacco: pres and ceo Souza Cruz (Brazilian subsid) 1991 (vice-pres 1989), regnl dir Latin American and the Caribbean 1996, memb Bd 2002, chief operating offr 2004–; memb Getulio Vargas Fndn Bd Rio de Janeiro; *Recreations* opera, travelling, reading; *Style*— Antonio Monteiro de Castro, Esq; ✉ British American Tobacco plc, Globe House, 4 Temple Place, London WC2R 2PG (tel 020 7845 1931, fax 020 7845 2390)

MONTEITH, Brian; s of Donald Mcdonald Monteith, of Edinburgh, and Doreen Campbell, *née* Purves; *b* 8 January 1958; *Educ* Portobello HS, Heriot-Watt Univ; *m* 1 Sept 1984, Shirley Joyce, da of Peter Marshall; 2 s (Duncan Peter, Callum Douglas (twins) b 13 April 1988); *Career* nat chm Cons Students 1982–83, nat chm Scot Youngs Cons 1987–88; account exec Michael Forsyth Assoc London 1983–84 and 1985–86, Dunseath Stephen PR Edinburgh 1984–85, md Leith Communications Ltd 1986–91, PR dir Forth Marketing 1991–95, dir Communication Gp Scotland 1995–97, prop Dunedin PR 1997–99; MSP (Cons until 2005, then Ind) Scotland Mid and Fife 1999–2007; spokesman educn, culture and sport 1999–2003, spokesman fin, local govt and public servs 2003–05, convenor Audit Ctee Scot Parl 2003–07; fndr Cons Against Apartheid 1988, fndr Tuesday Club 1996; fndr and campaign mangr No No Campaign 1997; *Recreations* association football, books of John Buchan, buildings of David Bryce, visual and performing arts; *Style*— Brian Monteith, Esq; ✉ 8 Mountcastle Terrace, Edinburgh EH8 1SP (tel 0131 468 4381)

MONTGOMERIE, Colin; OBE (2005, MBE 1998); s of James Montgomerie, sec of Royal Troon Golf Club; *b* 23 June 1963; *m* June 1990 (m dis 2006), Eimear, *née* Wilson; 2 da (Olivia Rose b March 1993, Venetia Grace b Jan 1996), 1 s (Cameron Stuart b May 1998); *Career* professional golfer; amateur victories: Scottish Amateur Stroke-play Championship 1985, Scottish Amateur Championship 1987; tournament victories since turning professional 1987: Portuguese Open 1989, Scandinavian Masters 1991, 1999 and 2001, Dutch Open 1993, Volvo Masters 1993 and 2002, Spanish Open 1994, English Open 1994, German Open 1994 and 1995, Trophee Lancome 1995, Dubai Desert Classic 1996, Irish Open 1996, 1997 and 2001, European Masters 1996, Sun City Million Dollar Challenge 1996, European Grand Prix 1997, King Hassan II Trophy 1997, World Cup (Individual) 1997, Andersen Consulting World Champion 1997, PGA Championship 1998, 1999 and 2000, German Masters 1998, British Masters 1998, Benson and Hedges International Open 1999, Standard Life Loch Lomond Invitational 1999, Int Open Munich 1999, World Matchplay Championships Wentworth 1999, French Open Paris 2000, Skins Game USA 2000, Ericsson Australian Masters 2001, TCL Classic 2002, Macau Open 2003, European Open Ireland 2007; US Open: third 1992, second 1994 and 1997; second The Open R&A 2005; US PGA 1995 (second); Tournament Players Championship 1996 (second); team memb: Eisenhower Trophy (amateur) 1984 and 1986, Walker Cup (amateur) 1985 and 1987, Alfred Dunhill Cup 1988, 1991, 1992, 1993, 1994, 1995 (winners), 1996, 1997, 1998, 1999 and 2000, World Cup 1988, 1991, 1992, 1993, 1997, 1998 and 1999, Ryder Cup 1991, 1993, 1995 (winners), 1997 (winners), 1999, 2002 (winners), 2004 (winners) and 2006 (winners), UBS Cup 2003; Henry Cotton Rookie of the Year 1988, winner European Order of Merit 1993, 1994, 1995, 1996, 1997, 1998 and 1999; *Recreations* motor cars, music, DIY; *Style*— Colin Montgomerie, Esq, OBE; ✉ c/o IMG, Pier House, Strand on the Green, London W4 3NN

MONTGOMERIE, Lorna Burnett (Mrs John Anderson); da of late (James) Fraser Montgomerie, of Helensburgh, Dunbartonshire, and Jane Burnett Sangster (Jean), *née* McCulloch; *b* 23 October 1953; *Educ* St George's Sch Montreal, North London Collegiate Sch Edgware, Churchill Coll Cambridge (MA), Coll of Law Lancaster Gate; *m* 8 July 1983, John Venner Anderson, s of late Prof John Anderson, of Park Langley, Beckenham, Kent; 1 s, 1 da (twins b 15 July 1992); *Career* admitted slr 1978, asst slr Biddle & Co 1978–80, annotator Halsbury's Statutes 1981, ed Encyclopaedia of Forms and Precedents (4 edn) 1981–85; Butterworths Ltd: R&D mangr 1985–89, editorial systems mangr 1989–93, ed Statutory Materials 1993–2000; articles written for: Dance 1986–87, The New Law Journal 1987–88, Holborn Report and Articles in Holborn (for Holborn Law Soc) 1989–92; memb: Ctee of Holborn Law Soc 1983–97, London Legal Educn Ctee (as rep for Holborn Law Soc) 1988–89, Law Soc Panel monitoring articles in Holborn Area 1987–2000; hon auditor Holborn Law Soc 2001–02; memb Law Soc 1978; *Recreations* reading, DIY, house renovation, sailing; *Style*— Ms Lorna Montgomerie; ✉ e-mail lorna.montgomerie@bcs.org.uk

MONTGOMERY, Alexander Jamieson (Alex); s of Walter Montgomery, of Eastbourne, and Helen, *née* Jamieson; *b* 12 August 1943; *Educ* Hyndland Sr Sch Glasgow; *m* 9 June 1970, Anne, da of James Robertson; 2 da (Helen Robertson b 16 June 1972, Katie Elizabeth b 24 Jan 1974); *Career* sports writer; various jobs Glasgow 1959–61, football reporter Sunday Post and Weekly News Glasgow/Newcastle/Manchester 1963–68, news reporter Sunday Express 1968, sports reporter Hayter's Sports Agency 1968–70, sports reporter Daily Mail 1970–71; The Sun: football reporter 1971–83, chief football writer 1983–92, football feature writer 1992–93; chief football news reporter Today 1993–95, chief football reporter News of the World 1996, currently with Mail on Sunday; chm Football Writers' Assoc 1994–95 (vice-chm 1993); dir AM Consultancy Ltd; *Recreations* sport, music; *Clubs* Royal Cwlth; *Style*— Mr Alex Montgomery; ✉ 36 Downside Close, Eastbourne, East Sussex BN20 8EL (mobile 07785 250439, e-mail vi22@dial.pipex.com)

MONTGOMERY, Archdeacon of; *see:* Griffith, Ven David Vaughan

MONTGOMERY, (Hugh) Bryan Greville; s of Hugh Roger Greville Montgomery, MC, and Molly Audrey Montgomery, OBE, *née* Neele; *b* 26 March 1929; *Educ* Repton, Lincoln Coll Oxford (MA); *Career* fndr memb Oxford Univ Wine and Food Soc, conslt and advsr on trade fairs and developing countries for UN, conslt Int Garden Festival Liverpool 1984, dir Andry Montgomery gp of cos (organisers, mangrs and conslts in exhibitions); chm: Br Assoc of Exhibition Organisers 1970–72, Int Ctee American Nat Assoc of Exposition Mangrs 1980–82 and 1990–92, Br Exhibition Promotion Cncl 1981–83; pres Union des Foires Int 1994–97 (vice-pres 1987–93); memb: Cncl Design and Industries Assoc 1983–85, Advsy Bd Inst of Hotel Mgmnt Montreux 1986–2001, London Regnl Ctee CBI 1987–89, Br Overseas Trade Bd 1990–93; chm: Interbuild Fund 1972–2004, Tstees Supply of Equipment to Charity Hosps Overseas (ECHO) 1978–89, Br Architectural Library Tst 1989–99, The Building Museum 1988–2000, Bd World Trade Centres Assoc 2000– (memb 1996–); vice-chm Bldg Conservation Tst 1979–94; dir Centre for Exhibition Industry Research USA 1998–2001; fndr: World Acad 1987–2001, The Montgomery Sculpture Tst, World Trade Center Novosibirsk; tstee: The Cubitt Tst 1982–98, Music for the World 1990–92, Thames Festival Tst 2002–, Mitchell City of London Charity and Educnl Fndn; hon treas Contemporary Art Soc 1980–82, cncllr Acad of St Martin-in-the-Fields Concert Soc 1986–2000; CGLI: memb Exec Ctee 1974–2003, chm Int Ctee 1997–2000; memb Exec Ctee Nat Fund for Res into Crippling Diseases 1970–91, memb Chancellor's Court of Benefactors Univ of Oxford 1999, Fleming fell Lincoln Coll Oxford 1996; chm The Montgomery Network; govr Guildhall Sch of Music and Drama 2001–04; councilman City of London (Dowgate Ward) 1999–2004; Liveryman Worshipful Co of Tylers and Bricklayers 1952 (Master 1980–81, tstee Charitable and Pension Tsts 1981–2000), Master Worshipful Co of World Traders 1995; voted Siberian Foreign Businessman in Novosibirsk 1993; Silver Jubilee Medal 1977, Pro Arte Hungaria Medal 1991, Brooch of the City of Utrecht 1992, UFI Gold Medal 1998; Hon Dr Humane Letters Endicott Coll 2003; Hon FRIBA 2000, Hon FCGLI 2003; *Books* Industrial Fairs and Developing Countries (UNIDO, 1975), Going into Trade Fairs (UNCTAD/GATT, 1982), Exhibition Planning and Design (1989, trans Russian 1994 and Chinese 2000); publisher and contrib Great Exhibitions: 150 Years; also contrib to int Trade Forum; *Recreations* collecting contemporary sculpture; *Clubs* Oxford and Cambridge, City Livery; *Style*— Bryan Montgomery, Esq; ✉ 9 Manchester Square, London W1U 3PL (tel 020 7886 3123, fax 020 7224 5270, e-mail bryan.montgomery@montex.co.uk); Snells Farm, Amersham Common, Buckinghamshire HP7 9QN

MONTGOMERY, Clare Patricia; QC (1996); da of Dr Stephen Ross Montgomery, of Bath, and Ann Margaret, *née* Barlow; *b* 29 April 1958; *Educ* Millfield, UCL (LLB); *m* 14 Dec 1991, Victor Stefan Melleney; 2 da (Natasha b 27 Dec 1994, Anna b 3 June 1997); *Career* called to the Bar Gray's Inn 1980, recorder 1999–, dep judge of the High Ct 2003–; capt Br Women's Foil Team 1992–96; *Style*— Miss Clare Montgomery, QC; ✉ Matrix Chambers Gray's Inn, London WC1R 5LN (tel 020 7404 3447, fax 020 7404 3448, e-mail claremontgomery@matrixlaw.co.uk)

MONTGOMERY, Sir (Basil Henry) David; 9 Bt (UK 1801), of Stanhope, Peeblesshire, JP (Kinross-shire 1966), CVO (2007), DL (Kinross 1960 and Perth 1975); s of Lt-Col Henry Keith Purvis-Russell Montgomery, OBE (d 1954), suc uncle, Sir Basil Russell Purvis-Russell-Hamilton-Montgomery, 8 Bt (d 1964); *b* 20 March 1931; *Educ* Eton; *m* 1956, Delia, da of Adm Sir (John) Peter Lorne Reid, GCB, CVO; 2 s (1 decd) (James David Keith b 1957), 4 da (Caroline Jean (Mrs Nicholas J K Liddle) b 1959, Davina Lucy (Mrs Humphrey M Butler) b 1961, Iona Margaret (Mrs Benjamin Romer-Lee) b 1972, Laura Elizabeth (Mrs David Redvers) b 1974); *Heir* s, James Montgomery; *Career* Tayside Regnl Cncl 1974–79, vice-pres Convention of Scottish Local Authorities (COSLA) 1978–79, Nature Conservancy Cncl 1974–79, chm Forestry Commission 1979–89, Lord-Lt of Perth and Kinross 1995–2006; Hon LLD Dundee 1977; *Style*— Sir David Montgomery, Bt, CVO; ✉ Home Farm, Kinross KY13 8EU (tel 01577 863416, e-mail david@thehomefarm.co.uk)

MONTGOMERY, David; *b* 8 February 1937, Brooklyn, NYC; *Educ* Midwood HS, Juilliard Sch of Music; *m* 1 (m dis); 2 da; m 2, 1982, Martine King; 1 s, 1 da; *Career* former musician; professional photographer 1964–; worked for: Jocelyn Stevens at Queen Magazine, The Sunday Times Magazine, Vogue, Tatler, Harpers & Queen, Rolling Stone, New York Times; has photographed: HM Queen Elizabeth II, HM Queen Elizabeth The Queen Mother, Lord Home, Lord Callaghan, Sir Edward Heath, Lady Thatcher, King Hussein of Jordan, The Duke and Duchess of York plus innumerable personalities; winner many int awards; *Recreations* gardening, photography, contemporary guitar; *Style*— David Montgomery, Esq; ✉ c/o M & M Management, Studio B, 11 Edith Grove, London SW10 (tel 020 7823 3723, fax 020 7351 3714)

MONTGOMERY, David John; s of William John Montgomery, and Margaret Jean, *née* Flaherty; *b* 6 November 1948; *Educ* Bangor GS, Queen's Univ Belfast (BA); *m* 1, 1971 (m dis 1987), Susan Frances Buchanan, da of James Francis Buchanan Russell, QC; m 2, 1989 (m dis 1997), Heidi, da of Dr Edward Kingstone, of McMaster, Ontario; m 3, 1997, Sophie, formerly w of 3 Earl of Woolton, *qv*, and da of 3 Baron Birdwood, *qv*; 1 s (b 15 July 2001); *Career* asst chief sub ed Daily Mirror 1978–80 (sub ed 1973–78), chief sub ed The Sun 1980–82, asst ed Sunday People 1982–84, ed News of the World 1985–87, ed and md Today 1987–91 (Newspaper of the Year 1988); md News UK 1987–91; chief exec Mirror Group plc 1992–99; dir: News Group Newspapers 1986–91, Satellite TV plc 1986–91, London Live Television 1991–99, Caledonian Newspaper Publishing Ltd 1992, Newspaper Publishing 1994–98, Donohue Inc 1992–95, Scottish Television 1995–99, Press Assoc 1996–99; chm: TRI-MEX Gp Ltd 1999–2002, MECOM Gp plc 2000, YAVA 2000–02, Integrated Educn Fund Devpt Bd NI 2000, African Lakes plc 2000–07, Campaign for Peace and Democratic Reconstruction for NI 2002, Team Northern Ireland 2002, West 175 Media Inc 2002–06, Berliner Verlag (Germany) 2005, Media Gp Limburg (Netherlands) 2006; *Style*— David Montgomery, Esq; ✉ 15 Collingham Gardens, London SW5 0HS (tel 020 7370 3106, fax 020 7244 7864, e-mail dmontgomery@tri-mex.com)

MONTGOMERY, Rev Prof John Warwick; Baron of Kiltartan and Lord of Morris, Comte de St-Germain de Montgommery; s of Maurice Warwick Montgomery (d 1993), and Harriet Genevieve, *née* Smith (d 1986); *b* 18 October 1931; *Career* academic, barr (Middle Temple, Lincoln's Inn, US Supreme Court Bar and Paris Bar), theologian; ordained to ministry Lutheran Church 1958; assoc prof Dept of History Wilfred Laurier Univ Ontario 1960–64, prof of history, prof of Christian thought and dir European Seminar Prog Trinity Evangelical Divinity School Illinois 1964–74, prof of law and theology Sch of Law George Mason Univ Virginia 1974–75, theological conslt Christian Legal Soc 1975–76, dir of studies International Inst of Human Rights Strasbourg 1979–81; fndr dean, prof of jurisprudence and dir European Prog Sch of Law Simon Greenleaf Univ California 1980–88, distinguished prof of theology and law Faith Evangelical Lutheran Seminary Washington State 1989–91; Univ of Beds: princ lectr in law 1991–92, reader in law 1992–93, prof of law and humanities 1993–97, prof emeritus 1997–; distinguished prof of apologetics and law and vice-pres of academic affairs (UK and Europe) Trinity Coll and Theological Seminary Indiana 1997–2007, distinguished prof of law Regent Univ Virginia 1997–99, distinguished prof of philosophy and Christian thought Patrick Henry Coll Virginia 2007–; sr counsel European Centre for Law and Justice Strasbourg 1997–2001; visiting prof: Concordia Theological Seminary Illinois 1964–67, De Paul Univ Chicago 1967–70, Concordia Univ Irvine California 2006; hon pres Academic Bd Int Inst for Religious Freedom Germany 2005–; memb: ALA, European Acad of Arts, Sciences and Humanities, Lawyers' Christian Fellowship (hon vice-pres 1995–), National Conference of Univ Profs, California, Virginia, DC and Washington State Bar Assocs, Int Bar Assoc, World Assoc of Law Profs, American Soc of Int Law, Union Internationale des Avocats, American Historical Assoc, Presbyterian Historical Soc (NI), Heraldry Soc, Soc of Genealogists, Tyndale Fellowship, American Theological Library Assoc, Evangelical Theology Soc, Tolkien Soc, C S Lewis Soc, Creation Research Soc, Stair Soc (Scotland), Int Wine and Food Soc, Chaîne des Rôtisseurs, Académie Internationale des Gourmets et des Traditions Gastronomiques, Club Prosper Montagné Paris, Soc des Amis des Arts Strasbourg, Sherlock Holmes Soc; fell: American Scientific Affiliation, Trinity Coll Indiana, Victoria Inst London (hon vice-pres 2004–), Soc for Advanced Legal Studies; Freeman City of London, Freeman and Liveryman Worshipful Co of Scriveners; FRSA; *Publications* books incl: Slaughter of the Innocents (1981), The Marxist Approach to Human Rights: Analysis and Critique (1984), Human Rights and Human Dignity (1987), Evidence for Faith: Deciding the God Question (1991), Giant in Chains: China Today and Tomorrow (1994), Law and Morality: Friends or Foes (1994), Jésus: la raison rejoint l'histoire (with C Cranfield and D Kilgour, 1995), Christians in the Public Square (with C Cranfield and D Kilgour, 1996), Conflicts of Law (1997), The Transcendental Holmes (2000), The Repression of Evangelism in Greece (2001), Christ our Advocate (2002), Tractatus Logico-Theologicus (2002), History, Law and Christianity (2002), Heraldic Aspects of the German Reformation (2003), The Church: Blessing or Curse? (2004); author of articles in numerous learned jls; *Films* incl: Is Christianity Credible? (1968), In Search of Noah's Ark (1977), Defending the Biblical Gospel (1985); *Recreations* 16th and 17th century rare books, antique Citroën cars, Macintosh computers; *Clubs* Athenaeum; *Style*— The Rev Prof Dr John Warwick Montgomery; ✉ No 9, 4 Crane Court, Fleet Street, London EC4A 2EJ (tel 020 7583 1210); 2 rue de Rome, 67000 Strasbourg, France (tel 00 33 3 88 61 08 82)

MONTGOMERY, Richard John; s of Basil Richard Montgomery, of Tonbridge, Kent, and Mary Elizabeth, *née* Goddard; *b* 5 May 1955; *Educ* Tonbridge, Univ of Newcastle upon Tyne (MB BS); *m* 3 July 1982, Angela, da of John Todd, of Newcastle upon Tyne; 1 s (Duncan Richard b 16 Nov 1991), 3 da (Clare Louise b 20 Sept 1987, Esme Helen b 16 Feb 1993, Eleanor Frances b 29 Nov 1995); *Career* demonstrator in anatomy Univ of Newcastle Med Sch 1979–80; post grad trg Northern Region: surgery 1980–83, orthopaedic surgery 1983–88; orthopaedic research fell Mayo Clinic Rochester Minnesota USA 1986–87, conslt in traumatic and orthopaedic surgery N and S Tees Health Dist 1989–91, conslt in traumatic and orthopaedic surgery S Tees Health Dist 1991–; hon clinical lectr Faculty of Med Univ of Newcastle upon Tyne 1996–; Univ of Teesside: hon lectr Sch of Human Studies 1996–, visiting fell Sch of Health and Social Care 2002–; memb Panel of Examiners Intercollegiate Speciality Bd for Trauma and Orthopaedic Surgery 2002–; memb: Br Soc for Children's Orthopaedic Surgery (hon treas 2006–), Br Limb Reconstruction Soc (hon treas 2002–), Br Assoc for Surgery of the Knee, Br Orthopaedic Assoc, BMA; FRCSEd 1983 (memb Panel of Examiners 2001–); *Recreations* sailing; *Style*— Richard Montgomery, Esq; ✉ The James Cook University Hospital, Middlesbrough, Teesside TS4 3BW (tel 01642 850850)

MONTGOMERY CUNINGHAME, Sir John Christopher Foggo; 12 Bt (NS 1672), of Corsehill, Ayrshire; s of Col Sir Thomas Andrew Alexander Montgomery Cuninghame, 10 Bt, DSO, JP (d 1945) and his 2 w, Nancy Macaulay, *née* Foggo; suc bro Sir William Andrew Malcolm Martin Oliphant Montgomery Cuninghame, 11 Bt (d 1959); *b* 24 July 1935; *Educ* Fettes, Worcester Coll Oxford; *m* 9 Sept 1964, Laura Violet, 2 da of Sir Godfrey Nicholson, 1 Bt (d 1991); 3 da (Christian Elizabeth (Mrs David McDonald) b 1967, Georgiana Rose (Mrs Rageh Omaar) b 1969, Elizabeth Clara (Mrs Ben Brabyn) b 1971); *Heir* none; *Career* Nat Serv 2 Lt Rifle Bde; dir: Primentia Inc, Global Sourcing Inc, Mannin Industries and other cos; *Clubs* Boodle's, Pratt's; *Style*— Sir John Montgomery Cuninghame, Bt; ✉ The Old Rectory, Brightwalton, Berkshire RG20 7BL

MONTGOMERY OF ALAMEIN, 2 Viscount (UK 1946); David Bernard Montgomery; CMG (2000), CBE (1975); o s of 1 Viscount Montgomery of Alamein, KG, GCB, DSO (d 1976), and Elizabeth, *née* Hobart (d 1937); *b* 18 August 1928; *Educ* Winchester, Trinity Coll Cambridge; *m* 1, 27 Feb 1953 (m dis 1967), Mary Raymond, yr da of Sir Charles Connell (d 1973); 1 s, 1 da; m 2, 30 Jan 1970, Tessa, da of Lt-Gen Sir Frederick A M Browning, GCVO, KBE, CB, DSO (d 1965), and Lady Browning, DBE (Daphne du Maurier, the writer, d 1989), and former w of Maj Peter de Zulueta; *Heir* s, Hon Henry Montgomery; *Career* sat as Cons peer in House of Lords 1976–99, elected ind (crossbench) peer 2005–; dir Yardley International 1963–74, md Terimar Services Ltd (overseas trade consultancy) 1974–2000, chm Baring Puma Fund 1991–2002; memb Editorial Advsy Bd Vision Interamericana 1974–94; cncllr RBC&K 1974–78; chm: Hispanic and Luso Brasilian Cncl Canning House 1978–80 (pres 1987–94), Antofagasta (Chile) and Bolivia Railway Co and subsids 1980–82; vice-pres Brazilian C of C GB 1983– (chm 1980–82), chm European Atlantic Group 1992–94 (pres 1994–97); non-exec dir: Korn/Ferry Int 1977–93, Northern Engrg Industries 1980–87; patron D-Day and Normandy Fellowship 1980–94, Eighth Army Veterans Assoc 1984–2002; patron Restaurateurs Assoc of GB 1990–99 (pres 1982–90); pres: Centre for International Briefing Farnham Castle 1983–2003, Univ of Cambridge Engrgs Assoc 2001–06; Anglo-Argentine Soc 1976–87, Redgrave Theatre Farnham 1978–90, Anglo-Belgian Soc 1994–2006; Liveryman Worshipful Co of Mercers; Gran Oficial Orden Bernardo O'Higgins (Chile) 1989, Gran Oficial Orden Libertador San Martin (Argentina) 1992, Grande Oficial Orden Nacional Cruzeiro do Sul (Brazil) 1993, Encomienda Orden de Isabel la Catolica (Spain) 1993, Commanders Cross Order of Merit (Germany) 1993, Encomienda Orden del Aguila Azteca (Mexico) 1994, Commander Order of Leopold II (Belguim) 1997, Gran Cruz Orden de San Carlos (Colombia) 1998, Gran Ofical Orden del Libertador (Venezuela) 1999; *Books* The Lonely Leader - Monty 1944–45 (with Alistair Horne, 1994); *Clubs* Garrick, Canning; *Style*— The Rt Hon Viscount Montgomery of Alamein, CMG, CBE; ✉ 2/97 Onslow Square, London SW7 3LU (tel 020 7589 8747, fax 020 7589 5020)

MONTROSE, 8 Duke of (S 1707); Sir James Graham; 11 Bt (S 1625), of Braco; also Lord Graham (S 1445), Earl of Montrose (S 1505), Marquess of Montrose (S 1644, new charter granted 1706), Marquess of Graham and Buchanan, Earl of Kincardine, Viscount Dundaff, Lord Aberuthven, Mugdock and Fintrie (all S 1707), Earl Graham and Baron Graham (GB 1722); also Hereditary Sheriff of Dunbartonshire; s of 7 Duke of Montrose (d 1992), and his 1 w, Isobel Veronica, *née* Sellar (d 1990); *b* 6 April 1935, Salisbury, Rhodesia; *Educ* Loretto; *m* 1970, Catherine Elizabeth MacDonnell, yst da of Capt Norman Andrew Thompson Young (d 1942), Queen's Own Cameron Highlanders of Canada; 1 da (Lady Hermione Elizabeth b 1971), 2 s (James Alexander Norman, Marquess of Graham b 1973, Lord Ronald John Christopher b 1975); *Heir* s, Marquess of Graham; *Career* farmer and landowner; Capt Queen's Body Guard for Scotland (Royal Co of Archers) 2006– (Ensign 2001–03, Lt 2003–06); sits as Cons in House of Lords (elected hereditary peer 1999–), oppn whip 2001–, oppn spokesman for Scottish affrs; memb Cncl NFU of Scotland 1981–86 and 1987–90 (vice-chm Loch Lomond and Trossachs Working Pty 1991–93), pres Royal Highland and Agricultural Soc of Scotland 1997–98; chm Buchanan Community Cncl 1982–93; OStJ 1978; *Clubs* Royal Scottish Pipers' Soc, Royal Highland Agric Soc, The Farmers; *Style*— His Grace the Duke of Montrose; ✉ Montrose Estates Ltd, Buchanan Castle, Drymen, Glasgow G63 0HY (tel and fax 01360 870382); House of Lords, London SW1A 0PW (tel 020 7219 3000, fax 020 7219 5979, e-mail montrosej@parliament.uk)

MOODY, Prof (Anthony) David; s of Edward Tabrum Moody, of Dunedin, NZ, and Nora, *née* Gordon; *b* 21 January 1932; *Educ* St Patrick's Coll Wellington, Canterbury Coll Univ of NZ (MA), Univ of Oxford (MA); *Career* Shirtcliffe fell Univ of NZ 1953–55, asst info offr UNHCR Geneva 1957–58, sr lectr Univ of Melbourne 1958–64, Nuffield Fndn travelling fell 1965, memb Dept of English and Related Literature Univ of York 1966–99 (emeritus prof 2000–); fell English Assoc (FEA); *Books* Virginia Woolf (1963), Shakespeare: 'The Merchant of Venice' (1964), 'The Waste Land' In Different Voices (ed, 1972), Thomas Stearns Eliot: Poet (1979 and 1994), At the Antipodes: Homage to Paul Valéry (1982), News Odes: The El Salvador Sequence (1984), The Cambridge Companion to T S Eliot (ed, 1994), Tracing T S Eliot's Spirit: Essays (1996), Ezra Pound: Poet, A Portrait of the Man and His Work - Vol 1, the Young Genius 1885–1920 (2007); *Recreations* listening, looking, hill walking; *Style*— Prof A David Moody; ✉ Church Green House, Old Church Lane, Pateley Bridge, North Yorkshire HG3 5LZ

MOODY, Lewis Walton; MBE (2004); *b* 12 June 1978, Ascot, Berks; *Educ* Oakham Sch; *Career* rugby union player (flanker); currently with Leicester Tigers RUFC (winners Madrid Sevens 1997, winners four successive Premiership titles 1999–2002, winners Heineken Cup 2001 and 2002); England: 46 caps, debut v Canada 2001, ranked no 1 team in world 2003, winners Six Nations Championship 2003 (Grand Slam), winners World Cup Aust 2003, memb squad World Cup France 2007; memb Br & I Lions tour squad NZ 2005 (2 Test caps); Zurich England Young Player of the Season 2001/02; *Style*— Mr Lewis Moody, MBE; ✉ c/o Leicester Tigers, Aylestone Road, Leicester LE2 7TR

MOODY, Nicola; *Educ* Saffron Walden Co HS, Cambridge Coll of Arts and Educn, Univ of York (BA), Middlesex Poly (Dip Film and TV); *Career* researcher rising to dir BBC Manchester 1987–88, documentaries dir Diverse Productions 1988, dir, prodr and dep ed (documentaries and feature) BBC TV London 1988–94, ed Reportage BBC Manchester 1994–96, exec prodr factual series 1995–97, commissioning exec then head of factual commissioning Ind Commissioning Gp BBC London 1997–2000, controller factual commissioning BBC TV 2000–03, acting controller BBC4 2003, cmmr documentaries and contemporary factual BBC TV 2003–05, dir of factual progs Optomen TV 2005–; memb RTS 1999; *Recreations* writing, film, walking; *Style*— Ms Nicola Moody; ✉ Optomen Television Ltd, 1 Valentine Place, London SE1 8QH

MOODY, Philip Edward; s of Frederick Osborne Moody, and Hilda Laura, *née* Frost; *b* 28 July 1954; *Educ* Bentley GS Calne; *Career* CA; articled clerk Monahan & Co Chippenham 1972–82; Solomon Hare: fndr ptnr Chippenham 1983–88, sr ptnr and lead corporate finance ptnr Bristol 1989–2005, managing ptnr Bristol 2005–07; dir Centaur Grain Ltd 1990–, corp devpt dir Dairy Farmers of Britain Ltd 2003–, head of corporate finance Smith & Williamson 2005–, dir English Farming Food Patnerships Ltd; FCA 1990 (ACA 1980), ATII 1982; *Recreations* Formula 1, walking, photography, snooker, cricket; *Style*— Philip Moody, Esq; ✉ Solomon Hare LLP, Oakfield House, Oakfield Grove, Clifton, Bristol BS8 2BN (tel 0117 933 3211, e-mail philip_moody@solomonhare.co.uk)

MOODY-STUART, Sir Mark; KCMG (2000); *b* 15 September 1940, Antigua; *Educ* Univ of Cambridge (BA, PhD); *m* Judy; 3 s, 1 da; *Career* Royal Dutch/Shell Group: joined Shell Internationale Petroleum Maatschappij BV as geologist 1966, worked as geologist in Spain, Oman and Brunei 1966–72, chief geologist Australia 1972–76, i/c North Sea oil

M

exploration teams 1976–78, servs mangr Brunei 1978–79, mangr Western Div Shell Petroleum Development Co of Nigeria 1979–82, gen mangr Shell Group of Cos Turkey 1982–86, chm and chief exec Shell Cos in Malaysia 1986–90, gp exploration and prodn coordinator 1990–94, dir Shell International Petroleum Co 1991–2001, a gp md 1991–2001, chm Shell Transport and Trading Co plc 1997–2001 (an md 1991–97), non-exec dir 2001–05; chm Anglo American plc 2002–, dir Accenture 2001–, non-exec dir HSBC Holdings plc 2001–; chm Business Action for Sustainable Devpt 2001–02, co-chm G8 Renewable Energy Taskforce 2000–01, memb UN Sec Gen's Advsy Cncl for the Global Compact 2001–04, vice-chair UN Global Compact Bd and chm Global Compact Forum 2006–; pres Liverpool Sch of Tropical Med 2001–, chm Int Advsy Cncl SOAS 2004–; govr Nuffield Hosps 2000–; FGS (pres 2002–04), FRGS; *Recreations* sailing, travel; *Style—* Sir Mark Moody-Stuart, KCMG; ✉ Anglo American plc, 20 Carlton House Terrace, London SW1Y 5AN (tel 020 7968 8709)

MOON, Doug; s of Charles Douglas Moon (d 1975), and Lydia Jane Llewellyn, *née* Barnes; *b* 17 August 1950, Preston, Lancs; *Educ* Open Univ (BA), Leeds Metropolitan Univ (Cert, Dip); *m* 15 July 1972, Elizabeth Emily, *née* Lewthwaite; 1 da (Mellissa Kay b 2 Aug 1979), 2 s (Andrew Duncan b 26 Feb 1984, Stuart Gordon b 24 Nov 1990); *Career* prison offr HMP Preston 1974, HM Borstal Huntercombe 1974, hosp offr HMP Oxford 1978–82, hosp sr offr HMP Grendon 1982–88, hosp princ offr HMP Wormwood Scrubs 1988–92, i/c healthcare HMP Belmarsh 1992–94, head of regimes/dep govr HMP Cookham Wood 1996–97, mangr then head of prisoner mgmnt HMP Elmley 1997–99, staff offr to the area mangr South Coast Area 1999–2001, staff offr to the Area Mangr London Area 2001–02, dep govr HMP Dartmoor 2002–03, sr mangr and area lead on resettlement for S W Area prisons 2003–05, govr HMP Erlestoke 2005–; memb Wilts Criminal Justice Bd; *Style—* Doug Moon, Esq; ✉ HMP Erlestoke, Devizes, Wiltshire SN10 5TU (tel 01380 814402, e-mail douglas.moonDA@hmps.gsi.gov.uk)

MOON, Madeleine; MP; da of Albert Edward Ironside, and Hilda, *née* Greener; *b* 27 March 1950, Sunderland; *m* 2 June 1983, Stephen John Moon; 1 s (David Stephen b 16 May 1984); *Career* social worker Care Standards Inspectorate until 2005; former Mayor Porthcawl, cncllr Porthcawl 1992–, rep Bridgend CBC on Sports Cncl for Wales and Tourism S and W Wales Ctee, Nat Chair Br Resorts Assoc 1999–2001; MP (Lab) Bridgend 2005–; *Style—* Mrs Madeleine Moon, MP; ✉ House of Commons, London SW1A 0AA

MOON, Michael (Mick); s of Donald Charles Moon, and Marjorie, *née* Metcalfe; *b* 9 November 1937; *Educ* Shoreham GS, Chelsea Sch of Art, RCA; *m* Anjum, da of Abdul Khalid Khan; 2 s (Timur b 26 Aug 1977, Adam Khalid b 9 Feb 1982); *Career* artist; sr lectr in painting Slade Sch of Art 1973–90; *Solo Exhibitions* Waddington Galleries 1969, 1970, 1972, 1978, 1984, 1986 and 1992, Tate Gallery 1976, Dolan Maxwell Philadelphia 1986, Pace Prints NY 1987, Kass Meridien Gallery Chicago 1992, Alan Cristea Gallery London 1996, Serge Sorokko Gallery San Francisco 1996; *Group Exhibitions* Young Contemporaries Exhbn 1963, Caulfield Hodgkin Moon (Paris) 1972, La Peinture Anglaise d'Aujourd'hui (Musée d'Art Paris) 1973, British Painting (Hayward Gallery) 1974, Recent Purchases of the Arts Cncl (Serpentine Gallery) 1983, Perspecta Survey of Work in Australia 1983, American and European Monoprints (Pace Gallery NYC) 1987; major Arts Cncl award 1980, first prize John Moores Exhbn 1984, Gulbenkian Print Award; *Work in Public Collections* Art Gallery of NSW Sydney, Arts Cncl Collection, Scottish Nat Gallery, Tate Gallery, Univ Coll Gallery, V&A; RA 1994; *Style—* Mick Moon, Esq, RA; ✉ c/o Alan Cristea Gallery, 31 Cork Street, London W1X 2NU (tel 020 7439 1866, fax 020 7734 1549)

MOON, Peter Geoffrey; s of Roland Charles Moon, of Gosport, and Bernice Moon; *b* 4 November 1949; *Educ* Brockenhurst GS, UCL (BSc (Econ)); *m* 31 May 1975, Susan Elizabeth Williams; 3 c (Richard David, Katherine Helen (twins) b 5 Aug 1978, Simon Edward b 26 Aug 1980); *Career* Central Bd of Fin Church of England 1972–75, Slater Walker Securities 1975–78, National Provident Institution 1978–85, British Airways Pensions 1985–92, Universities Superannuation Scheme 1992– (chief investment offr); dir: MBNA Europe, Scottish American Investment Co; advsr: Teesside Superannuation Fund, London Pension Fund Authy; AIIMR; *Style—* Peter Moon; ✉ The Universities Superannuation Scheme Ltd, 13th Floor, 99 Bishopsgate, London EC2M 3XD (tel 020 7972 0300, fax 020 7628 0062, e-mail pmoon@uss.co.uk)

MOON, Sir Roger; 6 Bt (UK 1887), of Copsewood, Stoke, Co Warwick; s of Jasper Moon, OBE (d 1975, gs of 1 Bt); suc bro, Sir Edward Moon, MC, 5 Bt, 1988; *b* 17 November 1914; *Educ* Sedbergh; *m* 16 Dec 1950, Meg (d 2000), da of late Col Arthur Mainwaring Maxwell, DSO, MC; 3 da (Sarah Corinna b 1951, Gillian Adèle (Mrs Johnston) b 1954, Patricia Isolda (Mrs Hogg) b 1955); *Heir* bro, Humphrey Moon; *Recreations* gardening; *Style—* Sir Roger Moon, Bt; ✉ The Barn House, Wykey, Ruyton-XI-Towns, Shropshire SY4 1JA (tel 01939 260354)

MOONEY, Bel; da of Edward Mooney, and Gladys, *née* Norbury; *b* 8 October 1946; *Educ* Aigburth Vale Girls' HS Liverpool, Trowbridge Girls' HS, UCL (BA); *m* 1968 (m dis 2006), Jonathan Dimbleby, *qv*, s of Richard Dimbleby, CBE (d 1965); 1 s (Daniel Richard b 1974), 1 da (Katharine Rose b 1980); *Career* asst to the ed then contributing ed Nova magazine 1971–75, freelance contrib (The Guardian, The Times, The Observer, New Statesman, Sunday Times, Daily Express, Daily Mail amongst others) 1972–; columnist: Cosmopolitan, The Mirror, Sunday Times, The Listener, The Times; TV presenter 1980–86 (Mothers by Daughters (C4), Fathers by Sons (C4), Dora Russell (BBC2), Ellen Wilkinson (BBC2)), presenter Radio 4 1985–2002 (Women: Equal Sex?, American Authors, Turning Points, A Perspective for Living, Devout Sceptics); ed Proof Magazine 2000–01; dir Friends of Great Ormond Street 1993–97, vice-pres Bath Festivals Tst 1997–; Hon DLitt Univ of Bath 1998; fell UCL 1994, hon fell Liverpool John Moores Univ 2002; *Non-Fiction Books* The Year of the Child (1979), Differences of Opinion (1984), Bel Mooney's Somerset (1989), Perspectives for Living (1992), Devout Sceptics (2003); *Novels* The Windsurf Boy (1983), The Anderson Question (1985), The Fourth of July (1988), Lost Footsteps (1993), Intimate Letters (1997), The Invasion of Sand (2005); *Children's Books* Liza's Yellow Boat (also illustrated by the author, 1980), I Don't Want To! (1985), The Stove Haunting (1986), I Can't Find It! (1988), It's Not Fair (1989), A Flower of Jet (1990), But You Promised! (1990), Why Not? (1990), I Know! (1991), I'm Scared (1994), The Voices of Silence (1994), I Wish! (1995), Why Me? (1996), I'm Bored (1997), Joining the Rainbow (1997), The Green Man (1997), It's Not My Fault (1999), So What! (2002), Kitty's Friends (2003), Mr Tubs is Lost! (2004), Who Loves Mr Tubs? (2006), Big Dog Bonnie (2007), Best Dog Bonnie (2007); *Satire* Father Kissmass and Mother Claws (with Gerald Scarfe, 1985); *Anthology* From This Day Forward (1989); *Recreations* literature, art, music, friends, churches; *Style—* Miss Bel Mooney; ✉ c/o David Higham Associates, 5 Lower John Street, London W1 (tel 020 7437 7888, website www.belmooney.co.uk)

MOONEY, Kevin Michael; s of John Fergal Mooney (d 1984), and Bridget Mooney (d 1986); *b* 14 November 1945, Hammersmith, London; *Educ* Cardinal Vaughan Sch Kensington, Univ of Bristol (LLB); *m* 1 May 1972, Maureen; 2 s (Christopher James b 9 Aug 1974, Benjamin John b 7 Sept 1976), 1 da (Charlotte Elizabeth b 28 March 1979); *Career* admitted slr 1971; Simmons & Simmons: slr 1971–73, ptnr 1973–, memb Bd 1999–2005; pres European Patent Lawyers Assoc 2003–; *Recreations* farming in Majorca, supporting QPR FC; *Style—* Kevin Mooney, Esq; ✉ Simmons & Simmons, CityPoint, One Ropemaker Street, London EC2Y 9SS (tel 020 7628 2020, fax 020 7628 2070, e-mail kevin.mooney@simmons-simmons.com)

MOONIE, Baron (Life Peer UK 2005), of Bennochy in Fife; Dr Lewis George Moonie; *b* 25 February 1947; *Educ* Grove Acad Dundee, Univ of St Andrews (MB ChB), Univ of Edinburgh (MSc); *m*; 2 c; *Career* jr med posts 1970–75, DPM 1975, sr med advsr and clinical pharmacologist in the pharmaceutical indust in Holland, Switzerland and Edinburgh 1976–80, conslt in public health Fife Health Bd 1984–87 (trainee in community med 1980–84), MP (Lab) Kirkcaldy 1987–2005; memb Treasy Select Ctee 1988–89; oppn spokesman: trade and industry 1989–92, science and technol 1992–94, industry 1994–95, nat heritage 1995–97; Parly under-sec of state MOD 2000–; memb Liaison Select Ctee 1997–; non-exec dir AEA Technology 2004–; MFCM 1984, MRCPsych 1979; *Style—* The Rt Hon the Lord Moonie; ✉ House of Lords, London SW1A 0PW

MOONMAN, Prof Eric; OBE (1991); s of Borach Moonman (d 1953), and Leah, *née* Bernstein (d 1959); *b* 29 April 1929; *Educ* Christ Church Southport, Univ of Manchester (MSc), Univ of Liverpool (Dip Social Sci); *m* m 1 (m dis); 2 s (Daniel b 10 July 1966, Joshua b 27 Jan 1972), 1 da (Natasha b 19 April 1968); m 2, 11 Feb 2001, Gillian Louise, da of Joseph Mayer, and Muriel Mayer; *Career* Nat Serv Kings Liverpool Regt 1951–53; human rels advsr Br Inst Mgmnt 1956–62, leader of Stepney Cncl 1958–62, memb Tower Hamlets Cncl 1963–67; MP: Basildon 1966–70, Billericay 1974–79; govr BFI 1978–83, dir Gp Rels Educn Tst 1979–88, chm Islington HA 1980–90, memb Bloomsbury and Islington DHA 1990–93; HM treas Toynbee Hall 1979–93, sr vice-pres Bd of Deps of Br Jews 1986–91 and 1994–2000, visiting prof of health mgmnt City Univ 1990–; dir Natural History Museum Tst 1990–92, chair Friends of Natural History Museum 2007–; chm Essex Radio 1991–2001; conslt Int Red Cross Namibia and Zimbabwe 1992–95, chair Continuing Care Appeals Panel City of Liverpool 1996–, memb Advsy Bd Centre for Counter Terrorism Studies, Potomac Inst Washington; FIMgt 1959; *Books* The Manager and the Organisation (1961), Communications in an Expanding Organisation (1970), Reluctant Partnership (1971), Alternative Government (1984), Violent Society (1987), Learning to Live in the Violent Society (2006); *Recreations* cinema, theatre, football (watching), tennis (playing); *Style—* Prof Eric Moonman, OBE; ✉ 1 Beacon Hill, London N7 9LY (tel 01704 532367)

MOOR, Philip Drury; QC (2001); s of late Rev David Moor, and Evangeline, *née* White; *b* 15 July 1959; *Educ* Canford Sch, Pembroke Coll Oxford; *m* 18 July 1987, Gillian Elizabeth, *née* Stark; 2 da (Alice Elizabeth b 24 May 1992, Emily Ruth b 9 Sept 1995); *Career* called to the Bar Inner Temple 1982 (bencher 2004); recorder of the Crown Court 2003–, head of chambers 1 Hare Court 2007; chm Family Law Bar Assoc 2004–05 (vice-chm 2002–2003, actg treas 2000–01); memb: Gen Cncl of the Bar 1987–89 and 2004–05, Cncl of Legal Educn 1988–91 (memb Bd of Examiners 1989–92), Phillips Ctee on Financing Pupillage 1989, Professional Standards Ctee 2002–03 (vice-chm 2003); *Books* contrib to Family Law; *Recreations* cricket, association football; *Clubs* MCC (assoc memb); *Style—* Philip Moor, Esq, QC; ✉ 1 Hare Court, Temple, London EC4Y 7BE (tel 020 7797 7070, fax 020 7797 7435, e-mail moor@1hc.com)

MOORCOCK, Michael John; s of Arthur Edward Moorcock, of Worthing, W Sussex, and June, *née* Taylor; *b* 18 December 1939; *Educ* Michael Hall Sch Forest Row, Pitman's Coll Croydon; *m* 1, 25 Oct 1962 (m dis 1978), Hilary Denham Bailey; 2 da (Sophie Elizabeth b 3 Sept 1963, Katherine Helen b 5 Sept 1964), 1 s (Max Edward b 24 Feb 1971); m 2, 7 May 1978 (m dis 1983), Jill Riches; m 3, 23 Sept 1983, Linda Mullens Steele; *Career* author 1956–; ed: Tarzan Adventures 1957–, Fleetway Publications 1959–, Liberal Party 1961–, New Worlds 1964–; awards incl: August Derleth Award (four times, 1971–75), Nebula Award 1968, World Fantasy Award 1979, Guardian Fiction Prize 1977, World Fantasy Lifetime Achievement Award 2000; memb: Womankind Worldwide, Amnesty Int, PEN Int Royal Overseas League, Soc of Authors; *Books* over 80 books incl: Byzantium Endures (1981), The Laughter of Carthage (1984), Mother London (1988), Jerusalem Commands (1992), Blood (1994), Fabulous Harbours (1995), The War Amongst the Angels (1996), Tales from the Texas Woods (1997), King of the City (2000), London Bone (2001), The Dream Thief's Daughter (2002), The Skrayling Tree (2003), The Lives and Times of Jerry Cornelius (2003), Wizardry and Wild Romance (2004), The Vengeance of Rome (2006), The Metatemporal Detective (2007); omnibus novels reissued 1992 and 1993: Von Bek, The Eternal Champion, Corum, Sailing to Utopia, The Nomad of the Time Streams, The Dancers at the End of Time, Elric of Melniboné, The New Nature of the Catastrophe, The Prince with the Silver Hand, Legends from the End of Time, Stormbringer, Earl Aubec, Count Brass, Gloriana, The Brothel in Rosenstrasse, Behold the Man, Breakfast in the Ruins, Jerry Cornelius Quartet, A Cornelius Calendar; ed of numerous anthologies, collections and short stories; *Recreations* camel racing, mountaineering; *Style—* Michael Moorcock, Esq; ✉ Old Circle Squared, PO Box 1230, Lost Pines, Texas 78602, USA (e-mail mjm@multiverse.org); Chez Agence Hoffman, 77 boulevard St Michel, 75005 Paris, France

MOORCROFT, David Robert; OBE (1999, MBE 1983); s of Robert Moorcroft, of Coventry, and Mildred, *née* Hardy; *b* 10 April 1953; *Educ* Woodlands Comp Sch, Tile Hill Coll of Further Educn, Loughborough Univ (BEd); *m* Linda Ann, da of John Ward; 1 s (Paul David b 4 May 1981), 1 da (Lucy Ann b 19 April 1985); *Career* former int athlete; chief exec UK Athletics (formerly British Athletic Federation) 1997–2007; sr GB debut 1973, AAA 1500m champion 1978, UK 1500m and 5000m champion 1980; other achievements incl: seventh 1500m Olympic Games Montreal 1976, Gold medal 1500m Cwlth Games Edmonton 1978, Bronze medal 1500m Euro Championships Prague 1978, semi-finalist 5000m Olympic Games Moscow 1980, Gold medal 5000m Europa Cup Zagreb 1981, Gold medal 5000m Cwlth Games Brisbane 1982, Bronze medal Euro Championships Athens 1982, finalist 5000m Olympic Games LA 1984; records: world 5000m 13:00:41 Oslo 1982, Euro 3000m 7:32:79 Crystal Palace 1982; school teacher 1976–81, dir charitable tst 1981–, memb commentary teams BBC TV and Radio 1983–; *Style—* David Moorcroft, Esq, OBE

MOORE, Prof Adrian William; s of Victor George Moore, of Wilmslow, Cheshire, and Audrey Elizabeth, *née* Wallis; *b* 29 December 1956, Kettering, Northants; *Educ* Manchester Grammar, King's Coll Cambridge (MA), Balliol Coll Oxford (BPhil, John Locke Prize, DPhil); *Career* lectr UC Oxford 1982–85, jr research fell King's Coll Cambridge 1985–88, tutorial fell St Hugh's Coll Oxford 1988–, prof of philosophy Univ of Oxford 2004– (lectr 1988–2004); memb: Editorial Ctee European Jl of Philosophy 2003–, Exec Ctee Mind Assoc 2005–, Exec Ctee Br Philosophical Assoc 2005–; Leverhulme maj research fell 2006–; *Publications* Meaning and Reference (ed, 1993), Infinity (ed, 1993), Points of View (1997), The Infinite (1990, 2 edn 2001), Noble in Reason, Infinite in Faculty: Themes and Variations in Kant's Moral and Religious Philosophy (2003), Bernard Williams: Philosophy as a Humanistic Discipline (ed, 2006); *Recreations* lifelong Manchester City FC supporter; *Style—* Prof Adrian Moore; ✉ St Hugh's College, Oxford OX2 6LE (tel 01865 274953, fax 01865 274912, e-mail adrian.moore@philosophy.ox.ac.uk)

MOORE, Austin; s of Michael Moore, of Whatton, Notts, and Shirley, *née* Hutchins; *b* 5 February 1963, Leeds; *Educ* Leeds GS, Univ of Manchester (LLB); *Children* 2 da (Lucy Ann b 19 March 1994, Sarah Elizabeth b 4 Oct 1995), 1 s (James Augustin b 29 Sept 1998); *Career* admitted slr 1992; slr specialising in corporate law and corporate finance; ptnr HBJ Gateley Wareing; memb Cncl Notts Law Soc 1998–, memb Law Soc; chm Notts Multiple Sclerosis Soc 1996–2000; *Publications* The Owner-Managed Business, Business Sale; *Recreations* drums and music; *Clubs* Nottingham; *Style—* Austin Moore, Esq; ✉ 177A Melton Road, West Bridgford, Nottingham NG2 6JL (tel 0115 846 5007, e-mail austin_moore4@hotmail.com); HBJ Gateley Wareing LLP, City Gate East, Tollhouse Hill, Nottingham NG1 5FS (tel 0115 983 8216, fax 0115 983 8201, e-mail amoore@hbj-gw.com)

MOORE, Prof Brian Cecil Joseph; *b* 10 February 1946; *Educ* Sir Walter St John's GS Battersea, St Catharine's Coll Cambridge (exhibitioner, MA), Univ of Cambridge (PhD); *Career* lectr in psychology Univ of Reading 1971–73, Fulbright-Hays sr scholar and visiting prof Dept of Psychology Brooklyn Coll City Univ NY 1973–74, lectr in psychology Univ of Reading 1974–77; Univ of Cambridge: lectr in experimental psychology 1977–89, reader in auditory perception 1989–95, prof of auditory perception 1995–; fell Wolfson Coll Cambridge 1983–; Univ of Calif Berkeley: visiting researcher 1985, visiting prof Dept of Psychology 1990; visiting conslt prof Dept of Bioengineering Univ of Ulster 1991–93; pres Assoc of Independent Hearing Healthcare Professionals; memb: Experimental Psychology Soc, Cambridge Philosophical Soc, Br Soc of Audiology, American Speech-Language-Hearing Assoc, Audio Engrg Soc, Acoustical Soc of Japan, American Acad of Audiology, American Auditory Soc, Assoc for Research in Otolaryngology; memb Editorial Bd: Int Jl of Audiology, Jl Acoustical Soc of Japan, Jl Audiology and Neuro-otology, Hearing Research; sometime memb various MRC ctees and advsy gps 1979–95 (incl Hearing Research Ctee 1986–94); T S Littler prize Br Soc of Audiology 1983 and 2006, Silver Medal Acoustical Soc of America 2003, Int Award in Hearing American Acad of Audiology 2004, Award of Merit Assoc for Research in Otolaryngology 2008; fell Acoustical Soc of America 1985, Van Houten fell Inst for Perception Research Eindhoven 1994, hon fell Belgian Soc of Audiology 1997, hon fell Br Soc of Hearing Aid Audiologists 1999, FMedSci 2001, FRS 2002; *Books* An Introduction to the Psychology of Hearing (1977, 5 edn 2003), Frequency Selectivity in Hearing (ed, 1986), Auditory Frequency Selectivity (jt ed, 1986), Hearing (ed, 1995), Perceptual Consequences of Cochlear Damage (1995), Cochlear Hearing Loss (1998, 2 edn 2007), New Developments in Hearing and balance (jt ed, 2002); also author of numerous book chapters, papers and articles in learned jls; *Style*— Prof Brian Moore; ✉ Department of Experimental Psychology, University of Cambridge, Downing Street, Cambridge CB2 3EB (tel 01223 333574, fax 01223 333564, e-mail bcjm@cam.ac.uk)

MOORE, Charles Hilary; s of Richard Gillachrist Moore, and Ann Hilary, *née* Miles; *b* 31 October 1956; *Educ* Eton, Trinity Coll Cambridge (BA); *m* 1981, Caroline Mary (former fell Peterhouse Cambridge), da of Ralph Lambert Baxter, of Etchingham Sussex; 2 c (William, Katharine (twins) b 1 April 1990); *Career* journalist and author; editorial staff Daily Telegraph 1979, ldr writer Daily Telegraph 1981–83, asst ed and political columnist The Spectator 1983–84, ed The Spectator 1984–90, weekly columnist The Daily Express 1987–90, fortnightly column Another Voice The Spectator 1990–95, dep ed The Daily Telegraph 1990–92, ed The Sunday Telegraph 1992–95, ed The Daily Telegraph 1995–2003, gp consltg ed The Telegraph Gp 2004–, weekly columnist The Daily Telegraph and The Spectator 2004–; chm Policy Exchange 2005–; memb Cncl Benenden Sch 2000–, tstee: T E Utley Meml Fund, Resources for Autism 2005–; *Publications* 1936 (ed with C Hawtree, 1986), The Church in Crisis (with A N Wilson and Gavin Stamp, 1986), A Tory Seer - The Selected Journalism of T E Utley (ed with Simon Heffer, 1989); *Clubs* Beefsteak, White's; *Style*— Charles Moore, Esq

MOORE, Christopher M; o s of Sir Harry Moore, CBE (d 2001); *b* 1 December 1944; *Educ* Winchester, Pembroke Coll Cambridge (MA); *m* 2 Sept 1972, Charlotte C, da of J Glessing, of Montague, Hankham, E Sussex; 3 s (Tercel R, Wilaf M, Frederic C); *Career* investment banking/venture capital/businessman; Price Waterhouse 1966–70, Robert Fleming inc 1970–72, Lazards 1972–73; dir: Jardine Fleming and Co Ltd 1973–76, Robert Fleming and Co Ltd 1978–95, Robert Fleming Holdings Ltd 1986–95, Stop Loss Mutual Insurance Association Ltd 1992–2000, TriVest VCT plc 2001–, Matrix Income & Growth 4 VCT plc 2002–, Matrix Income & Growth 3 VCT plc 2005–; chm: Fleming Ventures Ltd 1992–2003, Moore Corporation 1995–, Calderburn plc 1996–99, Oxonica 2004–; sr advsr to Chm of Lloyd's 1996–2000; chm Fight for Sight; vice-chm Bletchley Park Tst; FCA; *Recreations* country sports, agriculture, flying, tennis, music, books; *Clubs* White's, Pratt's, Leander, Farmers'; *Style*— Christopher Moore, Esq; ✉ Thornborough Grounds, Buckingham MK18 2AB (tel 01280 812170)

MOORE, Prof David Moresby; s of Moresby George Moore (d 1979), of Barnard Castle, Co Durham, and Elizabeth, *née* Grange (d 1994); *b* 26 July 1933; *Educ* Barnard Castle Sch, Univ Coll Durham (BSc, PhD, DSc); *m* 26 July 1957, Ida Elizabeth, da of Herbert Shaw (d 1956), of Carlisle, Cumberland; 2 s (Wayne Peter b July 1961, Lloyd Randal b Sept 1969); *Career* res offr CSIRO Canberra 1957–59, res botanist UCLA 1959–61, lectr in botany Univ of Leicester 1961–68, prof of botany Univ of Reading 1976–94 (reader in plant taxonomy 1968–76, prof emeritus 1994–); pres Systematics Assoc 1979–82, sec gen Flora Europaea 1985–89; ed Flora de Chile 1987–, chm Editorial Ctee Lichen Flora of GB and I; memb: Soc Botany Argentina, Botanical Soc of Br; Claudio Gay medal Univ Concepción Chile 1987; *Books* Flora Europaea (1963–93), Vascular Flora of Falkland Islands (1968), Plant Cytogenetics (1977), Green Planet (1982), Flora of Tierra del Fuego (1983), Flora Europaea Checklist and Chromosome Index (1983), Current Concepts in Plant Taxonomy (1984), La Transecta Botánica de Patagonia Austral (1984), Flora of the British Isles (3 edn 1987, revised 1990), Garden Earth (1991); *Recreations* walking, reading; *Style*— Prof David Moore; ✉ 26 Eric Avenue, Emmer Green, Reading, Berkshire RG4 8QX (tel 0118 947 2132)

MOORE, Prof Derek William; s of William McPherson Moore (d 1979), and Elsie Marjorie, *née* Patterson (d 1969); *b* 19 April 1931; *Educ* South Shields Boy's HS, Univ of Cambridge (MA, PhD); *Career* lectr in maths Univ of Bristol 1960, sr postdoctoral res fell Nat Acad of Sciences 1964; Imperial Coll London: sr lectr 1967, reader in theoretical fluid mechanics 1968, prof of applied mathematics 1973–96, prof emeritus and sr research fell 1996–2003; Sherman Fairchild Distinguished Scholar Caltech 1986–87, Sr Whitehead Prize London Mathematical Soc 2001; hon memb American Acad of Arts and Sciences 1985; FRS 1990; *Recreations* jazz saxophone; *Style*— Prof Derek Moore; ✉ Department of Mathematics, Imperial College, 180 Queens Gate, London SW7 2BZ (tel 020 7594 8501)

MOORE, Fionna Patricia; da of Maj Samuel James Moore, and Margaret Patricia Moore, *née* Boyd; *b* 18 May 1950; *Educ* Croydon HS for Girls (GPDST), UCL (BSc), UCH Med Sch (MB BS); *m* 12 April 1980, Richard Philip Ward; 2 s (Jonathan b 1982, Patrick b 1988), 2 da (Victoria b 1975, Jennifer b 1985); *Career* registrar in gen surgery St James and St George's Hosps 1980–81, Bayer res fell UCH 1981–83 (registrar in surgery 1978–80), sr registrar in accident and emergency med Ealing Central Middx and Hammersmith Hosps 1983–85; conslt in accident and emergency med: UCH and Middx Hosp 1985–94, John Radcliffe Coll Oxford 1994–96, Hammersmith Hosp NHS Tst 1996–; currently med dir London Ambulance Service; memb RSM, FRCS, FRCSEd, FFAEM; *Recreations* reading, music, walking; *Style*— Miss Fionna Moore

MOORE, Jamie Edward; s of Gary Moore, the racehorse trainer, and Jayne, *née* Workmen; bro of Ryan Moore, the champion flat jockey; *b* 31 January 1985, Brighton, E Sussex; *Educ* Cardinal Newman Sch Hove; *Partner* Lucie Smith; *Career* Nat Hunt jockey 2001–; champion conditional jockey 2003–04; *Style*— Jamie Moore, Esq

MOORE, Jane; da of Prof John Moore, of Oxford, and Patricia, *née* Richardson; *b* 17 May 1962; *Educ* Worcester Girls' GS, South Glamorgan Inst of HE Cardiff (Dip); *Career* journalist; trainee reporter Solihull 1981–83, news reporter Birmingham Post and Mail 1983–86, freelance reporter The People 1986–, pop columnist The Sun 1986–87, freelance researcher Thames News 1987–88; Today: feature writer 1988, Royal corr 1989, dep news ed 1989, feature ed 1990; features ed The Mirror 1993–95, women's ed and columnist The Sun 1995–99; columnist The Sun 2000–, writer The Sunday Times 2000–; co-presenter: Loose Women (ITV) 2000–, Crimewatch Daily (BBC) 2001; regular presenter on This Morning (ITV) 2002–; presenter Breakfast Show LBC Radio 2003–04; authored documentaries: The Beckhams (Sky One) 2004, Spoilt Children (Channel 4) 2004, Mothers Who Leave (Sky One) 2004, Supermarket Secrets (Channel 4) 2005, Dispatches - What's Really in Your Christmas Dinner? 2005, Dispatches - Fast Food 2006, Grumpy Old Women 2005–06; *Novels* Fourplay, The Ex Files, Dot. Homme, The Second Wives Club; *Recreations* photography; *Style*— Miss Jane Moore; ✉ The Sun, 1 Virginia Street, London E1 9XP (tel 020 7782 4000, fax 020 7782 4063, e-mail jane.moore@the-sun.co.uk)

MOORE, John Edward; s of late Sqdn Ldr Joseph Enos Moore (d 1995), of Marlow, Bucks, and Audrey Sheila, *née* Matthews (d 1997); *b* 15 November 1947; *Educ* Royal GS High Wycombe, Univ of London (LLB); *m* 1, 12 April 1971 (m dis 1998), Diana, da of John Horend Dixon, MBE, of Ealing; 3 s (James b 1974, Alexander b 1976, Thomas b 1988); m 2, 1 May 1999, Lucy, da of George Tsourous, of N Wales; 1 da (Matilda b 2000), 1 s (Henry b 2004); *Career* civilian gliding instr RAF(VR)T 1967–77; admitted slr 1973; Macfarlanes: joined 1979, head property dept 1986–94, currently ptnr in charge healthcare; lectr and author of articles on agric law, public and private sector partnerships, commercial property, and property jt ventures; memb: Agric Law Assoc, City of London Slrs Co, Law Soc; *Recreations* flying; *Style*— John Moore, Esq; ✉ Messrs Macfarlanes, 10 Norwich Street, London EC4A 1BD (tel 020 7831 9222, fax 020 7831 9607, telex 296381)

MOORE, Dr Kevin Charles; s of Dr Donald Charles Moore (d 1989), and Nellie Partington (d 1985); *b* 25 January 1941; *Educ* Giggleswick Sch, Univ of Manchester Med Sch (MB ChB); *m* 23 Feb 1972, Jillian Margaret, da of Frank Bromley (d 1984); 1 da (Alison b 1972); *Career* conslt anaesthetist Oldham 1973–2001, chm Med Staff Ctee Oldham 1981–85, chm Rochdale Private Surgical Unit 1983–88, dir Highfield Private Hosp Rochdale 1988–91; vice-pres Int Laser Therapy Assoc 1988–94, treas Br Med Laser Assoc 1987–98, treas World Assoc of Laser Therapy 1994–; memb Oldham HA 1987–90; chm: Governing Cncl Dr Kershaw's Hospice Oldham 1992– (memb 1982–92, med dir 1994–), Med Advsy Ctee BMI, Highfield Hosp 1991–97, Highfield M R Scanning plc 1992–99; FFARCS 1972; *Recreations* horse riding, carriage driving; *Style*— Dr Kevin Moore; ✉ 4 The Wells, Stock Lane, Halifax, West Yorkshire HX2 7QP (tel 01422 345636, e-mail kevin.moore@zen.co.uk); Department of Anaesthesia, The Royal Oldham Hospital, Rochdale Road, Oldham, Lancashire OL1 2JH (tel 0161 627 8828)

MOORE, Martin Luke; QC (2002); s of Brig Peter Moore, DSO**, MC, and (Enid) Rosemary, *née* Stokes; *b* 25 April 1960, Aldershot, Hants; *Educ* Winchester, Lincoln Coll Oxford; *m* 21 Sept 1985, Caroline Mary, *née* Mason; 3 da (Alexandra Emily b 1989, Laura Charlotte b 1991, Serena Frances b 1995); *Career* called to the Bar Lincoln's Inn 1982; barr specialising in company law; memb Erskine Chambers 1983–; memb: Commercial Bar Association, Chancery Bar Assoc, Insolvency Lawyers' Assoc, SE Circuit; *Recreations* equestrianism; *Clubs* Naval and Military; *Style*— Martin Moore, Esq, QC; ✉ Erskine Chambers, 33 Chancery Lane, London WC2A 1EN (tel 020 7242 5532, website www.erkine-chambers.co.uk)

MOORE, Michael; s of Gerald Edward Moore (d 1975), of Yangon, Myanmar, and Shwe Mu Tha Soe; *Educ* Methodist Eng HS Yangon, Hackney Downs Sch London, Univ of Leicester (BSc), Univ of Aberdeen (MLitt), Nat Coll for Hypnosis & Psychotherapy, UK Training Centre for Neuro-Linguistic Programming; *Career* pilot RAFVR; memb Contact Counselling Servs: Univ of Aberdeen 1978–79, Keele Univ 1979–81; res and admin asst Cmmn for Int Justice and Peace 1981–82; psychologist and specialist in human performance and conflict resolution ('Building Integrity Into Achievement') 1982–; assoc Powerfax Learning Systems Ltd; freelance journalist, guest speaker on human performance and conflict resolution; auditor Southwark Metropolitan Tbnl 1998; memb: Br Psychological Soc 1987, Assoc of Neuro-Linguistic Programming 1987, CEDR 1998–; *Recreations* philosophy, comparative religion, languages, TA, flying; *Style*— Michael Moore, Esq; ✉ 130 Harley Street, London W1N 1AH (tel 020 7935 6558)

MOORE, Vice Adm Sir Michael Antony Claes; KBE (1997), LVO (1982); s of Lt A D W Moore, RN (d 1942), and Ebba Agneta, *née* Wachtmeister (d 1998); *b* 6 January 1942; *Educ* Wellington, RNC Dartmouth; *m* Penelope Moore, JP, *née* Lawson; 1 s, 3 da; *Career* Royal Navy: Midshipman 1960–62, Cdr 1975–80, Capt 1980–90, Rear Adm 1990–94, Vice Adm 1994–98, ret 1998; CO: HMS Beachampton, HMS Tartar, HMS Andromeda and 8 Frigate Sqdn; COS COMNAVSOUTH Naples; chief exec IMechE 1998–2007; chm Forces Pension Soc; memb Royal Swedish Military Sciences, yr bro Trinity House; Hon FIMechE; *Style*— Vice Adm Sir Michael Moore, KBE, LVO; ✉ c/o Churchill Cottage, Castle Street, Portchester, Hampshire PO16 9QW

MOORE, Michael Kevin; MP; s of Rev W Haisley Moore, and Jill, *née* Moorhead; *b* 3 June 1965; *Educ* Strathallan Sch, Jedburgh GS, Univ of Edinburgh (MA); *m* 2004, Alison Louise, *née* Hughes; *Career* research asst to Archy Kirkwood, MP 1987–88, Coopers & Lybrand Edinburgh (latterly a mangr in corp fin practice) 1988–97; MP (Lib Dem): Tweeddale, Ettrick and Lauderdale 1997–2005, Berwickshire, Roxburgh and Selkirk 2005–; memb Scottish Affrs Select Ctee 1997–99, Lib Dem spokesman on tport then on Scotland until 2001, dep Lib Dem spokesman for foreign affrs 2001–05, Lib Dem defence spokesman 2005–06, foreign affrs spokesman 2006–; dep ldr Scot Lib Dem Pty 2003–; govr and vice-chm Westminster Fndn for Democracy 2002–05, memb Cncl RIIA 2004–; memb: Amnesty Int, Charter 88, ICAS 1991–; *Recreations* jazz, film, music, hill walking, rugby; *Style*— Michael Moore, Esq, MP; ✉ House of Commons, London SW1A 0AA (tel 020 7219 2236, fax 020 7219 0263, e-mail michaelmooremp@parliament.uk)

MOORE, Mike; s of Jack Francis Moore, BEM, of Epsom, Surrey, and Joan Florence, *née* Walker; *b* 6 January 1954; *Educ* Bideford Sch of Art and Design, Reading Sch of Art and Design; *m* Helen; 1 s (Harry b 13 July 1990), 1 da (Sophie b 28 June 1992); *Career* photographer: Thomson Regnl Newspapers 1976–79, London Evening Standard 1980–85, The Today Newspaper 1986–93, Daily Mirror 1993–; *Awards* Midland Bank Press Awards commendation 1977 and 1978, World Press Photo Fndn Gold Medal 1978, Br Press Awards commendations 1981 and 1991, Ilford Press Awards commendation 1984 and 1991, Royal Photographer of the Year 1987, Press Photographer of the Year 1987, Kodak Press Awards commendation (two) 1991, Nikon Press Awards commendation 1991, News Photographer of the Year 1991, Gulf War Medal 1991, Photographer of the Year (UK Press Gazette) 1997, Royal Photographer of the Year and Feature Photographer of the Year (UK Picture Eds' Guild) 1997, Photographer of the Year (Amnesty Int) 2000, World Press Award 2004; *Books* Desert War (1991); *Style*— Mike Moore, Esq; ✉ The Daily Mirror Picture Desk, 1 Canada Square Canary Wharf, London E14 5AP (tel 020 7293 3851, mobile 07710 613936)

MOORE, Nicholas Alan (Nick); s of Dr John M Moore (d 2005), and Jill, *née* Maycock (d 1995); *b* 16 July 1962; *Educ* Rugby, Magdalene Coll Cambridge (MA); *m* 3 October 1987, Jane, *née* Clarke; 2 da (Natasha Louise b 24 Sept 1992, Charlotte Sarah b 24 Jan 1996); *Career* various copywriting positions 1985–89, copywriter and dep creative dir Wunderman London 1989–92; creative dir: Sutch Webster WMGO 1992–95, Barraclough Hall Woolston Gray (latterly Proximity London) 1995–2000, TBWA/GGT 2000–04; exec creative dir TEQUILA/London 2005–06, chief creative offr Wunderman NY 2006–; full memb D&AD, MIDM; awards: BDMA, DMA, Caples, Echo; *Recreations* wine, family, garden, poetry, sailing; *Style*— Nick Moore, Esq; ✉ Wunderman New York, 285 Madison Avenue, New York, NY 10017-6486, USA (tel 00 1 212 941 3270, e-mail nick.moore@wunderman.com)

MOORE, Dr (Sir) Norman Winfrid; 3 Bt (UK 1919), of Hancox, Whatlington, Sussex (has established his claim but does not use title); s of Sir Alan Hilary Moore, 2 Bt, MB (d 1959); *b* 24 February 1923; *Educ* Eton, Trinity Coll Cambridge (BA); *m* 14 July 1950,

M

Janet, PhD, o da of Paul Singer; 1 s (Peter Alan Cutlack b 1951), 2 da (Caroline Mary Phyllis b 1953, Helena Meriel (Mrs David Alexander) b 1957); *Heir* s, Peter Moore; *Career* Lt RA, served 1942–45 War; asst lectr and lectr Univ of Bristol 1949–53, princ scientific offr Nature Conservancy Cncl 1958–65, sr princ scientific offr 1965–83, ret; visiting prof Wye Coll London 1979–83; *Books* Dragonflies (with Philip S Corbet and Cynthia Longfield, 1960), Hedges (with E Pollard and M D Hooper, 1974), The Bird of Time: The Science and Politics of Nature Conservation (1987), Oaks, Dragonflies and People: Creating a Small Nature Reserve and Relating Its Story to Wider Conservation Issues (2002); *Style*— Dr Norman Moore; ⌧ The Farm House, 117 Boxworth End, Swavesey, Cambridge CB24 4RA

MOORE, Sir Patrick (CALDWELL-); kt (2001), CBE (1989, OBE 1968); s of Capt Charles Caldwell-Moore, MC (d 1947), and Gertrude Lilian, *née* White (d 1981); *b* 4 March 1923; *Educ* privately; *Career* served WWII RAF 1940–45, Flt Lt, navigator with Bomber Cmd; dir Armagh Planetarium 1965–68; author, broadcaster, astronomer; vice-pres Br Astronomical Assoc (pres 1982–84); Hon DSc: Lancaster Univ 1979, Hatfield Poly 1989, Univ of Birmingham 1990, Keele Univ 1994, Univ of Leicester 1996, Univ of Portsmouth 1997, Univ of Glamorgan 2000, Sheffield Hallam Univ 2001, Trinity Coll Dublin 2002; Hon FInstP, FRAS 1945, FRSA 1949, FRS; hon memb various foreign scientific socs; *Books* over 150 books, mainly astronomical; *Recreations* cricket, chess, tennis, music (xylophone player); *Clubs* Athenaeum, Sussex CCC, Lord's Taverners; *Style*— Sir Patrick Moore, CBE, FRS; ⌧ Farthings, West Street, Selsey, West Sussex PO20 9AD (tel 01243 603668)

MOORE, Peter David; s of Frederick Cecil Moore, and Joan Lambert *née* Wickham; *b* 5 June 1945; *Educ* King George V GS Southport; *m* 28 April 1973, Susan Janet, da of Duncan Ferguson Ure; 1 da (Philippa Jane b 1 Jan 1976), 1 s (Stephen David b 5 May 1978); *Career* Grant Thornton 1963–69, Arthur Andersen 1969–71, Sterling Treasury Dealer Bankers Trust Co 1971–72; dir Trio Holdings plc (holding co of Martin Brokers Group Ltd) 1979–2005 (co sec 1972–79), dir GGS Holdings Ltd 2001–03; dir Richmond Vikings Ltd; FCA; *Recreations* sporting; *Style*— Peter Moore, Esq, FCA; ⌧ c/o Richmond Vikings Limited, The Athletic Ground, Kew Foot Road, Richmond TW9 2SS (tel 020 8940 0397)

MOORE, Prof Peter Gerald; TD (1963); s of Leonard Jiggens Moore (d 1998), and Ruby Silvester, *née* Wilburn (d 1978); *b* 5 April 1928; *Educ* KCS Wimbledon, UCL (BSc, PhD, Rosa Morison medallist), Princeton Univ (Harkness fell); *m* 27 Sept 1958, Sonja Enevoldson, da of William Ivor Thomas, of Cooden (d 1973); 1 da (Penelope (Mrs Lawrenson) b 1960), 2 s (Richard b 1963, Charles b 1967); *Career* sr under-offr Mons Cadet Sch 1948–49, 2 Lt 3 Regt RHA 1949–51, 2 Lt (later Lt then Capt) 290 Field Regt (City of London) RA TA 1951–61, Capt (later Maj) 254 Field Regt RA TA 1961–65; lectr UCL 1951–56, asst econ advsr NCB 1956–59, head statistical servs Reed Paper Group 1959–65; London Business Sch: prof of statistics 1965–2000, dep princ 1972–84, princ 1984–89, hon fell 1993; pt/t ptnr Duncan C Fraser 1974–77; pt/t dir: Copeman Paterson Ltd 1984–89, Elf Petroleum UK plc 1989–94; memb: Drs and Dentists Renumeration Body 1971–89, Ctee on 1971 Census Security 1971–73, UGC 1978–84 (vice-chm 1980–83); conslt: Wilson Ctee on Financial Institutions 1977–80, Pugh-Roberts Associates Cambridge MA 1989–95; memb Cncl: Univ of Sci and Technol Hong Kong 1986–92, UCL 1989–2004 (vice-chm 1998–2001); fell UCL 1988, Gresham prof of rhetoric Gresham Coll 1992–95; Freeman City of London 1964; Liveryman Worshipful Co of Tallow Chandlers (memb Ct of Assts 1987–, Master 1994–95, Dep Master 1996–97); Hon DSc Heriot-Watt Univ 1985; FRSS (Guy medallist 1970, Chambers medallist 1995, pres 1989–91), FIA 1956 (pres 1984–86), CIMgt 1985; *Books* incl: Statistics and the Manager (1966), Anatomy of Decisions (1976), Reason By Numbers (1980), The Business of Risk (1983), Basic Operational Research (1986); numerous articles in professional jls; *Recreations* walking, opera, travelling; *Clubs* Athenaeum, Cordwainer Ward; *Style*— Prof Peter Moore, TD; ⌧ 3 Chartway, The Vine, Sevenoaks, Kent TN13 3RU (tel 01732 451 936)

MOORE, Philip John; s of late Cecil Moore, of Stamford Bridge, York, and Marjorie, *née* Brewer; *b* 30 September 1943; *Educ* Maidstone GS, RCM; *m* 1, 9 Nov 1968 (m dis 1979); 1 s (Thomas), 2 da (Sophia, Bianca); *Career* asst music master Eton 1965–68, asst organist Canterbury Cathedral 1968–74, organist and master of the choristers Guildford Cathedral 1974–82, organist and master of the music York Minster 1983–; memb: RCM Union 1962, Br Acad of Composers and Songwriters 1987, Performing Rights Soc 1988; BMus (Hons) Dunelm; FRCO 1962, GRSM, ARCM, FRSCM, FGCM; *Recreations* collecting Imari and old fountain pens, malt whisky, cooking; *Style*— Philip Moore, Esq; ⌧ 1 Minster Court, York YO1 7JJ (tel 01904 557206, fax 01904 557204, e-mail philipm@yorkminster.org)

MOORE, Philip Wynford; TD (1993); s of Cecil Philip John Moore, of Potters Bar, Herts, and Christine Margaret Moore; *b* 5 January 1960, Welwyn Garden City, Herts; *Educ* St Albans Sch, Clare Coll Cambridge (MA); *m* 29 April 1995, Amanda, *née* Lawson; 2 da (Georgina Emily b 7 Feb 1998, Victoria Lucy b 16 Feb 2000); *Career* Coopers & Lybrand (now PricewaterhouseCoopers): ptnr i/c UK life actuarial servs 1989–95, ldr of insurance consulting practice E Asia 1995–98; finance dir and actuary NPI 1998–2000, corp dir of finance and head of M&A AMP (UK) plc 2000–03; Friends Provident plc: gp finance dir 2003–06, gp chief exec 2007–; non-exec dir F&C Asset Mgmnt plc; Freeman City of London, Liveryman Worshipful Co of Actuaries; FIA 1988; *Recreations* private flying, travel; *Clubs* HAC; *Style*— Philip Moore, Esq, TD; ⌧ Friends Provident plc, 100 Wood Street, London EC2V 7AN (tel 0845 641 7831, fax 020 7796 4720, e-mail philip.moore@friendsprovident.co.uk)

MOORE, Richard Hobart John deCourcy; s of Hobart Harold deCourcy Moore (d 1981), and Elizabeth Helen, *née* Tod; *b* 31 August 1949; *Educ* Stowe; *m* 30 April 1977, Lucy Annabelle, da of Victor Sefton-Smith, and Barbette, *née* Salt (now Lady Millais); 1 s (Francis Richard Hobart deCourcy b 25 June 1985), 1 da (Natasha Elizabeth Victoria b 1 Nov 1993); *Career* Moore Stephens: articled clerk 1968–72, CA 1972, ptnr 1975–, sr ptnr 1989–; Freeman City of London 1974, Liveryman Worshipful Co of Vintners, Liveryman Worshipful Co of Shipwrights (memb Ct of Assts); FCA 1979 (ACA 1972); *Recreations* real tennis, cricket; *Clubs* MCC, Boodle's, Harbour, Hurlingham; *Style*— Richard Moore, Esq; ⌧ 11 Chelsea Park Gardens, London SW3 6AF (tel 020 7352 7594); Moore Stephens, St Paul's House, Warwick Lane, London EC4P 4BN (tel 020 7248 4499)

MOORE, Prof Robert Samuel; s of late Douglas Kenneth Moore, of Rhos-on-Sea, and late Kathleen Phyllis Moore; *b* 3 June 1936; *Educ* Beckenham and Penge Co GS, RNC Dartmouth, Univ of Hull (BA), Univ of Durham (PhD); *m* 16 Aug 1969, Lindy Ruth, da of late Sir Alan Parker, of Shenstone, Sutton-cum-Beckingham; 1 s (David Kenneth b 1974), 1 da (Heloise Kathryn b 1976); *Career* RN 1952–61; sociology lectr Univ of Durham 1965–69, sr lectr in sociology Univ of Aberdeen 1970–75, reader in sociology 1975–77, prof of sociology 1977–89, Eleanor Rathbone prof of sociology Univ of Liverpool 1989–2001 (emeritus prof 2001–); vice-pres Aberdeen City Anti Apartheid, chm Grampian Community Relations Cncl until 1989; memb: Assoc Univ Teachers, CND, Br Sociological Assoc 1964–, Br Assoc 1965–; FRSA, AcSS; *Books* Race, Community and Conflict (with John Rex, 1967), Pitmen, Preachers and Politics (1970), Slamming the Door (with Tina Wallace, 1975), Racism and Black Resistance in Britain (1975), The Social Impact of Oil (1982), Women in the North Sea Oil Industry (with Peter Wybrow, 1985), Ethnic Statistics and the 1991 Census (1995), Positive Action in Action: equal opportunities and declining opportunities in Merseyside (1997); *Recreations* gardening, photography; *Style*— Prof Robert Moore; ⌧ The University of Liverpool, Eleanor Rathbone Building, Bedford Street South, Liverpool L69 7ZA (tel 01352 714456, fax 0151 794 2997, e-mail rsmoore@liverpool.ac.uk)

MOORE, Sir Roger George; KBE (2003, CBE 1999); *b* 14 October 1927; *Educ* Battersea GS, RADA; *m* 1 (m dis 1953), Doorn van Steyn; m 2 (m dis 1969), Dorothy Squires; m 3, Luisa Mattioli; 2 s, 1 da; *Career* actor; chm Stars Organisation for Spastics 1973–76, UNICEF special ambass 1991–; *Television* Ivanhoe 1958, The Alaskans 1959, Maverick 1960, The Saint 1962–68, The Persuaders 1972–73, The Muppet Show 1980, The Wedding of Prince Andrew and Sarah Ferguson (ABC-TV) 1986, Happy Anniversary 007 (ABC-TV) 1987, The Dame Edna Experience Christmas Show (LWT) 1987, James Bond - 30th Anniversary (LWT) 1992, The Man Who Wouldn't Die (Universal) 1992, Best Ever Bond 2002; *Film* extra in Caesar and Cleopatra 1945, Trottie True 1949, The Last Time I Saw Paris 1954, Interrupted Melody 1955, The King's Thief 1955, Diane 1956, The Miracle 1959, Gold of the Seven Saints 1961, Rachel Cade 1961, Rape of the Sabines 1961, No Man's Land 1961, Crossplot 1969, The Man Who Haunted Himself 1970, Gold 1974, That Lucky Touch (Who Needs Friends?) 1975, Shout at the Devil 1975, Street People (Sicilian Cross) 1975, Sherlock Holmes in New York 1976, Wild Geese 1977, Escape to Athena 1978, North Sea Hi-jack 1979, The Sea Wolves 1979/80, Sunday Lovers 1980, The Cannonball Run 1980, Curse of the Pink Panther 1982, The Naked Face 1983, Bed & Breakfast 1989, Bullseye 1989, Fire, Ice and Dynamite 1990, The Quest 1995, cameo role Spiceworld The Movie 1997, The Enemy 2001, Boat Trip 2002; as Cdr James Bond: Live and Let Die 1973, The Man with the Golden Gun 1974, The Spy Who Loved Me 1976, Moonraker 1978, For Your Eyes Only 1980/81, Octopussy 1982, A View to a Kill 1984; *Awards* nominated: Golden Globe World Film Favourite Award (USA) 1980, Man of the Year Award Friars Club of NY 1986, Bambi Lifetime Achievement Award (Germany) 1990; *Publications* James Bond Diary (1973); *Style*— Sir Roger Moore, KBE

MOORE, Rowan William Gillachrist; s of Richard Gillachrist Moore, of Battle, E Sussex, and Ann Hilary, *née* Miles; *b* 22 March 1961; *Educ* Westminster, St John's Coll Cambridge (BA, DipArch); *m* 3 Aug 1991, Elizabeth Black Treip; 2 da (Helena Rose Rebecca, Stella Hannah Hilary); *Career* ptnr Zombory-Moldovan Moore Architects 1990–2005; dir Architecture Fndn 2002–; architecture critic Daily Telegraph 1993–98, architecture critic Evening Standard 1998–, ed Blueprint 1994–97; *Books* Vertigo, The Strange New World of the Contemporary City (1999), Building Tate Modern (2000), The New Art Gallery Walsall (2003); *Style*— Rowan Moore, Esq; ⌧ Architecture Foundation, 2a Kingsway Place, Sans Walk, London EC1R 0LS (tel 020 7253 3334, fax 020 7253 3335, e-mail rowan@architecturefoundation.org.uk)

MOORE, Sean; *b* 30 July 1968; *Educ* Oakdale Comp Sch (played trumpet in S Wales jazz orch); *Family* 1 c; *Career* pop musician; drummer with Manic Street Preachers; signed to Sony 1991–; *Albums* New Art Riot (EP, 1989), Generation Terrorists (1991), Gold Against the Soul (1993), The Holy Bible (1994), Everything Must Go (1996), This Is My Truth Tell Me Yours (1998), Know Your Enemy (2001), Forever Delayed (2002), Lipstick Traces (2003); *Singles* Motown Junk (1990), You Love Us (1990), Stay Beautiful (1991), Love's Sweet Exile (1991), Slash 'N' Burn (1992), Motorcycle Emptiness (1992), Suicide is Painless (1992), Little Baby Nothing (1992), From Despair to Where (1993), La Tristesse Durera (1993), Roses in the Hospital (1993), Life Becoming a Landslide (1994), Faster (1994), Revol (1994), She is Suffering (1994), Design for Life (1996), Everything Must Go (1996), Kevin Carter (1996), Australia (1996), If You Tolerate This Your Children Will Be Next (UK no 1, 1998), The Everlasting (1998), You Stole The Sun From My Heart (1999), Tsunami (1999), The Masses Against The Classes (UK no 1, 2000), So Why So Sad (2001), Found That Soul (2001); *Awards* Best Band Brit Awards 1997, Best Album Brit Awards (for Everything Must Go) 1997, Best Band Brit Awards 1999, Best Album Brit Awards (for This Is My Truth Tell Me Yours) 1999; *Style*— Sean Moore; ⌧ c/o Terri Hall, Hall or Nothing, 11 Poplar Mews, Uxbridge Road, London W12 (tel 020 8740 6288, fax 020 8749 5982)

MOORE, Stephen; s of Stanley Moore (d 1992), of Highgate, London, and Mary Elisabeth, *née* Bruce-Anderson (d 1978); *b* 11 December 1937; *Educ* Archbishop Tenison's GS London, Central Sch of Speech and Drama (Lawrence Olivier Award); *m* 1, Barbara Mognaz; 3 c (Robyn, Guy, Hedda); m 2, Celestine Randall; 1 da (Charlotte); m 3, Beth Morris; m 4, Noelyn George; 1 da (Sophie Martha George-Moore); *Career* actor; prof stage debut 1959 as 1st Immigration Officer in A View from the Bridge (Theatre Royal Windsor), London stage debut 1959 as William in As You Like It (Old Vic Theatre Co); many radio plays, dramas and short stories incl The Hitch Hiker's Guide to the Galaxy; *Theatre* numerous appearances; Old Vic Theatre Co 1959–61 incl: A Midsummer Night's Dream, Dr Faustus, Twelfth Night, The White Devil, Saint Joan, Romeo and Juliet, Mourning Becomes Electra; Theatre Royal Windsor 1959–1968 incl: Pride and Prejudice, Present Laughter, An Ideal Husband, The Importance of Being Ernest; Mermaid Theatre 1962–67 incl: The Plough and the Stars, The Good Soldier Schweyk, The Trojan Wars, The Fight for Barbara; Royal Court 1963–72 incl: Julius Caesar, Ojections to Sex and Violence, Action, Treats; Colchester Rep Co 1967–68 incl: A Day In The Life of Joe Egg, Spring and Port Wine (also dir), Forget-Me-Not Lane; Bristol Old Vic 1969–71 incl: Major Barbara, Macbeth, A Streetcar Named Desire, Woyzeck, The Iceman Cometh, Who's Afraid of Virginia Woolf; RSC 1973–86 incl: Section Nine, Peter Pan, Henry VIII, Twelfth Night, All's Well That Ends Well, Poppy, Mother Courage, A Penny for a Song; RNT 1977–1998 incl: Bedroom Farce, State of Revolution, Plenty, The Romans in Britain, The Life of Galileo, Love for Love, The Threepenny Opera, Dalliance, A Small Family Business, Sister Feelings, The Shaughraun, Peer Gynt, Piano, An Enemy of the People, The Cherry Orchard, The President of an Empty Room; West End appearances incl: Hughie and Others (Duchess) 1963, It's a Two Foot Six Inches Above The Ground World (Wyndham's) 1970, Treats (Mayfair) 1976, New Found Land (Arts Theatre) 1977, Bedroom Farce (Prince of Wales, also Broadway) 1978, The Hardshoulder (Aldwych) 1983, Paris Match (Garrick) 1989, Reflected Glory (Vaudeville) 1992, Disposing of the Body (Hampstead) 1999, The Cherry Orchard (National Theatre) 2001, My Fair Lady (Theatre Royal Drury Lane) 2003, Festen (Lyric) 2004–05, The History Boys (Wyndham's) 2006–07; *Television* debut in 1962 as Georges in Dinner With the Family (BBC); since then over 200 appearance incl: Three Men in a Boat, Brideshead Revisited, The Secret Diary - The Growing Pains of Adrian Mole, Rock Follies, Middlemarch, Solo, Just Between Ourselves, Small World, Soldiers Talking Cleanly, Love on A Gunboat, Just William, The Last Place on Earth, Love on a Branchline, The Beat Goes On, The Queen's Nose (4 series), The Missing Postman, Leprechauns, Silent Witness, Ready When You Are Mr McGill, Foyles War, The Brief; guest appearances with Fry and Laurie, Dawn French, Emma Thompson, Rowan Atkinson, Lenny Henry, Alexei Sayle and Harry Enfield; *Film* roles incl: Young Man in The White Bus, Major Steele in A Bridge Too Far, Michael in White Bird, Guy in Diversion, Howard in Singleton's Pluck, Mr Jolly in Clockwise, Roscoe in Under Suspicion, MacKenzie in Brassed Off; *Awards* winner of SWET Award for Best Actor in a Revival for A Doll's House (RSC) 1982; 1983 SWET Award nominations incl: Best Actor in a Musical, Best Supporting Actor, Best Actor in a Revival; Tony Award nomination for Broadway prodn of All's Well That Ends Well 1983; *Recreations* supporter Chelsea FC, motor cycling, music, computing; *Style*— Stephen Moore, Esq; ⌧ c/o Markham & Froggatt Ltd, Julian House, 4 Windmill Street, London W1P 1HF (tel 020 7636 4412, fax 020 7637 5233, e-mail himself@stephenmoore.co.uk, website www.stephenmoore.co.uk)

MOORE, Stuart Alfred; JP (Gtr Manchester 1996), DL (Gtr Manchester 2007); s of Alfred Moore (d 1995), and Kathleen, *née* Dodd (d 1986); *b* 9 October 1939; *Educ* Stockport Sch,

Univ of Manchester (BA, MA, DSocSc, Cobden Prize); *m* 1966, Diana Mary, da of Laurence Thomas Michael Connery, of Ashton-under-Lyne; 2 s (Christopher John b 1967, Michael Stuart b 1970), 1 da (Lucy Jane b 1968); *Career* Univ of Manchester: computer offr 1960–64, research associate 1964–66, lectr 1966–74, sr lectr 1974–92, Robert Ottley prof of quantitative studies 1992–99, dir Research Support Unit Faculty of Econ and Social Studies 1970–80, dean Faculty of Econ and Social Studies 1980–83, pro-vice-chllr 1985–90, actg vice-chllr 1990–92, dep vice-chllr 1990–96, pro-vice-chllr 1996–99, chm of Convocation 2000–04; chm: Central Manchester Healthcare NHS Tst 1991–2001, Stockport Primary Care Tst 2001–06, City of Manchester Magistrates' Bench 2006–; author of various academic pubns; *Recreations* music, gardening, photography, travel, detective stories; *Style*— Prof S A Moore, DL; ✉ City of Manchester Magistrates' Court, Crown Square, Manchester M60 1PR (tel 0161 830 4260)

MOORE, Terence (Terry); CBE (1993); s of Arthur Doncaster Moore, and Dorothy Irene Gladys, *née* Godwin; *b* 24 December 1931; *Educ* Strand Sch Univ of London (BScEcon), Harvard Business Sch; *m* 17 Sept 1955, Tessa Catherine, da of Ernest Walter Wynne; 2 s (Simon Jeremy b 1961, Adam Gavin b 1965), 1 da (Anna Louise b 1968); *Career* Nat Serv Army; mktg, fin and economics appts Shell International 1948–64, economist Locana Corp 1964–65; Conoco Ltd: economist, mangr econ planning, gen mangr and dir 1965–74, dep md Mktg Ops 1974–79, md Supply and Trading 1979–86, gp md/ceo 1986–95, conslt 1995–; non-exec dir John Fisher plc 1998–2003; pres Oil Industries Club 1989–90 and 2003–; dir and hon sec Inst Petroleum 1995–2003; dir Conoco Pension Fund Ltd 1995–2003; govr Greenwich Theatre 1992–98; ACII, AICS, FInstPet 1996, FEI 2003; *Recreations* theatre, reading, music; *Style*— Terry Moore, Esq, CBE; ✉ 67 Merchant Court, Thorpes Yard, 61 Wapping Wall, London E1W 3SJ (tel and fax 020 7481 0853, e-mail t.moore@talktalk.net)

MOORE, Brig W H (Bill); CBE; *m* Jane; 2 s; *Career* operational experience incl: NI, Falklands Campaign, Sierra Leone, UN serv; memb Directing Staff Army Staff Coll 1994, cmd 7 Para Regt RHA 1996 (previously cmd artillery batty), Col Force Devpt Directorate Gen of Doctrine and Devpt 1998, Higher Command and Staff Course 2000, ACOS (Ops) Sierra Leone 2001, cmd 19 Mech Bde 2001, cmd Jt Task Force Sierra Leone (Operation Keeling) 2003, cmd 19 Mech Bde Iraq 2003, DEC Ground Manoeuvre MOD 2004–; coach and mgr under 15 cricket Wilts 2000 and 2001; FIMgt; *Recreations* mountain marathons, hockey, hill walking, skiing, cricket; *Style*— Brig Bill Moore, CBE; ✉ MOD Level 2, Zone 1, Main Building, Whitehall, London SW1A 2HB (tel 020 8218 3001, e-mail bill.moore423@mod.uk)

MOORE, Sir William Roger Clotworthy; 3 Bt (UK 1932), of Moore Lodge, Co Antrim; TD (1963), DL (Co Antrim 1990); s of Sir William Samson Moore, DL, JP, 2 Bt (d 1978), and Ethel Coburn Gordon (d 1973); *b* 17 May 1927; *Educ* Marlborough, RMC Sandhurst; *m* May 1954, Gillian, da of John Brown, of Co Antrim; 1 s (Richard William b 1955), 1 da (Belinda Jane b 1956); *Heir* s, Richard Moore; *Career* Lt Royal Inniskilling Fusiliers 1945, Maj North Irish Horse 1956; Grand Juror Co Antrim 1952–68, High Sheriff Co Antrim 1964; BBC broadcaster 1964–66; prison visitor 1965–71, chm Bd of Visitors HM Prison Castledillon Co Armagh 1971–72, memb Parole Bd for Scotland 1981–83; *Recreations* shooting, golf, country pursuits; *Clubs* Kildare St Univ (Dublin); *Style*— Sir William Moore, Bt, TD, DL; ✉ Moore Lodge, Ballymoney, Co Antrim BT53 7NT

MOORE-BICK, Maj-Gen John D; CBE 1997 (OBE 1991); s of John Ninian Moore-Bick (d 2001), and Kathleen Margaret, *née* Beall (d 2003); bro of Martin James Moore-Bick (Hon Mr Justice Moore-Bick), *qv*; *b* 10 October 1949; *Educ* Univ of Oxford (MA); *m*; 1 da; *Career* early serv with Royal Marines Germany, Falkland Islands, Norway and NI, Führungsakademie der Bundeswehr 1979–82, asst to chm NATO Mil Ctee Brussels 1987–89, Regtl Cdr Germany and Gulf War 1989–91, Branch Col MOD 1991–94, Higher Command and Staff Course 1994, chief engr NATO Implementation Force Bosnia 1994–96, dir Princ MOD Directorate 1997–99, ldr study team Defence Postgrad Acad 1999, mil advsr to High Rep Bosnia and Herzegovina 2000, GOC UK Support Command Germany 2001–, special defence advsr to Govt of Serbia and Montenegro 2003–; Hon Col 39 Regt Royal Signals, Col Cmdt RE; vice-chm Skinners' Sch; memb Ct of Assts Worshipful Co of Skinners (Renter Warden 2003); FICE 1997, FIL; *Style*— Maj-Gen John Moore-Bick, CBE; ✉ c/o Defence Section, British Embassy Belgrade, c/o Foreign & Commonwealth Office, King Charles Street, London SW1A 2AH (tel 01580 831926, e-mail kestral4@bfgnet.de)

MOORE-BICK, Rt Hon Lord Justice; Rt Hon Sir Martin James; kt (1995), PC (2005); s of John Ninian Moore-Bick (d 2001), and Kathleen Margaret, *née* Beall (d 2003); bro of Maj-Gen John Moore-Bick, CBE, , *qv*; *b* 6 December 1946; *Educ* Skinners Sch Tunbridge Wells, Christ's Coll Cambridge (MA); *m* 3 Aug 1974, Tessa Penelope, da of George Michael Gee; 2 da (Catherine b 1977, Elizabeth b 1977), 2 s (Christopher b 1980, Matthew b 1983); *Career* called to the Bar Inner Temple 1969 (bencher 1992), recorder of the Crown Court 1990–95, judge of the High Court of Justice (Queen's Bench Div) 1995–2005, Lord Justice of Appeal 2005–, dep head of civil justice 2007–; chm Legal Servs Consultancy Panel 2005–; *Recreations* music, literature, gardening; *Style*— The Rt Hon Lord Justice Moore-Bick; ✉ Royal Courts of Justice, Strand, London WC2A 2LL

MOORE-GILLON, Dr John Christopher; *b* 2 January 1953; *Educ* Tiffin Sch, St Catharine's Coll Cambridge, St Thomas' Hosp Med Sch; *m* 1980, Victoria Kirby, FRCS; 1 s (Edwin b 1984), 2 da (Olivia b 1986, Claudia b 1994); *Career* conslt physician: Dept of Respiratory Med St Bartholomew's Hosp 1988–, King Edward VII's Hosp for Offrs 2005–; pres Br Lung Fndn 2001– (chm 1994–99), hon sec Br Thoracic Soc 1992–94; Liveryman Worshipful Soc of Apothecaries (memb Ct of Assts); *Publications* author of book chapters, invited review articles and original scientific papers on respiratory medicine; *Clubs* Trygone, Athenaeum; *Style*— Dr John Moore-Gillon, MD, FRCP; ✉ Department of Respiratory Medicine, St Bartholomew's Hospital, West Smithfield, London EC1A 7BE (tel 020 7601 8441, fax 020 7601 8437)

MOORE OF LOWER MARSH, Baron (Life Peer UK 1992), of Lower Marsh in the London Borough of Lambeth; John Edward Michael Moore; PC (1986); s of Edward O Moore, of Brighton; *b* 26 November 1937; *Educ* Licensed Victuallers' Sch Slough, LSE (BSc, chm Cons Assoc 1958–59, pres Students' Union 1959–60); *m* 1962, Sheila Sarah, da of Richard Tillotson, of Illinois, USA; 1 da (Hon Stephanie b 1968), 2 s (Hon Martin b 1970, Hon Richard b 1972); *Career* Nat Serv Royal Sussex Regt Korea 1955–57; worked in banking and stockbroking and took part in Democratic politics in Chicago 1961–65; cncllr (Cons) London Borough of Merton 1971–74, MP (Cons) Croydon Central Feb 1974–92; vice-chm Cons Pty 1975–79, Parly under sec Energy 1979–83, econ sec Treasy June-Oct 1983, fin sec Treasy (responsibilities incl taxation and privatisation) 1983–86; sec of state for: Tport 1986–87, Health and Social Servs 1987–88, Social Security 1988–89; chm: Dean Witter International Ltd 1975–79 (dir 1968–79), Credit Suisse Asset Management 1992–2000 (dir 1991–2000), Energy Saving Trust Ltd 1992–95 (pres 1995–2001), Rolls-Royce plc 2003–05 (dir 1994, dep chm 1996–2003); dir: Gartmore Investment Management Group Ltd 1990–91, Monitor Company Inc USA 1991– (chm Monitor Europe 1991–), Swiss American Corporation 1992–96, GTECH Corporation 1992–2001, Blue Circle Industries plc 1993–2001, Camelot Holdings Ltd 1993–94, Camelot Group plc 1994–98, Central European Growth Fund plc 1995–2000, BEA Associates 1996–98, TIG Holdings Inc 1997–99, Private Client Bank Zurich 1999–2004; memb: Advsy Bd Marvin & Palmer Associates Inc USA 1989– (dir 1994–), Supervisory Bd ITT Automotive Europe GmbH 1994–97, Advsy Bd Sir Alexander Gibb & Co 1990–95; memb Cncl IOD 1991–2002; memb Ct of Govrs LSE 1977–2002; *Recreations* sport; *Clubs* RAC; *Style*— The Rt Hon Lord Moore of Lower Marsh, PC

MOORE OF WOLVERCOTE, Baron (Life Peer UK 1986), of Wolvercote in the City of Oxford; Philip Brian Cecil Moore; GCB (1985, KCB 1980, CB 1973), GCVO (1983, KCVO 1976), CMG (1966), QSO (1986), PC (1977); s of Cecil Moore, ICS (d 1950), and Alice Mona, *née* Bath (d 1967); *b* 6 April 1921; *Educ* Dragon Sch Oxford, Cheltenham Coll, BNC Oxford; *m* 28 Aug 1945, Joanna Ursula, da of Capt M E Greenop, DCLI (d 1972); 2 da (Hon Sally Jane (Hon Mrs Leachman) b 9 June 1949, Hon Jill Georgina (Hon Mrs Gabriel) b 2 Dec 1951); *Career* served WW II RAF Bomber Cmd, and POW; PPS to First Lord of the Admty 1957–58 (asst private sec 1950–51), dep high cmmr Singapore 1963–65 (dep UK cmmr 1961–63), chief of PR MOD 1965–66, private sec to HM The Queen and keeper of the Queen's Archives 1977–86 (dep private sec 1972–77, asst private sec 1966–72), a permanent lord in waiting to HM The Queen 1990–; former chm Tstees King George VI and Queen Elizabeth Fndn of St Catharines, vice-pres SPCK; hon fell BNC Oxford 1981; *Recreations* golf, shooting, fishing; *Clubs* MCC; *Style*— The Rt Hon Lord Moore of Wolvercote, PC, GCB, GCVO, CMG, QSO; ✉ Apartment 64, Hampton Court Palace, Surrey KT8 9AU (tel 020 8943 4695)

MOOREHEAD, Caroline; OBE (2005); *b* 28 October 1944; *Educ* French Lycées London and Rome, Sorbonne, Univ of London (BA); *m*; 2 c; *Career* child psychologist Rome 1967–68, reporter Time Magazine Rome 1968–69, feature writer Daily Telegraph Magazine 1969–70, features ed TES 1970–73, specialist in human rights and feature writer The Times 1973–88, human rights corr and feature contrib The Independent 1988–93; contribs and reviews for TES, TLS, London Review of Books, Spectator, New Statesman, New Society, Listener, Literary Review, Sunday Telegraph, Harpers, Departures, Traveler (US); memb: Wolfenden Ctee on Voluntary Work 1977, London Library Ctee 1990–94, Human Rights Mission Eminent Persons to Moscow 1990, Exec Ctee PEN 1993–96 (memb Writers in Prison Ctee 1989–96), Cncl RSL 1995–, Cncl Soc of Authors 1996–, Ctee Redress Tst; tstee and memb Cncl Index on Censorship 1990–, tstee Br Inst of Human Rights, conslt various refugee ctees, judge various literary and human rights prizes; FRSL; *Television* script writer: Forty Minutes Troublesome People (also presenter, BBC) 1987, Prisoners of Conscience (also assoc prodr, two 10–part series BBC) 1988–91, Children and Human Rights (UN film), Human Rights, Human Wrongs (also prodr 1992–); *Books* trans of novel and 3 art books from French and Italian 1967–70, Fortune's Hostages (1980), Sidney Bernstein: A Biography (1983), Freya Stark: A Biography (1985), Troublesome People (1987), Beyond the Rim of the World: The Letters of Freya Stark (ed, 1988), Betrayed: Children in Today's World (1989), Bertrand Russell: A Life (1993), The Lost Treasures of Troy (1994), Dunant's Dream: War, Switzerland and the Red Cross (1997), Iris Origo, Marchesa of Val D'Orcia (2000), Martha Gellhorn: A Life (2003),The Collected Letters of Martha Gellhorn (ed, 2006); *Pamphlets* incl: Working Children (Anti-slavery Soc, 1987), Children of Namibia (Oxfam, 1988), A Guide to Human Rights (BBC, 1992); *Style*— Ms Caroline Moorehead, OBE, FRSL; ✉ 89 Gloucester Avenue, London NW1 8LB; c/o Clare Alexander, Gillon Aitken Associates, 18–21 Cavage Place, London SW10 9PT

MOORES, Sir Peter; kt (2003), CBE (1991), DL (Lancashire 1992); s of Sir John Moores, CBE (d 1993), and late Ruby, *née* Knowles; *b* 9 April 1932; *Educ* Eton, ChCh Oxford; *m* 1960 (m dis), Luciana (d 1994), da of Salvatore Pinto, of Naples; 1 da (Donatella), 1 s (Alexis); *Career* dir Singer and Friedlander 1972–92, chm The Littlewoods Organisation 1977–80 (dir 1965–93); tstee Tate Gallery 1978–85, govr BBC 1981–83; fndr patron Peter Moores Fndn 1964, fndr Compton Verney House Tst 1993; Hon MA ChCh Oxford, Gold Medal of the Italian Republic 1974; hon fell RNCM 1985; *Recreations* opera, shooting; *Style*— Sir Peter Moores, CBE, DL; ✉ Parbold Hall, Wigan, Lancashire WN8 7TG

MOORHEAD, Prof John; s of Patrick Moorhead (d 1960), and Mary, *née* Ashurst; *b* 1 December 1932; *Educ* St Edward's Coll Liverpool, Univ of Liverpool Med Sch (MB ChB), Georgetown Univ Hosp Washington DC; *m* 20 June 1967, Anna; 1 da (Alison b 25 Sept 1973); *Career* asst prof Georgetown Univ Hosp Washington DC 1964–67, conslt nephrologist Royal Free Hosp 1967–, sec gen Int Soc of Nephrology 1975–82, prof of renal med Royal Free Hosp Sch of Med and UCL 1993–, med dir Royal Free Hosp 1993–, chm and med dir Hosp of St John and St Elizabeth 1997–2000, emeritus prof Royal Free and UC Sch of Med 1998–; dir and tstee Hosp Mgmnt Tst 2002, princ tstee J F Moorhead Research Tst; formerly: special tstee Royal Free Hosp, tstee Peter Samuel Research Tst; FRCP; *Publications* author of 1 book and over 300 papers on subjects incl: progressive kidney disease, especially as influence by lipids and lipoproteins, molecular cell biology of progressive renal disease, organisational evolution; *Recreations* music, piano, painting (oils); *Style*— Prof John Moorhead; ✉ The Royal Free Hospital, Department of Nephrology and Transplantation, Pond Street, London NW3 2QG (tel 020 7830 2930, fax 020 7830 2125)

MOORHOUSE, Geoffrey; s of William Heald (d 1971), and Gladys (d 2001), *née* Hoyle; step s of Richard Moorhouse (d 1998); *b* 29 November 1931; *Educ* Bury GS; *m* 1, May 1956 (m dis 1974), Janet Marion, da of Alec Murray (d 1978), of Christchurch, NZ; 2 da (Jane b 1960, Brigid b 1965 d 1981), 2 s (Andrew b 1961, Michael b 1966); m 2, Sept 1974 (m dis 1978), Barbara Jane, *née* Woodward; m 3, June 1983 (m dis 1996), Marilyn Isobel, *née* Edwards; *Career* coder RN 1950–52; journalist 1952–70 (chief features writer Manchester Guardian 1963–70), rode camels 2,000 miles across the Sahara 1972–73, worked as deep-sea fisherman out of Gloucester MA 1976–77, author; Hon DLitt Univ of Warwick 2006; FRGS 1972–95, FRSL 1982; *Books* The Other England (1964), Against All Reason (1969), Calcutta (1971), The Missionaries (1973), The Fearful Void (1974), The Diplomats (1977), The Boat and The Town (1979), The Best-Loved Game (1979, Cricket Soc Award), India Britannica (1983), Lord's (1983), To the Frontier (1984, Thomas Cook Award), Imperial City (1988), At the George (1989), Apples in the Snow (1990), Hell's Foundations - A Town, its Myths and Gallipoli (1992), OM: an Indian Pilgrimage (1993), A People's Game: the Centenary History of Rugby League 1895–1995 (1995), Sun Dancing: a Medieval Vision (1997, nominated Booker Prize), Sydney (1999), The Pilgrimage of Grace: the rebellion that shook Henry VIII's throne (2002), Great Harry's Navy: How Henry VIII Gave England Seapower (2005), The Last Office: 31st December 1539 (2008); *Recreations* listening to music, gardening, hill walking, looking at buildings, watching cricket and Bolton Wanderers FC; *Clubs* Lancashire CCC; *Style*— Geoffrey Moorhouse, FRSL; ✉ Park House, Gayle, Hawes, North Yorkshire DL8 3RT (tel and fax 01969 667456)

MOORIN, Eur Ing Raymond Leslie; s of Joseph Wilson Moorin (d 1957), and Edith, *née* Waterston (d 1985); *b* 1 March 1939; *Educ* Emanuel Sch, Wandsworth Tech Coll, Borough Poly; *m* 14 Aug 1965, (Victoria) Wendy, da of Edwin McCleod Miller, of Merseyside; 3 s (Robert b 1966, Patrick b 1969, Matthew b 1971); *Career* bldg servs engr Slough BC 1964–70, mechanical and electrical engr Dept of Educn & Science 1970–72, assoc HL Dawson and Assocs 1972–73, sr ptnr Multi Building Services Design Partnership 1973–; CEng, MEI (MInstE 1968), MIMechE 1969, MInstR 1972, FCIBSE 1975; *Recreations* golf, squash, tennis; *Style*— Eur Ing Raymond Moorin; ✉ Lyndale, 21 Coates Lane, High Wycombe, Buckinghamshire HP13 5EY (tel 01494 533147); tel 01494 474712, fax 01494 474738

MOORSOM, Patrick William Pierre; s of Frederick William Moorsom (d 1971), of Dinas Powys, Glamorgan, and Jeanne Juliette, *née* Phelippon; *b* 30 October 1942; *Educ* Downside, Jesus Coll Cambridge (MA, Squash blue); *m* 14 Sept 1965, Dominique Ann, da of Andre Leroy; 1 s (Pierre Frederick Andre), 3 da (Natasha Juliet, Sophie Ann, Stephanie Helene); *Career* CA Arthur Andersen & Co 1965–69; dir: Rothschild

M

Intercontinental Bank 1969–78, Barclays Merchant Bank 1978–81; md Cayzer Ltd 1981–87, vice-chm Guinness Mahon & Co Ltd 1987–91; chm: Regent Inns plc 1989–95, Brown, Shipley & Co Ltd 1996–2006, Westhouse Securities LLP 2004–; FCA 1971; *Style*— Patrick Moorsom, Esq; ✉ 37 Sterndale Road, London W14 0HT (tel 020 7602 9437)

MOOS, Khursheed Francis; OBE (1995); s of Jehangir Dhanjishah Moos (d 1973), and Maria Gerritje, *née* Tulp; *b* 1 November 1934; *Educ* Dulwich Coll, Univ of London (BDS, MB BS), Guy's Hosp, Westminster Hosp; *m* 23 June 1962, Katharine, da of George Stewart Addison (d 1952); 2 s (Christopher b 1964, John b 1968), 1 da (Hilary b 1966); *Career* Nat Serv RADC 1959–61, Lt 1959, Capt 1960; registrar in oral surgery Mount Vernon Hosp Middx 1966–67, sr registrar in oral surgery Univ of Wales Cardiff Dental Sch 1967–69; conslt oral surgn: South Warwicks, Coventry, E Birmingham Hosps 1969–74; conslt oral and maxillofacial surgn Plastic and Maxillofacial Unit Canniesburn Hosp Glasgow 1974–99, advsr and civilian conslt oral surgn to RN 1976–99; Univ of Glasgow: hon prof of oral and maxillofacial surgery 1992–, hon sr research fell 2002–; visiting prof Univ of Otago NZ 1988; fellowship examiner: RCSEd, RCPSGlas, RCSI; pres: BAOMS 1991–92, Craniofacial Soc of GB 1994–95; dean Dental Faculty RCPSGlas 1992–95; chm: Special Advsy Ctee in Oral Surgery and Oral Med 1985–89, Intercollegiate Speciality Advsy Bd in Oral and Maxillofacial Surgery 1995–98; memb: Bd Indian Med Assoc (UK) 1999–2001 (pres 1998–99), Euro Assoc Cranio Maxillofacial Surgery, Int Assoc Oral Maxillofacial Surgery; memb: BAOMS 1964, BDA 1958, BMA 1964, RSM 1965; *Books* Surgery of the Mouth and Jaws (contrib, 1985), Companion to Dental Studies (contrib, 1986), Plastic Surgery in Infancy and Childhood (contrib, 1988), Operative Maxillofacial Surgery (contrib, 1998), Oral & Maxillofacial Surgery (contrib, 1999), Oral & Maxillofacial Surgery - Orthognathic Surgery (contrib, 2000), Textbook of General and Oral Surgery (contrib, 2003), Oral and Maxillofacial Diseases (jt ed and contrib, 2004); *Recreations* dental history, music, natural history, philately, eastern philosophy, gardening; *Style*— Prof Khursheed F Moos, OBE; ✉ Department of Oral and Maxillofacial Surgery, Glasgow Dental Hospital and School, 378 Sauchiehall Street, Glasgow G2 3JZ (tel and fax 0141 211 9824)

MORAES, Claude; MEP (Lab); s of Mr H I Moraes, and Theresa, *née* Aranha; *Educ* St Modan's HS Stirling, Univ of Dundee (LLB), Birkbeck Coll London (MSc), LSE; *Career* political advsr to Dr John Reid MP and Paul Boateng MP House of Commons 1987–89, nat offr TUC 1989–92, rep Euro TUC, dir JCWI 1992–; chief exec Immigrants' Aid Tst, cmmr Cmmn for Racial Equality 1998–99; Parly candidate (Lab) Harrow West 1992; MEP (Lab) London 1999–; vice-pres Educn Action International, former memb Cncl Liberty (NCCL), tstee Toynbee Hall East London; FRSA 1998; *Publications* Social Work and Minorities: European Perspectives (co-author 1998), The Politics of Migration (co-author, 2003), Immigratie e Italiani (co-author, 2004), Perspectives on Migration (contirb, 2005), European Civic Index (contrib, 2005); articles on human rights issues in journals and newspapers; *Recreations* film (memb BFI), Scottish literature, chess, listening to BBC Radio 4, 5 and the World Service; *Style*— Claude Moraes, Esq, MEP; ✉ tel 00 3 22 284 5553, website www.claudemoraes.net

MORAN, Andrew Gerard; QC (1994); s of Francis Michael Moran (d 1979), of Widnes, and Winifrede, *née* Plant (d 1971); *b* 19 October 1953; *Educ* West Park GS St Helens, BRNC Dartmouth, Balliol Coll Oxford (BA); *m* 17 Feb 1977, Carole Jane, da of James Sullivan; 6 s (Michael b 1978, James b 1980, Peter b 1984, Kevin b 1987, John b 1989, Matthew b 1995), 1 da (Claire Louise b 1982); *Career* Univ Cadetship RN, Offr and Merchant Navy Deck Offr 1972; called to the Bar Gray's Inn 1976 (bencher 2005), dep High Ct judge; recorder of the Crown Ct; arbitrator Singapore Chamber of Maritime Arbitration; chm Disciplinary Tribunal Int Petroleum Exchange; memb Commercial Bar Assoc; *Recreations* travel, sport, walking, sailing; *Style*— Andrew Moran, Esq, QC; ✉ 7 Harrington Street, Liverpool L2 9YH (tel 0151 242 0700); Stone Chambers, 4 Field Court, Gray's Inn, London WC1R 5EF (tel 020 7440 6900); St John's Building, 24A-28 St John Street, Manchester M3 4DJ (tel 0161 214 1500, e-mail agmqc@aol.com)

MORAN, Brendan John; s of Peter Moran, of Kilmihil, Co Clare, and Teresa, *née* Morrissey (d 1959); *b* 21 July 1957; *Educ* Laken Nat Sch, Christian Brothers Sch Kilrush, UC Cork (MCh, MB BCh, BAO); *m* 4 May 1985, Dr Karina Kirby; 1 s (Shane b 14 Jan 1986), 1 da (Suzanne b 28 June 1987); *Career* sr registrar: Basingstoke Dist Hosp 1993–94, Royal Hants County Hosp 1994–95, Univ of Southampton Hosps 1995; conslt surgn N Hants Hosp Basingstoke 1995–, dir UK Pseudomyxoma Nat Referral Centre; memb Bd and Ctee: Assoc of Coloproctology of GB and I, Assoc of Surgns of GB and I, Nutrition Soc, Section of Surgery RSM, Section of Coloproctology RSM (memb Cncl), Surgical Assoc for Clinical Research in Europe (SACRE); tstee: Wessex Cancer Tst, Kingston Tst; numerous contribs to nat and int meetings 1994–, numerous lectures 2002–; accredited clinical nutritionist 1991; Espen-Abbott Fellowship European Soc of Parenteral & Enteral Nutrition 1989, Alfano Award for Colorectal Cancer Surgery American Soc of Abdominal Surgns 2002; European Sch of Oncology colorectal fellowship 1994, RSM Section of Coloproctology travelling fellowship 1992 and 1995, European travelling fell Br Jl of Surgery 1995, Assoc of Coloproctology of GB & I American travelling fell 2000; FRCSI 1984, FRCSI (Gen) 1995, FRCS 1997; *Publications* reg reviewer: The Br Jl of Surgery, Techniques in Coloproctology, Colorectal Disease, Cancer, Gut; author of numerous chapters and articles in various pubns; *Style*— Brendan Moran, Esq; ✉ The North Hampshire Hospital, Basingstoke, Hampshire RG24 9NA

MORAN, Air Marshal Christopher Hugh (Chris); OBE (1997), MVO (1993); s of Edward Moran (d 1991), and Margaret, *née* Hewitt (d 1984); *b* 28 April 1956; *Educ* Bishop Ullathorne Sch Coventry, UMIST (BSc), KCL (MA); *m* 26 April 1980, Elizabeth Jane, *née* Goodwin; 2 da (Jennifer b 20 Nov 1983, Lucy b 20 Aug 1986), 1 s (Thomas b 15 Sept 1993); *Career* pilot trg RAF Coll Cranwell 1977–78, 4 (Army Co-operation) Sqdn RAF Gütersloh 1980–85, qualified weapons instr (Harrier) 1983, exchange duties Marine Attack Sqdn (VMA) 542 US Marine Corps 1985–87, 233 (Harrier) Operational Conversion Unit 1987–91, advanced cmd and staff course RAF Coll Bracknell 1991, equerry to HRH The Duke of Edinburgh 1992–93, OC 4 (Army Co-operation) Sqdn RAF Laarbruch 1994–96, OC RAF Wittering 1997–98, higher cmd and staff course Jt Servs Cmd and Staff Coll (JSCSC) 1999, divnl dir JSCSC 1999–2000, Dir of Air Staff MOD 2000–02, jt staff Pentagon 2002–03, AOC No 1 Gp 2003–05, Asst Chief of Air Staff 2005–07, Dep Cdr Allied Jt Force Cmd Brunssum 2007–; memb Bd CAA 2005–07; pres RAF Triathlon; QCVSA 1991; *Recreations* skiing, sailing, triathlon; *Clubs* RAF, Yealm Yacht; *Style*— Air Marshal Chris Moran, OBE, MVO

MORAN, Christopher John; s of Thomas Moran (d 1977), and Iva Mary, *née* Alcock (d 1989); *b* 16 January 1948, London; *Educ* Owens GS; *m* 1981 (m dis 1999), Helen Elisabeth Taylor; 2 s (Charles, Jamie (twins) b 31 Jan 1988); *Career* chm Christopher Moran Gp of Cos 1970–; tstee: UCL Hosps Charitable Fndn 1999– (chm 2003–), Cncl of Christians and Jews Exec Ctee 2003–, Mary Rose Tst 2004–; chm Finance Bd LSO 2004–; chm: Co-operation Ireland (GB) 2004–, Co-operation Ireland 2006–; dir C&UCO Properties Ltd 2006–; memb: Consultative Ctee Dulwich Picture Gallery 1993–96, Advsy Bd Thames 1994–97; FRSA 2005; *Recreations* architecture, opera, art, politics, country pursuits; *Style*— Christopher Moran, Esq; ✉ c/o Crosby Hall, Cheyne Walk, London SW3 5AZ

MORAN, David John; *b* 22 August 1959; *m* 1993, Carol Ann Marquis; *Career* diplomat; exec offr Office of Telecommunications (Oftel) DTI 1985, entered FCO 1985; ODA: higher exec offr Zimbabwe Africa Gen Section 1985–86, higher exec offr Finance Dept 1986–87, spokesman News Dept 1987–88; second sec Nairobi 1988–91, head IMF/Debt Section Economic Relations Dept FCO 1991–93, first sec (Know How Fund) Moscow 1993–96; FCO: head France and Switzerland Section Western European Dept 1996–98, head Justice and Home Affrs Section EU Dept (Internal) 1998–99, head Charter of Rights Section EU Dept (Internal) 1999–2000; dep perm rep UK Delgn to OECD Paris 2001–05, ambass to Uzbekistan 2005–07; *Style*— David Moran, Esq; ✉ c/o Foreign & Commonwealth Office, King Charles Street, London SW1A 2AH

MORAN, Dylan; *Career* comedian, actor, writer and performer; weekly columnist The Irish Times 1995–96; *Live Performances* incl: Edinburgh Festival 1996, 1998 and 1999 (Perrier Award 1996), Gurgling for Money (UK tour) 1997, Murphy's Cat Laughs (Kilkenny Festival) 1997, Hay Literary Festival 1997 and 2001, Black Books (Channel 4 Sitcom Festival) 1998, Just for Laughs (Montreal Comedy Festival) 1998, Vancouver Comedy Festival 1998, Ready, Steady...Cough (UK tour) 2000, Monster (UK tour) 2003, Monster II (UK tour) 2004, Like Totally (UK tour) 2006; *Television* How Do You Want Me 1998 and 1999, Black Books 2000 and 2001 (Bronze Rose of Montreux for Best Sitcom 2001, BAFTA Best Sitcom 2001), Black Books 3 2004; *Film* Notting Hill 1999, The Actors 2003, Shaun of the Dead 2004, A Cock and Bull Story 2005; *Style*— Dylan Moran, Esq; ✉ c/o PBJ Management Ltd, 7 Soho Street, London W1D 3DQ (tel 020 7287 1112, fax 020 7287 1191)

MORAN, Dr John Denton; RD (1977); s of Paul Francis Moran (d 1989), of Marine Gate, Brighton, and Mary, *née* Denton (d 1997); *b* 3 November 1940; *Educ* Downside, Univ of London, St George's Hosp London (MB BS), Guy's Hosp London (LDS, RCS, DFFP, Dip), Univ of Surrey (Dip, MSc); *m* 16 June 1973, Jane, da of Gen Sir Malcolm Cartwright-Taylor, KCB (d 1969); 2 da (Iona b 16 Sept 1973, Louise b 18 March 1975), 1 s (Paul b 29 Jan 1976); *Career* RNR: Surgn Sub Lt (dental) 1962, Surgn Lt (dental) 1964, Surgn Lt Cdr (dental) 1969, dental offr HMS Centaur RN 1965, med and dental offr White City and Jamaica Rd RMR, resigned 1979; dental house surgn Bart's 1964, med house surgn ENT Dept St George's Hosp Tooting 1970, med house physician Christchurch and Boscombe Hosps Bournemouth 1971, GP Brandon Manitoba Canada 1972, private dental practice Harley St 1973–; hon conslt dental surgn to retired RN offrs 1999–; MO: Margaret Pyke Centre 1974, Marie Stopes 1978–96, Menopause Clinic 1979–96; Freeman City of London 1979, Liveryman Worshipful Co of Barber Surgns 1980; memb BMA, FRSM; *Recreations* golf, shooting, skiing, walking, bridge; *Clubs* RAC, Royal Ashdown; *Style*— Dr John Moran, RD; ✉ Belvedere Farm, Cinder Hill Lane, Horsted Keynes, West Sussex RH17 7BA (tel 01825 790246); 30A Wimpole Street, London W1G 8YA (tel 020 7935 4870)

MORAN, 2 Baron (UK 1943); (Richard) John McMoran Wilson; KCMG (1981, CMG 1970); s of 1 Baron, MC (d 1977), formerly Dr (then Sir) Charles McMoran Wilson, and Dorothy, *née* Dufton (d 1983); *b* 22 September 1924; *Educ* Eton, King's Coll Cambridge; *m* 29 Dec 1948, Shirley Rowntree, eldest da of late George James Harris, MC, of Bossall Hall, York; 2 s, 1 da; *Heir* s, Hon James Wilson; *Career* served WWII RNVR, HMS Belfast, motor torpedo boats and HM destroyer Oribi; entered Foreign Service 1945, served in Ankara, Tel-Aviv, Rio de Janeiro, Washington and South Africa, head West African Dept Foreign Office 1968–73 (concurrently non-resident ambass to Chad 1970–73); ambass to: Hungary 1973–76, Portugal 1976–81; high cmmr to Canada 1981–84; sits as cross-bencher in House of Lords, elected hereditary peer 1999; chm All-Pty Conservation Gp of both Houses of Parliament 1993–2000; Euro Communities Ctee House of Lords: memb Industry Sub-Ctee 1984–86, memb Environment Sub-Ctee 1986–91, memb Agric Sub-Ctee 1991–95 and 1997–2000; other House of Lords ctees: memb Sub-Ctee of the Sci and Technol Ctee on the Scientific Base of the Nature Conservancy Cncl 1990–, memb Sub-Ctee of the Sci and Technol Ctee on Fish Stocks 1995–, Sub-Ctee on the 1996 Inter-Governmental Conf 1995–; pres: Welsh Salmon and Trout Anglers Assoc 1988–95 and 2001–, Radnorshire Wildlife Tst 1994–; vice-pres RSPB 1996–97 (memb Cncl 1989–94); exec vice-pres Salmon and Trout Assoc 2000– (chm 1997–2000); chm: Wildlife and Countryside Link 1990–95, Regnl Fisheries Advsy Ctee, Welsh Region Nat Rivers Authy 1989–94, Jt Fisheries Policy and Legislation Working Gp (The Moran Ctee) 1997–; vice-chm Atlantic Salmon Tst; Grand Cross Order of the Infante Portugal 1978; *Books* as John Wilson: CB: A Life of Sir Henry Campbell-Bannerman (Whitbread award for biography 1973), Fairfax (1985); *Recreations* fishing, fly-tying, bird watching; *Clubs* Flyfishers' (pres 1987–88), Beefsteak; *Style*— The Rt Hon Lord Moran, KCMG; ✉ House of Lords, London SW1A 0PW

MORAN, Margaret; MP; *b* 1955; *Educ* St Ursula's HS Greenwich, St Mary's Coll Twickenham, Univ of Birmingham (BSocSc); *Career* chief exec Housing for Women until 1997; MP (Lab) Luton S 1997–; PPS to: sec of state for Tport 1997–98, Rt Hon Mo Mowlam, MP, 1999–2001, Rt Hon Baroness Morgan of Huyton 2001–02, Rt Hon Andrew Smith, MP, *qv* 2002–; memb NI Select Ctee 1997, chm Parly Lab Housing Gp, chm PLP Parly Affairs Ctee, sec PLP NI Ctee; assoc memb Br-Irish Parly Gp 1997; currently memb various All-Pty Parly Gps and Parly Backbench Ctees incl Info Technol, Environment and NI; chair EURIM; sometime: cncllr and ldr Lewisham Cncl, dep chm Assoc of Metropolitan Authorities (chm Housing Ctee); govr: Denbigh Infants and Junior Sch, Cardinal Newman HS; chair APPG Domestic Violence, chair and fndr Luton Irish Forum; memb Ct Univ of Luton; *Recreations* visiting historic sites, walking, almost anything Irish, eating (especially curry); *Style*— Ms Margaret Moran, MP; ✉ House of Commons, London SW1A 0AA (tel 020 7219 5049, fax 020 7219 5094, e-mail moranm@parliament.uk, website www.margaretmoran.org); constituency office: 93 Castle Street, Luton LU1 3AN (tel 01582 731882, fax 01582 731882)

MORAN, Michael Edward (Mike); s of Edward Moran, of Barkingside, Essex, and Iris Jean, *née* Munn; *b* 16 February 1960; *Educ* Buckhurst Hill Co HS, Ealing Coll of HE (BA, Dip MRS); *m* 1, 8 Dec 1984 (m dis 2000), Sonya Caroline; 1 s (Oliver Eduard b 1 Jan 1989), 2 da (Rebecca b 15 April 1991, Gabriella b 27 Sept 1992); m 2, 15 April 2000, Janet Mary; 1 da (Gina Elizabeth b 6 April 2001), 1 s (Sean Edward b 27 June 2005); *Career* Ford Motor Company Ltd 1982–96: sales and after sales experience Ford of Britain 1982–89, mangr of trg Ford of Europe Brussels 1989–90, fleet sales/mktg Ford of Britain 1990–93, dir of sales and mktg Ford of Spain Madrid 1994–96; mktg dir Toyota (GB) plc 1996–99, commercial dir Toyota (GB) plc 1999–2003, worldwide dir of marketing and strategy RWE Thames Water plc 2003–04, chm RWE España 2003–04, dir ESSBIO Chile 2003–04, fndr and managing ptnr The Orchard Consultancy Ltd 2004–; memb Govt Advsy Ctee on Advtg; memb Mktg Gp of GB, memb MRS 1982, FRSA, fell Marketing Soc, FIMI; *Recreations* golf, motor sports; *Clubs* Solu; *Style*— Mike Moran, Esq; ✉ The Orchard Consultancy, Orchard House, New Road, Stanton Harcourt, Witney OX29 5RT (tel 01865 880020, fax 01865 881888)

MORAN, Tom; s of Michael Moran, and Brigid Gillick; *b* 16 November 1955, Dublin; *Educ* UC Dublin (BA, MA, DipEd), Inst of Public Administration Dublin (Cert); *m* 1979, Elizabeth, *née* O'Byrne; 4 s (Andrew, Conor, Declan, Barry); *Career* secdy sch teacher 1978–80, administrative offr then asst princ offr Irish Dept of Agriculture 1980–89, agriculture attaché to France and OECD Irish Embassy Paris 1989–92; Irish Dept of Agriculture: asst sec gen 1992–2005, sec gen 2005–; *Style*— Tom Moran, Esq; ✉ Irish Department for Agriculture & Food, Agriculture House, Kildare Street, Dublin 2, Ireland (tel 0035 3 607 2184)

MORAY, 20 Earl of (S 1562); Douglas John Moray Stuart; also Lord Abernethy and Strathearn (S 1562), Lord Doune (S 1581), Lord St Colme (S 1611), and Baron Stuart of Castle Stuart (GB 1796); s of 19 Earl of Moray (d 1974; himself 11 in descent from 1 Earl, an illegitimate s of James V of Scotland, Regent of Scotland from 1567 until his murder in 1570 by Hamilton of Bothwellhaugh), and Mabel Helen Maud (May) (d 1968), only child of late Benjamin 'Matabele' Wilson, of Battlefields, Southern Rhodesia; *b* 13

February 1928; *Educ* Trinity Coll Cambridge (BA), Hilton Coll Natal; *m* 27 Jan 1964, Lady Malvina Dorothea Murray, er da of 7 Earl of Mansfield (d 1971); 1 s (John Douglas Stuart, Lord Doune b 1966), 1 da (Lady Louisa b 1968); *Heir* s, Lord Doune; *Career* JP Perthshire 1968–96; FRICS; *Clubs* New (Edinburgh); *Style*— The Rt Hon the Earl of Moray; ✉ Doune Park, Doune, Perthshire FK16 6HA (tel 01786 841333); Darnaway Castle, Forres, Moray IV36 2ST (tel 01309 672101)

MORCOM, Christopher; QC (1991); s of (Alfred) Rupert Morcom (d 1996), of Ombersley, Worcs, and Mary, *née* Carslake (d 1994); *b* 4 February 1939; *Educ* Sherborne (music exhibitioner), Trinity Coll Cambridge (exhibitioner, MA); *m* 3 Sept 1966, Diane, da of late Jose A Toledo; 2 da (Charmian b 19 Jan 1968, Melanie Carmen b 3 March 1972), 1 s (Darrell Kenneth b 15 Feb 1969); *Career* called to the Bar Middle Temple 1963 (Harmsworth entrance exhibitioner, Astbury scholar, bencher 1996); head of chambers 1985–2006; chm: Competition Law Assoc 1985–99, Bar Musical Soc 1991–; memb Standing Advsy Ctee on Industrial Property 1990–2001; pres Ligue Internationale du Droit de la Concurrence (LIDC) 1996–98 (vice-pres 1994–96, hon pres 2000–); *Books* Service Marks - A Guide to the New Law (1987), A Guide to the Trade Marks Act 1994 (1994), The Modern Law of Trade Marks (jtly, 2000, 2 edn 2005); *Recreations* music, walking; *Clubs* Athenaeum; *Style*— Christopher Morcom, Esq, QC; ✉ Hogarth Chambers, 5 New Square, Lincoln's Inn, London WC2A 3RJ (tel 020 7404 0404, fax 020 7404 0505, e-mail barristers@hogarthchambers.com)

MORCOS, Prof Sameh Kamel; *b* 19 April 1949; *Educ* Maronite Sch Cairo, Univ of Cairo (MB BCh); *Career* radiologist; pre-registration house jobs Cairo Univ Teaching Hosps 1971–72, resident in gen surgery and orthopaedics Benha Gen Hosp Egypt 1972–73; SHO: in orthopaedics and casualty Bedford Gen Hosp England 1973, in casualty Noble's Hosp IOM 1973–74, in orthopaedics Queen Mary's Hosp for Children Carshalton Surrey 1974–75, in orthopaedics Rowley Bristow Orthopaedic Hosp Pyrford Surrey and St Peter's Hosp Chertsey Surrey 1975–76, in surgical rotation Taunton and Somerset Hosps 1976–78; sr registrar in radiodiagnosis Sheffield Teaching Hosps 1981–83 (registrar 1978–81), conslt radiologist Northern Gen Hosp Sheffield UK 1983–; prof Univ of Sheffield 2005– (hon reader 2003–05); recipient: Graham-Hodgson scholarship RCR 1987, Flude meml prize BIR 1993, Nuclear Electric Research travel bursary 1994, Barclay's prize BIR 1997, Barclay's medal BIR 2004; assoc ed Br Jl of Radiology (BJR) 2002–, author of numerous articles in learned jls; European Soc of Urogenital Radiology (ESUR): sec and treas 2000–04, pres elect 2004–06, pres 2006–; memb BMA (chm Sheffield Div 1991–92); hon fell Overseas Doctors Assoc 1988 (memb Nat Exec Ctee 1982–93), chm Sheffield Dist Div of Radiology 1992–95; ECF MG (USA) 1974, FRCS (Glasgow) 1978, DMRD (London) 1981, fell Faculty of Radiologists RCS (Dublin) 1982, FRCR (London) 1982; *Style*— Prof Sameh Morcos; ✉ Northern General Hospital, Herries Road, Sheffield S5 7AU (tel 0114 271 4339, fax 0114 261 1791, e-mail sameh.morcos@sth.nhs.uk)

MORDAUNT, Sir Richard Nigel Charles; 14 Bt (E 1611), of Massingham Parva, Norfolk; s of Lt-Col Sir Nigel John Mordaunt, 13 Bt, MBE (d 1979); *b* 12 May 1940; *Educ* Wellington; *m* 1964, Myriam Atchia; 1 da (Michele b 1965), 1 s (Kim John b 1966); *Heir* s, Kim Mordaunt; *Style*— Sir Richard Mordaunt, Bt; ✉ 1/11 Motherwell Street, South Yarra, Melbourne, Victoria 3141, Australia

MORDAUNT, Terence Charles; s of Archibald Raleigh Mordaunt (d 1995), of Reigate, Surrey, and Diana Patricia, *née* Gresty (d 1994); *b* 22 May 1947; *Educ* Wells Cathedral Sch; *m* 3 April 1973 (m dis 1993); 1 da (Sharon b 13 May 1975), 1 s (Jonathan b 29 June 1978); partner, Julia Grassick; *Career* trainee navigator Blue Funnel Line 1965, navigation offr John Swire & Sons 1968–73, obtained Master's ticket 1973, operations mgmnt Saguenay Shipping 1974–76, distribution mangr Alcan UK 1976–82, mktg dir Port of Tyne 1982–83, commercial dir Bellway plc 1983–87, founded First Corporate Consultants 1987, purchased Port of Bristol 1991, chm Bristol Port Co 1991–; chm UK Major Ports Group; memb: Nautical Inst, Inst of Chartered Shipbrokers, Soc of Merchant Venturers; tstee SS Great Britain Tst; patron Outward Bound; Hon LLD Univ of Bristol; *Recreations* sailing, hill walking, gardens; *Style*— Terence Mordaunt, Esq; ✉ The Bristol Port Company, St Andrew's House, St Andrew's Road, Avonmouth, Bristol BS11 9DQ (tel 0117 982 0000, fax 0117 982 5931, e-mail exec@bristolport.co.uk)

MORDEN, Jessica; MP; *b* 29 May 1968; *Educ* Croesyceiliog Comp, Univ of Birmingham; *Career* MP (Lab) Newport E 2005–; general sec Welsh Lab Pty; memb GMB; *Style*— Jessica Morden, MP; ✉ House of Commons, London SW1A 0AA (tel 020 7219 6135, e-mail mordenj@parliament.uk)

MORE-MOLYNEUX, Maj James Robert; OBE (1983), DL; s of Brig-Gen Francis More-Molyneux Longbourne, CMG, DSO, and Gwendoline, da of Adm Sir Robert More-Molyneux, GCB; *b* 17 June 1920; *Educ* Eton, Univ of Cambridge; *m* 1948, Susan, da of Capt Frederick Bellinger; 1 s (Michael George); *Career* WWII, Italy; landowner; fndr: Loseley Dairy Products Ltd, Guildway Ltd, Loseley Christian Tst, Loseley Christian Cancer Centre; memb Lambeth Partnership; High Sheriff Surrey 1974, Vice Lord-Lt Surrey 1982–96; Bledisloe Gold Medal for Landowners 1984; *Books* The Loseley Challenge (1995), The Spark of God (2000); *Clubs* Farmers'; *Style*— Maj James More-Molyneux, OBE, DL; ✉ Nursery Wing, Loseley Park, Guildford, Surrey GU3 1HS (tel 01483 566090); estate office (tel 01483 304440, fax 01483 302036)

MORE-MOLYNEUX, Michael George; DL (Surrey 2000); s of Maj James More-Molyneux, OBE, DL, *qv*, of Loseley Park, Surrey, and Susan *née* Bellinger; *b* 3 September 1951; *Educ* Milton Abbey, RAC Cirencester (DipAg, Dip Advanced Farm Mgmnt); *m* July 1980, Sarah, da of Christopher Westmacott (d 1998); 3 s (Alexander b 1982, Christopher b 1985 d 1997, Tristram b 1986), 1 da (Katrina b 1983); *Career* Loseley Dairy Products: managing ptnr 1980–87, chm 1988–91; currently managing ptnr Loseley Park Farms; chm Guildford Business Forum - Rural Gp; govr QE Fndn for Disabled (pres 2000–01); chm Surrey branch CLA; vice-pres: The Children's Hospice Assoc for SE (CHASE), Surrey branch SSAFA-Forces Help, Loseley and Guildway Charitable Tst; High Sheriff Surrey 2000; *Recreations* art galleries, skiing, countryside, marathon running, travel; *Clubs* Farmers'; *Style*— Michael More-Molyneux, Esq, DL; ✉ Estate Office, Loseley Park, Guildford, Surrey GU3 1HS (tel 01483 405111, fax 01483 302036, e-mail partners@loseley-park.com)

MORE NISBETT, Patrea Evelyn; da of David Agar MacDonald (d 1967), of Dorset, and Elisabeth May, *née* Ferguson; *b* 2 March 1944; *Educ* Cranborne Chase, Sorbonne, House of Citizenship Bucks; *m* 2 March 1968, George Alan More Nisbett, s of Surgn Cdr John Graham More Nisbett (d 1991), of Mid Lothian; 3 s (William David Hamilton b 1979, Alexander Talbot John b 1982, Charles Neilson George b 1984); *Career* writer and broadcaster; Harpers and Queen Magazine, contrib Sloane Ranger Handbook, assoc ed The Good Schools Guide, Gap and University Guides; also advsr to travel indust; *Style*— Mrs Patrea Evelyn More Nisbett; ✉ 43 Godfrey Street, London SW3 3SX (tel 020 7352 3259, mobile 077 6742 1046, e-mail patrea@patrea.freeserve.co.uk); The Drum, Gilmerton, Edinburgh EH17 8RX (tel 0131 664 7215, fax 0131 658 1944)

MOREAN PHILLIP, HE Glenda Patricia; da of Fitzroy Haig Bushell (d 1972), and Enid Olga, *née* Moore; *b* 14 January 1944, Trinidad; *m* Oscar Adrian Phillip; 1 s (b 16 Dec 1976); *Career* Trinidadian diplomat; admitted slr Trinidad 1974 (first Trinidad and Tobago born female slr), sr counsel 2003; slr in private practice 1974–2001 (latterly head of firm), attorney-at-law in private practice 1986–2001, judge Supreme Court of Trinidad and Tobago 1999–2000, senator Trinidad and Tobago, attorney-gen Trinidad and Tobago 2001–03, high cmmr to UK 2003–; assoc tutor Faculty of Hugh Wooding Law Sch Univ of the WI 1986–87; memb Law Assoc of Trinidad and Tobago (pres 1989–91, memb Disciplinary Ctee 1992–95 and 1998–99); chm Nursing Cmmn 1980–81, cmmr Public Utilities Cmmn 1981–86, dep chm Airports Authy of Trinidad and Tobago 1993–96; pres Tennis Assoc of Trinidad and Tobago 1991–97; hon pres Blind Welfare Assoc of Trinidad and Tobago 1994–; memb Grenada Bar Assoc; *Style*— HE Mrs Glenda Morean Phillip; ✉ Office of the High Commissioner for the Republic of Trinidad and Tobago, 42 Belgrave Square, London SW1X 8NT

MORELAND, Robert John; s of Samuel John Moreland, MC, TD (d 1998), and Norah Molly, *née* Haines (d 1980); *b* 21 August 1941; *Educ* Glasgow Acad, Dean Close Sch Cheltenham, Univ of Nottingham (BA), Univ of Warwick; *Career* civil servant Canada 1966–72, mgmnt conslt Touche Ross & Co 1974–; MEP (EDG) Staffs 1979–84; memb Econ and Social Ctee of Euro Community 1986–98 (chm Section on Regnl Policy and Town Planning 1990–98); Westminster City Cncl: cncllr Knightsbridge Ward 1990–98, dep chief whip 1991–93, chief whip 1993–94, chm of the environment 1994–95, chm of planning and the environment 1995–97; dep chm London Research Centre 1996–98, chm London Europe Soc 2000– (dep chm 1997–2000), cncllr Gloucester City Cncl 2001–02, treas European Movement 2003–; tstee Albert Meml Tst 1996–2000, chm of govrs Archbishop Tenison's Secdy Sch 2003– (govr 1993–); *Books* Transport for Europe (jtly 1983), The European Union and Global Climate Change (jtly with The Rt Hon J S Gummer, MP, 2000); *Recreations* swimming, skiing, golf, watching cricket; *Clubs* MCC, Glos CCC; *Style*— Robert Moreland, Esq; ✉ 3 The Firs, Heathville Road, Gloucester GL1 3EW (tel 01452 522612); 7 Vauxhall Walk, London SE11 5JT (e-mail r.moreland@virgin.net)

MORENO, Glen Richard; s of John Richard Moreno (d 2003), and Ellen Oberg Moreno; *b* 24 July 1943, San Jose, CA; *Educ* Stanford Univ (BA), Harvard Law Sch (JD); *m* 26 March 1966, Cheryl Eschbach; *Career* sr positions in Europe and Asia incl gp exec dir and memb Policy Ctee Citigroup 1969–87, pres Fidelity International 1987–91 (dir 1987–), non-exec chm Pearson plc 2005–; sr ind non-exec dir Man Gp plc 1994–; tstee Prince of Liechtenstein Fndn 1999–, govr Ditchley Fndn; *Recreations* cattle breeding, wine making, shooting, fishing; *Clubs* Farmers'; *Style*— Glen Moreno, Esq; ✉ Neala, 100 Neala Lane, Madison, Virginia 22727, USA (tel 00 1 540 948 4529, e-mail grmoreno@msn.com); 3 Whitehall Court, London SW1A 2EL (tel 020 7930 9103); Pearson plc, 80 Strand, London WC2R 0RL (tel 020 7010 2304)

MORGAN, Alan William; s of Alfred Charles Morgan, ISO (d 2003), of Stoke Bishop, Bristol, and Eliza Dora, *née* Sproul-Cran (d 2004); *b* 4 October 1951; *Educ* Clifton (scholar), Trinity Coll Oxford (scholar, MA), Harvard Business Sch (MBA); *m* 17 Oct 1981, Janet Cullis, da of Rainier Campbell Connolly, FRCS, of London; 2 s (Campbell b 1983, Edward b 1986), 1 da (Georgina b 1988); *Career* called to the Bar Middle Temple 1974; Brandts 1974–76, Harvard Business Sch 1976–78, McKinsey & Co 1978–2006 (ptnr 1984, head UK Fin Servs Practice 1986–96, dir 1991, head Euro Fin Services Practice 1996–2001, head ME Fin Servs Practice 2001–06), co-fndr MMC Ventures (Devpt Capital) 1999–, co-fndr and pres Olivant & Co 2006–; non-exec dir City of London Sinfonia 2007–; memb Chllr's Ct of Benefactors Univ of Oxford; visiting fell Nuffield Coll Oxford; govr St Paul's Sch, tstee St Paul's Sch Gen Charitable Tst; memb Cncl Clifton Coll; FRSA; *Recreations* horse racing, golf, theatre, books, walking; *Clubs* Brooks's, Hurlingham, Glos CCC, Harvard Club of New York; *Style*— Alan Morgan, Esq; ✉ Olivant Advisers Limited, 2 Basil Street, London SW3 1AA (tel 020 7225 4100, fax 020 7225 4141, e-mail alan.morgan@olivant.com)

MORGAN, Rt Rev Alan Wyndham; *see:* Sherwood, Bishop of

MORGAN, Alasdair; MSP; s of Alexander Morgan (d 1980), and Emily, *née* Wood (d 2003); *b* 21 April 1945; *Educ* Breadalbane Acad Aberfeldy, Univ of Glasgow (MA), Open Univ (BA); *m* 28 Aug 1969, Anne, *née* Gilfillan; 2 da (Gillian b 3 March 1974, Fiona b 28 Aug 1977); *Career* SNP: nat treasurer 1983–90, sr vice-convener 1990–91, nat sec 1992–97, vice-pres 1997–2004, chief whip and business mangr 2005–; MP (SNP) Galloway and Upper Nithsdale 1997–2001, MSP (SNP) Galloway and Upper Nithsdale 1999–2003, MSP (SNP) South of Scotland 2003–; memb Trade and Industry Select Ctee House of Commons 1997–2001; Scottish Parl: memb and vice-convener Rural Affairs Ctee 1999–2000, convener Justice 1 Ctee 2000–01, memb Fin Ctee 2001–03 and 2004–05, convener Enterprise and Culture Ctee 2003–04, memb Subordinate Legislation Ctee 2003–04; *Recreations* hill walking, cycling; *Style*— Alasdair Morgan, Esq, MSP; ✉ Nether Cottage, Crocketford, Dumfries DG2 8RA (tel 0870 240 7268); The Scottish Parliament, Edinburgh EH99 1SP (tel 0845 278 1999, e-mail alasdair.morgan.msp@scottish.parliament.uk, website www.amorgan.org.uk)

MORGAN, Most Rev Dr Barry Cennydd; *see:* Wales, Archbishop of

MORGAN, Brian David Gwynne; *b* 2 March 1935; *Educ* Univ of London (MB BS, MRCS LRCP); *m*; 3 c; *Career* sr conslt plastic surgn: UCH 1972–98, Regnl Plastic Surgery Unit Mount Vernon Hosp Northwood 1972–98; hon conslt King Edward VII Hosp for Officers and St Luke's Hosp for the Clergy, ret; Emlyn Lewis meml lecture 1994; pres Plastic Surgery Section RSM 1984, sec Br Assoc of Plastic Surgns 1984–86, treas Br Assoc of Aesthetic Plastic Surgns 1985–87; memb Cncl RCS 1991– (chm Ct of Examiners 1988–), tstee Hunterian Collection RCS; hon archivist Antony Wallace Archive Br Assoc of Plastic, Reconstructive and Aesthetic Surgns; pres Rickmansworth and District Residents' Assoc; fell UCL 1992; FRCS 1962, FRCOphth 1995; *Books* Essentials of Plastic and Reconstructive Surgery (1986); author of chapters in various text-books; *Recreations* painting in watercolours and oils, sailing; *Style*— B D G Morgan, Esq; ✉ e-mail bmorgan@mailbox.co.uk

MORGAN, Vice Adm Sir (Charles) Christopher; KBE (1996); s of Capt Horace Leslie Morgan, CMG, DSO, RN (d 1973), and Kathleen Hilda, *née* Bellhouse (d 1972); *b* 11 March 1939; *Educ* Clifton; *m* 14 Feb 1970, Susan Caroline, da of William Sturge Goodbody (d 1962); 3 da (Kirsty Joanna b 26 Aug 1970, Victoria Kate b 26 Nov 1972, Juliet Anne b 5 Dec 1978); *Career* initial trg BRNC Dartmouth 1957–59, served HMS Paladin first Cod War Iceland 1959–60, Amphibious Warfare Sqn Persian Gulf 1960–62 (incl Kuwait crisis 1961), 2 i/c HMS Woolaston 1962–64 (incl Brunei rebellion and Indonesia confrontation), Flag Lt to C-in-C Home Fleet 1964–66, i/c HMS Greatford 1966 (active serv Singapore), Specialist Navigation Course HMS Dryad 1966–67, exchange serv Royal Australian Navy 1967–69, Sqn Navigation Offr to Capt F4 HMS Juno 1970–72, Advanced Navigation Course 1973, Flag Navigating Offr to FOF1/FOF2 HMS Tiger and Blake 1973–76, Cdr i/c HMS Eskimo 1976–78, attended Nat Def Coll 1978–79, Cdr Sea Trg Portland 1979–81, Capt Operational Requirements Div MOD 1981–83, RCDS 1984, Capt 5 Destroyer Sqn (i/c HMS Southampton) 1986–87, on staff of JSDC 1987–89, Rear Adm Naval Sec 1990–92, Vice Adm 1992, Flag Offr Scotland, Northern England and NI (FOSNNI) 1992–96, ret; DG UK Chamber of Shipping 1997–; govr: Clifton Coll 1993–, Tancred's Charities 1997–; pres RN Lawn Tennis Assoc 1990–96, vice-pres RN Rugby Union 1993–96, chm Navy Club 1998– (ctee memb 1990–96), chm The Royal Navy Benevolent Society for Officers 1998– (tstee 1996–); Yr Bro Trinity House 1977, elected Honourable Co of Master Mariners 1999, Freeman Citizen and Master Mariner of London 1999, Liveryman Worshipful Co of Shipwrights 2000; FIMgt 1980, FRIN 1996 (MRIN 1990); *Recreations* golf, tennis, skiing, wine, gardening, reading; *Clubs* Army and Navy, Royal N Devon Golf, Sherborne Golf; *Style*— Vice Adm Sir Christopher Morgan, KBE; ✉ Chamber of Shipping, Carthusian Court, 12 Carthusian Street, London EC1M 6EB (tel 020 7417 8400)

MORGAN, Christopher; s of Geoffrey Morgan (d 1991), of Ashtead, Surrey, and Bertha Florence, *née* Jaffe (d 1948); *b* 6 October 1937; *Educ* Oundle, St John's Coll Cambridge (MA), Univ of Heidelberg; *m* 18 Sept 1971, Pamela Rosamund, da of John Kellock Laurence, of Ham Common, Surrey; 2 da (Juliette Rachel b 1973, Claudia Lucy b 1974),

M

1 s (James Edward Laurence b 1977); *Career* PricewaterhouseCoopers (formerly Deloitte): articled 1959, ptnr 1973–92; hon treas DrugScope (formerly Inst for the Study of Drug Dependence) 1992–2006; non-exec dir GE Life Group Ltd 1994–97; chm Rayner and Keeler Ltd 2003– (non-exec dir 1996–); *Recreations* piano, walking, rowing; *Clubs* Barnes Music Soc, Dacre Boat; *Style*— Christopher Morgan, Esq; ✉ 13 Laurel Road, London SW13 0EE (tel and fax 020 8878 4620)

MORGAN, (Frederick) David; s of Frederick Barlow Morgan (d 1976), and Caroline, *née* Constable (d 1999); *b* 6 October 1937, Tredegar; *Educ* Thomas Richards Tech Sch Tredegar, Henley Mgmnt Coll; *m* 27 Feb 1960, Ann, da of Spencer Cruickshank; 1 s (William Jonathan b 11 Aug 1969); *Career* chm: Glamorgan CCC 1994–98, First Class Forum (ECB) 1997–2002, ECB 2003–; dir Int Cricket Council 2003–; commercial dir European Electrical Steels 1991–2000; memb Exec Ctee Friends of St Woolos Cathedral, memb Newport Devpt Bd; pres elect Int Cricket Cncl 2007; Chllr's Medal Univ of Glamorgan 2004; *Recreations* wine, cricket, church liturgy and music, travel; *Clubs* MCC, Glamorgan CCC, Worcester CCC; *Style*— David Morgan, Esq; ✉ The England and Wales Cricket Board, Lord's Cricket Ground, London NW8 8QZ (tel 01633 420578 or 020 7432 1221, fax 01633 420497, e-mail david.morgan@ecb.co.uk)

MORGAN, David George; RD; s of Frederick David Morgan (d 1981), and Betty Suzanne, *née* Henderson; *b* 21 September 1946; *Educ* Forres Acad, Univ of St Andrews (BSc); *m* 1, 17 May 1969, Helen, *née* Campell; 1 s (Hamish Robert David b 1 Feb 1971), 1 da (Fiona Helen Ruby b 22 Oct 1974); m 2, 21 July 1989, Ruth Mary Morgan, JP, da of John Culpan (d 1999); *Career* Pilot Offr RAFVR 1964–68; Lt Cdr RNR 1975–89; Cooperative Insurance Society 1968–71, Royal Liver Friendly Society 1974–78, asst gen mangr Ideal Insurance Company Ltd 1978–84, pensions mangr AE Pensions 1984–85, pensions mangr Nestlé Rowntree Pensions 1985–93, head of gp pensions Nestlé UK 1993–98, chief exec Coal Pension Trustees Services (British Coal Pensions) 1998–2007; Nat Assoc of Pension Funds: memb Cncl 1990–96, chm Yorks Gp 1991–93, vice-chm 1995–96, memb Investment Cncl 1998–2007 (chm 2006–07); memb Takeover Panel 2006–07; pres Birmingham Actuarial Soc 1982–83, FIA 1970; *Recreations* reading, walking; *Style*— David Morgan, Esq, RD; ✉ Coldwell House, Coldwell Hill, Oughtibridge, Sheffield S35 0FY (tel 0114 286 3040, e-mail david_ruth_morgan@hotmail.com)

MORGAN, His Hon David Glyn; s of Dr Richard Glyn Morgan, MC (d 1972), and Nancy, *née* Griffiths (d 1984); *b* 31 March 1933; *Educ* Newport HS, Mill Hill Sch, Merton Coll Oxford (MA); *m* 1959, Ailsa Murray, da of Archibald McPherson Strang; 3 da (Sian Louise, Catherine Mary (Mrs Phillip Mould), Sara Elen); *Career* Nat Serv cmmnd Queen's Bays (2 Dragoon Gds) 1955 (served Jordan and Libya), Capt AER, Dep Col 1 Queen's Dragoon Gds 1976; mgmnt trainee General Motors (GB) Ltd 1956; called to the Bar Middle Temple 1958, asst recorder Cardiff 1971, recorder of the Crown Court 1974–84, asst cmmr Local Govt Boundary Cmmn for Wales 1976–83, asst cmmr Parly Boundary Cmmn for Wales (Gwent & Powys) and for Review of Euro Assembly Constituencies 1983–84, circuit judge (Wales & Chester Circuit) 1984–2001 (dep circuit judge 2001–), assigned judge Newport Co Court 1988–, designated children and family judge 1991–; hon pres Royal Nat Eisteddfod (Newport) 1988, memb Hon Soc of Cymmrodorion; *Recreations* fishing, country pursuits, opera; *Clubs* Cavalry and Guards', Cardiff & County; *Style*— His Hon David Glyn Morgan; ✉ Newport County Court, Olympia House (3rd Floor), Upper Dock Street, Newport, Gwent NP9 1PQ (tel 01633 227150)

MORGAN, David Llewellyn; eld s of David Bernard Morgan, JP (d 1955), of Cardiff, and Eleanor Mary, *née* Walker (d 2004); *b* 5 October 1932; *Educ* Charterhouse, Trinity Coll Cambridge (MA); *Career* admitted slr 1959; asst slr Herbert Smith 1963–65, conslt Richards Butler 1993–2006 (asst slr 1959–63, ptnr 1965–93); non-exec dir Deymel Investments Ltd 1966–2005 (chm 1977–2005); Liveryman: Worshipful Co of Clockmakers 1963, City of London Slrs Co; memb: Law Soc 1959, City of London Law Soc; *Clubs* Travellers, White's, City Univ, Cardiff and County; *Style*— D Ll Morgan, Esq; ✉ Flat 15, 52 Pont Street, London SW1X 0AE (tel 020 7589 3538)

MORGAN, Prof David Rhys; s of Philip Haydn Percival Morgan (d 1974), and Annie Irene, *née* Rees (d 1981); *b* 22 May 1937; *Educ* Queen Elizabeth GS Carmarthen, Jesus Coll Oxford (MA), Emmanuel Coll Cambridge (PhD); *m* 27 July 1963, Sally Lewis, da of Colton Theodore Lewis (d 1984), of Binghamton, NY, USA; 2 s (Christopher b 18 July 1968, Timothy b 18 Sept 1970), 1 da (Siân b 28 June 1973); *Career* Nat Serv RAF 1955–57; Univ of Liverpool: lectr 1965, sr lectr 1973, reader 1987, dean Social and Environmental Studies Faculty 1988–94, prof 1989– (now emeritus), head Sch of Politics and Communication Studies 1995–96; visiting prof: SUNY Albany 1974–75, George Washington Univ Washington DC 1981–82, Rhodes Coll Memphis 1986; guest scholar Brookings Inst Washington DC 1978 and 1979; memb: Cncl of American Political Sci Assoc 1986–88, Exec Ctee Political Studies Assoc UK 1988–94; FRHistS 1981; *Books* Suffragists and Democrats (1972), Suffragists and Liberals (1975), City Politics and the Press (with Harvey Cox, 1973), The Capitol Press Corps (1978), The Flacks of Washington (1986), The European Parliament, Mass Media and the Search for Power and Influence (1999); *Recreations* walking, travel, short story writing; *Style*— Prof David Morgan; ✉ e-mail morgan@delfryn.demon.co.uk

MORGAN, David Treharne; MBE (2003), TD (1983); s of Maj Hugh Treharne Morgan, OBE, TD (d 1996), of Crowborough, E Sussex, and Betty Gladys Boys, *née* Schreiber; *b* 21 October 1941; *Educ* Dragon Sch Oxford, Winchester, Innsbruck Univ; *m* 7 July 1973, Heather, da of William Thomson (d 1953), of Steilston House, Dumfries; 1 da (Claire b 2 Aug 1979); *Career* TA; joined HAC 1964, cmmnd 2 Lt 1975, transferred RCT 1977, Lt Movement Control Offr 1977, Capt 2 i/c 282 MC Sqdn 1979, Maj Cmdg 281 MC Sqdn 1984, Lt Col Liaison Offr to MOD (Netherlands) 1988, Lt Col Liaison Offr All Arms Liaison Unit RLC until 1996, ret; admitted slr 1970; ptnr: R A Roberts 1973–83, Wright Son & Pepper 1987–2000; practising as David T Morgan Slrs 2000–; pres Holborn Law Soc 1998–99, pres Fedn of European Bars (memb Cmmn on Ethics) 2002–03, memb Cncl Law Soc of Eng and Wales 2005–; chm: North Norfolk Railway plc 1973–92 and 2001– (dir 1969–), Swindon Historic Castings Ltd, The South Yorkshire Railway Ltd, Heritage Railway Assoc, Heritage Afloat; dir: Great Central Railway plc, The Solent Steam Packet Ltd, Maritime Tst, West Somerset Railway plc 1982– (and vice-chm); former dir Eden Valley Railway Tst (until 2001); pres Fedecrail (European Fedn of Museum and Tourist Railways) 1992; dep pres Transport Tst (former chm), memb Railway Heritage Ctee 1996–2000, vice-pres Severn Valley Railway; tstee Cutty Sark Tst; treas The Trauma Fndn; Freeman City of London 1982, Liveryman Worshipful Co of Glaziers; memb Law Soc 1970, FInstD, MCIT; *Recreations* skiing, sailing, preserved railways; *Clubs* Norfolk; *Style*— David Morgan, Esq, MBE, TD; ✉ 7 Cheyne Place, London SW3 4HH (tel 020 7352 6077); David T Morgan Solicitors, 9 Gray's Inn Square, London WC1R 5JF (tel 020 7404 2646, fax 020 7404 2890, e-mail davidtmorgan21@hotmail.com)

MORGAN, His Hon Judge David Wynn; s of Arthur Islwyn Lewis Morgan, of Allt-yr-yn, Gwent, and Mary, *née* Wynn; *Educ* Kingswood Sch Bath, Balliol Coll Oxford (BA); *m* 25 Sept 1982, Marian Elena, o da of late David Richard Lewis; 1 da (Catherine Lowri b 1 July 1986), 1 s (Huw Alexander b 4 June 1988); *Career* called to the Bar Gray's Inn 1977, in practice 1978–2000, recorder of the Crown Court 1995–2000, circuit judge (Wales & Chester Circuit) 2000–; memb Parole Bd 2002–; *Recreations* walking, opera, reading, Pembrokeshire; *Style*— His Hon Judge David Wynn Morgan; ✉ The Law Courts, Cathays Park, Cardiff CF10 3PG (tel 029 2041 4400, fax 029 2041 4445, e-mail dwynnmorgan@lix.compulink.co.uk)

MORGAN, Prof Derec Llwyd; s of Ewart Lloyd Morgan (d 1970), and Margaret, *née* Jones (d 1984); *b* 15 November 1943; *Educ* Amman Valley GS, UCNW Bangor (BA), Jesus Coll Oxford (DPhil), Univ of Wales (DLitt); *m* 1965, Jane, da of Richard Edwards; 1 da (Elin b 17 Dec 1966); *Career* research fell Univ of Wales 1967–69, lectr UCW Aberystwyth 1969–74; UCNW Bangor: sr lectr then reader 1975–89, dir Research Centre Wales 1985–89; UCW Aberystwyth: prof of Welsh 1989–95, vice-princ 1994–95, vice-chllr and princ 1995–2004; sr vice-chllr Fed Univ of Wales 2001–2004; non-exec dir: Royal Mail for Wales and the Marches 1996–2000, Menter A Busnes 1997–2000; memb: Gen Advsy Cncl BBC 1984–90, Broadcasting Cncl for Wales 1990–95, Bd of Celtic Studies Univ of Wales 1990–95, Ct and Cncl Nat Library of Wales 1995–2007, Governing Body Inst of Grassland and Environmental Research 1995–2004, Ind Television Cmmn 1999–2003, Governing Bd Royal Welsh Coll of Music and Drama 2000–2003; Royal Nat Eisteddfod of Wales: chm Cncl 1979–82 and 1985–86, pres Ct 1989–93; chm Exec Ctee Nat Eisteddfod Ynys Môn 1983; chm Celtic Film and Television Festival 2000; chm Kyffin Williams Tst 2006–; chm Rowntree Cmmn on Rural Housing in Wales 2007–08; Welsh Arts Cncl Literature Prize 1971, Ellis Jones Griffith Prize 1982; hon fell Univ of Wales Bangor 1996, hon fell Jesus Coll Oxford 1999 (supernumerary fell 1997–98 and 2003–04); Hon DUniv Wales; hon memb Gorsedd of the Bards 1999; *Publications* Y Tân Melys (1966), Pryderi (1970), Barddoniaeth Thomas Gwynn Jones: Astudiaeth (1972), Kate Roberts (1974, 2 edn 1991), Cerddi '75 (ed, 1975), Iliad Homer (1976), Adnabod Deg (ed, 1977), Gwna yn Llawen, Wr Ieuanc (1987), Y Diwygiad Mawr (1981, trans, The Great Awakening in Wales, 1988, reprint 1999), Williams Pantycelyn (1983), Pobl Pantycelyn (1986), Glas y Nef: Cerddi ac Emynau John Roberts Llanfwrog (ed, 1987), Cefn y Byd (1987), Emynau Williams Pantycelyn (ed, 1991), Meddwl a Dychymyg Williams Pantycelyn (ed, 1991), Charles Edwards (1994), Y Beibl a Llenyddiaeth Gymraeg (1998), John Roberts Llanfwrog: Pregethwr, Bardd, Emynydd (1999), Nid hwn mo'r llyfr terfynol: Hanes Llenyddiaeth Thomas Parry (2004), Kyffin: A Celebration (2007); *Recreations* gardening, cricket, Swansea City FC, reading; *Clubs* Premier, Glamorgan CCC, Llangefni RFC; *Style*— Prof Derec Llwyd Morgan; ✉ Carrog Uchaf, Tregaian, Anglesey LL77 7UE

MORGAN, Derek William Charles; OBE (1997), DL (Mid Glamorgan 1992); s of Thomas Brinley Morgan (d 1978), of Neath, and Brenda Vanessa, *née* Megraw (d 1992); *b* 28 November 1934; *Educ* Neath GS, Univ of Nottingham (BA); *m* 17 Aug 1963, Anne Yvette, da of Evan Morgan Davies (d 1977), of Bridgend; 2 da (Siân, Louise); *Career* Nat Serv RE 1956–58; mangr Littlewoods Ltd 1958–61, plant mangr Ilford Ltd 1961–67, dir PA Consulting Group 1967–90, dir Business Action Team (Birmingham) Ltd 1988–90, chm API 1991–2003, dir Moulded Foams (Wales) Ltd 1991–99, HSBC Venture and Enterprise Funds (Gen Ptnr Wales) Ltd 1999–; non-exec dir: Morganite Electrical Carbon Ltd 1982–2003, Corgi Toys Ltd 1987–89; memb: Neath Devpt Partnership 1981–88, Welsh Health Common Servs Authy 1982–90, Mid Glamorgan HA 1987–92, Wales Regnl Cncl CBI 1987–97, Birmingham Chamber of Industry and Commerce 1987–90, BT Advsy Forum for Wales 1991– (chm), Cncl Univ of Wales Coll of Med 1995–99; dir Wales Mgmnt Cncl 2000–02; chm: Ogwr Partnership Tst 1988–95, Artificial Limb and Appliance Serv Ctee for Wales 1988–90, PA Pension Scheme 1988–2002, Mid Glamorgan Educn Business Partnership 1989–95, Welsh Wildlife Appeal 1989–93, Bridgend & Dist NHS Tst 1992–95, Prince's Youth Business Tst S Wales 1993–2000, Princess of Wales Hosp Brigend Macmillan Cancer Appeal 1993–96, Univ Hosp of Wales Healthcare NHS Tst 1995–99, Technology Means Business-Wales@TEB 1999–2001, Business in Focus/Cardiff and Vale Enterprise Tst Ltd 1999–, Br Heart Fndn Cardiff 2000–01; vice-chm Mid Glamorgan TEC1990–95; govr: UC Swansea 1982–98, Univ of Wales 1997–, Howell's Sch Llandaff 2000–; pres Cardiff C of C and Industry 1990–91, chm St David's Hall and New Theatre Tst 1990–98, memb All Wales e-Crime Steering Gp 2005–, chm ESU S Wales 2006–; High Sheriff Mid Glamorgan 1988–89; Freeman City of London 1986, Liveryman Worshipful Co of Tin Plate (Wire) Workers 1986, Liveryman Welsh Livery Guild 1993; Hon Dr Univ of Glamorgan 1995; FIMC 1976, CIMgt 1996 (FIMgt 1979); *Recreations* walking, wine, reading, cricket; *Clubs* Cardiff and Co (Cardiff); *Style*— Derek Morgan, Esq, OBE, DL; ✉ Erw Graig, Merthyr Mawr, Bridgend CF32 0NU

MORGAN, Prof Edwin George; OBE (1982); s of Stanley Morgan (d 1965), and Madge, *née* Arnott (d 1970); *b* 27 April 1920, Glasgow; *Educ* Rutherglen Acad, Glasgow HS, Univ of Glasgow (MA); *Career* war serv RAMC Middle East 1940–46; titular prof of English Univ of Glasgow 1975–80 (now emeritus); Poet Laureate for Glasgow 1999–2005, Nat Poet for Scotland 2004–; Queen's Gold Medal for Poetry 2000; Hon DLitt: Loughborough Univ 1981, Univ of Glasgow 1990, Univ of Edinburgh 1991, Univ of St Andrews 2000, Heriot-Watt Univ 2000, Glasgow Caledonian Univ 2005; Hon DUniv: Stirling 1989, Waikato 1992; Hon MUniv Open Univ 1992; Order of Merit (Hungary) 1997; *Poetry* Collected Poems (1990), Cyrano de Bergerac (1992), Collected Translations (1996), New Selected Poems (2000), Cathures (2002), Love and a Life (2003), Tales from Baron Munchausen (2004); *Style*— Prof Edwin Morgan, OBE; ✉ Clarence Court, 234 Crow Road, Broomhill, Glasgow G11 7PD (tel 0141 357 7229)

MORGAN, (Mair) Eluned; MEP (Lab) Wales; da of Canon Bob Morgan, and Elaine, *née* Evans; *b* 16 February 1967; *Educ* Ysgol Gyfun Gymraeg Glantaf, United World Coll of the Atlantic (scholar), Univ of Strasbourg, Complutense Univ Madrid, Univ of Hull (BA); *Career* stagiaire Euro Parl 1990, S4C 1991, Agenda TV 1992, TV documentary researcher BBC Wales 1993; MEP (Lab): Wales Mid and W 1994–99, Wales 1999–, spokesperson Socialist Gp on Euro Parl Budget and Budget Control Ctees; *Style*— Ms Eluned Morgan, MEP; ✉ c/o European Parliament, Rue Wiertz, B-1047 Brussels, Belgium; Labour European Office, The Coal Exchange, Mount Stuart Square, Cardiff CF10 6RB (tel 029 2048 5303, fax 020 2048 4534, e-mail emorgan@welshlabourmeps.org.uk, website www.elunedmorgan.org.uk)

MORGAN, Fay (Mrs Roger Oates); da of Phillip Hughues Morgan, of Goodwick, Dyfed, and Iris Friend, *née* John; *b* 18 December 1946; *Educ* Bishopswood Secdy Sch, Hornsey Coll of Art (DipAD), RCA (MDes); *m* 31 July 1976, Roger Kendrew Oates, *qv*, s of William Oates; 1 s (Daniel Morgan Oates b 25 Jan 1979); *Career* textile designer; set up own studio London 1970–75, dir Weavers Workshop Edinburgh 1973–75, pt/t lectr Goldsmiths Coll London 1975–79, memb Governing Body Herefordshire Coll of Art and Design 1989–95; Morgan Oates Partnership at the House in the Yard Ledbury 1975–86, Morgan & Oates Ltd 1986–97 (designing for own label and clients incl Ralph Lauren, Christian Dior, Sonia Rykiel, Donna Karan and Laura Ashley), sr ptnr Roger Oates Design Associates 1987–98, dir Roger Oates Design Co Ltd 1998–; work in exhibitions incl: The Craftsman's Art (V&A Museum) 1973, The House in the Yard Textiles from the Workshop of Fay Morgan and Roger Oates (Welsh Arts Cncl Cardiff and tour) 1978, Tufted Rugs (Environment London) 1980, Texstyles (Crafts Cncl London and tour) 1984–85, Design Awards (Lloyd's Building London) 1988; awarded: USA ROSCOE award 1984, British Design award 1988, Duke of Edinburgh's certificate for services to design; contrib various TV prodns, IdFX Magazine Decorex Award Best Contempory Product 1998; FRSA; *Books* Clothes Without Patterns (1977); *Style*— Mrs Fay Morgan; ✉ Roger Oates Design Company Ltd, The Long Barn, Eastnor, Ledbury, Herefordshire HR8 1EL (tel 01531 632718, fax 01531 631361, e-mail design@rogeroates.com, website www.rogeroates.com); Roger Oates Design, 1 Munro Terrace, Cheyne Walk, London SW10 0DL (tel 020 7351 2288, fax 020 7351 6841)

MORGAN, Fidelis; da of Peter N Horswill, of Kenya, and Fidelis, *née* Morgan (d 2001); *b* 8 August 1952; *Educ* Farnborough Hill Convent, Upper Chine Sch, Univ of Birmingham

(BA); *Career* actress and writer; nominated Most Promising Playwright in Plays & Players 1986, LIPA'96 (co-winner); *Theatre* incl: Clara Hibbert in The Vortex (Garrick and Glasgow Citizens), Angustias in The House of Bernarda Alba (Nottingham Playhouse), Crawshaw in Savages (W Yorkshire Playhouse), title role in Arturo Ui (Liverpool Everyman), Ruth Fischer in Berlin Days/Hollywood Nights (The Place and tour); Glasgow Citizens Theatre: Queen Elizabeth in Mary Stuart, Ruth in Blithe Spirit, Anna in Anna Karenina, title role in The Mother, Kath in Entertaining Mr Sloane, Andree in A Waste of Time, Charlotte in Chéri, Mrs Peachum in Threepenny Opera; *Television* appearances incl: Jeeves and Wooster, Mr Majeika, As Time Goes By; *Books* incl: The Female Wits (1981), A Woman of No Character (1986), Bluff Your Way in Theatre (1986), The Well Known Trouble-Maker (1988), A Misogynist's Source Book (1989), The Female Tatler (1991), The Years Between (1994), My Dark Rosaleen (1994), Wicked (1995), Unnatural Fire (2000), The Rival Queens (2001), The Ambitious Stepmother (2002), Fortune's Slave (2003); *Plays* Pamela (with Giles Havergal, 1985), Hangover Square (1990), Fragments from the Life Marie Antoinette (with Jill Benedict, 1997); *Recreations* music, cooking, throwing parties; *Style*— Fidelis Morgan; ✉ c/o Sally Hope Associates, 108 Leonard Street, London EC2A 4XS (tel 020 7613 5353, fax 020 7613 4848, e-mail sally@sallyhope.biz, website www.fidelismorgan.com); c/o Lisa Queen, Suite 704, 850 7th Avenue, New York, NY 10019, USA (tel 00 1 212 974 8333, e-mail lqueen@queenliterary.com)

MORGAN, Gareth Dylan; s of Dr Edward Morgan, of Codsall, S Staffs, and Enfys Magdalene Grace, *née* Jones; *b* 11 September 1968, Aberystwyth; *Educ* Victoria Univ of Manchester (BSc); *m* 1999 (m dis 2004), Helen Louise; 1 da (Katherine Grace b 28 April 2001); partner, Sandra Cristina Campos; 1 da (Jocelyn Faith b 25 Aug 2005); *Career* with Army Weapons Div British Aerospace 1987–91, reporter Mercury Press Agency 1992–93, reporter then chief reporter Daily Star 1993–99, reporter Sunday Mirror 1999, asst ed Daily Star 2000–03, ed Daily Star Sunday 2003–; *Recreations* rugby, beer, chips and gravy; *Style*— Gareth Morgan, Esq; ✉ The Northern & Shell Building, 10 Lower Thames Street, London EC3R 6EN (tel 0871 520 7233, e-mail gareth.morgan@dailystar.co.uk)

MORGAN, (John) Gwynfryn (Gwyn); OBE (1999); s of Arthur Glyndwr Morgan (d 1964), Mary, *née* Walters (d 1963); *b* 16 February 1934; *Educ* Aberdare GS, UCW Aberystwyth (BA, MA, DipEd); *Family* divorced; 4 c (Sian b 2 Jan 1964, Gregory b 24 Dec 1974, Eliot b 22 Sept 1979, Joanna b 23 Aug 1977); *Career* pres NUS 1960–62, sec gen Int Student Conferences 1962–65, dep gen sec Br Lab Pty 1968–72 (int sec 1965–68); chef de cabinet Rt Hon George Thomson EC Cmmn 1973–75, head EC office Wales 1975–79, head press and info EC delgn Canada 1979–83, head EC representation Turkey 1983–87, head EC delgn Israel 1987–93, head EC delgn Thailand (covering Thailand, Cambodia, Malaysia, Myanmar (Burma), Laos and Vietnam) 1993–95, head SE Asia Div EC Brussels 1995–99, EU chief observer: Indonesian election 1999, Ivory Coast election 2000; author of numerous articles in political jls; assoc prof Univ of Guelph Canada, chm European Inst for Asian Studies (Brussels); vice-pres London Welsh Rugby Club; fell Royal Cwlth Soc, fell Univ of Wales Aberystwyth; commandeur d'honneur Chaîne des Rotisseurs; *Recreations* rugby, cricket, crosswords, wine tasting; *Clubs* Reform, Cardiff and Co, MCC, Hon Soc of Cymmrodorion; *Style*— Gwyn Morgan, Esq; ✉ 14 Ravenscroft Road, London W4 5EQ (tel 020 8994 4218, fax 020 7460 7091)

MORGAN, Howard James; s of Thomas James Morgan, of N Wales, and Olive Victoria, *née* Oldnall; *b* 21 April 1949; *Educ* Fairfax HS Sutton Coldfield, Univ of Newcastle upon Tyne (MA); *m* 1, 27 Aug 1977 (m dis), Susan Ann, da of Alexander Sandilands; 2 s (Alexander James b 26 May 1985, Rupert Thomas Oldnall b 23 March 1991), 1 da (Romilly Grace Victoria b 27 March 1989); m 2, 4 June 2004, Sarah Jane, da of Roger Milligan; 2 s (Perseus Aubrey William Roger (twin) b 27 Sept 2001, Samuel Ronald Mackenzie b 10 Sept 2005), 1 da (Velvet Rose Luna Talullah Vanda (twin) b 27 Sept 2001); *Career* artist; numerous Royal and private cmmns incl: HM The Queen, HM The Queen of the Netherlands (Unilever Tricentennial celebrations), HRH Prince Michael of Kent (for Mark Masons), TRH The Prince and Princess of Hanover, Dame Antoinette Sibley NPG, Mr and Mrs Neill McConnell (USA) 1992, Chelsea Arts Club (for Absolut Vodka) 1994, Lady Bell, Mr & Mrs Nick Mason 1996, Mr & Mrs Matt Handbury 1996, Mr & Mrs Shaun Woodward 1997, Sarah Von Hallé 1998, Mr and Mrs Bernard Carl 1998, Marqués de Caltójar Tulio O'Neill Castrillo 1999, Mrs J L Thornton 1999, Mr and Mrs Mike Cottman family and friends 2001, children of Christopher Carter, children of Barbara Winkworth, black and white picture of Fleur Gibbs; perm display of work Nat Portrait Gallery including: Paul Maurice Dirac, Herbert Howells, Francis Crick and Tom Stoppard; Portrait Painting Prize RSPP 2004; memb RSPP 1986; *Subject Work* incl: Shanty Pictures (In Plymouth Towne, A Drop of Nelson's Blood... and Mingulay) 1990–91, Golden Gate Quartet 1994, Monticello watercolours of Jefferson's House (for Civilization magazine) 1994, Snow White Triptych, Cinderella Triptych 1995, Ladies in Hats 1996–98, Mozart Opera pictures (Figaro, Magic Flute, Cosi Fan Tutte, Don Giovanni) 1999–2000, Strauss's Der Rosenkavalier 1999, Dinner Party 1999, Theseus and Ariadne Triptych 2001, The Quiet American 2002; *Exhibitions* incl: Anthony Mould 1983, Claridges 1984, Richmond Gallery 1986–87, 1988, 1989, 1990, 1991 and 1995 (including Difficult Red, Le Soirée du Comte Frederiqúe de la Chasseur, Dinner Party-Tiananmen Square, etc), Cadogan Contemporary Watercolours 1988, 1989, 1990, 1991 and 1995, Thomas Agnew 1989, 1996 and 1998, Park Walk Gallery (lithography) 1990, Leighton House Exhibition 1993, Sara Stewart watercolours 1998, Opera pictures 2001, Eaton Gallery (studio party) 2003, David Messum Cork Street 2006; *Recreations* riding, 1938 Citroën, books; *Clubs* Chelsea Arts, Beefsteak; *Style*— Howard Morgan, Esq; ✉ Studio 401 1/2, Wandsworth Road, Battersea, London SW8 2JP (tel 020 7720 1181, e-mail howard@howard-morgan.co.uk, website www.howard-morgan.co.uk); 12 Rectory Grove, Clapham Old Town, London SW4 0EA (website www.myspace.com/howardjmorgan)

MORGAN, His Hon Judge Hugh Marsden; s of Hugh Thomas Morgan (d 1986), of Cyncoed, Cardiff, and Irene, *née* Rees (d 1969); *b* 17 March 1940; *Educ* Cardiff HS, Magdalen Coll Oxford (demy, BCL, MA); *m* 18 March 1967, Amanda Jane, da of John Hubert Morton Tapley (d 1987), of Temple Cloud, Bath, Somerset; 2 s (Richard b 1972, Charles b 1978), 1 da (Zoë b 1975); *Career* called to the Bar Gray's Inn 1964, in practice on SE Circuit, recorder of the Crown Court 1987–95, circuit judge (SE Circuit) 1995–; memb: Matrimonial Causes Rule Ctee 1989–91, Family Proceedings Rule Ctee 1991–93, Fees and Legal Aid Ctee Senate and Bar Cncl 1976–82, Ctee of Family Law Bar Assoc 1976–89, Wine Ctee SE Circuit 1986–88; *Recreations* gardening, reading, listening; *Style*— His Hon Judge Hugh Morgan

MORGAN, Dr Janet; *see:* Balfour of Burleigh, Lady

MORGAN, Sir John Albert Leigh; KCMG (1989, CMG 1982); s of John Edward Rowland Morgan, and Ivy Ann Ashton; *b* 21 June 1929; *Educ* LSE (BSc Econ); *m* 1, 1961 (m dis 1976), Hon Fionn Frances Bride O'Neill, da of 3 Baron O'Neill (d 1944); 1 s, 2 da; m 2, 1976, Angela Mary Eleanor, da of Patrick Warre Rathbone; 1 s, 1 da; *Career* served Army 1947–49, cmmnd 1948; HM Dip Serv 1951–89: served in Moscow (twice), Peking and Rio de Janeiro, head Far Eastern Dept FCO 1970–72, head Cultural Relations Dept FCO 1972–80, ambass and consul-gen Korea 1980–83, ambass Poland 1983–86, ambass Mexico 1986–89, ret; md (int relations) Maxwell Communications Corp 1989–90, dir Christie's 1993–95; chm: INVESCO (formerly Drayton) Korea Trust plc 1993–99 (dir 1991–99), East European Development Trust 1994–, Gulf International Minerals Vancouver 1996–2003, Ceiba Investments Ltd Cuba 2002–; dir: INVESCO Europe Ltd 1994–99, INVESCO Japan Discovery Trust 1994–2005; dir and co sec Global Tote Ltd 1999–; pres: Int Fedn of the Phonographic Industry 1990–93, Actions Asie Emergent (Paris) 1996–2001, Anglo Korean Soc 2002 (chm 1990–95); tstee: Br Museum 1991–99, Br Museum Devpt Tst 1991 (tstee emeritus 2001–); dir Royal Philharmonic Orch 1992–95 (chm RPO Devpt Tst 1993–95); LSE: govr 1971–95 and 1997–2002, chm LSE Fndn 1994–96; vice-chm South Bank Foundation Ltd 1995–2003; Hon LLD Mexican Inst of Int Law, Hon DSc (Politics) Univ of Korea, hon fell LSE; FRSA, FRAS; Order of the Aztec Eagle (Mexico) 1994, Order of Diplomatic Merit (1st Class) Korea 1999; *Clubs* Travellers; *Style*— Sir John Morgan, KCMG; ✉ 41 Hugh Street, London SW1V 1QJ (tel 020 7821 1037); Beaumont Cottage, South Brewham, Somerset BA10 0JZ (tel 01749 850606)

MORGAN, His Hon John Ambrose; s of Joseph Michael Morgan (d 1973), of Liverpool, and Monica Mary, *née* Horan (d 1994); *b* 22 September 1934; *Educ* St Edward's Coll Liverpool, Univ of Liverpool (Emmott meml scholar, Alsopp prizewinner, LLB); *m* 19 Dec 1970, Rosalie Mary, da of Harold Edward Tyson (d 1995), and Jane Tyson, *née* Railston (d 1977); 2 s (Matthew Jardine b 24 Nov 1972, Benedict Edward b 20 June 1974); *Career* Nat Serv RAF 1958–60; articled to Town Clerk Bootle, asst slr Preston Corp 1960–62, asst slr Liverpool Corp 1962–64, slr with J Frodsham & Sons Prescot, St Helens and Widnes 1964–70; called to the Bar Grays Inn 1970; practised at the Bar Northern Circuit 1970–90, dep stipendiary magistrate 1982–90, recorder 1988–90 (asst recorder 1983–88), circuit judge (Northern Circuit) 1990–2003 (dep circuit judge 2003–); chm Govrs St Edward's Coll 1986–95; pres Liverpool RFC 1980–82 (former player 1st XV); *Recreations* golf, amateur operatics, rugby football (writing and broadcasting); *Clubs* Athenaeum (Liverpool), Woolton Golf, Liverpool St Helens Rugby, Sefton Park CC (pres 2003–), Liverpool Bar CC (pres 1993–); *Style*— His Hon John Morgan; ✉ e-mail john.morgan11@virgin.net

MORGAN, John Christopher; s of Ieuan Gwyn Jones Morgan, of Winchester, and late Gwen, *née* Littlechild; *b* 31 December 1955; *Educ* Peter Symonds Coll Winchester, Univ of Reading (BSc), Open Univ (MBA); *m* 1 Sept 1984, Rosalind Jane, da of John Kendrew; 2 s (James b 1986, Charles b 1988), 1 da (Anna b 1989); *Career* Morgan Sindall plc: chief exec 1977–2000, exec chm 2000–; non-exec chm Genetix Group plc 2000, non-exec dir Newfound NV 2006–; FRICS; *Recreations* sailing; *Clubs* Mudeford Sailing; *Style*— John Morgan, Esq; ✉ Morgan Sindall plc, 77 Newman Street, London W1T 3EW

MORGAN, John White; s of John White Morgan (d 1973), of Bridge of Allan, and Catherine, *née* Halliday (d 2000); *b* 11 March 1946; *Educ* Greenock Acad; *m* Morag Nicol, da of William McFarlane; 2 da (Megan Sarah b 14 Sept 1973, Erika Catherine b 11 Jan 1977); *Career* md: Simpson & Gemmell 1972–78, Woolward Royds 1978–80, Morgan Associates 1980–89; chief exec The Morgan Partnership 1999–2001 (md 1990–93, chm and md 1993–99), chm and chief exec Merle Ltd 2001; dir The Entrepreneurial Exchange; memb Incorporation of Maltmen; MInstM 1980; *Recreations* internet gallery, chess sets, Highland Games, Robert Burns, Town of Stirling, football, public speaking; *Clubs* Old Manor Burns (chm); *Style*— John W Morgan, Esq

MORGAN, Jonathan; AM; s of Barrie Morgan, and Linda, *née* Griffiths, of Cardiff; *b* 12 November 1974; *Educ* Bishop of Llandaff Church-in-Wales Sch Cardiff, Univ of Wales Cardiff (LLB, MScEcon); *Career* Euro Funding offr Coleg Glan Hafren Cardiff; memb Cons Pty 1991–, memb Nat Assembly for Wales (Cons) South Wales Central 1999–, Cons spokesman on Health and Social Services, business mangr Welsh Cons Gp; dir The Nat Assemb for Wales Broadcasting Co Ltd; FRSA 1999–2001; *Recreations* music, golf, theatre; *Clubs* Merthyr Cons, County Cons (Cardiff); *Style*— Jonathan Morgan, Esq, AM; ✉ National Assembly for Wales, Cardiff Bay, Cardiff CF99 1NA (tel 029 2089 8734, fax 029 2089 8335, mobile 07968 447856)

MORGAN, Julie; MP; *Career* MP (Lab) Cardiff North 1997–; *Style*— Ms Julie Morgan, MP; ✉ House of Commons, London SW1A 0AA (tel 020 7219 3000)

MORGAN, Kenneth; OBE (1978); s of Albert Edward Morgan (d 1975), of Bristol, and Lily Maud, *née* Stafford (d 1995); *b* 3 November 1928; *Educ* Stockport GS; *m* 1950, Margaret Cynthia, da of Roland Ellis Wilson (d 1981), of Stockport; 3 da (Helen (Mrs J E Brown), Sarah Caroline (Mrs N J Martin), Jane Charlotte (Jenny (Mrs J C Hawke)); *Career* Lt RAOC 1946–49 (Egypt and Palestine); successively journalist with Stockport Express, Kemsley Newspapers and Exchange Telegraph Co until 1962; NUJ: Central London sec 1962–66, nat organiser 1966–70, gen sec 1970–77; Press Cncl: consultative memb 1970–77, jt sec 1977–78, dep dir and conciliator 1978–79, dir 1980–90; dir Press Complaints Cmmn 1991, conslt on press freedom and press ethics 1992–; assoc press fell Wolfson Coll Cambridge 1998–; cnsllr Bureau Int Fedn of Journalists Brussels 1970–78; memb: Exec Ctee Nat Fedn of Professional Workers 1970–77, Jt Standing Ctee Nat Newspaper Industry 1976–77, Br Ctee Journalists in Europe 1977–2003, Pro Tem Ctee World Assoc of Press Cncls 1989–92; dir Reuters Founders Share Co 1984–99; tstee: Reuters 1984–99, Journalists' Copyright Fund 1995– (chm of tstees 1996–); conslt: The Thomson Fndn 1991–, Nat Media Cmmn Ghana 1995–99, Fiji Media Cncl 1998, The Media Tst Mauritius 1998, govt Sierra Leone 1998, Ind Media Cmmn Sierra Leone 2003–04, Botswana Press Cncl 2004; conducted (with John Prescott Thomas) review for Cabinet of media legislation in Fiji 1996–97; govr ESU 1992–99, hon sec ESU of the Cwlth 1993–99; Methodist Recorder (Wesley) Lecture 1989, Br Cncl and Cncl of Europe lectures, Central and West Africa, Papua New Guinea, Fiji, Spain, Japan, Russia, Greece and Germany; memb C of E Gen Synod Communications Ctee Press Panel 1981–90, assoc Int Press Inst 1980, FRSA; *Publications* Press Conduct in the Sutcliffe Case (1983), New Connexions: The Power to Inform (with D Christie, 1989), Future Media Legislation and Regulation for the Republic of the Fiji Islands (with J Prescott Thomas, 1996), A Press Council for Mauritius? Safeguarding Freedom, Responsibility and Redress for Mauritius and its Media (1999); contrib: El Poder Judicial en le Conjunto de los Poderes del Estado y de la Sociedad, Media Freedom and Accountability (1989), The Independence of the Journalist, Is de Klant of de Krant Koning (1990), Beyond the Courtroom: Alternatives for Resolving Press Disputes (1991), Allmänhetens Pressombudsman Årsberattelser (1992), Sir Zelman Cowen: a Life in the Law (1997), Arsenal for Democracy (Media Accountability Systems) (2002); *Recreations* theatre, history, inland waterways, travel; *Style*— Kenneth Morgan Esq, OBE; ✉ 151 Overhill Road, Dulwich, London SE22 0PT (tel 020 8693 6585)

MORGAN, Prof Kenneth; s of Idris Morgan (d 1995), of Llanelli, and Megan Elizabeth, *née* Richards; *b* 9 June 1945; *Educ* Llanelli Boys' GS, Univ of Bristol (BSc, PhD, DSc); *m* 7 April 1969, Elizabeth Margaret, da of William Harrison (d 1989); 2 s (Gareth b 1970, David Kenneth b 1972); *Career* scientific offr Mathematical Physics Div UKAEA AWRE Aldermaston 1969–72, lectr Dept of Mathematics Univ of Exeter 1972–75; Univ of Wales Swansea: lectr Dept of Civil Engrg 1975–84, sr lectr 1984–86, reader 1986–88, prof 1988–89; Zaharoff prof of aviation Dept of Aeronautics Imperial Coll London 1989–91; Univ of Wales Swansea: prof Dept of Civil Engrg 1991–2002 (head of dept 1991–96), dean of engrg 1997–2000, prof Sch of Engrg 2002–, head Civil and Computational Engrg Centre 2003–; visiting scientist Jt Research Centre of the EC Ispra Italy 1980, visiting research scientist Inst for Computer Applications in Sci and Engrg (ICASE) NASA Langley Research Center Hampton VA 1985; visiting research prof: Old Dominion Univ Norfolk VA 1986–87, Univ of Virginia Charlottesville 1988–92; govr Ysgol Gynradd Gymraeg Bryn-y-Môr Swansea 2000–; memb: Cncl Int Assoc for Computational Mechanics (IACM) 1993–, Mgmnt Bd Euro Ctee for Computational Methods in the Applied Scis (ECCOMAS) 1993–, Inter Research Cncl High Performance Computing Mgmnt Ctee (IHMC) 1995–98; Special Achievement Award NASA Langley Research

M

Center 1989; Computational Mechanics Award of the Int Assoc for Computational Mechanics 1998; hon fell Int Soc for Computational Fluid Dynamics (ISCFD) 2003, fell Int Assoc for Computational Mechanics 2004; CMath, CEng, FIMA 1978, FICE 1993, FREng 1997; *Publications* Finite Elements and Approximation (co-author, 1983), The Finite Element Method in Heat Transfer Analysis (co-author, 1996); *Recreations* Llanelli Scarlets Rugby Club, cynghanedd; *Style*— Prof Kenneth Morgan, FREng; ✉ 137 Pennard Drive, Southgate, Swansea SA3 2DW (tel 01792 233887); School of Engineering, University of Wales Swansea, Swansea SA2 8PP (tel 01792 295515, fax 01792 295676, e-mail k.morgan@swansea.ac.uk)

MORGAN, Baron (Life Peer UK 2000), of Aberdyfi in the County of Gwynedd; Prof Kenneth Owen; s of David James Morgan (d 1978), of Aberystwyth, and Margaret, *née* Owen (d 1989); *b* 16 May 1934; *Educ* Univ Coll Sch, Oriel Coll Oxford (MA, DPhil, DLitt); *m* 4 Jan 1973, Jane (d 1992), da of Jessica Keeler, of Wrexham; 1 s (Hon David Keir Ewart b 4 July 1974), 1 da (Hon Katherine Louise b 22 Sept 1977); *Career* lectr in history Univ Coll Swansea 1958–66 (sr lectr 1965–66), visiting fell American Cncl of Learned Socs Univ of Columbia NY 1962–63, fell and praelector in modern history and politics The Queen's Coll Oxford 1966–89, lectr Univ of Oxford 1967–89 and 1995–; vice-chllr Univ of Wales Aberystwyth 1989–95, sr vice-chllr Univ of Wales 1993–95, research prof Univ of Wales Aberystwyth 1995–99; visiting prof: Columbia Univ 1965, Univ of Cape Town 1997, Univ of the Witwatersrand 1997–2000, Univ of Bristol 2000; visiting lectr Univ of texas Austin 1994, 1999 and 2007; BBC political commentator on elections, radio and TV 1964–79; ed: Welsh History Review 1965–2003, 20th Century British History 1994–99; memb: Bd Celtic Studies 1972–2003, Welsh Political Archive 1985–, Cncl Nat Library of Wales 1989–95, Lords Select Ctee on the Constitution 2001–04, Fabian Soc Ctee on the Monarchy 2002–03; hon fell Univ of Wales Swansea 1985, supernumerary fell Jesus Coll Oxford 1991–92; hon fell: The Queens' Coll Oxford 1992, Univ of Wales Cardiff 1997, Trinity Coll Carmarthen 1998, Oriel Coll Oxford 2003; Hon DLitt: Univ of Wales 1997, Univ of Glamorgan 1997, Univ of Greenwich 2004; FRHistS 1964, FBA 1983; *Books* Wales in British Politics 1868–1922 (1963, 3 edn 1980), David Lloyd George - Welsh Radical as World Statesman (1963, 2 edn 1964), Freedom or Sacrilege? (1966), Keir Hardie (1967), The Age of Lloyd George (1971, 3 edn 1983), Lloyd George - Family Letters 1885–1936 (1973), Lloyd George (1974), Keir Hardie - Radical and Socialist (1975), Consensus and Disunity - the Lloyd George Coalition Government 1918–1922 (1979), Portrait of a Progressive - the Political Career of Christopher, Viscount Addison (with Jane Morgan, 1980), Rebirth of a Nation - Wales 1880–1980 (1981), David Lloyd George 1863–1945 (1981), Welsh Society and Nationhood - Historical Essays (jt ed, 1984), The Oxford Illustrated History of Britain (ed, 1984, many edns), Labour in Power 1945–1951 (1984), Labour People - Leaders and Lieutenants, Hardie to Kinnock (1987), The Oxford History of Britain (ed, 1988, many edns), The Red Dragon and the Red Flag - The Cases of James Griffiths and Aneurin Bevan (1989), The People's Peace - British History since 1945 (1990, latest edn 2001), Modern Wales, Politics, Places and People (1995), Young Oxford History of Britain and Ireland (ed, 1996), Callaghan: A Life (1997), Crime, Protest and Police in British Society (jt ed, 1999), The Twentieth Century (2001), The Great Reform Act (2001), Michael Foot: A Life (2007); *Recreations* architecture, music, sport, travel; *Clubs* Reform, Middx CCC; *Style*— Prof the Rt Hon the Lord Morgan, FBA; ✉ The Croft, 63 Millwood End, Long Hanborough, Witney, Oxfordshire OX29 8BP (tel 01993 881341)

MORGAN, Marilynne Ann; CB (1996); da of J Emlyn Williams (d 1984), and Roma Elizabeth, *née* Ellis (d 1992); *b* 22 June 1946; *Educ* Gads Hill Place Sch, Bedford Coll (BA); *m* 26 Sept 1970, Nicholas Alan Morgan, eld s of Rear Adm Sir Patrick Morgan, KCVO, CB, DSC (d 1989); *Career* called to the Bar Middle Temple 1972 (bencher 2002); DHSS: legal asst 1973, sr legal asst 1978, asst slr 1982, princ asst slr (grade 3) 1985–91; DOE: dep slr 1991–92, slr and legal advsr (grade 2) 1992–97, sr dir Legal and Corp Servs Gp 1996–97; the slr DWP (formerly DSS) and Dept of Health 1997–2004, head Law and Special Policy Gp DWP (formerly DSS), non-exec dir Treasy Slr's Dept 2004–; contrib articles to learned jls; chm: Legal Section First Div Assoc 1984–86 (vice-chm 1983–84), Departmental Task Force 1994–95; memb Gen Cncl of the Bar 1986–92; tstee/dir Alzheimer's Soc 2003–; *Books* Halsbury's Laws of England (contrib 4 edn), Vaughan's Law of the European Communities (contrib, 1990); *Recreations* homely pursuits; *Clubs* Univ Women's, Royal Commonwealth; *Style*— Mrs Marilynne A Morgan, CB; ✉ c/o The University Women's Club, 2 Audley Square, South Audley Street, London W1K 1DB

MORGAN, Neil Christopher; s of Ernest Morgan, of Morriston, Swansea, and Myra, *née* John; *b* 28 January 1967, Morriston, Swansea; *Educ* Ystalyfera Comp Swansea, Aberystwyth Univ (LLB), Coll of Law Chester; *m* 19 Sept 1998, Allison, *née* Cox; 1 da (Emily Ceri b 13 Dec 1999), 1 s (Daniel William b 1 Oct 2004); *Career* slr specialising in property litigation; articled clerk Edwards Geldard Slrs 1989–91, asst slr Hugh James Jones & Jenkins 1991–96, ptnr and head Property Litigation Dept Hugh James Slrs 1996–; memb Ctee S Wales and SW Branch Property Litigation Assoc; author of various articles in the legal press; memb Law Soc 1991; *Recreations* most sports, especially football; *Style*— Neil Morgan, Esq; ✉ Hugh James Solicitors, Hodge House, 114–116 St Mary Street, Cardiff CF10 1DY (tel 029 2066 0589, fax 029 20391165, e-mail neil.morgan@hughjames.com)

MORGAN, Hon Mr Justice; Sir Paul Hyacinth; kt (2007); s of Daniel Morgan (d 1977), of Londonderry, and Veronica Mary, *née* Elder (d 2000); *b* 17 August 1952; *Educ* St Columbs Coll Londonderry, Peterhouse Cambridge (scholar), Lincoln's Inn (Hardwicke scholar, Droop scholar); *m* 19 April 1980, Sheila Ruth, da of Arthur Reginald Harvey; 3 s (Daniel Arthur b 17 Oct 1982, Edwin Hugh Rory b 22 Oct 1985, Leo Robert b 26 Sept 1987); *Career* called to the Bar 1975 (bencher 2001), joined chambers of Ronald Bernstein QC at 11 King's Bench Walk Temple (which removed to Falcon Chambers), QC 1992, judge of the High Court of Justice 2007– (dep High Court Judge 2001–07); dep chm Agricultural Land Tbnl 1999–; *Publications* incl: Megarry on Rent Acts (jt ed, 11 edn 1988), Woodfall on Landlord and Tenant (jt ed, 28 edn 1994), Gale on Easements (jt ed, 17 edn 2002), Fisher & Lightwood's Law of Mortgage (jt ed, 12 edn 2006); *Style*— The Hon Mr Justice Morgan; ✉ Royal Courts of Justice, Strand, London WC2A 2LL

MORGAN, Paul William David; s of Evan John Morgan (d 1987), and Sonia Myfanwy Morgan, of Blackwood, Gwent, S Wales; *b* 12 November 1948; *Educ* Pengam GS, Ealing Sch of Business (BA); *m* 29 Dec 1988, Linda Anne, *née* Jenner; 2 s (Matthew John b 9 Feb 1989, Alexander David b 25 July 1994); *Career* brand mangr: Res Projects Smiths Industries 1971–72 (mktg trainee Clock and Watch Div 1967–71), Snacks Div United Biscuits 1972–74; RHM Foods: brand mangr 1975–77, sr brand mangr 1977–79, mktg mangr 1979–81, sr mktg mangr 1981–84; The Brand Development Company: mktg dir 1984–86, jt managing ptnr 1986–89, md 1989–; memb: Mktg Soc 1987, Market Research Soc 1995; *Recreations* sport, reading, music; *Clubs* Brentham Lawn Tennis, Ealing RFC, Beaconsfield Tennis; *Style*— Paul Morgan, Esq; ✉ Rose Cottage, Andrew Hill Lane, Hedgerley, Buckinghamshire SL2 3UL; The Brand Development Company, 50 Long Acre, London WC2E 9JR (tel 020 7497 9727, fax 020 7497 3581)

MORGAN, Peter William Lloyd; MBE (2003); s of Matthew Morgan (d 1974), of Sketty, Swansea, and Margaret Gwynneth Morgan; *b* 9 May 1936; *Educ* Llandovery Coll, Trinity Hall Cambridge (MA); *m* 18 April 1964, Elisabeth Susanne, da of William Edward Davis; 3 da (Justine Elisabeth b 9 Aug 1965, Penelope Susanne b 4 March 1967, Gabrielle Margaret b 11 Sept 1969); *Career* IBM: joined 1959, sales dir London 1971, gp dir mktg IBM Europe, Middle East and Africa (Paris based) 1975, dir IBM UK 1983–87, dir IBM UK Holdings 1987–89; DG Inst of Directors 1989–94; chm: South Wales Electricity plc (Swalec) 1996 (non-exec dir 1989–95), NPI (formerly National Provident Institution) 1996–99 (non-exec dir 1990–95, dep chm 1995), Pace Micro Technology plc 1996–2000, Baltimore Technologies plc 2000–2003 (dep chm 1998–2000), Technetix plc 2002–, Strategic Thought Group plc 2004–, IXICO Ltd 2006–; non-exec dir: Oxford Instruments plc 2000–, Hyder Consulting plc 2002–; memb Economic and Social Ctee European Community 1994–2002 and 2006–; memb Lloyd's 1987 (elected memb Cncl 2000), dir Assoc of Lloyd's Membs (ALM); vice-pres London Welsh Male Voice Choir; Master Worshipful Co of Information Technologists 2002, Liveryman Welsh Livery Guild 2005; *Books* Alarming Drum (2005); *Recreations* gardening, skiing, wine, history, dog walking; *Clubs* Oxford and Cambridge; *Style*— Peter Morgan, Esq, MBE; ✉ Cleeves, Weydown Road, Haslemere, Surrey GU27 1DT (tel 01428 642757, e-mail petermorgan@cleeves2.demon.co.uk)

MORGAN, Piers; s of Anthony Glynne Pughe-Morgan, and Gabrielle Georgina Sybille, *née* Oliver; *b* 30 March 1965; *Educ* Chailey Sch, Lewes Priory Sixth Form Coll, Harlow Journalism Coll; *m* 13 July 1991, Marion Elizabeth, da of Niall Shalloe; 3 s (Spencer William b 26 July 1993, Stanley Christopher b 18 June 1997, Albert b 11 Dec 2000); *Career* reporter Surrey and S London Newspapers 1987–89, showbiz ed The Sun 1989–94; ed: News of the World 1994–95, The Mirror 1995–2004; co-prop Press Gazette 2005–; presenter: Morgan and Platell (Channel 4) 2004–05, You Can't Fire Me I'm Famous (BBC 1) 2006–; judge: America's Got Talent (NBC) 2006–, Britain's Got Talent (ITV 1) 2007–; *Books* Private Lives of the Stars (1990), Secret Lives of the Stars (1991), Phillip Schofield - To Dream a Dream (1992), Take That - Our Story (1993), Take That - On The Road (1994), The Insider (2005), Don't You Know Who I Am? (2007); *Recreations* cricket, Arsenal FC; *Clubs* Tramp, Newick Cricket; *Style*— Piers Morgan, Esq; ✉ c/o James Grant Media, 94 Strand on the Green, London W4 3NN (tel 020 8742 4950)

MORGAN, Rt Hon (Hywel) Rhodri; PC (2000), AM; s of T J Morgan (d 1986), and Huana, *née* Rees; *b* 29 September 1939; *Educ* Whitchurch GS Cardiff, St John's Coll Oxford (open exhibitioner, BA), Harvard Univ (Williams scholar, MA); *m* 1967, Julie, da of Jack Edwards; 1 s (Stuart), 2 da (Mari, Siani); *Career* tutor-organiser WEA SE Wales region 1963–65; res offr: Cardiff City Planning Dept 1965–66, Planning Div Welsh Office 1966–68 and 1970–72, DoE 1968–70; econ advsr DTI 1972–74, industrial devpt offr S Glamorgan CC 1974–80, head EEC Office for Wales 1980–87; MP 1987–2001, memb Nat Assembly for Wales (Lab) Cardiff W 1999–; House of Commons: oppn front bench spokesman on Energy 1988–92, oppn front bench spokesman on Welsh Affrs 1992–97, chm Select Ctee on Public Administration 1997–2001; National Assembly for Wales: sec for econ devpt and Europe 1999–2000, first min 2000–; memb Dept of Energy Severn Barrage Ctee 1978–81; *Books* Cardiff: Half and Half a Capital (1994); *Recreations* tennis, dolphin watching, wood-carving, barbecue cooking; *Clubs* Canton Labour, Canton Rugby, Fairwater Rugby; *Style*— The Rt Hon Rhodri Morgan, AM; ✉ Lower House, Michaelston-le-Pit, Dinas Powys, Glamorgan CF64 4HE (tel 029 2051 4262); National Assembly for Wales, Cardiff Bay, Cardiff CF99 1NA

MORGAN, Robert John; s of late Ioan Brynfab Morgan, of Woodford Green, Essex, and late Doris Eileen Morgan; *b* 19 February 1941; *Educ* Forest Sch, St Peter's Coll Oxford, Guy's Hosp London (Golding-Bird scholar); *m* 29 Jan 1977, Anita Joan, da of John Richardson; 2 s (William Ioan James, Henry Christopher George), 1 da (Jessica Rhiannon); *Career* various jr appointments Guy's Hosp, Guildford Hosps and The London Hosp 1967–75, sr registrar in urology St Peter's Hosps 1975–78, sr lectr in urology Inst of Urology London and hon conslt urologist St Peter's Hosps 1978–81, conslt urological surgn Whittington and Royal Free Hosps 1981–88, hon sr lectr in surgery UCH Med Sch 1982–88; currently: emeritus conslt urological surgn Royal Free Hosp, lectr in surgery Univ of London, hon sr lectr in surgery Royal Free and UC Sch of Med, hon conslt urological surgn St Luke's Hosp for the Clergy, King Edward VII Hosp for Officers and the Hosp of St John and St Elizabeth London; pres Sec of Urology RSM 2003–04; hon memb American Urological Assoc; memb various med socs incl Br Assoc of Urological Surgns (hon sec and memb Cncl 1989–93); Liveryman Worshipful Soc of Apothecaries; *Publications* papers on adult and paediatric urology; *Recreations* reading, fishing, sailing; *Clubs* Travellers; *Style*— Robert J Morgan, Esq; ✉ 5 Devonshire Place, London W1G 6HL (tel 020 7486 3345, fax 020 7486 1873)

MORGAN, Robin Richard; s of Raymond Morgan, and Jean Edith Bennett; *b* 16 September 1953; *Educ* King Edward VI GS Stourbridge; *m* 31 July 1977 (m dis 2000), Ruth Winefride Mary; 2 s, 1 da; *Career* journalist and author; County Express Stourbridge 1971–73, Evening Echo Hemel Hempstead 1973–78; Sunday Times: reporter 1979–83, dep news ed 1983–85, ed Insight 1985–87, features ed 1987–89; ed Sunday Express 1989–91, ed Sunday Times Magazine 1991–93, editorial dir designate Reader's Digest 1993–95, ed Sunday Times Magazine 1995–, contrib ed GQ 1999–; Campaigning Journalist of the Year 1983 (commended 1982); *Books* The Falklands War (co-author, 1982), Rainbow Warrior (co-author, 1986), Bullion (co-author, 1988), Manpower (ed, 1988), Ambush (co-author, 1989), 1000 Makers of the Cinema (co-ed); *Recreations* US politics, modern American literature, travel, cinema; *Style*— Robin Morgan, Esq; ✉ Sunday Times, 1 Pennington Street, Wapping, London E98 1ST (tel 020 7782 7380)

MORGAN, Prof Rodney Emrys (Rod); s of William Emrys Morgan (d 1976), of Ystalfera, Glamorgan, and Jesmine Lilian, *née* Reed; *b* 16 February 1942; *Educ* Haberdashers' Aske's, Paston GS, Univ of Southampton (BSc, Dip Social Studies); *m* 19 August 1966, Karin Birgitta, da of Folke Mortimer Lang, of Växjö, Sweden; 3 s (Magnus Rodney b 4 Oct 1968, Tobias Mortimer b 26 Feb 1970, Benjamin Emrys Folke b 20 July 1972); *Career* sr lectr in criminology Univ of Bath 1981–89 (lectr 1972–81); Univ of Bristol: prof of criminal justice 1990–2001 (prof emeritus 2001–), dean Faculty of Law 1992–95; HM chief inspr Probation Serv for Eng and Wales 2001–04, chair Youth Justice Bd for Eng and Wales 2004–07; visiting fell Univ of Oxford 1985–87; visiting prof: Univ of W Australia 1991, Harvard Univ 1996; assessor to Lord Justice Woolf's inquiry into prison riots 1990–91; expert advsr to: Amnesty Int on custodial conditions 1986–, Cncl of Europe on custodial conditions 1989–; memb: ind inquiry into role and responsibilities of the police 1993–95, Avon and Somerset Police Authy 1997–2001, Parole Bd 1998–2001, numerous ctees concerned with criminal justice policy; memb Br Soc of Criminology; JP City of Bath 1974–95; *Books* A Taste of Prison (1976), The Future of the Prison System (1980), Prisons and Accountability (1985), Coming to Terms with Policing (1989), The Oxford Handbook of Criminology (1994, 3 edn 2002), The Politics of Sentencing Reform (1995), The Future of Policing (1997), Preventing Torture (1998), Protecting Prisoners (1999), Combating Torture (2001); memb editorial ctees of various learned jls; *Recreations* sailing, theatre, gardening; *Style*— Prof Rod Morgan; ✉ Beech House, Lansdown Road, Bath BA1 5EG (tel 01225 316676)

MORGAN, Terry Keith; s of Keith Morgan (d 1985), of Cwmbran, Gwent, and Ivy Margaret, *née* Went; *b* 28 December 1948; *Educ* Croesycelliog Secdy Modern, Newport & Monmouth Tech Coll (HND), Univ of Birmingham (MSc); *m* 22 Aug 1970, Ann Elizabeth, da of Kingsley Jones; 1 da (Rebecca Elizabeth b 24 April 1978), 1 s (Rhys Keith b 16 June 1980); *Career* Lucas Girling: craft apprentice 1965–68, student apprentice 1968–72, prodn engr 1972–78, prod engr 1978–80; res mangr Leyland Vehicles 1980–83, mfrg mangr Leyland Bus 1983–85; Land Rover Ltd: prodn dir Range Rover 1985–87, prodn ops dir 1987–89; Rover Group: ops dir 1989–90, md Land Rover Vehicles 1991–94; md Royal Ordnance Div British Aerospace Defence Ltd 1994–96, dir of personnel British Aerospace plc 1997–2001, gp managing dir ops BAE Systems; ceo Tube Lines 2002–; non-exec dir NAAFI 2000–; chm: Central England Training & Enterprise Cncl, Solihull Chamber of Commerce and Industry; memb: Bd Investors in People UK, Solihull Health Authy, Exec Industrial Soc, Qualification Curriculum Authy (QCA) 2001–; Silver Medal Inst of Mgmnt; MIMfgE 1975, FIEE 1994, FREng 1995; *Recreations* golf, rugby; *Clubs* Copt Heath Golf; *Style*— Terry Morgan, Esq, FREng; ✉ 51 Lady Byron Lane, Knowle, Solihull, West Midlands B93 9AX (tel 01564 777560); Tube Lines, 30 The South Colonnade, Canary Wharf, London E14 5EU

MORGAN, Dr Thomas Clifford Naunton; s of Sir Clifford Naunton Morgan (d 1986), and Ena Muriel, *née* Evans (d 1993); *b* 9 March 1948; *Educ* Harrow, St Bartholomew's Hosp Med Sch London (MB BS); *m* 16 June 1974, Dr Rosemary Naunton Morgan, da of Maj Arthur William Hayward Bradstreet (d 1987), of Buxted, E Sussex; 3 da (Nicola Anne b 3 Dec 1977, Katherine Lucy b 24 Aug 1981, Louise Polly b 8 Oct 1985); *Career* house surgn 1974; conslt radiologist W Middx Univ Hosp 1988–; Freeman City of London 1974, Liveryman Worshipful Co of Barbers 1974; memb: BMA, MDU; LRCP, FRCS 1978 (MRCS), FRCR 1987; *Recreations* shooting, tennis, windsurfing; *Clubs* Roehampton; *Style*— Dr Thomas Naunton Morgan; ✉ 3 Campion Road, Putney, London SW15 6NN (tel 020 8789 5211, tom.nauntonmorgan@btinternet.com); West Middlesex University Hospital NHS Trust, Isleworth TW7 6AF (tel 020 8565 5865)

MORGAN, Prof (David) Vernon; s of David Vernon Grenville Morgan (d 1941), and Isobel Lovina, *née* Emanuel (d 1996); *b* 13 July 1941; *Educ* Llanelli Boys' GS, Univ of Wales Aberystwyth (BSc), Gonville & Caius Coll Cambridge (PhD), Univ of Leeds (DSc); *m* 31 July 1965, Jean, da of Francis Anderson (d 1979); 1 da (Suzanne b 22 Jan 1969), 1 s (Dyfrig b 3 Sept 1973); *Career* Cavendish Laboratory Cambridge: Univ of Wales fell 1966–68, Harwell fell 1968–70; Univ of Leeds: lectr 1970–77, sr lectr 1977–80, reader 1980–85; Univ of Wales Cardiff: prof of microelectronics 1985–, head Sch of Electrical & Systems Engrg 1992–94, head Cardiff Sch of Engrg 1995–2002, distinguished research prof 2002–; visiting prof Cornell Univ 1978 and 1979; vice-pres IOP 1992–96; IEE: chm Books Publication Ctee, memb Accreditation Ctee; memb MOD Electronic Materials and Devices Ctee; hon fell Univ of Wales Aberystwyth 2006; FIEE, FInstP, FCGI 1988, FREng 1996; Papal Cross Pro Ecclesia et Pontifica 2004; *Books* Introduction to Semiconductor Microtechnology (1983), Gallium Arsenide for Device and Integrated Circuits (1986); *Recreations* golf, hill walking; *Style*— Prof Vernon Morgan, FREng; ✉ Cardiff School of Engineering, Queen's Building, PO Box 925, University of Wales, Cardiff CF2 1XH (tel 029 2087 4424, fax 029 2087 4292)

MORGAN, Zoe Jeanette; da of Malcolm Knight, and Jeanette, *née* Mitchelson; *Educ* Felixstowe Coll, Braintree Coll of FE (vice-pres student union and govr), Univ of Newcastle upon Tyne (BSc); *m* James Neale Morgan; *Career* dir of mktg Hasbro 1993–94, dir of mktg and merchandise AG Stanley 1994–96, dir of mktg and merchandise Halfords 1996–99, mktg dir Boots plc 2000–02, mktg dir HBOS Retail 2003–04, dir of mktg The Co-operative Gp 2004–; memb: Mktg Soc 1990, Industry and Parly Tst 1997, Women's Advtg Club of London (WACL) 2001; memb many wildlife and conservation charities; memb Worshipful Co of Marketors 2006; *Recreations* natural history, woodlands and wildlife preservation, organic gardening; *Style*— Mrs Zoe Morgan

MORGAN-GILES, Rear Adm Sir Morgan Charles; kt (1985), DSO (1944), OBE (1943, MBE 1942), GM (1942), DL (Hants 1983); s of F C Morgan-Giles, OBE (Naval Architect, d 1964), of Teignmouth, Devon, and Ivy Carus-Wilson (d 1936); *b* 19 June 1914; *Educ* Clifton; *m* 1, 11 May 1946, Pamela (d 1966), da of Philip Bushell, of Sydney, Aust; 4 da (Penelope (Mrs Cartwright) b 1947, Melita (m Hon Victor Lampson, now 3 Baron Killearn, *qv*) b 1951, Camilla (m John, er s of Sir Eric Drake, CBE, DL (d 1996)) b 1953 d 1988, Alexandra (m Col Edward Bolitho, OBE) b 1958), 2 s (Philip b 1949, Rodney (m Sarah, da of Maj Sir Hereward Wake, 14 Bt, MC, DL, *qv*) b 1955); m 2, 1968, Mrs Marigold Steel (d 1995), da of late Percy Lowe; *Career* Cadet RN 1932, China Station 1933–35, HMS Echo 1936, torpedo specialist 1938; WWII: Atlantic convoys, Norway, Med, West Desert and Tobruk Garrison 1941, attached RAF 1942, sr naval offr Vis (Dalmatia) and liaison with Commandos and Marshal Tito's Partisan Forces 1943–44, RN Staff Coll 1945, Force W Bangkok and Far East 1945, HMS Norfolk 1946; Trieste 1948–49, i/c HMS Chieftain 1950–51, Admty 1953–54, Capt Chief of Intelligence Staff Far East 1954–56, Capt (D) Dartmouth Trg Sqdn 1957–58, Capt HMS Vernon 1959–60, i/c HMS Belfast Far East Station 1961–62, Adm Pres RN Coll Greenwich 1962, ret at own request 1964; MP (Cons) Winchester 1964–79; vice-chm Cons Def Ctee 1965–75, chm HMS Belfast Tst 1971–78, life vice-pres RNLI 1989– (memb Mgmnt Ctee 1971–); Prime Warden Worshipful Co of Shipwrights 1987–88 (Freeman 1965–); Partisan Star Yugoslavia 1953; *Recreations* sailing, country pursuits; *Clubs* Royal Yacht Sqdn; *Style*— Rear Adm Sir Morgan Morgan-Giles, DSO, OBE, GM, DL; ✉ The Anchor House, Little Sodbury Manor, Chipping Sodbury, Gloucestershire BS37 6QA (tel 01454 327485/312232); c/o Upton Park, Alresford, Hampshire SO24 9DX (tel 01962 732443)

MORGAN-JONES, Rhydian James; s of Gwyn William Morgan-Jones (d 1964), and Hon (Mary) Lorraine, *née* Berry (later Hon Mrs Smith-Bingham, d 1986); *b* 27 October 1944, Windsor, Berks; *m* 1974 (m dis 1979), Patricia Mary Bird (d 2004); partner, Lady Rose Diana Musker, *née* Lambton; 1 da (Katie Jane b 1 Dec 1979); *Career* racehorse breeder for Flat and Nat Hunt racing; joined Br Bloodstock Agency 1972; chm: Thoroughbred Breeders' Assoc, Br Horseracing and Standards Tst, Industry Committee (Horseracing) Ltd; memb Bd BHB (chm Finance and Audit Ctees); formerly: chm Fedn of Bloodstock Agents, sec Bloodstock and Racehorse Industries Confedn, founding sec Horseracing Advsy Cncl; advsr Juddmonte Farms; dir Small Breed Bantam (Chicken) Assoc; Pigley Revial Fund for Exotic Breeds 1984; dir Animal Rights Glos, chm Vegan Soc Glos; memb Right to Ramble Assoc; FCA 1967; *Recreations* racing, golf, country sports, nargleing in Northumberland; *Clubs* White's, Portland, Madame Jojo's; *Style*— Rhydian Morgan-Jones, Esq; ✉ c/o Pauline Fordham, 20 Oakley Street, London SW3 5NT

MORGAN OF HUYTON, Baroness (Life Peer UK 2001), of Huyton in the County of Merseyside; Sally Morgan; da of Albert Edward Morgan; *b* 28 June 1959; *Educ* Belvedere Girls' Sch Liverpool, Univ of Durham (BA), Univ of London (PGCE, MA); *m* 1984, John Lyons; 2 s; *Career* secdy sch teacher 1981–85; Lab Pty: student organiser 1985–87, sr targeting offr 1987–93, dir of campaigns and elections 1993–95; head of pty liaison for ldr HM Oppn 1995–97, political sec to PM 1997–2001, min of state Cabinet Office 2001, dir of govt relations PM's Office 2001–05; non-exec dir Carphone Warehouse plc, Southern Cross Healthcare plc; memb Advsy Panel Lloyds Pharmacy; memb Bd Olympic Delivery Authy; advsr to Bd ARK; *Style*— The Baroness Morgan of Huyton

MORGAN WILLIAMS, Hugh Richard Vaughan; s of Hugh Morgan Williams (d 1980), of Canford Magna, Dorset, and Jean, *née* Crocker (d 1967); *b* 29 January 1953; *Educ* Aiglon Coll Switzerland, Canford Sch, Grey Coll Durham (BA); *m* 1982, Anna Louise, da of Peter Terry; 3 da (Sophie b 1984, Madeleine b 1987, Keira b 1998), 1 s (Oliver b 1991); *Career* trainee journalist Metro Radio Newcastle 1974–75, journalist LBC 1975–81, news ed Radio Tees 1981–85, fndr dir rising to chm Canford Gp plc 1985–; assoc dir Sovereign Strategy Ltd 2002–, non-exec chm Laser Broadcasting Ltd; chm: NE Regnl Investment Fund Ltd 1999–, Galaxy Radio NE 1999–2003, Capital NE 2002–, NE Econommic Forum 2006–; fndr dir Minster Sound Radio; CBI: regnl chm (NE) 1995–98, chm Small and Medium Enterprises Nat Cncl 2004–06, memb Econ Affrs Ctee; vice-chm Small and Medium Enterprises Ctee UNICE, memb Bd One NE 1998–2001; chm Nat Language Trg Orgn 1998–2003, govr Centre for Info on Language Trg (CILT) Nat Centre for Languages 2003–, memb Govt Steering Gp for Languages; tstee: Int Centre for Life Newcastle, Cowesby Tst; memb Bd Univ of Durham 2006–; memb Cncl: St John's Coll Durham, Univ of Durham; govr Queen Mary's Sch Topcliffe; runner-up NE Businessman of the Year, semi-finalist Entrepreneur of the Year, Smaller Companies Export Award, DTI Languages for Export Award (twice), FT Exporter of the Year; FInstD; *Publications* Variations on a Recipe (series of cookery books, 1980), Improving Regional Competitiveness - The Business Agenda for the North (1996), Nuffield Languages Inquiry (co-author, 2001); *Recreations* skiing, tennis, reading, theatre, opera; *Clubs* Northern Counties; *Style*— Hugh Morgan Williams, Esq; ✉ Canford Group plc, Crowther Road, Washington, Tyne & Wear NE38 0BW (tel 0191 418 1000, fax 0191 418 1001, e-mail hw@canford.co.uk)

MORGANS, (John) Barrie; *b* 9 November 1941; *Educ* Dyffryn GS Port Talbot, Swansea Tech Coll; *m*; 1 s, 2 da; *Career* fin mangr British Steel until 1964 (joined 1957), fin mangr British Rail 1965–67; IBM: cost accountant then pricing mangr 1967–71, fin mangr Southern Area IBM Europe Paris 1971–73, controller IBM UK Ltd 1975–78, dir of fin 1978–86, dir of fin and planning 1986–92, dir of quality and mgmnt servs 1992–95, chief exec IBM UK Ltd 1995–96, chm and chief exec IBM UK Ltd 1996–97, dir IBM United United Kingdom Holdings Ltd until 1997; non-exec chm: Plasmon plc 1999–, Azlan Gp plc 1997–, Telemedic Holdings plc, IBM Pensions Trust Ltd; non-exec dir: Legal & General Gp plc 1997–, Psion plc 1998–, 1... Ltd 2000–; chm of govrs Chichester Coll of Technol; FCCA, FRSA; *Recreations* good wine, food, skiing, travel; *Style*— J Barrie Morgans, Esq

MORGENSTERN, Philip Louis; s of Maurice Joseph Morgenstern (d 1966), and Celia, *née* Hausmann (d 1999); *b* 15 January 1932; *Educ* St Paul's, Univ of London (BA); *m* 1961, Estelle Pamela, da of Jakoba Erenberg; 2 da (Ava Miriam b 18 Oct 1963, Deborah Sarah b 15 April 1972), 2 s (Neil Hardy Iain b 31 March 1965, Matthew Joseph b 6 Jan 1968); *Career* Nicholson Graham & Jones: articled clerk 1954, ptnr 1962, sr ptnr 1981–95; sec GB-Sasakawa Foundation 1986–97; tstee: Inst of Jewish Studies 1989 (chm 1999), Jewish Law Publication Fund, Kessler Fndn; Freeman City of London; *Recreations* hermeneutic and rhetorical exegesis of ancient texts, music, art history; *Style*— Philip Morgenstern, Esq; ✉ c/o Kirkpatrick & Lockhart Preston Gates Ellis LLP, 110 Cannon Street, London EC4N 6AR (tel 020 7648 9000, fax 020 7648 9001)

MORIARTY, Gerald Evelyn; QC (1974); s of Lt Col Gerald Ruadh Moriarty (d 1981), and Eileen, *née* Moloney (d 1978); *b* 23 August 1928; *Educ* Downside, St John's Coll Oxford (MA); *m* 17 June 1961, Judith Mary, da of Hon William Robert Atkin (d 1984); 4 s (Michael b 25 Aug 1962, Matthew b 12 Aug 1963, Thomas b 20 Jan 1966, John b 12 Jan 1973); *Career* called to the Bar Lincoln's Inn 1951, recorder 1976–98, chm exam in public Bedfordshire Structure Plan 1978, bencher 1983, memb Gen Cncl of the Bar 1986–90; *Recreations* golf, reading; *Clubs* Reform; *Style*— Gerald Moriarty, Esq, QC; ✉ 15 Campden Street, London W8 7EP

MORIARTY, Hon Mr Justice Michael Anthony; s of Dr James Moriarty (d 1975), of Belfast and Dublin, and Nora, *née* Diamond (d 1992); *b* 10 August 1946, Belfast; *Educ* Blackrock Coll Dublin, UC Dublin (BCL, Dip European Law), King's Inns Dublin; *m* 1980, Mary Irvine; 1 s (Mark b 1 Oct 1983), 2 da (Clare b 31 Aug 1986, Aoife b 2 Aug 1988); *Career* called to the Bar: King's Inns Dublin 1968, Middle Temple London 1981; barr-at-law 1968–82, sr counsel 1982–87, circuit judge 1987–96, judge of the High Court of Ireland 1996–; chm Lord Mayor's Cmmn on Crime in Dublin 1995, chm and sole memb Tbnl of Inquiry into Payments to Charles Haughey and Michael Lowry 1997; *Recreations* music (especially opera), sport (especially cricket), wine; *Clubs* Fitzwilliam Lawn Tennis (Dublin), Pembroke Cricket (Dublin); *Style*— The Hon Mr Justice Michael Moriarty; ✉ The High Court, Four Courts, Inns Quay, Dublin 7, Ireland; Tribunal of Inquiry, Upper Yard, Dublin Castle, Dublin 2, Ireland

MORIARTY, Stephen; QC (1999); s of George William Moriarty, and Dorothy Violet, *née* Edwards; *b* 14 April 1955; *Educ* Chichester HS for Boys, BNC Oxford (BA, Proxime Accessit Prize 1977, BCL 1978, Vinerian Scholarship 1978); *m* 1989, Dr Susan Clare Stanford; *Career* Univ of Oxford: fell and tutor in law Exeter Coll 1979–86, lectr in law 1979–86; called to the Bar 1986, practising barr 1987–; memb Middle Temple 1976; *Recreations* theatre, opera; *Clubs* Reform; *Style*— Stephen Moriarty, Esq, QC; ✉ Fountain Court Chambers, Temple, London EC4Y 9DH (tel 020 7583 3335, fax 020 7353 0329, e-mail smoriarty@fountaincourt.co.uk)

MORISON, Hugh; CBE (2002); s of Archibald Ian Morison, of Felpham, W Sussex, and Enid Rose, *née* Mawer; *b* 22 November 1943; *Educ* Chichester HS for Boys, St Catherine's Coll Oxford (MA); *m* 1, 1971 (m dis 1993), Marion, da of Fred Aubrey Smithers, of Lincoln; 2 da (Emma b 1972, Lucy b 1975); m 2, 1993, Ilona, da of Sandor Roth, of Budapest; *Career* Civil Serv SO 1966–93: under sec Scottish Home and Health Dept 1984–88, Industry Dept for Scotland 1988–93; chief exec Scotch Whisky Assoc 1994–2003; pres European Confedn of Spirits Producers 2001–03, chm Scottish Business and Biodiversity Gp 1999–2003; non-exec dir Praban Na Linne Ltd 2005–06; memb: Health Appointments Advsy Ctee (Scotland) 1994–2000, Exec Ctee Barony Housing Assoc Ltd 1996– (chm 2005–); chm Letterfearn Moorings Assoc 2001–; govr UHI Millennium Inst 2004–; FRSA; *Recreations* hill walking, sailing, literature, archaeology; *Clubs* New (Edinburgh), Royal Commonwealth Soc; *Style*— Hugh Morison, Esq, CBE; ✉ 12 Sunbury Place, Edinburgh EH4 3BY (tel 0131 225 6568, e-mail hugh.morison@at-inform.com)

MORISON, Hon Mr Justice; Sir Thomas Richard Atkin Morison; kt (1993); s of late Harold Thomas Brash Morison, of London, and Hon Nancy Morison, *née* Atkin (d 1978); gs of Lord Atkin (Baron Atkin of Aberdovey) and Lord Morison; *b* 15 January 1939; *Educ* Winchester, Univ of Oxford; *m* 1963 (m dis 1993), Judith Rachel Walton, da of Rev R J W Morris, OBE, of Shaftesbury; 1 s (Ben b 1969), 1 da (Lucy b 1967); *Career* called to the Bar Gray's Inn 1960, QC 1979, judge of the High Court of Justice (Queen's Bench Div) 1993–, judge Employment Appeal Tbnl 1994–; Liveryman Worshipful Co of Grocers; *Recreations* sailing; *Clubs* Oriental; *Style*— The Hon Mr Justice Morison; ✉ Royal Courts of Justice, Strand, London WC2A 2LL

MORITZ, Michael; *b* Cardiff; *Educ* Univ of Oxford; *Career* venture capitalist; early career as journalist (incl head San Francisco bureau Time magazine late 1970s) then held various positions with Time Warner and founded Technologic Ptnrs, with Sequoia Capital 1986–; currently dir: Flextronics, Google, Saba Software; formerly founding dir: Agile Software, Global Center, LinkExchange, eGroups, NeoMagic, Quote.com, Visigenic, CenterRun, PayPal, Yahoo!; hon student ChCh Oxford; *Style*— Michael Moritz, Esq; ✉ Sequoia Capital, 3000 Sand Hill Road, Building 4, Suite 180, Menlo Park, CA 94025, USA

MORLAND, Miles Quintin; s of Cdr Henry Morland, RN, and Vivienne Yzabel Suzanne Nicholson Walters, *née* Hogg; *b* 18 December 1943; *Educ* Radley, Lincoln Coll Oxford; *m* 10 March 1972 (m dis 2003), Guislaine, da of Guy Vincent Chastenet de la Maisoneuve; 2 da (Katherine Natasha b 29 Aug 1973, Georgia Susanna b 18 Dec 1976); *Career* md The First Boston Corp 1983–89; chm: Blakeney Management 1989–, Devpt Ptnrs LLP Indochina Capital Vietnam Hldgs Ltd 2007–, Ukraine Opportunity Tst plc 2007–; dir: East Europe Devpt Fund, SABMiller plc, SW Energy, Dubai Gp; *Publications* The Man Who Broke Out of the Bank (1992); *Recreations* beachcombing, visiting places where you can't drink the tapwater; *Clubs* Leander, Boodle's; *Style*— Miles Morland, Esq; ✉ 29 Chelsea Wharf, Lots Road, London SW10 0QJ

MORLEY, David Howard; s of Glyn Morley, of Ludlow, Shropshire, and Yvonne, *née* Auvache; *b* 21 September 1956; *Educ* Queens Park HS Chester, St John's Coll Cambridge;

M

m 4 Sept 1982, Susan Diana, da of Denis C Radcliffe, of Huxley, nr Chester, Cheshire; 2 s (William b 27 Jan 1987, Thomas b 13 April 1989), 2 da (Emma b 20 May 1985, Rachael b 11 Jan 1992); *Career* admitted slr 1982, managing ptnr Allen & Overy 2003– (ptnr 1988–); memb Law Soc; *Style*— David Morley, Esq; ✉ Allen & Overy, One New Change, London EC4M 9QQ (tel 020 7330 3000, fax 020 7330 9999, e-mail david.morley@allenovery.com)

MORLEY, Rt Hon Elliot Anthony; PC (2007), MP; s of Anthony Morley, of Ormskirk, Lancs, and Margaret, *née* Walsh (d 1985); *b* 6 July 1952; *Educ* St Margaret's HS Liverpool, Hull Coll of Educn (CertEd, BEd); *m* 20 Oct 1975, Patricia Winnifrid Broderick, da of Chief Supt Matthew Hunt, QPM, of Yarm; 1 da (Kathryn b 1981), 1 s (Jonathan b 1985); *Career* teacher 1975–87, head of special needs Greatfield Senior HS; cncllr Hull City Cncl 1979–86 (chm Tport Ctee 1981–85); MP (Lab): Glanford and Scunthorpe 1987–97, Scunthorpe 1997–; oppn spokesman on food agric and rural affairs with responsibility for fisheries and animal welfare 1989–97; Parly sec MAFF 1997–2001, Parly under-sec of state DEFRA 2001–03, min of state for the environment 2003–06; vice-pres Steel Action Assoc of Drainage Authorities; vice-pres RSPCA, vice-pres Wildlife Link, tstee Born Free Fndn, pres Humber and North Lincs RSPCA; former memb Cncl: RSPB, Br Tst for Ornithology; hon fell Lincoln Univ; Hon FICE; *Recreations* ornithology, travel, conservation, countryside issues; *Clubs* Kinsley Labour; *Style*— The Rt Hon Elliot Morley, MP; ✉ House of Commons, London SW1A 0AA (tel 020 7219 3000, Parly office 01724 842000)

MORLEY, 6 Earl of (UK 1815); Lt-Col Sir John St Aubyn Parker; KCVO (1998), JP (Plymouth 1972); Viscount Boringdon (UK 1815), Baron Boringdon (GB 1784); s of Hon John Holford Parker (d 1955); suc unc, 5 Earl, 1962; *b* 29 May 1923; *Educ* Eton; *m* 1955, Johanna Katherine, da of Sir John Molesworth-St Aubyn, 14 Bt, CBE; 1 s (Mark Lionel, Viscount Boringdon b 1956), 1 da (Lady Venetia Katherine b 1960); *Heir* s, Viscount Boringdon; *Career* 2 Lt KRRC 1942, transferred to Royal Fus 1947; served: NW Europe 1944–45, Palestine and Egypt 1945–48, Korea 1952–53, ME 1953–55 and 1956; Staff Coll Camberley 1957, cmd 1 Bn Royal Fus 1965–67, Lt-Col, ret 1970; pres: Plymouth Inc Chamber of Trade and Commerce 1970–, W Country Tourist Bd 1971–89, Fedn of C of C and Traders Assocs of Co of Cornwall 1972–79; chm Farm Industry Ltd Truro 1970–86; regnl dir Devon and Cornwall Regnl Bd Lloyds Bank 1971–91; dir: Lloyds Bank Ltd 1974–78, Lloyds Bank UK Management Ltd 1978–85; chm Plymouth Sound Ltd 1974–94; govr: Seale-Hayne Agric Coll 1973–92, Plymouth Poly 1975–82 (chm 1977–82); memb Devon and Cornwall Regnl Ctee Nat Tst 1969–84; HM Lord-Lt Devon 1982–98 (DL 1973, Vice Lord-Lt 1978–82); pres: Cncl of Order of St John for Devon 1979–98, Devon Co FA 1979–87; Hon Col: Devon ACF 1978–87, 4 Bn Devonshire and Dorset Regt 1987–92; KStJ; *Style*— The Rt Hon the Earl of Morley, KCVO; ✉ Pound House, Buckland Monachorum, Yelverton, Devon PL20 7LJ (tel 01822 853162)

MORLEY, Dr (William) Neil; RD (1969, clasp 1979); s of Eric Morley, JP (d 1964), of Bradford, W Yorks, and Barbara, *née* Mitchell (d 1986); *b* 16 February 1930; *Educ* Merchiston Castle Sch Edinburgh, Univ of Edinburgh (MB ChB); *m* 13 March 1958, Patricia (d 2003), da of Walter McDonald; 1 da (Carolyn b 1961), 3 s (David b 1963, Alistair b 1964, Christopher b 1966); *Career* Surgn Lt HMS Falcon 1955–57, served Malta, Surgn Lt Cdr RNR 1959–84; conslt dermatologist Gtr Glasgow Health Bd 1963–95, civil conslt to RN in Scotland 1979–95; memb Med Appeal Tbnl ITS 1979–99; memb Incorporation of Barbers of Glasgow 1987; FRCPEd 1970, FRCPGlas 1977, FRSM; *Books* Colour Atlas of Paediatric Dermatology; *Recreations* golf, fishing; *Clubs* Glasgow GC; *Style*— Dr Neil Morley, RD; ✉ 5 Great Western Terrace, Glasgow G12 0UP (tel 0141 334 3017)

MORLEY, Paul Robert; s of Leslie Ronald Morley (d 1977), and Dilys, *née* Young; *b* 26 March 1957; *Educ* Stockport GS, Stockport Coll of Technol; *partner* Elizabeth Levy; 1 da (Madeleine Amber b 7 January 1992); *Career* writer NME 1976–83, dir Zang Tuum Tumb Records, A&R and art dir Frankie Goes to Hollywood (incl Relax, biggest selling single of 1980s), fndr memb Art of Noise, conslt Island Records 1990–92 (exec prodr Vic Reeves, qv, no 1 single Dizzy); contrib ed: Blitz Magazine 1983–87, Esquire Magazine 1991–99; TV critic: New Statesman 1987–89, The Guardian 1991–94, GQ Magazine 1998–99; regular contrib to nat newspapers, TV documentaries and radio arts progs; co-fndr Service prodn co 2002; conslt Palm Pictures 2002–; hon memb Peter Cook Appreciation Soc; *Television* fndr presenter The Late Show (BBC2) 1989–91, writer and presenter The Thing Is...(Channel 4) 1989–92, panellist Newsnight Review (BBC2) 2001–, writer and dir arts documentaries for BBC, ITV and Channel 4 (incl Omnibus on Reeves and Mortimer); *Publications* Ask: The Chatter of Pop (1986), Nothing (2000); contrib: Faber Book of Pop, The Penguin Book of Rock and Roll Journalism; *Recreations* listening, looking, reading, philosophy, hotels, internet, music, waiting; *Style*— Paul Morley, Esq; ✉ David Goodwin Associates, 55 Monmouth Street, London WC2H 5DG (tel 020 7240 9992, fax 020 7395 6110, e-mail assistant@davidgodwinassociates.co.uk)

MORONY, Elizabeth Rachel Anne; da of Eric Gent, and Monica, *née* Jukes; *b* 2 May 1968; *Educ* Chislehurst and Sidcup GS, Wadham Coll Oxford (MA); *m* 8 May 1993, Matthew Morony; 2 s (George Lovett b 21 Feb 1997, Henry Thomas b 10 June 1999); *Career* slr; ptnr Clifford Chance 2000–; *Recreations* tennis, gardening, family; *Clubs* Roehampton Tennis; *Style*— Mrs Elizabeth Morony; ✉ Clifford Chance LLP, 10 Upper Bank Street, London E14 5JJ (tel 020 7006 1000, fax 020 7006 5555, e-mail elizabeth.morony@cliffordchance.com)

MORPETH, Iain Cardean Spottiswoode; TD (1991); s of Sir Douglas Spottiswoode Morpeth, TD, of Shamley Green, Surrey, and Anne Rutherford, *née* Bell; *b* 28 December 1953; *Educ* Fettes, Univ of Bristol (LLB); *m* 30 June 1979, Angela Susan, da of Sir Thomas Gordon Devitt, 2 Bt (d 1995), of Colchester, Essex; 3 s (Richard Douglas Gordon b 18 Nov 1985, Duncan Hugh Sinclair b 1 Dec 1987, James Rutherford Thomas b 17 Oct 1992), 1 da (Catherine Louise Nicholl b 10 Feb 1990); *Career* admitted slr 1978, ptnr Clifford Chance 1988– (currently head Real Estate Funds and Investment Banking Gp); memb: Law Soc, Int Bar Assoc, Investment Property Forum, British Property Fedn, memb Editorial Bd Jl of Property Fin; Liveryman and memb Ct of Assts Worshipful Co of Slrs 1993; *Publications* Property Joint Ventures, Structures and Precedents (contrib); *Recreations* fishing, skiing, hill walking; *Style*— Iain Morpeth, Esq; ✉ Clifford Chance, 10 Upper Bank Street, London E14 5JJ (tel 020 7600 1000, fax 020 7600 5555, e-mail iain.morpeth@cliffordchance.com)

MORPHET, John Charles; s of William Morphet (d 1999), and Peggy, *née* Maddock (d 1999); *b* 22 November 1954, Preston; *Educ* Bentham GS; *m* 8 June 2002, Victoria, *née* Green, 3 s (Matthew b 7 May 1974, James b 21 Aug 1977, William b 7 Dec 1989), 2 da (Rebecca b 9 Dec 1986, Madison b 20 Aug 2003); *Career* worked on family estate; fndr: South Lakeland Caravans 1988, South Lakeland Caravans Ltd 1996, Lake District Leisure Pursuits Ltd 2002, Pure Leisure 2004 (including Royal Westmoreland, Barbados, Spain and Cyprus lodge devpts); Fast Track 100 Award for 3 years; *Recreations* golf, farming, fishing; *Style*— John Morphet, Esq; ✉ Pure Leisure, South Lakeland House, Yealand Redmayne, Carnforth CA5 9RN (tel 01524 781918, fax 01524 782243, email jm@pureleisuregroup.com)

MORPHET, Richard Edward; CBE (1998); s of Horace Morphet (d 1987), and Eleanor, *née* Shaw; *b* 2 October 1938; *Educ* Bootham Sch York, LSE (BA); *m* 1965, Sally, *née* Richmond; 2 da (Selina b 1967, Thea b 1969); *Career* Fine Arts Dept British Council 1963–66; Tate Gallery: asst keeper 1966–73, dep keeper 1973–86, keeper of the Modern Collection 1986–98; *Publications* author of numerous magazine articles; curator of exhibitions and author of catalogues on numerous individual artists and of others on

themes incl: The Hard Won Image (Tate Gallery, 1984), Encounters: New Art from Old (National Gallery, 2000); *Style*— Richard Morphet, CBE; fax 020 7820 1610

MORPURGO, Michael Andrew Bridge; OBE (2006, MBE 1999); s of Tony Van Bridge (d 2005), and Catherine, *née* Cammaerts; step s of Jack Morpurgo (d 2002); *b* 5 October 1943, St Albans; *Educ* King's Sch Canterbury, RMA Sandhurst, KCL; *m* Clare Lane; 2 s (Sebastian b 1964, Horatio b 1967), 1 da (Rosalind b 1968); *Career* writer; early career as primary sch teacher, fndr (with wife) Farms for City Children 1976–; children's laureate 2003–05, Author of the Year 2005; Chevalier des Arts et des Letteres (France) 2004; *Publications* incl: It Never Rained: Five Stories (1974), Living Poets (1974), Long Way Home (1975), Thatcher Jones (1975), The Story-Teller (1976), Friend or Foe (1977), Do All You Dare (1978), What Shall We Do with It? (1978), All Around the Year (with Ted Hughes, 1979), Love at First Sight (1979), That's How (1979), The Day I Took the Bull by the Horn (1979), The Ghost-Fish (1979), The Marble Crusher and Other Stories (1980), The Nine Lives of Montezuma (1980), Miss Wirtle's Revenge (1981), The White Horse of Zennor: And Other Stories from below the Eagle's Nest (1982), War Horse (1982), Twist of Gold (1983), Little Foxes (1984), Why the Whales Came (1985), Words of Songs (libretto, music by Phyllis Tate, 1985), Tom's Sausage Lion (1986), Conker (1987), Jo-Jo, the Melon Monkey (1987), King of the Cloud Forests (1988, Prix Sorciere (France) 1993), Mossop's Last Chance (with Shoo Rayner, 1988), My Friend Walter (1988), Albertine, Goose Queen (with Shoo Rayner, 1989), Mr. Nobody's Eyes (1989), Jigger's Day Off (with Shoo Rayner, 1990), Waiting for Anya (1990, shortlist Carnegie Medal 1991), And Pigs Might Fly! (with Shoo Rayner, 1991), Colly's Barn (1991), The Sandman and the Turtles (1992), Martians at Mudpuddle Farm (with Shoo Rayner, 1992), The King in the Forest (1993), The War of Jenkins' Ear (1993), Arthur, High King of Britain (1994, shortlist Carnegie Medal 1995), Ghostly Haunts (ed, 1994), Snakes and Ladders (1994), The Dancing Bear (1994), Blodin the Beast (1995), Muck and Magic: Tales from the Countryside (ed, 1995), Mum's the Word (with Shoo Rayner, 1995), Stories from Mudpuddle Farm (with Shoo Rayner, 1995), The Wreck of the Zanzibar (1995, Whitbread Children's Book Award 1995, shortlist Carnegie Medal 1996), Beyond the Rainbow Warrior: A Collection of Stories to Celebrate 25 Years of Greenpeace (co-ed, 1996), Robin of Sherwood (1996), Sam's Duck (1996), The Butterfly Lion (1996, Gold Award Nestlé Smarties Book Prize 1996), The Ghost of Grania O'Malley (1996), Farm Boy (1997), Cockadoodle-doo, Mr Sultana! (1998), Escape from Shangri-La (1998), Joan of Arc (1998), Red Eyes at Night (1998), Wartman (1998), Animal Stories (ed, 1999), Kensuke's Kingdom (1999, Red House Children's Book Award 2000, Prix Sorciere (France) 2001), The Rainbow Bear (1999), Wombat Goes Walkabout (1999, Prix Sorciere (France) 1999), Billy the Kid (2000), Black Queen (2000), Dear Olly (2000), From Hereabout Hill (2000), The Kingfisher Book of Classic Boy Stories: A Treasury of Favourites from Children's Literature (ed, 2000), The Silver Swan (2000), Who's a Big Bully Then? (2000), More Muck and Magic (2001), Out of the Ashes (2001, shortlist WH Smith Award for Children's Literature 2002), Toro! Toro! (2001), Because a Fire Was in My Head: 101 Poems to Remember (ed, 2002), Cool! (2002, shortlist Blue Peter Book Award: The Book I Couldn't Put Down 2003), Mr. Skip (2002), The Kingfisher Treasury of Classic Stories (co-ed, 2002), The Last Wolf (2002, Bronze Award Nestlé Smarties Book Prize 2002), The Sleeping Sword (2002), Gentle Giant (2003), Private Peaceful (2003, shortlist Carnegie Medal 2003, shortlist Whitbread Children's Book Award 2003, Red House Children's Book Award 2004), Cock Crow (co-ed, 2004), Cockadoodle-doo Mr Sultana! (with Holly Swain, 2004), Orchard Book of Aesop's Fables (ed, 2004), Sir Gawain and the Green Knight (2004), War: Stories of Conflict (ed, 2005); *Style*— Michael Morpurgo, Esq, OBE; ✉ c/o David Higham Associates, 5–8 Lower John Street, Golden Square, London W1F 9HA (www.michaelmorpurgo.org)

MORPURGO DAVIES, Prof Anna Elbina Laura Margherita; Hon DBE (2001); da of Augusto Morpurgo (d 1939), and Maria, *née* Castelnuovo (d 1991), of Rome; *b* 21 June 1937; *Educ* Liceo-Ginnasio Giulio Cesare Rome, Univ of Rome (MA); *m* 8 Sept 1962 (m dis 1978), John Kenyon Davies; s of Harold Davies; *Career* assistente in classical philology Univ of Rome 1959–61, jr fell Center for Hellenic Studies Washington DC 1961–62, lectr in classical philology Univ of Oxford 1964–71, fell St Hilda's Coll Oxford 1966–71, prof of comparative philology Univ of Oxford 1971–2004 (Diebold prof of comparative philology 2003–04, prof emeritus 2004–), fell Somerville Coll Oxford 1971–2004 (emeritus fell 2004–); visiting prof: Univ of Pennsylvania 1971, Yale Univ 1977, Univ of Calif Berkeley 2006 and 2007; Collitz prof Linguistic Soc of America 1975, Semple lectr Univ of Cincinnati 1983, TBL Webster prof Stanford Univ 1988, Jackson lectr Harvard Univ 1990; Sather prof of classical literature Univ of Calif Berkeley 2000; delegate OUP 1992–2004; pres Br Philological Soc 1976–80 (hon vice-pres 1980–); foreign hon memb American Acad of Arts & Sciences 1986, corresponding memb Oesterreichische Akademie der Wissenschaften (Wien) 1988, hon memb Linguistic Soc of America 1993, memb Academia Europaea 1989, foreign memb American Philosophical Soc 1991, corresponding memb Académie des inscriptions et belles-lettres, Institut de France 1992, Bayerische Akademie der Wissenschaften 1998; Premio Linceo per la Linguistica Accademia dei Lincei 1996; hon fell St Hilda's Coll Oxford 1972; Hon DLitt Univ of St Andrews 1981; FSA 1974, FBA 1985; *Books* Mycenaeae Graecitatis Lexicon (1963), Studies in Greek, Italic and Indo-European Linguistics offered to L R Palmer (ed with W Meid, 1976), Linear B/A 1984 Survey (ed with Y Duhoux, 1985), La Linguistica dell' Ottocento (1996), Nineteenth Century Linguistics (1998); numerous articles in Br and foreign periodicals; Festschrift: Indo-European Perspectives, Studies in honour of Anna Morpurgo Davies (ed by J H W Penney, 2004); *Style*— Prof Anna Morpurgo Davies, DBE, FSA, FBA; ✉ 22 Yarnells Hill, Oxford OX2 9BD; Somerville College, Oxford OX2 6HD (e-mail anna.davies@some.ox.ac.uk)

MORRELL, Frances Maine; da of Frank Galleway, and Beatrice Galleway; *b* 28 December 1937; *Educ* Queen Anne Sch York, Univ of Hull (BA), Univ of London (MA); *m* 1964, Brian Morrell; 1 da; *Career* policy advsr to: Sec of State for Indust, Sec of State for Energy 1974–79; leader ILEA 1983–87, memb GLC Islington S and Finsbury 1981–86; sec Speaker's Cmmn on Citizenship 1988–91, exec dir Inst for Citizenship Studies 1992–93, dir of studies Euro Citizenship 1999 Project 1994–99; chair Arts Inform 1993–97, jt chief exec Arts Inform 1997–, chair London Sch Arts Service 2005–; memb LSE Grad Sch 1996–; memb Bd and dep chair Islington Festival 2000–, memb Bd King's Head Theatre 2000–; FRIBA 2005; *Books* From the Electors of Bristol: a study of constituents' grievances, A Ten Year Industrial Strategy for Britain (with Benn and Cripps), A Planned Energy Policy for Britain (with Benn and Cripps), Manifesto: A radical strategy for Britain's future (jtly), Children of the Future: The Battle For Britain's Schools (1989); *Style*— Mrs Frances Morrell

MORRELL, Paul Dring; s of David Dring Morrell (d 2007), of Malta, and Joan Hannah, *née* Rankin; *b* 28 February 1948; *Educ* Oundle, Univ of Reading (BSc); *m* 8 April 1978, Shirley, *née* Betney; *Career* Davis Langdon LLP (formerly Davis Langdon & Everest): joined 1971, ptnr 1976, sr ptnr 1998–2003, ret 2007; cmmr and dep chair CABE; govr and memb Bd Royal Shakespeare Co, chair Siobhan Davis Dance Co; FRICS 1975, Hon FRIBA 1999; *Books* The Commercial Offices Handbook (2003); *Recreations* sailing, ballet, opera; *Style*— Paul Morrell, Esq; ✉ 4 Caithness Road, London W14 0JB (tel 020 7602 6082, e-mail paul.morrell@davislangdon.com)

MORRELL, Peter John; s of Arthur Markham Morrell (d 1984), of Oxford, and Geraldine Doris, *née* Harvey (d 1992), of Devon; *b* 28 February 1931; *Educ* numerous schs (latterly Worthing HS), Kingston upon Thames Coll of Art (NDD), RCA (life drawing and life painting prizes, ARCA); *m* 1, 1958, Yvonne Nichol; m 2, 1964, Margaret Froud; 1 s (Steven b 1967), 1 da (Nicola b 1971); m 3, 1981, Helene Halstuch, of New York; *Career* artist; pt/t lectr in fine art painting: Maidstone Coll of Art 1961–62, Sir John Cass Sch of Art 1962–65, Hornsey Coll of Art 1962–70, St Martin's Coll of Art 1969–70, Central Sch of Art and Design 1970–92; instigated summer schs at Central Sch of Art and Design 1986; numerous solo and gp exhbns, work in numerous private and public collections; memb London Gp 1990–; RWS 1983; *Awards* Br Cncl Prize 1955, Arts Cncl Prize 1959, Prix de Rome in Painting 1959; *Style*— Peter Morrell, Esq; ✉ 19 Tremeadow Terrace, Hayle, Cornwall TR27 4AF (tel 01736 755051)

MORRELL, His Hon Judge Peter Richard; s of Frank Richard Morrell (d 1974), of Dane End, Herts, and Florence Ethel, *née* Gleave (d 1992); *b* 25 May 1944; *Educ* Westminster, UC Oxford (MA); *m* 6 June 1970, (Helen) Mary Vint, da of Capt William Norman Collins, of Peterborough; 2 da (Helen b 1971, Harriet b 1976); *Career* admitted slr 1970; called to the Bar Gray's Inn 1974; recorder of the Crown Court 1990–92, circuit judge (Midland & Oxford Circuit) 1992–; reader Dio of Peterborough 2005–; Parly candidate Ilkeston 1974; *Recreations* shooting, fishing, photography, Spain; *Style*— His Hon Judge Morrell; ✉ Leicester Crown Court, Wellington Street, Leicester LE1 6HG (tel 0116 222 3434)

MORRILL, Rev Prof John Stephen; s of William Henry Morrill, of Hale, Cheshire, and Marjorie, *née* Ashton; *b* 12 June 1946; *Educ* Altrincham GS for Boys, Trinity Coll Oxford (MA, DPhil); *m* 27 July 1968, Frances Dreda Mary, *née* Mead (d 2007); 4 da (Rachel Clare (Mrs Finch) b 18 Jan 1973, Ruth Mary b 11 Nov 1978, Naomi Catharine b 27 May 1981, Clare Margaret b 27 Nov 1983); *Career* research fell Trinity Coll Oxford 1970–74; lectr in history: St Catherine's Coll Oxford 1973–74, Univ of Stirling 1974–75; Univ of Cambridge: lectr in history 1975–92, reader in early modern history 1992–98, prof of Br and Irish history 1998–; fell Selwyn Coll Cambridge 1975– (sr tutor 1987–92, vice-master 1994–); ordained to the permanent diaconate RC diocese of East Anglia 1996; Br Acad: chair Public Understanding and Activities Ctee 1997–, memb Cncl 1999–, vice-pres 2001–; AHRB: convenor History Panel 1999–2002, tstee 2000–03, memb Bd 2000–04; Ford's lectr in Br history Univ of Oxford 2006; centenary fell Historical Assoc 2006; hon fell Trinity Coll Oxford 2006; Hon DLitt UEA 2002, Hon DUniv Surrey 2002; FRHistS 1977 (vice-pres 1992–96), FBA 1996; *Publications* author and ed of 17 books on Br and Irish history principally concerning the 16th and 17th centuries, and author of more than 60 essays and articles; *Recreations* classical music, travel, malt whisky; *Style*— Rev Prof John Morrill; ✉ 1 Bradfords Close, Bottisham, Cambridgeshire CB25 9DQ (tel 01223 811822); Selwyn College, Cambridge CB3 9DQ (tel 01223 335895, fax 01223 335837, e-mail jsm1000@cam.ac.uk)

MORRIS, *see also:* Temple-Morris

MORRIS, Abigail; da of Geoffrey Morris, and Audrey, *née* Wolfson; *Educ* Woodhouse Sch Finchley, Camden Sch, Sidney Sussex Coll Cambridge (MA); *m* David Evans; 3 da; *Career* fndr and artistic dir Trouble & Strife Theatre Co 1984–90, artistic dir Soho Theatre Co 1992–, artistic dir of team which designed, raised money for and built new Soho Theatre and Writers' Centre Dean Street (opened 2000); Judith E Wilson visting fell in drama Univ of Cambridge 1990–91; *Productions* for Trouble & Strife Theatre Co: Present Continuous, Now and at the Hour of our Death (co-author), Next to You I Lie (co-author); Soho Theatre Co prodns incl: Tulip Futures, Kindertransport (also Manhattan Theatre Club and West End), Rock Station (Cockpit Theatre), The Station, Be My Baby, Stop Kiss, Navy Pier, Kiss Me Like You Mean It, Office (also Lyceum Theatre Edinburgh), Protection, Wrong Place, Colder than Here, A Night at the Dogs; freelance credits incl: Leave it to Me (Arts Theatre), Noyes Fluddle (Albert Hall), Julius Caesar Jones (Sadler's Wells Theatre); *Awards* Fringe First 1986 and 1987, Time Out Award 1988 and 1993, London Fringe Award 1994, Empty Space Award 1996; *Recreations* swimming, running, family, watching football, Jewish Learning; *Clubs* Cally Masters, Tri London; *Style*— Ms Abigail Morris; ✉ c/o Soho Theatre, 21 Dean Street, London W1D 3NE

MORRIS, Albert (Bert); *b* 21 October 1934; *Educ* Skerrys Coll Liverpool, MIT; *m* Patricia, *née* Lane (d 2005); 1 s (Jonathan), 1 da (Ailsa); *Career* National Westminster Bank plc: head of money transmission 1979–83, gen mangr Mgmnt Servs 1985–88 (dep gen mangr 1983–85), dir 1989–94, chief exec Support Servs 1989–92, dep gp chief exec 1992–94, ret; dir: Westments Ltd 1985–94, Eftpos UK Ltd 1987–94, National Westminster Life Assurance Ltd 1992–94, APACS (Admin) Ltd; sr advsr IBOS (international electronic bank payment system) 1995–96; non-exec dir Regent Associates Ltd 1999; exec chm Lorien plc 1998–; chm: BACS Ltd 1985–94, Metroline plc 1997–2003, Centre-file Ltd; non-exec chm Macro 4 plc 2000–; chm Office of the Banking Ombudsman 1985–87, sometime memb Cncl Chartered Inst of Bankers, non-exec memb Bd DSS 1993–97; former hon treas The Kingwood Tst (resigned 2000); Freeman City of London 1992, Liveryman Worshipful Co of Info Technologists (also tstee); CCMI, FCIB, FRSA; *Recreations* golf, politics; *Style*— Bert Morris, Esq

MORRIS, Alfred Cosier; CBE (2003), DL (Glos 2002); s of Stanley Bernard Morris (d 1970), of Anlaby, E Yorks, and Jennie, *née* Fletcher (d 1994); *b* 12 November 1941; *Educ* Hymers Coll Hull, Lancaster Univ (MA); *m* 26 Sept 1970, Annette, da of Eamonn and May Donovan, of Cork, Ireland; 1 da (Jessica b 24 April 1980); *Career* articled clerk Oliver Mackrill 1958–63, co sec fin controller and dir various cos 1963–71, sr Leverhulme res fell in univ planning and orgn Univ of Sussex 1971–74, visiting lectr in fin mgmnt Univ of Warwick 1973, gp mgmnt accountant Arthur Guinness Ltd 1974–76, sr mgmnt conslt Deloitte Haskins & Sells 1976–77, fin advsr subsids of Arthur Guinness 1977–80, acting dir South Bank Poly 1985–86 (dep dir 1980–85), dir Bristol Poly 1986–92, vice-chllr UWE 1992–2005; memb: HE Quality Cncl 1992–94, HE Funding Cncl for Wales 1992–2000, FE Funding Cncl for England 1997–99; advsr House of Commons Select Ctee on Educn Sci and Arts 1980–83; chm Audit Ctee e-Universities Holding Co 2002–06; dir Bristol and West plc (formerly Bristol and West Building Soc) 1992–2002; chm: Bristol Old Vic Tst 1992–94, Patrons of the Bristol Old Vic Ltd 1993–, N Bristol NHS Tst 2006–; memb: SW Arts 1994–2000, SW E RDA 1998–2002, Gtr Bristol Fndn 1999–2003 (chm 1999–2000), Exec Ctee Dolphin Soc; dir SW Urban Regeneration Fund (SURF); tstee: Bristol Cathedral Tst, Patrons of the Royal West of Eng Acad 2000–05, Glos Community Fndn 2006–, Bristol Old Vic Theatre Sch 2006–, Bristol Charities 2006–; patron: Davar 1999–, Fast Track Tst 2000–, Bristol Drugs Project 2002; pres City Acad Bristol 2003–05; fell Humberside Coll; Hon LLD: Univ of Bristol, UWE 2006; High Sheriff Glos 2006–07; FCA 1963, FSS, hon fell RWA 2001; *Books* Resources and Higher Education (jt ed and contrib, 1982); *Recreations* tennis, windsurfing, sailing; *Style*— Alfred Morris, Esq, CBE, DL; ✉ Park Court, Sodbury Common, Old Sodbury BS37 6PX (tel 01454 319900)

MORRIS, Sir Allan Lindsay; 11 Bt (UK 1806), of Clasemont, Glamorganshire; s of Sir Robert Byng Morris (d 1999), and Christine Kathleen, *née* Field; *b* 27 November 1961; *m* 1986, Cheronne Denise, eld da of Dale Whitford of Goonhavern, Cornwall; 1 da (Chelsea Alana b 29 Aug 1992), 2 s (Sennen John b 5 June 1995, Chace James b 18 Sept 1997); *Heir* s, Sennen Morris; *Style*— Sir Allan Morris, Bt

MORRIS, Prof Alun Owen; OBE (2000); s of Arthur Morris (d 1969), of Ruthin, and Jennie, *née* Owen; *b* 17 August 1935; *Educ* Brynhyfryd Sch Ruthin, UCNW Bangor (BSc, PhD); *m* 1, 16 April 1960, Margaret Erina (d 1987), da of Rev William Jones, of Caernarfon; 2 da (Lowri b 1962, Angharad b 1971), 1 s (Iwan b 1964); m 2, 11 April 1992, Mary, da of Moses Jones, of Aberystwyth; *Career* Univ of Wales Aberystwyth: asst lectr 1959–61, lectr 1961–66, sr lectr 1966–69, prof 1969–2000, vice-princ 1986–90, emeritus prof 2000–; London Mathematical Soc: memb Cncl 1974–78, jt ed 1983–88, vice-pres 1993–94, treas 1994–2002; chm Higher Educn Section Jt Mathematical Cncl 1993–95, memb Mathematics Ctee UGC 1986–89, advsr to Univ Funding Cncl 1989–93; memb: London Mathematical Soc 1960, American Mathematical Soc 1962; *Books* Linear Algebra - An Introduction (1978, 2 edn 1982); *Style*— Prof Alun Morris, OBE; ✉ Hiraethog, Cae Melyn, Aberystwyth, Ceredigion SY23 2HA (tel and fax 01970 623464, e-mail alun@morris25.fsnet.co.uk); Institute of Mathematical and Physical Sciences, University of Wales, Aberystwyth, Ceredigion SY23 3BZ

MORRIS, Amanda Claire; da of David Ellis, and Shirley, *née* Springate; *b* 2 December 1962, Haslemere, Surrey; *Educ* Horsham HS for Girls, Collyers Sixth Form Coll, Univ of Warwick (LLB), Guildford Coll of Law, Nottingham Law Sch (Dip); *m* 29 May 2004, Michael Crehan; *Career* slr Thomas Eggar Verrall Bowles 1992–97, ptnr Sherwin Oliver 1999–2001 (sr slr 1997–99), ptnr Blake Lapthorn Tarlo Lyons 2001–; memb Law Soc 1994; *Publications* Neighbour Disputes: A concise guide to the law and practice (2006); *Recreations* amateur dramatics and operatic singing, vintage car touring and trials, skiing, mountain biking; *Clubs* Vintage Sports Car, Ulster Vintage Car, Petersfield Hilights Soc, Petersfield Operatic Soc; *Style*— Ms Amanda Morris; ✉ Blake Lapthorn Tarlo Lyons, Harbour Court, Compass Road, North Harbour, Portsmouth PO6 4ST (tel 023 9222 1122, fax 023 9222 1124, e-mail amanda.morris@bllaw.co.uk)

MORRIS, Andrew; *Educ* Architectural Association (Dip Arch), Croydon Technical Coll (ONC/HNC); *Career* architect; architectural asst: Dept of the Environment 1969–72, H G Huckle & Partners Architects 1972–75; Crysalis Architects 1980–81, conslt to Alan Stanton Architects 1981–82; Richard Rogers Partnership: conslt 1981–82, joined 1982, job architect (on Richard Rogers' house) 1983–85, dir 1994–, sr dir 2000–; dir: Reading Construction Forum, Design and Build Fndn; *Projects* incl: Coin Street London, Lloyds of London, Centre Commercial St Herblain Nantes France, Reuters, Blackwall Yard London, Royal Docks London, Christopher Columbus Centre Baltimore USA, Harbour Place Seattle USA, Channel 4 TV HQ London, Heathrow Terminal 1 Airside devpt, Euopier devpt Heathrow Airport; co-dir responsible for design co-ordination and mgmnt of conslt team on: Heathrow Terminal 1 Airside and Europier schemes, redevelopment of Lloyds Register of Shipping, office devpt 88 Wood St London, Designer Retail Outlet Centre Ashford Kent, Millennium Experience Greenwich, Terminal 5 Heathrow Airport, Europe House/K2 St Katherine Docks London, San Francisco Bus Terminal, Elan HQ Dublin; *Style*— Andrew Morris, Esq

MORRIS, Andrew Bernard; s of Samuel Cyril Morris, and Golda, *née* Berkowitz; *b* 16 October 1952; *Educ* Christ's Coll GS, Coll for the Distributive Trades (HND Business Studies), Harvard Business Sch (Mgmnt Prog); *m* 29 June 1976, Jennifer Amanda, da of late Arthur Leslie Maizner; 2 da (Amy Louise b 10 June 1979, Sophie Victoria b 5 Oct 1981), 1 s (Ben Oliver b 24 Sept 1987); *Career* apprentice rising to sales role City Industrial Ltd (family shopfitting co) 1973–76, jt md Jontique (City Industrial subsid) 1976–80, sales and mktg dir City Industrial Ltd 1981–85, md Business Design Centre 1989–99 (bd dir 1986–89), chief exec Earls Court & Olympia 1999–2004, chief-exec NEC Gp Ltd 2004–; *Recreations* family, contemporary art, running, cycling, tennis, film, theatre, food and drink; *Style*— Andrew B Morris; ✉ NEC Group Ltd, National Exhibition Centre, Birmingham B40 1NT (tel 0121 767 3334, fax 0121 767 3865, e-mail andrew.morris@necgroup.co.uk)

MORRIS, Anthony; s of Francis Victor Morris (d 1964), and Winifred Morris, *née* Cooper (d 1978); *b* 2 August 1938; *Educ* Oxford Sch of Art (Dip Design), Royal Acad Schs (David Murray scholar, Leverhulme scholar, RAS Cert); *m* 1970, Aileen Sybil, *née* Griffiths; *Career* portraitist; one man exhbn Medici Gall London 1981; RP 1971, NEAC 1994; *Commissions* Prof Myers in Bodelian Library 1964, Lord Perry of Walton 1970, The Hon Thomas Iremonger, MP 1973, Prof K P Liddelow 1986, Sir Sacheverll Sitwell, Bt, CBE, The Rt Rev David Halsey, Bishop of Carlisle 1989, Rev Kenneth Loveless, MBE, RNR, 1993, Maj-Gen Ian Sprackling, OBE, Prof Sir Roy Meadow, pres Royal Coll of Paediatrics and Child Health, The Rt Hon Sir Robert Megarry, FBA; *Recreations* painting and sculpture, classical music and opera, wildlife and conservation; *Style*— Anthony Morris, Esq, RP, NEAC, FRSA; ✉ Church House, Clodock, Longtown, Herefordshire HR2 0NY (tel and fax 01873 860267); c/o The Royal Society of Portrait Painters, 17 Carlton House Terrace, London SW1Y 5BD (tel 020 7930 6844, fax 020 7839 7830)

M

MORRIS, Prof Anthony Isaac; s of Moshe Morris (d 1991), of Manchester, and Betty, *née* Harris (d 1977); *b* 18 August 1946; *Educ* Salford GS, Univ of Manchester (BSc, MSc, MB ChB, MD); *m* 16 Sept 1972, (Joan) Sheila, da of Eric Broadhurst (d 1970); 2 s (Daniel b 19 Feb 1976, David b 2 Aug 1978); *Career* sr house offr Manchester Royal Infirmary 1971–72 (house offr 1970–71), med registrar Whittington and UCH London 1972–74, lectr in med Univ of Manchester 1974–79, res fell in hepatology Univ of Pittsburgh USA 1978–79, sr lectr in med Univ of Liverpool 1979–85, conslt physician and gastroenterologist 1985–, post clinical dir of gastroenterology 1995–2002; dir endoscopy trg Mersey Sch of Endoscopy (Nat Endoscopy Trg Centre) and Royal Liverpool Hosp; past chm Jt Advsy Gp on Gastrointestinal Endoscopy; hon prof Dept of Medicine Univ of Liverpool; pres Br Soc of Gastroenterology (educn offr and past vice-pres Endoscopy Ctee); FRCP 1985 (MRCP 1972); *Books* ECG'S for Examinations (1975), Illustrated Case Histories in Gastroenterology (1994), Clinician's Manual on Gastro-Oesophageal Reflux Disease (1994); *Recreations* sailing, music; *Style*— Prof Anthony Morris; ✉ 7 Cromptons Lane, Calderstones, Liverpool L18 3EU; 52 Link Unit, Royal Liverpool University Hospital, Prescot Street, Liverpool L7 8XP (tel 0151 706 3554)

MORRIS, His Hon Judge Anthony Paul; QC (1991); s of Isaac Morris Morris (d 1966), and Margaret Miriam, *née* Hassan; *b* 6 March 1948; *Educ* Manchester Grammar, Keble Coll Oxford (MA); *m* 26 Sept 1975, Jennifer Morys (Jennie), da of Maurice George Foley (d 1962); 2 s (Guy b 1977, Charles b 1980); *Career* called to the Bar Gray's Inn 1970 (bencher 2001), recorder of the Crown Court 1988–2003, circuit judge (SE Circuit) 2003–; *Recreations* travel, the arts, sport incl cycling across Europe, visiting 'the theatre of dreams'; *Style*— His Hon Judge Morris, QC; ✉ Central Criminal Court, Old Bailey, London EC4M 7EH

MORRIS, Candida Frances (Candy); da of Philip John Butcher (d 2001), and Faith Layland, *née* Parker; *b* 3 February 1956; *Educ* Manchester HS for Girls, St Hilda's Coll Oxford (scholar, MA), Inst of Health Service Mgmnt (Dip); *m* 26 Oct 1985, Stanley David Morris; *Career* nat administrative trainee NW Regnl HA 1977–80, dep hosp administrator Fairfield Gen Hosp 1980–83, dep sector administrator S Trafford Hosp 1983–84, princ asst administrator rising to asst unit gen mangr Stepping Hill Hosp 1984–89, unit gen mangr Grimsby HA 1989–92; chief exec: Scunthorpe and Goole Hosps Tst 1992–2000, W Sussex HA 2000–02, E Surrey HA 2001–02, Kent and Medway Strategic HA 2002–06, NHS SE Coast 2006–; frequent speaker at healthcare confs; formerly: memb Lord Chllr's Humberside Advsy Sub-Ctee on Magistrates, memb N Lincs Partnership, govr John Leggott Sixth Form Coll; FCMI; *Recreations* travel, good company; *Style*— Mrs Candy Morris; ✉ 179 Comptons Lane, Horsham, West Sussex RH13 6BW (tel 01403 264739, fax 01403 275970, mobile 07850 814786); South East Coast Strategic Health Authority, York House, Massetts Road, Horley RH6 7DE (tel 01293 778808, e-mail candy.morris@southeastcoast.nhs.uk)

MORRIS, Prof Christopher David; s of late David Richard Christopher Morris, of Doncaster, and Ethel Margaret, *née* Back; *b* 14 April 1946; *Educ* Queen Elizabeth's GS Blackburn, Grey Coll Durham (BA), Worcester Coll Oxford (DipEd); *m* 21 July 1981 (sep 2004), Colleen Elizabeth, da of William and Mary Batey; *Career* asst lectr in history and archaeology Hockerill Coll of Educn Bishop's Stortford 1968–72; Univ of Durham: lectr in archaeology Dept of Archaeology 1972–81, sr lectr 1981–88, reader in viking archaeology 1988–90; Univ of Glasgow: prof of archaeology 1990–2006, vice-princ 2000–06; cmmr Royal Cmmn on the Ancient and Historical Monuments of Scotland (RCAHMS) 1999– (vice-chair 2005–), memb Ancient Monuments Bd for Scotland 1990–2001; FSA Scot 1974, FSA 1981, MIFA 1984, FRHistS 1996, FRSE 1996, FRSA 1998; *Publications* incl: The Birsay Bay Project (Vol 1 1989, Vol 2 1996), Norse and Later Subsistence and Settlement in the North Atlantic (ed, 1992), The Viking Age in Caithness, Orkney and the North Atlantic (ed, 1993), Freswick Links. A Norse Settlement in Caithness (1995); *Recreations* opera, music, running, walking; *Style*— Prof Christopher Morris, FSA, FRSE

MORRIS, His Hon Judge David Griffiths; s of Capt Thomas Griffiths Morris, and Margaret Eileen Morris; *b* 10 March 1940; *Educ* Abingdon Sch, KCL (LLB); *m* May 1971, Carolyn Mary, *née* Miller; 1 da (Hannah Bethan b April 1975), 1 s (Owen Thomas b January 1977); *Career* called to the Bar Lincoln's Inn 1965 (bencher 1999); asst recorder 1979–84, head chambers Cardiff 1984–94 (local jr 1981–87, recorder 1984–94), circuit judge (Wales & Chester Circuit) 1994–; memb: Gwent Probation Bd 1998–, Gwent Courts Bd 2004–; fndr memb: Llanmaes Community Cncl 1982–84, Llantwit Major Round Table, Llantwit Major 41 Club, Llantwit Major Rotary Club (pres 1984–85); pres Pontypool RFC 1997– (sr vice-pres 1993–97); *Recreations* rugby union football, cricket, swimming, theatre, reading, gardening; *Clubs* Cardiff and County, United Services Mess Cardiff; *Style*— His Hon Judge David Morris; ✉ Bryn Hafren, Newport Road, Castleton, Cardiff CF3 2UN (e-mail calmorris@amserve.com or dmorris@lix.compulink.co.uk)

MORRIS, David Scott; s of John Hilary Morris (d 1994), of Bow Brickhill, Bucks, and Frances Deans, *née* Cooper (d 1995); *b* 20 December 1940; *Educ* Westmont Sch IOW, Royal Liberty GS Romford; *m* 23 Oct 1965, Jennifer Lois, da of Alan George Skinner (d 1986), of Sydney, Aust; 1 da (Catriona Lucy Scott b 1967); *Career* admitted slr 1965; HM coroner: for Huntingdon 1987–99, for Beds 1992–, for S and W Cambs 1999–; legal memb Mental Health Review Tbnl 1989–; pres: Milton Keynes and Dist Law Soc 1985–86, Beds Law Soc 1987–88, Berks, Bucks and Oxon Inc Law Soc 2003–04, E Anglian Coroners Soc 2003–07; memb Law Soc; FInstD; *Recreations* travel, gardening, cycling, walking; *Clubs* Carlton; *Style*— David S Morris, Esq; ✉ The Old Vicarage, Granborough, Buckinghamshire MK18 3NT (tel 01296 670217, fax 01296 670543); Coroners Office, 8 Goldington Road, Bedford MK40 3NF (tel 01234 273012, fax 01234 273014, e-mail davids.morris@ukonline.co.uk)

MORRIS, Sir Derek James; kt (2003); s of Denis William Morris, and Olive Margaret, *née* Collison; *b* 23 December 1945; *Educ* Harrow County GS, St Edmund Hall Oxford (MA), Nuffield Coll Oxford (DPhil); *m* 4 Oct 1975, Susan Mary, da of Walter Whittles; 2 s (Alastair Henry Whittles b 14 Nov 1981, Roderick William Tudor b 6 July 1984); *Career* research fell Centre for Business and Industrial Studies Univ of Warwick 1969–70; Univ of Oxford: fell and tutor Oriel Coll and CUF lectr in economics 1970–98, Sir John Hicks research fell 1991–92, reader in economics 1996–98, provost Oriel Coll 2004–; chm of tstees OUP Pension Fund 2006–, non-exec dir Lucida plc 2007–; economic dir NEDO 1981–84, dir and chm Oxford Economic Forecasting Ltd 1984–98, chm Competition Cmmn (formerly Monopolies and Mergers Cmmn) 1998–2004 (memb 1991, dep chm 1995–98), chm Morris Review of Actuarial Profession 2004–05; visiting prof Univ of Calif Irvine 1986–87; hon fell: St Edmund Hall Oxford, TCD; Hon Dr: UC Dublin, UEA, Cranfield Univ; memb Royal Economic Soc 1985–; *Books* The Economic System in the UK (ed, 1977, 3 edn 1985), Industrial Economics: Theory and Evidence (1979), Unquoted Companies (1984), Strategic Behaviour and Industrial Competition (ed), Industrial Economics and Organisation (1991), State Owned Enterprises and Economic Reform in China 1979–87; *Recreations* skiing, walking, history, watching rugby; *Clubs* Reform, Oxford and Cambridge; *Style*— Sir Derek Morris; ✉ Oriel College, Oxford OX1 4EW (tel 01865 276543)

MORRIS, Dr Desmond John; s of Capt Harry Howe Morris (d 1942), and Dorothy Marjorie Fuller, *née* Hunt (d 1996); *b* 24 January 1928; *Educ* Dauntsey's Sch West Lavington, Univ of Birmingham (BSc), Univ of Oxford (DPhil); *m* 1952, Ramona Joy, da of Windsor Baulch, of Marlborough, Wiltshire; 1 s (Jason b 1968); *Career* zoological res worker Univ of Oxford 1954–56, head of Granada TV and Film Unit at Zoological Soc of London 1956–59, curator of mammals at Zoological Soc of London 1959–67, dir Inst of Contemporary Arts 1967–68, res fell Wolfson Coll Oxford 1973–81; Hon DSc Univ of Reading; TV series: Zootime (weekly, 1956–67), Life (fortnightly, 1965–67), The Human Race (1982), The Animals Roadshow (1987–89), The Animal Contract (1989), Animal Country (1991–96), The Human Animal (1994), The Human Sexes (1997); one man (paintings) shows: Swindon Art Centre 1948, London Gallery 1950, Ashmolean Museum Oxford 1952, Stooshnoff Fine Art London 1974, Quadrangle Gallery Oxford 1976, Lasson Gallery London 1976, Public Art Gallery Swindon 1977 and 1993, Galerie d'Eendt Amsterdam 1978, Mayor Gallery London 1987, 1989, 1991, 1994, 1997, 1999, 2002 and 2004, Shippee Gallery New York 1988, Keats Gallery Knokke 1988, Galerie Michele Heyraud Paris 1991, Public Art Galleries Stoke and Nottingham 1996, Charleston Gallery Sussex 1997, Buxton Public Art Gallery 1997, Clayton Gallery Newcastle 1998, Keitelman Gallery Brussels 1998, Van der Velde Gallery Antwerp 1998; Art Consultancy Witteveen Amsterdam 1999 and 2002, Galerie Pack-Huys Meckelen 2001, MOMA Ostend 2002, Solomon Gall Dublin 2003; *Books* The Reproductive Behaviour of the Ten-spined Stickleback (1958), The Story of Congo (1958), Curious Creatures (1961), The Biology of Art (1962), Apes and Monkeys (1964), The Big Cats (1965), The Mammals, a Guide to the Living Species (1965), Men and Snakes (with Ramona Morris, 1965), Men and Apes (with Ramona Morris, 1966), Men and Pandas (with Ramona Morris, 1966), Zootime (1966), Primate Ethology (ed, 1967), The Naked Ape (1967), The Human Zoo (1969), Patterns of Reproductive Behaviour (1970), Intimate Behaviour (1971), Manwatching, a Field-guide to Human Behaviour (1977), Gestures, their Origins and Distribution (jtly, 1979), Animal Days (autobiography, 1979), The Soccer Tribe (1981), Inrock (fiction, 1983), The Book of Ages (1983), The Art of Ancient Cyprus (1985), Bodywatching, a Field-guide to the Human Species (1985), The Illustrated Naked Ape (1986), Catwatching (1986), Dogwatching (1986), The Secret Surrealist (1987), Catlore (1987), The Animals Roadshow (1988), Horsewatching (1988), The Animal Contract (1990), Animalwatching (1990), Babywatching (1991), Christmas Watching (1992), The World of Animals (1993), The Naked Ape Triology (1994), The Human Animal (1994), The Illustrated Catwatching (1994), Bodytalk: a World Guide to Gestures (1994), Illustrated Babywatching (1995), Illustrated Dogwatching (1996), Catworld, a Feline Encyclopedia (1996), The Human Sexes (1997), Illustrated Horse Watching (1998), Cool Cats (1999), Body Guards (1999), The Naked Eye (2000), Dogs: A Dictionary of Dog Breeds (2001), People Watching (2002), The Nature of Happiness (2004), The Naked Woman (2004), Watching: Encounters with Humans and Other Animals (2006), Fantastic Cats (2006); *Recreations* book collecting, archaeology; *Style*— Dr Desmond Morris; ✉ c/o Jonathan Cape, 20 Vauxhall Bridge Road, London SW1V 2SA; (fax 01865 512103)

MORRIS, (George) Eryl; *b* 16 August 1943; *Educ* LSE (BSc), Harvard Business Sch (MBA); *m*; 1 da; *Career* Courtaulds plc 1970–98: md International Red Hand Marine Coatings 1973–76 (commercial dir 1971, gen mangr 1972), chm and chief exec International Paint Bd 1984–87 (memb Bd 1974–76, dep gp md 1976–78, gp md 1978–84), main bd exec dir 1981–98, responsible for Films and Packaging 1987–92, responsible for Coatings, Packaging and devpt of Courtaulds in the Far East 1992–95, memb Gp Exec 1986–98, dep chief exec Courtaulds plc 1995–98; chm: Safetynet Gp Ltd 1999–2000, Airinmar Ltd 2000–, HPI Ltd 2001–; non-exec dir: Manweb plc 1990–95, Courtaulds Textiles plc 1995–99, Blagden plc 1998–2000, Enodis plc 1998–, AWG plc 2000–, Mill Digital Media Ltd 2001–; FCA 1968; *Style*— Eryl Morris; ✉ Broad Oak, Devonshire Avenue, Amersham, Buckinghamshire HP6 5JE (tel 07899 798783, fax 01494 729303, e-mail erylmorris@hotmail.com)

MORRIS, Frank; s of Michael Joseph Morris (d 1981), of Uttoxeter, Staffs, and Mary Agnes, *née* Lavin (d 2006); *b* 13 July 1948; *Educ* St Joseph's Coll Stoke-on-Trent, Imperial Coll London (BSc, full colours, Union Gen Award for social activities); *m* 6 Sept 1969 (m dis 2005), Ann Jeanette, da of Robert McIlquham; 1 s (David John b 21 Jan 1972); *Career* asst exec engr PO Research Station Dollis Hill London 1967–74, exec engr PO Engineering 1974–79, design and devpt dir Kent Process Control Luton 1983–89 (design mangr 1979–83), associate director and manager of consulting practice Cambridge Consultants Ltd 1995–2001 (divnl mangr 1990–95); fndr Vecta Consulting Ltd 2001–; govr The Highfield Sch Letchworth 1986–98 (chm of govrs 1988–95), dir Letchworth Community Educn Tst 1997–98; assoc City and Guilds of London Inst, chartered electrical engr, FIET, sr memb Instrument Soc of America; *Style*— Frank Morris, Esq; ✉ tel 07768 713084, e-mail frank.morris@vecta5.com, website www.vecta5.com

MORRIS, Harvey James; s of Kenneth Montague Morris (d 1969), and Mary, *née* Hutchison (d 1992); *b* 3 April 1946; *Educ* Wilson's GS Camberwell, Queens' Coll Cambridge (BA, MA); *m* 1976 (sep 1991), Sarah Margaret Perry; 2 s (Jack b and d 1981, Joseph b 1983), 1 da (Rose b 1985); *Career* gen reporter: Walthamstow Guardian 1969–71, East Anglian Daily Times Ipswich 1971–72; sub ed Associated Press London 1972–73; Reuters 1973–86: news ed Latin America 1976–79, chief corr Teheran 1979–80, actg chief corr Beirut 1980, dip corr 1981–83, energy corr 1984, political corr 1984–86; The Independent: asst foreign ed 1986–88, Middle East ed 1988–90, dep foreign ed 1990–92, foreign ed 1992–94; ed Geneva Post Switzerland 1994–95; sr ed Bloomberg News London 1995–97, devpt manager Latin American Newsletters 1997–; fndr ed Tower Magazine on-line 1996–; FT: Sunday news ed 1997, currently chief corr Jerusalem; *Publications* No Friends But the Mountains: The Tragic History of the Kurds (co-author, 1992); *Style*— Harvey Morris, Esq

MORRIS, Ingrid Mary; da of Robert W Morris, and Edith, *née* Bundy; *b* 10 October 1945; *Educ* Nat Cathedral Sch for Girls Washington DC, Herts and Essex HS Bishop's Stortford, Architectural Assoc Sch of Architecture (AADipl, SADG); *m* 1 s (Vasiles b 1981); *Career* architect; estab Bone and Morris private practice with Jeanne Bone 1976 (formerly with McNab and Jamieson 1968–69, Piano and Rogers 1972–74); former memb Co of Women in Architecture 1974–76; visiting lectr: Royal Univ of Malta 1974–77, Univ of Queensland 1982; memb Cncl Architectural Assoc 1985–1999 (hon librarian 1985–97), RIBA rep on ARCUK Educn Ctee 1987, RIBA assessor RIBA Housing Awards Northern Region 1988; external examiner: Architectural and Engrg degree course Univ of Westminster 1993–95, Part III courses Univ of Westminster and Univ of North London 1996–98, Univ of Plymouth 1996–2000, UCL 2001–; memb AA, RIBA; *Recreations* swimming, skiing, painting; *Clubs* Arts, Architecture, Chelsea Arts; *Style*— Miss Ingrid Morris; ✉ Bone and Morris, 37 Mossop Street, London SW3 2NB (tel 020 7589 8535)

MORRIS, Jack Anthony; OBE (2005); s of Samuel Cyril Morris, of London, and Golda, *née* Berkovitch, of London; *b* 23 June 1956; *Educ* Christ's Coll GS; *m* 1 Nov 1983, Susan Anne, da of Harry Lee, of London; 1 da (Emily Kate b 14 May 1985), 2 s (Robert Edward b 27 May 1987, Harry Samuel b 18 March 1993); *Career* chm: Business Design Centre Gp Ltd 1992– (dep chm 1985–91), Portland Design Assocs Ltd 1992–2005 (dir 1988–91), Citycentral Estates Ltd 1992– (dir 1981–91), North London Area CBI 1994–99 (memb London Region Cncl 1993–99), City North Islington Ltd 2003–; dir Earls Court & Olympia Gp Ltd 1999–2004; tstee: The Morris Charitable Tst 1989– (chm), Islington Building Preservation Tst 1997–, Anne Frank Tst UK 2000–04; special advsr to Bd City and Inner London North TEC 1993–95; memb: Mayor of London's Skills and Employment Bd 2006–, Ministerial Standing Gp on Further Educn 2006–; govr: North London Coll 1992–93, City & Islington Coll 1992–, London Met Univ 1996–99; chm City & Islington Coll 1996– (vice-chm 1992–96); freeperson London Borough of Islington 2003–; FInstD 1988, FRSA 2007; *Recreations* cycling, classic cinema and film music, piano, collecting vintage radios, Spanish culture, charity and voluntary work; *Style*— Jack Morris, OBE; ✉ The Business Design Centre, Upper Street, Islington, London N1 0QH (tel 020 7359 3535, fax 020 7226 0590)

MORRIS, Dr Jackie Evelyn; da of Prof Norman Morris, *qv*, and Lucy, *née* Rivlin; *b* 26 June 1948; *Educ* Camden Sch for Girls London, St Mary's Hosp Med Sch Univ of London (MB BS); *m* 1974, Dr Martin Howard Seifert, *qv*; 1 da (Victoria Charlotte b 1975), 1 s (Benjamin William D'Avigdor b 1978); *Career* house appts St Mary's Hosp and Hillingdon Hosp Uxbridge, subsequently SHO (rotation med) Central Middx Hosp 1972–74, med registrar St Mary's Hosp Paddington 1974–75, pt/t sr registrar in geriatric med UCH London 1975–79; conslt physician: St Mary's Hosp 1979–85, Royal Free Hosp 1985–2004 (seconded Dept of Health 1992–94); Frohlich visiting prof UCLA 1987; hon dep sec and sec Br Geriatrics Soc 1984–89; RSM: pres Geriatrics and Gerontology Section 1996 (hon sec 1991–94), dep chm RSM Academic Bd 1997–2000; expert assessor GMC; pres Central London Branch Parkinson's Disease Soc 1991–, chm Age Concern London 1994–97, chair Policy Ctee Br Geriatrics Soc 2005–07 (chair Primary and Continuing Care Special Interest Gp 2001–05); memb Editorial Bd: Br Jl of Hosp Med 1984–90, RSM Jl 1992–96; examiner RCP Dip in Geriatric Med 1996–; memb: Disability Living Allowance Bd 1994–95, Arthritis Care Services Ctee 1994–95, N Thames Geriatric Trg Ctee (chm Educn Sub-Ctee 1996–2004); FRCP 1990, FRSA 2002; *Publications* articles on community problems of elderly people; *Recreations* reading, friends, music, children, husband, cooking; *Style*— Dr Jackie Morris; ✉ 23 Balcombe Street, Dorset Square, London NW1 6HE

MORRIS, (Catharine) Jan; CBE (1999); *b* 2 October 1926; *Educ* Univ of Oxford (MA); *Career* author; memb Gorsedd of Bards Nat Eisteddfod of Wales; fell yr Academi Gymreig; Hon DLitt: Univ of Wales, Univ of Glamorgan; hon fell: UCW Aberystwyth, UCW Bangor; hon student ChCh Oxford; Hon FRIBA, FRSL; *Books* Venice (1960), Spain (1964), Oxford (1965), The Pax Britannica Trilogy (1973–78), Conundrum (1974), The Venetian Empire (1980), The Matter of Wales (1984), Last Letters from Hav (1985), Among the Cities (1985), Manhattan '45 (1987), Hong Kong (1988), Pleasures of a Tangled Life (1989), Sydney (1992), O Canada! (1992), A Machynlleth Triad (1993), Fisher's Face (1995), 50 Years of Europe (1997), Lincoln (1999), Trieste and the Meaning of Nowhere (2001), A Writer's World (2003), Hav (2006); The Oxford Book of Oxford (ed, 1978), Travels with Virginia Woolf (ed, 1993); 6 books of collected travel essays; *Style*— Ms Jan Morris, CBE, FRSL; ✉ Trefan Morys, Llanystumdwy, Gwynedd LL52 0LP (tel 01766 522222, fax 01766 522426, e-mail janmorris1@msn.com)

MORRIS, John Colin; s of John B Morris (d 1977), of Reading, Berks, and Joan, *née* Davis; *b* 12 April 1946; *Educ* Leighton Park Sch Reading (head of house, capt rugby and cricket), St Edmund Hall Oxford (BA); *m* 1972, Penny, da of Laurence J Halling; 2 s (Andrew b 1 Oct 1975, Christopher b 21 March 1977), 1 da (Ruth (twin) b 21 March 1977); *Career* teacher and housemaster Woolverstone Hall nr Ipswich 1969–80; Hymers Coll Hull: head of history 1980–86 (also sr master and rugby and cricket coach), dep head 1986–90, headmaster 1990–2006; memb: HMC 1990, SHA 1990; memb various educnl bodies in Hull; sec Baptist Church, memb Rotary Club of Hull; *Recreations* sport (golf), gardening, walking; *Style*— John Morris, Esq

MORRIS, Judith Anne; da of Harold Morris (d 1986), of London, and Eve, *née* Sutton; *b* 23 August 1948; *Educ* Buckingham Gate Sch, Camden HS for Girls, City Univ London (BSc,

MSc); *Career* sr sessional optometrist Contact Lens Dept Moorfields Eye Hosp London 1971–94; Inst of Optometry London: sr lectr 1983–91, dir 1991–2001, head of contact lenses 2001–; assoc dir of contact lens teaching City Univ 2001–; pres Br Contact Lens Assoc 1983–84 (ed jl of Br Contact Lens Assoc 1984–89), pres Coll of Optometrists 1989–90 (memb Cncl and examiner 1980–2006), EMEA pres Int Assoc of Contact Lens Educators 1998–; elected memb Gen Optical Cncl 1997–2006; memb Lambeth Southwark and Lewisham FPC 1988–90; Freeman City of London 1972, Liveryman Worshipful Co of Spectacle Makers 1992; FBCO 1971; *Recreations* theatre, ballet, bridge; *Style*— Miss Judith Morris; ✉ 9 Cosway Street, London NW1 5NR (tel 020 7724 1176)

MORRIS, Mali; *b* 5 February 1945; *Educ* Univ of Newcastle upon Tyne (BA), Univ of Reading (MFA); *Career* artist; more than 20 solo shows since 1979, recently in London, NY and Tokyo; many gp exhbns incl: Whitechapel Gall, Serpentine Gall, Barbican, Hayward Gall; int shows: France, Belgium, Luxembourg, Netherlands, Cyprus, USA, Eastern Europe, Canada, Brazil, Botswana, Japan; public collections incl: Arts Cncl of GB, Br Cncl, Contemporary Art Soc, The Whitworth Art Gallery Manchester, Lloyd's of London, Nat Museum Gaborone; lectured and examined widely incl: Chelsea Coll of Art and Design, Univ of the Arts London, RCA, Slade Sch of Art; *Awards* Hatton scholar 1968, Arts Cncl Award 1976, GLAA Major Award 1979, Elephant Tst Award, Univ of Reading Res Award 1983, Lorne Award 1994–95, Daiwa Award 2000, Br Cncl Travel Awards 2000, Chelsea Coll of Art and Design Awards 2000–05; *Publications* Mali Morris Paintings (1994), Mali Morris Recent Paintings (2002); *Style*— Mali Morris; ✉ website www.malimorris.co.uk

MORRIS, Margaret Faith; da of Claud Morris, of Penzance, Cornwall, and Patricia Morris; *b* 4 November 1955; *Educ* Laban (BA), Principia Coll USA, Queens Coll London; *m* 29 Sept 2000, Matthew James Tomkinson; *Career* choreographer, dancer, dir, dance educator; soloist Murray Louis Dance Co 1982–1990; artistic dir Phoenix Dance Co 1991–97; choreographer/dir: Institute Theatre Co, Transitions Dance Co, Phoenix Dance Co, Intoto Dance Co, various films and theatre; artistic advsr Transitions Dance Co; mgmnt consIt: Alta Associates, Shapiro & Smith Dance NY, Nikolais and Louis Dance, Adzido Dance Co 1999–2001; Inspector of Professional Dance and Drama Trg Schs (FEFC and Ofsted) 2001–02; arts and dance educn consIt; dance teacher: Laban Centre, London Contemporary Dance Sch, Coker Colls USA, Transitions Dance Co, Diversions Dance Co, Phoenix Dance Co; choreography lectr and teacher: Japan (Tamagawa Univ), Israel, Russia, USA; various contribs to jls; chair Bonnie Bird Choreography Fund, dir Dance UK; advsr Dance Panel Arts Cncl of England; memb: Dance UK, Equity (USA), American Guild of Musical Artists (AGMA), Dance Critics Assoc; *Awards* New Choreographers Award, Gulbenkian Rockefeller Fndn Award; *Recreations* singing, scuba diving; *Style*— Margaret Morris; ✉ 67 Calbourne Road, London SW12 8LS (tel 020 8673 0470, e-mail maggiemorris@btinternet.com)

MORRIS, Martin John; s of Norman Ernest Morris, and Margaret Joan Morris; *Educ* Dauntsey's Sch West Lavington, St Luke's Coll Exeter (BEd), Open Univ (BA); *Career* teacher and sports coach Sedbergh Sch 1978–89 (master i/c cricket 1981–89), Master of Fryer and teacher Leighton Park Sch Reading 1989–95 (also i/c cricket), headmaster Catteral Hall Sch Giggleswick 1995–2000, headmaster Kingham Hill Sch 2000–; memb IAPS 1995–2000 (memb Sports and Recreation Ctee), memb Ctee SHMIS 2000; govr: Dormer House Sch Moreton-in-Marsh, Arnold Lodge Sch Leamington Spa; memb: RSPB, Evangelical Alliance, Christians in Sport, Fell-Runners Assoc; MInstD 2001; *Recreations* sport, particularly cricket, rugby, hockey, golf, road, cross and fell-running, bird watching, walking; *Clubs* Shipton-under-Wychwood Cricket, Cryptics Cricket; *Style*— Martin Morris, Esq; ✉ The Warden's House, Kingham Hill School, Kingham, Chipping Norton, Oxfordshire OX7 6TH (tel 01608 658234, 01608 658999, fax 01608 658658, e-mail headmaster@kingham-hill.oxon.sch.uk)

MORRIS, 3 Baron (UK 1918); Michael David Morris; er twin s of 2 Baron Morris (d 1975), and Jean Beatrice, *née* Maitland-Makgill-Crichton (d 1989, having m 2, Baron Salmon (Life Peer)); *b* 9 December 1937; *Educ* Downside; *m* 1, 1959, Denise Eleanor, da of Morley Richards; m 2, 1962, Jennifer, da of Tristram Gilbert; 2 da; m 3, 1980, Juliet Susan, twin da of Anthony Buckingham; 2 s, 1 da; m 4, 1999, Nicola Mary, da of Colin Morgan Watkins; *Heir* s, Hon Thomas Morris; *Career* sat as Cons in House of Lords; FCA; *Style*— The Rt Hon the Lord Morris

MORRIS, Dr Norma Frances; da of Henry Albert Bevis (d 1984), of Chadwell Heath, Essex, and Lilian Eliza, *née* Flexon (d 1993); *b* 17 April 1935; *Educ* Ilford Co HS, UCL (BA, MA, George Smith prize), Univ of Twente Netherlands (PhD); *m* 14 July 1960, Samuel Francis Morris, s of Samuel Morris (d 1969), of London; 2 da (Jane Albertine b 1965, Anne Caroline b 1970), 1 s (John Stephen b 1967); *Career* TEFL Paris 1956–57, asst lectr Univ of Hull 1959–60; MRC: various admin appts 1960–76, estab offr 1976–78, head of accommodation and industrial liaison 1978–84, head of fin 1984–89, admin sec 1989–95; research fell UCL 1995–; chm Gen Chiropractic Cncl 1998–2002; memb and dep chm Nat Biological Standards Bd 1990–98; memb: Int Sociological Assoc, Br Acupuncture Accreditation Bd 2004; tstee Patient's Assoc 2004–06; FRSM; *Publications* articles in academic jls on sci and regulatory policy; *Recreations* canoeing, opera, edible fungi; *Style*— Dr Norma Morris; ✉ Department of Science and Technology Studies, University College London, Gower Street, London WC1E 6BT (tel 020 7679 3703, fax 020 7679 2328, e-mail norma.morris@ucl.ac.uk)

MORRIS, Prof Norman Frederick; s of Frederick William Morris (d 1974), of Luton, Beds, and Evelyn, *née* Biggs (d 1971); *b* 26 February 1920; *Educ* Dunstable Sch, St Mary's Hosp Med Sch Univ of London (MB BS); *m* 2 June 1944, Lucia Xenia (Lucy), da of Dr Benjamin Rivlin (d 1964), of Stratford, London; 2 s (David, Nicholas), 2 da (Dr Jackie Morris, *qv*, Vanessa); *Career* Sqdn Ldr RAFVR (Med Section) 1946–48; res surgical offr East Ham Meml Hosp 1945–46 (dep res 1944–45), sr registrar Dept of Obstetrics & Gynaecology Royal Postgrad Med Sch 1950–53 (departmental reader 1956–58), sr lectr Dept of Obstetrics & Gynaecology UCH 1953–56, prof of obstetrics and gynaecology Charing Cross Hosp Med Sch 1958–85, med dir IVF Unit Cromwell Hosp 1986–97 (dir Dept of Postgraduate Med Educn 1997–2005); Univ of London: dean Faculty of Med 1971–76, dep vice-chllr 1974–80, emeritus prof of obstetrics and gynaecology 1985–; dep chm NW Thames HA 1976–80; sec gen Cwlth Health Fndn 1994; fndr and pres Int Soc of Psychosomatic Obstetrics and Gynaecology 1972–80; chm Br Soc of Psychosomatic Obstetrics and Gynaecology and Andrology 1988–94 (hon pres 1994–), chm Cwlth Health Devpt Programme 1990–2000; tstee and chm Scientific Ctee Little Fndn 1992–; hon memb: Societas Gynaecologa et Obstetrica Italica 1979, Aust Soc of Psychosomatic Obstetrics and Gynaecology 1981; fell RSM (pres Section of Obstetrics and Gynaecology 1979), FRCOG; govr St Paul's Sch for Boys and Girls 1975–90, treas Int Soc for the Investigation of Stress 1990–; *Books* The Baby Book (1953–90), Sterilisation of Men and Women (1976); author of numerous articles in medical press 1956–; *Recreations* travelling, music, reading; *Clubs* Athenaeum; *Style*— Prof Norman Morris; ✉ Flat 3, The Etons, 13 Eton Avenue, London NW3 3EL (tel and fax 020 7431 4626, e-mail profgynmorris@aol.com)

MORRIS, Paul Christopher Early; s of Christopher John Morris, of Kensington, London, and (Alice) Ruth, *née* Early (d 1997); *b* 21 September 1950; *Educ* Westminster Abbey Choir Sch, Westminster, UCNW Bangor (BA); *m* 1991, Rosemary Kinross; 2 s (Nicholas Paul Makumbi b 16 Oct 1992, Benedict Patrick Mulira b 31 Oct 1994); *Career* organist and choirmaster Christ Church Llanfairfechan N Wales 1970–73; admitted slr 1978, ptnr Winckworth Sherwood (formerly Winckworth & Pemberton) 1981– (asst slr 1978–81, sr ptnr 2003); slr: Southwark Diocesan Bd of Fin, London Diocesan Fund; registrar: Diocese of Southwark, Diocese of London; chapter clerk Southwark Cathedral; hon slr St Luke's Hosp for the Clergy; Freeman City of London 1984; Liveryman: Worshipful Co of Wheelwrights 1984, Worshipful Co of Weavers 1993; *Recreations* music; *Clubs* Athenaeum, Oriental; *Style*— Paul Morris, Esq; ✉ Winckworth Sherwood, The Old Deanery, Deans Court, London EC4V 5AA (tel 020 7593 5000, fax 020 7248 3221)

MORRIS, Paul David; s of Reginald Morris (d 1981), of Leicester and IOM, and Patricia, *née* Sayle (d 1999); *b* 10 September 1955; *Educ* Ramsey GS IOM, Univ of Sheffield (LLB); *m* 28 Aug 1982, Joy Anne, *née* Turner; *Career* admitted slr 1997, advocate Manx Bar 1981; sr ptnr Morris Maddrell 1985–99, ptnr Dickinson Cruickshank 1999– (sr ptnr 2005–); memb: IOM Law Soc 1981 (pres 2001–03), Law Soc of Eng and Wales 1997; tstee Manx Aviation Preservation Soc; *Recreations* golf, cricket, aviation, archaeology; *Clubs* MCC, Ramsey Golf (pres); *Style*— Paul Morris, Esq; ✉ Dickinson Cruickshank, 33 Athol Street, Douglas, Isle of Man IM1 1LB

MORRIS, Prof Peter Edwin; s of Stewart Silvester Morris, and Doris Maud, *née* Wilson; *b* 13 November 1947; *Educ* Weston-super-Mare GS, Univ of Exeter (BA, PhD); *m* 17 Sept 1976, Priscilla Jane, da of Ronald Kelley, of Costa Di Vaghia, 20122 Quenza, Corse Du Sud, France; 2 da (Lucy b 1979, Susan b 1988); *Career* lectr in psychology Open Univ 1972–74, prof of psychology and personal chair Lancaster Univ 1989– (lectr 1974–84, sr lectr 1984–89, head of Psychology Dept 1987–93); memb Exec Ctee Save Br Sci 1986–88; Br Psychological Soc: hon gen sec 1983–86, chm Scientific Affrs Bd 1988–89, pres elect 1989–90, pres 1990–91, vice-pres 1991–92, chm Jt Ctee for Funding in Higher Educn 1991–; memb Experimental Psychology Soc, FBPsS, CPsychol, FRSA; *Books* Visual Imagery and Consciousness (jtly, 1983), Cognition in Action (1987, 2 edn 1994); ed: Aspects of Memory (1978), Practical Aspects of Memory (1978), Applied Problems in Memory (1979), Everyday Memory, Actions and Absentmindedness (1984), Modelling Cognition (1987), Practical Aspects of Memory: Current Research and Issues (2 vols, 1988), Aspects of Memory: The Practical Aspects (1992), The Psychology of Memory (3 vols, 1993), Theoretical Aspects of Memory (1994); *Recreations* fell walking, local history, bird watching, gardening; *Style*— Prof Peter Morris; ✉ Psychology Department, Lancaster University, Lancaster LA1 4YF (tel 01524 593885, telex 65111 Lancuf G, fax 01524 841710)

MORRIS, Peter John; s of Eric Charles Morris, and Joan Morris, of Carmarthen; *b* 29 April 1958; *Educ* Queen Elizabeth GS Carmarthen, Univ of Exeter (BA), Poly of Central London (MBA); *m* Angela, da of Michael Sadlo; 1 s (Alexander b 6 May 1991), 1 da (Sarah b 10 Aug 1993); *Career* gen mgmnt posts NHS SW and SE England 1980–86; assoc mangr Leicester Royal Infirmary: Accident and Trauma Unit 1986–89, Med Unit 1989–91; assoc gen mangr Univ Hosp of Wales Cardiff 1991–94, dir of business and contracting Northern Gen Hosp NHS Tst 1994–98, chief exec The Ipswich Hosp NHS Tst 1998–2002, chief exec S Manchester Univ Hosps NHS Tst 2002–; FHSM 1988; *Recreations* golf, sailing; *Clubs* Bramhall Park Golf; *Style*— Peter Morris, Esq; ✉ South Manchester University Hospitals NHS Trust, Wythenshawe Hospital, Southmoor Road, Manchester M23 9LT (tel 0161 291 2023, e-mail peter.morris@smuht.nwest.nhs.uk)

MORRIS, (Thomas) Richard; s of Capt Thomas Griffiths Morris, and Margaret Eileen, *née* Osborne; *b* 29 October 1945; *Educ* Abingdon Sch, Univ of Birmingham (LLB); *m* 18 Oct 1975, Vanessa Jane; 1 s (Nicholas b 30 April 1979), 1 da (Miriam b 12 Feb 1978); *Career* Lt 6 QEO Gurkha Rifles 1969–71, served Malaysia, Hong Kong, Nepal, India, Capt 6 Queens Regt (Vol) 1971–75; articled clerk Norton Rose London 1971–73, admitted slr 1974, ptnr D J Freeman London 1987–91, in practice T R Morris slrs 1991–99; occasional contribs Estates Times Magazine, Architects Journal; hon ward clerk Ward of Bishopsgate London 1986–; Freeman City of London 1981, Liveryman Worshipful Co of Slrs 1981, Liveryman Worshipful Co of Glovers 2003; memb: Law Soc, Inst of Export; *Recreations* squash, swimming, gardening; *Clubs* City Livery, Anglo-Portuguese Soc; *Style*— Richard Morris, Esq; ✉ The Forge, The Street, Stratfield Mortimer, Berkshire RG7 3PB (tel 0118 933 3274, e-mail trmllb@hotmail.com)

MORRIS, Richard Francis Maxwell; s of Maxwell Morris (d 1996), of Pulborough, W Sussex, and Freda, *née* Abelson (d 1981); *b* 11 September 1944; *Educ* Eton, New Coll Oxford (MA), Coll of Law London; *m* 1, 1974 (m dis 1978), Sarah Quill; m 2, 1983, Marian Sperling; 2 da (Harriet b 1984, Jessica b 1986); *Career* slr Farrer & Co 1967–71, dep head Sterling Banking Dept Grindlay Brandts Ltd 1971–75, gen mangr Corp Fin S G Warburg & Co Ltd 1975–79; Hodder & Stoughton Holdings Ltd: fin dir then md Educational & Academic Publishing 1979–89, jt md 1989–91; chief exec Associated Board of the Royal Schools of Music 1993–; dir: Southern Radio plc (formerly Invicta Sound plc) 1984–92, The Lancet Ltd 1986–91; md Edward Arnold (Publishers) Ltd 1987–91; memb: Governing Body Kent Opera 1985–90, Exec Ctee Music Educn Cncl 1995– (chair 1998–2001); fndr Almaviva Opera 1989, tstee Cncl for Dance Educn and Trg 1999–2005; govr: Kent Music Sch 2001–, The Yehudi Menuhin Sch 2004–; Hon RCM, Hon RNCM, Hon FRAM; *Recreations* singing, golf, poetry, visual arts; *Clubs* Athenaeum; *Style*— Richard Morris, Esq; ✉ Associated Board of the Royal Schools of Music, 24 Portland Place, London W1B 1LU (tel 020 7467 8225, fax 020 7467 8224, e-mail chiefexec@abrsm.ac.uk)

MORRIS, Prof Richard Graham Michael; CBE (2007); s of Robert Walter Morris, of Old Harlow, Essex, and Edith Mary, *née* Bundy (d 1996); *b* 27 June 1948; *Educ* St Alban's Sch Washington DC, Marlborough, Univ of Cambridge (BA), Univ of Sussex (DPhil); *m* 18 May 1985, Hilary Ann, da of Ian D Lewis; 2 da (Louise Edith b 4 June 1988, Josephine Claire b 26 March 1991); *Career* Addison-Wheeler res fell Univ of Durham 1973–75, sr scientific offr British Museum 1975–77, res Science and Features Dept BBC TV 1977, lectr Univ of St Andrews 1977–86; Univ of Edinburgh: reader 1988–93, prof of neuroscience and dir Centre for Neuroscience 1993–97, chm Dept of Neuroscience 1998–2002, dir Centre for Cognitive and Neural Systems, Royal Soc/Wolfson prof of neuroscience 2006–; MRC res fell 1983–86, visiting prof MIT 1991, adjunct prof Univ of Trondheim 2001–; Segerfalk lectr Univ of Lund 1991, BNA Decade of Int Brain lectr 1998, Zotterman lectr Karolinska Inst 1999, Edwards lectr Univ of Seattle 2002, American Alumnus lectr Univ of St Andrews 2003; memb: MRC Neurosciences Grants Ctee 1981–85, MRC Neurosciences Bd 1993–97, MRC Strategy Developments Gp 2000–, Editorial Advsy Bd Trends in Neurosciences, Editorial Bd Learning and Memory, Experimental Psychology Soc (hon sec 1985–89), Brain Res Assoc (chm 1990–94), European Neuroscience Assoc, European Brain and Behaviour Soc; pres Fedn of European Neuroscience Socs 2006–; Henry Dryerre Prize RSE 2000, BNA Neuroscientist of the Year Award 2003; FRSE 1994, FRS 1997, FMedSci 1998, FAAAS 2004, fell American Assoc for the Advancement of Science 2005; *Publications* Parallel Distributed Processing: Implications for Psychology and Neurobiology (ed, 1990), Neuroscience: Science of the Brain (1994, 2 edn 2003), Long-term Potentiation (ed, 2004), The Hippocampus Book (ed, 2006); academic papers on memory and its brain mechanisms; *Recreations* sailing; *Clubs* Royal Yachting Assoc, Port Edgar Sailing; *Style*— Prof Richard Morris, CBE, FRS, FRSE, FMedSci; ✉ Centre for Cognitive and Neural Systems, University of Edinburgh, 1 George Square, Edinburgh EH8 9JZ (tel 0131 650 3518, fax 0131 651 1835, e-mail r.g.m.morris@ed.ac.uk)

MORRIS, Richard Keith; OBE (2003); s of John Richard Morris, and Elsie Myra, *née* Wearne; *b* 8 October 1947; *Educ* Denstone Coll, Pembroke Coll Oxford (MA, pres Univ Opera Club), Univ of York (BPhil); *m* 1971, Jane Hilda, da of David Holmes Whiteley; 2 s (David Edward b 27 Feb 1972, Henry John b 23 July 1982), 1 da (Eva Judith Ann b 21 July 1974); *Career* res asst York Minster excavations 1971–74, res offr Cncl for British

M

Archaeology 1978–88 (churches offr 1975–78), lectr Univ of York 1988–91, dir Cncl for British Archaeology 1991–99, dir Inst for Medieval Studies Univ of Leeds 2003–; hon visiting prof Dept of Archaeology Univ of York 1995–; cmmr English Heritage 1996–; hon vice-pres Cncl for British Archeology 2001–, hon memb Inst of Field Archeologists 2001–; runner up Yorkshire Post Best First Book Award 1979, Educnl Film/Video for Archaeology Channel 4 Award 1988, Frend Medallist Soc of Antiquaries 1992; writer/composer 1999–; FSA 1982, MIFA 1986; *Books* Cathedrals and Abbeys of England and Wales (1979), The Church in British Archaeology (1983), Churches in the Landscape (1989), Guy Gibson (jtly, 1994), Cheshire VC OM (2000), The Triumph of Time (2008); *Recreations* opera, natural history, aviation history; *Style*— Richard Morris, Esq; ✉ 13 Hollins Road, Harrogate, North Yorkshire HG1 2JF

MORRIS, Richard Nicholas; s of Rev D S Morris, and Mrs V A Morris; *Educ* Queen Elizabeth's Hosp Bristol, St Catharine's Coll Cambridge (MA); *Career* advertising exec; DDB London 1988–, currently business devpt dir; *Recreations* football, hill walking, skiing, gardening; *Style*— Richard Morris, Esq; ✉ DDB London, 12 Bishops Bridge Road, London W2 6AA (tel 020 7258 3979, fax 020 7402 4871, e-mail richard.morris@ddb-europe.com)

MORRIS, Prof Robert John (Bob); *b* 12 October 1943; *Educ* Acklam Hall GS Middlesbrough, Keble Coll Oxford (BA), Nuffield Coll Oxford (DPhil); *m* Barbara Anne; 1 s (George b 1969), 1 da (Helen b 1971); *Career* Univ of Edinburgh: lectr in economic history 1968–80, sr lectr 1980–91, prof of economic and social history 1991–; pres European Assoc of Urban Historians 2000–02; convenor Press Cmmn Univ of Edinburgh 2000–; FRHistS 1990; *Books* Cholera (1974), Class and Class Consciousness in the Industrial Revolution (1976), Class, Sect and Party 1820–1850 (1988), Men, Women and Property in England 1780–1870 (2004), and various other pubns; *Recreations* growing vegetables; *Style*— Prof Bob Morris; ✉ School of History and Classics, Economic and Social History, University of Edinburgh, William Robertson Building, George Square, Edinburgh EH8 9JY (tel 0131 650 3834, fax 0131 6645, e-mail rjmorris@ed.ac.uk)

MORRIS, Robert Vernon (Robin); s of Harold Vernon Morris, MRCVS (d 1986), of Hereford, and Dorothy Agnes, *née* Foulkes (d 1994); *b* 27 May 1932; *Educ* St Mary's Coll Bitterne Park Southampton, LSE (LLB); *m* 19 Sept 1959, Patricia Margaret, da of Thomas Norman Trevor (d 1968), of Gloucester; 3 s (Nicholas b 1960, Timothy b 1963, James b 1965), 1 da (Sally b 1970); *Career* Nat Serv 1956–58, Intelligence Corps GCHQ Cheltenham; slr Supreme Court 1957, sr ptnr Rowberry Morris Glos (and assoc offices); chm: Social Security Appeal Tbnl (Wales and SW) 1980–99, Glos Legal Assoc 1985–88, Child Support Appeal Tbnls (Wales and SW) 1993–99; legally qualified panel memb Appeals Serv 1999–2006; chm House of Tailor of Gloucester plc 2006–; sec Glos Historic Bldgs 1980–, pres Glos Rotary Club 1981–82, chm Glos Civic Tst 1983–, cdr St John Ambulance Glos 1988–94; chm: Cncl Order of St John Glos 1994–98, Order of St John Visitation Ctee 1998–2000; memb: Chapter Gen Order of St John 1996–2000, Priory Chapter of England and the Islands 2001– (alternate memb Glos 2000), Law Soc; Paul Harris fell 2005; KJStJ 1996 (OStJ 1986, CStJ 1991); *Recreations* jogging, inner city conservation; *Clubs* LSE, Army and Navy; *Style*— Robin Morris, Esq; ✉ The Court House, Church Street, Newent, Gloucestershire GL18 1AB (tel 01531 822526, mobile 07074 301903, e-mail rvm@rowmor.co.uk); Morroway House, Station Road, Gloucester GL1 1DW (tel 01452 301903, fax 01452 411115, telex DX 7500 Gloucester)

MORRIS, Simon James; s of Kenneth Stapleton Morris, of Cape Town, South Africa, and Grace, *née* Skitmore; *b* 24 January 1958; *Educ* Aberdour Sch, Whitgift Sch, Gonville & Caius Coll Cambridge (MA), Birkbeck Coll London (PhD); *Career* admitted slr 1982; ptnr CMS Cameron McKenna LLP (formerly Cameron Markby Hewitt) 1988–; memb Cncl London Topographical Soc 1983–; *Books* Financial Services: Regulating Investment Business (1989, 2 edn 1995), Highgate Archway: Gateway to the City (with Towyn Mason, 2000); *Recreations* history of London; *Style*— Simon Morris, Esq; ✉ CMS Cameron McKenna LLP, 160 Aldersgate Street, London EC1A 4DD (tel 020 7367 3000, fax 020 7367 2000, e-mail simon.morris@cms-cmck.com)

MORRIS, Trevor John; s of Peter Morris, of E Grinsted, and Dorothy, *née* Haines; *b* 13 July 1955; *Educ* Drayton Manor GS, Univ of Exeter (BA); *m* 21 May 1982, Claire, *née* Laven; 2 da (Olivia b 27 Oct 1988, Flora b 22 August 1991); *Career* asst to mktg dir Fenwick of Bond Street 1977–79, mktg servs mangr OEM plc 1979–81; The Quentin Bell Organisation: campaign dir 1982–84, md 1984–, chm 1998–; chm Good Relations Gp 2000–, chm QBO Bell Pottinger 2002; visiting prof Univ of Westminster 2005–; *Recreations* reading, theatre, football; *Clubs* 2 Brydges Place; *Style*— Trevor Morris, Esq; ✉ Department of Journalism and Mass Communication, School of Media, Arts and Design, University of Westminster, Harrow Campus, Watford Road, Harrow HA1 3TP (tel 07771 810984, e-mail trevor.j.morris@btinternet.com)

MORRIS, HE Warwick; *b* 10 August 1948; *m* 1972, Pamela Jean, *née* Mitchell; 1 s, 2 da; *Career* diplomat; entered HM Dip Serv 1969, posted Paris 1972, language trg and second sec Seoul 1975, second sec FCO 1979, first sec (commercial) Mexico City 1984, first sec and head of Chancery Seoul 1988, first sec then cnsllr FCO 1991, cnsllr (commercial and economic) New Delhi 1995, RCDS 1999, ambass to Vietnam 2000–03, ambass to South Korea 2003–; *Style*— HE Mr Warwick Morris; ✉ c/o Foreign & Commonwealth Office (Seoul), King Charles Street, London SW1A 2AH

MORRIS, Very Rev William James; KCVO (1995), JP (Glasgow 1971); o s of William John Morris, and Eliza Cecilia Cameron Johnson; *b* 22 August 1925; *Educ* Cardiff HS, Univ of Wales (BA, BD), Univ of Edinburgh (PhD); *m* 1952, Jean Daveena Ogilvy Morris, CBE (d 2005), o da of Rev David Porter Howie, of Kilmarnock, Ayrshire; 1 s; *Career* ordained 1951; minister: St David's Buckhaven 1953–57, Peterhead Old Parish 1957–67; chaplain HM Prison Peterhead 1963–67; memb Convocation Univ of Strathclyde, chm Cncl Soc of Friends of Glasgow Cathedral 1967–2002, minister of Glasgow Cathedral 1967–2005 (minister emeritus 2005–); chaplain: to HM The Queen in Scotland 1969–96 (extra chaplain 1996–), to the Lord High Cmmr to Gen Assembly of Church of Scotland 1975–76, to the Queen's Body Guard for Scotland (Royal Co of Archers) 1994–2007; Dean of the Chapel Royal in Scotland 1991–96; memb: IBA Scotland 1979–84, Bd of Govrs Jordanhill Coll of Educn 1983–91; hon pres City of Glasgow Soc of Social Serv; hon memb: Rotary Clubs of Dennistoun and Glasgow, Royal Scottish Automobile Club, RNVR Club; chaplain Strathclyde Police; hon vice-pres Glasgow Bn The Boys' Bde; pres Saint Andrew Soc (Glasgow); Hon LLD Univ of Strathclyde 1974, Hon DD Univ of Glasgow 1979, Hon DLitt Glasgow Caledonian Univ 2003; Hon FRCPS Glasgow; hon memb Royal Faculty of Procurators in Glasgow; ChStJ; *Books* A Walk Through Glasgow Cathedral (1986), Amazing Graces (2001); *Recreations* gardening; *Clubs* New (Edinburgh); *Style*— The Very Rev William Morris, KCVO; ✉ 1 Whitehill Grove, Newton Mearns, Glasgow G77 5DH (tel 0141 639 6327)

MORRIS OF ABERAVON, Baron (Life Peer UK 2001), of Aberavon in the County of West Glamorgan and of Ceredigion in the County of Dyfed; Sir John Morris; KG (2003), kt (1999), PC (1970), QC (1973); s of late D W Morris, of Talybont, Cardiganshire, and late Mrs M O A Morris (later Mrs Lewis); *b* 1931; *Educ* Ardwyn Aberystwyth, Univ Coll of Wales Aberystwyth, Gonville & Caius Coll Cambridge, Acad of Int Law The Hague; *m* 1959, Margaret, da of Edward Lewis, OBE, JP, of Llandysul; 3 da; *Career* served Royal Welch Fusiliers and Welch Regt; called to the Bar Gray's Inn 1954 (Holker sr exhibitioner 1955–58), bencher 1985; legal advsr Farmers' Union of Wales 1955–57, recorder of the Crown Court (SE Circuit) 1982–97; MP (Lab) Aberavon 1959–2001, Parly sec Miny of Power 1964–66, jt Parly sec for tport 1966–68, min for defence (equipment) 1968–70, sec of state for Wales 1974–79, oppn spokesman on legal affrs and shadow attorney-gen 1979–81 and 1983–96; attorney-gen 1997–99; memb: UK Delgn Consultative Assembly Cncl of Europe and WEU 1963–64, N Atlantic Assembly 1970–74; chllr Univ of Glamorgan 2001–; pres London Welsh Assoc 2001–; HM Lord-Lt Dyfed 2003–06; Hon LLD Univ of Wales 1983; hon fell: Gonville & Caius Coll Cambridge, UC Aberystwyth, UC Swansea, Trinity Coll Carmarthen; *Style*— The Rt Hon the Lord Morris of Aberavon, KG, PC, QC

MORRIS OF BALGONIE AND EDDERGOLL, Yr, Stuart Gordon Cathal; s of Raymond Stanley Morris of Balgonie and Eddergoll, and Margaret Newton Morris, *née* Stuart; matriculated arms (Morris of Balgonie and Eddergoll quartered with Stuart) Court of the Lord Lyon Edinburgh 1987; *b* 17 April 1965; *Educ* Bell-Baxter HS, Elmwood Coll, Univ of Birmingham; *Career* historian, armorist, author; Scottish Castles Assoc: fndr memb, memb Cncl 1996–, sec 1997–2003, chm 2003–05, vice-chm 2005–; fndr memb Heraldry Soc of Scotland, memb The Stewart Soc 1981 (memb Cncl 1998–2006), memb Ctee Markinch Heritage Gp 2004–; Lt Col and ADC to HE the Govr of the State of Georgia 1991, Col Commonwealth of Kentucky 1999; dir: Balgonie Castle Enterprises, Theobald-Hicks, Morris & Gifford; Freeman City of London 2001, Liveryman Worshipful Co of Meadmakers 1982; FSA Scot 1983, FRSA 1990 (assoc 1986); Cdr Order of Polonia Restituta 1990, SBStJ 2003, Companion Order of Malta; *Recreations* archery, heraldry, genealogy, historical researching, painting; *Style*— The Younger of Balgonie and Eddergoll; ✉ Balgonie Castle, by Markinch, Fife KY7 6HQ (tel 01592 750119, fax 01592 753103, e-mail sbalgonie@yahoo.co.uk, website www.balgonie-castle.com)

MORRIS OF BOLTON, Baroness (Life Peer UK 2004), of Bolton in the County of Greater Manchester; Patricia Morris; OBE (1997); da of James Sydney Whittaker (d 1994), and Alice, *née* Redington (d 2004); *b* 16 January 1953, Bolton, Lancs; *Educ* Bolton Sch Girls' Div, Clifton Coll of Educn, Didsbury Coll of Educn; *m* 1978, His Hon Judge William Patrick Morris; 1 s (Hon Jonathan William Basil b 1983), 1 da (Hon Katharine Elizabeth b 1985); *Career* PA to the Northern Regnl Dir Slater Walker Ltd 1974–75, PA to the Chevalier Dr Harry D Schultz 1975, fund mangr PPS 1975–77, tech analyst Foster & Braithwaite 1977–78, tech analyst Charlton, Seal, Dimmock & Co 1979–83, policy and political advsr to Cons MEP 1999–2001, vice-chm Cons Pty 2001–05; sits as Cons in House of Lords 2004–, oppn whip 2004–, oppn spokesman on children, families and women 2005–, oppn spokesman on educn and skills 2006–; Parly candidate (Cons) Oldham Central & Royton 1992; memb Ctee Patrons and Assocs of Manchester City Art Galleries 1982–94, memb Manchester North Valuation and Community Charge Tbnl 1988–92, chm Bolton Cancer Res Campaign 1992–95, govr and tstee Bolton Sch 1992–, dep chm Salford Royal Hosps NHS Tst 1993–97, memb Bd of Mgmnt Bolton Lads' & Girls' Club 1994–97 (dir 1997–2002), advsr to Abbot of Ampleforth 1998–2004, pres Nat Benevolent Instn 2006–, patron Oxford Parent Infant Project (OXPIP) 2006–, tstee The Disability Partnership 2007–, co-chair Women in Public Policy 2007–; *Recreations* reading, football, country pursuits, cinema; *Clubs* Special Forces; *Style*— The Baroness Morris of Bolton, OBE; ✉ House of Lords, London SW1A 0PW (tel 020 7219 3000)

MORRIS OF HANDSWORTH, Baron (Life Peer 2006), of Handsworth in the County of West Midlands; Sir William Manuel (Bill) Morris; kt (2003); *b* 19 October 1938, Jamaica; *Educ* Mizpah Sch Jamaica, Handsworth Tech Coll; *m* Minetta (d 1990); 2 s (Garry, Clyde); *Career* arrived in UK from Jamaica 1954, joined Hardy Spicers c1955, memb TGWU 1958, shop steward 1963, memb TGWU Gen Exec Cncl 1971–72; TGWU (employed): Nottingham/Derby dist organiser 1973–76, Northampton dist sec 1976–79, nat sec Passenger Servs Trade Gp 1979–86, dep gen sec 1986–91, gen sec 1991–2003; memb Exec Bd Int Transport Workers' Fedn 1986–2003, memb Gen Cncl and Exec Ctee TUC 1988–2003, pres TUC 2000–01, memb Cncl ACAS 1997–2003; non-exec dir Bank of England 1998–2006; chm Morris Inquiry 2004; past chm Conf Arrangements Ctee Lab Pty; memb: Cmmn for Racial Equality 1977–87, Prince of Wales Youth Business Tst 1987–90, Employment Appeals Tbnl 1988–, Economic and Social Affrs Ctee EC 1990–92, New Deal Taskforce 1997–99, Royal Cmmn on Reform of House of Lords 1999, Cmmn for Integrated Tport 1999–2005, ARB 2001–05, Panel of Mergers and Take Overs 2005–; memb Gen Advsy Bd: IBA 1981–86, BBC 1987–88; non-exec dir ECB 2004–; chllr: Univ of Technol Jamaica 2000–, Staffordshire Univ 2004–; hon degrees: Southbank Univ, Open Univ, Leeds Metropolitan Univ, Univ of Westminster, Greenwich Univ, Teesside Univ, Thames Valley Univ, UC of Northampton, Staffordshire Univ, Middlesex Univ, Univ of Warwick, Univ of Birmingham, Univ of Luton, Univ of Technol Jamaica, Univ of Nottingham; FRSA, FCGI; OJ 2002; *Recreations* family life, walking, gardening, music; *Style*— The Rt Hon the Lord Morris of Handsworth, OJ; ✉ House of Lords, London SW1A 0PW (website www.billmorris.info)

MORRIS OF MANCHESTER, Baron (Life Peer UK 1997), of Manchester in the County of Greater Manchester; Alfred Morris; PC (1979), AO (1991), QSO (1989); s of George Henry Morris, and Jessie, *née* Murphy; *b* 23 March 1928; *Educ* Ruskin Coll Oxford, St Catherine's Coll Oxford, Univ of Manchester; *m* 1950, Irene Jones; 2 s, 2 da; *Career* former schoolmaster and univ lectr; Parly candidate (Lab & Co-op) Liverpool Garston 1951, MP (Lab & Co-op) Manchester Wythenshawe 1964–97; PPS to: Min of Agric Fisheries and Food 1964–67, Lord Pres of the Cncl and ldr of House of Commons 1968–70; UK delg to UN Gen Assembly 1965; Parly advsr to the Police Fedn 1970–74, memb Gen Advsy Cncl BBC 1968–74 and 1983–97; chm PLP Food and Agric Gp 1971–74 (vice-chm 1970–71), Britain's first min for disabled people 1974–79; chm World Planning Gp appointed to draft Charter for the 1980s for disabled people worldwide 1979–80 and Charter for the New Millennium 1998–2000; co-opted memb United States Congressional Ctee of Inquiry into Gulf War Illnesses 2001–; oppn front bench spokesman: on social servs 1979–81 (and 1970–74), for disabled people 1981–92; chm: Co-op Parly Gp 1982–84, Anzac Gp of MPs and Peers 1982–97 (pres 1997–); jt treas Br-American Parly Gp 1983–97; piloted Chronically Sick and Disabled Persons Act 1970 through Parl as a private memb, also the Food and Drugs (Milk) Act 1970 and the Police Act 1972; first recipient of Field Marshal Lord Harding award for distinguished serv to the disabled 1971; Louis Braille Meml award for outstanding servs to the blind 1972; Henry H Kessler Prize awarded quinquennially for inspired leadership and historic achievements for people with disabilities around the World 2000; tstee: Hallé Orch, Crisis at Christmas, Earl Snowdon's Fund for Handicapped Students; chm Managing Tstees of Parly Contributory Pension Scheme and of House of Commons Members' Fund 1983–97; vice-pres Parly and Sci Ctee 1991– (chm 1988–91), appointed to Select Ctee on Privileges 1994–97; pres: Co-op Congress 1995, Soc of Chiropodists and Podiatrists 1998, Haemophilia Soc 1999; govr St Dunstan's 1989; Earl Snowdon Award 1997, AA Award 1998, People of the Year Award for lifetime achievement 2000; Paul Harris fell of Rotary International 1993; Hon DUniv Salford 1997, Hon LLD Univ of Manchester 1998; hon fell Manchester Metropolitan Univ 1990, hon fell Assoc of Building Engineers 2000; hon assoc BVA 1982; *Books* Human Relations in Industry (1960), VAT: A Tax on the Consumer (1970), Parliamentary Scrutiny by Committee (1971); author of numerous publications on the problems and needs of disabled people; *Recreations* gardening, tennis, snooker and chess; *Style*— The Rt Hon the Lord Morris of Manchester, PC, AO, QSO; ✉ House of Lords, London SW1A 0PW

MORRIS OF YARDLEY, Baroness (Life Peer UK 2005), of Yardley in the County of West Midlands; Estelle Morris; PC (1999); da of Charles Morris, former MP, and Pauline Morris; *b* 17 June 1952; *Educ* Whalley Range HS, Coventry Coll of Educn; *Career* teacher Sidney Stringer Sch and Community Coll 1974–92; cncllr Warwick DC 1979–91 (ldr Lab Gp

1982–89); MP (Lab) Birmingham Yardley 1992–2005; oppn whip 1994–95, oppn spokesperson on educn 1995–97, Parly under-sec of state (school standards) DfEE 1997–98, min of state for school standards 1998–2001, sec of state for educn and skills 2001–02, min of state for the arts 2003–05; *Style—* The Rt the Lady Morris of Yardley, PC

MORRISON, Alasdair; s of Alexander Morrison (d 1999), of North Uist, Western Isles, and Marion, *née* MacLeod; *b* 18 November 1968; *Educ* Paible Sch North Uist, Nicolson Inst Isle of Lewis; *m* 23 June 1995, Erica, da of Donald Alex MacPherson; 2 c (Ceitidh b 8 Jan 1999, Donald Alex b 29 June 2001); *Career* journalist BBC 1989–98, ed An Gaidheal Ur (Gaelic language newspaper) 1997–99, MSP (Lab) Western Isles 1999–2007; Scot Parl: dep min for Highlands and Islands, Gaelic and Tourism 1999–2001, memb Justice Ctee 2001–, memb Rural Devpt Ctee 2001–; *Style—* Alasdair Morrison, Esq

MORRISON, Anne Catherine; da of George Charles Morrison (d 1993), and Persis Mae, *née* Ross; *b* 18 August 1959; *Educ* Richmond Lodge Sch Belfast, Churchill Coll Cambridge (MA); *m* 1989, Robert John Jarvis Johnstone, s of Robert Johnstone (d 1974); 1 da (Alice Emily b 21 May 1993); *Career* BBC TV: trainee 1981–83, researcher and dir Documentary Features Dept 1983–87, prodr Holiday 1987–88, series prodr Crimewatch UK 1988–90, chief asst Documentary Features Dept 1990–92, exec prodr Taking Liberties and Rough Justice 1992, dep head Features Dept 1992–94, head Features Dept 1994–96; BBC Prodn: head Consumer and Leisure Dept 1996–98, head Features and Events Dept 1998–2000, controller Leisure and Factual Entertainment 2000–01, controller General Factual Gp 2001–03, controller Documentaries and Contemporary Factual 2003–06, controller Network Production 2006–; *Recreations* reading, running, genealogy, gardening; *Style—* Ms Anne Morrison

MORRISON, Hon Antoinette Sara Frances Sibell; da of 2 Viscount Long (ka 1944), and Frances Laura, *née* Charteris (d 1990); *b* 9 August 1934; *Educ* England, France; *m* 1954 (m dis), Hon Sir Charles Andrew Morrison; 1 s, 1 da; *Career* dir General Electric Co 1975–98; non-exec dir: Abbey National Building Society 1979–95, The Fourth Channel Television Co 1980–85, Imperial Group 1982–86, Carlton Television Ltd 1991–99, New Millennium Experience Co 1997–2001; chm: NCVO 1977–81 (vice-chm 1970–77), Charter European Trust plc 1993–2002; memb: Cncl Policy Studies Inst 1983–93, UK Round Table for Sustainable Devpt 1995–98, HEPI Advsy Bd 2006–; former memb: Nat Consumer Cncl, The Volunteer Centre, Wilts CC (until 1970), Cncl Family Policy Studies Centre; dir Nat Radiological Protection Bd 1989–97; dep pres WWF Int 2000–05, chm WWF-UK 1998–2001 (tstee 1996–); govr Wiltshire Coll 1993–; pro-chllr and chm Univ of Bath 1999–2005; hon fell Imperial Coll London 1993 (govr 1986–2002), Hon DBA Coventry Univ 1994, Hon LLD De Montfort Univ 1998, Hon DSc Univ of Buckingham 1999; FCGI 2005; *Style—* The Hon Sara Morrison; ✉ 16 Groom Place, London SW1X 7BA; Wyndham's Farm, Wedhampton, Devizes, Wiltshire SN10 3QE

MORRISON, Dr (Philip) Blake; s of Arthur Blakemore Morrison (d 1991), of Skipton, N Yorks, and Agnes, *née* O'Shea (d 1997); *b* 8 October 1950; *Educ* Ermysted's GS Skipton, Univ of Nottingham (BA), McMaster Univ (MA), UCL (PhD); *m* 1976, Katherine Ann, da of Robert C Drake; 2 s (Seth Nicholas b 1981, Gabriel Eli b 1989), 1 da (Aphra Grace b 1984); *Career* various pt/t teaching posts 1976–81 (Open Univ, Goldsmiths Coll London, Furzedown Coll), poetry and fiction ed TLS 1978–81, dep literary ed Observer 1981–86 (literary ed 1986–89); Independent on Sunday: literary ed 1990–94, staff writer 1994–95; prof of creative and life writing Goldsmiths Coll London 2003–; poet; chm Poetry Book Soc 1984–87, memb Mgmnt Bd Poetry Soc 1980–83; FRSL 1990; *Awards* Eric Gregory Award, Somerset Maugham Award, Dylan Thomas Meml Prize, EM Forster Award, Volvo/Waterstone's Award for Non-Fiction 1993, J R Ackerley Prize 1994; *Books* The Movement (1980), Dark Glasses (1984), The Ballad of the Yorkshire Ripper (1987), The Yellow House (children's book, 1987), And When Did You Last See Your Father? (memoir, 1993), The Cracked Pot (play, 1996), As If (non-fiction, 1997), Too True (stories and essays, 1998), Dr Ox's Experiment (libretto, 1998), Selected Poems (1999), The Justification of Johann Gutenberg (2000), G (libretto, 2002), Things My Mother Never Told Me (non-fiction, 2002), Oedipus (trans, 2003), Antigone (trans, 2003), The Man With Two Gaffers (play, 2006), South of the River (novel, 2007), Elephant & Castle (libretto, 2007), Lisa's Sex Strike (play, 2007); *Recreations* tennis, football, running; *Style—* Dr Blake Morrison; ✉ c/o PFD, 34–43 Russell Street, London WC2B 5HA (tel 020 7344 1000, fax 020 7836 9541)

MORRISON, Dennis John; s of Leonard Tait Morrison, of Sale, Cheshire, and Alice, *née* Hutson; *b* 20 May 1942; *Educ* Ashton upon Mersey Boys Sch, Lymm GS, Univ of Manchester (BA, Dip Town and Country Planning); *m* 18 March 1967, Frances Joan (Polly), da of Frank Pollard, of Roundhay, Leeds; 1 s (Duncan John b 1971), 1 da (Rosalyn Jane b 1973); *Career* planning offr Lancashire CC 1966–70, sr planning offr Welsh Office Cardiff 1970–75, reg superintending planner DOE Manchester 1975–81, head NW Enterprise Unit DOE Manchester 1981–84, regnl controller Merseyside Task Force Liverpool 1984–89, regnl dir E Midlands Region DOE and Tport Nottingham 1989–94, dir Environment and Tport Govt Office for the E Midlands 1994–97, regnl dir Govt Office for Merseyside 1997–98, regnl dir Govt Office for the E Midlands 1998–2003; memb Advsy Bd Highways Agency 2000–03; special prof Faculty of the Built Environment Univ of Nottingham 2000–; non-exec dir Independent Decision Makers Ltd 2002–; memb Exec Ctee Liverpool Anglican Cathedral; dir and tstee Arkwright Soc; Freeman Burgess of the Altrincham Court LEET; MRTPI, FRGS; *Recreations* antiquarian horologist, collector of antiquarian books, gardening, hill walking; *Clubs* Altrincham 41; *Style—* Dennis Morrison, Esq; ✉ e-mail dennisandpolly@ortelius.freeserve.co.uk

MORRISON, Fiona Jane; da of John Black (Ian) Morrison (d 1994), and Marion Lilian Morgan (now Mrs Bicknell); *b* 2 May 1957, Stevenage, Herts; *Educ* Dauntsey's Sch Devizes, Selwyn Coll Cambridge (MA, Rowing blues, pres Cambridge Univ Women's Boat Club); *m* 14 July 1984, Dr Eivind James Dullforce (d 2006); *Career* Lane Clark & Peacock: actuarial trainee 1979–82, staff actuary 1982–84, ptnr 1984–; Inst of Actuaries: memb Cncl 2001–, memb Pensions Bd 2001– (dep chm 2006–), chm Pensions Guidance Ctee 2002–06 (memb 1996–2006), hon sec 2004–06; Liveryman Worshipful Co of Actuaries, tstee Co of Actuaries Charitable Tst 2004–; FIA 1984, fell Soc of Actuaries in Ireland; *Recreations* ski touring, rowing; *Clubs* Lansdowne, Leander; *Style—* Miss Fiona Morrison; ✉ Lane Clark & Peacock LLP, 30 Old Burlington Street, London W1S 3NN (tel 020 7439 2266, fax 020 7439 0183, e-mail fiona.morrison@lcp.uk.com)

MORRISON, Frances Margaret (Fran); da of Lt Cdr William Morrison, OBE, RNVR, of Cove, Scotland, and Hilary Mary, *née* Wootton; *Educ* Queen's Park Sch Glasgow, Univ of St Andrews (MA); *m* 1984 (m dis); 2 s (Adam b 1984, Dominic b 1986); *Career* broadcaster and media conslt, tobacco and oil industry communications mangr; news and current affrs reporter/presenter BBC Radio and TV, first woman presenter of BBC TV's Newsnight at its launch 1979; reporter/presenter BBC TV: Nationwide 1981–83, 60 Minutes 1983–84; reporter BBC TV Watchdog 1984–85, reporter various documentary progs BBC TV 1978–86, presenter various arts and music progs BBC TV 1978–86; reporter/presenter Thames TV, Channel 4, Sky TV and BBC Radio Womans Hour 1986–91; media conslt 1986–91, freelance journalist 1978–91, head of media rels and communications Shell UK Ltd 1991–99; British American Tobacco plc: mangr external communications 1999–2000, head corp communications; MIPR, FRSA 1992; *Recreations* travel, theatre, visual arts; *Style—* Ms Fran Morrison; ✉ c/o British American Tobacco, Globe House, Temple Place, London WC2R 2PG (tel 020 7845 1000)

MORRISON, Sir (Alexander) Fraser; kt (1998), CBE (1993); s of late Alexander Ferrier Sharp Morrison, and Catherine Colina, *née* Fraser; *b* 20 March 1948; *Educ* Tain Royal Acad, Univ of Edinburgh (BSc); *m* 23 Sept 1972, Patricia Janice, da of late Peter David Murphy; 1 s (Alexander Peter b 13 Jan 1974), 2 da (Claire Catherine b 6 June 1975, Sarah-Jane b 21 Aug 1977); *Career* Morrison Construction Group: dir 1970–76, md 1976–84, chm and md 1984–96, exec chm 1996–2000; dir: Shand Ltd 1978–89, Alexander Shand Holdings Ltd 1982–86; chm: Teasses Capital Ltd 2003–, Ramco Hldgs Ltd 2005–; dep chm Clydesdale Bank plc 1999–2004 (non-exec dir 1994–99), memb Bd Yorkshire Bank plc 1999–2004; FCEC: chm Scotland 1991–92, chm 1993–94, vice-pres 1994–96; dir Chief Execs Orgn 2003; chm: Highlands and Islands Enterprise 1992–98 (dir 1991–92), Univ of Highlands and Islands Project 1997–2001; Hon DTech 1995 and 1997; Hon DUniv Open 2000; CEng, MIHT, FRSA 1990, FICE 1993, FScotvec 1994, FCIOB 1995; *Recreations* golf, skiing, shooting, opera, art; *Style—* Sir Fraser Morrison, CBE; ✉ Teasses House, Leven, Fife KY8 5PG (tel 01334 828048, fax 01334 828 049)

MORRISON, (William) Garth; CBE (1994), JP (2001); s of Walter Courtenay Morrison (d 1993), of Gullane, E Lothian, and Audrey Elizabeth, *née* Gilbert (d 2000); *b* 8 April 1943; *Educ* Pembroke Coll Cambridge, Pangbourne Coll (Queen's Gold medal), RNC Dartmouth (Queen's Telescope), RNEC Manadon (Queen's Sword), RNC Greenwich; *m* 25 July 1970, Gillian, da of Stanley Cheetham, of Oldham, Lancs; 2 s (Alastair b 22 Nov 1972, Christopher b 15 May 1974), 1 da (Clare (twin) b 15 May 1974); *Career* served RN 1961–73 (ret Lt); farmer in family partnership 1973–, dir Top Hat Holdings (formerly Scotfresh Ltd) 1975–97; The Scout Assoc: area cmmr E Lothian 1973–81, chief cmmr Scotland 1981–88, chief scout UK and dependent territories 1988–96, vice-pres 1996–, hon pres Scottish Cncl 2001–; memb World Scout Ctee 1991–2002; chm: E and Midlothian NHS Tst 1993–98, Royal Infirmary of Edinburgh NHS Tst 1998–99, Lothian Primary Care NHS Tst 1999–2004, Lamp of Lothian Collegiate Tst 2001– (tstee 1978–2001); vice-pres Cwlth Youth Exchange Cncl 1997–; memb: Lothian and Borders Ctee of Royal Jubilee and Prince's Tsts 1979–86, Scot Community Educn Cncl 1988–95 (hon fell 1995), Nat Lottery Charities Bd 1995–99; tstee MacRobert Tsts 1998– (chm 2007–); HM Lord-Lt E Lothian 2001– (DL 1984–2001); MIEE 1973; *Books* chapter in The Scottish Juvenile Justice System (ed Martin and Murray, 1982); *Recreations* golf, sailing, scouting; *Style—* W Garth Morrison, Esq, CBE; ✉ West Fenton, North Berwick, East Lothian EH39 5AL (tel 01620 842154); W Courtenay Morrison & Co, West Fenton, North Berwick, East Lothian EH39 5AL (tel 01620 842154, fax 01620 842052, e-mail garthm@westfenton.co.uk)

MORRISON, Prof George Chalmers; s of Donald Crerar Morrison (d 1956), of Bearsden, Glasgow, and Annie Sibbald, *née* Johnston (d 1984); *b* 14 May 1930; *Educ* Bearsden Acad, Univ of Glasgow (BSc, PhD); *m* 7 Oct 1961, Prudence, da of Albert Donald Valentine Knowers (d 1975), of Lymington, Hants; 3 da (Leslie b 25 Aug 1962, Vanessa b 10 Jan 1965, Nicola b 24 Dec 1965); *Career* res assoc Univ of Chicago 1957–60, princ scientific offr AERE Harwell 1961–65 (res fell 1954–57), scientist Argonne Nat Laboratory Illinois 1965–73; Univ of Birmingham: prof 1973–97 (chair of nuclear structure), dep dean Faculty of Sci 1985–88, dean Faculty of Sci 1988–91, head Sch of Physics and Space Res 1990–97, prof emeritus 1997–; SERC: memb Nuclear Structure Ctee 1974–78, 1982–86 and 1991–94, chm 1992–94, memb Nuclear Physics Bd 1984–87 and 1992–94, memb Physics Ctee 1984–87, chm Nuclear Physics Ctee 1994; memb: Working Gp on Nuclear Physics Euro Sci Fndn 1981–84, Bd Nuclear Physics Div Euro Physical Soc 1984–92, Nuclear Physics Euro Co-ord Ctee 1993–97, Exec Ctee Euro Physical Soc Cncl 1993–98 (Cncl delg 1991–98); sci ed Europhys News 2000– (chm Editorial Bd 1998–); FInstP, FAPS, FEPS; *Recreations* golf, walking, philately; *Clubs* Harborne Golf; *Style—* Prof George Morrison; ✉ 184 Lordswood Road, Harborne, Birmingham B17 8QH (tel 0121 427 3248); School of Physics and Astronomy, The University of Birmingham, Edgbaston, Birmingham B15 2TT (tel 0121 414 4651, fax 0121 414 4577, e-mail g.c.morrison@bham.ac.uk)

MORRISON, Graham; s of Robert Morrison (d 2000), and Robina Sandison, née Wilson; *b* 2 February 1951; *Educ* Brighton Coll, Jesus Coll Cambridge (MA, DipArch, Brancusi award); *m* 1, 20 Feb 1973 (m dis 1996); 1 da (Laura b 16 Sept 1981), 1 s (Alan b 6 Nov 1984); m 2, 11 July 2001, M R Lovric; *Career* architect; co-fndr (with Bob Allies, *qv*) Allies and Morrison 1983 (Architectural Practice of the Year Award Building Awards 2004); architects to Royal Festival Hall 1994–98; other projects incl: The Clove Bldg (RIBA Award 1991), Pierhead Liverpool 1995, Sarum Hall Sch (RIBA Award 1996, Civic Tst Award 1996), Nunnery Square Sheffield (RIBA Award 1996), Rosalind Franklin Bldg Newnham Coll Cambridge (RIBA Award 1996), Br Embassy Dublin (RIBA Award 1997), Abbey Mills Pumping Station Stratford (RIBA Award 1997), Rutherford Info Servs Bldg Goldsmiths Coll London (RIBA Award 1998), Blackburn House London (RIBA Award 2000), Blackwell House Cumbria (RIBA Award 2003, Civic Tst Award 2003), extension to Horniman Museum London (Civic Tst Award 2004, RIBA Award 2004), 85 Southwark Street London (Civic Tst Award 2004, Building of the Year Award RIBA London 2004, Corporate Workplace Building Br Cncl for Offices Awards 2004); exhibitions: New British Architecture (Japan) 1994, Retrospective (USA Schs of Architecture) 1996–98; memb: Nat Cncl RIBA 1992–95 (dir RIBA Jl 1994–98), Architecture Advsy Ctee Arts Cncl of England 1997–98, Royal Fine Art Cmmn 1998–99, CABE Design Review Ctee 2000–04, London Advsy Ctee English Heritage 2001–; external examiner Univ of Portsmouth 2003–05, visiting prof Univ of Nottingham 2004–05; RIBA 1976; *Publications* Allies and Morrison (Univ of Michigan Architectural Papers, 1996); *Recreations* blues music, Venice; *Style—* Graham Morrison, Esq; ✉ 5 Winchester Wharf, 4 Clink Street, Southwark, London SE1 9DL (tel 020 7357 8468); Allies and Morrison, 85 Southwark Street, London SE1 0HX (tel 020 7921 0100, fax 020 7921 0101, e-mail gmorrison@alliesandmorrison.co.uk)

MORRISON, His Hon Judge Howard Andrew Clive; CBE (2007, OBE 1988), QC (2001); s of Howard Edward Morrison (d 1986), and Roma, *née* Wilkinson (d 1998); *b* 20 July 1949, Kent; *Educ* Univ of London (LLB), Inns of Court Sch of Law; *m* 1980, Kathryn Margaret, *née* Moore; 1 da (Sarah Elizabeth), 1 s (Edward Howard James); *Career* called to the Bar: Gray's Inn 1977, Fiji 1988, Eastern Caribbean 1990; VSO: vol Ghana 1968–69, desk offr Zambia and Malawi 1975–76; practising barr Midland and Oxford Circuit 1977–85, resident magistrate then chief magistrate Fiji and sr magistrate Tuvalu 1985–87, locum attorney-gen Anguilla 1988–89, practising barr Midland and Oxford Circuit 1989–2004, def barr UN War Crimes Tbnls The Hague and Arusha 1998–2004, circuit judge 2004–, sr judge Sovereign Base Areas Cyprus 2007; lectr in int law, advocacy teacher/trainer Gray's Inn 1994, Holding Redlich distinguished visiting fell Monash Univ 2007; author of numerous legal articles on int criminal law; Bar Cncl: memb Race Rels Ctee 1996–2002, memb Equal Opportunities Ctee 2002–03; memb: Int Bar Assoc, Cwlth Judges and Magistrates Assoc, Br Inst for Int and Comparative Law; Subalt Queen's Regt and Parachute Regt (TAVR) then RARO 1970–99; FRGS 1991; *Recreations* travel, scuba diving, sailing, flying; *Clubs* Portsmouth Offshore Gp; *Style—* His Hon Judge Morrison, CBE, QC; ✉ 36 Bedford Row, London WC1R 4JH (tel 020 7421 8000)

MORRISON, Hon Hugh; s of 2 Baron Margadale (d 2003), of Wilts, and Clare, *née* Barclay; *b* 7 November 1960, London; *Educ* Eton, Ealing Coll of HE (BA); *m* 1, Jan 1986 (m dis), Jane, *née* Jenks; 1 s (Geordie Anthony b 29 Sept 1989), 1 da (Amber Belinda b 14 Sept 1993); m 2, Aug 2004, Mary Dorothy Wordsworth, *née* Drysdale; *Career* racehorse trainer 1997–, horses trained incl Pastoral Pursuits (champion sprinter 2005) and Alcazar (Group One winner); dir Islay Estates Co Ltd 1989; *Recreations* country sports; *Clubs* White's;

M

Style— The Hon Hugh Morrison; ✉ Summerdown, East Ilsely, Newbury, Berkshire RG20 7LB (tel 01635 281678, fax 01635 281746, e-mail hughie@hughiemorrison.co.uk)

MORRISON, (William) Ivan; s of William Morrison, of Coleraine, NI, and Wilhelmina, *née* Stirling; *b* 15 March 1949; *Educ* Royal Sch Dungannon, Univ of Glasgow (BVMS, PhD); *m* 14 March 1974, Sheila Jean, da of James Orr; 3 s (Liam James b 17 Aug 1974, Neil Ivan b 29 May 1977, Euan Thomas b 22 Oct 1979), 1 da (Karen Sarah b 3 Nov 1982); *Career* Int Lab for Research on Animal Diseases Nairobi: postdoctoral research fell 1975–77, scientist 1978–85, sr scientist and prog leader 1985–89; head Div of Immunology and Pathology Inst for Animal Health 1990–2002, prof of immunology Royal (Dick) Sch of Vet Studies Univ of Edinburgh 2002–; visiting prof: Univ of Glasgow 1996, Univ of Bristol 1999; scientific advsr to: Wellcome Tst, DFID (formerly ODA), DEFRA (formerly MAFF), Horserace Betting Levy Board; MRCVS 1972, FRCPath 1996 (MRCPath 1986), FRSE 1997; *Awards* Pfizer Award 1990, Wellcome Tst Medal for Vet Research 1991, Distinguished Vet Immunologist Award American Assoc of Vet Immunologists 1994, RASE Bledisloe Award 2001; *Publications* The Ruminant Immune System in Health and Disease (ed, 1986), Cell-Mediated Immunity in Ruminants (jtly ed, 1994); author of over 150 articles in scientific jls; *Style—* Professor Ivan Morrison, FRSE; ✉ Centre for Tropical Veterinary Medicine, Royal (Dick) School of Veterinary Studies, The University of Edinburgh, Easter Bush Veterinary Centre, Roslin, Midlothian EH25 9RG (tel 0131 650 6216, e-mail ivan.morrison@ed.ac.uk)

MORRISON, James Fyffe Thomson; s of John Morrison (d 1952), and Margaret Morrison (d 1984); *b* 11 April 1932; *Educ* Hillhead HS Glasgow, Glasgow Sch of Art (DA), Jordanhill Coll of Educn; *m* 12 April 1955, Dorothy Jean Allison, da of James Barclay McCormack; 1 s (John Coull b 25 Aug 1959), 1 da (Judith Kate b 10 Aug 1961); *Career* oil and watercolour painter; travels and paints extensively in the Arctic, Southern Africa and France; visiting artist Hospitalfield House 1962 and 1963, head of dept Duncan of Jordanstone Coll of Art 1978–87 (lectr 1965–78); presenter Scope (BBC) 1976–, writer and presenter A Scottish Picture Show (STV) 1988; memb: Soc of Scottish Artists 1963 (Cncl 1964–67), Bd of Govrs Duncan Jordanstone Coll of Art 1988–; Torrance Award RGI 1958, Arts Cncl Travelling Award 1968; Hon DUniv Stirling 1986; RSW 1968, RSA 1992 (ARSA 1973); *Solo Exhibitions* McClure Gallery 1959, Scottish Gallery 1959, 1989, 1992, 1994, 1997, 1999 and 2002, Reid Gall 1962, Vaughan Coll Leicester 1968, Richard Demarco Gallery 1968, Compass Gallery 1970, Galleria Vaccarino 1971, Steiger Gallery 1973, Düsseldorf Kunstmesse 1974, Edinburgh Festival Exhbn (Scottish Gallery) 1978, Thackeray Gallery 1979, 1981, 1985, 1995, 1997 and 2000, Fine Art Soc 1986, Waddington and Sheill Gallery 1987, Perth Festival Exhbn (Perth Museum and Art Gallery) 1988, Talbot Rice Gallery (Univ of Edinburgh) 1995, Macaulay Gallery 1989, William Hardie Gallery 1990, Riverside Gallery 1991; *Work in Various Collections* incl: Duke of Edinburgh, Scottish Arts Cncl, Aberdeen Art Gallery, Dundee Museum and Art Gallery, Kelvingrove Art Gallery and Museum, Perth Museum and Art Gallery, Bank of Scotland, Univ of Edinburgh, Tayside Educn Ctee, British Linen Bank, Grampian Television, Clydesdale Bank, Univ of Glasgow, BBC, Low and Bonar plc, Glaxo Wellcome, Conoco, SISIS Equipment Ltd, IBM, Robert Fleming Holdings Ltd; numerous works in private collections in USA, Britain, Canada and Europe; *Publications* Aff the Squerr (2 edn 1990), Paris in Winter (1992); *Recreations* playing the recorder in a chamber group; *Style—* James Morrison, RSA; ✉ Craigview House, Usan, Montrose, Angus, Tayside DD10 9SD (tel and fax 01674 672639); The Scottish Gallery, 16 Dundas Street, Edinburgh

MORRISON, Jasper; s of Alec Morrison, and Dinah, *née* Herbert; *b* 11 November 1959, London; *Educ* Bryanston, Kingston Poly, RCA; *m* 2004, Ruth, *née* Donaghey; *Career* designer; opened: Office for Design London 1986, Paris studio 2002; designs for leading Italian mfrs incl: Alessi, Cappellini, Flos, Vitra, Rosenthal, Rowenta; designer Hannover Tram for Üstra 1997, furnished public spaces in Tate Modern London 2000; Designer of the Year Paris Design Fair 2000; RDI 2001; *Publications* Designs, Projects & Drawings 1981–89 (1990), A World Without Words (ed, 1992, 2 edn 1998), A Book of Spoons (ed, 1997), A Tram for Hanover (1998), International Design Yearbook (ed, 1999), Everything but the Walls (2002 and 2006), Super Normal (2007); *Style—* Jasper Morrison, Esq; ✉ Jasper Morrison Ltd, 51 Hoxton Square, London N1 6PB (e-mail mail@jaspermorrison.com)

MORRISON, John; s of Thomas Patrick Morrison, and Marie, *née* Boylan; *b* 6 March 1949; *Educ* St Edward's Coll Liverpool, St Catherine's Coll Oxford (BA); *m* 29 Feb 1980, Judith, da of Ronald Lee, of Bury, Lancs; 1 s (Nicholas b 1981), 1 da (Joanna b 1984); *Career* news trainee BBC 1971, scriptwriter ITN 1973, prog ed Channel 4 News 1982, features ed The Independent 1986, ed Newsnight BBC 1987, ed Assignment BBC 1990, ed Six O'Clock News BBC 1993–95, managing ed BBC News 1995–96, ed BBC TV News 1996–97, exec ed Core News BBC TV 1997–99, head of ops BBC World Service News 1999–2000, ed BBC World News Service News and Current Affairs 2000–02; Morrison Media Consultants 2002–; *Style—* John Morrison, Esq; ✉ e-mail john@morrisonmedia.co.uk

MORRISON, Hon (Dame) Mary Anne; DCVO (1982, CVO 1970); does not use style of Dame; da of 1 Baron Margadale (d 1996); *b* 17 May 1937; *Educ* Heathfield Sch Ascot, abroad; *Career* woman of the bedchamber to HM The Queen 1960–; *Style—* The Hon Mary Morrison, DCVO; ✉ tel 01747 820231

MORRISON, Michael John; s of John Percy Morrison, JP, and Kathleen Morrison; *b* 31 March 1939; *Educ* Fettes, St Catharine's Coll Cambridge (MA, LLB); *m* 11 Sept 1965, June; 1 s (Nicholas James b 21 Dec 1967), 1 da (Louise Charlotte b 23 June 1971); *Career* admitted slr 1965; ptnr Parker Garrett 1969–82; sr ptnr: Taylor Garrett 1988 (ptnr 1982–88), Taylor Joynson Garrett 1989–99; chm: Yuills Ltd 1975–, Bride (Exel) Ltd 1997–, Skelton Gp Ltd 2000–; dir: Leif Hoegh UK Ltd 1978–, Norwegian American Cruises UK Ltd 1980–87; memb Law Soc; *Recreations* golf, squash; *Clubs* Moor Park Golf, Melton Mowbray GC; *Style—* Michael Morrison, Esq; ✉ Yuills Ltd, 104 Park Street, London W1K 6NF (tel 020 7499 8447)

MORRISON, Sheriff Nigel Murray Paton; QC (Scot 1988); s of David Paton Morrison (d 1968), of Edinburgh, and Dilys Trenholm Pritchard or Morrison (d 1995); *b* 18 March 1948; *Educ* Rannoch Sch; *Career* called to the Bar Inner Temple 1972, admitted to Scot Bar 1975; asst ed Session Cases 1976–82, asst clerk to Rules Cncl 1978–84, clerk of faculty Faculty of Advocates 1979–86, standing jr counsel to Scot Devpt Dept (planning) 1982–86, temp sheriff 1982–96, Sheriff of Lothian and Borders 1996–, dir of Judicial Studies 2000–04; chm Social Security Appeal Tbnl 1982–91, counsel to Sec of State under the Private Legislation Procedure (Scot) Act (1936) 1986–96, first counsel to Lord Pres of Court of Session 1989–96 (jr and second counsel 1984–89), chm Med Appeal Tbnl 1991–96; tstee Nat Library of Scotland 1989–99; memb Faculty of Advocates; *Publications* contrib to: Stair Memorial Encyclopaedia of the Laws of Scotland, Macphail on Sheriff Court Practice (2 edn); princ author Green's Annotated Rules of the Court of Session; ed Sentencing Practice; *Recreations* being taken for walks by my dogs, music, riding, Scottish country dancing; *Clubs* New (Edinburgh); *Style—* Sheriff Nigel Morrison, QC; ✉ Sheriff's Chambers, Sheriff Court House, 27 Chambers Street, Edinburgh EH1 1LB (tel 0131 225 2525, fax 0131 225 4422)

MORRISON, Richard Duncan; s of Donald Melville Morrison, and Winifred Mary, *née* Stocks; *b* 24 July 1954; *Educ* Univ Coll Sch, Magdalene Coll Cambridge (MA); *m* 1977, Marian, da of Joseph Plant; 2 s (Philip b 1984, Edmund b 1988), 1 da (Katharine b 1985); *Career* asst ed Classical Music Magazine 1977–84, dep ed Early Music Magazine 1985–89; The Times: music critic 1984–89, dep arts ed 1989–90, arts ed 1990–99, columnist 1999–; FRSA 1995; *Recreations* walking, playing the organ; *Style—* Richard Morrison, Esq; ✉ 11 Sunningfields Crescent, London NW4 4RD (tel 020 8202 8028); The Times, 1 Pennington Street, London E1 9XN (tel 020 7782 5038, fax 020 7782 5748, e-mail richard.morrison@thetimes.co.uk)

MORRISON, Robert Charles (Bob); Dr Robert Bruce Morrison, of Bucklebury, Reading, and Christine Davidson, *née* Henry; *b* 22 June 1961; *Educ* St Edward's Sch Tilehurst, Abingdon Sch; *m* 20 July 1985, Hazel Ann, da of (William) John Rudd; 1 s (Simon b 1995); *Career* Radio 210: music presenter 1979–80, trainee journalist 1980–82, journalist 1982–85, sports ed 1985–90, head of news and sport 1990–96; owner First Eleven Sport (sports publicity and promotion co) 1988–; *Recreations* reading, computer programming, transport, photography; *Style—* Bob Morrison, Esq; ✉ First Eleven Sport, PO Box 11, Reading, Berkshire RG6 3DT (tel 0870 741 5117, fax 0870 741 5119, e-mail enquiries@firsteleven.co.uk)

MORRISON, Prof Ronald; s of David Morrison, of Airdrie, and Catherine, *née* Turner (d 1958); *b* 15 April 1946; *Educ* Eastbank Acad, Univ of Strathclyde (BSc), Univ of Glasgow (MSc), Univ of St Andrews (PhD); *m* 17 Oct 1975, Ann Margaret, da of Alistair MacDonald, of Edinburgh; 1 s (David b 1979), 1 da (Catriona b 1981); *Career* prof of software engrg Univ of St Andrews 1985– (sr res fell 1971–72, lectr 1972–84, reader 1984–85); pres Scottish Cross Country Union 1986–87, pres Scottish Athletics Fedn 1997–99 (vice-pres 1995–97); MBCS, CEng, FRSE; *Books* Davie & Morrison Recursive Descent Compiling (jtly, 1981), Cole & Morrison Introduction to S-Algol Programming (jtly, 1982), Sommerville & Morrison Software Development with Ada (jtly, 1987), Atkinson, Burneman & Morrison Data Types and Persistence (1988), Hull, Morrison, Stemple Database Programming Languages (1989), Albamo, Morrison Persistent Object Systems (1993), Morrison, Kennedy Advances in Databases (1996), Morrison, Jorden & Atkinson Advances in Persistent Object Systems (1998); *Recreations* golf, athletics, cross-country running; *Clubs* St Andrews Golf, Fife Athletic, Grail Golfing Soc; *Style—* Prof Ronald Morrison; ✉ School of Computer Science, University of St Andrews, North Haugh, St Andrews, Fife KY16 9SS (tel 01334 463254, fax 01334 463278, e-mail ron@dcs.st-and.ac.uk)

MORRISON, Stephen Roger (Steve); s of Hyman Michael Morrison, and Rebecca, *née* Zolkwer; *b* 3 March 1947; *Educ* Univ of Edinburgh, Nat Film Sch; *m* 1979, Gayle Valerie, *née* Broughall; *Career* Granada Television: joined to set up Northern Documentary Unit 1974, subsequently prodr/dir World in Action, head of regnl progs then head of features and documentaries until 1987, dir of progs 1987–92, md 1993–94; md: Granada Broadcasting 1992, LWT 1994–96; dep chief exec TV Div Granada Group plc 1995, ceo Granada Media plc 1996–2001 (chief operating offr 1996), ceo Granada plc 2001–02; chm Granada Sky Broadcasting 1996–2002; chief exec Granada Film (fndr mid 1980s); Granada network credits incl: The Spanish Civil War, Disappearing World, China, Scully (comedy-drama), The Road to 1984, 28–Up (fourth Seven-Up series); Granada film credits incl: prodr The Magic Toyshop and The Fruit Machine, exec prodr My Left Foot (two Oscars), The Field (Oscar nomination) and Jack & Sarah; chm North West Vision 2003–, chief exec All3Media 2003–; memb Bd: British Screen Advsy Cncl, Edinburgh Int Film Festival; govr NFTS; dir British Screen Finance; FRTS 1998; *Recreations* reading, films and theatre, talking and dining, touring delicatessens; *Clubs* Garrick; *Style—* Steve Morrison, Esq

MORRISON, Susan; da of Glen Wilkinson, and Eileen Iris, *née* Greenwood; *b* 1 July 1960; *Educ* Balderstone HS Rochdale, Loughborough Univ (BSc); *m* (m dis); 1 da; *Career* joined Prison Serv 1981; served at: HMP Holloway, HM YOI Glen Parva, HMP Liverpool N Regnl Office 1981–90; head of residence HMP Leeds 1990–93, secondment to area mangr's office 1993–94, head of throughcare HMP Styal 1994–99, dep govr HMP Manchester 1999–2001, govr HMP Buckley Hall 2001–; Butler Tst Award for outstanding contribution to the quality of prison care 1997; *Recreations* gardening, cooking, singing, theatre, swimming; *Style—* Mrs Susan Morrison; ✉ HMP Buckley Hall, Buckley Hall Road, Rochdale, Lancashire OL12 9DP (tel 01706 514300)

MORRISON-BELL, Sir William Hollin Dayrell; 4 Bt (UK 1905), of Otterburn Hall, Elsdon, Northumberland; s of Capt Sir Charles Reginald Francis Morrison-Bell, 3 Bt (d 1967), and Prudence Caroline, *née* Davies; *b* 21 June 1956; *Educ* Eton, St Edmund Hall Oxford; *m* 6 Oct 1984, Cynthia Hélène Marie, yr da of Teddy White, of Switzerland; 1 s (Thomas Charles Edward b 13 Feb 1985); *Heir* s, Thomas Morrison-Bell; *Career* solicitor; legal advsr for Air Products plc; *Style—* Sir William Morrison-Bell, Bt; ✉ 106 Bishop's Road, London SW6 7AR (tel 020 7736 4940); Highgreen, Tarset, Hexham, Northumberland (tel 01434 240223); Air Products plc, Hersham Place, Molesey Road, Walton on Thames, Surrey KT12 4RZ

MORRISON-LOW, Eur Ing Sir James Richard; 3 Bt (UK 1908), of Kilmaron, Co Fife; DL (Fife 1978); s of Sir Walter John Morrison-Low, 2 Bt, JP (d 1955; assumed by deed poll the additional surname of Morrison 1924), and Dorothy Ruth, *née* de Quincey (d 1946); Sir James Low, 1 Bt, was Lord Provost of Dundee 1893–96; *b* 3 August 1925; *Educ* Harrow, Merchiston Castle Sch Edinburgh, Faraday House (Dip); *m* 1953, Ann Rawson, da of Air Cdre Robert Gordon, CB, CMG, DSO (d 1954); 3 da (Alison Dorothy b 1955, Jean Elspeth (Mrs Larry Keim) b 1957, Susan Elizabeth (Mrs Graham Latham) b 1963), 1 s (Richard Walter b 1959); *Heir* s, Richard Morrison-Low; *Career* served Royal Corps of Signals 1943–47, Capt; dir Osborne & Hunter Ltd Glasgow 1956–89 (electrical engineer 1952), ptnr Kilmaron Electrical Co 1982–99; tstee: Cupar TSB 1958–78, Fife Area Bd TSB 1978–82; dir Nat Inspection Cncl for Electrical Installation Contracting 1982–88, pres Electrical Contractors Assoc of Scotland 1982–84; memb: Technical Ctee Assoc Internationale des Enterprises d'Equipment Electrique 1981–95, Wiring Regulations Ctee Inst of Electrical Engrs 1982–95; chm: Scottish Traction Engine Soc 1961–63, Fife Area Scout Cncl 1966–84; Hon Pipe Maj of Royal Scottish Pipers' Soc 1981–83; CEng, MIEE, FInstD 1982, Eur Ing 1990; *Recreations* piping, shooting, fishing, steam rollers and traction engines; *Clubs* New (Edinburgh); *Style—* Eur Ing Sir James Morrison-Low, Bt, DL; ✉ Kilmaron House, Cupar, Fife KY15 4NE (tel 01334 652248)

MORRISSEY, Caroline Susan; da of Philip John Stanley, of Woking, Surrey, and Rita Dagmar, *née* Hillwood (d 1992); *b* 29 January 1955; *Educ* Woking Co GS for Girls, W London Coll, Lancaster Univ (BEd); *Partner* Franz Andres; 3 da (Corrina Marie b 19 Oct 1980, Astrid Zoe b 1 Dec 1983, Frances Amy b 30 April 1987), 1 s (Andri Niculin b 25 July 1995); *Career* teacher: Brown Rigg Sch 1979–80, Inlingua Sch Switzerland 1981–83; British Council: educnl and cultural asst Berne 1984–91, dir Switzerland 1995– (mangr 1991–95); *Recreations* photography; *Style—* Ms Caroline Morrissey; ✉ The British Council, British Embassy, Thunstrasse 50, 3000 Berne 15, Switzerland

MORRISSEY, David; *b* 21 June 1964; *Educ* RADA; *Career* actor and dir; co dir Tubedale Films; patron: Merseyside Unity Theatre, Merseyside Fact Centre; *Theatre* credits incl: King John (RSC), Peer Gynt (RNT), Much Ado About Nothing (Queen's), Three Days of Rain (Donmar); *Television* credits incl: Framed, Finney, The One That Got Away, Holding On (nominated BAFTA Award), Our Mutual Friend, Big Cat, Pure Wickedness, Sweet Revenge (dir), State of Play (nominated BAFTA Award), Murder, Linda Green, The Deal (RTS Award), Blackpool, Cape Wrath, Sense and Sensibility, One Summer; *Film* Drowning By Numbers, Waterland, The Commissioner, Hilary and Jackie, Fanny and Elvis, The Suicide Club, A Secret Audience (dir), Some Voices, Born Romantic, Bring me your Love (dir), Captain Corelli's Mandolin, Out Of Control, This Little Life, Passer-By (dir, nominated Best New Dir BAFTA Awards)), The Reaping, The Other Boleyn Girl,

The Waterhorse; *Style*— David Morrissey, Esq; ✉ Tubedale Films, c/o Barley Mow Centre, 10 Barley Mow Passage, Chiswick, London W4 4PH (tel 020 8994 6477)

MORRISSEY, Michael Peter; s of Peter Anthony Morrissey (d 2007), of Langshott Wood, Surrey, and Sheila Margaret, *née* Berrett (d 1984); *b* 15 August 1959; *Educ* Worth Sch Sussex, RMA Sandhurst; *m* 30 May 1987, Sally-Anne, da of Derek Harris (d 1996), of St Buryan, Cornwall; 3 da (Rosie Henrietta b 16 Aug 1990, Olivia Mary b 27 March 1996, Francesca Sophie b 26 Oct 1998), 1 s (Hugo William b 18 March 1993); *Career* enlisted 1977; Irish Guards: cmmnd 2 Lt 1978, Lt 1980, Capt 1983, Maj 1988, Co Cmd 1 Irish Guards; serv: Cyprus, Kenya, NI, Belize, Canada, Germany; Thornton Management Ltd London 1989–91, Mercury Asset Management 1991– (now Merrill Lynch Investment Managers), dir Mercury Investment Services 1994–2002, dir Mercury Fund Managers 1998–2002, Liontrust Asset Mgmnt 2002–, dir Liontrust Investment Funds Ltd 2002–; *Recreations* shooting, riding, rugby, cricket; *Clubs* Cavalry and Guards; *Style*— Michael Morrissey, Esq; ✉ Home Farm, Kineton, Guiting Power, Gloucestershire GL54 5UG; Liontrust Asset Management, 2 Savoy Court, London WC2R 0BR (tel 020 7412 1768, e-mail mickey@liontrust.co.uk)

MORROCCO, Leon; s of Alberto Morrocco (d 1998), and Vera Cockburn, *née* Mercer; *b* 4 April 1942; *Educ* Duncan of Jordanstone Coll of Art Dundee, Slade Sch of Art, Edinburgh Coll of Art; *Career* lectr in painting Edinburgh Coll of Art 1965–68, Academia di Brera Milan (Italian Govt scholarship) 1968–69, lectr in painting Glasgow Sch of Art 1969–79, head Dept of Fine Art Chisholm Inst Melbourne 1979–84, lectr in drawing Ballarat Univ Coll Victoria 1991–92; ARSA 1971, RGI 1996; *Solo Exhibitions* Douglas and Foulis Gallery Edinburgh 1965, French Inst Gallery Edinburgh, Traverse Theatre Gallery Edinburgh 1965, The Scottish Gallery Edinburgh 1971 and 1975, The Loomshop Gallery Edinburgh 1973, Univ of St Andrews 1976, Stirling Gallery 1978, Greenock Arts Centre 1978, Univ of Strathclyde 1978, Glasgow Sch of Art 1979, Stuart Gertsman Galleries Melbourne 1982, Australian Galleries Melbourne 1984, 1986, 1992 and 2003, Bonython-Meadmore Gallery Sydney 1988, Australian Galleries Sydney 1989 and 2003, Portland Gallery London 1991 and 1993, Roger Billcliffe Fine Art Glasgow 1993, 1994 and 1998, Open Eye Gallery Edinburgh 1993, 1995, 1997, 2001, 2003 and 2005, Loomshop Gallery Fife 1994, John Martin of London 1996, 1998, 2000 and 2003, Scottish Painting (Chelsea Gallery Palo Alto) 2005, Salon d'Automne Paris 2005, Havana (John Martin Gallery London) 2006, Lalique NY 2007, The Sketchbooks of Leon Morrocco (Open Eye Gallery Edinburgh) 2007; *Work in Collections* HRH Princess Margaret, The Scottish Nat Gallery of Modern Art, Univ of Liverpool, Univ of Strathclyde, Scottish Arts Cncl, Scottish Educn Dept, Leeds Art Gallery, Lillie Art Gallery, Australian Govt Collection, Queensland Govt Collection, United Distillers plc, Touche-Ross plc; *Awards* Andrew Grant Travelling Scholarship 1965, Royal Scottish Acad Latimer Award 1970, Guthrie Award 1971, Royal Bank of Scotland Painting Award 1999; ARSA 1972, RGI 1995; *Style*— Leon Morrocco, RSA, RGI; ✉ 99 St James's Lane, Muswell Hill, London N10 3RJ (tel 020 8883 3774)

MORROW, His Hon Judge Graham Eric; QC (1996); s of George Eric Morrow, of Liverpool, and Freda, *née* Duckett; *b* 14 June 1951; *Educ* Liverpool Coll, Univ of Newcastle upon Tyne (LLB); *m* 31 Jan 1987, Rosalind Nola, da of Samuel Ellis; 1 s (Philip Ellis b 24 July 1987), 2 step da (Erika Suzanne Patrick b 11 May 1971, Lisa Danielle Patrick 6 Oct 1973); *Career* called to the Bar Lincoln's Inn 1974, recorder 1997–2006, circuit judge (Northern Circuit) 2006–; *Recreations* skiing, cricket, hockey; *Style*— His Hon Judge Morrow, QC; ✉ The Queen Elizabeth II Law Courts, Derby Square, Liverpool L2 1XA

MORSE, Christopher George John (Robin); s of John Morse, of Swansea, and Margaret, *née* Maliphant; *b* 28 June 1947; *Educ* Malvern Coll, Wadham Coll Oxford (MA, BCL); *m* 26 March 1983, Louise Angela, da of Ronald Stott (d 1974), of Mirfield, W Yorks; 1 s (Richard b 24 May 1985); *Career* called to the Bar 1971; visiting prof: John Marshall Law Sch Chicago 1979–80, Leuven Univ 1982; King's Coll London: lectr in law 1971–88, reader in law 1988–92, prof of law 1992–, dean and head of Sch of Law 1992–93 and 1997–2002, FKC 2000; *Books* Torts in Private International Law (1978), The Conflict of Laws (ed, 11 edn 1987, 12 edn 1993, 13 edn 2000, 14 edn 2006), Benjamin's Sale of Goods (ed, 3 edn 1987, 4 edn 1992, 5 edn 1997, 6 edn 2002, 7 edn 2006), Public Policy in Transnational Relationships (1991), Chitty on Contracts (ed, 27 edn 1994, 28 edn 1999, 29 edn 2004); *Recreations* travel, Swansea City AFC; *Style*— Prof Robin Morse; ✉ School of Law, King's College, London WC2R 2LS (tel 020 7836 5454, fax 020 7873 2465)

MORSE, David Thomas; s of Thomas Walter Morse (d 1984), of London, and Emily Annie, *née* Garrett (d 2003); *b* 10 November 1943; *Educ* Royal Ballet Sch (White Lodge); *m* 9 Oct 1971, Marion, da of Charles Arnold Browell Tait, OBE; *Career* ballet dancer; with the Royal Ballet 1961–65; princ character artist Birmingham Royal Ballet (formerly Sadler's Wells Royal Ballet) 1989–, concurrently video archivist 1998–; roles with co incl: the Rake in The Rake's Progress, Jasper in Pineapple Poll, Hilarion in Giselle, Polichinelle in Meadow of Proverbs, Punch in Punch and the Street Party, The Dago and Popular Song in Façade, Bootface in The Lady and the Fool, Widow Simone in La Fille Mal Gardée, Carabosse in The Sleeping Beauty, Henry Hobson in Hobson's Choice, Dr Coppelias in Coppélia, Lord Capulet in Romeo and Juliet, the Merchant in Beauty and the Beast; choreography incl the works Pandora and Birdscape for Sadler's Wells; awarded Polish ballet's bicentennial medal of honour; *Recreations* photography, reading, music; *Style*— David Morse, Esq; ✉ Birmingham Royal Ballet, Birmingham Hippodrome Theatre, Thorp Street, Birmingham B5 4AU (tel 0121 245 3500)

MORSE, John Frederick; s of late Leonard John Morse, and late Flossie, *née* Bishop; *b* 4 September 1944, Swansea; *Educ* Bishop Gore GS Swansea, Coll of Law Guildford; *m* 13 July 1970, Andrea, *née* Morris; 1 s (James Edward b 25 Oct 1971), 2 da (Rachel Jane b 7 March 1973, Natalie Alexandra b 17 March 1975); *Career* admitted slr 1967; fndr and sr ptnr John Morse Slrs 1971–; tstee Gwalia Housing Tst; memb: Law Soc 1967–, Swansea and Dist Law Soc 1967– (pres 1999); *Recreations* golf, horse racing, skiing; *Clubs* Royal Porthcawl Golf, Langland Bay Golf, Beechwood (Swansea), Bristol Channel Yacht; *Style*— John Morse, Esq; ✉ Blaen Coed, Cilonnen, Gower, Swansea SA4 3UP (tel 01792 872307); John Morse Solicitors, St Helen's House, 156 St Helen's Road, Swansea SA1 4DG (tel and fax 01792 648111, fax 01792 648028, e-mail mail@johnmorse.co.uk)

MORT, District Judge Paul Collins; s of James Mort, and Myrtle Kathleen Mort; *Educ* Bootham Sch York, Univ of Manchester (LLB), Coll of Law Guildford; *Career* asst slr 1974–76, partner in private practice 1976–2000, district judge (NE Circuit) 2000–; memb Law Soc; *Recreations* riding, swimming, amateur dramatics; *Style*— District Judge Mort; ✉ Sheffield Combined Court Centre, The Law Courts, 50 West Bar, Sheffield S3 8PH

MORTADA, HE Jihad; *m* Rima; *Career* Lebanese diplomat; ambass to the Ct of St James's 1999–; *Style*— HE Mr Jihad Mortada; ✉ Embassy of Lebanon, 15–21 Palace Garden Mews, London W8 4RB

MORTENSEN, Neil James McCready; s of Peter John McCready Mortensen, of Laleham, Middx, and Rhoda, *née* Bamber; *b* 16 October 1949; *Educ* Hampton Sch, Univ of Birmingham (MB ChB), Univ of Bristol (MD); *m* 16 June 1973, Jane Alison, da of Lt-Col Paul Baker, of Shortlands, Kent; 2 da (Gemma b 1977, Chloe b 1981), 1 s (James b 1979); *Career* conslt sr lectr Univ of Bristol and Dept of Surgery Bristol Royal Infirmary 1983–86, conslt surgn John Radcliffe Hosp Oxford 1986–, reader in surgery Univ of Oxford 1994–2000, prof of colorectal surgery Univ of Oxford 2000–, fell Green Coll Oxford 2005– (memb 1987), memb Intercollegiate Bd in Gen Surgery 2003–; memb: Ctee Surgical Section Br Soc of Gastroenterology 1987–, Cncl Br Soc of Gastroenterology 1992–; pres Assoc of Coloproctology Great Britain and Ireland 2002–03 (memb Cncl 1995–99), pres Coloproctology Section RSM 2003–04, hon treas Surgical Res Soc; co-ed Int Jl of Colo Rectal Disease 1985–, assoc ed Dis Col Rect; chair Br Jl of Surgery Soc 2004– (treas 1996–2004), memb Editorial Ctee Br Jl of Surgery; FRCS 1980; *Books* Colo Rectal Cancer (1989), An Atlas of Rectal Ultrasound (1991), Restorative Proctocolectomy (1993), Controversies in Inflammatory Bowel Disease (2001); *Recreations* tennis, farming; *Style*— Neil Mortensen, Esq; ✉ Department of Colorectal Surgery, John Radcliffe Hospital, Oxford OX3 9DU (tel 01865 220926)

MORTIMER, Dr Andrew Joseph; s of Stanley Joseph Mortimer (d 1960), and Grace Wilkinson, *née* Armorey (d 2006); *b* 11 October 1948; *Educ* Barnard Castle Sch, Univ of Newcastle upon Tyne (BSc, MB BS, MD); *m* 1, 30 June 1973 (m dis 2003), Janet Mary, da of Kenneth Harry Levis (d 1993); 3 s (Sam b 3 Feb 1975, Tom b 21 April 1978, Joe b 25 Aug 1989); m 2, Sept 2004, Susan Howard; *Career* SHO in obstetrics and gynaecology Hexham Gen Hosp 1974–75 (house offr in med and surgery 1973–74), vocational trainee in family med Musgrove Park Hosp Taunton 1975–78; Nuffield Dept of Anaesthetics Radcliffe Infirmary Oxford: SHO in anaesthesia Jan-July 1979, registrar in anaesthesia 1979–80, MRC research trg fell Dec 1980–84; sr registrar Oxfordshire RHA 1984–87 (hon sr registrar 1980–84), conslt anaesthetist (with special interest in intensive care) S Manchester Univ Hosps NHS Tst 1987–, hon clinical lectr Univ of Manchester 1988–; memb: Multi-Centre Research Ethics Ctee 1997–2000, Steering Ctee Nat Confidential Enquiry into Patient Outcome and Death 1998–2001, Steering Ctee of Serious Hazards of Transfusion 1999–, Steering Ctee Nat Comparative Audit of Blood Transfusion RCP 2004–; Royal Coll of Anathaesthetists: elected memb Cncl 1997 and 2003–07, chm Examinations Ctee 2002–04, Final FRCA 2002–04, jt treas and chm Finance Ctee 2002–05; invited lectr at home and abroad; memb Health Fndn 2000–05; DObstRCOG, FRCA; *Books* A Handbook of Clinical Anaesthesia (ed Section on Vascular Anaesthesia, 1996), Guide to the Final FRCA (ed); author of numerous papers in learned jls; *Recreations* running, skiing, mountain biking, swimming; *Style*— Dr Andrew Mortimer; ✉ Department of Anaesthesia, University Hospital of South Manchester, Baguley House, Southmoor Road, Wythenshawe, Manchester M23 9LT (tel 0161 291 5710, fax 0161 291 5909, e-mail marie.oliver@smtr.nhs.uk)

MORTIMER, Prof Ann Margaret; da of Harry Mortimer, of Beeford, E Yorks, and Muriel, *née* Wood; *b* 11 May 1957; *Educ* Heckmondwike GS, Univ of Leicester (MB ChB, BSc), Univ of Leeds (MMedSc); *Family* 2 s (Benjamin Hugo, Jeremy Alexander), 1 da (Lucille Jacinthe); *Career* lectr in psychiatry Univ of Leeds 1986–88, conslt psychiatrist St Luke's Hosp Huddersfield 1988, sr lectr in psychiatry Charing Cross and Westminster Med Sch (Univ of London) 1991–95, foundation chair in psychiatry Postgraduate Med Sch Univ of Hull 1995–; FRCPsych 1999 (MRCPsych 1985), MD 2004; *Books* Managing Negative Symptoms of Schizophrenia (2001); numerous other pubns on schizophrenia; *Recreations* skiing, piano playing, gardening; *Style*— Prof Ann M Mortimer; ✉ Department of Psychiatry, Hertford Building, The University of Hull, Cottingham Road, Hull HU6 7RX (tel 01482 464565, fax 01482 464569)

MORTIMER, Edward James; s of Rt Rev Robert Cecil Mortimer, DD, Bishop of Exeter 1949–73 (d 1976), and Mary Hope, *née* Walker (d 1992); *b* 22 December 1943; *Educ* Summer Fields Oxford, Eton, Balliol Coll Oxford; *m* 1968, Elizabeth Anne, da of John Zanetti; 2 s (Horatio b 1970, Matthew b 1973), 2 da (Frances b 1978, Phoebe b 1980); *Career* asst d'Anglais Lycée Faidherbe St Louis-du-Sénégal 1962, fell All Souls Coll Oxford 1965–72 and 1984–86, foreign specialist and leader writer The Times 1973–85 (asst Paris corr 1967–70), sr assoc Carnegie Endowment (NY) 1980–81, series conslt Roosevelt's Children (Channel 4) 1985–87, foreign affairs ed Financial Times 1987–98; research assoc IISS 1990–91, hon prof Dept of Govt and Int Rels Univ of Warwick 1993–98, chief speechwriter to the Sec-Gen UN 1998–, dir of communications in the office of Sec-Gen UN 2001–; winner first David Watt Meml Prize 1988, European Press Prize 1993 (jtly); Hon DLitt Univ of Exeter 1999; hon fell Balliol Coll Oxford 2004–; *Publications* France and the Africans (1969), Eurocommunism, Myth or Reality (1979), Faith and Power, The Politics of Islam (1982), Rise of the French Communist Party (1984), Roosevelt's Children (1987), European Security After the Cold War (IISS Adelphi paper, 1992), People, Nation & State (1999); *Recreations* conversation, travel, family life; *Clubs* Beefsteak, Groucho; *Style*— Edward Mortimer, Esq; ✉ Room S-3850 A, Executive Office of the Secretary General, United Nations, New York, NY 10017, USA (fax 00 1 212 963 5965)

MORTIMER, Emily; *m* Alessandro Nivola; 1 s (Sam); *Career* actress; *Television* The Glass Virgin 1995, Sharpe's Sword 1995; Silent Witness: Heartstones 1996, Lord of Misrule 1996; A Dance to the Music of Time 1997, Midsomer Murders 1998, Coming Home 1998, Cider with Rosie 1998, Noah's Ark 1999, *Films* Ghost and the Darkness 1996, The Last of the High Kings 1996, The Saint 1997, Elizabeth 1998, Notting Hill 1999, Love's Labour's Lost 1999, Scream 3 1999, Killing Joe 1999, The Kid 2000, The Sleeping Dictionary 2001, The 51st State 2001, Lovely & Amazing 2001, A Foreign Affair 2003, Nobody Needs to Know 2003, The Sleeping Dictionary 2003, Young Adam 2003, Bright Young Things 2003, Dear Frankie 2004; *Style*— Ms Emily Mortimer; ✉ c/o Harriet Robinson, ICM Ltd, Oxford House, 76 Oxford Street, London W1D 1BS

MORTIMER, Sir John Clifford; kt (1998), CBE (1986), QC (1966); s of Clifford Mortimer, and Kathleen May, *née* Smith; *b* 21 April 1923; *Educ* Harrow, BNC Oxford; *m* 1 (m dis), Penelope Ruth, *née* Fletcher (d 1999); 1 s (Jeremy), 1 da (Sally); m 2, Penelope, *née* Gollop; 2 da (Emily, Rosie); *Career* barrister, playwright and author; called to the Bar Inner Temple 1948 (bencher 1975); plays incl: The Dock Brief (1958), What Shall We Tell Caroline (1958), The Wrong Side of the Park (1960), Two Stars for Comfort (1962), The Judge (1967), Voyage Round My Father (1970, filmed 1982), I Claudius (1972, adapted from Robert Graves), Collaborators (1973), The Bells of Hell (1977), Naked Justice (2000), Hock and Soda Water (2001); film script John Mary (1970); television scripts incl: Brideshead Revisited (1981), Edwin (1984), Under the Hammer (1993); works of fiction incl: Charade (1947), Three Winters (1956), Will Shakespeare and Entertainment (1977), Rumpole of the Bailey (1978, BAFTA Writer of the Year Award), The Trials of Rumpole (1979), Rumpole's Return (1980, televised), Regina vs Rumpole (1981), Rumpole for the Defence (1982), Rumpole and the Golden Thread (1983, televised), Paradise Postponed (1985, televised 1986), Rumpole's Last Case (1987), Summers Lease (1988, televised 1989), Rumpole and the Age of Miracles (1989), Titmuss Regained (1990, televised 1991), Rumpole À La Carte (1990), Dunster (1992), Rumpole on Trial (1992), Rumpole and the Angel of Death (1995), Felix in the Underworld (1997), The Sound of Trumpets (1998), Rumpole Rests His Case (2001), Rumpole and the Primrose Path (2002), Quite Honestly (2006); trans incl: A Flea in Her Ear (1965), The Lady From Maxim's (1977), A Little Hotel on the Side (for Nat Theatre) 1984, Die Fledermaus (for Covent Garden Opera) 1988; interviews incl: In Character (1983), Character Parts (1986); autobiography: Clinging to the Wreckage (1982, Yorkshire Post Book of the Year), Murderers and other Friends (1994), The Summer of a Dormouse (2000), Where There's a Will (2003); Christmas Carol (dramatised) RSC 1994; ed The Oxford Book of Villains (1992); pres Royal Court Theatre Tst 2004–, memb Nat Theatre Bd 1968–89; chm: Royal Court Theatre 1990–2000, RSL 1990–; pres Howard League of Penal Reform 1992–; pres Berks Bucks & Oxon Naturalists Tst 1984–90; writers award BAFTA; Hon DLitt Susquehanna Univ 1985, Hon LLD Exeter 1986, Hon DLitt St Andrews 1987, Hon DLitt Nottingham 1988, Hon DUniv Brunel 1990; Italia Prize 1958; FRSL; *Recreations* working, gardening, opera; *Clubs* Garrick; *Style*— Sir John Mortimer, CBE, QC; ✉ c/o PFD, Drury House, 34–43 Russell Street, London WC2B 5HA (tel 020 7352 4446, fax 020 7352 7356)

M

MORTIMER, Katharine Mary Hope; da of Rt Rev Robert Cecil Mortimer, DD, Bishop of Exeter 1949–73 (d 1976), and Mary Hope, *née* Walker (d 1992); *b* 28 May 1946; *Educ* St Mary and St Anne Abbots Bromley, Somerville Coll Oxford (BA, BPhil); *m* 1, 7 July 1973 (m dis 1986), John Noel Nicholson, s of Rev John Malcolm Nicholson (d 1982); 1 s (Andrew Robert b 1982); m 2, 19 May 1990, Robert Michael Dean, s of Daniel Dean (d 1994); *Career* dir: National Bus Company (non-exec) 1979–91, N M Rothschild & Sons Ltd 1985–89 (non-exec 1988–89), Centre for Econ Policy Res (non-exec) 1986–91, N M Rothschild Asset Management (Holdings) 1987–89 (non-exec 1988–89); seconded as dir of policy Securities and Investments Bd 1985–87, chief exec Walker Books Ltd 1988–89, ind conslt 1989–, fin sector advsr to the UK Know How Fund 1989–97; non-exec dir Pennon Gp plc 2000–, govr Imperial Coll of Sci and Technol 1987–91, tstee Inst for Public Policy Res 1989–92; memb: Cncl ESRC 1984–86, Governing Body Inst of Devpt Studies Sussex 1983–95, BBC General Advsy Cncl 1987–91, Royal Cmmn for the Exhibition of 1851 1987–2002, Bd of the Crown Agents 1990–97, Cncl Crown Agents Fndn 1997–, Competition Cmmn (formerly Monopolies and Mergers Cmmn) 1995–2001; non-exec dir: Crown Agents Financial Services Ltd 1990–, Crown Agents Asset Management Ltd 1990–2007, British Nuclear Fuels plc 1992–2000; *Style*— Miss Katharine Mortimer; ✉ Lower Corscombe, Okehampton, Devon EX20 1SD (tel 01837 840431, e-mail katemortimer@waitrose.com)

MORTIMER, Robert (Bob); *b* 23 May 1959; *Career* comedian, part of comedy duo with Vic Reeves, *qv*; *Television* Vic Reeves Big Night Out 1990 and 1991, Weekenders (both Channel 4) 1992, The Smell of Reeves and Mortimer (3 series, BBC) 1993, 1995 and 1998 (BAFTA Award for Originality 1992, Best Live Performance British Comedy Awards 1992, Best Comedy Series British Comedy Awards 1994), A Night in with Vic and Bob (Boxing Day Special) 1993, Shooting Stars 1995, 1996, 1998, 2002 and 2003 (Best Entertainment Prog RTS Award 1996, Silver Rose of Montreux 1996, BAFTA Award for Best Light Entertainment 1997), A Nose Through Nature 1995, It's Ulrika (BBC) 1997, Families at War (BBC) 1998 and 1999, Bang Bang, It's Reeves and Mortimer (BBC) 1999, Randall and Hopkirk (Deceased) (BBC1) 2000 and 2001, Surrealissimo - The Trial of Dali (BBC 2 and BBC 4) 2002, Celebrity Boxing (BBC 2) 2002, Celebrity Mastermind (BBC 2) 2002, Catterick (BBC 3) 2004, All Star Comedy Show (ITV) 2004; *Film* Churchill: The Hollywood Year 2003; *Tours* Vic Reeves Big Night Out 1990 and 1991, The Smell of Reeves and Mortimer 1994, The Smell of Reeves and Moritmer: The Weathercock Tour 1995, Shooting Stars (nat tour) 1996, Shooting Stars/Fast Show Live (Labatt's Apollo) 1998; *Video* Shooting Stars - Unviewed & Nude 1996, Shooting Stars - Unpicked and Unplucked 1997; *Recordings* Dizzy (single, UK no 1), I Will Cure You (album), I'm A Believer (single), Let's Dance (single, with Middlesbrough FC); *Books* Big Night In (1991), Smell of Reeves and Mortimer (1993), Shooting Stars (1996); subject of Reeves & Mortimer (by Bruce Dessau, 1998); *Style*— Bob Mortimer; ✉ c/o PBJ Management Ltd, 7 Soho Street, London W1D 3DQ (tel 020 7287 1112, fax 020 7287 1191, e-mail general@pbjmgt.co.uk, website www.pbjmgt.co.uk)

MORTIMER, Tim; *b* 6 December 1957; *Educ* West of England Coll of Art (BA Graphic Design, DipAD); *m* Virginia Lana; *Career* account mangr Boase Massimi Pollit 1979–83, account dir/assoc dir KMP/KHBB 1983–86, account dir FCO 1986–88; Generator: joined as bd account dir 1988, md 1989, md Advertising Options 1994–95, fndr ptnr Mortimer Whittaker O'Sullivan 1995–; *Recreations* fitness and Formula 1; *Style*— Tim Mortimer, Esq

MORTIMORE, Prof Peter John; OBE (1993); s of late Claude Mortimore, of Richmond, Surrey, and Rose, *née* Townsend; *b* 17 January 1942; *Educ* Chiswick GS, Univ of London (BSc, MSc, PhD); *m* 19 April 1965, Jo Marie, da of Michael Hargaden (d 1986), of Monmouth, Gwent; 3 da (Joanna b 1966, Rebecca b 1967, Claudia b 1968); *Career* teacher secdy sch 1964–73; res offr Inst of Psychiatry 1975–78, memb HMI 1978, dir of research and statistics ILEA 1979–85, asst educn offr (sec) ILEA 1985–88, prof and dir Sch of Educn Lancaster Univ 1988–90; Univ of London: prof of educn 1990–, dir Inst of Educn 1994–2000 (dep dir 1990–94), pro-vice-chllr 1999–2000; conslt OECD 2003–05; memb: Br Psychological Soc, Assoc for Child Psychology and Psychiatry, Br Educnl Research Assoc, American Educnl Research Assoc; fell Birkbeck Coll London 2001; Hon DLitt 1998; FBPsS 1988, FRSA 1990, FCP 1994, AcSS 2000; *Books* Fifteen Thousand Hours (co-author, 1979), Behaviour Problems in Schools (1984), Helpful Servant not Dominating Master (1986), School Matters (1988), The Primary Head (1991), The Secondary Head (1991), Managing Associate Staff (1993), Planning Matters (1995), Living Education (1997), Forging Links (1997), The Road to Improvement (1998), Understanding Pedagogy (jtly, 1999), Culture of Change (jtly, 2000), Improving School Effectiveness (jtly, 2001), An Education System for the 21st Century: Which Way Forward? (2006); *Recreations* music, theatre, walking; *Style*— Prof Peter Mortimore, OBE; ✉ c/o Institute of Education, University of London, 20 Bedford Way, London WC1H 0AL (tel 020 7612 6004, fax 020 7612 6089)

MORTIMORE, Simon Anthony; QC (1991); s of Robert Anthony Mortimore (d 1995), and Katharine Elizabeth, *née* Mackenzie Caine (d 1986); *b* 12 April 1950; *Educ* Westminster, Univ of Exeter (LLB); *m* 26 March 1983, Fiona Elizabeth, da of Bernard Maurice Jacobson (d 1988); 1 da (Laura Alexandra b 21 Feb 1985), 1 s (Edward Robert b 20 Jan 1988); *Career* called to the Bar Inner Temple 1972; dep bankruptcy registrar High Court 1987–99; CEDR accredited mediator 1997–; memb ACCA Disciplinary and Regulatory Ctee 2003–; *Books* Bullen Leake & Jacobs Precedents of Pleading (contrib 13 edn, 1990), Insolvency of Banks - Managing the Risks (contrib, 1996); *Recreations* golf; *Clubs* Hurlingham, Royal St George's Golf, Rye Golf; *Style*— Simon Mortimore, Esq, QC; ✉ 3–4 South Square, Gray's Inn, London WC1R 5HP (tel 020 7696 9900, fax 020 7696 9911)

MORTON, (John) Andrew; s of John Douglas Morton (d 1975), of Nutfield, Surrey, and Anne Marjorie, *née* Gray; *b* 5 July 1943; *Educ* Charterhouse, Merton Coll Oxford (BA); *m* 6 Dec 1975, Angela Fern Gage, da of Cdr Leonard Gage Wheeler, RN (d 1997); 1 da (Fiona Anne b 1978); *Career* Univ of Oxford Air Sqdn RAFVR 1963–65; admitted slr 1968; ptnr Allen & Overy 1973–2000 (asst slr 1968–73); conslt Mundays Slrs, dir Bowater Europe Ltd; *Recreations* sailing, golf, skiing; *Clubs* Army & Navy, Offshore Cruising, Royal Wimbledon Golf, Royal Yacht Squadron; *Style*— Andrew Morton, Esq; ✉ Mundays Solicitors, Cedar House, 78 Portsmouth Road, Cobham, Surrey KT11 1AN

MORTON, His Hon Judge (David) Christopher; s of Rev Alexander Francis Morton (d 1991), and Esther Ann, *née* Williams (d 2005); *b* 1 December 1943; *Educ* Worksop Coll, Fitzwilliam Coll Cambridge (BA, LLB); *m* Aug 1970, Sandra Jo, da of Alvin Kobes, of Nebraska; 1 da (Sarah Ceinwen b 8 April 1973), 3 s (Geraint Deiniol James b 28 April 1976, Emlyn David Gruffydd b 22 April 1980, Rhys Benjamin Hywel b 13 June 1982); *Career* called to the Bar Inner Temple 1968; recorder of the Crown Court 1988–92, circuit judge (Wales & Chester Circuit) 1992–; *Recreations* family, railways; *Clubs* Royal Over-Seas League; *Style*— His Hon Judge Morton; ✉ The Crown Court, St Helen's Road, Swansea SA1 4PF (tel 01792 637000)

MORTON, 21 Earl of (S 1458); John Charles Sholto Douglas; also Lord Aberdour (no actual cr, but designation of the eld s & h, incorporated with the Earldom in a charter of 1638, where the Earls of Morton are described as *domini Abirdour*); head of the male line of the Douglas family worldwide; s of Hon Charles William Sholto Douglas (d 1960, 2 s of 19 Earl of Morton); suc cous, 20 Earl 1976; *b* 19 March 1927; *m* 1949, Mary Sheila, da of late Rev Canon John Stanley Gibbs, MC, of Didmarton House, Badminton, Glos; 2 s, 1 da; *Heir* s, Lord Aberdour; *Career* ptnr Dalmahoy Farms, chm Edinburgh Polo Club; Lord Lt West Lothian (DL 1982); *Clubs* Edinburgh Polo, Dalmahoy Country, Farmers'; *Style*— The Rt Hon the Earl of Morton; ✉ The Old Mansion House, Dalmahoy, Kirknewton EH27 8EB (tel 0131 333 1331)

MORTON, Ralph Nicholas; s of John Frank Morton, and Nancy Margaret, *née* White; *b* 19 September 1958; *Educ* Alleyn's Sch Dulwich, Westfield Coll London (BA); *m* 26 May 1984, Alison Ellenor, da of Robert George Sharpe (d 1987); 1 s (Matthew James b 25 May 1992), 1 da (Sarah-Ellen b 25 Feb 1996); *Career* Autosport 1982–86, What Car? 1986–94 (ed 1992–94), ed-in-chief Haymarket motoring special projects 1994–98; fndr: Mortonmedia 1998, Business Car Manager 2006; ed www.businesscarmanager.co.uk, ed automanager, ed Driving Business; contrib: Fleet News, FT; memb Ctee Guild of Motoring Writers 1993–98; *Recreations* swimming, tennis; *Clubs* Harlequins RFC; *Style*— Ralph Morton, Esq; ✉ Business Car Manager Limited, 95 Station Road, Hampton, Middlesex TW12 2BD (tel 020 8783 0999, e-mail editor@businesscarmanager.co.uk, website www.businesscarmanager.co.uk)

MORTON, Dr Richard Emile; s of Donald Morton, and Mary, *née* Wilkinson; *b* 10 November 1949; *Educ* Bexley GS, St John's Coll Oxford (BA, BM BCh), UCH; *m* 1 May 1976, April Joy Georgina, da of William Milne (d 1979); 1 s (Robert William), 2 da (Alice Elizabeth, Lucy Jenniffer); *Career* registrar in paediatrics Hosp for Sick Children Gt Ormond St, sr registrar in paediatrics London Hosp and Queen Elizabeth Hosp for Children Hackney, conslt paediatrician Derbyshire Children's Hosp; chm Umbrella, sec BPA Child Disability and Devpt Gp; FRCP; *Recreations* family, music, running; *Style*— Dr Richard Morton

MORTON, Robert Edward; s of Charles Morton, and Yvonne, *née* Galea; *b* 20 May 1956; *Educ* Canford Sch, Oriel Coll Oxford (MA); *m* 12 Dec 1981; 2 da (Caroline b 13 Aug 1983, Georgina b 21 Jan 1985); *Career* res analyst: Simon & Coates 1978–83, de Zoete & Bevan 1983–86 (ptnr 1986); dir and head Conglomerates and Support Services Res Teams: Barclays de Zoete Wedd 1986–92; dir Charterhouse Securities 1992–99; exec dir and head Support Services Team WestLB Panmure 1999–2003, head Support Services Team Investec Securities 2004–; MSI; *Recreations* squash, music, sailing; *Clubs* RAC; *Style*— Robert Morton, Esq; ✉ 28 Cambridge Street, Pimlico, London SW1V 4QH (tel 020 7828 7955, e-mail robert.morton@investec.co.uk)

MORTON, Samantha; *b* Nottingham; *Career* actress; ambass Save the Children UK; *Theatre* Star-Gazey Pie and Sauerkraut (Royal Court) 1995, Ashes and Sand (Royal Court) 1995; *Television* incl: Boon 1986, Soldier Soldier 1991, Cracker 1993, Band of Gold 1995, Jane Eyre 1997, The History of Tom Jones 1997, Emma 1997, Max & Ruby 2002, Longford 2006; *Films* incl: The Future Lasts a Long Time 1996, Under the Skin 1997, This is the Sea 1998, Pandaemonium 1999, Sweet and Lowdown 1999 (nomination Best Supporting Actress Acad Awards), Jesus' Son 1999, Dreaming of Joseph Lees 1999, The Last Yellow 1999, Eden 2000, Morvern Callar 2002, Minority Report 2002, In America 2002 (nomination Best Actress Acad Awards), Code 46 2003, Enduring Love 2004, The Libertine 2004, River Queen 2004, LAssie 2005, Expired 2006, The Golden Age 2003, Mr Lonely 2006; *Style*— Ms Samantha Morton

MORTON JACK, His Hon Judge David; s of Col William Andrew Morton Jack, OBE (d 1950), of Lemonfield, Co Galway, and Margery Elizabeth Happell (d 1978); *b* 5 November 1936; *Educ* Stowe, Trinity Coll Oxford (MA); *m* 1972, Elvira Rosemary, da of Francis Gallo Rentoul, of London; 4 s (Edward b 1975, Richard b 1977, Henry b 1979, George b 1981); *Career* 2 Lt Royal Irish Fusiliers 1955–57 (Lt AER 1957–60); called to the Bar Lincoln's Inn, in practice SE Circuit 1962–86, recorder of the Crown Ct 1979–86, circuit judge (SE Circuit) 1986–; *Recreations* fishing, shooting, reading, music; *Style*— His Hon Judge David Morton Jack; ✉ Oxford Combined Court Centre, The Law Courts, St Aldates, Oxford OX1 1TL

MORTON-SANER, Anthea Katherine; da of Robert Morton-Saner, and Katharine Mary, *née* Gordon; *Career* literary agent 1975–2006; dir: Curtis Brown Gp Ltd 1986–2002, Curtis Brown Australia plc 1986–2002; *Recreations* gardening, reading, travelling; *Clubs* Lansdowne; *Style*— Miss Anthea Morton-Saner; ✉ e-mail antheams@supanet.com

MOSBACHER, Michael Oliver; s of Ottmar Mosbacher (d 2001), and Renate Mosbacher (d 1998); *b* 14 July 1972, NY; *Educ* Univ of Exeter (BA, MA); *m* 22 Feb 2003, Amanda; *Career* Social Affairs Unit: prog offr 1996–2001, dep dir 2001–04, dir 2004–; *Publications* Another Country (ed, 1999), Marketing the Revolution: The New Anti-Capitalism and the Attack upon Corporate Brands (2002), Understanding Anti-Americanism (contrib, 2004); *Style*— Michael Mosbacher, Esq; ✉ The Social Affairs Unit, 314–322 Regent Street, London W1B 5SA (tel 020 7637 4356, fax 020 7436 8530, e-mail mosbacher@socialaffairsunit.org.uk)

MOSELEY, Dr Ivan Frederick; s of Frederick Clarence Moseley (d 1994), and Edith Sophia, *née* Smith (d 1987); *b* 29 May 1940; *Educ* Latymer Upper Sch, St Mary's Hosp Med Sch Univ of London (BSc, MB BS, DMRD, MD), Centre for the Study of Philosophy and Health Care UC Swansea (PhD), Royal Northern Coll of Music (MMus), Royal Holloway Univ of London; *m* 22 April 1967, Mary Cheyne Thomson, da of George Malcolm (d 1991), of Royston, Cambs; 1 da (Hannah b 1968), 1 s (James b 1978); *Career* house offr: St Mary's Hosp Paddington 1965–66, Whittington Hosp 1967; SHO: Royal Marsden Hosp 1967–68, London Chest Hosp 1968; sr registrar in radiology Bart's 1970–72 (registrar 1968–70), clinical assoc fell Mount Zion Hosp and postdoctoral scholar Univ of Calif San Francisco 1972–73; consultant radiologist: National Hosp Queen Sq London 1975–2000 (sr registrar 1973–75, dir of radiology 1994–2000), Wellington Hosp London 1975–87, Moorfields Eye Hosp London 1984–2000 (dir of radiology 1987–2000), London MRI Centre 1987–; hon conslt Royal Surrey Co Hosp Guildford 1988–92; Br Cncl visiting prof Université de Nancy 1978; visiting prof: Univ of Calif San Francisco 1982, Univ of Hong Kong 1988, Univ of Auckland 1988, Univ of Sydney 1995; Br rep Euro Union of Med Specialists 1988–2000; Wellcome Tst scholar Univ of West Indies Jamaica 1964, CIBA/INSERM scholar Hôpital Lariboisiére Paris 1974, Euro Soc of Neuroradiology prize 1976; ed Neuroradiology 1993–2005; memb: Br Soc of Neuroradiologists 1975 (sec 1986–90, pres 1998–2000), European Soc of Neuroradiology 1976 (chair Cncl of Nat Delegates 1997–2000), BIR 1978, European Soc for Philosophy of Med and Health Care 1992; hon memb Japanese Soc of Neuroradiology 2002; memb: Southwold Sailors Reading Room Assoc 1997–, Turner Soc (sec 2003–); FFR 1972, FRCR 1975, FRSM 1980 (pres Section of Clinical Neurosciences 1999–2000), FRCP 1985 (MRCP); *Books* Computer Tomographie des Kopfes (contrib, 1978), Computerized Tomography in Neuro-Ophthalmology (contrib, 1982), Diagnostic Imaging in Neurological Disease (1986), Magnetic Resonance Imaging in Diseases of the Nervous System (1988), Introduction to Magnetic Resonance Imaging of the Brain (contrib, 1998); *Recreations* music, wine, bullfighting, graphic arts; *Clubs* Arts (dir 1999–2003 and 2005–), Club Taurino of London (sec gen 1985–90, pres 1990–2003 and 2006–); *Style*— Dr Ivan Moseley; ✉ 65 St Mary's Grove, London W4 3LW (tel 020 8995 5668)

MOSER, Baron (Life Peer UK 2001), of Regents Park in the London Borough of Camden; Sir Claus Adolf Moser; KCB (1973), CBE (1965); s of Dr Ernest Moser, and Lotte Moser; *b* 24 November 1922; *Educ* Frensham Heights Sch, LSE; *m* 1949, Mary Oxlin; 1 s, 2 da; *Career* LSE: asst lectr 1946–49, lectr 1949–55, reader 1955–61, prof of social statistics 1961–70, visiting prof 1970–75; statistical advsr Ctee for Higher Educn 1961–64, dir Central Statistical Office and head Govt Statistical Serv 1967–78, visiting fell Nuffield Coll Oxford 1972–80, pres Royal Statistical Soc 1978–80; memb: Governing Body Royal Acad of Music 1967–79; chm Bd of Dirs Royal Opera House Covent Garden 1974–87, vice-chm NM Rothschild & Sons 1978–84 (dir 1984–90); dir: Economist Intelligence Unit 1979–83, The Economist 1979–93, Equity and Law Life Assurance Society 1980–87,

Octopus Publishing Group 1982–88; chm Askonas Holt Ltd (formerly Howard Holt) 1990–2002; warden Wadham Coll Oxford 1984–93, chllr Keele Univ 1986–2002; tstee: Br Museum 1988–2001, London Philharmonic Orch 1988–2000; pres Br Assoc for the Advancement of Science 1989–90; hon fell LSE; Hon DSc: Univ of Southampton, Univ of Leeds, City Univ London, Univ of Sussex, Univ of Wales, Liverpool; Hon DUniv: Keele, Surrey, York, Edinburgh, Open Univ; Hon DTech Brunel Univ; FBA 1969, Hon FRAM; Cdr de l'Ordre National du Mérite (France); *Style*— The Lord Moser, KCB, CBE, FBA; ✉ 3 Regent's Park Terrace, London NW1 7EE (tel 020 7485 1619)

MOSES, Colin John; *b* 13 September 1962; *Educ* Woodhouse Grove Sch Bradford, Univ of Sheffield (BArch, DipArch); *Career* currently dir RMJM Ltd; *Style*— Colin Moses, Esq; ✉ RMJM, 5 Westbrook Centre, Milton Road, Cambridge CB4 1TGCB1 5EP (tel 01223 417150, fax 01223 417155, e-mail c.moses@rmjm.com)

MOSES, Geoffrey Haydn; *s* of Canon Haydn Moses (d 1983), of Llanelli Vicarage, Dyfed, and Beryl Mary, *née* Lloyd; *b* 24 September 1952; *Educ* Ystalyfera GS, Emmanuel Coll Cambridge (BA, Cricket blue), KCL (PGCE); *m* 24 July 1981, Anne Elizabeth, da of Harry Mason; 1 *s* (Timothy *b* 1 Dec 1994), 1 da (Lucy *b* 27 Nov 1996); *Career* bass; princ singer WNO 1978–82; *Performances* Barber of Seville (WNO 1978, Scottish Opera 1984, Hamburg State Opera 1984), Tales of Hoffman (Royal Opera House Covent Garden) 1981, Don Giovanni (Glyndebourne Touring Opera 1982, Kent Opera 1983), Madame Butterfly (Opera North) 1983, Arabella (Glyndebourne Festival Opera) 1983, Simon Boccanegra (Belgian Opera) 1983, Salome (Netherlands Opera) 1988, Falstaff (WNO 1988–92, touring NY, Paris, Milan and Tokyo), La Favorita, Tristan & Isolde, Eugene Onegin and Lucia di Lammermoor (all WNO 1993), Peter Grimes (Glyndebourne Festival) 1994; concerts and recitals at: Gothenburg, Frankfurt Alte Oper, Royal Festival Hall, Royal Albert Hall; debut Deutche Opera Berlin (I Puritani) 1991, debut Opera de Nancy (Somnambula) 1991, Hong Kong Festival (Marriage of Figaro) 1991, Faust Nabucco (ENO) 1996, Die Meistersingers (Covent Garden) 1997, debut Rape of Lucretia (Caen) 1998, La Traviata (tour to Baden Baden with Covent Garden) 1998, debut Peter Grimes (Strasbourg) 1999, world premier The Last Supper (Berlin Staatsoper) 2000, Verdi Requiem (Berlin Philharmonie) 2000, A Midsummer Night's Dream (Glyndebourne Festival Opera) 2001, debut Seville (Collatinus in Rape of Lucretia) 2002, debut La Fenice Venice (Midsummer Night's Dream) 2004, Glyndebourne Festival 2006, Rocco in Fidelio (Dublin) 2006, Gremin in Eugene Onegin (English Touring Opera) 2007, Raimondo in Lucia di Lammermore (Dublin) 2007; *Recreations* walking, cricket, reading, wine; *Style*— Geoffrey Moses, Esq; ✉ Music International, 13 Ardilaun Road, London N5 2QR

MOSES, Very Rev Dr John Henry; KCVO (2006); *s* of Henry William Moses (d 1975), of London, and Ada Elizabeth Moses (d 1997); *b* 12 January 1938; *Educ* Ealing GS, Univ of Nottingham, Trinity Hall Cambridge, Lincoln Theol Coll (BA, PhD, Gladstone Meml Prize); *m* 25 July 1964, Susan Elizabeth, da of James Wainwright (d 1980), of London; 1 *s* (Richard), 2 da (Rachel, Catherine); *Career* asst curate St Andrew's Bedford 1964–70, rector Coventry East Team Ministry 1970–77, examining chaplain to Bishop of Coventry 1972–77, rural dean Coventry East 1973–77, archdeacon of Southend 1977–82, provost of Chelmsford 1982–96, dean of St Paul's 1996–2006 (dean emeritus 2006–); dean of Order of St Michael & St George and of Order of British Empire 1996–2006, select preacher Univ of Oxford 2004–05; memb General Synod 1985–2005; church cmmr 1988–2006; chm Cncl of Centre for the Study of Theology Univ of Essex 1987–96, rector Anglia Poly Univ 1992–96; visiting fell Wolfson Coll Cambridge 1987; vice-pres City of London Festival 1997–2006, Freeman City of London 1997, Liveryman Worshipful Co of Feltmakers 1998, Liveryman Worshipful Co of Plaisterers 1999, Hon Freeman Worshipful Co of Water Conservators 2000, Hon Liveryman Worshipgul Co of Masons 2005; Hon Dr Anglia Poly Univ 1997; Order of Al Istiqlal (Jordan) 2002, OStJ 2003; *Publications* The Sacrifice of God (1992), A Broad and Living Way (1995), The Desert (1997), One Equall Light (2003), The Language of Love (2007); *Clubs* Athenaeum; *Style*— The Very Rev Dr John Moses, KCVO; ✉ Chestnut House, Burgage, Southwell, Nottinghamshire NG25 OEP (tel and fax 01636 814880, e-mail johnandsusanmoses@btinternet.com)

MOSESSON, John Gunnar; *s* of Torsten Johannes Mosesson (d 1974); *b* 9 July 1938; *Educ* Frensham Heights Sch, Keele Univ (BA), Royal Coll of Music (ARCM); *m* 1, 1968 (m dis 1980), Jennifer Davies; 1 da (Gaël *b* 1970), 2 *s* (Dargan *b* 1972, Truan *b* 1976); *m* 2, 1985 (m dis 1990), Ruth Marland; *m* 3, 1990, Baroness Anne, da of Baron Jack Anstruther Carl Knutson Bonde; 1 da (Cecilia *b* 1991); *Career* John Laing Res and Devpt 1959–61, Univ 1961–65; md T F Sampson Ltd 1965; chm: T F Sampson Ltd 1974–, Stramit International 1982– (md 1974–82); dep chm Green Resources Development Ltd Beijing 2000–; chm Glas Restaurant London; vice-pres Friends Aldeburgh Fndn 1985–; *Recreations* music, tennis, golf; *Clubs* Chelsea Arts, Aldeburgh Golf; *Style*— John Mosesson, Esq; ✉ Marygold, Aldeburgh, Suffolk IP15 5HF (tel 01728 453323, fax 01728 454686); Stramit International Ltd, Creeting Road, Stowmarket, Suffolk IP14 5BA (tel 01449 613564, fax 01449 678381)

MOSEY, Roger; *s* of late Geoffrey Swain Mosey, of Washingborough, Lincoln, and Marie, *née* Pilkington; *b* 4 January 1958; *Educ* Bradford GS, Wadham Coll Oxford (MA), INSEAD (AMP); *Career* with Pennine Radio Ltd Bradford 1979–80; BBC: reporter BBC Radio Lincolnshire 1980–82, prodr BBC Radio Northampton 1982–83, prodr The Week in Westminster BBC Radio 4 1983–84, prodr Today 1984–86, prodr BBC New York Bureau 1986–87, ed PM 1987–89, ed The World at One 1989–93, ed The Today Programme 1993–96, exec ed Radio 4 current affairs progs 1996, controller Radio 5 Live 1996–2000 (acting dir of continuous news 1999–2000), head of TV news 2000–05, dir BBC Sport 2005–; author of book reviews for The Guardian and columns for The Business; memb: RTS, BAFTA; One World Broadcasting Tst Award 1990, Br Environment and Media Award 1990, 1991 and 1995, Sony Gold Award 1994, Broadcasting Press Guild Radio Prog of the Year 1995, Best Speech-Based Breakfast Show Sony Radio Awards 1995, Voice of the Listener & Viewer Award for Outstanding Radio Prog 1996, Sony Gold Award Station of the Year (Radio 5) 1998; fell Radio Acad 1999; *Recreations* travel, cinema, reading political biographies and thrillers, watching football; *Style*— Roger Mosey, Esq; ✉ BBC Television Centre, London W12 7RJ (tel 020 8225 6644, e-mail roger.mosey@bbc.co.uk)

MOSIMANN, Anton; OBE (2004); *s* of Otto Albert Mosimann (d 1996), and Olga, *née* Von Burg (d 1966); *b* 23 February 1947; *m* 13 April 1973, Kathrin, da of Jakob Roth; 2 *s* (Philipp Anton *b* 1975, Mark Andreas *b* 1977); *Career* chef; apprentice Hotel Baeren Twann Switzerland 1962–64, commis entremétier Palace Hotel Villars 1964–65, commis garde-manger Cavalieri Hilton Rome 1965, commis saucier Hotel Waldhaus Sils-Maria Switzerland 1965–66, chef tournant/chef saucier/sous chef Queen Elizabeth Hotel Montreal 1966–67, chef de froid/sous chef Canadian Pavilion EXPO '67 Montreal; chef tournant: Palace Hotel Montreux 1969, Palace Hotel St Moritz 1969–70; exec chef Swiss Pavilion Expo 70 Osaka Japan 1970, chef entremétier Palace Hotel Lausanne 1970–71; sous chef: Palace Hotel Lucerne summer seasons 1971–73, Kulm Hotel St Moritz winter seasons 1972–73 and 1973–74 (chef restaurateur 1971–72); commis pâtissier Palace Hotel Gstaad 1974–75, dir of cuisine Dorchester London 1986–88 (mâitre chef des cuisines 1975), chef patron Mosimann's London 1988–; chm: Mosimann's Ltd, Mosimann's Party Sevice 1990–, The Mosimann Acad 1995–, Créative Chefs 1996–; request TV and radio appearances incl: Anton Goes to Switzerland (BBC) 1985 (Glenfiddich Award), Anton Mosimann - Naturally (Channel 4) 1991 and 1994, co-presenter My Favourite Nosh (BBC) 1996, Natürlich, Leichtes Kochen (Swiss TV) 1997, Mosimann's Culinary Switzerland (Swiss TV) 1998; Royal Warrant Holder for Catering to HRH Prince of Wales 2000, pres

Royal Warrant Holders Assoc 2006; hon prof Thames Valley Univ, invited as guest speaker Oxford Union 1997; winner of numerous gold medals and awards worldwide incl Chef of the Year 1985 and Restaurauteur of the Year 2000; Freeman City of London 1999; Hon Dr Culinary Arts Johnson and Wales Univ SC, Hon DSc Bournemouth Univ 1998; La Croix de Chevalier du Mérite Agricole, Officier National Ordre du Merite Agricole (France) 2006; *Books* Cuisine à la Carte (1981), The Great Seafood Book (1985), Cuisine Naturelle (1985), Anton Mosimann's Fish Cuisine (1988), The Art of Anton Mosimann (1989), Cooking with Mosimann (1989), Anton Mosimann - Naturally (1991), The Essential Mosimann (1993), Mosimann's World (1996), Mosimann's Fresh (2006); *Recreations* participating in the Peking to Paris Rally 2007, classic cars, collecting antiquarian cookery books, enjoying fine wine, passionate about food and travel; *Clubs* Reform, Garrick; *Style*— Anton Mosimann, Esq, OBE; ✉ Mosimann's, 11B West Halkin Street, Belgrave Square, London SW1X 8JL (tel 020 7235 9625, fax 020 7245 6354, e-mail amosimann@mosimann.com)

MOSLEY, Max Rufus; 4 *s* (but only 2 by his 2 w, Diana (Hon Lady Mosley)) of Sir Oswald Mosley, 6 Bt; *b* 13 April 1940; *Educ* ChCh Oxford (sec Oxford Union 1960); *m* 1960, Jean Marjorie, er da of James Taylor; 2 *s* (Alexander *b* 1970, Patrick *b* 1972); *Career* called to the Bar Gray's Inn 1964; dir March Cars Ltd, co-fndr March Grand Prix Team; former Formula Two racing driver; chair Mfrs Cmmn Fedn Internationale du Sport Automobile (FISA) 1986–91; pres: FISA 1991–93, FIA 1993–; legal advsr to Formula One Constructors Assoc; chair European New Car Assesment Prog 1997–2004; Supervisory Bd ERTICO Intelligent Transport Systems Europe: vice-chair 1999–2001, chair 2001–04, pres and spokesperson 2004–07, hon memb 2007–; hon pres: European Parl Automobile Users Gp 1994–99, Nat Road Safety Cncl Armenia 2005; co-fndr EU Cmmn: eSafety Forum 2003, CARS 21 High Level Gp 2005; fndr memb Institut du Cerveau et de la Moelle épinière France 2005; patron eSafety Aware 2006–; Gold medal Castrol/Inst of the Motor Industry 2000, Gold medal Quattroruote Premio Speciale per la sicurezza stradale (Italy) 2001, Der Goldene VdM-Dieselring (Germany) 2001; hon pres Nat Road Safety Cncl of Armenia 2006; Hon DCL Univ of Northumbria 2005; Order of Merit (Italy) 1994, Order of Madarski Kannik, First Degree (Bulgaria) 2000, Order of Merit (Romania) 2004, Huesped Ilustre de Quito (Ecuador) 2005, Chevalier de la Légion d'Honneur (France) 2006, Commandeur de l'Ordre de Saint Charles (Monaco) 2006; *Recreations* snowboarding, walking; *Style*— Max Mosley, Esq; ✉ 8 Place de la Concorde, 75008 Paris, France (tel 00 331 43 12 44 55)

MOSLEY, Nicholas; *see:* Ravensdale, 3 Baron

MOSS, Prof (Jennifer) Ann; da of John Shakespeare Poole (d 1945), and Dorothy Kathleen Beese, *née* Sills (d 1988); *b* 21 January 1938; *Educ* Barr's Hill GS Coventry, Newnham Coll Cambridge (MA, PhD); *Children* 2 da (Imogen *b* 1963, Abigail *b* 1965); *Career* asst lectr UC of North Wales 1963–64; Univ of Durham: resident tutor and pt/t lectr Trevelyan Coll 1966–79, univ lectr in French 1979–85, sr lectr 1985–88, reader 1988–96, prof of French 1996–2003; FBA 1998; *Books* Ovid in Renaissance France (1982), Poetry and Fable (1984), Printed Commonplace Books and the Structuring of Renaissance Thought (1996), Latin Commentaries on Ovid from the Renaissance (1998), Les recueils de lieux communs: apprendre à penser à la Renaissance (2002), Renaissance Truth and the Latin Language Turn (2003); *Recreations* children and grandchildren; *Style*— Prof Ann Moss, FBA; ✉ 7 Mountjoy Crescent, Durham DH1 3BA (tel 0191 383 0672, e-mail ann.moss@btinternet.com)

MOSS, His Hon Judge Christopher John; QC (1994); *s* of John Gordon (Jack) Moss (d 1984), of Kingston upon Thames, Surrey, and Joyce Mirren (Joy), *née* Stephany (d 2003); *b* 4 August 1948; *Educ* Bryanston, UCL (LLB); *m* 1, 11 Dec 1971 (m dis 1987), Gail Susan, da of late Frederick Pearson; 2 da (Melanie Jane *b* 17 Feb 1975, Rebecca Caroline *b* 1 Sept 1980), 1 *s* (Nicholas John *b* 17 Sept 1977); *m* 2, 31 March 1988 (m dis 1997), Tracy Louise, da of Geoffrey Levy; 1 *s* (Aaron Geoffrey *b* 2 Oct 1989), 1 da (Liberty Michele *b* 10 April 1992); *m* 3, 9 July 1999, Lisa Annette, da of Barry O'Dwyer; 2 da (Caitlin Philomena Joy *b* 5 March 2001, Mirren Lisa *b* 3 March 2003); *Career* called to the Bar Gray's Inn 1972; recorder of the Crown Court 1993, circuit judge (SE Circuit) 2002–; memb Criminal Bar Assoc 1980–; *Recreations* playing the piano and piano accordion; *Style*— His Hon Judge Moss, QC; ✉ Central Criminal Court, Old Bailey, London EC4M 7EH (tel 020 7248 3277)

MOSS, David John; *s* of John Henry Moss (d 2003), and Doris Fenna (d 2005); *b* 23 May 1947; *Educ* Sevenoaks Sch, St John's Coll Cambridge (MA), Central London Poly (DMS); *m* 24 May 1975, Susan Elizabeth, da of Reginald Victor Runnalls (d 1982); 3 *s* (Oliver Richard, Benjamin Roland (twins) *b* 21 April 1976, Jonathan Edward *b* 1 Dec 1980); *Career* mgmnt accountant Philips 1970–73 (mgmnt trainee 1968–70), asst fin offr St Thomas' Hosp 1973–74; dist fin offr: Enfield 1974–79, E Dorset 1979–85; unit gen mangr: Poole Gen Hosp 1985–88, Southampton Gen Hosp 1988–90; gen mangr Southampton Univ Hosps 1990–93, chief exec Southampton Univ Hosps NHS Tst 1993–2004; chm UK Univ Hosps Forum 2001–03, memb Audit Cmmn 2001–, dep dir of workforce Dept of Health 2003–07; memb CIPFA 1979, memb Inst of Healthcare Mgmnt 1979, FCMA 1981, FRSA 1994, FCMI (FIMgt 1984); *Books* Managing Nursing (co-author, 1984); *Recreations* history, golf, walking, opera, tennis, cricket; *Style*— David Moss, Esq; ✉ 41 Pinewood Road, Ferndown, Dorset BH22 9RP (>e-mail < davidmoss56@hotmail.com)

MOSS, David Reginald; *s* of Frank Moss, and Iris, *née* Thornton; *b* 11 March 1949; *Educ* Stockport Sch, Faculty of Art and Design Liverpool Poly (DipAD, RSA bursary); *m* 10 Aug 1971, Pauline Althea, da of Edward Scott Jones; 3 *s* (Robin James *b* 10 Nov 1973, Andrew Thornton, Laurence Scott (twins) *b* 20 Sept 1978); *Career* visualiser Clough Howard & Richards 1971–73; Brunning Advertising Liverpool: sr visualiser 1973–74, art dir 1974–75, creative controller 1975–76, creative dir 1977; exec prodr Five Cities Films 1977–79, bd account dir Michael Bungey DFS Liverpool 1979–85, account dir Brunning Advertising Yorkshire 1985–86; fndr dir: Quadrant Advertising and Marketing 1986–98, Insite-Webmedia 1998–2001; chm PSA Film Productions 2001–; memb Manchester Publicity Assoc, MIPA; *Recreations* photography, golf; *Clubs* Woolton Golf; *Style*— David Moss, Esq; ✉ 18 Menlove Gardens South, Liverpool L18 2EL (tel and fax 0151 722 9205, e-mail david@psa.u-net.com)

MOSS, Gabriel Stephen; QC (1989); *b* 8 September 1949; *Educ* Univ of Oxford (Eldon scholar, MA, BCL); *m* 1979, Judith; 1 da; *Career* called to the Bar Lincoln's Inn 1974 (Hardwicke and Cassel scholarships, bencher 1998); in practice specialising in business and fin law, dep judge of the High Court 2001–; fndr memb Bd Insolvency Res Unit KCL (now at Univ of Sussex) 1991–; called to the Bar Gibraltar; memb: Editorial Bd Insolvency Intelligence 1991– (chm 1994–), Insolvency Law Sub-Ctee of the Consumer and Commercial Law Ctee Law Soc 1991–, Insolvency Ctee of Justice 1993–, Advsy Ed Bd Receivers Administrators and Liquidators Quarterly 1993–, Insolvency Lawyers' Assoc 1999–, UK Insolvency Serv Review Panel (considering changes to Eng Law and practice in the light of EU Insolvency Regulation) 2000–, Editorial Bd Int Insolvency Review 2000–, Int Insolvency Inst 2001–; Insol Europe: assoc memb 1996–2001, memb 2001–; formerly: lectr Univ of Connecticut Law Sch, pt/t lectr/tutor Univ of Oxford, LSE and Cncl of Legal Educn; fell Soc of Advanced Legal Studies Inst of Advanced Legal Studies Univ of London 1998; *Books* Rowlatt on Principal and Surety (jt ed, 4 edn 1982, 5 edn 1999), Law of Receivers of Companies (jtly, 1986, 3 edn 2000), Ryde on Rating (contrib, 1990), Insolvency of Banks (jt author of chapter 6, Cross-Border Issues, 1996), Cross-Frontier Insolvency of Insurance Companies (jtly, 2001), The EC Regulation on Insolvency Proceedings (jtly, 2002); *Recreations* foreign travel, tennis; *Style*— Gabriel

Moss, Esq, QC; ✉ 3–4 South Square, Gray's Inn, London WC1R 5HP (tel 020 7696 9900, fax 020 7696 9911, e-mail clerks@southsquare.com)

MOSS, Kate; da of Peter Edward Moss, and Linda Rosina, *née* Shephard; *b* 16 January 1974, Croydon; *Educ* Riddlesdown HS Croydon; *Children* 1 da (Lila Grace b 29 Sept 2002); *Career* fashion model; first appeared on cover of British Vogue 1993, first cover girl of Russian Vogue; exclusive worldwide contract with Calvin Klein 1992–2000 (campaigns incl: Calvin Klein Obsession fragrance 1993, CK One fragrance 1994); various worldwide campaigns incl: Dolce & Gabbana, Katherine Hamnett, Versace and Versace Versus, Yves Saint Laurent, Louis Vuitton, Gucci, Rimmel London, Celine; appeared in the film Unzipped 1996; Fashion Personality of the Year British Fashion Awards 1995, Model of the Year British Fashion Awards 2001; *Books* Kate (1995); *Style*— Miss Kate Moss; ✉ c/o Storm Model Management, 5 Jubilee Place, London SW3 3TD (tel 020 7352 2278)

MOSS, Malcolm Douglas; MP; s of Norman Moss (d 1976), and Annie, *née* Gay (d 1996); *b* 6 March 1943; *Educ* Audenshaw GS, St John's Coll Cambridge (MA, CertEd); *m* 1, 28 Dec 1965, Vivien Lorraine (d 1997), da of Albert Peake (d 1964); 2 da (Alison Claire b 1969, Sarah Nicole b 1972); m 2, 12 May 2000, Sonya Alexandra McFarlin, *née* Evans; 1 step s (Justin), 1 step da (Kate); *Career* asst master then head of Geography and Economics Dept Blundell's Sch Tiverton 1966–70, gen mangr Barwick Associates 1972–74 (insurance conslt 1971–72), co-fndr and dir Mandrake (Insurance and Finance Brokers) Ltd 1974–94 (chm 1986–92, changed name to Mandrake Associates Ltd 1988), chm Mandrake Group plc 1986–88; dir: Mandrake (Insurance Services) Ltd 1976–81, Mandrake Collinge Ltd 1977–86, Mandrake (Insurance Advisory Service) Ltd 1978, Mandrake (Financial Management) Ltd 1985–87, Fens Business Enterprises Trust Ltd 1983–94 (chm 1983–87); MP (Cons) Cambs NE 1987–; memb Select Ctee on Energy 1988–91, PPS to Tristan Garel-Jones as min of state FCO 1991–93, PPS to Sir Patrick Mayhew as sec of state for NI 1993–94, Parly under-sec of state NI Office 1994–97; oppn whip 1997, oppn frontbench shadow min for NI 1997–99, oppn frontbench spokesman for agric, fisheries and food 1999–2001, oppn frontbench spokesman on tport, local govt and the regions 2001–02, shadow min for culture, media and sport 2002–06, memb Foreign Affrs Select Ctee 2006–; vice-chm Cons Backbench Energy Ctee 1989–92 (jt sec 1987–89); cncllr: Wisbech Town Cncl 1979–87, Fenland DC 1983–87, Cambs CC 1985–87; *Recreations* amateur dramatics, tennis, skiing; *Clubs* Lords and Commons Tennis and Ski; *Style*— Malcolm Moss, Esq, MP; ✉ House of Commons, London SW1A 0AA (tel 020 7219 6933, secretary 020 7219 1426, e-mail mossm@parliament.uk); business: 111 High Street, March, Cambridgeshire PE15 (tel 01354 656541); website malcmoss.easynet.co.uk

MOSS, Montague George; s of Harry Neville Moss (d 1982), and Ida Sophia, *née* Woolf (d 1971); *b* 21 April 1924; *Educ* Harrow, New Coll Oxford; *m* 28 Sept 1955, Jane, da of David Levi (d 1994); 1 da (Joanna b 15 Aug 1956), 2 s (Andrew b 7 Feb 1958, David b 15 Sept 1959); *Career* served Army 1943–47, cmmnd KRRC 1944, demobbed as Capt; Moss Bros Gp plc: dir 1953–87, chm 1981–87, pres 1987–; pres: Fedn of Merchant Tailors of GB 1965–66 and 1985–86, Tailors Benevolent Inst 1980–; Freeman City of London 1948, Liveryman Worshipful Co of Carmen 1949; *Recreations* public speaking, music; *Clubs* Jesters, Old Harrovian Eton Fives; *Style*— Montague Moss, Esq; ✉ 4 Melina Place, London NW8 9SA (tel 020 7286 0114); Moss Bros, Covent Garden, London WC2E 8JD (tel 020 7240 4062, fax 020 7379 5652)

MOSS, His Hon Judge Peter Jonathan; s of Capt John Cottam Moss (d 1997), and Joyce Alison, *née* Blunn (d 1977); *b* 29 March 1951; *Educ* Charterhouse; *m* (m dis 2003), Rosanne Marilyn, da of late Alexander James Houston, of Emsworth, Hants; 3 s (Alexander b 28 Oct 1981, Ben b 14 Nov 1983, Patrick b 22 April 1987); *Career* called to the Bar Lincoln's Inn 1976; asst recorder 1999, recorder 2000, circuit judge (SE Circuit) 2004–; memb Mental Health Review Tbnl 1994–; Freeman City of London 1985, Liveryman Worshipful Co of Clockmakers 1987; *Recreations* golf, windsurfing, skiing, cricket, fishing, motorcycling, fun; *Clubs* New Zealand Golf, MCC; *Style*— His Hon Judge Peter Moss; ✉ Woolwich Crown Court, 2 Belmarsh Road, London SE28 0EY

MOSS, His Hon Judge Ronald Trevor; s of Maurice Moss, and Sarah, *née* Camlett; *b* 1 October 1942; *Educ* Univ of Nottingham (BA); *m* 28 March 1971, Cindy, da of Archie Fiddleman; 1 s (Andrew b 18 Dec 1972), 1 da (Clare b 14 Nov 1974); *Career* admitted slr 1968, ptnr Moss Beachley slrs 1972–84, metropolitan stipendiary magistrate 1984–93, chm Youth Ct 1986–93, chm Family Ct 1991–93, memb Inner London Probation Ctee 1991–93, circuit judge (SE Circuit) 1993–; resident judge: Luton Crown Court 2001–05, Harrow Crown Court 2005–; *Recreations* golf, bridge, watching association football (Watford FC); *Clubs* Moor Park Golf; *Style*— His Hon Judge Moss; ✉ Harrow Crown Court, Hailsham Drive, Harrow HA1 4TU

MOSS, Stephen Raymond; s of Raymond Moss, and Catherine, *née* Croome; *b* 30 July 1957; *Educ* Hartridge HS Newport, Balliol Coll Oxford (BA), Univ of London (MA); *m* 1984, Helen Mary Bonnick; 1 s (Timothy b 1986); *Career* worked previously in magazine and book publishing; The Guardian: sometime dep arts ed and dep features ed 1989–95, literary ed 1995–98, feature writer 1999–; *Recreations* cricket, chess, riding; *Style*— Stephen Moss, Esq; ✉ c/o The Guardian, 119 Farringdon Road, London EC1R 3ER (tel 020 7278 2332, fax 020 7239 9935, e-mail stephen.moss@guardian.co.uk)

MOSS, Sir Stirling; kt (2000), OBE (1957); s of Alfred Moss, and Aileen Moss; *b* 17 September 1929; *Educ* Haileybury and ISC; *m* 1, 1957 (m dis 1960), Kathleen, da of F Stuart Molson, of Canada; m 2, 1964 (m dis 1968), Elaine, da of A Barbarino, of New York; 1 da; m 3, 1980, Susan, da of Stuart Paine of London; 1 s; *Career* racing driver 1947–62; learnt to drive aged 6, built own Cooper-Alta 1953, Br Nat Champion 1950–52, 1954–59 and 1961; winner: Tourist Trophy 1950–51, 1955 and 1958–61, Coupe des Alpes 1952–54, Alpine Gold Cup 1954, Italian Mille Miglia 1955 (only Englishman to win); competed in 529 races, rallies, sprints, land speed records and endurance runs, completed 387 and won 211; Grand Prix and successes incl: Targa Florio 1955, Br 1955 and 1957, Italian 1956–57 and 1959, NZ 1956 and 1959, Monaco 1956 and 1960–61, Leguna Seca 1960–61, US 1959–60, Aust 1956, Bari 1956, Pesara 1957, Swedish 1957, Dutch 1958, Argentinian 1958, Moroccan 1958, Buenos Aires 1958, Melbourne 1958, Villareal 1958, Caen 1958, Portuguese 1959, South African 1960, Cuban 1960, Austrian 1960, Cape Town 1960, Watkins Glen 1960, German 1961, Modena 1961; Driver of the Year 1954 and 1961, holder of 1500cc World speed record driving MG EX181 at 240mph; md Stirling Moss Ltd; dir: Designs Unlimited Ltd, SM Design & Interior Decorating Co, Hankoe Stove Enamelling Ltd; former dir of racing Johnson's Wax; judge: Miss World (4 times), Miss Universe 1974; former demonstrator Dunlop Rubber Co (travelled across India and Malaysia); conslt incl work for: Ferodo Opel Germany and Chrysler Aust; has given numerous lecture tours across US and in UK, NZ, Aust and Hong Kong; *Books* Stirling Moss's Book of Motor Sport (1955), In the Track of Speed (1957), Stirling Moss's Second Book of Motor Sport (1958), Le Mans (1959), My Favourite Car Stories (1960), A Turn at the Wheel (1961), All But My Life (1963), Design and Behaviour of the Racing Car (1964), How to Watch Motor Racing (1975), Motor Racing and All That (1980), My Cars, My Career (1987), Fangio, A Pirelli Album (1991), Great Drives in the Lakes (1993), Motor Racing Masterpieces (1994); *Recreations* historic motor racing, cruising, work, model making, designing; *Clubs* Br Racing Drivers', Br Automobile Racing, Br Racing and Sports Car, Road Racing Drivers of America, 200mph, RAC, International des Anciens Pilotes des Grand Prix; chm or pres of 36 motoring clubs; *Style*— Sir Stirling Moss, OBE; ✉ 46 Shepherd Street, London W1J 7JN (tel 020 7499 7967, 020 7499 3727, fax 020 7499 4104)

MOSS, Stuart; s of Morris Moss (d 1976), of London, and Bertha Moss; *b* 31 December 1944; *Educ* Grocers' Co Sch, Regent St Poly (DipArch); *m* 1, 24 June 1973 (m dis 1985), Layn Sandra, da of Ronald Feldman, of London; 2 s (Lucas Ryan b 1974, Daniel Miles b 1979), 1 da (Zoë Anastasia b 1982); m 2, 1993, Lesley Ben Evan; 1 s (Jacob Jeffrey b 7 Aug 1993); *Career* qualified as chartered architect 1972; assoc with Robert Turner Architects 1973–75, formed partnership with John Bennett 1975–84, formed Moss & Co Architects 1985–; author of various articles written for architectural magazines; RIBA, MRIAI; *Recreations* the visual arts, reading, travel; *Style*— Stuart Moss, Esq; ✉ Moss & Co Architects, 11 Broadbent Close, Highgate High Street, London N6 5JW (tel 020 8348 4888, fax 020 8348 4877)

MOSSE, Katharine Louise (Kate); da of Richard Hugh Mosse, of Chichester, W Sussex, and Barbara Mary, *née* Towlson; *b* 20 October 1961; *Educ* Chichester HS for Girls, New Coll Oxford (MA); *Partner* Greg Charles Mosse, *né* Dunk; 1 da (Martha b 25 Feb 1990), 1 s (Felix b 8 Oct 1992); *Career* various positions rising to ed dir Random House (UK) 1985–92; co-fndr Orange Prize for Fiction (chair Judging Panel 1996, hon dir 1998–); memb: Arts for Everyone (A4E) Panel Arts Cncl of England, Labour Party; former memb: Women in Publishing, Women in Management in Publishing, NUJ; former dep dir Chichester Festival Theatre; presenter Saturday Review BBC Radio 4; judge: Asham Award 1999, Business & Sponsorship Awards Financial Times 1999; European Woman of Achievement for Contribution to the Arts 2000; *Books* Becoming a Mother (1993 and 1997), The House: A Year in the Life of the Royal Opera House Covent Garden (1996), Eskimo Kissing (novel, 1996), Crucifix Lane (novel, 1998), Labyrinth (novel, 2005); *Recreations* theatre, literature, classical music, swimming, politics, walking; *Style*— Ms Kate Mosse; ✉ c/o Mark Lucas, Lucas Alexander Whitley Ltd, Elsinore House, 77 Fulham Palace Road, London W6 8JA

MOSSOP, James; s of James Mossop (d 1943), and Emma, *née* Wilson (d 1965); *b* 2 August 1936; *Educ* Barrow-in-Furness GS; *m* 1, 1958 (m dis 1975), June, *née* Large; 1 da (Judith Lyn b 1959), 1 s (John James b 1960); m 2, Prof Sandra Holtby, OBE; *Career* sports writer; North Western Evening Mail Barrow-in-Furness 1954–61 (jr reporter, sr reporter, sub-ed, dep sports ed), sports sub-ed Daily Mail Manchester 1961–63, sports writer Sunday Express (Manchester) 1963–74, chief sports writer Sunday Express 1974–96, sports feature writer Sunday Telegraph 1996–; major assignments incl: Olympic Games 1976, 1980, 1984, 1988, 1992, 1996, 2000 and 2004, football World Cup 1966, 1970, 1978, 1982, 1986, 1990, 1994, 1998 and 2006, numerous golf, boxing, motor racing, athletics and cricket events; commended Br Press Awards 1980 and 1982, Minet Olympic Sports Writer of the Year Br Sports Journalism Awards 1993; memb: Sports Writers' Assoc, Assoc of Golf Writers, Boxing Writers' Club, Football Writers' Assoc; *Recreations* golf, horse racing; *Clubs* Ashton-on-Mersey Golf, European Golf (Wicklow Ireland); *Style*— James Mossop, Esq; ✉ mobile 07710 908362, e-mail jmossop@compuserve.com

MOSTYN, 6 Baron (UK 1831); Llewellyn Roger Lloyd-Mostyn; 7 Bt (GB 1778); s of 5 Baron Mostyn, MC, by his 1 w Yvonne (later Lady Wrixon-Becher; d 2004); *b* 26 September 1948; *Educ* Eton, Inns of Court Sch of Law; *m* 1974, Denise Suzanne, da of Roger Duvanel, an artist, of France; 1 da (Alexandra Stephanie b 1975), 1 s (Gregory Philip Roger b 1984); *Heir* s, Gregory Lloyd Mostyn; *Career* late Capt Army Legal Servs; called to the Bar Middle Temple 1973 (practising Criminal Bar), pt/t teacher at Bromley Coll of Technol; *Recreations* literature, history, classical music, tennis, sport, rugger; *Style*— The Rt Hon the Lord Mostyn; ✉ 9 Anderson Street, London SW3 (tel 020 7584 3059); c/o 184–185 Temple Buildings, The Temple, London EC4

MOSTYN, Nicholas Anthony Joseph Ghislain; QC (1997); of Jerome Mostyn, of Salisbury, Wilts, and Mary Learoyd, *née* Medlicott; *b* 13 July 1957; *Educ* Ampleforth, Univ of Bristol (LLB); *m* 1981, Lucy Willis; 3 s (Henry b 1987, Gregory b 1995, Charlie b 1998), 1 da (Daisy b 1989); *Career* called to the Bar Middle Temple 1980 (bencher 2005), recorder 2000 (asst recorder 1997), dep judge of the High Court 2000; Knight of Honour and Devotion SMO Malta 2003; *Publications* Child's Pay (1993, 3rd edn 2002), At a Glance (15 edn 2006); *Recreations* Southampton FC, Wagner, skiing; *Clubs* MCC; *Style*— Nicholas Mostyn, Esq, QC; ✉ 1 Hare Court, Temple, London EC4Y 7BE (tel 020 7797 7070, fax 020 7797 7435, e-mail nmostyn@compuserve.com)

MOSTYN, (Sir) William Basil John; *de jure* 15 Bt (E 1670), of Talacre, Flintshire, but claim has not yet been submitted for entry on the Official Roll of the Baronetage; o s of Sir Jeremy John Anthony Mostyn, 14 Bt (d 1988), and Cristina Beatrice Maria, o da of Marchese Pier-Paolo Vladimiro Orengo; sr male rep of Tudor Trevor, Lord of Hereford (10 cent); *b* 15 October 1975; *Heir* unc, Trevor Mostyn; *Style*— William Mostyn, Esq; ✉ The Coach House, Lower Heyford, Oxfordshire

MOTHERWELL, Bishop of (RC) 1983–; Rt Rev Joseph Devine; s of Joseph Devine (d 1989), and Christina, *née* Murphy (d 1981); *b* 7 August 1937; *Educ* Blairs Coll Aberdeen, St Peter's Coll Dumbarton, Pontificial Scots Coll Rome, Gregorian Univ Rome (PhD); *Career* personal sec to Archbishop of Glasgow 1964–66, lectr in philosophy St Peter's Coll Dumbarton 1966–74, chaplain Univ of Glasgow 1974–77, auxiliary bishop Glasgow 1977–83; Papal Bene Merenti 1962; *Recreations* reading, music, soccer; *Style*— The Rt Rev the Bishop of Motherwell; ✉ Bishop's House, 22 Wellhall Road, Hamilton ML3 9BS (tel 01698 423058)

MOTION, Andrew; s of Lt-Col A R Motion, of Braintree, Essex, and C G Motion (d 1982); *b* 26 October 1952; *Educ* Radley, UC Oxford; *m* 1985, Jan Dalley, *qv*, da of C M Dalley, of Maldon, Essex; 2 s (Andrew Jesse b 26 July 1986, Lucas Edward b 19 May 1988), 1 da (Sidonie Gillian Elizabeth (twin) b 19 May 1988); *Career* Poet Laureate 1999; currently prof of creative writing Royal Holloway Univ of London; formerly: poetry ed Chatto & Windus, ed Poetry Review; freelance writer; prizes incl: Avon Observer prize 1982; memb Arts Cncl of England (currently chm Lit Panel); Hon DLitt: Univ of Hull, Univ of Exeter, Brunel Univ, Anglia Poly Univ, Open Univ, Sheffield Hallam Univ; hon fell UC Oxford; FRSL 1984, FRSA 2000; *Poetry* incl: The Pleasure Steamers (1978), The Penguin Book of Contemporary British Poetry (ed with Blake Morrison, 1982), Dangerous Play (John Llewelyn Rhys prize, 1984), Natural Causes (Dylan Thomas prize, 1988), Love in a Life (1991), Salt Water (1997), Selected Poems (1998), Public Property (2002); *Writings* incl: The Lamberts (Somerset Maugham award 1987), Philip Larkin: A Writer's Life (Whitbread award for biography, 1993), Keats (1997), Wainewright the Poisoner (2000), The Invention of Dr Cake (2003); *Style*— Prof Andrew Motion, FRSL

MOTSON, John Walker; OBE (2001); s of Rev William Motson (d 1992), of Worthing, W Sussex, and Gwendoline Mary Motson (d 1991); *b* 10 July 1945; *Educ* Culford Sch Bury St Edmunds, NCTJ (Cert); *m* 1976, (Jennifer) Anne, da of Cyril Jobling (d 1991), and Marion Jobling; 1 s (Frederick James b 4 Feb 1986); *Career* football commentator and reporter; news and sports reporter Barnet Press 1963–67, sports writer and sub ed Morning Telegraph Sheffield 1967–68, freelance BBC Radio Sheffield 1968, presenter, reporter and commentator (football, boxing, tennis) BBC Network Radio Sports Dept 1968–71, football commentator and reporter BBC TV (incl Match of the Day, Sportsnight, Grandstand and other outside broadcasts) 1971–; major events as commentator: all World Cups 1974– (incl finals 1982–, commentator on record fifth World Cup Final Japan 2002), all Euro Championships 1976– (incl finals 1980–), FA Cup Final annually 1977– (commentator on record 25th FA Cup Final BBC 2004); writer and narrator over 20 football videos for BBC Enterprises 1987–, also numerous club histories and Match of the Day compilations; voted nation's favourite commentator Carling-Net website 1998;

Books Second to None: Great Teams of Post-War Soccer (1972), The History of the European Cup (with John Rowlinson, 1980), Match of the Day: the Complete Record (1992, reprinted 1994), Motty's Diary (1996), Motty's Year 2004 (2004), Motson's National Obsession (2004), Motson's FA Cup Odyssey (2005), Motson's World Cup Extravaganza (2006); *Recreations* running (half marathons and 10km races), reading novels, theatre, cinema, watching sport; *Style*— John Motson, Esq, OBE; ✉ c/o Jane Morgan Management, Thames Wharf Studios, Rainville Road, London W6 9HA (tel 020 7386 5345, fax 020 7386 0338, e-mail enquiries@janemorganmgt.com)

MOTT, Sir John Harmar; 3 Bt (UK 1930), of Ditchling, Co Sussex; s of Sir Adrian Spear Mott, 2 Bt (d 1964), and Mary Katherine, *née* Stanton (d 1972); *b* 21 July 1922; *Educ* Radley, New Coll Oxford (MA, BM BCh), Middx Hosp; *m* 1950, Elizabeth, da of Hugh Carson, FRCS (d 1981), of Selly Oak, Birmingham; 1 s (David Hugh b 1952), 2 da (Jennifer (Mrs Robert A Buckey) b 1954, Alison Mary b 1958); *Heir* s, David Mott; *Career* served 1939–45 RAF, Flying Offr 1943–46, Far East; qualified med practitioner 1951; regnl med offr DHSS 1969–84, ret; MRCGP; *Recreations* photography, classical archaeology and history; *Style*— Sir John Mott, Bt; ✉ Staniford, Brookside, Kingsley, Cheshire WA6 8BG (tel 01928 788123)

MOTT, His Hon Michael Duncan; s of Francis John Mott (d 1979), and Gwendolen, *née* Mayhew (d 2005); *b* 8 December 1940; *Educ* Rugby, Gonville & Caius Coll Cambridge (MA); *m* 19 Dec 1970, Phyllis Ann, da of V James Gavin, of Dubuque, Iowa, USA; 2 s (Timothy b 1972, Jonathan b 1975); *Career* called to the Bar Inner Temple 1963; in chambers Birmingham 1964–69, resident magistrate Kenya 1969–71, in practice Midland & Oxford circuit 1972–85, dep circuit judge 1976–80, recorder 1980–85, circuit judge (Midland Circuit) 1985–2006; parish cncllr 1982–86, parish organist 1984–; *Recreations* music, travel, skiing, tennis; *Clubs* Cambridge Union; *Style*— His Hon Michael Mott; ✉ c/o Midland Regional Office, HMCS, Temple Court, Bull Street, Birmingham B4 6WF (tel 0121 681 3205)

MOTT, Philip Charles; QC (1991); s of Charles Kynaston Mott (d 1981), of Taunton, Somerset, and Elsa, *née* Smith (d 2000); *b* 20 April 1948; *Educ* King's Coll Taunton, Worcester Coll Oxford (MA); *m* 19 Nov 1977, Penelope Ann, da of Edward Caffery; 2 da (Sarah b 1981, Catherine b 1983); *Career* called to the Bar Inner Temple 1970; practising Western Circuit 1970–, recorder of the Crown Court 1987–, dep judge of the High Court 1998–, ldr Western Circuit 2004–07; chm Restricted Patients Panel Mental Health Review Tbnl 2000–; memb: Bar Legal Services Ctee 2004–05, Advocacy Trg Cncl 2004–, Bar Carter Response Gp 2005–; vice-chm Bar Policy & Res Gp 2006–07; *Recreations* the countryside, growing trees, sailing; *Clubs* Bar Yacht, Percuil Sailing; *Style*— Philip Mott, Esq, QC; ✉ Outer Temple Chambers, 222 Strand, London WC2R 1BA (tel 020 7353 6381, fax 020 7583 1786, e-mail philip.mottqc@outertemple.com)

MOTT, Susan Jane (Sue); da of Dennis Charles Mott, and Jean, *née*, Taylor; *Educ* Woodhouse GS London, Univ of Nottingham (BA); *Children* 1 s (Tom), 1 da (Jeannie); *Career* journalist; trainee Hull Daily Mail 1979–81, freelance journalist NY Daily News and San Francisco Chronicle 1982–85; sports feature writer: The Australian 1985–86, Sunday Times 1986–94, Daily Telegraph 1994–; TV presenter On the Line (BBC) 1987–91; Sports Feature Writer of the Year 1995 (highly commended 1999 and 2001), highly commended UK Press Awards 1999; *Publications* Girl's Guide to Ball Games (1996, shortlisted William Hill Sports Book Awards); *Recreations* Arsenal FC, tennis; *Clubs* Henham Tennis, Dover Street Wine Bar; *Style*— Ms Sue Mott; ✉ The Daily Telegraph, 1 Canada Square, Canary Wharf, London E14 5DT (tel 020 7538 5000)

MOTT, Toby Victor; s of James Mott, of London, and Patricia, *née* Stark; *b* 12 January 1964; *Career* artist; founding memb Grey Orgn (artists' gp) 1983–90, curator of exhbns Coins Coffee Shop London 1996–; dir DEF COM Ltd 1998– (supplying products incl fashion, homeware and stationery, under Toby Pimlico and Toby Studio brands); involved with numerous charities *Solo Exhibitions* Jean Louis Pierson Gallery San Francisco 1993, Survey (Thomas Solomon's Garage LA) 1993, Lost in Music (Tri Gallery LA) 1995, Maureen Paley Interim Art London 1995, London 1997 (Maureen Paley Interim Art London) 1997, Totally London (designed London bus for mayor Ken Livingstone) 2004; *Group Exhibitions* Riot Furniture (Furniture of the Twentieth Century NY) 1991, Casual Ceremony (White Columns NY) 1991, Scraping By (Project Box LA) 1994, Elements of Mystery, Motifs of Lunacy (PS1 Museum NY) 1994, Given Space (Canute's Pavillion Ocean Village Southampton) 1994, Candy Man II (Building C - Tower Bridge London) 1994, House of Styles (Tri Gallery LA) 1995, Action Station, Exploring Open Systems (Santa Monica Museum of Art) 1995, Greatest Hits (Tri Gallery LA) 1995, Sick (152c Brick Lane London) 1995, Affinità (Castello di Rivara Torino) 1996, Loosy (Galerie Philippe Rizzo Paris) 1996, Flag (Clink Street London) 1996, Some Drawings: from London (Princelet Street London) 1996, Vocimiecontemporanee (Sala 1 Rome) 1997, Host (Tramway Glasgow) 1998, The Road (Espace Culturel François Mitterand Beauvais) 1998, The Forest (Tabernacle London) 1998, Klega's Flat (Sali Gia Gallery London) 1999, Temple of Diana (Blue Gallery London) 1999, Big Blue, Century City (Tate Modern) 2001, Copy (Roth Horowitz NY) 2002, Let There Be Light (B&B Italia London) 2003, Sirreal (Redux Gallery London) 2004; *Recreations* poetry, long country walks, gardening; *Style*— Toby Mott, Esq; ✉ 7 Powis Mews, London W11 1JN (tel 020 7727 7244, fax 020 7221 5695, e-mail toby@tobypimlico.com)

MOTTERSHEAD, Christopher Alan Leigh (Chris); s of Alan Mottershead, and Elvene Mottershead; *b* 24 September 1958; *Educ* Cowbridge Sch, Univ of Warwick (BA); *m* Vivienne; 3 da (Olivia b 25 Oct 1992, Lily b 20 July 1994, Holly b 25 April 1996), 1 s (Joseph b 14 Dec 1998); *Career* grad trainee Wales Gas 1980–84, prodn control mangr, accounts mangr and fin accountant Business Forms Div Burroughs Machines Ltd 1984–86, fin controller Sterilin/Motil Plastics Ltd 1987–88, fin dir Avon Inflatables Ltd 1988–90, gp fin dir Aspro Travel & Inter European Airways 1990–93; Airtours plc: md Airtours Holidays 1998–2000 (fin dir 1993–97, dep md and fin dir 1997–98), pres and ceo N American Leisure Gp 2000–01; md TUI UK (Thomson Holidays, Lunn Poly, Travelhouse and Portland) 2001–04, gp ceo Travelzest plc 2005; ACMA 1985; *Style*— Chris Mottershead, Esq

MOTTERSHEAD, Derek Stuart; s of Alan Mottershead (d 1954), of Blackpool, and Irene, *née* Huyton; *b* 2 September 1947; *Educ* Royal Masonic Sch Bushey, Univ of Manchester (BSc); *m* 1, 1 Sept 1969 (m dis 1988), Jean, da of James Arthur Wright, of Nelson, Lancs; 3 da (Gillian b 30 May 1964, Sarah b 11 April 1972, Lucy b 17 Feb 1982); m 2, 5 June 1993, Jacqui, da of Michael Martin, of Aspley Guise, Beds; *Career* mktg dir Pretty Polly Ltd (winner Br Mktg awards 3 consecutive years) 1976–80, Euro mktg dir Lee Apparel UK Ltd (subsid Vanity Fair Corp America) 1980–82, mktg dir Lee Cooper Ltd 1982–84, md All-time Sportswear UK Ltd 1984–87, md Prontaprint plc 1987–92 (chm Prontaprint Communications Ltd, md Prontaprint International Ltd, jt gp md Continuous Stationery plc), jt md Prontaprint Group plc 1992–93, chm and md Prontaprint Ltd, chm and md The Franchise Option 1993–, md Bang and Olufsen UK Ltd 1994–; chm Br Franchise Assoc 1992–93, vice-pres Br Small Business Bureau; memb: Br Inst of Mktg, IOD; *Recreations* private aviation, golf, shooting; *Style*— Derek Mottershead, Esq; ✉ Bang and Olufsen UK Ltd, Unit 630, Wharfedale Road, Winnersh, Wokingham, Berkshire (tel 0118 969 2288, fax 0118 969 3388, e-mail dmt@bang-olufsen.dk)

MOTTISTONE, 4 Baron (UK 1933); David Peter Seely; CBE (1984); 4 s of 1 Baron Mottistone, CB, CMG, DSO, TD, PC (d 1947; himself 3 s of Sir Charles Seely, 1 Bt), by his 2 w, Hon Evelyn Izmé Murray, JP, da of 10 Lord and 1 Viscount Elibank and widow of George Nicholson (s of Sir Charles Nicholson, 1 Bt) by whom she was mother of Sir John Nicholson, 2 Bt; Lord Mottistone succeeded his half-bro, 3 Baron, 1966; *b* 16 December 1920, (HRH The Duke of Windsor stood sponsor); *Educ* RNC Dartmouth; *m* 1944, Anthea Christine, da of Victor McMullan, of Co Down; 2 s, 3 da (1 decd); *Heir* s, Hon Peter Seely (HRH The Duke of Edinburgh stood sponsor); *Career* sat as Cons in House of Lords until Nov 1999; Cdr RN 1955, Capt RN 1960 (D) 24 Escort Sqdn 1963–65; ret at own request 1967; dir personnel trg Radio Rentals Ltd 1967–69, dir Distributive Industry Trg Bd 1969–75; dir Cake and Biscuit Alliance 1975–81, Parly advsr Biscuit, Cake, Chocolate and Confectionary Alliance 1981–99 (export sec 1981–83); DL IOW 1981, HM Lord-Lt IOW 1986–95, Govr IOW 1992–95; KStJ 1989; pres East Wessex TAVRA 1990–93, chm of tstees SANE 1987–99; Hon DLitt Bournemouth Univ 1993; FIEE, FIPM; *Clubs* Royal Yacht Sqdn, Royal Cruising, Royal Naval Sailing Assoc, Island Sailing, Royal Cwlth Soc, House of Lords Yacht (Cdre 1985–98); *Style*— The Rt Hon the Lord Mottistone, CBE; ✉ Old Parsonage, Mottistone, Isle of Wight PO30 4EE (tel and fax 01983 740264)

MOTTRAM, Sir Richard Clive; GCB (2006, KCB 1998); s of John Mottram (d 1991), of Chislehurst, Kent, and Florence Bertha, *née* Yates; *b* 23 April 1946; *Educ* King Edward VI Camp Hill Sch Birmingham, Keele Univ (BA); *m* 24 July 1971, Dr Fiona Margaret Mottram, da of Keith David Erskine (d 1974) and Audrey, *née* Skinner (d 2003); 3 s (Keith b 1974, David b 1981, Thomas b 1985), 1 da (Ruth b 1977); *Career* Home Civil Serv, assigned MOD 1968, Cabinet Office 1975–77, private sec to Perm Under Sec of State MOD 1979–81, private sec to Sec of State for Def 1982–86, asst under sec MOD 1986–89, dep under sec (policy) MOD 1989–92; perm sec: Office of Public Service and Science 1992–95, MOD 1995–98, DETR 1998–2001, DTLR 2001–02, Dept for Work and Pensions 2002–05; prem sec Intelligence, Security and Resilience Cabinet Office and chair Jt Intelligence Ctee 2005–; pres Cwlth Assoc for Public Admin and Mgmnt 2000–02 (vice-pres 1998–2000); govr: Ditchley Fndn 1996–, Ashridge Mgmnt Coll 1998–; memb Acad of Learned Socs for the Social Services 1999–; Hon DLitt Keele Univ 1996; *Recreations* theatre, cinema; *Style*— Sir Richard Mottram, GCB

MOULD, Christopher Peter; s of Peter Sidney Mould (d 1998), of Pembrokeshire, and Phyllida Charlotte Elaine, *née* Ormond; *b* 30 November 1958; *Educ* Royal GS High Wycombe, Magdalen Coll Oxford (BA), LSE (MSc); *m* 18 Aug 1979, Angela Geraldine, da of Roger Ellis Druce; 4 da (Hannah Elizabeth b 26 Dec 1984, Verity Ruth b 20 June 1986, Alicia Ellen Joy b 27 April 1990, Madeleine Grace b 4 June 1993); *Career* fund raiser LEPRA 1982, planning asst NE Thames RHA 1982–83, planning mangr Southend Health Authy 1983–86, hosp mangr Southend Hosp 1986–88, gen mangr Community and Mental Health Servs S Beds Health Authy 1989–91 (gen mangr Mental Health 1988–89), chief exec (designate) S Beds Community Health Care NHS Tst 1991–92, dist gen mangr Salisbury Health Authy and chief exec Salisbury Health Care 1992–94, chief exec Salisbury Health Care NHS Tst 1994–98 and 1999–2003, prog dir Prog Cmmn for Strategic Change in Wiltshire and Swindon (health care) 1998–99 (on secondment); dir Nat Police Trg 2001–02, chief exec Centrex (Central Police Trg and Devpt Authy) 2002–03; conslt in strategy and organizational change; chair and memb various police ctees and bds until 2004; chm Healthwork UK (Health Care National Trg Orgn) 1998–2001; prog dir: Postgrad Medical Educn and Trg Bd 2004–05, V (Nat Youth Vol Charity) 2006–07; chm Fndn Redlynch C of E Primary Sch 2005–06 (govr 1994–2002); tstee Ffald y Brenin Tst 1994–, tstee and dir Trussell Tst 2004–; appraisal fellowship Nuffield Prov Hosps Tst, 4th prize RIPA/Hay Award for Managerial Innovation 1989; MHSM, DipHSM; *Recreations* jazz guitar, hockey, running, Christian preaching; *Style*— Chris Mould, Esq; ✉ Ash Grove House, Church Hill, Lover, Salisbury, Wiltshire SP5 2PL (tel 01725 510468, mobile 07881 624887, e-mail chris@chrismould.co.uk)

MOULTON, Jonathan Paul (Jon); s of Douglas Cecil Moulton (d 1992), of Stoke-on-Trent, and Elsie Turner Moulton (d 1984); *b* 15 October 1950; *Educ* Hanley HS, Lancaster Univ (BA); *m* 13 Aug 1973, Pauline Marie, da of Stanley Dunn, of Stoke-on-Trent; 1 da (Rebecca Clare b 1978), 1 s (Spencer Jonathan b 1980); *Career* mangr Coopers & Lybrand 1972–80; Citicorp Venture Capital: dir NY 1980–81, gen mangr London 1981–85, managing ptnr Schroder Ventures 1985–94; dir Apax & Co 1994–97, managing ptnr Alchemy Partners 1997–, chm A G Stanley plc 1997–98; non-exec dir: Haden MacLellan Holdings plc 1987–2000, Appledore Holdings Ltd 1990–93, Ushers Holdings plc 1991–98, R J B Mining plc 1992–94, Unicorn Abrasives plc 1995–97, Prestige Holdings Ltd 1995–99, United Texon plc 1995–98, Brands Hatch Leisure Holdings plc 1995–98, Phoenix IT Services Ltd 1997, USM Group Holdings Ltd 1997–2000, Ashmore Group plc 1999–, Wardle Storeys plc 2000–01, Aardvark TMC Ltd 2001–04, Datapoint 2001–, Cedar plc 2002–; chm: British Allergy Fndn 1996–99, Airborne Systems Gp Ltd 2001–, Riverdeep 2003–04, Tattershall Castle Group Ltd 2005–; dep chm Parker Pen Ltd 1986–97; tstee UK Stem Cell Fndn 2005–; Corporate Finance Qualification (ICAEW); FCA 1983, FIMgt, fell Soc of Turnaround Professionals; *Recreations* chess, fishing; *Style*— Jon Moulton, Esq; ✉ The Mount, Church Street, Shoreham, Sevenoaks, Kent TN14 7SD (tel 01959 524008, fax 01959 525809)

MOUNFIELD, Dr Peter Reginald; s of Reginald Howard Mounfield (d 1969), of Benllech, Gwynedd, and Irene, *née* Williams (d 1992); *b* 15 February 1935; *Educ* Canon Slade GS Bolton, Univ of Nottingham (BA, PhD); *m* 12 Sept 1959, Patricia, da of Ernest John Jarrett (d 1991); 2 s (John, David); *Career* asst lectr then lectr Dept of Geography and Anthropology Univ Coll of Wales Aberystwyth 1958–68, lectr then sr lectr Univ of Leicester 1968– (head Dept of Geography 1988–91); visiting assoc prof Dept of Geography and Regnl Planning Univ of Cincinnati Ohio USA 1966–67, sr Fulbright scholar 1966–67, sr visiting res fell Jesus Coll Oxford 1988; *Books* World Nuclear Power (1991), Victoria County History of Northamptonshire (Industry and Transport) (contrib footwear and leather chapters, 2007); *Recreations* lawn bowls, gardening, bridge; *Clubs* RGS; *Style*— Dr Peter Mounfield; ✉ Department of Geography, University of Leicester, University Road, Leicester LE1 7RH (tel 0116 252 3840, fax 0116 252 3854, e-mail pandp@mounfield.wanadoo.co.uk)

MOUNSEY-HEYSHAM, Giles Herchard; s of Maj Richard Herchard Gubbins Mounsey-Heysham (d 1960), of Castletown, Rockcliffe, Carlisle, and Mrs Isobel Margaret Rowcliffe; *b* 15 August 1948; *Educ* Gordonstoun, RAC Cirencester; *m* 24 April 1982, Penelope Auriol, da of William Anthony Twiston-Davies (see Debrett's Peerage and Baronetage, Archdale, Bt); 3 s (Toby b 23 Jan 1984, Benjamin b 3 March 1986, Rory b 2 Feb 1989), 1 da (Anna b 29 May 1991); *Career* chartered surveyor; Smiths Gore 1970–72, Cluttons 1973– (ptnr 1976); memb Ct of Assts Worshipful Co of Grocers; FRICS 1982 (memb 1972); *Recreations* music, walking, travelling, motorbiking, golf; *Clubs* Boodle's, Pratt's; *Style*— Giles Mounsey-Heysham, Esq; ✉ Castletown Estate Office, Rockcliffe, Carlisle CA6 4BN (tel 01228 674792, fax 01228 674464)

MOUNT, (Sir) (William Robert) Ferdinand; 3 Bt (UK 1921), of Wasing Place, Reading, Berks, but does not use his title; s of Robert Francis Mount (d 1969, 2 s of Sir William Arthur Mount, 1 Bt, CBE), and his 1 w, Lady Julia Agnes Cynthia Pakenham (d 1956), da of 5 Earl of Longford; suc unc, Sir William Malcolm Mount, 2 Bt (d 1993); *b* 2 July 1939; *Educ* Eton, Vienna Univ, ChCh Oxford; *m* 1968, Julia Margaret, twin da of Archibald Julian Lucas; 2 s (and 1 s decd), 1 da; *Heir* s, William Mount; *Career* former CRD desk offr (home affrs and health and social security); former chief ldr writer Daily Mail, columnist The Standard 1980–82, political correspondent The Spectator to 1982; head PM's Policy Unit 1982–84, literary ed The Spectator 1984–85, columnist Daily Telegraph 1985–90, ed Times Literary Supplement 1991–2002, columnist Sunday Times 2002–04, columnist Daily Telegraph 2005–; FRSL 1991 (memb Cncl 2002); *Books* The Theatre of Politics

M

(1972), The Man Who Rode Ampersand (1975), The Clique (1978), The Subversive Family (1982), The Selkirk Strip (1987), Of Love And Asthma (1991, Hawthornden Prize 1992), The British Constitution Now (1992), Umbrella (1994), The Liquidator (1995), Jem (and Sam) (1998), Fairness (2001), Heads You Win (2004), Mind the Gap (2004); *Style—* Ferdinand Mount, Esq, FRSL; ✉ 17 Ripplevale Grove, London N1 1HS (tel 020 7607 5398)

MOUNT, Paul Morrow; s of Ernest Edward Mount, and Elsie Gertrude, *née* Morrow; *b* 8 June 1922; *Educ* Newton Abbot GS, Paignton Sch of Art, RCA; *m* 1, 1947 (m dis), Jeanne Rosemary Martin; 1 s (Martin b 1950), 1 da (Margaret b 1956); m 2, 1978, June Sylvia, da of Lt Col William George Hilary Miles, RM; *Career* served WWII with Friends' Ambulance Unit, attached to 13 Bn Med, 2 Div Blindee (Free French); initiated and ran Art Dept Yaba Nigeria 1955–61, freelance sculptor 1962–; cmmns incl: Br Steel Corp, Fibreglass Ltd St Helens, York House Bristol, CRS and Leo supermarkets, Swiss Embassy Tafawa Balewa Square, Chase Manhattan Bank Lagos, Bauchi Meml Nigeria, cabinet offices Accra; exhbn en Permanence New Art Centre Roche Court and Beaux Arts W1; memb Penwith Soc; ARCA 1948, RWA; *Novels* Agnes Holbrook (under pseudonym Andrew Morrow, 2002), A Ticket to the Garden (2004), Alice Cantier (2006); *Recreations* music; *Style—* Paul Mount, Esq; ✉ Nancherrow Studio, St Just, Penzance, Cornwall TR19 7LA (tel 01736 788 552)

MOUNT EDGCUMBE, 8 Earl of (GB 1789); Robert Charles Edgcumbe; also Viscount Mount Edgcumbe and Valletort (GB 1781) and Baron Edgcumbe of Mount Edgcumbe (GB 1742); s of George Aubrey Valletort Edgcumbe (d 1977, bro of 7 Earl, who d 1982) and his 1 w, Meta, da of late Charles Robert Lhoyer, of Nancy, France; descended from Sir Richard Edgcombe (d 1489), a supporter of Henry Tudor, Earl of Richmond (later Henry VII), who was knighted on the field of Bosworth, and later became a PC and comptroller of the Household; *b* 1 June 1939; *m* 1960 (m dis 1988), Joan Ivy, da of Ernest Wall, of Otorohanga, NZ; 5 da; *Heir* half bro, Piers Edgcumbe; *Career* farmer; ex mangr Lands and Survey Dept NZ; landowner (2200 acres); *Style—* The Rt Hon The Earl of Mount Edgcumbe; ✉ Empacombe House, Mount Edgcumbe, Cornwall PL10 1HZ

MOUNTBATTEN, Lord Ivar Alexander Michael; yr s of 3 Marquess of Milford Haven, OBE, DSC (d 1970), and Janet, Marchioness of Milford Haven; *b* 9 March 1963; *Educ* Gordonstoun, Middlebury Coll Vermont USA (BA); *m* 23 April 1994, Penelope Ann Vere, da of Colin Thompson, of Warminster, Wilts; 3 da (Ella Louise Georgina b 20 March 1996, Alexandra Nada Victoria b 8 May 1998, Louise Xenia Rosie b 30 July 2002); *Career* Monarch Resources Venezuela 1987–88; dir: Delta Minerals Corp Bermuda 1988–, AEI Redifusion 1995–98, AEI Music Inc 1998–2001; md Crown Self-Storage Ltd 1999–; chm Int Corporate Protection Ltd 2000–03; chm Regain, The Tst for Sporting Tetraplegics 1997– (tstee 1994–97); hon pres: Haverhill RNA 1996–, 1451 (Haverhill) Squadron ATC 1996–; tstee Coldharbour Mill Museum 1998–2006; *Recreations* skiing, windsurfing, flying, shooting; *Style—* The Lord Ivar Mountbatten; ✉ Bridwell Park, Uffculme, Devon EX15 3BU (tel 01884 840890, fax 01884 840950)

MOUNTBATTEN OF BURMA, Countess (UK 1947); Patricia Edwina Victoria Knatchbull; CBE (1991), CD (1976), DL (Kent 1973); also Viscountess Mountbatten of Burma (UK 1946), Baroness Romsey (UK 1947); da of Adm of the Fleet 1 Earl Mountbatten of Burma, KG, GCB, OM, GCSI, GCIE, GCVO, DSO, PC, FRS (assas 1979), and Hon Edwina Ashley, CI, GBE, DCVO (d 1960, da of 1 and last Baron Mount Temple, himself gs of 7 Earl of Shaftesbury, the philanthropist); Edwina's mother was Maud, da of Sir Ernest Cassel, the banker and friend of Edward VII; *b* 14 February 1924; *Educ* Malta, England, NYC; *m* 26 Oct 1946, 7 Baron Brabourne, CBE (d 2005); 4 s (and 1 twin s k 1979, with his gf), 2 da; *Heir* s, 8 Baron Brabourne, *qv*; *Career* served 1943–46 WRNS; Col-in-Chief Princess Patricia's Canadian Light Inf 1974–2007; JP Kent 1971–94, Vice Lord-Lt Kent 1984–2000; pres: Shaftesbury Homes and Arethusa, Kent Branch Save the Children, Kent Branch Relate, Friends of Cassel Hosp and of William Harvey Hosp, The Kent Community Housing Tst; dep pres BRCS; vice-pres: NSPCC, Kent Rural Community Cncl, SSAFA - Forces Help, FPA, Nat Childbirth Tst, Royal Life Saving Soc, Shaftesbury Soc, Royal Coll of Nursing, Nat Soc for Cancer Relief, Royal Nat Coll for the Blind; hon pres: British Maritime Charitable Fndn, Child Bereavement Tst; hon vice-pres Soc for Nautical Research; tstee: Sir Ernest Cassel Educn Tst, Edwina Mountbatten Tst; patron: Legion of Frontiersmen of the Commonwealth, Commando Assoc, Royal Naval Commando Assoc, VAD (RN) Assoc, Nurses' Welfare Tst, SOS Children's Villages UK, Compassionate Friends, HMS Kelly Reunion Assoc, East Kent Hospices, Kent Cncl on Drug Addiction, Mote House Cheshire Home, Kent Handicapped Orphans' Caring Assoc, Chatham Dockyard Hist Soc, Ashford Samaritans, Ashford Umbrella Club, T S Churchill Sea Cadets Ashford; vice-patron Burma Star Assoc; tstee Mountbatten Meml Tst; Hon DCL Univ of Kent 2000; DStJ 1981; *Style—* The Rt Hon the Countess Mountbatten of Burma, CBE, CD, DL; ✉ Newhouse, Mersham, Ashford, Kent TN25 6NQ (tel 01233 503636, fax 01233 502244, b@knatchbull.com)

MOUNTEVANS, 3 Baron (UK 1945); (Edward Patrick) Broke Andvord Evans; s of 2 Baron Mountevans (d 1974); *b* 1 February 1943; *Educ* Rugby, Trinity Coll Oxford; *m* 1974, Johanna, da of Antonius Keyzer, of The Hague; *Heir* bro, Hon Jeffrey Evans; *Career* Lt ret 74 MC regt RCT, AER 1960–66; joined management of Consolidated Gold Fields Ltd 1966; joined BTA 1972, mangr Sweden and Finland 1973, mangr Promotion Services 1976, asst marketing mangr 1982–90, railway and tourism conslt 1990, ret; *Recreations* reading, travel; *Style—* The Rt Hon the Lord Mountevans

MOUNTFORD, Kali Carol Jean; MP; *b* 12 January 1954; *Educ* Crewe GS for Girls, Crewe and Alsager Coll (BA); *Career* civil servant with Dept of Employment 1975–96, MP (Lab) Colne Valley 1997–; cncllr Sheffield City Cncl 1992–96; *Clubs* Honley Socialist, Marsden Socialist; *Style—* Ms Kali Mountford, MP; ✉ House of Commons, London SW1A 0AA (tel 020 7219 4507, fax 020 7219 1256)

MOUNTFORD, Margaret Rose; da of James Ross Gamble, of Holywood, NI, and Kathleen Margaret, *née* Stevenson; *b* 24 November 1951; *Educ* Strathearn Sch Belfast, Girton Coll Cambridge (MA), UCL (MA); *Career* admitted slr 1976, ptnr Herbert Smith 1983–99 (latterly jt head of corp finance); non-exec dir: Georgica plc, Amstrad plc 1999–; appearances as memb of the bd The Apprentice (BBC2) 2005–; Liveryman Worshipful Co of Solicitors; memb Law Soc; *Recreations* travel, opera, wine; *Style—* Ms Margaret Mountford

MOUNTFORD, Philip; *b* 26 February 1965; *Career* mgmnt trainee rising to buying and merchandise dir Simpson Piccadilly 1984–96, retail dir (Europe and UK) Daks Simpson Gp 1996–97, sales and mktg dir Nautica Europe 1997–99, md Wholesale Div (UK and Scandinavia) Gianni Versace 1999–2002, chief exec Moss Bros Gp plc 2004– (gp trading dir 2002–04); *Style—* Philip Mountford, Esq; ✉ Moss Bros Group plc, 8 St Johns Hill, London SW11 1SA

MOUNTFORD, Roger Philip; s of Stanley W A Mountford (d 1984), of Leatherhead, Surrey, and Evelyn Mary Richardson (d 1979); *b* 5 June 1948; *Educ* Kingston GS, LSE (BSc), Stanford Grad Sch of Business (Sloan fell, MS); *m* 24 July 1981, Jane Rosemary, da of Rev Canon Eric Edwin Stanton, hon Canon of Canterbury (d 1984); 3 da (Laura Jane b 1983, Annabel Louise b 1985, Nicola Mary b 1989); *Career* PA to Rt Hon Edward Heath 1969–70 and during 1970 and 1974 gen elections, nat chm Fedn of Cons Students 1970–71, memb Carlton Club Political Ctee 1990–96; merchant banker; Hambros Bank Ltd 1971–98 (dir 1984–98); md: Hambro Pacific Ltd Hong Kong 1983–89, SG Hambros 1998–2000; chm: Civil Aviation Authy Pension Scheme 2003–, Enterprise LSE Ltd 2004–, Hg Capital Tst plc 2005– (non-exec dir 2004–), Housing Finance Corp 2007–; non-exec dir: Thames Valley Housing Assoc 2002–, Civil Aviation Authy 2003–; govr and chm of fin Cobham Hall 1995–; Freeman City of London 1974, Liveryman Worshipful Co of Stationers and Newspaper Makers 1992; *Recreations* opera, music, theatre, tennis; *Clubs* Carlton, Hong Kong, Royal Hong Kong Jockey, London Capital (hon bd of advsrs); *Style—* Roger Mountford, Esq; ✉ Hookstile House, Godstone, Surrey RH9 8JH (tel 01342 893198)

MOUNTFORD, (John) Toby; s of John Dennis Mountford, of Thames Ditton, Surrey, and Wendy, *née* Gowlland; *b* 4 November 1954; *Educ* Wellington, Univ of Durham (BSc); *m* 18 Oct 2003, Carolina, *née* Van Oordt; 1 s (Benjamin Alexander b 13 March 2006); *Career* articled clerk then chartered accountant Price Waterhouse London 1976–80, mgmnt accountant Int Div Beecham Pharmaceuticals 1980–81, fin PR dir Streets Financial Ltd 1981–87, dir Citigate Dewe Rogerson (formerly Citigate Communications Ltd) 1987–; ACA 1980; *Books* Practice Development - A Guide to Marketing Techniques for Accountants (1985); *Recreations* skiing, walking, swimming, theatre; *Clubs* Hurlingham; *Style—* Toby Mountford, Esq; ✉ Citigate Dewe Rogerson Ltd, 3 London Wall Buildings, London Wall, London EC2M 5SY (tel 020 7638 9571, fax 020 7628 3444, e-mail toby.mountford@citigatedr.co.uk)

MOUNTGARRET, 18 Viscount (I 1550); Piers James Richard Butler; also Baron Mountgarret (UK 1911); s of 17 Viscount (d 2004); *b* 15 April 1961; *Educ* Eton, Univ of St Andrews; *m* 2 Sept 1995, Laura Brown Gary, da of Mrs Albert Dickens Williams, Jr, of Lake Forest, Illinois, USA; 1 da (Hon Alexa b 16 Feb 1997); *Clubs* White's, Union (New York); *Style—* The Rt Hon the Viscount Mountgarret; ✉ 44 Stanmer Street, London SW11 3EG (tel 01488 658229)

MOURBY, Adrian Roy Bradshaw; s of Roy Mourby, of Welshpool, Montgomeryshire, and Peggy, *née* Bradshaw; *Educ* King Edward VI Camp Hill Sch Birmingham, Univ of Wales (BA), Univ of Bristol Film Sch (postgrad); *m* 1, 19 July 1980 (m dis 1998), Katharine Mary, da of John Richard Trevena Nicholas (d 1971), of West Penwith, Cornwall; 1 da (Miranda Jane b 1987), 1 s (John James b 1990); m 2, 20 March 2004, Kathryn du Bois, da of Martin Connor Miller, of Washington State, USA; *Career* BBC TV and Radio 1979–92; currently writer and prodr; columnist Times Educnl Supplement 1998–2002; writer: 8 broadcast plays, numerous radio talks, two Radio 4 comedy series Whatever Happened to...?, Silkies, Men of Letters, Mr Handel & Mr Congreve (stageplay, Valletta) 2002 (also Buxton 2003); writer, prodr and presenter of BBC independent documentary Nimrod, contrib talks and entertainments to Radio 3 Proms 1994–97 and Christmas on Radio 4 1993, 1995 and 1997, prog essayist Covent Garden, ENO and WNO 1996–, co-artistic dir Celebrating Handel 2002, co-artistic dir Oxford Millennium Opera 2004–; opera prodr: Semele (Malta), Cosi fan tutte (Oxford Millennium Opera) 2004, The Grave's a Fine and Pleasant Place 2005 (with Ian Hogg), Marriage of Figaro (Oxford and Blewbury Festival) 2006; creator Tristan & Matilda (cartoon series) 2003; regualr contrib Independent on Sunday; *Awards* Smith-Kline Award for Radio Journalism 1983, commendation Sony Radio Awards 1985, BAFTA/Cymru Best English Drama Award 1991, Celtic Film Festival Best Short Drama Award 1994, Sony Silver Award for Radio Writing 1995; others from Francisco Film Festival 1993 and NY Int Radio Festival 1994; Canadian Travel Awards 1998; *Books* We Think the World of Him (novel, 1996), The Four of Us (novel, 1997), Whatever happened to....? (1998), Wishdaughter (novel, 2004), A Guide Book to Venice (2007); *Recreations* eating, drinking, talking, architecture, travel, opera, films; *Clubs* British Guild of Travel Writers; *Style—* Adrian Mourby; ✉ 24 Cox's Ground, Oxford OX2 6PX (e-mail mail@adrianmourby.com)

MOUTAFIAN, Princess Helena; MBE (1976); da of Prince Alexei Gagarin (d 1938), and Countess Ana Phillipovitz (d 1944); *b* 2 May 1930; *m* 14 Jan 1955, Artin Moutafian (d 1992), s of Nikogos Moutafian (d Armenia 1914); 2 s (Nicholas b 6 Nov 1958, Mark b 21 Dec 1960); *Career* vice-pres Help the Aged (pres Ladies' Ctee), fndr pres Anglo-Russian Children Appeal, vice-pres Ladies' Ctee European-Atlantic Gp, hon vice-pres Women's Cncl, life patron NSPCC, patron Cwlth Countries' League; tstee European-Atlantic Gp; vice-pres and tstee Byron Soc; memb: Br Assoc of Women Entrepreneurs, Int PEN, Inst of Journalists, Pilgrims 1990–, Rotary Club of London 1998–; awarded Silver Medal of Grollo d'Ore for paintings of Venice; fell Soil Assoc; FRGS, FRZS; Croix de Chevalier (Ordre de la Courtoisie Française) 1976, Etoile Civique (Grande Médaille de Vermeil de la Ville de Paris) 1977, Freedom City of Paris 1977, DStJ 1990, Russian decoration for service to humanity; *Recreations* painting, writing; *Clubs* English Speaking Union, Lansdowne; *Style—* Princess Helena Moutafian, MBE; ✉ 18 Burgess Hill, Hampstead, London NW2 2DA

MOVERLEY SMITH, Stephen Philip; QC (2002); s of Philip Smith, of Lustleigh, N Devon, and Carol, *née* Moverley; *b* 10 January 1960, Frimley, Surrey; *Educ* Reading Sch, Pembroke Coll Oxford (MA); *m* 8 Sept 1990, Caroline, *née* Topping; 3 s (Benjamin b 25 Sept 1995, Rupert, Theodore (twins) b 5 Dec 1997); *Career* called to the Bar: Middle Temple 1985, Eastern Caribbean Supreme Court 1995; practising barr specialising in int company and commercial litigation, currently memb of chambers 24 Old Buildings; jr counsel to the Crown (Chancery) 1992–2001; *Style—* Stephen Moverley Smith, Esq, QC; ✉ 24 Old Buildings, Lincoln's Inn, London WC2A 3VP (tel 020 7404 0946, fax 020 7405 1360, e-mail sms@xxiv.co.uk)

MOWAT, David McIvor; JP (Edinburgh 1968); s of Ian McIvor Mowat (d 1985), and Mary Isabelle Simpson, *née* Steel; *b* 12 March 1939; *Educ* Edinburgh Acad, Univ of Edinburgh (MA), Open Univ (BA); *m* 20 June 1964, (Elinor) Anne, da of Eric Edward Birtwistle (d 1974); 3 da (Sarah Jane b 4 Sept 1965, Anna Katherine (Kate) b 25 April 1967, Julia Claire b 9 Jan 1969); *Career* journalist, broadcaster, co dir; chief exec Edinburgh Chamber of Commerce and Manufactures 1968–90, pres Br C of C Execs 1987–89; md Iatros Ltd; dir: St Andrews Golf Club (Manufacturing) Ltd; FRSA 1986; *Style—* David Mowat, Esq; ✉ 37 Orchard Road South, Edinburgh EH4 3JA (tel 0131 332 6865); Iatros Ltd, Dundee (fax 01382 562583)

MOWAT, Magnus Charles; s of John F M Mowat, MBE (d 1988), of Ellesmere, Shropshire and Elizabeth Rebecca, *née* Murray (d 1977); *b* 5 April 1940; *Educ* Haileybury; *m* 27 April 1968, Mary Lynette St Lo, da of Alan D Stoddart (d 1994), of Taunton, Somerset; 3 s (Charles b 15 April 1969, Alexander b 27 June 1970, Hugh b 7 June 1973); *Career* CA; Peat Marwick Mitchell & Co 1959–67, Hill Samuel & Co Ltd 1968–70, ptnr Illingworth & Henriques Stockbrokers 1970–84, dir Barclays de Zoete Wedd Ltd 1984–90; non-exec dir Woodward Corp; chm of govrs Kings Coll Taunton; Liveryman Worshipful Co of World Traders; FCA 1964; *Recreations* shooting, gardening, music; *Clubs* East India; *Style—* Magnus Mowat, Esq; ✉ Westcott Farm, Brompton Ralph, Taunton, Somerset TA4 2SF (tel 01984 623 274)

MOWAT, Her Hon Judge Mary Jane Stormont; da of late Duncan Mackay Stormont Mowat, and late Jane Archibald Mowat, *née* Milne; *b* 7 July 1948; *Educ* Sherborne Sch for Girls, Lady Margaret Hall Oxford (MA), Inns of Court Sch of Law; *m* Prof the Hon Nicholas Michael John Woodhouse, s of 5 Baron Terrington; 1 s (Thomas Duncan b 4 Feb 1987); *Career* called to the Bar Inner Temple 1973; circuit judge (SE Circuit) 1996–; *Recreations* music, walking, riding, reading; *Style—* Her Hon Judge Mowat; ✉ Reading Crown Court, Old Shire Hall, The Forbury, Reading RG1 3EH

MOWBRAY, Sir John Robert; 6 Bt (UK 1880), of Warennes Wood, Berkshire; JP (W Suffolk 1972), DL (Suffolk 1993); s of Sir George Robert Mowbray, 5 Bt, KBE (d 1969), and Diana Margaret, *née* Hughes (d 1996); *b* 1 March 1932; *Educ* Eton, New Coll Oxford; *m* 1957, Lavinia Mary, da of Lt-Col Francis Edgar Hugonin, OBE, JP, RA; 3 da (Mary Clare (Mrs James D Delevingne) b 1959, Teresa Jane b 1961, Katherine Diana (Mrs David Chastel de Boinville) b 1965); *Heir* none; *Style*— Sir John Mowbray, Bt, DL; ✉ The Hill House, Duffs Hill, Glemsford, Suffolk CO10 7PP (tel 01787 281930, fax 01787 282352)

MOWL, Colin John; CB (2004); s of Arthur Sidney Mowl (d 1993), and Ada, *née* Bartlett (d 1993); *b* 19 October 1947; *Educ* Lawrence Sheriff Sch Rugby, LSE (MSc); *m* 27 June 1980, Kathleen Patricia, da of Michael Joseph Gallagher; 1 s (Thomas b 24 Oct 1983), 1 da (Sophie b 27 June 1985); *Career* econ asst Miny of Tport 1970–72; HM Treasy: sr econ asst 1972–74, econ advsr 1974–83, seconded as res mangr Forex Research Ltd 1983, sr econ advsr 1983–90, head Macro Economic Analysis and Forecast Gp 1990–94, dep dir Macroeconomic Policy and Prospects 1995, dep dir Budget and Public Finances 1995–2002; dir Macroeconomics and Labour Market Office for National Statistics 2002–; *Recreations* most sport (now only as a spectator), family; *Style*— Colin Mowl, Esq, CB

MOWSCHENSON, Terence Rennie; QC (1995); s of Henry Mowschenson (d 1994), and Hanny Mowschenson (d 1992); *b* 7 June 1953; *Educ* Peterhouse, Queen Mary Coll London (LLB), Exeter Coll Oxford (BCL); *m* 10 Oct 1992, Judith Angela, da of Christopher Strang; *Career* called to the Bar Middle Temple 1977 (bencher 2003); memb Chambers of Edward Nugee QC, asst recorder 1995–2000, recorder 2000–, dep judge of the High Court 2003; chm: Financial Services and Markets Act Tbnl 2001, Pensions Tbnl 2004; chm Barristers' Benevolent Assoc 1999–, memb Chancery and Commercial Bar Assocs; FCIArb 1991; *Recreations* opera; *Clubs* RAC; *Style*— Terence Mowschenson, Esq, QC; ✉ Wilberforce Chambers, 8 New Square, Lincoln's Inn, London WC2A 3QP (tel 020 7306 0101, fax 020 7306 0095)

MOXHAM, Prof John; s of Wilson Moxham (d 1949), and Marie, *née* Blande; *b* 9 December 1944; *Educ* Prince Henry's GS Evesham, LSE (BSc), UCH (MB BS, MD); *m* 4 June 1978, Nicola Dawn, da of (Alec William) Larry Seaman; 3 da (Jessica Hannah b 4 May 1980, Madeleine Emily b 15 Dec 1985, Rose Harriet b 20 Dec 1988); *Career* conslt physician King's Coll Hosp 1982, dean Faculty of Clinical Med King's Coll Sch of Med and Dentistry 1997–98, dean King's Denmarkhill Campus 1998–; author of numerous papers, chapters and reviews on respiratory physiology; FRCP 1987 (MRCP 1975); *Recreations* my wonderful daughters; *Clubs* The Lord Lyndhurst; *Style*— Prof John Moxham

MOXLEY, Raymond James (Ray); s of Rev Henry Roberts Moxley (d 1953), of Oxford, and Ruby Alice, *née* Gems (d 1972); *b* 28 July 1923; *Educ* Caterham Sch, Oxford Sch of Architecture; *m* 1, 12 Oct 1949 (m dis 1972), Jacqueline Marjorie, da of Orlando Beater (d 1954), of Standlake, Oxon; 1 s (Mike b 1950), 2 da (Caroline b 1956, Alison b 1959); m 2, 16 Oct 1999, Ann Barbara, da of Ewart March, of Clifton, Bristol; *Career* trooper RHG 1942; RE: joined 1943, cmmnd 1944, Capt 1945, demobbed 1946; architect; fndr own practice 1953–65, dir and chm Moxley Jenner & Partners (London) Ltd 1986–99 (fndr ptnr 1965); originating designer Lateral BM Schooner Cruising Catermarans 2000–; visiting lectr 1953–75: Univ of Bristol Sch of Architecture, Univ of Reading, Univ of Manchester; lectr: W of Eng Coll of Art 1965–69, Bristol Poly 1969–71; RIBA: assessor regnl awards 1968, rep Ct of Univ of Bath 1968–69, memb Cncl 1972–78, first hon librarian 1975–77, vice-pres 1973–75; DOE Housing Awards: assessor E Midlands Region 1977, chm SE Region 1979, chm London Region 1980; chm: Bristol Bldg and Design Centre 1965–70, Assoc of Conslt Architects 1974–77, Soc for Advanced Methods of Mgmnt 1978, London Assoc of Conslt Architects 1984–86; pres Bristol and Somerset Soc of Architects 1968–69, vice-pres Design and Industries Assoc 1989; hon fell UWE 1989; Freeman City of London 1975, Liveryman Worshipful Co of Chartered Architects; FRIBA, FRSA, RWA; *Books* Building Construction Vol 1 (23 edn); ed: Build International (1973–74), The Architects Guide to Fee Negotiation (1983), ACA Illustrated Directory of Architects (1983 and 1984), Architects Eye, Building Management by Professionals; *Recreations* piano, sailing; *Clubs* Royal Western Yacht, RAC, Cargreen Yacht (past cdre); *Style*— Ray Moxley, Esq; ✉ 10 The Belvedere, Chelsea Harbour, London SW10 0XA (tel 020 7352 2813, fax 020 7352 1847); March House, Cargreen, Saltash, Cornwall PL12 6PA (tel 01752 845338, fax 01752 845173)

MOXON, Prof (Edward) Richard; s of Gerald Richard Moxon, CBE (d 1980), and Margaret, *née* Forster Mohun; *b* 16 July 1941; *Educ* Shrewsbury, St John's Coll Cambridge (BChir); *m* 20 Oct 1973, Marianne, da of Prof George Graham; 2 s (Christopher Alan b 1978, Timothy Stewart b 1987), 1 da (Sarah Graham b 1981); *Career* sr house offr Hosp for Sick Children 1969, res fell Children's Hosp Med Centre Boston USA 1971–74 (asst resident paediatric 1970), asst prof of paediatrics Johns Hopkins Univ Hosp Baltimore USA 1974–78 (assoc prof and Eudowood chief of paediatric infectious diseases 1978–84), prof of paediatrics Univ of Oxford 1984–; *Recreations* sport, music, literature; *Style*— Prof Richard Moxon; ✉ Department of Paediatrics, John Radcliffe Hospital, Headington OX3 9DU

MOXON-BROWNE, Prof Edward; s of Kendall Edward Moxon-Browne, and Sheila Heron, *née* Weatherbe; bro of Robert Moxon Browne, QC, *qv*; *Educ* Gordonstoun, St Andrews Univ (MA Medieval History), Univ of Pennsylvania (MA Int Rels); *Career* lectr in int rels US Int Univ 1970–72, lectr, sr lectr then reader in political sci Queen's Univ of Belfast 1973–91, Jean Monnet chair of Euro integration Univ of Limerick 1992–; Univ of Limerick: dir Centre for European Studies, memb Bd Centre for Criminal Justice; memb Editorial Bd: Regional and Federal Studies, Contemporary Politics; external examiner: Queen's Univ of Belfast, South Bank Univ; memb: RIIA, Int Studies Assoc, Euro Community Studies Assoc; *Books* Nation, Class and Creed in Northern Ireland (1983), Political Change in Spain (1989), European Terrorism (ed, 1993), The Police, Public Order and the State (co-author, 2 edn, 1996), A Future for Peacekeeping (ed, 1997), Who are the Europeans? (ed, 1999); also author of numerous contrib to various learned pubns; *Style*— Prof Edward Moxon-Browne; ✉ University of Limerick, Limerick, Ireland (tel 00 353 61 202202, fax 00 353 61 330316, e-mail edward.moxon-browne@ul.ie)

MOXON BROWNE, Robert William; QC (1990); s of late Kendall Edward Moxon-Browne, and Sheila Heron, *née* Weatherbe; bro of Prof Edward Moxon-Browne, *qv*; *b* 26 June 1946; *Educ* Gordonstoun, Univ Coll Oxford (BA); *m* 26 June 1968, Kerstin Elizabet, da of Oscar Warne; 1 da (Emily Kendall b 20 Oct 1973), 1 s (James Weatherbe b 7 April 1977); *Career* called to the Bar Gray's Inn 1969, in practice specialising in commercial and insurance law on Western Circuit and in London, recorder 1991–, dep judge of Technol and Construction Ct 1992–, dep judge of the High Court 1998; *Recreations* theatre, gardening, cooking; *Style*— Robert Moxon Browne, Esq, QC; ✉ 2 Temple Gardens, London EC4Y 9AY (tel 020 7583 6041, fax 020 7583 2094)

MOYES, James Christopher (Jim); *b* 29 April 1943; *Educ* Maidstone Coll of Art, Univ of Kent (BA), Slade Sch of Fine Art London (MA); *m* 1, 1969 (m dis 1981), Elizabeth McKee; 1 da (Sara Jo b 1969); m 2, 1987 (m dis 2000), Joanna Margaret, da of Col David E G Price (decd); 2 da (Beatrice Oliphant b 1987, Clementine b 1990); *Career* laboratory asst and quality control technician Watneys Laboratories 1959–64, merchant marine 1964–66, artist and gallery asst 1971–, fndr Momart plc (int fine art serv co, Royal Warrant holder), estab Momart fellowship (artist in residence Tate Gallery Liverpool), former dir Momart Ltd (Royal Warrant reassigned); lectr in art handling techniques; practising artist in all media; former memb Ctee Contemporary Art Soc; *Recreations* art exhibitions and other arts related activities; *Style*— Jim Moyes, Esq; ✉ Unit 4, Ropewalk Mews, 118 Middleton Road, London E8 4LP (tel 020 7241 4007, fax 020 7241 3172); Studio (tel 020 7241 4007, fax 020 7241 3172)

MOYLE, Andrew; s of Peter Moyle, of Sydney, Aust, and Anne, *née* Mavin; *b* 28 May 1964, Aust; *Educ* Univ of Melbourne (LLB, BComm); *m* 26 Feb 1994, Julie A, *née* Duffey; 2 da (Eliza b 23 June 1997, Alice b 15 Aug 2002), 1 s (Sam b 6 April 2000); *Career* slr; ptnr: Freehill Hollingdale and Page 1996, Shaw Pittman 1996–2003; Latham and Watkins: ptnr 2003–, managing ptnr 2006–; memb Law Soc; *Recreations* skiing; *Clubs* Australia; *Style*— Andrew Moyle, Esq; ✉ Latham and Watkins, 99 Bishopsgate, London EC2M 3XF (tel 020 7710 1000, fax 020 7374 4460, e-mail andrew.moyle@lw.com)

MOYNE, 3 Baron (UK 1932); Jonathan Bryan Guinness; s of 2 Baron Moyne (d 1992), and his 1 w, Hon Diana, *née* Freeman Mitford (da of 2 Baron Redesdale and who subsequently m Sir Oswald Mosley, 6 Bt; d 2003); *b* 16 March 1930; *Educ* Eton (King's Scholar), Trinity Coll Oxford (MA); *m* 1, 1951 (m dis 1963), Ingrid Olivia Georgia, da of late Maj Guy Richard Charles Wyndham, MC (ggs of 1 Baron Leconfield); 2 s (Hon Jasper Jonathan Richard b 1954, Hon Valentine Guy Bryan b 1959), 1 da (Hon Catherine Ingrid (Hon Mrs Hesketh) b 1952); m 2, 1964, Mrs Suzanne Phillips, da of Harold William Denis Lisney, of Gerona, Spain, and formerly w of Timothy Phillips; 1 s (Hon Sebastian Walter Denis b 1964), 1 da (Hon Daphne Suzannah Diana Joan (Hon Mrs Niarchos) b 1967); further children by Susan Mary Taylor; 1 s (Thomas Julian Guinness-Taylor b 1986), 2 da (Diana Rose Guinness-Taylor b 1981, Aster Mary Guinness-Taylor b 1984); *Heir* s, Hon Jasper Guinness; *Career* dir: A Guinness Son & Co 1961–88, Leopold Joseph & Sons 1963–91; former Reuters journalist, chm Monday Club 1970–72; *Style*— The Rt Hon Lord Moyne; ✉ South Wing, Rodmarton Manor, Rodmarton, Cirencester, Gloucestershire GL7 6PF

MOYNIHAN, 4 Baron (UK 1929); Sir Colin Berkeley Moynihan; 4 Bt (UK 1922); s of 2 Baron Moynihan, OBE, TD (d 1965), and June Elizabeth, *née* Hopkins; suc half-bro 3 Baron (d 1991), (claim to barony admitted by Ctee for Privileges House of Lords 1997); *b* 13 September 1955; *Educ* Monmouth, UC Oxford (MA, Rowing and Boxing double blue, pres Oxford Union); *m* 7 March 1992, Gaynor-Louise, only da of Paul G Metcalf, of Healing, S Humberside; 2 s (Hon Nicholas Ewan Berkeley b 31 March 1994, Hon George Edward Berkeley b 4 June 1995), 1 da (Hon India Isabella Sarah b 2 Sept 1997); *Heir* s, Hon Nicholas Moynihan; *Career* personal asst to chm Tate & Lyle Ltd 1978–80, mangr Tate & Lyle Agribusiness 1980–82, chief exec Ridgways Tea and Coffee Merchants 1980–83, MP (Cons) Lewisham E 1983–92, jt md Independent Power Corp plc and affiliates 1996–2001, dir Rowan Gp of Companies, exec chm and md Consort Resources Gp of Companies 1999–2003, chm Clipper Windpower Europe Ltd 2001–07, chm Spectron Gp plc 2004–05, chm Ocean Power Delivery Ltd 2007–; chm BOA 2005–, memb Organising Ctee London 2012 Olympics 2005–; political asst to Foreign Sec 1983, PPS to Rt Hon Kenneth Clarke as Min of Health and PMG 1986–87, Parly under-sec of state DOE and min for sport 1987–90, Parly under-sec of state Dept of Energy 1990–92, oppn sr spokesman on foreign and Cwlth affrs House of Lords 1997–2000, a shadow min for sport 2003–05; chm: All-Pty Gp on Afghanistan 1984, Govt Inner City Working Gp on Sport and Recreation 1988, Govt Review Gp on Sport for the Disabled 1989, Govt Renewable Energy Advsy Gp 1991–97; vice-chm Cons Backbenchers Sports Ctee; memb: Bow Gp 1978 (chm Bow Gp Industry Ctee 1985–87), Paddington Cons Mgmnt Ctee 1980–81; sec: Major Spectator Sports Ctee CCPR 1979–87, CCPR Enquiry into Sponsorship of Sport 1982–83, Cons Foreign and Cwlth Affairs Ctee 1985; memb Sports Cncl 1982–85, govr Sports Aid Fndn (London and SE) 1980–82; steward British Boxing Bd of Control 1979–87; tstee: OUBC 1980–83, Sports Aid Tst 1983–87; fndr memb Worldwatch Inst Europe 1991; dir Canterbury Festival 1999–2001; rowing achievements incl: Gold medal World Championships 1978, Silver medal Olympic Games Moscow 1980, Silver medal World Championships 1981; Freeman City of London 1978, Liveryman Worshipful Co of Haberdashers (memb Ct of Assts); *Recreations* collecting Nonesuch books, music, sport; *Clubs* Brooks's, Vincent's (Oxford); *Style*— The Lord Moynihan; ✉ House of Lords, London SW1A 0PW (e-mail c.moynihan@cmagroup.org.uk)

MOYNIHAN, Jon; OBE (1994); s of Sir Noel Moynihan (d 1993), of Herstmonceux, E Sussex, and Margaret, *née* Lovelace (d 1989); *b* 21 June 1948, Cambridge; *Educ* Balliol Coll Oxford (MA), N London Poly (MSc), MIT (SM); *m* Dec 20 1980, Patricia Underwood, *née* Gilbert; *Career* worked for War on Want and Save the Children India and Bangladesh 1971–1972; Roche Products 1972–1976, McKinsey & Co Amsterdam 1977–79, Strategic Planning Assocs Washington DC 1979–81, First Manhattan Gp NY 1982–92; exec chm PA Consltg Gp (formerly ceo rising to chm and ceo) 1992–; chm: First Manhattan Gp NY 1982–92, Ubinetics Ltd 1999–2005, Meridica Ltd 2000–04, Aegate Ltd 2004–, Procserve Ltd 2006–, Aditon Ltd 2006–; chm Balliol Campaign Bd, chm Helen Bamber Fndn, tstee Chelsea Festival; memb: Dean's Cncl Sloan Sch MIT, Dean's Business Advsy Forum Saïd Business Sch; fndn fell Balliol Coll Oxford; *Clubs* Travellers, MCC; *Style*— Jon Moynihan, Esq, OBE; ✉ PA Consulting Group, 123 Buckingham Palace Road, London (tel 020 7333 5001, fax 020 7333 5112, e-mail jon.moynihan@paconsulting.com)

MS DYNAMITE, *see:* McLean-Daley, Niomi

MUCHEMI, HE Joseph Kirugumi; s of Jason Kirugumi (d 1978), and Rachel Nyambura (d 1954); *b* 1 January 1942, Nyeri, Kenya; *Educ* Univ of London (BA), Univ of Pittsburgh (Dip Mgmnt); *m* 20 Dec 1975, Cecilia; 2 da (Rachel Mona Nyambura b 4 Oct 1976, Elizabeth Gathoni b 9 Nov 1981), 1 s (David Muchemi b 3 April 1978); *Career* Kenyan diplomat; with E African community 1967–74, various posts rising to perm sec Kenyan Govt Serv 1977–84, md banking and fin instn 1984–90, conslt of fin and admin 1991–2003, high cmmr to UK 2004– (concurrently ambass to Ireland and Switzerland); involved with numerous social orgns; *Recreations* reading, touring, walking; *Clubs* Rotary; *Style*— HE Mr Joseph K Muchemi; ✉ Kenya High Commission, 45 Portland Place, London W1B 1AS

MUCKLE, David Sutherland; s of John Leslie Muckle, and Ruth, *née* Sutherland; *b* 30 August 1939; *Educ* Univ of Durham (MB BS), Univs of Oxford and Newcastle upon Tyne (MS MD); *m* Christine; 2 da (Carolyn Jane b 22 July 1964, Deborah Christine b 17 July 1966); *Career* research assoc Univ of Durham 1963; orthopaedic surgn: Radcliffe Infirmary Oxford, Oxford United FC and Univ of Oxford 1970–77, Cleveland AHA 1977–95; held various visiting professorships in Japan, Caribbean and USA 1977–82, visiting prof Univ of Teesside 1994; examiner RCS(Ed) 1989–; med advsr to the FA, UEFA and FIFA; MO: UEFA Nations Cup Final Gothenburg 1992, Euro 96 Final Wembley 1996; winner President's Prize in Orthopaedic Research 1973–74; author of various articles on biochemistry of soft tissue injuries, femoral neck fractures and cancer oncology; memb: Br Orthopaedic Research Soc 1973, Br Orthopaedic Assoc 1974, RGS 1984; Hon Dip Sports Med The Scottish Royal Colls 1997; FRCS, FRCSEd; *Non-Fiction Publications* A Doctor's Look at Life and History (1970), Sports Injuries (1971), Femoral Neck Fractures (1977), Injuries in Sport (1977), An Outline of Orthopaedic Practice (1985), An Outline of Fractures and Dislocations (1985) *Novels* The Sower Went Forth Sowing (2002); A Country Doctor: Vol 1 - On Distant Fells (2003), Vol 2 - The Holly Blue (2003), Vol 3 - A Child at War (2003); A Highland Story - Written on Glass (2005); *Poems* The Call of Dusk (2002), Such Happiness is Life (2002), Endangered Species (2004); *Recreations* natural history, classical English literature, sport in general, breeding rare farm animals, fell walking, astronomy; *Style*— David S Muckle, Esq; ✉ Marden House, Heathwaite, North Yorkshire DL6 3DS; Park View Medical Clinic, Middlesbrough TS4 2NS (tel 01642 242357)

MUCKLOW, Rupert Jeremy; s of Albert Mucklow, and Gillian, *née* Bullock; *b* 27 April 1963, Stourbridge, W Midlands; *Educ* Millfield (head boy, rugby capt), Boston Univ (BSc); *m* 18 Sept 1993, Diana, *née* Mullett; *Career* surveyor; Chesshire Gibson 1986–88, Grimley J R Eve 1988–90, A & J Mucklow Gp plc: investment surveyor 1990–96, md 1996–2004, chm 2004–; memb Investment Property Forum; *Recreations* golf, horse racing, sailing; *Clubs* Blackwell Golf; *Style*— Rupert Mucklow, Esq; ✉ A & J Mucklow Group plc, 60 Whitehall Road, Halesowen, West Midlands B63 3JS

M

MUDDIMAN, Noel; CBE (1992, OBE 1985); step s of Arthur George Muddiman (d 1976), and s of Flora May, *née* Holdsworth; *b* 17 December 1943; *Educ* Borden GS, RMA Sandhurst; *m* 25 Oct 1969, Patricia Anne, *née* Sevage; 2 s (Andrew Robert b 1 April 1973, Matthew b 21 July 1980); *Career* served Army until 1995 (joined 1963), CO 25 Regt Royal Corps of Transport; head of Personnel and Logistics Falkland Is 1985–86, princ logistic planner Br Forces Germany 1987–90, cdr Tport and Movements BAOR 1990–92, cdr Logistic Support Gp (Middle East) March-Aug 1991, RCDS 1992, cmdt Army Sch of Mechanical Tport 1992–95, ret Army (with rank of Brig) 1995; dir CF Solutions Ltd 2004–; vice-chm Charity Investors Gp 2002–, memb Advsy Bd Charinco and Charishare 2001– (chm 2007–), memb Motability (charity) 2004– (dir 1995–2004); Freedom of Oerlinghausen (Germany) 1984, Norwegian Gulf Medal (with Clasp) 1992; *Books* Blackadder's War (jtly, 1995); *Recreations* gardening, photography, philately; *Clubs* RASC/RCT Officers', Movement Control Officers'; *Style*— Noel Muddiman, Esq, CBE; ✉ c/o Motability, Goodman House, Station Approach, Harlow, Essex CM20 2ET (tel 01279 303414, fax 01279 632002)

MUDIE, Colin Crichton; *b* Edinburgh; *Educ* Scotland and England; *m* Rosemary Horder; 1 s (Colin Maxwell); *Career* naval architect and yacht designer; design apprentice: British Power Boat Co Hythe Southampton, Laurent Giles & Partners yacht designers Lymington; fndr independent design firm (partnerd by w): Westminster London 1958–68, Lymington 1968–; designs incl sail trg vessels, special reproduction, expedition and exploration boats, power boats, sailing yachts, motor cruisers, motor sailers, workboats, pilot boats and dinghies; design work incl: TS Royalist (23 metre brig for Sea Cadet Corps) 1971, STS Lord Nelson (43 metre barque for the Jubilee Sailing Tst) 1986, STS Young Endeavour (35 metre brigantine - official gift of the British nation to Australia to mark the 1988 Bicentennial) 1987, HMRB Zinat al Bihaar (50 metre dhow (Baghla)) 1988, KLD Tunas Samudera (35 metre brigantine for the Royal Malaysian Navy) 1989, Aileach (12 metre birlinn which re-enacted Lord of the Isles voyages 1991 and 1992) 1991, Matthew (reconstruction of vessel which retraced John Cabot's 1497 historic voyage from Bristol to Newfoundland in 1997) 1995, INV Tarangini (43 metre barque for Indian Navy) 1995; Dunbrody, built in Ireland (36 metre reproduction of an 1845 barque) 1998, Jockey Club Huan (40 metre Chinese junk) 2005; for Tim Severin: Brendan (11 metre curragh) 1975, Sohar (20 metre dhow) 1980, Argo (16.5 metre galley) 1984; Winston Churchill fell 1968, Lloyd's Award (for best design and construction for the sail trg brig Royalist) 1971, RINA Small Craft Medal (for outstanding contribs to the Small Craft Indust) 1984, Br Design Cncl Award (for sail trg barque Lord Nelson) 1993; past memb: Hovercraft Ctee CAA Air Requirements Bd, Marine Technol Ctee and Mech and Electrical Engrg Requirements Bd Dept of Indust, Mary Rose Structure Advsy Panel, Steering Ctee Yacht and Boat Design Course Southampton Inst of HE; a life vice-pres RNLI; RDI 1995, CEng, FRINA, Hon FRIN, FRSA; *Books* Motor Boats and Boating, Power Boats, Sopranino (with Patrick Ellam), The Story of the Sailing Ship (with Rosemary Mudie), Power Yachts (with Rosemary Mudie), The Sailing Ship (with Rosemary Mudie), Sailing Ships; also author of various conf papers and pubns; *Recreations* sailing, model boats, books; *Clubs* Royal Lymington Yacht, Royal Ocean Racing, Ocean Cruising, Square Rigger; *Style*— Colin Mudie, Esq; ✉ Bywater Lodge, Undershore Road, Lymington, Hampshire SO41 5SB

MUDIE, George; MP; *Career* MP (Lab) Leeds East 1992–; formerly treas HM Household (dep chief whip), Parly under sec Dept for Educn and Employment 1998–; *Style*— George Mudie, Esq, MP; ✉ House of Commons, London SW1A 0AA (tel 020 7219 3000)

MUEHLE, Henrik; *b* 15 June 1968; *Educ* Usdorfschool Frechen Germany, Commercial Sch Bergisch-Gladbach Germany, Tech Sch for Hotel Business Garmisch-Partenkirchen Germany; *Career* mgmnt trainee Hotel and Casino Imperial Palace Annecy 1991–1992, front office mangr Millennium Hotel Charles-de-Gaulle Paris 1993–94 (reception mangr 1992–93), front of house mangr Hotel Copthorne Windsor 1994–96, front office mangr Holiday Inn Republique Paris 1996–97, ops mangr Hotel L'Horizon Jersey 1998–2000, dep gen mangr Tylney Hall Hotel Rotherwick 2000–02, gen mangr The Capital Hotel Knightsbridge 2002–; PDP Yield Mgmnt Cornell Univ 1999; *Awards* for Tylney Hall: IIP achieved June 2000, Golden Ribbon 2000 and 2001, Hotel of the Year 2000, Southern England Hotel of the Year 2002, SEB England 2002, Michelin Award 5 Black Houses 2002; for The Capital: 2 Michelin Stars, Golden Ribbon 2002, runner-up Hotel of the Year 2002/2003 LTB, RAC 5 Star Townhouse Award 2003/2004, AA 5 Red Star Townhouse Award 2003/2004; *Style*— Henrik Muehle, Esq; ✉ The Capital Hotel, 22–24 Basil Street, Knightsbridge, London SW3 1AT (tel 020 7591 1207)

MUGGERIDGE, Sara Ann (Sally); da of John Raymond Muggeridge, MBE, FICE, CEng (d 2001), and Sylvia, *née* Jenkins; niece of Malcolm Muggeridge (d 1990), the journalist and author; *b* 10 September 1949; *Educ* South Hampstead HS, Westfield Coll, Univ of London (BA), Henley Mgmnt Coll (MBA); *m* 19 July 1969, Lt Richard David Williams; 2 da (Philippa Ann b 1973, Georgina Elizabeth b 1977), 1 s (Jonathan Roland b 1982); *Career* mktg mangr BT plc 1985–91; Cable & Wireless plc: mktg dir Mercury Communications 1991–93, mgmnt devpt dir 1993–96, HR dir Asia 1996–99; mgmnt devpt dir Pearson plc 1999–2003, chief exec Industry and Parliament Tst 2003–; pres CIM Singapore 1996–98, exec vice-pres CIM UK 1999–2004, memb Senate CIM 2007–; memb Professional Accreditation Ctee IOD 2006–; tstee: Tutu Fndn UK, Fndn for Church Leadership; int pres Malcolm Muggeridge Soc; memb Cncl Univ of Kent; Voluntary Sector Acheiver Woman of the Year Awards 2007; Freeman City of London, Liveryman, chair Awards and memb Ct of Assts Worshipful Co of Marketors; FCIM 1988, FRSA 1995, fell IPT 1995, chartered fell CIPD; *Recreations* jogging, cycling, country walks; *Clubs* Royal Over-Seas League, Farmers; *Style*— Ms Sally Muggeridge; ✉ Industry and Parliament Trust, Suite 101, 3 Whitehall Court, London SW1A 2EL (tel 020 7839 9400, fax 020 7839 9401, e-mail sallymuggeridge@ipt.org.uk)

MUIR, Prof Alexander Laird; s of Andrew Muir (d 1982), of Crieff, and Helena, *née* Bauld; *b* 12 April 1937; *Educ* Morrisons Acad Crieff, Fettes, Univ of Edinburgh (MB ChB, MD); *m* Berenice, da of Edward Snelgrove; 1 da (Alicia b 19 Nov 1972), 1 s (Andrew b 18 Sept 1974); *Career* house surgn Leeds Gen Infirmary and house physician Edinburgh Royal Infirmary 1961–62, SHO Leeds General Infirmary 1962–63, British Antarctic Survey 1963–65, asst lectr rising to lectr Dept of Med Univ of Edinburgh 1965–70, MRC travelling fell McGill Univ Montreal 1970–71, lectr Dept of Med Univ of Edinburgh 1971–73, conslt physician Manchester Royal Infirmary 1973–74, sr lectr rising to reader Dept of Med Univ of Edinburgh 1974–89, postgrad dean of med Univ of Edinburgh 1990–99; physician to HM The Queen in Scotland 1985–96, hon physician to the Army in Scotland 1986–97; FRCPEd 1976 (MRCPEd, vice-pres 1994–97), FRCR 1986, FRCSEd 1994, FRCP 1999; *Recreations* reading, golf, sailing, skiing; *Style*— Prof Alexander Muir; ✉ Tigh na Darroch, St Fillans, Perthshire PH6 2NG

MUIR, Jim; s of John Muir-Long Muir (d 1963), and Constance Jeannie, *née* Gilmour; *b* 3 June 1948; *Educ* Sedbergh, Univ of Cambridge (BA, Wright Prize); *m* 1, 1968, Carleen, *née* Batstone; 2 s (Judd b 1970, Joseph b 1972); m 2, 1986, Joumana, *née* Sayegh; 2 da (Shona b 1986, Diyala b 1992); *Career* ed Frank Cass & Co publishers 1970–74, Beirut corr Inter Press Service (IPS) 1975–78, freelance corr in Beirut for BBC and others 1978–80, freelance corr in Cyprus for BBC, Sunday Times, Daily Telegraph, Christian Science Monitor, National Public Radio (US) and Middle East International 1980–95 (covering Lebanon and Middle East, also covering Afghanistan and Bosnia 1993–94), BBC Middle East corr based Cairo 1995–99, BBC Tehran corr 1999–; *Recreations* ornithology, squash, travel, hill walking; *Style*— Jim Muir, Esq; ✉ via Room 410SE, BBC Bush House, London WC2B 4PH (e-mail jim.muir@bbc.co.uk)

MUIR, Dr Keith William; s of William John Muir, and Jean Bulloch, *née* Shanks; *Educ* Univ of Aberdeen (MB ChB, MD), Univ of Glasgow (MSc); *Career* conslt neurologist S Glasgow Univ Hosps NHS Tst 1999–2001, sr lectr in neurology Univ of Glasgow 2001–; memb Assoc of Br Neurologists 2000; MRCP 1992, FRCPGlas 2002; *Style*— Dr Keith Muir; ✉ Institute of Neurological Sciences, Southern General Hospital, Glasgow G51 4TF (tel 0141 201 1100, fax 0141 201 2510)

MUIR, Dr Richard Ernest; s of Kenneth Richard Muir, of Birstwith, Harrogate, and Edna Violet, *née* Huggall; *b* 18 June 1943; *Educ* Univ of Aberdeen (MA, PhD); *m* 13 Oct 1978, Nina Bina-Kumari, da of Indrajit Rajpal; *Career* lectr in geography Trinity Coll Dublin 1970–71, lectr and sr lectr in geography Cambridge Coll of Art and Technol 1971–80, freelance author and photographer 1981–94, sr lectr in geography UC of Ripon and York St John 1994–2001; co-fndr and ed LANDSCAPES jl 2000–, ed Nat Tst Histories, ed Countryside Cmmn Nat Parks; hon research fell in Geography and Environment Univ of Aberdeen 2001–; Yorks Arts Literary Award 1982–83; hon life memb Yorks Dales Soc 2005; various articles in Observer, Sunday Times, Geographical Magazine, NY Times; memb: FOE, CPRE, Yorks Dales Soc; *Books* Modern Political Geography (1975), Geography Politics and Behaviour (1980), The English Village (1980), Riddles in The British Landscape (1981), The Shell Guide to Reading The Landscape (1981), The Lost Villages of Britain (1982), History From The Air (1983), Visions of The Past (with C Taylor, 1983), The National Trust Guide to Prehistoric and Roman Britain (with H Welfare, 1983), A Traveller's History of Britain and Ireland (1984), The Shell Countryside Book (with E Duffey, 1984), The National Trust Guide to Dark Age and Medieval Britain (1985), The National Trust Guide to Rivers of Britain (with N Muir, 1986), Landscape and Nature Photography (1986), Old Yorkshire (1987), Hedgerows (with N Muir, 1988), The Countryside Encyclopaedia (1988), Fields (with N Muir, 1989), Portraits of the Past (1989), Barleybridge (1990), Castles and Strongholds (1990), The Dales of Yorkshire (1991), The Villages of England (1992), Coastlines (1993), Political Geography: A New Introduction (1997), The Yorkshire Countryside: A Landscape History (1997), Approaches to Landscape (1999), New Reading the Landscapes (1999), Landscape Detective (2001), Landscape Encyclopaedia (2004), Ancient Trees, Living Landscapes (2005), Be Your Own Landscape Detective 92007), How to Read a Village (2007); *Recreations* historical and environmental issues relating to British landscape, landscape photography; *Style*— Dr Richard Muir; ✉ e-mail richard.muir1@btinternet.com, website www.richardmuir.net

MUIR, (Sir) Richard James Kay; 4 Bt (UK 1892), of Deanston, Perthshire (does not use title); s of Sir John Harling Muir, 3 Bt, TD (d 1994), and Elizabeth Mary, *née* Dundas; *b* 25 May 1939; *m* 1, 1965 (m dis 1974), Susan Elizabeth, da of George Albert Gardener, of Calcutta and Leamington Spa; 2 da (Louisa Jane b 1967, Catherine Elizabeth b 1968); m 2, 1975, Lady Linda Mary Cole, da of 6 Earl of Enniskillen (d 1989); 2 da (Daisy Mary b 1977, Anna Charlotte b 1979); *Heir* bro, Ian Muir; *Style*— Richard Muir, Esq; ✉ Park House, Blair Drummond, by Stirling, Perthshire

MUIR MACKENZIE, Sir Alexander Alwyne Brinton; 7 Bt (UK 1805), of Delvine, Perthshire; s of Sir Robert Henry Muir Mackenzie, 6 Bt (d 1970), and Charmian Cecil de Vere, *née* Brinton (d 1962); *b* 8 December 1955; *Educ* Eton, Trinity Coll Cambridge; *m* 1984, Susan Carolyn, yst da of John David Henzell Hayter, of Holwell, Dorset; 1 da (Georgina Mary b 1987), 1 s (Archie Robert David b 17 Feb 1989); *Heir* s, Archie Muir Mackenzie; *Style*— Sir Alexander Muir Mackenzie, Bt; ✉ New House Farm, Lydlinch, Sturminster Newton, Dorset DT10 2JB

MUIR WOOD, Prof David; s of Sir Alan Marshall Muir Wood, FREng, FRS, and Winifred Leyton, *née* Lanagan; *b* 17 March 1949; *Educ* Royal GS High Wycombe, Peterhouse Cambridge (MA, PhD); *m* 7 Sept 1978, Helen Rosamond, *née* Piddington; 2 s (Alan Jamie b 8 May 1980, Andrew Peter b 25 May 1982); *Career* William Stone research fell Peterhouse Cambridge 1973–75, Royal Soc research fell Norwegian Geotechnical Inst Oslo 1975, lectr Univ of Cambridge and fell Emmanuel Coll Cambridge 1975–87; Univ of Glasgow: prof of civil engrg 1987–95, head of dept 1991–93, dean of engrg 1993–94; Univ of Bristol: prof of civil engrg 1995–, head Dept of Civil Engrg 1997–2002, dean of engrg 2003–07; MTS visiting prof of geomechanics Univ of Minnesota 2000, Fndn for Promotion of Industrial Science visiting prof Univ of Tokyo 2003; conslt: Geotechnical Consulting Gp 1983–, Babtie Gp Glasgow 1997– (Royal Soc industry fell 1995–96); chm Scottish Geotechnical Gp 1991–93; memb American Soc of Civil Engrs 1997; hon ed Géotechnique 1991–93, elder Cairns Church of Scotland Milngavie 1993–98, British Geotechnical Soc Prize (with C P Wroth, 1978), 20th Bjerrum lectr Norway 2005; FICE 1992, FREng 1998; *Books* Pressuremeter testing: Methods and Interpretation (with R J Mair, *qv*, 1987), Soil behaviour and critical state soil mechanics (1990), Geotechnical Modelling (2004); also author of numerous learned articles in professional jls; *Recreations* hill walking, music, opera, travel; *Style*— Prof David Muir Wood, FREng; ✉ Leigh Lodge, Church Road, Abbots Leigh, Bristol BS8 3QP (tel 01275 375563, e-mail muirwood@talk21.com); Department of Civil Engineering, Queen's Building, University Walk, Bristol BS8 1TR (tel 0117 928 7709, fax 0117 921 0318, e-mail d.muir-wood@bristol.ac.uk)

MUIRHEAD, Alastair William (Sandy); s of William Calliope Muirhead, OBE (d 1983), and Joan Andrade, *née* Sutherland; *b* 12 September 1953; *Educ* Tonbridge, St John's Coll Oxford (BA); *m* 19 April 1980, Linda Anne, da of Robert Johnson, of Wakefield; 3 da (Joanna b 19 Feb 1983, Nicola b 12 March 1985, Catriona b 16 Aug 1989); *Career* Price Waterhouse 1976–80, Saudi International Bank 1980–84; md: Charterhouse Bank Ltd 1984–96, DLJ Euro Investment Banking Gp; dir D L J Phoenix Private Equity Ltd 1996–2001; ptnr: The Phoenix Partnership 1996–99, Phoenix Equity Ptnrs 2001–; non-exec dir Partnership Assurance Holdings Ltd 2005–; memb Business Bd RHS 2005–; MA(Hons) Univ of Oxford; ACA; *Recreations* fly fishing, gardening, hill walking; *Style*— Sandy Muirhead

MUIRHEAD-ALLWOOD, Sarah Kathryn; formerly William Forster Gillespie Muirhead, name changed by deed poll to Muirhead-Allwood 1956; name changed by statutory declaration 1996; c of Maj W R Muirhead (d 1946), and Joyce, *née* Forster; *b* 4 January 1947; *Educ* Wellington, St Thomas' Hosp Med Sch (BSc, MB BS, LRCP); *m* 1983; 2 s (William Ritchie b 12 Sept 1984, James Miles b 3 July 1986); *Career* St Thomas' Hosp: house surgn 1971–72, SHO 1972–73, anatomy demonstrator 1973; SHO Stoke Mandeville Hosp 1973–74; registrar: UCH 1974–77, Charing Cross Hosp 1977–78; sr registrar 1978–84 (Queen Mary's Hosp Roehampton, Westminster Hosp, Royal Nat Orthopaedic Hosp, UCH); conslt orthopaedic surgn: Whittington Hosp 1984, Royal Nat Orthopaedic Hosp 1991, King Edward VII's Hosp for Offrs; hon sr clinical lectr UCL 1984; hon conslt: St Luke's Hosp for the Clergy 1984, Hosp of St John and St Elizabeth; memb: Br Orthopaedic Assoc 1980, BMA 1983, Br Hip Soc 1989, European Hip Soc 1993; FRCS; *Books* contrib: Joint Replacement - State of the Art (1990), Recent Advances in Orthopaedic Surgery (1991), Grays Anatomy (1995); *Recreations* sailing, golf; *Style*— Miss Sarah Muirhead-Allwood; ✉ The London Hip Unit, 4th Floor, 30 Devonshire Street, London W1G 6PU (tel 020 7908 3709, fax 020 7636 5758, e-mail smuirheadallwood@compuserve.com)

MUKARJI, Dr Daleep; s of Anand Kumar Mukarji (d 1974), and Shirin, *née* Warris (d 2001); *b* 22 February 1946, Lahore, India; *Educ* Medical Coll Vellore India (MBBS), LSHTM (DTPH), LSE (MSc); *m* 22 Feb 1974, Azra, *née* Latifi; 1 s (Armaan Anand b 2 April 1979), 2 da (Nitika Shirin b 6 April 1983, Diya Sabiha b 4 April 1984); *Career* dir Rural

Unit for Health and Social Affrs (RUHSA) Vellore India 1977–84, gen sec Christian Medical Assoc of India (CMAI) Delhi 1985–94, sec for health, community and justice World Cncl of Churches Geneva 1994–98, dir Christian Aid 1998–; memb: APRODEV, Trade Justice Movement, ACT Int, Guy Chester Centre; B C Roy Nat Award India; Hon DLL Aberdeen Univ 2006; fell Christian Acad of Medical Sciences India; *Recreations* music, drama, theatre, walks; *Style*— Dr Daleep Mukarji; ✉ Christian Aid, PO Box 100, London SE1 7RT (tel 020 7523 2356, e-mail dmukarji@christian-aid.org)

MUKHAMEDOV, Irek; s of Djavdat Rasulievich Mukhamedov, of Kazan, USSR, and Rashida Nizamovna, *née* Fatkulina; *b* 8 March 1960; *Educ* Moscow Ballet Sch; *m* 23 March 1990, Maria, da of Leonid Kovbas; 1 da (Alexandra Chulpan b 22 Aug 1990), 1 s (Maxim b 25 Jan 1996); *Career* ballet dancer; soloist Moscow Classical Ballet 1978–81, former princ dancer Bolshoi Ballet, currently dancer Royal Ballet; *Performances* with Bolshoi incl: Spartakus, Don Quixote, Ivan the Terrible, Golden Age, Romeo and Juliet, Raymonda, Giselle, Nutcracker, Swan Lake; with Royal Ballet incl: La Bayadère, Manon (2 roles), Nutcracker, Raymonda, Winter Dreams, The Judas Tree, Prince Rudolf in Mayerling; other performances incl: Roland Petit's Cyrano de Bergerac, Nureyev's Sleeping Beauty (Grand Opera Paris and Vienna Opera), Nureyev's Don Quixote (Flanders Ballet), Balanchine's Apollo (Vienna); *Awards* incl: Grand Prix Moscow IV competition, Gandersen Best Dancer in the World, Laurence Olivier Best Acting Prize, Evening Standard Ballet Award 1993; *Recreations* dedication to art of ballet, family; *Style*— Irek Mukhamedov, Esq; ✉ The Quintus Group, 535 King's Road, London SW10 0SZ (tel 020 7351 7499)

MULCAHY, Sir Geoffrey John; kt (1993); s of late Maurice Frederick Mulcahy; *b* 7 February 1942; *Educ* King's Sch Worcester, Univ of Manchester, Harvard Univ (MBA); *m* 1964, Valerie Elizabeth, *née* Ison; 1 s, 1 da; *Career* labour relations, mktg and planning Esso Corporation, fin dir British Sugar Corporation Ltd 1977–82; Kingfisher plc (formerly Woolworth Holdings plc): dir 1983–2002, gp md 1984–86, chief exec 1986–93 and 1995–2002, chm 1990–95, exec chm 1993–95; non-exec dir: Bass plc 1989–2002, BNP UK Holdings Ltd 1994–2002, Instore plc 2005–07; formerly non-exec dir: BT plc, Eurotunnel until 1995; *Recreations* squash, sailing; *Clubs* RAC, Royal Southern Yacht, Lansdowne, Royal Thames Yacht; *Style*— Sir Geoffrey Mulcahy; ✉ 31 Eaton Terrace, London SW1W 8TP

MULDOON, Prof Paul Benedict; s of Patrick Muldoon (d 1985), and Brigid, *née* Regan (d 1974); *b* 20 June 1951; *Educ* St Patrick's Coll Armagh, Queen's Univ Belfast (BA); *Career* prodr Arts Progs (Radio) BBC Northern Ireland (sr prodr 1978–85), TV prodr BBC Northern Ireland 1985–86, Judith E Wilson visiting fell Univ of Cambridge 1986–87, creative writing fell UEA 1987, pt/t teacher Writing Div Sch of the Arts Colombia Univ 1987–88, pt/t teacher Creative Writing Prog Princeton Univ 1987–88, writer in residence 92nd Street 'Y' New York 1988, Roberta Holloway lectr Univ of Calif Berkeley 1989, visiting prof Univ of Massachusetts Amherst 1989–90; Princeton Univ: lectr 1990–95, dir Creative Writing Prog 1993–2002, prof 1995–98, Howard G B Clark prof in the Humanities 1998–; fell Hertford Coll Oxford 1999–2004, prof of poetry Univ of Oxford 1999–2004; memb Aosdána (Irish Acad of Artists); memb American Acad of Arts and Sciences 2000; FRSL 1981, *Awards* Eric Gregory Award 1972, Sir Geoffrey Faber Meml Award 1980 and 1991, John Simon Guggenheim Meml Fellowship 1990, shortlisted Aristeion Euro Translation Prize 1994, shortlisted Forward Poetry Prize 1994, T S Eliot Prize 1994, American Acad of Arts and Letters Award for Literature 1996, Pulitzer Prize for Poetry 2003; *Poetry* Knowing My Place (1971), New Weather (1973), Spirit of Dawn (1975), Mules (1977), Names and Addresses (1978), Immram (1980), Why Brownlee Left (1980), Out of Siberia (1982), Quoof (1983), The Wishbone (1984), Selected Poems 1968–83 (1986), Meeting the British (1987), Madoc: A Mystery (1990), Selected Poems 1968–86 (1987 and 1993), Incantata (1994), The Prince of the Quotidian (1994), The Annals of Chile (1994), New Selected Poems 1968–94 (1996), Kerry Slides (1996), Hay (1998), Poems 1968–98 (2001), Moy Sand and Gravel (2002), Horse Latitudes (2006); *Drama* Monkeys (TV play, BBC 1989), Shining Brow (opera, 1993), Six Honest Serving Men (play, 1995), Bandanna (opera, 1999); *Childrens* The Last Thesaurus (1995), The O-O's Party (1981 and 1997), The Noctuary of Narcissus Batt (1997); *Edited* The Scrake of Dawn (1979), The Faber Book of Contemporary Irish Poetry (1986), The Essential Byron (1989), The Faber Book of Beasts (1997); *Other Work* To Ireland, I (criticism, 2000); numerous recordings and readings, anthologies and translations and interviews and criticisms; *Style*— Prof Paul Muldoon, FRSL

MULFORD, Dr David Campbell; s of Robert Lewis Mulford (d 1950), of Rockford, Illinois, and Theodora Moellenhauer Mulford Countryman (d 1988); *b* 27 June 1937; *Educ* Lawrence Univ Wisconsin (BA Econ cum laude), Univ of Cape Town (Rotary Fndn Int Fellowship), Boston Univ (Woodrow Wilson Fellowship, MA), St Antony's Coll Oxford (Technical Co-operation Grant, Ford Fndn Fellowship, DPhil); *m* 19 Oct 1985, Jeannie, *née* Simmons; 2 s (Ian, Edward); *Career* special asst to sec and under sec Treasy White House 1965–66, md and head Int Fin White Weld & Co Inc 1966–84 (seconded to Saudi Arabian Monetary Agency 1974–84); under sec and asst sec Treasy for Int Affairs USA 1984–92; major appts 1984–92 incl: sr int econ policy official Treasy, US dep for co-ordination of econ policies with other G7 nations, head admin Yen/Dollar negotiations with Japan, sr advsr on fin assistance to Russia, ldr int debt strategy, devpt and implementation of Baker/Brady Plans and Pres Bush's Enterprise Initiative for Americas, ldr US Delegation estab of EBRD and G7 negotiations to reduce Poland's official bilateral debt; vice-chm Credit Suisse First Boston Inc 1992– (memb exec Bd), chm International Credit Suisse First Boston (Europe) Ltd 1993–; Hon PhD Law Lawrence Univ 1984, Legion d'Honneur 1990, distinguished Alumni Award Boston Univ 1992, Alexander Hamilton Award US Treasy 1992, Order of May for Merit Argentina 1993, Officer's Cross Medal of Merit Poland 1995; memb: Cncl on Foreign Rels, Centre for Strategic and Int Studies Washington DC, White House Fellows Assoc, RIIA; *Books* Northern Rhodesia General Election (1962), Zambia - The Politics of Independence (1967); *Recreations* golf, running; *Clubs* Metropolitan (Washington DC); *Style*— Dr David C Mulford

MULGAN, Dr Geoffrey J (Geoff); CBE (2004); *b* 28 August 1961; *Educ* Univ of Oxford (BA), PCL (PhD); *Career* investment exec Greater London Enterprise Bd 1984–86, Harkness fell MIT 1986–88, lectr Poly of Central London and memb Comedia consulting gp 1988–90, policy advsr to Gordon Brown MP 1990–92, fell BFI 1992–93, fndr and dir Demos (independent think-tank) 1993–97, memb PM's Policy Unit 1997–2000, dir Performance and Innovation Unit (PIU) Cabinet Office 2000–02, dir PM's Strategy Unit 2001–04, head of policy PM's Office 2003–04, dir The Young Fndn 2004–; visiting prof: UCL, LSE, Melbourne Univ; dir/tstee: Photographers Gallery, Crime Concern, Political Quarterly, The Work Fndn, The Design Council; contrib numerous articles to pubns incl The Times, Financial Times, Guardian, Independent, New Statesman; *Books* Saturday Night or Sunday Morning (with Ken Worpole, 1987), The Question of Quality (ed, 1990), Communication and Control (1991), The Hollywood of Europe (ed BBC monograph series, 1993), Reconnecting Taxation (with Robin Murray, 1993), Politics in an Antipolitical Age (1994), Connexity (1997), Good and Bad Power (2006); *Style*— Dr Geoff Mulgan, CBE

MULHOLLAND, Clare; OBE (1998); da of James Mulholland (d 1969), of Glasgow, and Elizabeth, *née* Lochrin (d 1998); *b* 17 June 1939; *Educ* Notre Dame HS Glasgow, Univ of Glasgow (MA); *Career* with ICI 1961–64, Granada Television 1964–65, TWW Ltd 1965–68, HTV Ltd 1968–71; Independent Television Cmmn (Independent Broadcasting Authy until 1990): regnl exec Bristol 1971–78, regnl offr Midlands 1978–82, dep dir of TV 1983–90, dir of progs 1991–96, dep chief exec 1996–97; int broadcasting conslt 1998–2007; vice-chair Communications Regulatory Agency (Independent Media Cmmn until 2001) Bosnia and Herzegovina 1998–2005; tstee Scottish Film Prodn Fund 1984–90, memb Arts Cncl of GB 1986–94, chm Film Video and Broadcasting Panel 1986–94, memb Film Advsy Panel Arts Cncl of England 1997–2000; FRTS 1988; *Recreations* theatre, cinema, travel; *Style*— Miss Clare Mulholland, OBE

MULHOLLAND, Dr (Hugh) Connor; s of William Hugh Mulholland (d 1987), of Belfast, and Agnes, *née* Connor (d 1995); *b* 10 September 1938; *Educ* Campbell Coll Belfast (sr scholar), Queen's Univ Belfast (BSc, MB BCh, BAO); *m* 18 Dec 1968, (Hannah Eileen) Sandra, da of Frederick William Hedgecock (d 1984), of Belfast; 2 s (Michael b 1969, Gareth b 1975), 1 da (Shona 1972); *Career* asst prof Dept of Med Christian Med Coll Univ of Punjab 1969–71; res fellowship: NI Hosp Authy 1972–74, Ontario Heart Fndn 1974–76; conslt paediatric cardiologist Royal Belfast Hosp for Sick Children 1976–2003; Royal Gp of Hosps: co chm Regnl Med Cardiology Centre 1983–93, clinical dir cardiology and cardiothoracic surgn 1990–97, clinical dir paediatrics 1995–96, assoc med dir 1999–2002, dep med dir 2002–03; med mgmnt conslt 2003–; memb Bd Regulation and Quality Improvement Authy DHSS 2005–; assoc Beeches Mgmnt Centre Belfast; pres Irish Paediatric Cardiology Assoc 2001–, memb Cncl Br Paediatric Cardiology Assoc 1999–2003; memb: NY Acad of Scis, Br Cardiac Soc, Irish Cardiac Soc (pres 1998–2000), Assoc of Euro Paediatric Cardiologists, Ulster Paediatric Assoc (pres 1991–92), BMA, Belfast City YMCA, Children's Heart Tst NI, Bridge Community Tst (chm 2005–), Br Assoc of Med Mangrs; FRCPE 1979, FESC; *Recreations* hill walking, reading, photography; *Style*— Dr Connor Mulholland; ✉ 31 Deramore Drive, Belfast BT9 5JR (tel 028 9066 6266)

MULHOLLAND, Greg; MP; *b* 31 August 1970; *Educ* Univ of York (BA, MA); *Career* account handler sales promotion and events 1997–2002, cncllr (Lib Dem) Headingley 2003–05, MP (Lib Dem) Leeds NW 2005–; *Style*— Greg Mulholland, MP; ✉ House of Commons, London SW1A 0AA (website www.gregmulholland.org)

MULHOLLAND, John Peter Patrick; s of John Llewellyn Mulholland (d 1989, eld s of Hon Alfred John Mulholland, himself s of 1 Baron Dunleath), and Helen, *née* Moss (d 1993); *b* 2 September 1929; *Educ* Berkhamsted Sch, SSEES Univ of London (BA), Trinity Coll Dublin (BL), RAC Cirencester (Dip Advanced Farm Mgmnt); *m* 15 Dec 1973, Rosemary Kathleen Vaughan, da of Charles Hawkins, MC, of Cirencester, Glos; 2 s (John Charles b 1975, James Patrick b 1977); *Career* freelance journalist 1955–: Latin American corr News Chronicle 1959–61, prog organiser BBC External Serv 1963–69, numerous articles on fin and tax; called to the Bar: Middle Temple 1969, King's Inns Dublin 1975; in practice: Southampton and London 1969–, Repub of Ireland 1975–; sr lectr in law Royal Agric Coll 1980–88; memb: Chancery Bar Assoc 1970, Lincoln's Inn 1971; MRAC 1980, ACIArb 1992; *Books* Practical Puppetry (1961), Brazil 1968 (1968), Ploughing of Rights of Way (jtly, 1988), The Northern Dilemma (2006); *Recreations* hunting, shooting, equestrian sports; *Style*— John Mulholland, Esq; ✉ Drimbane, Curry, Co Sligo, Eire (tel 00 353 94 92 54358); 17 Old Buildings, Lincoln's Inn, London WC2A 3UP (tel 020 7405 9653)

MULHOLLAND, Prof Robert Charles; s of Philip Mulholland (d 1965), and Eileen, *née* Dwyer; *b* 4 December 1934; *Educ* Prior Park Coll Bath, London Hosp Med Sch; *m* 5 June 1965, Elizabeth, da of George Kennedy (d 1960); 2 s (Andrew b 19 Dec 1967, Seamus b 9 April 1969), 1 da (Sarah (twin) b 9 April 1969); *Career* Aust Navy 1959–61; sr house offr Royal Nat Orthopaedic Hosp 1965, registrar Bart's 1965–67, registrar and sr registrar Robert Jones and Agnes Hunt Orthopaedic Hosp 1967–72, instr and on faculty Univ of Washington Seattle 1969–71, conslt orthopaedic surgn Spinal Disorders Unit Nottingham Univ Hosp 1972–2000, emeritus conslt spinal surgeon Nottingham Univ Hosp, special prof in orthopaedic and accident surgery Univ of Nottingham; pres: Soc of Back Pain Res 1981–84, Int Soc for Study of the Lumbar Spine 1990–91, Br Orthopaedic Spinal Soc 1997–2000; author pubns on aspects of low back pain and problems of the lumbar spine; memb: RSM, Br Orthopaedic Assoc; FRCS; *Books* Back Pain Methods of Clinical Investigation and Assessment (ed with D Hukins, 1986); *Recreations* sailing; *Style*— Prof Robert Mulholland

MULLALLY, Rev Dame Sarah Elisabeth; DBE (2005); da of Michael Frederick Mills Bowser, and Ann Dorothy, *née* Mills; *b* 26 March 1962; *Educ* Winston Churchill Sch Woking, Woking Sixth Form Coll, Southbank Poly (BSc, MSc, RGN), Univ of Kent (DipTh), Heythrop Coll Univ of London (MA); *m* 11 July 1987, Eamonn James Mullally; 1 da (Grace Emily Louise b 9 Sept 1991), 1 s (Liam Timothy Cullam b 12 Dec 1995); *Career* staff nurse St Thomas' Hosp 1984–87 (clinical teacher 1987), staff nurse Royal Marsden Hosp 1987–88, ward sister Westminster Hosp 1988–90, sr nurse Riverside HA 1990–92, asst chief nurse Riverside Hosps 1992–94, dir of nursing and dep chief exec Chelsea and Westminster Healthcare Tst 1994–99, chief nursing offr and dir of patient experience Dept of Heath 1999–2004; non-exec dir Royal Marsden Fndn Hosp 2005–; ind govr London South Bank Univ; stipendiary curate Battersea Fields C of E, team rector Sutton 2006–; hon fell London South Bank Univ 2001; Hon Dr: Bournemouth Univ 2001, Univ of Wolverhampton 2004, Hertfordshire Univ 2005, hon fell Canterbury Christ Church Univ 2006; *Style*— The Rev Dame Sarah Mullally

MULLEN, Larry, Jr; s of Larry Mullen, of Dublin, and Maureen Mullen; *b* 31 October 1961; *Educ* Mount Temple Sch; *Partner* Ann Acheson; *Career* drummer and fndr memb U2 1978– (with Bono, The Edge, and Adam Clayton, *qqv*); first U2 release U23 (EP) 1979; *Albums* Boy 1980, October 1981, War 1983 (entered UK chart at no 1), Under A Blood Red Sky 1983 (live album), The Unforgettable Fire 1984 (entered UK charts at no 1), Wide Awake in America 1985, The Joshua Tree 1987 (entered UK charts at no 1, fastest selling album ever in UK, Album of the Year Grammy Awards 1987), The Joshua Tree Singles 1988, Rattle & Hum 1988 (entered UK charts at no 1), Achtung Baby 1991, Zooropa 1993 (no 1 in 18 countries, Best Alternative Album Grammy Awards 1993), Pop 1997 (no 1), The Best of 1980–1990 1998, All That You Can't Leave Behind 2000 (no 1, Best Rock Album Grammy Awards 2002), The Best of 1990–2000 2002, How To Dismantle An Atomic Bomb 2004 (Album of the Year and Best Rock Album Grammy Awards 2006); *Singles* incl: Fire 1981, New Year's Day (first UK Top Ten hit) 1983, Pride (In the Name of Love) 1984, Unforgettable Fire 1985, With or Without You 1987, I Still Haven't Found What I'm Looking For 1987, Where The Streets Have No Name 1987 (Best Video Grammy Awards 1989), Desire (first UK no 1 single) 1988 (Best Rock Performance Grammy Awards 1989), Angel of Harlem 1988, When Love Comes to Town 1989, All I Want Is You 1989, Night & Day (for AIDS benefit LP Red Hot & Blue) 1990, The Fly (UK no 1) 1991, Stay 1993, Discotheque (UK no 1) 1997, Staring at the Sun 1997, Sweetest Thing 1998, Beautiful Day (UK no 1) 2000 (Record of the Year, Song of the Year and Best Rock Performance by a Duo or Group with Vocal Grammy Awards 2001), Stuck in a Moment You Can't Get Out Of 2001 (Best Song by a Pop Duo or Group Grammy Awards 2002), Elevation 2001 (Best Rock Performance by a Duo or Group with Vocal Grammy Awards 2002), Walk On 2001 (Record of the Year Grammy Awards 2002), Electrical Storm 2002, Vertigo (UK no 1) 2004 (Best Rock Performance by a Duo or Group with Vocal, Best Rock Song and Best Short Form Music Video Grammy Awards 2005), Sometimes You Can't Make It On Your Own (UK no 1) 2005 (Song of the Year, Best Rock Duo or Group Vocal and Best Rock Song Grammy Awards 2006); *Film* Rattle & Hum 1988; *Tours* incl: UK, US, Belgium and Holland 1980, UK, US, Ireland and Europe 1981–83, Aust, NZ and Europe 1984, A Conspiracy of Hope (Amnesty International Tour) 1986, Joshua Tree tour 1987, Rattle & Hum tour 1988, Zoo TV tour (played to 5 million people) 1992–93, Popmart Tour 1997–98, Elevation 2001 tour 2001,

M

Vertigo tour 2005; also appeared at: Live Aid 1985 (Best Live Aid Performance Rolling Stone Readers' Poll 1986), Self Aid Dublin, Smile Jamaica (Dominion Theatre, in aid of hurricane disaster relief) 1988, New Year's Eve concert Dublin (broadcast live to Europe and USSR) 1989; performed at venues incl: Wembley Stadium, Madison Square Garden NY, Longest Day Festival Milton Keynes Bowl, Croke Park Dublin, Sun Devil Stadium AZ; *Awards* Best Band Rolling Stone Readers' Poll 1986 (also jt winner Critics' Poll), Band of the Year Rolling Stone Writers' Poll 1984, Best International Act BPI Awards 1989 and 1990, Best Live Act BPI Awards 1993, Best International Group Brit Awards 2001, Outstanding Contribution to the Music Industry Brit Awards 2001, Outstanding Song Collection Ivor Novello Awards 2003, Golden Globe Award (for Hands that Built America) 2003, Oscar nomination (for Hands that Built America) 2003; *Style—* Larry Mullen, Jr; ✉ c/o Regine Moylett Publicity, 2C Woodstock Studios, Woodstock Grove, London W12 8LE (tel 020 8749 7999)

MULLEN, Dr Richard; s of Dr Richard W Mullen, of Paterson, NJ, and Eleanor Wild Mullen; *b* 25 May 1945; *Educ* Seton Hall Univ (BA), Fordham Univ (MA), St Edmund Hall Oxford (DPhil); *Career* tutor in history and politics Univ of Oxford and Univ of London 1969–78, literary ed Christian World 1978–79, historical advsr CBS TV 1981, author numerous historical and literary features for BBC Radio 1981–, ed Contemporary Review 1991–; edited: The Pamphleteer 1813–28 (29 vols, 1978), Frances Trollope Domestic Manners of the Americans (1984), Malachi's Cove and Other Stories and Essays by Anthony Trollope (1985); BBC documentaries and features incl progs on Queen Victoria, Anthony Trollope, Charles Lamb, John Galsworthy, William Pitt, Lord Palmerston, Scott Fitzgerald, Edward Fitzgerald; Weaver fellowship 1972; *Books* Victoria: Portrait of a Queen (with James Munson, 1987), Anthony Trollope: A Victorian in His World (1990, winner Yorkshire Post Book of the Year award 1991), The Sayings of Anthony Trollope (1992), Anthony Trollope: A Pocket Anthology, Birds of Passage: Five Englishwomen in Search of America, The Penguin Companion to Trollope (with James Munson); *Recreations* music, walking, reading; *Style—* Dr Richard Mullen; ✉ 2 Butts Road, Horspath, Oxfordshire OX33 1RH (tel 01865 874286, e-mail richardmullen@contemporaryreview.co.uk)

MULLENS, Lt-Gen Sir Anthony Richard Guy; KCB (1989), OBE (1978, MBE 1974); s of Brig Guy John de Wette Mullens, OBE (d 1981), and Gwendoline Joan, *née* Maclean (d 1996); *b* 10 May 1936; *Educ* Eton, RMA Sandhurst; *m* 31 Oct 1964, Dawn Elizabeth Hermione, da of Lt-Col John Walter Pease (d 1983); *Career* cmmnd 4th/7th Royal Dragoon Gds 1956, ADC to Cdr 1st Br Corps 1958–60, Adj 1963, Staff Coll Camberley 1967–68, MOD 1968–70, regtl duty 1970–72, Bde Maj 1972, dir staff Staff Coll 1973–76, CO 4th/7th Royal Dragoon Gds 1976–78, HQ BAOR 1978–80, Cdr 7th Armd Brigade 1980–82, Mil Sec Dept MOD 1982–85, GOC 1st Armd Div 1985–87, ACDS Operational Requirements (Land Systems) MOD 1987–89, DCDS (Systems) MOD 1989–92; Col Royal Dragoon Gds 1994–99, Hon Col Eton Coll CCF 2001–07; conslt to British Rail on personnel and equipment 1992–95, assoc Varley Walker (HR Conslts) 1994–; tstee Army Museums Ogilby Tst 1997–2007; pres 7th Armd Div Thetford Forest Meml Assoc 1998–, pres 7th Armd Div Officers Club 2000–05; church warden 1997–2003, memb Alpheton PC 1999–2003; Liveryman Worshipful Co of Coachmakers & Coach Harness Makers 1977, Renter Warden Worshipful Co of Armourers and Brasiers 1996 (Liveryman 1974, memb Ct of Assts 1993); MInstD 1992–2002; Niedersachsen Verdienstkreuz (am Bande 1982, First Class 1987); *Recreations* travel, riding, skiing; *Clubs* Cavalry and Guards'; *Style—* Lt-Gen Sir Anthony Mullens, KCB, OBE; ✉ 81 Cranmer Court, Sloane Avenue, London SW3 3HH (tel 020 7584 3239, e-mail mullens@btinternet.com)

MULLER, Franz Joseph; QC (1978); s of Wilhelm Muller (d 1982), and Anne Maria Muller, *née* Ravens (d 1989); *b* 19 November 1938; *Educ* Mount St Mary's Coll, Univ of Sheffield (LLB); *m* 1985, Helena, da of Mieczyslaw Bartosz; 2 s (Julian b 1986, Henry b 1988); *Career* called to the Bar Gray's Inn 1961 (bencher 1994), called to the NI Bar 1982; graduate apprentice United Steel Cos 1960–61, commercial assoc Workington Iron & Steel Co Ltd 1961–63; commenced practice at the Bar 1964, recorder of the Crown Court 1977–, head of chambers; non-exec dir: Richards of Sheffield (Holdings) plc 1969–77, Satinsteel Ltd 1970–77, Rodgers Wostenholm Ltd 1975–77; memb SCR UC Durham 1981; *Recreations* fell walking, listening to music, skiing; *Style—* Franz Muller, Esq, QC; ✉ Slade Hooton Hall, Laughton en le Morthen, South Yorkshire S25 1YQ

MULLER, Dr Ralph Louis Junius; s of Carl Muller (d 1937), and Sarah Muller (d 1982); *b* 30 June 1933; *Educ* Summerhill Sch, Univ of London (BSc, PhD, DSc); *m* 1, 1958 (m dis), Gretta, da of Vernon Shearer; 1 da (Karen b 16 Oct 1959), 1 s (Julian b 7 Aug 1961); m 2, 1979, Annie (d 1998), da of Rafael Badilla; 1 da (Harriet b 2 Oct 1981), 1 s (Barnaby b 29 March 1985); *Career* scientific offr ODM 1959–61, lectr in parasitology Univ of Ibadan 1962–66, hon sr lectr LSHTM (sr lectr 1966–80), dir Int Inst of Parasitology 1981–93; hon sec Br Soc for Parasitology 1995–98 (hon memb 1998–); pres Euro Fedn of Parasitologists 1988–92, sec Int Filariasis Assoc 1978–; ed Advances in Parasitology; FRSTM&H 1968, FIBiol 1974; *Books* Worms and Disease (1975, 2 edn 2001), Bibliography of Onchocerciasis (1987), Medical Parasitology (1990); *Recreations* beekeeping, photography, pen collecting; *Style—* Dr Ralph Muller; ✉ 22 Cranbrook Drive, St Albans, Hertfordshire AL4 0SS (tel 01727 769322, fax 01727 769322, e-mail ralphmuller@hotmail.co.uk); London School of Hygiene and Tropical Medicine, Keppel Street, London WC1E 7HT

MULLIGAN, (Margaret) Mary; MSP; *b* 12 February 1960; *Educ* Univ of Manchester (BA); *m* 15 May 1982, John Mulligan; 2 s, 1 da; *Career* personnel offr BHS 1981–82, retail mangr Edinburgh Woollen Mill 1982–86; memb Edinburgh DC 1988–96, memb City of Edinburgh Cncl 1995–99, MSP (Lab) Linlithgow 1999–; Scottish Parl: dep min for health and community care 2001–03, dep min for communities 2003–04; *Style—* Mrs Mary Mulligan, MSP; ✉ The Scottish Parliament, Edinburgh EH99 1SP (tel 0131 348 5799, fax 0131 348 5967, e-mail mary.mulligan.msp@scottish.parliament.uk)

MULLIGAN, Tracy Dima; da of Frederick George Mulligan (d 1994), of Esher, Surrey, and Gladys, *née* Egerton; *b* 6 May 1962; *Educ* Chelsea Sch of Art (BTec), Kingston Univ (BA), St Martin's Sch of Art (BA); *Career* fashion designer; early career experience as hair stylist with The Ginger Group and Sanrizz London 1978–83, subsequent experience as sales asst with fashion retailers Joseph and Browns; asst womenswear designer Daniel Hechter Paris 1991; fndr ptnr Sonnentag Mulligan 1991–96; consultancy for: Stirling Gp M&S 1995, French Connection 1996–97, Scapa of Scotland 1997, ICB Japan 1999–2000; Mulligan (own label): launched catwalk show London Fashion Week 1998, eight collections, Womens and Menswear, sold to int designer stores 1998–2002; catwalk show and talk at Br Embassy for Br Cncl Elle Bangkok Fashion week 2000; touring exhibition Fabric of Fashion-Exhibition@Crafts Cncl 2000–02; visiting lectr in fashion: Central St Martin's 1994, 1995, 1997 and 2001, Univ of Central England 1996, RCA 1998–2001, London Coll of Fashion 2002; sr lectr in fashion Univ of Westminster 2001–02; gp finalist Jigsaw Womenswear Competition 1988, finalist Garroulds Corp Clothing Competition 1989, finalist ICRF Design Competition and Charity Fashion Show 1989; selected to show during London Fashion Week (Harvey Nichols) and sponsored by BFC to exhibit at Br Fashion Week (Ritz Hotel) 1993, sponsored by Harvey Nichols/Perrier for catwalk show 1994, sponsored by Stirling Group plc for catwalk show 1994, sponsored by DTI for catwalk show in Osaka and to exhibit in Tokyo 1994, sponsored by Marks and Spencer for catwalk show and stand Oct 1995; nominated: British Design/New Generation Lloyds Bank British Fashion Awards 1993, 1994 and 1995; speaker Addressing Dressing (with Sally Brampton and Betty Jackson) ICA Fashion Talks 1993; *Recreations* meditation, travel, swimming; *Style—* Ms Tracy Mulligan

MULLIN, Christopher John (Chris); MP; s of Leslie Mullin, and Teresa, *née* Foley; *b* 12 December 1947; *Educ* St Joseph's Coll Birkfield, Univ of Hull (LLB); *m* 1987, Nguyen Thi Ngoc, da of Nguyen Tang Minh, of Kontum, Vietnam; 2 da (Sarah b 2 Nov 1989, Emma b 18 June 1995); *Career* trainee scheme Mirror Group Newspapers 1969–71, freelance journalist 1972–74, BBC World Service 1974–78, freelance 1978–82, ed Tribune 1982–84, author 1984–87; Parly candidate (Lab): N Devon 1970, Kingston upon Thames 1974; MP (Lab) Sunderland S 1987–; chm Home Affairs Select Ctee 1997–99 and 2001–03 (memb 1992–99); Parly under sec of state: DETR 1999–2001, Dept of Int Devpt 2001, FCO 2003–05; *Publications* The Tibetans (1981), How to Select or Reselect your MP (1981), A Very British Coup (1982), The Last Man Out of Saigon (1986), Error of Judgement - The Truth about the Birmingham Pub Bombings (1986), The Year of the Fire Monkey (1991); *Recreations* walking, gardening; *Style—* Chris Mullin, Esq, MP; ✉ House of Commons, London SW1A 0AA; tel 0191 567 2848, fax 0191 510 1063

MULLIN, Geoffrey Kenneth (Geoff); s of Kenneth Mullin (d 1986), of Garstang, Lancs, and Lily, *née* Butcher (d 1976); *b* 11 September 1942; *Educ* Burnage GS for Boys Manchester, Royal Victoria Coll of Music (Dip); *m* 1, 5 Dec 1970 (m dis 1989), Caroline Moira, da of William Frederick Irving Stephenson (d 1988), of Henley, Oxon; 1 da (Crystal b 1973); m 2, 8 July 1999, Lesley, da of Anthony McCann (d 1979), of Didcot, Oxon; *Career* schoolteacher 1960–61, civil servant 1962–64, professional musician, singer, songwriter with recordings for DECCA and CBS 1964–68; advertising mangr and journalist 1968–70: Record Mirror, Music Week, Billboard; freelance prodr with BBC 1970–73, record prodr for various artists incl Marmalade and the Troggs 1970–73; prodr BBC Radio Two 1973–94: Simon Bates 1973–74, Jack Jackson, Terry Wogan 1975–79, David Hamilton 1979–80, Kenny Everett 1980–82, Sounds of the Sixties (Keith Fordyce) 1983–84, Ken Bruce 1985–86, Your Hundred Best Tunes (Alan Keith) 1987, Anne Robinson, Michael Aspel, The Earl Spencer, Wally Whyton, Maureen Lipman, Sue Cook, Brian Blessed and Anna Raeburn 1988–90, Jimmy Young, Terry Wogan and Glen Campbell's A to Z of Country Music 1991, Brian Hayes Breakfast Show 1992, Country Music Assoc Awards Show 1992, Radio 2 Country Season 1992, Buddy Concert for Nat Music Day 1992, Michael Aspel Xmas Special 1992, Wake Up to Wogan 1993, Elizabeth Power 1993, Beatles Day with George Martin 1993, Sarah Kennedy 1993, Country Style (BBC World Serv) 1993, Michael Aspel Sunday Show 1994 (Gold Sony Radio Award, Best Breakfast Show for Non-Contemporary Music 1994); head of music Melody FM (formerly Melody Radio) 1994–97: VJ Day Music Thames Relay 1995, Ella Fitzgerald Special Tribute (with David Jacobs, CBE); head music policy BBC Radio 2 1997–2001; music radio conslt 2001–; judge: Sony Awards 1995, Brit Awards 1998, Song for Europe 1998; memb: Ctee Music and Radio Conf 1995, 1996 and 1997, Radio Acad; *Recreations* squash, badminton, skiing, reading, travel, music, films, theatre; *Style—* Geoffrey Mullin, Esq; ✉ 11 Lancaster Road, St Albans, Hertfordshire AL1 4EP (tel 01727 848222, e-mail geoffmullin@btinternet.com)

MULLIN, Prof Tom; s of Joseph Michael Mullin (d 1991), and Elsie, *née* Fynney; *b* 5 September 1949, Broxburn, Lothian; *Educ* Napier Coll Edinburgh, Univ of Edinburgh (PhD); *m* 21 Nov 1970, Sylvia Janet; 1 da (Zoe Elizabeth b 26 April 1971), 1 s (Graham b 7 Sept 1974); *Career* scientific asst then scientific offr Naval Construction Research Establishment 1966–75, postdoctoral research asst Imperial Coll London and Univ of Oxford 1979–82, research fell Clarendon Lab Univ of Oxford 1982–91, research fell Wolfson Coll Oxford 1987–91 (jr research fell 1982–87), univ lectr in physics and fell Linacre Coll Oxford 1991–96, prof of physics Schuster Lab Univ of Manchester 1996–, dir Manchester Centre for Nonlinear Dynamics 2002–; sr fell ESPRC 2002– (advanced fell 1982–87); memb: Mathematics Coll EPSRC, UK Panel Int Union of Theoretical and Applied Mechanics (IUTAM); memb Editorial Bd Proceedings of the Royal Society A; several invited lectures; author of numerous articles; FRSE 2004; *Recreations* cycling, fell walking, music; *Style—* Prof Tom Mullin; ✉ Department of Physics and Astronomy, University of Manchester, Manchester M13 9PL (tel 0161 275 4070, fax 0161 275 4056, e-mail tom.mullin@man.ac.uk)

MULLINER, Stephen Nigel; s of Dr Gerald Norman Mulliner (d 2001), and Kathleen Wilma, *née* Ritchie; *b* 4 September 1953; *Educ* Downside, Emmanuel Coll Cambridge (MA, LLB), Inns of Court Sch of Law; *m* 18 Aug 1979, Sarah Lucinda, da of Lt-Col John Arthur Speirs, of Coombe Bissett, Wilts; 2 s (Andrew b 1983, Jonathan b 1985), 2 da (Lucy b 1983, Charlotte b 1989); *Career* called to the Bar 1978; assoc dir Swiss Bank Corporation Investment Banking Ltd 1987–89, gen mangr Tokai International Ltd 1989–91, gen mangr Arbitrage and Derivatives Dept Tokai Capital Markets Ltd 1991–98, exec dir Tokai Derivative Products Ltd 1995–98, md Witherden Financial Services Ltd 1999–2001, head of performance mgmnt Old Mutual plc 2001–; non-exec chm JS Real Estate plc (formerly James Smith Estates plc) 1989–2007 (non-exec dir 1988); Br Open Croquet champion 1988, 1990 and 2000, President's Cup winner 1981, 1983, 1986, 1987 and 1992, Men's champion 1985 and 1986, World Invitation Singles champion 1986 1987, 1988, 1999 and 2000, Br Open Doubles champion 1980, 1981, 1984, 1986, 1988, 1994 and 1997, Euro Open champion 1993, 1994, 1995 and 1998, 2nd World Championships 1997; vice-pres Croquet Assoc 2002– (chm 1990–92); *Books* The World of Croquet (1987), Play The Game - Croquet (1989); *Recreations* croquet, golf, tennis, real tennis, running; *Style—* Stephen Mulliner, Esq

MULLINS, Anthony Roy (Tony); s of Royston George Mullins (d 1985), and Evelyn Hilda Mullins; *b* 20 September 1939; *Educ* Loughton Sch, SW Essex Tech Coll, London Sch of Printing; *m* 1, 1964 (m dis 1995), Patricia Janet Stone; 2 s (John b 1969, Benjamin b 1973), 1 da (Nicola b 1971); m 2, Julie Elizabeth, da of Dr and Mrs Peter Hacking; *Career* art asst Sunday Times Magazine 1962–64, art ed The Observer Magazine 1967–76, art dir The Observer Newspaper 1976–95 (Focus Newspaper of the Year Design Award 1995), art dir The Design Desk 1995–; *Recreations* theatre; *Style—* Tony Mullins, FISTD; ✉ 29 Weybourne Street, London SW18 4HG (tel 0208944 8339, fax 020 8944 8449, e-mail tonym@designdesk.demon.co.uk)

MUMFORD, Prof David; *b* 11 June 1937, Three Bridges, W Sussex; *Educ* Harvard Coll (BA), Harvard Univ (PhD); *Career* Harvard Univ: instr and research fell in mathematics 1961–62, asst prof 1962–63, assoc prof 1963–67, prof 1967–77, Higgins prof of mathematics 1977–97, chm Dept of Mathematics 1981–84; prof Div of Applied Mathematics Brown Univ 1996–; visiting prof: Univ of Tokyo 1962–63, Tata Inst of Fundamental Research 1967–68 and 1978–79, Inst des Hautes Etudes Scientifiques Paris 1976–77, Inst Henri Poincare Paris 1998; Nuffield prof Univ of Warwick 1970–71, Rothschild prof Isaac Newton Inst Univ of Cambridge 1993; pres Int Mathematical Union 1995–98 (vice-pres 1991–94); Fields medal Int Congress of Mathematics Vancouver 1974; Hon DSc: Univ of Warwick 1983, Norwegian Univ of Science and Technol 2000, Rockefeller Univ 2001; fell Nat Acad of Sciences 1975, hon fell Tata Inst of Fundamental Research 1978, MacArthur Fndn fell 1987–92, foreign memb Accademia Nazionale dei Lincei Rome 1991, hon memb London Mathematical Soc 1995, fell American Philosopical Soc 1997; *Publications* Lectures on Curves on Surfaces (jtly, 1964), Geometric Invariant Theory (1965, 3 edn (jtly) 1994), Abelian Varieties (1970, 2 edn 1974), Toroidal Embeddings I (jtly, 1973), Curves and their Jacobians (1975), Smooth Compactification of Locally Symmetric Varieties (jtly, 1975), Algebraic Geometry I: Complex Projective Varieties (1976), Tata Lectures on Theta (jtly, Part I 1982, Part II 1983, Part III 1991), Filtering, Segmentation and Depth (jtly, 1993), Two and Three Dimensional Patterns of the Face (jtly, 1999), Mathematics: Frontiers and Perspectives (contrib, 2000), Indra's Pearls (jtly, 2002); writer of numerous articles on algebraic geometry and on vision; *Style—* Prof David Mumford; ✉ Division of Applied Mathematics, Brown University,

Box F, Providence, RI 02912, USA (tel 00 1 401 863 3441, fax 00 1 401 863 1355, e-mail david_mumford@brown.edu)

MUMFORD, Peter Taylor; s of John Stanley Mumford, and Doreen, *née* Taylor; *b* 12 December 1946; *Educ* Rutlish GS, Wimbledon Sch of Art, Central Sch of Art; *m* 1, Mary David Becket (decd); 3 s (Daniel b 1972, Luke b 1975, Samuel b 1982); m 2, Tana Marie Lester; 1 da (Théa Rose b 1995); *Career* director and lighting designer; extensive work throughout Britain and Europe in dance, drama and opera; memb: Assoc of Lighting Designers, United Scenic Artists (USA); *Theatre* most recent designs for Opera North incl: Madam Butterfly, Tanhauser, The Return of Ulysses, Luisa Miller; for RNT designs incl: Volpone, Mother Courage, Richard II, Stanley (also Broadway), The Invention of Love; for Birmingham Royal Ballet designs incl: Nutcracker Sweeties, Carmina Burana, Edward II (also Stuttgart Ballet); for RSC designs incl: Learned Ladies, Wallenstein, Ion, Goodnight Children Everywhere, Henry V, Camino Real; other designs incl: The Dolls House (Thelma Holt Prodns and Broadway), The Marriage of Figaro (Sydney Opera House), Mr Wordly Wise, Fearful Symmetries, Two Part Invention (all Royal Ballet), Symphony in C, Simon Boccanegra (both Munich Opera), The School for Wives, The Winter Guest (both Almeida Theatre), The Strip (Royal Court Theatre Upstairs); *Television* credits as dir incl: Swan Lake (1996, Adventures in Motion Pictures for BBC (winner The Crystal Award and Emmy nomination 1997)), Sound on Film (1996, The Music Practice/Andy Sheppard for BBC/ACE), Dance for the Camera III (BBC/ACE), Natural Selection (BBC Wales), White Bird Featherless (Siobhan Davies Dance Co for BBC), White Man Sleeps (winner Dance Screen Best Studio Adaptation) and Wyoming (both Siobhan Davies Dance Co for Channel Four), Heaven Ablaze in His Breast (for BBC 2 (winner Opera Screen/London Dance and Time Out Performance Award)), Dancehouse (1990, 12 pt series for BBC 2 (Special Jury mention at Dance Screen and Video Dance Grand Prix and NY Film Festival Finalist Award)), 48 Preludes and Fugues (dir 24 short films, lighting dir for remaining 24 films, BBC 2); *Awards* first lighting designer to win Olivier Award for Outstanding Achievement in Dance 1995 for lighting the Royal Ballet's Fearful Symmetries and Siobhan Davies Dance Co's The Glass Blew In, Olivier nomination RNT (Volpone, Richard II and Mother Courage) 1996, Olivier nomination Hamlet and Private Lives (RSC) 2000, winner Irish Times Award for Best Lighting Design for Iphigenia (Abbey Theatre Dublin) 2001, winner Olivier Award for Best Lighting Designer for Bacchai (NT) 2003; *Publications* Lighting Dance 1993; *Recreations* riding, sailing, fishing; *Style*— Peter Mumford; ✉ c/o Harriet Cruickshank, 97 Old South Lambeth Road, London SW8 1XU (tel 020 7735 2933, fax 020 7820 1081)

MUMMERY, *see also:* Lockhart-Mummery

MUMMERY, Rt Hon Lord Justice; Rt Hon Sir John Frank; kt (1989), PC (1996); s of late Frank Stanley Mummery (d 2002), of Bridge, Kent, and Ruth, *née* Coleman (d 2001); *b* 5 September 1938; *Educ* Oakleigh House, Dover Co GS, Pembroke Coll Oxford (MA, BCL); *m* 11 March 1967, Elizabeth Anne Lamond, da of Dr Glyn Lackie (d 1985), of Edinburgh; 1 da (Joanna b 1968), 1 s (David b 1974); *Career* Nat Serv Border Regt RAEC 1957–59; called to the Bar Gray's Inn 1964 (bencher 1985, treas 2005); counsel attorney gen in charity matters 1977–81, jr treasy counsel Chancery 1981–89, recorder 1989, judge of the High Court of Justice (Chancery Div) 1989–96, a Lord Justice of Appeal 1996–; pres: Employment Appeal Tbnl 1993–96, Security Services Tbnl 2000–, Intelligence Services Tbnl 2000–, Investigatory Powers Tbnl 2000–, Cncl of the Inns of Court 2000–03; memb Legal Advsy Cmmn of Gen Synod of C of E 1988–, chm Clergy Discipline Cmmn 2004–, pres Clergy Discipline Tbnl 2004–, judge Court of Ecclesiastical Cases Reserved 2006–; chm of tstees CAB Royal Courts of Justice 2003–; govr Inns of Court Sch of Law 1996–2001; chm Charity Law Unit Univ of Liverpool; tstee Wye Rural Museum Tst 2007–; hon pres of employment Law Bar Assoc, hon pres Charity Law Assoc, hon memb Soc of Legal Scholars; hon fell: Pembroke Coll Oxford 1989, Soc for Advanced Legal Studies; Hon LLD: De Montfort Univ, City Univ; *Books* Copinger and Skone James on Copyright (jt ed 13 edn, 1991); *Recreations* walks with family, friends and alone; *Style*— The Rt Hon Sir John Mummery; ✉ c/o Royal Courts of Justice, Strand, London WC2A 2LL

MUNASINGHE, (Leelananda) Sepala; s of Lairis Appu Munasinghe (d 1992), of Kurunegala, Sri Lanka, and Joslyn, *née* Samarasinghe (d 1990); *b* 2 January 1937; *Educ* Trinity Coll Kandy Sri Lanka; *m* 21 May 1964, Dorothea Brunhildis, da of Wilhelm Karger (d 1968), of Ostbevern, Germany; 2 da (Karin b 1965, Gitanjali b 1968); *Career* called to the Bar Lincoln's Inn 1963; advocate Supreme Court of Ceylon 1964, attorney at law Supreme Court of Sri Lanka 1972; chm: Social Security Appeals Tbnl 1986–99, Disability Appeals Tbnl 1991–99 (both UK); asst cmmr Parly Boundary Cmmn for England 1992–95, special adjudicator Immigration Appeals Authy 1995–98; govr Waldegrave Sch for Girls 1980–83, memb Birmingham City Cncl Public Inquiry into Handsworth Riots 1986; *Recreations* cooking, reading, travelling; *Clubs* Capri (Colombo); *Style*— Sepala Munasinghe, Esq; ✉ 50 Impasse des Deportes, 34370 Maraussan, Languedoc, France

MUNDAY, Barry; s of Philip John Munday, of Marple, Cheshire, and Stella Frances Munday; *b* 19 November 1945; *Educ* Heles Sch Exeter, Poly of N London (DipArch); *m* 1; 1 da (Zoe b 9 Aug 1973), 1 s (Leo b 30 June 1976); m 2, 25 Sept 1985, Jane Elizabeth, *née* Jagot; *Career* architect; Powell and Moya 1965–73; Phippen Randall and Parkes (PRP): joined 1973, dir 1983, chm 2001–, chair Business Devpt Gp, dir PRP Project Services; projects incl: Broadfield Site 5 Crawley, Binfield Triangle Bracknell, Private Finance Initiative Manchester, New Cross City, Hurlingham Club London; memb Bd The Housing Forum 2002– (memb Nat Review Panel for Housing Forum Demonstration Projects), founding dir Architects in Housing (now Design for Homes), memb Br Urban Regeneration Assoc; occasional lectr Kingston Univ; memb Worshipful Co of Architects; RIBA 1973, MFB 1998; *Publications* High Density Housing in Europe: Lessons For London (2002); various articles and opinion pieces in Building, Housing Today, Inside Housing, The Guardian and The Times; *Recreations* golf, painting, reading, music, walking, French culture; *Clubs* RAC, Chelsea FC; *Style*— Barry Munday, Esq; ✉ PRP Architects, 10 Lindsey Street, London EC1A 9HP (tel 020 7653 1200, fax 020 7653 1201, e-mail barry.munday@prparchitects.co.uk)

MUNDAY, Peter James; s of Frederick Lewis James Munday (d 1987), of Esher, Surrey, and Lily Charlotte Rebecca, *née* Fowler (d 1998); *b* 31 October 1938; *m* 1 (m dis 1984), Inger Kristina Fagersjo; 1 da (Lisa Kristina b 1975); m 2, 22 Dec 1984, Linda Ann (Lin), da of Leslie Breckon, of Cardiff; 2 da (Emma Sophie b 1986, Zara Jane b 1989); *Career* Nat Serv RCS 1957–59; admitted slr 1968, NP 1975; sr ptnr Mundays 1976– (ptnr 1968–); tstee: Princess Alice Hospice Esher, Esher War Meml Property Fund, Friends of St George's Church Esher, Hospice Educn Centre Tst; Freeman City of London, Liveryman Worshipful Co of Bakers; memb: Law Soc 1968, Notaries Soc 1975; *Recreations* hockey, squash, cricket; *Clubs* MCC; *Style*— Peter Munday, Esq; ✉ Pinewood Lodge, Warren Lane, Oxshott, Surrey KT22 0ST (tel 01932 590500); Mundays, Cedar House, 78 Portsmouth Road, Cobham, Surrey KT11 1AN

MUNDELL, David Gordon; MP; s of Dorah Mundell; *b* 27 May 1962; *Educ* Lockerbie Acad, Univ of Edinburgh (LLB), Univ of Strathclyde (MBA); *m* Lynda Jane, *née* Carmichael; 2 s (Oliver Gordon Watson b 1 Dec 1989, Lewis Kenneth David b 16 Dec 1994); 1 da (Eve Margaret b 21 Aug 1991); *Career* sr corp lawyer Biggart Baillie and Gifford Slrs Glasgow 1989–91, gp legal advsr BT Scotland 1991–98, head of national affairs BT Scotland 1998–99; MSP (Cons) Scotland S 1999–2005, MP (Cons) Dumfriesshire, Clydesdale and Tweeddale 2005–, shadow sec of state for Scotland 2006–; House of Commons: memb Select Ctee on Scottish Affrs 2005–, vice-chair All-Pty Scotch Whisky and Spirits Gp 2005–; memb: Law Soc of Scotland, Law Soc of England and Wales; *Recreations* family and friends, cycling, travel; *Style*— David Mundell, Esq, MP; ✉ House of Commons, London SW1A 0AA

MUNDY, Prof Anthony Richard (Tony); s of Peter Gordon Mundy, of London, and Betty, *née* Hall; *b* 25 April 1948, London; *Educ* Mill Hill Sch, Univ of Paris, St Mary's Hosp Medical Sch London and Univ of London (MB BS, MS); *m* 20 Sept 1975 (m dis 1992), Marilyn June, da of Edward Ashton, of South Ockendon, Essex; 1 da (Emily b 1977), 1 s (Harry b 1986); partner, Debra Ann, da of late Owen Hendley; 1 da (Katie b 1995); *Career* trg in gen surgery and urology Guys Hosp London, CO and conslt surgn Force Base Hosp Muscat Oman 1977–78, conslt urological surgn Lewisham Hosp 1981–86, sr lectr in urology Inst of Urology and UMDS 1981–91; prof of urology Univ of London at Guy's Hosp and Inst of Urology 1991–, dir Inst of Urology and Nephrology, clinical dir of urology and nephrology UCL Hosps 1994–2000, med dir for medicine and surgery UCL Hosps 2000–; conslt urological surgn: Guy's Hosp 1981–99, St Peter's Hosps UCL Hosps 1986–; visiting conslt urologist St Luke's Hosp Malta 1984–; hon conslt urological surgeon Nat Hosp for Neurology and Neurosurgery 1995–; chm Specialist Advsy Ctee in Urology 1996–99, hon civilian conslt urological surgn RN; pres Cncl Br Assoc of Urological Surgns 2006– (vice-pres 2004–06), memb Cncl RCS, memb Exec Ctee Euro Assoc of Urology, memb Exec Ctee Br Jl of Urology, Urological Res, memb Jt Ctee on Higher Surgical Trg 1996–99, memb Bd Euro Urological Scholarship Fndn 1996–99, memb Scientific Ctee Br Urological Fndn, fndn memb Soc of Genito-Urinary Reconstructive Surgeons, examiner and memb Intercollegiate Bd FRCS (Urology); Sir Ernest Finch visiting prof Sheffield 1994; Bodo von Garelts lectr Stockholm 1995, C E Alken lectr Dusseldorf 1999, Ian Aird lectr Imperial Coll London 1999, Grey Turner lectr Newcastle 1999, Rovsing lectr Copenhagen 2000; St Peter's Medal Br Assoc of Urological Surgeons 2002, Hunterian Oration RCS 2007; convener and fndr memb Urological Research Soc and Assoc of Academic Urologists; hon memb Urological Soc of Australia, Holland, Malaysia and Singapore, and South Africa; FRCS 1975, FRCP 1996 (MRCP 1974); *Books* Urodynamics - Principles Practice and Application (1984, 2 edn 1994), Scientific Basis of Urology (1986, 2 edn 2000), Current Operative Surgery-Urology (1988), The Neuropathic Bladder in Childhood (1990), Urodynamic and Reconstructive Surgery of the Lower Urinary tract (1992); author of 155 pubns on lower urinary tract function and dysfunction and reconstructive urology; *Recreations* sailing, food, wine, history; *Style*— Prof Tony Mundy; ✉ UCL Hospitals, 2nd Floor Central, 250 Euston Road, London NW1 2PG (e-mail tony.mundy@uclh.nhs.uk)

MUNIR, Dr (Ashley) Edward; s of Hon Sir Mehmed Munir, CBE (d 1957), and Lady Vessime Munir, *née* Ziai (d 1979); *b* 14 February 1934; *Educ* Brentwood, St John's Coll Cambridge (MA), King's Coll London (MPhil, PhD); *m* 6 June 1960, Sureyya, da of Shukri Dormen, of Istanbul, Turkey; 1 s (Simon b 24 Oct 1964); *Career* called to the Bar Gray's Inn 1956; crown counsel 1960–64, legal asst Govt Legal Serv 1964, under sec MAFF 1982, resumed practice at the Bar 1993; *Books* Perinatal Rights (1983), Fisheries after Factortame (1991), Mentally Disordered Offenders (1993); *Recreations* walking, playing the double-bass, listening to music; *Style*— Dr Edward Munir; ✉ 5 St Andrew's Hill, London EC4V 5BY (tel 020 7332 5400, fax 020 7489 7847)

MUNKENBECK, Alfred Hedges III; s of Alfred Hedges Munkenbeck Jr, of Old Greenwich, CT, and Adelaide Celina, *née* Rickert; *b* 26 March 1947; *Educ* Le Rosey Rolle Switzerland, The Canterbury Sch New Milford CT, Dartmouth Coll Hanover NH (BA), Harvard Univ (MArch); *m* 1992, Paula Reed; 1 da (Chloe Adelaide b 25 June 1993), 2 s (Alfred Hedges IV b 30 Oct 1995, Finn John b 6 May 1998); *Career* architect; worked with James Stirling Architects on Stuttgart Contemporary Art Museum 1977–80, urban design conslt for Yanbu and MOIT new towns, Umm al Qura Univ and Royal palaces Saudi Arabia 1980–85; sr ptnr Munkenbeck & Marshall 1985–; projects incl: office buildings at 11 Leadenhall St City of London and 87 Lancaster Rd Notting Hill, Roche Court Art Gallery, Mount Stuart Visitor Centre, Jerwood Space Rehearsal Studios, Grand Rapids Art Museum MI, Metro Photographic Clerkenwell, private houses for Charles Saatchi, Norman Parkinson and 43 The Bishops Avenue in London, apartment buildings at Gainsborough Studios Hackney and Paddington Basin; lectr in architectural design: Univ of Cambridge, Kingston Univ, The AA; assessor Civic Trust Awards, memb RIBA Urbanism and Planning Gp; RIBA 1980; *Awards* RFAC Building of the Year commendation 1992 and 1999, Kensington and Chelsea Environmental Award 1992, Civic Trust Award 1999, RIBA Stephen Lawrence Award 1999; *Recreations* skiing, sailing, sandcastles; *Clubs* The Architecture; *Style*— Alfred Munkenbeck, Esq

M

MUNN, Prof Charles William; OBE (2005); s of David Shearer Munn (d 1968), of Glasgow, and Elizabeth McCowan, *née* Renfrew (d 2001); *b* 26 May 1948; *Educ* Queens Park Secdy Sch Glasgow, Univ of Strathclyde (BA), Univ of Glasgow (PhD), Jordanhill Coll of Educn (CertEd); *m* 1 Sept 1973, Andrea, da of David Cuthbertson and Violet Cuthbertson; 1 s (David Stuart b 19 Aug 1977), 1 da (Kirsten Elizabeth b 8 April 1981); *Career* clerk and teller various Glasgow branches British Linen Bank 1964–67, student 1967–75, lectr Dept of Finance and Accountancy Glasgow Coll of Technol (now Glasgow Caledonian Univ) 1975–78, lectr then sr lectr Dept of Econ History Univ of Glasgow 1978–88, chief exec Chartered Inst of Bankers in Scotland 1988–2007; pres The European Bank Training Network 2003–05 (chm Professional Standards Ctee 1998–2003), chm Quality Assurance Agency for HE (Scotland) 2003– (memb UK Bd 2003–, chm Audit Ctee 2005–), exec i/c Ctee of Scottish Clearing Bankers 2003–07, chm Customer Contact Assoc Standards Cncl 2005–; memb Scottish Qualifications Authy 1997–2001; visiting prof Univ of Paisley 2000; hon prof Dept of Accountancy and Fin Univ of Dundee 2002–; FCIBS 1993, FRSA 1993; *Books* The Scottish Provincial Banking Companies 1747–1864 (1981), Banking in Scotland (1982), The Clydesdale Bank: The First 150 Years (1988), Ethics, Integrity and Reputation (with N Gallagher, 2001); *Recreations* reading, writing, golf; *Clubs* New (Edinburgh), New Golf (St Andrews), Aberdour Golf; *Style*— Prof Charles W Munn, OBE; ✉ 1 Ross Avenue, Dalgety Bay, Fife KY11 9YN (tel 01383 824567, e-mail charles.munn@btinternet.com)

MUNN, Margaret Patricia (Meg); MP; da of Reginald Edward Munn (d 2002), and Lillian, *née* Seward; *b* 24 August 1959; *Educ* Rowlinson Comp Sch Sheffield, Univ of York (BA), Univ of Nottingham (MA), Open Univ (Certificate in Mgmnt Studies, DMS); *m* 26 May 1989, Dennis Clifford Bates, s of late Ernest Edward Bates; *Career* social work asst Berks 1981–84, social worker Notts 1986–90, sr social worker Notts 1990–92, dist mangr Barnsley Social Servs 1992–96, children servs mangr Wakefield Social Servs 1996–99, asst dir York Social Servs 1999–2000; MP (Lab/Co-op) Sheffield Heeley 2001–; Parly under sec for state for women and equality Dept for Trade and Industry 2005–06, Parly under sec of state for women and equality Dept for Communities and Local Govt 2006–07, Parly under sec of state FCO 2007–; *Style*— Ms Meg Munn, MP; ✉ House of Commons, London SW1A 0AA (tel 020 7219 8316, fax 020 7219 1793, e-mail munnm@parliament.uk); Constituency Office, Barkers Pool House, Burgess Street, Sheffield S1 2HF (tel 0114 263 4004, fax 0114 263 4334, website www.megmunnmp.org.uk)

MUNN, Prof Robert William; s of William Anderson Munn (d 1989), and Kathleen Maud, *née* Bishop (d 1981); *b* 16 January 1945; *Educ* Huish's GS Taunton, Univ of Bristol (BSc, PhD), Victoria Univ of Manchester (DSc); *m* 24 June 1967, Patricia Lorna, da of Robert William Moyle (d 1965); 1 s (Nicholas b 1971), 1 da (Philippa b 1974); *Career* postdoctorate fell Nat Res Cncl of Canada 1968–70, ICI postdoctoral fell Univ of

Edinburgh 1970–71, visiting fell ANU 1982; UMIST (now Univ of Manchester): lectr 1971–80, reader 1980–84, prof of chemical physics 1984–, vice-princ 1987–90, dean 1994–99; vice-pres for teaching and learning Univ of Manchester 2004–07; co-ordinating ed Jl of Molecular Electronics 1985–91, assoc ed Advanced Materials for Optics and Electronics 1992–2000, numerous pubns in scientific jls; CChem 1987, CPhys 1987, CSci 2004, FRSC, FInstP, FHEA 2007; *Books* Molecular Electromagnetism (with A Hinchliffe), Magnetism and Optics of Molecular Crystals (with J W Rohleder); *Recreations* guitar, singing; *Style—* Prof Robert Munn; ✉ Office of the President, University of Manchester, Manchester M13 9PL (tel 0161 306 6030, fax 0161 306 6031, e-mail bob.munn@manchester.ac.uk)

MUNRO, Sir Alan Gordon; KCMG (1990, CMG 1984); s of Sir Gordon Munro, KCMG, MC, and Lilian Muriel, *née* Beit; *b* 17 August 1935; *Educ* Wellington, Clare Coll Cambridge (MA); *m* 1962, Rosemary Grania, da of Cdr N A Bacon; 2 s (twins), 2 da; *Career* HM Dip Serv: consul-gen Rio de Janeiro 1974–77, head of East African Dept FCO 1977–78, head of Middle East Dept 1979, head of Personnel Operations Dept 1979–81, dir of ME Def Sales MOD 1981–83, ambass to Algeria 1984–87, dep under sec of state FCO 1987–89, ambass to Saudi Arabia 1989–93; vice-chm Bd British Red Cross 1994–2002, advsr Tate & Lyle plc, non-exec dir Middle East International Ltd, dir Schroder Asseily Ltd 1993–2003; vice-chm Arab-Br C of C; chm: Beit Tst for Central Africa, Red Cross Order of St John Ctee, Saudi-Br Soc, Soc for Algerian Studies; MIPM; *Books* An Arabian Affair (Arab Storm): Politics and Diplomacy Behind the Gulf War (1996 and 2006); *Recreations* Middle East travel, conservation, history, gardens; *Clubs* Travellers; *Style—* Sir Alan Munro, KCMG

MUNRO, Colin Andrew; CMG (2002); s of Capt Frederick Bertram Munro (d 1963), and Jane Eliza, *née* Taylor (d 1998); *b* 24 October 1946; *Educ* George Watson's Coll Edinburgh, Univ of Edinburgh (MA), KCL (MA); *m* 1967, Ehrengard Maria, da of Rudolf Heinrich (d 1981); 2 s (Peter b 25 Dec 1967, Richard b 27 Jan 1978); *Career* asst princ Bd of Inland Revenue 1968–69, third sec FCO 1969–71, third then second sec Bonn 1971–73, second then first sec Kuala Lumpur 1973–77, FCO 1977, private sec to Min of State 1979–80, head of Chancery Bucharest 1981–82, FCO 1983, dep head Western Euro Dept 1985, dep head of mission E Berlin 1987–90, consul-gen Frankfurt 1990, head OSCE Cncl of Europe Dept 1993–97, ambass to Croatia 1997–2000, dep high rep Bosnia and Herzegovina (based in Mostar) 2001, RCDS 2002, UK perm rep to Orgn for Security and Co-operation in Europe 2003–07; tstee Accord Int; *Publications* contribs to journals of Prince Albert Society, Coburg, Vienna Univ and Inst of Contemporary British History; *Recreations* history, sports especially hockey, cricket, skiing; *Clubs* Reform, RAC, Rotary, Wien Nord Ost, Royal Selangor (Kuala Lumpur); *Style—* Colin A Munro, Esq, CMG

MUNRO, Prof Colin Roy; s of James Smith Munro (d 1970), and Isabel, *née* Thomson (d 1993); *b* 17 May 1949; *Educ* Aberdeen GS, Univ of Aberdeen (LLB), Open Univ (BA); *m* 10 April 1976, Ruth Elizabeth, da of Dr Thomas Leonard Cheesbrough Pratt; 1 s (Philip Edward b 12 Dec 1980), 1 da (Sally Joanna b 22 Sept 1982); *Career* lectr in law: Univ of Birmingham 1971–72, Univ of Durham 1972–80; reader in law and dean Sch of Law Univ of Essex 1984–85 (sr lectr 1980–84), prof of law Univ of Manchester 1985–90 (dean Faculty of Law 1986–88), prof of constitutional law Univ of Edinburgh 1990– (dean Faculty of Law 1992–94); memb: Soc of Legal Scholars 1971–, Scottish Media Lawyers Soc 1995–, Consultative Cncl Br Bd of Film Classification 2000–, Advtg Advsy Ctee 2005–; *Books* Thalidomide: The Legal Aftermath (with H Teff, 1976), Television, Censorship and the Law (1979), Studies in Constitutional Law (1987, 2 edn 1999), Sentencing, Judicial Discretion and Training (with M Wasik, 1992), Devolution and the Scotland Bill (with C Himsworth, 1998), The Scotland Act 1998 (with C Himsworth, 1999, 2 edn 2000); *Recreations* sport, film and theatre, beer and skittles; *Style—* Prof Colin Munro; ✉ University of Edinburgh, Old College, South Bridge, Edinburgh EH8 9YL (tel 0131 650 2047, fax 0131 662 0724)

MUNRO, Dr Dowling Donald; s of John Munro (d 1980), of Great Missenden, Bucks, and Etta Mansfield, *née* Cottrell (d 1992); *b* 29 May 1931; *Educ* Merchant Taylor's Sch Crosby, Royal Free Hosp Sch of Med London (MD); *m* 1, 7 Sept 1962, Pamela Grace (d 1977); 2 da (Fiona b 1964, Janet b 1966); m 2, 22 March 1980, Isabella Sinclair, da of Alexander Baillie Macdonald (d 1954), of Lanarkshire; 2 step da (Jane Tillotson b 1964, Helen White b 1967); *Career* Capt RAMC Cyprus; US public health res fell in dermatology Western Reserve Univ of Cleveland OH 1964; conslt dermatologist: Bart's 1968–93, Harley Street 1968–2000; civilian conslt dermatologist RN 1981–; asst surgn St John Ambulance Buckinghamshire 1997–2003; pubns in med jls incl British Jl of Dermatology; *Books* Steroids and the Skin (ed, 1976); *Recreations* horticulture, ornithology; *Clubs* RSM; *Style—* Dr Dowling D Munro; ✉ 18 Upper Hollis, Great Missenden, Buckinghamshire HP16 9HP (tel 01494 864683)

MUNRO, Graeme Neil; CVO (2005); s of Daniel Munro (d 1985), and Nancy Kirkwood, *née* Smith; *b* 28 August 1944; *Educ* Daniel Stewart's Coll Edinburgh, Univ of St Andrews (Ramsay residential scholar, MA); *m* 1972, Nicola Susan Munro, *qv*, da of late Ernest Derek Wells; 1 da (Rachel Helen Nicola b 1976), 1 s (Keith Alexander b 1981); *Career* Scottish Devpt Dept SO: asst princ 1968–70, seconded to Falkirk Town Cncl 1970–71, private sec to Sec 1971–72, princ 1972–79, asst sec 1979–90, dir Historic Buildings and Monuments 1990–91, dir and chief exec Historic Scotland 1991–2004; FSA Scot 1990; *Recreations* walking, gardening, travel, local history, voluntary work in conservation and Third World fields; *Style—* Graeme Munro, Esq, CVO

MUNRO, Dr John Forbes; OBE; s of John Bennet Lorimer Munro, CBE, CMG (d 1993), and Gladys Maie Forbes, *née* Simmons (d 1965); *b* 25 June 1933; *Educ* Univ of Edinburgh (MB ChB), Open Univ (BA); *m* Elizabeth Jean Durell, da of Dr James Colin Caird, OBE (d 1990); 3 da (Patricia Jane Mary b 1960, Elizabeth Ann Caird b 1962, Jennifer Kathleen Margaret b 1965); *Career* conslt physician Eastern Gen Hosp 1968–92; Univ of Edinburgh: pt/t sr lectr Dept of Med Western Gen Hosp 1971–92, hon fell 1992–2000, clinical teaching fell 2000–02; registrar RCPEd 1993–97; Cullen prize RCPEd 1994; hon fell Coll of Physicians and Surgns Bangladesh 1995; FRCP, FRCPEd, FRCPGlas; *Books* Macleod's Clinical Examination (co-ed, 10 edn 2000); *Recreations* contemporary art, gardening; *Style—* Dr John Munro, OBE; ✉ Backhill, Carberry, Musselburgh, East Lothian EH21 8QD (tel 0131 663 4935)

MUNRO, Neil; s of Neil Munro, and Alexina Munro; *Educ* Nicolson Inst Stornoway, Univ of Edinburgh (MA); *Career* journalist; West Highland Free Press: reporter 1974, ed 1974–75; TES Scotland: reporter 1975–77, dep ed 1977–2001, ed 2001–; *Recreations* cycling, walking, reading, swimming; *Style—* Neil Munro, Esq; ✉ Times Educational Supplement Scotland, Scott House, 10 South St Andrew Street, Edinburgh EH2 2AZ (tel 0131 557 1133, fax 0131 558 1155, e-mail neil.munro@tes.co.uk)

MUNRO, Neil Christopher; CBE (2003); s of Alan Main Munro (d 1999), and Jean Elizabeth, *née* Kelly; *b* 25 July 1947; *Educ* Wallasey GS, St John's Coll Oxford (MA); *m* 18 Dec 1987, C A V Smith, da of Angus Smith (decd); 2 da (Alice Elizabeth Jane b 12 Jan 1989, Victoria Anne Frances b 23 Jan 1995); *Career* Bd of Inland Revenue: joined 1970, various jobs in tax policy and mgmnt, seconded CBI head Taxation Dept 1978–80, project dir Nottingham Relocation 1989–95, dep dir of personnel 1991–94, dir of mgmnt services 1994–96, dir Tax Law Rewrite Project 1996–2001, dir Revenue Policy Corporate Services 2001–05, dir Better Guidance Prog 2005–06, head Customer Contact Transformation Prog 2006; MCIPD 1993; *Recreations* modern literature, music, cricket, cooking; *Clubs* MCC; *Style—* Neil Munro, Esq, CBE

MUNRO, Nicola Susan; CB (2006); da of Ernest Derek Wells (d 1972), and Barbara Gurney Wells; *b* 11 January 1948; *Educ* Harrogate GS, Univ of Warwick (BA); *m* 1972, Graeme Neil Munro, *qv*, s of Daniel Munro; 1 da (Rachel Helen Nicola b 7 Sept 1976), 1 s (Keith Alexander b 30 Sept 1981); *Career* Scottish Office: various posts in health, educn, criminal justice, civil law and personnel 1970–86, head Hosp Specialist Services Div Dept of Health 1986–89, head Urban and Local Econ Policy Div Industry Dept 1989–92, head 5–14 Curriculum and Careers Div Educn and Industry Dept 1992–95, under sec for public health policy Health Dept Scottish Exec 1995–2000, head Environment Gp Rural Affairs Dept Scottish Exec 2000–01, head Devpt Dept Scottish Exec 2001–07; *Recreations* family, travel, gardening, theatre, natural and built heritage; *Style—* Mrs Nicola Munro, CB

MUNRO, Robert Malcolm; s of Malcolm William Munro (d 1975), of Chelmsford, and Sheila Mary, *née* Lamont (d 1983); *b* 16 May 1937; *Educ* Trinity, Mid-Essex Tech Coll, Manchester Business Sch; *m* 25 March 1961, Irene Mavis, da of late William David Percy, of Chelmsford; 2 s (Nigel Robert b 1964, Philip Spencer b 1966); *Career* branch mangr Lloyds & Scottish Finance Ltd 1958–68, asst gen mangr ELCO (Hambros Bank) 1968–72, md Williams & Glyn's Leasing Co Ltd 1972–80, dir Nordic Bank Ltd 1980–83, exec dir The Union Discount Company of London plc 1983–90, banking and leasing conslt Munro Associates 1990–; chm: Int Ctee ELA 1976–81, VRL Publishing Ltd 1993–2003, Field Solutions Ltd, Park Finance Gp Ltd 2002–06; dep chm Mid Essex Hosp Servs NHS Tst 1992–98; memb: Mgmnt Ctee ELA 1973–90, Cncl LEASEUROPE 1976–81; *Books* The Leasing Handbook (with D R Soper, 1992); *Recreations* tennis, golf, music, theatre; *Style—* Robert Munro, Esq

MUNRO OF LINDERTIS, Sir Alasdair Thomas Ian; 6 Bt (UK 1825), of Lindertis, Forfarshire; s of Sir (Thomas) Torquil Alphonso Munro of Lindertis, 5 Bt, JP (d 1985), and his 1 w, Beatrice Maude (d 1974), da of Robert Sanderson Whitaker, of Villa Sofia, Palermo; *b* 6 July 1927; *Educ* Landon Sch USA, Georgetown Univ Washington DC, Univ of Pennsylvania, IMEDE Lausanne Switzerland; *m* 1954, Marguerite Lillian, da of late Franklin R Loy, of Dayton, Ohio, USA; 1 da (Karen Fiona (Mrs Robert D Macmichael, Jr) b 1956), 1 s (Keith Gordon b 1959); *Heir* s, Keith Munro; *Career* importer of Scottish Antiques; dir St Andrew's Soc of Vermont; *Style—* Sir Alasdair Munro of Lindertis, Bt; ✉ River Ridge, Box 940, Waitsfield, Vermont 05673, USA

MURCH, Fiona Margaret; *see:* Stourton, Fiona Margaret

MURCHISON, Prof Duncan George; s of John Kenneth Murchison (d 1934), and Maude Gertrude Mitchell Murchison, *née* Tordoff (d 1964); *b* 13 January 1928; *Educ* Glasgow HS, Morrisons Acad Crieff, Univ of Durham (BSc, PhD); *m* 1, 23 July 1953 (m dis 1981), Dorothy Jean, da of Edward Charlton (d 1961); 2 s (Roderick b 28 June 1957, Torquil b 22 Sept 1959), 2 da (Kate b 10 March 1962, Rona b 10 March 1962 (d 1962)); m 2, 27 July 1982 (m dis 1993), Gail Adrienne, da of Robert Hermon (d 1960); 2 da (Hanna b 28 Oct 1981, Rosie b 26 July 1988), 1 s (Peter b 23 Feb 1984); *Career* lectr Univ of Durham 1960–64; Univ of Newcastle upon Tyne: lectr 1964–68, sr lectr 1968–71, reader in geochemistry 1971–76, personal prof 1976–93 (now emeritus), dean Faculty of Science 1980–83, head Dept of Geology 1982–86, pro-vice-chllr 1986–93 (acting vice-chllr 1991); author of numerous publications in fields of reflected light microscopy, organic petrology and geochemistry; pres: Royal Microscopical Soc 1976–78, Int Cmmn on Coal Petrology 1979–83; treas Geological Soc of London 2000–06 (vice-pres 1995–97); Hon FRMS, FGS, FRSE 1973; *Recreations* fishing, philately, photography; *Style—* Prof Duncan Murchison, FRSE; ✉ School of Civil Engineering and Geosciences, Drummond Building, University of Newcastle upon Tyne, Newcastle upon Tyne NE1 7RU (tel and fax 0191 281 8703, e-mail duncan@dmurchison.freeserve.co.uk)

MURCHISON, Lilian Elizabeth; da of John Alexander Murchison (d 1958), of Alness, Ross and Cromarty, and Mary Nicholson, *née* MacIver (d 1996); *b* 29 April 1936; *Educ* Invergordon Acad, Univ of Edinburgh (MB ChB), Univ of Glasgow (PhD); *Career* memb scientific staff MRC Atheroma Res Unit Glasgow 1963–68, sr tutor Royal Victoria Hosp Belfast 1969–71, lectr Dept of Therapeutics and Clinical Pharmacology Univ of Aberdeen 1971–76, conslt physician and hon clinical sr lectr Aberdeen Royal Infirmary 1976–2000, ret; chm Aberdeen Gomel Tst, memb Perth Soroptimist Int, fell RSPB, fndr Friends of Scottish Monuments, memb Nat Tst (Scotland); FRCPEd 1981, FRCP 1987 (MRCP(UK) 1970), FFCS; *Recreations* overseas travel, hill walking; *Style—* Miss Lilian Murchison; ✉ 35 Lynedoch Road, Scone, Perth PH2 6RJ (tel 01738 553651, e-mail lilian.murchison@btinternet.com)

MURDIN, Prof Paul Geoffrey; OBE (1988); s of Robert Samuel Frederick Rodham Murdin, and Ethel, *née* Chubb; *b* 5 January 1942; *Educ* Trinity Sch of John Whitgift, Wadham Coll Oxford (BA), Univ of Rochester NY (PhD); *m* 8 Aug 1964, Lesley Carol, da of Frederick Milburn; 2 s (Benedict Neil b 1966, Alexander Nicholas b 1970), 1 da (Louisa Jane b 1974); *Career* princ scientific offr Royal Greenwich Observatory 1974–75 (sr res fell 1971–74), princ res scientist Anglo-Australian Observatory 1975–78; Royal Greenwich Observatory: princ scientific offr 1978–81, sr princ scientific offr and head La Palma Ops Dept 1981–87, head Astronomy Dept 1987–91, dep dir 1990–91 and 1993–94; dir and head Royal Observatory Edinburgh 1991–93; head of Astronomy Div Particle Physics and Astronomy Res Cncl 1994–2001, dir Sci and Microgravity Br Nat Space Centre 1994–2001; sr fell Inst of Astronomy Cambridge 2001–; visiting prof Liverpool John Moores Univ 2002–; pres Euro Astronomical Soc 1994–97; memb: Bd of Tstees Nat Maritime Museum 1990–2001, Int Astronomical Union, Academia Europaea; FRAS (memb Cncl 1994–2001, vice-pres 2000–01, treas 2001–), FInstP; *Books* Astronomers Telescope (1962), Radio Waves From Space (1964), New Astronomy (1978), Catalogue of the Universe (1979), Colours of the Stars (1984), End in Fire (1990), Encyclopedia of Astronomy and Astrophysics (2001), Firefly Encyclopedia of Astronomy (2004); *Style—* Prof Paul Murdin, OBE; ✉ Institute of Astronomy, Madingley Road, Cambridge CB3 0HA (tel 01223 337548, fax 01223 337523, e-mail paul@murdin.com)

MURDOCH, Andrew James; s of James Clive Leonard Murdoch (d 1981), and Adela Marjorie, *née* Gepp; *b* 16 November 1949; *Educ* Charterhouse, Pembroke Coll Cambridge (MA); *m* 1972, Lynn Hilary, da of Vernon Cecil Thompson; 1 s (Simon Scott b 16 April 1976), 1 da (Hilary Caroline Noel b 17 Dec 1979); *Career* architect; HKPA 1973–78, Eric Lyons Cunningham Partnership 1978–79, Cambridge Design 1979–80, John S Bonnington Partnership 1980–84, Fitzroy Robinson Ltd (formerly The Fitzroy Robinson Partnership) 1984– (currently dir); RIBA; *Recreations* painting, golf; *Clubs* Royal Ashdown Forest Golf; *Style—* Andrew Murdoch, Esq

MURDOCH, Elisabeth; da of Rupert Murdoch, *qv*, and Anna Maria, *née* Torv; *Educ* Vassar Coll Poughkeepsie NY; *Children* 3 da (Anna, Cornelia, Charlotte), 1 s (Samson); *Career* Nine Network Australia: presentation and promotions asst 1990–91, researcher and prodr 1991–93; mangr of programming and promotion Fox TV LA 1993, prog dir KSTU Fox 13 Salt Lake City 1993–94, dir of prog acquisitions FX Cable Network LA 1994–95, pres and ceo EP Communications 1995–96 (Peabody Award for Broadcast Excellence 1995); BSkyB Ltd: general mangr Broadcasting Dept 1996, dir of programming 1996–98, md Sky Networks 1998–2000; chm and chief exec Shine Ltd 2001–; *Style—* Ms Elisabeth Murdoch; ✉ Shine Ltd, 140–142 Kensington Church Street, London W8 4BN (tel 020 7985 7013)

MURDOCH, His Hon Judge Gordon Stuart; QC (1995); s of Ian William Murdoch (d 1978), and Margaret Henderson McLaren, *née* Scott (d 1974); *b* 7 June 1947; *Educ* Falkirk HS, Sidney Sussex Coll Cambridge (MA, LLB); *m* 27 Dec 1976, Sally Kay, da of Henry Cummings, of Ludlow, Salop; 2 s (Thomas b 1979, Alexander b 1982); *Career* called to the Bar Inner Temple 1970; recorder of the Crown Court 1995–2002 (asst recorder

1991–95), circuit judge (SE Circuit) 2002–; *Recreations* music, walking; *Style*— His Hon Judge Murdoch, QC; ✉ Canterbury County Court, The Law Courts, Chaucer Road, Canterbury, Kent CT1 1ZA

MURDOCH, John Derek Walter; s of James Duncan Murdoch, OBE (d 1979), and Elsie Elisabeth, *née* Hardman (d 1989); *b* 1 April 1945; *Educ* Shrewsbury, Magdalen Coll Oxford (BA), KCL (MPhil); *m* 1, 9 Sept 1967 (m dis 1986), Prudence Helen, da of late Brig WR Smijth-Windham, CBE, DSO, of Pitney, Somerset; 1 s (Thomas Duncan b 1970), 2 da (Clarissa Helen b 1972, Rosamond Elsie b 1977); m 2, 9 Nov 1990, Susan Barbara, da of late Alan Lambert, of Little Bookham, Surrey; *Career* asst keeper Dept of Art City Museum and Art Gallery Birmingham 1969–73; V&A: dep keeper Dept of Paintings 1977–85 (asst keeper 1973–77), keeper dept of prints drawings photographs and paintings 1986–89, asst dir in charge of collections 1989–93; dir Courtauld Inst Galleries 1993–2002, dir Huntington Art Collections Calif 2002–; tstee: The William Morris Gallery Walthamstow 1975–2002 (dep chm 1997–2002), Wordsworth Library and Museum Dove Cottage 1982–2002; *Books* David Cox (1970), Byron (1974), Forty-Two English Watercolours (1977), The English Miniature (1981), Discovery of the Lake District (1984), Painters and The Derby China Works (1987), Seventeenth Century Miniatures in the Collection of the V&A (1997); *Style*— John Murdoch, Esq

MURDOCH, Dr Peter Stevenson; s of John Duncan Murdoch, TD (d 1988), and Zoe Mann, *née* Hannay (d 1987); *b* 16 October 1950; *Educ* Haileybury, Guy's Hosp Med Sch (MB BS); *m* 28 Dec 1974, Sarah, da of Tor Ingemar Lundegard; 2 s (Neil b 1976, John b 1979); *Career* med supt Presbyterian Jt Hosp Uburu Nigeria 1975–81, sr registrar in geriatric med Royal Victoria Hosp Edinburgh 1981–82; conslt physician in geriatric med: Falkirk and Dist Royal Infirmary 1983–, Stirling Royal Infirmary 2005–; assoc med dir NHS Forth Valley, tstee Dementia Servs Devpt Tst; Hon DUniv Univ of Stirling 2006; FRCPEd 1987, FRCPGlas 1993; *Style*— Dr Peter Murdoch; ✉ 4 Abercromby Place, Stirling, Falkirk FK8 2QP (tel 01786 473087); Falkirk and District Royal Infirmary, Falkirk FK1 5QE (tel 01324 624000, e-mail peter.murdoch@fvah.scot.nhs.uk)

MURDOCH, (Keith) Rupert; AC (1984); only s of Sir Keith Murdoch, sometime chm and md The Herald & Weekly Times Ltd, Melbourne Herald, Sun-News Pictorial, Weekly Times (d 1952), by his w Dame Elisabeth Murdoch, AC, DBE; *b* 11 March 1931; *Educ* Geelong GS, Worcester Coll Oxford (MA); *m* 1, 1956 (m dis); 1 da (Prue); m 2, 1967 (m dis 1999), Anna Maria, da of J Torv, of Scotland; 2 s (Lachlan Murdoch, James Murdoch), 1 da (Elisabeth Murdoch, *qv*); m 3, Wendi Deng; 2 da (Grace Helen b 2001, Chloe b 2003); *Career* publisher; chm and ceo News Corporation, chm and pres News America Publishing Inc, chm and ceo 20th Century Fox until 1996 (currently dir); dir: News International, HarperCollins Publishers Ltd 1989–, British Sky Broadcasting plc 1990–; UK newspapers owned incl The Sun and The Times; hon fell Worcester Coll Oxford 1982–; *Style*— Rupert Murdoch, AC; ✉ c/o News America Inc, 1211 Avenue of the Americas, New York 10036, USA; Times Newspapers Limited, PO Box 495, Virginia Street, London E1 9XY

MURDOCH, Stuart Lee; s of Robert Gordon Murdoch, of Ayr, and Norma Margaret, *née* Massey; *Educ* Belmont Acad Ayr; *Career* singer/songwriter; founding memb Belle and Sebastian 1996; winner (one-eighth) Best Newcomer Brit Awards 1998; memb Hyndland Church Choir; *Albums* Tigermilk (1996), If You're Feeling Sinister (1996), The Boy With The Arab Strap (1998), Fold Your Hands Child, You Walk Like A Peasant (2000), Storytelling (2002), Dear Catastrophe Waitress (2003); *Singles* Dog on Wheels (1997), Lazy Line Painter Jane (1997), 3... 6... 9... Seconds of Light (1997), This is Just a Modern Rock Song (1998), Legal Man (2000); *Recreations* football; *Style*— Stuart Murdoch, Esq

MURDOCK, Christopher; s of Dr Charles Rutherford Murdock (d 1968), and Eirene Nolan, *née* Baird (d 2001); *b* 15 August 1946; *Educ* Brackenber House Belfast, Portora Royal Sch Enniskillen; *m* 31 Jan 1970, Dorothy Rosemary Richardson; 2 s (Christopher Jeremy b 1973, Antony John b 1975), 1 da (Rosemary Sarah Alexandra b 1980); *Career* joined NHS 1965, asst dist admin offr Armagh and Dungannon Dist 1974–75, dist personnel offr S Belfast Dist 1975–76, asst dist admin offr E Belfast and Castlereagh Dist 1976–84; gp admin Purdysburn Unit of Mgmnt 1984–89, sr mangr Eastern Health and Social Services Bd 1989–98; Fold Housing Assoc: memb Bd 1998–, chm Care Services Ctee 1999–, chm Audit Ctee 2001–, vice-chm Bd 2003–; dir: Fold Housing Tst and Shepherdcare Ltd 1998–, Fold Housing Assoc (Ireland) 2002–; chief exec (on consultancy basis) The Commandery of Ards in NI of the Most Venerable Order of the Hospital of St.John of Jerusalem and St.John Ambulance in NI 2001, tstee and dir (training and marketing) The Commandery of Ards in NI of the Most Venerable Order of the Hospital of St.John of Jerusalem and St.John Ambulance in NI 2005–; commercial mangr: Eventing Ireland N Region 2000–02, Necarne Int Horse Trials 2000–03; patron Ulster Operatic Co, memb Friends of the Ulster Orch; MIHM, DipHSM, MCMI; OStJ 2006; *Recreations* photography and video, Donegal (Inishowen), wines; *Clubs* IEC Wine Society, NI Wine and Spirit Inst; *Style*— Christopher Murdock, Esq; ✉ Ballyhomra House, Comber Road, Hillsborough, Co Down BT26 6NA (tel 028 9266 2992, e-mail c.murdock@btinternet.com); Ballybrack Lodge, Moville, Co Donegal, Ireland

MURE, Kenneth Nisbet; QC (Scot 1989); s of late Robert Mure, and late Katherine Mure; *b* 11 April 1947; *Educ* Glasgow HS, Univ of Glasgow (MA, LLB); *Career* admitted to the Scots Bar 1975, called to the English Bar Gray's Inn 1990; lectr in Law Faculty Univ of Glasgow 1971–83; temp sheriff Scotland 1982–99; memb: CICAP 2000–, VAT Tribunal 2003–; FTII 1971; *Style*— Kenneth Mure, Esq, QC; ✉ Advocates' Library, Edinburgh EH1 1RF (tel 0131 226 5071)

MURFIN, Dr David Edward; s of Leslie Walter Murfin (d 1989), and Elizabeth Ann, *née* Jones (d 1984); *b* 15 June 1946; *Educ* Gowerton Boys' GS Swansea, KCL (MB BS, DRCOG), St George's Hosp London, Univ of Wales (MPhil); *m* 1972, Ann Margaret, da of Mervyn Henry Lewis; 1 da (Rhian Nicola b 5 Dec 1973), 1 s (Owen David b 16 April 1976); *Career* house surgn St George's Hosp London 1970–71, house physician Peterborough Dist Hosp 1971; SHO: in obstetrics St Paul's Hosp Cheltenham 1971–72, in paediatrics Oldchurch Hosp Romford 1972, in paediatrics and casualty Queen Elizabeth Hosp Barbados 1972–73, in psychiatry Swansea 1974; princ in gen practice 1974–2006; RCGP: memb SW Wales Faculty 1976–, faculty sec 1981–86, faculty chm 1987–90, faculty rep on Cncl 1984–90 and 1993–96, chm Servs to Membs and Faculties Div 1987–90, memb Editorial Bd 1988–2006, hon ed Connection 1993–96, vice-chm Cncl 1994–96; gen practice trainer 1980–96, gen practice advsr to Assoc of the Br Pharmaceutical Industry 1991–2006, memb Standing Advsy Ctee on Medicines for Children 1996–2001; author of various pubns in learned jls; FRCGP 1985 (MRCGP); *Recreations* reading, walking, cycling; *Style*— Dr David Murfin; ✉ Longmeadow, 30 Llandeilo Road, Llandybie, Ammanford, Carms SA18 3JB (tel 01269 850 914, e-mail david@murfind.freeserve.co.uk)

MURFITT, Catriona Anne Campbell; da of Dr Alfred Ian Campbell Murfitt (d 1983), and Anne, *née* Ritchie (d 1998); *b* 16 January 1958; *Educ* St Mary's Sch Ascot, Leicester Poly Sch of Law (BA); *Career* called to the Bar Gray's Inn 1981; in practice SE Circuit 1982–, asst recorder 1998, recorder 2000; FRSA; *Recreations* skiing, gardening, art, sacred choral music; *Style*— Miss Catriona Murfitt; ✉ 1 Hare Court, Temple, London EC4Y 7BE (tel 020 7797 7070, e-mail murfitt@1hc.com, website www.1hc.com)

MURIE, John Andrew; s of John Andrew Murie, of Airdrie, and Jessie, *née* Sutherland; *b* 7 August 1949; *Educ* Univ of Glasgow (BSc, MB ChB, MD), Univ of Minnesota, Univ of Oxford (MA); *m* 7 Sept 1977, Edythe, da of James Munn, of Glasgow; 1 da (Emma Jane b 1986); *Career* clinical reader in surgery Univ of Oxford 1984–89, conslt surgn John Radcliffe Hosp Oxford 1984–89, fell Green Coll Oxford 1984–89, clinical dir of surgery Royal Infirmary Edinburgh 1995–2000 (conslt surgn 1989–), hon sr lectr in surgery Univ of Edinburgh 1989–; ed-in-chief Br Jl of Surgery 2002– (review ed 1989–96, jt sr ed 1996–2002); hon editorial sec Assoc of Surgeons of GB and Ireland 1996–99; memb Cncl: Vascular Soc of GB and I 1998–2001, RCPSGlas 1998–2005; FRCPS 1979, FRCSEd 1993; *Recreations* golf, swimming, food and wine; *Style*— John Murie, Esq; ✉ 8 Dalhousie Crescent, Eskbank, Edinburgh EH22 3DP (tel 0131 663 5676); Department of Surgery, The Royal Infirmary, Old Dalkeith Road, Edinburgh EH16 4SA (tel 0131 242 1059, fax 0131 242 1055); BUPA, Murrayfield Hospital, 122 Corstorphine Road, Edinburgh EH12 6UD (tel 0131 334 0363, fax 0131 334 7338, e-mail jamurie@hotmail.com)

MURNAGHAN, Dermot John; s of Vincent Patrick George Murnaghan, of Wisbech, and Wendy, *née* Bush; *b* 26 December 1957; *Educ* Sullivan Upper Sch Holywood Co Down, Univ of Sussex (BA, MA), City Univ (Postgrad Dip Journalism); *m* Maria, da of Patrick Keegan; 1 da (Kitty Niamh b 13 March 1992); *Career* reporter: Coventry Evening Telegraph 1984–85, The Business Programme (Channel 4) 1985–88; corr/presenter Euro Business Channel 1988–89, presenter Channel 4 Daily 1989–90, newscaster ITN 1990–2002, presenter The Big Story (ITV) 1993–2002, presenter Breakfast (BBC 1) 2002–; *Documentaries* A Whale of a Mess (Channel 4), Against the Odds (Channel 4); *Recreations* racing, tennis, running, theatre; *Style*— Dermot Murnaghan, Esq

MURPHY, Alan Denis; s of James Denis Murphy (d 1984), of Norwich, and Ruby Lilian, *née* Aaron (d 1995); *b* 13 March 1939; *Educ* St Joseph's Coll Beulah Hill, Rugby Coll of Engrg (Dip Electrical Engrg); *m* 23 Feb 1963, Kay Anita, da of Cecil Wakelin; 1 s (Neil Andrew b 27 June 1965), 1 da (Nicola Joanne b 29 June 1969); *Career* commercial engr AEI (Rugby) Ltd steelworks automation Port Talbot 1961–62, devpt engrg GEC (Telecoms) Ltd Coventry 1962–66, project engr Elliott Process Automation Leicester 1966–69, gen mangr Leicester Automation Centre Leicester Poly (now de Montfort Univ) 1969–73, conslt PA Management Birmingham 1973–75, gp mangr PA Technology Cambridge 1976–78; Cambridge Consultants Ltd advanced mfrg technol: gp mangr 1978–81, mktg mangr 1981–83, bd/mktg dir 1983–; FIEE 1984, FIMC 1986; *Publications* Packaging for the Environment (co-author, 1991); *Recreations* music, golf, building and restoring classic cars; *Clubs* Girton Golf; *Style*— Alan Murphy, Esq; ✉ Cambridge Consultants, Science Park, Milton Road, Cambridge CB4 0DW (tel 01223 420024, fax 01223 423373, mobile 077 8535 1452)

MURPHY, Sheriff Andrew John; s of Robert James Murphy, of Glasgow, and Robina, *née* Scott; *b* 16 January 1946; *Educ* Allan Glen's Sch Glasgow, Univ of Edinburgh (MA, LLB); *m* 20 Nov 1980, Susan Margaret, da of Dr Peter Dewar Thomson, OBE, of Dingwall; 2 s (Patrick Andrew Sean b 1983, Simon Peter Scott b 1987), 2 da (Lucy Jane Robina b 1978, Sarah Belle Margaret b 1979); *Career* 2 Lt RA (TA) 1971–73, Flt Lt RAF 1973–75; admitted Faculty of Advocates and called to the Bar Scotland 1970, called to the Bar Middle Temple 1990; crown counsel Hong Kong 1975–79, standing jr counsel to Registrar Gen for Scotland 1982–85, temp Sheriff 1983–85; Sheriff: of Grampian Highlands and Islands at Peterhead and Banff 1985–91, of Tayside Central and Fife at Falkirk 1991–; *Style*— Sheriff Andrew Murphy; ✉ Sheriff's Chambers, Sheriff Court House, Main Street, Camelon, Falkirk FK1 4AR

MURPHY, (Peter) Anthony (Tony); s of (Peter) Anthony (Tony) Murphy Sr (d 2005), and Lily McCartan Murphy; *b* 9 July 1971, Ireland; *Educ* Queen's Univ Belfast (LLB); *Partner* Patrick Brindle (civil partnership, 2006); *Career* slr; B M Birnberg & Co 1996–98, Bindman & Partners 1998– (ptnr 2005–); memb Law Soc 1998; *Style*— Tony Murphy, Esq; ✉ Bindman & Partners, 275 Gray's Inn Rd, London WC1X 8QB

MURPHY, Prof Brian; s of James Murphy (d 1987), of Huddersfield, and Winifred Helen, *née* Ellis (d 1990); *b* 20 May 1940; *Educ* Rotherham GS, Lancaster Univ (MSc), Open Univ (BA); *m* 18 Dec 1982, Vivienne; *Career* rating and auditing asst Rotherham Co Borough 1956–61, accountancy and auditing asst Castleford BC 1961–63, head of Accountancy Section West Riding CC 1963–64, sr accountant Oxford CBC 1964–66, lectr in management accountancy Worcester Tech Coll 1966–69; Univ of Huddersfield (formerly Huddersfield Poly): sr lectr in management accountancy 1969–70, princ lectr 1970–71, head of Accountancy Div 1971–72, head Dept of Accountancy and Fin 1972–87, prof (for life) 1987–; md BWD Rensburg Unit Tst Mangrs Ltd 1988–96; dir: Conscious Visions Ltd 1997–, Conscious Properties Ltd 1999–; former dir Clifton Language Servs Ltd; former dir and co sec: Double M Construction Ltd, Daleside Devpts Ltd; lectr, examiner and conslt 1997–; rotarian 1978–; memb: Inst of Public Finance and Accountancy 1963, Chartered Inst of Cost and Management Accountants 1971; fell Assoc of Certified Accountants 1982; MSI 1992; *Books* Management Accounting (3 edn, 1986); *Recreations* golf, classic cars, cycling; *Style*— Prof Brian Murphy; fax 01484 300786

MURPHY, Brian Arthur; s of Arthur Albert Murphy (d 1982), and Constance Margaret, *née* Young (d 2001); *b* 3 May 1951; *Educ* Emanuel Sch London, Keble Coll Oxford (BA); *m* 30 April 1977, Jane (d 2005), da of John Champion Stevenson, of Atherstone, Warks; 1 s (Giles b 10 March 1980), 1 da (Leila b 14 June 1982); *Career* slr, dep head legal servs Allied Lyons plc 1982, sr assoc Ashurst Morris Crisp 1989; Freeman City of London, Liveryman Worshipful Co of Founders; memb Law Soc 1976; *Clubs* Ski Club of GB; *Style*— Brian Murphy, Esq; ✉ The Old Rectory, Little Brickhill, Buckinghamshire MK17 9NA (tel 020 7638 1111, fax 020 7638 1112)

MURPHY, Brian Gordon; s of Albert Gordon Murphy, and Doris Edna Murphy; *b* 18 October 1940; *Educ* Mill Hill Sch; *m* 3 Nov 1973, Judith Ann, da of Frederick Robert Parkinson; *Career* admitted slr 1966, ptnr Knapp Fishers Westminster 1968–87, ptnr Farrer and Co Lincoln's Inn Fields 1987–92, building societies ombudsman 1992–99; pt/t employment tribunal chm 1991–92 and 2001–03; memb Cncl Incorporated Cncl of Law Reporting for England and Wales 1992–96; Law Soc: memb Cncl 1982–93, chm Employment Law Ctee 1987–90; pres City of Westminster Law Soc 1983–84; *Recreations* golf, theatre, photography, travel; *Clubs* Phyllis Court (Henley); *Style*— Brian Murphy, Esq; ✉ Phyllis Court, Henley-on-Thames RG9 2HT

MURPHY, Catherine; TD; da of Colm Murnane (d 1996), of Dublin, and Eileen, *née* Byrne; *b* 1 September 1953, Dublin; *Educ* Dominican Convent Ballyfermott, Coll of Commerce Rathmines, Institute of Public Administration Ireland (Dip); *m* 27 Aug 1974, Derek Murphy; 1 s (Alan b 2 Aug 1977), 1 da (Yvonne b 25 March 1980); *Career* town cncllr Leixlip 1988–2005, co cncllr Kildare 1991–2005, TD (Ind) Co Kildare 2005–; *Recreations* researching genealogy, sport (spectator); *Style*— Ms Catherine Murphy, TD; ✉ 49 Main Street, Leixlip, Co Kildare, Ireland (tel 00 353 1624 3052, fax 00 353 1624 7276, e-mail catherine.murphy@oir.ie); Dáil Éireann, Leinster House, Kildare Street, Dublin 2, Ireland (tel 00 353 1618 4411, fax 00 353 1618 4507)

MURPHY, Conor; MP, MLA; *Educ* St Colman's Coll, Univ of Ulster, Queen's Univ Belfast; *m* Catherine; 1 s, 1 da; *Career* cncllr Newry and Mourne DC 1989–97; memb NI Assembly 1998– (ldr Pty Gp), MP (Sinn Féin) Newry and Armagh 2005– (Parly candidate (Sinn Féin) Newry and Armagh 2001); *Style*— Conor Murphy, Esq, MP, MLA; ✉ House of Commons, London SW1A 0AA

MURPHY, Denis; MP; *Career* MP (Lab) Wansbeck 1997–; *Style*— Denis Murphy, Esq, MP; ✉ House of Commons, London SW1A 0AA (tel 020 7219 3000)

MURPHY, Baroness (Life Peer UK 2004), of Aldgate in the City of London; Prof Elaine Murphy; da of Roger Lawson (d 1978), of Nottingham, and Nell, *née* Allitt; *b* 16 January 1947; *Educ* West Bridgford GS Nottingham, Univ of Manchester Med Sch (MB ChB, MD), Univ of London (PhD); *m* 1, 1969 (m dis 2001), John Matthew Murphy, s of Daniel Murphy (d 1975), of Ilford, Essex; m 2, 2001, Michael Alfred Robb; *Career* psychiatric trg London Teaching Hosps, subsequently research registrar Bedford Coll London, conslt

M

psychiatrist NE Thames RHA 1981–83, prof of old age psychiatry Univ of London 1983–96; vice-chm Mental Health Act Cmmn 1987–94; chm: City and Hackney Community Servs NHS Tst 1995–98, E London and the City HA 1998–2002, NE London SHA 2002–06; chm Cncl St George's Univ of London 2006–; crossbench peer House of Lords 2004–; Dr (hc): Univ of Stirling 1993, City Univ 2006, Univ of London 2007; FRCPsych; *Books* After the Asylums (1991), Dementia and Mental Illness in Older People (1986 (as Dementia and Mental Illness in the Old), 2 edn 1993), The Falling Shadow (with Blom-Cooper and Hally, 1995); *Recreations* Italy, Norfolk, social history; *Style*— The Rt Hon the Baroness Murphy; ✉ House of Lords, London SW1A 0PH

MURPHY, Gerald James; JP; s of James Murphy (d 1956), and Agnes Murphy, *née* Youles (d 2004); *Educ* Finchley GS, AA Sch of Architecture (AADipl); *m* 17 June 2005, Fiona, *née* Brown; 2 step da; *Career* fndr ptnr architectural practice Gerald Murphy & Ptnrs 1962, after amalgamation sr ptnr Gerald Murphy Burles Newton & Ptnrs; ptnr A:Kitekts 2002–; works of note incl: Brentwood Cathedral, New Docklands Church, conversion of Wembley Stadium for Pope's visit; vice-chm Enfield & Haringey HA 1993–, non-exec Haringey Teaching Primary Care Tst; Cons Pty candidate 1973–78, chm London N Euro Constituency Cncl 1978–84, former int pres Serra Int, vice-chm Issues Ctee Catholic Union of GB; Freeman City of London; ARIBA, ACIArb; KCSG, Knight Grand Cross Religious Order of the Holy Sepulchre of Jerusalem, Knight Military and Hospitaller Order of St Lazarus of Jerusalem; *Recreations* filming, painting; *Style*— Gerald J Murphy, KCSG; ✉ 8 Highgate High Street, London N6 5JL (tel 020 8341 1277)

MURPHY, Gerard; *Career* actor; assoc dir Independent Radio Drama Co; *Theatre*; as assoc artist of RSC: Juno and the Paycock, The Witch of Edmonton, Henry IV Parts I and II, Country Dancing, A Midsummer Night's Dream, Two Noble Kinsmen, The Balcony, The Maids, Deathwatch, Speculators, Doctor Faustus, The Taming of the Shrew, The Theban Plays; as dir work incl: Deathwatch (co-dir, RSC Barbican), The Maids (co-dir, RSC Barbican), Edward II (RSC Swan Theatre Stratford-upon-Avon and Barbican London); other performances as actor incl: Pericles (Theatre Royal Stratford East), The White Devil (Greenwich), The Devil and the Good Lord (Lyric Hammersmith), Phaedra (Old Vic and West End), The Saxon Shore (Almeida), Easter (Haymarket Leicester), Broken Nails (St Peter's Cathedral Belfast), Dreaming (West End) 1999, Twelfth Night (Birmingham Rep) 2000, Hamlet (Birmingham Rep) 2000, A Moon For The Misbegotten (Manchester Royal Exchange) 2001, Who's Afraid Of Virginia Woolf (Bristol Old Vic) 2002, Henry The Fourth Parts I & II (Bristol Old Vic) 2002, Waiting For Godot (Northampton Royal and Derngate Theatres) 2003, The White Crow (Mercury Studio Colchester) 2003, The Weir (Northampton Royal and Derngate Theatres) 2003, A Small Family Business (West Yorkshire Playhouse) 2003; *Television* incl: Catchpenny Twist (BBC), The Best of Friends (BBC), The Plough and the Stars (BBC), My Son, My Son (BBC series), Facing The Sun (Thames), Keats (2 plays, BBC), Charteris and Caldicott (BBC series), Silver Nemesis (Dr Who 25th anniversary series), McCallum (STV), Taggart (STV), The Governor II; *Radio* for BBC Radio 3 incl: In The Jungle of the Cities, Julius Caesar, The Fool, Auden - Lyric and Form (poetry readings), Shelley, The Real Don Juan, Blue Glass and the Sun God; for BBC Radio 4 incl: The Lord of the Rings, The Elephant Man, Dada and Co, The Devil and the God Almighty, Danton's Death, The Drunkard, Monday, Tuesday, Ball The Wall, Woman in Blue, Seize The Fire, The Belle of Belfast City, Children of the Dead End, Prisoners of Honour, Balleylenon, Barry Lyndon, Something Misunderstood, The Nuremberg Trials; for Independent Radio Drama Co: Heart of Darkness, Valley of Fear; *Film* incl: Sacred Hearts, Girl In A Swing, Waterworld, Commission; *Style*— Gerard Murphy, Esq

MURPHY, Hugh Patrick; s of Patrick Joseph Murphy (d 1996), and Agnes Murphy (d 1973); *b* 16 December 1948, Leicester; *Educ* Ratcliffe Coll; *m* 21 April 1976, Margaret, *née* Tiernan; 2 s (Patrick b 10 March 1977, Joseph b 24 Sept 1978), 1 da (Mary b 25 March 1981); *Career* Murphy Brothers Ltd: joined 1965 as apprentice mechanic on earth moving machinery, then driving and supervisor on opencast coal sites; Charles Street Building (Leicester) Ltd: mangr 1970, dir and shareholder 1973, chm and ceo 1996–, largest shareholder 2001; patron Leics C of C; *Recreations* rugby union, soccer, music, theatre; *Style*— Hugh Murphy, Esq; ✉ Charles Street Buildings Limited, 856 Melton Road, Thurmaston, Leicester LE4 8BT (tel 0116 269 3443, fax 0116 269 3346, e-mail enquiries@csbgroup.co.uk)

MURPHY, Ian Patrick; QC (1992); s of Patrick Murphy, of Cardiff, and Irene Grace, *née* Hooper; *b* 1 July 1949; *Educ* St Illtyd's Coll Cardiff, LSE (LLB); *m* 31 Aug 1974, Penelope Gay, da of Gerald Hugh-Smith (d 1965), of Hove, E Sussex; 2 da (Anna b 1982, Charlotte b 1984); *Career* chartering clerk Baltic Exchange 1970–71; called to the Bar Middle Temple 1972 (bencher 2001); recorder of the Crown Court 1990– (asst recorder 1986–90), head of chambers 1998–; *Recreations* golf, skiing, rugby and cricket; *Clubs* Royal Porthcawl GC, Cardiff County; *Style*— Ian Murphy, Esq, QC; ✉ Chambers, 9 Park Place, Cardiff CF10 3DP (tel 029 2038 2731, fax 029 2022 2542)

MURPHY, Jim; MP; *b* 23 August 1967; *Educ* Milnerton HS Cape Town, Univ of Strathclyde; *m*; 2 c; *Career* pres: NUS Scotland 1992–94, NUS 1994–96 (concurrently dir Endsleigh Insurance Services); special projects mangr Scottish Lab Pty 1996–97; MP (Lab) Eastwood 1997–; PPS to Rt Hon Helen Liddell, MP, *qv*, 2001–02, asst Govt whip 2002–03, Lords Cmmr (Govt Whip) 2003–05, Parly sec Cabinet Office 2005–06, min of state Dept for Work and Pensions 2006–; memb Public Accounts Select Ctee 1999–2001; chm Lab Friends of Israel 2001–02; *Recreations* sport, cinema, travelling around Scotland; *Style*— Jim Murphy, Esq, MP; ✉ House of Commons, London SW1A 0AA (tel 020 7219 3000, e-mail murphyj@parliament.uk)

MURPHY, John Michael Murphy; *b* 7 September 1945; *Career* artist; *Solo Exhibitions* Serpentine Gallery London 1971, MOMA Oxford 1972, Jack Wendler Gallery London 1973, Selected Works (MOMA Oxford) 1975, Nature Morte - Collected Works (The New Gallery ICA London) 1976, An Art of Exchange - Featuring The Picture Frame or Egg Note (Barry Barker Gallery London) 1976, The Work of Art Is...AJ JM (Barry Barker Gallery London) 1977, Galerie Arno Kohnen Düsseldorf 1978, Desire Not Geometry (Barry Barker Gallery London) 1979, Lesson on Money (Art Projects Melbourne) 1980, Objects of Desire (Piwna Warsaw) 1980, John Murphy (Arts Cncl of NI Gallery Belfast) 1981, (D) (E) (L) (T) (A) (The Orchard Gallery Dery) 1982, The Nocturnal Inscription Represents... (Vereniging voor het Museum van Hedendaagse Kunst Gent) 1983, Beyond the Fixing of Appearances (Serpentine Gallery London) 1984, Stuck in the Milky Way (Lisson Gallery London) 1985, Whitechapel Art Gallery London 1987–88, Arnolfini Gallery Bristol 1988, Instruments of Attack (Galerie Yvon Lambert Paris) 1988, Galeria Marga Paz Madrid 1988, Phoenix - Sagitta - Horologium - Reticulum - Libra - Ursa Major (Asher/Faure Gallery LA) 1989, Silent Vertigo (Lisson Gallery London) 1990, John Weber Gallery NY 1991, Christine Burgin Gallery NY 1991, Remains to be Seen (John Weber Gallery NYC) 1992, No Representation, No Intention, No Trace (Galerie Yvon Lambert Paris) 1992, The Sense of Resemblance (Lisson Gallery London) 1992, The Tone that Calls the Song (Galerie Bruges la Morte Bruges) 1992, Lisson Gallery London 1996, A Portrait of the Artist as a Deaf Man (Douglas Hyde Gallery Dublin) 1996, Galerie de Luxembourg 1996, Villa Arson Nice 1997, A Different Constellation (Galerie Yvon Lambert Paris) 1998, On the Incline of Our Tongue (Galerie Erna Hécey Luxembourg) 1998, The Way Up and the Way Down (Southampton City Art Gallery) 1999, Of Voyages (Galerie Erna Hécey Luxembourg) 2003; *Group Exhibitions* incl: London Now in Berlin (Akademie der Künste Berlin) 1971, Drawing (MOMA Oxford) 1972, Contemporary Art Society Recent Acquisitions (Gulbenkian Hall RCA Gallery London) 1975, Eight British Artists (C A Y C Buenos Aires) 1976, Art - Museum des Geldes (Stadliche Kunsthalle Düsseldorf) 1978, Europa '79 (Kunst der 80er Jahre Stuttgart) 1979, Lang'uages (Third Eye Centre Glasgow) 1979, British Art 1940–80 (Hayward Gallery London) 1980, Through the Summer (Lisson Gallery London) 1981, Collazione Inglese (Scuola di San Pasquale Venice) 1982, Who's Afraid of Red Yellow and Blue (Arnolfini Gallery Bristol) 1985, L'Indifferent (Jon Hansard Gallery Southampton) 1985, Falls the Shadow Recent British and European Art (Hayward Gallery London) 1986, Aperto '86 XLII Biennale di Venezia 1986, Made in London (Jack Shainman Gallery Washington DC and NY) 1987–88, British Art - the Literate Link (Asher/Faure Gallery LA) 1988, Blasphemies Ecstasies Cries (Serpentine Gallery London) 1989, Now for the Future - Purchases for the Arts Council Collection since 1984 (Hayward Gallery London) 1990, De Pictura (Galerie Bruges la morte Brugge) 1990, John Weber Gallery NY 1991, Les Couleurs de l'argent (Musée de la Poste Paris) 1991, Out of Sight, Out of Mind (Lisson Gallery London) 1993, The Sublime Void (or the Memory of the Imagination) (Koninklijke Museum voor Schone Kunsten Antwerpen) 1993, Paula Rego John Murphy and Avis Newman (Saatchi Gallery London) 1996, Das Abenteuer Der Malerei (Kunstverein für die Rheinlande, Westfalen, Düsseldorf and Stuttgart) 1996, À Vendre (Galerie Erna Hécey), A Conversation Piece (MOMA Oxford) 1999, Larmes Blanches: Un Hommage á James Lee Byars (Trafic Frac Haute Normandie) 1999, Acquisitions from the Nineties (Tate Britain) 2000, East Wing Collection No 5 Looking With/Out (Courtauld Inst London) 2000, Stanze del Cammino di Mezzo (with John Murphy, Ettore Spalletti and Franz West, Casa Masaccio San Giovanni Valdarno) 2001–02, Le Regard de L'Autre Dialogue Entre les Collections du Franc-Normandie et du Musée des Beaux-Art de Rouen (Musée des Beaux-Art de Rouen) 2002; work represented in: numerous articles and reviews for both nat and trade magazines, exhibition catalogues and books incl New British Art in the Saatchi Collection (Allistair Hicks, 1989); *Style*— John Murphy, Esq; ✉ c/o Lisson Gallery, 67 Lisson Street, London NW1 5DA (tel 020 7724 2739, fax 020 7724 7124)

MURPHY, John Terence; s of Francis Joseph Murphy, of Blandford St Mary, Dorset, and Barbara Pauline, *née* Daft; *b* 16 January 1948; *Educ* Downside, Magdalen Coll Oxford (MA); *m* 11 Sept 1981, Jocelyn, da of Joseph Wang (d 1986), of Honiara, Guadalcanal, Solomon Islands; 1 da (Georgia Elizabeth b 1988); *Career* admitted slr 1971; ptnr: Crawley & de Reya 1976–78, Bartletts de Reya 1978–88, Theodore Goddard 1988–92; chm The International Business Library Ltd 1993–; memb: Law Soc Working Pty on Central and E Europe, Int Cncl for New Initiatives in East/West Cooperation, Int C of C Ctee on E Euro Rels; vice-chm Br-Polish Legal Assoc; memb: Br Advsy Bd to Know How Fund, Pan-European Inst Advsy Bd; *Books* Joint Ventures in Poland (1987), Joint Ventures in the Soviet Union (1988), Joint Ventures in Poland: The New Legislation (1990), Joint Ventures in Hungary (1990), Investment in CIS (1991), International Business Glossary (1994), Negotiating International Business Acquisitions (1997); *Recreations* sailing, swimming, music, reading; *Clubs* RNVR Yacht, Law Soc Yacht, Cruising Association, E Europe Business; *Style*— John Murphy, Esq; ✉ 94 Bromfelde Road, London SW4 6PS (tel 020 7622 0229, fax 020 7498 5155)

MURPHY, Liz; da of James Murphy (d 1981), and Elizabeth, *née* Mair; *b* 14 November 1959; *Educ* Sacred Heart HS Paisley, St Margaret's Secdy Sch Paisley, Napier Coll of Commerce (NCTJ Proficiency Cert, ESSO Student Journalist of the Year Special Prize, NCTJ Year Prize); *m* 19 Sept 1992, Steven Le Comber, s of Peter Le Comber; 2 da (Rachel b 1997, Eleanor b 2000); *Career* reporter and features writer Paisley Daily Express 1978–83; features writer: Evening Express Aberdeen 1983–85, Woman's Own London 1985–87; features ed Best 1988–90 (dep features ed 1987–88), assoc ed Me 1990, dep ed Best 1990–92, ed TV Times 1994–99, freelance showbusiness writer and editorial conslt 1999–2001, project ed Bauer 2001–02, conslt Good Housekeeping 2002, ed Sky The Magazine 2002–04, editorial conslt 2005–; Young Journalist of the Year for 1984 Scottish Press Awards 1985; memb BSME 1994; *Recreations* watching TV (especially soaps); *Style*— Ms Liz Murphy; ✉ mobile 07889 152808, e-mail liz.murphy@virgin.net

MURPHY, Michael; s of Francis Murphy (d 1989), and Dorothy Byrne, *née* Kenny (d 1998); *b* 12 February 1954; *Educ* Lourdes Secdy Sch Glasgow, Napier Coll Edinburgh; *m* 29 May 1982 (m dis), Carolynne Dawn, da of Derrick Thomas Evans; 2 s ((Michael) Stuart b 1984, Lewis Kwong Sang b 1995), 1 da (Kimberley Jane b 1987); *Career* journalist Johnston Newspaper Gp 1972–76, press offr Greater Glasgow Passenger Transport Gp 1976–78, PRO Ind Coope Scotland 1978–93, md PR Consultants Scotland, chm The PR Centre Ltd; ceo Shandwick Hong Kong Ltd 1994–98, chief exec Shandwick Asia 1995–98, chief exec Shandwick Europe 1998–2001, dep ceo Shandwick Int 1999–2001, chief exec Hatch-Group 2001–03, ceo Trimedia Int 2003–; non-exec dir Think London, tstee Action on Addiction; FIPR, FSA Scot; *Recreations* keeping fit, reading; *Style*— Michael Murphy, Esq

MURPHY, Michael; *b* 25 January 1965; *Educ* Harvard Univ Grad Sch of Business Admin; *m*; 2 da; *Career* trainee mangr Currys Ltd 1981–83, field sales rep Multi-Broadcast 1983–84, advertisement sales exec rising to advertisement mangr and gen mangr SE London & Kentish Mercury Gp 1984–93, gp advertisement mangr Oxford & County Newspapers 1993–95, md Free Press Gp 1995–96; FT Gp: UK sales devpt dir 1996, dir FT UK 1996–98, worldwide commercial dir 1998–99, md FT Business 1999–2002, chief operating offr internet businesses 2000–01, chief operating offr FT 2001–02, ceo Friends Reunited 2003–; non-exec dir: Datamonitor plc 2003–, Multimap 2006–; *Recreations* golf, swimming, football; *Style*— Michael Murphy, Esq; ✉ Friends Reunited, Unit 2, Oxted Chambers, 185–187 Station Road East, Oxted, Surrey RH8 0QE

MURPHY, Prof Michael Furber; s of Arthur Furber Murphy (d 1989), and Dr Jean Marjorie Frazer; *b* 2 May 1951; *Educ* Malvern Coll, St Bartholomew's Hosp (MB BS, MD); *m* 1 Sept 1984, Dr (Elizabeth) Sarah Green, da of Prof L L Green, of Wirral, Merseyside; 1 s (James Nicholas Furber b 16 March 1993), 1 da (Anna Cordelia Furber b 16 May 1995); *Career* house physician St Bartholomew's Hosp 1974; sr house offr in med: St Leonard's Hosp, Brompton Hosp and Nat Heart Hosp 1975–78; St Bartholomew's Hosp: registrar in haematology 1978–79, sr registrar 1979–84, sr lectr and hon conslt 1985–96; lead conslt and clinical dir Nat Blood Serv Oxford and conslt haematologist John Radcliffe Hosp Oxford 1996–, prof of blood transfusion Univ of Oxford 2004–; sec Br Ctee for Standards in Haematology 1992–95, sec Nat Blood Transfusion Ctee 2002–; memb Blood Transfusion Task Force Br Ctee for Standards in Haematology 1995–2001; scientific memb Biomedical Excellence for Safer Transfusion Research Collaborative 1999–; Kenneth Goldsmith award Br Blood Transfusion Soc 1994; FRCP 1993 (MRCP 1976), FRCPath 1994 (MRCPath 1982); *Books* Practical Transfusion Medicine (co-ed, 2001 and 2005); *Publications* original articles and reviews on clinical aspects of transfusion medicine; *Recreations* surfing, golf, wine tasting; *Style*— Prof Michael Murphy; ✉ Church Farm, Upper Lambourn, Hungerford, Berkshire RG17 8RG (tel 01488 72770); National Blood Service, John Radcliffe Hospital, Headington, Oxford OX3 9BQ (tel 01865 447902, fax 01865 447915, e-mail mike.murphy@nhsbt.nhs.uk)

MURPHY, His Hon Judge Michael Joseph Adrian; QC (1993); s of Patrick Joseph Murphy, of Hirwaun, Mid Glamorgan, and Frances Murphy (d 1990); *b* 1 October 1949; *Educ* Aberdare Boys GS, Univ of Sheffield (LLB, MA); *m* 1973, Rosemary Dorothy, *née* Aitken; 3 s (Peter Michael b 1976, Matthew Gareth b 1978, John Owen b 1982), 1 da (Mary Frances b 1980); *Career* called to the Bar Inner Temple 1973; recorder 1989–, circuit judge (NE Circuit) 1999–; *Style*— His Hon Judge Murphy, QC; ✉ Sheffield Combined Courts Centre, The Law Courts, 50 West Bar, Sheffield S3 8PH (tel 0114 2812400)

MURPHY, Rt Hon Paul Peter; PC (1999), MP; s of Ronald Murphy, and Marjorie Murphy (d 1984); *b* 25 November 1948; *Educ* St Francis RC Sch Abersychan, W Monmouth Sch Pontypool, Oriel Coll Oxford (MA); *Career* lectr in history and politics Ebbw Vale Coll of Further Educn 1971–87; memb Torfaen Borough 1973–87, MP (Lab) Torfaen 1987–; oppn spokesman on: Welsh affrs 1988–94, NI 1994–95, foreign affrs 1995, defence 1995–97; min of state NI Office 1997–99, sec of state for Wales 1999–2002, sec of state for NI 2002–2005, chair Intelligence and Security Ctee 2005–; hon fell Oriel Coll Oxford 2000; *Recreations* music; *Style*— The Rt Hon Paul Murphy, MP; ✉ House of Commons, London SW1A 0AA

MURPHY, Penelope Gay; da of Gerald Hugh-Smith (d 1965), of Hove, E Sussex, and Pamela Daphne, *née* Miller; *b* 28 October 1949; *Educ* Brighton & Hove HS, LSE (LLB); *m* 31 Aug 1974, Ian Patrick, QC, s of Patrick Murphy, of Cardiff; 2 da (Anna b 1982, Charlotte b 1984); *Career* court clerk Dir of Public Prosecutions Old Bailey 1971–73, admitted slr 1976, ptnr Geldards LLP (formerly Edwards Geldard of Cardiff) 1977–; treas S Wales Branch Assoc of Women Slrs 1984–; memb Law Soc 1976–; *Recreations* family life, theatre, travel, tennis; *Style*— Mrs Penelope Murphy; ✉ 3 Llandaff Chase, Llandaff, Cardiff CF5 2NA; Geldards LLP, Dumfries House, Dumfries Place, Cardiff CF10 3ZF (tel 029 2039 1891, fax 029 2023 7268, e-mail penny.murphy@geldards.co.uk)

MURPHY, Richard; s of Sir William Murphy, KCMG, LLD (d 1965), and Betty Mary, *née* Ormsby, MBE (d 1995); *b* 6 August 1927, Milford, Kilmaine, Co Mayo, Ireland; *Educ* King's Sch Canterbury, Wellington, Magdalen Coll Oxford (MA), Sorbonne; *m* 1955 (m dis 1959), Patricia Avis; 1 da (Emily); *Career* poet; visiting poet or writer in residence: Univ of Reading 1968, Univ of Hull 1969, Colgate Univ NY 1971, Bard Coll NY 1972, Princeton Univ 1974–75, Univ of Iowa 1976–77, Syracuse Univ NY 1977–78, Catholic Univ of America Washington DC 1983, Pacific Lutheran Univ Tacoma WA 1985, Wichita State Univ KS 1987, Tulsa Univ OK 1992, 1994, 1996 and 1998; memb Aosdána 1982; FRSL 1969; *Awards* AE Meml Award for Poetry 1951, First Prize Guinness Awards 1962, Br Arts Cncl Award 1967 and 1976, Irish Arts Cncl Award 1980, American Irish Fndn Literary Award 1983, Translation Award Poetry Book Soc 1989, Soc of Authors Fndn Award 2002; *Publications* The Archaeology of Love (1955), Sailing to an Island (1963, Poetry Book Soc Choice), The Battle of Aughrim (1968, Poetry Book Soc Recommendation), High Island (1974), High Island: New and Selected Poems (1975), Selected Poems (1979), Care (1982), The Price of Stone (1985, Poetry Book Soc Recommendation), The Price of Stone and Earlier Poems (1985), New Selected Poems (1989), The Mirror Wall (1989, Poetry Book Soc Translation Award), The Mayo Anthology (ed, 1990), Collected Poems (2000), The Kick - A Memoir (hardback, 2002), The Kick - A Life Among Writers (paperback, 2003); poems published in numerous literary magazines; subject of Richard Murphy: Poet of Two Traditions (collection of essays, 1977), included in Oxford Companion to English Lit (1985); *Style*— Richard Murphy, Esq; ✉ 61 Saratoga, 69 Forest Drive, La Lucia, Durban 4051, South Africa (tel and fax 00 27 31 562 9710, e-mail rmurphy@iafrica.com); 144 Glendale Estate, Leixlip, Co Kildare, Ireland (tel and fax 00 353 1 624 6089)

MURPHY, Roisin; da of Michael Murphy, of Wexford, Eire, and Rose Kavanagh, of Arklow, Eire; *b* 5 July 1973, Dublin; *Educ* St Mary's Secdy Sch Stockport, North Area Coll Stockport; *Career* singer/songwriter Moloko; extensive touring worldwide; Best Female Humo magazine 2003, Best Live Act TMF 2003; *Albums* Do You Like My Tight Sweater? 1995, I Am Not A Doctor 1998, Things To Make And Do 2000, Statues 2003, Ruby Blue (solo album) 2005; *Video* 11,000 Clicks 2004; *Recreations* art, ballet, mountain walking, dancing; *Style*— Ms Roisin Murphy; ✉ c/o Graham Peacock Management, PO Box 84, Hove, East Sussex BN3 6YP (tel 01273 777409, fax 01273 777809, e-mail gpmanage@aol.com)

MURPHY, Shaun Peter; s of Tony Murphy, of Stanwick, Northants, and Jean, *née* Fulham; *b* 10 August 1982, Harlow, Essex; *Educ* Huxlow Sch Irthlingborough, educn at home; *m* 16 July 2005, Clare Louise, *née* Llewellyn; *Career* professional snooker player 1998–; winner: Benson & Hedges Championship 2000, Embassy World Championship 2005, Malta Cup 2007; ranked 3 in the world 2007/08; memb: World Snooker Assoc, World Professional Billiards and Snooker Assoc (WPBSA); World Snooker Young Player of the Year 2001, World Snooker Newcomer of the Year 2001; *Recreations* golf, piano, tennis, ten pin bowling, cars, cinema; *Clubs* 147 Snooker (Sheffield); *Style*— Shaun Murphy, Esq; ✉ Champions UK plc, Meadow End, Leake Road, Costock, Loughborough LE12 6XA (tel 01509 852927, fax 01509 853378, e-mail info@championsukplc.com)

MURPHY, Stuart; *Educ* Clare Coll Cambridge; *Career* early positions as researcher then asst prodr BBC 1995, series prodr MTV 1996, prodr The Big Breakfast (Planet 24) 1996, strategic devpt mangr Ind Commissioning Gp BBC 1997, broadcast devpt exec BBC 1997, channel ed UK Play 1997–99, head of programming BBC Choice 1999–2001, controller BBC Choice 2001–03, controller BBC Three 2003–05 (also memb BBC TV Mgmnt Bd), creative dir RDF Media 2005–; *Style*— Stuart Murphy, Esq; ✉ RDF Media, The Gloucester Building, Kensington Village, Avonmore Road, London W14 8RF

MURPHY, Vernon Leslie; s of Sir Leslie Murphy, of Barton-on-Sea, Hants, and Marjorie Iris Murphy (d 1991); *b* 28 July 1944; *Educ* Westminster, Gonville & Caius Coll Cambridge (MA); *m* Sept 1974, Joan Bridget Mary, da of Thomas Anthony Leonard; 2 da (Olivia Bridget b 26 Jan 1978, Juliet Rosemary b 19 March 1982); *Career* British Airports Authority: joined as graduate trainee 1966, asst to Chief Exec 1969–71, successively dep mangr Terminal 2 Heathrow, sales mangr Heathrow Airport then gen mangr Terminal 1 Heathrow until 1980, gen mangr Aberdeen Airport 1980–84, dep md Gatwick Airport Ltd 1984–88, md Glasgow Airport Ltd 1988–92, md Scottish Airports 1988–99, chm Scottish Airports 1992–2001, regnl dir BAA Airports 1999–2001; dir Australia Pacific Airport Co 1999–2004, pres BAA Italia 2000–01, md BAA Rail 2001–05, chm BAA Int 2002–03; chm Heathrow Express 2001–06; non-exec dir Nat Air Traffic Solutions 2003–04; dep chm Renfrewshire Enterprise Co 1991–99, chm Scottish Chambers of Commerce 2000–03; Keeper of the Quaich 1995; FCIT 1984, FRSA 1995, FILT 1998; *Recreations* cricket, music, steam trains; *Clubs* RAC, MCC; *Style*— Vernon Murphy, Esq; ✉ Lissadell, Manor Lane, Gerrards Cross, Buckinghamshire SL9 7NS

MURPHY-O'CONNOR, Most Rev Cormac; *see:* Westminster, Archbishop (RC) of

MURRAY, Dr Andrew Christopher; s of Andrew Murray (d 1984), and Bridget, *née* Geraghty; *b* 9 June 1955; *Educ* Bishop Ullathorne Comp Sch, Queens' Coll Cambridge (BA), Univ of Warwick (PGCE), Boston Univ (MA), Univ of Manchester (PhD); *m* July 1984, Valerie, *née* Clark; 2 s (Edward b 1987, Richard b 1994), 2 da (Katherine b 1989, Elizabeth b 1991); *Career* lectr in history Univ of Botswana 1984–88; Br Cncl: asst dir Malawi 1988–92, asst dir Romania 1992–95, asst dir Poland 1995–99, dir Br Cncl Seminars 1999–2004, mangr Knowledge and Learning Prog 2004–05, mangr UK Change Prog 2005–; FRSA 2001; *Books* A Historical Dictionary of Botswana (1989), People's Rights: The Case of Bayei Separatism (1990); *Recreations* tennis, squash, supporting Coventry City FC; *Style*— Dr Andrew Murray; ✉ British Council, 10 Spring Gardens, London SW1A 2BN (tel 020 7389 6229, e-mail andrew.murray@britishcouncil.org)

MURRAY, Braham Sydney; s of Sam Goldstein, and Gertie Murray; *Educ* Clifton, UC Oxford; *Career* artistic dir Century Theatre 1965–67, founding dir '69 Theatre Co 1968–75, founding artistic dir Royal Exchange Theatre Co 1975–; memb NW Arts Bd 1994–2000, Hon BA Manchester Met Univ 1996; *Theatre* Royal Exchange Theatre Co: The Dybbuk, Riddley Walker, The Nerd, Leaping Ginger, Andy Capp, The Three Musketeers, Court in the Act!, Your Home in the West (Mobil Prize), The Odd Women, The Brothers Karamazov, Hamlet, Maybe (with Vanessa Redgrave, *qv*), Smoke, The Count of Monte Cristo, Unidentified Human Remains and the True Nature of Love, Private Lives, Miss Julie, The Candidate, Peer Gynt, Bats (co-writer), Snap-Shots, The Ghost Train Tattoo, Snake in Fridge (world premiere), Loot, Hedda Gabler, Time and the Conways, Othello, Cold Meat Party, Hobson's Choice, The Happiest Days of Your Life, Antony and Cleopatra; '69 Theatre Co (all prodns transferred to London): Charley's Aunt, Mary Rose, Endgame, Erb, Catch My Soul, She Stoops to Conquer; West End: The Good Companions (with Judi Dench, *qv*, and John Mills), The Black Mikado, The Cabinet Minister, Lady Windermere's Fan; other prodns incl: Hang Down Your Head and Die (Oxford, West End and Broadway), Uncle Vanya (Circle in the Square Theatre NY) 1995, Resurrection (world premiere Houston Grand Opera, Boston and Calif) 1999; *Recreations* food, wine, reading; *Style*— Braham Murray, Esq; ✉ Royal Exchange Theatre, St Ann's Square, Manchester M2 7DH (tel 0161 615 6704, fax 0161 832 0881, mobile 07967 103 782, e-mail braham.murray@royalexchange.co.uk)

MURRAY, Colin Keith; s of Brig George Murray, CBE, DSO, MC (d 1983), and Betty, *née* Wheeler (d 1982); *b* 18 June 1932; *Educ* Wellington; *m* 1 Feb 1964, Precelly, da of Col David Davies-Scourfield, MC (d 1998); 1 s, 2 da; *Career* Seaforth Highlanders and 1 Bn King's African Rifles 1950–52, TA 1952–64; CT Bowring & Co Ltd 1953–63, R J Kiln & Co Ltd 1963–95 (chm 1985–95); memb Cncl Lloyd's 1983–86 and 1989–92 (dep chm 1989–90), chm Lloyd's Volunteer Forces Fund 1990–95; dir Kiln Capital plc 1994–98, tstee Equitas Holdings Ltd 1996–2001; pres Youth Clubs Hants and IOW 1996–2006, chm Trust in Children 1994–2004, chm Friends of Music in Winchester, dir St Joseph's Soc 1985–2006, govr St John the Baptist Primary Sch Andover; Lt City of London 1993; High Sheriff Hants 2002–03; Liveryman Worshipful Co of Insurers; *Recreations* music, bridge, gardening, country sports; *Clubs* Boodle's, Flyfishers', The City; *Style*— Colin Murray, Esq; ✉ The Long House, Hurstbourne Priors, Whitchurch, Hampshire RG28 7SB (tel 01256 892606, fax 01256 893969)

MURRAY, Sir David Edward; kt (2007); s of David Ian Murray (d 1975), and Roma Murray; *b* 14 October 1951; *Educ* Fettes, Broughton HS; *m* 22 July 1972, Louise Violet (decd); 2 s (David Douglas b 1973, Keith Andrew b 1975); *Career* fndr and chm Murray International Holdings and subsidiaries 1976–, chm Glasgow Rangers Football Club plc 1988–2002 and 2004– (hon chm 2002–04); estab The Murray Fndn 1997 (Queen's Award for Voluntary Serv 2006); chm UK 2000 Scotland 1987–88, govr Clifton Hall Sch 1987–89; commercial devpt conslt Scottish Rugby Union 1997–2006; Hon Dr of Business Heriot-Watt Univ 1986; *Recreations* collecting and producing wine, watching sport; *Style*— Sir David Murray; ✉ 9 Charlotte Square, Edinburgh EH2 4DR (tel 0131 317 7000, fax 0131 317 7111)

MURRAY, Denis James; OBE (1997); s of Dr James Murray (d 1956), of Evesham, Worcs, and Helen, *née* McKeever (d 1977); *b* 7 May 1951; *Educ* St Malachy's Coll Belfast, Trinity Coll Dublin (BA); *m* 22 April 1978, Joyce, *née* Linehan; 2 da (Claire b 26 Oct 1981, Sophie b 17 Dec 1986), 2 s (Gavin b 6 June 1984, James b 19 Aug 1989); *Career* reporter Belfast Telegraph 1974–77 (graduate trainee 1974), reporter RTE 1977–82; BBC: Dublin corr 1982–84, Northern Ireland political corr 1984–88, Ireland corr 1988–; Journalist of the Year TV Sports and Journalism Awards 1997; *Recreations* playing and watching sport, books, music; *Style*— Denis Murray, Esq, OBE; ✉ c/o BBC Broadcasting House, Ormeau Avenue, Belfast BT2 8HQ (tel 028 9033 8000, fax 028 9033 8806, mobile 078 3187 7000)

MURRAY, Diana Mary; JP (E Lothian 2000); da of Keith Gordon George Collyer, of Sale Green, Worcs, and (Joyce) Mary, *née* Cottrell; *b* 14 September 1952, Birmingham; *Educ* King Edward VI Camphill Sch for Girls Kings Heath, Univ of Cambridge (MA); *m* 14 Feb 1987, Robin Francis Murray; 2 da (Katharine Mary b 4 June 1988, Clare Frances b 6 Oct 1989); *Career* Royal Cmmn on the Ancient and Historical Monuments of Scot: res asst 1976–83, head Nat Monuments Record of Scot (NMRS) Recording Section 1983–90, curator Archaeology Record 1990–95, curator depute NMRS 1995–2004, sec (chief exec) 2004–; chm Inst of Field Archaeologists 1995–96 (sec Scot Gp 1985–92, hon sec 1993–95); memb: Cncl Soc of Antiquaries of Scot 1984–87, Exec Ctee Cncl for Scot Archaeology 1993–96, Cncl Nat Tst for Scot 2003– (non-exec dir 2004), Bd Scot Coastal Archaeological and Environmental Tst 2003–04, Cncl Soc of Antiquaries of London 2004–; ldr E Lothian Young Archaeologists Club 1998–2001; memb Dirleton Sch Bd 1995–96 and 2001–03, chm Dirleton Village Assoc 1996–2001; FSA Scot 1977, MIFA 1984, FSA 1986; *Publications* specialist pubns on archaeology and heritage info data mgmnt; *Recreations* choral singing, gardening, family, reading, renovating new house in Dirleton; *Style*— Mrs Diana Murray, JP; ✉ The Rowans, 15 Manse Road, Dirleton, East Lothian EH39 5EL (e-mail diana.murray@rowanberry.co.uk); Royal Commission on the Ancient and Historical Monuments of Scotland, John Sinclair House, 16 Bernard Terrace, Edinburgh EH8 9NX (tel 0131 662 1456, fax 0131 662 1477, e-mail diana.murray@rcahms.gov.uk)

MURRAY, Dr Elaine Kildare; MSP; da of Kenneth Gordon Murray, of Prestwick, and Patricia Murray, *née* Kildare; *b* 22 December 1954; *Educ* Mary Erskine Sch, Univ of Edinburgh (BSc), Univ of Cambridge (PhD); *m* 1986, Jeff Leaver, s of John Leaver (decd); 2 s (Alex b 6 Jan 1986, Richard b 20 Dec 1989), 1 da (Elspeth b 4 Jan 1988); *Career* postdoctoral res fell: Cavendish Lab Cambridge 1979–82, Royal Free Hosp London 1982–83; sr sci offr Inst of Food Res Reading 1984–87; asst to Alex Smith MEP 1989–93, cncllr Strathclyde Regnl Cncl 1994–96, cncllr South Ayrshire Cncl 1995–99 (convenor Educnl Services Ctee); MSP (Lab) Dumfries 1999–; dep min for Tourism, Culture and Sport 2001–; assoc lectr Open Univ Scotland 1992–99; *Recreations* reading, cooking, gardening, music, horse riding; *Style*— Dr Elaine Murray, MSP; ✉ The Scottish Parliament, Holyrood, Edinburgh EH99 1SP (tel 0131 348 5826, fax 0131 348 5834, mobile 07919 392049, e-mail elaine.murray.msp@scottish.parliament.uk); 5 Friar's Vennel, Dumfries DG1 2RQ (tel 01387 279205, fax 01387 279206)

MURRAY, (Ian) Gordon; s of William Gordon Murray (d 1984), and Rosemary Morrison, *née* Irvine; *b* 18 June 1946; *Educ* Glenwood HS Durban, Natal Tech Coll (Dip Mech Engrg, Arthur May prize); *m* 4 June 1970, Stella Lynne, da of Victor Gane; 1 s (Christopher Dylan b 23 Jan 1978); *Career* motorsport designer; design draughtsman South Africa 1964–69, moved to England 1969; Brabham: design draughtsman 1970–73, chief designer 1973–74, tech dir 1974–86; tech dir: McLaren International 1986–90, McLaren Cars Ltd 1990–2004; Gordon Murray Design Ltd 2007–; dir TAG McLaren Group 1990–; achievements as designer: 51 grand prix wins, 4 World Drivers' Formula One Championships, 2 World Constructors' Formula One Championships, McLaren F1 (fastest road car in the world), McLaren F1 GTR (winner Le Mans 1995, Global Endurance GT series, European Endurance GT series, GT World Championship 1996, All Japan GT Championship 1996, GT Class 24 hr Le Mans 1997); winner various awards for motorsport design; memb: South African Inst of Mech Engrs, Inst of Engrg Designers; hon prof Durban Inst of Technol; *Recreations* motor sport, music, art; *Style*— Gordon Murray, Esq; ✉ Gordon Murray Design Limited, Wharfside, Broadford Park, Shalford GU4 8EP

MURRAY, Rt Rev Ian; *see:* Argyll and the Isles, Bishop of

MURRAY, James David George; s of George Murray, and Susan, *née* Tullis; *b* 11 February 1970, Newcastle upon Tyne; *Educ* Shiplake Coll Henley-on-Thames, Cambridge Business Studies Coll; *Partner* Natasha Forrest-Hay; *Career* trainee engr Lamont Telecommunications 1989–90, trainee project mgmnt/sales Rapid Telecom 1990–92, Lynton Europe Ltd 1992–94, co-fndr and ceo Alternative Networks plc 1994–; Young Entrepreneur of the Year regnl and nat winner 2005; *Recreations* cars, supporting Newcastle United FC; *Style*— James Murray, Esq; ✉ Alternative Networks plc, Chatfield

M

Court, 56 Chatfield Road, London SW11 3UL (tel 0870 190 7006, fax 0870 190 7602, e-mail jmurray@alternativenetworks.com)

MURRAY, Jennifer Susan (Jenni); OBE (1999); da of Alvin Bailey, of Barnsley, S Yorks, and Winifred, *née* Jones; *b* 12 May 1950; *Educ* Barnsley Girls' HS, Univ of Hull (BA); *m* 1, (m dis), Brian Murray; partner, David Forgham-Bailey; 2 s (Edward Louis b 1983, Charles Edgar b 1987); *Career* prodr and presenter BBC Radio Bristol 1973–76, presenter and reporter BBC TV South 1977–82; presenter: Newsnight (BBC TV Lime Grove) 1983–85, Today (BBC Radio 4) 1986–87, Woman's Hour (BBC Radio 4) 1987–, This Sunday (Granada TV), Turning World (BBC Radio 4) 1998–2001, The Message (BBC Radio 4) 2001–; documentary films for TV incl: The Duchy of Cornwall, Everyman, Stand by Your Man, Breaking the Chain, Here's Looking At You; contrib: The Guardian, The Independent on Sunday, Daily Mail, The Observer, The Times, The Express and various magazines; columnist Manchester Evening News; trg public speaking presentation; vice-pres FPA, vice-pres Parkinson's Disease Soc, memb Bd The Women's Library; visiting prof London Inst; Hon DLitt Univ of Bradford, Hon DUniv Open Univ; *Books* The Woman's Hour, Is It Me, or Is It Hot in Here?, That's My Boy!; *Recreations* horses, books, swimming, the children; *Style*— Ms Jenni Murray, OBE; ✉ Woman's Hour, BBC Broadcasting House, London W1A 1AA (tel 020 7580 4468); agent Speakeasy (tel 0116 240 4101), literary agent Barbara Levy (tel 020 7435 9046)

MURRAY, John Joseph; s of Kevin Thomas Murray (d 2000), of Bridge of Weir, Renfrewshire, and Mary, *née* Leahy (d 1973); *b* 10 May 1953; *Educ* Fort Augustus Abbey Sch, Caledonian Univ, Univ of Leeds (LLB), Coll of Law Guildford; *Career* admitted slr 1979; articled clerk Smallpeice & Merriman 1977–79, ptnr Nabarro Nathanson 1986– (asst slr 1979); chm Tax and Legislation Sub-Ctee 1994–97, memb Ctee Assoc of Pensioneer Trustees 1991–97 and 2003–05, memb Pensions Ctee of the Assoc of Corp Tstees 2000–, memb Ctee Assoc of Member-Directed Pension Schemes 2005–; memb: Law Soc, Assoc of Pension Lawyers; assoc fell Soc for Advanced Legal Studies; memb Ctee: American Civil War Round Table (UK), Western Front Assoc, Friends of Kensal Green Cemetary, Amnesty Int; FRSA 2005; *Publications* Encyclopedia of Forms and Precedents (5 edn), contrib Vol 31 Pensions, Pensions Law Handbook (contrib, 2000, 6 edn 2004); articles in Pensions World, Pension Dimension, Journal of Pensions Management and Marketing, Professional Pensions, Crossfire; *Recreations* reading, travel, music, sport; *Style*— John Murray, Esq; ✉ Nabarro Nathanson, Lacon House, Theobalds Road, London WC1X 8RW (tel 020 7524 6327, fax 020 7524 6524, e-mail j.murray@nabarro.com)

MURRAY, Prof John Joseph; CBE (1997); s of John Gerald Murray (d 1980), of Bradford, W Yorks, and Margaret Sheila, *née* Parle (d 1979); *b* 28 December 1941; *Educ* St Bedes GS Bradford, Univ of Leeds (BDS, MDS, PhD); *m* 28 March 1967, Valerie (d 2002), da of Harry Allen (d 1969), of Heanor, Derbys; 2 s (Mark b 14 March 1975, Christopher b 3 Nov 1976); *Career* res fell in children's dentistry Univ of Leeds 1966–70, reader Inst of Dental Surgery Univ of London 1975–77 (sr lectr in children's dentistry 1970–75); Univ of Newcastle upon Tyne: prof of child dental health 1977–1992, dental postgrad sub dean 1982–92, dean of dentistry 1992–2002; asst scientific ed Br Dental Jl 1985–92, pres Br Paedodontic Soc 1985 (conslt advsr to chief med offr 1982–92); Dept of Health: memb Standing Dental Advsy Ctee 1980– (chm 1992–), memb Ctee on Continuing Educn Trg 1985–95, memb Clinical Standards Advsy Gp (CSAG) 1992–98, chm CSAG Cleft Lip and Palate Ctee 1995–98, Children's Task Force 2002; chm Educn Ctee GDC 1999–2003, memb Exec Cncl Dental Deans and Directors 1999–2002; clinical dir Dental Directorate Newcastle upon Tyne NHS Hosps 1995–2002; memb: BDA, GDC, Acad of Med Sciences, Int Assoc Paediatric Dentristry (chm Organising Ctee 1999); IADR Trendley Dean Research Award 1997, Colyer Gold Medal FDS RCS; Hon MFPHM 1998; FDS RCS 1973, MCCD RCS 1989; *Books* The Acid Etch Technique in Paedodontics and Orthodontics (jtly), Fluorides in Caries Prevention (1976, 2 and 3 edns jtly 1982 and 1991), Prevention of Oral Disease (ed, 1983, 4 edn 2003); *Recreations* golf, bridge, photography; *Clubs* Ponteland Golf (capt 2006); *Style*— Prof John Murray, CBE; ✉ 6 Regency Way, Darras Hall, Ponteland, Newcastle upon Tyne NE20 9AU (tel 01661 871 035, fax 0191 222 6137, e-mail j.murray@ncl.ac.uk)

MURRAY, Jorian Mark; s of Michael Murray (d 2005), of London, and Rosemary Murray (d 1991); *b* 1 September 1961; *Educ* Westminster City Sch, Univ of London (BA), Harvard Business Sch (AMP); *m* 2 Sept 1989, Deborah, da of Geoff Scott; 2 s (Joseph b 22 July 1994, George b 21 Jan 2001), 1 da (Eleanor b 29 Jan 1997); *Career* Lasky's Hi-Fi 1986, Publicis 1988, successively account dir, head of dept and md DDB London 1992 (IPA Effectiveness Agency of the Year 1992–2006), founding ptnr Dye Holloway Murray LLP 2007; memb Mktg Soc 2002; MIPA 1989, MInstD 2007; *Recreations* watching and playing football (season ticket Arsenal FC), gym, dog walking; *Clubs* Home House; *Style*— Jorian Murray, Esq; ✉ Dye Holloway Murray LLP, 30–32 Southampton Street, London WC2E 7RA (tel 020 7240 0603, e-mail jorian@dhmlondon.com)

MURRAY, Kevin Ian; s of Ian Campbell Murray (d 1994), and Shirley Esme Gladys Maud, *née* Edwards; *b* 9 June 1954, Rhodesia; *Educ* Hyde Park HS Johannesburg; *m* 4 Feb 1978, Elisabeth Anne Mary, da of Maj-Gen William Leonard Whalley, CB; 1 s (Jason Nicholas b 14 Aug 1979), 1 da (Kirstin Leigh b 27 Jan 1981); *Career* Nat Serv SA Inf 1971–72, active serv (annual civilian force tours of duty) Transvaal Scot Regt 1972–82; The Star Johannesburg 1973–81, gp pubns ed and PR exec Barlow Rand Ltd Johannesburg 1981–82, managing ed Leadership SA magazine rising to dir of mktg and advtg Churchill Murray Publications 1982–85, md Kestrel Publications rising to md Shearwater Communications Services 1985–88, PR mangr Bayer UK Ltd rising to gp PR mangr all Bayer plc cos in UK 1988–92, dir of corp communications UKAEA and dir of corp affrs/memb Mgmnt Ctee AEA Technology 1992–96, dir of communications British Airways plc 1996–98, sr conslt rising to chm Bell Pottinger Communications 1998–, chm PR Div Chime Communications plc 2003–; FCIPR, MInstD, FRSA; *Recreations* golf, theatre, travel; *Style*— Kevin Murray, Esq; ✉ Chime Communications, 14 Curzon Street, London W1J 5HN (tel 020 7495 4044, e-mail kmurray@chime.plc.uk)

MURRAY, Martin Charles; s of Brian Murray, of Crosby, and Muriel Gertrude, *née* Spence; *b* 13 April 1955; *Educ* Merchant Taylors', Emmanuel Coll Cambridge (MA, LLB), Harvard Univ (LLM); *Career* admitted slr 1981; Clifford Chance 1979–83, Enodis plc 1983–86, Hanson plc 1986–97, company sec and gen counsel The Energy Gp plc 1997–99, gp company sec Old Mutual plc 1999–; tstee: Ralph Vaughan Williams Soc, Braga Santos Fndn; memb Law Soc; *Recreations* wine, food, music, opera, travel; *Style*— Martin Murray, Esq; ✉ Flat 3, The Old Sorting Office, 37 Station Road, Barnes, London SW13 0LF; Old Mutual plc, 5th Floor, Old Mutual Place, 2 Lambeth Hill, London EC4V 4GG (tel 020 7002 7109, fax 020 7002 7209, e-mail martin.murray@omg.co.uk)

MURRAY, Prof Maxwell; s of Maxwell Murray (d 1981), and Martha Letham, *née* Davidson (d 2001); *b* 3 May 1939; *Educ* Shawlands Acad, Univ of Glasgow (BVMS, PhD, DVM); *m* 8 Sept 1976, Christine Madelaine, da of Maj Ronald Lewis Allen, of Glasgow; 2 da (Katie b 1978, Kirsty b 1983), 1 s (Maxwell b 1979); *Career* lectr in vet pathology Univ of Nairobi 1963–65, sr scientist Int Lab for Research on Animal Diseases Nairobi 1975–85; Univ of Glasgow: lectr in vet pathology 1965–74, sr lectr 1974–75, prof of vet med 1985–2003, emeritus prof of vet med and hon sr research fell 2003–; FRCPath 1984, FRSE 1984; *Books* Current Trends in Immunology and Genetics and their Implications for Parasitic Diseases (1978), Livestock Productivity and Trypanotolerance: Network Training Manual (1983); *Recreations* family, football, music, quantification of inspiration, deprivation in Africa; *Style*— Prof Maxwell Murray, FRSE; ✉ 21 Ledcameroch Road, Bearsden, Glasgow G61 4AE (tel and fax 0141 942 6476, e-mail m.murray@vet.gla.ac.uk)

MURRAY, Michael Thomas (Mike); s of Robert Murray, and Anne Clark, *née* Leech; *b* 13 October 1945; *Educ* Bedlington GS; *m* 1968, Else Birgitta Margareta, *née* Paues; 1 s, 1 da; *Career* diplomat; entered HM Dip Serv 1964, posted Prague 1967, posted Vienna 1971, vice-consul (commercial) Frankfurt 1973, second sec (devpt) Khartoum 1977, FCO 1980–83, first sec and head of Chancery Banjul 1983, FCO 1988–95, first sec (devpt and economic) Lusaka 1995, dep consul-gen Chicago 1999, ambass to Eritrea 2002–06, ret; memb Advsy Bd Tynedale Enterprise Project; *Recreations* living lightly, coarse/chemical free horticulture, golf; *Clubs* Alnmouth Golf, Laholms Golf; *Style*— Mike Murray, Esq

MURRAY, Neil Alastair Charles; s of Alastair Richardson Murray, of Wimbledon, London, and Patricia Stella Ray, *née* Jones; *b* 25 February 1954; *Educ* King George V Sch Hong Kong, Univ of Southampton (LLB), City Univ (MA); *m* 1 Sept 1984 (m dis 1998), Patricia Susan, da of John Herbert Mulholland, of Connecticut, USA; 1 s (James b 4 July 1987), 1 da (Stephanie b 18 June 1989); *Career* admitted slr 1980; Boodle Hatfield & Co London 1978–80, Legal Dept ICI 1980, Norton Rose 1980–85, ptnr Travers Smith Braithwaite (now Travers Smith) 1987– (joined 1985); Freeman Worshipful Co of Slrs; memb Law Soc; *Recreations* music, golf, skiing, fitness; *Clubs* City of London; *Style*— Neil Murray, Esq; ✉ Travers Smith, 10 Snow Hill, London EC1A 2AL (tel 020 7295 3000, fax 020 7295 3500)

MURRAY, Nicholas Julyan Edward; s of Sir (Francis) Ralph Hay Murray, KCMG, CB (d 1986), of Whaddon Hall Mews, Whaddon, Bucks, and Mauricette, *née* Countess von Kuenburg (d 1996); *b* 7 March 1939; *Educ* Bedford Sch, English Sch Cairo, Univ of St Andrews (MA); *m* 14 July 1973, Caroline Anne, da of Capt A McClintock, of Glenbower, Coolbawn, Nenagh, Co Tipperary, Ireland; 1 da (Anstice Aileen Thérèse b 22 Jan 1981); *Career* S H Benson Ltd 1962–71 (dir 1968), dir Ogilvy Benson & Mather Ltd 1971–72, md Murray Parry & Ptnrs 1972–81, dir Woodyer Hutson Chapman 1981–86, md Conzept Int Mgmnt Business Devpt Conslts 1986–97, chief exec Galileo Brand Architecture Ltd 1997–; memb and professional advsr Bd of Trade (missions Tokyo 1968, San Francisco 1969); chm Friends of the Vale of Aylesbury 1987–92 (memb ctee 1975–, vice-chm 1985); FInstD; *Books* Chronicle of the Villages of the Vale of Aylesbury (1986); *Recreations* sailing; *Clubs* Sussex Yacht, Lough Derg Yacht; *Style*— Nicholas Murray, Esq; ✉ 38 Perrers Road, London W6

MURRAY, Prof Noreen Elizabeth; CBE (2002); da of John and Lilian Grace Parker; *b* 26 February 1935; *Educ* King's Coll London (BSc), Univ of Birmingham (PhD); *m* 1958, Kenneth Murray; *Career* res assoc: Stanford Univ 1960–64, Univ of Cambridge 1964–67, Molecular Genetics Unit MRC Edinburgh 1968–74; Dept of Molecular Biology Univ of Edinburgh: successively lectr, sr lectr, reader 1974–88, prof of molecular genetics 1988–2002, emeritus prof 2003–; scientist European Molecular Biology Laboratory Heidelberg 1980–82; memb: Royal Cmmn for the Exhbn of 1851 2002–, Science and Technol Honours Ctee 2005–; pres Genetical Soc 1987–90; memb: EMBO, Genetics Soc USA; tstee Darwin Tst of Edinburgh 1990–; author of original res papers and reviews of genetics and molecular biology; Gabor Medal Royal Soc 1989, AstraZeneca Award Biochemical Soc 2005; Hon DSc: UMIST, Univ of Birmingham, Univ of Warwick; fell KCL; FRS 1982, FRSE 1989; *Recreations* gardening; *Clubs* Athenaeum; *Style*— Prof Noreen Murray, CBE, FRS, FRSE; ✉ Institute of Cell Biology, University of Edinburgh, Mayfield Road, Edinburgh EH9 3JR (tel 0131 650 5374, e-mail noreen.murray@ed.ac.uk)

MURRAY, Norman Loch; s of Thomas Loch Murray, of Cumnock, Ayrshire, and May Fox, *née* Davidson; *b* 17 March 1948; *Educ* George Watson's Coll Edinburgh, Heriot-Watt Univ (BA), Harvard Grad Sch of Business Admin (PMD); *m* 17 March 1973, Pamela Anne, da of George Low; 2 s (Niall, Andrew); *Career* Scottish and Newcastle Breweries plc Edinburgh 1971–73, Arthur Young & Co Edinburgh 1973–77, Peat Marwick Mitchell & Co Hong Kong 1977–80, The Royal Bank of Scotland plc Edinburgh 1980–85, dir Charterhouse Development Capital Ltd 1985–89; Private Equity Business Morgan Grenfell Development Capital Ltd: dep chief exec 1989–96, chief exec 1996–98, chm 1996–98; dir: Morgan Grenfell Development Capital France SA 1995–98, Morgan Grenfell Asset Mgmnt 1996–98, Deutsche Morgan Grenfell Devpt Capital Italy SA 1996–98, Deutsche Morgan Grenfell Private Equity Asia Fund Ltd 1997–98; chm Cairn Energy plc 2002– (dir 1999–2002); dir: Penta Capital 2000–, Robert Wiseman Dairies plc 2003–, Greene King plc 2004–; non-exec dir: Burn Stewart Distillers plc 1988–90, Taunton Cider plc 1991–92, Bristow Helicopter Group Ltd 1991–96, EuroDollar (Holdings) plc 1993–94, Glasgow Income Tst 1999–2003; chm Br Venture Capital Assoc (memb Cncl) 1997–98, pres ICAS 2006– (memb Cncl 1992–98, convenor Fin and General Purposes Ctee); memb Co of Merchants of City of Edinburgh; CA 1976; FRSA; *Books* Making Corporate Reports Valuable (jtly, 1988); *Recreations* squash, golf, climbing; *Clubs* Luffness New Golf, Watsonian, Harvard Business School, Royal Hong Kong Yacht; *Style*— Norman Murray, Esq

MURRAY, Peter; OBE (1996); *b* 1941, Middlesbrough; *Educ* Teesside Coll of Art, Univ of Leeds; *Career* teacher and curator; exhibited extensively until 1975 (paintings, drawings and prints in several public and private collections); taught in general, further and higher educn, lectr/visiting tutor to colls, polys and univs throughout Britain and abroad, formerly princ lectr responsible for postgrad studies Bretton Hall Coll W Yorks; fndr and exec dir Yorkshire Sculpture Park (pioneering the siting and exhibiting of sculpture in the open air) 1977–; organised maj open air exhibitions incl: Henry Moore and Landscape (largest ever open Henry Moore exhibition), Scultura - Carving from Carrara, Massa and Pietrasanta 1988, Emile Antoine Bourdelle - Pioneer of the Future 1989, Contemporary Stone Carving from Zimbabwe, Lynn Chadwick 1991–92, Phillip King, Barry Flanagan 1992, Jorgen Haugen Sorenson Retrospective and Fritz Wotruba 1993, Elizabeth Frink Meml 1994, Ed Paolozzi 70th Birthday Exhbn 1994, Kan Yasuda 1994; organiser and dir first Open Air Sculpture Symposium in Britain 1983, made presentations at Int Sculpture Confs USA 1982, Japan 1984 and San Francisco 1994; sponsored by: French Govt to visit Paris and northern France 1984, Canadian Govt to visit Canada 1981 and 1986, Br Cncl to visit India 1988, Zimbabwe 1990, Thailand 1991, N America 1992, 1993 and 1994, Germany 1993 and Austria 1993; estab: Artist Residences, Public Sculpture Workshops, Educn and Outreach Prog, Access Sculpture Trail at Yorks Sculpture Park; author of reviews for arts jls, contrib to several Radio and TV progs incl Review of Jacob Epstein exhibition BBC Radio 4 Kaleidoscope 1987, contrib to catalogues for exhibitions for other galleries and organisations nationally and internationally; hon fell RCA 1989; *Publications* incl: Sculpture Parks in Britain (Studio International, 1983), Sculpture Parks - Origins & Aims (Arts Review Yearbook, 1983), Zimbabwe Carving (Arts Review Yearbook, 1990); *Style*— Peter Murray, Esq, OBE; ✉ Yorkshire Sculpture Park, Bretton Hall College, West Bretton, Wakefield, West Yorkshire WF4 4LG (tel 01924 830579)

MURRAY, Peter Gerald Stewart; s of Stewart Hay Murray (d 1988), and Freda, *née* Woodland (d 2000); *b* 6 April 1944; *Educ* King's Coll Taunton, Royal West of England Acad Sch of Architecture, Univ of Bristol, AA Sch of Architecture London; *m* Jane Rosetta, da of Alexander Wood; 2 s (Rupert Hay b 28 May 1969, William Alexander b 21 April 1972), 2 da (Sophie Elizabeth b 12 Oct 1977, Alice Adelaide b 31 Aug 1981); *Career* freelance journalist and designer 1967–70 (design corr for Nova Magazine, Domus, Town Magazine); Architectural Design magazine: art ed 1970–72, tech ed 1972–74; ed Building Design 1974–79, ed RIBA Jl and RIBA Transactions 1979–84, md RIBA Magazines Ltd 1979–84, fndr Wordsearch Ltd 1983, launched Blueprint magazine 1983;

fndr: Blueprint Monographs book series 1986, Blueprint Extras book series 1989, Eye Magazine, The Int Review of Graphic Design 1990, Design Review (jl of the Chartered Soc of Designers) 1991; publisher Tate Magazine and Perspectives Magazine 1993; fndr Wordsearch Communications 1995; architectural advsr St Hugh's Coll Oxford 1996; dir London Architecture Biennale 2004, 2006 and 2008, fndr dir New London Architecture 2005–; ed Pidgeon Digital 2007–; lectr in architecture and design; RIBA: ex officio memb Policy Ctee 1978–83, memb Events Ctee 1978–83, Library Ctee 1981–83, Mktg Ctee 1985–87, Br Architectural Library Ctee 2001–04; Architectural Assoc: memb Cncl 1987–90, hon sec 1989–90; exhibitions at the Royal Academy: New Architecture - The Work of Foster Rogers Stirling 1986, Living Bridges: Inhabited Bridges Past, Present and Future 1996, Beyond Minimalism - The Work of Tadao Ando 1998; chm Int Building Press 1976–78 (pres 1978–83); sec Architecture Club 1978–; memb Bedford Park Soc Ctee 1998 (hon sec and dep chm 2000–), memb Royal Acad Architecture Ctee 1997–; tstee: Bannister Fletcher 1984–86, Sarah Matheson Tst; chm BBC Design Awards Panel 1994; memb Selection Panel: Nat Portrait Gall extension 1987, Inland Revenue HQ Nottingham 1991, The Crown Estate 1995, Br Cncl for Offices Awards 1998; D&AD Silver Medal 1973, Publisher of the Year PPA 1991, Property Mktg Awards 1993, 1994, 1995, 1998 and 1999; FRSA 1989, Hon FRIBA 1999; *Books* A Village in Wiltshire (1975), The Lloyds Building (1980), Ove Arup & Partners (1981), SOM: Reality before Reality (1982), YRM: On Making a Building (1983), BDP: Expressing Corporate Personality (1983), Modern Architecture in Britain (1984), Harry Seidler: Towers in the City (1985), Contemporary British Architects (1993), Living Bridges: The Inhabited Bridge Past, Present and Future (1996), New Urban Environments (1998), Understanding Plans (1998), New Architects (1998), The Saga of Sydney Opera House (2003), Architecture and Commerce (2004); *Recreations* tennis, cycling, painting, looking at architecture; *Clubs* Architecture, Hurlingham, Athenaeum; *Style*— Peter Murray, Esq; ✉ Wordsearch, 85 Clerkenwell Road, London EC1R 5AR (e-mail peter.murray@wordsearch.co.uk)

MURRAY, Rob; s of Prof John Murray, of Botley, Hants, and Jeanne, *née* Faith (d 1998); *b* 29 November 1963, Bristol; *Educ* Exeter Coll Oxford (scholar, BA), Vrije Univ Brussels (Flemish Govt scholar, LLM); *m* 28 Dec 1990, Sarah, *née* Giles; 1 s (Tom b 21 April 1995), 1 da (Gracie b 18 March 1997); *Career* admitted slr 1989; slr Commercial Dept then EC Unit Clifford Chance 1989–96 (articled clerk 1987–89), ptnr and head of EU/competition Bond Pearce 1996–2000, dir EU/Competition Gp and Legal Risk Mgmnt Gp KLegal 2000–02, ptnr and head EU/Competition Gp DLA 2002–04; memb Competition Cmmn Reporting Panel 2005–; md Foreverafter Ltd 2004–, dir Cornelia Properties Ltd 2004–; memb Law Soc; *Style*— Rob Murray, Esq; ✉ Competition Commission, Victoria House, Southampton Row, London WC1B 4AD (tel 020 7271 0100, fax 020 7271 0367)

MURRAY, Prof Robin MacGregor; s of James Alistair Campbell Murray (d 1979), of Glasgow, and Helen, *née* MacGregor (d 1992); *b* 31 January 1944; *Educ* Royal HS Edinburgh, Univ of Glasgow (MB ChB, MD), Univ of London (MPhil, DSc); *m* Shelagh, da of Frank Harris; 1 s (Graham Keith b 8 Feb 1972), 1 da (Claire Alison b 22 May 1978); *Career* SHO and registrar: Dept of Med Univ of Glasgow 1969–72, Maudsley Hosp 1972–76; Inst of Psychiatry: sr lectr 1978, dean 1982, prof of psychological med 1989–99, prof of psychiatry 1999–; visiting fell Nat Inst of Mental Health Washington 1976, pres Assoc of European Psychiatrists 1995–96; *Style*— Prof Robin Murray; ✉ Division of Psychological Medicine, Institute of Psychiatry, DeCrespigny Park, London SE5 8AF (tel 020 7703 6091)

MURRAY, Sir Rowland William; 15 Bt (NS 1630), of Dunerne, Fifeshire; s of Sir Rowland William Patrick Murray, 14 Bt (d 1994), and his 1 w Josephine Margaret, *née* Murphy (d 1989); *b* 22 September 1947; *Educ* Georgia State Univ; *m* 1970, Nancy Diane, da of George C Newberry, of New Smyrna Beach, Florida; 1 da (Ryan McCabe b 10 Feb 1974), 1 s (Rowland William b 1979); *Heir* s, Rowland Murray; *Career* memb Bd of Tstees Marist Sch Atlanta Georgia; *Clubs* Brookwood Midtown Atlanta Rotary, Ansley Golf; *Style*— Sir Rowland Murray, Bt

MURRAY, Simon Anthony; s of Dr Frank Murray (d 1962), and Rosemary de Meza, *née* Williams (d 1997); *b* 31 August 1951; *Educ* St Andrews HS Malawi, Hampton GS, Welbeck Coll, Imperial Coll London (Unwin Medal); *m* 1983 (m dis 2004), Lindsay; 3 c (Maxim b 1986, Jenevora b 1988, Calum b 1992); *Career* dir Ove Arup & Partners 1990–94, md gp technical services BAA plc 1994–98, dir major projects and investment Railtrack plc 1998–2001, conslt 2001–; non-exec dir: Ascot Authy (Holdings) Ltd 2000–06, Manchester Airport Developments Ltd 2002–04; chm: Construction Round Table 1997, Geoffrey Osbourne Ltd 2003–; memb EPSRC, FCGI 1999, FICE 2001 (MICE 1978); *Recreations* reading, windsurfing, keeping fit; *Style*— Simon Murray, Esq; ✉ 150 Langton Way, London SE3 7JS (tel 020 8858 2235, mobile 07904 103956, e-mail samurray1951@aol.com)

MURRAY, Susan E; *b* 16 January 1957; *m*; 1 step da; *Career* Marshall Sellers 1976–78, Butler Dennis & Garland 1978–79, mktg trainee Colgate Palmolive UK Ltd 1979–82, md (Desserts) General Foods (UK) Ltd 1987–89 (various product and mktg mangr positions 1982–87), dir of mktg Duracell 1989–92, dir Int Marketing IDV Ltd 1992–95, pres and ceo Pierre Smirnoff Co Ltd 1995–98, sales and mktg dir then chief exec Littlewoods Stores Ltd 1998–2004; non-exec dir: Enterprise Inns 2004–, Imperial Tobacco Gp 2004–, SSL International 2005–; dir and memb Cncl Advtg Standards Authy; memb: Women in Advertising and Communications, Forum UK; FRSA; *Recreations* walking, music, theatre; *Style*— Mrs Susan Murray

MURRAY, Thomas Kenneth (Tom); WS (1982); s of Charles Murray, of Edinburgh, and Audrey, *née* Haddon; *b* 25 June 1958; *Educ* Sedbergh, Univ of Dundee (LLB); *m* 12 Sept 1986, Sophie, da of Alexander Mackenzie; 3 da (Millie b 21 Sept 1989, Katie b 20 March 1991, Flora b 30 Dec 1993); *Career* slr; ptnr Gillespie Macandrew 1983–; chm Br Hallmarking Cncl 2004– (memb 1991–); memb Investor Protection Ctee and Practising Cert Ctee Law Soc of Scotland; chm Trefoil House 2002–; memb Kyle of Sutherland Dist Fishery Bd; Purse Bearer to Lord High Cmmr to Gen Assembly Church of Scotland 2003–, memb Queen's Body Guard for Scotland (Royal Co of Archers), clerk Incorporation of Goldsmiths City of Edinburgh; *Recreations* fishing, golf; *Clubs* New (Edinburgh), Hon Co of Edinburgh Golfers; *Style*— Tom Murray, Esq, WS; ✉ Gillespie Macandrew LLP, 5 Atholl Cresent, Edinburgh EH3 8EJ (tel 0131 225 1677, fax 0131 225 4519, e-mail tom.murray@gillespiemacandrew.co.uk)

MURRAY-LEACH, Roger; s of Robert Murray-Leach (d 1949), of Salop, and Mary Barbara, *née* Caisley (d 1986); *b* 25 June 1943; *Educ* Aldenham, AA Sch of Architecture; *m* 1, 1 June 1968 (m dis), Sandra Elizabeth, da of John Tallent, of Hereford; 1 da (Tamsin b 13 April 1972), 1 s (Robert b 17 Feb 1978), 1 adopted s (Jon James (JJ) b 20 April 1974); m 2, 2 Sept 1995, Dale Mackenzie, da of Tom Tillotson (d 1998), of Oxon; *Career* production designer and interior designer; films incl: Local Hero 1983, Defence of the Realm 1986, A Fish Called Wanda 1988, Fierce Creatures 1996; dir Fishworks plc 2000–04; Freeman: City of London 1969, Worshipful Co of Haberdashers 1970; *Recreations* riding, skiing; *Style*— Roger Murray-Leach, Esq; ✉ e-mail roger@rm-l.com

MURRAY-LESLIE, Dr Christian Francis Victor; s of Francis Murray-Leslie, of Boxnoor, Herts, and Nancy Joan, *née* Brenthall (d 1947); *b* 12 July 1944; *Educ* Hemel Hempstead GS, Middlesex Hosp Med Sch (MB BS); *m* 7 June 1972, Margaret Ann, da of Arthur Charles Harmer, of Hartshorne, Derbys; 2 s (Nicholas John b 1972, Robin Charles b 1974), 1 da (Catherine Arbella b 1980); *Career* registrar in med 1971–72, registrar in med and cardiology 1972–73, lectr and res asst 1973–74, sr registrar in rheumatology and rehabilitation Univ of Leeds 1974–77, conslt in rheumatology and rehabilitation med Derbyshire Royal Infirmary 1977, conslt i/c Nat Demonstration Centre in Rehabilitation Derby 1980, clinical dir Orthotics and Disability Res Centre Derby 1980, visiting prof Loughborough Univ 1988; dir Derby Disabled Driving Centre, past chm Assoc of Driver Educn of People With Disabilities; memb: BMA, Br Soc Rehabilitation Med (hon sec), Soc for Res in Rehabilitation; *Books* Recent Advances in Rheumatology (contrib); author of papers on driving for disabled people; *Recreations* walking, birdwatching, gardening, music; *Style*— Dr Christian Murray-Leslie; ✉ Derbyshire Royal Infirmary, London Road, Derby DE1 2QY (tel 01332 347141)

MURRAY-LYON, Dr Iain Malcolm; s of Ranald Malcolm Murray-Lyon (d 1970), of Edinburgh, and Jennipher, *née* Dryburgh (d 2003); *b* 28 August 1940; *Educ* Loretto, Univ of Edinburgh (BSc, MB ChB, MD); *m* 7 Nov 1981, Teresa Elvira, da of Antonio Gonzalez Montero, of Buenos Aires; 1 da (Caroline Claire b 1982), 1 s (Andrew Malcolm b 1984); *Career* hon sr lectr Liver Unit KCH 1972–74; conslt physician and gastroenterologist: Charing Cross Hosp 1974–2002, Chelsea Westminster Hosp 1993–; hon conslt physician: Hosp of St John & St Elizabeth 1976–2003, King Edward VII Hosp for Offrs 1990–; author of over 150 pubns in the areas of liver disease and gastroenterology; former: censor Royal Coll of Physicians, chm Liver Section Br Soc of Gastroenterology, sec Br Assoc for Study of the Liver (memb); Liveryman Worshipful Soc of Apothecaries; FRCP 1980, FRCPE 1980; *Recreations* golf, skiing, tennis; *Clubs* Brooks's, Hurlingham; *Style*— Dr Iain Murray-Lyon; ✉ 12 St James's Gardens, London W11 4RD (tel 020 7602 1806); 149 Harley Street, London W1G 6DE (tel 020 7935 6747/4444, fax 020 7935 7017, e-mail i.m-lyon@lonclin.co.uk)

MURRAY OF BLACKBARONY, Sir Nigel Andrew Digby; 15 Bt (NS 1628), of Blackbarony, Peeblesshire; s of Sir Alan John Digby Murray of Blackbarony, 14 Bt (d 1978), and Mabel Elisabeth, *née* Schiele; *b* 15 August 1944; *Educ* St Paul's Sch Argentina, Salesian Agric Tech Sch, RAC Cirencester; *m* 1980, Diana Margaret, da of Robert Campbell Bray; 1 s (Alexander Nigel Robert b 1981), 2 da (Rachel Elisabeth Vanda Digby b 1982, Evelyn Caroline Digby b 1987); *Heir* s, Alexander Murray; *Career* farms own land (crops, dairy, bees); private pilot's licence from Midland Sch of Flying at Castle Donnington; landowner; *Recreations* tennis, golf, rowing, camping, mountain walking, fishing; *Style*— Sir Nigel Murray of Blackbarony, Bt; ✉ Establecimiento Tinamú, CC 115, 2624 Arias, Provincia de Córdoba, Argentina (tel 00 54 0468 40031)

MURRAY OF OCHTERTYRE, Sir Patrick Ian Keith; 12 Bt (NS 1673), of Ochtertyre, Perthshire; s of Sir William Patrick Keith Murray of Ochtertyre, 11 Bt (d 1977), and Susan Elizabeth Hudson, *née* Jones; *b* 22 March 1965; *Educ* Christ Coll Brecon, LAMDA; *Heir* kinsman, Maj Peter Keith-Murray; *Style*— Sir Patrick Murray of Ochtertyre, Bt

MURRAY-PHILIPSON, Robin Hylton; OBE (2002), DL (Leics 1994); s of Hylton Ralph Murray-Philipson, MP (d 1934), and Monica Lloyd, *née* Beasley-Robinson (d 1994); *b* 5 June 1927; *Educ* Eton; *m* Oct 1954, Catherine Cornelia (Nini), da of late Brig Robert Tilney, CBE, DSO, TD, DL; 3 da (Cornelia b 1955, Suzie b 1961, Kate b 1963), 1 s (Hylton b 1959); *Career* Lt Grenadier Guards 1945–48; owner: Executive Travel Ltd 1957–75, Executive Helicopters Ltd 1960–64; dir: Helicopter Sales Ltd 1960–70, Trans World Helicopters Ltd 1967–72; md Serenissima Travel Ltd 1973–86; pt/t Marie Curie Cancer Care 1986–94 (patron Marie Curie Cancer Care Leics 1994–98); jt rep National Art Collections Fund (Leics and Rutland) 1986–99; memb Ctee Leics Clubs for Young People 1995–; memb Ctee National Crimebeat 1997–, memb Ctee Leics Crimestoppers 1996–, fndr and chm Leics and Rutland Crimebeat Ltd; High Sheriff Leics 1993–94; *Recreations* shooting, tennis, travel; *Clubs* White's; *Style*— Robin Murray-Philipson, Esq, OBE, DL; ✉ The Garden House, Blaston, Market Harborough, Leicestershire LE16 8DE (tel 01858 555233, fax 01858 555724); 31 Astell Street, London SW3 3RT (tel 020 7352 1250)

MURRAY-SMITH, Prof David James; *b* 20 October 1941; *Educ* Aberdeen GS, Univ of Aberdeen (BSc Eng, MSc), Univ of Glasgow (PhD); *m* Effie, *née* Macphail; 2 s (Roderick William b 1969, Gordon David b 1972); *Career* engr Inertial Systems Dept Ferranti UK Edinburgh 1964–65; Univ of Glasgow: asst 1965–67, lectr 1967–77, sr lectr 1977–83, reader 1983–85, prof of engrg systems and control Dept of Electronics and Electrical Engrg 1985–2005, dean Faculty of Engrg 1997–2001, prof emeritus 2005–; MInstMC, FIEE; *Publications* Continuous System Stimulation (1995); over 100 jl and conference papers; *Style*— Prof David Murray-Smith; ✉ Department of Electronics and Electrical Engineering, University of Glasgow, Rankine Building, Glasgow G12 8LT (tel 0141 330 5222, fax 0141 330 6004, e-mail d.murray-smith@elec.gla.ac.uk)

MURRELL, David Brian; s of William Percy John Murrell (d 1988), of Minehead, Somerset, and Muriel Mary Elizabeth, *née* Stevens (d 1988); *b* 7 February 1946; *Educ* Taunton Sch; *m* 29 Nov 1969, Sheila Mary, da of Lt Alured Francis Fairlie-Clarke (d 1984), of Norton Fitzwarren, Somerset; 1 s (Alan b 1970), 2 da (Deborah b 1972, Julia b 1974); *Career* qualified as CA with Amherst and Shapland of Minehead 1967; KPMG: joined 1968, ptnr 1981–99, head of UK and global media and entertainment industry practice 1984–99, chm UK and Euro info communications and entertainment practice 1994–97, chm UK and global mktg 1995–97, chm UK alumni programme 1993–99; dir Renscombe Properties Ltd 2000–, sr ind dir Chrysalis Gp plc 2003– (non-exec dir 2000–03); sr ptnr: Target Films 2000–03, Jasper Films 2001–; chm City Boardroom and City Golf Bar 2000–06, chm Casa Catalina Bar and Restaurant 2007–; barker Variety Club, pres Cinema and TV Benevolent Fund 2007– (dir 2003–07); memb: BAFTA, RTS, Mktg Soc; FCA 1978 (ACA 1968), fell Radio Acad; *Publications* author of numerous articles on finance and tax in leading media and entertainment industry trade magazines; *Recreations* golf, photography, classic car trials, racehorse owning; *Clubs* West Hill Golf, Old Tauntonians London Golfing Soc (chm), Wooden Spoon Soc, Soho House, Motor Cycling; *Style*— David Murrell, Esq; ✉ Casa Catalina Bar and Restaurant, 8 Bride Court, London EC4Y 3DU (tel 020 7353 6431, fax 01932 858815)

MURRELL, Prof John; MBE (2004); s of George Henry Murrell, and Anne, *née* Rock; *b* 12 December 1933; *Educ* Lawrence Sheriff Sch Rugby, Coll of St Mark and St John London (CertEd), Birkbeck Coll London (BA), Chelsea Coll London (MEd); *m* 14 May 1960, Anne Amy Helen, *née* Prees; 1 s (Richard Anthony), 1 da (Laura Helen); *Career* Nat Serv RAF 1952–54, VRT RAF 1960–67; mathematics teacher 1958–68; Homerton Coll Cambridge: lectr 1968, sr lectr 1970, princ lectr 1975, dir of postgrad studies 1976, George Peabody prof of educn and human devpt (jtly with George Peabody Coll) 1992–2001 (emeritus 2001–), postgrad tutor 2001–04, sometime sec to Coll Cncl; Faculty of Educn Univ of Cambridge: memb Faculty Bd, memb Degree Ctee Faculty Bd, examiner in educational theory, teaching practice and res methods; George Peabody Coll Nashville USA: visiting scholar 1984, visiting lectr summer sch 1986, scholar in residence 1990; trg conslt Judicial Studies Bd and Lord Chllr's Dept 1994–, conslt Advsy Cncl Industrial Soc 2020 Vision Project 1996–98, conslt Local Advsy Ctee BBC 1996–2000, trg conslt GMC 1997–2000; designed and taught courses on trg and educn, delivered numerous guest lectures; former chm Cambridge and Huntingdon Nurse Educn Ctee, former memb Working Parties of the Lord Chancellor's Office, former memb Educn Ctee School of Physiotherapy Addenbrooke's Hosp Cambridge; memb Regnl Cncl Duke of Edinburgh's Award 1992–2003, memb Working Pty of the Lord Chllr's Office on Equality in the Lay Magistracy and the Gen Cmmrs of Income Tax 2000–; *Publications* Nurse Training: An Enterprise in Curriculum Development at St Thomas' Hospital London (with Hazel O Allen, 1978), Handbook for the Training of Magistrates (jtly, 1989), Tribunals Training Handbook (2005); numerous essays, articles and research papers published in learned jls; *Recreations* golf, fly fishing, Anglo-American history; *Clubs* RAF, Royal

Commonwealth Soc, Gog Magog Golf; *Style—* Prof John Murrell, MBE; ✉ tel 01223 354042, e-mail jm150@hermes.cam.ac.uk

MURRISON, Dr Andrew William; MP; s of late William Murrison, RD, and Marion, *née* Horn; *Educ* Harwich County HS, The Harwich Sch, Univ of Bristol (MB ChB, MD), Univ of Cambridge (DPH); *Career* MO (Surgeon Cdr) RN 1981–2000 (recalled 2003), former princ MO HM Naval Base Portsmouth, conslt occupational physician 1996–99, locum conslt occupational physician Glos Royal Hosp 2000–01; MP (Cons) Westbury 2001–, shadow health min 2003–; Gilbert Blane Medal 1996; hon research registrar Southampton Gen Hosp 1990–93; memb Faculty of Occupational Med RCP 1996 (assoc 1993); *Publications* various biomedical pubns; *Recreations* sailing, skiing; *Style—* Dr Andrew Murrison, MP; ✉ House of Commons, London SW1A 0AA; Constituency Office, Lovemead House, Roundstone Street, Trowbridge BA14 8DG (tel 01225 358584)

MURSELL, Rt Rev (Alfred) Gordon; *see:* Stafford, Bishop of

MURTON, HE Dr John Evan; s of Anthony Stewart Murton, of Cowbridge, Vale of Glamorgan, and Marion Elizabeth, *née* Heale; *b* 18 March 1972, Aldershot, Hants; *Educ* Cowbridge Comp Sch, Sidney Sussex Coll Cambridge (scholar (twice), MA), Darwin Coll Cambridge (PhD, Audrey Richards UK African Studies Assoc Prize), Univ of Nairobi; *m* 19 Dec 1998, Sarah Elizabeth, *née* Harvey; 2 s (Theodore Harvey b 28 Nov 2002, Raphael Dominic b 28 Nov 2006), 1 da (Annabella Grace b 14 Oct 2004); *Career* diplomat; teacher Kawondera Secdy Sch Zimbabwe 1990–91, UN Dept FCO 1997–98, Japanese language trg FCO 1998–2000, second sec then first sec Br Embassy Tokyo 2000–04, dep dir Sec Gen's Private Office NATO Brussels 2004–07, high cmmr to Republic of Mauritius 2007– (concurrently non-resident ambass to Madagascar and Comoros) 2007–; *Recreations* hiking, skiing, cooking; *Style—* HE Dr John Murton; ✉ British High Commission, Les Cascades Building, Edith Cavell Street, Port Louis, Mauritius (tel 00 230 202 9400, e-mail john.murton@fco.gov.uk)

MURTON OF LINDISFARNE, Baron (Life Peer UK 1979), of Hexham in the County of Northumberland; (Henry) Oscar Murton; OBE (1946), TD (1947, clasp 1951), PC (1976), JP (Poole 1963); o s of late Henry Edgar Crossley Murton, of Hexham, Northumberland; *b* 8 May 1914; *Educ* Uppingham; *m* 1, 1939, Constance (d 1977), da of late Fergus O'Loughlin Connell, of Low Fell, Co Durham; 1 s (Hon (Henry) Peter John Connell b 1941), 1 da (Hon Melanie Frances Isobel Connell (Hon Mrs Vickery) b 1946 d 1986); m 2, 1979, Pauline Teresa, yst da of late Thomas Keenan, JP, of Johannesburg, South Africa; *Career* serv Royal Northumberland Fus (TA) 1934–50, Staff Coll Camberley 1939, Lt-Col Gen Staff 1942–46; md Dept Stores NE England 1949–57; MP (Cons) Poole 1964–79, asst govt whip 1971–72, lord cmmr Treasy 1972–73, dep chm Ways and Means 1973–76 (chm and dep speaker 1976–79), dep chm of Ctees House of Lords 1981–2004, dep speaker 1983–2004; *Recreations* sailing, painting; *Style—* The Rt Hon the Lord Murton of Lindisfarne, OBE, TD, PC; ✉ 49 Carlisle Mansions, Carlisle Place, London SW1P 1HY (tel 020 7834 8226)

MUSCATELLI, Prof Vito Antonio (Anton); s of Ambrogio Muscatelli, of London, and Rosellina, *née* Defonte; *b* 1 January 1962, Bari, Italy; *Educ* HS of Glasgow, Univ of Glasgow (MA, PhD, Logan Prize); *m* 1986, Elaine, *née* Flood; 1 da (Anna Rosa b 1990), 1 s (Ambrogio Roberto b 1999); *Career* Univ of Glasgow: lectr 1984–80, sr lectr 1990–92, prof of economics 1992–94, Daniel Jack prof of economics 1994–, dean Faculty of Social Sciences 2000–04, vice-princ (strategy and budgeting then strategy and advancement) 2004–; research fell CES-info Research Inst Munich 1999–; visiting prof: Univ of Parma 1989, Catholic Univ Milan 1991 and 1997–98, Univ of Bari 1995–2004, Univ of Pavia 1997–98, Tel-Aviv Univ 2001, Univ of Brescia 2003–04; princ and vice-chllr Heriot-Watt Univ 2007–; memb: Advsy Panel of Economic Conslts to Sec of State for Scotland 1998–2000, Economics and Econometrics Panel HEFCE Research Assessment Exercise 2001, Cncl Royal Economic Soc 2002–, Research Grants Bd ESRC 2002–; ed Scottish Jl of Political Economy 1990–2003; memb Bd of Govrs HS of Glasgow 2000–, dir GU Hldgs 2004–; FRSA 1995, FRSE 2003, AcSS 2004; *Books* Macroeconomic Theory and Stabilisation Policy (jtly, 1988), Economic and Political Institutions in Economic Policy (ed, 1996), Fiscal Policies, Monetary Policies and Labour Markets: Key Aspects of European Macroeconomic Policies after Monetary Unification (jt ed, 2003); *Recreations* football, music, literature; *Style—* Prof Anton Muscatelli; ✉ Heriot-Watt University, Edinburgh EH14 4AS (tel 0131 451 3360, fax 0131 451 3330, e-mail a.muscatelli@hw.ac.uk)

MUSGRAVE, Sir Christopher Patrick Charles; 15 Bt (E 1611), of Hartley Castle, Westmorland; s of Sir Charles Musgrave, 14 Bt (d 1970), and Olive Louise Avril, *née* Cringle; *b* 14 April 1949; *m* 1, 1978 (m dis 1992); 2 da (Helena b 1981, Antonia b 1987); m 2, 1995, Carol, da of Geoffrey Lawson, of Chandler's Ford, Hants; *Heir* bro, Julian Musgrave; *Recreations* drawing, painting, model making, gardening, animals; *Style—* Sir Christopher Musgrave, Bt; ✉ Barn Farm, Bunns Lane, Hambledon, Hampshire PO7 4QH

MUSGRAVE, Mark Jonathan; s of Sir (Frank) Cyril Musgrave, KCB (d 1986), of Flixton, Suffolk, and Jean Elsie, *née* Soulsby (d 1993); *b* 6 October 1952; *Educ* Haileybury; *m* 1 Sept 1979, Belinda Joan, da of John Hugh Clerk (d 1976), of Kingston, Jamaica; 2 s (William b 1984, George b 1988), 1 da (Chloe b 1987); *Career* admitted slr 1977; Speechly Bircham: ptnr 1981–, personnel ptnr 1988–91, dep managing ptnr 1989–90, fin ptnr 1992–95, managing ptnr 1995–98; dir Devoran Trustees Ltd 1991–; memb: Law Soc 1977, Justinians 1989–2001, New England Co 1993–2001; tstee and treas Nat Hosp Devpt Fndn 1999–; *Recreations* sport, gardening, travel; *Style—* Mark Musgrave, Esq; ✉ Pitchards House, Halstead, Essex CO9 1JH (tel 01787 472393); Speechly Bircham, 6 St Andrew Street, London EC4A 3LX (tel 020 7427 6400)

MUSGRAVE, Thea (Mrs Peter Mark); CBE (2002); da of James P Musgrave (d 1971), of Edinburgh, and Joan, *née* Hacking (d 1997); *b* 27 May 1928; *Educ* Moreton Hall Oswestry, Univ of Edinburgh (MusB), private study in Paris with Nadia Boulanger; *m* 2 Oct 1971, Peter Mark, s of Irving Mark (d 1987), of Sarasota, Florida; *Career* composer; active as conductor of own work; performances at festivals: Edinburgh, Warsaw, Aldeburgh, Cheltenham, Zagreb, Florence Maggio Musicale, Venice Biennale; numerous broadcastings and recordings; distinguished prof Queen's Coll City Univ NY; hon fell New Hall Cambridge 1973; Hon Doctorates: Cncl Nat Academic Awards 1976, Smith Coll USA 1979, Old Dominion Univ Norfolk Virginia 1980, Univ of Glasgow 1995; *Orchestral works* incl: Beauty and the Beast (ballet) 1968–69, Concerto for Clarinet and Orchestra (cmmnd Royal Philharmonic Soc in assoc with Calouste Gulbenkian Fndn) 1968, Horn Concerto 1971, Viola Concerto (cmmnd BBC) 1973, Peripeteia (cmmnd RPO) 1981, The Seasons (cmmnd Acad of St Martin's in the Fields) 1988, Song of the Enchanter (cmmnd Helsinki Philharmonic) 1990, Autumn Sonata (cmmnd Victoria Soames) 1993, Journey Through a Japanese Landscape (cmmnd Br Assoc of Symphonic Bands and Wind Ensembles and Consortium of Music Colleges) 1993–94, Helios (cmmnd St Magnus Festival) 1994, Phoenix Rising (cmmnd BBC) 1997; *Chamber and instrumental works* incl: Chamber Concerto No 1 1962, Chamber Concerto No 2 1966, Chamber Concerto No 3 1966, Space Play (cmmnd Serge Koussevitzky Music Fndn) 1974, Pierrot 1985, Wind Quintet (cmmnd Barlow Endowment for music composition) 1992, Postcards from Spain (cmmd Sam Dorsey & Tidewater Classical Guitar Soc) 1995, Lamenting With Ariadne 2001; *Vocal and choral music* incl: Rorate Coeli 1973, For the Time Being: Advent 1986, Midnight (cmmnd Laura Lane & Nova Singers) 1992, Wild Winter (cmmnd Lichfield Festival) 1993, On the Underground Set No 1: On Gratitude, Love & Madness (cmmnd Canzonetta) 1994, On the Underground Set No 2: The Strange and the Exotic (cmmnd Ithaca Coll) 1994, On the Underground Set No 3: A Medieval Summer (cmmnd Ionian Singers) 1995; *Operas* incl: The Voice of Ariadne (cmmnd Royal Opera House) 1973, Mary Queen of Scots (cmmnd Scottish Opera) 1975–77, A Christmas Carol (cmmnd Virginia Opera Assoc) 1978–79, Harriet, An Occurrence at Owl Creek Bridge (cmmnd BBC) 1981, Harriet The Woman Called Moses (cmmnd jtly Royal Opera House and Virginia Opera Assoc) 1984, Simón Bolívar (cmmnd Los Angeles Music Center and Scottish Opera) 1989–92, Pontalba: A Louisianna Legacy (New Orleans Opera) 2003; *Style—* Miss Thea Musgrave, CBE; ✉ c/o Novello & Co Ltd, 8–9 Frith Street, London W1V

MUSGROVE, Harold John; s of Harold John Musgrove (d 1984), and Francis, *née* Clements (d 1983); *b* 19 November 1930; *Educ* King Edward GS Birmingham, Birmingham Tech Coll; *m* 1959, Jacqueline; 2 s (Michael b 1963, James b 1972), 2 da (Sarah b 1969, Laura b 1970); *Career* cmmnd navigator RAF 1954; various positions Austin Motor Co 1954–63, memb sr mgmnt Truck and Bus Gp Leyland Motor Corp 1963–78; Austin Morris Ltd: dir of mfrg 1978–79, md 1979–80, chm and md 1980–81, chm Light Medium Cars Gp 1981–82; chm and chief exec Austin Rover Group 1982–86, chm Power Supplies and Lighting Gp Chloride plc 1991–92 (chm Industrial Battery Sector 1988–91); dir: Chloride plc 1989–92, Metalrax Gp 1987–2003; chm: W Midland Ambulance Tst 1992–94, Birmingham Heartlands & Solihull Hosp NHS Tst 1994–99, Worcs Acute Hosp NHS Tst 1999–2002; pres: Birmingham C of C 1987–88, Aston Villa FC 1986–96; Midlander of the Year Award 1980, Instn of Prodn Engrs Int Award 1981, The Soc of Engrs Churchill Medal 1982; Dr (hc) Univ of Birmingham 2000; FIMI 1985; *Recreations* golf, soccer; *Style—* Harold John Musgrove, Esq; ✉ The Lodge, Laverton, Broadway, Worcestershire WR12 7NA

MUSHIN, Alan Spencer; s of Dr Louis Mushin (d 1984); *b* 31 January 1938; *Educ* Haberdashers' Aske's, London Hosp Med Coll (MB BS); *m* 27 Feb 1972, Joan Carolyn, da of Dr Simon Behrman, of London; 1 da (Rosalind b 1974), 1 s (James b 1976); *Career* conslt ophthalmic surgn: Moorfield Eye Hosp London, Royal London Hosp and Queen Elizabeth Hosp for Children; sec European Paediatric Ophthalmology Soc; Freeman City of London; fell American Acad of Ophthalmology; FRSM, FRCS, FRCOphth, FRCPCH; *Publications* papers on paediatric ophthalmology; *Recreations* photography, philately, gardening; *Clubs* Savage; *Style—* Alan S Mushin, Esq; ✉ 935 Finchley Road, London NW11 7PE (tel 020 8455 7212); 82 Harley Street, London W1N 1AE (tel 020 7580 3116, fax 020 7580 6998, e-mail almushin@hotmail.com)

MUSKERRY, 9 Baron (I 1781); Sir Robert Fitzmaurice Deane; 14 Bt (I 1710); s of 8 Baron Muskerry (d 14 Oct 1988), and Betty Fairbridge, *née* Palmer (d 20 Aug 1988); *b* 26 March 1948; *Educ* Sandford Park Sch Dublin, Trinity Coll Dublin (BA, BAI); *m* 1975, Rita Brink, of Pietermaritzburg, South Africa; 2 da (Hon Nicola b 1976, Hon Catherine b 1978), 1 s (Hon Jonathan Fitzmaurice b 1986); *Heir* s, Hon Jonathan Deane; *Career* shipyard mangr Dorbyl Marine, dir Dorbyl Marine Ltd; md: Stride Ltd, Bridco Ltd; currently md Elgin Brown and Hamer (Pty) Ltd; *Style—* The Rt Hon Lord Muskerry; ✉ 725 Ridge Road, Berea, Durban 4001, South Africa (e-mail rfd@iafrica.com)

MUSTERS, Patrick Havelock Auchmuty; s of Patrick Thorvald Auchmuty Musters, DFC, RA (d 2003), of Rutland, and Nancy Stella, *née* Havelock-Allan; *b* 20 July 1952, Kuala Lumpur, Malaya; *Educ* Allhallows Sch Lyme Regis, Univ of London; *m* 1991 (m dis 1996), Lavinia Stephanie, *née* Moore; *Career* admitted slr 1977, appointed Higher Court advocate 1994; fndr Twitchen & Musters (now BTMK LLP) 1981–; memb: Law Soc, Br Acad of Forensic Sciences, London Criminal Courts Slrs Assoc; *Publications* Law Soc's Handbook on Road Traffic Offences; *Recreations* golf, rugby, other people's fine wine; *Clubs* Thorpe Hall Golf, Royal Cinque Ports Golf; *Style—* Patrick Musters, Esq; ✉ BTMK LLP, County Chambers, 25–27 Weston Road, Southend-on-Sea, Essex SS1 1BB (tel 01702 339222, fax 01702 331563, e-mail patrick.musters@btmk.co.uk)

MUSTILL, Baron (Life Peer UK 1992), of Pateley Bridge in the County of North Yorkshire; Sir Michael John Mustill; kt (1978), PC (1985); s of Clement William Mustill; *b* 10 May 1931; *Educ* Oundle, St John's Coll Cambridge; *m* 1, 1960 (m dis 1983), Beryl Reid Davies; 2 c; m 2, Caroline Phillips; 1 step da; *Career* called to the Bar Gray's Inn 1955, QC 1968, recorder of the Crown Court 1972–78, judge High Court of Justice (Queen's Bench Div) 1978–85, a Lord Justice of Appeal 1985–91, a Lord of Appeal in Ordinary 1991–97; chm Civil Serv Appeal Tbnl 1971–78; dir City Disputes Panel 1998–; Liveryman Worshipful Co of Grocers; FBA 1996; *Style—* The Rt Hon Lord Mustill, FBA; ✉ House of Lords, London SW1A 0PW

MUSTOE, Nicholas (Nick); s of Raymond Mustoe, of Claygate, Surrey, and Maureen, *née* Pringle; *b* 7 July 1961; *Educ* Wimbledon Coll, Esher Coll, Coll of Distributive Trades; *Career* fndr Mustoe Merriman Herring Levy Ltd (now Mustoes) 1993–; *Recreations* sport, horseracing, cars; *Style—* Nick Mustoe, Esq; ✉ Mustoes, 2–4 Bucknall Street, London WC2H 8LA (tel 020 7379 9999, fax 020 7379 8487)

MUSTON, (Frederick Charles) Lee; s of Howard Alfred Paul Muston, and Rose Amelia Muston, of Chaddesden, Derby; *b* 13 September 1943; *Educ* Bemrose GS, Bishop Lonsdale Coll, Open Univ (BA, CertEd); *m* 20 Aug 1966, Irene Mary, *née* Barker; 1 s (Nicholas John b 17 Oct 1971), 1 da (Jena Victoria b 20 Dec 1973); *Career* asst teacher Darwin Co Secdy Sch Breadsall Derby 1965–67, head Liberal Studies Dept Spondon House Sch Derby 1967–70, head Humanities Dept Cranbourne Sch Basingstoke 1970–74, dep headmaster Larkmead Sch Abingdon 1974–80, headteacher Middleton Park HS Leeds 1980–84, headteacher Fakenham HS 1984–2001, chair N Norfolk PCT 2002–; *Recreations* rugby, cricket, poetry, cooking; *Style—* Lee Muston, Esq; ✉ Kelling Hospital, High Kelling, Norfolk (tel 01263 710611)

MUTTRAM, Roderick Ian; s of Wilfred Reginald Muttram DSC RN (d 1977), and Dorothy May, *née* Best (d 1977); *b* 15 January 1952; *Educ* St Bartholomew's GS Newbury, Abingdon Coll of Technol (ONC), Reading Tech Coll (HNC), Victoria Univ of Manchester (BSc), Manchester Poly (DMS); *m* 10 Aug 1974, Jane Elisabeth, *née* Sinkinson; 4 da (Claire Sarah-Jane b 10 Dec 1985, Jennifer Karen-Anne b 20 April 1988, Rebecca Helen-Louise b 22 Feb 1990, Caroline Laura-Elisabeth b 16 July 1992); *Career* asst scientific offr UK AEA 1969–76, dep chief engr Chloride Lorival Ltd 1978–80 (project engr 1976–78); Ferranti Instrumentation Ltd: asst project engr design 1980–82, gp ldr electronic design 1982, asst chief engr 1982–83, chief engr 1983–86, gen mangr Weapons Equipment Div 1986–89, dir gp engrg and quality 1989–90; dir and gen mangr Defence Systems Div Thorn EMI Electronics Ltd 1990–93, dir safety and standards Railtrack plc 1997–2000 (dir electrical engrg and control systems 1994–97), chief exec Railway Safety 2000–03, dir AEIF 2001–03 and 2004–06, ind engrg and safety conslt 2003; Bombadier Transportation (UK) Ltd: vice-pres technol, rail controls and communications networks and railway standards and regulations 2003–04, vice-pres project mgmnt and ops improvement 2004–07, vice-pres quality and safety 2007–; chm Supervisory Bd European Rail Research Inst Dutch Research Fndn, chm Bd Rail Industry Trg Cncl (RITC) Ltd 2001–03, vice-chm European Rail Research Advsy Cncl (ERRAC) 2004; Liveryman Worshipful Co of Engrs 2005 (Freeman 2004); CEng, MIMgt 1980, MInstD 1994, FIET (FIEE 1994), FIRSE 1995, MCIT 1998, FREng 2002; *Recreations* rifle shooting, DIY, vehicle restoration; *Style—* Roderick I Muttram, Esq, FREng; ✉ The Cottage, The Street, Ewhurst, Cranleigh, Surrey GU6 7QA (tel 01483 277218, fax 01483 277218, mobile 07860 340123, e-mail rmuttram@aol.com); Bombadier Transportation (UK) Ltd, St Giles House, 10 Church Street, Reading, Berkshire RG1 2SD (tel 0118 953 8043, fax 0118 953 8483, mobile 07919 305076, e-mail rod.muttram@uk.transport.bombadier.com)

MUTTUKUMARU, Christopher; CB (2006); s of late Maj-Gen Anton Muttukumaru, OBE, ADC, of Canberra, and Margaret Vasanthi, *née* Ratnarajah; *b* 11 December 1951; *Educ* Xavier Coll Melbourne, Jesus Coll Oxford (MA); *m* 15 May 1976, Ann Elisabeth, da of Dr and Mrs John Tutton; 2 s (Timothy b 27 June 1982, Nicholas 25 March 1984); *Career* called to the Bar Gray's Inn 1974, practised at the Bar 1976–83; Treasy Slrs Dept (TSD) 1983–88, law officers' dept 1988–91, head of employment litigation section TSD 1991–92, sec to Sir Richard Scott's Inquiry into exports of defence and defence related equipment to Iraq 1992–96, dep legal advsr Min of Defence TSD 1996–98, memb UK delegation to diplomatic conf on establishment of the International Criminal Ct, legal advsr to DCMS TSD 1998–99, dir Legal (Commercial, Environment, Housing and Local Govt) DETR 1999–2001, dir Legal (Tport) DTLR 2001–02, legal advsr and legal services dir Legal DfT 2002–; memb Editorial Advsy Bd Nottingham Law Jl; vice-chair Governing Body Eltham Coll London; *Publications* contrib to learned jls and books incl: The Quality of Fairness is not Constrained (1996), The International Criminal Court, The Making of the Rome Statute (1999); *Recreations* reading, 10000 maniacs, running, sunflowers, photography; *Style*— Christopher Muttukumaru, Esq, CB; ✉ DfT, Great Minster House, 76 Marsham Street, London SW1P 4DR (tel 020 7944 4770, fax 020 7944 2224, e-mail christopher.muttukumaru@dft.gsi.gov.uk)

MYDDELTON, Prof David Roderic; s of Dr Geoffrey Cheadle Myddelton, of Glutieres-sur-Ollon, Switzerland, and Jacqueline Esther, *née* Nathan; *b* 11 April 1940; *Educ* Eton, Harvard Business Sch (MBA); *m* 28 April 1986 (m dis 1998), Hatherley Angela d'Abo; 1 step da (Louisa b 1974), 1 step s (Charles b 1975); *Career* CA 1961; lectr fin and accounting Cranfield 1965–69, lectr accounting London Business Sch 1969–72, prof of fin and accounting Cranfield Sch of Mgmnt 1972–2005; tstee Inst of Economic Affrs (chm 2001–); ACIS 1966, FCA 1971; *Books* The Power to Destroy (1969, 2 edn 1994), The Meaning of Company Accounts (1971, 8 edn 2005), On A Cloth Untrue (1984), The Economy And Business Decisions (1984), Essential Management Accounting (1987, 2 edn 1992), Accounting and Financial Decisions (1991), The Essence of Financial Management (1994), Accountants without Standards? (1995), Managing Business Finance (2000), Unshackling Accountants (2004); *Recreations* crossword puzzles, jigsaw puzzles; *Style*— Prof D R Myddelton; ✉ 20 Nightingale Lodge, Admiral Walk, London W9 3TW (tel 020 7286 9945)

MYERS, Andrew; s of Gordon Elliot Myers, CMG, and Wendy Myers; *b* 1964; *Educ* Haberdashers' Aske's, UC Oxford; *m* 1993, Dr Kathryn Myers; *Career* slr Travers Smith Braithwaite 1991–2001, ptnr Howes Percival 2001–; Alfred Syrett Prize 1991; memb Law Soc 1993; memb Welwyn Hatfield Deanery Synod; *Style*— Andrew Myers, Esq; ✉ Howes Percival LLP, 252 Upper Third Street, Grafton Gate East, Central Milton Keynes MK9 1DZ (tel 01908 672682, fax 01908 247575, e-mail andrew.myers@howespercival.com)

MYERS, Bernard Ian; s of Edward Nathan Myers (d 1986), and Isabel Violet, *née* Viner (d 2000); *b* 2 April 1944; *Educ* Hendon Co GS, LSE (BSc Econ); *m* 17 Sept 1967, Sandra Hannah, da of Samuel Barc (d 1980); 2 da (Lara b 1969, Lyndsey b 1974), 1 s (Andrew b 1972); *Career* accountant 1962–72, merchant banker 1972–; directorships incl: Shield Tst Ltd 1976–96, N M Rothschild & Sons Ltd 1976–97 (md gp fin and overseas 1988–96), Rothschilds Continuation Holdings AG 1983–99, Rothschilds Continuation Ltd 1984–, Smith New Court plc 1985–95, Rothschild North America Inc 1987–99, Fairacre Property Holdings Ltd 1999–2004, Rothschild Group Companies (non-exec); chm: Lambert Fenchurch plc 1998–99, Rothschild Tst Co Ltd 1998–2005, Industrial Dwelling Soc (1885) Ltd 1997–, Enable Holidays Ltd 2005–; non-exec dir Moss Bross Group plc 2001–; FCA; *Recreations* opera, golf, theatre; *Style*— Bernard I Myers, Esq; ✉ Rothschilds Continuation Ltd, New Court, St Swithin's Lane, London EC4P 4DU (tel 020 7280 5031, fax 020 7283 4278, e-mail bernie.myers@rothschild.co.uk)

MYERS, Ian David; s of Stuart Charles Myers, of Oxshott, Surrey, and Enid, *née* Alexander; *b* 3 August 1956; *Educ* Latymer Upper Sch, Pembroke Coll Oxford (MA); *m* 1976, Helen Rosemary, *née* Bennett; 1 da (Anastasia Tiffany b 2 July 1979), 2 s (Nikolai James Elliot b 23 April 1982, Anatoly Cornelius Constantine Wreyland b 18 Dec 1987); *Career* White Weld & Co London 1977–78 (NY office 1976–77), dir PaineWebber Inc 1989–2000, chm PaineWebber International (UK) Ltd 1990–2000 (joined 1978, dir 1987), md UBS Warburg 2000–2003, md SG Cowen 2003–; *Style*— Ian Myers, Esq; ✉ Cowen International Limited, 11th Floor, 1 Snowden Street, London EC2A 2DQ

MYERS, Prof Norman; CMG (1998); s of John Myers (d 1963), of Whitewell, Lancs, and Gladys, *née* Haworth (d 1994); *b* 24 August 1934; *Educ* Clitheroe Royal GS, Keble Coll Oxford (MA), Univ of Calif Berkeley (PhD); *m* 11 Dec 1965, Dorothy Mary, da of Frank Halliman (d 1966), of Nairobi, Kenya; 2 da (Malindi b 3 Oct 1970, Mara b 13 Aug 1973); *Career* Nat Serv RA 1952–53 (invalided out); dist offr Overseas Admin Kenya 1958–60, teacher Delamere Boys' Sch Nairobi 1961–64, professional wildlife photographer and TV film-maker E Africa 1965–68, conslt in environment and devpt 1972–; res and projects in over 80 countries incl assignments for: World Bank, UN agencies, Nat Acad of US, OECD, EEC, World Cmmn Environment and Devpt; foreign assoc US Nat Acad of Scis, Pew scholar in conservation and environment, hon visiting fell Green Coll Oxford, external fell Saïd Business Sch Univ of Oxford, chm and visiting prof of int environment Univ of Utrecht, adjunct prof Duke Univ; visiting prof: Harvard Univ, Cornell Univ, Univ of Michigan, Univ of Texas, Stanford Univ, Univ of Kent, Univ of Cape Town; Hitchcock prof Univ of Calif Berkeley 1998; Regents lectr Univ of Calif; author over 300 papers in professional jls; memb Bd of Dirs of 16 orgns; fell: World Acad Arts and Sci 1988, American Assoc for the Advancement of Science 1990; ambass WWF (UK); hon degree Univ of Kent 2003; FRSA 1993, FLS 1993; *Awards* Gold medal and Order of Golden Ark World Wildlife Fund International, Gold medal of New York Zoological Soc, Global 500 Roll of Honour UN Environment Programme, Special Achievement award International Environment Protection Sierra Club US, Distinguished Achievement award Soc for Conservation Biology, Gold medal San Diego Zoological Soc, jt recipient Volvo Environment Prize 1992, UN Sasakawa Environment Prize 1995, Blue Planet Prize 2001; *Books* The Long African Day (1972), The Sinking Ark (1979), Conversion of Tropical Moist Forests (1980), A Wealth of Wild Species (1983), The Primary Source: Tropical Forests and Our Future (1984 and 1992), The Gaia Atlas of Planet Management (1986 and 1993), Future Worlds: Challenge and Opportunity in an Age of Change (1990), Population, Resources and the Environment: The Critical Challenges (1991), Tropical Forests and Climate (ed, 1992), Ultimate Security: The Environmental Basis of Political Stability (1993, 2 edn 1996), Scarcity or Abundance: A Debate on the Environment (with J L Simon, 1994), Environmental Exodus: An Emergent Crisis in the Global Arena (with J Kent, 1995), Perverse Subsidies: Tax $s Undercutting our Economies and Environments Alike (with J Kent, 1998 and 2001), The Gaian Corporation: A Greenprint for Business at the Millennium (Japanese edn, 1999), Biodiversity Hotspots (with R A and C R Mittermeier, 2000), The New Consumers: The Influence of Affluence on the Environment (with J Kent, 2004), The New Gaia Atlas of Planet Management (with J Kent, 2005); *Recreations* marathon running, professional photography, mountaineering; *Clubs* Achilles; *Style*— Prof Norman Myers, CMG; ✉ Upper Meadow, Douglas Downes Close, Headington, Oxford OX3 8FS (tel 01865 750387, fax 01865 741538, e-mail myers1n@aol.com)

MYERS, Sidney Albert; s of Gordon Myers, of London, and Leonora, *née* Wilson; *b* 21 May 1958, London; *Educ* St Paul's, Worcester Coll Oxford (BA); *m* 2 April 1995, Lorraine, *née* Viner; 1 da (Rosine Alex b 26 Nov 1996), 1 s (Samuel Edward b 1 July 1999); *Career* Allen & Overy LLP: articled clerk 1982–84, assoc 1984–90, ptnr 1991–, head Regulatory Investigations Gp 1998–; memb Lawyers Consultative Gp FSA; memb Law Soc 1984; *Recreations* family, sport; *Clubs* MCC; *Style*— Sidney Myers, Esq; ✉ Allen & Overy LLP, One New Change, London EC4M 9QQ (tel 020 7330 4819, fax 020 7330 9999, e-mail sidney.myers@allenovery.com)

MYERSCOUGH, Ishbel; da of Henry Ferdinand Myerscough, of London, and Elizabeth Cricthton Fraser; *b* 5 November 1968; *Educ* Highbury Hill HS, City of London Sch for Girls, Glasgow Sch of Art (BA), Slade Sch of Art (postgrad with distinction); *Career* artist; cmmns incl portrait of Helen Mirren for the Nat Portrait Gallery and Graham Gooch for the MCC; *Exhibitions* incl: Van Gogh Self-Portrait Exhbn (Burrell Collection Glasgow) 1990–91, RSA Student Exhbns Edinburgh 1990 and 1991, Nat Portrait Gallery Portrait Competition Exhbn 1990, 1991, 1992 and 1995, one man show Turtle Quay Art Centre London 1992 and 1996, RGI 131st Annual Exhbn McLellan Gallery Glasgow 1992, ROI annual show Mall Gallery London 1994, Treasures of the Nat Portrait Gallery (touring show Japan) 1995–96, Group Realist Show Berlin 1995, British Figurative Art (pt 1) Flowers East 1997, one man show Cork Street Gallery London 2000, Being Present (Jerwood Space London) 2004; *Awards* incl: John and Mabel Craig Bequest 1990 and 1991, Elizabeth Greenshields Fndn award 1991, 1993 and 1999, first prize in gp Hunting/Observer plc Prize for Art 1992, Nat Portrait Gallery BP Portrait Awards 1st prize 1995 (commended 1991 and 1993, 3rd prize 1992), National Westminster Bank prize for Art 3rd prize, Rootstein Hopkins Travel award to NY 1996, Robert and Susan Summers Connecticut residency 1996 and 1997; *Style*— Miss Ishbel Myerscough; ✉ Anthony Mould Ltd, 173 New Bond Street, London W1Y 9PF (tel 020 7491 4627, fax 020 7355 3865)

MYERSCOUGH, Morag Crichton; da of Henry Ferdinand Myerscough and Elizabeth Crichton Myerscough, of London; *b* 3 December 1963; *Educ* Highbury Hill HS, St Martin's Sch of Art (BA), Royal Coll of Art (MA); *Career* graphic designer; sr designer Lamb & Shirley 1988–90, independent designer 1990–93 (incl 6 months in Milan at Studio De Lucchi), fndr designer/dir Studio Myerscough 1993–; clients incl: Barbican Centre (Barbican Foyer Signale 2001–), Architecture Fndn, Derwent Valley Hldgs plc, Design Museum, Cmmn for Architecture and the Built Environment (CABE), RIBA, GLA, Design Cncl, Sci Museum, Br Cncl, Arts Cncl, British Land Company plc; external examiner MA Communications Central St Martins; graphic design conslt Conran Design Partnership 1996–; exhbns incl: Memphis Remembered (Design Museum) 2001, Rock Style: Fashion, Attitude & Style (Barbican) 2001, Architectural Odyssey (RIBA) 2001, Web Wizards (Design Museum) 2002, London Living City (RIBA); touring exhbns incl: Curation/Design 'Millennium Products' (Br Cncl and Design Cncl), 12 for 2000 (Br Cncl), Design Against Crime (Design Cncl) 2001, Expo E3 - 'State of Play' British Pavilion (Br Cncl LA) 2003, Hometime (Br Cncl China tour) 2003–04, European Design Biennial (Design Museum) 2003–04; owner 'Her House' Gallery 2002–; launched Hel Lamp (with Luke Morgan) and other products; lectr/judge: Germany, Norway, Canada, Switzerland, UK; Silver Award D&AD 1998, Design Week Award 2003; *Publications* incl: Myerscough Caravan (2003); *Style*— Ms Morag Myerscough

MYERSCOUGH-JONES, (Arthur) David; s of Frederick Cecil Sidney Jones, and Lilian Dorothy Jones; *b* 15 September 1934; *Educ* Bickerton House Sch Southport, Southport Sch of Art, Central Sch of Art (DA); *m* 23 Feb 1963, (Ursula Theodora Joy) Pelo, da of Charles Graham Cumpston (d 1968), of Pooley Bridge, Cumbria; 3 da (Frances b 21 Feb 1966, Ellen b 21 July 1971, Madeleine b 15 Sept 1974), 1 s (Richard b 23 June 1969); *Career* theatre designer; Citizens Theatre Glasgow 1958–60, Baikie Charivari (Edinburgh Festival) 1959, Gay Landscape (Royal Court) 1959; res designer Mermaid Theatre London 1960–65; transfers to W End: Alfie, All in Good Time, Emil and the Detectives, Lock Up Your Daughters (new prodn) 1961; BBC TV sr designer 1965–90; prodns incl: Peter Grimes 1969, Winterreise 1970, Owen Wingrave (B Britten world premiere) 1971, Louise, Alceste and Faerie Queene (London Opera Centre and Sadlers Wells) 1972, La Traviata, The Marriage of Figaro, The Flying Dutchman (Royal TV Soc Award) 1976, Therese Raquin (BAFTA Design Award, D&AD Gold and Silver awards) 1983, Orde Wingate Trilogy, The Beggars Opera, Cosi Fan Tutte, A Midsummer Night's Dream and All's Well That Ends Well (Jonathan Miller), The Theban Plays (ACE Nominations for Art Direction Los Angeles) 1988 and 1989; prodns for BBC TV incl: How Many Miles to Babylon, Virtuoso, The Master Builder, Metamorphosis, Bomber Harris, Circles of Deceit; adapted Trevor Nunn's RSC prodn of Othello for television; freelance prodn designer 1990–; prodns: Stagelands 1992, La Bohème (Bath City Opera) 1992, The Hawk (feature film, Initial/BBC), Il Trovatore and Il Barbiere di Siviglia (Festival Opera Walnut Creek Calif) 1993, La Traviata and The Turn of the Screw (Bath and Wessex Opera) 1993, The Rime of the Ancient Mariner (BBC) 1994, Young Jung (BBC) 1994, Don Giovanni and Rigoletto (Bath and Wessex Opera and Opera Northern Ireland) 1994, You Never Can Tell 1995 and Cold Comfort Farm 1996 (all Michael Friend Theatre Prodns), Educating Rita and Oleanna (Norwich Playhouse) 1997; exhibition of theatre and TV designs Theatre Royal Bath 1997, retrospective exhibitions in Lormes and Avallon 2004–05, designs for Peter Grimes (BBC TV 1969) exhibited as part of Aldeburgh Festival Exhbn 2005; Enoch Arden (Tennyson music by Richard Strauss) for Compagnie de la Hulotte, Burgundy 2000; memb: BAFTA 1980–2005, Wagner Soc of GB; FCSD 1985–2005; *Recreations* music, opera and painting; *Style*— David Myerscough-Jones, Esq; ✉ 10 rue Alphonse de Neuville, 62500 St Omer, Pas de Calais, France

MYERSON, Prof Jeremy; *Educ* Univ of Hull, RCA (MA); *Career* design writer, editor and broadcaster; with The Stage 1970s, design journalist 1980s, fndr ed Design Week 1986–89, ind author, researcher and curator in design 1990s; prof of contemporary design De Montford Univ 1995–98, prof of design studies and co-dir Helen Hamlyn Research Centre RCA 1999–, dir Innovation RCA 2004–; FRSA; *Exhibitions* curator: Doing a Dyson (Design Museum London) 1996, Look Inside: New British Interiors for People (Br Cncl touring show) 1998, Rewind: 40 Years of Design and Advertising from the D&AD (V&A) 2002; *Publications* Gordon Russell: Designer of Furniture (1992), Design Renaissance (ed, 1994), New Public Architecture (1996), Making the Lowry (2000), The 21st Century Office (2003), Space To Work (2006); *Style*— Prof Jeremy Myerson; ✉ Helen Hamlyn Research Centre, Royal College of Art, Kensington Gore, London SW7 2EU

MYERSON, Dr Keith Roger; s of Alexander Myerson, and Maxine, *née* Pearson; *b* 1 February 1950, Liverpool; *Educ* Quarry Bank HS Liverpool, Univ of Liverpool (MB, ChB); *m* 18 Dec 1981, Stella, *née* Brooks; 1 da (Alice Heather b 3 May 1984), 1 s (Peter Edward b 19 March 1986); *Career* house offr St Helen's Hosp Lancs 1973–74, SHO in clinical measurement Middx Hosp 1976–77, SHO in anaesthetics Plymouth 1977–78, registrar in anaesthetics Southampton 1979–81, sr registrar Bristol and SW region 1981–87, sr registrar Flinders Univ Adelaide 1982–83, conslt in anaesthesia and intensive care med Eastbourne Dist Gen Hosp 1987–; sr perf assessor GMC, chair Clinical Question Gp Royal Coll of Anaesthetics, memb Postgrad Medical Educn and Trg Bd Workplace Based Assessment Ctee 2004–05; ed Bulletin of the Royal Coll of Anaesthetists 2004–, editorials writer Anaesthesia; memb Cncl Royal Coll of Anaesthetists 2003; *Recreations* music, sailing, skiing; *Clubs* Kellog's Noddy; *Style*— Dr Keith Myerson; ✉ Department of Anaesthetics, Eastbourne District General Hospital, Kings Drive, Eastbourne, East Sussex BN21 2JD (tel 01323 417400, fax 01323 413805, e-mail keith.myerson@esht.nhs.uk)

MYKURA, Hamish Finlayson; s of Walter Mykura (d 1988), and Alison, *née* Edmond; *b* 28 March 1962, Edinburgh; *Educ* George Heriot's Sch Edinburgh, Univ of Aberdeen (MA),

Univ of Manchester (PhD); *m* 26 July 1997, Janey, *née* Walker; 2 da (Anna, Ingrid (twins) b 20 March 2000); *Career* prodn trainee BBC 1989–91, documentaries prodr BBC Radio 1991–92, prodr and dir BBC TV 1992–2000, dir Blakeway Productions 2000–01; Channel 4: commissioning ed for history 2001–03, head of history, science and religion 2003–07, head of specialist factual progs 2007–; FRSA; *Recreations* skiing, hill walking, travel writing; *Style*— Hamish Mykura, Esq; ✉ Channel 4, 124 Horseferry Road, London SW1P 2TX (tel 020 7306 1036, e-mail hmykura@channel4.co.uk)

MYLNE, Nigel James; QC (1984); s of Maj Harold James Mylne (10 Royal Hussars, d 1942), and Dorothy Evelyn Hogg, *née* Safford (d 1985); *b* 11 June 1939; *Educ* Eton; *m* 1, 4 April 1967 (m dis 1978), Julie Felicity Selena, da of Cdr Christopher Phillpotts, RN (d 1982); 1 da (Jessica b 1968), 2 s (Jonathan b 1969, Dominic b 1972); m 2, 18 Jan 1980 (m dis 1997), Mrs Judy Camilla Wilson, da of Maj Francis Gawain Hamilton Monteith (d 1975); 1 s (James b 1981); *Career* Nat Serv 2 Lt 10 Royal Hussars; called to the Bar Middle Temple 1963 (bencher 1995); recorder of the Crown Court 1983–, head of chambers 1997–99, pres Mental Health Review Tbnl 1999–, immigration judge 2005– (immigration adjudicator 1997–2005); Liveryman Worshipful Co of Haberdashers; *Recreations* beekeeping; *Clubs* Pratt's; *Style*— Nigel Mylne, Esq, QC; ✉ Langleys, Brixton Deverill, Wiltshire BA12 7EJ (tel 01985 840992, fax 01985 840351, e-mail nmylneswalker@aol.com)

MYLVAHAN, Dr Natarajan; s of Nurani Natarajan, and Saraswathy; *b* 29 June 1948; *Educ* Sri Lanka (MB BS, MD, DCH, LRCP); *m* 4 July 1976, Kalpana, da of K Ranganathan; 1 s (Kailash Natarajan Mylvahan); *Career* registrar in med Mansfield Dist and Gen Hosp Notts 1979–80, sr registrar in geriatrics St Mary's Gp Paddington London 1980–82, conslt physician for elderly Derby City General Hosp Tst 1982–; MRCS, FRCP; *Style*— Dr Natarajan Mylvahan; ✉ Hawksworth, 54 Ford Lane, Allestree, Derby DE3 2EW (tel 01332 553370, e-mail rajmyl@hotmail.com); Derby City General Hospital Trust, London Road, Derby (tel 01332 340131)

MYNERS, Paul; CBE (2003); *b* 1 April 1948; *m* 1995, Alison A I Macleod; 1 s (Bartholomew Piers Trevelyan b Feb 1996), 1 da (Talitha Phoebe Molly b April 1998); *Career* with N M Rothschild 1974–85 (latterly bd memb), chief exec and exec chm Gartmore Investment Management plc 1987–96 (joined as chief exec 1985), with NatWest Gp (following acquisition of Gartmore) 1996–2000 (exec dir 1997–2000), chm Gartmore plc 2000–01; non-exec chm: Guardian Media Gp plc 2000–, Marks and Spencer plc 2004–06 (non-exec dir 2002–06), Land Securities Gp plc 2007– (non-exec dir 2006–), Aspen Insurance Holdings Ltd; non-exec dir: PowerGen plc until 1996 (sometime non-exec dep chm), English & Scottish Investors Ltd, Orange plc, Bank of NY, mmO2 2001–; led HM Treasy's Review of Institutional Investment, chm Low Pay Cmmn 2006–, chm Personal Accounts Delivery Authy 2007–; former chm Assoc of Investment Cos, chm Investment Ctee Lloyd's of London; memb: City Disputes Panel, Financial Reporting Cncl, Ct of Dirs Bank of England 2005–; memb Advsy Bd: London Symphony Orch, Nat Maritime Museum Cornwall; tstee: Royal Acad, Glyndebourne, Tate (chair 2004–); FRSA; *Style*— Paul Myners, Esq, CBE

MYNORS, Sir Richard Baskerville; 2 Bt (UK 1964), of Treago, Co Hereford; s of Sir Humphrey Charles Baskerville Mynors, 1 Bt (d 1989); *b* 5 May 1947; *Educ* Marlborough, Corpus Christi Coll Cambridge; *m* 1970, Fiona Bridget, da of late Rt Rev George Edmund Reindorp; 3 da (Alexandra Fiona (Mrs Stephen Herbert) b 1975, Frances Veronica (Mrs Michael Tomlinson-Mynors) b 1978, Victoria Jane b 1983); *Heir* none; *Career* schoolmaster and asst dir of music King's Sch Macclesfield 1970–73; dir of music: Wolverhampton G S 1973–81, Merchant Taylors' Sch Crosby 1981–88, Belmont Abbey Sch Hereford 1988–90; landowner and freelance musician 1990–; fell Woodward Corporation (Midland Div) 1995–; *Recreations* gardening, DIY, organ building, viticulture; *Style*— Sir Richard Mynors, Bt; ✉ Treago, St Weonards, Hereford HR2 8QB (tel and fax 01981 580208, e-mail fiona.mynors@cmail.co.uk)

N

NAGANO, Kent; *Career* conductor; studied with Seiji Ozawa, Pierre Boulez, Leonard Bernstein; music dir Opera de Lyon 1989–98, assoc princ guest conductor LSO 1990–, music dir Hallé Orch 1992–99, also music dir Berkeley Symphony Orch Calif, artistic dir and princ conductor Deutsches Sinfonie-Orchester Berlin and princ conductor LA Opera; winner first Seaver National Endowment for the Arts Award 1984; premieres incl: Messiaen's The Transfiguration (USA), St François d'Assise (Paris Opera), John Adams's The Death of Klinghoffer (Brussels) 1991; other performances incl: Berg's Wozzec, Strauss's Salome (with Paris Opera), Strauss's Elektra (La Scala), John Adams's Nixon in China, Weill's Mahagonny (Los Angeles Opera), Milhaud's Christopher Columbus (San Francisco Opera), Poulenc's Dialogues des Carmelites (debut with Metropolitan Opera New York) 1994, Stravinsky's Oedipus Rex and Symphony of Psalms (Salzburg Festival) 1994, St François d'Assise (Salzburg Festival) 1998; *Recordings* incl: Prokofiev's Love for Three Oranges (Gramophone Magazine Record of the Year 1990, Best Opera Recording Award 1990, nominated Grammy Award 1990), Poulenc's Dialogues des Carmelites (Gramophone Opera Award 1993), John Adams's The Death of Klinghoffer (nominated Grammy Award 1993), Busoni's Turandot (nominated Grammy Award 1995), Floyd's Susannah (Grammy Award 1995), Britten's Billy Budd (with Hallé Orchestra) 1998; *Style*— Kent Nagano, Esq; ✉ c/o Van Walsum Management, 4 Addison Bridge Place, London W14 8XP (tel 020 7371 4343, fax 020 7371 4344)

NAGELSZTAJN, Michael James; s of Chajm Nagelsztajn, of Newcastle upon Tyne, and Cecelia, *née* Cooney; *b* 13 April 1955; *Educ* St Mary's Tech Sch Newcastle upon Tyne, Univ of Sheffield (BA, Dip Arch); *m* 16 Oct 1976, Judith, *née* Jennings; 2 s (Adam b 19 March 1982, Peter b 22 June 1985), 1 da (Hannah b 14 March 1989); *Career* fndr ptnr NSP Architects Nottingham 1988–89, project dir Benoy Ltd 1989–2000, dir S-P Architects 2000–, dir i/c media village for Olympic Games Athens 2004; memb Nottingham Ambassadors; memb ARB 1985, RIBA 1985; *Recreations* food and wine, keep-fit, football and rugby; *Style*— Michael Nagelsztajn, Esq; ✉ 16 Hillcrest Gardens, Burton Joyce, Nottingham NG14 5DE (tel 0115 9314283, mobile 07989 555109); 9 Weekday Cross, The Lace Market, Nottingham NG1 2GB (tel 0115 9415369, fax 01159 475955, e-mail miken@s-p.ltd.co.uk)

NAGGAR, Guy Anthony; s of Albert Naggar, of Italy, and Marjorie, *née* Smouha; *b* 14 October 1940; *Educ* Ecole Centrale des Arts et Manufactures Paris; *m* 6 Dec 1964, Hon Marion, da of Baron Samuel of Wych Cross (Life Baron, d 1987); 2 s (Albert b 15 July 1967, Jonathan b 24 Jan 1971), 1 da (Diane b 11 May 1969); *Career* dir Banque Financière de la Cité Geneva 1970–88, dep chm Charterhouse Bank 1976–81, dir Charterhouse Group Ltd 1980–81; chm: Dawnay Day Int 2001–, Austin Reed; *Style*— Guy Naggar, Esq

NAGLER, Neville Anthony; s of Gerald Joseph Nagler (d 1999), of London, and Sylvia, *née* Vernon; *b* 2 January 1945; *Educ* St George's Sch Mill Hill, Christ's Coll Finchley, Jesus Coll Cambridge (scholar, MA, history prizes); *m* 28 Feb 1971, Judy Maxine, da of Jack Leon Mordant; 1 da (Danielle b 25 June 1973), 1 s (Tristan b 11 March 1976); *Career* HM Treasy: joined 1967, private sec to Chllr of Exchequer 1970–71, princ 1972–75; Home Office: princ (firearms and contingency planning) Police Dept 1975–77, princ (police powers and procedures) Police Dept 1977–80, asst sec (race rels policy) Community Rels Dept 1980–83, head of Drugs and Extradition Policy Dept (concurrently UK rep to US Cmmn on Narcotic Drugs, chm Cncl of Europe Drug Co-operation Gp) 1983–88, head of Fin Div (responsible for local govt servs) 1988–91; DG Bd of Deps of British Jews 1991–2007; Haldane Essay Prize 1979, Cert of Appreciation UN Drug Enforcement Admin 1988, Cert in Public Services Mgmnt 2000; *Recreations* music appreciation, wine making, DIY/home improvements; *Style*— Neville Nagler, Esq

NAHUM, Peter John; s of Denis E Nahum, and Allison Faith, *née* Cooke; *b* 19 January 1947; *Educ* Sherborne; *m* 29 Aug 1987, Renate Angelika, da of Herr Ewald Meiser, of Germany; *Career* dir Peter Wilson's Sotheby's 1966–84; regular contrib as painting expert Antiques Roadshow 1980–2002 (discovered lost Richard Dadd painting 1986, subsequently sold to Br Museum); currently art dealer and publisher The Leicester Galleries St James's London, also website and web portal builder; memb: BADA, Society of London Art Dealers (SLAD), Confederation Internationale de Negociants en Oeuvres d'Art (CINOA); FRSA; *Books* Prices of Victorian Painting Drawings and Watercolours (1976), Monograms of Victorian and Edwardian Artists (1976), Cross Section, British Art in the 20th Century (1988), British Art From the 20th Century (1989), Burne-Jones, The Pre-Raphaelites & Their Century (1989), Burne-Jones: A Quest for Love (1993), Fairy Folk in Fairy Land (1997), Pre-Raphaelite. Symbolist. Visionary (2001), Medieval to Modern (2003), My Secret Book From the World of Tolkien (2007); *Recreations* gardening, sailing, photography, theatre, travel, walking; *Style*— Peter Nahum, Esq; ✉ 5 Ryder Street, London SW1Y 6PY (tel 020 7930 6059, fax 020 7930 4678, e-mail peternahum@leicestergalleries.com, website www.leicestergalleries.com)

NAIPAUL, Sir Vidiadhar Surajprasad (Vidia); kt (1990); *b* 1932; *Educ* UC Oxford (BA); *m* 1, 1955, Patricia Ann Hale (d 1996); m 2, 1996, Nadira Khannum Alvi; *Career* author; awards incl: David Cohen British Literature Prize 1993, Nobel Prize for Literature 2001; Hon DLitt: Univ of Cambridge 1983, Univ of London 1988, Univ of Oxford 1992; CLit 1994; *Books* The Mystic Masseur (winner of John Llewelyn Rhys Memorial prize, 1958), A House for Mr Biswas (1961), In A Free State (winner of Booker prize, 1971), A Bend in the River (1979), The Return of Eva Peron (1980), Among the Believers (1981), The Enigma of Arrival (1987), A Turn in the South (1989), India: A Million Mutinies Now (1990), A Way in the World (1994), Beyond Belief (1998), Half a Life (2001); *Style*— Sir Vidia Naipaul; ✉ c/o Gillon Aitken Associates, 18–21 Cavaye Place, London SW10 9PT (tel 020 7351 7561, fax 020 7376 3594)

NAIRN, Andrew; s of Capt Andrew Nairn, MC (d 1971), of Glasgow, and Margaret Cornfoot, *née* Turner (d 1972); *b* 31 July 1944; *Educ* Strathallan Sch; *m* 1, 1970 (m dis 1983), Susan Anne, da of Richard Alphonse Napier (d 1997); 1 da (Penelope Margaret b 1976), 1 s (Jonathan Richard b 1981); m 2, 1983, Glynis Vivienne, *née* Sweet; 1 step s (Barnaby Craggs b 1971), 1 step da (Charlotte Craggs b 1974); *Career* trainee chartered accountant Thomson Jackson Gourlay and Taylor 1962–67; Baker Tilly: joined 1967, ptnr 1970–2004, London region managing ptnr 1990–93, conslt 2004–; England and Wales area sec and treas ICAS until 1999; dir Booker Prize Trading Ltd 2002–, co sec and dir Colebream Estates Ltd 2004–; tstee Caza Azul Tst 2003–; dep chm Dulwich Cons Assoc 1978; MICAS; *Recreations* fly fishing, golf; *Clubs* Garrick, Union Soc of the City of Westminster (hon sec 1995–, chm 2005–06), Society of Bookmen (hon sec 2004–07); *Style*— Andrew Nairn, Esq, CA; ✉ 52 Redhill Wood, New Ash Green, Kent DA3 8QP (tel 01474 873 724); Baker Tilly, 2 Bloomsbury Street, London WC1B 3ST (tel 020 7413 5100, fax 020 7413 5122)

NAIRN, Nicholas (Nick); s of James and Irene Nairn, of Lochend House, Port of Mentieth, Stirling; *b* 12 January 1959; *Educ* McLaren HS, Glasgow Nautical Coll; *m* 1, 30 Jan 1986 (m dis), Fiona, da of Hector Macdonald; m 2, 16 June 2001, Holly, da of Rodger Anderson; 1 da (Daisy Skye b 27 Sept 2002); *Career* served Merchant Navy 1976–83 (third navigating offr 1980–83); fndr, chef and formerly dir Braeval restaurant by Aberfoyle Stirling 1986–97 (renovation 1984–86), fndr, chef and dir Nairns (Glasgow) 1998–2003, fndr Nairns Cook Sch 2000–, fndr Nairns Anywhere 2000–, owner Nick Nairn Enterprise 1995–; chef conslt Tesco; conslt: Foodfest Scottish Exhbn Centre 2001 and 2002, Aquascot Seafarms, Weber Barbecues, Royal Bank of Scotland, Salton Europe, Scottish Exec Healthy Eating Campaign; launched Baxter's with Nick Nairn range of sauces 2000, launched Nick Nairn Cookware (Best Cookware and Bakeware Housewares Industry Awards 2002); presenter: Ready Steady Cook (BBC2) 1995–, Wild Harvest with Nick Nairn (BBC2) 1996, Who'll do the Pudding? (BBC1) 1996, Wild Harvest 2 with Nick Nairn (BBC2) 1997, Island Harvest (BBC2) 1998 (Silver Ladle for Best TV Show Jacobs Creek World Food Media Awards), Celebrity Ready Steady Cook (BBC1) 1998–, Back to Basics with Nick Nairn (Carlton) 2000, Kitchen Invaders 2000, So You Think You're A Good Driver (BBC1) 2002, Nick Nairn and the Dinner Ladies (BBC Scotland) 2003; regular contrib: Food and Drink, Masterchef, Junior Masterchef and Carlton Daily, Good Food Live, Saturday Kitchen; columnist and contrib: Sunday Mail 1997–2000, BBC Good Food Magazine 1997–, Sunday Herald 2000–01, Sunday Herald Magazine 2000–, Scots Magazine 2000–03; fndr memb: Scottish Chefs' Assoc 1993 (memb Advsy Bd), Scottish Martell Cordon Bleu Assoc 1994; memb Masterchefs of GB 1992; hon pres Scottish Chefs Nat Cookery Centre; patron Queen Margaret Univ Coll; *Awards* Scottish Field/Bollinger Newcomer of the Year 1987, Acorn award Caterer and Hotelkeeper Magazine 1988, Scottish Field/Carlton Best Restaurant in Category 1988, Michelin Red M award 1990, Scottish Field/Charles Heidsieck Scottish Restaurant of the Year 1990, Good Food Guide County Restaurant of the Year 1991, Michelin Star 1991–, 3 AA Rosettes 1991–, Macallan/Decanter Scottish Restaurant of the Year 1992, Scottish Field/Bowmore Restaurant of the Year 1992, 4/5 Good Food Guide 1996, Thistle Award Scottish Tourist Board 1998, Michelin Bib Gourmand 1998, Glenfiddich Spirit of Scotland Award 2000, Personality of the Year Food Processing Awards 2002; *Books* incl: Wild Harvest with Nick Nairn (1996), Wild Harvest 2 (1997), Meat, Poultry and Game (1997), Nick Nairn Cooks The Main Course (with video, 1998), Island Harvest (1998), Nick Nairn Cooks Desserts (with video, 1998), Tower Pressure Cooker recipe Book (1999), Nick Nairn Top 100 Salmon Recipes (2002), New Scottish Cookery (2003), Nick Nairn's Top 100 Chicken Recipes (2004); contrib to numerous cookery books; *Recreations* hill walking, mountain biking, windsurfing, wine, eating in!; *Style*— Nick Nairn, Esq; ✉ Nick Nairn Enterprise, Port of Menteith, Stirling FK8 3JZ (tel 01877 389 900 fax 01877 385643, e-mail info@nairncookschool.co.uk, website www.nairnscookschool.com)

NAIRN-BRIGGS, Very Rev George Peter; DL (West Yorkshire 2006); s of Fredrick Nairn-Briggs (d 1980), and Gladys Lilian Nairn-Briggs (d 1999); *b* 5 July 1945; *Educ* Slough Tech HS, KCL (AKC), St Augustine's Coll Canterbury; *m* 1968, Candida, da of William Vickery; 1 da (Rebekah b 1970), 1 s (Edmund b 1972); *Career* local authy housing 1963–64, press offr MAFF 1964–66; ordained: deacon 1970, priest 1971; curate: St Laurence Catford 1970–73, St Saviour Raynes Park 1973–75; vicar: Christ the King Salfords 1975–81, St Peter St Helier 1981–87; Bishop's advsr for social responsibility Wakefield 1987–97, canon residentiary Wakefield Cathedral 1992–97, provost of Wakefield 1997–2000, dean of Wakefield 2000–; dep prolocutor Convocation of York 1995–2006; memb Gen Synod C of E 1980– (memb Bd for Social Responsibility 1985–2001, memb Panel of Chm 1997–2004), memb C of E Marriage Law Working Gp 2003–; chm Churches Regnl Cmmn for Yorkshire and the Humber 1998–2002, memb Exec Assoc of English Cathedrals 2000–, church cmmr 2004; memb: Wakefield City Centre Partnership 1995–2006, Wakefield Standards Ctee 1999– (ind chair 2004), Wakefield Local Strategic Partnership 2001–03, Yorks Regnl Cultural Consortium 2002–07, Mid-Yorks Hosp Tst Bd 2002–04; fndn govr Cathedral Sch 1997–, govr Bretton Hall Coll 1999–2001, govr Wakefield Coll 2002–06; chm various local charitable trusts; Freeman City of Wakefield; *Publications* Love in Action (1986), Serving Two Masters (1988), It Happens in the Family (1992); *Recreations* reading, buying antiques, travel; *Style*— The Very Rev the Dean of Wakefield, DL; ✉ The Deanery, 1 Cathedral Close, Margaret Street, Wakefield WF1 2DP (tel 01924 210005, fax 01924 210009, e-mail dean@wakefield-cathedral.org.uk)

NAIRNE, Alexander Robert (Sandy); s of Rt Hon Sir Patrick Dalmahoy Nairne, KCB, MC, of Chilson, Oxon, and Penelope Chauncy, *née* Bridges; *b* 8 June 1953; *Educ* Radley, UC Oxford (MA, memb Isis Boat Crew); *partner* Prof Sylvia Elizabeth Tickner (Lisa); 1 s (Kit b 1984), 1 da (Eleanor b 1987); *Career* asst dir: MOMA Oxford 1974–76, Modern Collection Tate Gallery London 1976–79; dir of exhibitions ICA London 1980–84, freelance curator and writer 1984–87, dir of visual arts Arts Cncl of GB London 1987–92, sr research fell Getty Grant Prog 1992–93; Tate Gallery: dir of public and regnl servs 1994–98, dir of nat progs 1998–2001, dir progs 2001–02; dir Nat Portrait Gallery 2002–; chair Fourth Plinth Commissioning Gp 2003–; memb: Exec Ctee Art Galleries Assoc 1976–81, Exec Ctee Gtr London Arts 1983–86, Art and Architecture Advsy Panel RSA 1990–95, Fabric Advsy Ctee St Paul's Cathedral 1997–; advsr Works of Art Ctee Br Library 1989–91; govr Univ of Middx 1996–2003 (dep chair 1999–2001); memb Cncl: Br Sch at Rome 2001–, RCA 2001–; Hon Dr Middx Univ 2005, hon fell UC Oxford 2006; *Books* British Sculpture in the Twentieth Century (jt ed, 1981), Picturing the System (jt ed, 1981), State of the Art (1987), Thinking About Exhibitions (jt ed, 1996), The Portrait Now (2006); *Recreations* racing punting; *Clubs* Chelsea Arts; *Style*— Sandy Nairne, Esq; ✉ c/o National Portrait Gallery, St Martin's Place, London WC2H 0HE

NAIRNE, Andrew; s of Sir Patrick Nairne, of Oxon, and Penelope Chauncy, née Bridges; bro of Sandy Nairne, *qv*; *b* 10 February 1960, Guildford, Surrey; *Educ* Radley, Univ of St Andrews; *m* 1 July 1995, Nicola Dandridge; 2 s (Matthew b 5 Oct 1996, Patrick b 29 April 1998); *Career* asst curator Kettle's Yard Cambridge 1984, dep dir Ikon Gall Birmingham 1985, exhbns dir Centre for Contemporary Arts (CCA) Glasgow 1986–92, visual arts dir Scottish Arts Cncl 1992–97, dir Dundee Contemporary Arts 1997–2001,

N

dir Modern Art Oxford 2001–; visiting fell Nuffield Coll Oxford, memb Ct Oxford Brookes Univ; FRSA; *Recreations* running; *Style*— Andrew Nairne, Esq; ✉ 61 Southmoor Road, Oxford OX2 6RF (tel 01865 554220, e-mail andnic@nairne.f9.co.uk); Modern Art Oxford, 30 Pembroke Street, Oxford OX1 1BP (tel 01865 722733, fax 01865 722573, e-mail andrew.nairne@modernartoxford.org.uk)

NAISH, John Alexander; s of William Henry Naish (d 1987), and Elizabeth Lyon, *née* Pirie (d 1993); *b* 12 April 1948; *Educ* Queen Elizabeth's Hosp Bristol, Dr Challoner's GS Amersham, City of London Coll (BA); *m* 18 Sept 1982, Bonnie Kam Pik, da of Pham Tak, of Hong Kong; 2 s (William b 3 April 1987, Henry b 3 Aug 1989); *Career* dir Hill Samuel Bank Ltd 1985–93, dir Investment Banking Asia Pacific NatWest Markets 1994–97, sr conslt Penna 1997–; exec dir: Willis 1997–, LCF Rothschild Securities 1998–, Neat Concepts Ltd 2002–; memb Cncl Japan Soc 1998–2005; FCIB 1983; *Recreations* golf, astronomy, music; *Clubs* Oriental, Royal Over-Seas League, Tokyo; *Style*— John Naish, Esq; ✉ 12 Waldegrave Gardens, Strawberry Hill, Twickenham, Middlesex TW1 4PG (tel 020 8892 7953, e-mail johnnaish@btinternet.com)

NAPIER, Sir Charles Joseph; 6 Bt (UK 1867), of Merrion Square, Dublin; o s of Sir Robert (Robin) Surtees Napier, 5 Bt (d 1994), and Jennifer Beryl, *née* Daw (now Mrs Donald Black); *b* 15 April 1973; *Educ* Eton, Univ of Edinburgh (MA); *m* 5 July 2003, Imelda Blanche Elisabeth, er da of late John Trafford, of Bayswater, London; 1 s (Finnian John Lennox (Finn) b 14 Feb 2006); *Heir* s, Finn Napier; *Career* MIND 1997–98, appeal dir Downside Settlement 1998–99 (memb Mgmnt Ctee 2000–), assoc The Policy Partnership 1999–2006, account dir PPS Gp 2006–, assoc dir Quintus Public Affrs 2006; cncllr (Lab) London Borough of Hammersmith and Fulham 2002–06; govr Peterborough Primary Sch Fulham 2000–; *Recreations* watching and playing sport; *Clubs* Flyfishers'; *Style*— Sir Charles Napier, Bt; ✉ 35 Warbeck Road, London W12 8NS

NAPIER, Christopher Lennox; s of Capt Lennox William Napier, DSO, DSC, RN (d 2001), and Elizabeth Eve, *née* Lindsay (d 1996); *b* 5 December 1944; *Educ* Sherborne, Britannia RNC Dartmouth; *m* 1971, Susan Margaret, da of Ian McLauchlan (d 1985); 1 s (James b 1972), 1 da (Georgina b 1976); *Career* joined BRNC Dartmouth 1962, qualified submarines 1966, ret as Lt Cdr 1976; Clifford Turner: articled clerk 1976–78, admitted slr 1979, slr 1979–83, ptnr 1983–87; ptnr Clifford Chance 1987–99; mediator and facilitator 1999–; vice-chm CPRE, chm Hants CPRE; pres Petersfield Soc; vice-chm Drum Housing Assoc, chm South Downs Advsy Forum, memb South Downs Jt Ctee; Freeman City of London, Liveryman City of London Slrs' Co; memb: Law Soc, UKELA; FRSA; *Recreations* walking, reading, skiing, sailing; *Style*— Christopher Napier; ✉ Kimpton House, Durford Wood, Petersfield, Hampshire GU31 5AS (tel 01730 893272, e-mail christopher.napier@cliffordchance.com)

NAPIER, Iain John Grant; *b* 10 April 1949; *m*; 3 c; *Career* Whitbread plc 1972–77, Ford Motor Co 1977–89 (latterly fleet sales dir Ford of Britain), Bass plc 1989–2000 (positions incl chief exec Bass Brewers and Bass International Brewers 1996–2001), vice-pres UK and Ireland and memb Exec Ctee Interbrew SA 2000–01, chief exec Taylor Woodrow plc 2002–06; non-exec chm: Imperial Tobacco Gp plc 2007– (non-exec dir 2000–, jt vice-chm 2004–06), McBride plc 2007–; non-exec dir: Perry Gp 1996–2001, Henderson Investors plc 1997–99, St Modwens Properties plc 2001–02, BOC Gp plc 2004, Collins Stewart plc 2007–; ACMA; *Recreations* rugby, walking; *Style*— Iain Napier, Esq

NAPIER, John; s of James Edward Thomas Napier, and Florence Emma, *née* Godbold; *b* 1 March 1944; *Educ* Hornsey Coll of Art, Central Sch of Art & Crafts; *m* 1 (m dis 1985), Andreane Neofitou; 1 s (Julian b 1965), 1 da (Elise b 1968); m 2 (m dis 1995), Donna King; 1 s (James b 1984), 1 da (Jessica b 1988); *Career* set designer; assoc designer RSC; hon fell London Inst 2001; RDI 1996; *Theatre and Film* 150 film, musical and theatrical prodns incl: The Ruling Class 1968, The Fun War 1968, Muzeeka 1968, George Frederick 1968, Turista 1968, Cancer 1969, Isabel's a Jezebel 1969, Mister 1970, The Foursome 1970, The Lovers of Viorne 1970, Lear 1970, Jump 1971, Sam Sam 1971, Big Wolf 1971, The Devils (ENO) 1972, Equus (NT) 1972, The Party 1972, Knuckle 1973, Kings & Clowns 1974, The Travelling Music Show 1974, Hedda Gabler (RSC) 1974, Much Ado About Nothing 1975, The Comedy of Errors (RSC) 1975, King Lear (RSC) 1975, Macbeth (RSC) 1975, A Midsummer Night's Dream 1976, As You Like It 1976, The Merry Wives of Windsor 1977, Twelfth Night 1977, Three Sisters 1977, Once in a Lifetime 1977, Lohengrin (Royal Opera House, SWET Award), The Greeks (RSC) 1979, Nicholas Nickleby (RSC, SWET and Tony Awards) 1979, Cats (Tony Award) 1980, Henry IV Parts I and II 1981, Peter Pan (RSC) 1981, Idomeneo (Glyndebourne) 1982, Macbeth (Royal Opera House) 1983, Starlight Express (Tony Award 1987) 1984, Les Misérables (Tony Award 1987) 1985, Time (Dominion) 1986, Captain EO (Disney film starring Michael Jackson) 1987, Miss Saigon 1989, Siegfried and Roy (The Mirage Las Vegas) 1989, Children of Eden 1990, Hook (Steven Spielberg film) 1991, Trelawny of the Wells (RNT) 1993, Sunset Boulevard 1993 (Tony Award 1995), Burning Blue (Haymarket (Olivier Award for Best Set Design 1996)) 1995, The Tower (Almeida) 1995, Who's Afraid of Virginia Woolf? (Almeida and Aldwych) 1996, Jane Eyre (Toronto) 1996, Jesus Christ Superstar (Lyceum) 1996, An Enemy of the People (RNT) 1997, Peter Pan (RNT) 1997, Martin Guerre (UK tour) 1998, Candide (RNT) 1999, Jane Eyre (NY) 2000, Nabucco (Met Opera) 2001, South Pacific (RNT) 2001, Skellig 2003, Aladdin 2004 and 2005, Equus 2007; *Recreations* photography; *Style*— John Napier, Esq; ✉ c/o Macnaughton Lord 2000 Ltd, 19 Margravine Gardens, London W6 8RL (tel 020 8741 0606, fax 020 8741 7443)

NAPIER, John Alan; s of William Arthur Napier, of Sudbury, and Barbara Eileen, *née* Chatten (d 1962); *b* 22 August 1942; *Educ* Colchester Royal GS, N E Essex Tech Coll, Emmanuel Coll Cambridge (BA); *m* 1, 24 June 1961 (m dis), Gillian Joyce, *née* Reed; 2 s (Stephen Paul b 1 Dec 1961, Russell John b 15 Sept 1965), 1 da (Karen Clare b 3 Oct 1963); m 2, 12 March 1992, Caroline Mary Elizabeth, da of Charles Jarvis; 1 da (Amelia Caroline b 17 Sept 1992); *Career* jr and middle mangr Int Publishing Corp and Reed Int 1960–69, md Index Printers 1969–72, md QB Newspapers 1972–76, exec dir (Aust) James Hardie Industries 1976–86, gp md AGB plc 1986–90, md Hays plc 1991–98; chm: Booker plc 1998–2000, Kelda Gp plc 2000–, Royal & Sun Alliance Insurance Gp plc 2003–; bd memb Yorkshire Forward 2002–; chm Yorks and Humber Rural Affrs Forum 2000–; *Recreations* rural matters, outdoor activities, people and philosophy; *Style*— John Napier, Esq

NAPIER, (Thomas) Michael; CBE (2005); s of Montague Keith Napier (d 1975), and Mary, *née* Mather (d 1954); *b* 11 June 1946; *Educ* Loughborough GS, Hulme Hall Univ of Manchester (open exhibition, First XV Rugby); *m* 27 Dec 1969, Denise Christine; 2 da (Holly Danielle b 26 June 1973, Amy Abigail b 9 June 1975), 1 s (Frederick John b 31 Oct 1980); *Career* articled clerk Malcolm H Moss Moss Toone & Deane Loughborough 1968–70, asst slr W H Thompson Manchester 1970–72, sr ptnr Irwin Mitchell Sheffield, Leeds, Birmingham, Newcastle upon Tyne, Manchester, Marbella and London 1983– (ptnr Sheffield 1973), jt sr ptnr Pannone Napier 1985–94; visiting prof of gp litigation and disaster law Nottingham Law Sch 1992–; pro bono envoy to attorney-gen; editorial conslt: Personal and Medical Injuries Law Letter, Medical Law Review; Mental Health Act Cmmn: cmmr 1983–92, jt vice-chm 1985–88, chm NE region 1985–89; former pres S Yorks Medico-Legal Soc, memb Governing Bd Assoc of Trial Lawyers of America 1990–97, pres Assoc of Personal Injury Lawyers 1994–96; chm Hosp Advsy Ctee Rampton Hosp 1992–96; consulting ed Litigation Funding; memb: Cncl JUSTICE 1995–, Civil Justice Cncl 1998–; tstee Thalidomide Tst; Freeman Co of Cutlers in Hallamshire 1992; Hon LLD Univ of Sheffield, Hon LLD Nottingham Law Sch; memb Law Soc 1970 (memb Cncl 1993–, pres 2000–01); *Recreations* mountain biking in Norfolk; *Clubs* Athenaeum; *Style*— Michael Napier, Esq, CBE; ✉ Windmill Hill, Great Walsingham, Norfolk (tel 01328 820213); Irwin Mitchell, 150 Holborn, London EC1N 2NS

NAPIER, Robert Stewart; s of Andrew Napier (d 1967), and Lilian V, *née* Ritchie (d 2000); *b* 21 July 1947; *Educ* Sedbergh, Sidney Sussex Coll Cambridge (MA), Harvard Business Sch (AMP); *m* 17 Dec 1977, Patricia Gray Stewart; 1 da (Catriona Rose Stewart b 1984); *Career* Rio Tinto Zinc Corp 1969–73, Brandts Ltd 1973–75, Fisons Ltd 1975–81; Redland plc: fin dir 1981–87, gp md 1987–97, chief exec 1991–97; chief exec WWF-UK 1999–2007; chm Met Office 2006–; non-exec dir: United Biscuits (Holdings) plc 1992–2000, Rentokil Initial plc 1996–99, Anglia Water Services Ltd 2002–, English Partnerships 2004–; pres Nat Cncl of Building Materials Prodrs 1996–99; *Style*— Robert Napier, Esq

NAPIER AND ETTRICK, 14 Lord (Napier S 1627) and 5 Baron (Ettrick UK 1872); Chief of the name of Napier, and 23 of Merchistoun; Sir Francis Nigel Napier; 11 Bt (Nova Scotia 1666), of Thirlestane, KCVO (1992, CVO 1985, LVO 1980), DL (Selkirkshire 1974, Ettrick and Lauderdale 1975); eld s of 13 Lord Napier and Ettrick, TD, JP, DL (d 1954, twelfth in descent from first Lord, himself s of John Napier of Merchistoun, the inventor of logarithms), and Violet Muir, *née* Newson (d 1992); the Napiers of Merchistoun are co-heirs general of the ancient Celtic Earls of Lennox; *b* 5 December 1930; *Educ* Eton, RMA Sandhurst; *m* 1958, Delia Mary, da of Maj Archibald D B Pearson; 2 da (Hon Louisa (Hon Mrs Morrison) b 1961, Hon Georgina (Hon Mrs Walker) b 1969), 2 s (Hon Francis, Master of Napier b 1962, Hon Nicholas b 1971); *Heir* s, Master of Napier; *Career* Maj Scots Gds (R of O), Malaya 1950–51 (invalided); Adjt 1 Bn Scots Gds 1955–57; equerry to HRH the late Duke of Gloucester 1958–60 (ret 1960), in the City 1960–62, dep ceremonial and protocol sec Cwlth Rels Office 1962–68; sat as ind peer in House in Lords 1973–99; Cons whip House of Lords 1970–71, private sec, comptroller and equerry to HRH The Princess Margaret, Countess of Snowdon 1973–98 (treas and equerry 1998–2002); pres St John Ambulance Assoc and Bde London Dist 1975–83; memb Queen's Body Guard for Scotland (Royal Co of Archers) 1953–; handed over the Instruments of Independence to Tuvalu (Ellice Islands) on behalf of HM The Queen 1979; memb: Standing Cncl of Scottish Chiefs, Exec Ctee Standing Cncl of the Baronetage; Liveryman Worshipful Co of Grocers 1963; Hon DLitt Napier Univ 1993; KStJ 1991 (CStJ 1988, OStJ 1982); *Clubs* Turf, Pratt's, Pitt; *Style*— Major the Lord Napier and Ettrick, KCVO, DL; ✉ Down House, Wylye, Wiltshire BA12 0QN

NAPIER OF MAGDALA, 6 Baron (UK 1868), in Abyssinia and of Caryngton, Co Chester; Robert Alan Napier; eld s of 5 Baron Napier of Magdala, OBE (d 1987), and Elizabeth Marian, *née* Hunt; *b* 6 September 1940; *Educ* Winchester, St John's Coll Cambridge (MA); *m* 4 Jan 1964, Frances Clare, er da of late Alan Frank Skinner, OBE, of Woolpit, Suffolk; 1 da (Hon Frances Catherine b 2 July 1964), 1 s (Hon James Robert b 29 Jan 1966); *Heir* s, Hon James Napier; *Career* with Northern Res & Engrg Corp 1962–66; Alfred Holt & Co: joined 1966, dir Ocean Fleets 1973–76, md Cory Towage 1976–79, co mangr Elder Dempster (Nigeria) 1979–82; chief exec Alexandra Towing 1983–85, port dir Manchester Ship Canal Co 1986–87, ports conslt 1988–, dir Motion Poster plc 2000–02 (chm 2002); ind memb House of Lords 1988–99, chm All-Pty Coastal Gp 1998–99; *Recreations* sailing, playing the cello, trout fishing; *Clubs* Leander; *Style*— The Rt Hon Lord Napier of Magdala; ✉ The Coach House, Kingsbury Street, Marlborough, Wiltshire SN8 1HU (tel and fax 01672 512333)

NAPIER OF MERCHISTOUN, Sir John Archibald Lennox; 14 Bt (NS 1627), of Merchistoun; s of Sir William Archibald Napier of Merchistoun, 13 Bt (d 1990), and Kathleen Mabel, *née* Greaves; descended from John Napier, inventor of logarithms; *b* 6 December 1946; *Educ* St Stithians, Univ of the Witwatersrand (BSc, MSc, PhD); *m* 9 Dec 1969, Erica Susan, da of late Kurt Kingsfield, of Johannesburg, South Africa; 1 da (Natalie Ann b 1973), 1 s (Hugh Robert Lennox b 1977); *Heir* s, Hugh Napier; *Career* res engr; fell SA Inst of Mining and Metallurgy; *Clubs* Johannesburg Country; *Style*— Sir John Napier of Merchistoun, Bt; ✉ Merchistoun, PO Box 65177, Benmore 2010, Transvaal, South Africa (tel 00 27 11 783 2611)

NAQVI, Syed (Zakir Husain) Haider; s of Syed Ather Husain Naqvi (d 1954), and Saghir Fatima, *née* Rizvi (d 1997); *b* 14 October 1949; *Educ* Karachi Univ (BCom, MA Econ); *m* Marja-Liisa, da of Paavo Ilmari Nyyssönen, of Sorsakoski, Finland; 2 da (Chantal Samreen b 1980, Sabrina Yasmin b 1986); *Career* chartered accountant; internal auditor Philip Industries (UK) Ltd 1975–77, gp fin controller London Export Corporation (Holdings) Ltd 1977–78, ptnr Haider Naqvi & Co Chartered Accountants 1978–; fndr HELPs Group; FCA 1973, FCCA, FCIS 1974; *Recreations* Urdu poetry, snooker, chess; *Style*— Syed Haider Naqvi, Esq; ✉ Concept House, 225 Hale Lane, Edgware, Middlesex HA8 9QF (tel 020 8958 8015, fax 020 8958 8535, e-mail shn@haider-naqvi.co.uk)

NARBETT, Roger David; s of (William) John Narbett, of Queens Hotel Belbroughton, and Sheila Mary, *née* Hudson; *b* 4 May 1960; *Educ* Smethwick Hall Boys Sch, Halesowen Coll (City & Guilds); *m* 1 Oct 1988, Joanne, da of Thomas Marshall; 1 s (Oliver Daniel b 5 March 1989), 1 da (Simone Victoria b 15 Aug 1991); *Career* chef; Savoy Hotel London 1979–81, The Waterside Inn Bray Berks 1981–82, Le Gavroche London 1982–83, Les Frères Troisgros Roanne France May-July 1983; chef/ptnr (with father): The Bell Inn Belbroughton Worcs 1983–88, Sloans Restaurant Edgbaston 1986–92; exec sous chef Dorchester Hotel London 1992–94, exec chef The Lygon Arms Broadway Worcs 1994–98, exec chef The Hyatt Regency 1998–; chef England Football Team 1989–; chm Regnl Finals Nestle Toque D'Or Student Competition 1989–; memb Restaurateurs Assoc of GB, memb Food and Cookery Assoc, master chef Craft Guild of Chefs, memb Académie Culinaire de France; *Awards* winner Taste of England Competition 1979, finalist Commis Chef of the Year Académie Culinaire de France 1983, Young Chef of the Year Restaurateurs Assoc of GB 1985, winner 30 under 30 Acorn Awards 1987, Chef of the Year Craft Guild of Chefs 1990 (runner up 1988), Meilleur Ouvrier de Grande Bretagne 1991, UK finalist Pierre Taittinger Int Culinary Prize 1992, finalist Wedgwood Chef and Potter Competition 1996; *Recreations* health and fitness, music, fine wines, agriculture; *Style*— Roger Narbett, Esq; ✉ The Hyatt Regency Birmingham, 2 Bridge Street, Birmingham B1 2JZ (tel 0121 632 1651)

NAREY, Martin James; s of John Narey, and Ellenor Narey; *b* 5 August 1955; *Educ* Sheffield Poly (BA); *m* 1978, Jan Goudy; 1 s, 1 da; *Career* asst govr HM Young Offender Inst Deerbolt 1982–86, asst govr HM Prison Frankland 1986–90, govr IV Prison Service HQ 1990–91; Home Office: private sec to min of state 1991–92, Criminal Policy Dept 1992–94, Coordination of Computerisation in the Criminal Justice System 1994–96, head Crime Prevention Agency 1996; Reviewer of Delay in the Criminal Justice System 1996–97; HM Prison Service: head of security policy 1997–98, dir of regimes 1998–99, DG 1999–2003; Home Office: second perm sec 2002–03, cmmr for correctional servs and perm sec for HR 2003, chief exec Nat Offender Mgmnt Service 2004–05; chief exec Barnardo's 2005–; visiting prof Sheffield Hallam Univ; Gold medal Chartered Mgmnt Inst 2003; Hon Dr Sheffield Hallam Univ 2003; *Publications* review of delay in criminal justice system, report on an investigation at the Maze Prison; *Recreations* planning holidays, watching Middlesbrough FC; *Style*— Martin Narey

NARGOLWALA, Kaikhushru Shiavax; s of Shivax D Nargolwala (d 1986), and Dhun S Nargolwala; *b* 22 April 1950; *m* 8 July 1973, Aparna, da of M G Kaul; *Career* CA Peat Marwick Mitchell & Co UK 1970–76; Bank of America: various mgmnt roles in UK 1976–84, head of US High Technology Industry Gp 1984–89, sr vice-pres and sr credit offr Asia 1990–93, gp exec vice-pres and head of Asia Wholesale Banking Gp 1993–95; gp exec dir Standard Chartered Bank 1999– (gp head of corp banking sales 1998–99); non-exec dir Tate & Lyle 2004–; ACA 1975, FCA 1981; *Recreations* reading, music, technology; *Clubs* Tower (Singapore), Tanglin (Singapore), Oriental (London); *Style*— Kai Nargolwala, Esq; ✉ Standard Chartered Bank, 6 Battery Road, 8th Floor, Singapore 049909 (tel 65 531 8088, fax 65 334 0427, e-mail kai.nargolwala@sg.standardchartered.com)

NARULA, Prof Antony Ajay Pall (Tony); s of Yash Pall Narula (d 2003), and Prakash, *née* Varma; *b* 14 November 1955, Burma; *Educ* Epsom Coll, Trinity Hall Cambridge (MA), Univ of London (MB, BChir); *m* Aug 1985, Charlotte, *née* Beech; 1 da (Alexandra Devina Isabelle b 8 April 1986), 2 s (Maximilian Henry Anish b 29 March 1993, Henry Robin Anil b 24 Sept 1995); *Career* conslt surgn: Univ Hosp Leicester 1989–2001, St Mary's Hosp London 2001–; hon prof Middlesex Univ 2003–; elected tstee RCS 2004–; NHS Beacon Award 1999; FRCS 1984, FRCSEd 2001; *Publications* Clinical ENT: an illustrated textbook (1992, 2 edn 1999); *Clubs* RAC; *Style*— Prof Tony Narula; ✉ 4 Albion Close, London W2 2AT (tel 020 7723 3690, e-mail tony.narula@btinternet.com); ENT Department, St Mary's Hospital, Praed Street, London W2 1NY

NASEBY, Baron (Life Peer UK 1997), of Sandy in the County of Bedfordshire; Rt Hon Michael Wolfgang Laurence Morris; PC (1994); s of late Cyril Laurence Morris; *b* 25 November 1936; *Educ* Bedford Sch, St Catharine's Coll Cambridge (MA); *m* 1960, Ann Phyllis, da of Percy Appleby (d 1973); 2 s (Hon Julian b 1961, Hon Jocelyn b 1972), 1 da (Hon Susannah b 1965); *Career* Nat Serv pilot offr RAF and NATO Wings; dir Benton & Bowles (advertising agency) 1971–81, fndr proprietor AM International Public Affairs Consultants 1976–92; Parly candidate (Cons) Islington N 1966, MP (Cons) Northampton S Feb 1974–97; PPS to Min of State NI Office 1979–81, chm Ways and Means Ctee and dep speaker 1992–97; memb: Public Accounts Ctee 1979–92, Cncl of Europe and WEU 1983–91, Speaker's Panel of Chairmen 1984–92; chm Br-Sri Lanka Parly Gp, chm Br-Maldives Parly Gp; chm: PSP Euro Med Charity 1993–2001, Tunbridge Wells Equitable Friendly Soc 1998–2005, Northants Victoria Co History 1994–; former chm Br Singapore Parly Gp, Br Malaysia Gp, Br Burma Gp; former vice-chm Br-Indonesia Gp; former treas: Br-Thailand Gp, Br-Asian Gp; chm Invesco Recovery Tst 1998–, non-exec dir Mansell plc 1998–2003; fndr prop Julius International Consultants 1997–; chm Bedford Sch 1989–2002 (govr 1982–); chm Confradia del Vino Chileno; Chamberlain Ordre des Coteaux de Champagne, Chevalier Confrérie des Chavaliers du Tastevin; *Recreations* field sports, cricket, golf (former capt Parly Golf Soc), shooting, tennis, heritage, forestry, budgerigars; *Clubs* Carlton, George Row (Northampton), John O'Gaunt Golf, Port Stanley Golf, MCC, Northampton CCC (patron), All England Lawn Tennis, Royal St George's Golf, Lord's Taverners, La Commanderie de Bordeaux a Londres; *Style*— The Rt Hon the Lord Naseby, PC; ✉ Caesar's Camp, Sandy, Bedfordshire SG19 2AD (tel 01767 680388)

NASH, Prof Andrew Samuel; s of Rev Samuel George Hall Nash (d 1993), of Cambridge, and Kathleen Grace, *née* Wells (d 1996); *b* 1 August 1944; *Educ* Judd Sch Tonbridge, Southend on Sea Municipal Coll, Univ of Glasgow (BVMS, Silver medal for clinical med, PhD); *m* 1 Nov 1968, Rosemary Truscott, da of Rev John Harris Hamilton (d 1997); 1 da (Heather Jane b 14 Oct 1971), 1 s (Graham Paul b 26 June 1975); *Career* veterinary asst in gen practice Ilfracombe 1967–72; Univ of Glasgow Veterinary Sch: house physician 1973–75, lectr 1975–85, sr lectr 1985–92, titular prof Dept of Veterinary Med 1992–95, dir of the Veterinary Hosp 1993–96, prof of small animal med 1995–, vice-dean for student affairs 1995–99, dir Student Support Services 1999–2001; Univ of Glasgow: senate assessor on Univ Ct 1999–2001, clerk of senate 2002–08, vice-princ for learning and teaching 2002–04; recognised specialist in small animal internal diseases (RCVS) 1993–2002; diplomate Euro Coll of Veterinary Internal Med 1995–; dir Glasgow Dog & Cat Home 1982–95, memb Bd and convenor Animal Welfare Centres Ctee Scottish Soc for the Prevention of Cruelty to Animals (SSPCA) 1995–2003, hon memb Soft-Coated Wheaten Terrier Club of GB 1988–, hon pres The Scottish Cat Club 1990–99, pres Euro Soc for Veterinary Nephrology and Urology 1992–94; organist Sandyford-Henderson Meml Church of Scot 1994–; MRCVS 1967; memb: BVA (W of Scot) 1973–2003, Assoc of Veterinary Teachers and Res Workers 1974–2003, Br Small Animal Veterinary Assoc 1993–; Dip Euro Coll of Veterinary Internal Med 1995; CBiol 1993, FIBiol 1993; *Publications* author of numerous book chapters and papers published in veterinary jls; *Style*— Prof Andrew Nash; ✉ Senate Office, University of Glasgow, Glasgow G12 8QQ (tel 0141 330 4242, fax 0141 330 4021, e-mail a.nash@admin.gla.ac.uk)

NASH, Prof Anthony Aubrey; s of Alfred Nash (d 1967), of Coalville, Leics, and Mabel Evelyn, *née* Garrett; *b* 6 March 1949; *Educ* Newbridge Secdy Modern Coalville, Loughborough Coll, Queen Elizabeth Coll London (BSc), Univ of Birmingham (MSc, PhD); *m* 1979, Marion Eileen, da of Eric James Bazeley; 4 da (Laura Amy b 25 Feb 1980, Ruth Ellen b 23 Jan 1983, Esther Jane b 29 April 1985, Hannah Bethan b 24 Feb 1990); *Career* lectr Dept of Pathology Univ of Cambridge 1989–94 (research assoc 1977–84), prof and head Dept of Vet Pathology Univ of Edinburgh 1994–; Eleanor Roosevelt fell 1989–90; memb: Cncl of Soc for Gen Microbiology 2001–, BBSRC 2002–, Soc for Gen Microbiology, Br Soc of Immunology; FMedSci 1999, FRSE 2005; *Books* Mims Pathogenesis of Infectious Disease (1995); *Style*— Prof Anthony Nash; ✉ Department of Veterinary Pathology, University of Edinburgh, Summerhall, Edinburgh EH9 1QH (tel 0130 650 6164, fax 0130 650 6511, e-mail tony.nash@ed.ac.uk)

NASH, Christopher Arthur Haseltine; s of Arthur Edward Nash, and Patricia, *née* Haseltine; *b* 16 August 1955; *Educ* Eastbourne GS, Eastbourne Coll of Art and Design, Univ of Bristol (BA, DipArch), Royal Western Acad Sch of Arch; *m* 1981, Sarah Patricia, *née* Woodgate; 1 s (Edward Thomas Woodgate b 1990), 1 da (Poppy Margot Lillian b 1992); *Career* architect; Form Structures Ltd Bristol 1976–77, Rock Townsend London 1978–81, dir then md Grimshaw Architects LLP (formerly Nicholas Grimshaw & Partners Ltd) (dir various projects incl new airside centre for Zürich Airport, Euro Inst of Health and Med Sciences Univ of Surrey, RAC Regnl Control Centre Bristol, and Stansted Airport Masterplan); memb Architectural Ctee Steel Construction Inst; numerous public lectures at home and abroad; assessor: Civic Tst Awards 1993–2006, Corus Students' Competition 1994–, Structural Steel Awards 2005–; memb ARCUK 1981, RIBA 1981, MInstD 1996; *Recreations* sailing (yachtmaster); *Clubs* Seahorse Sailing; *Style*— Christopher Nash, Esq; ✉ Grimshaw Architects LLP, 57 Clerkenwell Road, London EC1M 5NG (tel 020 7291 4141, fax 020 7291 4194, e-mail chris.nash@grimshaw-architects.com)

NASH, David Harwood; s of Victor Nash, of Welwyn, Herts, and Anne, *née* Richardson; *Educ* St Albans Sch; *m* 1, Susan Margaret (d 1991), da of John Charlesworth Haldane; 1 s (James Harwood), 2 da (Charlotte Louise Harwood, Annabel Haldane); m, Valerie Conroy Scott; *Career* ptnr: Binder Hamlyn 1966–76, Pannell Kerr Forster (and predecessor firms) 1977–91, Nash & Co, chartered accountants 1991–; dir: Pelham Investment Property plc 1990, South West Peninsular Properties Ltd 2002; Liveryman Worshipful Co of Farriers; FCA; *Recreations* skiing, sailing, tennis; *Clubs* Royal Thames Yacht, MCC, Harlequin Football; *Style*— David Nash, Esq; ✉ Highclose Farm, Hungerford, Berkshire RG17 0SP (tel 01488 680616, fax 01488 680643)

NASH, David John; s of Herbert John Nash, of Swanage, Dorset, and Daphne Diana, *née* Wedekind; *b* 12 May 1942; *Educ* Ashdown House, Marlborough, Université de Neuchâtel; *m* 1, 1966, Judith, *née* Small; 1 da (Sarah b 30 Jan 1970); m 2, 1986, Lucy Mitchell-Innes, 2 da (Josephine Clare b 14 Nov 1987, Isobel Daphne 16 April 1990); *Career* Sotheby's: London 1961–63, asst rep NY 1963–66 dir 1966–78, dir Painting Dept Sotheby's USA 1978–89, sr vice-pres and worldwide dir of Impressionist and Modern Painting Dept 1989–96; dir Mitchell-Innes & Nash Fine Art Consultants and Dealers 1996–; memb Art Advsy Panel US Internal Revenue Serv 1984–; *Style*— David Nash, Esq; ✉ 1060 Fifth Avenue, New York City, New York 10021, USA; Mitchell-Innes & Nash, 1018 Madison Avenue, New York City, New York 10021, USA (tel 00 1 212 744 7400)

NASH, Prof David John; OBE (2004); s of Lt-Col W C E Nash (d 1984), of Maentwrog, N Wales, and D L Nash (d 1994); *b* 14 November 1945; *Educ* Brighton Coll, Kingston Coll of Art, Chelsea Sch of Art; *m* 1972, Claire, da of Walter Langdown; 2 s (William b 1973, Jack b 1977); *Career* artist; sculpture, environmental projects and works on paper exhibited worldwide; work in over 100 public collections incl: Tate Gallery London, Guggenheim Museum NY, Metropolitan Museum of Art Tokyo; Hon Dr of Art and Design Kingston Univ 1999, Hon Dr of Humanities Univ of Glamorgan 2002; hon fell Univ of Wales Cardiff 2004; RA 1999; *Books* Forms into Time (1996, reprinted 2001), The Sculpture of David Nash (1996, reprinted 1999), Black and Light (2001), The Return of Art to Nature (2003); *Style*— Prof David Nash, OBE, RA; ✉ c/o Annely Juda Fine Art, 23 Dering Street, London W1S 1AW (tel 020 7629 7578)

NASH, David P; *Career* formerly with ICI plc and Cadbury Schweppes plc; Grand Metropolitan plc: main bd dir 1989–96, gp fin dir 1989–93, chm and chief exec Food and Retailing Sector 1993–96; formerly chm: Kenwood Appliances plc 1996–2001, General Healthcare Group Ltd, Amicus Healthcare Group Ltd; non-exec dir: Sun Life and Provincial Holdings plc, Cable & Wireless plc, AXA UK plc; formerly non-exec dir: The Energy Group plc, IMRO; hon treas Prince of Wales Business Leaders Forum; *Style*— David Nash, Esq

NASH, His Hon Judge (Timothy Michael) Ellison; s of Denis Frederick Ellison Nash, of Bickley, Kent, and Joan Mary, *née* Andrew; *b* 10 December 1939; *Educ* Dulwich Coll; *m* 1965, Gael, da of Dr A M Roy; 2 s (Matthew (decd), Oliver b 15 Feb 1971), 1 da (Charlotte b 12 June 1973); *Career* called to the Bar Gray's Inn 1964; standing counsel: DHSS 1974–79, DTI 1976–90; recorder 1990–94 (asst recorder 1987–89), circuit judge 1994–; chm Home Office Police Appeals Tbnl 1988–94, legal assessor to GMC 1989–94, examiner Dio of Canterbury 1990–94; special constable Met Police 1961–79; *Style*— His Hon Judge Ellison Nash

NASH, Eric Stanley; s of Stanley Noah Nash (d 1975), of Paulton, Somerset, and Ina Louisa Nash (d 1978); *b* 17 May 1944; *Educ* Midsomer Norton GS, Univ of Bristol (BDS), Univ of Wales (MSc); *m* 14 June 1969, Enid Dorothy, da of Walter Perry, of Farrington Gurney, Avon; 2 s (Richard John b 10 Oct 1981, Michael James b 8 June 1983); *Career* jr posts: Bristol Hosps 1967–68, United Cardiff Hosps 1968–72; lectr Univ of Wales Coll of Med 1973–79, conslt oral and maxillofacial surgn North Glamorgan NHS Tst, clinical dir North Glamorgan NHS Tst; lectr and author of articles in Br Jl of Oral Surgery; memb Welsh Dental Ctee; dir Dental Postgrad Educn for Wales 1991–; memb: CESU (Wales), Peer Review, MEDMEC (Wales), Dental Manpower Sub Ctee, COPDEND (UK); FDS, RCS, fell Assoc of Oral and Maxillofacial Surgery 1979; FRSM; *Recreations* church organisation, playing the organ, music; *Style*— Eric Nash, Esq; ✉ Mendip House, 43 Penlline Road, Whitchurch, Cardiff, South Glamorgan CF14 2AB (tel 029 2062 7548); Oral Surgery Department, Prince Charles Hospital, Merthyr Tydfil, Mid Glamorgan; Room 130, Dental School, University of Wales College of Medicine, Heath Park, Cardiff (tel 029 2074 2594)

NASH, John Alfred Stoddard; s of Lewis John Alfred Maurice Nash, and Josephine Karen, *née* Stoddard (d 1962); *b* 22 March 1949; *Educ* Milton Abbey, CCC Oxford (MA); *m* 6 Aug 1983, Caroline Jennifer, da of Geoffrey Hamilton Paul (d 1985); 1 da (Josephine b 1984), 1 s (Charles b 1985); *Career* asst dir Lazard Brothers and Co Ltd 1975–83, md Advent Ltd 1986 (joined 1983), chm British Venture Capital Association 1988–89, chm Sovereign Capital Ptnrs LLP 1989–, chm Care UK plc; *Recreations* golf, tennis, skiing; *Clubs* Turf; *Style*— John Nash, Esq; ✉ Sovereign Capital Partners LLP, 25 Buckingham Gate, London SW1E 6LD

NASH, John Roderick (Roddy); s of Robert William Nash, and Joan, *née* Chapman; *b* 18 June 1948; *Educ* Michaelhouse Balgowan, Middx Hosp Med Sch (MB BS, MD); *m* 11 May 1974, Rosemary Anne, da of Rev Robert Charles Poston, of Stokeby Nayland; 2 s (James b 1976, Mark b 1977); *Career* lectr in surgery Univ of Leicester 1975–84, conslt surgn S Derbyshire Health Authy 1984–, chief exec Derbyshire Royal Infirmary NHS Tst 1997–98; FRCSEd 1977, FRCS 1988; *Recreations* trout fishing; *Style*— Roddy Nash, Esq

NASH, Ronald Peter; CMG (2004), LVO (1983); s of John Henry Nash, and Jean Carmichael, *née* McIlwraith; *Educ* Harefield Secdy Modern Sch, Southall Grammar Tech Sch, Southall GS, Univ of Manchester (BA); *Career* entered HM Dip Serv 1970; served: Moscow, Vienna, New Delhi, Colombo; ambass to Nepal 1999–2003, ambass to Afghanistan 2002–03, high cmmr to Trinidad and Tobago 2004–06; MCIL; *Recreations* tennis; *Style*— Mr Ronald Nash, CMG, LVO; ✉ 175 Hirings Hill, Chesham, Buckinghamshire HP5 2PN

NASH, Stephanie Joy; da of Alfred Raymond Nash (d 1973), and Mary, *née* Spencer; *b* 20 March 1959; *Educ* Oldfields Hall Sch for Girls Uttoxeter, Sch of St Mary & St Anne Abbots Bromley (Duke of Edinburgh Gold award), St Martin's Sch of Art (BA); *Partner* Anthony Colin Michael, *qv*; 2 s (Montgomery Louis Spencer b 6 May 1996, Nelson Bartholomew Edwin b 28 Nov 1998), 1 da (Astor Elizabeth Pearl b 8 Jan 2003); *Career* Island Records: graphic designer 1981–86, art dir 1986–88; full-time ptnr Michael Nash Associates 1988– (fndr ptnr 1984); initially designers of record sleeves for artists incl Neneh Cherry, Fluke, Etienne Daho and Seal, subsequently cmmns for fashion designers Marc Jacobs, Jasper Conran, Issey Miyake, Jil Sander and Philip Treacy, etc, graphic designers for Harvey Nichols own brand food products 1992–, packaging designers for Egg (fashion retail outlet) 1994; memb AGI, FRSA; *Awards* (for Harvey Nichols food packaging) Gold Award D&AD for the Most Outstanding Packing Range 1993, Silver Award D&AD for the Most Outstanding Packaging - Individual Pack 1994, Art Dirs' Club of Europe Award 1994, CSD Minerva Award for Graphic Design 1994 and NY Festivals Gold Medal and Grand Award 1994; Silver Award D&AD for Compact Disc Packaging for Massive Attack 1995, Silver Award D&AD for Packaging Range for UTH Menswear 2001, Silver Award D&AD for John Galliano Packaging; various music industry awards; *Style*— Miss Stephanie Nash; ✉ Michael Nash Associates, 42–44 Newman Street, London W1P 3PA (tel 020 7631 3370, fax 020 7637 9629, e-mail stephanie@michaelnash.co.uk)

NASH, Dr Timothy Paul (Tim); s of Flt Lt Laurence Nash (d 1970), and Margaret Ellen, *née* Davis (d 1985); *b* 13 August 1946; *Educ* Changi GS, Andover GS, UCH Med Sch London (MB BS); *m* 18 Oct 1969, Bridget Eleanor, da of William Albert Harrison, of Tonbridge; 3 da (Deborah b 23 Feb 1972, Rebecca b 24 April 1974, Juliette b 3 April 1980), 1 s (Matthew b 2 Dec 1981); *Career* conslt in anaesthetics and pain mgmnt Basingstoke and N Hants Health Authy 1976–94, conslt in pain medicine The Walton Centre for Neurology and Neurosurgery Liverpool 1995–2007 (dir 1998–2002), Mersey regnl advsr in Pain Mgmnt Royal Coll of Anaesthetists; hon sr lectr Univ of Liverpool 1999– (hon clinical lectr 1995–99, dir Pain Studies 1997–2006), visiting prof Kwong Wah Hosp Hong Kong 1999; ed Frontiers of Pain 1988–92, asst ed The Pain Clinic 1989–95; pres The Pain Soc 1994–97 (fndr ed IPS Forum 1982–85, sec 1985–88); chm: Pain Speciality Working Gp NHS Clinical Terms Project 1992–95, Task Force on Educnl Standards (memb Cncl), European Fedn of Chapters, Int Assoc for the Study of Pain 1995–99 (also memb task forces on taxonomy and data retrieval); memb Cncl Nat Back Pain Assoc 1994–2000; tstee Pain Relief Fndn 2007–; contrib World of Pain (TV documentary) 2002; memb: BMA, RSM, Assoc of Anaesthetists; hon memb The Pain Soc; FFARCS 1974; *Publications* contrib to: Pain (1985, 1986, 1993 and 2002), Chronic Non-Cancer Pain (1987), The Pain Clinic (1987, 1990, 1992 and 2001), British Medical Journal (1988, 1998), British Journal of Hospital Medicine (1991), Medicine International (1991 and 1995), International

Journal of Pain Therapy (1993), Read Codes (3 version, 1994), Anaesthesia Review 12 (1995), Management of Pain - A World Perspective (1996, 1998), Health and Healing the Natural Way: Managing Pain (1998), Acta Neurologica Scandinavia (1999), Pain Digest (1999), Prescriber (1999), Alternative Answers: Pain (1999), Clinical Pain Management (2002), Palliative Medicine (2003), British Journal of Anaesthesia (2005); *Recreations* music, reading, hiking, badminton, cricket; *Style—* Dr Tim Nash; ✉ The Walton Centre for Neurology and Neurosurgery, Lower Lane, Fazakerley, Liverpool L9 7LJ (tel 0151 529 5749, fax 0151 529 5486, e-mail nashtp@liv.ac.uk)

NASH, Prof William Frederick; CBE (1987); s of William Henry Nash (d 1960), and Doris, *née* Jenkins; *b* 28 January 1925; *Educ* Amman Valley GS, UCW Swansea (BSc, MSc), Univ of Manchester (PhD); *m* 18 Aug 1951, (Gladys) Christabel, da of Stephen Williams (d 1942); 1 da (Sian Christabel (Mrs Crosby) b 16 May 1959), 1 s (Dylan Llywellyn b 16 April 1962); *Career* res physicist Metropolitan Vickers Manchester 1945–48; Univ of Nottingham: asst lectr, lectr, sr lectr 1950–64, reader in physics 1964–74, prof of physics 1974–90 (prof emeritus 1991), pro-vice-chllr 1974–80, head Dept of Physics 1981–84; author of over 100 articles on cosmic rays and astrophysics; chm Home Defence Scientific Advsy Ctee 1973–95, chief regnl science advsr Number 3 Regn Home Defence 1962–95, chm E Midlands Univs Military Educn Ctee 1973–90, memb Astronomy and Space Research Bd SERC 1980–84; tstee govr Queen Elizabeth's (1561) Endowed Sch Mansfield 1962–; Queen's Silver Jubilee Medal 1977; non-resident memb Hugh Stewart Hall SCR 1962–; CPhys, FInstP, FRAS, FRSA; *Recreations* rugby (played when young), operatic singing, walking, travel; *Style—* Prof William Nash, CBE; ✉ 6 Spean Drive, Aspley Hall, Nottingham NG8 3NQ (tel 0115 929 6607); Department of Physics, University of Nottingham, University Park, Nottingham NG7 2RD (mobile 07979 335723)

NASON, Col Ian Geoffrey; s of Lt Col C F Nason, OBE (d 1988), of Guernsey, and Eleanor Ethel May, *née* Carey; *b* 11 November 1936; *Educ* Wellington; *m* 31 Dec 1960, Anne Mary, da of Lt-Col J W McKergow (d 1961), of NZ; 2 da (Julia Anne b 24 Aug 1962, Sara Anne Catherine b 24 July 1964), 2 s (Andrew John Fortescue b 18 Oct 1965, James Henry Fortescue b 18 Nov 1970); *Career* cmmnd Seaforth Highlanders 1956, Staff Coll Canada 1967, Nat Def Coll 1977, cmd 1 Bn Queen's Own Highlanders 1977–79, instr Nigerian Staff Coll 1979–81, COS HQ Br Forces Falkland Islands 1983, Col Cdr RMA Sandhurst 1984–86, DA Br High Cmmn 1987–91; civil servant HQ Land Cmd 1992–2003, asst John Morgan Hire Co 2003–; chm Army Ornithological Soc 1994–2000; Chief Aku-Tubo of Bakana Island Rivers State Nigeria; *Books* Enjoy Nigeria (1991, 2 edn 1993); *Recreations* African bird photography, golf, travel; *Clubs* Salisbury and South Wilts Golf (vice-capt srs section); *Style—* Col Ian Nason; ✉ Mount Sorrel Farm, Broad Chalke, Salisbury, Wiltshire SP5 5HQ (tel 01722 780296, e-mail nasonam@aol.com)

NATHAN, Dr Anthony Wayne; s of Murray Nathan (decd), of London, and Pamela Simone, *née* Spack; *b* 10 September 1952; *Educ* Haberdashers' Aske's, Middx Hosp Med Sch (MB BS, MD); *m* 11 July 1975, Alison Jane, da of late John Dick Campbell; 1 da (Emma Michelle b 4 March 1979), 1 s (Mark b 9 Feb 1981); *Career* house physician Middx Hosp London 1975–76, house surgn in neurosurgery The Royal Infirmary Sheffield Feb-July 1976, SHO in gen med and clinical pharmacology Hammersmith Hosp London 1976–77, SHO in cardiology Brompton Hosp London Feb-July 1977, SHO in renal and transplant med Guy's Hosp London 1977–78, registrar in gen med Royal Free Hosp London March 1978–79; Bart's: registrar in cardiology 1979–81, hon sr registrar in cardiology 1981–87, conslt cardiologist 1987–; currently conslt cardiologist Barts & the London NHS Tst; former sec Br Pacing and Electrophysiology Group, former sr ed Jl of Electrophysiology; currently contrib papers to various other learned jls; Int Cardiac Pacing Soc Award for Scientific Excellence 1983; memb: Br Cardiac Soc, Br Cardiovascular Interventional Soc, Br Med Laser Assoc, Br Pacing and Electrophysiology Gp, Euro Laser Assoc, Int Soc for Heart Transplantation, N American Soc of Pacing and Electrophysiology (memb Advsy Cncl); hon memb Spanish Soc of Cardiology, fndr fell Euro Soc of Cardiology, Fell American Coll of Cardiology, FRCP 1992; *Recreations* sub-aqua diving, skiing, football, theatre, modern British art; *Style—* Dr Anthony W Nathan; ✉ Department of Cardiology, St Bartholomew's Hospital, West Smithfield, London EC1A 7BE (tel 020 7601 7810); BUPA Hospital Bushey, Heathbourne Road, Bushey, Hertfordshire WD23 1RD (tel 020 8420 4471, fax 020 8420 4472); 84 Harley Street, London W1G 7HW (e-mail anthony.nathan@btinternet.com)

NATHAN, Clemens Neumann; s of Kurt Arthur Nathan (d 1958), of London, and Dr Else Nathan, *née* Kanin; *b* 24 August 1933; *Educ* Berkhamsted Sch, Scottish Coll of Textiles, Heriott-Watt Univ, Univ of Leeds; *m* 4 June 1963, (Barbara) Rachel, da of Geoffrey H Whitehill (d 1971), of London; 2 da (Jennifer Ruth b 13 May 1964, Elizabeth Rebecca b 18 Oct 1970), 1 s (Richard Abraham b 15 Dec 1965); *Career* conslt textile technologist on bd of various textile orgns, govt advsr; vice-pres Anglo Jewish Assoc (pres 1983–89), jt chm CCJO (UN NGO); chm Christian Jewish Rels Cambridge 1998–2003, vice-pres Centre for German-Jewish Studies Univ of Sussex; presidential advsr Alliance Israelite Universelle; former vice-pres Textile Inst, memb Int Cncl; author on mktg and textiles; Textile Inst Medal (for servs to textile industry and Inst) 1987; hon fell Shenkar Coll of Technol Israel 1994, hon fell Centre for Jewish-Christian Relations Cambridge, visiting fell SSEES Univ of London; Freeman City of London, Liveryman Worshipful Co of Glovers; CTex, FTI, FRAI, FRSA; Cavaliere Al Merito Della Republica Italiana, Israel Econ Cncl Medal, Grosse Ehrenzeichen Austria; *Recreations* swimming, mountaineering, art, history, music; *Clubs* Athenaeum; *Style—* Clemens Nathan, Esq; ✉ Flat 10, Cambridge Terrace, London NW1 4JL (e-mail clemens@newnathan.com)

NATHAN, Ian L B; s of Christopher Nathan, of Stevenage, and Patricia, *née* Lowe; *b* 17 July 1969; *Educ* John Hampden GS High Wycombe, UC Cardiff (BSc), Watford Coll (Dip Publishing); *Career* freelance film journalist and broadcaster 1990–94; Empire: staff writer 1994–95, reviews ed 1995–96, features ed 1996, ed 1996–99, assoc ed 1999–, awards prodr 1999–, Empire TV prodr 1999–, nominated for PPA Consumer Magazine of the Year 1998; contrib: The Times, Arena, Mail on Sunday, Q; *Recreations* travelling, sport, literature; *Style—* Ian Nathan, Esq; ✉ Endeavour House, 189 Shaftesbury Avenue, London WC2 4JG (tel 020 7859 8612, fax 020 7859 8613, e-mail ian.nathan@emap.com and ilbn_uk@yahoo.co.uk)

NATHAN, Janet; *b* 31 March 1938, London; *Educ* St Martin's Sch of Art London; *m* 1999, Patrick Caulfield; *Career* artist; *Solo Exhibitions* Newcastle Poly Art Gallery 1979, Air Gallery London 1981, Ikon Gallery Birmingham 1982, Ferens Art Gallery Hull 1982, Riverside Studios London 1983, Howard Gardens Gallery Cardiff 1983, Mappin Art Gallery Sheffield 1984, Windsor Old Ct Windsor 1986, Warwick Arts Tst London 1988, Hampstead Theatre 1991, The Gallery at John Jones 1992, Chelsea Arts Club London 1993, Reed's Wharf Gallery London 1995, Concourse Gallery Barbican Centre London 1997, Metropole Arts Centre Folkestone 1997, Graves Art Gallery Sheffield 1997, Gardner Arts Centre Brighton 1997, The Customs House South Shields 1997, Tiempos Modernos Madrid 1997, British Airways Terminal 1 1999–2002, Aalders Gallerie France 2006; *Group Exhibitions* incl: The British Art Show (Arts Cncl touring, Arnolfini Bristol, Newcastle upon Tyne and Mappin Art Gallery Sheffield), Painted Constructions (ICA London) 1980, Royal Acad Summer Exhbn 1980–2002, Art and the Sea (Third Eye Centre Glasgow 1981 and ICA London 1982), 10 London Artists (Scandinavian tour) 1983, Coloured Constructions (Ikon Gallery Birmingham and touring), Whitechapel Open Exhbn 1983 and 1984, Leicestershire Exhbn (annually) 1983–93, TWSA Touring Exhbn 1984, The London Group (Morley Coll and RCA) 1984–2000, Crawford Centre for the Arts (Univ of St Andrews) 1985, Scarborough Festival 1985, Art on a Plate (Serpentine Gallery London) 1987, John Moores 15 Exhbn 1987, London Group Members Exhbn 1981–93, London Group (RCA) 1990, Riverside One London 1990, The Discerning Eye (invited by Sir Roger de Gray, PRA) Exhbn London 1990, Redfern Gallery London 1992, Leicestershire Exhbn 1993, London Group (London Inst and Barbican) 1993, Bruton Street Gallery 1993, RGI Glasgow 1993, Summer Exhbn (William Jackson Gallery) 1994, London Group 1994, 1995, 1996, 2000, 2003, 2004 and 2005, Contemporary British Artists (Smiths Galleries London and Business Design Centre London) 1995, John Moores 19 Exhbn 1995, Cross Currents (Reeds Wharf and Barbican) 1996, Angela Flowers Small Works 1997, RCA Br Art Fair 1998, Olympia Art Fair 1999, Aalders Gallery France 2000, Walk Gallery 2003, RA Summer Exhbn 2004, 2005 and 2006; *Work in Collections* Walker Art Gallery Liverpool, ICI HQ Millbank, Exchange House Broadgate, Leics Educn Authy, HRH The Princess Margaret, Lord Snowdon, Lonrho Group, Smiths Industries, Unilever House, Pentland Industries, Coopers & Lybrand, Chelsea and Westminster Hosp, Arts Cncl GB, Br Cncl, private collections in Britain, America and Europe; *Style—* Ms Janet Nathan; ✉ 19 Belsize Square, London NW3 4HT (tel 020 7431 1188, website www.janetnathan.com)

NATHAN, Michael Ronald; s of Maj Cyril H Nathan (d 1977), of Chiddingfold, Surrey, and Violet, *née* Simon (d 1974); *b* 20 July 1927; *Educ* St Cyprian's Sch, Charterhouse; *m* 21 Oct 1984, Jennifer Madelin Nathan, MBE, da of Mr Eric Abrahams; *Career* articled clerk Whinney Smith & Whinney 1948–51, ptnr Baker Tilly (and predecessor firms) 1953–90 (conslt 1990–2007); pres Stepney Jewish (B'nai B'rith) Clubs & Settlement 1978–95 (hon treas 1954–95), memb Cncl Guild of Glass Engravers 1981– (chm 1982–85 and 1993–94, pres 1994–2001, hon fell 2005), hon treas Assoc for Jewish Youth 1954–95, hon treas Jewish Welfare Bd 1959–69, memb Advsy Cncl Jewish Youth Fund 1955–95, chm United Charities Fund Liberal Jewish Synagogue 1962–2007; Master Worshipful Co of Glass Sellers 1973–74 (tstee Charity Fund 1974–); FCA 1958 (ACA 1951); *Recreations* art, glass (especially modern glass engraving), music, reading, gardening, cricket, entertaining family and friends; *Clubs* The Samuel Pepys; *Style—* Michael Nathan, Esq; ✉ c/o Baker Tilly, 2 Bloomsbury Street, London WC1B 3ST (tel 020 7413 5100)

NATHAN, Peter Geoffrey; OBE (1999), DL (Gtr London 1991); s of Maj Cyril H Nathan, FCA (d 1977), of Chiddingfold, Surrey, and Violet, *née* Simon (d 1974); *b* 27 July 1929; *Educ* Summer Fields, Charterhouse, Oriel Coll Oxford (MA), Univ of Paris (Dip Etudes de Civilisation Française); *m* 14 May 1970, Caroline Monica, da of Lt Cdr Anthony C Mullen, RINVR (d 1991); 2 s (Hugo, Anthony), 2 da (Arabella, Venetia); *Career* writer RN 1948–49; admitted slr 1958; Herbert Oppenheimer Nathan & Vandyk 1954–88 (ptnr 1959–88); conslt: Boodle Hatfield 1988–92, Wood & Awdry 1992–2000; govr Sports Aid Fndn Ltd 1999–2002, hon pres Sports Aid London 2003– (chm 1999–2002); London Playing Fields Soc: chm 1984–97, vice-pres 1997–, dep chm Peter May Meml Appeal 1995–97; vice-pres Croydon Playing Fields Soc 1996–; Nat Heritage Sec's ministerial nominee London Cncl for Sport and Recreation 1992–95; tstee Oriel Coll Devpt Tst until 1996 (patron 1996–), chm Oriel Law Soc until 1996, chm Oriel Law Fellowship Appeal until 1996; chm Chiddingfold Branch of Farnham Cons Assoc 1965–70; memb: Community Health Cncl for Kensington, Chelsea and Westminster representing Royal Borough of Kensington and Chelsea 1974–78, Cncl British Heart Fndn 1976–93, Cncl Anglo-Swiss Soc 1988–2005, Ct City Univ 1989–93, Livery Consultative Ctee Corp of London 1994–97; successively memb Post Office User Area Cncls for City of London and London W2–W14 1988–93; chm Butterflies CC 1986–93 (hon treas 1961–86); recipient Nat Playing Fields Assoc Pres's Cert for servs to the playing fields movement 1992; Freeman City of London 1961, Master Worshipful Co of Gold and Silver Wyre Drawers 1989 (memb Ct of Assts, chm Tercentenary 1993 Exhbn Ctee); hon memb Geographical Assoc; memb Law Soc; *Recreations* sport, reading, wine, opera; *Clubs* MCC, Vincent's (Oxford), Jesters, Oriental, City Univ; *Style—* P G Nathan, Esq, OBE, DL; ✉ Kites Nest House, Bourton, Dorset SP8 5AZ

NATHAN, Philip Charles; MBE (2001); s of Denis William Nathan, of South Woodham Ferrers, Essex, and Grace Pauline, *née* Brennan; *b* 11 May 1951; *Educ* Alexandra Park Sch; *Career* stockbroker; dir Charles Stanley & Co Ltd; Lions Clubs Int: former pres Rayleigh, South Woodham Ferrers Essex, dist govr E Anglia 1995–96, chm Cncl of Govrs Br Isles and Ireland 1996–97, int dir 1999–2001, Int Bd appointee 2002–03; chm Medicalert Fndn; memb: Stock Exchange Veterans' Club Ctee (charity steward), Stock Exchange Benevolent Fund Ctee, Lime Street Ward Club; Freeman City of London; FSI, MInstD; *Clubs* City of London; *Style—* Philip Nathan, Esq, MBE; ✉ Charles Stanley & Co Ltd, 25 Luke Street, London EC2A 4AR (tel 020 7667 2266, fax 020 7551 0362, mobile 077 8538 0069, e-mail phil.nathan@charles-stanley.co.uk)

NATHAN, 2 Baron (UK 1940); Capt Roger Carol Michael Nathan; s of 1 Baron, PC (d 1963); *b* 5 December 1922; *Educ* Stowe, New Coll Oxford; *m* 1950, Philippa, da of Maj Joseph Bernard Solomon, MC, of Pulborough, W Sussex; 1 s, 2 da; *Heir* s, Hon Rupert Nathan; *Career* served WWII, Capt 17/21 Lancers (despatches, wounded twice); slr; sr ptnr Herbert Oppenheimer Nathan & Vandyk until 1986, conslt Denton Hall Burgin and Warrens until 1992; hon assoc memb Bar Assoc of City of NY; pres Jewish Welfare Bd 1967–71, hon pres Central Br Fund for Jewish Relief and Rehabilitation 1977– (chm 1971–77), vice-pres RSA 1977– (chm 1975–77); vice-chm Cancer Res Campaign 1987– (chm Exec Ctee 1970–75, treas 1979–87); memb Royal Cmmn on Environmental Pollution 1979–89; memb (House of Lords): Select Ctee on Euro Communities 1983–88 and 1990–93, Privileges Ctee 1992–99, Select Ctee on Sci and Technol 1995–99, Sub Ctee on E Euro Union Law and Instns 1995–99; chm (House of Lords): Environment Sub Ctee 1983–87 and 1990–92, Select Ctee on Murder and Life Imprisonment 1988–89, Animal Procedures Ctee 1990–93; pres: UK Environmental Law Assoc 1987–92, Nat Soc for Clean Air 1987–89, Soc of Sussex Downsmen 1987–93, Weald and Downland Open Air Museum 1994–97; chm: Inst of Environment Assessment 1990–91, Ct of Discipline Univ of Cambridge 1989–92, S Downs Conservation Bd 1992–97; memb Cncl Univ of Sussex 1989–98; Master Worshipful Co of Gardeners 1963; Hon LLD Univ of Sussex; FSA, FRSA, FRGS; *Publications* The Spice of Life (memoir, 2003); *Clubs* Athenaeum, Cavalry and Guards'; *Style—* The Rt Hon the Lord Nathan; ✉ Collyers Farm, Lickfold, Petworth, West Sussex GU28 9DU (tel 01798 861284, fax 01798 861619, e-mail nathan@dial.pipex.com)

NATHAN, Sara Catherine; da of Derek Maurice Nathan, of New Malden, Surrey, and Mary Catherine, *née* Lavine; *Educ* Wimbledon HS, New Hall Cambridge (BA, vice-pres Cambridge Union), Stanford Univ (Harkness fell); *m* 15 July 1984, Malcolm John Singer, dir of music Yehudi Menuhin Sch, s of Gerald Singer, of Finchley, London; 1 da (Rachel Fonya b 23 Jan 1989), 1 s (Jonathan Joseph b 5 June 1991); *Career* BBC: news trainee 1980–82, prodr/sr prodr BBC News and Current Affrs (on News, Newsnight, Breakfast Time and The Money Programme) 1982–87, output ed Breakfast News and Newsnight 1989–92, results ed Gen Election 1992, asst to Jenny Abramsky as ed News & Current Affrs Radio/controller Radio 5 Live 1992–93, ed The Magazine (Radio 5 Live) 1994–95; ed Channel Four News ITN 1995–97, freelance journalist 1998–; ed: TUC Live '98 (BBC2) 1998, The State of Israel (Channel 4) 1998; media columnist The Scotsman 1999–2000; chair Animal Procedures Ctee 2006–; memb: Human Fertilization and Embryology Authy 1998–2005, Bar Cncl 1998–2004, BAFTA, Radio Authy 1999–2003, Gambling Review Body 2000–01, Criminal Injuries Compensation Appeal Panel 2000–06, Regulatory Decisions Ctee FSA 2001–, Bd Ofcom 2002–, Judicial Appts Cmmn 2006–; chair Children's First Cmmn Lambeth 2000–02; cmmr Marshall Scholarships; memb (premium rate regulator) Ind Ctee for the Supervision of Standards of Telephone Info Servs

(ICSTIS) 2002–; Sony Radio Awards: Gold for Best Response to a News Event 1995, Silver for Best Topical Phone-in 1995; *Recreations* theatre, cinema; *Style*— Ms Sara Nathan; ✉ tel 020 8992 2318, fax 020 8896 2556, e-mail sara@natsing.co.uk or sara.nathan@ofcom.org.uk

NATKIEL, Rod; s of Daniel Natkiel (d 1986), and Marjorie Jessie, *née* Pinkham (d 1988); *b* 30 January 1952; *Educ* Kingston GS, Univ of Bristol (BA), Univ of Birmingham (MBA); *m* 6 Nov 1976, Janet Ruth; 2 s (Rory b 29 Aug 1978, Alastair b 6 March 1981); *Career* Arts Cncl Bursary trainee dir 1976, assoc dir and resident musical dir Contact Theatre Manchester 1975–78, dir/prodr BBC TV Light Entertainment Dept Scotland 1978–84, freelance exec prodr/dir in entertainment, drama, news and current affairs 1984–92, prodn exec Birmingham Media Devpt Agency 1992–93, head of network TV BBC Midlands and East (Pebble Mill) 1992–96, head of network prodn BBC Birmingham 1996–99, md and head of prodn Rod Natkiel Associates 1999–; visiting prof of television studies Univ of Central England 1993–99; chm: Variety Club Midlands 1997–2000, W Midlands Arts 1997–2002; memb Arts Cncl of England 1997–98; tstee Variety Club of GB 1999–; chair Screen W Midlands 2001–03; *Recreations* squash, cricket, cinema, theatre, DIY; *Style*— Rod Natkiel, Esq; ✉ Rod Natkiel Associates Ltd, 5 Vesey Road, Sutton Coldfield, West Midlands B73 5NP (tel 0121 355 2197, fax 0121 355 8033, e-mail rod@rodnatkiel.co.uk)

NAUGHTIE, (Alexander) James; s of Alexander Naughtie (d 1973), and Isabella, *née* Milne (d 1994); *b* 9 August 1951; *Educ* Keith GS, Univ of Aberdeen (MA), Syracuse Univ NY (MA); *m* 1986, Eleanor, *née* Updale; 1 s (Andrew b 22 Sept 1987), 2 da (Catherine b 24 Feb 1989, Flora b 25 Jan 1991); *Career* journalist: The Press and Journal 1975–77, The Scotsman 1977–84; chief political corr The Guardian 1984–88; presenter: The World at One (BBC Radio) 1988–94, BBC Proms 1991–, Today Programme (BBC Radio) 1994–, Book Club (BBC Radio) 1998–; contrib to newspapers and magazines; Laurence Stern fell The Washington Post 1981, Sony Radio Personality of the Year 1991; memb Cncl Edinburgh Int Festival 2003–; Hon LLD Univ of Aberdeen 1991, Hon LLD Univ of St Andrews 2001, Hon DUniv Stirling 2001, Hon Dr Napier Univ 2002, Hon Dr Glasgow Caledonian Univ 2002; *Books* The Rivals (2001), The Accidental American (2004); *Recreations* books, opera; *Clubs* Travellers, Garrick; *Style*— James Naughtie; ✉ The Today Programme, BBC News Centre, London W12 7RJ (fax 020 8940 7047, e-mail james.naughtie@bbc.co.uk)

NAUGHTON, Philip Anthony; QC (1988); s of Francis Naughton, of Littlehampton, W Sussex, and Madeleine, *née* Wales; *b* 18 May 1943; *Educ* Wimbledon Coll, Univ of Nottingham (LLB); *m* 6 July 1968, Barbara Jane, da of Prof F E Bruce, of Esher, Surrey; 1 da (Charlotte b 8 Sept 1972), 2 s (Sebastian b 18 March 1974, Felix b 24 April 1978); *Career* in industry 1964–71; called to the Bar Gray's Inn 1970 (bencher 1997); *Recreations* walking, fishing, sailing, theatre, music; *Style*— Philip Naughton, Esq, QC; ✉ 3 Serjeants' Inn, London EC4Y 1BQ (tel 020 7427 5000, fax 020 7353 0425, e-mail philipnaughton@3serjeantsinn.com)

NAWRAT, Christopher John (Chris); s of Stanislaw Jerzy Nawrat (d 1976), of London, and Margaret Jane Patricia, *née* Maguire; *b* 6 February 1949; *Educ* Salesian Coll London, Univ of Edinburgh, Univ of Essex (BA); *m* 26 July 1975, Christine Patricia (d 1996), da of Daniel Patrick Boyle; *Career* sports journalist Morning Star 1979–81, ed National Student 1981–83; The Sunday Times: columnist (Inside Track) 1983–85, dep sports ed 1986–88, sports ed 1988–94; Channel 4: internet sports ed 1996–2001, internet sports investigative ed 2001–02, ed-in-chief eleven magazine 2002–04, conslt Sporting Talk 2002–03; Pools Forecaster of the Year 1979–80, Sports Reporter of the Year (special joint award with Nick Pitt) 1984–85, Sports Pages Design Award Nat Sunday Newspapers 1987, 1988 and 1990, New Media Age best entertainment site on internet 1997; memb: NUJ, Sports Writers' Assoc; *Books* The Sunday Times Chronicle of Twentieth Century Sport (with Steve Hutchings and Greg Struthers, 1992, 3 edn 1997), The Traveller's Food and Wine Guide to Spain and Portugal (with Christine Boyle, 1994), The Sunday Times Illustrated History of Football (with Steve Hutchings, 1994, 5 edn 1998), Football Inside the Game (1998); *Recreations* literature, cinema, cooking, television, Spain; *Clubs* Reform, Sports Journalists Assoc; *Style*— Chris Nawrat, Esq; ✉ 4 Hawksmoor Mews, 200 Cable Street, London E1 0DG (tel 020 7791 2507, e-mail cnawrat@sky.com)

NAYLER, Georgina Ruth; da of Dennis Victor Nayler, and Yvonne Dorothy, *née* Loader; *b* 16 March 1959; *Educ* Brentwood Co HS, Univ of Warwick (BA); *Partner* Simon Stillwell; 1 s, 1 da; *Career* Nat Heritage Memorial Fund: joined 1982, asst dir 1986, dep dir 1988, dir 1989–95; dir The Pilgrim Trust 1996–; memb Historic Buildings Cncl for Scotland 1990–96; *Recreations* gardening; *Style*— Miss Georgina Nayler; ✉ The Pilgrim Trust, Cowley House, 9 Little College Street, London SW1P 3SH

NAYLOR, Allan Peter; s of Geoffrey Alan Naylor (d 2000), of West Kirby, Wirral, and Joyce Ethel, *née* Chappell; *b* 21 December 1952; *Educ* Calday Grange GS; *m* 18 Oct 1975, (Margaret) Joan, da of Thomas Stanley Wilson (d 1980); 1 s (Stephen John b 12 Nov 1981), 1 da (Rachel Anne b 10 Sept 1985); *Career* articled clerk Stacey Williams CAs Liverpool 1971–75, mangr Pannell Kerr Forster (after merger) 1975–80, fin controller then fin dir Outlook (Glass & Aluminum) Ltd 1980–84, ptnr Leonard Batty & Son Halifax 1985–89 (PA to sr ptnr 1984–85), ptnr i/c Halifax Office Revell Ward (following merger) 1989–93, in sole practice 1993–, business conslt APN Business Conslts Ltd 2005–; tstee Rowntree Mackintosh Fund for Calderdale, local advsr Prince of Wales Tst; *Recreations* golf, rugby; *Style*— Allan P Naylor, Esq; ✉ 10 Bolehill Park, Hove Edge, Brighouse, West Yorkshire HD6 2RS (tel 01484 721286); 8 King Cross Street, Halifax HX1 2SH (tel 01422 348212, fax 01422 330166, e-mail apn@allanpnaylor.co.uk)

NAYLOR, David Malcolm Broadley; s of Frank Broadley Naylor (d 1968), of Guiseley, W Yorks, and Joyce, *née* Clarke (d 1990); *b* 2 July 1944; *Educ* Rossall Sch Fleetwood; *m* 1 (m dis); 2 s (James b 7 June 1971, Robert b 28 April 1973); m 2, Valerie Ann, *née* Sutcliffe; 2 step c (Craig b 29 June 1969, Sonia b 7 March 1973); *Career* articled clerk Smithson Blackburn & Co Leeds 1961–66, qualified chartered accountant 1966; Grant Thornton (formerly Thornton Baker): joined 1966, ptnr 1976–, managing ptnr Leeds office 1981–90, memb Policy Bd 1987–90, managing ptnr NE Region 1990–94, sr ptnr NE Region 1994–, head Int Business Centre Leeds 1998–; treas and memb Cncl Leeds C of C 1994–2001 (memb Cncl 1978–90); ACA 1966; *Recreations* collection and restoration of vintage MG sports cars, model railways, DIY; *Clubs* Leeds, MG Car, Naylor Car; *Style*— David Naylor, Esq; ✉ Borrowdale Court, 76A Filey Road, Scarborough, North Yorkshire YO11 3AY(tel 01723 366109)

NAYLOR, Douglas Rodger (Doug); s of Leslie Naylor, of Manchester, and Isabella Graham Barclay, *née* McLaughlan; *b* 31 December 1955; *Educ* Chethams Hosp Sch of Music Manchester, Univ of Liverpool; *m* 7 June 1986, Linda Jane, da of Dr Richard Arthur de Keler Glover; 2 s (Richard Duncan Glover b 20 Nov 1986, Matthew Lawrence b 9 Jan 1990); *Career* screenwriter, producer and director; writer for series incl: Son of Cliche (BBC Radio 4, Sony Award for Best Comedy, Ondas Award), Carrott's Lib (BBC TV, BAFTA Award), Three of a Kind (BBC TV, BAFTA Award), Spitting Image (a head writer and prodr, ITV, Montreux Rose and International Emmy awards); co-creator, prodr and writer (with Rob Grant): Red Dwarf (6 series, BBC2, various awards incl International Emmy for Best Popular Arts Prog 1994, British Comedy Awards Best Sitcom on BBC 1994), Red Dwarf VII and VIII (writer and exec prodr), The 10%ers (2 series Carlton TV/ITV Network, Silver Medal NY Festival 1994) 1993–; co-fndr Grant Naylor Productions Ltd; memb: Performing Rights Soc, BAFTA; *Books* Red Dwarf: Infinity Welcomes Careful Drivers (with Rob Grant, 1989), Red Dwarf: Better than Life (with Rob Grant, 1990), Red Dwarf: Last Human (1995); *Recreations* film and theatre, reading, golf; *Style*— Doug Naylor, Esq; ✉ Grant Naylor Productions Ltd, Suite 2034/6, The Orson Welles Building, Shepperton Studios, Studios Road, Shepperton, Middlesex TW17 0QD (tel 01932 592552, fax 01932 592484)

NAYLOR, (Charles) John; OBE (1993); s of Arthur Edgar Naylor, MBE (d 1984), and Elizabeth Mary Naylor (d 1991); *b* 17 August 1943; *Educ* Royal GS Newcastle upon Tyne, Haberdashers' Aske's, Clare Coll Cambridge (MA); *m* 1968, Margery; 2 s; *Career* jr and sr exec posts in industry 1965–75, dir YMCA Nat Centre Lakeside Cumbria 1975–80, dep nat sec Nat Cncl of YMCA's 1980–82, nat sec Nat Cncl of YMCA's 1982–93, chief exec Carnegie UK Tst 1993–2003; chm Assoc of Heads of Outdoor Centres 1979–80, fndr chm Scottish Grant Making Tsts Gp 1993–96, chm of tstees Brathay Exploration Group 1995–2000 (tstee 2000–), vice-chm Nat Cncl for Vol Youth Servs 1985–88, treas The Tomorrow Project 2000–, memb Devpt Grants Bd Scout Assoc 2002–05 (chm 2005–), chm Scottish Ctee Community Fund 2004–06 (memb 2003–04), memb UK Bd Big Lottery Fund 2004–06, chair Office of the Scottish Charity Regulator (OSCR) 2006–; cmmr Scottish Charities Law Review 2000–01; chm and memb: various European and world YMCA Ctees 1976–93, various Dept of Educn and Sci youth serv related ctees and advsy gps 1985–91; elder Crammond Kirk 1998–; FRSA, CIMgt; *Recreations* the outdoors (particularly mountains), golf, theatre and other performing arts; *Clubs* Bruntsfield Links Golfing Soc; *Style*— C John Naylor, Esq, OBE; ✉ Orchard House, 25B Cramond Glebe Road, Edinburgh EH4 6NT

NAYLOR, Prof Malcolm Neville; RD (1967), DL (1992); s of Roland B Naylor, MBE (d 1969), of Walsall, Staffs, and Mabel Louisa, *née* Neville (d 1976); *b* 30 January 1926; *Educ* Queen Mary's Sch Walsall, Univ of Glasgow, Univ of Birmingham (BSc, BDS), Univ of London (PhD); *m* 10 Jan 1956, (Doreen) Mary, da of Horace E Jackson, CBE (d 1966), of Gerrards Cross, Bucks; 1 s (Andrew b 1960); *Career* RNVR and RNR 1943–77: Seaman Offr 1943–47, served HMS Suffolk; dental offr 1954–77, ret as Surgn Capt (D) and princ dental surgn RNR; civil conslt dental surgn RN 1969–91, jr hosp appts Birmingham and Dundee 1954–59; Guy's Hosp Dental Sch and Univ of London: res fell 1959–62, sr lectr in preventive dentistry 1962–66, reader 1966–70, hon conslt 1966–91, prof of preventive dentistry 1970–91, head of Dept of Periodontology and Preventive Dentistry 1980–91; hon sr res fell Inst of Dental Surgery 1991–; res hon affiliate Forsyth Dental Center Boston 1975–; chm: Cncl Mil Educn Ctees of Univs of UK 1982–89, Mil Educn Ctee Univ of London 1979–91, Bd of Studies in Dentistry 1989–91 (dep chm 1986–89); memb Bd of Govrs UMDS 1987–91; memb Sea Cadet Assoc Cncl 1976–94, chm Sea Cadet Sport cncl 1975–, vice-chm Bacons Sch 1978–90, chm of govrs St Saviour's and St Olave's Sch 1987–, tstee St Olave's and St Saviour's GS Fndn 1984– (warden 1997–99); govr: Whitelands Coll 1972–96, Roehampton Inst for Higher Educn 1976–96, Wye Coll London 1991–2000; lay reader C of E 1974–; Queen's hon dental surgn 1976; Hon Col Univ of London OTC 1979–94; rep DL Borough of Lambeth 1994–2004; Freeman City of London 1981, Hon Liveryman Worshipful Co of Bakers 1981; memb: BDA 1955 (Tomes medallist 1987), IADR Br Div 1959 (treas Br Div 1974–90, pres 1990–92); patron Soc Cosmetic Scientists 1996– (Silver Medallist 1978, hon life memb 2000); FDSRCS (England) 1958, FRSM 1959 (pres Odontology Section 1984–85), Hon FDS RCPS (Glasgow) 1992; *Recreations* sailing (cruising off-shore), home and family; *Clubs* RYA, RN Sailing Assoc; *Style*— Prof Malcolm N Naylor, RD*, DL; ✉ Institute of Dental Surgery, Eastman Dental Hospital, 256 Gray's Inn Road, London WC1X 8LD (tel 020 7915 1193, fax 020 7915 2012)

NAYLOR, Martin James; s of James Naylor (d 1989), of Morley, W Yorks, and Lilian Farrar (d 1990); *b* 11 October 1944; *Educ* Dewsbury and Batley Tech and Art Sch, Leeds Art Coll, RCA (MA); *m* 17 Sept 1996, Dr Liliana Maler; *Career* artist; living and working in Argentina 1993–; art advsr Psychology Dept Univ of Leeds 1966–67; lectr: Lancaster Poly 1970–71, RCA 1972–78, Hornsey Coll of Art 1972–73, Wimbledon Art Sch 1972–73; visiting prof: École Nationale des Arts Décoratifs Nice 1972–73, École Nationale des Beaux Arts Bourges 1976; tutor RCA 1974–75 and 1977–84, assoc visiting lectr Chelsea Sch of Art 1974–75, head Sculpture Dept Hornsey Coll of Art 1977–84 (pt/t lectr 1974–75), artist in residence Cité Internationale des Arts Paris 1982, artist in residence Altos de Chavon La Romana Dominican Repub 1985, artist in residence/sr visiting fell Br Sch at Rome 1987, artist in residence MOMA Buenos Aires 1993, visiting artist The New York Studio Sch NYC 1993; Freedom of the City of La Plata Buenos Aires 1993; FRSA 1989; *Solo Exhibitions* incl: Rowan Gallery London 1973–80, Works on Paper - Paris 1982 (Juda Rowan Gallery) 1983, Newcastle Poly Art Gallery 1983, Between Discipline and Desire (Galerie Artem Quimper France) 1985, Galeria Principal (Altos de Chavon La Romana Dominican Repub) 1985, La Galeria Santo Domingo 1986, Serpentine Gallery London 1986, Leeds Art Gallery 1986, Walker Art Gallery Liverpool 1987, James Mayor Gallery London, Galerie Léger Malmö Sweden 1988, Galerie Art Now Gothenberg Sweden, Between Discipline and Desire (Centro Cuidad de Buenos Aires Argentina, Museo Nacional de Artes Plasticas Uruguay, Museo de Arte Moderna Rio de Janeiro Brazil) 1990, Museo de Arte São Paulo Brazil, Yale Center for Br Art 1992, Sonoma Museum of Fine Art Calif, MOMA Buenos Aires 1993, Estudio Lisenbeg Buenos Aires 1993, Palacio Municipal La Plata Buenos Aires 1993, Museo de Arte Moderno Mendoza 1994, Museum of Contemporary Art Cordoba Argentina 1994, Charles Cowles Gallery NY 1995, AAA Gallery NY 1995, Fundation Perez Celis Buenos Aires, Important Mischief (Centro Cultural Borges Buenos Aires) 1996, Galeria Achimboldo Buenos Aires, The Thirteen Stations (Centro Cultural Recoleta Buenos Aires) 2000, Centro Cultural Cordoba Spain 2001, Centro Jose Guerrero Granada Spain 2001; *Work in Public Collections* Aerolineas Argentinea, Altos de Chavon Fndn Dominican Republic, Amerada Hess Corp NY, Arnolfini Collection Tst Bristol, Arts Cncl of GB, Bradford City Art Gallery, Br Cncl, Contemporary Art Soc London, Eastern Arts Assoc, Govt Art Collection, Hatton Gallery Newcastle, Iwaki MOMA Japan, Leeds City Art Gallery, Leicestershire Educn Authy, Manchester City Art Gallery, National Collection of Brazil Rio de Janeiro, Tate Gallery London, Unilever London, V&A Museum London, Walker Art Gallery Liverpool, Museet Moderna Stockholm Sweden, Contemporary Drawings Collection Br Museum London, Fitzwilliam Museum Cambridge, Museo del Parco Centro Internazionale di Scultura All'Aperto Portofino Italy, Important Mischief: British Sculpture from 1960–80 (Henry Moore Fndn Leeds); *Awards* Peter Stuyvesant Fndn prize 1969, Arts Cncl award 1971, Gregory fell in sculpture Univ of Leeds 1973, jt first prize Art into Landscape Serpentine Gallery 1974, Gulbenkian Fndn Visual Arts award 1975, prizewinner John Moores Liverpool Exhibition 11 1978, Arts Cncl of GB award 1979, Lorne Bequest Univ of London 1984, purchase grant Elephant Tst 1984, Henry Moore Fndn award 1985, Henry Moore Tst award 1992, Br Cncl award 1992; *Recreations* art; *Style*— Martin Naylor, Esq; ✉ Home: Esmeralda 1355 (p 4, D 6), Cap Fed 1007, Buenos Aires, Argentina (tel and fax 541 14327 1366, e-mail cyclops@icatel.net); Studio: Esmeralda 865 p.b.4, Buenos Aires, Argentina (tel 541 14314 0283); 11A Westbere Road, London NW2 3SP

NAYLOR, Robert Antony; s of Francis Thomas Naylor, of Reading, and Kathleen Mary, *née* Donellan; *b* 13 November 1949; *Educ* Salesian Coll Oxford, Presentation Coll Reading, Univ of London (BSc); *m* 9 Nov 1974, Jane Karen, da of Charles Evans; 1 s (James Richard), 1 da (Victoria Jane); *Career* grad mgmnt trainee NW Thames RHA 1972–74, hosp sec Nat Hosp for Nervous Diseases London 1974–77, sector admin Kent AHA 1977–79, dist admin Enfield DHA 1979–84, gen mangr E Birmingham Hosp 1986–90, chief exec Birmingham Heartlands Hosp NHS Tst 1991–2000, chief exec UCL Hosps 2000–; AHSM; *Recreations* golf, scuba diving; *Style*— Robert Naylor, Esq; ✉ 4 Chester

N

Terrace, Regent's Park, London NW1 4ND; University College London Hospitals, 2nd Floor Central, 250 Euston Road, London NW1 2PG

NAYLOR, (Andrew) Ross; s of Robert Charles Naylor, and Patricia Mary, *née* Goodall; *Educ* Merchiston Castle Sch Edinburgh, Univ of Aberdeen (first bursar, MB ChB, MD); *m* 1982, May Bruce, *née* MacPherson; 1 s (Iain Bruce), 1 da (Sarah May); *Career* basic surgical trg Aberdeen and Edinburgh Royal Infirmary 1981–91, higher surgical trg Leicester Royal Infirmary 1991–93; conslt vascular surgn: Aberdeen Royal Infirmary 1993–95, Leicester Royal Infirmary 1995–; Hunterian prof of surgery RCS 2002, hon prof of surgery Univ of Leicester 2003 (hon reader in surgery 2002); memb Editorial Bd: Br Jl of Surgery 2000–, Jl of Vascular Surgery 2003–, European Jl of Vascular and Endovascular Surgery 2006–; memb: R&D Ctee UK Stroke Assoc 1993–2002, Cncl Vascular Soc of GB and I; Wilfred Card Medal 1990; memb: GMC 1981–, European Vascular Soc 1990–, Vascular Surgical Soc 1990–, Medical and Dental Defence Union of Scotland 1991–, Br Vascular Fndn 1994–98; FRCSEd 1986, FRCS 1994; *Publications* Carotid Artery Surgery: A Problem-Based Approach (ed); author of 30 book chapters and 220 pubns in peer-reviewed jls; *Recreations* golf, gardening, skiing; *Style*— Ross Naylor, Esq; ✉ Department of Surgery, Clinical Sciences Building, Leicester Royal Infirmary, Leicester LE2 7LX (tel 0116 252 3252, fax 0116 252 3179)

NAYLOR-LEYLAND, Sir Philip Vyvian; 4 Bt (UK 1895), of Hyde Park House, Albert Gate, Co London; s of Sir Vivyan Edward Naylor-Leyland, 3 Bt (d 1987), and Hon Elizabeth Anne Marie Gabrielle Fitzalan-Howard (d 1997), da of 2 Viscount Fitzalan of Derwent; *b* 9 August 1953; *Educ* Eton, Sandhurst, New York Univ, RAC Cirencester; *m* 1980, Lady Isabella Lambton, 5 and yst da of Antony Claud Frederick Lambton (6 Earl of Durham, who disclaimed his peerage 1970); 4 s (Thomas Philip b 1982, George Antony b 1989, Edward Claud b 1993, William Rufus Luke b 1999), 2 da (Violet Mary b 1983, Beatrix Rose Elizabeth b 1998); *Heir* s, Thomas Naylor-Leyland; *Career* Lt LG (ret); pres National Coursing Club 1988–, chm Peterborough Royal Foxhound Show Soc 1995– (vice-chm 1989–95); dir: Milton (Peterborough) Estates Co, Nantclwyd Farms Ltd; jt master Fitzwilliam (Milton) Hunt 1987–; *Recreations* hunting, coursing, shooting, golf; *Clubs* White's, The Air Squadron; *Style*— Sir Philip Naylor-Leyland, Bt; ✉ Milton, Peterborough, Cambridgeshire; Nantclwyd Hall, Ruthin, Denbighshire LL15 2PR

NAYSMITH, Dr (John) Douglas (Doug); MP; s of late James Hamilton Naysmith, and late Wilhelmina, *née* Vass; *b* 1 April 1941; *Educ* George Heriot's Sch Edinburgh, Univ of Edinburgh (BSc, PhD), Yale Univ (postdoctoral fell); *m* 1966 (sep), Margaret Caroline, da of Sidney Hill; 1 s (Stephen b 1968), 1 da (Catherine b 1973); *Career* technician Civil Serv 1958–61, research asst Univ of Edinburgh Med Sch 1965–69, med scientist Beecham Research Labs 1969–72; Univ of Bristol: successively research asst, fell then lectr Dept of Pathology 1972–94, with Registrars Office 1994–97; MP (Lab/Co-op) Bristol NW 1997–; cncllr Bristol City Cncl 1981–98; chm Bristol Port Authy 1986–91, pres Socialist Health Assoc 1990–97 (vice-pres 1997–2000); memb Br Soc for Immunology 1966; FIBiol; FRSM; *Recreations* theatre, films, football, paddle steamer preservation; *Style*— Dr Doug Naysmith, MP; ✉ Unit 6, Greenway Business Centre, Doncaster Road, Southmead, Bristol BS10 5PY (tel 0117 950 2385, fax 0117 950 5302); House of Commons, London SW1A 0AA (tel 020 7219 4187, fax 020 7219 2602, e-mail naysmithd@parliament.uk, website www.epolitix.com/webminster/doug-naysmith.htm)

NAZIR-ALI, Rt Rev Dr Michael; *see:* Rochester, Bishop of

NEAL, Prof Alan Christopher; s of Harold Joseph Neal, of Bath, and Gladys May, *née* Lovelock; *b* 9 January 1950; *Educ* City of Bath Boys' Sch, Univ of Warwick (LLB), LSE (LLM), Univ of Stockholm Sweden (DGLS); *m* 30 July 1981, Alessandra, da of Dr Alessandro Tadini (d 1974), of Lucca, Italy; 1 s (James Alexander b 1984), 1 da (Francesca Jane b 1986); *Career* called to the Bar Gray's Inn 1975; in practice Midland & Oxford Circuit; pt/t chm Employment Tbnls 1995–, convenor Euro Assoc of Labour Court Judges 1996–; ed-in-chief The International Journal of Comparative Labour Law and Industrial Relations 1984–95, prof of law Univ of Leicester 1988–2000 (lectr 1976–86, sr lectr 1986–88); Univ of Warwick: prof of law 2000–, dir Employment Law Research Unit 2002–; visiting prof: Salford Univ 1992–, Univ of Paris I (Sorbonne) 1993–96; *Books* A Perspective on Labour Law (1982), Law and the Weaker Party (ed, 5 vols 1981–92), Collective Agreements and Collective Bargaining (1984), European Communities Health and Safety Legislation (1992), Developing the Social Dimension in an Enlarged European Union (1995), Fundamental Social Rights at Work in the European Community (1999), European Labour Law and Social Policy (1999, 2nd edn 2002), European Social Policy and the Nordic Countries (2000); *Recreations* hockey (formerly Somerset and Warwickshire), skiing, music; *Style*— Prof Alan C Neal; ✉ School of Law, The University of Warwick, Coventry CV4 7AL (tel 024 7652 3205 (direct) and 024 7652 3098 (sec), fax 024 7652 4105, e-mail alan.neal@warwick.ac.uk); Barristers' Chambers, 2 New Street, Leicester LE1 5NA (tel 0116 262 5906, fax 0116 251 2023)

NEAL, Dr Anthony James; *b* 18 October 1961; *Educ* Roan GS for Boys London, St Thomas' Hosp Med Sch London (MB BS, MD); *m*; 3 c; *Career* house surgn St Thomas' Hosp London, house physician Queen Mary's Hosp Sidcup, SHO (vocational trg scheme in gen med) Colchester gp of hosps 1986–88, SHO (radiotherapy and oncology) Essex Co Hosp Colchester 1988, lectr and hon registrar in med oncology Royal London Hosp 1988, registrar in gen med Newham gp of hosps 1989, registrar in radiotherapy and oncology Royal London Hosp1989–92, clinical res fell Inst of Cancer Res and hon sr registrar Royal Marsden NHS Tst 1993–94, sr registrar in clinical oncology Royal Marsden NHS Tst 1994–96 (conslt 1996–99), hon sr lectr Inst of Cancer Res 1996–2000, conslt in clinical oncology Royal Surrey Co Hosp Guildford, recognised teacher Univ of London 1996–2000, clinical tutor Univ of London and Royal Marsden Hosp 1999, RCR tutor St Luke's Cancer Centre Guildford 2000–; examiner for dip in clinical oncology Faculty of Med Univ of London 1998; chm Postgrad Med Educn Ctee 1999, oncology advsr Thames Cancer Registry 1996–99, memb Pan-Thames Clinical Oncology Specialist Registrar Appointments Ctee, memb Speciality Trg Ctee Pan-Thames Clinical Oncology Rotation; chm Royal Marsden NHS Tst Radiotherapy Quality Assurance Ctee 1996–99; involved in numerous clinical trial activities; memb Editorial Bd: CME Breast Jl 1999–; referee for peer review pubns in jls: Radiotherapy & Oncology, Clinical Oncology, Br Jl of Radiology, Br Jl of Cancer, The Breast; memb: American Soc of Clinical Oncology, Euro Soc of Therapeutic Radiology and Oncology (ESTRO), Br Oncological Assoc, Med Protection Soc; MRCP 1988, FRCR 1992; *Awards* ICI Travel Award 1993, runner up Finzi Jr Radiologist Prize RSM 1993, ESTRO Philips Fellowship 1994 (funded study at Dept of Radiation Oncology Univ of Michigan), ESTRO Travelling Grant 1994, Amgen-Roche Jr Investigator Award 1994, Br Oncological Assoc Award 1994, Pfizer Academic Travel Award 1994, ESTRO Varian Physics Res Award 1994, Lilly Oncology Award 1995; *Publications* Clinical Oncology - A Textbook for Students (with P J Hoskin, 1994), Clinical Oncology - Basic Principles and Practice (with P J Hoskin, 3 edn 2003); *Recreations* photography, tennis, golf, computing and IT, personal fitness training, family-orientated activities; *Style*— Dr Anthony Neal; ✉ St Luke's Cancer Centre, Royal Surrey County Hospital, Guildford, Surrey GU2 5XX (tel and fax 01483 406767, e-mail anthony.neal@royalsurrey.nhs.uk)

NEAL, Prof David Edgar; s of Norman Neal, of Ripon, N Yorks, and Beth Neal; *b* 9 March 1951; *Educ* Prince Henry's GS Otley, UCL, UCH Med Sch (BSc, MB BS), Univ of London (MS); *m* 27 July 1972, Deborah Mary, *née* Heyworth; 3 da (Rebecca b 29 June 1976, Emily b 17 June 1978, Miriam b 22 August 1980); *Career* house physician and surgeon W Suffolk Hosp, Bury St Edmunds Hosp and Stoke Mandeville Hosp 1975–76, SHO UCH 1977, registrar in gen surgery and urology Kettering Hosp 1977–79, surgical registrar Gen Infirmary Leeds 1979–80, clinical lectr in gen surgery Univ Dept of Surgery Gen Infirmary Leeds 1982–83; Univ of Newcastle upon Tyne: Leech-Green first asst in urology (hon sr registrar) Dept of Surgery 1983–88, sr lectr in urological surgery (hon conslt urologist) Dept of Surgery (also at Dept of Urology Freeman Hosp) 1988–92, head Dept of Surgery 1992–98, head Sch of Surgery 1992–98, head Sch of Surgical and Reproductive Sci 1992–98, dir of research Faculty of Med 1998–2001, prof of surgery and hon conslt urologist Dept of Surgery the Med Sch (and Newcastle upon Tyne Hosps NHS Tst) 1992–2002, chm Jt Research Exec (also at Newcastle upon Tyne Hosps NHS Tst) 2000–02; prof of cancer research (surgical oncology) Addenbrooke's Hosp Univ of Cambridge 2002–; chm Urological Site Specific Gp W Anglia Cancer Network 2003–, advsr Nat Dir of Cancer Services 2003–; memb: Cncl RCS, American Assoc of Genito-urinary Surgns (overseas memb) 1998–, Clinical Standards Gp for Urological Cancers 2003–, CR UK Health Policy Advsy Gp 2003–; St Peter's Medal Br Assoc of Urological Surgns 2001; FRCS 1980, FRCSEd (ad hominem) 1994, FMed Sci 1998; *Publications* author of various articles in professional jls; *Recreations* motor cycles, guitar playing; *Style*— Prof David Neal; ✉ Oncology Centre, Box 193, Addenbrooke's Hospital, Cambridge CB2 2QQ (tel 01223 331940, fax 01223 763120, e-mail den22@cam.ac.uk)

NEAL, Gub Matthew Michael; s of Michael David Neal, and Barbara Lisette, *née* Carter; *b* 24 January 1959; *Educ* Eton, Univ of Exeter (BA), Univ of Calif Berkeley (postgrad directing course, exchange scholarship); *m* 1991, Anna, da of Glynne Price (d 2004); 2 s (William b 8 Nov 1993, Isaac b May 1998), 1 da (Phoebe Agnes b 1 March 1996); *Career* prodr London Int Festival of Theatre 1981–84, floor mangr BBC TV 1985–87, script ed BBC TV 1987–89, television drama prodr 1989–; fndr Gub Neal Productions Ltd 1995, controller of drama Granada TV 1995–97, head of drama Channel 4 1997–2000, fndr Box TV Ltd 2000–; prodr films and series incl: Medics (Granada TV) 1990, The Cloning of Joanna May (Granada) 1991, Angels (Granada) 1991, The Humming Bird Tree (BBC Films) 1992, Cracker (Granada) 1993, Bad Boys (BBC Films) 1994; exec prodr: Hillsborough (Granada) 1996, Moll Flanders, Prime Suspect V; other credits incl: Sunday (Channel 4) 2001 (winner Grand Prix Italia), Swallow (Channel 4) 2001, Trust (BBC 1) 2002, Gunpowder Treason and Plot (BBC 2) 2003; memb: BAFTA, Equity; *Awards* Best Film Award (for The Humming Bird Tree) Rheims TV Festival 1993; for Cracker: RTS Award for Best Series 1994, American Cable Ace Award 1995, BAFTA Best Series nomination 1994, Prix Italia nomination 1995; US Emmy Best Mini Series (for Prime Suspect V); *Recreations* walking, motorbiking, skiing, cycling, art history, photography; *Clubs* Teatro; *Style*— Gub Neal, Esq

NEAL, Harry Morton; CBE (1991); s of Godfrey French Neal (d 1985), and Janet Bryce Morton (d 1960); *b* 21 November 1931; *Educ* Uppingham, Univ of London (BSc), City and Guilds Coll; *m* 1954, Cecilia Elizabeth, da of Col Mervyn Crawford, DSO (d 1977); 1 s (Michael b 1956), 3 da (Camilla (Mrs Edward Cottrell) b 1960, Janet (Mrs Rupert Ryle-Hodges) b 1961, Alexandra (Mrs Rupert Asquith) b 1967); *Career* Flying Offr RAF 1953; Harry Neal Ltd (bldg and civil engrg contractors): md 1963–86, chm 1985–; dir: Connaught Hotel Ltd 1966–97 (chm 1980–94), Savoy Hotel 1982–93; chm: St Anselm Devpt Co Ltd 1985–; memb Lloyd's; vice-pres C&G 1999–2004 (memb Cncl 1970–2004, chm Cncl 1979–91); pres: City and Guilds Coll Assoc 1994–95, City and Guilds Assoc 2006–; memb: Technician Educn Cncl 1982–83, Business and Technology Educn Cncl 1983–94, Ct City Univ 1982–91, Mgmnt Ctee Courtauld Inst of Art 1983–99, Delegacy St Mary's Hosp Med Sch 1993–97; memb Bd of Govrs: Willesden Tech Coll 1983–86, Imperial Coll London 1988–2001, Francis Holland Sch 1988–2006 (vice-chm 1996–2005); memb Cncl Univ of Herts 2006–; tstee: Buckminster Estate 1969–2005, Samuel Courtauld Tst 1989–2006, HRH Prince of Wales Inst of Architecture 1991–99 (memb Bd of Advsrs 1993–99); pres Middx W Co Scout Cncl 1983–; pres Herts Agric Soc 2004; High Sheriff Herts 1999–2000; Liveryman Worshipful Co of Carpenters (Master 1997); hon fell Courtauld Inst of Art 2007–; FIC, FCGI, FCIOB, FRSA; Chevalier de Tastevin 1981; *Recreations* gardening; *Style*— Harry Neal, Esq, CBE; ✉ Great Sarratt Hall, Sarratt, Rickmansworth, Hertfordshire WD3 4PD

NEAL, Nicholas Geoffrey; s of Francis Richard Neal, and Sheila Rosemary, *née* Bennett; *b* 6 June 1949; *Educ* Cardiff HS, Univ of Wales (LLB), Bristol Law Sch; *Career* asst clerk to the Justices Cardiff 1971–74, admitted as slr 1973; S Glamorgan CC: asst slr 1974–80, asst county slr 1980–87, chief slr 1987–92; dep chief exec and legal advsr Land Authy for Wales 1992–98; Welsh Devpt Agency: md Land Div 1998–2001, exec dir 2001–02, exec dir Land Devpt and Legal Servs 2002–; hon slr: S Glamorgan Community Foundation, Cardiff Action for Single Homeless, Norwegian Church Preservation Tst; memb Bd of Visitors Cardiff Prison 1984–92; memb Law Soc 1975–, memb Soc of City Secs 1980–92; *Recreations* badminton, opera, reading; *Style*— Nicholas Neal, Esq; ✉ Welsh Development Agency, Principality House, The Friary, Cardiff CF10 3FE

NEAL-STURGESS, Prof Clive; *b* 13 April 1942; *Educ* Higham Lane Secdy Modern Nuneaton, King Edward VI GS Nuneaton, Nuneaton Tech Coll (ONC), Lanchester Poly Coventry (BSc), Univ of Birmingham (PhD, Avery Res Prize); *Career* project engr Clarkson International 1965–67; Univ of Birmingham: sr lectr Dept of Mechanical Engrg 1985–89 (Chubb res fell 1971–73, lectr 1973–85), Jaguar prof of automotive engrg Sch of Manufacturing & Mechanical Engrg 1989– (dir of res 1990–92, dir Automotive Engrg Centre 1992–93 and 1997–, dir of undergrad studies 1993–97, jt head 2001–); chm Materials Gp IMechE 1986–92, chm Birmingham Centre Automobile Div IMechE, res grant assessor FORESIGHT EPSRC and Australian Res Cncl, QAA specialist assessor 1996–98; external examiner: Dept of Engrg Univ of Reading 1990–93, Mech Engrg Univ of Mauritius 1995–99, Univ of Hertfordshire 1999–; memb: BCFG Ctee 1980–85, Res Policy Ctee IMechE 1986–, Technical Policy Bd IMechE 1986–92, Cncl Inst of Metals 1989–91, Br Cncl LINK Co-ordinator Univ of Mauritius 1995–, Euro Tport Safety Cncl, Qualifications Panel IMechE 2000–, Engrg Cncl SARTOR Monitoring Gp 1999–, Engrg Integrity Soc, memb Engrg Professors Cncl; memb Ed Bd: Proc IMechE Jl of Materials: Design & Applications, Jl of Materials Processing Technol, Int Jl of Machine Tools Manufacturing, Jl of Res Univ of Mauritius; CEng 1981, FIMechE 1987 (MIMechE), FIM 1995, FRSA; *Publications* author/co-author of over 140 papers and 3 books; *Recreations* golf, renovating a Tudor grade II listed building; *Clubs* Royal Over-Seas League; *Style*— Prof Clive Neal-Sturgess; ✉ School of Engineering, The University of Birmingham, Edgbaston, Birmingham B15 2TT (tel 0121 414 4144, fax 0121 414 3688, e-mail c.e.n.sturgess@bham.ac.uk)

NEALE, Frank Leslie George; s of Hugh Neale, and Mona, *née* Clarkson; *b* 25 August 1950; *Educ* King Henry VIII Sch Coventry, St John's Coll Cambridge (MA), Manchester Business Sch (MBA); *m* 16 June 1976, Helen, da of Ronald Carter; 3 s (Michael James b 29 May 1979, Jeremy John Simon b 20 Jan 1985, Rory William b 1 Jan 1989); *Career* Econ Intelligence Unit 1973–77, PA Mgmnt Consits 1977–83, Citicorp Venture Capital 1983–88, ptnr IRRfc; dir: Northern 2 VCT plc, Northern Investors Co plc 2007–, Bison Gp Ltd; former vice-chm Cncl Br Venture Capital Assoc; dir Jonzi D Prodns; dir Eating Disorders Assoc; MIMC, FRSA; *Recreations* ballet, swimming, reading; *Clubs* Watford FC Supporters'; *Style*— Frank Neale, Esq; ✉ 53 Chandos Place, London WC2N 4HS (tel 020 7812 6599, fax 020 7812 6596)

NEALE, Mark; s of Sir Alan Neale (d 1995), and Joan, *née* Frost (d 2003); *b* 7 July 1957; *Educ* Highgate Sch, The Queen's Coll Oxford (BA); *m* 27 Aug 1988, Xanthe, *née* Lunghi; 1 da (Catherine b 25 Jan 1994), 1 s (Daniel b 22 Dec 1996); *Career* civil servant; head: Assessment Div DfE 1991–95, Spending Div HM Treasy 1995–98, Structural

Unemployment Policy Div DfEE 1998–2000; fin dir Employment Serv 2000–01, dir for children and housing DWP 2001–03, DG security, int and organised crime Home Office 2003–05, DG budget, tax, welfare HM Treasy 2005–; *Style*— Mark Neale, Esq; ✉ HM Treasury, 1 Horseguards Road, London SW1A 2HQ (tel 020 7270 5939, e-mail mark.neale@hm-treasury.gov.uk)

NEAME, Robert Harry Beale; CBE (1999), DL (Kent 1992); s of Jasper Beale Neame (d 1961), and Violet Evelyn, *née* Cobb (d 1976); The Neame family have been resident in E Kent and can be traced back 500 years; *b* 25 February 1934; *Educ* Harrow; *m* 1, 1961, Sally Elizabeth, *née* Corben; 2 s (Jonathan, Richard (decd)), 2 da (Charlotte, Sarah); m 2, 1974, Yvonne Mary, *née* Mackenzie; 1 da (Moray); *Career* cmmnd 17/21 Lancers 1953–55 (army racquets champion 1954); chm Shepherd Neame Ltd 1971– (joined 1956, dir 1957, mktg dir 1961), former dir and chm Faversham Laundry Co, regnl dir National Westminster Bank plc 1982–92; dir: Kent Econ Devpt Bd 1984–89, Folkestone Racecourse 1984–99 (chm 1989); local dir Royal Insurance (UK) Ltd 1971–2000; non-exec dir Merrydown Cider 1997–2004; memb Faversham CC 1965–89, ldr Kent CC 1982–84; High Sheriff Kent 2001–02; vice-pres SE Eng Tourist Bd 1990– (chm 1979–90), chm Int Union of Local Authorities 1986–89, chm Kent Ambassador 2002–; memb: Rural Devpt Ctee SEEDA 1999–, Assoc of Brewing; pres Kent CCC 2003; Master Worshipful Co of Brewers 1999–2000; *Recreations* shooting, riding, cricket, golf, squash, racquets; *Clubs* MCC, I Zingari, Butterflies, Escorts, Jesters, Band of Brothers, Press, Royal St George's, Free Foresters; *Style*— Robert Neame, Esq, CBE, DL; ✉ Dane Court Farmhouse, Kits Hill, Selling, Faversham, Kent (tel 01227 752284); c/o Shepherd Neame Ltd, 17 Court Street, Faversham, Kent ME13 7AX (tel 01795 532206)

NEARY, Martin Gerard James; LVO (1998); s of Leonard Walter Neary (d 1996), of Walton-on-Thames, Surrey, and Jeanne Marguerite, *née* Thébault; *b* 28 March 1940; *Educ* City of London Sch, Chapel Royal Choir, Gonville & Caius Coll Cambridge (organ scholar, MA); *m* 22 April 1967, Penelope Jane, da of Sir Brian Warren (d 1996), of London, and Dame Josephine Barnes, DBE (d 1999); 2 da (Nicola b 1969, Alice b 1972), 1 s (Thomas b 1974); *Career* prof of organ Trinity Coll London 1963–72, organist and master of music St Margaret's Westminster 1965–71; conductor: Twickenham Musical Soc 1966–72, St Margaret's Westminster Singers 1967–71, Waynflete Singers 1972–87, RSCM Millennium Youth Choir 1999–2001, Paulist Choristers of California 1999–2003, English Chamber Singers 1999–; organist and master of the music Winchester Cathedral 1972–87, organist and master of the choristers Westminster Abbey 1988–98, lectr in church music Royal Acad of Music 1989–, dir of music First Congregational Church LA 2001–02, artistic dir LA Bach Festival 2002; guest conductor: Academy of Ancient Music, Bournemouth Symphony Orchestra, English Chamber Orchestra, London Symphony Orchestra, Winchester Baroque Ensemble 1982–87, Westminster Baroque Ensemble 1988, Brandenburg Orchestra 1991; 12 foreign tours with Winchester Cathedral Choir 1978–87, toured America (thrice), France (twice), Germany, Hungary, Switzerland, Norway, Russia and Ukraine with Westminster Abbey Choir 1988–97; dir Southern Cathedrals Festival 1972, 1975, 1978, 1981, 1984 and 1987; many organ recitals and broadcasts in UK, Europe, America, Aust, NZ, Korea and India, has conducted premières of music by many Br composers especially Jonathan Harrey and John Tavener, numerous recordings incl Purcell Music for Queen Mary; pres: Cathedral Organists' Assoc 1985–88, Royal Coll of Organists 1988–90 and 1996–98, Organists' Benevolent League 1988–, John Carpenter Club 1997–98; chm Herbert Howells Soc 1993–; Grammy Award nomination 1996; hon citizen Texas 1971; Hon DMus Univ of Southampton 1997; Hon FTCL 1969, Hon RAM 1988; FRCO 1963, FRSCM 1997; Knight of the Order of St Lazarus of Jerusalem (KLJ) 2001; *Books* Early French Organ Music (ed 2 vols, 1975); several compositions incl May The Grace (for Royal Golden Wedding), O Worship the Lord, and numerous arrangements of carols and hymns; *Recreations* watching cricket, visiting Test Match grounds throughout the world; *Clubs* Garrick, Middx CCC; *Style*— Dr Martin Neary, LVO; ✉ 44 Radipole Road, Fulham, London SW6 5DL (tel 020 7736 5268, e-mail martin@mneary.co.uk)

NEATE, Francis Webb; s of Francis Webb Neate (d 1982), of Kew, Surrey, and Fiona L M, *née* O'Brien (d 2003); *b* 13 May 1940; *Educ* St Wilfrid's Sch Seaford, St Paul's, BNC Oxford (BA), Univ of Chicago Law Sch (JD); *m* 25 Aug 1962, Patricia Ann, da of Anthony Vincent Hugh Mulligan (d 1984), of Putney, London; 2 da (Polly b 1966, Emily b 1973), 2 s (Vincent b 1968, Patrick b 1970); *Career* assoc Davis Polk & Wardwell NY 1963; admitted slr 1966; Slaughter and May: articled clerk 1964–66, asst slr 1966–71, ptnr 1972–97; gp legal advsr Schroders plc 1997–2004, of counsel Kirkland & Ellis LLP 2004–; pres Int Bar Assoc; memb: Law Soc, City of London Slrs' Co; *Recreations* cricket, reading, family; *Clubs* MCC, Berkshire CCC, Richmond CC, Falkland CC; *Style*— Francis Neate, Esq; ✉ Kirkland & Ellis International LLP, 30 St Mary Axe, London EC3A 8AF (tel 020 7469 2000)

NEATH, Gavin Ellis; CBE (2007); s of Ronald William Neath (d 2002), of Portsmouth, and Frances Gillian, *née* Davis; *b* 5 April 1953, Mbulu, Tanzania; *Educ* Warwick Sch, Univ of Manchester (BA), Univ of Warwick (MSc), Stanford Univ; *m* 6 Jan 1979, Ann Elizabeth; 3 da (Gemma Louise b 1983, Georgia Beatrice b 1986, Nancy Sian b 1990); *Career* Unilever: joined as grad trainee 1977, various sales and mktg roles Lever Bros UK 1977–85, mktg dir Lever France 1985–90, category dir laundry Lever Europe 1990–94, md Lever Ponds SA 1994–98, chm Unilever Bestfoods UK 1999–2004, chm Unilever UK 2004–; pres Food and Drink Fedn 2005–; *Recreations* theatre, cinema, squash, tennis; *Clubs* St Margarets Film (hon sec); *Style*— Gavin Neath, Esq, CBE; ✉ Unilever UK, Walton Court, Station Avenue, Walton-on-Thames, Surrey KT12 1UP (tel 01932 261510, e-mail gavin.neath@unilever.com)

NEAVE, Prof Guy Richard Irvine; s of Lt Cdr Arundel Richard York Neave, DSC (d 1977), and Barbara Marie, *née* Liardet (d 1979); *b* 27 December 1941; *Educ* Kings Sch Worcester, Univ of London (BA, PhD); *m* 6 Dec 1986, Martine Gabriele Thérèse, da of Claude Herlant, of Woluwe Saint Pierre, Belgium; 2 c (Joel, Magali (twins) b 3 Aug 1988); *Career* lectr in history Wales 1967–69, research fell Univ of Edinburgh 1969–75, prof of comparative and gen educn Amsterdam 1978–80, directeur de recherche Paris 1981–85 (maitre de recherche 1975–78), prof of comparative educn Univ of London 1986–90, prof Centre for Higher Educn Policy Studies Univeriteit Twente Enschede 2000–; hon vice-pres Soc for Research in Higher Educn, foreign memb Nat Acad of Educn USA 1999–, pres Euro Assoc for Institutional Research 2001–03; ed Higher Educn Policy, jt ed European Jl of Educn 1980–91; fell Cwlth of Aust Fellowship 1993; FRSA 1987; *Books* How They Fared (1975), An Improper Sixth Year (jtly, 1976), Modèles d'Egalité (1976), The EEC And Education (1985), La Communidad Europea Y La Educación (1987), Prometheus Bound (jtly, 1991), The Teaching Nation (1992), Encyclopedia of Higher Education (jt ed-in-chief, 4 vols, 1992), Government and Higher Education Relationships across Three Continents: The Winds of Change (jtly, 1994), The Complete Encyclopedia of Education (CD-Rom, jt ed-in-chief, 1999), Higher Education and the Nation-State (jtly, 2001), Abiding Issues, Changing Perspectives: Visions of the University across a Half Century (ed, 2001), La Universidad Contemporanea: historia y politicas, Barcelona (2001); *Recreations* jogging, bricolage; *Clubs* Anglo-Belgian; *Style*— Prof Guy Neave; ✉ 31 Square Saint Germain, F78100 Saint Germain En Laye, France; International Association of Universities, 1 rue Miollis, F75732 Paris Cedex 15, France (tel 00 33 1 45 68 48 07, fax 00 33 1 47 34 76 05)

NEAVE, Sir Paul Arundell; 7 Bt (GB 1795), of Dagnam Park, Essex; s of Sir Arundell Thomas Clifton Neave, 6 Bt (d 1992), and Richenda Alice Ione (d 1994), da of Sir Robert Joshua Paul, 5 Bt (d 1955); *b* 13 December 1948; *Educ* Eton; *m* 1976, Coralie Jane Louise, da of Sir Robert George Caldwell Kinahan, ERD (d 1997), of Castle Upton, Templepatrick, Co Antrim; 2 s (Frederick Paul Kinahan b 25 Jan 1981, Julian Robin Kinahan b 1983); *Heir* s, Frederick Neave; *Career* stockbroker; dir Rensburg Sheppards plc; MSI (memb Stock Exchange 1980); *Recreations* gardening; *Clubs* Boodle's; *Style*— Sir Paul Neave, Bt; ✉ Queen's House, Monk Sherborne, Hampshire RG26 5HH

NEBHRAJANI, Sharmila; da of Vir Tirathdas Nebhrajani, of London, and Jayantee, *née* Chanda; *b* 30 March 1966, London; *Educ* St Anne's Coll Oxford (MA); *m* Peter Charles Wallace; 1 s (Alexander), 1 da (Anamika); *Career* strategy conslt Coopers & Lybrand 1988, strategic planning mangr Cable & Wireless plc 1993, asst dir Media Corp Fin Gp Price Waterhouse 1995; BBC: sr strategy advsr 1996, head of corporate planning 1997–2002, chief operating offr Future Media and Technol 2002–; dep chair Human Fertilisation and Embryology Authy 1998–, memb Human Tissue Authy, memb Olympic Lottery Distributor; Yale world fell 2007; memb ICAEW 1991; *Style*— Ms Sharmila Nebhrajani; ✉ BBC Broadcast Centre, Wood Lane, London W12 7TP

NEEDELL, Timothy Richard (Tiff); s of Anthony Fairey Needell (d 1994), and Diana May, *née* Pelly (d 1988); *b* 29 October 1951; *Educ* Ottershaw Boarding Sch, City Univ (BSc); *m* 17 Dec 1988, Patricia Louise (Patsy), da of Leslie Arthur Rowles; 3 s (Jack Michael b 23 Jan 1992, Harry Alexander b 25 Feb 1996, George Frederick b 27 Dec 1998); *Career* racing driver, TV presenter and writer; formerly structural design engr George Wimpey & Co Ltd; racing driver: Formula Ford 1600 1971–76 (Townsend Thoresen champion 1975), Formula Ford 2000 1975–76, Formula 3 1976–78, Formula 2 and Formula Atlantic 1977–84, Br Formula One 1979, Grand Prix with Team Ensign 1980, World Endurance Sportscars 1981–92 (third Le Mans 24–hr race 1990), British Touring Cars 1993–94, GT Championships 1995–; joined BBC TV motor racing commentary team 1981, contrib Top Gear (BBC TV) 1987–2001, contrib Fifth Gear (five) 2002–; *Recreations* golf; *Clubs* British Racing Drivers; *Style*— Tiff Needell, Esq; ✉ c/o Blackburn Sachs Associates, 2–4 Noel Street, London W1F 8GB (tel 020 7292 7555, fax 020 7292 7576, e-mail presenters@blackburnsachsassociates.com)

NEEDHAM, Andrew James (Andy); s of Paul Needham, and Sandra, *née* Mylne; *b* 25 August 1971; *Educ* Castle Hall GS Mirfield, Huddersfield Tech Coll; *Career* chef; Savoy Hotel London 1988–91, Le Pré Catalan Paris 1992–93, La Cinlianella Lumbardia Italy 1993–94, Aubergine 1994–95, Zafferano 1995– (1 Michelin star 2001–); *Style*— Andy Needham, Esq; ✉ Zafferano, 15 Lowndes Street, Belgravia, London SW1X 9EY

NEEDHAM, Ed; *b* 5 August 1964; *Educ* Melbourne Village Coll, Hills Road Coll Cambridge, Univ of Sussex (BA); *Career* ed FHM 1997–99, ed-in-chief FHM (USA) 1999–2002, managing ed Rolling Stone Magazine 2002–; Ed of the Year PPA Awards 1998, BSME Men's Magazine Ed of the Year 1998; *Recreations* poker, movies, restaurants; *Clubs* Soho House; *Style*— Ed Needham

NEEDHAM, Richard Joseph; s of Douglas Martyn William Needham (d 1999), of Wigginton, Herts, and Vera Gwenllian, *née* Bowen; *b* 2 July 1946; *Educ* Berkhamsted Sch, Poly of N London (BSc, DipArch); *m* 11 Dec 1976, Rosalyn Jill, da of Leslie James Attryde (d 2001), of Wigginton, Herts; 2 s (Robert b 29 Nov 1981, Edward b 16 Nov 1985); *Career* with John Penton Chartered Architect St Albans (specialising in design for disabled) 1974–77, ptnr Melvin Lansley & Mark Chartered Architects 1988–90 (joined 1977, assoc 1981), conslt Hurd Rolland Partnership (incorporating Melvin Lansley & Mark) 1990– (specialising in construction technol, bldg litigation, conservation and failure investigation); memb Cons Pty; ARCUK 1975, RIBA 1981, MBAE 1989; *Recreations* photography, walking, cycling, reading, gardening; *Style*— Richard Needham, Esq; ✉ Hurd Rolland Partnership, 32 Fitzroy Square, London W1T 6EX (tel 020 7387 9595)

NEEDHAM, Sheila June; da of Steven Ellis Needham (d 1981), and Grace Kathleen, *née* Tarrant (d 1987); *b* 22 June 1937; *Educ* Sutton HS; *Career* held several secretarial positions in London and USA 1955–71; dir Scribe-Ex Ltd 1965–74, fndr and md Needham Printers Ltd 1974–92, md Needhams Design & Print Ltd 1993–99, md Needham Griffin Ltd 2000–; govr Haberdashers' Aske's Hatcham Coll 1990–2002; vice-pres City of London Branch Inst of Mgmnt (formerly BIM) 1995–2002 (chm 1993–95); pres: NE Dist London Printing Assoc 1981, Farringdon Ward Club 1984–85; Freeman City of London, Freeman Worshipful Co of Haberdashers 2002, Liveryman Worshipful Co of Stationers and Newspaper Makers 1979; FRSA, FInstD; *Recreations* gardening, reading, entertaining, theatre, travel, hill walking; *Clubs* City Livery, Forum UK, Wynkyn de Worde Soc; *Style*— Miss Sheila J Needham; ✉ 67 Roupell Street, London SE1 8SS (tel 020 7633 0917, fax 020 7633 0715, e-mail sheila@needhamgriffin.co.uk)

N

NEELY, William Robert Nicholas (Bill); s of William John Neely (d 1960), and Lucy Patricia, *née* Larney (d 2000); *b* 21 May 1959; *Educ* St Malachy's Coll Belfast, Queen's Univ Belfast (BA); *m* 5 June 1988, Marion, da of John Kerr; 2 da (Sarah Caroline Kerr b 20 June 1989, Emma Sophie Kerr b 6 May 1998); *Career* reporter News & Current Affairs BBC: NI 1981–87, London 1987–88; reporter/presenter Sky News 1989; ITN: reporter 1989–90, Washington corr 1991–96, Europe corr 1997–2002, int ed 2002–; *Recreations* wine, poetry, football; *Style*— Bill Neely, Esq

NEESON, Sean; MLA; s of Patrick Neeson (d 1992), and Mary Ann, *née* McGlinchey (d 1986); *b* 6 February 1946; *Educ* Queen's Univ Belfast (BA), St Joseph's Coll of Educn Belfast (DipEd), Univ of Ulster (DipM); *m* 23 Aug 1978, Ann Caroline, da of Patrick Henderson; 2 da (Claire b 13 Nov 1979, Ciara b 11 July 1983), 2 s (Peter b 16 July 1981, John b 31 Aug 1986); *Career* head of history St Comgall's Coll Larne 1968–84; cncllr Carrickfergus BC 1977– (mayor 1993–94); memb NI Assembly 1982–86, MLA (Alliance) E Antrim 1998–; ldr Alliance Pty 1998–2001; del: Brooke-Mayhew Talks 1991, NI Forum for Political Dialogue 1996–98, Castle Buildings Talks 1996–98; chairperson NI Assembly and Business Tst 2002, memb Br-Irish Parly Body 2000–, memb Congress of Local and Regnl Authorities in Europe 2002–; md Neeson Mktg Enterprises 1990–96; memb: Bd Nat Museums and Galleries NI, Bd NI Centre in Euro, Nat Historic Ships Ctee 2001–, UK Nat Historic Ships Ctee 2002–, Bd NI Museums Cncl 2003–; *Publications* Growth and Development of Carrickfergus (1969), Carrickfergus Harbour (1985), numerous contribs to pubns on maritime heritage; *Recreations* promotion and development of maritime heritage in NI; *Style*— Sean Neeson, Esq, MLA; ✉ 44 Milebush Park, Carrickfergus, Co Antrim BT38 7RR (tel 028 9336 4105, fax 028 9336 6133); Northern Ireland Assembly, Parliament Buildings, Stormont Estate, Belfast BT4 3XX (tel 028 9052 1314, fax 028 9052 1313, e-mail allianceparty@cix.co.uk)

NEIDPATH, Lord; James Donald Charteris; DL (Glos 2006); full title Lord Douglas of Neidpath, Lyne and Munard; s and h of 12 Earl of Wemyss and (8 of) March, KT, JP, *qv*; *b* 22 June 1948; *Educ* Eton, UC Oxford (BA), St Antony's Coll Oxford (DPhil), RAC Cirencester (Dip Rural Estate Mgmnt); *m* 1, 1983 (m dis 1988), Catherine Ingrid, da of Hon Jonathan Bryan Guinness, later 3 Baron Moyne; 1 s (Hon (Francis) Richard b 1984), 1 da (Hon Mary Olivia b 1987); m 2, 1995, Amanda Claire Marion, yst da of Basil Percy Terence Feilding (d 1986); *Heir* s, Hon Francis Charteris; *Career* page of honour to HM Queen Elizabeth The Queen Mother 1962–64, memb Queen's Body Guard for Scotland (Royal Co of Archers); land agent; MRICS; *Publications* The Singapore Naval Base and the Defence of Britain's Eastern Empire 1919–41 (1981); historical reviews in The Spectator, Literary Review and Field; *Recreations* history, landscape restoration; *Clubs* Brooks's, Pratt's, Puffins, Ognisko Polskie; *Style*— Lord Neidpath, DL; ✉ Stanway, Cheltenham, Gloucestershire GL54 5PQ (tel 01386 584469, fax 01386 584688, e-mail jdcn@btconnect.com)

NEIGHBOUR, Dr Roger Harvey; s of late Kenneth George Neighbour, and late Eileen Nora, *née* Roberts; *b* 9 June 1947, Berkhamsted, Herts; *Educ* Watford GS for Boys, King's Coll Cambridge (MA), St Thomas' Hosp Medical Sch (MB BChir), Watford Vocational Trg Scheme; *Career* princ in gen practice Vine House Health Centre 1975–2003; trainer in gen practice 1977–94, course organiser Watford Vocational Training Scheme 1979–86; pres RCGP 2003–06, MRCGP examiner 1984– (convenor Panel of MRCGP examiners 1997–2002); columnist: Educn for Gen Practice 1990–2001, Br Jl of Gen Practice 2002–03; author of numerous articles in medical trade jls and papers on vocational trg, family therapy, the MRCGP examination, medical assessment, foetal memory and Franz Schubert; RCGP: George Abercrombie Award 2001, Richard Scott lectr 2001, George Swift lectr 2001; Hon DSc Univ of Hertfordshire 2004; inaugural fell Assoc of Course Organisers 1988; DObstRCOG 1975, FRCGP 1987 (MRCGP 1975), Hon FRCP 2004; *Publications* The Inner Consultation (1987, 2 edn 2004), The Inner Apprentice (1992, 2 edn 2004), The MRCGP Examination (contrib, 2000), The Successful GP Registrar's Companion (co-author, 2003), The Management Handbook for Primary Care (contrib, 2004), I'm Too Hot Now (2005); *Recreations* playing the violin, the music of Schubert, France, writing, armchair philosophy, trying to give up golf; *Style*— Dr Roger Neighbour; ✉ Argowan, Bell Lane, Bedmond, Hertfordshire WD5 0QS; Apartment 26, La Falaise d'Hacqueville, 52 rue Saint Gaud, 50400 Granville, France

NEIL, Alex; MSP; s of Alexander Neil (d 2001), of Ayr, and Margaret Neil (d 1977); *b* 22 August 1951; *Educ* Dalmellington HS, Ayr Acad, Univ of Dundee (MA); *m* 1978, Isabella, *née* Kerr; 1 s (Michael b 1 Dec 1979); *Career* project ldr Manpower Service Cmmn Project Univ of Glasgow 1977–79; Digital Equipment Corp Ayr and USA: mktg rep 1979–80, mktg and admin mangr 1981–82, logistics mangr 1982–83; mktg mangr Future Technology Systems Beith 1983, dir Cumnock and Doon Enterprise Tst (CADET) 1983–88, chief exec The Prince's Scottish Business Tst (PSYBT) 1988–90, dir Development Options Ltd 1988–89, md EES Consultants Ltd 1990–95; freelance advsr econ and business 1995–; MSP (SNP) Scotland Central 1999–, oppn spokesperson on Social Security 1999–2000, chm Enterprise and Lifelong Learning Ctee 2000–03, memb Standards Ctee 2003–04, currently chm Enterprise, Culture and Sport Ctee; *Recreations* golf, reading, travel; *Style*— Alex Neil, Esq, MSP, MIED; ✉ The Scottish Parliament, Edinburgh EH99 1SP (tel 0131 348 5703, mobile 07899 876139, e-mail alex.neil.msp@scottish.parliament.uk)

NEIL, Andrew Ferguson; s of Maj James Neil (d 1987), and Mary, *née* Ferguson (d 1993); *b* 21 May 1949; *Educ* Paisley GS, Univ of Glasgow (MA); *Career* Cons Res Dept 1971–72, UK ed The Economist 1982–83 (UK and US corr 1973–81), ed The Sunday Times 1983–94, exec chm Sky TV 1988–90, exec ed Fox News (New York) June-Dec 1994, freelance broadcaster, writer, lectr and media conslt 1994–, columnist The Sunday Times and Daily Mail 1994–96, contrib ed Vanity Fair 1994–, publisher ed-in-chief and chief exec Press Holdings Ltd (The Scotsman, Scotland on Sunday, Edinburgh Evening News, Scotsman.com) 1996–2006, chief exec The Business 1999–, chief exec The Spectator and Apollo 2004–, chm World Media Rights 2005–, chm ITP Dubai 2006–; co-presenter: The Midnight Hour (BBC 2) 1994–98, Conference Talk (BBC 2) 1996–99, Thursday Night Live (Carlton TV) 1997–2000, Despatch Box (BBC 2) 1998–2002; presenter: The Andrew Neil Show (BBC 2) 1995–96, The Sunday Breakfast Programme (BBC Radio 5 Live) 1998–2000, The Daily Politics (BBC 2) 2003–, This Week with Andrew Neil (BBC 1) 2003–, Straight Talk with Andrew Neil (BBC News 24) 2006–; lord rector Univ of St Andrews 1999–2002; FRSA 1997; *Books* The Cable Revolution (1982), Full Disclosure (autobiography, 1996), British Excellence (1998); *Recreations* dining out in London, NY, Dubai and Côte d'Azur, cycling; *Clubs* RAC; *Style*— Andrew Neil, Esq; ✉ Glenburn Enterprises, PO Box 584, London SW7 3QY (tel and fax 020 7581 1655, e-mail afneil@aol.com)

NEIL, Prof James Charles; s of Charles Neil (d 1960) and Margaret, *née* Bishop (d 2003); *b* 6 January 1953; *Educ* Allan Glen's Sch Glasgow, Univ of Glasgow (BSc, PhD); *m* 1975, Una Anne Dunlop, *née* Murray; 2 da (Ailsa b 1981, Lucy 1986), 1 s (Charles b 1983); *Career* Univ of Southern Calif 1979–81, Beatson Inst for Cancer Research 1987–1992, prof of virology and molecular oncology Univ of Glasgow 1992–; memb: Soc of Gen Microbiology 1975, Human Genome Orgn 1996; Lievre fell American Cancer Soc 1981; FRSE 1997; *Publications* author of numerous papers and articles in scientific jls and books on virology; *Recreations* music, racket sports; *Style*— Prof James Neil, FRSE; ✉ University of Glasgow, Molecular Oncology Laboratory, Institute of Comparative Medicine, Bearsden, Glasgow G61 1QH (tel 0141 330 2365, fax 0141 330 2271, e-mail j.c.neil@vet.gla.ac.uk)

NEILAND, Prof Brendan Robert; s of Arthur Neiland (d 1990), and Joan Agnes Bessie, *née* Whiley; *b* 23 October 1941; *Educ* Lowestoft Co GS Birmingham, St Philips GS Birmingham, St Augustine's Seminary Co Cavan Eire, Birmingham Coll of Art (dip), RCA (MA); *m* 1970, Hilary Vivienne, da of late Morris Salter; 2 da (Naomi b 23 Aug 1974, Lucy 17 Feb 1977); *Career* artist; gallery artist: Angela Flowers Gallery 1970–78, Fischer Fine Art 1978–92, Redfern Gallery 1992–; pt/t teaching: Manchester Art Coll 1969–73, Brighton Art Coll 1983–; prof Univ of Brighton 1996–; keeper Royal Acad of Arts 1998–2004; co-operated in making of video Commissioned Art and Professional Practice (dir Gavin Nettleton 1991); lectr Buildings Within Buildings, Reflections on Paintings RIBA 1989; hon fell Royal Soc of Painters and Etchers 1998; FRSA 1996; *Solo Exhibitions* Flowers Gallery 1971–72 and 1974–76, Fischer Fine Art 1979–84 and 1987–91, Tate Gallery 1988, RIBA Galleries 1989, Redfern Gallery London 1993, 1997 and 2006, touring show (Gardner Art Centre Brighton, Milton Keynes Exhbn Gallery, N Centre for Contemporary Art Sunderland, Stafford Art Gallery, Grundy Art Gallery Blackpool) 1992–, Reading Coll Reading 1993, Friends Room RA 1997, Brighton Univ 1997, Loughborough Univ 1998, Keele Univ 1998, Turlej Gallery Krakow 2006, Sharjah Museum UAE 2006; *Group Exhibitions* Bradford Int Print Biennale 1970, 1972, 1974, 1976, 1982 and 1986, From Britain '75 Helsinki Finland 1975, Arts Cncl Gallery Hayward 1976, Eight British Realists Meisel Gallery NYC 1983, Pintura Británica Municipal Museum Madrid 1983, Images et Imaginaires d'Architecture Centre Georges Pompidou Paris 1984, Artists in National Parts V&A and touring UK and USA 1988, Printmaking from Britain Moscow 1989, The New Patrons NACF Christie's London 1992, RA Summer Exhbn 1979–81 and 1986–92, five paintings for InterCity 225 (later used for posters) 1990–91 and others; *Commissions* incl: A T Kearney, Aukett, BAA, BMW Gp, Univ of Brighton, CapitaLand Singapore, English Heritage, Enron, Great Western, Intercity, Loughborough Univ, Mazda, Nat Bank of Dubai, Rolls Royce, Rover, Royal Mail, Scot Rail, Waterloo Int; *Awards* CAS Purchase Prize Northern Young Contemporaries 1968, Arthur Tooth's Prize Young Contemporaries 1969, Silver Medal RCA 1969, Minton Scholarship 1969, Arts Cncl Minor Award 1972, John Moores XI Prizewinner 1978, scholar Crabtree Fndn 1982, Daler Rowney Award RA Summer Exhbn 1989; *Recreations* listening to the Radio 4 cricket commentary, drinking fine wines; *Clubs* Chelsea Arts; *Style*— Prof Brendan Neiland; ✉ 2 Granard Road, London SW12 8UL (tel and fax 020 8673 4597, website www.brendanneiland.com); 3 rue du Moulin de Crêpé, Courçon, 17170 La Greve sur Mignon, France (tel 00 33 5 46 01 62 97); c/o Redfern Gallery, 20 Cork Street, London W1X 2HL (tel 020 7734 1732/0578, fax 020 7494 2908)

NEILL, Rt Hon Sir Brian Thomas; kt (1978), PC (1985); s of Sir Thomas Neill, JP (d 1937); bro of Baron Neill of Bladen, QC (Life Peer), *qv*; *b* 2 August 1923; *Educ* Highgate Sch, CCC Oxford (MA); *m* 1956, Sally Margaret Backus; 3 s; *Career* served WWII Rifle Bde; called to the Bar Inner Temple 1949; QC 1968, recorder of the Crown Court 1972–78, judge of the High Court of Justice (Queen's Bench Div) 1978–84, a Lord Justice of Appeal 1985–96, ret; pres Court of Appeal for Gibraltar 1998–2003 (Justice of Appeal 1997); chm: Ctee on Rhodesia Travel Restrictions 1973–78, Civil Mediation Cncl 2003–; chm of tstees Lord Slynn of Hadley European Law Fndn 2003–; memb Court of Assts Worshipful Co of Turners (Master 1980–81); hon fell CCC Oxford 1986; *Style*— The Rt Hon Sir Brian Neill; ✉ 20 Essex Street, London WC2R 3AL

NEILL, John Mitchell; CBE (1994); s of Justin Bernard Neill, and Johanna Elisabeth, *née* Bastiaans; *b* 21 July 1947; *Educ* George Heriott Sch Edinburgh, Univ of Strathclyde (BA, MBA, DBA); *m* 24 May 1975, Jacqueline Anne, da of Phillip Brown (d 1985); 2 s (Richard John b 19 July 1979, Alexander James b 4 Nov 1982); *Career* mktg mangr Europe AC Delco 1972–73 (planning mangr 1969–71), sales and mktg dir British Leyland Parts & KD Div 1976 (merchandising mangr 1974–75); md: Leyland Car Parts Div 1977–78, BL Components 1979–80, Unipart Group 1981–82; gp md Unipart Gp Ltd 1983–86, gp chief exec Unipart Gp of Cos 1987–; non-exec dir: Bank of England 1996–2003, Royal Mail plc, Charter plc; SMMT: memb Cncl, memb Exec Ctee, dir Industry Forum, pres 2000–01 (also sometime vice-pres); vice-pres: Inst of Motor Industry, BEN; memb: Cncl Business in the Community Bd, Alumni Bd Univ of Strathclyde; tstee Nat Motor Museum; FInstM; *Recreations* tennis, skiing; *Style*— John M Neill, Esq, CBE; ✉ UGC Ltd, Unipart House, Cowley, Oxford OX4 2PG (tel 01865 778966, fax 01865 383790)

NEILL, Robert James MacGillivray (Bob); MP; s of John MacGillivray Neill, of Ilford, Essex, and Elsie May, *née* Chaston; *b* 24 June 1952; *Educ* Abbs Cross Sch Hornchurch Essex, LSE (LLB); *Career* called to the Bar: Middle Temple 1975, King's Inns Dublin 1992; memb: Havering London Borough Cncl 1974–90 (chief whip), GLC for Romford (Cons) 1985–86; GLA: memb London Assembly (Cons) Bexley and Bromley 2000–08, ldr Cons Gp 2000–02, chair Planning and Spatial Devpt Ctee 2001–02; MP (Cons) Bromley and Chislehurst 2006–, shadow min for London 2007–; first ldr London Fire & Civil Defence Authy 1985–87, oppn spokesman Fire and Public Protection Ctee Assoc of Met Authorities; chm Gtr London Cons Political Centre 1990–93; Nat Union of Cons & Unionists Assocs: dep chm Gtr London Area 1993–96, chm Gtr London Area 1996–98, regnl chm Gtr London Conservatives 1996–99; memb UK delgn Ctee of the Regions EU 2000–08; memb London Regnl Arts Cncl; author of various articles and pamphlets on civil def, legal affrs and small businesses; *Recreations* sailing, travel, opera; *Clubs* St Stephen's Constitutional, Bar Yacht; *Style*— Bob Neill, Esq, MP; ✉ House of Commons, London SW1A 0AA (tel 020 7219 8169, fax 020 7219 8089, e-mail neillb@parliament.uk)

NEILL, Robert Moore; s of Charles Neill (d 1991), of Donaghadee, NI, and Elizabeth Ida, *née* Moore; *b* 16 September 1950; *Educ* Campbell Coll Belfast, Queen's Univ Belfast (LLB); *Career* admitted slr: England and Wales 1976, Hong Kong 1987; Herbert Smith: articled clerk 1974–76, ptnr 1984–2004, sr litigation ptnr Hong Kong Office 1987–90; accredited mediator Centre for Dispute Resolution; *Recreations* sailing, tennis, theatre, travel; *Clubs* RAC, Royal Hong Kong Yacht; *Style*— Robert Neill, Esq

NEILL, Rose Mary Margaret; da of Roger Henry James Neill (d 1979), and Doreen Elizabeth, *née* Morrice; *b* 29 November 1958; *Educ* Mount Sch York, City and E London Coll; *m* 1, 22 Feb 1985 (m dis 1997), (Robert) John Magill, s of Thomas Stewart Magill (d 1987); 2 s (Roger Thomas b 23 June 1986, Henry Harley Peter b 11 Sept 1988); m 2, 23 Dec 2000, Ivan Wilson, s of Richard Wilson; *Career* television newscaster, sports presenter and gen prog presenter; Ulster TV Ltd 1978–86; BBC Belfast 1986–: co presenter main evening news prog, newscaster and writer for other daily bulletins; regular broadcaster Pick of the Week radio prog, host of hour long chat show BBC Radio, writer and presenter various TV documentaries, travel corr; involved in annual Children in Need TV presentation and Royal Dublin Horse Show; memb Ctee NI Mother and Baby appeal, hon patron Ulster Cancer Res Campaign; *Recreations* hunting, skiing (water and snow), sailing, travelling, tennis; *Clubs* Royal Ulster Yacht, Strangford Lough Yacht, E Down Fox Hounds, Windsor Lawn Tennis; *Style*— Miss Rose Neill; ✉ BBC, Broadcasting House, Ormeau Avenue, Belfast BT2 8HQ (tel 028 9033 8000, e-mail rose.neill@bbc.co.uk)

NEILL, (James) Ruary Drummond; s of Thomas Neill (d 1969), and Elsie Margaret Wilson, *née* Sharp; *b* 9 January 1959; *Educ* Gresham's, Univ of London (BA); *m* 5 Sept 1987, Hilary Jane Vipan, da of Peter Harvey Bourne; 1 da (Georgina Kim Jane b 13 Feb 1990), 1 s (Tom Callum Ruary b 21 Jan 1993); *Career* Chartered Bank Abu Dhabi UAE 1981–83, Chartered Bank Hong Kong 1983–85, Rowe & Pitman then Warburg Securities London 1985–88; Schroder Securities Ltd: joined 1988, dir 1990–94, head of int sales Asian Div 1993–94; md Schroder Securities (Hong Kong) Ltd 1990–93, md UBS 2003– (exec dir 1994–2003); fndn govr Albury Primary Sch 1999–2003; *Recreations* shooting, farming, reading; *Clubs* Travellers; *Style*— Ruary Neill, Esq; ✉ UBS, 1 Finsbury Avenue, London EC2M 2PP (tel 020 7568 4681, fax 020 7247 3456)

NEILL OF BLADEN, Baron (Life Peer UK 1997), of Briantspuddle in the County of Dorset; Sir (Francis) Patrick Neill; kt (1983), QC (1966); s of Sir Thomas Neill, JP (d 1937); bro of Rt Hon Sir Brian Neill, *qv*; *b* 8 August 1926; *Educ* Highgate Sch, Magdalen Coll Oxford; *m* 1954, Caroline Susan, da of Sir Piers Debenham, 2 Bt (d 1964); 4 s, 2 da; *Career* served Rifle Bde 1944–47; called to the Bar Gray's Inn 1951 (bencher 1971, treas 1990); jt head of chambers; judge of Courts of Appeal of Jersey and Guernsey 1977–94; chm Press Cncl 1978–83, first chm Cncl for Securities Industry 1978–85, chm DTI Ctee of Inquiry into Regulatory Arrangements at Lloyd's 1986–87, chm Ctee on Standards in Public Life 1997–; warden All Souls Coll Oxford 1977–95 (fell 1950–77), vice-chllr Univ of Oxford 1985–89; *Style*— The Rt Hon Lord Neill of Bladen, QC

NEILSON, John Stuart; s of Ian Neilson (d 2006), and Dr Betty Neilson; *b* 31 May 1959; *Educ* St Paul's, CCC Cambridge (BA, ICE Prize); *m* 1985, Alison, *née* Green; 1 s (Alistair b 1991), 1 da (Laura b 1993); *Career* Dept of Energy: joined 1980, second private sec to Sec of State for Energy 1983–85, seconded to Economic Secretariat Cabinet Office 1988–89, princ private sec to Sec of State for Energy 1989–92; DTI: private sec to Min of Energy 1992–93, dir UK Communications Policy 1993–97, dir Aerospace and Defence Industries Policy 1997–2000; md customers & supply Ofgem 2000–05, gp dir Research Base Office of Science and Innovation DTI 2005–07, dir Research Base Dept of Innovation, Univs and Skills 2007–; *Style*— John Neilson, Esq; ✉ Department of Innovation, Universities and Skills, 66–74 Victoria Street, London SW1E 6SW (tel 020 7215 0183, e-mail john.neilson@dius.gsi.gov.uk)

NELIGAN, His Hon Judge John Oliver; s of Desmond Neligan (d 1993), of NZ, and Penelope Anne, *née* Mason (d 1996); *b* 21 June 1944; *Educ* Brickwall Sch Northiam; *m* May 1971, Mary Brigid, *née* Daniel; 2 da (Fiona Claire b Oct 1974, Caroline Mary b Jan 1977), 1 s (Andrew James b Jan 1978); *Career* admitted slr 1969, called to the Bar Middle Temple 1975; in practice Western Circuit 1975–96, recorder 1994–96, circuit judge (Western Circuit) 1996–; legal memb Mental Health Review Tbnl 2001–; *Recreations* walking, gardening, painting; *Style*— His Hon Judge John Neligan; ✉ c/o Exeter Crown and County Courts, Southernhay Gardens, Exeter EX1 1UH

NELIGAN, Timothy Patrick Moore; s of Moore Dermot Neligan (d 1977), of Worthing, W Sussex, and Margaret Joan, *née* Cockell (d 1975); *b* 16 June 1934; *Educ* Tonbridge; *m* 30 Nov 1957, Felicity Caroline, da of Norman Rycroft, of Thornton Hough, Cheshire; 2 da (Henrietta b 1958, Kate b 1959), 2 s (Patrick b 1963, Timothy b 1963); *Career* pupil Capt H Ryan Price racehorse trainer 1953–55, exec Agric Div ICI 1955–57, brewer and mangr Arthur Guinness (Park Royal) Ltd 1957–73, dir Goodwood Racecourse Ltd 1973–77, md United Racecourses Ltd 1977–94; Freeman City of London 1980, Liveryman Worshipful Co of Farriers (Master 1990–91, memb Ct of Assts); MInstM 1973, MCIM 1989; OStJ 1990; *Books* The Epsom Derby (with Roger Mortimer, 1984), The Derby (with Alastair

Burnet, 1993); *Recreations* fishing, travel; *Style—* Timothy Neligan, Esq; ✉ Sheepdown, Angel Street, Petworth, West Sussex GU28 0BN (tel 01798 342497)

NELMES, Dianne Gwenllian; da of late James Allen Nelmes, and Celandine, *née* Kimber; *Educ* The Holt Girls' GS Wokingham, Univ of Newcastle upon Tyne (BA); *m* 17 May 1986, Ian McBride, s of Robert McBride; *Career* pres Newcastle Univ Students' Union 1973–74, graduate trainee Thomson Newspapers 1974–78 (variously sr news reporter, municipal corr and property reporter The Journal Newcastle), regional journalist and on-screen reporter/presenter BBC TV North East 1978–83; Granada Television: dep news ed Granada News 1983, researcher World in Action 1984; prodr/dir Brass Tacks BBC News & Current Affrs 1987–88; rejoined Granada Television as launch ed This Morning 1988, exec prodr Entertainment Dept 1989–92; dir of news and current affrs Meridian Broadcasting (from start of franchise) 1992; Granada Television: rejoined Granada as exec prodr World in Action 1992, head of factual progs 1993–94, controller of factual progs 1994–95, dir of programming Granada Satellite Television 1995–97; ITV: controller of daytime progs 1998–2000, controller of documentaries and features 2000–03; dir daytime and lifestyle programming Granada 2003–; trustee Refuge; memb BAFTA, FRTS, FRSA; *Recreations* canal boating, cookery, walking; *Style—* Ms Dianne Nelmes; ✉ ITV Productions, The London Television Centre, Upper Ground, London SE1 9LT (tel 020 7261 3936, fax 020 7261 8140)

NELSON, Alan David; s of W S A Nelson, of Harrowlands Park, Surrey, and Olive Violet, *née* Hillman; *b* 6 June 1954; *Educ* Sir Bernard Lovell Boys' Sch, Prince of Wales Coll Dover; *m* 13 Sept 1985, Margaret Pauline, da of William Kennefick (d 1991), of Co Cork, Ireland; 3 da (Diana Alice b 1992, Corinna b 1995, Elizabeth b 1997); *Career* art dealer Lane Fine Art 1974–; memb: BADA, LAPADA; *Recreations* yachting, golf; *Clubs* East Cork Golf; *Style—* Alan Nelson, Esq; ✉ Loughane, County Cork, Rep of Ireland; Lane Fine Art, 123 New Bond Street, London W1 (tel 020 7499 5020, fax 020 7495 2496, e-mail ad@nelso.screaming.net)

NELSON, (Richard) Anthony; s of late Gp Capt R Gordon Nelson, and Mrs J M Nelson; *b* 11 June 1948; *Educ* Harrow, Christ's Coll Cambridge (MA); *m* 1974, Caroline Victoria, da of B A Butler; 1 da (Charlotte-Anne b 1979), 1 s (Carlton b 1981); *Career* Parly candidate (Cons) Leeds E Feb 1974, MP (Cons) Chichester Oct 1974–97; memb Select Ctees on: Sci and Technol 1975–79, Televising Proceedings of the House 1988–91; PPS to: min for housing and construction 1979–83, min for armed forces 1983–85; economic sec to HM Treasy 1992–94, min of state at the Treasy 1994–95, min of state DTI 1995–97; chm: Southern Water plc 2002–04, Gateway to London 2002–; vice-chm Citi 1997–; dir Chichester Festival Theatre 1982–92; FRSA; *Recreations* music, rugby; *Style—* Anthony Nelson, Esq; ✉ Citigroup Centre, 33 Canada Square, Canary Wharf, London E14 5LB (tel 020 7986 6000)

NELSON, David Brian; s of Victor Harry Nelson (d 1987), of Leicester, and Edna Mary, *née* Elliot (d 1987); *b* 15 April 1951; *Educ* Longslade Sch Birstall, Loughborough Coll of Art, Hornsey Coll of Art (DipAD), Royal Coll of Art (MA, travelling scholar Northern Italy); *m* 13 Aug 1977, Caroline Georgette, da of John Weston Evans; 2 da (Aimee Jacqueline b 17 Oct 1979, Bibiana Christina b 9 Nov 1983); *Career* architect; dir Foster and Partners (formerly Sir Norman Foster & Partners) 1984– (joined 1976), dep chm 2004–; former projects incl: Hongkong and Shanghai Bank 1979–85 (latterly project ldr), American Air Museum Duxford Cambridge (winner of the BSkyB/Royal Fine Art Cmmn Bldg of the Year award and RIBA Stirling Prize for Architecture 1998), Millennium Tower 1989, Century Tower Tokyo 1991, Bilbao Metro System Spain 1995, ptnr i/c Canary Wharf Station (Jubilee Line) 1999 and Reichstag New German Parliament Berlin, Clark Center Stanford Univ, Technology Centre McLaren UK, Petronas Univ Malaysia 2004, Supreme Ct Singapore 2005, Repsol HQ Madrid, 126 Philip Street Sydney, Regent Place Sydney; Hon FRIBA 2002; *Style—* David Nelson, Esq; ✉ Foster & Partners, Riverside Three, 22 Hester Road, London SW11 4AN (tel 020 7738 0455, fax 020 7738 1107/1108, website www.fosterandpartners.com)

NELSON, Dr Elizabeth Hawkins; OBE (1997); da of Harry Dadmun Nelson (d 1965), of Summit, NJ, and Gretchen, *née* Hawkins (d 1984); *b* 27 January 1931; *Educ* Hanover HS NH, Middlebury Coll VT (BA), Inst of Psychiatry Univ of London (PhD); *m* 1, 1960 (m dis 1972), Ivan Piercy; 1 da (Catherine b 15 Sept 1961), 2 s (Christopher b 5 March 1963, Nicholas b 3 Aug 1965); *m* 2, 26 July 1975 (m dis 1998), Claude Jacob Esterson, s of Elias Esterson; *Career* fndr dir and chm Taylor Nelson Group 1965–92; chm Addison Consultancy Group plc 1989–91, chm Taylor Nelson AGB 1992, chief exec Princess Royal Tst for Carers 1992–96; chm UK Ecolabelling Bd 1992–98, memb Pay Review Body Doctors and Dentists 1992–97; chm Richmond, Twickenham, Roehampton Healthcare NHS Tst 1997–99; chair: Univ of Surrey Roehampton (formerly Roehampton Inst) 1996–2001, SW London Community NHS Tst 1999–2002, Exec Ctee Well Being RCOG 2002–04, Stargate Capital Investment Gp Ltd 2004–; dir Chronic Granulomatous Disorder Research Tst 2004–; non-exec dir: The Royal Bank of Scotland plc 1987–97, Bright Talk Ltd 2004–; past pres World Assoc of Public Opinion Res 1990–92, vice-chair and memb Cncl Open Univ 1992–2001, dir US Open Univ 1998–2001; tstee Immigrant Advsy Service 2005–; govr Wimbledon Sch of Art; memb: Consumer Ctee Meat to Livestock Cmmn 1998–, Cncl City & Guilds 1998–, Quality Assurance Agency 1999–, First Forum (UK), Int Women's Forum UK; Hon DSc City Univ 1993, Hon Dr Open Univ 2003, hon fell City & Guilds 1994, hon fell Univ of Roehampton 2003; FRSA; *Recreations* bridge, choral singing, opera; *Style—* Dr Elizabeth Nelson, OBE; ✉ 57 Home Park Road, Wimbledon, London SW19 (tel 020 8946 2317, fax 020 8879 0280, car 078 8554 6905, e-mail liznlson53@aol.com)

NELSON, Hon James Jonathan; yr s of 2 Baron Nelson of Stafford (d 1995); *b* 17 June 1947; *Educ* Ampleforth, McGill Univ Montreal (BCom); *m* 18 Nov 1977, Lucilla Mary, da of Roger Gopsill Brown, of Albrighton, Salop; 3 da (Camilla Amy b 1982, Lara Kitty b 1986, Eloise Violet b 1988); *Career* commercial banking offr Morgan Guaranty Tst Co of New York 1969–73, dir Foreign & Colonial Management Ltd 1974–2001, md and dir Foreign & Colonial Ventures Ltd 1985–2001, ptnr Graphite Captial 2001–, chm PIFC Group 2002–; non-exec dir: Intermediate Capital Group plc 2001–, Henderson Smaller Companies Investment Trust 2002–; chm Br Venture Capital Assoc 1999–2000; Freeman City of London 1986, Liveryman Worshipful Co of Goldsmiths 1989; *Recreations* golf, tennis, skiing, shooting, fishing; *Clubs* Boodle's, Hurlingham, New Zealand; *Style—* The Hon James Nelson

NELSON, Sir Jamie Charles Vernon Hope; 4 Bt (UK 1912), of Acton Park, Acton, of Denbigh; eldest s of Sir William Vernon Hope Nelson, 3 Bt, OBE (d 1991), and Hon Elizabeth-Ann Bevil Cary, da of 14 Viscount Falkland; *b* 23 October 1949; *Educ* Redrice; *m* 25 June 1983, Maralynn Pyatt, da of late Albert Pyatt Hedge, of Audenshaw, Lincs; 1 s (Liam Chester b 1982); *Heir* bro, Dominic Nelson; *Career* forester, teacher; *Style—* Sir Jamie Nelson, Bt; ✉ tel and fax 01460 72369

NELSON, Prof Dame Janet Laughland (Jinty); DBE (2006); da of William Wilson Muir (d 1965), and Elizabeth Barnes, *née* Laughland (d 1991); *b* 28 March 1942; *Educ* Keswick Sch Cumbria, Newnham Coll Cambridge (BA, PhD); *m* 1965, Howard George Horatio Nelson; 1 da (Elizabeth Muir b 1972), 1 s (William Horatio b 1974); *Career* King's Coll London: lectr 1970–87, reader 1987–92, prof 1992–, dir Centre for Late Antique and Medieval Studies 1994–2000; pres Ecclesiastical History Society 1993–94 (memb 1969–); pres Royal Historical Soc 2000–; vice-pres Br Acad 1999–2001; memb AUT 1970–; memb: Confraternity of St James 1990–; corresponding fell Medieval Acad of America 2000–, fell KCL 2001–; FRHistS 1981, FBA 1996; *Books* Politics and Ritual in the Early Middle Ages (1986), The Annals of St Bertin (1991), Charles the Bald (1992), The Frankish World (1996), Rulers and Rulership in Early Medieval Europe (1999), The Medieval World (ed, with P Linehan, 2001), Courts, Elites and Gendered Power in Early Medieval Europe (2007); *Recreations* music, walking, looking after grandchildren Elias, Ruth and Martha; *Style—* Prof Dame Jinty Nelson, FBA; ✉ 71 Oglander Road, London SE15 4DD; Department of History, King's College London, Strand, London WC2R 2LS (tel 020 7848 1086, fax 020 7848 2052, e-mail janet.nelson@kcl.ac.uk)

NELSON, John Frederick; *b* 26 July 1947; *Educ* Marlborough; *m*; 3 c; *Career* Kleinwort Benson: joined (corp fin) 1971, a vice-pres Kleinwort Benson Inc NY 1973–75, dir Kleinwort Benson Ltd 1980–86; Lazard Brothers & Co Ltd: md 1986–98, vice-chm 1990–98; chm Credit Suisse First Boston Europe Ltd 1999–2002; non-exec chm Hammerson plc 2005– (non-exec dir 2004–), non-exec dep chm Kingfisher plc 2002–; non-exec dir: Woolwich plc 1998–2000, BT Gp plc 2002–; chm London Investment Banking Assoc (LIBA) 2001–02; dir ENO 2002–; FCA (ACA 1970); *Style—* John Nelson, Esq

NELSON, John Graeme; s of Charles Nelson (d 1985), and Jean, *née* Blackstock; *b* 19 June 1947; *Educ* Aylesbury GS, Slough GS, Univ of Manchester (BA); *m* 19 June 1971, Pauline Viola, da of Stanley Arthur Dickinson (d 2002), of Hayes, Kent; 2 s (Andrew b 1973, Ian b 1976), 1 da (Clare b 1979); *Career* BR: management trainee Western Region 1968–71, asst station mangr Liverpool St 1971–73, area passenger mangr Shenfield 1973–77, passenger sales offr Leeds 1977–79, passenger mangr Sheffield Div 1979–81, PA to chief exec BRB 1981–82, parcels mangr Southern Region 1982–84, nat business mangr Red Star Parcels 1984–87, gen mangr Eastern Region 1987–92, dir InterCity E Coast Main Line 1991–92, md Network SouthEast 1992–94, md British Rail South and East 1994–97, mgmnt conslt First Class Partnerships 1997– (chm 2000); dir: First Class Insight Ltd 1997–2002, Renaissance Trains Ltd 1999–, Hull Trains 1999–; memb Bd: M40 Trains 1998–2002, Laing Rail 2002–06, Wrexham Shropshire and Marylebone Railway 2006–; chm: N Yorks Ambulance Serv NHS Tst 1997–99, Tees E and N Yorks Ambulance Serv NHS Tst 1999–2002, ctee advising Govt on use of defibrillators in public places 1999–2001; memb Advsy Bd: Nat Railway Museum 2006–, Yorks Rail Acad 2007–; former memb: London Regnl Cncl CBI, Cncl London C of C, Br Tport Police Ctee; *Recreations* piano, football, painting, psephology; *Style—* John Nelson, Esq; ✉ First Class Partnerships, 32 St Paul's Square, York YO24 4BD (tel 01904 638659, e-mail fcp@easynet.co.uk)

NELSON, Nigel David; s of David Gordon Nelson (d 1978), and Iris May, *née* Phillips (d 2001); *b* 16 April 1954; *Educ* Sutton Valence; *Children* 3 s (Marcus, Dominic, Hallam), 2 da (Nicolette, Cordelia); *Career* reporter: Kent Evening Post 1972–75 (crime reporter 1973–75), Daily Mail 1975–79 (royal reporter 1978, New York corr 1978–79); freelance US corr 1979–82, feature writer Sunday Mirror 1982–86, political ed The Sunday People 1986–; memb NUJ; *Books* The Porton Phial (1991); *Recreations* eating, drinking and being merry; *Clubs* Parliamentary Sports; *Style—* Nigel Nelson, Esq; ✉ The Sunday People, 1 Canada Square, Canary Wharf, London E14 5AP (tel 020 7293 3059, fax 020 7293 3517, e-mail nigel.nelson@people.co.uk)

NELSON, Paul Maurice; s of Aubrey Nelson, of Swiss Cottage, London, and Myrtle, *née* Herman; *b* 22 August 1956; *Educ* Latymer Upper Sch, CCC Cambridge (BA, MA); *m* 1 May 1983, Dora Jennifer Lawson; 2 c (Saul b 1992, Joel b 1995); *Career* ptnr Linklaters 1987– (articled clerk 1979–81, asst slr 1981–87); memb Law Soc 1981; *Style—* Paul Nelson, Esq; ✉ Linklaters, One Silk Street, London EC2Y 8HQ (tel 020 7456 2000, fax 020 7456 2222, e-mail paul.nelson@linklaters.com)

NELSON, 9 Earl (UK 1805); Peter John Horatio Nelson; also Baron Nelson of the Nile and of Hilborough (UK 1801) and Viscount Merton of Trafalgar and of Merton (UK 1805); s of Capt Hon John Nelson, RA (5 s of 5 Earl and yr bro of 6, 7 and 8 Earls); Lord Nelson (suc uncle, 8 Earl, Sept 1981) is fifth in descent from the 2 Earl; the 2 Earl's mother Susannah was sister to the 1 Earl and his yr bro, the celebrated naval hero; Horatio Nelson's Barony of Nelson (GB) and Viscountcy of Nelson (UK) were extinguished with him, but his Barony of Nelson of the Nile and of Hilborough have descended to the present Peer along with his er bro's Earldom and Viscountcy (the two last titles being created, like the aforesaid Barony, with special remainder to ensure the survival of dignities honouring one of Britain's greatest sons); the Admiral's Dukedom of Brontë, however, passed, through the marriage of the 1 Earl's da Charlotte with the 2 Baron Bridport, to the Viscounts Bridport; *b* 9 October 1941; *Educ* St Joseph's Coll Ipswich, Nat Inst of Agric; *m* 1, 1969, Maureen Diana, da of Edward Patrick Quinn, of Kilkenny; 1 s (Simon John Horatio, Viscount Merton b 1971) (and 1 s, Peter Francis Horatio b and d 1970), 1 da (Lady Deborah Jane Mary b 1974); m 2, Sept 1992, Tracy Cowie; 1 s (Hon Edward James Horatio b 1994); *Heir* s, Viscount Merton; *Career* pres: Royal Naval Commando Assoc, Nelson Soc; vice-pres Jubilee Sailing Tst; hon life memb: Royal Naval Assoc, Royal Naval Museum; pres Int Fingerprint Soc; *Clubs* St James's; *Style—* The Rt Hon the Earl Nelson

NELSON, Prof Philip Arthur; s of David Nelson, of Kings Somborne, Hants, and Brenda, *née* Sneath; *b* 22 June 1952; *Educ* Colchester Royal GS, Univ of Southampton (BSc, PhD); *m* 4 Aug 1979, Jennifer, *née* Mills; 2 s (Benjamin b 23 April 1983, Samuel b 14 Sept 1985); *Career* research devpt and consltg engr Sound Attenuators Ltd Colchester 1978–82; Inst of Sound and Vibration Research Faculty of Engrg and Applied Sci Univ of Southampton: lectr 1982–88, sr lectr 1988–94, prof of acoustics 1994–, dir 2001–05; dep vice-chllr Univ of Southampton 2005–; dir: Adaptive Control Ltd, Adaptive Audio Ltd, Opsodis Ltd, Univ of Southampton Science Park Ltd; conslt: Br Aerospace, Lotus Engrg, Short Bros, Tek Gp Ltd, EA Technol Ltd, Yamaha Corp, Ultra Electronics, Rolls-Royce plc; memb Cncl Inst of Acoustics 1991–2000, pres Int Cmmn for Acoustics 2004– (UK rep 1998–), memb CBI SE Regnl Cncl; keynote lectr at int confs in Tokyo, Yokohama, Blacksburg, Chicago, Liverpool, Atlanta, Eindhoven, Copenhagen and Hawaii; Tyndall Medal Inst of Acoustics (jtly) 1992, Rayleigh Medal Inst of Acoustics 2002; distinguished corresponding memb Int Inst of Noise Control Engrs 1995; fell Acoustical Soc of America 2002 (memb 1990), CEng 1992, FIMechE 1997 (MIMechE 1993), FIOA 1997, MIEEE, FREng 2002; *Publications* Active Control of Sound (with S J Elliott, 1992), Active Control of Vibration (with C R Fuller and S J Elliott, 1996); author of more than 100 sci pubns in refereed jls, and more than 200 other pubns; *Recreations* golf; *Clubs* Hockley Golf; *Style—* Prof Philip Nelson, FREng; ✉ 3 Montfort Heights, Halterworth Lane, Romsey, Hampshire SO51 9LP (tel 01794 515936); Institute of Sound and Vibration Research, University of Southampton, Highfield, Southampton SO17 1BJ (tel 023 8059 2367, fax 023 8059 1390, e-mail pan@isvr.soton.ac.uk)

NELSON, Richard William; s of Cyril Aubrey Nelson (d 1971), and (Gillian) Mary Withers; *b* 14 June 1950, Nottingham; *Educ* Nottingham HS, Univ of Bristol (LLB); *m* 29 April 1978, Elizabeth Mary, *née* Cope; 1 s (William Henry b 18 Nov 1987), 1 da (Charlotte Louise b 11 March 1990); *Career* admitted slr 1975; asst slr J & A Bright Richards & Flewitt, slr Freeth Cartwright & Sketchley 1977–83 (ptnr 1980–83), sr ptnr and fndr Nelson Johnson & Hastings Slrs 1983–2003, princ Richard Nelson Business Defence Slrs 2003–; dir: Industrial Automation Ltd, Homeland Videos Ltd, Evocell Ltd, Stellarview Ltd, North Lodge Enterprises Ltd; govr Trent Coll, dir Trent College Ltd, dir Trent College Trading Ltd; sec Serious Fraud Assoc, fndr memb Complex Crime Practitioners Gp, memb Criminal Business Ctee Notts Law Soc, memb and ctee memb Slrs Assistance Scheme; former vice-chair Notts Hospice; memb Law Soc 1975; FRSA; *Recreations* sport (rugby and fishing in particular), comedy; *Style—* Richard Nelson, Esq; ✉ Richard

N

Nelson Business Defence Solicitors, North Star House, 6 The Midway, Nottingham NG7 2TS (tel 0115 986 3636, fax 0115 986 2626, e-mail richardnelson@rnbds.co.uk)

NELSON, Hon Mr Justice; Sir Robert Franklyn Nelson; kt (1996); s of late Clarence William Nelson, of North Rigton, N Yorks, and late Lucie Margaret, *née* Kirkby; *b* 19 September 1942; *Educ* Repton, St John's Coll Cambridge (MA); *m* 14 Sept 1968, Anne-Marie Sabina, da of late Francis William George Hall, and late Vera Evelyn Iris, of Hook Green, Wilmington, Kent; 2 s (Joshua *b* 1970, Bartholomew *b* 1973); *Career* called to the Bar Middle Temple 1965, QC 1985, recorder 1986–96, bencher 1993, a judge of the High Court of Justice (Queen's Bench Div) 1996–; *Recreations* opera, cricket, golf; *Style—* The Hon Mr Justice Nelson; ⊠ Royal Courts of Justice, Strand, London WC2

NELSON-JONES, John Austen; s of late Dr Archibald Nelson-Jones, of Putney, London, and Constance Vera, *née* Riley (d 1996); *b* 26 July 1934; *Educ* Repton, Trinity Coll Oxford; *m* 31 Aug 1963, Helene, da of John George William Wood (d 1976); 2 s (Michael, Martin); *Career* Nat Serv 2 Lt 1 Regt RHA 1954–55; admitted slr 1963, ptnr Field Fisher and Martineau 1968–89, managing ptnr Field Fisher Waterhouse 1991–98; ind cncllr London Borough of Merton 1998–2006; memb Cncl: Nat Consumer Cncl 1987–92 (chm Legal Advsy Panel), City Technol Tst 1987–97; memb Bd Job Ownership Ltd 1986–95, res sec Bow Group 1968 and 1969, taxation ed Law Soc Gazette 1972–80; memb: Law Soc 1963, Int Bar Assoc 1982 (chm Travel and Tourism Law Ctee 1987–91); FRSA 1991; *Books* Nelson-Jones Practical Tax Saving (3 edn, 1976), Employee Ownership (1987), Package Holiday Law and Contracts (3 edn, 1993); contrib numerous articles to professional jls; *Recreations* golf, walking, music, reading; *Clubs* Hurlingham; *Style—* John Nelson-Jones, Esq; ⊠ 22 Melrose Road, Merton Park, London SW19 3HG (tel 020 8542 1686)

NELSON-JONES, Rodney Michael; s of Dr Archibald Nelson-Jones (d 1995), and Constance Vera, *née* Riley (d 1996); *b* 11 February 1947; *Educ* Repton, Hertford Coll Oxford (MA); *m* 21 Sept 1988, Kusum, da of Babulal Keshavji, of Derby; 1 s; *Career* admitted slr 1975; Prothero & Prothero 1973–77, L Bingham & Co 1977–83, ptnr i/c Personal Injury Litigation Dept Field Fisher Waterhouse 1983–; memb: M1 Air Crash Steering Ctee 1989–93, Richard Grand Soc; Assoc of Personal Injury Lawyers (APIL) Award for Outstanding Achievement 2002; *Books* co-author: Product Liability - The New Law Under The Consumer Protection Act 1987 (2 edn 1988), Personal Injury Limitation Law (1994, 2 edn 2007), Medical Negligence Case Law (2 edn 1995), Schedules of Loss (2002, 2 edn 2005); sole author: Computing Personal Injury Damages (1997, 4 edn 2001), Multipliers (1998), Butterworths Personal Injury Damages Statistics (1999, 8 edn 2006), Butterworths Monthly Multiplier Tables (2006); contrib: Butterworths Personal Injury Litigation Service (1988), Structured Settlements - A Practical Guide (1993, 2 edn 1997), The Medical Accidents Handbook (1998); *Periodicals* Personal Injury Interest Calculation (annually, 1980–), Nelson-Jones and Nuttall's Tax and Interest Tables (5 edn 1992), Special Damages Statistics (1994, 5 edn 1998); *Recreations* classical music, tennis, travel; *Style—* Rodney Nelson-Jones, Esq; ⊠ 36 Pattison Road, London NW2 2HH; Field Fisher Waterhouse, 35 Vine Street, London EC3N 2AA (tel 020 7861 4022, e-mail rodney.nelson-jones@ffw.com)

NEMONE, *née* Nemone Metaxas; *Educ* Univ of Manchester; *Career* DJ; former res asst in psychiatric ward; voiceovers for Kiss 102, presenter and prodr The Word Kiss 105 1997; presenter: Morning Show (Galaxy 102 FM), Network Chill Out Show, Galaxy Chart (Manchester radio); DJ Early Breakfast Show Radio 1 2000–; master of ceremonies Top of the Pops Awards 2001 and 2002, presenter Glastonbury BBC Radio 5 Live 2005; TV presenter: Turn it Up Loud (BBC Choice), Radio 1 TV (BBC Choice), X Games Grandstand (BBC 1); TV voiceover work: Planet Pop (Channel 4), Singles (Granada), Queer as Folk (video), Gatecrashers (ITV2), The Tour of Duty (Radio 1), Sing When You're Winning (Radio 1), My Big Fat Greek Dream (BBC 3), MTV, Rapture; *Recreations* running, sky-diving, abseiling, water skiing; *Style—* Nemone; ⊠ c/o John Noel Management, 10A Belmont Street, London NW1 8HH (tel 020 7428 8400, fax 020 7428 8401)

NEOFITOU, Andreane (Andy); *Career* costume designer; *Theatre* The Far Pavilions (West End), Les Miserables (London and worldwide, Tony nomination for Best Costumes), Miss Saigon (London and worldwide), Grease (West End and tour), Martin Guerre (West Yorkshire Playhouse, UK and US tours), The Baker's Wife (West End), Jane Eyre (Toronto and Broadway), Timon of Athens (Young Vic), Peter Pan (RNT), Miss Julie (Athens), Nabucco (Met Opera NY); RSC prodns incl: Nicholas Nickleby, Fair Maid of the West, The Merchant of Venice, The Changeling, Peter Pan, Hedda Gabler; *Films* Still Life, Rosencrantz and Guildenstern are Dead; *Style—* Ms Andy Neofitou; ⊠ c/o Stella Richards Management, 42 Hazlebury Road, London SW6 2ND (tel 020 7736 7786, fax 020 7731 5082)

NEOPTOLEMOS, Prof John Phitoyiannis; *b* 30 June 1951; *Educ* Owen's GS N London, Churchill Coll Cambridge, Guy's Hosp London (MA, MB BChir), Univ of Leicester (MD); *m* 2 Feb 1974, Linda Joan, da of Richard Blaylock, of Kenton, Newcastle upon Tyne; 1 s (Ptolemy *b* 11 Aug 1978), 1 da (Eleni *b* 12 May 1981); *Career* Guy's Hosp London 1976–77, Leicester Royal Infirmary 1978–84 and 1986–87, UCSD San Diego 1984–85, sr lectr then reader Univ Dept of Surgery Birmingham and conslt surgn City Hosp 1987–94, prof of surgery Queen Elizabeth Hosp Birmingham 1994–96, prof of surgery and head Div of Surgery and Oncology Univ of Liverpool Royal Liverpool Univ Hosp 1996–, head Sch of Cancer Studies Univ of Liverpool 2005–; Hunterian prof of surgery RCS 1987–88; scientific contribs to aetiology, diagnosis and treatment of diseases of the pancreas, bilary tree and liver; chm: European Study Gp for Pancreatic Cancer 1991–, NCRI Pancreas Cancer Subgroup 2004–; memb: Ctee Surgical Research Soc 1994–98, World Cncl Int Hepato-Pancreato-Bilary Assoc 1995–98, Scientific Ctee United European Gastroenterology Fedn 2002–06 (memb Cncl 1997–2002); pres: Pancreatic Soc of GB and I 1994–95 (memb Ctee 1987–90), Int Assoc of Pancreatology 2000–02 (memb World Cncl 1996–2004); sec European Pancreatic Club 1996–2002 (memb Cncl 1995–2002), treas European Digestive Surgery 1997–2004; Rodney Smith prize 1987, Moynihan travelling fell Assoc of Surgns of GB and I 1988; FRCS, FMedSci 2007; *Recreations* latin and ballroom dancing, squash; *Clubs* Heswell Squash (memb ctee 1999–2004); *Style—* Prof John P Neoptolemos; ⊠ Division of Surgery and Oncology, The Duncan Building, Daulby Street, Liverpool L69 3GA (tel 0151 706 4175, fax 0151 706 5798, e-mail j.p.neoptolemos@liv.ac.uk)

NESBITT, Prof Robert William; s of Thomas Dodgson Nesbitt (d 1977), of Blyth, Northumberland, and Mary Florence Nesbitt (d 1983); *b* 26 September 1936; *Educ* Blyth GS, Univ of Durham (BSc, PhD); *m* 24 Oct 1959, Catherine, da of Peter Robertson (d 1976), of Blyth, Northumberland; 3 da (Carolyn Anne *b* 1960, Joanne Louise *b* 1964, Jacqueline Clare *b* 1969); *Career* geologist Greenland Geological Survey 1958–59; Univ of Adelaide: lectr 1962–68, sr lectr 1968–72, reader 1972–80; visiting res fell Yale Univ 1968, visiting prof Université de Rennes 1979–92, dean of sci Univ of Southampton 1987–90 (prof of geology 1980–); subject advsr Univ Funding Cncl 1985–93; hon corr Geological Soc of Australia, chm Ctee of Heads of Geoscience Dept 1992, memb Cncl Geological Soc London 1994–97; FGS (Aust) 1976, FGS 1980; *Recreations* golf; *Style—* Prof Robert Nesbitt; ⊠ School of Ocean and Earth Science, Southampton Oceanography Centre, University of Southampton, Empress Dock, Southampton SO14 3ZH (tel 023 8059 2037, fax 023 8059 3052, e-mail rwn2@soc.soton.ac.uk)

NESSLING, Paul William Downs; s of late Herbert William Nessling, and Mary Alice, *née* Perry; *b* 26 September 1945; *Educ* Latymer Upper Sch; *m* 1975, Kathryn Lynne, *née* Freeman; 1 da; *Career* mgmnt trainee Midland Bank 1963–64, buyer BAT 1965–66, with

DTI 1967–75, on secondment to FCO as third sec Chicago 1970, asst private sec to Sec of State DTI 1972–74, private sec to Min of Prices 1974–75, on secondment to FCO as second sec Bahrain 1975–79; HM Dip Serv: second sec FCO 1979–81, second sec Lisbon 1981–82, HM consul Warsaw 1982–84, head of Chancery Aden 1984, first sec (aid) and dep UK perm rep to UN Environment Programme (UNEP) Nairobi 1984–87, first sec FCO 1987–89, first sec (commercial) Harare 1989–93, first sec (commercial) Muscat 1993–96, first sec Sarajevo 1996–97, dep dir Jt Export Promotion Directorate FCO 1997–98, dep high cmmr Lusaka 1998–2001, high cmmr to the Kingdom of Tonga and consul for Pacific Islands under American Sovereignty South of the Equator 2002–06; *Recreations* current affairs, tennis, travelling, reading, walking; *Style—* Paul Nessling, Esq; ⊠ c/o Foreign & Commonwealth Office, King Charles Street, London SW1A 2AH (e-mail pknessling@yahoo.co.uk)

NETHERCOT, Prof David Arthur; OBE (2006); s of Arthur Owen Martin Nethercot (d 1980), and Dorothy May, *née* Bearman (d 1996); *b* 26 April 1946; *Educ* Minchenden GS, Univ of Wales (BSc, PhD, DSc, Page prize and medal); *m* 3 Aug 1968, Hedd Dwynwen, da of John Byron Evans; 2 da (Susanna Kate *b* 29 Dec 1971, Emily Victoria *b* 4 March 1975); *Career* ICI fell Univ of Wales 1970–71, lectr and reader Univ of Sheffield 1971–89; Univ of Nottingham: prof of civil engrg 1989–99, head of dept 1994–99; Imperial Coll London: prof of civil engrg 1999–, head Dept of Civil and Environmental Engrg 1999–; visiting prof: Japan Soc for Promotion of Science Univ of Nagoya 1980, Swiss Federal Inst of Technology Lausanne 1990; chm and memb Ctee: BSI, EPSRC, IABSE; memb Cncl Steel Construction Inst 1992–, chm Jt Bd of Moderators 1996–98 (memb 1993–99); FIStructE 1989 (memb 1976, memb Cncl 1986–89 and 1991–96, vice-pres 2000–03, pres 2003–04); FREng 1993 (memb Cncl 2000–03), FICE 1995, FCGI 2001, FRSA 2002; *Awards* ICE: Miller Prize 1971, Telford Premium 1991; IStructE: Oscar Faber Bronze medal 1989, Murray Buxton Prize 1992, Henry Adams dip 1994, 1998 and 2006; *Books* Design for Structural Stability (1985), Limit States Design of Structural Steelwork (2001); author of over 400 papers on structural engineering; *Recreations* sport; *Style—* Prof D A Nethercot, OBE, FREng; ⊠ 132 Queens Road, London SW19 8LS (tel 020 8542 2349); Department of Civil and Environmental Engineering, Imperial College London, Imperial College Road, London SW7 2A2 (tel 020 7594 6097, fax 020 7594 6042, e-mail d.nethercot@imperial.ac.uk)

NETHERTHORPE, 3 Baron (UK 1959); James Frederick Turner; s of 2 Baron Netherthorpe (d 1982); *b* 7 January 1964; *Educ* Harrow; *m* 10 Dec 1989, (Elizabeth) Curran, da of Edward William Fahan, of Redding, Connecticut, USA; 2 s (Hon Andrew James Edward *b* 24 March 1993, Hon John Patrick William *b* 24 May 2001), 2 da (Hon Megan Anna Curran *b* 19 Nov 1994, Hon Nell Katherine Elizabeth *b* 10 June 1997); *Heir* s, Hon Andrew Turner; *Style—* The Rt Hon the Lord Netherthorpe; ⊠ Boothby Hall, Boothby Pagnell, Grantham, Lincolnshire NG33 4DQ (tel 01476 585374)

NETHERTON, Derek Nigel Donald; s of John Gordon Netherton, of London, and Beryl Agnes, *née* Freeman; *b* 4 January 1945; *Educ* Charterhouse, King's Coll Cambridge (MA); *Children* 4 s (Charles *b* 1981, George *b* 1984, Patrick, David (twins) *b* 1987); *Career* dir J Henry Schroder 1981–96; non-exec dir: St James's Place Capital 1996–, Next 1996–2008, Plantation & General Investments 1997–, Hiscox plc 1999–2006, Greggs plc 2002– (non-exec chm 2002–); FIA; *Style—* Derek Netherton, Esq

NETTEL, Julian Philip; s of Leopold Nettel (d 1990), and Clare, *née* Carter (d 2000); *b* 23 October 1953; *Educ* Sutton GS, Univ of Bristol (BA); *m* 9 Aug 1980, Caroline Gillian, *née* Mawhood; 2 s (Thomas Alexander *b* 7 July 1984, Edward Philip *b* 17 May 1987); *Career* hosp sec Westminster Hosp 1983–86, gen mangr Whittington Royal Northern Hosps 1986–1990, divnl mangr King's Coll and Dulwich Hosps 1990–93, exec in res Univ of Ottawa Ontario 1992–93, chief exec Ealing Hosp NHS Tst 1994–99, chief exec St Mary's NHS Tst London 1999–; Inst of Healthcare Mgmnt 1978; govr Wimbledon Sch of Art; *Recreations* painting, jazz, cricket, golf, cycling; *Clubs* Roehampton, Royal Anglo-Belgian; *Style—* Julian Nettel, Esq; ⊠ St Mary's NHS Trust, Praed Street, London W2 1NY (tel 020 7886 1327, fax 020 7886 1017, e-mail julian.nettel@st-marys.nhs.uk)

NETTLE, David Richard; s of Gerald Nettle, of Redruth, and Viola, *née* Tregenza; *b* 10 June 1956; *Educ* Redruth GS, Royal Coll of Music; *Career* concert pianist; worldwide appearances with Richard Markham, *qv*, as Nettle-Markham Piano Duo: North American debut 1979, London debut (Wigmore Hall) 1982, Far East tour 1983, Middle East tours 1983 and 1985, African and Aust tours 1992/93, regular US tours, frequent performances at princ Euro festivals incl BBC Proms; *Recordings* incl: The Rite of Spring and Petrushka (1984), The Planets (1985), Dyson's The Blacksmiths (1987), Delius and Grainger Folksongs (1988), Rossini's Petite Messe Solennelle (1990), Carnival of the Animals (1991), Nettle & Markham in England (1993), Arnold-Piano Duet Concerto (1993), Nettle & Markham in America (1994), Arnold-2 Piano Concerto (1994), Nettle & Markham in France (1996), Complete 2–Piano Works of Brahms (2006); *Awards* Norris prize 1977, Music Retailers' Assoc Award Award for best chamber music record 1985; *Recreations* travel, cooking, wining and dining, tennis, chess, photography, languages, writing; *Style—* David Nettle, Esq; ⊠ The Old Power House, Atherton Street, London SW11 2JE (tel 020 7738 2765, e-mail nettleandmarkham@aol.com, website www.nettleandmarkham.com)

NETTLES, John; *Career* actor; early stage work incl plays at Royal Court, Traverse Theatre Edinburgh and Theatre 69; *Repertory* Northcott Theatre Exeter: Jimmy Porter in Look Back in Anger, Feste in Twelfth Night, Vladimir in Waiting For Godot, Mompesson in Roses of Eyam, Tranio in The Taming of the Shrew; Bristol Old Vic: Thersites in Troillus and Cressida, Sganarelle in Don Juan, Harold in The Philanthropist, Joey in Butley, Alwa in Lulu, Ed in Entertaining Mr Sloane; Crucible Theatre Sheffield: Charles Surface in School for Scandal; Derby Playhouse: Leonard in Time and Time Again, Brian in A Day in the Death of Joe Egg; RSC: Florizel in A Winter's Tale, Thersites in Troilus and Cressida, Maxwell in Destiny, Godber in That Good Between Us, Kung Tu in The Bundle, Von Lieres in A Miserable Death, Detective in The Factory Birds, Priest in Frozen Assets, Bassanio in The Merchant of Venice, Lucio in Measure For Measure, Thompson in The Churchill Play, Harry Thunder in Wild Oats, Alexei Tourbin in The White Guard, Ernest in Once in a Lifetime, La Ronde, The Hollow Crown (USA tour), Leontes in The Winter's Tale, Page in The Merry Wives of Windsor, Caesar in Antony and Cleopatra, Merecraft in The Devil is an Ass, Julius Caesar; *Other Theatre* incl: Lord Foppington in The Relapse (Old Vic), title role in Butley (Fortune Theatre); *Pantomine* Abanazar in Aladdin (Theatre Royal Bath), Sheriff of Nottingham in Babes in the Wood (Palace Theatre Manchester), Bluebeard the Pirate in Robinson Crusoe (Theatre Royal Plymouth and New Theatre Cardiff), King Rat in Dick Whittington (Palace Theatre Manchester, Wimbledon and Leeds); *Television* LWT incl: Black Beauty, Holding On; BBC incl: The Liver Birds, The Merchant of Venice, Bergerac, Bergerac Special, Hands Across the Sea; other credits incl: Submarine (narrator, series), A Family at War, Dickens of London, Boon (guest lead role), Midsomer Murders; *Books* Nudity in a Public Place (semi-autobiographical, 1991); *Style—* John Nettles, Esq; ⊠ c/o Saraband Associates, 265 Liverpool Road, London N1 1LX (tel 020 7609 5313, fax 020 7609 2370)

NETTLETON, Charles; s of Travers Dering Nettleton, and Margrit, *née* Schill; *Educ* Dover Coll, Peterhouse Cambridge (exhibitioner, MA); *Career* William Collins Publishers 1980–86; Hodder & Stoughton Publishers: sales and mktg dir H & S 1991–93, dep md Headline 1993–96, md religious books 1996–2002, md children's books 2002–; *Recreations* family, singing, mountain biking; *Style—* Charles Nettleton, Esq; ⊠ Hodder Headline

Ltd, 338 Euston Road, London NW1 3BH (tel 020 7873 6000, fax 020 7873 6024, e-mail charles.nettleton@hodder.co.uk)

NEUBERG, Roger Wolfe; s of Klaus Neuberg, of London, and Herta, *née* Hausler (d 1986); *b* 24 May 1941; *Educ* Hendon Co GS, Middx Hosp Med Sch (MB BS); *m* 16 Aug 1964, Ruth Denise, da of Manning Ephron (d 1984), of Bournemouth; 2 s (Guy b 1966, Kim b 1967); *Career* conslt obstetrician and gynaecologist; registrar Middx Hosp and Hosp for Women; sr registrar: John Radcliffe Hosp Oxford and Royal Berkshire Hosp; conslt and dir of infertility servs Leicester Royal Infirmary, clinical inspr HFEA; memb: Br Fertility Soc, Assoc of Broadcasting Doctors; obstetrician memb Exec Ctee and regnl advsy faculty rep ALSO(UK) (Advanced Life Support Obstetrics), instr MOET (Mgmnt of Obstetric Emergencies and Trauma); LRCP 1965, MRCS 1965, FRCOG 1983; *Books* So You Want to Have a Baby (1985, 4 edn 1996), Infertility (1991, 2 edn 1994), Obstetrics: A Practical Manual (1995); *Recreations* aikido, gardening; *Style*— Roger Neuberg, Esq; ✉ 9 Barrington Road, Stoneygate, Leicester LE2 2RA (tel 0116 255 3933, e-mail roger@neuberg.fsnet.co.uk); Women's Hospital, Leicester Royal Infirmary, Leicester (tel 0116 258 6426)

NEUBERGER, Prof James Max; s of Prof Albert Neuberger, CBE (d 1996), of London, and Lilian Ida, *née* Dreyfus; *b* 4 November 1949; *Educ* Westminster, ChCh Oxford (MA, BM BCh, DM); *m* 14 Sept 1979, Belinda Patricia, da of Patrick Joseph Keogh, of Manchester; 2 s (Oliver b 1980, Edmund b 1984), 2 da (Francesca b 1982, Octavia b 1988); *Career* sr lectr in med KCH London 1980–86, conslt physician Queen Elizabeth Hosp Birmingham 1986– (assoc med dir for R&D), prof of med Univ of Birmingham 1999; FRCP 1991 (MRCP 1977); *Books* Liver Annual (1988), Immunology of Liver Transplantation (1993), Liver Transplantation (1994); *Recreations* fishing, gardening, reading; *Style*— Prof James Neuberger; ✉ The Moat House, Radford Road, Alvechurch, Worcestershire B48 7ST (tel 0121 445 1773); Queen Elizabeth Hospital, Edgbaston, Birmingham B15 2TH (tel 0121 472 1311, e-mail j.m.neuberger@bham.ac.uk)

NEUBERGER, Baroness (Life Peer UK 2004), of Primrose Hill in the London Borough of Camden; Rabbi Julia Babette Sarah Neuberger; DBE (2004); da of Walter Manfred Schwab (d 1996), of London, and Alice, *née* Rosenthal (d 2001); *b* 27 February 1950; *Educ* S Hampstead HS for Girls, Newnham Coll Cambridge, Leo Baeck Coll London; *m* 17 Sept 1973, Anthony John Neuberger, s of Prof Albert Neuberger, CBE (d 1996), of London; 1 da (Hon Harriet b 16 June 1979), 1 s (Hon Matthew b 2 July 1981); *Career* rabbi S London Liberal Synagogue 1977–89, visiting fell King's Fund Inst 1989–91, visiting and Harkness fell Harvard Med Sch 1991–92, chair Camden and Islington Community Health Servs NHS Tst 1992–97, chief exec The King's Fund 1997–2004; fell King's Fund Coll London 1992–97, chllr Univ of Ulster 1994–2000; tstee Imperial War Museum 1999–2006; memb: HFEA 1990–95, Ethics Ctee BMA 1992–94, GMC 1993–2001, MRC 1995–2000, Library Cmmn 1995–97; Civil Service cmmr 2001–02, memb Ctee on Standards in Public Life (Wicks Ctee) 2001–04; memb Cncl: UCL 1993–96, Save the Children Fund 1994–96; vice-pres Patients' Assoc 1992–97, tstee Runnymede Tst 1990–97; regular broadcaster; Hon Dr: Univ of Humberside, Univ of Ulster, Univ of Stirling, City Univ, Oxford Brookes Univ, Univ of Teesside, Univ of Nottingham, Open Univ, Queen's Univ Belfast, Sheffield Hallam Univ, Univ of Aberdeen, Univ of London 2006; hon fell Mansfield Coll Oxford 1997; Hon FCGI 1998, Hon FRCP 2004, Hon FRCGP 2006, Hon FRCPsych 2007; *Books* The Story of Judaism (for children, 1986), Caring for Dying People of Different Faiths (1987, 3 edn 2004), Days of Decision (ed, 1987), Whatever's Happening to Women (1991), A Necessary End (ed with John White, 1991), The Things That Matter (ed, 1993), Ethics and Healthcare: Research Ethics Ctees in the UK (1992), On Being Jewish (1995), Dying Well: A guide to enabling a good death (1999, 2 edn 2004), Hidden Assets: Values and decision-making in the NHS (ed with Bill New, 2002), The Moral State We're In (2005); *Style*— The Rt Hon the Lady Neuberger, DBE; ✉ House of Lords, London SW1A 0PW

NEUBERGER, Dr Michael Samuel; s of Prof Albert Neuberger, CBE, FRS (d 1996), of London, and Lilian Ida, *née* Dreyfus; *b* 2 November 1953; *Educ* Westminster, Trinity Coll Cambridge (scholar, MA), Imperial Coll London (PhD); *m* 6 Sept 1991, Dr Gillian Anne Pyman; 2 da (Saskia b 5 Sept 1992, Lydia b 18 May 1994), 2 s (Thomas b 26 March 1997, Benjamin b 20 Feb 2002); *Career* SRC postdoctoral fell Univ of London 1977–79, EMBO fell Inst of Genetics Univ of Cologne 1979–80; Univ of Cambridge: res fell Trinity Coll 1977–81, memb of staff MRC Laboratory of Molecular Biology 1980– (jt head Div of Protein and Nucleic Acid Chemistry 2002–), fell and dir of studies in cell biology and biochemistry Trinity Coll 1985–, hon prof of molecular immunology 2002–; int research scholar Howard Hughes Med Inst 1992–98; memb EMBO 1989; FRS 1993, FMedSci 2000; *Style*— Prof Michael Neuberger, FRS; ✉ MRC Laboratory of Molecular Biology, Hills Road, Cambridge CB2 2QH (tel 01223 402245, fax 01223 412178, e-mail msn@mrc-lmb.cam.ac.uk)

NEUBERGER OF ABBOTSBURY, Baron (Life Peer UK 2007), of Abbotsbury in the County of Dorset; Sir David Edmond Neuberger; kt (1996), PC (2004); s of Prof Albert Neuberger, CBE, FRS (d 1996), and Lilian Ida, *née* Dreyfus; *b* 10 January 1948; *Educ* Westminster, ChCh Oxford; *m* Angela, da of late Brig Peter Holdsworth; 1 da (Jessica b 1977), 2 s (Nicholas b 1979, Max b 1981); *Career* N M Rothschild & Sons 1970–73, called to the Bar Lincoln's Inn 1974 (bencher 1993), QC 1987, recorder 1990–96, former jt head of Falcon chambers, judge of the High Court of Justice (Chancery Div) 1996–2004, Chancery supervising judge (Midlands, Wales & Chester, and Western Circuits) 2001–04, Lord Justice of Appeal 2004–07, judge i/c modernisation 2004–, Lord of Appeal in Ordinary 2007–; chm Advsy Ctee on Spoilation of Art during the Holocaust 1997–; chm of tstees Schizophrenia Tst 1997–; govr London Inst 2000–; *Clubs* Garrick; *Style*— The Rt Hon the Lord Neuberger of Abbotsbury; ✉ House of Lords, London SW1A 0PW

NEUMANN, Daniela; da of Isaaco Aronne Neumann (d 1997), and Renate, *née* Fromm; *b* 11 November 1966, Hong Kong; *Educ* St Christopher Sch Letchworth, Nat Westminster Press Journalism Coll Hastings (NCTJ); *Career* early career as newspaper reporter and sub-ed, then TV researcher; controller ITV2 2002–06 (also ed Factual ITV1), head of factual entertainment and features Wall to Wall Prodns 2006–; memb BAFTA; *Television* prodr London Tonight (London News Network); assoc prodr: Michael Winner's True Crimes (and scriptwriter), Somalia Special, War Against the Mafia; prodr and dir: Special Operations 1994–95, Speakeasy does the Business 1995, Cops, Missing, Ibiza Uncovered 1997, The London Programme 1998, Airline 1998–99, Hello Mum 1999, Blagging Britain 2000–01; series prodr: Des Res 1987, Dinner Dates 1997, Friday Night Fever 1997–98; series ed: Crime Monthly 1995, Crime Net 1996; dir: Emmerdale 1999–2000, Brookside 2000, The Bill 2000; exec prodr Reps in Ibiza 2001; *Style*— Ms Daniela Neumann; ✉ tel 07710 214828

NEVILE, Christopher William Kenneth; s of Kenneth Nevile (d 1960), of Swinderby, Lincs, and Elizabeth Mary, *née* Brown; *b* 27 April 1957; *Educ* St Hugh's Wood Hall SPA, Rugby, Univ of Exeter (LLB); *m* Sept 1993, Charlotte Brodie (Charlie), da of Dr Jeremy Lee-Potter, *qv*, of Stoborough, Dorset, and Lynda Lee-Potter; 1 s (Kit Brodie Kenneth b 9 Oct 1995), 1 da (Mia Brodie Calypso b 20 Jan 1999); *Career* stockbroker; assoc dir Scrimgeour Vickers until 1987; dir Adams & Nevile Ltd 1987–95; md Granville Private Banking 1995–2000, dir Granville plc 1997–2000, md Nevile Merriam Investment Mgmnt 2000–03, dir Principal Investment Management 2003–, dir Granville Bank, md Granville Pension Mgmnt; *Recreations* fishing, riding, music, cricket; *Clubs* Holmes Place (Barbican); *Style*— Christopher W K Nevile, Esq; ✉ e-mail chris.nevile@principalinvestment.co.uk

NEVILL, Amanda Elizabeth; *b* 21 March 1957; *Educ* Bar Convent York, British Inst France; *m* 3 May 1980 (m dis 1986), Dominic John Nevill, s of John Nevill, of Folkstone, Kent; 2 da; *Career* Rowan Gallery London 1978–79, Francis Kyle Gallery London 1979–80, Bath Int Festival Contemporary Art Fair 1980–84, sec Royal Photographic Soc Bath 1990–94 (admin 1985), head Nat Museum of Photography, Film & Television 1994–2003, dir BFI 2003–; Hon DLitt Univ of Bradford 2000; Hon FRPS, FRSA 1996; *Style*— Amanda Nevill; ✉ British Film Institute, 21 Stephen Street, London W1T 1LN

NEVILL, Prof Bernard Richard; s of R G Nevill (d 1941); *b* 24 September 1934; *Educ* privately, St Martin's Sch of Art, RCA; *Career* lectr: Shoreditch Coll 1954–56, Central Sch Art and Design 1957–60, St Martin's Sch of Art and RCA 1959–74; freelance illustrator 1956–60 (incl Good Housekeeping, Woman's Journal, Vogue, Harpers Bazaar), freelance journalist 1956–60 (incl Vogue, Sketch), designer then design dir Liberty Prints 1961–71, memb Advsy Panel Nat Dip Design 1964–66, art critic Vogue 1965–66, govr Croydon Coll Art 1966–67, designer and design dir Ten Cate Holland 1969–71, design conslt Cantoni Italy 1971–84, prof of textile design RCA 1984–89 (fell 1985); commissions and collections incl: Cotton Board Manchester 1950, For Liberty 1961–71, Verve 1960, Cravate, Islamic 1963, Jazz 1964, Tango 1966, Renaissance 1967, Chameleon 1969, Cantoni Casa 1971–84, Int Wool Secretariat 1975–77, English Country House Collection for Sekers Int 1981–82, Romanex de Boussac France 1982–87, Unitika Co Ltd Japan 1990–, Pierre Frey France 1991–, collection of furnishing textiles for Château de Bagnols France 1991–, collections of dress and furnishing textiles designed for DMC Texunion France 1992–, KBC Germany; designed costumes for: films (Genevieve 1953, Next to No Time 1955, The Admirable Crichton 1957), musicals (Marigold 1958), opera (Cosi fan Tutte Glyndebourne 1960); redesigned Long Gallery, British Embassy Washington 1982; cmmnd to restore interiors of Eastnor Castle Herefordshire 1990–, presently rebuilding the remaining wing and restoring the landscape of Fonthill Abbey; memb: Victorian Soc, Chelsea Soc; FRSA 1966–77, FSIA 1970–87, FCSD 1987; *Recreations* admiring well-built walls and buildings, passionate conservationist and environmentalist, tree worshipper; *Style*— Prof Bernard Nevill; ✉ Fonthill Abbey, Salisbury, Wiltshire SP3 6QR

NEVILL, John Robert Ralph Austin; s of Frederick Reginald Nevill (d 1949), of Newbury, Berks, and Jeanne, *née* Fageol (d 1975); *b* 15 February 1928; *Educ* Ampleforth; *m* 30 July 1955, Ann Margaret Mary, da of Archibald Corble (d 1944), of Cookham, Berks; 2 da (Cecilia b 1956, Caroline b 1960), 4 s (Dominic b 1957, Ralph b 1959, Christopher b 1962, Anthony b 1966); *Career* Lt DCLI 1947–48; dir: Nevill Developments 1956–, The Nevill Gallery; formerly: chm and pres SE Region ESU, chm and vice-pres Canterbury and E Kent Branch ESU, dir Family Housing Assoc Folkestone Area, memb Ctee SE Arts Assoc; memb Ctee Canterbury Arts Cncl; hon memb Rutherford Coll Univ of Kent at Canterbury; judge Flowers City Campaign and Children's Flower Soc; memb Hon Soc of Gray's Inn 1951; supporter Army Benevolent Fund; Freeman City of London, Liveryman and former memb Ct of Assts Worshipful Co of Gardeners; Knight of Honour and Devotion Br Assoc SMOM; *Recreations* travelling, fishing, photography, painting; *Clubs* Athenaeum, ESU; *Style*— John Nevill, Esq; ✉ 5 Tite Street, London SW3 4JU (tel 020 7352 7368); 8 Radnor Cliff, Folkestone, Kent CT20 2JN (tel 01303 248403); Nevill Gallery, 43 St Peter's Sreet, Canterbury, Kent CT1 2BG (tel 01227 765291, e-mail enquiries@nevillgallery.com, website www.nevillgallery.com)

NEVILLE, Dr Adam Matthew; CBE (1994), TD (1963); *b* 5 February 1923; *Educ* Univ of London (BSc, MSc, PhD, DSc), Univ of Leeds (DSc); *m* 29 March 1952, Mary Hallam, *née* Cousins; 1 da (Elizabeth Louise (Dame Elizabeth Neville, DBE, QPM, *qv*) b 5 Feb 1953), 1 s (Adam Andrew b 11 May 1955); *Career* War Serv Middle East and Italy, Maj RETA; practising and academic engr 1950–, prof of civil engrg Univ of Leeds 1968–78, princ and vice-chllr Univ of Dundee 1978–87, conslt and arbitrator 1987–, ptnr A & M Neville Engineering 1987–; pres Concrete Soc 1974–75, chm Ctee of Princs of Scottish Univs 1984–86, pres Cncl of Europe Ctee on Univs 1984–86; memb Advsy Cncl Br Library 1989–94, memb Nat Academies Policy Advsy Gp 1992–97, vice-pres Royal Acad of Engineering (formerly Fellowship of Engineering) 1992–95; Freeman City of London 1977; memb: Bonnetmaker Craft of Dundee 1979; Hon LLD Univ of St Andrews 1987, Hon LLD Univ of Dundee 1998, Hon Dr Applied Science Sherbrooke Univ Canada 1999; hon fell Queen Mary Univ of London 1996; hon memb American Concrete Inst 1986, hon memb The Concrete Soc 2000, hon memb Brazilian Concrete Inst 2007; Gold Medal The Concrete Soc; FICE, FIStructE, FRSE 1979, FREng 1986; OStJ 1983; *Books* Properties of Concrete (1963, 4 edn 1995), Basic Statistical Methods (with J B Kennedy, 1964, 3 edn 1986), Creep of Concrete: Plain, Reinforced and Prestressed (1970), Structural Analysis: A Unified Classical and Matrix Approach (with A Ghali, 1977, 5 edn 2003), Hardened Concrete: Physical and Mechanical Aspects (1971), High Alumina Cement Concrete (1975), Creep of Plain and Structural Concrete (with W H Dilger and J J Brooks, 1983), Concrete Technology (with J J Brooks, 1987), Neville on Concrete (2003, 2 edn 2007), Concrete: Neville's Insights and Issues (2006); *Recreations* skiing (reminiscing), travel; *Clubs* Athenaeum, New (Edinburgh), Travelers' Century (LA); *Style*— Dr Adam Neville, CBE, TD, FRSE, FREng

NEVILLE, Dan; TD; s of Thomas Neville (d 1967), of Kiltannan Croagh, Co Limerick, and Esther, *née* Giltenane (d 2004); *b* Co Limerick Ireland; *Educ* Univ of Limerick, NUI Cork; *m* 1974, Goretti, *née* O'Callaghan; 2 s (Thomas, Daniel), 2 da (Maria, Maeve); *Career* memb Seanad Eireann (Fine Gael) Lab Panel 1989–1997, TD (Fine Gael) Limerick West 1997–; memb Limerick CC 1985–2003; memb Mid-Western Health Bd 1992–99; pres Irish Assoc of Suicidology, dir Irish Palatine Assoc; Magill Campaigning Politician of the Year 2005; *Style*— Dan Neville, Esq, TD; ✉ Kiltannan Croagh, Co Limerick, Ireland (tel 00 353 61 396351, e-mail dan.neville@oireachtas.ie, www.danneville.ie); Main St, Rathkeale, Co Limerick, Ireland (tel 00 353 69 63610)

NEVILLE, Dame Elizabeth Louise; DBE (2003), QPM (1996); da of Dr Adam Neville, CBE, *qv*, of London, and Dr Mary Hallam, *née* Cousins; *b* 5 February 1953; *Educ* Univ of Oxford (MA), Univ of London (PhD); *Family* 1 s (Matthew Edward Burbeck b 1983), 1 da (Katherine Mary Burbeck b 1985); m 18 Jan 2003, Nicholas David Cox; *Career* joined Metropolitan Police 1973, transferred Thames Valley Police 1986, Asst Chief Constable Sussex Police 1991–94, Dep Chief Constable Northants Police 1994–97, Chief Constable Wilts Constabulary 1997–2004, fell Univ of Northampton 2004–; non-exec dir Serious Fraud Office, Policy Authy memb Civil Nuclear Constabulary, ind complaints assessor Driver Vehicle and Operator Gp Dept for Tport, complaints adjudicator Assets Recovery Agency; dir Ajay Shopfit Ltd; tstee: Cumberland Lodge, Wiltshire Bobby Van; patron Swindon Sanctuary, govr Stonar Sch Wiltshire; hon fell St Hilda's Coll Oxford 2006; Hon LLD Southampton Solent Univ 2004; FRSA; *Recreations* skiing, cycling, riding, walking, sailing, opera; *Clubs* Reform; *Style*— Dame Elizabeth Neville, DBE, QPM

NEVILLE, Gary; *b* 18 February 1975; *Educ* Elton HS Bury; *Career* professional footballer; Manchester United: Sch of Excellence 1986, signed schoolboy forms 1989, trainee 1991, first team debut European Cup v Torpedo Moscow 1992, League debut v Coventry May 1994, over 400 appearances, Premier League champions 1996, 1997, 1999, 2000, 2001, 2003 and 2007, winners FA Cup 1996, 1999 and 2004 (runners up 1995 and 2005), winners European Champions League 1999; England: 85 full caps, debut v Japan 1995, memb squad European Championships 1996, 2000 and 2004, memb squad World Cup 1998 and 2006; *Recreations* golf; *Style*— Gary Neville; ✉ c/o Manchester United FC, Old Trafford, Manchester M16 0RA

NEVILLE, Prof (Alexander) Munro; s of Alexander Munro Neville (d 1983), of Troon, and Georgina Stewart, *née* Gerrard (d 1989); *b* 24 March 1935; *Educ* Univ of Glasgow (MB ChB, PhD, MD), Harvard Univ, Univ of London (DSc); *m* 5 Sept 1961, Anne Margaret Stroyan (d 2000), da of Dr Hugh Black (d 1975), of Paisley; 1 da (Judeth b 25 Nov 1963),

N

1 s (Munro b 26 Nov 1964); *Career* sr lectr in pathology Univ of Glasgow 1967–70, res fell Inst of Cancer Res MRC London 1970–73, prof of pathology Univ of London 1973–85; Ludwig Inst for Cancer Res: dir 1975–85, dir Zurich and London 1985–92, sci sec and assoc dir 1992–2005, vice-pres 2004–05; treas RCPath 1993–98; FRCPath 1979 (MRCPath 1969), FIBiol 1997; *Recreations* golf, gardening, history; *Clubs* Banstead Downs; *Style*— Prof Munro Neville; ✉ 6 Woodlands Park, Boxhill, Tadworth, Surrey KT20 7JL (tel 01737 844113, e-mail munro.neville@lineone.net)

NEVILLE, Philip (Phil); *b* 21 January 1977; *Educ* Elton HS Bury; *Career* professional footballer; clubs: Manchester United FC 1988–2005 (Sch of Excellence 1988, signed schoolboy forms 1990, trainee 1993, first team debut 1995, over 300 appearances, Premier League champions 1996, 1997, 1999, 2000, 2001 and 2003, FA Cup winners 1996, 1999 and 2004 (finalists 1995 and 2005), winners European Champions League 1999), Everton FC 2005–; England: 50 caps, full debut v China 1996, memb squad European Championships 2000 and 2004; *Recreations* golf, cricket; *Style*— Phil Neville

NEVILLE-JONES, Dame (Lilian) Pauline; DCMG (1996, CMG 1987); da of Roland Neville-Jones, RAMC (ka 1941), and Cecilia Emily Millicent Winn, *née* Rath, step da of Dr John Michael Winn; *b* 2 November 1939; *Educ* Leeds Girls' HS, Lady Margaret Hall Oxford (BA); *Career* HM Dip Serv 1963–96: joined FCO 1963, third sec Salisbury Rhodesia 1964–65, third sec (later second sec) Singapore 1965–68, FCO 1968–71 (dealing with Med), first sec Washington 1971–75, dep chef de cabinet (later chef de cabinet) to Christopher Tugendhat, Cmmn of Euro Communities Brussels 1977–82, sabbatical RIIA London and Institut Français des Relations Internationales Paris 1982–83, head of policy planning staff FCO 1983–87, min (econ) Bonn Embassy 1987–91 (min 1988–91), dep under sec for overseas and defence Cabinet Office 1991–94, chm Jt Intelligence Ctee 1993–94, political dir FCO 1994–96; sr advsr to Carl Bildt, High Rep for the Civilian Peace Implementation for Bosnia Feb-July 1996; head of global business strategy NatWest Markets 1996–98, chm NatWest Markets France 1996–98, vice-chm Hawkpoint Partners (memb of Natwest Gp) 1998–2000; chm Qinetiq Gp plc 2003–06; a govr BBC 1998–2004; head Cons Pty Nat and Int Security Policy Gp 2006–, shadow security min and nat security adsvr to Ldr of the Oppn 2007–; chm Information Assurance Advsy Cncl 2003–; memb: Cncl IISS 1996–, Cncl City Univ 1997–2003 (currently memb Advsy Cncl), Cncl Univ of Oxford 2003–06; Hon DUniv Open Univ 1998, Hon DSc (Econ) Univ of London 1999; *Recreations* cooking, gardening, antiques; *Style*— Dame Pauline Neville-Jones, DCMG

NEVILLE-ROLFE, Lucy Jeanne; CMG (2005); da of Edmund Neville-Rolfe, and late Margaret Elizabeth, *née* Evans (d 2006); sis of Marianne Neville-Rolfe, CB, *qv*; *b* 2 January 1953; *Educ* St Mary's Shaftesbury and Cambridge, Somerville Coll Oxford (MA); *m* Sir Richard John Packer, KCB, *qv*; 4 s (Thomas Edmund b 21 June 1981, William Henry b 17 Aug 1984, Harold Charles b 24 Nov 1988, Samuel Inigo b 19 August 1994); *Career* MAFF 1973–92: private sec to Rt Hon John Silkin MP 1977–79, European Community policy on Sheepmeat and Milk 1979–86, head Land Use and Tenure Div 1986–89, Food Safety Act Div 1989–90, head Personnel 1990–92; memb Prime Minister's Policy Unit 1992–94, dir Deregulation Unit Cabinet Office (formerly DTI) 1995–97, memb Bd FCO 2000–05; Tesco plc: gp dir of corp affrs 1997–2006, co sec 2004–06, exec dir corp legal affrs 2006–; non-exec dir: John Laing Construction 1991–92, Holloway White Allom 1991–92; dep chm Br Retail Consortium; memb: CBI Economics Ctee, CBI Europe Ctee, ESRC Panel on Cultures of Consumption, Bd UNICE Task Force on Enlargement 1999–2004, Dep PM's Local Govt Funding Ctee 2003–04, Sec of State's Panel on Monitoring the Economy, Foresight Obesity Project, China-Britain Business Cncl, Corporate Leaders Gp on Climate Change 2005; vice-pres EuroCommerce; hon fell Somerville Coll Oxford; *Recreations* cricket, racing, gardening, art, architecture, theatre; *Style*— Miss Lucy Neville-Rolfe, CMG; ✉ Tesco plc, Tesco House, Delamare Road, Cheshunt, Hertfordshire EN8 9SL (tel 01992 632222, fax 01992 630794, e-mail lucy.neville-rolfe@uk.tesco.com)

NEVILLE-ROLFE, Marianne Teresa; CB (2000); da of Edmund Neville-Rolfe, of Ark Farm, Tisbury, Wiltshire, and Margaret Elizabeth, *née* Evans (d 2006); sis of Lucy Neville-Rolfe, CMG, *qv*; *b* 9 October 1944; *Educ* St Mary's Convent Shaftesbury, Lady Margaret Hall Oxford (BA); *m* 1, 16 Sept 1972 (m dis 1992), David William John Blake, *qv*; m 2, 29 Sept 2001, Peter Andrew Hill; *Career* with CBI 1965–73 (head Brussels Office 1971–72); DTI: princ 1973, asst sec 1982, grade 3 under sec 1987; chief exec Civil Service Coll 1990–94, also prog dir Top Mgmnt Prog until 1994, regnl dir Govt Office for NW 1994–99, chief exec New East Manchester Ltd 1999–2000, dir SE England Devpt Agency (SEEDA) 2000–04, dir P & M Hill Conslts Ltd 2004–; memb Bd of Govrs Univ of Bolton 2005–; *Style*— Ms Marianne Neville-Rolfe, CB; ✉ Angle Croft, Somerford Booths, Congleton, Cheshire CW12 2JU

NEVIN, Charles William; s of John Francis Nevin (d 1991), of St Helens, Lancs, and Jean Emmie, *née* Davey; *b* 27 March 1951; *Educ* Mount St Mary's Coll, UC Oxford; *m* 1988, Liv Barbara, da of William Bernard O'Hanlon and Inger Luise, *née* Bye; 2 s (Jack Cristian Diaz O'Hanlon b 1991, William Luis Arturo Gatica O'Hanlon b 1994); *Career* Granada Television 1974–75, Liverpool Daily Post and Echo 1975–79, Daily and Sunday Telegraph 1979–88; freelance writer 1988–; *Publications* Lancashire, Where Women Die of Love (2004); *Recreations* watching Rugby League and going to the foot of our stairs; *Clubs* Berkshire Press, St Helens Bowling (country memb); *Style*— Charles Nevin; ✉ Rock House, Great Elm, Somerset BA11 3NY (e-mail cnevin@nevinsltd.co.uk)

NEWALL, Christopher Stirling; s of late Peter Stirling Newall, and Rosemary, *née* Marriage; *b* 8 April 1951; *Educ* The Downs Sch, Abbotsholme Sch, Courtauld Inst London (BA); *m* 10 Oct 1985, Jenifer Hylda, da of late Sir Derek Ryan, 3 Bt; 2 s (Alfred Stirling b 8 Feb 1987, George Stirling b 20 Jan 1990); *Career* writer and art historian; conslt Dept of Victorian Paintings Sotheby's 1994–; research fell Univ of Northumbria 1996–98; assoc ed Oxford DNB 1997–2003; sec Ruskin Today (centenary events programme) 2000; Companion of Guild of St George 1995; *Books* Victorian Watercolours (1987), The Art of Lord Leighton (1990), The Grosvenor Gallery Exhibitions (1995); exhbn catalogues: George Price Boyce (Tate Gallery 1987), Victorian Landscape Watercolors (contrib, Yale Center for British Art 1992), Victorian Painting (contrib, Neue Pinakothek Munich and Prado Madrid 1993), John William Inchbold (Leeds City Art Gallery 1993), Frederic Leighton (contrib, Royal Acad of Arts 1996), The Age of Rossetti, Burne-Jones & Watts - Symbolism in Britain 1860–1910 (contrib, Tate Gallery 1997), La Era Victoriana (contrib, Museo Nacional de San Carlos Mexico City), The Victorian Imagination (Bunkamura Museum of Art Tokyo and touring 1998), Espejismos del Medio Oriente: Delacroix a Moreau (contrib, Museo Nacional de San Carlos Mexico City 1999–2000), Pre-Raphaelites Exhibition - from Manchester City Art Galleries and other Collections (MOMA Shiga and touring 2000), John Brett: a Pre-Raphaelite on the Shores of Wales (Nat Museum of Wales 2003), Pre-Raphaelite Vision: Truth to Nature (jtly, Tate Britain (co-curated with Allen Staley) 2004), The Poetry of Truth: Alfred William Hunt and the Art of Landscape (Ashmolean Museum Oxford and Yale Center for British Art New Haven 2004–05); *Style*— Christopher Newall, Esq; ✉ 17 Lonsdale Square, London N1 1EN

NEWALL, 2 Baron (UK 1946); Francis Storer Eaton Newall; DL (London); s of Marshal of the RAF 1 Baron Newall, GCB, OM, GCMG, CBE, AM (d 1963, Chief of Air Staff during Battle of Britain); *b* 23 June 1930; *Educ* Eton, RMA Sandhurst; *m* 1956, Pamela, da of Hugh Rowcliffe, TD (d 1978), by his 1 w, Margaret (da of Sir Henry Farrington, 6 Bt); 2 s, 1 da; *Heir* s, Hon Richard Newall; *Career* took Cons whip House of Lords; Capt 11 Hussars, served Germany, Malaya, Singapore, NI; adj Royal Glos Hussars; conslt and company dir; Cons whip and oppn front bench spokesman House of Lords 1976–79, fndr memb House of Lords All-Pty Def Study Gp, delg WEU and Cncl of Europe 1983–98, responsible for Farriers Registration Acts and Betting and Gaming Amendment (Greyhound Racing) Acts; led Parly visits to Cyprus, Oman, Bahrain, Qatar, Morocco; fndr Turfed Out Peers Soc (TOPS); chm: New Muscovy Co 2002–, Code Circus Ltd 2004–; chm Br Greyhound Racing Bd 1985–97, pres Soc for Protection of Animals Abroad (SPANA), chm Br Moroccan Soc 2000–05; friend of Romania; Liveryman Worshipful Co of Farriers, memb Ct of Assts Worshipful Co of Merchant Taylors; *Recreations* shooting, tennis, travel; *Clubs* Cavalry and Guards'; *Style*— The Rt Hon the Lord Newall, DL; ✉ Wotton Underwood, Aylesbury, Buckinghamshire (tel 01844 238376, fax 01844 237153, e-mail newallf@btconnect.com)

NEWALL, Sir Paul Henry; kt (1994), TD (1967), JP (City of London 1981), DL (Greater London 1977); s of Leopold Newall (d 1956), and Frances Evelyn, *née* Bean (d 1981); *b* 17 September 1934; *Educ* Harrow, Magdalene Coll Cambridge (MA); *m* 1 March 1969, Penelope Moyra, da of late Sir Julian Ridsdale, CBE; 2 s (Rupert b 1971, Jamie b 1973); *Career* Nat Serv 1953–55: cmmnd Royal Fusiliers, served Egypt and Sudan; TA 1955–70: Maj 1961, cmd City of London Co 5 Bn RRF 1967–70; chm City of London TA & VRA 1986–89, vice-chm TAVRA for Gtr London 1989–95, Hon Col The London Regt 1995–2001; ptnr Loeb Rhoades & Co 1971–77; overseas dir: Shearson Loeb Rhoades (UK) 1979–81, Shearson American Express (UK) 1981–84; dir Shearson Lehman International Ltd 1985–93; exec dir: Shearson Lehman Hutton Securities 1988–90, Lehman Bros Securities 1990–92; sr advsr Lehman Bros 1992–98; non-exec dir Guardian Royal Exchange plc 1995–99; vice-pres Inst of Export 1995–2002, chm UK/Korea Forum for the Future 1999–; pro-chllr and chm of cncl City Univ 1997–2003; pres Fedn of Old Comrades Assocs of the London Territorial and Aux Units 2003–; tstee: Army Benevolent Fund 1998–2007, City of London Endowment Tst for St Paul's Cathedral 1993–2004, Morden Coll 1990–2004, Int Bankers' Charitable Tst; patron Samaritans Nat Appeal 1989–93, vice-pres City of London Br Red Cross 1986–, churchwarden St Stephen Walbrook 1981–2005; memb: Friends of St Paul's Cathedral, City Heritage Soc, UK-Japan 21st Century Gp, Anglo-Korean Soc, Royal Soc for Asian Affairs, Partnership Korea Advsy Gp; hon rep for City of Seoul, hon visiting magistrate HM Tower of London 1988–, hon citizen Georgia USA 1994; City of London: one of HM's Lts 1975–, elected Ct of Common Cncl 1980–81, Alderman (Walbrook Ward) 1981–2005, Sheriff 1989–90, Lord Mayor of London 1993–94; memb Guild of Freemen of the City of London 1988– (memb Ct 1988–91), fndr master Guild Int Bankers 2001; memb Hon Co of Freeman of the City of London of N America; Liveryman Worshipful Co of Gold and Silver Wyre Drawers 1980–2005, Master Worshipful Co of Bakers 1990–91; Hon Freeman Worshipful Co of Fuellers, Hon Freeman and Liveryman Worshipful Co of Marketors; pres Assoc of Livery Masters 1993/94–; hon memb Incorporation of Bakers of Glasgow and Burgess of the City of Glasgow 1995–; Hon DLitt City Univ 1993; Order of Dip Merit (first class) Korea 1999, KStJ; *Books* Japan and the City of London (1996); *Recreations* fencing, fly fishing, water skiing, tennis, trees; *Clubs* City Livery, Walbrook Ward, United Wards, East India, MCC, Pilgrims; *Style*— Sir Paul Newall, TD, DL; ✉ Grove Park, Yoxford, Saxmundham, Suffolk IP17 3HX

NEWARK, Archdeacon of; *see:* Peyton, Ven Nigel

NEWARK, Quentin; s of Derek Newark, and Jean, *née* Thornhill; *b* 24 September 1961; *Educ* Purley HS for Boys, Kingston Poly (fndn course), Brighton Poly (BA); *Career* book designer: Mitchell Beazley Publishers 1985, Faber and Faber Publishers 1985–86; Pentagram Design: sr designer 1986–91, clients incl Faber and Faber, Santa Barbara Museum of Art, Washington Museum of Art, Asea Brown Boveri, V&A Museum (identity and signage); Atelier Design (partnership with John Powner): formed 1991, projects incl Br Rail exhibition on the environment, The Encyclopaedia of the 21st Century for Mitchell Beazley, work for Philips, Wiggins Teape and Arthur Anderson; memb 02 int environmental design gp; memb Sign Design Inst; lectured at Pembroke Coll Oxford and Epsom Sch of Art and Design; *Style*— Quentin Newark, Esq; ✉ 37 Kenilworth Road, London E3 5RH (tel 020 8981 6612); The Old Piano Factory, 5 Charlton Kings Road, London NW5 2SB

NEWBERRY, Patrick John (Pat); s of Thomas Newberry, of Salcombe, Devon, and Jean, *née* Knill (d 1997); *b* 14 October 1956, Glos; *Educ* Bristol Cathedral Sch, Univ of Southampton (BSc); *m* 19 July 1980, Elizabeth Jane, da of Peter Ware, of Church Knowle, Dorset, and Margaret Maud Lancelyn Green; 3 s (Nicholas Peter Knill b 10 April 1984, John Alfred Lancelyn b 26 May 1986, Edwin Gilbert Knill b 21 Nov 1989), 1 da (Nancy Harriet Lancelyn b 16 June 1995); *Career* chartered accountant 1980; Coopers & Lybrand: ptnr 1988–98, head Fin Servs Business Devpt Gp 1995–97; PricewaterhouseCoopers: ptnr 1998–, global ldr of insurance consulting 1998–2001, head of UK financial servs consulting and memb Mgmnt Consulting Bd 2001–03, UK financial servs advsy ldr 2003–, memb Supervisory Bd 2003–; memb Cncl Manufacturing Consultancies Assoc; author of numerous articles in financial press; FRSA; *Recreations* sailing, book collecting, Cornish history; *Clubs* Salcombe Yacht; *Style*— Pat Newberry, Esq; ✉ Kitlands East Lodge, Coldharbour, Surrey RH5 4LN (tel 01306 711946); PricewaterhouseCoopers LLP, Southwark Towers, 32 London Bridge Street, London SE1 9SY (tel 020 7212 4659, e-mail pat.j.newberry@uk.pwc.com)

NEWBERY, Chris; s of Sqdn Ldr James Newbery, DFC, and Daphne, *née* Wass; *b* 10 December 1949; *Educ* Kent Coll Canterbury, Univ of Leicester (BA, Grad Cert in Museum Studies), NVQ Cultural Heritage Mgmnt (awarded by Qualifications for Industry); *Career* res asst London Museum Kensington Palace 1972–75, sr asst keeper Museum of London Barbican 1975–78, curator Chichester District Museums 1978–81, curator Newport Museum and Art Gallery Gwent 1981–83, London museums offr Area Museum Service for SE Eng 1983–85, dep dir Museums and Galleries Cmmn 1985–95, dir Museum Trg Inst 1995–97, dir Royal Marines Museum 1998–; sec Int Cncl of Museums Ctee for the Trg of Personnel 1995–98; tstee: Museum of Richmond 1987–95, Nat Football Museum 1996–2002; memb: Museums Assoc, ICOM; fell Museums Assoc 1990 (Dip 1974); *Recreations* badminton, travel; *Style*— Chris Newbery, Esq; ✉ Royal Marines Museum, Southsea, Hampshire PO4 9PX (tel 02392 819385, fax 02392 838420, e-mail chris.newbery@royalmarinesmuseum.co.uk)

NEWBERY, Prof David Michael; s of the late Alan Newbery, of Gosport, Hants, and Betty Newbery; *b* 1 June 1943; *Educ* Portsmouth GS, Trinity Coll Cambridge (scholar, MA, PhD), ScD; *m* 1975, Dr Terri Apter, da of Dr Nathaniel Apter; 2 da (Miranda b 1979, Julia b 1983); *Career* economist Treasy Tanzanian Govt 1965–66; Univ of Cambridge: asst lectr 1966–71, lectr 1971–86, reader in economics 1986–88, dir Dept of Applied Economics 1988–2003, prof of applied economics 1988–, professorial fell Churchill Coll 1988– (teaching fell 1965–88); res assoc Cowles Fndn Yale Univ 1969, assoc prof Stanford Univ 1976–77, visiting prof Princeton Univ 1985, visiting scholar IMF 1987, Ford visiting prof Univ of Calif Berkeley 1987–88, sr res fell Inst for Policy Reform 1990–95; div chief Public Economics Div World Bank 1981–83; memb Environmental Economics Academic Panel DEFRA (formerly DETR) 1992–, pres Euro Economic Assoc 1996; Frisch medal Econometric Soc 1990, Harry Johnson prize Canadian Economics Assoc 1993; fell: Centre for Economic Policy Res 1984–, Econometric Soc 1989; FBA 1991; *Books* Project Appraisal in Practice (jtly, 1976), The Theory of Commodity Price Stabilization: a study in the economics of risk (with J E Stiglitz, 1981), The Theory of Taxation for Developing Countries (ed, 1987), Hungary, An Economy in Transition (ed, 1993), Tax and Benefit Reform in Central and Eastern Europe (ed, 1995), Privatization, Restructuring and

Regulation of Network Utilities (2000); *Recreations* skiing; *Style*— Prof David Newbery, FBA; ✉ Faculty of Economics, University of Cambridge, Sidgwick Avenue, Cambridge CB3 9DE (tel 01223 335248, fax 01223 335299, e-mail dmgn@econ.cam.ac.uk)

NEWBIGGING, David Kennedy; OBE (1982), DL (Wilts 1993); s of David Locke Newbigging, CBE, MC (d 1948), and Lucy Margaret Newbigging (d 1970); *b* 19 January 1934; *Educ* Oundle; *m* 1968, Carolyn Susan, da of Geoffrey Band (d 1974); 1 s, 2 da; *Career* 2 Lt Nat Serv KOSB; Jardine Matheson & Co Ltd: joined 1954, dir 1967, md 1970, chm and sr md 1975–83; chm: Hongkong & Kowloon Wharf & Godown Co Ltd 1970–80, Hong Kong Land 1975–83 (also md), Hongkong Electric Holdings Ltd 1982–83 (dir 1975–83), Jardine Fleming Holdings Ltd 1975–83, Hong Kong Tourist Assoc 1977–82, Hong Kong General C of C 1980–82, Rentokil Gp plc 1987–94 (dir 1986–94), Redfearn plc 1988, NM UK Limited 1990–93, Ivory and Sime plc 1992–95 (dir 1987–91), Maritime Tport Services Ltd 1993–95, Faupel plc 1994– (dir 1989–93), Equitas Holdings Limited 1995–98, Equitas Management Services Limited 1995–98, Equitas Reinsurance Limited 1995–98, Equitas Limited 1996–98, Friends Provident plc (formerly Friends Provident Life Office) 1998–2005 (dir 1993, dep chm 1996–98), Thistle Hotels plc 1999–2003, Talbot Holdings Ltd 2003–07, Synesis Life Ltd 2006–; dep chm: Provincial Gp plc 1985–91 (dir 1984–91), Benchmark Gp plc 1996–2004; dir: Hongkong & Shanghai Banking Corp 1975–83, Hongkong Telephone Co Ltd 1975–83, Rennies Consolidated Holdings Ltd 1975–83, Provincial Insurance plc 1984–86, Provincial Life Assurance Co Ltd 1984–86, The British Coal Corp (formerly the National Coal Bd) 1984–87, CIN Management Ltd 1985–87, United Meridian Corp (USA) 1987–98, Wah Kwong Shipping Holdings Ltd (Hong Kong) 1992–99, Market Bd Corp of Lloyd's 1993–95, Merrill Lynch & Co Inc 1996–2007, Ocean Energy Inc (USA) 1998–2003, Paccar Inc (USA) 1999–2006; memb: Int Cncl Morgan Guaranty Tst Co of NY 1977–85, Hongkong Legislative Cncl 1978–82, Hongkong Exec Cncl 1980–84; chm Cancer Research UK 2004– (dep chm Cncl of Tstees 2002–04); tstee UK Tst for Nature Conservation in Nepal (formerly King Mahendra UK Tst for Nature Conservation) 1988–; chm: Wilts Community Fndn 1991–97, Cncl The Mission to Seafarers 1993– (vice-chm Cncl and chm Exec Ctee 1986–93); High Sheriff Wilts 2003–04; Liveryman Worshipful Co of Grocers; *Recreations* Chinese art, most outdoor sports; *Clubs* Boodle's, Hongkong (Hong Kong), Hong Kong Jockey, The Bohemian (San Francisco); *Style*— David Newbigging, Esq, OBE, DL; ✉ 4th Floor, 61 Lincoln's Inn Fields, London WC2A 3PX (tel 020 7061 8178, fax 020 7061 8411)

NEWBOLD, Prof Robert Frank; s of Francis James Newbold, of Oxon, and Aileen Mary, *née* Bird; *b* 5 February 1950; *Educ* Abingdon Sch, Aston Univ (BSc), Univ of London (PhD, DSc); *m* 1972, Ann, da of Thomas Hood; *Career* Inst of Cancer Research London 1973–87 (res fell 1973–84), scientific dir Ludwig Inst for Cancer Research Sydney Aust 1987–89; Brunel Univ: head Dept of Biology and Biochemistry 1991–2001, dean Faculty of Science 1996–99, dir Brunel Inst of Cancer Genetics and Pharmacogenomics 2000–, dean Faculty of Life Sciences 2001–04; memb: Govt ctees on mutagenicity and carcinogenicity of chemicals in food, consumer products and the environment 1991–2000, Advsy Bd UICC Fellowship Int Union Against Cancer (UICC-WHO) 2003–; co-ordinator multinational EU framework (FP) projects on molecular mechanisms of human cancer devpt for FP3 1992–95, FP4 1996–99, FP5 2000–04, and FP6 2004–; tstee Hillingdon Hosp Post Grad Centre 1996–2004; memb Bd of Eds Int Jl of Cancer 2005–, author of numerous scientific papers on cancer genetics and carcinogenesis in learned jls; CBiol, FIBiol 1990, FRSM 1993, FRCPath 2001, FRSA 2002; *Recreations* jazz and blues guitar, motor sport, natural history, country pursuits; *Style*— Prof Robert Newbold; ✉ Faculty of Health Sciences, Brunel University, Uxbridge, Middlesex UB8 3PH (tel 01895 266290, fax 01895 269787, e-mail robert.newbold@brunel.ac.uk)

NEWBOLD, Yve Monica; da of Thomas Peter Radcliffe (d 1963), and Anne Gertrude, *née* Flynn; *b* 6 July 1940; *Educ* Blessed Sacrament Convent Hove, Univ of London (LLB), Coll of Law; *m* 1958, Anthony Newbold; 1 da (Lorraine b 1959), 3 s (Timothy b 1960, Jonathan b 1964, Toby b 1965); *Career* admitted slr 1970, staff lawyer IBM (UK) 1968–71, chief staff counsel Rank Xerox 1972–79, int counsel Xerox Corporation USA 1979–82, euro counsel Walt Disney Productions Ltd 1982–86, co sec Hanson plc 1986–95, chief exec Pro Ned Ltd 1995–97, ptnr Heidrick and Struggles 1998–2000; non-exec dir: British Telecommunications plc 1991–97, Coutts & Co 1994–97; chair Ethical Trading Initiative 1999–2002; chair Inst of Global Ethics 2005–, govr London Business Sch 1990–98; memb: Community Support Ctee 1997–, Advsy Bd Henderson SRI 2001–05, Advsy Bd FTSE4Good 2003–; former memb Sr Salary Review Body; *Style*— Mrs Yve Newbold; ✉ 6 Park Village West, London NW1 4AE (tel 020 7383 2816)

NEWBON, Gary; s of Jack Newbon (d 1982), and Preeva, *née* Cooklin; *b* 15 March 1945; *Educ* Culford Sch Bury St Edmunds; *m* 26 Oct 1973, Katharine Janet, da of Bernard While (d 1982), of Birmingham; 1 da (Claire Rosalie b 5 June 1975), 2 s (Laurence Jon, Neil Christie (twins) b 16 Aug 1977); *Career* journalist Jeacock's News Agency Cambridge 1964–67; sports writer Hayter's Sports Agency, sports presenter Westward TV Plymouth 1968–71; ATV Network Ltd: sports presenter 1971–74, sports presenter and ed 1974–81; controller of sport Central TV and Carlton TV 1982–2004, presenter Sky Sports 2004–; ITV reporter: Olympic Games 1972, 1980 and 1988, World Cup Soccer 1974, 1982, 1986, 1990, 1994, 1998 and 2002; memb: Lord's Taverners, Variety Club of GB; nat patron Deafblind UK; Officer de l'Ordre des Coteaux de Champagne; *Books* Over the Sticks and Under Starters Orders (with late Michael Ayres, 1970 and 1971); *Recreations* jazz, blues, rock and roll, drinking champagne and wine; *Clubs* Garrick, Groucho; *Style*— Gary Newbon, Esq; ✉ tel 07836 513958, fax 0121 764 4502, e-mail gary@primeticketuk.com

NEWBOROUGH, 8 Baron (I 1776); Robert Vaughan Wynn; 10 Bt (GB 1742); s of 7 Baron Newborough, DSC (d 1998), of Rhug, Corwen, N Wales, by his 1 w, Rosamund, da of late Maj Robert Barbour, of Bolesworth Castle, Tattenhall, Cheshire; *b* 11 August 1949; *Educ* Milton Abbey; *m* 1, 1981, Mrs Sheila Christine Wilson, da of William A Massey; 1 da (Hon Lucinda Rosamond b 1982); m 2, 16 April 1988, Mrs Susan E Hall, da of late Andrew Lloyd, of Malta; *Career* landowner and organic farmer; dir: Peplow Training and Recruitment Services Ltd, Legends Park Ltd; *Recreations* skiing, sailing; *Style*— The Rt Hon the Lord Newborough; ✉ Peplow Hall, Peplow, Market Drayton, Shropshire TF9 3JP

NEWBURGH, 12 Earl of (S 1660); Filippo Giambattista Francesco Aldo Maria Rospigliosi; also Viscount Kynnaird and Lord Levingston (S 1660), Prince Rospigliosi (HRE 1668 by Emperor Leopold I and Papal 1854 by Pope Pius IX), 14 Prince of Castiglione (by the Sicilian cr of 1602, and a further cr of the kingdom of Italy 1897), 11 Duke of Zagarolo (Papal 1668), Marquis of Giuliana (Sicily 1543, It 1897), Count of Chiusa (Sic 1535, It 1897), Baron di Valcorrente e della Miraglia (Sic 1780, It 1897), Lord (Signore) of Aidone, Burgio, Contessa, and Trappeto (1854), conscribed Roman Noble (1854), and Patrician of Venice (1667), Genoa (1786) and Pistoia; s of 11 Earl of Newburgh (d 1986), and Donna Giulia, da of Don Guido Carlo dei Duchi Visconti di Modrone, Count of Lonate Pozzolo; *b* 4 July 1942; *m* 1972, Baronessa Donna Luisa, da of Count Annibale Caccia Dominioni; 1 da (Princess Benedetta Francesca Maria (Countess Piero Albertario) b 1974); *Heir* da, Mistress of Newburgh; *Style*— The Prince Rospigliosi; ✉ Piazza St Ambrogio 16, 20123 Milan, Italy

NEWBY, Prof Sir Howard Joseph; kt (2000), CBE (1995); s of Alfred Joseph Newby, and Constance Annie, *née* Potts; *b* 10 December 1947; *Educ* John Port GS Etwall, Atlantic Coll Glamorgan, Univ of Essex (BA, PhD); *m* 1, 4 July 1970 (m dis 2003), Janet Elizabeth; 2 s (Stephen b 1980, Jake b 1983); m 2, May 2005, Sheila; *Career* Univ of Essex: lectr in sociology 1972–75, sr lectr 1975–79, reader 1979–83, prof of sociology 1983–88; dir ESRC Data Archive 1983–88, chm ESRC 1988–94, vice-chllr Univ of Southampton 1994–2001, chief exec HEFCE 2001–06, vice-chllr UWE 2006–; prof of sociology and rural sociology Univ of Wisconsin Madison USA 1980–83; visiting appts: Univ of NSW Sydney 1976, Univ of Newcastle upon Tyne 1983–84; chm Centre for Exploitation of Science and Technol 1995–99; pres UUK 1999–2001; *Books* incl: The Deferential Worker (1977), Green and Pleasant Land? (2 edn, 1985), Country Life (1987), The Countryside in Question (1988); jtly: Community Studies (1971), Property Paternalism and Power (1978), The Problem of Sociology (1983), Social Class in Modern Britain (1988); *Recreations* family life, gardening, Derby County, railways; *Clubs* Athenaeum; *Style*— Sir Howard Newby, CBE; ✉ University of the West of England, Coldharbour Lane, Bristol BS16 1QY

NEWBY, Baron (Life Peer UK 1997), of Rothwell in the County of West Yorkshire; Richard Mark (Dick) Newby; OBE (1990); s of Frank and Kathleen Newby, of Rothwell; *b* 14 February 1953; *Educ* Rothwell GS, St Catherine's Coll Oxford (MA); *m* 1978, Hon Ailsa Ballantyne Thomson, da of Baron Thomson of Monifieth, KT, PC; 2 s (Hon Mark George b 1985, Hon Roger James Swift b 1987); *Career* HM Customs and Excise: joined 1974, private sec to Perm Sec 1977–79, princ Planning Unit 1979–81; dir of corp affairs Rosehaugh plc 1988–92, dir Matrix Communications Consultancy Ltd 1992–99, chm Reform Publications Ltd 1993–, dir Flagship Gp 1999–2001, chm Live Consultancy 2001–; nat sec SDP 1981–88, dir of external communications Lib Dem Gen Election Team 1996–97, sits as Lib Dem peer in House of Lords, Treasy spokesman 1997–, COS to Rt Hon Charles Kennedy, MP, *qv* 1999–2006; tstee: Allachy Tst, Coltstaple Tst; chair Int Devpt through Sport (IDS); *Recreations* football, tennis, cricket, reading; *Clubs* MCC; *Style*— The Rt Hon the Lord Newby, OBE; ✉ House of Lords, London SW1A 0PW (mobile 07802 887606, e-mail newbyr@parliament.uk)

NEWCASTLE, Bishop of 1997–; Rt Rev (John) Martin Wharton; s of John Wharton, of Dalton-in-Furness, Cumbria, and Marjorie Elizabeth, *née* Skinner (d 1962); *b* 6 August 1944; *Educ* Ulverston GS, Univ of Durham (BA), Univ of Oxford (MA); *m* 29 Aug 1970, Marlene Olive; 1 da (Joanna Helen b 17 Nov 1972), 2 s (Andrew Benjamin b 1 March 1974, Mark Richard b 6 March 1978); *Career* Martins Bank Ltd 1960–64; ordained: deacon 1972, priest 1973; curate: St Peter Spring Hill Birmingham 1972–75, St John the Baptist Croydon 1975–77; dir of pastoral studies Ripon Coll Cuddesdon 1977–83, curate All Saints Cuddesdon 1979–83, sec Bd of Min and Trg Dio of Bradford 1983–92, residentiary canon Bradford Cathedral 1992, area bishop of Kingston 1992–97; memb House of Lords 2002–; *Books* Knowing Me, Knowing You (with Malcolm Goldsmith, 1993); *Recreations* sport; *Clubs* Lancs CCC; *Style*— The Rt Rev the Lord Bishop of Newcastle; ✉ Bishop's House, 29 Moor Road South, Newcastle upon Tyne NE3 1PA (tel 0191 285 2220, fax 0191 284 6933)

NEWCOMBE, Barry; s of Ronald William Newcombe (d 1991), of Northampton, and Doris May, *née* Underwood (d 1991); *b* 21 December 1939; *Educ* Northampton GS; *m* 30 Dec 1967, Maureen, da of Douglas Brooks; 1 da (Kerry Margaret b 18 June 1968), 1 s (Andrew James b 1 Nov 1970); *Career* sports writer; trainee journalist then rugby corr Chronicle and Echo Northampton 1957–64, staff writer Hayters's Agency 1964–65; rugby and tennis corr: Evening Standard 1965–84, Sunday Express 1984–96; sports reporter Daily Express 1996–97, currently freelance journalist, chief exec Hayters's Agency 1999–2001; UK Olympic press attaché: Sydney 2000, Athens 2004; pres Rugby Writers' Club, chm Sports Journalists' Assoc, tchm Lawn Tennis Writers' Assoc, former press offr Teddington Soc; *Books* Carling's England (1991), Upfront with Jeff Probyn (1993), Lawrence Dallaglio - Diary of a Season (1997); *Recreations* woodland studies; *Style*— Barry Newcombe, Esq; ✉ Springwood, Sands Road, Runfold, Surrey GU10 1PX (tel 01252 782668, e-mail barrynewcombe@gmail.com)

NEWCOME, Rt Rev James William Scobie; *see:* Bishop of Penrith

NEWELL, Prof Alan Francis; MBE (2000); *b* 1 March 1941; *Educ* St Philip's GS, Univ of Birmingham; *m* 31 July 1965, Margaret Eleanor, *née* Morgan; 2 da (Anna b 1968, Catherine b 1969), 1 s (David b 1976); *Career* res engr Standard Telecommunication Laboratories 1965–69, lectr in electronics Univ of Southampton 1969–80; Univ of Dundee: NCR prof of electronics and microcomputer systems and dir Microcomputer Centre 1980–, dep princ 1993–95, head of Applied Computer Studies Div Dept of Mathematics and Computer Science 1995–97, head Dept of Applied Computing 1997–2002, prof 2002–; hon fell Coll of Speech and Language Therapists; FIEE, FBCS, FRSE 1992; *Recreations* family life, sailing; *Clubs* Wormit Boating; *Style*— Prof Alan Newell, MBE, FRSE; ✉ Applied Computing, The University, Dundee DD1 4HN (tel 01382 344145, fax 01382 345509, e-mail afn@computing.dundee.ac.uk)

N

NEWELL, Christopher William Paul; s of Lt-Col Nicolas Gambier Newell (d 1980), and Edith Alice, *née* Edgill (d 1984); *b* 30 November 1950; *Educ* Wellington, Univ of Southampton (LLB); *m* 1998, Teresa Mary; 1 da (Natalie Bridget Rosie b 2003); *Career* called to the Bar Middle Temple 1973, in private practice 1973–75, legal asst then sr legal asst Dept of DPP 1978–79, sr legal asst Law Offr's Dept 1979–83, sr legal asst Dept of DPP 1983–86, asst DPP 1986, branch crown prosecutor CPS 1986–87, asst legal sec Law Offr's Dept 1987–89; CPS: dir of HQ casework 1989–93, dir of casework 1993–96, dir of casework evaluation 1996–98, dir of casework 1998–2005, princ legal advsr to DPP 2005–; vice-chair Centre for Accessible Environments 2004–; sr vice-chair Criminal Law Ctee Int Bar Assoc 2002; tstee: Crime Reduction Initiatives 2001, Nat Deaf Children's Soc 2001, Centre for Accessible Environments 2001; *Recreations* sport, travel; *Clubs* RAC; *Style*— Christopher Newell, Esq; ✉ Crown Prosecution Service, 50 Ludgate Hill, London EC4M 7EX (tel 020 7796 8554, fax 020 7796 8680)

NEWELL, David Richard; s of late Dick Newell, and Davida, *née* Juleff; *b* 21 September 1951; *Educ* Shrewsbury, Univ of Birmingham (LLB), Univ of Southampton (MPhil); *m* 1978, Cora Sue, *née* Feingold; 1 da (Rebecca); *Career* admitted slr 1978 (articles Lawford & Co 1976–78); Univ of Leicester: lectr in law 1978–86, postgrad tutor 1979–84, dir employment law postgrad prog 1983–86; Newspaper Soc: head of govt and legal affrs 1984–96, dir 1997– (dep dir 1992–97); sec Parly and Legal Ctee Guild of Editors 1984–97; dir: ABC 1997–, Press Standards Bd of Fin 1997–, Advtg Standards Bd of Fin 1998–, Publishers NTO 2001–, Newspaper Publishers Assoc 2007–; memb: Confedn of Communication and Info Industries 1984–, Ctee of Advtg Practice 1984–, Ctees Advtg Assoc 1984–, Employment and Media Ctees Law Soc 1990–97, Cncl Campaign for Freedom of Info 1990– (Award for campaigning against official secrecy 1989), Advtg Law Gp 1995–, UK Assizes Gp 1995–, Bd Euro Newspapers Publishers' Assoc 1996– (chm Legal Framework Ctee 1995–98), CPU 1997–, Cncl World Assoc of Newspapers 1997–, Cncl CBI 1999–; judge Press Awards 1999–; Special Award UK Press Gazette 1988; hon legal advsr Leicester Legal Advice Centre 1979–84; *Publications* The New Employment Legislation: a guide to the Employment Acts 1980 and 1983 (1983), Understanding Recruitment Law (1984), How to Study Law (jtly, 1986, 4 edn 2000), Financial Advertising Law (jtly, 1989), Aspects of Employment Law (jtly, 1990), Law for Journalists (jtly, 1991), Tolleys Employment Law (jtly, 1994, 2 edn 2000), The Law of Journalism (jtly, 1995), Copinger on Copyright (contrib, 1998); res papers and articles on employment law, media and legal policy issues; *Recreations* country and seaside walks, sailing, tennis; *Style*— David Newell, Esq; ✉ Newspaper Society, St Andrews House, 18–20 St Andrews Street, London EC4A 3AY (tel 020 7632 7410, e-mail ns@newspapersoc.org.uk)

NEWELL, Donald; s of Stephen Newell (d 1982), and Ida Laura, *née* Hatch (d 1992); *b* 31 August 1942, Turnford, Herts; *Educ* Cheshunt GS; *m* 22 June 1968, Rosemary, *née* Litler-Jones; 1 s (Simon b 12 July 1971), 2 da (Sarah b 3 Oct 1973, Alexandra b 18 Nov 1978); *Career* Hillier Parker May and Rowden: managing ptnr 1986–90, sr ptnr 1990–98;

chm EMEA Div CBRichard Ellis Servs Inc 1998–2000; non-exec dir: London Merchant Securities plc 1998–2007, Derwent London plc 2007–; fndr memb British Cncl for Offices (pres 1992–93); FRICS 1968; *Recreations* travel and sport; *Clubs* Bucks, MCC; *Style—* Donald Newell, Esq; ✉ e-mail newelldon@aol.com

NEWELL, (Priscilla) Jane; OBE (1997), JP (Liverpool 1993, Inner London 1995); da of (Arthur Ronald) Michael Watts, of Weymouth, Dorset, and Sylvia Margaret Scarfe, *née* McNabb; *b* 13 April 1944; *Educ* Merrow Grange Convent Guildford, Guildford Tech Coll, Victoria Univ of Wellington NZ (BA, sr scholar, postgrad scholar); *m* 1, 22 Jan 1977, Prof Kenneth Wyatt Newell (d 1990); m 2, 12 April 2007, Lord Cuckney, *qv*; *Career* int civil servant WHO 1965–77, linguistics tutor Victoria Univ of Wellington and tutor to Chinese exchange students NZ Miny of Foreign Affrs 1982–83, school administrator and sec Voluntary Funds Ctee Liverpool Sch of Tropical Med 1984–92, non-service assessor Assessment and Consultancy Unit Home Office 1994–; tstee GlaxoSmithKline Pension Plan (formerly Glaxo-Wellcome Pension Plan) 1994–2004; chm: United Utilities Pension Scheme 1998–2005, Electricity Supply Pension Scheme (UU Gp) 1998–2005, Dixons Gp Retirement and Employee Security Scheme 2004–07 (tstee 1996–), Royal Mail Pension Plan 2005–; non-exec dir: United Utilities plc 1996–2006, Synesis Life Ltd 2007–; fndr tstee Maxwell Pensioners Tst 1992 (chm 1995–97), tstee Common Purpose Charitable Tst 1995–2000; non-exec dir Royal Liverpool Univ Hosp Tst 1992–95, dep chm Glaxo Tstee Companies 1994–96; vice-pres Liverpool Sch of Tropical Med 1997– (chm 1995–97), pro-chllr and chair Bd of Govrs London South Bank Univ 1999– (govr 1996–); *Recreations* gardening, walking, music; *Clubs* Royal Cwlth Soc, Athenaeum; *Style—* Jane Newell, OBE; ✉ c/o Royal Mail Pension Trustees Ltd, Lloyds Chambers, Portsoken Street, London E1 8PP (tel 020 7977 7781, fax 020 7977 7782)

NEWELL, Michael Cormac (Mike); *b* 28 March 1942; *Educ* Univ of Cambridge (MA); *m*; 1 da, 1 s; *Career* television and film director; Granada TV 1963–69, subsequently freelance dir of TV dramas; dir Fifty Cannon Entertainment; *Television films* incl The Melancholy Hussar (TV film, BBC) 1973, Baa Baa Black Sheep (Granada) 1974, Gift of Friendship (YTV) 1974, Lost Your Tongue (Granada) 1974, Brassneck (Play for Today, BBC) 1975, Ready When You Are Mr McGill (Granada) 1975 (BAFTA nominee, ITC entry for Monte Carlo Festival), Of The Fields Lately (offical entry Prague Festival) 1975, Destiny (BBC) 1977, Mr & Mrs Bureaucrat (BBC) 1977, Tales Out of School - Birth of a Nation (CBC) 1982, Blood Feud (3 pt mini-series) 1982–83 (Emmy nomination), Common Ground (CBS) 1990; *Films* incl: The Man in the Iron Mask (ITC) 1976, The Awakening (Orion) 1977, Bad Blood 1980, Dance with a Stranger 1984 (Prix de la Jeunesse Directors Fortnight Cannes), The Good Father 1985 (Prix Italia), Amazing Grace and Chuck 1986, Soursweet 1987, Enchanted April 1991, Into the West 1992, Four Weddings and a Funeral 1994 (David Lean Award for Best Achievement in Dir and Best Film BAFTA Awards, Lloyd's Bank People's Vote Most Popular Film, Cesar for Best Foreign Film, London Film Critics' Circle Br Film of the Year & Br Dir of the Year, also Academy Award nominee for Best Film & DGA nominee for Best Dir of a Feature Film), An Awfully Big Adventure 1995 (official entry Directors Fortnight Cannes), Donnie Brasco 1997, Pushing Tin 1998, Mona Lisa Smile 2003, Harry Potter and the Goblet of Fire 2005, Love in the Time of Cholera 2007; as exec prodr: Best Laid Plans 1999, High Fidelity 2000, Traffic 2000; *Style—* Mike Newell, Esq

NEWEY, Adrian Martin; s of Richard Martin Newey, of Stratford-on-Avon, Warks, and Joan Edwina, *née* Calvert; *b* 26 December 1958; *Educ* Repton, Leamington Coll of FE (OND), Univ of Southampton (BSc); *m* 1, 13 Aug 1983 (m dis 1991), Amanda, *née* Hitchens; 2 da (Charlotte Katie b 28 Aug 1986, Hannah Louise b 3 Feb 1989); m 2, 1 Aug 1992, Marigold Phillippa, da of Peter Proudfoot; 1 da (Imogen Victoria b 30 Aug 1993), 1 s (Harrison William Innes b 25 July 1998); *Career* race car designer; aerodynamicist Formula One project Fittipaldi 1980–82; March Engineering: race engr Formula 2 1982, designer American series sports racing car 1982–84 (won championship 1983 and 1984), designer and race engr Indycars USA 1984–87 (won Indianapolis 500 each year); tech dir Formula 1 March Racing 1987–90, chief designer Formula One Williams Grand Prix Engineering 1990–97 (won Drivers' Championship 1992, 1993, 1996 and 1997, Constructors' Championship 1992, 1993, 1994, 1996 and 1997), tech dir Formula 1 McLaren International Ltd 1997–2006 (won Drivers' Championship 1998 and 1999, and Constructors' Championship 1998), chief technical offr Red Bull Formula 1 team 2006–; Hon DTech Robert Gordon Univ, Hon DSc Univ of Southampton; *Recreations* skiing, waterskiing, tennis; *Clubs* BRDC, VSCC; *Style—* Adrian Newey, Esq

NEWEY, Guy Richard; QC (2001); s of His Hon John Newey, QC (d 1994), and Mollie Patricia, *née* Chalk; *b* 21 January 1959; *Educ* Tonbridge, Queens' Coll Cambridge (MA, LLM), Cncl of Legal Educn; *m* 2 Aug 1986, Angela Clare, da of Hugh Ross Neilson; 1 s (Timothy Guy b 31 March 1989), 3 da (Emma Katherine, Natasha Clare (twins) b 18 Oct 1990, Elspeth Patricia Irene b 21 Sept 1994); *Career* in practice Chancery Bar 1983–; jr counsel to the Crown (Chancery/A Panel) 1990–2001, jr counsel to the charity commissioners 1991–2001, actg deemster IOM 2003–, inspr into the affrs of MG Rover 2005–, dep High Court judge 2006–; govr New Beacon Sch Sevenoaks; *Publications* Directors' Disqualification (contrib), Civil Court Service (contrib); *Style—* Guy Newey, Esq, QC; ✉ Westmead, 29 Serpentine Road, Sevenoaks, Kent TN13 3XR (tel 01732 458579); Maitland Chambers, 7 Stone Buildings, Lincoln's Inn, London WC2A 3SZ (tel 020 7406 1200, fax 020 7406 1300, e-mail gnewey@maitlandchambers.com)

NEWING, Prof Angela; JP; da of James Grainger (d 1964), and Mabel, *née* Steel (d 1975); *Educ* Univ of Bristol (BSc, MSc), Columbia Pacific Univ CA (PhD); *m* 1965, Peter Newing; *Career* basic grade physicist Royal Sussex County Hosp 1960–65, teacher of physics, mathematics and games Chipping Campden Comp Sch 1968, sr grade physicist Cheltenham Gen Hosp 1968–81 (princ grade 1981–89, top grade dir of med physics for Glos 1989–2000), first dir Glos Royal & Cranfield Univ Inst of Med Sciences 1994–96, visiting prof of med physics Cranfield Univ 1994–, supervisor of res students; papers published in numerous learned jls, ed HPA Bulletin 1980–93, lectr; memb bd Hosp Physicists' Assoc & Inst of Physics & Engrg in Med (IPEM) 1980–83, 1986–88 and 1991–94; IPEM: external assessor training scheme 1988–2001, memb Training and Assessment Bd 1986–95, registrar of training scheme 1986–88, memb Radiotherapy Physics Topic Gp 1988–91, memb Inst of Physics Benevolent Fund Ctee 1988–92 and 1995–2001, chm Jt Accreditation Panel for Post-Graduate Training Centres 1989–94, chm Training & Educn Ctee 1991–92, tstee IOP Mayneord Philips Bequest 1993–2003 (chm tstees 1995–97 and 2001–02), Dept of Health assessor for Sr NHS posts 1994–2001, sec Radiology History & Heritage Tst 1997–2000, non-exec dir Royal Nat Hosp for Rheumatic Diseases Bath Somerset 2000–06; chm N Glos Bench 2003–06, dep chm Glos Co Bench 2007–; dep chm Liquor Licensing and Betting Ctee 2001–06; mathematical puzzle setter for Sunday Times and Daily Telegraph, memb BBC Radio 4 panel for Puzzle Panel; fell Inst of Physics, fell IPEM; FRSM, FIEE, CPhys; *Recreations* maze designer, campanologist, collector of mechanical puzzles; *Style—* Prof Angela Newing; ✉ 'Jubilate', Blakewell Mead, Painswick, Gloucestershire GL6 6UR (tel 01452 814360, e-mail profnewing@btinternet.com)

NEWLAND, Prof Adrian Charles; *b* 26 August 1949; *Educ* City of Norwich Sch, Downing Coll Cambridge (MA), London Hosp Med Coll (MB BCh); *m* 1973, Joanna Mary, da of Prof Thurstan Shaw, CBE, FSA, FBA; 1 da (Emily Ruth b 1978), 1 s (Thomas William Derek b 1980); *Career* prof of haematology Bart's and The Royal London Sch of Med and Dentistry 1992– (centre lead for haematology Inst of Cellular and Molecular Sci), concurrently dir NE Thames Cancer Network and dir of pathology Bart's and the London NHS Tst, dir of research Bart's and the London NHS Tst 1997–2001; chm Jt Ctee of Higher Med Trg (Haematology) 1991–2001; memb: Med Research Cncl Leukaemia Trials Ctee 1991–, Med and Scientific Panel Leukaemia Research Fund 1992–95 (Bhagwan Singh travelling fell 1993, memb of Coll Exec); chm Assoc of Profs in Haematology 1993–; pres Br Soc for Haematology 1998–99 (scientific sec 1989–95), pres RCPath 2005– (memb Cncl 1993–96 and 1999–2002, vice-pres 2002–05); chm Intercollege Cmmn on Haematology, Trg and Educn Ctee of the Int Soc of Haematology, memb DOH Commissioning Gp for Blood, memb Med Ctee and patron Thalassaemia Soc; med advsr: Leukaemia Care Soc, ITP Patient Support Assoc; FRCPath 1991, FRCP 1992; *Publications* author of numerous pubns in the field of haematology incl 16 books or chapters in books; *Recreations* fine wine, walking, foreign travel; *Clubs* Athenaeum, MCC; *Style—* Prof Adrian Newland; ✉ 41 Elmwood Road, Dulwich, London SE24 9NS (tel 020 7274 3295); Department of Haematology, Royal London Hospital, Whitechapel, London E1 1BB (tel 020 3246 0338, fax 020 3246 0351, e-mail a.c.newland@qmul.ac.uk)

NEWLAND, Prof David Edward; s of Robert William Newland (d 1979), of Knebworth, Herts, and Marion Amelia, *née* Dearman (d 1993); *b* 8 May 1936; *Educ* Alleyne's Sch Stevenage, Selwyn Coll Cambridge (MA, ScD), MIT (ScD); *m* 18 July 1959, Patricia Frances, da of Philip Mayne, of Marton, N Yorks; 2 s (Andrew David William b 1961, Richard David Philip b 1963); *Career* English Electric Co London 1957–61, instr and asst prof MIT 1961–64, lectr (later sr lectr) Imperial Coll London 1964–67, prof of mechanical engrg Univ of Sheffield 1967–76; Univ of Cambridge: prof of engrg (1875) 1976–2003, prof emeritus 2003–, fell Selwyn Coll 1976–, head Dept of Engrg 1996–2002, dep vice-chllr 1999–2003; dir Cambridge-MIT Inst 2000–02; memb Royal Cmmn on Environmental Pollution 1984–89, visitor Tport and Road Res Laboratory 1990–92, memb Engrg Cncl Working Party on Engrs and Risk Issues 1991–94, tech advsr London Millennium Bridge Tst 2000–01; memb Cncl Royal Acad of Engrg 1985–88; govr St Paul's Schs 1978–93, churchwarden Ickleton 1979–87; Freeman City of London 2000, Liveryman Worshipful Co of Engrs 2001; Hon DEng Univ of Sheffield 1997; FREng 1982, FIMechE, FIEE; *Books* An Introduction to Random Vibrations, Spectral and Wavelet Analysis (1975, 3 edn, 1993), Mechanical Vibration Analysis and Computation (1989), Discover Butterflies (2006); *Recreations* music, photography, golf, bell ringing; *Clubs* Athenaeum; *Style—* Prof David Newland, FREng; ✉ Department of Engineering, University of Cambridge, Trumpington Street, Cambridge CB2 1PZ (tel 01799 530268, fax 01799 531146, e-mail den@eng.cam.ac.uk)

NEWLAND, Martin Laurence; s of Edward Newland, of France, and Elena, *née* Martini; *b* 26 October 1961, Port Harcourt, Nigeria; *Educ* Downside, Goldsmiths Coll London (BA), Heythrop Coll London (MTh); *m* 18 July 1987, Bénédicte, *née* Smets; 4 c (Evelyn b 25 Aug 1990, Raphael b 23 Jan 1994, Otto b 20 Dec 1996, Gabriel b 20 Aug 2002); *Career* news ed Catholic Herald 1986–88, successively reporter, news ed and home ed Daily Telegraph 1989–98, dep ed National Post Canada 1998–2003, ed Daily Telegraph 2003–05; *Recreations* music, fitness, martial arts; *Style—* Martin Newland, Esq

NEWLAND, Peter John; s of Alec John Newland (d 2000), of Stratford-upon-Avon, and Mary Monica, *née* Leahy (d 1995); *b* 30 March 1943; *Educ* Douai Sch; *m* 29 June 1969, Philippa Ernestine Marshall, da of Philip Marshall Healey (d 1996); 3 da (Isabel Louise Cave b 12 June 1971, Joanna Lucy Mackenzie b 20 July 1974, Susannah Elizabeth b 29 March 1981); *Career* articled clerk Clement Keys & Son Birmingham 1960–66, qualified chartered accountant 1966, Peat Marwick Mitchell & Co Birmingham 1966–68, fin planner Unbrako Limited Coventry 1968–70, mangr Arthur Young McClelland Moores & Co Birmingham 1970–75, ptnr Ernst & Young Bristol 1975–93, dir of fin and admin John Cabot CTC 1993–2006, ret; *Recreations* golf, tennis, bridge; *Style—* Peter Newland, Esq; ✉ Charlecote, 8 Badminton Gardens, Bath BA1 2XS (tel 01225 315143)

NEWLANDS, David Baxter; s of George Frederick Newlands (d 1981), and Helen Frederica Newlands; *b* 13 September 1946; *Educ* Edinburgh Acad; *m* 31 March 1973, Susan Helena, da of Ernest Ferguson Milne, OBE, of Walton on the Hill, Surrey; 2 da (Katharine b 11 Jan 1977, Jennifer b 17 Nov 1978), 2 s (Edward b 27 June 1981, Andrew b 27 Sept 1983); *Career* ptnr Touche Ross and Co 1977–86 (joined 1963), fin dir Saatchi and Saatchi plc 1986–89, fin dir GEC plc 1989–97; non-exec chm: Paypoint 1998–, Prospect Investment Mgmnt 1999–, Britax International plc 2000–01 (non-exec dir 1999–2001), Tomkins plc 2000– (non-exec dir 1999–), Kesa Electricals 2003–, Open Business Exchange 2004–; non-exec dir: Weir Gp 1997–2003, Global Software Services 1998–2004, London Regnl Transport 1999–2001, Standard Life Assurance Co 1999–; chm of tstees SeeAbility 2001–; FCA 1969; *Recreations* golf, bridge; *Clubs* RAC, Walton Heath Golf, Sutton and Epsom RFC; *Style—* David Newlands, Esq

NEWLANDS, Prof George McLeod; s of George Newlands (d 1973), of Perth, and Mary Newlands; *b* 12 July 1941; *Educ* Perth Acad, Univ of Edinburgh (MA, BD, PhD), Univ of Heidelberg, Churchill Coll Cambridge (MA), Univ of Edinburgh (DLitt); *m* 1 Sept 1967, (Mary) Elizabeth, da of Rev Prof Ronald S Wallace, of Edinburgh; 3 s (Stewart b 1971, Murray b 1974, Craig b 1977); *Career* minister Church of Scotland, priest C of E; lectr in divinity Univ of Glasgow 1969–73, univ lectr in divinity Univ of Cambridge 1973–86, fell Wolfson Coll Cambridge 1975–82, fell and dean Trinity Hall Cambridge 1982–86, prof of divinity Univ of Glasgow 1986– (dean Faculty of Divinity 1988–90), princ Trinity Coll 1991–97 and 2002–; *Books* Hilary of Poitiers (1978), Theology of the Love of God (1980), The Church of God (1984), Making Christian Decisions (1985), God in Christian Perspective (1994), Generosity and the Christian Future (1997), Scottish Christianity in the Modern World (2000), John and Donald Baillie: Transatlantic Theology (2002), The Transformative Imagination (2004), Believing in the Text (jt ed, 2004), Fifty Key Christian Thinkers (jt ed, 2004), Traces of Liberality (2006), Christ and Human Rights (2006), The God of Love and Human Divinity: Essays for George Newlands (2007); *Recreations* walking, music; *Clubs* New (Edinburgh); *Style—* Prof George Newlands; ✉ Faculty of Divinity, The University, Glasgow G12 8QQ (tel 0141 339 8855, e-mail g.newlands@divinity.gla.ac.uk)

NEWLANDS OF LAURISTON, William Alexander; s of Frank Newlands (d 1971), of Ballinluig, Perthshire, and Annie Shand-Henderson (d 1986); the family is descended from Jasper Newlands of that Ilk (in record 1469); Lauriston Castle first recorded 1243, Glenfiddich award 1992; granted the arms of Newlands by Lyon Court 1987; matriculated as feudal baron 2003; *b* 5 November 1934; *Educ* Dollar Acad, Robert Gordon's Coll Aberdeen, Churchill fell 1968; *m* 1, 1960 (m dis 1976), Kathleen Cook; 2 da (Fiona b 1960, Riona b 1962), 1 s (Hamish Newlands of Lauriston Yr b 1965); m 2, 1985, Dorothy Walker, *qv*; *Career* Far East Air Force 1953–55; formerly with: Game Conservancy, Int Union for Conservation of Nature (Morges, Switzerland); travel ed (as Willy Newlands) Daily Mail 1982–92; ed and presenter Scots Away (TV series) 1993; London ed Alliance Press Features 1994–, columnist The Field 2002–; Travel Writer of the Year 1983–84 and 1987–88; FSA Scot; *Books* incl: Hobby Farm: Ideas for the New Countryside (2006); *Style—* William Newlands of Lauriston; ✉ tel 020 7351 6468; Lauriston Castle, St Cyrus, Kincardineshire (tel 01674 850488, e-mail wnewlands@aol.com); Alliance Press Features, 405 Kings Road, Chelsea, London SW10 0BB

NEWLYN, Prof Lucy Anne; da of Prof Walter T Newlyn (d 2002), and Doreen Harrington Newlyn; *b* 16 September 1956, Uganda; *Educ* Lawnswood HS Leeds, Lady Margaret Hall Oxford (open scholar, BA, DPhil); *m* 3 Jan 1991, Martin Slater; 1 da (Emma b 1995); *Career* Univ of Oxford: lectr Lincoln Coll, Lady Margaret Hall, Mansfield Coll and ChCh 1981–86, official fell and tutor in English St Edmund Hall 1986– (stipendiary lectr 1984–86), CUF lectr in English 1986–, prof of English language and lit 2004–; hon prof

Dept of English Univ of Wales Aberystwyth; Rose Mary Crawshay Prize Br Acad 2001; *Books* incl: Coleridge, Wordsworth and the Language of Allusion (1986), Paradise Lost and the Romantic Reader (1993), Reading, Writing and Romanticism: The Anxiety of Reception (2000), Ginnel (2005); *Recreations* swimming, gardening; *Style*— Prof Lucy Newlyn; ✉ 53 Latimer Road, Oxford OX3 7PG (tel 01865 435020); St Edmund Hall, Oxford OX1 4AR (tel 01865 279081, e-mail lucy.newlyn@seh.ox.ac.uk)

NEWMAN, Andrew William; s of Alistair John Newman, and Geraldine Elizabeth Maguire, *née* Long; *b* 4 November 1969; *Educ* St Paul's, UCL (BSc); *m* 31 Aug 2002, Terry Louise, *née* Burgess; 2 s (Frederick Ralph Stanley b 9 Dec 2000, William Robert Shrek b 22 May 2003); *Career* TV writer and prodr 1993–98 (shows incl The Word The Big Breakfast, Brass Eye, The Sunday Show The Eleven O'Clock Show and Ali G), commissioning ed entertainment Channel 4 1998–99, head of programmes E4 1999–2001, controller of entertainment Channel 5 2001–03; Channel 4: head of entertainment 2003–06, head of entertainment and comedy 2006–; *Recreations* collecting vintage fashion, obsessively watching television, magic; *Style*— Andrew Newman, Esq

NEWMAN, Catherine Mary; QC (1995); da of Dr Ernest Newman (d 1971), of London, and Josephine, *née* McLaughlin (d 1991); *b* 7 February 1954; *Educ* Convent of The Sacred Heart HS, UCL (LLB); *m* 1982, Ian Gouldsbrough; 1 s (Charles b 1987), 1 da (Mary Hope b 1991); *Career* called to the Bar Middle Temple (Harmsworth scholar 1979, bencher 2002), currently recorder; Lt-Bailiff of the Royal Court of Guernsey; chm Inns of Court and Bar Educnl Tst 2005–; memb: Bar Cncl 1987–90, Legal Services Cmmn Public Advsy Panel 2000–; hon sec Chancery Bar Assoc 1989–94; *Style*— Miss Catherine Newman, QC; ✉ Maitland Chambers, 7 Stone Buildings, Lincoln's Inn, London WC2A 3SZ (tel 020 7406 1200, fax 020 7406 1300)

NEWMAN, Derek Anthony; s of Maurice John Newman, of Ashtead, Surrey, and Christine Newman, *née* Grieve; *b* 7 April 1944; *Educ* Chorlton GS Manchester, City Univ (MBA); *m* 1968, Patricia Ann Wynne; 3 c (Michelle b 15 March 1972, David b 14 Jan 1975, Lisa b 3 Nov 1977); *Career* audit mangr Touche Ross 1968–73 (articled clerk 1965–68), fin controller First National Finance Ltd 1973–75; Chemical Bank: fin controller 1975–76, vice-pres fin 1976–78, vice-pres and head of corp fin NY 1978–81, vice-pres fin insts 1981–85; Canadian Imperial Bank of Commerce: gen mangr UK and Ireland 1985–86, sr vice-pres Europe, Africa and ME 1987–90 (vice-pres 1986–87), head of Europe 1990–91, chief executive CIBC/Wood Gundy Group Europe 1990–91; chief operating offr Summit Group plc 1991–94; chief fin offr: Nomura Securities plc, IBJ-Nomura Financial Products plc; FCA; *Recreations* windsurfing, golf, swimming; *Clubs* RAC; *Style*— Derek Newman, Esq; ✉ tel 07803 628845

NEWMAN, Sir Francis Hugh Cecil; 4 Bt (UK 1912), of Cecil Lodge, Newmarket, Co Cambridge; s of Sir Gerard Robert Henry Sigismund Newman, 3 Bt (d 1987), and Caroline Philippa, *née* Neville (now Mrs Andrew Crawshaw); *b* 12 June 1963; *Educ* Eton, Univ of Pennsylvania; *m* 18 Dec 1990, Katharine M, yr da of (Cecil Ralph) Timothy Edwards (d 1996), of Upton Bishop, Herefords; 3 s (Thomas Ralph Gerard b 7 Jan 1993, Arthur Guy Hugh b 28 April 1996, Louis Timothy Geoffrey b 4 April 2002), 1 da (Lily May Violet b 22 May 1994); *Heir* s, Thomas Newman; *Career* N M Rothschild Asset Mgmnt Ltd, vice-chm Galloway Group Ltd, ceo Cadweb Ltd; vice-pres Royston Dist Scouts; *Recreations* shooting, family, farming, visual arts; *Clubs* Eton Vikings, Turf, Penn; *Style*— Sir Francis Newman, Bt; ✉ Burloes Hall, Royston, Hertfordshire SG8 9NE (tel 01763 242150, fax 01763 243958, e-mail francis.newman@cadweb.co.uk)

NEWMAN, Sir Geoffrey Robert; 6 Bt (UK 1836), of Mamhead, Devonshire; s of Sir Ralph Alured Newman, 5 Bt (d 1968), and Hon Ann Rosemary Hope Newman, *née* Hope-Morley; *b* 2 June 1947; *Educ* Heatherdown Sch, Kelly Coll; *m* 1980, Mary Elizabeth, yr da of Col Sir Martin St John Valentine Gibbs, KCVO, CB, DSO, TD (d 1992); 3 da (Frances Joyce b 1983, Elsie Laura b 1987, Louisa Bridget b 1990), 1 s (Robert Melvil b 1985); *Heir* s, Robert Newman; *Career* 1 Bn Grenadier Gds 1967–70, Lt T&AVR until 1979; Daniel Greenaway & Sons Ltd 1973–75; memb Transglobe Expedition 1977–79; dir Blackpool Sands (Devon) Utilities Co Ltd 1970–; prodn controller Wadlow Grosvenor International 1980–90 (corporate film and video prodn); walk leader/guide The Wayfarers 1990–; vice-chm and dir Dartmouth & District Tourism Services Ltd 1992–; pres Dartmouth and Kingswear Soc 2001–, chm Dartmouth Swimming Pool 1998–, chm Marine Conservation Soc 2001–02, memb Devon Assoc of Tourist Attractions 1995–; FRGS; *Style*— Sir Geoffrey Newman, Bt

NEWMAN, Hon Mr Justice; Sir George Michael Newman; kt (1995); s of Wilfred James Newman (d 1970), of Seaford, E Sussex, and Celia Beatrice Lily, *née* Browne (d 1977); *b* 4 July 1941; *Educ* Lewes Co GS, St Catharine's Coll Cambridge; *m* 1966, Hilary Alice Gibbs, da of late Robert Gibbs Chandler, of Battle, E Sussex; 2 s (Benedict b 1968, Matthew b 1970), 1 da (Clarissa b 1971); *Career* called to the Bar Middle Temple 1965 (bencher 1989); recorder of the Crown Court 1985–95, a judge of the High Court of Justice (Queen's Bench Div) 1995–; FRSA 1991, fell Inst of Advanced Legal Studies 1999; *Recreations* tennis, skiing, walking; *Style*— The Hon Mr Justice Newman; ✉ The Royal Courts of Justice, Strand, London WC2A 2LL

NEWMAN, Iain Bernard; s of Rev David Newman, and Anne, *née* Taylor; *b* 5 January 1966, Yateley, Hants; *Educ* St Bees Sch Cumbria, Mansfield Coll Oxford (BA); *m* 30 July 1994, Victoria, *née* Chesworth; 1 da (Anna b 16 March 1998), 2 s (Peter b 5 Nov 2000, Mark b 9 Jan 2002); *Career* slr; Nabarro Nathanson: trainee 1988–90, assoc 1991–97, ptnr 1997–; memb Law Soc; *Recreations* children, cricket, rugby; *Style*— Iain Newman, Esq; ✉ Nabarro Nathanson, Lacon House, 84 Theobald's Road, London WC1X 8RW (tel 020 7524 6423, fax 020 7868 3423, e-mail i.newman@nabarro.com)

NEWMAN, John Arthur; s of C Gordon Newman, and Ruth, *née* Seabrook; *b* 12 December 1946; *Educ* St Albans Sch, St John's Coll Cambridge (MA); *m* 1 (m dis); m 2, Freya Darvall; 2 s (Alexander John b 18 May 1971, Michael Christopher b 22 Dec 1973), 1 da (Eloïse Freya b 20 May 1999); *Career* articled clerk Cooper Bros & Co 1967, Arthur Andersen & Co 1971, international tax mangr Touche Ross & Co 1973, ptnr Smith & Williamson 1994–2004; chm Equitable Members Action Gp Ltd 2006–; memb: Main Ctee LSCA 1979–87 and 1993–96, Cncl ICAEW 1987–93 and 1995–97; Assoc of Accounting Technicians: memb Cncl 1989–99, vice-pres 1995–96, pres 1996–97; MAAT, FCA; *Publications* UK/US Double Tax Agreement (1980), Controlled Foreign Corporations (1985); *Recreations* hellenophile; *Style*— John A Newman, Esq; ✉ 1 Ritherdon Road, London SW17 8QE (tel 020 8767 8167, fax 020 8672 0604, e-mail john.newman@londonsw17.org.uk)

NEWMAN, Dr John Howard; s of Edward Howard Newman (d 1975), of Sevenoaks, Kent, and Mary Newman (d 1993); *b* 14 June 1943; *Educ* Clare Coll Cambridge (MA), Guys Hosp Med Sch (MB BChir); *m* 31 July 1971, (Elizabeth) Anne, da of David Reynolds Cox (d 1994), of Torquay; 2 s (Bruce b 1973, Ian b 1979), 1 da (Rachel b 1975); *Career* conslt orthopaedic surgn: Bristol Royal Infirmary 1978–, Avon Orthopaedic Centre 1994–; former memb: Specialist Advsy Ctee in Orthopaedics, Overseas Doctors' Trg Ctee; ed The Knee 2000–05; Hunterian prof 2007; chm Brinckman Tst 2000–04; pres Grateful Soc 2007–08; memb: RCS, BOA (Cncl 1992–94), BASK (pres 1998–2000), BMA, Nat Jt Registry; FRCS 1971; *Recreations* real tennis, bridge, golf, watersports; *Style*— Dr John Newman; ✉ 2 Clifton Park, Bristol (tel 0117 906 4213, fax 0117 973 0887, e-mail newmancorner@doctors.org.uk)

NEWMAN, Kevin; *b* 1957; *Educ* Keele Univ (BA), Univ of Essex (MA); *m* Cathy; 2 s (Benjamin b 1989, Joshua b 1991), 1 da (Naomi b 1996); *Career* trainee programmer rising to sr project mangr Mars Group Services 1981–85; Woolworths plc: joined as info centre mangr 1985, then business systems mangr, dir of Mgmnt Info Systems (i/c all gp IT) until 1989; First Direct: i/c systems devpt prior to launch 1989, ops dir 1990–91, chief exec 1991–97; dir global distribution Citibank NY 1997–; *Recreations* squash, golf, running, gym workout, skiing, American football; *Style*— Kevin Newman, Esq; ✉ Citibank, NA Global Consumer Citibanking, One Court Square, 40th Floor, Long Island City, NY 11120, USA (tel 718 248 4754, fax 718 248 5303)

NEWMAN, Dr Lotte Therese (Mrs N E Aronsohn); CBE (1998, OBE 1991); da of Dr George Newman (d 1976), of London, and Dr Tilly Meyer (d 1966); *b* 22 January 1929; *Educ* N London Collegiate Sch, Univ of Birmingham (BSc), KCL and Westminster Hosp Med Schs (MB BS, LRCP, MRCS); *m* 1959, Norman Edward Aronsohn, s of Solomon Aronsohn; 1 da (Simone b 9 April 1960), 3 s (Simon b 22 May 1961, David b 29 Aug 1963, Alex b 14 Oct 1965); *Career* successively: casualty offr Westminster Hosp, paediatric house offr Westminster Children's Hosp, SHO St Stephen's Hosp, SHO in obstetrics and gynaecology Hillingdon Hosp, GP locum Edgware and Queensway; in gen practice 1960–; med advsr St John Ambulance Nat HQ 1999–2003; chm GMC Registration Ctee 1997–98; memb: Advsy Ctee on Breast Cancer Screening 1987–99, Disability Rights Forum 1998–; Purkinje medal Czechoslovak Soc of Gen Practice 1987, Sir David Bruce lecture and medal (first female lectr) RAMC 1989, Mackenzie lecture and medal RCGP 1991, Baron der Heyden de Lancey meml award 1992; Lotte Newman prize instituted by N London Faculty RCGP; first woman pres Int Soc of Gen Practice 1994–97, first Euro vice-pres World Orgn of Nat Colleges and Academies of Gen Practice (WONCA); pres London Jewish Med Soc 1998–99, memb Bd of Deputies of British Jews 1998–2006 (memb Defence and Group Relations Ctee, chm Circumcision Working Gp); Freeman City of London 1987, Liveryman Worshipful Soc of Apothecaries 1987; memb and chm Registration Ctee GMC 1984–98, memb BMA 1985 (fell 1999); fell Royal NZ Coll Gen Practice 1998; FRCGP 1977 (MRCGP 1967, pres 1994–97), FRSM 1977; *Recreations* spending time with family, listening to music, boating; *Clubs* RAC; *Style*— Dr Lotte Newman, CBE, FRCGP; ✉ The White House, 1 Ardwick Road, London NW2 2BX (tel 020 7435 6630, fax 020 7435 6672, e-mail jh44@dial.pipex.com)

NEWMAN, Michael Henry; s of Henry Ernest Newman, of Wimbledon, London, and Rhoda May, *née* Symonds (d 1986); *b* 19 October 1945; *Educ* Whitgift Sch; *m* 15 Jan 1977, Jennifer Mary, da of Matthew McCargo Roger (d 1977), of Glasgow; *Career* CA 1968; chief exec Britannia Arrow Holdings plc 1979–86 (dir from 1977), dep chm National Employers Life Assurance Co Ltd 1983–86, dir Singer & Friedlander 1984–86, chief exec Prudential Corporation Asia Ltd 1989–90, sr mgmnt Prudential Corporation plc 1990–92, business conslt 1993–2000, devpt dir Life Old Mutual plc 2000–01, chm Old Mutual Strategic Interests 2002–; *Recreations* travel, gardening; *Clubs* Reform, Singapore Town; *Style*— Michael Newman, Esq; ✉ 37 Wool Road, Wimbledon, London SW20 0HN (tel 020 8947 9756, fax 020 8944 7323)

NEWMAN, Paul; s of Christopher William Newman (d 2002), and Nesta, *née* Morgan (d 1997); *b* 5 March 1958, Wales; *Educ* Clare Coll Cambridge (MA), City Univ London (Dip), Cncl of Legal Educn London; *m* 17 Oct 1987, Veronica, *née* Grant; 2 s (David b 18 Jan 1993, Jonathan b 25 Dec 2000); *Career* called to the Bar Gray's Inn 1982 (pupil master); barr specialising in construction law, mediation and arbitration; barr in private practice Manchester 1986–88, with slrs practice Cardiff 1990–2006 (latterly with Hugh James), resumed practice as barr Bristol 2006–; memb: CIArb, Talk Mediation, Wales Baltic Soc, Br-Lithuanian Soc; highly commended Hudson Prize for Construction Law 1997; accredited adjudicator and mediator; FCIArb 1999, assoc Chartered Inst of Linguists 2005; *Publications* author, co-author and contrib to numerous titles on construction law and dispute resolution; regular contrib: Slrs Jl, Legal Executive, Construction Law, Tottel's Construction Newsletter; *Recreations* outdoors, family, reading, theatre, travel; *Style*— Paul Newman, Esq; ✉ 77 Roath Court Road, Cardiff CF24 3SF; 3 Paper Buildings (Bristol), Hanover House, 47 Corn Street, Bristol BS1 1HT (tel 0117 928 1520, fax 0117 928 1525, e-mail paul.newman@3paper.co.uk)

NEWMAN, Paul Stephen; s of Gordon Patrick Newman, of Bexhill, E Sussex, and Maureen Winifred, *née* Lee; *b* 16 October 1954; *Educ* Caterham Sch, Univ of Southampton (BA); *m* 3 Sept 1983, Rosemary Jane; 1 da (Katy Mary b 8 Sept 1985); *Career* Mirror Gp Newspapers trg scheme 1977–79, sports ed Barnet Press 1979–80, sub ed Daily Mail 1980–81, various posts on sports desk culminating in asst sports ed The Times 1981–90; The Independent: dep sports ed 1990–91, sports ed 1991–2004, chief sports feature writer 2004–, tennis corr 2006–; chm Crystal Palace Supporters' Tst, dir Crystal Palace Youth Tst; *Recreations* tennis, Crystal Palace FC, France; *Style*— Paul Newman, Esq; ✉ The Independent, 191 Marsh Wall, London E14 9RS (tel 020 7005 2847, fax 020 7005 2894, e-mail p.newman@independent.co.uk)

NEWMAN, Prof Ronald Charles (Ron); s of Charles Henry Newman (d 1983), and Margaret Victoria May, *née* Cooper (d 1985); *b* 10 December 1931; *Educ* Tottenham GS, Imperial Coll London (BSc, DIC, PhD); *m* 7 April 1956, Jill Laura, da of Robert Charles Weeks (d 1949); 2 da (Susan Laura (Mrs Lee) b 1959, Vivienne Heather (Mrs Cadman) b 1962); *Career* research scientist AEI Central Research Lab Aldermaston Court 1955–63, sr research scientist AEI Research Lab Rugby 1964; Univ of Reading: lectr J J Thomson Physical Lab 1964–69, reader 1969–75, prof 1975–88, visiting prof 1989–2006; prof and assoc dir IRC semi-conductor materials Imperial Coll London 1989–99, emeritus prof and sr research investigator Imperial Coll London 1999–2006, visiting prof UMIST 2000–2005; memb EPSRC Coll Functional Materials 1996–97, vice-chm MPI Fachbeirat Halle 1996–99; memb Br Assoc for Crystal Growth until 2006; ARCS, FInstP, FRS 1998; *Books* Infrared Studies of Crystal Defects (1973); *Recreations* music, foreign travel; *Style*— Prof Ron Newman, FRS; ✉ Maiden Oak, 23 Betchworth Avenue, Earley, Reading, Berkshire RG6 7RH (tel 0118 966 3816); Centre for Electronic Materials and Devices, The Blackett Laboratory, Imperial College London, Prince Consort Road, London SW7 2BZ (tel 020 7594 6692, fax 020 7581 3817, e-mail r.newman@ic.ac.uk)

NEWMAN, Vice Adm Sir Roy Thomas; KCB (1992, CB 1991), JP (SE Hants 1996), DL (Hants 2001); *Educ* Queen Elizabeth's GS Barnet; *m*; 4 s; *Career* joined RN 1954, specialised in anti-submarine warfare (ASW) 1963, instr HMS Dolphin Submarine Sch, served ASW frigate HMS Hardy, joined Submarine Serv 1966, served HMS Otus and Warspite, instr Jt ASW Sch Londonderry, cmd submarine HMS Onyx; Cdr 1971, 2 i/c HMS London, Nat Defence Coll course 1972, various appts on staff of Flag Offr Submarines and MOD, cmd ASW frigate HMS Naiad; Capt 1979, Operational Requirements Dept MOD Central Staff Directorate, cmd HMS Dolphin, 1 Submarine Sqdn and Submarine Sch 1981, involved in evacuation of UK troops from Lebanon 1984, Capt 7 Frigate Sqdn and cmd HMS Cleopatra, Dir Naval Warfare MOD 1986–88; Rear Adm 1988, Flag Offr Sea Trg 1988–90, Dep Cdr Fleet and COS to C-in-C Fleet 1990–92, Naval Dep to Jt Cdr Operation Granby RAF High Wycombe 1991; Vice Adm 1991, Flag Offr Plymouth and Cdr Central Sub Area Eastern Atlantic 1992–96; responsible for 50th anniversary commemoration of the Battle of the Atlantic May 1993; pres Royal Naval Assoc 1996–2001 (vice-patron 2001); chm Bd of Tstees RN Submarine Museum 1999–2005; govr St John's Primary Sch Rowlands Castle 1999–2003; Liveryman City of London 1989, Liveryman Worshipful Co of Shipwrights 1996, Yr Bro Trinity House 1997; *Clubs* Broad Halfpenny Brigands CC (pres 1995–), Army and Navy, Pall Mall; *Style*— Vice Adm Sir Roy Newman, KCB, JP, DL; ✉ Foxdenton, 16 Links Lane, Rowlands Castle, Hampshire PO9 6AE

NEWMAN TURNER, Roger Geoffrey; s of Frank Newman Turner (d 1964), of Letchworth, Herts, and Lorna Mary, *née* Clarke (d 1976); *b* 29 April 1940; *Educ* Sidcot Sch, Br Coll of Naturopathy and Osteopathy (Naturopathic Dip, Dip Osteopathy), Br Coll of

N

Acupuncture (Licentiate Dip Acupuncture, BAc); *m* 1966, Birgid, da of Carl Rath, of Stuttgart; 1 da (Nicole b 1966), 1 s (Julian b 1968); *Career* naturopath, osteopath and acupuncturist in private practice 1963–; sec Res Soc for Natural Therapeutics 1966–75, ed Br Jl of Acupuncture 1982–93, pres Br Acupuncture Assoc 1990–92, chm Res Cncl for Complementary Med 1993–97 (tstee 1983–); memb Register of Naturopaths, memb Gen Osteopathic Cncl; fell Br Acupuncture Cncl, fell Br Naturopathic Assoc; *Books* incl: First Aid Nature's Way (1969), Diets to Help Hay Fever and Asthma (1970), Diets to Help Heart Disorders (1971), Diets to Help Control Cholesterol (1978), Naturopathic Medicine (1984, re-issued 2000), Self Help for Angina (1987), Hay Fever Handbook (1988), Banish Back Pain (1989); *Recreations* acting, singing, theatre, opera, cricket; *Style*— Roger Newman Turner, Esq; ✉ 1 Harley Street, London W1G 9QD (tel 020 7436 1446, website www.naturomed.co.uk)

NEWMARCH, Michael George (Mick); s of George Langdon Newmarch, and Phyllis Georgina, *née* Crandon; *b* 19 May 1938; *Educ* Tottenham Co GS, Univ of London (BSc external); *m* 10 Oct 1959, Audrey Ann, da of Cecil Clark; 1 s (Timothy b 1963), 2 da (Kate b 1966, Joanne b 1971); *Career* The Prudential Corporation: joined Economic Intelligence Dept Prudential Assurance Co Ltd 1955, sr asst investment mangr 1976–78, dep investment mangr 1979–80, investment mangr and ceo Prudential Portfolio Managers Ltd 1981–89, chief exec Prudential Corporation 1990–95, chm Prudential Assurance Company 1990–95, chm Prudential Portfolio Managers 1990–95; md PricewaterhouseCoopers 1997–99; non-exec dir: Celltech Gp plc 1996–, Bourne End Properties plc 1997–2000, Weston Medical 1999–2003; vice-chm Princess Royal Tst for Carers 1995–, tstee Berks Community Tst 1996–2003 (currently chm); memb: Advsy Cncl Orch of the Age of Enlightenment 1995–, Gen Cncl Univ of Reading 1999–; *Recreations* salmon-fishing, fly-tying, music, opera, cinema, bridge; *Clubs* Flyfishers, RAC; *Style*— Mick Newmarch, Esq

NEWMARK, Brooks; MP; s of Howard Newmark (d 1964), and Gilda Gourlay, *née* Rames; *b* 8 May 1958, Norwalk, CT; *Educ* Harvard Coll (AB), Worcester Coll Oxford, Harvard Business Sch (MBA); *m* 6 July 1985, Lucy, *née* Keegan; 4 s (Benjamin b 31 July 1988, Sam b 19 Dec 1990, Max b 3 Nov 1992, Zachary b 10 July 1997), 1 da (Lily b 24 May 1994); *Career* vice-pres Shearson Lehman Brothers Inc 1984–87, dir Newmark Brothers Ltd 1987–92, dir Stellican Ltd 1992–98, ptnr Apollo Mgmnt LP 1998–2005; chair Southwark and Bermondsey Cons Assoc 1990–93; Parly candidate (Cons): Newcastle upon Tyne Central 1997, Braintree 2001; MP (Cons) Braintree 2005–; *Recreations* running, skiing, football (Newcastle United supporter); *Clubs* Beefsteak, Boodle's, Cresta, White's; *Style*— Brooks Newmark, Esq, MP; ✉ House of Commons, London SW1A 0AA

NEWRY AND MORNE, Viscount; Robert Francis John; s and h of 6 Earl of Kilmorey, PC, *qv*; *b* 30 May 1966; *Educ* Eton, Lady Margaret Hall Oxford, Imperial Coll London (MBA); *m* 13 April 1991, Laura Mary, o da of Michael Tregaskis, of Cosham, Hants; 1 da (Hon Julia Helen Mary b 11 March 1997), 1 s (Hon Thomas Francis Michael b 25 Sept 1998); *Career* prodn controller Bissell 1988–89, sales mangr Lewmar Marine 1990–92, business devpt mangr Inchcape Pacific 1994–97; dir Inchcape NRG 1997–99, dir ops Gilman Office Automation 1999–2001; dir: Morne Consultancy 2000–02, Network Programs Europe 2001–02, Newfield IT Ltd 2003–; assoc dir Ricoh UK Ltd 2001–03; *Style*— Viscount Newry and Morne

NEWSOME, Dr Roy; s of Norman Newsome (d 1959), of Elland, W Yorks, and Minnie, *née* Crompton (d 1971); *b* 17 July 1930; *Educ* Elland C of E Sch, Halifax Tech Coll, Univ of Durham (BMus), Univ of Salford (PhD); *m* 18 Dec 1954, Muriel, da of William Wilson; 2 s (Neil Michael b 21 July 1960, Martin John b 14 July 1963); *Career* brass band personality, conductor, adjudicator, composer; conducting appts incl: Black Dyke Mills Band 1966–77, Besses o' th' Barn 1978–85, Fairey Engineering Band 1986–89, Sun Life Band 1989–96; music dir Nat Youth Brass Band of GB 1984–2000, presenter of Listen To The Band (BBC Radio 2) 1986–94, head of band studies and band musicianship UC Salford 1976–89 (awarded Hon Grad Dip Band Musicianship in recognition of outstanding contrib to band music throughout the world 1989); conductor laureate and research fell Univ of Salford; pres Nat Assoc of Brass Band Conductors 1992–; has circa 100 published compositions and arrangements incl Concerto for Piano and Brass Band first performed at the Royal Albert Hall; music advsr Brass in Concert Championships; adjudicated major brass band contests and nat championships in: UK, Switzerland, Holland, Belgium, Norway, USA, Aust, NZ; author of books on band history; Silver medal Worshipful Co of Musicians for services to brass bands 1976, Masters Dedicated Service Award All England Masters Championships 2000, British Bandsman Life Achievement Award 2005; FRCO, ARCM; *Recreations* motoring, reading, good food and wine; *Style*— Dr Roy Newsome; ✉ 17 Belmont Drive, Seddons Farm, Bury, Lancashire BL8 2HU (tel and fax 0161 764 2009)

NEWSON-SMITH, Sir Peter Frank Graham; 3 Bt (UK 1944), of Totteridge, Co Hertford; s of Sir John Kenneth Newson-Smith, 2 Bt (d 1997), and his 1 w, Vera Margaret Greenhouse Allt (d 2001); paternal gf was Lord Mayor of London; maternal gf was Dr Greenhouse Allt, CBE, princ of Trinity Coll of Music London; *b* 8 May 1947; *Educ* Dover Coll, Trinity Coll of Music; *m* 1974, Mary-Ann, da of Cyril C Collins, of Old Woodstock, Oxon, and formerly w of Anthony Owens; 1 s (Oliver Nicholas Peter b 1975), 1 da (Emma Jo b 1977); *Heir* s, Oliver Newson-Smith; *Career* dir of music Clayesmore Preparatory Sch until 2003; hon treas MMA 2002–06, chm Young Musicians of Muscat Adjudication Panel 2002–; Freeman City of London 1969, Liveryman Worshipful Co of Musicians 1971; *Recreations* gardening, sailing; *Style*— Sir Peter Newson-Smith, Bt; ✉ Lovells Court, Burton Street, Marnhull, Sturminster Newton, Dorset DT10 1JJ (tel 01258 820652, fax 01258 820487, e-mail peternewson@gmail.com)

NEWTH, Jonathan Gildon; s of Terence Conrad Newth (d 1994), of Appledore, Devon, and Winifred Gertrude Mary, *née* Lack (d 1991); *b* 6 March 1939; *Educ* Aldenham, Central Sch of Speech and Drama; *m* 1, 1964 (m dis 1978), Joanna, da of Dr S V Brookes; 2 s (Benjamin b 1965, Daniel b 1968); m 2, 1979, Gay, da of R A Wilde; 3 da (Rosalind b 1980, Eliza b 1982, Charlotte b 1988), 1 s (George b 1985); *Career* actor; *Theatre* Open Air Theatre Regents Park: Lysander in A Midsummer Night's Dream 1966, Camillo in A Winters Tale 1988, Quince in A Midsummer Night's Dream 1988; RSC: Bonaventure in 'Tis Pity She's a Whore 1991–92, Capulet in Romeo and Juliet 1991–92, Player King in Hamlet 1992–93, Duke Frederick and Duke Senior in As You Like It 2005–06; other roles incl: The School for Scandal (Theatre Royal Haymarket and USA) 1962–63, The Creeper (St Martins) 1965, Robert in Meeting At Night (Duke of York's) 1972, Richard in Rents (Lyric Hammersmith) 1982, Col Tallboys in Too True to be Good 1986, Fred in The Viewing (Greenwich) 1987, Bill Coles in Other Peoples Money (Lyric) 1990, Leonato in Much Ado About Nothing (Queens) 1993, Mr Bennet in Pride and Prejudice (nat tour) 1995, Vertigo (Theatre Royal Windsor) 1998, Brovik in The Master Builder (English touring theatre) 1999, Clive in The Circle (Oxford Stage Co) 2000, David Bliss in Hay Fever (Oxford Stage Co) 2001, Tiresias/Shepherd in King Oedipus (Paphos Int Theatre Festival) 2002, Sir Horace Broughton in Office Games (Pleasance Theatre) 2003, Prospero in The Tempest (Theatre Royal Bury St Edmunds and touring) 2004; The Expedition of Humphry Clinker (own adaptation, first performance Bath Literature Festival) 2003, Lord Burleigh in Mary Stuart (Nuffield Theatre) 2004; *Television* incl: Lord Rochford in The Six Wives of Henry VIII 1968, Capt Blamey in Poldark 1972, Brig Jefferson in Tenko 1984, Josh in Fainthearted Feminist 1984, Boustead in Voyage Around My Father 1984, Russell in After Henry 1987–92, Matthew Pocket in Great Expectations 1988, Dr Eliot in Casualty 1996, Don Luis & Francisco in Don Juan (English touring theatre) 1999; *Radio* incl: Green Mansions and The Siege of Krishnapur (Book At Bedtime); *Film* incl: Far from the Madding Crowd, Yellow Dog, Pope John Paul II, North Sea Hi-Jack, Accounts, Judge in Incognito, A Secret Audience, The Affair of the Necklace; *Style*— Jonathan Newth, Esq; ✉ c/o Caroline Dawson Associates, 125 Gloucester Road, London SW7 4TE (tel 020 7373 3323, fax 020 7373 1110)

NEWTON, Air Vice Marshal Barry Hamilton; CB (1988), CVO (2002), OBE (1975); s of Bernard Hamilton Newton, FCA (d 1932), of Southgate, Middx, and Dorothy Mary Newton, *née* Thomas (d 1979); *b* 1 April 1932; *Educ* Highgate Sch, RAF Coll Cranwell; *m* 1959, Lavinia, da of Col John James Aitken, CMG, DSO, OBE (d 1946), of Taunton, Somerset; 1 s (Charles), 1 da (Melanie); *Career* cmmnd RAF 1953, 109 (Canberras) Sqdn 1954–55, 76 (Canberras) Sqdn nuclear weapon trials Aust and Christmas Is 1955–58 (QCVSA); advanced instr (Vampires) RAF Coll Cranwell 1959–61, OC 2 Sqdn 6 FTS 1962–64, RAF Staff Coll 1965, PSO to COMTWOATAF/CINC RAF Germany 1966–69, OC Ops Wing RAF Cottesmore 1969–71, Air Warfare Coll 1971, Defence Policy Staff MOD 1971–73, Directing Staff NDC 1974–75; Cabinet Office 1975–78; asst dir Defence Policy 1978–79, Cabinet Office 1979–81, Air Cdre Flying Trg HQ RAF Support Cmd 1982–83, sr dir Staff RCDS 1984–86, Cmdt JSDC Greenwich 1986–88, sr dir Staff (Forward Plans) RCDS 1988–89; ADC to HM The Queen 1982–83, Gentleman Usher to HM The Queen 1989–2002, Extra Gentleman Usher to HM The Queen 2002–; vice-chm Cncl TAVRA 1989–99, Hon Air Cdre 606 (Chiltern) Sqdn RAuxAF 1996–, Hon Inspr Gen RAuxAF 2000, pres UK Reserve Forces Assoc 2005–; Freeman City of London 2002, Hon Freeman Worshipful Co of Lightmongers 2002; *Recreations* country pursuits, military history; *Clubs* RAF; *Style*— Air Vice Marshal B H Newton, CB, CVO, OBE; ✉ c/o National Westminster Bank plc, 48 Blue Boar Row, Salisbury, Wiltshire SP1 1DF

NEWTON, Christopher John; s of Henry Newton (d 1975), of Leicester and London, and Florence Alice, *née* Wilton (d 1978); *b* 24 June 1936; *Educ* Market Bosworth GS, Royal Ballet Sch Sadler's Wells; *Career* joined Royal Ballet Co Corps de Ballet 1954–1970 (soloist 1958–70), joined Faculty of US Int Univ San Diego CA to teach dance notation and repertoire 1970–73; Royal Ballet: re-joined as dance notator and repetiteur 1973–80, ballet master 1980–88, artistic co-ordinator 1988; has re-produced ballets of Frederick Ashton, Antony Tudor, Rudolph Nureyev and Roland Petit 1970–88 for American Ballet Theatre, Joffrey Ballet, SF Ballet, Paris Opera Ballet and Deutsch Oper Ballet of Berlin, also staged own production of Swan Lake - Act III for Pennsylvania Ballet, re-produced and staged Frederick Ashton's 3 act ballet Ondine from incomplete film records 1988 (created in 1958 and last performed in 1966), re-produced Polotsvian Dances from Prince Igor for National Youth Ballet for VE Day celebrations Hyde Park 1995, re-constructed and staged Frederick Ashton's 3 act ballet Sylvia 2004 (created in 1952 and last performed in 1965), reconstructed in part Frederick Ashton's coronation ballet Homage to the Queen in celebration of Queen Elizabeth II's 80th Birthday 2006, co-produced new prodn of The Sleeping Beauty 2006; MRAD, AIChor; *Recreations* textile crafts; *Style*— Christopher Newton, Esq; ✉ Royal Ballet Company, Royal Opera House, Covent Garden, London WC2E 9DD (tel 020 7212 9668, e-mail christopher.newton@roh.org.uk)

NEWTON, David Alexander; s of Alexander Newton (decd), of Eye, Suffolk, and Hazel, *née* Little; *b* 6 October 1942; *Educ* Morecambe GS; *m* 6 March 1965, Kathleen Mary, da of George Ernest Moore; 1 da (Rebecca b 8 Dec 1965), 1 s (Stewart Alexander b 17 Sept 1967); *Career* trainee Provincial Insurance Co 1958–61, mgmnt trainee J Bibby & Sons 1961–66, area mangr Cobb Breeding Co 1966–68, gen mangr Anglian Hatcheries 1968–71, agric dir Sovereign Group 1971–81; Hillsdown Group: md Ross Poultry 1981–82, chm Ross Group 1982–85, chm and ceo Buxted Ltd 1983–87, dep chm Maple Leaf Foods Canada 1992–95 (pres and ceo 1987–92), ceo Hillsdown Group 1993–96 (chief operating offr 1992–93); chm: Carrs Milling plc, Firstan Ltd, Meadow Foods Ltd; chm Muntons Maltings plc, non-exec dir Bernard Matthews plc; ptnr K&D Partnership; dir various group cos 1982–92; CIM, FInstD, FRSA; *Recreations* golf, watching sports, music; *Clubs* Diss Golf; *Style*— David Newton, Esq; ✉ Falcon House, Mellis, Eye, Suffolk IP23 8DS (tel 01379 783561, e-mail dnewton@btclick.com)

NEWTON, Derek Henry; s of Sidney Wellington Newton (d 1976), of Worthing, W Sussex, and Sylvia May, *née* West (d 1959); *b* 14 March 1933; *Educ* Emanuel Sch; *m* 18 May 1957, Judith Ann (d 1995), da of Rowland Hart (d 1973); 2 da (Katherine Jane (Mrs Smith) b 3 Sept 1960, Amanda Jean (Mrs Roberts) b 4 Nov 1962); *Career* Nat Serv Lt RA 1952–54; insurance broker; chm: C E Heath plc 1983–87, Flanagan & Co 1998–99; dir: Glaxo Trustees Ltd 1980–92, Glaxo Pharmaceuticals Trustees Ltd 1980–92, Glaxo Insurance (Bermuda) Ltd 1980–93, Clarges Pharmaceuticals Trustees Ltd 1985–92; govr BUPA Medical Research & Development Ltd 1981–95; cncllr for Oxshott and Stoke D'Abernon Esher UDC 1968–71; Liveryman Worshipful Co of Insurers; FCII 1957; *Recreations* cricket, golf; *Clubs* Surrey CCC (chm 1979–94, pres 2004), MCC, RAC, Burhill Golf; *Style*— Derek Newton, Esq; ✉ Pantiles, Meadway, Oxshott, Surrey KT22 0LZ (tel 01372 842273, fax 01372 843913, e-mail derekhnewton@hotmail.com)

NEWTON, Prof Ian; OBE (1999); s of Haydn Edwin Newton (d 1980), of Chesterfield, Derbys, and Nellie, *née* Stubbs (d 1986); *b* 17 January 1940; *Educ* Chesterfield Boys' GS, Univ of Bristol (BSc), Univ of Oxford (DPhil, DSc); *m* 21 July 1962, Halina Teresa, da of Edward Bialkowski; 2 s (Michael Peter b 1965, Robert Edward b 1967), 1 da (Diana Catherine b 1969); *Career* postdoctoral research Univ of Oxford 1964–67; Nature Conservancy Edinburgh: research on waterfowl populations 1967–71, research on birds of prey 1971–79; Inst of Terrestrial Ecology: head of Pollution Research Unit 1979–84, special merit post grade 5 1992– (grade 6 1984–92); visiting prof in ornithology Univ of Oxford 1994–; Union Medal Br Ornithologists Union 1988, Gold Medal Br Ecological Soc 1989, Medal RSPB 1991, President's Award Raptor Research Fndn 1993, Marsh Award in Conservation Biology Zoological Soc 1995, Elliott Cowes Award American Ornithologists Union 1995; memb: Br Ecological Soc (pres 1994–95), Br Ornithologists' Union 1984 (vice-pres 1989–93, pres 1999–2003); hon fell American Ornithologists Union, memb RSPB (chm Conservation Ctee 1997–2003, chm Cncl 2003–); hon memb: Br Ecological Soc 1999, Sociedad Española de Ornithogia 2004; FRS 1993, FRSE 1994; *Books* Finches (1972), Population Ecology of Raptors (1979), The Sparrowhawk (1986), Lifetime Reproduction in Birds (ed, 1989), Population Limitation in Birds (1998), The Speciation and Biogeography of Birds (2003); *Recreations* walking, travel, fruit growing; *Style*— Prof Ian Newton, OBE, FRS, FRSE; ✉ Centre for Ecology and Hydrology, Monks Wood, Abbots Ripton, Huntingdon, Cambridgeshire PE28 2LS (tel 01487 772552, fax 01487 773467, e-mail ine@ceh.ac.uk)

NEWTON, Sir Kenneth Garnar; 3 Bt (UK 1924), of Beckenham, Co Kent; OBE (1969, MBE 1944), TD; s of Sir Edgar Henry Newton, 2 Bt (d 1971); *b* 4 June 1918; *Educ* Wellington; *m* 1944, Margaret Isabel (d 1979), da of Rev Dr George Blair, of Dundee; 2 s (John Garnar b 1945, Peter Blair b 1950); *Heir* s, John Newton; *Career* served WWII, Lt-Col 1944; gen cmmr for Income Tax 1961–93; md Garnar Booth plc 1961–83 (chm 1972–87); pres: Br Leather Fedn 1968–69, Int Cncl of Tanners 1972–78; Master: Worshipful Co of Leathersellers 1977–78, Worshipful Co of Feltmakers 1983–84; chm Bd of Govrs Colfe's Sch 1982–93; *Style*— Sir Kenneth Newton, Bt, OBE, TD; ✉ Oaklands, Harborough Gorse, West Chiltington, West Sussex RH20 2RU

NEWTON, Mark Robert; s of Robert William Banner Newton (d 1982), and Cicely Kathleen, *née* Radmall (d 1989); *b* 2 June 1954; *Educ* Eton, RAC Cirencester; *m* 12 May 1979, Diana Sarah, da of Maj Sir Robert David Black, 3 Bt, of Goring-on-Thames, Oxon; 2 s (William David Rupert b 7 Dec 1989, James Robert George b 3 Nov 1993); *Career* chartered surveyor; ptnr Fisher German 1985–; memb Langtons Ward Harborough DC 1995–2003;

chm Midlands Branch Royal Forestry Soc 1994–95; regnl rep Leics and Rutland Branch Nat Art Collections Fund 2000–; memb: Game Conservancy (chm Leics Branch Game Conservancy Tst 1995–97), CLA (chm Leics and Rutland Branch 2004–07), Historic House Assoc; tstee Henry Smiths Charity 1999–; High Sheriff Leics 2006–07; FRICS 1986; *Recreations* fishing, shooting; *Style*— Mark Newton, Esq, FRICS; ✉ The Old Rectory, Church Langton, Leicestershire LE16 7SX (tel 01858 545600); Fisher German, 40 High Street, Market Harborough, Leicestershire LE16 7NX (tel 01858 411215, fax 01858 410207, mobile 07860 514474, e-mail mark.newton@fishergerman.co.uk)

NEWTON, Sir (Harry) Michael Rex; 3 Bt (UK 1900), of The Wood, Sydenham Hill, Lewisham, Kent, and Kottingham House, Burton-on-Trent, Co Stafford; s of Sir Harry Kottingham Newton, 2 Bt, OBE (d 1951), and Myrtle Irene, *née* Grantham (d 1977); *b* 7 February 1923; *Educ* Eastbourne Coll; *m* 1958, Pauline Jane (d 2002), o da of Richard John Frederick Howgill, CBE, of Sullington Warren, W Sussex; 1 s (George Peter Howgill b 1962), 3 (adopted) da (Lucinda Jane b 1964, (Julia) Kate, Jennifer Anne (twins) b 1967); *Heir* s, Rev George Newton; *Career* served 1941–46 with KRRC; dir Thomas Parsons & Sons Ltd; memb Ct of Assts Worshipful Co of Girdlers (past Master); Freeman City of London; winner of 1953 Fastnet Race; *Clubs* Royal Ocean Racing; *Style*— Sir Michael Newton, Bt; ✉ c/o George Newton, 2 Cranmore Lane, Aldershot GU11 3AS (tel 01252 320618)

NEWTON, (John) Nigel; s of Peter Leigh Newton, and Anne St Aubyn Newton; *b* 16 June 1955, San Francisco; *Educ* Deerfield Acad Mass, Selwyn Coll Cambridge (MA); *m* 1981, Joanna Elizabeth, *née* Hastings-Trew; 1 s, 2 da; *Career* asst sales dir Macmillan 1976–78, sales dir then dep md Sidgwick & Jackson 1978–86, chm and chief exec Bloomsbury Publishing plc (co-fndr 1986); supporter: Garrick Charitable Tst, Asham Tst; memb Communications Ctee Catholic Bishops Conf; *Recreations* walking, travel, tennis; *Clubs* Hurlingham, Garrick; *Style*— Nigel Newton, Esq; ✉ Bloomsbury Publishing plc, 36 Soho Square, London W1D 3HB (tel 020 7494 2111, e-mail nigel_newton@bloomsbury.com)

NEWTON, Prof Ray William; *b* 8 December 1944; *Educ* Univ of Edinburgh (MB, MRCP); *Career* formerly med registrar Royal Infirmary Edinburgh, conslt physician Ninwells Hosp and Med Sch 1977– (hon prof Dept of Med), postgraduate dean East of Scotland 1999–2003; conslt i/c Dundee Diabetic Serv; NHS: memb Scottish Med & Scientific Advsy Ctee 1998 (chm Div of Med 1989–92), clinical dir of med 1994–96; RCPEd: Tayside regnl advsr 1983–99, memb Educn Ctee 1990–, memb Overseas Ctee 1990–, memb Cncl 1992–98; visiting clinical tutor Queen Elizabeth Hosp Hong Kong 1988; chm: Jt Royal Colls Working Gp on SHO Trg 1993, Jt Colls Review on Doctors in Basic Med Trg 1995; chm: Scottish Study Gp for the Care of the Young Diabetic 1989–91, Scottish Implementation Task Force on Care in Childhood and Adolescence 1994; dir of Telemedicine Initiative Scotland Scottish Med Exec 1999; memb Cncl Med and Dental Defence Union of Scotland 1998, memb Br Diabetic Assoc; FRCPEd 1981 (memb Cncl 1992–98), FRCPGlas 1995; *Books* Endocrinology - The New Medicine (jt ed, 1983), Diabetes in Childhood and Adolescence (jtly, 1995); author of numour book chapters and pubns on diabetes and endocrinology; *Clubs* Royal and Ancient Golf (St Andrews); *Style*— Prof Ray Newton; ✉ Department of Medicine, Ninewells Hospital, Dundee DD1 9SY (tel 01382 660111)

NEWTON, 5 Baron (UK 1892); Richard Thomas Legh; s of 4 Baron Newton (d 1992), and Priscilla, *née* Egerton-Warburton (now Mrs Frederick Fryer); *b* 11 January 1950; *Educ* Eton, ChCh Oxford; *m* 1978, Rosemary Whitfoot, da of Herbert Whitfoot Clarke, of Eastbourne; 1 da (Alessandra Mary b 24 Aug 1978), 1 s (Piers Richard b 25 Oct 1979); *Heir* s, Hon Piers Legh; *Career* slr, gen cmmr of Income Tax 1983–; cncllr Wealden DC 1987–99; memb Sussex Downs Cons Bd 1992–95 and 1997–98; *Style*— The Rt Hon the Lord Newton; ✉ Laughton Park Farm, Laughton, Lewes, East Sussex BN8 6BU (tel 01825 840627, fax 01825 841048)

NEWTON, Rodney Stephen; s of Amos Bernard Newton (d 1981), of Birmingham, and Winifred Nellie, *née* York (d 1999); *b* 31 July 1945; *Educ* King's Heath HS Birmingham, Lordwood Boys' Sch Birmingham, Birmingham Sch of Music; *m* 19 Sept 1970 (m dis 1999), Jennifer Kathleen, da of Denis Williams, of Halesowen, Worcs; 2 s (Matthew b 15 Sept 1977, Christopher b 24 April 1980); *Career* orchestral timpanist, percussionist, composer, arranger, conductor, music publisher, lectr and writer 1967–; BBC trg orchestra 1967–70, ENO orchestra 1974–85, promotion mangr United Music Publishers 1979–82, music conslt London Int Film Sch 1988–, princ lectr in film music composition London Coll of Music 1997–2000 (lectr in composition and orchestration 1995–97), visiting lectr in film music Royal Acad of Music 1995–98; co-ordinator of light music Williams Fairey Band 1997–2004, composer-in-residence 2004–05; music assoc Cory Band 2004–; features ed British Bandsman magazine 2001–; gen ed Prima Vista Musikk 2006–; compositions in: 12 symphonies, 5 string quartets, flute concerto, tuba concerto, music for brass band, wind band, chamber and vocal works; film and TV scores incl: The Pyrates, The Watch House (BBC TV), Lucinda Lambton's A-Z of Britain (BBC TV), Theatre of Paint (BEU Prodns), Change at Clapham Junction (Thames TV); commercial recordings incl: Variations for Percussion, Four Spanish Impressions, Capriccio, Heroes and Warriors, Five Greek Sketches, Seascapes, Phantasm, Prince Bishops, The Defenders, Dick Turpin's Ride to York, The King of Elfland's Daughter; memb: Br Acad of Composers and Songwriters, Wagner Soc, Knights of St Columba; hon memb Birmingham Conservatoire 1996; *Recreations* reading, cinema, eating out; *Style*— Rodney Newton; ✉ c/o London Film School, 24 Shelton Street, London WC2H 9HP (fax 020 7497 3718, e-mail film.school@lfs.org.uk)

NEWTON, Stewart Worth; *b* 31 October 1941; *m* Jannion; 3 da (Catherine, Antonia, Lucy); *Career* investment mgmnt; formerly with: Touche Ross Chartered Accountants, W Greenwell stockbrokers, Ivory & Sime plc; fndr Newton Investment Management, ret 2002; chm The Real Return Holding Co Ltd 2003–; non-exec dir: HSBC Holdings plc 2002–, Flying Brands Ltd 2006–; memb: Investment Ctee Wellcome Tst, Xfi Advsy Bd Univ of Exeter, Advsy Bd East Asia Inst Univ of Cambridge, Cambridge Investment Bd 2006; FCA; *Style*— Stewart Newton, Esq

NEWTON, Sir (Charles) Wilfrid; kt (1993), CBE (1988); s of Gore Mansfield Newton (d 1966), of Durban, South Africa, and Catherine, *née* Knox Darcus (d 1972); *b* 11 December 1928; *Educ* Highlands N HS Johannesburg, Univ of the Witwatersrand (Cert Theory of Accountancy); *m* 6 Feb 1954, Felicity Mary Lynn, da of John Lynn Thomas (d 1973), of Johannesburg, South Africa; 2 s (Gavin b 1957, Thomas b 1964), 2 da (Tessa (Mrs Newton) b 1958, Glynis (Mrs Murphy) b 1960); *Career* Samuel Thomson & Young Chartered Accountants South Africa 1947–55; Mobil Oil Corporation: territory accounting and fin mangr South Africa 1955–62, controller Mobil Sekiyu KK Tokyo 1962–63, fin mangr and dep gen mangr E Africa Nairobi 1963–65, fin dir Mobil Sekiyu KK Tokyo and chief fin offr Mobil interests Japan 1965–68; Turner and Newall: fin dir 1968, md of fin and planning 1974, md of plastics, chemicals and mining 1976, gp md 1979, chief exec 1982–83; chm: Mass Transit Railway Corp Hong Kong 1983–89, London Regional Transport 1989–94, London Underground Ltd 1989–94, Raglan Properties plc 1994–99, Jacobs Hldgs plc 1994–2001, Mount City Hldgs Ltd 1994–, G Maunsell International Ltd 1996–99; non-exec dir: Hongkong Bank 1986–92, HSBC Hldgs plc 1990–99, Midland Bank plc 1992–99, Sketchley plc 1991–99; memb Transvaal Soc of Accountants 1956, memb Pres's Ctee CBI 1990–94; Freeman City of London, memb Worshipful Co of Horners; fndr memb Inst of Chartered Accountants of South Africa 1979, CCIM 1974, fell Hong Kong Mgmnt Assoc 1987, hon fell Hong Kong Inst of Engrs 1994; FCIT 1989, FRSA 1990, Hon FREng 1993; *Recreations* sailing, reading, current affairs, economics; *Clubs* Wanderers' (Johannesburg), Carlton, Hong Kong, Royal Hong Kong Yacht, Aberdeen Boat, Royal Lymington Yacht; *Style*— Sir Wilfrid Newton, CBE, Hon FREng; ✉ Newtons Gate, 12 Ramley Road, Pennington, Lymington, Hampshire SO41 8GQ (tel 01590 679750, fax 01590 677990, e-mail wandfnewton@btinternet.com)

NEWTON DUNN, William Francis (Bill); MEP (Lib Dem) East Midlands; s of Lt-Col Owen Frank Newton Dunn, OBE (d 1995), and Barbara Mary, *née* Brooke (d 1995); *b* 3 October 1941; *Educ* Marlborough, Gonville & Caius Cambridge (MA), INSEAD Business Sch Fontainebleau (MBA); *m* 17 Oct 1970, Anna Terez Arki; 1 s (Thomas b 1973), 1 da (Daisy b 1976); *Career* MEP: (Cons) Lincolnshire 1979–94, (Cons) E Midlands 1999–2000, (Lib Dem) E Midlands 2000–; chm and jt ldr Cons MEPs 1993–94 (dep ldr 1991–93), chm Lib Dem MEPs 2002–; formerly with Fisons Fertilisers; *Books* Greater in Europe (1986), Big Wing (1992), The Man Who Was John Bull (1996), The Devil Knew Not (2000), Europe Needs an FBI (2004); *Style*— Bill Newton Dunn, Esq, MEP; ✉ 10 Church Lane, Navenby, Lincoln LN5 0EG (tel 01522 810812, e-mail bill.newtondunn@europarl.europa.eu,website www.newton-dunn.com)

NEWTON OF BRAINTREE, Baron (Life Peer UK 1997), of Coggeshall in the County of Essex; Rt Hon Antony Harold (Tony) Newton; PC (1988), OBE (1972); s of Harold Newton, of Dovercourt, Harwich; *b* 29 August 1937; *Educ* Friends' Sch Saffron Walden, Trinity Coll Oxford; *m* 1, 1962 (m dis 1986), Janet Dianne, er da of Phillip Huxley, of Sidcup; 2 da; m 2, 1986, Mrs Patricia Gilthorpe; 1 step s, 2 step da; *Career* pres Oxford Univ Cons Assoc 1958, pres Oxford Union 1959, sometime vice-chm Fedn of Univ Cons and Unionist Assocs; economist, former sec and res sec Bow Gp, asst dir CRD 1970–74 (head Econ Section 1965–70); Parly candidate (Cons) Sheffield Brightside 1970, MP (Cons) Braintree Feb 1974–97, asst govt whip 1979–81, a Lord Cmmr of the Treasy (govt whip) 1981–82, Parly under sec DHSS 1982, min for the disabled 1983–84, min for social security and the disabled 1984–86, min for health 1986–88, Chllr of the Duchy of Lancaster and min for trade and indust 1988–89, sec of state for social security DSS 1989–92, Lord Pres of the Cncl and ldr of the House of Commons 1992–97; chm NE Essex Mental Health NHS Tst 1997–; dir of professional standards IOD 1998–; *Style*— The Rt Hon Lord Newton of Braintree, OBE; ✉ House of Lords, London SW1A 0PW

NEYROUD, Peter William; QPM (2004); s of John Arthur Lucien Neyroud, of Winchester, Hants, and Penelope Mary Anne, *née* Edwards; *b* 12 August 1959; *Educ* Winchester, Oriel Coll Oxford (MA), Univ of Portsmouth (MSc), Wolfson Coll Cambridge (Dip Applied Criminology); *m* 16 Aug 1986, Sarah, *née* Longman; 2 s, 2 da; *Career* Police Constable rising to Detective Supt then dir of intelligence Hampshire Constabulary 1980–97; West Mercia Constabulary: Asst Chief Constable (Support) 1998–2000, Asst Chief Constable (Territorial Policing) 2000, Dep Chief Constable 2000–02; Chief Constable Thames Valley Police 2002–05, chief exec Nat Policing Improvement Agency 2006–; ACPO: memb 1998, portfolio holder Police Use of Firearms 2000–02, former vice-chm Human Rights Ctee, lead on Criminal Justice 2000–04, vice-pres 2004–06; memb: Cncl Justice 1997–2006, Sentencing Guideline Cncl 2004; ind reviewer Parole Bd 2006–; Home Office Police Research Award for Multi-Agency Approaches to Racial Harassment 1990, Gary P Hayes Award US Police Executive Research Forum 2004; FRSA 2000; *Publications* Policing, Ethics and Human Rights (2001), Public Participation in Policing (2001), Police Ethics for the 21st Century (in The Handbook of Policing, 2003); *Recreations* running, writing, gardening and reading; *Style*— Peter Neyroud, Esq, QPM

NG, Dr Weng Cheong; s of Kam Sooi Ng, and Ng-Sung Ngan-Lui; *b* 18 September 1943; *Educ* Methodist Boys' Sch Penang, Univ of Singapore (MB BS), Royal Coll of Physicians and Surgeons (DPath), Univ of London (DCP), Univ of Mahidol (DTM&H); *m* 25 Sept 1971, Chew Pek Choo, da of Chew Poh Leang; 1 s (Paul b 4 Jan 1979); *Career* MO: Rural Health Trg Sch Jitra Malaysia 1970–71, Inst of Med Res Kuala Lumpur Malaysia 1971–75; registrar Gen Infirmary Salisbury 1978; sr registrar: Southampton and Poole Gen Hosps 1978–80, Pathology Dept Singapore 1981–83; conslt histopathologist Princess Margaret Hosp Swindon 1983–; memb: Assoc of Clinical Pathologists, Br Soc of Clinical Cytology, BMA; MRCPath 1979, FCAP 1982, FRCPath 1991; *Recreations* chess, music, swimming; *Style*— Dr Weng Cheong Ng; ✉ Pathology Department, Princess Margaret Hospital, Okus Road, Swindon, Wiltshire SN1 4JU (tel 01793 426336)

NIBLETT, His Hon Judge Anthony Ian; s of Albert William Niblett (d 2001), and Jessie Alma, *née* McMickan; *b* 11 June 1954; *Educ* Varndean GS Brighton, Univ of Birmingham (LLB), Coll of Law; *m* 12 Oct 1991, Valerie Ann, da of Robert Ranger; 1 da, 1 s; *Career* called to the Bar Inner Temple 1976, in practice SE Circuit 1977–2002, recorder 1998–2002 (asst recorder 1993–98), circuit judge (SE Circuit) 2002–; memb: SE Area Legal Aid Ctee 1988–2002, Professional Conduct Ctee Bar Cncl 1993–97, SE Circuit Ctee 1995–98 and 2000–02; jr Sussex Bar Mess 1986–95, govr Varndean Coll Brighton 1997–2003; *Recreations* travel, history, gardening; *Clubs* Travellers; *Style*— His Hon Judge Niblett; ✉ The Law Courts, High Street, Lewes, East Sussex BN7 1YB

NICE, Sir Geoffrey; kt (2007), QC (1990); s of William Charles Nice (d 1992), and Mahala Anne, *née* Tarryer (d 1982); *b* 21 October 1945; *Educ* St Dunstan's Coll Catford, Keble Coll Oxford; *m* 1974, Philippa, da of Kemlo Abbot Cronin Gross, OBE; 3 da (Amelia b 1975, Tabitha b 1976, Mahalah b 1980); *Career* barr; recorder Crown Court 1987–; memb Criminal Injuries Compensation Bd 1995–2001; bencher Inner Temple 1996, sr trial attorney Int Criminal Tbnl for the former Yugoslavia 1998–2001, princ trial attorney Milosevic Trial 2002–06; memb Bd Indict 2001–04; Parly candidate (SDP/Lib Alliance) Dover 1983 and 1987; *Clubs* Reform; *Style*— Sir Geoffrey Nice, QC; ✉ 1 Temple Gardens, Temple, London EC4Y 9BB (tel 020 7583 1315)

NICHOL, David Brett; s of Philip George Nichol (d 1974), of Gullane, E Lothian, and Kathleen, *née* Brett (d 2000); *b* 20 April 1945; *Educ* Sedbergh; *m* 22 July 1977, Judith Mary, da of Godfrey Arthur Parker (d 1966), of Godalming, Surrey; 4 da (Alexandra b 1979, Tessa b 1981, Leonie b 1982, Flora b 1986); *Career* CA; Deloitte & Co 1962–68, County Bank London 1968–70, Martin Corpn Australia 1970–71, W I Carr Hong Kong 1971–72, dir Ivory & Sime plc 1972–92, md Ivory & Sime Asia Ltd 1989–91, ptnr Rossie House Investment Management 1992–; chm Pacific Assets Trust plc 2004– (non-exec dir 1985); tstee Royal Botanic Gdns Edinburgh 1986–89; FCA; *Recreations* shooting, skiing, golf; *Clubs* New (Edinburgh), R&A, Hon Co of Edinburgh Golfers, Shek-o (Hong Kong); *Style*— David Nichol, Esq; ✉ Rossie House Investment Management, Forgandenny, Perth PH2 9EH (tel 01738 813223, fax 01738 813256, e-mail davidnichol@rossiehouse.com)

NICHOL, Prof Sir Duncan Kirkbride; kt (1993), CBE (1989); s of James Nichol (d 1989), and Mabel Nichol (d 1984); *b* 30 May 1941; *Educ* Bradford GS, Univ of St Andrews (MA); *m* 18 March 1972, Elizabeth Elliott Mitchell, da of Herbert Wilkinson (d 1967), of Blackpool; 1 s (Andrew b 1973), 1 da (Rachael b 1977); *Career* hosp sec Manchester Royal Infirmary 1969–73, dep gp sec and acting gp sec Univ Hosp Mgmnt Ctee of S Manchester 1973–74, dist admin S Manchester Dist 1974–77, area admin Salford DHA 1977–81, regnl gen mangr Mersey RHA 1984–89 (regnl admin 1981–84), ceo NHS Mgmnt Exec 1989–94; prof and dir Health Servs Mgmnt Unit Victoria Univ of Manchester 1995–98; chm: Clinical Pathology Accreditation 2000–, Primary Insurance Gp 2001–; non-exec dir: BUPA 1994–, Correctional Services Strategy Bd 2000–06; cmmr for judicial appts 2001–06, chm Parole Bd for Eng and Wales 2004–, chm QC Selection Panel 2005–; memb Central Health Servs Cncl 1980–81, pres IMSM 1984–85, chm Kings Fund Educn Ctee 1991–94, govr Henley Mgmnt Coll 1993–98; Hon DLitt Univ of Salford 1991; CIMgt

N

1988, FHSM 1990; *Recreations* golf, walking; *Style—* Prof Sir Duncan Nichol, CBE; ✉ 1 Pipers Close, Heswell, Wirral, Merseyside CH60 9LJ (tel 0151 342 2699)

NICHOL, Ian James; s of Thomas Nichol (d 1989), and Joan Lena May, *née* Lambourne (d 2005); *b* 20 December 1954, Kingston upon Thames, Surrey; *Educ* Tiffin Boys Sch Kingston upon Thames, Solihull Sch, Queens' Coll Cambridge (scholar, MA, Penny White prize); *m* 16 March 1996, Valerie Mary, *née* Piper; *Career* various accountancy and tax appts 1977–88, ptnr Touche Ross & Co 1988–92, ptnr and head of profit-related pay practice PricewaterhouseCoopers (formerly Coopers & Lybrand) 1992–2001, princ Ian Nichol Training 2001–; cmmr Criminal Cases Review Cmmn 2003–, cmmr Press Complaints Cmmn 2006–; tstee and memb Cncl Assoc of Taxation Technicians 2002–04; memb: ICAEW 1980, Chartered Inst of Taxation 1981; *Publications* Employment Tax Essentials (contributing ed, 2001–03), Tax Planning for Family and Owner-Managed Companies (co-author, 2002); *Recreations* food, wine and spirits, avoiding exercise, public speaking; *Style—* Ian Nichol; ✉ The Criminal Cases Review Commission, Alpha Tower, Suffolk Street Queensway, Birmingham B1 1TT (tel 0121 633 1800, fax 0121 633 1823, mobile 07971 862180, e-mail ijnichol@btinternet.com)

NICHOLAS, Mark Charles Jefford; s of Peter Jefford Nicholas (d 1968), and Anne Evelyn (stage name Loxley, m Brian Widlake, TV and radio presenter incl Money Programme and World at One); *b* 29 September 1959; *Educ* Bradfield Coll; *Career* professional cricketer Hampshire CCC 1977–95: debut 1978, awarded county cap 1982, capt 1984–95; honours: winner John Player Sunday League 1986, winner Benson & Hedges Cup 1988 and 1992, winner NatWest Trophy 1992; capt: 4 unofficial Test matches v Sri Lanka 1986, 3 unofficial Test matches v Zimbabwe 1990, 10 unofficial one day Ints, England under 25 v NZ 1986, England Counties tour Zimbabwe 1985, MCC v Aust 1985 (scored 115 not out); Advtg Dept The Observer 1980, PR conslt Hill & Knowlton (UK) Ltd 1987–88, publisher various cricket magazines, TV and radio commentator, journalist Daily Telegraph, presenter and commentator Sky TV until 1999, presenter and commentator Channel 4 1999–; RTS Sports Presenter of the Year 2000; host Survivor (ITV, series) 2002, co-host Richard and Judy (Granada TV) 2003; *Recreations* music, theatre, golf (golf handicap 6, caddie Euro tour 1992), food and wine; *Style—* Mark Nicholas, Esq; ✉ c/o The Daily Telegraph, 1 Canada Square, Canary Wharf, London E14 5DT

NICHOLAS, Dr Michael Bernard; s of Bernard Victor Herbert Nicholas (d 1975), and Dorothy, *née* Gilfillan (d 2001); *b* 31 August 1938; *Educ* City of London Sch, Trinity Coll of Music (jr exhibitioner), Jesus Coll Oxford (organ scholar, MA); *m* 1975, Heather Grant, *née* Rowdon; 2 s (Mark Alexander, Benjamin William (twins) b 1976); *Career* organist and choirmaster Louth Parish Church Lincs 1960–64, organist and choirmaster St Matthew's Church Northampton 1965–71, organist and master of the choristers Norwich Cathedral 1971–94, chief exec Royal Coll of Organists 1994–97; dir of music: King Edward VI GS Lincs 1960–64, Northampton GS 1965–71; pt/t lectr in music UEA 1971–94, organist and dir of music All Saints' Church Blackheath 1995–99, currently dir of music St Mary-le-Tower Ipswich; conductor: Louth Choral and Orchestral Soc 1960–64, Northampton Bach Choir and Orch 1965–71, St Matthew's Singers 1965–71, Norwich Philharmonic Chorus 1972–94, Allegri Singers 1994–2000; organist emeritus Norwich Cathedral 1995; a vice-pres: The Organ Club, Church Music Soc; memb: Cncl RSCM 1978–87, Cncl RCO 1980–94 and 1998–2004, Cncl Guild of Church Musicians; Hon DMus UEA 1995; FRCO 1958 (CHM (Choirmaster) 1964), Hon FGCM 1995; *Music Publications* Sightsinging (RSCM, 1966), From the Rising of the Sun (Elkin 1979), Versicles and Responses (Novello, 1988), various choral pieces and arrangements; *Recreations* bridge, walking, reading, wine; *Clubs* Athenaeum, Ipswich and Suffolk; *Style—* Dr Michael Nicholas; ✉ Cansell Grove Farmhouse, Poy Street Green, Rattlesden, Bury St Edmunds, Suffolk IP30 0SR

NICHOLAS, Paul Denzil; s of Walter Denzil Nicholas, of Herts, and Eileen, *née* Whelan (d 2002); *b* 24 April 1946, London; *Educ* Mill Hill Sch, Emmanuel Coll Cambridge (BA, LLB); *m* 1970, Elsa Marion, da of Ian Dashwood Moir; 1 s (Harry Denzil b 1976), 1 da (Elisabeth Anne b 1979); *Career* admitted slr 1970; Reynolds Porter Chamberlain (formerly Reynolds Porter): articled 1968–70, asst slr 1970–72, ptnr 1972–, sr ptnr 2004–; non-exec dir: Brit Syndicates Ltd, Brit Insurance Ltd; govr Lockers Park Sch Tst Ltd 1989–, tstee SW Herts Hospice Charitable Tst 1990–; *Recreations* golf; *Clubs* Ashridge Golf, Old Millhillians; *Style—* Paul Nicholas, Esq; ✉ Reynolds Porter Chamberlain, Chichester House, 278–282 High Holborn, London WC1V 7HA (tel 020 7242 2877, fax 020 7242 1431)

NICHOLAS, Peter William; s of Stanley Watkin Nicholas (d 1988), and Martha Elizabeth, *née* Griffiths (d 1985); *b* 5 July 1934; *Educ* Ebbw Vale County GS, Cardiff Coll of Art (NDD), RCA; *m* 1, Marjorie, *née* Nash (decd); 1 s (Saul), 2 da (Ruth and Rachel); m 2, Ann, *née* Maine; 1 s (Reuben); *Career* sculptor and academic; Nat Serv 1956–58; lectr in sculpture and drawing studies Newport Art Sch Gwent 1963, head of Fndn Studies at Newport until 1980, head of sch Faculty of Art and Design at Swansea until 1988; lectured in West Virginia 1992; assoc lectr UCW Swansea 1997; *Selected Exhibitions* Woodlands Gall London 1992, Sculpture Int touring exhbn 1993, Pangolin Gall Gloucestershire 1994, Wales Art Fair Cardiff 1995, The Albany Gall Cardif 1996, Chelsea Art Fair London 1997, Art '97 London 1997, Compton Cassey Gall Gloucestershire 1998, Watercolur Soc of Wales Penarth 1998, Wales Drawing Biennale '99 touring exhbn 1999, Newport Museum and Art Gall 1999, Sculpture Bretagne in Brittany France and Wales 2000; commissions incl: Guto The Running Man 1991, Mari Llwyd 1992, Mother Sea 1993, water sculpture for Aberystwyth 1997, meml sculpture to Eddie Thomas 1998, The Manvers Book 1998, Giant and Child bronze 1999–2000, cmmn for the Celtic Manor Resort 2001, public sculpture Weston-super-Mare 2002, portrait bronze of John Charles, CBE, commemorative medal for Dylan Thomas 2003, cmmn bronze meml to Ivor Novello (Cardiff Bay) 2006, numerous carvings; work incl in collections in UK, Europe and USA; dir Sculpture at Margam, fndr memb Welsh Sculpture Tst (now Art Works Wales); memb Watercolour Soc of Wales 1996; FRBS 1993, ARCA; *Style—* Peter Nicholas, Esq; ✉ Craig-y-Don, Horton, Gower, Swansea SA3 1LB (tel 01792 390511, e-mail peter.nicholas@yahoo.co.uk); c/o Jonathan Poole, Compton Cassey Galleries, Cassey Compton House, Cassey Compton, Withington, Cheltenham, Gloucestershire GL54 4DE

NICHOLL, His Hon Anthony John David; s of Brig David William Dillwyn Nicholl (d 1972), and P M Nicholl, *née* Dunne (d 1975); *b* 3 May 1935; *Educ* Eton, Pembroke Coll Oxford, Wycliffe Hall Oxford (Dip); *m* 1961, Hermione Mary, da of William Harcourt Palmer Landon (d 1978) and Enid Landon, *née* Robertson (d 1998); 1 s (William b 19 May 1962), 2 da (Charlotte b 30 Oct 1963, Lucy b 4 June 1967); *Career* called to the Bar Lincoln's Inn 1958; in practice London 1958–61 and Birmingham 1961–88, head of chambers 1976–87, recorder Crown Court 1978–88, chm Fountain Court Chambers Birmingham 1984–88, circuit judge (Midland & Oxford Circuit) 1988–2003; reader Diocese of Coventry 2003–; *Recreations* history, theology, walking, listening to music, motoring; *Style—* His Hon Anthony Nicholl; ✉ Black Martin Farm, Ettington, Stratford-on-Avon, Warwickshire CV37 7PB

NICHOLLS, Dr Christine Stephanie; da of Christopher James Metcalfe (d 1986), of Mombasa, Kenya, and Olive, *née* Kennedy (d 1982); *b* 23 January 1943; *Educ* Kenya HS, Lady Margaret Hall Oxford (MA), St Antony's Coll Oxford (DPhil); *m* 12 March 1966, Anthony James Nicholls, s of Ernest Alfred Nicholls (d 1981), of Carshalton, Surrey; 1 s (Alexander b 1970), 2 da (Caroline b 1972, Isabel b 1974); *Career* Henry Charles Chapman res fell Inst of Cwlth Studies Univ of London 1968–69, freelance writer BBC 1970–74; *Books* The Swahili Coast (1971), Cataract (with Philip Awdry, 1985), Dictionary of National Biography (jt ed 1977, ed twentieth century supplements 1989–95), Power - A Political History of the Twentieth Century (1990), Missing Persons (1993), Hutchinson Encyclopaedia of Biography (ed, 1996), David Livingstone (1998), A History of St Antony's College Oxford 1950–2000 (2000), Elspeth Huxley (2002), Red Strangers: The White Tribe of Kenya (2005); *Recreations* reading novels, playing the flute; *Style—* Dr Christine Nicholls; ✉ 27 Davenant Road, Oxford OX2 8BU (tel 01865 511320, e-mail christine.nicholls@lineone.net)

NICHOLLS, Clive Victor; QC (1982); s of Alfred Charles Victor Nicholls, and Lilian Mary, *née* May; *b* 29 August 1932; *Educ* Brighton Coll, TCD (MA, LLB), Sidney Sussex Coll Cambridge (BA, LLM); *m* 23 July 1960, Alison Virginia, da of late Leonard Arthur Oliver; 3 s (Jeremy Oliver b 1962, James Colin Oliver b 1967, John Patrick Oliver b 1969), 3 da (Jacqueline Alison b 1963, Judie Victoria b 1965, Jill Caroline b 1965); *Career* called to the Bar Gray's Inn 1957 (bencher 1989); recorder of the Crown Court 1984–98, head of chambers; barr Supreme Court of the Australian Capital Territory 1991; tstee and former chm Bob Champion Cancer Tst; patron Multiple Birth Assoc; *Publications* The Law of Extradition and Mutual Assistance (co-author, 2002); *Recreations* sailing, fly fishing; *Style—* Clive Nicholls, Esq, QC; ✉ 3 Raymond Buildings, Gray's Inn, London WC1R 5BH (tel 020 7400 6400, fax 020 7400 6464)

NICHOLLS, Colin Alfred Arthur; QC (1981); s of Alfred Charles Victor Nicholls (d 1987), and Lilian Mary, *née* May (d 1990); *b* 29 August 1932; *Educ* Brighton Coll, Univ of Dublin (MA, LLB); *m* 23 Oct 1976, Clarissa Allison Spenlove, da of Clive Dixon (d 1976); 2 s (Benjamin Clive b 30 Aug 1977, Jonathan Charles b 6 Jan 1979); *Career* called to the Bar Gray's Inn (Albion Richardson Award) 1957 (bencher 1989); recorder of the Crown Ct 1983–99; pres Cwlth Lawyers' Assoc 2003–05 (vice-pres 1985–96, hon treas 1997–2003, hon sec 1999–2003); tstee Cwlth Human Rights Initiative 1998–2007, tstee Cwlth Law Conf Fndn 2003–07; patron Multiple Births Fndn, govr Fedn of Br Artists 2001–; hon memb Historical Soc TCD 1958– (auditor 1956); fell Soc of Advanced Legal Studies; *Publications* Corruption and the Misuse of Public Office (jtly, 2006); *Recreations* painting (exhibitor RHA, ROI); *Clubs* Garrick, Royal Cwlth Soc; *Style—* Colin Nicholls, Esq, QC; ✉ 3 Raymond Buildings, Gray's Inn, London WC1R 5BH (tel 020 7400 6400, fax 020 7400 6464)

NICHOLLS, David Alan; CB (1989), CMG (1984); s of Thomas Edward Nicholls (d 1971), and Beatrice Winifred Nicholls (d 1992); *Educ* Cheshunt GS, St John's Coll Cambridge (MA); *m* 1955, Margaret; 2 da (Amanda, Camilla); *Career* entered Home Civil Serv 1954; asst sec MOD 1969–75, Cabinet Office 1975–77, under sec MOD 1977–80, asst sec-gen NATO 1980–84, dep under sec MOD 1984–90; defence conslt; visiting fell Magdalene Coll Cambridge 1989–90, sr Pol-Mil assoc Inst for Foreign Policy Analysis 1990–; memb Visiting Ctee Royal Coll of Art 1991–93; hon sr lectr Univ of Birmingham 1992–2000; assoc fell RIIA 1990–92, memb Cncl London C of C and Indust 1994–2005; chm Soc for Italic Handwriting 1995–96; *Recreations* sketching; *Clubs* Nat Lib; *Style—* David Nicholls, Esq, CB, CMG; ✉ c/o HSBC Bank, Church Stretton, Shropshire SY6 6BT

NICHOLLS, David Andrew; s of Gordon Robert Nicholls (d 1973), of Deal, Kent, and Maureen Rachel, *née* Waddon (d 2004); *b* 15 January 1957; *Educ* Walmer Secdy Sch Deal, Thanet Tech Coll Broadstairs, Westminster Coll London (City and Guilds); *Children* 2 s (Daniel Gordon Charles b March 1985, Dean Stephen Robert b Oct 1989); *Career* chef de partie Waldorf Hotel London 1975–76, successively chef tournant, saucier then gardemanger Dorchester Hotel London 1976–79, chef saucier then sous chef Hotel Intercontinental London 1979–81, chef/dir The Old Lodge Restaurant Limpsfield Surrey 1981–83, head chef Waltons Restaurant London 1983–86; exec chef: Britannia Intercontinental Hotel London 1986–89, Royal Garden Hotel London 1989–92; exec head chef Ritz Hotel London 1992–98, exec chef and dir of food & beverage Mandarin Oriental Hyde Park Hotel 1998–; memb: British Div Toques Blance, Guild de Fromagers France; hon memb Chain de Rotisseurs; chm: Académie Culinaire de France Grande Bretagne (Affiliates), Exec Chefs Worldwide Soc (UK Div); chm and fndr Nicholls Spinal Injury Fndn 2005; *Recreations* golf, squash, gardening; *Style—* David Nicholls, Esq; ✉ Mandarin Oriental Hyde Park Hotel, 66 Knightsbridge, London SW1X 7LA (tel 020 7235 2000, fax 020 7201 3811, e-mail dnicholl@mohg.com)

NICHOLLS, Prof (Ralph) John; s of Clifton Wilson Nicholls (d 1991), and Muriel Morten, *née* Heathcote; *b* 20 May 1943, Wilby, Northants; *Educ* Felsted, Gonville & Caius Coll Cambridge (BA), London Hosp Med Sch (scholar), Univ of Cambridge (MB BChir, MChir); *m* 1966, Stella Mary; 4 c (b 1967, 1969, 1972 and 1977); *Career* The London Hosp: lectr in surgery Surgical Unit 1972, sr registrar 1974–76; clinical asst Chirurgische Universitatsklinik Heidelberg (Alexander von Humboldt fell) 1976–77, resident surgical offr St Mark's Hosp 1978, conslt surgn St Mark's Hosp and sr lectr (ICRF) St Bartholomew's Hosp 1978–82, conslt surgn St Thomas' Hosp 1982–93; currently: visiting prof of colorectal surgery Imperial Coll London, emeritus conslt surgn St Mark's Hosp, civilian advsr in surgery RAF, conslt Policlinico di Monza Italy; past pres Section of Coloproctology RSM, past pres Assoc of Coloproctology of GB and I, pres Euro Assoc of Coloproctology, sec Euro Bd of Coloproctology; memb: Br Soc of Gastroenterology, Swiss Soc for Gastroenterology; past memb Specialist Advsy Ctee in Gen Surgery; ed Colorectal Disease; memb Academie Nationale de Chirugie; hon memb: French Soc of Proctology, Chilean Soc of Surgery, Spanish Soc of Surgery, Italian Soc of Colorectal Surgery, Assoc Française de Chirurgie, hon fell Brasilian Coll of Surgns, Hon FRCSEd, Hon FRCSGlas, FRCS (Halett prize); *Books* Colorectal Disease: An Introduction for Surgeons and Physicians (jt ed, 1981), Coloproctology: Diagnosis and Outpatient Management (with R E Glass, 1985), Restorative Proctocolectomy (ed with N J McC Mortensen and D C C Bartolo, 1993), Colon and Rectal Surgery (ed with R R Dozois, 1997); contrib various book chapters and author of numerous pubns in learned jls; *Recreations* history, languages, walking, music; *Clubs* Athenaeum, St Alban's; *Style—* Prof John Nicholls; ✉ 149 Harley Street, London W1G 6DE (tel 020 7935 0924, e-mail j.nicholls@thelondonclinic.co.uk)

NICHOLLS, Prof John Graham; s of late Dr Nicolai Nicholls, and Charlotte, *née* Kaphan (d 1994); *b* 19 December 1929; *Educ* Berkhamsted Sch, KCL (BSc), UCL (PhD), Charing Cross Hosp (MB BS); *m* 22 Oct 1988, Nancy Venable; 2 s (Julian b 11 May 1964, Stephen b 7 June 1966); *Career* house offr Casualty and Radiotherapy Charing Cross Hosp 1956–57, Beit meml fell UCL 1957–60, departmental demonstrator Dept of Physiology Oxford 1960–62, assoc prof of physiology Yale Med Sch 1965–68, assoc prof of neurobiology Harvard Med Sch 1968–73 (res assoc 1962–65), prof of neurobiology Stanford Med Sch 1973–83, prof of pharmacology Biocenter 1983, currently visiting prof Int Sch for Advanced Studies Trieste; FRS 1988; *Books* The Search for Connexions (1987), From Neuron to Brain (3 edn with A R Martin and B G Wallace, 1992); *Recreations* music, literature, S American history; *Clubs* Athenaeum; *Style—* Prof John Nicholls, FRS

NICHOLLS, Rt Rev John (Jack); *see:* Sheffield, Bishop of

NICHOLLS, Jonathan Clive; s of David and Jill Nicholls; *b* 27 October 1957; *Educ* Uppingham, Univ of Manchester (BA Economics and Accountancy), Harvard Business Sch (PMD); *Career* auditor Peat Marwick Mitchell & Co 1979–83, chief accountant P S Refson & Co (merchant bank) 1983–85; Abbey National Building Society: mangr Fin Servs 1985–86, commercial mangr Business Devpt 1987–88; dir Corp Fin and Capital Markets Abbey National Treasury Services plc 1988–94, dir and dep chief exec Abbey National Treasury Services plc and dep treas Abbey National plc 1994–96, finance dir Hanson plc 1998–2006 (treas 1996–98), finance dir Old Mutual plc 2006–; non-exec dir

Man Gp plc 2004–; ACA 1982, FCT 1989; *Recreations* sailing, skiing, cycling, travel, food and wine, opera; *Style*— Jonathan Nicholls, Esq

NICHOLLS, Mark Patrick; s of Patrick Nicholls, and Patricia, *née* Dickson; *b* 5 May 1949, Gloucester; *Educ* Oundle, Christ's Coll Cambridge; *m* 8 July 1978, Catherine, *née* Betts; 5 c; *Career* admitted slr 1974; Linklaters 1972–76, dir and head corp fin SG Warburg Gp plc 1976–96, chief exec private equity gp Royal Bank of Scotland 1996–2003, dep chm Venture Production plc 2004–, chm EcoSecurities Gp plc 2005–; non-exec dir: City of London Investment Tst plc 1997–, Bovis Homes Gp plc until 2007, Alexander Forbes Ltd (South Africa), Portman Building Soc; chm St Mary's Paddington Charitable Tst, protector Nat Lottery Fair Share Fund; *Recreations* golf, tennis; *Style*— Mark Nicholls, Esq

NICHOLLS, Robert Michael (Bob); CBE (1995); s of Herbert Edgar Nicholls (d 1977), and Bennetta L'Estrange, *née* Burges (d 2002); *b* 28 July 1939; *Educ* Hampton Sch, UCW (BA, treas Students' Union, dep ldr expedition to Kurdistan), Univ of Manchester (DSA); *m* 9 Dec 1961, Dr Deirin Deirdre O'Sullivan, da of Dr Frank O'Sullivan (d 1955); 4 s (Kevin Paul b 1965, Clive Ranulf John b 1967, Liam Dougal b 1969, Alec Eoin b 1971); *Career* house govr St Stephen's Hosp Chelsea 1966–68, asst clerk of the govrs St Thomas' Hosp 1968–72, dep gp sec Southampton Univ Hosp Mgmnt Ctee 1972–74, dist admin Southampton and SW Hants Health Dist 1974–77, area admin Newcastle Area HA 1977–81, regnl admin S Western Regnl HA 1981–85, dist gen mangr Southmead Health Dist 1985–88, chief exec Oxford Regnl HA 1988–93, seconded as exec dir London Implementation Gp NHS Mgmnt Exec 1993–96, health mgmnt conslt 1996–2004, chm Nat Clinical Assessment Authy 2003–05, NHS regnl appts cmmr for London 2005–; health assoc conslt Br Cncl 1997–2005; non-exec dir Nestor Healthcare 1997–2003 (sr non-exec dir 2001–03); memb: Inst of Health Serv Mangrs (former memb Cncl, nat pres 1983–84), King's Fund Educn Ctee 1974–79, Health Educn Cncl 1984–87, Calman Ctee on Med Trg 1993, GMC 1996–2005 (chair Preliminary Proceedings Ctee 1999–2003), Clinical Advsy Bd Oxford Univ Med Sch 2001–; assoc fell Templeton Coll Oxford 1996–2001; FHSM 1993 (AHSM 1965); *Books* Resources in Medicine (contrib, 1970), Working with People (contrib, 1983), Rationing of Health Care in Medicine (contrib, 1993), Doctors in Society (contrib, 2005); *Recreations* cricket, golf, walking, bird watching, opera, jazz; *Clubs* Lensbury, Studley Wood Golf; *Style*— Bob Nicholls, Esq, CBE; ✉ Maple Lodge, 62A Queens Road, Thame OX9 3NQ (tel 01844 261748, e-mail rmnicholls@btinternet.com)

NICHOLLS, Simon; s of James Derrick Nicholls (d 1981), and Marcia Ann, *née* Bacon (d 1996); *b* 25 November 1955, Shropshire; *Educ* Bridgnorth GS, Wolverhampton Poly, Coll of Law Chester; *m* 15 May 1982, Juliet, *née* Price; 2 da (Grace Edith b 16 July 1992, Isabelle Florence b 2 Oct 1995); *Career* slr specialising in criminal defence; asst slr then ptnr Overbury Steward and Eaton Solicitors 1980–96, fndr and ptnr Nicholls and Co 1996–99, ptnr Belmores (following merger) 1999–; memb Law Society 1980; *Recreations* riding a customised Harley Davidson, running, skiing; *Clubs* Final Chapter Motorcycle Gang, Norwich City FC; *Style*— Simon Nicholls, Esq; ✉ 164 Saint Clements Hill, Norwich NR3 4DG (tel 01603 499995, e-mail nicholls.co@netcom.co.uk); Belmores Solicitors, 40 Crown Road, Norwich NR1 3DX (tel 01603 499999, fax 01603 499998, e-mail enquiries@belmores-solicitors.co.uk)

NICHOLLS, Susan Frances (Sue) (Hon Mrs Eden); da of Baron Harmar-Nicholls, JP (Life Peer and 1 Bt, d 2000); *b* 23 November 1943; *m* 6 July 1993, Mark Eden, the actor/writer; *Career* actress; trained RADA; early theatre work nationwide, appeared in London Assurance (RSC); numerous TV roles incl: Crossroads, The Fall and Rise of Reginald Perrin, Rent-a-Ghost, Up the Elephant and Round the Castle, Audrey Roberts in Coronation Street 1979–; *Style*— Sue Nicholls

NICHOLLS OF BIRKENHEAD, Baron (Life Peer UK 1994), of Stoke D'Abernon in the County of Surrey; Sir Donald James Nicholls; kt (1983), PC (1986); yr s of late William Greenhow Nicholls and late Eleanor Jane Nicholls; *b* 25 January 1933; *Educ* Birkenhead Sch, Univ of Liverpool (LLB), Trinity Hall Cambridge (MA, LLB); *m* 1960, Jennifer Mary, yr da of late W E C Thomas, MB, BCh, MRCOG, JP; 2 s, 1 da; *Career* called to the Bar Middle Temple 1958 (bencher 1981, treas 1997), QC 1974, judge of the High Court of Justice (Chancery Div) 1983–86; Lord Justice of Appeal 1986–91; vice-chllr of the Supreme Court 1991–94; Lord of Appeal in Ordinary 1994–, second sr Lord of Appeal 2002–; non-perm memb Hong Kong Court of Final Appeal 1998–2004; *Clubs* Athenaeum (tstee); *Style*— The Rt Hon the Lord Nicholls of Birkenhead, PC; ✉ House of Lords, London SW1A 0PW

NICHOLS, Dinah Alison; CB (1995); da of Sydney Hirst Nichols (d 1982), and Elsie Freda, *née* Pratt; *b* 28 September 1943; *Educ* Wyggeston GS for Girls Leicester, Bedford Coll London (Reid arts scholar, BA); *Career* Miny of Tport: asst princ 1965–69, Winston Churchill Meml fellowship to study tport in Japan 1969, asst private sec to the Min of Tport 1969–70, princ Railways Policy 1970–74; princ Cabinet Office 1974–77, asst sec (Radioactive Waste) DOE 1977–80, asst sec (Ports) Dept of Tport 1980–81, asst sec (Inner Cities) DOE 1981–83, princ private sec to the Sec of State for Tport 1983–85; DOE (latterly DETR then DEFRA): dir Admin Resources 1985–88, under sec (Water) 1988–91, dep sec (Property and Construction) 1991–93, dep sec (Housing and Construction) 1994–96, DG Environment 1996–2002; non-exec dir: John Laing ETE 1987–90, Anglian Water plc 1992–95, Include 1995–2000, Shires Smaller Companies plc 1999–, Pennon Gp plc 2003–; memb Commonwealth War Graves Cmmn 1993–96, cmmr Crown Estate 2003–, chair National Forest Co; dir Toynbee Housing Assoc 1996–, chm Toynbee Partnership Housing Assoc 2002–, chm Groundwork Camden & Islington 2004–; tstee: Travel Fndn 2003–, Environmental Campaigns 2005–; hon fell Royal Holloway Coll 1997, FRSA; *Recreations* mountain and fell walking, choral singing, music, theatre, travel; *Clubs* Swiss Alpine; *Style*— Ms Dinah Nichols, CB

NICHOLS, Jeremy Gareth Lane; *b* 20 May 1943; *Educ* Lancing, Fitzwilliam Coll Cambridge (MA, Athletics half blue), Univ of Perugia (Dip Teaching); *m* 1 s (Rupert), 3 da (Lucy, Victoria, Emma); *Career* house tutor Rugby Sch 1966–67; Eton Coll: asst Eng master 1967–89, house master 1980–89, master i/c of soccer and first XI coach 1969–79, second cricket XI coach and master i/c 1974–79, Exchange Scheme Gilman Sch Baltimore Maryland 1979–80 (elected to Cum Laude Soc); headmaster Stowe Sch 1989–2003; advsr tstee Manor Charitable Tst Villiers Park 1989–2003; fndr chm Assoc of Educnl Guardians for Int Students; former memb Educn and Trg Sector Overseas Project Bd DTI; fndr memb and former pres Foundation Bd Model European Parliament; govr: Aysgarth Sch Yorks, Wellesley House Kent; FCollP, FRSA; *Recreations* outdoor pursuits, sport, music and old cars; *Clubs* Free Foresters CC, I Zingari CC, Corinthian Casuals AFC, Hawks' (Cambridge), Lansdowne, Public Schools; *Style*— Jeremy Nichols, Esq; ✉ e-mail upperlookout@connectfree.co.uk

NICHOLS, (Peter) John; s of late Peter Nichols, of Bowdon, Cheshire, and Edith Nan, *née* Rhodes; *b* 24 December 1949; *Educ* Shrewsbury, Univ of Leicester (BSc); *m* 15 Sept 1973, Elaine Mary, da of late William H W Chadwick; 2 s (James b 1979, Matthew b 1982), 1 da (Katharine b 1986); *Career* Nichols plc: joined 1970–, dir 1978–86, md 1986–99, chm 1999–; *Recreations* golf, sailing, skiing; *Clubs* Ringway Golf, Nefyn Golf, South Caernarvonshire Yacht, Bowdon Lawn Tennis; *Style*— John Nichols, Esq; ✉ Hatton Cottage, Hatton, Cheshire WA4 5NY; Nichols plc, Laurel House, Ashton Road, Newton Le Willows, Lancashire WA12 0HH (tel 01925 222222, fax 01925 222233, mobile 07764 933194, e-mail john.nichols@nicholsplc.co.uk)

NICHOLS, HE John Roland; s of Richard Alan Nichols, of Peaslake, Surrey, and Katherine Louisa, *née* Barham (d 1992); *b* 13 November 1951, Hampton, Middx; *Educ* Latymer Upper Sch, Univ of Surrey (BSc); *m* 8 Oct 1983, Suzanne Angela, da of James Harry Davies, MBE, RA (ret), and Helen Christine Davies, JP; 1 s (Richard James b 27 July 1987), 1 da (Elizabeth Ann b 12 Aug 1989); *Career* admitted slr 1977 (articled clerk 1975–77); joined HM Dip Serv 1977, S Asian Dept FCO 1977–79, Hungarian language trg and second (later first) sec (political/economic) Budapest 1979–82, first sec Energy Science and Space Dept FCO 1982–85, first sec (commercial) Brasilia 1985–89, asst head Commercial Relations and Exports Dept FCO (later FCO/DTI Jt Directorate) 1989–91, asst head Arms Control and Disarmament Dept FCO 1991–93, dep high cmmr Dhaka 1993–95, consul-gen Geneva 1995–97, dep head of mission and dir of trade promotion Berne 1997–2000, on secondment as actg chief exec British Invisibles (later Int Fin Services London) 2000, on secondment as dep chief exec and dir of govt liaison and communications Int Fin Services London 2001, ambass to Hungary 2003–; chm Bd Int Sch of Berne 1998–2000; *Style*— HE Mr John Nichols; ✉ British Embassy, Harmincad Utca 6, 1051 Budapest, Hungary (tel 00 36 1 429 6211, fax 00 36 1 429 6301, e-mail john.nichols@fco.gov.uk)

NICHOLS, Peter Richard; s of Richard George (d 1965), of Bristol, and Violet Annie Ladysmith Poole (d 1992); *b* 31 July 1927; *Educ* Bristol GS, Bristol Old Vic Theatre Sch; *m* 1960, Thelma, da of George Reginald Reed, of Bristol (d 1995); 1 s (Daniel), 3 da (Abigail d 1971, Louise, Catherine); *Career* actor, teacher, journalist, playwright and director; visiting writer Nat Inst of Educn Singapore 1994; FRSL; *Screen and Stage* plays incl: The Gorge (TV), A Day in the Death of Joe Egg (stage and screen), Forget-me-not Lane (stage), Privates on Parade (stage and screen), Passion Play (stage), Poppy (stage musical), Blue Murder (writer and dir, Show of Strength Co Bristol) 1995 (nat tour 1996), So Long Life (Show of Strength Co Bristol and nat tour) 2000; *Awards* 4 Evening Standard Drama, 2 Oliviers, Critics' Circle, Tony, Ivor Novello Award for Best British Musical (for Poppy); *Publications* Feeling You're Behind (autobiography, 1984), Diary 1969–77; author of various papers; *Recreations* reading his own diary, complaining about cars and muzak; *Style*— Peter Nichols, Esq, FRSL

NICHOLS, Sir Richard Everard; kt (1998); *b* 26 April 1938; *Educ* Christ's Hosp; *m* 19 March 1966, Shelagh, *née* Loveband; 2 s (Jonathan, Tom), 1 da (Victoria); *Career* Nat Serv cmmnd RE 1956–58; slr; articles 1958–63: Sedgwick Turner Sworder & Wilson Slrs Watford, Speechly Mumford & Soames Lincoln's Inn; asst slr Gunston & Smart Hong Kong 1963–64, ptnr Norman E Kelly & Son Slrs Watford 1965–76 (asst slr 1964–65), sr ptnr Kelly Nichols & Blayney (now Sedgwick Kelly) 1976–2002; chllr Ulster Univ 2000–, memb Cncl City Univ; chm St John Ambulance City of London Centre, Almoner Christ's Hosp 1984–2005 (chm Audit Ctee); hon memb Baltic Exchange; memb Herts Law Soc; govr The Irish Soc 2000–05; pres Rickmansworth and Sarratt Branch Cancer Research Campaign, vice-pres Br Diabetic Assoc, memb NCH Action for Children; Hon Col 101 (City of London) Engr Regt 1997; City of London: elected memb Common Cncl for Ward of Candlewick 1983, elected to Ct of Aldermen 1984, Sheriff 1994–95, Lord Mayor of London 1997–98; memb Ct of Assts Worshipful Co of Salters 1980 (Master 1988–89), Liveryman Worshipful Co of Solicitors 1984; KStJ 1997; *Recreations* music, coarse gardening, wine, travel, farming; *Clubs* East India, Amicables; *Style*— Sir Richard Nichols

NICHOLS, Richard Stephen; s of Basil Nichols, and Jean Nichols; *b* 18 May 1965; *Educ* Royal GS Newcastle upon Tyne, St Catharine's Coll Cambridge (MA); *m* 3 June 1995, Deborah Rachel Cantrell; 1 s (Mark b 15 July 1998), 1 da (Louise b 30 Aug 2000); *Career* with Price Waterhouse (London) 1987–94, sr fin analyst British Gas plc 1994–96, dep gp fin dir Citigate Communications Gp Ltd 1996–97; Incepta Gp plc: dep gp fin dir 1997–98, gp fin dir 1998–2001, chief exec 2001–; ACA; *Recreations* golf, tennis, Newcastle United FC; *Clubs* Harpenden Golf, Woburn Golf and Country, Brocket Hall Golf, Harpenden Lawn Tennis; *Style*— Richard Nichols, Esq; ✉ Incepta Group plc, 3 London Wall Buildings, London Wall, London EC2M 5SY (tel 020 7282 2800, fax 020 7256 7542)

N

NICHOLS, Roger David Edward; s of Edward Compton Lowther Nichols (d 1945), and Dorothy Norah, *née* West (d 1994); *b* 6 April 1939; *Educ* Harrow, Worcester Coll Oxford (open exhibitioner, BA); *m* 11 April 1964, Sarah, eld da of Antony Bydder Edwards; 2 s (Thomas Edward b 7 March 1965, Jeremy Owen b 22 Aug 1966), 1 da (Olwen Beatrice b 5 May 1969); *Career* asst master St Michael's Coll Tenbury 1966–73, lectr Open Univ 1974–80, lectr Univ of Birmingham 1974–80; freelance writer and broadcaster 1980–; FRCO 1964; Chevalier de la Légion d'Honneur 2006; *Books* Debussy (1972), Messiaen (1975), Ravel (1977), Debussy Letters (ed and trans, 1987), Ravel Remembered (1987), Pelléas et Mélisande (with R Langham Smith, 1989), Debussy Remembered (1992), Conversations with Madeleine Milhaud (1996), Mendelssohn Remembered (1997), The Life of Debussy (1998), The Harlequin Years (2002); *Recreations* playing chamber music, walking the Welsh hills; *Style*— Roger Nichols, Esq; ✉ The School House, The Square, Kington, Herefordshire HR5 3BA (tel 01544 231742, e-mail roger@nicholsnet.org)

NICHOLS, Steven Leslie (Steve); s of Ralph William Nichols, and Josephine Mary, *née* Beaumont; *b* 7 March 1958; *Educ* Lowestoft GS, Univ of Surrey (BSc), Coll of Acupuncture Leamington Spa, Univ of Stirling (MSc); *m* Christine Anne, *née* Davies (d 1988); *Career* games consultant; fndr Aztral Games 1982–; publisher and ed Games Monthly 1988–89, sales and tech dir Quorum Game Development Ltd 1990; inventor and publisher/mfr over 50 board games; fndr Post-Human Movement, assoc memb Inst of Reprographic Technol 1986, memb British Psychological Soc 1993–; *Books* The Primal Eye - A Crash Course in the Evolution of Intelligence (1987); *Recreations* shogi, tennis, computing, chess; *Style*— Steve Nichols, Esq; ✉ 54 Wykebeck Mount, Leeds LS9 0HW (tel 0113 225 0635, e-mail steve@multisell.com)

NICHOLS, Most Rev Vincent Gerard; *see:* Birmingham, Archbishop of (RC)

NICHOLSON, Sir Bryan Hubert; kt (1987), GBE (2005); s of Reginald Hubert Nicholson (d 1977); *b* 6 June 1932; *Educ* Palmers Sch Grays, Oriel Coll Oxford; *m* 1956, Mary Elizabeth, da of Albert Cyril Harrison; 2 c; *Career* Nat Serv Lt; dir Sperry Rand (Australia) Pty Ltd 1966–69, dir Sperry Rand Ltd UK 1969–72; chm: Rank Xerox (UK) Ltd 1980–84 (dir 1972–84, dir Rank Xerox Ltd 1977–87), Manpower Services Cmmn 1984–87, The Post Office (also chief exec) 1987–92, BUPA 1992–2001, Varity Europe Ltd 1993–96, Cookson Gp plc 1998–2003, GOAL plc 2001–05, Financial Reporting Cncl 2001–05 (memb 1993–98 and 2001–05, dep chm 1993–96); non-exec dir: Evode Group plc 1981–84, Baker Perkins Holdings plc 1982–84, GKN plc 1991–2000, LucasVarity plc 1996–99, Equitas Holdings Ltd 1996–2005, Newsquest plc 1997–99; CBI: chm Educn and Trg Affrs Ctee 1990–93, dep pres 1993–94, pres 1994–96; chm: Nationalised Industries Chairmen's Gp 1988–90, CNAA 1988–91, Nat Cncl for Vocational Qualifications 1990–93, The Industrial Soc 1990–93; memb: NEDC 1985–92; dir Accountancy Fndn 2000–04 (chm 2003–04), tstee Int Accoutnig Standards Ctee Fndn 2006–; pro-chllr and chm Cncl Open Univ 1996–2004, chllr Sheffield Hallam Univ 1992–2001; pres Nat Centre for Young People with Epilepsy 2005–; Hon FCGI; *Recreations* tennis, bridge; *Clubs* Oxford and Cambridge (chm 1995–97); *Style*— Sir Bryan Nicholson, GBE; ✉ Point Piper, Lilley Drive, Kingswood, Surrey KT20 6JA

NICHOLSON, Sir Charles Christian; 3 Bt (UK 1912), of Harrington Gdns, Royal Borough of Kensington; s of Sir John Norris Nicholson, 2 Bt, KBE, CIE (d 1993), and (Vittoria) Vivien, *née* Trewhella (d 1991); *b* 15 December 1941; *Educ* Ampleforth, Magdalen Coll Oxford; *m* 1975, Martha Rodman, da of Col Stuart Warren Don, and wid of Niall Hamilton Anstruther-Gough-Calthorpe; *Heir* bro, James Nicholson; *Clubs* Brooks's,

Pratt's, RYS; *Style*— Sir Charles Nicholson, Bt; ✉ Turners Green Farm, Elvetham, Hook, Hampshire RG27 8BE

NICHOLSON, Clive Anthony Holme; s of Dennis Thomas Holme Nicholson, MBE, of Barnet, Herts, and Eileen Blanche, *née* Fitkin; *b* 24 February 1947; *Educ* Merchant Taylors'; *m* 12 Dec 1970 (m dis 2003), Patricia Mary, da of Ernest Johnson (d 1979), of Lancaster; 3 da (Amanda b 5 Dec 1972, Zoe b 27 May 1975, Gemma b 8 Aug 1981); *Career* CA; Deloitte & Co Lusaka Zambia 1970–72; Saffery Champness (formerly Safferys) 1972– (ptnr 1975–, managing ptnr 1990–2002); Liveryman Worshipful Co of Merchant Taylors 1974; FCA 1979, FHKSA 1985; *Style*— Clive A H Nicholson, Esq; ✉ 30 Shrewsbury Avenue, East Sheen, London SW14 8JZ; Saffery Champness, Lion House, Red Lion Street, London WC1R 4GB (tel 020 7841 4000, fax 020 7841 4100)

NICHOLSON, David John; s of John Madison Nicholson, of Guildford, Surrey, and Jean Nicholson; *b* 8 August 1953; *Educ* King's Sch Tynemouth, Westminster Coll (HND, Student of the Year); *m* 23 Sept 1978, Patricia Alexandra, *qv*, da of Donald Young, of Gosforth, Newcastle upon Tyne; *Career* mgmnt roles Centre and Crest Hotels 1975–82 (Centre Hotels Trainee of the Year 1975), regnl mangr First Leisure Corp 1982–87, jt prop Holbeck Ghyll Country House Hotel 1988– (4 AA Red Stars, 3 AA Rosettes,1 Michelin Star 2000–, Cumbria Tourist Bd Hotel of the Year 2000–01, Northern Hospitality Awards Best Hotel 2006, Cumbria Restaurant of the Year Good Food Guide Special Awards 2007, Taittinger Wine List of the Year Condé Nast Johansens Awards of Excellence 2007); pres Lakes Hospitality Assoc 2002–04 (former chm), memb Bd Pride of Britain, memb Small Luxury Hotels of the World; Master Innholder 1997; Freedom City of London; FHCIMA; *Recreations* golf, lifelong supporter of Sunderland AFC, dining out, wine, travelling; *Clubs* Windermere Golf; *Style*— David Nicholson, Esq; ✉ Holbeck Ghyll Country House Hotel, Holbeck Lane, Windermere, Lake District, Cumbria LA23 1LU (tel 01539 432375, fax 01539 444431, e-mail david@holbeckghyll.com)

NICHOLSON, Rev Prof Ernest Wilson; s of Ernest Tedford Nicholson (d 1977), Veronica Muriel, *née* Wilson (d 1963); *b* 26 September 1938; *Educ* Portadown Coll, Trinity Coll Dublin (BA, MA), Univ of Glasgow (PhD), Univ of Cambridge (BD, DD), Univ of Oxford (DD by incorporation); *m* 5 April 1962, Hazel, da of Samuel John Jackson; 1 s (Peter), 3 da (Rosalind, Kathryn, Jane); *Career* lectr in Hebrew and Semitic languages Trinity Coll Dublin 1962–67; Univ of Cambridge: lectr in divinity 1967–79, fell Wolfson Coll 1967–69, fell and chaplain Pembroke Coll 1969–79, dean 1973–79; Univ of Oxford: Oriel prof of the interpretation of Holy Scripture and fell Oriel Coll 1979–90, provost Oriel Coll 1990–2003, pro-vice-chllr Univ of Oxford 1993–2003; chm Jardine Fndn 1993–2000; hon fell: Oriel Coll Oxford, Trinity Coll Dublin, Wolfson Coll Cambridge, St Peter's Coll Oxford; FBA 1987; Cdr of the Order of Merit of the Italian Republic; *Recreations* music, walking; *Style*— The Rev Prof Ernest Nicholson, FBA; ✉ 39A Blenheim Drive, Oxford OX2 8DJ

NICHOLSON, Sheriff Principal (Charles) Gordon Brown; CBE (2002), QC (Scot 1982); s of William Addison Nicholson, OBE (d 1987), of Edinburgh, and Jean Brown (d 1967); *b* 11 September 1935; *Educ* George Watson's Coll Edinburgh, Univ of Edinburgh (MA, LLB); *m* 1963, Hazel Mary, da of Robert Riddle Nixon (d 1976); 2 s (David, Robin); *Career* called to the Bar Scotland 1961, advocate depute 1968–70; Sheriff of Dumfries and Galloway at Dumfries 1970–76, Sheriff of Lothian and Borders 1976–82, cmmr Scot Law Cmmn 1982–90, Sheriff Princ of Lothian and Borders and Sheriff of Chancery 1990–2002, temp judge High Court of Justiciary 2002–; hon pres Scottish Assoc for Study of Delinquency 1988–2002, hon pres Victim Support Scotland 1989–2005; cmmr Northern Lighthouse Bd 1990–2002 (vice-chm 1993–94, chm 1994–95), chm Ctee on Liquor Licensing Law in Scotland 2001–03; *Books* The Law and Practice of Sentencing in Scotland 1981 (supplement 1985, 2 edn 1992), Sheriff Court Practice (gen ed, 2 edn 1998); *Recreations* music; *Clubs* New (Edinburgh); *Style*— Sheriff Principal Gordon Nicholson, CBE, QC; ✉ Back O'Redfern, 24C Colinton Road, Edinburgh EH10 5DX (tel 0131 447 4300, e-mail g.nicholson199@btinternet.com)

NICHOLSON, Graham Beattie; s of John Arthur Nicholson (d 1975), and Ena Patricia Nicholson; *b* 22 February 1949; *Educ* Bloxham Sch, Trinity Hall Cambridge; *Children* 1 da (Vanessa b 1978); *Career* slr; Freshfields (now Freshfields Bruckhaus Deringer): NY office 1979–80, ptnr 1980–, Singapore office 1980–83, managing ptnr Co Dept 1986–90, managing ptnr 1990–93; memb City of London Slrs' Co 1983; memb Law Soc; dir City of London Sinfonia; *Recreations* music, sailing, racquet sports; *Style*— Graham Nicholson, Esq; ✉ Freshfields Bruckhaus Deringer, Whitefriars, 65 Fleet Street, London EC4Y 1HS (tel 020 7936 4000, e-mail graham.nicholson@freshfields.com)

NICHOLSON, James Frederick (Jim); MEP (UUP) N Ireland; s of Thomas Richard Nicholson (d 1987), of Ballyards, Armagh, and Matilda, *née* Morrow (d 1984); *b* 29 January 1945; *m* 30 Nov 1968, Elizabeth, *née* Gibson; 6 s, 1 da; *Career* elected: Armagh Dist Cncl 1975–97, NI Assembly 1982–86; MP 1983–85; MEP (UUP) N Ireland 1989–; farmer; *Recreations* walking, football; *Style*— Jim Nicholson, Esq, MEP; ✉ 3 Glengall Street, Belfast BT12 5AE (tel 028 9043 9431, fax 028 9024 6738)

NICHOLSON, Jeremy Dawson; s of Maj Rodney Scholfield Nicholson, of Birdham, and Leta, *née* Dawson; *b* 14 March 1945; *Educ* Wellington; *m* 15 June 1968, Sarah Helen, da of Michael Richards; 2 s (Anthony Charles b 31 May 1969, Michael Dawson b 21 May 1973), 1 da (Charlotte Helen b 23 March 1971); *Career* Josolyne Layton-Bennett (formerly Layton-Bennett Billingham & Co): articled clerk 1964–68, mangr 1971–75, ptnr 1975–81; ptnr: Arthur Young 1981–89, Ernst & Young 1989–2004; FCA 1979 (ACA 1968); *Recreations* golf, theatre, music; *Clubs* MCC, Caledonian; *Style*— Jeremy Nicholson, Esq

NICHOLSON, Lindsay; da of Anthony Cuthbertson-Nicholson, and Sheila Rose, *née* Pigram; *Educ* UCL (BSc), NCTJ; *Career* journalist; trainee Mirror Gp Newspapers 1978–82, health and beauty ed Honey 1983–85, features ed Best 1987, asst ed Woman 1992–95, ed-in-chief Prima 1995, ed-in-chief Good Housekeeping 1999–, editorial dir National Magazine Co 2006–; chairwoman: BSME 1997, PTC Ed Ctee 2002–04, Women in Journalism 2002–04; PPA Ed of the Year (consumer magazines) 1999, PPA Magazine of the Year 2006; tstee Home-Start 2000–, patron The WAY (Widowed and Young) Fndn 2007–; hon visiting prof City Univ 2007–; *Recreations* dressage, ballet; *Clubs* Groucho; *Style*— Ms Lindsay Nicholson; ✉ The National Magazine Company, 72 Broadwick Street, London W1F 9EP (tel 020 7439 5247, fax 020 7439 5591, e-mail lindsay.nicholson@natmags.co.uk)

NICHOLSON, Malcolm G C; *b* 4 March 1949; *Educ* Haileybury, Univ of Cambridge (BA, LLB), Brussels (Dip en Droit Européen); *m* Diana Fay Nicholson; 2 s (James, Peter), 4 da (Claire, Laura, Briony, Emily); *Career* ptnr Slaughter and May 1981– (specialising in European, Regulatory and Commercial Law); *Style*— Malcolm Nicholson, Esq; ✉ Slaughter and May, 1 Bunhill Row, London EC1Y 8YY (tel 020 7600 1200)

NICHOLSON, Rt Hon Sir (James) Michael Anthony; kt (1988), PC (1995); s of Cyril Anthony de Lacy Nicholson, QC, DL (d 1963), of Beech Hill, Ardmore, Co Londonderry, and Eleanor Gerad, *née* Caffrey (d 1972); *b* 4 February 1933; *Educ* Downside, Trinity Coll Cambridge (MA); *m* 7 July 1973, Augusta Mary Ada, da of Thomas F Doyle (d 1979), and Elizabeth Doyle (d 1994), of Ardmanagh, Passage West, Co Cork; 2 da (Emma b 10 Jan 1975, Tessa b 26 July 1978), 1 s (Thomas b 7 May 1977); *Career* called to the Bar: NI 1956 (bencher 1978, treas 1990), Gray's Inn 1962 (hon bencher 1994), Ireland 1975; QC 1971; chm Bar Cncl 1983–85; judge High Court of Justice NI 1986–95; Lord Justice of Appeal NI 1995–2006; chm Mental Health Review Tbnl 1973–76; memb Standing Advsy Cmmn on Human Rights in NI 1976–78; pres: ICU 1978, NWICU 1986–93; High Sheriff Co Londonderry 1972; *Recreations* cricket, chess; *Clubs* MCC; *Style*— Sir Michael Nicholson; ✉ Royal Courts of Justice, Chichester Street, Belfast BT1 3JF (tel 028 9023 5111, fax 028 9023 6838, e-mail mnicholson.rcj@courtsni.gov.uk)

NICHOLSON, Michael Thomas; OBE (1991); s of Maj Allan Alfred Nicholson, RE (d 1956), of Romford, and Doris Alice, *née* Reid (d 1963); *b* 9 January 1937; *Educ* Prince Rupert Wilhelmshaven Germany, Univ of Leicester (BA); *m* Diana; 2 s (Tom b 17 Jan 1972, William b 19 May 1973), 1 adopted da (Natasha b 7 Oct 1982); *Career* served RAF 1955–57; political writer DC Thompson 1962–63; ITN: foreign corr 1963–82 and 1985–, bureau corr Southern Africa 1976–81, newscaster 1982–85, Washington corr Channel 4 1989; currently: corr Tonight prog (ITV), contrib Radio 4; wars covered incl: Nigeria/Biafra 1968–69, Ulster 1968–75, Vietnam 1969–75, Cambodia (incl invasion of Laos) 1972–75, Jordan (incl Dawson's Field and Black September) 1970, Indo-Pakistan War 1971, Yom Kippur War 1973, Rhodesian War 1973–80, invasion of Cyprus 1974, Beirut Lebanon 1975, Angolan Civil War 1975–78, Falklands War (awarded Falklands medal) 1982, Gulf War (awarded Gulf medal) 1991; Hon MA Univ of Leicester; FRGS 1983, fell Royal Cwlth Soc 1983; *Awards* American Emmy nomination 1969, British Broadcasting Guild award 1974, RTS award 1974, Silver Nymph award (for Vietnam report) Monte Carlo Film Festival 1975, RTS Reporter of the Year (for Angola 1979, for Falklands 1983, for Yugoslavia 1992), BAFTA Richard Dimbleby award 1983, VALA award 1983, RTS Journalist of the Year 1991; *Books* Partridge Kite (1978), Red Joker (1979), December Ultimatum (1981), Across The Limpopo (1985), Pilgrims Rest (1987), A Measure of Danger (1991), Natasha's Story (1993,basis of film Welcome to Sarajevo); *Recreations* tennis, sailing; *Style*— Michael Nicholson, Esq, OBE; ✉ c/o PFD, 34 Russell Street, London WC2B 5HA (tel 020 7344 1000)

NICHOLSON, Patricia Alexandra; da of Donald Young, of Gosforth, Newcastle upon Tyne, and Margaret, *née* Bailes; *b* 2 December 1955, Newcastle upon Tyne; *Educ* La Sagesse Convent Sch, Westminster Coll (HND), Garnet (CertEd); *m* 23 Sept 1978, David John Nicholson, *qv*, s of Jack Nicholson; *Career* grad mgmnt trainee Grand Met Hotels 1977–78, trg exec Centre Hotels 1978–80, lectr S Warks Coll of FE 1981–87, jt prop Holbeck Ghyll Country House Hotel 1988– (4 AA Red Stars, 3 AA Rosettes, Michelin Star 2000, Cumbria Tourist Bds Hotel of the Year 2000–01, Best Hotel Northern Hospitality Awards 2006, Cumbria Restaurant of the Year Good Food Guide Special Awards 2007, Taittinger Wine List of the Year Condé Nast Johansens Awards of Excellence 2007); vice-chm Kendal Coll Consultative Ctee, memb Ctee Cumbria Tourist Bd Devpt Workforce, memb Small Luxury Hotels of the World, memb Pride of Britain; MHCIMA; *Recreations* golf, watching football, dining out, wine and food appreciation, cooking, walking the dogs; *Clubs* Windermere Golf; *Style*— Mrs Patricia Nicholson; ✉ Holbeck Ghyll Country House Hotel, Holbeck Lane, Windermere, Lake District, Cumbria LA23 1LU (tel 01539 432375, fax 01539 434743)

NICHOLSON, Sir Paul Douglas; kt (1993); eld s of Frank Douglas Nicholson, TD, DL (d 1984), and Pauline, yr da of Maj Sir Thomas Lawson-Tancred, 9 Bt; *b* 7 March 1938; *Educ* Harrow, Clare Coll Cambridge; *m* 1970, Sarah, 4 and yst da of Sir Edmund Bacon, 13 and 14 Bt, KG, KBE, TD (d 1982), of Raveningham Hall, Norfolk; 1 da; *Career* Lt Coldstream Guards 1956–58; chartered accountant Price Waterhouse 1964; chm Vaux Group plc 1976–99 (exec 1965, dir 1967); non-exec dir: Tyne Tees TV plc 1981–1997, Northern Development Company 1987–99, Northern Electric plc 1990–1997, Yorkshire Tyne Tees TV Holdings plc 1992–1997, The Scottish Investment Trust plc 1998–2005, Steelite International 2000–02; chm: Northern Region CBI 1977–79, Northern Bd Nat Enterprise Bd 1979–84, Northern Investors Ltd 1984–89, Tyne & Wear Devpt Corp 1987–98, Brewers and Licensed Retailers' Assoc 1994–96; pres: North East C of C 1995–96, Co Durham Fndn 2002– (chm 1995–2002); High Sheriff Co Durham 1980–81, HM Lord-Lt Co Durham 1997– (DL 1980–97); Liveryman: Worshipful Co of Grocers, Worshipful Co of Brewers; *Publications* Brewer at Bay (2003); *Recreations* shooting, deerstalking, driving horses (pres Coaching Club 1990–97); *Clubs* Boodle's, Pratt's, Northern Counties; *Style*— Sir Paul Nicholson; ✉ Quarry Hill, Brancepeth, Durham DH7 8DW (tel 0191 378 2455, fax 0191 378 3015, e-mail sirpdn@aol.com)

NICHOLSON, Peter Charles; CBE (2004); s of Charles Arthur Nicholson (d 1993), and Kathleen Mary, *née* Carr (d 1998); *b* 10 April 1934; *Educ* Cheltenham Coll; *m* 1, Tessa, *née* Clarke (d 1980); 1 da (Jane Elizabeth b 1961), 2 s (Charles Edward b 1963, David George b 1965); m 2, 1981, Lesley-Jane, *née* Wynne-Williams; *Career* naval architect Fleet Air Arm 1952–54; dir: Camper & Nicholsons Ltd 1965–88 (chm 1969–88), Crest Nicholson plc 1972–2002 (exec 1972–88, non-exec 1988–2002), Original 106 FM Ltd 2005–; chm Carisbrooke Shipping plc 1990–1999; non-exec dir: Lloyds Bank plc 1990–95, MIF Ltd 1993–2001, TEN Ltd 2001–, Lloyds TSB Group plc 1995–2000, Solent Regional Radio Ltd 1996–2000 (chm 2000); younger bro Trinity House, chm RNLI 2000–04, Br delg IYRU 1969–94, tstee Br Marine Industries Fedn 1988–; pres: Solent Cruising and Racing Assoc 2004–, Solent Protection Soc 2005–; *Recreations* yachting, skiing, golf; *Clubs* Royal Yacht Sqdn (Cdre 1996–2001), Royal Thames Yacht (Rear Cdre 1980–83), RORC, Royal Southern Yacht, Ski Club of GB, Stoneham Golf; *Style*— Peter Nicholson, Esq, CBE; ✉ Mere House, Hamble, Southampton SO31 4JB (tel 023 8045 5019, fax 023 8045 5834)

NICHOLSON, Robin Alaster; CBE (1999); s of Gerald Hugh Nicholson (d 1970), of Bayford, and Margaret Evelyn, *née* Hanbury (d 2000); *b* 27 July 1944; *Educ* Eton, Magdalene Coll Cambridge (MA), UCL (MSc), RIBA Sch (design prize); *m* 1, 18 Dec 1969, Fiona Mary, *née* Bird; 3 s (Zachary Luke b 7 March 1971, Solomon Rufus Seb b 13 Sept 1974, Caspian Ned b 5 June 1978); m 2, 18 June 2005, Isobel, *née* Dawson; 1 da (Beatrice Elizabeth Louisa b 22 Jan 2007); *Career* architect; Evan Walker Associates Toronto 1967, James Stirling Chartered Architects London 1969–73, Boza Lührs and Muzard Santiago Chile 1973, UCL 1974–76, Poly of N London 1976–79, Edward Cullinan Architects 1979–; visiting fell Univ of Wales 1984; memb Cncl RIBA 1991–97 (vice-pres 1992–94); chm: Construction Industry Cncl 1998–2000 (vice-chm 1997–98 and 2000–01), Cmmn for Architecture and the Built Environment (CABE) 2002–; memb The Edge; RIBA, FRSA, Hon FIStructE 2002; *Recreations* gardening, building; *Style*— Robin Nicholson, Esq, CBE; ✉ Edward Cullinan Architects, 1 Baldwin Terrace, London N1 7RU (tel 020 7704 1975, fax 020 7354 2739, e-mail robin.nicholson@ecarch.co.uk)

NICHOLSON, Sir Robin Buchanan; kt (1985); s of late Carroll Nicholson and Nancy Esther Nicholson (d 1993); *b* 12 August 1934; *Educ* Oundle, St Catharine's Coll Cambridge (PhD); *m* 1, 1958, Elizabeth Mary (d 1988), da of Sir Sydney Caffyn; 1 s, 2 da; m 2, Yvonne, *née* Appleby; *Career* Univ of Cambridge: demonstrator in metallurgy 1960, lectr in metallurgy 1964, fell Christ's Coll 1962–66 (hon fell 1984); prof of metallurgy Univ of Manchester 1966; md Inco Europe 1976–81 (dir 1975–81), chief sci advsr Cabinet Office 1981–85; exec dir Pilkington plc 1986–96; non-exec dir: Rolls Royce plc 1986–2005, BP plc 1987–2005; memb SRC 1978–81, Cncl Univ of Exeter 2005–; Liveryman Worshipful Co of Goldsmiths; FRS 1978, FREng 1980, FIM, MInstP; *Clubs* MCC; *Style*— Sir Robin Nicholson, FREng, FRS

NICHOLSON, Roy Knollys Ellard; s of Basil Ellard Nicholson (d 1985), and Gilda Gwendolyn, *née* Maurice-Green; *b* 4 December 1946; *Educ* Oundle, Bachschule Schloss Rettershof Königstein im Taunus Germany; *m* 1976, Bridget Mary, da of Paul Patterson Davis; 2 s (Tim Paul b 1978, Andrew Charles b 1980); *Career* KPMG (formerly Peat Marwick Mitchell & Co): ptnr 1984–2002, currently corp fin vice-chm; memb Cncl Soc of Share & Business Valuers; FCA; *Recreations* golf; *Clubs* Walton Heath Golf, Royal West Norfolk Golf (treas); *Style*— Roy Nicholson, Esq; ✉ KPMG Corporate Finance, 8 Salisbury Square, London EC4Y 8BB (tel 020 7311 1000, fax 020 7694 6410)

NICHOLSON, Vanessa-Mae Vanakorn; *b* 27 October 1978; *Educ* Francis Holland Sch for Girls, Central Conservatoire Beijing, Royal Coll of Music; *Career* violinist; live performances worldwide incl: Times Square NY, Kremlin Palace Moscow, Paralympics opening ceremony Salt Lake City 2002, Buckingham Palace, Soweto township SA, venues in USA, Middle East, China, SE Asia, Russia, Kazakstan, UK, Europe, Baltic States, Mexico and S America; actress: Arabian Nights (TV) 2000, Gangs of New York (film) 2002; model for Jean Paul Gaultier Paris Fashion Week; patron: Red Cross, RSPCA; *Albums* The Violin Player 1995, The Classical Album 1 1996 (Best-Selling Classical Artiste World Music Awards), Storm 1997, China Girl (The Classical Album 2) 1998, The Original Four Seasons 1998, The Classical Collection - Part 1 2000, Subject to Change 2001, The Best of Vanessa Mae 2002, Choreography 2004; *Style*— Miss Vanessa-Mae Nicholson

NICHOLSON OF WINTERBOURNE, Baroness (Life Peer UK 1997), of Winterbourne in the Royal County of Berkshire; Emma Harriet Nicholson; MEP (Lib Dem) SE England; 3 da of Sir Godfrey Nicholson, 1 and last Bt (d 1991), and Lady Katharine Constance, *née* Lindsay (d 1972), da of 27 Earl of Crawford and Balcarres; *b* 16 October 1941; *Educ* Portsdown Lodge Sch, St Mary's Sch Wantage, Royal Acad of Music (LRAM, ARCM); *m* 9 May 1987, Sir Michael Harris Caine (d 1999), s of Sir Sydney Caine, KCMG; 2 step c, 1 ward; *Career* computer software programmer and engr ITC (now ICL) 1962–66, computer conslt John Tyzack & Ptnrs 1967–69, computer and gen mgmnt conslt McLintock Mann and Whinney Murray 1969–73; dir of fundraising Save the Children Fund 1977–85 (joined 1974), fndr and memb Bd Stichting Redt de Kinderen (Netherlands) 1982–88, fndr and memb Comité d'Honneur Sauvez Les Enfants (France) 1983; conslt 1985–87: World Assoc of Girl Guides and Girl Scouts, The Duke of Edinburgh's Award Scheme, Foster Parents Plan UK, Westminster Children's Hosp; Parly candidate (Cons) Blyth Valley 1979, MP (Cons until Dec 1995, whereafter Lib Dem) Devon W and Torridge 1987–97; vice-chm Cons Party (with special responsibility for women) 1983–87, PPS to Michael Jack as min of state 1992–95 (successively at Home Office, MAFF and HM Treasy), sec Lib Dem spokesperson on human rights and overseas aid 1996–97; MEP (Lib Dem) SE England 1999–; Euro Parl: rapporteur for Romiania and Iraq, vice-chm Foreign Affairs, Human Rights, Common Security and Def Ctee, Women's Rights and Equal Opportunities Ctee, substitute memb Ctee for Agric and Rural Affairs and EP/Romania Jt Parly Ctee, memb Stability Pact Parly Forum, European Mediterranian Parly Forum, Mashreq Delegation and Delegation for Kyrgyzstan, Kazakhastan, Uzbekistan, Tajikistan, Turkmenistan and Mongolia; WHO special envoy for Health, Peace and Devpt 2002–; WHO visiting fell St Antony's Coll Oxford 1995–96 (sr assoc memb 1997–98, 1998–99 and 2001–); All-Pty Parly Gps: former chm Br Iraq Gp, chm Oman Gp, chm Kuwait Gp, co-chm UNA Advsy Gp, co dep chm Br Iranian Gp, treas Saudi Arabia Gp, treas Romanian Children Gp, former treas Positive European Gp, treas Br Caribbean Gp, sec Syrian Gp, sec Human Rights Gp, fndr and former chm Euro Information Market Gp; memb Cncl: UNICEF, Howard League for Penal Reform, Media Soc, Industry Churches Forum, Africa 95; memb: Euro Standing Ctee A, Standing Ctee on Statutory Instruments, Select Ctee on Employment 1990–91, Conservative Backbench Environment Ctee 1990–91 (sec and subsequently chm), Bd MRC 1991–94, Lib Dem Foreign Affairs team in House of Lords; patron: Cities in Schools, The Manningford Tst; chm: AMAR Int Charitable Fndn 1995– (fndr 1991–), Iraqi Humanitarian Relief Ctee until 1996 (also vice-patron until 1996), Access for Disabled People to Arts Premises Today (ADAPT) until 1996 (currently tstee and vice-patron), Blind in Business 1993–95, Emily Trust Appeal Ctee (chm 1993–95), UNA Advsy Gp UNESCO (co-chm, chm 1998–), Int Year of the Disabled UNESCO; vice-chm: European Movement, Relatives' Assoc (memb of mgmnt Bd); pres numerous charitable orgns in Devon; vice-pres: Assoc of Dist Cncls, Br Tinnitus Assoc, Nat Assoc for Maternal and Child Welfare, Small Farmers' Assoc, Br Leprosy Relief Assoc (LEPRA), The Little Fndn, The Child Psycotherapy Tst, The Missing Persons Hotline; patron numerous charitable and other orgns incl: Int Ctee for a Free Iraq, Ecaterina Iliescu Meml Lecture, Br Deaf Accord, Nat Deaf Blind and Rubella Assoc, AMANA (soc to promote understanding of Islam), Soc for the Freedom of the City of London Municipality, Freedom Cncl, Reading Industrial Therapy Orgn, Women into IT Fndn, Women's Engrg Soc, Women's Business Assoc, Federal Tst for Educn and Res, Devon Daycare Tst, Sense South West, Opera South West, PHAB South West, Deaf Educn through Listening and Talking (DELTA), Nat Music and Disability Information Service; vice-pres Methodist Homes for the Elderly; formerly dir Shelter; tstee: Covent Garden Cancer Res Tst, Motor Neurone Disease Assoc, World Meml Fund for Disaster Relief; memb: Mgmnt Bd European Movement, Guild of Mgmnt Conslts, Forum UK, RIIA, Centre for Policy Studies, Inst of Economic Affrs, Cncl for Arab-Br Understanding, Prince of Wales Advsy Tst on Disability, Advsy Cncl Justis Legal Databases, Exeter Univ Devpt Ctee, Br Romanian Assoc, West Regnl Assoc for the Deaf, Editorial Panel 300 Group, Advsy Bd Women of Tomorrow Awards, London Business Women's Network, Appeal Ctee Royal Acad of Music, Advsy Cncl United World Fndn, Advsy Cncl Centre for Adoptive Identity Studies Univ of E London; Hon Dr: Univ of North London, Univ of Timosoara; Freeman Worshipful Co of Info Technologists; fell Industry and Parliament Tst, fell Federal Tst for Education and Res; FRSA 1990; *Books* Why Does the West Forget? (1993), Secret Society: Inside and Outside the Conservative Party (1996); author of various articles and pamphlets; *Recreations* music (organ, piano, cello and singing), chess, walking, reading; *Clubs* Reform; *Style*— The Rt Hon Baroness Nicholson of Winterbourne, MEP; ✉ House of Lords, London SW1A 0PW

NICKELL, Prof Stephen John; CBE (2007); s of John Edward Hilary Nickell (d 1962) and Phyllis, *née* Vicary (d 1975); *b* 25 April 1944; *Educ* Merchant Taylors', Pembroke Coll Cambridge (scholarship, BA), LSE (MSc, Ely Devons prize); *m* 25 June 1976, Susan Elizabeth, da of Peter Nicholas Pegden, of Bridlington, E Yorks; 1 da (Katherine Jane b 30 Sept 1979), 1 s (William Thomas b 16 Oct 1981); *Career* mathematics teacher Hendon Co Sch 1965–68; prof of economics: LSE 1979–84 (lectr 1970–77, reader 1977–79), (and dir) Inst of Economics and Statistics Univ of Oxford 1984–98; professorial fell Nuffield Coll Oxford 1984–98, school prof of economics LSE 1998–2005, warden Nuffield Coll Oxford 2006–; memb Bank of England Monetary Policy Ctee 2000–06; chm Research Grants Bd ESRC 1990–94 (also memb); pres: European Assoc of Labour Economists 1999–2002, Royal Economic Soc 2001–04 (memb Cncl 1984–94); hon fell: Nuffield Coll Oxford 2003, Pembroke Coll Cambridge 2006; hon memb: American Economic Assoc 1997, American Acad of Arts and Sciences 2006; fell Econometric Soc 1980 (memb Cncl 1987–93), FBA 1993; *Books* The Investment Decisions of Firms (1978), The Rise in Unemployment (ed, 1987), Unemployment (1991), The Unemployment Crisis (1994), The Performance of Companies (1995); *Recreations* reading, cricket; *Style*— Prof Stephen Nickell, CBE, FBA; ✉ e-mail steve.nickell@nuffield.ox.ac.uk

NICKLIN, Stephen Richard; s of Richard Patrick Nicklin (d 1982), of Rugby, Warks, and Elsie Joan, *née* Crisp; *b* 20 April 1952; *Educ* Sloane GS; *m* 3 March 1979, (Mary) Theresa, da of Vincent O'Shea (d 1995), Collooney, Co Sligo; 3 s (Edward b 1981, Anthony, Luke (twins) b 1988), 1 da (Emily b 1985); *Career* BBC 1970; unit mangr: Newsnight BBC 1984–87, American Elections BBC 1984, Election 87 BBC 1985–87; ITN: unit mangr Channel 4 News 1987–89, editorial mangr 1989–91, home news mangr 1991–93, input mangr 1993–94, gen mangr ITV Dept 1994–95, resource mangr 1996–97, head of commercial resources 1997–, health & safety mangr 2000; chartered memb Inst of Occupational Health and Safety (CMIOSH), memb Int Inst of Risk and Safety Mgmnt (MIIRSM); *Style*— Stephen Nicklin, Esq; ✉ ITN Ltd, 200 Gray's Inn Road, London WC1X 8XZ (tel 020 7833 3000, e-mail steve.nicklin@itn.co.uk)

NICKOLLS, Malcolm Charles; s of Capt Charles Nickolls (d 1985), and Lillian Rose, *née* Taylor; *b* 20 March 1944; *Educ* Rickmansworth GS, Univ of London (LLB), Brighton Coll of Art (DipArch), Thames Poly (Dip Landscape Architecture); *m* 26 Aug 1967, Mary Delia Margaret, da of Ronald Edward Groves, CBE; 2 da (Joanna Helen b 8 Nov 1973, Deborah Sally b 31 Aug 1976); *Career* architect and landscape architect; currently in private practice; princ building J Paul Getty Jr Conservation Centre (Nat Film Archive); ARCUK (now ARB): memb Cncl 1979–, hon offr 1982–, chair Professional Purposes 1982–92, vice-chair Cncl 1992–94, chair Cncl 1994–97, memb Bd 2000; RIBA: memb Cncl 1989–96, chair Discipline Ctee 1992–94; external examiner: Univ of Brighton 1998–, Univ of Northumbria 2001–; MCIArb 1976, MLI 1977, FRSA 1989; *Recreations* cycling, computers, technology, science, invention; *Clubs* Mensa; *Style*— Malcolm Nickolls, Esq; ✉ 27 Rickfords Hill, Aylesbury, Buckinghamshire HP20 2RT (tel 01296 397272, e-mail malcolm@nickolls.com)

NICKSON, Baron (Life Peer UK 1994), of Renagour in the District of Stirling; Sir David Wigley Nickson; KBE (1987, CBE 1981), DL (Stirling and Falkirk 1982); s of Geoffrey Wigley Nickson (d 1983), and Janet Mary, *née* Dobie (d 1994); *b* 27 November 1929; *Educ* Eton, RMA Sandhurst; *m* 18 Oct 1952, (Helen) Louise, da of late Lt-Col Louis Latrobe Cockcraft, DSO, MVO; 3 da (Hon Felicity (Hon Mrs James Lewis) b 3 Nov 1955, Hon Lucy (Hon Mrs Melfort Campbell) b 8 July 1959, Hon Rosemary (Hon Mrs Alastair Campbell) b 11 Feb 1963); *Career* regular cmmn Coldstream Gds 1949–54; William Collins plc: joined 1954, dir 1959–76, vice-chm and gp md 1976–83; dir Radio Clyde Ltd 1981–85; Scottish & Newcastle plc: dir 1981–95, dep chm 1982, chm 1983–89; chm Clydesdale Bank plc 1991–98 (dir 1981–98, dep chm 1990–91), dep chm General Accident plc 1993–98 (dir 1971–98); dir: Edinburgh Investment Trust plc 1981–94, Hambros plc 1988–98, National Australia Bank 1991–96; pres CBI 1986–88 (chm for Scot 1979–81); chm: Countryside Cmmn for Scot 1983–85, Senior Salaries Review Body 1989–95, Scottish Devpt Agency 1989–91, Scottish Enterprise 1990–93, sec of state for Scotland's Task Force for Scottish Salmon 1997; pres Assoc of Scottish Salmon Fishing Boards 1996–; memb: Scottish Ind Devpt Advsy Bd 1974–79, Scottish Econ Cncl 1979–91, NEDC 1985–88; chm Atlantic Salmon Tst 1988–95; chllr Glasgow Caledonian Univ 1993–2002; Capt Queen's Body Guard for Scotland (Royal Co of Archers); Vice Lord-Lt Stirling and Falkirk 1997–;2005 Hon Dr: Univ of Stirling, Napier Univ, Paisley Univ, Glasgow Caledonian Univ; FRSE 1987; *Recreations* fishing, shooting, stalking, bird-watching, countryside; *Clubs* Boodle's, Flyfishers'; *Style*— The Rt Hon Lord Nickson, KBE, DL, FRSE; ✉ The River House, Doune, Perthshire FK6 6DA (tel 01786 841614)

NICOL, Andrew George Lindsay; QC (1995); s of Duncan Rennie Nicol (d 1991), and Margaret, *née* Mason (d 1967); *b* 9 May 1951; *Educ* City of London Freemen's Sch, Selwyn Coll Cambridge (BA, LLB), Harvard Law Sch (LLM); *m* 2005; *Children* 2 s; *Career* special asst to dir Housing and Community Dept State of Calif 1975–76, asst Allen Allen & Hemsley Slrs Sydney 1976–77, lectr in law LSE 1977–87; called to the Bar Middle Temple 1978 (bencher 2004), asst recorder 1998–2000, recorder 2000–, dep judge High Ct 2003–; chair Immigration Law Practitioners' Assoc 1997–2000; *Books* Subjects, Citizens, Aliens and Others (with Ann Dummett, 1990), Robertson and Nicol on Media Law (with G Robertson QC, 1992, 4 edn 2002), Media Law and Human Rights (with G Millar QC and Andrew Sharland, 2001); *Recreations* family, walking, sailing; *Style*— Andrew Nicol, Esq, QC; ✉ Doughty Street Chambers, 10 Doughty Street, London WC1N 2PL (tel 020 7404 1313, fax 020 7404 2283)

NICOL, Angus Sebastian Torquil Eyers; s of Henry James Nicol (d 1977), and Phyllis Mary, *née* Eyers (d 1999); *b* 11 April 1933; *Educ* RNC Dartmouth; *m* 20 April 1968, Eleanor Denise, da of Lt Cdr William Lefevre Brodrick (ka 1943); 2 da (Catharine Sophia b 1968, Augusta Devorgilla Margaret b 1972); *Career* RN (ret as Sub-Lt 1956), served HMS Euryalus, HM MMS 1635, HMS Brocklesby, and HMS Coquette; literary ed Cassell & Co 1956–61; called to the Bar Middle Temple 1963, recorder 1982–98; adjudicator and special adjudicator Immigration Appellate Authy 1998–2002; chm: Disciplinary Ctee Potato Mktg Bd 1988–, VAT and Duties Tbnl 1988–2005, SE Area Legal Aid Ctee 1991; memb Appeal Ctee Taxation Disciplinary Bd 2006–; author of poems and short stories in Gaelic; piping corr The Times 1979–; fndr memb and first vice-chm The Monday Club 1961, dir The Highland Soc of London 1981– (sec 1982–), sr steward The Argyllshire Gathering 1983 and 1998, lectr in Gaelic Central London Adult Educn Inst 1982–96, conductor London Gaelic Choir 1985–91, pres Scottish Piping Soc of London 2006–; tstee: Argyllshire Gathering Piping Tst 1984–, Urras Clann Mhic Neacail 1987–; memb: Cncl Gaelic Soc of London 1989–, Gaelic Soc of Inverness, Piobaireachd Soc; chieftain Clan MacNicol and cmmr for all the Territories of GB S of the River Tweed and for Europe; FSA Scot; *Recreations* shooting, fishing, sailing, music, gastronomy, Gaelic literature; *Style*— Angus Nicol, Esq (also Aonghas MacNeacail); ✉ 5 Paper Buildings, Temple, London EC4Y 7HB (tel 020 7815 3200)

NICOL, Michael John; s of John Chalfont Nicol, of Barnet, Herts, and Jean Etta, *née* Crawley; *b* 8 May 1940; *Educ* Queen Elizabeth's Sch Barnet, Univ of London (LLB); *m* (m dis 1985), Carol Ann, *née* Howie; 3 da (Kate b 1969, Amanda b 1971, Lucy b 1975); *Career* admitted slr 1963; currently conslt Wedlake Bell; dir City of London PR Gp plc; tstee Family Holiday Assoc; memb Law Soc 1963; *Recreations* bridge, badminton, croquet; *Clubs* MCC; *Style*— Michael Nicol, Esq; ✉ Wedlake Bell, 16 Bedford Street, Covent Garden, London WC2E 9HE (tel 020 7395 3000, fax 020 7836 9966)

NICOL, Prof Richard Charles; s of George Richard Nicol, and Alice, *née* Ardley; *b* 14 July 1948; *Educ* UCL (BSc(Eng), PhD); *m*; 2 c; *Career* British Telecommunications plc: joined 1970, head univ research prog 1989–92, head of research 1998–2001; fndr and chief exec Fynntek Ltd 2001–; dir: CMI@Adastral Park 2003–06, Suffolk Devpt Agency; memb: ESPRC IT and Telecommunications Coll, HEFCE Reserch Ratings Panel for Electrical and Electronic Engrg Depts in UK Academia 1996 and 2001, Corp Suffolk Coll (vice-chm), Bd Suffolk Learning and Skills Cncl, Cncl Univ of Essex; visiting prof Univ of Essex; CEng, FREng, FIEE; *Recreations* gardening, sailing, DIY, football (watching Ipswich Town FC); *Clubs* Ipswich and Suffolk; *Style*— Dr Richard Nicol; ✉ Fynntek Ltd, High Storrs, Hall Lane, Witnesham, Ipswich, Suffolk IP6 9HN (tel 01473 785710, e-mail r@fynntek.com)

NICOL, Stuart Malcolm; s of James Nicol (d 2000), and Mavis Betty, *née* Gay; *b* 10 October 1957, Kano, Nigeria; *Educ* Hurst Community Sch Baughurst, Berkshire Coll of Art and Design, West Bromwich Poly (Cert); *m* 5 Nov 1983 (m dis 1996); partner, Arlene Melville; *Career* photographer: London Evening Standard 1978–86, Sunday Times 1986–88, Sunday Telegraph 1988–89; picture ed The European newspaper 1990–92, conslt ed colour reproduction The Times 1992, photographer Daily Mirror 1993–95, picture ed Daily Record 1995–2005, gp picture ed Press Assoc 2006–; memb Guild of Picture Eds; Br Young Photographer of the Year 1978, Br Photographer of the Year 1988; *Recreations* golf; *Clubs* Balmore Golf; *Style*— Stuart Nicol, Esq; ✉ PA Group Photos, 292 Vauxhall Bridge Road, London SW1V 1AE (tel 020 7963 7155, fax 020 7963 7191, e-mail stuart.nicol@pressassociation.co.uk)

NICOL, Baroness (Life Peer UK 1983), of Newnham in the County of Cambridgeshire; (Olive Mary) Wendy Nicol; JP (1972); da of James Rowe-Hunter (d 1962), and Harriet Hannah (d 1932); *b* 21 March 1923; *Educ* Cahir Sch Ireland; *m* 1947, Dr Alexander Douglas Ian Nicol, CBE, s of Alexander Nicol (d 1962); 2 s (Hon Adrian Timothy b 1949, Hon Colin Douglas b 1950), 1 da (Hon Jane Lesley (Hon Mrs John) b 1954); *Career* Civil

N

Serv 1943–48; cncllr Cambridge City Cncl 1972–82 (chm Environment Ctee 1978–82), Cambridge City Bench 1972–86; memb: Supplementary Benefits Tbnl 1976–78, Careers Serv Consultative Panel 1978–81; oppn dep chief whip House of Lords 1987–89 (oppn whip 1983–87), dep speaker House of Lords 1995–2002, memb Bd Parly Office of Sci and Technol 1998–2000; spokesman on natural environment 1983–92; memb Select Ctee on: Euro Communities 1986–91, Sci and Technol 1990–93, Europe 1993–96 (memb Environment and Social Affairs Sub-Ctee), Sustainable Devpt 1994–95, Use of Animals in Scientific Procedures 2001–02; memb Sci and Tech Sub-Ctee on Mgmnt of Nuclear Waste 1998–99; memb Ecclesiastical Ctee 1990–96; chm All-Pty Retail Gp 1997–98; public serv in many and varied areas; hon fell Inst of Waste Mgmnt; FRGS 1990; *Recreations* reading, walking, gardening; *Style*— The Rt Hon the Lady Nicol; ✉ House of Lords, London SW1A 0PW

NICOLAIDES, Prof Kypros Herodotou; s of Dr Herodotos Nicolaides, of Paphos, Cyprus, and Antigoni, *née* Theodotos; *b* 9 April 1953; *Educ* The English Sch Nicosia, KCL (BSc), King's Coll Hosp Med Sch (MB BS); *Career* house offr in gen surgery Eastbourne Gen Hosp 1979, house offr in obstetrics and gynaecology KCH 1980 (house offr in gen med 1979–80), med offr Cyprus Nat Gd 1980; SHO in obstetrics and gynaecology: City Hosp Nottingham 1981–82, Queen's Univ Hosp Nottingham 1982; prof of fetal med (personal chair) and conslt in obstetrics KCH Sch of Med 1992– (res fell and hon registrar 1982–83, lectr and hon registrar 1983–86, sr lectr and hon sr registrar 1986–89, sr lectr and conslt 1989–92), dir Harris Birthright Res Centre for Fetal Med KCH Sch of Med 1989– (dep dir 1986–89); RCOG rep Working Pty on the Recognition and Mgmnt of Fetal Abnormalities 1988; memb: SE Thames Regnl Specialist Subctee in Genetics 1989–92, Euro Ctee on Doppler Technol in Perinatal Med 1989, Med Advsy Bd of the Toxoplasmosis Tst 1989–, Advsy Bd for Support After Termination for Abnormality 1991–, Euro Inst of Prenatal Diagnosis Dexeus Univ Inst 1991, Jt WHO and World Fedn of Haemophilia Study Gp on the Control of Haemophilia 1992, SELCA Diabetes Forum Gp 1992; memb Editorial Bds: Fetal Diagnosis and Therapy, Ultrasound in Obstetrics and Gynaecology, Israeli Jl of Obstetrics and Gynaecology, Turkish Jl of Obstetrics and Gynaecology, Progresos en Diagnostico Prenatal, Jl of Maternal-Fetal Med, References on Gynecologie Obstetrique, Ultrasound; pres Cyprus Assoc of Perinatology 1990; memb: Int Fetoscopy Gp 1982, Int Fetal Surgery and Med Soc 1984, Panhellenic Soc of Perinatology 1985, The Neonatal Soc 1988, Asociación Espanola de Diagnostico Prenatal 1989, Indian Soc for Prenatal Diagnosis and Therapy 1989, Soc for Research into Hydrocephalus and Spina Bifida 1989, Euro Soc of Paediatric Urology 1990, Int Soc of the Fetus as a Patient 1991, Devptal Pathology Soc 1992; MRCOG 1984; *Publications* author of invited papers and review articles, and ed of various chapters in med reference books; *Style*— Prof Kyprianos Nicolaides; ✉ Harris Birthright Research Centre for Foetal Medicine, King's College Hospital Medical School, Denmark Hill, London SE5 9RS (tel 020 7346 3040, fax 020 7738 3740)

NICOLI, Eric Luciano; CBE (2006); s of Virgilio Nicoli (d 1978), and Ida, *née* Zanga (d 1990); *b* 5 August 1950; *Educ* Diss GS Norfolk, King's Coll London (BSc); *m* 1977, Rosalind, *née* West; 1 s, 1 da; *Career* mktg posts Rowntree Mackintosh 1972–80; United Biscuits: joined 1980, mktg dir UK biscuits 1981, gp business planning dir 1984, md frozen foods 1985, md brands 1986–89, memb Bd 1989–99, chief exec European ops 1989–91, gp chief exec 1991–99; EMI Gp plc (formerly THORN EMI plc): non-exec dir 1993–99, exec chm 1999–2006, ceo 2007; non-exec chm: HMV Gp plc 2001–04, Tussauds Gp 2001–, Vue Entertainment 2006–; chm EMI Music Sound Fndn, chm Per Cent Club 1992–, dep chm BITC 1992–2003, tstee Comic Relief 1999–, memb Bd Creative and Cultural Skills; CIMgt; *Recreations* sport, music, food; *Style*— Eric Nicoli, Esq, CBE

NICOLLE, Frederick Villeneuve; s of Arthur Villeneuve Nicolle (d 1971), of St Peters House, Jersey, and Alice, *née* Cobbold (d 1981); *b* 11 March 1931; *Educ* Eton, Univ of Cambridge (BA, MB BChir, MChir); *m* 1957, Helia Immaculata Stuart-Walker, da of Edward Alan Walker, and Lady Mary, *née* Chrichton-Stuart; 2 da (Miranda b 1958, Edwina b 1961), 1 s (Hugo b 1963); *Career* McLoughlan fell 1964, conslt plastic surgn Montreal Gen Hosp and Montreal Children's Hosp and lectr Faculty of Med McGill Univ Montreal 1964–69, conslt plastic surgn Hammersmith Hosp London and sr lectr in surgery Univ of London and the Royal Postgrad Med Sch London 1970–81, in full time private practice in aesthetic and reconstructive plastic surgery 1982–; pres Br Assoc of Aesthetic Plastic Surgery 1984–86, pres Chelsea Clinical Soc 1986, treas Int Soc of Aesthetic Plastic Surgery 1986–92, pres Int Alpine Surgical Soc; memb: Br Assoc of Plastic Surgery, Br Assoc of Aesthetic Plastic Surgery, Int Soc of Aesthetic Surgery, American Soc of Aesthetic Plastic Surgery; FRCS 1963; *Books* The Care of the Rheumatoid Hand (1975), Surgery of the Rheumatoid Hand (1979), Breast Augmentation (1977), Some Methods of Improving Results of Reduction Mammoplasty and Mastopexy (1983), The Hand (1985), Aesthetic Rhinoplasty (1994); *Recreations* painting, skiing, shooting, fishing, tennis; *Clubs* White's; *Style*— F V Nicolle, Esq

NICOLLE, Robert Arthur Bethune (Bobby); s of Arthur Villeneuve Nicolle (d 1970), of Jersey, and Alice Margarite, *née* Cobbold (d 1980); *b* 24 September 1934; *Educ* Eton, Trinity Coll Cambridge (MA); *m* 21 Jan 1963, Anne Carolyn, da of Sir Anthony Kershaw, MC, MP, of Badminton, Glos; 2 s (Darcy b 1965, Harry b 1971), 1 da (Fiona (Mrs Jonathan Norbury) b 1967); *Career* Lt Grenadier Gds active serv Cyprus 1957–58; joined Kleinwort Sons & Co merchant bankers 1958; formerly dir Kleinwort Benson Ltd 1973–89, dir Matheson Investment Ltd 1989–2000; treas IRIS Fund 1973–97, dir Colonial Mutual Life Insurance of Aust 1975–96; special tstee: St Thomas' Hosp 1981–99, Guy's Hosp 1996–99; advsr Worldwide Fund for Nature in Switzerland (formerly World Wildlife Fund) 1988–92; treas: HOST (Hosting for Overseas Students) 1992–98, Nightingale Fund 1993–2005, Countryside Alliance 2000–02; Master Worshipful Co of Tallow Chandlers 1998–99; *Recreations* skiing, shooting, fox hunting, stalking, watercolour painting; *Clubs* White's; *Style*— R A B Nicolle, Esq; ✉ The Tithe Barn, Didmarton, Badminton GL9 1DT (tel 01454 238484)

NICOLLS, Andrew Darsie; s of Simon Hugh Nicolls (d 1964), and Pat Pell, *née* Van Den Bergh; *b* 2 December 1962; *Educ* Radley, UC Cardiff; *Partner* E J O Wilson; *Career* with Barclays DeZoete Wedd 1985–92, dir Ludgate Communications 1995–98, founding ptnr Penrose Financial 1998–; patron Lighthouse, memb Ctee Terrence Higgins Tst; *Books* Tartanware (with Princess Ira von Furstenberg); *Recreations* interior design, fitness, travel; *Style*— Andrew Nicolls, Esq; ✉ Penrose Financial, 30–34 Moorgate, London EC2R 6PJ (tel 020 7786 4888, fax 020 7786 4889, e-mail andrewn@penrose.co.uk)

NICOLSON, Fiona; da of Edward James Hart, of Helensburgh, and Margaret McLean, *née* Wilson; *b* 22 June 1954; *Educ* Glasgow HS for Girls, Jordanhill Coll of Educn Univ of Glasgow (MA, LLB, DipLP, teaching cert); *m* 2, 10 April 1996, Francis Hugh Binnie, s of late Dr H Binnie; 2 c from prev m (Alexander David Nicolson b 28 Sept 1976, Anna Fiona Jane Nicolson b 17 April 1978); *Career* ptnr and head Intellectual Property Gp Bird Semple Fyfe Ireland 1991–93 (slr and assoc 1986–91), ptnr and head Intellectual Property and Technol Dept Maclay Murray & Spens 1994–; non-exec dir: St Andrews Clinics for Children, Law Soc of Scotland (memb 1986–); past pres Licensing Execs Soc Britain and Ireland; chair: Int Intellectual Property Maintenance Ctee Licensing Execs Soc, Accreditation Panel for Intellectual Property Law Soc, Lexmundi Intellectual Property Practice Gp; memb: Steering Gp Hillington Innovation Centre Glasgow, Scot Ctee BioIndustry Assoc, Med Research Scotland; *Publications* A Directory of Technology Transfer Services in Scotland (co-ed, 1992); *Recreations* yoga, cycling, travel; *Style*— Ms Fiona Nicolson; ✉ Maclay Murray & Spens, 151 St Vincent Street, Glasgow G2 5NJ (tel 0141 303 2360, fax 0141 248 5819, e-mail fmmn@maclaymurrayspens.uk)

NICOLSON, Rebecca; da of Nigel Nicolson, OBE (d 2004), and Philippa, *née* Tennyson d'Eyncourt; *Educ* St Paul's Girls' Sch, St Hugh's Coll Oxford; *Career* features ed The Observer 1990–92, ed Observer Magazine 1992–93, features ed The Spectator 1993–95, dep ed (review) Sunday Telegraph 1995–98, dep ed Independent on Sunday 1998–99; currently publisher Short Books; *Recreations* horse racing, gardening; *Style*— Ms Rebecca Nicolson; ✉ Short Books, 3A Exmouth Market, Pine Street, London EC1R 0JH (tel 020 7833 9429, fax 020 7833 9500, mobile 07770 235117, e-mail rebecca@shortbooks.biz)

NICOLSON, Sanders Nairn; s of William Holmes Nicolson (d 1966), of Glasgow, and Eleanor Mary, *née* Dunlop; *b* 23 July 1944; *Educ* Glasgow HS for Boys, Gordonstoun, Regent St Poly London; *Children* 1 s (Jamie Nairn Nicolson-Gray b 13 May 1986), 1 da (Rosanna Cailin Nicolson-Gray b 14 Dec 1988); *Career* starving artist, gardener and dish washer 1966–68, self-taught fashion photographer Foto Partners 1968–71, freelance photographer 1971–; clients incl: Next, Barbour, Stella Artois, Goretex, Boots, Max Factor, De Beers; solo exhibitions incl: Waves (Pentax Gallery London) 1979, Maske (The Association Gallery London) 1989; judge: Assoc of Photographers Awards 1996, D&AD Awards 2002; recipient: Assoc of Photographers (formerly AFAEP) Awards 1984, 1986, 1989, 1993, 1997, 1998 and 2002, D&AD Awards; *Recreations* fly fishing, gardening, music, food and wine, painting, photography; *Style*— Sanders Nicolson, Esq; ✉ Charity House, 14/15 Perseverance Works, 38 Kingsland Road, London E2 8DD (tel 020 7739 6987, fax 020 7729 4056, e-mail mail@sandersnicolson.com, website www.sandersnicolson.com)

NICOLSON, Seamus; *b* 23 February 1971; *Educ* Kingston Univ (BA), RCA (MA); *Career* photographer; photographed Vivienne Westwood advtg campaign 2004; Individual Artist Award London Arts Bd 1998, finalist Mandarina Duck Prize 2000; *Solo Exhibitions* Galerie Peter Borchardt Hamburg 1998, The Agency Contemporary Art London 1998, 2000, 2001 and 2004, Galeria Alberto Peola Turin 2000 and 2002, Galeria Metropolitana Barcelona 2001, The Agency Contemporary London 2003, Van Ram Gallery Gent 2004; *Group Exhibitions* Becks New Contemporaries (Camden Art Centre London) 1997, Art Forum Berlin (The Agency Berlin) 1997, Modern Narrative (Arts Sway Gallery Lymington) 1997, Supa Store (Cornerhouse Manchester) 1997, Group Show (UP & CO Gallery NY) 1997, Three Out Of Camden (Galerie Dorothee de Pauw Brussels) 1998, Shoreditch Biennial London 1998, Photofest Arles 1998, The Agency Contemporary Art Basel 1998, Sorted (Ikon Gallery London) 1998, John Kobal Prize (Nat Portrait Gallery London) 1998, Remix (Musée des Beaux Arts Nantes) 1998, Silence (Galeria Alberto Peola Turin) 1999, Berlin Artforum 1999, Surveying the Landscape (Lombard Freid NY) 1999, Tales of The Cities (The Agency London) 1999, Art Cologne 1999 and 2000, Bologna Artfair 2000, I'm Really Really Sorry (Luciano Inga-Pin Milan) 2000, Psychosoma (Lombard Freid NY) 2000, Artissima 00 Turin 2000, ARCO Agency Gallery UK Pavilion Madrid 2001, Night on Earth (Kunsthalle Muenster) 2001, Neue Welt (Frankfurter Kunstverein Frankfurt) 2001, The Centenery Development (Tate Britain London) 2001, Air Guitar (Milton Keynes Gallery) 2002, Shopping (Schirn Kunsthalle Frankfurt) 2002, Tate Liverpool 2002–03, MOMA Sao Paolo 2004, Stranger then Fiction (Leeds) 2003, British Photography (Huis Marseilles Amsterdam) 2004; *Style*— Seamus Nicolson, Esq

NIELSEN, Beverley; da of Dr Stanley Nielsen, of Leigh, and Ethel Mary, *née* Jenkins; *b* 25 January 1960; *Educ* Trinity Coll Dublin (BA), Michael Smurfit Grad Sch of Mgmnt UC Dublin; *m* 1992, J Robert Emmerson, s of Dr R Emmerson; 2 s (Niels Robert Stanley b 26 Sept 1994, Charles Christian William b 16 Dec 1997), 1 da (Amelia Catherine b 25 July 1999); *Career* CBI: policy advsr European Affrs Gp until 1982, dep mangr Brussels 1982–84; sales and mktg co-ordinator Liz Leveque Fashions Inc NY 1984–85, PR offr Flora Kung Inc NY 1985–86, fashion asst Vogue magazine NY 1985–86, mktg exec Visnews Ltd London 1986–87, institutional equity dealer National City Brokers Dublin 1987–89, broadcast sales exec CNN Int Sales Ltd London 1989–91; CBI: asst dir North West 1992–95, dir West Midlands 1995–2000, customer rels and mktg dir 2000–01; chief exec Heart of England Tourist Bd 2001–03; Aga Foodservice Gp plc: non-exec dir 2001–03, md Fired Earth 2003, retail dir Aga, special projects dir 2005; fndr dir Midlands Excellence Ltd 1996–97, dir West Midlands Enterprise Ltd 1997–99, vice-chm West Midlands IOD 2006; non-exec dir: 100.7 Heart FM 1996–, 102.2 Galaxy Radio 1999–, Chrysalis Radio, Unicorn Tourism Ltd 2001–; princ fell Warwick Manufacturing Gp Univ of Warwick 2000–; memb: Midlands Advsy Cncl on Arts and Business 1996–, Cncl Univ of Birmingham 1997–2000, Advsy Bd Aston Business Sch 1999–2000, Chllr's Forum Coventry Univ, Chllr's Forum Staffordshire Univ 1999–2001; govr UC Worcester 1999–2002; Businesswoman of the Year Variety Club Midlands 1998; Hon MA Coventry Univ 1999; *Style*— Ms Beverley Nielsen

NIELSEN, Kester Carl (Kes) (KOEFOED-); s of Christian Koefoed-Nielsen, of Herts, and Mary Hayward, *née* Wright; *b* 9 December 1972, Newcastle upon Tyne; *Educ* Brockenhurst Coll Hants, Manchester Metropolitan Univ (BA); *m* 18 Sept 1999, Gaynor, *née* Finlan; 2 da (Kate b 19 Nov 1999, Sylvie b 27 Aug 2002); *Career* bookseller Waterstone's 1994–2000, non-fiction mktg mangr Waterstone's HQ 2000–01, fiction buyer WH Smith HQ 2001–04, dir of book buying Amazon.co.uk 2004–; memb Books Mktg Soc; *Recreations* gardening, country walks, good friends, good food, music, a drink or two; *Style*— Kes Nielsen, Esq; ✉ Amazon.co.uk, Patriot Court, 1–9 The Grove, Slough SL1 1QP (tel 020 8636 9225, e-mail kes@amazon.co.uk)

NIENOW, Prof Alvin William; s of Alvin William Nienow (d 1969), and Mary May, *née* Hawthorn (d 1968); *b* 19 June 1937; *Educ* St Clement Dane's GS, UCL (BSc, PhD, DSc); *m* 29 Aug 1959, Helen Mary; 1 da (Fiona Mary b 1961), 2 s (Gary John b 1963, Peter William b 1965); *Career* chem engr various industries 1958–63, hon research fell UCL 1980– (lectr and sr lectr 1963–80); Univ of Birmingham: prof of chemical engrg 1980–89, prof of biochemical engrg 1989–2004, emeritus prof 2004–; memb Rhône Poulenc Conseil Technologique 1988–2000 (pres 1998–2000); sr visiting fellowship Japanese Soc for Promotion of Sci 1986, hon visiting prof Sichuan Union Univ China 1996; Moulton medallist IChemE 1984, Jan E Purkyne medal Czech Acad of Science 1993, Donald Medal Inst of Chem Engrs 2000; author and co-author of over 400 papers in chem and biochem engrg jls and conf proceedings; ed (Euro and Africa) Jl of Chemical Engrg Japan 2001–05; memb Ed Bd: Canadian Jl of Chemical Engrg (int advsr) 1989–2005, Biotechnology and Bioengineering 2003–; SERC: chm Chem Engrg Sub Ctee 1981–83, memb Biotechnology Directorate Ctee 1990–93, memb Engrg Bd 1991–94; Inst of Chem Engrs: memb Cncl and hon librarian 1984–88, rep on Euro Fedn of Chem Engrs Sci Advsy Ctee 1987–94, memb Euro Fedn Biotechnology Bioreactor Performance Working Party 1988–; AFRC: memb Cncl, memb Food Res Ctee and chm Engrg Advsy Gp 1987–89, Food Res Grants Bd 1988–91; BBSRC: Planning and Resource Ctee, Engrg and Physical Sciences Ctee 1994–96; memb Advsy Ctee Czech Triennial Int Chem Engrg Congress 1986–2002, memb DTI Mgmnt Gp LINK in Biochem Engrg 1988–2002, memb Standing Ctee for Engrg Royal Acad of Engrg 1996–99, memb Governing Body Silsoe Research Inst 1996–98, speaker Inst Engrs Australia Chemical Coll Bd 1999; Lifetime Contribution Award European Fedn of Chemical Engrs Working Pty on Mixing 2003; FIChemE 1980 (MIChemE 1964), FREng 1985; *Books* Mixing in the Process Industries (1985, 2 edn 1993, paperback edn 1997); *Recreations* sport, travel, dancing; *Clubs* MCC, Athenaeum, Edgbaston Priory, Reading Cricket and Hockey; *Style*— Prof Alvin W Nienow, FREng;

✉ Department of Chemical Engineering, The University of Birmingham, Birmingham B15 2TT (tel 0121 414 5325, fax 0121 141 5324, e-mail a.w.nienow@bham.ac.uk)

NIGHTINGALE, Annie; MBE (2001); da of Basil John Nightingale, and Celia, *née* Winter; *Educ* St Catherine's Convent Twickenham, Lady Eleanor Holles Sch, Univ of Westminster; *Career* broadcaster; presenter: BBC Radio 1 1970–, Old Grey Whistle Test (BBC TV) 1978–82; columnist: Daily Express, Sunday Mirror; feature writer: Cosmopolitan magazine, Punch magazine; reporter and feature writer Brighton Evening Argus; ambass Prince's Tst; BASCA Gold Award for Services to Music 1992, Women of the Year Lifetime Achievement Award 1998, Muzik Magazine Caner of the Year Award 2001, inducted into Radio Acad Hall of Fame 2004, Best Radio Show Int Breaks Poll Awards 2006 and 2007; *Publications* Chase the Fade (1982), Wicked Speed (2000); Annie on One (compilation CD 1995), Y4K Annie Nightingale Presents (compilation CD, 2007); *Clubs* Cobden, The End; *Style*— Ms Annie Nightingale, MBE; ✉ BBC, Yalding House, 152–156 Great Portland Street, London W1N 4DJ (tel 020 7765 4762, e-mail annie.nightingale@bbc.co.uk, website www.myspace.com/djannienightingale)

NIGHTINGALE, Caroline Ann; *see:* Slocock, Caroline Ann

NIGHTINGALE, Sir Charles Manners Gamaliel; 17 Bt (E 1628), of Newport Pond, Essex; s of Sir Charles Athelstan Nightingale, 16 Bt (d 1977), and (Evelyn) Nadine Frances, *née* Diggens (d 1995); *b* 21 February 1947; *Educ* St Paul's, Open Univ (BA); *Heir* 2 cous, Edward Nightingale; *Career* Grade 7 Dept of Health 1996–2007; *Style*— Sir Charles Nightingale, Bt; ✉ 16 Unity Grove, Harrogate, North Yorkshire HG1 2AQ

NIGHTINGALE, Neil; *Educ* Collyer's GS Horsham, Wadham Coll Oxford (MA); *Career* BBC: joined as researcher 1983, prodr BBC Natural History Unit 1989–95 (credits incl: Natural World, Wildlife on One, Lost Worlds Vanished Lives, The Private Life of Plants (Emmy Award 1995)), ed The Natural World 1995–2001 (RTS Best Documentary Series), ed Wildlife Specials 2001–03 (winner BAFTA Awards), exec prodr Wild Africa, Wild Down Under, Congo and Wild Battlefields, head BBC Natural History Unit 2003–; tstee: Wildscreen Tst, BBC Wildlife Fund; *Publications* New Guinea, An Island Apart (1992), Wild Down Under (2003); *Recreations* sailing, scuba diving; *Style*— Neil Nightingale; ✉ BBC Natural History Unit, Whiteladies Road, Bristol BS8 2LR (tel 01179 742114)

NIGHTINGALE, Richard Mervyn; s of Edward Humphrey Nightingale, CMG (d 1996), of Nunjoro Farm, Naivasha, Kenya, E Africa, and Evelyn Mary, *née* Ray; *b* 9 July 1954; *Educ* Rugby, Emmanuel Coll Cambridge (MA, DipArch); *Career* architect; with practices in Nairobi, London and Hong Kong 1977–81, Colin St John Wilson and Partners 1981–85, estab partnership with Hugh Cullum as Cullum and Nightingale Architects 1985; articles published in: Architects Journal, Building Design, International Architect, Interni, Baumeister, Building Magazine, Perspectives in Architecture, Architectural Review; work exhibited at: Royal Acad, RIBA, Fitzwilliam Museum Cambridge, Building Centre London, Br Cncl Nairobi; tstee Southwark Festival 1996–2002; RIBA; FRSA 1999; *Building work published* House in Hampstead (1988), New British High Commission Nairobi (1989 and 1997), New Teaching Space North Westminster Sch (1991), Extensions Central Sch of Speech and Drama (1994, 1998), Harley Davidson Showroom (2000), New Eden House Bequia (2003), Embassy Theatre London (2003), Guludo Eco-Resort Mozambique (2005), British High Commission Kampala (2006); *Style*— Richard Nightingale, Esq; ✉ 30A Parkhill Road, London NW3 (tel 020 7482 1213); Cullum and Nightingale Architects Ltd, 26 Harrison Street, London WC1H 8JW (tel 020 7383 4466, fax 020 7383 4465, e-mail r@richardnightingale.com)

NIGHTINGALE OF CROMARTY, John Bartholomew Wakelyn; Baron of Cromarty (feudal); er s Michael David Nightingale of Cromarty, OBE (d 1998); *b* 7 September 1960; *Educ* Winchester, Magdalen Coll Oxford (MA, DPhil); *m* 24 December 1996, Lucy Charlotte, da of Dr Patrick Drummond Fergusson (d 1997); 1 s (Thomas b 1999); *Career* Harmsworth sr res scholar Merton Coll Oxford 1984–86; fell Magdalen Coll Oxford 1986– (tutor in modern history 1993–), fell Winchester Coll 2002–; chm: Black Isle Civic Tst 1993–, Cromarty Arts Tst 1998–; tstee: Cromarty Harbour Tst, Wye Rural Museum Tst 1999–; *Publications* Monasteries and Patrons in the Gorze Reform (2001); also articles on medieval history; *Recreations* woodland management, restoration of old buildings; *Clubs* Athenaeum; *Style*— John Nightingale; ✉ Cromarty House, Ross and Cromarty IVII 8XS; 25 West Square, London SE11 4SP

NIGHY, William Francis (Bill); s of Alfred Martin Nighy, and Catherine Josephine, *née* Whittaker; *b* 1949; *Educ* John Fisher GS Surrey, Guildford Sch of Acting; *Career* actor; *Theatre* RNT productions incl: Illuminatus!!!, A Map of the World, Skylight, Pravda, King Lear, The Seagull, Arcadia, Mean Tears, Blue/Orange; other productions incl: Rudy in The Milk Train Doesn't Stop Here Any More (professional debut, Watermill Theatre Newbury), Betrayal (Almeida), A Kind of Alaska (Donmar Warehouse), Landscape and Silence (Chester Gateway), Illuminations (Lyric Hammersmith), Speak Now (Traverse Theatre Edinburgh), The Warp (ICA), The Vertical Hour (Music Box Theatre NY); *Television* Soldiers Talking Cleanly, Deasey's Desperate, Dreams of Leaving, Easter 2016, The Last Place on Earth, Antonia and Jane, The Men's Room, Absolute Hell, The Maitlands, Longitude, People Like Us, Auf Wiedersehen Pet, The Lost Prince, Ready When You Are Mr McGill, State of Play, The Young Visiters, The Girl in the Cafe, Gideon's Daughter; *Radio* The Lord of the Rings, Bleak House, Little Dorrit, Strangers on a Train, The Mind Body Problem, Beaumarchais, Pravda, Skylight, Arcadia, Romeo and Juliet, The Libertine, The Information, People Like Us, No Commitments, Death of the Heart; *Film* Still Crazy, Blow Dry, Lucky Break, Fairy Tale, The Lawless Heart, Indian Summer, I Capture the Castle, Underworld, Love Actually, Enduring Love, Shaun of the Dead, Hitchhiker's Guide to the Galaxy, Notes on a Scandal, Pirates of the Caribbean: Dead Man's Chest, Pirates of the Caribbean: To the Ends of the Earth; *Awards* Barclays Theatre Managers Award 1997, Peter Sellers Evening Standard Comedy Award 1999 and 2004, LA Critics Circle Best Suppporting Actor 2004, London Critics Circle Best Supporting Actor 2004, BAFTA Best Supporting Actor 2004, BAFTA Best Actor 2004 (for State of Play), Golden Globe Best Actor 2007 (for Gideon's Daughter); *Recreations* books, walks, rhythm and blues, air guitar; *Style*— Bill Nighy, Esq; ✉ c/o Markham & Froggatt Ltd, Julian House, 4 Windmill Street, London W1P 1HF (tel 020 7636 4412)

NIMMO, Ian Alister; *b* 14 October 1934; *Educ* Royal Sch of Dunkeld, Breadalbane Acad; *m* 11 July 1959, Grace Paul; 1 da (Wendy b 1960), 2 s (Alasdair b 1962, Struan b 1973); *Career* Nat Serv 2 Lt RSF 1955–57; ed: The Weekly Scotsman 1963–66, Teesside Evening Gazette 1970–76, Edinburgh Evening News 1976–89; editorial conslt and author 1989–, sr conslt Shanghai Daily China 1999; vice-pres Newspaper Press Fund, chm Acad Bd Scotland's Story 2000; FSA Scot; *Books* Robert Burns (1965), Portrait of Edinburgh (1968), The Bold Adventure (1969), Scotland at War (1989), The Commonwealth Games (1989), Edinburgh: The New Town (1991), Edinburgh's Green Heritage (1996), Walking with Murder (2005); also writer Rythms of the Celts (scottish musical; performed: Waterfront Concert Hall Belfast 1997, Edinburgh Playhouse 1998); *Recreations* the outdoors, fly fishing, painting, writing; *Clubs* Scottish Arts, Robert Louis Stevenson (chm); *Style*— Ian Nimmo, Esq; ✉ The Yett, Whim Farm, Lamancha, By West Linton, Peeblesshire EH46 7BD (tel 01968 675457, fax 01968 675457, e-mail iannimmoscotland@aol.com)

NIMMO, Prof Walter Sneddon; *b* 2 April 1947; *Educ* Bathgate Acad, Univ of Edinburgh (BSc, MB ChB, MD, MRCP); *Children* 1 s (Thomas William John b 21 Aug 1976), 1 da (Kathryn Margaret b 7 Nov 1980); *Career* Sir Stanley Davidson lectr in clinical pharmacology Univ of Edinburgh 1973–76, lectr in anaesthesia Univ of Edinburgh 1977–79, sr lectr in anaesthesia Univ of Glasgow 1979–84, prof of anaesthesia Univ of Sheffield 1984–88, chm and chief exec Inveresk Clinical Research 1988–96, chief exec Inveresk Research 1996–2004; non-exec dir Aberforth Smaller Companies Trust plc 2004–; FRCA 1977, FRCP 1984, FANZCA 1988, FRCPEd 1988, FRCPGlas 1988, FFPM 1993, FRSE 2000; *Books* editor of 11 textbooks in anaesthesia, clinical measurement and drug absorption, author of over 100 papers in academic jls; *Recreations* songwriter, cabaret performer; *Clubs* New (Edinburgh), Royal Burgess Golf (Edinburgh); *Style*— Prof Walter Nimmo

NIMMO SMITH, Rt Hon Lord; William Austin Nimmo Smith; PC (2005); s of Dr Robert Herman Nimmo Smith (d 1991), and Ann, *née* Wood; *b* 6 November 1942; *Educ* Eton, Balliol Coll Oxford (BA), Univ of Edinburgh (LLB); *m* 1968, Dr Jennifer, da of Rev David Main; 1 da (Harriet b 1972), 1 s (Alexander b 1974); *Career* admitted to Faculty of Advocates 1969, standing jr counsel to Dept of Employment 1977–82, QC (Scot) 1982, advocate depute 1983–86, chm Med Appeal Tbnls 1986–91, temp judge Court of Session 1995–96, Senator Coll of Justice in Scotland (Lord of Cncl and Session and Lord Cmmr of Justiciary) 1996– (Outer House 1996–2005, First Div Inner House 2005–); chm Cncl Cockburn Assoc (Edinburgh Civic Tst) 1996–2001; pt/t memb Scot Law Cmmn 1988–96; *Recreations* mountaineering, music; *Style*— The Rt Hon Lord Nimmo Smith; ✉ Supreme Courts, Parliament House, Edinburgh EH1 1RQ (tel 0131 225 2595)

NISBET, Andrew; s of Peter Nisbet, and Mary, *née* Lalonde; *b* 21 August 1960, Weston-super-Mare, Somerset; *Educ* St Dunstan's, Kings Coll Taunton; *m* 6 July 1985, Anne Marie, *née* West; 1 s (Joseph Peter b 2 March 1988), 1 da (Emily Rose b 8 Sept 1990); *Career* Peter Nisbet Ltd 1978–83, Nisbets plc 1983–; chm Young Bristol; govr Colston Girls' Sch; memb Soc of Merchant Venturers; *Recreations* family, music, sailing, travel; *Clubs* Clifton; *Style*— Andrew Nisbet, Esq

NISBET, Prof Hugh Barr; s of Thomas Nisbet (d 1977), of Edinburgh, and Lucy Mary, *née* Hainsworth; *b* 24 August 1940; *Educ* Dollar Acad, Univ of Edinburgh (MA, PhD); *m* 1, 26 Dec 1962 (m dis 1981), Monika Luise Ingeborg, da of Wilhelm Otto Uecker, of Guben, Germany; 2 s (Arnold b 1966, Marcus b 1968); m 2, 24 Nov 1995, Angela Maureen Parker, da of Cecil Chapman, of Great Yarmouth; *Career* reader Univ of Bristol 1972–73 (asst lectr 1965–67, lectr 1967–72), prof of German Univ of St Andrews 1974–81, prof of modern languages (German) and fell Sidney Sussex Coll Cambridge 1982–; memb: Ctee Modern Humanities Res Assoc 1972–84, Gen Teaching Cncl Scotland 1978–81, Bd of Govrs Dollar Acad 1978–81, Cncl English Goethe Soc 1978–, Ctee Goethe-Gesellschaft 1991–95, Nat Cncl for Modern Languages 1983–90; pres Br Soc Eighteenth Century Studies 1986–88 (vice-pres 1984–86), tstee Kurt Hahn Tst 1988–95; *Books* Herder and the Philosophy and History of Science (1970), Goethe and the Scientific Tradition (1972); *Recreations* music, art history; *Style*— Prof H B Nisbet; ✉ Sidney Sussex College, Cambridge CB2 3HU (tel 01223 338877)

NISH, David Thomas; s of Thomas Nish, and Jean C M, *née* Scott; *Educ* Paisley GS, Univ of Glasgow; *Career* ptnr Price Waterhouse 1993–97; ScottishPower plc: dep fin dir 1997–99, fin dir 1999–2005, gp dir Infrastructure Divison 2005–; memb Scottish Cncl CBI, former memb Urgent Issue Task Force of the Accounts Standards Bd (UITF); non-exec dir: Northern Foods plc, Royal Scottish Nat Orch; Scottish Fin Dir of the Year 2001CAS 1984; *Recreations* tennis, golf, family; *Clubs* Kilmalcolm Golf; *Style*— David Nish, Esq; ✉ ScottishPower plc, 1 Atlantic Quay, Robertson Street, Glasgow G2 8SP (tel 0141 636 4505, fax 0141 636 4580, e-mail david.nish@scottishpower.com)

NISSEN, George Maitland; CBE (1987); s of Col Peter Norman Nissen (d 1930), and Lauretta, *née* Maitland (d 1954); *b* 29 March 1930; *Educ* Eton, Trinity Coll Cambridge; *m* 1956, Jane Edmunds, *née* Bird; 2 s, 2 da; *Career* KRRC 2/Lt, Royal Greenjackets TA Capt; memb Stock Exchange 1956–73 (dep chm 1978–81), memb Cncl Int Stock Exchange 1973–91, sr ptnr Pember & Boyle 1982–86, dir Morgan Grenfell Gp 1985–87, chm Foreign & Colonial Emerging Markets Tst 1987–99, chm Investment Mgmnt Regulatory Orgn 1989–92, chm Liberty Syndicate Management (Lloyd's) 1997–2002; chm: The Book Guild 1993–, Ffestiniog Railway Co 2001–03, Friends of Chiswick House 2001–; Hon FRAM 1996; *Recreations* music, railways, walking; *Clubs* Brooks's, Beefsteak; *Style*— George Nissen, Esq, CBE; ✉ Swan House, Chiswick Mall, London W4 2PS (tel 020 8995 8306, fax 020 8742 8198)

NIVEN, Dr Alastair Neil Robertson; OBE (2001); s of Harold Robertson Niven (d 1999), and Elizabeth Isobel Robertson, *née* Mair (d 1993); *b* 25 February 1944; *Educ* Dulwich Coll, Univ of Cambridge (MA), Univ of Ghana (MA), Univ of Leeds (PhD); *m* 22 Aug 1970, Helen Margaret, da of Claude William Trow (d 1983); 1 da (Isabella b 1981), 1 s (Alexander b 1985); *Career* lectr: Univ of Ghana 1968–69, Univ of Leeds 1969–70, Univ of Stirling 1970–78; dir gen Africa Centre London 1978–84, Chapman fell Inst of Cwlth Studies Univ of London 1984–85, special asst to Sec Gen Assoc of Cwlth Univs 1985–87, dir of literature Arts Cncl of GB 1987–97 (Arts Cncl of England since 1994), dir of literature Br Cncl 1997–2001, princ King George VI and Queen Elizabeth Fndn of St Catharine's Cumberland Lodge Windsor 2001–; chm: Public Schs Debating Assoc England and Wales 1961–62, Literature Panel Gtr London Arts Assoc 1981–84, UK Cncl for Overseas Student Affrs 1987–92, Southern Africa Book Devpt Educnl Tst 1997–2003; pres English PEN 2003–; judge of the Booker Prize 1994, chm of jury Stakis Prize for Scottish Writer of the Year 1998, chm of jury English Speaking Union Marsh Prize for Biography 1999, 2001 and 2003; *Books* D H Lawrence: The Novels (1978), The Yoke of Pity: The Fictional Writings of Mulk Raj Anand (1978), D H Lawrence (1980), The Commonwealth of Univs (with Sir Hugh W Springer, 1987), Under Another Sky: The Commonwealth Poetry Prize Anthology (ed, 1987), Enigmas and Arrivals: An Anthology of Commonwealth Writing (co-ed with Michael Schmidt, 1997); *Recreations* theatre, travel, dog walking; *Clubs* Royal Cwlth Soc, Garrick; *Style*— Dr Alastair Niven, OBE; ✉ Eden House, 28 Weathercock Lane, Woburn Sands, Buckinghamshire MK17 8NT (tel and fax 01908 582310); Cumberland Lodge, The Great Park, Windsor, Berkshire SL4 2HP (tel 01784 432316, fax 01784 497799, e-mail aniven@cumberlandlodge.ac.uk)

NIX, Prof John Sydney; s of John William Nix (d 1968), of London, and Eleanor Elizabeth, *née* Stears (d 1978); *b* 27 July 1927; *Educ* Brockley Co Sch, UC of the SW (BScEcon), Univ of Cambridge (MA); *m* 1, 7 Oct 1950, Mavis Marian (d 2004), da of George Cooper, of Teignmouth, Devon; 2 da (Alison Mary b 23 July 1952, Jennifer Ann b 7 May 1959), 1 s (Robert David John b 10 Jan 1955); m 2, 13 May 2005, Sue, *née* Clement; *Career* Instr Lt RN 1948–51; sr res offr Farm Econs Branch Univ of Cambridge 1957–61 (1951–61); Wye Coll London: farm mgmnt liaison offr and lectr 1961–70, sr tutor 1970–72, sr lectr 1972–75, head Farm Business Unit 1974–89, reader 1975–82, prof of farm business mgmnt (personal chair) 1982–89, emeritus prof 1989, fell 1995; fndr memb Farm Mgmnt Assoc 1965; prog advsr Southern TV 1966–81; chm: Editorial Ctee of Farm Management (CMA) 1971–95, Bd of Farm Mgmnt (BIM) 1979–81; pres: Agric Economics Soc 1990–91, Kingshay Farming Tst 1991–96, Assoc of Ind Crop Conslts 1993–97, Guild of Agric Journalists 2000–02; Nat Award for Outstanding Contrib to Advancement of Mgmnt in Agric CBIM (now CIMgt) 1982, Agric Communicators Award (first recipient) 1999, The Farmers' Club Cup 2004; author of numerous articles for jls, memb various nat study gps and advsy ctees; Liveryman Worshipful Co of Farmers 1999; CIMgt 1983, FRSA 1984, FRAgS 1985, FIAgrM 1993; *Books* Farm Planning and Control (with C S Barnard, 2 edn 1979), Farm Mechanisation For Profit (with W Butterworth, 1983), Land and Estate Management (4 edn 2003), Farm Management Pocketbook (36 edn 2005); *Recreations* rugby, cricket, old films, reading the papers; *Clubs* Farmers'; *Style*— Prof John Nix; ✉ Imperial College London, Wye Campus, Wye, Ashford, Kent TN25 5AH (tel 020 7594 2855, fax 020 7594 2838, e-mail j.nix@imperial.ac.uk)

N

NIXON, David; s of David Nixon, of Chatham, Ontario, and Alice, *née* Charvill; *b* Windsor, Ontario; *Educ* Nat Ballet Sch of Canada (Peter Dwyer scholarship, Canada Cncl grant); *m* 29 June 1985, Yoko Ichino; *Career* princ dancer: Nat Ballet of Canada, Deutsche Oper Berlin, Bayerisches Staatsballett Munich; guest artist: Hamburg Ballet, Staatsoper Ballet Berlin, Komische Oper Berlin, Birmingham Royal Ballet, Royal Winnipeg Ballet; guest choreographer: Royal Winnipeg Ballet, Cape Town City Ballet; dir: BalletMet Columbus OH 1995–2001, Northern Ballet Theatre 2001–; Best Male Dancer of the Year Munich, Dir of the Year Dance Europe 2004 and 2007; *Style—* David Nixon, Esq; ✉ Northern Ballet Theatre, West Park Centre, Spen Lane, Leeds LS16 5BE (tel 0113 274 5355)

NIXON, Sir Edwin Ronald; kt (1984), CBE (1974), DL (Hants 1987); s of William Archdale Nixon, and Ethel, *née* Corrigan; *b* 21 June 1925; *Educ* Alderman Newton's Sch Leicester, Selwyn Coll Cambridge (MA); *m* 1, 1952, Joan Lilian, *née* Hill (d 1995); 1 s (Christopher), 1 da (Carol); m 2, 1997, Bridget Diana, *née* Rogers; *Career* IBM UK Holdings Ltd: chief exec 1965–85, chm 1979–90; chm: Monteverdi Tst 1971–2001, NatWest Gp Pensions Tst 1992–98, Leicester BioSciences Ltd 1996–2000, ret; dir: NatWest Bank plc 1975–96 (dep chm 1987–96), Royal Insurance plc 1980–88, Amersham International plc 1987–96 (chm 1988–96); memb Cncl: Electronic Engrg Assoc 1965–76, Fndn for Automation and Employment 1967–77, Business in the Community 1981–88; memb Cncl for Industry and HE 1986–97; CBI: chm Standing Ctee on Mktg 1971–78, memb Cncl 1971–96, memb Ctee on Industrial Policy 1978–85, memb President's Ctee 1986–88; memb Ctee of Awards for Harkness Fellowships 1976–82, memb Cncl Fndn for Mgmnt Educn 1973–84, chm Bd for Pre-Vocational Educn 1983–87; dir ROH Covent Garden 1984–87, chm ROH Devpt Tst 1984–87 (tstee 1980); vice-pres Int String Quartet Competition 1980–; memb Advsy Cncl New Oxford English Dictionary 1985–89; vice-pres Opportunities for People with Disabilities 1980–2004, memb Cncl Prince's Tst 1987–96, memb Cncl Lloyds of London Tercentenary Fndn 1987–; memb: Study Cmmn on the Family 1979–83, Chichester Cathedral Devpt Tst 1986–96, Boxgrove Priory Tst 2001–; chm Cncl Univ of Leicester 1992–98; memb Cncl: Westfield Coll London 1969–82 (vice-chm 1980–82), Oxford Centre for Mgmnt Studies (now Templeton Coll Oxford) 1973–83, Manchester Business Sch 1974–86 (chm 1979–86), Civil Serv Staff Coll Sunningdale 1979–91, Open Univ 1986–92; govr United World Coll of the Atlantic 1977–, vice-pres Chartered Inst of Mktg 1985–96; hon tstee Inst of Economic Affrs 1992 (tstee 1986–92); Liveryman Worshipful Co of Marketors; hon fell: Selwyn Coll Cambridge 1983, Westfield Coll London 1983, Portsmouth Poly 1986, Leeds Poly 1991; Hon DSc Aston Univ 1985, Hon DUniv Stirling 1985, Hon DTech Brunel Univ 1986, Hon LLD Victoria Univ of Manchester 1987, Hon LLD Univ of Leicester 1990, Hon DTech CNAA 1991; *Recreations* music, reading; *Clubs* Athenaeum; *Style—* Sir Edwin Nixon, CBE, DL; ✉ Starkes Heath, Rogate, Petersfield, Hampshire GU31 5EJ (tel and fax 01730 821504)

NIXON, Prof James Robert; s of Dr Robert Samuel Nixon, of Bangor, Co Down, and Veda, *née* McKee; *b* 2 September 1943; *Educ* Bangor GS, Trinity Coll Dublin (MB BCh, BAO, MA), Univ of Liverpool (MChOrth); *m* 23 June 1967, Katherine, da of Ronald Stoddart Nesbitt, of Dublin; 1 da (Holly b 1968), 1 s (Alexander b 1972); *Career* formerly: conslt orthopaedic surgn Belfast City Hosp, med dir Green Park Healthcare Tst Belfast; currently: pt/t conslt orthopaedic surgn Musgrave Park Hosp, hon prof of orthopaedic surgery Queen's Univ Belfast; examiner: RCS Ireland, FRCS in Orthopaedics (FRCSOrth); pres Br Hip Soc 2002–03 (vice-pres 2000–02), pres NI Medico-Legal Soc 2001–02, sec Irish Orthopaedic Assoc; chm RYA NI 1983–86; FRCSI 1971, FRCS 1972; *Recreations* sailing, fishing; *Clubs* Royal Ulster Yacht, Irish Cruising, Royal Cruising; *Style—* Prof James Nixon; ✉ Withers Orthopaedic Centre, Musgrave Park Hospital, Belfast BT9 7JB (tel 028 9066 9501, e-mail jamesnixon@btconnect.com)

NIXON, John Edwin; s of late Edwin Nixon, and Dorothy, *née* Hall; *b* 5 December 1948; *Educ* Univ of Edinburgh Med Sch (MB ChB, ChM), Univ of Oxford (MA), FRCS; *m* Bridget Anne, da of late Dr S John Coulson, of Stratton-on-the-Fosse, Somerset; 1 s (David John b 1976), 2 da (Susannah Jane b 1980, Natasha Elizabeth b 1985); *Career* clinical reader in orthopaedic surgery Univ of Oxford, hon conslt orthopaedic surgn Nuffield Orthopaedic Centre, former conslt orthopaedic surgn KCH; currently conslt orthopaedic surgn Charing Cross and Hammersmith Hosp, sr examiner Univ of London, external examiner Univ of Oxford, Univ of Nottingham and KCL, hon sr lectr Imperial Coll Sch of Med, past fell Green Coll Oxford; ed and pt author int reference work on Spinal Stenosis, also numerous pubns on joint replacement, arthroscopy, trauma, foot surgery and spinal surgery and spinal biomechanics; past pres W London Medicochirurgical Soc; memb: BMA, memb SICOT; fell: Girdlestone Orthopaedic Soc, Br Assoc of Spinal Surgeons, Br Assoc of Children's Orthopaedic Surgery, Br Assoc of Surgns of the Knee, Chelsea Clinical Soc, Royal Instn, Br Orthopaedic Assoc; FRSM; *Recreations* family, travel, sailing (yachtmaster ocean), skiing, theatre; *Clubs* Athenaeum, Royal Lymington Yacht, Royal Dart Yacht, Little Ship Club; *Style—* John E Nixon, FRCS; ✉ The London Clinic, 5 Devonshire Place, London W1G 6HL (tel 020 7616 7693); Charing Cross Hospital, Fulham Palace Road, London W6 (tel 020 7487 5020, car 07860 267861)

NIXON, Prof John Forster; s of Edward Forster Nixon, MBE (d 1989), and Mary, *née* Lytton (d 1993); *b* 27 January 1937; *Educ* Whitehaven GS, Univ of Manchester (BSc, PhD, DSc), Univ of Cambridge, Univ of Southern Calif; *m* 19 Nov 1960, Kim, da of John Thomas Smith (d 1987); 1 da ((Susan) Joanna Forster b 16 July 1964), 1 s (Jonathan Forster b 23 March 1966); *Career* ICI research fell Cambridge 1962–64, lectr in chemistry Univ of St Andrews 1964–66; Univ of Sussex: lectr in chemistry 1966, reader 1975, prof 1986–2002, dean Sch of Chemistry 1989–92, research prof 2002–; Royal Soc Leverhulme sr research fell 1993–94, visiting fell Research Sch of Chemistry ANU Canberra 2004; visiting prof: Victoria Univ Canada 1971, Simon Fraser Univ Canada 1976, Indian Inst of Sci Bangalore 2001–02 and 2004–05; titular memb Inorganic Nomenclature Cmmn IUPAC 1986–88; memb: Inorganic Chemistry Panel SERC 1986–89, Editorial Bd Phosphorus, Sulphur, Silicon Jl 1989–, Dalton Cncl 1994–97, Scientific Advsy Bd Internet Jl of Chemistry 1997–2000, EPSRC 2001–, Bd of Dirs Main Gp Chemistry Ctee, Int Bd of Phosphorus Chemistry; FRS 1994; *Awards* Royal Soc of Chemistry: Corday-Morgan medal and prize 1973, Main Gp Element prize and medal 1985, Tilden lectureship and prize 1992, Alexander von Humboldt prize 2001–02, Ludwig Mond lectr and medal winner RSC 2002–03, Geza Zemplen medal Budapest Inst of Technol 2003; *Publications* Phosphorus: The Carbon Copy (jly, 1998); over 350 contribs to a variety of chemistry jls; *Recreations* playing tennis, badminton, squash, walking, theatre, watching cricket; *Style—* Prof John Nixon, FRS; ✉ Chemistry Department, School of Life Sciences, University of Sussex, Brighton, East Sussex BN1 9QJ (tel 01273 678536, fax 01273 677196); Juggs Barn, The Street, Kingston, Lewes, East Sussex (tel 01273 483993)

NIXON, Sir Simon Michael Christopher; 5 Bt (UK 1906), of Roebuck Grove, Milltown, Co Dublin, and Merrion Square, City of Dublin; s of Cecil Dominic Henry Joseph Nixon, MC (d 1994), and Brenda, *née* Lewis; suc uncle, Rev Father Sir Kenneth Michael John Basil Nixon, SJ, 4 Bt (d 1997); *b* 19 May 1957; *Heir* bro, Michael Nixon; *Style—* Sir Simon Nixon, Bt; ✉ Salt Winds, Torridge Road, Appledore, North Devon

NOAH, Prof Norman David; s of Jack David Noah (d 2002), of Wallington, Surrey, and Jane Rachel, *née* Samuel (d 1961); *b* 7 July 1939; *Educ* Burma, India and London, St Thomas' Hosp Med Sch London (MB BS); *m* 7 March 1971, Veronica Hilary, da of Bruno Kiwi; 2 s (Benedict Joel David b 16 April 1974, Joshua Luke Alexander b 2 July 1975), 1 da (Olivia Rachel Emma b 16 Feb 1979); *Career* house surgn Worthing Hosp 1964; St Thomas' Hosp: house physician 1964–65, SHO 1965–66, registrar 1966; SHO West End Hosp for Neurology and Neurosurgery 1967–68, research asst Dept of Experimental Pathology Cardiothoracic Inst The Brompton Hosp and registrar Paddington and Kensington Chest Clinic and St Charles' Hosp London 1968–70, sr epidemiologist Epidemiological Research Lab Central Public Health Lab London 1971–76, hon community physician Brent and Harrow AHA 1977–78, conslt epidemiologist Communicable Disease Surveillance Centre 1977–89, hon sr lectr Dept of Clinical Epidemiology and Social Med Royal Free Hosp Sch of Med 1979–89, hon conslt in control of infection Shenley Hosp 1983–89, prof and head Dept of Public Health and Epidemiology King's Coll Hosp Sch of Med and Dentistry 1989–98, dir of public health King's Healthcare 1989–98, prof of epidemiology and public health LSHTM 1998–; distinguished visitor Dept of Public Health and Primary Care Royal Free Hosp Sch of Med 1989–94, conslt in communicable disease Thames Region NRA Environment Agency 1989–2000, conslt Acupuncture Cncl of GB 1990–, hon conslt Communicable Disease Surveillance Centre 1993–98, conslt epidemiologist PHLS Communicable Disease Surveillance Centre Colindale 1998–2003, visiting prof Istituto di Igiene Univ of Rome 1996, 1998, 1999, 2000, 2001 and 2002; jt conslt to WHO/Int Epidemiological Assoc on epidemiology 1987, advsr to Aust Nat Univ Canberra on formation of CDSC/CDC type centre for surveillance of infectious diseases 1989, chm WHO meeting on acute respiratory infections Geneva 1990, advsr to WHO and Govt of China on the surveillance and control of infectious diseases March 1995; sec and memb Exec Cncl Int Epidemiological Assoc 1993–96; external examiner: Univ of Manchester 1992–95, Royal London Hosp Sch of Med 1996–2000, Dept of Public Health Univ of Glasgow 1996–2002, Kuwait Nat Univ 1997, UCL 2004; memb: MRC Sub-Ctee on Respiratory Syncytial Virus 1980–94, Med Advsy Ctee Nat Meningitis Tst 1987–2002, RCP Working Pty on Prevention 1988–91, Specialist Advsy Ctee and Educn Ctee FPHM 1993–96, Med Advsy Ctee Br Liver Tst 1994–98; editorial rep and memb Cncl Section of Epidemiology and Community Med RSM 1981–96, sr ed and managing ed Epidemiology and Infection 2002–; author of various books and book chapters and numerous original and leading articles in learned jls; MFCM, FFPH, FRCP (MRCP); *Recreations* cricket, music, food and wine, travel, hoarding (magpie syndrome) and oniomania; *Clubs* MCC; *Style—* Prof Norman Noah; ✉ Orley Rise, Orley Farm Road, Harrow-on-the-Hill, Middlesex HA1 3PE (tel 020 8422 2649); Department of Infectious and Tropical Diseases, London School of Hygiene and Tropical Medicine, Keppel Street, London WC1E 7HT (tel 020 7299 4767, e-mail norman.noah@lshtm.ac.uk)

NOAKES, Michael; s of Basil Henry Noakes (d 1969), of Horley and then Reigate, Surrey, and Mary Josephine, *née* Gerard (d 1989); *b* 28 October 1933; *Educ* Downside, Reigate Sch of Art, RA Schs London; *m* 9 July 1960, Dr Vivien Noakes, FRSL, *qv*, the writer, da of Marcus Langley (d 1977), of Reigate, Surrey; 1 da (Anya b 1961), 2 s (Jonathan b 1963, Benedict b 1965); *Career* Nat Serv 1954–56, Subaltern; portrait and landscape painter; numerous TV and radio appearances on art subjects; subject of: Portrait BBC 2 (with Eric Morley, 1977 and 1978), Changing Places BBC1 (with Jak, 1989); art corr Town & Around BBC 1964–68; ROI: elected memb 1964, vice-pres 1968–72, pres 1972–78, hon memb Cncl 1978–, fell 1996–; RP: elected memb 1967, memb Cncl 1969–72, 1972–74, 1978–80, 1993–95, 2004 and 2006–07; dir Fedn of Br Artists 1981–83 (govr 1972–81); hon memb: Nat Soc, United Soc; former chm Contemporary Portrait Soc, former pres Soc of Catholic Artists; judge Miss World Contest 1976; platinum disc award (for record sleeve Portrait of Sinatra, 1977); Freeman City of London; former FRSA; *Exhibitions* RA, ROI, RBA, RSMA, RP, Nat Soc, Young Contemporaries, Contemporary Portrait Soc, Grosvenor and Upper Grosvenor Galleries, Grafton Galleries (also New Grafton, Upper Grafton), Woodstock Galleries, RGI, Christie's, Tryon; *Represented in Collections of* HM The Queen, Royal Collection Windsor, Prince of Wales, Br Museum, Nat Portrait Gallery Perm Collection, numerous univs, House of Commons, Frank Sinatra, Guildhall London; *Portraits* incl: The Queen and most other members of the Royal Family, Pope Benedict XVI, President Clinton, Margaret Thatcher (when PM), and numerous other figures from service, academic, business and theatre life, as well as many sitters whose portraits were commissioned by their families; *Group Portraits* incl: Queen Elizabeth The Queen Mother opening Overlord Embroidery to public view (with The Duke of Norfolk, Princess Alice Countess of Athlone, Earl Mountbatten, and others), The Princess Royal being admitted to Livery of Worshipful Co of Woolmen, The Five Lords of Appeal in Ordinary for the Middle Temple (Lord Cross, Lord Diplock, Lord Salmon, Lord Wilberforce, Lord Simon), a commission for the Corporation of London to mark the Royal Silver Wedding featuring all senior members of the Royal Family at that time; designer of a £5 coin to mark the 50th birthday of The Prince of Wales 1998; *Books* A Professional Approach to Oil Painting (1968), contrib to various journals and books on art subjects; illustrator The Daily Life of the Queen: an Artist's Diary (by Vivien Noakes); *Recreations* idling; *Clubs* Garrick; *Style—* Michael Noakes; ✉ Eaton Heights, Eaton Road, Malvern WR14 4PE (tel 01684 575530, e-mail michael@michael-noakes.co.uk, website www.michael-noakes.co.uk)

NOAKES, Baroness (Life Peer UK 2000), of Goudhurst in the County of Kent; Dame Sheila Valerie Noakes; DBE (1996); da of Albert Frederick Masters, and Iris Sheila, *née* Ratcliffe; *b* 23 June 1949; *Educ* Eltham Hill GS, Univ of Bristol (LLB); *m* 3 Aug 1985, (Colin) Barry Noakes, s of Stuart Noakes, of Brenchley; *Career* KPMG: joined 1970, ptnr 1983–2000; seconded to: HM Treasy as accounting/commercial advsr 1979–81, Dept of Health as fin dir on NHS Mgmnt Exec 1988–91; sr non-exec dir Court of the Bank of England 1994–2001; memb: London Soc of CAs 1984–88, Cncl ICAEW 1987–2002 (pres 1999–2000); memb: Ctee of Enquiry MAFF 1988–2000, Mgmnt Bd of Inland Revenue 1992–99, NHS Policy Bd 1992–95, Private Fin Panel 1993–97, Bd of Companions Inst of Mgmnt 1997–2002, Public Services Productivity Panel 1998–2000, Cncl Inst of Business Ethics 1998–2003; memb Bd: ENO 2000–, Carpetright plc 2001–, Hanson plc 2001–, SThree plc 2001–07, John Laing plc 2002–04, The Racing Tst 2002–04, Social Market Fndn 2002–05, ICI plc 2004–; cmmr of Public Works Loan Bd 1995–2001; Cons front bench spokesman House of Lords: work and pensions 2001–, health 2001–03, treasy 2003–; tstee Reuters Founder Share Co Ltd 1998–; govr London Business Sch 1998–2001; memb Cncl: Marlborough Coll 2000–02, Eastbourne Coll 2000–04; Hon DBA London Guildhall Univ, Hon LLD Univ of Bristol, Hon DSc Univ of Buckingham; FCA; *Books* Tolley's Stamp Duties (1980); *Recreations* skiing, horse racing, opera, early classical music; *Style—* Baroness Noakes, DBE; ✉ House of Lords, London SW1A 0PW (tel 020 7219 5230, fax 020 7219 4215, e-mail noakess@parliament.uk)

NOAKES, Vivien; da of Marcus Langley (d 1977), and Helen, *née* Oldfield Box (d 1983); *b* 16 February 1937; *Educ* Manchester Coll Oxford, Somerville Coll Oxford (sr scholar, DPhil); *m* 9 July 1960, Michael Noakes, *qv*, s of Basil Noakes (d 1969); 1 da (Anya b 19 June 1961), 2 s (Jonathan b 15 May 1963, Benedict b 9 Feb 1965); *Career* writer; lectr Somerville Coll Oxford 1995–96; Philip and Frances Hofer lectr Harvard Univ 1988; guest curator of the maj exhibition Edward Lear at the Royal Acad of Arts and Nat Academy of Design NY 1985; judge: RSL Winifred Holtby Award 1999–2002, RSL W H Heinemann Award 1999–2003; FRSL; *Books* Edward Lear: The Life of a Wanderer (1968, 4 edn 2004), For Lovers of Edward Lear (ed, 1978), Scenes from Victorian Life (ed, 1979), Edward Lear 1812–1888: the catalogue of the Royal Academy Exhibition (1985), Selected Letters of Edward Lear (ed, 1988), The Painter Edward Lear (1991), The Imperial War Museum Catalogue of Isaac Rosenburg (1998), The Daily Life of the Queen: An Artists Diary (2000), Edward Lear: The Complete Verse and other Nonsense (ed, 2001, re-issued as The Complete Nonsense and Other Verse, 2002), The Poems and Plays of Isaac

Rosenberg (ed, 2004), Voices of Silence: The Alternative Book of First World War Poetry (ed, 2006); *Recreations* friends, reading, cooking; *Style—* Vivien Noakes; ✉ Eaton Heights, Eaton Road, Malvern, Worcestershire WR14 4PE (tel 01684 575530, e-mail mail@vivien-noakes.co.uk)

NOBBS, David Gordon; s of (Cyril) Gordon Nobbs (d 1968), and Gwendoline, *née* Williams (d 1995); *b* 13 March 1935; *Educ* Marlborough, St John's Coll Cambridge (BA); *m* 1, 1968 (m dis 1998), Mary Jane, da of Daniel Alfred Emmanuel Blatchford (d 1980); 2 step s (David b 1953, Christopher b 1955), 1 step da (Kim b 1957); m 2, 1998, Susan, da of Jack Bray; 1 step da (Briget b 1964); *Career* writer 1960–; reporter Sheffield Star 1958–60; Br Comedy Award for Top Br TV Comedy Screenwriter 1990; *Television* series incl: The Fall and Rise of Reginald Perrin (three series) 1976–78, Fairly Secret Army, A Bit of a Do 1989, Rich Tea and Sympathy 1991, The Life and Times of Henry Pratt (adapted from Second From Last in the Sack Race) 1992, Love on a Branch Line 1994, The Legacy of Reginald Perrin 1996; TV films incl: Stalag Luft 1993, Gentlemen's Relish 2001; contrib to: That Was the Week the Was, The Two Ronnies, The Frost Report, Sez Les, and others; *Plays* incl: Our Young Mr Wignall 1976, Cupid's Darts 1981, Dogfood Dan and the Carmarthen Cowboy 1982; *Books* The Itinerant Lodger (1965), Ostrich Country (1968), A Piece of the Sky is Missing (1969), The Death of Reginald Perrin (1975, later retitled The Fall and Rise of Reginald Perrin), The Return of Reginald Perrin (1977), The Better World of Reginald Perrin (1978), Second From Last in the Sack Race (1983), A Bit of a Do (1986), Pratt of the Argus (1988), Fair Do's (1990), The Cucumber Man (1994), The Legacy of Reginald Perrin (1995), Going Gently (2000), I Didn't Get Where I Am Today (2003), Sex and Other Changes (2004), Pratt à Manger (2006), Cupid's Dart (2007); *Recreations* the arts, eating, drinking, travel, bridge and cricket; *Style—* David Nobbs, Esq; ✉ c/o Jonathan Clowes Ltd, Iron Bridge House, Bridge Approach, London NW1 8BD (tel 020 7722 7674, fax 020 7722 7677, e-mail david.nobbs@virgin.net)

NOBES, Prof Christopher William; s of Harold Alfred Nobes, and Beryl Muriel, *née* Ramsay; *b* 20 March 1950; *Educ* Portsmouth GS, Univ of Exeter (BA, PhD); *m* 27 March 1982 (m dis 1988); *Career* head internal audit Hambro Life Assurance 1973–75, lectr Univ of Exeter 1975–82; prof of accounting: Univ of Strathclyde 1982–86, Univ of Reading 1987–2007, Royal Holloway Univ of London 2007–; memb Accounting Standards Ctee UK and Ireland 1987–90, vice-chm Accounting Ctee Fédération des Experts Comptables Européens, UK rep on Bd of Int Accounting Standards Ctee 1993–2001; FCCA 1973; *Books* incl: Comparative International Accounting (1981, 9 edn 2006), Accountants' Liability in the 1980's (with E P Minnis 1985), Issues in Multinational Accounting (with R H Parker 1988), Interpreting European Financial Statements (1994), Pocket Accounting (2002); contribs incl: The Fourth Directive and the United Kingdom (1984), Imputation Systems of Corporation Tax within the EEC (1984, 1985); *Style—* Prof Christopher Nobes; ✉ Department of Management, Royal Holloway, University of London, Egham, Surrey TW20 0EX

NOBLE, Adrian Keith; s of William John Noble (d 1987), of Chichester, W Sussex, and Violet Ena, *née* Wells (d 2003); *b* 19 July 1950; *Educ* Chichester HS, Univ of Bristol (BA), Drama Centre London; *m* June 1991, Joanne, *née* Pearce; 1 s, 1 da; *Career* assoc dir Bristol Old Vic Co 1976–80; RSC: assoc dir 1981–89, artistic dir 1991–2003 (artistic dir elect 1990); guest dir Manchester Royal Exchange Theatre Co; visiting prof London Inst 2001; Hon DLitt: Univ of Birmingham 1994, Univ of Bristol 1996, Univ of Exeter 1999, Univ of Warwick 2001; hon bencher Middle Temple 2001; *Theatre* prodns Stratford incl: King Lear 1993, A Midsummer Night's Dream 1994, Romeo and Juliet 1995, The Cherry Orchard 1995, Cymbeline 1997, The Lion, the Witch and the Wardrobe 1998, The Seagull 1999, The Secret Garden 2000; Chitty Chitty Bang Bang (London Palladium) 2002; *Opera* The Fairy Queen (Aix en Provence) 1989 (Grand Prix des Critiques), Il Retour d'Ulysses (Aix en Provence) 2000 (Grand Prix des Critiques), Magic Flute (Glyndebourne) 2004, Cosi fan Tutti (Opera de Lyon) 2006; *Films* A Midsummer Night's Dream 1996; *Awards* 12 nominations Olivier Awards; *Style—* Adrian Noble, Esq; ✉ c/o ICM, Oxford House, 76 Oxford Street, London W1D 1BS (tel 020 7636 6565)

NOBLE, Alexandra; *Educ* Wycombe Abbey, Univ of Florence, Univ of Sussex, (BA); *Career* curatorial asst Dept of Prints and Drawings V&A 1980–84, exhbns organiser The Photographers' Gall London 1984–88, exhbn organiser Nat Touring Exhibitions Hayward Gall/South Bank Centre London 1988–94, curator Eric and Salome Estorick Fndn London 1994–99, dir Estorick Collection of Modern Italian Art London 2000–01; retrained as integrative psychotherapist 2002–06, currently working in private practice and for The Place2Be; memb Editorial Ctee Ten Eight magazine 1985–86, memb Gtr London Arts Advsy Gp 1986–87, memb Organising Ctee 1st Rotterdam Arts Biennale 1987–88, advsr Compton Verney Exhbns Ctee; ed various fine art and photography pubns 1984–94, author of various articles in art jls; occasional lectr: Christie's Educn, RCA, Univ of Cambridge, Birkbeck Coll London; Winston Churchill travelling fell to USA 1982; *Style—* Ms Alexandra Noble; ✉ 48A Chalcot Road, London NW1 8LS (tel 020 7586 5484)

NOBLE, Rt Rev Brian Michael; *see:* Shrewsbury, Bishop of (RC)

NOBLE, Sir David Brunel; 6 Bt (UK 1902), of Ardmore and Ardardan Noble, Cardross, Co Dumbarton; er s of Sir Marc Brunel Noble, 5 Bt, CBE (d 1991), and Jennifer Lorna (Jane), *née* Mein-Austin; *b* 25 December 1961; *Educ* Eton, Univ of Greenwich (BA); *m* 1, 26 Sept 1987 (m dis 1993), Virginia Ann, yr da of late Roderick Lancaster Wetherall, MBE, of St Mary's Platt, Kent; 2 s (Roderick Lancaster Brunel b 8 Dec 1988, Alexander David b 28 Feb 1990); m 2, 29 Oct 1993, Stephanie, da of Daniel Digby, of Rainham, Kent; 3 s (Connor Daniel b 2 Jan 1993, Drew Marc (twin) b 2 Jan 1993 d 10 Jan 1993, Piers William Brunel b 29 Oct 2002), 1 da (Megan Lorna Annette b 2 June 1995); *Heir* s, Roderick Noble; *Style—* Sir David Noble, Bt; ✉ Meridian Court, 4 Wheelers Lane, Linton, Maidstone, Kent ME17 4BL

NOBLE, Prof Denis; CBE (1998); s of George Noble (Flt Lt RFC, d 1957), and Ethel, *née* Rutherford; *b* 16 November 1936; *Educ* Emanuel Sch London, UCL (BSc, PhD); *m* Jan 1965, Susan Jennifer, da of Flt Lt Leslie H Barfield; 1 da (Penelope Jean b 27 Aug 1967), 1 adopted s (Julian Aidan b 29 Aug 1970); *Career* asst lectr in physiology UCL 1961–64, tutorial fell Balliol Coll Oxford 1963–84, praefectus of Holywell Manor 1971–89, Burdon Sanderson prof of cardiovascular physiology Univ of Oxford 1984–2004 (emeritus prof 2004–); fell UCL 1986; fndr dir: Oxsoft Ltd 1984–, Physiome Sciences Inc 1994–2003; numerous appearances on radio and TV, various articles published in nat press; foreign sec Physiological Soc 1986–92 (hon sec 1974–80), chm Int Congress of Physiological Sciences 1993; sec-gen Int Union of Physiological Sciences 1994–2001; memb Founding Gp Save British Science; Gold Medal Br Heart Fndn 1985, Pierre Rijlant Prize Royal Acad of Med Belgium 1991, Pavlov Medal Russian Acad of Sciences 2004, Mackenzie Medal Br Cardiac Soc 2005; correspondant étranger de l'Académie Royale de Medecine de Belgique; hon memb: American Physiological Soc 1996, Japanese Physiological Soc 1998; Hon DSc Univ of Sheffield 2004, Doctorat (hc) Université de Bordeaux 2005; FRS 1979, Hon FRCP 1994 (Hon MRCP 1988), FMedSci 1998; *Books* The Initiation of the Heart Beat (1975), Electric Current Flow in Excitable Cells (1975), Goals, No Goals and Own Goals (1989), Sodium-Calcium Exchange (1989), The Logic of Life (1993), Ethics of Life (1997), The Music of Life (2006); *Recreations* foreign languages, guitar; *Style—* Prof Denis Noble, CBE, FRS; ✉ University Laboratory of Physiology, Parks Road, Oxford OX1 3PT (tel 01865 272533, fax 01865 272554, e-mail denis.noble@dpag.ox.ac.uk)

NOBLE, Sir Iain Andrew; 3 Bt (UK 1923), OBE, of Ardkinglas and Eilean Iarmain, Isle of Skye; er s of Sir Andrew Napier Noble, 2 Bt, KCMG, diplomat (d 1987), and Sigrid, *née* Michelet; *b* 8 September 1935; *Educ* Shanghai, Buenos Aires, Eton, Univ of Oxford (MA); *m* 27 Oct 1990, Lucilla Charlotte James, da of Col Hector Andrew Courtney Mackenzie of Dalmore, OBE, MC, TD, JP, DL (d 1988), of The House of Rosskeen, Invergordon, Ross-shire; *Heir* bro, Timothy Noble, *qv*; *Career* Nat Serv 1954–56, 2 Lt Intelligence Corps 1956–59, 2 Lt Argyll and Sutherland Highlanders (TA); exec Scottish Cncl (Devpt and Indust) Edinburgh 1964–69; entrepreneur; jt fndr and md Noble Grossart Ltd (merchant bankers) Edinburgh 1969–72; fndr and chm: Seaforth Maritime plc Aberdeen (offshore oil servs) 1972–77, Pràban na Linne Ltd ('The Gaelic Whiskies') 1976–, Lennox Oil Co plc Edinburgh 1980–85, Noble Gp Ltd Edinburgh (merchant bankers) 1980–2000 (also ceo until 1990), Noble Asset Managers 1985–97; chm Skye Bridge Ltd 1994–96, chm and ceo Sir Iain Noble & Partners Ltd Edinburgh (fin advsrs) 2000–; fndr and dir: Adam & Co plc (private bankers) 1983–93; dir Premium Tst plc (investment trust) 1993–2002; prop Fearann Eilean Iarmain (property business) in Skye 1972–; dep chm Traversee Theatre Co 1966–69; memb Ct Univ of Edinburgh 1970–72; fndr and tstee Sabhal Mor Ostaig (Gaelic Coll) Sleat Isle of Skye 1973–83 (chm 1973–75); tstee: Nat Museums of Scotland 1987–91, Nat Museum of Scotland Charitable Tst 1989–; pres The Saltire Soc 1992–96; fndr chm Scots Australian Cncl and Tst 1990–99; memb The Securities Assoc (now SFA) 1988–2000; Scotsman of the Year (Knights Templar Award) 1982; Keeper of the Quaich 2000; *Recreations* comhradh agus ceol le deagh chompanaich, restoring old buildings and ancient woodlands, Scottish history, traditional Gaelic and Scottish music, political theory; *Clubs* New (Edinburgh); *Style—* Sir Iain Noble of Ardkinglas and Eilean Iarmain, Bt, OBE; ✉ Eilean Iarmain, Sleite, An t-Eilean Sgitheanach IV43 8QR (tel 01471 833266, fax 01471 833260)

NOBLE, James Douglas Campbell; s of Capt Frederick Burnaby Noble, RN (d 1946), and Elsie Mackintosh, *née* Mackintosh (d 1962); *b* 20 April 1921; *Educ* Bradfield Coll, Canford Sch; *m* 1, 25 Aug 1956, Patricia Jean, da of Harold Strange Taylor-Young, FRCS (d 1988), and Nancy Seymour (d 1993); 3 da (Sarah b 1957, Charlotte b 1960, Diana b 1961), 1 s (Robert b 1965); m 2, 15 April 1978, Teresa Jane, da of Lt-Col Douglas Forster, DSO (d 1983) 11 Hussars (Prince Albert's Own), and Joan Forster (d 1992); *Career* The Royal Sussex Regt 1940, cmmnd The Argyll & Sutherland Highlanders 1940, 2 Bn A&SH Singapore 1941, Malayan Campaign 1941–42, ADC to Maj-Gen ACM Paris and Maj-Gen William Key 11 Div 1941–42, POW Thailand 1942–45, ret 1946; Investment Dept Kleinwort Sons & Co 1946–52, memb Stock Exchange London 1953–82; ptnr: Fielding Newson & Smith & Co 1953–62, Colegrave & Co 1962–73, Kitcat & Aitken 1973–81; H M Tennent Ltd: fin dir 1958–73, chm 1973–77; investment advsr to King George V's Pension Fund for Actors and Actresses (1911) 1960–82; memb: Bd of Visitors and Local Review Bd HMP Chelmsford 1972–87, Ctee Stars Orgn for Spastics 1974–76, Investment Ctee Peterhouse Cambridge 1983–85; tstee: Royal Ballet Benevolent Fund 1978–84, Cambridge HA Tst Fndn 1986–88; official speaker: Far East POWs Assoc E Anglia Branch 1984–99, Burma Star Herts Cambs and Essex Borders Branch 1980–; lectr: 22 Special Air Services Regt Courses Stirling Lines Hereford 1985–91, Staff Coll Camberley Realities of War Conf 1989–92; lectr on leadership RMA Sandhurst 1995–2003; fndr memb and tstee A Company of Speakers (Christian charitable tst) 1989–2000; vice-pres Christian Education Movement 2000–03; UK Templeton Individual Award for pioneering in religion 1992; *Recreations* walking, reading, writing, correspondence, conversation, travel, preaching, lecturing; *Clubs* The Cryptics CC, The Free Foresters CC, The Arabs CC, The Bradfield Waifs CC, Hawks' (Cambridge); *Style—* James Noble, Esq; ✉ 1 Dalegarth, Hurst Park Avenue, Milton Road, Cambridge CB4 2AG (tel 01223 312277)

NOBLE, Prof Mark Ian Munro; s of Leslie Ewart Noble (d 1985), of Sunbury, Surrey, and Jessie Munro, *née* Wilson (d 1993); *b* 6 September 1935; *Educ* Hampton GS, Bart's Med Coll London (DSc, PhD, MD); *m* 1985, Dr A J Drake-Holland; 3 c; *Career* sr fell Cardiovascular Research Inst San Francisco 1966–68, sr lectr and conslt physician Charing Cross Hosp Med Sch London 1971–73 (lectr Dept of Med 1968–71), sr investigator Midhurst Med Research Inst Midhurst W Sussex 1973–83, Boerhaave prof of med Univ of Leiden 1982, prof of cardiovascular med Imperial Coll Sch of Med at Charing Cross Hosp (Charing Cross and Westminster Med Sch until merger 1997) 1989–, hon conslt physician Hammersmith Hosps NHS Tst (research dir for cardiology) and Chelsea and Westminster Hosp 1989–, visiting prof Nat Heart and Lung Inst London 1989–; FRCP, FESC; *Books* The Cardiac Cycle (1979), Cardiac Metabolism (jtly, 1983), Starling's Law of the Heart Revisited (jtly, 1988), The Interval-Force Relationship of the Heart: Bowditch Revisited (jtly, 1992); numerous book chapters and full original papers; *Recreations* opera, gardening, classical music; *Clubs* RSM; *Style—* Prof Mark Noble

NOBLE, Prof Michael William John; OBE; s of William John Noble (d 1987), and Violet, *née* Wells (d 2003); *b* 25 January 1948, Isleworth, Middlesex; *Educ* Magdalen Coll Oxford (BA, MSc), Coll of Law; *m* 1; 2 s (Stefan b 16 Dec 1980, David b 1 Oct 1984); m 2, 21 June 2004, Gemma, *née* Wright; *Career* admitted slr 1974; articled clerk, asst slr then ptnr Ferguson Bricknell & Co 1971–81, community welfare rights lawyer Barton Project Oxford 1981–83 and 1985–86; Univ of Oxford: student unit supervisor and researcher Dept of Social and Admin Studies 1986–91, lectr then reader in social policy 1991–2004, prof of social policy 2004–, dir Social Disadvantage Research Centre, dir Centre for the Analysis of South African Social Policy; memb: Law Soc, Social Policy Assoc; FRSS; *Publications* incl: Welsh Index of Multiple Deprivation (2000), Measuring Multiple Deprivation at the Small Area Level: The indices of deprivation 2000 (2000), The Northern Ireland Multiple Deprivation Measure (2001 and 2005), Changing Fortunes: Geographic patterns of income deprivation in the late 1990s (2001), Growing Together or Growing Apart? Geographic Patterns of Change in IS and JSA-IB Claimants in England 1995–2000 (2002), Scottish Index of Deprivation (2003), Older People Count: The Help the Aged Income Index for older people in England and Wales 2003 (2003), The English Indices of Deprivation (2004), The Provincial Indices of Multiple Deprivation for South Africa 2001 (2006); *Style—* Prof Michael Noble, OBE; ✉ Department of Social Policy and Social Work, University of Oxford, Barnett House, Wellington Square, Oxford OX1 2ER (tel 01865 270325, fax 01865 270324, e-mail michael.noble@socres.ox.ac.uk)

NOBLE, Tim; s of David Noble, and Mary Noble; *b* 1966; *Educ* Cheltenham Art Coll, Nottingham Poly (BA), RCA (MA); *Career* artist; collaborator with Sue Webster, *qv*; residency Dean Clough Halifax 1989–92; *Two-Person Exhibitions* British Rubbish (Independent Art Space London) 1996, Home Chance (Rivington St London) 1997, Vague Us (Habitat London) 1998, WOW (Modern Art London) 1998, The New Barbarians (Chisenhale Gallery London) 1999, I Love You (Deitch Projects NY) 2000, British Wildife (Modern Art London) 2000, Masters of the Universe (Deste Fndn Athens) 2000, Instant Gratification (Gagosian Gallery Beverly Hills) 2001, Ghastly Arrangements (Milton Keynes Gallery) 2002, Black Magic (MW Projects London) 2002, Real Life is Rubbish (Statements at Art Basel Miami) 2002, PS1/MOMA (Long Island City NY) 2003, Modern Art is Dead (Modern Art London) 2004, Noble & Webster (MFA Boston) 2004, The New Barbarians (CAC Málaga) 2005, The Joy of Sex (Kukje Gallery Seoul) 2005, The Glory Hole (Bortolami Dayan NY) 2005; *Group Exhibitions* incl: Lift (Brick Lane London) 1993, Hijack (NY London and Berlin) 1994, Fete Worse Than Death (Hoxton Square London) 1994, Absolut Art (RCA London) 1994, Self Storage (Artangel London) 1995, Hanging Picnic (Hoxton Sq London) 1995, Fools Rain (ICA London) 1996, Turning the Tables (Chisenhale Gallery London) 1997, Livestock Market (London) 1997, Sex and the British (Galerie Thaddaeus Ropac Salzburg and Paris) 2000, Man-Body in Art from 1950 to 2000 (ARKEN Copenhagen) 2000, Apocalypse (Royal Acad of Art London) 2000, Tattoo Show (Modern Art London) 2001, Form Follows Fiction (Castello di Rivoli Turin) 2001, Casino

2001 (SMAK Ghent) 2002, 2001 A Space Oddity (A22 Projects London) 2001, Shortcuts (Nicosia Municipal Arts Centre Cyprus) 2001, Art Crazy Nation (Milton Keynes Gallery) 2002, State of Play (Serpentine Gallery London) 2004, New Blood (Saatchi Gallery London) 2004, Monument To Now (Dakis Joannou Collection Athens) 2004, Masquerade (MCA Sydney) 2006; *Clubs* Colony Room; *Style*— Tim Noble, Esq; ✉ c/o Modern Art, 10 Vyner Street, London E2 9DG (tel 020 8980 7742, e-mail info@modernartinc.com)

NOBLE, Timothy Peter; yr s of Sir Andrew Napier Noble, 2 Bt, KCMG (d 1987); hp of bro Sir Iain Andrew Noble, 3 Bt, *qv*; *b* 21 December 1943; *Educ* Eton, UC Oxford (MA), INSEAD Fontainebleau (MBA); *m* 1976, Elizabeth Mary, da of late Alexander Wallace Aitken; 1 da (Sasha Heidi Elizabeth b 1978), 2 s (Lorne Andrew Wallace b 1980, Andrew Iain Brunel b 1984); *Career* called to the Bar Gray's Inn 1969; exec dir Lyle Shipping plc Glasgow 1976–83, chm Noble Group Ltd Edinburgh 2000– (chief exec 1983–2000); chm: Palmaris Capital plc, Darnaway Venture Capital plc; dir: Scottish Friendly Assurance Soc Ltd, Martin Energy Ltd; *Clubs* New (Edinburgh); *Style*— Timothy Noble, Esq; ✉ Ardnahane, Barnton Avenue, Edinburgh EH4 6JJ; Noble Group Ltd, 76 George Street, Edinburgh EH2 3BU (tel 0131 225 9677, fax 0131 225 5479)

NOBLETT, Ven William Alexander; s of Joseph Henry Noblett, and Hilda Florence Noblett; *Educ* HS Dublin, Salisbury and Wells Theol Coll, Univ of Southampton (BTh), Univ of Oxford (MTh); *Career* ordained: deacon 1978, priest 1979; curate Sholing Southampton 1978–80, rector Ardamine Union 1980–82, chaplain RAF 1982–84, vicar Middlesbrough St Thomas 1984–87; chaplain HMP: Wakefield 1987–93, Norwich 1993–97, Full Sutton 1997–2001; chaplain-gen and archdeacon to HM Prisons 2001–, canon of York Minster 2001–, chaplain to HM The Queen 2005–; FRSA 2004; *Books* Prayers for People in Prison (1998); *Recreations* family life, running, reading, music; *Style*— The Ven William Noblett; ✉ Room 410, Abel House, John Islip Street, London SW1P 4LH (tel 020 7217 8201, fax 020 7217 8844)

NOEL, Lady Celestria; *see:* Hales, Lady Celestria Magdalen Mary

NOEL, Hon Gerard Eyre; s of 4 Earl of Gainsborough, OBE (d 1927); *b* 1926; *Educ* Georgetown USA, Exeter Coll Oxford; *m* 1958, Adele Julie Patricia, da of late Maj V N B Were and Mrs M J Were, OBE; 2 s, 1 da; *Career* called to the Bar Inner Temple 1952; author, journalist and lectr; Catholic Herald: ed 1971–83, editorial dir 1983–; contested (Lib) Argyll 1959; vice-pres Cncl of Christians and Jews 2003 (hon treas 1974–79); sr research fell St Anne's Coll Oxford 1993–97; Freeman City of London, Liveryman Worshipful Co of Stationers and Newspapermakers; FRSL; *Publications* author of 25 books, incl: Paul VI, The Path from Rome, Goldwater, Harold Wilson, Princess Alice, The Great Lock-Out of 1926, The Anatomy of the Catholic Church, Ena, Spain's English Queen; also various translations; *Clubs* Pratt's, Garrick, White's; *Style*— The Hon Gerard Noel, FRSL; ✉ Westington Mill, Chipping Campden, Gloucestershire GL55 6EB

NOEL, Hon Thomas; s of 5 Earl of Gainsborough; *b* 9 March 1958; *Educ* Ampleforth, RAC Cirencester (MRAC 1980); *Career* Savills 1981–83, Humberts 1983–84; dir: Bride Hall plc 1987– (joined 1984, now non-exec dir), Barnsdale Lodge Ltd 1989–, First City Air; chm and chief exec Metropolitan Realty Tst (UK) Ltd 1984–; memb: CLA, Royal Forestry Soc; FRICS 1982; *Recreations* shooting, skiing, flying fixed and rotary aircraft (vintage and modern); *Clubs* Pratt's, The Air Squadron; *Style*— The Hon Thomas Noel; ✉ Bride Hall plc, 49 Hays Mews, London W1 (tel 020 7493 3996, fax 020 7499 4388)

NOEL-BUXTON, 3 Baron (UK 1930); Martin Connal Noel-Buxton; s of 2 Baron Noel-Buxton (d 1980), by his 1 w, Nancy, *née* Connal; *b* 8 December 1940; *Educ* Bryanston, Balliol Coll Oxford; *m* 1, 1964 (m dis 1968), Miranda Mary (d 1979), da of Maj Hugo Atherton Chisenhale-Marsh (d 1996), of Epping, Essex; m 2, 1972 (m dis 1982), Sarah Margaret Surridge (who m, 1982, Peter E W Adam), da of Neil Charles Wolseley Barrett TD (d 2006), of Teddington, Middx; 1 s (Hon Charles Connal b 1975), 1 da (Hon Lucy Margaret b 1977); m 3, 1986, Mrs Abigail Marie Granger, da of Eric Philip Richard Clent; 1 da (Hon Antonia Helen Isabella b 11 Dec 1989); *Heir* s, Hon Charles Noel-Buxton; *Career* slr 1966; *Style*— The Rt Hon the Lord Noel-Buxton

NOEST, Peter J; s of Maj A J F Noest, of Dulwich, and Maria Gerbrands-Noest; *b* 12 June 1948; *Educ* St George's Coll Weybridge, RAC Cirencester; *m* 1, (m dis 1993), Lisabeth Penelope Moody; 1 s (Timothy Peter b 1974), 1 da (Lisa Jane b 1976); m 2, 1993, Jocelyn Claire (d 2003), yr da of Alan Douglas Spencer (d 2000); 1 s (Thomas Andrew Spencer b 1995); *Career* chartered surveyor (land agency and general practice); Knight Frank & Rutley: ptnr Amsterdam 1972–77, ptnr London 1977–81, full equity ptnr 1981, resigned 1983; sr commercial ptnr Hampton & Son 1984–88; md: Capital Consultancy Group 1993–, P H Gillingham (Investments) Ltd 1986–, Cotswold Land and Estates Ltd 2000–, P H Gillingham Gp Ltd 2003–; dir Lambert Smith Hampton 1988–92; FRICS; *Books* contributor to Office Development, Estates Gazette (1985); *Recreations* shooting, hunting, photography, farming, conservation, forestry, travel, wine; *Clubs* Turf; *Style*— Peter Noest, Esq; ✉ The Manor Farmhouse, Withington, Cheltenham, Gloucestershire GL54 4BG

NOGAMI, HE Yoshiji; s of Hiroshi Nogami (d 1998), and Masako, *née* Sakai (d 2002); *b* 19 June 1942; *Educ* Univ of Tokyo (BA); *m* 20 Dec 1978, Geraldine Ann, *née* Woods McDermott; 3 s (Masao Sean b 1979, Haruo Justin b 1982, Kazuo Anthony b 1984); *Career* Japanese diplomat; joined Miny of Foreign Affrs 1966, economic cnsllr Washington 1985–88, actg dir Japan Inst for Int Affrs 1988–91, dep DG Middle East and African Affrs Bureau 1991–93, dep DG Foreign Policy Bureau 1993–94, consul-gen Hong Kong 1994–96, DG Economic Affairs Bureau 1996–97, ambass to OECD 1997–99, dep min for foreign affrs 1999–01, vice-min for foreign affrs 2001–02, sr visiting fell RIIA 2002–04, ambass to the Ct of St James's 2004–; Officeier de la Légion d'Honneur (France); *Clubs* Athenaeum, Travellers, RAC, Brocket Hall; *Style*— HE Mr Yoshiji Nogami; ✉ Embassy of Japan, 101–104 Piccadilly, London W1J 7JT

NOGUERA, Anthony; *b* 17 July 1969, Cheltenham, Glos; *Educ* Whitefriars Sch Cheltenham, Univ of Birmingham; *m* Lucy Anne, *née* Mallon; 1 s (Louis b 25 Oct 2001), 1 da (Madalena b 31 Jan 2004); *Career* fomer ed various music magazines, sr features writer Sky magazine 1998–99, ed FHM 1999–2001 (joined as features ed 1995), ed-in-chief FHM Int 1999–2001, ed-in-chief Arena 2001–05, ed-in-chief Emap East (men's div) Arena, Zoo, Arena Homme-Plus 2005–; ed largest selling single issue of a Br monthly magazine ever FHM July 2000 (1.2 million copies); Emap Ed of the Year 1999, Ed of the Year BSME 2000; *Recreations* Jeet Kune Do (brown belt); *Style*— Anthony Noguera, Esq; ✉ Emap, Mappin House, 4 Winsley Street, London W1W 8HF

NOKES, David Leonard; s of Anthony John Nokes, and Ethel Murray, *née* Smith; *b* 11 March 1948; *Educ* KCS Wimbledon, Christ's Coll Cambridge (open scholar, BA, PhD); *Career* Adelaide Stoll res scholar Christ's Coll Cambridge 1969; King's Coll London: lectr in English 1973–88, reader in Eng lit 1988–98, prof of English 1998–; regular reviewer for TLS, The Spectator, BBC Radio, The Sunday Times; memb Br Soc for Eighteenth-Century Studies (treas 1982–83); FRSL 1994; *Books* Jonathan Swift, A Hypocrite Reversed (1985, James Tait Black Meml Prize for biography), Raillery and Rage, A Study of 18th Century Satire (1987), Joseph Andrews, A Master Study (1987), John Gay, A Profession of Friendship (1995), Jane Austen (1997), the Nightingale Papers (2005); *Television* No Country for Old Men: The Long Exile of Jonathan Swift (BBC Omnibus film) 1981, co-writer Clarissa (BBC serial adapted from Richardson's novel) 1991, The Count of Solar (BBC Screen Two) 1992, The Tenant of Wildfell Hall (BBC serial adapted from Anne Bronte's novel) 1996, Frankenstein: Birth of a Monster 2003; *Radio* The Man on the Heath 2005; *Recreations* reading, writing; *Clubs* The Johnson; *Style*— Prof David Nokes, FRSL; ✉ Department of English, King's College, University of London, Strand, London WC2R 2LS (tel 020 7848 2185)

NOLAN, Benjamin; QC (1992); s of Benjamin Nolan (d 1951), and Jane, *née* Mercer (d 2001); *b* 19 July 1948; *Educ* St Joseph's Coll Blackpool, Newcastle upon Tyne Poly, Univ of London (LLB); *Children* 2 da (Georgina b 19 Aug 1978, Katharine b 29 Nov 1980); *Career* called to the Bar 1971; recorder 1989–, head of chambers 1998–2003, dep judge of the High Court 1998–; *Recreations* travel, cooking, swimming, walking; *Style*— Benjamin Nolan, Esq, QC; ✉ Broad Chare Chambers, 33 Broad Chare, Newcastle upon Tyne NE1 3DQ (tel 0191 232 0541, e-mail bnqc@aol.com)

NOLAN, Hon Michael Alfred Anthony; s of Baron Nolan, PC, DL (Life Peer), and Margaret, *née* Noyes; *b* 17 June 1955; *Educ* Ampleforth, St Benet's Hall Oxford (MA), City Univ (Dip Law); *m* 26 May 1984, Adeline Mei Choo, da of Henry S H Oh, of Singapore; 2 s (Hugh b 1986, Felix b 1992), 1 da (Sophia Min b 1989); *Career* called to the Bar Middle Temple 1981; contrib to Atkins Court Forms (Arbitration, Carriers, Commercial Court, Insurance); memb: Commercial Bar Assoc (exec 1998–2001), London Common Law and Commercial Bar Assoc; *Recreations* swimming, tennis, skiing, books, plays, films, opera; *Clubs* Oxford Union, Millennium, Hurlingham, MCC; *Style*— The Hon Michael Nolan; ✉ Quadrant Chambers, Quadrant House, 10 Fleet Street, London EC4Y 1AU (tel 020 7583 4444, fax 020 7583 4445, e-mail info@quadrantchambers.com)

NOLAN, Dr Philip Michael Gerard (Phil); s of Philip Nolan (d 1979), and Mary, *née* Corrigan; *b* 15 October 1953; *Educ* Queen's Univ Belfast (BSc, PhD), London Business Sch (MBA); *m* 27 May 1978, Josephine, da of Andrew Monaghan; 2 s (Andrew b 2 Oct 1991, Christopher b 23 June 1994); *Career* lectr in geology Univ of Ulster 1979–81; geologist BP 1981–87, commercial and planning roles Head Office BP Exploration 1987–93, magr acquisitions and disposals BP Exploration 1993–95, md (secondment from BP) Interconnector (UK) Ltd 1995, dir Transco E Area BG plc 1996, md Transco 1997, appointed BG Bd 1998; chief exec: Transco BG plc 1998–2000, Lattice Gp plc 2000–02, eircom Ltd 2002–06; chm Infinis 2007–; non-exec dir: De La Rue plc 2001–, Providence Resources plc, Ulster Bank Ltd; *Recreations* walking, golf, listening to music, reading, watching football; *Style*— Dr Phil Nolan

NOON, Jamie Darren; s of Russ Noon, and Kath, *née* Wakefield; *b* 9 May 1979, Goole, E Yorks; *Educ* Northumbria Univ (BSc), Vocational Trg Charitable Tst (Dip); *m* 16 July 2004, Rachel, *née* Littlewood; 1 s (Lewis Benjamin b 18 Feb 2005), 1 da (Elodie Grace b 7 Oct 2006); *Career* rugby union player; with Newcastle Falcons 1998– (winners Tetley Bitter Cup 2001, Powergen Cup 2004); England: 26 caps, debut v Canada 2001, memb squad World Cup 2007; *Recreations* fly fishing, squash, football, reading; *Style*— Jamie Noon, Esq; ✉ Newcastle Falcons, Kingston Park Stadium, Brunton Road, Newcastle upon Tyne NE13 8AF

NOON, Paul; s of Thomas Noon, of Orpington, Kent, and Barbara, *née* Grocott; *b* 1 December 1952, Crewe, Cheshire; *m* 12 Feb 1977, Eileen, *née* Smith; 2 da (Helen b 7 Jan 1981, Alice b 2 Feb 1986); *Career* Prospect (formerly Inst of Professional Civil Servants, then Inst of Professional Mangrs and Specialists): negotiator 1974–99, gen sec 1999–; chair Cncl of Civil Service Unions 2001–03; TUC Gen Cncl: memb 2001–, memb Exec Ctee 2002–; *Style*— Paul Noon, Esq; ✉ 3 Warwick Close, Bexley, Kent DA5 3NL (tel 01322 550968); Prospect, 75–79 York Road, London SE1 7A6 (tel 020 7902 6704, e-mail paul.noon@prospect.org.uk)

NORBURY, Peter; s of Harold Norbury (d 1987), and Mabel Victoria, *née* Whittaker (d 1984); *b* 12 January 1953, Manchester; *Educ* Manchester Grammar, Univ of Sheffield (LLB), Coll of Law; *m* 11 April 1987, Elizabeth, *née* Standley; 2 s (Robert Edward b 21 May 1988, Michael Peter b 1 Oct 1990); *Career* admitted slr 1978; slr specialising in employment law; ptnr Eversheds 1984–; chm Wigan Warriors Rugby League Club 1998–99, chm Disciplinary Ctee Rugby Football League; memb: Law Soc 1978, Employment Lawyers Assoc, Industrial Soc; *Recreations* cricket, football, golf, rugby league; *Style*— Peter Norbury, Esq; ✉ Eversheds, Eversheds House, 70 Great Bridgewater Street, Manchester M1 5ES (tel 0161 831 8000, fax 0161 831 8888, e-mail peternorbury@eversheds.com)

NORDEN, Denis; CBE (1980); s of George Norden (d 1977), and Jenny Norden (d 1979); *b* 6 February 1922; *Educ* City of London Sch; *m* 1943, Avril Rosen; 1 s (Nicolas), 1 da (Maggie); *Career* writer and broadcaster; collaborated with Frank Muir (d 1998), 1947–64, solo TV and film writer 1964–; co-author (with Frank Muir): Take It From Here (radio series), Whacko! (TV series); panellist: My Word! (radio series) 1956–93, My Music (TV and radio series) 1967–92; author of film screenplays incl Buona Sera Mrs Campbell; writer and presenter: Looks Familiar (Thames TV) 1973–86, It'll be Alright on the Night (nos 1–21, LWT) 1977–2005, Denis Norden's Laughter File (nos 1–13), Denis Norden's Trailer Cinema 1992, Laughter by Royal Command 1993, 40 Years of ITV Laughter (Parts 1, 2 and 3) 1995, A Right Royal Song and Dance 1996, All the Best from Denis Norden (ITV) 2006; Lifetime Achievement Award Writers Guild of GB 1999, admitted to RTS Hall of Fame 2000; *Books* My Word (series with Frank Muir), The Utterly Ultimate My Word Collection, Coming To You Live (with Sybil Harper and Norma Gilbert); *Recreations* loitering; *Clubs* Odeon Saturday Morning; *Style*— Denis Norden, Esq, CBE; ✉ Whitefields, Dean Bottom, South Darenth, Kent DA4 9JX (tel 01474 703027)

NORFOLK, 18 Duke of (Premier E Dukedom 1483 with precedence 1397); Edward William Fitzalan Howard; DL (W Sussex) 2002; also Earl of Arundel (E 1139 if the claim by tenure, which was admitted by the Crown in 1433, is recognised; otherwise 1292; either way, the Premier E Earldom), Baron Beaumont (E 1309), Baron Maltravers (E 1330), Earl of Surrey (E 1483), Baron FitzAlan, Baron Clun, Baron Oswaldestre (all E 1627), Earl of Norfolk (E 1644), and Baron Howard of Glossop (UK 1869); Earl Marshal and Hereditary Marshal of England (1672); s of 17 Duke of Norfolk, KG, CB, CBE, MC, DL (d 2002); *b* 2 December 1956; *Educ* Ampleforth, Lincoln Coll Oxford; *m* 27 June 1987, Georgina Susan, yr da of John Temple Gore; 3 s (Henry Miles, Earl of Arundel and Surrey b 3 Dec 1987, Lord Thomas Jack b 14 March 1992, Lord Philip b 14 July 1996), 2 da (Lady Rachel Rose b 10 June 1989, Lady Isabel Serena b 7 Feb 1994); *Heir* s, Earl of Arundel and Surrey; *Career* chm: Sigas Ltd 1979–88, Parkwood Group Ltd 1989–2002; Dep Earl Marshal of England 2000–02; Liveryman Worshipful Co of Fishmongers; *Recreations* motor racing, skiing, shooting; *Clubs* British Racing Drivers (Silverstone); *Style*— His Grace the Duke of Norfolk; ✉ Arundel Castle, Arundel, West Sussex (tel 01903 883400)

NORGROVE, David; s of Douglas Norgrove, and Ann Norgrove; *b* 23 January 1948; *Educ* Christ's Hosp, Exeter Coll Oxford (BA), Emmanuel Coll Cambridge (DipEcon), LSE (MSc); *m* 1977, Jenny Stoker; 1 s, 2 da; *Career* HM Treasy 1972–85 (seconded to First Nat Bank of Chicago 1978–80), private sec to PM 1985–88, Marks & Spencer 1988–2004 (exec dir and chair Pensions Fund Tstees 2000–04), chair Pensions Regulator 2005–; non-exec dir Strategic Rail Authy 2002–04; tstee: Hanover Tst 1993–2000, Media Tst 1998–2003, Mencap 2000–03, Br Museum 2004–; *Style*— David Norgrove; ✉ The Pensions Regulator, Napier House, Trafalgar Place, Brighton BN1 4DW (tel 01273 627612, fax 01273 627630, e-mail david.norgrove@thepensionsregulator.gov.uk)

NORMAL, Henry; *Career* comedy writer; co-prop Baby Cow Prodns (with Steve Coogan); co-writer: Paul Calf Video Diary 1994, Three Fights, Two Weddings and a Funeral 1994, Coogan's Run 1995, The Tony Ferrino Phenomenon 1997, The Parole Officer 2002; co-writer and assoc prodr: The Mrs Merton Show 1996 and 1997, Mrs Merton and Malcolm 1997, The Royle Family 1998; co-creator and co-writer The Man Who Thinks

He's It 1998; exec prodr: Marion and Geoff 2000, Combat Sheet 2001 (script ed), Human Remains 2001 (script ed), Dr Terrible's House of Horrible 2001 (co-writer), 24 Hour Party People 2002, The Sketch Show 2002 (script ed), The Private Life of Samuel Pepys 2003, Whine Gums 2003, Posh and Becks' Big Impression 2003, Marion and Geoff 2 2003, Cruise of the Gods 2003, I Am Not An Animal 2004, The Keith Baret Show 2004, The Mighty Boosh 2004, Nighty Night 2004; BAFTA Award 1994, 1996, 1997, 2002 and 2003, Br Comedy Award 1996 and 1998, Silver Rose of Montreux 1997, South Bank Award 1998, Banff Rockie Award 2001; *Style—* Henry Normal, Esq; ✉ Baby Cow Productions, 77 Oxford Street, London W1D 2ES

NORMAN, Archibald John (Archie); *b* 1 May 1954; *Career* formerly: with Citibank NA, ptnr McKinsey & Co Ltd (joined 1979); fin dir Kingfisher plc 1986–91, chm Chartwell Land plc until 1991, chief exec Asda plc 1991–96 (chm 1997–2000), non-exec chm French plc 1999–2001, chm Energis 2002–; non-exec dir: British Rail (now Railtrack) 1992–2000, Holmes Place 2003–; sr advsr Lazard 2004–; MP (Cons) Tunbridge Wells 1997–2005; chief exec and dep chm Cons Pty 1997–99; shadow min for Europe 1999–2000, shadow sec for environment, tport and the regions 2000–01; *Style—* Archie Norman, Esq

NORMAN, Barry Leslie; CBE (1998); s of Leslie Norman (d 1993; film prodr (Mandy, The Cruel Sea) and dir (Dunkirk, The Long and the Short and the Tall)), and Elizabeth, *née* Crafford (d 1999); *b* 21 August 1933; *Educ* Highgate Sch; *m* 1957, Diana, da of late Arthur Narracott; 2 da (Samantha, Emma); *Career* author and broadcaster; dir Film Finance Corp 1980–85; writer and presenter BBC TV: Film '73–'81 and '83–'98, The Hollywood Greats 1977–79 and 1984–85, Talking Pictures 1988; writer and presenter Sky TV 1998–2001; presenter BBC Radio 4: Today 1974–76, Going Places 1977–81, Breakaway 1979–80, The Chip Shop 1984, How Far Can You Go 1990; govr BFI 1996–2001; winner: Richard Dimbleby award BAFTA 1980, Publishing Magazine award for Columnist of the Year Radio Times 1990, special award London Film Critics Circle 1995, Special Achievement award Guild of Provincial Film Writers 1995; Hon DLitt: UEA 1991, Univ of Hertfordshire 1996; *Books* fiction: The Matter of Mandrake, The Hounds of Sparta, End Product, To Nick A Good Body, A Series of Defeats, Have A Nice Day, Sticky Wicket, The Birdog Tape (Chapmans, 1992), The Mickey Mouse Affair (1995), Death on Sunset (1998); non-fiction: Tales of the Redundance Kid, The Hollywood Greats, Film Greats, The Movie Greats, Talking Pictures, 100 Best Films of the Century (1992 and 1998), Barry and Emma Norman's Family Video Guide (1994), And Why Not? (2002); *Recreations* cricket; *Clubs* Groucho, Lord's Taverners, MCC; *Style—* Barry Norman, Esq, CBE; ✉ c/o Curtis Brown, 4th Floor, Haymarket House, 28–29 Haymarket, London SW1Y 4SP (tel 020 7396 6600)

NORMAN, David Mark; s of Lt-Col Mark Richard Norman, CBE (d 1994), of Much Hadham, Herts, and Helen, *née* Bryan; *b* 30 January 1941; *Educ* Eton, McGill Univ Montreal (BA), Harvard Business Sch (MBA); *m* 9 July 1966, Diana Anne, da of John Vincent Sheffield, CBE, of Whitchurch, Hants; 3 da (Anna b 1967, Isabella b 1971, Davina b 1981), 1 s (Jonathan b 1972); *Career* Norcros Ltd 1967–77 (dir of ops and main bd dir 1975–77), chief exec Norcros Printing & Packaging 1971–75, md Russell Reynolds Associates Inc 1978–82 (exec dir 1977–78); chm: Norman Resources Ltd 1982–83, Norman Broadbent International Ltd 1983–98, BNB Resources plc 1987–98, Norlan Resources Ltd 1998–; non-exec dir Alex Brown & Sons Inc Baltimore 1992–96; govr: Royal Ballet Sch 1980– (chm 2000–), Royal Ballet 1996–2005; tstee and chm Finance Ctee Royal Botanic Gardens Kew 2002–; chm Tennis and Rackets Assoc 1982–97; *Recreations* golf, tennis, rackets, classical music, opera, ballet; *Clubs* Boodle's, All England Lawn Tennis and Croquet, Queen's; *Style—* David Norman, Esq; ✉ Burkham House, Alton, Hampshire GU34 5RS (tel 01256 381211); office (tel 020 7235 5031, fax 020 7235 5036, e-mail dmnorman2@aol.com)

NORMAN, Jeremy Gordon; yr s of Roland Frank Holdway Norman (d 1958), of London, and Muriel (Peggy) Harvard, *née* Johnson (later Mrs Sim, d 1997); *b* 18 May 1947; *Educ* St Andrew's Eastbourne, Harrow, Univ of Cambridge (MA); *Partner* since 1978 (civil partnership 21 Dec 2005), Derek Norton Frost, *qv*; *Career* chm and md Burke's Peerage Ltd 1974–83; started and owned night clubs: Embassy 1978–80, Heaven 1979–83, eMbargo 1989–91, Leopard Lounge 1997–98; chm and md Soho Gyms Group 1994–; dir: Blakenhall & Co Ltd (t/a The Furniture Cave), Citychance Ltd (property), Ovalhouse Ltd; formerly dir: Pasta Pasta, La Reserve Wines; fndr tstee Nat Aids Tst (resigned 1989), fndr chm CRUSAID (resigned 1987); *Publications* No Make-Up: Straight Tales from a Queer Life (autobiography, 2006); *Recreations* boats, weight training, natural history; *Clubs* Mark's, Pitt (Cambridge, hon treas); *Style—* Jeremy Norman, Esq; ✉ Moreton Yard, London SW1V 2NT; The Furniture Cave, 533 King's Road, London SW10 OTZ (tel 020 7828 1776, fax 020 7976 5059, e-mail jeremy@sohogyms.com)

NORMAN, Sir Mark Annesley; 3 Bt (UK 1915), of Honeyhanger, Parish of Shottermill, Co Surrey; s of Air Cdre Sir (Henry) Nigel St Valery Norman, 2 Bt, CBE (d 1943), and Lady Perkins (d 1986); *b* 8 February 1927; *Educ* Winchester, RMA; *m* 1953, Joanna Camilla, da of Lt-Col Ian James Kilgour and Aura (ggda of Gen Sir George Walker, 1 Bt, GCB, KCTS); 2 s (Nigel James b 5 Feb 1956, Antony Rory b 9 Sept 1963), 1 da (Lucinda Fay b 7 Dec 1965); *Heir* s, Nigel James Norman, *qv* b 5 Feb 1956; *Career* late Lt Coldstream Gds and Flying Offr 601 (Co of London) Sqdn RAuxAF, mangr and dir aviation and shipping companies 1948–88; High Sheriff Oxfordshire 1983/84, Hon Air Cdre 4624 (Co of Oxford) Movements Sqdn RAuxAF 1984–2000; chm St Luke's Oxford 1986–88; patron and churchwarden St Peter's Church Wilcote; DL Oxfordshire 1985–2003; *Recreations* gardening, workshop, offshore motor cruising; *Clubs* RAF, Royal Southern Yacht; *Style—* Sir Mark Norman, Bt, DL; ✉ Wilcote Manor, Wilcote, Chipping Norton, Oxfordshire OX7 3EB (tel 01993 868357, fax 01993 868032)

NORMAN, Nigel James; s and h of Sir Mark Annesley Norman, 3 Bt, DL, *qv*; *b* 5 February 1956; *m* 1, 1985 (m dis 1989), Joanna Rosemary Jane, da of Michael Montagu George Naylor-Leyland, MC, of Coates, Glos; m 2, 1994, Juliet Clare Louise, da of Richard Lloyd Baxendale, of Aston Rowant, Oxon; 3 s (Antony b 10 March 1995, Mark b 26 May 1996, Harry b 28 June 2002), 1 da (Sophie b 11 Sept 1997); *Career* 13/18 Royal Hussars (QMO), (dispatches 1979), Sultan of Oman's Armoured Regt, ret Maj 1983; with Morgan Grenfell Asset Management Ltd (dir Morgan Grenfell International Funds Management Ltd 1990–2000), md Deutsche Asset Management Ltd 2002–05, head Middle East and Africa Aberdeen Asset Management 2005–; *Clubs* White's, Annabel's, Pratt's; *Style—* Nigel Norman, Esq; ✉ Wilcote Manor, Wilcote, Chipping Norton, Oxfordshire OX7 3EB

NORMAN, Robert David (Rob); s of Malcolm Norman (d 1971), of London, and Angela Frances, *née* Cymbalist; *b* 30 March 1960; *Educ* UCS, Pinner VI Form Coll, Trent Poly (BA); *m* 1, 1986; m 2, 1996, Katherine Jane Helen, da of Stanley Marber; *Career* mgmnt trainee Texaco UK 1978–79, software mktg mangr Data Communications Corp 1983–84, media planner/buyer Colman RSCG 1985–86 (media trainee 1984), account dir CIA Group plc 1987 (sr media planner 1986), exec media dir WM Media Ltd (jt venture between CIA Group plc and Woollams Moira Gaskin O'Malley Ltd) 1990–94 (dir 1988–89), head of Euro Interactive Media Div CIA Group plc 1994–97 (conslt 1997–), sr vice-pres Prisma Sports and Media 1997–; currently: ceo Outrider Worldwide, ptnr CIA Worldwide, chm Mediaedge:cia UK; chm Sutton Jones Multimedia; MInstD 1989; *Recreations* bobsleighing (completed Cresta Run), collecting antiquarian cookery books, pop art, supporting Tottenham Hotspur FC, opera; *Style—* Rob Norman, Esq

NORMAN, Prof (Kenneth) Roy; s of Clement Norman (d 1978), and Peggy, *née* Nichols (d 1980); *b* 21 July 1925; *Educ* Taunton Sch, Downing Coll Cambridge (BA, MA); *m* 12 Aug 1953, Pamela Norman, da of George Raymont; 1 s (Timothy), 1 da (Felicity); *Career* WWII Lt RA, served Br and Indian Armies; fell and tutor Downing Coll Cambridge 1952–64; Univ of Cambridge: lectr 1955–78, reader 1978–90, prof of Indian studies 1990–92, prof emeritus of Indian studies 1992–; foreign memb Royal Danish Acad 1983; FBA 1985; *Books* Elders Verses I (1969, 2 edn 2007), Elders Verses II (1971), Pali Literature (1983), The Group of Discourses (1984, 2 edn 2001), Collected Papers I (1990), Collected Papers II (1991), Collected Papers III (1992), The Group of Discourses II (1992), Collected Papers IV (1993), Collected Papers V (1994), Collected Papers VI (1996), The Word of the Doctrine (1997), A Philological Approach to Buddhism (1997), Poems of Early Buddhist Monks (1997), The Patimokkha (with W Pruitt, 2001), Collected Papers VII (2001), Kankhavitarani (with W Pruitt, 2003), Collected papers VIII (2007); *Recreations* reading, pottery; *Style—* Prof K R Norman, FBA; ✉ 6 Huttles Green, Shepreth, Royston, Hertfordshire SG8 6PR (tel 01763 260541)

NORMANBY, 5 Marquess of (UK 1838); Constantine Edmund Walter Phipps; also Baron Mulgrave (I 1767), Baron Mulgrave (GB 1794), Earl of Mulgrave and Viscount Normanby (UK 1812); s of 4 Marquess of Normanby, KG, CBE (d 1994), and Hon Grania Maeve Rosaura Guinness, da of 1 Baron Moyne, DSO, TD, PC; *b* 24 February 1954; *Educ* Eton, Worcester Coll Oxford, City Univ; *m* 1990, Nicola, da of Milton Shulman (d 2004); 1 da (Lady Sibylla Victoria Evelyn b 6 Aug 1992), 2 s (John Samuel Constantine, Earl of Mulgrave b 26 Nov 1994, Lord Thomas Henry Winston b 3 June 1997), 1 other da (Pandora Aoife Lazuli McCormick b 12 Dec 1984); *Heir* s, Earl of Mulgrave; *Career* writer, co dir; *Publications* (as Constantine Phipps) Careful with the Sharks (1985), Among the Thin Ghosts (1989); *Clubs* Travellers, Garrick; *Style—* The Most Hon the Marquess of Normanby; ✉ Mulgrave Castle, Whitby, North Yorkshire YO21 3RJ

NORMANTON, 6 Earl of (I 1806); Shaun James Christian Welbore Ellis Agar; also Baron Mendip (GB 1794), Baron Somerton (I 1795 & UK 1873, which sits as), and Viscount Somerton (I 1800); s of 5 Earl of Normanton (d 1967), and his 2 w, Lady Fiona Pratt, da of 4 Marquess Camden; *b* 21 August 1945; *Educ* Eton; *m* 29 April 1970 (m dis 2000), Victoria Susan, da of Jack Beard (d 1989), of Ringwood, Hants; 2 da (Lady Portia Caroline (Lady Portia Baker) b 1976, Lady Marisa Charlotte b 1979), 1 s (James Shaun Christian Welbore Ellis, Viscount Somerton b 1982); *Heir* s, Viscount Somerton; *Career* Capt Blues & Royals until 1972; farmer (7,000 acres in Hants); *Recreations* shooting, skiing, scuba diving, powerboat racing; *Clubs* White's, Royal Yacht Sqdn; *Style—* The Rt Hon the Earl of Normanton; ✉ Somerley, Ringwood, Hampshire BH24 3PL (tel 01425 473253; office: 01425 473621)

NORMINGTON, David John; KCB (2005, CB 2000); s of Ronald Normington (d 1976), and Kathleen Williams, *née* Towler; *b* 18 October 1951; *Educ* Bradford GS, CCC Oxford (MA); *m* 30 March 1985, Winifred Anne Charlotte, *née* Harris, CBE; *Career* Dept for Educn and Employment (formerly Dept of Employment): joined 1973, private sec to Permanent Sec 1976–77, head Employment Policy Div 1977–79, head Industrial Rels Div 1979–82, area magr Manpower Servs Cmmn 1982–83, princ private sec to Sec of State for Employment 1983–84, regnl dir employment service (London and S East) 1987–89, dir of strategy and employment policy 1989–92, dir personnel and development 1992–95, dir Personnel and Support Servs 1995–97, DG Strategy Int and Analytical Servs 1997–98, DG Schools 1998–2001; perm sec: DfES 2001–05, Home Office 2006–; *Recreations* cricket, tennis, watching ballet, gardening; *Style—* Sir David Normington, KCB; ✉ Home Office, Queen Anne's Gate, London SW1H 9AT

NORRIE, 2 Baron (UK 1957); George Willoughby Moke; s of 1 Baron Norrie, GCMG, GCVO, CB, DSO, MC (d 1977), and Jocelyn Helen (d 1938), da of Richard Henry Gosling, of Hawthorn Hill; *b* 27 April 1936; *Educ* Eton, RMA Sandhurst; *m* 1, 1964 (m dis 1997), Celia Marguerite, JP, da of Major John Pelham Mann, MC, of New Orleans, USA; 2 da (Hon Clare b 1966, Hon Julia b 1968), 1 s (Hon Mark Willoughby John b 1972); m 2, Mrs Pamela Ann (Annie) McCaffry, da of Sir Arthur Ralph Wilmot, 7 Bt (d 1942); *Heir* s, Mark Norrie; *Career* cmmnd 11 Hussars (PAO) 1956, ADC to C in C ME Cmd 1960–61, GSO3 (int) 4 Gds Bde 1967–69, ret 1970; dir: Fairfield Nurseries (Hermitage) Ltd 1976–89, Int Garden Centre (Br Gp) Ltd 1984–86, Conservation Practice Ltd 1988–91, Hilliers (Fairfield) Ltd 1989–97; advsr: S Grundon (Waste) Ltd 1991–2001, CH2M Hill Ltd 1994–96; memb House of Lords EC Ctee (Environment) 1988–92; pres: Newbury Branch Royal Br Legion 1971–96, Br Tst for Conservation Volunteers 1987–, Int Cultural Exchange 1988–2000, Nat Kidney Fedn 1994–2001, Commercial Travellers Benevolent Inst 1992–; vice-pres: Cncl for Nat Parks 1991–, Tree Cncl 1991–; patron: Age Resouce 1991–, Faure-Alderson Romanian Appeal 1993–2001, Janki Fndn 1997–; UK patron Royal Life Saving Soc 1994– (memb Cwlth Cncl 1999–); memb Cncl Winston Churchill Meml Tst 1993–; Green Ribbon Political Award for Services to the Environment House of Lords 1993; Freeman City of London 1999; *Clubs* MCC, White's, Cavalry and Guards'; *Style—* The Rt Hon the Lord Norrie; ✉ Holehouse, Penpot, Tornhill, Dumfries DG3 4AP (tel 01848 600303)

NORRINGTON, Ian Arthur; s of Charles Arthur Norrington (d 2001), and Georgina Marina, *née* Beardmore (d 1974); *b* 1 October 1936; *Educ* Downside; *m* 21 Sept 1968, Brigitte Maria, *née* Albrecht; 1 s (Christopher Charles b 1972), 1 da (Antonia Jane b 1974); *Career* Midshipman RNVR served Home and Med Fleets 1955–57, Sub Lt RNVR 1957, Lt RNR 1958; De Beers Consolidated Mines Ltd (The Diamond Trading Co Ltd) 1957–71: ptnr W I Carr Sons and Co 1971–79, ptnr Grieveson Grant and Co 1979–86, dir Kleinwort Benson Securities Ltd 1986–90, conslt Fiduciary Trust International Ltd 1990–91, assoc Walker Crips Weddle Beck plc 1991–; vice-pres St Gregory's Soc (Downside Old Boys) 1996– (pres 1993–96); Liveryman Worshipful Co of Goldsmiths; memb Stock Exchange 1974–92, MSI (Dip); *Recreations* fishing, shooting; *Clubs* Flyfishers', MCC; *Style—* Ian Norrington, Esq; ✉ Flat 2, 18 Waterden Road, Guildford, Surrey GU1 2AY

NORRINGTON, Sir Roger Arthur Carver; kt (1997), CBE (1990, OBE 1980); s of late Sir Arthur Norrington, and late Edith Joyce, *née* Carver; *b* 16 March 1934; *Educ* Westminster, Clare Coll Cambridge (BA); *m* 1, 1964 (m dis 1982), Susan Elizabeth McLean, *née* May; 1 s, 1 da; m 2, 1986, Karalyn Mary, *née* Lawrence; 1 s; *Career* conductor music dir Schütz Choir of London 1962–, freelance singer 1962–72, princ conductor Kent Opera 1966–84, currently chief conductor Radio Symphony Orchestra Stuttgart, Camerata Academica Salzburg 1997–; musical dir: London Classical players 1978–97, Orchestra of St Lukes NY 1990–94; co-dir Early Opera Project 1984–, princ conductor Bournemouth Sinfonietta 1985–89, co-dir Historic Arts 1986–; debuts: Br 1962, BBC radio 1964, TV 1967, Germany Austria Denmark and Finland 1966, Portugal 1970, Italy 1971, France and Belgium 1972, USA 1974, Holland 1975, Switzerland 1976; guest conductor for many Br and Foreign Orchs appearing at: Covent Garden, The Coliseum, The Proms, NY, Boston, San Francisco, Paris, Vienna and elsewhere; regular broadcasts at home and abroad, numerous recordings, occasional contrib to various musical jls; Prince Consort prof Royal Coll of Music; Hon DUniv York 1991, Hon DMus Univ of Kent 1994; hon fell Clare Coll Cambridge 1991; FRCM, Hon RAM; Cavaliere Order al Merita della Repubblica Italiana 1981; *Style—* Sir Roger Norrington, CBE

NORRIS, Alan John; s of Jesse Oliver Norris (d 1980), of Newport, Gwent, and Queenie Iris Norris; *b* 7 June 1942; *Educ* St Julian's Newport, Newport and Monmouthshire Coll of Advanced Technol (HNC, Dip); *m* 1, 31 July 1965 (m dis 1969), Jane Margot Inkin, da of Vernon Dixon; m 2, 14 June 1975 (m dis 2001), Penelope Catherine, da of Lt-Col (William) Edwin Daniel (d 1974); 1 s (Oliver William Edwin b 28 June 1982); m 3, 7 Feb 2005, Juliet Quartermain; 1 da (Genevieve Louise b 11 Dec 1998), 1 s Elliot Jonathan b 11 July 2001); *Career* graduate trainee to orgn and method offr Alcan 1960–66, princ orgn and method offr Osram (GEC) 1966–67, latterly systems and programming mangr United

N

Glass (formerly sr systems analyst, computer ops mangr) 1967–76, London branch mangr Computer People 1976–79, chm and chief exec Gatton Consltg Gp (formerly Computastaff Gp) 1979–98, chm Customer Behaviour Dynamics (CBD) 2000–; owner Hotel Caprice Wengen; Freeman City of London, Liveryman Worshipful Co of Information Technologists; MInstM 1968; *Recreations* skiing, swimming, golf, travel, wine, meteorology, psychology; *Clubs* RAC; *Style—* Alan Norris, Esq; ✉ Woodlands House, Chestnut Close, Warren Drive, Kingswood, Surrey KT20 6QB (tel 01737 833678, fax 01737 833550, e-mail ajnmail@aol.com); Hotel Caprice, CH 3823, Wengen, Switzerland (tel 00 41 33 856 0606, fax 00 41 33 856 0607, e-mail hotel@caprice-wengen.ch, website www.caprice-wengen.ch)

NORRIS, His Hon Judge Alastair Hubert; QC (1997); s of Hubert John Norris, and Margaret Murray, *née* Savage (d 1992); *b* 17 December 1950; *Educ* Pate's GS Cheltenham, St John's Coll Cambridge; *m* 1982, Patricia Lesley Rachel, da of Leslie Mark White; 2 da (Frances b 12 June 1986, Meredith b 21 May 1990), 1 s (Edmund b 10 July 1992); *Career* called to the Bar Lincoln's Inn 1973, asst recorder 1998, recorder 2000, circuit judge (Midland Circuit) 2001–; chm Haven Green Housing Assoc; FCIArb 1991; *Recreations* sailing; *Clubs* Gloucestershire CCC, Teifi Boating (Cardigan); *Style—* His Hon Judge Norris, QC

NORRIS, Prof Christopher Charles; s of Charles Frederick Norris (d 1979), of Leigh-on-Sea, Essex, and Edith Eliza, *née* Ward; *b* 6 November 1947; *Educ* East Ham GS, Univ of London (BA, PhD); *m* 17 April 1971, Alison, da of Thomas W Newton and Kathleen, *née* Davidson, of Fakenham, Norfolk; 2 da (Clare Tamasin b 1978, Jennifer Mary b 1983); *Career* lectr Univ of Duisburg W Germany 1974–76, asst ed Books and Bookmen 1976–77; Univ of Wales: lectr 1978–85, reader 1985–87, personal chair 1987–97, distinguished research prof 1997–; visiting prof: Univ of Calif Berkeley 1986, City Univ of NY 1988, Tulane Univ 1992, Dartmouth Coll New Hampshire 1994, Univ of Santiago de Compestela 1997–; assoc fell Dept of Philosophy Univ of Warwick 1990–; vice-pres British Soc of Aesthetics 1993–96, pres Welsh Inst for Philosophy 2003–; *Books* incl: William Empson and the Philosophy of Literary Criticism (1978), Deconstruction: Theory and Practice (1982), Shostakovich: the man and his music (ed, 1982), The Deconstructive Turn: Essays in the Rhetoric of Philosophy (1983), Inside the Myth: George Orwell - views from the left (ed, 1984), The Contest of Faculties: Philosophy and Theory after Deconstruction (1985), Derrida (1987), Post-Structuralist Readings of English Poetry (ed, 1987), Paul de Man: Deconstruction and the Critique of Aesthetic Ideology (1988), What Is Deconstruction? (jtly, 1988), Deconstruction and the Interests of Theory (1989), Music and the Politics of Culture (ed, 1989), What's Wrong with Postmodernism (1990), Spinoza and the Origins of Modern Critical Theory (1991), Uncritical Theory: Postmodernism, Intellectuals and the Gulf War (1992), The Truth About Postmodernism (1993), William Empson: the critical achievement (ed, 1993), Truth and the Ethics of Criticism (1994), Reclaiming Truth: contribution to a critique of cultural relativism (1996), Resources of Realism: prospects for post analytic philosophy (1996), New Idols of the Cave: on the Limits of Anti-realism (1997), Against Relativism: Philosophy of Science, Deconstruction and Critical Theory (1997), Quantum Theory and the Flight from Realism: philosophical responses to quantum mechanics (2000), Minding the Gap: epistemology and philosophy of science in the two traditions (2000), Deconstruction and the Unfinished Project of Modernity (2000), The Cambridge History of Literary Criticism Vol 9: philosophical, psychological and historical approaches (ed, 2001), Truth Matters: realism, anti-realism and response-dependence (2002), Hilary Putnam: realism, reason, and the uses of uncertainty (2002), Jacques Derrida (ed, 4 vols, 2003), Philosophy of Language and the Challenge to Scientific Realism (2004), Language, Logic and Epistemology (2004), Epistemology: Key concepts (2005), On Truth and Meaning (2006), Platonism, Music and the Listener's Share (2006), Fiction, Philosophy and Possible Worlds (2007); Critics of the Twentieth Century (gen ed); *Recreations* music (memb Côr Cochion, Cardiff), travel, model aircraft; *Style—* Prof Christopher Norris; ✉ 14 Belle Vue Terrace, Penarth, Vale of Glamorgan CF64 1DB (tel 029 2021 4555); Philosophy Section, University of Cardiff, PO Box 94, Cardiff CF10 3EU (tel 029 2087 5412, telex 498635, fax 029 2087 4618, e-mail norrisc@cardiff.ac.uk)

NORRIS, Dan; MP; s of David Norris, and June Norris; *b* 28 January 1960; *Educ* state schs, Univ of Sussex; *Career* former: child protection social worker, freelance researcher/author; MP (Lab) Wansdyke 1997–; asst Govt whip 2001–03, PPS to Rt Hon Peter Hain MP (as Sec of State for NI) 2006–; hon fell Sch of Cultural and Community Studies Univ of Sussex; *Publications* author of various works on the mgmnt and reduction of violence; *Recreations* photography; *Style—* Dan Norris, Esq, MP

NORRIS, David Owen; s of Albert Norris, of Long Buckby, Northants, and Margaret Amy, *née* Owen; *b* 16 June 1953; *Educ* Daventry GS, Royal Acad of Music, Keble Coll Oxford (MA); *Children* 2 s (Barnaby William b 1987, Josiah George b 1989); *Career* pianist; prof: Royal Acad of Music 1978–89, Royal Coll of Music 1999–; dir: Petworth Festival 1986–92, Cardiff Festival 1992–95; chm Steans Inst Chicago 1991–98, Gresham prof of music 1993–97; Univ of Southampton: AHRB fell in creative and performing arts 2000–, prof 2007–; visiting prof RCM 2007–; radio presenter; premiere recordings: Elgar Concerto, Lambert Concerto, Elgar Complete Piano Music, Dyson Complete Piano and Chamber Music, Quilter Duets and Piano Music, Schbert Kosegarten Liederspiel; first Gilmore Artist 1991; hon fell Keble Coll Oxford; FRAM, FRCO; *Clubs* Savile; *Style—* David Owen Norris, Esq; ✉ 17 Manor Road, Andover, Hampshire SP10 3JS (website www.davidowennorris.com)

NORRIS, Senator David Patrick Bernard Fitz-Patrick; s of John Bernard Norris (d 1950), of Dublin and Leopoldville, and Aida Margaret, *née* Fitz-Patrick (d 1967); *b* 31 July 1944, Leopoldville, Belgian Congo (now Kinshasa, Democratic Republic of the Congo); *Educ* St Andrew's Coll the HS Dublin, Reade Pianoforte Sch, TCD; *Career* sr lectr in English and coll tutor TCD 1968–94; memb (senator) Seanad Éireann (Ind) Univ of Dublin 1987–, memb Jt Ctee on Foreign Affrs; memb: Irish Fedn of Univ Teachers, Royal Dublin Soc, Nat Union of Journalists, Amnesty Int, Irish Actors Equity, Royal Zoological Soc of Ireland; hon life memb: Univ Philosophy Soc, Coll Historical Soc; life memb: Friends of St Patrick's Cathedral (memb Bd), Dublin Univ Central Athletics Ctee, TCD Assoc; chm: Friends of the Library TCD, James Joyce Cultural Centre (also fndr), N G George's St Preservation Soc (also fndr); vice-pres Children of Ireland Peace Garden Tst; Gold and Silver Medals Univ Philosophical Soc, Gold Medal Brazilian Acad of Letters; broadcaster and author of articles on various literary, sociological and legal topics, speaker at int scholarly gatherings; *Publications* James Joyce's Dublin (1982), Proceedings of the International James Joyce Symposium (1984), James Joyce for Beginners (1992), Joyce in the Hibernian Metropolis (co-ed, 1996); *Recreations* swimming, marathon running, music, reading, travel; *Style—* Senator David Norris; ✉ Seanad Éireann, Leinster House, Kildare Street, Dublin 2, Ireland (tel 00 353 1 618 3104, e-mail info@senatordavidnorris.ie)

NORRIS, Brig His Hon Judge (Alaric) Philip; OBE (1982); s of late Charles Henry Norris, and late Maud Frances, *née* Neild; *b* 20 September 1942; *Educ* Sir William Turner's Sch Coatham, Queens' Coll Cambridge (MA); *m* 1 April 1967, Pamela Margaret, *née* Parker; 3 s (Adam b 19 Sept 1969, Benjamin b 21 Jan 1972, Toby b 10 Feb 1975); *Career* admitted slr 1968, cmmnd Army Legal Servs 1970, served BAOR, NEARELF, Berlin, MOD, SHAPE, NI, UKLF, USA, Geneva, ret Army (in rank of Brig) 1995; asst recorder then recorder of the Crown Court 1988–95, circuit judge (SE Circuit) 1995–; Liveryman Worshipful Co of Fruiterers 2005; *Recreations* a bit of all sorts, but not golf; *Style—* Brig His Hon Judge Norris, OBE; ✉ c/o Woolwich Crown Court, 2 Belmarsh Road, London SE28 0EY

NORRIS, Steven John; s of John Francis Birkett Norris, and Eileen Winifred, *née* Walsh; *b* 24 May 1945; *Educ* Liverpool Inst HS, Worcester Coll Oxford (MA); *m* 1, 23 Aug 1969 (m dis), Peta Veronica, da of Rear Adm Peter Cecil-Gibson, CB; 2 s; m 2, Emma Courtney; 1 s; *Career* MP (Cons): Oxford E 1983–87, Epping Forest 1988–97; memb Select Ctee on Social Servs 1985, PPS to Home Sec 1990–92, Parly under-sec of state Dept of Transport (min for transport, London local transport and road safety) 1992–96; mayoral candidate (Cons) London 2000 and 2004; chm Jarvis plc 2003–, AMT-Sybex 2005–; DG Road Haulage Assoc 1997–99; cncllr Berks CC 1977–85, memb Berks Area Health Authy 1979–82, vice-chm W Berks DHA 1982–85; patron: Transport 2000 from 1996, Sustrans 1996–; chm Nat Cycling Strategy Bd 2001–04; former fndr Alcohol and Drug Addiction Prevention and Treatment Tst; fndr and former chm: The Crime Concern Trust Ltd, The Grant Maintained Schs Tst; hon memb Cyclists' Touring Club 1996–; Freeman City of London; Liveryman: Worshipful Co of Coachmakers and Coach Harness Makers, Worshipful Co of Watermen and Lightermen of the River Thames; Companion Inst of Civil Engrs, FIHT, FIMI, FCIT; *Recreations* reading; *Clubs* Brooks's, RAC; *Style—* Steven Norris, Esq

NORRIS, William John; QC (1997); s of John Phillips Norris, QGM, of Salisbury, Wilts, and Joan Hattersley, *née* Barnes; *b* 3 October 1951; *Educ* Sherborne, New Coll Oxford (MA); *m* 3 Oct 1987, Lesley Jacqueline, da of Douglas Osborne, of Hythe, Kent; 2 da (Charlotte Louise b 15 Oct 1988, Emily Clare b 6 Oct 1990); *Career* called to the Bar Middle Temple 1974; former amateur jockey; *Books* Kemp and Kemp: The Quantum of Damages (gen ed), The Collected Letters of C W Catte (ed), Perhaps it will brighten up later (2004); *Recreations* racing, sailing, cricket; *Clubs* Royal Cruising, Royal Lym Yacht, Lobsters; *Style—* William Norris, Esq, QC; ✉ 39 Essex Street, London WC2R 3AT

NORRIS, William Vernon Wentworth; s of William Henry Norris, of Shepperton-on-Thames, Middx, and Eileen Louise, *née* Willmott; *b* 11 May 1937; *Educ* Bedford Sch; *m* 1, 10 Oct 1960 (m dis 1982), Penelope Anne, da of Herbert James Dimmock (d 1987), of Brookwood, Surrey; 1 da (Sally b 1962), 1 s (Richard b 1965); m 2, 5 May 1982, Catherine, da of Bernard James Knowles; 1 da (Katie b 1982); *Career* admitted slr 1959; lectr Gibson & Weldon 1959–61, Allen & Overy 1961–97 (ptnr 1964–97); called to the Bar Lincoln's Inn 1997; chm UK Taxation Disciplinary Ctee 2001–; past chm Law Soc Revenue Law Ctee; govr Christ's Hosp, memb Addington Soc; FTII 1994; *Recreations* poetry; *Style—* William V W Norris, Esq; ✉ Maitland Chambers, 7 Stone Buildings, Lincoln's Inn, London WC2A 3SZ (tel 020 7406 1200, fax 020 7406 1300)

NORRISS, Air Marshal Sir Peter Coulson; KBE (2000), CB (1996), AFC (1977); s of Arthur Kenworthy Norriss, and Marjorie Evelyn, *née* Coulson; *b* 22 April 1944; *Educ* Beverley GS, Magdalene Coll Cambridge (MA), Harvard Business Sch (AMP); *m* 7 August 1971, Lesley Jean, *née* McColl; 2 s (Mark Alastair b 6 Feb 1973, Angus John b 26 Aug 1974), 1 da (Katie Elizabeth b 15 Feb 1977); *Career* RAF; joined 1966, flying instr RAF Coll Cranwell 1969–71; Buccaneer: pilot 1972–74, chief flying instr 1974–76; personal air sec to Parly Under Sec 1977–79, Sqn Cdr Buccaneer XVI 1980–83, head RAF Presentation Team 1984, Tornado and Victor Station Cdr RAF Marham 1985–87, Dep Dir subsequently Dir Operational Requirements 1988–91, DG Air Procurement 1991–98, Dep Chief Defence Procurement 1998–2000, def conslt 2001–; chm Microturbo Ltd 2002–, non-exec dir Chemring Gp plc 2004–; patron Cambridge UAS; FRAeS (pres 2003–04); *Recreations* golf, skiing, tennis; *Clubs* RAF; *Style—* Sir Peter Norriss, KBE, CB, AFC; ✉ e-mail peter.norriss@hedgeapple.co.uk

NORTH, Prof John David; s of John Ernest North (d 1988), of Cheltenham, Glos, and Gertrude Anne North (d 1989); *b* 19 May 1934; *Educ* Batley GS, Merton Coll Oxford (MA, DPhil, DLitt), Univ of London (BSc); *m* 6 April 1957, Marion Jean Pizzey, da of J H Pizzey, of Bournemouth, Dorset; 3 c (Richard b 1961, Julian b 1962, Rachel b 1965); *Career* Univ of Oxford: Nuffield res fell in history and philosophy of science 1963–68, Museum of History of Science 1968–77; prof of history of philosophy and the exact sciences Univ of Groningen The Netherlands 1977–99; sr res assoc Museum of History of Science Univ of Oxford 2002–; memb Royal Dutch Acad, foreign memb Royal Danish Acad, memb Academia Leopoldina (Halle, Germany); Acad Int d'Hist des Sciences: secrétaire perpétuel honoraire, Médaille Alexandre Koyré 1989; FBA; Knight of the Order of the Netherlands Lion 1999; *Books* The Measure of the Universe (1965, 1967 and 1990), Richard of Wallingford (1976), Horoscopes and History (1986), Chaucer's Universe (1988 and 1990), The Universal Frame (1989), Stars, Minds and Fate (1989), The Fontana History of Astronomy and Cosmology (1994), Stonehenge: Neolithic Man and the Cosmos (1996), The Ambassadors Secret: Holbein and the World of the Renaissance (2001 and 2004), God's Clockmaker: Richard of Wallingford and the Invention of Time (2005); *Style—* Prof John North, FBA; ✉ 28 Chalfont Road, Oxford OX2 6TH (tel 01865 558458)

NORTH, Sir (William) Jonathan Frederick; 2 Bt (UK 1920), of Southwell, Co Nottingham; s of Hon John Montagu William North (d 1987, s of 8 Earl of Guilford), and late 1 w, Muriel Norton, *née* Hicking; suc (under special remainder) his maternal gf, Sir William Norton Hicking, 1 Bt, 1947; *b* 6 February 1931; *Educ* Marlborough; *m* 1956, Sara Virginia, da of late Air Chief Marshal Sir (James) Donald Innes Hardman, GBE, KCB, DFC; 2 da (Charlotte Amelia (Mrs Mathew Tester) b 1958, Harriet Cordelia Henrietta (Mrs Thomas Thistlethwayte) b 1963), 1 s (Jeremy William Francis b 1960); *Heir* s, Jeremy North; *Style—* Sir Jonathan North, Bt; ✉ Frogmore, Weston-under-Penyard, Herefordshire HR9 5TQ

NORTH, Sir Peter Machin; kt (1998), CBE (1989), Hon QC (1993); s of Geoffrey Machin North (d 1974), and Freda Brunt, *née* Smith (d 1991); *b* 30 August 1936; *Educ* Oakham Sch, Keble Coll Oxford; *m* 1960, Stephanie Mary North, OBE, DL, eld da of Thomas L Chadwick (d 1963); 1 da (Jane Amanda b 1962), 2 s (Nicholas Machin b 1964, James William Thomas b 1971); *Career* Lt Royal Leics Regt Cyprus 1955–56; teaching asst Northwestern Univ Sch of Law Chicago 1960–61; lectr: UCW Aberystwyth 1961–63, Univ of Nottingham 1963–65; tutor in law Keble Coll Oxford 1965–76 (fell 1965–84), law cmmr for Eng and Wales 1976–84, princ Jesus Coll Oxford 1984–2005, vice-chllr Univ of Oxford 1993–97; chm: Road Traffic Law Review 1985–88, Ind Review of Parades and Marches in NI 1996–97, Ind Ctee for the Supervision of Standards of Telephone Information Services 1999–2006, Fin Ctee OUP 2005–; vice-chm Ashmolean Museum Oxford 2006– (visitor 2004–); hon fell: Jesus Coll Oxford, Keble Coll Oxford, Univ of Wales Bangor, Trinity Coll Carmarthen, Univ of Wales Aberystwyth; Hon LLD: Univ of Reading, Univ of Nottingham, Univ of Aberdeen, Univ of New Brunswick; Hon Dr of Humane Letters Univ of Arizona; hon bencher Inner Temple; FBA; *Recreations* locking; *Style—* Sir Peter North, CBE, QC, FBA; ✉ Jesus College, Oxford OX1 3DW

NORTH, Richard Conway; s of Frederick Jack North (d 1966), and Megan Wyn, *née* Gruffydd (d 2001); *b* 20 January 1950; *Educ* Marlborough, Sidney Sussex Coll Cambridge; *m* 29 July 1978, Lindsay Jean, *née* Buchanan; 3 da (Louise Gwendoline Melissa b 9 July 1982, Charlotte Elizabeth Clare b 24 July 1984, Victoria Alexandra Emma b 24 April 1986); *Career* Coopers and Lybrand: joined 1971, seconded to NY 1976–78, seconded to Midland Bank plc 1981–82, ptnr 1983–91; gp fin dir Burton Gp plc 1991–94, gp fin dir Six Continents plc 1994–2003, ceo InterContinental Hotels Gp plc 2003–04; chm: Britvic Soft Drinks 1996–, Woolworths 2007–; non-exec dir: The Bristol Hotel Co Inc 1997–98, Asda plc 1997–99, Leeds United plc 1998–2002, FelCor Lodging Tst 1998–, Logica plc 2002–04, Majid Al Fatteim Gp LLC 2006–; memb: Senate ICAEW 1991–2000, Hundred Gp Ctee 1996–2000, Exec Ctee World Travel and Tourism Cncl 2004–; FCA 1981 (ACA 1976), FCT 1993; *Recreations* golf, tennis, sailing, soccer, opera; *Clubs* Athenaeum, Burhill Golf, Buckinghamshire Golf, Hurlingham; *Style—* Richard North, Esq

NORTH WEST EUROPE, Archdeacon of; *see:* Allen, Ven Geoffrey Gordon

NORTHAM, Jeremy Philip; s of John Northam, and Rachel Northam; *b* 1 December 1961; *Educ* King's Coll Sch Cambridge, Bristol GS, Bedford Coll (BA); *Career* actor; *Theatre* incl: National Theatre 1989–91: The Voysey Inheritance, Hamlet, The Shaughraun, The School for Scandal; RSC 1992–94: Love Labour's Lost, The Country Wife, The Gift of the Gorgon; other credits incl: The Three Sisters 1991, The Way of the World 1992, Certain Young Men (Almeida) 1999, Old Times (Donmar) 2004; *Television* incl: Journey's End 1988, Piece of Cake 1988, A Fatal Inversion 1991, Poirot 1993, A Village Affair 1994, The Tribe 1997, Martin & Lewis 2002; *Films* incl: Wuthering Heights 1992, Soft Top Hard Shoulder 1992, Voices 1994, Carrington 1995, The Net 1995, Emma 1996, Mimic 1997, Amistad 1997, The Misadventures of Margaret 1998, Gloria 1999, The Winslow Boy 1999, An Ideal Husband 1999, Happy Texas 1999, The Golden Bowl 2000, Possession 2001, Enigma 2001, Gosford Park 2001, The Singing Detective 2002, Cypher 2002, Stroke of Genius 2003, Guy X 2004; *Awards* incl: Olivier Award Most Promising Newcomer 1990, Evening Standard Film Actor 2000, Film Critic's Circle British Actor Award 2000; *Style*— Jeremy Northam, Esq; ✉ c/o Harriet Robinson, ICM, Oxford House, 76 Oxford Street, London W1D 1BS

NORTHAMPTON, 7 Marquess of (UK 1812); Spencer Douglas David Compton; DL (Northants 1979); also Earl of Northampton (UK 1618), Earl Compton, and Baron Wilmington (both UK 1812); patron of 9 livings; s of 6 Marquess of Northampton, DSO (d 1978), and his 2 w, Virginia (d 1997), yst da of David Rimington Heaton, DSO, of Brookfield, Crownhill, S Devon; *b* 2 April 1946; *Educ* Eton; *m* 1, 1967 (m dis 1973), Henriette Luisa Maria, o da of late Baron Adolph William Carel Bentinck, sometime Netherlands ambass to France; 1 s, 1 da; m 2, 1974 (m dis 1977), Annette Marie, da of Charles Anthony Russell Smallwood; m 3, 1977 (m dis 1983), Rosemary Ashley Morritt, o da of P G M Hancock, of Truro, and formerly w of Hon Charles Dawson-Damer (bro of 7 Earl of Portarlington); 1 da; m 4, 1985 (m dis 1989), Hannelore Ellen (Fritzi), da of late Hermann Erhardt, of Landsberg-am-Lech, and formerly w of Hon Michael Pearson (now 4 Viscount Cowdray); 1 da; m 5, 1990, Mrs Pamela Kyprios; *Heir* s, Earl Compton; *Career* landowner; proprietor of Compton Wynyates (built 1480–1520) and former proprietor of Castle Ashby (constructed 1574, with an Inigo Jones frontage of 1635, remains in the Compton family); Pro Grand Master United Grand Lodge of England 2001–; *Recreations* Freemasonry; *Clubs* Turf; *Style*— The Most Hon the Marquess of Northampton, DL; ✉ Compton Wynyates, Tysoe, Warwick CV35 0UD

NORTHBOURNE, 5 Baron (UK 1884); Sir Christopher George Walter James; 6 Bt (GB 1791); only s of 4 Baron Northbourne (d 1982), of Northbourne Court, Kent, and Katharine Louise (d 1980), yr da of late George Nickerson, of Boston, Mass, and his w Ellen (d 1950), who m as her 2 husb Rear Adm Hon Sir Horace Hood, KCB, MVO, DSO (ka Jutland 1916), and was by him mother of 6 and 7 Viscounts Hood; *b* 18 February 1926; *Educ* Eton, Magdalen Coll Oxford (MA); *m* 29 July 1959, Marie-Sygne, da of Henri Louis Claudel and gda of Paul Claudel, poet and diplomat; 3 s (Hon Charles Walter Henri b 14 June 1960, Hon Anthony Christopher Walter Paul b 14 Jan 1963, Hon Sebastian Richard Edward Cuthbert b 7 March 1966), 1 da (Hon Ophelia Mary Katherine Christine Aliki b 23 Aug 1969); *Heir* s, Hon Charles James; *Career* farmer; chm: Betteshanger Farms Ltd 1975–, Kent Salads Ltd 1987–92; dir: Anglo Indonesian Corp 1971–96, Chillington Corp plc 1986–96, Center Parcs Ltd 1987–96, Center Parcs plc 1988–96; regnl dir Lloyds Bank plc 1986–90; sits as Ind in House of Lords (special interests agric, educn, children's affairs); FRICS; *Clubs* Brooks's, Royal Yacht Squadron; *Style*— The Rt Hon the Lord Northbourne; ✉ Coldharbour, Northbourne, Kent CT14 0LP (tel 01304 611277, fax 01304 611128); 69 Eaton Place, London SW1X (tel 020 7235 6790)

NORTHBROOK, 6 Baron (UK 1866), of Stratton, Co Hants; Sir Francis Thomas Baring; 8 Bt (GB 1793); o s of 5 Baron Northbrook (d 1990), and Rowena Margaret, da of Brig-Gen Sir William Henry Manning, GCMG, KBE, CB (d 1932); *b* 21 February 1954; *Educ* Winchester, Univ of Bristol; *m* 27 June 1987 (m dis 2006), Amelia Sarah Elizabeth, er da of Dr Reginald David Taylor, of Hursley, Hants; 3 da (Hon Arabella Constance Elizabeth b 1989, Hon Venetia Harriet Anne b 1991, Hon Cosima Evelyn Maud b 1994); *Heir* (to Baronetcy only) kinsman, Peter Baring; *Career* trainee accountant Dixon Wilson Ltd 1976–80, Baring Brothers & Co Ltd 1981–89, investment mangr Taylor-Young Investment Management Ltd 1990–93, investment mangr Smith & Williamson 1993–95, dir Mars Asset Management Ltd 1996–2006; chm Dido Films Ltd 2002–; landowner; oppn whip 1999–2000; tstee: Winchester Med Tst 1990–97, CLA (Hants Ctee) 1999–2000, Fortune Forum 2006–; *Recreations* cricket, tennis, skiing, shooting, fishing; *Clubs* White's, Pratt's; *Style*— The Rt Hon Lord Northbrook; ✉ House of Lords, London SW1A 0PW

NORTHCOTT, Montague Walter Desmond; s of Cdr W C Northcott, JP, DL, RNR (d 1965), and Irene Violet, *née* Lay (d 1972); *b* 25 April 1931; *Educ* Harrow; *m* 24 Aug 1966, Annie Margaret Durrance; 1 s (Richard Walter Montague b 1967), 1 da (Joanna Rosemary Marion b 1969); *Career* Royal Navy 1949–51; Cunard Steamship Co 1951–67, Hogg Robinson Travel 1968–96; underwriting member of Lloyd's 1977–95; tstee Northcott Fndn; govr: Haberdashers' Aske's Schs 1972–82, Jones GS Fndn 1985–88; chm St Andrews Church Little Berkhamsted Restoration Appeal 1987–91; Master: Worshipful Co of Haberdashers 1985, Worshipful Co of Painter-Stainers 1989; Liveryman Worshipful Co of Loriners; *Recreations* painting, geneology, golf, swimming, gardening; *Clubs* RAC, City Livery; *Style*— Montague Northcott, Esq; ✉ 11 Watton House, Watton-at-Stone, Hertfordshire SG14 3NZ

NORTHEDGE, Richard; *b* 3 September 1950; *Career* journalist; Estates Times 1973–76, property ed Investors Chronicle 1976–78, property ed Evening Standard 1978–80; Daily Telegraph: columnist 1980–83, personal fin ed 1983–86, dep City ed 1986–98; dep ed Sunday Business 1998–2001, exec ed The Business 2001–02, freelance writer and columnist 2002–; contrib: Sunday Telegraph, Spectator, CityAM; Services Journalist of the Year 1999, Banking Journalist of the Year 2003; *Publications* Consumers' Guide to Personal Equity Plans; *Style*— Richard Northedge, Esq; ✉ tel 020 7602 8277, e-mail richardnorthedge@yahoo.co.uk

NORTHESK, 14 Earl of (S 1647); David John MacRae Carnegie; also Lord Rosehill and Inglismaldie (S precedence 1639); s of 13 Earl of Northesk (d 1994), and his 1 w, Jean Margaret, *née* MacRae (d 1989); *b* 3 November 1954; *Educ* Eton, UCL; *m* 1979, Jacqueline, da of David Reid, of Cascais, Portugal; 1 s (Alexander Robert MacRae, Lord Rosehill b 16 Nov 1980 d 2001), 3 da (Lady Sarah Louise Mary b 29 Oct 1982, Lady Fiona Jean Elizabeth b 24 March 1987, Lady Sophie Margaret Jean b 9 Jan 1990); *Heir* kinsman, Patrick Carnegy, *qv*; *Career* company dir; Cons Pty whip House of Lords 1999–2002; *Recreations* gardening, shooting; *Clubs* Kennel; *Style*— The Rt Hon the Earl of Northesk; ✉ House of Lords, London SW1A 0PW

NORTHFIELD, Baron (Life Peer UK 1975), of Telford in the County of Shropshire; (William) Donald Chapman; s of William Henry Chapman, of Barnsley, S Yorks; *b* 25 November 1923; *Educ* Barnsley GS, Emmanuel Coll Cambridge (MA); *Career* sits as Lab peer in House of Lords; formerly memb Cambridge Borough Cncl, gen sec Fabian Soc 1949–53, MP (Lab) Birmingham (Northfield) 1951–70; res fell Nuffield Coll Oxford 1971–73, visiting fell Centre for Contemporary European Studies Univ of Sussex 1973; chm: HM Devpt Cmmrs 1974–80, Telford New Town Devpt Corpn 1975–87, Consortium Devpts Ltd 1985–91; co dir; economist, writer; *Style*— The Rt Hon the Lord Northfield; ✉ House of Lords, London SW1A 0PW

NORTHFIELD, Prof Timothy Clive (Tim); *b* 16 February 1935; *Educ* Radley, Peterhouse Cambridge/Guy's Hosp Med Sch London (MA, MB BChir, MD, Beddard Prize), Goldsmiths Coll London (MA pt/t), DSc; *m*; 2 c; *Career* Nat Serv 2 Lt RA BAOR 1953–55; SHO in med Guy's Hosp 1963–64 (pre-registration house offr 1962–63), registrar in gastroenterology Central Middx Hosp 1965–67 (SHO in gastroenterology 1965), MRC research fell Depts of Biochemistry and Chemistry and of Med Guy's Hosp Med Sch 1968–69, sr registrar in med and in gastroenterology Guy's Hosp 1970–74 (registrar in med 1969–70); St George's Hosp: conslt physician and gastroenterologist 1974–98, head Norman Tanner Gastroenterology Unit 1976–98, memb '3 Wise Men' Ctee 1992–98, head Gastroenterology Serv Delivery Unit 1994–98; St George's Hosp Med Sch: sr lectr in med 1974–83, reader in med 1983–88, prof of gastroenterology 1988–98 (and med 1998), head Div of Biochemical Med 1988–96, head Div of Gastroenterology, Endocrinology and Metabolism 1996–98, currently emeritus prof of med and gastroenterology; SW Thames RHA: organiser Gastroenterology Teaching Day and Norman Tanner Lecture 1976–98, chm SW Thames Gut Club 1987–98, rep for Br Soc of Gastroenterology 1995–98, specialty advsr for RCP 1995–98, chm Trg Ctee in Gastroenterology 1996–98; memb RCP Ctee: providing nat guidlines for mgmnt of acute gastrointestinal bleeding 1992, defining nat guidelines for transfusion med 1992; chm Steering Ctee for Nat Audit of Acute Gastrointestinal Bleeding 1993–98, pres Int Advanced Course in Gastroenterology (BPMF) 1996–99; numerous invited lectures at home and abroad; memb Editorial Bd Alimentary Pharmacology and Therapeutics 1987–; hon treas Domestic Building Res Gp 2000–; RSM: memb Cncl 1987–89, pres Section of Measurement in Med 1987–89 (vice-pres 1994–98); memb: Br Soc of Gastroenterology, Pancreatic Soc of GB and I (pres 1987–89), Med Research Soc, Br and Euro Assocs for the Study of the Liver, Int Gastro-Surgical Club; FRCP 1977 (MRCP 1965); *Awards* incl: postgrad research prize 1967, MRC travelling fellowship 1971, Eli Lilly Prize Med Research Soc 1984, Hopkins Endoscopy Prize Br Soc of Gastroenterology 1987, Hosp Dr of the Year Award in Gastroenterology 1995; *Books* Bile Acids in Health and Disease (jt ed, 1988), Helicobacter Pylori Infection (jt ed, 1993), Bile Acids in Hepatobiliary Disease (jt ed, 2000); author of numerous original articles in peer reviewed jls; *Recreations* local history, the history of buildings and history relating to biographies and travel in foreign countries (memb Domestic Building Research Gp and Bourne Local History Soc); *Style*— Prof Tim Northfield; ✉ St George's Hospital Medical School, Cranmer Terrace, London SW17 0RE (tel 01737 553209, fax 01737 551560)

NORTHMORE-BALL, Martin Dacre; s of Dr Godfrey Dacre Jennings Ball (d 2001), of Warminster, Wilts, and Judith Marion, *née* Northmore (d 1979); *b* 14 February 1943; *Educ* Clifton, King's Coll Cambridge (MA), St Thomas' Hosp Med Sch (MB BChir); *m* 26 July 1969, Averina Constance Frances, da of Prof Sir Francis Gerald William Knowles, 6 Bt (d 1974), of Avebury Manor, Wilts; 2 s (Dacre b 1970 d 1975, Lawrence b 1986), 1 da (Laetitia b 1976); *Career* registrar Charing Cross and King's Coll Hosps 1973–76, sr registrar Addenbrooke's Hosp Cambridge 1979–81 (registrar 1975–78), clinical fell Univ of Toronto 1978–79; currently: hon conslt orthopaedic surgn Robert Jones and Agnes Hunt Orthopaedic Hosp Oswestry, sr clinical lectr Keele Univ 1995–2001; memb Editorial Bd Hip International; memb: BMA, European Hip Soc; fndr memb Br Hip Soc; FRCS 1973, FBOA, CIMechE; *Recreations* study of antiquities, books, travel; *Style*— Martin Northmore-Ball, Esq; ✉ Higher Grange, Ellesmere, Shropshire SY12 9DH (tel 01691 623110, fax 01691 623131); The Robert Jones and Agnes Hunt Orthopaedic Hospital, Oswestry, Shropshire SY10 7AG

NORTHOVER, James Walter Edward; s of Maurice Alexander Northover (d 1975), and Gladys Mary, *née* Frost (d 1981); *b* 19 November 1946; *Educ* Ardingly, Kingston Coll of Art, London Coll of Printing (DipAD, BA); *m* 1975, Gillian Mary Denise, da of John Thomas Kinsman; 2 da (Sophie b 1979, Romy b 1982), 1 s (Maxim b 1984); *Career* sr designer Conran Design Group 1970–72, assoc dir Fitch & Co 1972–75, md Lloyd Northover (graphic design, corp identity and design mgmnt conslts) 1975–93, chm Lloyd Northover 1993– (formerly Citigate Lloyd Northover), dir Citigate Bass Yager (USA) 1997–2000, dir Citigate Asia 1997–2003; chm Incepta Middle East 2003–06; current and former clients incl: BAA, Barbican Centre, Barclays de Zoete Wedd, Belfast City Cncl, Br Cncl, BRS, BUPA, Centro, China Light & Power, Courtaulds, Dept for Educn and Skills, Dubai International Financial Centre, Exxon, HMSO, Hong Kong Mass Transit Railway Corporation, John Lewis Partnership, Land Transport Authority of Singapore, Millennium Commission, National Savings and Investments, Tesco, Univ of the Arts London; avsry bd memb: Zero One Digital Media Creative Learning Lab London, London Coll of Communication Information Environments Res Unit; Design Effectiveness Awards 1989 (Grand Prix), 1992, 1998 and 2001; lectr at business and design confs, author of various articles for business and design media; memb: D&AD Assoc, Design Mgmnt Inst, International Inst of Information Design (IIID); FCSD, FRSA, FISTD; *Style*— Jim Northover; ✉ Lloyd Northover, 30 Great Pulteney Street, London W1F 9NN (tel 020 7534 5600, e-mail jim.northover@lloydnorthover.com)

NORTHOVER, Baroness (Life Peer UK 2000), of Cissbury in the County of West Sussex; Lindsay Patricia Northover; da of (Maurice Colin) Charles Granshaw, of Worthing, W Sussex, and Patricia Winifred, *née* Jackson; *b* 21 August 1954; *Educ* Brighton and Hove HS, St Anne's Coll Oxford (MA), Bryn Mawr Coll and Univ of Pennsylvania (MA, PhD); *m* 1988, John Martin Alban Northover, s of (William) Joseph Northover; 2 s (Thomas Charles b 23 Jan 1989, Joseph Mark b 9 Nov 1990), 1 da (Louisa Alice Lindsay b 28 March 1993); *Career* research fell UCL and St Mark's Hosp London 1980–83, research fell St Thomas' Hosp Med Sch London 1983–84, lectr in history of modern med Wellcome Inst and UCL 1984–91; chair Women Lib Dems 1992–95; House of Lords: Lib Dem spokesperson on health 2000–02, Lib Dem spokesperson on int devpt 2002–, memb Select Ctee of Embryonic Stem Cell Research 2001–02, memb Select Ctee on the EU and Sub-Ctee on Foreign Affrs, Defence and Int Devpt 2003–04; vice-chair All Party Gp on Aid, Debt and Trade, sec All Party Gp on Overseas Devpt; exec memb Cwlth Parly Assoc of UK; memb Cncl ODI; patron Breast Cancer Campaign, tstee Bryn Mawr Coll Assoc GB; *Publications* author and co-author of various academic books and articles; *Style*— The Baroness Northover; ✉ House of Lords, London SW1A 0PW

NORTHRIDGE, Nigel; *b* 31 January 1956; *Educ* Sullivan Upper Sch, NI Poly; *m* Linda Elizabeth; 1 s (Richard b 3 March 1984), 2 da (Kate b 30 May 1986, Emma b 31 Aug 1991); *Career* Gallaher Ltd: joined as trainee mangr 1976, asst brand mangr 1981–84, mktg mangr 1984–86, divnl dir Iberia 1986–89, gen mangr Europe 1989–90, bd dir Gallaher Int Ltd 1989–90, md Gallaher (Dublin) Ltd 1990–94, sales and mktg dir and memb Bd Gallaher Tobacco Ltd 1994, chief exec Gallaher Gp plc 2000–; non-exec dir: Aggreko plc, Paddy Power plc; *Style*— Nigel Northridge, Esq

NORTHROP, Antony Patrick Clinton; *Educ* King's Sch Canterbury, Univ of Oxford; *m* Hilary; 2 s (Augustus, Joshua), 1 da (Elektra); *Career* former md Lazard Brothers, fndr md Touchstone Securities Ltd; *Style*— Antony Northrop, Esq; ✉ e-mail apcn@touchstone-securities.com

NORTHUMBERLAND, 12 Duke of; Sir Ralph George Algernon Percy; 15 Bt (E 1660), DL (1997); also Baron Percy (GB 1723), Earl of Northumberland and Baron Warkworth (GB 1749), Earl Percy (GB 1776), Earl of Beverly (GB 1790), and Lord Lovaine, Baron of Alnwick (GB 1784); 2 s of 10 Duke of Northumberland, KG, GCVO, TD, PC (d 1988); suc bro 11 Duke of Northumberland (d 1995); *b* 16 November 1956; *Educ* Eton, ChCh Oxford; *m* 1979, (Isobel) Jane Miller, da of John Walter Maxwell Miller Richard, of Edinburgh; 2 da (Lady Catherine Sarah b 1982, Lady Melissa Jane b 1987), 2 s (George Dominic, Earl Percy b 1984, Lord Max Ralph b 1990); *Heir* s, Earl Percy; *Career* chartered surveyor, landowner; MRICS; *Recreations* shooting, fishing, painting, skiing, tennis,

N

snooker; *Style*— His Grace the Duke of Northumberland, DL; ✉ Alnwick Castle, Northumberland NE66 1NG; Syon House, Brentford, Middlesex TW8 8JF

NORTON, Col (Ian) Geoffrey; TD (1963), JP (1973), DL (S Yorks 1979); s of Cyril Needham Norton, MBE (d 1979), of Sheffield, and Winifred Mary, *née* Creswick (d 1973); *b* 8 June 1931; *Educ* Stowe; *m* 4 April 1961, Eileen, da of Ernest Hughes (d 1996); *Career* Nat Serv 1949–51, cmmnd RASC 1950, TA 1951–76, Hallamshire Bn York and Lancaster Regt 1951–67, Yorks Volunteers 1967–72, cmd 1 Bn Yorks Volunteers 1970–72, Dep Cdr (TAVR) NE Dist 1973–76, Regtl Col Yorkshire Volunteers, ADC to HM The Queen 1973–78; Hon Col: 1 Bn Yorkshire Vols 1989–93, Univ of Sheffield OTC 1990–96, 4th/5th Bn The Green Howards 1993–94; vice-pres York and Lancaster Regt 1993–2007; chm: John Norton and Son (Sheffield) Ltd 1976–97 (md 1965–76), Shirley Aldred and Co Ltd 1976–94 (dir 1959–76); pres SSAFA Forces Help S Yorks 2007–, treas SSAFA Forces Help Sheffield 1993–2002; chm: Yorks and Humberside TAVR Assoc 1985–91, Friends of Sheffield Children's Hosp 1979–85, St George's Chapel Sheffield Cathedral 1982–2006, Sheffield Def Studies Dining Club 1992–97; High Sheriff S Yorks 2000–01; *Recreations* pottering in the garden, music, reading; *Style*— Col Geoffrey Norton, TD, DL; ✉ 22 Cortworth Road, Sheffield S11 9LP (tel 0114 236 6304)

NORTON, Hilary Sharon Braverman (known professionally as Hilary Blume); da of Henry Braverman (d 1986), of London, and Muriel, *née* Millin (d 2005); *b* 9 January 1945; *Educ* LSE, Univ of Sussex; *m* 1, 5 Sept 1965 (m dis 1977), Prof Stuart Blume; 2 s (Toby b 22 Aug 1972, Joby b 12 July 1975); m 2, 25 July 1977, Michael Aslan Norton, OBE, s of Richard Michael Norton (d 1985); 1 da (Poppy b 15 June 1978); *Career* dir Charities Advsy Tst 1982–, dir Greenway Hotels India; co-chm Finnart House Tst; cmmr National Lottery Cmmn 1999–2000; patron Trees for London; FRSA 2002 (memb Cncl 2004–); *Books* Fund-raising: A Comprehensive Handbook, The Charity Trading Handbook, The Museum Trading Handbook, Charity Christmas Cards, Charity Shop Handbook; *Style*— Mrs Michael Norton; ✉ Charities Advisory Trust, Radius Works, Back Lane, London NW3 1HL (tel 020 7794 9835, fax 020 7431 3739)

NORTON, (Michael) James; s of Christopher Stephen Norton, of Birchington, Kent, and Lilian Ivy, *née* Buckley; *b* 15 December 1952; *Educ* Roan Sch for Boys Blackheath (exhibitioner), Univ of Sheffield (BEng, Mappin medal); *m* 29 May 1976, Barbara, da of Joseph Leslie Foster; 1 s (Stephen b 26 July 1979); *Career* Exec engr Computer Systems Div Post Office (Telecoms) 1974–81; British Telecom: head of gp Systems Evolution and Standards Dept 1981–83, seconded to IT Standards Unit DTI 1983, head of section SESD 1983–84, sr mangr Advanced Networks Mktg BT National Networks 1984–86, sr mangr Int Business Devpt BT International 1986–87; dir Vendor Consultancy Practice Butler Cox plc 1987–90, dir of mktg Cable & Wireless Europe 1990–93, chief exec Radiocommunications Agency DTI 1993–98, dir Electronic Commerce Team, Performance & Innovation Unit, Cabinet Office 1999, head of e-Business Policy IOD 1999–2001, chm Deutsche Telekom Ltd 2001–02, sr policy advsr e-Business and e-Government IOD 2004–; non-exec dir: Securicor plc 2000–02, Telemetrix plc 2000–04, 3i European Technology Trust 2000–04, F&C Capital and Income Tst 2001–; sr independent dir Zetex plc 2004–; memb: Bd Parly Office of Sci and Technol 2001–, Strategic Stakeholder Gp Nat Hi-Tech Crime Unit 2005–06, Cncl Parly IT Ctee 2005–; visiting prof of electrical engineering Univ of Sheffield 1998–; chartered dir 2005; FIEE 1997 (AMIEE 1974), FRSA 1995, FInstD 2001, DEng Univ of Sheffield 2003; *Recreations* reading, music, amateur radio; *Style*— James Norton, Esq; ✉ 179b Kimbolton Road, Bedford MK41 8DR (tel 01234 325844, e-mail j.norton@dial.pipex.com, website www.profjimnorton.com)

NORTON, 8 Baron (UK 1878); James Nigel Arden Adderley; er s of 7 Baron Norton, OBE (d 1993), and Betty Margaret, *née* Hannah; *b* 2 June 1947; *Educ* Downside; *m* 1, 1971 (m dis 1989); 1 s (Hon Edward), 1 da (Hon Olivia Fleur Elizabeth); m 2, 23 April 1997, Frances Elizabeth Prioleau, yr da of George Frederick Rothwell; 1 da (Hon Alexandra Mary Evelyn); *Heir* s, Hon Edward Adderley; *Career* FCA 1970; *Recreations* flying, skiing, music; *Style*— The Rt Hon the Lord Norton; ✉ Chalet Petrus, Rue de Patier 24, 1936 Verbier, Switzerland

NORTON, John Charles; *b* 22 April 1937; *Educ* Dulwich Coll, UC Oxford (MA); *m* 1962, Dianne, *née* Lloyd; 2 s (James b 1963, Adam b 1968), 1 da (Emma b 1966); *Career* ptnr Arthur Andersen 1971–95 (joined 1961), dir and hon treas Arab-Br C of C 1995–, dir SOCO International plc 1997–; memb Oil Indust Accounting Ctee; govr Dulwich Coll 1998–; FCA 1974 (ACA 1964), FInstPet 1975; *Recreations* opera, rugby, golf, travel; *Clubs* Brooks's, Vincent's (Oxford); *Style*— John Norton, Esq

NORTON, John Lindsey; s of Frederick Raymond Norton (d 1981), and Doris Ann, *née* Jobson (d 1988); *b* 21 May 1935; *Educ* Winchester, Univ of Cambridge (MA); *m* 10 Oct 1959, Judith Ann, da of Brig Arthur Bird; 3 da (Bridget Ann b 6 Dec 1960, Claire Elizabeth b 25 May 1963, Sophie b 6 April 1965); *Career* Binder Hamlyn: joined 1963, ptnr (specialist in taxation, fin advice) 1966, nat managing ptnr 1981–87, chm BDO Binder (int firm) 1987–91, sr ptnr Binder Hamlyn 1992–96; chm Thames Valley Power Ltd 1995–, chm Barking Power Ltd 1995–97 and 1999– (dep chm 1997–99), dir H P Bulmer Holdings plc 1997–2003; chm NSPCC 1995–2001 (treas 1991–95); FCA; *Recreations* gardening, walking, music, theatre, a little golf; *Style*— John Norton, Esq; ✉ c/o Barking Power Ltd, Chequers Lane, Dagenham, Essex RM9 6PF (tel 020 8984 5000, fax 020 8984 5001, e-mail johnnorton@clara.co.uk)

NORTON, Richard William Fisher; s of Richard Glover Norton (d 2003), and Philippa Margaret, *née* Fisher (d 1995); *b* 4 October 1959; *Educ* Summer Fields, Radley; *m* 1987, Caroline Nicola Amy, da of Col Charles Taylor, MC, and Diana Elizabeth, *née* Gott; 2 da (Victoria b 1992, Lucinda b 1994); *Career* slr Linklaters & Paines 1983–87, slr and ptnr Charles Russell 1987–; *Recreations* golf, shooting and dogs; *Clubs* MCC, Annabel's, Cavalry and Guards, St Enedoc Golf, Wychwood Golf; *Style*— Richard Norton, Esq; ✉ Shawswell Grange, Rendcomb, Gloucestershire GL7 7HD; Compass House, Lypiatt Road, Cheltenham, Gloucestershire GL50 2QJ

NORTON, Robert; s of Ernest Robert Norton (d 1981), and Elsie Margaret, *née* Nix (d 1981); *b* 6 January 1941; *Educ* Downing Coll Cambridge, St Thomas' Hosp Med Sch (MA, MB BChir); *m* 29 July 1967, Ann Venetta Anderson, da of Romeo Alfredo Pazzi (d 1967); 2 s (Andrew b 20 Nov 1968, Christopher b 26 July 1970), 1 da (Colette b 23 Nov 1972); *Career* sr registrar in cardiothoracic surgery Edinburgh Royal Infirmary and City Hosps 1976–80; conslt cardiothoracic surgn West Midlands Regnl Health Authy 1980–; memb: Soc of Cardiothoracic Surgns, Br Cardiac Soc, Euro Soc of Cardiothoracic Surgns; Intercollegiate Bd examiner 1992–; FRCS 1972; *Style*— Robert Norton, Esq; ✉ Northfield, 6 Amherst Road, Kenilworth, Warwickshire CV8 1AH (tel 01926 57870); Walsgrave Hospital, Coventry CV2 2DX (tel 024 7660 2020); Priory Hospital, Edgbaston, Birmingham B5 7UG (tel 0121 440 2323)

NORTON, Prof Trevor Alan; s of Alan Norton, and Agnes, *née* Walsh; *b* 28 July 1940; *Educ* Blyth GS, Univ of Liverpool (BSc, PhD); *m* 26 July 1968, Win Marian; 1 da (Rachel Jane b 1971), 1 s (Paul Martin b 1974); *Career* regius prof of marine biology Bergen 1981, titular prof of botany Univ of Glasgow 1982–83, prof of marine biology Univ of Liverpool 1983–2005 (emeritus prof 2005–), dir Port Erin Marine Laboratory 1983–2005; author of 200 research pubns; pres: Br Phycological Soc 1989–91, Int Phycological Soc 1991–93; chm Aquatic Life Sciences NERC 1988–90, memb Cncl Marine Biological Assoc UK; FRSE 1985, FIBiol 1987; *Books* The Zonation of Rocky Shores (in The Ecology of Rocky Coasts, 1985), An Atlas of the Seaweeds of Britain and Ireland (1986), Marine Ecology in Biology of the Red Algae (1990), The Exploitable Living Resources of the Irish Sea (1990), Stars Beneath the Sea (1999), Reflections on a Summer Sea (2001), Out of the Past (2003), Under Water to get out of the Rain (2005); *Recreations* writing, gardening, watching movies; *Style*— Prof Trevor Norton, FRSE

NORTON-GRIFFITHS, Sir John; 3 Bt (UK 1922), of Wonham, Betchworth, Co Surrey; s of Maj Sir Peter Norton-Griffiths, 2 Bt (d 1983), and Kathryn, *née* Schrafft (d 1980); *b* 4 October 1938; *Educ* Eton; *m* 1964, Marilyn Margaret, da of Norman Grimley, of S Blundellsands, Liverpool; *Heir* bro, Dr Michael Norton-Griffiths; *Career* Sub-Lt RN; chartered accountant, pres Main Street Computers Inc 1980–; FCA; *Style*— Sir John Norton-Griffiths, Bt

NORTON OF LOUTH, Baron (Life Peer UK 1998), of Louth in the County of Lincolnshire; Prof Philip Norton; s of George Ernest Norton (d 1987), and Ena Dawson, *née* Ingham (d 2005); *b* 5 March 1951; *Educ* Univ of Sheffield (BA, PhD), Univ of Pennsylvania (MA); *Career* Univ of Hull: lectr in politics 1977–82, sr lectr in politics 1982–84, reader in politics 1984–86, prof of govt 1986– (youngest prof of politics in UK), dir Centre for Legislative Studies 1992–; chm: Cmmn to Strengthen Parliament 1999–2000, Cons Academic Gp 2000–, House of Lords Select Ctee on the Constitution 2001–04; memb Exec Ctee: Study of Parl Gp 1981–93, Political Studies Assoc of UK 1983–89, Br Politics Gp in USA 1983–95 (pres 1988–90), Res Ctee of Legislative Specialists Int Political Science Assoc 1991– (co-chair 1994–2003); pres Politics Assoc 1993–, memb Cncl Hansard Soc 1997–, vice-pres UK Political Studies Assoc 1999–, tstee History of Parliament 2000–; assoc ed Political Studies 1987–93, ed Jl of Legislative Studies 1995–; chm Standards Ctee Kingston upon Hull City Cncl 1999–2003; FRSA 1995, AcSS 2001; *Books* incl: The Commons in Perspective (1981), Conservatives and Conservatism (jtly, 1981), The Constitution in Flux (1982), The British Polity (1984, 4 edn 2001), Legislatures (ed, 1990), Back from Westminster (jtly, 1993), Does Parliament Matter? (1993), The Conservative Party (ed, 1996), Parliaments in Contemporary Western Europe (ed 3 vols, 1998–2002), Parliament in British Politics (2005), Politics UK (jtly, 6 edn 2006); *Recreations* tabletennis, walking; *Clubs* Royal Cwlth Soc, Royal Over-Seas League; *Style*— Prof the Rt Hon the Lord Norton of Louth; ✉ Department of Politics, University of Hull, Hull HU6 7RX (tel 01482 465863, fax 01482 466208, e-mail p.norton@hull.ac.uk); House of Lords, London SW1A 0PW (e-mail nortonp@parliament.uk)

NORTON-TAYLOR, Richard Seymour; *b* 6 June 1944; *Educ* King's Sch Canterbury, Hertford Coll Oxford (BA), Coll of Europe Bruges; *Career* freelance journalist; positions 1969–73 incl: EEC corr Washington Post, writer The Economist, writer Financial Times, broadcaster BBC Brussels; The Guardian: corr Brussels 1973–75, corr Whitehall 1975–85, security and intelligence corr 1985–; contrib to various radio and TV progs on the intelligence services; Freedom of Information Campaign Journalist of the Year 1986, Freedom of Information Campaign Special Award 1995; *Books* Whose Land Is It Anyway (1981), The Ponting Affair (1985), Blacklist (1988), In Defence Of The Realm? (1990), GCHQ: A Conflict of Loyalties 1984–1991, Truth is a Difficult Concept: Inside the Scott Inquiry (1995), Knee Deep in Dishonour: The Scott Report and its Aftermath (1996), Sleaze, The Corruption of Parliament (contrib, 1997), The Hutton Inquiry and its Impact (2004); *Plays* Half The Picture (1994, (based on Scott arms to Iraq inquiry)), Nuremberg (1996), The Colour of Justice (1999), Justifying War (2003), Bloody Sunday (2005, Olivier Award for Outstanding Theatre Production 2006), Called to Account (2007); *Clubs* National Liberal; *Style*— Richard Norton-Taylor, Esq; ✉ The Guardian, 119 Farringdon Road, London EC1R 3ER (tel 020 7278 2332, fax 020 7239 9787, e-mail richard.norton-taylor@guardian.co.uk)

NORWICH, Archdeacon of; *see:* Offer, Ven Clifford

NORWICH, 71 Bishop of (cr 1094) 1999–; Rt Rev Graham Richard James; s of late Lionel Dennis James, and (Florence Edith) May, *née* James; *b* 19 January 1951; *Educ* Northampton GS, Lancaster Univ (BA), Univ of Oxford (DipTh), Cuddesdon Theol Coll (CertTheol); *m* 21 Jan 1978, Julie Anne, da of Stanley William Freemantle; 2 da (Rebecca Alice b 5 Oct 1980, Victoria Rachel b 1983 d 1984), 1 s (Dominic Richard b 12 April 1985); *Career* ordained: deacon 1975, priest 1976; asst curate Christ the Carpenter Peterborough 1975–78, priest-in-charge later team vicar Christ the King Digswell Welwyn Garden City 1979–83, selection sec/sec for continuing ministerial educn 1983–85, sr selection sec ACCM 1985–87, chaplain to the Archbishop of Canterbury 1987–93, bishop of St Germans 1993–99; chair: Rural Bishops' Panel 2001–06, Central Religious Advsy Ctee to BBC and Ofcom 2004–, Miny Div C of E 2006–; memb Archbishop's Cncl 2006–; memb Bd Countryside Agency 2001–06, pres Royal Norfolk Agric Assoc 2005–06; memb House of Lords 2004–; *Books* Say One for Me (contrib, 1991), New Soundings (ed, 1997); *Recreations* theatre, walking, secondhand bookshops; *Clubs* Athenaeum, Norfolk; *Style*— The Rt Rev the Lord Bishop of Norwich; ✉ Bishop's House, Norwich, Norfolk NR3 1SB (tel 01603 629001, fax 01603 761613, e-mail bishop@bishopofnorwich.org)

NORWICH, 2 Viscount (UK 1952); John Julius Cooper; CVO (1993); s of 1 Viscount Norwich, GCMG, DSO, PC (Duff Cooper), sec of State for War 1935–37, First Lord of Admiralty 1937–38, min of Info 1940–41, and ambass to France 1944–47, and Lady Diana Cooper, *née* Manners (d 1986); *b* 15 September 1929; *Educ* Upper Canada Coll Toronto, Eton, Univ of Strasbourg, New Coll Oxford; *m* 1, 1952 (m dis 1985), Anne Frances May, da of Hon Sir Bede Clifford, GCMG, CB, MVO (yst s of 10 Baron Clifford of Chudleigh), and Alice, *née* Gundry, of Cleveland, Ohio; 1 s, 1 da; m 2, 1989, Mary (Mollie), da of 1 Baron Sherfield, GCB, GCMG, and former w of Hon Hugo John Laurence Philipps (later 3 Baron Milford); *Heir* s, Hon Jason Cooper; *Career* author, broadcaster (as 'John Julius Norwich'); with FO 1952–64; former chm Venice in Peril Fund, chm World Monuments Fund UK; maker of some thirty programmes (historical or art-historical) for television; FRSL, FRGS, FRSA; Ordine al Merito della Repubblica Italiana, Ordine della Solidarictà Italiana; *Books* two-volume history of Norman Sicily: The Normans in the South, The Kingdom in the Sun (published in one volume as The Normans in Sicily, 1992); two-volume history of Venice: The Rise to Empire, The Greatness and the Fall; Mount Athos, Sahara, The Architecture of Southern England, Fifty Years of Glyndebourne; three-volume History of Byzantium: The Early Centuries, The Apogee, The Decline and Fall; Shakespeare's Kings, Paradise of Cities, Christmas Crackers, More Christmas Crackers, Still More Christmas Crackers, The Middle Sea (History of the Mediterranean), Treasures of Britain (ed); *Recreations* Venice, commonplace books, nightclub piano; *Clubs* Beefsteak; *Style*— The Rt Hon the Viscount Norwich, CVO; ✉ 24 Blomfield Road, London W9 1AD (tel 020 7286 5050, fax 020 7266 2561, e-mail jjnorwich@dial.pipex.com)

NORWOOD, Graham Michael Mark; *b* 24 October 1956; *Educ* St Boniface's Coll Plymouth (head pupil), S Glamorgan Inst Cardiff (NCTJ Cert), Univ Coll Swansea; *m*; *Career* joined BBC as news trainee 1979, sub-ed BBC Radio News 1980–81, sub-ed BBC TV News 1981, BBC Ceefax 1981–90 (ed 1990–94), special asst to head BBC Newsgathering 1995–98, chief asst BBC Entertainment 1998–; secondments to develop teletext services for: RTE Dublin 1983, KTTV Los Angeles 1984, Hungarian Teletext 1989, Singapore Broadcasting Corp 1992; also seconded to relaunch of BBC Breakfast News 1989; BBC rep on Teletext Working Gp European Broadcasting Union; *Recreations* media, motor sport, cinema, theatre, writing; *Style*— Graham Norwood

NOSSITER, Prof Thomas Johnson (Tom); s of Alfred Nossiter (d 1989), of Stockton-on-Tees, and Margaret, *née* Hume; *b* 24 December 1937; *Educ* Stockton GS, Exeter Coll Oxford (BA), Nuffield Coll Oxford (DPhil); *m* Jean Mary, da of Irvin Clay, of Marsden, W Yorks; 2 s (Thomas b 1976, William b 1978); *Career* Nat Serv Royal Signals 1956–58; LSE: lectr 1973–77, sr lectr 1977–83, reader 1983–87, chm Bd of Studies in Economics 1984–85, dean Graduate Sch 1986–89, prof of govt 1989–94, prof emeritus 1996–; academic govr LSE 1988–92 (chm Bd of Examiners BSc External 1980–, chm Working Party on Revision of BSc External 1983); visiting professorship Univ of Leeds 1994–; state guest Kerala India 1977, visiting prof of politics Kerala India 1973, 1977 and 1983, state guest W Bengal 1983, visiting res fell and acting dir Centre for TV Res Univ of Leeds (lectr in social studies 1964); cmmnd evidence to Peacock Ctee 1986; dir Sangam Books London; conslt to UN Office on Somalia 1996; co-fndr Newlay Conservation Soc Leeds; chair Horsforth Town Cncl Ctee 1997–, Leeds city cncllr 1999–2000, Horsforth town cncllr 1999–; memb: Political Studies Assoc RIIA, BASAS; hon citizen Tralee 1991; *Books* ed: Imagination and Precision in the Social Sciences (1971), Influence, Opinion and Political Idioms in Reformed England (1975), Communism in Kerala (1982), Research on Range and Quality of Broadcasting Services (1986), Marxist State Goverments in India (1988), Broadcasting Finance in Transition (with J G Blumler, 1991), Local Quasi National Administrative Structures in Somaliland (1996); *Recreations* gardening, walking; *Style—* Prof Tom Nossiter; ✉ 38 Newlay Lane, Horsforth, Leeds LS18 4LE; University of Leeds, Leeds LS2 9JT (tel and fax 0113 258 2126); London School of Economics and Political Science, Houghton Street, London WC2A 2AE

NOTLEY, Somerled MacDonald; s of Lt Col George Harry Norman Notley, of Kirkcaldy, Fife, and Catherine, *née* MacDonald; *b* 30 March 1954; *Educ* George Watson's Coll Edinburgh, Univ of Edinburgh (LLB); *Career* apprentice Menzies Dougal & Milligan 1977–79; slr: Church of Scotland 1979–80, Standard Life Assurance Co 1980–81; Brodies: legal asst 1981–87, assoc 1987–89, ptnr 1989–; memb: Law Soc, Soc of Writers to HM Signet 1993, Notary Public 2004, Agricultural Law Assoc 2005; *Recreations* angling, skiing, music, reading, antiques; *Style—* Somerled Notley, Esq; ✉ Brodies WS, 15 Atholl Crescent, Edinburgh EH3 8HA (tel 0131 228 3777, e-mail somerled.notley@brodies.co.uk)

NOTTINGHAM, Bishop of 2000–; Rt Rev Malcolm Patrick McMahon; s of Patrick McMahon (d 1987), and Sarah, *née* Watson (d 1982); *b* 14 June 1949, London; *Educ* St Aloysius' Coll Highgate, UMIST (BSc, pres Students Union), Heythrop Coll Univ of London (BD, MTh); *Career* with London Transport 1971–76, joined Dominican Order 1976, ordained priest 1982, asst priest 1982–88, parish priest St Dominic's Newcastle upon Tyne 1989, prior St Dominic's Priory London 1989–92, prior provincial 1992–2000; *Recreations* golf, reading novels; *Clubs* Notts Co Golf; *Style—* The Rt Rev the Bishop of Nottingham; ✉ Bishop's House, 27 Cavendish Road East, The Park, Nottingham NG7 1BB (tel 0115 947 4786, e-mail bishop.secretary@nrcdt.org.uk)

NOULTON, John David; s of John Noulton (d 1993), of London, and Kathleen, *née* Sheehan; *b* 5 January 1939; *Educ* Clapham Coll; *m* 7 Oct 1961, Anne Elizabeth, da of Edward Byrne (d 1985); 3 s (Mark John b 1963, Stephen Anthony b 1965, Simon Anthony b 1966), 1 da (Jane Antonina b 1968); *Career* asst princ Dept of Tport 1970–72, princ DOE 1972–76, private sec to Min of State Rt Hon Denis Howell, MP 1976–78, sec Property Servs Agency 1978–81, under sec Dept of Tport 1985–89 (asst sec 1981–85); dir British Channel Tunnel Co plc 1982–89, chm Channel Tunnel Intergovernmental Cmmn 1989, dir Marine and Ports 1989, admin dir Transmanche Link 1989–92, dir public affairs Eurotunnel plc 1992–2004, advsr to Chm London Olympic Devpt Ctee 2005–06; tstee Franco-British Cncl 2003–; MCIT 1986, companion memb ICE 1994; *Recreations* walking, Mediterranean gardening, boating, writing, music; *Style—* John Noulton, Esq; ✉ 74 Garricks House, Wadbrook Street, Kingston-upon-Thames KT1 1HS (tel 020 8546 3855, e-mail johnnoulton@aol.com)

NOURSE, Christopher Stuart; s of Rev John Nourse (d 2006), of Devon, and Helen Jane Macdonald, *née* Allison (d 1992); *b* 13 August 1946; *Educ* Hurstpierpoint Coll, Univ of Edinburgh (LLB), Middle Temple; *Career* legal exec Life Offices Assoc 1970–72; various arts managerial positions: ROH, English Opera Gp, Royal Ballet New Gp 1972–76; gen mangr Sadler's Wells Royal Ballet 1976–90, admin dir Birmingham Royal Ballet 1990–91, asst to gen dir ROH 1991–96, admin dir ROH Tst 1996–97, exec dir Rambert Dance Co 1997–2001, md English Nat Ballet 2001–03; arts and dance conslt 2005–; admin Nat Dance Awards 2005–; dir and vice-chm London Dance Network 1998–2000; tstee: Nat Youth Dance Tst 2002–06, Youth Dance England 2004–, Dancers Pension Scheme 2006–; project mangr A Statue for Oscar Wilde appeal launch Nat Portrait Gallery 1997; FRSA 1998; *Publications* 'To Birmingham and beyond' in About the House (book, 1989), 'Parting Company' in Opera House (magazine, 1997); *Recreations* the performing and visual arts, music, eating out, the Orient, the countryside; *Style—* Christopher Nourse, Esq; ✉ 55 Queen's Gate, London SW7 5JW

NOURSE, Rt Hon Sir Martin Charles; kt (1980), PC (1985); s of late Henry Edward Nourse, MD, MRCP, of Cambridge, and Ethel Millicent, da of Rt Hon Sir Charles Henry Sargant, Lord Justice of Appeal; *b* 3 April 1932; *Educ* Winchester, CCC Cambridge; *m* 1972, Lavinia, da of late Cdr David Malim; 1 da (Charlotte b 1975), 1 s (Harry b 1977); *Career* 2 Lt (Nat Service) Rifle Bde 1951–52, London Rifle Bde Rangers (TA) 1952–55, Lt 1953; called to the Bar Lincoln's Inn 1956 (bencher 1978, treas 2001); memb Gen Cncl of the Bar 1964–68, jr counsel to Bd of Trade in Chancery Matters 1967–70, QC 1970, attorney-gen Duchy of Lancaster 1976–80, judge of the Courts of Appeal of Jersey and Guernsey 1977–80, judge of the High Court of Justice (Chancery Div) 1980–85, a Lord Justice of Appeal 1985–2001, vice-pres Court of Appeal (Civil Div) 2000–01, acting Master of the Rolls June-Oct 2000; pres Cncl of Inns of Court 1992–95; hon fell CCC Cambridge 1988, fell Winchester Coll 1993–2006; *Style—* The Rt Hon Sir Martin Nourse; ✉ Dullingham House, Dullingham, Newmarket, Suffolk CB8 9UP

NOWELL, Jonathan Charles Peter; s of David Charles Nowell, and Joan Nowell; *Educ* Stamford Sch, Westfield Coll London (BA); *Career* publishing dir Pearl & Dean Gp 1987–91, publisher motoring titles EMAP 1991–95, publisher and gp md J Whitaker & Sons Ltd 1995–, pres Nielsen Book Div VNU 2001–; memb: Publishers Assoc, Booksellers Assoc, PPA, Soc of Bookmen, Book Industry Study Gp (US); *Recreations* ex-player and ardent rugby fan, fishing (coarse and game), wine, cricket; *Clubs* Groucho, Soho House; *Style—* Jonathan Nowell, Esq; ✉ 5 Midhurst Avenue, London N10 3EP (e-mail jcpnowell@yahoo.co.uk); Endeavour House, 189 Shaftesbury Avenue, London WC2H 8TJ (tel 020 7420 6000)

NOWELL, Peter Jack; s of Roger Nowell (d 1991), of Reading, and Suzanne Elisabeth Nowell (d 1995); *b* 13 October 1948; *Educ* Reading Sch, LSE (MSc); *m* 1 May 1976, Wendy Margaret, da of Raymond Bonfield (d 1986); 2 da (Lucy b 1977, Emma b 1980); *Career* equity fund mangr Prudential Assurance Co Ltd 1971–81, fixed income dir Prudential Portfolio Managers 1982–87, chief exec Prudential Corporate Pensions 1988–90, gp chief actuary Prudential Corporation plc 1991–99; assoc Bacon & Woodrow 1999–2000; dir: B & W Deloitte 2001–02, Univ Life 2003–; chm RNPFN Supervisory Bd; FIA 1974; *Recreations* skiing; *Style—* Peter Nowell, Esq; ✉ 19 Pheasant Walk, Chalfont St Peter, Buckinghamshire SL9 0PW (tel 01494 873099, fax 01494 872697)

NUDD, Prof Graham Raymond; s of Raymond Charles Nudd (d 1966), and Eva May, *née* Ayling (d 1989); *b* 18 March 1940; *Educ* Collyers Sch Horsham, Univ of Southampton (BSc, PhD); *m* 1966, Laura Mary, *née* Brandram-Adams; 1 da (Alison Elizabeth b 1974); *Career* with Bendix Aerospace System Michigan USA 1966–68, head of info sci Hughes Res Laboratories Calif 1968–84; Univ of Warwick: Lucas prof of electronics and computer sci 1984–85, chm Computer Science Dept 1984–2006, prof of computer sci 1985–; nominated for Defense Sci Bd 1984, panellist NASA Review Ctee on Robotics and Machine Intelligence, sr memb IEEE (fndr VLSI Signal Processing Chapter); memb: Aerospace Advsy Panel ESPRIT, Microelectronic Facilities Sub-Ctee SERC, Working Gp on IT SERC, Ed Panel VLSI Signal Processing Jl; conslt: GEC, Marconi, Hughes Aircraft Co, RSRE; FIEE, FREng; *Publications* author of over 100 publications on computer and electronics systems; *Recreations* boating, rural preservation, living quietly in the Cotswolds; *Style—* Prof Graham Nudd, FREng; ✉ Department of Computer Science, University of Warwick, Coventry CV4 7AL (tel 02476 523366, e-mail grn@dcs.warwick.ac.uk)

NUGEE, Christopher George; QC (1998); s of Edward Nugee, Esq, TD, QC, *qv*, and Rachel *née* Makower; *b* 23 January 1959; *Educ* Radley, CCC Oxford (BA), City Univ (Dip Law); *m* 1991, Emily Thornberry, MP, *qv*, da of Cedric and Sallie Thornberry; 2 s (Felix Henry b 10 Dec 1991, Patrick George b 8 July 1999), 1 da (Rose Elizabeth b 2 Oct 1993); *Career* called to the Bar Inner Temple 1983 (Queen Elizabeth scholarship, bencher 2003); in practice at Chancery Bar 1984–, Eldon law scholar 1984, recorder 2002–, dep judge of the High Court 2003–; memb: Bar Cncl 1991–93 (Professional Conduct Ctee 1992–96), Assoc of Pension Lawyers Main Ctee 1998–2002; *Recreations* cycling, my family; *Style—* Christopher Nugee, Esq, QC; ✉ Wilberforce Chambers, 8 New Square, Lincoln's Inn, London WC2A 3QP (tel 020 7306 0102, fax 020 7306 0095)

NUGEE, Edward George; TD (1964), QC (1977); s of Brig George Travers Nugee, CBE, DSO, MC (d 1977), and Violet Mary Brooks, *née* Richards (d 1997), of Henley-on-Thames, Oxon; *b* 9 August 1928; *Educ* Radley, Worcester Coll Oxford (MA), Eldon Law Scholarship 1953; *m* 1 Dec 1955, Rachel Elizabeth Nugee, JP, da of Lt-Col John Moritz Makower, MBE, MC (d 1989), of Henley-on-Thames, Oxon; 4 s (John b 1956, Christopher Nugee, Esq, QC, *qv*, b 1959, Andrew b 1961, Richard b 1963); *Career* Nat Serv RA 1947–49 (office of COS Far East Land Forces, Singapore 1948–49), TA serv Intelligence Corps 100 APIU 1950–64, ret Capt 1964; called to the Bar Inner Temple 1955 (bencher 1976, treas 1996) ad eundem Lincoln's Inn 1968, head of chambers Wilberforce Chambers 1976–2006; poor man's lawyer Lewisham CAB 1954–72, dep High Ct judge 1982–97; memb: Bar Cncl 1961–65, CAB Advsy Ctee Family Welfare Assoc 1969–72, Ctee Gtr London CAB 1972–74, Mgmnt Ctee Forest Hill Advice Centre 1972–76, Cncl Legal Educn 1967–90 (chm bd of studies 1976–82), Common Professional Examination Bd 1976–89 (chm 1981–87), Advsy Ctee on Legal Educn 1971–90, Inst of Conveyancers 1971– (pres 1986–87), Assoc of Pension Lawyers 1992–; jr counsel to Land Cmmn 1967–71, counsel for litigation under Commons' Registration Act (1965) 1968–77; conveyancing counsel 1972–77 to: Treasy, WO, MAFF, Forestry Cmmn, MOD, DOE; Lord Chllr's Law Reform Ctee 1973–; conveyancing counsel of the Ct 1976–77; chm Ctee of Inquiry into Mgmnt of Privately Owned Blocks of Flats 1984–85; church cmmr 1990–2001 (memb Bd of Govrs 1993–2001), memb Legal Advsy Cmmn of Gen Synod 2002–; chm govrs Brambletye Sch 1972–77, memb Cncl Radley Coll 1975–95, churchwarden Hampstead Parish Church 1979–83, tstee Lambeth Palace Library 1999–2001, hon treas and tstee Temple Music Tst 1997–; *Books* Nathan on the Charities Act 1960 (jtly, 1962), Halsbury's Laws of England (jt ed, Landlord and Tenant 3 edn 1958, Real Property 3 edn 1960, 4 edn 1982, 4 edn reissue 1998); *Recreations* travel, history, church and family life; *Style—* Edward Nugee, Esq, TD, QC; ✉ 35 The Panoramic, 12 Pond Street, Hampstead, London NW3 2PS (tel 020 7435 9204); Wilberforce Chambers, 8 New Square, Lincoln's Inn, London WC2A 3QP (tel 020 7306 0102, fax 020 7306 0095, e-mail enugee@wilberforce.co.uk)

NUGENT, Sir John Edwin Lavallin; 7 Bt (I 1795), of Ballinlough Castle, Westmeath; 4 Count Nugent (Austrian Empire); er s of Sir Hugh Charles Nugent, 6 Bt (d 1983), and Margaret Mary Lavallin, *née* Puxley (d 2004); *b* 16 March 1933; *Educ* Eton; *m* 1959, Penelope Anne, er da of Brig Richard Nigel Hanbury, CBE, TD, DL (d 1972); 1 s (Nicholas Myles John b 1967), 1 da (Grania Clare b 1969); *Heir* s, Nicholas Nugent; *Career* Lt Irish Gds; formerly JP Berks, High Sheriff Berks 1981; *Recreations* gardening, shooting, fishing; *Style—* Sir John Nugent, Bt; ✉ The Steward's House, Ballinlough Castle, Clonmellon, Navan, Co Meath, Ireland (tel 00 353 46 9433135)

NUGENT, Sir (Walter) Richard Middleton; 6 Bt (UK 1831), of Donore, Westmeath; s of Sir Peter Walter James Nugent, 5 Bt; *b* 15 November 1947; *Educ* Downside; *m* 1985, Okabe Kayoko; *Career* with PricewaterhouseCoopers (formerly Deloitte, Plender Griffiths & Co) 1967–74, chief fin offr IMS Japan Kabushiki Kaisha 1991–2003, ret; FCA 1970; *Clubs* Lansdowne, Kildare St and Univ (Dublin); *Style—* Sir Richard Nugent, Bt; ✉ 61–6 Yaguchi-dai, Naka-ku, Yokohama, 231, Japan (e-mail nugentwr@gol.com)

NUGENT, Sir Robin George Colborne; 5 Bt (UK 1806), of Waddesdon, Berkshire; s of Capt Sir (George) Guy Bulwer Nugent, 4 Bt (d 1970), and Maisie Esther, *née* Bigsby (d 1992); *b* 11 July 1925; *Educ* Eton, RWA Sch of Architecture; *m* 1, 1947 (m dis 1967), Ursula Mary, da of Lt-Gen Sir Herbert Fothergill Cooke, KCB, KBE, CSI, DSO (d 1936); 2 s (Christopher George b 1949, Patrick Guy b 1959), 1 da (Philippa Mary b 1951); m 2, 1967, Victoria Anna Irmgard, da of Dr Peter Cartellieri; *Heir* s, Christopher Nugent; *Career* Lt Grenadier Gds 1944–48; ARIBA; *Style—* Sir Robin Nugent, Bt

NUÑEZ, Marianela; da of Norberto Nuñez, and Elena Clarijo de Nuñez; *b* 23 March 1982, Buenos Aires, Argentina; *Educ* Teatro Colón Ballet Sch, Royal Ballet Sch; *Career* ballet dancer; princ Royal Ballet 2002– (joined 1999); *Performances* incl: Kitri, Swanilda, Sugar Plum Fairy, Gamzatti, Nikiya, Aurora, Lilac Fairy, Olga in Onegin, Myrtha, Mitzi Caspar, Princess Louise and Lescaut's Mistress in Mayerling, Polyhymnia, Lykanion, Raymonda Act III, Monotones I, Agon, The Vertiginous Thrill of Exactitude, This House Will Burn, The Leaves Are Fading, Sinfonietta, The Four Temperaments, Diana and Actaeon pas de deux, La Nuit in Les Saisons, Acheron's Dream; *Style—* Miss Marianela Nuñez; ✉ c/o The Royal Ballet, Royal Opera House, Covent Garden, London WC2E 9DD

NUNN, Christopher Leslie; s of Walter Leslie Nunn (d 1990), and Beatrice Rose, *née* Jones (d 1989); *b* 14 March 1943; *Educ* Highgate Sch, LSE (BScEcon); *m* 15 Nov 1969, Lynne Margaret Rochelle, da of Cdr Richard Hosking Hughes (d 1994); 2 s (Richard b 1974, Peter b 1978); *Career* Arthur Andersen: joined 1965, qualified CA 1968, London office 1965–76, ptnr 1976, head of audit div Birmingham 1976–80, head of audit gp London 1980–90, i/c UK tech gp and risk mgmnt and compliance 1990–; memb urgent issues task force Accounting Standards Bd 1994–; FCA (memb Auditing Ctee 1994–); *Style—* Christopher Nunn, Esq

NUNN, Michael; s of Reginald Edward Nunn, and Shirley Louise, *née* Morrison; *b* 1 July 1967; *Educ* Bush Davies Sch, Royal Ballet Sch; *m* Belinda Hatley; 1 s (George Jacob Nunn b 27 Sept 2003); *Career* dancer; with Royal Ballet 1987–99 (first soloist 1997–99), fndr memb K Ballet 1999, fndr (with William Trevitt , *qv*) George Piper Dances 2001; *Performances* Sir Kenneth MacMillan repertoire: cr The Friend in The Judas Tree, Romeo and Benvolio in Romeo and Juliet, Offertoire in Requiem, The Brother in My Brother, My Sisters, Des Grieux and The Gaoler in Manon, Bethena Waltz in Elite Syncopations, Crown Prince Rudolf in Mayerling, The Boy in The Invitation, one of the Four Officers and Anna's Husband in Anastasia, The King of the East in The Prince of the Pagodas, Kulygin in Winter Dreams, The Orange Boy in La Fin du Jour, second movement in Concerto; Sir Frederick Ashton repertoire: Beliaev in A Month in the Country, The Prince in Cinderella, white pas de deux in Les Patineurs, Dorkon in Daphnis and Chloe, pas de deux in Birthday Offering, Elgar in Enigma Variations, Thais pas de deux, Monotones II, Symphonic Variations; cr roles: lead in William Tuckett's Present Histories, role in Matthew Hart's Fanfare, Act II sextet in Twyla Tharp's Mr Worldly Wise, lead couple in Christopher Wheeldon's Souvenir, part II in Page's Two Part Invention, The Ringmaster in Sawdust and Tinsel, Glen Tetley's Amores; other roles incl: Albrecht in Giselle, Suitor, Prince Florimund and Gold variation in The Sleeping Beauty, Rag Mazurka Boy in Nijinska's Les Biches, Mazurka and pas de deux in Fokine's Les Sylphides, pas de trois in Balanchine's Agon, fourth movement in Symphony in C, pas de trois in David Bintley's Galanteries, Mars in The Planets, first princ man in Cheating,

Lying, Stealing, The Man in Dream of Angels, first section in William Forsythe's In the Middle Somewhat Elevated, leading man in Steptext, William Tuckett's A Shropshire Lad (Dance Bites tour 1995), Ashley Page's Pursuit, Room of Cooks (Dance Bites tour 1997), Herman Schmerman, Twyla Tharp's Push Comes to Shove, Consort Lessons; television appearances with Royal Ballet: La Valse (Channel 4), 1997 Farewell Gala (Channel 4), The Judas Tree (Channel 4), The Ancient Mariner (BBC2), featured in The House (BBC2); perfs with George Piper Dances incl: Steptext, Sigue, Truly great thing, Critical Mass and Torsion, other mens wives, Approximate Sonata I, V, Mesmerics, restaged Halleloo, choreographed Moments of Plastic Jubilation; also with William Trevitt: co-filmed and co-directed Ballet Boyz and Ballet Boyz II - The Next Step (Channel 4), presented 4Dance (Channel 4) 2003 and 2004, created Critic's Choice ***** (featuring Matthew Bourne, *qv*, Michael Clark, Akram Khan, *qv*, Russell Maliphant, *qv* and Christopher Wheeldon) 2004, Broken Fall (commissioned by Russell Malipahnt, premiered ROH) 2004, dir and choreographer Naked (premiered at Sadler's Wells) 2005; *Awards* nominated South Bank Show Dance Award 2001 and 2003, nomination (for Memerics) Best New Dance Production Laurence Olivier Award 2004, winner (for Broken Fall) Best New Dance Production Laurence Olivier Award 2004; *Recreations* Film, Travel, Music, Literature; *Style—* Michael Nunn, Esq; ✉ George Piper Dances, Sadler's Wells, Rosebery Avenue, London EC1R 4TN (tel 020 7863 8238, e-mail michael@gpdances.com)

NUNN, Sir Trevor Robert; kt (2002), CBE (1978); s of Robert Alexander Nunn, and Dorothy May, *née* Piper; *b* 14 January 1940; *Educ* Northgate GS Ipswich, Downing Coll Cambridge (BA), Univ of Newcastle upon Tyne (MA); *m* 1, 1969 (m dis 1986), Janet Suzman, *qv*; 1 s (Joshua b 1980); m 2, 1986 (m dis 1991), Sharon Lee, *née* Hill; 2 da (Laurie b 1986, Amy b 1989); m 3, 1994, Imogen Stubbs, *qv*; 1 da (Ellie b 1991), 1 s (Jesse b 1996); *Career* theatre and film director; RSC: assoc dir 1964–68, chief exec and artistic dir 1968–78, chief exec and jt artistic dir 1978–86; artistic dir RNT 1997–2003; memb Arts Council 1994–96; *Theatre and Film* Belgrade Theatre Coventry: The Caucasian Chalk Circle, Peer Gynt, Around the World in Eighty Days (musical); RSC: The Revenger's Tragedy, The Relapse, The Alchemist, Henry V, The Taming of the Shrew, King Lear, Much Ado About Nothing, The Winter's Tale, Henry VIII, Hamlet, Antony and Cleopatra (also for ATV, BAFTA Award for Best Single Play Prodn), Hedda Gabler (also as a film), Macbeth (also for Thames TV), Coriolanus, Julius Caesar, Titus Andronicus, Romeo and Juliet, The Comedy of Errors (also for ATV, musical version - Ivor Novello Award for Best British Musical, SWET Award for Best Musical), The Alchemist, As You Like It, Once in a Life-time (Plays and Players London Theatre Critics' Award - Best Production, New Standard Drama Awards - Sydney Edwards Award for Best Director), Three Sisters, Nicholas Nickleby (New Standard Drama Awards - Sydney Edwards for Best Director, SWET Award for Best Director, Drama Review London Theatre Critics' Award - Best Production, Tony Award - Best Director, special citation as Outstanding Broadway Production in All Categories, Emmy Award - Best Best TV Serial; shown on TV in London and NY, with John Caird), Juno and the Paycock (Drama Review London Theatre Critics' Award - Best Revival), Henry IV Parts I and II, All's Well That Ends Well, Peter Pan (with John Caird), Les Miserables (London and Worldwide, with John Caird), Fair Maid of the West, Othello (also for BBC TV), The Blue Angel (Stratford 1991, Globe 1992), Measure for Measure (Stratford) 1991 (Young Vic) 1992; freelance dir: Cats (worldwide, Tony Award - Best Director of a Musical) 1981, Idomeneo (Glyndebourne Opera) 1982, Starlight Express (London and NY) 1984, Lady Jane (film) 1985, Chess (London and NY) 1986, Porgy and Bess (Glyndebourne Opera 1986, Royal Opera House 1992), Aspects of Love (London and NY) 1989, The Baker's Wife 1989, Timon of Athens (Young Vic Theatre, Evening Standard Award for Best Dir) 1991, Cosi Fan Tutte (Glyndebourne Opera) 1991, Heartbreak House (Yvonne Arnaud Guildford and Haymarket) 1992, Arcadia (RNT 1993, Haymarket 1994, NY 1995), Sunset Boulevard (London and Los Angeles 1993, NY 1994), Twelfth Night (film) 1996, The Lady From the Sea 2003, Richard II (Old Vic) 2005; RNT: Enemy of the People 1997, Mutabilitie 1997, Not About Nightingales 1998, Oklahoma! 1998, Betrayal 1998, Troilus and Cressida 1999, Merchant of Venice 1999, Summerfolk 1999, Albert Speer 2000, The Cherry Orchard 2000, My Fair Lady 2001, South Pacific 2001, A Streetcar Named Desire 2002, Sophie's Choice 2002, Anything Goes 2002, Love's Labour's Lost 2003, Skellig 2003, Hamlet 2004, We Happy Few 2004; *Books* A; *Style—* Sir Trevor Nunn, CBE; ✉ 49B British Grove, London W4 2NL (tel 020 8563 7273)

NUNNELEY, Sir Charles Kenneth Roylance; kt (2003); s of Robin Michael Charles Nunneley (d 2005), of Holt, Norfolk, and Patricia Mary, *née* Roylance (d 1999), of Harrietsham, Kent; *b* 3 April 1936; *Educ* Eton; *m* 1961, Catherine Elizabeth Armstrong, da of Sir Denys Burton Buckley, MBE (d 1998), of London; 1 s (Luke b 1963), 3 da (Alice b 1964, Clare b 1967, Frances b 1969); *Career* 2 Lt Scots Gds, served chiefly BAOR; merchant banker; Robert Fleming Holdings: dir 1968–96, dep chm 1986–96, former chm or dir of various other Fleming gp cos; chm: Save & Prosper Gp (Fleming subsid) 1989–96, Fleming Income & Capital Investment Tst 1992–2002, Nationwide Building Society 1996–2002 (dir 1994–2002), Monks Investment Tst 1996–2005 (dir 1977–2005), Nationwide Fndn 1997–2001, JP Morgan Income and Capital Investment Tst 2002–07, Edinburgh Fund Managers Gp 2003; dep chm Clerical Medical & General Life Assurance Society 1978–96 (dir 1974–96); dir: Macmillan Ltd 1982–95, HM Publishers Holdings 1995–96; chm: Institutional Fund Mangrs' Assoc 1989–92, IMRO 1992–97 (dir 1986–97), Nat Tst 1996–2003 (chm Fin Ctee 1991–96, memb Cncl 1992–2003, memb Exec Ctee 1992–2003); chm Cncl N Wessex Downs Area of Outstanding Natural Beauty 2004–; govr Oundle Sch 1975–99; memb Ct of Assts Worshipful Co of Grocers 1975– (Master 1982–83); CA 1961; *Recreations* walking, theatre, photography; *Style—* Sir Charles Nunneley; ✉ 4 Grenville Place, London SW7 4RU (tel 020 7341 9710)

NUNNERLEY, Dr Heather Bell; *Educ* Calder High Sch, Univ of Liverpool (state scholar, MB ChB, DCH, DObst RCOG); *Career* house physician then house surgn Royal Southern Hosp Liverpool 1956–57; SHO: in child health Alder Hey Children's Hosp Liverpool 1957–58, in obstetrics Mill Road Maternity Hosp Liverpool 1958–59; in gen practice Stafford 1959–65 (princ 1960–65); King's Coll Hosp: trainee registrar in radiology 1965–67, sr registrar in radiology 1967–74 (Br Inst of Radiology scholarship to Stockholm 1972), gp conslt in radiology 1974–86, dir Dept of Diagnostic Radiology 1986–96, care gp dir of diagnostic radiology and nuclear med 1987–96; chm Ravensbourne NHS Tst 1998–; dir SE London Breast Screening Serv 1987–98 (chm 1993–97); Royal Coll of Radiologists: memb Faculty Bd of Radiodiagnosis 1984–86, memb Cncl 1986–89, past vice-pres Mammography Gp, chm Clinical Dirs' Gp 1992–96; chm: Regional Higher Awards Ctee SE Thames 1991–94, Conslts' Ctee King's Healthcare 1993–95, S Thames (E) Regional Radiology Speciality Ctee, Ravensbourne NHS Tst; currently non-exec memb Bd of Queen Marys NHS Tst Sidcup; formerly pres Radiology Section RSM, memb Advsy Gp in Radiology to Dept of Health 1988–92; recognised teacher Univ of London, former examiner for final fellowship Royal Coll of Radiologists in London and overseas; author of various articles in learned jls and text books; FRCR, FRCP; *Style—* Dr Heather B Nunnerley; ✉ 6 The Tudors, 10 Court Downs Road, Beckenham, Kent BR3 6LR

NURNBERG, Andrew John; s of Walter Nurnberg, OBE (d 1991), and Rita, *née* Kern (d 2001); *b* 16 October 1947; *Educ* St Benedict's Sch Ealing, Univ of London (BA); *m* 22 Oct 1983, Harriet Goodman; 1 s (Alexander b 31 May 1985), 1 da (Lucy b 10 Sept 1987); *Career* literary agent Robert Harben Literary Agency 1973–77; fndr Andrew Nurnberg Assocs 1977 (offices in London, Moscow, Prague, Warsaw, Budapest, Sofia, Riga, Beijing and Taipei); Br Cncl scholarship Moscow State Univ 1968–69; vice-pres Assoc of Authors' Agents 1991; memb Finance Ctee: St Etheldreda's Church London 1982–87, St Patrick's Catholic Church London 1993–; *Publications* The Green Frog Service (with M Raeburn and L Voronikhina, 1995) author of various articles; *Recreations* mountain climbing, cooking, music, reading; *Clubs* Reform, Alpine; *Style—* Andrew Nurnberg, Esq; ✉ Andrew Nurnberg Associates Ltd, Clerkenwell House, 45–47 Clerkenwell Green, London EC1R 0QX (tel 020 7417 8800, fax 020 7417 8812)

NURSE, Dr Sir Paul Maxime; kt (1999); *b* 25 January 1949; *Educ* Harrow County GS, Univ of Birmingham (BSc, John Humphrey's Meml Prize), UEA (PhD); *m*; 2 da; *Career* research fell: Dept of Zoology Univ of Edinburgh 1974–78, Sch of Biology Univ of Sussex 1980–84; head of Cell Cycle Control Laboratory ICRF London 1984–87, Iveagh prof of microbiology Univ of Oxford 1987–91, Napier research prof of the Royal Soc Univ of Oxford 1991–93, DG ICRF 1996–2002 (previously dir of lab research), ceo Cancer Research UK 2002–03, pres Rockefeller Univ NY 2004–; visiting prof Univ of Copenhagen 1981; author of over 100 pubns in learned jls; speaker at over 200 seminars in research insts worldwide, speaker chm and organiser at over 30 int meetings and confs dealing with yeast molecular biology and genetics and cell cycle and growth control; pres UK Genetical Soc 1990–94, memb EMBO 1987; FRS 1989, memb Academia Europaea 1992, foreign assoc US Nat Acad of Sciences 1995; *Awards* Fleming lectr Soc of Gen Microbiology 1985, Florey lectr Royal Soc 1990, Marjory Stephenson lectr Soc of Gen Microbiology 1990, CIBA Medal UK Biochemical Soc 1991, Louis Jeantet Prize for Medicine Switzerland 1992, Gairdner Fndn Int Award 1992, Royal Soc Wellcome Medal 1993, Jimenez Diaz Meml Award Spain 1993, Rosenstiel Award and Medal USA 1993, Dunham lectr Harvard Univ 1994, Purkyne Medal Czech Republic 1994, Pezcoller Award for Oncology Research Italy 1995, Bradshaw lectr RCP London 1995, Royal Soc Royal Medal 1995, Dr Josef Steiner Prize Switzerland 1996, Dr H P Heineken Prize for Biochemistry and Biophysics The Netherlands 1996, General Motors Cancer Research Fndn Alfred P Sloan Jr Prize and Medal USA 1997, Albert Lasker Basic Med Research Award USA 1998, Nobel Prize in Physiology or Medicine 2001 (jtly with Leland H Hartwell and Dr Sir Tim Hunt, FRS, *qv*), Romanes Lecture 2003, Royal Society Copley Medal 2005; fell American Acad of Arts and Sciences 2006; *Style—* Dr Sir Paul Nurse, FRS; ✉ Office of the President, Rockefeller University, 1230 York Avenue, New York NY 10021–6399, USA (tel 00 1 212 327 8080)

NURSTEN, Prof Harry Erwin; s of Sergius Nursten (d 1950), of Ilkley, and Helene, *née* Breslauer (d 1971); *Educ* Ilkley GS, Univ of Leeds (BSc, PhD, DSc); *m* 23 Dec 1950, Jean Patricia, da of Arnold Frobisher (d 1972), of Leeds, and Hilda, *née* Wood (d 1991); *Career* Bradford Dyers' Assoc research fell Dept of Colour Chemistry Univ of Leeds 1949–52, lectr in dyeing and textile chemistry Nottingham and Dist Tech Coll 1952–54; Univ of Leeds: lectr Dept of Leather Industries 1955–65, assoc lectr Dept of Organic Chemistry 1962–65, sr lectr Procter Dept 1965–70, reader Procter Dept 1970–76; Univ of Reading: prof of food science 1976–92, head of dept 1976–86, head Dept of Food Science and Technol 1986–89, head Sub-Dept of Food Science 1989–91, prof emeritus 1992–; MIT: research assoc Dept of Nutrition, Food Science and Technol 1961–62, fell Sch for Advanced Study 1962; visiting prof: Dept of Food Science and Technol Univ of Calif Davis 1966, Inst of Food, Nutrition and Family Science Univ of Zimbabwe 1994; memb ARC/MRC Ctee on Food and Nutrition Research Working Pty on Non-Nutritive Constituents of Foods 1971–73; Bill Littlejohn Meml Medallion lectr Br Soc of Flavourists 1974; pres Soc of Leather Technologists and Chemists 1974–76, chief examiner Inst of Food Science and Technol 1982–90 (examiner 1978–81); Br Cncl assignments to: Malaysia 1982 and 1988, Portugal 1988 and 1990, Cyprus 1990, Zimbabwe 1991; Senior Medal of Food Chemistry Gp RSC 1996; memb: Soc of Dyers and Colourists 1945, Soc of Chemical Industry 1951, Chemical Soc 1951, Sigma Xi 1962, FRIC 1957, FIFST 1972, inaugural fell Soc of Leather Technologists and Chemists 1986 (memb 1955); *Books* Azo and Diazo Chemistry (trans, 1961), Progress in Flavour Research (ed jtly, 1979), Chemistry of Tea Infusions incl: Chemical and Biological Properties of Tea Infusions (1997), Flavours and Off-Flavours in Milk and Dairy Products incl: Advanced Dairy Chemistry Vol 3 (1997), The Maillard Reaction in Foods and Medicine (ed jtly, 1998), Capillary Electrophoresis for Food Analysis: Method Development (jtly, 2000), The Maillard Reaction in Food and Nutrition incl: Flavour 2000, Perception, Release, Evaluation, Formation, Acceptance, Nutrition/Health (2001), The Maillard Reaction, Chemistry, Biochemistry and Implications (2005), Gastronomy: The Ultimate Flavour Science (2006); numerous scientific papers; *Style—* Prof Harry Nursten; ✉ Department of Food Biosciences, University of Reading, Whiteknights, PO Box 226, Reading RG6 6AP (tel 0118 931 6725, fax 0118 931 0080, e-mail h.e.nursten@reading.ac.uk)

NUSSEY, Dr Ian David; OBE (1988); s of Dr Adolph Marcus Nussey (d 1993), and Susannah Rayner Nussey (d 1981); *b* 4 April 1936; *Educ* Bromsgrove Sch, Downing Coll Cambridge (MA, Engrg Assoc prize), Univ of Birmingham (PhD); *m* 1976, Gillian Patricia, da of Dr Thomas Russell and Enid Stanley Stevens; 2 da (Emma Frances Guest (step da) b 1966, Jessica Clare b 1977); *Career* Lucas Industries 1958–62, IBM United Kingdom Ltd 1963– (chm Technical Consultancy Gp 1991–98, vice-pres IBM Acad of Technol 1998–99, Univ Relations 2000–); contrib to various jls associated with mfrg and info technol; various public service appts; visiting prof: Loughborough Univ 1973–76, Univ of Newcastle upon Tyne 1976–2002, Univ of Salford 1983–94, Univ of Wales Cardiff 1986–; memb Cncl Univ of Warwick 1989–2002; vice-pres: Inst of Mfrg Engrs 1990–91, IEE 1995–98 (chm Mfrg Div 1991–92); memb: Senate Engrg Cncl 1996–97, Cncl Royal Acad of Engrg 2005–; Sargent Award Soc of Mfrg Engrs USA 1988, Viscount Nuffield Silver Medal IEE 2000, Chllr's Medal Univ of Warwick 2006; hon fell Cardiff Univ 2007; Freeman City of London, Liveryman Worshipful Co of Engrs 1983; FREng 1985, Hon FIET, FIMechE, FBCS, FSME, FRSA; *Recreations* gardening, theatre-going, hillside conservation, skiing, golf; *Clubs* Athenaeum; *Style—* Dr Ian Nussey, OBE, FREng; ✉ Cidermill Farm House, Ardens Grafton, Alcester, Warwickshire B49 6DS (tel 01789 773356); IBM United Kingdom Ltd, PO Box 31, Warwick CV34 5JL (tel 01789 773356)

NUTKINS, Terry; *Career* television personality specialising in marine and other animals; worked with elephants London Zoo aged 8, with otters for naturalist and author Gavin Maxwell aged 12; presenter on BBC: Animal Magic (with Johnny Morris) 1980–85 (advsr on dolphin filming 1977), Really Wild Show 1985– (winner BAFTA Award), Really Wild Roadshows 1990–, Animal Corner (Radio 4) 1987–90, Growing Up Wild 1993, 1994 and 1995, own weekly prog Radio 5 1993, Really Useful Show 1996–98, Watchdog Value for Money 1997, Wildways (Radio Scotland) 2002; also presenter: Disney Club (Family Channel) 1997, Attractions (Channel 5) 1997, Brilliant Creatures (Children's ITV) 1998, 1999 and 2000, wildlife features Gloria Hunniford Show (Channel 5) 2001; prodr and presenter commercial videos for Sea Life Centres Notts County Cncl 1994 and 1995, narrator Really Wild Animal Tape (audio cassette) 1995, played Baron Hardup in Roy Hudd's Cinderella, after-dinner speaker on wildlife and the environment; author of various articles on natural history for Watch, BBC Wildlife, Countryside and other magazines; *Books* Nutkins on Pets (1989); *Style—* Terry Nutkins, Esq; ✉ c/o John Miles Organisation, Cadbury Camp Lane, Clapton-in-Gordano, Bristol BS20 9SB (tel 01275 854675, fax 01275 810186)

NUTTALL, Christopher Guy; s of Derek Reginald Nuttall, of Northwich, Cheshire, and Doris Joan Bentley, *née* Johnson; *b* 16 August 1957; *Educ* Sir John Deane's GS Northwich, UCL (BA); *m* 1993, Nishanthri Wickramasinghe, of Colombo, Sri Lanka; 1 da (Constance Geneva b 16 Oct 1995), 1 s (Kesara Calvin b 2 March 1998); *Career* journalist; Warrington Guardian Series newspapers 1978–81; BBC: journalist 1982–99, foreign corr BBC World

Serv 1988, Sri Lanka corr 1988–90, Washington corr BBC World Serv 1991–93, foreign affrs corr BBC World Serv 1994–95, Ankara corr BBC World Serv 1995–97, world ed BBC News Online 1997–98, internet corr BBC News 1998–99; internet ed Sunday Business 1999, sr writer Industry Standard Europe 2000, sr reporter FT 2001–, IT corr 2003–; Global Communications Journalist of the Year 2000; *Recreations* cycling, cinema, computers; *Style*— Christopher Nuttall, Esq; ✉ Financial Times, 251 Post Street, San Francisco, CA 94108 USA (tel 00 1 415 445 5602, e-mail chris.nuttall@ft.com)

NUTTING, David Anthony; DL (Essex 1988); yr s of Rt Hon Sir (Harold) Anthony Nutting, 3 Bt (d 1999); *b* 13 September 1944; *Educ* Eton, Trinity Coll Cambridge (MA); *m* 25 April 1974, Tessa Anne, o da of Sir Nigel John Mordaunt, 13 Bt, MBE (d 1979); 3 da (Belinda b 18 Aug 1975, Serena b 24 Nov 1977, Alexandra b 27 Dec 1978); *Career* chm: Select Sires Ltd 1982–89, Bridge Farm Dairies Ltd 1987–95, Strutt & Parker (Farms) Ltd 1987–; dir Lavenham Fen Farms Ltd; chm: Essex Agric Soc 1985–90, Br Cattle Breeders Club 1978–79; memb Advsy Bd Inst of Animal Physiology 1983–86; pres Holstein Friesian Soc 1990; tstee Cambridge Univ Veterinary Sch Tst 1994; Freeman Worshipful Co of Farmers 1975; *Recreations* fishing, shooting, racing; *Style*— David Nutting, Esq, DL; ✉ Peverel House, Hatfield Peverel, Chelmsford, Essex CM3 2JF (tel 01245 383100, fax 01245 383111)

NUTTING, Sir John Grenfell; 4 Bt (UK 1902), of St Helens, Booterstown, Co Dublin, QC (1995); s of Rt Hon Sir (Harold) Anthony Nutting, 3 Bt (d 1999); *b* 28 August 1942; *Educ* Eton, McGill Univ Montreal (BA); *m* 1973, Diane, da of Capt Duncan Kirk, and widow of 2 Earl Beatty; 1 da (Victoria Emily b 1975), 1 s (James Edward Sebastian b 1977), 1 step s, 1 step da; *Heir* s, James Nutting; *Career* called to the Bar Middle Temple 1968, bencher 1991; first sr treasy counsel 1993–95 (jr treasy counsel 1981, first jr treasy counsel 1987–88, sr treasy counsel 1988–93), recorder of the Crown Court 1986–, judge of the Cts of Appeal of Jersey and Guernsey 1995–, cmmr for Interception of Communications (Jersey and Guernsey) 1998–2005, dep judge of the High Court (Queen's Bench and Chancery Div) 1998–, cmmr for Regulation of Investigatory Powers (Jersey and Guernsey) 2004–; memb Bar Cncl 1976–80 and 1986–87, chm Young Bar 1978–79, vice-chm Criminal Bar Assoc 1995–97; memb Lord Chllr's Advsy Ctee on Legal Educn and Conduct 1997–99; pres NE Milton Keynes Cons Assoc 1990–93; chm: Helmsdale River Bd 2001–, Helmsdale Dist Salmon Fishery Bd 2001–; memb Appointments Panel Ind Supervisory Authy for Hunting 2001–05; patron Philharmonia Orch 2001–; FRPSL 1970; *Clubs* White's, Pratt's, Mark's; *Style*— Sir John Nutting, Bt, QC; ✉ 3 Raymond Buildings, Gray's Inn, London WC1R 5BH; Achentoul, Kinbrace, Sutherland KW11 6UB; Chicheley Hall, Newport Pagnell, Buckinghamshire MK16 9JJ; K3, Albany, Piccadilly, London W1J 0AY

NUTTING, Peter Robert; JP (Inner London 1978), DL (Surrey 2000); s of Capt Arthur Ronald Stansmore Nutting, OBE, MC (d 1964), of North Breache Manor, Ewhurst, Surrey, and Patricia Elizabeth, *née* Jameson; *b* 22 October 1935; *Educ* Eton; *m* 1965, Cecilia Hester Marie-Louise, da of Cosmo Re Russell, of Lenham, Kent; 2 s, 1 da; *Career* Lt Irish Gds, Suez Canal 1955–56; stockbroker; ptnr W I Carr & Sons Co 1963–67, last chm E & J Burke Ltd 1965–68 (gf, Sir John Nutting, 1 Bt, was first chm); chm: Hampden Agencies Ltd, Telecom Plus plc; conslt and dir of a number of public and private cos; former memb Cncl Lloyd's; High Sheriff Surrey 1999; Liveryman Worshipful Co of Gunmakers; *Recreations* shooting, golf, sailing; *Clubs* Royal Yacht Squadron, Boodle's, Pratt's, MCC, Swinley Forest Golf; *Style*— Peter Nutting, Esq, JP, DL; ✉ Field House, Bentworth, near Alton, Hampshire GU34 5RP

NYE, Robert Thomas; s of Oswald William Nye (d 1990), of Southend-on-Sea, Essex, and Frances Dorothy, *née* Weller (d 2000); *b* 15 March 1939; *Educ* Southend HS; *m* 1, 1959 (m dis 1967), Judith Pratt; 3 s (Jack, Taliesin, Malory); m 2, 1968, Aileen, da of Robert Campbell (d 1972), of Beith, Ayrshire; 1 da (Rebecca), 1 step s (Owen), 1 step da (Sharon); *Career* poet, novelist and critic; gen literary reviewer The Scotsman 1962–, reviewer of new fiction The Guardian 1966–92, poetry ed The Scotsman 1967–, poetry critic The Times 1971–96, gen literary reviewer The Times 1996–2003; FRSL 1977; *Awards* Eric Gregory award 1963, Scottish Arts Cncl bursary 1970 and 1973 and publication award 1970 and 1976, James Kennaway meml award 1970, Guardian Fiction prize 1976, Hawthornden prize 1977, Soc of Authors' travelling scholarship 1991, Authors' Fndn Award 2003, Cholmondeley Award 2007; *Poems* Juvenilia 1 (1961), Juvenilia 2 (1963), Darker Ends (1969), Agnus Dei (1973), Two Prayers (1974), Five Dreams (1974), Divisions on a Ground (1976), A Collection of Poems 1955–88 (1989), 14 Poèmes (1994), Henry James and other Poems (1995), Collected Poems (1995), The Rain and the Glass: 99 Poems, New and Selected (2005), Sixteen Poems (2005); *Novels* Doubtfire (1967), Falstaff (1976), Merlin (1978), Faust (1980), The Voyage of the Destiny (1982), The Memoirs of Lord Byron (1989), The Life and Death of My Lord Gilles de Rais (1990), Mrs Shakespeare: The Complete Works (1993), The Late Mr Shakespeare (1998); *Short Stories* Tales I Told My Mother (1969), The Facts of Life and Other Fictions (1983); *Editions* A Choice of Sir Walter Ralegh's Verse (1972), William Barnes of Dorset: A Selection of his Poems (1973), A Choice of Swinburne's Verse (1973), The Faber Book of Sonnets (1976), The English Sermon 1750–1850 (1976), PEN New Poetry 1 (1986), First Awakenings: The Early Poems of Laura Riding (with Elizabeth Friedmann and Alan J Clark, 1992), A Selection of the Poems of Laura Riding (1994), Some Poems by Ernest Dawson (2006), Poems by Thomas Chatterton (2007); *Plays* Sawney Bean (with William Watson, 1970), The Seven Deadly Sins: A Mask (1974), Penthesilea, Fugue and Sisters (1975); *Stories for Children* March Has Horse's Ears (1966), Taliesin (1966), Beowulf (1968), Wishing Gold (1970), Poor Pumpkin (1971), Once Upon Three Times (1978), Out of the World and Back Again (1977), The Bird of the Golden Land (1980), Harry Pay the Pirate (1981), Three Tales (1983), Lord Fox and Other Spine-Chilling Tales (1997); *Recreations* gambling; *Style*— Robert Nye, Esq; ✉ c/o Vivienne Schuster, Curtis Brown, Haymarket House, 28–29 Haymarket, London SW1Y 4SP (tel 020 7393 4400, fax 020 7393 4401/02, e-mail cb@curtisbrown.co.uk)

NYMAN, Bernard Martin; s of Raymond Nyman (d 2006), and Jean, *née* Geffner (d 1984); *b* 27 February 1954; *Educ* Royal Liberty Sch Gidea Park, Univ of Sheffield (BA); *m* July 1986, Carole Gloria, da of Harold Stern (d 2006); 2 da (Jessica b 29 Nov 1988, Ella b 9 June 1993); *Career* articled clerk Wedlake Bell London 1977–79, admitted slr 1979, slr Rubinstein Callingham 1979–83, ptnr Rubinstein Callingham 1983–94 (merged with Manches & Co), ptnr Manches & Co 1994–98 (specialising in intellectual property law and defamation with particular reference to print and electronic publishing industry), sole prop B M Nyman & Co 1999–; tstee: The Enid Blyton Tst for Children 2000–, The Cleft Lip and Palate Assoc 2003–; memb: Law Soc 1979; *Publications* The Encyclopaedia of Forms and Precedents (Copyright section Vol 21 (2), 1999), Adams: Character Merchandising (contrib, 2 edn 1996), Copinger & Skone James on Copyright (contrib, 14 edn 1999, supplement 2002, 15 edn 2005, supplement 2006), Entertainment Law Review (regular contrib); *Recreations* jazz, films, theatre, family, cricket; *Style*— Bernard Nyman, Esq; ✉ B M Nyman & Co, 181 Creighton Avenue, London N2 9BN (tel 020 8365 3060, fax 020 8883 5151, e-mail bernie.nyman@iname.com, website www.bmnyman.co.uk)

NYMAN, Dr Cyril Richard; s of James Nyman (d 1955), and Rose Caroline, *née* James (d 1992); *b* 19 May 1943; *Educ* Malmesbury GS, Univ of London (MB BS, LRCP, MRCS); *m* 6 June 1970, Jill Elizabeth, da of Robert Charles Ricketts (d 2005), and Phyllis, *née* Craig (d 1977); 1 da (Sarah b 1976); *Career* HS Professorial Surgical Unit St Mary's Hosp London 1968, registrar gen and thoracic med St Thomas' Hosp London 1971–75, sr registrar cardiorespiratory med St Mary's Hosp 1975–79, conslt physician in cardiorespiratory med Pilgrim Hosp Lincs 1979–; clinical tutor Univ of Leicester; chm Pilgrim Scanner Appeal (raised £7 million for CT scanners, MRI and cardiorespiratory equipment); pres: Pilgrim Heart and Lung Fund, Boston Branch Br Heart Fndn, Pilgrim Heart Support Gp; life pres Lincolnshire & Nottinghamshire Ambucopter Appeal; memb: Br Lung Fndn, Br Cardiac Soc, Br Thoracic Soc, Br Soc of Echocardiography; awarded: Illuminated Scroll Boston for services to community 1992, Boston Standard New Year Honours Award 2003, Civic Pride Award Boston 2005, Paul Harris Fell Award Rotary Int 2006; fell: Euro Soc of Cardiology, American Coll of Cardiology; DRCOG 1970, FRCP 1987 (MRCP 1971), FESC 2000, FACC 2001; *Books* Some Common Medical Disorders (1988), Heart and Lung Disease (1989); *Recreations* swimming, jogging, shooting, archery, music; *Clubs* Boston Swimming, Harlequin FC, Skegness RFC (vice-pres), Boston Rotary, Boston and County; *Style*— Dr Cyril R Nyman; ✉ Pilgrim Hospital, Sibsey Road, Boston, Lincolnshire PE21 9QS (tel 01205 364801, fax 01205 359257, e-mail cnyman2@compuserve.com)

NYMAN, Michael; *b* 23 March 1944, London; *Educ* Royal Acad of Music (BMus), KCL; *Career* composer and musician; fndr MN Records 2005; music critic The Listener, The New Statesman, The Spectator and Studio International 1968–78 (introduced the word 'minimalism' as a description of music); actor Subterrain 2001; composer in residence Badisches Stadtstheater Karlsruhe 2002–; subject of Homage to Michael Nyman RomaEuropa Festival Rome 2001; Flaiano Award for contribution to film 2001; *Film Scores* Keep It Up Downstairs 1976, 1–100 1977, A Walk through H 1977, Vertical Features Remake 1978, The Falls 1980, The Draughtsman's Contract 1982, Brimstone and Treacle 1982, Frozen Music 1983, Nelly's Version 1983, The Cold Room 1984, A Zed and Two Noughts 1985, Ballet Méchanique 1986, Drowning by Numbers 1987, Monsieur Hire 1989, The Cook, The Thief, His Wife & Her Lover 1989, Le Mari de la Coiffeuse (The Hairdresser's Husband) 1991, Les Enfants Volants 1991, Prospero's Books 1991, Songbook 1992, The Piano 1992, A La Folie (Six Days, Six Nights) 1994, Carrington 1994, The Diary of Anne Frank 1995, The Ogre (Der Unhold) 1996, Gattaca 1997, The End of the Affair 1999, Wonderland 1999, Ravenous (with Damon Albarn, *qv*) 1999, Acts Without Words 1 2000, The Claim 2000, That Sinking Feeling 2000, 24 Heures de la Vie d'une Femme 2002, The Actors 2002, Nathalie 2004, Detroit: Ruin of a City 2005, 9 Songs 2005, A Cock and Bull Story 2005, The Libertine 2005; *Other Recordings* Michael Nyman Band: Decay Music 1976, English Experimental Music 1977, Masterwork Samples 1979, From Brussels With Love 1980, Miniatures 1980, Michael Nyman 1981, Mozart 1981, The Kiss and Other Movements 1985, The Man who Mistook his Wife for a Hat 1987, And Do They Do/Zoo Caprices 1989, La Traversée de Paris 1989, Out of the Ruins 1989, The Nyman/Greenaway Soundtracks 1989, String Quartet Nos 1–3 1991, The Essential Michael Nyman Band 1992, Michael Nyman for Yohji Yamamoto 1993, Time will Pronounce 1993, Michael Nyman - Live 1994, Noises, Sounds and Sweet Airs 1994, Taking a Line for a Second Walk 1994, The Piano Concerto/MGV 1994, Plus que Tango 1995, The Piano Concerto/On the Fiddle/Prospero's Books 1995, The Piano Concerto and other Themes 1995, After Extra Time 1996, Century XXI UK N-Z 1996, Concertos 1997, Enemy Zero 1997, The Very Best of Michael Nyman 1997, An Eye for a Difference 1998, Federico Garcia Lorca - De Granada a la Luna 1998, Practical Magic 1998, Strong on Oaks, Strong on the Causes of Oaks 1998, The Piano Concerto/Where the Bee Dances 1998, The Suit and the Photograph 1998, Twentieth Century Blues - The Songs of Noel Coward 1998, Michael Nyman Band Live in Concert 1999, Nyman & Greenaway 1999, The Commissar Vanishes 1999, Miniatures 2 2000, The Very Best of Michael Nyman Film Music 1980–2001 2001, Facing Goya 2002, String Quartets Nos 2–4 2002, Sangam - Michael Nyman meets Indian Masters 2003; performed by other artists: The Fourth Wall 1981, Beyond Modernism 1991, Bow Out 1992, Piano Circus 1992, Saxophone Works 1992, Contini/Interzone 1993, The Contemporary Trumpet 1993, First & Foremost 1995, Saxophone Songbook 1995, Visions 1995, Meeting Point 1996, Cinema Emotion 1997, Pick it Up 1997, Duo Dilemme - Nouvelle Musique pour Saxophone & Piano 1998, The English Patient and other arthouse classics 1998, Art House Café 2 1999, The Golden Section/Wallace Collection 1999, Ahn Trio - Ahn-Plugged 2000, Overture to Orpheus/Elaine Funaro 2001, Ahn Trio - Groovebox 2002, The Piano Sings 2005, Man and Boy: Dada 2005, The Piano 2005, The Draughtsman's Contract 2005, Nyman/Greenway Revisited 2005, The Libertine 2005, Six Celan Songs/The Ballad of Kastriot Rexhepi 2006, Acts of Beauty/Exit No Exit 2006, Nyman Brass 2006, Love Counts 2007; *Publications* George Frederic Handel - Concerto Grosso, B Minor for String Orchestra, Op 6, No 12 (ed, 1968), Down by the Greenwood Side, A Dramatic Pastoral (author of libretto for work by Sir Harrison Birtwistle, CH, *qv*, 1971), Henry Purcell - Come Let Us Drink - Catches, Compleat, Pleasant and Divertive (ed, 1972), George Frederic Handel - 12 Grand Concertos, Opus 6 (ed, 1973), Bentham and Hooker (1973), Experimental Music - Cage and Beyond (1974, 2 edn with a foreword by Brian Eno, *qv* 1999), Henry Purcell - Complete Catches (ed, 1995); author of numerous articles; *Style*— Michael Nyman, Esq; ✉ Michael Nyman Ltd, 5 Milner Place, London N1 1TN (tel 020 7226 3188, fax 020 7689 0824, website www.michaelnyman.com)

OAKE, Robin; QPM (1997); s of Leslie Ernest Oake (d 1987), and Florence Thelma (d 1994); *b* 25 June 1937; *Educ* Reigate GS, UCL (LLB); *m* 1961, Christine Mary, da of James Arthur Murray; 1 s (Stephen Robin b 21 April 1962 d 14 Jan 2003), 2 da (Judi Christine Rigby b 14 August 1963, Sue Elizabeth Hutchinson b 1 May 1965); *Career* exec Prison Cmmn 1954–57, constable rising to chief inspr Met Police 1957–78, superintendent rising to asst chief constable Gtr Manchester Police 1978–86, chief constable IOM Constabulary 1986–1999 (2 years secondment Bramshill Police Staff Coll Hants); leadership course RMC Sandhurst 1977; pres CMI, pres IOM Boxing, vice-pres Christian Police Assoc; cdr St John Ambulance IOM, chm and dir Age Concern, chm Cwlth Games Assoc, lay preacher; MIPR, FCMI; KStJ 2002 (OStJ 1996); *Publications* This Is It: History of Christian Police Association (1975), Forgive - The Forgotton 'F' Word; *Recreations* rugby, athletics, cricket, golf; *Clubs* St John London; *Style*— Robin Oake, Esq, QPM; ✉ Mamre, The Chase, Ballakillowey, Colby, Isle of Man IM9 4BL

OAKELEY, Dr Henry Francis; s of Rowland Henry Oakeley, of Chipping Campden, Glos, and Diana Margaret, *née* Hayward (d 2001); *b* 22 July 1941; *Educ* Clifton, St Thomas' Hosp Med Sch Univ of London (MB BS); *m* 20 Jan 1968 (m dis 1988), Penelope Susan, da of late Dr Wilfred Barlow; 2 s (Matthew Thomas b 15 Dec 1968, Edward James b 29 March 1970), 1 da (Rachel Mary b 15 Jan 1973); *Career* house offr and SHO St Thomas' Hosp, Nat Hosp Queen Sq and Frenchay Hosp 1965–69, registrar St Thomas' Hosp, Maudsley Hosp and St George's Hosp 1970–72, sr registrar Maudsley Hosp 1972–73, conslt psychiatrist St Thomas' Hosp 1973–96, ret; holder nat scientific collection of Lycastes and Anguloas for which awarded: RHS Gold medals Chelsea 1990, 1991, 1992, Holford medal 1991, 1992 and 2001, Brickell medal 2003, Westonbirt Medal 2005, Victoria Medal of Honour 2006; RHS: chm Orchid Ctee, chm Orchid Registration Advsy Ctee, chm Bursaries Ctee; pres Orchid Soc of GB, assoc Royal Botanic Gardens Kew, research assoc Singapore Botanical Gardens; memb: Advsy Ctee Chelsea Physic Garden, Br Orchid Cncl, IUCN, SS Orchid Gp; tstee European Orchid Cncl; Freeman City of London 1980, Liveryman Worshipful Soc of Apothecaries 1974; fell S London Botanic Inst, garden fell RCP, MRCPsych 1972, FRCP 1989 (MRCP 1969), FLS 1993; *Publications* Richard Oakeley, Royalist and Country Gentleman 1580–1653 (1989), Lycaste Species, The Essential Guide (1993), Oakeley's War 1899–1902 (jtly with R H Oakeley, 2005), many articles on lycastes and anguloas in jls incl Orchid Soc of GB Jl, American Orchid Soc Bulletin, Orchid Review, Die Orchideen, Orchid Digest; *Recreations* orchids; *Style*— Dr Henry Oakeley; ✉ 77 Copers Cope Road, Beckenham, Kent BR3 1NR (tel 020 8658 0358, fax 020 8658 0359, e-mail henry.oakeley@virgin.net)

OAKELEY, Sir John Digby Atholl; 8 Bt (GB 1790), of Shrewsbury; s of Sir (Edward) Atholl Oakeley, 7 Bt (d 1987); *b* 27 November 1932; *Educ* by private tutor; *m* 1958, Maureen Frances, da of John Cox (d 1965), of Hamble, Hants; 1 da (Marina Anne (Mrs Robert Gordon) b 1961), 1 s (Robert John Atholl b 13 Aug 1963); *Heir* s, Robert Oakeley; *Career* former md Dehler Yachts UK, now ret; winner 20 Nat, 3 Euro and 2 World Championships in various sailing craft, rep GB in the Americas Cup and in Olympic Games (sailing); author; *Books* Winning, Downwind Sailing, Sailing Manual; *Recreations* sailing (yacht 'Twilight'); *Clubs* RAF Yacht; *Style*— Sir John Oakeley, Bt; ✉ 10 Bursledon Heights, Long Lane, Bursledon, Hampshire SO3 8DB (tel 023 8040 2484)

OAKENFOLD, Paul; s of Peter Oakenfold, and Sheila Nicholson Oakenfold; *b* 30 August 1967; *Educ* Westminster Tech Coll; *Career* DJ; head: A&R Polo Records, A&R Profile Records; UK rep Def Jam Records; fndr and owner Perfecto Records; club nights incl: Funhouse 1984, The Project 1987, Spectrum 1987, Future 1988, Land Of Oz 1990, Cream, Liverpool (residency) 1997–99, Home (London, residency) 1999; supported U2 on world tour; also recorded as: Electra 1988–89, Movement 98 1990, B Real 1993, [State Of] Grace 1993–97, Rise 1994, Perfecto Allstarz 1995, Virus 1995–97, Planet Perfecto 1997–, Perfecto FC 2000, Bunker 2000, Element Four 2000; Biggest DJ in the World Guinness Book of World Records 1999; involved with Nat Literacy Tst, Cancer Research World DJ Day; *Albums* incl: Voyage Into Trance 1995 (re-released 2001), Fluoro 1996, Live In Oslo 1997, Global Underground: New York 1998, Tranceport 1998, Resident: Two Years of Oakenfold at Cream 1999, Perfecto Presents Another World 2000, Travelling 2000, Swordfish: The Album 2001, Perfecto Presents: Paul Oakenfold in Ibiza 2001, Bust A Groove 2002, Bunkka 2002, Great Wall 2003, Greatest Remixes 2004, Creamfields 2004, Paul Oakenfold: Greatest hits and remixes 2007; *Awards* DJ of the Year Dance Acad Awards 2002, BAFTA Award 2002, Grammy Award 2002, Award for Swordfish BMI Film and Television Awards 2002, Int DJ of the Year Dance Acad Awards 2003, DJ of the Year Dance Music Festival 2003; *Recreations* football; *Style*— Paul Oakenfold, Esq

OAKES, Sir Christopher; 3 Bt (UK 1939), of Nassau, Bahama Islands; s of Sir Sydney Oakes, 2 Bt (d 1966); *b* 10 July 1949; *Educ* Bredon Tewkesbury, Georgia Military Acad USA; *m* 1978, Julie Dawn, da of Donovan Cowan, of Canada; 1 da (Greta Anna Eunice b 1979), 1 s (Victor b 1983); *Heir* s, Victor Oakes; *Style*— Sir Christopher Oakes, Bt; ✉ Site 15, Comp 18 RR7, Vernon, BC V1T 7Z3, Canada

OAKES, Robin Geoffrey; s of Geoffrey Albert Oakes (d 1999), of Norwich, and Doris Florence, *née* Catton (d 2003); *b* 18 February 1946; *Educ* City of Norwich Sch, Univ of Birmingham (BCom); *m* 16 Aug 1969, Lorna Hazel, da of Albert O'Neill (d 2001); 3 da (Claire Lorna b 8 April 1972, Helen Esther b 1 July 1974, Juliet Elizabeth b 14 Aug 1980); *Career* articled clerk Coopers & Lybrand 1968–71 (later gp audit mangr); Mazars LLP (formerly Neville Russell then Mazars Neville Russell): joined as nat audit and accounts tech mangr 1981–83, sr mangr 1983–84, ptnr 1985–99, sr ptnr London regn 1999–2006, ret 2007; conslt and non-exec dir 2007–; seminar speaker and author of various articles; FCA 1979 (ACA 1971); *Books* An Industry and Accounting Guide: Insurance Brokers (1990, 4 edn 2006); *Recreations* charity trustee, church leadership, family, garden; *Clubs* Lloyds; *Style*— Robin Oakes, Esq; ✉ Mazars LPP, 24 Bevis Marks, London EC3A 7NR (tel 020 7377 1000, fax 020 7377 8931, e-mail robin.oakes@mazars.co.uk)

OAKESHOTT OF SEAGROVE BAY, Baron (Life Peer UK 2000), of Seagrove Bay in the County of Isle of Wight; Matthew Alan; s of Keith Robertson Oakeshott, CMG (d 1974), of Horsham, W Sussex, and Jill Oakeshott, *née* Clutterbuck; *b* 10 January 1947; *Educ* Charterhouse, UC Oxford, Nuffield Coll Oxford (scholar, MA); *m* 1976, Dr Philippa Poulton, MD, da of Dr Christopher Poulton; 2 s (Joseph Andrew b 1979, Luke Christopher b 1985), 1 da (Rachel Jill b 1982); *Career* economist Kenya Miny of Fin and Econ Planning 1968–70, special advsr to Rt Hon Roy Jenkins, MP 1972–76, investment mangr then dir Warburg Investment Mgmnt Ltd 1976–81, investment mangr Courtaulds Pension Fund 1981–85, fndr and jt md OLIM Ltd 1986–; jt investment dir Value & Income Tst plc 1986–; city cncllr Oxford 1972–76; Parly candidate: (Lab) Horsham and Crawley Oct 1974, (SDP/Lib Alliance) Cambridge 1983; memb SDP Nat Ctee 1981–82, memb Cncl Britain in Europe; a Lib Dem Treasy spokesman House of Lords 2001–, Lib Dem Pensions spokesman House of Lords 2002–; *Books* By-Elections in British Politics (contrib, 1973); *Recreations* music, elections, supporting Arsenal; *Style*— The Rt Hon the Lord Oakeshott of Seagrove Bay; ✉ OLIM Ltd, Pollen House, 10–12 Cork Street, London W1X 1PD (tel 020 7439 4400)

OAKHAM, Archdeacon of; *see:* Painter, Ven David Scott

OAKLEY, Prof Celia Mary; da of Arthur Howard Oakley (d 1963), of Guildford, Surrey, and Minnie Isabel, *née* Stevenson (d 1989); *b* 14 May 1931; *Educ* Berkhamsted Sch, Royal Free Hosp Sch of Med UCL (LRCP, MB BS, MD, Winifred Ladds prize in physiology, Walter Culverwell prize in anatomy, Edward Hanson prize in physiology, AM Bird prize for pre-clinical studies, Proxime Accessit Univ Gold medal, Helen Prideaux prize for the pre-registration year); *m* 11 June 1960, Dr Ronald Blackwood Pridie, s of George Pridie (d 2000); 2 da (Susan b 1961, Alison b 1965), 1 s (Peter b 1968 (decd)); *Career* house physician: Royal Free Hosp 1955 (house surgn 1954), Brompton Hosp 1955; res pathologist Royal Free Hosp 1956, house physician to the Cardiac Dept Brompton Hosp 1957, house physician and sr house offr Nat Hosp for Nervous Diseases 1957, registrar Dept of Med Hammersmith Hosp 1957–60, res fell Cardiopulmonary Laboratory Univ of Rochester and Strong Meml Hosp USA 1960–61; Hammersmith Hosp and Imperial Coll Sch of Med at Hammersmith Hosp (The Royal Postgrad Med Sch until merger 1997): sr registrar Dept of Med (Cardiology) and tutor in med 1961–63, asst lectr in med 1963–64, lectr in med and hon conslt physician 1965–67, sr lectr in med (Cardiology) 1967–74, emeritus prof of cardiology 1996; hon conslt cardiologist St Mary's Hosp London; examiner MRCP 1982–98; Univ of London: recognised teacher 1969, examiner Dip in Cardiology 1984–; memb: Cncl Br Cardiac Soc 1977–80, Cncl RCP 1978–81 (censor 1988–90), Cncl Thoracic Soc 1978–81, Transplant Advsy Panel Dept of Health 1982–88, Ctee on Safety of Med 1992–95; author of numerous med articles in learned jls; memb Editorial Bd: Jl of Internal Med 1990–, Int Jl of Cardiology 1990–; memb: Assoc of Physicians of GB and I, Br Cardiac Soc, Euro Soc of Cardiology, American Coll of Cardiology, MRS, Int Med Soc, RSM (past vice-pres Clinic Section), BMA, Int Soc and Fedn of Cardiology (past chm Cncl on Cardiomyopathies and memb Scientific Bd); hon memb Pakistan, Colombian, Venezuelan, Chilean, Peruvian, Hellenic, Portuguese and South African Socs of Cardiology; MRCS; fell American Coll of Cardiology 1970, founding fell Euro Soc of Cardiology 1988, FRCP (MRCP); *Recreations* country pursuits, travelling; *Clubs* RCP; *Style*— Prof Celia M Oakley; ✉ Long Crendon Manor, Long Crendon, Buckinghamshire HP18 9DZ (tel 01844 208246, fax 01844 202968); Hammersmith Hospital, Du Cane Road, London W12 0NN (tel 020 8383 3141, fax 020 8740 8373, e-mail oakleypridie@aol.com)

OAKLEY, Christopher John; CBE (1999); s of Ronald Oakley (d 1965), of Tunbridge Wells, Kent, and Joyce Barbara, *née* Tolhurst (d 1996); *b* 11 November 1941; *Educ* The Skinners Sch Tunbridge Wells; *m* 1 (m dis 1986), Linda Margaret, da of William John Edward Viney, of Tunbridge Wells, Kent; 1 s, 2 da; m 2 (m dis 2003), Moira Jean, da of H Martingale; 1 s, 2 step da; m 3, Lisa, da of J Hanson, of Ottery St Mary, Devon; 1 step da; *Career* dep ed Yorkshire Post 1976–81, ed Lancashire Evening Post 1981–83; dir: Lancashire Evening Post Ltd 1982–83, Liverpool Echo, Liverpool Daily Post and Echo Ltd 1983–89; ed-in-chief/md Birmingham Post and Mail Ltd 1989–91, gp chief exec Midland Independent Newspapers Ltd 1991–97, regnl md Mirror Gp Newspapers 1997–98, chief exec Regional Independent Media 1998–2002, chm and chief exec HRM Partnership Ltd 2002–04, chm and chief exec Comm VA MEF, chm Newsco-Insider Ltd 2002; pres: Guild of British Newspaper Editors 1990–91, Newspaper Soc 1997–98; patron Hollybank Tst 1999, tstee Royal Armouries 2002; fell Univ of Central Lancs 1998; *Style*— Christopher Oakley, Esq, CBE; ✉ Comm VA MEF, Dreve des Pins 40, B-1420 Braine-l'Alleud, Belguim (e-mail ochris829@aol.com)

OAKLEY, Dr (George) David Gastineau; s of Douglas Edward Oakley, and Barbara Mary, *née* Earle; *b* 26 April 1948; *Educ* Rugby, Univ of Cambridge (MB BChir, MA), Westminster Med Sch; *m* 29 Sept 1979, Clare Elizabeth, da of Christopher Brent-Smith; 1 s (Sam b 1982), 1 da (Charlotte b 1988); *Career* former sr house offr and registrar City General Hosp Stoke-on-Trent, registrar cardiology Hammersmith Hosp 1977–79; Northern Gen Hosp Tst Sheffield: sr registrar 1979–84, currently conslt cardiologist N Trent Regnl Health Authy (hon appointment Univ of Sheffield); articles: ischaemic heart disease, pregnancy and heart disease, athletes hearts; memb: Br Cardiac Soc, Ctee Br Heart Fndn; FRCP 1988 (MRCP 1975); *Recreations* music, skiing; *Style*— Dr David Oakley; ✉ Department of Cardiology, Northern General Hospital Trust, Sheffield S5 7AU (tel 0114 243 4343 ext 4953)

OAKLEY, Geoffrey Michael Whittall; s of Harold Whittall Oakley, of St Martins, Guernsey, and Hazel Louise, *née* Peters; *b* 22 April 1953; *Educ* Oundle; *m* 3 April 1987, Joanna Helen, da of Fred Morgan Hodges, of Harborne, Birmingham; 2 da (Georgina Louise b 1987, Olivia Sarah Helen b 1990), 1 s (Nicholas Frederick James b 1989); *Career* ptnr Margetts & Addenbrooke 1977–86; dir: National Investment Group plc 1986–90, Capel-Cure Myers Capital Management 1990–98, Portway Investments Ltd (formerly J A Main) 1996; non-exec dir: Aero Needles Group plc 1976–84, Margetts Financial Services Ltd 1985; pres Br Jewellery and Giftware Fedn 2003–04; govr Birmingham Royal Inst for the Blind; tstee Birmingham Botanical Gardens and Glasshouses; FSI (memb Stock Exchange 1976), memb Int Stock Exchange 1986; *Recreations* theatre, local history, antiques; *Style*— Geoffrey Oakley, Esq; ✉ St Mary's Close, 10 St Mary's Road, Harborne, Birmingham B17 0HA (tel 0121 427 7150); Portway Investments Limited, 20 Portway Road, Oldbury, West Midlands B69 2BY

OAKLEY, Michael Dudley; s of Lt Cdr (George) Eric Oakley, RN (d 1996), of Clifton-on-Teme, Worcs, and Dr Margaret Dorothy Dudley, *née* Brown (d 1993); *b* 5 November 1944; *Educ* Oundle, Coll of Law; *m* 7 Oct 1967, Jennifer Catherine, da of Richard Percy Lazenby (d 1987), of Bulmer, York; 2 da (Catherine b 2 Nov 1969, Victoria b 6 Nov 1971), 1 s (William b 3 Oct 1973); *Career* slr; former ptnr Oakleys, currently conslt Crombie Wilkinson; HM coroner N Yorks 1979–, NP 1985–, chm Appeals Tbnl 1992–, immigration judge 2001–; pres Coroners Soc of Eng and Wales 2004–05; lay memb Gen Synod C of E representing Diocese of York 1980–95; memb: Working Party on

Ordination of Women to the Priesthood, Cathedral Statutes Cmmn, various legislative revision ctees, panel of chm of Gen Synod; clerk and co sec Queen Margaret's Sch (York) Ltd; pres Yorkshire Law Soc 1991–92; Master Merchant Taylors' Co of York 1998–99; *Recreations* tennis, golf, fishing, shooting; *Style*— Michael Oakley, Esq; ✉ Rose Cottage, Oswaldkirk, York YO62 5XT (tel 01439 788339, fax 01439 788037, mob 07860 789957, e-mail moakleyrosecott@aol.com)

OAKLEY, Robin Francis Leigh; OBE (2001); s of Joseph Henry Oakley, of East Molesey, Surrey, and Alice Barbara Oakley; *b* 20 August 1941; *Educ* Wellington, BNC Oxford (MA); *m* 4 June 1966, Carolyn Susan Germaine, da of late Leonard Rumball; 1 da (Annabel Louise Germaine b 19 July 1971), 1 s (Alexander Guy Leigh b 12 Aug 1973); *Career* political corr Liverpool Daily Post 1967–70 (feature writer then sub ed 1964–67), Crossbencher columnist then asst ed Sunday Express 1970–79, political ed and asst ed Now! magazine 1979–81, asst ed Daily Mail 1981–86, political ed The Times 1986–92, political ed BBC 1992–2000, European political ed CNN 2000–; racing columnist The Spectator 1995–, racing writer for various pubns incl FT; *Publications* Valley of the Racehorse (2000), Inside Track (2001); *Recreations* theatre, horse racing, swimming, bird watching; *Clubs* RAC; *Style*— Robin Oakley, Esq, OBE; ✉ 17 West Square, Kennington, London SE11 4SN (tel 020 7582 9654, e-mail robin.oakley@cnn.com)

OAKS, Agnes; da of Juhan Oks, of Estonia, and Valentina, *née* Troffimova; *b* 29 May 1970; *Educ* Tallin Ballet Sch, Vaganova Inst Moscow; *m* 1990, Thomas Edur, *qv*, s of Enn Edur; *Career* Estonia State Ballet School: Coppélia 1987, Paquita 1988; Estonia State Opera Ballet: Sleeping Beauty 1989, Swan Lake 1990, Romeo and Juliet 1990; princ rising to sr princ English National Ballet 1990–96 and Birmingham Royal Ballet 1996–97, principal guest artist English National Ballet 1997–; credits incl: Hynd's Coppélia 1990, Ben Stevenson's The Nutcracker 1990, Les Sylphide 1990, 3 Preludes 1990, Our Waltzes 1991, Sanguine Fan 1991, Bianca in Taming of the Shrew, Olga in Eugene Onegin, Our Waltzes, Apollo, Cinderella, Études, Four Last Songs, Sphinx, Hynd's Sleeping Beauty (world premiere), Raissa Struchkova's Swan Lake (world premiere), Impromptu, Spectre de la Rose 1992, cr title role Derek Deane's Giselle 1994, Paquita 1994, Romeo and Juliet 1995, Dream Alice in Alice in Wonderland 1995, Christopher Dean's Encounters 1996, Peter Wright's Swan Lake, Peter Wright's Nutcracker, David Bintley's Nutcracker Sweeties, Peter Wright's Sleeping Beauty; freelance 1997–; performances incl: Sleeping Beauty (Estonian Opera), Nutcracker (São Paulo and Tokyo), Sleeping Beauty (Chile) 1997, Romeo and Juliet (Royal Albert Hall) 1998, Cinderella (Zurich) 2000, Tchaikovsky pas de deux 2000, Sleeping Beauty (Royal Albert Hall) 2000, Wedding Journey (Estonia) 2001, Swan Lake (Cape Town) 2001, Veronica Paeper's Romeo and Juliet (Cape Town) 2002, Don Quixote (Cape Town) 2003, Wayne McGregor's duet 2 Human (Sadlers Wells) 2003, Michael Corder's Melody on the Move (Sadlers Wells) 2003, Ashton's Cinderella (Het Ballet Amsterdam) 2005, Kenneth Macmillan's Sleeping Beauty 2005, The Nutcracker (Rome Opera) 2005, Elizabeth Triegaardt's Sleeping Beauty (Cape Town) 2006, Wayne Eagling's Duet 2006, David Dawson's A Million Kisses to my Skin 2007 (Sadlers Wells); Best Couple (with Thomas Edur) Int Ballet Competition Jackson Mississippi 1990, Dancer of the Year Dance International magazine 2000–01, Best Partnership Award (with Thomas Edur) London Critics' Circle 2002, Laurence Olivier Award for Outstanding Achievement in Dance 2004; patron British Ballet Orgn (BBO); Third Class Order of the White Star (Estonia) 2001; *Recreations* walking, travel; *Style*— Ms Agnes Oaks; ✉ c/o Continental Classics, 19 Tierney Road, London SW2 4QL

OAKSEY, 2 Baron (UK 1947), and 4 Baron Trevethin (UK 1921); John Geoffrey Tristram Lawrence; OBE; known as Lord Oaksey; s of 3 and 1 Baron Trevethin and Oaksey, DSO, TD (d 1971); *b* 21 March 1929; *Educ* Eton, New Coll Oxford, Yale Law Sch; *m* 1, 1959 (m dis 1987), Victoria Mary, da of Maj John Dennistoun, MBE (d 1980); 1 s (Hon Patrick John Tristram b 1960), 1 da (Hon Sara Victoria b 1961); m 2, 7 March 1988, Mrs Rachel Crocker; *Heir* s, Hon Patrick Lawrence; *Career* Lt 9 Lancers and P/O RAFVR; racing corr to: Daily Telegraph (as 'Marlborough') 1957–94, Sunday Telegraph 1961–88, Horse and Hound (as 'Audax') 1959–88; columnist Racing Post 1988–90; TV racing commentator (World of Sport, Channel 4 Racing) 1969–2002; JP 1976–99; pres: Beverley Race Club, Cheltenham and Three Counties Race Club, Horses and Ponies Protection Assoc (HAPPA); pres Injured Jockeys' Fund 2002– (tstee 1964–); Daily Telegraph Order of Merit Cartier Racing Awards 2003; *Publications* History of Steeplechasing, The Story of Mill Reef, Oaksey on Racing, Mince Pie for Starters; *Recreations* riding, skiing; *Clubs* Brooks's; *Style*— The Rt Hon the Lord Oaksey, OBE; ✉ Hill Farm, Oaksey, Malmesbury, Wiltshire SN16 9HS (tel 01666 577303, fax 01666 577962, e-mail coaksey@freenetname.co.uk)

OATEN, Mark; MP; s of Ivor Oaten, and Audrey, *née* Matthews; *b* 8 March 1964; *Educ* Dip PR, BA; *m* Belinda, da of Bob Fordham; 2 da (Alice b 20 June 1996, Milly b 22 June 1999); *Career* dir Oasis Radio 1992–95, md Westminster Public Relations 1994–97; MP (Lib Dem) Winchester 1997–; PPS to Charles Kennedy, MP, *qv*, 1999–2001, chm Lib Dem Parly Pty 2001–; Lib Dem spokesman: disabilities 1997–99, foreign affrs and defence (Europe) 2000–01, Cabinet Office 2001–03; shadow home sec Lib Dem 2003–06; memb Select Ctee for Public Admin 1999–2001; chm All Pty Prisoners of War Gp 1997–2000, co-chm All Pty Adoption Gp 2000–, sec All Pty Euro Union Accession Gp 2000–, treas Human Rights Gp 2000–; memb Lib Dem Social Security & Welfare Team 1997–; cnclr Watford BC 1986–94; *Recreations* gardening, cinema, swimming; *Style*— Mark Oaten, MP; ✉ House of Commons, London SW1A 0AA (tel 020 7219 3000, fax 020 7219 2389, e-mail oatenm@parliament.uk)

OATEN, Michael John; s of Frederick Atkins Oaten (d 1991), and Lilian May, *née* Lock; *b* 1 May 1943; *Educ* Egham Sch, LSE (BSc); *m* Susan Wendy, *née* Precious; 2 s (Simon b 18 April 1977, Marcus b 1 Nov 1983), 2 da (Nicola b 30 Sept 1978, Sarah b 30 Sept 1982); *Career* articled clerk Rooke Lane & Co CA's 1961–62; Arthur Andersen & Co: articled clerk 1965–67, sr clerk 1967–70, mangr Audit 1970–76, ptnr 1976–2002, managing ptnr SE Asia Singapore 1980–84, dir of Educn Consulting and Change Mgmnt 1985–89, head of Corp Fin 1986–2002, global md of Corp Fin 1992–2002; md Barons Financial Services SA 2002–; FCA 1967; *Books* Obtaining A Quotation For French Companies On The London Stock Exchange (1975), Banking In Singapore (1983); *Recreations* skiing, riding, tennis, travel, walking up mountains; *Clubs* Tanglin (Singapore); *Style*— Michael Oaten, Esq; ✉ Barons Financial Services SA, ICC (H-Ground Floor) Route de Pri-Bois 20, Case Postale 103, CH-1215 Geneva 15, Switzerland

OATES, (John) Keith; s of John Alfred Oates (d 1983), of Bispham, Blackpool, Lancs, and Katherine Mary, *née* Hole; *b* 3 July 1942; *Educ* King's Sch Chester, Arnold Sch Blackpool, LSE (BSc), UMIST (Dip Tech), Univ of Bristol (MSc); *m* 25 May 1968, Helen Mary, da of Donald Charles Matthew Blake (d 1985), of Sale, Cheshire; 1 s (Jake b 1976), 3 da (Cathee b 1970, Kirsten b 1971, Felicity b 1982); *Career* work study trainee Reed Paper Gp 1965–66, budgets and planning mangr IBM UK Ltd 1966–73, gp fin controller Rolls Royce Ltd 1973–74, controller Black & Decker Europe 1974–78, vice-pres (fin) Thyssen Bornemisza 1978–84; Marks & Spencer plc: fin dir 1984–91, dir international ops, expenditure/fin activities, estates and store devpt 1991–99, dep chm 1994–99; currently sr advsr Coutts Bank Monaco; a dir FSA 1998–2001; non-exec dir: John Laing Plc 1987–89, BT plc 1994–2000, Guinness plc 1995–97, Diageo plc (following merger between Guinness plc and Grand Metropolitan plc) 1997–2004; former memb: Cncl CBI, Bd of Govrs BBC 1988–93, Bd London First, Sports Cncl of Great Britain; memb 100 Gp of Chartered Accountants 1985–94; memb Cncl (govr) Wycombe Abbey Sch 1995–, pres UMIST Assoc 1996–; FCT 1982, CIMgt 1992, FRSA; *Recreations* spectator sports (association football, athletics, boxing and cricket), skiing, tennis; *Clubs* Supporter de l'Association Sportive de Monaco, Tennis Club de Monaco; *Style*— Keith Oates, Esq

OATES, Laurence Campbell; CB (2006); s of Stanley Oates (d 1995), and Norah, *née* Meek (d 1984); *b* 14 May 1946; *Educ* Beckenham and Penge GS, Univ of Bristol (LLB); *m* 26 Oct 1968, Brenda Lilian, da of John Trevor Hardwick, of Stourbridge, W Midlands; 1 da (Marianne Louise b 1972), 1 s (Adrian Laurence b 1974); *Career* called to the Bar Middle Temple 1968, in practice 1969–76; legal advsr Dept of Employment involved in industrial relations law reform 1977–80, legal sec Law Offrs' Dept advising on civil and constitutional law 1981–84, asst treasy slr Dept of Transport advising on civil aviation law 1984–88, under sec and head Legal and Law Reform Gp Lord Chllr's Dept 1989–92, circuit admin Midland & Oxford Circuit 1992–94, assoc head Policy Gp Lord Chllr's Dept 1995–96, dir Magistrates' Courts Gp Lord Chllr's Dept 1996–99, official slr to the Supreme Court 1999–2006 (public tstee 2001–06); *Recreations* music, golf; *Style*— Laurence Oates, Esq, CB; ✉ The Official Solicitor and Public Trustee Office, 81 Chancery Lane, London WC2A 1DD (tel 020 7911 7116)

OATES, Roger Kendrew; s of William Oates (d 1987), and Mary Dorothy, *née* Mayne (d 1957); *b* 25 June 1946; *Educ* Thirsk Sch, York Sch of Art, Farnham Sch of Art (DipAD), Kidderminster Coll; *m* 31 July 1976, Fay Morgan, *qv*, da of Phillip Hughes Morgan; 1 s (Daniel Morgan Oates b 25 Jan 1979); *Career* textile designer; set up own studio Ledbury Herefords 1971–75, dir and chm Craftsman's Mark Ltd 1971–75, lectr at numerous colls of art England and Aust 1971–75; Morgan Oates partnership at The House in the Yard Ledbury 1975–86, Morgan & Oates Co Ltd 1986–97 (designing for own label and clients incl Ralph Lauren, Christian Dior, Sonia Rykiel, Donna Karan and Laura Ashley); sr ptnr Roger Oates Design Associates partnership 1987–98, dir Roger Oates Design Co Ltd 1998–; work in exhibitions incl: The Craftsman's Art (V&A Museum) 1973, The House in the Yard - Textiles from the Workshop of Fay Morgan & Roger Oates (Welsh Arts Council Cardiff and tour) 1978, Tufted Rugs (Environment London) 1980, Texstyles (Crafts Council London and tour) 1984–85, Design Awards (Lloyd's Building London) 1988; awarded: USA ROSCOE Award 1984, British Design Award 1988, Duke of Edinburgh's certificate for services to design; contrib various TV prodns; FRSA; *Style*— Roger Oates, Esq; ✉ Roger Oates Design Company Ltd, The Long Barn, Eastnor, Ledbury, Herefordshire HR8 1EL (tel 01531 632718, fax 01531 631361, e-mail director@rogeroates.com, website www.rogeroates.com); Roger Oates Design Company Ltd, 1 Munro Terrace, Cheyne Walk, London SW10 0DL (tel 020 7351 2288, fax 020 7351 6841)

OATLEY, Neil Vernon; s of Ronald Stanley Oatley, of Istead Rise, Kent, and Audrey Helen, *née* Munday; *b* 12 June 1954; *Educ* Gravesend GS, Loughborough Univ (BTech); *m* 7 July 2001, Peta Geraldine Brown; *Career* race car designer (Formula One); engr Williams Grand Prix Engineering 1977–84, designer Formula One Race Car Engineering 1984–86; McLaren International: designer 1986–, chief designer 1989–2002, exec dir of engrg 2002–06, dir of design and devpt 2006–; *Recreations* music (rock and classical), motorcycling, reading; *Style*— Neil Oatley, Esq; ✉ Culvers, Littleworth Road, Seale, Surrey GU10 1JN (tel 01252 782210); McLaren Racing Ltd, McLaren Technology Centre, Chertsey Road, Woking, Surrey GU21 4YH (tel 01483 261000, fax 01483 215572)

OBERTELLI, Ricci; *Educ* Hotel Mgmnt and Catering trg course Italy; *Career* hotelier; extensive experience in London including Claridge's, The Savoy and The Ritz, subsequently various mgmnt positions rising to sales and mktg dir Four Seasons Inn on the Park; The Dorchester: mangr rising to dir and gen mangr 1986–95 (responsible for complete refurbishment 1988–90), dir of operations Dorchester Gp 1997–, global devpt dir 2004–; dep nat delegate for GB Euro Hotel Mangrs Assoc; Master Innholder; memb: Chaîne des Rotisseurs, Réunion des Gastronomes, Ordre des Coteaux de Champagne, Acad of Food and Wine Serv, Inst of Dirs; FCIMA; *Style*— Ricci Obertelli, Esq; ✉ Dorchester Collection, 3 Tilney Street, London W1K 1JB (tel 020 7629 4848, fax 020 7355 4649, e-mail robertelli@dorchestergrouphotels.com, website www.dorchestercollection.com)

OBHOLZER, Dr Anton Meinhard; s of Anton Max Karl Obholzer (d 1985), of Cape Town, South Africa, and Eva Maria Clarissa, *née* von Hartungen (d 1985); *b* 16 November 1938; *Educ* Christian Brothers' Coll Kimberley, Univ of Stellenbosch (BSc), Univ of Cape Town (MB ChB, DPM); *m* 16 Feb 1963, Annabel Harriet Barbara, da of Dr Christopher Jarvis Molteno; 1 da (Clarissa Judith b 9 Dec 1966), 2 s (Anton Manfred b 29 June 1968, Rupert John b 27 March 1970); *Career* conslt child psychiatrist Child Guidance Trg Centre 1975–80; conslt psychiatrist Tavistock Clinic 1980– (chm 1985–93), chief exec Tavistock and Portman NHS Tst 1993–; hon prof: Univ of Vienna 1994, Univ of Klagenfurt 1994, Univ of Innsbruck 1994; memb Br Psycho Analytical Soc, FRCPsych (memb Cncl 1991–97); *Books* with M Baraitser: Cape Country Furniture (1978), Town Furniture of the Cape (1985), The Cape House and its Interior (1987), Cape Antique Furniture (2004); The Unconscious at Work (ed with Vega Roberts, 1994); *Style*— Dr Anton Obholzer; ✉ Tavistock and Portman NHS Trust, 120 Belsize Lane, London NW3 5BA (tel 020 7435 7111, fax 020 7447 3709)

OBOLENSKY, Prince Nikolai (Nick); s of Prince Michael Obolensky (d 1995), of Madrid, Spain, and Anne, *née* Helbronner (d 1980); descends from Rurik who conquered Russia in 860s; *b* 7 June 1956; *Educ* Harrow, RMA Sandhurst, Univ of Durham (BA), IMEDE Lausanne (MBA, valedictorian); *m* 1987, Charlotte Isabella, *née* Sharpe; 2 da (Isabella b 28 Oct 1993, Larissa b 7 Sept 1995), 1 s (Alexei b 24 Nov 1990); *Career* Maj 17/21 Lancers 1986– (cmmnd 1976, Lt 1978, Capt 1981), ret 1988; Ernst & Young CAs: conslt 1989, sr conslt 1990, managing conslt 1991; Gateway/Somerfield Foodmarkets: exec co-ordinator of change prog 1991, launch dir of new fascias 1992, devpt dir 1993; md Rurikof & Co 1993–98, ptnr Harding & Yorke 1994–96, UK ptnr The Vth Dimension Partnership 1996–; devpt dir The Centre for Tomorrow's Co 1995–97; ceo: Tomorrow's Co Enterprise Ltd 1997–2000, Tomorrow's Co Ltd 2000–01, Musikline Ltd 2001–; ceo and chm Your Release Ltd 2001–; assoc prof of leadership Nyenrode Univ, Netherlands Business Sch 1999– (MBA Professor of the Year 2001–02 and 2002–03), visiting prof for Leadership INSEAD France 2002–; fell CMD London Business Sch 2003; hon fell Centre for Leadership Studies Univ of Exeter; FCMC, FRGS, FRSA, MInstD; *Books* Practical Business Re-engineering: Tools and Techniques for Achieving Effective Change (1994), A Strategy for the Ecu (jtly 1990), Management Consultancy - a handbook for best practice (jtly, 1998), RSA: On Work and Leadership (jtly, 2001); *Recreations* mountaineering, flying, skiing; *Clubs* Lansdowne; *Style*— Prince Nikolai Obolensky; ✉ c/o National Westminster Bank, 315 Station Road, Harrow, Middlesex HA1 2AD (fax 01225 849149, e-mail nickobolensky@compuserve.com)

OBORN, Peter Mill; s of Gerald Oborn, and Pauline, *née* Scott (d 2001); *b* 27 October 1955; *Educ* Melville Coll Edinburgh, Edinburgh Coll of Art/Heriot-Watt Univ (BArch, MArch); *Partner* Amanda Reekie; *Career* architect; Abbey Hanson Rowe: regnl mangr Manama Bahrain 1986–87, estab London office 1988, fixed share ptnr 1992–94, equity ptnr 1994–; current projects incl: major housing estate refurbishments incl Mozart and Wellington Estates Acton, numerous lottery sports projects, new HQ National Bank of Bahrain, Asprey refurbishment New Bond St; memb Sports Cncl Panel of Expert Advisers for the Lottery Sports Fund; also involved with: Community Bldg in Britain, Permaculture Assoc; RIBA, ARIAS; *Recreations* horse riding; *Clubs* Arts; *Style*— Peter Oborn, Esq; ✉ Aedas AHR, 5–8 Hardwick Street, London EC1R 4RB (tel 020 7837 9789, fax 020 7837 9678)

O

OBORNE, Brig John Douglas; OBE (1989); s of Lt-Col Tom D Oborne, DSO (d 1985), and Elsie Cottrill, *née* Booth (d 1992); *b* 29 February 1928; *Educ* Wellington, RMA Sandhurst; *m* 9 Oct 1954, Margaret Elizabeth, da of Cdr A R P Brown (d 1973); 3 s (Peter Alan b 1957, Nicholas David b 1961, James Richard b 1963); *Career* Br Army cmmnd into 4/7 Royal Dragoon Gds 1948; Staff Coll Camberley 1961, Jt Servs Staff Coll 1968, Br Liaison Offr US Army Armor Centre Fort Knox 1969–71, chief instr Junior Div Staff Coll 1971–73, cdr Br Army Trg Team in Sudan 1973–75, def advsr Br High Cmmn India 1977–80, vice-pres Regular Cmmns Bd 1980–82; ADC to HM The Queen 1980–82; Def Attaché Br Embassy Dublin 1984–89, Br sec British-Irish Inter-Parly Body 1990–2004; First Class Order of the Nile (Sudan) 1975; *Clubs* Cavalry and Guards'; *Style—* Brig John Oborne, OBE; ✉ Horningsham, Warminster, Wiltshire BA12 7LX (e-mail johnoborne@gawab.com)

O'BOYLE, Patrick John; s of James O'Boyle, of Glasgow, and Elizabeth, *née* Dunlop (d 1980); *b* 12 April 1941; *Educ* St Aloysius Coll Glasgow, Univ of Glasgow (MB ChB); *m* 4 Sept 1968, Emilia Maria, *née* Galli; 1 da (Marie-Claire b 16 Aug 1971), 1 s (Stephen James b 26 Sept 1973); *Career* lectr Univ of Leeds 1972–74, sr urological registrar Liverpool 1974–79, conslt urologist Somerset 1979–2002 (chm SW Region Urological Ctee 1993–99), ret; pioneer of micro video endoscopic operating techniques and laser surgery, author of numerous pubns on devpts in technology applicable to surgery; chair Taunton Deane Cncl for Voluntary Service 2004; ChM Univ of Liverpool; memb: RSM (memb Cncl), Br Assoc of Urological Surgns (memb Cncl); FRCSEd; *Recreations* golf, skiing, sailing; *Clubs* Taunton and Pickeridge; *Style—* Patrick O'Boyle, Esq; ✉ Wild Oak Cottage, Wild Oak Lane, Trull, Taunton TA3 7JS (tel 01823 278057)

O'BRIEN, Barry John; s of John O'Brien, and Patricia, *née* Barry; *b* 27 October 1952; *Educ* St Illtyd's Coll Cardiff, UCL (LLB); *m* 29 Sept 1984, Susan Margaret; 2 s (William James, Thomas Barry), 1 da (Joanna Elizabeth); *Career* slr Slaughter and May 1978–83 (articled clerk 1976–78), ptnr Freshfields Bruckhaus Deringer (formerly Freshfields) 1986– (slr 1983–86); Liveryman Worshipful Co Slrs; memb Law Soc; *Recreations* sport; *Style—* Barry J O'Brien, Esq; ✉ 9 Highbury Terrace, London N5 (tel 020 7359 2354); Freshfields Bruckhaus Deringer, 65 Fleet Street, London EC4 (tel 020 7936 4000)

O'BRIEN, HE Basil G; CMG (1996); s of late Cyril O'Brien, and late Kathleen *née* Brownrigg; *b* 5 December 1940; *Educ* St John's Coll Nassau, Univ Tutorial Coll London, London Inst of World Affairs Univ of London (Dip Int Affairs); *m* Marlene Devika, *née* Chand; 2 c (David Krishna b 26 May 1967, Tariq Jeremy b 29 August 1973); *Career* higher exec offr Miny of External Affairs 1969–70, asst sec Cabinet Office then dep perm sec 1970–78, perm sec Miny of Tourism 1978–86, perm sec Miny of Foreign Affairs 1986–89, perm sec Miny of Agric Trade and Industry 1989, perm sec Miny of Educn 1993–94, sec to Cabinet and head of Public Service 1994–99, high cmmr to UK and ambass to EU, Belgium, France, Germany and Italy 1999–, rep International Maritime Organisation (IMO); dir: The Bahamas Hotel Trg Coll, Bahamasair Holdings Co; memb: Anglican Central Educn Authy, Int Club of Sr Persons in Travel Industry (SKAL); chm Bd of Govrs St John's Coll; *Recreations* walking, swimming, gardening; *Clubs* RAC, Chaîne des Rôtisseurs; *Style—* HE Mr Basil O'Brien; ✉ Bahamas High Commission, 10 Chesterfield Street, London W1J 5JL (tel 020 7408 4488, fax 020 7499 9937, e-mail information@bahamashc/on.net)

O'BRIEN, Conor Cruise; s of Francis Cruise O'Brien, and Katherine, *née* Sheehy; *b* 3 November 1917; *Educ* Sandford Park Sch Dublin, Trinity Coll Dublin (BA, PhD); *m* 1, 1939 (m dis 1962), Christine Foster; 1 s, 2 da; m 2, 1962, Máire Mac Entee; 1 adopted s, 1 adopted da; *Career* Dept of External Affrs Ireland: entered 1944, cnsllr Paris 1955–56, head of UN Section and memb Irish Delgn to UN 1956–60, asst sec 1960, rep of Sec Gen of UN in Katanga 1961; vice-chllr Univ of Ghana 1962–65, Albert Schweitzer prof of humanities NY Univ 1965–69, TD (Lab) Dublin NE 1969–77 (min for posts and telegraphs 1973–77), memb Senate Republic of Ireland 1977–79, ed-in-chief The Observer 1979–81; contributing ed The Atlantic (Boston), contrib The Independent and The Irish Independent; pro-chllr Univ of Dublin 1973–, visiting fell Nuffield Coll Oxford 1973–75, fell St Catherine's Coll Oxford 1978–81, visiting prof and Montgomery fell Dartmouth Coll 1984–85, sr research fell Nat Centre for the Humanities Durham NC 1993; Valiant for Truth Media Award 1979; Hon DLitt: Univ of Bradford 1971, Univ of Ghana 1974, Univ of Edinburgh 1976, Nice Univ 1978, Coleraine 1981, Queen's Univ Belfast 1984; MRIA, FRSL 1984; *Books* Maria Cross (under pseudonym Donat O'Donnell 1952, reprinted under own name 1963), Parnell and his Party (1957), The Shaping of Modern Ireland (ed, 1959), To Katanga and Back (1962), Conflicting Concepts of the UN (1964), Writers and Politics (1965), The UN: Sacred Drama (1967), Murderous Angels (1968), Power and Consciousness (ed, 1969), Conor Cruise O'Brien Introduces Ireland (1969), Edmund Burke: Reflections on the Revolution in France (ed, 1969), Camus (1969), A Concise History of Ireland (with Máire Cruise O'Brien, 1972, revd edn 1993), The Suspecting Glance (1972), States of Ireland (1972), Herod (1978), Neighbours: the Ewart-Biggs memorial lectures 1978–79 (1980), The Siege: the Saga of Israel and Zionism (1986), Passion and Cunning (1988), God Land: Reflections on Religion and Nationalism (1988), The Great Melody: A Thematic Biography of Edmund Burke (1992), Ancestral Voices: Religion and Nationalism in Ireland (1994); *Recreations* travelling; *Clubs* Athenaeum; *Style—* Conor Cruise O'Brien, Esq, FRSL; ✉ Whitewater, Howth Summit, Dublin, Ireland (tel 00 353 1 8322474)

O'BRIEN, Prof Denis Patrick; s of Patrick Kevin O'Brien (d 1944), of Welwyn, Herts, and Dorothy Elizabeth, *née* Crisp (d 1985); *b* 24 May 1939; *Educ* Douai Sch, UCL (BSc Econ), Queen's Univ Belfast (PhD); *m* 1, 5 Aug 1961, Eileen Patricia (d 1985), da of Martin O'Brien (d 1987), of Bognor Regis, W Sussex; 1 s (Martin Michael), 2 da (Ann Elizabeth, Alison Mary); m 2, 11 Sept 1993, Julia, da of John Brian Stapleton, of Gosport, Hants; 1 da (Juliet Florence); *Career* reader in economics Queen's Univ Belfast 1970–72 (asst lectr 1963–65, lectr 1965–70), prof of economics Univ of Durham 1972–97 (emeritus prof 1998–); memb Cncl Royal Economic Soc 1978–83; distinguished fell History of Economics Soc 2003; FBA; *Books* J R McCulloch (1970), The Correspondence of Lord Overstone (3 vol, 1971), Competition in British Industry (jtly, 1974), The Classical Economists (1975), Competition Policy, Profitability and Growth (jtly, 1979), Pioneers of Modern Economics in Britain (jtly, 1981), Authorship Puzzles in The History of Economics: A Statistical Approach (jtly, 1982), Lionel Robbins (1988), Thomas Joplin and Classical Macroeconomics (1993), Methodology, Money and the Firm (2 vols, 1994), The Classical Economists Revisited (2004), History of Economic Thought as an Intellectual Discipline (2007); *Recreations* the violin; *Style—* Prof D P O'Brien, FBA; ✉ Department of Economics, University of Durham, 23–26 Old Elvet, Durham DH1 3HY (tel 0191 334 6579)

O'BRIEN, Dermod Patrick; QC (1983); s of Lt Dermod Donatus O'Brien (d 1939), and Helen Doreen Lesley, *née* Scott O'Connor (d 1971); *b* 23 November 1939; *Educ* Ampleforth, St Catherine's Coll Oxford (MA); *m* 1974 (m dis 2003), Zoë Susan, da of Roderick Edward Norris, of Sussex; 2 s (Edward b 1977, Timothy b 1980); *Career* called to the Bar: Inner Temple 1962 (bencher 1993), NI 2002; recorder of the Crown Court (Western Circuit) 1978–2005; head of chambers 1999–2003; govr Milton Abbey Sch 1992–; landowner; *Recreations* fishing, shooting, skiing; *Clubs* Boodle's; *Style—* Dermod P O'Brien, Esq, QC; ✉ 2 Temple Gardens, Temple, London EC4Y 9AY (tel 020 7822 1200, fax 020 7822 1300, e-mail dobrien@2tg.co.uk)

O'BRIEN, Desmond Leonard; CBE (1999), QPM; s of Joseph O'Brien (d 1972), of Belfast, and Adelaide, *née* Cadden (d 1959); *b* 31 March 1934; *Educ* St Mary's Secdy Sch Belfast, Brunel Univ; *m* 1975, Susan, da of Albert Fradley; 2 da (Kathrine b 5 Oct 1976 d 11 Oct 1976, Tamsin Lucinda b 28 Oct 1978); *Career* supt RUC 1953–73, chief supt Police Staff Coll Bramshill 1973–75, chief supt RUC 1975–78, asst chief constable Greater Manchester Police 1978–83, dep chief constable Kent Co Police 1983–89, chief constable British Transport Police 1989–97; memb ACPO 1978; *Recreations* country activities, walking, fly fishing; *Style—* Desmond O'Brien, Esq, CBE, QPM; ✉ c/o British Transport Police, 25 Camden Road, London NW1 9LN (tel 020 7830 8854, fax 020 7830 8944)

O'BRIEN, Most Rev Keith Michael Patrick; *see:* St Andrews and Edinburgh, Archbishop of (RC)

O'BRIEN, Dr (John) Michael; s of Peter O'Brien (d 1977), of Melton Mowbray, Leics, and Nellie, *née* Harrap (d 1975); *b* 30 December 1935; *Educ* Stockport GS, Univ of Manchester Med Sch (MB ChB, pres Univ Boat Club, sec Univ Athletic Union), Univ of Liverpool (DPH, Trevor Lloyd Hughes gold medal and prize); *m* 1960, Constance Amy, da of Albert Edward Dalton (d 1955); 2 da (Sarah Jane b 1963, Rachel Elizabeth b 1964); *Career* house offr posts Manchester Royal Infirmary and St Mary's Hosp Manchester 1962, tutor in clinical surgery (hon registrar) Manchester Royal Infirmary 1963, princ in gen practice Kidsgrove 1964 and 1965, med inspr of aliens and Cwlth immigrants 1966–81, dep med offr of health and dep princ sch med offr Kingston upon Hull 1969 and 1970 (actg sr asst med offr 1968), dep port med offr Hull and Goole Port HA 1969–70, dep county med offr and dep princ sch med offr Durham CC 1970–74 (pt/t factory doctor 1971–73), area med offr Durham AHA 1974–81; Northern RHA: regional specialist in community med 1981–85, actg postgrad dean 1984–85; E Anglian RHA: regional dir of public health 1985–93, exec dir 1990–93; postgraduate advsr in public health med Northern and Yorkshire RHA 1994–97, chm Standing Clinical Advsy Gp Newcastle and N Tyneside HA 1994–96, memb Cncl Univ of Newcastle upon Tyne 1994–99 (hon sr research assoc Dept of Med 1994–98), chm Northumberland HA 1995–2002; pres: Faculty of Public Health Med 1992–95 (vice-pres 1989–92), Soc of Public Health 1995–96; memb various working parties for Govt depts incl Working Pty on Health of the Nation and the Med Profession 1995; sr memb Hughes Hall Cambridge 1987–93, assoc lectr MB and DPH Courses Univ of Cambridge Clinical Sch 1989–93; chm: Bd of Mgmnt Inst of Public Health Cambridge 1991–93, Public Health Med Consultative Ctee 1992–94, Northern Cancer Network Steering Gp 1996–98; vice-chm Conf of Colls 1993–95, memb Cncl Royal Inst of Public Health 1997–2004 (chm 1999–2002); author of numerous pubns in professional and academic jls; QHP 1990–93; FFPHM RCP 1980, FRCP 1990 (memb Cncl 1992–95), FRCPath 1992, Hon FFOM 1993, FRCPE 1996, Hon FFPHMI 1997, Hon FRIPH 2003 (vice-pres 2003–); *Recreations* gardening; *Style—* Dr Michael O'Brien; ✉ Catbells, 2 Ullswater Drive, Great Warford, Alderley Edge, Cheshire SH9 7WB (tel and fax 01565 872948, e-mail jm.obrien@btinternet.com); The Royal Institute of Public Health, 28 Portland Place, London W1B 1DE (tel 020 7580 2731, fax 0207580 6157)

O'BRIEN, Michael Anthony (Mike); s of Dr Donal O'Brien (d 1999), and Patricia Mary, *née* Dowdall (d 1990); *b* 7 September 1950; *Educ* The Oratory Sch Reading, Trinity Coll Dublin (BA, BAI); *m* 7 Sept 1971, Robin Patricia Antonia, da of Roger Greene (d 1954), of Wellington Quay, Dublin; 4 da (Louise b 1974, Pippa b 1976, Tara b 1977, Alice b 1987); *Career* qualified chartered accountant; asst dir C T Bowring & Co (Lloyd's brokers) 1975–78, gp fin controller Mining Investment Corp Ltd 1978–79, chief exec Anglo Int Mining Corp Ltd 1979–82, chm and chief exec Loupiptar plc and subsids 1982–91, chief exec Healthcare Gp Ltd and subsids, chm United Healthcare Ltd; memb S of England Agric Soc; FCA; *Recreations* racing, horses, ponies, swimming; *Style—* Mike O'Brien, Esq; ✉ Beresford House, Plumpton Green, Lewes, East Sussex BN8 4EN (tel 01273 891205, fax 01273 891445, e-mail mikeobrien@unitedhealthcare.co.uk)

O'BRIEN, Michael (Mike); MP, QC; *m*; 2 da; *Career* MP (Lab) Warks N 1992–; oppn spokesman on treasy and economic affrs 1995–96, oppn spokesman on the City 1996–97, Parly under-sec of state Home Office 1997–2001, Parly under sec FCO 2002–03, min of state for trade and investment DTI 2003–04, min of state for energy and e-commerce 2004–05, slr gen 2005–; parly advsr to: Police Fedn 1993–95, CPOSA 2001–02; *Style—* Mike O'Brien, Esq, MP, QC; ✉ House of Commons, London SW1A 0AA (tel 020 7219 3000); Constituency Office, 92 King Street, Bedworth (tel 024 7631 5084)

O'BRIEN, Prof Patrick Karl; s of William Patrick O'Brien, of Coggeshall, Essex, and Elizabeth, *née* Stockhausen; *b* 12 August 1932; *m* 15 April 1959, Cassy, da of Charles Cobham; 2 da (Karen b 18 Nov 1964, Helen b 18 Nov 1966), 1 s (Stephen b 23 March 1972); *Career* Univ of London: res fell 1960–63, lectr 1963–70, reader in economics and econ history 1967–70, univ reader in econ history and professorial fell St Antony's Coll Oxford 1984–90 (univ lectr in econ history and faculty fell 1970–84), prof of econ history and dir of the Inst of Historical Research (IHR) Univ of London 1990–98; centennial prof of econ history LSE 1999; pres Econ History Soc 1998–2001; Hon DUniv: Carlos III Madrid 1999, Uppsala 2000; FRHistS, FAE, FBA, FRSA; *Books* The Revolution in Egypt's Economic System (1966), The New Economic History of the Railways (1977), Economic Development in Britain and France 1780–1914: Two Paths to the Twentieth Century (jtly with C Keyder), Productivity in the Economics of Europe in the 19th and 20th Centuries (jt ed, 1983), Railways and the Economic Development of Western Europe 1914–1930 (ed, 1983), International Productivity Comparisons 1750–1939 (ed, 1986), The Economic Effects of the Civil War (1988), The Industrial Revolution and British Society (ed with R Quinalt, 1993), The Industrial Revolution in Europe (ed, 1994), The Costs and Benefits of European Imperialism (ed with L Prados de la Escosura, 1998), Industrialization, 4 Vols (ed, 1998), Atlas of World History (ed, 2000), Urban Achievement in Early Modern Europe (jt ed, 2001), The Hegemonies: Britain 1846–1914 and the United States 1941–1989 (ed with A Clesse, 2002), The Political Economy of British Historical Experience 1688–2002 (ed with D Winch, 2002); contrib to numerous learned jls; *Recreations* art history, walking; *Style—* Prof Patrick O'Brien, FBA; ✉ 66 St Bernard Road's, Oxford OX2 6EJ; London School of Economics and Political Science, Houghton Street, Aldwych, London WC2A 2AE (tel 020 7955 6586, e-mail p.o'brien@lse.ac.uk)

O'BRIEN, His Hon Judge Patrick William; s of William Columba O'Brien, of Melksham, Wilts, and Ethel Minnie, *née* Austin; *b* 20 June 1945; *Educ* St Joseph's Acad Blackheath, Queens' Coll Cambridge (MA, LLM); *m* 23 May 1970, Antoinette Magdeleine, da of Louis Wattebot; 1 s (Nicholas William Wattebot O'Brien b 11 Oct 1971), 2 da (Dr Charlotte Clementine Wattebot O'Brien b 11 Aug 1973, Juliet Gisela Magdeleine Wattebot O'Brien b 11 April 1975); *Career* called to the Bar Lincoln's Inn 1968 (Mansfield scholar, additional bencher 2003); in practice in chambers of Lord Havers 1970–91, recorder 1987–91 (asst recorder 1984–87), circuit judge (SE Circuit) 1991–; *Publications* Great Oxford (contrib, 2004); *Recreations* music, cricket; *Clubs* MCC, Highgate CC, Great Canfield CC, Norfolk; *Style—* His Hon Judge O'Brien; ✉ Cambridge County Court, 197 East Road, Cambridge CB1 1BA (tel 01223 224500)

O'BRIEN, Richard; s of Alec James Morley-Smith, of Tauranga, New Zealand, and Doreen Mary, *née* O'Brien; *m* 1, 1971 (m dis 1979), Kimi Wong; 1 s (Linus b 1 May 1972); m 2, 1982, Jane Elizabeth Moss; 1 s (Joshua b 22 June 1983), 1 da (Amelia b 9 Jan 1989); *Career* actor, presenter and writer 1967–; dir Druidcrest Music Publishing; memb: Equity, Publishing Rights Soc; *Theatre* incl: Robert and Elizabeth, Gulliver's Travels, Hair, Jesus Christ Superstar; four prodns at Royal Court Theatre (writer of two incl The Rocky Horror Show), Mephistopheles Smith in Disgracefully Yours, performed in Chitty Chitty Bang Bang (London Palladium) 2002; *Television* A Hymn for Jim (writer, BBC), The Crystal Maze (presenter, Channel 4) 1987–93, The Ink Thief (actor, Tyne Tees for ITV) 1993; *Film* The Rocky Horror Picture Show, Dark City, Spice World, Ever After,

Dungeons and Dragons 1999, Mumbo Jumbo 2000; *Albums* Absolut O'Brien (jazz) 1999; *Awards* for Rocky Horror Show: Evening Standard Award for Best Musical of 1973, Plays and Players Award for Best Musical of 1973, Golden Scroll Award from The Academy of Science Fiction, Fantasy and Horror Films; *Recreations* work; *Clubs* The Chelsea Arts, The Gothic Soc, Groucho; *Style—* Richard O'Brien, Esq; ✉ c/o Jonathan Altaras Associates Ltd, 1st Floor, 11 Garrick Street, London WC2E 9AR (tel 020 7836 8722, fax 020 7836 6066)

O'BRIEN, Prof (Patrick Michael) Shaughn; s of Patrick Michael O'Brien (d 1978), and Joan, *née* Edleston (d 1999); *b* 1 April 1948; *Educ* Pontypridd Boys' GS, Univ of Wales, Welsh Nat Sch of Med (MB BCh, MD); *m* 10 Aug 1985, Sandra Louise, da of Edward Arthur Norman (d 1979), of Henley-on-Thames, Oxon; 1 s (James b 1986), 1 da (Louise b 1988); *Career* lectr and hon sr registrar Univ of Nottingham 1979–84, sr lectr and hon conslt in obstetrics and gynaecology Royal Free Hosp Sch of Med London 1984–89; Keele Univ: fndn prof of obstetrics and gynaecology 1989–, memb Senate 1996–99, memb Cncl 1996–99 and 2001–04, chm Educn Ctee Sch of Postgraduate Med 1996–; N Staffs Hosps: conslt obstetrician and gynaecologist 1989–, postgraduate clinical tutor 1996–2000; RCOG: publications offr 1996–99, memb Scientific Advsy Ctee 1996–99, convenor of study groups 1996–99, chm Publications Editorial Ctee 1996–99, fndr ed-in-chief The Obstetrician and Gynaecologist 1998–2004, memb Cncl 1999–, memb Fin and Exec Gp 2001–02, vice-pres 2004–07; chm N Staffs Med Inst 2002–04 (hon sec 2001–02); author of numerous papers in learned jls on premenstrual syndrome, menopause, fetal monitoring, pregnancy hypertension, labour, prostaglandins, disorders of the menstrual cyle, menorrhagia, renin angiotensin system, selective serotonin reuptake inhibitors; computerised Measurement of Disorders of the Menstrual Cycle (2001); devised and published: The Menstrual Pictogram (2002), Menstrual Symptometrics (2002), The Premenstrual Disorders: PMS and PMDD (2007), Introduction to Research Methodology (2007); FRCOG 1991 (MRCOG 1979); *Books* Premenstrual Syndrome (1987), Problems of Early Pregnancy (1997), Evidence-based Fertility Treatment (1998), Gene Identification, Manipulation and Therapy (1998), Fetal Programming: Intrauterine Influences on Adult Disease (1999), Hormones and Cancer (1999), Introduction to Research Methodology for Specialists and Trainees (1999), Placenta: Basic Science and Clinical Practice (2000), Disorders of the Menstrual Cycle (2000), Psychological Disorders in Obstetrics and Gynaecology for the MRCOG and Beyond (2006); RCOG Yearbook of Obstetrics and Gynaecology: vol 5 (1997), vol 6 (1998), vol 7 (1999), vol 8 Millennium Edition (2000); *Recreations* music, jazz, clarinet, saxophone, skiing, tennis; *Clubs* RSM; *Style—* Prof P M S O'Brien; ✉ Cardington House, Shrewsbury, SY1 1ES; Keele University, Academic Obstetrics & Gynaecology, Maternity Hospital, University Hospital of North Staffordshire, Stoke-on-Trent, Staffordshire ST4 6QG (tel and fax 01782 552472, e-mail shaughn.obrien@uhns.nhs.uk)

O'BRIEN, (Robert) Stephen; CBE (1987); s of Robert Henry O'Brien (d 1969), and Clare Winifred, *née* Edwards (d 1975); *b* 14 August 1936; *Educ* Sherborne; *m* 1, 1958 (m dis 1989), Zoe O'Brien; 2 s (Dermot b 1962, Paul b 1969), 2 da (Rachel b 1965, Louise b 1966); m 2, 30 June 1989, Meriel, *née* Barclay; *Career* Charles Fulton and Co Ltd: joined 1956, dir 1964, chm 1970–82; chief exec: Business in the Community 1983–92 (vice-chm 1992–2005, vice-pres 2005–), London First 1992–2002 (jt pres 2005–, vice-chm London First Centre); chm Foreign Exchange & Currency Deposit Assoc 1968–72; chm: Christian Action 1976–88, Fullemploy Gp 1973–91, UK 2000 1988–91, London Regnl Cncl Prince's Tst 1999–2006, Tower Hamlets PCT 2005–; dir: Prince of Wales Int Business Leaders' Forum, Greenwich Theatre 1999; tstee Prince's Youth Business Tst 1987–97, tstee and vice-chm Church Urban Fund 1994–2002; memb Bd of Govrs Univ of East London 2005– (chm 1999–2005); ordained deacon 1971, hon curate St Lawrence Jewry 1973–82; Hon LLD Univ of Liverpool 1994, Hon DSc City Univ 2000; Hon DUniv: Middx 2001, East London 2005; FRSA (memb Cncl 1987–91); *Recreations* gardening, cooking, tapestry; *Style—* Stephen O'Brien, Esq, CBE; ✉ London First, 1 Hobhouse Court, Suffolk Street, London SW1Y 4HH (tel 020 7665 1500, fax 020 7665 1501)

O'BRIEN, Stephen; MP; s of David O'Brien, and Rothy O'Brien; *b* 1 April 1957; *Educ* Sedbergh (music scholar), Emmanuel Coll Cambridge (MA), Coll of Law Chester; *m* 1986, Gemma, *née* Townshend; 2 s (James, Angus), 1 da (Clara); *Career* slr Freshfields 1981–88; Redland plc: exec asst to Bd 1988–89, dir gp operating cos 1989–98, dir gp fin/hldg cos 1989–98, dir gp res and devpt 1989–98, dir Corp Planning 1989–94, gp ctee memb 1990–98, gp sec 1991–98, dir corp affrs 1994–98, exec dir 1994–98, dep chm and exec dir Redland Tile & Brick Ltd (NI) 1995–98; int business conslt 1998–; MP (Cons) Eddisbury 1999– (by-election); PPS to Rt Hon Francis Maude, MP 2000, PPS to Rt Hon Earl of Ancram, DL, QC, MP 2000–01, oppn whip 2001–02, shadow min for the Treasy 2002–03, shadow sec of state for industry 2003–05, shadow min for skills and higher educn 2005, shadow min for health 2005–; memb: Educn Select Ctee 1999–2001, Environment, Food and Rural Affrs Select Ctee 2001–; sec Cons Pty Backbench Ctee on Trade and Industry 1999–2001, sec Cons Pty Backbench Ctee on NI 1999–2001, actg dir Cons Pty Ldr's Office 2001; memb: Br-American Gp 1999–, Int Parly Union 1999–, Cwlth Parly Assoc 1999–; assoc memb Br-Irish Inter-Parly Body 2000–; Parly advsr: ICSA 2000–, Manufacturing Technols Assoc 2005–; Cons Pty: special advsr (construction sector) Cons Business Liaison Unit 1998–2001, chm Chichester Cons Assoc 1998–99 (hon vice-chm 1999–), memb Nat Membership Ctee 1999–2001, Parly rep Westminster Candidates Assoc 2000–01 (memb Exec Ctee 1998–99); UK Building Materials Prodrs (BMP) 1995–99 (memb Ctee of Mgmnt, memb President's Strategy Ctee and chm Public and Parly Affrs Ctee), CBI 1995–98 (memb SE Regnl Cncl, memb Int Investment Panel); non-exec dir Univ of Cambridge Careers Serv Syndicate 1992–99; fndr memb Brazil-UK Jt Business Cncl 1994–; memb Cncl Scot Business in the Community 1995–98; dir City of London Sinfonia 2001–; tstee Reigate Priory Museum 1992–98, bd tstee Liverpool Sch of Tropical Medicine 2006–, non-exec dir Small Business Research Tst 2006–; chm Malaria Consortium (UK) 2007–; memb Law Soc; FICSA 1997; *Recreations* music, fell-walking, golf; *Clubs* Winsford Constitutional & Conservative, Cheshire Pitt, Ebernoe Cricket (vice-pres); *Style—* Stephen O'Brien, Esq, MP; ✉ House of Commons, London SW1A 0AA (tel 020 7219 6315, fax 020 7219 0584, e-mail obriens@parliament.uk)

O'BRIEN, Timothy Brian; s of Brian Palliser Tighe O'Brien (d 1966), and Elinor Laura, *née* Mackenzie (d 2002); *b* 8 March 1929; *Educ* Wellington, CCC Cambridge (MA), Yale Univ; *m* 22 Nov 1997, Jenny Jones; *Career* designer; BBC Design Dept 1954, Assoc Rediffusion 1955–56, head of design ABC TV 1956–65, theatrical designer (in partnership with Tazeena Firth 1961–79); prodns incl: Love's Labour's Lost (RSC) 1990, War and Peace (Kirov St Petersburg) 1991, Eugene Onegin (ROH) 1993, The Merry Wives of Windsor (RNT) 1995, Outis (La Scala Milan) 1996, Twelfth Night (Clwyd) 1999, Macbeth (Clwyd) 2000, Romeo and Juliet (Clwyd) 2002, Werther (Sao Carlos Lisbon) 2004, Ulysses Comes Home (Birmingham Opera Co) 2005, Das Rheingold (Sao Carlos Lisbon) 2006, Die Walküre (Sao Carlos Lisbon) 2007; chm Soc of Br Theatre Designers 1984–91; Gold Medal for set design Prague Quadriennale 1975, jt winner Golden Triga for best national exhibit Prague Quadriennale 1991; Master Faculty of Royal Designers for Industry 1999–2001; RDI 1991; *Recreations* sailing; *Style—* Timothy O'Brien, Esq; ✉ Flat 3, 97 Cambridge Street, London SW1V 4PY (tel 020 7630 1388, fax 020 7821 1447); The Level, Blackbridge Road, Freshwater Bay, Isle of Wight PO40 9QP (tel 01983 721752, fax 01983 721023, e-mail all@highwaterjones.com)

O'BRIEN, Tony; s of Padraig O'Brien (d 2002), and Sheila, *née* Crowe (d 2005); *b* 17 January 1951; *Educ* Univ of Cambridge (MA), Univ of Manchester (Dip Teaching English Overseas, PGCE), Inst of Educn Univ of London (MA); *m* 1975, Yolanda, *née* Lange; 3 da (Becci b 1978, Emily b 1980, Anna b 1984); *Career* VSO Aswan Egypt 1971–73, lectr Univ of Tabriz Iran 1975–77; Br Cncl: dir of studies Morocco 1978–82, conslt London 1982–86, dir English language centres Singapore and Hong Kong 1986–94, dir Morocco 1994–97, dir (ELT) and devpt dir knowledge and learning centres 1997–2002, dir Sri Lanka 2002–06, dir Poland 2006–; author of numerous articles for professional pubns 1975–2002; tstee Int House London 1997–2001; founding fell Br Inst of ELT 1999; *Books* Nucleus: Medicine (1980), Teacher Development, Evaluation and Teacher Profiles in TESOL (1986); *Recreations* travel, food, bird-watching, tennis; *Clubs* Commonwealth; *Style—* Tony O'Brien, Esq; ✉ c/o FCO (Warsaw), King Charles Street, London SW1A 2AH (tel 00 48 226 955 920, mobile 00 48 602 726 185, e-mail tony.obrien@britishcouncil.org)

O'CATHAIN, Baroness (Life Peer UK 1991), of The Barbican in the City of London; Detta Bishop; OBE (1983); da of Caoimhghin O'Cathain (d 1986), of Dublin, and Margaret, *née* Prior (d 1977); *b* 3 February 1938; *Educ* Laurel Hill Limerick, UC Dublin (BA); *m* 4 June 1968, William Ernest John Bishop (d 2001), s of William Bishop (d 1968), of Bristol; *Career* former md mktg Milk Mktg Board, md Barbican Centre 1990–95; dir Midland Bank plc 1984–93; non-exec dir: Tesco plc 1985–2000, Sears plc 1987–94, British Airways plc 1993–2004, BET plc 1994–96, BNP Paribas Holdings (UK) Ltd 1995–2005, Thistle Hotels plc 1996–2003, South East Water plc 1998–, William Baird plc 2000–02, Alders plc 2000–03; pres CIM 1998–2001 (vice-pres 1996–98); *Recreations* reading, walking, swimming, gardening, music; *Style—* The Baroness O'Cathain, OBE; ✉ House of Lords, London SW1A 0PW (tel 020 7219 0662, e-mail ocathaind@parliament.uk)

O'CEALLAIGH, HE Dáithí; *b* 24 February 1945; *Educ* UC Dublin (BA); *m* Antoinette, *née* Reilly; 1 da (Clíona), 1 s (Rónan); *Career* teacher Zambia 1968–71; first sec: Dept of Foreign Affrs 1974 (third sec 1973), Embassy of Ireland Moscow 1975–77, Embassy of Ireland London 1977–82, Anglo-Irish Div HQ 1982–85, cnsllr: Anglo-Irish Div HQ 1985, Anglo-Irish Secretariat Maryfield 1985–87; consul -gen NY 1987–93, ambass to Finland and Estonia 1993–98, asst sec Admin Div HQ 1998–2000, second sec-gen Anglo-Irish Div HQ 2000–01, ambass to the Ct of St James's 2001–; *Recreations* bird watching, cinema, history, theatre, jazz; *Style—* HE Mr Dáithí O'Ceallaigh; ✉ Embassy of Ireland, 17 Grosvenor Place, London SW1X 7HR (tel 020 7235 8483, fax 020 7235 2851)

OCEAN, Humphrey; s of Capt Maurice Erdeswick Butler-Bowdon, OBE (d 1984), and Anne, *née* Darlington (d 1999); *b* 22 June 1951; *Educ* Ampleforth, Canterbury Coll of Art (BA); *m* 3 March 1982, Miranda, da of Dr Michael Argyle, of Oxford; 2 da (Ruby b 1982, Beatrice b 1986); *Career* artist; visiting prof in painting and drawing Univ of the Arts London 2002–; Imperial Tobacco Portrait Award 1982, Wellcome Sci-Art Award 1998; hon fell Kent Inst of Art and Design (KIAD); RA 2004; *Solo Exhibitions* incl: Nat Portrait Gallery 1984, Ferens Art Gallery Hull 1986–87, Double-Portrait (Tate Gallery Liverpool) 1991–92, urbasuburba (Whitworth Art Gallery Manchester and tour) 1997–98, The Painter's Eye (Nat Portrait Gallery) 1999, how's my driving (Dulwich Picture Gallery) 2003; *Work in Collections* British Council, Imperial War Museum, Scot Nat Portrait Gallery, Ferens Art Gallery, Southwark Collection, Nat Portrait Gallery, Wolverhampton Art Gallery, Royal Library, Nat Maritime Museum, Port Authy Zeebrugge, Whitworth Art Gallery Manchester, Victoria & Albert Museum; *Commissions for Portraits* incl: Philip Larkin, Paul McCartney, A J Ayer, Graham Greene, Lord Callaghan, Lord Whitelaw, Tony Benn; *Books* The Ocean View (1982), Big Mouth: The Amazon Speaks (1990), Zeebrugge by Humphrey Ocean (2002); *Style—* Humphrey Ocean, Esq, RA; ✉ 22 Marmora Road, London SE22 0RX (tel 020 8693 8387, studio tel and fax 020 8761 7400)

O'CONNELL, Bernard John; s of William O'Connell, and Dorothy, *née* Veale; *b* 22 November 1942; *Educ* St Brendan's Coll, Univ of Sheffield; *m* 12 Feb 1966, Mary Jacqueline, da of Capt Norman Clark (d 1959); 1 s (James b 1967), 1 da (Anna b 1971); *Career* consumer res mangr Cadbury's 1967–69, mktg mangr Imperial Tobacco 1969–72, chm and md Market Solutions 1973–78, md Noble Whelan O'Connell 1978–84, chm The O'Connell Partnership 1984–97, vice-chm Momentum Integrated Communications 1998–2000, chm Volcano Group 2001–03; mktg awards: Silver 1975, Gold 1975 and 1977, Grand Prix 1977; *Recreations* golf, sailing, music; *Clubs* Chartridge Park Golf, Savile; *Style—* Bernard O'Connell, Esq; ✉ Woodland Court, Long Park, Chesham Bois, Amersham, Buckinghamshire HP6 5LG

O'CONNELL, Dr David Henry Anthony; s of late David Andrew O'Connell, and late Ellen Mary, *née* Paul; *b* 26 February 1955; *Educ* Presentation Brothers Coll Cork, UC Cork (MB BCh, BAO), DRCOG, MICGP; *Career* family doctor, house physician and house surgn Royal Hosp Wolverhampton 1978–79, GP registrar St Bartholomew's and Hackney Hosp Vocational Trg Scheme 1979–82, family doctor 1982–; chm dist jr exec City and Hackney Health Dist 1980–81, med advsr and memb Mgmnt Ctee St Wilfrid's Residential Home Chelsea 1984–2003, dir of various med cos 1990–, memb Exec Ctee, sec Audit Sub-Ctee and chm Insurance Sub-Ctee Independent Doctors' Forum, memb Cncl RSH 1994–97, co-fndr and chm London Irish Med Assoc 2000–; author of various contribs to popular med jls; Freeman City of London, Liveryman Worshipful Soc of Apothecaries 1995 (Yeoman 1985); memb BMA 1978; fell: Med Soc of London 1985, Chelsea Clinic Soc 1985; FRSM 1982; FRIPHH 1993, FRSH 1994; Knight of Magistral Grace Sovereign Mil Order of Malta 1993 (Cross of Merit 1987, Bronze Medal 1994), Knight Order of St Maurice and St Lazarus 2001; *Publications* Jetlag - How to Beat It (1998); *Recreations* wine and travel; *Clubs* RAC, Seychelles Yacht, Carlton; *Style—* Dr David H A O'Connell; ✉ Fortress House, Kosta Popadopoulou St 15, Akrounta, Cyprus 4522 (tel 00 797 641 7591, e-mail oconnell@cytanet.com.cy)

O'CONNELL, Sir Maurice James Donagh MacCarthy; 7 Bt (UK 1869), of Lakeview, Killarney, Co Kerry, and of Ballybeggan, Tralee, Co Kerry; er s of Sir Morgan Donal Conail O'Connell, 6 Bt (d 1989), and Elizabeth, *née* MacCarthy-O'Leary; *b* 10 June 1958; *Educ* Ampleforth; *m* 11 Sept 1993, Francesca Susan, o da of Clive Raleigh (d 2004), of Hong Kong; 1 s (Morgan Daniel Clive MacCarthy b 17 Nov 2003); *Heir* s, Morgan Daniel Clive MacCarthy O'Connell; *Style—* Sir Maurice O'Connell, Bt; ✉ Lakeview House, Killarney, County Kerry, Republic of Ireland

O'CONNOR, Bridget Anne (Biddie); da of John O'Connor (d 1994), of Manchester, and Joan Mears (d 1984); *b* 28 April 1958, Chesterfield, Derbys; *Educ* St Helena Sch Chesterfield, St Hugh's Coll Oxford (BA), Sidney Sussex Coll Cambridge (PGCE); *m* 8 Jan 1982, Simon Salem; *Career* asst teacher (classics) Francis Holland Sch Clarence Gate 1981–83, teacher and head Classics Dept Old Palace Sch of John Whitgift Croydon 1983–90, head of dept, head of sixth form and dep head Haberdashers' Aske's Sch for Girls Elstree 1991–2002, headmistress Loughborough HS 2002–; *Recreations* reading, cookery, walking, visiting galleries, art; *Style—* Miss Biddie O'Connor; ✉ Loughborough High School, Burton Walks, Loughborough, Leicestershire LE11 2DU (tel 01509 212348, fax 01509 215720, e-mail admin@loughhs.leics.sch.uk)

O'CONNOR, Denis Francis; CBE (2002), QPM (1996); s of Denis O'Connor (d 1978), and Ellen, *née* Walsh (d 1961); *b* 21 May 1949, Ireland; *Educ* Univ of Southampton (BEd), Cranfield Univ (MSc); *m* 3 April 1972, Louise, *née* Harvey; 2 da (Tanya b 1976, Annabel b 1983), 1 s (Denis b 1978); *Career* Met Police Serv 1968–70 and 1974–85, Supt Surrey Police 1985–88, Chief Supt Met Police Serv 1989–91, Asst Chief Constable Surrey Police 1991–93, Dep Chief Constable Kent Police 1993–97, Asst Cmmr Met Police Serv 1997–2000, Chief Constable Surrey Police 2000–04, HM Inspr of Constabulary 2004–; *Recreations* walking, reading, trying to keep up with my children; *Style—* Denis O'Connor, Esq, CBE, QPM

O'CONNOR, Des; *b* 12 January 1932; *Career* entertainer and chat-show host; former Butlin's Red Coat; Lifetime Achievement Special Recognition Award Nat TV Awards 2003; *Theatre* professional debut Palace Theatre Newcastle 1953, compere Sunday Night at the London Palladium, completed 1,000th performance at London Palladium in his own show, one-man show UK, Canada and Australia since 1980, pantomime Cinderella (London Palladium 1985), numerous Royal Show appearances (incl host Royal Variety Performance 1997); Canada and USA: headlined three seasons London Palladium Show in Toronto and Ottawa, seasons at The Royal York Hotel and Royal Alexandra Theatre, two all-star galas at The MGM Grand Hotel Las Vegas; Australia: theatre and cabaret performances over many years, broke all box office records St George's League Club Sydney 1975, appeared at Sydney Opera House; *Television* host: Spot the Tune 1958, own series since 1963, two series screened US then worldwide 1975, Des O'Connor Tonight 1977– (awarded Nat TV Awards Most Popular Talk Show 1995 and 1997), Des O'Connor Now 1985, TV Times Awards ceremony 1989–90 and 1990–91, Take Your Pick 1992, 1994 and 1996, Pot of Gold 1993 and 1995, An Audience with Des O'Connor 2001, Des O'Connor on Des O'Connor 2001, The Way They Were 2001, Fame in the Family 2000–, Today With Des And Mel 2002– (RTS Programme Award for Best Daytime Programme 2003), Des O'Connor Comedy Tonight 2003, host Countdown 2007–; *Recordings* first record Careless Hands reached number one in charts and sold over one million copies 1967, numerous hit singles and albums released since, album Des O'Connor sold over 250,000 copies 1984, released Sky Boat Song with Roger Whittaker entering Top Twenty charts 1986, album Portrait for Columbia (Gold on release) 1992; *Books* Bananas Can't Fly (autobiography, 2001); *Style*— Des O'Connor, Esq; ✉ c/o Lake-Smith Griffin Associates, Walter House, 418 Strand, London WC2R 0PT (tel 020 7836 1020, fax 020 7836 1040, website www.des-oconnor.com)

O'CONNOR, Joseph Victor; s of John Oliver Vincent O'Connor, of Dublin, and Joanna Marie, *née* O'Grady (d 1985); *b* 20 September 1963; *Educ* Blackrock Coll Dublin, UC Dublin (BA, MA), UC Oxford, Univ of Leeds (MA); *m* 1998, Anne-Marie *née* Casey, of London; 2 s (James Casey b 24 July 2000, Marcus Casey b 16 May 2004); *Career* writer; fndr memb Amnesty Educn Tst (Ireland); *Awards* Hennessy First Fiction Award 1989, New Irish Writer of the Year 1989, Travel Writing Award Time Out Magazine 1990, special Jury Prize (for A Stone of the Heart) Cork Int Film Festival 1992, shortlisted Whitbread Prize 1992, Macaulay fell Irish Arts Cncl 1993, shortlisted Sunday Independent Irish Novel of the Year Award 2002, New York Times Notable Book of the Year 2003, Prix Littéraire Européen Madeleine Zepter 2004, Premio Giuseppi Acerbi for New Literature 2004, Hennessy/Sunday Tribune Hall of Fame Literary Award 2004, nominated Dublin Int IMPAC Literary Award 2004, American Library Assoc Notable Book Award 2004, Neilsen-Bookscan Golden Book Award 2005, Premio Napoli 2005, fell Cullman Centre for Scholars and Writers New York Library 2005; *Fiction* Cowboys and Indians (1991), True Believers (short stories, 1991), Desperadoes (1994), The Salesman (1997), Inishowen (2000), The Comedian (novella, 2000), Star of the Sea (2002); *Filmscripts* A Stone of the Heart (1992), The Long Way Home (1993), Ailsa (1993); *Stage Plays* Red Roses and Petrol (1995), The Weeping of Angels (1997), True Believers (1999); *Other* Even the Olives Are Bleeding: the Life and Times of Charles Donnelly (1992), The Secret World of the Irish Male (1994), Sweet Liberty: Travels in Irish America (1996), The Irish Male at Home and Abroad (1996), The Last of the Irish Males (2001), Yeats is Dead: A Serial Novel by Fifteen Irish Writers for Amnesty International (ed, 2001); *Style*—Joseph O'Connor, Esq; ✉ c/o Blake Friedmann Literary Agency, 122 Arlington Road, London NW1 7HP (tel 020 7284 0408, e-mail carole@blakefriedmann.co.uk)

O'CONNOR, Patrick Michael Joseph; QC (1993); *b* 7 August 1949; *Educ* St Francis Xavier's Sch Liverpool, UCL; *m* 1986; 2 da; *Career* called to the Bar Inner Temple 1970; author of articles in Criminal Law Review and other journals; *Books* Justice in Error (contrib, 1993); *Style*— Patrick O'Connor, Esq, QC; ✉ 10–11 Doughty Street, London WC1N 2PL (tel 020 7404 1313, fax 020 7404 2283/4, e-mail p.oconnor@doughtystreet.co.uk, website www.doughtystreet.co.uk)

O'CONOR DON, Desmond Roderic O'Conor; er son of Denis Armar, O'Conor Don, Prince of Connacht (d 2000), and Elizabeth, *née* Marris (now Mrs Elizabeth Cameron); *b* 22 September 1938; *Educ* Sherborne; *m* 23 May 1964, Virginia Anne, da of late Sir Michael Williams, KCMG, and Joy, *née* Holdsworth Hunt; 2 da (Emma Joy (Mrs Mark Leveson-Gower) b 17 April 1965, Denise Sarah (Mrs Wheeler) b 8 Dec 1970), 1 s (Philip Hugh b 17 Feb 1967); *Heir* s, Philip O'Conor; *Career* Bank of London and Montreal Ltd Guatemala and Honduras 1960–64, J Henry Schroder Wagg & Co Ltd London 1964–79, dir Schroders Int Ltd London 1977–79; KleinwortBenson Ltd London: dir 1979–1998, gp dir 1989–98, sr conslt 1998–2002; sr advsr: Latin American Capital Partners IILC NY until 2004, Darby Latin American Mezzanine Fund LP Washington until 2004; UK ceo and head London Office Antofagasta plc and dir of subsids 2004–; non-exec dir: Foreign and Colonial Latin American Investment Tst plc 1998–2006, Merrill Lynch Latin American Investment Tst plc 2006–; chm: Int Fin Servs London Latin American Advsy Gp 2000–, Br Chilean C of C 2003–; chm Sailors and Soldiers Home Eastbourne; memb Standing Cncl of Irish Chiefs and Chieftans Dublin, vice-pres Irish Genealogical Soc; Knight Cdr Order of Bernardo O'Higgins (Chile) 2006; *Recreations* tennis, walking, shooting; *Clubs* Kildare Street and Univ (Dublin), Cavalry and Guards', City of London; *Style*— O'Conor Don; ✉ Horsegrove House, Rotherfield, East Sussex TN6 3LU (tel 01892 852667, fax 01892 853699, e-mail d.oconor@dial.pipex.com)

ODAM, Prof George Neville; s of George Odam (d 1979), of Beccles, Suffolk, and Muriel, *née* Tawell (d 1964); *b* 30 September 1938; *Educ* Sir John Leman Sch, Univ of Manchester (BA), Univ of London (Music Teachers' Cert), Univ of Southampton (BMus, MPhil); *m* 15 April 1963, Penelope Anne Lloyd, da of Oliver Lloyd Smith (d 1979), of Beccles, Suffolk; 1 s (Timothy b 1964), 1 da (Joanna b 1966); *Career* composer; Totton GS Hants 1961–65, Bath Spa Univ Coll (formerly Bath Coll of Higher Educn) 1966– (prof of music educn 1993–99); GSMD: research fell in teaching and learning 1999–, head of research and staff devpt 2003–; compositions: Cantata for Christmas 1967, Angry Arrow 1969, St George and the Dragon 1970, Tutankhamun 1971, Inca 1975, Robin Hood 1978, Peredur (opera) 1979, Concerto for piano and timpani 1980, Baba Yaga 1984, Morning Service in G 2001, Evening Service in F 2002; fndr and conductor Nat Scouts and Guides Symphony Orch, chm UK Cncl for Music Educn and Trg 1988–91, vice-chm SEAC Music Ctee, chm MusicSpace UK 2004–; memb: ISM (warden of MES 1986–87), SW Arts Bd 1994– (chm Educn Steering Gp Ctee 1988–94); chm Nat Music & Disability Info Serv 1991–94; Music Industries Assoc Award for Outstanding Servs to Music Educn 1994; *Books* Silver Burdett and Ginn Music Books 1–4 (1989), The Sounding Symbol (1995), The Sounds of Music Books 1–7 (1996), Seeking the Soul: The Music of Alfred Schnittke (ed, 2001), Britten: Voice and Piano (preface, 2003), The Reflective Conservatoire (ed, 2005); *Recreations* drawing and painting, computer graphics and DTP, poetry, travel; *Style*— Prof George Odam; ✉ Bramble House, The Street, Farmborough, Bath, Somerset BA2 0AL (tel 01761 470182); Guildhall School of Music and Drama, Silk Street, London EC2Y 8DT (tel 020 7382 2370, e-mail george.odam@gsmd.ac.uk)

O'DAY, Prudence Anne (Prue); da of Dr Kevin John O'Day (d 1961), of Melbourne, and Bernadette Anne Hay (d 1983), of London; *b* 12 June 1946; *Educ* Mandeville Hall Melbourne, UCL, Westminster Coll; *m* 16 Jan 1971, Donald William Sievwright Anderson; 1 s (William Sievwright b 23 April 1975), 1 da (Amelia (Amy) b 11 Feb 1977); *Career* managed London Graphic Arts Gallery 1966–68, work with Ira Gale (Rembrandt expert) 1968–69, volunteer ICA Galleries 1968–69, researcher and buyer London Arts Gallery 1969–71, fndr (with husband) Anderson O'Day (formerly 20th Century Prints) 1971 (dir 1986–) and Anderson O'Day Gallery 1986–95; art conslt 1971–; curator survey exhbn of British prints Brooklyn Museum NYC 1974; co-fndr and treas Portobello Galleries Assoc 1986–, co-fndr Portobello Contemporary Art Festival 1986, co-fndr and sec Portobello Arts trust 1988–; memb: Steering Ctee Art Works for London Lighthouse 1993 1991, Selection Panel Cleveland Drawing Biennale 1991, Bd Landscape Fndn 1999; tstee The Showroom Gallery E London 2004; *Books* Prints & Drawings Fifteenth to Twentieth Century (1969), Ian Jones - Exhibition Catalogue (1991); *Recreations* politics, theatre, dance, contemporary art, literature and music, cinema, gardening, birdwatching, swimming, tennis and most sports as a spectator; *Clubs* Chelsea Arts; *Style*— Ms Prue O'Day; ✉ Anderson O'Day Fine Art, 5 St Quintin Avenue, London W10 6NX (tel 020 8969 8085)

ODDIE, Bill; *b* 7 July 1941; *Educ* Halesowen GS, King Edward's Sch Birmingham, Pembroke Coll Cambridge; *m* 1, Jean Hart; 2 da (Kate b 1968, Bonnie b 1971); m 2, Laura Beaumont; 1 da (Rose b 1985); *Career* writer and performer; memb: cncl RSPB, Wildfowl and Wetland's Tst, The Worldwide Fund for Nature; pres Northumberland Wildlife Tst; rep: Birdlife Int, Friends of The Earth, Plantlife, RSNC; *Theatre* as writer/performer incl: Cambridge Circus (transfered from Cambridge Footlights to London, NZ, USA), TW3 (touring co); as performer incl: Cousin Kevin in Tommy, Koko in Mikado (ENO), Childrens Variety Show (London Palladium); one pantomime as performer, one as writer; *Television* as writer/performer incl: TW3 (first appearances), The Braden Beat, BBC3, Twice A Fortnight (first series, co-writer Graeme Garden, *qv*, BBC), Then Broaden Your Mind (with Graeme Garden and Tim Brooke-Taylor, *qv*), The Goodies (co-writer Graeme Garden, eight series, 3 specials, twice winner Silver Rose of Montreux), From the Top (Central); with co-writer Laura Beaumont: The Bubblegum Brigade (HTV); as writer incl: scripts for That Was the Week That Was, numerous sketches for TW3, Ronnie Barker, Tommy Cooper etc; with Graeme Garden incl: Doctor In the House (50 episodes), At Large, The Astronauts (Central), Jim Henson's Animal Show (scripts and songs); as presenter incl: The Saturday Banana (Southern), Time for a Story (Granada), Fax (3 series, BBC), Ask Oddie (2 series, HTV), Festival (BBC); as narrator incl: Tubby the Tuba, The Snowman, Peter and the Wolf; numerous voice overs for commercials and animations; Wildlife progs incl: Oddie in Paradise (Papua New Guinea), The Great Bird Race, The Bird Business, For the Birds (USA cable), Bird in the Nest (BBC), Birding with Bill Oddie (three series, 1997, 1998 and 2000), Bill Oddie Goes Wild (three series, BBC), Bill Oddie's How to Watch Wildlife (BBC), Springwatch with Bill Oddie (BBC); guest appearance The Detectives (with Jasper Carrott and Robert Powell); *Radio* I'm Sorry I'll Read That Again (co-writer Graeme Garden, over 100 shows, BBC); as presenter incl: Breakaway (BBC), numerous shows on Jazz FM and GLR; *Recordings* with The Goodies: 5 top ten singles incl The Funky Gibbon, The Inbetweenies (both silver), 3 albums (1 silver); From the Top; *Books* as writer, illustrator and photographer incl: Bill Oddie's Little Black Bird Book, Gone Birding, Follow that Bird, Gripping Yarns, Bird Watching with Bill Oddie, Bird Watching for Under Tens, Bill Oddie's Colouring Guides, Bill Oddie's How to Watch Wildlife; numerous articles for magazine and newspapers; numerous Goodies Books with Graeme Garden and Tim Brooke-Taylor; with Laura Beaumont The Toilet Book (UK and worldwide); *Recreations* sports, drums, percussion, saxophone, music; *Style*— Bill Oddie; ✉ c/o All Electric Productions, PO Box 1805, Andover, Hampshire SP10 3ZN (tel 01264 361924, fax 01264 337014); voice overs c/o Yakkity Yak (tel 020 7430 2600)

ODDIE, Christopher Peter; s of late Alfred Birtwistle Oddie, of Lancs, and late Elsie Mary, *née* Bateman; *b* 26 September 1948; *Educ* King Edward VII Sch Lytham; *m* 12 June 1971, Gail, da of late Maj Horace George Ablett; 2 s (Simon Christopher b 19 Sept 1975, Matthew David b 1 July 1979); *Career* CA 1978; articled clerk T & H P Bee Preston 1967–72; ptnr: Tyson Westall CAs Lancs 1973–76, Grant Thornton CAs 1976–86; sr ptnr Lonsdale and Partners CAs Lancaster and branches 1986–2005; chm: Hanse Yachts UK Ltd, Fjord Boats UK Ltd 2005–; FICA; *Recreations* sailing; *Clubs* Royal Southern Yacht Club; *Style*— Christopher Oddie, Esq; ✉ 2 Low Chambers, Brigsteer, Kendal LA8 8DP (tel 01539 568737); Hanse Yachts UK Ltd, Gillys Landings, Glebe Road, Bowness on Windermere, Cumbria LA23 3HE (e-mail chris@hanseyachts.co.uk)

ODDIE, Elaine Anne; OBE (2003); da of Brian John Cory, of Hartley, Kent, and Molly Cory; *b* 11 February 1955; *Educ* Gravesend Girls' Sch, King's Coll Cambridge (MA); *m* 3 July 1976 (m dis), Alan James Oddie; *Career* articled clerk Brebner Allen & Trapp 1976–79, fin accountant Yardley International Ltd 1979–82; ptnr Mason Charlesworth & Co 1982–89, ptnr Morison Stoneham 1989–2000, dir Tenon 2000–03, ptnr NSO Associates LLP 2003–; memb N Thames Gas Consumers' Cncl 1981–84, pres S Essex Soc of Chartered Accountants 1990–91, pres Chelmsford Chamber of Commerce 1997–99 and 2001–03, chair Essex Chambers of Commerce 2003–; memb Cncl ICAEW 1991–2001, chair Eastern England Industrial Devpt Bd 2000–04; tstee Helen Rollason HEAL Cancer Charity 2004–; govr Chelmsford Coll 2001–; memb Exec Ctee Squash Rackets Assoc 1994–2002, treas Road Runners Club 2003–; FCA 1989 (ACA 1979); *Recreations* squash, running; *Style*— Ms Elaine Oddie, OBE; ✉ 7 Bellway Court, Grosvenor Road, Westcliff-on-Sea, Essex SS0 8EP; NSO Associates LLP, 75 Springfield Road, Chelmsford, Essex CM2 6JB (tel 01245 455400, fax 01245 494177, e-mail elaine.oddie@nso-associates.co.uk)

ODDY, Christine; da of Eric Lawson Oddy, and Audrey Mary, *née* Latham; *b* 20 September 1955; *Educ* UCL (LLB), Institut d'Études Européenes Brussels (licenciée spéciale en droit Européen, Belgian Govt scholar, Walter Page Hine travel scholar, Cncl of Europe travel scholar), Birkbeck Coll London (MScEcon); *Career* stagiaire at European Cmmn Brussels 1979–80, articled clerk 1980–82, admitted slr 1982, charity worker 1982–83, law lectr City of London Poly 1984–89, assoc fell Dept of Sociology Univ of Warwick, freelance lectr and Euro conslt 1999–, pt/t lectr London Met Univ 1999–, pt/t lectr Univ of Warwick 1999–; dir Coventry Univ 2002–; MEP (Lab): Midlands Central 1989–94, Coventry and Warks N 1994–99; memb Inst for Employment Rights; memb Editorial Bd Int Jl of Discrimination and the Law; memb: Bentham Soc, Haldane Soc, Industrial Law Soc, Law Soc; Law Soc rep Home Office Review of the Rehabilitation of Offenders Act 2001–02, memb Employment Ctee Law Soc 1996–; memb Bd of Govrs Coventry Univ 2002–05; dir Coventry Refugee Centre 2002–; vice-pres Coventry Older People's Forum 1996–, co-chair Saving Sight in S Asia (SAARC), patron Vocaleyes; hon fell Professional Business and Tech Mgmnt; MRIIA, FRSA; *Recreations* arts, cinema, theatre and wine; *Clubs* English Speaking Union; *Style*— Ms Christine Oddy; ✉ 33 Longfellow Road, Coventry CV2 5HD (tel 024 7645 6856); 105A Queen's Court, Queensway, London W2 4QR (tel 020 7229 5228)

ODDY, Jason Matthew; s of Noel Carter Oddy, and Joy Oddy; *Educ* Marlborough, UCL (MA); *Career* photographer and writer: The Independent, Modern Painters, Art Review, The AA Files, The Observer, Aperture (US), Portfolio, Nest (US); *Solo Exhibitions* The Henry Peacock Gallery London 1999 and 2000, Architectural Assoc 2000, Yossi Milo Gallery NY 2000, The Photographers' Gallery London 2001, 2003 and 2006, Royal Pump Rooms Museum Leamington Spa 2002, Galerie Serieuze Zaken Amsterdam 2002, Frederieke Taylor Gallery NY 2002 and 2004, Gallerie Vassie Amsterdam 2005, Univ of Herts Galleries 2007, Catalyst Arts Belfast 2007; *Style*— Jason Oddy, Esq; ✉ The Photographers' Gallery, 5 Great Newport Street, London WC2H 7HY (tel 020 7831 1772, e-mail info@jasonoddy.com)

O'DELL, June Patricia; OBE (1990); da of Lt Leonard Frederick Vickery (d 1940), and Myra Sarah, *née* Soden (d 1972); *b* 9 June 1929; *Educ* Edgehill Girls' Coll Bideford N Devon, Plymouth Tech Coll; *m* 9 Feb 1951 (m dis 1963), Ronald Desmond O'Dell; 1 s (Richard Patrick b 27 Feb 1952), 2 da (Caroline b 16 Nov 1955, Alison Julia b 27 July 1957); *Career* princ Chesneys Estate Agents 1965–88, nat pres UK Fedn of Business and Professional Women 1983–85, chair Int Fedn of Business and Professional Women Employment Ctee 1983–87, dep chair Equal Opportunities Cmmn 1986–90, memb Euro Advsy Ctee for Equal Treatment Between Women and Men 1986–90, dir Eachdale Developments 1988–97; non-exec dir Aylesbury Vale Community Care Health Tst 1992–98; RSA: memb Women's Advsy Gp 1985–95, memb Cncl 1992–97, chm Fellowship and Marketing Ctee 1994–97, memb Women's Forum 1996–99; memb: Women's Fin Panel National and Provincial Building Society 1988–95, Authorised Conveyancing Practitioners Bd 1991–94, Lord Chllr's Legal Aid Advsy Ctee 1992–94, Bd Probus Women's Housing Soc 1992– (vice-chm 1996–98, chair 1998–); tstee Women Returners Network 1994–96; govr Sir William Ramsay Sch 2002–05; FRSA 1987; *Recreations* opera, music, reading, theatre, the countryside, watching equestrian events; *Style*— Mrs June O'Dell, OBE; ✉ Gable End, High Street, Great Missenden, Buckinghamshire HP16 9AA (tel 01494 890185, fax 01494 865268)

ODELL, Prof Peter Randon; s of Frank James Odell (d 1978), of Coalville, Leics, and Grace Edna, *née* Randon (d 1954); *b* 1 July 1930; *Educ* King Edward VII GS Coalville, Univ of Birmingham (BA, PhD, W A Cadbury Prize, univ grad scholarship), Fletcher Sch of Law and Diplomacy Tufts Univ (AM); *m* 17 Aug 1957, Jean Mary, da of Ewan John McKintosh (d 1991), of Isle of Man; 2 s (Nigel Peter b 1958, Mark John b 1965), 2 da (Deborah Grace b 1960, Susannah Mary b 1967); *Career* RAF Educn Offr 1954–57, Flying Offr 1954–56, Flt Lt 1956–57; economist Shell International Petroleum Company Ltd 1958–61, sr lectr in economic geography LSE 1966–68 (lectr 1961–66), prof of economic geography Netherlands Sch of Economics 1968–73; Erasmus Univ Rotterdam: prof of economic geography 1973–81, prof of int energy studies 1982–91, prof emeritus 1992–; visiting prof: Coll of Europe Bruges 1984–90, LSE 1985–2001, Univ of Plymouth 1997–2003; Killam visiting fell Univ of Calgary 1989, visiting scholar Univ of Cambridge 1996–2000; special advsr to Sec of State for Energy 1977–79, specialist advsr House of Commons Select Ctee 2001–02; Int Assoc for Energy Econs Prize for Outstanding Contrib to Energy Economics 1991, Royal Scottish Geographical Soc Centenary Medal 1993, OPEC Biennial Award; Euro Parly candidate (SLD) Suffolk and SE Cambs 1989; memb Int Assoc for Energy Economics, RIIA; FRSA, FRGS, FEI; *Books* An Economic Geography of Oil (1963), Natural Gas in Western Europe - A Case Study in the Economic Geography of Energy Resources (1969), Oil and World Power - A Geographical Interpretation (1970, 8 edn 1986), Economies and Societies in Latin America - A Geographical Interpretation (with D A Preston, 1973, 2 edn 1978), The North Sea Oil Province: A Simulation of its Development 1969–2029 (with K E Rosing, 1975), The West European Energy Economy - The Case for Self-Sufficiency (1976), The Pressures of Oil - A Strategy for Economic Revival (with L Vallenilla, 1978), The Future of Oil (with K E Rosing, 1980, 2 edn 1983), The International Oil Industry (with J Rees, 1987), Global and Regional Energy Supplies (1991), Energy in Europe: Resources and Choices (1998), Fossil Fuel Resources in the 21st Century (1999), International Oil and Gas, Crises and Controversies 1961–2000 vol 1: Global Issues (2001) International Oil and Gas, Crises and Controversies 1961–2000 vol 2: Europe's Entanglement (2002), Why Carbon Fuels will Dominate the 21st Century's Energy Economy (2004); *Recreations* mountain walking, local history, performing and visual arts; *Clubs* Ipswich and Suffolk; *Style*— Prof Peter Odell; ✉ 7 Constitution Hill, Ipswich IP1 3RG (tel 01473 253376, fax 01473 259125)

ODGERS, Sir Graeme David William; kt (1997), DL (Kent 2002); s of William Arthur Odgers (d 1950), and Elizabeth Minty, *née* Rennie (d 1987); *b* 10 March 1934; *Educ* St John's Coll Johannesburg, Gonville & Caius Coll Cambridge, Harvard Business Sch (MBA); *m* 1957, Diana Patricia, *née* Berge; 1 s (John), 2 da (Mary, Juliet) and 1 da decd; *Career* dir Keith Shipton & Co Ltd 1965–72, chm Odgers & Co (mgmnt conslts) 1970–74, C T Bowring (Insurance) Holdings Ltd 1972–74, dir Industry Devpt Unit DOI 1974–77, assoc dir (fin) GEC 1977–78, gp md Tarmac plc 1983–86 (gp fin dir 1979–83); BT: pt/t memb Bd 1983–86, UK govt dir 1984–86, dep chm and chief fin offr 1986–87, gp md 1987–90; non-exec dir: Dalgety 1987–93, National and Provincial Building Society 1990–93, Scottish and Southern Electric plc 1998–2004; chief exec Alfred McAlpine plc 1990–93; chm: Monopolies and Mergers Cmmn 1993–97, Locate in Kent 1998–2006, Kent Economic Bd 2001–; Hon Dr: Univ of Greenwich 2004, Univ of Kent 2005; *Recreations* golf; *Clubs* Wilderness, Carlton; *Style*— Sir Graeme Odgers, DL; ✉ 5 The Coach House, Springwood Park, Tonbridge, Kent TN11 9LZ

ODLING-SMEE, John Charles; CMG (2005); s of Rev Charles William Odling-Smee (d 1990), and Katharine Hamilton, *née* Aitchison (d 1997); *b* 13 April 1943; *Educ* Durham Sch, St John's Coll Cambridge (MA); *m* 1996, Carmela Veneroso; *Career* res offr Inst of Economics and Statistics Univ of Oxford 1968–71 and 1972–73, fell in economics Oriel Coll Oxford 1966–70, economic res offr Govt of Ghana 1971–72, sr res offr Centre for Urban Economics LSE 1973–75, economic advsr Central Policy Review Staff 1975–77, sr economic advsr HM Treasy 1977–80, sr economist IMF 1981–82, dep chief economic advsr HM Treasy 1989–90 (under sec in economics 1982–89), dept dir IMF 1992–2003 (sr advsr 1990–91), ret 2004; author of articles in learned jls; *Books* British Economic Growth 1855–1973 (with R C O Matthews and C H Feinstein, 1982); *Style*— John Odling-Smee; ✉ 3506 Garfield Street NW, Washington DC 20007, USA (tel 00 1 202 338 3471)

ODONE, Cristina; da of Augusto Odone, of Washington DC, and Ulla Sjöström Odone; *b* 11 November 1960; *Educ* Nat Cathedral Sch Washington, St Clare's Hall Oxford, Worcester Coll Oxford (BA); *m* Edward Lucas; 1 da (Isabella b 6 Aug 2003); *Career* freelance journalist 1982–83 (articles published in Cosmopolitan, Harper's & Queen, TES, Daily Telegraph, Company, The Independent); journalist: The Catholic Herald 1983–85, The Times Diary 1986; conslt Odone Assocs Washington DC (lobbyists at World Bank on behalf of euro cos) 1987–92, ed The Catholic Herald 1992–96, TV critic The Daily Telegraph 1996–98, dep ed New Statesman 1998–; *Books* The Shrine (novel, 1996), A Perfect Wife (novel, 1997); *Recreations* reading, walking, travelling, entertaining; *Style*— Miss Cristina Odone

O'DONNELL, Sir Augustine Thomas (Gus); KCB (2005, CB 1994); s of James O'Donnell, and Helen, *née* McLean; *b* 1 October 1952; *Educ* Salesian Coll London, Univ of Warwick (BA), Nuffield Coll Oxford (MPhil, Soccer blue); *m* 1979, Melanie Joan Elizabeth, *née* Timmis; 1 da (Kirstin Elizabeth b 3 Nov 1990); *Career* lectr in political economy Univ of Glasgow 1975–79, economist HM Treasy 1979–85, first sec Br Embassy Washington DC 1985–88, sr econ advsr HM Treasy 1988–89, press sec to the Chllr 1989–90, press sec to the PM 1990–94, dep dir HM Treasy and UK rep EU Monetary Ctee 1994–97, min (econ) Br Embassy Washington and UK exec dir IMF and World Bank Gp 1997, dir of macroeconomic policy and prospect directorate/head UK Govt Economic Service 1997–2000, md macroeconomic policy and int fin HM Treasy 2000–02, Chllr's G7 dep 2000–02, perm sec HM Treasy 2002–05, sec to the Cabinet and head of the Home Civil Serv 2005–; *Recreations* golf, tennis, soccer, cricket, bridge, whitewater rafting; *Style*— Sir Gus O'Donnell, KCB

O'DONNELL, Sir Christopher; kt (2003); *Educ* Imperial Coll London (BSc(Eng)), London Business Sch (MBA); *m* Mia; 4 c; *Career* early career with Davy Ashmore, Vickers Medical and C R Bard Inc; Smith & Nephew plc: joined as md Medical Div 1988, memb Bd 1992–, dep chief exec 1996–97, chief exec 1997–; non-exec dir BOC Gp plc 2001–06; co-chair Healthcare Industries Task Force; MIMechE, CEng; *Style*— Sir Christopher O'Donnell; ✉ Smith & Nephew plc, 15 Adam Street, London WC2N 6LA

O'DONNELL, Hugh; s of John O'Donnell of Ireland, and Jean O'Donnell; *Educ* Camberwell Coll of Art, Falmouth Coll of Art (BA), Birmingham Coll of Art (HDip AD, prize Sir Whitworth Wallace Tst), RCA; *m* Tina Eden; 1 da (Kristie b 1983); *Career* artist; *Solo Exhibitions* incl: Works on Paper (Nishimura Gallery Tokyo) 1976, Air Gallery London 1977, Paintings and Drawings (Ikon Gallery Birmingham) 1979, Rahr-West Museum Wisconsin 1983, Marlborough Gallery (London 1985, NY 1986 and 1987), Works on Paper and Monoprints (Marlborough Gallery NY) 1984, Works on Paper (Marlborough Graphics London) 1984, Paintings (Marlborough Gallery NY) 1987, Paintings (Eva Cohen Gallery Chicago 1990, Hokin Gallery Palm Beach Florida 1989), Paintings and Works on Paper (Eva Cohen Gallery Chicago) 1990, Paintings (Marlborough Gallery NY) 1991, The Lake Series (Denise Cade Gallery NY 1992, Jan Abrams Gallery LA 1994, Freedman Gallery Pennsylvania 1995, Art Museum Univ of Memphis 1995), The Body Echo Project (Freedman Gallery Pennsylvania 1995, Art Museum Univ of Memphis 1995); *Group Exhibitions* incl: first exhibition 1972, Br Art Now (Guggenheim Museum NY) 1980, Decorative Arts Award 1988 (designs for jewels - collaboration with Ros Conway, Sotheby's London MOMA), Kyoto Japan, Arte & Alchimia (XLII Venice Biennale) 1986, The Question of Drawing (South Campus Gallery Miami, travelled) 1989, Works on Paper: Amenoff, Barth, O'Donnell (Tomoko Liguori Gallery NY) 1990, Marlborough en Pelaires (Centre Cultural Contemporani Pelaires Palma de Mallorca) 1990, Drawings Only (Denise Cade Gallery NY) 1992, Innovations in Collaborative Print Making: Kenneth Tyler 1963–92 (Yokohama Museum of Art and tour of Japan) 1992–93, Drawing in Black and White: Selections from the Permanent Collection (MOMA NY) 1993, First Thoughts: Working Drawings by Seven Artists (Bristol-Myers Squibb Co Princeton) 1993, Selection of Prints from Graphics Studio (Greenfield Gallery LA) 1993, Works on Paper (Margret Biederman Gallery Munich) 1994, The Computer in the Studio (DeCordova Museum and Sculpture Park Lincoln MA) 1994, Works Selected by Dore Ashton (Bill Maynes Gallery NY) 1994–95, An American Passion: The Kasen Summer Collection of Contemporary British Painting (McLellan Galleries Glasgow) 1994–95; selected public collections: Br Cncl UK, Solomon R Guggenheim Museum NY, London Contempory Arts Soc, Met MOMA NY, MOMA NY, V&A, Arts Cncl of GB, Virginia Museum of Fine Arts, Nat Gallery of Art Washington DC; Purchase award Arts Cncl of GB 1978 (Arts Cncl award 1978); set and costume designs for: Red Steps (London Contemporary Dance Theatre), Drawn Breath (Siobhan Davies Dance Company, 1989 Digit Dance award); numerous appearances on American television; *Style*— Hugh O'Donnell, Esq; ✉ 34 Shearer Road, Washington, CT 06793, USA (tel 00 1 203 860 868 9770, fax 00 1 203 860 868 9717)

O'DONNELL, James Anthony; s of Dr James Joseph Gerard O'Donnell (d 1978), and Dr Gillian Anne O'Donnell; *b* 15 August 1961; *Educ* Westcliff HS, Royal Coll of Music, Jesus Coll Cambridge (organ scholar, open scholar in music, MA); *Career* master of music Westminster Cathedral 1988–99 (asst master 1982–88); organist and master of the chorists Westminster Abbey 2000–; Royal Acad of Music: lectr in church music studies 1990–, prof of organ 1997–2004, visiting prof 2004–; RCO Performer of the Year 1987, Gramophone Record of the Year and Best Choral Record 1998, Royal Philharmonic Soc Award (with the choir of Westminster Cathedral) 1998; memb Cncl RCO 1989–2003; Hon RAM 2001, Hon FGCM 2001; FRCO 1983, FRSCM 2000; KCSG (Papal) 1999; *Recreations* opera, food and wine; *Clubs* Athenaeum; *Style*— James O'Donnell, Esq; ✉ The Chapter Office, Westminster Abbey, 20 Dean's Yard, London SW1P 3PA (tel 020 7654 4854, fax 020 7233 2072, e-mail music@westminster-abbey.org)

O'DONOGHUE, (James) Bernard; s of Bartholomew James O'Donoghue (d 1962), of Cullen, Co Cork, and Mary Josephine, *née* McNulty (d 1979); *b* 14 December 1945; *Educ* Coláiste Pádraig Millstreet Co Cork, St Bede's Coll Manchester, Lincoln Coll Oxford (BA, BPhil); *m* 23 July 1977, Heather O'Donoghue, Vigfusson-Rausing reader in old Icelandic Univ of Oxford and fell of Linacre Coll Oxford, da of Roderick MacKinnon, and Sheila MacKinnon; 2 da (Ellen Mary b 11 Sept 1978, Josephine Sheila b 26 Dec 1986), 1 s (Thomas Roderick b 4 Jan 1981); *Career* writer; trainee systems analyst IBM (UK) 1968–69; tutor in English language and Medieval literature Magdalen Coll Oxford 1971–95, fell in English Wadham Coll Oxford 1995–; memb AUT 1971–; fell English Assoc, FRSL 1999; *Books* The Courtly Love Tradition (1982), Seamus Heaney and the Language of Poetry (1994), Oxford Irish Quotations (ed, 1999), Sir Gawain and the Green Knight (trans, 2006); *Poetry* Razorblades and Pencils (1984), Poaching Rights (1987), The Absent Signifier (1990), The Weakness (1991, Southern Arts Award), Gunpowder (1995, Whitbread Poetry Prize), Here Nor There (1999), Outliving (2003); *Recreations* classical and Irish music, Manchester City FC; *Style*— Bernard O'Donoghue, Esq; ✉ 14 Hill Top Road, Oxford OX4 1PB (tel 01865 243662); Wadham College, Oxford OX1 3PN

O'DONOGHUE, Daniel; s of Daniel O'Donoghue (d 1994), of Knockroe, Castlerea, Roscommon, Eire, and Sabina, *née* Carey (d 1976); *b* 27 March 1947; *Educ* St Bede's Coll Manchester, Univ of Sheffield (BEng); *m* 1 April 1972, Suzanne Lynne Andromeda, da of Harold Hamer Holman; 3 s (Timothy Peter Joseph b 4 Dec 1977, James Edward Michael b 27 Aug 1980, Alexander Daniel Hogarth b 13 Sept 1982), 1 da (Johanna Morgan Driella b 12 Jan 1985); *Career* advtg exec; trainee GUS 1968–69; market res mangr Europe Rowntree 1973–76 (market res offr 1969–73), marketing offr Shepherd Building 1976–77, account planner Ogilvy Benson Mather 1977–79; planning dir: CDP/Aspect 1979–82, McCormicks 1982–87; Publicis (formerly McCormicks): planning dir 1987–88, vice-chm 1988–91, jt chief exec 1991–97, dep gp chm 1997–99, worldwide strategic planning dir 2000–, dir QMP Publicis Ireland; chm Andromeda Boru; memb: Educn Cncl D&AD; memb MRS 1973, FIPA (chm Bibliography Ctee 1989–90, memb Cncl 1989–93); *Recreations* fine art collecting, football; *Clubs* Soho House; *Style*— Daniel O'Donoghue, Esq; ✉ Hautbois Hall, Little Hautbois, Coltishall, Norwich, Norfolk NR12 7JR; Publicis Ltd, 82 Baker Street, London W1U 6AE (tel 020 7935 4426, fax 020 7935 7251, e-mail dan.o'donoghue@publicis.co.uk)

O'DONOGHUE, Denise; OBE (1999); da of late Micheal O'Donoghue, and late Maura O'Donoghue; *Educ* St Dominic's Girls' Sch, Univ of York (BA); *Career* with Coopers & Lybrand 1979–81, dir IPPA 1981–83, with Holmes Assocs 1983–86, md Hat Trick Productions Ltd 1986–, md Hat Trick Films Ltd 1995–; numerous awards incl: RTS, BAFTA, Press Guild, Emmy; CCMI (CIMgt 1998), FRTS 1998; *Style*— Ms Denise O'Donoghue, OBE; ✉ Hat Trick Productions, 10 Livonia Street, London W1F 8AF (tel 020 7434 2451)

O'DONOGHUE, Hugh Eugene (Hughie); s of Daniel O'Donoghue (d 1994), and Sabina Carey (d 1976); *b* 5 July 1953; *Educ* St Augustine's RC GS Manchester, Trinity and All Saints' Colls Leeds, Goldsmiths Coll London (MA, CertEd); *m* 18 May 1974, Clare, da of Thomas Patrick Reynolds (d 1987); 2 s (Matthew Thomas b 12 Nov 1974, Vincent John Domhnall b 26 July 1987), 1 da (Kathryn Sabina b 20 July 1985); *Career* artist; solo exhibitions incl: Air Gallery London 1984, Nat Gallery London 1985, Fabian Carlsson Gallery London 1986 and 1989, Galleria Carini Florence Italy 1987, Art Now Gallery Gothenburg Sweden 1987, Kilkenny Festival 1991, Gallery Helmut Pabst Frankfurt 1991, Thirteen Drawings from the Human Body (Jill George Gallery) 1993, A Painted Passion (Atlantis Upper Gallery London) 1993, Eigse Carlow 1995, Via Crucis (Haus der Kunst Munich) 1997, A Line of Retreat (Purdy Hicks Gallery London, Galerie Helmut Pabst Frankfurt) 1997, Carborundum Prints (Galerie Karl Pfeffere Munich, Cartwright Hall Bradford, Rubicon Gallery Dublin) 1997, Corp, Paintings and Drawings of the human

O

body 1984–1998 (Irish MOMA Dublin, Whitworth Art Gallery Manchester) 1998–99, Episodes from the Passion (RHA Gallagher Gallery Dublin) 1999, Niobes Children (Galerie Karl Pfefferle Munich) 1999, Musik alter Zeiten (Ancient Music) (Galerie Helmut Pabst Frankfurt) 2000, Naming the Fields (Rubicon Gallery Dublin) 2001, Navigation (Mayo General Hosp) 2001, Richer Dust: Carborundum Prints and related paintings and drawings 1995–2000 (Fitzwilliam Museum Cambridge, Djanogly Art Gallery Nottingham, Abbot Hall Gallery Kendal, Victoria Art Gallery Bath) 2001–2002, Ten Years: Panting Memory and the human form (Model Arts and Niland Gallery Sligo) 2002, Course of the Diver (Galerie Karl Pfefferle Munich, Purdy Hicks Gallery London) 2002, Richer Dust (Gas Hall Gallery Birmingham) 2003, Painting Caserta Red (Imperial War Museum London, Imperial War Museum Manchester) 2003; gp exhibitions incl: Whitechapel Open (Whitechapel Art Gallery London) 1982, 1983, 1986, 1988 and 1992, 10 Years at Air (Air Gallery London) 1984, Works on Paper (Anthony Reynolds Gallery London and Galleria Carini Florence Italy) 1986, New Year New Work (Fabian Carlsson Gallery London) 1987, Nuovi Territori dell Arte: Europa/America (Francavilla al Mare Abruzzo) 1987, The Romantic Tradition in Contemporary British Painting (Sala de Exposiciones Murcia, Circulo de Bellas Artes Madrid, Ikon Gallery Birmingham) 1988, Landscape and Beyond (Cleveland Gallery Middlesbrough) 1988, Ways of Telling (Oriel Mostyn Llandudno) 1989, Drawing '89 Cleveland 9th Int Drawing Biennale (prizewinner), School of London 1989, Works on Paper (Odette Gilbert Gallery London) 1989, Roads to Abstraction (Whitworth Art Gallery Manchester) 1990, The Forces of Nature - Landscape as Metaphor (Manchester City Art Galleries) 1990, Drawing Show 11 (Jill George Gallery London) 1990, Ten Artists in Residence (National Gallery London) 1991, The Figure Laid Bare (Pomeroy Purdy Gallery London) 1992, The Man, the Form and the Spirit (Connaught Brown London) 1992, Whitechapel Open Exhibition Part One (invited artist) (Whitechapel Art Gallery London) 1992, Six British Artists (De Serpentini Gallery Rome) 1992, The Figure Laid Bare (Pomeroy Purdy Galley London) 1992, Paint Marks (Kettles Yard Cambridge, and tour) 1994, Credo (Purdy Hicks Gallery London) 1994, Famine (Claremorris County Mayo) 1995, Andata e Ritorno: British Artists in Italy 1980–96 (Royal Albert Memorial Museum Exeter) 1996, Natural Forms (Reeds Wharf Gallery London) 1996, Last Dreams of the Millenium: The re-emergence of British Romantic Painting (Univ Art Gallery Calif State Univ Stanislaus, Main Art Gallery Calif State Univ Fullerton, Univ of Hawaii Manoa) 1997–98, When Time began to Rant and Rage: Figurative Painting from 20th Century Ireland (Walker Art Gallery Liverpool, Berkley Art Museum Univ of Calif, Grey Art Gallery NY, Univ of Michigan Museum of Art Ann Arbour) 1999, Graphic! British Prints Now (Yale Center for British Art New Haven) 1999, Geschichte und Erinnerung in der Kunst der Gegenwart (History and Memory in Contemporary Art) (Schirn Kunsthalle Frankfurt) 2000, Five Centuries of Genius: European Master Printmaking (Art Gallery of S Aust Adelaide) 2000, The Times of Our Lives: Endings (Whitworth Art Gallery Manchester) 2000, An Artists Century: Master Works and Self Portraits of 20th Century Irish Artists (RHA Gallagher Gallery Dublin) 2000, Drawing Parallels (Waterhall Gallery of Modern Art Birmingham) 2002–03, The Journey (Whitworth Art Gallery Manchester) 2002–03, Contemporary Prints (Ashmolean Museum Oxford) 2003; work in numerous public collections incl: Arts Cncl of GB, Arts Cncl of NSW Adelaide, Ashmolean Museum Oxford, Birmingham Museums and Art Gallerys, British Museum London, Cartwright Hall Bradford, Cleveland County Museums Middlesbrough, Djanogly Art Gallery Univ of Nottingham, Ferens Art Gallery Hull, The Fitzwilliam Museum Cambridge, Huddersfield Art Gallery, Hugh Lane Gallery Dublin, Hunterian Art Gallery Glasgow, Imperial War Museum London, Irish MOMA Dublin, Nat Gallery London, Trinity Coll Dublin, Univ of Birmingham, Univ Coll Cork, Univ of Michigan Museum of Art Ann Arbour, Victoria Art Gallery Bath, Whitworth Art Gallery Manchester, Yale Center for Br Art; *Awards* Artist's awards Lincolnshire and Humberside Arts Assoc 1977, 1978 and 1979, Artist in Industry fellowship Yorkshire Arts Assoc 1983, artist in residence Nat Gallery London (Nat Gallery and Arts Cncl of GB) 1984, artist in residence St John's Coll Oxford 2000; *Publications* incl: Hughie O'Donoghue Paintings and Drawings 1983–86 (1986), Hughie O'Donoghue Opera 1986–87 (1987), Crow Paintings Hughie O'Donoghue (1989), Fires (1989), Thirteen Drawings from the Human Body (1993), Via Crucis (1997), A Line of Retreat (1997), Hughie O'Donoghue a catalogue 1979–97 (1998), Episodes from the Passion (1998), Niobes Children (1998), Music alter Zeiten (2000), Smoke Signals (2000), Richer Dust: Carborundum Prints and Related Paintings and Drawings 1995–2000 (Craig Hartley, 2003), Hughie O'Donoghue: Painting, Memory, Myth (James Hamilton, 2003); *Style*— Hughie O'Donoghue, Esq; ✉ Kilfane Glebe, Thomastown, Co Kilkenny, Ireland; c/o Purdy Hicks Gallery, 65 Hopton Street, London SE1 9GZ (tel 020 7401 9229)

O'DONOGHUE, Gen Sir Kevin; KCB (2005), CBE (1996); s of Philip James O'Donoghue (d 1982), and Winifred, *née* Gibson (d 2002); *b* 9 December 1947; *Educ* Eastbourne Coll, UMIST (BSc), Higher Command and Staff Course (1990), NATO Defence Coll (1993); *m* 1973, Jean Monkman; 3 da (Karen Elizabeth b 1976, Joanne Louise b 1978, Sarah Jennifer b 1981); *Career* cmmd RE 1969, instr RMA Sandurst 1976, Staff Coll Canada 1978, MA to CGS 1980, OC 4 Field Sqn RE 1982, Directing Staff Staff Coll Camberley 1984, CO 25 Engr Regt 1986, Cmd Corps RE 1990, Cmd Engr ACE Rapid Reaction Corps 1992, Dir Staff Ops SHAPE 1993, Chief of Staff HQ QMG 1996–99, ACGS 1999–2001, UK Mil rep NATO and EU 2001–02, DCDS (Health) 2002–04, Chief of Defence Logistics 2005–07, Chief of Defence Materiel 2007–; Chief Royal Engr 2004–; Hon Col 75 Engr Regt (V) 2001–04, Col Royal Glos, Berks and Wilts Regt 2001–07, Col Comdt RE 2002–, Hon Col Cmdt Royal Logistics Corps 2007–; Hon Dr of Science Cranfield Univ 2007; *Recreations* military history, gardening; *Clubs* National Liberal, Army and Navy; *Style*— Gen Sir Kevin O'Donoghue, KCB, CBE; ✉ Defence Equipment and Support, Ministry of Defence, Zone G, Level 5, Main Building, Whitehall, London SW1A 2HB

O'DONOGHUE, Rt Rev Patrick; *see:* Lancaster, Bishop of (RC)

O'DONOGHUE, (Michael) Peter Desmond; s of Michael John O'Donoghue, of Sevenoaks, Kent, and Elizabeth Anne Hawkins, *née* Borley; *b* 5 October 1971, Sevenoaks, Kent; *Educ* Dulwich Coll, Gonville & Caius Coll Cambridge (MA); *m* 7 Sept 2002, Dr Catherine Ann Wolfe; 1 s (Thomas Michael Wolfe b 25 Nov 2004); *Career* ind genealogist, historian and researcher 1994–2003, research asst Coll of Arms 1994–2005, Bluemantle Pursuivant of Arms 2005–; jt ed The Coat of Arms (jl of Heraldry Soc); Freeman: City of London, Armourers' and Brasiers' Co; *Publications* The Electrical Contractors' Association 1901–2001 (2001); *Style*— Peter O'Donoghue, Esq, Bluemantle Pursuivant; ✉ College of Arms, Queen Victoria Street, London EC4V 4BT (tel 020 7332 0776, e-mail bluemantle@college-of-arms.gov.uk)

O'DONOGHUE, Rodney Charles (Rod); s of George Albert O'Donoghue (d 1988), and Doris Ada, *née* Matthews (d 2001); *b* 10 June 1938; *Educ* Merchant Taylors; *m* 17 Oct 1964, Kay Patricia, da of Clifford Montague Lewis; 2 s (Mark Christopher b 20 Feb 1970, Richard James b 24 Sept 1977), 1 da (Kerry Frances b 26 July 1974); *Career* articled clerk Singleton Fabian & Co CAs 1956–61, audit staff Monkhouse Stoneham & Co 1961–63, fin dir Kimberly-Clark Ltd 1965–72 (asst fin mangr 1963–65), gp controller Rank Xerox Group 1972–83, gp fin dir Pritchard Services Group 1983–86, exec dir Inchcape plc 1986–98 (gp fin dir 1986–97); historian, genealogist and writer 1998–; fndr Worldwide O'Donoghue Soc; FCA (ACA 1961); *Books* O'Donoghue - People and Places (1999); *Publications* contrib regular articles in O'Donoghue Soc jl; *Recreations* nature, golf, walking; *Style*— Rod O'Donoghue, Esq; ✉ 30 Canonbury Park South, London N1 2FN (e-mail rod@odonoghue.co.uk, website www.odonoghue.co.uk)

O'DONOVAN, Hugh; *b* 19 August 1952; *Educ* Univ of Oxford (BA); *Career* called to the Bar 1975; admitted slr 1988; barr in private practice 1975–85, barr Knapp-Fishers 1985–87, ptnr Richards Butler 1989–91 (barr 1987–88), ptnr Denton Wilde Sapte 1991–2004 (head of aviation regulatory and commercial law), barr Quadrant Chambers 2004–; *Publications* Halisbury's Laws of England (co-author of Aviation title, 2003); *Style*— Hugh O'Donovan, Esq; ✉ Quadrant Chambers, Quadrant House, 10 Fleet Street, London EC4Y 1AU (tel 020 7583 4444, fax 020 7583 4455, e-mail hugh.odonovan@quadrantchambers.com)

O'DONOVAN, Prof Katherine; da of Prof John O'Donovan, TD (d 1982), of Dublin, and Kathleen, *née* Mahon (d 1991); *b* 7 February 1942; *Educ* Nat Univ of Ireland (BCL), Univ of Strasbourg (Diplôme de Droit Comparé), Harvard Law Sch (LLM), Univ of Kent (PhD); *m* 5 June 1971, Julian Davey, s of F V Davey, of Fernhurst, W Sussex; 1 da (Julia b 4 Nov 1979); *Career* lectr in law: Queen's Univ Belfast 1965–69, Haile Sellassie I Univ Ethiopia 1969–72, Univ of Sussex 1972–73, Univ of Kent 1973–79, Univ of Malaya 1979–81, Univ of Kent 1981–85, Univ of Hong Kong 1985–88, Univ of Kent 1988–95; prof of law Queen Mary Univ of London (formerly Queen Mary & Westfield Coll) 1995–; visiting prof Univ of Paris, Jean Monnet fell Euro Univ Inst Florence 1991–92; ed Social and Legal Studies; memb: Cwlth Soc, Int Soc on Family Law, Cncl Soc of Public Teachers of Law, Nat Tst, RSPB; govr Canterbury Sch; *Books* Sexual Divisions in Law (1985), Equality and Sex Discrimination Law (1988), Family Law Matters (1993), Human Rights and Legal History (2000); *Clubs* Hong Kong, Cwlth Tst; *Style*— Prof Katherine O'Donovan; ✉ Faculty of Law, Queen Mary, University of London, Mile End Road, London E1 4NS (tel 020 7755 3276, e-mail k.odonovan@qmul.ac.uk)

O'DONOVAN, Rev Prof Oliver Michael Timothy; *b* 28 June 1945; *m* 1978, Joan Lockwood; 2 s (Matthew Augustine b 1981, Paul Jeremiah b 1986); *Career* ordained: deacon 1972, priest 1973; tutor Wycliffe Hall Oxford 1972–77, hon asst curate St Helen's Abingdon 1972–76, prof of systematic theology Wycliffe Coll Toronto Sch of Theology 1972–82 (asst 1977–81, assoc 1981–82), memb Church of England Bd for Social Responsibility 1976–77 and 1982–85, examining chaplain to Bishop of Toronto and memb Candidates Ctee of Diocese of Toronto 1978–82; Univ of Oxford: regius prof of moral and pastoral theology and canon of ChCh 1982–2006, dir of grad studies Faculty of Theology 1995–99, librarian ChCh 2002–06; prof of Christian ethics and practical theology Univ of Edinburgh 2006–; McCarthy visiting prof Gregorian Univ Rome 2001; pres Soc for Study of Christian Ethics 1997–2000; chm Bd Faculty of Theolgy Univ of Oxford 1990–92; memb: Canadian Anglican-Roman Catholic Dialogue 1979–82, Jt Orthodox-Anglican Doctrinal Discussions 1982–85, Archbishop of Canterbury's Gp on the Law of Affinity 1982–84, Working Pty on Human Fertilization and Embryology of the Church of England Bd for Social Responsibility 1982–85, Mgmnt Ctee Ian Ramsey Centre St Cross Coll Oxford 1983–89, Anglican Roman Catholic Int Cmmn 1985–90, Cncl Wycliffe Hall Oxford 1985–95, House of Bishops' Working Gp on Marriage in Church after Divorce 1996–98, Church of England Doctrine Cmmn 1996–97, Faith and Order Advsy Gp Archbishops' Cncl 2004–, Gen Synod C of E 2005–06; Chevasse lectr Wycliffe Hall Oxford 1985, Church of Ireland Theological lectr Queen's Univ Belfast 1986 and 2006, pastoral theology lectr Univ of Durham 1987, select preacher Univ of Oxford 1982, 1987, 1988 and 1993, Assize preacher Birmingham Cathedral 1988, Hulsean preacher Univ of Cambridge 1989; visiting lectr St Patrick's Coll Maynooth Ireland 1989, Payton lectr Fuller Theological Seminary Passadena Calif 1989, Paddock lectr Gen Theological Seminary NY 1990–, Hulsean lectr Univ of Cambridge 1994, Hooker lectr McMaster Univ Ontario 1996, Cheung Siu Kwai lectr St John's Coll Hong Kong 2002, Bampton lectr Univ of Oxford 2003; FBA 2000; *Books* The Problem of Self-Love in Saint Augustine (1980), Begotten or Made? (1984), Resurrection and Moral Order (1986), On the Thirty Nine Articles: a Conversation with Tudor Christianity (1986), Peace and Certainty; a theological essay on deterrence (1989), The Desire of the Nations: rediscovering the roots of political theology (1996), From Irenaens to Grotius (with Joan Lockwood O'Donovan, 1999), Common Objects of Love: moral reflection and the shaping of community (2002), The Just War Revisited (2003), Bonds of Imperfection: Christian politics past and present (jtly, 2004), The Ways of Judgment (2005); *Recreations* music, walking; *Style*— The Rev Prof Oliver O'Donovan; ✉ New College, Mound Place, Edinburgh EH1 2LX (tel 0131 650 8953)

O'DONOVAN, Timothy Charles Melville (Tim); s of John Conan Marshall Thornton O'Donovan (d 1964), of London, and Enid Muriel Liddell (d 1958); *b* 10 February 1932; *Educ* Marlborough; *m* 19 Sept 1958, Veronica Alacoque, da of Leslie White (d 1981), of Hawkley, Hants; 2 s (Michael b 1962, Richard b 1966); *Career* Nat Serv with Life Gds 1950–52; dir Common Cause Ltd 1964–95, chm Eckersley Hicks & Co Ltd Lloyd's Brokers 1979–84, dir of public affrs Bain Clarkson 1987–91; chm: A Princess for Wales Exhibition 1981, Pollution Abatement Technol Award Scheme 1983–87, Better Environment Awards for Industry 1987–92; hon sec Soc of the Friends of St George's and Descendants of the Knights of the Garter 1992–2002; vice-capt of lay stewards St George's Chapel Windsor Castle 1993– (steward 1978, dep vice-capt 1983–93); tstee The Environment Fndn 1985–, div pres Windsor Div St John's Ambulance 2001–; Berkshire rep NACF 2003–; memb The Queen's Birthday Ctee 1986; exhibitions organised: E-II-R - A Celebration 1986, Sixty Years a Queen (Windsor Castle) 1987, Ninety Memorable Years to Celebrate The Queen Mother's 90th birthday, The Queen is Crowned (Windsor Castle) 1993, Prince Philip His Life and Work (1996), The Queen at Windsor (2002); author of annual survey of Royal Family duties since 1979 in The Times and Illustrated London News; memb President's Club Thames Hospicecare Windsor; FRSA 1984; *Books* Above The Law?; *Recreations* watching cricket, photography, collecting royal memorabilia, reading the Court Circular; *Clubs* MCC; *Style*— Tim O'Donovan, Esq, FRSA; ✉ Mariners, 11 The Avenue, Datchet, Berkshire SL3 9DH

O'DOWD, Sir David Joseph; kt (1999), CBE (1995), QPM (1988), DL (Northants 2002); s of Michael Joseph O'Dowd (d 1972), of Oadby, Leics, and Helen, *née* Merrin; *b* 20 February 1942; *Educ* Gartree HS Oadby, Univ of Leicester (Dip Social Studies), Open Univ (BA), Aston Univ (MSc), FBI Nat Acad USA; *m* 7 Sept 1963, Carole Ann, da of Charles Albert Watson, of Leicester; 1 da (Sharon Marie b 3 Dec 1964), 1 s (Andrew David b 29 Jan 1967); *Career* Sgt, Inspr and Chief Inspr CID Leicester City Police 1961, Supt W Midlands Police Coventry and Birmingham 1977; head of traffic policing, dir of complaints and discipline Investigation Bureau and head of strategic planning and policy Analysis Unit Metropolitan Police New Scotland Yard 1984; Chief Constable Northants Police 1986–93 (Asst Chief Constable head of operations 1982), HM Inspr of Constabulary 1993–96, HM Chief Inspr of Constabulary 1996–2001, law enforcement conslt 2001–; dep chair British Transport Police Authy 2004–; Cabinet Office Top Mgmnt Prog 1986, rep Br Chief Constables Nat Exec Inst FBI Acad Washington 1988; visiting teaching fell Mgmnt Centre Aston Univ Birmingham, visiting prof Bristol Business Sch UWE; chair Victim Support Northants; Hon DSc Aston Univ; fell Univ of Northampton; High Sheriff Northants 2006–07; CCMI (CIMgt) 1988; OStJ 1988; *Recreations* golf, gardening, skiing; *Style*— Sir David J O'Dowd, CBE, QPM, DL

O'DRISCOLL, Michael; s of Michael James O'Driscoll, of Hemingbrough, N Yorks, and Esther O'Driscoll; *b* 6 August 1939; *Educ* Archbishop Holgate's GS York, Univ of Leeds (MB, ChB), Univ of Bristol (MCh); *m* 28 Nov 1966, Susan Leah, da of Sam Lewis (d 1982), of Leeds; 2 s (Daniel b 1 July 1968, Gavin b 9 Aug 1969), 1 da (Philippa b 11 May 1972); *Career* offr's trg corps parachute section Univ of Leeds 1957–62; lectr orthopaedics Univ of Bristol 1969–77, visiting orthopaedic surgn Hebden Green Special Sch Winsford, conslt orthopaedic surgn Robert Jones and Agnes Hunt Orthopaedic Hosp Shropshire and Leighton Hosp Cheshire until 1996, currently consIt orthopaedic surgn South Cheshire Private Hosp; memb: Fortress Study Gp, Back Pain Soc; patron Darren Kennerley Tst; FRCS 1967, memb SICOT 1983; *Recreations* fell walking, travelling, study of fortification, architecture, tanks and aircraft; *Clubs* Old Oswestrians; *Style—* Michael O'Driscoll

O'DRISCOLL, Suzanne Elizabeth; da of William George O'Driscoll, of Blackthorn, Oxon, and Cynthia Anne, *née* Wright; *b* 7 June 1955; *Educ* St Joseph's Convent Reading, Berkshire Coll of Art, Central Sch of Art and Design London (BA), Slade Sch of Fine Art UCL (MND, Boise travelling scholarship to Mexico and Guatemala); *Career* artist; work in various collections; artist in residence: Bracknell Sch Berkshire 1987, Rhos y Gwalian Wales 1987, Maidenhead Teachers Centre 1988; featured in Assessment and Evaluation in the Arts 1987; Edwin Austin Meml Rome scholarship 1993/94; *Solo Exhibitions* incl: Air Gallery 1984, South Hill Park Art Centre Bracknell 1987, Anderson O'Day Gallery London 1987 and 1989, Solomon Gallery Dublin 1992, CCA Galleries Oxford 1993, Rostra Gallery Bath 2000, Forest Art Centre New Milton 2002; *Group Exhibitions* incl: Three Decades of Artists from Inner London Art Schs 1953–83 (Royal Acad London) 1983, St John's Smith Square 1985, Space Artists (B P London) 1985, Air Gallery Picture Fair 1986, Anderson O'Day Gallery London 1986, Open Studio Show Berry St London 1987, Heads (Anderson O'Day Gallery London) 1987, Contemporary Arts Soc Market London annually 1987–, Oxford Gallery 1988, Drawing Show (Thumb Gallery London) 1988, Fish Exhibition (South Hill Park Bracknell) 1988, Int Contemporary Art Fair London 1989 and 1990, Bath Contemporary Arts Fair 1989 and 2000, Painting of the Week (Channel 4 TV) 1989, Works on Paper (Thumb Gallery London) 1990, Encounters (Oxford Gallery) 1991, Art for a Fairer World OXFAM touring 1992, Archer Exhbn London 1992, Subtitles Mostra (Br Sch at Rome) 1994, Cairn Gallery 1999, (Equinox) Nailsworth (CCA Galleries) 1999, Rostra Gallery Bath 1999, 2000 and 2001, New Landscapes (CCA Galleries) 2000, Taurus Gallery Oxford 2000 and 2001; *Commissions* for: Southampton Gen Hosp 1985, Harold Wood Gen Hosp1986, Radcliffe Infirmary Oxford 1986, RA Baileys Dublin 1994, UDV UK 2000, flowerbed design Abingdon (Year of the Artist) 2001, Accenture 2001, J Sainsbury plc 2001, Pernod Richard (Abelour Distillery), Chivas Bros London 2003 and 2004; *Style—* Ms Suzanne O'Driscoll; ✉ The Studio, Ash Barn House, Blackthorn, Bicester, Oxfordshire OX25 1TG (tel 01869 323992)

OERTON, Robert Edward; *b* 12 November 1964; *Educ* Royal Forest of Dean GS, Univ of Bath (BSc, Drake & Skull award), Univ of Canberra (MBA); *Career* grad project mgmnt trainee Taylor Woodrow Construction Ltd 1988–91, project engr AMEC Construction Pty Ltd Aust 1991–92, newspaper sales mangr Federal Capital Press of Aust 1992–98, ops dir The Good Book Guide Ltd 1998–99, ceo Murdoch Books UK Ltd 1999–; MIMgt; *Style—* Robert Oerton, Esq

OF MAR, *see:* Mar

O'FARRELL, Maggie; *b* 1972, NI; *Career* writer; previously worked as journalist; *Books* After You'd Gone (2000, Betty Trask Award), My Lover's Lover (2002), The Distance Between Us (2004, Somerset Maugham Award), The Vanishing Act of Esme Lennox (2006); ✉ c/o A M Heath & Co Limited, 6 Warwick Court, London WC1R 5DJ

O'FERRALL, Rev Patrick Charles Kenneth; OBE (1989); s of Rev Kenneth John Spence O'Ferrall (d 1977), and Isoult May, *née* Bennett (d 1977); *b* 27 May 1934; *Educ* Winchester, New Coll Oxford (MA); *m* 1, Mary Dorothea (d 1997), da of Maj Cyril Edward Lugard (d 1970), and Katharine Isabel Beatrice, *née* Carroll (d 1981); 2 da (Nicola Maeve (Mrs Slynn) b 7 Dec 1961, Katharine Susannah (Mrs Bach) b 16 Oct 1965), 1 s (Mark Edward Cormac b 29 Feb 1964); m 2, 1999, Mrs Wendy Elizabeth Barnett, eld da of Peter Gilmore (d 2002); *Career* Nat Serv 2 Lt Royal Fusiliers 1952–54; various positions Iraq Petroleum Group (incl in Abu Dhabi, Qatar, Oman and Beirut) 1958–70, BP area co-ordinator for Abu Dhabi Marine Areas Ltd and BP Eastern Agencies 1971–73, Total CFP 1974–77; Total Oil Marine plc: joined as commercial mangr 1970, dir Gas Gathering Pipeline (North Sea) Ltd 1977–78, dir TOMEC (responsible for co-ordination of Alwyn North project) 1983, projects co-ordination mangr 1985–90; chm Lloyd's Register of Shipping 1993–99 (dep chm 1991); memb Offshore Industry Advsy Bd 1991–94; lay reader C of E 1961–2000; ordained: deacon 2000, priest 2001; curate Sts Peter and Paul Godalming 2000–07, hon asst priest 2007–; chm City Branch Outward Bound Assoc 1993–96, pres Godalming and Dist C of C 2003–04; pres Aldgate Ward Club 1998 (jr vice-pres 1996), hon chaplain The Baltic Exchange and Aldgate Ward Club 2001–; elected memb Ct of Common Cncl Corp of London 1996–2001; Master Worshipful Co of Coachmakers and Coach Harness Makers 1993–94, Liveryman Worshipful Co of Shipwrights 1992, Hon Liveryman Worshipful Co of Master Mariners 1993–99; FRSA 1993, CIMgt 1994, Hon FREng 2000; *Recreations* tennis, golf, crosswords, violin playing and singing, walking, wine; *Clubs* MCC, RSA; *Style—* The Rev Patrick O'Ferrall, OBE; ✉ Catteshall Grange, Catteshall Road, Godalming, Surrey GU7 1LZ (tel 01483 410134, fax 01483 414161, e-mail patrick@oferrall.co.uk)

OFFEN, Nigel; *Educ* St Bartholomew's Hosp London; *Career* post-graduate trg in hosps in and around London incl Royal London Hosp, consIt gen surgn Whipps Cross Hosp 1976–90 (pt/t unit gen mangr 1988–90), subsequent appt as regional lead in clinical audit and quality improvement NE Thames RHA, chief exec Essex Rivers Healthcare NHS Tst 1993–99, head of clinical quality Eastern Regnl Office of NHS Exec 1999–; chm Br Assoc of Med Mangrs, formerly memb Clinical Outcomes Gp; *Style—* Nigel Offen, Esq; ✉ 83 Drury Road, Colchester CO2 7UU

OFFER, Prof Avner; *Educ* Hebrew Univ of Jerusalem (BA), St Antony's Coll Oxford, Univ of Oxford (DPhil); *Career* jr research fell Merton Coll Oxford 1976–78; Univ of York: lectr in economic and social history 1979–90, reader in economic and social history 1990–91; sr fell Center for Historical Analysis Rutgers Univ USA 1991, professorial fell and reader in recent social and economic history Nuffield Coll Oxford 1992–2000, fell All Souls Coll Oxford 2000–, Chichele prof of economic history Univ of Oxford 2000–; Hartley research fell Univ of Southampton 1981–82, visiting assoc Clare Hall Cambridge 1984, research fell Inst of Advanced Studies ANU 1985–88, sr visiting fell Remarque Inst NYU 1999; memb: Advsy Bd History of the London Co Cncl 1983–85, Editorial Bd Rural History 1989–94, Editorial Bd Jl of Mktg History; author of numerous articles in learned jls incl: The Public Historian, Modern Law Review, Economic History Review, Historical Jl, Past and Present, Jl of Contemporary History; numerous invited talks and lectures internationally; memb: ESRC Bd for Post-Grad Trg in Economics and Social History (also research training referee), ESRC Sociology History, Anthropology and Geography Research Coll, Economics and Economics History Section Ctee Br Acad, Comité Scientifique Centre de Recherch Historial de la Grande Guerre (France), Ctee Social History Soc 1992–99, Cncl and Exec Ctee Economic History Soc 2001–; govr History of Advtg Tst 1996–98; FBA 2000, AcSS 2003; *Books* incl: Property and Politics 1870–1914: Landownership, Law, Ideology and Urban Development in England (1981), The First World War: An Agrarian Interpretation (1989, Trevor Reese Meml Prize for Imperial and Cwlth History 1992), In Pursuit of the Quality of Life (ed, 1996), Why is the Public Sector so Large in Market Societies? The Political Economy of Prudence in the UK, c1879–2000 (2003), The Challenge of Affluence: Self-control and Well-being in the United States and Britain since 1950 (2006); *Style—* Prof Avner Offer; ✉ All Souls College, Oxford OX1 4AL (tel 01865 279379, fax 01865 279299, e-mail avner.offer@all-souls.ox.ac.uk)

OFFER, Ven Clifford Jocelyn; s of Rev Canon Clifford Jesse Offer (d 1964), of Ightham, Kent, and Jocelyn Mary, *née* Kerr; *b* 10 August 1943; *Educ* King's Sch Canterbury, St Peter's Coll Oxford (sent down), Univ of Exeter (BA), Westcott House Theol Coll; *m* 1980, Dr Catherine Mary Lloyd, da of Dr George Marner Lloyd; 2 da (Isabel Mary b 28 Sept 1981, Rebecca Catherine b 11 Oct 1985); *Career* curate of Bromley Parish Church 1969–74, team vicar Parish of Southampton (City Centre) 1974–83, team rector of Hitchin 1983–93, archdeacon of Norwich and canon librarian of Norwich Cathedral 1994–, dir Norwich Diocesan Bd of Fin 1996–; chm: Norwich Advsy Bd of Mission and Miny 1994–98 and 2000–03, Norwich Course Mgmnt Ctee 1998–2003, Norwich Bd of Miny 2003–; memb: Gen Synod C of E 1998–2005, Ctee Centre for East Anglian Studies 1999–; Bishop's Selector, Warden of Readers; Assoc Community of St Egidio; FRSA; *Books* King Offa in Hitchin (1992), In Search of Clofesho (2002); *Recreations* model making, tennis, medieval and saxon history, collecting Merchant Navy Livery Co buttons; *Clubs* Norfolk; *Style—* The Ven the Archdeacon of Norwich; ✉ 26 The Close, Norwich, Norfolk NR1 4DZ (tel 01603 620375)

OFFORD, Prof Robin Ewart; s of Frank Etchelles Offord (d 1994), and Eileen Elisabeth, *née* Plunkett, of Brent, Essex; *b* 28 June 1940; *Educ* Owen's Sch, Peterhouse Cambridge (MA, PhD); *m* 3 July 1963, Valerie Edna, da of Ronald Wheatley (d 1971); 1 s (Alan b 1964), 2 da (Jane b 1967, Alice b 1973); *Career* fell UC Oxford 1968–73 (univ lectr in molecular biophysics 1972–80), fell and tutor in biochemistry ChCh Oxford 1973–80; Université de Genève: prof and dir Département de Biochimie Médicale 1980–2004, dir Département de Biologie Structurale et Bioinformatique 2004–05, emeritus prof 2005–; pres Sch of Basic Med Geneva 1994–2001 (vice-pres 1992–94), jt fndr Swiss Inst Bioinformatics; dir Geneva Bioinformatics SA 1998–2000, jt fndr, pres and exec vice-chm GeneProt Inc 2000–01, founding pres and exec dir Mintaka Fndn for Medical Research 2005–; chm: Dutch Govt Panel on Proteomics 2002, Int Scientific Cncl Netherlands Proteomics Centre 2003–, Advsy Bd of Geneva Biosciences Incubator 2003–; ed Biochemical Journal 1972–79; memb: local ctees of Christian Aid 1970–80, editorial bds of various scientific jls 1972–, various ctees and bds of the UK MRC and UK Miny of Health 1976–80, Comité Scientifique de la Fondation Jeantet de Médecine 1985–88; jt sci fndr: Gryphon Sciences Corporation S San Francisco 1994, Ciphergen Inc; sec American Peptide Soc 2003– (memb Cncl 1999–); shared L'agefi (fin jl) Man of the Year Switzerland award 2002, Makineni Prize Lectr American Peptide Soc 2005; *Books* A Guidebook to Biochemistry (with M D Yudkin, 1971, various new edns and foreign translations 1972–), Comprehensible Biochemistry (with M D Yudkin, 1973), Biochemistry (1975, Spanish translation 1976), Semisynthetic Peptides and Proteins (with C di Bello, 1977), Simple Macromolecules (1979), Macromolecular Complexes (1979), Semisynthetic Proteins (1980); *Recreations* comparative linguistics, scuba diving (PADI master scuba diver trainer), windsurfing, cross-country skiing; *Style—* Prof Robin Offord; ✉ Département de Biochimie Médicale, Centre Médical Universitaire, 1211 Genève 4, Suisse (tel 00 41 223 79 54 70, fax 00 41 22 346 87 58, e-mail robin.offord@medicine.unige.ch)

OFILI, Christopher (Chris); *b* 1968; *Educ* Thameside Coll of Technol (Fndn Course), Chelsea Sch of Art (BA), Hochschule der Kunst Berlin, RCA (MA); *Career* artist; tstee Tate Gallery 2003–05; hon fell Univ of the Arts London 2004; *Solo Exhibitions* Paintings and Drawings (Kepler Gallery London) 1991, Gavin Brown's Enterprise NY 1995, Afrodizzia (Victoria Miro Gallery London) 1996, Pimpin ain't easy but it sure is fun (Contemporary Fine Art Berlin) 1997, Southampton City Art Gallery 1998, Serpentine Gallery London 1998, Whitworth Art Gallery Manchester 1998–99, Afrobiotics (Gavin Brown's Enterprise NY) 1999, Chris Ofili Drawings (Victoria Miro Gallery London) 2000, Watercolours (Gallery Side 2 Tokyo) 2001, Freedom One Day (Victoria Miro Gallery London) 2002, Within Reach (50th Venice Biennale) 2003, Afro Muses (The Studio Museum Harlem NY) 2005, The Blue Rider (Contemporary Fine Arts Berlin) 2005, The Upper Room (Tate Britain London) 2005–07, The Blue Rider Extended Remix (kestnergesellschaft Hanover) 2006; *Group Exhibitions* incl: BP Portrait Award (National Portrait Gallery) 1990 and 1991, BT New Contemporaries (Cornherhouse Gallery Manchester and tour) 1993–94, About Vision: New British Painting in the 1990s (cmmnd by Absolut Vodka, MOMA Oxford and tour) 1995–96, Belladonna (ICA London) 1997, Pictura Britannica (Museum of Contemporary Art Sydney and tour) 1997–, Sensation: Young British Artists from the Saatchi Collection (Royal Acad London and tour) 1997–98, 20th John Moores Liverpool Exhibition of Contemporary Painting (Walker Art Gallery Liverpool) 1997, Carnegie International (Carnegie Museum of Art Pittsburgh) 1999–2000, 6th International Istanbul Biennial 1997, Trouble Spot Painting (Museum voor Hedendaagse Kunst Antwerp) 1999, Dimensions Variable (Br Cncl touring exhibition incl Helsinki City Art Museum, Stockholm Royal Acad of Free Arts and Prague Nat Gallery of Modern Art) 1997–2000, The Jerwood Fndn Painting Prize (Jerwood Gallery London) 1998, The Turner Prize (Tate Gallery London) 1998, Sydney Biennale 2000, Painting at the Edge of the World (Walker Arts Center Minneapolis) 2001–, Form Follows Fiction (Castello di Rivoli Turin) 2001–, Public Offerings (Museum of Contemporary Art LA) 2001–02, One Planet under a groove: Hip Hop and Contemporary Art (Bronx Museum of the Arts NY touring to Walker Arts Center Minneapolis and Spelman Museum of Fine Art Atlanta) 2001–02, Cavepainting (Santa Monica Museum of Art) 2002, drawing now: eight propositions (MOMA QNS NY) 2002–03, Paradise (National Gallery, Laing Art Gallery Newcastle upon Tyne and City Museum and Art Gallery Bristol) 2003, Fabulism (Joslyn Art Museum Omaha) 2004, Monument to Now (The Dakis Joannou Collection DESTE Fndn for Contemporary Art Athens) 2004, Artists & Prints (MOMA NY) 2005, Getting Emotional ICA Boston 2005, Translation (Palais de Tokyo Paris) 2005; *Awards* Christopher Head drawing scholarship 1989, Erasmus exchange to Berlin 1992, Br Cncl travel scholarship Zimbabwe 1992, second prizewinner Tokyo Print Biennale 1993, Wingate Young Artist Award 1996, Turner Prize 1998, South Bank Show Award - Visual Arts 2004; *Style—* Chris Ofili, Esq

O'FLYNN, Patrick James; s of Patrick J J O'Flynn, and Mary, *née* Stebbing; *b* 29 August 1965; *Educ* Parkside Community Coll Cambridge, Long Rd Sixth Form Coll Cambridge, King's Coll Cambridge (BA), City Univ (Dip Journalism); *m* 1997, Carole Ann, da of John Radbone; 1 da (Phoebe b 20 May 1997), 1 s (Raphael b 11 March 1999); *Career* journalist; reporter: Hull Daily Mail 1989–92, Birmingham Post 1992–93; political corr Birmingham Post 1993–96, dep political ed Sunday Express 1996–97, political ed Daily Express 2000– (chief political corr 1998–2000); Yorkshire Journalist of the Year 1991–92; *Style—* Patrick O'Flynn, Esq; ✉ Room 11, Press Gallery, House of Commons, London SW1A 0AA (tel 020 7219 6764, e-mail patrick.o'flynn@express.co.uk)

OGBORN, Anthony Douglas Ronald (Tony); s of late Dr Ronald Sherrington Ogborn, of Sutton Coldfield, and Margery Mary, *née* Norris; *b* 22 December 1938; *Educ* King Edward's Sch Birmingham, UC Oxford (MA, BM BCh); *m* 5 Aug 1967, Monica, da of late Oswald Faithfull Shipton; 1 s (Ian b 1969); *Career* sr registrar in obstetrics and gynaecology Northampton and Hammersmith Hosps 1973–77; Bedford Hosp: consIt obstetrician and gynaecologist 1977–2003, now hon consIt, chm Project Team for new Maternity Unit opened by HM The Queen Nov 1997; visiting gynaecologist Maadi Mil Hosp Cairo 1992–2006; treas NW Thames Regnl Ctee Hosp Med Servs 1980–86; memb: N Beds HA 1982–86, NW Thames Region Perinatal Working Pty 1982–89, N Beds Dist Advsy Bd 1988–90; FRCOG 1982 (MRCOG 1969); *Recreations* Egyptology, gardening, photography, Heron dinghy sailing (Nat Champion 2000); *Clubs* Priory Sailing (Bedford); *Style—* Tony Ogborn, Esq; ✉ 10A Rotten Row, Riseley, Bedfordshire MK44 1EJ (tel 01234 708010)

OGDEN, Sir Peter James; kt (2005); s of James Platt Ogden (d 1994), and Frances Ogden; *b* 26 May 1947; *Educ* Rochdale GS, Univ of Durham (BSc, PhD), Harvard Business Sch (MBA); *m* 22 Aug 1970, Catherine Rose, da of Harold Blincoe; 1 da (Tiffany b 1 Oct 1975), 2 s (Cameron b 9 Oct 1977, Edward b 18 Aug 1981); *Career* exec dir Merrill Lynch International Bank Ltd 1976–81; md: Merrill Lynch White Weld Capital Markets Group 1976–81, Morgan Stanley & Co 1981–87 (advsy dir 1987–95); chm: Computacenter Ltd 1981–98 (non-exec dir 1998–), Dealogic Ltd 1988–, Omnia Ltd 1996–2003; non-exec dir: Abbey National plc 1996–2004, Psion Ltd 1999–2005; visiting prof Dept of Physics Univ of Durham 2003; fndr, chm and tstee The Ogden Trust 1999– (projects funded incl The Ogden Centre for Fundamental Physics at Durham University); memb Durham Univ Devpt Cncl, govr Westminster Sch 2003–; hon fell Hughes Hall Cambridge 1999; Hon MA Univ of Cambridge 2001, Hon DCL Univ of Durham 2002; Hon FInstP 2000, Hon CPhys 2000; *Style*— Sir Peter Ogden

OGILVIE, Dame Bridget Margaret; AC (2007), DBE (1996); da of late John Mylne Ogilvie, and Margaret Beryl, *née* McRae; *b* 24 March 1938; *Educ* New England Girls' Sch, Univ of New England (BRurSc), Univ of Cambridge (PhD, ScD); *Career* worked in Parasitology Div Nat Inst for Med Research 1963–81, Ian McMaster fell Animal Health Div CSIRO 1971–72; Wellcome Trust: co-ordinator Tropical Med Prog 1979–81, dep sec and asst dir 1981–84, dep dir Science 1984–89, dir Science Progs 1989–91, the dir 1991–98; visiting prof Dept of Biology Imperial Coll London 1985–92, visiting prof UCL 1998–; chm: AstraZeneca Science Teaching Tst 1998–2006, Assoc of Med Research Charities 2002–07, Governing Body Lister Inst 2002–; vice-chm Sense about Science 2003–, memb UK Cncl for Science and Technol 1993–2000, memb Advsy Ctee for Science, Technol and Business The British Library 1999–2002; tstee: Science Museum 1992–2003, Nat Endowment for Science, Technology and the Arts (NESTA) 1998–2002, Scottish Science Tst 1998–2002, Cancer Research UK (formerly Cancer Research Campaign) 2001–; chm Ctee of the Public Understanding of Science 1998–2002, chm Governing Body Inst of Animal Health 1998–2003, chm Medicines for Malaria Venture (MMV) 1999–2006; contrib to numerous scientific papers and jls; non-exec dir: Lloyds TSB Group plc 1995–2000, Zeneca Group plc 1997–99, Astra Zeneca 1999–2006, Manchester Technol Fund 1999–2004; High Steward Univ of Cambridge 2000–; Distinguished Alumni Award Univ of New England 1994, Lloyd of Kilgerran Prize 1994, Australian Soc of Med Research Medal 2000, Kilby Award 2003, Duncan Davies Meml Medal 2004, Ralph Doherty Meml Medal Qld Inst of Med Res 2006; Hon DSc: Univ of Nottingham 1994, Univ of Salford 1994, Univ of Westminster 1994, Univ of Glasgow 1995, Univ of Bristol 1995, Aust Nat Univ 1995, Univ of Buckingham 1996, Nat Univ of Ireland 1996, Oxford Brookes Univ 1996, Nottingham Trent Univ 1996, Univ of Greenwich 1997, Univ of Auckland 1998, Univ of Durham 1998, Univ of Kent 1998, Imperial Coll of Science, Technol and Med London 1999, Univ of Exeter 1999, Univ of Leicester 2000, Univ of Manchester 2001, Univ of St Andrews 2001, Univ of Wollongong 2005; Hon MD Univ of Newcastle upon Tyne 1996, Hon LLD Univ of Dublin 1996, Hon LLD Univ of Leicester 2000, Hon Dr Univ of Edinburgh 1997; hon fell: UCL 1993, Girton Coll Cambridge 1993, St Edmund's Coll Cambridge 1999; hon memb: Br Soc for Parasitology 1990, American Soc of Parasitologists 1992, Br Veterinary Assoc; hon assoc RCVS 1993; fndn hon fell RVC 1994, Hon FRCP 1996 (Hon MRCP 1992), Hon FIBiol 1998, Hon FRSM 1999; FIBiol 1985, FRCPath 1992, FMedSci 1998, FRS 2003, hon fell BAAS 2006 (hon memb 2005); *Style*— Dame Bridget Ogilvie, AC, DBE; ✉ University College London, Medical School Administration, Gower Street, London WC1E 6BT (tel 020 7679 4602)

OGILVIE-LAING OF KINKELL, Gerald; *b* 11 February 1936; *Educ* Berkhamsted Sch, RMA Sandhurst, St Martin's Sch of Art (NDD); *m* 1, 1962 (m dis 1967), Jennifer Anne Redway; 1 da (Yseult (Mrs Hughes) b 8 April 1962); m 2, 1969 (m dis 1985), Galina Vasilievna Golikova; 2 s (Farquhar Piotr b 12 March 1970, Alexander Gerald Vassily b 2 Feb 1972); m 3, 1988, Adaline Havemeyer, *née* Frelinghuysen; 2 s (Titus Christian Havemeyer Oberon b 21 June 1991, Clovis Quintus Frelinghuysen Endymion b 1993); *Career* sculptor and artist; cmmnd 5 Fus (Royal Northumberland Fus) 1955–60; artist in residence Aspen Inst for Humanistic Studies CO 1966; visiting prof: Univ of New Mexico 1976–77, Columbia Univ NY 1986–87; work in collections of: National Gallery, Tate Gallery, V&A, Nat Portrait Gall, Whitney Museum, MOMA NY, Smithsonian Washington DC; maj cmmns incl: Callanish Univ of Strathclyde, Wise and Foolish Virgins Edinburgh, Fountain of Sabrina Bristol, Conan Doyle Meml Edinburgh, Axis Mundi Edinburgh, Bank Station London (dragons), Twickenham Rugby Stadium (four sculptures), portrait bust of Sir Paul Getty Nat Gall London, Von Clemm Memorial Canary Wharf, Glass Virgins Edinburgh, Batsman Lord's Cricket Ground London, Fallon Sq Mercat Cross Inverness; Civic Tst Award 1971; memb: Ctee Scot Arts Cncl 1978–80, Royal Fine Art Cmmn for Scot 1987–95; FRBS; *Books* Kinkell: The Reconstruction of a Scottish Castle (1974, 2 edn 1984); *Clubs* Chelsea Arts, Academy; *Style*— Gerald Ogilvie-Laing of Kinkell; ✉ Kinkell Castle, Ross-shire IV7 8AT (tel 01349 861485, e-mail kinkell@btinternet.com, website www.geraldlaing.com)

OGILVY, Sir Francis Gilbert Arthur; 14 Bt (NS 1626), of Inverquharity, Forfarshire; o s of Sir David John Wilfrid Ogilvy, 13 Bt (d 1992), and Penelope Mary Ursula, *née* Hills; *b* 22 April 1969; *Educ* Edinburgh Acad, Glenalmond, RAC Cirencester, Univ of Reading (BSc); *m* 12 Oct 1996, Dorothy Margaret, eldest da of Rev Jock Stein, and Rev Margaret Stein, of Kincardine, by Alloa; 3 s (Robert David b 8 July 1999, Calum John b 24 Sept 2001, Hamish Walter b 9 Aug 2003), 1 da (Elspeth Katherine b 16 Oct 2005); *Heir* s, Robert Ogilvy; *Career* chartered surveyor; MRICS; *Style*— Sir Francis Ogilvy, Bt; ✉ Winton House, Pencaitland, East Lothian EH34 5AT (tel 01875 340222, e-mail f.ogilvy@wintonhouse.co.uk)

OGILVY, Hon James Donald Diarmid; s of 12 Earl of Airlie, KT, GCVO, MC, and Lady Alexandra Coke, da of 3 Earl of Leicester; *b* 28 June 1934; *Educ* Eton; *m* 1, 1959, (Magda) June, da of Robert Ducas, of New York; 2 da (Laura Jane b 1960, Emma Louise b 1962), 2 s (Shamus Diarmid Ducas b 1966, Diarmid James Ducas b 1970); m 2, 1980, Lady Caroline, *née* Child-Villiers, da of 9 Earl of Jersey and former w of Viscount Melgund, MBE (now 6 Earl of Minto), and Hon John Stuart (s of 1 Viscount Stuart of Findhorn); *Career* Lt Scots Gds 1952–54; page of honour to HM King George VI 1947–51; ptnr Rowe & Pitman 1962–86, chm Rowan Investment Managers 1972–86, chm Mercury Rowan Mullens 1986–88, vice-chm Mercury Asset Management plc 1986–88, chief exec Foreign & Colonial Management Ltd 1988–97 (chm 1997–98); non-exec chm Sutherlands Holdings Ltd 1998–2000; chm: Museum of Garden History (tstee) 2000–, webweekends.co.uk 2000–; dir: Foreign & Colonial Investment Trust 1990–98, Foreign & Colonial Emerging Markets Investment Trust plc 1996–2000, Berkshire Capital Corp 1999–; govr Queen Charlotte's and Chelsea Hosps 1966–76, chm Inst of Obstetrics and Gynaecology 1983–86; memb Queen's Body Guard for Scotland (Royal Co of Archers); *Clubs* White's, Pratt's; *Style*— The Hon James Ogilvy; ✉ Sedgebrook Manor, Sedgebrook, Grantham, Lincolnshire NG32 2EU (tel 01949 842337); 20 Stack House, Cundy Street, London SW1W 9JS (tel 020 7881 0925)

OGILVY-WEDDERBURN, Sir Andrew John Alexander; 7 Bt (UK 1803), of Balindean, Perthshire; descended from Sir Alexander Wedderburn, 4 Bt (S 1704), of Blackness, who served as a volunteer in Lord Ogilvy's Regiment at the Battle of Culloden (1746) where he was taken prisoner and executed, and his estate forfeited. His descendants continued to assume the title until Sir David (7 Bt, but for the attainder) was cr Bt in the present UK creation, with special remainder to the heirs male of the 4 Bt of the original creation; s of Cdr Sir (John) Peter Ogilvy-Wedderburn, 6 Bt (d 1977), and Elizabeth Katharine, *née* Cox; *b* 4 August 1952; *Educ* Gordonstoun; *m* 1984, Gillian Meade, da of Richard Boyle Adderley, MBE, of Pickering, N Yorks; 1 da (Katherine b 1985), 3 s (Peter Robert Alexander, Geordie Richard Andrew (twins) b 1987, Sam b 1990 d 1992); *Heir* s, Peter Ogilvy-Wedderburn; *Career* Army Offr; CO 1 Black Watch 1994–96, Queen's Commendation for Valuable Serv 1996, ret 2004; dir Army Benevolent Fund Scotland; *Recreations* bobsleighing (memb British Bobsleigh Team 1974–80, British Olympic Bobsleigh Team Innsbruck 1976 and Lake Placid 1980, British 2 man bobsleigh champion 1976–77 and 1978–79), skiing, shooting; *Clubs* New; *Style*— Sir Andrew Ogilvy-Wedderburn, Bt; ✉ Silvie, Alyth, Blairgowrie, Perthshire PH11 8NA (tel 01828 633522)

OGLESBY, Michael John; s of George Oglesby, and Alice, *née* Godfrey; *b* 5 June 1939, Scunthorpe, Lincs; *Educ* De Aston Sch Market Rasen, Aston Univ (BSc), Univ of Manchester (LLD); *m* 15 Aug 1964, Jean Davies, *née* McLauchlan; 1 s (Christopher George b 9 Sept 1967), 1 da (Katherine Jane b 4 March 1969); *Career* dir Lyon Gp 1971–73, ceo Bruntwood Estates Ltd 1977–98, chm Bruntwood Ltd 1998–; chm: Bd of Govrs RNCM, Manchester Cancer Res Centre, MIDAS; High Sheriff Gtr Manchester 2007–08; *Recreations* theatre, classical music, sailing, skiing, hill walking; *Style*— Michael Oglesby, Esq; ✉ Bruntwood Limited, City Tower, Piccadilly Plaza, Manchester M1 4BD (tel 0161 238 7134, fax 0161 237 1799, e-mail michael.oglesby@bruntwood.co.uk)

OGNALL, Hon Sir Harry; kt (1986), DL (W Yorks 2000); s of late Leo Ognall, and Cecilia Ognall; *b* 9 January 1934; *Educ* Leeds GS, Lincoln Coll Oxford (MA), Univ of Virginia (LLM); *m* 1; 2 s, 1 da; m 2, 1977, Elizabeth Young; 2 step s; *Career* called to the Bar Gray's Inn 1958 (bencher 1983); joined NE Circuit, recorder of the Crown Court 1972–86, QC 1973, judge of the High Court of Justice (Queen's Bench Div) 1986–2000, memb Criminal Injuries Compensation Bd 1976, arbitrator Motor Insurers' Bureau Agreement 1979–85, memb Senate of Inns of Ct 1980–83 (memb Planning Ctee and Professional Conduct Ctee), chm Criminal Ctee Judicial Studies Bd 1986–89, memb Parole Bd England & Wales 1989–91 (vice-chm 1990–91), judicial memb Proscribed Orgns Appeal Cmmn 2001–; chm EWitness Ltd 2000–05; tstee Martin House Children's Hospice; *Recreations* photography, golf, music, grandchildren; *Clubs* Ilkley Golf, Ganton Golf, Ilkley Bowling; *Style*— The Hon Sir Harry Ognall, DL

OGORKIEWICZ, Prof Richard Marian; s of Col Marian Anthony Ogorkiewicz (d 1962), of Poland, and Waldyna, *née* Pryfer (d 1986); *b* 2 May 1926; *Educ* SRW Sch Warsaw, Lycée de C Norwid Paris, George Heriot's Sch Edinburgh, Imperial Coll London (BSc, MSc); *m* 2005, Jocelyn Marie Bernier; *Career* devpt engr: Ford Motor Co 1952–55, Humber Ltd 1955–57; lectr in mech engrg Imperial Coll London 1957–85, conslt to various cos involved with armoured fighting vehicles 1972–; consulting ed Int Defense Review 1988–; visiting prof RMCS; memb various sci advsy ctees: Miny of Aviation 1964–70, Miny of Technol 1967–71, MOD 1972–2006; pres Friends of the Tank Museum Dorset 1987–93 (tstee 1993–); FIMechE 1970; *Books* Armour (1960), Design and Development of Fighting Vehicles (1968), Armoured Forces (1970), Technology of Tanks 2 vols (1991); *Recreations* gardening, walking; *Style*— Prof Richard Ogorkiewicz; ✉ 18 Temple Sheen, East Sheen, London SW14 7RP (tel 020 8876 5149)

O'GRADY, Frances; *b* 9 November 1959, Oxford; *Family* 2 c; *Career* early career with TGWU; TUC: joined 1994, subsequently campaigns offr then dir New Unionism project, head Orgn and Servs Dept 1998–2003, dep gen sec 2003–; formerly memb: Local Govt Pay Cmmn, Royal Mail Nat Partnership Bd, Modern Apprenticeship Advsy Ctee; currently memb: Bd IPPR, UK Skills Bd, Nat Employment Panel, LSC Nat Cncl, Low Pay Cmmn; *Style*— Ms Frances O'Grady; ✉ Trades Union Congress, Congress House, Great Russell Street, London WC1B 3LS (tel 020 7467 1249, fax 020 7467 1277, e-mail fogrady@tuc.org.uk)

OGSTON, Hamish MacGregor; s of Robert Davidson Ogston, and Pauline Jeannette Ogston; *Educ* Cranleigh Sch, Univ of Manchester (BSc); *Career* co-fndr and chair Countdown plc 1970, co-fndr and dir Supreme Awards 1977–79, co-fndr and dir Guinness World of Records 1979–82, co-fndr and chm CPP Gp plc 1980–, investor in mktg rights to World Cup 1982, launched Sportsworld Gp plc 1982; Ernst & Young Entrepeneur of the Year Financial Services Award 2000; Outstanding Alumnus of the Year Award Univ of Manchester 2002; FRSA, FRGS; *Recreations* travel, skiing, sailing, music, friends; *Style*— Hamish Ogston, Esq

OGUS, Prof Anthony Ian; CBE (2002); s of Samuel Joseph Ogus (d 1981), of Blackheath, and Sadie Phyllis, *née* Green; *b* 30 August 1945; *Educ* St Dunstan's Coll, Magdalen Coll Oxford (MA, BCL); *m* 1, 26 July 1980, Catherine (d 1998), da of Marc Klein (d 1975), of Strasbourg; m 2, 27 July 2001, Helen Margaret Legard, da of Ernest Edwin Legard Owens (d 2004), of Northallerton; *Career* asst lectr Univ of Leicester 1967–69, tutorial fell Mansfield Coll Oxford 1969–75, sr res fell Centre for Socio-Legal Studies Oxford; prof: Univ of Newcastle upon Tyne 1978–87, Faculty of Law Univ of Manchester 1987–; memb Social Security Advsy Ctee 1993–; *Books* Law of Damages (1973), Law of Social Security (with E M Barendt, 1978, 5 edn, 2002), Policing Pollution (with G M Richardson and P Burrows, 1983), Readings in the Economics of Law and Regulation (with C Veljanovski, 1984), Regulation: Legal Form and Economic Theory (1994, reprinted 2004), Controlling the Regulators (with J Froud and others, 1998), Économie Du Droit: Le Cas Français (with M Faure, 2002), Costs and Cautionary Tales (2006); *Recreations* theatre, music, reading, cycling, walking; *Clubs* Oxford and Cambridge; *Style*— Prof Anthony Ogus, CBE; ✉ School of Law, University of Manchester, Oxford Road, Manchester M13 9PL (tel 0161 275 3572, fax 0161 275 3579, e-mail anthony.ogus@manchester.ac.uk)

OGUS, Hugh Joseph; s of Louis Ogus (d 1951), of London, and Anne, *née* Goldstein (d 1986); *b* 23 January 1934; *Educ* Central Fndn Sch London, QMC London (BA); *m* 14 Aug 1960, Mavis, da of Michael Mendel (d 1971), of London; 1 s (Simon b 1964), 1 da (Deborah b 1967); *Career* various jr mgmnt posts Philips Electrical Ltd 1957–67, commercial dir Salamandre Metalworks Ltd 1968–73, chm and md Poselco Ltd 1984–94 (md 1973–84), dir Cryselco Ltd 1992–93, chm Fusebox Ltd 1990–2000, dir Galaxy Consultancy Ltd 2000–, non-exec chm DSG Asia (Hong Kong-based) 2000–; memb Cncl: Light Industry Fedn 1977–2000 (pres 1982–83), CIBSE 1986–89 and 1993–96 (chm Lighting Div 1993–94, vice-pres 1994–96); fndr chm Lighting Educn Tst 1995; chm of govrs: Mill Hill Oral Sch for Deaf Children 1987–89 (treas 1977–87), Mary Hare GS for the Deaf 1992– (vice-chm of govrs 1984–92, chm of fin 1980–94); vice-chm of govrs London Sch of Foreign Trade 1982–87; hon vice-pres (former chm) 4th Hendon Scouts and Guides; Freeman City of London 1983, Liveryman Worshipful Co of Lightmongers (Master 1994–95); CEng, FCIBSE; *Recreations* music, travel, swimming, horology; *Style*— Hugh J Ogus, Esq; ✉ Oakhills, 10 Spring Lake, Stanmore, Middlesex HA7 3BX (tel and fax 020 8954 0657); e-mail hughogus@dsgasia.com, website www.dsgasia.com; website www.maryhare.org.uk; website www.lighting-education-trust.org

OH, Justin; s of Teh Seng Oh; *b* 18 June 1966; *Educ* St Martins Sch of Art (BA), Royal Coll of Art (Courtalds bursary, MA); *Career* fashion designer; designer: Charles Jourdan Paris 1989 (ready-to-wear), Courtalds plc 1990, Yohji Yamamoto Tokyo 1990; conslt designer French Connection 1991, established own Justin Oh label 1995, designed all-in-ones for The Boat Race 1997, cnslt womenswear wovens Joseph 2007–; memb: London Inst Members Assoc, Inst of Chartered Designers; *Fashion Shows* Yohji Yamamoto (Paris, 1990), London Fashion Week 1995–; *Style*— Justin Oh, Esq; ✉ 14A Clerkenwell Green, London EC1R 0DP (tel 020 7336 6988, e-mail admin@justinoh.co.uk)

O'HAGAN, Antony Richard (Tony); TD (1976, 1 Clasp 1982, 2 Clasp 1988), DL (Gtr London 2005); s of Capt Desmond O'Hagan, CMG (d 2001), of Kiambu, Kenya, and Pamela Jane, *née* Symes-Thompson; *b* 3 October 1942; *Educ* Wellington; *m* 6 Dec 1975 (m dis 1999), Caroline Jessica, da of Walter Herbert Franklin (d 1987), of Great Rissington, Glos; 1 da (Clare Pamela b 6 Sept 1976), 1 s (Richard Franklin b 19 Oct 1979); m 2, 21 Sept 2001, Julia, da of late Brian Henry Jennings; *Career* HAC: non-cmmnd serv 1962–67, 2 Lt 1967, Capt 1975, Maj 1982, Capt Co of Pikemen and Musketeers 2005– (pikeman 1984–); TA watch keeper 3 Armd Div HQ RA 1984–91; mangr Coopers & Lybrand 1972–73, gp accountant Hays Wharf Group 1973–76, fin accountant Freemans Mail Order 1977–82, fin dir St Martin's Property Corporation Ltd 1986–2001 (chief accountant 1982–85); rep ptnr Pool of London Partnership 1996–2001; pres NE Area St John Ambulance 2003– (pres Edmonton Div 1997–2002); vice-pres HAC 1990–92 (treas 1987–90, memb Ct of Assts 1978–); tstee: Chindits Old Comrades Assoc 1989–, Vitalise (formerly Winged Fellowship Tst) 2003–06; tstee and treasurer London Bridge Museum and Educnl Tst 1999–2006; chm Civilian Ctee 329 Sqdn ATC 1997–2003, chm London Wing Civilian Ctee ATC 2004–; clerk Ward of Bridge and Bridge Without 1996–2005; representative DL London Borough of Barking and Daganham 2005; Freeman City of London 1979, Liveryman Worshipful Co of Fanmakers 1980 (memb Ct of Assts 1994–, Master 2006, chm Charity Ctee 1995–2005); FCA 1978; SBStJ 2003; *Recreations* tennis, swimming, skiing, fishing, gardening; *Clubs* Army and Navy; *Style—* A R O'Hagan, Esq, TD, DL; ✉ 50 Dunbar Wharf, 124 Narrow Street, Limehouse, London E14 8BB (tel and fax 020 7531 8943, e-mail arohagan@hotmail.com)

O'HAGAN, 4 Baron (UK 1870); Charles Towneley Strachey; s of Hon Anthony Strachey (d 1955), who assumed surname Strachey *vice* Towneley-O'Hagan 1938 and added forename Towneley; he was s of 3 Baron O'Hagan (d 1961) by his 1 w, Hon Frances Strachey (da of 1 Baron Strachie); *b* 6 September 1945; *Educ* Eton, New Coll Oxford; *m* 1, 1967 (m dis 1984), HSH Princess Tamara, former w of Lt Cdr Thomas Smith-Dorrien-Smith, of Tresco Abbey, Isles of Scilly, and er da of HSH Prince Michael Imeretinsky (of the Princely family of Bagration, sometime rulers of an independent Georgia), RAFVR, of Menton; 1 da (Hon Nino (m Harry Bradbeer, *qv*) b 1968); m 2, 1985 (m dis 1995), Mrs Mary Claire Parsons, only da of Rev Leslie Roose-Francis, of Blisland, Cornwall; 1 da (Hon Antonia b 1986); m 3, 1995, Mrs Elizabeth Lesley Eve Macnamara, o da of late Hubert Smith, of Exeter; *Heir* bro, Hon Richard Strachey; *Career* page of honour to HM The Queen 1959–62; MEP (Ind) 1973–75, MEP (Cons) Devon 1979–94; sat as Cons in House of Lords, cons whip and front bench spokesman in the House of Lords 1977–79; Liveryman Worshipful Co of Mercers; *Clubs* Pratt's; *Style—* The Rt Hon the Lord O'Hagan; ✉ The Granary, Beaford, Winkleigh, Devon EX19 8AB

O'HAGAN, Simon Timothy Byard; s of Maj Alan Bernard O'Hagan, of Langley, Maidstone, Kent, and Heather Mary Byard, *née* White; *b* 25 September 1957; *Educ* King's Sch Rochester, Univ of Birmingham (BA); *m* 6 May 1989, Lindsay Carol, da of Laurence Frederick John Bray; 2 da (Isabel Clare b 23 Dec 1990, Eleanor Catherine b 8 Nov 1993); *Career* journalist: The Kent Messenger 1978–81, The Times 1982–89, The Independent on Sunday 1990–2006; asst ed The Independent 2006–; *Style—* Simon O'Hagan, Esq; ✉ The Independent, 191 Marsh Wall, London E14 9RS (tel 020 7005 2394, fax 020 7005 2628, e-mail s.ohagan@independent.co.uk)

O'HANLON, Ardal; s of Rory O' Hanlon, and Teresa, *née* Ward; *Career* stand-up comic; fndr memb Comedy Cellar Dublin; Hackney Empire New Act of the Year 1994, Top TV Comedy Newcomer Br Comedy Awards 1996, Best Comedy Actor BAFTA 1998; patron Aisling Return to Ireland Project, hon pres Edinburgh Univs and Heriot-Watt Celtic Supporters Club; *Television* Father Dougal in Father Ted (C4), George/Thermoman in My Hero (BBC 1), Eamonn in Big Bad World (ITV); presenter Stand-Up Show (BBC 1); *Books* Talk of the Town (1997); *Recreations* sleeping; *Style—* Ardal O'Hanlon, Esq; ✉ Dawn Sedgwick Management, 3 Goodwins Court, London WC2N 4LL (tel 020 7240 0404, e-mail dawnsedgwick@compuserve.com)

O'HANLON, Redmond Douglas; s of Canon William Douglas O'Hanlon, of Swanage, Dorset, and Philippa Katherine O'Hanlon; *b* 5 June 1947; *Educ* Marlborough, Merton Coll Oxford (MA, MPhil, DPhil); *m* 6 April 1967, Belinda Margaret, da of Desmond Ingham Harty; 1 da (Puffin Annabelinda b 26 Feb 1985), 1 s (Galen Redmond b 2 Aug 1988); *Career* writer; St Antony's Coll Oxford: sr scholar 1971–72, Alistair Horne res fell 1972–73, sr visitor 1985–89, sr assoc memb 1989–95; ed natural history TLS 1981–95; memb: Literature Panel Arts Cncl 1971–74, Soc for the History of Natural History 1982, Br Ornithological Union 1986; Le Prix de L'Astrolabe 1989; FRGS 1984, FRSL 1993; *Books* Charles Darwin 1809–1882: A Centennial Commemorative (contrib, 1982), Joseph Conrad and Charles Darwin: The Influence of Scientific Thought on Conrad's Fiction (1984), Into the Heart of Borneo (1984), In Trouble Again, A Journey between the Orinoco and the Amazon (1988), Congo Journey (1996, Best Non-Fiction Book American Libraries Assoc 1997), Trawler, A Journey through the North Atlantic (2003); *Recreations* pond-watching by torchlight; *Clubs* Rainforest; *Style—* Redmond O'Hanlon, Esq, FRSL; ✉ c/o PFD, Drury House, 34–43 Russell Street, London WC2B 5HA (tel 020 7344 1020, fax 020 7836 9539)

O'HARA, Edward; MP; s of Robert Edward O'Hara, and Clara, *née* Davies; *b* 1 October 1937; *Educ* Liverpool Collegiate Sch, Magdalen Coll Oxford (MA), Univ of London (DipEd (Adv), PGCE); *m* 1962, Lillian, da of Thomas Hopkins; 2 s, 1 da; *Career* asst teacher: Perse Sch Cambridge 1962–65, Birkenhead Sch 1966–70; lectr and princ lectr C F Mott Coll of Educn 1970–74, princ lectr, sr tutor and dean of postgrad studies City of Liverpool Coll of Higher Educn 1974–83, head of curriculum studies Sch of Educn and Community Studies Liverpool Poly 1983–90; MP (Lab) Knowsley S 1990–, co-chm All-Pty Gp for Ageing and Older People, chm Anglo Greek Gp; memb Knowsley BC 1975–91 (memb all standing ctees, chm Libraries and Arts, Finance, Youth, Educn and Econ, Devpt and Planning Ctees), memb Educn and Planning and Econ Devpt Ctees AMA; memb: Bd of Management NFER 1986–90, Euro Assoc of Teachers, Socialist Educn Assoc; memb: Labour Movement in Europe, Perm Ctee Assembly of Euro Regions 1987–90; Merseyside delegate to Régions Européennes de Tradition Industrielle 1989–90; tstee Community Devpt Fndn 1992–2004 (chm 1997–2004), memb Fabian Soc, memb Co-op Pty, memb Bd of Mgmnt Royal Liverpool Philharmonic Soc 1987–90, memb Social Educn Assoc; corresponding memb Fndn for Hellenic Culture; pres Knowsley S Juniors FC 1997–, vice-pres TS Iron Duke Huyton 1994–, vice-chm National Wildflower Centre Devpt Tst 1996–; patron Knowsley Arts Tst; govr: Knowsley Community Coll, Prescot County Primary Sch; *Recreations* music (classical/jazz/folk especially Rembetiko), reading, theatre, travel, Greek language and culture; *Clubs* Halewood Labour; *Style—* Edward O'Hara, Esq, MP; ✉ House of Commons, London SW1A 0AA (tel 020 7219 4538/5232, fax 020 7219 4952, e-mail oharae@parliament.uk)

O'HARE, Kevin Patrick; s of Michael J O'Hare, and Anne Veronica, *née* O'Callaghan; bro of Michael O'Hare, *qv*; *Educ* White Lodge (Royal Ballet Lower Sch), The Royal Ballet Upper Sch, Royal Danish Ballet; *Career* former ballet dancer with Birmingham Royal Ballet (formerly Sadler's Wells Royal Ballet): first soloist 1989, principal dancer 1990; roles incl: Prince Sigfried in Swan Lake, Albrecht in Giselle, The Poet in Les Syphides, Colas in La Fille Mal Gardée, The Prince in Sleeping Beauty, Oberon in A Midsummer Night's Dream, Man in Two Pigeons, Edward in Edward II; dances principal roles in ballets by Ashton, Balanchine, Bintley and Macmillan, created roles in ballets by David Bintley, Graham Lustig and William Tukett, debut as Romeo in new prodn of Macmillan's Romeo and Juliet 1992, guest appearance with Royal Ballet Covent Garden 1992, and in Milan, Brussels, Hong Kong, China, Japan, Holland and Poland; ret from dancing 2000, trainee co mangr RSC 2000, co mangr Birmingham Royal Ballet 2001–; organized the international charity gala Stepping Heals at Birmingham Hippodrome 1997, organized an evening of new dance works Changing Stages MAC Birmingham 1998; govr Royal Ballet Sch 2000–; memb jury of many ballet awards incl Young Br Dancer of the Year and Prix de Lausanne; *Style—* Kevin O'Hare, Esq

O'HARE, Michael James; s of Michael Joseph O'Hare, and Anne Veronica, *née* O'Callaghan; bro of Kevin O'Hare, *qv*; *b* 7 December 1960; *Educ* Marist Coll Hull, The Royal Ballet Sch; *m* 1996, Julie Ann, *née* Francis; 1 da (Georgia Mai b 28 April 1998); *Career* ballet dancer; The Birmingham Royal Ballet (formerly Sadler's Wells Royal Ballet): joined 1980, soloist 1984, princ 1987–2002, asst ballet master 2002– (teacher 2000–); sometime teacher: Royal Ballet Sch 1997–, Yorkshire Ballet Assembly 1997–; performed a wide range of princ roles within repertoire (character, demi-character and classical) in ballets by: Ashton, MacMillan, Balanchine, De Valois, Cranko and others; the first dancer to perform all three male roles (Alain, Colas and Widow Simone) in Ashton's La Fille Mal Gardée; has danced numerous seasons at Sadler's Wells, the ROH Covent Garden and The Birmingham Hippodrome and has toured extensively worldwide; has worked with numerous younger choreographers; created role of Will Mossop in Hobson's Choice with choreographer David Bintley (first performance Royal Opera House 1989 and shown on BBC 2 1990); performances incl: Eros in Sylvia (David Bintley), Satan in Job (De Valois Ballet, at Coventry Cathedral), La Fille Mal Gardée (at Teatro Regio Torino), The Prodigal Son (Balanchine), The Prince in The Sleeping Beauty, Carmina Burana and the role of Gabriel Oak in Far From the Madding Crowd (both David Bintley) 1996, Edward in Edward II (David Bintley), Mr O'Reilly in The Prospect Before Us (De Valois), Richard III in Shakespeare Suite (David Bintley), Arthur in Arthur Part I and Part II (David Bintley), Hoofer in Slaughter on 10th Avenue (Balanchine), Drosselmeyer in The Nutcracker (Sir Peter Wright), Dr Coppelius in Coppélia (Sir Peter Wright), Widow Simone in La Fille Mal Gardée (Frederick Ashton), The Merchant in Beauty and the Beast 2006, Kostchei in the Firebird 2006, Widow Simone in La Fille Mal Gardee 2006, Lord Capulet in Romeo and Juliet 2006; *Style—* Michael O'Hare, Esq; ✉ The Birmingham Royal Ballet, Birmingham Hippodrome, Thorp Street, Birmingham B5 4AU (tel 0121 622 2555)

O'HIGGINS, Prof Paul; s of Richard Leo O'Higgins, MC, MRCVS (d 1973), of Uxbridge, Middx, and Elizabeth, *née* Deane (d 1984); *b* 5 October 1927; *Educ* St Columba's Coll Rathfarnham, TCD (MA, LLD), Clare Coll Cambridge (MA, PhD, LLD); *m* May 1951, Rachel Elizabeth, da of late Prof Alan Dudley Bush, of Radlett, Herts; 3 da (Maeve b 16 Feb 1953, Siobhan b 21 Sept 1956, Niav b 23 April 1964), 1 s (Niall b 29 May 1961); *Career* called to the Bar: King's Inns Dublin 1957, Lincoln's Inn 1959; Barstow scholar Inns of Court Sch of Law 1958; Univ of Cambridge: fell Christ's Coll 1959– (vice-master 1992–95), univ lectr 1965–79, reader in labour law 1979–84; lectr in labour law Cncl of Legal Educn and Inns of Court Sch of Law 1976–84, regius prof of laws TCD 1984–87 (hon prof of law 1992–); prof of law: KCL 1987–92 (emeritus prof 1992), Univ of Kent, Monash Univ, Univ of Belfast, Nat Univ of Ireland Galway, Tilburg Univ; visiting prof of law City Univ 1992–96; memb Office of Manpower Economics Advsy Ctee on Equal Pay 1970–72; occasional conslt to EC and Int Labour Orgn on employment law (drafted current Lesotho's Labour Code); chm Cambridge branch: Nat Cncl for Civil Liberties 1970–78, Assoc of Univ Teachers 1971–75; memb: Bureau European Inst of Social Security 1970–95, Staff Side Panel Civil Serv Arbitration Tbnl 1972–84; pres: Irish Branch Cambridge Soc 1999–, Trinity Coll Dublin Assoc Cambridge Branch 2003–; patron Cambridge Univ Grad Soc 1972–84, tstee Cambridge Union Soc 1973–84, elector Finley Fellowships Darwin Coll Cambridge 1990–; vice-pres: Inst of Safety and Public Protection 1973–, Haldane Soc 1981–, Inst of Employment Rights 1989–; govr Br Inst of Human Rights 1988–98, treas Alan Bush Music Tst 1997–, memb Exec Ctee Int Soc for Labour Law and Social Legislation 1985–; Joseph L Andrews Bibliographical Award of the American Assoc of Law Libraries 1987; hon fell Trinity College Dublin 1996; MRIA 1986, memb Acad of European Private Lawyers 1994, hon memb Irish Soc for Lab Law 1997; *Books* Bibliography of Periodical Literature Relating to Irish Law (1966, supplements 1975 and 1983), Public Employee Trade Unionism in the UK - The Legal Framework (with Ann Arbor, 1971), Censorship in Britain (1972), A Bibliography of British & Irish Labour Law (1975), Workers' Rights (1976), Employment Law (4 edn 1981), Labour Law in Great Britain and Ireland to 1978 (1981), Discrimination in Employment in Northern Ireland (1984), A Bibliography of Irish Trials and other Legal Proceedings (1986), A Bibliography of the Literature on British & Irish Social Security Law (1986), The Common Law Tradition - Essays in Irish Legal History (1990), Lessons from Northern Ireland (1991), A Bibliography of British and Irish Labour Law 1979–90 (1995); *Recreations* travel, talk, wine; *Clubs* Royal Dublin Soc; *Style—* Prof Paul O'Higgins; ✉ Christ's College, St Andrew's Street, Cambridge CB2 3BU (tel 01223 334900, fax 01223 334967)

OHLSON, Sir Brian Eric Christopher; 3 Bt (UK 1920), of Scarborough, North Riding of Co of Yorkshire; s of Sir Eric James Ohlson, 2 Bt (d 1983), and Marjorie Joan, *née* Roosmale-Cocq; *b* 27 July 1936; *Educ* Harrow, RMA Sandhurst; *Heir* bro, Peter Ohlson; *Career* cmmnd Coldstream Gds 1956, Capt, ret 1961; money broker; *Recreations* safaris, sport of kings, cricket, theatre, bridge, bowls, real tennis; *Clubs* Hurlingham, MCC, Queen's; *Style—* Sir Brian Ohlson, Bt; ✉ 1 Courtfield Gardens, London SW5 0PA

O'HORA, Ronan; s of Desmond O'Hora, and Gertrude, *née* Maguire; *b* 9 January 1964; *Educ* St Bede's Coll Manchester, RNCM; *m* 5 Jan 1991, Hannah Alice, *née* Bell; *Career* concert pianist; London concerto debut with Philharmonia Barbican Hall 1989, London recital debut Wigmore Hall 1989, US debut with Florida Philharmonic Orch Miami 1990; played with orchs incl: Royal Philharmonic, London Philharmonic, BBC Symphony and Philharmonic Orchs, Acad of St Martin-in-the-Field's, Hallé Orch, Royal Liverpool Philharmonic, Tonhalle Orch of Zurich, Indianapolis Symphony Orch; played concertos and recitals in numerous countries incl: Germany, France, Switzerland, Holland, Italy, Scandinavia, Belgium, Austria, Yugoslavia, Poland, Ireland, Portugal, Canada, Czechoslovakia; sr tutor RNCM 1996–99; head of keyboard studies Guildhall Sch of Music and Drama 1999–; *Awards* Silver Medal Worshipful Co of Musicians 1984, Dayas Gold Medal 1984, Stefania Niekrasz Prize 1985; *Recordings* Britten Music for Two Pianos (with Stephen Hough), concertos by Grieg, Tchaikovsky and Mozart with the RPO, solo recordings of Chopin, Schubert and Debussy; numerous recordings for broadcasting cos incl: BBC TV and Radio, Netherlands TV and Radio, Polish TV, Czech TV; *Recreations* theatre; *Style—* Ronan O'Hora, Esq; ✉ c/o Guildhall School of Music and Drama, Silk Street, Barbican, London EC2Y 8DT (tel 020 7628 2571)

O'KANE, Maggie; s of Peter O'Kane, of Skerries, Co Dublin, and Maura, *née* McNeil; *Educ* Assumption Convent Ballynahinch Co Down, Loreto Convent Balbriggan Co Dublin, Coll of Commerce Dublin, UC Dublin (BA), Inst de Journaliste en Europe Paris; *m* John Mullin; 2 c (Billy, Ruby); *Career* reporter Magill Magazine Ireland 1980–82, journalist Sunday Tribune Ireland 1982–84, TV reporter Irish television 1984–89, scholarship to Journalistes En Europe Fndn Paris 1989, covered E Europe for Irish Times and RTE 1989–90, Gulf War for The Irish Times, freelance 1991– (working for Mail on Sunday, The Guardian, The Economist and Sunday Times in Beirut, Kuwait, N Iraq, Croatia and Bosnia), currently special corr The Guardian and editorial dir Guardian Films; television progs incl: documentary on Haiti (BBC) 1995, documentary on anniversary of Gulf War (Channel 4) 1996, documentary on Third World debt; *Awards* Journalist of the Year What the Papers Say Awards 1992, Journalist of the Year and Foreign Corr (jt) British Press Awards 1992, Foreign Corr (jt) of the Year Amnesty Int 1993, Br TV Documentary

O

Award (for Bloody Bosnia) Channel 4 1993, runner-up RTS Reporter of the Year 1993, James Cameron Award for int and domestic reporting 1996, runner-up Int Foreign Corr Amnesty Int 1998, shortlisted Foreign Corr of the Year 2000, European Journalist of the Year 2002; *Style—* Ms Maggie O'Kane; ✉ GuardianFilms, 119 Farringdon Road London EC1R 3ER (tel 020 7278 2332, fax 020 7239 9787)

O'KEEFFE, Bartholomew (Batt); TD; s of Daniel O'Keeffe (d 1979), of Cullen, Co Cork, and Ellen, *née* O'Connell (d 1989); *b* 2 April 1945, Co Cork; *Educ* St Brendan's Coll Killarney, UC Cork; *m* Oct 1970, Mary, *ée* Murphy; 1 s (Mark), 3 da (Elaine, Hilda, Patrice); *Career* formerly lectr in communications and gen studies; TD (Fianna Fáil) Cork South Central 1987–89, memb (senator) Seanad Éireann (Fianna Fáil) Lab panel 1989–92, TD (Fianna Fáil) Cork South Central 1992–; min of state Dept of the Environment, Heritage and Local Govt 2004–07, min for housing, urban renewal and devpt areas Dept of the Environment, Heritage and Local Govt 2007–; *Style—* Batt O'Keeffe, Esq, TD; ✉ 8 Westcliffe, Ballincollig, Co Cork, Ireland (tel 00 353 21 4871393, e-mail batt_okeeffe@environ.ie)

O'KELLY, Declan; s of John O'Kelly (d 1945), and Mary, *née* Doherty (d 1967); *b* 7 November 1939, Claudy, Co Derry; *Educ* Victoria Univ of Manchester (CertEd), Open Univ (BA), Univ of Ulster (MSc); *m* 11 July 1968, Mary, *née* Bradley; 3 da (Mary Louise b 11 April 1969, Veronica Patricia b 27 Nov 1971, Susan Anne b 17 Oct 1980), 1 s (John Francis b 4 Nov 1977); *Career* princ St Patrick's & St Brigid's Claudy Co Derry 1975–88, sr advsr Cncl for Catholic Maintained Schs 1988–97, founding princ Lumen Christi Coll Derry 1997–2003; memb (min of educn nominee) NI Cncl for Educnl Devpt 1980–87, pres NI Branch NAHT 1979; *Recreations* fishing, golf, reading; *Clubs* City of Derry Golf; *Style—* Declan O'Kelly, Esq; ✉ 27 Drummond Park, Derry, Northern Ireland BT48 8PH (tel 02871 353193, e-mail declanokelly@tiscali.co.uk)

OKRI, Ben; OBE (2001); s of Silver Okri, and Grace Okri; *b* 15 March 1959; *Educ* Univ of Essex; *Career* author and poet; broadcaster and presenter BBC 1983–85, poetry ed W Africa 1983–86, fell commoner Trinity Coll Cambridge 1991–93; one of 200 leaders of tomorrow World Economic Forum 1993; memb: Soc of Authors, PEN International, Cncl RSL 1999–2004, Bd RNT 1999–2006; Hon DLit: Univ of Westminster 1997, Univ of Essex 2002, Univ of Exeter 2004; FRSL 1997, FRSA 2003; *Awards* Cwlth Prize for Africa 1987, Paris Review Prize for Fiction 1987, Booker Prize 1991, Premio Letterario Internazionale Chianti Ruffino-Antico Fattore 1993, Premio Grinzane Cavour 1994, Crystal Award 1995, Premio Palmi 2000; *Books* Flowers and Shadows (novel, 1980), The Landscapes Within (novel, 1982), Incidents at the Shrine (stories, 1986), Stars of the New Curfew (stories, 1988), The Famished Road (novel, 1991), An African Elegy (poems, 1992), Songs of Enchantment (novel, 1993), Astonishing the Gods (novel, 1995), Birds of Heaven (essays, 1996), Dangerous Love (novel, 1996), A Way of Being Free (essays, 1997), Infinite Riches (novel, 1998), Mental Fight (poetry, 1999), In Arcadia (novel, 2002), Starbrook (novel, 2007); *Recreations* music, art, theatre, cinema, martial arts, good conversation, dancing and silence; *Style—* Ben Okri, Esq, OBE, FRSL; ✉ c/o Orion Publishing Group, Orion House, 5 Upper St Martin's Lane, London WC2H 9EA (tel 020 7240 3444, fax 020 7240 4822)

OLDENBURG, HH Duke Friedrich August Nikolaus Udo Peter Philipp of; elder s of HH Duke Peter of Oldenburg (2 s of HRH Nikolaus, Hereditary Grand Duke of Oldenburg, descended from Egilmar I, Count of Aldenburg, who was living in 1108; Hereditary Grand Duke Nikolaus m HSH Princess Helene of Waldeck and Pyrmont, whose paternal grandmother was HSH Princess Helene of Nassau; Princess Helene of Nassau's paternal gf's mother was Princess Caroline of Orange, whose mother was Princess Anne (Princess Royal), eldest da of King George II of Great Britain), by his w HSH Princess Gertrud, 2 da of HSH Udo, 6 Prince zu Löwenstein-Wertheim-Freudenberg; *b* 26 September 1952; *m* 9 Jan 1982, Belinda, da of Maj (Alison) Digby Tatham Warter, DSO (d 1993), of Nanyuki, Kenya, and Jane, *née* Boyd (whose mother was Lady Mary Egerton, o da of 5 Earl of Wilton); 3 da (Anastasia (Daisy) b 10 Oct 1982, Alice b 15 April 1986, Cara b 14 June 1993); *Career* businessman and farmer; *Style—* His Highness Duke Friedrich August of Oldenburg; ✉ Anstey Hall, Anstey, Buntingford, Hertfordshire SG9 0BY (tel 01763 848254, fax 01763 848048, e-mail fao@farmline.com); Lensahnerhof, D23738 Lensahn, Germany

OLDERSHAW, Dr Paul John; s of Harold Oldershaw (d 1981), and Irene, *née* Summerlin (d 1999); *b* 23 September 1947; *Educ* Henry Mellish GS Nottingham, Emmanuel Coll Cambridge (exhibitioner and scholar in natural scis, MB BChir, MA, MD, Colin McKenzie prize, Albert Hopkinson award, Peake prize), St Thomas' Hosp Med Sch; *Career* jr hosp appts St Thomas', St Peter's and Brompton Hosps 1973–75, rotating med registrar Worthing Gen Hosp (gen med) and St Thomas' Hosp (gen med and nephrology) 1975–77, Br Heart Fndn research fell St Thomas' Hosp Med Unit 1977–79, cardiac registrar Brompton Hosp 1979–81, sr registrar Cardiac Dept St George's Hosp 1981–82; Royal Brompton Nat Heart and Lung Hosp: conslt cardiologist 1982–, dir of cardiology 1992–; Br Cardiac Soc: memb Cncl 1986–90, sec 1988–92, chm Pubns Ctee 1990–93, memb Prog and Meetings Ctee 1991–95; Br Heart Fndn: memb Educn Ctee 1986–90, memb Factfile Ctee 1986–90; Euro Soc of Cardiology: memb Scientific Exec Ctee 1990–, memb Valvular Heart Disease Working Pty 1992–; memb Adult Congenital Heart Disease Working Pty Br Cardiac Soc 1993–; numerous post-graduate awards incl Br Heart Fndn Research Award (with Andrew Bishop) to study right ventricular function using impedance catheterisation 1993–; memb Editorial Bds: Br Heart Jl 1986–90, Int Jl of Cardiology 1986–92, Euro Heart Jl 1990–; referee: BMJ, Lancet; memb: Med Research Soc 1977, Br Cardiac Soc 1981; FRCP 1990 (MRCP 1975), FESC 1991 (MESC 1982), FACC 1991 (MACC 1982); *Books* A Practice of Cardiac Catheterisation (with D Mendel, 1986), Textbook of Adult and Paediatric Echocardiography and Doppler Echocardiography (with M St John Sutton, 1989), Cardiology Dictionary (with R A Anderson and J R Dawson, 1990), A Practical Guide to Congenital Heart Disease in Adults (with A Redington and D F Shore, 1994); author of numerous pubns in academic jls; *Recreations* opera, wine; *Style—* Dr Paul Oldershaw; ✉ 76 Carlton Hill, St John's Wood, London NW8 (tel 020 7625 6829); Royal Brompton Hospital, Sydney Street, London SW3 6NP (tel 020 7352 8121, fax 020 7351 8629)

OLDFATHER, Irene; MSP; *Educ* Univ of Strathclyde (BA, MSc), Univ of Arizona; *Career* MSP (Lab) Cunninghame South 1999–; Scot Parl: vice-chm European Ctee 2003– (former chm), convenor Cross-Pty Gp on Tobacco Control, memb Cross-Pty Animal Welfare Gp, memb European Ctee of Regions 2002–, vice-pres Co Regions Socialist Gp 2002–; former: chm Convention of Scottish Local Authorities Task Gp on Economic and Monetary Union, vice-chm West of Scotland Euro Consortium, vice-chm Ayrshire Int, memb Ayrshire Educn Business Partnership, memb and Euro spokesperson North Ayrshire Cncl; researcher Dumbarton Cncl on Alcohol 1976–77, lectr Univ of Arizona 1977–78, res offr Strathclyde Regnl Cncl 1978–79, various posts Glasgow Dist Cncl Housing Dept 1979–90, political researcher for Alex Smith MEP 1990–98, freelance writer and broadcaster 1994–98; *Publications* numerous articles and research papers on subjects incl devolution, European monetary union, and the Common Agric Policy; *Style—* Irene Oldfather, MSP; ✉ The Scottish Parliament, Holyrood, Edinburgh EH99 1SP (tel 0131 348 5769, fax 0131 348 5778); Constituency: Sovereign House, Academy Road, Irvine KA12 8RL (tel 01294 313078, fax 01294 313605)

OLDFIELD, Bruce; OBE (1990); *b* 14 July 1950; *Educ* Spennymoor GS Durham, Ripon GS, Sheffield Poly (DipEd), Ravensbourne Coll of Art, St Martin's Coll of Art; *Career* fashion designer; designed for Henri Bendel NY and other stores 1973–74, freelance cmmns incl film wardrobe for Charlotte Rampling 1974–75, first collection 1975, estab couture div 1978, opened London boutique and redeveloped ready-to-wear collection with couture collection 1984–, Br rep Aust Bicentennial Wool Collection Fashion Show Sydney Opera House 1988; lectures: Fashion Inst NY 1977, LA County Mus 1983, Int Design Conference Aspen Colorado 1986; vice-pres Barnardos 1998–, memb Panel Whitbread Literary Awards 1987, organised Bruce Oldfield for Barnardos gala evenings attended by HRH The Princess of Wales 1985 and 1988, govr London Inst 1999–2002; Northern Personality of the Year Variety Club 1985, subject of TV documentary A Journey into Fashion (Tyne Tees TV) 1990, tstee Royal Acad of Arts 2000–02; hon fell: Sheffield Hallam Univ 1987, RCA 1990, Hatfield Coll Durham 1991; Hon DCL Univ of Northumbria at Newcastle 2001, DUniv UCE 2005; *Books* Bruce Oldfield's Season (contrib, 1987), Bruce Oldfield: an autobiography (2004); *Recreations* reading, music, films, driving; *Style—* Bruce Oldfield, Esq, OBE; ✉ c/o Bruce Oldfield Ltd, 27 Beauchamp Place, London SW3 1NJ (tel 020 7584 1363, fax 020 7761 0351, e-mail hq@bruceoldfield.com, website www.bruceoldfield.com)

OLDFIELD, Michael Gordon (Mike); s of Raymond Henry Oldfield, of Stuttgart, Germany, and Maureen Bernadine, *née* Liston (d 1976); *b* 15 May 1953; *Educ* Highlands Sch Reading, Hornchurch GS Essex, St Edward's Reading, Presentation Coll Reading; *Partner* 1; 2 s (Dougal b 17 Sept 1981, Luke b 11 April 1986), 1 da (Molly b 30 Nov 1979); ptnr 2; 1 s (Noah b 8 March 1990), 1 da (Greta b 28 April 1988); *Career* musician; first recording with sister Sally Oldfield 1969, 3 recordings with Kevin Ayres 1970–72; solo albums: Tubular Bells 1973, Hergest Ridge 1974, Ommadawn 1975, Incantations 1978, Platinum 1979, QE2 1980, Five Miles Out 1982, Crises 1983, The Killing Fields 1984, Discovery 1984, Islands 1987, Earth Moving 1989, Amarok 1990, Heaven's Open 1991, Tubular Bells II 1992, The Songs of Distant Earth 1994, Voyager 1996, Tubular Bells III 1998, Guitars 1999, The Millennium Bell 1999, Light and Shade; various major tours incl two world tours; 50 Gold and 15 Platinum discs worldwide, Grammy award, Golden Globe, Ivor Novello and BAFTA nominations; Freeman City of London; involved with Blue Peter Cambodian Appeal and hostage release work; *Recreations* skiing, cycling, squash; *Style—* Mike Oldfield, Esq

OLDHAM, Gavin David Redvers; s of David George Redvers Oldham, of Bucks, and Penelope Barbara, *née* Royle; *b* 5 May 1949; *Educ* Eton, Trinity Coll Cambridge (MA); *m* 17 May 1975, Virginia Russell, da of late Rodney Fryer Russell, of Dorset, and Elisabeth Jane, *née* Shettle; *Career* CSE Aircraft Services Ltd 1971–76, ptnr Wedd Durlacher Mordaunt & Co 1984–86 (joined 1976), secretariat Barclays de Zoete Wedd 1984–86, chm Barclayshare Ltd 1989–90 (chief exec 1986–89); chief exec The Share Centre Ltd 1990–, chief exec Share plc 2000–, chm The Share Fndn 2005–; chm Christian Ethical Investment Group 2003–, dir West Highland Air Transport Ltd 1998–, tstee Personal Finance Educn Gp 2003–; memb Economic Research Cncl 1989–; church cmmr; memb: Gen Synod (House of Laity) for Dio of Oxford, Financial Ctee (Archbishops' Cncl); MInstD, FSI; *Clubs* Leander; *Style—* Gavin Oldham, Esq; ✉ Oxford House, Oxford Road, Aylesbury, Buckinghamshire HP21 8SZ (tel 01296 439100, fax 01296 414410, e-mail ceo@share.co.uk)

OLDING, Prof Simon; s of Roy Edward Olding, of Dawlish, Devon, and Rita Frances, *née* Heard; *b* 9 March 1954; *Educ* Hele's GS Exeter, Fitzwilliam Coll Cambridge (Leathersellers scholar, MA), Univ of Edinburgh (PhD); *m* July 1990, Isabel, da of Noel Hughes; 2 da (Mabel, Madeleine); *Career* asst keeper for ceramics Glasgow Museums and Art Galleries 1980–82 (grad trainee 1979–80), asst curator (art) Salisbury Museum 1982–85, London museums offr and asst dir for museum devpt Area Museums Serv for SE England 1985–89, head of arts and museums Bournemouth Borough Cncl 1989–98, dir of policy and research Heritage Lottery Fund 1998–2002, dir Crafts Study Centre UC for the Creative Arts 2002–; pres Walford Mill Craft Centre; memb Bd The Study Gallery, memb Bd George Dannatt Tst; hon fell The Arts Inst at Bournemouth 2000; FMA 1991 (AMA 1982, Trevor Walden prize), FRSA 1994, FTS 2002; *Books* Michael Cullimore (1986), A Vision of Dartmoor (jtly, 1990), Exploring Museums - London (1991), Marcus Tate Photographs (1993), Russell-Cotes Commissions (1994), So Fair a House (1997), Martyn Brewster (1997), Emma Stibbon (1998), London Museums and Collections (co-ed, 1998), Essays for the Opening of the Crafts Study Centre (co-ed, 2004), Magdalene Odundo (jtly, 2004), John Hinchcliffe (2006), Peter Thursby (jtly, 2007); *Recreations* the arts; *Style—* Prof Simon Olding; ✉ Crafts Study Centre, Falkner Road, Farnham, Surrey GU9 7DS (tel 01252 891450)

OLDMAN, Gary; *b* 21 March 1958, New Cross, London; *Educ* Rose Bruford Drama Coll (BA); *m* 1, Lesley *née* Manville; 1 s (Alfie); m 2, Uma Thurman; m 3, Donya Fiorentino; 2 s (Gulliver Flynn b 20 Aug 1999, Charlie); *Career* actor; performed in various plays Royal Court Theatre and RSC 1984–87; *Theatre* incl The Pope's Wedding (Royal Court) 1995; *Television* Mean Time 1981, The Firm 1988, Jesus 1999; *Films* incl: Sid and Nancy 1986, Prick Up Your Ears 1986, Tracks 29 1988, Criminal Law 1988, Rosencrantz and Guildenstern are Dead 1990, State of Grace 1990, JFK 1991, Dracula 1992, True Romance 1993, Romeo is Bleeding 1993, Immortal Beloved 1994, Leon 1994, Murder in the First 1994, Basquiat 1996, Fifth Element 1997, Air Force One 1997, Lost in Space 1998, The Contender 2000 (also exec prodr), Nobody's Baby 2001, Interstate 60 2001, Hannibal 2001, Tiptoes 2003, Sin 2003, Harry Potter and the Prisoner of Azkaban 2004; wrote, directed and co-produced Nil By Mouth 1997, produced Plunkett & Macleane 1999; *Awards* Time Out's Fringe Award for Best Newcomer 1985; BAFTA: Best Actor nomination for Prick Up Your Ears 1988, Best British Film, Best British Screenplay; Channel Four Director's Award at the 51st Edinburgh Festival; *Style—* Gary Oldman, Esq

OLDRIDGE, John Norman Leslie; *b* 26 January 1947; *Educ* Oundle, Oxford Sch of Architecture (DipArch); *Career* currently sr ptnr Chapman Taylor Partners (joined 1973, assoc 1977, ptnr 1987); RIBA 1977, memb Ordre des Architectes 1990; *Recreations* offshore sailing; *Clubs* Royal Yacht Squadron, Royal Southampton Yacht; *Style—* John Oldridge, Esq

OLDWORTH, Richard Anthony; s of Anthony Gilbert Frederick Oldworth, and Patricia, *née* Thompson; *b* 5 June 1957; *Educ* Radley, City of London Poly; *m*; 3 da; *Career* chartered accountant; Peat Marwick Mitchell 1976–80, corp finance exec County Bank 1980–83, Bisgood Bishop & Co 1983–84, chief exec Buchanan Communications 1984–; ACA 1980; *Recreations* flying, motorsport; *Clubs* City of London, Royal Solent Yacht, Helicopter Club of GB, Historic Sports Car; *Style—* Richard Oldworth, Esq; ✉ Buchanan Communications Ltd, 45 Moorfields, London EC27 9AE (tel 0207 466 5000, fax 0207 466 5001)

O'LEARY, Dermot; s of Sean O'Leary, and Maria O'Leary; *Educ* St Benedict's RC Sch, Colchester Sixth Form Coll, Univ of Middlesex (BA); *Career* runner and devpt researcher Barraclough Carey 1995–96; researcher 1996–97: Chapter One, Dove Prodns, Princess Prodns; TV presenter 1997– (progs incl T4, Barfly Sessions, Big Brother's Little Brother, Big Breakfast, Top of the Pops, TFI Friday and SAS - Are You Tough Enough?); presenter and assoc prodr: Recovered 2001–, Dermot's Sporting Buddies 2001–; owner Murfia Prodns 2001–; columnist Sky magazine 2000–; Best Newcomer Irish World 2000, TV Personality of the Year GQ 2001, Elle Style Award 2001; patron Everyman 2002–; worked with charities incl: NSPCC, Centrepoint, Terrence Higgins Tst, CAFOD, Cinemagic; *Recreations* diving and all things oceanic, learning to speak Italian, boxing, marathon running; *Style—* Dermot O'Leary, Esq

OLINS, Rufus; s of Wally Olins, *qv*, and Renate, *née* Steinert; *b* 24 February 1961; *Educ* UCS London, Univ of York (BA); *m* 30 Sept 1995, Sara, *née* Scott; 1 da (Eliza b 23 Nov

1996), 1 s (Clem b 15 Feb 1999); *Career* Campaign 1986–89, Sunday Times 1989–94, Eastern Express Hong Kong 1994–95, Sunday Times 1996–98; Management Today: ed 1998–99, ed-in-chief and publishing dir 1999–2000; Haymarket Management Publications Ltd: publishing dir 2001–02, md 2003–06; md Haymarket Brand Media 2006–; memb: Advsy Cncl RSA, Devpt Bd Nat Portrait Gallery, Bd Almeida Theatre; vice-patron Working Families, govr Salusbury Sch; *Recreations* cinema, cooking, tennis, cycling; *Style*— Rufus Olins, Esq; ✉ Haymarket Brand Media, 174 Hammersmith Road, London W6 7JP (tel 020 8267 4956, fax 020 7267 4966, e-mail rufus.olins@haynet.com)

OLINS, Wallace (Wally); CBE (1999); s of Alfred Olins (d 1970), and Rachel, *née* Muscovitch (d 1961); *b* 19 December 1930; *Educ* Highgate Sch, St Peter's Coll Oxford (MA); *m* 1, 1957 (m dis 1989), Maria Renate Olga Laura Steinert; 1 da ((Sarah) Edwina b 1959), 2 s (Rufus Laurence, *qv*, b 1961, Benjamin Toby b 1967); m 2, 1990, Dornie; 1 da (Harriet Rachel Hildegard); *Career* Nat Serv 1950–51; SH Benson (now part of Ogilvy & Mather): joined 1954, in India latterly as md Bombay 1957–62; md Caps Design London 1962–64, jt fndr Greers Gross Olins 1964, jt fndr (with Michael Wolff) Wolff Olins 1965 (chm until 1997), chm Saffron Brand Consultants 2001–; visiting lectr in design mgmnt London Business Sch 1984–89; visiting prof Mgmnt Sch: Imperial Coll London 1987–91, Lancaster Univ 1991–, Duxx Mexico 1995–2002, Copenhagen Business Sch 1993–, Saïd Business Sch Oxford 2002–; vice-pres CSD 1982–85, chm Design Dimension Educnl Tst 1987–94; dir Health Educn Authy 1996–99, dir Glasgow Year of Design and Architecture 1999; nominated Prince Philip Designers Prize 1999, awarded Bicentenary Medal RSA 2000, awarded D&AD President's Award 2003; memb Cncl RSA 1989–95; FCSD; *Books* The Corporate Personality (1978), The Wolff Olins Guide to Corporate Identity (1983), The Wolff Olins Guide to Design Management (1985), Corporate Identity (1989), International Corporate Identity (1995), The New Guide to Identity (1996), Trading Identities (1999), On Brand (2003); *Recreations* looking at buildings, shopping for books, theatre, old cars; *Clubs* Groucho; *Style*— Wally Olins, CBE; ✉ 3 Jacob's Well Mews, London W1U 3DU (tel 020 7190 3500, 020 7190 3501, e-mail wally@wallyolins.com, website www.wallyolins.com)

OLISA, Kenneth Aphunezi (Ken); *b* 13 October 1951; *Educ* High Pavement GS Nottingham, Fitzwilliam Coll Cambridge (IBM scholar, MA); *m*; 2 da; *Career* systems engr rising to product mktg mangr IBM (UK) Ltd 1974–81, various sr mktg positions rising to vice-pres worldwide mktg then md Wang (UK) Ltd and latterly sr vice-pres and gen mangr EMEA Wang Laboratories Inc 1981–92; Interregnum plc: fndr chm and ceo 1992–2006, non-exec chm 2006–; chm: Metapraxis Ltd 1993–2004, DMA-TEK Ltd 1994–98; dir: BDO Stoy Hayward Consulting 1994–97, Voss Net plc 1994–97, ProMetrics Gp Ltd 1994–97, Thumb Candy Ltd 1994–97, Pro-Bel Ltd 1995–96, Lambeth Healthcare NHS Tst 1995–99, Geoconference Ltd 1996–2000, CallCentric Ltd 1997–2000, Open Text Corp 1998–, uDate.com Ltd 2000–03, Datapoint 2000–02, Adaptive Inc 2002–, Yospace Technologies Ltd 2003–, Biowisdom 2004–, Reuters plc 2004–; cmmr Postal Servs Cmmn 2000–04; chm Thames Reach Bondway 1994–, dir Fitzwilliam Society Tst Ltd 1994–, govr Peabody Tst 1998–; Br Venture Capital Assoc/Real Deals Private Equity Personality of the Year 2003; Freeman City of London, Liveryman Worshipful Co of Info Technologists; FRSA; *Style*— Ken Olisa, Esq; ✉ Interregnum plc, 22–23 Old Burlington Street, London W1S 2JJ (tel 020 7494 3080, fax 020 7494 3090, e-mail ken.olisa@interregnum.com)

OLIVE, Prof David Ian; CBE (2002); s of Ernest Edward Olive (ka 1944), and Lilian Emma, *née* Chambers (d 1992); *b* 16 April 1937; *Educ* Edinburgh Royal HS, Univ of Edinburgh (MA), Univ of Cambridge (BA, PhD); *m* 15 April 1963, Jenifer Mary, da of William G Tutton; 2 da (Katharine Alice b 1964, Rosalind Mary b 1966); *Career* fell Churchill Coll Cambridge 1963–70, lectr DAMTP Cambridge 1965–71, staff memb CERN Geneva 1971–77, lectr Imperial Coll London 1977–92, prof Univ of Swansea 1992–2002; visiting prof Univ of Virginia 1982–83, visiting prof Univ of Geneva 1986, Kramers prof Univ of Utrecht 2000, Miller prof Univ of Calif Berkeley 2004; memb NATO ASI panel 1995–99; Dirac Medal and Prize of ICTP Trieste 1997 (jtly with Dr P Goddard, *qv*); FRS 1987; *Books* Analytic S-Matrix (with R J Eden, P V Landshoff and J C Polkinghorne, *qv*, 1965), Kac Moody and Virasoro Algebras (with P Goddard, 1988), Paul Dirac: The Man and His Work (with P Goddard, Sir Michael Atiyah, *qv*, M Jacob and A Pais, 1998), Duality And Supersymmetric Theories (with P West, 1999); *Recreations* golf, listening to music; *Clubs* Pennard Golf; *Style*— Prof David Olive, CBE, FRS; ✉ Department of Physics, University of Wales Swansea, Swansea SA2 8PP (tel 01792 295842, e-mail d.i.olive@swan.ac.uk)

OLIVEIRA, Prof David Benjamin Graeme; s of Anthony Benjamin Oliveira (d 1983), and Pamela Avril, *née* Maitland-Heriot; *b* 11 September 1955; *Educ* CCC Cambridge (Smyth scholar, MB BChir, MA), Westminster Hosp Med Sch London, PhD (London); *m* 14 April 1984, Patricia Margaret, da of Gp Capt J E F Williams, CBE; 2 s (Benjamin b 30 April 1985, Samuel b 26 May 1987), 1 da (Amelia b 24 Nov 1988); *Career* house physician then house surgn Westminster Hosp London 1979–80; SHO: Hammersmith Hosp London 1980–81, Nat Hosp for Nervous Diseases Queen Square 1981, Brompton Hosp London 1981–82, Renal Unit Guy's Hosp London 1982; registrar rotation Ealing Hosp then Renal Unit Hammersmith Hosp 1982–84, MRC trg fell UCL 1984–87; Univ of Cambridge: Lister Inst research fell Sch of Clinical Med 1987–95, univ lectr 1995; Addenbrooke's Hosp Cambridge: sr registrar in nephrology 1990–91, hon conslt physician 1991–95; fndn prof of renal med St George's Hosp Med Sch 1995–; memb Lister Inst of Preventive Med; assoc ed Clinical and Experiment Immunology; author of numerous articles in learned jls; FRCP; *Recreations* bridge, natural history (especially insects), computers; *Style*— Prof David Oliveira; ✉ Division of Renal Medicine, St George's Hospital Medical School, Cranmer Terrace, Tooting, London SW17 0RE (tel 020 8725 5035, e-mail doliveir@sghms.ac.uk)

OLIVER, Hon David Keightley Rideal; QC (1986); o s of Baron Oliver of Aylmerton, PC (Life Peer), *qv*, and his 1 w, Mary Chichester, *née* Rideal (d 1985); *b* 4 June 1949; *Educ* Westminster, Trinity Hall Cambridge (BA), Université Libre de Bruxelles (Lic Special en Droit Européen); *m* 1, 5 April 1972 (m dis 1987), Maria Luisa, da of Juan Mirasierras, of Avenida Reina Vitoria, Madrid, Spain; 2 s (Daniel b 1974, Thomas b 1976); m 2, 20 Feb 1988, Judith Britannia Caroline, da of David Henry John Griffiths Powell; 2 s (Rhodri b 1990, Alexander Rollo Tristram b 1993); *Career* called to the Bar Lincoln's Inn 1972 (bencher 1994); standing counsel to DG of Fair Trading 1980–86; *Recreations* gardening, bird watching, rough shooting, horse racing, tennis; *Style*— The Hon David Oliver, QC; ✉ Erskine Chambers, 30 Lincoln's Inn Field, London WC2A 3PF (tel 020 7242 5532, fax 020 7831 0125)

OLIVER, Prof (Ann) Dawn; da of Ernest Gordon Borrett Taylor (d 1989), and Ann Zoë Mieke Taylor (d 1961); *b* 7 June 1942; *Educ* Notting Hill and Ealing HS, Newnham Coll Cambridge (MA, PhD); *m* 6 Jan 1967, Sir Stephen J L Oliver, *qv*, s of Capt P D Oliver, RN (d 1979); 2 da (Rebecca b 1969, Rosemary b 1972), 1 s (Adam b 1970); *Career* called to the Bar Middle Temple 1965 (bencher 1996); in practice 1965–69, conslt Legal Action Gp 1973–76, assoc memb Blackstone Chambers Temple 1994–2002; UCL: lectr in law 1976–88, sr lectr 1988–90, reader in public law 1990–93, prof of constitutional law 1993–, dean of the faculty and head of dept 1993–98 and 2007; memb: Inst of Public Policy Res working gp on a constitution for the UK 1990–91, Hansard Soc Cmmn on Election Campaigns 1990–91, Study of Parliament Gp 1992–, Justice Working Party on Interventions in Public Interest Cases 1994–95, Advsy Bd Constitution Unit 1995–, Royal Cmmn on Reform of House of Lords 1999, Fabian Soc Cmmn on the Future of the Monarchy 2002–03, Animal Procedures Ctee 2003–; chair Advtg Advsy Ctee ITC 1999–2003; ed Public Law 1993–2001; assoc fell Newnham Coll Cambridge 1996–99; hon fell Soc of Advanced Legal Studies 1997, hon fell UCL 2001; FBA 2005; *Books* The Changing Constitution (ed with J L Jowell, 1985, 6 edn 2007), Cohabitation - The Legal Implications (1987), New Directions in Judicial Review (ed with J L Jowell, 1988), Economical with the Truth - The Law and the Media in a Democracy (ed with D Kingsford Smith, 1989), Government in the United Kingdom: The Search for Accountability, Effectiveness and Citizenship (1991), The Foundations of Citizenship (with D Heater, 1994), Public Service Reforms (with G Drewry, 1996), Halsbury's Laws of England Constitutional Law (4 edn, ed with Lord Lester of Herne Hill, QC, 1996), The Law and Parliament (ed with G Drewry, 1998), Common Values and the Public - Private Divide (1999), Constitutional Reform in the UK (2003); *Style*— Professor Dawn Oliver; ✉ University College London, Law Faculty, Bentham House, Endsleigh Gardens, London WC1H 0EG (tel 020 7679 1409, fax 020 7979 1424, e-mail d.oliver@ucl.ac.uk)

OLIVER, Dr Ian Thomas; s of Thomas Oliver, GM (d 1967), and Mary Elizabeth, *née* Burton (d 2000); *b* 24 January 1940; *Educ* Hampton GS, Univ of Nottingham (LLB, MPhil), Univ of Strathclyde (PhD); *m* 22 Feb 1964, Elsie, *née* Chalmers; 1 da (Stephanie Katherine b 20 Dec 1965), 2 s (Guy Thomas b 29 Sept 1967, Craig Stewart b 15 May 1969); *Career* Offr RAF 1959–61; Constable rising to Supt Metropolitan Police 1961–77, awarded Cwlth Fndn bursary to Kenya 1972, asst Chief Constable Mgmnt Servs Northumbria Police 1978–79 (Chief Supt 1977–78), Chief Constable Central Scotland Police 1979–90, Chief Constable Grampian Police 1990–98; awarded Winston Churchill Travelling Fellowship to North America (drugs educn progs) 1986, visiting lectr Univ of Teeside 2001; drug trg conslt Aberdeen Coll of FE 2005–; memb: various ctees IACP 1982–98 (int vice-pres 1997–98), Editorial Bd Criminal Law Review 1989–98, Home Sec's Firearms Consultative Ctee 1989–98, Steering Gp for Royalty Protection Home Office 1990–98, Service Authy for Nat Criminal Intelligence Service 1997–98, Bd Int Scientific and Medical Forum on Drug Abuse 1999–, Inst on Global Drug Policy 2001–, Advsy Bd EURAD (Europe Against Drugs) 2007–; chm Crime Ctee ACPO Scotland 1997–98 (pres 1983–84 and 1993–94); conslt UN Drug Control Programme; columnist Aberdeen Press & Journal 2001–05, memb Editorial Bd Jl of Global Drug Policy and Practice 2005; memb: Int Criminal Justice Symposium SUNY 1982, L'Ordre de Bon Temps Nova Scotia 1985; chm Nat Police Lifeboat Appeal Ctee 1990–92; tstee Mayor of Bulawayo's Children's Fund 2005; QPM 1984; FRSA 1993; *Books* The Metropolitan Police Approach to the Prosecution of Juvenile Offenders (1977), Police, Government and Accountability (1987, 2 edn 1996), Drug Affliction: What you need to know (2006); *Clubs* RAF; *Style*— Dr Ian Oliver; ✉ e-mail snowbird@ifb.co.uk

OLIVER, Jamie Trevor; MBE (2003); *b* May 1975; *Educ* Westminster Catering Coll; *m* 2000, Jools; 2 da (Poppy Honey b 18 March 2002, Daisy Boo b 10 April 2003); *Career* formerly: chef in France, head pastry chef Neal Street Restaurant London, chef River Café London, conslt chef Monte's London; currently proprietor Fifteen London (fndr 2002); touring cookery show Happy Days Tour (UK, Aust and NZ) 2001; former columnist GQ magazine, former feature writer The Times Magazine; advsr Sainsbury's, designer of own cook and tableware for Royal Worcester and cookware for Tefal; *Television* The Naked Chef (three series, BBC), Jamie's Kitchen (Channel 4) 2002, Jamie's School Dinners (Channel 4) 2005, Jamie's Chef (Channel 4) 2007; *Awards* incl: GQ Man of the Year 2000, GQ Best Chef Award in the USA, Most Stylish Male TV Personality award Elle Style Awards 2000, TV Quick Award for Best TV Cook 2000, BAFTA (for The Naked Chef) 2001, Tatler Best Restaurant Award (for Fifteen) 2003, Academy Award of Excellence Tio Pepe Carlton London Restaurant Awards 2003, Time Out Special Award for Outstanding Achievement 2003, Glenfiddich Food and Drink Awards 2003; *Books* The Naked Chef (1999), The Return of The Naked Chef (2000, WH Smith Book Award 2001), Happy Days with The Naked Chef (2001), Jamie's Kitchen (2003, WH Smith Book Award), Jamie's Dinners (2004), Something for the Weekend (2005); *Style*— Jamie Oliver, Esq, MBE; ✉ c/o The Outside Organisation, 177–178 Tottenham Court Road, London W1T 7PD (tel 020 7436 3633, fax 020 7436 3632)

OLIVER, Rt Rev John Keith; s of Walter Keith Oliver (d 1977), of Danehill, E Sussex, and Ivy, *née* Nightingale (d 1981); *b* 14 April 1935; *Educ* Westminster, Gonville & Caius Coll Cambridge (MA, MLitt); *m* 16 Sept 1961, Meriel, da of Sir Alan Moore, Bt (d 1959), of Battle, E Sussex; 2 s (Thomas b 1964, Henry b 1968), 1 da (Mary b 1971 d 2002); *Career* curate Hilborough Gp of Parishes Norfolk 1964–68, chaplain and asst master Eton Coll 1968–72; team rector: S Molton Gp 1973–82 (rural dean 1974–80), Central Exeter 1982–85; archdeacon of Sherborne, canon of Salisbury and priest-in-charge W Stafford 1985–90, bishop of Hereford 1990–2003, hon asst bishop Diocese of Swansea and Brecon 2004–; chaplian Royal Agric Benevolent Inst 2003– (tstee 2005–); chm C of E's Advsy Bd of Min 1993–98; chm Rural Support Network (West Midlands) 2003–07, tstee Marches Energy Agency 2004–, memb NI Office Cmmn of Inquiry into murder of Billy Wright 2004–; memb House of Lords 1997–2003; *Recreations* railways, music, architecture, walking, motorcycling; *Clubs* Oxford and Cambridge, Herefordshire CCC, Farmers'; *Style*— The Rt Rev John Oliver; ✉ The Old Vicarage, Glascwm, Powys LD1 5SE

OLIVER, Keith Edward; *b* 5 September 1956, London; *Career* slr specialising in commercial, regulatory and insolvency litigation; Peters & Peters: joined as trainee, ptnr 1983, sr ptnr 2005–, head of commercial litigation/commercial fraud; vice-pres d'honneur Assoc Internationale des Jeunes Avocats (AIJA), founding past pres AIJA Commercial Fraud Cmmn; memb: Int Bar Assoc, Br Italian Lawyers' Assoc; *Recreations* the arts, football (playing and spectating), wine appreciation; *Style*— Keith Oliver, Esq; ✉ 101 West City One, 6 Naoroji Street, London WC1X 0GD; Peters & Peters, 15 Fetter Lane, London EC4A 1BW (tel 020 7822 7722, fax 020 7822 7788, e-mail keoliver@petersandpeters.com)

OLIVER, Mark Leo; s of Rudolf Oliver, of London, and Anita, *née* Levinson; *b* 19 September 1963; *Educ* Orange Hill HS, Hertford Coll Oxford (BA); *m* (m dis), Victoria Rosalind, *née* Pugh; *Career* econ analyst National Economic Research Associates 1985–87 (work incl conslt to Peacock Ctee on funding of the BBC), conslt and media gp mangr Deloitte Haskins & Sells Consultancy 1987–89; BBC Policy and Planning Unit: business analyst 1989–90, business policy advsr to BBC Bd of Mgmnt (on corp strategy and operational efficiency and effectiveness) 1990–93, chief advsr (corp strategy) 1993–95; md Oliver & Ohlbaum Associates Ltd 1995–; *Style*— Mark Oliver, Esq; ✉ Oliver & Ohlbaum Associates Ltd, 5 Lambton Place, London W11 2SH (tel 020 7313 5900, fax 020 7985 0645)

OLIVER, Sir (James) Michael Yorrick; kt (2003), DL (2004), JP (1987); s of Sqdn Ldr George Leonard Jack Oliver (d 1984), of Mallorca, and Patricia Rosamund, *née* Douglas; *b* 13 July 1940; *Educ* Brunswick Sch, Wellington; *m* 22 June 1963, Sally Elizabeth Honor, da of George Gerhard Exner (d 1965), of London W1; 2 da (Sophia Tugela Rosamund b 14 Oct 1969, Justine Umthandi Electra b 29 Dec 1971); *Career* asst mangr Rediffusion Ltd Leicester 1959–63, mangr Helios Ltd Johannesburg 1965–70; ptnr Kitcat & Aitken 1977–86 (joined 1970), dir Kitcat Aitken & Co 1986–90, md Carr Kitcat & Aitken 1990–93; dir Lloyds Investment Managers Ltd 1994–98; dir: Oliver's Wharf Management Co 1970–2003, Gabhaig Hydro Power Co 1988–2000, Highland Light & Power 1994–2001, Hill Samuel UK Emerging Companies Investment Tst 1995–2000, The Central & Eastern European Fund 1995– (chm), The Euro-Spain Fund 1996–2005, The Portugal Growth Fund Ltd 1996–2001, The European Growth Fund 2001–, Goldstone Resources Ltd 2004– (chm); tstee: UK Growth & Income Fund, The Income Plus Fund (chm), Zenex Tst; Alderman Ward of Bishopsgate 1987– (memb Common Cncl 1980–87), Sheriff City of London 1997–98, Lord Mayor of London 2001–02; chllr City Univ 2001–02; govr:

O

Bishopsgate Fndn, King Edward's Sch Witley, Christ's Hosp 1979–2006, Univ of East London 1999–2003; chm: Cncl of Tstees The Museum in Docklands 1993–, City of London Centre St John Ambulance 1998–; memb: City of London Archaeological Tst, Ctee City of London Historical Soc; memb Ct of Assts Worshipful Co of Ironmongers (Master 1991–92); Hon LLD, Hon DLitt; FSI; KStJ; *Recreations* archaeology, travel; *Clubs* City of London, City Livery; *Style*— Alderman Sir Michael Oliver; ✉ Paradise Barns, Bucks Lane, Little Eversden, Cambridge CB23 7HL (mobile 07970 616636, e-mail olivers@petticoat.demon.co.uk)

OLIVER, Dr Raymond; s of Joseph Oliver (d 1995), and Ethel Margaret, *née* Anderson (d 1993); *b* 26 November 1951; *Educ* Beath HS, Heriot-Watt Univ (BSc, PhD); *m* 20 July 1974, Darina Maria, da of late Ondrej Čurilla; 1 da (Clara Cecilia b 8 July 1977), 1 s (Peter Duncan b 12 Aug 1983); *Career* ICI: process engr Runcorn 1974–81, sr process engr Billingham 1981–86, engrg assoc 1986–89, conslt ICI Explosives Canada 1987–97, co research assoc 1989–90, mangr Particle Process Engrg Gp 1990–94, ICI fell 1994–2004; non-exec dir Cenamps 2003– (science and strategy advsr 2004–); visiting prof: Univ of Nottingham 1996–, Univ of Leeds 2003–; memb: Royal Acad of Engrg/Royal Soc Working Gp on Nanoscience and Nanomanufacturing 2003–04, Royal Soc 'Science in Soc' Working Gp 2004–; chair Industrial Liaison Ctee Univ of Newcastle upon Tyne, memb Industrial Liaison Ctee UCL; Hon DEng Heriot-Watt Univ 2001; FIChemE 1995, CEng 1995, FREng 1998; *Publications* incl: Granulation (book, 1981), Jet Induced Emulsification (paper, 1991); *Recreations* theatre, travel, golf, contemporary music, the art of gatecrashing a good party; *Style*— Dr Raymond Oliver, FREng; ✉ Cenamps, Fabrian Centre, Atmel Way, Newcastle upon Tyne NE28 9NZ (tel 0191 280 4290, e-mail raymond.oliver@cenamps.com)

OLIVER, Rt Rev Stephen John; *see:* Stepney, Bishop of

OLIVER, Sir Stephen John Lindsay; kt (2007), QC; s of Phillip Daniel Oliver (Capt RN, d 1979), of Carlton, and Audrey Mary Taylor (d 2001); *b* 14 November 1938; *Educ* Rugby, Oriel Coll Oxford (MA); *m* 1967, Prof (Ann) Dawn Oliver, *qv*, da of Gordon Taylor (d 1989); 2 da (Rebecca b 1969, Rosemary b 1972), 1 s (Adam b 1970); *Career* RNVR (submariner) 1957–59; barr; bencher 1987, asst Parly boundary cmmr, recorder 1989–91, circuit judge SE Circuit 1991–92, presiding special cmmr 1992–; pres: VAT Tbnls 1992–94, VAT and Duties Tbnls 1994–, Financial Services and Markets Tbnl 2001–, Pensions Regulator Tbnl 2005–; chm Blackheath Concert Halls 1986–92, memb Cncl London Sinfonietta 1993–; tstee: Britten-Pears Fndn 2001–, TaxAid 2006–; Hon FCInstT 1997; *Recreations* music, golf; *Clubs* Groucho; *Style*— Sir Stephen Oliver, QC; ✉ 15 Bedford Avenue, London WC1B 3AS (tel 020 7612 9662, fax 020 8852 4686, e-mail stephen.oliver@judiciary.gsi.gov.uk)

OLIVER, Timothy Patrick (CAMROUX-); s of Wing Cdr George Leonard, DFC, AFC (d 1984), and Patricia Rosamund, *née* Douglas; *b* 2 March 1944; *Educ* Christ's Hosp; *m* 18 July 1966, Susan Elizabeth, da of Maj Frederick Wilson Hanham, of Bucks; 2 s (James Richard b Sept 1967, Charles Guy b 1 April 1970), 1 da (Alexa Kate Louise b 25 Dec 1974); *Career* asst gen mangr IGI (SA) 1969–71; dir: Manson Byng Gp 1971–, Hampden Russell plc 1987–; chm: Hampden Insurance Holdings Ltd 1973–, Market Run-Off Services plc 1984–, Hampden plc 1993–; memb Lloyd's 1977; chm Historic Houses Assoc Thames and Chilterns 2001–04; Freeman City of London 1966, Master Worshipful Co of Ironmongers 2002; FRGS 1963, FInstD; *Recreations* shooting, fishing, skiing, tennis, dogs; *Clubs* Brook's, City of London, City Livery Yacht; *Style*— Tim Oliver, Esq; ✉ Hampden House, Great Hampden, Buckinghamshire HP16 9RD (tel 01494 488888, fax 01494 488686); Hampden plc, 42 Crutched Friars, London EC3N 2AP (tel 01494 489000, mobile 07775 501248, e-mail tim.oliver@hampden.co.uk)

OLIVER, Vaughan William; s of Ernest Oliver, and Doreen, *née* Tindale; *b* 12 September 1957; *Educ* Ferryhill GS, Newcastle upon Tyne Poly (BA); *Career* graphic designer, art dir; packaging designer: Benchmark 1980, Michael Peters Gp 1981; record cover designer (under name 23 Envelope, with Nigel Grierson), 4AD (record co) 1983–88, freelance (under name v23, with Chris Bigg) 1988–98, ptnr v23 (with Chris Bigg) 1998–; record covers for gps incl: Cocteau Twins, Heidi Berry, His Name is Alive, Lush, Pixies, The Psychedelic Furs, This Mortal Coil, The Breeders, David Sylvian; gp exhibitions incl: British Design, New Traditions (Boymans Museum Rotterdam) 1989, Pictures of Rock (Denmark) 1990, British Design 1790–1990 (Calif) 1990, Best of British Design (Tokyo) 1990, The Art of Selling Songs 1690–1990 (V&A) 1991; solo exhibitions: Exhibition/Exposition (Nantes, St Brieuc 1990, Paris 1991), Expo 23 (Tokyo) 1991, Glove (Osaka) 1992 and (Tokyo) 1993, 13 Year Itch (ICA London) 1993, This Rimy River (LA and UK) 1994, Is Minty a Man? (Newcastle upon Tyne) 1996; other design work includes: book jackets (Serpents Tail, Picador), book design (Tokyo Salamander, Shinro Ohtake), freelance music projects (Virgin, RCA, East West), TV title sequences for BBC2 (Snub TV, Gimme 8), conf publicity (Kingston Poly, V&A Museum), fashion catalogue (John Galliano, Aspesi), TV station identity, design and direction (Documania, Canal Plus, Madrid), posters (Angelin Preljocaj, Paris and Young Vic London), TV advert (Microsoft); memb Assoc of Music Indust Designers (AMID); *Style*— Vaughan Oliver, Esq; ✉ v23, Crombie Mews, 11A Abercrombie Street, London SW11 2JB (tel 020 7978 6636/4860, fax 020 7978 5552)

OLIVER-BELLASIS, Hugh Richard; s of Lt-Col John Oliver-Bellasis, DSO, JP, DL (d 1979), and Anne Mary, *née* Bates (d 2006); *b* 11 April 1945; *Educ* Winchester, RMA Sandhurst; *m* 7 Aug 1971, Daphne Phoebe, da of Christopher Parsons, of Hatchwood House, Odiham; 2 da (Joanna (Mrs Andrew Runciman) b 8 April 1975, Nicola b 12 June 1978); *Career* 2 Lt Royal Fusiliers City of London Regt 1964, Welsh Gds 1970, Maj 1977 (ret); dir Manydown Co Ltd 1964–2007, farmer 1980–2007; Parish Cncl 1980–2001; pres Br Crop Prodn Cncl 2003–07; chm Br Deer Soc 1986–96, vice-chm Game Conservancy Tst 1999–; tstee RASE 2003– (memb Cncl 1983); memb Grasshoppers' Assoc 1989; Freeman City of London 1967; Liveryman: Worshipful Co of Merchant Taylors 1971 (memb Ct of Assts 1998, Master 2006–07), Worshipful Co of Gunmakers 1990; FRAgS 1992 (ARAgS 1990); *Recreations* field sports, wine, food, motor racing; *Clubs* Army and Navy, Boodle's, Farmers', MCC; *Style*— Hugh Oliver-Bellasis, Esq; ✉ Wootton House, Wootton St Lawrence, Basingstoke, Hampshire RG23 8PE (tel 01256 781145, fax 01256 782666, e-mail ho-b@chui.org.uk)

OLIVER-JONES, His Hon Judge Stephen; QC (1996); s of Arthur William Jones (d 2002), of King's Stanley, Glos, and Kathleen, *née* Woodcock (d 1993); *b* 6 July 1947; *Educ* Marling Sch Stroud, Univ Coll Durham (BA); *m* 16 Dec 1972, Margaret Anne, da of Ronald Thomas Richardson; 1 da (Claire Felicity b 22 March 1979), 1 s (Robin Stephen b 19 March 1982); *Career* lectr in law Durham Tech Coll 1968–70, called to the Bar Inner Temple 1970, recorder 1993 (asst recorder 1988), circuit judge (Midland & Oxford Circuit) 2000–, designated civil judge Coventry and Walsall 2001–; memb: Mental Health Review Tbnl 2000–, Civil Procedure Rule Ctee 2002–; *Recreations* fly fishing; *Style*— His Hon Judge Oliver-Jones, QC; ✉ Coventry Combined Court, 140 Much Park Street, Coventry CV1 2SN

OLIVER OF AYLMERTON, Baron (Life Peer UK 1986), of Aylmerton in the County of Norfolk; Peter Raymond Oliver; kt (1974), PC (1980); s of David Thomas Oliver (d 1947), and Alice Maud, da of George Kirby; *b* 7 March 1921; *Educ* The Leys Sch Cambridge, Trinity Hall Cambridge (hon fellow 1980); *m* 1, 1945, Mary Chichester (d 1985), da of Sir Eric Keightley Rideal, MBE, FRS; 1 s (Hon David Keightley Rideal, *qv*, b 1949), 1 da (Hon Sarah Chichester b 1951); m 2, 1987, Wendy Anne, widow of Ivon Lloyd Lewis Jones; *Career* called to the Bar Lincoln's Inn 1948; QC 1965; High Court Judge (Chancery) 1974–80; Lord Justice of Appeal 1980–86; memb Restrictive Practices Court 1976–80; chm Review Body on High Court Chancery Div 1979–81; memb Supreme Court Rule Ctee 1982–85; Lord of Appeal in Ordinary 1986–92; *Style*— The Rt Hon Lord Oliver of Aylmerton, PC; ✉ House of Lords, London SW1A 0PW

OLIVIER, Joan Sheila Ross; *b* 30 April 1941; *Educ* Morrisons Acad Crieff, Rosa Bassett Streatham, Queen Mary Coll London (BA), Hughes Hall Cambridge (PGCE); *m* 16 Aug 1966, John Eric Hordern Olivier; 1 s (James Maximilian Dering b 6 July 1978); *Career* Camden Sch for Girls: history teacher 1964–67, head History Dept 1967–73, schs examination supervisor 1970–73; Lady Margaret Sch London: dep head 1973–84, headmistress 1984–2006; Lady Margaret featured in The Independent's Good Sch Guide and Evening Standard's Best State Schs in London; *Recreations* bad bridge; *Style*— Mrs Joan Olivier

OLIVIERI, René; s of Hal W Bowen (d 2000), and Dixie Ann Olivieri, *née* Mann (d 1995); *b* 1 May 1953, Everett, WA; *Educ* Univ of Oregon (BA), Univ of Stuttgart (scholar), Johns Hopkins Univ (MA); *m* 2004, Dr Anne Luetcke-Olivieri; 1 step s (Julius Luetcke b 15 July 1993), 1 step da (Katharina Luise Luetcke b 29 Nov 1994); *Career* ed MIT Press 1978–80; Blackwell Publishers: econs publisher 1980–83, editorial dir 1983–85, dep md 1985–88, md 1988–2000; ceo Blackwell Publishing Ltd 2000–; chm: InfoSource Inc 1990–2000, Polity Press 1995–2000, Marston Book Distributors 1998–2000; tstee Tubney Charitable Tst 2002–; memb Cncl: Assoc of Learned and Professional Soc Publishers, Soc of Bookmen, Publishers' Assoc, Scientific, Technical and Medical Publishers' Assoc; *Recreations* tennis, skiing, scuba diving, pilates, music, literature, theatre; *Style*— René Olivieri, Esq; ✉ Blackwell Publishing Ltd, 9600 Garsington Road, Oxford OX4 2DQ (tel 01865 476119, fax 01865 476774, e-mail reneolivieri@blackwellpublishing.com)

OLLERENSHAW, Dame Kathleen Mary; DBE (1971), DL (1987); da of Charles Timpson, JP (d 1967), and Mary Elizabeth, *née* Stops (d 1954); *b* 1 October 1912, Manchester; *Educ* Ladybarn House Sch Manchester, St Leonards Sch St Andrews, Somerville Coll Oxford (MA, DPhil); *m* 1939, Col Robert Ollerenshaw, ERD, TD, JP, DL (d 1986): 1 s (decd), 1 da (decd); *Career* chm: Assoc of Governing Bodies of Girls' Public Schs 1963–69, Manchester Educn Ctee 1967–70, Manchester Poly 1968–72 (hon fell 1978), Ct RNCM 1968–86 (companion 1978), Educn Ctee Assoc of Municipal Corporations 1968–71; author of numerous res papers in mathematical jls; Manchester CC 1956–81: Alderman 1970–74, Lord Mayor 1975–76, dep Lord Mayor 1976–77, ldr Cons opposition 1977–79, Hon Alderman 1981–; vice-pres Br Assoc for Commercial and Industrial Educn (memb delgn to USSR 1963); memb: Central Advsy Cncl on Educn in England 1960–63, CNAA 1964–74, SSRC 1971–75, Layfield Ctee of Enquiry into Local Govt Fin 1974–76; pres: St Leonards Sch St Andrews 1976–2003, Manchester Technol Assoc 1981 (hon memb 1976–), Manchester Statistical Soc 1983–85; hon res fell Dept of Computer Science Univ of Manchester 1998–2003; hon memb Manchester Literary and Philosophical Soc 1981; dep pro-chllr Lancaster Univ 1978–91 (memb Ct 1991–), pro-chllr Univ of Salford 1983–89; dir Manchester Ind Radio Ltd 1972–83; memb Manchester Astronomical Soc 1990– (hon vice-pres 1994–); Hon Col Manchester and Salford Univ OTC 1977–81; patron Museum of Science and Industry Manchester 2004–; chm Cncl Order of St John Greater Manchester 1974–89, memb Chapter General Order of St John 1978–96; Mancunian of the Year Jr C of C 1977, Wome's Hour Interview BBC Radio 4 Pick of the Year 2004; hon fell: Somerville Coll Oxford 1978, City and Guilds London Inst 1980 (memb Educn Ctee 1960–73), UMIST 1987 (vice-pres 1977–86); Freeman City of Manchester 1984; Hon DSc Univ of Salford 1975, Hon LLD Univ of Manchester 1976, Hon DSc CNAA 1976, Hon DSc Lancaster Univ 1992, Hon LLD Univ of Liverpool 1994; Inst of Mathematics and its Applications Catherine Richards Prize for mathematical research articles in Mathematics Today 2006; Hon FIMA 1990 (FIMA 1964, memb Cncl 1972, pres 1979–80), FCP FCGI; CMath; DStJ 1983 (CStJ 1978); *Books* Education of Girls (1958), The Girls' Schools (1967), Returning to Teaching (1974), The Lord Mayor's Party (1976), First Citizen (1977), Most-Perfect Pandiagonal Magic Squares, their Construction and Enumeration (with David Brée, 1998), To Talk of Many Things (autobiography, 2004), Constructing Magic Squares of Arbitrarily Large Size (2006); *Recreations* astronomy; *Style*— Dame Kathleen Ollerenshaw, DBE, DL; ✉ 2 Pine Road, Didsbury, Manchester M20 6UY (tel 0161 445 2948, e-mail kmo@mighty-micro.co.uk)

OLLERENSHAW, Stephen Christopher; s of Roy Ollerenshaw, of Padstow, Cornwall, and Kim, *née* Hartland (d 1991); *b* 9 April 1970, Birmingham; *Educ* Sollihull Sch, Univ of Essex (BA, MA), Coll of Law Guildford, Univ of Birmingham; *Career* slr specialising in IT law; slr: Osborne Clarke 1997–98 (trainee slr 1995–97), Wragge & Co 1998–2002; co-founding ptnr Technology Law Alliance Slrs 2003–; author of various pubns in legal and IT press, business mentor with various univs; memb Law Soc; *Recreations* motor racing, football, guitar, ornithology; *Style*— Stephen Ollerenshaw, Esq; ✉ Technology Law Alliance, 2nd Floor, 3 Brindley Place, Birmingham B1 2JB (tel 0870 730 5552, fax 0870 199 1361, e-mail stephen.ollerenshaw@tlawa.co.uk)

OLLEY, Martin Burgess; s of Robert William Olley (d 1969), of Sheringham, Norfolk, and Dorothy Lillian Alexander, *née* Burgess (d 1941); *b* 11 August 1932; *Educ* Gresham's, Coll of Estate Mgmnt London; *m* 1 (m dis 1971), Averil Rosemary Phyllis, *née* Cann; 2 s (Clive Matthew Burgess b 1961, Edward Martin Burgess b 1967), 1 da (Lucy Ann Burgess b 1963); m 2, 1980, Moira Bernadette, da of Joseph Kelly (d 1968); *Career* RAF 1950–52; Norwich Union: London Estates mangr 1973–80, Norwich estates mangr 1980–82, chief estates mangr 1983–; memb Gen Cncl Br Property Fedn, former pres Norwich Wanderers CC; Freeman City of London 1974, Liveryman Worshipful Co of Woolmen 1978; FRICS; *Recreations* golf, boating, squash, tennis, walking; *Clubs* RAC, Norfolk Broads Yacht; *Style*— Martin Olley, Esq; ✉ 1 Marston Lane, Eaton, Norwich, Norfolk NR4 6LZ (tel 01603 456495); 55 Netheravon Road, Chiswick, London W4 2NA (tel 020 8994 1392); Norwich Union Real Estate Managers Ltd, Sentinel House, 37 Surrey Street, Norwich NR1 3PW (tel 01603 682256, fax 01603 683950)

OLLIFF, Barry Martin; s of Clarence Martin William Olliff, and Patricia Joan, *née* Greenley; *b* 31 December 1944; *Educ* Hinchley Wood County Secdy Sch; *m* Margaret Ann, da of Francis Samuel Thomas Cleave; 1 s (Andrew James), 1 da (Samantha Claire); *Career* various appts in investment depts of: Rowe Swann & Co Stockbrokers 1962–63, Denny Bros/Pinchin Denny Stockjobbers 1963–79, Laing & Cruickshank Stockbrokers 1979–86 (dir 1983–86); md Olliff & Partners plc 1987–97; md: City of London Unit Trust Managers 1991–, City of London Investment Gp 1997–; MSI; *Recreations* cricket, skiing; *Style*— Barry Olliff, Esq; ✉ City of London Investment Management, 10 Eastcheap, London EC3M 1AJ (tel 020 7711 0771, fax 020 7711 0772)

OLNER, William John (Bill); MP; s of late C William Olner, and Lillian Olner; *b* 9 May 1942; *Educ* Atherstone Secdy Modern Sch, N Warks Tech Coll; *m* 10 March 1962, Gillian, da of David Everitt; *Career* apprentice engr Armstrong Siddeley Motors, skilled machinist Rolls Royce Coventry until 1992, AEU branch sec 1972–92; MP (Lab, AEU sponsored until 1997) Nuneaton 1992–; House of Commons: memb Select Ctee for Environment 1995–97, memb Select Ctee for Environment, Tport and the Regions 1997–2001, memb Foreign Affrs Select Ctee 2001–06, memb ODPM Select Ctee 2006–; Nuneaton BC: cncllr 1971–93, chm Planning Ctee 1974–76, chm Policy and Resources Ctee 1982–86, chm Environmental Health Ctee 1990–92, dep ldr 1980–82, ldr 1982–86; *Recreations* working for local hospice, walking, current affairs, television; *Style*— Bill Olner, Esq, MP; ✉ House of Commons, London SW1A 0AA

O'LOAN, Nuala Patricia; *b* 20 December 1951, Bishop's Stortford, Herts; *Educ* Convent of the Holy Child Harrogate, KCL (LLB), Coll of Law London; *m* Declan O'Loan; 5 s; *Career*

slr Supreme Court of Eng and Wales 1976–, lectr in law Ulster Poly 1976–80; Univ of Ulster: lectr in law 1984–92, Jean Monnet chair in European law 1992–99, sr lectr in law 1992–2000; Police Ombudsman for NI 2000–, special cmmr Cmmn for Racial Equality 2004–05; chm NI Consumer Cncl for Electricity 1997–2000; memb: Energy and Tport Gp Gen Consumer Cncl for NI 1991–96 (convenor 1994–96), UK Domestic Coal Consumer Cncl 1992–95, Ministerial Working Gp on the Green Economy 1993–95, N Health and Social Servs Bd 1993–97 (convenor for complaints 1996–97), Police Authy for NI 1997–99; expert memb European Cmmn Consumers Consultative Cncl 1994–95; lay visitor to RUC Stations 1991–97; *Publications* author of more than 50 pubns on consumer law, policing and other issues; *Recreations* reading, music; *Style*— Mrs Nuala O'Loan; ✉ Police Ombudsman for Northern Ireland, New Cathedral Buildings, St Anne's Square, 11 Church Street, Belfast BT1 1PG (tel 028 9082 8600, fax 028 9082 8615, e-mail info@policeombudsman.org, website www.policeombudsman.org)

O'LOGHLEN, Sir Colman Michael; 6 Bt (UK 1838), of Drumconora, Ennis; s of Henry Ross O'Loghlen (d 1944), and Doris Irene, *née* Horne; suc uncle, Sir Charles Hugh Ross O'Loghlen, 5 Bt (d 1951); *b* 6 April 1916; *Educ* Xavier Coll Melbourne, Univ of Melbourne (LLB); *m* 1939, Margaret, da of Francis O'Halloran, of Melbourne; 2 da (Margaret b 1940, Janet b 1942), 6 s (Michael b 1945, Bryan b 1946, Ross b 1948, Hugh b 1952, 2 others); *Heir* s, Michael O'Loghlen; *Career* served 1942–45 with AIF New Guinea, Capt 1945; stipendiary magistrate Lae New Guinea, former actg judge of Supreme Court of Territory of Papua and New Guinea; *Style*— Sir Colman O'Loghlen, Bt

OLSEN, John Richard; s of (Lawrence) Nigel Guy Olsen, of Saffron Walden, Essex, and Rosemary Elizabeth, *née* Kies; *b* 7 January 1964; *Educ* Charterhouse, Univ of Durham (BA Archaeology); *m* 9 May 1992, Juliet Mary; 2 da (Lucy b 15 Dec 1993, Samantha b 24 Jan 1998), 1 s (Jack b 30 Aug 1995); *Career* PR exec; Broad Street Associates PR 1986–89, Shandwick Consultants 1990–97 (latterly dir), fndr and managing ptnr The Hogarth Partnership 1997–; *Recreations* family, sailing, golf; *Style*— John Olsen, Esq; ✉ St Breward, Rickford, Worplesdon, Surrey GU3 3PH (tel 01483 235188); The Hogarth Partnership, No 1 London Bridge, London SE1 9BG (tel 020 7357 9477, e-mail jolsen@hogarthpr.co.uk)

OLVER, Richard (Dick); *b* 1947; *Career* BP: joined 1973, vice-pres BP Pipelines Inc BP N America 1979, divnl mangr for new technology 1983, divnl mangr of corp planning 1985, gen mangr (gas) BP Exploration Europe 1988, head of corporate strategy and COS to the Chm 1990, chief exec BP Exploration USA 1992, dep chief exec BP Exploration 1995, dir of exploration and prodn BP 1998 and BP Amoco plc 1999–2002, dep gp chief exec BP plc 2003–04; non-exec chm BAE Systems plc 2004–, non-exec dir Reuters Gp plc 1997– (sr ind non-exec dir 2004–); DSc (hc) City Univ 2004; CEng, MICE, FREng; *Style*— Richard Olver, Esq

OLYMPITIS, Emmanuel John; s of John Emmanuel Olympitis, and Argyro, *née* Theodorou; *b* 19 December 1948; *Educ* King's Sch Canterbury, UCL (LLB); *m* 1, 26 Oct 1979 (m dis 1983), Jan Cushing; 1 s (John); m 2, 1 Dec 1995, Emily Clare, da of Michael John Benjamin Todhunter, *qv*; 2 s (Michael, Alexander (twins)), 1 da (Olympia); *Career* chief exec and dir Aitken Hume International plc 1986–89; chm Johnson & Higgins Ltd 1993–96, gp md Johnson & Higgins Holdings Ltd 1992–96; chm: Pacific Media plc 1999–2004 (non-exec dir 2004–), Bella Media plc 2003–04, Lyra Investments Ltd 2004–; dir Norman 95 SpA; memb: GB Int Fencing Squad 1966–70, Kent County Fencing Team 1966–70 (foil and épée champion 1966); *Books* By Victories Undone (1988); *Recreations* writing, sailing; *Clubs* Turf, Special Forces; *Style*— Emmanuel Olympitis, Esq; ✉ 23 Warwick Square, London SW1V 2AB (tel 020 7828 4343, fax 020 7828 5353); Kalymnos, Dodecanese Islands, Greece

O'MALLEY, His Hon Judge Stephen Keppel; DL (Somerset 1998); *b* 21 July 1940; *Educ* Ampleforth, Wadham Coll Oxford; *m* 1963, Frances Mary, da of Stewart Ryan; 4 s, 2 da; *Career* called to the Bar Inner Temple 1962; recorder 1978–89, circuit judge (Western Circuit) 1989–; wine treas Western Circuit 1986–89; co-fndr Bar European Gp 1977; *Books* European Civil Practice (1989); *Style*— His Hon Judge O'Malley, DL; ✉ Taunton Crown Court, Taunton, Somerset TA1 4EU

OMAND, Sir David Bruce; GCB (2004, KCB 2000); s of James Bruce Omand (d 1980), and Esther, *née* Dewar; *b* 15 April 1947; *Educ* Glasgow Acad, CCC Cambridge (fndn scholar, BA), Open Univ (Dip Mathematics); *m* Feb 1971, Elizabeth Marjorie, da of Geoffrey Wales (d 1990); 1 da (Helen b 1975), 1 s (Duncan b 1978); *Career* joined GCHQ 1969; MOD: asst princ 1970, private sec to Chief Procurement Exec 1973, asst private sec to Sec of State for Def 1973–75 and 1979–80, princ 1975, asst sec 1981, private sec to Sec of State for Def 1981–82, seconded as def cnsllr to FCO Delgn to Nato Brussels 1985–88, under sec grade 3 1988, asst under sec of state (Mgmnt Strategy) 1988–91, asst under sec of state (Programmes) 1991–92, dep under-sec of state (Policy) 1992–96; head of GCHQ 1996–97, perm sec Home Office 1998–2001; Cabinet Office: chair Centre for Mgmnt and Policy Studies 2001–, security and intelligence co-ordinator and perm sec 2002–05; memb Jt Intelligence Ctee 1993–97 and 2002–05; currently visiting prof of war studies KCL; tstee Natural History Museum 2006–; *Recreations* hill walking, opera; *Clubs* Reform; *Style*— Sir David Omand, GCB; ✉ Reform Club, 104 Pall Mall, London SW1Y 5EW

O'MARA, Kate; *b* 10 August 1939; *Children* 1 s (Dickon b 3 Jan 1963); *Career* actress 1963–; fndr and dir The British Actors Theatre Co 1987–; patron: Thorndike Theatre Leatherhead, Theatre Royal Portsmouth, Guildford Sch of Acting, The Brewhouse Theatre Taunton; vice-pres The Royal Mail Charity - Mailshot; numerous TV and film appearances; *Theatre* seasons incl: The Flora Robson Playhouse 1963–64, The Shakespeare for Schools Co 1964, The New Theatre Bromley 1965, The Ashcroft Theatre Croydon 1965; credits incl: Jessica in The Merchant of Venice (Stockton-on-Tees) 1963, Lydia Languish in The Rivals (Welsh National Theatre Co) 1965–66, The Italian Girl (Wyndhams) 1968, The Spoils of Poynton (Mayfair) 1970, Love for Love (Watford) 1971, An Ideal Husband (Watford) 1971, Of Mice and Men (New Theatre Bromley) 1972, Suddenly At Home (Fortune) 1972–73, Elvira in Blithe Spirit (Bristol Old Vic) 1974, Sherlock's Last Case (Open Space Theatre) 1974, Hedda Gabler (Harrogate) 1976, Louka in Arms and The Man (Hong Kong Festival) 1976–77, Kate in The Taming of the Shrew (Ludlow Festival) 1978, Rosaline in Love's Labour's Lost (Thorndike) 1978, Cyrene in Rattle of A Simple Man (tour) 1978, Cleopatra in Antony and Cleopatra (Thorndike) 1979, Lena in Misalliance (Birmingham Rep) 1979, T S Eliot's The Elder Statesman (Birmingham Rep) 1979, The Crucifer of Blood (Haymarket London) 1979, Night and Day (post-London tour) 1980, Beatrice in Much Ado About Nothing (New Shakespeare Co) 1981, Kate in The Taming of the Shrew (New Shakespeare Co) 1982, Titania/Hippolyta in A Midsummer Night's Dream (New Shakespeare Co) 1982, Cleopatra in Antony and Cleopatra (Nottingham Playhouse) 1982, Millamant in The Way of the World (Nottingham Playhouse) 1982, Duet for One (post-London tour and former Yugoslavia) 1982, Lady Macbeth in An Evening with the Macbeths (Mercury Colchester) 1983, The Merry Wives of Windsor (New Shakespeare Co) 1984, Light Up the Sky (Old Vic) 1985, Goneril in King Lear (Compass Theatre Co) 1987, Light Up the Sky (Globe) 1987, Kate in The Taming of the Shrew (Jerash Festival Jordan) 1988, Berinthia in The Relapse (tour and Mermaid Theatre London) 1988–89, The Last Englishman (Orange Tree Richmond) 1990, Martha in Who's Afraid of Virginia Woolf 1990, Lilli Vanessi in Kiss Me Kate (RSC Remount tour) 1991, Lady Fanciful in The Provoked Wife (RNT Studio) 1992, Rosabel in Venus Oberved (Chichester Festival) 1992, Jacky Lane in King Lear In New York (Chichester Festival) 1992, Eve in Cain (Chichester Festival/Minerva Theatre) 1992, Mrs Cheveley in An Ideal Husband (Peter Hall Co) 1994, Kiss and Tell (author and actress, tour) 1994, Maria Wislake in On Approval (Peter Hall Co) 1994, premiere of Bernard Shaw's The Simpleton of The Unexpected Isles (Orange Tree Richmond) 1995, Rachel in My Cousin Rachel (tour and Vienna, nominated Best Actress Manchester Evening News Awards) 1996, Mrs Cheveley in An Ideal Husband (Haymarket Theatre Royal) 1997, Madame Alexandra in Colombe (Salisbury Playhouse) 1999, Gertrude Lawrence in Noel and Gertie (nat tour) 1999, Passport to Pimlico (nat tour) 2000, The Crime at Blossoms (dir and actress, Brewhouse Theatre Taunton) 2001, The Rape of the Belt (dir, Brewhouse Theatre Taunton) 2001, The Dresser (prodr, Brewhouse Theatre Taunton) 2001, Rachel Arbuthnot in A Woman of No Importance (nat tour) 2002, The Rivals (prodr and actress, nat tour) 2002, Mary Queen of Scots in Shadow in the Sun (author and dir, tour) 2003, Eloise de Kestournel in The Marquise (tour) 2003, Helen Irving in We Happy Few (Gielgud Theatre London) 2004; British Actors Theatre Co credits incl: Kate in The Taming of the Shrew (tour) 1987, Rosalind in As You Like It (tour) 1989, Cleopatra in Antony and Cleopatra (tour) 1989, Olivia in Twelfth Night (also director) 1996; *Books* Game Plan: A Modern Woman's Survival Kit (lifestyle, 1990), When She Was Bad (novel, 1992), Goodtime Girl (novel, 1993), Vamp Until Ready (autobiography, 2003); *Recreations* walking, classical music, reading, home decorating; *Style*— Ms Kate O'Mara; ✉ c/o Narrow Road, 21–22 Poland Street, London W1V 3DD (tel 020 7434 0406, fax 020 7439 1237)

ONDAATJE, Sir (Philip) Christopher; kt (2003), OC (1993), CBE (2000); s of Philip Mervyn Ondaatje, of Sri Lanka, and Doris, *née* Gratiaen; bro of Michael Ondaatje, *qv*; *b* 1933, Kandy, Sri Lanka; *Educ* St Thomas' Coll Ceylon, Blundell's; *Career* Nat and Grindlays Bank London 1951–55, Burns Bros & Denton Toronto 1955–56, Montrealer Magazine and Canada Month Magazine 1956–57, Maclean-Hunter Publishing Co Ltd Montreal 1957–62, The Financial Post Toronto 1963–65, Pitfield Mackay Ross & Co Ltd Toronto 1965–69; fndr and former chm: The Pagurian Corp Ltd 1967–89, Loewen Ondaatje McCutcheon & Co Ltd 1970–88; former vice-chm Hees Int Bancorp Inc; fndr: The Ondaatje Fndn Canada, The Ondaatje Fndn Bermuda, The Ondaatje Hall Tst England, The Ondaatje Prize for Portraiture (in assoc with RSPP), RSL Ondaatje Prize; hon govr Art Gallery of Nova Scotia; tstee: Nat Portrait Gall, Pearson Coll Canada; memb Advsy Bd: RSPP, Lakefield Coll Sch Ontario; govr emeritus Blundell's Sch; memb Canadian Olympic Bob-Sled Team 1964; LLD (hc) Dalhousie Univ 1994, Hon DLitt Univ of Buckingham 2003, Hon DLitt Univ of Exeter 2003; FRSL, FRGS; *Books* The Prime Ministers of Canada 1867–1967, The Prime Ministers of Canada 1867–1985, Olympic Victory (1964), Leopard in the Afternoon (1989), The Man-Eater of Punanai (1992), Sindh Revisted (1996), Journey to the Source of the Nile (1998), Hemingway in Africa (2003), Woolf in Ceylon (2005), The Power of Paper (2007); *Clubs* Travellers, Somerset CCC (life memb), Lyford Cay (Bahamas), MCC; *Style*— Sir Christopher Ondaatje, Esq, OC, CBE

ONDAATJE, (Philip) Michael; s of Philip Mervyn Ondaatje, of Sri Lanka, and Doris, *née* Gratiaen; bro of Christopher Ondaatje, *qv*; *b* 12 September 1943; *Educ* St Thomas' Coll Sri Lanka, Dulwich Coll, Bishop's Univ Quebec, Univ of Toronto (BA), Queen's Univ Ontario (MA); *Career* prof English Dept Glendon Coll York Univ Toronto 1970–; ed Coach House Press 1970–94; Booker Prize for Fiction 1992; *Books* The Dainty Monsters (1967), The Man with Seven Toes (1969), The Collected Works of Billy The Kid (1970), The Broken Ark: A Book of Beasts (ed, 1971), Rat Jelly (1973), Coming Through Slaughter (1976), Personal Fictions: Stories by Munro, Wiebe, Thomas, and Blaise (ed, 1977), Elimination Dance (1978), There's a Trick with a Knife I'm Learning to Do (1979), The Long Poem Anthology (ed, 1979), Tin Roof (1982), Claude Glass (1982), Running in the Family (memoir, 1982), Secular Love (1984), In the Skin of a Lion (1987), From Ink Lake: Canadian Stories (ed, 1990), The Brick Reader (co-ed, 1991), The Cinnamon Peeler (poetry, 1991), The English Patient (1992, made into film 1996), Handwriting (1998), Lost Classics (co-ed, 2000), Anil's Ghost (2000), The Conversations: Walter Murch and the Art of Editing Film (2002), The Story (2005), Divisadero (2007); *Style*— Michael Ondaatje, Esq

O'NEIL, William A; CMG (2004), CM (1995); *Educ* Univ of Toronto; *m*; 3 c; *Career* various engrg positions Federal Dept of Tport 1949–55, successively div engr, regnl dir and dir of construction St Lawrence Seaway Authy 1955–71, cmmr Canadian Coast Guard and dep admin Canadian Marine Transportation Admin (CMTA) Federal Dept of Tport 1975–80 (dep admin Marine Servs CMTA 1971–75); St Lawrence Seaway Authy 1980–90: pres and ceo, dir Canarctic Shipping Company, pres Seaway International Bridge Corporation, memb Bd Thousand Islands Bridge Authy; sec-gen International Maritime Organisation (IMO) 1990– (Canadian rep to Cncl 1972–90, chm Cncl 1980–90); Canadian delg Permanent International Assoc of Navigation Congresses 1984–90, chm Canadian Ctee Lloyd's Register of Shipping 1987–88, memb Bd Int Maritime Bureau 1991–, chm Governing Body Int Maritime Law Inst 1991–; Nat Union of Marine Aviation and Shipping Tport Offrs (NUMAST): hon memb 1995, NUMAST Award 1995; hon titular memb Comité Maritime International 2001; hon memb: Canadian Maritime Law Assoc 1989, Hon Co of Master Mariners 1990, Int Maritime Pilots' Assoc 1991, Soc of Naval Architects and Marine Engrs Singapore 1992, Int Fedn of Shipmasters Assocs 1993, Int Assoc of Lighthouse Authorities 1994, Soc of Naval Architects and Marine Engrs USA 1995, Co of Master Mariners India 1998; chllr World Maritime Univ 1991– (memb Bd of Govrs and Exec Ctee 1983–90); Hon Dip Canadian Coast Guard Coll 1990, Hon Cdre Canadian Coast Guard 1981; Distinguished Public Service Award US Govt 1980, Admiral's Medal Canada 1994, Commander Ordre National des Cèdres Lebanon 1995, SEATRADE Personality of the Year Award 1995, Gold Medal Professional Engrs Ontario 1995, memb Engrg Alumni Hall of Distinction Univ of Toronto 1996, Silver Bell Award Seamen's Church Inst NY 1997, Orden Vasco Nunez de Balboa en el Grado de Gran Cruz Panama 1998, Connecticut Maritime Assoc Cdre Award USA 1998, Dioscuri Prize Lega Navale Italiana Agrigento Italy 1998, Vice Adm 'Jerry' Land Medal of the Soc of Naval Architects and Marine Engrs USA 1999, Halert C Shepheard Award USA 2000, medal for distinguished services to the DG for maritime affrs Colombia 2001, Communications and IT in Shipping (CITIS) 2002 Lifetime Achievement Award 2002, Golden Jubilee Medal Canada 2002, 15 November 1817 Medal Uruguay 2002; Freeman (hc) Worshipful Co of Shipwrights 2002; Hon LLD: Univ of Malta 1993, Meml Univ of Newfoundland Canada 1996; Hon DSc Nottingham Trent Univ 1994; Dr jur (hc) Korea Maritime Univ 2002; memb: Assoc of Professional Engrs of Ontario (Engrg Medal for engrg achievement 1972), American Soc of Civil Engrs; hon memb Baltic Exchange 1999; foreign memb Royal Acad of Engrg 1994, hon fell Nautical Inst UK 1996, Hon FRIN 1999, FILT, FRSA, FREng 1994, Hon FRINA 1998; *Style*— William A O'Neil, Esq, CMG, CM, FREng; ✉ 4 Albert Embankment, London SE1 7SR (tel 020 7587 3100, fax 020 7587 3210, e-mail secretary-general@imo.org)

O'NEILL, Dr Brendan Richard; s of Dr John C O'Neill, of St Helens, Lancs; *b* 6 December 1948; *Educ* West Park GS St Helen's, Churchill Coll Cambridge (MA), UEA (PhD); *m* 21 July 1979, Margaret; 2 da (Katherine b 15 May 1980, Elizabeth b 13 May 1982), 1 s (John b 10 Aug 1984); *Career* grad trainee Ford Motor Co Brentwood 1973–75, various fin appts Leyland Vehicles Ltd 1975–81, gp audit mangr BICC Ltd 1981–83, gp fin controller Midland Bank plc 1986–87 (joined 1983); Guinness plc: dir of fin control 1987, fin dir United Distillers 1987–91, regnl md Int Region (Central and S America, Middle E and Africa) United Distillers 1991–93, md Guinness Brewing Worldwide and main bd dir Guinness plc 1993–98, also chm GUD Pension Fund Tst Ltd; ICI plc: chief operating offr 1998–99, chief exec 1999–2003; chm RAC Pension Fund; non-exec dir: Tyco International 2003–, Rank Gp plc 2004–, Aegis Gp plc 2005–, Endurance Specialty Holdings, Watson

O

Wyatt Worldwide Inc; memb Cncl Cancer Research UK; FCMA (memb Cncl ICMA 1987–90); *Style—* Dr Brendan O'Neill

O'NEILL, Dennis James; CBE (2000); s of Dr William Patrick O'Neill (d 1986), of Pontarddulais, S Wales, and Eva Ann, *née* Rees; *b* 25 February 1948; *Educ* Gowerton GS, studied singing privately with Frederick Cox in London and Campogalliani, Mantova, Ricci in Rome; *m* 1, 4 April 1970 (m dis 1987), Margaret Ruth, da of Rev Edward Collins, of Old Harlow, Essex; 1 da (Clare b 21 July 1977), 1 s (Sean b 22 Dec 1979); m 2, 11 Jan 1988, Ellen, da of Hans Einar Folkestad, of Tybakken, Norway; *Career* tenor and broadcaster; operatic debuts: Royal Opera House Covent Garden 1979 (annually thereafter), Metropolitan Opera NYC 1986, Vienna State Opera 1981, Hamburg State Opera 1981, San Francisco 1984, Chicago Lyric 1985, Paris Opera 1986, Deutche Oper Berlin 1989, Bayerische Staatsoper 1992 (annually thereafter); many recordings; presenter Dennis O'Neill BBC 2; pres Friends of WNO, fndr Dennis O'Neill Bursary; hon fell Univ of Wales; FTCL, ARCM, FWCMD; *Recreations* cookery; *Style—* Dennis O'Neill, Esq, CBE; ✉ c/o Ingpen & Williams Ltd, 7 St George's Court, 131 Putney Bridge Road, London SW15 2PA (tel 020 8874 3222, fax 020 8877 3113)

O'NEILL, Derham Charles; s of Charles Daniel O'Neill (d 1984), and Phyllis, *née* Derham (d 1983); *b* 4 July 1943; *Educ* St Mary's Coll Crosby, Univ of Manchester (LLB), Manchester Business Sch (MBA); *m* 5 Aug 1967, Patricia, da of William Kay (d 1963); 1 da (Katharine Alexandra b 1975), 1 s (Derham Aidan b 1977); *Career* admitted slr 1968; md Brown Shipley Fund Mgmnt Ltd 1979–80, corp fin ptnr Clifford Turner (now Clifford Chance) 1981–97, investment banking, private equity and pension issues advsr 1997–; non-exec dir of cos incl Georgica plc 2007–; memb AIM Appeals Ctee London Stock Exchange 1996–2003; *Books* Management Buyouts (contrib, 1988); *Recreations* writing poetry, short stories and novels, windsurfing, skiing, swimming, moral philosophy; *Style—* Derham O'Neill, Esq; ✉ Clifford Chance, 10 Upper Bank Street, London E14 5JJ (tel 020 7600 1000, fax 020 7600 5555, e-mail derham_oneill@msn.com)

O'NEILL, Eamonn Patrick; s of Edward O'Neill, of Co Offaly, Ireland, and Bridget, *née* O'Reilly; *b* 25 March 1967; *Educ* St Aidan's HS Wishaw, Univ of Strathclyde (BA); *m* 21 Sept 1991, Sarah, da of Prof David Kellam Sterling; *Career* investigative journalist and writer; freelance journalist 1989–90, researcher rising to prodr and dir Scottish Television 1990–95, prodr network factual progs Scottish Television Enterprises 1995, contributing ed Esquire 1998, lectr in journalism Univ of Strathclyde; prodr various documentaries Channel 4; contrib to newspapers and magazines incl The Herald 2003–; nominated BAFTA Documentary Award for The Truth of Christmas Island (Dispatches strand) 1991; runner-up: British Press Awards Feature Writer of the Year 2005, Paul Foot Award for Investigative Journalism 2005; memb NUJ; *Books* No Risk Involved (1991), Outlaws (1998), Matadors (1999); *Recreations* running, reading, writing, wife, family; *Clubs* Frontline; *Style—* Eamonn O'Neill Esq; ✉ website www.eamonnoneill.net

O'NEILL, (Dr) (Terence) James (Jim); s of Terence O'Neill (d 2004), and Kathleen, *née* Simpson (d 1997); *b* 17 March 1957, Manchester; *Educ* Univ of Sheffield (BA, MA), Univ of Surrey (PhD); *m* 18 June 1983, Caroline; 2 c; *Career* Bank of America 1982–83, Marine Midland Bank 1983–88, Swiss Bank Corporation 1988–95, Goldman Sachs 1995– (currently md and head of global economics research); non-exec dir Manchester United plc 2004–05; author of numerous articles on economic matters particularly on exchange rates; creator of BRICs acronym (standing for Brazil, Russia, India and China); chm Shine Tst; *Recreations* sport, travel, cinema; *Style—* Jim O'Neill, Esq; ✉ Goldman Sachs International, Peterborough Court, 133 Fleet Street, London EC4A 2BB (tel 020 7774 2699, fax 020 7774 2643, e-mail jim.oneill@gs.com)

O'NEILL, John Joseph (Jonjo); s of Thomas O'Neill, and Margaret O'Neill; *b* 13 April 1952; *Educ* Castletownroche Nat Sch; *m* 1997, Jacqueline, *née* Bellamy; 3 s, 2 da; *Career* jockey and racehorse trainer; nat hunt jockey 1969–87, winner 901 races, champion jockey 1977–78 (winner record 149 races) and 1979–80, winner Cheltenham Gold Cup 1979 and 1986, Champion Hurdle 1980 and 1984; trainer 1987–, trained over 600 winners incl Gipsy Fiddler (Windsor Castle Stakes Royal Ascot) and winners at Cheltenham Nat Hunt Festival, Aintree Festival and Punchestown; trained 14 winners at Cheltenham Nat Hunt Festival incl: Danny Conners, Front Line, Master Tern, Rith Dubh, Inching Closer, Sudden Shock, Spectroscope, Creon, Native Emperor, Iris's Gift, Black Jack Ketchum, Butler's Cabin, Wichita Lineman, Drombeag; trained 16 winners at Aintree Festival incl: Radiation, Sudden Shock, Quazar, Carbury Cross, Intersky Falcon, Master Tern, Clan Royal, Iris's Gift (twice), Classic Native, Rhinestone Cowboy, Black Jack Ketchum, Refinement, Exotic Dancer, Two Miles West, Albertas Run; three winners at Punchestown: Quazar, Predator, Refinement; Ireland's People of the Year Award 1986; *Style—* Jonjo O'Neill, Esq; ✉ Jackdaws Castle, Temple Guiting, Cheltenham, Gloucestershire GL54 5XU (tel 01386 584209, fax 01386 584219, e-mail jonjo@jonjooneillracing.com)

O'NEILL, Prof Paul Anthony; s of Joseph O'Neill, and Jean, *née* Bradbury; *b* 14 March 1955; *Educ* St Thomas Aquinas GS Leeds, Univ of Manchester (BSc, MB ChB, MD); *m* 1978, Jo, *née* Beeston; 1 s (David b 5 Oct 1986), 1 da (Alice b 19 May 1990); *Career* house physician Univ Hosp of S Manchester 1979, house surgn Manchester Royal Infirmary 1980, SHO Univ Hosp of S Manchester 1981–82, res fell Manchester Royal Infirmary and ICI Pharmaceuticals 1982–84, registrar Bristol Royal Infirmary 1984–86, lectr Univ Dept of Geriatric Med Manchester 1986–89, hon conslt in geriatric med Univ of Manchester 1989–, sr lectr and hon conslt in geriatric med S Manchester Univ Hosps NHS Tst 1992–2000, prof of med educn Univ of Manchester 2000–06 (assoc dean of med undergrad studies 1998–2004, dir of educn 2004–06), head Manchester Med Sch 2006–; educn fell and memb Faculty Harvard Macy Prog 1999–, examiner RCP 1999–; subject reviewer Quality Assurance Agency 1998–2002, Quality Assurance of Basic Med Educn (QABME) visitor GMC 2004–; ldr Physicians as Educators prog RCP 1999; memb: Br Geriatrics Soc 1986–, Cncl Assoc for the Study of Med Educn (ASME) 1994–; Norman Exton Smith Prize Br Geriatrics Soc 1990, Elizabeth Brown Prize Br Geriatrics Soc 1991, Dhole Bequest Br Geriatrics Soc 1991, Nat Teaching and Learning Fellowship 2001; FRCP 1994 (MRCP 1982); *Publications* Master of Medicine (jtly, 1997, 2 edn 2001), Clinical Skills and OSCE (jtly, 2000); author of numerous articles, papers and chapters in books; *Recreations* cooking, gardening, Bonsai trees, walking, windsurfing and sailing; *Style—* Prof Paul O'Neill; ✉ Faculty of Medical and Human Sciences, Stopford Building, University of Manchester, Oxford Road, Manchester M13 9PL (tel 0161 275 7792, e-mail mdxaspao@fsl.scg.man.ac.uk)

O'NEILL, 4 Baron (UK 1868); Raymond Arthur Clanaboy O'Neill; TD (1970); s of 3 Baron O'Neill (ka Italy 1944); the O'Neills stem from the oldest traceable family in Europe; *b* 1 September 1933; *Educ* Eton, RAC Cirencester; *m* 11 June 1963, Georgina Mary, da of late Lord George Montagu Douglas Scott (3 s of 7 Duke of Buccleuch), of Weekley, Northants; 3 s (Hon Shane b 25 July 1965, Hon Tyrone b 24 June 1966, Hon Rory b 20 Dec 1968); *Heir* s, Hon Shane O'Neill; *Career* short service cmmn 11 Hussars Prince Albert's Own 1952–53, joined NI Horse (TA) 1954; Maj cmdg D (N Irish Horse) Sqdn The Royal Yeomanry Regt 1967–69, cmdg N Irish Horse Cadres 1969–71, RARO 1971; Hon Col: D Sqdn (RYR) 1986–91, 69 (N Irish Horse) Signals Sqdn (V) 1988–93; dir: Shanes Developments Ltd, Shanes Castle Estates Co; chm: Ulster Countryside Ctee 1971–75, NI Tourist Bd 1975–80; former dir Romney Hythe & Dymchurch Railway plc; tstee Ulster Folk and Tport Museum 1969–90 (vice-chm 1987–90); pres: The Railway Preservation Soc of Ireland 1964–, NI Assoc of Youth Clubs (Youth Action) 1968–, The Royal Ulster Agric Soc 1984–86 (chm Fin Ctee 1974–83); memb: NT Ctee for NI 1980–91 (chm 1981–91), Cncl for Nature Conservation and Countryside 1989–92; cmmr Museums and Galleries Cmmn 1987–94; chm: NI Museums Advsy Ctee 1989–91, NI Museums Cncl 1993–98; memb Bd Nat Gallery of Ireland 1993–97; HM Lord-Lt Co Antrim 1994– (DL 1967); *Recreations* railways, vintage motoring, gardening, shooting, walking, swimming; *Clubs* Turf; *Style—* The Rt Hon the Lord O'Neill, TD; ✉ Shanes Castle, Antrim BT41 4NE (tel 028 94463264, fax 028 94468457); Conigre House, Calne, Wiltshire

O'NEILL, Prof Robert John; AO (1988); s of Joseph Henry O'Neill (d 1982), of Melbourne, Australia, and Janet Gibbon, *née* Grant (d 2004); *b* 5 November 1936; *Educ* Scotch Coll Melbourne, Royal Mil Coll of Aust, Univ of Melbourne (B E Rankine prize in mgmnt), BNC Oxford (Rhodes scholar, MA, DPhil); *m* 23 Oct 1965, Sally Margaret, da of Donald Frank Burnard, of Adelaide, Aust; 2 da (Katherine Melinda b 1968, Jennifer Louisa b 1971); *Career* Aust Army 1955–68: staff cadet 1955–58, Lt 1958–62, Capt 1962–67 (active serv Vietnam 1966–67, despatches 1967), Maj 1967–68; lectr in mil history Royal Mil Coll of Aust 1967–69, sr fell Dept of Int Relations Res Sch of Pacific Studies Aust Nat Univ 1969 (professorial fell 1977–82), head Strategic and Defence Studies Centre Aust Nat Univ 1971–82, conslt to Aust Govt and expert witness before various Parly Ctee enquiries 1969–82, dir IISS London 1982–87 (memb Cncl 1977–82 and 1992–2001, vice-chm 1994–96, chm 1996–2001), Chichele prof of the history of war Univ of Oxford and fell All Souls Coll 1987–2001, co-dir All Souls Foreign Policy Studies Prog 1989–2001, ret; chm: Delegacy for Mil Instruction Univ of Oxford 1990–2000, Imperial War Museum 1998–2001 (tstee 1990–2001, dep chm 1996–98), Cncl Aust Strategic Policy Inst Canberra 2000–; dep chm Cncl Grad Sch of Govt Univ of Sydney 2003–; pres Rylstone and District Historical Soc 2003–07; planning dir US Studies Centre Univ of Sydney 2006–07; memb: Bd Int Peace Acad New York 1990–2001, Salzburg Seminar 1992–97, Advsy Bd Investment Co of America LA 1987–, Cwlth Sec Gen's Advsy Gp on Security of Small States 1984–85, The Rhodes Tst 1995–2001, Canberra Cmmn on the Elimination of Nuclear Weapons 1995–96, Bd Lowy Inst for Int Policy Sydney 2003–; govr Ditchley Fndn 1989–2001, cmmr Cwlth War Graves Cmmn 1991–2001; Armed Servs ed Australian Dictionary of Biography 1971–2001; non-exec dir: The Shell Transport and Trading Company plc 1992–2002, Capital World Growth and Income Fund Inc LA 1992–, Capital Income Builder Inc LA 1992–; memb Advsy Bd Investment Co of America Inc LA 1988–; Hon Col 5 (Vol) Bn Royal Green Jackets 1993–99; hon fell BNC Oxford 1990; fell Acad of Social Sciences in Australia 1978, FIE(Aust) 1981–96, FRHistS 1989; *Books* The German Army and the Nazi Party 1933–39 (1966), Vietnam Task (1968), General Giap: Politician and Strategist (1969), The Strategic Nuclear Balance (ed, 1975), Insecurity: the Spread of Weapons in the Indian and Pacific Oceans (ed, 1978), New Directions in Strategic Thinking (ed with David Horner, 1981), Australia in the Korean War 1950–53 (Vol 1 1981, Vol 2 1985), Security in East Asia (ed, 1984), The Conduct of East-West Relations in the 1980s (ed, 1985), New Technology and Western Security Policy (ed, 1985), Doctrine, the Alliance and Arms Control (ed, 1986), East Asia, The West and International Security (ed, 1987), Hedley Bull on Arms Control (ed with David N Schwartz, 1987), Prospects for Security in the Mediterranean (ed, 1988), The West and the Third World (ed with John Vincent, 1990), Securing Peace in Europe 1945–62 (ed with Beatrice Heuser, 1992), War Strategy and International Politics (ed with Lawrence Freedman and Paul Hayes, 1992), Alternative Nuclear Futures (ed with John Baylis, 1999); *Recreations* walking, local history; *Style—* Prof Robert O'Neill, AO; ✉ Long Gully, Rylstone, NSW 2849, Australia (e-mail rjoneill@winsoft.net.au)

O'NEILL, Sally Jane; QC (1997); da of Maj John O'Neill RA (ret) (d 1971), and Frances Agnes, *née* Riley; *b* 30 September 1953; *m* 1986, David Bloss Kingsbury; *Career* called to the Bar Gray's Inn 1976 (bencher 2002); asst recorder 1997, recorder 2000; *Recreations* gardening, tennis, skiing, sailing, bulldogs; *Style—* Miss Sally O'Neill, QC; ✉ Furnival Chambers, 32 Furnival Street, London EC4A 1JQ (tel 020 7405 3232, fax 020 7405 3322)

O'NEILL, Shirley; da of Patrick O'Neill, of Atherstone, Warks, and Betty, *née* Ford; *b* 21 August 1947; *Educ* Nuneaton Sch of Art, Walthamstow Coll of Art, The Royal Acad Sch; *Career* artist; gp exhbns: as a memb of The Wapping Studio Collective of Artists 1975–84, summer show at Serpentine Gallery 1982, Francis Graham Gallery 1988; first solo exhibition Francis Graham-Dixon Gallery 1989; *Recreations* travelling, photography; *Style—* Miss Shirley O'Neill; ✉ 52 Albert Street, Whitstable, Kent CT5 1HS

O'NEILL, Terence Patrick (Terry); s of Leonard Victor O'Neill (d 1980), of Cork, Ireland, and Josephine Mary, *née* Gallagher (d 1978); *b* 30 July 1938; *Educ* Gunnersbury GS; *m* 1, Vera Day; 1 s (Keegan Alexander), 1 da (Sarah Jane); m 2, Faye Dunaway; 1 s (Liam Walker); *Career* professional jazz drummer since 1952 in leading London clubs incl The Flamingo, The Florida and The Mapleton; Nat Serv PT instr; professional photographer: took first published pictures of The Beatles and The Rolling Stones, photographic biographer of emerging 60s personalities incl Jean Shrimpton, Terence Stamp and Michael Caine, became int celebrity photographer to politicians, royalty and rock and pop stars, work published in 52 countries (average 500 front covers per annum); *Books* Legends, Celebrity; *Recreations* music, reading, cooking, all sport; *Style—* Terry O'Neill, Esq

O'NEILL OF BENGARVE, Baroness (Life Peer 1999), of The Braid in the County of Antrim; Onora Sylvia; CBE (1995); da of Sir Con Douglas Walter O'Neill, KCMG (d 1988), and Rosemary Margaret, *née* Prichard, now Lady Garvey; *b* 23 August 1941; *Educ* St Paul's Girls' Sch, Somerville Coll Oxford (scholar, MA), Harvard Univ (PhD); *m* 1963 (m dis 1974), Edward John Nell, s of Edward John Nell; 2 s (Hon Adam Edward O'Neill b 1967, Hon Jacob Rowan b 1969); *Career* asst then assoc prof Barnard Coll Columbia Univ NYC 1970–77, lectr then prof of philosophy Univ of Essex 1978–92, princ Newnham Coll Cambridge 1992–2006, pres British Acad 2005–; visiting appts: Australian Nat Univ 1984, Univ of Santa Clara 1985, Wissenschaftskolleg Berlin 1989–90; pres Aristotelian Soc 1988–89; chm Nuffield Cncl on Bioethics 1996–98; Nuffield Fndn: tstee 1997–, chm 1998–; memb Human Genetics Advsy Cmmn 1996–99 (chm 1999); foreign hon memb: American Acad of Arts & Sciences 1993, Austrian Acad of Scis 2002, Norwegian Acad 2006; foreign memb American Philosophical Soc 2003; FBA 1993, FMedSci 2002, Hon MRIA 2003, Hon FRS 2007; *Books* Acting on Principle (1976), Faces of Hunger (1986), Constructions of Reason (1989), Towards Justice and Virtue (1996), Bounds of Justice (2000), Autonomy and Trust in Bioethics (2002), A Question of Trust (2002), Rethinking Informed Consent in Bioethics (jtly, 2007); *Recreations* walking and talking; *Style—* The Rt Hon Baroness O'Neill of Bengarve, CBE, PBA; ✉ British Academy, Carlton House Terrace, London SW1Y 5AH (tel 020 7969 5200, fax 020 7969 5300)

O'NEILL OF CLACKMANNAN, Baron (Life Peer UK 2005), of Clackmannan in Clackmannanshire; Martin John O'Neill; *b* 6 January 1945; *Educ* Trinity Acad Edinburgh, Heriot-Watt Univ, Moray House Educn Coll Edinburgh (pres Scottish Union of Students); *m* 1973, Elaine Samuel; 2 s; *Career* former insurance clerk, asst examiner Scottish Estate Duty Office, secondary schoolteacher, tutor Open Univ; MP (Lab): Stirlingshire E and Clackmannan 1979–83, Clackmannan 1983–97, Ochil 1997–2005; memb Select Ctee on Scottish Affrs 1979–80; oppn front bench spokesman on: Scottish Affrs 1980–84, defence and disarmament 1984–88; princ oppn spokesman on: defence 1988–92, energy 1992–95; chm Trade and Industry Select Ctee 1995–; *Style—* The Lord O'Neill of Clackmannan; ✉ House of Lords, London SW1A 0PW

ONIONS, Jeffery Peter; QC (1998); s of Derrick Onions (d 2005), and Violet, *née* Bond (d 1975); *b* 22 August 1957; *Educ* St Albans (Abbey) Sch, St John's Coll Cambridge (MA, LLM, Hockey blue); *m* 29 Aug 1987, Sally Louise, da of Roy Hine; 1 da (Grace b 8 Aug 1992); *Career* called to the Bar Middle Temple 1981 (Astbury scholar); elected memb Bar Cncl 1987–89; memb: Townley Gp Br Museum, ROH Tst; *Recreations* cricket, wine, opera; *Clubs* MCC, Hawks' (Cambridge), Surrey CCC, Middlesex CCC, 1890; *Style*— Jeffery Onions, Esq, QC; ✉ 1 Essex Court, Temple, London EC4Y 9AR (tel 020 7583 2000, fax 020 7583 0118)

O'NIONS, Prof Sir (Robert) Keith; kt (1999); *b* 26 September 1944; *Educ* Univ of Nottingham (BSc), Univ of Alberta (PhD); *m*; 3 da; *Career* postdoctoral fell Univ of Alberta 1969, Unger Verlesen fell Univ of Oslo 1970, lectr in geochemistry Univ of Oxford 1972–75 (demonstrator in petrology 1971–72), assoc prof then prof of geology Columbia Univ NY 1975–79, Royal Soc research prof Univ of Cambridge 1979–95, official fell Clare Hall Cambridge 1980–95, prof of the physics and chemistry of minerals Univ of Oxford 1995–2003 (head Dept of Earth Sciences 1995–99), professorial fell St Hugh's Coll Oxford 1995–2003 (hon fell 2004–), fell Wolfson Coll Oxford 2004–; memb Cncl of Science and Technol 1998–2000, chief scientific advsr MOD 2000–04, DG Research Cncls Office of Science and Technol/DTI 2004–; Sherman Fairchild distinguished scholar Caltech 1988; author of numerous articles in learned jls and chapters in books; NERC: memb Earth Sciences Ctee 1985–90, memb Earth Sciences Technol Bd 1996–99, chm Br Geological Survey Audit 1998; gen sec Cncl European Union of Geosciences 1985–87, pres European Assoc of Geochemistry 1992–95, memb Cncl Royal Soc 1994–95, cncllr Geochemical Soc 1997–2000, memb Jury Institut Universitaire de France 1997–99; chm Bd of Tstees Natural History Museum 2003– (memb 1995–); J B Macelwane Award American Geophysical Union 1979, Bigsby Medal Geological Soc of London 1983, Hallimond lectr Mineralogical Soc 1985, UK-Canada Rutherford lectr Royal Soc 1986, William Smith lectr Geological Soc of London 1986, Ingerson lectr Geological Soc of America 1990, Arthur Holmes Medal European Union of Geosciences 1995, Lyell Medal Geological Soc of London 1995, Jaeger-Hales lectr ANU 1998, Urey Medal European Assoc of Geochemistry 2001, Bruce Preller prize lectr RSE 2004; MA (by incorporation): Univ of Cambridge 1980, Univ of Oxford 1995; hon fell Univ of Cardiff 2000; Hon DSc Heriot-Watt Univ 2004; fell American Geophysical Union 1980, memb Norwegian Acad of Science and Letters 1980, memb Academia Europaea 1990, hon fell Indian Acad of Sciences 1998, foreign fell Indian Nat Science Acad 2001; FRS 1983, Geochemistry fell 1997, FInstP 1999, Hon FREng 2005; *Style*— Prof Sir Keith O'Nions, FRS; ✉ Department of Trade and Industry, Office of Science and Technology, Room 469, 1 Victoria Street, London SW1H 0ET (tel 020 7215 5000, fax 020 7215 0313, e-mail keith.onions@dti.gsi.gov.uk)

ONIONS, His Hon Judge Robin William; s of late Ernest Onions, DFC, and late Edith Margaret Onions; *Educ* Priory GS Shrewsbury, LSE (LLB); *Career* admitted slr 1973, sr ptnr Lanyon Bowdler (formerly J C H Bowdler & Sons) 1993–2000 (ptnr 1977–2000), slr advocate 1995, asst recorder 1992, recorder 1995, circuit judge (Midland Circuit) 2000–; memb Law Soc; *Recreations* cricket, football, travel, walking, gardening, keeping fit; *Clubs* Shrewsbury Town FC, Cound Cricket (vice-pres); *Style*— His Hon Judge Onions; ✉ Wolverhampton Crown Court, Pipers Row, Wolverhampton WV1 3LQ (tel 01902 481000, fax 01902 481001, mobile 07868 791012)

ONSLOW, Sir John Roger Wilmot; 8 Bt (GB 1797), of Althain, Lancashire; s of Sir Richard Wilmot Onslow, 7 Bt, TD (d 1963); *b* 21 July 1932; *Educ* Cheltenham; *m* 1, 1955 (m dis 1973), Catherine Zoia, da of Henry Atherton Greenway, of The Manor, Compton Abdale, nr Cheltenham; 1 da (Joanna Elizabeth b 1956), 1 s (Richard Paul Atherton b 1958); m 2, 1976, Susan Fay (d 1998), 2 da of E M Hughes, of Frankston, Vic, Aust; *Heir* s, Richard Onslow; *Style*— Sir John Onslow, Bt; ✉ 85 Leila Road, Ormond, Victoria 3163, Australia (tel 61 3 9578 9535, fax 61 3 9578 5675)

ONSLOW, 7 Earl of (UK 1801); Sir Michael William Copplestone Dillon Onslow; 11 Bt (E 1674, of 2 cr, with precedency 1660); also Baron Onslow (GB 1716), Baron Cranley (GB 1776), and Viscount Cranley (UK 1801); high steward of Guildford; s of 6 Earl, KBE, MC, TD (d 1971), and Pamela, Countess of Onslow; *b* 28 February 1938; *Educ* Eton, Sorbonne; *m* 1964, Robin, o da of Maj Robert Lee Bullard III, of Atlanta, Ga (Lady Onslow's mother subsequently m Lord Aberconway as his 2 w); 1 s (Rupert, Viscount Cranley b 1967), 2 da (Lady Arabella b 1970, Lady Charlotte b 1977); *Heir* s, Viscount Cranley; *Career* sits as Conservative in House of Lords (elected memb 2000); Lloyd's underwriter; farmer (800 acres in Surrey); served Life Gds M East; sometime govr UC Buckingham, govr Royal GS Guildford; *Style*— The Rt Hon the Earl of Onslow; ✉ Temple Court, Clandon Park, Guildford, Surrey GU4 7RQ (tel 01483 222754)

ONSLOW, Hon Richard; s of Rt Hon Lord Onslow of Woking, KCMG, PC (Life Peer, d 2001), and Lady June Hay (d 2002); *b* 27 June 1956; *Educ* Harrow, Univ of Oxford (MA), City Univ (DPL); *m* 27 July 1985, Phyllida (d 2000), da of Michael Moore, OBE, of Lindsey, Suffolk; 1 s (Thomas), 1 da (Isabella); *Career* called to the Bar Inner Temple 1982, recorder of the Crown Court 2005; *Recreations* shooting, fishing, real tennis, cricket, commentating at Tarrant Gunville Horse Show; *Clubs* MCC, Stragglers of Asia Cricket, Lords and Commons Cricket, Canford Real Tennis, Usk Valley Casting; *Style*— The Hon Richard Onslow; ✉ 2 King's Bench Walk, Temple, London EC4 (tel 020 7353 1746)

ONSLOW-COLE, Julia Elizabeth; da of Michael Onslow-Cole (d 1986), and Joy Elizabeth Watson, OBE, JP, of Peacemarsh, Dorset; *b* 30 September 1959, London; *m* 12 April 1986, Neil Howard Thomas, FRCP, FRCPCH, DCH, s of Howard Donald Thomas; 4 da; *Career* ptnr CMS Cameron McKenna (also head of global immigration business practice); memb: Cncl Int Bar Assoc (former chair Immigration Ctee, chair UN and Other World Orgns Ctee, sec Educnl Tst), Advsy Panel Office of the Immigration Services Cmmr; former sec Immigration Law Practitioners' Assoc; memb: American Immigration Lawyers Assoc, UK Assoc of European Law; FSALS; *Publications* contributing co-ed: Butterworths Immigration Law Service, Sweet & Maxwell's Immigration Law and Practice, Macdonald's Immigration Law and Practice; *Style*— Ms Julia Onslow-Cole

ONWIN, Glen; *b* 1947; *Educ* Edinburgh Coll of Art (DA), Moray House Coll of Educn; *Career* artist; art teacher Edinburgh 1972–79; visiting lectr: Glasgow Sch of Art 1979, Duncan of Jordanstone Coll of Art 1980, Grays Sch of Art Aberdeen 1983, Edinburgh Coll of Art pt/t lectr 1979–87; Edinburgh Coll of Art Sch of Drawing and Painting: lectr 1987–94, dir of postgrad studies 1992–, sr lectr 1994–; worked Scottish Arts Cncl Studio Amsterdam 1979; memb Bd New 57 Gall 1974–84; exhbn selector Scottish Art Now 1982; Scottish Arts Cncl 1972; *Solo Exhibitions* Scottish Arts Cncl Gallery 1975, Serpentine Gallery London 1975, Arnolfini Gallery Bristol 1978, ICA London 1978, Third Eye Glasgow 1979, Fruit Market Gallery Edinburgh 1979, AIR Gallery London 1982, Crawford Arts Centre St Andrews 1989, Space-Ex Exeter 1989, John Hansard Gallery Southampton 1991, As Above so Below (Square Chapel Halifax, an installation with The Henry Moore Sculpture Trust), Flammable Solid Flammable Liquid (Tramway Glasgow, site specific installation) 1994, and others; *Group Exhibitions* Video Exhibition (Serpentine Gallery) 1975, Scottish Sculpture (Kelvingrove Museum Glasgow) 1975, Ulster Museum of Art Belfast 1976, Aspects of Landscape (British Cncl touring exhbn) 1976, Works on Paper (RA) 1977, Scottish Nat Gallery of Modern Art Edinburgh 1978, Invited Artists (RSA Festival Exhbn) 1979, Un Certain Art Anglais (ARC Musee d'Art Moderne Paris) 1979, JP2 Palais des Beaux Arts Brussels 1979, Demarcations (Demarco Gallery Edinburgh) 1984, City Arts Centre Edinburgh 1985, Sarajevo Winter Festival Sarajevo 1988, Scottish Art Since 1900 (Scottish Nat Gallery of Modern Art 1989 and Barbican 1990), Fruitmarket Open (Fruitmarket Gallery Edinburgh) 1990, From Art to Archaeology (S Bank Centre touring) 1991–92, A Quality of Light (St Ives Cornwall) 1997, Working Drafts (Envisioning the Human Genome Exhbn 2/10 Gallery London) 2002, An Turas (collaborative architecture/sculpture structure Isle of Tiree) 2003, Place of Origin (collaborative sculpture/landscape project Kemney Aberdeenshire) 2003–; *Public Collections* British Cncl, Contemporary Arts Soc, Scottish Arts Cncl, Scottish Nat Gallery of Modern Art, Univ of Salford, Arts Cncl of GB, Kelvingrove Museum, City Art Centre Edinburgh, Whitworth Art Gallery Manchester, Tate Gallery; *Style*— Glen Onwin, Esq; ✉ 77 Duke Street, Leith, Edinburgh EH6 8HN (e-mail g.onwin@eca.ac.uk)

OPENSHAW, David Kay; s of Frank Kay Openshaw, of Nelson, Lancs, and Florence Openshaw; *b* October 1946; *Educ* Nelson GS, Wadham Coll Oxford, Univ of Bradford Mgmnt Centre; *m* Jacqueline; 1 da (Jane), 1 s (Tom); *Career* ops dir Volvo UK 1980–85, md Lex Specialist Car Group 1986–90, vice-pres Lex Electronics USA 1990–91, md Motorway Tyres and Accessories Ltd 1992–97, mgmnt conslt 1997–; non-exec dir Thames Valley Enterprise 1996–97; croquet player: memb Harrow Oak Croquet Club 1971– (capt 1976–), memb GB team 1979–2002 (capt 1982–94 and 1999–2002); honours incl: Br Open champion 1979, 1981 and 1985, Br mens champion 1981, 1991 and 1995, US Open champion 1991, Canadian Open champion 1991, runner-up World Championship 1991, Br Mixed Doubles champion 2002 and 2003 (with Kathleen Priestley), Scottish Open champion 2006; GB rep: v Aust and NZ 1979, 1982, 1986, 1990, 1993 and 2000, v USA 1985, 1987, 1988, 1989, 1990, 1991, 1992, 1993, 1994, 1997, 1999, 2000 and 2002, v Ireland 2000; record for longest winning sequence of matches (39) May-Aug 1981; pres World Croquet Fedn 2003–; chess player: rep Lancs 1966–70, capt Oxford Univ 1968; *Style*— David Openshaw, Esq

OPENSHAW, Hon Mr Justice; Sir (Charles) Peter Lawford; kt (2005), DL (Lancs 2000); s of His Hon Judge William Harrison Openshaw, DL (d 1981), of Broughton, Lancs, and Elisabeth Joyce Emily, *née* Lawford; *b* 21 December 1947; *Educ* Harrow, St Catharine's Coll Cambridge (MA); *m* 15 Dec 1979, Caroline Jane Swift, QC (Hon Mrs Justice Swift), *qv*, da of Vincent Seymour Swift, of Brookhouse, Lancs; 1 da (Alexandra b 1984), 1 s (Henry b 1986); *Career* called to the Bar Inner Temple 1970 (bencher 2003); practised on Northern Circuit, junior 1973, asst recorder 1984–88, recorder 1988–99, QC 1991, sr circuit judge (Northern Circuit) 1999–2005, hon recorder Preston 1999–2005, judge of the High Court of Justice (Queen's Bench Div) 2005–; *Recreations* fishing, gardening, country life; *Style*— The Hon Mr Justice Openshaw, DL

OPIE, Alan John; s of Jack Opie (d 1985), and Doris Winifred, *née* Bennetts; *b* 22 March 1945; *Educ* Truro Sch, Guildhall Sch of Music and Drama (AGSM), London Opera Centre (Cinzano scholar); *m* 18 April 1970, Kathleen Ann, da of Ernest Smales; 1 s (James Alexander b 1976), 1 da (Helen Louise b 1979); *Career* princ baritone ENO 1973–96; performed with: Royal Opera, Glyndebourne Festival Opera, Scottish Opera, Opera North, Eng Opera Gp, Chicago Lyric Opera, Bayreuth Festival, Paris Opera, Netherlands Opera, Brussels Opera, Hong Kong Festival, Buxton Festival, Stadtsoper Berlin, Bavarian State Opera, Wexford Festival, NY Met Opera, BBC Symphony Chorus and Orch (BBC Proms) 1996, La Scala Milan 1996, Gothenburg Symphony Orch (BBC Proms) 1997; concerts in: UK, Europe, USA and Australia; recordings with: CBS, EMI, Decca, Hyperion, Chandos; Grammy winner 1997 and 1998, Olivier Award nomination for outstanding achievement in opera for Falstaff 1998; *Recreations* golf; *Clubs* Leatherhead Golf; *Style*— Alan Opie, Esq

OPIE, Julian Gilbert; s of Roger G Opie, and Norma Opie; *b* 12 December 1958, London; *Educ* Magdalen Coll Sch Oxford, Chelsea Sch of Art, Goldsmiths Sch of Art London; *m* Christine; 2 da (Elena, Padmini); *Career* artist; solo exhbns: Lisson Gallery London 1983, 1996, 2000, 2001 and 2004, ICA London 1985, Kunsthalle Berlin 1991, Kohji Ogura Gallery Tokyo 1991, Wiener Secession Vienna 1992, Hayward Gall London 1993, Kunstverein Hanover 1994, Tramway Glasgow 1994, Barbara Thumm Gallery Berlin 1999, 2002 and 2004, Morrisson Judd London 1999, Meymac Centre d'Art Contemporain Abbaye St Andre France 2000, Alan Cristea London 2000, 2003 and 2006, Ikon Gallery Birmingham 2001, Patrick de Brock Gallery Knokke 2001 and 2004, Atelier Augarten Galerie Belvedere Vienna 2002, Barbara Krakow Gallery Boston MA 2002 and 2007, Mario Sequeira Gallery Braga 2002 and 2005, Rebecca Camhi Gallery Athens 2002, Galerie Bob Van Orsouw Zurich 2003 and 2006, Neues Museum Nuremberg 2003, Galerie Krobath Wimmer Vienna 2004, MCA Chicago 2004, Wetterling Gallery Stockholm 2004, Gallery Valentina Bonomo Rome 2005, Gallery MGM Oslo 2005, Scai the Bathouse Tokyo 2005, La Chocolateria Santiago de Compostela 2005, ICA Boston MA 2005–06, Museum of Indianapolis 2006, CAC Malaga 2006, Julian Opie in the 90s (King's Lynn Art Centre) 2007, San Diego Museum of Art 2007, Tokyo Met Museum of Photography 2008, Mie Prefecture Museum Japan 2008; cmmns incl cover design for Blur: The Best of 2000 (winner Music Week CADS 2007); works in public collections: Aberdeen Art Gallery, Arts Cncl of GB, Banque Bruxelles Lambert, Carnegie Museum Pittsburgh, Collection Essl Vienna, Contemporary Art Soc, Daimler Chrysler Berlin, Dresdner Bank Berlin, Deutsche Bank Frankfurt, Daros Collection Zurich, Fonds Nat d'Art Contemporain France, Fundacion Caja de Pensiones Madrid, Gana Art Centre Seoul, Gjensidige Oslo, ICA Boston, Institut Valenciá d'Art Modern, Kunsthalle Bern, Kunsthaus Bregenz, Kunsthaus Zurich, Kresge Art Museum Michigan State Univ, Lenbachhaus Städtische Galerie Munich, Maison Europeene de la Photographie Paris, Museet for Samtidskunst Oslo, Museo d'Arte Contemporanea Prato, Museum of Fine Arts Boston, Museum of Modern Art NY, Neue Galerie Sammlung Ludwig, Neues Museum Nuremberg, Nat Gall of Victoria Melbourne, Nat Portrait Gallery London, Stedelijk Museum Amsterdam, Br Cncl, Br Museum, Calouste Gulbenkian Fndn Portugal, Govt Art Collection London, Israel Museum Jerusalem, Museum of Contemporary Art of Leon, Nat Museum of Art Osaka, Takamatsu City Museum of Art Japan, Tate Gallery London, V&A, Wadsworth Atheneum; Sargant fell British Sch Rome 1995–96, residency at Atelier Calder Sache France 1996; *Style*— Julian Opie, Esq; ✉ c/o Lisson Gallery, 52–54 Bell Street, London NW1 5DA (website www.lisson.co.uk)

O

ÖPIK, Lembit; MP; *b* 2 March 1965; *Educ* Royal Belfast Academical Instn, Univ of Bristol (BA, pres Students' Union); *Career* memb NUS Nat Exec 1987–88; Procter & Gamble Ltd: successively brand asst, asst brand mangr, corporate trg and orgn devpt mangr, global human resources trg mangr 1988–97; cncllr Newcastle upon Tyne City Cncl 1992–97; Parly candidate Newcastle Central 1992, Euro Parl candidate Northumbria 1994; MP (Lib Dem) Montgomeryshire 1997–; Lib Dem Parly spokesman for Wales and NI 1997–2007 (spokesperson for Youth Affrs 1997–2002), Lib Dem Parly spokesperson for Business, Enterprise and Regulatory Reform 2007–; memb Lib Dem Welsh Affrs Team 1997–, ldr Welsh Lib Dems 2001–; pres Motor Neuron Disease Assc 2006–; *Recreations* windsurfing, aviation, motorcycles, astronomy, cinema; *Style*— Lembit Öpik, MP; ✉ Montgomeryshire Liberal Democrats, 3 Park Street, Newtown, Powys (tel 01686 625527, fax 01686 628891, e-mail montgomeryldp@cix.co.uk); House of Commons, London SW1A 0AA (tel 020 7219 1144, fax 020 7219 2210, e-mail opikl@parliament.uk)

OPPEN, Richard John Stuart; s of Arthur Harrie Oppen (d 1976), and Muriel Evelyn, *née* Dent (d 1984); *b* 29 January 1937; *Educ* City of London Sch; *m* 1 June 1963, Wendy, da of Leslie William Day Suffield (d 1979); 1 s (James b 11 July 1969), 1 da (Lucy b 27 Jan 1972); *Career* Nat Serv 3 Carabiniers (3DG) 1955–57; dir Galbraiths Ltd 1984–88, md Berge Y Cia (UK) Ltd 1989–; memb Baltic Exchange 1959; hon advsr Officers' Assoc; Freeman City of London 1980, Liveryman Worshipful Co of Shipwrights 1982, Freeman Worshipful Co of Watermen and Lightermen 1995; *Recreations* country pursuits, observing people; *Clubs* Army and Navy; *Style*— Richard Oppen, Esq; ✉ 7 Church Row, Plaxtol, Kent (tel 01732 810311); Berge Y Cia (UK) Ltd, 47 Albemarle Street, London W1S 4JW (tel 020 7499 3186, fax 020 7495 4808, telex 261675)

OPPENHEIM, (James) Nicholas; *b* 15 June 1947; *Educ* Edinburgh Acad, Univ of Columbia; *Career* dir: Kellock plc 1976–86 and 1988–97, Sterling Credit Group plc 1980–82, Argyle Trust plc 1982–91, The Smaller Companies International Trust plc 1982–89, Sterling

Trust plc (formerly Dewey Warren Holdings Ltd) 1983–91, Courtwell Group plc 1986–90, Northern Leisure 1987–99 (former vice-chm, non-exec dir 1999); *Style*— Nicholas Oppenheim, Esq; ✉ 33 King Street, London SW1Y 6RJ (tel 020 7623 9021, fax 020 7606 3025)

OPPENHEIM-BARNES, Baroness (Life Peer UK 1989), of Gloucester in the County of Gloucestershire; Sally Oppenheim-Barnes; PC (1979); da of late Mark and Jeanette Viner, of Sheffield; *b* 26 July 1930; *Educ* Sheffield HS; *m* 1, 1949, Henry M Oppenheim (d 1980); 2 da (Hon Carolyn (Hon Mrs Selman) b 1951, Hon Rose Anne (Hon Mrs Mattick) b 1955), 1 s (Hon Phillip b 1956); m 2, 1984, John Barnes (d 2004); *Career* MP (Cons) Gloucester 1970–87 (when her s Philip was elected MP 1983, it was the first time that both a mother and son sat in the same Parl); formerly social worker with ILEA; chm Cons Parly Prices and Consumer Protection Ctee 1973–74 (vice-chm 1971–73), front bench oppn spokesman (seat in Shadow Cabinet) Prices and Consumer Protection 1974–79, min state (consumer affrs) Dept of Trade 1979–82, chm Ctee of Enquiry into Pedestrian Safety at Public Road Level Crossings 1982–; non-exec dir: Boots Co Main Bd 1982–93, Fleming High Income Investment Tst 1989–96, HFC Bank plc 1990–98; memb House of Commons Ctee of Privileges, pres Br Red Cross Soc Glos Dist; chm Nat Consumer Cncl 1987–89; Nat Waterway Museum Tst until 1990; *Recreations* tennis, bridge; *Clubs* Glos Cons; *Style*— The Baroness Oppenheim-Barnes, PC

OPPENHEIMER, His Hon Judge Michael Anthony; s of Felix Oppenheimer (d 1962), of Highgate, London, and Ingeborg Hanna Oppenheimer (d 2001); *b* 22 September 1946; *Educ* Westminster, LSE (LLB); *m* 14 April 1973, Nicola Anne Oppenheimer, *qv*, da of Basil Vincent Brotherton (d 1961), of Pinner, Middx; 1 da (Rebecca Anne Julia b 14 April 1978), 1 s (James Felix Vincent b 15 Oct 1980); *Career* called to the Bar Middle Temple 1970 (Blackstone exhibitioner); memb SE Circuit, asst recorder 1985, recorder 1989, circuit judge (SE Circuit) 1991–; chm Bar Disciplinary Tbnl; *Recreations* cinema, theatre, books, wine and food, performing and listening to music; *Clubs* Athenaeum; *Style*— His Hon Judge Michael Oppenheimer; ✉ c/o The Athenaeum, 107 Pall Mall, London SW1Y 5ER

OPPENHEIMER, Sir Michael Bernard Grenville; 3 Bt (UK 1921), of Stoke Poges, Co Bucks; s of Sir Michael Oppenheimer, 2 Bt (d 1933 in a flying accident), and Caroline, da of Sir Robert Harvey, 2 and last Bt (d 1972); *b* 27 May 1924; *Educ* Charterhouse, ChCh Oxford (MA, BLitt); *m* 1947, (Laetitia) Helen, er da of Sir Hugh Lucas-Tooth, 1 Bt; 3 da (Henrietta Laetitia Grenville (Mrs Adam L Scott) b 1954, Matilda Magdalen Grenville (Mrs Neil G A King) b 1956, Xanthe Jennifer Grenville (Hon Mrs Ivo A R Mosley) b 1958); *Heir* none; *Career* served WWII, Middle East and Italy, SA Artillery, Lt; lectr in politics: Lincoln Coll Oxford 1955–68, Magdalen Coll Oxford 1966–68; *Books* The Monuments of Italy (2002, 6 vols); *Clubs* Victoria (Jersey); *Style*— Sir Michael Oppenheimer, Bt; ✉ L'Aiguillon, Grouville, Jersey JE3 9AP (tel 01534 854466)

OPPENHEIMER, Nicola Anne; da of Basil Vincent Brotherton (d 1961), and Joan Pamela, *née* Green (d 2003); *b* 30 September 1950; *Educ* St Margaret's Sch Bushey, QMC London (LLB); *m* 14 April 1973, His Hon Judge Michael Oppenheimer, *qv*; 1 da (Rebecca Anne Julia b 14 April 1978), 1 s (James Felix Vincent b 15 Oct 1980); *Career* called to the Bar Middle Temple 1972; Lord Chancellor's Dept: legal asst Criminal Appeal Office 1973–77, sr legal asst 1978–85, Judicial Appointments Div 1985–87, head Personnel Mgmnt Div 1987–91, head Legal Servs and Agencies Div 1991–93, princ estab and fin offr 1993–96; Cabinet Office: princ estab and fin offr 1996–2000, fell Knowledge Mgmnt Centre for Mgmnt and Policy Studies 2000–2001; ptnr Odgers Ray & Berndtson 2001–; tstee: The English Concert, The Early Opera Co 2005–; memb Devpt Bd: Royal Acad of Music, LAMDA; *Recreations* early music, theatre, skiing, walking; *Style*— Mrs Nicola Oppenheimer; ✉ Odgers Ray & Berndtson, 11 Hanover Square, London W1S 1JJ (tel 020 7529 1111, e-mail nicky.oppenheimer@odgers.com)

OPPENHEIMER, Peter Morris; s of Friedrich Rudolf Oppenheimer (d 1994), of London, and Charlotte Oppenheimer (d 1996); *b* 16 April 1938; *Educ* Haberdashers' Aske's, The Queen's Coll Oxford (MA); *m* 30 July 1964, Catherine Violet Rosalie Pasternak, da of Eliot Trevor Oakeshott Slater, CBE, MD (d 1983); 2 s (Daniel b 1967, Joseph b 1971), 1 da (Tamara b 1973); *Career* Nat Serv RN 1956–58, ret Lt Cdr RNR 1978; Bank for International Settlements 1961–64, res fell and actg investment bursar Nuffield Coll Oxford 1964–67, fell in economics ChCh Oxford 1967–, visiting prof int fin London Graduate Sch of Business Studies 1977–78, chief economist Shell Int Petroleum Co 1985–86, pres Oxford Centre for Hebrew and Jewish Studies (OCHJS) 2000–; chm Jewish Chronicle newspaper 2001–04; Freeman Worshipful Co of Haberdashers 1987; *Books* Russia's Post-Communist Economy (co-ed and contrib, 2001); *Recreations* swimming, skiing, theatre, opera, music; *Style*— Peter Oppenheimer, Esq; ✉ 6 Linton Road, Oxford OX2 6UG (tel 01865 558226); OCHJS, Yarnton Manor, Oxford OX5 1PY (tel 01865 377946, fax 01865 375079, mobile 07785 543169)

OPPETIT, Bernard; s of Marcel Oppetit, of Paris, France, and Jacqueline, *née* Barail; *b* 5 August 1956, Algiers, Algeria; *Educ* Ecole Polytechnique Paris; *m* 26 Oct 1985, Anne, *née* Brisset, 3 s (Octave b 28 Sept 1986, Ernest b 10 Dec 1990, Gabriel b 21 Jan 1992), 1 da (Alice b 10 Nov 1987); *Career* Paribas: joined Paris 1979, vice-pres NY 1987–95, md London 1995–2000; chm and ceo Centaurus Capital 2000–; *Recreations* music, sailing; *Style*— Bernard Oppetit, Esq; ✉ Centaurus Capital, 33 Cavendish Square, London W1G 0PW (tel 020 7852 3821, fax 020 7852 3850, e-mail bernard@centaurus-capital.com)

O'PREY, Prof Paul; s of Desmond O'Prey, and Ada, *née* Reid; *b* 2 April 1956, Southampton; *Educ* St George Sch Southampton, King Edward VI Sch Southampton, Keble Coll Oxford, Univ of Bristol (PhD); *m* Maria Pilar, *née* Garcia Navarro; 1 s (Llorenç b 8 Sept 1979), 1 da (Mireia b 1 March 1987); *Career* sec to Robert Graves 1977–81; Univ of Bristol: English tutor 1989–93, warden Goldney Hall 1989–2004, sr warden 1993–95, dir of res devpt 1995–99, dir of res and enterprise 1999–2002, dir of academic affrs 2002–04; Univ of Roehampton: prof of modern lit 2004–, vice-chllr 2004–; dir: London Higher, HE Careers Serv Unit; govr Putney HS for Girls; *Publications* In Broken Images: Selected Letters of Robert Graves 1914–46 (1982), Joseph Conrad, Heart of Darkness (ed,1983), Between Moon and Moon: Selected Letters of Robert Graves 1946–1972 (1989), Robert Graves: Selected Poems (ed, 1986), The Reader's Guide to Graham Greene (1988), The House of Ulloa (1990), Robert Graves: Collected Writings on Poetry (1995); various chapters in books and articles in jls; *Clubs* Athenaeum; *Style*— Prof Paul O'Prey; ✉ Vice-Chancellor's Office, Roehampton University, Roehampton Lane, London SW15 5PH (tel 020 8392 3101, e-mail paul.oprey@roehampton.ac.uk)

O'RAHILLY, Prof Stephen; *b* 1 April 1958; *Educ* Nat Univ of Ireland (scholar, MB BCh, BAO, MD, D K O'Donovan medal in med, Coleman Saunder's medal in paediatrics); *Career* surgical house offr Mater Hosp Dublin 1982 (med house offr 1981–82); med SHO: Bart's 1982–83, Hammersmith Hosp 1983–84; research fell in endocrinology Univ of Oxford 1984–87, hon registrar and Br Diabetic Assoc Redcliffe-Maud fell Nuffield Dept of Clinical Med Radcliffe Infirmary 1986–87; clinical registrar in endocrinology: John Radcliffe Hosp Oxford 1987–88, Radcliffe Infirmary Oxford 1989–91; MRC travelling fell Harvard Med Sch Div of Endocriniology Beth Israel Hosp Boston Mass 1989–91, hon conslt physician Addenbrooke's Hosp Cambridge 1994–; Univ of Cambridge: Wellcome sr research fell in clinical sci 1991–95, prof of metabolic med Depts of Med and Clinical Biochemistry 1996–2002, prof of clinical biochemistry and med 2002–; SmithKline Beecham visiting prof SKB Philadelphia PA 1995, R D Lawrence lectr Br Diabetic Assoc 1996, visiting prof Univ of Witwatersrand Johannesburg SA 1996, Bayer lectr Bichemical Soc UC Dublin 1997, lectr Univ of Washington 1999, Clinical Endocrinology Tst lectr 1999; Rufus Cole lectr Rockefeller Univ 2000, McCallum lectr Univ Toronto 2000, Kroc lectr Univ of Massachusetts 2007; memb: Research Ctee Br Diabetic Assoc 1996–, Wellcome Tst Clinical Interest Gp 1996– (chm 1999–); assoc ed Diabetologia 1995–98, scientific ed Jl of Endocrinology 1996–2004, memb Editorial Bd Clinical Endocrinology 1997–2000; invited lectures at regnl, nat and int meetings; memb: Br Diabetic Assoc, American Diabetes Assoc, Euro Assoc for the Study of Diabetes, Soc for Endocrinology, Endocrine Soc (USA), Biochemical Soc, Assoc of Physicians of GB; hon memb American Assoc of Physicians 2004, fell Pembroke Coll Cambridge 2007–; Soc of Endocrinology Medallist 2000, Graham Bull Prize RCP, Heinrich Wieland Prize 2002, Carl Gottschalk Award Univ of Carolina 2003, Rolf Luft Award Karolinska Inst 2005, Solomon Benson Award Mt Sinai Med Sch NY 2007, Clinical Investigator Award Endocrine Soc USA 2007, Feldberg Prize 2007; FRCPI 1996 (MRCPI 983), FRCP 1996 (MRCP 1984), FMedSci 1999, FRCPath 2002, FRS 2003; *Style*— Prof Stephen O'Rahilly; ✉ University of Cambridge, Department of Clinical Biochemistry, Box 232, Addenbrooke's Hospital, Hills Road, Cambridge CB2 2QQ (e-mail so104@medschl.cam.ac.uk)

ORAM, Douglas Richard; s of Alfred Richard Oram (d 1980), of London, and Gladys, *née* Lungley (d 1955); *b* 29 March 1942; *Educ* Licensed Victuallers' Sch, Southgate Co GS, Hendon Tech Coll; *m* 24 Sept 1966, Jannet Adyne, da of Ascensio Joseph Echevarria (d 1988), and Obdulia Ines, *née* Irureta (d 1992), of Villajoyosa, Spain; 2 s (Somerset b 17 March 1981, Sebastian b 12 Nov 1982); *Career* purchasing mangr then dir Centre Hotels (Cranston) Ltd 1965–75, purchasing mangr The Dorchester 1975–78, purchasing dir Comfort Hotels Int 1978–85, gp purchasing mangr Metropole Hotels 1985–96, freelance purchasing conslt 1996–2004, ret; former chm PM Club London; chm: Twenty-Eleven Soc, PM Tst; former vice-chm Child Growth Fndn; vice-pres Hospitality Action; former tstee Sheffield Children's Hospital Limb Inequality Service; memb and former hon sec: Old Metronians Assoc, Champagne Acad Old Boys' Assoc; former dir Telecommunications Numbering and Addressing Bd Ltd; former chm: Membership Servs Ctee BHRCA, Champagne Acad, 5th Hampstead Scout Gp; former co-ordinator Bone Dysplasia Gp; former memb: Bd of Mgmnt Hotel and Catering Benevolent Assoc, POUNC, Camden Lay Visitors' Panel, Advsy Ctee on Telecommunications for England; FHCIMA 1984, MCIPS 1988; Officier de l'Ordre des Coteaux de Champagne; *Books* A Leg Lengthening Diary - One Family's Experiences (with Jannet Oram, 1994); *Clubs* Royal Over-Seas League; *Style*— Douglas Oram, Esq; ✉ 38 Hillfield Road, London NW6 1PZ (tel 020 7435 8021, fax 020 7431 2467, e-mail droram@bulldoghome.com)

ORANMORE AND BROWNE, 5 Baron (I 1836) Dominick Geoffrey Thomas Browne; *see:* Mereworth, 3 Baron (UK 1926)

ORCHARD, Dr Robin Theodore; s of George William Orchard (d 1991), of Bexley Heath, Kent, and Christobel Edith Orchard; *b* 4 October 1940; *Educ* Chislehurst and Sidcup GS, Charing Cross Hosp Med Sch Univ of London (MB BS); *m* 5 June 1965, Ann Seymour, da of Dr Thomas Seymour Jones (d 1986), of Wimborne, Dorset; 2 s (Timothy, Christopher), 2 da (Kathryn, Elizabeth); *Career* sr registrar Charing Cross Hosp WC2 and W6 1970–74, sr lectr in med Royal Dental Hosp 1976–82, post grad clinical tutor St Helier Hosp 1978–86; conslt physician 1974–: St Helier Hosp Carshalton, Sutton Hosp, St Anthony's Hosp N Cheam; hon sr lectr St George's Hosp Med Sch 1982–, Univ of London examiner in medicine and dental surgery 1982–; churchwarden St John's Selsdon Sy 1982–87, memb Addington Deanery Synod 1988–; Univ memb Croydon D H A 1987–90, med dir St Helier Hosp Tst 1991–99, memb Cncl St George's Hosp Med Sch 1991–99; FRCP 1982, FRSM, MRCS; *Recreations* cricket, golf, C of E, Italian wine; *Style*— Dr Robin Orchard; ✉ St Helier Hospital, Wrythe Lane, Carshalton SM5 1AA (tel 020 8644 4343)

ORCHARD, Stephen; s of Leslie Orchard, of Oldham, and Ellen, *née* Cassells; *b* 13 April 1958; *Educ* Chadderton GS, St Peter's Coll Oxford, Nat Broadcasting Sch (scholar); *Career* CQSW Barnet House Univ of Oxford 1980–82, social worker High Wycombe SSD 1982–85; GWR Radio: broadcaster 1985–92, prog controller 1988–92, station dir 1992–94, gp prog dir GWR Group plc 1994–97, gp prog dir Classic FM 1997, ops dir Local Radio Div GWR 1998–2005, ops dir and bd memb GCap Media (following merger) 2005–; memb Equity 1986; *Style*— Stephen Orchard, Esq

ORCHARD-LISLE, Mervyn Christopher; s of Ulric Lock Orchard-Lisle (d 1955), and Thelma Julie Spelman, *née* Burdett (d 2000); *b* 6 June 1946; *Educ* Marlborough, Univ of Newcastle upon Tyne (BA, BArch); *m* 24 March 1979, Angela Jane, da of Edmund Louis Saunders (d 1996); 1 da (Lucy b 1983), 1 s (Alexander b 1985); *Career* chartered architect in private practice 1973–, sr ptnr Gotelee Orchard-Lisle; RIBA 1973; *Recreations* watercolours, books, motor cars, family life; *Style*— Mervyn Orchard-Lisle, Esq; ✉ The Old Rectory, Monksilver, Taunton, Somerset TA4 4HY (tel 01984 656550); Gotelee Orchard-Lisle, 3 Cromwell Place, Northbrook Street, Newbury, Berkshire RG14 1AF (tel 01635 36600, fax 01635 31421, e-mail mol@go-l.co.uk)

ORCHARD-LISLE, Paul David; CBE (1988), TD (1971), DL (Gtr London 1986–, rep DL City of Westminster 2007–); s of Mervyn George Orchard-Lisle, MBE (d 2007), and Phyllis Yvonne, *née* Jones (d 1975); *b* 3 August 1938; *Educ* Marlborough, Trinity Hall Cambridge (MA); *Career* chartered surveyor, sr ptnr Healey & Baker 1988–99, non-exec chm Healey & Baker Financial 1990–2001, chm Healey & Baker Investment Advisors Inc 1999–2001; memb Bd Europa Capital Partners 1999–2005; chm: Cambridge Univ Estate Mgmnt Devpt Fund 1999–2005, Falcon Property Tst 2003–, Slough Estates plc 2005–06; dir: Income Tst Standard Life 2003–, Trinity Capital plc 2006–; pres RICS 1985–86, chm RICS Fndn 2003–05; Brig (TA) UKLF 1985; chm Royal Artillery Museum 2002–06; Cwlth War Graves cmmr 1999–2004; tstee: The Church Schools Fndn 2001–, Florence Nightingale Museum 2004–, Crafts Cncl 2004–05; govr: Harrow Sch 1987–99, West Buckland Sch 1985–2005 (chm of govrs 2000–05, pres 2006–), Marlborough Coll 1990–2006 (chm Cncl 2001–06); pres Cncl Univ of Reading 1992–2003; Liveryman Worshipful Co of Chartered Surveyors; Hon DSc City Univ 1998, Hon LLD Univ of Reading; hon fell Trinity Hall Cambridge; FRICS; *Recreations* golf; *Clubs* Athenaeum; *Style*— Paul Orchard-Lisle, Esq, CBE, TD, DL; ✉ 30 Mount Row, London W1K 3SH (tel 020 7499 6470, e-mail pdol@ukonline.co.uk)

ORDE, *see also:* Campbell-Orde

ORDE, His Hon Denis Alan; s of John Orde, CBE (d 1992), of Littlehoughton Hall, Northumberland, and Charlotte Lilian Orde (d 1975); *b* 28 August 1932; *Educ* Univ of Oxford (MA); *m* 1961, Jennifer Jane, da of Dr John Longworth (d 1982), of Masham, N Yorks; 2 da (Georgina Jane, Philippa Denise); *Career* served Army 1950–52, cmmnd 2 Lt 1951; Capt RA 1958 (TA) 1952–64; called to the Bar Inner Temple 1956 (pupil studentship 1956, Profumo prize 1959, bencher 1998), recorder of the Crown Court 1972–79, head of chambers 1979, circuit judge sitting in Crown Court NE and London 1979–2001, liaison judge to Magistrates 1983–97, resident (designated) judge of a Crown Court 1986–2001 (dep circuit judge 2001–05), dep judge of the High Court 1983–2005; pres Mental Health Review Tbnl (restricted cases) 2001–; chm Criminal Justice Liaison Ctee for Northumberland, Tyne & Wear and Durham 1995–2000, chm Criminal Justice Strategy Ctee for County of Durham 2000–2001; memb Chollerton PCC 1980–91, life vice-pres Northumberland Lawn Tennis Assoc 1982–, memb Lord Chllr's Co Advsy Ctee 1986–2001, ex-officio govr Christ's Hosp Sherburn 1993–98; pres OUCA 1954; *Books* Nelson's Mediterranean Command (1997); contrib to New Dictionary of Nat Biography (1999), In the Shadow of Nelson (2008); *Recreations* writing, family history, cricket, listening to music, biography, travel in France, writing; *Clubs* Northern Counties, OUCC; *Style*— His Hon Denis Orde; ✉ Chollerton Grange, Chollerton, Hexham,

Northumberland NE46 4TG; Aristotle Court, 75 Plater Drive, Oxford Waterside, Oxford OX2 6QY

ORDE, Sir Hugh Stephen Roden; kt (2005), OBE (2001); s of Thomas Henry Egil Orde, and Stella Mary Orde; *b* 27 August 1958; *Educ* Univ of Kent (BA); *m* 1985, Kathleen Helen; 1 s (b 12 April 1986); *Career* joined Met Police 1977, Sgt Brixton 1982, Police Staff Coll 1983, Inspr Greenwich 1984–90 (Bramshill Sch 1984–87), Staff Offr to Dep Asst Cmmr SW London (Chief Inspr) 1990, Chief Inspr Hounslow 1991–93, Supt Territorial Support Gp 1993–95, Detective Chief Supt Major Crimes SW Area 1995–98, Cdr Crime S London 1998, Dep Asst Cmmr (Cmmr's Command) 1999–2002, Chief Constable Police Serv NI 2002–; *Recreations* marathon running, wine, gardening; *Style*— Sir Hugh Orde, OBE; ✉ Police Service of Northern Ireland, 65 Knock Road, Belfast BT5 6LE (tel 028 9056 1613, fax 028 9056 1645, e-mail comsec1@psni.police.uk)

O'REILLY, Prof Sir John James; kt (2007); s of Patrick William O'Reilly (d 1969), of Bromsgrove, Worcs, and Dorothy Anne Lewis (d 1968); *b* 1 December 1946; *Educ* Sacred Heart Coll Droitwich, Brunel Univ (BTech, DSc), Univ of Essex (PhD); *m* Lesley, da of W Johnson; *Career* Ultra Electronics Ltd 1969–72, sr lectr Univ of Essex 1972–85, researcher PO Res Centre 1978–79, prof of electronic engrg and head of dept Univ of Wales at Bangor 1985–93, princ research fell BT Laboratories 1993–94, chair of telecommunications UCL 1994–2001, head Dept of Electronic and Electrical Engrg UCL 1997–2001, chief exec EPSRC 2001–06, vice-chllr Cranfield Univ 2006–; chief exec/dep chm IDB Ltd 1985–94, chm Cast Ltd 2005–; chm UK Network Interoperability Consultative Ctee 1996–, memb Oftel Tech Experts Advsy Gp 1996–2003, chm SERC Communications and Distributed Systems Ctee, memb SERC/DTI Info Technol Advsy Bd 1991–94, memb OST ITEC Tecnol Foresight Panel 1994–99, memb Technol Strategy Bd DTI 2004–06; IEE: memb Cncl 1998–, chm Electronics and Communications Div 1999–2000 (dep chm 1998–99), memb Bd of Tstees 2001–05, vice-pres 2001–02, dep pres 2002–04, pres 2004–05; memb Cncl Royal Acad of Engrg 2000–03; CEng, CPhys, FIET (FIEE 1988, MIEE 1983), FInstP, FREng 1993, Hon FIChemE 2004; *Books* Telecommunication Principles (1984, 2 edn 1989), Optimisation Methods in Electronics and Communications (1984), Problems of Randomness in Communications Engineering (1984); *Recreations* music, theatre, cooking; *Style*— Prof Sir John O'Reilly, FREng; ✉ Cranfield University, Cranfield, Bedfordshire MK43 0AL (tel 01234 754013, fax 01234 752583, e-mail john.oreilly@cranfield.ac.uk)

O'REILLY, Most Rev Philip Leo; *see:* Kilmore, Bishop of (RC)

OREL, Dr Harold; s of late Saul Orel, and late Sarah Wicker Orel; *b* 31 March 1926, Boston, MA; *Educ* Univ of New Hampshire (BA), Univ of Michigan (MA, PhD); *m* 25 May 1951, Charlyn, da of late Leslie O Hawkins; 1 da (Sara Elinor b 2 July 1962), 1 s (Timothy Ralston b 23 July 1963); *Career* instr Univ of Maryland 1952–56 (overseas prog Germany, Austria and GB 1954–55); Univ of Kansas: assoc prof 1957–63, prof 1963–74, distinguished prof 1974–97 (now emeritus); pres American Ctee of Irish Studies, vice-pres Thomas Hardy Soc; orations at Poet's Corner Westminster Abbey 1978 and 1990; invited to give lectures in numerous countries; memb Discussion Club Univ of Kansas; Higuchi Achievement (Humanities) Award 1990; FRSL 1986; *Publications* The World of Victorian Humour (ed, 1961), Six Studies in Nineteenth-Century English Literature and Thought (ed with George J Worth, 1962), Thomas Hardy's Epic-Drama: A Study of 'The Dynasts' (1963), Thomas Hardy's Personal Writings: Prefaces, Literary Opinions, Reminiscences (ed, 1966), The Development of William Butler Yeats, 1885–1900 (1968), British Poetry 1880–1920: Edwardian Voices (ed with Paul Wiley, 1969), The Nineteenth-Century Writer and his Audience (ed with George J Worth, 1969), English Romantic Poets and the Enlightenment: Nine Essays on a Literary Relationship - Studies in Voltaire and the Eighteenth Century, Vol CIII (1973), Irish History and Culture: Aspects of a People's Heritage (ed, 1976), The Final Years of Thomas Hardy, 1912–1928 (1976), The Dynasts, by Thomas Hardy: New Wessex Edition (ed, 1978), The Scottish World (ed with Marilyn Stokstad and Henry Snyder, 1981), Rudyard Kipling: Interviews and Recollections, Vols 1–2 (ed, 1983), Victorian Literary Critics: George Henry Lewes, Walter Bagehot, Richard Holt Hutton, Leslie Stephen, Andrew Lang, George Saintsbury, Edmund Gosse (1984), The Literary Achievement of Rebecca West (1985), The Victorian Short Story (1986), The Unknown Thomas Hardy: Lesser Known Aspects of Hardy's Life and Career (1987), Victorian Short Stories: An Anthology (ed, 1987), Critical Essays on Rudyard Kipling (ed, 1989), A Kipling Chronology (1990), Victorian Short Stories 2: The Trials of Love (ed, 1990), Sir Arthur Conan Doyle: Interviews and Recollections (ed, 1991), Popular Fiction in England, 1914–1918 (1991), Critical Essays on Sir Arthur Conan Doyle (ed, 1992), Gilbert and Sullivan: Interviews and Recollections (ed, 1994), Critical Essays on Thomas Hardy's Poetry (ed, 1995), The Historical Novel from Scott to Sabatini: Changing Attitudes Toward a Literary Genre, 1814–1920 (1995), The Brontës: Interviews and Recollections (ed, 1997), Charles Darwin: Interviews and Recollections (ed, 1999), William Wordsworth: Interviews and Recollections (ed, 2006); *Recreations* travel, photography; *Style*— Dr Harold Orel, FRSL; ✉ 713 Schwarz Road, Lawrence, Kansas 66049, USA (tel 00 1 785 842 0375, e-mail horel@ku.edu)

ORGA (D'ARCY-ORGA), (Husnu) Ates; s of Capt Irfan Orga (d 1970), of Wadhurst, E Sussex, and Margaret Veronica, *née* D'Arcy-Wright (d 1974); *b* 6 November 1944; *Educ* Univ of Durham (BMus), Trinity Coll of Music (FTCL); *m* 1, 23 Nov 1974 (m dis 1991), Josephine, da of Walter Richard Sidney Prior, of Ticehurst, E Sussex; 1 da (Chloë Louise b 20 October 1980), 1 s (Alexander b 19 December 1983); m 2, 8 May 1992 (m dis 1996), Ruth Frances, da of Harry Davis, of Hod Hasharon, Israel; 1 da (Francesca Hélène b 18 September 1993); *Career* prog annotator London Sinfonietta 1968–73, music info and presentation asst BBC Music Div London 1971–75, ind record, radio and video prodr 1972–, lectr in music and concert dir Univ of Surrey 1975–90, artistic dir Inst of Armenian Music London 1976–80, princ prog annotator LSO 1976–81, dir Ateş Orga Associates 1990–; examiner: Univ of Cambridge Local Examinations 1978–85, Assoc Bd Royal Schools of Music 1981–96, Univ of Malta 1993–95; artistic conslt Sutton Place Heritage Tst Guildford 1983–86, artistic advsr Acad of the London Mozarteum 1988–89, record prodr and conslt Collins Classics 1988–90, music dir V&A Club 1988, record prodr Hyperion 1990–95, Naxos/Marco Polo 1994–, music prodr Music and the Mind (C4) 1996; special projects conslt The Entertainment Corporation 1990, special projects dir Georgina Ivor Associates 1991–95; artistic dir: MusicArmenia 78 London 1978, Yvonne Arnaud Theatre Appeal Concerts 1985, Liszt and His Contemporaries, Beethoven Plus, The Gallic Muse, Mainly Schumann Festivals Guildford 1986–89, Guildford 91 Int Music Festival 1991, Piano Masterworks (Nikolai Demidenko) Belfast 1991–92 and Wigmore Hall London 1993, Virtuoso Romantics (Marc-André Hamelin) Wigmore Hall London 1994, Vienna Nights (Medici String Quartet) St John's Smith Square 1995; memb Jury: Br Liszt Piano Competition Guildford 1976, Alkan Centenary Piano Competition Croydon 1988, RPS Music Awards 1991–93; contrib: International Music Guide, The Listener, The Literary Review, Music and Musicians International, The Musical Times, Records and Recording, Hi Fi News, BBC Music Magazine, Gramophone International, Piano Quaterly, The Independent, The Ultimate Encyclopedia of Classical Music (1995), The Ultimate Encyclopedia of Musical Instruments (1996), BBC Music Magazine Top 1000 CD's Guide (1996); music panel chm SE Arts Regnl Arts Assoc 1985–88 (vice-chm 1984), memb Univ of S California Sch of Performing Arts Int Advsy Cncl on Armenian Musical Studies 1980–81; Royal Philharmonic Soc Music Award (Best Concert Series) 1993; *Books* The Proms (1974), Chopin: His Life and Times (1976), Beethoven: His Life and Times (1978), Records and Recording Classical Guides (1977–78), Portrait of a Turkish Family (Afterword, 1988); contrib to: All About The Symphony Orchestra (1967), The Music Lover's Companion (1971), Contemporary Art in Malta (1973), London Sinfonietta Schoenberg/Gerhard South Bank Series (1973), Time Remembered (1981); music publications: Chopin Three Piano Pieces (1968), Beethoven Sonata in C WoO 51 (1978); CD Anthologies: New York Legends (1996–98), Discover The Classics 2 (1997), Brahms Piano Works and Concertos (1997); *Recreations* music occidental and oriental, food, watching people, matters Eastern European; *Style*— Ates Orga, Esq

ORGAN, (Harold) Bryan; s of Harold Victor and Helen Dorothy Organ; *b* 31 August 1935; *Educ* Loughborough Coll of Art, Royal Acad Schs London; *m* Sandra Mary Mills; *Career* artist; lectr in drawing and painting Loughborough 1959–65; solo exhibitions: Leicester, London, New York, Baukunst Cologne, Turin; represented: Kunsthalle, Darmstadt, Mostra Mercatao d'Arte Contemporánea Florence, 3rd Int Exhibitions of Drawing Germany, São Paulo Museum of Art; works in private and public collections in England, France, Germany, Italy, Switzerland, USA, Canada, Brazil; portraits include: Sir Michael Tippett, David Hicks, Mary Quant, Princess Margaret, Elton John, Harold Macmillan, The Prince of Wales, The Princess of Wales, Lord Denning, James Callaghan, The Duke of Edinburgh, President Mitterand, Richard Attenborough, Roy Jenkins; Hon MA Loughborough Univ, Hon DLitt Univ of Leicester, Hon DLitt Loughborough Univ; *Publications* work incl in variouspubns incl: Picturing People, The Portrait Now, The Art Book, The 20th Century Art Book; *Style*— Bryan Organ, Esq; ✉ c/o Redfern Gallery, 20 Cork Street, London W1X 2HL

O'RIORDAN, Rear Adm John Patrick Bruce (Paddy); CBE (1982), DL (Northants 1997); s of Surgn Capt Timothy Joseph O'Riordan, RN (d 1966), of Bergh Apton, Norwich, and Bertha Carson, *née* Young (d 1983); *b* 15 January 1936; *Educ* Kelly Coll; *m* 15 Aug 1959, Jane, da of John Alexander Mitchell (d 1996), of Kirkcudbright, Scotland; 2 da (Susie (Mrs Graham) b 1960, Katherine (Mrs Beattie) b 1966), 1 s (Tim b 1965); *Career* Nat Serv, midshipman RNVR 1954, transferred RN, cmd HMS Porpoise 1968–69 and HMS Dreadnought 1972–74; cmd: Submarine Sea Trg Orgn 1976–78, RCDS 1979, guided missile destroyer HMS Glasgow 1980–81 (disaster relief ops St Lucia after Hurricane Allen 1980); asst COS policy to Supreme Allied Cdr Atlantic Virginia USA 1982–84, dir naval warfare MOD 1984–86 (ADC to HM the Queen 1985), Rear Adm mil dep cmdt NATO Def Coll Rome 1986–89; chief exec St Andrew's Gp of Hosps Northampton 1990–2000; chm NXD O'Riordan Bond Holdings Ltd 1999–; dir: Workbridge Enterprises 1990–2000, Ind Healthcare Assoc 1993–2000; chm: SSAFA - Forces Help Northants 1996–2000, Dumfriesshire and Stewartry 2000–, Scottish Resources Ctee 2006–; JP (Northants) 1991–2000; FIMgt 1985; *Recreations* sailing, sketching, rugby football, country pursuits; *Clubs* The Royal Navy of 1765 and 1785, Army and Navy, Royal Yacht Sqdn, RNSA; *Style*— Rear Adm Paddy O'Riordan, CBE, DL; ✉ Nether Crae, Mossdale, Kirkcudbrightshire DG7 2NL (tel 01644 450644, fax 01644 450233); Mole Cottage, 45 Church Lane, Kislingbury, Northamptonshire NN7 4AD

O'RIORDAN, Prof Timothy (Tim); DL (Norfolk 1998); s of Kevin Denis O'Riordan (d 2000), and Norah Joyce, *née* Lucas (d 1996); *b* 21 February 1942; *Educ* George Heriot's Sch Edinburgh, Univ of Edinburgh (MA), Cornell Univ (MS), Univ of Cambridge (PhD); *m* 18 May 1968, Ann Morison, da of Elmsley Philip (d 1992); 2 da (Katharine Louise b 24 Jan 1977, Alice Janet b 31 May 1979); *Career* asst prof Dept of Geography Simon Fraser Univ Burnaby BC 1967–70 (assoc prof 1970–74); UEA: reader Sch of Environmental Scis 1974–80, prof 1980–2005, prof emeritus 2006–; assoc dir Centre for Social and Economic Research on the Global Environment 1991–2001; memb: Broads Authy (chm Environment Ctee 1989–98), ESRC (chm Environment Working Gp 1981–90), Dow Chemical Corporate Environmental Advsy Ctee 1992–98, Core Faculty HRH The Prince of Wales's Business and Environment Prog 1994–, Environmental Advsy Bd Eastern Gp plc 1996–, Lord Provost of Edinburgh's Cmmn on Sustainable Devpt 1998, UK Sustainable Devpt Cmmn 2000–08, Cncl Soil Assoc 2005–; advsr to HRH The Pricne of Wales's Accounting for Sustainability Project; pres Norfolk Branch CPRE; FBA 2000; *Books* Progress in Resource Management (1971), Environmentalism (1976, 1981), Sizewell B: An Anatomy of the Inquiry (1988), The Greening of the Machinery of Government (1990), Interpreting the Precautionary Principle (1994), Environmental Science for Environmental Management (1994), Politics of Climate Change: A European Perspective (1996), Ecotaxation (1997), The Transition to Sustainability: A European Perspective (1998), Environmental Science for Environmental Management (2 edn 1999), Globalism, Localism and Identity (2000), Reinterpreting the Precautionary Principle (2001), Biodiversity, Sustainability and Human Communities (2002); *Recreations* classical music (double bass playing); *Style*— Prof Tim O'Riordan, DL, FBA; ✉ Wheatlands, Hethersett Lane, Colney, Norwich NR4 7TT (tel 01603 810534); School of Environmental Sciences, University of East Anglia, Norwich NR4 7TJ (tel 01603 592840, fax 01603 250558, e-mail t.oriordan@uea.ac.uk)

ORKNEY, 9 Earl of (S 1696); (Oliver) Peter St John Fitz-Maurice; also Viscount Kirkwall and Lord Dechmont (both S 1696); s of Lt-Col Frederick Oliver St John, DSO, MC (d 1977), and gs of late Sir Frederick Robert St John, KCMG (yst s of late Hon Ferdinand St John, 2 s of 3 Viscount Bolingbroke and St John); through Sir Frederick's w, Isabella Fitz-Maurice (gda of 5 Earl of Orkney); suc kinsman, 8 Earl, 1998 (has not yet established his right to the peerages); *b* 27 February 1938; *Educ* Univ of Lausanne, Univ of British Columbia (BA, Int Student of the Year 1958), LSE (MA), Univ of London (PhD); *m* 1, 1963 (m dis 1985), Mary Juliet, da of W G Scott-Brown; 3 da (Lady Juliet Elizabeth b 1964, Lady Nicola Jane b 1966, Lady Lucy Margaret b 1972), 1 s (Oliver Robert, Viscount Kirkwall and Master of Orkney b 1969); m 2, 1985, Mary Barbara Huck, da of Dr D B Albertson; 1 step s (Anthony Cameron St John), 3 step da (Dawn Marie, Caroline Jane, Erin Katherine); *Heir* s, Viscount Kirkwall and Master of Orkney; *Career* lectr UCL 1963–64; Univ of Manitoba: lectr 1964–66, asst prof 1966–72, assoc prof 1972–98, prof of political scis 1998–; visiting prof: Carleton Univ 1981–82, Canadian Forces Base Lahr 1985, 1990 and 1991, Univ of Victoria 1987 and 2002; reg quarterly lectr USAF Special Ops Sch Revolutionary Warfare Course Hurlburt Field FL 1994–; numerous lectures, speeches, seminars, symposia and radio & TV commentaries on intelligence, terrorism, insurgency, foreign policy, air piracy, Algeria and the Middle East 1977–; conslt: Canadian Armed Forces, Air Canada, CBC Radio, USAF Special Ops Sch FL; memb Advsy Ctee on Acad Relations Dept of External Affairs Canada 1980–90, dir Counter Terror Study Centre 1985–94, pres Agassiz Inst for the Study of Conflict 1993–, chair Foreign Affairs Canadian Govt Scholarship Ctee 1998–; Social Scis and Humanities Res Cncl (SSHRC) Grant 1982, Univ of Manitoba Outreach Award 1996, Olive Beatrice Stanton Award for Teaching Excellence 1997; memb: RIIA 1962, Canadian Inst of Int Affrs 1964 (pres Winnipeg Branch 1971–73, chm Winnipeg Branch 1973–74 and 1996–99), UN Assoc of Canada 1980, Canadian Assoc for the Study of Intelligence & Security 1986 (Prairie rep 1996), UN Assoc 1991; memb Advsy Bd Winnipeg Cameron Highlanders 2000; patron Orkney Homecoming 1999; *Books* Fireproof House to Third Option (1977), Mackenzie King to Philosopher King (1984), Air Piracy, Airport Security and International Terrorism: Winning the War Against Hijackers (1991); *Recreations* tennis, squash, swimming, boating, cycling, heritage and photography; *Style*— The Rt Hon the Earl of Orkney; ✉ 595 Gertrude Avenue, Winnipeg, Manitoba, Canada, R3L 0M9 (tel 00 1 204 284 1089, fax 00 1 204 453 3615, e-mail hrtland@mts.net)

ORLEBAR, Christopher John Dugmore; s of Col John H R Orlebar, OBE (d 1989), of St Helens, IOW, and Louise, *née* Crowe (d 1997); *b* 4 February 1945; *Educ* Rugby, Univ of Southampton, Coll of Air Trg Hamble; *m* 5 Feb 1972, Nicola Dorothy Mary, er da of Dr

O

Leslie Ford (d 1987), of Sheringham, Norfolk; 1 s (Edward b 1977), 1 da (Caroline b 1979); *Career* Cadet Pilot Southampton Univ Air Sqdn 1964–66, trainee pilot Coll of Air Trg Hamble 1967–69, First Offr and Navigator VC10 (awarded basic Instr Trg Course), CAA course Stansted for examiner/instr 1973, Sr First Offr Concorde 1976–86, appointed examiner/instr to Concorde Fleet, chartered 2 Concordes for celebration of 50 anniversary of Schneider Trophy 1981; organised BBC documentary on Concorde in QED series 1983, writer and presenter BBC TV series Jet Trail 1984, initiator and conslt Faster than a Speeding Bullet (Channel 4 Equinox) 1989, tech conslt Channel 4 documentary on Air Traffic Control in Equinox series 1993; Capt Boeing 737: BA 1986–2000, trg capt 1994–, Maersk Air Ltd 2000–01; Freeman City of London 1975, Liveryman Guild of Air Pilots and Air Navigators; FRAeS (MRAeS 1984); *Books* The Concorde Story (1986, 6 edn 2004); *Recreations* family, photography, music, sailing, canoeing, tennis, gardening; *Clubs* Air League; *Style*— Captain Christopher Orlebar, FRAeS; ✉ Holt Cottage, Fairoak Lane, Oxshott, Surrey KT22 0TW (tel 01372 842100, e-mail chris.orlebar@ntlworld.com)

ORMAN, Dr Stanley; s of Jack Orman (d 1974), and Ettie, *née* Steiner (d 1984); *b* 6 February 1935; *Educ* Hackney Downs GS, King's Coll London (BSc, PhD); *m* 1960, Helen, da of Joseph Hourman (d 1982); 1 s (David b 1961), 2 da (Ann b 1963, Lynn b 1969); *Career* Fulbright scholar, postdoctoral research Brandeis Univ, research in materials science 1961–74, chief weapon system engr Chevaline 1981–82, min and cnsllr Br Embassy Washington 1982–84, under sec MOD 1984, DG Strategic Def Initiative Participation Office 1986–90 (dep dir Awre Aldermaston 1984–86); chief exec GTS Inc Washington 1990–96, chief exec Orman Assoc Inc 1996–; Jelf medallist King's Coll London 1957; *Publications* Faith in G.O.D.S - Stability in the Nuclear Age (1991); author of over 170 other pubns on materials, science and defence issues; *Recreations* reading, designing bow ties, woodwork, embroidery; *Style*— Dr Stanley Orman; ✉ 11420 Strand Drive #104, Rockville, Maryland 20852, USA (tel 00 1 240 221 3689, e-mail stanleyo1@comcast.net)

ORME, Prof Michael Christopher L'Estrange; s of Christopher Robert L'Estrange Orme, TD (d 1979), of Poole, Dorset, and Muriel Evelyn Janet, *née* Thomson (d 2005); *b* 13 June 1940; *Educ* Sherborne, Univ of Cambridge (MA, MB BChir, MD); *m* 15 April 1967, (Joan) Patricia, da of Stanley Abbott, OBE (d 2004), of Coulsdon, Surrey; 1 s (Robert Martin b 10 July 1969); *Career* Univ of Liverpool: sr lectr clinical pharmacology 1975–81, reader 1981–84, prof pharmacology and therapeutics 1984–2001 (ret), dean of Faculty of Med 1991–96; dir of educn and trg NW Regnl Office NHS Exec 1996–2001; hon conslt physician Liverpool HA; memb GMC 1994–96; sec: Clinical Pharmacology Section Br Pharmacological Soc 1982–88, Clinical Section Int Union of Pharmacology 1987–92; chm Euro Assoc of Clinical Pharmacology and Therapeutics 2003–07 (hon sec 1993–2003); govr Birkenhead School Ltd 1991–2005; Hon DSc Univ of Salford 2000, Hon MD Int Med Univ Malaysia 2004; FRCP 1980, FMedSci 1998, Hon FRCGP 1998, FFPHM 2000; *Books* Medicines - The Self Help Guide (1988), Human Lactation (1989), Therapeutic Drugs (1991); *Recreations* sailing, astronomy; *Clubs* RSM; *Style*— Prof Michael Orme; ✉ Lark House, Clapton-on-the-Hill, Cheltenham, Gloucestershire GL54 2LG (tel 01451 822238, fax 01451 822688, e-mail morme@eandthome.demon.co.uk)

ORME, Prof Nicholas; s of Edward Howell Orme, and Kathleen, *née* Plowright (d 1971); *Educ* Bristol Cathedral Sch, Magdalen Coll Oxford (MA, DPhil, DLitt); *m* 4 July 1981, Rona, da of James S Monro; 1 da (Verity b 1984); *Career* Univ of Exeter: lectr 1964–81, reader in history 1981–88, prof of history 1988–2007 (emeritus prof 2007–), Nuffield Fndn res fell 1991–92, Leverhulme Tst res fell 1993–94; visiting appointments: Merton Coll Oxford, St John's Coll Oxford, Univ of Arizona, Univ of Minneapolis, Univ of Victoria (BC); past pres Devon History Soc, vice-pres Devon and Cornwall Record Soc; past pres Bristol and Gloucestershire Archaeological Soc, past pres Somerset Archaeological Soc, past chm Exeter Cathedral Fabric Advsy Ctee; lay canon Truro Cathedral 2005; corresponding fell Medieval Acad of America 2003; FRHistS 1979, FSA 1985; *Books* English Schools in the Middle Ages (1973), Education in the West of England (1976), The Minor Clergy of Exeter Cathedral (1980), Early British Swimming (1983), From Childhood to Chivalry (1984), Exeter Cathedral As It Was (1986), Education and Society in Medieval and Renaissance England (1989), John Lydgate, Table Manners for Children (ed, 1989), Unity and Variety: A History of the Church in Devon and Cornwall (ed, 1991), Nicholas Roscarrock's Lives of the Saints (ed, 1992), The First English Hospitals 1070–1570 (with Margaret Webster, 1995), White Bird Flying (1995), English Church Dedications (1996), Education in Early Tudor England (1998), The Saints of Cornwall (2000), Medieval Children (2001), Death and Memory in Medieval Exeter (with David Lepine, 2003), The Survey of Cornwall by Richard Carew (2004), Medieval Schools (2006), Cornish Wills 1342–1540 (2007); *Style*— Prof Nicholas Orme; ✉ Department of History, University of Exeter, Amory Building, Rennes Drive, Exeter EX4 4RJ

ORME, His Hon Judge Robert Thomas Neil; s of Thomas Elsmore Orme, and Iris Marguerita Orme; *b* 25 January 1947; *Educ* Denstone Coll, UCL (LLB); *m* 1971, Angela Mary, *née* Stokes; 1 s, 1 da; *Career* called to the Bar Gray's Inn 1970; recorder 1988–92 (asst recorder 1984–88), circuit judge (Midland & Oxford Circuit) 1992–; a pres Mental Health Review Tbnls 2001–; memb W Midlands Probation Ctee 1996–2001, memb W Midlands Probation Bd 2001–; chm Moseley Soc 1993–, govr Denstone Coll 2000–; *Recreations* opera, theatre, conservation; *Style*— His Hon Judge Orme; ✉ Queen Elizabeth II Law Courts, Birmingham B4 7NA (tel 0121 681 3300)

ORMEROD, Ben; s of John Ormerod, and Paula Taylor; *b* 24 October 1958; *Educ* St Christopher's Sch Letchworth, Central Sch of Speech and Drama; *m* m, 2002, Aïcha Kossoko; *Career* lighting designer; began career with Andrew Visnevski's Cherub Co; other cos incl: Kick Theatre, Buick of Sighs, ATC, Cheek by Jowl, 7:84 Scotland, Théâtre de Complicité, Major Road; designed lighting for The Calico Museum Ahmedabad; *Theatre* for RNT incl: Bent, Accidental Death of an Anarchist, The Winter's Tale, Uncle Vanya, Remembrance of Things Past; RSC incl: The Revenger's Tragedy, The Two Gentlemen of Verona, Henry V, Julius Caesar; for Leicester Haymarket incl: Krapp's Last Tape (also Riverside Studios) 1990, Our Country's Good 1991; for West Yorkshire Playhouse incl: Life is a Dream 1992, Betrayal 1994; for English Touring Theatre incl: Hamlet (also Donmar Warehouse) 1993, No Man's Land 1994, A Doll's House 1994, Hedda Gabler (also Donmar Warehouse) 1996, The Seagull (also Donmar Warehouse) 1997; other credits incl: Pal Joey (Bristol Old Vic) 1991, A View from the Bridge (Sheffield Crucible) 1991, Cyrano de Bergerac (Vembo Theatre, Athens) 1992, Coriolanus (Rennaissance, Chichester Festival) 1992, Macbeth (Tzeni Karezi, Athens) 1994, The Winslow Boy (Plymouth Theatre Royal, tour, The Globe) 1994, Casement (Moving Theatre at Riverside Studios) 1995, A Crocodile Looking at Birds (Lyric Hammersmith) 1995, The Government Inspector (Tzeni Karezi Theatre, Athens) 1995, Hamlet (OSC) 1996, The Beauty Queen of Leenane (Druid Theatre Co and Royal Court) 1996, Silence Silence Silence (Mladinsko Theatre, Ljubljana) 1996, Oedipus Tyrannus (Epidaurus) 1996, Passing Places (Edinburgh) 1997, Leenane Trilogy (Druid and Royal Court) 1997, Man with Connections (Porta Theatre Athens), The Wake and The Colleen Bawn (Abbey Theatre Dublin) 1998, The Beauty Queen of Leenane (Broadway) 1998, The Freedom of the City (Abbey Theatre Dublin and Lincoln Center, New York) 1999, The Master Builder (English Touring Theatre) 1999, The Country Boy (Druid Theatre Co) 1999, God's Plenty (Rambert) 1999, Measure for Measure (Library Theatre Manchester) 2000, Death of a Salesman (Birmingham Rep) 2000, The House (Abbey Dublin) 2000, Pera Palas (Gate Theatre London) 2000, Abandonment and Shetland Saga (Traverse Edinburgh) 2000, Andromache (Living Pictures) 2000, The Circle (Oxford Stage Co) 2000, Rose Rage (Newbury) 2001, See Blue Through (Ballet Gulbenkian Lisbon) 2001, The Father (Theatro Synchrono Athens) 2001, Made in China (Peacock Dublin), Macbeth (Ludlow Castle) 2001, A Streetcar Named Desire (Northern Ballet Theatre) 2001, Putting it Together (Chichester) 2001, The Caretaker (ETT) 2001, Murder (Gate Theatre London) 2001, The Nest (Living Pictures) 2001, Ibi l'ohun (Brest) 2001, Ghosts (ETT) 2002, Rose Rage (Theatre Royal Haymarket) 2002, Journey to the West (Tara Arts) 2002, The Constant Wife (Apollo and Lyric Theatres London) 2002, Enemy of the People (Theatr Clwyd) 2002, Babes in Arms (Guildhall Sch) 2002, The Circle (nat tour) 2002, Macbeth (Albery) 2002; *Opera* credits incl: La Voix Humaine and Savitri (Aix-en-Provence) 1990, Punch and Judy (Aldeburgh Festival) 1991, The Turn of the Screw (Bath and Wessex Opera) 1993, The Wildman (Aldeburgh Festival) 1995, The Mask of Orpheus (QEH/BBCSO) 1996, Beatrice Cenci (Spitalfields Opera) 1998, The Coronation of Poppea (Purcell Quartet tour of Japan) 1998; Baa Baa Black Sheep (Opera North and BBC 2); *Awards* TMA Best Design Award for Life is a Dream (jtly with Neil Warmington and Mic Pool); *Style*— Ben Ormerod, Esq; ✉ mobile 077 8595 4000

ORMEROD, Paul; s of John Ormerod, of Rochdale, Lancs, and Doris, *née* Parker (d 2000); *b* 20 March 1950; *Educ* Manchester Grammar, Christ's Coll Cambridge (MA), St Catherine's Coll Oxford (MPhil); *m* 1975, Pamela, da of Sidney Meadows; 1 s (Andrew Whitworth b 3 Sept 1982); *Career* economist and author; res offr NIESR 1973–80, dir of economics Henley Centre for Forecasting, currently dir Volterra Consulting; *Books* The Death of Economics (1994), Butterfly Economics (1998), Why Most Things Fail (2005); *Style*— Paul Ormerod, Esq; ✉ Volterra Consulting, Sheen Elms, 135c Sheen Lane, London SW14 8AE

ORMOND, Prof Leonée; *née* Jasper; *b* 27 August 1940; *Educ* Ware GS for Girls, St Anne's Coll Oxford (BA), Univ of Birmingham (MA); *m* 11 May 1963, Richard Louis Ormond, CBE, *qv*, s of Conrad Ormond (d 1979); 2 s (Augustus b 1972, Marcus b 1974); *Career* KCL: asst lectr 1965–68, lectr 1968–85, sr lectr 1985–89, reader in English 1989–96, prof of Victorian studies 1996–2006 (prof emerita 2006–); chair Tennyson Res Pubns Bd, tstee G F Watts Gallery Compton Surrey; pres Dickens Fellowship, fell English Assoc; FRSA; *Books* George Du Maurier (1969), Lord Leighton (with Richard Ormond, 1975), J M Barrie (1987), Alfred Tennyson: a Literary Life (1993); *Recreations* mountain walking; *Clubs* Univ Women's; *Style*— Prof Leonée Ormond; ✉ English Department, King's College, Strand, London WC2R 2LS

ORMOND, Richard Louis; CBE (2001); s of Conrad Eric Ormond (d 1979), of Old Rectory, Cleggan, Co Galway, and Dorothea Charlotte (d 1987), da of Sir Alexander Gibbons, 7 Bt; *b* 16 January 1939; *Educ* Marlborough, Brown Univ RI, ChCh Oxford (MA); *m* 11 May 1963, Prof Leonée Ormond, *qv*; 2 s (Augustus b 1972, Marcus b 1974); *Career* dep dir Nat Portrait Gallery 1975–83 (asst keeper 1965–75), dir Nat Maritime Museum 1986–2000 (head of Picture Dept 1983–86), Kress prof Nat Gallery of Art Washington DC 2001–02, dir Sargent Catalogue Raisonné Project 2000–; dep chm Museums Training Inst 1994–97; chm of tstees Watts Gallery Compton, chm Friends of Leighton House, tstee Mariners Museum Newport News VA; *Books* J S Sargent (1970), Early Victorian Portraits in the National Portrait Gallery (1973), Lord Leighton (with Leonée Ormond, 1975), Sir Edwin Landseer (1982), The Great Age of Sail (1986), F X Winterhalter and the Courts of Europe (1987), Frederic, Lord Leighton (jtly, 1996), Sargent Abroad (jtly, 1997), John Singer Sargent: The Early Portraits (with Elaine Kilmurray, 1998), John Singer Sargent (ed with Elaine Kilmurray, 1998), John Singer Sargent: Portraits of the 1890s (with Elaine Kilmurray, 2002), John Singer Sargent: The Later Portraits (with Elaine Kilmurray, 2003), John Singer Sargent: Figures and Landscapes, 1874–1882 (with Elaine Kilmurray, 2006), Sargent's Venice (jtly, 2006), Rule Britannia (with James Taylor, 2007); *Recreations* cycling, opera, theatre; *Clubs* Garrick; *Style*— Richard Ormond, Esq, CBE; ✉ 8 Holly Terrace, London N6 6LX

O'RORKE, His Hon Judge Richard Charles Colomb; s of Charles Howard Colomb O'Rorke (d 1986), and Jacqueline, *née* Prickett; *b* 4 June 1944; *Educ* Blundell's, Exeter Coll Oxford (open exhibitioner, MA); *m* 1966, Jane Elizabeth Phoebe, da of His Hon Judge Rowe Harding; 3 da (Kate b 1966, Rachel b 1969, Imogen b 1972), 1 s (Owen b 1978); *Career* called to the Bar Inner Temple 1968; in practice 1970–94, recorder (Midland & Oxford Circuit) 1987–94, circuit judge (Midland & Oxford Circuit) 1994–; *Recreations* gardening, Japanese art and culture; *Style*— His Hon Judge O'Rorke

ORR, Prof Christopher John (Chris); *b* 8 April 1943; *Educ* Beckenham & Penge GS, RCA (MA); *Career* artist 1967–; exhibited internationally; RA 1995, FRCA; *Work in Collections* Arts Cncl of GB, Br Cncl, V&A, RA, Science Museum, Ulster Folk & Tport Museum, Govt Art Collection, British Museum; *Books* Chris Orr's John Ruskin (1976), Many Mansions (1990), The Small Titanic (1994), Happy Days (1999), Semi-antics (2001), The Disguise Factory (2003); *Style*— Prof Chris Orr, RA; ✉ 7 Bristle Hill, Buckingham MK18 1EZ (tel and fax 01280 815255, e-mail chrisorr@aol.com, website www.chrisorr-ra.co.uk)

ORR, Deborah Jane; da of John Scott Orr, of Motherwell, and Winifred Meta, *née* Avis; *b* 23 September 1962; *Educ* Garrion Acad Wishaw, Univ of St Andrews (MA); *m* 1997, William Woodard (Will) Self, *qv*; 2 s (Ivan William Scott b Sept 1997, Luther James David b Aug 2001); *Career* dep ed City Limits magazine and contrib New Statesman until 1990, ed Guardian Weekend 1993–98 (joined The Guardian 1990), freelance journalist 1998–, currently columnist The Independent; *Style*— Ms Deborah Orr

ORR, Gordon Inglis; s of John Inglis Orr (d 1993), of Broughty Ferry, Scotland, and Doris May, *née* Hoyle (d 1959); *b* 13 December 1946; *Educ* Audely Park Sch, S Devon Coll of Art (RSA bursary), Kingston Coll of Art (BA); *m* 1981, Susan Mary, yst da of James Hervey Hall; 1 da (Jenny Susanah Inglis b 1982), 1 s (Jonathon Inglis b 1985); *Career* interior designer Conran Design Group 1970–73, creative dir (interior design) Shuttleworth Farmer Orr Design Consultants 1973–76 (projects incl creation of Virgin Records retail chain), md Shuttleworth Orr Design Consultants London and Maclaren Orr Design Consultants Edinburgh 1976–83, creative dir (interiors) DIA Interiors (Lopex Gp) 1984–86, jt md Sparkes Orr Design Consultants London 1986– (devpt of subsid companies Lighting Design House, Swain Communications and Rawcliffe & Associates since 1992), chm Robson Design Associates Bristol 1990–95; major design projects incl: Somerfield (new trading concept of Gateway) 1989–90 (winner Retail Environments category Design Week Awards 1991), Dales (new discount trading concept for Asda) 1992–93, Shoe Express (new discount trading concept for BSC) 1993; FRSA 1966, FInstD 1978; *Recreations* sailing, opera, Scottish country dance; *Style*— Gordon Orr, Esq

ORR EWING, Sir Archibald Donald; 6 Bt (UK 1886), of Ballikinrain, Stirlingshire, and Lennoxbank, Co Dumbarton; s of Sir Ronald Archibald Orr Ewing, 5 Bt (d 2002); *b* 20 December 1938; *Educ* Gordonstoun, Trinity Coll Dublin (BA); *m* 1, 1965 (m dis 1972), Venetia Elizabeth, da of Maj Richard Turner; m 2, 1972, Nicola Jean-Anne, da of Reginald Baron (Barry) Black (d 1996), of Fovant, Wilts, and (Eloise) Jean Horatia, *née* Innes-Ker (d 1996), niece of 8 Duke of Roxburghe; 1 s (Alastair Frederick Archibald b 26 May 1982); *Heir* s, Alastair Orr Ewing; *Career* landowner; memb Queen's Body Guard for Scotland (Royal Co of Archers); grand master mason of Scotland 1999–2004; *Recreations* shooting, fishing, opera, theatre; *Clubs* New (Edinburgh); *Style*— Sir Archibald Orr Ewing, Bt; ✉ Cardross, Port of Menteith, by Stirling FK8 3JY (tel and fax 01877 385223, e-mail adoewing@lineone.net)

ORR EWING, Maj Edward Stuart; CVO (2007); s of Capt David Orr Ewing, DSO, DL (d 1964, s of Charles Orr Ewing, MP Ayr, 5 s of Sir Archibald Orr Ewing, 1 Bt), and Mary, da of late Benjamin Noaks, of Nylstroom, SA; *b* 28 September 1931; *Educ* Sherborne; *m* 1, 1958 (m dis 1981), Fiona Anne Bowman, da of Anthony Hobart Farquhar, of Hastingwood House (*see* Burke's Landed Gentry 18 edn 1965); 2 da (Jane b 1961, Victoria b 1962), 1 s (Alastair b 1964); m 2, 1981, Diana Mary, da of William Smith Waters, OBE, of Dalston, Cumbria; *Career* serv The Black Watch 1950–69, Maj; landowner and farmer 1969–; HM Lord-Lt Wigtown 1989– (DL 1970); *Recreations* country pursuits; *Clubs* New (Edinburgh); *Style—* Major Edward Orr Ewing, CVO; ✉ Dunskey, Portpatrick, Wigtownshire DG9 8TJ (tel 01776 810211)

ORR-EWING, Hon Sir (Alistair) Simon; 2 Bt (UK 1963); eldest s of Baron Orr-Ewing, OBE (Life Peer and 1 Bt, d 1999); *b* 10 June 1940; *Educ* Harrow, Trinity Coll Oxford (MA); *m* 1968, Victoria, da of Keith Cameron (d 1981), of Fifield House, Oxon; 2 s (Archie Cameron b 1969, James Alexander b 1971), 1 da (Georgina Victoria b 1974); *Career* chartered surveyor; cncllr RBK&C 1982–90, chm Town Planning Ctee 1986–88; Lloyd's underwriter 1986–93; FRICS; *Recreations* skiing, tennis, shooting; *Clubs* MCC, Boodle's; *Style—* The Hon Sir Simon Orr-Ewing, Bt; ✉ 29 St James's Gardens, London W11 4RF (tel 020 7602 4513)

ORRELL, His Hon Judge James Francis Freestone; s of Francis Orrell (d 1994), of Rangemore, Staffs, and Marion Margaret, *née* Freestone (d 1988); *b* 19 March 1944; *Educ* Ratcliffe Coll, Univ of York (BA); *m* 1 Aug 1970, Margaret Catherine, da of Albert Bernard Benedict Hawcroft, of Derby; 2 s (James Benedict John b 27 Nov 1971, Patrick George Francis b 22 Jan 1981); *Career* called to the Bar Gray's Inn 1968, in practice Midland & Oxford Circuit 1969–89, recorder 1988–89, circuit judge (Midland Circuit) 1989–; *Recreations* walking, reading; *Clubs* Burton; *Style—* His Hon Judge Orrell; ✉ c/o Derby Combined Court Centre, The Morledge, Derby DE1 2XE (tel 01332 31841, e-mail hhjudgejames.orrell@judiciary.gsi.gov.uk)

ORRELL-JONES, Keith; s of Francis George (d 1984), and Elsie (d 1988); *b* 15 July 1937; *Educ* Newcastle HS, St John's Coll Cambridge (MA); *m* 1961, Hilary; 4 s (Justin b 1963, Duncan b 1965, Richard b 1967, Sebastian b 1969); *Career* ARC Ltd (subsid of Consolidated gold Fields plc): joined as area mangr 1972, pres ARC America 1981, memb main bd 1982, chief exec 1987–89; former dir Consolidated Gold Fields 1989; pres Blue Circle America 1990–92, gp chief exec Blue Circle Industries plc 1992–99 (dir 1990–99), chm FKI plc 1999–2004; non-exec chm Smiths Industries plc 1998–2004 (non-exec dir 1992–2004); CIM 1992; *Recreations* game fishing, shooting, art, opera; *Clubs* RAC; *Style—* Keith Orrell-Jones, Esq

ORTON, Giles Anthony Christopher; s of late Dr Francis John Orton, of Sheffield, and Helen Davina Orton; *b* 18 August 1959, Nacton, Suffolk; *Educ* King Edward VII Sch Sheffield, The Queen's Coll Oxford (Hastings exhibitioner, MA), Chester Coll of Law; *m* 11 April 1987, (Kathryn) Jane, *née* Robinson; 3 s (Hugh b 16 Nov 1989, Ralph b 21 Oct 1991, Guy b 9 Nov 1996); *Career* slr DLA 1983–87 (trainee slr 1981–83); Eversheds: joined 1987, ptnr 1989–, head of litigation (East Midlands) 1994–2001, head of pensions 2001–06, head of pensions litigation 2006–; chm Pensions Ctee Assoc of Corporate Tstees 2003–06; memb: Law Soc 1983–, Assoc of Pension Lawyers 1994– (chm Litigation Ctee 1998–); memb Derby City Cncl 1988–92; *Recreations* country pursuits, sailing, gardening, bridge (bridge columnist in Professional Pensions magazine); *Clubs* Carlton; *Style—* Giles Orton, Esq; ✉ Brun Meadows, Brun Lane, Kirk Langley, Ashbourne, Derbyshire DE6 4LU (tel 01332 824233, e-mail gilesorton@fastmail.fm); Eversheds LLP, Senator House, 85 Queen Victoria Street, London EC4V 4JL (tel 020 7919 4739, fax 020 7849 8744, e-mail gilesorton@eversheds.com)

OSBORN, Prof Marilyn Jean; da of William Hoggan, of Meopham, Kent, and Jean, *née* Bruce (d 1999); *b* 30 October 1943; *Educ* LSE (BSc), Univ of Bristol (PhD); *m* 25 July 1968, Dr Albert Osborn (d 1998), s of Albert Osborn, and Henrietta Osborn; 2 s (Steven James b 5 July 1971, Richard Paul b 16 Sept 1974); *Career* pt/t tutor in sociology of educn Open Univ 1972–79, pt/t tutor in sociology for med students Dept of Mental Health Univ of Bristol 1973–79, research assoc Nat Inst of Adult Continuing Educn Leicester 1979–87, Canadian studies project offr Canadian High Cmmn London 1987–88, sr scientific offr ESRC 1988–89, prof of educn and dir of research Grad Sch of Educn Univ of Bristol 1989– (previously reader, sr research fell, dir MPhil/PhD prog and co-dir Centre for Int and Comparative Studies); examiner and reviewer: ESRC Studentship (ESRC), Social Sciences and Humanities Research Cncl (SSHRC), European Science Fndn (ESF); memb Editorial Bd COMPARE, memb Scientific Ctee Politiques d'Education et de Formation (jl); memb: BERA, Br Assoc for Int and Comparative Educn (BAICE), Comparative Educn Soc in Europe (CESE); *Publications* Learning from Comparing, Vol 2: Policy, Professionals and Development (jt ed, 2000), What Pupils Say: Changing Policy and Practice in Primary Education (jtly, 2000), What Teachers Do: Changing Policy and Practice in Primary Education (jtly, 2000), Promoting Quality in Learning: A Comparative Study in England and France (jtly, 2001), A World of Difference? Comparing Learners Across Europe (jtly, 2003); also author of book chapters and jl articles; *Recreations* walking, theatre, cinema, reading fiction and biographies; *Clubs* Royal Over-Seas League; *Style—* Prof Marilyn Osborn; ✉ Graduate School of Education, University of Bristol, 35 Berkeley Square, Bristol BS8 1JA (tel 0117 928 7073, fax 0117 925 1537, e-mail marilyn.osborn@bristol.ac.uk)

OSBORN, Neil Frank; s of George James Osborn, of Hemel Hempstead, Herts, and Georgina Rose, *née* Nash; *b* 24 October 1949; *Educ* St Albans Sch, Worcester Coll Oxford (MA); *m* 15 April 1975, Holly Louise, da of Lt-Col George Francis Smith, of McLean, VA; *Career* reporter The Daily Progress Charlottesville VA 1972–74, freelance reporter Lloyd's List and Liverpool Daily Post 1975–77, sr ed Institutional Investor NY 1978–83, US ed Euromoney NY 1983–85, ed Euromoney London 1985–90, publisher Euromoney 1990–; dir: Euromoney Inc 1985–, Euromoney Institutional Investor plc (formerly Euromoney Publications) 1988–; non-exec dir RBC Information Systems Moscow 2002–; memb Exec Bd Family Welfare Assoc 1994–2002; *Clubs* Carlton; *Style—* Neil Osborn, Esq; ✉ Flat 4, 16 Wetherby Gardens, London SW5 0JP; Euromoney Institutional Investor plc, Nestor House, Playhouse Yard, London EC4V 5EX (tel 020 7779 8888, fax 020 7779 8653, e-mail nosborn@euromoneyplc.com)

OSBORN, Sir Richard Henry Danvers; 9 Bt (E 1662), of Chicksands, Beds; s of Sir Danvers Lionel Rouse Osborn, 8 Bt (d 1983), and Constance Violette, *née* Rooke (d 1988); *b* 12 August 1958; *Educ* Eton; *m* 25 Feb 2006, Belinda Mary Elworthy; 1 da (Lara Constance Elizabeth b 20 June 2006); *Heir* kinsman, William Osborn; *Career* Christie's 1978–83, ind fine paintings conslt P & D Colnaghi Ltd 1984–87, dir Paul Mitchell Ltd (picture conservation and framing) 1991–2002, Richard Osborn Fine Art (fine art consultancy); *Recreations* real tennis, shooting, racing, golf; *Clubs* Turf, MCC, Queen's, Pratt's, NZ Golf; *Style—* Sir Richard Osborn, Bt; ✉ 48 Lessar Avenue, London SW4 9HQ; Richard Osborn Fine Art, 68 St James's Street, London SW1A 1PH

OSBORN, Shane Edward; s of Anthony Osborn (d 1985), and Patricia Osborn, of Perth, Aust; *b* Perth, Aust; *Educ* Willeton Sr HS Perth (HS Cert), Bently Tech Coll Perth (Dip Cookery); *Career* chef; sous chef rising to head chef Pied à Terre London 1998–; 8 out of 10 Good Food Guide 2001–, 2 Michelin Stars 2003–; *Publications* Starters (2004); *Recreations* cycling, diving, mountaineering, skydiving; *Style—* Shane Osborn, Esq; ✉ Pied à Terre, 34 Charlotte Street, London W1T 2NH (tel 020 7916 0787, fax 020 7916 1171, mobile 07736 638923)

OSBORNE, Charles Thomas; s of Vincent Lloyd Osborne; *b* 24 November 1927; *Educ* Brisbane State HS; *m* 1970 (m dis 1975), Marie Korbelarova; civil partnership, 9 Jan 2006, Kenneth Thomson; *Career* author; lit dir Arts Cncl of GB 1971–86, chief theatre critic Daily Telegraph 1987–91; memb: PEN, Royal Philharmonic Soc; Hon DUniv Griffith Univ Brisbane; FRSL 1996; *Books* The Complete Operas of Verdi (1969), The Concert Song Companion (1974), Wagner and His World (1977), The Complete Operas of Mozart (1978), W H Auden - the Life of a Poet (1979), Klemperer Stories (with Kenneth Thomson, 1980), The Complete Operas of Puccini (1981), Dictionary of the Opera (1983), Giving It Away - memoirs (1986), Verdi: a Life in the Theatre (1987), The Complete Operas of Richard Strauss (1988), The Complete Operas of Richard Wagner (1990), The Bel Canto Operas (1994), The Pink Danube (1998), The Opera Lover's Companion (2004), Agatha Christie: Murder in Three Stages (2007); *Recreations* travel; *Clubs* Savile; *Style—* Charles Osborne, Esq, FRSL; ✉ 125 St George's Road, London SE1 6HY (tel 020 7928 1534)

OSBORNE, Clive Maxwell Lawton; s of Raymond Peter Osborne (d 1997), of Newcastle-under-Lyme, and Eileen Mary Lawton; *b* 20 July 1955; *Educ* Newcastle HS, ChCh Oxford (MA); *m* Oct 1985, Ursula Frances Amanda, da of Francis Eric Futcher; 1 da (Georgina Rosamund Lawton b 1988), 1 s (Thomas Francis Lawton b 1991); *Career* called to the Bar Gray's Inn, joined Home Office 1980, asst legal advsr Home Office 1991–97, legal dir DTI 1997–99, asst legal advsr NI Office 1999–2001, dep legal advsr Home Office and NI Office 2001–05, legal advsr Serious Organised Crime Agency 2005–; *Style—* Clive Osborne, Esq; ✉ PO Box 8000, London SE11 5EN

OSBORNE, David Francis; s of William Henry Osborne (d 1969), of Surrey, and Beatrice Irene, *née* Hinge; *b* 24 October 1937; *Educ* Dulwich Coll, Jesus Coll Oxford (MA); *Children* 1 s (Martin b 1965), 2 da (Katharine b 1967, Juliet b 1968); *Career* Unilever Ltd 1960–66, PA International Management Consultants 1966–82, Hill Samuel & Co Ltd 1982–87, dir Electra Investment Tst plc 1981–96, dir Electra Fleming Ltd 1987–97; chm: Corporate Ventures Ltd 1996–99, Akhter Group 1997–99, Italian Private Equity Fund 1998–, Art Work Investment Ltd 2003–; dir B& S Equities (Lugano), dir Dinimia (Spain) 1997–; MIMgt, MICMA, MIMC; *Recreations* cricket, golf, gardening, reading, travel, languages, opera, bridge; *Clubs* MCC, Oxford and Cambridge; *Style—* David Osborne, Esq; ✉ Mayflower Cottage, Lower Assendon, Oxfordshire RG9 6AH (tel 01491 572004)

OSBORNE, Dr Denis Gordon; CMG (1990); s of Alfred Gordon Osborne (d 1993), of Wooburn Common, Bucks, and Frances Agnes Osborne (d 1998); *b* 17 September 1932; *Educ* Dr Challoner's GS Amersham, Univ of Durham (BSc, PhD); *m* 16 May 1970, Christine Susannah, da of Percy Rae Shepherd (d 1987); 2 da (Ruth b 1971, Sally b 1973); *Career* lectr in physics: Univ of Durham 1957, Fourah Bay Coll Freetown SA 1958, Univ of Ghana 1958–64; Univ of Dar es Salaam: reader in physics 1964–66, prof of physics 1966–71, dean of sci 1968–70; conslt World Bank: Malaysia 1971, Ethiopia 1972, res fell in physics UCL 1971–72; ODA London: princ 1972–80, asst sec natural resources 1980–84, asst sec Eastern and Western Africa 1984–87; high cmmr to Malawi 1987–90; research advsr RIPA International 1990–92; conslt and advsr on governance and devpt 1992–; assoc Inst for Devpt Policy and Mgmnt Univ of Manchester 1997–, sr res assoc Inst of Advanced Legal Studies Univ of London 1999–; author of papers on geophysics, technol, educn and devpt; reader St Mary's Church Elham; CPhys, FInstP 1966; *Books* Way Out: Some Parables of Science and Faith (1977); *Recreations* reading, writing, walking; *Clubs* Athenaeum; *Style—* Dr Denis Osborne, CMG; ✉ The Arc, North Elham, Kent CT4 6NH (tel 01303 840540, fax 01303 840541, e-mail do@governance.org.uk)

OSBORNE, Douglas Leonard; s of Leonard Osborne (d 1948), of Lincoln, and Gladys Ellen, *née* Ward; *b* 19 October 1940; *Educ* Royal Masonic Schs; *m* 22 March 1969, Barbara Helen, da of Ronald Bartrop; 1 s (Daniel James b 25 June 1972), 1 da (Emma Jane b 27 Aug 1974); *Career* Action for Blind People (formerly London Assoc for the Blind): asst sec 1965–76, dep dir 1976–79, dir 1979–83; chief exec Leukaemia Research Fund 1989–2007 (admin 1983–89), ret; advsr on charity matters ICSA, memb Cncl Metropolitan Soc for the Blind; FCIS 1985 (ACIS 1967); *Books* The Charities Manual (ed jtly, 1986, Supplements 1–32, 2005); *Recreations* music, rugby football, swimming, cooking, travel; *Style—* Mr Douglas Osborne; ✉ c/o Leukaemia Research Fund, 43 Great Ormond Street, London WC1N 3JJ (tel 020 7405 0101, fax 020 7405 3139)

OSBORNE, George Gideon Oliver; MP; s and h of Sir Peter Osborne, 17 Bt, *qv*, and Lady Osborne, *née* Felicity Loxton-Peacock; *b* 23 May 1971, London; *Educ* St Paul's, Davidson Coll NC (Dean Rusk scholar), Magdalen Coll Oxford (scholar, MA, ed Isis); *m* 1998, Hon Frances Victoria, da of Baron Howell of Guildford, PC (Life Peer), *qv*; 1s (Luke Benedict b 2001), 1 da (Liberty Kate b 2003); *Career* head of political section Cons Research Dept 1994–95, special advsr MAFF 1995–97, sec to the shadow cabinet and political sec to the Ldr of the Oppn 1997–2001, MP (Cons) Tatton 2001–; oppn whip 2003, oppn Treasy spokesman 2003–04, shadow chief sec of the Treasy 2004–05, shadow Chancellor of the Exchequer 2005–; memb Public Accounts Ctee House of Commons 2001–03; vice-pres E Cheshire Hospice, hon pres Br Youth Cncl, tstee Arts & Business; *Recreations* walking in the Peak District, film, theatre; *Style—* George Osborne, Esq, MP; ✉ House of Commons, London SW1A 0AA (tel 020 7219 8214)

OSBORNE, Georgiana Louise; JP (2001); da of Richard Douglas Moore, and June Louise, *née* Peachey; *Educ* Wellington Diocesan Sch for Girls (Nga Tawa) Marton NZ, Victoria Univ of Wellington (BA), Univ of Lausanne (Philips overseas scholar); *Career* dep pres Angus Branch Br Red Cross 1991–98, pres Tayside Branch Br Red Cross 1999–2004 (patron 2004–); Badge of Hon for Distinguished Serv Br Red Cross Soc 1996, Badge of Hon for Outstanding Serv Br Red Cross Soc 2004; tstee Angus Coll 2004 (patron 2003); HM Lord-Lt Angus 2001–; OStJ; *Recreations* music, the arts, tennis, golf, skiing; *Style—* Mrs Georgiana L Osborne; ✉ Balmadies, Guthrie, Forfar, Angus DD8 2SH (tel and fax 01307 818242)

OSBORNE, Ven Hayward John; s of Ernest Osborne, and Francis Joy, *née* Perman; *Educ* Sevenoaks Sch, New Coll Oxford (MA), King's Coll Cambridge (PGCE), Wescott House Theol Coll Cambridge; *Career* curate Bromley Parish Church 1973–77, team vicar Halesowen 1977–83, team rector St Barnabas Worcester 1983–88, vicar St Mary Moseley 1988–2001, area dean Moseley 1994–2001, hon canon Birmingham Cathedral 2000, archdeacon of Birmingham 2001–; memb Gen Synod 1988–; *Style—* The Ven the Archdeacon of Birmingham; ✉ Diocesan Office, 175 Harborne Park Road, Birmingham B17 0BH (tel 0121 426 0441, e-mail archdeaconofbham@birmingham.anglican.org)

OSBORNE, Prof John; s of Leonard Osborne (d 1948), and Gladys Ellen, *née* Ward (d 1996); *b* 31 December 1938; *Educ* Royal Masonic Sch, UC Swansea (BA), Univ of Munich, Univ of Cambridge (PhD), Univ of Wales (DLitt); *m* 7 Sept 1962, Janet Elizabeth, da of Alan George Hart, of Hove, E Sussex; 3 da (Helen b 1966, Josephine b 1968, Mary b 1975), 1 s (Luke b 1979); *Career* lectr in German Univ of Southampton 1965–68, lectr and reader in German Univ of Sussex 1968–79, prof of German Univ of Warwick 1979–; Alexander von Humboldt res fell Univ of Göttingen 1972–73, 1976–77 and 1992, visiting prof Univ of Metz 1985–86; memb Cncl English Goethe Soc; *Books* The Naturalist Drama in Germany (1971), J M R Lenz: The Renunciation of Heroism (1975), Die Meininger: Texte zur Rezeption (1980), Meyer or Fontane? (1983), The Meiningen Court Theatre (1988), Vom Nutzen der Geschichte (1994), Gerhart Hauptmann and the Naturalist Drama (1998), Theodor Fontane: Vor den Romanen (1999); *Recreations* listening to music, travel, swimming; *Style—* Prof John Osborne; ✉ Department of German Studies, University of Warwick, Coventry CV4 7AL (tel 024 7652 4419)

OSBORNE, John Leslie; s of Frederick James Osborne, of Lampeter, Wales, and May Doris, *née* Brown; *b* 20 March 1942; *Educ* The London Hosp Med Coll (MB BS); *Family* 2 da (Clare b 1969, Julia b 1981), 2 s (Andrew b 1972, James b 1979); m Oct 1997, Dr Bee Osborne (d 2005), *née* Eppel; *Career* lectr in obstetrics and gynaecology Inst of Obstetrics and Gynaecology 1974–79; currently conslt obstetrician and gynaecologist UCHL; formerly conslt obstetrics and gynaecology Queen Charlotte's and Chelsea Hosps; hon sr lectr: Inst of Urology, Inst of Obstetrics and Gynaecology; Freeman Worshipful Soc Apothecaries; chm: Elizabeth Garrett Anderson Appeals Tst, ASAP Women's Health;

O

FRCOG 1985 (MRCOG 1973), memb RSM; *Recreations* music, photography, old cars (Bentley); *Clubs* Bentley Drivers'; *Style—* John Osborne, Esq; ✉ Second Floor Consulting Suite, 214 Great Portland Street, London W1W 5QN (tel 020 8995 0019, fax 020 7387 7066)

OSBORNE, John Michael; s of Claudius Hase Osborne, and Irene Oliver, *née* Chaffé; *b* 30 October 1953; *Educ* Whitchurch GS, Univ of Sheffield (BSc); *m* 2 July 1983, Helen Elizabeth, da of Richard Derek Gommo; 1 da (Claire Hannah b 11 April 1986), 1 s (Nicholas John b 14 April 1988); *Career* Equity & Law: joined 1975, devpt mangr 1986, planning mangr 1986–88, mangr Equity & Law Home Loans 1988–92, mangr and dir Equity & Law Unit Trust 1990–98, actuary 1990–92, head of business devpt 1992–98, head of finance and operations AXA Assurance 1998–2000; established Hase Osborne Asset Mgmnt (ind fin advsrs, formerly Twigden Osborne Asset Mgmnt) 2000–; FIA 1981; *Recreations* golf, tennis; *Style—* John Osborne, Esq; ✉ Hase Osborne Asset Management, Chiltern Court, Back Street, Wendover, Buckinghamshire HP22 6EP (tel 01296 620950)

OSBORNE, Rt Hon Lord; Kenneth Hilton Osborne; PC (2001), QC (Scot) 1976; s of Kenneth Osborne and Evelyn Alice, *née* Hilton; *b* 9 July 1937; *Educ* Larchfield Sch Helensburgh, Merchiston Castle Sch Edinburgh, Univ of Edinburgh; *m* 1964, Clare Ann Louise Lewis; 1 s, 1 da; *Career* admitted to Faculty of Advocates in Scotland 1962, standing jr counsel to Min of Def (Navy) in Scot 1974–76, advocate-depute 1982–84, senator Coll of Justice in Scot 1990–; chm: Disciplinary Ctee Potato Mktg Bd 1975–90, Legal Aid Ctee Supreme Ct 1979–81, Med Appeal Tbnls Scot 1988–90, Local Govt Boundary Cmmn for Scot 1990–2000; pt/t legal memb Lands Tbnl for Scot 1985–87; *Clubs* New (Edinburgh); *Style—* The Rt Hon Lord Osborne, QC; ✉ 42 India Street, Edinburgh EH3 6HB (tel and fax 0131 225 3094, e-mail kenneth.osborne@btinternet.com); Primrose Cottage, Bridgend of Lintrathen, by Kirriemuir, Angus DD8 5JH (tel 01575 560316)

OSBORNE, Sir Peter George; 17 Bt (I 1629), of Ballintaylor, Co Tipperary; s of Lt-Col Sir George Francis Osborne, 16 Bt, MC (d 1960), and Mary, *née* Horn (d 1987); Richard Osborne cr 1 Bt of Ireland 1629, and supported Parl against the crown; 2, 7, 8, 9 and 11 Bts were MPs (8 Bt, PC); *b* 29 June 1943; *Educ* Wellington, ChCh Oxford; *m* 1968, Felicity, da of late Grantley Loxton-Peacock; 4 s (George Gideon Oliver, b 1971, Benedict George b 1973, Adam Peter b 1976, Theo Grantley b 1985); *Heir* s, George Osborne, MP, *qv*; *Career* chm Osborne & Little plc; *Clubs* White's; *Style—* Sir Peter Osborne, Bt; ✉ 67 Lansdowne Road, London W11 2LG

OSBORNE, Richard Ellerker; s of William Harold Osborne (d 1984), and Georgina Mary, *née* Farrow (d 1997); *b* 22 February 1943; *Educ* Worksop Coll, Univ of Bristol (BA, MLitt); *m* 18 Jan 1986, Hailz-Emily, da of Michael Ewart Wrigley, of Streetly, W Midlands; 1 s (Harry George Ellerker b 6 May 1992); *Career* head of English Bradfield Coll 1982–88 (teacher 1967–88, head 6th form gen studies 1979–88); contrib: Records and Recording 1967–73, Gramophone 1974–, Opera, The Spectator, Times Literary Supplement; music critic The Oldie; presenter BBC Radio 3 1989–98; chm Music Section Critics' Circle 1984–87; *Books* Rossini (1986), Conversations with Karajan (1989), Karajan: a Life in Music (1998), Till I End My Song: Music at Eton 1440–1940 (2002), Rossini: His Life and Works (2007); *Recreations* food and wine, cricket, fell walking; *Style—* Richard Osborne, Esq; ✉ 2 Vaughan Copse, Eton, Berkshire SL4 6HL (tel 01753 671368, e-mail h.osborne@etoncollege.org.uk)

OSBORNE, Robert (Bob); s of Walter Richard Osborne and Maud Osborne; *b* 18 April 1948; *Educ* Sedgehill Sch London, Univ of Warwick (BSc), Imperial Coll London (MSc, DIC); *m* 1970, Madeline, *née* Chatterton; 2 da (Tamsin b 20 March 1978, Jessica b 22 July 1981); *Career* dir Moon Enterprises (concert promotions) 1970, teacher 1970–71, commissioning ed mathematics and science Penguin Education 1971–74, commissioning ed rising to dep md Hutchinson Educational 1974–84, publishing dir then dep md Heinemann Educational Books 1984–88, md Harcourt UK Schools Publishing 1988–2004; strategic devpt dir Pearson Edexcel 2004–; educational publishing conslt 2006–; *Recreations* France, music, travel; *Style—* Bob Osborne; ✉ e-mail bob@bobosborne.co.uk

OSBORNE, Roy Paul; s of Gilbert William Osborne, and Jean Mary Osborne, of Cumnor, Oxford; *Educ* Magdalen Coll Sch Oxford; *m* 1977, Vivienne, *née* Gentry; 2 da (Lauren Claire b 1983, Melanie Kate b 1984); *Career* HM Dip Serv: Oslo 1972–74, immigration offr Islamabad 1974–78, vice-consul Rome 1978–80, Western Euro Dept FCO 1981–83, asst private sec to Min of State FCO 1983–85, second later first sec Yaoundé Cameroon 1985–88, first sec (Press and Info) Madrid 1989–93, Drugs and Int Crime Dept FCO 1993–97, ambass to Nicaragua 1997–2000, dep head Overseas Territories Dept 2001–04, dir trade and investment Berne 2005–; memb various conservation ogrns; fell RSPB; *Recreations* birdwatching, travel, environmental conservation, languages, gardening, jogging; *Style—* Roy Osborne; ✉ c/o Foreign & Commonwealth Office (Berne), King Charles Street, London SW1A 2AH (tel 00 41 (0) 31 359 7721, fax 00 41 (0) 31 359 7701, e-mail roy.osborne@fco.gov.uk)

OSBORNE, Sandra; MP; *b* 23 February 1956; *Educ* Camphill Sr Secdy Sch, Univ of Strathclyde (MSc), Jordanhill Coll (Dip Community Educn); *Career* cncllr Kyle and Carrick DC 1990–95, cncllr S Ayrshire Cncl 1994–97, women's aid worker Kilmarnock (for 15 years) until 1997, convenor Housing and Social Work Community Services until 1997; MP (Lab) Ayr 1997–; PPS to: Rt Hon Brian Wilson, *qv*, until 2001, Rt Hon George Foulkes, MP, *qv*, 2001–02, Rt Hon Helen Liddell, MP, *qv*, 2002–03; *Style—* Ms Sandra Osborne, MP; ✉ Constituency Office, Damside, Ayr KA8 8ER (tel 01292 262906, fax 01292 885661)

OSEI, HE Isaac; s of Nana Osei Nkwantabisa (d 1991), and Eunice Rosina, *née* Inkumsah; *b* 29 March 1951; *Educ* Achimota Sch, Univ of Ghana Legon (BSc), Univ of Colorado, Williams Coll (MA); *m* Marian Fofo; 4 c (Nana Akwasi, Paapa Inkumsah, Nana Adoma, Nana Akua Afriyie); *Career* Ghanaian diplomat; asst econ planning offr Miny of Fin and Econ Planning 1973–77, chief Commercial Ops Dept Ghana Tourist Devpt Co Ltd 1978–82, fndr and managing conslt Ghanexim Economic Consits Ltd 1982–99, dir EK Osei & Co Ltd 1984–1994, dir Kas Products Ltd 1985–1992, md Intravenous Infusions Ltd 1999–2001; high cmmr to UK 2001–06, ceo Ghana Cocoa Brand 2006–; chair Bd of Govrs Cwlth Secretariat 2002–04; sometime conslt: Govt of Ghana, USAID, World Bank, Japan Int Co-operation Agency, UNCTAD, DFID; nat pres Ghana UN Students Assoc (GUNSA) 1971–72; *Style—* HE Mr Isaac Osei; ✉ e-mail ikeosei@email.com)

OSERS, Dr Ewald; s of Paul Osers (d 1923), of Prague, and Fini, *née* Anders (d 1942); *b* 13 May 1917; *Educ* schs in Prague, Prague Univ, Univ of London (BA); *m* 3 June 1942, Mary, da of Arthur Harman (d 1959); 1 da (Ann Margaret b 1947), 1 s (Richard b 1951); *Career* translator/writer; BBC 1939–77, chm Translators' Assoc 1971, 1980–81 and 1983–84, chm Translators' Guild 1975–79; vice-pres Int Fedn of Translators 1977–81 and 1984–87; Schlegel-Tieck Prize 1971, CB Nathhorst Prize 1977, Josef Dobrovsky Medal 1980, Gold Pin of Honour of the German Translators' Assoc, Silver Pegasus of the Bulgarian Writers' Union 1983, Dilia Medal Czechoslovakia 1986, European Poetry Translation Prize 1987, Vitezslav Nezval Medal of the Czech Literary Fndn 1987, P-F Caillé Medal 1987, Golden Pen of the Macedonian Translators' Union 1988, Austrian Translation Prize 1989, Medal of Merit of the Czech Republic 1997, Franz Kafka Medal 1998, John Sykes Award for Excellence 2001, Jan Masaryk Gratias Agit Award 2001, Premia Bohemica Prize Czech Writers' Community 2001; Hon PhD Olomouc Univ 1990; FRSL 1984, FITI; Officer's Cross of the Order of Merit of the Federal Republic of Germany 1991; *Books* Wish You Were Here (poems, 1976), Arrive Where We Started (poems, 1995), Golden City (poems, 2004), Snows of Yesteryear (memoirs, 2007); translator of over 150 books, 45 of them poetry; *Recreations* music, skiing; *Style—* Dr Ewald Osers, FRSL; ✉ 33 Reades Lane, Sonning Common, Reading RG4 9LL (tel 0118 972 3196, fax 0118 972 4950, e-mail osers@aol.com)

OSGERBY, Jay; s of Paul Osgerby, of Oxon, and Wendy, *née* Hickman; *b* 23 October 1969, Oxford; *Educ* Ravensbourne Coll London (BA), RCA (MA); *m* 27 May 2000, Helen Louise; 1 da (Eva Jasmine b 28 Oct 2002), 1 da (Sophia Elizabeth b 1 Oct 2005); *Career* designer; fndr (with Edward Barber, *qv*) BarberOsgerby 1996–, founding dir and co-owner (with Edward Barber) Universal Design Studio Ltd 2001–; clients incl: Magis, Flos, Bute, Authentics, Venini, Isokon, Coca Cola, Levi's, Swarovski, Stella McCartney, Cappellini; commissioned to design furniture for De La Warr Pavilion Bexhill on Sea, RIBA, Portsmouth Cathedral; exhibited at: Sotheby's London, MOMA NY, Int Furniture Fair NY, Haute Definition Paris, Musée de la Mode et du Textil Paris, Design Museum London, Crafts Cncl London, Design Miami/Basel; work in permanent collections V&A London and Met Museum of Art NY; visiting tutor: Ravenbourne Coll London, Oxford Brookes Univ; MCSD 2003, FRSA 2005; *Awards* incl: Best New Designer ICFF NY 1998, shortlisted for Compasso d'Oro 2004, Jerwood Prize for Applied Arts 2004, winner Furniture Designer of the Year Blueprint Mgazine 2005, Best Furniture Design Award Design Week 2003 and 2004, Best Product Red Dot Awards 2006, Designer of the Future (with Established & Sons) Basel 2006; RDI 2007; *Style—* Jay Osgerby, Esq; ✉ 35 Charlotte Road, London EC2A 3PG (tel 020 7033 3884, fax 020 7033 3882)

O'SHEA, Chris; s of Frank Christopher Patrick O'Shea (d 1997), and Lucy Alice O'Shea (d 1990); *b* 5 December 1947; *Educ* The Hewett Sch Norwich; *m* 15 Nov 1969, Suzanne, da of Peter Edwards; 1 da (Alice b 10 March 1975), 2 s (Peter b 7 Dec 1978, Timothy b 23 May 1980); *Career* various advtg agencies 1963–75, writer Abbott Mead Vickers 1975–84, copy chief then exec creative dir Lowe Howard-Spink 1984–89, exec creative dir Chiat Day 1989–91, fndr ptnr and creative dir Banks Hoggins O'Shea 1991–98, jt exec creative dir and dep chm Banks Hoggins O'Shea/FCB (following merger) 1998–2004, estab HOW 2004 (merged with MCBD 2006); award-winning work for various clients incl Waitrose, Heineken, Cow & Gate and Australian Tourist Cmmn; pres Creative Circle 1998–2000, chm IPA Directors Forum 1999–2002, memb Exec Ctee D&AD 1999–2001; pres and non-exec dir Radio Advertising Bureau Ariels Fndn 2003–; *Awards* 1 Gold (D&AD), 2 Gold, 2 Silver and 2 Bronze (Cannes), 6 Silver (Campaign Press), 2 Gold, 1 Silver and 3 Bronze (BTA), 2 Silver (Campaign Poster Awards), 1 Gold (Br Cinema Awards), 7 Gold (Clio), 2 Gold, 1 Silver and 2 Bronze (Creative Circle), 2 Gold (Int Broadcasting Awards), 5 Gold (Int Festival NY), 2 Gold (Eurobest Awards), 2 Gold (Irish TV Festival), 1 Silver (One Show Awards); *Recreations* family and sleeping; *Style—* Chris O'Shea; ✉ tel 01277 372766, e-mail thefamilyoshea@btinternet.com

O'SHEA, Prof Michael Roland; s of Capt Jack Arthur O'Shea, and Ellen, *née* Hughes; *b* 5 April 1947; *Educ* Forest Hill Sch London, Univ of Leicester (BSc), Univ of Southampton (PhD); *m* 1977 (m dis 1991), Barbara, *née* Moore; 1 da (Linda b 1978 d 1990); *Career* Univ of Calif Berkeley: NATO fell 1971–73, NIH fell 1973–75; SRC fell Univ of Cambridge 1975–77, asst prof Univ of Southern Calif Los Angeles 1977–79, assoc prof Brain Research Inst Univ of Chicago 1979–85, prof of neurobiology Univ of Geneva 1985–88, prof of molecular cell biology Univ of London 1988–91; Univ of Sussex: dir Interdisciplinary Research Centre Sussex Centre for Neuroscience 1991–, dir Centre for Computational Neuroscience and Robotics 1996–; author of numerous papers on neuroscience in learned jls; memb: NSPCC, Soc for Neuroscience; *Recreations* classical music, mountaineering, modern poetry, the public understanding of science, triathlons, restoration of classic Lotus, gardens; *Clubs* Club Lotus; *Style—* Prof Michael O'Shea; ✉ 29 Eldred Avenue, Brighton, East Sussex BN1 5EB; School of Life Sciences, University of Sussex, Falmer, Brighton BN1 9QG

O'SHEA, Prof Timothy; *b* 1949, Hamburg, Germany; *Educ* Univ of Sussex, Univ of Leeds; *Career* fndr Computer Assisted Learning Research Gp Open Univ, research fell Dept of Artificial Intelligence Univ of Edinburgh 1974–78, master Birkbeck Coll London 1998–2001, pro-vice-chllr Univ of London 2001–02, princ Univ of Edinburgh 2002–; convener Research and Commercialisation Ctee Universities Scotland, memb Governing Body Roslin Inst; memb Bd: Intermediary Technology Institute Scotland Ltd, British Cncl; FRSE 2004; *Style—* Prof Timothy O'Shea; ✉ The Principal's Office, The University of Edinburgh, Old College, South Bridge, Edinburgh EH8 9YL

OSLER, Douglas Alexander; CB (2002); *b* 11 October 1942; *Educ* Royal HS Edinburgh, Univ of Edinburgh (MA), Moray House Coll of Educn; *m* 11 July 1973, Wendy Isobel, *née* Cochrane; 1 s (Martin b 29 June 1974), 1 da (Helen b 8 Aug 1977); *Career* teacher Liberton HS Edinburgh, princ teacher of history Dunfermline HS until 1974; HM Inspectorate of Schools: joined 1974, Western Div Glasgow (seconded to Scot Econ Planning Dept), dist inspr Highlands Western Isles and Orkney Northern Div 1984–87, chief inspr 1987–92, dep sr chief inspr 1992–96, HM sr chief inspr of Educn for Scotland 1996–2002; visiting prof Univ of Strathclyde 2003–05; Interim Scottish Prisons Complaints cmmr 2003; pres Standing Int Conferences of Central and General Inspectorates 1999–2001, chm Statutory Inquiry NI 2004–05, ind reviewer Scottish Courts Serv 2005; chm of cmmrs South Eastern Educn and Library Bd NI 2006–; memb: Br Cncl Scotland 1992–2000, ESU (fell to USA 1966); Intern Visitor Program Fellowship to USA 1989; KSG 2000; *Recreations* travel, golf; *Clubs* Rotary Int, Luffness Golf, ESU; *Style—* Mr Douglas Osler, CB, KSG; ✉ e-mail douglas@osler71.freeserve.co.uk

OSMAN, David Antony; s of Colin Alfred Earnest Osman, of Cockfosters, Herts, and Grace Florence, *née* White; *b* 13 April 1953; *Educ* Minchenden GS, Univ of Nottingham (BA); *m* 4 Sept 1976, Helen, da of Randall Jones-Pugh, of Roch, Dyfed; 2 da (Caroline b 5 Nov 1984, Nicola b 23 Jan 1988); *Career* dir RP Publishing Co Ltd 1975–78 (non-exec dir 1978–95), non-exec dir RP Typesetters Co Ltd 1980–96; UK economist Joseph/Carr Sebag & Co 1978–82, UK and int economist Laing & Cruickshank 1982–84, int economist James Capel & Co 1984–91; stockbroker: Sassoon (Europe) Ltd 1991–92, Smith New Court Far East/Merrill Lynch 1992–99; dir Cojent Ltd 1999–, economist and stockbroker SCS (UK) Ltd 1999–2005, economist and stockbroker UOB Kay Hian (UK) Ltd 2005–; fndr memb Enfield SDP 1981–87, SDP/Lib Alliance Pty candidate for Upminster 1983, vice-chm City SDP 1984–88 (fndr memb and sec), fndr and memb Enfield Lib Democrats 1988–; memb Soc of Business Economists, MSI; *Recreations* chess, cycling, golf, snooker; *Clubs* Old Minchendenians Golf Soc; *Style—* David Osman, Esq; ✉ 10 Old Park Ridings, Winchmore Hill, London N21 2EU (tel 020 8360 4343); UOB Kay Him (UK) Limited, 14 Austin Friars, London EC2N 2HE (tel 020 7972 0880, fax 020 7972 0882)

OSMAN, Mat; *Career* bassist; fndr memb Suede 1989–; singles: The Drowners 1992, Metal Mickey 1992, Animal Nitrate 1993, So Young 1993, Stay Together 1994, We are the Pigs 1994, The Wild Ones 1994, New Generation 1995, Trash 1996, Beautiful Ones 1996, Saturday Night 1997, Lazy 1997, Film Star 1997, Electricity 1999, She's in Fashion 1999, Everything Will Flow 1999, Can't Get Enough 1999, Positivity 2002; albums: Suede 1993 (UK no 1), Dog Man Star 1994, Coming Up 1996 (UK no 1), Sci-Fi Lullabies 1997 (compilation), Head Music 1999 (UK no 1), A New Morning 2002; Mercury Music Award 1993; *Style—* Mat Osman, Esq; ✉ c/o Charlie Charlton, Interceptor Enterprises, First Floor, 98 White Lion Street, London N1 9PF (tel 020 7278 8001, e-mail info@interceptor.co.uk)

OSTLER, Catherine Emma; da of John Ramsdell Ostler (d 1998), and Patricia Ann, *née* Leonard; *Educ* Cheltenham Ladies Coll (scholar), St Hilda's Coll Oxford (scholar, MA); *m* 13 Sept 2003, Albert Nathaniel Read, s of Piers Paul Read, FRSL, *qv*; 2 da (Clementine Margaret b 14 March 2003, Angelica Albertine b 6 March 2007), 1 s (Nathaniel John

Basil b 10 Dec 2004); *Career* features ed Tatler 1994, features writer Mail on Sunday 1994–96; ed: The Express Saturday Magazine 1996–99, The Times Weekend 1999–2000, peoplenews.com 2000–01, ES Magazine 2002–; *Style*— Ms Catherine Ostler; ✉ ES Magazine, Northcliffe House, 2 Derry Street, London W8 5EE (tel 020 7938 6727)

OSTRIKER, Prof Jeremiah P; *b* 13 April 1937, New York; *Educ* Harvard Univ (AB), Univ of Chicago (PhD); *Career* postdoctoral fell Univ of Cambridge 1964–65; Princeton Univ: research assoc and lectr 1965–66, asst prof 1966–68, assoc prof 1968–71, prof 1971–, chm Dept of Astrophysical Sciences and dir Princeton Univ Observatory 1979–95, Charles A Young prof of astronomy 1982–2002, provost 1995–2001; Plumian prof of astronomy and experimental philosophy Inst of Astronomy Univ of Cambridge 2001–; visiting prof Harvard Univ 1984–85, Regents fell Smithsonian Inst 1984–85, visiting Miller prof Univ of Calif Berkeley 1990; tstee and memb Editorial Bd Princeton Univ Press 1982–84 and 1986, tstee American Museum of Nat History 1997–; American Astronomical Soc: memb 1963–, memb Cncl 1978–80, chm Ctee on Astronomy and Public Policy 1988–89; IAU: memb 1966–, US rep 1978–81, pres Cmmn 48 High Energy 1991–94 (vice-pres 1988–91); Nat Acad of Sciences: memb Exec Ctee of Decennial Surveys 1969–73, 1978–83 and 1988–91, memb 1974–, astronomy rep Class Membership Ctee 1977, 1978, 1987, 1988 and 1993, memb Assembly of Mathematical and Physical Sciences 1977–80, memb Cmmn on Physical Sciences, Mathematics and Resources 1987–91, memb Ctee on Astronomy and Astrophysics 1992–95, memb Cncl 1992–95, memb Bd of Govrs 1993–95, memb Audit Ctee 1994–95; memb American Philosophical Soc 1994–, assoc memb RAS 1994–, foreign memb Royal Netherlands Acad of Arts and Sciences 1999–; Helen B Warner Prize American Astronomical Soc 1972, Henry Norris Russell Prize American Astronomical Soc 1980, Vainu Bappu Meml Award Indian Nat Sci Acad 1993, Karl Schwarzschild Medal Astronomische Gesellschaft 1999, US Nat Medal of Sci 2000, Golden Plate Award American Acad of Achievement 2001, Gold Medal Royal Astronomical Soc 2004; Nat Sci Fndn Fellowship 1960–65, Alfred P Sloan Fellowship 1970–72, Sherman Fairchild Fellowship Californian Instn of Technology 1977, Regents Fellowship Smithsonian Inst 1985; Hon DSc Univ of Chicago 1992; fell AAAS 1992 (memb 1975); *Style*— Prof Jeremiah Ostriker; ✉ Clare College, Cambridge CB2 1TL; Institute of Astronomy, Madingley Road, Cambridge CB3 0HA

O'SULLEVAN, Sir Peter John; kt (1997), CBE (1991, OBE 1977); s of late Col John Joseph O'Sullevan, DSO; *b* 3 March 1918; *Educ* Hawtreys, Charterhouse, Coll Alpin Switzerland; *m* 1951, Patricia, da of late Frank Duckworth of Manitoba, Canada; *Career* racing commentator BBC TV 1946–97 (incl Aust, SA, Italy, USA), racing corr Daily Express 1950–86; patron: Int League for the Protection of Horses, Brooke Hosp for Animals, Thoroughbred Rehabilitation Centre, Compassion in World Farming; *Books* Calling The Horses (autobiography, 1989, on audio cassette 1996); *Recreations* racehorses, travel, reading, art, food and wine; *Style*— Sir Peter O'Sullevan, CBE; ✉ 37 Cranmer Court, Sloane Avenue, London SW3 3HW (tel 020 7584 2781)

O'SULLIVAN, Bernard Gerard; s of Dr Jeremiah O'Sullivan (d 2000), and Margret Winifred, *née* O'Leary; *b* 3 December 1958; *Educ* St Gregory's GS Manchester, Blackpool Coll of FE; *m* 31 March 2001, Clare Gillian, da of Clarence William Street; *Career* photographer; Manchester Royal Eye Hosp 1982–83, Macclesfield Silk Heritage 1984–85, Mac of Manchester 1986–89, Photographic Images 1989–91, prop Inside-Out Photography 1991–; BIPP Nat Commercial Photographer of the Year 1997, BIPP NW Regn Architectural Award 1989, 1992, 1998, 1999, 2001 and 2004, BIPP NW Regn Photographer of the Year 2003; Cdre Fairfield Golf and Sailing Club 1994 and 1995; ABIPP 1991; *Recreations* walking, reading, cooking; *Style*— Bernard O'Sullivan, Esq; ✉ 14 Sibson Road, Chorlton-cum-Hardy, Manchester M21 9RH (tel 0161 860 5769, mobile 07831 344722); Inside-Out Photography, Unit 11 Wharf Parade, Lower Wharf Street, Ashton-under-Lyne OL6 7PE (tel 0161 339 3385, fax 0161 339 3386, e-mail info@insideoutphoto.co.uk)

O'SULLIVAN, Eddie; *b* 21 November 1958, Youghal, Co Cork; *Educ* Christian Bros Sch Youghal, Thomond Coll Limerick; *Career* rugby union coach; former rugby player Youghal, Garryowen, Munster and Ireland A, early coaching positions Monivea, Ballinasloe and Blackrock Coll, teacher Holy Rosary Coll Mountbellow 1981–88, rugby devpt offr Ireland Rugby Football Union (IRFU) 1988, asst coach then coach Connacht 1988–95, coach Ireland nat under 21 team 1995–97, asst coach US Eagles (nat team), nat tech dir USA Rugby and coach Buccaneers RFC 1997–99, coach Ireland nat team 2001– (asst coach 1999–2001, winners Triple Crown 2004), coach British and Irish Lions tour to NZ 2005; *Style*— Mr Eddie O'Sullivan; ✉ Irish Rugby Football Union, 62 Lansdowne Road, Dublin 4, Ireland

O'SULLIVAN, John Conor; s of James Vincent O'Sullivan (d 1976), of Harley St, London, and Maura O'Connor; *b* 25 September 1932; *Educ* Ampleforth, Oriel Coll Oxford (MA), Westminster Hosp Med Sch (BM BCh); *m* 26 April 1958, Maureen, da of Douglas Charles Mitchell (d 1977), of Wembley; 3 da (Marika b 1959, Claire b 1960, Catherine b 1962), 1 s (Hugh b 1966); *Career* Nat Serv RAMC 1960–62, dep asst dir Med Serv HQ London dist, T/Maj 1961; conslt obstetrician and gynaecologist Central Middx Hosp 1974–86, conslt in gynaecological oncology Hammersmith Hosp 1976–84, conslt gynaecologist Cromwell Hosp 1982–2003 (emeritus conslt 2003–), sr lectr Royal Postgrad Sch Inst of Obstetrics and Gynaecology 1984–92; Freeman City of London 1955, Liveryman Worshipful Soc of Apothecaries; FRCS 1967, FRCOG 1983; *Recreations* golf, skiing; *Clubs* Royal Wimbledon Golf (Capt 1999); *Style*— John O'Sullivan, Esq; ✉ 96 Arthur Road, Wimbledon, London SW19 7DT (tel 020 8946 6242); 8 Pennant Mews, London W8 5JN (tel 020 7580 6966/ 020 7460 5780, fax 020 7580 6966)

O'SULLIVAN, Michael Joseph; s of Patrick Joseph O'Sullivan, and Mary Elizabeth, *née* Herbert; *b* 21 December 1958; *Educ* St Philip's Coll Birmingham, BNC Oxford (BA), Wolfson Coll Cambridge (MPhil); *m* 17 July 1989, Moira, da of late James McDonald Boyd Grant; 2 da (Kira b 2 Oct 1990, Lara b 1 May 1992), 1 s (James b 23 June 1994); *Career* VSO English teacher Xiangtan China 1982–84; Br Cncl: asst dir Beijing 1987–90, UK corp planner 1991–93, dir S China 1993–95, head of corporate planning 1995–97, policy dir Asia Pacific 1997–2000, dir China 2000–; *Style*— Michael O'Sullivan, Esq

O'SULLIVAN, Patrick H P; *b* 15 April 1949; *Educ* TCD, LSE; *m*; 3 c; *Career* audit sr and articled clerk Arthur Andersen & Co Dublin 1971–74; Bank of America NT & SA: vice-pres/section mangr Bank of America London 1975–82, vice-pres/mangr Bank America Int Miami 1982–83, chief fin offr US Wholesale Banking LA 1983–85, pres Bank America World Trade Corp San Francisco 1985, vice-pres Sales and Mktg Germany 1987; gen mangr BA Futures Inc 1987–88, exec dir and fin controller Goldman Sachs 1988–89 (chm New Products Ctee), int md Financial Guaranty Insurance Co 1990–93; Barclays/BZW: head Int Banking & Structured Fin 1994–96, chief operating offr BZW 1996–97; chief exec Eagle Star Insurance Co Ltd 1997–2002, gp fin dir Zurich Financial Services 2002–; memb IASB Working Gp on FRS Accounting, memb Pilgrims Soc; FCA 1985; *Style*— Patrick O'Sullivan, Esq

O'SULLIVAN, Ronnie; *b* 5 December 1975, Chigwell, Essex; *Career* professional snooker player 1992–; ranked 1 in world 2002–; scorer fastest professional 147 maximum break (5 minutes 20 seconds) 1997; tournament winner: UK Championship 1993, 1997 and 2001, British Open 1994, B&H Masters 1995 and 2005, Asian Classic 1996, German Open 1996, Regal Masters 1998, 2000 and 2002, Liverpool Victoria Charity Challenge 1998, Regal Scottish Open 1998, 2000 and 2002, China Open 1999 and 2000, TSN Champions Cup 2000, Embassy World Championship 2001 and 2004, Citywest Irish Masters 2001, 2003 and 2005, Matchroom Premier League 2001, 2002, 2004, 2005 and 2006, Welsh Open 2004 and 2005, Totesport Grand Prix 2004, Saga Insurance Masters 2007; *Recreations* watching Arsenal FC; *Style*— Ronnie O'Sullivan, Esq (The Rocket)

O'SULLIVAN, Sally Angela; da of Albert James Lorraine (d 1995), of Jersey, Channel Islands, and Joan, *née* Crawley (d 1969); *b* 26 July 1949; *Educ* Ancaster House Sch Bexhill-on-Sea, Trinity Coll Dublin; *m* 2 Oct 1980, Charles Martin Wilson; 1 s (Luke b 18 Dec 1981), 1 da (Lily b 21 Aug 1985), 1 step da (Emma b 18 July 1970); *Career* freelance writer 1971–77, dep ed Women's World 1977–78, freelance writer NY 1978–80; women's ed: Daily Record 1980–81, Sunday Standard 1981–82; ed Options 1982–88, launch ed and originator Country Homes & Interiors 1986; ed: She 1989, Harpers & Queen 1989–91; ed-in-chief: Good Housekeeping 1991–95, Ideal Home, Woman & Home, Homes & Gardens, Country Homes & Interiors and Homes & Ideas 1995–98; launch ed: Living Etc, 25 Beautiful Homes; chief exec Cabal Communications 1998–2003, editorial dir Highbury House 2003–; Magazine Ed of the Year 1986 and 1994; memb: Broadcasting Standards Cmmn 1994–, Foresight Retail and Consumer Services Panel 1999–2001; non-exec dir: London Transport 1995–2000, Anglia Water 1996–2000; *Books* Things My Mother Never Told Me, Looking Good; *Recreations* family, riding, farming; *Style*— Sally O'Sullivan; ✉ Highbury House, Jordan House, Brunswick Place, London N1 6EB

OSWALD, Admiral of the Fleet Sir (John) Julian Robertson; GCB (1989, KCB 1987); s of Capt George Hamilton Oswald, RN (d 1971), of Newmore, Invergordon, and Margaret Elliot, *née* Robertson (d 1949); *b* 11 August 1933; *Educ* Beaudesert Park Sch, BRNC Dartmouth, RCDS; *m* 25 Jan 1958, Veronica Therese Dorette, da of Eric James Thompson, OBE (d 1975); 2 s (Timothy b 1958, Christopher b 1960), 3 da (Elisabeth b 1963, Victoria b 1967, Samantha b 1970); *Career* Cadet RN 1947–51, Midshipman 1952–53 (HM Ships Vanguard and Verulam), Sub Lt 1953–55 (HMS Theseus), Lt 1955–63 (HM Ships Newfoundland, Jewel, Excellent (gunnery specialist course), Victorious and Yarnton), Lt Cdr 1963–68 (HM Ships Excellent, Naiad, MOD (Naval Plans)), Cdr 1969–73 (HMS Bacchante, MOD (Def Policy Staff)), Capt 1974–82 MOD (Asst Dir Def Policy), RCDS, HMS Newcastle, RN Presentation Team BRNC Dartmouth, Rear Adm 1982–86, ACDS (Programmes), ACDS (Policy and Nuclear), Vice Adm 1986–87 (Flag Offr Third Flotilla and Cdr ASW Striking Force), Adm (C-in-C Fleet, Allied C-in-C Channel, C-in-C Eastern Atlantic 1987–89), First Sea Lord and Chief of Naval Staff 1989–93; First and Princ ADC to HM The Queen 1989–93; dir: SEMA Group plc 1993–2001 (non-exec chm 1999–2001), James Fisher & Sons plc 1993–2002, Marine and General Mutual Life Assurance Co 1994–2006; chm AeroSystems Int 1995–2005; pres: Frinton Soc 1990–99, Destroyer Club 1992–99, Assoc of RN Officers 1993–2003, Sea Cadet Assoc 1994–2003, Officers' Assoc 1996–2003; vice-pres: RUSI 1993–2004 (actg chm 2002–04), Forces Pension Soc 1995–; vice-pres Maritime Tst, chm Green Issues 1990–, Nat Historic Ships Ctee 1994–2004, Ends of the Earth Club 1997–2004; tstee: Nat Maritime Museum 1994–2004, Cutty Sark Tst 2001–; govr Univ of Portsmouth 1994–2000; memb: Cncl White Ensign Assoc 1993–2003, Advsy Cncl Assoc of MBAs 1997–2001; Liveryman Worshipful Co of Shipwrights (Asst Emeritus); Hon MBA 1992, Hon DL 2000; MInstD, FRSA; *Recreations* fishing, family, stamps; *Clubs* Mensa, Army and Navy; *Style*— Admiral of the Fleet Sir Julian Oswald, GCB; ✉ c/o Naval Secretary, Victory Building, HM Naval Base, Portsmouth, Hampshire PO1 3LS (tel 023 9272 7401)

OSWALD, Sir (William Richard) Michael; KCVO (1998, CVO 1988, LVO 1979); s of Lt-Col William Alexander Hugh Oswald, ERD (d 1974), of Weybridge, Surrey, and Rose-Marie, *née* Leahy (d 1985); *b* 21 April 1934; *Educ* Eton, King's Coll Cambridge (MA); *m* 21 April 1958, The Lady Angela Mary Rose, CVO, da of 6 Marquess of Exeter, KCMG (d 1981); 1 da (Katharine Davina Mary (Mrs Alexander Matheson) b 1959), 1 s (William Alexander Michael b 1962); *Career* 2 Lt 1 Bn King's Own Royal Regt 1953, BAOR and Korea, Lt 8 Bn Royal Fusiliers (TA) 1955, Capt 1958–61; mangr Lordship and Egerton Studs Newmarket 1962–69, dir The Royal Studs 1997–98 (mangr 1970–97), racing mangr for HM Queen Elizabeth The Queen Mother 1970–2002, Nat Hunt racing advsr to HM The Queen 2002–; pres The Thoroughbred Breeders Assoc 1997–2001 (memb Cncl 1964–2001); chm Bloodstock Industry Ctee Animal Health Tst 1986–2002; tstee Br Veterinary Assoc Tst 1998–2004; Liveryman Worshipful Co of Shipwrights; Hon DSc De Montfort Univ 1997; Hon Air Cdre 2620 Co of Norfolk Sqdn RAuxAF 2001–; *Recreations* painting, military history; *Clubs* Army and Navy, Jockey; *Style*— Sir Michael Oswald, KCVO; ✉ 6 St Olave's Court, St Petersburgh Place, London W2 4JY (tel 020 7229 0773); The Old Rectory, Weasenham St Peter, King's Lynn, Norfolk PE32 2TB (tel 01328 838311)

OTAKA, Tadaaki; Hon CBE (1997); s of Hisatada Otaka, conductor and composer, and Misaoko Otaka; *b* 8 November 1947; *Educ* Toho Gakuen Sch of Music (second prize Min-On Conducting Competition), Vienna Hochschule (Austrian State scholar); *m* 1978, Yukiko; *Career* conductor; began playing violin aged 5, studied conducting under Prof Hideo Saito and Prof Hans Swarowsky, student at NHK (Japanese Broadcasting Corp) Symphony Orch 1968–70; professional broadcasting debut 1971 with NHK Symphony Orch (asst conductor various int tours 1969–73), NY debut 1985 with American Symphony Orch; perm conductor Tokyo Philharmonic Orch 1971–91 (conductor laureate 1991–), conductor NHK New Year Opera Concert annually 1980–, chief conductor Sapporo Symphony Orch 1981–, princ conductor BBC Nat Orch of Wales 1987–95 (conductor laureate 1996–), chief conductor Yomiuri Nippon Symphony Orch 1992–, music advsr and princ conductor Kioi Sinfonietta Japan 1995–, dir Britten-Pears Orch 1998–2001; made various int tours incl: Vienna, Czechoslovakia, Germany, Russia, Indonesia, Australia, N America, Far East (BBC NOW); worked with other orchs incl: London Philharmonic, City of Birmingham Symphony, Royal Liverpool Philharmonic, Hallé, London Symphony, BBC Symphony, Brno State Philharmonic, Vancouver Symphony, Oregon Symphony, Helsinki Philharmonic, Turku Philharmonic, Orchestre National de Lille, Dresden Philharmonic, Polish Nat Radio Symphony, Hong Kong Philharmonic, Melbourne Symphony, Sydney Symphony, Rotterdam Philharmonic, Oslo Philharmonic, Bamberg Symphony, Strasbourg Philharmonic; opera: Salome (Welsh Nat Opera) 1991; various recordings with BBC Welsh Symphony Orch, Britten's Peter Grimes with Yomiuri Nippon Symphony Orch; Suntory Music Award 1992, Hon Doctorate Univ of Wales 1993; *Recreations* fishing, tennis, cooking; *Style*— Mr Tadaaki Otaka, CBE; ✉ c/o Askonas Holt, Lonsdale Chambers, 27 Chancery Lane, London WC2A 1PF (tel 020 7400 1700, fax 020 7400 1799, e-mail info@askonasholt.co.uk)

O'TOOLE, Senator Joseph John; s of Michael O'Toole (d 2001), and Teresa, *née* Moriarty; *b* 20 July 1947; *Educ* Christian Bros Sch Dingle, St Patrick's Coll of Educn Dublin, NUI Maynooth; *m* 27 June 1971, Joan, *née* Lynam; 3 da (Sorcha b 1972, Aoife b 1976, Áine b 1982), 2 s (Duncan 1973, Ruadhán b 1977); *Career* teacher 1967–77, sch princ 1977–87; memb (senator) Seanad Éireann (Ind) NUI 1987–; gen sec Irish Nat Teachers Orgn 1990–2001, pres Irish Congress of Trade Unions 2001–03; vice-chair Personal Injuries Assessment Bd; memb: Irish Audit and Accounting Supervisory Authy, Leinster House Cmmn, Parly Jt Ctee on Finance and Public Serv, Bd Co-Operation Ireland; *Books* Looking Under Stones (autobiography, 2002); *Recreations* boating, reading, walking; *Style*— Senator Joseph O'Toole; ✉ Thornton, Kilsallaghan, Co Dublin, Ireland (tel 00 353 1 8351 338, website www.joeotoole.net); Seanad Eireann, Leinster House, Kildare Street, Dublin 2, Ireland (tel 00 353 1 6183 786, fax 00 353 1 6184 625, e-mail jotoole@oireachtas.ie)

O'TOOLE, Peter; s of Patrick Joseph O'Toole; *b* 2 August 1932, 1932; *Educ* RADA; *m* 1959 (m dis 1979) Sian Phillips, *qv*; 2 da; *Career* actor; with Bristol Old Vic Co 1955–58, assoc dir Old Vic Co 1980; Hon Oscar for Lifetime Achievement 2003; *Theatre* incl: Major

Barbara (Old Vic) 1956, Oh My Papa! (Garrick) 1957, The Long and the Short and the Tall (Royal Court and New) 1959, season with Shakespeare Memorial Theatre Company (Stratford-on-Avon) 1960, Baal (Phoenix) 1963, Hamlet (NT) 1963, Ride a Cock Horse (Piccadilly) 1965, Juno and the Paycock, Man and Superman, Pictures in the Hallway (Gaiety, Dublin) 1966, Waiting for Godot, Happy Days (Abbey, Dublin) 1969, Uncle Vanya, Plunder, The Apple Cart, Judgement (Bristol Old Vic) 1973, Uncle Vanya, Present Laughter (Chicago) 1978, Macbeth (Old Vic) 1980, Man and Superman (Haymarket) 1982, Pygmalion (Shaftesbury) 1984, Yvonne Arnaud (Guildford and NY) 1987, The Apple Cart (Haymarket) 1986, Jeffrey Bernard is Unwell (Apollo) 1989, Our Song (Apollo (Variety Club Best Stage Actor Award)) 1992; Television incl: Rogue Male 1976, Strumpet City 1979, Masada 1981, Svengali 1982, Pygmalion 1983, Kim 1983, Banshee 1986, The Dark Angel 1989, Coming Home 1998, Joan of Arc 1999, Hitler: The Rise of Evil 2003, Imperium: Augustus 2003, Casanova 2005; Films incl: Kidnapped 1959, The Day They Robbed the Bank of England 1959, The Savage Innocents 1960, Lawrence of Arabia 1962 (nomination Best Actor Oscars), Becket 1963, Lord Jim 1964, What's New Pussycat 1965, How to Steal a Million 1966, The Bible...in the Beginning 1966, The Night of the Generals 1967, Great Catherine 1968, The Lion in Winter 1968, Goodbye Mr Chips 1969, Brotherly Love 1970, Murphy's War 1971, Under Milk Wood 1971, The Ruling Class 1972, Man of La Mancha 1972, Rosebud 1975, Man Friday 1975, Foxtrot 1975, The Stunt Man 1977, Coup d'Etat 1977, Zulu Dawn 1978, Power Play 1978, The Antagonists 1981, My Favorite Year 1981, Supergirl 1983, Club Paradise 1986, The Last Emperor 1987, High Spirits 1988, Creator 1990, The Manor 1999, Molokai: The Story of Father Damien 1999, Jeffrey Bernard Is Unwell 1999, Global Heresy 2002, The Final Curtain 2002, Bright Young Things 2003, Troy 2004, Lassie 2005, Romeo and Me 2006, Venus 2006 (nomination Best Actor Award Oscars 2007), One Night with the King 2006; Books Loitering With Intent (autobiography, 1992), Loitering With Intent: The Apprentice (vol 2 of autobiography, 1996); Clubs Garrick; Style— Peter O'Toole Esq

OTTAWAY, Richard Geoffrey James; MP; s of Prof Christopher Wyndham Ottaway (d 1977), and Grace Ottaway; b 24 May 1945; Educ Backwell Sch, Univ of Bristol (LLB); m 1982, Nicola Evelyn, da of John Kisch, CMG; Career Lt RN, Lt Cdr RNR; admitted slr 1977, ptnr Wm A Crump Slrs 1981–87; MP (Cons): Nottingham N 1983–87, Croydon S 1992–; PPS to Baroness Young and Tim Renton, MP as Mins of State at FCO 1985–87, PPS to Michael Heseltine, MP as Pres of the Bd of Trade and then as Dep PM 1992–95, asst Govt whip 1995–96, a Lord Cmmr HM Treasy (Govt whip) 1996–97, oppn whip and spokesman for London 1997–98, shadow local govt min and shadow min for London 1998, oppn defence spokesman 1999, shadow Paymaster Gen 2000, shadow secretary of state for the environment 2004–; chm: All Pty Gp on Population and Devpt 1992–95, All Pty Singapore Gp 1997–2000, All Pty Malaysia Gp 1999–; memb Intelligence and Secuirty Ctee 2005–; dir Coastal Europe 1988–95; Books Road to Reform, Thoughts for a Third Term (jtly, 1987), Less People, Less Pollution (1990); Recreations yacht racing, jazz, skiing; Clubs Royal Corinthian Yacht, Island Sailing; Style— Richard Ottaway, Esq, MP; ✉ House of Commons, London SW1A 0AA (tel 020 7219 3000)

OTTER, Robert George (Robin); s of Francis Lewis Otter, MC (d 1946), of Ottershaw, Surrey, and Helen, née Stephens (d 1988); b 25 February 1926; Educ Marlborough, UC Oxford (MA); m 16 Dec 1958, Elisabeth Ann, da of Eric Reginald St Aubrey Davies, MBE (d 1986); 2 s (Robert b 1960, David b 1966), 1 da (Lisette b 1968); Career RNVR 1944–47, cmmnd 1945, RNC Greenwich, served HMS Pretoria Castle Western Approaches and HMS Pincher 5 MSF FE 1945–46; dist offr/cmmr Kenya Colony Colonial Admin Serv 1951–62 (despatches 1957), slr and ptnr Moore, Brown & Dixon Tewkesbury 1963–96, conslt 1996–; govr: Abbey Sch Tewkesbury 1973–2000, Alderman Knight Sch Tewkesbury 1980–, Three Counties Agric Soc; fndr memb: Gloucester Cattle Soc (chm 1973–75, memb Cncl 1975–95), Rare Breeds Survival Tst (memb Cncl 1973–82 and 1994–97); Parly candidate (Lib) 1966, 1970 and 1974, Euro Parly candidate 1979 (vice-chm NEC 1976–80); memb: Law Soc, Glos & Wilts Law Soc, Glos Diocesan and Tewkesbury Deanery Synods 1969–95 (chm 1986–95), Cncl Friends of Tewkesbury Abbey 1966–, Exec Ctee Tewkesbury Civic Soc (chm 1996–98); tstee St Lazarus Charitable Tst 1995–2004 (chm 2002–04); fell Chemical Soc (FCS) 1946–53; Books Law - A Modern Introduction (contrib, ed Paul Denham, 1983, 1989, 1994 and 1999 edns); Tales of Gloucesters (contrib, 2001); Recreations judge and breeder of Gloucester cattle; Clubs Royal Cwlth Soc, RSA, Mombasa (Kenya), Oxford Union; Style— Robin Otter, Esq; ✉ Kemerton Grange, Tewkesbury, Gloucestershire GL20 7JE (tel 01386 725253, fax 01684 295147)

OTTLEY, Robert Jeremy Mark Linn; Career dir Greenwell Montagu Stockbrokers 1968–92, investment mgmnt dir HSBC Investment Management (formerly James Capel) 1992–2001; chm The Zero Preference Growth Tst; dir: Atlantis Asia Recovery Fund plc, JPMorgan Elect plc; Style— Robert Ottley; ✉ e-mail rlo@ottley.co.uk

OTTO-JONES, John Alcwyn; s of Col Thomas Otto-Jones, CBE, TD, DL (d 1953), of Bredwardine, Herefords, and Kathleen Mary, née Hale (d 1979); b 7 February 1930; Educ Christ Coll Brecon, Univ of Cardiff (BA), Wadham Coll Oxford (MA); m 1 Oct 1960, Bridget Mary, da of Ernest Jackson, of Mansfield, Notts; 1 s (Justin b 1963), 1 da (Candida b 1966); Career cmmnd RAEC 1950; admitted slr, ptnr then sr ptnr Gaskell Rhys & Otto-Jones 1962–96; Under Sheriff Glamorgan 1985–97; Recreations vintage cars, reading; Clubs Cardiff and County; Style— John Otto-Jones, Esq; ✉ The Court, St Nicholas, Vale of Glamorgan CF5 6SH

OTTON, The Rt Hon Sir Philip (Howard); kt (1983), PC (1995); s of late Henry Albert Otton, of Kenilworth, Warks, and Leah Otton (d 1995); b 28 May 1933; Educ Bablake Sch Coventry, Univ of Birmingham (LLB); m 1965, Helen Margaret, da of late P W Bates; 2 s (Charles, Christian), 1 da (Sophie (Mrs Euan Ambrose)); Career called to the Bar Gray's Inn 1955 (bencher 1983), dep chm Beds QS 1970–72, jr counsel to the Treasy (Personal Injuries) 1970–75, recorder of the Crown Court 1972–83, QC 1975, govr Nat Heart and Chest Hosps 1979–84, judge of the High Court of Justice (Queen's Bench Div) 1983–95; a Lord Justice of Appeal 1995–2001; surveillance cmmr 2001–; presiding judge: Midland & Oxford Circuit 1986–88, Official Referees' Court 1991–94; Justice of Appeal Gibraltar 2003–, judge Qatar Civil and Commercial Court 2007–; hon legal advsr Office of St James's 2001–; visitor Univ of Essex 2001–05; dir Equitable Life Assurance Soc 2001–04; chm: Royal Brompton & Nat Heart & Lung Hosps SHA 1991–98, Nat Heart & Lung Inst 1991–95, Royal Brompton & Harefield NHS Tst 1998–2001; pres: Soc of Construction Law 1995–2004, Bar Disability Panel 1996–98, Professional Negligence Bar Assoc 1997–2001, Personal Injury Bar Assoc 1998–2001, Holdsworth Club Univ of Birmingham 2000–01; tstee Migraine Tst 1992–99, Berith Fndn 1993–; govr Imperial Coll Sch of Med 1996–2001, govr FA Premier League 2004–; Hon LLD Nottingham Trent Univ 1997, Hon DU Univ of Essex 2006, Hon LLD Univ of Birmingham 2007; Award of Merit City of Coventry 2005; fell American Law Inst 2000–; FCIArb 1995, accredited mediator 2001–; Recreations theatre, opera, travel; Clubs Garrick, Pilgrims; Style— The Rt Hon Sir Philip Otton; ✉ 20 Essex Street, London WC2R 3AL (e-mail clerks@20essexst.com)

OTWAY, Mark McRae; s of Henry Arthur McRae Otway, of Surrey, and Ann, née Ingman; b 4 October 1948; Educ Dulwich Coll, Churchill Coll Cambridge (MA); m 10 July 1973, Amanda Mary, da of Roland Stafford; 2 s (Miles Daniel b 1983, Paul David b 1985); Career Andersen Consulting 1982–2002 (joined 1970, mangr 1975, ptnr 1982); currently: sales and transition advsr Inaltus Ltd, chm ALS Consulting Ltd; Recreations sailing, music, theatre; Clubs Royal Lymington Yacht; Style— Mark Otway, Esq

OUGHTON, Douglas Robert; b 1942; Educ Univ of Bristol (MSc); Career Oscar Faber: joined as engr 1967, responsible for major projects in UK, Asia, Egypt and Nigeria, later dir, currently conslt Faber Maunsell Ltd; CIBSE: pres 2002–03, memb Cncl 1995–98 and 2000–06, memb Bd 2005–06, memb Tech Pubns Ctee 1975–85, memb External Affrs Ctee 1986–89, memb Professional Practices Ctee 1992–94, chm Patrons Ctee 1999–2001, chm Educn Trg and Membership Ctee 2003–06; Engrg Cncl rep UNESCO Sci Ctee 2000–03; memb: Cncl Building Servs Research and Info Assoc 1975–87, Br Standards Mech Engrg Standards Ctee 1980–84, Building Design and Construction Ctee CIRIA 1984–90; chm Euro Intelligent Building Gp 1992–95; author of numerous papers for professional jls; CEng, FCIBSE, FREng 1995; Books Heating and Air Conditioning of Buildings; Style— Douglas Oughton, Esq, FREng; ✉ Faber Maunsell Ltd, Marlborough House, Upper Marlborough Road, St Albans, Hertfordshire AL1 3UT (tel 020 8784 5784, fax 020 8784 5700, e-mail doug.oughton@fabermaunsell.com)

OULTON, Claire; da of Prof Leslie Zisman, and Sally Zisman; Educ Lady Eleanor Holles Sch, Somerville Coll Oxford (MA), KCL (PGCE); m; 2 c; Career teacher Benenden Sch 1984–88, head of history Charterhouse 1988–94, headmistress St Catherine's Sch Bramley 1994–2000, headmistress Benenden Sch 2000–; Recreations reading, gardening, cooking, mainly family; Style— Mrs Claire Oulton; ✉ Benenden School, Benenden, Cranbrook, Kent TN17 4AA (tel 01580 240592, fax 01580 240280, e-mail cmo@benenden.kent.sch.uk)

OULTON, Therese; da of Robert Oulton, and Matilda, née Glover; b 20 April 1953; Educ St Martin's Sch of Art London, RCA London; Career artist; shortlisted Turner Prize; Solo Exhibitions incl: Peterborough City Museum and Art Gallery 1984, Fool's Gold: New Paintings (Gimpel Fils London) 1984, Recent Painting (MOMA Oxford) 1985, Marlborough Graphics London 1987, 1989, 1992, 1994 and 1998, Marlborough Fine Art London 1987, 1990, 1991, 1992, 1997, 2000 and 2003, New Paintings (Hirschl & Adler (Modern) NY) 1989, Marking Time (LA Louver Gallery) 1994, Recent Paintings (Marlborough Gallery NY) 1994, Illuminations (Oxford Gallery) 1999; Public Collections Arts Cncl of GB, British Cncl, British Museum, Fitzwilliam Museum Cambridge, Metropolitan Museum of Art NY, Museum of Fine Art Boston, National Gallery of Victoria Melbourne, Tate Britain, V&A, Yale Center for British Art; Style— Ms Therese Oulton

OUNSLEY, Margaret Mary; da of Laurence Kelly, and Maureen Reid; b 30 August 1958; Educ Cardinal Newman RC Comp Sch Luton, Luton VI Form Coll, Bulmershe Coll of HE (BEd); m 1980, Robert Ounsley; 2 s (Thomas b 8 Oct 1985, James 2 Oct 1987); Career teacher 1980–85, co-ordinator Southern Region Nat Local Govt Forum Against Poverty (NLGFAP) 1994–97, political offr Lab Gp Local Govt Assoc 1997–99, political advsr to Govt chief whip House of Lords 2000–; memb Reading BC 1990–94; memb: Lab Pty, Child Poverty Action Gp, Greenpeace; Publications Talking of Coley (1989), The Politics of Poverty (jtly, 1995); Recreations badminton, walking, reading, talking; Style— Ms Margaret Ounsley; ✉ House of Lords, London SW1A 0PW (tel 020 7219 1115, e-mail ounsleym@parliament.uk)

OUSELEY, Hon Mr Justice; Sir Duncan Brian Walter Ouseley; kt (2001); s of Maurice Henry Ouseley (d 1978), Margaret Helen Irene, née Vagts (d 1997); b 24 February 1950; Educ Trinity Sch Croydon, Fitzwilliam Coll Cambridge (MA, exhibitioner) UCL (LLM); m 27 April 1974, Suzannah Valerie, née Price; 3 s (Daniel b 18 Jan 1979, Jonathan b 24 May 1980, Robert b 2 March 1988); Career called to the Bar Gray's Inn 1973 (Atkin scholar 1972, bencher 2000); jr counsel to Crown Common Law 1986–92, QC 1992 (NI 1997), recorder 1994–2000 (asst recorder 1991–94), jt head of chambers 4–5 Gray's Inn Square 2000, dep judge of the High Court 2000, judge of the High Court of Justice (Queen's Bench Div) 2000–; pres Immigration Appeal Tribunal 2003–05, chm Special Immigration Appeal Cmmn 2003–06; chm examination in public of: Shropshire Structure Plan First Alterations 1985, Hampshire Structure Plan 1991; vice-chm Planning and Environmental Bar Assoc 2000; Recreations family, sport, music, wine; Clubs Garrick; Style— The Hon Mr Justice Ouseley; ✉ Royal Courts of Justice, Strand, London WC2A 2LL

OUSELEY, Baron (Life Peer UK 2001), of Peckham Rye in the London Borough of Southwark; Sir Herman George Ouseley; kt (1997); s of Johnny Ouseley, and Daphne Coggins, of Guyana; b 24 March 1945; Educ William Penn Sch Dulwich; Career town planning mangr 1963–70, social care mangr for elderly 1970–73, community relations exec 1973–79, race relations policy advsr Lambeth BC 1979–81, dir Policy Unit GLC 1981–84, asst ceo London Borough of Lambeth 1984–86, chief exec ILEA 1988–90 (dir of educn 1986–88), chief exec London Borough of Lambeth 1990–93, chm Cmmn for Racial Equality 1993–2000, Different Realities Partnership Ltd 2000–06; non-exec dir: Focus Consultancy Ltd, Brooknight Security Ltd; chm Policy Research Inst on Ageing and Ethnicity, memb Cncl Inst of Race Relations 1986–; pres Local Govt Assoc 2002–05; chm: Kick It Out 1993–, Preset Educn and Employment Charitable Tst 1997–; tstee Manchester United Fndn 2006–; patron: Presentation Housing Assoc 1990–, Daneford Tst 2001–, Nat Black Police Assoc 2007–; Publications The System (1981); various pamphlets and articles on aspects of equality and local government; Style— The Lord Ouseley

OUSTON, Hugh Anfield; s of Philip Anfield Ouston, of St Andrews, Fife, and Elizabeth, née Banbury; b 4 April 1952; Educ Trinity Coll Glenalmond, ChCh Oxford (MA), Univ of Aberdeen (DipEd), Aberdeen Coll of Educn (CertEd); m 28 July 1988, Yvonne Caroline, da of Ernest Young; 2 s (Philip b 7 June 1990, Adam b 28 Feb 1994), 2 da (Jessica b 27 April 1992, Louise b 20 Jan 1996); Career history teacher Portree HS 1977; North Berwick HS: history teacher 1977–82, APT guidance 1982–84; princ teacher of history Beeslack HS 1984–92, asst head teacher Dunbar GS 1992–97, devpt offr History Higher Still 1994–96, dep princ George Watson's Coll Edinburgh 1997–2004, head of coll Robert Gordon's Coll Aberdeen 2004–; Recreations bird watching, gardening, hill walking, sailing, poetry; Clubs Royal Northern and Univ (Aberdeen); Style— Hugh Ouston, Esq; ✉ Robert Gordon's College, Schoolhill, Aberdeen AB10 1FE (tel 01224 646346, fax 01224 630301, e-mail h.ouston@rgc.aberdeen.sch.uk)

OUTLAW, Nathan Daniel; s of Clive Outlaw, of Maidstone, Kent, and Sharon, née Munn; b 7 March 1978; Maidstone, Kent; Educ Holmsdale Sch Snodland, Thanet Tech Coll; m 6 Oct 2001, Rachel, née Morris; 1 s (Jacob Anthony b 6 May 2003); Career chef: Hotel Intercontinental Hyde Park Corner London 1996–97, Chavot Restaurant Fulham London 1997–98; second chef: Seafood Restaurant Padstow Cornwall 1998–99, Lords of the Manor Glos 1999–2001; head chef The Vineyard at Stockcross Berks 2001–03, prop and chef Black Pig Rock Cornwall 2003–; chef conslt to Morris Gp Cornwall; nat finalist Roux Scholarship 2001, second place Young Chef and Young Waiter of GB 2002, Michelin Star 2004; Style— Nathan Outlaw, Esq

OUTRAM, Sir Alan James; 5 Bt (UK 1858); s of late James Ian Outram (gs of 2 Bt), and late Evelyn Mary, née Littlehales; suc gt unc, Sir Francis Davidson Outram, 4 Bt, OBE, 1945; Lt-Gen Sir James Outram, GCB, KBE, received Baronetcy 1858 for service in Persia and India; b 15 May 1937; Educ Marlborough, St Edmund Hall Oxford (MA); m 1976, Victoria Jean, da of late George Dickson Paton; 1 da (Alison Catharine b 1977), 1 s (Douglas Benjamin James b 1979); Heir s, Douglas Outram; Career schoolmaster Harrow Sch (ret); Hon Lt-Col TA & VR; pres Dorset LTA 1995–2005 (vice-pres 2005–); Recreations bridge, golf, tennis, cycling; Clubs Vincent's (Oxford); Style— Sir Alan Outram, Bt; ✉ Chase House, Moorside, Sturminster Newton, Dorset DT10 1HQ

OUTRAM, Christopher David; s of Joseph Outram (d 1972), and Vera Anne, née Ogden; b 4 April 1949; Educ King's GS, Atlantic Coll, Univ of Birmingham (BSc, BComm, Economics prize, Engineering prize), INSEAD Business Sch (MBA); m (m dis), Anne

Marie, da of Noel Leslie Costain; 2 da (Sophie Marie Elizabeth b 26 Sept 1981, Verity Clementine b 24 Nov 1983); *Career* Mobil Oil Company 1972–73, Air Products 1973–74, mktg mangr CCL Systems 1974–76, INSEAD Business Sch 1976–77, strategy conslt Boston Consulting Group 1977–79, strategic planning dir Van Gelder Papier 1979–81, strategy conslt Booz Allen & Hamilton 1981–86 (vice-pres 1986), fndr and ptnr OC&C Strategy Consultants 1986– (chm 1986–2005); non-exec dir Action Leisure plc 1999–; dir PTRC; *Recreations* learning piano and golf and other leisure activities, reading, travelling; *Clubs* RAC; *Style—* Christopher Outram, Esq; ✉ OC&C Strategy Consultants, The OC&C Building, 233 Shaftesbury Avenue, London WC2H 8EE (tel 020 7010 8000, fax 020 7010 8100, e-mail chris.outram@occstrategy.com)

OVENDEN, Graham Stuart; s of Henry Ovenden (d 1986), of Winchester, Hants, and Gwendoline Dorothy, *née* Hill (d 1988); *b* 11 February 1943; *Educ* Itchen GS, Southampton Coll of Art, Royal Coll of Music (ARCM), Royal Coll of Art (ARCA, MA); *m* 1 March 1969, Ann Dinah, da of George Walter Gilmore (d 1963), of Upper Winchendon, Bucks; 1 s (Edmund Dante b 1972), 1 da (Emily Alice b 1976); *Career* painter, poet, art historian; numerous exhibitions incl Tate Gallery and Royal Acad, one-man shows in most major western countries; fndr memb The Brotherhood of Ruralists 1976, fndr memb SW Acad of Fine and Applied Arts; *Books* Illustrators of Alice (1971), Victorian Children (with Robert Melville, 1972), Pre-Raphaelite Photography (1972), Hill and Adamson Photographs (1973), Alphonse Mucha Photographs (1973), Clementina Lady Hawarden (1973), Victorian Erotic Photography (1973), Aspects of Lolita (1975), A Victorian Family Album (with Lord David Cecil, 1976), Satirical Poems and Others (1983), The Marble Mirror (poetry, 1984), Lewis Carroll Photographer (1984), Monograph - Graham Ovenden (with essays by Laurie Lee, Clive Wainwright, Robert Melville and others, 1987), Sold With All Faults (poetry, 1991), Graham Ovenden - Childhood Streets (Photographs 1956–64) (1998); *Recreations* music, architecture; *Style—* Graham Ovenden, Esq; ✉ Barley Splatt, Panters Bridge, Mount, Cornwall

OVENDEN, Rev Canon John Anthony; LVO (2007); s of Edward Clifford Lewis Ovenden (d 1996), and Marjorie Mabel Ovenden (d 2006); *b* 26 May 1945; *Educ* chorister St Paul's Cathedral, Ardingly (music scholar), Borough Rd Coll of Educn, Salisbury & Wells Theol Coll, Open Univ (BA), King's Coll London (MA); *m* 27 July 1974, Christine, da of John Broadhurst; 2 s (Julian, Nicholas), 1 da (Anne-Clare); *Career* ordained: deacon 1974, priest 1975; curate: Handsworth (Sheffield) 1974–77, Isfield (Chichester) 1977–80, Uckfield 1977–80; priest i/c Stuntney (Ely) 1980–85, minor canon, precentor and sacrist Ely Cathedral 1980–85, vicar St Mary's Primrose Hill London 1985–98, canon of St George's Chapel Windsor Castle and chaplain in the Great Park 1998–, chaplain to HM The Queen 2002; Freeman City of London; *Publications* Christians and Muslims in the Commonwealth (contrib); contrib Affirming Catholicism Magazine; *Recreations* sport, theatre, walking; *Style—* The Rev Canon John Ovenden, LVO; ✉ Chaplain's Lodge, The Great Park, Windsor, Berkshire SL4 2HP (tel 01784 432434)

OVENSTONE, Dr Irene Margaret Kinnear; da of David Ovenstone (d 1951), and Edith Margaret Ovenstone (d 1984); *b* 25 October 1929; *Educ* Harris Acad Dundee, Univ of St Andrews (MB ChB, DPH), Univ of Leeds (DPM), Univ of Dundee (MD); *Career* asst MO of health Huddersfield 1957–61, registrar Huddersfield 1961–64, sr registrar in psychiatry Westminster Hosp London 1964–68, memb Scientific Staff and hon lectr MRC Unit for Epidemiological Studies in Psychiatry Edinburgh 1969–72, clinical teacher and conslt psychiatrist specialising in psychiatry of old age Univ of Nottingham 1973–94, sec and chm Nottingham Area Psychiatric Div 1974–79, emeritus conslt Nottingham City Hosp NHS Tst 1994, locum conslt psychiatrist in gen psychiatry Mansfield and Newark 1994–2004; memb Working Parties on: Psychiatric Nurse Educn 1974, Drug Custody and Admin 1977, Home for Elderly Project Notts Social Services Dept 1981; chm Notts Health Care Planning Team for Elderly 1981–82; memb: Mental Health Tbnls 1981–, Mental Health Cmmn 1983–86, Health Advsy Service 1989, Expert Witness Inst 1999–; author of papers on suicidal behaviour, marital neurosis, admissions to old people's homes in Nottingham; FRCPsych 1979 (MRCPsych 1973); *Recreations* ballet, music, theatre, archeology, art, wildlife; *Style—* Dr Irene Ovenstone; ✉ 10 Moor Road, Calverton, Nottingham NG14 6FW (tel 0115 847 7970, fax 0115 847 7975)

OVERBEEKE, Aernout Albert; *b* 17 May 1951, Utrecht, Netherlands; *Career* fashion photographer 1970–80, advertising photographer 1980–, dir film commercials 1996–; *Solo Exhibitions* Mississippi (Amsterdam and Geneva) 1988, Geneva 1991, Portraits (Naarden) 1993, Hoorn 1994, Garden of Eden (Amsterdam) 1994, Durgerdam Netherlands 1994, Portraits (Cobra Museum Amstelveen) 1998, Rouen 1999, London 2000, Amsterdam 2001, LA 2001; *Work in Collections* Cobra Museum Astelveen Netherlands, Haags Gemeente Mueum Den Haag Netherlands; *Awards* Photographers Assoc of the Netherlands (PANL): PANL/Kodak Award 1994 and 1995, Silver award 1994, 1995 and 2000, merit awards 1995 and 2000, Members Choice award 2000; Assoc of Photographers: Gold award 1997, Silver award 1994, 1995, 1996 and 1997; Netherlands Art Dir's Club awards 1990 and 1995, German Art Dir's Club Bronze award 1992, 1994 and 1995, European Art Dir's Club Gold award 1995, Gold Clio award 1998, nomination Best Photography European Advtg Awards 2001; *Publications* author of an article The Newest Dutch Master (Graphis, 1990); *Style—* Aernout Overbeeke, Esq; ✉ Coen Cuserhof 39, 2012 GZ Haarlem, The Netherlands (tel 00 31 23 5324000, fax 00 31 23 5320323); c/o Freddie Brazil, 312 Golden House, 29 Great Pulteney Street, London W1R 3DD (tel 020 7494 4623, fax 020 7287 1255)

OVERSBY-POWELL, David John; s of George Herbert Oversby-Powell (d 1975), of Cranleigh, Surrey, and Eileen Mary Veronica, *née* Cornhill (d 2002); *b* 13 September 1947; *Educ* Scotus Acad Edinburgh, John Fisher Sch Purley; *m* 10 June 1972, Jennifer Merlyn Isobel, da of Percival Sidney Bamber; 1 s (James David b 5 May 1981), 1 da (Kate Louise b 4 Feb 1984); *Career* trainee surveyor Hunts CC 1969, insurance inspr and local mangr Guardian Royal Exchange Bedford 1974–77 (insurance clerk 1970–73), pensions mangr Borg-Warner Ltd 1980–89 (asst insurance mangr 1977–79), gp pensions admin mangr AXA UK plc 2000– (formerly remuneration and benefits mangr AXA Insurance plc); ACII 1973; *Recreations* oil painting, watercolour painting, hill walking; *Style—* David Oversby-Powell, Esq; ✉ AXA UK plc, 107 Cheapside, London EC2V 6DU (tel 020 7645 1645, fax 020 7645 1641)

OVERY, Paul Vivian; s of Arthur Frederick Overy (d 1992), of Hampstead, London, and Joan Vivien, *née* Major (d 1987); *b* 14 February 1940; *Educ* UCS London, King's Coll Cambridge (MA); *m* 1992, Theresa Ann Gronberg; *Career* art critic: The Listener 1966–68 and 1978–82, Financial Times 1968–71; book reviews ed New Society 1970–71, chief art critic The Times 1973–78, tutor in cultural history RCA London 1975–87, art critic The International Herald Tribune 1980–82, freelance art critic 1982–, contributing ed The Journal of Art 1990–91; reader in history and theory of modernism Middlesex Univ 1997–2005 (currently sr research fell); exhibitions incl: 18 Artists from Hungary (Third Eye Centre Glasgow) 1985, Rietveld Furniture & the Schröder House (Warwick Univ Arts Centre) 1990, Whitworth Gallery Manchester, Collins Gallery Glasgow, City Art Gallery Southampton, Nat MOMA Dublin 1991, Royal Festival Hall London 1991, Josef Albers (Nat MOMA Dublin and touring) 1994; Italian Govt scholar to Italy 1970, Leverhulme res fell Paris 1984–85; memb: Assoc Internationale des Critiques d'Art 1967, NUJ 1970, Assoc of Art Historians 1987; *Books* Kandinsky: The Language of the Eye (1969), De Stijl (1969), Concepts of Modern Art (contrib, 1974), The New Art History (contrib, 1986), The Rietveld Schröder House (jtly, 1988), De Stijl (1991), The Complete Rietveld Furniture (jtly, 1993), Investigating Modern Art (contrib, 1996), Art and Cubism (contrib, 1997), Norman Foster: 30 Colours (jtly, 1998), Cosmopolitan Modernisms (jtly, 2005), Modern Period Room (contrib, 2006); *Recreations* reading, walking; *Style—* Paul Overy, Esq; ✉ 92 South Hill Park, London NW3 2SN (tel 020 7435 8725); c/o Andrew Hewson, Johnson and Alcock, Clerkenwell House, 47 Clerkenwell Green, London EC1R 0HT (tel 020 7251 0125, fax 020 7251 2172)

OVERY, Prof Richard James; s of James Herbert Overy, and Margaret Grace, *née* Sutherland; *b* 23 December 1947; *Educ* Sexey's Blackford GS, Gonville & Caius Cambridge (MA, PhD); *m* 1, 1969 (m dis 1976), Tessa, *née* Coles; 2 da (Emma Gabrielle b 14 Oct 1969, Rebecca Lucy b 28 Sept 1972), 1 s (Jonathan Frederick b 10 July 1974); m 2, 1979 (m dis 1992), Jane, *née*Ellwood; m 3, 1992 (m dis 2004), Kim, *née* Turner; 2 da (Alexandra Elizabeth b 7 July 1993, Clementine Jann b 31 March 1998); *Career* Univ of Cambridge: research fell Churchill Coll 1972–73, coll lectr Queens' Coll 1973–79, univ asst lectr 1976–79; KCL: lectr 1980–88, reader 1988–92, prof of modern history 1992–2004; prof of history Univ of Exeter 2004–; T S Ashton prize 1983, Cass prize 1987, Samuel Eliot Morison prize 2001, Wolfson prize 2005, Hessell-Tiltman Prize 2005; tstee RAF Museum 1999–2003; hon fell Centre for Second World War Experience; FRHS 1997, FBA 2000, FKC 2003, FRSA 2006; *Publications* The Air War 1939–1945 (1980), Goering (1984), The Road to War (1989), War and Economy in the Third Reich (1994), Why the Allies Won (1995), Russia's War (1998), The Times History of the 20th Century (1998), The Battle (2000), Interrogations (2001), The Dictators: Hitler's Germany, Stalin's Russia (2004), Times History of the World (gen ed, 5, 6 and 7 edns); *Recreations* opera, twentieth century art, running, football; *Clubs* The Academy; *Style—* Prof Richard Overy; ✉ Department of History, University of Exeter, Amory Building, Rennes Drive, Exeter EX9 4RJ (tel 01392 263291, e-mail r.overy@ex.ac.uk)

OWEN, Albert; MP; s of late William Owen, of Holyhead, and late Doreen, *née* Woods; *b* 10 August 1959; *Educ* Holyhead Comp Sch, Coleg Harlech (Dip Industrial Rels & Welsh Studies), Univ of York (BA); *m* Angela Margaret, da of John James Magee; 2 da (Rachel Lynne b 10 Jan 1985, Fiona Angela b 18 July 1986); *Career* merchant seafarer 1975–92, in fulltime educn 1992–97, mangr Centre for the Unwaged 1997–2001; MP (Lab) Ynys Môn 2001–, memb Welsh Affrs Select Ctee 2001–05, memb Accomodation and Works Ctee 2001–05; memb Holyhead Town Cncl 1997–99; chair Anglesey Regeneration Partnership 1999–, dir Ynys Môn Homeless Forum, chair Ctee Community Hall, memb Ctee Workers' Educnl Assoc (N Wales) until 2001; govr Coleg Harlech until 2001; *Recreations* cycling, hill walking, cooking, gardening; *Clubs* Holyhead Sailing (hon memb); *Style—* Albert Owen, Esq, MP; ✉ House of Commons, London SW1A 0AA; 18 Thomas Street, (Ty Cledwyn) Holyhead, Isle of Anglesey LL65 1RR (tel 01407 765750, fax 01407 764336, e-mail owena@parliament.uk)

OWEN, (Alfred) David; OBE (1997); s of Sir Alfred George Beech Owen, CBE (d 1975), and Eileen Kathleen Genevieve, *née* McMullan (d 1995); *b* 26 September 1936; *Educ* Brocksford Hall, Oundle, Emmanuel Coll Cambridge (MA); *m* 1966, Ethne Margaret, da of Frank H Sowman, of Solihull; 2 s, 1 da; *Career* Nat Serv Lt RASC; chm Rubery Owen Group; dir: National Exhibition Centre Ltd 1982–2006, Welconstruct Group Ltd 2001–, Severn Valley Railway (Holdings) plc, Darlaston Housing Tst 2001–, Walsall Housing Regeneration Community Agency 2005–; warden Birmingham Assay Office 1999–2005; memb BOTB 1979–83; pres: Birmingham C of C 1980–81, Comitè de Liaison de la Construction d'Equipments et de Pièces d'Automobiles 1988–90, Commercial Trailer Assoc 1992–2004, Comitè de Liaison de la Construction de Carrosseries et de Remorques 1998–99; vice-pres SMMT 1987–90 (hon treas 2001–); chm of tstees Charles Hayward Fndn 2004–, tstee Community Development Fndn 1978–97; Liveryman Worshipful Co of Coachmakers and Coach Harness Makers; Hon DSc Aston Univ 1988; Hon DUniv Central England 2000; *Recreations* industrial archaeology, ornithology, walking, photography, music; *Clubs* National; *Style—* A David Owen, Esq, OBE; ✉ Mill Dam House, Mill Lane, Aldridge, Walsall WS9 0NB; Rubery Owen Holdings Ltd, PO Box 10, Darlaston, Wednesbury, West Midlands WS10 8JD (tel 0121 526 3131, fax 0121 526 2869, e-mail david.owen@ruberyowen.com)

OWEN, Baron (Life Peer UK 1992), of the City of Plymouth; David Anthony Llewellyn Owen; CH (1994), PC (1976); s of Dr John William Morris Owen (d 1994), and Molly Owen (d 2001); *b* 2 July 1938; *Educ* Bradfield Coll, Sidney Sussex Coll Cambridge, St Thomas' Hosp London (BA, MB BChir, MA); *m* 1968, Deborah (Mrs Deborah Owen, literary agent), da of late Kyrill Schabert, of Long Island, NY; 2 s (Tristan Llewellyn b 1970, Gareth Schabert b 1972), 1 da (Lucy Mary b 1979); *Career* St Thomas' Hosp: house appts 1962–64, neurological and psychiatric registrar 1964–66, res fell med unit 1966–68; contested (Lab) Torrington 1964, MP (Lab) Plymouth Sutton 1966–74, MP (Lab until 1981, SDP 1981–92) Plymouth Devonport 1974–92; PPS to MOD (Admin) 1967, Parly under sec of state for def (RN) 1968–70, resigned over EEC 1972, Parly under sec of state DHSS 1974, min of state DHSS 1974–76 and FCO 1976–77, sec of state for foreign and Cwlth affairs 1977–79, oppn spokesman on energy 1979–81; fndr memb SDP 1981, chm SDP Parly Ctee 1981–82, dep leader SDP 1982–83, elected SDP Leader following resignation of Rt Hon Roy Jenkins after election 1983, resigned over merger with Liberals 1987, re-elected SDP leader 1988–90; memb: Palme Cmmn on Disarmament and Security Issues 1980–89, Ind Cmmn on Int Humanitarian Issues 1983–86, Carnegie Cmmn on Preventing Deadly Conflict 1994–99, Eminent Persons Gp on Curbing Illicit Trafficking of Small Arms and Light Weapons 2000–02; EU co-chm Steering Ctee Int Conf on Former Yugoslavia 1992–95; chm: Humanitas 1990–2001, New Europe 1999–2005, Europe-Steel plc 2000–07, Yukos Int 2002–05; exec chm Global Natural Energy plc 1995–2006, dir Intelligent Energy 2003–05; non-exec dir: Coats Viyella plc 1994–2001, Abbott Laboratories 1995; dir Centre of Int Health and Co-operation 1990–; chllr Univ of Liverpool 1996–; sits as Independent Social Democrat Cross Bench Peer in House of Lords; pres Enham Tst, pres Nat Marine Aquarium, patron Greenham Common Tst; hon fell: Sidney Sussex Coll Cambridge 1977, King's Coll, St Thomas' Hosp; FRCP; *Books* A Unified Health Service (1968), The Politics of Defence (1972), In Sickness and in Health (1976), Human Rights (1978), Face The Future (1981), A Future That Will Work (1984), A United Kingdom (1986), Personally Speaking (to Kenneth Harris) (1987), Our NHS (1988), Time to Declare (autobiography, 1991), Seven Ages (an anthology of poetry, 1992), Balkan Odyssey (1995), the Hubris Syndrome (2007); *Style—* The Rt Hon Lord Owen, CH, FRCP; ✉ 78 Narrow Street, Limehouse, London E14 8BP (tel 020 7987 5441, e-mail lordowen@nildram.co.uk); House of Lords, London SW1A 0PW (fax 01442 876108)

OWEN, His Hon Judge (Francis) David Lloyd; TD (1967); s of Robert Charles Lloyd Owen, of Dolgellau, Meirionnydd, and Jane Ellen, *née* Francis; *b* 24 October 1933; *Educ* Wrekin Coll; *m* 28 Oct 1965, Jennifer Nan, da of Richard Eric Knowles Rowlands, of Mickle Trafford, Cheshire; 2 da (Charis Jane b 7 May 1971, Anna Clare b 2 June 1974); *Career* Nat Serv 1952–54, cmmnd 22nd (Cheshire) Regt 1953, TA 1954–67, Maj 1963; admitted slr 1961; practising slr 1961–66, called to the Bar Gray's Inn 1967; practising Northern Circuit, actg stipendiary magistrate 1981, dep circuit judge, asst recorder 1977–88, recorder 1988–91, circuit judge (Northern Circuit) 1991–; *Recreations* country pursuits, walking, genealogy; *Clubs* Grosvenor (Chester), Royal Over-Seas (London and Edinburgh); *Style—* His Hon Judge Owen, TD; ✉ The Courts of Justice, Crown Square, Manchester M60 9DF

OWEN, Prof (David) Gareth; s of Oscar Vivian Owen (d 1988), and Mary Gwladys, *née* Davies (d 1961); *b* 6 November 1940; *Educ* Christ Coll Brecon, Downing Coll Cambridge (MA, PhD), Univ of London (BD); *m* 2 July 1966, Ann Valerie, da of Stanley Wilfred Owen Wright (d 1988); 2 da (Ceridwen b 1969, Rachel b 1971); *Career* graduate engr

O

John Laing & Son 1966–67, sr engr Marconi Space and Defence Systems Portsmouth 1970–72; Heriot-Watt Univ: lectr Dept of Civil Engrg 1972–75, sr lectr Dept of Offshore Engrg 1977, head of dept 1981–91, prof of offshore engrg 1986–, seconded to Scottish Higher Educn Funding Cncl 1992–95, dir of quality 1995–96, dean of engrg 1996–99, asst princ 1997–99, vice-princ 1999–2001, head Sch of Textiles and Design 2002–; visiting assoc prof Univ of New Hampshire 1976; pres: Edinburgh and Leith Petroleum Club 1991–92, Scottish Oil Club 1999–2001; FICE, CEng, FRSA; *Recreations* music, travel, languages; *Style*— Prof D Gareth Owen; ✉ 7 Oak Lane, Edinburgh EH12 6XH (tel 0131 339 1740, e-mail dgarethowen@blueyonder.co.uk)

OWEN, Gordon Michael William; CBE (1991); s of Christopher Knowles Owen, and Margaret Joyce Milward, *née* Spencer (d 1986); *b* 9 December 1937; *Educ* Cranbrook Sch; *m* 1, 1963 (m dis 2001), Jennifer Pearl, da of Basil John Bradford; 1 da (Alison Carole b 29 Jan 1966), 1 s (Timothy Derek b 14 Feb 1969); m 2, 2001, Tina Elizabeth Davies; *Career* Cable & Wireless plc: joined 1954, md subsid co Mercury Communications Ltd 1984–90, dir 1986–91, jt md 1987, dep chief exec 1988, gp md 1990–91, chm Mercury Communications 1990–91; chm: Energis plc 1992–2002, Peterstar (Russia) 1992–94, MacIntyre Care 1993–2003, Yeoman Group plc 1995–2004, Acorn Group plc 1996–99, Waste Gas Technology 1997–2004, NXT plc 2001–05; non-exec dir: Portals Group plc 1988–95, London Electricity plc 1990–97, Olivetti SpA 1996–2002; chm: Acad St Martins in the Field Orchestra 1999–2003, Acad Concerts Soc; FIEE; *Recreations* golf (poor!), sailing, bee-keeping; *Style*— Gordon M W Owen, Esq, CBE; ✉ Sutton End House, Sutton End, West Sussex RH 20 1PY

OWEN, (John) Graham; s of (John) Hugh Owen, of Bridgend, and Mair Eluned, *née* Evans; *b* 30 August 1952; *Educ* Epsom Coll, Guy's Hosp (BDS, LDS, RCS); *m* Belle Steadman, da of Harry Mooney (d 1985), of Hounslow; 3 s (Robert b 28 Dec 1981, Jonathan b 27 June 1984, Martin b 17 Oct 1986), 1 da (Annabelle b 7 Feb 1983); *Career* Guy's Hosp: house offr 1977, SHO 1978, lectr in maxillofacial and oral surgery 1978–80 (pt/t 1980–); hon sec Dental Soc of London 1990–97 (pres 1997–98), memb: Br Dental Assoc, Assoc of Dental Implantology; memb Wales in London Soc; FRSM 1996; *Recreations* golf, rugby, cricket; *Clubs* Surrey CCC, Athenaeum, Wychwood Golf, Westerham Golf, Beckenham RFC; *Style*— Graham Owen, Esq; ✉ High View, 339 Main Road, Westerham Hill, Kent TN16 2HP (tel and fax 01959 573180); 142 Gipsy Hill, London SE19 1PW (tel 020 8761 8818); 86 Harley Street, London W1G 7HP (tel 020 7935 8084)

OWEN, John Aubrey; s of Douglas Aubrey Owen (d 1964), and Patricia Joan, *née* Griggs (d 1968); *b* 1 August 1945; *Educ* City of London Sch, St Catharine's Coll Cambridge (MA); *m* 8 May 1971, Julia Margaret, da of Thomas Gordon Jones (d 1993), of Shrewsbury, Salop; 1 s (Charles Aubrey b 1972), 1 da (Lucy Margaret b 1975); *Career* joined Miny of Tport 1969, asst private sec to Min for Tport Industries 1972, DOE 1972–75, Dept of Tport 1975–78, seconded to Cambs CC 1978–80; DOE: joined 1980, regnl dir Northern Regnl Office DOE and Dept of Tport 1987–91, dir of personnel mgmnt 1991–95, dir Skills, Enterprise and Regeneration Govt Office for London 1995–2001; sr ptnr Inside Advice 2001–; chm Mosaic Homes (formerly New Islington and Hackney Housing Assoc) 2002–06, dep chm Family Mosaic 2006–; MInstD; *Recreations* gardening, opera, singing; *Clubs* Middx CCC, Welwyn Garden City Music Soc; *Style*— John Owen, Esq; ✉ 33 Valley Road, Welwyn Garden City, Hertfordshire AL8 7DH (tel 01707 321768, e-mail johna.owen@ntlworld.com)

OWEN, John Wyn; CB (1994); s of Idwal Wyn Owen (d 1984), of Bangor, and Myfi, *née* Hughes; *b* 15 May 1942; *Educ* Friars Sch Bangor, St John's Coll Cambridge (BA, MA), King's Fund Hosp Admin Staff Coll (FHSM Dip HSM); *m* 1 April 1967, Elizabeth Ann, da of William MacFarlane (d 1980), of Bangor; 1 da (Sian b 1971), 1 s (Dafydd b 1974); *Career* hosp sec Glantawe HMC Swansea 1967–70, staff trg offr Welsh Hosp Bd Cardiff 1968–70, divnl admin Univ Hosp of Wales HMC Cardiff 1970–72, asst clerk St Thomas' Hosp London 1972–74, admin St Thomas' Health Dist 1974–79; exec dir United Medical Enterprises London 1979–85; dir: Allied Medical Group London 1979–85, Br Nursing Cooperations London 1979–85, Allied Med Gp Healthcare Canada 1982–85, Allied Shanning London 1983–85; chm Welsh Health Common Servs Authy 1985–94, dir Welsh NHS 1985–94, DG NSW Health Dept Sydney 1994–97, chm Australian Health Ministers' Advsy Cncl 1995–97, dep chm Strategic Planning and Evaluation Ctee Nat Health & Research Cncl 1995–97; chm CMG DOH London 1999; sec Nuffield Tst London 1997–2005, chm Univ of Wales Inst Cardiff 2005–; visiting fell LSE 1997–, sr assoc Judge Inst of Mgmnt Studies Univ of Cambridge 1997–, adjunct prof of public health Univ of Sydney Aust; memb: Personnel Standards Lead Body 1992–94, Cncl Univ of Wales Coll of Med 1997–; dir Madariaga European Fndn Brussels 2005–, non-exec dir UK Health Protection Agency 2006–; tstee: Florence Nightingale Museum Tst 1983–90, Mgmnt Advsy Serv 1986–90; jt sec London branch Cambridge Soc 1997–; organist United Free Church Cowbridge 1985; fell: Univ Coll of Wales Aberystwyth, Univ Coll of Wales Bangor, Australian Coll of Health Service Execs; memb Inst of Med (USA); hon memb Gorsedd of Bards; Hon DUniv Glamorgan 1999, Hon DSc City Univ 2004; FHSM, FRSM, Hon FFPM, Hon FRSA, Hon MRCP; *Recreations* organ playing, opera, travel; *Clubs* Athenaeum; *Style*— John Wyn Owen, Esq, CB; ✉ Newton Farm, Cowbridge, South Glamorgan CF7 7RZ (tel 01446 775113); University of Wales Institute, PO Box 377, Western Avenue, Cardiff CF5 2SG (tel 02920 416072, fax 02920 416914, e-mail johnwynowen@uwic.ac.uk)

OWEN, Michael James; s of Colin Owen, of Church Village, Mid Glamorgan, and Susan Rosemary, *née* Hopkins; *b* 7 November 1980, Church Village, Mid Glamorgan; *Educ* Bryn Celynnog Comp Sch Pontypridd; *m* 4 July 2004, Lucy Jayne; 2 da (Ellie Beth b 2 Aug 2002, Olivia Louise b 13 June 2005); *Career* rugby union player; clubs: Pontypridd 1998–2003 (joined as youth player, winners Principality Cup and finalists Parker Pen Shield 2002), Newport Gwent Dragons 2004–; Wales: 33 caps (6 as capt), debut v South Africa 2002, winners Grand Slam 2005; memb British and Irish Lions touring squad New Zealand 2005 (capt v Argentina); *Style*— Mr Michael Owen; ✉ c/o Newport Gwent Dragons, Rodney Parade, Newport, Gwent NP19 0UU

OWEN, Michael James; s of Terry Owen, and Janette Owen; *b* 14 December 1979; *m* 24 June 2005, Louise Bonsall; 1 da (Gemma Rose); *Career* professional footballer; clubs: Liverpool FC until 2004 (joined club aged 11, memb winning Youth Cup team 1995/96, scored on Premiership debut v Wimbledon 1997, Premiership Golden Boot 1997/98 (23 goals), Worthington Cup 2001, FA Cup 2001, UEFA Cup 2001, FA Charity Shield 2001, European Super Cup 2001), FC Real Madrid 2004–05, Newcastle United FC 2005–; England: 84 full caps (38 goals), debut v Chile Feb 1998, memb squad World Cup 1998, 2002 and 2006, memb squad European Championships 2000 and 2004; Young Player of the Year PFA Awards 1998, BBC Sports Personality of the Year 1998, European Footballer of the Year 2001; *Recreations* golf (handicap of 8), snooker, table tennis, my Staffordshire Bull Terrier (Bomber); *Style*— Michael Owen, Esq; ✉ c/o SFX Sports Group (Europe) Ltd, 9 Hockley Court, 2401 Stratford Road, Hockley Heath, West Midlands B94 6NW (tel 01564 786780, fax 01564 786789)

OWEN, Prof Michael John (Mike); s of Dr John Robson Owen, of Emsworth, Hants, and Mary Gillian, *née* Dowsett; *b* 24 November 1955, Birmingham; *Educ* Sherborne, Univ of Birmingham (BSc, PhD, MB ChB, Marjorie Hutching's Prize in Psychiatry); *m* 28 Sept 1985, Dr Deborah Cohen; 1 da (Laura b 30 May 1987), 2 s (Joe b 13 July 1989, Rob b 13 Feb 1992); *Career* house physician Queen Alexandra Hosp Portsmouth 1983–84, house surgn Dept of Neurosurgery Queen Elizabeth Hosp Birmingham 1984, SHO Div of Psychiatry Northwick Park Hosp and Clinical Research Centre Harrow 1984–85, registrar then sr registrar Bethlem Royal and Maudsley Hosps London 1985–90, research worker Genetics Section Inst of Psychiatry London 1986–87, MRC trg fell St Mary's Hosp Med Sch London 1987–90, hon lectr Inst of Psychiatry London 1988–90; hon conslt psychiatrist: S Glamorgan HA 1987–90, Univ Hosp Wales 1990– (clinical dir of psychiatry 1994–99); Univ of Wales Coll of Med Cardiff: sr lectr Dept of Psychological Med and Inst of Med Genetics 1990–95, prof of neuropsychiatric genetics 1995–98, prof of psychological med 1998–, head Dept of Psychological Med 1998–, memb Mgmnt Bd and Mgmnt Bd Exec 1999–2004, pro-vice-chllr for research 2001–04, chair Div of Community Specialities 2002– (vice-chair 2000–02); examiner Univs of: London, Antwerp, Helsinki, Lille, Bristol, Birmingham, Southampton; memb Editorial Bd: Human Molecular Genetics, Molecular Psychiatry, Archives of Gen Psychiatry, Schizophrenia Research, International Jl of Neuropsychopharmacology, Annals of Med, Psychiatric Genetics; reviewer for jls incl: Nature, Nature Med, Nature Genetics, Human Molecular Genetics, Molecular Psychiatry, Br Jl of Psychiatry, Psychological Med; keynote lectures incl: distinguished guest lectr Trinity Coll Dublin 2001, distinguished visiting prof NYU Sch of Med 2002, Eli Lilly lectr RCPsych 2002; memb: Research Ctee Mental Health Fndn 1993–96, Neurosciences and Mental Health Grants Ctee MRC 1995–97, Links with Industry Grants Ctee MRC 1995–2001, Special Ctee on Univ Psychiatry 1996–2002, Med and Scientific Advsy Bd Alzheimer Disease Soc 1996–, Advsy Bd MRC 1997–2000, Working Pty on Ethics in Research RCPsych 1999, Neurosciences and Mental Health Bd MRC 2000–04, Cncl Acad of Med Sciences 2001–04, Ctee of Scientists Human Frontier Science Prog; pres Int Soc of Psychiatric Genetics 2000–05 (memb Bd of Dirs 1993–); FRCPsych 1997 (MRCPsych 1987), FMedSci 1999; *Publications* Seminars in Psychiatric Genetics (jtly, 1994), Psychiaric Genetics and Genomics (jt ed, 2002); author of numerous contribs to academic jls; *Style*— Prof Mike Owen; ✉ Department of Psychological Medicine, Wales College of Medicine, Cardiff University, Heath Park, Cardiff CF14 4XN (tel 029 2074 3248, fax 029 2074 6554, e-mail owenmj@cf.ac.uk)

OWEN, Nicholas David Arundel; s of Tom Owen (d 1981), and Diana Owen; *b* 10 February 1947; *m* Brenda; 1 da (Rebecca b 22 Dec 1969), 1 s (Anthony b 2 Oct 1976); 1 step da (Justine b 26 April 1972), 1 step s Daniel b 10 Oct 1974); *Career* journalist: Surrey Mirror 1964–68, London Evening Standard 1968–70, Daily Telegraph 1970–72, Financial Times 1972–79, Now! Magazine 1979–81; reporter and presenter BBC Television News 1981–84, presenter ITN 1984–; *Books* History of the British Trolleybus (1972); *Recreations* reading, bridge, golf, piano; *Style*— Nicholas Owen, Esq; ✉ ITN Ltd, 200 Gray's Inn Road, London WC1X 8XZ (tel 020 7833 3000, e-mail nicholas.owen@itn.co.uk)

OWEN, Peter Francis; CB (1990); s of Arthur Owen (d 1988), and Violet, Winifred, *née* Morris; *b* 4 September 1940; *Educ* Liverpool Inst, Univ of Liverpool (BA); *m* 27 July 1963, Ann, da of William Henry Preece (d 1974); 1 s (David b 8 April 1969), 1 da (Poppy b 13 Sept 1973); *Career* joined Miny of Public Bldg and Works 1964, Cabinet Office and private sec to successive Ministers of Housing and Construction 1971–74, asst sec housing policy review DOE 1974–77, asst sec local govt fin DOE 1977–80, regnl dir Northern and Yorks and Humberside Regions DOE and Dept of Tport 1980–82, dir rural affrs DOE 1982–83, under sec local govt fin policy DOE 1983–86, dep sec housing and construction DOE 1986–90, dep sec Cabinet Office 1990–94, dep sec DFE 1994–95, DG of Schs DFEE 1995–98; sec gen ICAEW 2002–03 (exec dir 1998–2002); *Recreations* gardening, French, classical guitar; *Style*— Peter Owen, Esq, CB

OWEN, Dr Richard Charles; s of Alfred Roy Warren Owen (d 1978), of Rottingdean, E Sussex, and Florence Mary, *née* Walker; *b* 14 July 1947; *Educ* Varndean GS, Univ of Nottingham (BA), LSE (MSc, PhD), Stanford Univ (Harkness scholarship); *m* 1 May 1982, Julia Anne, da of Clive Raymond Crosse; 2 da (Eleanor Owen b 2 May 1983, Isabel Owen b 2 May 1983), 1 s (Laurence b 22 Aug 1988); *Career* script writer and prodr BBC External Servs 1973–79, asst prodr BBC TV Current Affrs 1979–80; The Times: leader writer 1980–82, Moscow corr 1982–85, Brussels corr 1985–88, Jerusalem corr 1988–91, dep foreign ed 1991–92, foreign ed 1992–96, Rome corr 1996–; *Books* Letters from Moscow (1985), Crisis in the Kremlin (1986), The Times Guide to 1992, Britain in a Europe without Frontiers (1990), The Times Guide to World Organisations (1996); *Style*— Dr Richard Owen; ✉ The Times, 1 Pennington Street, London E1 9BD (tel 020 7782 5234)

OWEN, Robert Frank; QC (1996); s of Tudor Owen (d 1994), of Clwyd, and (Alice) Pat, *née* Ferris; *b* 31 May 1953; *Educ* St Asaph GS, Prestatyn HS, PCL (Univ of London external LLB); *m* 24 May 1980, Anna Elizabeth, da of Richard Shaw; 3 s (Jonathan Robert b 31 Jan 1982, William Tudor b 25 May 1985, Thomas Rufus b 7 March 1989); *Career* called to the Bar Gray's Inn 1977, currently asst recorder; *Recreations* walking, gardening, sport; *Style*— R F Owen, Esq, QC; ✉ 24 The Ropewalk, Ropewalk Chambers, Nottingham NG1 5EF (e-mail rowen@ropewalk.co.uk)

OWEN, Robert John Vernon; s of David Tudor Owen (d 1987), and Marjorie Eugenie, *née* Burgess; *b* 14 September 1965, Wolverhampton; *Educ* Malvern Coll, Queen Mary Coll Univ of London (BA), Guildford Coll of Law; *m* 26 May 1995, Laura Joanna, *née* Baxter; 2 s (Patrick David Vernon b 1 Dec 1996, (Oliver) Harry Royce b 15 July 1998), 1 da (Freya Laura b 15 May 2000); *Career* Bircham Dyson Bell LLP (formerly Bircham & Co): trainee slr 1987–89, asst slr 1989–91, ptnr 1991–; Roll A Parly agent 1991; memb: Law Soc 1989, Soc of Parly Agents 1991; *Recreations* skiing, sailing, rugby, running, cycling, gardening; *Clubs* RAC, Bosham Sailing; *Style*— Robert Owen, Esq; ✉ 138 Rosendale Road, West Dulwich, London SE21 8LG (tel 020 8761 9706); Bircham Dyson Bell LLP, 50 Broadway, London SW1H 0BL (tel 020 7227 7076, fax 020 7233 1351, e-mail robbieowen@bdb-law.co.uk)

OWEN, Hon Mr Justice; Sir Robert Michael Owen; kt (2001); s of Gwynne Llewellyn Owen (d 1986), of Fowey, Cornwall and Phoebe Constance Owen; *b* 19 September 1944; *Educ* Durham Sch, Univ of Exeter (LLB); *m* 9 Aug 1969, Sara Josephine, da of Sir Algernon Rumbold, KCMG, CIE; 2 s (Thomas b 10 Nov 1973, Huw b 4 Jan 1976); *Career* called to the Bar Inner Temple 1968 (bencher 1995); recorder 1987, QC 1988, dep judge of the High Court 1994, judge of the High Court of Justice (Queen's Bench Div) 2001–, presiding judge Western Circuit 2005–; chm London Common Law and Commercial Bar Assoc 1993–95 (vice-chm 1991–93), chm Gen Cncl of the Bar 1997 (vice-chm 1996), govr Coll of Law 1998–2004; chm VCJD Tst 2002–, chm Consultative Ctee Fowey Harbour Cmmn 2006–; assoc fell Inst of Advanced Legal Studies 1998, FRSA 1998; *Clubs* Travellers, MCC, Royal Fowey Yacht; *Style*— The Hon Mr Justice Owen

OWEN, Prof (David) Roger Jones; s of Evan William Owen (d 1952), of Llanelli, and Margaret, *née* Jones (d 1990); *b* 27 May 1942; *Educ* Llanelli Boys' GS, UC Swansea (BSc, MSc), Northwestern Univ USA (PhD), Univ of Wales (DSc); *m* 12 Feb 1964, Janet Mary, da of William James Pugh (d 1983), of Llanelli; 2 da (Kathryn b 1967, Lisa b 1970); *Career* prof Univ of Wales 1982, dir Inst for Numerical Methods in Engrg Univ of Wales Swansea 1987–98; chm Rockfield Software Ltd, dir Pineridge Press Ltd; author of numerous pubns; memb: Cncl Nat Assoc On Finite Element Methods and Standards, various EPSRC ctees; Hon Dr: Univ of Porto Portugal 1998, ENS Cachan France 2007; FICE 1983, FREng 1996; *Books* with E Hinton: Finite Element Programming (1977), An Introduction to Finite Element Computations (1979), Finite Elements in Plasticity (1980), A Simple Guide to Finite Elements (1980), Engineering Fracture Mechanics: Numerical Methods and Applications (1983); *Recreations* flying, golf, tennis; *Clubs* Langland Bay Golf, Swansea; *Style*— Prof Roger Owen, FREng; ✉ Civil and Computational Engineering Centre, University of Wales Swansea, Singleton Park, Swansea SA2 9PP (tel 01792 295252, fax 01792 295676, e-mail d.r.j.owen@swansea.ac.uk)

OWEN, Tudor Wyn; s of Abel Rhys Owen (d 1974), of Aberdare, Glamorgan, and Mair, *née* Jenkins (d 2004); *b* 16 May 1951; *Educ* Aberdare GS, KCL (LLB); *Career* called to the Bar Gray's Inn 1974; in practice SE Circuit, recorder of the Crown Court 1991; inspr DTI 1989; memb: Ctee Criminal Bar Assoc 1987–91 (treas 1988–91), Gen Cncl of the Bar 1988–94, Bar Professional Conduct Ctee 1989–91, Bar Public Affairs Ctee 1990–91, Bar Ctee 1990–92 (vice-chm 1991–92), Gen Mgmnt Ctee 1992–93, Professional Standards Ctee 1992–93, SE Circuit Ctee 1992–96; FRAeS 2002; *Recreations* motor racing, flying helicopters and WWII fighter aircraft, shooting, skiing, riding the Cresta Run, music; *Clubs* Garrick, St Moritz Tobogganing; *Style—* Tudor Owen, Esq; ✉ Chambers, 9–12 Bell Yard, London WC2A 2LF (tel 020 7400 1800, fax 020 7404 1405, DX 390 Chancery Lane)

OWEN-JONES, David Roderic; s of (John) Eryl Owen-Jones, CBE, JP, DL (d 2000), and Mabel Clara, *née* McIlvride (d 2000); *b* 16 March 1949; *Educ* Llandovery Coll, UCL (LLB, LLM); *Career* called to the Bar Inner Temple 1972, ad eundem Lincoln's Inn 1993; in practice SE Circuit; Wales & Chester circuit, recorder of the Crown Court; memb Lord Chancellor's Advsy Ctee on the Appointments of JPs for Inner London 1986–91, actg Met stipendiary magistrate 1991–93; Parly candidate: (Lib) Carmarthen Div Feb and Oct 1974, (Lib Alliance) Rugby and Kenilworth 1983 and 1987; govr Int Students Tst 1981–84 and 1992– (tstee 1981–), vice-chm Assoc of Lib Dem Lawyers; FRSA 1984; *Books* The Prosecutorial Process in England and Wales (jtly); *Recreations* theatre, historical biography; *Clubs* Nat Lib (tstee, chm 1988–91), Reform; *Style—* David Owen-Jones, Esq; ✉ 17 Albert Bridge Road, London SW11 4 PX (tel 020 7622 1280); 3 Temple Gardens, Temple, London EC4Y 9AU (tel 020 7583 1155)

OWEN-SMITH, Dr Brian David; s of Cyril Robert Smith, OBE (d 1993), and Margaret Jane, *née* Hughes (d 1994); *b* 29 May 1938; *Educ* Dulwich Coll, Queens' Coll Cambridge (MA, MB BChir), Guy's Hosp London (DPhys, Med, DSpMed); *m* 24 Sept 1966, Hon Rose Magdalen Ponsonby, da of 2 Baron Ponsonby of Shulbrede (d 1976); 1 s (Timothy Clive b 25 April 1968), 1 da (Emma Elizabeth Jane b 22 Aug 1971); *Career* Lilly fell in clinical pharmacology Indiana Univ USA 1970, sr registrar rheumatic diseases Royal Nat Hosp Bath 1972; currently emeritus conslt in rheumatology St Richard's Hosp Chichester W Sussex, fell Hunterian Soc (pres 1999–), memb Chichester Soc; Freeman: City of London, Worshipful Soc of Apothecaries; Dip in Philosphy of Med Soc of Apothecaries (DPMSA), DHMSA; LRCP, MRCS, FRCP; *Recreations* squash, tennis, sailing; *Clubs* RSM; *Style—* Dr Brian Owen-Smith; ✉ 48 Westgate, Chichester PO19 3EU (tel 01243 786688, e-mail brosmith@lineone.net)

OWENS, Prof David Howard; s of Maurice Owens, of Derby, and Joan, *née* Browes; *b* 23 April 1948; *Educ* Dronfield Henry Fanshawe, Imperial Coll London (BSc, PhD); *m* 18 July 1969, Rosemary, da of John Cecil Frost, of Sheffield; 1 s (Benjamin David b 1976), 1 da (Penelope Rosemary Jane b 1979); *Career* scientific offr UKAEA Atomic Energy Estab Winfrith 1969–73, reader in control engrg Univ of Sheffield 1982 (lectr 1973, sr lectr 1981), prof of dynamics and control Univ of Strathclyde 1988–90 (prof of engrg mathematics 1985); Univ of Exeter: prof of systems and control engrg 1990–99, dir Sch of Engrg 1995–98, head Sch of Engrg and Computer Sci 1998–99; chm Exeter Enterprises Ltd 1998–99; Univ of Sheffield: prof of control and systems engrg 1999–, head dept Automatic Control and Systems Engrg 1999–, dean Faculty of Engrg 2002–06; dir Iter8 Control Systems Ltd 2007–; ctee work and conference orgn: IEE, IMechE, IMA, Health and Safety Cmmn, UK Automatic Control Cncl (chm 1999–2002); FIMA 1976, FIEE 1996 (MIEE 1979), MIEEE 1990, FIMechE 2001; *Books* Feedback and Multivariable Systems (1978), Multivariable and Optimal Systems (1981), Analysis and Control of Multipass Processes (jtly, 1982), Stability Analysis of Linear Repetitive Processes (jtly, 1992), Control Systems Theory and Applications for Linear Repetitive Processes (jtly, 2007); *Recreations* sketching, reading, guitar; *Style—* Prof David Owens; ✉ Department of Automatic Control and Systems Engineering, University of Sheffield, Mappin Street, Sheffield S1 3JD

OWENS, Graham Wynford; s of Wynford Owens (d 1996), of New Barnet, Herts, and Muriel, *née* Knibb (d 2002); *b* 23 February 1943; *Educ* Queen Elizabeth Sch Barnet, Univ of Bristol (BSc), Imperial Coll London (MSc, DIC, PhD); *m* 15 Aug 1970, Margaret Anne, *née* Muggridge; 2 da (Emma Jane b 3 April 1971, Lucy Alexandra b 2 Feb 1974), 1 s (Andrew Graham b 5 July 1972); *Career* UN volunteer Tanzania 1964–65; John Laing & Sons 1965–68, Flint & Neill (consulting engrs) 1968–69, lectr rising to sr lectr Imperial Coll London 1973–86 (postgrad study 1969–73), dir Steel Construction Inst 1992– (asst dir 1986–92); IStructE: vice-pres and memb Cncl, Oscar Faber Medal 1987 and 1998, Oscar Faber Award 1992; MICE 1969, FIStructE 1996, FRSA 1998, FREng 2003; *Publications* Structural Steelwork Connections (jtly, 1989), Structural Steel Design (jt ed, 1988), Steel Designers Manual (jt ed, 5 edn 1992, 6 edn 2002); author of 47 papers in refereed jls and at int confs; *Recreations* sailing, fishing, restoring antique furniture, reading; *Style—* Dr Graham Owens; ✉ Apsley House, Thicket Grove, Maidenhead, Berkshire SL6 4LW (tel 01628 623281); The Steel Construction Institute, Silwood Park, Ascot, Berkshire SL5 7QN (tel 01344 636525, fax 01344 636570, mobile 07831 719421, e-mail g.owens@steel-sci.com)

OWENS, John Ridland; s of Dr Ridland Owens (d 1968), of Lymington, and Elsie, *née* Smith (d 1990); *b* 21 May 1932; *Educ* Merchant Taylors', St John's Coll Oxford (Sir Thomas White scholar, MA); *m* 1, 1958 (m dis 1981), Susan Lilian, da of Cdr G R Pilcher, RN, of Yelverton; 1 da (Elizabeth Clare b 1 July 1960), 2 s (David Ridland b 23 Feb 1962, James Graham b 27 Sept 1966); m 2, 27 Sept 1985, Cynthia Rose, da of Sir Archibald Finlayson Forbes, GBE (d 1989); 1 s (Thomas Alasdair Ridland b 29 June 1987); *Career* Nat Serv 2 Lt RA served Germany 1951–52, Lt TA 1952–57, Gunner HAC 1957–61; section mangr ICI Ltd 1955–67 (founded Stokesley Civic Soc and the Civic Tst for the NE), md Cape Asbestos Fibres Ltd 1967–72, DG Dairy Trade Fedn 1973–83 (vice-pres Assoc Industrie Laitière du Marché Commun, dir Nat Dairy Cncl, memb Food and Drink Indust Cncl, founded Nat Dairy Museum), dep DG CBI 1983–90, DG Building Employers' Confedn 1990–92, memb Bd UK Skills 1990–92; chm: Owens Associates (ind conslt in strategic advice and govt rels) 1993–2005, Haringey Healthcare NHS Tst 1993–99, CBI Market Testing Gp 1994–97, Do It Even Better Ltd 2001–03; memb Tst Cncl and chm Procurement and Facilities Mgmnt Gp NAHAT (now NHS Confedn) 1995–97; memb: Bd PRONED 1983–90, Indust Ctee RSA 1984–87, Assoc of Business Sponsorship of the Arts Cncl 1986–95, Advsy Bd RA 1987–91, Cncl City and Guilds Inst 1988–94, Ct City Univ 1988–2005, Cncl Franco-Br Cncl 1989–90, Cncl RSA 1995–2001; practising painter etcher exhibiting in the Prince of Wales Drawing Sch, Mall Gallery, Painters Hall, Chelsea Art Soc and St Paul's Cathedral; govr Merchant Taylors' Sch 1996–2005 (vice-chm of govrs), govr Middlesex Univ 1999–2002 (memb Audit and HR Ctees); memb Armed Forces Art Soc; Freeman City of London, Liveryman Worshipful Co of Merchant Taylors (memb Ct of Assts, Master 2002–03), Freeman Worshipful Co of Painter-Stainers; *Publications* Marketing in the NHS - Putting Patients First (1993), Strategic Procurement for the NHS - Working with Suppliers (1996); *Recreations* painting, drawing, walking; *Clubs* Reform; *Style—* John R Owens, Esq

OWENS, Matthew; *b* 17 January 1971; *Educ* Chetham's Sch of Music Manchester, The Queen's Coll Oxford (John Betts organ scholar, MA, dir chapel choir), RNCM (MusM, PPRNCM), Sweelinck Conservatorium Amsterdam; *Career* organist, conductor and composer; tutor in organ studies and choral directing studies RNCM and tutor in organ and academic studies Chetham's Sch of Music Manchester 1994–2001, sub-organist Manchester Cathedral 1996–99, organist and master of the music St Mary's Episcopal Cathedral Edinburgh and tutor in organ studies St Mary's Music Sch Edinburgh 1999–2004, organist and master of the choristers Wells Cathedral 2005–, tutor in organ studies Wells Cathedral Sch 2006–; musical dir RNCM Chamber Choir 1993–94, musical dir, organist and singer Daily Service (BBC Radio 4) 1993–99, asst and assoc conductor Nat Youth Choir of GB 1993–2000, artistic dir and conductor Exon Singers 1997–, fndr and artistic dir Cathedral Cmmns 2005–; guest conductor: Orch of St Mary's Music Sch Edinburgh 1999–2004, BT Scottish Ensemble 1999–2001, Hungarian Nat Philharmonic Orch 2002, Sarum Orch 2005–, Devon Baroque 2005–, Wells Cathedral Sch Chamber Orch 2005–; composer 2000–; dir and tutor of organ workshops Edinburgh Organ Acad, Edinburgh Soc of Organists, Incorporated Assoc of Organists and Soc for the Promotion of New Music 1997–, dir Edinburgh Cathedral Course Royal Sch of Church Music (RSCM) 2004, examiner Royal Coll of Organists 2004–, dir Canterbury Cathedral Course RSCM 2006; pres Edinburgh Soc of Organists 2004; numerous recordings as conductor and solo organist; broadcasts and recitals in UK and overseas; author of articles in Choir & Organ and Organists' Review 1996–2005, assoc ed Friends of Cathedral Music Magazine 2005–; 13 prizes Royal Coll of Organists, Silver medal Worshipful Co of Musicians 1994; FRCO 1994 (ARCO 1994); *Style—* Matthew Owens, Esq; ✉ Wells Cathedral Music Office, Chain Gate, Cathedral Green, Wells, Somerset BA5 2UE (tel 01749 674483)

OWERS, Anne Elizabeth; CBE (2001); da of William Spark (d 1963), and Annie Smailes, *née* Knox (d 1969); *b* 23 June 1947; *Educ* Washington GS Co Durham, Girton Coll Cambridge (scholar, BA); *m* 1, 1968 (m dis 1997); 2 s (Nicholas William b 7 Dec 1970, Matthew Jonathan b 18 July 1972), 1 da (Rebecca Mary b 2 June 1974); m 2, 2005, Edmund Stephen Cook; *Career* teacher/researcher Zambia 1968–71, advice worker S London 1974–81, gen sec Jt Cncl for the Welfare of Immigrants 1986–92 (research offr 1981–86), dir Justice 1992–2001, HM chief inspr of prisons 2001–; memb C of E Race and Community Relations Ctee 1990–94, chair of tstees Refugee Legal Centre 1994–97; memb: Advsy Cncl NCVO, Lord Chancellor's Advsy Ctee on Legal Educn and Conduct 1997–99, Crown Office Review Team 1999–2000, Home Office Task Force on Implementation of the Human Rights Act 1999–2001, Legal Services Consultative Panel 2000–01; Hon Dr Univ of Essex; hon fell: Southwark Univ, Lucy Cavendish Coll Cambridge; *Books* Human Rights in the UK (contrib, 1990), Strangers and Citizens (contrib, 1994), Humane Prisons (contrib, 2006); *Recreations* theatre, music, friends and family; *Style—* Ms Anne Owers, CBE

OWSLEY-BROWN, Matthew Charles; s of Rev Michael Cunningsby Brown, and Elaine, *née* Owen; *b* 5 July 1962; *Educ* St John's Sch Leatherhead, Godalming Sixth Form Coll, Westminster Coll; *m*; 2 c; *Career* chef; formerly mktg exhibitions mangr Heinemann Educnl Books 1982–85; commis chef The Brasserie 1985, pt/t commis chef Inn on the Lake 1986–89, first commis chef Mosimann's 1989–90, sous chef Corney & Barrow 1990–93, chef de partie The Seafood Restaurant 1993–94, head chef and co-fndr The Stepping Stone Restaurant 1994–95; Fifth Floor Café Harvey Nichols: sous chef 1995–96, head chef 1996–2000; head chef Noble Rot 2000–01, chef and prop Fishes 2001–; *Recreations* photography, cycling, surfing, sailing, cooking; *Style—* Matthew Owsley-Brown, Esq; ✉ Fishes, Market Place, Burnham Market, Norfolk PE31 8HE (tel 01328 738588)

OWUSU, Elsie Margaret Akua; OBE (2003); da of Paul Kofi Owusu (d 1971), and Joyce Ophelia, *née* Biney; *b* 9 December 1953; *Educ* AA Sch of Architecture; *Children* 1 da (Kesewa Hennessy b 13 Dec 1971); *Career* architect; in private practice Elsie Owusu Architects 1986–, ptnr Feilden and Mawson LLP 2006–; arts projects incl: International Centre for Performing Arts, Contemporary African Art Gallery Greenwich, Global Trade Centre Offices and gallery space; major projects incl: International Centre for Performing Arts, Contemporary African Art Gallery, Global Trade Centre, E London Black Women's Centre, Palatine Road Centre Hackney, UK Supreme Ct interior design, Lagos Bus Rapid Transit System, Accra Bus Rapid Transit System; numerous housing schemes incl: Ebony House Neasden, Lido Square Haringey, Rendlesham Road Hackney, John Kallis Court Oxford, Mulgrave Street Development Liverpool, Hughes House Oxford; community centres incl East London Black Women's Centre; lectr in architecture Poly of N London and of E London 1986–90; fndr memb and chair Soc of Black Architects 1990–92, chair Housing Corpn Race in Housing Gp 1991–92, fndn memb Black Int Construction Orgn 1996–, acting chair Aduna 2006–, ambass Creative Partnerships 2006–; memb: Architects' Team: Solon SE Housing Assoc 1981–85, Women's Design Serv 1985–86, Exec Ctee Fedn of Black Housing Orgns 1994–96 (sec 1987), Educnl Visiting Bd RIBA 1995–97, Creative Britain Panel Design Cncl 1997, Cncl Nat Tst 2001–04, Bd Arts Cncl England 2002–, Enabling Panel Cmmn for Architecture and the Built Environment 2003–; assessor: Civic Tst Awards 1997, Design Cncl Millennium Products Awards 1998–; vice-pres Women's Tport Seminar 2005–; cmmr Haringey Employment Cmmn 1996; govr: Middx Univ 1998, Coll of NE London 1998–2000; various TV appearances incl: presenter Who Pays the Piper (Channel 5 series on architecture) 1997, presenter and panel memb Zeitgeist (Channel 4) 1998; RIBA; *Publications* Accommodating Diversity (jtly, 1993), Building E=Quality (ed and jt author, 1996); *Recreations* walking, reading, drawing, dreaming; *Style—* Ms Elsie Owusu, OBE

OXBURGH, Baron (Life Peer UK 1999), of Liverpool in the County of Merseyside; Sir (Ernest) Ronald Oxburgh; KBE (1992); *b* 2 November 1934; *Educ* Liverpool Inst, UC Oxford (BA), Princeton Univ (Sir John Dill fell, Class of 1897 fell, PhD); *m* 1958; 3 c; *Career* Univ of Oxford: demonstrator and lectr in geology 1960–78, official fell and tutor St Edmund Hall 1964–78 (admissions tutor 1965–77), vice-chm then chm Faculty of Physical Scis 1975–78; Univ of Cambridge: professorial fell Trinity Hall 1978–82, prof of mineralogy and petrology 1978–91, head Dept of Mineralogy and Petrology 1978–80, head Dept of Earth Sciences 1980–88, pres Queens' Coll 1982–89, hon prof Dept of Earth Scis Univ of Cambridge 2001–; chief scientific advsr MOD 1988–93 (chm inquiry into safety of UK nuclear weapons 1991), rector ICSTM 1993–2001; visiting prof: Caltech 1967–68, Cornell Univ 1967–68, 1973–74 and 1986, Stanford Univ 1973–74; Sherman Fairchild distinguished visiting scholar Caltech 1985–86, Allan Cox distinguished visiting prof Stanford Univ 1987; chm: Royal Soc Working Pty on Support of Geophysics 1984–85, Univ Grants Ctee Review of Earth Sciences 1986–87, UK Inter-agency Ctee on the Environment and Global Change 1994–97, Non-Exec Bd Centre for Defence Analysis 1995–97, Int Panel to review future of med educn Singapore 2000–01, SETNET 2002–05; assessor Advsy Bd for the Research Cncls 1988–90; memb: Cncl Royal Soc 1987–89, Advsy Cncl for Sci and Technol 1988–92, SERC 1988–93, NERC 1988–93, Univ and Polys Grants Ctee for Hong Kong 1989–2002, Conseil Scientifique pour l'Enseignement Superieur Paris 1992–94, Cmmn of Inquiry on the future of Oxford Univ 1994–97, EPSRC Users' Panel 1994–97, Cncl for Industry and HE 1994–2000, Cncl Parly Office on Sci and Technol 1995–, Nat Academies Policy Advsy Gp Working Pty on the future of the res base 1995–96, Nat Ctee of Inquiry into HE (Dearing Ctee) 1996–97, Cncl Fndn for Sci and Technol 1996–, Int Academic Advsy Panel Singapore 1997–2002, Conseil d'Administration Ecole Polytechnique France 1997–2002, Cncl Asian Univ of Sci and Technol 1997, Conseil Nat de la Sci Miny of Educn, Research and Technol France 1998–, House of Lords Select Ctee on Sci and Technol 1999– (chm 2001–05), Nat Econ Devpt Bd for Singapore 2001; sometime memb: Cncl Geological Soc, Editorial Bd Geological Soc, Editorial Bd Jl of Geophysical Research, Editorial Bd Sci and Public Affrs, Governing Body Northern House Sch Oxford, A C Irvine Fund Tstees, NERC Geological Scis Trg Awards Ctee (also chm), NERC Univ Affrs Ctee, Mgmnt Ctee Oxford Colls' Admissions Office, various ctees of Royal Soc and Univ of London; non-exec dir:

O

Hammersmith Hosps NHS Tst 1994–97, UK Nirex Ltd 1996–97, Shell Transport & Trading Co plc 1996– (chm 2004–05); advsr Climate Change Capital 2005–; tstee Nat History Museum 1993– (chm of tstees 1999–2002); memb: Cncl RCA 1993–2001, Cncl Winston Churchill Tst 1995–, Ct Univ of Leicester 1996–2000; foreign corr: Geologische Bundesanstalt Austria 1969, Geological Soc of Vienna 1972; advsr Low Carbon Accelerator 2006–, chm D1Oils plc 2007–, chm 2OC 2007–; Lyell Fund Award Geological Soc of London 1969, Bigsby Medal Geological Soc 1979, Sir Peter Kent lecture Geological Soc 1995; dr (hc): Univ of Paris VI-VII 1986, Univ of Leicester 1990, Loughborough Univ 1991, Univ of Edinburgh 1994, Univ of Birmingham 1996, Univ of Liverpool 1996, Univ of Southampton 2003, Lingnan Univ Hong Kong 2006, Liverpool JOhn Moores Univ 2006, Univ of Newcastle 2007; hon fell: Trinity Hall Cambridge 1982, University Coll Oxford 1983, St Edmund Hall Oxford 1986, Queens' Coll Cambridge 1992, City & Guilds of London Inst 1996; pres: Euro Union of Geosciences 1985–87 (former chm Editorial Bd), Br Assoc for the Advancement of Sci 1995–96, Geological Soc of London 2000–02; corresponding memb: Venezuelan Acad of Scis 1989, Australian Acad of Scis 1999; memb Deutsche Akademie der Naturforscher Leopoldina 1994, foreign assoc US Acad of Sci 2001; fell Geological Soc of America 1971, fell American Geophysical Union 1981, fndn memb Academia Europaea 1988; Hon FIMechE 1993, Hon FREng 2000; FRS 1978; Amigo de Venezuela 1995, Officier dans l'Ordre des Palmes Académiques 1995; *Publications* author of numerous articles and papers published in learned jls; *Recreations* mountaineering, orienteering, theatre, reading, repairing old cars; *Style—* The Rt Hon the Lord Oxburgh, KBE; ✉ House of Lords, London SW1A 0PW (e-mail oxburghe@parliament.uk)

OXFORD, 42 Bishop of (1542) 2007–; Rt Rev John Lawrence Pritchard; patron of over 116 livings and the Archdeaconries of Oxford, Buckingham and Berks; the Bishopric was originally endowed with lands of dissolved monasteries by Henry VIII, but in Elizabeth I's reign many of these were removed from it; s of Neil Lawrence Pritchard (d 1999), of Lyndhurst, Hants, and Winifred Mary Coverdale, *née* Savill (d 1991); *b* 22 April 1948; *Educ* Arnold Sch Blackpool, St Peter's Coll Oxford (MA, DipTh), Ridley Hall Cambridge (Cert Pastoral Theol), St John's Coll Durham (MLitt); *m* 1972, Susan Wendy, da of George Edward Claridge; 2 da (Amanda Kate b 27 May 1976, Nicola Clare b 3 Nov 1977); *Career* asst curate St Martin's in the Bull Ring Birmingham 1972–76, diocesan youth chaplain and asst dir of religious educn Bath and Wells Dio 1976–79, vicar Wilton Parish Taunton 1980–88, warden Cranmer Hall St John's Coll Durham 1993–96 (dir of pastoral studies 1989–93), archdeacon of Canterbury 1996–2001, bishop of Jarrow 2002–07; memb: Gen Synod C of E 1999–2001, Bd Church Army 2005–; pres Guild of Health 2005–; *Books* Practical Theology in Action (1996), The Intercessions Handbook (1997), Beginning Again (2000), Living the Gospel Stories Today (2001), How to Pray (2002), The Second Intercessions Handbook (2004), Living Easter Through the Year (2005), How to Explain your Faith (2006), The Life and Work of a Priest (2007); *Recreations* fell walking, photography, music, travel, reading, writing, cricket; *Style—* The Rt Rev the Bishop of Oxford; ✉ Bishop's House, 27 Linton Road, Oxford OX2 6UL (tel 01865 208222, e-mail bishopoxon@oxford.anglican.org)

OXFORD AND ASQUITH, 2 Earl of (UK 1925); Sir Julian Edward George Asquith; KCMG (1964, CMG 1961); also Viscount Asquith (UK 1925); s of Raymond Asquith (ka the Somme 1916; s of the Lib PM, Rt Hon Sir Herbert Henry Asquith, KG, later 1 Earl (d 1928)), and Katharine Frances (d 1976), da of Sir John Horner, KCVO (d 1927); *b* 22 April 1916; *Educ* Ampleforth, Balliol Coll Oxford (MA); *m* 28 Aug 1947, Anne Mary Celestine, CStJ (d 1998), da of late Sir Michael Palairet, KCMG; 2 s, 3 da; *Heir* s, Viscount Asquith, OBE; *Career* 2 Lt RE 1940; sat as Independent in House of Lords until 1999; asst dist cmmr Palestine Admin 1942–48, dep chief sec Br Admin Tripolitania 1949, dir of the Interior Tripolitanian Govt 1951, advsr to PM of Libya 1952, admin sec Zanzibar 1955, admin St Lucia 1958–61, govr and C-in-C Seychelles 1962–67, and cmmr Br Indian Ocean Territory 1965–67, constitutional cmmr Cayman Islands 1971, constitutional cmmr Turks and Caicos Islands 1973–74; KStJ; *Style—* The Rt Hon the Earl of Oxford and Asquith, KCMG; ✉ The Manor House, Mells, Frome, Somerset BA11 3PN (tel 01373 812324)

OXLEY, Julian Christopher; s of Horace Oxley (d 1958), of Newnham-on-Severn, Glos, and Lilian Alexandra Frances, *née* Harris (d 1985); *b* 23 November 1938; *Educ* Clifton (open scholar), Oriel Coll Oxford (organ scholar, MA); *m* 1, 1964, Carolyn, *née* Simpson; 2 da (Vivienne b 1966, Suzanne b 1967), 1 s (Martin b 1971); *m* 2, 1979, Carol, *née* Heath; 1 da (Joanna b 1985), 2 step da (Lisa b 1960, Sarah b 1964); *Career* articled clerk Deloitte Haskins & Sells (Chartered Accountants) 1961–64 (audit mangr 1964–66), chief accountant and sec Pressweld Ltd 1966–68, fin dir and sec Williams & James Ltd (later plc) 1971–84 (fin controller 1968–71), DG The Guide Dogs for the Blind Assoc 1989–96 (dir of admin and sec 1984–89); chm Int Fedn of Guide Dog Schools 1990–97; dir Heatherwood and Wexham Park Hosps Tst 1999–2006; tstee Nat Confedn of Parent Teacher Assocs (NCPTA) 2002– (chm 2004–); FCA 1965; *Recreations* music, old furniture, railway signalling; *Style—* Julian Oxley, Esq; ✉ Holden Fold, Lower Dawlish Water, Devon EX7 0QN (tel 01626 866877, fax 01626 866685, e-mail julian.oxley@btinternet.com)

ÖZVEREN, Ali Evrenay; s of Hamdi Özveren (d 1992), of Ankara, Turkey, and Zehra, *née* Zincirci (d 1992); *b* 6 October 1945; *Educ* Ankara Coll, Dept of Architecture Middle East Tech Univ Ankara (BArch); *m* 13 Nov 1976, Susan Catherine, da of Arthur Frank William Gimbert; 1 s (Jan Emil b 28 Dec 1979); *Career* GMW Architects London: joined as architectural asst 1970, completed univ educn in Turkey, assoc 1979, ptnr 1984, a sr ptnr 1991, conslt 2005, md GMW Architects Istanbul 2005–; built projects in London incl: Royal Mail (S London Postal Sorting Office Battersea), Wates City of London Properties (City Tower Basinghall St), Vestey Estates (34 Leadenhall St), Sun Alliance Group Properties (1 King William St), Land Securities (Regis House King William/Monument St), Gt Portland Estates (95 New Cavendish St); award-winning overseas projects incl: Wholesale Food Market Dubai, Retail Food Market Dubai, New Int Terminal Istanbul Atatürk Airport, New Domestic and Int Terminals Ankara Esenboga Airport and Mugla Dalaman Airport Turkey, Cerruti Hotel Istanbul; registered memb Chamber of Architects of Turkey 1971; FCSD 1992, FRSA 1995; *Recreations* modern art, travel, opera; *Style—* Ali Özveren, Esq; ✉ GMW Architects, PO Box 1613, 239 Kensington High Street, London W8 6SL (tel 020 7937 8020, fax 020 7937 5815, e-mail ali.ozveren@gmw-architects.com)

P

PACE, Franco Giustino; s of Edmondo Pace (d 1959); *b* 28 September 1927; *Educ* Bologna Univ (doctorate in industrial engrg), Milan Univ (postgrad specialisation in chemistry); *m* 1955, Maria Vittoria, da of Dr Ing Salvatore Picchetti, of Italy; 1 s (Valerio); *Career* chm: Montefibre UK Ltd 1974–89, Acna UK Ltd 1976–88, Cedar Service UK Ltd 1982–88, Internike Ltd 1984–88, Selm International Ltd 1986–88, Rubber and Chemicals Ltd 1989–2001, Euroil Exploration Ltd 1989–, Ausimont UK Ltd 1991–2003; dir: Montedison UK Ltd 1973–89, Polyamide Intermediates Ltd 1974–83, Farmitalia Carlo Erba Ltd 1990–93, Himont UK Subsidiary Ltd 1987–95, Montell Milton Keynes Ltd 1987–95, Accademia Italiana 1989–91; Italian C of C for GB: vice-pres 1981–88, sec-gen 1988–94; Commendatore al merito della Repubblica Italiana 1987; *Clubs* Hurlingham; *Style—* Franco G Pace, Esq; ✉ 10 Kensington Court Gardens, London W8 5QE (tel 020 7937 7143); Euroil Exploration Limited, 93–99 Upper Richmond Road, Putney, London SW15 2TG (tel 020 8788 0224, fax 020 8780 2871)

PACHACHI, Reema; da of Dr Adnan Pachachi, and Selwa Ali, *née* Jawdat; *b* 10 April 1951; *Educ* Brearley Sch NY, UN Sch NY, Central Sch of Art & Design (BA), RCA (MA, Anstruther award); *m* 14 Dec 1977, John William Dennis; 2 s (Said b 26 Jan 1981, Kareem b 23 May 1986), 1 da (Aisha b 23 Nov 1983); *Career* jewellery designer; visiting lectr Central St Martin's and Dundee Coll of Art; opened own shop 1994, sells collections internationally through major department stores and fashion boutiques, creates individual pieces for private customers; designer and creative dir De Beers 2002–04 *Exhibitions* Passing Out (Goldsmiths' Hall London) 1979, Arnolfini Gallery Bristol 1979, Ehrman Gallery London 1980, Artwear NY 1980, New Faces (Br Crafts Centre London) 1981, Jugend Gestaltet Munich 1981, Loot (Goldsmiths' Hall London) 1981, British Women Artists (House of Commons) 1981, Dazzle (NT) 1981–82, New Ashgate Gallery Farnham Surrey 1982, Byzantium Gallery NY 1982 (Christmas Exhbn) and 1993 (Spring/Christmas Exhbn), Nat Assoc of Decorative & Fine Art Socs' Clothes and Jewellery Show 1985, Precious Elements (Usher Gallery Lincoln) 1986, Sotheby's Decorative Arts Award Exhbn London 1988, History of Contemporary Jewellery Exhbn (Sheehan Gallery Washington) 1991; exhibits twice a year during London Fashion week; work in permanent collection of Crafts Cncl of GB (listed in their Index of Excellence); jewellery designs for Arabella Pollen and Geoffrey Beene; took part in a major 18ct gold project with Engelhard-Clal and World Gold Cncl; *Recreations* reading, dancing, swimming; *Style—* Ms Reema Pachachi

PACK, Stephen Howard John; s of Leonard Pack (d 1992), of London, and Isabel, *née* Heiser; *b* 26 April 1950; *Educ* Univ of Manchester (MA); *m* Cheryl, da of Albert Klyne; 1 da (Susannah b 15 Nov 1976), 1 s (Anthony b 12 Feb 1979); *Career* ptnr PricewaterhouseCoopers (formerly Price Waterhouse before merger) 1984– (joined 1972); FCA 1975; *Style—* Stephen Pack, Esq; ✉ PricewaterhouseCoopers, Southwark Towers, 32 London Bridge Street, London SE1 9SY (tel 020 7804 2828, e-mail steve.pack@uk.pwc.com)

PACKARD, Richard Bruce Selig; s of John Jacob Packard (d 1992), of Delray Beach, Florida, and (Priscilla) Lilian, *née* Joseph; *b* 20 February 1947; *Educ* Harrow, Middlesex Hosp Med Sch (MD, DO); *m* 1, 21 March 1974 (m dis 1986), Veronica Susan, da of Michael Bird, CBE (d 1991), of Esher, Surrey; 2 s (Rupert Alexander b 1978, Hugo Philip b 1980), 1 da (Elvira Rose b 1984); m 2, 24 April 1986, Fiona Catherine, da of Walter F Kinnear (d 1997), of Kilspindie, Perthshire; 1 s (Ian Charles b 1990), 1 da (Lucy Catherine b 1992); *Career* specialist trg in ophthalmology; house surgn in ophthalmology Middx Hosp 1970; held various jr med appointments 1971–75, res surgical offr Moorfields Eye Hosp 1975–78, sr registrar in ophthalmology Charing Cross Hosp Fulham 1978–82, conslt ophthalmic surgn and clinical dir Prince Charles Eye Unit King Edward VII Hosp Windsor 1982–; clinical services unit dir of ophthalmology Berkshire 2004–; currently chm Cyclotron Tst for Cancer Treatment; past chm Oxford RHA Ophthalmology Sub-Ctee, UK rep Int Med Panel for the Advance of Cataract Treatment 1992–; memb American Acad of Ophthalmology, memb Cataract Clinical Ctee American Soc of Cataract and Refractive Surgery, memb Bd Euro Soc of Cataract and Refractive Surgery; FRCS 1976, FRCOphth 1991; *Books* Cataract and Lens Implant Surgery (jtly, 1985), Emergency Surgery (jtly, 1986), Manual of Cataract and Lens Implant Surgery (jtly, 1991), Phacoemulsification (jtly, 1994), Phaco 2000 (jtly, 1997), Complicated Phaco (jtly, 2000), Principles of Practice (jtly, 2002), Mastering the Art of Bimanual Microincisional Phaco Emulsification (jtly, 2005); *Recreations* fly fishing, wine, music; *Clubs* Garrick, MCC; *Style—* Richard Packard, Esq; ✉ Arnott Eye Associates, 22A Harley Street, London W1G 9BP (tel 020 7580 1074 and 020 7580 8792, fax 020 7255 1524, e-mail post@arnotteye.com, website www.arnotteye.com)

PACKER, Jane; da of Maurice Packer, of Chadwell St Mary, and Brenda Packer; *b* 22 September 1959, Chadwell St Mary; *m* 20 July 1990, Gary Wallis; 2 c (Rebby b 28 Aug 1991, Lola b 9 Sept 1993); *Career* florist; opened Jane Packer Flowers: James Street London 1981, St John's Wood London 1994, Marylebone London 1995, NY 2001, Seoul S Korea 2001 and 2002, Tokyo 2001 and 2002; opened Jane Packer Sch of Flowers: London 1989, Tokyo 1990; launched: branded products 1990, ceramics 1995 (winner Top Drawer exhbn award London 1995), fragrance, ceramics and glassware 2000, International Greetings stationary 2004; conslt M&S horticulture 1987–2000, part of Designers At Debenhams 2001–; lectr tours: Europe 1988–89, USA 1989 and 1995, Japan 1991–98, UK 1996–98, France 1998; Spring lectr Cultural Centre Tokyo 1993; keynote speaker: American Soc of Perfumers NY 2002, Walters Museum Baltimore 2004, Hortifair Amsterdam 2004; Jane Packer Tulip developed by Vandershoot Holland 1997; Prince Phillip Medal 2005; *Commissions* incl: bridal flowers for HRH the Duke and Duchess of York 1986, BBC TV 1992; Marks and Spencer at RHS Hampton Court Flower Show: stand 1991–92 (award winner 1991–92), garden 1993–98, (RHS Gold Medal winner 1993–97, RHS Silver Medal 1998); *Television* reg appearances on BBC, ITV, Carlton, GMTV, Thames and American television 1986–; reg appearance Good Morning (BBC) 1995; subject of documentary (BBC) 1996, presenter The Flower Show (BBC) 1998, Big in Japan (six part series, BBC Style) 1999; *Publications* Celebrating With Flowers (1986), Flowers For All Seasons: Spring, Summer, Autumn, Winter (four part work, 1989), New Flower Arranging (1993), A Complete Guide (1994), Living With Flowers (1995), Fast Flowers 1998, Flowers, Design, Philosophy (1999), World Flowers (2003), Colour (2007); *Style—* Ms Jane Packer; ✉ 32–34 New Cavendish Street, London W1G 8UE (tel 020 7935 0787, fax 020 7935 2135, e-mail office@janepacker.com)

PACKER, Rt Rev John Richard; *see:* Ripon and Leeds, Bishop of

PACKER, Sir Richard John; KCB (2000); s of George Charles Packer (d 1979), and Dorothy May Packer (d 1993); *b* 18 August 1944; *Educ* City of London Sch, Univ of Manchester (BSc, MSc); *m* 1, Alison Mary, *née* Sellwood; 2 s (James b 1969, George b 1971), 1 da (Rachel b 1973); m 2, Lucy Jeanne Neville-Rolfe, CMG, *qv*, da of Edmund Neville-Rolfe, of Tisbury, Wilts; 4 s (Thomas b 1981, William b 1984, Harry b 1988, Samuel b 1994); *Career* MAFF: joined 1967, asst princ, first sec Office of UK Representative to EC 1973–76, princ private sec Minister 1976–78, asst sec 1979, under sec 1985, dep sec 1989, perm sec 1993–2000; dir ABM Chemicals 1985–86, non-exec dir Arla Foods (UK) plc 2002–07; jt ed Source Public Mgmnt Jl 2001–02; *Publications* The Politics of BSE (2006); *Recreations* many sporting and intellectual interests; *Style—* Sir Richard Packer, KCB; ✉ 113 St George's Road, London SE1 6HY (tel 020 7928 6819)

PACKER, Robin John; s of Edwin James Packer, and Alma, *née* Lodge; *b* 6 May 1948; *Educ* Catford Sch; *m* 1 Aug 1970, Diane Irana, da of Kenneth Derek Jones; 2 da (Melanie b 28 Dec 1973, Natalie b 1 Aug 1977); *Career* de Zoete & Gordon 1964–66, Govett Sons 1966–74, Cazenove 1974–76; Wood MacKenzie & Co: joined 1976, ptnr 1984–87, dir 1986–87; joined UBS Phillips & Drew 1987, currently a md UK equities Warburg Dillon Read (formerly UBS Ltd); memb local Cons Assoc; MSI; *Recreations* golf, game fishing; *Style—* Robin Packer, Esq; ✉ Southfields, Telegraph Hill, Higham by Rochester, Kent ME3 7NW (tel 01634 721420); Warburg Dillon Read, 100 Liverpool Street, London EC2 (direct tel 020 7901 1386)

PACKER, William John; s of Rex Packer, and Molly, *née* Wornham; *b* 19 August 1940; *Educ* Windsor GS, Wimbledon Coll of Art, Brighton Coll of Art; *m* 1965, Ursula Mary Clare, er da of Thomas Winn; 3 da (Charlotte, Claudia, Katherine); *Career* painter and art critic; first exhibited Royal Acad 1963, numerous exhibitions since incl one-man exhibitions Piers Feetham Gallery 1996, 2001 and 2004, two-man show (with William Feaver) Piers Feetham Gallery 2005; art critic Financial Times 1974–; selector of several exhibitions including Arts Cncl's first Br Art Show 1979–80; served on juries of many open exhibitions incl: John Moores Liverpool Exhibition, John Player Portrait Award, Hunting Prize; teacher 1964–67, pt/t art school teacher 1967–77; memb: Fine Art Bd CNAA 1976–83 (special advsr 1983–87), Advsy Ctee to Govt Art Collection 1977–84, Crafts Cncl 1980–87, Cncl AGBI, Cncl Nat Tst Fndn for Art, New English Art Club; Hon FRCA, Hon RBA, Hon FRBS; *Books* The Art of Vogue Covers (1980), Fashion Drawing in Vogue (1983), Henry Moore, A Pictorial Biography (1985), René Bouët-Willaumez (1989), Carl Erickson (1989), John Houston (2003), Tai-Shan Schierenberg (2005); *Recreations* bookshops; *Clubs* Chelsea Arts, Garrick; *Style—* William Packer, Esq; ✉ 60 Trinity Gardens, London SW9 8DR

PACKHAM, Jenny; da of Colin Packham, of Southampton, and Marion Rita, *née* Smith; *b* 11 March 1965; *Educ* Bitterne Park Sch Southampton, Southampton Art Coll (DA TEC) St Martin Sch of Art London (BA, RSA bursary award and fellowship); *Partner* Mathew John Anderson; 2 da (Georgia Packham Anderson b 8 Nov 1993, Isabella Packham Anderson b 3 Jan 1998); *Career* fashion designer specialising in catwalk, evening and bridal wear; clients incl: Harrods, Selfridges, Liberty, Saks, H Lorenzo & Kitsons (USA), Podium and Style Boutique (Russia), The Link (Singapore), Swank Shop (Hong Kong); eight Condè Nast Brides and Setting Up Home awards incl: New Designer Award 1993, Informal Award 1996, New Direction Award 1996, New Glamour Couture Award 1997; winner: Weddings Abroad 1998, Slim Silhouette 1998, British Bridal Award Informal 1999; FRSA; *Recreations* contemporary American art, travel, yoga, scuba diving, extreme sports; *Style—* Ms Jenny Packham; ✉ Jenny Packham London Ltd, Unit A, Spectrum House, 32–34 Gordon House Road, London NW5 1LB (tel 020 7267 1864)

PACKMAN, Martin John; s of Ivan Desmond Packman, of Addington, Surrey, and Joan Emily, *née* Cook (d 1982); *b* 29 April 1949; *Educ* Simon Langton GS Canterbury, Lancaster Univ (MA); *m* 17 Dec 1978 (m dis), Lyn, da of James Green, of Holt, Norfolk; 1 s (Myles b 1980), 1 da (Charlotte b 1984); *Career* corp fin dir Baring Bros International Ltd 1987–98 (joined 1984), a md Société Générale 1998–; tstee Nat Motor Museum Beaulieu; FCA 1973; *Books* UK Companies Operating Overseas - Tax and Financing Strategies (jtly, 1981); *Recreations* tennis, opera; *Style—* Martin Packman, Esq; ✉ 14 Fore Street, Old Hatfield, Hertfordshire AL9 5AH (tel 01707 259752); Societe Generale, SG House, 41 Tower Hill, London EC3N 4SG (tel 020 7676 642)

PACKSHAW, Charles Max; s of Savile Packshaw (d 1969), and Muriel, *née* Newton; *b* 30 January 1952; *Educ* Westminster, Univ of Bristol (BSc), London Business Sch (MSc); *m* 9 July 1983, Helena Mary, da of Peter Youngman; 2 s (Harry b 1984, Edward b 1987), 1 da (Olivia b 1989); *Career* with Costain 1973–78, sr conslt Cresap 1980–84, md Lazard Bros Co Ltd (joined 1984) until 2002, head of UK corp fin HSBC Bank plc 2002–; non-exec dir: City Centre Restaurants plc 1996–2001, Diagonal plc 2002–04; CEng, MICE 1978; *Style—* Charles Packshaw, Esq

PADGHAM, Hugh Charles; s of Charles Arthur Padgham, of Aylesbury, Bucks, and Ursula Mary, *née* Samuelson; *b* 15 February 1955; *Educ* The Beacon Sch Chesham Bois, St Edward's Sch Oxford; *Career* asst Advision Studios 1974–75, engr/asst Lansdowne Studios 1975–77, engr Townhouse Studios 1977–80, record prodr and engr 1980–; produced and engineered: Split Enz' Conflicting Emotions (A&M 1980) and Time and Tide (A&M 1982), The Police's Ghost in The Machine (A&M 1981, Platinum disc) and Synchronicity (A&M 1983, Platinum disc), Phil Collins' Face Value (Virgin 1983, 6 Platinum discs), No Jacket Required (Virgin 1985, Platinum disc), Hello I Must Be Going (Virgin 1988, Platinum disc) and But Seriously (Virgin 1989, 8 Platinum discs), Genesis' Genesis (Virgin 1983, 2 Platinum discs) and Invisible Touch (Virgin 1986, 4 Platinum discs), XTC's English Settlement (Virgin 1983, Silver disc), Human League's Hysteria (Virgin 1984, Gold disc), David Bowie's Tonight (EMI 1985, Gold disc), Paul Young's Between Two Fires (CBS 1986, Platinum disc), Paul McCartney's Press To Play (Parlaphone 1988, Gold disc), tracks from Julia Fordham's Porcelain (Circa 1989, Silver disc) and Julia Fordham (Circa 1988, Gold disc), Sting's The Soul Cages (A&M 1991) and Ten Summoner's Tales (A&M 1993), Melissa Etheridge's Yes I Am (Island 1993, Grammy 1995), Billy Pilgrim's (debut album, Atlantic 1994), Melissa Etheridge's Your Little Secret (Island Records 1995), Phil Collins' Dance into the Light (Atlantic/EW 1996), Bee Gees' 3 Tracks (A&M 1996), Beth Hart Band's Immortal (Lava/143 Records 1996), Sting's Mercury Falling (A&M 1996), Clannad's Lore (BMG/Atlantic 1996), Miyazawa's Sixteenth Moon (EMI Japan 1997), Kami Lyle's Blue Cinderella (MCA USA 1997);

P

engineered: XTC's Drums and Wires (Virgin 1979) and Black Sea (Virgin 1980), Genesis' Abacab (Virgin 1983, Gold disc), Peter Gabriel's The Third (Virgin 1986, Gold disc); mixed and produced McFly debut album 2003–04; mixed numerous singles/tracks incl: Hall and Oates' H2O (RCA 1982, Platinum disc), Sting's Nothing Like The Sun (A&M 1987, Platinum disc), Phil Collins' In The Air Tonight (Virgin 1988 remix, Gold disc), remix of Joan Armatrading's Love & Affection (A&M 1991), Trisha Yearwood's Walkaway Joe (MCA Int 1994), Self's Breakfast with Girls (Dreamworks/Spongebath 1998), McFly's Room on the Third Floor (debut album 2004, 2 Platinum discs); worked with various other artists incl: Mansun, Sheryl Crow, Tin Machine, Psychedelic Furs, Robbie Nevil, Kim Richey, Mark Joseph, The Tragically Hip; *Awards* Best British Producer Music Week Awards 1985 and 1990, Producer of the Year and Album of the Year Grammy Awards 1985, Best Producer nomination BPI Awards 1985 and 1986, Brit Awards Best Single 1989, Record of the Year Grammy Award 1990, Best Engineer Grammy Awards 1994, Billboard Tribute 1997; *Recreations* motor racing, tennis, cricket, skiing; *Style*— Hugh Padgham, Esq; ✉ c/o Universal Music Management, Bond House, 347–353 Chiswick High Road, London W4 4HA (tel 020 8742 5460, e-mail hughpadgham@compuserve.com)

PADMORE, Elaine Marguirite; da of Alfred Padmore (d 1971), and Florence, *née* Stockman; *b* 3 February 1947; *Educ* Newland HS Hull, Arnold Girls' Sch Blackpool, Univ of Birmingham (MA, BMus), Guildhall Sch of Music London; *Career* musician, singer, prodr, writer and broadcaster; ed Music Dept OUP 1970–71, lectr in opera Royal Acad of Music 1972–85, radio prodr Music Dept BBC 1971–76, chief prodr opera BBC Radio 1976–82, announcer BBC Radio 3 1982–90; artistic dir: Wexford Festival Opera 1982–94, Classical Productions (UK) Ltd 1990–92, London Opera Festival 1991, Opera Ireland (formerly Dublin Grand Opera Soc) 1991–93, Royal Danish Opera 1993–2000; dir of opera ROH 2000–; Sunday Independent Award for servs to music in Ireland 1987; Knight of the Order of the Dannebrog (Denmark) 1994; *Books* Wagner (Great Composers series), New Grove Dictionary of Music and Musicians (contrib); *Recreations* gardening, cats; *Style*— Miss Elaine Padmore; ✉ Royal Opera House, Covent Garden, London WC2E 9DD

PADMORE, Peter Sheldon; s of Sheldon Leslie Padmore (d 1994), of Lyndhurst, Hants, and Eileen Mary, *née* Staley (d 1979); *b* 17 September 1940; *Educ* Southwell Minster GS, Brockenhurst Co HS; *m* 19 Feb 1966, Jennifer Christobel, da of Harry Arthur Rice-Adams (d 1996); 1 s (Robert Sheldon), 1 da (Jane Elizabeth); *Career* PricewaterhouseCoopers (formerly Price Waterhouse before merger): joined 1967, ptnr 1976–, managing ptnr Southampton 1992–2000; govr Pilgrims' Sch 2005–; FCA, MIPA; *Recreations* golf, gardening, music; *Clubs* MCC, Reform, Royal Southampton Yacht; *Style*— Peter Padmore, Esq; ✉ Downsway, Dummer, Basingstoke, Hampshire (tel 01256 397226)

PADOVAN, John Mario Faskally; s of Dr Umberto Mario Padovan (d 1966); *b* 7 May 1938; *Educ* St George's Coll Weybridge, King's Coll London (LLB), Keble Coll Oxford (BCL); *m* 1963, Sally Kay; 3 s; *Career* chartered accountant Price Waterhouse 1963; County Bank Ltd: chief exec 1976–83, dep chm 1982, chm 1984; exec dep chm Hambros Bank Ltd 1984–86, dep chm Barclays de Zoete Wedd Ltd 1986–91; chm: AAH plc 1993–95 (dep chm 1992), Gardner Merchant Services Group Ltd 1993–95, Furniture Village plc 1998–2001, Schroder Split Fund plc 2000– (dir 1993–2000), Williams Lea Group Ltd 2001–04 (non-exec dir 1992–97, dep chm 1997–2000), Dawnay, Day Property Finance Group 2004–; dir: Tesco plc 1982–94, de Zoete & Bevan Ltd 1986–92, The Hartstone Group plc 1991–97, Whitbread plc 1992–2002, Evans of Leeds plc 1993–99 (chm 1997–99), Broadgate Properties plc 1994–96, Interserve plc 1996–2005 (dep chm 2003–05), Findel plc 1996–, HFC Bank plc 1997–2003; memb Ct of Assts Worshipful Co of Drapers (Master 1999–2000); *Style*— John Padovan, Esq; ✉ 15 Lord North Street, London SW1P 3LD

PAGAN, Hugh Edmund; s of Francis Edmund Pagan (d 2002), of London, and Margaret Jocelyn, *née* Neel (d 1971); *b* 4 October 1944; *Educ* Westminster, ChCh Oxford (MA); *m* 15 Feb 1974, Jill, da of Robert William Charles Catling, of Manchester; 2 s (Robert Edmund b 1974, Thomas Helier b 1978); *Career* antiquarian bookseller; dir B Weinreb Architectural Books Ltd 1978–87, md Hugh Pagan Ltd 1987–; jt ed Br Numismatic Jl 1971–76; Br Numismatic Soc: memb Cncl 1969–76 and 1979–, pres 1984–88, vice-pres 1992–, John Sanford Saltus Gold medal 1989; vice-chm Prep/Organising Ctee Int Numismatic Congress London 1986, memb Br Acad Ctee for Sylloge of Coinage of the Br Isles 1988–; fell Royal Numismatic Soc 1976 (memb Cncl 1981–84), FSA 1986; *Publications* Royal Numismatic Soc 150th Anniversary publication (jtly, 1986), contrib to volumes on Anglo-Saxon coinage, contrib articles in British Numismatic Journal; *Recreations* British political history; *Clubs* Garrick; *Style*— Hugh Pagan, Esq, FSA

PAGAN, Jill Catling; da of Robert William Charles Catling (d 1967), of Manchester, and Edna Catling (d 1978); *Educ* Loreburn Coll, Inns of Court Sch of Law; *m* 15 Feb 1974, Hugh Edmund, s of Francis Edmund Pagan, of Albany, London; 2 s (Robert b 27 Dec 1974, Thomas b 17 Jan 1978); *Career* called to the Bar Inner Temple 1972; int tax conslt: Tansley Witt & Co 1975–79, Thomson McLintock KMG 1980–82; practised at Revenue Bar 1982–89, int tax conslt J F Chown & Co Ltd 1989–92, memb Panel of Experts IMF 1992–, conslt OECD 1993; dir Hugh Pagan Ltd 1987–; contrib ed International Tax Report 1982–95, founding ed Inner Temple Yearbook; author numerous articles on int fin, int and UK taxation; memb Bar Liaison Ctee Inner Temple 1985–90, memb Ctee UK Branch Int Fiscal Assoc 1985–98; *Books* Taxation Aspects of Currency Fluctuations (1983, 2 edn 1992), Transfer Pricing Strategy in a Global Economy (with J Scott Wilkie, 1993); *Recreations* family, tennis, travel; *Style*— Mrs Jill Pagan; ✉ 1 Trevor Street, Knightsbridge, London SW7 1DU (tel 020 7581 9733, e-mail jill@hughpagan.com)

PAGE, Adrienne May; QC (1999); da of late Gwythian Lloyd Page, and Betty, *née* Spring; *b* 14 July 1952; *Educ* Godolphin Sch Salisbury, Univ of Kent at Canterbury (BA); *m* 1983 (m dis 2007), Anthony Crichton Waldeck, s of Ivor Waldeck; 1 step s, 1 step da; *Career* called to the Bar Middle Temple 1974 (bencher 2003); practising barrister specialising in defamation, recorder (SE Circuit) 1999–2004; *Recreations* gardening; *Clubs* Beaulieu River Sailing; *Style*— Miss Adrienne Page, QC; ✉ 5 Raymond Buildings, Gray's Inn, London WC1R 5BP (tel 020 7242 2902, fax 020 7831 2686)

PAGE, Prof Alan Chisholm; s of Samuel Chisholm Page, of Broughty Ferry, and Betsy Johnston, *née* Melville; *b* 7 April 1952; *Educ* Grove Acad Broughty Ferry, Univ of Edinburgh (LLB), City Univ (PhD); *m* 16 Aug 1975, Sheila Duffus, da of Ian Dunlop Melville, of Glasgow; 1 s (Michael b 1983), 1 da (Rebecca b 1986); *Career* lectr in law Univ of Cardiff 1975–80; Univ of Dundee: sr lectr in law 1980–85, head Dept of Public Law 1981–86, prof of public law 1985–, head Dept of Law 1985–95 and 2004–06, dean Faculty of Law 1986–89, dean Sch of Law 2006–; memb Tax Law Review Ctee 1994–2004, lead assessor in law Scottish HE Funding Cncl 1995–96; *Books* Legislation (2 edn, 1990), Investor Protection (1992), The Executive in the Constitution (1999); *Recreations* mountaineering; *Style*— Prof Alan Page; ✉ Westlands, Westfield Road, Cupar, Fife (tel 01334 655576); School of Law, University of Dundee, Dundee DD1 4HN (tel 01382 384633, fax 01382 226905, e-mail a.c.page@dundee.ac.uk)

PAGE, Ashley John; *né* Laverty; OBE (2006); s of John Henry Laverty, of Gillingham, Kent, and Sheila Rachael, *née* Medhurst; *b* 9 August 1956; *Educ* St Andrew's Rochester, Royal Ballet Lower and Upper Sch; *m* Nicola Roberts; 1 s (Jordan Paris Gower Page b 14 July 1994), 1 da (Audrey Sabrina b 10 July 1998); *Career* Royal Ballet: joined 1976 (after trg with Educnl Unit Ballet for All 1975), soloist 1980, principal dancer 1984; roles incl many created specially by resident & visiting choreographers plus a wide variety within Royal Ballet's repertoire; professional choreographer initially with Royal Ballet Covent Garden 1984–, sr research fell Froebel Coll Roehampton Inst 1997–2001, artistic dir Scottish Ballet 2002–; first professional work A Broken Set of Rules (Royal Ballet) 1984, established as choreographer with leading composers, theatre and fashion designers, fine artists and sculptors; extensive work with Rambert Dance Co, and in Paris, Amsterdam, Istanbul and Ankara; other work incl: Fearful Symmetries (Royal Ballet) 1994 (winner Time Out Dance Award 1994 and Olivier Award for best new dance prodn 1994), Room of Cooks (nominated for Olivier Award for best new dance prodn 1998); *Style*— Ashley Page, Esq, OBE; ✉ Scottish Ballet, 261 West Princes Street, Glasgow G4 9EE (tel 0141 331 2931)

PAGE, Ben; s of Charles Page, of Exeter, and Elizabeth, *née* Barrett; *b* 9 January 1965, Exeter; *Educ* Exeter Coll, St John's Coll Oxford (BA); *m* 1994, Janet, *née* Pritchard; 1 s (Horace b 16 Aug 1995); *Career* MIL (later NOP) 1986–87; MORI: researcher and mangr 1987–95, dir/ptnr 1995–2000, dir MORI Social Research Inst 2001–05, chm Ipsos MORI Social Research Inst and md Ipsos MORI Public Affrs 2006–; memb Editorial Bd Int Jl of Market Research; cmmr CABE, memb Bd INVOLVE; prize for best research for business improvement Br Market Research Assoc 2001, Silver medal Market Research Soc 2005; memb: Social Research Assoc 2002–, Market Research Soc 2004–; FRSA 2003; *Recreations* Italy, art history, architecture, skateboarding, jazz; *Clubs* Bay 66 Skate Park, Ronnie Scott's; *Style*— Ben Page, Esq; ✉ Ipsos MORI, 79 Borough Road, London SE1 1FY (tel 020 7347 3242, fax 020 7347 3804, e-mail ben.page@mori.com)

PAGE, Dr Christopher Howard; s of Ewert Lacey Page, and Marie Victoria, *née* Graham; *b* 8 April 1952; *Educ* Sir George Monoux Sch, Univ of Oxford (MA), Univ of York (DPhil); *m* 1, 15 Sept 1975 (m dis 2003), Régine, *née* Fourcade; m 2, 18 Sept 2004, Anne, *née* Dunan; *Career* currently reader in medieval music and literature Univ of Cambridge, fell Sidney Sussex Coll Cambridge (formerly fell Jesus Coll Oxford); presenter Radio 3 series Spirit of the Age; ldr of the ensemble Gothic Voices and prodr of acclaimed records; Gramophone Early Music Records of the Year: Hildegard of Bingen 1983 (also Guardian Choral Record of the Year), The Service of Venus and Mars 1988, A Song for Francesca (1989); chm Nat Early Music Assoc, chm Plainsong and Medieval Music Soc, fell Fellowship of Makers and Restorers of Historical Instruments; *Books* Voices and Instruments of the Middle Ages (1987), Sequences of Hildegard of Bingen (1986), The Owl and the Nightingale (1989), Summa Musice (1991), Discarding Images (1994); *Recreations* research and performance; *Style*— Dr Christopher Page; ✉ Sidney Sussex College, Cambridge CB2 3HU

PAGE, Christopher John (Chris); s of Albert Harold Page (d 1987), and Doris May, *née* Clarke (d 2005); *b* 28 May 1947; *Educ* Eton House Sch, South Bank Poly (DipArch); *m* 7 July 1979, Janice Anne, da of late Andrew John Sharman, of Wickford, Essex; 1 s (Richard b 1981), 1 da (Jacqueline b 1984); *Career* architect/program mangr; md: Atlanta Program Management 1986–, Atlanta Interiors 1987–; chm Atlanta Signs, ptnr Chris Page Associates; *Recreations* sailing, sketching, pre-history in UK; *Clubs* Eton House Old Boys, Thorpe Bay Yacht; *Style*— Chris Page, Esq; ✉ 35 Challacombe, Thorpe Bay, Essex SS1 3TY (tel 01702 585710, fax 01702 300647, e-mail chrispage@blueyonder.co.uk, website www.worldarchitects.tv); Raycastle Centre, 12 Devonshire Square, London EC2M 4TE; 87A Calle Pinsa, Pollenca 07470, Mallorca, Spain

PAGE, David Norman; s of Bernard Page, of Edinburgh, and Catherine Page, *née* Adam; *b* 4 September 1957; *Educ* Bearsden Acad Strathclyde, Univ of Strathclyde (BSc, BArch); *Career* sr ptnr Page\Park Architects 1981–; lectr Dept of Architecture and Building Science Univ of Strathclyde 1982–94; hon prof Edinburgh Coll of Art, Hon Dr Univ of Strathclyde 2004; RSA; *Style*— David N Page, Esq; ✉ Page\Park Architects, The Italian Centre, 49 Cochrane Street, Glasgow (tel 0141 552 0686)

PAGE, Dianne; da of William John Griffiths Bryce, of Walton, Warks, and Audrey Jean, *née* Smith; *b* 14 May 1946; *Educ* Regis Sch Tettenhall, Wolverhampton Poly (Dip); *Career* Sulzer Brothers Switzerland 1965–66, Alusuisse UK 1966–72, Tower Housewares 1972–80, md Barkers Public Relations 1980–2002, exec chm McCann-Erickson Public Relations 2002–; chm Inst of Consumer Sciences; FIPR; *Books* Pressure Cooking Explained (1979), Slow Cooking Explained (1982), Food Processors Explained (1984); *Recreations* painting, theatre, opera; *Style*— Mrs Dianne Page; ✉ McCann-Erickson Public Relations, McCann House, Highlands Road, Solihull B90 4WE (tel 0121 713 3500)

PAGE, Prof Edward Charles; s of Edward Charles Page (d 1998), and Winifred Victoria Page; *b* 19 October 1953; *Educ* William Ellis GS, Kingston Poly (BA), Univ of Strathclyde (MSc, PhD); *m* Christine Mary, da of Henry Batty; 1 s (Martin Edward b 4 Oct 1979), 2 da (Miriam Victoria b 16 May 1984, Florence Carmel b 9 May 1987); *Career* lectr Univ of Strathclyde 1978–81, successively lectr, sr lectr, reader and prof of politics Univ of Hull 1981–2001, Sidney and Beatrice Webb prof of public policy LSE 2001–; visiting assoc prof Texas A&M Univ 1986–87; dir Future Governance Prog ESRC 1998–2004; FBA 2001; *Books* Political Authority and Bureaucratic Power: A Comparative Analysis (2 edn, 1992), Governing the New Europe (co-ed, 1995), People Who Run Europe (1997), Bureaucratic Elites in Western Europe (1999), Governing By Numbers: Delegated Legislation and Everyday Policy Making (2001), Policy Bureaucracy: Government with a Cast of Thousands (co-author, 2005); *Recreations* jazz; *Style*— Prof Edward Page; ✉ Department of Government, London School of Economics and Political Science, Houghton Street, London WC2A 2AE (tel 020 7849 4269, fax 020 7831 1707, e-mail e.c.page@lse.ac.uk)

PAGE, Emma; *Educ* Univ of Oxford (MA); *Children* 2 s, 1 da; *Career* detective writer; *Books* Final Moments (1987), A Violent End (1988), Deadlock (1991), Mortal Remains (1992), In The Event of My Death (1994), Murder Comes Calling (1995), Hard Evidence (1996), Intent to Kill (1998), Say it with Murder (2000) and others; *Style*— Ms Emma Page; ✉ c/o Constable Publishers, 3 The Lanchesters, 162 Fulham Palace Road, London W6 9ER (tel 020 8741 3663, fax 020 8748 7562)

PAGE, Gordon Francis de Courcy; CBE (2000), DL (Dorset 2006); s of Sir Frederick William Page, CBE (d 2005), and Lady Kathleen de Courcy Page (d 1993); *b* 17 November 1943; *Educ* Cheltenham Coll, St Catharine's Coll Cambridge (MA); *m* 29 March 1969, Judi, *née* Mays; 2 da (Rebecca b 28 March 1970, Fiona b 27 Sept 1973), 2 s (Damian b 30 Jan 1972, Christopher (twin) b 27 Sept 1973); *Career* with Rolls Royce plc 1962–89; Cobham plc: md flight refuelling 1990, gp dep chief exec 1991, gp chief exec 1992, chm 2001–; non-exec chm: FKI plc 2004–, Hamworthy plc 2004–; pres SBAC 1997–98 and 2002–03, chm Industrial Advsy Bd DTI; chm Bournemouth, Dorset and Poole Economic Partnership 2000–, govr Canford Sch 2003–; Hon DSc Cranfield Univ 2003; FInstD 1990, FRAeS 1994 (pres 2006), CCMI 1996 (pres 2002–03), FRSA 1999; *Recreations* theatre, gardening, classic cars; *Style*— Gordon Page, Esq, CBE, DL; ✉ Avon Reach, The Close, Avon Castle, Ringwood, Hampshire BH24 2BJ (tel 01425 475365, fax 01425 475680, mobile 07768 715501, e-mail gordon.page@btinternet.com); Cobham plc, Brook Road, Wimborne, Dorset BH21 2BJ (tel 01202 857448, fax 01202 842115, e-mail gordon.page@cobham.com)

PAGE, Prof (John) Graham; s of George Ronald Page (d 1966), and Lilian Alice, *née* Kay (d 1982); *b* 16 February 1943; *Educ* Robert Gordon's Coll Aberdeen, Univ of Aberdeen (MB ChB); *m* 30 Aug 1969, Sandra; 1 s (Andrew b 11 Jan 1972), 2 da (Caroline b 12 April 1974, Alison b 21 March 1977); *Career* prof of emergency med Aberdeen Royal Infirmary 1981– (house physician and surgn 1968–69, surgical registrar 1970–78), hon sr lectr in surgery Univ of Aberdeen 1981– (terminable lectr in pathology 1969–70), research fell Harvard Univ 1974–75, hon conslt Br Antarctic Survey Med Unit 1983–97;

memb: BMA, Edinburgh Royal Coll Surgns, Euro Undersea Baromedical Assoc; FRCS 1972, ChM 1977, FFOM 1998; *Books* with K L G Mills and R Morton: A Colour Atlas of Cardiopulmonary Resuscitation (1986), A Colour Atlas of Plaster Techniques (1986), A Colour Atlas and Text of Emergencies (1995); *Recreations* skiing, sailing; *Style*— Prof Graham Page; ✉ 16 Kingswood Avenue, Kingswells, Aberdeen AB15 8AE (tel 01224 742945); Aberdeen Royal Infirmary, Grampian University Hospitals Trust, Accident and Emergency Department, Aberdeen AB25 2ZN (tel 01224 681818 ext 53306, fax 01224 550718)

PAGE, Howard William Barrett; QC (1987); *b* 11 February 1943; *Educ* Radley, Trinity Hall Cambridge (MA, LLB); *m* Helen Joanna Page, LVO, *née* Shotter, 3 c; *Career* called to the Bar 1967, bencher Lincoln's Inn; dep pres Lloyd's Appeal Tbnl, cmmr Royal Court of Jersey; *Style*— Howard Page, QC; ✉ 6 New Square, Lincoln's Inn, London WC2A 3QS (tel 020 7242 6105, fax 020 7405 4004, e-mail clerks@serlecourt.co.uk, website www.serlecourt.co.uk)

PAGE, Sir (Arthur) John; kt (1984); s of Sir Arthur Page, QC (d 1958), late Chief Justice of Burma, and Margaret Page, K-i-H, *née* Symes Thompson; *b* 16 September 1919; *Educ* Harrow, Magdalene Coll Cambridge; *m* 9 Dec 1950, Anne Gertrude, da of Charles Micklem, DSO, JP, DL (d 1957); 4 s (Hugo b 1951, Nathaniel, Henry (twins) b 1953, Rupert b 1963); *Career* served WWII, gunner RA 1939, Maj Norfolk Yeo 1945, served ME (wounded), France and Ger; contested (Cons) Eton and Slough Gen Election 1959, MP (Cons) Harrow 1960–87, chm Cons Parly Lab Affairs Ctee 1970–74 (sec 1960–61, vice-chm 1964–69), memb Br Delegn to Cncl of Europe and WEU 1972–87; dir: Long & Hambly Ltd 1960–81, N Surrey Water Co 1988–98; chm: Frederick Clarke (Furnishings) Ltd 1955–88, Colne Valley Water Co 1987–90 (dir 1984–90), Three Valleys Water plc 1990–2001, Cncl for Ind Educn 1974–80, Groundwork Hertfordshire 1993–98; pres: Independent Schools Assoc 1971–83, Water Companies Assoc 1986–89; vice-pres British Insurance Brokers Assoc 1980–, elected substitute pres (Int) Inter-Parly Union 1983; Freeman City of London, Liveryman Worshipful Co of Grocers 1970; *Recreations* painting, politics, defending the Monarchy; *Clubs* Brooks's, MCC; *Style*— Sir John Page; ✉ Hitcham Lodge, Taplow, Maidenhead, Berkshire SL6 0HG (tel 01628 605056, fax 01628 666241)

PAGE, Michael Brian; s of James Gourlay Page, of Chester-le-Street, Co Durham, and Mary Jane, *née* McTeague; *b* 14 April 1937; *Educ* Chester-le-Street GS, Aston Univ (BSc Eng); *m* 1961, Jennifer Grace Elizabeth, da of Joseph Victor Wetton (d 1966); 3 da (Joanna b 1966, Kathryn b 1968, Sally b 1971); *Career* sales dir Brush Electrical Machines Ltd 1977–84; chm Hawker Siddeley Power Engrg Inc (USA) 1984–90, dir Hawker Siddeley Electric Ltd 1986–90, md Hawker Siddeley Power Engrg Ltd & assoc companies 1984–90 (conslt 1990–92), chm Hopyard Foundries Ltd 1992–97, dir Acorn Power Development (UK) Ltd 1997–, non-exec dir Leicester City West Primary Care Tst 2001–06; md: Allied Insulators Ltd 1992–97, Doulton Insulators Ltd 1992–97; cncllr: Charnwood BC 1999–2007, Leics CC 2001– (chm Pension Bd); govr: Wyggeston's Hosp, Hall Sch Glenfield; CEng, FIEE; *Recreations* golf, chess; *Clubs* Rothley Park Golf; *Style*— Michael Page, Esq; ✉ Blue Haze, 90 Station Road, Cropston, Leicestershire LE7 7HE (tel 0116 236 2527, fax 0116 236 7066, e-mail brianpage001@aol.com)

PAGE, Roy Malcolm; s of Alec Page (d 1980), and Janet, *née* Hutton (d 2003); *b* 24 June 1950, Surbiton, Surrey; *Educ* Wymondham HS, Thetford GS, Univ of Portsmouth (BSc), Univ of Reading (PGCE), Nat Coll for Sch Leadership (NPQH); *m* Aug 1973, Marilyn; 1 s (James Anthony b 2 April 1977), 1 da (Katie Louise b 24 April 1980); *Career* Royal GS High Wycombe: teacher of mathematics 1972, housemaster 1982, dep headmaster 1989, sr dep headmaster 2001, headmaster 2006; memb: Nat Tst, RSPB, RHS; memb ASCL; *Recreations* hockey, cricket, golf, rugby, fitness, bird watching; *Clubs* Rotary (Princes Risborough); *Style*— Roy Page, Esq; ✉ Royal Grammar School, Amersham Road, High Wycombe, Buckinghamshire HP13 6QT (tel 01494 551403, fax 01494 551419, e-mail rmp@rgshw.com)

PAGE, Stephen Alexander; s of James Cornish Page, and Frances, *née* Drake; *Educ* Bromsgrove Sch, Univ of Bristol (BA); *Career* Fourth Estate Ltd: sales and mktg dir and dep md 1994–2000, md 2000; gp sales and mktg dir HarperCollins 2000–01, chief exec and publisher Faber & Faber 2001–; *Recreations* music (listening and playing tabla and drums), theatre, literature, poetry, cooking, film, parenting; *Style*— Stephen Page; ✉ Faber & Faber Ltd, 3 Queen Square, London WC1N 3AU (tel 020 7465 7603, fax 020 7465 0034, e-mail stephen.page@faber.co.uk)

PAGE, Prof Trevor Francis; s of Cyril Francis Page (d 1980), of Lichfield, Staffs, and Gladys Mary, *née* Boston; *b* 6 January 1946; *Educ* King Edward VI GS Lichfield, Jesus Coll Cambridge (MA, PhD); *m* 7 Aug 1971, Andrea Gail, da of Cyril James Jones, of Cambridge; 1 s (Matthew Nicholas James b 1976), 1 da (Victoria Sophie Louise b 1979); *Career* Univ of Cambridge: SRC res fell 1971–72, demonstrator in metallurgy and materials sci 1972–76, lectr 1976–86, fndn fell Robinson Coll 1976–86; Univ of Newcastle upon Tyne: Cookson Gp prof of engrg materials 1987–, head Material Div 1989–, pro-vice-chllr (research) 2000–04, pro-vice-chllr (external affrs and research liaison) 2004–; author of numerous scientific papers, reviews and encyclopaedia articles on materials sci, the applications of microscopy, the devpt of ceramic materials and surface engrg, tribology, nanotechnology and nano-mechanics; EPSRC: Structural Materials Coll 1995–; memb Materials Research Soc USA 1995–; chm Tyne & Wear Metallurgical Soc 1988–90; fell: Royal Microscopical Soc 1971, Inst of Metals 1984, Inst of Ceramics 1987; FIM 1991, FInstP 2002, CEng; *Recreations* family, classical music, opera, theatre, cinema, food and wine, photography, gardening; *Clubs* Athenaeum; *Style*— Prof Trevor Page; ✉ Executive Office, 6 Kensington Terrace, The University of Newcastle upon Tyne, Newcastle upon Tyne NE1 7RU (tel 0191 222 7701, fax 0191 222 8480, e-mail t.f.page@ncl.ac.uk)

PAGE WOOD, Sir Anthony John; 8 Bt (UK 1837), of Hatherley House, Gloucestershire; s of Sir David John Hatherley Page Wood, 7 Bt (d 1955); *b* 6 February 1951; *Educ* Harrow; *Heir* kinsman, Lt-Col Matthew Evelyn Wood; *Career* dir Société Générale Strauss Turnbull (London) 1982–2001; *Style*— Sir Anthony Page Wood, Bt; ✉ 77 Dovehouse Street, London SW3

PAGET, His Hon Judge David Christopher John; QC (1994); s of Henry Paget (d 1993), of Johannesburg, South Africa, and Dorothy, *née* Colenutt (d 2005); *b* 3 February 1942; *Educ* St John' s Coll Johannesburg, Inns of Court Sch of Law; *m* 21 March 1968, Dallas Wendy, da of Brian Thomas Hill (d 2000), and Jean Ursula, *née* Furmedge (d 1986); 2 da (Henrietta b 1975, Alexandra b 1987); *Career* called to the Bar Inner Temple 1967 (bencher 2003); sr prosecuting counsel to the Crown Central Criminal Court 1989–94 (jr prosecuting counsel 1982, first jr 1988), recorder of Crown Court 1986–97, circuit judge (SE Circuit) 1997–, perm judge Central Criminal Court 1998–; Freeman City of London 1999, Liveryman Worshipful Co of Coopers 1999; *Recreations* walking, bird watching, listening to music; *Clubs* Garrick; *Style*— His Hon Judge Paget, QC; ✉ c/o Central Criminal Court, Old Bailey, London EC4M 7EH

PAGET, Henry James; s and h of Lt-Col Sir Julian Tolver Paget, 4 Bt, CVO, *qv*; *b* 2 February 1959; *Educ* Radley; *m* 8 Sept 1993, Mrs Margrete E Varvill, da of late Halfdan Lynner; 1 s (Bernard Halfdan b 4 July 1994), 1 da (Daphne Ampuria b 9 Sept 1996); *Career* Coldstream Guards; sr ptnr St James's Place; *Recreations* fishing, shooting and property renovation; *Style*— Henry Paget, Esq; ✉ Glenlivet House, by Ballindalloch, Banffshire AB37 9DJ (tel 01807 590358)

PAGET, Lt-Col Sir Julian Tolver; 4 Bt (UK 1871), of Harewood Place, Middlesex, CVO (1984); s of Gen Sir Bernard Charles Tolver Paget, GCB, DSO, MC (d 1961); suc unc, Sir James Francis Paget, 3 Bt (d 1972); *b* 11 July 1921; *Educ* Radley, ChCh Oxford (MA); *m* 1954, Diana Frances, da of late Frederick Spencer Herbert Farmer, of Lymington, Hants; 1 da (Olivia Jane (Mrs Nigel Cox) b 1957); 1 s (Henry James b 1959); *Heir* s, Henry Paget, *qv*; *Career* joined Coldstream Gds 1940, served NW Europe 1944–45, ret as Lt-Col 1968; Extra Gentleman Usher to HM The Queen 1991– (Gentleman Usher 1971–91); author; *Books* Counter-Insurgency Campaigning (1967), Last Post-Aden 1964–67 (1969), The Story of the Guards (1976), The Pageantry of Britain (1979), The Yeomen of the Guard (1985), Wellington's Peninsular War (1990), Hougoumont: the Key to Victory at Waterloo (1992), Second to None: The Coldstream Guards 1650–2000 (ed); *Clubs* Cavalry and Guards', Flyfishers'; *Style*— Lt-Col Sir Julian Paget, Bt, CVO; ✉ 35 Courtenay Place, Lymington, Hampshire SO41 3NQ (tel 01590 673363)

PAGET, Sir Richard Herbert; 4 Bt (UK 1886), of Cranmore Hall, Co Somerset; s of Sir John Starr Paget, 3 Bt (d 1992), and Nancy Mary, JP (d 1999), da of late Lt-Col Francis Woodbine Parish, DSO, MC, 60 Rifles; *b* 17 February 1957; *Educ* Eton; *m* 1985, Richenda Rachel, da of Rev Preb John Theodore Cameron Bucke Collins, formerly vicar of Holy Trinity, Brompton; 3 da (Emma Rachel b 17 June 1986, (Richenda) Elizabeth b 29 Dec 1988, Camilla Mary b 5 May 1991); *Heir* bro, David Paget; *Career* computer sales and marketing, outplacement consultancy, currently business devpt mangr Somerset Creative Marketing Ltd, non-exec dir SFM Technology; pres Paget Gorman Signed Speech Soc; Liveryman Worshipful Co of Grocers; *Recreations* tennis, cricket, parachuting, carriage driving; *Style*— Sir Richard Paget, Bt; ✉ Burridge Heath Farm, Little Bedwyn, Marlborough, Wiltshire SN8 3JR (tel 01672 870194)

PAGET-WILKES, Ven Michael Jocelyn James; s of Rev Sqdn Ldr A H Paget-Wilkes (d 1956), of Freshford, nr Bath, and Bridget, *née* Perkins; *b* 11 December 1941; *Educ* Dean Close Sch Cheltenham, Harper Adams Agric Coll (NDA), London Coll of Divinity (ALCD); *m* 12 July 1969, (Ruth) Gillian, da of Dillon Macnamara (d 1967), of Dublin; 2 da (Jessica b 1972, Claire b 1973), 1 s (Rory b 1977); *Career* agric extension offr Lindi Tanzania 1964–66; curate All Saints Wandsworth 1969–74; vicar: St James Hatcham London 1974–82, St Matthews Rugby 1982–90; archdeacon of Warwick 1990–; *Books* The Church and the Land (1968), Inside Out (1976), Poverty Revolution and the Church (1981); *Recreations* squash, gardening, tennis, skiing; *Style*— The Ven the Archdeacon of Warwick; ✉ 10 Northumberland Road, Leamington Spa, Warwickshire CV32 6HA (tel 01926 313337); Cathedral and Diocesan Offices, 1 Hill Top, Coventry CV1 5AB (tel 024 7652 1200)

PAGNAMENTA, Peter John; s of Charles Francis Pagnamenta, of Richmond, and Daphne Isabel, *née* Kay (d 1990); *b* 12 April 1941; *Educ* Shrewsbury, Trinity Hall Cambridge; *m* 13 April 1966, Sybil, da of Frances Howard Healy, of NY; 1 da (Zoe b 1969), 1 s (Robin b 1973); *Career* independent TV prodr; BBC: joined 1964, asst prodr Tonight 1965, prodr 24 Hours 1966, prodr New York office 1968, ed 24 Hours 1971, ed Midweek 1972, ed Panorama 1975; dir news and current affairs Thames Television 1977; BBC: prodr All Our Working Lives 1984, ed Real Lives series 1984, head Current Affairs Group 1985, prodr Nippon 1990, prodr People's Century (26 part series) 1995–96; fndr Pagnamenta Assocs 1997; *Books* All Our Working Lives (jtly, 1984), The Hidden Hall (ed, 2005), Sword and Blossom (jtly, 2006); *Style*— Peter Pagnamenta; ✉ 145 Elgin Crescent, London W11 2JH

PAGNI, Patrick Robert Marie; s of Robert Pagni, of Ville D'Avray, France, and Eliane, *née* Sanouiller; *b* 15 July 1949; *Educ* Ecole St Louis de Gonzague Paris, Université Paris IX Dauphine (Master in Management), Harvard Univ (MBA); *m* 2 Oct 1978, Viviane, da of Andre Guyot; *Career* Société Générale: joined 1970, asst mangr Paris 1974, dep branch mangr Paris 1976, vice-pres NY Branch 1979, regnl mangr Western US 1981, gen mangr Hong Kong Branch 1984, UK gen mangr 1992–95, UK chief exec 1995–98; Société Générale Strauss Turnbull Securities: exec dir 1988, chief exec 1990–92, UK chief exec 1995–98, dep chm 1998–; chief exec SG Hambros 1998; exec dir and head of strategic planning SG Paris 1999–; *Recreations* photography; *Clubs* Hong Kong Jockey, City of London; *Style*— Patrick Pagni, Esq; ✉ Société Générale, Exchange House, Primrose Street, London EC2A 2HT (tel 020 7762 4444, fax 020 7638 6503)

PAHOR, Dr Ahmes Labib; s of Prof Pahor Labib (d 1994), of Cairo; *b* 15 September 1942, Cairo; *Educ* Cairo Univ (MB BCh, DLO), Ain Shams Univ Cairo (DMScPath), RCS(Ed) (Cert of Higher Surgical Trg in ENT), ECFMG (Philadelphia), Inst of Higher Coptic Studies Cairo (MA), DHMSA (Soc of Apothecaries London), Cert of Specialist Trg (EU), Radboud Univ Nijmegen Holland (PhD); *Career* intern Cairo Univ Hosp 1964–65, SHO Miny of Health Cairo 1965–66, asst researcher (demonstrator) Pathology and Cytology Dept Nat Research Centre Miny of Scientific Research Cairo 1966–70, clinical attachment Surgical Dept Moyle Hosp Larne Co Antrim 1970, SHO ENT Dept Waveney Hosp Ballymena, SHO Birmingham and Midland ENT Hosp 1972, registrar Eye and Ear Clinic Royal Victoria Hosp Belfast and Belfast City Hosp 1972–74, sr registrar at various Midlands hosps 1974–78, conslt ENT surgeon City Hosp Dudley Rd (Sandwell and West Birmingham HA - teaching) 1978–2002 (hon conslt 2002–), conslt ENT surgn Priory Hosp Birmingham; hon sr clinical lectr Med Sch Univ of Birmingham; memb: Ethical Ctee Sandwell Dist Gen Hosp 1981–92, Regnl Aural Servs Ctee, Regnl ENT Registrars and Sr Registrars Ctee 1987–2002; co-fndr, co-organiser and tutor: Temporal Bone Surgery Course Birmingham 1980–89, Combined Univs Advanced Otology Course 1987–2002; lectr on operating Selly Oak Hosp Birmingham; examiner: Midland Inst of Otology Dip for Nurses 1979–89, fellowship examination (ENT) RCS(Ed), Occulus fellowship (Eye) Exams Birmingham Midland Eye Hosp; author of articles and papers in professional jls and pubns in English and Arabic; many lectures to professional bodies worldwide incl Inst d'Egypte Cairo 1981 and RSM London 1995; fndr sec British Soc for the History of ENT; memb: NY Acad of Scis, BMA, RSM, BAOL, Midland Inst of Otology (hon librarian 1996–2001), Br Paediatric Otolaryngology Soc, Otology Research Soc, Soc of Authors 1979–82, Medical Writers' Gp 1980, Irish Otolaryngology Soc, European Rhinologic Soc, Int Hist of Medicine Soc, Int Hippocratic Fndn of Kos Greece, Int Assoc of Coptic Studies, Birmingham History of Medicine Soc, Br Soc History of Medicine, Advsy Bd Otolaryngology RCS(Ed); fndr memb Imhotep Scientific Soc Cairo; memb: Sandwell Social Evening Ctee, Rotary Club Birmingham (memb Int Ctee); Freeman City of London, Liveryman Worshipful Soc of Apothecaries; MRCS, LRCP, FRCSEd, FICS; *Recreations* travelling, reading, writing, golf, Tai Chi; *Style*— Dr Ahmes L Pahor; ✉ 34 Ingham Way, Harborne, Birmingham B17 8SN (e-mail ahmes@postmaster.co.uk, website www.pyramids3.netfirms.com)

PAICE, Prof Elisabeth Willemien; da of Ervin Ross Marlin, of Berkhamsted, Herts, and Hilda van Stockum, HRHA; *b* 23 April 1945; *Educ* Int Sch Geneva, Trinity Coll Dublin, Westminster Med Sch (BA, MB BCh, BAO); *m* 6 July 1968, Clifford Charles Dudley, s of Owen Paice (d 1973); 1 s (Matthew b 1972), 2 da (Katharine b 1973, Joanna b 1977); *Career* sr registrar: Stoke Mandeville Hosp 1977–78, High Wycombe Hosp 1978–79, UCH 1980–82; conslt rheumatologist Whittington Hosp 1982–95, hon sr lectr UCL, assoc dean postgrad med NT(E) 1992–95, dean dir postgrad med and dental educn Univ of London 1995–; visiting prof Faculty of Clinical Sciences UCL 2002; memb Br Soc of Rheumatology; MA 1995; FRCP 1989 (DipMedEd 1994), ILTM 2002; *Style*— Prof Elisabeth Paice; ✉ London Deanery, Stewart House, 32 Russell Square, London WC1B 5DN (tel 020 7866 3237, e-mail epaice@londondeanery.ac.uk)

P

PAICE, James Edward Thornton; MP; s of late Edward Percival Paice, and Winifred Mary, *née* Thornton; *b* 24 April 1949; *Educ* Framlingham Coll, Writtle Agric Coll (NDA); *m* 6 Jan 1973, Ava Barbara, da of late Robert Stewart Patterson, of Earl Soham, Suffolk; 2 s (Gordon b 1976, James b 1977); *Career* gen mangr/exec dir Framlingham Mgmnt and Training Services Ltd 1985–87 (non-exec dir 1987–89), non-exec dir United Framlingham Farmers Ltd 1989–94; MP (Cons) Cambs SE 1987–, memb Select Ctee on Employment 1987–89; PPS to: min of state for Agric 1989–90, to min for Agric, Fisheries and Food then sec of state for the Environment 1990–94; Parly under sec of state: Dept of Employment 1994–95, DfEE 1995–97; oppn frontbench spokesman on agric, fisheries and food 1997–2001, shadow min Home Office 2001–04, shadow agriculture min 2004–; *Recreations* the countryside, shooting; *Style—* James Paice, Esq, MP; ✉ House of Commons, London SW1A 0AA (tel 020 7219 4101)

PAIGE, Elaine; OBE (1995); da of Eric Bickerstaff, of London; *b* 5 March 1948; *Career* actress and singer since 1968; *Theatre* musicals incl: created role of Eva Peron in Evita (London stage) 1978, created role of Grizabella in Cats 1981, created role of Florence in Chess 1986, Reno Sweeney in Anything Goes 1989, Edith Piaf in Piaf (West End and tour) 1993, Norma Desmond in Sunset Boulevard (London 1995, Broadway 1996–97), Celimène in The Misanthrope (Peter Hall Theatre Co) 1998, Anna in The King and I (London Palladium) 2000–01, Where There's a Will (Peter Hall Theatre Co UK tour) 2003, Mrs Lovett in Sweeney Todd (NYC Opera) 2004, title role in The Drowsy Chaperone (Novello Theatre); *Television* incl: Love Story, The Lady Killers, Phyllis Dixey, View of Harry Clark, Unexplained Laughter, Boston Pops (PBS); *Films* incl: Oliver, Whatever Happened to What's His Name; *Recordings* incl: Stages (triple platinum) 1983, Cinema (gold) 1984, Chess 1985, I Know Him So Well (duet with Barbara Dickson, No 1 Hit Single) 1985, Love Hurts (platinum) 1985, Christmas 1986, Memories (compilation album, platinum) 1987, The Queen Album (8th consecutive gold album) 1988, Love Can Do That 1991, Romance and the Stage 1993, Elaine Paige - Piaf 1994, Encore 1995, On Reflection 1998, A Collection 2003, Centre Stage 2004, Essential Musicals 2006; concerts in: Australia, New Zealand, South Africa, Middle East, Far East, USA and Europe; UK concert tours 1985, 1987, 1991, 1993 1994, 2004 and 2006; *Awards* Show Business Personality of the Year Variety Club of GB Award (for Evita), Swet Award for Best Actress in a Musical (for Evita), Rear of the Year Award 1984, Recording Artiste of the Year Variety Club of GB (for album Christmas), Head of the Year Award! 1987, Br Academy of Songwriters, Composers and Authors Gold Badge of Merit 1993, Variety Club Award for Actress of the Year 1995, Olivier Award nomination for Outstanding Performance of the Year by an Actress in a Musical (for Chess and Anything Goes), Olivier Award nomination for Best Actress in a Musical (for Piaf and Sunset Boulevard), HMV Lifetime Achievement Award 1996, Nat Operatic & Dramatic Assoc Lifetime Achievement Award 1999, Drama Desk Award nomination for Outstanding Featured Actress in a Musical (for Sweeney Todd); *Recreations* skiing, antiques, tennis; *Style—* Miss Elaine Paige, OBE; ✉ Michael Storrs Music Ltd, CSS Stellar plc, 11 Maiden Lane, London WC2E 7NA (tel 020 7078 1458, fax 020 7078 1456, e-mail msm@css-stellar.com)

PAIN, Jacqualyn Christina Mary; da of J K Pain, of Oxford, and J W Pain, *née* Underwood; *b* 31 August 1957; *Educ* Sch of St Helen and St Katharine Abingdon, Univ of Wales (BA, MA), Univ of London (MA, PGCE), Univ of Leicester (MBA); *Career* teacher: Tiffin Girls' Sch Kingston upon Thames 1981–83, Old Palace Sch Croydon 1983–84, James Allen's Girls' Sch London 1984–96; on secondment Inst of Educn Univ of London 1992–94, dep head Northwood Coll 1996–2000, head Henrietta Barnett Sch London 2000–05, head St Albans HS for Girls 2005–; tstee Dame Henrietta Barnett Tst, govr Northwood Coll; MInstD; *Recreations* running, gym; *Clubs* Univ Women's; *Style—* Ms Jacqualyn Pain; ✉ St Albans High School for Girls, Townsend Avenue, St Albans, Hertfordshire AL1 3SJ

PAIN, Richard; s of Sir Peter Richard Pain, of Loen, St Catherines Rd, Frimley, Surrey, and Lady Barbara Florence Maud Pain, *née* Riggs; *b* 23 September 1942; *Educ* Westminster; *m* 6 Oct 1973, Adrienne Joyce, da of Myles Joseph Esmonde, of Longfield, Kent; 1 da (Catherine b 1975), 1 s (Peter b 1977); *Career* slr; ptnr Hyman Isaacs Lewis and Mills 1967–74, ptnr Beachcroft Hyman Isaacs 1974–88, ptnr Beachcroft Stanleys 1988–99, ptnr Beachcroft LLP (formerly Beachcroft Wansbroughs) 1999–2003 (conslt 2003–); memb City of London Law Soc; *Recreations* cricket, tennis; *Style—* Richard Pain, Esq; ✉ Beachcroft LLP, 100 Fetter Lane, London EC4A 1BN (tel 020 7894 6623, fax 020 7894 6660, e-mail rpain@bwlaw.co.uk)

PAINE, Sir Christopher Hammon; kt (1995); s of Maj John Hammon Paine (d 1987), of Great Coxwell, Oxon, and Hon Mrs J Shedden, MBE, *née* Vestey (d 1991); *b* 28 August 1935; *Educ* Eton, Merton Coll Oxford (MA, MSc, DM); *m* 3 Nov 1959, Susan, da of late D Martin, of Bridgwater, Somerset; 2 s (Edward b 1960, Simon b 1964), 2 da (Lucy b 1962, Alice b 1968); *Career* conslt in radiotherapy and oncology Oxford 1970–95 (hon conslt 1996–), dir clinical studies Univ of Oxford 1980–84, gen mangr Oxfordshire HA 1984–88; chm RSM Support Servsices Ltd 2005–, non-exec dir Medicsight Inc 2005–; memb Med Advsy Bd: Int Hosps Gp 1996–, Weill Cornell Med Coll in Qatar 2002–; pres: RCR 1992–95, RSM 1996–98, BMA 2000–01; med dir Advsy Ctee for Distinction Awards 1994–99; tstee The London Clinic 1999–; Liveryman Worshipful Soc of Apothecaries; FRCP, FRCR, Hon FRSCEd, hon fell Faculty of Radiologists Royal Coll of Surgns Ireland, hon fell Hong Kong Coll of Radiologists; *Recreations* gardening; *Clubs* Farmers'; *Style—* Sir Christopher Paine; ✉ The Avenue, Wotton Underwood, Aylesbury, Buckinghamshire HP18 0RP (tel 01296 770742, fax 01296 770318)

PAINE, Graham Ernest Harley; s of late Harley Joseph Paine, of Kingston on Thames, Surrey, and Ninette, *née* Sutch; *b* 2 September 1954; *Educ* Dulwich Coll, Univ of Bristol (LLB); *Career* admitted slr 1980; ptnr Wilde Sapte 1984–2000 (articled clerk 1978–80, asst slr 1980–84), ptnr Denton Wilde Sapte 2000–; licensed insolvency practitioner; memb: Assoc of Business Recovery Professionals (R 3), Law Soc, Insolvency Lawyers Assoc; *Recreations* golf, skiing, theatre, swimming; *Style—* Graham Paine, Esq; ✉ Denton Wilde Sapte, 1 Fleet Place, London EC4M 7WS (tel 020 7246 7000, fax 020 7246 7777, e-mail graham.paine@dentonwildesapte.com)

PAINES, Alison Jane Sargent; da of Eric Sargent Roberts (d 1969), and Audrey Lilian May, *née* Rosevear; *b* 27 July 1955, London; *Educ* Notting Hill & Ealing HS GDST, Girton Coll Cambridge (MA), Coll of Law Lancaster Gate; *m* 11 May 1985, Nicholas Paul Billot Paines, *qv*; 1 s (Rupert b 8 Sept 1986), 3 da (Emily b 10 June 1989, Katherine b 14 Aug 1992, Victoria b 7 June 1998); *Career* slr; articled clerk then asst slr Crossman Block & Keith 1979–88; Withers LLP: asst slr 1988–91, ptnr 1991–, head of charities practice 2000–; govr Godolphin & Latymer Sch 2002; memb Exec Ctee Charity Law Assoc 1995– (dep chair 2004–); *Publications* Practical Trust Precedents (contrib), Tolley's Charities Manual (contrib), The Law & Practice of International Charitable Giving (2007); *Style—* Mrs Alison Paines; ✉ Withers LLP, 16 Old Bailey, London EC4M 7EG (tel 020 7597 6057, fax 020 7597 6543, e-mail alison.paines@withersworldwide.com)

PAINES, Nicholas Paul Billot; QC (1997); s of Anthony John Cooper Paines (d 2004), and Anne, *née* Billot; *b* 29 June 1955; *Educ* Downside, Univ of Oxford (MA), Université Libre de Bruxelles (Licence Spéciale en Droit Européen); *m* 11 May 1985, Alison Jane, *qv*, da of Eric Sargent Roberts (d 1969); 1 s (Rupert b 1986), 3 da (Emily b 1989, Katherine b 1992, Victoria b 1998); *Career* called to the Bar: Gray's Inn 1978, NI 1996; practising barr 1980–, recorder 2003–; dep social security cmmr 2000–; memb Bar Cncl 1991–96, treas Bar European Gp 2001– (chm 1996–98); jt gen ed Common Market Law Reports; memb: Cncl St Christopher's Fellowship 1984–2002, Supplementary Panel of Counsel to the Crown (Common Law) 1993–97; *Books* Halsbury's Laws of England (contrib), Vaughan Law of the European Communities (contrib); *Recreations* family life; *Style—* Nicholas Paines, Esq, QC; ✉ Monckton Chambers, 1–2 Raymond Buildings, Gray's Inn, London WC1R 5NR (tel 020 7405 7211, fax 020 7405 2084)

PAINTER, Ven David Scott; s of Frank Painter (d 1954), and Winifred Ellen, *née* Bibbings (d 1980); *b* 3 October 1944; *Educ* Queen Elizabeth's Sch Crediton, Trinity Coll of Music London (LTCL, LTCL (Music Ed)), Worcester Coll Oxford (MA, CertEd); *Career* ordained priest 1971; chaplain to Archbishop of Canterbury 1976–80, vicar of Roehampton 1980–91, canon Southwark Cathedral and diocesan dir of ordinands 1991–2000, archdeacon of Oakham and canon residentiary Peterborough Cathedral 2000–; *Recreations* music, country walking, crossword puzzles; *Clubs* RSM; *Style—* The Ven the Archdeacon of Oakham; ✉ 7 Minster Precincts, Peterborough, Cambridgeshire PE1 1XS (tel 01733 891360, fax 01733 554524, mobile 07976 687059, e-mail david.painter@peterborough-cathedral.org.uk)

PAINTING, Norman George; OBE (1976); s of Harry George Painting, and Maud Painting; *b* 23 April 1924; *Educ* Leamington Coll, King Edward VI Sch Nuneaton, Univ of Birmingham (BA), ChCh Oxford; *Career* Anglo-Saxon tutor Exeter Coll Oxford 1946–48, writer and dir BBC 1949–50, freelance writer, dir and performer 1945–; world's longest serving actor in a daily radio serial (Guinness record) as Philip Archer in The Archers 1950–, other radio work incl team capt Gardening Quiz BBC Radio 4 and a castaway on Desert Island Discs BBC Radio 4 2000; writing credits incl approx 1,200 episodes of The Archers (as Bruno Milna), numerous TV films, radio scripts, plays and articles; TV appearances incl: chm TV quiz The Garden Game 1977–82, Wogan, Stop the Week, Quote Unquote, On the Air, subject of This is Your Life 1991, celebrity guest Countdown 1992–, Through the Keyhole 1993, judge Master Chef 1996; vice-pres Tree Cncl, vice-pres Royal Agric Benevolent Inst; patron: Age Concern Warwickshire, First Steps to Freedom (Help for Phobics) 1991–; tstee: Warwickshire and Coventry Historic Churches Tst (chm 1979–82), Birmingham Tst for People with Epilepsy; hon life govr RASE 1976, temp hon memb High Table ChCh Oxford 1985–; Hon MA Univ of Birmingham 1989; life fell RHS; life memb: CPRE, Nat Tst; *Books* Stories of the Saints (with M Day, 1956), More Stories of the Saints (with M Day, 1957), St Antony - The Man Who Found Himself (with M Day, 1958), Forever Ambridge (1975 and 1980), Reluctant Archer (autobiography, 1982); *Recreations* music, poetry, swimming, gardens, being quiet; *Style—* Norman Painting, Esq, OBE; ✉ c/o BBC Broadcasting House, London W1A 1AA

PAISLEY, Rt Hon Rev Ian Richard Kyle; PC (2005), MP, MLA; s of late Rev J Kyle Paisley; *b* 6 April 1926; *Educ* Ballymena Model Sch, Ballymena Tech HS, S Wales Bible Coll, Reformed Presbyterian Theol Coll Belfast; *m* 1956, Eileen Emily Cassells; 2 s, 3 da; *Career* ordained 1946, minister Martyrs Memorial Free Presbyterian Church Belfast 1946–; MP (Protestant Unionist then DUP) Antrim N 1970–, Protestant Unionist memb Northern Ireland Parliament (Stormont) for Bannside 1970–72, MEP (DUP) Northern Ireland 1979–2004, DUP memb Northern Ireland Assembly for N Antrim 1982–86 and 1998–; co-fndr and ldr DUP 1971–; memb: Int Cultural Soc of Korea; FRGS; *Books* History of 59 Revival, Christian Foundations (1960, 2 edn 1985), Exposition of Epistle to Romans (1968, 2 edn 1985), Massacre of St Bartholomew (1972), Ulster the Facts (1981), No Pope Here (1982), Paisley's Pocket Preacher (1987), Be Sure - 7 rules for public speaking (1987); *Style—* The Rt Hon Rev Ian Paisley, MP, MLA; ✉ House of Commons, London SW1A 0AA; The Parsonage, 17 Cyprus Avenue, Belfast BT5 5NT

PAISLEY, Ian Richard Kyle; MLA; s of Rt Hon Ian Paisley, MP, MLA , *qv*, and Eileen Emily, *née* Cassells (Baroness Paisley of St George's (Life Peer)); *b* 12 December 1966; *Educ* Shaftesbury House Coll, Methodist Coll Belfast, Queen's Univ Belfast; *m* 25 June 1990, Fiona Margaret Elizabeth, da of James Wilson Currie; 2 da (Emily Fiona Elizabeth b 1994, Lucy Jane b 1996), 2 s (Thomas Ian James b 2001, Matthew Ian Richard b 2004); *Career* press offr DUP 1989–96, memb NI Forum 1996–98, MLA (DUP) Antrim N 1998–, memb Police Bd NI 2001–07; Royal Humane Soc Award for Bravery; *Publications* Reasonable Doubt (1992), Peace Process (1998), Ian Paisley - A Life in Photographs (2004); *Style—* Ian Paisley, Esq, MLA

PAISLEY, Bishop of (RC) 1988–; Rt Rev John Aloysius Mone; s of Arthur Mone (d 1964), and Elizabeth, *née* Dunn (d 1979); *b* 22 June 1929; *Educ* Holyrood Secdy Sch, Sulpician Seminaries in France of Issy-les-Moulineaux and Paris, Institut Catholique Paris; *Career* ordained priest Glasgow 1952, St Ninian's Glasgow 1952–75, Our Lady and St George 1975–79, St Joseph's Tollcross 1979–84, dir min to priests prog 1982–84, bishop of Abercorn and bishop auxiliary of Glasgow 1984–88; Scottish nat chaplain Girl Guides 1971–; chm: Scottish Catholic Int Aid Fund 1974–75 (pres/treas 1985–), Scottish Marriage Advsy Cncl 1982–84; pres: Justice and Peace Cmmn 1987–, Social Care Cmmn 1996–; *Recreations* golf, piano playing; *Clubs* Hamilton Golf; *Style—* The Rt Rev the Bishop of Paisley; ✉ Diocesan Offices, Diocesan Centre, Cathedral Precincts, Incle Street, Paisley PA1 1HR (e-mail diocesanoffice@paisleydiocese.org.uk)

PAJARES, Ramon; OBE (2000); s of Juan Antonio Pajares Garcia (d 1954), of Jaen, Spain, and Rosario Salazar (d 1964); *b* 6 July 1935; *Educ* sr sch Jaen, Madrid Inst of Hotel and Tourism Studies; *m* 13 July 1963, Jean Kathleen, 2 da (Sofia Ramona b 14 June 1967, Maria del Rosario b 25 Aug 1969), 1 s (Roberto Javier b 17 March 1971); *Career* Nat Serv Spanish Navy 1955–57; Hotel Ritz Barcelona 1954–55, Hotel San Jorge Playa de Aro 1957, Hotel Parque Llavaneras 1957–59, Mansion Hotel Eastbourne 1959–61, Kleiner Reisen Koblenz 1961, Hotel Feldbergerhof Feldberg 1961–62, Le Vieux Manoir Morat 1962, Hotel Reina Isabel Las Palmas 1965–69, food and beverage dir Inn on the Park 1969–71, gen mangr San Antonio Lanzarote 1972–74, gen mangr Inn on the Park London 1975–94, md The Savoy Group 1994–99; memb: Académie Culinaire de France 1971–, Bd of Fells Skäl 1972, Cookery and Food Assoc 1973, Confrérie de la Chaîne des Rotisseurs 1978–, Confrèrie des Chevaliers du Sacavin 1979–, Caballeros del Vino 1987; Freeman City of London 1988; FHCIMA 1982, Master Innholder 1988; Officier de L'Ordre des Coteaux de Champagne, Chevalier du Tastevin 1982; *Awards* medal of Merito Civil awarded by HM King of Spain 1984, Hotelier of the Year award of Br Hotel and Catering Industry 1984, Personalité de l'Année for The Hotel Indust 1986, medal of Oficial de la Orden de Isabel la Católica awarded by HM King of Spain 1989, Caterer and Hotel Keeper Special Award 1997, European Hotel Design and Devpt Lifetime Achievement Award 1998, Hotels Magazine Hotelier of the World Award 1998, Waterford Wedgwood Hospitality Award 1999, British Travel Industry Hall of Fame Award 1999, Silver medal for services to tourism awarded by Spanish Govt 2000; *Style—* Ramon Pajares, Esq, OBE

PAKENHAM, Hon Kevin John Toussaint; yst s of 7 Earl of Longford, KG, PC (d 2001), and Elizabeth, Countess of Longford, CBE (d 2002); *b* 1 November 1947; *Educ* Ampleforth, New Coll Oxford (MA), St Antony's Coll Oxford (MPhil); *Career* Rothschild Intercontinental Bank 1972–75, American Express Bank 1975–83, md Foreign & Colonial Management 1983–88; chief exec: John Govett Ltd 1988–2000, AIB Asset Management Ltd 1997–2000; md Putnam Lovell NBF Securities Inc 2000–; tstee Ireland Fund of GB; *Clubs* MCC, Hurlingham, Rye Golf; *Style—* Kevin Pakenham; ✉ Putnam Lovell NBF Securities Inc, 130 Jermyn Street, London SW1Y 4PL (tel 020 7478 1600, e-mail kpakenham@plnbf.com)

PAKENHAM, Hon Sir Michael Aidan; KBE (2003), CMG (1993); 3 s of 7 Earl of Longford, KG, PC (d 2001), and Elizabeth, Countess of Longford, CBE (d 2002); *b* 3 November 1943; *Educ* Ampleforth, Trinity Coll Cambridge, Rice Univ Texas; *m* 1980, Meta (Mimi)

Landreth, da of William Conway Doak, of Maryland, USA; 2 da (Alexandra b 1981, Clio b 1985), 2 step da (Lisa, Lindsay); *Career* reporter Washington Post 1965; HM Dip Serv 1965–2003: Nairobi 1966, Warsaw 1967, FCO 1970, asst private sec later private sec to the Chllr of the Duchy of Lancaster 1971, on secondment to Cabinet Office 1972 (first sec 1972), UK Delgn CSCE Geneva 1974, first sec New Delhi 1974, Washington 1978, cnsllr FCO 1983, cnsllr (external rels) UK rep to EU Brussels 1987, HM ambass and consul-gen Luxembourg 1991–94, min Br Embassy Paris 1994–97, head of defence and overseas affrs secretariat Cabinet Office 1997–99, chm Jt Intelligence Ctee Cabinet Office 1997–2000, intelligence co-ordinator Cabinet Office 1999–2000, HM ambass Warsaw 2001–03, chm Pakenvest Int 2004–; sr advsr Access Industries 2004–; conslt: Signet Multimanager 2004–06, Thales Int 2004–06; tstee Chevening Estate 2005–; memb Cncl KCL 2005–; *Recreations* tennis, golf, reading, museums; *Clubs* MCC, Garrick, Beefsteak, Rye Golf, Pitt; *Style*— The Hon Sir Michael Pakenham, KBE, CMG; ✉ c/o Cope House, 15B Kensington Palace Gardens, London W8 4QG (tel 020 7908 9966)

PAKENHAM, Thomas Frank Dermot; *see:* Longford, 8 Earl of

PALACHE, Robert; s of Ralph Palache, of London, and Rosalind, *née* Simons; *b* 11 November 1957; *Educ* JFS Sch, Magdalene Coll Cambridge (MA); *Family* 2 da (Abigail b 22 Aug 1984, Dora b 24 May 1987); *Career* slr Coward Chance 1982–87, ptnr Clifford Chance 1988–98 (slr 1987), dir and jt head Securitisation Div Nomura International plc 1998–2001, md and head of real estate, corporate securitization and infrastructure finance Barclays Capital 2001–06, md Global Capital Markets Div Morgan Stanley 2006–; FRSA; *Recreations* reading, sports and theatre; *Clubs* City of London; *Style*— Robert Palache, Esq

PALASTANGA, Prof Nigel Peter; s of Joseph Peter Palastanga (d 2000), of Cwmbran, Wales, and Mildred Joan Palastanga (d 1988); *b* 10 May 1947; *Educ* Sladen Sch Kidderminster, RAMC Apprentices' Coll Ash Vale, Army Sch of Physiotherapy Woolwich, King's Coll Hosp Sch of Physiotherapy London, Open Univ (BA), NE London Poly (DMS), Univ of London (MA); *m* 1 April 1976, Dorothy Barbara; 1 da (Hazel b 24 Feb 1977), 1 s (Tom b 30 Jan 1981); *Career* physiotherapist (RAMC) Royal Herbert Hosp Woolwich 1969–71, student physiotherapy teacher KCH London 1971–73, teacher Army Sch of Physiotherapy Woolwich 1973–76, asst princ Sch of Physiotherapy Addenbrooke's Hosp Cambridge 1980–88 (physiotherapy teacher 1976–80), princ Cardiff Sch of Physiotherapy 1988–2005, dean Sch of Healthcare Studies Univ of Wales Coll of Med Cardiff 1995–2002, pro-vice-chllr Univ of Wales Coll of Med 1999–2005, pro-vice-chllr Cardiff Univ 2004–; non-exec memb Bro Morgannwg NHS Tst Bd; fell: Chartered Soc of Physiotherapy, Higher Educn Acad; *Books* Clayton's Electrotherapy (8 edn 1982, 9 edn 1986), Modern Manual Therapy (2 edn 1995), Anatomy and Human Movement (1989, 5 edn 2006); *Recreations* sailing, walking, rugby; *Style*— Prof Nigel Palastanga; ✉ Vice-Chancellor's Office, Cardiff University, Park Place, Cardiff CF10 3AT

PALIN, Michael Edward; CBE (2000); s of late Edward Palin, and late Mary Palin; *b* 5 May 1943; *Educ* Shrewsbury, BNC Oxford (BA); *m* 16 April 1966, Helen Margaret, *née* Gibbins; 2 s (Thomas Edward b 8 Oct 1968, William Michael b 19 Nov 1970), 1 da (Rachel Mary b 13 Jan 1975); *Career* actor and writer; winner Michael Balcon Award for Outstanding Contribution to Cinema (jtly with Monty Python team) 1987, BBC Personality of the Year TRIC Awards 1998, Lifetime Achievement Award Br Comedy Awards 2002, BAFTA Special Award 2005; *Theatre* playwright The Weekend (Strand Theatre) 1994; *Television* actor and writer: Monty Python's Flying Circus (BBC) 1969–74, Ripping Yarns (BBC) 1976–80; actor: Three Men in a Boat (BBC) 1975, GBH (Channel Four) 1991; presenter and writer of expedition series: Around the World in 80 Days (BBC) 1989, Pole to Pole (BBC) 1992, Full Circle With Michael Palin (BBC) 1997 (Most Popular Documentary Series Nat TV Awards), Michael Palin's Hemingway Adventure (BBC) 1999, Sahara with Michael Palin 2002, Himalaya 2004 (Best Presenter Award RTS); presenter: Palin's Column (Channel Four) 1994, Palin on Redpath (BBC) 1997, The Bright Side of Life (BBC) 2000, The Ladies Who Loved Matisse 2003, Michael Palin and the Mystery of Hammershoi 2005; *Films* actor and writer: And Now for Something Completely Different 1970, Monty Python and The Holy Grail 1974, Monty Python's Life of Brian 1979, Time Bandits 1980, Monty Python's The Meaning of Life 1982, American Friends 1991; actor: Jabberwocky 1976, A Private Function 1984, Brazil 1985, A Fish Called Wanda 1988 (Best Supporting Actor BAFTA Awards); actor, writer and co-prodr The Missionary 1983, Fierce Creatures 1997; *Books* Monty Python's Big Red Book (jtly, 1970), Monty Python's Brand New Book (jtly, 1973), Dr Fegg's Encyclopedia of All World Knowledge (jtly, 1984), Limericks (1985), Around the World in 80 Days (1989), Pole to Pole (1992), Pole To Pole - The Photographs (jtly, 1994), The Weekend (1994), Hemingway's Chair (novel, 1995), Full Circle (1997), Full Circle - The Photographs (1997), Michael Palin's Hemingway Adventure (1999), Sahara (2002), The Pythons Autobiography by the Pythons (jtly, 2003), Himalaya (2004, TV & Film Book of the Year Br Book Awards), Michael Palin Diaries 1969–79: The Python Years (2006); for children: Small Harry and the Toothache Pills (1981), The Mirrorstone (1986), The Cyril Stories (1986); co-writer Ripping Yarns (1978) and More Ripping Yarns (1980); *Clubs* Athenaeum; *Style*— Michael Palin, Esq, CBE; ✉ c/o Mayday Management, 34 Tavistock Street, London WC2E 7PB (tel 020 7497 1100, fax 020 7497 1133)

PALING, Robert Roy; s of Reginald Roy Paling (d 1978), and Margery Emily, *née* Lyford (d 2004); *b* 10 June 1940; *Educ* Shrivenham Sch, Faringdon Sch, The Coll Swindon; *m* 20 Feb 1965, Judith Dow, da of Reginald Albert Sheppard (d 1985); 1 da (Portia Dow (Mrs Duncan Trow) b 1968); *Career* sr conveyancing exec Lemon & Co Slrs Swindon 1980–96 (conslt 1996–); ptnr Dow Sheppard Relocation 1996–; cmmr for oaths 1994–2004; compiled Mortgage Guide for CBI Employee Relocation Cncl 1988; sr Jt-Master Shrivenham Beagles 1969–2004; memb: Old Berks Hunt, Assoc of Masters of Harriers and Beagles 1970, Soc Licensed Conveyancers 1987–2004; assoc Inst of Legal Execs 1965–2004, tstee The Roman Research Tst 1991–98, vice-pres Shrivenham FC 2006–; *Recreations* hunting, cross country riding, shooting, polo; *Clubs* Cavalry and Guards', Cirencester Park Polo, Edgeworth Polo, Defence Acad Golf; *Style*— Robert Paling, Esq; ✉ Orchard House, High Street, Shrivenham, Swindon, Wiltshire SN6 8AW (tel 01793 782789)

PALLANT, John; s of Dennis Pallant, of Southsea, Hants, and Doreen, *née* Hirst; *b* 10 August 1955; *Educ* St John's Coll Southsea, Univ of Reading (BA); *Career* copywriter: Griffin & George Ltd 1977, Acroyd Westwood Associates 1977, Boase Massimi Pollitt 1978, Collett Dickenson Pearce 1980, Gold Greenless Trott 1982; copywriter and creative gp head Boase Massimi Pollitt 1983; Saatchi & Saatchi: copywriter 1988, gp head 1991, dep creative dir and Exec Bd dir 1995, creative dir 1996–97, jt exec creative dir 1997–98, dep exec creative dir 1999–2003, European creative dir 2003–; *Awards* D & AD awards (for TV, press, public service and poster campaigns): Gold 1985, Silver 1981 (two), 1985 (three), 1989 and 1992; Br TV awards: Silver 1981, Gold 1992; Cannes Int Advtg awards: Silver 1981, Bronze 1988, Gold 1992; Campaign Press awards: Gold 1985, Silver 1985 (two), 1989 and 1990; Campaign Poster awards: Gold 1985, Silver 1983, 1985 (two), 1990 (two); Independent Radio awards Silver 1990; NY One Show awards Gold and Best of Show award 1992 and Silver 1997; IMSA Int Advtg awards Grand Prix for cinema 1992; *Style*— John Pallant, Esq; ✉ Saatchi & Saatchi, 80 Charlotte Street, London W1A 1AQ (tel 020 7636 5060 ext 3501, fax 020 7637 8489)

PALLETT, Julian Charles; s of Trevor William Pallett, and Hilary, *née* Williams; *Educ* Waverley GS Birmingham, Wadham Coll Oxford (MA); *Career* slr; Wragge & Co LLP: articled clerk 1981–83, asst slr/assoc 1983–90, ptnr (banking, restructuring and corporate recovery) 1990–; memb: Law Soc 1983, Birmingham Law Soc 1983; chm Birmingham Ctee, tstee Ironbridge Gorge Museum Devpt Tst, chair of govrs Univ of Worcester; *Recreations* music, history, architecture, running; *Style*— Julian Pallett, Esq; ✉ Wragge & Co LLP, 55 Colmore Row, Birmingham B3 2AS (tel 0870 733 0588, e-mail julian_pallett@wragge.com)

PALLEY, Eall Marcon (Marc); s of Dr Ahrn Palley (d 1993), of Zimbabwe, and Dr Claire Palley, *née* Swait; *b* 2 May 1954; *Educ* Clifton Coll, St John's Coll Oxford (MA); *m* 28 July 1979, Sabina Mary, da of Maj-Gen F W E Fursdon; 3 s (Charles b 9 Dec 1982, Frederick b 6 June 1985, Harry b 15 May 1988); *Career* admitted slr 1978; Allen & Overy 1976–85, ptnr Berwin Leighton Paisner 1985– (currently head Banking and Capital Markets Gp); *Style*— Marc Palley, Esq; ✉ Berwin Leighton Paisner LLP, Adelaide House, London Bridge, London EC4R 9HA (tel 020 7760 1000, fax 020 7760 1111, e-mail marc.palley@blplaw.com)

PALLISER, Charles; *b* 11 December 1947; *Educ* Exeter Coll Oxford (BA), Wolfson Coll Oxford (BLitt); *Career* author; lectr: Dept of Eng Studies Univ of Strathclyde 1974–90, Univ of Rutgers (spring semester) 1986; *Publications* The Journal of Simon Owen (BBC radio play, 1982), The Quincunx (1989, Sue Kaufman prize for first fiction 1991), The Sensationist (1991), Obsessions - Writing (1991), Betrayals (1994), The Unburied (1999); also various scholarly articles published on George Eliot, Henry James and William Faulkner; *Style*— Charles Palliser, Esq; ✉ c/o Giles Gordon, Curtis Brown, 28/29 Haymarket, London SW1Y 4SP (0202 396 6600)

PALLISER, Prof David Michael; s of Herbert Leslie Palliser (d 1973), and Doris Violet, *née* Brown (d 1969); *b* 10 September 1939; *Educ* Bootham Sch York, Worcester Coll Oxford (MA, DPhil); *Career* asst princ Home Civil Serv 1961–64, res fell Keele Univ 1967–73, successively lectr, sr lectr and reader in economic history Univ of Birmingham 1974–85, G F Grant prof of history Univ of Hull 1985–94, prof of medieval history Univ of Leeds 1994–2004; hon visiting prof in history Univ of York; memb Int Cmmn for the History of Towns 1998–; FRHistS 1974, FSA 1977; *Books* The Staffordshire Landscape (1976), Tudor York (1979), York (jtly, 1980), The Age of Elizabeth (1983, 2 edn 1992), The Cambridge Urban History of Britain, vol 1 (ed, 2000), The Diocesan Population Returns for 1563 and 1603 (jtly, 2005), Towns and Local Communities in Medieval and Early Modern England (2006); *Style*— Prof D M Palliser, FSA

PALLISER, Rt Hon Sir (Arthur) Michael; GCMG (1977, KCMG 1973, CMG 1966), PC (1983); s of Adm Sir Arthur Palliser, KCB, DSC (d 1956), and Margaret Eva, *née* King-Salter (d 1993); *b* 9 April 1922; *Educ* Wellington, Merton Coll Oxford (MA); *m* 1948, Marie Marguerite (d 2000), da of Paul-Henri Spaak (d 1972), sometime PM of Belgium and sec-gen NATO; 3 s; *Career* late Capt Coldstream Gds (despatches); entered FO 1947, private sec to PM 1966, min Paris 1969, ambass and head of UK Delgn to EEC Brussels 1971, ambass and UK perm rep to EEC 1973–75, perm under sec and head of Dip Serv FCO 1975–82; appointed PM's special advsr during Falklands Crisis 1982; assoc fell Harvard Univ Center for Int Affrs 1982; non-exec dir: United Biscuits (Holdings) 1983–89, Ibec Inc (later Arbor Acres Farm Inc) 1983–91, Booker McConnell (later Booker plc) 1983–92, BAT Industries 1983–92, Eagle Star Holdings 1983–92, Shell Transport and Trading 1983–92, Samuel Montagu & Co Ltd 1983–96 (chm 1984–93, vice-chm 1993–96), XCL Ltd 1994–2000; dep chm: Midland Bank plc 1987–91, British Invisibles 1987–95; chm: Cncl Int Inst for Strategic Studies 1983–90, City and E London Confedn of Medicine and Dentistry 1989–95, Major Projects Assoc 1994–98; vice-chm Salzburg Global Seminar 1995–; memb: Cncl Royal Inst of Int Affairs 1982–89, Bd Royal Nat Theatre 1988–96, Br Overseas Trade Bd 1992–96; pres: Br Section Int Social Servs 1982–95, China Britain Trade Gp (CBTG) 1992–96; memb: Security Cmmn 1983–92, Trilateral Cmmn 1982–96; govr Wellington Coll 1982–92; hon fell: Merton Coll Oxford 1986, Queen Mary & Westfield Coll London (now Queen Mary Univ of London) 1990; FRSA 1983; Chevalier Order of Orange Nassau 1944, Commandeur Légion d'Honneur 1996 (Chevalier 1957); *Recreations* travel, theatre; *Clubs* Buck's; *Style*— The Rt Hon Sir Michael Palliser, GCMG; ✉ 12B Wedderburn Road, London NW3 5QG (tel 020 7794 0440, fax 020 7916 2163)

PALMANO, Cindy; da of Roger Rennels Palmano, and Jean Frances Palmano; *b* 30 January 1963; *Educ* Enfield Chace Sch for Girls, Central Sch of Art; *Children* 1 s (Buster Luke Meeuwissen Palmano b 23 Dec 1987); *Career* photographer; work represented in the Nat Portrait Gallery and Nat Museum of Photography; magazine work incl: American, English Spanish and German Vogue, Tatler, Harpers & Queen, Face, Sunday Times, Vanity, Vanity Fair, Country Life; advtg work for clients incl: Fendi, Calugia & Giannelli, Jasper Conran, Georgina Godley, Fendissme, Shiseido International, Merloni, Tom Dixon, Kodak International, The Wool Board, Harvey Nichols, Debenham's, Pommery Champagne, Principals, Ignis, Kiss FM, Harrods; dir of music video for Tori Amos (four nominations MTV awards 1992), art dir 3 album campaigns for Tori Amos; *Exhibitions* 20th Century Aquisitions (Nat Portrait Gallery) 1986, First Int Photography Biennial (Nat Museum of Bradford) 1987, Fashion and Surrealism (NY Inst of Technol) 1988, The Photographers Gallery 1989, British Cncl 1989 and 1992, Arles 1991, Bliss (RCA) 1992, Positive View (Saatchi Gallery) 1994; *Style*— Miss Cindy Palmano; ✉ (tel 020 7490 0630, fax 020 7490 3113)

PALMER, 4 Baron (UK 1933), of Reading, Co Berks; Sir Adrian Bailie Nottage Palmer; 4 Bt (UK 1916); s of Col the Hon Sir Gordon William Nottage Palmer, KCVO, OBE, TD (d 1989), and Lorna Eveline Hope Palmer, DL, *née* Bailie (d 2004); suc uncle, 3 Baron Palmer (d 1990); *b* 8 October 1951; *Educ* Eton, Univ of Edinburgh; *m* 1, 7 May 1977 (m dis 2004), Cornelia Dorothy Katharine, da of Rohan Nicholas Wadham, DFC, of Exning, Suffolk; 2 s (Hon Hugo Bailie Rohan b 1980, Hon George Gordon Nottage b 1985), 1 da (Hon Edwina Laura Marguerite b 1982); m 2, Feb 2006, Loraine McMurrey; *Heir* s, Hon Hugo Palmer; *Career* mangr Assoc Biscuits Belgium 1974–77; farmer; sec Royal Caledonian Hunt 1989–2005, chm Historic Houses Assoc for Scotland 1994–99 (vice-chm 1993–94); memb Cncl: Historic Houses Assoc for Scotland 1980–99, Historic Houses Assoc 1981–99, Scottish Landowners Fedn 1987–93; Scottish rep European Landowning Orgn 1986–92, chm Country Sports Defence Tst 1994–; pres Br Assoc of Biofuels (BABFO) 2001–; memb Queen's Body Guard for Scotland (Royal Co of Archers) 1990–96; elected hereditary peer House of Lords 1999–; *Recreations* hunting, shooting, tennis, gardening; *Clubs* New (Edinburgh), Pratt's; *Style*— The Rt Hon the Lord Palmer; ✉ Manderston, Duns, Berwickshire TD11 3PP (tel 01361 883450, fax 01361 882010)

PALMER, Adrian Oliver; QC (1992); s of Richard Palmer, and Patricia, *née* Gambling; *b* 20 August 1950; *Educ* Clifton, St John's Coll Cambridge; *m* 1974, Rosemary, da of Mortimer Shaw; 1 da (Emily b 10 March 1978), 1 s (William b 8 Sept 1982); *Career* called to the Bar 1972, recorder (Western Circuit) 1992; dep High Ct Judge 1999, head of chambers; PNBA, PIBA; *Recreations* gardens, sheep, walking; *Style*— Adrian Palmer, Esq, QC; ✉ Guildhall Chambers, 22–26 Broad Street, Bristol BS1 2HG (tel 0117 930 9000, fax 0117 930 3800, e-mail adrian.palmer@guildhallchambers.co.uk)

PALMER, Prof Andrew Clennel; s of Gerald Basil Coote Palmer (d 2004), and Muriel Gertrude, *née* Howes (d 1982); *b* 26 May 1938; *Educ* Royal Liberty Sch Romford, Univ of Cambridge (MA), Brown Univ USA (PhD); *m* 10 Aug 1963, Jane Rhiannon, da of George Ewart Evans; 1 da (Emily Abigail b 18 Sept 1971); *Career* lectr in mechanical engrg Univ of Liverpool 1965–67, lectr in engrg Univ of Cambridge 1967–75, chief engr R J Brown and Associates 1975–79, prof of civil engrg UMIST 1979–82, vice-pres engrg R J Brown and Associates 1982–85, md Andrew Palmer and Associates 1985–93, tech dir SAIC Ltd 1993–96; Jafar research prof of petroleum engrg Univ of Cambridge 1996–2005, Keppel prof Nat Univ of Singapore 2006–; visiting prof Harvard Univ

P

2002–03; pres Pipeline Industries Guild 1998–2000; CEng, memb Soc of Petroleum Engrs, FICE 1986, FREng 1990, FRS 1994; *Books* Structural Mechanics (1976), Subsea Pipeline Engineering (with R A King, 2004), Dimensional Analysis and Intelligent Experimentation (2007); *Recreations* cooking, travel, languages, glassblowing; *Clubs* Athenaeum; *Style*— Prof Andrew Palmer, FRS, FREng; ✉ #12–06 Block C, 111 Clementi Road, Singapore 129792 (tel 00 65 6775 7934, e-mail acp24@eng.cam.ac.uk)

PALMER, Andrew William; s of Victor Cecil Frederick Palmer (d 1991), of Singapore and Malaysia, and Joan, *née* Webster; *b* 14 October 1953; *Educ* Dulwich Coll; *m* 29 Nov 1975, Jane Caroline, da of Clyde Townrow; 2 s (Nicholas b 13 Sept 1982, Daniel b 6 Dec 1983); *Career* Brewer & Co (chartered accountants) 1973–77, Deloitte Haskins & Sells (chartered accountants) London and Oman 1977–82, Providence Capitol Life Assurance Co Ltd 1983–86, Commercial Union 1986–88; Legal & General Group plc: fin dir Investment Mgmnt 1988–91, fin dir Life & Pensions 1991–94, md Servs 1994–99, gp dir Servs 1996–99, gp dir Corporate 1999–2000, gp dir Fin 2001–; chm Audit Ctee and non-exec dir Slough Estates 2004–; FCA 1977; *Recreations* fly fishing, opera; *Style*— Andrew Palmer, Esq; ✉ Legal & General Group plc, Temple Court, 11 Queen Victoria Street, London EC4N 4TP (tel 020 7528 6200, fax 020 7528 6229, e-mail andrew.palmer@group.landg.com)

PALMER, Lt-Gen Anthony Malcolm Douglas; CB (2005), CBE (1998); s of late Anthony George Douglas Palmer, and Joan Aileen Palmer; *b* 13 March 1949; *Educ* Winchester, RMA Sandhurst; *m* 29 April 1972, Harriet Ann, da of late Brig Sir Ian Jardine, Bt, OBE; 2 s (Edward b 14 April 1975, Henry b 5 May 1982), 1 da (Alice b 25 Dec 1976); *Career* CO 2 Royal Green Jackets 1988–90, Cdr 8 Inf Bde 1992–94; dir Army Plans MOD 1996–99, DG Army Training and Recruiting 1999–2002, Dep Cdr Operation Stabilisation Force Bosnia 2002, DCDS (Personnel) 2002–05; *Recreations* music, bridge, fishing, golf, tennis; *Clubs* Army and Navy; *Style*— Lt-Gen Anthony Palmer, CB, CBE; ✉ c/o Army and Navy Club, 36 Pall Mall, London SW1Y 5JN

PALMER, Anthony Wheeler; QC (1979); s of late Philip Palmer; *b* 30 December 1936; *Educ* Wrekin Coll; *m* Jacqueline, da of late Reginald Fortnum, of Taunton; 1 s, 2 da; *Career* barr Gray's Inn 1962, recorder of the Crown Court 1980–2002; *Style*— Anthony Palmer, Esq, QC; ✉ 17 Warwick Avenue, Coventry CV5 6DJ

PALMER, Caroline Ann (Cally); CBE (2006); da of Christopher Palmer, of Calgary, Canada, and Ann, *née* Atkinson; *Educ* Woking Girls' GS, Univ of London (BA), London Business Sch (MSc); *m* 4 Oct 1986, Ian Julian Makowski, s of Julian Makowski; 2 s (Christopher b 24 Oct 1994, Julian b 6 June 1996), 1 da (Alexandra (twin) b 6 June 1996); *Career* Gen Mgmnt Trg Scheme SE Thames RHA 1980–83; SW Surrey RHA: hosp admin Haslemere & Dist Hosp March–Aug 1983, asst unit admin St Luke's Hosp 1983–85; Royal Free Hampstead NHS Tst (formerly Royal Free Hosp): dep gen mangr Acute Unit 1987–90 (assoc unit admin 1985–87), gen mangr Tst Implementation 1990–91, gen mangr Lawn Road Div 1991–94, dir of servs/dep chief exec 1994–98; chief exec Royal Marsden NHS Tst 1998–; sec to Tstees Royal Marsden Hosp Cancer Fund, dir RMH Cancer Fund Trading Co Ltd; memb: Cncl Inst of Cancer Research, London Business Sch Alumni Assoc; MHSM 1983; *Recreations* music, ballet, art; *Style*— Miss Cally Palmer, CBE; ✉ The Royal Marsden NHS Trust, Fulham Road, London SW3 6JJ (tel 020 7352 8171, fax 020 7376 4809)

PALMER, Dr Christopher Ralph; s of Ralph George Palmer, of Northwood, and Joy E R Palmer, *née* Herd; *b* 11 August 1961, Maidstone, Kent; *Educ* Latymer Upper Sch, Merton Coll Oxford (MA), Univ of North Carolina Chapel Hill (MS, PhD); *m* 30 Dec 1989, Cathy-Joan, *née* MacDonald; 2 da (Laura b 29 March 1994, Carolyn b 3 March 1997), 1 s (David b 18 May 2001); *Career* teaching asst Dept of Statistics Univ of N Carolina Chapel Hill 1982–88, postdoctoral res fell Dept of Biostatistics Harvard Univ 1988–89, lectr Dept of Applied Statistics Univ of Reading 1989–91, medical statistician Univ of Cambridge 1991–96, dir Centre for Applied Medical Statistics Univ of Cambridge 1996–; memb: Soc for Clinical Trials 1986, Royal Statistical Soc 1989, Int Soc of Clinical Biostatistics 1993, World Assoc of Medical Eds 1997, RSA 2001; statistical reviewer The Lancet 1993–, dep or actg ed Statistics in Medicine 1996–2000, memb Editorial Bd Statistical Methods in Medical Research 2005–; *Books* Encyclopaedic Companion to Medical Statistics (ed with B Everitt, 2005); *Recreations* Sundays: church and family; *Style*— Dr Christopher Palmer; ✉ Centre for Applied Medical Statistics, University of Cambridge, Department of Public Health and Primary Care, Institute of Public Health, Robinson Way, Cambridge CB2 0SR (tel 01223 330308, fax 01223 330330, e-mail chris.palmer@medschl.cam.ac.uk)

PALMER, David Vereker; DL (Bucks 1995); s of Brig Julian William Palmer (d 1977), and Lena Elizabeth, *née* Vereker (d 1941); *b* 9 December 1926; *Educ* Stowe; *m* 10 June 1950, Mildred (Millie), da of Edward Asbury O'Neal (d 1977), of Alabama, USA; 3 da (Melanie (Mrs Rendall) b 29 June 1951, Alice (Mrs Parsons) b 12 May 1959, Katherine (Mrs Bentley) b 21 Feb 1962); *Career* Capt Life Gds 1944–49, served in Europe and ME; mangr NY office Edward Lumley & Sons 1953–59 (joined 1949); Willis Faber & Dumas Ltd: joined 1959, dir 1961, chief exec 1978, chm 1982, ret 1988; chm Syndicate Capital Tst plc 1993–96; cmmr Royal Hosp Chelsea 1980–88, pres Insurance Inst of London 1985–86, chm Br Insurance and Investment Brokers' Assoc 1987–89; tstee Tower Hill Improvement Tst; High Sheriff Bucks 1993–94; Freeman City of London 1980, memb Worshipful Co of Insurers (Master 1982); ACII 1950, memb Lloyd's 1953; *Recreations* farming, shooting; *Clubs* City of London, Cavalry and Guards'; *Style*— David Palmer, Esq, DL; ✉ Burrow Farm, Hambleden, Henley on Thames, Oxfordshire RG9 6LT (tel 01491 571256, fax 01491 571267)

PALMER, Duncan Roderick; *b* 14 November 1958; *Educ* Leys Sch Cambridge, Westminster Coll (HND), Havard Business Sch (PMD); *Career* actg food and beverage mangr The Dubai International 1982–83 (asst food and beverage mangr 1981–82), res mangr Mandarin Oriental Macau 1984–86 (food and beverage mangr 1983–84), mangr Mandarin Oriental Manila 1986–88, res mangr The Oriental Bangkok 1988–89; gen mangr: Mandarin Oriental Jakarta 1989–95, The Savoy 1995–97, The Connaught 1997–2002, The Sukhothai Bangkok 2002–04; md The Langham Hotel London 2004–; Freeman City of London; Master Innholder, MHCIMA; *Style*— Duncan Palmer, Esq; ✉ Langham Hotel, 1c Portland Place, Regent Street, London W1B 1JA (tel 020 7636 1000, fax 020 7436 1346)

PALMER, Felicity Joan; CBE (1993); *Educ* Erith GS, Guildhall Sch of Music and Drama (AGSM, FGSM), Hochschule für Musik Munich; *Career* mezzo-soprano; Kathleen Ferrier Meml Prize 1970; major appearances at concerts in: Britain, America, Belgium, France, Germany, Italy, Spain, Poland, Czechoslovakia, Russia; operatic appearances: London and throughout England, La Scala Milan, Paris, Bordeaux, Houston, Chicago, NY, San Francisco, Geneva, Amsterdam, Toronto, Leipzig, Madrid, Berne, Zürich, Frankfurt, Hanover, Vienna, Munich, Berlin, Tokyo; peformances incl: Last Night of the Proms 1987, First Night of the Proms 1999; recordings with maj record cos incl recital records and two Victorian ballad records; *Style*— Miss Felicity Palmer, CBE; ✉ c/o Intermusica, 16 Duncan Terrace, London N1 8BZ

PALMER, Geoffrey; OBE (2005); *b* 4 June 1927; *Educ* Highgate Sch; *Career* actor; *Theatre* incl: Difference of Opinion (Garrick), West of Suez (Royal Court), Savages (Royal Court), On Approval (Haymarket), Eden End (NT), Private Lives (Globe), St Joan (Old Vic), Tishoo (Wyndhams), Kafka's Dick (Royal Court), Piano (NT); *Television* incl: The Fall and Rise of Reginald Perrin, Butterflies, The Insurance Man, The Last Song, Absurd Person Singular, Fairly Secret Army, Seasons Greetings, A Question of Attribution, As Time Goes By, Alice Through the Looking Glass; *Films* incl: O Lucky Man, The Honorary Consul, Clockwise, A Zed and Two Noughts, A Fish Called Wanda, The Madness of George III, Her Majesty Mrs Brown, Tomorrow Never Dies, Anna and the King, Peter Pan, Piccadilly Jim; *Recreations* fly fishing; *Clubs* Garrick; *Style*— Geoffrey Palmer, Esq, OBE

PALMER, Sir Geoffrey Christopher John; 12 Bt (E 1660), of Carlton, Northamptonshire; s of Lt-Col Sir Geoffrey Frederick Neill Palmer, 11 Bt (d 1951), and Cicely Kathleen, *née* Radmall (d 1989); *b* 30 June 1936; *Educ* Eton; *m* 1957, Clarissa Mary, DL (Leics 1994), eldest da of Stephen Francis Villiers-Smith; 4 da (Sophia Mary (Mrs Michael H W Neal) b 1959, Celina Lucinda (Mrs William A M Francklin) b 1961, Isabella Anne (Mrs David W R Harrington) b 1962, Rosanna Jane (Mrs Edward J G Peel) b 1967); *Heir* bro, Jeremy Palmer; *Career* is a patron of two livings; agent Burberrys Ltd in Sweden, Norway and Finland 1971–94; *Recreations* shooting, golf, Falkland Islands philately; *Clubs* MCC, I Zingari, Free Foresters, Eton Ramblers, XL, Gentlemen of Leicestershire, Gentlemen of Lincolnshire, Butterflies, Frogs, Derby Friars CC, Northants Amateurs, Old Etonian Golfing Soc, Home House; *Style*— Sir Geoffrey Palmer, Bt; ✉ Carlton Curlieu Hall, Leicestershire LE8 0PH (tel 0116 259 2656)

PALMER, Prof Godfrey Henry Oliver (Geoff); OBE (2003); s of Aubrey George Palmer (d 1985), of Jamaica and NY, and Ivy Georgina, *née* Larmond; *b* 9 April 1940, Jamaica; *Educ* Shelbourne Rd Secdy Modern London, Highbury Co Sch London, Univ of Leicester (BSc), Univ of Edinburgh (PhD), Heriot-Watt Univ (DSc); *m* 20 June 1969, (Margaret) Ann; 3 c; *Career* jr lab technician 1957–61, sr scientist Brewing Res Fndn 1968, inventor barley abrasion process for accelerating malt prodn in indust 1969, cereal conslt to various cos 1979, prof Heriot-Watt Univ 1992– (reader 1988–92); Kyoto Univ Japan: visiting prof and res scholar 1991, research assessor (food and sci) 1995; chm Scottish Section Inst of Brewing 1990–92; course chm Chivas Regel Acad 1992; convenor Church of Scotland Educn Ctee (dealing with multicultural educn) 1988–90, memb Edinburgh Lothian Community Relations Ctee 1989, chm E Mid Lothian Borders of Scot Ctee (involved in multicultural approach to racial incidence) 1990, chm Mid and E Lothian Race Relations Working Gps; memb Mgmnt Ctee Hanover Housing Ctee 2000; Edinburgh Science Festival Lecture (on ethnic foods) 2000; Chemist Award of Sci Distinction American Soc of Brewing 1998, Sir William Darling's Edinburgh Cncl's Good Citizen Award 2002; C B Fell Inst Biol; Fell Brewers Guild 1999; Fell Inst of Brewing 1985; FRSA 1997; *Books* Cereal Science and Technology (1989), contrib Reader's Digest: Complete Guide to Cooking (1989), Mr White and the Ravens (illustrated short story, 2001), The Enlightenment - To Celebrate our Common Humanity (pamphlet, 2003); *Recreations* reading, charity work, television; *Clubs* Staff, Univ of Edinburgh; *Style*— Prof Geoff Palmer, OBE; ✉ 23 Waulkmill Drive, Penicuik, Midlothian (tel 01968 675148); Department of Biological Sciences, International Centre for Brewing & Distilling, Heriot-Watt University, Riccarton, Edinburgh (tel 0131 449 5111)

PALMER, Hon Henry William; s of Viscount Wolmer (ka 1942; s of 3 Earl of Selborne), and Priscilla, *née* Egerton-Warburton, and bro of 4 Earl; *b* 12 July 1941; *Educ* Eton, ChCh Oxford (MA); *m* 1968, Minette, da of Sir Patrick William Donner, of Hurstbourne Park, Hants; 3 s (Benjamin Matthew b 1970, Robert Henry b 1972, Charles William b 1978), 1 da (Laura Cecilia b 1976); *Career* Ford Motor Co 1963–66, Associated Industrial Consultants 1966–68, chm The Centre for Interfirm Comparison 1985– (joined 1968, dep dir 1975); dir: Blackmoor Estate Ltd, Legh of Lyme Ltd; tstee Portman Estate; govr: St Paul's Sch 1989–, St Paul's Girls' Sch 1989– (dep chm 1996–2001, chm 2001–); Master Worshipful Co of Mercers 1992; FCMI; *Recreations* gardening, genealogy; *Clubs* Farmers'; *Style*— The Hon Henry Palmer; ✉ Burhunt Farm, Selborne, Alton, Hampshire GU34 3LP (tel and fax 01420 511209, e-mail harry@burhunt.com)

PALMER, Howard William Arthur; QC (1999); s of William Alexander Palmer, CBE, DL, of Bussock Wood, Newbury, and Cherry Ann, *née* Gibbs; *b* 24 June 1954; *Educ* Eton (scholarship, 1st Cricket XI), UC Oxford (MA), Coll of Law; *m* 1983, Catherine Margaret, da of late Brig T G H Jackson; 3 da (Laura b 11 March 1984, Emily b 25 Jan 1986, Harriet b 14 May 1991), 1 s (Thomas b 15 April 1988); *Career* called to the Bar 1977; lectr in law King's Coll London 1977–78, barrister-at-law 1978, recorder of the Crown Court 2006–; *Recreations* cricket, country sports, theatre; *Clubs* MCC, Berkshire CCC; *Style*— Howard Palmer, Esq, QC; ✉ 2 Temple Gardens, Temple, London EC4Y 9AY (tel 020 7822 1200, fax 020 7822 1300, e-mail hpalmer@2templegardens.co.uk)

PALMER, John; *Career* Euro ed The Guardian 1975–97 (formerly business ed, chief econ ldr writer, industrial ed); political dir European Policy Centre Brussels 1997–; secondments: dir Gtr London Enterprise Bd 1983–86, memb Bd London Tport 1985–86; author, experienced radio tv broadcaster; *Style*— John Palmer, Esq; ✉ 74 Stretton Mansions, Glaisher Street, London SE8 3JP (tel 020 8691 6551, e-mail john.anthony.palmer@gmail.com)

PALMER, Sir John Edward Somerset; 8 Bt (GB 1791); s of Sir John Palmer, 7 Bt, DL (d 1963); *b* 27 October 1926; *Educ* Canford, Pembroke Coll Cambridge, Univ of Durham; *m* 1956, Dione Catharine, da of Charles Duncan Skinner; 1 s, 1 da; *Heir* s, Robert Palmer; *Career* Lt RA serv India; Colonial Agric Serv N Nigeria 1952–61; R A Lister & Co Ltd Dursley Glos 1962–63, min Overseas Devpt 1964–68, ind conslt 1969–79, dir W S Atkins Agriculture 1979–88; *Recreations* sailing, fishing, shooting; *Style*— Sir John Palmer, Bt; ✉ Court Barton, Feniton, Honiton, Devon EX14 3BD (tel 01404 851020)

PALMER, Prof Keith Francis; s of Frank Palmer (d 1987), of Cardiff, and Gwenda Evelyn, *née* Merrick; *b* 26 July 1947; *Educ* Howardian HS Cardiff, Univ of Birmingham (BSc, PhD), Univ of Cambridge (Dip Devpt Econ); *m* 10 Aug 1974, Penelope Ann, *née* McDonagh; 4 da (Alexandra b 1977, Georgia b 1979, Katherine b 1981, Megan b 1982); *Career* NATO postdoctoral res fell Lamont Geophysical Observatory NY 1971–73, first asst sec (fin) Miny Fin Papua New Guinea 1974–78, with IMF/World Bank 1978–84, vice-chm investment banking N M Rothschild & Sons Ltd 1997– (dir corp fin 1984–93, md corp fin 1993–97, non-exec 2002–); chm Cambridge Economic Policy Associates Ltd; p/t prof of econ Univ of Dundee 1997–; chm Emerging Africa Infrastructure Fund; non-exec dir: Guy's and St Thomas' Hosp Tst, International Virtual Medical School Ltd; tstee: Cancer Research UK (also treas), Kirkhouse Tst, Guy's and St Thomas' Charitable Fndn; *Recreations* geology, music, running; *Style*— Prof Keith Palmer; ✉ N M Rothschild & Sons Ltd, New Court, St Swithins Lane, London EC4 4DU (tel 020 7280 5000, e-mail palmerk@dial.pipex.com)

PALMER, Malcolm John Frederick; *b* 22 October 1933; *Educ* Charterhouse, Queens' Coll Cambridge (MA); *m* 3 Nov 1962, Rachel M Phillips; 2 s (James b 10 Sept 1963, Stephen b 18 Jan 1965), 1 da (Melanie Ruth (Mrs Peter D Pryor) b 21 Feb 1968); *Career* Nat Serv REME 1952–54; articled Linklaters & Paines 1957–60, asst slr Rickerby & Mellersh Cheltenham 1960–62; Baker & McKenzie: asst slr London 1962–63, conslt Chicago 1963–65, ptnr London 1965–75, sr ptnr Hong Kong 1975–81, ptnr London 1981–93, chm London Mgmnt Ctee 1987–91; dep special cmmr and pt/t chm VAT and Duties Tbnl 1992–2006, memb Advsy Ctee Control Risks Gp 1996–2002, chm Disciplinary Appeals Ctee Chartered Inst of Taxation 2002–; dir Myasthenia Gravis Assoc 2004–05; memb Law Soc 1960; *Recreations* bridge, bowls, buying and occasionally reading books; *Clubs* Reform, Hurlingham, RAC; *Style*— Malcolm Palmer, Esq; ✉ Woodsford Square, London W14 8DP (tel 020 7602 6736)

PALMER, Sir (Charles) Mark; 5 Bt (UK 1886), of Grinkle Park, Co York, and of Newcastle upon Tyne; s of Sir Anthony Frederick Mark Palmer, 4 Bt (ka 1941), and Lady (Henriette Alice) Abel Smith; *b* 21 November 1941, posthumously; *Educ* Eton; *m* 1976, Hon

Catherine Elizabeth Tennant, da of 2 Baron Glenconner (d 1983); 1 da (Iris Henriette b 1977), 1 s (Arthur Morris b 9 March 1981); *Heir* s, Arthur Palmer; *Career* was a page of honour to HM The Queen 1956–59; *Style—* Sir Mark Palmer, Bt; ✉ Mill Hill Farm, Sherborne, Northleach, Gloucestershire GL54 3DU (tel 0145 14 395)

PALMER, Martin Giles; s of Rev Derek George Palmer, and Celilie June, *née* Goddard; *b* 14 October 1953; *Educ* Hartcliff Comp Sch Bristol, Commonweal Comp Sch Swindon, Selwyn Coll Cambridge (MA); *m* 1, 27 Sept 1975 (m dis 2005), Sandra Ann, da of Rudi Fischer, of Aust; 1 s (James Richard b 25 June 1978), 1 da (Elizabeth Francis b 8 Dec 1981); m 2, 2 Sept 2006, Victoria Finlay; *Career* Church Missionary Soc vol Christian Children's Home Hong Kong 1972–73, nat pres Student Christian Movement while student of theol and religious studies Cambridge 1973–76, res work on Hong Kong for World Cncl of Churches Prog to Combat Racism and Hong Kong Res Project 1976–77, regnl organiser Christian Educn Movement Gtr Manchester 1977–79, fndr dir Centre for the Study of Religion and Educn in the Inner City Manchester 1977–83, dir Int Consultancy on Religion, Educn and Culture (clients incl WWF) 1983–, fndr dir Sacred Land Project 1997–; religious advsr to HRH Prince Philip (pres WWF Int) 1986–; fndr: Christian Stateman magazine 1978–, International Labour Reports magazine 1983–; co fndr: International Sacred Literature Tst 1990, Sacred Earth Drama 1991; sec gen Alliance of Religions and Conservation 1995–; special advsr to UN Sec-Gen on climate change and the faiths 2007–; lectr worldwide, contrib to various magazines and papers and to radio and TV progs incl being religious corr for This Sunday (ITV) 1993; Sandford Award for Religious Radio 1996; *Books* incl: Faiths and Festivals (1984), Worlds of Difference (1985), Genesis or Nemesis (1988), Contemporary I Ching (1989), Taoism (1991), Dancing to Armageddon (1992), Living Christianity (1993), Tao Te Ching (1993), Chuang Tzu (1995), Sacred Britain (co-author, 1997), The Jesus Sutras (2001), Sacred History of Britain (2002), Faith and Conservation (co-author, 2003), The Times: Mapping History - World Religions (ed, 2004), Atlas of Religion (co-author, 2007); *Recreations* brass rubbing, numismatics, cooking, icons, anything Chinese; *Style—* Martin Palmer; ✉ ICOREC, The House, Kelston Park, Bath BA1 9AE (e-mail martinp@arcworld.org)

PALMER, Dr Nicholas (Nick); MP; s of Reginald Palmer, and Irena, *née* Markin; *b* 5 February 1950; *Educ* various int schs, MIT, Copenhagen, Birkbeck Coll London (PhD); *m* 5 Feb 2000, Fiona Hunter; *Career* artificial intelligence research 1975–76, computing project ldr Ciba-Geigy Switzerland 1977–82, clinical trial computing package developer MRC 1982–85, various managerial jobs Ciba-Geigy (later Novartis) Switzerland 1985–97 (ultimately head Internet Dept); MP (Lab) Broxtowe 1997–; Parly candidate (Lab) Chelsea 1983, Euro Parly candidate (Lab) E Sussex and S Kent 1995; Parly private sec to Malcolm Wicks, MP, *qv*; sec Assoc Parly Internet Gp; vice-chair Assoc Parly Animal Welfare Gp; memb Lab Animal Welfare Soc; *Recreations* postal gaming; *Style—* Dr Nick Palmer, MP; ✉ House of Commons, London SW1A 0AA (tel 020 7219 2553, constituency tel 0115 943 0721, e-mail palmern@parliament.uk)

PALMER, Prof Nigel Fenton; s of James Terence Palmer, and Constance May, *née* Fenton; *b* 28 October 1946; *Educ* Hyde Co GS, Worcester Coll Oxford (MA, DPhil); *m* 1974, Susan Patricia, *née* Aldred; 1 da (Rachel Louise b 1975), 1 s (Rupert Oliver b 1979); *Career* lectr in German Univ of Durham 1970–76; Univ of Oxford: lectr in Medieval German 1976–90, reader in German 1990–92, prof of German medieval and linguistic studies 1992–; fell St Edmund Hall Oxford 1992–; fell Humboldt Fndn; Humboldt Research Prize 2007; FBA 1997; *Publications* Visio Tnugdali (1982), Deutsche Handschriften 1100–1400 (ed, 1988), Latein und Volkssprache im Deutschen Mittlelatter (ed, 1992), Die lateinisch-deutschen Blockbücher des Berlin-Breslauer Sammelbandes (1992), Zisterzienser und ihre Bücher: Die mittelalterliche Bibliotheksgeschichte von Kloster Eberbach im Rheingau (1998); *Style—* Prof Nigel F Palmer, FBA; ✉ St Edmund Hall, Oxford OX1 4AR (e-mail nigel.palmer@seh.ox.ac.uk)

PALMER, Prof Norman Ernest; CBE (2006); s of Norman George Palmer, of Grays, Essex, and Muriel, *née* Walker; *b* 16 August 1948; *Educ* Palmer's Endowed Sch Grays, Magdalen Coll Oxford (Ford fndn scholar, exhibitioner, MA, Shepherd Prize, BCL); *m* 1, 1971 (m dis), Judith Ann Weeks; 1 da (Victoria Olivia b 1974); m 2, 1994, Ruth Redmond-Cooper; 1 da (Lilian Mary Rose b 1999); *Career* called to the Bar Gray's Inn 1973, in practice SE Circuit, head of chambers 2 Field Ct 1992–99; law reform cmmr Tasmania 1976–77; prof of law: Univ of Reading 1981–84 (head Dept of Law 1982–84), Univ of Essex 1985–90 (dean Faculty of Law 1985–88), Univ of Southampton 1990–91 (concurrently dep dean Faculty of Law); UCL: prof of commercial law 1991–2001, acad dir Inst for Philanthropy 2000–01, prof of the law of art and cultural property 2001–04 (emeritus prof 2004–), visiting prof of law KCL 2005–; E W Turner Meml lectr and visiting prof of law Univ of Tasmania 1999; Mallesons visiting fell Univ of Western Aust 1993, Ross Parsons visiting prof Univ of Sydney 1990 and 1991; sec and jt dir Int Cultural Property Soc 1990–95, princ academic advsr Inst of Art and Law 1995–, accredited mediator Centre for Dispute Resolution 1999–, jt dir ArtResolve 2000–; chm: Ministerial Advsy Panel on Illicit Trade in Cultural Objects 2000–05, Treasure Valuation Ctee 2001–, Departmental Working Gp on Human Remains in Public Collections 2001–03; pres Fndn for Int Cultural Diplomacy 2006–; memb: Treasure Trove Reviewing Ctee 1996–97, Standing Conference on Portable Antiquities and Portable Antiquities Working Gp 1996–, Treasure Valuation Ctee 1997–, Spoliation Advsy Panel 2000–; ed-in-chief: Int Jl of Cultural Property 1990–95, Art Antiquity and Law 1996–; DUniv (hc) Geneva 2005; FRSA 1999, Hon RICS 2004, FSA 2005; *Publications* Bailment (1979, 2 edn 1991), Halsbury's Laws of England (contrib, 1984–99), Emden's Construction Law (5 vols, jtly 1990), Product Liability in the Construction Industry (with E McKendrick, 1993), Interests in Goods (ed with E McKendrick and contrib, 1993, 2 edn 1998), Butterworth's Manual of Construction Law (with Ruth Redmond-Cooper and S Bickford-Smith, 1993), Encyclopaedia of Forms and Precedents (contrib, 1994, 2000 and 2004), Laws of Australia (contrib, 1995), Art Loans (1997), The Recovery of Stolen Art (with Ruth Redmond-Cooper, Prof A Hudson and Sir Anthony Mason, 1998), Museums and the Holocaust: Law, Principles and Practice (2000), English Private Law (contrib, 2000 and 2004, 2 edn 2007); also author of numerous papers in various learned journals and periodicals; *Recreations* literature, archaeology, collecting antique motor cars, memorial verse; *Style—* Prof Norman Palmer, CBE; ✉ 3 Stone Buildings, Lincolns Inn, London WC2A 3XL (tel 020 7242 4937, e-mail npalmer@3sblaw.co.uk)

PALMER, Richard John; OBE (2004), JP (1961), DL (Berks 1994); s of Reginald Howard Reed Palmer (d 1970); *b* 5 November 1926; *Educ* Eton; *m* 1951, Hon Sarah Faith Georgina Spencer, da of 1 Viscount Churchill, GCVO (d 1934); 3 s, 1 da; *Career* served Grenadier Guards Lt 1944–48; chm Thames Valley Broadcasting plc; vice-pres Berks Assoc of Young People; vice-pres YMCA Eng; High Sheriff Berks 1979–80; *Recreations* shooting, fishing; *Clubs* White's; *Style—* Richard Palmer, Esq, OBE, DL; ✉ Queen Anne's Mead, Swallowfield, Berkshire RG7 1ST (tel 0118 988 3264, fax 0118 988 5167)

PALMER, Prof Richard M; *Educ* Univ of London (BDS, PhD); *Career* lectr Royal Dental Hosp London 1978–85, currently prof and head of restorative dentistry GKT Dental Inst KCL; pres British Soc of Periodontology 2003–04; memb: Assoc of Dental Implantology, British Soc of Periodontology, European Assoc of Osseointegration, Int Assoc for Dental Research; Colgate Prize 1986, Colyer Prize RSM 1986; FDSRCS 1979, FDSRCSE 1997; *Style—* Prof Richard M Palmer; ✉ GKT Dental Institute, Guy's Tower, King's College London, Guy's Hospital, London SE1 9RT

PALMER, Richard William (Dick); CBE (2006, OBE 1986); s of Richard Victor Palmer (d 1983), of Llangwm, Pembs, and Mary Ellen, *née* Sambrook (d 1984); *b* 13 April 1933; *Educ* Haverfordwest GS, Trinity Coll Carmarthen, Chester Coll, Univ of Leicester (MEd); *Career* sports administrator; sec gen Br Students' Sports Fedn 1964–72 (pres 1979–86), organising sec World Univ Cross Country Championship 1970 and World Univ Judo Championship 1971; gen sec: Cwlth Games Cncl for England 1977–86, British Olympic Assoc 1977–97 (exec vice-pres 1997–), conslt to IOC 1998–; dep chef de mission GB Olympic teams Innsbruck and Montreal 1976; chef de mission GB Olympic teams: Lake Placid and Moscow 1980, Sarajevo and LA 1984, Calgary and Seoul 1988, Albertville and Barcelona 1992, Lillehammer 1994, Atlanta 1996; gen team mangr Eng Cwlth Games teams: Edmonton 1978, Brisbane 1982, Edinburgh 1986; chm Confederation of British Sport 1978–79; memb: IOC Cmmn for New Sources of Fin 1981–95, Exec Bd Euro Nat Olympic Ctees 1989–98, IOC Cmmn for 1996 Olympic Games Atlanta and 2000 Olympic Games Sydney; pres British Inst of Sports Administrators 1997–2004, tstee Sports Coach UK 1997–, tstee Br Olympic Fndn 1997–, memb Sports Cncl for Wales 2006–; chm Assoc of Nat Olympic Ctees Cmmn for Olympic Games 1982–88 and 1992–99; tech dir London 2012 Bid; lectr and tutor MEMES prog; Sports Writers Assoc Award 1996, Award of Merit Assoc of Nat Olympic Ctees, Olympic Order 1998, Emlyn Jones Award 2003; formerly rugby and athletics rep Pembrokeshire (club capt); Freeman of Pembroke; FRSA; *Clubs* East India (life memb), Scribes, Cardiff Co, Fullwell and Haverfordwest Golf, Llangwm Boat; *Style—* Dick Palmer, Esq, CBE; ✉ British Olympic Association, 1 Wandsworth Plain, London SW18 1EH (tel 020 8871 2677, fax 020 8871 9104, e-mail richard.palmer@boa.org.uk)

PALMER, Prof Robert Leslie; s of Reginald John Freeman Palmer (d 1987), of Leamington Spa, and Marion May, *née* Sims (d 1988); *b* 15 March 1944; *Educ* Warwick Sch, St George's Med Sch Univ of London (MB BS); *m* 19 July 1969, Mary Violet, da of Frank Carter, of Stamford Hill, London; 1 da (Rebecca b 23 Oct 1971); *Career* res worker and hon lectr St George's Hosp Med Sch Univ of London 1971–73, lectr in psychiatry St Mary's Hosp Med Sch 1974–75; Univ of Leicester: sr lectr in psychiatry 1975–2005, conslt psychiatrist and hon prof of psychiatry 2005–; ed European Eating Disorders Review 1996–; author of papers on psychiatry and psychosomatic med especially clinical eating disorders; former examiner: for membership RCPsych, Univ of London final MB examination, Nat Univ of Singapore M Med Sci; MRCPsych 1972, FRCPsych 1984; *Books* Anorexia Nervosa: a guide for sufferers and their families (1980 and 1989), Helping People with Eating Disorders (2000); *Recreations* reading, jogging, birdwatching; *Style—* Prof Robert Palmer; ✉ University Department of Psychiatry, Brandon Mental Health Unit, Leicester General Hospital, Gwendolen Road, Leicester LE5 4PW (tel 0116 225 6211, fax 0116 225 6235, e-mail rlp@le.ac.uk)

PALMER, Prof Stuart Beaumont; s of Frank Beaumont Palmer (d 1990), and Florence Beryl, *née* Wilkinson (d 1995); *b* 6 May 1943; *Educ* Ilkeston GS, Univ of Sheffield (BSc, PhD, DSc); *m* 1966, Susan Mary, da of Arthur Clay; 2 s (Richard Stuart b 30 May 1967, Anthony John b 7 May 1969), 1 da (Katherine Mary b 20 Dec 1973); *Career* reader in applied physics Univ of Hull 1967–87; Univ of Warwick: prof of experimental physics 1987–, chm Physics Dept 1989–2001, pro-vice-chllr 1995–2001, acting vice-chllr 2001, dep vice-chllr 2001–; visiting prof: Univ of Grenoble 1982–83, Queen's Univ Ontario 1986; ed-in-chief Nondestructive Testing and Evaluation (jl); FInstP 1978, FInstNDT 1982, FIEE 1992, CEng 1992, FRSA 1999, FREng 2000; *Publications* Advanced University Physics (with M S Rogalski, 1995, 2 edn 2005), Quantum Physics (with M S Rogalski, 1999), Solid State Physics (with M S Rogalski, 2000), Encyclopaedia Britannica (ed Physics section, 1968–89); also author of over 270 research papers; *Recreations* tennis, sailing, music; *Clubs* Athenaeum, Hull Sailing, Coventry Flying, Warwick Tennis; *Style—* Prof Stuart Palmer; ✉ Max Gate, Forrest Road, Kenilworth, Warwickshire CV8 1LT; University of Warwick, Coventry, Warwickshire CV4 8UW (tel 024 7657 4004, e-mail s.b.palmer@warwick.ac.uk)

PALMER, Dr Timothy Noel (Tim); s of Alfred Henry Palmer (d 1987), of Oxshott, Surrey, and Anne Josephine, *née* Hayes (d 2001); *b* 31 December 1952, Kingston upon Thames, Surrey; *Educ* Wimbledon Coll, Univ of Bristol (BSc), Wolfson Coll Oxford (DPhil, DSc); *m* 21 Oct 1978, Gillian, da of Philip Dyer; 3 s (Samuel James b 27 Jan 1985, Gregory Thomas b 19 Nov 1988, Brendan George b 13 Sept 1993); *Career* visiting scientist Univ of Washington 1981–82, PSO Meteorological Office 1978–86, div head European Centre for Medium-Range Weather Forecasts 1986–; co-ordinator EU Provost and Demeter Climate Projects, co-chair UN/World Meteorological Orgn (WMO) Clivar Scientific Steering Gp; memb External Advsy Bd: Earth Inst Columbia Univ, Hadley Centre; lead author Third Assessment Report Intergovernmental Panel on Climate Change, also author of numerous pubns in peer-reviewed scientific literature; Royal Soc Esso Energy Award, Royal Meteorological Soc Buchan Award, American Meteorological Soc Charney Award; fell American Meteorological Soc, FRMetS 1978, FRS 2003, memb Academia Europaea 2004; *Recreations* golf, cycling, skiing, playing guitar; *Clubs* W Berks Golf; *Style—* Dr Tim Palmer; ✉ European Centre for Medium-Range Weather Forecasts, Shinfield Park, Reading, Berkshire RG2 9AX (tel 0118 949 9600, fax 0118 986 9450, e-mail tim.palmer@ecmwf.int)

PALMER, (Ann) Veronica Margaret; OBE (1993, MBE 1977); da of late Luke Murray, of Trim, Co Meath, Ireland, and Mary, *née* Neville; *b* 20 March 1940; *Educ* Convent of Mercy Trim; *m* Barrie Palmer, s of Arthur Alfred Palmer, and Dorothy Palmer; 3 da (Judith, Susan, Linda); *Career* student teacher 1958–61; RAF 1961–78, ret as Sqdn Ldr 1978; Parly sec Brewers' Soc 1981–88, DG Confedn of Passenger Transport UK 1989–2001, chm NI Transport Holding Co 2005– (dir 2002–); non-exec dir Arriva plc 2001–; memb Cmmn for Integrated Transport 1999–2002, memb Bd BTA 2000–03; Freeman City of London, Liveryman Worshipful Co of Carmen 1997; FRSA 1993, FCIT 1993; *Recreations* hill walking, reading, theatre and horse racing; *Clubs* RAF; *Style—* Mrs Veronica Palmer, OBE; ✉ Tully House, Beachamwell Road, Cockley Cley, Norfolk PE37 8AR (tel 01760 725496)

PALMER, William Alexander; CBE (1983), DL (Berks 1992); s of Reginald Howard Reed Palmer, MC, DL (d 1970), of Hurst Grove, Berks, and Lena Florence, *née* Cobham (d 1981); *b* 21 June 1925; *Educ* Eton; *m* 1949, Cherry Ann, da of late Arthur Gibbs (d 1945), of London; 2 s, 2 da; *Career* serv Grenadier Gds 1943–47, Capt, serv NW Europe and Palestine; dir Huntley & Palmers Ltd 1951 (chm 1980–83), dir Huntley & Palmers Foods plc 1971–83, chm Huntley Boorne & Stevens Ltd until 1983; pres: Flour Milling and Baking Res Assoc 1971–84, Royal Warrant Holders' Assoc 1976–77; chm Cake & Biscuit Alliance 1980–83; High Sheriff Berks 1974–75; vice-pres Univ of Reading 1995–98 (treas 1982–95); Hon LLD 2003; *Recreations* shooting, tennis, gardening; *Clubs* Cavalry and Guards'; *Style—* William Palmer, Esq, CBE, DL; ✉ Bussock Wood, Snelsmore Common, Newbury, Berkshire RG14 3BT (tel 01635 248203); Latheronwheel House, Caithness KW5 6DW (tel 01593 741206)

PALOMBA, Louise J; *Educ* Leicester Poly, Univ of Cambridge; *Career* architect; Leonard Manasseh Partnership 1985–86, Panter Hudspith Architects 1989–91, Richard Rogers Partnership 1990–; *Projects* incl: Channel 4 TV HQ, Daiwa I, Strasbourg Ct of Human Rights, Bordeaux Law Cts, Thames Valley Univ Learning Resource Centre, Daiwa II, Lloyds Register of Shipping, Heathrow Airport Terminal 5, Madrid Airport Spain; *Style—* Ms Louise Palomba; ✉ Richard Rogers Partnership, Thames Wharf, Rainville Road, London W6 9HA

PALUMBO, Baron (Life Peer UK 1991), of Walbrook in the City of London; Peter Garth Palumbo; s of late Rudolph Palumbo, and Elsie Palumbo; *b* 20 July 1935; *Educ* Eton, Worcester Coll Oxford (MA); *m* 1, 1959, Denia (d 1986), da of late Maj Lionel Wigram;

P

1 s, 2 da; m 2, 1986, Hayat, er da of late Kamel Morowa; 2 da (Hon Petra Louise b 1989, Hon Lana Rose b 1991), 1 s (Hon Philip Rudolph b 1992); *Career* chm: Tate Gallery Fndn 1986–87, Painshill Park Tst Appeal 1986–96, Arts Cncl of GB 1989–94, Serpentine Gallery 1994–; tstee: Mies van der Rohe Archive 1977–, Tate Gallery 1978–85, Whitechapel Art Gallery Fndn 1981–87, Natural History Museum 1994–2004, Design Museum 1995–2005; memb Cncl Royal Albert Hall 1995–99, chm jury Pritzker Architecture Prize 2004–; tstee and hon treas Writers' and Scholars' Educnl Tst 1984–99, dir and memb Bd Andy Warhol Fndn for the Visual Arts 1994–97; chllr Univ of Portsmouth 1992–2000; govr: LSE 1976–94, Royal Shakespeare Theatre 1995–2000, Whitgift Sch 2002–; Patronage of the Arts Award Cranbrook Acad of Arts Detroit 2002; Liveryman Worshipful Co of Salters; Hon DLitt Univ of Portsmouth 1993; Hon FRIBA, Hon FFB 1994, Hon FIStructE 1994; Nat Order of the Southern Cross (Federal Repub of Brazil) 1993; *Recreations* music, travel, gardening, reading; *Clubs* White's, Pratt's, Athenaeum, Garrick, Knickerbocker; *Style*— The Lord Palumbo; ✉ 2 Astell Street, London SW3 3RU (tel 020 7351 7371)

PANAYI, Prof Gabriel Stavros; s of Stavros Panayi, of Cyprus, and Maria, *née* Tarsides; *b* 9 November 1940; *Educ* Royal GS Lancaster, Gonville & Caius Coll Cambridge (Sir Lionel Whitby Medal), St Mary's Hosp Med Sch London (ScD, MD, Max-Bonn Pathology Medal); *m* 11 March 1973, Alexandra, da of Alexander Jourrou; 2 s (Stavros b 5 July 1977, Alexander b 8 Feb 1982); *Career* house physician Queen Elizabeth Hosp Welwyn Garden City 1965–66, house surgn St Mary's Hosp London 1966, SHO in medicine Gen Hosp Nottingham 1966, SHO in pathology Central Middx Hosp London 1967, jr res fell MRC St Mary's and Kennedy Inst of Rheumatology London 1967–69, clinical res fell Northern Gen Hosp Edinburgh 1970–73; GKT (formerly UMDS): Arthritis and Rheumatism Cncl (ARC) lectr 1973–76, ARC sr lectr 1976–80, ARC prof of rheumatology 1980–; RSM: former sec Exec Ctee Section for Medicine, Experimental Medicine and Therapeutics, pres Section for Clinical Immunology and Allergy; former memb Exec Ctee Heberden Soc; BSR: pres 2000–02, memb Exec Ctee, Heberden orator; Kave Berglund lectr Univ of Lund, Nana Svartz Lectr Swedish Acad of Med; memb: BSI, AASI, American Coll of Rheumatology; FRCP; *Books* Annual Research Review of Rheumatoid Arthritis (1977–81), Immunopathogenesis of Rheumatoid Arthritis (1979), Essential Rheumatology for Nurses and Therapists (1980), Scientific Basis of Rheumatology (1982), Seronegative Spondyloarthropathies Clinics in Rheumatic Diseases (1985), Immunogenetics (1985); *Recreations* photography, painting, reading; *Style*— Prof Gabriel Panayi; ✉ Departmetn of Rheumatology, King's College London School of Medicine at Guy's, King's and St Thomas', Guy's Hospital, London SE1 9RT (tel 020 7188 5880, fax 020 7188 5883, e-mail gabriel.panayi@kcl.ac.uk)

PANAYIOTOU, Panos; *b* 1953; *m* 1973, Svanhvit Olafsdottir; 1 da (Astria Lydia b 1985); *Career* architect; Scott Brownrigg & Turner Ltd: joined 1982, dir 1990, memb Bd of Dirs 1993, currently design dir; work incl: Lulu Leisure Island Abu Dhabi, designs and implementation for refurbishment of Berkeley Square House London 1981, design and implementation 7 Dials residential devpt Fairfield Court Covent Garden 1988, designs for Digital's Southern Logistics Centre Reading 1988, design and implementation for offices and residential devpt Orange Street London 1989, design and implementation Jardin House Crutched Friars City of London, design and implementation BP Engineering HQ Uxbridge, concept design BBC HQ White City, masterplanning and design concept Camden Goods Yard, design proposals and implementation of office devpt Denison House Victoria London 1990, masterplan major office and retail park Athens 1994, Mythos Park (theme park) Athens 1995, leisure and sports resort Mallorca 1997, design and implementation for Elysium Resort Hotel Paphos, Napa Plaza Hotel Ayia Napa, Amathus Vacation Resort Cyprus; RIBA 1981, ARCUK 1981; *Style*— Panos Panayiotou; ✉ Scott Brownrigg & Turner Ltd, Tower House, 10 Southampton Street, Covent Garden, London WC2E 7HA (tel 020 7240 7766, fax 020 7836 3556, e-mail panos@scottbrownrigg.com, website www.sbt.co.uk)

PANCHENKO, Oxana; da of Vladimir Borisovitch Panchenko (d 1988), of Ukraine, and Valentina Timofeyerna, *née* Nychoroshkova; *b* 28 November 1970; *Educ* Kiev Ballet Sch; *m* 7 April 1995, Jeremy Seth Gilbert, s of Terry Gilbert; *Career* dancer; Kiev Opera House 1988–90, sr soloist with English Nat Ballet 1990–93, Munich Ballet 1993–95, modelling work 1995–97, City Ballet of London 1997 and 2000, Wayne Sleep's Aspects of Dance 1999, K Ballet 2001, George Piper Dances 2001–, Adventures in Motion Pictures 2003–04; featured in The Rough Guide to Choreography (Channel 4) 2004; *Performances* with Kiev Opera House: Two Friends of Kitri in Don Quixote, Swan Lake, Ophelia in Hamlet, Juliet in Romeo and Juliet, Effirn in La Sylphide, roles in La Bayadere; with English Nat Ballet: Olga in Onegin, Bianca in The Taming of the Shrew, Zivia in Romeo and Juliet by Ashton, Act III Pas de Trois in La Bayadere, Peasant Pas de Deux and Myrtha in Giselle, Big Swans and Pas de Trois in Swan Lake, Apollo by Balanchine, Snow Queen, Mirlitons and Arabian Dance in The Nutcracker, the Waltz in Les Sylphides, Zobeide in Sherherazade, White Girls in Etudes, Pas de Quatre in Raymonda, Autumn Fairy in Cinderella; with Munich Ballet: princ roles in Sinfonietta and Svadebka by Kylian, Brief Fling by Twyla Tharp, Symphony in C by Balanchine, Complete Consort by Bintley, Swan Lake, Giselle, The Nutcracker, Don Quixote, A Midsummer Night's Dream; with City Ballet of London: princ role in The Sleeping Beauty, princ role in Sinfonietta Giocosa, Five Tangos by Hans Van Manen, Entre Dos Aguas by Robert North, solo in TBA by Christopher Hampson, *qv*, Ghost of Christmas Past in Christmas Carol by Christopher Hampson; with Wayne Sleep's Aspects of Dance: Dineresade by Christopher Hampson, solo in Dragon Fly, Pas de Deux in Sleeping Beauty, Canciones by Christopher Hampson; with K Ballet: Rhapsody by Ashton, Six Faces by Adam Cooper; with George Piper Dances: Steptext by William Forsythe, Sigue by Paul Lightfoot, Moments of Plastic Jubilation by Michael Nunn, *qv*, and William Trevitt, *qv*, Truly Great Thing by Charles Linehan, Lady Barnard in Other Mens Wives by Matthew Hart, *qv*, Mesmerics by Christopher Wheeldon, Trio by Russell Maliphant, *qv*, Ophelia in Non Exuent by Cathy Marston, Approximate Sonata I, V by William Forsythe, Broken Fall by Russell Maliphant, Follow By William Trevitt; The Queen in Swan Lake (with Adventures in Motion Pictures) 2003–04; *Awards* Outstanding Performance Time Out Award 2001 (for Steptext), Outstanding Female Classical Artist Critics Circle National Dance Award 2003; *Recreations* travel, music, reading, yoga, films, dogs; *Style*— Mrs Oxana Panchenko; ✉ George Piper Dances, 12 Harley Street, London W1G 9PG (tel 020 7637 5505, fax 020 7323 6480, e-mail info@gpdances.com)

PANDE, Dr Shiv Kumar; MBE (1989), JP (Liverpool 1982), DL (Merseyside 2002); *b* Jawad, India; *Educ* HS Bombay, Inter-Sci Jai Hind Coll Bombay, Vikram Univ Ujjian (MB BS), Univ of Indore (MS); *Career* hosp appts Indore, Gwalior and Bombay 1963–70 (lectr in surgery Med Coll Jabalpur 1968–71), SHO A&E Dept Royal Albert Edward Infirmary Wigan 1971; registrar in cardiothoracic surgery: London Chest Hosp 1972, Royal Liverpool Children's, Broadgreen and Fazakerley Hosps Liverpool 1972–74; A&E med asst various Liverpool hosps 1974, clinical med offr Child Health and Family Planning St Helens and Knowsley HA 1974–95, princ in gen practice Liverpool 1976– (trainee 1974–75, locum/ptnr 1975–76); chm int seminars Delhi (Family Planning in India) 1990 and Cairo (Recent Advances in Treatment of AIDS) 1992; memb GMC 1994– (treas 1999–), assoc memb Fitness to Pracice Panel GMC 2003–; Overseas Doctors Assoc: nat vice-chm 1987–93, chm Merseyside and Cheshire Div 1994–96, nat gen sec 1996–; sec (N region) Indo-Br Assoc 1982–; advsr and presenter This is your Right? (Granada TV) 1980–92; memb Advsy Panel: Radio Merseyside 1982–87, BBC North TV 1983–88; interviewed variously for local, nat and int press, radio and TV; fndr memb Inter Faith Merseyside; memb (N Region) BAFTA, memb Med Journalists Assoc/Assoc of Broadcasting; Lloyds TSB Asian Jewel Award 2004; FRIPHH 1988, MFCH 1990, FRCGP 2003 (MRCGP 1996); *Recreations* cricket (doctor on duty at One Day Internationals and Test Matches at Lancs CCC since 1984), fundraising for charity; *Style*— Dr Shiv Pande, MBE; ✉ e-mail shiv.pande@talk21.com.uk and shivpande@yahoo.com, website www.merseyworld.com/iba/

PANDOR, Dr Shabir Ahmed Gulam; s of Gulam Mahomed Pandor, of Lusaka, Zambia, and Khadija Badat; *b* 1 January 1955; *Educ* Epsom Coll, UCL (LDS RCS, BDS), MFGDP(UK), DDFHom; *m* 17 Dec 1985, (Maria) Suzy, da of Burghart Ferenc (d 1991), of Budapest, Hungary; 1 da (Aneesa b 21 Jan 1988); *Career* assoc dentist in practice: Chatham Kent 1980–81, Kingsway London 1979–80 and 1981–85; in own surgery Harley St 1985–; memb: BDA 1979, Faculty of Gen Dental Practioners (UK), British Endodontic Soc, British Homeopathic Dental Assoc, Br Med Acupuncture Soc, Int Assoc of Oral Med and Toxicology (IAOMT), Biological Dentistry, European Soc for Oral Laser Applications (ESOLA); *Recreations* golf, complementary med; *Style*— Dr Shabir Pandor; ✉ 44 Harley Street, London W1G 9PS (tel 020 7580 1076, fax 020 7580 8702, e-mail sapandor@aol.com)

PANESAR, Mudhsuden Singh (Monty); *b* 25 April 1982, Luton; *Educ* Stopsley HS Bedford, Loughborough Univ; *Career* cricketer; with Northants CCC (first team debut 2001); England: 20 Test caps, 25 one day int appearances, one Twenty20 appearance, Test debut v India 2006, memb touring squad Australia 2006–07, memb squad World Cup 2007, ranked 6th best test match bowler in the world 2007; *Style*— Monty Panesar, Esq

PANFORD, Frank; QC (1999); s of Frank Essansoh Martin Panford (d 1993), and Susanna, *née* Holdbrook-Smith (d 1996); *b* 23 January 1949; *Educ* Holborn Coll of Law (LLB), Univ of Cambridge (LLB), Hague Acad of Int Law (Diplôme de Droit Privé); *m* 1, 1979 (m dis 1985), Hilary Anne Luper; m 2, 1994, Najma Khanzada, da of Kabir Khan; 3 da (Lisa Esi b 1983, Safi-Ullah Kwame b 1998, Nur Ato Kwamena 1999); *Career* called to the Bar Middle Temple 1972, lectr in law Univ of Westminster 1974–94, legal advsr/film examiner Br Bd of Film Classification 1984–90, practising barrister 1992–; *Recreations* african politics, music, cooking, travel; *Style*— Frank Panford, Esq, QC; ✉ Doughty Street Chambers, 11 Doughty Street, London WC1N 2PG (tel 020 7404 1313, fax 020 7404 2283)

PANK, Edward Charles; s of Charles Clifford Pank (d 1974), of Norwich, and Marjorie Eira, *née* Bringloe (d 1988); *b* 5 June 1945; *Educ* Framlingham Coll, Trinity Hall Cambridge (MA), St Thomas' Hosp Univ of London (MB BS); *m* 17 Sept 1983, (Judith) Clare, da of Anthony Pethick Sommerville (d 1988), of Minchinhampton; *Career* admitted slr 1969; early career as merchant banker (incl dir Slater Walker Ltd 1974–76), subsequently medical dir St Thomas's Hosp London and Queen Elizabeth Hosp King's Lynn, co slr and sec ICAP plc (formerly Exco International plc) 1987–2003; non-exec dir: Bestpark Int Ltd 2004–, West Norfolk NHS Primary Care Tst 2004–; Liveryman Worshipful Soc of Apothecaries 1986; MRCS, LRCP; *Style*— Edward Pank, Esq

PANNICK, David Philip; QC (1992); s of Maurice Arthur Pannick (d 2000), of London, and Rita Lois, *née* Cushcat; *b* 7 March 1956; *Educ* Bancroft's Sch, Hertford Coll Oxford (MA, BCL); *m* 1, Denise (d 1999), da of Maurice Sloam; 2 s (Samuel b 1983, Joel b 1985), 1 da (Shula b 1988); m 2, Nathalie, da of David Trager-Lewis; 1 da (Katie b 2005), 1 s (James b 2007); *Career* called to the Bar Gray's Inn 1978, jr counsel to the Crown Common Law 1988–92; fell All Souls Coll Oxford 1978–, hon fell Hertford Coll Oxford 2004–; *Books* Judges (1987), Advocates (1992), Human Rights Law and Practice (with Lord Lester of Herne Hill, 1999 and 2004); *Recreations* cinema, watching television, supporting Arsenal FC; *Style*— David Pannick, Esq, QC; ✉ Blackstone Chambers, Blackstone House, Temple, London EC4Y 9BW (tel 020 7583 1770, fax 020 7822 7222)

PANNONE, Rodger John; DL; s of Cyril John Alfred Pannone (d 1982), and Violet Maud, *née* Weekes (d 1987); *b* 20 April 1943; *Educ* St Brendan's Coll Bristol, Manchester Coll of Law, London Coll of Law; *m* 13 Aug 1966, Patricia Jane, da of William Todd; 2 s (Mark b 24 Oct 1969, Richard b 7 Oct 1971), 1 da (Elizabeth b 19 July 1979); *Career* admitted slr 1969; conslt and former sr ptnr Pannone & Partners; Law Soc of Eng and Wales: memb Cncl 1978–96, dep vice-pres 1991–92, vice-pres 1992–93, pres 1993–94; chm Coll of Law 1999–2005; memb Lord Chllr's Advsy Ctee on Civil Justice 1985–88, former memb Supreme Court Rule Ctee; chm Renovo plc 2006–, non-exec dir Cooperative Legal Services Ltd 2006–; chm Manchester Concert Hall Ltd 1994–, chm Cncl Univ of Manchester 2000–04; vice-pres: Acad of Experts 1992–, Manchester Community Tst 1992–; hon fell: Manchester Met Univ 1994, Univ of Birmingham; Hon DLitt Univ of Salford 1993, LLD (hc) Nottingham Trent Univ 1993, Hon LittD Univ of Manchester 2004; hon life memb Canadian Bar; FRSA 1993; *Recreations* fell walking, wine and food, travelling; *Clubs* St James's (Manchester), Wyresdale Anglers; *Style*— Rodger Pannone, Esq, DL; ✉ Pannone LLP, 123 Deansgate, Manchester M3 2BU (tel 0161 909 3000, 0161 909 4444, e-mail rodger.pannone@pannone.co.uk)

PANTON, Dr Francis Harry; CBE (1997, MBE (Mil) 1948); s of George Emerson Panton; *b* 25 May 1923; *Educ* City Sch Lincoln, Univ of Nottingham (PhD), Univ of Kent (PhD); *m* 1, 1952, Audrey Mary, *née* Lane (d 1989); 2 s; m 2, 1995, Pauline Joyce Dean; *Career* MOD: asst chief sci advsr (nuclear) 1969–76, dir Propellants Explosives and Rocket Motors Estab Waltham Abbey and Westcott 1976–80, head of Rocket Motor Exec 1976–80; dir Royal Armament R&D Estab Fort Halstead 1980–84; conslt: Cabinet Office 1985–97, MOD 1984–99; chm: Mgmnt Ctee Canterbury Archaeological Tst 1985–2000, Dover Bronze Age Boat Tst 1994–2006; vice-pres and hon librarian Kent Archaeological Soc; FRSC, FRAeS, FRSA; *Recreations* local history, bridge; *Clubs* Reform; *Style*— Dr Francis Panton, CBE; ✉ tel and fax 01795 472218

PANTON, Janice; MBE (1999); da of Peter White (d 1963), of NY, and Ellen Lynch, *née* Peters (d 2000); *b* 22 January 1948; *Educ* Univ of Westminster (MA); *m* 30 July 1977, Roger Huntley, s of Albert Kenneth Panton; 2 s (Stuart Roger b 28 Sept 1978, Kevin Huntley b 31 May 1980); *Career* pt/t teacher 1981–85, legal sec to 1989, sec to Baroness Hamwee, GLA, *qv*, 1991; head Montserrat Govt UK Office, pt/t vol co-ordinator Montserrat Aid Ctee 1995–98; tstee: Montserrat Aid Ctee 1989–, Montserrat Fndn, Refuge; *Publications* Waiting on the Volcano (1996); *Recreations* music, gardening, reading; *Style*— Mrs Janice Panton, MBE; ✉ 13 Hyde Park Gardens, Winchmore Hill, London N21 2PN (tel 020 8360 2392, e-mail janicepanton@yahoo.co.uk); Monserrat Government UK Office, 180–186 Kings Cross Road, London WC1X 9DE (tel 020 7520 2622, fax 020 7520 2624, e-mail j.panton@montserratgov.co.uk)

PANTON-LEWIS, Catherine Rita; da of John Panton, MBE, of Larbert, Stirlingshire, and Elizabeth Renwick, *née* Seaton; *b* 14 June 1955; *Educ* Larbert HS, Univ of Edinburgh (MA), Thames Valley Univ (Postgrad Dip Hospitality Mgmnt); *m* 11 April 1991, Philip Lewis, of Llandybie, Dyfed; *Career* golfer; Scot girls champion 1969, Br amateur champion 1976, Scot Sportswoman of the Year 1976, E of Scot women's champion 1976; memb Br World Cup Amateur Team 1976, Vagliano Team 1977, played on USLPGA Tour 1983–85, qualified to play on US Women Sr Golf Tour 2004; winner: 1979 Women's Professional Golf Tour Order of Merit, 14 tournaments on the Ladies European Tour incl Portugese Open in 1986 and 1987 and Scot Women's Open in 1988, United Insurance section Ladies' Barbados Open 1993, Southern England Student Sports Assoc Championships 1994; exec dir McDonald's WPGA Championship of Europe 1996–99, events mangr Ronald McDonald House Charities Grand Banquet and Golf Cup 2000–02, staff pro The Berkshire Golf Club 2002–; dep chairwoman Women's PGA; memb: PGA (advanced fell), LET 1978, US Legends' Tour (formerly US Women Srs' Golf Assoc); *Recreations* reading, current affairs, stock market, cinema, horse racing, golf, su doku; *Clubs* Glenbervie Golf, Pitlochry Golf, Silloth Golf, The Berkshire; *Style*— Mrs Catherine Panton-Lewis

PAPADAKIS, Prof Andreas Constantine; s of Constantine Paul Papadakis (d 1992), of Nicosia, Cyprus, and Natalia Christou (d 1978); *b* 17 June 1938; *Educ* Faraday House (DFH), Imperial Coll London (DIC), Brunel Univ (PhD); *Career* publisher; ed: Architectural Design 1977–92, Art and Design 1985–92; md Academy Gp Ltd 1987–92 (imprint Academy Edns, founded 1968); dir Hellenic Centre London 1993–94, chm Hellenic Inst Royal Holloway Univ of London 1994–97, fndr Hellenic Inst Tstp; visiting prof Faculty of Architecture Univ of Lisbon Portugal, visiting prof History and Classics Depts Royal Holloway Univ of London 1995–97; ed New Architecture 1997–; md Papadakis Publishing 1996–, md New Architecture Gp Ltd 1998–; fndr and jt organiser Academy Forum at the Tate 1987–89, pres Academy Forum RA 1990–92, fndr and jt organiser Annual Acad Architecture Lecture Royal Acad of Arts 1990–92; curator: Theory and Experimentation - An Intellectual Extravaganza (RIBA and Whiteleys of Bayswater) 1992, Exhbn of Drawings for the Queen's Gallery Buckingham Palace at Belgravia 2002, Exhbn Warlamis: Poetic Architecture 2005; pres Windsor Hellenic Soc 1994–98, memb Cncl for Hellenes Abroad 1995–98 (co-ordinator for educn and religion (Europe)); chm Chapel of the Greek Orthodox Archdiocese 2000–; Archbishop's rep at Greek communities in GB; Archon Protonotarios of the Ecumenical Patriarchate; *Books* edited jointly: Post Modern Design (1989), Deconstruction Omnibus (1989), New Classicism Omnibus (1990), Deconstruction Pocket Guide (1990), Decade of Architectural Design (1991), New Art - An International Survey (1991), The Free Spirit Omnibus Volume (1992); sole ed: Theory and Experimentation (1992), Modern Classical Architecture (1996); numerous articles and editorials on architecture, art and the environment incl: Religion, Philosophy and Architecture Venice Biennale (1992), Architecture and City Form (1995), Philosophy and Architecture - A Partnership for the Future? (1996), The End of Innovation in Architecture (1997), The Architecture of Catastrophe (1998), Innovation: From Experimentation to Realisation (2003); *Recreations* horseriding; *Clubs* Carlton; *Style*— Prof Andreas C Papadakis; ✉ 16 Grosvenor Place, Belgravia, London SW1X 7HH (tel 020 7823 2323, fax 020 7823 2322, e-mail papadakis@newarchitecture.net, website newarchitecture.net); Dauntsey Park, Dauntsey, Chippenham, Wiltshire SN15 4HT

PAPHITI, Brig Anthony Steve; s of Serghios Anthony Paphiti, of Melton Mowbray, Leics, and Dorothy Lilian, *née* Wilson; *b* 12 May 1952; *Educ* King Edward VII GS Melton Mowbray, Univ of Leeds (LLB), Cncl of Legal Educn; *m* 1978, Ingrid, *née* Timm; 2 da (Anja Maria b 7 Feb 1980, Sophie Louise b 17 April 1982); *Career* called to the Bar Inner Temple 1975; pupillage at 9 & 10 King's Bench Walk 1976–77, in private practice 1977–81; Army Legal Servs: joined 1981, legal offr HQ BAOR 1981–83, legal offr HQ 4 Div 1983–86, legal offr HQ 3 Div 1986–87, OIC Criminal Injuries Compensation Cell 1987–89, Cdr Legal HQ 4 Div 1989–92, first legal advsr to NATO HQ ARRC 1992–95, memb MOU Negotiating Team, legal advsr to Cdr for Support Croatia and author Tech Arrangements between NATO and Croatia 1995–96, Cdr Legal HQ 1 (UK) Armd Div 1996–97, Col Prosecutions Germany 1997–2000, Brig Advsy 2001–02 and 2005–06, Brig Prosecutions 2002–06, currently military law consIt; mentioned in despatches 1990; co-vice chm Employed Barrs' Ctee Bar Cncl 2006; memb: Int Soc for Mil Law and the Law of War, Inter-Agency Judicial Appts Working Gp 2002; *Recreations* cycling, walking, gardening, music; *Style*— Brig Anthony Paphiti; ✉ c/o Directorate of Army Legal Services, Trenchard Lines, Upavon, Wiltshire SN9 6BE (tel 07802 416935, e-mail anthony@aspals.com)

PAPPANO, Antonio; s of Pasquale Pappano (d 2004), and Carmela Maria Scinto; *b* 30 December 1959, Epping, Essex; *Educ* Pimlico Sch, Central HS Bridgepoint CT; *m* 27 Feb 1995, Pamela Bullock; *Career* conductor; early career: rehearsal pianist NYC Opera, repetiteur and asst conductor numerous theatres incl NY City Opera, Gran Teatro del Liceu (Barcelona), Frankfurt Opera, Lyric Opera of Chicago and Bayreuth Festival; musical dir: Norske Opera Oslo 1990–92, Théâtre Royal de la Monnaie Belgium 1992–2002, ROH 2002–, Accademia Nazionale di Santa Cecilia Rome 2005–; principal guest conductor Israel Philharmonic Orchestra 1997; conductor of orchs worldwide incl: Boston Symphony Orch, Chicago Symphony Orch, Cleveland Orch, LA Philharmonic Orch, NY Philharmonic Orch, Berlin Philharmonic Orch, Concergebouw Orch, LSO, Orchestre de Paris, Munich Philharmonic Orch; conducted prodns at Royal de la Monnaie incl: Salome, Un ballo in maschera, Die Meistersinger von Nürnberg, Carmen, Otello (Verdi), Peter Grimes, La traviata, Tristan und Isolde, Le nozze di Figaro, Der Rosenkavalier, Il trittico, Erwartung/Verklärte Nacht, Pelléas et Mélisande, Don Carlos, Aida; conducted prodns at ROH incl: Ariadne auf Naxos, Wozzeck, Falstaff, Madama Butterfly, Pagliacci, Don Giovanni, Aida, Lady Macbeth of Mtsensk, Faust (Gounod), Peter Grimes, La Gioconda, Werther, Das Rheingold, Die Walküre, Un ballo in maschera, Otello; Artist of the Year Gramophone Magazine 2000, Conductor of the Year Royal Philharmonic Soc 2005; *Recordings* Don Carlos (CD and video), La bohème, La rondine (Best Recording of the Year Gramophone Magazine), Il trittico, Werther, Manon, Tosca, Il trovatore, Wintermdrchen, The Turn of the Screw, Tristan & Isolde; with soloists incl: Placido Domingo, Han-Na Chang, Maxim Vengerov, Leif Ove Andsnes, Ian Bostridge; *Clubs* Garrick; *Style*— Antonio Pappano, Esq; ✉ c/o IMG Artists, 44 rue Blanche, 75009 Paris, France (tel 00 33 1 44 31 44 00, fax 00 33 1 44 31 44 01, e-mail pwiggins@imgartists.com)

PARASKEVA, Janet; da of Antonis Paraskeva, and Doris Amanda, *née* Fowler (d 1986); *b* 26 May 1946; *Educ* Worcester Coll, Open Univ (BA); *m* (m dis 1988), Alan Richard Derek Hunt; 2 da (Amanda Joanne b 10 Feb 1970, Suzanna Maria b 19 Nov 1971); *Career* science teacher Shenley Court Comp Sch 1967–69, mathematics teacher St Thomas Aquinas GS 1969–71, pt/t Bromsgrove Club for the Mentally Handicapped 1969–71, dir Friday Toys 1970–73, sr youth worker Fillongley Youth Centre 1972–74, pt/t lectr N Warks Inst of Educn 1973–74, field work co-ordinator Warks Assoc of Youth Clubs 1973–74, projects offr NAYC (now Youth UK) 1974–78, head Youth Work Unit Nat Youth Bureau 1978–81, dist inspr (Youth and Adult) ILEA 1981–83, HMI (Youth and Community) DES 1983–88; dir: Nat Youth Bureau 1988–90, Nat Youth Agency 1990–95, Nat Lottery Charities Bd for England 1995–2000; chief exec Law Soc 2000–05, first civil serv cmmr 2005–; chair Olympic Lottery Distributor 2006–; memb Youth Justice Bd for England and Wales 1998–2000, ind memb Consumer Cncl for Water 2005–, non-exec dir Serious Organised Crime Agency 2005–, non-exec dir Assets Recovery Agency 2007–; JP 1993–2000; non-exec dir Fosse Community Health Tst 1992–99; Robert Schuman Silver Medal for European Unity 1978; various contribs to TES, educnl and legal pubns; Hon LLD Univ of Brighton 2006; *Style*— Ms Janet Paraskeva; ✉ First Civil Service Commissioner, Office of the Civil Service Commission, 35 Great Smith Street, London SW1P 3BQ

PARAVICINI, Nicolas Vincent Somerset; DL (Powys 2006); s of Col Vincent Rudolph Paravicini, TD (d 1989), and Elizabeth Mary (Liza) Maugham (Baroness Glendevon, d 1998); *b* 19 October 1937; *Educ* Eton, RMA Sandhurst; *m* 1, 4 April 1966 (m dis 1986), Mary Ann Parker Bowles; 2 s (Charles b 1968, Derek b 1979), 1 da (Elizabeth Ann (Mrs Robert Hall) b 1970); m 2, 18 Dec 1986 (Susan Rose) Sukie, da of Lt Alan Phipps, RN (ka 1943), and Hon Lady Maclean; *Career* The Life Gds 1957–69, served Aden, Oman, Cyprus and Malaysia, Adj 1963–65, ADC to C-in-C Far East 1965–66, ret Maj; dir Joseph Sebag & Co 1972–79, chm A Sarasin & Co Ltd 1980–89, md Sarasin (UK) Ltd 1983–89, chm and chief exec Sarasin Investment Management Ltd 1983–90, conslt Bank Sarasin & Co 1990–, chief exec MacIntyre Investments Ltd 1990–92, chief exec Ely Place Investments Ltd 1992–98; memb London Stock Exchange 1972–80; pres: Brecknockshire Agric Soc 1998–99, SSAFA Powys 2002–; dir Christ Coll Fndn 2002–, dep chm Investment Ctee Rep Body Church in Wales 2006– (memb 2001–); tstee Nat Heart & Lung Inst 2004–; Freeman City of London 1984; *Recreations* shooting, skiing; *Clubs* White's, Pratt's, Cardiff and County, Corviglia Ski; *Style*— Nicolas Paravicini, Esq, DL; ✉ Glyn Celyn House, Brecon, Powys LD3 0TY (tel 01874 624836, fax 01874 611471)

PARBHOO, Santilal Parag; s of Parag Parbhoo (d 1964), of Cape Town, South Africa, and Jasoda Pemi, *née* Ramjee (d 1961); *b* 16 January 1937; *Educ* Livingstone HS Cape Town, Univ of Cape Town (MB ChB), Queen's Univ Belfast (PhD); *m* 8 Jan 1969, (Constance) Ann, da of William Joseph Cedric Craig, of Belfast, NI; 2 s (Mark b 20 July 1970, Alan b 18 Feb 1977), 1 da (Kathryn b 1 Feb 1974); *Career* house surgn New Somerset Hosp Cape Town 1961, sr house surgn Edendale Hosp Pietermaritzburg 1961–62, tutor and registrar Royal Victoria Hosp Belfast 1964–65 (clinical asst 1962–64); surgical registrar: NI Hosp 1965–68, Frenchay Hosp Bristol 1973–74; conslt and sr lectr Royal Free Hosp and Sch London 1974–91 (research fell and lectr 1968–72); conslt: Bristol Myers Oncology UK 1984–86, Hosp of St John and St Elizabeth London 1991–; Royal Free Hosp London: chm Div of Surgery 1987–89, conslt surgn (gen and breast) 1991–2001, hon conslt surgn 2001–; chm Surgical Bd of Studies Royal Free Hosp Sch of Med 1984–91; chm Royal Free Breast Cancer Tst, dir Cancerkin London 1987–; exec memb Int Soc of Lymphology; memb: Gujerati Arya Assoc London, Sci Advsy Ctee UK Breast Cancer Forum 2002–; past memb Med Advsy Ctee Women's Nationwide Cancer Control Campaign; NATO int research travelling fell 1991–92; hon memb Argentinian Coll of Vascular and Lymphatic Surgery 2002–; hon fell: Hong Kong Soc of Surgns, Egyptian Soc of Hepatology 1989 (medal received 1989); fell: Br Assoc for Surgical Oncology, Assoc of Surgns of GB and I; FRCS 1967, FRCS (Eng); *Books* Bone Metastasis: Monitoring and Treatment (with B A Stoll, 1983), Scintimammography: A Guide to Good Practice (with J Buscombe and J Hill, 1998); *Recreations* walking, gardening, philately; *Clubs* Retired Consultant Staff (RFH); *Style*— Santilal Parbhoo, Esq; ✉ Brampton House, Hospital of St John and St Elizabeth, 60 Grove End Road, London NW8 9NH (tel 020 7266 4272, fax 020 7078 3898, e-mail spparbhoo@doctors.org.uk)

PARDOE, His Hon Judge Alan Douglas William; QC (1988); s of William Douglas Ronald Pardoe (d 1985), and Grace Irene, *née* Jones (d 1996); *b* 16 August 1943; *Educ* Victoria Sch Kurseong India, Oldbury GS, St Catharine's Coll Cambridge (MA, LLB, Winchester reading prize); *Career* Hardwicke scholar Lincoln's Inn 1964, lectr in law Univ of Exeter 1965–70, visiting lectr in law Univ of Auckland NZ 1970, lectr in law Univ of Sussex 1970–74; called to the Bar Lincoln's Inn 1971 (bencher 1998); in practice 1973–2003, recorder 1990–2003, circuit judge (SE Circuit) 2003–; *Recreations* mountain walking, cooking; *Clubs* Travellers; *Style*— His Hon Judge Pardoe, QC; ✉ Snaresbrook Crown Court, 75 Hollybush Hill, London E11 1QW

PAREKH, Baron (Life Peer UK 2000), of Kingston upon Hull in the East Riding of Yorkshire; Prof Bhikhu Chhotalal; s of Chhotalal Ranchhoddas Parekh, of Washington DC, USA, and Gajaraben Parekh; *b* 4 January 1935; *Educ* HDS HS India, Univ of Bombay (BA, MA), Univ of London (PhD); *m* 14 April 1959, Pramila, da of Kanaiyalal Keshavlal Dalal, of Baroda, India; 3 s; *Career* tutor LSE 1962–63, lectr Univ of Glasgow 1963–64; Univ of Hull: successively lectr, sr lectr then reader 1964–82, prof of politics 1982–2000, emeritus prof 2000–; centennial prof LSE 2001–03, prof of political philosophy Univ of Westminster 2001–; vice-chllr Univ of Baroda 1981–84 (lectr 1957–59); visiting prof: Univ of Br Columbia 1967–68, Concordia Univ Montreal 1974–75, McGill Univ Montreal 1976–77, Harvard Univ 1996, Univ of Pompeau Fabra Barcelona 1997, Univ of Pennsylvania 1998, Ecole des Hautes Etudes en Sciences Sociales Paris 2000; guest prof Inst of Advanced Studies Vienna 1997; adjunct fell Centre for the Study of Developing Socs Delhi India 1990–; chm: Nat Survey of the Ethnic Minorities in Britain Advsy Ctee 1993–97, Cmmn on the Future of Multi-Ethnic Britain 1998–; dep chm Cmmn for Racial Equality 1985–90, memb Nat Cmmn on Equal Opportunities CVCP 1994–99; tstee: Runnymede Tst 1986–2003, Inst for Public Policy Research 1988–96, Gandhi Fndn 1988–, Inst of Cwlth Studies 1991–97; Asian of the Year 1991, BBC Special Lifetime Achievement Award for Asians 1999, Sir Isiah Berlin Prize for Lifetime Contribution to Political Studies 2003; pres: Acad of Learned Socs for the Social Sciences 2004–, Br Assoc of South Asian Studies 2004–; fell Asiatic Soc Bombay 2004; hon prof Univ of Wales Aberystwyth; recipient of hon doctorates from 8 univs; FRSA 1990, FBA 2003; Pravasi Bharatiya Samman (India) 2005, Padma Bhushan (India) 2007; *Books* incl: Hannah Arendt (1981), Karl Marx's Theory of Ideology (1982), Contemporary Political Thinkers (1982), Gandhi's Political Philosophy (1989), Colonialism, Tradition and Reform (1989), Critical Assessments of Jeremy Bentham (4 vols, 1993), Decolonisation of Imagination (1996), Crisis and Change in Contemporary India (1996), Gandhi (1997), Rethinking Multiculturalism (2000); *Recreations* reading, walking, music; *Style*— The Rt Hon The Lord Parekh; ✉ 211 Victoria Avenue, Hull HU5 3EF (tel 01482 345530); House of Lords, London SW1A 0AW

PARFECT, Maj John Herbert; MBE (1957); s of George Frederick Parfect (d 1970), and Hedwig, *née* Jordi (d 1948); *b* 9 April 1924; *Educ* Brentwood Sch, Univ of Manchester, Columbia Univ NY; *m* 14 Aug 1948, (Mercia) Heather, da of Brig John Lawrence Maxwell, CBE, MC (d 1972); 4 da (Penelope b 1951, Wendy b 1952, Jane b 1954, Louise b 1958), 1 s (Jeremy John b 1963); *Career* WWII cmmnd RE serv Sicily and Italy 1943; serv: Bengal Sappers and Miners India 1945–47, Gurkha Engrs Malaya 1948–50, 6 Armd Div Engrs BAOR 1951–53, Staff Coll Camberley 1954, GSO2 Northern Cmd York 1955–57, OC 40 Field Sqdn Cyprus 1957–58, ret 1958; personnel mangr ICI 1958–81, self employed fin planning conslt Allied Dunbar 1981–90; memb N Yorks CC 1977–93, chm N Yorks Police Authy 1986–93; FIPD; *Recreations* beagling, military history, investments; *Clubs* Naval and Military; *Style*— Maj John Parfect, MBE; ✉ Colville Hall, Coxwold, York YO61 4AB (tel 01347 868305)

PARFITT, Andrew (Andy); *b* 24 September 1958; *Educ* Bristol Old Vic Theatre Sch; *m* Laura; 2 da (Lucy Sarah b 11 July 1998, Eva Kathryn b 5 April 2001); *Career* studio mangr BBC then prodr/presenter BFBS; BBC: rejoined as educn prodr, successively features prodr Radio 4, asst ed Radio 5, chief asst to controller of Radio 1, ed commissioning and planning Radio 1, managing ed Radio 1 1994–96, dep controller Radio 1 1996–98, controller Radio 1 1998–, controller 1 Xtra BBC; grad Wharton Advanced Mgmnt Prog 2000; winner Sony Creative Award; fell Radio Acad; *Style*— Andy Parfitt, Esq

PARFITT, David John; s of late William Arnold Parfitt, and Maureen, *née* Collinson; *b* 8 July 1958; *Educ* Bede GS Sunderland, Barbara Speake Stage Sch London; *m* 1, 1988 (m dis 1993), Susan Coates; 1 s (William Michael b 6 Sept 1990); m 2, 1996, Elizabeth Ann Barron; 2 s (Thomas Richard b 23 Aug 1998, Max Christopher b 18 May 2001); *Career* prodr 1985– (actor 1970–88); co-fndr: Renaissance Theatre Co 1987–, Renaissance Films 1988–92, Trademark Films 2000–, Trademark Theatre Co 2000–; memb Bd of Tstees BAFTA 2000–, chair of film BAFTA 2004–; tstee Chicken Shed Theatre Co 1997–, patron Royalty Theatre Sunderland 1999–; Hon Dr of Arts Univ of Sunderland 1999, Hon Dr Drama RSAMD 2001; *Theatre* for Renaissance Theatre Co Tradework as prodr: Tell Me Honestly (Not the RSC Stratford and London) 1985, John Sessions at the Eleventh Hour 1986, Romeo & Juliet 1986, Public Enemy 1987, Napoleon 1987, Renaissance Nights 1987, Twelfth Night 1988, Much Ado About Nothing, Hamlet and As You Like It (West End and nat tour) 1988, Look Back in Anger (West End and nat tour) 1989, Napoleon, The American Story (West End and nat tour) 1989, Scenes from a Marriage (West End) 1990, A Midsummer Night's Dream and King Lear (West End, nat tour and world tour) 1990, Travelling Tales (West End and nat tour) 1991, Uncle Vanya (West End and nat tour) 1991, Coriolanus (Chichester Festival) 1992, Les Liaisons Dangereuses (West End) 2004, Elling (Bush Theatre) 2007; *Television* assoc prodr: Twelfth Night (Thames Television/Renaissance Theatre Co) 1988, Look Back in Anger (First Choice/Renaissance Theatre Co) 1989; *Film* Henry V 1988 (assc prodr), Peter's Friends 1992 (line prodr), Swan Song 1992 (nomination Best Live Action Short American Acad Awards), Much Ado About Nothing 1993, Frankenstein 1994 (co-prodr), The Madness of King George 1995 (Best Br Film BAFTA Awards), Twelfth Night 1996, The Wings of the Dove 1997, Shakespeare in Love 1999 (7 American Acad Awards incl Best Picture, 4 BAFTA Awards incl Best Film), Gangs of New York 2001 (prodn consit), I Capture the Castle 2002, Chasing Liberty 2004; *Style*— David Parfitt, Esq; ✉ Trademark Films, 11 Trinity Rise, London SW2 2QP (tel 020 7240 5585, e-mail mail@trademarkfilms.co.uk)

PARFITT, Judy Catherine Clare; da of Laurence Hamilton Parfitt (d 1973), and Catherine Coulton; *Educ* Notre Dame Convent, RADA; *m* 25 Aug 1963, Anthony Francis Steedman, s of Baron Anthony Ward; 1 s (David Lawrence b 29 Sept 1964); *Career* actress; *Theatre* incl: D H Lawrence trilogy (Royal Court), Annie in A Hotel in Amsterdam 1968, Queen Mary in Vivat! Vivat! Regina! (Piccadilly) 1970, Family Dance (Criterion), Cleopatra (Young Vic), Duchess of Malfi (Royal Court), Ranyevskya in The Cherry Orchard (Riverside Studios) 1978, Eleanor in Passion Play (Wyndham's) 1980, A Dream of People (RSC), Molière's The Sisterhood and Valentine's Day, Mrs Birling in An Inspector Calls (RNT prodn at Aldwych) 1993, Night Must Fall (Lyceum Theatre Broadway) 1999, Therese Raquin (RNT); *Television* numerous prodns incl: Villette, E Nesbit in The Edwardians 1973, Lady Constance Lytton in Shoulder to Shoulder, Malice Aforethought 1979, Pride and Prejudice, Death of a Princess, You Never Can Tell, Alice Through The Looking Glass, Post Mortem, Angel Pavement, Secret Orchards, Jewel in the Crown 1984 (BAFTA Best Actress nomination), The Charmer 1987, The Charmings (USA series), Hilda Spearpoint in The Gravy Train 1989 and The Gravy Train Goes East 1992, The Borrowers (BBC), Lifeboat (BBC), Inspector Alleyn (BBC), September (mini-series), Harriet Collard in The Blackheath Poisonings (TV film), Loving (Screen Two), Heavy Weather (BBC), The Final Act (Granada), Element of Doubt, Holding the Baby, Berkley Square, ER, The Hunt, Murder in Mind, Hearts of Gold, Death on the Nile (ITV), The Long Firm (BBC), Funland (BBC 3); *Film* incl: Gertrude in Hamlet, Madam Sarti in Galileo, Getting it Right, Diamond Skulls, Maurice 1986, Vera Donovan in Dolores Claiborne, Lady Mount-Temple in Wilde, The Ruby Ring, Queen Marie in Ever After, The Bourne Identity, Maria Thinns in The Girl with a Pearl Earring (BAFTA Best Supporting Film Actress nomination), Asylum; *Recreations* needlepoint, gardening, antiques, talking; *Style*— Miss Judy Parfitt; ✉ c/o Conway van Gelder Ltd, 18–21 Jermyn Street, London SW1Y 6HP (tel 020 7287 0077, fax 020 7287 1940)

PARFORD, Simon William; s of Lt-Cdr John Littleton Parford, RN (ret), MBE, of Plymouth, and Barbara Daphne, *née* Hawton; *b* 12 November 1958, Singapore; *Educ* Plymouth Coll, Birmingham Poly, Guildford Law Coll; *m* 5 Sept 1987, Karen, *née* Jones; 1 s (Alexander John b 25 March 1991), 1 da (Chloe Jillian b 5 March 1995); *Career* admitted slr 1983; Wolferstans: articled clerk 1981–83, slr 1983, ptnr 1988–, head Clinical Negligence Dept 1991–; tstee Headway Plymouth 1992–; memb: Law Soc 1983, Plymouth Law Soc 1983, Assoc of Personal Injury Lawyers (APIL) 1993; *Recreations* watching rugby, drinking wine, playing tennis; *Clubs* OPM (Old Plymothians and Mannameadians), Plymouth Albion RFC; *Style*— Simon Parford, Esq; ✉ Wolferstans, 60–66 North Hill, Plymouth PL4 8EP (tel 01752 292217, e-mail sparford@wolferstans.com)

PARHAM, HE Philip John; s of John Carey Parham of Ladymead, S Ascot, and Christian Mary, *née* Fitzherbert; *b* 14 August 1960, Nairobi, Kenya; *Educ* Eton (King's scholar), ChCh Oxford (MA); *m* 7 Sept 1985, Kasia, *née* Giedroyc; 2 da (Mary 16 June 1986, Elizabeth 28 Sept 1994), 5 s (Joseph 19 Feb 1988, Francis-Christian 17 June 1989, Anthony 27 Oct 1990, Charles 16 April 1992, John 22 Jan 1996); *Career* Morgan Grenfell 1983–89, Barclays de Zoete Wedd 1989–93 (dir 1992–93), S Asia Dept FCO 1993–94, private sec to Parly Under Sec of State FCO 1995, policy planning staff FCO 1995–96, first sec Br Embassy Washington 1996–2000, dir trade and investment Br Embassy Riyadh 2000–03, head Iraq Ops Unit FCO 2003–04, head Counter-Terrorism Policy Dept FCO 2004–06, high cmmr Dar es Salaam 2006–; Liveryman Worshipful Co of Skinners; *Recreations* gardening, theology, genealogy, the parentage of Mary Anne Smythe; *Style*— HE Mr Philip Parham; ✉ c/o FCO (Dar es Salaam), King Charles Street, London SW1A 2AH (e-mail philip.parham@fco.gov.uk)

PARIKH, Anu; da of late Debesh Chandra Das, of Calcutta, India, and late Kamala, *née* Nag; *b* 16 March 1947; *Educ* Convent of Jesus and Mary New Delhi, Univ of Delhi (BA), KCL (LLB); *m* 15 Feb 1972, Bharat Amritlal Parikh, s of Amritlal Vithaldas Parikh, of Calcutta, India; *Career* formerly practising barr Middle Temple, now slr; dir Grosvenor House Trading Ltd; formerly sub ed Atkins Court Forms for Butterworths Ltd; memb: Jt Cncl of Welfare for Immigrants, Law Soc; *Recreations* reading, gardening, theatres; *Style*— Mrs Anu Parikh; ✉ Grosvenor House Trading Ltd, Dalton House, Windsor Avenue, London SW19 2RR; Collison & Co Solicitors, 1–3 Hildreth Street, London SW12 9RQ

PARIS, Andrew Martin Ingledew; s of Vernon Patrick Paris (d 1999), of Sussex, and Heather Constance Ingledew, *née* Dear; *b* 27 November 1940; *Educ* London Hosp Med Coll (MB BS); *Family* 1 da (Claire Elizabeth Ingledew); m 24 Dec 1975, Susan Philippa da of Perys Goodwin Jenkins (d 1969), of London; *Career* conslt urological surgn The Royal London Hosp 1972–2005, conslt urological surgn St Bartholomew's Hosp 1994–2005, emeritus consulting urological surgn The Royal London and St Bartolomew's Hosps 2005–, clinical dir of surgery Barts and the London NHS Tst 1979–2002; hon conslt surgn The Italian Hosp 1979–90; hon surgn St John Ambulance Air Wing (fndr memb); chm Marie Celeste Samaritan Soc 2006–, tstee Longship Museum 2004–; Freeman City of London 1984, Master Worshipful Soc of Apothecaries 2007 (memb Ct of Assts); FRCS 1971, FRSM (vice-pres Section of Urology 1988 and 1989); OStJ 1985; *Recreations* sailing, skiing, beekeeping; *Clubs* Athenaeum, Aldeburgh Yacht; *Style*— Andrew Paris, Esq; ✉ The Old Vicarage, Aldringham Cum Thorpe, Suffolk IP16 4QF

PARISH, Neil Quentin Gordon; MEP (Cons) SW England; s of Reginald and Kathleen Parish; *b* 26 May 1956; *Educ* Brymore Sch; *m* 1981, Susan Gail; 1 s (Jonathan), 1 da (Harriet); *Career* farmer; cncllr Pawlett PC 1980–95, cncllr Sedgemoor DC 1983–95 (dep ldr 1989), cncllr Somerset CC 1989–93, Parly candidate (Cons) Torfaen (Pontypool and Cwmbran) 1997; MEP (Cons) SW England 1999–; memb: EU Agric Ctee, Fisheries Ctee, Environment Ctee; Cons agric and fisheries spokesman 2001; chm Aust and NZ EU Delegation 2004–; memb Pawlett Parish Cncl 1980–99; *Recreations* swimming, walking; *Style*— Neil Parish, Esq, MEP; ✉ c/o Bridgwater Conservative Office, 16 Northgate, Bridgwater, Somerset TA6 3EU (tel 01278 423110, fax 01278 431034)

PARISH, Prof Richard; s of Leslie Thomas Parish, FCCA, and Winifred Alice Parish; *b* 11 October 1951; *Educ* Univ of London (BSc external), South Bank Poly (Dip Health Educn), Huddersfield Univ (MEd); *m* 1976, Joan Margaret, *née* Shepherd; 1 s, 1 da; *Career* dir of health promotion Stockport HA 1980–85, head of progs Heartbeat Wales and sr lectr WNSM 1985–87, dir of ops Health Promotion Authy for Wales 1987–90, princ and chief exec Humberside Coll of Health 1990–96, prof of public health and dir health and community studies Sheffield Hallam Univ 1996–97, prof and head of health studies Univ of York 1997–99, regnl dir (educn and trg) NHS Eastern Region 1999, chief exec Health Devpt Agency 2000–; FRSH 1988, CBiol 1989, MIBiol 1989, MIPR 1989, MHSM 1991, Hon MFPHM 2001; *Publications* author of pubns on health promotion and health policy; *Recreations* photography, rambling, cycling; *Style*— Prof Richard Parish; ✉ Health Development Agency, Holborn Gate, 330 High Holborn, London WC1V 7BA (tel 020 7430 0850, e-mail richardparish@hda-online.org.uk)

PARISH, Prof Richard John; s of late John Alfred Parish, and late Dorothy Evelyn, *née* Turner; *Educ* Cranbrook Sch, Univ of Newcastle upon Tyne (BA), Keble Coll Oxford (DPhil, MA); *Career* lectr Univ of Liverpool 1973–76; Univ of Oxford: lectr in French 1976–95, prof of French 1996–, chm Sub-Faculty of French 1997–2000, pro-proctor 1998–99; St Catherine's Coll Oxford: fell and tutor 1976–, sr tutor 1991–95, vice-master 1997–2000; memb Exec Ctee Soc for French Studies 2003–; external assessor Govt of Ireland HE Authy 1998–2002; Officier dans l'Ordre des Palmes Académiques (France) 2001; *Books* Pascal's Letters Provinciales: A Study in Polemic (1989), Racine: The Limits of Tragedy (1993), Scarron: Le Roman Comique (1991); editor of various editions, author of articles and reviews; *Recreations* music, Pevsnering, wine; *Clubs* Athenaeum; *Style*— Prof Richard Parish; ✉ St Catherine's College, Oxford OX1 3UJ (tel 01865 271700, fax 01865 271768, e-mail richard.parish@stcatz.ox.ac.uk)

PARK, Sir Andrew Edward Wilson; kt (1997); s of late Dennis Edward Park; *b* 27 January 1939; *Educ* Leeds GS, UC Oxford; *m* 1962, Ann Margaret Woodhead; 2 s (and 1 s decd), 1 da; *Career* called to the Bar Lincoln's Inn 1964, bencher 1986, in practice at Revenue Bar 1965–97, recorder of the Crown Ct 1989–95, judge of the High Ct of Justice (Chancery Div) 1997–2006; chm: Taxation and Retirement Benefits Ctee of the Bar Cncl 1978–82, Revenue Bar Assoc 1987–92; treas Senate of the Inns of Court and Bar 1982–85; *Style*— Sir Andrew Park; ✉ Loseberry, 30 Hare Lane, Claygate, Surrey KT10 9BU

PARK, Dr Gilbert Richard; TD (1985); *b* 17 May 1950; *Educ* Univ of Edinburgh (BSc, MB ChB, MD, MA); *Partner* Maire Shelly; *Career* Dept of Orthopaedic Surgery Royal Infirmary Edinburgh 1974, Dept of Med Bangor Gen Hosp 1974; Dept of Anaesthesia: Royal Infirmary Edinburgh 1975–80, Univ of Edinburgh 1980–83; dir of intensive care research and conslt in anaesthesia Addenbrooke's Hosp Cambridge; non-exec dir UK Transplant; sec gen World FEdn Socs of Intensive and Critical Care Medicine; TA: offr cadet 1968–74, Lt 1974–75, Capt 1975–80, Maj 1980–93; Hon MA Cambridge 1987, Hon Dr of Med Sci Univ of Pleven Bulgaria 1997; hon fell Bulgarian Soc of Anaesthetists 1996; FRCA, FFARCS, LFPS; *Books* Intensive Care: A Handbook (1988), The Management of Acute Pain (1991, 2 edn 2001), Sedation and Analgesia (1993), Anaesthesia and Intensive Care for Patients with Liver Disease (1994), Sedation and Analgesia in the Critically Ill (1995), A Colour Atlas of Critical and Intensive Care (1995), Fighting for Life (1996), How to Prescribe Drugs in the Critically Ill (1996), Algorithms for Rational Prescribing in the Critically Ill (1997), Tricks and Traps (1998), Fluid Balance and Volume Resuscitation for Beginners (1999), Septic Shock (2000), Pharmacology in the Critically Ill (2001), Top Tips in Intensive Care (2002); photographer for many magazines and calendars; *Recreations* writing, photography, motorcycling; *Style*— Dr G Park; ✉ The John Farman Intensive Care Unit, Addenbrooke's Hospital, Cambridge CB2 2QQ (tel 01223 217897, fax 01223 217223, e-mail gilbert.park@addenbrookes.nhs.uk, website www.gilbert-park-photography.com)

PARK, (James) Graham; CBE; s of James Park, OBE, JP (d 1959), of Salford, and Joan Clay, *née* Sharp (d 1987); *b* 27 April 1941; *Educ* Malvern Coll, Univ of Manchester (LLB); *m* 28 June 1969, Susan, da of Dr Charles Sydney Douglas Don (d 1973), of Manchester; 1 s (James b 1973); *Career* slr, ptnr H L F Berry & Co 1969–2003, conslt 2004–; Parly candidate (Cons) 1974 and 1979, chm Altrincham Sale Constituency Cons Assoc 1983–87, chm NW Area Cons 1992–95, nat vice-pres 1995–98, pres Nat Convention Cons Pty 1998–99, chm Cons Pty Conference 1998, Cons Pty Compliance Offr, chm Cons Pty Constitutional Ctee 2000–06; memb: Ct Univ of Salford 1987–97, Parole Bd 1996–2002 and 2003–, Criminal Injuries Compensation Appeal Panel 2000–, Mental Health Review Tbnl 2003–; *Recreations* cricket, motor racing; *Style*— Graham Park, Esq, CBE; ✉ HLF Berry & Co, 758 Oldham Road, Failsworth, Manchester M35 9XB (tel 0161 681 4005)

PARK, Ian Grahame; CBE (1995); s of William Park (d 1982), and Christina Wilson, *née* Scott; *b* 15 May 1935; *Educ* Lancaster Royal GS, Queens' Coll Cambridge; *m* 1965, Anne, da of Edward Turner (d 1979); 1 s (Adam); *Career* Nat Serv cmmnd Manchester Regt 1954–56; chm Northcliffe Newspapers Group 1995–2003 (md 1982–95), dir Associated Newspapers Holdings 1983–95, dir Daily Mail and General Trust 1994–; md and ed-in-chief Liverpool Daily Post and Echo 1972–82, asst literary ed Sunday Times 1960–63; dir: Reuters 1978–82 and 1988–94, Press Assoc 1978–83 (chm 1978–79 and 1979–80); pres Newspaper Soc 1980–81; *Clubs* Reform; *Style*— Ian Park, Esq, CBE; ✉ Northcliffe Newspapers Group, 2 Derry Street, London W8 5TT (tel 020 7400 1454)

PARK, District Judge John Kenneth; s of Robert Croasdale Park, and Muriel Joan Hymers Park, *née* Kennedy; *Educ* St Peter's Sch York, Liverpool Poly; *Career* solicitor 1973–2001, district judge 2002–; memb Law Soc 1973; FCIArb 1996; *Style*— District Judge Park; ✉ c/o Northern Circuit Office, The Court Service, 15 Quay Street, Manchester M60 9FD

PARK, Nicholas Wulstan (Nick); CBE (1997); *b* 1958; *Educ* Sheffield Sch of Art, Nat Film and TV Sch; *Career* producer/director of animated films; dir Aardman Animations (joined 1985); work incl: A Grand Day Out (BBC2) 1989 (BAFTA Best Animated Short 1990, Academy Award nomination 1990), Creature Comforts (Channel 4) 1990 (winner Academy Award for Best Animated Short 1990) and subsequent adaptation for series of 13 Heat Electric commercials (winners of various D&AD and other advtg industry awards), The Wrong Trousers (BBC2) 1993 (winner Academy Award for Best Animated Short and BAFTA Award for Best Short Animated Film 1994), A Close Shave 1995 (BAFTA for Best Animated Film 1995, Emmy for Best Popular Arts Programme 1996, four British Animation Awards 1996, Academy Award 1996), Chicken Run (with Pete Lord) 2000 (winner of many awards), Wallace & Gromit: The Curse of the Were-Rabbit 2005 (Academy Award 2006, Best Feature Film Children's BAFTA Awards 2006); *Style*— Nick Park, Esq, CBE

PARK, William Dennis; s of Edward Park (d 1954), of Cockermouth, Cumbria, and Fanny Moyra, *née* Walker (d 1986); *b* 28 May 1934; *Educ* St Bees Cumbria; *m* 1 Jan 1959, Valerie Margaret, da of Wallace Rutherford Bayne, MD (d 1956), of Barrow-in-Furness, Cumbria; 1 s (Adam b 9 July 1961), 1 da (Claire (Mrs Sutcliffe) b 9 Jan 1963); *Career* Nat Serv RAOC, RASC 1955–57 (Army Legal Aid 1956–57); admitted slr 1955, ptnr Morrison & Masters Swindon 1961–66, sr litigation ptnr Linklaters & Paines London 1971–92; former pres London Slrs' Litigation Assoc, memb Cncl London Int Arbitration Tst, memb Cncl and Ctee of Mgmnt Br Inst of Int & Comparative Law, memb Bd of London Int Ct of Arbitration 1988–92, UK memb Ct of Arbitration of the Int Chamber of Commerce Paris 1991–93; memb various bodies associated with Lake Dist and local agriculture, subcriber to fell and beagle packs; Lord of the Manors of Whicham and Whitbeck Cumbria; memb: City of London Slrs' Co, Law Soc 1955; FCIArb 1991 (ACIArb 1980); *Books* Hire Purchase and Credit Sales (1958), Collection of Debts (1962), Discovery of Documents (1966), Documentary Evidence (1985), International Commercial Litigation (1990); *Recreations* Cumbrian history, country pursuits; *Style*— William Park, Esq; ✉ Routenbeck House, Routenbeck, Cumbria CA13 9YN

PARK OF MONMOUTH, Baroness (Life Peer UK 1990), of Broadway in the County of Hereford and Worcester; Daphne Margaret Sybil Désirée Park; CMG (1971), OBE (1960); da of John Alexander Park (d 1952), and Doreen Gwynneth Park (d 1982); *b* 1 September 1921; *Educ* Rosa Bassett Sch, Somerville Coll Oxford, Newnham Coll Cambridge; *Career*

WTS (FANY) 1943–47 (Allied Cmmn for Austria 1946–48); FO 1948, second sec Moscow 1954, first sec Consul Leopoldville 1959–61, first sec Zambia 1964–67, consul-gen Hanoi 1969–70, chargé d'affaires Ulaanbaatar 1972, FCO 1973–79; princ Somerville Coll Oxford 1980–89, pro-vice-chllr Univ of Oxford; govr BBC 1982–87, dir Devpt Tst Zoological Soc of London 1989–90, chm Legal Aid Advsy Ctee to Lord Chllr 1984–90, chm Royal Cmmn on the Historical Monuments of England 1989–94, memb Bd Sheffield Devpt Corp 1989–92, memb Advsy Bd Zimbabwe Defence and Advsy Fund UK 2004–, former memb Br Library Bd; pres: Soc for the Promotion of the Trg of Women until 2006, Mil Commentators' Circle 2003–; govr Ditchley Fndn; tstee: The Jardine Educn Fndn 1990–98, Lucy Faithfull Travel Scholarship Fund; patron: Action Gp 2001, Disabled Police Officers Assoc NI 2001–, Britain Sasakawa Fndn 2002– (memb Bd 1994–2001); a vice-patron Atlantic Cncl Appeal; Hon LLD: Univ of Bristol 1988, Mount Holyoke Coll 1992; fell Chatham House (RIIA); *Recreations* good talk, politics and difficult places; *Clubs* Naval and Military, Cwlth Tst, Special Forces; *Style*— The Baroness Park of Monmouth, CMG, OBE; ✉ House of Lords, London SW1A 0PW

PARKER, Alan; s of Sir Peter Parker, KBE, LVO (d 2002), and Gillian, *née* Rowe-Dutton; *b* 3 May 1956; *m* 1, 22 March 1977 (m dis), Caroline Louise, da of Thaddeus Gordon, of Yates; 1 s (Samuel b 1 Oct 1982), 3 da (Jessica Alexandra b 18 Aug 1984, Natasha Rose b 11 Dec 1987, Flora Liberty b 28 Feb 1991); m 2, 9 March 2007, Jane Hermione, da of Blaise Hardman, and Caroline Hardman; 1 s (William Peter Blaise b 27 June 2005); *Career* dep md Broad Street Associates 1982–87, sr ptnr then chm Brunswick Group 1987–; *Recreations* friends; *Style*— Alan Parker, Esq; ✉ Brunswick Group LLP, 16 Lincoln's Inn Fields, London WC2A 3ED (tel 020 396 5332, fax 020 7396 7456)

PARKER, Alan; s of Frederick Parker, and Edith, *née* Cavell; *b* 26 August 1944; *Educ* Royal Acad of Music; *m* Stephanie, *née* Moore; 1 da (Jessica b 6 May 1979), 1 s (Josh b 25 Nov 1980); *Career* composer; worked with many leading performers incl: Dusty Springfield, Neil Diamond, John Denver, David Bowie, John Lennon, Paul McCartney; fndr memb: Blue Mink, The Congregation; involved with Lady Taverners (charity); FRSA; *Television and Documentaries*; over 80 prodns incl: Underwater Coast (BBC), The Way We Used To Live (YTV), The Outsiders (Channel 4), River Journeys (BBC), De-Beers Diamond Day, BMW (promo film), Esso (promo film), Horses in Our Blood (YTV), Westland Helicopters, Westland Aerospace, Men on Violence (LWT), Van der Valk (Thames), Jupiter Moon (BSkyB), Minder (Thames), Red Fox (LWT), Man & Animal (Carlton), Catherine Cookson's The Round Tower, Catherine Cookson's Colour Blind, Bomber (ITV), Tough Love (ITV), Victoria and Albert (BBC), The Swap (ITV), The Cry (ITV), Walking With Cavemen (BBC), The Crooked Man (ITV), D-Day (BBC), Marian Again (ITV), Fallen Angel (ITV); *Films* over 20 features incl: Jaws 3D (Universal, nominated Oscar 1985), Frankenstein (HBO), Mixed Doubles, American Gothic (Brent Walker), Philby Burgess & McClean (Granada), Nolan (Granada), The Glory Boys (YTV), Mirage (Granada), Sea of Serpents (Brent Walker), Out of Time (Alexandra), Voice of the Heart (Portman), To Be the Best (Gemmy), The Ice Man (MGM), Wild Justice (Berlusconi), What's Eating Gilbert Grape (Paramount), The Phoenix and the Magic Carpet (Miramax), Rhodes (Zenith/BBC, nominated Ivor Novello 1997), Hostile Waters (HBO/BBC), Up on the Roof (Granada Films/Rank), Oktober (Carnival), The Unknown Soldier (Carlton), Nancherrow (LWT), Diana Queen of Hearts (NBC), Victoria and Albert (BBC), The Swap (ITV), The Cry (ITV), Stormbreaker; *Jingles* 28 jingles and campaigns incl: Kellogg's Branflakes, Wrangler Jeans, Levis Jeans, Volkswagen Jetta & Polo, Heinz, Citröen, Ford Fiesta & Ford Cars (Germany), Tuborg Lager, Tango, Partners Against Crime (dir Mike Newell, ITV), Kronung Coffee; *Recreations* shooting, tennis, antiques; *Style*— Alan Parker, Esq, FRSA; ✉ c/o SMA Talent, The Cottage, Church Street, Fressingfield, Suffolk IP21 5PA (tel 01379 586734)

PARKER, Sir Alan William; kt (2002), CBE (1995); *b* 14 February 1944, London; *m* 1 (m dis), Annie Inglis; 4 c; m 2, Lisa Moran; 1 c; *Career* filmmaker; early career as advtg copywriter with Collett Dickinson Pearce; chm UK Film Cncl 1999–2004, former chm Bd of Govrs BFI, founding memb Directors Guild of GB; Michael Balcon Award BAFTA 1985; *Films* incl: The Evacuees 1975 (Best Dir BAFTA), Bugsy Malone 1976 (Best Screenplay BAFTA), Midnight Express 1978 (Best Dir BAFTA, Oscar and Golden Globe nominations for Best Dir), Fame 1980, Shoot the Moon 1982, Birdy 1984 (Grand Prix Special du Jury Cannes Film Festival), Angel Heart 1987, Mississippi Burning 1988 (Oscar, BAFTA and Golden Globe nominations for Best Dir), Come See the Paradise 1990, The Commitments 1990 (Best Dir BAFTA), The Road to Wellville 1994, Evita 1996 (BAFTA nomination Best Adapted Screenplay, Golden Globe nomination Best Dir), Angela's Ashes 1999, The Life of David Gale 2003; *Style*— Sir Alan Parker, CBE

PARKER, Prof Andrew; s of John Humphrey Parker, and Doreen May, *née* Jones; *b* 4 January 1954, Burnley; *Educ* Clare Coll Cambridge (BA, PhD); *Career* Univ of Oxford: Beit meml fell Physiology Dept 1979–80, Rudolph and Ann Rork Light res fell St Catherine's Coll and Physiology Dept 1980–83, official fell St Catherine's Coll 1985–90, official fell and tutor in physiology St John's Coll 1990–, prof of physiology 1996– (univ lectr 1985–96), memb Sci Ctee MRC Res Centre in Brain and Behaviour 1991–93, memb Sci Ctee McDonnell-Pew Centre for Cognitive Neuroscience 1994– (actg dir 1995–96), course dir grad prog in neuroscience 2000–; visiting scientist MIT Artificial Intelligence Lab USA 1984, visiting scientist Schlumberger Palo Alto Res Calif 1985; memb: Neuroscience Grants Panel The Wellcome Tst 1992–97, Advsy Bd MRC 1997–, Jl Ethics Panel Physiological Soc 2000–, Editorial Bd Vision Research 2000–, Organising Ctee Euro Conf on Visual Perception 1998; acted as referee for papers in numerous jls; visiting scholar Getty Res Inst LA 2002; memb Faculty of 1000 2001–; 21st Century Scientist Award James S McDonnell Fndn 2000–; *Publications* more than 55 papers in various leading jls incl Nature, Annual Review of Neuroscience and Jl of Neuroscience; *Style*— Prof Andrew Parker; ✉ University Laboratory of Physiology, Parks Road, Oxford OX1 3PT (tel 01865 272504 (department), 01865 277362 (college), fax 01865 272543, e-mail andrew.parker@physiol.ox.ac.uk)

PARKER, Andrew John Cunningham; s of John Bertram Parker, of Suffolk, and Sally Elizabeth, *née* Warnes; *b* 13 February 1959, Bedford; *Educ* King Edward VI Sch Norwich, CCC Cambridge (MA); *m* 20 Sept 1986, Sonia Denise, *née* Hobbs; 1 s (Charles Thomas Andrew); *Career* admitted slr 1983; slr: Daynes Chittock & Back 1983–90, Pengilly & Ridge 1990–91; slr then ptnr Keeble Hawson 1991–94, ptnr Irwin Mitchell 1994–97, ptnr Wansbroughs Willey Hargrave (subsequently Beachcroft Wansbroughs, now Beachcroft LLP) 1997– (currently head of strategic litigation); pres Forum of Insurance Lawyers 2000–01; memb: Civil Procedure Rule Ctee 2003–, Court of Appeal Civil Users Gp, Costs Practitioners Gp, Ctee London Slrs Litigation Assoc; *Recreations* travel, family, cricket; *Style*— Andrew Parker, Esq; ✉ Beachcroft LLP, 100 Fetter Lane, London EC4A 1BN (tel 020 7242 1011, fax 020 7894 6240, e-mail aparker@beachcroft.co.uk)

PARKER, Barrie Charles; s of Stanley Charles Digby Parker, of Southampton, Hants, and Betty Doreen, *née* Calverley; *b* 2 October 1940; *Educ* City of London Sch, Charing Cross Med Sch, Univ of London (MB BS); *m* 27 April 1968, Ann Teressa, da of William Rae Ferguson (d 1981), of Coventry, Warks; *Career* sr registrar Charing Cross and Royal Nat Orthopaedic Hosps 1973–76; conslt orthopaedic surgn: Kingston Hosp 1976–2003 (clinical tutor 1981–86), SW London Elective Orthopaedic Centre Epsom 2004–05; med dir: Kingston Hosp NHS Tst 1994–2001, SW London Elective Orthopaedic Centre Epsom 2003–05; pres Kingston and Richmond Div BMA 1978–79; former memb Kingston and Esher HA, former regnl advsr orthopaedics RCS England, Oxshott Heath conservator; FRCS 1970, FRSM 1974, FBOA; *Recreations* rugby football, swimming, skiing and water skiing; *Clubs* London Irish RFC, Kingston Med, RAC; *Style*— Barrie Parker, Esq; ✉ Delaval, 2 Redruth Gardens, Claygate, Surrey KT10 0HD

PARKER, Bruce Rodney Wingate; s of Robert Parker (d 1988), and Doris Maud, *née* Wingate (d 1995); *b* 20 July 1941; *Educ* Elizabeth Coll Guernsey, Univ of Wales (BA), Univ of Reading (DipEd); *m* 1, 1967 (m dis 1985), Anne Dorey; 2 s (James b 9 Aug 1968, Charles b 4 Aug 1974), 1 da (Sarah (m Huw Thomas, *qv*, b 28 Dec 1969); m 2, 2002, Suzanne Stevens; 1 step s (Rupert); *Career* house master Elizabeth Coll Guernsey 1964–67, BBC News and Current Affrs reporter, presenter and prodr 1967–; progs incl: Nationwide, Antiques Roadshow, Mainstream, Badger Watch, South Today; political corr BBC South 1991–98, political ed 1998–2003, presenter BBC South of Westminster 1992–2003, frequent contribs to numerous radio and TV progs; RTS Reporter of the Year 1982, RTS Industry Achievement Award 1997, BBC DG's Special Award 2002; former memb Educn Advsy Ctee Hampshire CC, former chm of govrs Harestock Sch Winchester; tstee Gibson Fleming Tst Guernsey; *Books* Everybody's Soapbox (with Nigel Farrell, 1983); *Recreations* travel, gardening, rifle-shooting, writing; *Clubs* Cwlth Rifle, London and Middx Rifle, N London Rifle; *Style*— Bruce Parker, Esq; ✉ Bridge Cottage, Appleshaw, Hampshire SP11 9BH (tel 01264 772251, e-mail bruceparker@tiscali.co.uk); 2 Place Felix Poullan, 06230 Villefranche Sur Mer, France (tel 00 04 93 76 64 34)

PARKER, Cameron Holdsworth; CVO (2007), OBE (1993); s of George Cameron Parker, MBE (d 1967), of Monifieth, Angus, and Mary Stevenson, *née* Houston (d 1985); *b* 14 April 1932; *Educ* Morrisons Acad Crieff, Univ of Glasgow (BSc); *m* 1, 20 July 1957, Elizabeth Margaret (d 1985), da of Andrew Sydney Grey Thomson (d 1957), of Dundee; 3 s (David b 1958, Michael b 1960, John b 1964); m 2, 23 May 1986, Marlyne, da of William Honeyman (d 1966), of Glasgow; *Career* chm John G Kincaid & Co Ltd 1976–80 (md 1967–80), chm and chief exec Scott Lithgow Ltd 1980–83, bd memb Br Shipbuilders Ltd 1977–80 and 1981–83, vice-chm Lithgows Ltd 1991–97 (md 1984–92); dir: Campbeltown Shipyard Ltd 1984–94, J Fleming Engineering Ltd 1984–94, Lithgow Electronics Ltd 1984–94, Malak Off & Wm Moore Ltd 1984–94, McKinlay & Blair Ltd 1984–94, Prosper Engineering Ltd 1984–94, A Kenneth & Sons Ltd 1985–94, Landcatch Ltd 1985–94, Glasgow Iron and Steel Co Ltd 1985–94, Argyll and Clyde Health Bd 1991–95, Scottish Homes 1992–96, Clyde Shaw Ltd 1992–94; memb Cncl CBI Scotland 1986–92; HM Lord-Lt Renfrewshire 1998–2007 (DL 1993–98); pres SSAFA Forces Help Renfrewshire 1998–2007, hon pres Accord Hospice Paisley 1998–2007; Freeman City of London, Liveryman Worshipful Co of Shipwrights 1981; Hon DUniv Paisley 2003; FIMarEST 1965; *Recreations* golf, gardening; *Style*— Cameron Parker, Esq, CVO, OBE; ✉ The Heath House, Rowantreehill Road, Kilmacolm, Renfrewshire PA13 4PE (tel 01505 873197)

PARKER, Cornelia; da of Frank Parker, and Irmgarde Clothilde Maria Diesch; *b* 14 July 1956; *Educ* Gloucestershire Coll of Art and Design, Wolverhampton Poly (BA), Univ of Reading (MFA); *m Children* 1 da (b 2001); *Career* sculptor; numerous awards, commissions, projects and residencies including residency at ArtPace Foundation for Contemporary Art San Antonio Texas (solo exhibition) 1997; Hon DUniv Wolverhapmton 2000; *Solo Exhibitions* incl: Chisenhale Gallery London 1991, Deitch Projects New York 1998, Serpentine Gallery London 1998, ICA Boston 2000, Chicago Arts Club 2000, Aspen Museum of Art Colorado 2000, Philadelphia ICA 2000, Galleria Civica d'Arte Moderna Italy 2001, D'Amelio Terras NY 2003, Guy Bartschi Geneva 2003; *Group Exhibitions* incl: The British Art Show (Mclennan Galleries Glasgow, Leeds City Art Gallery, Hayward Gallery) 1990, São Paulo Bienal Brazil 1994, The Maybe - collaboration with Tilda Swinton (Serpentine Gallery) 1995, Turner Prize (Tate Gallery) 1997, Material Culture (Hayward Gallery) 1997, New Art from Britain (Kunstraum Innsbruck) 1998, 1st Melbourne Int Biennial 1999, Postmark: An Abstract Effect (Site Santa Fe) 1999, Violent Incident (Tate Gallery Liverpool) 1999, Interventions (Milkwaukee Art Museum) 2000, Between Cinema and a Hard Place (Tate Modern) 2000, Anteprima Bovisa Milano Europa 2000, New Collections Displays 1900 to the Present (Tate Britain) 2001–02, New Collection Displays: Truths and Fictions (Tate Liverpool) 2002, Days Like These (Tate Triennial Tate Britain) 2003; *Collections* include: Tate Gallery and various private and public collections in Europe and the USA; *Commissions* major permanent sculpture for British Galleries V&A 2001; *Publications* Cornelia Parker (with B Ferguson and J Morgan, 2000); *Style*— Ms Cornelia Parker; ✉ Frith Street Gallery, 59–60 Frith Street, London W1V 5TA (tel 020 7494 1550, fax 020 7287 3733, e-mail info@frithstreetgallery.com)

PARKER, Prof David; s of Joseph William Parker, of Chester-le-Street, Co Durham, and Mary, *née* Hill (d 1988); *b* 30 July 1956, Leadgate, Co Durham; *Educ* Durham Johnston Secdy Sch, King Edward VI GS Stafford, ChCh Oxford (open exhibitioner, MA, Clifford Smith Prize), Hertford Coll Oxford (Carreras sr studentship, DPhil); *m* 27 July 1979, Fiona Mary, *née* MacEwan; 2 da (Eleanor Francoise b 4 Jan 1983, Julia Rose b 4 Aug 1984), 1 s (Philip James b 13 March 1988); *Career* Univ of Durham: lectr in chemistry 1982–89, sr lectr 1989–92, prof of chemistry 1992–, head Dept of Chemistry 1995–98 and 2003–06; visiting prof Université Louis Pasteur Strasbourg 1995, visiting prof Monash Univ 1998; chm RSC UK Supramolecular and Macrocycles Gp 1996–2000, chm Perkin 2 Scientific Editorial Bd 1996–2000, chm Chemical Soc Reviews Editorial Bd 2002–07; memb: Perkin Cncl RSC 1990–93 and 1996–99, RSC-FCMG/BCMG Ctee 1993–96, NECRC Scientific Ctee 1994–98; Coll Lectureship Hertford Coll Oxford 1979, NATO Fellowship 1980–81, Hickinbottom Fellowship RSC 1988–89, Royal Soc Leverhulme Tst Sr Research Fellowship 1998–99, Tilden Lectureship and Silver Medal RSC 2003–04; Corday-Morgan Medal and Prize RSC 1987, ICI Prize in Organic Chemistry 1991, Inderdisciplinary Award RSC 1995, Inaugural IBC Award in Supramolecular Science and Technol 2000, Inaugural RSC Award in Supramolecular Chemistry 2002; memb American Chemical Soc 1980–; CChem 1978, FRSC 1978, FRS 2002; *Recreations* cricket, golf; *Clubs* Durham City Cricket, Brancepeth Castle Golf; *Style*— Prof David Parker; ✉ Department of Chemistry, University of Durham, South Road, Durham DH1 3LE (tel 0191 334 2033, fax 0191 384 4737, e-mail david.parker@dur.ac.uk)

PARKER, Prof David; *b* 28 September 1949; *Educ* Univ of Hull (BSc), Univ of Salford (MSc), Cranfield Sch of Mgmnt (PhD); *Career* sr lectr Univ of Birmingham Business Sch 1993–97; prof of business economics and strategy: Aston Univ Business Sch 1997–2003, Sch of Mgmnt Cranfield Univ 2003–; visiting prof and memb Advsy Bd Centre for the Study of Regulated Industries Univ of Bath 1996–, visiting prof and dir of regulation research prog Centre for Research on Regulation and Competition Victoria Univ of Manchester (now Univ of Manchester) 2000–; memb Competition Cmmn (formerly Monopolies and Mergers Cmmn) 1999–; official historian of privatisation UK Govt; assoc conslt Public Administration International 2001–; numerous advsy and trg appts around the world incl economic advsr Office of Utilities Regulation Jamaica 2002–; MIMgt 1988, FRSA 1998, FBAM 2001, AcSS 2003; *Publications* incl: The Impact of Privatisation: Ownership and Corporate Performance in the UK (jtly, 1997), Privatisation and Supply Chain Management (jtly, 1999), Privatisation and Corporate Performance (ed, 2000), Globalisation and the Sustainability of Development in Latin America: Perspectives on the New Economic Order (jt ed, 2002), International Handbook on Privatisation (jt ed, 2003), Leading Issues in Competition, Regulation and Development (jtly, 2003), International Handbook of Economic Regulation (jtly, 2005); *Style*— Prof David Parker; ✉ Cranfield School of Management, Cranfield, Bedford MK43 0AL (tel 01234 751122, fax 01234 751806, e-mail david.parker@cranfield.ac.uk)

PARKER, Diana; da of Howard Parker (d 1967), and Avis Parker (d 1991); *b* 30 October 1957, Gosforth, Newcastle upon Tyne; *Educ* Univ of Cambridge (MA, MPhil); *m* 16 March

P

1991, Dr John Landers; *Career* admitted slr; specialises in family law; chm Withers LLP 1999–; memb: Law Soc, Int Acad of Matrimonial Lawyers; tstee: Inst for Philanthropy, Common Purpose; *Recreations* allotments; *Style*— Ms Diana Parker; ✉ Withers LLP, 16 Old Bailey, London EC4M 7EG (tel 020 7597 6198, fax 020 7597 6543, e-mail diana.parker@withersworldwide.com)

PARKER, Elinor Sheila Halling; da of Joseph Patrick Anthony Cheek (d 1994), of New Malden, Surrey, and Joan Sheila Maude, *née* Halling (d 1996); *b* 21 September 1940; *Educ* Grey Coat Hosp Westminster, Univ of Sheffield (BDS); *m* 24 Sept 1966, Dr David Parker, s of Hubert Robert Parker (d 1990), of Maidstone, Kent; 1 s (Daniel b 1969), 1 da (Clare b 1972); *Career* asst lectr Univ of Sheffield 1966–68; gen dental practioner: Kuala Lumpur 1969–74, New Malden 1975–87, Hersham 1987–; assoc ed Br Dental Jl 1992–2002; memb: Mgmnt Ctee Kingston Women's Centre 1984–87, Women's Ctee Kingston BC 1987–88, Br Dental Editors' Forum 1987–2003, Editorial Bd The Probe 1990–92, Bd SW Thames Div Faculty of Gen Dental Surgery 1993–2000; chm: Govrs Tiffin Girls' Sch 1987–88, Women in Dentistry 1989–90 (ed 1986–93, pres 2000–03); memb in Gen Dental Practice of Faculty of Gen Dental Practice Royal Coll of Surgns 1992; chm Kingston and District Section BDA 1997–98; memb BDA; *Recreations* writing, badminton, music; *Clubs* Kingston Feminists; *Style*— Dr Elinor Parker; ✉ 16 Alric Avenue, New Malden, Surrey KT3 4JN (tel 020 8949 2596, e-mail eshparker@aol.com); 5 The Green, Hersham, Walton-on-Thames, Surrey KT12 4HW (tel 01932 248348, fax 01932 888248,website www.hershamdentalpractice.co.uk)

PARKER, Sir Eric Wilson; kt (1991); s of Wilson Parker (d 1983), and Edith Gladys, *née* Wellings (d 1998); *b* 8 June 1933; *Educ* The Priory GS for Boys Shrewsbury; *m* 12 Nov 1955, Marlene Teresa, da of Michael Neale (d 1941); 2 s (Ian, Charles), 2 da (Karen, Sally Jane); *Career* Nat Serv RAPC Cyprus 1956–58; articled clerk with Wheeler Whittingham & Kent (CAs) 1950–55; with Taylor Woodrow 1958–64; Trafalgar House plc: joined 1965, fin dir 1969, dep md 1973, md 1977, chief exec 1983–92, dep chm 1988–93; chm Caradon plc (now Novar plc) 1998–99, non-exec dir International Real Estates plc (formerly Criterion Properties) 1998–; dir: Kvaener Tstees (KEPS) Ltd 2001–, Trafalgar House Pension Tstee (formerly Kvaerner Tstees (KPF) Ltd) 2002–, Job Partners 2000–02; non-exec chm Albert Goodwin plc 2003–; quartermaster gen conslt and memb Advsy Bd MOD 1997–2000; pres Race Horse Owners Assoc 1999–2001 (dir 1994–), dir: British Horse Racing Bd 1999–2004, Horserace Betting Levy Bd (HBLB) 2000–04, Horserace Totaliser Bd 2000–, National Stud 2005–; memb Lloyds; patron Teenage Cancer Tst; FCA 1967 (ACA 1956), CIMgt; *Recreations* racehorse owner and breeder (Crimbourne Stud), golf, tennis, cricket, wine; *Clubs* RAC, West Sussex Golf, MCC; *Style*— Sir Eric Parker; ✉ Crimbourne House, Wisborough Green, Billingshurst, West Sussex RH14 0HR (tel 01403 700400, fax 01403 700776)

PARKER, Prof (Noel) Geoffrey; s of late Derek Geoffrey Parker, and Kathleen Betsy, *née* Symon; *b* 25 December 1943; *Educ* Nottingham HS, Christ's Coll Cambridge (MA, PhD, LittD); *Children* 3 s, 1 da; *Career* fell Christ's Coll Cambridge 1968–72; Univ of St Andrews: reader in modern history 1978–82 (lectr 1972–78), prof of early modern history 1982–86; visiting prof: Vrije Universiteit Brussels 1975, Univ of British Columbia Vancouver 1979–80, Keio Univ Tokyo 1984; Lees Knowles lectr in mil history Univ of Cambridge 1984, Charles E Nowell distinguished prof of history Univ of Illinois at Urbana-Champaign 1986–93 (chm of dept 1989–91), Robert A Lovett prof of mil and naval history Yale Univ 1993–96, Andreas Dorpalen prof of history Ohio State Univ 1997–; British Acad Exchange fell Newberry Library Chicago 1981, corresponding fell Spanish Royal Acad of History 1988–, J S Guggenheim Fndn fell 2001–02, H T Guggenheim sr fell 2002–03; Hon Doctorate in history and letters Vrije Universiteit Brussels 1990, Hon Dr Katholieke Universiteit Brussels 2005; foreign memb: Academia Hispano-Americana Cadiz 2004, Koninklijke Akademie voor Wetenschappen Amsterdam 2005; FBA 1984; Encomienda Order of Isabel the Catholic (Spain) 1988, Caballero Gran Cruz Order of Isabel the Catholic (Spain) 1992, Caballero Gran Cruz Order of Alfonso the Wise (Spain) 1996; *Awards* American Military Inst Best Book of the Year award for The Military Revolution (*see* Books) 1989, Dexter Prize for the best book published 1987–90 on the hist of technol for The Military Revolution 1990, Samuel Eliot Morrison Prize for teaching and publishing in the field of military history 1999, Alumni Assoc Distinguished Teaching Award Ohio State Univ 2006; *Books* The Army of Flanders and The Spanish Road 1567–1659 (1972, 2 edn 2004), The Dutch Revolt (1977, 3 edn 1985), Philip II (1978, 4 edn 2001), Europe in Crisis 1598–1648 (1979, 3 edn 2001), Spain and the Netherlands 1559–1659 (1979, 2 edn 1990), The Thirty Years' War (1984, 3 edn 1997), The World - An Illustrated History (ed 1986, 4 edn 1995), The Military Revolution - Military Innovation and the Rise of the West 1500–1800 (1988, 4 edn 2000), The Spanish Armada (with Colin Martin 1988, 4 edn 1999), The Cambridge Illustrated History of Warfare (ed, 1995, 3 edn 2008), The Times Compact History of the World (ed, 1995, 4 edn 2005), Spain, Europe and the Atlantic World - Essays in Honour of John H Elliott (ed, 1995), The Reader's Companion to Military History (ed, 1996), The Grand Strategy of Philip II (1998, 2 edn 1999), Success is Never Final. Empire, War and Faith in Early Modern Europe (2002); author of numerous articles and reviews and ed numerous other books; *Recreations* travel, archaeology; *Style*— Prof Geoffrey Parker; ✉ The Ohio State University, 106 Dulles Hall, 230 West 17th Avenue, Columbus, Ohio 43210–1367, USA (tel 00 1 614 292 2674, fax 00 1 614 292 2282)

PARKER, Prof Geoffrey Alan; s of Alan Parker (d 1989), and Gertrude Ethel, *née* Hill (d 1992); *b* 24 May 1944; *Educ* Lymm GS Cheshire, Univ of Bristol (BSc, Rose Bracher prize for biology, PhD), King's Coll Cambridge (MA); *m* 29 July 1967, Susan Mary (d 1994), da of Harold Alfred William Wallis; 1 da ((Nicola) Claire b 27 Aug 1973), 1 s (Alan Leslie b 4 April 1977); m 2, 25 Oct 1997, Carol Elizabeth, da of Harold Emmett; 1 step da (Maxine Sylvia b 18 July 1983); *Career* Univ of Liverpool: asst lectr in zoology 1968–69, lectr 1969–76, sr lectr 1976–80, reader 1980–89, prof Dept of Environmental and Evolutionary Biology 1989–96, prof Sch of Biological Scis 1996–; sr research fell King's Coll Research Centre Cambridge 1978–79, Nuffield Science research fell Univ of Liverpool 1982–83, SERC sr research fell Univ of Liverpool 1990–95; memb Editorial Bd: Heredity 1983–88, Ethology, Ecology and Evolution 1989–95, American Naturalist 1991–92, Journal of Evolutionary Biology 1991–96, Proceedings of the Royal Society of London, Series B 1991–97; consulting ed Animal Behaviour 1977–78 and 1980–82; memb Cncl: Assoc for Study of Animal Behaviour 1979–82 (memb 1976–), Int Soc for Behavioural Ecology 1986–88 (memb 1986–); memb: Br Ecological Soc 1965–, American Soc of Naturalists 1978–92, European Soc for Evolutionary Biology 1991–; Niko Tinbergen lectr Assoc for the Study of Animal Behaviour 1995, medal of Assoc for the Study of Animal Behaviour 2002, Animal Behaviour Soc Distinguished Animal Behaviourist Award 2003, Spallanzani medal Biology of Spermatozoa conf 2005, Frink medal Zoological Soc of London 2005, W D Hamilton lectr Int Soc for Behavioural Ecology 2006; FRS 1989; *Books* Evolution of Sibling Rivalry (co-author, 1997); also author of numerous scientific articles in learned jls; *Recreations* breeding, showing and judging exhibition bantams (Supreme Champion, Nat Poultry Club GB show 1997), playing jazz clarinet (mainly Dixieland) in local bands; *Clubs* Partridge & Pencilled Wyandotte (hon sec and treas 1987–94, pres 2003–), Poultry Club of GB (memb Cncl 1986–90, pres 2003–06), Plymouth Rock (vice-pres 2002–07); *Style*— Prof Geoffrey Parker, FRS; ✉ School of Biological Sciences, Biosciences Building, University of Liverpool, Liverpool L69 7ZB (tel 0151 795 4524)

PARKER, Prof Eur Ing Graham Alexander; s of Joe Parker (d 1964), of Nuneaton, and Margaretta Annie, *née* Mawbey (d 1985); *b* 20 November 1935; *Educ* King Edward VI GS Nuneaton, Univ of Birmingham (BSc, PhD, CEng, Eur Ing); *m* 7 Nov 1959 (m dis 2001), Janet Ada, da of Cecil Parsons (d 1963), of Nuneaton, Warks; 2 da (Joanne Marie b 1966, Louise Alessandra b 1968); *Career* Hawker-Siddeley Dynamics Ltd 1957–60, Cincinnati Milacron Inc USA 1963–64, Univ of Birmingham 1964–68, currently prof of mech engrg Univ of Surrey (joined 1968); govr Charterhouse Sch; Freeman City of London 1998, Liveryman Worshipful Co of Engineers 1999; memb Mfrg Systems Div IMechE; FIMechE, memb ASME; *Books* Fluidics - Components and Circuits (with K Foster, 1970), A Guide to Fluidics (contrib 1971); *Recreations* tennis, walking; *Style*— Prof Eur Ing Graham Parker; ✉ Chinthurst Cottage, Wonersh Common, Guildford, Surrey GU5 0PP (tel 01483 898973, fax 01483 893542); School of Engineering, University of Surrey, Guildford, Surrey GU2 7XH (tel 01483 689283, fax 01483 306039, e-mail g.parker@surrey.ac.uk)

PARKER, Prof Howard John; s of John Raymond Parker, and Doreen, *née* Taylor; *b* 2 November 1948; *Educ* Birkenhead Sch, Univ of Liverpool (BA, MA, PhD); *m* Linda; 2 s (James b 1977, Ben b 1980); *Career* reader in social work studies Univ of Liverpool 1987–88 (research fell 1972–74, lectr in applied social studies 1974–79, sr lectr in social work studies 1980–86), appointed prof of social work Univ of Manchester 1988 (now emeritus prof); seconded on research work: to Home Office Res and Planning 1985, to Wirral Borough Cncl 1986; conducted research into alcohol and crime, youth culture and drug use; advsr on drugs policies in local, regnl and Govt depts (especially Home Office and Health Educn Authy 1993–2000), advsr on drugs policy Denmark and Iran 2001, non-exec dir Nat Care Standards Cmmn; QuADs conslt developing drug treatment 2001–04; conslt Police Services Drug Treatment Agencies, conducted Ind Review NI Alcohol and Drug Strategies 2005; lecture tour Aust 2006; *Books* View from the Boys (1974), Social Work and the Courts (1979), Receiving Juvenile Justice (1981), Living with Heroin (1988), Unmasking the Magistrates (1989), Drugs Futures: changing patterns of drug use amongst English youth (1995), Illegal Leisure: The normalisation of adolescent recreational drug use (1998), Dancing on Drugs: risk, health and hedonism is the British club scene (2000), UK Drugs Unlimited (2001); *Style*— Prof Howard Parker; ✉ School of Law, University of Manchester, Manchester M13 9PL (e-mail howard.parker@manchester.ac.uk)

PARKER, James Mavin (Jim); s of James Robertson Parker (d 1983), of Hartlepool, Cleveland, and Margaret, *née* Mavin; *b* 18 December 1934; *Educ* Guildhall Sch of Music and Drama; *m* 1; 1 da (Louise b 1964); m 2, 2 Aug 1969, Pauline Ann, da of John George, of Reading, Berks; 2 da (Claire b 1974, Amy b 1976); *Career* musician 4/7 Dragoon Gds; composer and conductor, joined Barrow Poets 1963; composed music for: Banana Blush (John Betjeman), Captain Beaky (Jeremy Lloyd); printed music: Follow the Star (Wally K Daly), Ground Force and other pieces (brass band), The Golden Section (brass quintet), All Jazzed Up (various instruments and piano), The Music of Jim Parker (various instruments and piano); childrens musicals: five Childrens Musicals (Tom Stanier), English Towns (flute and piano), A Londoner in New York (suite for brass), All Jazzed Up (oboe and piano), Mississippi Five (woodwind quintet); clarinet concerto, Light Fantastic (suite for brass), Mexican Wildlife (for brass quintet), Boulevard (for woodwind quintet); film and TV music: Mapp and Lucia, Wynne and Penkovsky, Good Behaviour, The Making of Modern London, Girl Shy (Harold Lloyd), The Blot, Wish Me Luck, Anything More Would be Greedy, Parnell and the Englishwoman, Soldier Soldier, The House of Eliott, Body and Soul, Goggle Eyes, House of Cards, To Play The King (BAFTA Award for Best TV Music 1993), The Final Cut, Moll Flanders (BAFTA Award for Best TV Music 1996), Tom Jones (BAFTA Award for Best TV Music 1997), A Rather English Marriage (BAFTA Award for Best TV Music 1998), Lost For Words, The Midsomer Murders, Foyle's War, Born and Bred; Hon GSM 1985; GSM (Silver medal) 1959, LRAM 1959; *Recreations* twentieth century art, literature; *Style*— Jim Parker, Esq; ✉ 16 Laurel Road, London SW13 0EE (tel and fax 020 8876 8442)

PARKER, Sir (Thomas) John; kt (2001); s of Robert Parker (d 1957), and Margaret Elizabeth, *née* Bell; *b* 8 April 1942; *Educ* Belfast Coll of Technol, Queen's Univ Belfast; *m* July 1967, Emma Elizabeth, da of Alexander Blair, of Ballymena, NI; 1 s (Graham b 31 July 1970), 1 da (Fiona b 1 June 1972); *Career* shipbuilder and engr; Harland & Wolff Ltd: memb Ship Design Team 1963–69, ship prodn mangr 1969–71, prodn drawing office mangr 1971–72, gen mangr Sales and Projects Dept 1972–74; md Austin & Pickersgill (shipbuilders) Sunderland 1974–78, dep chief exec British Shipbuilders Corp 1980–83 (bd memb for shipbuilding mktg and ops 1978–80), chm and chief exec Harland & Wolff plc (became Harland & Wolff Holdings plc) 1983–93 (non-exec dir 1993–96); chm: Babcock Int Gp plc 1994–2000 (dep chm and chief exec 1993–94), Lattice Gp plc (following demerger from BG Gp) 2000–02 (non-exec dir BG Gp plc 1997–2000), Firth Rixon 2001–03 (dep chm 1999–2001), RMC Gp 2002–04 (dep chm 2001–02), National Grid Transco plc (following Lattice's merger with National Grid) 2002–, Peninsular and Oriental Steam Navigation Co (P&O) 2005– (dep chm Feb-May 2005); dir: QUBIS Ltd Belfast 1984–93, British Coal Corp 1986–93, AS Quatro Norway 1989–93, AS Cinco Norway 1989–93, GKN plc 1993–2003, P&O Princess Cruises 2000–03, Brambles Industries plc 2001–03, Carnival Corp and Carnival plc (formerly P&O Princess Cruises) 2003–; vice-pres Engrg Employers Fedn; memb: Cncl RINA 1978–80 and 1982– (vice-pres 1985, pres 1996–99), Int Ctee Bureau Veritas Paris 1981–97, Gen Ctee Lloyd's Register of Shipping 1983– (chm Technical Ctee 1996–2001), Industry Devpt Bd NI 1983–87, Br Ctee Det Norske Veritas Oslo 1984–94, Ctee of Mgmnt RNLI 1998–, Smeatonian Soc of Civil Engrgs; Worshipful Co of Shipwrights (Liveryman 1978, prime warden 2000–02); Hon DSc: Queen's Univ of Belfast 1985, Univ of Ulster 1992, Univ of Abertay 1997, Univ of Surrey 2001; Hon ScD TCD 1986; FRINA 1978, FIMarE 1979, FREng 1982; *Recreations* sailing, reading, music, the countryside; *Clubs* Royal Ulster Yacht, Royal Thames Yacht; *Style*— Sir John Parker, FREng; ✉ National Grid plc, 1–3 Strand, London WC2N 5EH

PARKER, Dr John Richard; s of Richard Robert Parker (d 1987), and Elsie Winifred, *née* Curtis (d 2005); *b* 5 November 1933; *Educ* SE London Tech Coll, Regent St Poly (DipArch), UCL (DipTP), Central London Poly (PhD); *m* 1959, Valerie Barbara Mary, da of Edward James Troupe Duguid (d 1952); 1 s (Jonathan b 1965), 1 da (Joanna b 1968); *Career* Nat Serv 2 Lt RE served Canal Zone Cyprus 1952–54, TA (Lt) 1954–64; private commercial architects firms 1954–59, architect LCC 1961–64, gp leader urban design London Borough of Lambeth 1964–70, head central area team GLC 1970–86; fndr and dir Greater London Consultants (urban design and planning conslts) 1986–, princ John Parker Associates (architectural and planning conslts) 1990–; originator of devpt nr tport interchanges related to pedestrian movement 1967–86, project mangr Piccadilly Circus redevpt 1972–86, originator London's Canal Way Parks and Walk 1978–86, planning conslt for Addis Ababa 1986, vol advsr VSO (formerly BESO (Br Exec Servs Overseas)) China and Bulgaria 1997–, conslt to Cncl of Europe 2003–; author of various pubns on subjects incl urban design, environmental planning, pedestrians and security; memb: Urban Design Gp 1978–, Pedestrians Assoc 1983–, Soc of Expert Witnesses 1996–2004, Int Devpt Forum 1990–2004 (chm 2000–04), RTPI Int Devpt Network 2004– (leader 2004–); tstee Jubilee Walkway Tst 2002–, memb Catemian Assoc 1977–; Winston Churchill fell 1967, RIBA Pearce Edwards Award 1969, Br Cncl Anglo-Soviet Award 1988; ARIBA, FRTPI, FRSA; *Books* Piccadilly Circus: From Controversy to Reconstruction (1980); *Recreations* tennis, golf, drawing, yoga, tai chi; *Clubs* Royal Cwlth, Shortlands Golf, Catford Wanderers Sports (former chm); *Style*— Dr John Parker;

✉ John Parker Associates, 4 The Heights, Foxgrove Road, Beckenham, Kent BR3 5BY (tel and fax 020 8658 6076, e-mail jpa@btinternet.com); Greater London Consultants, c/o Inside Out Architecture, Cole Street Studios, 6–8 Cole Street, London SE1 4YH (tel 020 7367 6831, fax 020 7378 7784, e-mail glc@btinternet.com)

PARKER, John Robert; s of John Thomas Parker, and Jennie, *née* Hardman (d 1997); *b* 30 April 1953; *Educ* Lancaster Royal GS, Hertford Coll Oxford (MA); *m* 1975, Fiona Jayne, *née* Rae; 1 s (Philip b 1979), 1 da (Claire b 1981); *Career* accountant Price Waterhouse 1975–79; Building Design Partnership: mgmnt accountant 1979–85, chief accountant 1985–89, equity ptnr (fin and admin ptnr) 1989–97, fin dir 1997–; FCA 1979; *Recreations* church work (memb UK Christians in Sci Assoc), reading (incl interest in sci devpts), walking; *Clubs* RAC; *Style—* John Parker, Esq; ✉ Building Design Partnership Limited, PO Box 85, Sunlight House, Quay Street, Manchester M60 3JA (tel 0161 834 8441, fax 0161 8362116, e-mail jr-parker@bdp.co.uk)

PARKER, Rt Hon Sir Jonathan Frederic; kt (1991), PC (2000); s of Sir (Walter) Edmund Parker (d 1981), and Elizabeth Mary, *née* Butterfield (d 1984); *b* 8 December 1937; *Educ* Winchester, Magdalene Coll Cambridge (MA); *m* 1967, Maria-Belen, da of Thomas Ferrier Burns OBE; 3 s (James b 1968, Oliver b 1969, Peter b 1971), 1 da (Clare b 1972); *Career* called to the Bar Inner Temple 1962 (bencher 1985); QC 1979, recorder of the Crown Court 1989–91, attorney gen Duchy of Lancaster 1989–91, judge of the High Court of Justice (Chancery Division) 1991–2000, vice-chllr County Palatine of Lancaster 1994–98, a Lord Justice of Appeal 2000–07; *Recreations* painting, gardening; *Clubs* Garrick; *Style—* The Rt Hon Sir Jonathan Parker

PARKER, Judith Mary Frances; QC (1991); *Educ* Somerville Coll Oxford (BA); *Career* called to the Bar 1973; practising barr specialising in family law; dep High Ct judge Family Div 1995, recorder 2000– (asst recorder 1998–2000); memb: SE Circuit, Family Law Bar Assoc, Ctee Assoc of Lawyers for Children; chm Inter-County Adoption Lawyers Assoc; regular lectr on all aspects of family law; fell Int Acad of Matrimonal Lawyers; *Publications* Encyclopaedia of Financial Provision in Family Matters (contrib), Essential Family Practice (consltg ed); *Style—* Miss Judith Parker, QC; ✉ 1 King's Bench Walk, Temple, London EC4Y 7DB (tel 020 7936 1500, fax 020 796 1590, e-mail clerks@1kbw.co.uk)

PARKER, Keith John; OBE (1993); s of late Sydney John Parker, of Tywyn, Gwynedd, N Wales, and late Phyllis Mary, *née* Marsh; *b* 30 December 1940; *m* 25 Aug 1962, Marilyn Ann, da of William Frank Edwards; 1 s (Nicholas Edward b 18 July 1966); *Career* reporter: Wellington Journal and Shrewsbury News 1957–63, Express and Star Wolverhampton 1963–64; Shropshire Star: reporter, chief reporter, dep news ed 1964–72, ed and dir 1972–77; ed and dir Express and Star 1977–95, gen mangr Express and Star 1995, md Shropshire Newspapers Ltd 1996–2002, md Express and Star Ltd Wolverhampton 2002–05; dir Midland News Assoc Ltd 1996–2005, dep chm Telford Radio Ltd 1999–, chm Kidderminster Radio Ltd 2004–, dir MNA Broadcasting 2005–, chm Shrewsbury and Oswestry FM Ltd 2005–; pres Guild of Br Newspaper Editors 1988–89 (chm Parly and Legal Ctee 1991–94), pres Midlands Newspaper Soc 1999–2000, press memb PCC 1992–95; memb: Data Protection Tbnl 1996–2006, Parly Editorial and Regulatory Affrs Ctee Newspaper Soc 1997–2003; dir Shropshire C of C Trg and Enterprise 1997–2002, tstee Ironbridge Gorge Museum Devpt Tst 2000–02; *Style—* Keith Parker, Esq, OBE; ✉ 94 Wrottesley Road, Tettenhall, Wolverhampton WV6 8SJ (tel 01902 758595, e-mail keithjparker@btinternet.com)

PARKER, Malcolm Peter (Mal); s of William Harvey Parker (d 1999), of Navenby, Lincs, and Mary Jean, *née* Spinks; *b* 4 June 1946; *Educ* Kings Sch Grantham, Oxford Sch of Architecture; *m* 21 June 1975, Linda Diane, da of Emmanuel Theodore, of London; 2 da (Charlotte b 1982, Georgina b 1984); *Career* architect; Tom Hancock Assocs 1972–73, John Winter Assocs 1973–74, Pentagram 1974–76, Richard Ellis 1976–78, founding ptnr Dunthorne Parker 1978–; projects incl: offices for BUPA, Brooke-Bond, Capital Radio and Swiss Life, office investments for Rolls Royce, Rank Xerox, Windsor Life and General Motors Pension Funds, industrial parks, Royal Bank of Scotland branches, historic shopping schemes in Oxford, Colchester, High Wycombe and Bury St Edmunds, retail stores for J Sainsbury, hotels in Central London, recording studios for Nat Broadcasting Sch and Chrysalis Records, hostel for High Cmmr for Malaysia, restoration of Grade I listed bldgs Golden Cross in Oxford and Red Lion in Colchester and Grade II offices in Clifton, residential schemes in Whitehall and City of London for Royal Bank of Scotland; awards incl: Office Agents Soc Building of the Year 1999, Robertson Award, Ideas in Architecture Award, Oxford Preservation Tst Award, Royal Tunbridge Wells Civic Soc Conservation Award, Civic Tst Award; RIBA 1973, MCSD 1985; *Recreations* golf, skiing, sailing, walking, philately, theatre, opera, concerts; *Clubs* Reform; *Style—* Mal Parker, Esq; ✉ Dunthorne Parker, 16 Hampden Gurney Street, London W1H 5AL (tel 020 7258 0411, fax 020 7723 1329, e-mail mal.parker@dunthorneparker.co.uk, website www.dunthorneparker.co.uk)

PARKER, Martin; s of Leonard Parker, of Newcastle upon Tyne, and Winifred, *née* Callighan; *b* 20 June 1959, Newcastle upon Tyne; *Educ* Gosforth HS Newcastle upon Tyne, Univ of Leicester (LLB), Guildford Coll of Law; *m* 17 Dec 2005, Faye Louise, *née* Barker; 1 da; *Career* admitted slr 1983; slr: Harbottle & Lewis 1983–87, Northern Engineering Industries plc 1987–89; Northumbrian Water Group plc: joined 1990, head of gp legal services 1998–2003, co sec and head of legal affrs 2003–; dir NTC Northumberland Touring Theatre Co; *Recreations* tennis, theatre, Newcastle United FC; *Style—* Martin Parker; ✉ Northumbrian Water Group plc, Northumbria House, Abbey Road, Pity Me, Durham DH1 5FJ (tel 0191 301 6746, fax 0191 301 6705, e-mail martin.parker@nwl.co.uk)

PARKER, Maj Sir Michael John; KCVO (2000, CVO 1991), CBE (1996, MBE 1968); s of Capt S J Wilkins, and V S M Wilkins, *née* Parker; assumed his mother's maiden name in lieu of his father's patronymic by Deed Poll 1959; *b* 21 September 1941; *Educ* Dulwich Coll, Hereford Cathedral Sch, RMA Sandhurst; *m* February 2005, Emma Mary Baswell Purefoy, *née* Gilroy; *Career* Capt Queen's Own Hussars 1961–71, Maj TA Special List attached Queen's Own Hussars 1972–; deviser and prodr of large-scale civilian and mil events; antique dealer; vice-pres: Morriston Orpheus Choir, Queen Elizabeth The Queen Mother's Meml Fund, Support for Africa; patron: Chicken Shed Theatre Co, Brooklands SLD Sch; KStJ 1985 (OStJ 1982), Grand Offr Order of al Istiqlal (Jordan) 1987; *Main Productions* Becket 1963, Richard III (Berlin TV) 1964, Berlin Tattoo 1965, 1967, 1971, 1973, 1975, 1977, 1979, 1981, 1983, 1986, 1988 and 1992, British Week Brussels 1967, The Royal Tournament 1974–99, The Edinburgh Military Tattoo 1992–94, The Aldershot Army Display 1974, 1975, 1977, 1979, 1981 and 1983, Wembley Musical Pageant 1979, 1981 and 1985, over 30 other mil events around the world; *National Events* HM The Queen's Silver Jubilee Celebrations 1977, The Great Children's Party (Int Year of the Child) 1979, Carols for the Queen 1979, The Royal Fireworks 1981, The Great Children's Party Hyde Park 1985, HM Queen Elizabeth The Queen Mother's 90th Birthday Celebrations 1990, Economic Summit Spectacular (G7) Buckingham Palace 1991, HM The Queen's 40th Anniversary Celebration 1992; *Other Events* Son et Lumière on Horse Guards Parade 1983 and 1985, Americas Cup Newport 1983, King Hussein of Jordan's 50th Birthday Celebrations 1985, Royal Weddings 1987 and 1993 and Coronation Celebration 1988 and 1993, Joy to the World (Christmas celebration Royal Albert Hall) 1988–97, International Horse Shows Olympia, Wembley and Birmingham (variously), World Equestrian Games Stockholm, National Day Celebrations Oman (Royal Equestrian Day) 1990, Fortress Fantasia Gibraltar 1990, British National Day Expo'92 Seville Spain, P&O 150th Anniversary Celebration Greenwich 1992 (further 18 shows in Hong Kong, Cyprus, Jordan, USA, Canada, Germany and UK), Wedding of Prince Abdullah Bin Al Hussein of Jordan, Memphis in May International Festival Tattoo USA 1993 and 1994, Opening of The Queen Elizabeth Gate Hyde Park London 1993, Firework Display to mark opening of The Channel Tunnel Folkestone 1994, The Spirit of Normandy (Royal Albert Hall) 1994, Multi-media Show for Normandy 50th Celebration Portsmouth 1994, The Army Benevolent Fund Drumhead Serv 1994, Pavarotti International Horse Show Modena Italy 1993 and 1994, P&O ship naming Shekou China 1994, P&O ship namings Portsmouth and USA 1995, VE Day Celebrations Hyde Park and Buckingham Palace 1995, Jersey Liberation Fireworks 1995, VJ Day Celebrations Horseguards and Buckingham Palace 1995, Oriana Gala Sydney 1996, naming of Dawn Princess Fort Lauderdale 1997, The Countryside Rally Hyde Park 1997, Royal Windsor Horse Show 1998, Gala for naming of Grand Princess NY 1998, Unveiling Ceremony for the Albert Meml London 1998, Centenary Celebrations for King Abdul Aziz Riyadh Saudi Arabia 1999, Royal Military Tattoo 2000, HM Queen Elizabeth The Queen Mother's 100th Birthday Celebrations 2000, All the Queen's Horses Windsor 2002, The London Golden Jubilee Weekend Festival 2002 (incl National Beacon and Fireworks), Opening of Meml Gates Constitution Hill 2002, Opening of Memphis Symphony Orchestra Concert Hall 2003, Ship naming of Minerva II Port of London 2003, Not Forgotten Assoc Christmas Show St James's Palace 2003–, Music on Fire! Royal Military Acad Sandhurst Centenary Cavalcade Royal Welsh Agricultural Show 2004, Liberation Day Son et Lumière Jersey 2005, Royal Yacht Sqdn Cowes Trafalgar Celebration 2005, Glory of Wales Debbigh 2005; *Awards* Evening Standard Ambass for London 1995, Walpole Gold Medal for Excellence 2002, Walpole Award for Best Cultural Achievement 2002, CIB Communicator of the Year 2002, SPAM Lifetime Achievement Award 2002, RTS Derek Harper Technical Award; *Style—* Maj Sir Michael Parker, KCVO, CBE

PARKER, Mike Howard; s of Michael Harding Parker, and Margaret Elfrida, *née* Armstrong; *b* 24 April 1956; *Educ* Chelmer Valley HS Chelmsford; *m* 31 May 1980, Teresa Marie, *née* Soler (d 1990); 1 da (Laura Michelle b 4 Dec 1980); partner, Anna Marie Treacher; *Career* reporter Essex Chronicle 1973–77, freelance reporter 1977–82, reporter and feature writer News of the World 1982–87; Daily Star: reporter Jan-Sept 1987, night news ed 1987–88, dep news ed 1988–89, features ed 1989–94, asst ed 1994–; assignments covered in N and S America, W Indies, Africa, Middle East, Russia and throughout Europe; Nat Newspaper Consumer Journalist of the Year 1988; *Books* The World's Most Fantastic Freaks (1982); *Recreations* tennis, theatre, travel; *Style—* Mike Parker, Esq; ✉ The Daily Star, c/o Express Newspapers, Ludgate House, 245 Blackfriars Road, London SE1 9UX (tel 020 7928 8000, fax 020 7620 1641)

PARKER, Oliver Tom; s of Sir Peter Parker (d 2002), and Lady Jill Parker, *née* Rowe-Dutton; *b* 6 September 1960; *Educ* St Paul's; *Partner* Cassia Kidron; 1 da (Bel b 19 Aug 1996), 1 s (Otis Saxon b 12 Oct 2002), 1 step s (Cato Sandford b 25 May 1989); *Career* film dir, screenplay writer and actor; writer and dir: Othello 1996, An Ideal Husband 1999 (BAFTA nomination for Best Adapted Screenplay 1999), The Importance of Being Earnest 2002, Fade to Black 2006; dir I Really Hate My Job 2006, co-dir and co-prodr St Trinian's 2007; short films: A Little Loving 1994, The Short Cut 1994, Unsigned 1994; for TV: Billingsgate Alfie 1996, Copper Clive 1996, The Private Life of Samuel Peypes 2003; extensive stage, television and film acting roles; patron Big Arts Week; *Recreations* tennis, football; *Clubs* Groucho, Electric; *Style—* Oliver Parker, Esq; ✉ c/o Sue Rodgers, ICM, Oxford House, 76 Oxford Street, London W1D 1BS (tel 020 7636 6565)

PARKER, Sir (William) Peter Brian; 5 Bt (UK 1844), of Shenstone Lodge, Staffordshire; o s of Sir (William) Alan Parker, 4 Bt (d 1990), and Sheelagh Mary, *née* Stevenson; *b* 30 November 1950; *Educ* Eton; *m* 1976, Patricia Ann, da of late R and late Mrs D E Filtness, of Lea Cottage, Beckingham, Lincoln; 1 da (Lucy Emma b 1977), 1 s (John Malcolm b 1980); *Heir* s, John Parker; *Career* FCA; sr ptnr Stephenson Nuttall & Co Newark Notts; *Style—* Sir Peter Parker, Bt; ✉ Apricot Hall, Sutton-cum-Beckingham, Lincoln LN5 0RE

PARKER, Peter Robert Nevill; s of Edward Parker, and Patricia, *née* Sturridge; *b* 2 June 1954; *Educ* Canford Sch, UCL (BA); *Career* freelance literary journalist 1978–, author 1987–, columnist and diarist Hortus (gardening jl) 1990–2002, assoc ed Oxford DNB 1996–2004 (advsy ed 2006–); memb Exec Ctee PEN 1993–97, tstee PEN Literary Fndn 1993– (chair 1999–2000); memb: Ctee London Library 1999–2002 (chm Books Sub-Ctee 1999–2002 and 2004–07, tstee 2004–07), Cncl RSL 2004–; FRSL 1997; *Books* The Old Lie: The Great War and the Public-School Ethos (1987), Ackerley: A Life of J R Ackerley (1989), The Reader's Companion to the Twentieth-Century Novel (ed, 1994), The Reader's Companion to Twentieth-Century Writers (ed, 1995), Isherwood: A Life (2004); *Recreations* gardening; *Style—* Peter Parker, Esq, FRSL; ✉ Rogers, Coleridge & White, 20 Powis Mews, London W11 1JN (tel 020 7221 3717, fax 020 7229 9084)

PARKER, Peter William; TD (1966); s of William Nichol Parker (d 1978), of Burnley, and Muriel, *née* Constantine (d 1965); *b* 13 June 1933; *Educ* Winchester, New Coll Oxford (MA); *m* 5 Oct 1963, Janet Pusey (d 1998), da of Tom Rymer Till (d 1982), of Caerleon; 1 da (Lucy (Mrs Leverett) b 1966), 2 s (Tom b 1968, Daniel b 1971); *Career* Nat Serv; 2 Lt E Lancashire Regt 1952 (actg capt 1953), TA 4 E Lancashire Regt 1953–67 (Maj 1965); Phillips & Drew 1956–85: ptnr 1962, dep sr ptnr 1983; chm Phillips & Drew International Ltd 1980–85; memb: Cncl Inst of Actuaries 1977–82 and 1986–92 (vice-pres 1988–91), Cncl CGLI 1991–2007, Royal Patriotic Fund Corp 1991–, Ctee RUKBA 1996–2006, Investigation Ctee ICAEW 1999–2003; memb Archbishops' Review of Bishops' Needs and Resources 1999–2002, memb Pensions Bd C of E 2003–, church cmmr 2003–; tstee Tower of London Choral Fndn 1983–, govr Sidney Perry Fndn 1983– (chm 2004–), treas Egypt Exploration Soc 1988–2003, govr Music Therapy Charity 1989–; Liveryman Worshipful Co of Actuaries (Master 1989–90); Hon FCGI, FIA 1963, FSI; SBStJ; *Recreations* music, gardening, travel, typography; *Clubs* City of London, Naval and Military; *Style—* Peter Parker, Esq, TD; ✉ 1 Turner Drive, London NW11 6TX (tel 020 8458 2646, fax 020 8455 8498)

PARKER, Sir Richard William; *see:* Hyde Parker, Sir Richard William

PARKER, Richard William; s of Eric Parker, and Hope Margaret, *née* Martin; *b* 29 March 1942; *Educ* Bilton Grange, Uppingham, Seal Hayne Agric Coll; *m* 22 Sept 1966, Ruth Margaret, da of Charles Frederick Banks; *Career* joined family farming business 1964, currently dir; chm Blankney PC; former chm: Upper Witham Drainage Bd, Lincs Agric Soc; Liveryman Worshipful Co of Farmers; Freedom of London; High Sheriff Lincs 2000; MCIM; *Recreations* golf, squash, rugby, cricket, tennis, hockey; *Clubs* RAC (London); *Style—* Richard Parker, Esq; ✉ Blankney Estates Ltd, Estate Office, Blankney, Lincoln LN4 3AZ (tel 01526 320181, fax 01526 322521, mobile 07967 164301)

PARKER, Prof Robert Henry (Bob); s of Henry William Parker (d 1978), of London, and Gladys Mary, *née* Bunkell (d 1939); *b* 21 September 1932; *Educ* Paston Sch North Walsham, UCL (BScEcon); *m* 5 Oct 1955, (Marie) Agnelle Hilda, da of Antoine Yves Laval (d 1962), of Mauritius; 1 s (Michael b 1956), 1 da (Theresa b 1959); *Career* accountant Cassleton Elliott and Co Lagos Nigeria 1958–59, lectr in commerce Univ of Adelaide 1960–61, sr lectr in commerce Univ of W Aust 1962–66, P D Leake res fell LSE 1966, reader in mgmnt accounting Manchester Business Sch 1966–68, assoc prof of finance INSEAD Fontainebleau 1968–70; prof of accountancy: Univ of Dundee 1970–76, Univ of Exeter 1976–97 (prof emeritus 1997–); professorial fell Inst of CAs of Scotland 1991–96, ed Accounting and Business Research 1975–93; FCA 1968 (ACA 1958); *Books* Topics in Business Finance and Accounting (jtly, 1964), Readings in Concept and Measurement of Income (jtly, 1969, 2 edn 1986), Management Accounting - An Historical

P

Perspective (1969), Understanding Company Financial Statements (1972, 6 edn 2007), Accounting in Scotland - A Historical Bibliography (jtly, 1974, 2 edn 1976), The Evolution of Corporate Financial Reporting (jtly, 1979), British Accountants - A Biographical Sourcebook (1980), Accounting Thought and Education (jtly, 1980), Bibliographies for Accounting Historians (1980), Comparative International Accounting (jtly, 1981, 9 edn 2006), Macmillan Dictionary of Accounting (1984, 2 edn 1992), Papers on Accounting History (1984), The Development of the Accountancy Profession in Britain to the Early Twentieth Century (1986), Issues in Multinational Accounting (jtly, 1988), A Dictionary of Business Quotations (jtly, 1990), Accounting in Australia - Historical Essays (1990), Consolidation Accounting (jtly, 1991), Collins Dictionary of Business Quotations (jtly, 1991), Accounting History - Some British Contributions (jtly, 1994), Financial Reporting in the West Pacific Rim (jtly, 1994), An International View of True and Fair Accounting (jtly, 1994), Accounting History from the Renaissance to the Present (jtly, 1996), Milestones in the British Accounting Literature (jtly, 1996), Readings in True and Fair (jtly, 1996), Accounting in France/ La comptabilité en France: Historical Essays/Etudes historiques (jtly, 1996), Professional Accounting and Audit in Australia 1880–1900 (jtly, 1999); *Recreations* local history, genealogy; *Style—* Prof Bob Parker; ✉ St Catherines, New North Road, Exeter EX4 4AG (tel 01392 255154); School of Business and Economics, University of Exeter, Streatham Court, Exeter EX4 4PU (tel 01392 263201,, fax 01392 263210, e-mail r.h.parker@exeter.ac.uk)

PARKER, Robert John; s of Eric Robert Parker (d 1984), and Joan Marjorie Parker (d 1991); *b* 22 February 1952; *Educ* Whitgift Sch, St John's Coll Cambridge (MA); *m* 28 Aug 1982, Claudia Jane, da of Col Alexander Akerman; 3 s (Felix Alexander b 12 Feb 1987, Toby, Benjamin (twins) b 14 Oct 1991); *Career* asst dir NM Rothschild & Sons Ltd 1976–82, exec dir investment Credit Suisse First Boston Group 1982–94; Credit Suisse Asset Management Ltd: chief exec 1995–98, global head institutional business devpt 1997–2002, vice-chm 1998–, memb Chm's Bd and Investment Ctee; dir: Central European Growth Fund plc 1994–2000, Credit Suisse Asset Management Deutschland GmbH 1995–2001, Credit Suisse Asset Management France SA 1997–2001; Freeman City of London, Liveryman Worshipful Co of Farriers; *Style—* Robert Parker, Esq; ✉ Credit Suisse, One Cabot Square, London E14 4QJ

PARKER, Robert Stewart; CB (1998); s of Robert Arnold Parker, and Edna, *née* Baines; bro of Elizabeth Blackburn, QC, *qv*; *b* 13 January 1949; *Educ* Brentwood Sch, Trinity Coll Oxford (MA); *Career* called to the Bar Middle Temple 1975, ad eundem Lincoln's Inn 1977; Office of the Parly Counsel 1980, Law Cmmn 1985–87, dep Parly counsel 1987–92, Parly counsel 1992–; Freeman City of London 1984, Liveryman Worshipful Co of Wheelwrights 1984; MCMI (MIMgt 1984), FRSA 2000; *Books* Cases and Statutes on General Principles of Law (with C R Newton, 1980), The Best of Days? (contrib, 2000); *Recreations* the livery, cricket, bridge, books, music; *Clubs* Athenaeum, City Livery, Langbourn Ward, Horatian Soc, Kipling Soc, Royal Soc of St George (City of London), Edinburgh Walter Scott; *Style—* Robert Parker, Esq, CB, FRSA; ✉ Office of the Parliamentary Counsel, 36 Whitehall, London SW1A 2AY (tel 020 7210 3000)

PARKER, Prof Stella; da of James Parker (d 1976), and Gertrude, *née* Curley (d 1985); *b* 3 July 1944; *Educ* Brentwood Sch Southport, Imperial Coll London (BSc, PhD), Birkbeck Coll London (MSc), Garnett Coll London (CertEd); *m* (m dis); *Career* lectr Biology and Medical Lab Sci Hounslow Coll 1973–76, lectr Biological Educn and Medical Lab Sci Garnett Coll London 1976–83, seconded as advsy teacher Advanced Biology Alternative Learning Project 1978–80; City Univ: lectr continuing educn 1984–87, head Sch of Continuing Educn 1987–96, pro-vice-chllr 1993–96; Robert Peers chair in adult/continuing educn Univ of Nottingham 1997–; exec Univs Assoc of Continuing Educn 1987; co-opted memb City of London Educn Ctee; govr The City Lit 1995–; FRSA 1989; *Publications* jt ed ABAL Project books/manuals, also author of various pubns on sci and access; *Recreations* gentle exercise, Francophile; *Clubs* Reform; *Style—* Prof Stella Parker; ✉ School of Continuing Education, University of Nottingham, University Park, Nottingham NG7 2RD (tel 0115 951 4396, fax 0115 951 4397, e-mail stella.parker@nottingham.ac.uk)

PARKER, Timothy Charles (Tim); s of Clifford Parker (d 1999), and Eileen, *née* Jupp; *b* 19 June 1955, Aldershot, Hants; *Educ* Pembroke Coll Oxford (MA), London Business Sch (MSc); *m* 4 Aug 1984, Therese, *née* Moralis; 2 da (Louise b 14 Oct 1985, Josephine b 9 Dec 1997), 2 s (Antony b 7 March 1990, George b 21 Sept 1991); *Career* chief exec: Kenwood Appliances 1989–96, Clarks Shoes 1996–2002, Kwik-Fit 2002–04 (non-exec dep chm 2004–06), The AA 2004–; non-exec dir: Alliance Boots plc (formerly Boots Gp plc), Compass Gp plc 2007–; memb Bd Audit Cmmn; FRSA; *Recreations* music, running, reading; *Clubs* Reform; *Style—* Tim Parker, Esq; ✉ The AA, Fanum House, Basing View, Basingstoke, Hampshire RG21 4EA (tel 01256 491111)

PARKER-EATON, Robert George; OBE (1986, MBE (Mil) 1966); s of Leonard George Parker-Eaton (d 1956), of Wythall, nr Birmingham, and Phyllis Muriel, *née* Broome (d 1962); *b* 21 November 1931; *Educ* Solihull Sch, RAF Staff Coll; *m* 21 Dec 1962, Dorothy Elizabeth, da of Thomas Edgar Sharpe (d 1957), of Bletchley, Bucks; 2 s (Stephen Paul b 1963, Timothy Simon b 1968), 1 da (Sarah Frances b 1965); *Career* cmmnd supply branch RAF 1950, Wing Cdr 1966, controller civil air trooping MOD 1966–69, dep dir logistics prog Supreme Allied Cmd Atlantic 1969–72, OC air movements RAF Brize Norton 1972–74; Britannia Airways Ltd: controller customer servs 1974–78, dir customer servs and external affrs 1978–90, dep md 1990–; UK dir Ind Air Carriers Assoc (IACA) 1993–2000; chm UK Travel Retail Forum 2000–; memb: Exec Ctee Br Air Tport Assoc 1989–, Bd Int Travel Retail Confederation 2000–, Bd Airline Gp Ltd 2000–; awarded silver medal by Airport Operators' Assoc 1997; swimming rep: Cornwall 1955–56, Cumbria 1959–60, RAF 1959–69, Combined Services 1960–63, Berkshire 1961–62; FIMgt 1981 (MIMgt 1968), FCIT 1991 (MCIT 1982), FRAeS 1997; *Recreations* swimming, model railways, reading; *Style—* Robert Parker-Eaton, Esq, OBE; ✉ 1 Kiln Lane, Clophill, Bedford MK45 4DA (tel 01525 861128); Britannia Airways Ltd, Luton Airport, Luton, Bedfordshire (tel 01582 424155, fax 01582 428861, telex 82239)

PARKES, Timothy Charles; TD (1988); s of Frank Leonard Parkes (d 1955), of Leamington Spa, Warks, and Marie Joan Parkes, *née* Morris (d 1999); *b* 13 August 1954; *Educ* Royal Masonic Sch, Wadham Coll Oxford (MA); *m* 31 Aug 1985, Wendy Patricia, da of Maj Vincent Reginald Hook, of Ufford, Suffolk; 1 s (Charles Alexander Frederick b 1988), 2 da (Laura Claire Venetia b 1990, Eleanor Juliet Lucy b 1992); *Career* TACSC 1989 (Maj TA Royal Yeomanry 1984–90); admitted slr 1980; currently ptnr Herbert Smith; memb: Judicial Studies Bd Hong Kong 1990–95, Civil Court Users' Ctee Hong Kong 1993–95, Cncl Law Soc of Hong Kong 1993–95 and 2002–05, Law Soc Far East Ctee 1997–99, Oxford Univ Law Devpt Ctee, Wadham Coll Oxford Devpt Cncl; memb Law Soc of England and Wales; chm Kent and Sharpshooters Yeomanry Museum Tst 1997–2001; hon legal advsr Matilda Int Hosp Hong Kong 2002–05; Freeman Worshipful Co of Slrs 1982; FCIArb; *Recreations* tennis, painting, reading; *Clubs* Cavalry and Guards', Hong Kong, Royal Hong Kong Jockey; *Style—* Timothy Parkes, Esq, TD; ✉ Berghersh Place, Witnesham, Ipswich, Suffolk IP6 9EZ (tel 01473 785504, fax 01473 785159)

PARKIN, Catherine Elizabeth (Kate); da of Ian Stuart Parkin, of Alderton, Glos, and Elizabeth, *née* Downey; *b* 9 April 1959; *Educ* Tewkesbury Comp, Cheltenham GS, St Catherine's Coll Oxford (MA); *m* 29 Aug 1983, William John Urwick Hamilton, s of Mark Hamilton; 2 da (Susannah Elizabeth Rose b 18 April 1989, Mary Isabel Angelica b 19 April 1993); *Career* grad trainee Thomson Publishing 1980–81, editorial controller Macmillan London Ltd 1981–85; Transworld Publishers Ltd: ed 1985–86, sr ed 1986–87 editorial dir 1987–89; editorial dir Collins Publishers 1989–91; Random House UK: publishing dir Century 1991–93, publisher Century Arrow 1993–2000, md Century Hutchinson William Heinemann and Arrow 2000; with John Murray Publishers 2005–; coach Way Ahead Gp; *Recreations* reading, cooking, gardening, music; *Style—* Ms Kate Parkin

PARKIN, Ian Michael; s of George Harold Parkin (d 1996), of Worthing, W Sussex, and Ethel Mary, *née* Fullerton (d 2002); *b* 15 October 1946; *Educ* Dorking Co GS, Open Univ (BA); *m* 30 April 1977, Patricia Helen, da of Maj Frederick James Fowles, MC (d 1982); 2 s (Andrew b 1978, Richard b 1984), 1 da (Jennifer b 1981); *Career* CA; formerly: sr ptnr Pannell Kerr Forster CI 1979–90, sr ptnr Brownes CAs Jersey, dir Citadel Trust Ltd Jersey 1990–93, ptnr Moores Rowland Jersey 1993–95; dir: Compass Trust Company Ltd Jersey, Cater Allen Trust Company (Jersey) Ltd 1994–99, Chatsworth Property Services Ltd 1999–; FCA 1979; *Recreations* golf, reading; *Style—* Ian Parkin, Esq; ✉ Le Petit Jardin, La Rue a la Pendue, Millais, St Ouen, Jersey (tel 01534 483218, fax 01534 483795, e-mail parkin@jerseymail.co.uk)

PARKIN, Sara Lamb; OBE (2000); da of Dr George Lamb McEwan (d 1996), of Isle of Islay, Argyll, and Marie Munro, *née* Rankin; *b* 9 April 1946; *Educ* Barr's Hill GS Coventry, Bromsgrove Coll, Edinburgh Royal Infirmary (RGN), Univ of Michigan, Leeds Poly; *m* 30 June 1969, Donald Maxwell Parkin, s of Donald Harry Parkin (d 2001), of Lincolnshire, and Lesley Mary, *née* Tyson (d 2002); 2 s (Colin McEwan b 28 March 1974, Douglas Maxwell b 12 Sept 1975); *Career* staff nurse and ward sister Edinburgh Royal Infirmary 1970–74, nursing res asst and undergraduate tutor Univ of Edinburgh 1972–73, memb Cncl Brook Advsy Serv 1974–76, Leeds AHA 1976–80, self employed writer and speaker on green issues 1981–; Green Pty: memb Cncl 1980–81, int liaison sec 1983–90, chair of the Exec 1992; co-sec Euro Greens 1985–90 (ed Newsletter 1986–89); dir Forum For The Future 1995–; memb: Bd Environment Agency of England and Wales 2000–06, Bd Heads, Teachers and Industry Ltd 2002–, Cncl NERC 2003–, Bd Leadership Fndn for HE 2003–; Companion ICE,CInstE; *Publications* incl: Green Parties: An International Guide (1989), Green Light on Europe (ed, 1991), Green Futures (1991), The Life and Death of Petra Kelly (1994); also author of various nat and Euro Green Election manifestos; *Recreations* walking, gardening, theatre, opera; *Style—* Ms Sara Parkin, OBE; ✉ Forum for the Future, 19–23 Ironmonger Row, London EC1V 3QN (tel 020 7324 3676)

PARKINS, Brian James Michael; JP (Inner London 1989); s of Ronald Anthony Parkins (d 1979), of Ilford, Essex, and Adelaide Florence, *née* Percival; *b* 1 November 1938; *Educ* St Ignatius Coll London, KCH and Univ of London (BDS), Inst of Dental Surgery and RCS (LDS, FDS), Northwestern Univ Chicago (MS); *m* 1, 20 Oct 1966 (m dis 1980), Jill Elizabeth, da of James Dawson (d 1982), of Lytham St Annes, Lancs; 1 da ((Alison) Jane b 14 Nov 1967), 1 s (Richard Mark b 1 March 1971); m 2, 19 May 1988, Mary Saunders, *née* Burton; *Career* conslt dental surgn; sr clinical lectr Inst of Dental Surgery 1969–81, private practice 1970–, recognised teacher of the Univ of London 1972, conslt in restorative dentistry UCL and Middx Hosp Sch of Dentistry 1982–92; pres Br Soc for Restorative Dentistry 1987–88 (memb Cncl 1982–84); sec: American Dental Soc of London (pres 1996–97), American Dental Soc of Europe (pres 1993–94); examiner 1977–86: BDS, RCS for LDS Final Part III FDS and MGDS; retired memb: Acad of Expert Witnesses, Family Health Servs Appeal Authy (FHSAA); hon treas Dentist Provident Soc; hon memb American Dental Assoc; lay memb Mental Health Review Tbnl 1999–; fell: Pierre Fouchard Acad, American Coll of Dentists; *Recreations* reading, music, golf; *Style—* Brian Parkins, Esq; ✉ 4 Sussex Mews West, London W2 2SE (tel 020 7723 8766, e-mail ffredbear@bjpjp.co.uk)

PARKINS, Graham Charles; QC (1990); *Educ* Univ of London (LLB); *Career* called to the Bar Inner Temple 1972, recorder of the Crown Court 1989–; memb Criminal Bar Association, chm Norfolk Bar Mess; *Style—* Graham Parkins, Esq, QC; ✉ 18 Red Lion Court, London EC4A 3EB

PARKINSON, Baron (Life Peer UK 1992), of Carnforth in the County of Lancashire; Cecil Edward Parkinson; PC (1981); s of Sidney Parkinson, of Carnforth, Lancs; *b* 1 September 1931; *Educ* Royal Lancaster GS, Emmanuel Coll Cambridge; *m* 1957, Ann Mary, da of F A Jarvis, of Harpenden; 3 da (Hon Mary b 1959, Hon Emma (Hon Mrs Owrid) b 1961, Hon Joanna (Hon Mrs Bamber) b 1963); *Career* joined West Wake Price & Co 1956 (ptnr 1961–71); formerly with Metal Box Co, founded Parkinson Hart Securities Ltd 1967; chm: Hemel Hempstead Cons Assoc 1966–69, Herts 100 Club 1968–69; Parly candidate (Cons) Northampton 1970; MP (Cons): Enfield W Nov 1970–74, Herts S 1974–1983, Hertsmere 1983–92; sec Cons Parly Fin Ctee 1971–72, PPS to Michael Heseltine as min for Aerospace and Shipping DTI 1972–74, asst govt whip 1974, oppn whip 1974–76, oppn spokesman on trade 1976–79, min of state Dept of Trade 1979–81, chm Cons Pty and Paymaster-General 1981–83, chllr Duchy of Lancaster 1982–83, sec of state for trade and indust June-Oct 1983 (resigned), sec of state for energy 1987–89, sec of state for tport 1989–90, chm Cons Pty 1997–98; non-exec chm of various cos incl inTechnology and Huntswood; *Style—* The Rt Hon the Lord Parkinson, PC; ✉ House of Lords, London SW1A 0PW

PARKINSON, HE Howard; CVO (1998); s of Ronald Parkinson, of Manchester, and Doris, *née* Kenyon; *b* 29 March 1948, Manchester; *Educ* Openshaw Tech HS Manchester; *m* 1974, Linda, *née* Wood; 1 da (Suzanne b 1979), 1 s (Carl-Michael b 1982); *Career* Bd of Trade Liverpool 1967; entered HM Dip Serv 1969, floater duties Latin America (Honduras, Nicaragua, Panama, Ecuador and Paraguay) 1972, vice-consul Tegucigalpa 1974, vice-consul Buenos Aires 1975, second sec (commercial/aid) Maputo 1978, second later first sec FCO 1981, first sec (commercial) Lisbon 1985, first sec on loan to British Gas 1989, dep head (policy) Migration and Visa Dept FCO 1991, consul-gen and cnsllr Washington DC 1994, cnsllr (trade and investment) Kuala Lumpur 1997, dep high cmmr Mumbai 2001, high cmmr to Mozambique 2003–; *Style—* HE Mr Howard Parkinson, CVO; ✉ c/o Foreign & Commonwealth Office (Maputo), King Charles Street, London SW1A 2AH

PARKINSON, Malcolm Ross; s of F C D Parkinson (d 1983), and Alexa St Clair, *née* Ross; *b* 20 April 1948; *Educ* Sutton Valence; *m* 1972, Beatrice Maria, da of Prof C Schwaller; 1 da (Charlotte b 1978), 1 s (Alexander b 1981); *Career* trainee navigation offr Cunard then actg 4th offr T & J Brocklebank Ltd 1964–69, trainee account exec BBD&O Ltd 1969–72, account dir Leo Burnett Inc 1972–74, jt md DWK Ltd 1974–76, dir B & Q Ltd 1976–84, chief exec F W Woolworth Ltd 1984–87; dir: Woolworth Holdings plc 1984–87, James Latham plc 1992–, Powerbreaker plc 1992–97, Applied Chemicals Ltd 1992–97, gp chief exec Landmark Retail plc 1997–2000; md: Retail Corporation plc 1989–92, Siegel & Gale Ltd (UK, Europe, Africa and ME) 1993–96; chm: Imatronic Ltd 1989–93, Latham Timber Centres Ltd 1992–97, Cardionetics plc 1996–2001, Malross Management Ltd; govr Capel Manor Coll; memb Worshipful Co of Gardeners; fell Mktg Soc; *Recreations* sailing, shooting; *Clubs* Royal Thames Yacht, Reform; *Style—* Malcolm Parkinson, Esq; ✉ Malross Management Ltd, Estate Office, Claywood House, Sway, Hampshire SO41 6DA (tel 01590 683899)

PARKINSON, (Robert) Michael; s of Robert Scott Parkinson (d 1999), of Lancaster, and Rhoda, *née* Chirnside (d 1964); *b* 9 August 1944; *Educ* Wrekin Coll, Coll of Estate Mgmnt Univ of London (BSc); *m* 26 Oct 1968, Elizabeth Ann, da of Michael Moore (d 1998), of Lancaster; 2 s (Duncan b 27 Nov 1969, Andrew b 4 Sept 1971); *Career* ptnr Ingham & Yorke (chartered surveyors and land agents) 1971–, dir Marsden Building Soc 1984– (vice-chm 1994–2005); chm: Marsden Home Renovations Ltd 1991–2006, Marsden Homes (Pendle) Ltd 1994–2006; steward to the Honor of Clitheroe 1991–; FRICS 1976; *Recreations* mountaineering, country pursuits; *Clubs* Fell and Rock Climbing, Alpine, Univ of London Graduate Mountaineering, Rotary (Clitheroe), Clitheroe Ex-Tablers (41); *Style*— Michael Parkinson, Esq; ✉ Beechcroft, Back Commons, Clitheroe, Lancashire BB7 2DX (tel 01200 422660); Ingham & Yorke, Littlemoor, Clitheroe, Lancashire BB7 1HG (tel 01200 423655, fax 01200 429160)

PARKINSON, Michael; CBE (2000); *b* 28 March 1935, Yorkshire; *Educ* Barnsley GS; *m* 22 August 1959, Mary Heneghan; 3 s (Andrew, Nicholas, Michael); *Career* TV and radio presenter, journalist and writer; prodr/interviewer Granada TV 1964–68 (Granada's Scene, Granada in the North, World in Action, What The Papers Say), exec prodr and presenter LWT 1964–68; presenter: 24 Hours (BBC) 1964–68, Cinema (Granada TV) 1969–70, Tea Break and Where in the World (Thames TV) 1971; host: Parkinson (BBC) 1972–82 and 1998–2004 (Channel 10 and ABC Australia 1979–85), Parkinson (ITV) 2004–; co-fndr and presenter TV-AM 1983–84; presenter: Give Us A Clue (Thames TV) 1984–92, Desert Island Discs (BBC Radio 4) 1986–88; host: Parkinson One to One (Yorkshire TV) 1987–88, Parky (Thames TV) 1989, The Michael Parkinson Show (LBC) 1990–92; presenter: Help Squad (TVS) 1991–92, Ghostwatch (BBC) 1992, Parkinson on Sport (BBC Radio 5) 1994–97, Parkinson's Sunday Supplement (BBC Radio 2) 1996–; host Going For a Song (BBC) 1995–99; fndr Pavilion Books 1980; sometime columnist and feature writer: Sunday Times, Guardian, Daily Express, The People, The Listener, Daily Mirror, New Statesman, Mail on Sunday; currently columnist Daily Telegraph; Sports Feature Writer of the Year (British Sports Journalism Awards) 1995, Sports Writer of the Year British Press Awards 1998, Variety Club's Media Personality of the Year 1998, Sony Radio Award for Parkinson's Sunday Supplement 1998, Comic Heritage Gold Award for Special Contribution to the World of Entertainment 1998, Yorkshire Man of The Year 1998, BASCA Gold Award 1998, National Television Awards Most Popular Talk Show for Parkinson 1998, 1999, 2000 and 2001, Broadcasting Press Guild Award for Best Performance in Non-Acting Role 1999, Best Light Entertainment Performance BAFTA 1999, Media Soc Award for Distinguished Contribution to the Media 2000; Hon DUniv Humberside 1999; fell BFI 2000; *Books* Football Daft (1968), Cricket Mad (1969), Pictorial History of Westerns (with Clyde Jeavons, 1969), Sporting Fever (1974), Best - An Intimate Biography (1975), A-Z of Soccer (with Willis Hall, 1975), Bats in the Pavilion (1977), The Woofits (1980), Parkinson's Lore (1981), The Best of Parkinson (1982), Sporting Lives (1992), Sporting Profiles (1995), Michael Parkinson on Golf 1999, Michael Parkinson on Football (2001), Michael Parkinson on Cricket (2002); *Recreations* sport (particularly cricket and golf); *Style*— Michael Parkinson, Esq, CBE; ✉ CSS-Stellar Management Ltd, Drury House, 34–43 Russell Street, London WC2B 5HA

PARKINSON, Steven David; s of David K Parkinson, of Aberdeen, and Lilian, *née* Rannie; *b* 1 April 1967; *Educ* Robert Gordon's Coll Aberdeen, Queen Margaret Coll Edinburgh (Dip Drama; *Career* mktg mangr Scottish Opera tours 1989, prodn mangr P&O SS Canberra 1990, press and events offr National Garden Festival 1990, presenter Tyne Tees TV 1991; Metro Radio Group: charity fundraiser 1990, prodr Hallam FM Sheffield 1991–92, prog controller Great North Radio Newcastle 1992–94, prog controller Great Yorkshire Gold 1994–95, former head of marketing and promotions Hallam FM and Great Yorkshire Gold from 1995; Chrysalis plc: md Galaxy 101 Bristol 1996–, md Galaxy 105 Leeds 1996–, brand dir Galaxy Network, md Chrysalis Radio 2000, mktg dir Chrysalis Radio 2001–, md Heart 106.2 2001–; *Recreations* fencing, swimming, photography, theatre; *Style*— Steven Parkinson, Esq

PARKS, Timothy Harold (Tim); s of Harold James Parks (d 1980), and Joan Elizabeth, *née* MacDowell; *b* 19 December 1954; *Educ* Westminster City Sch London, Downing Coll Cambridge (BA), Harvard Univ (MA); *m* 15 Dec 1979, Rita Maria, *née* Baldassarre; 1 s (Michele Roberto b 3 June 1985), 1 da (Stefania Angela b 20 Jan 1988); *Career* writer; marketing exec Tek Translation & International Print London 1979–80, freelance teacher and translator Verona 1981–85, lettore Univ of Verona 1985–, visiting lectr Istituto Universitario di lingue Moderne Milan 1992–; memb Soc of Authors 1986–; *Fiction* Tongues of Flame (1985, Somerset Maugham award, Betty Trask award), Loving Roger (1986, John Llewellyn Rhys award), Home Thoughts (1987), Family Planning (1989), Cara Massimina (as John MacDowell, 1990), Goodness (1991), Shear (1993), Mimi's Ghost (1995), Europa (1997, shortlisted for Booker Prize), Destiny (1999), Judge Savage (2003), Rapids (2005), Talking About It (short stories, 2005), Cleaver (2006); numerous short stories; series of trans from Italian incl work by Calvino, Moravia, Tabucchi and Calasso; *Non-Fiction* Italian Neighbours (1992), An Italian Education (non-fiction, 1997), Translating Style: English Modernists and their Italian Translations (1997), Adultery and Other Diversions (essays, 1998), Hell and Back (essays, 2001), A Season with Verona (2002), Medici Money, Banking, Metaphysics and Art in Fifteenth Century Florence, a work of history (2005); numerous academic pubns; *Recreations* cycling, squash; *Style*— Tim Parks; ✉ website www.timparks.com

PARMINTER, Kate; da of James Henry Parminter, and June Rose Parminter; *b* 24 June 1964; *Educ* Millais Sch Horsham, Collyer's Sixth Form Coll, LMH Oxford (MA); *m* 9 July 1994, Neil Roger Sherlock; 2 da (Rose Vera Sherlock b 26 July 2000, Grace Francine Sherlock b 16 Aug 2003); *Career* grad mktg trainee The Nestlé Co Ltd 1986–88, Parly researcher for Simon Hughes MP 1988–89, sr account exec Juliette Hellman PR 1989–90; RSPCA: PR offr 1990–92, head of campaigns and events 1992–95, head of public affrs 1996–98, chm Campaign for the Protection of Hunted Animals 1997–98; dir CPRE 1998–2004; memb: Nat Consumer Cncl Policy Cmmn into Public Servs 2003–04, Nat Consumer Cncl Advsy Gp 2004–; tstee IPPR 2007–; cncllr Horsham DC 1987–95; memb: Lib Dems, National Trust; *Publications* Working For and Against Government in Pressure Group Politics in Modern Britain (1996), A Third Sector as well as a Third Way (jtly, 2001); *Recreations* Pre-Raphaelite paintings, walking, golf; *Clubs* National Liberal; *Style*— Ms Kate Parminter; ✉ 15B Quartermile Road, Godalming, Surrey GU7 1TG

PARMOOR, 4 Baron (UK 1914); (Frederick Alfred) Milo Cripps; s of 3 Baron Parmoor, DSO, TD, DL (d 1977), and of Violet Mary Geraldine (d 1983), da of Sir William Nelson, 1 Bt; *b* 18 June 1929; *Educ* Ampleforth, CCC Oxford; *Heir* kinsman, Seddon Cripps; *Style*— The Rt Hon the Lord Parmoor; ✉ Flat 26, 2 Mansfield Street, London W1G 9NF

PARNABY, Dr John; CBE (1987); s of John Banks Parnaby (d 1986), of Workington, Cumbria, and Mary Elizabeth Parnaby (d 1988); *b* 10 July 1937; *Educ* Univ of Durham (BSc), Univ of Glasgow (PhD); *m* 4 July 1959, Lilian, da of William Gambles Armstrong; 1 da (Susan Elisabeth b 1960), 3 s (John Mark b 1963, Christopher Stuart b 1966, Nicholas Gregory William b 1970); *Career* chm Aston Independent Hosp 2004–; former chm: Knowledge Process Software plc, Amchem Ltd, BPSE Ltd, Think Digital Solutions plc; formerly: gp dir Lucas Industries plc, chief exec Lucas Electronic Systems Ltd, chief exec Lucas Applied Technologies Ltd, chm Lucas Systems Engrg and Software Ltd, gen mangr Dunlop Diversified Products; formerly non-exec dir: Scottish Power plc, Jarvis plc, Molins plc; memb Cncl Royal Acad of Engrg, senator Engrg Cncl; past pres: Instn of Mfrg Engrs, IEE; former chm: Link Bd DTI, Engrg Bd CNAA, Electromechanical Engrg Bd EPSRC; author of over 60 papers in learned jls; Gold medal Instn of Mfrg Engrs, Faraday medal IEE, 2 Silver medals Rubber and Plastics Inst, Gold medal Inst of Purchasing and Supply; treas and chm Fin Cmmn Aston Univ 1999–, govr Bradford GS; hon prof Univ of Cambridge; hon fell: Coventry Poly 1989, Sheffield Poly 1991, Univ of Wales 1995; Hon DTech: Liverpool Poly 1990, CNAA 1990, Loughborough Univ 1991, Napier Univ 1997; Hon DSc: Univ of Hull 1991, Aston Univ 2002; Hon DUniv Open Univ 1992; Hon DEng: Univ of Bradford 1993, Univ of Newcastle upon Tyne 2000; Hon FIEE 1958, Hon FIMechE 1967, FREng 1988, FRSA; *Books* Minicomputers and Microcomputers in Engineering and Manufacture (1986), Manufacturing Systems Engineering Miniguide Handbook (1989, 2 edn 1992), Managing by Projects for Business Success (2003); *Recreations* field hockey, skiing, golf, yacht racing and cruising; *Clubs* Royal Southampton Yacht, Olton and West Warwickshire Hockey, Olton Golf; *Style*— Dr John Parnaby, CBE, FREng; ✉ Crest Edge, 4 Beechnut Lane, Solihull B91 2NW (tel and fax 0121 705 4348, e-mail drjparnaby@aol.com)

PARR, Anthony Stephen; s of Stephen Valentine Parr, of Preston, Lancs, and Brenda, *née* Carter-McGrath (d 1970); *b* 27 August 1949; *Educ* Balshaw's GS Leyland; *m* Jan 1985, Jannette Marie, da of Rudi Becker; 2 s (Jamie Anthony b 6 June 1986, Daniel Andrew b 14 June 1988), 1 da (Sally Jane b 26 June 1990); *Career* accountant Lancs CC 1967–72, accountant Shropshire CC 1973–77, asst treas Somerset CC 1977–85, treas Bristol and Weston Health Authy 1987–91 (dep treas 1985–87), chief exec South Devon Healthcare NHS Tst 1991–; CIPFA 1972; *Recreations* tennis, former rugby player; *Style*— Anthony Parr, Esq; ✉ South Devon Healthcare NHS Trust, Hengrave House, Torbay Hospital, Lawes Bridge, Torquay, Devon TQ2 7AA (tel 01803 655703, fax 01803 616334)

PARR, Christopher Serge (Chris); *b* 25 September 1943; *Educ* HS for Boys Chichester, The Queen's Coll Oxford (open scholar); *m* 23 Dec 1985, Anne Maria Devlin; 1 s (Connal Sebastian Devlin Parr b 23 Oct 1984); *Career* ABC trainee dir's bursary Nottingham Playhouse 1965–66, freelance theatre dir 1966–69, fell in theatre Univ of Bradford 1969–72, freelance (incl Royal Court Theatre) 1972–75, artistic dir Traverse Theatre Club 1975–81, prodr TV Drama BBC Northern Ireland, Pebble Mill, London and Scotland 1981–93, head of TV drama BBC Pebble Mill 1993–95; BBC TV: head of drama series 1995–96, exec prodr Drama Gp 1996–98; head of UK drama Thames Television (formerly Pearson Television) 1998–2002, formed (with Kenneth Trodd) Better Pictures 2003; *Awards* two RTS Serial Awards (for Nice Work and Children of the North), ACE Award (for The Rainbow), BAFTA Award (Drama Serial, for Takin' Over the Asylum), Celtic Film and TV Festival Drama Award (for Naming the Names), Michael Powell Award Edinburgh Festival (for You, Me and Marley); *Style*— Chris Parr, Esq

PARR, John Robert; s of Henry George Parr (d 1982), and Hilda Frances, *née* Pattison (d 1992); *b* 25 September 1934; *Educ* Dulwich Coll, Merton Coll Oxford (open scholar, MA); *m* June 1993, Prof Dolores O'Reilly, da of Charles Michael O'Reilly; 1 da; *Career* British Iron and Steel Fedn 1959–64 (dep sec 1963), princ Industrial Policy Div Dept of Economic Affairs 1965–67; British Steel Corp: joined 1968, co-ordinator European Community Affairs 1972–73; DG British Footwear Manufacturers Fedn 1973–76; General Secretariat of the Cncl of the European Communities: joined 1976, head of Div for Air Tport and Shipping 1986–89, hon dir 1989; DG Air Tport Users Cncl 1989–96; conslt on consumer affrs Int Air Tport Assoc 1996–98; chm: Airline-Consumer Forum Geneva 1995–98, Friends of the Ulster Orchestra 2007; band memb Ulster Orchestra 2007–; *Recreations* theatre, concert and opera-going, 20th century European history, Irish country life; *Style*— John Parr

PARR, Martin; s of Donald Parr (d 1999), and Joyce, *née* Watts; *b* 23 May 1952; *Educ* Surbiton GS, Manchester Poly (Dip Creative Photography); *m* 1980, Susie, da of Douglas Mitchell; 1 da (Ellen b 18 April 1986); *Career* photographer; visiting lectr: Nat Coll of Art and Design Dublin and Chelsea Sch of Art 1975–82, Sch of Documentary Photography Newport 1982–1984, W Surrey Coll of Art and Design 1983–90; visiting prof of photography Univ of Industrial Arts Helsinki 1990–92; memb Magnum Photo Agency 1994–; Arts Cncl of GB Photography Award 1975 and 1979; *Solo Exhibitions* incl: Home Sweet Home (Impressions Gallery York and Arnolfini Gallery Bristol) 1974, Beauty Spots (Impressions Gallery York and tour) 1976, Photographers' Gallery London 1977, Fotomania Gallery Barcelona 1978, The Non-Conformists (Camerawork London) 1981, Rural Irish Photographers (Neikrug Gallery NY) 1982, Bad Weather (Photographers' Gallery London and tour) 1982, International Photography Festival Malmo 1983, British Photographic Art (Geology Museum Beixing) 1984, A Fair Day (Orchard Gallery Derry and tour) 1984, George Eastman House Rochester 1985, Point of Sale (Salford City Art Gallery) 1986, The Last Resort (Serpentine Gallery London) 1986, Museum Folkwang Essen 1986, Arles Festival 1986, Fotograficentrum Stockholm 1986, Amsterdam Manifestation 1986, ICP Midtown NY 1987, Spending Time (Nat Centre of Photography Paris) 1987, Kodak Gallery Tokyo and Osaka 1988, The Cost of Living (RPS Bath and tour) 1989, Janet Borden NY 1991 and 1996, Gallery Jacques Gordat Paris 1991, Signs of the Times (Janet Borden NY) 1992, Kiek in de Kok Gallery Tallinn 1992, A Year in the Life of Chew Stoke (Chew Stoke Village Hall) 1993, Bored Couples (Gallery du Jour Paris and tour) 1993, Home and Abroad (Watershead Gallery Bristol and int tour) 1993, From A to B (27 Welcome Break service stations across UK) 1994, Curitiba Photo Festival 1994, Small World (Photographers' Gallery London) 1995, Small World and From A to B (Nat Centre of Photography Paris) 1995, Gallery du Jour Paris 1995 and 2000, West Bay (Rocket Gallery London) 1997, Ooh La La (Nat Museum of Photography Bradford) 1998, Japonais Endormis (Gallery du Jour Paris) 1998, Gallery Riis Oslo 1998, Common Sense (43 locations worldwide) 1999, Benidorm (Sprengel Museum Hanover) 1999, 20/21 Gallery Essen 2000, Autoportrait (Tom Blau Gallery London) 2000, Japonais Endormis (Kunsthalle Rotterdam) 2000, Kulturbeutel (Old Post Office Mitte Berlin) 2000, Think of England (Rocket Gallery London) 2001, Martin Parr: Photographic Works 1971–2000 (Barbican Art Gallery London) 2002; *Group Exhibitions* incl: Butlins by the Sea (Impressions Gallery York) 1972, Personal Views 1860–1977 (Br Cncl touring show) 1978, Art for Society (Whitechapel Art Gallery London) 1978, Three Perspectives on Photography (Hayward Gallery London) 1979, New Work in Britain (Photographers' Gallery London) 1981, Strategies - recent developments in British photography (John Hansard Gallery Southampton) 1982, Quelques Anglais (Centre Nationale de la Photographie Paris) 1985, British Contemporary Photography (Houston Foto Festival) 1986, New Documents (Museum of Contemporary Photography Chicago) 1986, Attitudes to Ireland (Orchard Gallery Derry) 1987, Mysterious Coincidences (Photographers' Gallery London) 1987, Inscriptions and Inventions (Br Cncl touring exhbn) 1987, A British View (Museum für Gestalturg Zurich) 1988, Through the Looking Glass, British Photography 1945–1989 (Barbican Centre London) 1989, The Art of Photography (Royal Acad London) 1989, Foto Biennale (Enschede) 1989, The Past and Present of Photography (MOMA Tokyo) 1990, British Photography from the Thatcher Years (MOMA NY) 1991, Voir la Suisse Autrement (Fribourg) 1991, Imagina (World Fair Seville) 1992, Photographs from the Real World (Lillehammer Art Museum) 1993, Sobre Santiago, Tres de Magnum (Santiago) 1993, European Photography Award 1985–1994 (Kultur Zentrum Bad Hamburg) 1994, Internationale Foto-Triennale (Esslingen) 1995, Zurich (Kunsthaus Zurich) 1997, Trois Grands Egyptiennes (Musée de la Photographie Charlleroi) 1997, No Sex Please, we're British (Shisheido Dept Store Tokyo) 1998, Our Turning World: Magnum Photographers 1989–1999 (Barbican Art Gallery London) 1999, Cruel & Tender (Tate Modern London) 2003; *Work in Public Collections* incl: Arts Cncl of GB, Union Bank of Finland Helsinki, Museum for Fotokunst Odense, V&A, George Eastman House Rochester, Bibliotheque Nationale Paris, MOMA NY, Philadelphia Museum of Art, MOMA Tokyo, Calderdale Cncl Halifax, Getty Museum Malibu, Walker Art Gallery Liverpool, Kodak France, Museum Folkwang Essen, Seagrams Collection NY, MOMA Tempere, Br Cncl London, Irish Arts Cncl, Australian Nat Gallery, Paris Audiovisual, Sprengel Museum Hannover, Yokohama Museum of Art, Tokyo Metropolitan Museum of Photography, San Francisco MOMA, Stedelijk Museum Amsterdam, Tate Modern London; *Books* Bad Weather (1982), A Fair Day (1984), The

P

Last Resort (1986, 2 edn 1998), The Actual Boot - the Photographic Postcard 1900–1920 (1986), The Cost of Living (1989), Signs of the Times (1992), Home and Abroad (1993), From A to B (1994), Small World (1995), West Bay (1997), Flowers (1999), Common Sense (1999), Boring Postcards (1999), Autoportrait (2000), Think of England (2000), Boring Postcards USA (2000), Langweilige Postkarten (2001), Phone Book (2002), 7 Communist Still Lives (2003), Fashion Magazine (2005), Mexico (2006), Parking Spaces (2007); subject of book Martin Parr by Val Williams (2002); *Clubs* Clifton Poker Sch; *Style*— Martin Parr, Esq; ✉ Magnum Photos, 63 gee Street, London EC1V 3RS (tel 020 7490 1771); Mosaic Films, 1A Flaxman Court, London W1F 0AU (tel 020 7287 0222)

PARRATT, Prof James Roy; s of James John Parratt, and Eunice Elizabeth Parratt; *b* 19 August 1933; *Educ* St Clement Danes Holborn Estate GS, Univ of London (BPharm, MSc, PhD, DSc (Med)), Univ of Strathclyde (DSc); *m* 7 Sept 1957, Pamela Joan Lyndon, da of Stanley Charles Marels; 2 s (Stephen John Lyndon b 14 March 1960, Jonathan Mark b 21 March 1969), 1 da (Deborah Joy b 3 Sept 1965); *Career* sr lectr Dept of Physiology Univ of Ibadan Nigeria 1958–66; Univ of Strathclyde: sr lectr then reader Dept of Pharmacology 1966–74, personal chair in pharmacology 1975, newly established chair in cardiovascular pharmacology 1983–, chm and head Dept of Physiology and Pharmacology 1986–90, emeritus prof 1998–, res prof 2001–; prof Dept of Pharmacology Albert Szent-Györgyi Med Univ Szeged Hungary 1996– (Hon MD 1989), emeritus fell Leverhulme Tst 2001–03, Albert Szent-Györgyi Res Fellowship Hungarian State Govt 2003; former chm Br Soc Cardiovascular Res; hon memb: Pharmacological Soc Hungary 1976, Slovak Medical and Cardiological Socs 1997, Czech Cardiological Soc 1998; Polish Physiological Soc Medal 1989, J Purkinje Gold Medal Acad of Scis of the Czech Republic 1995; memb Br Cardiac Soc, FRSE 1986, FIBiol, FRCPath, FRPharmS, FESC, fell Int Soc for Heart Res (FISHR); *Books* Early Arrhythmias Resulting From Myocardial Ischaemia; Mechanisms and Prevention by Drugs (1982), Calcium Movement and its Manipulation by Drugs (1984), Myocardial Response to Acute Injury (1992), Ischaemic Preconditioning (1996); *Recreations* music; *Style*— Prof James Parratt, FRSE; ✉ 10 St Germains, Bearsden, Glasgow G61 2RS (tel 0141 942 7164); Department of Physiology and Pharmacology, University of Strathclyde, Strathclyde Institute for Biomedical Sciences, 27 Taylor Street, Glasgow G4 0NR (tel 0141 548 2858, fax 0141 552 2562, telex 77472, e-mail pimjam.parratt@btinternet.com); Department of Pharmacology, Szent-Györgyi Albert Medical University, Dóm tér 12, Szeged, Hungary (tel 36 62 54 56 73, e-mail jr.parratt@phcol.szote.u-szeged.hu)

PARRIS, Matthew Francis; s of Leslie Francis Parris (decd), and Theresa Eunice, *née* Littler; *b* 7 August 1949; *Educ* Waterford Sch Swaziland, Clare Coll Cambridge, Yale Univ USA; *Career* author, journalist and broadcaster; FO 1974–76, Cons Research Dept 1976–79, MP (Cons) West Derbyshire 1979–86, presenter Weekend World LWT 1986–88, currently freelance broadcaster and columnist The Times and other jls; recipient of various journalistic awards and author of books on politics, humour and travel; *Publications* incl: Chance Witness: An Outsider's Life in Politics (2002), Castle in Spain: A mountain ruin and an impossible dream (2005); *Recreations* travelling; *Style*— Mr Matthew Parris; ✉ c/o The Times, 1 Virginia Street, London E1 9XN

PARRITT, Clive Anthony; s of Allan Edward Parritt, MBE (d 1998), and Peta, *née* Lloyd; *b* 11 April 1943; *Educ* privately; *m* 1, 28 Sept 1968 (m dis 1984), Valerie Joyce, da of Jesse Sears, of Reigate, Surrey; 2 s (James b 1977, Daniel b 1980); m 2, 5 Oct 1985, Deborah, da of Kenneth Jones, of Ashtead, Surrey; 2 s (Matthew b 1987, Thomas b 1989); *Career* CA; successively ptnr 1973–82: Fuller Jenks Beecroft, Mann Judd, Touche Ross & Co; Baker Tilly: ptnr 1982–2001, managing ptnr 1987–96, chm 1996–2001; chief exec The Business Exchange plc 2001–03 (dir 2001–2004); chm: Baronsmead Investment Trust plc 1994–98, Baronsmead VCT2 plc 1998–, BG Consulting Gp Ltd 2004–, dir: Herald Investment Trust plc 1994–2005, Harvard Managed Offices Ltd 2003–, Cardiomag Imaging Inc 2005–, London & Associated Properties plc 2006–, Baronsmed AIM VCT plc 2006–, F&C US Smaller Cos 2006–; memb Advsy Panel Enterprise and Deregulation Unit DTI 1986–88; memb: Nat Assoc of CA Students Soc 1965–67 (chm London Branch 1965–66), Cncl ICAEW 1983–; chm London Soc of CAs 1982–83 (treas 1980–82); chm Redhill and Reigate Round Table 1976–77; treas Br Theatre Assoc 1984–87; govr Arnold House Sch; Liveryman Worshipful Co of Chartered Accountants; FCA 1966, CF, FIIA, FRSA; *Recreations* theatre, entertaining, gardening; *Style*— Clive Parritt, Esq; ✉ 3 Howitt Road, London NW3 4LT (tel 020 7722 8551 (home), 020 7470 7233 (office), fax 020 7586 6777, e-mail clive@parritt.com)

PARROTT, Andrew Haden; s of Reginald Charles Parrott, BEM (d 1979), of Walsall, and Edith Dora Parrott; *b* 10 March 1947; *Educ* Queen Mary's GS Walsall, Merton Coll Oxford (open postmastership, BA); *m* 1 (m dis); m 2, 23 June 1986, Emily, da of William Payne Van Evera, of Duluth, MN; 1 da (Kate b 3 Aug 1995); *Career* conductor; fndr and artistic dir Taverner Choir, Consort and Players 1973–; music dir: London Mozart Players 2000–06, NY Collegium 2002–; guest conductor: Europe, Scandinavia, USA, Canada and others; appeared at festivals incl: Bath, BBC Proms, Edinburgh, Lucerne, Salzburg, Tanglewood; hon research fell Royal Holloway Univ of London, sr hon research fell Univ of Birmingham; memb Royal Musical Assoc; *Recordings* over 50 incl works by: Machant, Josquin, Taverner, Tallis, Gabrieli, Monteverdi, Purcell, Vivaldi, Bach, Handel, Mozart, Beethoven and twentieth-century composers; *Publications* New Oxford Book of Carols (jt ed), The Essential Bach Choir, various articles; *Style*— Andrew Parrott, Esq; ✉ c/o Allied Artists, 42 Montpelier Square, London SW7 1JZ (tel 020 7589 6243, fax 020 7581 5269, e-mail name@alliedartists.co.uk)

PARROTT, Graham Joseph; *b* 17 August 1949; *Career* memb Bd Granada Gp (merged to form ITV plc 2004) 1992–2004 (joined 1973), gp commercial dir and co sec ITV plc, chm ITV Pension Scheme 1990–; chm: The Local Radio Co plc 2004–07, Cancer Research Campaign Pension Scheme 2007–; dir: Elecrent Insurance Ltd, 1989–2004, ITN 1997–2004, GMTV Ltd 1999–2004; FCIS; *Style*— Graham Parrott, Esq; ✉ 39 Springfield Road, London NW8 0QJ (tel 07785 551908, e-mail gparrott@btconnect.com)

PARROY, Michael Picton; QC (1991); s of Leopold Gerald May Parroy (d 1982), and Elizabeth Mary, *née* Picton-Bayton (d 1979); *b* 22 October 1946; *Educ* Malvern Coll, BNC Oxford (MA); *m* 18 Nov 1978, Susan Patricia Blades Winter; *Career* called to the Bar Middle Temple 1969 (Winston Churchill exhibitioner, bencher 2001), recorder 1990– (asst recorder 1986), head of chambers 1995–2004; *Books* Halsbury's Law of England (co-author, 4 edn vol 40); *Recreations* dog walking, gardening; *Style*— Michael Parroy, Esq, QC; ✉ 3 Paper Buildings, Temple, London EC4Y 7EU (tel 020 7583 8055, fax 020 7353 6271)

PARRY, His Hon David Johnston; s of Kenneth Johnston Parry (d 1942), and Joyce Isobel, *née* Burt (now Mrs Cooper); *b* 26 August 1941; *Educ* Merchant Taylors', St Catharine's Coll Cambridge (MA), Higher Cts (Criminal Proceedings) Advocacy qualification 1994; *m* 20 April 1968, Mary, da of George Percy Harmer; 1 s (Andrew Kenneth b 4 Feb 1970), 3 da (Susanna b 25 Feb 1971, Annette b 26 Nov 1973, Marita b 12 July 1976); *Career* articled clerk Turberville Smith & Co Uxbridge, admitted slr 1968, ptnr (then co sr ptnr) Dixon Ward Slrs 1969–95; recorder 1991–95 (asst recorder 1986–91), circuit judge (SE Circuit) 1995–2002 (dep circuit judge 2003–); pt/t chm Ind Tbnl Serv 1993–96, admin Richmond and Twickenham Duty Slr Scheme 1990–95, patron Richmond Legal Advice Serv 1995– (co-chm 1969–95); Freeman City of London, Liveryman Worshipful Co of Merchant Taylors; memb: Law Soc, London Criminal Courts Slrs' Assoc; *Recreations* music, literature, theatre, travel, DIY and (whenever possible) lying in the sun doing nothing!; *Clubs* Old Merchant Taylors'; *Style*— His Hon David Parry

PARRY, Prof Eldryd Hugh Owen; OBE (1982); s of Owen Brynog Parry (d 1954), of Cardiff, and Constance Lilian, *née* Griffiths (d 1974); *b* 28 November 1930; *Educ* Shrewsbury, Emmanuel Coll Cambridge (MA, MD), WNSM; *m* 26 Aug 1960, Helen Madeline, da of (Arthur) Humphry House (late Maj RAC WWII, d 1955), of Wadham Coll, Oxford; 1 s (David b 1962), 3 da (Julia b 1964, Anna b 1965, Victoria b 1968); *Career* jr appts Cardiff Royal Infirmary, Nat Heart Hosp and Hammersmith Hosp 1956–65; assoc prof of med: Haile Sellassie I Univ Addis Ababa 1966–69, Ahmadu Bello Univ Zaria Nigeria 1969–77; foundation dean Faculty of Health Sciences Univ of Ilorin Nigeria 1977–80, dean Sch of Med Sciences Univ of Science and Technol Kumasi Ghana 1980–85, dir Wellcome Tropical Inst 1985–90, sr res fell LSHTM 1990–95 (hon prof 1995–), special prof Sch of Med and Surg Sciences Univ of Nottingham 1997–; chm Tropical Health and Educn Tst (THET) 1989–2007, memb Med and Dental Cncl Ghana 1980–85, memb Cncl All Nations Christian Coll 1986–99, founding memb Amoud Univ Faculty of Medicine and Surgery Somaliland 2006; Albert Cook meml lectr Kampala 1974; Frederick Murgatroyd Prize RCP 1974, Donald Mackay Medal 1998; hon fell: LSHTM 1997, Univ of Wales Coll of Med 2004; Hon DSc Univ of Kumasi 2003; fell W African Coll of Physicians 1976, fndn fell Ghana Coll of Physicians and Surgns 2003; FRCP 1970, Hon FRSTM&H 1993; *Books* Principles of Medicine in Africa (3 edn, 2004, RSM/Soc of Authors Prize, BMA first prize Public Health); *Recreations* tennis, Welsh furniture; *Style*— Prof Eldryd Parry, OBE; ✉ 21 Edenhurst Avenue, London SW6 3PD (e-mail eldryd@thet.org)

PARRY, Eric Owen; s of Eric Parry, CBE (d 1995), and Marion, *née* Baird; *b* 24 March 1952; *Educ* Shrewsbury, Univ of Newcastle upon Tyne (BA), Royal Coll of Art (MA), Architectural Assoc (AADipl); *m* 5 Sept 1981, Jane, *née* Sanders; 1 da (Anna Aurelia b 19 Aug 1986); *Career* fndr princ Eric Parry Architects Ltd 1983–; princ bldgs and architectural projects incl: W3 Stockley Park Heathrow 1991, Foundress Court (new court containing 90 student rooms and Master's Lodge) Pembroke Coll Cambridge 1995–97, new masterplan for Granta Park S Cambs 1996–97, head conslt for restoration of Mandarin Oriental Hyde Park Hotel London 1996–97, condominium of 30 luxury appartments Kuala Lumpur Malaysia 1996–97, 30 Finsbury Square 2000–02, 10 Paternoster Square The London Stock Exchange 2001–03, Royex House London Wall 2001–, St Martin-in-the-Fields 2002–, numerous private and smaller cmmns; lectr Univ of Cambridge 1983–97; visiting appts: Grad Sch of Design Harvard, Univ of Houston, Tokyo Inst of Technol; examiner at several schs of arch; chair RIBA Awards Gp 2002–04; memb: Cncl Architectural Assoc, Kettles Yard Ctee Cambridge, Arts Cncl of England Advsy Panels for Visual Arts, Exhbns and Architecture; RIBA 1983; *Publications* author/subject of Eric Parry Architects Vol I (2002) and various articles in professional jls; *Style*— Eric Parry, Esq

PARRY, Jann; da of John Hywel Parry (d 1992), of Cambridge, and Evelyn Florence, *née* Upton; *Educ* Kingsmead Coll Johannesburg, Univ of Cape Town (BA), Girton Coll Cambridge (BA, Cwlth scholar); *m* 15 April 1994, Richard Ruegg Kershaw; *Career* prodr BBC Radio World Service 1970–89; dance critic: The Listener 1981, The Spectator 1982 and 1995–96, The Observer 1983–2006; memb: Dance Panel Arts Cncl 1988–90, Exec Ctee Dance UK 1991–2000, Critics' Circle; *Style*— Ms Jann Parry; ✉ 82 Prince of Wales Mansions, Prince of Wales Drive, London SW11 4BL (tel and fax 020 7738 8732)

PARRY, John Kelsall; s of Edward Parry (d 1983), of Birmingham, and Kathleen Mary, *née* Allen; *b* 28 August 1936; *Educ* Loughborough GS, London Sch of Journalism (Dip); *m* 18 Dec 1960, Judy Valerie Cornwell, *qv*, da of late Darcy Nigel Barry Cornwell, of Gympie, Aust; 1 s (Edward Dylan Parry b 20 June 1965); *Career* reporter Evening Argus Brighton 1960–62, feature writer then William Hickey diarist Daily Express London 1962–67, reporter Tomorrow's World BBC TV 1967–70; BBC Radio News and Current Affrs: reporter and presenter World at One, PM and The World This Weekend 1971–82, arts corr 1982–95; writer for The Times, columnist The Spectator 1996–, ed Sculpture 1997–99; *Recreations* theatre, opera, cooking; *Clubs* Garrick; *Style*— John Parry, Esq

PARRY, Kevin Allen Huw; s of H L Parry (d 1983), and F E Parry, *née* Jones; *b* 29 January 1962; *Educ* Olchfa Swansea, Robinson Coll Cambridge (MA); *m* 28 May 2000, J C Parry, *née* Phillips; 1 da (Charlotte Elizabeth b 6 April 2001), 1 s (James David Hugh b 20 Sept 2002); *Career* KPMG: joined 1983, qualified CA 1986, ptnr 1994, managing ptnr 1998–99, memb UK Mgmnt Team London Bd 1998–99; chief exec Management Consulting Gp plc 2000–; non-exec dir: Schroders plc 2003– (chm Audit Ctee), Knight Frank 2004–; dep chm Royal Wanstead Fndn; memb ICAEW 1986, FCA; *Recreations* watching cricket and rugby; *Clubs* Oxford and Cambridge, IOD; *Style*— Kevin Parry, Esq; ✉ Management Consulting Group plc, Fleet Place House, 2 Fleet Place, London EC4M 7RF (tel 020 7710 5000, e-mail kparry@mcgplc.com)

PARRY, (George) Mervyn; s of late George Alwyn Parry, and late Aileen Maude, *née* Long; *b* 16 March 1951; *Educ* KCS Wimbledon, Downing Coll Cambridge (Squire scholar, BA, 3 Badminton half blue); *m* 1 Aug 1987, Jill Patricia, da of William Odiam; 2 da (Imogen Sophie b 21 June 1989, Annabel Rose b 1 Sept 1992); *Career* Allen & Overy: articled clerk 1973–75, asst slr 1975–85, ptnr 1985–; memb Law Soc 1973; *Recreations* photography, mountain walking, wine, opera, family, sport; *Style*— Mervyn Parry, Esq; ✉ Allen & Overy, One New Change, London EC4M 9QQ (tel 020 7330 3000, fax 020 7330 9999, e-mail mervyn.parry@allenovery.com)

PARRY, Richard Nicholas (Rick); s of Nicholas Albert Parry (d 1987), of Chester, and Kathleen Stewart, *née* Howard; *b* 23 February 1955; *Educ* Ellesmere Port GS, Univ of Liverpool (BSc); *m* 12 Aug 1978, Catherine Mary, da of Dr Malcolm Vivian John Seaborne; 3 s (James Robert b 27 Oct 1982, Thomas William b 3 April 1985, Jonathan Luke b 4 Nov 1994); *Career* trainee chartered accountant Arthur Young McClelland Moores 1976–79, mktg accountant Haulfryn Estate Co 1979–81, fin controller Hoseasons Holidays 1981–83, mgmnt conslt Arthur Young 1983–92, seconded (as full-time dir) Manchester Olympic Bid Ctee 1988–90, chief exec FA Premier League 1992–97, chief exec Liverpool FC 1998–; FCA 1979; *Recreations* watching sport; *Style*— Rick Parry, Esq; ✉ c/o Liverpool FC, Anfield Road, Anfield, Liverpool L4 0TH

PARRY, Roger; *b* 4 June 1953; *Educ* Sutton GS, Univ of Bristol (BSc), Jesus Coll Oxford (MLitt); *m* 1990, Johanna; 1 s (Benjamin b 1993); *Career* broadcaster BBC and ITV 1977–85, conslt McKinsey & Co 1985–88; devpt dir: WCRS Group 1988–90, Aegis Group 1990–94; pres Carat North America 1994–95; ceo: More Gp plc 1995–98, Clear Channel International 1998–2006; exec chm Media Square plc 2007–; chm: Johnston Press plc 2001–, Future plc 2001–, Mobile Streams plc 2005–, You Gov plc 2007–; chm Shakepeare's Globe Tst; *Books* People Businesses (1991), Enterprise (2003), Making Cities Work (2004); *Clubs* MCC, Hurlingham, Garrick; *Style*— Roger Parry, Esq; ✉ Media Square plc, Eldon House, 1 Dorset Street, London W1U 4EG (tel 020 7535 9950, e-mail roger@rogerparry.com)

PARRY, Stephen (Steve); s of David Harold Parry, and Pauline Parry; *b* 2 March 1977; *Educ* Liverpool Blue Coat Sch, Florida State Univ (BSc), Dip Mgmnt Devpt; *Career* swimmer; achievements in 200m butterfly incl: 15 nat titles, NCAA champion 1997, Bronze medal European Championships 1997 and 2000, Bronze medal Commonwealth Games 1998, sixth place Olympic Games Sydney 2000, ranked number one in world 2000, Br and Cwlth record holder (1 min 56.3 secs); Bronze medal 4x50m relay European Championships 2000, winner World Cup Melbourne and Shanghai 2002, European champion 2002, Bronze medal Olympic Games Athens 2004; tstee Liverpool Sports Partnership; *Recreations* golf, tennis, books; *Clubs* City of Manchester Aquatics, Stockport Metro; *Style*— Steve Parry, Esq

PARRY-JONES, Dr Richard; CBE (2005); *b* 15 September 1951, Wales; *Educ* Univ of Salford; *Career* engr; Ford Motor Co: joined 1969, mangr Small Car Programs 1982, exec engr Technological Research in Europe 1985, responsible for Vehicle Concepts 1986, dir Vehicle Concepts Engrg USA 1988, i/c Mfrg Ops Cologne Germany 1990, chief engr Vehicle Engrg 1991, vice-pres Small and Medium Car Vehicle Centre Europe 1994–97, vice-pres Global Product Devpt 1998–, chief technical offr 2001–, senior technical advisor Mazda, i/c Premier Performance Division 2002–; visiting prof Dept of Aeronautical and Automative Engrg Loughborough Univ 2001; memb: Engineering Technology Board (ETB), Advsy Bd Warwick Business Sch, Int Advsy Cncl Int Mgmnt Bd (IMB); Hon Dr Loughborough Univ 1995; FREng 1997, FIMechE; *Awards* Man of the Year Autocar 1994, Man of the Year Automobile USA 1997, Golden Gear Award Washington Automative Press Assoc 2001, Marketing Statesman of the Year Sales and Marketing Execs of Detroit 2001; *Style*— Dr Richard Parry-Jones, CBE, FREng

PARSLOE, John; s of (Charles) Guy Parsloe (d 1985), and (Mary) Zirphie (Munro), *née* Faiers (d 2001); *b* 14 October 1939; *Educ* Bradfield Coll, The Queen's Coll Oxford (MA); *m* 6 Oct 1973, (Helen) Margaret, da of Dr (Daniel) Arnold Rolfe (d 1985); 2 s (Thomas b 1974, William b 1979), 1 da (Alice b 1976); *Career* admitted slr 1971; formerly with Coward Chance and Lovell, White & King; dir: Mercury Asset Management plc (then Merrill Lynch Investment Managers) 1990–99 (conslt 1999–2001); memb Financial Servs and Markets Tbnl; *Clubs* Brooks's; *Style*— John Parsloe, Esq; ✉ e-mail j.parsloe@zen.co.uk

PARSONS, Charles Andrew (Charlie); s of Anthony Maxse Parsons (d 1999), and Rosamund, *née* Hurst; *b* 7 August 1958; *Educ* Tonbridge, Pembroke Coll Oxford (MA, pres JCR); *Career* reporter Ealing Gazette 1980–82, researcher London Weekend Television 1982–87, series ed Network 7 (Channel Four) 1988 (prodr 1987), series ed Club X (Channel Four) 1989; exec prodr for Planet 24 Productions Ltd (formerly 24 Hour Productions Ltd): The Word 1990, Handel's Messiah at The Point Dublin 1991, The Big Breakfast 1992–2002, Gaytime TV 1995–, Desire 1996–99; jt md Planet 24 Ltd 1992–99, ceo Castaway Television Ltd 2001–; exec prodr Keenen Ivory Wayans Show, exec prodr Survivor (UBS and ITV) 2001, prodr Never Forget 2007; media conslt 1999–; Freeman: City of London, Worshipful Co of Haberdashers; memb: RTS, BAFTA, IOD; *Awards* Royal Instn of Chartered Surveyors Best News Award for The London Programme 1985–86, BAFTA Originality Award 1987 and Gold Hugo Chicago Film Festival 1988 for Network 7, Silver Medal NY Int Film Festival for The Word 1991, RTS Best Team Award for The Big Breakfast 1992, Emmy for Survivor 2001, Special Class Outstanding Non-Fiction Programme Acad of Television Arts and Science USA; *Style*— Charlie Parsons, Esq; ✉ Castaway Television, 4th Floor, Aldwych House, London WC2E 4HN (e-mail charlie@castawaytelevision.com)

PARSONS, Prof Ian; s of Arthur Alan Parsons (d 1992), and Doris Marion, *née* Ivins (d 1942); *b* 5 September 1939; *Educ* Beckenham and Penge GS, Univ of Durham (BSc, PhD); *m* 8 Aug 1963, Brenda Mary, da of William Spence Reah (d 2003); 3 s (Mark Ian b 10 July 1967, John Richard, Andrew James (twins) b 8 March 1969); *Career* DSIR res fell Univ of Manchester 1963–64, personal prof Univ of Aberdeen 1983–88 (asst lectr 1964–65, lectr 1965–77, sr lectr 1977–83), prof of mineralogy Univ of Edinburgh 1988–2004 (head of dept 1993–96, emeritus prof 2004–); pres: Mineralogical Soc of Great Britain and Ireland 1994–96 (vice-pres 1980), Int Mineralogical Assoc 2002– (vice-pres 1998–2002); Schlumberger medal Mineralogical Soc 1993 (Hallimond lectr 1977); memb: Mineralogical Soc of Great Britain 1962, Mineralogical Soc of America 1980; FRSE 1984; *Books* Geological Excursion Guide to the Assynt District of Sutherland (with M R W Johnson, 1979), Origins of Igneous Layering (1987), Feldspars and their Reactions (1994); *Recreations* walking, skiing, music; *Style*— Prof Ian Parsons, FRSE; ✉ Grant Institute of Earth Science, University of Edinburgh, West Mains Road, Edinburgh EH9 3JW (tel 0131 650 8512, fax 0131 668 3184, e-mail ian.parsons@ed.ac.uk)

PARSONS, Sir John Christopher; KCVO (2002, CVO 1998, LVO 1992); s of late Arthur Christopher Parsons, of Odiham, Hants, and Veronica Rosetta de Courcy, *née* Glover; *b* 21 May 1946; *Educ* Harrow, Trinity Coll Cambridge (MA); *m* 20 Feb 1982, Hon Anne Constance Manningham-Buller, da of 1 Viscount Dilhorne, PC; 2 s (Michael b 1983, David b 1985), 1 da (Lilah b 1988); *Career* chartered accountant; Dowty Gp Ltd 1968–72, Peat Marwick Mitchell & Co 1972–85; asst treas to HM The Queen 1985–87, dep keeper of the Privy Purse and dep treas to HM The Queen 1988–2002, extra equerry to HM The Queen 2002–; dep dir (fin) Royal Collection 1992–93; lay memb Chapter Peterborough Cathedral 2001– (treas 2004–); govr Elstree Sch 1987– (vice-chm of govrs 2002–); tstee and treas Music in Country Churches 2006–, tstee Country Houses Fndn 2006–; FCA, FCMC; *Clubs* Brooks's, Pratt's; *Style*— Sir John Parsons, KCVO; ✉ The Old Rectory, Eydon, Daventry, Northamptonshire NN11 3QE

PARSONS, Nicholas; OBE (2004); s of Dr Paul Frederick Nigel Parsons (d 1981), of Hampstead, London, and Nell Louise, *née* Maggs (d 1980); *b* 10 October 1923; *Educ* St Paul's, Univ of Glasgow; *m* 1, 1954 (m dis 1989), Denise Pauline Rosalie, da of Claud Bryer; 1 da (Suzy Zuleika (Mrs James Buchanan) b 13 June 1958), 1 s (Justin Hugh b 24 Dec 1960); m 2, 1995, Ann Reynolds; *Career* actor, presenter, comedy performer; Variety Club Radio Personality of the Year 1967, entered in the Guinness Book of Records for longest after dinner humorous speech 1978; involved with children's charities incl The Lord's Taverners (past pres, memb Cncl and tstee) and NSPCC (govr), Barker of The Variety Club of GB; tstee: Aspire, Deaf Blind UK, Spring Centre, Breakthrough, Br Dyslexia Assoc, Br Stammering Assoc; memb: Soc of Stars, Sparks; ambass Childline; rector Univ of St Andrews 1988–91, Hon LLD Univ of St Andrews; *Theatre* The Hasty Heart (London), Jack in Charley's Aunt (Palace Theatre) 1947, Arsenic and Old Lace (tour) 1948, in repertory Bromley 1949–51, in cabaret 1951–65 (Quaglinos, Colony, Cafe de Paris, Blue Angel, Pigalle, Society), as comedian (Windmill Theatre) 1952, revues (London fringe theatres and Lyric Revue) 1953, 1st and 2nd Edition (Watergate Theatre) 1954, Swing Along with Arthur Haynes (Palladium) 1963, starred in Boeing Boeing (Duchess Theatre) 1967–68, Say Who You Are (Vaudeville Theatre) 1968, Uproar in the House (Whitehall Theatre) 1968, Darling I'm Home (tour) 1978, Stage Struck (tour) 1980, Keeping Down with the Joneses (tour) 1981, Charlie Girl (Victoria Palace and nat tour) 1987–88, the Narrator in Into the Woods (Stephen Sondheim musical, Phoenix Theatre) 1990–91, Rocky Horror Show (Duke of York's Theatre) 1994 and 1995 (tour 1996, 1998–99 and 2000), numerous pantomimes and 3 one-man shows (Edward Lear Show performed at Edinburgh Festival 1990, also touring 1995–2007), Nicholas Parsons A Laugh a Minute (tour and cruise ships), Nicholas Parsons Happy Hour (Edinburgh Fringe, annually) 2000–; *Television* comedy work in partnership with Eric Barker 1952–55, comedy partnership with Arthur Haynes 1956–66, Last Train to Surbiton (comedy series, BBC) 1966, Benny Hill Show 1969–70, host of Sale of the Century (Anglia TV) 1971–84 and The All New Alphabet Game (LWT Night Network) 1988, Mr Jolly Lives Next Door (for Comic Strip) 1988, The Curse of Fenric (Dr Who story, BBC) 1989, host of Laughlines (BSB) 1990, Just a Minute (Carlton TV) 1994 and 1995, Just a Minute (BBC) 1999; *Radio* since 1952 incl: various prodns for BBC Drama Repertory Company 1953, host Just a Minute 1967–2007, Listen to This Space (first radio satire show) 1967–92, How Pleasant to Know Mr Lear (solo show) 1995–96; *Film* Brothers-in-Law, Carlton Browne of the FO, Happy is the Bride, Don't Raise the Bridge Lower the River, Spy Story, Simon and Laura, Upstairs Downstairs, Too Many Crooks, Eyewitness, Carry On Regardless, Murder Ahoy; writer and dir of 5 comedy documentaries for cinema and TV for own production co; *Books* Egg on the Face (1985), The Straight Man - My Life in Comedy (autobiography, 1994); *Recreations* cricket, golf, gardening, photography; *Clubs* Garrick; *Style*— Nicholas Parsons, OBE; ✉ c/o Jean Diamond, Diamond Management, 31 Percy Street, London W1T 2DA (tel 020 7631 0400, fax 020 7631 0500); e-mail nicholas_parsons@btinternet.com

PARSONS, Peter Frank; s of Frank Leslie John Parsons, of Fleet, and Margaret, *née* Wing; *b* 24 August 1950; *Educ* Farnborough GS, City of London Coll; *Children* 2 da (Amy Carol b 18 July 1977, Zoe Gemma b 16 Oct 1978); *Career* chartered accountant; ptnr Temple Gothard 1977–85, nat dir business devpt Touche Ross (now Deloitte & Touche) 1995– (ptnr 1985–); FCA; *Style*— Peter Parsons, Esq; ✉ Deloitte & Touche, Stonecutter Court, 1 Stonecutter Street, London EC4A 3TR (tel 020 7936 3000, fax 020 7583 8517)

PARSONS, Prof Peter John; s of Robert John Parsons, and Ethel Ada, *née* Frary; *b* 24 September 1936; *Educ* Raynes Park Co GS, ChCh Oxford (Craven scholar, de Paravicini scholar, Derby scholar, Dixon and sr scholar, Passmore Edwards scholar, MA, Chancellor's prize for Latin verse, Gaisford prize for Greek verse); *m* 25 March 2006, Barbara Montagna Macleod (d 2006); *Career* Univ of Oxford: lectr in documentary papyrology 1960–65, lectr in papyrology 1965–89, regius prof of Greek 1989–2003, student of ChCh 1964–2003; J H Gray lectr Univ of Cambridge 1982, Heller lectr Univ of Calif Berkeley 1988; Hon PhD Bern 1985, Hon DLitt Milan 1993, Hon PhD Athens 1995; fell Academia Europaea 1990, FBA 1977; *Books* The Oxyrhynchus Papyri: XXXI (jtly, 1966), XXXIII and XXXIV (jtly, 1968), XLII (1973), LIV (jtly, 1987), LIX (jtly, 1992), LX (jtly, 1993), LXVI (jtly, 1999); Supplementum Hellenisticum (with H Lloyd-Jones, 1983), City of the Sharp-nosed Fish (2007); *Recreations* music, cinema, cooking, eating; *Style*— Prof Peter Parsons, FBA; ✉ Christ Church, Oxford OX1 1DP (tel 01865 288265, e-mail peter.parsons@classics.ox.ac.uk)

PARSONS, Robin Edward; s of Anthony Maxse Parsons (d 1999), and Rosamund, *née* Hurst; *b* 30 December 1948; *Educ* Uppingham, UCL (LLB); *m* 27 May 1972, Elizabeth Hamilton Floyd; 2 da (Sonia Katharine Elizabeth, Alexandra Geraldine); *Career* asst slr Coward Chance (now Clifford Chance) 1973–75 (articled clerk 1971–73); Cameron Markby Hewitt (now CMS Cameron McKenna): asst slr 1975–77, ptnr 1977–99, estab Paris Office 1980; ptnr Eversheds 1999–2000, ptnr Sidley Austin Brown & Wood 2000–; lectr at numerous legal conferences and seminars incl series given to Chartered Inst of Bankers 1988–96; memb Documentation Ctee Loan Markets Assoc; author of articles for legal jls; Freeman Worshipful Co of Haberdashers, Freeman Worshipful Co of Slrs; memb Law Soc (memb City of London Finance Law Ctee); *Recreations* tennis, squash, skiing, French; *Style*— Robin Parsons, Esq; ✉ Sidley Austin (UK) LLP, Woolgate Exchange, 25 Basinghall Street, London EC2V 5HA (tel 020 7360 3600, fax 020 7626 7937, e-mail rparsons@sidley.com)

PARSONS, Sandra Kay; da of John Kenneth Parsons, of London, and Kathleen, *née* Stirling; *b* 8 September 1961; *Educ* Archbishop Tennison's GS Croydon; *m* 22 Jan 1994, Dr Serge Nikolic, s of Ljubisa Nikolic; 1 da (Isabella b 1 Sept 1995), 1 s (Luke b 26 April 2001); *Career* journalist; reporter Luton News 1982–85, Wolverhampton Express and Star 1985–87, Today 1987–90, Daily Mail 1990–95, The Times 1995–; *Recreations* reading, my children; *Style*— Ms Sandra Parsons; ✉ The Times, 1 Pennington Street, London E98 1TT (tel 020 7782 5330)

PARSONS, Susie; da of Alfred Parsons, of East Grinstead, West Sussex, and Dorothy, *née* Barratt; *b* 29 April 1950, Cuckfield, West Sussex; *Educ* East Grinstead Co GS, Lancaster Univ (BA), KCL (PGCE); *Partner* Dave Perry; 1 s (Ben b 1976); *Career* educn offr then community educn dir Shelter 1974–77, housing projects offr N Kensington Law Centre 1977–81, chief offr Paddington and N Kensington Community Health Cncl 1981–84, gen mangr London Energy and Employment Network 1984–87, head of press, publicity and info London Borough of Hackney 1987–94, exec dir then chief exec London Lighthouse 1994–98, chief exec Cmmn for Racial Equality 1999–2001, ind mgmnt conslt 2001–02, chief exec Campaign for Learning 2002–05, md Susie Parsons Mgmnt Solutions Ltd 2005–; author of articles and pubns on health, social care, equality and lifelong learning; memb Bd Kensington & Chelsea Tenant Mgmnt Orgn; former memb Bd: ACEVO, Quality Standards Task Gp NCVO, Cncl Inst for Employment Studies; chair Bd Golborne Forum; FRSA 1996; *Publications* School and Community in the Inner City (jtly, 1977), Workout (jtly, 1979), London Energy Action Plan (1986), Good Practice Guide to District Heating (1988), Taking the Lead (1992), The Right Side of the Law (1993), 50/50: Equality for Women Managers by the Year 2000 (jtly, 1995), Learning to Learn in Schools (jtly, 2003 and 2005), Give Your Child a Better Chance (2003), Promoting Diversity in the Workplace (contrib, 2004), QCA Futures Programme (contrib, 2005), Learning to Learn for Life (jtly, 2005), Reinventing Education (contrib, 2005), Board Training (jt ed, 2005); *Style*— Ms Susie Parsons; ✉ 171 Oxford Gardens, London W10 6NE (tel 020 8969 7415, e-mail susie@spms.org.uk)

PARTINGTON, Ven Brian Harold; OBE (2002); s of Harold Partington, and Edith, *née* Hall; *b* 31 December 1936; *Educ* Burnage HS Manchester, Moor Park Coll Farnham, St Aidan's Coll Birkenhead; *m* 4 Aug 1962, Valerie, da of Sydney Fenton Nurton; 2 s (Andrew b 30 July 1964, David b 9 March 1968), 1 da (Sarah b 6 March 1966); *Career* Dio of Manchester: curate: Emmanuel Didsbury 1963–66, Deane 1966–68; Dio of Sodor and Man: vicar of Kirk Patrick 1968–96, Bishop's youth chaplain 1968–77, rural dean of Peel 1976–96, vicar of Foxdale and of St John's 1977–96, canon of St Patrick St German's Cathedral 1985–96, archdeacon of IOM 1996–2005 (archdeacon emeritus 2005–), vicar of St George Douglas 1996–2004; exec chm IOM Sports Cncl 1989–2003 (memb 1986–2003), vice-pres Hospice Care 1996– (chm 1988–96), chm Assoc of Manx Motor Clubs 2003–06, chm Int Island Games Assoc 2005– (vice-chm 2001–05); pres: IOM Cricket Assoc 1998–2006, IOM Hockey Assoc 1997–2006; *Recreations* golf, cricket, reading, travel; *Clubs* Peel Golf (capt 2006), St John's Cricket (IOM), Royal Cwlth Soc, Rotary, Pisces Swimming (pres 2005–), IOM Yacht (princ RYA Trg Section); *Style*— The Ven Brian Partington, OBE; ✉ Brambles, Kirk Patrick, Isle of Man IM5 3AH (tel 01624 844173, e-mail bpartington@mcb.net)

PARTINGTON, Prof (Thomas) Martin; CBE; s of Thomas Paullet Partington (d 1980), and Alice Emily Mary, *née* Jelly (d 1970); *b* 5 March 1944; *Educ* King's Sch Canterbury, Univ of Cambridge (BA, LLB); *m* 1, 15 Aug 1969 (m dis 1973), Marcia Carol, *née* Leavey; 1 s (Daniel b 1971); m 2, 21 Oct 1978, Daphne Isobel, *née* Scharenguivel; 1 s (Adam b 1979), 1 da (Hannah b 1980); *Career* lectr: Univ of Warwick 1969–73, LSE 1973–80; Brunel Univ: prof of law 1980–87, dean Faculty of Social Sciences 1985–87; Univ of Bristol: asst lectr 1966–69, prof of law 1987–2005, dean Faculty of Law 1988–92, pro-vice-chllr 1995–99, emeritus prof 2006–; called to the Bar Middle Temple 1984 (bencher 2006), in practice Arden Chambers London 1993–2000 and 2006–, Law Cmmr 2001–05; memb: Lord Chllr's Advsy Ctee on Legal Aid 1988–91, Law Soc Trg Ctee 1989–93, Judicial Studies Bd 1992–94, Cncl on Tbnls 1994–2000, Civil Justice Cncl 1998–2005, Public Legal Educn Taskforce 2006; special conslt Law Cmmn 2006–07, academic advsr Coll of Law 2006–; expert consultee: Leggatt Review of Tbnls 2000–01, Employment Tribunals Task Force 2002; chm: Ctee Heads of Univ Law Schs 1990–92, Socio-Legal Studies Assoc 1993–95, Social Security Appeal Tbnls 1990–94 (pt/t), Med Appeal Tbnls and Disability Appeal Tbnls 1992–94 (pt/t); non-exec dir United Bristol Hosp NHS Tst 1998–2000; FRSA 1999; *Books* Landlord and Tenant (1975), Housing Law: Cases, Materials and Commentary (with Jonathan Hill, 1991), Claim in Time (1994), Housing Law (with Andrew Arden and Caroline Hunter, 1994), Administrative Justice in the 21st Century (with Michael Harris, 1999), Introduction to the English Legal System (2006); *Recreations* music, walking, cooking, foreign travel; *Style*— Prof Martin Partington, CBE; ✉ 8 Clifton Hill, Bristol BS8 1BN (tel 0117 973 6294); Law Commission, Conquest House,

P

37/38 John Street, Theobalds Road, London WC1N 2BQ (tel 020 7453 1204, fax 020 7453 1297, e-mail martin.partington@lawcommission.gsi.gov.uk)

PARTINGTON, Robin Courtland; s of Dr James Ernest Partington (d 1967), of Bolton, and June, *née* Whittenbury; *b* 5 August 1960; *Educ* Bolton Sch Bolton, Univ of Liverpool Sch of Architecture (BA, BArch); *m* 22 Sept 1990, Sally Maurice, da of Maurice Owen Jones; 2 s (Oliver Courtland b 7 July 1997, Teilo Courtland b 24 Jan 2001); *Career* training (year out) Scott Brownrigg and Turner Guildford 1981–82; Foster & Partners (formerly Sir Norman Foster & Partners): joined 1984, assoc 1987, project dir 1988, dir 1992–; RIBA 1985, ARCUK 1985, RIAS 1996; *Recreations* sailing, shooting; *Style*— Robin Partington, Esq; ✉ Foster & Partners, Riverside 3, 22 Hester Road, London SW11 4AN (tel 020 7738 0455, fax 020 7738 1107/1108)

PARTON, Geoffrey Paul; s of Walter St John Parton (d 1962), and Betty Mary, *née* Herring; *b* 25 April 1947; *Educ* Belfairs HS; *m* 1973, Patrika Anne, da of John McClemont; 1 s (John Vivian Henry b 1981), 2 da (Hannah Mary b 1978, Frances Anne b 1980); *Career* dir Marlborough Fine Art London (joined 1969); numerous exhibitions organised incl those of R B Kitaj and Frank Auerbach; memb Exec Ctee Soc of London Art Dealers 1991–; *Style*— Geoffrey Parton, Esq; ✉ Marlborough Fine Art, 6 Albemarle Street, London W1S 4BY

PARTON, Nicholas George; s of Maj Michael Henry Parton, and Jean Mary, *née* Saxby; *b* 1 June 1954; *Educ* Haileybury, Grenoble Univ, Liverpool Poly (BA); *m* 12 Sept 1981, (Elizabeth) Querida, da of late John Wilfred da Cunha, of Churchill, Avon, and Janet, *née* Savatard; 3 da (Amy b 1983, Phoebe b 1986, Felicity b 1988), 2 s (Sam b 1984, John (Jack) b 1996); *Career* admitted slr 1979; articled clerk Bremmer Sons & Corlett 1977, Holman Fenwick & Willan 1980, Middleton Potts 1983; ptnr: Taylor Garrett 1985–89, Taylor Joynson Garrett 1989–92, Jackson Parton 1992–; memb Law Soc 1979; *Recreations* skiing and sailing; *Clubs* Trearddur Bay Sailing; *Style*— Nicholas Parton, Esq; ✉ 31 Ambleside Avenue, London SW16 1QE (tel 020 8769 0127, e-mail nickparton@aol.com); Pant y Llin, Ravenspoint Road, Trearddur Bay, Anglesey, North Wales (tel 01407 861099); Le Mazuet, Bellentre, Aime, Savoie, France; Jackson Parton, 5th Floor, 18 Mansell Street, London E1 8AA (tel 020 7702 0085, fax 020 7702 0858, e-mail mail@jacksonparton.com or n.parton@jacksonparton.com)

PARTRIDGE, Prof Derek; *b* 24 October 1945; *Educ* UCL (BSc), Imperial Coll London (DIC, PhD); *m* 27 Aug 1971, Mehrazar; 2 da (Mischa b 1974, Morgan b 1976); *Career* lectr in computer sci Univ of Nairobi Kenya 1972–74, asst prof, assoc prof then full prof Dept Computer Sci New Mexico State Univ USA 1975–86, prof of computer sci Univ of Exeter 1987– (head of dept 1989–94); visiting fell Univ of Essex 1981–82, visiting lectr Univ of Queensland 1983–84; involved with Nat Youth Theatre 1966–68; FRSA, AAAI, AISB; *Books* incl: Artificial Intelligence: Applications in the Future of Software Engineering (1986), Computers for Society (contrib, 1986), The Encyclopaedia of Microcomputers (contrib, 1988), Machine Learning (contrib, 1989), The Foundations of Artificial Intelligence: A Source Book (contrib, 1989); *Recreations* reading, writing, natural history, football; *Style*— Prof Derek Partridge

PARTRIDGE, Derek William; CMG (1987); s of Ernest Partridge (d 1984), of Wembley, Middx, and Ethel Elizabeth, *née* Buckingham (d 1985); *b* 15 May 1931; *Educ* Preston Manor Co GS Wembley; *Career* RAF 1949–51; HM Dip Serv: FO 1951–54, Oslo 1954–56, Jedda 1956, Khartoum 1957–60, Sofia 1960–62, Manila 1962–65, Djakarta 1965–67, FCO 1967–72, Brisbane 1972–74, Colombo 1974–77; FCO 1977–86, head Migration and Visa Dept 1981–83, head Nat and Treaty Dept 1983–86, high cmmr to Sierra Leone 1986–91; cncllr (Lib Dem) London Borough of Southwark 1994–2002; memb Royal African Soc; *Clubs* National Liberal; *Style*— Derek W Partridge, Esq, CMG; ✉ 16 Wolfe Crescent, Rotherhithe, London SE16 6SF

PARTRIDGE, Frank; s of late John and Flora Partridge, of Inverness; *b* 16 August 1953; *Educ* Abbey Sch Fort Augustus, Univ of Edinburgh (BA), UC Cardiff (Dip Journalism); *Career* BBC: presenter Newsbeat Radio One 1982–88, sports corr 1988–91, presenter PM Radio 4 1991–93; presenter with Sky Television 1993–; *Recreations* squash, swimming, cricket playing, watching and collecting; *Style*— Frank Partridge, Esq

PARTRIDGE, Ian Harold; CBE (1992); s of Harold William (d 1972), and Eugenia Emily, *née* Stinson (d 1992); *b* 12 June 1938; *Educ* New Coll Oxford (chorister), Clifton, RCM, Guild Sch of Music (LGSM); *m* 4 July 1959, Ann Pauline, da of William Maskell Glover (d 1965), of Bexhill, E Sussex; 2 s (Daniel b 1964, Jonathan b 1967); *Career* tenor; concert singer and recitalist, repertoire ranges from early baroque to new works; operatic debut as Iopas in Les Troyens (Covent Garden) 1969, title role in Britten's St Nicolas (Thames TV, winner Prix Italia 1977), regular appearances at London's concert halls with major orchestras and conductors and at int festivals throughout the world, frequent broadcaster on BBC Radio 3; more than 350 performances worldwide of An Evening with Queen Victoria (with Prunella Scales), given masterclasses on Lieder, English Song and Early Music at festivals incl Aldeburgh, Dartington, Trondheim and Vancouver; prof of singing RAM; chm RSM 1999–2001 (govr 1994–98 and 2005–), pres ISM 1996–97, dir PAMRA 1996–2002; Hon RAM 1996; *Recordings* incl: Schubert's Die Schöne Müllerin and Winterreise, Schumann Dichterliebe, Vaughan Williams' On Wenlock Edge, Warlock's The Curlew, Britten's Winter Words, Bach's St John Passion, Handel's Chandos Anthems, Bax Songs; *Recreations* theatre, bridge, horse racing; *Clubs* Garrick; *Style*— Ian Partridge, Esq, CBE; ✉ 127 Pepys Road, Wimbledon, London SW20 8NP (tel 020 8946 7140, website www.ianpartridge.co.uk)

PARTRIDGE, John Arthur; s of Claude Partridge (d 1958), of London, and Iris Florence, *née* Franks (d 1982); *b* 6 July 1929; *Educ* Elstree Sch, Harrow; *m* 1 (m dis), Hon Caroline Elizabeth Maud Cust, da of 6 Baron Brownlow (d 1978), of Belton House, Lincs; 2 s (Frank David Peregrine b 14 Sept 1955, Claude Edward b 29 Aug 1962), 1 da (Sophia Josephine (Mrs Anthony Waltham) b 12 May 1969); m 2, Rosemary FitzGibbon, da of Maj Robert Tyrrell (d 1975), of Litcham, Norfolk; *Career* ADC to Govr of S Aust Gen Lord Norrie 1952–53; chm and md Partridge Fine Art plc 1958–2005; *Recreations* hunting, fishing, shooting, gardening; *Clubs* Brooks's; *Style*— John Partridge, Esq; ✉ Prebendal House, Empingham, Rutland LE15 8PW (tel 01780 460234)

PARTRIDGE, Prof Linda; CBE (2003); da of George Albert Partridge, of Bath, and Ida, *née* Tucker; *b* 18 March 1950; *Educ* Convent of the Sacred Heart, Univ of Oxford (Christopher Welch scholar, BA, DPhil); *m* 1, 1983 (m dis 1990), V French; m 2, 1996, M J Morgan; *Career* NERC postdoctoral fell Univ of York 1974–76; Univ of Edinburgh: demonstrator 1976–78, lectr 1978–87, reader 1987–92, prof of evolutionary biology and Darwin research fell 1992–93; Weldon prof of biometry UCL 1994–, NERC research prof 1997–2002, BBSRC professorial fell 2002–; pres: Int Soc for Behavioural Ecology 1990–92, Assoc for the Study of Animal Behaviour 1995–97; memb: Genetical Soc (pres 2000–03), Br Ecological Soc; Frink Medal Zoological Soc of London 2000, Sewall Wright Prize American Soc of Naturalists 2002, Fndn IPSEN Longevity Prize 2004, Lord Cohen Medal British Soc for Research on Ageing 2004, Medal of Assoc for the Study of Animal Behaviour 2005; Hon DSc Univ of St Andrews 2004; memb: European Acad of Sciences 2004, EMBO 2005; FRSE 1992, FRS 1996, FMedSci 2004; *Recreations* gardening, sailing, tennis; *Style*— Prof Linda Partridge, CBE, FRS, FRSE

PARTRIDGE, Prof Martyn Richard; s of Maj Raymond John Bruce Partridge, RA, of Loughton, Essex, and Grace, *née* Darch; *b* 19 May 1948; *Educ* Pocklington Sch, Univ of Manchester (MB ChB, MD); *m* 23 June 1973, Rosemary Jane Emily, da of Lt (John) Dennis Radford, of Hove, E Sussex; 2 da (Judith Stephanie Louise b 10 June 1977, Philippa Rachel Jane b 26 Feb 1981), 1 s (Richard John Oliver b 15 Feb 1979); *Career* resident med offr Nat Heart Hosp London 1975–76, med registrar Royal Post Grad Med Sch London 1976–78, sr Jules Thorne res fell Middx Hosp 1978–80; sr med registrar: London Chest Hosp 1980–81, UCH 1981–82; conslt physician Whipps Cross Hosp London 1982–2001, prof of respiratory med Imperial Coll London Nat Heart and Lung Inst (NHLI) Charing Cross Hosp 2002–; author of various pubns of respiratory med and terminal care; chm British Thoracic Soc, chief med advsr Nat Asthma Campaign; FRCP, FRSM; *Recreations* travel, railways, music, church and family; *Style*— Prof Martyn Partridge; ✉ Imperial College of Science, Technology and Medicine, Faculty of Medicine, NHLI Division, Charing Cross Hospital Campus, St Dunstan's Road, London W6 8RP (tel 020 8846 7181, fax 020 8846 7999, e-mail m.r.partridge@imperial.ac.uk)

PASCO, Adam Gerhold; s of Cecil Filmer Pasco (d 1974), and Sheila Mary, *née* Gerhold; *b* 11 January 1957; *Educ* George Abbot Sch Guildford, NE Surrey Coll of Technology (Higher Nat Dip Applied Biology), Univ of Nottingham (BSc); *m* 8 August 1992, Jayne Petra, *née* Fisher; 1 da (Danielle Jean b 16 September 1994), 1 s (Luke Peter Graham b 10 October 1996); *Career* Garden Answers: tech ed 1982–84, ed 1984–88; ed Garden News 1988–90, launched BBC Gardeners' World Magazine 1991 (ed 1991–), gardening corr Daily Telegraph 1995–98, launched BBC Easy Gardening Magazine 2002 (ed 2002–03, editorial dir 2003–); memb Garden Writers' Guild 1992–; memb: Henry Doubleday Research Assoc, British Soc of Magazine Eds, Woodland Tst, RHS; *Publications* The Garden Manager (CD-ROM, 1998), The Collins Complete Garden Manual (1998), The Greenfingers Book (1999), Collins Gardeners' Calendar (2000); *Recreations* gardening, writing, walking, photography, cooking, travel, family life; *Style*— Adam Pasco, Esq; ✉ 43 Latham Avenue, Orton Longueville, Peterborough PE2 7AD; BBC Gardeners' World Magazine, Woodlands, 80 Wood Lane, London W12 0TT (tel 020 8433 3593, fax 020 8433 3986, e-mail adam.pasco@bbc.co.uk)

PASCO, Richard Edward; CBE (1977); s of Cecil George Pasco (d 1982), and Phyllis Irene, *née* Widdison (d 1991); *b* 18 July 1926; *Educ* KCS Wimbledon, Central Sch of Speech and Drama; *m* 1 (m dis), Greta, *née* Watson; 1 s; m 2, 1967, Barbara Leigh-Hunt, *qv*; *Career* actor; Army Serv 1944–48; many leading roles RSC, London, West End Theatre, film, radio and TV, concert and recital work; hon assoc artist RSC, RNT player; tstee Shakespeare's Birthplace Tst 1992, dir Royal Theatrical Fund 1995; *Recreations* music, gardening, reading; *Clubs* Garrick; *Style*— Richard Pasco, Esq, CBE; ✉ c/o Whitehall Artistes Ltd, 10 Lower Common South, London SW15 1BP (tel 020 8785 3737)

PASCOE, (Gerald) John; s of Rick Pascoe, and Roma Pascoe; *b* 19 January 1949; *Educ* St Brendan's Coll Bristol, Wimbledon Sch of Art (BA); *Career* asst designer Derby Playhouse and resident designer Bristol Old Vic and Sheffield Crucible 1971–74; teacher/lectr Prior Park Coll Bath and Univ of Bath 1974–79; designer/director for opera; credits for set design incl: Giulio Cesare (ENO, TV and video) 1979, Lucrezia Borgia (ROH and Teatro dell'Opera Rome) 1980, Alcina (also costumes, Sydney Opera House) 1980, Tosca (WNO) 1980, Giulio Cesare (San Francisco Opera and Grand Théatre De Genève Switzerland) 1981, Anna Bolena (Canadian Opera) 1984, Cosi fan tutte (Dallas Opera) 1984, Giulio Cesare (Metropolitan Opera) 1988, Orlando (Lyric Opera of Chicago and San Francisco Opera) 1985, Norma (also costumes, Santiago) 1986, Amahl (also costumes, ROH) 1986, Apollo et Hyacinthus (Cannes) 1990, Maria Golovin (Spoleto Festival) 1991, Tosca (Opera Nice) 1991, Anna Bolena (Washington Opera) 1993, Anna Bolena (San Francisco Opera) 1995, The Telephone/The Medium (Spoleto Festival) 2002, Don Pasquale (Michigan Opera Theater) 2002, Turandot (L'Opera de Quebec) 2003, Manon Lescaut (Washington Nat Opera) 2004, Democracy (Washington Nat Opera) 2005; credits as dir and/or design incl: La Bohème (Northern Ireland Opera) 1983 and 1992, Solomon (Göttingen Händel Festival) 1985, Platée (Spoleto Festival) 1987, Anna Bolena (ROH) 1987, Platée (Brooklyn Acad of Music) 1988, Norma (Michigan Opera Theatre and Opera Pacific) 1989, Maria Padilla (Opera Omaha) 1989, Don Giovanni (Michigan Opera and Opera Pacific) 1990, Dido and Aeneas 1991, La Boheme 1992, La Traviata 1993, Rigoletto 1994, Don Giovanni (Miami) 1997, Pretty Baby (world premier, New Orleans) 1997, Hänsel und Gretel (Chicago Opera Theater) 1998, Giulio Cesare (Metropolitan Opera) 1999, Lucia di Lammermoor (Connecticut Grand Opera) 1999, The Barber of Seville (Chicago Opera Theatre) 1999, Rigoletto (Connecticut Grand Opera) 1999, Giulio Cesare (Washington Opera) 2000, Don Pasquale (Virginia Opera) 2001, Il Barbieri di Siviglio (Virginia Opera) 2001, Don Giovanni (Washington Opera and Michigan Opera Theater) 2003; designed concert gowns for Renée Fleming (also costumes for La Traviata Metropolitan Opera House 2003) fndr The Bath & Wessex Opera (UK); interior decorating and murals for private clients incl: Renée Fleming, Michael Bolton; work featured in: Vogue, House & Gardens, Art & Antiques 1994, PBS (TV programme) 1996; *Recreations* listening to opera, rock climbing; *Style*— John Pascoe, Esq; ✉ c/o Robert Lombardo Associates, 61 West 62nd Street, Suite 6F, New York, NY 10023, USA (tel 00 1 212 586 4453)

PASCOE, Nigel Spencer Knight; QC (1988); s of Ernest Sydney Pascoe (d 1970), and Cynthia, *née* Holtom (d 1992); *b* 18 August 1940; *Educ* Epsom; *m* 1964, Elizabeth Anne, da of Bryan Walter; 4 da (Gillie, Jemma, Dimity, Miranda), 2 s (Hallam, Tristan); *Career* called to the Bar Inner Temple 1966 (bencher 1998); in practice Western Circuit (ldr 1995–98), recorder of the Crown Court 1979–; chm Bar Public Affrs Ctee 1997–98, pres Mental Health Review Tbnl 2001–; chm Editorial Bd Counsel 1999–2006; fndr ed All England Quarterly Law Cassettes; memb Hampshire CC 1979–83; The Trial of Penn and Mead (one man show, Edinburgh Fringe Festival) 1994, Merely Players (Shakespearean one man show) 2004; *Books* The Trial of Penn and Mead (1994); *Plays* The Nearly Man (1993), Pro Patria (1996), Who Killed William Rufus? (2000), Without Consent (2005), To Encourage the Others (2006); *Recreations* acting, cricket, theatre, writing, presenting legal anthologies with Elizabeth Pascoe, after dinner speaking; *Clubs* Garrick; *Style*— Nigel Pascoe, Esq, QC; ✉ 3 Pump Court, Upper Ground, Temple, London EC4Y 7AJ (tel 020 7353 0711)

PASSMORE, George; *b* 1942, Devon; *Educ* Dartington Hall Adult Educn Centre, Dartington Hall Coll of Art, Oxford Sch of Art, St Martin's Sch of Art; *Career* artist, in partnership with Gilbert Proesch, *qv*, since 1967; shortlisted Turner Prize 1984, Turner Prize 1986; Living Sculpture incl: The Red Sculpture, 3 Living Pieces, Underneath the Arches, Our New Sculpture, Reading from a Stick; *Selected Two Person Exhibitions* Snow Show (St Martins Sch of Art London) 1968, Shit and Cunt (Robert Fraser Gallery London) 1969, The Paintings (Whitechapel Art Gallery London, Kunstverein Dusseldorf, Koninklijk Museum voor Schone Kunsten Antwerp) 1971–72, Dusty Corners (Art Agency Tokyo) 1975, Photo-Pieces 1971–1980 (Stedelijk van Abbemuseum Eindhoven, Georges Pompidou Centre Paris, Kunsthalle Bern, Whitechapel Art Gallery London) 1980–81, Gilbert & George (touring, galleries incl: Contemporary Arts Museum Houston, The Solomon R Guggenheim Museum NY, Milwaukee Art Museum Milwaukee) 1984–85, Pictures 1982 to 85 (Hayward Gallery London, Lenbachaus Munich, Palacio de Velazquez Madrid) 1987, For AIDS Exhibition (Anthony d'Offay Gallery London) 1989, The Cosmological Pictures (touring, galleries incl: Palazzo delle Esposizioni Rome, Fundació Joan Miró Barcelona, Irish MOMA Dublin, Kunsthalle Zürich, Wiener Secession Vienna, Tate Gallery Liverpool) 1991–93, Gilbert & George China Exhibition (The Art Museum Shanghai, Nat Art Gallery Beijing) 1993, Shitty Naked Human World (Wolfsburg Kunstmuseum Germany) 1994, The Naked Shit Pictures (South London Art Gallery) 1995, New Testamental Pictures (Museo do Capodimonte Naples) 1998, Black White and Red 1971 to 1980 (James Cohan Gallery New York) 1998, The Rudimentary Pictures (inaugural exhibition, Milton Keynes Gallery) 1999, Nineteen Ninety Nine (Kunstmuseum

Bohn, Museum of Contemporary Art Chicago, Museum Moderner Kunst Vienna) 1999–2001, Enclosed and Enchanted (MOMA Oxford) 2000, New Horny Pictures (White Cube London) 2001, Gilbert & George: A Retrospective (Sch of Fine Art Athens, Kunsthaus Bregenz) 2002, The Dirty Words Pictures (Serpentine Gallery London) 2002, Thirteen Hooligan Pictures (Bernier/ Eliades Athens) 2004, 20 London E1 Pictures (Modern Art Museum St Etienne, Kestner Gesellschaft Hannover) 2004–05, Gilbert & George (British Pavilion Venice Biennale) 2005; *Work in Collections* incl: Arario Gallery Chungnam, Astrup Fearnley Museet fur Moderne Kunst Oslo, Denver Art Museum, Nat Portrait Gallery London, San Francisco MOMA, Tate Modern London; *Style*— George Passmore; ✉ White Cube, 48 Hoxton Square, London N1 6PB (tel 020 7930 5373, fax 020 7749 7480)

PASSMORE, Jeremy Cedric; s of John Passmore, and Pamela, *née* Dunkels; *b* 30 March 1952, Kent; *Educ* Cranleigh Sch, Trinity Coll Cambridge (open exhibitioner, MA); *m* 3 Sept 1977, Diana, *née* Willmott; 3 da (Sophia Katharine b 13 Sept 1981, Jennifer Melissa, Felicity Diana (twins) b 17 May 1985); *Career* slr; Frere Cholmeley: articled clerk 1975–77, slr 1977–79; Thomson Snell & Passmore: slr 1979–81, ptnr 1981–, head Private Client Dept 2003; memb: Charity Law Assoc, Law Soc, Inst of Financial Planning, Soc of Estates and Trust Practitioners; *Recreations* the arts, gardening, tennis, riding; *Style*— Jeremy Passmore, Esq; ✉ 1 The Old Riding School, Leyswood, Groombridge, Tunbridge Wells, Kent TN3 9PH (tel 01892 861015); Thomson Snell & Passmore, 3 Lonsdale Gardens, Tunbridge Wells, Kent TN1 1NX (tel 01892 701344, fax 01892 701122, e-mail jpassmore@ts-p.co.uk)

PATEL, Dr Chaitanya; CBE (1999); s of Bhupendra Patel (d 1997), and Ashru Patel (d 2004); *b* 14 September 1954; *Educ* Univ of Southampton; *Children* 2 da (Meera Jade b 7 Oct 1987, Hannah Anjuli b 5 March 1990); *Career* physician 1979–85, investment banker 1985–88; MRC research fell Pembroke Coll Oxford 1985; fndr chm Ct Cavendish 1988–96, chief exec Care First 1996–97; chief exec Westminster Health Care plc 1999–2002, ceo Priory Group 2002–; chm UK-Procure; Care Personality of the Year (Caring Times) 1999; memb Better Regulation Task Force 1997–2002; tstee: Inst for Public Policy Research (IPPR), Windsor Leadership Tst; Hon DUniv Open Univ; CCMI, FRSA, FRCP 1999 (MRCP); *Publications* Better Regulation Task Force reports: Long Term Care 1998, Early Education and Daycare 1998, Red Tape Affecting Head Teachers 2000; *Recreations* golf, music, reading, drawing, films; *Clubs* RAC, Queenwood Golf, Tyrells Wood Golf, Mark's, Mosimann's, Harry's; *Style*— Dr Chaitanya Patel, CBE; ✉ Priory Healthcare, Priory House, Randalls Way, Leatherhead, Surrey KT2 7TP (tel 01372 860403, fax 01372 860402)

PATEL, Dr Hasmukh Rambhai; s of Rambhai Patel, of London, and Shardaben Patel; *b* 1 January 1945; *Educ* King's Coll London, King's Coll Hosp Med Sch (MB BS, MRCS); *m* 16 July 1969, Mrudula Hasmukh, da of Revabhai Patel, of Baroda, India; 1 s (Veran b 31 July 1972), 1 da (Nesha b 7 May 1975); *Career* conslt paediatrician Joyce Green Hosp Dartford 1976–, clinical dir Dept of Paediatrics Darent Valley Hosp; clinical tutor Univ of London 1982–91, SE Thames regnl postgrad associate dean Univ of London 1991–96; chm Paediatric Trg Ctee S Thames Region 1996–98, memb GMC Fitness to Practice Panel, assessor Nat Clinical Assessment Serv; FRCPE 1985, FRCP 1986, FRCPCH; *Recreations* golf, travel, photography; *Style*— Dr Hasmukh Patel; ✉ 24A Claremont Road, Bickley, Bromley, Kent BR1 2JL (e-mail hrzp@hotmail.com); Children's Resource Centre, Darent Valley Hospital, Dartford, Kent DA2 8DA (tel 01322 428221)

PATEL, Prof Minoo Homi; s of Homi Edalji Patel, of Hounslow, Middlesex, and Doly Homi Patel; *b* 28 July 1949; *Educ* Univ of London (BSc, PhD); *m* Irene Veronica, da of Harry Kay, of Basildon, Essex; 2 s (Zubin Homi b 1973, Darren Lindsay b 1975); *Career* res engr Queen Mary Coll London 1973–76, UCL 1976–2002 (successively lectr, reader 1987–89, Kennedy prof of mechanical engrg 1989–2002, latterly head of dept), currently prof and head Sch of Engrg Cranfield Univ; dir: BPP Ocean Technology Ltd 1983–, Pamec Technology Ltd 1986–, BPP Technical Services Ltd 1989–, UCLi Ltd 1990–1995; FREng, FRINA, FIMechE, CEng; *Books* Dynamics of Offshore Structures (1989), Compliant Offshore Structures (1990); *Recreations* gliding, jogging; *Style*— Prof Minoo Patel, FREng; ✉ School of Engineering, Cranfield University, Cranfield, Bedfordshire MK43 0AL

PATEL, Baron (Life Peer UK 1999), of Dunkeld in Perth and Kinross; Prof Sir Narendra Babubhai (Naren); kt (1997); s of Babubhai Patel, of London, and Lalita Patel (d 1992); *b* 11 May 1938; *Educ* Univ of St Andrews (MB ChB), Univ of Lund Sweden (DM); *m* 25 Sept 1970, Helen, da of Wilfred Dally; 1 da (Hon Susan b 29 Nov 1971), 2 s (Hon Mark, Hon Neil (twins) b 18 May 1975); *Career* conslt obstetrician and hon prof Ninewells Hosp Univ of Dundee 1974–2003; author of pubns in areas of fetal growth, preterm labour, clinical audit and quality healthcare; MD (hc) Univ of Stellenbosch; former chm: Acad of Med Royal Colls, NHS Quality Improvement Scotland, Advsy Ctee Scientific Advances and Genetics; chm Steering Ctee Stem Cell MRC UK; chair Nat Patient Safety Agency 2005, vice-pres RSE 2006, chair UK Stem Cell Network; memb Science and Technol Ctee House of Lords 1999, memb Armed Forces Diversity Panel 1999; memb Cncl Stroke Assoc; Hon DSc: Napier Univ Edinburgh, Univ of Aberdeen, Univ of St Andrews; Hon LLD Univ of Dundee, Hon Dr Univ of Athens; FRCOG 1987 (MRCOG 1970), FMedSci, FRSE; Hon FRCPEd, Hon FRCPGlas, Hon FRCSEd, Hon FRCS(Eng), Hon FRCA, Hon FRCPI, Hon FRCGP, Hon FRCPsych, Hon FFPHM; hon fell: Royal Aust and NZ Coll of Obsetriticians and Gynaecologists, German, Canadian, Finnish, Argentine, Italian, Chilean and Thai Socs of Obstetrics and Gynaecology, Indian, Sri Lankan, American, Canadian, South African and Thai Colls of Obstetrics and Gynaecology; *Style*— The Rt Hon Lord Patel; ✉ Birkenbrae, Spoutwells, Dunkeld PH8 0AZ (tel 01350 727366, e-mail patel_naren@hotmail.com); Department of Obstetrics and Gynaecology, Ninewells Hospital, Dundee, Tayside DD1 9SY (tel 01382 632959, fax 01382 425515, e-mail naren.patel@tuht.scot.nhs.uk)

PATEL, Pankaj; MBE (2006); *b* Tanzania; *Educ* South Bank Univ (BA), RIBA (DipArch); *Career* architect; MacCormac Jamieson Pritchard, ptnr Patel Taylor Architects 1989–; prof Welsh Sch of Architecture Cardiff, sr lectr South Bank Univ, external examiner Oxford Brookes Univ, examiner Univ of Sheffield, advsr Government Off for London, memb CABE Design Review Ctee; *Competitions* incl: Sainsbury's supermarket 1987, sheltered accommodation Clywd Wales 1989, the city and the river Antwerp Belgium 1990, Choral and Music Centre Rhondda Heritage Park Wales 1990, Europan II Châteauroux France 1991, Peckham London 1991, Ayr Citadel 1993, Europan III Pierre-Bénite France 1994, Thames Barrier Park London 1995, Footbridge Balmaha Scotland 1996, Portland College Nottinghamshire 1998; *Awards* Royal Acad Summer Exhibition Non-members Award 1988, RIBA Architecture Award (for Arts Centre Wales) 1992, Geoffrey Gribble Conservation Award (for PACE Counselling Centre London) 1995, Glass and Glazing Award (for PACE Counselling Centre London) 1995, Saltire Geddes Planning Award (for Ayr Citadel Scotland) 1995, 4 RIBA Architecture Awards 2001 (for Thames Barrier, Benslow Music Sch, Peace Park Pavilion, Apartment, Battersea), Civic Tst Landscape Award 2002 (for Thames Barrier Park); *Style*— Pankaj Patel, Esq, MBE; ✉ Patel Taylor Architects, 53 Rawstorne Street, London EC1V 7NQ (tel 020 7278 2323, fax 020 7278 6242, e-mail pta@pateltaylor.co.uk)

PATEL OF BLACKBURN, Baron (Life Peer UK 2000), of Langho in the County of Lancashire; Adam Hafejee; s of Hafejee Ismail Patel (d 1996), and Aman Hafejee Patel; *b* 7 June 1940, Gujarat, India; *Educ* Univ of Baroda India (BCom); *m* 10 May 1964, Aysha; 4 s, 4 da; *Career* accountant Ivan Jacques Chartered Accountants Blackburn and accountant S & RD Thornton Chartered Accountants Preston 1967–74; chief internal auditor Zamtan Lusaka Zambia; md Comet Cash and Carry Co Ltd 1977–97; chm Blackburn and District Cwlth Friendship Soc 1966–67; fndr and gen sec Blackburn Indian Workers Assoc 1967–74 (pres 1977–); magistrate Divisional Petty Sessions of Blackburn 1984–95; fndr memb Blackburn Community Relations Cncl (now Blackburn with Darwen Racial Equality Cncl) subsequent treas, vice-chm and chm, currently hon vice-pres under presidency of Rt Hon Jack Straw, MP; chm UK Hagg Ctee, chm Br Hajj Delegation FCO 2001–; fndr chm and former pres Lancashire Cncl of Mosques 1989–; fndr dir Lancashire TEC until 1996, fndr dir Blackburn Partnership; non-exec dir Lancashire Enterprises plc (now Enterprises plc); exec memb Blackburn City Challenge and its Forward Strategy Gp 1993–98; memb: Labour Pty 1966–, NW Conciliation Ctee Race Relations Bd until 1974, Lancashire CC Standing Adsvy Cncl on Religious Educn, Ethnic Minority Panel of Blackburn, Hyndburn and Ribble Valley Health Tst, Home Secretary's Race Relations Advsy Forum, Christian/Muslim Inter-Faith Forum (jt chm); memb and tstee E Lancashire Racial Harrassment Partnership; chm and tstee W Brookhouse Community Centre Blackburn; one of five nat counsellors of Muslim Cncl of Br; special interests: educn, trg and re-training for life skills, all aspects of race and community relations, the economy, ethnic minority health concerns and religious understanding; pres E Lancashire Co Scout Cncl; govr Bolton Inst; *Recreations* community and social work, gardening, football, cricket; *Style*— The Rt Hon the Lord Patel of Blackburn; ✉ Snodworth Hall, Snodworth Road, Langho, Lancashire BB6 8DS (tel 01254 240346, fax 01254 249584, e-mail lordadampatel@hotmail.com)

PATERSON, Prof Alan Keith Gordon; s of Maj Albert Paterson (d 1946), of Kinmundy House, Aberdeenshire, and Helen, *née* Horne; *b* 8 March 1938; *Educ* Aberdeen GS, Univ of Aberdeen (MA), Univ of Cambridge (PhD); *m* 28 June 1965, Anna, da of Tage Holm, of Malmö, Sweden; 1 s (Andrew); *Career* lectr Queen Mary Coll London 1964–84, prof of Spanish Univ of St Andrews 1985–2001 (now emeritus, dean Faculty of Arts 1991–94); author of specialist pubns on theatre, poetry and prose of seventeenth century Spain; *Books* Tirso De Molina, La Venganza De Tamar (1967), Calderón, The Painter of His Dishonour (1992), Calderón de la Barca, El nuevo palacio del Retiro; *Recreations* cooking, hill walking, motorcycling; *Style*— Prof Alan Paterson; ✉ Spanish Department, The United College, St Andrews KY16 9AL (tel 01334 476161, fax 01334 476474, telex 9312110846 SAG)

PATERSON, Anthony John; s of John McLennan Paterson (d 1978), and Isobel Margaret, *née* Reichwald; *b* 16 May 1951; *Educ* Winchester, Worcester Coll Oxford (LLB); *Career* slr; special constable 1976–79; Parly candidate (Lib) for Finchley 1979, press offr Cons Bow Group 1983–84, Parly liaison offr 1984–85, res sec 1985–87, Parly candidate (Cons) Brent S 1987; currently immigration conslt; author of 3 Bow Group papers; sec Bow Group Environment Ctee; memb: Cncl World Wildlife Fund 1985–91, Exec Green Alliances 1987–90; *Books* The Green Conservative (1989); *Recreations* politics, reading, languages; *Style*— Anthony J Paterson, Esq; ✉ office: tel and fax 020 8748 8532

PATERSON, Bill; *b* 3 June 1945; *m* Nov 1984, Hildegard Maria Bechtler, *qv*; 1 s (Jack b 10 April 1985), 1 da (Anna b 28 Sept 1989); *Career* actor; FRSAMD; *Theatre* for 7:84 Theatre Co Scotland: incl: Willie Rough (Royal Lyceum), Great Northern Welly Boat Show (Edinburgh Festival), The Game's a Bogey, Little Red Hen and The Cheviot, The Stag and The Black Black Oil, Mongrel's Heart (Edinburgh Lyceum) 1994; London prodns incl: Treetops (Riverside), Writer's Cramp (Hampstead/Bush), Ella (ICA), Whose Life Is It Anyway? (Savoy), And Me Wi' A Bad Leg Tae (Royal Court), A Man With Connections (Royal Court/Traverse), Crime and Punishment (Lyric Hammersmith), Guys and Dolls (NT), title role in Schweyk In The Second World War (NT), Good Person of Sezuan (NT), Death and the Maiden (Royal Court/Duke of York's), Misery (Criterion) 1992–93, Ivanov (Almeida) 1997, Marriage Play (NT) 2001; *Television* for BBC: The Cheviot, The Stag and The Black Black Oil, Licking Hitler, The Vanishing Army, The Lost Tribe, United Kingdom, The Cherry Orchard, Smiley's People, Stan's Last Game, One of Ourselves, Lily My Love, The Singing Detective, The Interrogation of John, Yellowbacks, Tell Tale Hearts, Wall of Silence, Oliver's Travels, Ghostbusters of East Finchley, The Writing on the Wall; other credits incl: Aufwiedersehen Pet (Central), Traffik (Channel Four) 1993, Shrinks (Euston Films), God On The Rocks (Channel Four), The Crow Road 1996, Melissa 1997, Mr White Goes To Westminster 1997, Wives and Daughters 1999, Rebel Heart 2000, The Whistleblower 2001, Dr Zhivago 2002, Danielle Cable Eye Witness 2003, Sea of Souls 2003–06, Tell Me Lies 2004; *Radio* incl: Byline, A Man With Connections, Flowers in the Sky, Hiroshima The Movie, A Good Man in Africa, Hedda Gabler, The Caucasian Chalk Circle, Tales From the Backgreen (wrote and read); *Film* incl: The Ploughman's Lunch, The Killing Fields, Comfort and Joy, A Private Function, Defence of the Realm, Friendships Death, The Witches, Baron Munchausen, Truly Madly Deeply, Victory, Richard III, Hilary and Jackie 1998, Sunshine 1998, Crush 2001, Bright Young Things 2004, Ragtale 2005, Miss Potter 2006, Amazing Grace 2007; *Style*— Bill Paterson, Esq, FRSAMD; ✉ c/o Gordon and French, 12–13 Poland Street, London W1V 3DE (tel 020 7734 4818, fax 020 7734 4832)

PATERSON, Christopher Douglas (Chris); s of David D Paterson, and Lynn S Paterson; *b* 30 March 1978, Edinburgh; *Educ* Galashiels Acad, Moray House Inst of Educn (Dip PE Teaching); *Career* rugby union player; clubs: Gala RFC 1996–99 (as amateur, winners Melrose Sevens 1999, winners Scottish Cup 1999, Second Div champions), Edinburgh Rugby (formerly Edinburgh Reivers) 1999–; int: Scotland Schs 1996, Scotland U19 1997, Scotland U21 1998–99, Scotland A 1999, Scotland Sevens 1999, Scotland 1999– (61 caps, scored over 400 points, debut v Spain, capt Six Nations Championship 2004); Scotland Player of the Year 2003, Scotland Player of the World Cup 2003, World Try of the Year v South Africa 2003; *Style*— Chris Paterson, Esq; ✉ c/o Scottish Rugby Union, Murrayfield, Edinburgh EH12 5PJ

PATERSON, Christopher John; s of John Macdonald Paterson, and Mary Kathleen, *née* Body; *b* 9 January 1947; *Educ* Peterhouse S Rhodesia, Univ of Exeter (BA), Grad Intern Prog UN Geneva, Stanford Exec Prog; *m* 15 Dec 1973, Gillian Diana, da of Geoffrey Piper, of Christchurch, Dorset; 1 da (Sarah b 1978), 1 s (Timothy b 1981); *Career* Nat Serv Royal Rhodesia Regt 1965–66; Macmillan: joined 1970, publisher Nature 1980–81, md College Press Zimbabwe 1983–85, chm Macmillan Southern Africa 1983–, md Macmillan Press 1985–91, dir Macmillan Publishers Ltd 1989–, chm Macmillan Education 1999–; chm Int Bd Publishers Assoc 2000–06, vice-chm Southern Africa Business Assoc Exec 2002–05; memb: Chllr's Advsy Cncl Univ of Exeter 1994– (chm alumni funding 1994–2000), Singapore Br Business Cncl 1999–2004, Advsy Bd China Centre for English Languae Teaching and Research Beijing 2007–; govr Peterhouse Zimbabwe 2000–; *Recreations* gardening, running, rugby football, collecting Africana; *Clubs* Harare, Henley RFC; *Style*— Christopher Paterson, Esq; ✉ Macmillan Oxford, Between Towns Road, Oxford OX4 3PP (tel 01865 405728, fax 01865 405896, e-mail c.paterson@macmillan.com)

PATERSON, Don; s of Russell Leslie Paterson, of Dundee, and Jean Louise, *née* Cougan; *b* 30 October 1963; *Educ* Kirkton HS; *Career* poet and musician; writer in residence Univ of Dundee 1993, poetry ed Picador, lectr Sch of English Univ of St Andrews; Eric Gregory Award 1990, winner Arvon/Observer Poetry competition 1994; memb Jazz band Lammas; FRSL; *Recordings* Talisker 1987, Lammas 1992, Lammas: This Morning 1994, Lammas: The Broken Road 1995, Lammas: Sourcebook 1997, Sea Changes 1999; *Publications* Nil Nil (1993, Forward prize for Best First Collection, Scottish Arts Cncl Book Award), God's Gift to Women (1997, T S Eliot Award, Geoffrey Faber Memorial Prize, SAC Book

P

Award), The Eyes (1999, SAC Book Award), Landing Light (2003, Whitbread Poetry Prize Prize, T S Eliot Award), Book of Shadows (2004), Orpheus (2006); *Style—* Don Paterson, Esq; ✉ c/o Faber & Faber Ltd, 3 Queen Square, London WC1N 3AU (tel 020 7465 0045, fax 020 7465 0034)

PATERSON, Douglas Gordon James; s of Gordon Mellish Paterson, of Moor Park, Herts, and Anne Barbara Bolam, *née* Mason; *b* 24 October 1943; *Educ* George Watson's Coll Edinburgh, Univ Coll Sch, Univ of St Andrews (MA); *m* 29 May 1972, Pamela Jane, da of William Taylor Rollo (d 1984); 2 s (Christopher Douglas Mark b 18 Oct 1973, Nicholas Gordon William b 13 May 1975), 1 da (Alice Elspeth Jane b 21 March 1977); *Career* PricewaterhouseCoopers (formerly Coopers & Lybrand before merger): qualified CA 1968, Cologne office 1970–72, London office 1972–77, ptnr Switzerland 1977–79, ptnr UK 1979–2001; non-exec dir: Goldman Sachs Int Bank 2002, Close Brothers Gp plc 2004–, The Derivatives Consulting Gp Ltd 2007; vice-chm Br German Assoc; FCA 1968, ATII 1968; *Recreations* tennis, photography, walking, reading; *Clubs* Caledonian; *Style—* Douglas Paterson, Esq

PATERSON, Ewan Gill; s of Patrick Paterson of Redlynch, Wilts, and Pamela Paterson (d 1997); *b* 1 February 1963; *Educ* various schs in Africa and UK, Univ of Manchester (BSc, first XI football), Imperial Coll London (Britoil scholarship, MSc, first XI football); *m* 25 Aug 2001, Tricia Leslie, *née* Black; 1 da (Olivia Pamela b 2003), 1 s (James Gardiner b 2003); *Career* exploration geologist (North Sea) Exlog Inc 1984–85, advtg account handler McCann-Erickson Advertising 1987–88, advtg copywriter Yellowhammer Advertising 1988–90, copywriter Young & Rubican (incl campaigns for Pirelli and Colgate) 1990–95; BMP DDB (now DDB London): copywriter (campaigns incl London Transport, Volkswagen and The Guardian) 1995–2002, jt creative dir 2002–04; creative dir Bartle Bogle Hegarty 2004–06, exec creative dir CHI & Ptnrs (formerly Clemmow Hornby Inge) 2006–; judge: D&AD 1997, 2002, 2004 and 2006, CLIO Awards 2003; memb Lab Pty; *Awards* Br Television Awards Commercial of the Year (for Pirelli) 1996, Silver Pencil D&AD (for London Transport) 1998, Cannes Advtg Festival Gold Lion (for Volkswagen) 2001, Gold Campaign Poster Award (for Guardian) 2003, Grand Prix Cannes Advtg Festival (for Volkswagen) 2004, runner-up Agency of the Year Cannes Advtg Festival (DDB London) 2004, Silver Pencil D&AD (for Vodafone) 2006; *Clubs* Manchester City FC; *Style—* Ewan Paterson, Esq; ✉ CHI & Partners, 7 Rathbone Street, London W1T 1LY (tel 020 7462 8500, e-mail ewan.paterson@chiandpartners.com)

PATERSON, Gil; MSP; *Career* cncllr Strathclyde Regnl Cncl, exec vice-convenor Local Govt, exec vice-convenor Administration; MSP (SNP): Scotland Central 1999–2003, W of Scotland 2007–; *Style—* Gil Paterson, Esq, MSP

PATERSON, Graham Julian; s of Peter James Paterson, *qv*, and Beryl, *née* Johnson; *b* 7 June 1955; *Educ* Dulwich Coll, Magdalen Coll Oxford (BA); *Career* journalist Daily Telegraph 1977–86, ed 7 Days Section Sunday Telegraph 1988–89 (assoc ed 1987–88, home ed 1986–87); The Times: asst ed 1989–, chief asst to the ed and features ed 1993–95, foreign ed 1995–99, exec ed 1999–2001, home ed 2001–; *Clubs* Travellers; *Style—* Graham Paterson, Esq; ✉ The Times, 1 Pennington Street, London E98 1TT

PATERSON, Lt-Col Howard Cecil; TD (two clasps); s of Henry John Paterson (d 1969), of Romanno Bridge, Peeblesshire, and Margaret Isobel, *née* Eunson (d 1983); *b* 16 March 1920; *Educ* Daniel Stewart's Coll Edinburgh, Edinburgh Coll of Art; *m* 21 July 1945, Isabelle Mary Paterson, MBE, FSA Scot (d 2000), da of Frederick Augustus Edward Upton (d 1960), of Southampton; 1 s (Colin Howard b 7 Aug 1948); *Career* Lt-Col RA (TA), serv Europe, ret 1970; asst personnel mangr Jute Industries Ltd 1949–51, dep dir Scot Co Industry Devpt Tst 1951–66, sr dir Scot Tourist Bd 1966–81, ind tourism conslt 1981–; chm: Taste of Scot Scheme 1976–86, Scot Int Gathering Tst 1982–92, Trekking and Riding Soc of Scot 1995–2003 (vice-chm 1990–95, hon life pres 2003–); vice-chm: Scot Aircraft Collection Tst 1982–89 (chm 1989–90), John Buchan Soc 1988–95; life memb Nat Tst for Scotland (NTS); memb: Scot Lowland Reserve Forces and Cadets Assoc, Royal Artillery Assoc, Royal Artillery Instn, City of Edinburgh Artillery Officers' Assoc, Reserve Forces Assoc, Royal Artillery Heritage Campaign (fndr memb), Scot Landowners' Fedn, Countryside Alliance, BASC, Game Conservancy Tst, Royal Highland and Agricultural Soc, Historic Houses Assoc; life fell RSPB; FSA Scot; *Books* Tourism in Scotland (1969), Flavour of Edinburgh (with Catherine Brown, 1986); *Recreations* fishing, shooting, drawing and painting, writing, wild life study, food; *Clubs* Royal Scots, Scot Armed Forces Officers', Country Club UK; *Style—* Lt-Col Howard Paterson, TD; ✉ Dovewood, West Linton, Peeblesshire EH46 7DS (tel and fax 01968 660346)

PATERSON, Prof Ian; s of Angus Paterson (d 1986), and Violet Paterson (d 1978); *b* 4 May 1954, Dundee; *Educ* Kirkton HS Dundee, Univ of St Andrews (BSc), Univ of Cambridge (PhD); *m* 18 June 1977, Nina, *née* Kuan; *Career* research fell Christ's Coll Cambridge 1978–79, NATO/SERC postdoctoral research fell Columbia Univ NY 1979–80, lectr in chemistry UCL 1980–83; Univ of Cambridge: univ lectr Dept of Chemistry 1983–97, reader in organic chemistry 1997–2000, prof of organic chemistry 2001–; Jesus Coll Cambridge: teaching fell 1983–2001, dir of studies in chemistry 1991–97, professorial fell 2002–; visiting prof Univ of Rennes I France 1993; various consultancies with pharmaceutical cos; Hickinbottom fell RSC 1989–91; MRSC, FRS; *Awards* Meldola Medal and Prize RSC 1983, Pfizer Award in Chemistry (UK) 1990 and 1993, ICI (AstraZeneca) Award in Organic Chemistry (UK) 1990, Organic Reactions Lectr (USA) 1992, Merck Grant in Chemistry 1995–, Bader Prize RSC 1996, RSC Award in Synthetic Organic Chemistry 2001, Robert Robinson Lectureship Award RSC 2003, FRS 2005; *Publications* extensive pubns in jls incl Angewandte Chemie, Organic Letters and Jl of the American Chemical Soc; *Recreations* walking, gardening; *Style—* Prof Ian Paterson; ✉ Department of Chemistry, University of Cambridge, Lensfield Road, Cambridge CB2 1EW (tel 01223 336407, fax 01223 336362, e-mail ip100@cam.ac.uk)

PATERSON, Martin James Mower; s of John Mower Alexander Paterson, of Great Missenden, Bucks, and Miriam Daisy Ballinger Paterson; *b* 14 March 1951; *Educ* Oundle, Univ of Birmingham (BSc), Cranfield Inst of Technol (MBA), Inst of Mktg (DipM); *m* 9 July 1977 (m dis 1996), Anne Vivien, da of Vivian Erroll Bowyer, DSC; 2 s (David Mower Erroll, Andrew James), 1 da (Victoria Katharine); *Career* Metal Box 1973–81: graduate trainee 1973–74, devpt technician 1974–76, mfrg mangr 1975–78, works mangr Thailand 1978–81; Betec plc: dir and gen mangr Black and Luff Ltd 1981–82, divnl mfrg dir 1982–84; Cranfield Inst of Technol 1984–85, special assignments exec TI Group plc 1985–86, md Seals Div Aeroquip Ltd 1986–89, chm STS Ltd 1989–90, chm and chief exec Gallery Home Fashions Ltd 1991–2002, chm Manufacturing Investments Ltd 1991–; MIEE, MCIM, CEng; *Recreations* sailing; *Clubs* Royal Lymington Yacht, RORC; *Style—* Martin Paterson, Esq; ✉ Hobbles Green House, Hobbles Green, Cowlinge, Suffolk CB8 9HX (tel 01440 783255, fax 01440 783059, e-mail martin@manin.co.uk)

PATERSON, Maurice Dinsmore; s of Maurice Sidney Paterson (d 1977), of Glasgow, and Agnes Dinsmore, *née* Joss (d 1995); *b* 28 August 1941; *Educ* Glasgow HS; *m* 3 Oct 1967, Avril Grant, da of John Gordon Barclay (d 1984), of Glasgow; 2 s (Michael b 11 Sept 1970, Colin b 28 May 1974); *Career* Scottish Amicable: joined 1959, asst sec 1968, gen mangr sales and mktg 1978, dir 1985, dep md 1990–94; dir: LAUTRO 1990–94, Refuge Gp plc 1994–96, United Assurance plc 1996–98; chm Glasgow Life and Pensions Gp 1972–73; non-exec chm: Origo Services Ltd 1989–91, Intelligent Pensions Ltd 1998–; non-exec dir Student Loans Co Ltd 1999–2002; pres Insurance and Actuarial Soc of Glasgow 1987–88; FFA 1967 (memb Cncl 1996–99); *Recreations* golf, badminton, jogging, genealogy; *Clubs* Pollok Golf, Western Gailes Golf; *Style—* Maurice Paterson, Esq; ✉ 11 Briar Gardens, Glasgow G43 2TF (tel 0141 637 2690, fax 0870 160 2765, e-mail m.paterson@collinsactuaries.com)

PATERSON, Owen William; MP; s of late Alfred Dobell Paterson, and Cynthia Paterson; *b* 24 June 1956; *Educ* Radley, CCC Cambridge (MA), Nat Leathersellers Coll Northampton; *m* 1980, Hon Rose Ridley, da of 4 Viscount Ridley, KG, GCVO, TD, *qv*; 2 s (Felix b 1986, Ned b 1988), 1 da (Evie b 1992); *Career* md British Leather Co Ltd 1993–99; MP (Cons) Shropshire N 1997– (Parly candidate Wrexham 1992); PPS to Rt Hon Iain Duncan Smith, MP, *qv*, 2001–03; shadow min for agric 2003–05, shadow min of state for tport 2005–07, shadow sec of state for NI 2007–; co-chm Parly Manufacturing Industry Gp 1997–98; memb: Welsh Grand Ctee 1997–2000, Welsh Affrs Select Ctee 1997–2001, Inter-Parly Union 1997, Parly Waterways Gp 1997–, Cons Friends of Israel, Franco-Br Parly Relations Ctee 1997–, All-Pty Racing Gp, Cons Way Forward Gp, Euro Scrutiny Select Ctee 1999–2001, Agric Select Ctee 2000–01; pres COTANCE (Confedn of European Tanners) 1996–98; vice-chm All-Pty BBC Gp; dep chm Ellesmere Community Care Centre Tst 1991–97, memb Cncl Inst of Orthopaedics 1992–; Liveryman Worshipful Co of Leathersellers; *Style—* Owen Paterson, Esq, MP; ✉ House of Commons, London SW1A 0AA (tel 020 7219 5185, fax 020 7219 3955, e-mail patersono@parliament.uk)

PATERSON, Peter James; *b* 4 February 1931; *Educ* Spurgeon's Orphan Home, Balham and Tooting Sch of Commerce, LCC evening classes; *Children* 1 s (Graham Julian Paterson, *qv*); *Career* reporter: Fulham Gazette 1948–49, Fulham Chronicle 1951–52, Western Daily Press 1952–54; Parly reporter Exchange Telegraph News Agency 1954–59, industrial corr Daily Telegraph 1959–62, industrial corr Sunday Telegraph 1962–68, asst ed New Statesman 1968–70, political columnist Spectator 1970, TV critic Daily Mail 1987– (industrial ed 1985–87); *Books* The Selectorate (1967), Tired and Emotional - The Life of Lord George Brown (1993); *Recreations* dog walking, collecting old typewriters; *Clubs* Academy, Travellers; *Style—* Peter Paterson, Esq; ✉ Daily Mail, Northcliffe House, 2 Derry Street, London W8 5TT (tel 020 7938 6362, fax 020 7937 3251)

PATERSON, Ronald McNeill; s of Ian McNeill Paterson (d 1997), and Doris MacNicol, *née* Dunnett (d 1980); *b* 1 August 1950; *Educ* Hillhead HS Glasgow, Univ of Aberdeen (LLB); *m* 31 Dec 1988, Frances Ann Early, da of Hon Mr Justice Kenneth David Potter, QC (d 1986); *Career* CA 1974; ptnr Arthur Young 1982–89 (joined 1970), ptnr and dir of accounting Ernst & Young 1989–99; memb: Accounting Standards Ctee 1987–90, Urgent Issues Task Force Accounting Standards Bd 1991–99, Cncl ICAS 1998–2004, Fin Reporting Review Panel 1999–2005; treas Amateur Rowing Assoc 2002–; hon prof Univ of Glasgow 2001–04; *Books* UK GAAP - Generally Accepted Accounting Practice in the United Kingdom (jt author 1989), Off Balance Sheet Finance (1993); *Recreations* rowing, tennis, travel, music; *Clubs* Deeside Scullers; *Style—* Ronald Paterson, Esq; ✉ Church Orchard, Sheepscombe, Gloucestershire GL6 7RL (tel 01452 813338, e-mail ronpaterson@lineone.net)

PATERSON, Prof William Edgar; OBE (1999); s of William Edgar Paterson (d 1978), of Comrie, Perthshire, and Williamina, *née* McIntyre (d 2003); *b* 26 September 1941; *Educ* Morrison's Acad, Univ of St Andrews (MA, class medallist), LSE (S H Bailey scholar, MSc, PhD); *m* 1, 1964, Jacqueline, *née* Cramb (d 1974); 2 s (William b 1970, John b 1973); m 2, 1979, Phyllis MacDowell; 1 da (Alison b 1980), 1 step s (Colin b 1970), 1 step da (Catherine b 1975); *Career* lectr in int relations Univ of Aberdeen 1967–70; Univ of Warwick: Volkswagen lectr in German politics 1970–75, sr lectr 1975–82, reader 1982–89, prof and chm of dept 1989–90; Salvesen prof of European Insts and dir Europa Inst Univ of Edinburgh 1990–94, prof of German politics and fndn dir Inst for German Studies Univ of Birmingham 1994–; dir Königswinter Conf; chm: Assoc for the Study of German Politics 1974–76, Univ Assoc for Contemporary European Studies 1989–94, One Europe or Several Prog, German-British Forum 2005; memb: ESRC Research Priorities Bd 1994–99, Kuratorium Allianz Kultur Stiftung 2001–05, Advsy Bd Centre for Br Studies Humboldt-Univ Berlin; co-ed Jl of Common Market Studies 2003–, memb Editorial Bd Int Affairs; hon vice-pres Assoc for the Study of German Politics 2000; Lifetime Award Assoc for the Study of German Politics 2004, Lifetime Achievement Award in European Studies Univ Assoc for Contemporary European Studies 2007; assoc fell RIIA 1994; FRSE 1994, FRSA 1998, AcSS 2000; Officer's Cross of the Federal Republic of Germany 1999; *Publications* incl: Federal Republic of Germany and the European Community (jtly, 1987), Government and the Chemical Industry (jtly, 1988), The Kohl Chancellorship (co-eds, 1998), Germany's European Diplomacy (jtly, 2000), The Future of the German Economy (co-ed, 2000), Developments in German Politics III (jtly, 2003), Governance in Contemporary Germany (co-ed, 2005); author of numerous articles in learned jls; *Recreations* walking; *Style—* Prof William Paterson, OBE, AcSS, FRSE, FRSA; ✉ tel 0121 414 7183, fax 0121 414 7329, e-mail w.e.paterson@bham.ac.uk

PATERSON-BROWN, Dr June; CVO (2007), CBE (1991), JP (2000); da of Wing Cdr Thomas Clark Garden (d 1978), of Gorebridge, Midlothian, and Jean Martha Garden, BEM, *née* Mallace (d 1976); *b* 8 February 1932; *Educ* Esdaile Coll Edinburgh, Univ of Edinburgh Med Sch (MB ChB); *m* 29 March 1957, Peter Neville Paterson-Brown, s of Keith Paterson-Brown (d 1981), of Edinburgh; 3 s (Simon b 1958, Timothy b 1960, William b 1965), 1 da (Sara b 1959); *Career* med offr Family Planning and Well Woman Clinics Hawick 1960–85, non-exec dir Border TV plc 1979–2000; former memb Roxburghshire Co Educn Ctee; chm: Roxburghshire Co Youth Ctee, Roxburgh Dist Duke of Edinburgh Award Ctee; co cmmr: Roxburghshire Girl Guides Assocs 1971–77, Peeblesshire Girl Guides Assoc 1973–75; chief cmmr UK and Cwlth Girl Guides 1985–90 (Scot chief cmmr 1977–82); chm: Borders Region Children's Panel Advsy Ctee 1982–85, Scot Standing Conf Voluntary Youth Orgns 1982–85; vice-pres Guide Assoc 1991–; tstee: Prince's Tst 1980–94 (vice-chm Tst 1980–92), MacRoberts Tsts 1987–2002; Queen's Silver Jubilee Medal 1977, Queen's Golden Jubilee Medal 2002; Paul Harris fell Rotary Int 1990; HM Lord-Lt Roxburgh, Ettrick and Lauderdale 1998–2007 (DL 1990); *Recreations* golf, music, reading, fishing; *Clubs* Lansdowne; *Style—* Dr June Paterson-Brown, CVO, CBE; ✉ Norwood, Hawick, Roxburghshire TD9 7HP (tel 01450 372352, e-mail pbnorwood@btinternet.com)

PATEY, HE William Charters; CMG (2005); s of Maurice William Patey, of Edinburgh, and Christina Kinnell Patey; *b* 11 July 1953; *Educ* Trinity Acad Edinburgh, Univ of Dundee (MA); *m* 23 Sept 1978, Vanessa Carol, *née* Morrell; 2 s (William Rory b 7 Sept 1987, Thomas Morrell b 24 Feb 1991); *Career* joined FCO 1975, commercial attaché Abu Dhabi 1978–81, second sec (political) Tripoli 1981–84, FCO London 1984–88, head Political Section Canberra 1988–92, dep head UN Dept 1992–94, overseas inspr 1994–95, dep head of mission and consul-gen Riyadh 1995–98, head Middle East Dept 1998–2002, ambass to Sudan 2002–05, ambass to Iraq 2005–06, dir Comprehensive Spending Review Prog FCO 2006–07, ambass to Saudi Arabia 2007–; memb Anglo Omani Soc, patron Together for Sudan; tstee: Bishop Mubarak Fund, Kids 4 Kids; hon pres St Margaret's Film Club 1996; *Recreations* tennis, golf, diving, theatre, cinema; *Style—* HE Mr William Patey, CMG; ✉ c/o Foreign & Commonwealth Office (Riyadh), King Charles Street, London SW1A 2AH (e-mail william.patey@fco.gov.uk)

PATHY, Prof (Mohan Sankar) John; OBE (1991); s of Dr Conjeveram Pathy (d 1977), and Agnes Maud Victoria, *née* Purchel (d 1992); *b* 26 April 1923; *Educ* KCL, King's Coll Hosp London; *m* 27 Sept 1949, Norma Mary, da of John Gallwey (d 1959); 2 s (Aidan b 13 May 1951, Damian b 3 Nov 1963), 3 da (Anne b 21 April 1952, Sarah b 29 Nov 1956, Helen b 4 May 1959); *Career* asst physician Oxford Regnl Hosp Bd 1958–60, conslt physician in geriatric med S Glamorgan HA 1960–79, prof of geriatric med Univ of Wales Coll of Med 1979–90, emeritus prof Univ of Wales 1990, research dir Health Care

Research Unit St Woolos Hosp Newport 1991–2001, currently with Health R&D Associates; past memb: Exec Ctee Int Assoc of Gerontology, Scientific Ctee Fedn Int des Assoc de Personnes Agèes; pres Age Concern Wales; memb: BMA 1948, BGS 1958, BSRA 1976, American Geriatric Soc 1986; hon memb: Spanish Soc of Geriatrics and Gerontology 1997, Slovakian Soc of Medicine 1995, Medical Soc of Bohemia 1990, Bohemian Soc of Gerontology 1987; FRCPEd 1967, FRCP 1973, FRCPGlas 1997; *Books* Principles and Practice of Geriatric Medicine (1985, 4 edn 2006), Geriatric Medicine: Problems and Practice (1989); *Recreations* creative gardening; *Style*— Prof John Pathy, OBE; ✉ Mathern Lodge, Cefn Coed Crescent, Cardiff CF23 6AT (tel 029 2075 5476, fax 029 2076 5040, e-mail johnpathy@aol.com); Health Care Research Unit, St Woolos Hospital, Newport NP20 4SZ (tel 01633234234 ext 8305)

PATIENCE, His Hon Judge Andrew; QC (1990); s of William Edmund John Patience (d 1960), and Louise Mary (d 1998); *b* 28 April 1941; *Educ* Whitgift Sch Croydon, St John's Coll Oxford (MA); *m* 1975, (Jean) Adèle, *née* Williams (Her Hon Judge Williams), *qv*; 1 da (Louise b 1981), 1 s (David b 1984); *Career* called to the Bar Gray's Inn 1966; recorder of the Crown Court 1986–99, circuit judge (SE Circuit) 1999–, resident judge Maidstone Crown Court 2000–, hon recorder of Dover 2001–; *Recreations* mimicry, complaining, horse racing; *Clubs* Oxford and Cambridge; *Style*— His Hon Judge Patience, QC; ✉ The Law Courts, Barker Road, Maidstone, Kent ME16 8EQ

PATON, Andrew John; s of John William Davies Paton, of Birmingham, and Peggy Irene Lois Paton; *b* 15 March 1957, Birmingham; *Educ* Bishop Vesey's GS Sutton Coldfield, Univ of Exeter (LLB); *m* 18 Sept 1982, Catherine, *née* Andrews; 1 da (Hannah b 1987), 2 s (Tom b 1994, Rory b 1997); *Career* admitted slr 1981; ptnr Pinsent Masons 1986– (slr 1981–86); accredited mediator 1990, jt fndr Panel of Ind Mediators (PIM), chm Assoc of Midlands Mediators; author of numerous articles on mediation; dir ADR Net Ltd 1991–; memb Law Soc 1981, MCIArb 2003; *Recreations* sailing, tennis, golf; *Clubs* Edgbaston Priory Tennis, Barnt Green Sailing; *Style*— Andrew Paton, Esq; ✉ Pinsent Masons, 3 Colmore Circus, Birmingham B4 6BH (tel 0121 200 1050, fax 0121 626 1040, e-mail andrew.paton@pinsents.com)

PATON, Maureen Virginia; da of William Harney, and Blanche, *née* Adams (later Mrs Paton); *Educ* Watford Tech HS, Univ of Leicester (BA); *m* 21 May 1977, Liam Michael Maguire (d 2006), s of William Maguire; *Career* journalist and author; trainee with British Printing Corporation on various pubns, subsequently with IPC Business Press, The Express 1979–98; freelance feature writer on subjects incl arts, showbusiness and women's issues 1998–; contrib to pubns incl: You magazine, The Times, Daily Telegraph, The Independent, Daily Express, The Guardian, The Stage; memb: NUJ, Broadcasting Press Guild, Women In Journalism; *Books* Alan Rickman: The Unauthorised Biography, The Best of Women: The History of The Women of the Year Lunch & Assembly; *Recreations* films, reading, writing; *Style*— Maureen Paton; ✉ mobile 07775 888491, e-mail maurpaton@tiscali.co.uk

PATON WALSH, Gillian (Jill); CBE (1996); da of John Llewellyn Bliss (d 1979), and Patricia, *née* Dubern (d 1977); *b* 29 April 1937; *Educ* St Michael's Convent Sch N Finchley, St Anne's Coll Oxford (MA, DipEd); *m* 1 1961, Antony Edmund Paton Walsh (d 2003); 1 s (Edmund Alexander b 1963), 2 da (Margaret Anne b 1965, Helen Clare b 1966); m 2 2004, John Rowe Townsend; *Career* teacher Enfield Girls GS 1959–62, Arts Cncl Creative Writing Fellowship 1976–78, perm visiting faculty memb Centre for Children's Literature Simmons Coll Boston Mass 1978–86, Gertrude Clarke Whittall lectr Library of Congress 1978, judge Whitbread prize 1984, chm Cambridge Book Assoc 1987–89, ptnr Green Bay Pubns; memb: Ctee Children's Writers Gp, Mgmnt Ctee Soc of Authors; adjunct Br Bd memb Children's Literature New England, memb cncl Soc of Authors 1999; FRSL 1996; *Books* Hengest's Tale (1966), The Dolphin Crossing (1967), Wordhoard (1969), Fireweed (1970), Farewell, Great King (1972), Goldengrove (1972), Toolmaker (1973), The Dawnstone (1973), The Emperor's Winding Sheet (1974), The Butty Boy (1975), The Island Sunrise: Prehistoric Britain (1975), Unleaving (1976), Crossing to Salamis, The Walls of Athens, Persian Gold (1977–78), A Chance Child (1978), The Green Book (1981), Babylon (1982), Lost & Found (1984), A Parcel of Patterns (1984), Gaffer Samson's Luck (1985), Five Tides (1986), Lapsing (1986), Torch (1987), A School for Lovers (1989), Birdy and The Ghosties (1989), Can I Play? (1990), Grace (1991), When Grandma Came (1992), Matthew and The Seasingers (1992), The Wyndham Case (1993), Knowledge of Angels (1994, Booker Prize nominee), Pepi and the Secret Names (1994), A Piece of Justice (1995), Connie Came to Play (1995), Thomas and the Tinners (1995), The Serpentine Cave (1997), Thrones, Dominions (completion of Dorothy L Sayers novel, 1998), A Desert in Bohemia (2000), A Presumption of Death (based on notes by Dorothy L Sayers, 2002), Debts of Dishonour (2006), The Bad Quarto (2007); *Recreations* reading, walking, sewing, photography; *Clubs* Athenaeum; *Style*— Mrs Jill Paton Walsh, CBE, FRSL; ✉ c/o Bruce Hunter, David Higham Associates, 5–8 Lower John Street, Golden Square, London W1R 3PE

PATRICK, Andrew Graham McIntosh; s of Dr James McIntosh Patrick, OBE, RSA, ARE, RGI, LLD (d 1998), and Janet, *née* Watterston (d 1983); *b* 12 June 1934; *Educ* Harris Acad Dundee; *Career* The Fine Art Soc: joined 1954, dir 1966, md 1976–2003, dep chm 2003–; has presented hundreds of exhbns, mostly of Br artists but covering all aspects of the visual arts; memb: Exec Ctee Soc of London Art Dealers (chm 1983–86), Cncl The Br Antique Dealers' Assoc 1986–93, Curatorial Ctee Nat Tst for Scot 1986–89, Art in Lieu Panel 2001–; chm Decorative Arts Soc 2005–; *Recreations* collecting: pictures, Japanese prints, camels, etc; *Clubs* Marks, Royal Cwlth Soc, Garrick; *Style*— Andrew McIntosh Patrick, Esq; ✉ The Fine Art Society plc, 148 New Bond Street, London W1S 2JT (tel 020 7629 5116)

PATRICK, Andrew John; s of Patrick John Charles, of Hockley Heath, W Midlands, and Norma, *née* Harris (d 1987); *b* 23 November 1955; *Educ* Dartmouth HS, Univ of Birmingham (BA); *m* 3 Dec 1981, Petrice Janice, da of Edward Blackmore; 1 da (Joanna Norma b 8 Sept 1985), 1 s (Matthew John b 29 Jan 1988); *Career* actor 1975–76 (stage credits incl Black and White Minstrel Show, Another Bride Another Groom and The National Health, TV credits incl Angels, Penda's Fen, Looking for Clancy, Crossroads and Trinity Tales), asst mangr Birmingham Hippodrome Theatre 1976–78; British Film and TV Producers Assoc (now PACT): accountant 1978–80, asst sec 1980–83, sec 1983–86, dir Admin and Mktg 1986–88, dep chief exec 1988–91; chief exec: British Film Commission 1992–97, Film & Television Commission North West England 1997–; dir: Medicinema (registered charity), UK Screen Commission Network, British Film Advsy Group; memb: BAFTA 1992–, North West Cultural Consortium; *Recreations* board games, squash, football, watching cricket, cinema; *Style*— Andrew Patrick, Esq; ✉ Film & Television Commission North West England, 109 Mount Pleasant, Liverpool L3 5TF (tel 0151 708 8099, fax 0151 708 9859, e-mail andrewp@ftcnorthwest.co.uk)

PATRICK, Bruce Robertson; s of Francis Wheatly Patrick, of Edinburgh, and Isabel, *née* Spencer; *b* 26 November 1945; *Educ* Glasgow Acad, Edinburgh Acad, Exeter Coll Oxford (BA), Univ of Edinburgh (LLB, Green Prize for criminal law, Millar Prize for Scots law); *m* 9 Feb 1980, Hilary Jane, eld da of Richard Alan Sutton; 2 da (Ruth b 5 Nov 1980, Catherine b 4 July 1982), 1 s (Robert James b 9 July 1984); *Career* apprentice Mitchells Johnston Solicitors Glasgow 1971–73; asst: Maclay Murray & Spens Glasgow 1973–75, Coward Chance Solicitors London 1975–76; Maclay Murray & Spens: ptnr Company Dept 1976–2003 (Glasgow office 1976–77, Edinburgh office 1978–2003), managing ptnr 1991–94, sr ptnr 2000–03, conslt 2003–06; pt/t tutor in law Univ of Edinburgh 1980–84; completed Glasgow marathon 1985; non-exec dir Dunedin Enterprises Investment Tst plc 2003–; memb: Law Soc of Scotland 1973 (vice-convenor Company Law Ctee), Royal Faculty of Procurators Glasgow 1976, Soc of WS 1980; *Books* IBA Handbook on Maritime Law (contrib Scottish section, 1983); *Recreations* sailing, golf, hill walking, rugby (now spectator), occasional gardening; *Clubs* Luffness Golf, Prestwick Golf, Clyde Cruising; *Style*— Bruce Patrick, Esq

PATRICK, (Katherine) Emily (Mrs Michael Perry); da of William Pitt Patrick, of Folkestone, Kent, and Rosemary Martha, *née* Pulvertaft; *b* 4 October 1959; *Educ* Folkestone GS, Architectural Assoc, Univ of Cambridge (MA); *m* 16 Oct 1986, Michael Luke Perry, s of David Edward Perry, of Hitchin, Herts; 2 da (Beatrice Lillian b 9 Sept 1987, Isabel Eliza b 5 March 1990), 1 s (Alfred Oberon Patrick b 4 April 1994); *Career* artist; exhibited at: King St Gallery, Wraxall Gallery, Long & Ryle Int, Maine Gallery, Mall Galleries, Lefevre Gallery, The Nat Portrait Gallery, The Napier Gallery; one man shows at: Agnew's 1986, 1989, 1992 and 1995, 27 Cork Street 1997 and 2000, Hanover Sq Gallery NY 1997, 32 Dover St London 2002, 2005 and 2007; painted HRH The Princess of Wales, portrait for Royal Hants Regt 1987; first winner of Royal Soc of Portrait Painters' Caroll Prize 1988; FRSA 2001; *Recreations* walking; *Style*— Emily Patrick; ✉ e-mail mail@emilypatrick.com

PATRICK, Prof John Howard; s of George Edward Patrick (d 1994), of Shrewsbury, Shropshire, and Emmeline Swindells, *née* Brierley; *b* 17 June 1943; *Educ* Haberdashers' Aske's, St Thomas' Hosp Med Sch Univ of London; *m* 9 Sept 1972, Patricia, da of Geoffrey Thornton-Smith, of Wokingham, Berks; 3 da (Tamsyn b 1975, Abigail b 1977, Bryony b 1989); *Career* RAF 1963–72 (ret sqdn ldr); various house appts St Thomas' Hosp, sr lectr and hon conslt orthopaedic surgn Univ of Liverpool, past dir Orthotic Res and Locomotion Assessment Unit, conslt orthopaedic surgn 1980–, prof of orthopaedic engrg Univ of Wolverhampton 2005–; papers published in med jls incl British Medical Journal, memb Editorial Bd Gait and Posture; memb Int Standards Orgn; former Master Shrewsbury Drapers' Co; FRCS 1972; *Recreations* skiing, travel; *Clubs* RAF; *Style*— Prof John Patrick; ✉ Orthotic Research and Locomotion Assessment Unit, Robert Jones and Agnes Hunt Orthopaedic Hospital, Oswestry, Shropshire SY10 7AG (tel 01691 404236)

PATRICK, Keith Ian; s of Hubert Eric Patrick (d 1983), of Watford, and Edna May, *née* Hart; *b* 23 February 1952; *Educ* Watford Boys' GS, Watford Sch of Art, Hockerill Coll, Camberwell Sch of Art (BA); *m* 1989, Maria Teresa Lorés Bergua (Maite Lorés); 1 step s (Fabian Hutchinson b 25 July 1973), 1 step da (Anna Nuria Smythe b 4 May 1981); *Career* worked and exhibited as practising artist 1974–83, art critic 1983–; works published in numerous art jls at home and abroad, guest ed Studio International 1984, ed Art Line Magazine 1990–96, ed Contemporary Visual Arts Magazine 1996–2001, ed Contemporary Magazine 2001–03; curator of exhibitions incl: The Romantic Tradition in Contemporary British Painting (Spain and England touring) 1988, Romantic Visions (Camden Arts Centre) 1988, Critics' View (Royal Festival Hall) 1991, From Bacon to Now - The Outsider in British Figuration (Palazzo Vecchio Florence) 1991–92, Contemporary Br Sculpture - Henry Moore to the 90s (Spain and Portugal touring) 1995, Jaume Plensa: Up Close (Ljubljana) 2001–, Video London (Madrid, Barcelona) 2005, 2006 and 2007; Int Assoc of Art Critics: assoc 1984, sec Br Section 1986–89, pres Br Section 1991–94, vice-pres Int Section 1993–96; *Publications* Oil on Canvas (1997); *Style*— Keith Patrick, Esq; ✉ Passeig Sant Joan 204, 4a 1o, 08037 Barcelona, Spain (e-mail lores.patrick@virgin.net)

PATRICK, Peter Laurence; s of Anthony Frederick Herbert Patrick, of St Peters, Broadstairs, Kent, and Joyce Stanley, *née* Sowerby; *b* 11 July 1946; *Educ* Alleyne's Sch Stevenage, UC Durham (BA); *m* 22 April 1972, Teresa Mary Patrick, JP, da of William Roland Mills, MBE, of Billericay, Essex; 1 s (Edward William b 4 Nov 1973), 1 da (Frances Elizabeth b 10 July 1975); *Career* CA 1972; Price Waterhouse & Co: Newcastle 1967–70, London 1970–73, Paris 1973–76; computer audit mangr Howard Tilly & Co 1976–78, head of inspection Hambros Bank Ltd 1978–86, co sec Hambros plc and Hambros Bank Ltd 1986–98; ct sec HAC 1999–; cnclr Billericay E Basildon DC 1984–96 and 1998–2002; chm Fin Ctee Basildon DC 1992–95, vice-pres (finance) S Suffolk Cons Assoc; chm Towngate Theatre Co Basildon 1988–89, tstee Adventure Unlimited (Chelmsford Dio Youth Charity), tstee Essex Young Musicians' Tst; churchwarden and memb choir St Mary's Boxford; *Recreations* singing, gardening, politics, history, architecture; *Clubs* Carlton; *Style*— Peter Patrick, Esq; ✉ Amberley, Whitestreet Green, Boxford, Suffolk CO10 5JN (tel 01787 210346, office 020 7382 1530, e-mail ppat@btinternet.com)

PATTEN, Brian; *b* 7 February 1946; *Career* poet and author; Freeman City of Liverpool 2001; hon fell Liverpool John Moores Univ 2002; FRSL 2003; *Publications* poetry: Little Johnny's Confessions (1967), The Mersey Sound (with Adrian Henri and Roger McGough, 1967), Penguin Modern Poets (1967), Notes to the Hurrying Man (1969), The Irrelevant Song (1971), The Unreliable Nightingale (1973), Vanishing Trick (1976), The Shabby Angel (1978), Grave Gossip (1979), Love Poems (1981), Clares Countryside (1978), New Volume (1983), Storm Damage (1988), Grinning Jack (Selected Poems, 1990), Armada (1997), New Collected Love Poems (2007), Penguin Selected Poems (2007); novels: Mr Moon's Last Case (1975), The Story Giant (2001); plays: The Pig and the Junkle (1975), The Mouth Trap (with Roger McGough, 1982), Blind Love (1983), Gargling with Jelly - The Play! (1989); for younger readers: The Elephant and the Flower (1969), Jumping Mouse (1971), Emma's Doll (1976), The Sly Cormorant and the Fish (1977), Gangsters Ghosts and Dragonflies (ed, 1981), Gargling with Jelly (1985), Jimmy Tag-along (1988), Thawing Frozen Frogs (1990), The Puffin Book of Twentieth Century Children's Verse (ed, 1991), Grizzelda Frizzle (1992), The Magic Bicycle (1993), Impossible Parents (1994), The Utter Nutters (1994), The Puffin Book of Utterly Brilliant Verse (ed, 1998), Beowulf: a Retelling (1999), The Blue and Green Ark (1999), Little Hotchpotch (2000), Juggling with Gerbils (2000), Ben's Magic Telescope (2002), The Story Giant (2002), The Monsters' Guide to Choosing a Pet (with Roger McGough, 2004); *Clubs* Chelsea Arts; *Style*— Brian Patten, Esq; ✉ c/o Rogers, Coleridge and White, 20 Powis Mews, London W11 1JN (tel 020 7221 3717, fax 020 7229 9084)

PATTEN, Garry John; s of Henry John Patten, of Plymouth, Devon, and Mildred Lilian, *née* Rudge; *b* 22 February 1950; *Educ* Queen Elizabeth's Sch Crediton, New Univ of Ulster (BA); *m* 1; 2 s (James b 31 Aug 1976, Nicolas b 11 Sept 1979), 1 da (Susanna b 23 Aug 1989); m 2, 12 Oct 2002, Susan Janet, *née* Ross; *Career* admitted slr 1979; asst slr Tosswill & Co 1979–81, Office of the Dir of Public Prosecutions 1981–86; CPS: joined 1986, various positions incl head of fraud, dep chief crown prosecutor for CPS London and asst dir of casework services, dir of policy 1998–; *Recreations* tennis, golf; *Style*— Garry Patten, Esq; ✉ Crown Prosecution Service, 50 Ludgate Hill, London EC4M 7EX (tel 020 7796 8124)

PATTEN, H; s of Hubert Patten, of Birmingham, and Agnes, *née* Johnson (d 1986); *b* 20 January 1961; *Educ* Lea Mason C of E Sch Birmingham, Bournville Sch of Art and Craft Birmingham (City & Guilds Part 1), South Glamorgan Inst of Higher Educn Cardiff (BA), Univ of Legon Ghana; *m* 1 s (Kwesi Yaadi b 26 July 1987), 2 da (Mawuena Esi b 16 March 1986, Onayomi Ayokunle b 22 August 1994); *Career* dancer; Danse de L'Afrique 1982–86: fndr memb, princ male dancer, drummer English tour 1983, Moroccan tour 1984 organised and performed Midlands tour with Jean Binta Breeze 1985; participant Mayfest Festival Glasgow with Pepsi Poet and Benjamin Zephania 1983; Inst of African Studies Univ of Legon Ghana 1983: trg with Ghana National Danse Ensemble, tutor of Caribbean dance, participant in Accra and Hogbetsocho Festival Angola Volta Region; dep dir and community arts worker The CAVE (Community and Village Entertainment) Birmingham 1983–86; freelance artiste, tutor of Caribbean and African music and dance

P

and visual arts, painter, sculptor, photographer, storyteller 1986–; performer and teacher of dance Int Lit Festival Lecce Italy (for Cwlth Inst) 1990, lead dancer Adaniloro nat tour (with Sakoba Prodns) 1991; Adzido Pan African Dance Ensemble: joined 1986, re-joined 1987, In the Village of Africa tour 1987, Coming Home tour 1988, performances at Queen Elizabeth Festival Hall South Bank 1988, Edinburgh Festival 1988, performances at Sadler's Wells 1988, Irish tour 1989, Montpellier Dance, Festival France 1989, Under Africa Skies tour 1990, educn outreach liaison co-ordinator 1990; Dis Ya Set Up (dance, drama, story telling prodn, which toured nationally) prodr/choreographer/performer 1994, dance conslt Africa 95 (an int festival of African arts), Panafest (workshops, Ghana) 1994; Black Dance Development Trust: tstee Bd 1987, performed at first and second annual awards 1987 and 1989, planned and co-ordinated prog for Summer School III 1988, received Creativity in Music & Dance award 1989, East Midlands educn outreach devpt worker 1989; choreographer of: Carnival Fire (Third Dimension Theatre Co) 1987, Devil Going to Dance (Staunch Poets & Players) 1988, Mother Poem (Temba Theatre Co) 1989, Round Heads and Peak Heads (Tara Arts Theatre Co) 1989, Soul-Less-Game (Kokuma Performing Arts) 1989, Flying Costumes, Floating Tombs (by Keith Khan for London Int Festival of Arts) 1991 (Dance Umbrella award), Ina De Wildanis (one man theatre prodn touring nationally and internationally) 1992 (also prodr), Journey From Jourouvert (for Costume Designers Club and LIFT Festival) 1993 (designed and cmmnd making of costumes for Irie Dance Theatre Co in The Gambia), The Story Behind the Song - Torie Bac a De Song (Irie Dance Theatre) 1993; *Publications* involved with: UK Black by Karen Wheeler (music video) 1990, Black Voices film 1990, Ama (Efirititi Film Co) 1990; British Council sponsored tours: to Malawi (choreographed Ndakula prodn with Kwacha Cultural Troupe, led troupe on first nat tour) 1990, to Zambia (choreographed one hour showcase with Zambia National Dance Troupe and The Univ of Zambia Dance Ensemble) 1992, to Malawi (to work with Kwacha Cultural Troupe) and to Kenya 1993; research tour to Ghana, Senegal, The Gambia, Jamaica, Trinidad, Tobago, Carriacou and Greneda (with Irie Dance Theatre for The Story Behind the Song) 1992; also extensive teaching in UK and abroad, work with numerous nat and int tutors of African and Caribbean dance; Black Dance Devpt Tst Summer Schs 1 2 3 4 & 5; solo storytelling performance Guildhall Gloucester 1989; has exhibited extensively in Britain and the Caribbean; *Recreations* basketball, music, research into Folk Culture; *Style*— H Patten, Esq

PATTEN, James; s of James Arthur Patten (d 1973), and Edith Veronica Patten (d 1989); *b* 30 July 1936; *Educ* St Mary's Coll Liverpool, Trinity Coll of Music London (FTCL, GTCL, LTCL), Die Hochschule für Musik Berlin; *m* (m dis 1990); 3 s (Clovis, Dominic, Samuel); *Career* Duke of Wellington's Regt 1956–59; Die Hochschule Fur Music Berlin DAAD scholarship, Royal Philharmonic Composition Prize 1963, lectr in theory of music Ealing Coll of FE 1965–69, prof of composition Trinity Coll of Music London 1965–70; work for BBC 1969–76: Schools Radio inserts music Session I and II, Music Club, Omnibus (BBC2), Wednesday Play (BBC1); tutor Open Univ 1970–76, LSQ open competition prize 1976, freelance lectr and composer, music tutor and composer in residence Downside Sch 1981–90; pt/t lectr: Dept of Continuing Educn Univ of Bristol 1987–91, Wells Community Educn Dept 1991–93; visiting lectr Birmingham Conservatoire 1991–94, conductor Frome and Dist Choral Union 1992–2000; adjudicator: Frome Music Festival 1991–, Dorset Young Composers' Competition 1996–; compositions (publishers incl Kevin Mayhew Ltd and Bosworth Music Ltd) incl works for guitar, piano, string quartet, organ, various chamber ensembles, saxophone, solo cello, choir, orchestra and military band; recent performances incl: Stabat Mater (Omsk), in memory of an (Berlin), Pepper Place (Hong Kong); memb: Ctee SEAC 1989–92, Univ of Oxford Delegacy Music Panel (chief examiner and sr moderator A and AS Level Music) 1989–96, Horningham Parish Cncl 1979–90; PRS 1965; memb: Int Gustav Mahler Soc 1958, MCPS 1987, RSM 1987, Nat Fedn of Music Socs (SW Region) 1994, Br Acad of Composers and Songwriters, Int Samuel Beckett Soc, Friends of Stanley Spencer Gallery, Trinity Coll of Music Alumni, DAAD Alumni; *Recreations* reading; *Style*— James Patten, Esq; ✉ 1 Crown Cottages, Cats Ash, Shepton Mallet, Somerset BA4 5EL (tel 01749 344859, e-mail japatten@ukonline.co.uk, website www.jamespatten.co.uk)

PATTEN, Baron (Life Peer UK 1997), of Wincanton in the County of Somerset; John Haggitt Charles Patten; PC (1990); s of late Jack Patten, and late Maria Olga, *née* Sikora; *b* 17 July 1945; *Educ* Wimbledon Coll, Sidney Sussex Coll Cambridge (MA, PhD), Univ of Oxford (MA); *m* 1978, Louise Alexandra Virginia Patten, *qv*, da of late John Rowe; 1 da (Hon Mary-Claire b 10 June 1986); *Career* MP (Cons): Oxford 1979–83, Oxford W and Abingdon 1983–97 (ret); PPS to mins of state at the Home Office 1980–81; Parly under sec of state: NI Office 1981–83, DHSS 1983–85; min of state: for housing, urban affrs and construction 1985–87, Home Office 1987–92; sec of state for education 1992–94; non-exec dep chm CCF Charterhouse plc 2000–1, sr advsr Charterhouse Devpt Capital 2001–; advsr Lockheed Martin Overseas Corp 1997–, non-exec dir Lockheed Martin UK Holdings Ltd 1999–; memb Advsy Bd Thomas Goode & Co Ltd 1997–; fell Hertford Coll Oxford 1972–94, hon fell Harris Manchester Coll Oxford 1996; Liveryman Worshipful Co of Drapers; *Books* The Conservative Opportunity (with Lord Blake), Things to Come: The Tories in the 21st Century, Not Quite the Diplomat, and four other books; *Recreations* talking with my wife and daughter; *Style*— The Rt Hon the Lord Patten, PC; ✉ House of Lords, London SW1A 0PW

PATTEN, Lady; Louise Alexandra Patten; *b* 2 February 1954; *Educ* St Paul's Girls' Sch, St Hugh's Coll Oxford (MA); *m* 1978, Baron Patten, PC (Life Peer), *qv*; 1 da; *Career* with: Citibank NA 1977–81, Wells Fargo Bank NA 1981–85, PA Consulting Gp 1985–93; memb UK Advsy Bd Bain & Co 1997– (ptnr 1993–97); non-exec dir: Hilton Gp 1993–, Harveys Furnishings plc 1996–2000, Great Universal Stores 1997–, Somerfield plc 1998– (actg chm 1999–2000), Brixton plc 2001– (chm 2003–), Bradford & Bingley plc 2003–, Marks and Spencer Group plc 2006–; *Style*— The Lady Patten; ✉ c/o Bain & Co, 40 Strand, London WC2N 5HZ

PATTEN OF BARNES, Baron (Life Peer UK 2005), of Barnes in the London Borough of Richmond; Christopher Francis (Chris) Patten; CH (1998), PC (1989); s of late Francis Joseph Patten; *b* 12 May 1944; *Educ* St Benedict's Ealing, Balliol Coll Oxford; *m* 1971, (Mary) Lavender St Leger, da of late Maj John Thornton, by his late wife Joan Coulton, *née* Walker-Smith, sister of 1 Baron Broxbourne; 3 da (Hon Kate, Hon Laura, Hon Alice); *Career* CRD 1966–70, dir 1974–79; worked in Cabinet Office 1970–72, Home Office 1972, PA to Chm Cons Party 1972–74, MP (Cons) Bath 1979–92; PPS to: Norman St John-Stevas as Chllr Duchy of Lancaster and Ldr House of Commons 1979–81, Patrick Jenkin as Sec of State for Social Servs 1981; jt vice-chm Cons Fin Ctee 1981–83, under sec of state NI Office 1983–85; min of state DES 1985–86, min of state for overseas devpt 1986–89, sec of state for the environment 1989–90, chm Cons Pty and Chancellor of the Duchy of Lancaster 1990–92, govr and C-in-C of Hong Kong 1992–97; chm Independent Cmmn on Policing for NI 1998–99; EU cmmr for external affairs 1999–2004; chllr: Univ of Newcastle upon Tyne 1999, Univ of Oxford 2003–; non-exec dir Cadbury Schweppes plc 2005–; awarded several honorary degrees; distinguished hon fell Massey Coll Univ of Toronto 2005; Hon FRCPE 1994; *Books* East and West (1998); *Recreations* reading, tennis; *Clubs* Beefsteak, RAC, Oxford and Cambridge, Athenaeaum; *Style*— The Rt Hon the Lord Patten of Barnes, CH, PC

PATTENDEN, Prof Gerald; s of Albert James Pattenden, and Violet Eugene, *née* Smith; *b* 4 March 1940; *Educ* Brunel Univ, Univ of London (BSc, PhD, DSc); *m* 3 Aug 1969, Christine Frances, da of Charles Leo Doherty; 3 da (Caroline Sarah b 1971, Rebecca Jane b 1974, Katherine Rachael b 1977); *Career* lectr UC Cardiff 1966; Univ of Nottingham: lectr 1972, reader 1975, prof 1980, Sir Jesse Boot prof of organic chemistry 1988–2005, pro-vice-chllr 1997–2003, research prof 2005–; chem conslt; pres Perkin Div Royal Soc of Chemistry 1995–97; scientific ed J Chem Soc, Perkin Trans I 1995–98; also author of 450 res pubns and editor of over 20 books; memb Cncl Royal Soc; RSC honours incl: Corday-Morgan Medallist 1975, Simonsen Medal 1987, Tilden Medal 1991, Award for Synthetic Organic Chemistry 1992, Award for Heterocyclic Chemistry 1994, Pedler Medal 1995, Award in Natural Product Chemistry 1997, Hugo Müller lectr 2000, Robert Robinson lectr 2007; hon fell Queen Mary & Westfield Coll London; FRSC, CChem, FRS; *Recreations* sport, DIY, entertainment; *Style*— Prof Gerald Pattenden, FRS; ✉ School of Chemistry, University of Nottingham, Nottingham NG7 2RD (tel 0115 951 3530, fax 0115 951 3535, e-mail gp@nottingham.ac.uk)

PATTENDEN, Stephanie Jane; da of John Anthony Pattenden, and Patricia Marguerite Sadlier, *née* Harrison; *Educ* St Anne's Coll Sanderstead, St Aidan's Coll Durham (BSc), KCL (PGCE); *Career* maths teacher Harrow Co Girls' GS (latterly Lowlands Sixth Form Coll) 1973–75, maths teacher and second mistress St Paul's Girls' Sch 1975–85, head Maths Dept and Sixth Form The Lady Eleanor Holles Sch 1985–92, dep head S Hampstead HS 1992–97, headmistress Francis Holland Sch 1997–; memb Mathematical Assoc; *Recreations* music, hill walking, bell ringing; *Style*— Miss Stephanie Pattenden; ✉ Francis Holland School, 39 Graham Terrace, London SW1W 8JF (tel 020 7730 2971, fax 020 7823 4066, e-mail head@fhs-swl.org.uk)

PATTERSON, (George) Benjamin (Ben); s of Prof Eric James Patterson (d 1972), of Alphington Cross, Devon, and Dr Ethel Patterson, *née* Simkins (d 1993); *b* 21 April 1939; *Educ* Westminster, Trinity Coll Cambridge (MA), LSE; *m* 5 Dec 1970, Felicity Barbara Anne, da of Gordon W Raybould, of Sundridge, Kent; 1 s (Alexander b 6 Dec 1974), 1 da (Olivia b 15 April 1977); *Career* tutor Swinton Coll Masham 1961–65, ed CPC Monthly Report 1965–73, dep head European Parly London Office 1973–79, dir Wiltenbridge Ltd 1980–93; MEP (EDG until 1992, now EPP) Kent West 1979–94, spokesman on economic monetary and industrial policy 1984–89, bureau memb EDG/EPP 1989–94, vice-pres European Parl Econ, Monetary and Industrial Ctee 1992–94, Secretariat European Parliament 1994–2004; dir CJA Consultants Ltd 2005–; cncllr London Borough of Hammersmith 1968–71; MInstD; *Books* The Character of Conservatism (1973), Direct Elections to the European Parliament (1974), Vredeling and All That (1984), VAT: The Zero Rate Issue (1988), European Monetary Union (1991), A European Currency (1994), Options for a Definitive VAT System (1995), The Co-ordination of National Fiscal Policies (1996), The Consequences of Abolishing Duty Free (1997), Adjusting to Asymmetric Shocks (1998), The Feasibility of a 'Tobin Tax' (1999), Exchange Rates and Monetary Policy (2000), Tax Co-ordination in the EU (2002), Background to the Euro (2003), The Euro: Success or Failure (2006); *Recreations* walking; *Clubs* Bow Group, IOD; *Style*— Ben Patterson, Esq; ✉ Elm Hill House, Hawkhurst, Kent TN18 4XU (e-mail gb.patterson@btinternet.com); 38 Le Village, Montsigur 09300, Ariège, France (tel 00 33 5 61 64 01 19)

PATTERSON, Christina Mary; da of John Allan Patterson, and Anne Marie Patterson; *Educ* Guildford Co Sch, Univ of Durham (BA), UEA (MA); *Career* press officer A & C Black Ltd then press officer Faber and Faber 1988–90, programmer and presenter Lit Prog RFH 1990–98; The Poetry Soc: ran Poetry Places Scheme 1998–2000, dir 2000–03; dep literary ed The Independent 2004–07, assoc ed (comment) The Independent 2007–; freelance journalist for pubns incl The Observer, The Sunday Times and The Independent; chair of judges: Geoffrey Faber Memorial Prize 2000, Forward Poetry Prize 2001; *Publications* contrib to The Cambridge Guide to Women's Writing in English (1999), ed The Forward Book of Poetry (2002); *Recreations* reading, cinema, music, travel; *Style*— Ms Christina Patterson; ✉ Independent House, 191 Marsh Wall, London E14 9RS (tel 020 7005 2654, e-mail c.patterson@independent.co.uk)

PATTERSON, Frances Silvia; QC (1998); *Educ* Queen's Sch Chester, Univ of Leicester; *m* 1980, Dr Graham Nicholson; 3 c; *Career* called to the Bar Middle Temple 1977 (bencher 2005); head of chambers Kings Chambers (formerly 40 King Street) Manchester 2004– (joined 1979–), recorder 2000– (asst recorder 1997–2000); memb Law Reform Working Party on Planning and Environmental Law, Planning and Environment Bar Assoc, Administrative Law Bar Assoc; *Publications* contrib Journal of Planning Law; *Style*— Miss Frances Patterson, QC; ✉ Kings Chambers, 36 Young Street, Manchester M3 3FT

PATTERSON, Glenn; s of Phares Patterson, and Agnes Alexandra (Nessie), *née* Murphy; *b* 9 August 1961; *Educ* Methodist Coll Belfast, UEA (BA, MA); *Partner* Ali Fitzgibbon; *Career* writer; artist in the community Arts Cncl of NI 1989–91, creative writing fell UEA 1992, writer in residence UC Cork 1993–94, writer in residence Queen's Univ Belfast 1994–97, creative writing fell Seamus Heaney Centre for Poetry Queen's Univ Belfast 2005–; memb Arts Cncl NI 1996–99; Rooney Prize for Irish Literature 1988, secdy Betty Trask Award 1988; *Books* Burning Your Own (1988), Fat Lad (1992), Black Night at Big Thunder Mountain (1995), The International (1999), Number 5 (2003), That Which Was (2004), Lapsed Protestant (2006), The Third Party (2007); *Style*— Glenn Patterson; ✉ c/o Antony Harwood Ltd, 103 Walton Street, Oxford OX2 6EB (tel 01865 559615)

PATTERSON, Dr Linda Joyce; OBE (2000); da of Thomas William Matthew Patterson (d 1981), of Liverpool, and Mary Frances, *née* Ollerhead; *b* 12 April 1951; *Educ* Liverpool Inst HS for Girls, Middx Hosp Med Sch London (MB BS, MRCP); *Partner* Christopher Stephen Green; *Career* pre-registration house offr Stoke-on-Trent and Gloucester 1975–76, SHO/registrar in pathology Charing Cross Hosp 1976–77, SHO in gen med Manchester Royal Infirmary 1978–80, tutor in med Univ of Manchester 1980–82, sr registrar in gen and geriatric med Withington Hosp Manchester and Bolton 1982–84, asst prof of geriatric med Univ of Saskatchewan Canada 1985, conslt physician in geriatric med Burnley Gen Hosp 1986–, clinical dir of med for the elderly Burnley Gen Hosp 1992–95, med dir Burnley Health Care NHS Tst 1995–2000, med dir Cmmn for Health Improvement 2000–; King's Fund travelling scholar; memb: Standing Ctee of Membs RCP 1986–89, Geriatric Med Speciality Ctee RCP 1987–90 and 1994–, Audit Ctee Br Geriatrics Soc 1990–, NW Region Speciality Trg Ctee in Geriatric Med 1992–, Exec Ctee Manchester Med Soc 1993–, GMC 1994–99; FRCPE 1991, FRCP 1993; *Recreations* member of Labour Party, Medical Practitioners Union, Amicus, MEDACT, playing the piano and enjoying opera; *Style*— Dr Linda Patterson, OBE; ✉ Knott Hall, Charlestown, Hebden Bridge, West Yorkshire HX7 6PE (tel 01422 845390); Burnley General Hospital, Casterton Avenue, Burnley, Lancashire BB10 2PQ (tel 01282 474591, fax 01282 474444); Commission for Health Improvement, Finsbury Tower, 103–105 Bunhill Row, London EC1Y 8TG (tel 020 7448 9263, fax 020 7448 9222, e-mail linda.patterson@chi.nhs.uk)

PATTERSON, Dr Mark Jonathan David Damian Lister; s of Alfred Patterson (d 1972), and Frederica Georgina Mary Hammersley, *née* Lister Nicholson; *b* 2 March 1934; *m* 25 Oct 1958, Jane Teresa Mary Scott, da of David Dominic Scott Stokes, of London; 1 s (Damian b 1967), 2 da (Rebecca b 1972, Victoria b 1977); *Career* NHS, Univ of London and MRC 1959–67, conslt haematologist NHS and sr lectr Univ of London 1967–84; conslt haematologist: Bradford Royal Infirmary 1990–94, Royal Cornwall Hosps 1994–96, Leighton District Gen Hosp 1996–; hon conslt haematologist Manchester Royal Infirmary 1997–; Parly candidate (Cons) Ealing N 1974, memb GLC 1969–73 and 1977–81; memb Worshipful Soc of Apothecaries 1965; MB BS, MRCS, LRCP, MRCP; *Recreations* historic restoration of ancient buildings; *Style*— Dr Mark Patterson; ✉ Wolverton Manor, Shorwell, Newport, Isle of Wight PO30 3JS (tel 01983 740609, fax 01983 740977, e-mail markpatterson@btinternet.com)

PATTERSON, Neil Michael; s of Robin Shanks Patterson (d 1964), and Nancy Mearns, *née* Milne (d 1997); *b* 22 March 1951; *Educ* Trinity Coll Glenalmond, Watford Art Sch; *m* 23 July 1983, Doris Karen, da of Ceferino William Boll, of Saguier, Argentina; 1 s (Robin William); *Career* sr writer: Hall Advertising Edinburgh 1972, Saatchi & Saatchi 1973; exec creative dir: TBWA 1983–85, Young & Rubicam 1985–90; creative ptnr Mitchell Patterson Grime Mitchell (formerly Mitchell Patterson Aldred Mitchell) 1990–; river columnist: Trout & Salmon, Trout Fisherman, Fly-Fishing & Fly-Tying; *Television* The Take (Sky Sports); *Books* Chalkstream Chronicle, Distant Waters, The Complete Fly Fisher, The Art of the Trout Fly, The One That Got Away; *Recreations* fly fishing, guitar, cooking; *Clubs* Flyfishers, D & AD; *Style—* Neil Patterson, Esq; ✉ 18 Colet Gardens, London W14 9DH (tel 020 8563 7110); Wilderness Lodge, Elcot, Newbury, Berkshire RG20 8NH; Mitchell Patterson Grime Mitchell, 137 Regent Street, London W1R 8PG (tel 020 7734 8087, fax 020 7434 3081)

PATTERSON, Noel Anthony; s of Arthur Patterson (d 1975), and Doreen Violet, *née* Smith; *b* 29 December 1952; *Educ* Penarth GS, Univ of Wales Coll of Cardiff (BScEcon), LSE (MSc), Queens' Coll Cambridge (MPhil, coach Univ Amateur Boxing Club); *m* Janet Susan, da of Leonard George Frederick Boyle (d 2005); 3 s (Frederick James b 12 June 1990, Arthur Henri b 4 July 1994, Edmund Louis b 20 July 1997); *Career* furniture remover Lyon France 1974–75, exec offr PO Telecommunications London 1977–78, industrial rels offr Alcan Aluminium (UK) Ltd Rogerstone Gwent 1978–80; Mobil Oil Co Ltd: employee rels advsr London 1980–85, terminals mangr Midlands and West 1985–86, gen mangr Gatwick Refuelling Servs Gatwick 1986–87, industrial rels mangr Coryton Refinery 1987–88; employee rels mangr Watney Truman Ltd London 1988–89, human resources mangr Grand Metropolitan Brewing Ltd London 1989–91, employee rels mangr Courage Ltd London 1991–92, dir Patterson James Management Consulting 1993–95, assoc Harold Whitehead & Partners Ltd 1994–95; Matthew Clark plc: dir of personnel 1995–99, sales dir 1999–2000, regnl md 2000–01; HR dir Red Bull UK Ltd 2001–; memb Nat Examining Bd for Supervision and Mgmnt (steering ctee) 1994–98, lectr in mgmnt Richmond upon Thames Coll 1994; memb UK Warehousing Assoc (steering ctee) 1999; regular contrib to: Modern Management, Professional Manager, Progress and numerous other mgmnt jls; assoc Inst of Occupational Safety and Health (AIOSH), MCIM (dip), MInstD 1990, FCIPD 1990, FCMI (FIMgt 1990), FRSA 2004; *Recreations* reading, writing, sports and fatherhood; *Clubs* Richmond Golf, Glamorganshire Golf, London Welsh RFC; *Style—* Noel Patterson, Esq; ✉ 16 St Pauls Road, Richmond, Surrey TW9 2HH (tel 020 8948 2045, e-mail n.patterson@blueyonder.co.uk)

PATTERSON, Prof Paul Leslie; s of Leslie Patterson, of Exeter, and Lilian Anne, *née* Braund; *b* 15 June 1947; *Educ* RAM; *m* 12 Dec 1981, Hazel Rosemary, da of Dr Alexander Wilson, of Winchester; 1 da (Philippa b 1983), 1 s (Alastair b 1986); *Career* composer; dir twentieth century music Univ of Warwick 1976–81; Royal Acad of Music: prof of composition 1972–, head of composition 1985–97, Manson prof of composition 1997–; artistic dir: Exeter Festival 1991–97, PLG Young Composers' Forum 1998–; external examiner: London Coll of Music 1998–2002, RM Sch of Music 1998–2002, Royal Northern Coll of Music 2002–, Colchester Inst 2002–05; music advsr N Devon Festival 1999–2000; visiting prof of composition Christchurch Univ Canterbury 2000–; composer of large-scale choral music incl: Mass of the Sea, Stabat Mater, Te Deum, Requiem, Voices of Sleep, Little Red Riding Hood, Three Little Pigs, Orchestra on Parade, Magnificat Violin Concerto, Millennium Mass, Cello Concerto; other compositions incl: orchestral music, symphony, concertos, chamber music, organ music, film and TV music; performances world-wide by leading musicians; featured composer at festivals incl: Llandaff 1985, Greenwich 1985, PLG 1987, Cheltenham 1988, Three Choirs 1988, Patterson South Bank 1988, Peterborough 1989, Southwark 1989–91, Cheltenham 1990, Exeter 1991; BBC Radio 3 Composer of the Week June 1997; composer in residence: Eng Sinfonia Nottingham 1969–70, SE Arts Canterbury 1981–83, Truro Festival 1992–94, Nat Youth Orch 1997–, Presteigne Festival 2001; cmmns incl: BBC, RPO, LPO, Polish Chamber Orch, Kings Singers, Eng Chamber Orch, London Sinfonietta, Bach Choir, Acad of Saint Martins in the Field, Birmingham Symphony Orch, Nash Ensemble, LMP, OSJ, Residente Orch Holland/Zurich Chamber Orch, Basle Symphony Orch; recordings for: EMI, Hyperion, ASV, Priory, Pearl, Phillips; memb: Arts Cncl Recordings Ctee, BBC Reading Panel, RPS Award Panel; pres RAM Club 1992–94, pres and patron numerous choral socs and choirs; Leslie Boosey Award PRS/RPS 1996; FRAM 1982 (ARAM 1978), FRSA 1989, Hon FLCM 1998; Medal of Honour Miny of Culture Poland 1987; *Recreations* sailing, swimming, supporting Arsenal FC, computers; *Clubs* Brixham Yacht; *Style—* Prof Paul Patterson; ✉ 31 Cromwell Avenue, Highgate, London N6 5HN (tel 020 8348 3711); Royal Academy of Music, London NW1 5HT (tel 020 7873 7379, e-mail musicpp@hotmail.com)

PATTIE, Sir Geoffrey Edwin; kt (1987), PC (1987); o s of late Alfred Edwin Pattie, LDS, of Hove, E Sussex, and late Ada Olive, *née* Carr; *b* 17 January 1936; *Educ* Durham Sch, St Catharine's Coll Cambridge; *m* 1 Oct 1960, Tuëma Caroline, er da of Charles William Eyre-Maunsell (d 1989); 1 s (Andrew Edwin Charles b 1966), 1 da (Jessica Tuëma b 1963, decd); *Career* served TA Queen Victoria's Rifles, later Queen's Royal Rifles then 4 Royal Green Jackets (Capt, Hon Col 1996); called to the Bar Gray's Inn 1964; Parly candidate (Cons) Barking 1966 and 1970, MP (Cons) Chertsey and Walton Feb 1974–97; former memb GLC (Lambeth) and chm ILEA Fin Ctee; vice-chm: All-Pty Ctee on Mental Health 1977–79, Cons Parly Def Ctee 1978–79; Parly under-sec of state: for the RAF 1979–81, for defence procurement 1981–83; min of state: for defence procurement 1983–84, for industry and IT 1984–87; vice-chm (International) Cons Party 1990–97; dir Fairey Group 1987–93, dep chm Cambridge Instruments 1988–91; chm: CDP Nexus 1988–92, GEC Marconi 1996–99 (jt chm 1991–96); communications dir GEC plc 1998–99 (mktg dir 1997–98); sr ptnr Terrington Mgmnt 1999–; *Clubs* Reform, Royal Green Jackets; *Style—* The Rt Hon Sir Geoffrey Pattie

PATTISON, Rev Prof George Linsley; s of George William Pattison (d 1981), and Jean, *née* Allan; *b* 25 May 1950; *Educ* Perse Sch Cambridge, Univ of Edinburgh (MA, BD), Univ of Durham (PhD, DD); *m* 25 Feb 1971, Hilary Christine, da of Robert Gilchrist Cochrane; 2 da (Charlotte Ann b 14 April 1972, Elisabeth Linsley b 20 Feb 1980), 1 s (Neil John Robert b 15 Aug 1976); *Career* ordained: deacon 1977, priest 1978; curate St James Newcastle upon Tyne 1977–80, priest-in-charge St Philip and St James Kimblesworth Co Durham 1980–83, rector Badwell Ash Great Ashfield Hunston and Stowlangtoft with Langham 1983–91, dean of chapel King's Coll Cambridge 1991–2001; assoc prof Univ of Århus 2002–03, Lady Margaret prof Univ of Oxford 2004–, canon Christ Church Cathedral Oxford 2004–; ed Modern Believing 1994–98; visiting research prof Univ of Copenhagen 1997 and 2000, visiting prof Univ of Århus 2005–; memb Advsy Bd Søren Kierkegaard Research Centre Copenhagen; vice-pres Modern Churchpeople's Union; *Books* Art, Modernity and Faith (1991, 2 edn 1997), Kierkegaard: The Aesthetic and the Religious (1992, 2 edn 1999), Kierkegaard on Art and Communication (ed, 1993), Pains of Glass (with Wendy Beckett, 1995), Spirit and Tradition (with Stephen Platten, 1996), Agnosis: Theology in the Void (1996), Kierkegaard and the Crisis of Faith (1997), The End of Theology and the Task of Thinking about God (1998), 'Poor Paris!' Kirkegaard's Critique of the Spectacular City (1998), Kierkegaard: The Self in Society (ed with S Shakespeare, 1998), Anxious Angels (1999), the Later Heidegger (2000), A Short Course in the Philosophy of Religion (2001), Dostoevsky and the Christian Tradition (ed with D Thompson, 2001), Kierkegaard: Religion and the Nineteenth Century Crisis of Culture (2002), Kierkegaard's Upbuilding Discourses (2002), A Short Course in Christian Doctrine (2005), The Philosophy of Kierkegaard (2005), Thinking about God in an Age of Technology (2005); *Style—* The Rev Prof George Pattison; ✉ Priory House, Christ Church, Oxford OX1 1DP (e-mail george.pattison@theology.ox.ac.uk)

PATTISON, Michael Ambrose; CBE (1996); s of Osmond John Pattison (d 1997), and Eileen Susannah, *née* Cullen (d 1995); *b* 14 July 1946; *Educ* Sedbergh, Univ of Sussex; *m* 16 July 1975, Beverley Jean, da of Hugh E Webber (d 1988), of Florida, USA; 1 da (Jenni b 1977); *Career* civil serv: Miny of Overseas Devpt 1968, asst private sec to Min for Overseas Devpt 1970–72, first sec UK perm mission to the UN NY 1974–77, private sec to successive PMs 1979–82, estab offr ODA 1983–85; chief exec RICS 1985–95, dir The Sainsbury Family Charitable Tsts 1995–2006; dir: Surveyors Holdings Ltd 1985–95, Battersea Arts Centre Tst 1988–94; Univ of Greenwich: govr 1989–97, pro-chllr 1994–97; non-exec dir Ordnance Survey 1997–2001; memb Advsy Bd Univ of Nottingham Inst of Engrg Surveying and Space Geodesy 1990–95; hon visiting fell Dept of Valuation and Property Mgmnt City Univ 1990–, Hon DUniv Greenwich 1997; FRSA; *Recreations* golf, cricket, real tennis, local history, countryside, cinema; *Style—* Michael Pattison, Esq, CBE; ✉ 8 Bimport, Shaftesbury, Dorset SP7 8AX

PATTISSON, John Harmer; s of Frederick Edward Pattisson (d 1946), and Louise Mary, *née* Dalton (d 1973); *b* 24 April 1931; *Educ* Radley, Trinity Coll Oxford (MA); *m* 29 March 1958 (m dis 1975), Julia Jane, da of Maj Percy Montagu Nevile (d 1957); 2 s (Edward b 1960, William b 1963); *Career* Nat Serv 2 Lt Oxford & Bucks LI 1950–52, Capt TA 1952–63; Dawnay Day Group Ltd 1955–80 (dir 1964–69, md 1969–80); dir: Hanson Trust Ltd (formerly Wiles Group Ltd) 1960–74, Target Trust Group Ltd 1973–81, J Rothschild & Co Ltd 1980–81, Hanson plc 1981–89, New Court Property Fund Managers Ltd 1984–92, Imperial Group Pension Trust Ltd 1986–96 (chm 1989–96), Imperial Investments Ltd 1987–96 (chm 1989–96), Wassall plc 1988–2000, Allders plc 1993–2000 (chm 1994–2000), Blenheim Group plc 1994–96; chm Fife Gp plc 1997–99, vice-chm Northern Leisure plc 1999–2000; memb Cncl Radley Coll 1965–2005 (vice-chm 1992–2004), govr City Technol Coll Kingshurst 1988–99 (vice-chm 1988–97), memb Cncl Aims of Industry 1990–98, memb Cncl Technol Colleges Tst 1995–99, tstee The Literary Review Tst 1996–2007; hon fell: St Anne's Coll Oxford 1999, Trinity Coll Oxford 2000; FRSA 1995; *Clubs* Boodle's, City of London; *Style—* John H Pattisson, Esq; ✉ 19 Wyke Mark, Dean Lane, Winchester, Hampshire SO22 5DJ (tel 01962 813388, fax 01962 861663, e-mail johnpattisson@hotmail.com)

PATTMAN, Dr Richard Stewart; s of Robert Pearson Pattman, VRD (d 1998), and Joyce Mary, *née* Long (d 1989); *b* 19 April 1950; *Educ* Glasgow Acad, Sedbergh, Univ of Glasgow (MB ChB); *m* 27 April 1976, (Mary) Geraldine, da of John Purcell (d 1983), of Glasgow; 1 s (Stewart John b 1979); *Career* house offr and registrar in gen med Western Infirmary Gartnavel Glasgow 1976, sr registrar in genito-urinary med Royal Infirmary Glasgow 1976–79, conslt in genito-urinary med and clinical lectr to Univ of Newcastle upon Tyne 1979–; ed Oxford Handbook of GUM, HIV and AIDS; FRCPG 1986, FRCP 1991 (MRCP 1976), FFFP 2007 (MFFP 1995); *Recreations* gardening, fishing; *Style—* Dr Richard Pattman; ✉ Department of Genito-Urinary Medicine, Newcastle General Hospital, Westgate Road, Newcastle upon Tyne NE4 6BE (tel 0191 256 3256)

PATTON, Prof Michael Alexander; s of Henry Alexander Patton, of Donaghadee, and Margaret Murray, *née* Drennan; *b* 15 April 1950; *Educ* Campbell Coll Belfast, Pembroke Coll Cambridge (MA), Univ of Edinburgh (MB ChB, MSc); *m* 4 June 1977, Jaqueline Heidi, da of John Pickin, OBE, of Wyck Rissington, Glos; 1 s (Alistair b 10 April 1979), 1 da (Rebecca b 21 Sept 1983); *Career* dir Regnl Genetics Serv SW Thames RHA; St George's Hosp Med Sch: conslt 1986–, sr lectr 1986–92, reader 1992–98, prof 1998–; med advsr to various parent gps for inherited disease, med dir Scientific Ctee Birth Defects Fndn; examiner: Univ of London 1986–, RCPath 1990, Univ of Sheffield 1994, Univ of Manchester 1996 and 2001, Univ of Wales 1999; inspr Human Fertilisation and Embryology Authy 1991–96; chm Ethics Ctee RCPCH 2001–04 (memb 1996–2004), pres Medical Genetics Section RSM 2004–06; conslt TDL Genetics 2002–; memb: Exec Ctee London Genetic Knowledge Park 2002–07, Advsy Bd IKON Warwick Business Sch; Ctee Genetic Interest Gp, Ctee Clinical Genetic Soc; fndr memb Expert Witnesses Inst; hon visiting fell Green Coll Oxford; MInstD, FRCP 1993 (MRCP 1979), FRCPCH 1997; *Books* Contact a Family Directory (1992 and subsequent edns); *Recreations* skiing, sailing, watercolour painting; *Style—* Prof Michael Patton; ✉ 126 Woodlands Road, Little Bookham, Surrey KT23 4HJ (tel 01372 456327, fax 01372 453151); SW Thames Regional Genetic Service, St George's Hospital Medical School, Cranmer Terrace, London SW17 0RE (tel 020 8725 5335, fax 020 8725 3444, e-mail mpatton@sgul.ac.uk)

PAUK, Gyorgy; s of Imre Pauk (d 1944), and Magda Pauk; *b* 26 October 1936; *Educ* Franz Liszt Music Acad Budapest; *m* 19 July 1959, Susan, *née* Mautner; 1 s (Thomas b 19 April 1962), 1 da (Catherine b 13 June 1966); *Career* violinist; as the youngest pupil of the Franz Liszt Music Acad toured numerous countries incl Hungary and Eastern Europe; first prize winner: The Paganini Competition, Marguerite Long/Jacques Thibauld Competition, Munich Sonata Competition; London orchestral and recital debuts 1961; currently performs with maj orchestras of the world under such conductors as: Sir Colin Davies, Antal Dorati, Kondrashin, Lorin Maazel, Rozhdestvensky, Rattle, Previn, Tennstedt, Haitink, Sir George Solti; American debut with the Chicago Symphony Orch leading to subsequent return visits playing with: Cleveland Philadelphia, Los Angeles Philharmonic, Boston Symphony Orch; festival appearances incl: Aspen, Ravinia, Hollywood Bowl, Saratoga; many prizewinning recordings incl works by Bartók (new recording nominated for Grammy 1995), Schubert, Mozart and Brahms; prof of music Royal Acad of Music 1986– (hon memb), artistic dir Mozart Festival in London Wigmore Hall 1991; hon memb Guildhall Sch; awarded The Middle Cross of the Hungarian Republic 1999; *Style—* Gyorgy Pauk, Esq; ✉ c/o Royal Academy of Music, Marylebone Road, London NW1 5HT (tel 020 7873 7373)

PAUL, Alan; *b* 19 July 1954; *Educ* St Paul's, Univ Coll Oxford (MA); *m*; 3 s, 1 da; *Career* ptnr Allen & Overy 1985– (seconded to Panel on Takeovers and Mergers 1985–88); memb Law Soc; *Style—* Alan Paul, Esq

PAUL, Alan Roderick; CMG (1997); s of Roderick Ernest Paul (d 1969), and Hilda May, *née* Choules, of Surrey; *b* 13 May 1950; *Educ* Wallington HS for Boys, ChCh Oxford (scholar, MA), Univ of Cambridge, Univ of Hong Kong; *m* 1979, Rosana Yuen Ling Tam, da of Tam Sui Kwong; 1 da (Christina Mei-En b 1 Dec 1981), 1 s (Jonathan Wing-En b 30 Jan 1985); *Career* Chinese Language Trg Univ of Cambridge and Univ of Hong Kong 1973–75; HM Dip Service: FCO 1972–73 and 1975–77, first sec Beijing 1977–80, head of China section Far Eastern Dept FCO 1980–81, Euro Community Dept FCO 1982–84, head of Chancery The Hague 1984–87 Hong Kong Dept FCO head 1989–91 (dep head 1987–88), dep sr rep Sino Br Jt Liaison Gp 1991–97, sr Br rep Sino Br Jt Liaison Gp (with personal rank of ambass) 1997–99, head of Political and Economic Section of Br Consulate-Gen 1997–2000; dir Exec Access Ltd 2001– (ptnr 2004–); *Recreations* hill climbing, travel, music, literature; *Clubs* Hong Kong, Pacific (Kowloon); *Style—* Alan Paul, Esq, CMG; ✉ c/o Hong Kong Club, Central, Hong Kong (fax 00 852 2530 9357)

PAUL, George William; DL (Suffolk 1991); s of William Stuart Hamilton Paul (d 1984), of Freston Lodge, Ipswich, and Diana Violet Anne, *née* Martin; *b* 25 February 1940; *Educ* Harrow, Wye Coll London (BSc); *m* 1, 1963, Mary Annette (d 1989), da of Col Frank Mitchell, DSO, MC (d 1985); 2 s (Stuart, Oliver), 1 da (Bridget); m 2, 1991, Margaret Joyce, da of F J Hedges (d 1984); *Career* chm: Pauls plc 1985–95, Harrisons and Crosfield plc 1994–97 (chief exec 1987–94, dir 1985–97), Norwich Union 1994–2000 (dir 1990–2000), Jockey Club Estates Ltd 1991–2005, Agricola Holdings Ltd 1998–2000, JPMorgan Fleming Overseas Investment Tst 1998–, Agricola Group Ltd 2000–, Notcutts Ltd 2006–

P

(dir 1998–); dep chm: CGNU plc 2000–02, Aviva plc 2002–05; chm Essex and Suffolk Foxhounds (master 1978–85), High Sheriff Suffolk 1990; *Recreations* country pursuits, travel, sailing; *Clubs* Jockey, Boodle's, Farmers'; *Style*— George Paul, Esq, DL

PAUL, Eur Ing Prof John Poskitt; s of William Boag Paul (d 1962), of Old Kilpatrick, and Maude Meikle, *née* Poskitt (d 1972); *b* 26 June 1927; *Educ* Aberdeen GS, Allan Glens Sch Glasgow, Royal Tech Coll Glasgow (BSc, ARTC, PhD), Univ of Glasgow; *m* 7 Sept 1956, Elizabeth Richardson (d 2004), da of James Richardson Graham (d 1962), of Dalmuir; 2 da (Gillian Anne b 1960, Fiona Helen (Mrs David Williams) b 1968), 1 s (Graham William b 1962); *Career* Univ of Strathclyde: lectr in mechanical engrg 1952, sr lectr 1964, personal prof of bioengrg 1972, prof of bioengrg 1978–92 (now emeritus), head Bioengrg Unit 1980–92; visiting prof West Virginia Univ Morgantown 1969–70; Donald Julius Groen lectr Instn of Mech Engrs 1991; pres Int Soc of Biomechanics 1987–89; memb Ctee: BSI (chm Ctee for Bone and Joint Replacements), ISO (chm Ctee for Bone and Joint Replacements), CEN, MRC, SERC, SHHD, EPSRC, RSE, Royal Acad of Engrg; Medal of Honour Czechoslovak Soc for Mechanics 1990, Carl Hirsch lectr Karolinska Inst Stockholm 1995, Muybridge lectr Int Soc of Biomechanics 1997, Royal Acad of Engrg/Royal Soc of Edinburgh special lectr 1997, Strathclyder of the Year 1997, Marriner Medal Inst of Engrs and Shipbuilders in Scotland 2002; membre d'Honneur Societé de Biomecanique; FIMechE 1971, FISPO 1979, FRSA 1974, FBOA 1975, FRSE 1984, Eur Ing 1990, FIPEM 1991, FREng 1992; *Books* Disability (co-ed, 1979), Computing in Medicine (sr ed, 1982), Biomaterials in Artificial Organs (sr ed, 1984), Influence of New Technology in Medical Practice (sr ed, 1984), Total Knee Replacement (co-ed, 1988), Progress in Bioengineering (sr ed, 1989), Influence of New Technologies in Medical Practice (sr ed, 1991); 70 articles in refereed scientific jls, 80 conf abstracts and 8 book chapters; *Recreations* gardening, formerly rugby and refereeing; *Style*— Eur Ing Prof John P Paul, FRSE, CEng, FREng; ✉ 25 James Watt Road, Milngavie, Glasgow G62 7JX (tel 0141 956 3221, e-mail john.paul.1@btinternet.com); Bioengineering Unit, Wolfson Centre, University of Strathclyde, Glasgow G4 ONW (tel 0141 548 3030, fax 0141 552 6098, e-mail john.paul@strath.ac.uk)

PAUL, Julian Braithwaite; s of Michael Braithwaite Paul, MD (d 2000), of Newchurch, Staffs, and Patricia Elisabeth Ann, *née* Mumm; *b* 18 May 1945; *Educ* Wrekin Coll, St John's Coll Oxford (MA); *m* 3 Nov 1973, Diana, da of Ernest Trevor Davies (d 1981), of Epsom, Surrey; 2 da (Arabella b 1975, Henrietta b 1978), 1 s (Rupert b 1981); *Career* Arthur Andersen & Co Chartered Accountants 1966–71, Citibank NA 1971–74, dep md Banco Hispano Americano Ltd 1974–87, md Guinness Mahon & Co Ltd 1987–90; dep chm: Castle Communications plc 1991–97, Eagle Rock Entertainment Ltd 1997–; non-exec chm: Tele-Cine Cell Group plc 1994–98, Argonaut Games plc 2000–05, Cellcast plc 2005–; non-exec dir: Tiger Books International plc 1994–99, Entertainment Rights plc 1996–, Stagecoach Theatre Arts plc 2001–, Pilat Media Global plc 2002–, Ekay plc 2006–, Edge Performance VCT plc 2006–, Inspired Gaming Gp plc 2006–, Regent Orgn Ltd 2006–; chm of govrs Valence Sch Westerham 1987–; cncllr (Cons) Kent County Cncl (Sevenoaks W) 1985–93; FCA 1979; *Recreations* politics, travel; *Clubs* Carlton, Pilgrims; *Style*— Julian Paul, Esq; ✉ The Mount House, Brasted, Westerham, Kent TN16 1JB (tel 01959 563617, fax 01959 561296, e-mail jpaulco@webspeed.net)

PAUL, Dr (Peter) Michael; s of Thomas James Paul, of Woore, Salop, and Nora, *née* Wilcox; *b* 26 September 1947; *Educ* Queen Elizabeth GS Wakefield, St Andrews Univ (MB), Univ of Manchester (MB ChB); *m* 22 June 1974, Susan Margaret, da of Frank Pickles; *Career* house offr Wythenshaw Hosp Manchester 1973–74, SHO Casualty Dept Westminster Hosp London 1974, vocational trg scheme Aylesbury 1974–77, ptnr in practice White Bungalow Surgery Sunninghill 1977–86, private GP and med dir Gen Med Clinics plc London 1986–2003, private GP and sr ptnr MSA & Co 2003–; med offr Ascot Priory Convent 1977–86, memb Ctee and hon treas Thames Valley Faculty RCGP 1980–86, fndr and hon sec Independent Doctors Forum 1989–96, gen practice trainer, pt/t lectr Red Cross; memb Ctee Ascot Volunteer Bureau 1981–86; DObstRCOG, FPA Cert, MRCGP, memb BMA, FRSM; *Recreations* theatre, reading, walking; *Clubs* RAC; *Style*— Dr Michael Paul; ✉ 285A Kings Road, Chelsea, London SW3 5EW (tel 020 7351 6210); MSA & Company, 79 Harley Street, London W1G 8PZ (tel 0845 644 6672, e-mail michael.paul@msaco.co.uk)

PAUL, Nancy Catherine Trask; da of Frank Stone Trask (d 1983), of Deer Lodge, Montana, USA, and Cora Nichols (d 1964); *b* 1 June 1936; *Educ* Powell County HS, DL Montana, Univ of Montana USA (BA, MA); *m* 1, 17 Sept 1960 (m dis 1982), William J Paul, Jr; 2 s (William James Paul, III b 19 Nov 1962, Michael Justin Paul b 18 June 1971), 1 da (Elisa Anne Paul b 7 Sept 1969); m 2, 11 April 1992, David A Tyrell; *Career* lectr in psychology Univ of Montana 1958–60, assoc mgmnt prof Brunel Univ 1979–; dir: Paul Mgmnt Ltd 1979–89, Excel International Ltd 1989–; author of pubns on: the effects of divorce on men and women, orgns and work in the UK and USA; maker of numerous award winning videos; fndr memb Inst of Transactional Analysis, hon memb Int Inst of Transactional Analysis Assoc; memb: American Acad of Mgmnt, Int OD Network; *Books* The Right to Be You (1985), The Principles of Project Management (1991), Meetings, Your Guide to Making Them Work (1991); *Recreations* mountaineering, classical music; *Style*— Mrs Nancy Paul; ✉ Excel International, 2810 Contour Road, Missoula, Montana 59802, USA (tel and fax 00 1 406 549 4021)

PAUL, Philip; *Career* various news/editorial appts with regnl and nat newspapers until 1960, asst PRO CEGB 1960–68, assoc dir Eric White & Partners PR conslts 1968–70, dep dir of PR The Post Office 1970–76; dir of PR: RICS 1976–78, Royal Pharmaceutical Soc of GB 1978–86; freelance author, journalist and PR/public affrs conslt 1986–, chm Health and Med PR Assoc (HAMPRA) 1992–; memb: Chartered Inst of Journalists, Br Assoc of Journalists, Soc of Authors; DipCAM; FCIPR (MIPR 1960, FIPR 1986), FRSM; *Books* City Voyage: The Story of Erlebach & Co Ltd, Some Unseen Power: Diary of a Ghost Hunter, Murder Under the Microscope: The Story of Scotland Yard's Forensic Science Laboratory; *Recreations* video and still photography, target shooting, motor racing, thinking; *Style*— Philip Paul, Esq; ✉ Upper Benchwood, Guestling Thorn, Hastings, East Sussex TN35 4LU (tel 01424 812847, fax 01424 814625)

PAUL, Richard; *Educ* Bartlett Sch of Architecture and Planning (BSc, Dipl Arch); *Career* architect; Foster Associates: joined 1982, project dir 1985, main bd of dir 1988; Richard Rogers Partnership: joined 1991, assoc dir 1996; *Projects* incl: Hongkong and Shanghai Bank HQ, Century Tower, Stokley Park B3 bldg, King's Cross Masterplan, King's Cross rail terminal, ITN HQ, St Sebastian Convention and Congress Hall Spain, Hanseem Housing S Korea, Potsdamer Platz Masterplan Berlin Germany, Spandau Masterplan Berlin Germany, Treptow Germany, B4/B6 offices Berlin Germany, Saitama Arena, Seol Broadcasting System HQ South Korea, Nippon TV HQ Tokyo Japan, Baby Dome Greenwich, Rome Congress Hall Italy, Chiswick Park Masterplan London; *Style*— Richard Paul, Esq; ✉ Richard Rogers Partnership, Thames Wharf, Rainville Road, London W6 9HA

PAUL, Robert Cameron (Robin); CBE (1996); *b* 7 July 1935; *Educ* Rugby, CCC Cambridge (MA, MEng), UCL (Dip); *m* 1, 1 May 1965, Diana Kathleen, *née* Bruce (d 2001); 2 da (Caroline b 1966, Juliet b 1968); m 2, 12 July 2003, Catherine Frances, *née* Young; *Career* Nat Serv 2 Lt RE BAOR 1953–55; ICI 1959–86 (dep chm ICI Mond Div 1979), dep chm and md Albright & Wilson Ltd 1986–95, chief exec Albright & Wilson plc 1995–97; non-exec dir Courtaulds plc 1994–98; chm Crystal Faraday Partnership 2001–04; pres: Inst of Chemical Engrs 1990–91, Chemical Industries Assoc 1995–97; Hon DEng Univ of Birmingham; FREng 1990 (memb Cncl until 1994), FRAS 2006; *Recreations* music (piano), astronomy; *Clubs* Oriental, Wychwood Golf; *Style*— R C Paul, Esq, CBE, FREng; ✉ 2 Devonshire Place, London W8 5UD (tel 020 7938 4608)

PAUL, Baron (Life Peer UK 1996), of Marylebone in the City of Westminster; Swraj Paul; s of Payare Paul (d 1944), of Jalandhar, India, and Mongwati, *née* Lal; *b* 18 February 1931; *Educ* Univ of Punjab (BSc), MIT (BSc, MSc); *m* 1 Dec 1956, Aruna, da of Ramnath Vij, of Calcutta; 3 s (Hon Ambar, Hon Akash (twins) b 20 Dec 1957, Hon Angad b 6 June 1970), 2 da (Hon Anjli b 12 Nov 1959, Ambika b 1963 d 1968); *Career* dir family owned Apeejay-Surrendra Gp India 1952–66, came to England 1966, estab Natural Gas Tubes Ltd 1968; chm: Caparo Group Ltd 1978–, Caparo Industries plc 1980–, Caparo Inc USA 1988–; pro-chllr Thames Valley Univ 1998–2000, chllr Univ of Wolverhampton 1999–, chllr Univ of Westminster 2006–; memb Bd London Devpt Agency 2000–; Hon PhD American Coll of Switzerland 1986, Hon DSc Univ of Hull 1992, Hon DHL Chapman Univ California 1996, Hon Dr Univ of Bradford 1997, Hon DLit Univ of Westminster 1997, Hon DrUniv of Central England 1999, Hon DSc Univ of Birmingham 1999, Hon PhD Thames Valley Univ 2000, Hon DCS Univ of Hartford USA 2002, Hon Dr State Univ of Mgmnt Moscow 2002, Hon Dr Punjab Tech Univ Jalandhar 2005, Hon PhD Ambedkar Nat Inst of Technol India 2006; Order of Padma Bhushan India 1983; *Books* Indira Gandhi (1985), Beyond Boundaries (1998); *Clubs* MCC, RAC; India: Royal Calcutta Turf, Royal Calcutta Golf, Cricket of India (Bombay); *Style*— The Rt Hon Lord Paul; ✉ Caparo Group Ltd, Caparo House, 103 Baker Street, London W1U 6LN (tel 020 7486 1417, fax 020 7935 3242)

PAULSON, Prof Lawrence C; *b* 20 September 1955, Philadelphia, PA; *Educ* Caltech (BS, Motorola Project Award), Stanford Univ (PhD); *m*; 2 c; *Career* research asst Univ of Edinburgh 1982–83; Univ of Cambridge: asst dir of research 1983–93, lectr 1993–, reader in computational logic 1998–2002, prof of computational logic 2002–; fell Clare Coll Cambridge 1987– (memb Computer Ctee, dir of studies in computer science); delivered numerous lectures worldwide; *Publications* Logic and Computation: Interactive proof with Cambridge LCF (1987), ML for the Working Programmer (1991, 2 edn 1996), Isabelle: A Generic Theorem Prover (1994), Isabelle/HOL: A Proof Assistant for Higher-Order Logic (with Tobias Nipkow and Markus Wenzel, 2002); also numerous refereed articles in learned jls and unrefereed conf papers; *Style*— Prof Lawrence C Paulson; ✉ University of Cambridge Computer Laboratory, William Gates Building, Cambridge CB3 0FD (tel 01223 334623, fax 01223 334678, e-mail lp15@cam.ac.uk)

PAULSON-ELLIS, Jeremy David; s of Christian William Geoffrey Paulson-Ellis (d 1982), and Vivien Joan Paulson-Ellis (d 1966); *b* 21 September 1943; *Educ* Sherborne; *m* 27 April 1973, Jennifer Jill, da of Angus Harkness (d 1991); 1 da (Vivien b 1974), 2 s (Nicholas b 1976, Matthew b 1984); *Career* Citicorp Scrimgeour Vickers International Ltd (formerly Vickers da Costa & Co): joined 1964, ptnr 1970, dir 1974, chm 1985–88; chm: Genesis Investment Management LLP, JP Morgan Japan Investment Tst plc, Mekong Enterprise Fund II; dir: Genesis Emerging Markets Fund Ltd, Genesis Condor Fund Ltd, Genesis Chile Fund 1989–2005, Genesis Malaysia Maju Fund Ltd 1990–2006, Korea Asia Fund Ltd 1991–96, Second India Investment Fund Ltd 1992–2000, Vietnam Fund Ltd 1996–2004; memb Investment Advsy Cncl: Korea International Trust 1982–87, Seoul International Trust (chm) 1985–87, Thailand Fund 1986–88; ind memb Heathrow Airport Consultative Ctee 1984–88; MSI 1970; AMSIA; *Recreations* tennis, travel; *Style*— Jeremy Paulson-Ellis, Esq; ✉ Genesis Investment Management LLP, 21 Knightsbridge, London SW1X 7LY (tel 020 7201 7200, fax 020 7201 7400, e-mail paulsonellis@giml.co.uk)

PAUNCEFORT-DUNCOMBE, Sir Philip Digby; 4 Bt (UK 1859), of Great Brickhill, Buckinghamshire, DL (Bucks 1971); s of Maj Sir Everard Philip Digby Pauncefort-Duncombe, 3 Bt, DSO (d 1971); *b* 18 May 1927; *Educ* Stowe; *m* 4 April 1951, Rachel Moyra, yr da of Maj Henry Gerald Aylmer, gggs of 2 Baron Aylmer; 2 da (Diana (Mrs Jeremy D T West) b 1953, Charlotte b 1967), 1 s (David Philip Henry b 1956); *Heir* s, David Pauncefort-Duncombe; *Career* 2 Lt Grenadier Guards 1946, Hon Maj (ret 1960), RARO, County Cmdt Bucks ACF 1967–70, memb HM Body Guard of Hon Corps of Gentlemen-at-Arms 1979–97, Harbinger 1993–97; High Sheriff of Bucks 1987–88; pres St John Ambulance Bucks 1984–99; CStJ 1992 (OStJ 1986); *Clubs* Cavalry and Guards; *Style*— Sir Philip Pauncefort-Duncombe, Bt, DL; ✉ Church Close, Church Lane, Great Brickhill, Buckinghamshire MK17 9AE (tel 01525 261205, fax 01525 261505)

PAVORD, Anna; da of Arthur Vincent Pavord (d 1989), of Abergavenny, Gwent, and Christabel Frances, *née* Lewis (d 1978); *b* 20 September 1940; *Educ* Abergavenny HS for Girls, Univ of Leicester (BA); *m* Trevor David Oliver Ware, s of John Ronald Ware; 3 da (Oenone b 15 Dec 1967, Vanessa b 7 June 1970, Tilly b 8 Dec 1974); *Career* copywriter Lintas Advertising Agency 1962–63, Line-Up BBC TV 1963–70 (prodn asst rising to dir), contrib Observer 1970–92, gardening corr The Independent 1986–, assoc ed Gardens Illustrated 1993–; writer and presenter Flowering Passions (10-part series, Channel 4); Gold Veitch Meml Medal RHS) 1991; memb: Gardens Panel Nat Tst 1996–2006 (chm 2002–06), English Heritage Parks and Gardens Panel 2001–; Hon DLitt Univ of Leicester 2005; *Books* Foliage (1990), The Flowering Year (1991), Gardening Companion (1992), The Border Book (1994), The New Kitchen Garden (1996), The Tulip (1999), Plant Partners (2001), The Naming of Names (2005); *Recreations* gardening, sailing, rainforests in Central America, Evelyn Waugh, black and white films; *Style*— Ms Anna Pavord; ✉ The Independent, Independent House, 191 Marsh Wall, London E14 9RS (tel 020 7293 2000, fax 020 7293 2435)

PAWLAK, His Hon Judge Witold Expedyt; s of Felicjan Pawlak, and Jolanta Pawlak; *b* March 1947; *Educ* St Joseph's Coll Beulah Hill, Trinity Coll Cambridge (MA); *m* 1971, Susan, *née* Dimsdale; 1 da (Lucy b 28 Feb 1980), 1 s (Nicholas b 1 Jan 1984); *Career* called to the Bar Inner Temple 1970; circuit judge 2004–; *Style*— His Hon Judge Pawlak; ✉ Wood Green Crown Court, Woodall House, Lordship Lane, Wood Green, London N22 5LF (tel 020 8826 4100)

PAWLEY, Prof (Godfrey) Stuart; s of George Charles Pawley (d 1956), of Bolton, Lancs, and Winifred Mary, *née* Wardle (d 1989); *b* 22 June 1937; *Educ* Bolton Sch, Univ of Cambridge (MA, PhD); *m* 29 July 1961, Anthea Jean, da of Rev Alan Miller (d 1981), of Northwich, Cheshire; 2 s (Philip b 1963, Graham b 1967), 1 da (Alison b 1965); *Career* Univ of Edinburgh: lectr 1964–69, reader 1970–85, prof of computational physics 1985–2002, emeritus prof 2002–; guest prof Aarhus Univ Denmark 1969–70; FRSE 1975, FRS 1992; *Books* An Introduction to OCCAM-2 Programming (jtly); *Recreations* choral singing, hill walking; *Clubs* Scottish Rock Garden (Seed Reception Mangr); *Style*— Prof G Stuart Pawley, FRS, FRSE; ✉ School of Physics, Kings Buildings, University of Edinburgh, Edinburgh EH9 3JZ (fax 0131 650 7174)

PAWLOWSKI, Prof Mark; s of Kazimierz Pawlowski, of London, and Maria Zwienislawa, *née* Konkol; *b* 15 September 1953; *Educ* St Benedict's Sch Ealing, Univ of Warwick (LLB), Wadham Coll Oxford (BCL); *m* 19 April 1986, Lidia Maria, da of Capt Jerzy de Barbaro (of the Barbaro family, Venice); *Career* called to the Bar Middle Temple 1978; in practice at Chancery Bar 1980–91; Univ of Greenwich (formerly Thames Poly): pt/t lectr 1980–83, lectr 1983–84, sr lectr 1984–95, reader in property law 1995–99, prof of property law 1999–; visiting prof UCL 1990–, memb convocation Wadham Coll Oxford 1983; ed: Jl of Rent Review and Lease Renewal, Landlord and Tenant Review; author of numerous articles in learned jls on property, landlord and tenant law 1984–; Sweet & Maxwell Law prizewinner 1974; memb: Middle Temple, Soc of Public Teachers of Law, Assoc of Law Teachers, Br Polish Legal Assoc; ACIArb 1990; *Books* Casebook on Rent Review and Lease Renewal (with Diana Brahams, 1986), The Forfeiture of Leases (1993), Casebook on Landlord and Tenant Law (with James Brown, 1995), Law Q & A, Landlord and Tenant (with James Brown, 1995, 3 edn, 2005), The Doctrine of Proprietary Estoppel (1996), Leasing Commercial Premises (1999), Undue Influence and the Family Home (with James Brown, 2002), Kenilworth - Portrait of a Town & Castle (with John H Drew, 2003); *Recreations* tennis, gardening, walking, travel; *Style*— Prof Mark Pawlowski; ✉ Department of Law, University of Greenwich, Queen Mary Court, Greenwich Maritime Campus, 30 Park Row, London SE10 9LS (tel 020 8331 9040, fax 020 8331 8473, e-mail m.pawlowski@gre.ac.uk); Pepys' Chambers, 17 Fleet Street, London EC4Y 1AA (tel 020 7936 2710, fax 020 7936 2501)

PAWSEY, James Francis; s of Capt William John Pawsey (d 1941), of Coventry, and Mary Victoria, *née* Mumford (d 1958); *b* 21 August 1933; *Educ* Coventry Tech Sch, Coventry Tech Coll; *m* 1956, Cynthia Margaret, da of Arthur John Francis (d 1990), of Coventry; 6 s (Mark, Michael, Gregory, Clive, Philip, Adrian); *Career* MP (Cons): Rugby 1979–83, Rugby and Kenilworth 1983–97; memb Exec Ctee 1922 Ctee 1989–97; chm Select Ctee of the Parly Cmmn for Admin; PPS: DES 1982–83, DHSS 1983–84, NI Office 1984–86; vice-chm Int Parly Union, chm Cons Backbench Educn Ctee 1985–97, former chm W Midlands Gp of Cons MPs; memb: Rugby RDC 1964–73, Rugby Borough Cncl 1973–75, Warwickshire CC 1974–79; *Books* The Tringo Phenomenon; *Recreations* gardening; *Style*— James Pawsey, Esq

PAWSEY, John; s of Albert Pawsey, and Doris Pawsey; *Educ* Brentwood Sch (head of house, capt of cricket, Essex Co youth cricketer); *Career* managing ed Leslie Frewin Publishers 1965–69, assoc ed Reader's Digest 1969–71, dir Elm Tree Books Hamish Hamilton 1971–73, dir Mitchell Beazley Marketing Ltd 1973–76, prop John Pawsey Literary Agency 1981–; *Recreations* reading, writing, watching cricket; *Style*— John Pawsey, Esq

PAWSEY, Karol Anne; da of Hubert Sydney Pawsey, of Thurrock, Essex, and Kathleen Ada, *née* Jordan; *b* 26 July 1963; *Educ* Grays Sch Essex, Glos Coll of Art Cheltenham (BA, CNAA distinction for thesis); *Career* art dealer; with Fischer Fine Art London 1985–87, dir Curwen Gallery 1988–96 (joined 1987), gallery dir Theo Waddington Fine Art London 1996–; *Style*— Ms Karol Pawsey; ✉ 361 Queenstown Road, Battersea, London SW8 (tel 020 7627 1659); Theo Waddington Fine Art, 5A Cork Street, London W1X 1PB (tel 020 7494 1584, fax 020 7287 0926)

PAWSON, Anthony John Dalby; s of Donald Pawson, and Kathleen, *née* Goodwin; *b* 14 October 1946; *Educ* Kent Coll Canterbury, City Univ (BSc); *m* 1969, Kathleen, *née* Chisholm (d 2004); 1 s, 1 da; *Career* MOD: joined 1967, private sec to Chief of Air Staff 1978–80, first sec UK Delgn to NATO 1981–83, private sec to Sec of State for NI 1990–92, RCDS 1992, asst under sec of state (fleet support) 1993–95; under sec (overseas and defence) Cabinet Office 1995–97, DG mktg MOD 1997–98, DG defence export services MOD 1998–2003, DG of corporate communication 2003–04, dep chief of def intelligence 2004–; *Recreations* cricket, rugby; *Clubs* Tunbridge Wells Rugby, Borderers' Cricket; *Style*— Anthony Pawson, Esq

PAWSON, John; s of Jim Pawson (d 1990) and Winifred, *née* Ward (d 1991); *b* 6 May 1949; *Educ* Eton, AA Sch of Architecture; *m* 20 Sept 1989, Catherine, da of Frederick Berning; 2 s (Caius b 1986, Benedict b 1990); *Career* architect; former experience working in family's textile mill Yorks, subsequently lived in Japan for several years, returned to London as architectural student AA, in private architectural practice 1981–; projects incl: apartment for the writer Bruce Chatwin, flagship store for fashion designer Calvin Klein, airport lounges for Cathay Pacific Hong Kong, retail devpt 250 Brompton Rd London, Cistercian Monastery in Czech Repub; *Publications* subject of John Pawson (1992, updated and expanded edn 1998), Critic vol 3 (1996), minimum (1996, mini edn 1998), John Pawson Works (2000), Living and Eating (with Annie Bell, 2001), John Pawson - Themes and Projects (2002); *Style*— John Pawson, Esq; ✉ Unit B, 70–78 York Way, London N1 9AG (tel 020 7837 2929, fax 020 7837 4949, e-mail email@johnpawson.com)

PAXMAN, HE (Timothy) Giles; LVO (1989); s of Arthur Keith Paxman, and Joan McKay, *née* Dickson; bro of Jeremy Paxman, *qv*; *b* 15 November 1951; *m* 1980, Segolene Claude Marie; 3 da; *Career* diplomat; with DOE 1974–78, Ecole Nationale d'Administration Paris 1978–79, with Dept of Tport 1979–80, first sec UKREP Brussels 1980–84, EC Dept (External) FCO 1980–84, Southern European Dept FCO 1986–88, head of Chancery Singapore 1988–91, dep head Assessments Staff Cabinet Office 1991–93, cnsllr (economic and commercial affrs) Rome 1994–98, cnsllr (political and institutional affrs) UKREP Brussels 1999–2002, min and dep head of mission Paris 2002–05, ambass to Mexico 2005–; *Style*— HE Mr Giles Paxman, LVO; ✉ c/o Foreign & Commonwealth Office (Mexico City), King Charles Street, London SW1A 2AH

PAXMAN, Jeremy Dickson; s of Arthur Keith Paxman, formerly of Yorks, now resident Qld, Aust, and Joan McKay, *née* Dickson, of Yorks; bro of HE Giles Paxman, LVO, *qv*; *b* 11 May 1950; *Educ* Malvern Coll, St Catharine's Coll Cambridge (exhibitioner); *Career* journalist Northern Ireland 1974–77, BBC Tonight 1977–79, Panorama (BBC1) 1979–84; presenter: Six O'Clock News (BBC1) 1985–86, Breakfast Time (BBC1) 1986–89, Newsnight (BBC2) 1989–, Did You See? (BBC2) 1991–93, University Challenge (BBC2) 1994–, You Decide - with Paxman (BBC1) 1995–96, Start the Week (Radio 4) 1998–2002; numerous contribs to radio, newspapers and magazines; RTS Int Current Affairs Award 1984, Richard Dimbleby Award BAFTA 1996 and 2000, RTS Interviewer of the Year 1997 and 1998, Variety Club Media Personality of the Year 1999, RTS Journalism Presenter of the Year 2002; Hon PhD: Univ of Leeds 1999, Univ of Bradford 1999; hon fell: St Catharine's Coll Cambridge, St Edmund Hall Oxford; *Books* A Higher Form of Killing (jtly, 1982), Through the Volcanoes (1985), Friends in High Places (1990), Fish, Fishing and the Meaning of Life (1994), The English: A Portrait of a People (1998), The Political Animal: An Anatomy (2002), On Royalty (2006); *Recreations* fly fishing, mountains; *Style*— Jeremy Paxman, Esq; ✉ c/o Capel & Land Ltd, 29 Wardour Street, London W1D 6PS

PAY, Antony Charles; s of Arthur Morris Pay, of London, and Charlotte Pay; *b* 21 February 1945; *Educ* Leyton Co HS, Corpus Christi Coll Cambridge (MA), LRAM 1962; *m* 14 April 1980, Suki, da of Louis Towb, of Newcastle; 2 s (Sam b 24 April 1981, Mungo b 20 Aug 1984); *Career* principal clarinet and fndr memb London Sinfonietta 1968–83; principal clarinet: Royal Philharmonic Orch 1968–78, Acad of St Martin-in-the-Fields 1979–84; prof of Clarinet Guildhall Sch of Music and Drama 1982–90; memb: Nash Ensemble 1968–83, Tuckwell Wind Quintet 1973–77; soloist with many orchestras incl: RPO, LPO, Philharmonia, Berlin Radio Orch, San Francisco Symphony, RAI Torino, Acad of St Martin-in-the-Fields, London Sinfonietta; conducted: London Sinfonietta, Acad of St Martin-in-the-Fields, Philharmonia, Royal Philharmonic, San Diego Symphony, Stockholm Philharmonic, music teacher at: Accademia Perosi Biella Italy, Accademia Chigiana Siena Italy; numerous recordings of clarinet concerti and various chamber music discs; Hon RAM 1986; *Recreations* reading, computers; *Style*— Antony Pay, Esq; ✉ c/o Allied Artists, 42 Montpelier Square, London SW7 1JZ

PAYKEL, Prof Eugene Stern; s of Joshua Paykel (d 1962), and Eva, *née* Stern; *b* 9 September 1934; *Educ* Auckland GS NZ, Univ of Otago (MB ChB, MD), Univ of Cambridge (MD), Univ of London (DPM); *m* 7 July 1969, Margaret, da of John Melrose (d 1966); 2 s (Nicholas b 1971, Jonathan b 1973); *Career* registrar then sr registrar Maudsley Hosp London 1962–65, asst prof of psychiatry and co-dir (later dir) Depression Res Unit Yale Univ 1966–71, prof of psychiatry St George's Hosp Med Sch Univ of London 1977–85 (conslt and sr lectr 1971–75, reader 1975–77), prof of psychiatry Univ of Cambridge and fell Gonville & Caius Coll 1985–2001 (emeritus prof and emeritus fell 2001–); ed Psychological Med 1994–2006; pres Collegium Internationale Neuropsychopharmacologicum 2000–02; pres: Br Assoc for Psychopharmacology 1982–84 (hon sec 1979–82), Marcé Soc 1992–94; chief scientist advsr Mental Illness Res Liaison Gp DHSS 1984–88, memb Neuro Sciences Bd MRC 1981–85 and 1995–99, tstee Mental Health Fndn 1988–95, chm Jt Ctee on Higher Psychiatric Trg 1991–95 (hon sec 1988–90), chm Pharmacopsychiatry Section and regnl rep World Psychiatric Assoc 1992–99; ed Jl of Affective Disorders 1979–93; formerly examiner: Univ of Edinburgh, Univ of Nottingham, Univ of Manchester, Univ of London, Chinese Univ of Hong Kong; vice-pres RCPsych 1994–96 (examiner, chm Social and Community Psychiatry Section 1984–88, memb Cncl, memb Exec and Fin Ctee and various other ctees); Foundations Fund Prize for Res in Psychiatry 1978, second prize Anna Monika Stiftung 1985, ECNP-Lilly Clinical Neuroscience Award 2001; Maudsley lectr RCPsych 1988; MRCPEd 1960, FRCP 1977 (MRCP 1961), FRCPEd 1978, fndr FMedSci 1998, Hon FRCPsych 2001 (MRCPsych 1971, FRCPsych 1977); *Books* The Depressed Woman (1971), Psychopharmacology of Affective Disorders (1979), Monoamine Oxidase Inhibitors - the State of the Art (1981), Handbook of Affective Disorders (1982, 2 edn 1992), Community Psychiatric Nursing for Neurotic Patients (1983), Depression - an Integrated Approach (1989), Prevention in Psychiatry (1994); *Recreations* opera, music, theatre; *Style*— Prof Eugene Paykel; ✉ Department of Psychiatry, University of Cambridge, Douglas House, 18E Trumpington Road, Cambridge CB2 8AH (tel 01223 741930, fax 01223 741929)

PAYNE, Anthony Edward; s of Edward Alexander Payne (d 1958), and Muriel Margaret Elsie, *née* Stroud (d 1991); *b* 2 August 1936; *Educ* Dulwich Coll, Univ of Durham (BA); *m* 24 Sept 1966, Jane Marian, da of Gerald Manning (d 1987); *Career* composer; visiting Milhaud prof of music Mills Coll Oakland California 1983, teacher in composition NSW Conservatorium Sydney Aust 1986 and Univ of West Australia 1996; memb: Soc for the Promotion of New Music (chm 1969–71), Macnaghten Concerts Soc (chm 1965–67), Myra Hess Tst, Boise Mendelssohn Fndn, Br Acad of Composers and Songwriters, Musicians Benevolent Fund, RVW Tst; Hon DMus: Univ of Birmingham 2001, Kingston Univ 2003; FRCM 2005; *Works* incl: Phoenix Mass 1968–72, Paean (for solo piano) 1971, Concerto for Orchestra 1974, The World's Winter (for soprano and 8 players) 1976, String Quartet 1978, The Stones and Lonely Places Sing (for 7 players) 1979, The Song of the Clouds (for oboe and orchestra) 1980, A Day in the Life of a Mayfly (for 6 players) 1981, Evening Land (for soprano and piano) 1981, Spring's Shining Wake (for chamber orchestra) 1981, Songs and Seascapes (for strings) 1984, The Spirit's Harvest (for orchestra) 1985, The Song Streams in the Firmament (for 6 players) 1986, Half Heard in the Stillness (for orchestra) 1987, Consort Music for String Quintet 1987, Sea Change (for 7 players) 1988, Time's Arrow (for orchestra) 1990, Symphonies of Wind and Rain (for chamber orchestra) 1991, A Hidden Music (for chamber orchestra) 1992, The Seeds Long Hidden..... Orchestral Variations 1994, Empty Landscape - Heart's Ease (for 6 players) 1995, completion of Elgar's Third Symphony 1994–97, Piano Trio 1998, Scenes from The Woodlanders (for soprano and 4 players) 1999, Of Knots and Skeins (for violin and piano) 2000, Twixt Heaven and Charing Cross (for unaccompanied choir) 2001, Visions and Journeys (for orchestra) 2002, Poems of Edward Thomas (for soprano and 4 players) 2003, Storm Chorale (for solo violin) 2003, Horn Trio 2005, completion of Elgar's Sixth Pomp and Circumstance 2005, Windows on Eternity (for chamber orchestra) 2006, Piano Quintet 2007; *Books* Schoenberg (1968), Frank Bridge Radical and Conservative (1984), Elgar's Third Symphony, The Story of the Reconstruction (1998); *Recreations* films, British countryside; *Style*— Anthony Payne, Esq; ✉ 2 Wilton Square, London N1 3DL (tel 020 7359 1593, fax 020 7226 4369, e-mail paynecomp@yahoo.co.uk)

PAYNE, Prof Anthony Philip; s of Philip Charles Payne, and Pamela Burgoyne, *née* Daniels (d 1982); *b* 9 July 1947; *Educ* Eastbourne GS, Univ of Reading (BSc), Univ of Birmingham (PhD); *m* 28 July 1970, Ruth Mary, da of Donald Jack Beake; 2 s (Christopher Jeremy b 7 Nov 1977, Alexander Richard b 24 Jan 1980); *Career* MRC jr res fell Dept of Anatomy Univ of Birmingham 1971–73; Dept of Anatomy Univ of Glasgow: temp lectr 1973–76, lectr 1976–84, sr lectr 1984–94, head 1993– (acting head 1990–92), prof 1994–; memb Editorial Bd Jl of Anatomy 1993–; memb: The Anatomical Soc (memb Cncl 1993–), Euro Neuroscience Assoc, Soc for Endocrinology, Soc for the Study of Fertility; *Books* Social Behaviour in Vertebrates (1976), Animal Behaviour (consulting ed, 1976 and 1980); *Recreations* reading, ornithology; *Style*— Prof Anthony Payne; ✉ Neuroscience and Biomedical Systems, Institute of Biomedical and Life Sciences, Thomson Building, University of Glasgow, Glasgow G12 8QQ

PAYNE, Dr Christopher Charles; OBE (1997); s of Rupert George Payne (d 1990), and Evelyn Violet, *née* Abbott (d 1981); *b* 15 May 1946; *Educ* Bexley GS, Wadham Coll Oxford (minor scholar, MA, Christopher Welch scholar, sr scholar, DPhil); *m* 1 Sept 1969, Margaret Susan, da of William Roy Street; 1 da (Katherine Ruth b 11 Nov 1970), 1 s (Robert James b 22 Dec 1971); *Career* post doctoral fell Dept of Microbiology Univ of Otago NZ 1972–73, sr scientific offr NERC Unit of Invertebrate Virology Oxford 1973–77; Glasshouse Crops Res Inst (GCRI) Littlehampton: head Insect Virus Section 1977–83, head Entomology and Insect Pathology Dept 1983–87; head Crop and Environment Protection Div AFRC East Malling 1987–90, chief exec Horticulture Res Int Wellesbourne 1990–99; prof of horticulture and landscape Univ of Reading 1999–2003, visiting prof Sch of Plant Sciences Univ of Reading 2003–07, conslt and author 2003–; pres: Soc for Invertebrate Pathology 1992–94, Assoc of Applied Biologists 1995–96; hon prof: Dept of Biological Sciences Univ of Warwick 1991–99, Sch of Biological Sciences Univ of Birmingham 1995–99; chm Assured Produce Co 2001–06, dir Assured Food Standards 2003–06, sr exec Nat Horticultural Forum 2004–05; tstee Royal Botanic Gardens Kew 1997–2004; FIHort 1991; *Books* Dictionary and Directory of Animal, Plant and Bacterial Viruses (with F Brown and R Hull, 1989); *Recreations* cycling, walking, gardening, military history; *Clubs* Farmers', Cyclists' Touring; *Style*— Dr Chris Payne, OBE; ✉ Hall View, Natland, Kendal, Cumbria LA9 7QQ (tel 01539 561980, e-mail oldthatch@btinternet.com)

PAYNE, Prof David Neil; CBE (2004); *Career* dir Optoelectronics Res Centre Univ of Southampton; co-fndr and dir York Technology and the York Gp; co-fndr, dir and chm Southampton Photonics Inc (now SPI Lasers plc); res interests in optical communications 1969–; frequently invited speaker to major int confs especially in USA and Japan; holder of 23 patents; published over 538 papers; memb Royal Norwegian Soc of Sciences and Letters 2003; FRS 1992, FRSA, fell Optical Soc of America 1996, FREng 2005; *Awards* Electronics Divisional Bd Premium of IEE (5 times), Gyr and Landis Commemorative Prize (twice), best paper Euro Conf on Optical Communications, Academic Enterprise Award 1982, Queens Award for Industry 1986, Tobie Award, John Tyndall Award (USA) 1991, Rank Prize Fund 1991, Japanese Computers and Communications Prize 1993, Benjamin Franklin Medal (USA) 1998, ISI Certificiate for one of world's most cited authors 2000, Basic Research Award Eduard Rhein Fndn (Germany) 2001, Mountbatten Medal IEE 2001, Kelvin Medal of the Eight UK Engineering Institutions 2004; *Style*— Prof David Payne, CBE, FRS, FREng; ✉ Optoelectronics Research Centre, Building 46, University of Southampton, Southampton SO17 1BJ (tel 023 8059 4521, fax 023 8059 3142, e-mail dnp@orc.soton.ac.uk)

PAYNE, Ian Philip Milner; s of Philip Stuart Payne (d 1977), of Nottingham, and Joyce Marian Milner (1964); *b* 4 October 1944, Nottingham; *Educ* Oundle; *m* 22 July 1967, Julia Elizabeth; 1 s (Myles Philip Milner), 2 da (Nicola Elizabeth, Sara Louise); *Career* admitted slr 1968; Freeth Cartwright & Sketchley (now Freeth Cartwright LLP): ptnr 1972–, sr ptnr 1992–, also head Commercial Dept; memb Law Soc; *Recreations* skiing, golf, squash, tennis, music, shooting; *Clubs* RAC; *Style*— Ian Payne, Esq; ✉ Freeth Cartwright LLP,

P

Cumberland Court, 80 Mount Street, Nottingham NG1 6HH (tel 0115 935 0605, fax 0115 859 9642, e-mail ian.payne@freethcartwright.co.uk)

PAYNE, Jeremy John Ames; s of Cdr Douglas Edmund Payne, RN (d 1976), and Doreen Nancy, *née* Ames; *b* 10 March 1946; *Educ* Brentwood Sch; *m* 1, 1969, Lynn Peta, da of Sidney Roskams; m 2, 1974, Carole Joy, da of Roy Bailey; 1 da (Lisa Marie b 12 May 1976); m 3, 1982, Susan Rosemary, da of Sir Austin Bide; 2 s (Thomas James b 21 Dec 1982, William Jeremy b 19 June 1989); *Career* reporter West Essex Gazette 1964–66; with: NZ Broadcasting Corp 1966–68, Royal NZ Navy 1968–69, Caltex Oil Australia 1970–71; freelance journalist London 1972–74, TV presenter and prodr South Pacific TV 1974–79; with: HTV West News 1979–80, Anglia TV News and Current Affrs 1981–86; HTV West: ed of current affrs 1986–92, head of factual 1993–94, dir of progs 1995–97, md 1997–2000; md HTV Gp Ltd 2000–04, media conslt 2004–; memb Bd South West Screen 2000–06, vice-chm Culture South West 2002–06, tstee South West Film and Television Archive; memb Wilts CC Members Allowances Panel, jt pres Wilts Avon and Glos Red Cross*Awards* Ambrose Fleming Award for contribution to television, nominated NZ Feltex Award 1977, winner of NY Film and TV Awards for current affrs progs 1988 and 1992; *Recreations* walking, golf; *Style*— Jeremy Payne, Esq; ✉ South West Screen, St Bartholomews Court, Lewins Mead, Bristol, BS7 5BT

PAYNE, Keith Howard; s of Sydney William John Payne (d 1990), and Jean Emily, *née* Blower (d 1966); *b* 16 July 1937; *Educ* Shooters Hill GS; *m* 1, Dec 1972 (m dis); m 2, 23 Nov 1984, Tania Jeannette, da of Frank John Trevisani; 1 da (Francesca Jean b 13 April 1987); *Career* Nat Serv personal staff Dep SACEUR SHAPE Paris 1955–57; fin journalist The Times 1958–68 (first banking 1965–68); Charles Barker City 1968–91: dir 1970–74, asst md 1974–76, md 1976–80, dep chief exec and vice-chm 1980–84, dep chm 1984–91; dir Charles Barker Ltd 1988–92; dep chm: Georgeson & Co Ltd 1992–95, Tavistock Communications Ltd 1995–; Freedom Nova Scotia Province (following journalistic visit with The Times) 1965; MIPR; *Recreations* swimming, walking, theatre; *Style*— Keith Payne, Esq, MIPR; ✉ Tavistock Communications Limited, 1 Angel Court, London EC2R 7HX (tel 020 7600 2288, fax 020 7600 5084)

PAYNE, Michael Anthony; s of late Albert John Payne, and Beryl Kathleen Cavey, *née* Slater; *b* 2 September 1939; *Educ* Stowe, City of Westminster Coll, Open Univ (BA); *m* 1965, Elizabeth Harvieston, da of late Alan Brown, of Scotland; 1 da (Sophie b 1968), 1 s (Toby b 1970); *Career* Nat Serv 2 Lt Royal Regt of Artillery 1960–62, gunner HAC TA, Capt 254 FD Regt RA TA; co sec: Hill Samuel and Co (Jersey) Ltd 1978–88, Hill Samuel Jersey Ltd 1984–95, Hill Samuel Bank (Jersey) Ltd; dir: Hill Samuel (CI) Tst Co Ltd 1979–95, Hill Samuel Fund Mangrs (Jersey) Ltd 1982–95; mangr private clients Mourant du Feu & Jeune 1995–2004 (partnership sec 1998–2001); pres CI Dist Soc of Certified Accountants 1983–84; Hon ADC to Lieut Govr of Jersey 1990–95, memb CICB Jersey 1998–; FCCA, MCMI; *Recreations* historical reading, glass engraving; *Clubs* HAC, United (Jersey); *Style*— Michael Payne, Esq; ✉ 3 Ashley Close, Bagatelle Road, St Saviour, Jersey JE2 7TY (fax 01534 610789)

PAYNE, (Geoffrey John) Nicholas; s of John Laurence Payne (d 1961), and Dorothy Gwendoline, *née* Attenborough; *b* 4 January 1945; *Educ* Eton, Trinity Coll Cambridge (BA); *m* 6 Jan 1986, Linda Jane, da of Donald Wallace Adamson (d 1992), of Bristol; 2 s (Ralph John Anthony b 1986, Oliver Nicholas Pearsall b 1988); *Career* fin asst Royal Opera House 1968–70, subsid offr Arts Cncl of GB 1970–76, fin controller WNO 1976–82, gen admin Opera North 1982–93, artistic co-ordinator Leeds Festival 1990, dir Royal Opera 1993–98, gen dir ENO 1998–2002, dir Opera Europa 2003–; hon memb Guildhall Sch of Music and Drama, hon memb Royal Northern Coll of Music, Hon Dr Leeds Metropolitan Univ; *Style*— Nicholas Payne, Esq; ✉ tel 020 7713 9055, e-mail nicholas.payne@opera-europa.org)

PAYNE, Robert Gardiner; s of Dr Robert Orlando Payne (d 1989), and Frances Elisabeth, *née* Jackson (d 1987); *b* 12 July 1933; *Educ* Lady Barn House Sch, Packwood Haugh, Clifton, Trinity Hall Cambridge (MA); *m* 11 April 1964, Diana Catalina, da of Rupert Henry Marchington, of Alderley Edge, Cheshire; 2 da (Frances Patricia b 1967, Emily Diana b 1972), 1 s (Philip Robert b 1968); *Career* Nat Serv 2 Lt RA 1952–54; admitted slr 1961; ptnr: Skelton and Co (Manchester) 1963–66, March Pearson and Skelton 1966–91, Pannone March Pearson (now Pannone & Partners) 1992–2002; chm: Gaddum Centre, Edward Mayes Tst; *Recreations* opera, tennis, skiing, walking; *Style*— Robert Payne, Esq; ✉ Bradford Lodge, Bradford Lane, Over Alderley, Macclesfield, Cheshire SK10 4UE (tel 01625 583156)

PAYTON, Michael; s of Geoffrey Payton (d 1983), and Pamela Carey, *née* Miller-Kerr; *b* 8 June 1944, Llandrindod, Wells; *Educ* Felstead Sch (exhibitioner); *m* 25 Aug 1977, Sally; 2 da (Anna b 1 Feb 1978, Lucy b 17 Dec 1980); *Career* admitted slr 1966; sr ptnr Clyde & Co 1984– (ptnr 1971–); chm Slrs' Indemnity Mutual Insurance Assoc 1984–, chm Exec Ctee Br Maritime Law Assoc 1986–, memb Law Soc 1967–; Sr Ptnr of the Year Legal Business Awards 2004; *Recreations* France, horse racing; *Clubs* Garrick, MCC; *Style*— Michael Payton, Esq; ✉ Clyde & Co, 51 Eastcheap, London EC3M 1JP (tel 020 7623 1244, fax 020 7623 5457, e-mail michael.payton@clydeco.com)

PEACE, David Neil; s of Basil Dunford Peace, of Ossett, W Yorks, and Felicity Wilkinson, MBE; *b* 9 April 1967; *Educ* Batley GS, Wakefield Dist Coll, Manchester Poly (BA); *m* 1996, Izumi, *née* Goto; 1 s (George Basil b 1997), 1 da (Emi b 2000); *Career* writer; *Awards* Cognac Prix du Roman Noir 2002, Granta Best of Young British Novelists list 2003, James Tait Black Award 2004; *Books* Nineteen Seventy-Four (1999), Nineteen Seventy-Seven (2000), Nineteen Eighty (2001), Nineteen Eighty-Three (2002), GB84 (2004); *Style*— David Peace, Esq; ✉ c/o Mr William Miller, English Agency (Japan) Ltd, Tokyo, Japan; c/o Faber & Faber Ltd, 3 Queen Square, London WC1N 3AU

PEACE, John Wilfred; *Educ* RMA Sandhurst; *Career* joined Great Universal Stores plc 1970, co-fndr CCN Ltd 1980–96 (chief exec 1991–96), ceo Experian Ltd 1996–2000, memb Bd Great Universal Stores plc 1997–2006, gp chief exec GUS plc (formerly Great Universal Stores plc) 2000–06, chm Burberry 2002–, chm Experian (following demerger from GUS) 2006–; non-exec dir Standard Chartered plc 2007–; memb Pres's Ctee CBI; chm Bd of Govrs Nottingham Trent Univ; CCMI, FRSA; *Recreations* riding, golf; *Style*— John Peace, Esq; ✉ Experian, Talbot House, Talbot Street, Nottingham NG80 1TH

PEACE, Prof Richard Arthur; s of Herman Peace (d 1991), of Otley, W Yorks, and Dorothy, *née* Wall (d 1993); *b* 22 February 1933; *Educ* Ilkley GS, Keble Coll Oxford (MA, BLitt); *m* 18 Oct 1960, (Shirley Mary) Virginia, da of Capt William George Wright (d 1969), of London; 1 s (Henry Richard b 24 April 1964, d 25 Sept 1975), 2 da (Mary b 7 April 1967, Catherine b 14 Jan 1969); *Career* prof of Russian: Univ of Hull 1975–84, Univ of Bristol 1984–94 (lectr 1963, sr lectr 1972–75); prof emeritus Univ of Bristol 1994–; pres Br Univs Assoc of Slavists 1977–80; *Books* Dostoevsky: An Examination of The Major Novels (1971), The Enigma of Gogol (1981), Chekhov: A Study of The Four Major Plays (1983), Oblomov: A Critical Examination of Goncharov's Novel (1991), Dostoevsky's Notes from Underground (1993), Gogol: Village Evenings near Dikanka (introduction and bibliography, 1994), Gogol: Plays and Petersburg Tales (introduction, 1995), Dostoevsky: Crime and Punishment (introduction and notes, 1995), The Novels of Turgenev: Symbols and Emblems (2002, online at http://eis.bris.ac.uk/rurap/novelsof.htm), Fyodor Dostoevsky's Crime and Punishment: A Casebook (2006); *Recreations* fishing; *Style*— Prof Richard Peace; ✉ Department of Russian Studies, University of Bristol, 17 Woodland Road, Bristol BS8 1TE (tel 0117 930 3030 ext 3516, fax 0117 928 8188)

PEACH, Prof (Guthlac) Ceri Klaus; s of Wystan Adams Peach, and Charlotte Marianne, *née* Klaus; *b* 26 October 1939; *Educ* Howardian HS Cardiff, Merton Coll Oxford (MA, DPhil); *m* 1964, Susan Lesley, *née* Godfrey; 2 s, 1 da; *Career* Univ of Oxford: demonstrator 1964–66, faculty lectr in geography 1966–92, prof of social geography 1992–, head of dept Sch of Geography 1995–98; fell and tutor St Catherine's Coll Oxford 1969– (sometime dean, sr tutor and bursar, pro-master 1993–94); visiting fell Dept of Demography Australian Nat Univ 1973; visiting prof: Dept of Sociology Yale Univ 1977, Dept of Geography Univ of Br Columbia 1998, Dept of Sociology Harvard Univ 1998, Office of Population Research Princeton Univ 2006; Fulbright visiting prof Dept of Geography Univ of Calif Berkeley 1985; distinguished social geography scholar Assoc of American Geographers 2007; memb Univ of Oxford Hebdomadal Cncl 1996–2000; *Books* West Indian Migration to Britain: a social geography (1968), Urban Social Segregation (ed, 1975), Ethnic Segregation in Cities (co-ed, 1981), South Asians Overseas (co-ed, 1990), The Ethnic Minority Populations of Great Britain (1996), Islam in Europe (co-ed, 1997), Global Japan (co-ed, 2003); *Recreations* travelling, reading, computing; *Clubs* Leander; *Style*— Prof Ceri Peach; ✉ St Catherine's College, Oxford OX1 3UJ (tel 01865 271700)

PEACH, Sir Leonard Harry (Len); kt (1989); s of Harry Peach (d 1985), of Walsall, Staffs, and Beatrice Lilian, *née* Tuck (d 1978); *b* 17 December 1932; *Educ* Queen Mary's GS Walsall, Pembroke Coll Oxford (MA), LSE (Dip Personnel Mgmnt); *m* 15 March 1958, Doreen Lilian, da of John Roland Barker (d 1979), of West Molesey, Surrey; 2 s (Mark Philip b 1964, David John b 1967); *Career* Nat Serv 1951–53, 2 Lt 1 Bn S Lancs Regt 1952; Capt TA 5 Bn S Staffs Regt 1953–65; res asst to Randolph S Churchill 1956, various personnel mgmnt appts 1956–71; dir IBM: UK Rentals 1971–76, UK Holdings 1976–85 and 1989–92, Pensions Trust 1976–85 and 1989–92; gp dir personnel IBM (Europe, Africa, ME) 1972–75, dir of personnel and corp affrs IBM UK Ltd 1975–85 and 1989 (dir of personnel 1971–72), pres IPM 1983–85, seconded to DHSS as dir of personnel NHS Mgmnt Bd 1985–86, chief exec NHS Mgmnt Bd and memb NHS Supervisory Bd 1986–89; Civil Serv cmmr 1995–2001, cmmr for public appts (first appointee) 1995–99, cmmr for public appts in NI 1995–99; chm: Skillbase Ltd 1990–94, IPM PMS Ltd 1991, IPM Services Ltd 1991–94, IPD Enterprises Ltd 1992–98; dir: Nationwide Building Society 1990–93, Personal Investment Authy 1993–97, Coutts Consulting Group plc 1993–98; non-exec dir: Affinity Internet Holdings plc 2001–03, Appeals Serv 2004–06; chm: Policy Studies Inst 1991–2005, Police Complaints Authy 1992–95, Univ of Westminster 1993–99; dep chm Nationwide Pension Fund 1991–2003; chm: NHS Trg Authy 1986–91, Remuneration Ctee Scope 1995–2003, UKCC Cmmn on Educn for Nurses 1998–99, Inst of Continuing Professional Devpt 1998–, Quintin Hogg Tst 1999–, Regent St Polytechnic Tst 1999–, Discipline Bodies Selection Bd RICS 2001–06, Audit Ctee Appeals Serv 2004–06; dep chm: PIA Membership and Discipline Ctee 1996–2001, Regulatory Decisions Ctee FSA 2001–05; memb: Data Protection Tbnl 1985–99, Civilian Trg Bd MOD 1992–95, Civilian Personnel Bd MOD 1995–2001, Forensic Science Serv Remuneration Ctee 1998–2005, Audit Ctee DWP 2004–; pres: Manpower Soc 1991–97, Assoc of Business Schs 1991–99; govr Portsmouth GS 1976–2001; IPM President's Gold Medal 1988; Hon DSc Aston Univ, Hon DLitt Univ of Westminster, Hon DSc UWE 2000, Hon DCL Univ of Huddersfield 2000; hon fell: Thames Poly (now Univ of Greenwich), Pembroke Coll Oxford 1996; CCIPD 1983, Hon FFOM 1994; *Publications* Fitness for Practice: report on the Education and Training of Nurses, Midwives and Health Visitors (1999); published report for the Lord Chancellor on the Appointment Processes of Judges and Queen's Counsel in England and Wales (1999); *Recreations* opera, theatre, cricket, gardening; *Clubs* Oxford and Cambridge, Wentworth; *Style*— Sir Len Peach; ✉ Crossacres, Meadow Road, Wentworth, Virginia Water, Surrey GU25 4NH (tel 01344 842258, fax 01344 845294)

PEACOCK, Prof Sir Alan Turner; kt (1987), DSC (1945); s of Prof Alexander David Peacock (d 1976), and Clara Mary, *née* Turner (d 1983); *b* 26 June 1922; *Educ* Grove Acad, Dundee HS, Univ of St Andrews (MA); *m* 23 Feb 1944, Margaret Martha, da of Henry John Astell Burt (d 1960); 2 s (David Michael b 1945, Richard Alan b 1947); 1 da (Helen Mary Charlton b 1950); *Career* Lt RNVR 1943–45; reader in economics LSE 1951–56; prof of economics: Univ of Edinburgh 1956–62, Univ of York 1962–77, Univ of Buckingham 1978–84 (princ vice-chllr 1980–84); research prof of public fin Heriot-Watt Univ 1984–; chief econ advsr and dep sec DTI 1973–76, chm Ctee on Financing BBC 1985–86; chm Scottish Arts Cncl 1986–92, co-fndr and exec dir David Hume Inst Edinburgh 1985–90 (hon pres 2003–05), managing tstee IEA 1987–93, memb Panel of Econ Advsrs sec of state for Scotland 1987–91; non-exec dir Caledonian Bank 1990–96; hon doctorates: Stirling 1974, Zürich 1984, Buckingham 1986, Brunel 1989, St Andrews, Edinburgh, Dundee 1990, Catania 1991, York 1997, Lisbon 2000, Turin 2001; hon fell: LSE, IEA, Italian Acad of Arts and Scis 1996; hon memb RSM 1996; FBA 1979, FRSE 1989; *Books* numerous books and publications in professional journals mainly on economics topics and occasionally on music; *Recreations* trying to write serious music, wine spotting; *Clubs* Reform, New (Edinburgh); *Style*— Prof Sir Alan Peacock, DSC, FBA, FRSE; ✉ Flat 24, 5 Oswald Road, Edinburgh EH9 2HE (tel 0131 667 5677, e-mail pavone@blueyonder.co.uk); c/o David Hume Institute, 25 Buccleuch Place, Edinburgh EH8 9LN (tel and fax 0131 667 9609)

PEACOCK, Christopher Arden (Chris); s of Ralph Warren Peacock (d 1987), and Phyllis Emily Alice, *née* Hardwicke (d 1999); *b* 9 April 1945; *Educ* Wellington; *m* 1, 1968 (m dis); 2 da (Julie b 1971, Susannah b 1973); m 2, 1979; 3 c (Samantha b 1980, Charles b 1982, Thomas b 1986); *Career* Kemsley Whiteley Ferris 1963–66, Daniel Smith Briant & Done 1966–72; Jones Lang Wootton: joined 1972, ptnr 1974, chm and head Ptnr Agency 1988, managing ptnr Continent of Europe 1992–96, chief exec Jones Lang Wootton Europe 1996–97 (int chief exec 1997–99), pres and ceo Jones Lang LaSalle 2002–04 (pres, dep chief exec and chief operating offr 1999–2002); non-exec dir: Slough Estates 2004–, Land Locator Co 2005–, Howard de Walden Estates 2006–; Freeman City of London, memb Ct of Assts Worshipful Co of Pewterers; FRICS 1982 (ARICS 1970); *Recreations* golf, sailing, tennis, travel, shooting; *Clubs* Walton Heath Golf; *Style*— Chris Peacock, Esq

PEACOCK, Geraldine; CBE (2001); *b* 26 January 1948; *Educ* Redland HS for Girls Bristol, Univ of Durham (BA), Univ of Calif (Rotary Int fell), Univ of Newcastle upon Tyne (CQSW, Dip Applied Social Work Studies); *Career* 1969–1989: sr social work practitioner, lectr in social policy and social work theory and practice, trg conslt to govt depts and local authorities, dep dir London Trg for Care; chief exec: Nat Autistic Soc 1989–97, Guide Dogs for the Blind Association 1997–2003; chair Charity Cmmn 2004– (non-exec cmmr 2003–), interim chair Futurebuilders 2004–; civil serv cmmr 2001–; chm ACEVO 1996–2000 (vice-chm 1995–96, memb Exec Ctee), vice-chm The Int Fedn of Guide Dog Schs for the Blind 2001–; memb: Residential Homes Tbnl 1995–98, Cncl Industrial Soc 1996–2002, Social Investment Task Force 2000, Project Advsy Gp Performance and Innovation Unit (PIU) Voluntary Sector 2001, Advsy Ctee Active Community Unit Home Office; chm Voluntary Sector Women Leaders Network (Groundbreakers); tstee: NCVO 1999–2003, Inge Wakehurst Tst; voted Britain's most admired charity chief exec 2003; *Publications* Social Work and Received Ideas (with C Rojek and S Collins, 1989), The Haunt of Misery (with C Rojek and S Collins, 1990); author of numerous articles and conference papers; *Style*— Ms Geraldine Peacock, CBE; ✉ Futurebuilders, 1 Carlisle Avenue, London EC3N 2ES (tel 020 7680 7880, fax 020 7680 7881)

PEACOCK, Ian Douglas; OBE (1998); s of Andrew Inglis Peacock (d 1981), of Sevenoaks, Kent, and Minnie Maria, *née* King (d 1978); *b* 9 April 1934; *Educ* Sevenoaks Sch; *m* 21 July 1962, Joanna Hepburn, da of George Milne MacGregor (d 1993), of Strathaven, Lanarkshire; 1 s (Colin Michael b 8 Sept 1963), 1 da (Susan Jean b 2 May 1965); *Career*

PO RAF 1953–54, Flying Offr RAuxAF 1955–58; md: Slazenger Ltd 1976–83 (mktg dir 1973–76), Sports Mktg Surveys Ltd 1983–85; chief exec LTA 1986–96; vice-pres Golf Fndn 2003– (dir and memb Cncl 1984–, chm 1996–2003); chm: Golf Ball 1975–96, Torch Trophy Tst 1998–2006 (vice-pres 2006–); pres Br Sports and Allied Industries Fedn 1983–85; dir: Br Tennis Fndn 1997–, Wembley National Stadium Ltd (formerly English National Stadium Development Co) 1998–2002; tstee English National Stadium Tst 1998–; *Recreations* golf, painting; *Clubs* All England Lawn Tennis, RAF, Royal Ashdown Forest Golf, Queen's; *Style—* Ian Peacock, Esq, OBE; ✉ 135 More Close, St Paul's Court, West Kensington, London W14 9BW

PEACOCK, Ian Rex; s of Mervyn George Peacock, of Bristol, and Evelyn Joyce, *née* Gay; *b* 5 July 1947, Bristol; *Educ* Kingswood GS Bristol, Trinity Coll Cambridge (MA), Open Univ; *m* 31 March 1973, Alyanee, da of Lt-Gen Amnuay Chya-Rochana; 1 s (Christopher George Insree b 5 May 1982); *Career* mangr Economics and Statistics Dept Unilever 1968–73, economist Cripps Warburg Ltd 1973–75; Kleinwort Benson Gp: int loan admin 1975–76, asst mangr syndication 1976–78, mangr Banking Dept Hong Kong 1978–81, asst dir domestic banking 1981–85, dir North American banking NY 1985–87, dir LBO Unit and head of loan syndications 1987–1990, jt head of financing and gp dir 1990–94; BZW Ltd: co-head merchant banking NY 1994–96, chief operating offr Investment Banking Div 1996–97; special advsr Bank of England 1998–2000, dep chm Lombard Risk Mgmnt 2000–, non-exec chm MFI Furniture Gp plc 2000–06, chm Mothercare plc 2002–; sr advsr Close Brothers Corporate Finance 2005–; non-exec dir: Norwich and Peterborough Building Soc 1997–2005, i-documentsystems Gp plc 2000–04; chm Finance Advsy Ctee Westminster Abbey 2003–; tstee WRVS 2001–; *Clubs* Oxford and Cambridge; *Style—* Ian Peacock, Esq; ✉ Mothercare plc, Cherry Tree Road, Watford WD24 6SH (tel 01923 206001, fax 01923 255782, e-mail jane.vernol@mothercare.co.uk)

PEACOCK, Jonathan Mark; s of John Keith Peacock, of Stoke-on-Trent, and Gloria Theresa, *née* Martin; *b* 16 December 1961, Stoke-on-Trent; *Educ* St Joseph's Coll Trent Vale, Univ of Hull (LLB), UCL (LLM); *Partner* Julie Ann Lewis, *née* Miller; 1 s (Jacob b 14 July 1993), 1 da (Asha b 30 Oct 1999); *Career* admitted slr 1993; slr specialising in medical law and patients' rights; Shoosmiths & Harrison Solicitors 1989–95, Irwin Mitchell Solicitors 1996– (ptnr 1999); chair Grafton Manor Research and Ethics Ctee 2004–; tstee: Headway UK, Birmingham Citizens Advocacy (dep chair); memb Law Soc 1993; *Recreations* literary fiction, cinema, tennis, running; *Style—* Jonathan Peacock, Esq; ✉ Irwin Mitchell Solicitors, Imperial House, 31 Temple Street, Birmingham B2 5DB (tel 0121 214 5217, e-mail jonathan.peacock@irwinmitchell.com)

PEACOCK, Lynne Margaret; da of George Beare (d 1986), of London, and Elsie, *née* Humphries; *b* 26 December 1953; *Career* Woolwich (Building Soc) plc: mktg devpt mangr 1983–87, mktg mangr 1987–91, head of mktg 1991–94, gen mangr 1994–96, ops dir 1996–2000, chief-exec 2000–; formerly held mktg positions with Tate & Lyle and Unilever; *Style—* Ms Lynne Peacock; ✉ Woolwich plc, Watling Street, Bexleyheath DA6 7RR (tel 020 8298 5041)

PEACOCKE, Prof Christopher Arthur Bruce; s of Arthur Robert Peacocke, and Rosemary Winifred Mann; *b* 22 May 1950; *Educ* Magdalen Coll Sch Oxford, Exeter Coll Oxford (MA, BPhil, DPhil); *m* 3 Jan 1980, Teresa Anne, *née* Rosen; 1 s, 1 da; *Career* jr research fell The Queen's Coll Oxford 1973–75, prize fell All Souls Coll Oxford 1975–79, fell and tutor and CUF lectr in philosophy New Coll Oxford 1979–85, Susan Stebbing prof of philosophy KCL 1985–88; visiting prof: Univ of Calif Berkeley 1975, Univ of Michigan Ann Arbor 1978, UCLA 1981, Univ of Maryland 1987, NYU 1996–99; visiting fell ANU 1981, fell Centre for Advanced Study in the Behavioral Sciences Stanford 1983–84, Waynflete prof of metaphysical philosophy Univ of Oxford 1989–2000, fell Magdalen Coll Oxford 1989–2000, Leverhulme personal res prof 1996–2000, prof of philosophy NYU 2000–04, prof of philosophy Columbia Univ 2004–; Whitehead Lectures Harvard Univ 2001, Kant Lectures Stanford Univ 2003; Euro Soc for Philosophy and Psychology: memb Steering Ctee 1991–95, memb Advsy Bd 1995–99, memb Bd 1999–; papers on philosophy of mind, language and logic and metaphysics; pres Mind Assoc 1986; FBA 1990; *Books* Holistic Explanation: Action, Space, Interpretation (1979), Sense and Content (1983), Thoughts: an Essay on Content (1986), A Study of Concepts (1992), Being Known (1999), The Realm of Reason (2004); *Recreations* music, visual arts; *Style—* Prof Christopher Peacocke, FBA; ✉ Department of Philosophy, 708 Philosophy Hall, Columbia University, 1150 Amsterdam Avenue, MC4971, New York NY 10027

PEAFORD, Alan James; s of James William Thomas Peaford (d 1986), and Iris Maud, *née* Tustain; *b* 31 October 1952; *Educ* Ockendon Court, Harlow Coll, Cranfield (Mktg Mgmnt Dip); *m* 17 Dec 1978, Jane Elizabeth, da of John Donald Saxton; 2 da (Sara Jane b 20 Aug 1980, Victoria Lesley b 28 March 1985), 1 s (Thomas James Charles b 16 Feb 1982); *Career* journalist; Express Newspapers 1971–74, Westminster Press 1975–76, Times Newspapers 1977–, night ed Arab Times 1977–78, dep ed Gulf Daily News 1978–79, PR and communications mangr British Petroleum 1980–88, md Charles Barker 1988–90, chm Trident Communications 1990–2004, chm Aerocomm Ltd 2004–; dir Oddjobz Ltd; awards: Foreign Corr of the Year 1977, Safety Writer of the Year 1982, Aerospace Journalist of the Year (Airshows) 2001 and 2005; nat chm BAIE 1989–90 (memb 1981, fell 1986), memb Cncl Nat Youth Theatre 1999–; chm: Cornelia de Lange Syndrome Fndn 1990–, Treetops 2002–; pres Fedn of European Editors 1995–2000, pres BACB 2000–; FRSA; *Recreations* flying, golf, tennis, watching West Ham; *Clubs* IOD, Aviation, Ward of Cheap; *Style—* Alan Peaford, Esq

PEAKE, David Alphy Edward Raymond; s of Sir Harald Peake (d 1978), and his 1 w Resy, OBE, *née* Countess de Baillet Latour; *b* 27 September 1934; *Educ* Ampleforth, ChCh Oxford; *m* 1962, Susanna, da of Sir Cyril Kleinwort (d 1980); 1 s, 1 da; *Career* 2 Lt Royal Scots Greys 1953–55; chm: Hargreaves Group plc 1974–86, Kleinwort Benson Group plc 1989–93; dir: Kleinwort Benson Ltd 1971–93, BNP plc 1974–2005, Banque Nationale de Paris SA (now BNP Paribas SA) 1998–2004; chm BNP UK Holdings Ltd (now BNP Paribas UK Holdings Ltd) 1997–2005; dir: The British Library 1990–96, British Overseas Trade Bd 1993–96, Life Educn Centres 1994–; chm The Educn 2000 Tst (now The 21st Century Learning Initiative (UK)) 1994–; memb Cncl Goldsmiths Coll London 1997–2004; memb Ct of Assts Worshipful Co of Goldsmiths 1992 (Prime Warden 2003–04); *Clubs* Brooks's, Cavalry and Guards', Pratt's; *Style—* David Peake, Esq; ✉ Home Farm, Bourton-on-the-Hill, Moreton-in-Marsh, Gloucestershire GL56 9AF

PEAKER, Prof Malcolm; s of late Ronald Smith Peaker, of Stapleford, Nottingham, and Marian, *née* Tomasin; *b* 21 August 1943; *Educ* Henry Mellish GS Nottingham, Univ of Sheffield (BSc, DSc), Univ of Hong Kong (PhD); *m* 23 Oct 1965, Stephanie Jane, da of late Lt Cdr J G Large, DFC; 3 s (Christopher James Gordon, Alexander John, Nicholas Edward); *Career* ARC Inst of Animal Physiology 1968–78, head Dept of Physiology Hannah Res Inst 1978–81, dir and Hannah prof Univ of Glasgow 1981–2003; non-exec dir Edinburgh Instruments Ltd; Hon DSc Univ of Hong Kong; FZS 1969, FIBiol 1979, FRSE 1983, FRS 1996; *Books* Salt Glands in Birds and Reptiles (1975), Avian Physiology (ed, 1975), Comparative Aspects of Lactation (ed, 1977), Physiological Strategies in Lactation (ed, 1984), Intercellular Signalling in the Mammary Gland (ed, 1995), Biological Signalling and the Mammary Gland (ed, 1997); *Recreations* zoology, natural history, golf; *Clubs* Royal Troon Golf, Zoological; *Style—* Prof Malcolm Peaker, FRSE, FRS; ✉ 13 Upper Crofts, Alloway, Ayr KA7 4QX

PEARCE, (John) Allan Chaplin; yr s of late John William Ernest Pearce, and Irene, *née* Chaplin; bro of Baron Pearce (Life Peer, d 1990); *b* 21 October 1912; *Educ* Charterhouse, BNC Oxford; *m* 18 Nov 1948, Raffaella, da of Avv Umberto Baione, of Florence, Italy; 2 s (Laurence b 1949, Charles b 1952); *Career* cmd 4 Co of London Yeo, served N Africa and Italy 1941–44, Maj, Mil Mission to Italian Army Rome 1945–46; admitted slr 1947; sr ptnr Sandilands Williamson Hill & Co 1952–70, asst Legal Dept Church Cmmrs for England 1970–78; memb Ctee: Br Italian Soc 1967–92, Venice in Peril Fund 1970–99; Turner Soc (whose call for a Turner Gallery was answered in 1987): fndr memb and first chm 1975–77, vice-pres 1980–; Liveryman Worshipful Co of Skinners 1937, Freeman City of London; Cavaliere of the Order of Merit of the Italian Republic 1978; *Recreations* travel, opera, painting (exhibited Royal Acad of Arts); *Clubs* Travellers, Hurlingham; *Style—* Allan Pearce, Esq; ✉ 32 Brompton Square, London SW3 2AE

PEARCE, Brian Harold; CBE (1995), DL (Kent 2005); s of (John) Harold George Pearce (d 1982), of Sevenoaks, Kent, and Dorothy Elsie Pearce (d 1994); *b* 30 July 1931; *Educ* Tonbridge, UCL (BSc(Eng)); *m* 1, 3 Sept 1955, Jean Isabel, *née* Richardson (d 1985); 2 s (Nicholas Michael John b 1959, Jonathan Brian Miles b 1966), 1 da (Gillian Sarah (Mrs Mueller-Pearce) b 1961); m 2, 2 Aug 1988, Veronica Mary, *née* Maund, formerly Mrs Magraw; *Career* Nat Serv RE 1953–55 (cmmnd 2 Lt 1954); gp chm Pearce Signs Gp and subsids 1981–96 (joined 1955, gp md 1975); memb Bd London First 1992–96; dir: London First Centre 1992–98, Business Link London 1995–97; co-chm London Mfrg Gp (renamed Made in London) 1996–2003; pres London C of C and Industry 1994–96; former pres: Br Sign Assoc, Euro Fedn of Illuminated Signs; chm: Royal London Soc for the Blind 1993–2000, Stag Theatre Sevenoaks 1997–99, LCCI Commercial Educn Tst 1998–2000 (tstee 1993–2000); chm of tstees Royal Engineers Museum Fndn 1997–; govr New Beacon Sch Sevenoaks until 2005; Freeman City of London; hon fell Goldsmiths Coll London 1998, Hon Dr Open Univ 1998; *Recreations* sailing, flying (helicopter), country interests; *Clubs* RAC, Army and Navy; *Style—* Brian Pearce, Esq, CBE, DL; ✉ Hamptons Farmhouse, Hamptons, Shipbourne, Kent TN11 9SR (tel 01732 810547, fax 01732 810862, e-mail bhpea@talk21.com)

PEARCE, Caroline Jill; da of Charles Martin Mitchell, of Epsom, Surrey, and Audrey Joan, *née* Noyes; *b* 17 April 1973, Epsom, Surrey; *Educ* Parsons Mead Sch Ashtead, Epsom Coll, Univ of Cardiff (BSc Econ), Journalism Training Centre Mitcham; *m* 31 Aug 2001, Timothy Joseph John Pearce; 1 da (Gabriella Grace Anne b 9 Oct 2003), 1 s (Jake Alexander Kenneth b 24 May 2006); *Career* editorial asst The Lawyer Magazine Centaur Communications 1994; EMAP plc: sub ed Screen International 1994, prodn ed Screen International 1996; Global Professional Media Ltd: prodn ed Legal Week 1998, managing ed Legal Week 1999, gp managing ed 2000; gp managing ed Alternative Assets Div Incisive Media 2007; PPA Int Magazine of the Year (for Screen Int) 1997/8, PPA Weekly Business Magazine of the Year (for Legal Week) 2001/2 (shortlisted 2005), Incisive Media Awards Editorial Team of the Year (for Legal Week) 2006; *Recreations* swimming, theatre, film; *Style—* Mrs Caroline Pearce

PEARCE, Prof Eur Ing Christopher Michael; s of Glyndwr Pearce (d 1975), and Inis Mary, *née* Kenniford; *b* 23 October 1952; *Educ* Newent Sch, Univ of Bath (prizewinner, BSc); *m* 20 Sept 1975, Janice, da of Frank Holman; 2 da (Gillian Louise b 15 Aug 1980, Catherine Ruth b 29 Oct 1984); *Career* Dowty Group plc: apprentice 1970–74, designer and ldr Dowty Rotol Ltd 1974–79, propeller project engr Dowty Rotol Ltd 1979–84, gp trg mangr Dowty Gp plc 1984–86, chief engr Dowty Fuel Systems Ltd 1986–87, dir of engineering Dowty Fuel Systems Ltd 1987–89, dir of ops Dowty Fuel Systems Ltd 1989–90, dir and gen mangr Dowty Aerospace Hydraulics 1990–93, dir of Dowty Aerospace 1993–94; tech dir Ricardo Aerospace Ltd, Ricardo Hitec Ltd and Geschäftsfuhrer Ricardo Technology GmbH (Ricardo Group plc) 1994–97, tech and quality dir INBIS Gp Ltd and INBIS Ltd 1997–2006, tech dir Assystem SA 2006–, tech and quality dir Assystem UK Ltd 2006–; visiting fell Univ of Bristol, visiting prof Xi'an Jiaotong Univ (People's Republic of China), visiting prof Univ of Salford; Sir George Dowty prizewinner, Sir Roy Fedden prizewinner; CEng 1981, FREng 1993, MRAeS 1981, FIMechE 1991, FIET 2001; *Recreations* active church memb, fell walking, table tennis (former rep Univ of Bath); *Style—* Prof Eur Ing Christopher Pearce, FREng; ✉ Assystem SA, c/o 1 The Brooms, Emersons Green, Bristol BS16 7FD (tel 0117 987 4000, fax 0117 987 4088, e-mail cpearce@assystemuk.com)

PEARCE, Christopher Thomas; s of Thomas Neill Pearce, OBE (d 1994), of Worthing, and Stella Mary, *née* Rippon (d 1978); *b* 13 January 1941; *Educ* Christ's Hosp; *m* 1972, Jennifer Jane, da of Guy Stephen Carlton; 1 s (Marcus b 1976), 1 da (Tiffany b 1978); *Career* articled clerk Cole Dickin & Hills CAs 1960–65, CA Coopers & Lybrand London and New York 1965–70, with J Henry Schroder Wagg & Co Ltd and Schroder Group in London, Hong Kong and Brazil 1970–84 (dir 1981–84), dir County NatWest London 1984–87, fin dir Rentokil Initial plc (formerly Rentokil Group plc) 1987–2001; chm 100 Gp of Finance Dirs 1997–; FCA 1964; *Recreations* sailing, skiing, reading, music; *Style—* Christopher Pearce, Esq; ✉ Rentokil Initial plc, Felcourt, East Grinstead, West Sussex RH19 2JY (tel 01342 833022, fax 01342 326229)

PEARCE, Dave; s of Donald Pearce, and Edith Pearce; *b* 14 June 1963; *Educ* Esher Coll Surrey; *Partner* Fiona; *Career* presenter and prodr BBC Radio London/GLR 1983–90, Breakfast and Drivetime presenter Kiss 100 1990–95, presenter BBC Radio 1 1995–; UK and int club DJ 1985–; A&R dir: Polydor Records 1988–89, BMG Records 2000–; presenter and music conslt Behind The Beat (BBC) 1988, presenter The Dance Years (ITV) 2001; columnist: The Sun 1998–2000, Daily Star 2002–; music conslt film soundtrack SW9 2001 (winner Best Film Soundtrack Br Independent Film Awards 2001); memb Ctee: World DJ Funds, Nordoff Robbins Music Therapy; *Recordings* Dave Pearce Dance Anthems vols 1–5, various Euphoria dance mix albums; *Recreations* walking, cinema, collecting baseball caps; *Style—* Dave Pearce, Esq; ✉ c/o Wise Buddah Ltd, 74 Great Titchfield Street, London W1W 7QP (tel 020 7307 1607, fax 020 7307 1608)

PEARCE, Gareth David; s of Howard Spencer Pearce, of Cardiff, and Enid Norma, *née* Richards (d 1994); *b* 13 August 1953; *Educ* Abingdon Sch, Balliol Coll Oxford (MA); *m* Virginia Louise, da of late Desmond Campbell Miller; 4 da (Caroline, Emma, Davina, Leonora); *Career* CA: Peat Marwick Mitchell & Co 1975–81, Electra Investment Tst plc 1982–86, Smith & Williamson 1986– (gp md 1995–2000, exec chm 2000–); dir National Mutual Life Assurance Soc 1997–2002; FCA 1997 (ACA 1979); *Clubs* Hurlingham; *Style—* Gareth Pearce, Esq; ✉ Smith and Williamson, 25 Moorgate, London EC2R 6AY (tel 020 7637 5377, fax 020 7436 2889)

PEARCE, Howard John Stredder; CVO (1993); s of Ernest Victor Pearce, and Ida, *née* Booth; *Educ* City of London Sch, Pembroke Coll Cambridge (MA, LLB); *Career* joined FCO 1972, third sec Buenos Aires 1975–78, FCO 1978–83, first sec and head of Chancery Nairobi 1983–87, asst later dep head of personnel ops FCO 1987–90, dep head of mission Budapest 1991–94, fell Center for Int Affairs Harvard Univ 1994–95, head Central European Dept FCO 1996–99, high cmmr to Malta 1999–2002, govr of Falkland Islands and Cmmr for S Georgia and the S Sandwich Islands 2002–06; sr assoc memb St Antony's Coll Oxford; memb Exec Ctee VSO 1988–90; *Recreations* classical music, opera, reading, hill walking, travel; *Clubs* Oxford and Cambridge; *Style—* Howard Pearce, Esq, CVO

PEARCE, Sir (Daniel Norton) Idris; kt (1990), CBE (1982), TD (1972), DL (Greater London 1986); s of Lemuel George Douglas Pearce (d 1988), and Evelyn Mary Pearce (d 1987); *b* 28 November 1933; *Educ* West Buckland Sch, Coll of Estate Mgmnt; *m* 1963 (m dis), Ursula Langley; 2 da (Sara b 30 April 1965, Claire Mary (Mrs Simon C Thomsett) b 8 Dec 1968); *Career* chartered surveyor; Nat Serv RE 1957–59, cmd 135 Ind Topographic Sqdn TA 1970–73, Hon Col 1989–91; Richard Ellis: joined 1959, ptnr 1961, managing ptnr 1981–87, conslt 1992–2000; chm: English Estates 1989–94, Varsity Funding 1995–99,

P

Baffin UK Ltd 2001–02; dep chm Dusco Ltd 1992–2000; dir: Higgs & Hill plc (now Swan Hill Group plc) 1993–2000, Innisfree Ltd 1996–, Millenium & Copthorne plc 1996–, Regalian Properties plc 1997–2002, Resolution plc 1998–2002; RICS: memb Gen Cncl 1980–94, chm of Parly and public affairs 1984–89, memb Bd of Mgmnt 1984–91, vice-pres 1986–90, pres 1990–91; chm Int Assets Valuation Standards Ctee 1981–86; memb: Advsy Bd for Institutional Fin in New Towns 1974–80, Advsy Bd PSA 1981–86, Inquiry of Sec of State for Health and Social Security into Surplus Land in NHS 1982 (property advsr NHS 1985–89), Advsy Panel on Diplomatic Estate FCO 1985–95, Bd London First Centre 1992–2000; dep chm English Partnerships 1993–2001; HEFC: chm Wales 1992–96, memb England 1992–96; memb: Ct City Univ 1987–97, Univs Funding Cncl 1991–92, Fin Reporting Review Panel 1991–92, Cncl Univ of Reading 1997–99; Univ of Surrey: memb Cncl 1993–2004, pro-chllr 1994–2004 (pro-chllr emeritus 2004–), chm 1998–2002; chm Bd of Govrs Stanway Sch Dorking 1982–85, govr Peabody Tst 1992–2003, memb Cncl RCA 1997–; Gtr London TA&VRA: memb 1970–96, chm Works and Bldgs Sub-Ctee 1983–91, vice-chm 1991–94; cmmr Royal Hosp Chelsea 1995–2001; Parly candidate (Cons) Neath W Glam 1959; Freeman: Worshipful Co of Tylers and Bricklayers 1973 (Master 2000), Worshipful Co of Chartered Surveyors 1977; Hon DSc: City Univ 1991, Univ of Salford 1992, Oxford Poly 1991; Hon DEng UWE 1994, Hon DTech Univ of E London 1998, Hon DUniv Surrey 2004; hon fell: Coll of Estate Mgmnt 1987, Univ of Wales Cardiff 1998; centenary fell Thames Poly 1991, companion De Monfort Univ 1993; FRICS, FRSA; *Recreations* reading, opera, ballet, travel; *Clubs* Brooks's; *Style—* Sir Idris Pearce, CBE, TD, DL

PEARCE, Prof John Barber; s of Arnold Porteous Pearce (d 1979), and Ruth, *née* Parry; *b* 27 October 1940; *Educ* Michael Hall (Rudolph Steiner Sch), UCL, UCH (MB BS, DCH, MPhil); *m* 1965, (Jean) Mary, da of Derek Wynne Bogle; 3 da (Rachel Christina b 1 Dec 1966, Clare Judith b 10 Oct 1968, Anna Jane b 19 March 1971); *Career* postgrad: Bart's 1967–71, Maudsley Hosp 1971–75; conslt child and adolescent psychiatrist Guy's Hosp London 1975–87, sr lectr in child and adolescent psychiatry Univ of Leicester 1987–91, prof of child and adolescent psychiatry Univ of Nottingham 1991–99 (emeritus prof 1999–); formerly examiner (MSc in Human Communication) Univ of London, examiner (DCH) RCP 1989–99; RCPsych: formerly sec Child and Adolescent Psychiatry Speciality Advsy Ctee, formerly examiner membership exam, sec Child and Adolescent Section 1993–95 (formerly academic sec), memb Jt Ctee for Higher Psychiatric Trg 1993–99; regnl advsr Med Cncl on Alcoholism 1992–99; expert on childhood problems for nat and local radio and TV and for nat newspapers and mags, weekly columnist Nottingham Evening Post; memb: BMA, Br Paediatric Assoc, Assoc of Psychologists and Psychiatrists, Assoc for the Psychiatric Study of Adolescence; FRCPCH, FRCP, FRCPsych; *Books* The 'Kids Work Out' Guide for Parents (1987), Worries and Fears (1989), Bad Behaviour (1989), Tantrums and Tempers (1989), Fighting, Teasing and Bullying (1989), Food: Too Faddy Too Fat (1991), Family and Friends (1991), Bad Behaviour, Tantrums and Tempers (1993), Good Habits - Bad Habits (1994), Growth and Development - Too Fast Too Slow (1994), Baby and Toddler Sleep Programme (1997); also author of book chapters and scientific papers concerning childhood depression and suicide, the psychiatric consequences of physical illness, bullying and general child psychiatric topics; *Recreations* narrowboating and sailing, playing the cello occasionally, restoring anything, travelling with my wife; *Style—* Prof John Pearce; ✉ Thorneywood Unit, Porchester Road, Nottingham NG3 6LF (tel 0115 844 0502, e-mail johnbarberpearce@btinternet.com)

PEARCE, Jonathan; *b* 23 December 1959; *Educ* Univ of Birmingham (BA), National Broadcasting Sch; *m* Amanda; 2 3 (Sam b 1999, William b 2001, Elizabeth b 2003); *Career* freelance football reporter BBC Radio Bristol 1980–83; sports ed: Radio West Bristol 1983–84, Southern Sound Radio 1984, Radio West/GWR Bristol 1984–86, BBC Radio 2 Local Radio Network London 1986–87; sports ed and commentator Capital Radio 1987–2002, freelance reporter, commentator and presenter Sky TV 1991–97, football commentator Channel 5 TV 1997–2004, football commentator BBC Radio Five Live 2002–05; presenter: The Footballers Football Show (Sky TV) 1991–93, Sports Talk (Granada Talk TV) 1996–97, Up for the Cup (LWT) 1997, Robot Wars (BBC) 1997–2005, Jonathan Pearce's Football Night (Channel 5) 2000–04, BC Radio Five 6–0–6 2002–03, BBC Radio Five Mid-week Sport on Five 2003–05; commentator Match of the Day 2004–; several voice-overs for various video prodns, radio and TV ads; *Awards* New York Radio Festival Gold Medal 1990, 1992 and 1999 (Silver Medal 1991, Bronze Medal 1993), Best Sports Prog of the Year Sony Radio Awards 1990 and 1992, Best Sports Commentator Sony Radio Awards 1996, Variety Club Independent Radio Personality of the Year 1996; *Recreations* all sport (trained with Bristol City FC as a teenager); *Style—* Jonathan Pearce, Esq; ✉ Blackburn Sachs Associates, 2–4 Noel Street, London W1F 8GB (tel 020 7292 7555, fax 020 7292 7576)

PEARCE, Reynold (Ren); *Educ* Trent Poly Nottingham (BA Fashion), Central St Martin's Sch of Art London (MA); *Career* fashion designer; former asst to designers incl John Galliano and Roland Klein, fndr ptnr own label Pearce Fionda (with Andrew Fionda, *qv*) 1994–; New Generation Designers of the Year (Br Fashion Awards) 1995, Newcomers Award for Export (Br Knitting and Clothing Export Cncl/Fashion Weekly) 1995, World Young Designers Award (Int Apparel Fedn Istanbul) 1996, Glamour Category Award (Br Fashion Awards) 1997; worldwide stockists incl: Liberty, Harrods, Harvey Nichols and Selfridges (UK), Saks 5th Avenue and Bergdorf Goodman (USA), Lidia Shopping (Italy), CRC (Thailand), Brown Thomas (Ireland); gp exhbns incl: Design of the Times (RCA) 1996, The Cutting Edge of British Fashion 1947–1997 (V&A) 1997; *Style—* Ren Pearce

PEARCE, Prof Shirley Anne; CBE (2005); da of Derek Pearce, of Norfolk, and Nancy, *née* Ferris; *b* 19 February 1954, Cirencester; *Educ* Norwich HS for Girls, St Anne's Coll Oxford (BA), Inst of Psychiatry Univ of London (MPhil), Univ of London (PhD); *m* Aug 1980, Robert Pugh; 2 s (Jonathan Robert b 31 March 1988, Thomas George b 22 Sept 1985); *Career* clinical psychologist St Mary's Hosp London 1977–81, lectr then sr lectr in psychology UCL 1981–94, prof of health psychology UEA 1994–2006, pro-vice-chllr Health and Professional Schs UEA 2000–06, vice-chllr Loughborough Univ 2006–; cmmr Healthcare Cmmn; memb: Health Ctee Univs UK 2005–, Equality Challenge Unit 2006– (also dir), HEFCE Bd Strategic Advsy Ctee for Business and Community 2006–, E Midlands Regnl Sports Bd Sport England 2006–, FE-HE 2012 Steering Gp Univs UK 2006–, Cncl for Industry and HE, Bd of Tstees Youth Sport Tst 2007–, Bd Univs and Colls Employers Assoc 2007–; *Publications* The Practice of Behavioural Medicine (co-ed, 1989), Psychological Factors in Measurement of Pain (contrib, 2000); numerous articles in learned jls; *Recreations* running, gardening; *Style—* Prof Shirley Pearce, CBE; ✉ Loughborough University, Ashby Road, Loughborough LE11 3TU (tel 01509 222002, fax 01509 223900, e-mail s.pearce@lboro.ac.uk)

PEARCE, Prof Susan Mary; *b* 20 March 1942; *Educ* Wycombe HS for Girls, Somerville Coll Oxford (MA), Univ Southampton (PhD); *m*; *Career* curatorial asst Dept of Archaeology Nat Museums of Merseyside 1965; Exeter City Museum: curator of antiquities 1965–78, sr curator (dep dir post) 1978–84; tutor Univ of Exeter 1972–84; Dept of Museum Studies Univ of Leicester: sr lectr 1984–89, dir and head of dept 1989–96, dean of arts 1996–, personal professorship in museum studies 1992–; tutor and examiner dip of Museum Assoc 1976–79; visiting lectr: Dept of Rhetoric Univ of Calif Berkeley 1982, Dept of Museum Studies Univ of Brno Czechoslovakia 1988; memb: Area Archaeological Advsy Ctee 1976–81, Archaeology Advsy Ctee Exmoor Nat Park 1979–84, Nat Trust Archaeological Advsy Ctee 1979–84, Govt Ctee for Reviewing Works of Art for Export 1990–92, Scholarship Assessment Panel Cwlth Inst 1991–; sec, chm and pres Devon Archaeological Soc 1973–79, exec sec Devon Ctee for Rescue Archaeology 1978–83, chm Leicester Univ Press Ctee 1991–, treas and chm Museums Ethnographers Gp 1976–83; Museums Assoc: Cncl memb 1989–, vice-chair Educnl Bd 1989–, professional vice-pres 1990–92, pres 1992–; Winston Churchill Travelling Fellowship (to visit Central Arctic) 1975, Catherine and Leonard Woolley Fellship grant Somerville Coll Oxford (res Balearic Isles) 1984; FSA 1979, FMA 1980 (AMA 1973); *Books* The Kingdom of Dumnonia - Studies in History and Tradition in SW Britain AD 350–1150 (1978), The Archaeology of SW Britain (1981), The Early Church in W Britain and Ireland (ed, 1982), The Bronze Age Metalwork of SW Britain (pts 1 and 2, 1983), Museum Studies in Material Culture (ed, 1989), Archaeological Curatorship (1990), Objects of Knowledge (ed, 1990), Museum Economics and the Community (ed, 1991), Museum Studies Bibliography (ed, 1991), Museums and Europe (ed, 1992), Museums, Objects and Collections - A Cultural Study (1992), Museums and the Appropriation of Culture (ed, 1993), Art in Museums (ed, 1994), Collecting in the European Tradition (1995), Collecting in Contemporary Practice (1998); author of numerous papers for confs and jls; *Style—* Prof Susan M Pearce, FSA; ✉ Department of Museum Studies, University of Leicester, 105 Princess Road East, Leicester LE1 7LG (tel 0116 252 3963)

PEARCE-HIGGINS, His Hon Judge Daniel John; QC (1998); *b* 26 December 1949; *Educ* St Paul's, Univ of Bristol (BSc), Inns of Court Sch of Law; *Career* called to the Bar Middle Temple 1973; recorder 1999–2004 (asst recorder 1995–99), circuit judge (Midland Circuit) 2004–; memb Mental Health Tbnl 2000–; CEDR accredited mediator 1999–2004, FCIArb 1999–2004; *Style—* His Hon Judge Pearce-Higgins, QC

PEARCEY, Leonard Charles; s of Leonard Arthur Pearcey (d 1992), of Dorset, and Jessie Sinclair, *née* Millar (d 1965); *b* 6 June 1938; *Educ* Christ's Hosp, CCC Cambridge (MA); *Career* PA to md Hargreaves Group 1957–59, dir of studies Rapid Results Correspondence Coll 1962–63, teacher Wimbledon 1964–65, arts admin Harold Holt Ltd 1965–66, music dir Guildhall Sch of Music and Drama 1966–70; competition sec Int Violin Competition 1966–70, dir Merton Festival 1972–76; involved in numerous major arts and religious radio and TV programmes incl BBC Radio 2 Young Musician competition, Book at Bedtime, Music Now, The Arts This Week, Seeing and Believing, Meeting Place and Songs of Praise; own series as singer and guitarist (Gold disc 1990), composer of numerous songs and arrangements; dedicatee Peter Wishart Five Psalms 1968; film commentary Robert Graves House Deia 2006–; prodr and presenter: P&O cruise-ship naming ceremonies (incl NY with Sophia Loren and Olivia de Havilland), various other major presentations, conferences and award ceremonies, audio communication cassettes; admin BBC Radio Times Drama Awards and Comedy Awards 1972–90, stage co-ordinator and compere World Travel Market 1980–2006, dir Music at Leisure Series 1988–; ed Music Teacher Magazine 1980–85, feature columnist Classical Music Magazine 1979–85; Mayoress (sic) London Borough of Merton 1973–74; memb: Actors Equity, Mediterranean Garden Soc, Bath Preservation Tst; *Books* The Musician's Survival Kit (1979); *Recreations* travel; *Style—* Leonard Pearcey, Esq; ✉ Apartment 22, The Tramshed, Beehive Yard, Bath BA1 5BB

PEAREY, David Dacre; *b* 15 July 1948; *m* 1996, Susan Anne, *née* Knowles; 1 da; *Career* diplomat; first sec FCO 1983, dep high cmmr Kampala 1987, first sec then cnsllr FCO 1990, cnsllr (commercial and economic) Lagos 1995, dep high cmmr Karachi 2000, high cmmr to Malawi 2005–06, govr British Virgin Islands 2006–; *Style—* David Pearey, Esq; ✉ c/o Foreign & Commonwealth Office, King Charles Street, London SW1A 2AH

PEARL, David Alan (aka David Pearlman); s of Harry Pearlman (d 1974), and Blanche, *née* Tafel; *b* 25 October 1945, London; *Educ* state schs Tottenham; *m* 19 Jan 1982, Susan Jayne, *née* Kaye; 1 s (Howard b 4 Dec 1975), 2 da (Laura b 16 Nov 1982, Gabriella b 25 July 1987); *Career* entrepreneur; co-fndr Pearl & Coutts Ltd, fndr Structadene Ltd; charter fndr memb Duke of Edinburgh Award, supporter Nat Youth Theatre; *Recreations* buying property, occasionally watching Spurs (vice-pres); *Style—* David Pearl, Esq; ✉ Structadene Limited, 3rd Floor, 9 White Lion Street, London N1 9PD (tel 020 7843 3775, fax 020 7843 3799, e-mail david.p@pearl-coutts.co.uk)

PEARL, David Brian; s of Leonard Pearl (d 1983), past Lord Mayor of Westminster, and Rivka Chenevix-Trench; *b* 6 August 1944; *Educ* Wellington Coll; *m* 1972, Rosamond Mary Katharine, da of Lt Cdr C G de L'isle Bush (d 2003), of Frampton-upon-Severn, Glos; 2 s, 1 da; *Career* articled clerk Cooper Brothers (qualified CA); md: Meru Group Ltd 1972–76, Promotions House plc 1976–84; chm: London Securities plc 1984–94, Premier Asset Management plc 1995–97; currently: exec chm Garrison Investment Mgmnt Ltd, chm Pearl Investment Mgmnt Servs Ltd; non-exec dir Stanley Leisure plc 1995–2001; underwriting memb Lloyds of London 1977–90; vice-chm Medway Ports Authy (Dept of Tport appointment) 1987–93, chm The Crown Suppliers (Dept of Environment appointment) 1989–90; cncllr Westminster City Cncl 1974–82 (local sch govr, London Tourist Bd rep, dep Lord Mayor, chief whip); past chm: St Marylebone Cons Assoc, London Central Euro Cons Assoc, Cons Party Property Advsy Ctee SE Region; FCA; *Recreations* greyhound breeding, golf; *Clubs* White's, Reform, MCC, Royal St George's Golf, Sunningdale Golf; *Style—* David B Pearl, Esq, FCA; ✉ Blake House, 19c Town Range, Gibraltar

PEARL, His Hon Judge David Stephen; s of late Chaim Pearl, and Anita, *née* Newman; *b* 11 August 1944; *Educ* George Dixon's Sch Birmingham, Westminster City Sch, Univ of Birmingham (LLB), Queens' Coll Cambridge (LLM, MA, PhD); *m* 1, 7 April 1967 (m dis 1983), Susan, da of late Joseph Roer, of Croydon, Surrey; 3 s (Julian Kim b 1969, Daniel Benjamin Meir b 1971, Marcus Alexander Jethro b 1974); *m* 2, 4 Oct 1985, Gillian, da of late Ryszard Maciejewski, of Melbourn, Herts; 1 step s (Benjamin), 1 step da (Sarah); *Career* called to the Bar Gray's Inn 1968 (bencher 2002); fell and dir studies in law Fitzwilliam Coll Cambridge 1969–89 (life fell 1989), lectr Univ of Cambridge 1972–89, prof of law and dean Sch of Law UEA 1989–94 (hon prof 1995–), recorder of the Crown Court 1992–94 (asst recorder 1985–92), circuit judge 1994–; pt/t adjudicator Immigration Act 1980–92, pt/t chm Immigration Appeal Tbnl 1992–94, chief adjudicator Immigration Appeals 1994–97, pres Immigration Appeal Tbnl 1997–99; Judicial Studies Bd: memb Civil and Family Ctee 1994–96, memb Tbnls Ctee 1996–99 and 2004–, dir of studies 1999–2001; pres Care Standards Tbnl 2001, cmmr Judicial Appts Cmmn 2006–; Int Soc on Family Law: gen sec 1985–91, vice-pres 1991–97; asst dep coroner Cambridge 1978–89; city cncllr Cambridge 1972–74, co cncllr Cambs 1974–77; *Books* A Textbook on Muslim Personal Law (1979, with W Menski, 3 edn 1998), Social Welfare Law (with K Gray, 1981), Interpersonal Conflict of Laws (1981), Family Law and Society (with B Hoggett, 1983, 2 edn 1987, 3 edn 1991, 4 edn 1996, 5 edn 2002), Family Law and Immigrant Communities (1986), Blood Testing, Aids and DNA Profiling (with A Grubb, 1990), Frontiers of Family Law (jt ed with A Bainham, 1993), Butterworths Immigration Law Service (ed); *Recreations* helping wife with horses, goats and chickens; *Clubs* Reform; *Style—* His Hon Judge Pearl; ✉ Care Standards Tribunal, 18 Pocock Street, London SE1 0BW (tel 020 7960 0673, e-mail david.pearl.cstpresident@judiciary.gsi.gov.uk)

PEARLMAN, Joseph Joshua (Jerry); MBE; s of Samuel Myer Pearlman, MM (d 1981), and Sarah Rachael Pearlman (d 1983); *b* 26 April 1933; *Educ* Keighley Boys GS, King James VI GS Bishop Auckland, Univ of London (LLB); *m* 18 June 1962, Bernice; 2 da (Kate, Debbie); *Career* Nat Serv Lt RASC; admitted slr 1956; fndr Pearlman Grazin & Co 1958–95, conslt Zermansky & Ptnrs 2004–; advsr to Omukama of Bunyoro-Katara Uganda 1960–61; hon slr: Sikh temple Leeds 1965–2005, Etz Chaim Synagogue Leeds 1997–, Hindu temple Leeds 1998–2006; pres: Leeds and W Riding Medico Legal Soc

1975–76, Leeds Law Soc 1985–86; ministerial appointed memb Yorkshire Dales Nat Park Ctee 1983–92 and 1998–2007 (dep chm 2001–07, dep chm Planning Ctee 2000–02), memb Adjudication Ctee Slrs' Complaints Bureau 1986–88, chm Open Spaces Soc 1988, vice-chm Yorkshire Dales Millennium Tst 1996–98 (tstee 1996–), memb Nat Countryside Access Forum 1999–; vice-pres Ramblers' Assoc 2004– (pres W Riding area); Liveryman Patternmakers' Guild; *Recreations* rambling, eating, drinking; *Clubs* Royal Over-Seas League; *Style—* Jerry Pearlman, Esq, MBE; ✉ 10 Lakeland Crescent, Leeds LS17 7PR (tel 0113 267 1114); Zermansky & Partners, 10 Butts Court, Leeds LS1 5JS (tel 01132 459766, fax 01132 467465, e-mail jj@pearlman.co.uk)

PEARLMAN, Her Hon Judge Valerie Anne; da of Sidney Pearlman, and Marjorie Pearlman; *b* 6 August 1936; *Educ* Wycombe Abbey; *m* 1972; 1 s, 1 da; *Career* called to the Bar Lincoln's Inn 1958 (bencher 2002); recorder (SE Circuit) 1982–85, circuit judge (SE Circuit) 1985– (sr circuit judge 2003–); chm Home Sec's Advsy Bd on Restricted Patients 1991–98; memb: Parole Bd 1989–94, Civil and Family Ctee Judicial Studies Bd 1992–97, Mental Health Fndn Ctee on the Mentally Disordered Offender 1992–95, Cncl of Civil Judges 1998–2001; memb Cncl Marlborough Coll 1989–97, govr Godolphin & Latymer Sch 1998–2003; patron: Suzy Lamplugh Tst, Juvenile & Family Courts Soc (now Children Law UK) 2000–; *Style—* Her Hon Judge Pearlman; ✉ Royal Courts of Justice, Strand, London WC2A 2LL

PEARS, David; *b* 24 April 1968; *Educ* City of London Sch; *Career* landowner; with The William Pears Group; *Style—* David Pears, Esq

PEARSALL, Dr Fiona Jean Burns; da of Dr Ian Stewart Pearsall (d 1982), and Jean Dawson, *née* Burns; *b* 5 May 1963; *Educ* Craigholme Sch for Girls Glasgow, Hutchesons' GS Glasgow, Univ of Glasgow (MB ChB, MSc), FRCA (Dip), postgrad dip law; *Career* house offr (med and surgery) Western Infirmary Glasgow 1986–87, registrar (anaesthesia) Victoria Infirmary Glasgow 1988–91 (SHO (anaesthesia) 1987–88), research asst Univ of Glasgow 1991–93, SHO (anaesthesia) Western Infirmary Glasgow 1993; Glasgow Royal Infirmary: registrar (anaesthesia) 1993–94, sr registrar 1994–96, conslt anaesthetist 1996–; clinical dir Anaesthetics, ITU and Theatres N Glasgow Univ NHS Div 2004–; memb: GMC 1994–2003, Professional Conduct Ctee, BMA; medical screener; *Recreations* drawing and watercolour painting, music, ornithology; *Clubs* RSM; *Style—* Dr Fiona Pearsall; ✉ Directorate of Anaesthesia, Glasgow Royal Infirmary, Castle Street, Glasgow (tel 0141 211 4620/1, fax 0141 211 4622)

PEARSE, Dr Barbara Mary (Mrs M S Bretscher); *b* Wraysbury, Bucks; *Educ* UCL (BSc, PhD, Jack Drummond Prize for Biochemistry); *m* M S Bretscher; 1 da (Nicola b 15 Aug 1978), 1 s (Andrew Jonathan b 15 Sept 1981); *Career* MRC Lab of Molecular Biology: jr research fell 1972–74, jr Beit meml fell 1974–77, SRC advanced fell 1977–82, memb scientific staff 1982–; appointed to MRC 1981–82, visiting prof Dept of Cell Biology Stanford Med Centre USA 1984–85; fell UCL 1995, fell commoner Lucy Cavendish Coll Cambridge 1997; K M Stott Prize for scientific research Newnham Coll Cambridge 1979, EMBO Gold Medal and Prize 1987; memb EMBO 1982, FRS 1988; *Publications* author of numerous articles, chapters and contribs to books and jls; *Recreations* wild flowers, planting trees, fresh landscapes; *Style—* Dr Barbara Pearse; ✉ MRC Laboratory of Molecular Biology, Hills Road, Cambridge CB2 2QH (e-mail bulbeck@mrc-lmb.cam.ac.uk)

PEARSE, Lesley Margaret; da of Geoffrey Arthur Sargent, and Marie, *née* Glynn; *Educ* Northbrook C of E Sch London; *Children* 3 da (Lucy, Samantha, Joanne); *Career* writer; previously various dead-end jobs; memb: Romantic Writers Assoc, W Country Writers; pres (Bath and Wilts) NSPCC, patron Nat Parents' Assoc; *Books* Georgia (1993), Tara (1994), Charity (1995), Ellie (1996), Camellia (1997), Rosie (1998), Charlie (1999), Never Look Back (2000), Trust Me (2001), Father Unknown (2002), Till We Meet Again (2002), Remember Me (2003), Secrets (2004); *Recreations* gardening, reading, DIY; *Style—* Ms Lesley Pearse; ✉ c/o Darley Anderson, Estelle House, 11 Eustace Road, London SW6 1JB (tel 020 7385 6652)

PEARSE WHEATLEY, Robin John; s of John Edward Clive Wheatley, MC, JP (d 1998), and Rosemarie Joy, *née* Malet-Veale; *b* 23 May 1949; *Educ* Leys Sch Cambridge, Inns of Court Sch of Law; *m* 9 April 1979 (m dis 2003), Victoria Eugenia Perez de Ascanio y Zuleta de Reales, da of Nicolas Perez de Ascanio Ventoso, of Tenerife, Spain; 2 da (Victoria-Eugenia Amabel b 16 Dec 1983, Rafaela Eleanor b 11 Jan 1986), 1 s (Edward Victor Francisco de Borga b 23 Dec 1988); *Career* called to the Bar Inner Temple 1971, recorder of the Crown Court 1992– (asst recorder 1987–92); councillor RBK and C 1974–78; chm London Area Nat Fedn Self Employed and Small Business 1989–92; Cons Parly candidate Lewisham Deptford 1983, Cons Euro candidate London South Inner 1989; Knight of Grace Constantinian Order of St George; *Recreations* swimming, bridge; *Clubs* Annabel's, Hurlingham; *Style—* Robin Pearse Wheatley, Esq; ✉ 45 Slaidburn Street, London SW10 0JW; 2 Paper Buildings, London EC4Y 7ET (tel 020 7556 5500, fax 020 7583 3423)

PEARSON, Barrie; s of Albert James Pearson (d 1987), of Selby, N Yorks, and Mary Pearson (d 1980); *b* 22 August 1939; *Educ* King's Sch Pontefract, Univ of Nottingham (BSc); *m* 1, 1962 (m dis), Georgina Ann; 1 da (Philippa Jane Antonia b 1965), 1 s (Gavin Charles Livingstone b 1968); m 2, 1984, Catherine Campbell; *Career* Dexion-Comino Int Ltd 1960, The Plessey Co 1967, The De La Rue Co 1973; non-exec chm Info Transmission Ltd 1985–87, exec chm Livingstone Guarantee plc 1976–2001, chm Global M&A 2001–2002; non-exec dir: Universal Salvage plc 1995–98; fndr and chief exec Realization 2002–, chm Precision Corporate Finance Ltd 2007–; video films: Business Strategy 1989, Time Management 1990, for Accountancy TV 1993; *Books* Successful Acquisition of Unquoted Companies (1983, 4 edn 1999), Common Sense Business Strategy (1987), Common Sense Time Management for Personal Success (1988), Realising The Value of a Business (1989), The Profit Driven Manager (1990), The Shorter MBA (1991, 2 edn 2004), Manage Your Own Business (1991), How to Buy and Sell a Business (1995), Boost Your Company's Profits (1998), Selling An Unquoted Company Successfully (2002), The Book of Me, A Life Coaching Manual (2002), Exit Right (2004), Serious Money (2005), Trade Secrets of Business Disposals (2005); *Recreations* theatre, ballet, outstanding hotels, travel; *Style—* Barrie Pearson, Esq; ✉ Campbell House, Weston Turville, Buckinghamshire HP22 5RQ (tel 01296 613828)

PEARSON, David Charles; s of Eric Charles Pearson, of Cornwall, and Joan Esdaile, *née* Wyatt (d 1997); *b* 14 June 1950; *Educ* Manchester Grammar, Blake Sch Minnesota USA (American Field Service Scholar), New Coll Oxford (MA); *m* 17 Dec 1982, Carmen Libera, da of Sidney Chellew; 1 s (Andrew b 16 April 1976), 1 da (Michelle Valentina b 25 April 1984); *Career* unit sales mangr Procter & Gamble Ltd 1971–75; Mars Inc: area sales mangr Pedigree Petfoods 1976–78, product gp mangr Pedigree Petfoods 1978–80, int mktg mangr Kal Kan LA USA 1980–81, gen mangr Effem Chile 1981–83; ptnr and mktg dir Crombie Eustace Ltd 1983–84, dir and gen mangr Pillsbury UK Ltd 1984–88; Sony UK Ltd: md Consumer Products 1988–98, dep md and chm European Consumer Mktg 1992–93, regnl dir Consumer Sales North 1993–95, md UK Sales Co 1995–98, memb Mgmnt Bd Consumer Gp Europe 1996–98, md 1997–98; md International Brands Pentland Gp plc 1998–99, ceo NXT plc 2000–05, gp ceo QM Gp Ltd 2006–07; dir JPMorgan Japanese Investment Tst plc 2003–; chm Vividas Gp plc 2007–, chm innovITS Ltd 2007–; lectr at various mktg conferences 1989–; pres AFS International Scholarships UK 1971–74; winner Hall of Fame ITV Award for Mktg 1995; chm Mktg Soc Consumer Electrical/Electronics Sector 1993–98; asst dir CriticalEYE 2007–; memb: Mktg Soc 1978–80 and 1985–, CBI Mktg Strategy Gp 1988–93, Editorial Bd Jl of Brand Mgmnt 1993–, CBI Nat Cncl 1997–98; Duchy of Cornwall Market Advsy Gp 1991–96; LEA govr St Albans Girls' Sch 2002– (vice-chm 2003–06, chm 2006–), govr Univ of Beds 2006–; fell Mktg Soc 1995, FRSA 1995; *Publications* regular contrib to Marketing Magazine; *Recreations* opera, walking, Manchester United FC; *Clubs* Pastmasters, Procter & Gamble Old Boys, English Speaking Union; *Style—* David Pearson, Esq; ✉ 9 The Warren, Harpenden, Herts AL5 2NH (tel 01582 4762748, e-mail dcpearson@btclick.com)

PEARSON, Dr David John; s of Eric Pearson (d 1977), of Eccleston, Chester, and Winifed Mary Pearson (d 1988); *b* 29 January 1946; *Educ* Ampleforth, St George's Hosp Med Sch London (MB BS), Univ of Manchester (PhD); *Career* house offr St George's Hosp 1968, SHO Manchester Royal Infirmary 1970, visiting scientist US Public Health Serv 1977, asst prof of med Univ of W Virginia 1977, sr lectr in med Univ of Manchester 1979– (res fell 1972, lectr in med 1976), hon conslt physician Manchester NHS 1979– (currently Univ Hosp of South Manchester NHS Fndn Tst); author of numerous res papers on allergy, immunology, food and health; memb: Br Soc for Immunology, Br Soc for Allergy and Clinical Immunology, Soc for Free Radical Res; FRCP 1987; *Recreations* skiing, windsurfing, sailing; *Style—* Dr David Pearson; ✉ The Alexandra Hospital, Mill Lane, Cheadle SK8 2PX; Wythenshawe Hospital, Southmoor Road, Wythenshawe, Manchester M23 9LT

PEARSON, Dr Donald William Macintyre; s of William Clark Gilmour Pearson (d 1982), of New Cumnock, Ayshire, and Morag Macrae, *née* Macintyre (d 1961); *b* 5 September 1950; *Educ* Cumnock Acad Cumnock Ayrshire, Univ of Glasgow (BSc, MB ChB, MRCP); *m* 26 Aug 1972, Margaret Jessie Kennedy, da of James Harris, of Auchenleck, Ayrshire; 2 s (Andrew b 1979, Donald b 1984), 1 da (Gillian b 1977); *Career* registrar Univ Dept of Med Glasgow Royal Infirmary 1979–81, sr registrar in med diabetes and endocrinology Grampian Health Authy 1982–84, hon sr lectr Univ of Aberdeen 1984– (lectr in med 1981–82), conslt physician Aberdeen Royal Hosps NHS Tst 1984–; memb: Br Diabetic Assoc, Scottish Soc for Experimental Med, Aberdeen Medico-Chirurgical Soc, Scottish Soc of Physicians, BMA; MRCP 1979, FRCPGlas 1988, FRCPEd 1990; *Books* Carbohydrate Metabolism in Pregnancy and the New Born (ed with Sutherland and Stowers, 1989); *Recreations* golf; *Style—* Dr Donald Pearson; ✉ Diabetic Clinic, Woolman Hill, Aberdeen Royal Infirmary, Aberdeen (tel 01224 681818)

PEARSON, Dr Graham Scott; CB (1990); s of Ernest Reginald Pearson (d 1996), and Alice, *née* Maclachlan (d 1987); *b* 20 July 1935; *Educ* Woodhouse Grove Sch Bradford, Univ of St Andrews (BSc, PhD); *m* 10 Sept 1960, Susan Elizabeth Meriton, da of Dr John Meriton Benn, CB (d 1992); 2 s (Gavin b 1963, Douglas b 1965); *Career* Univ of Rochester NY 1960–62, princ scientific offr Rocket Propulsion Estab 1967–69 (sr sci offr Westcott 1962–67), explosives and propellants liaison offr Br Embassy Washington DC 1969–72, asst dir Naval Ordnance Servs Bath 1973–76, tech advsr explosives and safety Chevaline 1976–79, princ superintendent Perme Westcott 1979–80, dep dir 1 and 2 Rarde Fort Halstead 1980–83, DG R&D Royal Ordnance Factories 1983–84, dir Chemical Def Estab Porton Down 1984–91, DG and chief exec Chemical and Biological Def Estab MOD Porton Down 1991–95, asst chief scientific advsr (non-proliferation) MOD 1995; Univ of Bradford: hon sr visiting research fell in peace studies 1996–97, hon visiting prof in int security 1997–; CChem, FRSC 1985; *Books* The UNSCOM Saga: Chemical and Biological Weapons Non-Proliferation (1999), The Search for Iraq's Weapons of Mass Destruction: Inspection, Verification and Non-Proliferation (2005), Hidcote: The Garden and Lawrence Johnston (2007); contrib: Advances in Inorganic and Radiochemistry Vol 8 (1966), Advances in Photochemistry Vol 3 (1964), Oxidation and Combustion Reviews Vol 3 and 4 (2 edn, 1969), Biological Weapons: Weapons of the Future (1993), Non-Conventional Weapons Proliferation in the Middle East (1993), US Security in an Uncertain Era (1993), Control of Dual Threat Agents: The Vaccines for Peace Programme (1994), Weapons Proliferation in the 1990s (1995), Strengthening The Biological Weapons Convention: Key Points for the Fourth Review Conference (1996), Biological Weapons: Limiting the Threat (1999), Biological Warfare: Modern Offense and Defense (2000), Verification of the Biological and Toxin Weapons Convention (2000), Nuclear Disarmament: Obstacles to Banishing the Bomb (2000), Strengthening the Biological Weapons Convention: Key Points for the Fifth Review Conference (2001), Scientific and Technical Means of Distinguishing Between Natural and Other Outbreaks of Disease (2001), Maximising the Security and Development Benefits from the Biological and Toxin Weapons Convention (2002), The Implementation of Legally Binding Measures to Strengthen the Biological and Toxin Weapons Convention (2004), Deadly Cultures: Biological Weapons since 1945 (2006), Strengthening the Biological Weapons Convention: Key Points for the Sixth Review Conference (2006); *Recreations* reading, archival research, walking, photography, foreign travel; *Style—* Dr Graham S Pearson, CB; ✉ Department of Peace Studies, University of Bradford, Bradford, West Yorkshire BD7 1DP (tel 01274 234186, fax 01274 235240)

P

PEARSON, Ian; MP; *Educ* Brierley Hill GS, Balliol Coll Oxford (BA),Univ of Warwick (MA, PhD); *m*; 2 da, 1 s; *Career* auditor Price Waterhouse 1981–82, research offr Univ of Warwick 1983–87, dep dir Urban Trust 1987–88, sr conslt Victor Hausner & Assocs 1988–89, jt chief exec WMEB Group (West Midlands Enterprise Bd) 1992–94 (dir of mktg 1989–92); MP (Lab): Dudley W (by-election) 1994–97, Dudley S 1997–; PPS to Geoffrey Robinson, MP as Paymaster Gen 1997–98, asst Govt whip 2001–02, a Lord Cmmr (Govt whip) 2002, Parly under-sec of state NI Office 2002–05, min for trade 2005–06, min for climate change and environment 2006–; non-exec dir GLE (Greater London Enterprise) 1995–2000; chm Redhouse Tst 1997–2001; *Recreations* rugby, literature, architecture; *Style—* Ian Pearson, Esq, MP; ✉ House of Commons, London SW1A 0AA (tel 020 7219 3000)

PEARSON, (Hugh) John Hampden; s of Lt-Col Hugh Henry Pearson (d 1975), and Sybil Monica, *née* Dunn (d 1994); *b* 22 March 1947; *Educ* Charterhouse, King's Coll London (LLB); *m* 12 Oct 1974, Jacqueline Anne, da of Maj Harold Arthur Bird, of Goring, W Sussex; 2 da (Alice b 1976, Juliet b 1978), 1 s (Daniel b 1982); *Career* admitted slr 1971, Stephenson Harwood 1971–73, Coward Chance 1973–86; ptnr Lovells 1986–; treas South African Townships Health Fund 1989–2002, The Pensions Policy Inst 2002–; memb: City of London Slrs Co, Law Soc, Assoc of Pension Lawyers, Charity Law Assoc; *Recreations* reading, hill walking, tennis, bridge, opera; *Clubs* MCC, Roehampton; *Style—* John Pearson, Esq; ✉ 15 Howard's Lane, London SW15 6NX; Providence Cottage, Buckland Newton, Dorset DT2 7BU; Lovells, Atlantic House, Holborn Viaduct, London EC1A 2FG (tel 020 7296 2000, fax 020 7296 2001, e-mail john.pearson@lovells.com)

PEARSON, Luke Neil; s of Raymond Pearson, and Sheila, *née* Bevan; *b* 15 December 1967, Portsmouth; *Educ* Central St Martins Sch of Art London (BA), RCA (MA); *Partner* Ana Saenz Castellano; 1 da (Marta Ana); *Career* early career as sr designer Studio X (with Ross Lovegrove, *qv*); co-fndr (with Tom Lloyd, *qv*) PearsonLloyd 1997–; projects incl: first class seat for Virgin Atlantic Airways, Artemide, Knoll International, Magis, Walter Knoll; visiting lectr Royal Coll of Art (running Platform 6 with Michael Marriott); *Awards* incl: FX Designers of the Year 2002, Industrial Product Design Award Design Week Awards 2004; *Style—* Luke Pearson, Esq; ✉ Pearson Lloyd, 117 Drysdale Street, London N1 6ND (tel 020 7033 4440)

PEARSON, Maxwell John (Max); *b* 30 July 1959; *Educ* King's Sch Canterbury, Keele Univ; *m* 2 s; *Career* journalist and broadcaster; BBC radio: local radio 1982–84, prodr Today Prog (Radio 4) 1984–85; English language output ed UAE govt Dubai 1985–87, freelance corr NBC (USA) radio 1985–87, reporter (travelled by bicycle in Indian sub-continent with tape recorder) BBC World Serv, CBC Canada and ABC Aust 1987–88; presenter BBC radio 1988–; progs incl: Newshour (World Serv), The World Tonight (Radio Four),

The World Today (World Serv), live hosting of World Serv output from various locations worldwide incl elections and interviews with world ldrs; *Recreations* golf, tennis; *Style*— Max Pearson, Esq; ✉ Europe Team, The World Today, BBC World Service, Bush House, Strand, London WC2B 4PH

PEARSON, Sir (Francis) Nicholas Fraser; 2 Bt (UK 1964), of Gressingham, Co Palatine of Lancaster; o s of Sir Francis Fenwick Pearson, 1 Bt, MBE (d 1991), and Katharine Mary, *née* Fraser; *b* 28 August 1943; *Educ* Radley; *m* 1978, Henrietta, da of Cdr Henry Pasley-Tyler, of Coton Manor, Guilsborough, Northants; *Heir* none; *Career* 3 Bn RB 1961–69 (ADC to C-in-C Far East 1969); Cons party candidate Oldham W 1975–78; chm Euro-Asia Group Ltd 1994; dir: Virgin Atlantic Airlines Ltd 1988–92, Inter-Continental Hotels Group Ltd 1989–92, Saison Holdings BV 1990–92, Passport Hotels 1992, Ecofin Group Ltd 1993; chm The Temenos Acad, tstee Ruskin Fndn; *Recreations* shooting, fishing, tennis, opera; *Clubs* Carlton; *Style*— Sir Nicholas Pearson, Bt; ✉ 9 Upper Addison Gardens, Holland Park, London W14 8AL

PEARSON, Nicholas (Nick); *b* 24 March 1951; *Educ* King Edward Sch Birmingham, Lincoln Coll Oxford (BA); *m* 1982, Chooi Yong Fong; 1 s (Oliver b 1985), 1 da (Sarah b 1989); *Career* Herbert Smith & Co 1974–79; Baker & McKenzie: based Hong Kong 1979–88, ptnr 1982–, based London 1988–, currently head Global Dispute Resolution Dept and Civil Fraud Gp; insolvency practitioner 1990–; memb Law Soc; *Recreations* tennis, cricket, walking; *Clubs* MCC; *Style*— Nick Pearson, Esq; ✉ Baker & McKenzie, 100 New Bridge Street, London EC4V 6JA (tel 020 7919 1000, fax 020 7919 1999, e-mail nick.pearson@bakernet.com)

PEARSON, Richard John Crewdson; s of Maj R A R B Pearson (d 1983), and Evelyn Katherine, *née* Crewdson (d 2001); *b* 4 May 1940; *Educ* Packwood Haugh, St Edward's Oxford, Univ of St Andrews (MA); *m* 30 Nov 1968, Catriona Wallace, da of Robert S Angus; 1 s (Richard b 25 Sept 1971), 1 da (Sarah Catriona b 13 April 1973); *Career* CA; Pannell Kerr Forster: ptnr 1970–2005, sr ptnr London 1990–2005, chm 1990–99; cmmr of taxes 1988–; Freeman City of London, Liveryman Worshipful Co of Barbers 1971; FCA 1975 (ACA 1965); *Recreations* golf, walking, sporting and country pursuits; *Style*— Richard Pearson; ✉ pearson9@aol.com

PEARSON, Dr Richard Martin; s of late Leonard Louis Pearson, of Bournemouth, and late Anne, *née* Tobias; *Educ* Royal GS High Wycombe, Gonville & Caius Coll Cambridge, St Mary's Hosp London; *Career* house surgn Addenbrooke's Hosp Cambridge 1967, house physician St Mary's Hosp London 1968, res fell and registrar Hammersmith Hosp 1971–73, sr registrar Royal Free Hosp 1977–80; conslt physician: Victoria and Kilton Hosps Bassetlaw 1980–81, Queen's Hosp Romford and St Bartholomew's Hosps 1981–; FRCP; *Recreations* opera, keep fit, walking; *Clubs* Savile; *Style*— Dr Richard Pearson; ✉ 152 Harley Street, London W1G 7LH (tel 020 7935 3834, fax 020 7354 1501)

PEARSON, Sara Ann; da of John Vernon Henry Franklin, of Robertsbridge, E Sussex, and Jeanette Marguerite, *née* Webster; *b* 1 August 1953; *Educ* Rosary Priory Convent; *m* 4 Oct 1974 (m dis 1999); 2 da (Chloe Ann b 15 March 1978, Clementine Sara b 29 Nov 1985), 1 s (Charlie Jon Eric b 29 Oct 1979); *Career* Sunday Telegraph, fndr The SPA Way Ltd; *Recreations* buildings and doing building; *Style*— Mrs Sara Pearson; ✉ 62 Bourne Street, London SW1W 8JD (tel 07818 061328)

PEARSON LUND, Peter Graham; s of Douglas Pearson Lund, CBE (d 1974), and Honor Winifred (d 1996); *b* 9 September 1947; *Educ* Shiplake Coll Henley, Guildford Sch of Art; *m* 16 Nov 1968, Isabelle McLachlan; 2 s (Piers b 19 Oct 1969, Oliver b 10 Dec 1971); *Career* Tilney & Co 1969–70, Cazenove and Co 1970–73, Antony Gibbs 1973–75; md Henderson Unit Trust Management (dir Henderson Administration Ltd) 1975–85, Gartmore Fund Managers Ltd (dir Gartmore plc) 1985–96; principal Gartmore Fund Managers Ltd 1996–99; chief exec Rathbone Unit Trust Management Ltd 1999–, memb Bd Rathbone Bros plc 2005–; *Recreations* tennis, skiing, sailing; *Style*— Peter Pearson Lund, Esq; ✉ Rathbone Unit Trust Management Limited, 159 New Bond Street, London W1S 2UD

PEARSON OF RANNOCH, Baron (Life Peer UK 1990), of Bridge of Gaur in the District of Perth and Kinross; Malcolm Everard MacLaren Pearson; s of late Col John MacLaren Pearson; *b* 20 July 1942; *Educ* Eton; *m* 1, 1965 (m dis 1970), Francesca Frua, da of Giuseppe Frua de Angeli; 1 da (Hon Silvia Maria Francesca (Hon Mrs Le Marchant) b 1966); m 2, 1977 (m dis 1995), Hon (Francesca) Mary Charteris, o da of late Baron Charteris of Amisfield, GCB, GCVO, QSO, OBE, PC; 2 da (Hon Marina b 1980, Hon Zara Alexandra Mary b 1984); m 3, 1997, Caroline, da of Maj Hugh Launcelot St Vincent Rose; *Career* chm PWS Holdings plc; hon treas CNAA 1983–93; memb House of Lords Select Ctee on the European Communities 1991–96; hon pres of RESCARE (Nat Soc for Mentally Handicapped People in Residential Care) 1994–; hon pres The Register of Chinese Herbal Medicine 1998–; Hon LLD from CNAA; *Clubs* White's; *Style*— The Rt Hon the Lord Pearson of Rannoch; ✉ House of Lords, London SW1A 0PW

PEART, Susan Rhona; *Educ* Felixstowe Coll; *Career* Cosmopolitan magazine 1979–84, Daily Express 1984–87; ed: Sunday Express Magazine 1989–91 (dep ed 1987–89), Weekend Times 1992–93, YOU magazine 2001– (dep ed 1993–2001); runner up Catherine Pakenham Award 1981; chairwoman BSME (memb 1987); *Recreations* entertaining, theatre, films; *Style*— Ms Susan Peart; ✉ 1 Hollingbourne Road, Dulwich, London SE24 9NB (e-mail sue.peart@mailonsunday.co.uk)

PEASE, Alexander Michael; s of Nicholas Edwin Pease (d 1975), and Anne Raikes (d 1985); *b* 14 March 1956; *Educ* Malvern Coll, Mansfield Coll Oxford (MA); *m* 22 April 1989, Lucy Jane, da of (George) Anthony Slater, of Guildford, Surrey; 2 da (Claudia Catherine Anne b 14 April 1992, Marina Lily Jane b 16 July 1994); *Career* Allen & Overy: asst slr 1981, ptnr 1989–2005, chm Alumni Prog 2005–; memb: Law Soc, City of London Law Soc; *Clubs* Cavalry and Guards', Royal Green Jackets; *Style*— Alexander Pease, Esq; ✉ Allen & Overy, One New Change, London EC4M 9QQ (tel 020 7330 3000, fax 020 7330 9999, telex 8812081)

PEASE, Sir Richard Thorn; 3 Bt (UK 1920); s of Sir Richard Arthur Pease, 2 Bt (d 1969); *b* 20 May 1922; *Educ* Eton; *m* 9 March 1956, Anne, o da of Lt-Col Reginald Francis Heyworth (d 1941), and formerly w of David Henry Lewis Wigan; 1 s, 2 da; *Heir* s, Richard Pease; *Career* served WWII 60 Rifles 1941–46; vice-chm Barclays Bank Ltd 1970–82, vice-chm Barclays Bank UK Mgmnt 1971–82, chm Yorkshire Bank 1987–90; *Recreations* fishing; *Clubs* Brooks's, Pratt's, Army and Navy; *Style*— Sir Richard Pease, Bt; ✉ Hindley House, Stocksfield-on-Tyne, Northumberland (tel 01661 842361)

PEASE, Sir (Alfred) Vincent; 4 Bt (UK 1882), of Hutton Lowcross and Pinchinthorpe, Co York; s of Sir Alfred Edward Pease, 2 Bt (d 1939), of Pinchinthorpe House, Guisborough, Cleveland, and Emily Elizabeth, *née* Smith (d 1979); half-bro of Sir Edward Pease, 3 Bt (d 1963); *b* 2 April 1926; *Educ* Bootham Sch York, Durham Sch of Agric; *Heir* bro, J Gurney Pease; *Style*— Sir Vincent Pease, Bt

PEASE, William Simon; *see:* Wardington, 3 Baron

PEASNELL, Prof Kenneth Vincent (Ken); *b* 2 February 1945; *Educ* Univ of Sheffield (Postgrad Dip Business Studies), LSE (MSc), Lancaster Univ (PhD); *m*; 2 c; *Career* trainee accountant Melman Pryke & Co London 1961–67, fin analyst IBM (UK) Ltd 1968–69; Lancaster Univ: P D Leake res fell Dept of Accounting and Fin 1970–72, research fell ICRA 1972–75, lectr in accounting and fin 1976–77, Wolfson prof of accounting and fin 1977–87 and 1998–, head Dept of Accounting and Fin 1978–83, assoc dean Mgmnt Sch 1987–91 and 1994–97, research prof of accounting and dir ICRA 1987–97; memb Lancaster Univ: Fin Ctee 1980–83 and 1990–91, Academic Promotions Ctee 1986–87, Ctee for Research 1986–97, Ctee for Colleges 1991, Budgeting and Monitoring Ctee 1994–97, Senate 1978–83, 1990–91 and 1998–, Univ Cncl 1987–91; visiting prof: Dept of Accounting Univ of Sydney 1983–84, Graduate Sch of Business Stanford Univ April-July 1984; memb Editorial Bd: Accounting Review 1977–82 and 1989–93, Accounting and Business Res 1980–81, Journal of Business Fin and Accounting 1980–84; ed Accounting and Business Research 1993–, Issues in Accounting 1995–, Br Accounting Review 1998–2001; external examiner: Univ of Birmingham 1979–80, Univ of Bristol 1979–82, Univs of Manchester and Warwick 1981–83, Manchester Business Sch 1987–90, LSE 1993–; external assessor for professorial or readership appointments at numerous univs; memb Exec Ctee Cncl of Depts of Accounting Studies 1979–84, chm Assoc of Univ Teachers of Accounting 1981–82; ICAEW: memb Res Sub-Ctee of Tech and Res Ctee 1979–82, memb Tech Ctee 1985–87, memb Educn and Training Advsy Gp 1987–90; memb Academic Accountants' Panel Accounting Standards Bd 1990– (Accounting Standards Ctee 1987–90), academic advsr to Accounting Standards Ctee on Off-Balance Sheet Financing 1988–90, memb Business and Mgmnt Studies Sub-Ctee of Univ Grants Ctee 1984–89; Univs Funding Cncl: chm Accountancy Panel 1989, Accountancy Subject advsr 1989–91; dir and hon treas Dukes Playhouse Ltd 1988–93; Distinguished Academic of the Year Award Chartered Assoc of Cert Accountants and Br Accounting Assoc 1996; FCA 1975 (ACA 1967); *Publications* author of numerous articles in academic, professional and miscellaneous publications and contribs to books; British Financial Markets and Institutions (with C W R Ward, 1985, 2 edn with J Piesse and C W R Ward, 1995), Off-Balance Sheet Financing (with R A Yaansah, 1988), Discounting in Corporate Financial Reporting (with C J Lovejoy, M Y Talukdar and P A Taylor, 1989); *Style*— Prof Ken Peasnell; ✉ Management School, Lancaster University, Lancaster LA1 4YX (tel 01524 593977, fax 01524 594334, e-mail k.peasnell@lancaster.ac.uk)

PEAT, Adam Erskine; s of late Raymond B B Peat, and late Cynthia Elisabeth Peat; *b* 30 November 1948; *Educ* Stowmarket County GS, Pembroke Coll Oxford (open exhbn, MA); *m* 1973, Christine Janet, da of late James Huzzard Champion; 1 s (Andrew James b July 1979), 1 da (Joanna Jane b Nov 1982); *Career* Welsh Office: joined 1972, princ 1977, private sec to Sec of State 1982–83, asst sec 1984; acting dir CADW 1984–85, head Housing Div Welsh Office 1985–89, chief exec Housing for Wales 1989–98, dir Housing Dept Welsh Office 1998–99, dir Local Govt, Communities and Culture Gp Nat Assembly for Wales 1999–2003, ombudsman Public Services Wales 2003–; *Style*— Adam Peat, Esq; ✉ The Public Services Ombudsman for Wales, 1 Ffordd yr Hen Gae, Pencoed CF35 5LJ (tel 01656 641150, fax 01656 641199)

PEAT, Jeremy; *b* 1945; *m*; 2 da; *Career* econ advsr: Br Embassy Bangkok 1972–74, Govt of Botswana 1980–84, HM Treasy 1984–85, Scotland Office 1985–93, gp chief economist Royal Bank of Scotland 1993–2005; memb Bd of Govrs and nat govr for Scotland BBC 2005–06 (chm Audit Ctee 2005–), memb BBC Tst and nat tstee for Scotland 2006–; dir David Hume Inst 2005–; memb Competition Cmmn 2005–, memb Cncl Scottish Econ Soc; visiting prof Univ of Edinburgh Sch of Mgmnt, hon prof Heriot Watt Univ; Hon LLD Univ of Aberdeen; FCIBS, FRSE; *Style*— Jeremy Peat, Esq; ✉ BBC Scotland, Broadcasting House, Glasgow G12 8DG

PEAT, Sir Michael Charles Gerrard; KCVO; s of Sir Gerrard Peat, KCVO, and Margaret Peat; *b* 16 November 1949; *Educ* Eton, Trinity Coll Oxford (MA), INSEAD (MBA); *m* 1976, Deborah Sage, *née* Wood; 2 da, 1 s and 1 s decd; *Career* with KPMG 1972–93; joined Royal Household 1993, Keeper of the Privy Purse, Treasurer to HM The Queen and Receiver Gen of the Duchy of Lancaster 1996–2002, Private Sec to HRH The Prince of Wales 2002–; FCA; *Style*— Sir Michael Peat, KCVO; ✉ Clarence House, London SW1A 1BA (tel 020 7930 4832)

PEATTIE, Cathy; MSP; *Career* dir Cncl of Voluntary Service in Falkirk, convenor Cncl of Voluntary Service Scotland; MSP (Lab) Falkirk East 1999–; convenor: Equal Opportunities Ctee, Cross Pty Gp on the Media, Cross Pty Gp on Scottish Traditional Arts, Cross Pty Gp on Asthma, Cross Pty Gp on Men's Violence against Women and Children, Lab Trade Union Gp; co-convenor Cross Pty Gp on Women; former chair Scottish Lab Women's Ctee; memb Advsy Ctee of the Nat Asthma Campaign, former memb Rural Affairs Ctee; *Recreations* traditional music, singing; *Style*— Ms Cathy Peattie, MSP; ✉ Constituency Office, 5 Kerse Road, Grangemouth FK3 8HQ (tel 01324 666026, fax 01324 473951, e-mail mail@cathypeattiemsp.org.uk, website www.cathypeattiemsp.org.uk); The Scottish Parliament, Edinburgh EH99 1SP (tel 0131 348 5746, fax 0131 348 5750/5976, e-mail cathy.peattie.msp@scottish.parliament.uk)

PECK, Alan Charles Weston; s of Awdry Francis Weston Peck (d 1980), and Marjory, *née* Taylor; *b* 13 April 1949; *Educ* Sherborne, Univ of Oxford (BA); *m* 1974, Anne Carolyn, da of Sir Herbert Ingram, 3 Bt (d 1980); 1 da (Frances Miranda Weston b 17 Sept 1978), 1 s (Alexander Robin Weston b 12 Feb 1981); *Career* admitted slr 1974; Freshfields: joined 1972, ptnr 1980–86 and 1989–2004, managing ptnr 1993–96, chief exec 1996–2004; dir S G Warburg & Co Ltd 1986–88; *Recreations* shooting, fishing, gardening; *Clubs* Turf, MCC; *Style*— Alan Peck, Esq; ✉ Hingsdon, Netherbury, Bridport, Dorset DT6 5NQ

PECKHAM, Prof (Lady); Catherine Stevenson; CBE (1998); da of Dr Alexander King, CBE, CMG, of Paris, and Sarah Maskell, *née* Thompson; *b* 7 March 1937; *Educ* St Paul's Girls' Sch, Univ of London (MB BS, MD); *m* 7 Oct 1958, Prof Sir Michael John Peckham, *qv*, s of William Stuart Peckham (d 1981); 3 s (Alexander b 1962, Daniel Gavin b 1964, Robert Shannan b 1965); *Career* reader in community med Charing Cross Hosp Med Sch 1977–85, prof of paediatric epidemiology Inst of Child Health and hon conslt Hosp for Sick Children Great Ormond St 1985– (sr lectr and hon conslt 1975–77), hon conslt Public Health Laboratory 1985–; memb: US Fulbright Cmmn 1987–95, Med Advsy Ctee Br Cncl 1992–95, Advtg Standards Authy 1993–99, New Millennium Experience Co Bd 1998–99, Nuffield Cncl on Bioethics 1999–, Cncl Inst of Educn 1999–; FFPHM 1980, FRCP 1988, FRCPath 1992, FRCOG 1994, FMedSci 1998 (founding fell); *Recreations* flute; *Style*— Prof Catherine Peckham, CBE; ✉ Institute of Child Health, Guilford Street, London WC1

PECKHAM, Prof Sir Michael John; kt (1995); s of William Stuart Peckham (d 1981), and Gladys Mary, *née* Harris (d 1998); *b* 2 August 1935; *Educ* William Jones W Monmouthshire Sch, St Catharine's Coll Cambridge (MA, MD), UCH Med Sch; *m* 7 Oct 1958, Prof Catherine Stevenson Peckham, CBE, *qv*, da of Dr Alexander King, CMG, CBE, of London; 3 s (Alexander b 1962, Daniel Gavin b 1964, Robert Shannan b 1965); *Career* Capt RAMC 1960–62; clinical res cncl scholar MRC Paris 1965–67, dean Inst of Cancer Res London 1984–86 (sr lectr 1972–74, prof 1974–86), civilian conslt to RN 1975–86, dir Br Postgrad Med Fedn 1986–90, dir of res and devpt Dept of Health 1991–95, dir Sch of Public Policy UCL 1996–; chm Nat Educn Res Forum 1999–; special tstee Guy's Hosp & St Thomas' Hosp Bd of Special Tstees 1996–2000; pres: Euro Soc of Therapeutic Radiology and Oncology 1984–85, Br Oncology Assoc 1986–88, Fedn of Euro Cancer Socs 1989–91; ed-in-chief European Journal of Cancer 1990–95, fndr Bob Champion Cancer Tst; memb New Millennium Experience Co Bd 1998–99; former memb special health authy: Hosps for Sick Children Gt Ormond St, Brompton and Nat Heart Hosp, Hammersmith Hosp, Imperial Cancer Res Fund (vice-chm Cncl); artist: solo exhbns Oxford, London and Edinburgh 1965–; Hon DSc Loughborough Univ of Technol 1992; Dr (hc): Université de Franche-Compté Besançon 1991, Katholieke Universiteit Leuven 1993; hon fell St Catharine's Coll Cambridge 1998; foreign assoc memb Nat Acad of Sciences Inst of Med Washington 1994; FRCP, FRCR, FRCPath, FRCPG, FRCS; *Recreations* painting; *Style*— Prof Sir Michael Peckham; ✉ School of Public Policy, University College London, The Rubin Building, 29/30 Tavistock Square, London WC1H 9QU

PECORELLI, Giuseppe; s of Leopoldo Pecorelli, of Rivello, Italy, and Maria, *née* Sersale; *b* 30 April 1939, Rivello, Italy; *Educ* Giorgio Vasari Coll of Accountancy Arezzo Italy; *m* 28 Nov 1964, Penelope Ann, *née* Birch; 3 s (Daniel Leopoldo Enrico, Nicholas Luigi Paolo (twins) b 24 July 1966, Giuseppe Patrick 6 Jan 1970), 1 da (Marie-Louise Elizabetta b 13 June 1968); *Career* md Trusthouse Forte Hotels and main bd dir Forte plc 1965–85 (also sometime pres Travel Lodge USA), chief exec Ciga Hotels (owned by the Aga Khan) 1985–87, dir Sun Int 1987–90, fndr Exclusive Hotels 1988–; FHCIMA; *Recreations* golf, oil painting; *Clubs* North Hants Golf; *Style*— Giuseppe Pecorelli, Esq; ✉ Exclusive Hotels, Pennyhill Park Hotel & Spa, London Road, Bagshot, Surrey GU19 5EU (tel 01276 478428, fax 01276 452182, e-mail barbara@exclusivehotels.co.uk)

PEDDIE, Ian James Crofton; QC (1992); s of Lord Peddie, MBE, JP (Life Peer; d 1978), and Lady Hilda Peddie (d 1985); *b* 1945; *Educ* Gordonstoun, UCL (LLB); *m* 1976, Susan Renée, da of Edmund John Brampton Howes; 2 s (James, Thomas), 2 da (Kate, Nichola); *Career* called to the Bar Inner Temple 1971; recorder 1997– (asst recorder 1993–97); *Style*— Ian Peddie, QC; ✉ Garden Court Chambers, 57–60 Lincoln's Inn Fields, London WC2A 3LS (tel 020 7993 7600)

PEDELTY, Sir Mervyn Kay; kt (2005); s of William Hopper Pedelty (d 1977), and Muriel, *née* Kay; *b* 16 January 1949; *Educ* Felixstowe GS, Harvard Business Sch (AMP); *m* 1998, Jill, *née* Hughes; 1 s, 1 step da; *Career* with British Leyland Ltd 1973–76, divnl fin dir rising to divnl md Plantation Holdings Ltd (later Phicom plc) 1976–80, divnl md Gould Inc 1981–83, fin dir and asst md Abacus Electronics Holdings plc 1983–87, fin dir TSB Banking and Insurance 1987–92, chief exec (commercial ops) TSB Group plc 1992–95, ptnr LEK Consulting LLP 1995–97; chief exec: The Co-operative Bank plc 1997–2004, Co-operative Insurance Soc 2002–04, Co-operative Financial Services 2002–04; non-exec dir: Hiscox plc 2005–, Hiscox Insurance Co Ltd 2005–, Hiscox Ltd 2006–, Friends Provident plc 2006–; sr advsr Permira Advisers LLP 2005–; dep chair NW Business Leadership Team 2001–05, chair Policy Ctee FTSE4Good 2001–, chair Manchester Enterprises Gp 2002–05, dir ABI 2002–04; memb: BBA CEO's Ctee 2002–04, Employer Task Force on Pensions DWP, Co-operative Cmmn; tstee: Symphony Hall Birmingham, Triumph Over Phobia; Freeman City of London, Liveryman Worshipful Co of Tin Plate Workers Alias Wire Workers, memb Guild of Int Bankers; FCA 1976 (ACA 1971), FCIB 1992; *Recreations* charity and community work, the countryside and the environment, music, art, skiing; *Clubs* RAC; *Style*— Sir Mervyn Pedelty

PEDLER, Garth; s of Thomas Wakeham Pedler (d 1984), of Exeter, and Ruby, *née* Cornish (d 1996); *b* 21 February 1946; *Educ* King's Coll Taunton; *partner* Jane Domaille Palmer; *Career* with Touche Ross & Co 1969–73, now independent taxation conslt; contributor on fiscal matters: Sunday Telegraph 1991–96, Sunday Times 1993–97; developed Br's first fully funded annual omphalotic national rail timetable, centred on Totnes 1996–2003; memb Old Boys' Ctee King's Coll Taunton 1972–; FCA, ATII; *Books* The 9.5mm Vintage Film Encyclopaedia (ed and jt author), A prep school in Somerset: Kings College Taunton Junior School up to 1982 (ed and jt author), biography of Joan Morgan; contributor to Classic Images USA 1982–93; *Recreations* vintage film research, collections of hardback books and vintage films; *Style*— Garth Pedler, Esq; ✉ Hay Hill, Totnes, Devon TQ9 5LH

PEDLEY, Rt Rev (Geoffrey) Stephen Pedley; s of Rev Prebendary Geoffrey Heber Knight Pedley (d 1974), and Muriel, *née* Nixon (d 1972); *b* 13 September 1940; *Educ* Marlborough, Queens' Coll Cambridge (MA), Cuddesdon Theol Coll; *m* 9 Jan 1970, Mary Frances, da of Rev Canon Alexander Macdonald (d 1980); 2 s (Mark Alexander b 1974, Andrew Francis b 1976), 1 da (Philippa Rose b 1979); *Career* asst curate: Liverpool Parish Church 1966, Holy Trinity Coventry 1969; rector Kitwe Zambia 1971–77, vicar St Peter's Stockton 1977–88, QHC 1985, rector Whickham 1988–93, canon residentiary of Durham Cathedral 1993–98, bishop of Lancaster 1998–2006; *Style*— The Rt Rev Stephen Pedley

PEDLEY, Prof Timothy John; s of Richard Rodman Pedley (d 1973), and Jean Mary Mudie Pedley, *née* Evans (d 2002); *b* 23 March 1942; *Educ* Rugby, Trinity Coll Cambridge (Wrangler, Mayhew Prize, MA, PhD, ScD); *m* 1965, Avril Jennifer Martin Uden, da of B G Grant-Uden (d 1990); 2 s (Jonathan Richard b 1968, Simon Grant b 1969); *Career* post-doctoral fell Mechanics Dept Johns Hopkins Univ 1966–68, lectr Physiological Flow Studies Unit and Dept of Mathematics Imperial Coll London 1968–73; Dept of Applied Mathematics and Theoretical Physics (DAMTP) Univ of Cambridge: successively asst dir of research, lectr then reader in biological fluid dynamics 1973–89, G I Taylor prof of fluid mechanics 1996–, head 2000–05; prof of applied mathematics Univ of Leeds 1990–96 (head Dept of Applied Mathematics 1991–94); Gonville & Caius Coll Cambridge: fell and dir of applied mathematics 1973–89, professorial fell 1996–; pres: World Cncl for Biomechanics 2002–06, Inst of Maths and its Applications 2004–05, Cambridge Philosophical Soc 2006–07; ed Jl of Fluid Mechanics 2000–06; lectures: GI Taylor (Camridge) 1998, Clifford (Tulane Univ) 2002, Rutherford (Royal Soc and RSNZ) 2003, Talbot (Univ of Illinois) 2004, Prandtl Meml 2007; memb: American Soc of Mechanical Engrg 1990, Soc for Experimental Biology 1993, European Mechanics Soc 1994 (memb Cncl 1995–2000), Soc of Mathematical Biology 1990, London Mathematical Soc 1997, American Physical Soc 2001; sometime govr: Perse Sch Cambridge, Batley GS; Adams Prize Univ of Cambridge 1977; foreign assoc US Nat Acad of Engrg 1999; sr fell EPSRC 1995–2000; FIMA 1981, FRS 1995; fell American Inst of Med and Biological Engrg 2001, fell American Physical Soc 2005; *Books* Scale effects in animal locomotion (ed, 1977), The mechanics of the circulation (jtly, 1978), The fluid mechanics of large blood vessels (1980), Biological fluid dynamics (co-ed, 1995); *Recreations* bird watching, running, reading, crosswords; *Style*— Prof Timothy Pedley; ✉ Department of Applied Mathematics & Theoretical Physics, University of Cambridge, Centre for Mathematical Sciences, Wilberforce Road, Cambridge CB3 0WA (tel 01223 339842, fax 01223 760497, e-mail tjp3@damtp.cam.ac.uk)

PEEBLES, Robert Andrew (Andy); s of Robert Peebles (d 1961), and Mary Jean, *née* Simmonds (d 1992); *b* 13 December 1948; *Educ* Bishop's Stortford Coll, Bournemouth Coll of Tech; *Career* radio presenter: BBC Radio Manchester 1973, Piccadilly Radio Manchester 1974–78, BBC World Serv 1978–88, BBC Radio One 1978–92, BBC Schools Radio 1983–87, BBC Radio Sport 1983–, BBC Radio Lancashire 1992–99, BBC Radio Two 1997–2002, BBC Radio North 1999–2005, Jazz FM 2003–05, Smooth Radio 2004–; *Books* The Lennon Tapes (1981), The Elton John Tapes (1981); *Recreations* sport, cinema, photography; *Clubs* Lancashire CCC; *Style*— Andy Peebles, Esq; ✉ Smooth Radio, 8 Exchange Quay, Manchester M5 3EJ (tel 0845 050 1004)

PEEL, Fiona Natalie; OBE (2001); *Educ* St Thomas' Hosp London (SRN), Univ of Exeter (BA), Univ of Wales Cardiff (LLM); *m* 1973, Hon Robert Michael Arthur Peel; 3 da (Kathryn b 1978, Hermione b 1979, Eleanor b 1981); *Career* chair: Gwent Community Health NHS Tst 1993–98, Cancer Servs Coordinating Gp Wales 1997–, Gwent HA 1998–2003, Cardiff Local Health Bd 2006–; dir Gwent TEC 1994–98; memb: Cncl UWCM 1996–2003, Cncl Univ of Wales Cardiff 2000–03, Cncl Cardiff Univ 2004–; *Style*— Mrs Fiona Peel, OBE

PEEL, Jane Elizabeth; da of William Richard Peel (d 1994), and Josephine Irene, *née* Stewart (d 1995); *b* 4 October 1960; *Educ* Highbury Hill HS London, Harlow Tech Coll (NCTJ Cert), Fletcher Sch of Law and Diplomacy Medford MA; *Career* reporter Barnet Press/Enfield Gazette 1981–84, sr reporter Lincolnshire Echo 1984–85; BBC: reporter BBC Radio Lincolnshire 1985–86, news prodr BBC Essex 1986–87, news ed BBC Essex 1987–89, reporter BBC national radio 1989–90, home and legal affrs corr 1990–2001, news corr 2001–; *Recreations* running, waterskiing, snow skiing; *Style*— Ms Jane Peel; ✉ BBC News, Television Centre, Wood Lane, London W12 7RJ (tel 020 8624 9094, e-mail jane.peel@bbc.co.uk)

PEEL, Prof John David Yeadon; s of Prof Edwin Arthur Peel (d 1992), of Birmingham, and Nora Kathleen, *née* Yeadon (d 1988); *b* 13 November 1941; *Educ* King Edward's Sch Birmingham, Balliol Coll Oxford (MA), LSE (PhD), Univ of London (DLit); *m* 4 Sept 1969 (m dis 2000), Jennifer Christine Ferial, da of Maj Kenneth Nathaniel Pare; 3 s (David Nathaniel Yeadon b 16 March 1972, Timothy James Olatokunbo b 27 Jan 1974, Francis Edwin b 30 March 1977); *Career* asst lectr and lectr in sociology Univ of Nottingham 1966–70, lectr in sociology LSE 1970–73, visiting reader in sociology and anthropology Univ of Ife Nigeria 1973–75, Charles Booth prof of sociology Univ of Liverpool 1975–89 (dean of Faculty of Social and Environmental Studies 1985–88), visiting prof of anthropology and sociology Univ of Chicago 1982–83, prof of anthropology and sociology with reference to Africa SOAS Univ of London 1989–2007 (dean of undergraduate studies 1990–94, emeritus prof 2007–); ed Africa (jl of Int African Inst) 1979–86, gen ed Int African Library 1985–; writer of numerous scholarly articles in Africanist, anthropological and sociological jls; Amaury Talbot Prize for African Anthropology 1983 and 2000, Herskovits Award for African Studies (USA) 1984 and 2001; memb Assoc of Social Anthropologists 1979, pres African Studies Assoc of UK 1996–98; FBA 1991 (vice-pres 1999–2000); *Books* Aladura: A Religious Movement among the Yoruba (1968), Herbert Spencer: The Evolution of a Sociologist (1971), Ijeshas and Nigerians: The Incorporation of a Yoruba Kingdom (1983), Religious Encounter and the Making of the Yoruba (2000), Christianity and Social Change in Africa: Essays in Honor of J D Y Peel (festschrift, 2005); *Recreations* gardening, fell walking, old churches; *Style*— Prof J D Y Peel, FBA; ✉ Department of Anthropology and Sociology, School of Oriental and African Studies (University of London), Thornhaugh Street, London WC1H 0XG (tel 020 7898 4407, e-mail jp2@soas.ac.uk)

PEEL, Richard Martin; s of Robert Horace Peel, of Boston, Lincs and Joan Ella, *née* Martin; *b* 23 April 1952; *Educ* Boston GS, Lanchester Poly (BA); *m* 26 May 1984, Diane Joan, da of Laurie Almond, of Perth, Ontario, Canada; 1 da (Charlotte Emma b 1976); *Career* cricket corr Northampton Chronicle and Echo 1976–79 (journalist 1973–79), press offr Milton Keynes Devpt Corp 1979–83; BBC: press offr 1983, sr press offr 1983–85, chief press offr 1985–87, chief asst info 1987–88, head of publicity and PR BBC News and Current Affrs 1988–93, head of communications and info BBC News and Current Affrs 1993–96, controller of communication and info BBC News 1996–97, controller of mktg and communication BBC News 1997–98; dir corp affrs England and Wales Cricket Bd 1998–2000, dir of public affairs, nations and regions ITC 2000–03, communications advsr Ofcom 2003; md: Communications and Public Reporting The Audit Cmmn 2004–06, RPPR; sr ptnr HPL 2006–; memb: Media Soc, RTS, Radio Acad, London Business Sch Alumni; MCIM; *Recreations* walking, reading, music; *Clubs* Reform, Lord's Taverners, Cricket Writers; *Style*— Richard Peel, Esq; ✉ Lower Farm, Buckland, Buckinghamshire HP22 5HY (mobile 07768 045008, e-mail rppr@hotmail.co.uk)

PEEL, (Kenneth) Roger; s of Kenneth Galloway Peel (d 1966), and Elizabeth Margaret, *née* Watson (d 1989); *b* 9 September 1935; *Educ* Aireborough GS, Univ of Leeds Med Sch (MB ChB, FRCSEd, FRCOG); *m* 1959, Doreen; 2 s (Simon Charles b 19 Dec 1961, Andrew James b 15 April 1964); *Career* formerly GP and holder of jr hosp appts in obstetrics, gynaecology, urology and gen surgery, conslt obstetrician and gynaecologist St James's Univ Hosp and St Mary's Hosp 1968–72, surgn to the Hosp for Women Leeds and the Maternity Hosp Leeds 1968–80, conslt gynaecological surgn Gen Infirmary Leeds (with responsibilities in gynaecological oncology), sr clinical lectr Univ of Leeds 1968–99, assoc med dir The Leeds Teaching Hosp 1999–2000, conslt gynaecological surgeon Nuffield Hosp Leeds, ret; post graduate advsr in obstetrics and gynaecology Yorks region 1977–83, memb then chm Dept of Health Ctee on Gynaecological Cytology 1981–89, memb Cncl Royal Coll of Obstetricians and Gynaecologists 1984–90 and 1991–95 (sr vice-pres and overseas offr 1992–95), invited memb Cncl RCS 1990–92, memb GMC 1995–97; examiner and sometime external examiner to RCOG, Arab Bds, Coll of Physicians and Surgns of Pakistan and Univs of Khartoum and W Indies; Sims Black travelling prof to Pakistan, India, Sri Lanka and Nepal 1996; pres Central Yorks Scout County; fndr memb: Br Soc of Colposcopy and Cervical Pathology, Gynaecological Cancer Gp (later Br Gynaecological Cancer Soc); Freeman City of London, Liveryman Worshipful Soc of Apothecaries; memb BMA; *Publications* Dewhurst's Postgraduate Textbook of Obstetrics and Gynaecology (contrib chapters on gynaecological oncology, 1995); *Recreations* sailing, skiing, fell walking and vintage cars; *Style*— Roger Peel, Esq; ✉ Borrings Cottage, Hawkswick, Skipton, North Yorkshire BD23 5QA (tel 01756 770279)

PEEL, 3 Earl (UK 1929); Sir William James Robert Peel; 8 Bt (GB 1800), GCVO (2006), PC (2006), DL (N Yorks 1998); Viscount Peel (UK 1895) and Viscount Clanfield (UK 1929); s of 2 Earl Peel (d 1969, himself gs of 1 Viscount, who was in turn 5 s of Sir Robert Peel, 2 Bt, the distinguished statesman); *b* 3 October 1947; *Educ* Ampleforth, Tours Univ, RAC Cirencester; *m* 1, 1973, Veronica Naomi Livingston, da of Alastair Timpson; 1 s (Ashton Robert Gerard, Viscount Clanfield), 1 da (Lady Iona Joy Julia b 1978); m 2, 1989, Hon Charlotte Clementine, *née* Soames, da of Baron Soames, GCMG, GCVO, CH, CBE, PC (Life Peer, d 1987), and formerly w of (Alexander) Richard Hambro, *qv*; 1 da (Lady Antonia Mary Catherine b 14 Dec 1991); *Heir* s, Viscount Clanfield; *Career* pres The Game Conservancy Tst (formerly chm), chm The Standing Conference for Countryside Sports, former pres Yorkshire Wildlife Tst; memb: Prince's Cncl 1993–, Exec Ctee The Moorland Assoc, Cncl for English Nature, Bd The Countryside Movement, Bd Countryside Alliance; former memb Yorkshire Dales National Park Ctee, former pres Gun Trade Assoc; Lord Warden of the Stannaries and Keeper of the Privy Seal of the Duke of Cornwall 1994–2006, Lord Chamberlain to HM's Household 2006–, chllr Royal Victorian Order 2006–; *Style*— The Earl Peel, GCVO, DL; ✉ Eelmire, Masham, Ripon, North Yorkshire HG4 4PF

PEGDEN, His Hon Judge Jeffrey Vincent; QC (1996); s of George Vincent Pegden (d 1994), and Stella Blanche Katherine, *née* Maxted; *b* 24 June 1950; *Educ* Wallington County GS, Univ of Hull (LLB, pres Univ Law Soc); *m* 5 Sept 1981, Delia Mary, da of Paul and Lucy Coonan; 1 s (Oliver Roderick William b 30 May 1982), 1 da (Antonia Catherine Lucy b 15 Aug 1985); *Career* called to the Bar Inner Temple 1973 (bencher 2002); recorder 1996–2007, circuit judge (South Eastern Circuit) 2007–; Bar Cncl of England and Wales rep Criminal Bar Assoc 1993–95; memb: SE Circuit, Criminal Bar Assoc, Br Acad of Forensic Sciences, Crown Court Rules Ctee Home Office; Liveryman Worshipful Co of Clockmakers 2002; FRSA; *Recreations* music, reading, walking, gardening, sailing; *Style*— His Hon Judge Pegden, QC

PEGG, Jonathan; *b* 21 April 1973; *Career* literary agent Curtis Brown 1997–; *Style*— Jonathan Pegg, Esq; ✉ Curtis Brown Group Ltd, Haymarket House, 28–29 Haymarket, London SW1Y 4SP (e-mail jonnyp@curtisbrown.co.uk)

PEGG, Dr Michael Stuart; s of Gilbert Seaton Pegg, of Reigate, Surrey and Waldy Greta, *née* Jonsson; *b* 15 June 1948; *Educ* The GS Reigate, UCL, Westminster Med Sch (BSc, MB BS), Cardiff Law Sch (LLM); *m* 17 Jan 1983, Kaija Kaarina, da of Niilo Sarolehto, of Espoo, Finland; 1 da (Antonia Alexandra b 9 Aug 1984), 1 s (Justin William b 12 June 1986); *Career* conslt anaesthetist Royal Free Hosp 1981–, hon sr lectr Royal Free Hosp Med Sch 1981–; memb: BMA, Assoc of Anaesthetists; FRCA; *Style*— Dr Michael Pegg; ✉ Newstead, 3 Canons Close, Radlett, Hertfordshire WD7 7ER (tel 01923 856640, fax

P

01923 858430, e-mail m.pegg@btinternet.com); Department of Anaesthetics, Royal Free Hospital, Pond Street, London NW3 2QG

PEGG, Simon; *b* 14 February 1970, Glos; *Educ* Univ of Bristol; *Career* actor, writer, comedy performer; *Television* as actor incl: Faith in the Future 1995, Big Train (also writer) 1998, Spaced (also writer) 1999–2000, Hippies 1999, Band of Brothers 2001; *Film* as actor incl: Shaun of the Dead (also co-writer) 2004, Mission Impossible III 2006, The Big Nothing 2006, The Good Night 2006, Hot Fuzz (also writer) 2007; *Style*— Simon Pegg, Esq; ✉ c/o Dawn Sedgwick Management, 3 Goodwins Court, Covent Garden, London WC2N 4LL (tel 020 7240 0404, fax 020 7240 0415)

PEIN, Malcolm; s of Norman Pein, and Linda Pein (d 1990); *b* 14 August 1960; *Educ* Quarry Bank Comp, UCL (BSc); *m* 20 Jan 1991, Philippa, da of Leslie Vides; *Career* chess corr: The European 1990–91 and 1992–, Daily Telegraph 1991–; purchased Maxwell McMillan Chess & Bridge Ltd 1992 (publishing Chess Monthly and Bridge Monthly); conslt chess.ibm.com (Kasparov v Deep Blue chess computer) 1997; match dir Kramnik v Deep Fritz Bahrein 2002; Br jr chess champion 1977, int chess master 1985; *Books* Grunfeld Defence Exchange Variation (1981), Trends in the Marshall Attack (1991), Blumenfeld Gambit (1991), Bobby Fischer $5 Million Comeback (1992), Daily Telegraph Guide to Chess (1995); *Recreations* football, classical music, BBC World Service; *Style*— Malcolm Pein, Esq

PEIRSON, Richard; s of Geoffrey Peirson (d 1986), of Purley, Surrey, and Beryl Joyce, *née* Walder (d 1999); *b* 5 March 1949; *Educ* Purley GS, Univ of Liverpool (BSc); *m* 1, 31 May 1975 (m dis), Jennifer Margaret, da of late F E Fernie; 1 s (James Richard b 1978), 1 da (Caroline Jane b 1980); m 2, 16 Feb 1991, Victoria, da of R P Steiner; 2 s (Charles Hamilton b 1993, George Alexander b 1996); *Career* Arthur Andersen & Co 1970–72, Colegrave & Co 1972–73, J & A Scrimgeour Ltd 1973–75, Carr Sebag & Co (formerly W I Carr Sons & Co) 1975–82, Grieveson Grant & Co 1982–86, Kleinwort Benson Investment Management Ltd 1986–94, Framlington Investment Management Ltd 1994–; Liveryman Worshipful Co of Glaziers and Painters of Glass; MSI; *Recreations* tennis, interior design, reading, collecting watercolours; *Clubs* City of London; *Style*— Richard Peirson, Esq; ✉ 13 Kings Road, Richmond, Surrey TW10 6NN (tel 020 8940 2013); Axa Framlington Investment Management Ltd, 155 Bishopsgate, London EC2M 3XJ (tel 020 7374 4100, fax 020 7330 6570, e-mail richard.peirson@axaframlington.com)

PEISER, Graham Allan; s of Eric George Peiser (d 1991), of Bucks, and Honor, *née* Greenwood (d 1988); *b* 26 March 1940; *Educ* Aldenham, Coll of Estate Mgmnt; *m* 26 Sept 1970, Jennifer Ann, da of Dr John Richard Cooper; 2 da (Georgina b 1972, Lucy b 1976); *Career* chartered surveyor and arboriculturist; ptnr: Fuller Peiser 1970–91, Graham Peiser Properties 1991–, Hyrons Trees 1992–; Liveryman Worshipful Co of Glass Sellers; FRICS; *Style*— Graham A Peiser, Esq; ✉ Pear Tree Cottage, The Green, Sarratt, Rickmansworth, Hertfordshire WD3 6BL (tel 01923 269136, fax 01923 270625)

PELHAM, Dr Hugh Reginald Brentnall; s of Reginald Arthur Pelham, (d 1981), and Pauline Mary, *née* Brentnall; *b* 26 August 1954; *Educ* Marlborough, Christ's Coll Cambridge (MA, PhD); *m* 25 May 1996, Dr Mariann Bienz, *qv*; 1 s, 1 da; *Career* res fell Christ's Coll Cambridge 1978–84, postdoctoral fell Dept of Embryology Carnegie Inst of Washington Baltimore MD 1979–81; MRC Laboratory of Molecular Biology Cambridge: staff memb 1981–, head Cell Biology Div, dep dir 1996–2006, dir 2006–; visitor Univ of Zürich 1987–88; awards: Colworth medal Biochemical Soc 1988, EMBO medal 1989, Louis Jeantet prize for med 1991, King Faisal int prize for science 1996; memb: EMBO 1985, Academia Europaea 1990; FRS 1988, FMedSci 1998; *Style*— Dr Hugh Pelham, FRS; ✉ MRC Laboratory of Molecular Biology, Hills Road, Cambridge CB2 0QH (tel 01223 248011, fax 01223 249565, e-mail hp@mrc-lmb.cam.ac.uk)

PELHAM BURN, Angus Maitland; JP, DL (1978); s of Brig-Gen Henry Pelham Burn, CMG, DSO (d 1958), and Katherine Eileen, *née* Staveley-Hill (d 1989); *b* 13 December 1931; *Educ* Harrow, N of Scotland Coll of Agric; *m* 19 Dec 1959, Anne Rosdew, da of Sir Ian Algernon Forbes-Leith, 2 Bt, KT, MBE (d 1973); 4 da (Amanda b 1961, Lucy b 1963, Emily b 1964, Kate b 1966); *Career* Hudson's Bay Co 1951–58; chm and dir MacRobert Farms (Douneside) Ltd 1970–87, chm Pelett Administration Ltd 1973–95; dir: Aberdeen and Northern Marts Ltd 1970–86 (chm 1974–86), Aberdeen Meat Marketing Co Ltd 1973–86 (chm 1974–86), Bank of Scotland 1977–2000 (dir Aberdeen and North Local Bd chm 1973–2001), Prime Space Design Ltd 1981–87, Taw Meat Co 1984–86, Status Timber Systems 1986–90, Skeendale Ltd 1987–88, Abtrust Scotland Investment Co plc 1989–96, Dana Petroleum plc 1999–; chm: Aberdeen Asset Management plc (and predecessor firms) 1993–2000 (dir 1985–98), Scottish Provident Institution 1995–98 (dir 1975–, dep chm 1991–95), Global Philanthropic International Ltd 2002–, Oilcats Ltd 2005–06; memb: Kincardine CC 1967–75 (vice-convener 1973–75), Grampian Regnl Cncl 1974–94, Aberdeen Assoc for the Prevention of Cruelty to Animals 1975–96 (dir 1984–94, chm 1984–89), Accounts Cmmn 1980–94 (dep chm 1987–94), Cncl Winston Churchill Meml Tst 1984–93, Exec Cncl Scottish Veterans' Residences until 2002; chm: Aberdeen Airport Consultative Ctee 1986–2006, Order Ctee Order of St John (Aberdeen) Ltd 1992–97 (memb 1987–); tstee The Gordon Highlanders Regimental Tst until 2001, memb Gordon Highlanders Museum Mgmnt Ctee 1994–; memb Queen's Body Guard for Scotland (Royal Co of Archers) 1968–; general cmmr of income tax Kincardine Div 1997–2001; dir Lathallan Sch 2001–04; JP Kincardine and Deeside 1984–2004; Vice Lord-Lt Kincardineshire 1978–99; Liveryman Worshipful Co of Farmers until 1988; Hon LLD Robert Gordon Univ Aberdeen 1996; CStJ; *Recreations* vegetable gardening, photography; *Clubs* Royal Northern & Univ (Aberdeen), Sloane; *Style*— Angus Pelham Burn, Esq, JP, DL, LLD; ✉ Kennels Cottage, Dess, Aboyne, Aberdeenshire AB34 5AY (tel 01339 884445, fax 01339 884430, e-mail snow.bunting@virgin.net)

PELL, Gordon; *Educ* Wellington Coll, Univ of Southampton; *Career* with Lloyds Bank 1971–2000 (gp dir retail banking Lloyds TSB 1998–2000), chief exec retail markets Royal Bank of Scotland Gp 2000–, chief exec Coutts Gp 2002–; memb: Nat Employment Panel, Practitioner Panel FSA; dir Race for Opportunity; FCIB, FCIBS; *Recreations* riding, clay shooting; *Style*— Gordon Pell; ✉ 12th Floor, 280 Bishopsgate, London EC2M 4RB

PELLEGRINO, Prof Sergio; s of Arturo Pellegrino (d 2004), and Maria Bonavita; *Educ* Univ of Naples (Laurea), Univ of Cambridge (PhD); *m* 1984, Mariella Soprano; 1 da (Giulia b 4 Jan 1991); *Career* Univ of Cambridge: bye-fell Peterhouse 1983 (research studentship 1982–83), teaching fell CCC 1985–, lectr 1988 (asst lectr 1985), reader 1997, prof of structural engrg (personal chair) 2000–, dep head of dept 2005–; visiting researcher Inst for Space and Astronautical Science Tokyo and Nippon Telegraph and Telephone Corp Spacecraft Structures Lab Yokosuka 1987 and 1990, research fell Structures and Mechanisms Div European Space Technol Centre Netherlands 1992, visiting prof: Univ of Colorado Boulder 1997–98, Univ Teknology Malaysia 2002–04; assoc fell American Inst of Aeronautics and Astronautics, memb Int Assoc for Shell and Spatial Structures; CEng, MIStructE, MASCE; *Style*— Prof Sergio Pellegrino; ✉ Department of Engineering, Trumpington Street, Cambridge CB2 1PZ

PELLEW, Robin Anthony; OBE (2006); s of Cdr Anthony Pellew RN, (d 1993), and Margaret Critchley, *née* Cookson; *b* 27 September 1945; *Educ* Marlborough, Univ of Edinburgh (BSc), UCL (MSc), Univ of London (PhD); *m* 1974, Pamela, da of Dr Desmond MacLellan; 1 da (Sophie Harriet b 1979), 1 s (Toby James Pownoll b 1982); *Career* chief research scientist Serengeti Research Inst Tanzania 1972–78, research fell Physiology Lab Univ of Cambridge 1978–82, dir Biological Sciences Cambridge University Press 1985–87 (science ed Biological Sciences 1982–85), dir World Conservation Monitoring Centre Cambridge 1987–94, DG WWF-World Wide Fund for Nature (UK) 1994–98, chief exec Animal Health Tst Newmarket 1999–2001, chief exec Nat Tst for Scotland 2001–06; memb Cncl: RGS 1993–96, Conservation Science Ctee Zoological Soc of London 1996–, Round Table on Sustainable Development UK 1994–99; Busk Medal for Conservation RGS 1992; fell British Ecological Society 1982, FZS 1992, FRSA 1992; *Publications* author of numerous scientific papers and conservation articles in academic journals, magazines and newspapers; *Recreations* travel, wildlife; *Style*— Robin Pellew, Esq, OBE; ✉ 32 Selwyn Gardens, Cambridge CB3 9AY (tel 01223 327321)

PELLING, Andrew John; MP, AM; s of Anthony Adair Pelling, *qv*, and Margaret Rose, *née* Lightfoot (d 1986); *b* 20 August 1959; *Educ* Trinity Sch Croydon, New Coll Oxford; *Career* memb London Borough of Croydon 1982–2006 (chm Educn Ctee 1988–94, dep ldr of oppn 1998–2002, ldr of oppn 2002–05), memb London Assembly (Cons) Sutton and Croydon 2000– (chair Public Servs Ctee 2002–04, chair Budget Ctee 2007–08), MP (Cons) Croydon Central 2005– (memb Educn and Skills Select Ctee 2006–07); memb: Cncl for the Accreditation of Teacher Educn 1990–92, Bd London Devpt Agency 2000–04; *Style*— Andrew Pelling, Esq, MP, AM; ✉ House of Commons, London SW1A 0AA

PELLING, Anthony Adair; s of Brian Pelling, and Alice, *née* Lamb; *b* 3 May 1934; *Educ* Purley GS, LSE (BSc), NW Poly London, Wolverhampton Coll of Technol (MIPM); *m* 1, Margaret Rose, *née* Lightfoot (d 1978); 1 s (Andrew John, *qv*), 1 da (Sarah Margaret); m 2, Virginia, *née* Glen-Calvert; 1 da (Amanda d 2001); *Career* War Office 1955–57, NCB 1957–67; Civil Serv 1967–93: princ 1967–69, asst sec 1969–81, under sec 1981–93, dep dir Business in the Community 1981–83, dir Highways Contracts and Maintenance Dept of Tport 1983–85, dir Construction Industry, Sports and Recreation Directorates DOE 1985–87, dir London Region DOE 1987–91, dir Construction Policy Directorate DOE 1991–93; dir GJW Government Relations Ltd 1993–95, exec dir The Advocacy Gp Inc 1999–2001; conslt Trade and Regulatory Intelligence 1995–; dir: Cities in Schools, Croydon Business Venture 1982–95; memb Croydon Family Health Servs Authy 1989–95; pres Richmond ESU 1998–2000, chm Region IV US ESU 2000–02 (memb Nat Bd US ESU 2000–02), pres Byrd Theatre Fndn Richmond; *Clubs* Reform, Kiwanis Richmond VA; *Style*— Anthony Pelling; ✉ 70 West Square Drive, Richmond, VA 23238, USA (tel 00 1 804 784 8881, fax 00 1 804 784 8789, e-mail gjw1995pel@aol.com)

PELLING, Prof Christopher Brendan Reginald; s of Reginald Pelling (d 1990), of Cardiff, and Brenda, *née* Sadler (d 2000); *b* 14 December 1947, Newport, Gwent; *Educ* Cardiff HS, Balliol Coll Oxford (MA), ChCh Oxford; *m* 1973, Margaret Ann, *née* Giddy; 1 s (Charles b 1978), 1 da (Sally b 1983); *Career* research fell Peterhouse Cambridge 1972–74, McConnell Laing fell and praelector in classics UC Oxford 1975–2003 (lectr 1974–75), regius prof of Greek Univ of Oxford 2003–; *Books* Plutarch: Life of Antony (1988), Literary Texts and the Greek Historian (2000), Plutarch and History (2002); *Recreations* cricket, golf, music (especially Broadway), conviviality; *Clubs* MCC; *Style*— Prof Christopher Pelling; ✉ Christ Church, Oxford OX1 1DP

PELLING, Rowan Dorothy; da of Ronald Alfred Pelling, and Hazel, *née* Underwood (d 2003); *Educ* Walthamstow Hall Sevenoaks, St Hugh's Coll Oxford; *Career* editorial asst Private Eye then GQ, ed The Erotic Review 1997–, dir The Erotic Print Soc, dir Dedalus Ltd; columnist GQ and Independent on Sunday; *Books* The Erotic Review Bedside Companion (ed, 2000), The Decadent Handbook (ed, 2006); *Recreations* reading, buying shoes, growing broad beans, Formula 1, flirting; *Clubs* The Academy, Blacks; *Style*— Ms Rowan Pelling; ✉ EPS, 4th Floor, 1 Maddox Street, London W1S 2PZ (tel 020 7437 8887, fax 020 7437 3528, e-mail editrice@eroticreview.org)

PELLOW, Marti (né Mark McLachlan); *b* 23 March 1965, Clydebank; *Career* singer; lead singer with Wet Wet Wet 1983–1999 and 2004–, 14 top twenty singles incl 3 no 1's (With A Little Help from my Friends 1988, Goodnight Girl 1992, Love Is All Around 1994); albums with Wet Wet Wet: Popped In Souled Out (1987, UK no 1), The Memphis Sessions (1988, UK no 3), Holding Back The River (1989, UK no 2), High On The Happy Side (1992, UK no 1), End of Part One (compilation, 1994, UK no 1), Picture This (1995), 10 (1997); solo albums: Smile 2001, Between the Covers 2003, Moonlight over Memphis 2006; participated in: Prince's Trust Rock Gala 1988, 1989 and 1990, concert for Nelson Mandela's 70th birthday 1988, John Lennon Tribute concert 1990, Wet Wet Wet at The Royal Albert Hall (in aid of Nordoff-Robbins Music Therapy Tst) 1992, Party in the Park Hyde Park (in aid of Prince's Tst) 2000; Billy Flynn in Chicago (Adelphi Theatre London, Broadway and Tokyo) 2002 and 2004; TV appearances incl Just the Two of Us (BBC 1) 2007; *Style*— Marti Pellow, Esq; ✉ website www.martipellowofficial.com

PELLY, Derek Roland (Derk); s of Arthur Roland Pelly (d 1966), of Ballygate House, Beccles, Suffolk, and Phyllis Elsie, *née* Henderson (d 1973); *b* 12 June 1929; *Educ* Marlborough, Trinity Coll Cambridge (MA); *m* 20 June 1953, Susan, da of John Malcolm Roberts (d 1986), of Felpham, W Sussex; 2 da (Rosemary b 1955, Catherine b 1958), 1 s (Sam b 1960); *Career* 2 Lt RA 1947–49; Barclays Bank 1952–88: local dir Chelmsford Dist 1959–68 (asst to chm 1968–69), local dir Luton Dist 1969–79, dir Barclays Int 1974 (vice-chm 1977–86, chm 1986–87), dir Barclays plc 1974 (vice-chm 1984–86, dep chm 1986–88); dir Private Bank and Tst Co Ltd 1989–94, memb Ctee Family Assurance Soc 1988–91, chm City Commuter Gp 1987–88, dir Milton Keynes Devpt Corp 1976–85, memb Cncl Overseas Devpt Inst 1984–89; govr London House for Overseas Graduates 1985–91, treas Friends of Essex Churches 1989–96, memb Chelmsford Diocesan Bd of Fin 1989–96; JP Chelmsford 1965–68; FCIB; *Recreations* painting; *Style*— Derk Pelly, Esq; ✉ Kenbank, St John's Town of Dalry, Kirkcudbrightshire DG7 3TX (tel 01644 430424)

PELLY, Frances Elsie; da of Russell Steele Pelly (d 1993), and Agnes Mysie, *née* MacPherson; *b* 21 July 1947; *Educ* Morrison's Acad, Duncan of Jordanstone Coll of Art (Scottish Educn scholar, Carnegie scholar, DA), Moray House Coll of Educn (CertEd); *Career* sculptor; artist in residence: Stromness Acad 1990, Fort William Library 1991, RSA 1991; artist in industry Highland Park Distillery 1987, residency Lazonby Cumbria 1996, Cape Dorset Canada 1997; pt/t lectr Duncan of Jordanstone Coll of Art 1974–78, lectr Gray's Sch of Art 1979–83; RSA 1990; *Major Exhibitions* Scottish Sculpture Open 1983, 1989 and 1993, Paper, Wood and Stone (Collective Gall) 1985, Stirling Smith Biennial 1985 and 1987, Spring Fling 1986, retrospective (Crawford Art Centre) 1987, Artist in Industry Exhbn (Seagate Gall) 1987, Scottish Sculpture Tst (tour) 1988, Glasgow Garden Festival 1988, Ten Years On 1989, Directions in Scottish Sculpture (Barbican) 1990, Five Thousand Years of Orkney Art (tour) 1990, Nousts (tour) 1992, Scottish Sculpture Open No 7 (Kildrummy Castle) 1993, Scandex Exhbn (tour) 1994–96, Shoreline Exhbn (tour) 1995–96, New Work at the Yards St Magnus Festival (Kirkwall) 1996, Island (Crawfords Arts Centre St Andrews) 1996, RSA Festival Exhbn 1996, Poetry in Place Orkney 1999, Hansel 2002 Orkney, Shetland and Norway 2003, Plants and Stones Orkney 2003, Orkney Eight Norway 2003; *Work in Collections* Dundee Coll of Commerce, Fine Art Soc (Edinburgh and London), Scottish Arts Cncl, RSA, Royal Glasgow Concert Hall, Museum of Scotland, Fort William, Banff, Perth, Kirkwall, Glasgow; *Awards* Gleichen Award Royal British Sculptors 1970, Guthrie Award RSA 1971, Ottillie Helen Wallace Award RSA 1972, William J Macaulay Award RSA 1977, Benno Schotz Award Royal Glasgow Inst 1980, Gillies Award RSA 1982, Ireland Alloys Award RSA 1983; *Recreations* riding, gardening, studying wildlife, travelling; *Style*— Frances Pelly, RSA; ✉ Quoyblackie, Rendall, Orkney KW17 2HA (tel 01856 751464)

PELLY, Sir Richard John; 7 Bt (UK 1840), of Upton, Essex; s of Richard Heywood Pelly (d 1988), and Mary Elizabeth, *née* Luscombe; *b* 10 April 1951; *Educ* Wellington, Wadham Coll Oxford (BA); *m* 1983, Clare Gemma, da of late Harry Wilfred Dove, of Winchester, Hants; 3 s (Anthony Alwyne b 1984, James Richard b 1986, Harry Philip b 1988); *Heir* s, Anthony Pelly; *Career* with: Price Waterhouse & Co 1974–79, Birds Eye Walls Ltd

1979–81, New Century Software Ltd 1981–98; farmer 1991–; *Clubs* Farmers'; *Style*— Sir Richard Pelly, Bt; ✉ The Manor House, Preshaw, Upham, Southampton SO32 1HP

PEMBERTON, Antony Francis; DL (2001); s of Sir Francis William Wingate Pemberton, of Cambridge, and Diana Patricia Pemberton (d 1999); *b* 24 February 1942; *Educ* Eton, Trinity Coll Cambridge (MA); *m* 7 Jan 1967, Victoria Anne, da of Maj Antony Gibbs (d 2000); 2 s (Richard Francis Antony b 9 July 1970, Charles Jeremy b 23 June 1972); *Career* farmer and estate mangr 1964–; memb Cncl RASE; tstee: Nat Inst of Agric Botany Tst, Fund for Addenbrooke's, Addenbrooke's Recreational & Devpt Tst; Liveryman Worshipful Co of Farmers; High Sheriff Cambs 2000–01; FRAgS 1998; *Recreations* sailing, shooting, fishing; *Clubs* Farmers'; *Style*— Antony Pemberton, Esq, DL; ✉ Trumpington Hall, Cambridge CB2 9LH (tel 01223 841101, fax 01223 841143)

PEMBERTON, Dr James; s of Tom Winstanley Pemberton, of Sheffield, and Marjorie, *née* Chesney; *b* 21 December 1940; *Educ* King Edward VII Sch Sheffield, St Bartholomew's Hosp Med Sch (MB BS, MRCP, BSc scholarship, Hayward prize); *m* Sylvia Ann, *née* Finnigan; 4 c (Philippa Louise b 12 Sept 1968, Tom Winstanley b 12 Oct 1969, James Wentworth b 25 June 1971, Sam b 28 April 1981); *Career* St Bartholomew's Hosp: house physician 1968, house surgn 1969, registrar Pathology Dept 1970, registrar in med 1970–71, registrar in diagnostic radiology 1971–73; sr registrar in diagnostic radiology King's Coll Hosp 1973–74, conslt radiologist St Thomas' Hosp 1974–2001; admin head Radiology Dept Lambeth and S Western Hosps 1975–77; organiser Scientific Exhibition Jl Annual Congress of the Combined Royal Colls of UK, Netherlands and BIR 1978 and 1979; chm: Radiology Sub Ctee St Thomas' Hosp 1978–80 and 1984–86, Dist Working Pty on Jr Hosp Med and Dental Staff Hours of Work 1988; St Thomas' Hosp: chm Dist Working Pty on Junior Doctors' Rotas (Safety Nets), memb Dist Manpower Ctee 1986–92, chm Med and Surgical Offrs Ctee 1993–95, pres Sch of Radiography; memb: Regnl Manpower Ctee 1986–90, Regnl Radiology Specialists Sub-Ctee 1984–90; former pres Symposium Mammo Graphicum; memb BIR: Prog Ctee 1976–79, Med Ctee 1977–79 and 1990–92, Cncl 1990–93, Radiation Protection Ctee 1990–92; med lectr for: RCR, Br Cncl, FRCS Course and FRCR Course in Radiotherapy St Thomas' Hosp; author of numerous pubns in learned jls; MRCS 1967, LRCP 1967, DMRD 1972, FFR 1974, FRCR 1976; *Recreations* watching Arsenal FC, horseracing; *Style*— Dr James Pemberton; ✉ 18 Village Way, Dulwich, London SE21 7AN (tel 020 7737 2220)

PEMBERTON, Steve James; s of Derek James Pemberton (d 1998), and Margaret, *née* Catterall; *b* 1 September 1967; *Educ* Bretton Hall Coll (BA); *Partner* Alison Rowles; 2 s (Lucas James b 13 May 2000, Adam Elliot b 14 Jan 2006), 1 da (Madeleine Ann b 15 Feb 2003); *Career* actor and writer; Hon DLitt Univ of Huddersfield; *Theatre* The League of Gentlemen Are Behind You (Hammersmith Apollo and tour), A Local Show for Local People (Theatre Royal Drury Lane and tour) 2000–01, Marc in Art (Whitehall Theatre) 2002; *Television* The League of Gentlemen 1999, 2000 and 2002 (awards include BAFTA Best Comedy Series, RTS Award for Best Entertainment and Golden Rose of Montreux), The League of Gentlemen Christmas Special 2000, Gormenghast 2000, Shameless 2003, Poirot: Death on the Nile 2004, Blackpool 2004, The Last Detective 2005, Under the Greenwood Tree 2005, Hotel Babylon 2005, Benidorm 2007, The Bad Mother's Handbook 2007, Kingdom 2007; *Radio* On The Town With The League of Gentlemen 1997 (Sony Silver for Best Radio Comedy); *Film* Birthday Girl 2002, Churchill - The Hollywood Years 2003, The Life and Death of Peter Sellers 2003, The Hitchhiker's Guide to the Galaxy 2005, Match Point 2005, The League of Gentlemen's Apocalypse 2005, Lassie 2006, Free Jimmy 2006, I Could Never Be Your Woman 2006, Mr Bean's Holiday 2007; *Publications* A Local Book For Local People (2000), The League of Gentlemen: Scripts and That; *Style*— Steve Pemberton, Esq; ✉ c/o Caroline Chignell, PBJ Management Ltd, 7 Soho Street, London W1D 3DQ (tel 020 7287 1112); c/o Nicki van Gelder, Conway van Gelder, 18–21 Jermyn Street, London SW1Y 6HP (tel 020 7287 0077)

PEMBROKE, Dr Andrew Charles; s of Geoffrey Vernon Worth Pembroke (d 1983), of Bexhill-on-Sea, E Sussex, and Mary Constance, *née* Purkis (d 1978); *b* 1 June 1947; *Educ* Winchester (scholar), King's Coll Cambridge (scholar and sr scholar, MA, MB BChir), Bart's Med Coll; *m* 1977, Jacqueline Beatrice, da of Percival Henry Gage Hall; 3 s (Thomas Peter Ignatius b 1980, Charles Dominic b 1985, Theodore Philip Gervase b 1987), 2 da (Beatrice Mary b 1978, Olivia Constance b 1982); *Career* med registrar Hackney Hosp 1974–75, sr registrar in dermatology London Hosp 1975–78; conslt dermatologist: King's Coll Hosp 1981–94 (sr registrar in dermatology 1978–81), Bromley Hosps NHS Tst 1994–; hon treas: Br Assoc of Dermatologists 1987–92, Br Skin Fndn 1996–; chm SE Thames Regnl Specialty Sub-Ctee for Dermatology 1987–91; FRCP 1988; *Style*— Dr A C Pembroke; ✉ 28 Dartford Road, Sevenoaks, Kent TN13 3TQ (tel 01732 450197); 152 Harley Street, London W1N 1HH (tel 020 7935 2477)

PEMBROKE, Ann Marjorie Francesca; *Educ* Holy Trinity Convent, Sorbonne; *Career* Foreign Office London and Paris 1956–58, The Monotype Corp and Odhams Press 1958–60, Pembroke & Pembroke fin and legal recruitment conslts London 1969–; memb: Ct of Common Cncl City of London 1978– (representing Ward of Cheap), IOW Soc, Cncl St John Ambulance IOW, Keats House Consultative Ctee, RSL, Wynkyn de Worde Soc, FAO Assoc; govr City of London Sch; tstee: Dr Johnson's House, Dickens House Museum, City of London Archaeological Tst, Jane Austen Meml Tst, Clockmakers Museum; fndr Isle of Wight Heritage and Field Studies Centre 2000; Freeman City of London 1977, Liveryman Worshipful Co of Horners 1980; OStJ 1999; *Recreations* travel, horticulture, country pursuits; *Clubs* City Livery, Guildhall, Ward of Cheap, Royal Corinthian Yacht, Pepys; *Style*— Mrs A M F Pembroke; ✉ Pembroke & Pembroke, The Green House, 41–42 Clerkenwell Green, London EC1R 0DU

PENDER, 3 Baron (UK 1937); John Willoughby Denison-Pender; s of 2 Baron Pender, CBE (d 1965), and Camilla Lethbridge, da of late Willoughby Arthur Pemberton; *b* 6 May 1933; *Educ* Eton; *m* 1962, Julia, da of Richard Nevill Cannon, OBE, of Lewes, E Sussex; 2 da (Hon Emma Charlotte (Hon Mrs Brett) b 1964, Hon Mary Anne Louise (Hon Mrs Curtis Green) b 1965), 1 s (Hon Henry John Richard b 1968); *Heir* s, Hon Henry Denison-Pender; *Career* formerly Lt 10 Royal Hussars and Capt City of London Yeo; former dir Globe Trust Ltd, chm J J & D Frost plc; vice-pres The Royal Sch for Deaf Children 1992– (treas 1999–2004); sits as Cons in House of Lords; steward: Folkestone 1985–2003, Lingfield Park 1989–2003; *Recreations* golf, racing, gardening; *Clubs* White's, Pratt's; *Style*— The Rt Hon the Lord Pender; ✉ North Court, Tilmanstone, Kent CT14 0JP

PENDRY, Prof Sir John Brian; kt (2004); s of Frank Johnson Pendry (d 1978), and Kathleen, *née* Shaw (d 2001); *b* 4 July 1943; *Educ* Ashton-under-Lyne GS, Downing Coll Cambridge (MA, PhD); *m* 15 Jan 1977, Patricia, da of Frederick Gard, of London; *Career* res fell in physics Downing Coll Cambridge 1969–75, memb tech staff Bell Laboratories USA 1972–73, sr asst in res Cavendish Laboratory Cambridge 1973–75 (postdoctoral fell 1969–72), SPSO and head Theory Gp SERC Daresbury Laboratory 1975–81; Imperial Coll London: prof of theoretical solid state physics 1981–, assoc head Dept of Physics 1981–92, head Dept of Physics 1998–2001; dean Royal Coll of Sci 1993–96; chm Physics Sub-Panel RAE 2008; memb: Physics Ctee SERC (chm Panel Y) 1985–88, Sci Bd SERC 1992–93, Cncl Royal Soc 1992–94, Cncl PPARC 1998–2002; Cwlth scholarships cmmr 1998–2000; hon fell Downing Coll Cambridge 2005; FRS 1984, FInstP 1984, fell Optical Soc of America 2005; *Recreations* music, piano playing, gardening, photography; *Style*— Prof Sir John Pendry, FRS; ✉ Metchley, Knipp Hill, Cobham, Surrey KT11 2PE (tel 01932 864306); The Blackett Laboratory, Imperial College, London SW7 2AZ (tel 020 7594 7606, fax 020 7594 7604)

PENDRY, Baron (Life Peer UK 2001), of Stalybridge in the County of Greater Manchester; Thomas (Tom) Pendry; PC (2000); s of L E Pendry, of Broadstairs, Kent; *b* 10 June 1934; *Educ* St Augustine's Ramsgate, Univ of Oxford; *m* 1966 (sep 1983), Moira Anne, da of A E Smith, of Derby; 1 s, 1 da; *Career* electrical engr; Nat Serv RAF 1955–57; joined Lab Pty 1950, NUPE official 1960–70, memb Paddington Cncl 1962–65, chm Derby Lab Pty 1966; MP (Lab) Stalybridge and Hyde 1970–2001, oppn whip 1971–74, a Lord Cmmr of the Treasy (Govt whip) 1974–77 (resigned), Parly under sec of state NI Office 1978–79; oppn spokesman: on NI 1979–81, on overseas devpt 1981–82, on devolution and regnl affrs 1982, on Sport 1992; shadow min for sport and tourism 1992–97; chm: All-Pty Football Ctee 1980–92, PLP Sports Gp 1984–, All-Pty Tourism Ctee 1997–; co-chm All-Pty Jazz Ctee; pres Football Fndn 2003–, chm Football Tst 1998–2003, steward Br Boxing Bd of Control 1987–2003; Freeman Borough of Tameside 1975, Lordship of Mottram in Longdendale 1975; *Recreations* sports of all kinds; *Clubs* Stalybridge Labour, Vincent's (Oxford), Lord's Taverners, MCC; *Style*— The Rt Hon the Lord Pendry, PC; ✉ Alice House, Old Road, Stalybridge, Cheshire SK15 2RG

PENFOLD, Adrian Philip; s of Albert Penfold (d 1958), and Dorothy Jane, *née* Milner (d 1989); *b* 9 March 1952, Buckinghamshire; *Educ* Bedford Modern Sch, Univ of Essex (BA), Kingston Poly (Dip); *m* July 1976, Elspeth Anne, *née* Hemery; 3 s (Daniel Liam b 1978, James Geoffrey b 1981, Michael Leonard b 1984); *Career* planning asst Beds CC 1973, career grade planner then memb then ldr devpt control team London Borough of Hammersmith and Fulham 1976–88, planning exec then head central enterprise zone team London Docklands Devpt Corp 1988–90, asst devpt servs mangr then head of planning and design Dartford BC 1990–96; British Land Co plc: chief planner 1996–2001, head planning and environment 2001–, memb Bd and Devpt Bd British Land Corporation Ltd; memb Third Age Project, vice-chair Strategy Sub-Ctee West Euston Partnership; MRTPI 1978, FRSA; *Recreations* sport, walking, travel; *Clubs* Architecture; *Style*— Adrian Penfold, Esq; ✉ 11 Cliveden Road, Wimbledon, London SW19 3RD (tel 020 8715 7739, e-mail ea.penfold@blueyonder.co.uk); The British Land Company plc, York House, Seymour Street, London W1H 7LX (tel 020 7467 3481, e-mail adrian.penfold@britishland.com)

PENFOLD, Derek John; s of Joseph Penfold, of Tiverton, Devon, and Catherine, *née* O'Sullivan; *b* 17 July 1948; *Educ* Clapham Coll, City of Westminster Coll, NW London Poly (LLB); *Career* features ed Estates Times 1975–78, dep ed Estates Gazette 1978–86 (news ed 1978–80), property analyst Alexanders Laing & Cruickshank 1986–87; dir: Streets Communications 1987–89, Phillips Communications 1990–91, Derek Penfold Associates 1991–94; ed Estates Times 1994–96; dir: Publishing Business Ltd 1996–97, CMT International 1998–2001; communications dir HOK International Ltd 2005–; chm Greenwich Theatre 1976–87 (dir 1975–90), dir Greenwich Young People's Theatre 1980–88, former chm Greenwich Festival; London Borough of Greenwich cncllr 1971–78, (chm Leisure Ctee, chief whip); vice-pres The Story of Christmas Charity Appeal, tstee LandAid Charitable Tst; Freeman City of London; fell Land Inst; *Recreations* theatre, architecture; *Clubs* Wig & Pen, Globe Rowing, Walbrook and Broad Street Wards, Architecture, Tyburn Anglers, Volestranglers; *Style*— Derek Penfold, Esq; ✉ 89A Edith Road, London W14 0TJ (tel 020 7603 6495)

PENFOLD, Peter Alfred; CMG (1995), OBE (1986); s of Alfred Penfold (d 1991), and Florence Maud Penfold; *b* 27 February 1944; *Educ* Sutton Co GS; *m* 1, 1972 (m dis 1983), Margaret Quigley; 2 da (b 1963 and 1974), 2 s (b 1973 and 1980); m 2, 1992, Celia Dolores Koenig; *Career* Foreign Serv (later HM Dip Serv); joined 1963, Bonn 1965–68, Kaduna 1968–70, various posts Mexico City, Quito, San Juan, Montevideo, Asuncion and St Vincent 1970–72, Canberra 1972, FCO 1972–75, second sec Addis Ababa 1975–78, Port of Spain 1978–81, FCO 1981–84, dep high cmmr Kampala 1984–87, FCO 1987–91, govr Br Virgin Islands 1991–97, high cmmr to Sierra Leone 1997–2001, sr conflict advsr DfID 2001–02, int conslt 2003–; Queen's scout, Paramount Chief in Sierra Leone; chm UK Assoc for the Milton Margai Sch for the Blind Sierra Leone; *Recreations* travel, reading; *Style*— Peter Penfold, Esq, CMG, OBE

PENHALIGON, Susan; da of William Russell Penhaligon, of San Francisco, USA, and Muriel Jean Mickleborough; *Educ* The Collegiate Sch Winterbourne, Rustington House Sch, The Webber-Douglas Sch London; *Career* actress; *Theatre* Painting Churches (Nuffield Southampton), David Lodge's The Writing Game (Birmingham Rep), The Girl In Melony Klein (Palace Watford), A Doll's House (Palace Watford), The Three Sisters (Albery), The Maintenance Man (Comedy), Of Mice And Men (Southampton & Mermaid), The Formation Dancers (Yvonne Arnaud Theatre), Tom Stoppard's The Real Thing (Strand), Sylvia Plath's Three Women (Old Red Lion), Mrs Warren's Profession (Gardner Centre Brighton), The Cherry Orchard (Royal Exchange Manchester), The Lower Depths (Royal Exchange Manchester), Time And The Conways (Royal Exchange Manchester), Picasso's Four Little Girls (Open Space), Painting Churches (Nuffield Theatre Southampton), Abducting Diana (Edinburgh Festival), The Statement (Watermans Art Centre), Dangerous Corner (Whitehall), The Mysterious Mr Love (Comedy Theatre); *Television* Trouble In Mind, Fay Weldon's Heart Of The Country, Seven Faces Of Women, Andrew Davies' Fearless Frank, Phillip Saville's Dracula, Country Matters, Jonathan Miller's The Taming Of The Shrew, A Fine Romance, A Kind Of Loving, Bouquet Of Barbed Wire, Casualty, Ruth Rendell Mysteries, Junk; *Films* The Last Chapter, The Soldier Of The Queen, The Uncanny, The Confessional, Miracles Still Happen, No Sex Please We're British, Patrick, Nasty Habits, Leopard In The Snow, Under Milk Wood, The Land That Time Forgot, Private Road; *Publications* A Two Hander (collection of poems with Sara Kestleman, The Do-Not Press); *Style*— Ms Susan Penhaligon

PENKETT, Prof Stuart Arthur; s of Arthur Penkett (d 1963), of Leeds, and Ilene Maud, *née* Henshaw (d 1988); *b* 3 January 1939, Eccles; *Educ* Eccles GS, Univ of Leeds (BSc, PhD); *m* 2 June 1962, Marigold, *née* Gibbens; 2 da (Fiona Sally b 24 Feb 1968, Rebecca Gayle b 26 July 1973), 2 s (Clive Stuart b 11 Jun 1969, Christopher John b 18 Feb 1972); *Career* postdoctoral research fell Univ of Southern Calif 1963–65, Unilever Research Labs Welwyn 1965–68, Atomic Energy Research Estab Harwell 1968–85, Nat Center for Atmospheric Research Boulder 1985; UEA: NERC reader in atmospheric chemistry 1985–90, prof of atmospheric chemistry 1990–2004, emeritus prof 2004–; affiliate scientist Nat Center for Atmospheric Research Boulder 1997–2000; chm: NERC ACSOE Community Prog, IGBP IGAC Symposium Fuyi Yoshida; memb: Dept of Environment review gps on Stratospheric Ozone and Photochemical Oxidants, UK Meteorological Office Hadley Centre Scientific Advsy Gp, NERC Atmospheric Sceince Ctee, EU Jt Environment Centre Ispra, UN Environment Prog Assessment of Stratospheric Ozone; memb: US Nat Acad of Sciences, World Meteorological Orgn, European Science Fndn, European Research Cncl, Royal Soc; author of over 200 pubns since 1965, also many citations; Royal Meteorological Soc Gaskell Medal 1987, Elsevier Science Haagen-Smit Award 2003, Leverhulme emeritus fell 2005–06; memb Academia Europaea 1988, foreign memb Max Planck Soc 1987; FRMetS; *Recreations* walking, American geography and history, European history, architecture; *Style*— Prof Stuart Penkett; ✉ University of East Anglia, School of Environmental Sciences, Norwich NR4 7TJ (tel 01603 501051, e-mail m.penkett@uea.ac.uk)

PENMAN, John; s of John Penman, of Cumbernauld, and Sarah, *née* Welsh; *b* 10 January 1962; *Educ* St Gregory's Secdy Sch Glasgow, Greenfaulds HS Cumbernauld, Napier Coll Edinburgh; *m* 24 Oct 2003, Lucy Jane Patton; 1 da (Daisy b 15 Sept 1999); *Career* chief reporter Carlisle Evening News and Star 1987–91, asst new ed The Northern Echo

P

1991–94, dep news ed The Scotsman 1994–98 (political ed 1996–98), asst ed Daily Record 1998, new business dir Daily Record and Sunday Mail 1998–2000, ed-in-chief/md Business a.m. 2000–02, Business and Fin ed Scottish Daily Record 2003–05, ed-in-chief Scottish Business Insider 2003–05, business ed Scotland The Sunday Times 2005–; highly commended Campaigning Journalist of the Year Award 1992, Scottish Daily Newspaper of the Year 2000, runner-up UK Daily Newspaper of the Year 2000, Best Designed Newspaper Newspaper Awards 2001, UK Regnl Business and Fin Newspaper of the Year 2002, runner-up Business Journalist of the Year Scottish Press Awards 2006; memb SO Ctee on Media Regulation Scot Parl 1998; *Recreations* watching Partick Thistle FC, astronomy, walking, running; *Style*— John Penman, Esq; ✉ The Sunday Times, 124 Portman Street, Glasgow G41 (tel 0141 420 5267)

PENN, Christopher Arthur; s of Lt-Col Sir Eric Charles William Mackenzie Penn, GCVO, OBE, MC (d 1993), and Prudence Stewart-Wilson, da of Aubyn Wilson (d 1934); *b* 13 September 1950; *Educ* Eton; *m* 1976, Sabrina Mary, 2 da of Sir Timothy Colman, KG, DCL, of Bixley Manor, Norwich; 1 s (Rory b 1980), 1 da (Louisa b 1983); *Career* chartered surveyor; dir Jones Lang LaSalle; *Clubs* White's, Buck's; *Style*— Christopher Penn, Esq

PENN, David John; s of late Surgn Capt Eric Arthur Penn, DSC, of W Mersea, Essex, and late Catherine, *née* Dunnett; *b* 2 January 1945; *Educ* Dulwich Coll, St Catherine's Coll Oxford (MA); *m* 1993, Catherine Janet Davidson; 1 s (Alexander Eric Davidson b 12 Jan 1995), 1 da (Flora Catherine Davidson b 25 Jan 1999); *Career* keeper Imperial War Museum: Dept of Info Retrieval 1970–77, Dept of Firearms 1973–76, Dept of Exhibits and Firearms 1976–2005 (conslt 2005–); memb: Home Office Firearms Consultative Ctee 1989–2004 (chm 2000–04), National Historic Ships Ctee 1995–99; pres Arms and Armour Soc; vice-pres: Muzzle-Loaders Assoc of GB, Hist Breechloading Smallarms Assoc, BASC; sec Br Shooting Sports Cncl, conslt Fedn for European Socs of Arms Collectors; Freeman City of London 1982, Liveryman Worshipful Co of Gunmakers 1982; FSA 1989; *Books* Imperial War Museum Film Cataloguing Rules (with R B N Smither, 1976); *Recreations* shooting; *Style*— David Penn, Esq, FSA; ✉ 70 Holmdene Avenue, London SE24 9LE (tel 020 7274 4265)

PENNANT-REA, Rupert Lascelles; s of late Peter Athelwold Pennant-Rea, MBE, of Burford, Oxon, and late Pauline Elizabeth, *née* Creasy; *b* 23 January 1948; *Educ* Peterhouse Zimbabwe, TCD (BA), Univ of Manchester (MA); *Children* 1 da (Emily b 1982), 2 s (Rory b 1983, Edward b 1986); *Career* with Confedn of Irish Industry 1970–71, Gen & Municipal Workers Union 1972–73, Bank of England 1973–77; The Economist: economics corr 1977–81, economics ed 1981–85, ed 1986–93; dep govr Bank of England 1993–95; chm: The Stationery Office 1996–2005, PGI plc 1997–, Security Printing and Systems 1999–2006, Electra Kingsway VCT plc 2001–, Henderson Gp plc 2005–; non-exec dir: Sherritt Int 1995–2007, British American Tobacco plc 1995–2007, First Quantum Minerals 2001–, Gold Fields 2002–, Go-Ahead Gp plc 2002–, Financial News Gp 2003–07, The Economist Newspaper Ltd 2006–; chm The Shakespeare Schs Festival 2001–; *Books* Gold Foil (1978), Who Runs The Economy? (jtly, 1979), The Pocket Economist (jtly, 1982), The Economist Economics (jtly, 1986), Public Choice Analysis of Economic Policy (jt ed, 2000); *Recreations* music, tennis, fishing, family, golf; *Clubs* MCC, Reform, Harare; *Style*— Rupert Pennant-Rea, Esq; ✉ Henderson, 4 Broadgate, London EC2M 2DA

PENNEY, Penelope Anne; da of late Richard Chamberlain, and late (Lydia) Joan, *née* Kay; *b* 30 September 1942; *Educ* Chatelard Sch Les Avants Switzerland, Univ of Bristol (BA); *m* 27 July 1963, Rev William Affleck Penney, s of Robert Affleck Penney; 1 s (Christopher James Affleck b 25 Sept 1964), 2 da (Margaret Clare b 10 Feb 1966, Alison Joan b 27 April 1971); *Career* pt/t English teacher 1967–74, head of languages and communications Astor of Hever Sch Maidstone 1975–79; headmistress: Prendergast Sch Catford 1980–86, Putney HS GDST 1987–91, Haberdashers' Aske's Sch for Girls 1991–2005; educn conslt 2005–, educn advsr London Diocesan Bd for Schs 2005–; memb SHA 1980–, memb Teacher Induction Panel Ind Schs Cncl 1999–2002; GSA: memb 1987–, memb Professional Ctee 1991–94, chm London Region 1992–94, pres 1994–95, chm Inspections Ctee 2001–03; Freeman City of London 1993, Liveryman Worshipful Co of Haberdashers; MInstD 1991, FRSA 1994, FCMI (FIMgt 1994), FZS 2007; *Publications* Hearing the Squirrel's Heartbeat (2006); *Recreations* fast cars, grandparental duties, education; *Style*— Mrs Penelope Penney; ✉ 6 Devonshire Court, 26A Devonshire Street, London W1G 6PJ (e-mail p.a.penney@btinternet.com)

PENNING, Michael; MP; *b* 1957, London; *Educ* King Edmund Comp; *Career* Grenadier Guards (served NI, Kenya and Germany); sometime fireman; former political advsr Cons Shadow Cabinet under William Hague, former dep head of media Cons Pty; MP (Cons) Hemel Hempstead 2005– (Parly candidate (Cons) Thurrock 2001); *Style*— Michael Penning, Esq, MP; ✉ House of Commons, London SW1A 0AA

PENNINGTON, Prof (Thomas) Hugh; s of Thomas Wearing Pennington (d 1993), and Dorothy Pennington (d 1989); *b* 19 April 1938; *Educ* Lancaster Royal GS, St Thomas' Hosp Med Sch (MB BS, Clutton Medal, Bristowe Medal, Beaney Prize, Foord Caiger Prize, PhD); *m* 1965, Carolyn Ingram, da of George Beattie; 2 da; *Career* asst lectr med microbiology St Thomas' Hosp Medical Sch 1963–67, postdoctoral fell Univ of Wisconsin Madison 1967–68, lectr and sr lectr MRC Virology Unit and Dept of Virology Univ of Glasgow 1969–79, prof of bacteriology Univ of Aberdeen 1979–2003 (dean Faculty of Med 1987–92, emeritus prof 2003–); external examiner at several Br univs; chm: Expert Gp on the 1996 E.coli Outbreak in Central Scotland, Public Inquiry into 2005 E.coli Outbreak in S Wales 2006–; govr Rowett Research Inst 1980–88 and 1995–2004; memb: BBC Broadcasting Cncl for Scotland 2000–05 (vice-chair), Scottish Food Advsy Ctee Food Standards Agency 2000–05, BBC Rural Affairs Advsy Ctee, World Food Prog Tech Advsy Gp; pres Soc for Gen Microbiology 2003–06; Hon DSc: Lancaster Univ, Univ of Strathclyde, Univ of Aberdeen, Univ of Hull; FRCPath, FRCPEd, FMedSci, FRSE, FRSA; *Publications* Molecular Virology (with D A Ritchie, 1975), When Food Kills (2003); numerous papers on molecular virology, molecular epidemiology and the systematics of pathogenic bacteria, contrib London Review of Books; *Recreations* collecting books, dipterology; *Style*— Prof Hugh Pennington, FRSE; ✉ 13 Carlton Place, Aberdeen AB15 4BR (tel 01224 645136); Department of Medical Microbiology, University of Aberdeen, Medical School Buildings, Aberdeen AB25 2ZD (e-mail mmb036@abdn.ac.uk)

PENNINGTON, Michael Vivian Fyfe; s of Vivian Maynard Cecil Pennington (d 1984), and Euphemia Willock Fyfe (d 1987); *b* 7 June 1943; *Educ* Marlborough, Trinity Coll Cambridge (BA); *m* 10 Oct 1964 (m dis 1967), Katharine, da of Peter Barker; 1 s (Mark Dominic Fyfe b 12 Aug 1966); *Career* actor; memb RSC 1964–66; freelance, West End and TV plays 1966–73: The Judge, Hamlet, A Woman of No Importance, Savages; leading memb RSC 1974–81: Angelo in Measure for Measure, Mercutio in Romeo and Juliet, Edgar in King Lear, Berowne in Love's Labour's Lost, Mirabell in Way of the World, title role in Hippolytus, title role in Hamlet, Donal Davoren in Shadow of a Gunman; NT 1984: title role in Strider, Jaffier in Venice Preserved, solo performance of Anton Chekhov; subsequent credits: The Real Thing (West End) 1985, Oedipus The King (BBC) 1985; artistic dir English Shakespeare Co until 1993 (fndr and leading actor 1986–92, participated in four round the world tours); roles incl: Richard II, Henry V, Coriolanus, Leontes in The Winter's Tale, Macbeth; other credits: Summer's Lease (BBC) 1989, Playing with Trains (RSC Barbican) 1989, Vershinin in Three Sisters (Gate Theatre Dublin) 1990, Edward Damson in The Gift of the Gorgon (RSC Barbican and Wyndham's) 1993, Old Times and One for the Road (Dublin Pinter Festival), Claudius and the Ghost in Hamlet (Peter Hall Co) 1994, Taking Sides (Chichester Festival, Criterion) 1995, Archie Rice in The Entertainer (Hampstead) 1996; Old Vic 1997 incl: Waste, The Seagull, The Provoked Wife, Anton Chekhov; also Alceste in The Misanthrope and Domenico in Filumena (Piccadilly Theatre) 1998, Oscar Wilde in Gross Indecency (Gielgud Theatre) 1999, Timon in Timon of Athens (RSC Stratford and Barbican), Nandor in The Guardsman (Albery Theatre) 2000, Prentice in What the Butler Saw 2001, John in The Shawl 2001, Walter Burns in The Front Page (Chichester Theatre) 2002, title role in John Gabriel Borkman (English Touring Theatre) 2003, Dr Dorn in The Seagull (Edinburgh Festival) 2003, George III in The Madness of King George (W Yorks Playhouse) 2003, Cecil in When the Night Begins (Hampstead Theatre) 2004; dir Twelfth Night (English Shakespeare Co 1991, Haiyuza Co Tokyo 1993, Shakespeare Repertory Co Chicago 1996), A Midsummer Night's Dream (Regents Park Open Air Theatre) 2003; *Books* Rossya: A Journey Through Siberia (1977), English Shakespeare Company: The Story of the Wars of The Roses (1990), Hamlet: A User's Guide (1995), Twelfth Night: A User's Guide (1999), Are You There, Crocodile - Inventing Anton Chekhov (2002); *Recreations* reading, music; *Style*— Michael Pennington, Esq; ✉ c/o Cassie Mayer Ltd, 5 Old Garden House, The Lanterns, Bridge Lane, London SW11 3AD

PENNINGTON, Prof Robert Roland; s of Roland Alexander Pennington (d 1952), of Warley, W Midlands, and Elsie Davis (d 1977); *b* 22 April 1927; *Educ* Holly Lodge Smethwick, Univ of Birmingham (LLB, LLD); *m* 14 March 1968, Patricia Irene, da of Cecil Allen Rook (d 1968), of Alcester, Warwickshire; 1 da (Elisabeth Anne b 1974); *Career* admitted slr 1951; reader Law Soc's Sch of Law London 1955 (sr lectr 1951), memb Bd of Mgmnt Coll of Law London 1962; Univ of Birmingham sr lectr in law 1962–68, prof of commercial law 1968–94, emeritus prof 1994–; visiting prof Univ of London 1995–; govt advsr on co legislation Trinidad 1967 and Seychelles 1970, special legal advsr on commercial law harmonisation Cmmn of the Euro Communities 1973–79; Hon LLD Univ of Exeter 1994; memb Law Soc 1951; *Books* Company Law (1959, 8 edn 2001), Companies in the Common Market (1962, 3 edn as Companies in the European Communities 1982), The Investor and the Law (1967), Stannary Law - A History of the Mining Law of Cornwall and Devon (1973), Commercial Banking Law (1978), The Companies Acts 1980 and 1981 - A Practitioner's Manual (1983), Stock Exchange Listing - The New Requirements (1985), Britisches Gesellschaftsrecht, Jura Europa - Gesellschaftsrecht: Vereinigtes Königreich (1986), Directors' Personal Liability (1987), Company Liquidations - The Substantive Law, The Procedure (2 vols, 1987), The Law of the Investment Markets (1990), Corporate Insolvency Law (1990, 2 edn 1997), Small Private Companies (1998), The Re-organisation of Public and Private Companies' Share Capital (1999); *Recreations* travel, walking, history, archaeology; *Style*— Prof Robert Pennington; ✉ Gryphon House, Langley Road, Claverdon, Warwickshire (tel 0192 684 3235)

PENNY, Nicholas Beaver; s of Joseph Noel Bailey Penny, QC (d 1998), and Agnes Celia, *née* Roberts (d 1969); *b* 21 December 1949; *Educ* Shrewsbury, St Catharine's Coll Cambridge (MA), Courtauld Inst London (MA, PhD); *m* 1, 1971 (m dis), Anne Philomel, *née* Udy; 2 da (Caroline Emily, Elizabeth Joan (twins) b 26 Jan 1977); *m* 2, 1994, Mary Wall, *née* Crettier; *Career* Leverhulme fell Clare Coll Cambridge, lectr Dept of History of Art Univ of Manchester 1975–82, Slade prof of fine art Univ of Oxford 1980–81, sr res fell King's Coll Cambridge 1982–84, keeper of Western art Ashmolean Museum and professorial fell Balliol Coll Oxford 1984–89, Clore curator of Renaissance painting National Gallery London 1990–2002 (keeper 1998–2002); National Gallery of Art Washington DC: Andrew W Mellon prof Center for Advanced Studies in the Visual Arts 2000–02, sr curator of sculpture and decorative arts 2002–; Cavaliere dell'Ordine al merito della Repubblica Italiana 1990, memb American Acad of Arts and Sciences 2007; *Books* Church Monuments in Romantic England (1977), Piranesi (1978), Taste and the Antique (with Francis Haskell, 1981), Mourning (1981), The Arrogant Connoisseur (ed with Michael Clarke, 1982), Raphael (with Roger Jones, 1983), Reynolds (ed, 1986), Alfred and Winifred Turner (1988), Lucian Freud, Works on Paper (with Robert Flynn Johnson, 1988), Ruskin's Drawings (1988), From Giotto to Dürer (with Jill Dunkernon et al, 1991), European Sculpture in the Ashmoleam Museum: 1540 to the Present Day (1992), The Materials of Sculpture (1993), From Dürer to Veronese (with Jill Dunkerton et al, 1999), Art of the Renaissance Bronze (with Anthony Radcliffe, 2004), The Sixteenth Century Paintings in the National Gallery London: Paintings from Bergamo, Brescia and Cremona (2004); *Style*— Nicholas Penny, Esq; ✉ National Gallery of Art, 2000B South Club Drive, Landover, MD 20785, USA (fax 00 1 202 789 3194)

PENNY, Hon Peter George Worsley; s and h of 3 Viscount Marchwood, *qv*; *b* 8 October 1965; *Educ* Winchester; *m* 1995, Annabel C, yr da of Rex Cooper, of E Bergholt, Suffolk; 1 da (India Rose b 21 March 1997), 1 s (Kit b 8 Sept 1999); *Career* assoc dir The HMG Group plc 1990–92, md The Staveley Gp Ltd 1996–; *Recreations* racing, tennis, cricket, shooting; *Style*— The Hon Peter Penny

PENRHYN, 7 Baron (UK 1866); Simon Douglas-Pennant; s of Maj the Hon Nigel Douglas Pennant (d 2000), and Margaret, *née* Kirkham (d 1939); suc unc, 6 Baron Penrhyn, 2003; *b* 28 June 1938, Glasgow; *Educ* Eton, Clare Coll Cambridge (BA, Cricket blue); *m* 5 Oct 1963, Josephine, *née* Upcott; 2 da (Hon Sophie Margaret b 11 Dec 1964, Hon Harriet Josephine b 25 May 1972), 2 s (Hon Edward Sholto b 6 June 1966, Hon Hugo Charles b 21 April 1969); *Heir* s, Hon Edward Douglas-Pennant; *Career* main bd dir Brintons Ltd; *Recreations* travel, golf, gardening, music; *Clubs* MCC; *Style*— The Rt Hon the Lord Penrhyn

PENRITH, Bishop of 2002–; Rt Rev James William Scobie Newcome; *b* 24 July 1953, Aldershot; *Educ* Marlborough (exhibitioner), Trinity Coll Oxford (MA, exhibitioner, Laurence Binyon prize), Selwyn Coll Cambridge (MA, scholar), Ridley Hall Cambridge; *m* Sept 1977, Alison Margaret; 2 s (Edward John b 1984, Alexander Charles b 1988), 2 da (Clare Rosamonde b 1986, Anna Jane b 1991); *Career* ordained 1978; asst curate All Saints Leavesden 1978–82 (ATC chaplain), minister Bar Hill Church 1982–94, rural dean North Stowe Deanery 1993–94, residentiary canon Chester Cathedral 1994–2002; tutor Ridley Hall Cambridge 1983–94, diocesan dir of ordinands and lay ministry advsr 1994–2000, dir adult educn and trg Chester Dio 1996–2002, proctor in convocation Gen Synod 2000–02; chm Dio Bd for Ministry and Trg; pres Churches Together in Cumbria; C of E rep to Scot Episcopal Church Gen Synod, convenor NW bishops' meeting; numerous broadcasting and speaking engagements, various articles and contributions to reviews; memb Soc for Study of Christian Ethics, FRSA; *Publications* One in the Spirit, Ecumenical Ordination, An Alternative Way Ahead, Fostering Vocation in the Parish (1998), Setting the Church of England Free (chapter, 2003); *Recreations* squash (Trinity Oxford and Selwyn Cambridge 1st Fives), cross country running, hill walking, history of art, novels, films, cricket (St Albans, Ely and Chester Dio teams), restoring furniture; *Style*— The Rt Rev the Bishop of Penrith; ✉ Holm Croft, 13 Castle Road, Kendal, Cumbria LA9 7AU (tel 01539 727836)

PENROSE, John; MP; *b* 22 June 1964; *Educ* Ipswich Sch, Univ of Cambridge, Columbia Univ; *m* Dido Harding; *Career* risk mangr J P Morgan 1986–90, mgmnt conslt McKinsey and Co 1992–94, commercial dir Thomson Publishing 1995–96, md schs publishing Pearson plc 1996–2000, chm Logotron Ltd; Parly candidate (Cons): Ealing Southall 1997, Weston-super-Mare 2001; MP (Cons) Weston-super-Mare 2005–; *Style*— John Penrose, Esq, MP; ✉ House of Commons, London SW1A 0AA (e-mail john.penrose@weston-conservatives.co.uk, website www.weston-conservatives.co.uk)

PENROSE, Dr Richard James Jackson; s of Walter James Pace (d 1944), and Gertrude May, *née* Penrose (d 1981); name changed by deed poll 1968; *b* 12 October 1941; *Educ* Haberdashers' Aske's, Charing Cross Hosp Med Sch London (MB BS), DPM 1970; *m* 1 May 1976, Lynda Elisabeth, da of Dr Reginald John Alcock, of Kemble; 2 s (James b

1977, William b 1980); *Career* Charing Cross Hosp: house surgn in ENT 1966, house physician in gen med and neurology 1967, SHO in psychiatry 1968; sr registrar in psychiatry St George's Hosp London 1971–75 (SHO and registrar 1968–71); conslt psychiatrist: St George's Hosp 1975–89, West Park Hosp Epsom 1975–81, Springfield Hosp 1981–89, Epsom Gen Hosp 1989–97, The Priory Hosp Roehampton 1997–; visiting lectr Univ of Surrey 1999–; fndr memb Br Assoc for Psychopharmacology; LRCP, MRCS, MRCPsych 1973; *Books* various articles in jls on life events, brain haemorrhage, depression and drug treatment; *Recreations* music, gardening, reading; *Style*— Dr Richard Penrose; ✉ The Priory Hospital, Priory Lane, London SW15 5JJ (tel 020 8876 8261)

PENROSE, Prof Sir Roger; OM (2000), kt (1994); s of Prof Lionel S Penrose FRS (d 1972), and Dr Margaret, *née* Leathes (d 1989); *b* 8 August 1931; *Educ* UCL (BSc), St John's Coll Cambridge (PhD); *m* 1, 1958 (m dis 1980), Joan Isabel Wedge; 3 s (Christopher Shaun b 1963, Toby Nicholas b 1964, Eric Alexander b 1966); m 2, 1988, Vanessa Dee Thomas; 1 s (Maxwell Sebastian b 26 May 2000); *Career* conslt National Research Development Corporation London 1956–57, asst lectr in mathematics Bedford Coll London 1956–57, res fell St John's Coll Cambridge 1957–60; concurrently res fell 1959–61: Princeton Univ (NATO res fell), Syracuse Univ and Cornell Univ; res assoc Dept of Mathematics King's Coll London 1961–63, prof of applied mathematics Birkbeck Coll London 1967–73 (reader 1964–66), Rouse Ball prof of mathematics Wadham Coll Oxford 1973–98 (prof emeritus 1998–); prof of mathematics (pt/t) Rice Univ 1982–87, prof of physics and mathematics (pt/t) Syracuse Univ 1987–93, prof of physics and mathematics at Penn State Univ 1993–, Gresham prof of geometry Gresham Coll London 1998–; visiting assoc prof of mathematics and physics Univ of Texas 1963–64; visiting appts: Yeshiva Univ, Princeton Univ, Cornel Univ, Univ of Chicago, lectr at Battelle Inst Seattle; Adams Prize 1966, Dannie Heineman Prize 1971, Eddington Medal 1975, Gravity Research Fndn 1975, Royal Medal 1985, Wolf Prize (for physics) 1988, Dirac Medal and Prize 1989, Albert Einstein Medal 1990, Science Book Prize 1990, Naylor Prize 1991, Forder lectr 1992–93; hon degrees: Univ of New Brunswick 1992, Univ of Surrey 1993, Univ of Bath 1994, Univ of London 1995, Univ of Glasgow 1996, Univ of Essex 1996, Univ of St Andrews 1997, Univ of Santiniketan India 1998, Open Univ 1998, Univ of Southampton 2002; memb Cncl: Royal Society 1980–82, London Mathematical Society 1983–87, Inst of Mathematics and Its Applications 1982–85 and 1990–93; pres Int Soc for Gen Relativity and Gravitation 1992–95; memb Polish Acad Sciences 1996, US Nat Acad of Sciences; fell: Wadham Coll Oxford 1973–98 (emeritus fell 1998–), UCL 1975, Univ of Calif 1978, Birkbeck Coll London 1996; hon fell St John's Coll Cambridge 1987, hon fell Inst of Physics 1999; FRS 1972; *Books* Techniques of Different Topology in Relativity (1972), Spinors and Space Time (with W Rindler, vol 1, 1984, vol 2, 1986), The Emperor's New Mind (1989), Shadows of the Mind (1994), The Nature of Space and Time (with Stephen Hawking, 1996), The Large, the Small and the Human Mind (1997); also co-edited numerous learned books and many scientific articles in academic jls; *Style*— Prof Sir Roger Penrose, OM; ✉ Mathematical Institute, 24–29 St Giles, Oxford OX1 3LB (tel 01865 273546, fax 01865 273583, e-mail rouse@maths.ox.ac.uk)

PENROSE, Roger Ian; s of Edward Charles Penrose, of Plymouth, and Grace Feltis, *née* Bond; *b* 15 September 1953; *Educ* Plymouth Coll, Univ of Bath (BSc, BArch); *m* 7 Aug 1976, Janet Elaine, da of Richard Alan Harvey, RN; 2 s (Richard Merrick b 1984, Simon Tristan b 1987), 1 da (Laura Jane b 1989); *Career* princ Ian Penrose and Associates (chartered architects), md Ian Penrose Architects Ltd 1987–; *Recreations* motorcycling, sailing, cycle, swimming; *Clubs* OPM, IMTC, Royal Western Yatch Club of England; *Style*— R I Penrose, Esq; ✉ Ian Penrose Architects Ltd, The Park House, 13 Queens Terrace, Exeter EX4 4HR (tel 01392 253000)

PENRY-DAVEY, Hon Mr Justice; Sir David Herbert Penry-Davey; kt (1997); s of Samuel Saunders Watson Penry-Davey (d 1991), and Almary Lorna, *née* Patrick, of Rochester, Kent (d 2000); *b* 16 May 1942; *Educ* Hastings GS, King's Coll London (LLB); *m* 1970, Judith Ailsa Nancy, da of John Walter, of Morley St Botolph, Norfolk; 2 s (Matthew b 1972, James b 1979), 1 da (Caroline b 1974); *Career* called to the Bar Inner Temple 1965; recorder of the Crown Court 1986, QC 1988, ldr SE Circuit of the Bar 1992–95, chm Gen Cncl of the Bar 1996 (vice-chm 1995), judge of the High Court of Justice (Queen's Bench Div) 1997–, presiding judge Northern Circuit 2000–03; dep chm Security Vetting Appeals Panel 2004–; fell King's Coll London 1998–; *Recreations* music, golf, cycling; *Style*— The Hon Mr Justice Penry-Davey; ✉ c/o The Royal Courts of Justice, Strand, London WC2A 2LL

PENSON, Alan Anthony; *b* 30 January 1952; *Educ* Dulwich Coll, St Catharine's Coll Cambridge (MA); *m* 1976, Jane; 1 s (Alexander b 1983), 1 da (Mary b 1985); *Career* Price Waterhouse 1974–85, gp chief exec Clarke Hooper plc 1992 (fin dir 1986–92), gen mangr Interwood Marketing (UK) plc 1993, gp fin dir Grey Communications Group Ltd 1994–95, princ Penson Associates 1996–; FCA; *Style*— Alan Penson, Esq; ✉ Penson Associates, Fairfield House, Dodds Lane, Chalfont St Giles, Buckinghamshire HP8 4EL (tel 01494 778946, fax 0870 134 7896, e-mail alan@penson.co.uk)

PENTLAND, Dr Brian; s of George Hodge Pentland (d 1985), and Irvine Wilson, *née* Booth (d 1991); *b* 24 June 1949; *Educ* Gracemount Secdy Sch, Liberton HS, Univ of Edinburgh (BSc, MB ChB), Euro Bd of Physical Med and Rehabilitation (Dip); *m* 21 July 1973, Gillian Mary, da of Cecil John Duggua; 4 s (Malcolm Keith b 16 Sept 1977, Gordon Neil b 17 Nov 1978, Duncan Roy b 14 Dec 1981, Kenneth Brian b 1 March 1984); *Career* house physician Royal Infirmary Edinburgh 1974–75, house surgn West Cumberland Hosp Whitehaven Feb-July 1975, SHO Northern Gen Hosp Edinburgh 1975–76, registrar Ninewells and Kings Cross Hosps Dundee 1976–78, registrar Northern Gen Hosp Edinburgh Jan-Sept 1979, lectr in med neurology Univ of Edinburgh 1979–82, conslt neurologist (rehabilitation med) Astley Ainslie Hosp Edinburgh 1982–, dir Scottish Brain Injury Rehabilitation Serv Edinburgh 1991–, head Rehabilitation Studies Unit Univ of Edinburgh 1991–, head of rehabilitation servs Lothian Primary Care NHS Tst 1994–; visiting lectr Queen Margaret Coll Univ Edinburgh 1979–; memb Assoc of Br Neurologists 1982, Scottish Soc of Physicians 1986; hon prof Queen Margaret Univ 2005; MRCP, FRCPEd 1986; *Books* Parkinson's Disease: diagnosis and management (1986); over 150 published articles or chapters in scientific jls; *Recreations* hill walking, gardening; *Style*— Dr Brian Pentland; ✉ Astley Ainslie Hospital, Grange Loan, Edinburgh EH9 2HL (tel 0131 537 9039, fax 0131 537 9030)

PENTON, John Howard; MBE (1987); s of Richard Howard Penton (d 1961), and Ciceley Urmson, *née* Heinekey (d 1966); *b* 12 February 1938; *Educ* Merchant Taylors', AA Sch of Architecture (AADip), Open Univ (BA); *m* 1, 2 Nov 1963 (m dis 1997), (Elizabeth) Diana, da of (Henry) Harold King (d 1985); 1 da (Ciceley Rebecca Clare b 1975); m 2, 27 Dec 1997, Kristina Söderlind, da of Gustav Karlsson, of Uppsala, Sweden; *Career* chartered architect; designer, accessibility conslt and expert witness; assoc D E Pugh & Assocs 1963–72, fndr ptnr Penton Smart & Grimwade 1972–94, ind conslt 1994–; conslt: LT, English Tourist Bd, Irish Nat Rehabilitation Bd, Inst for Rehabilitation & Res Houston Texas, Perkins Inst for the Blind Boston, Nordic Ctee on Deaf/Blindness Dronninglund Denmark, ReHabAid Hong Kong, Leonard Cheshire Fndn, Healthgain (UK) Ltd, Norfolk and Norwich Univ NHS Tst, Hosp of St Cross Winchester, Claremont Fan Court Sch, St Albans Cathedral, St Paul's Cathedral, Westminster Cathedral; prof advsr Millennium Cmmn; res fell RIBA 1984–85, res fell Hull Sch of Architecture 1987–; fndr chm Herts and Beds Construction Industry Liaison Gp, former chm Herts Assoc of Architects, memb Eastern Regnl Cncl RIBA; fndr tstee and former chm Centre for Accessible Environments, fndr memb The Access Ctee for England, memb King's Fund Grants Ctee, memb Cncl of Europe Ctee CIB/W41 on co-ordinating European access standards; memb: Prince of Wales Advsy Gp on Disability, US President's Ctee on Employment of the Handicapped, Rehab Int (UN); memb Ct of Assts Worshipful Co of Merchant Taylors (chm Charities Ctee, Warden 1988 and 1991), Master Worshipful Co of Chartered Architects 1998–99; Hon MA De Montfort Univ 1999; RIBA, RIAS, ACIArb, FBEng, FCSD, FRSA; *Awards* DIA Melchett Award 1985, RIBA/DOE Housing and Special Housing, Civic Tst (several awards and commendations); *Books* A Handbook of Housing for Disabled People (1982), Providing Accessible Accommodation (1990), DfEE Building Bulletin 91: Access for Disabled People to School Buildings (1999), Widening the Eye of the Needle (1999, 2 edn 2001), Inclusion - a guide to the Disability Discrimination Act 1995 (1999); *Recreations* reading (history), sketching, travel, swimming, target rifle shooting, carving chessmen; *Clubs* Reform, AA; *Style*— John H Penton, Esq, MBE; ✉ 8 Spicer Street, St Albans, Hertfordshire AL3 4PQ (tel 01727 868873, fax 01727 852376); 17 College Place, St Albans, Hertfordshire AL3 4PU

PENTREATH, (Richard) John; s of John Alistair Dudley Pentreath (ka Burma 1945), and Mary Lena, *née* Gendall; *b* 28 December 1943; *Educ* Sir Humphry Davy GS, Univ of London (BSc, DSc), Univ of Auckland (Commonwealth scholar, PhD); *m* Elisabeth Amanda, *née* Leach; 2 da (Tamsin Sarah b 22 Feb 1971, Lamorna Kate b 7 Nov 1974); *Career* MAFF: Science Res Cncl fell 1969 and memb scientific staff 1969–89, head Radiobiological Res 1985–87, head Aquatic Environment Protection Div and Res Support Gp and dep dir Fisheries Res 1988–89; chief scientist and dir of water quality Nat Rivers Authy 1989–95, chief scientist and dir of environmental strategy Environment Agency 1995–2000, res prof Environmental Systems Science Centre Univ of Reading 2000–07, prof emeritus Univ of Reading 2007–; hon prof UEA 1996–, visiting prof Imperial Coll London 1997–2003; memb: Nat Environment Res Cncl 1992–98, Advsy Bd Centre for Social and Economic Res on the Global Environment 1994–2005, HE Funding Cncl Res Assessment Panel 1995–96 and 1999–2001, Cncl Marine Biological Assoc UK 1997–2000, Cncl Assoc for Schs Science Engrg and Technol (ASSET) 1998–99, Int Cmmn on Radiological Protection (ICRP) 2003–; chm ICRP Ctee on Environmental Protection 2005–; tstee Sir Alister Hardy Fndn for Ocean Science 2001–; ind memb Jt Nature Conservation Ctee 2000–06; pres: Cornwall Wildlife Tst 2003–, Cornwall Sustainable Building Tst 2005–; Hon DSc: Univ of Hertfordshire 1998, UWE 1999, Univ of Plymouth 2002; CBiol, FIBiol, FSRP; *Books* Nuclear Power, Man and the Environment (1980); *Recreations* visual arts, Cornish history, tall ship sailing; *Style*— Dr John Pentreath; ✉ Environmental Systems Science Centre, University of Reading, Whiteknights, PO Box 238, Reading RG6 6AL (tel 0118 931 8741)

PENTY, Prof Richard Vincent; s of Peter Penty (d 1991), and (Patricia) Janet, *née* Shelbourne (d 1987); *b* 9 September 1964; *Educ* Repton, Sidney Sussex Coll Cambridge; *m* 1 Aug 1992, Victoria, *née* Eve; 2 s (George b 29 May 1994, Edward b 22 June 1998), 1 da (Katherine b 19 June 1996); *Career* lectr Sch of Physics Univ of Bath 1990–95, lectr rising to prof Dept of Electrical and Electronic Engrg Univ of Bristol 1995–2001, prof Univ of Cambridge 2001–, fell Sidney Sussex Coll Cambridge 2002–; MIEE, MInstP, MIEEE; *Style*— Prof Richard Penty; ✉ Department of Engineering, University of Cambridge, Trumpington Street, Cambridge CB2 1PZ (tel 01223 748358, fax 01223 748342)

PEPINSTER, Catherine; da of Michel Joseph Pepinster (d 1974), and Winifred, *née* Jones; *b* 7 July 1959, London; *Educ* Univ of Manchester (BA), City Univ London (Dip), Heythrop Coll London (MA); *m* 2003, Kevin Charles Morley; *Career* local newspaper reporter Manchester and London 1981–85, property corr Sheffield Morning Telegraph 1985–86, chief reporter Estate Times 1986, news ed Building 1987–89, reporter The Observer 1989–90, news ed Time Out 1990–94; asst news ed The Independent 1994–95, news ed Independent on Sunday 1997–98 (dep news ed 1995–97), features ed The Independent 1998, exec ed The Independent of Sunday 2002–04 (asst ed 1999–2002), ed The Tablet 2004–; *Recreations* walking, reading, architecture, Belgian culture; *Clubs* Reform; *Style*— Ms Catherine Pepinster; ✉ The Tablet, 1 King Street Cloisters, Clifton Walk, London W6 0QZ (tel 020 8748 8484, fax 020 8748 1550, e-mail cpepinster@thetablet.co.uk)

PEPLOE, Guy; s of Denis Frederick Neil Peploe, RSA, and Elizabeth Marion, *née* Barr; *b* 25 January 1960; *Educ* The Edinburgh Acad, Univ of Aberdeen (MA); *Career* exhibition offr Royal Scottish Acad 1983, res asst Scottish Nat Gallery of Modern Art 1983–85, md The Scottish Gallery 1991– (dir 1984–); *Recreations* golf, mycology; *Style*— Guy Peploe, Esq; ✉ The Scottish Gallery, 16 Dundas Street, Edinburgh EH3 6HZ (tel 0131 558 1200, fax 0131 558 3900)

PEPPER, Prof Gordon Terry; CBE; s of Harold Terry Pepper (d 1973), and Jean Margaret Gordon, *née* Furness (d 1963); *b* 2 June 1934; *Educ* Repton, Trinity Coll Cambridge (MA); *m* 30 Aug 1958, Gillian Clare, da of Lt-Col William Helier Huelin (d 1978); 3 s (Alasdair b 1960, Harry b 1967, Mark b 1969), 1 da (Linda (Ninna) b 1961); *Career* Nat Serv cmmnd RCS 1952–54; Equity and Law Life Assurance Soc 1957–60; W Greenwell & Co: joined 1960, ptnr 1962, jt sr ptnr 1980; chm Greenwell Montagu & Co 1986–87, dir and sr advsr Midland Montagu (Holdings) Ltd 1987–90, chm Payton Pepper & Sons Ltd 1987–97 (dir 1986–97); City Univ Business Sch: dir Centre For Financial Markets 1988–98, prof 1991–98 (hon visiting prof 1987–90 and 1998–); dir Lombard Street Research Ltd 1998– (chm 2000–); memb: Ctee on Industry and Fin Nat Econ Devpt Cncl 1988–90, Econ and Social Res Cncl 1989–93; FIA 1961, FSIP; *Publications* Money, Credit and Inflation (1990), Money, Credit and Asset Prices (1994), Inside Thatcher's Monetarist Revolution (1998), Monetarism Under Thatcher: Lessons for the Future (with M Oliver, 2001), The Liquidity Theory of Asset Prices (with M Oliver, 2006), articles in various econ and fin jls; *Recreations* sailing, walking, family; *Clubs* Reform, Royal Ocean Racing, Royal Channel Islands Yacht; *Style*— Prof Gordon Pepper, CBE; ✉ Staddleden, Sissinghurst, Cranbrook, Kent TN17 2AN (tel 01580 712852, fax 01580 714853, e-mail gordonpepper@btopenworld.com)

PEPPER, Prof Sir Michael; kt (2006); s of Morris Pepper (d 1982), and Ruby, *née* Bloom (d 2006); *b* 10 August 1942; *Educ* St Marylebone GS, Univ of Reading (BSc, PhD); *m* Oct 1973, Dr Jeannette Denise, da of Albert Josse, of London; 2 da (Judith Leah, Ruth Jennifer); *Career* res physicist The Plessey Co Ltd 1969–82, res Cavendish Lab 1973–, princ res fell GEC plc 1982–87, prof of physics Univ of Cambridge 1987–; Warren res fell Royal Soc 1978–86, fell Trinity Coll Cambridge 1982–; jt md Toshiba Research Europe Ltd 1990–, jt fndr and dir TeraView Ltd 2001–; Guthrie Prize and Medal Inst of Physics 1985, Hewlett-Packard Europhysics Prize 1985, Hughes Medal of Royal Soc 1987, Mott Prize and Medal Inst of Physics 2000; various named lectures incl: Mountbatten meml lectr IEE 2003, Bakerian lectr Royal Soc 2004; Royal Medal Royal Soc 2005; ScD Univ of Cambridge 1989; FRS 1983; *Recreations* travel, music, walking, whisky tasting; *Clubs* Arsenal FC, Athenaeum; *Style*— Prof Sir Michael Pepper, FRS; ✉ Cavendish Laboratory, Madingley Road, Cambridge CB3 0HE (tel 01223 337330, fax 01223 337271, e-mail mp10000@cam.ac.uk); Toshiba Cambridge Research Laboratory, 260 Cambridge Science Park, Milton Road, Cambridge CB4 0WE (tel 01223 436900, fax 01223 436990)

PEPPERCORN, David James Creagh; s of James Kenneth Peppercorn (d 1991), and Ida Alice Knight (d 1985); *b* 25 August 1931; *Educ* Beaumont Coll, Trinity Coll Cambridge (MA); *m* 1, 11 April 1959, Susan Mary Sweeney; 3 da (Caroline b 1961, Sarah b 1963, Frances b 1964); m 2, 10 June 1977, Serena Sutcliffe, *qv*; *Career* int wine conslt; dir: Morgan Furze & Co Ltd 1958–74, Peter Dominic 1964–74, Gilbey Vintners 1969–74, Wine Standards Bd of the Vintners' Co 1987–93, French Wine Farmers Ltd 1993–99, AWM Fine Wine Fund Ltd 2000–03; memb Inst of Masters of Wine 1962 (chm 1968–70); judge

P

at Premier Concours Mondial (Budapest 1972); André Simon Meml Prize 1983; Liveryman Worshipful Co of Vintners 1952, memb Worshipful Co of Watermen and Lightermen of the River Thames; Chevalier de l'Ordre des Arts et des Lettres (France) 1988; *Books* Drinking Wine (with Bryan Cooper, 1979), Bordeaux (1982, 2 edn 1991), Pocket Guide to the Wines of Bordeaux (1986, 2000, 2002 and 2004, translated into German 1986, 2000 and 2002, French 1987 and 1993, Danish 1987, Swedish 1988, Japanese 1990 and 1999, also American edn 1987), Wine Report (Bordeaux Section, 2008); *Recreations* music, walking, travelling; *Clubs* Garrick, MCC, Saintsbury; *Style—* David Peppercorn, Esq, MW; ✉ 2 Bryanston Place, London W1H 2DE

PEPPIATT, Michael Henry; s of Edward George Peppiatt (d 1983), of Stocking Pelham, Herts, and Elsa Eugénie Peppiatt (d 1997); *b* 9 October 1941; *Educ* Brentwood Sch, Göttingen Univ, Trinity Hall Cambridge (MA, PhD); *m* 1989, Dr Jill Patricia Lloyd, *qv*, da of Peter Brown; 1 da (Clio Patricia b 16 Feb 1991), 1 s (Alexander Michael b 23 April 1994); *Career* art critic The Observer 1964, arts ed Réalités Paris 1966–68, art and literary ed Le Monde 1969–71; Paris arts corr: New York Times, Financial Times, Art International 1973–86; ed and publisher Art International 1987–; exhibition organiser: Sch of London (Louisiana Museum Humlebaek) 1987, Francis Bacon retrospective (Museo d'Arte Moderna Lugano) 1993, Ecole de Londres (Musée Maillol Paris) 1998, (Kunsthaus Vienna) 1999, Zoran Music Retrospective (Sainsbury Centre Norwich) 2000, Raymond Mason Retrospective (Musée Maillol Paris) 2000, Alberto Giacometti Retrospective (Sainsbury Centre Norwich) 2001, Fondation de l'Hermitage Lausanne 2002, Aristide Maillol Retrospective (IVAM Valencia) 2002, Christian Schad Retrospective (with Jill Lloyd, Musée Maillol Paris) 2002, (Neue Galerie New York) 2003, Francis Bacon Retrospective (IVAM Valencia) 2003, Musée Maillol Paris 2004, Antoni Tàpies (Centro Cultural Banco do Brasil São Paulo) 2005; memb: Soc of Authors, Royal Soc of Lit; *Publications* Imagination's Chamber - Artists and Their Studios (1983), School of London (1987), Francis Bacon: Anatomy of an Enigma (1996), Entretiens avec Francis Bacon (1998), Entretiens avec Zoran Music (1999), Francis Bacon à l'atelier (2000), Alberto Giacometti in Postwar Paris (2001), L'Atelier d'Alberto Giacometti (2003), Francis Bacon: The Sacred and the Profane (2003), Les dilemmes de Jean Dubuffet (2006), Francis Bacon in the 1950s (2006); *Clubs* Jeu de Paume (Paris), RAC, The Academy; *Style—* Michael Peppiatt, Esq; ✉ 56 St James's Gardens, London W11 4RA (tel 020 7460 8626, fax 020 7603 6249, e-mail m.peppiatt@zen.co.uk)

PERAHIA, Murray; *b* New York; *Educ* Mannes Coll; *Career* pianist and conductor; studied with Mieczyslaw Horszowski; winner Leeds Int Piano Competition 1972; co-dir Aldeburgh Festival 1981–89 (first concert appearance 1973); Hon FRCM, Hon RAM; princ guest conductor Acad of St Martin in the Fields; recitals in NY, London, Berlin, Zurich, Vienna; orchs played with incl: Berlin Philharmonic, Philharmonia Orch, Acad of St Martin in the Fields, Israel Philharmonic, Chicago Symphony, Met Orch (Carnegie Hall); *Recordings*exclusive Sony recording artist; complete Mozart piano concertos (directing English Chamber Orch), complete Beethoven concertos (with Concertgebouw Orch under Bernard Haitink), Mendelssohn and Chopin concertos, Schubert's Winterreise (with Peter Pears and Dietrich Fischer-Dieskau), Bartok's Sonata for Two Pianos and Percussion (with Sir Georg Solti, winner 1989 Grammy Award), Brahms' G minor Quartet (with Amadeus Quartet), Chopin's Études (winner Grammy Award 2002); *Style—* Murray Perahia, Esq; ✉ c/o Askonas Holt, Lonsdale Chambers, 27 Chancery Lane, London WC2A 1PF (e-mail info@askonasholt.co.uk)

PERCEVAL, John Dudley Charles Ascelin; s of Lt-Col John Francis George Perceval (d 1981), of Vancouver, BC, and Diana Madeleine Scott, *née* Pearce; *b* 8 April 1942; *Educ* Eton; *m* 11 Sept 1971, Tessa Mary, da of Geoffrey Bruce Dawson, OBE, MC (d 1984), of Caerleon; 2 s (Oliver Charles b 1972, Christopher Geoffrey John b 1978), 1 da (Candida Mary b 1974); *Career* Unilever 1961–69, Save & Prosper Group Ltd 1969–95 (exec dir 1985–95), Omnium Communications Limited 1995–2005; *Style—* John Perceval, Esq; ✉ The Forge House, Monk Sherborne, Tadley, Hampshire RG26 5HS (tel 01256 850073)

PERCHARD, Peter John; s of Stanley Dreluad Perchard, of London, and Shirley Gwendoline, *née* Twyman, of Worcester Park, Surrey; *b* 4 November 1943; *Educ* Sevenoaks Sch, Bromley Tech Coll; *m* 1, 19 March 1966, Paula Bennett; 1 da (Lorna Melanie b 27 April 1967); m 2, 2 March 1983, Lorraine Eve, da of Thomas Victor Frederick Cooper; 1 s (Oliver James b 10 Aug 1983), 1 da (Lucy Grace b 11 Aug 1985); *Career* copy ed George Newnes Ltd 1962–64, advtg/features New Musical Express 1964–66, Penguin Books Ltd 1967–85 (sometime exhibitions mangr, fieldwork mangr, mktg prodn mangr); The Cricketer: joined as dep ed 1986, exec ed 1988, managing ed 1991–98, ed 1998–2003; co-author and prodr Virgin Warrior (rock opera, Epsom Playhouse) 1986; memb Performing Right Soc 1976; *Books* Cricket (1988); *Recreations* cricket, football, tennis, theatre, music, song writing, books, cinema, photography, eating out; *Clubs* Cricket Writers'; *Style—* Peter Perchard, Esq; ✉ 21 Burgh Heath Road, Epsom, Surrey KT17 4LP (tel 01372 813401, mobile 07785 220895, e-mail p.perchard@ntlworld.com)

PERCIVAL, Anthony Henry; s of William Potter Percival (d 1996), and Iris, *née* Hiller (d 1973); *b* 11 January 1940; *Educ* Felsted; *m* 30 May 1964, Sally Angela, da of Owen Buckland; 2 s (Jonathan Clive b 14 July 1966, James Owen b 28 Dec 1968), 1 da (Anna Catherine b 19 April 1977); *Career* PricewaterhouseCoopers (formerly Deloitte Haskins & Sells then Coopers & Lybrand): articled clerk 1957–62, ptnr 1966–95, ptnr in charge London Audit Div 1982–87, managing ptnr Deloitte Haskins & Sells Singapore 1988–90; Kingfisher plc: gp fin dir 1995–98, exec dir 1998–2002; non-exec dir: British Standards Institution, Royal London UK Equity and Income Tst plc; Liveryman Worshipful Co of Chartered Accountants; FCA 1973 (ACA 1963); *Recreations* tennis, theatre, gardening; *Style—* Anthony Percival, Esq

PERCIVAL, John; MBE (2002); s of late Cecil Ernest Percival and late Mua Phoebe, *née* Milchard; *b* 16 March 1927; *Educ* Sir George Monoux GS Walthamstow, St Catherine's Coll Oxford (MA); *m* 1, 1953 (m dis), Betty, *née* Thorne-Large; m 2, 1972, Judith, *née* Cruickshank; *Career* dance critic: The Times 1965–97, The Independent 1997–; Dance & Dancers magazine: contrib 1950–, assoc ed 1964–80, ed 1981–; London corr Ballet Review (NY) 1996–; contrib numerous other dance magazines and newspapers incl Dance Now, Ballet Annual, Ballett (Germany) and Dance Magazine (NY); writer of commentary for I Am A Dancer (film starring Nureyev); memb and past pres The Critics' Circle; *Books* Antony Tudor, Modern Ballet, The World of Diaghilev, Experimental Dance, Nureyev, Facts About A Ballet Company, Theatre In My Blood (biog of John Cranko), Men Dancing (with Nigel Gosling); *Style—* John Percival, MBE; ✉ 36 Great James Street, London WC1N 3HB (tel and fax 020 7405 0267, e-mail jpcritical@aol.com); office: tel and fax 020 7813 1049

PERCIVAL, Michael John; s of John William Percival (d 1971), of Northampton, and Margery Edith, *née* Crawford; *b* 11 July 1943; *Educ* Berkhamsted Sch; *m* 11 June 1966, Jean Margaret, da of Vincent Everard Dainty, of Northampton; 3 da (Katie b 1968, Alison b 1970, Linda b 1973); *Career* admitted slr London 1966, ptnr Howes Percival Slrs (sr ptnr 1984–2005); memb Cncl of Northants Law Soc 1982–94 (pres 1992–93), pres Northampton and Dist Branch MS Soc 1988; govr Northampton HS for Girls 1993–2005; registrar High Ct and Co Ct 1983–88, memb Northampton DHA 1987–90, clerk to Gen Cmmrs of Taxes for Northampton Dist 1 and 2 1988–2001; memb Law Soc 1966–2005; *Recreations* rugby, tennis, sailing; *Style—* Michael Percival, Esq

PERCY, Humphrey Richard; s of Adrian John Percy, of Tunbridge Wells, Kent, and Maisie, *née* Gardner; *b* 2 October 1956; *Educ* Winchester; *m* 27 April 1985, Suzanne Patricia Spencer, da of Maj Bruce Holford-Walker, of London; 2 s (Luke, Christopher), 2 da (Daisy, Emma); *Career* J Henry Schroder Wagg & Co Ltd 1974–80, dir Barclays Merchant Bank Ltd 1985–86 (joined 1980); Barclays de Zoete Wedd Ltd: dir 1986–94, dep treas 1986–89, md and head Swaps and Options Gp Europe 1989–92, md and global head of foreign exchange Barclays Bank plc 1992–94, divnl md Barclays Bank plc 1992–94; exec dir Strategic Asset Management Ltd Bermuda 1994–95; Westdeutsche Landesbank Girozentrale (WestLB): gen mangr London 1995–2002, md and head of European treasury 1995–96, md and global head of treasury 1997–2000, chief exec and head of global financial markets 2000–02, dir of various WestLB cos; chm and fndr SGM-Foreign Exchange Ltd 2002–, global head of futures ICAP plc 2004, chief exec House of London and The Middle East plc; dir: Core 12 LLC, Sloane LLC, Moorgate LLC, Trophy LV Fund, Trophy LV Master Fund; memb Int Advsy Ctee Thomas Cook 1996–97; MCIB; *Recreations* walking, skiing, reading, travel, wine, history; *Clubs* Capital, Knole; *Style—* Humphrey Percy, Esq; ✉ House of London and The Middle East plc, Sherborne House, Cannon Street, London EC4N 5AT

PERCY, Prof John Pitkeathly (Ian); CBE (1997); s of John Percy (d 1984), of Edinburgh, and Helen Glass, *née* Pitkeathly (d 1988); *b* 16 January 1942; *Educ* Edinburgh Acad, Univ of Edinburgh; *m* 26 June 1965, Sheila Isobel, da of Roy Toshack Horn (d 1957), of Edinburgh; 2 da (Jill Sheila b 12 April 1969, Sally Charlotte b 24 Dec 1972); *Career* chartered accountant; asst Graham Smart & Annan 1960–68, ptnr Martin Currie & Scott 1969–71; Grant Thornton: ptnr 1971–95, London managing ptnr 1981–88, Scottish sr ptnr 1991–95; chm: Kiln plc 2002–05, Companies House 2002–06 (memb Steering Bd 1995–2001); dep chm: Scottish Provident Institution 1993–2001, The Weir Group plc 2005– (non-exec dir 1996–), Ricardo plc 2000–; non-exec dir: Deutsche (Scotland) Ltd 1992–2001, William Wilson Holdings Ltd 1993–2005, Cala Group Ltd 2001–; chm: Accounts Cmmn for Scotland 1992–2001, ICMG Corporate Governance Cmmn until 2001; vice-chm UK Auditing Practices Bd 1991–2001, UK memb Int Audit Practices Cmmn 1995–2000, memb Scottish Legal Aid Bd 2000–06; pres ICAS 1990–91; hon prof of accountancy Univ of Aberdeen; chm of govrs The Edinburgh Acad 1992–2000; chm Queen Margaret Univ Edinburgh 2004–; elder St Cuthbert's Church of Scotland 1966; Freeman: City of London 1982, Worshipful Co of Painter-Stainers 1982; Hon LLD Univ of Aberdeen 1999; CA 1967, MAE 1989, FRSA 1989, CIMgt 2001; *Recreations* golf, trout fishing; *Clubs* Hon Co of Edinburgh Golfers, R&A, RAC, New (Edinburgh), Caledonian; *Style—* Prof Ian Percy, CBE; ✉ 30 Midmar Drive, Edinburgh EH10 6BU (tel 0131 452 8641, fax 0131 447 6233)

PERCY, Keith Edward; s of Cyril Edward Percy, of London, and Joyce Rose Percy; *b* 22 January 1945; *Educ* Wanstead Co HS, Univ of Manchester (BA); *m* 14 Feb 1970, (Rosemary) Pamela, da of Thomas William Drake, of London; 1 da (Elizabeth b 1974), 1 s (Nicholas b 1977); *Career* head research Phillips & Drew 1976–83 (joined 1967), exec chm Phillips & Drew Fund Management 1983–90; chief exec: UBS Asset Management (UK) Ltd 1989–90, Morgan Grenfell Asset Management Ltd 1990–96, exec chm SG Asset Management 1999–; dir: Standard Life Equity Income Tst 1991–, Brunner Investment Tst plc 2004– (chm 2005–), JP Morgan Japanese Investment Tst 2004–, Henderson Smaller Cos Investment Tst plc 2006–; chm RAW Communications Ltd 1998–2003; non-exec dir: Smiths Industries Med Systems 1977–2000, IMRO 1987–95; memb Cncl Soc of Investment Analysts 1976–87, chm FTSE Actuaries Share Indices Steering Ctee, dir FTSE Int 1995–96; *Recreations* tennis, rugby, music, theatre, travel; *Clubs* The City; *Style—* Keith E Percy, Esq

PERCY, Rev Canon Prof Martyn; s of Roy Percy, and Sylvia, *née* Owens; *b* 31 July 1962; *Educ* Merchant Taylor's Sch Northwood, Univ of Bristol (BA), Univ of Durham, KCL (PhD), Univ of Sheffield (MEd), Univ of Oxford (MA); *m* 1989, Emma Bray; 2 s (Ben b 1993, Joe b 1996); *Career* publisher 1984–88; ordained: deacon 1990, priest 1991; curate St Andrew's Bedford 1990–94, chaplain and dir of theology and religious studies Christ's Coll Cambridge 1994–97, dir of studies Sidney Sussex Coll Cambridge 1995–97, dir Lincoln Theological Inst for the Study of Religion and Soc 1997–2004, reader Univ of Sheffield 2000–03 (sr lectr 1997–2000, memb Ethics Ctee 1999–2004), prof of theology and ministry Hartford Seminary Connecticut 2002–, reader Univ of Manchester 2003–04, princ Ripon Coll Cuddesdon Oxford 2004–, prof of theological education KCL 2004–, canon theologian Sheffield Cathedral 2004– (hon canon 1997–2004); memb Cncl and dir ASA 2000–06 (sr ind dir 2003–06), memb Ind Complaints Panel Portman Gp 2006–; memb Diocesan Synod: St Albans 1993–94, Sheffield 1997–2004; occasional contrib to The Guardian, The Independent, BBC World Service and Radio 4; chair Cliff Coll Cncl 2002–06, fndr and co-chair Soc for the Study of Anglicanism 2003–; patron St Francis Children's Soc 1997– (memb Panel 1994–97); Freeman City of London 1989; FRSA 2000; *Publications* Words, Wonders and Power: Understanding Contemporary Christian Fundamentalism and Revivalism (1996), Intimate Affairs: Spirituality and Sexuality in Perspective (ed, 1997), Power and the Church: Ecclesiology in an Age of Transition (1998), Richard Hooker: An Introduction (1999), Previous Convictions: Studies in Religious Conversion (ed, 2000), Managing the Church? Order and Organisation in a Secular Age (co-ed, 2000), Calling Time: Religion, Society and Change at the Turn of the Millennium (ed, 2000), Restoring the Image: Essays in Honour of David Martin (co-ed, 2001), Darkness Yielding (co-ed, 2001), Fundamentalism, Church and Society (co-ed, 2002), Salt of the Earth: Religious Resilience in a Secular Age (2002), The Character of Wisdom: Essays in Honour of Wesley Carr (co-ed, 2004), Why Liberal Churches are Growing (co-ed, 2005), Engaging Contemporary Culture: Christianity, Theology and the Concrete Church (2005), Clergy: The Origin of Species (2006); *Recreations* reading, cinema, listening to jazz; *Clubs* Athenaeum; *Style—* The Rev Canon Prof Martyn Percy; ✉ Ripon College, Cuddesdon, Oxford OX44 9EX (tel 01865 874404, fax 01865 875 431, e-mail mpercy@ripon-cuddesdon.ac.uk)

PERCY, His Hon Rodney Algernon; 3 s of late Hugh James Percy, of Alnwick; *b* 15 May 1924; *Educ* Uppingham, BNC Oxford (MA); *m* 1948, Mary Allen (d 2002), da of late J E Benbow, of Aberystwyth; 1 s, 3 da; *Career* Lt RCS 1942–46, served Burma, India, Malaya and Java; called to the Bar Middle Temple 1950, ad eundum Lincoln's Inn 1987; dep coroner N Northumberland 1957–64, asst recorder Sheffield QS 1964–67, dep chm Co Durham QS 1966–71, recorder of the Crown Court 1972–79, circuit judge (NE Circuit) 1979–93; fndr memb and hon pres Conciliation Serv for Northumberland and Tyneside 1982–93, pres Northumberland and Tyneside Marriage Guidance Cncl 1983–87; Caravan Park op 1993–99; *Publications* ed: Charlesworth on Negligence (4 edn 1962, 5 edn 1971, 6 edn 1977), Charlesworth & Percy on Negligence (7 edn 1983, 8 edn 1990, 9 edn 1996, conslt ed 10 edn 2001 and 11 edn 2006); *Recreations* golf, gardening, hill walking, beachcombing, King Charles Cavalier spaniels; *Style—* His Hon Rodney Percy; ✉ Brookside, Lesbury, Alnwick, Northumberland NE66 3AT (tel 01665 830326, fax 01665 830000)

PERCY-DAVIS, Sarah Anne; da of Guy Harvey, of Bromsgrove, Worcs, and Jane, *née* Taylor; *b* 2 October 1971; *Educ* The Alice Ottley Sch Worcester, Br Inst Florence, Oxford Brookes Univ (BA), Christie's Education (RSA Dip Fine and Decorative Art); *m* 18 Sept 2004, Nicholas Percy-Davis; *Career* Phillips Fine Art Auctioneers: ceramics porter 1994, saleroom mangr Picture Dept 1994–95, head of Picture Dept 1997–98; picture specialist and jt head Regular Auction Dept Sotheby's 1998–2000; prodr Brando Quilici Prodns Rome 2000–03; produced documentaries for Discovery Channel incl: Ultimate Guide: Iceman, Ultimate Guide: Volcano, Iceman the Sequel, John Paul II: His Life and Legacy; prodr Atlantic Prodns London 2003–04; produced documentaries for Discovery Channel, Channel 5, BBC Worldwide, La 7 and Spiegel incl: Mysterious Death of Cleopatra,

Mystery of the Tibetan Mummy; chief exec LAPADA 2004–; *Style*— Mrs Sarah Percy-Davis; ✉ LAPADA, 535 Kings Road, Chelsea, London SW10 0SZ (tel 020 7823 3511, fax 020 7823 3522, mobile 07970 870703, e-mail spercy-davis@lapada.org)

PERCY-ROBB, Prof Iain Walter; s of Capt Ian Ernest Percy-Robb (d 1967), and Margaret Drysdale Carrick, *née* Galbraith (d 1991); *b* 8 December 1935; *Educ* George Watson's Coll Edinburgh, Univ of Edinburgh (MB ChB, PhD); *m* 22 May 1961, Margaret Elizabeth, da of Dr Ronald Leslie Cormie (d 1997), of Glasgow; 2 s (Michael Iain b 1964, Stephen Leslie b 1966), 2 da (Jane Elizabeth b 1962, Claire Margaret b 1971); *Career* MRC int travelling res fell Cornell Univ 1972–73; Univ of Edinburgh: res scholar 1963–65, lectr 1965–68, sr lectr 1968–76, reader 1976–84; prof of pathological biochemistry Univ of Glasgow 1984– (assoc dean of educn Faculty of Med); chm Informed Software Ltd 1987–97; memb Scot Swimming Team Empire and Cwlth Games Cardiff 1958; FRCPE, FRCPath; *Books* Lecture Notes on Clinical Chemistry (jtly, 1984), Diseases of the Gastrointestinal Tract and Liver (jtly, 1989), Muir's Textbook of Pathology (jtly, 1992); *Recreations* golf; *Clubs* Royal Burgess Golfing Soc (Edinburgh), The Glasgow GC; *Style*— Prof Iain Percy-Robb

PEREGO, Monica; *b* Monza, Italy; *Educ* Immagine Danza Milan, Royal Ballet Sch (scholar); *Career* ballerina; with Birmingham Royal Ballet 1991–92, princ Eng Nat Ballet 1997–2002 (joined 1992), freelance 2002–; first prize Benetton Dance Competition 1990; Best Classical Dancer Leonida Massine Award 1999, Int Dancer La Ginestra d'Oro Award 2003; *Ballet* prodns with Birmingham Royal Ballet and ENB incl: Swan Lake, Sleeping Beauty, Giselle, Romeo & Juliet, Nutcracker, Cinderella, Don Quixote, Who Cares?; freelance performances with: K-Ballet, Royal Swedish Operan, Tokyo City Ballet, Shanghai Ballet, Balletto di Roma, Balletto di Puglia, Balletto del Sud; *Galas* 50th Wings Birthday Gala in memory of Diana, Princess of Wales (Her Majesty's Theatre), Festival of Genazo Rome, Birthday Offering in homage to HRH Princess Margaret (Sadler's Wells), Dame Beryl's Evening (Sadler's Wells), Stars of English National Ballet Spain, Spoleto Festival, Bolle and Friends; *Style*— Ms Monica Perego; ✉ Via della Guerrina 18c, 20052 Monza, Milan, Italy (tel 00 39 039 837341, e-mail monica@monicaperego.com, website www.monicaperego.com)

PEREIRA, Dr (Raul) Scott; s of Dr Helio Gelli Pereira, FRS (d 1994), and Dr Marguerite Pereira, *née* Scott (d 1988); *b* 14 April 1948; *Educ* Mill Hill Sch, Trinity Coll Cambridge, Univ of Oxford Med Sch; *m* 14 April 1972, Hilary Glen, da of Prof Vernon Rycroft Pickles, of Oxford; 1 s (Thomas b 1979), 1 da (Penelope b 1977); *Career* pathology trainee Northwick Park Hosp Harrow 1973–76, res sr registrar Westminster Hosp and Med Sch 1976–79, clinical scientist MRC Clinical Res Centre Harrow 1979–83, res fell West Middlesex Univ Hosp 1983–86; conslt and sr lectr in immunology: St Helier Hosp, Carshalton and St George's Hosp Med Sch Tooting 1986–96; sr lectr and conslt immunologist Chelsea & Westminster Hosp (Imperial Coll Sch of Med) 1996–2000; dir of clinical audit and effectiveness Royal Coll of Pathologists 2000–; vice-pres Residential Boat Owners' Assoc; *Recreations* offshore cruising, boating; *Style*— Dr Scott Pereira

PEREIRA GRAY, Prof Sir Denis John; kt (1999), OBE (1981); s of Dr Sydney Joseph Pereira Gray (d 1975), of Exeter, and Alice Evelyn, *née* Cole (d 1999); *b* 2 October 1935; *Educ* Exeter Sch, St John's Coll Cambridge (MA, MB BChir), Bart's Med Sch; *m* 28 April 1962, Jill Margaret, da of Frank Carruthers Hoyte (d 1976), of Exeter; 1 s (Peter b 1963), 3 da (Penelope b 1965, Elizabeth b 1968, Jennifer b 1970); *Career* in gen med practice 1962–2000, prof of gen practice Univ of Exeter 1986–2001 (sr lectr 1973–86), regnl advsr in gen practice Univ of Bristol 1975–96, conslt advsr in gen practice to CMO DHSS 1984–87, dir Postgrad Med Sch Exeter 1987–97, assoc med postgrad dean Univ of Bristol 1992–96, dir of postgrad gen practice educn (SW Region) 1996–2000; elected memb: Cncl RCGP 1991–2000 (chm 1987–90, pres 1997–2000), GMC 1994–2003; pres: Soc of Med Illustrators 1997–2000, Soc for the Social History of Med 1999; chm: Acad of Med Royal Colls 2000–02 (vice-chm 1998–2000), Nuffield Tst 2003–06 (governing tstee 1994–); ed Med Annual 1983–87, hon ed RCGP journal 1972–80 and pubns 1976–2000; chm Jt Ctee on Postgrad Trg for Gen Practice 1994–97; Hunterian Soc Gold Medal 1966 and 1969, Sir Charles Hastings Prize 1967 and 1970, James Mackenzie Lecture 1977, George Abercrombie Award 1978, Gale Memorial Lecture 1979, RCGP Fndn Cncl Award 1980, Sir Harry Platt Prize 1981, Haliburton Hume Memorial Lecture 1988, McConaghey Memorial Lecture 1988, Northcott Memorial Lecture 1988, Harvard Davis Lecture 1988, Murray Scott Lecture 1990, Harben Lecture 1994, Sally Irvine Lecture 1995, annual address Royal Soc of Health 1997, Albert Wander Lecture RSM 1998, Andrew Smith Memorial Lecture 1998, Reading Oration 1998, Sir David Bruce Lecture 1999, Tom Stewart Lecture 2000, Purves Oration 2000, Frans Huygen Lecture (The Netherlands) 2001, Long Fox Lecture 2002, Deakin Lecture (Aust) 2005; hon fell Queen Mary Univ of London, Hon DSc De Montfort Univ, Hon DM Univ of Nottingham 2003; hon memb Cuban Family Practitioners Assoc 2000, hon memb Polish Coll of GPs 2000, foreign memb Inst of Med USA 2000; FRCGP 1973 (MRCGP 1967), FRSA 1989, Hon FRSH 1997, FRCP 1999, Hon FFPH 2000, Hon FIHSM 2000, Hon FRCPI 2001; *Publications* Running a Practice (jtly, 1978), Training for General Practice (1981), Forty Years On: The Story of the First 40 Years of the Royal College of General Practitioners (ed, 1992); author of articles in The Lancet, BMJ, British Journal of General Practice, Medical Education; *Recreations* reading, walking; *Clubs* RSM, Royal Over-Seas League; *Style*— Prof Sir Denis Pereira Gray, OBE; ✉ Alford House, 9 Marlborough Road, Exeter, Devon EX2 4TJ (tel 01392 218080); University of Exeter, Smeall Building, Peninsula Medical School, St Luke's Campus, Exeter EX1 2LU

PERERA, Dr Bernard Sarath; s of Vincent Perera (d 1985), of Colombo, Sri Lanka, and Patricia, *née* Fernando; *b* 20 February 1942; *Educ* St Joseph's Coll Colombo, Univ of Ceylon (MB BS), Univ of Manchester (DipBact); *m* 1, 1 June 1971, late Dr Piyaseeli Perera, da of Piyasena Jayatilake, of Colombo, Sri Lanka; 1 s (Shamira b 10 Aug 1973), 1 da (Lakshika b 7 June 1975); m 2, 6 July 1996, Dr Indra Ariyawansa; *Career* registrar Med Res Inst Colombo 1972–75, registrar in pathology Manchester Royal Infirmary 1976–78, sr registrar Northwest Regnl HA 1978–82; conslt microbiologist: Scarborough Hosp 1983, Royal Oldham Hosp 1984–2006 (ret); memb: BMA, Assoc of Med Microbiologists, Assoc of Clinical Pathologists, Manchester Med Soc; FFPathRCPI 1985, FRCPath 2000; *Clubs* St Joseph's Coll Old Boys', Sri Lankan Doctors'; *Style*— Dr Bernard S Perera; ✉ 10 Winchester Close, Rochdale, Oldham OL11 5NE (e-mail bsperera@yahoo.com)

PERERA, Prof Katharine Mary; da of Arnold Lacey, of Wallasey, and Eileen, *née* Haylock; *b* 12 December 1943; *Educ* Wallasey HS for Girls, Bedford Coll London (BA), Univ of Manchester (MA, PhD); *m* 1967, Suria Perera; *Career* VSO Malaysia 1965–66, teacher Merseyside 1967–72, lectr Padgate Coll of HE 1973–76; Univ of Manchester: lectr 1977–91, prof 1991–, sr pro-vice-chllr 2000– (pro-vice-chllr 1994–); non-exec dir Salford Royal Hosps NHS Tst 1999–, chair of govrs Withington Girls' Sch 1998–, govr NE Wales Inst of HE 2001–, memb bd Leadership Fndn for HE 2003–; *Books* Children's Writing and Reading (1984), Understanding Language (1987), Growing Points in Child Language (1994); *Recreations* walking, reading, music (memb Hallé Concerts Soc); *Style*— Prof Katharine Perera; ✉ School of English and Linguistics, University of Manchester, Oxford Road, Manchester M13 9PL (tel 0161 275 3190, fax 0161 275 3187, e-mail k.perera@man.ac.uk)

PERGANT, Jean-Jacques; s of Jean Pergant (d 1974), and Anne-Marie, *née* François; *b* 24 February 1949; *Educ* Coll Episcopal St Etienne Strasbourg, Lycée Technique Hotelier de Strasbourg, McGill Univ Mgmnt Inst Montreal (Sr Mgmnt Prog), Exec TV Workshop NY (media trg), Nottingham Trent Univ (Cert Enterprise Mgmnt); *m*; 2 c; *Career* hotelier; served French Forces 1969–70; various jr managerial positions in hotel business London, Paris and Canary Islands 1968–74, various mgmnt positions within Four Seasons Hotels and Resorts Gp 1974–91 (latterly gen mangr Four Seasons Hotel Ottawa 1986–91), gen mangr Hanbury Manor Hotel, Golf & Country Club 1991–94, gen mangr The Berkeley Hotel (Savoy Gp) London 1994–2002, sr vice-pres and md Savoy Gp 2002–04, pres Boca Raton Resort & Club FL 2004–05, pres LXR Luxury Resorts 2005–; chm West One Hotel Managers Gp London 2000; memb: London Divnl Ctee Br Hospitality Assoc, HCIMA; Officier/Maitre de Table La Chaîne des Rotisseurs, Grand Officier L'Ordre Illustre des Chevaliers de Meduse, Cdr La Commanderie de Bordeaux, Chev Chancellerie Franco-Britannique; *Recreations* triathlons, photography, watercolours, the visual arts; *Style*— Jean-Jacques Pergant, Esq; ✉ LXR Luxury Resorts, WHM LLC, 501 East Camino Real, Boca Raton, Florida 33432, USA

PERHAM, Rt Rev Michael Francis; *see:* Gloucester, Bishop of

PERHAM, Prof Richard Nelson; s of Cyril Richard William Perham (d 1948), of London, and Helen Harrow, *née* Thornton (d 1992); *b* 27 April 1937; *Educ* Latymer Upper Sch, St John's Coll Cambridge (MA, PhD, ScD), MRC Lab of Molecular Biology Cambridge (MRC scholar); *m* 22 Dec 1969, Dr Nancy Jane Lane, OBE, *qv*, da of Maj Temple Haviland Lane; 1 da (Temple Helen Gilbert b 1970), 1 s (Quentin Richard Haviland b 1973); *Career* Nat Serv RN 1956–58; fell St John's Coll Cambridge 1964–2004 and 2007– (research fell 1964–67, tutor 1967–77), Helen Hay Whitney fell Yale Univ 1966–67; Univ of Cambridge: lectr in biochemistry 1969–77 (demonstrator 1964–69), reader in biochemistry of macromolecular structures 1977–89, head of dept 1985–96, chm Cambridge Centre for Molecular Recognition 1988–92, prof of structural biochemistry 1989–2004, master St John's Coll 2004–07 (pres 1983–87); memb Sci Bd SERC 1985–90; chm Biological Sci Ctee SERC 1987–90, chm Scientific Advsy Ctee Lister Inst of Preventive Med 2000–06, pres Section D BAAS 1987–88, tstee Novartis (formerly CIBA) Fndn 2002– (memb Exec Cncl 1989–2002), memb Marshall Cmmn (FCO London) 1999–2005 (vice-chair 2004–05); Drapers visiting prof Univ of South Wales 1972; Fogarty int scholar NIH USA 1990–93, Max Planck Prize 1993, Novartis Medal and Prize Biochemical Soc 1998, Silver Medal Italian Biochemical Soc 2000; memb: Biochemical Soc 1965, EMBO 1983, Royal Instn of GB 1986; syndic Cambridge Univ Press 1988–2004, pres Lady Margaret Boat Club 1990–97 and 2004–07; chm of govrs Latymer Upper Sch 2005–, govr Shrewsbury Sch 2004–07; EMBO Fell Max-Planck-Institut für Medizinische Forschung Heidelberg 1971; FRS 1984, FRSA 1988, memb Academia Europaea 1992, FMedSci 2005; *Books* Instrumentation in Amino Acid Sequence Analysis (ed, 1975), numerous papers in scientific jls; *Recreations* gardening, theatre, rowing, nosing around in antique shops; *Clubs* Hawks' (Cambridge), Oxford and Cambridge; *Style*— Prof Richard Perham, FRS, FMedSci; ✉ St John's College, Cambridge CB2 1TP (tel 01223 338600)

PERKIN, (George) David; s of Alan Spencer Perkin (d 1996), of Leeds, and Vera Perkin (d 1958); *Educ* Leeds Modern Sch, Pembroke Coll Cambridge (BA, MB BChir), KCH; *m* 11 July 1964, Louise Ann, da of Sqdn Ldr John Boston, of Sevenoaks; 2 s (Michael b 1968, Matthew b 1971), 1 da (Emma b 1969); *Career* conslt neurologist Hillingdon Hosp 1977–2001, conslt neurologist Charing Cross Hosp 1977–2006; co-chm RCP Speciality Question Group 1998–2002, memb RCP Part II Examining Bd 1994–2003; FRCP 1985 (MRCP 1969), FRSM; *Books* Optic Neuritis and its Differential Diagnosis (1978), Basic Neurology (1986), Atlas of Clinical Neurology (1986, 2 edn 1993), Diagnostic Tests in Neurology (1988), Clinical Examination (1993, 3 edn 2003), Color Atlas and Text of Neurology (1998, 2 edn 2002), Clinical Examination (1992, 4 edn 2007); *Recreations* reading, music, bridge; *Style*— Dr David Perkin; ✉ Charing Cross Hospital, Fulham Palace Road, London W6 8RF (tel 020 8846 1153, fax 020 8846 7487, mobile 07967 975138, e-mail d.perkin@ic.ac.uk)

PERKINS, *see also:* Steele-Perkins

PERKINS, Alice Elizabeth; CB (2002); da of Derrick Leslie John Perkins (d 1965), and Elsa Rose, *née* Rink (d 1986); *b* 24 May 1949; *Educ* North London Collegiate Sch, St Anne's Coll Oxford (BA); *m* 10 Nov 1978, Rt Hon Jack Straw, MP, *qv*; 1 s (William David John Straw b 21 Sept 1980), 1 da (Charlotte Alice b 18 Aug 1982); *Career* DSS (formerly DHSS): joined as admin trainee 1971, private sec to Min of State 1974–75, princ 1975, asst to Chm of Supp Benefits Cmmn 1975–77, asst sec 1984–90, under sec and dir of personnel 1990–93; HM Treasy: head Def and Material Gp 1993–95, dep dir of public spending 1995–98; dir of corp mgmnt Dept of Health 1998–2000; head Corp Devpt Gp Cabinet Office 2001–05; non-exec dir: Littlewoods Organisation plc 1997–2000, Taylor Nelson Sofres plc 2005–, BAA plc 2006–; *Recreations* gardening, riding, looking at pictures; *Style*— Ms Alice Perkins, CB

PERKINS, David Charles Langrigge; s of Charles Samuel Perkins, OBE (d 1987), of Newcastle upon Tyne, and Victoria Alexandra Ryan (d 1991); *b* 31 May 1943; *Educ* Uppingham, Univ of Newcastle upon Tyne (LLB); *m* 1, 1971 (m dis 2000), Sandra Margaret, da of Frank Gerard Buck; 4 s (Benedict William Charles Heritage b 21 June 1972, Rory Philip Francis b 12 Oct 1979, Guy Ranulf David Westbury b 27 Jan 1983, Rupert Alexander David Langrigge b 19 Nov 1973 d 1981), 1 da (Davina Helen Alexandra b 20 May 1978); m 2, 29 Nov 2003, Marie-Ann Strömbäck; *Career* admitted slr 1969; Theodore Goddard & Co 1967–72, Clifford-Turner 1972–87, ptnr Clifford Chance 1987–2003, ptnr Milbank, Tweed, Hadley & McCloy 2003–; arbitrator and mediator WIPO; memb Cncl: The Intellectual Property Inst, The Intellectual Property Lawyers Orgn (TIPLO), Br Gp Union of Euro Practitioners in Industrial Property, Common Law Inst of Intellectual Property; memb: Law Soc, City of London Slrs' Co, Intellectual Property Lawyers' Assoc (IPLA), Int Bar Assoc, Euro Communities Trade Mark Practitioners' Assoc, Association Internationale pour la Protection de la Propriété Industrielle (AIPPI), American Bar Assoc, Intellectual Propery Advsy Ctee (IPAC); assoc memb: Chartered Inst of Patent Agents, Inst of Trade Mark Agents; foreign memb: Int Trade Mark Assoc, American Intellectual Property Law Assoc, American Bar Assoc; *Publications* incl: Rights of Employee Inventors in the United Kingdom under the Patents Act 1977 (1979), Know-How/Confidential Information: an EEC Perspective (1984), Intellectual Property Protection for Biotechnology (1983), Copyright and Industrial Designs (1985), Intellectual Property and the EEC: 1992 (1988), EEC Aspects of Patent/Anti-Trust (1989), Intellectual Property Aspects of 1992 (1989), Transnational Legal Practice in Europe (1991), Foreign Principles of Intellectual Property/Anti-Trust (1992), Proving Patent Infringement in the United Kingdom (1993), The European Community's draft Technology Transfer Regulation (1995), Foreign Principles of Intellectual Property/Anti-Trust (with M van Kerckhove, 1995), A New EC Block Exemption for Patent Licenses and Know-How Licenses (with M van Kerckhove, 1996), Patent Infringement and Forum Shopping in Europe (1996), Claim Interpretation: the United Kingdom and Germany - A Comparative Study (with D Rosenberg, 1996), The WIPO Perspective on Resolution of Intellectual Property Disputes (1996), The EU Technology Transfer Block Exemption for Patent and Know-How Licenses (1996), Trade Mark Developments in 1996 (with Helen Bolton, 1997), Protection of Global Creativity & Ingenuity at the Millennium - Enforcement of Intellectual Property Rights in the European Union (1997), European Union Exhaustion of Rights (with M van Kerckhove, 1997), No Bolar in Europe: No Patent Term Erosion (1997), Alternative Dispute Resolution of Intellectual Property Disputes (1997), International Exhaustion of Intellectual Property Rights (1998), Super Generic Drugs & Patent Busting (with Duncan Curley, 1998), Patent Protection in Europe (1998), Patent Law Development in the European Union as they affect the Pharmaceutical Industry (1998), International Exhaustion of Intellectual Property Rights (1998), Three Dimensional Trade Marks in

Europe (1999), Exhaustion of Intellectual Property Rights (1999), Exhaustion of Intellectual Property Rights - The EU Perspective (with Marleen van Kerckhove and David Rosenberg, 1999), Discovery in Foreign Jurisdictions: Enforcing Judgments Abroad (with David Rosenberg, 1999), The Latest Developments in EU Licensing Law (with Marleen van Kerckhove, 2000), Third Patent System for Europe? (2001), European Community and Exhaustion of Intellectual Property Rights: Shades of Grey (with Marleen van Kerckhove, 2001), The Role of Alternative Dispute Resolution in Patent Disputes (2002), Compulsory Licensing in Europe (2002), Patent Litigation in England and Wales (with Justin Lambert, 2002, Business Method Patents in Europe (2002), Patent Litigation in the United Kingdom (2003), Arbitration of Disputes involving IPRS (2003), European Community Case Law Update on Exhaustion of Rights and Refusal to License (2003), European Union Technology Transfer Block Exemption (2003), Intellectual Property and the Essential Facilities Doctrine (2004), Forum Shopping in Europe - A United Kingdom Perspective (2004); *Recreations* golf, tennis; *Clubs* Northumberland Golf, Northern RFC, Hurlingham; *Style*— David Perkins, Esq; ✉ Milbank, Tweed, Hadley & McCloy, 10 Gresham Street, London EC2V 7JD (tel 020 7615 3000, fax 020 7615 3100, e-mail dperkins@milbank.com)

PERKINS, Geoffrey Howard; s of Wilfred Jack Perkins, and Peggy, *née* Patterson; *b* 22 February 1953; *Educ* Harrow Co GS, Lincoln Coll Oxford (exhibitioner, MA); *m* 1986, Lisa Braun; 1 da (Charlotte b 1988), 1 s (Arthur b 1989); *Career* writer, producer and performer; dir Hat Trick Productions Ltd 1988–95 (whose output incl Have I Got News For You, Whose Line Is It Anyway and Drop The Dead Donkey), head of comedy BBC TV 1995–; former prodr of over 20 programmes and 200 individual shows incl The Hitch-Hikers Guide to the Galaxy for BBC Radio Light Entertainment; TV prodn credits: Spitting Image (Central) 1986–88, Saturday Live and Friday Night Live (Channel 4), Norbert Smith - A Life (Hat Trick/Channel 4, also co-writer (Int Emmy, Banff Light Entertainment Award, Silver Rose of Montreux)), Ben Elton - The Man From Auntie (BBC1), Harry Enfield's Television Programme (2 series, BBC2), Game On (Hat Trick/BBC 2), A Very Open Prison (Hat Trick/BBC2) 1995, Father Ted (Hat Trick/Channel 4 (BAFTA - Best Comedy 1995)), The Thin Blue Line (Tiger Aspect/BBC1); exec prodr Blackadder Back & Forth (Tiger Aspect for the Millennium Dome); writer: Stand By Your Man (for series About Face, awarded American Blue Riband), Radio Active 1980–87 (BBC Radio (BPG, Sony and Premier Onda Barcelona awards)), Uncyclopaedia of Rock (Capital Radio, also prodr) 1986–87 (Monaco Radio award 1986), KYTV (BBC2) 1989–92 (Grand Prix and Silver Rose of Montreux 1992); performer: Radio Active (BBC Radio 4), KYTV (BBC2); *Style*— Geoffrey Perkins, Esq; ✉ Tiger Aspect, 7 Soho Square, London W1D 3DQ

PERKINS, Dr Harvey John; *b* 21 October 1943, Skipton, N Yorks; *Educ* Accrington GS, Accrington Coll of FE, Univ of Wales Cardiff (state scholar, BSc), Univ of Waterloo Canada (Commonwealth scholar, MASc), Univ of Cambridge (PhD); *Career* engrg apprentice English Electric Co Ltd 1960–62; GEC plc: res engr GEC Engrg Lab 1967–74, asst chief engr Ruston Gas Turbines Ltd 1974–75, md Napier Turbochargers Ltd 1975–80, asst md GEC Ruston Gas Turbines Ltd 1983–86 (tech dir 1980–83), md GEC Diesels Ltd 1986–89; ALSTOM (formerly GEC Alsthom): md GEC Alsthom Diesels Ltd 1989–97, md GEC Alsthom Industrial Corp Gp 1997–98, pres ALSTOM Industry Sector 1998–2000; conslt 2000– (incl business advsr Univ of Essex); fell Pembroke Coll Cambridge 1970–74; FIMarEst, FREng 1986; *Recreations* sailing; *Style*— Dr Harvey Perkins; ✉ Gatehouse, 2 New Road, Manningtree, Essex CO11 2AE

PERKINS, Ian Richard Brice; s of Francis Layton Perkins, CBE, DSC (d 1994), of London, and Josephine Louise, *née* Brice (d 1999); *b* 15 November 1949; *Educ* Charterhouse; *m* 5 April 1975, Melissa Anne, da of Sir John Milne; 2 da (Lisa Elizabeth b 5 Feb 1980, Tania Catherine Brice 29 Jan 1982), 1 s (Roderick John Bloomfield b 2 Oct 1984); *Career* W I Carr 1968–70 and 1971–72, Fergusson Bros Johannesburg 1970–71, Greenshields Inc 1972–79; James Capel and Co: joined 1979, pres James Capel Inc NY 1986–88, dir 1988–91; ceo King & Shaxson Holdings plc 1994–97 (dir 1991–97), dir Gerrard Group plc 1997–2000; chm: Gerrard & King Ltd 1997–99, GNI Ltd 2001–03 (ceo 1999–2001), King & Shaxson Ltd 2003–, ILEX Asset Mgmnt 2005–; dir: King & Shaxson Bond Brokers 1996–, Lombard Street Research 1998–; Freeman City of London 1973, memb Ct of Assts Worshipful Co of Skinners (Freeman 1975); *Recreations* golf, tennis, skiing; *Clubs* Boodle's, The Berkshire, Honourable Co of Edinburgh Golfers (Muirfield), Swinley Forest, Leopard Creek; *Style*— Ian Perkins, Esq; ✉ Moth House, Brown Candover, Alresford, Hampshire SO24 9TT (tel 01256 389260)

PERKINS, Prof John Douglas; CBE (2007); s of Douglas Herbert Perkins (d 1997), of Kent, and Isobel Mary Perkins; *b* 18 March 1950; *Educ* Royal GS Guildford, Univ of London (BSc, MA, PhD, FCGI, DIC, Dip TCDHE, Hinchley Meml Medal); *m* 11 June 1975 (m dis 1992), Chantal Marie, da of Claude Paul Ernest Lestavel; 1 s (Matthew John b 1987); *Career* univ demonstrator in chemical engrg Univ of Cambridge 1973–77, seconded to ICI Agric Div as res engr 1975–76, sr lectr in chemical engrg Imperial Coll London 1983–85 (lectr 1977–83), ICI prof of process systems engrg Univ of Sydney 1985–88; Imperial Coll London: prof of chemical engrg 1988–99, dir Centre for Process Systems Engrg 1992–98, head Dept of Chemical Engrg 1996–2001, Courtaulds prof of chemical engrg 2000–04, princ Faculty of Engrg 2001–04; vice-pres and dean of engrg and physical sciences Univ of Manchester 2004–; memb Foresight Manufacturing Panel Office of Science and Technol 1994–99; CEng, CSci, CMath; fell Inst of Mathematics and its Applications 1992 (assoc fell 1976), FIChemE 1986 (memb Cncl 1997–, dep pres 1999–2000, pres 2000–01), FREng 1993, FCGI 1996, FRSA; *Recreations* orienteering, reading; *Style*— Prof John Perkins, CBE, FREng; ✉ Room B1, Sackville Street Building, PO Box 88, Sackville Street, Manchester M60 1QD (tel 0161 306 9111, fax 0161 306 9109, e-mail john.perkins@manchester.ac.uk)

PERKINS, Dame Mary Lesley; DBE (2007); da of (George) Leslie Bebbington (d 1985), and Eileen Hilda Constance, *née* Mawditt (d 1965); *b* 14 February 1944, Bristol; *Educ* Fairfield GS Bristol, Cardiff Univ; *m* 25 March 1967, Douglas John David Perkins; 2 da (Cathryn Llywella b 14 Oct 1967, Juliette Mary b 16 Oct 1968), 1 s (John Douglas b 4 Aug 1972); *Career* owner and optometrist Bebbington and Perkins 1966–80 (sold 23 stores 1980), fndr Specsavers 1984 (initially jt owner with husband, now ptnr and memb Bd), fndr Specsavers HearCare; memb Gen Optical Cncl 1966; dir Guernsey Trg Agency, dir Women's Refuge Guernsey, pres Age Concern Guernsey, govr Ladies' Coll Guernsey; Liveryman Worshipful Co of Spectacle Makers; Community and Vocational Service Award Rotary Intl 2005; hon fell Cardiff Univ 2005; FBOA 1967; *Recreations* choir, walking, yoga, seven grandchildren; *Style*— Dame Mary Perkins, DBE; ✉ Specsavers Optical Group Ltd, La Villiaze, St Andrews, Guernsey GY6 8YP (tel 01481 234811, fax 01481 233714, e-mail maryp@gg.specsavers.com)

PERKINS, Michael John; s of Phillip John Broad Perkins, OBE, DL (d 1982), of Lymington, Hants, and Jane Mary, *née* Hope; *b* 31 January 1942; *Educ* Eton, RNC Dartmouth; *m* 9 Nov 1968, Nicola Margaret, da of Air Cdre William Vernon Anthony Denney, of Amersham, Bucks; 1 s (Robert b 1971), 1 da (Caroline b 1973); *Career* RN 1961–66, Sub Lt 1963, Lt 1965; sr ptnr Westlake Clark & Co Chartered Accountants 1996–99 (ptnr 1981–99), dir NEWSCOM plc 1981–2000, dir New Milton Property 2002–; treas: New Forest Assoc 1997–, New Forest Agric Show Soc 2001–07; Freeman City of London 1964, Liveryman Worshipful Co of Haberdashers 1964; CA (Canada) 1973, FCIS 1982; *Recreations* sailing, skiing, shooting, fly fishing; *Clubs* Royal Lymington Yacht, Royal Naval Sailing Assoc; *Style*— Michael Perkins, Esq; ✉ Critchells Farmhouse, Lockerley, Romsey, Hampshire SO51 0JD (tel 01794 340281, e-mail perkins.lockerley@tiscali.co.uk)

PEROWNE, Adm Sir James Francis; KBE (Mil) (2000, OBE (Mil) 1983); s of Lt Cdr John Herbert Francis Perowne (d 1999), and (Mary) Joy, *née* Dibb (d 2006); *b* 29 July 1947; *Educ* Sherborne, BRNC Dartmouth; *m* 1, 22 May 1971 (m dis 1990), Susan Anne, da of Cdr Peter John Holloway, of Western Australia; 4 s (Julian b 1972, Samuel b 1975, Roger b 1977, Timothy b 1977); m 2, 15 Feb 1992, Caroline Nicola, da of Dr T Grimson, of Co Durham; *Career* CO: HMS Opportune 1976–77, HMS Superb 1981–83, HMS Boxer 1986–88, asst dir Underwater Warfare MOD 1988–90, Second Submarine Sqdn 1990–92, HMS Norfolk and 6 Frigate Sqdn 1992–94; Sr Naval Memb RCDS 1995–96, Flag Offr Submarines, Cdr Submarines Eastern Atlantic and North West Europe and COS (Ops) to C-in-C Fleet 1996–98, Dep Supreme Allied Cdr Atlantic 1998–2002; pres: Submariners' Assoc 2002–, Assoc of Royal Navy Offrs and Royal Navy Benevolent Soc for Offrs 2003–; chm: Central Region Ctee Watervoice 2002–05, Consumer Cncl for Water Midlands Region 2005–; memb: Judiciary Review Bd DCA 2006–, Fitness to Practice Panels GMC 2006–; tstee Br Forces Fndn 2002–, chm Cncl Queen Mother Meml Fund 2003–06, chm James Caird Soc 2006–; *Recreations* canal boating, golf, gardening; *Clubs* RN; *Style*— Adm Sir James Perowne, KBE; ✉ c/o ARNO, 70 Porchester Terrace, Bayswater, London W2 3TP (e-mail jamesperowne@aol.com)

PERRAUD, Michel Bernard; s of René Perraud (d 1989), and Jeanne, *née* Brebion; *b* 30 January 1957; *Children* 1 s (Cédric b 16 Dec 1985), 1 da (Sabrina b 23 Oct 1987); *Career* French Nat Serv 1978–79; chef; apprentice Restaurant Dagorno Paris 1975–77; commis de cuisine: Hotel St Paul Noirmoutier 1977, Restaurant Chez Albert Cassis 1977–78; chef de partie: Hotel St Paul Noirmoutier 1979, Restaurant Trois Gros Roanne 1979–80; demi-chef de partie Restaurant Taillevent Paris 1980–81; chef de cuisine: Hotel St Paul Noirmoutier 1981, Restaurant Le Bressan London 1981, Waterside Inn Restaurant Bray Berks 1982–87; assistant de direction conseiller en sous vide Ecole de Cuisine Georges Pralus Briennon 1988, chef de cuisine Les Alouettes Restaurant Claygate Surrey 1988–92, chef des chefs Le Cordon Blue London 1992, opened own restaurant Fleur de Sel 1994; memb Académie Culinaire de France in UK 1983–; *Awards* first prize Mouton Cadet Rothschild Menu Competition 1983–84, 3 Michelin Stars (Waterside Inn) 1985, 1 Michelin Star (Les Alouettes) 1990, 1 Michelin Star (Fleur de Sel) 1995, Diplôme MOGB (Meilleur Ouvrier de Grande Bretagne) 1987; *Style*— Michel Perraud; ✉ Fleur de Sel, Manleys Hill, Storrington, West Sussex, RH20 4BT

PERRETT, Amanda Jill; da of Guy Harwood, the racehorse trainer, and Gillian, *née* Lawson; *b* 31 December 1969, London; *m* 2 July 1995, Mark Edward Perrett, the former jockey; 1 s (Ryan Phillip b 4 March 2006); *Career* racehorse trainer; former jockey, more than 100 winners in flat and Nat Hunt races, first female jockey to ride in Champion Hurdle (Cheltenham Festival); trainer (succeeding f, Guy) Coombelands Stables 1996–, trained more than 300 winners, horses incl Indian Lodge, Tungsten Strike, Tillerman and Carnival Dancer; *Style*— Mrs Amanda Perrett; ✉ Coombelands Racing Stables, Pulborough, West Sussex RH20 1BP (tel 01798 873011, fax 01798 875163, e-mail aperrett@coombelands-stables.com)

PERRIAM, Wendy Angela; da of Edward Francis Leopold Brech, of Esher, Surrey, and Irene Ella, *née* Thompson; *b* 23 February 1940; *Educ* Combe Bank Convent, St Anne's Coll Oxford (MA), LSE; *m* 1, 22 Aug 1964, Christopher Hugh Tyack, s of Dr Norman Tyack; 1 da (Pauline Maria b 31 Dec 1965); m 2, 29 July 1974, John Alan Perriam, s of John Perriam; *Career* author and creative writing tutor; formerly copywriter: Colman Prentis & Varley, Notley & Pritchard Wood; various articles and stories published in magazines and newspapers incl: She, Cosmopolitan, For Women, Woman's Jl, The Lady, Image, Penthouse, Esquire, Sunday Times, Daily Telegraph, Daily Mail, Evening Standard, Independent, Daily Express; poems and stories included in: Arts Cncl Anthology, SE Arts anthologies, Seven Deadly Sins, Best Short Stories, The Picador Book of Erotic Prose, The Literary Comparison to Sex and Second Penguin Book of Modern Women's Short Stories; memb: Soc of Authors, PEN, Br Actors Equity; *Books* Absinthe for Elevenses (1980, reissued 1991), Cuckoo (1981, reissued 1992), After Purple (1982, reissued 1993), Born of Woman (1983, reissued 1993), The Stillness The Dancing (1985, reissued 1994), Sin City (1987, reissued 1994), Devils, for a Change (1989), Fifty-Minute Hour (1990), Bird Inside (1992), Michael, Michael (1993), Breaking and Entering (1994), Coupling (1996), Second Skin (1998), Lying (2000), Dreams, Demons and Desire (2001), Tread Softly (2002), Virgin in the Gym and Other Stories (2004), Laughter Class and Other Stories (2006), The Biggest Female in the World and Other Stories (2007); *Style*— Wendy Perriam; ✉ c/o Jonathan Lloyd, Curtis Brown, 4th Floor, Haymarket House, 28–29 Haymarket, London SW1Y 4SP (tel 020 7396 6600, website www.wendyperriam.com)

PERRIN, Charles John; CBE (2004); s of Sir Michael Perrin, CBE (d 1988), of London, and Nancy May, *née* Curzon (d 1992); *b* 1 May 1940; *Educ* Winchester, New Coll Oxford; *m* 1966, Gillian Margaret, da of late Rev M Hughes-Thomas (d 1969); 2 da (Felicity Margaret Roche b 1970, Nicola May Roche b 1973); *Career* Hambros Bank Ltd: joined 1963, dir 1973, dep chm 1986–98, chief exec 1995–98; former dir: Hambros plc, Hambro Pacific Ltd Hong Kong, Harland & Wolff plc Belfast (non-exec 1984–89); memb Exec Ctee UK Ctee UNICEF 1970–91 (vice-chm 1972–91); hon treas UK Assoc for Int Year of the Child 1979; vice-chm Royal Brompton & Harefield NHS Tst 1998–; memb: Royal Brompton Nat Heart and Lung Hosps SHA 1993–94, Cncl Univ of London 1994–, Queen Mary & Westfield Coll London 1997– (hon treas 1999–), Central Sch of Speech & Drama 2006–; chm MRC Pension Tst 2004–; tstee: Medical Research Fndn 2006–, The Nuffield Tst 2006–; govr: Queen Anne's Sch Caversham 1981–2006, London Hosp Med Coll 1991–95; Liveryman Worshipful Co of Shipwrights; hon fell New Coll Oxford 1999, Hon MRCP 1999; *Clubs* Athenaeum; *Style*— Charles Perrin, Esq, CBE

PERRING, Sir John Raymond; 2 Bt (UK 1963), of Frensham Manor, Surrey; TD (1965); s of Sir Ralph Edgar Perring, 1 Bt (d 1998), by his late w Ethel Mary, da of Henry Theophilus Johnson, of Putney; *b* 7 July 1931; *Educ* Stowe; *m* 1961, Ella Christine, da of late Maj Anthony George Pelham; 2 s (John Simon Pelham b 1962, Mark Ralph Pelham b 1965), 2 da (Emma (Mrs Christian Heyman) b 1963, Anna (Mrs Edward Standish) b 1968); *Heir* s, John Perring; *Career* chm: Perring Furnishings Ltd 1981–88, Perrings Finance Ltd 1986–2007, Ranyard Nursing Home 1992–2001; cncl memb Retail Consortium 1972–91 (hon treas 1973–78); Master: Worshipful Co of Furniture Makers 1978–79, Merchant Taylors' Co 1988–89 and 1994–95; one of HM Lieutenants of the City of London 1963–, Sheriff City of London 1991–92; chm Wimbledon Decorative and Fine Arts Soc 1999–2002, pres Old Stoic Soc 2002–03, pres Bishopsgate Ward Club 1997–98, govr Bishopsgate Fndn 1992–2002; OStJ, FRSA; *Style*— Sir John Perring, Bt, TD

PERRINS, Robert Charles Grenville (Rob); *b* 5 April 1965; *Educ* Marlborough, Aston Univ; *m* Vanessa, *née* Gullis; 2 s (Ralph b 26 April 2000, Humphrey b 23 Nov 2001); *Career* CA 1992; Ernst & Young 1987–91, Shanks 1991–94; Berkeley Gp: joined 1994, md Berkeley Homes plc 2001–02, gp fin dir 2002–; *Style*— Rob Perrins, Esq; ✉ The Berkeley Group plc, Berkeley House, 19 Portsmouth Road, Cobham, Surrey KT11 1JG (tel 01932 868555, fax 01932 860403, e-mail rob.perrins@berkeleygroup.co.uk)

PERROTT, Prof Ronald Henry; *b* 27 December 1942; *Educ* Queen's Univ Belfast (BSc, PhD); *m* 4 April 1974, Valerie Mary Perrott; 1 s (Simon b 2 March 1976); *Career* prof of software engrg: Univ of Wisconsin 1968–69, NASA Res Centre Calif 1977–78, CERN Geneva 1984–85, Queen's Univ Belfast 1985–; memb: EC Working Gp on High Performance Computing, IT Advsy Bd to DTI and SERC, EU IST Monitoring Panel, OST Informatics

Ctee; ed Jl of Scientific Programming; NI BCS IT Professional of the Year 1993; fell US Assoc for Computing Machinery 1997; FBCS, FRSA, FIEEE 2004; *Books* Operating Systems Techniques (1972), Software Engineering (1978), Pascal for Fortran Programmers (1983), Parallel Programming (1987), Software for Parallel Computers (1991); *Recreations* skiing, squash; *Style*— Prof Ronald Perrott; ✉ Department of Computer Science, The Queen's University of Belfast, Belfast BT7 1NN (tel 028 9097 5463, fax 028 9097 5666, e-mail r.perrott@qub.ac.uk)

PERRY, Adam; *b* 14 October 1958; *Career* broadcasting prodn; Yorkshire TV 1978–86, Central TV 1986–94, Carlton Productions 1994–96, head of regnl productions and special events Channel 5 1996–2001, creative dir World of Wonder 2001–06, head of progs and campaigns Community Channel 2007–; dir Birmingham Int Film and TV Festival 1994–98; memb RTS; *Style*— Adam Perry, Esq

PERRY, Hon Alan Malcolm; s of Baron Perry of Walton (Life Peer, d 2003), and Anne Elizabeth, *née* Grant; *b* 6 February 1950; *Educ* George Heriot's Sch Edinburgh, Trinity Coll Oxford (MA); *m* 1976, Naomi Melanie, da of Dr Abraham Freedman, MD, FRCP, of London; 3 s (Daniel b 1980, Guy b 1982, Edmund b 1986); *Career* Harmsworth scholar, admitted slr 1982, currently ptnr D J Freeman; *Recreations* painting, making music, gardening; *Style*— The Hon Alan Perry; ✉ 43 Meadway, London NW11 7AX; D J Freeman, 43 Fetter Lane, London EC4A 1NA (tel 020 7583 4055, telex 894579)

PERRY, David Gordon; s of Elliott Gordon Perry (d 1994), of Kemble, Glos, and Lois Evelyn, *née* Allen; *b* 26 December 1937; *Educ* Clifton, Christ's Coll Cambridge (Rugby blue); *m* 16 Sept 1961, Dorne Mary, da of Edwin Timson Busby (d 1980), of Braybrooke, Leics; 4 da (Belinda b 1963, Philippa b 1964, Rebecca b 1967, Joanna b 1970); *Career* Nat Serv 2 Lt Parachute Regt 1956–58; Br Printing Corp (BPC) Ltd: md Fell & Briant Ltd (subsid) 1966–78, chief exec Packaging and Paper Products Div 1978–81, dir 1981; John Waddington plc: md 1981–88, chief exec 1988–92, chm 1993–97; chm Anglian Gp plc 1996–2001; non-exec dir: Dewhirst Group plc 1992–2001, National and Provincial Building Soc 1993–96, Kelda Gp plc 1996–2000, Euler Hermes UK plc, Bellway plc 1999–, Minorplanet Systems plc (chm 2005–07); fifteen caps England Rugby XV 1963–66 (capt 1965); Liveryman Worshipful Co of Makers of Playing Cards; CIMgt 1986, FIP; *Recreations* golf, music; *Clubs* Oxford and Cambridge, MCC; *Style*— David Perry, Esq; ✉ Deighton House, York Road, Deighton, York YO19 6HQ

PERRY, George Cox; s of George Cox Perry (d 1962), of Berkhamsted, Herts, and Hortense Irene Emily Sadler (d 1983); *b* 7 January 1935; *Educ* Tiffin Sch, Trinity Coll Cambridge (MA, ed Varsity); *m* 1 (m dis 1976), Susanne Puddefoot; m 2, 1976, Frances Nicola, da of Sidney Murray Scott (d 1987); 1 s (Matthew Richard Scott b 1977); *Career* advtg (creative) T Eaton Co Montreal 1957, sub ed The Sphere 1957–58, copywriter J Walter Thompson 1958–62; Sunday Times: sub ed 1962–63, asst to the ed (magazine) 1963–65, projects ed 1965–69, asst ed 1967–77, sr ed 1977–85, films ed 1985–98; chief exec: Cameo Editions 1998–2000, Boulevard Classics 2000–05; chm Forever Ealing 2000–02; managing ed Crossbow 1965–70; dir Cinema City 1970; film critic: The Illustrated London News 1982–88 and 1992–99, Jazz-FM 1990–92; presenter Radio 2 Arts 1990–97; chm (film) The Critics' Circle 1991–94 (vice-chm 1987–91), pres The Critics' Circle 1998–2000 (vice-pres 1996–98); juror Carl Foreman Award BAFTA 1998–2005; *Books* incl: The Films of Alfred Hitchcock (1965), The Penguin Book of Comics (1967), The Great British Picture Show (1974), Movies from the Mansion (1976), Forever Ealing (1981), Life of Python (1983), Rupert - A Bear's Life (1985), Bluebell (adapted as BBC drama serial, 1986), The Complete Phantom of the Opera (1987), Sunset Boulevard: from Movie to Musical (1993), The Life of Python (1994), Director's Cuts: Steven Spielberg (1998), Magic Movie Moments (2000), London in the Sixties (2001), Paris in the Sixties (2001), New York in the Sixties (2001), San Francisco in the Sixties (2001), Héros d'Hollywood (with Matthew Perry, 2002), Films Cultes (with Matthew Perry, 2002), James Dean (2005), Bogie (with Richard Schickel, 2006); *Recreations* walking, talking, watching movies, travelling, taking pictures; *Style*— George Perry, Esq; ✉ 7 Roehampton Lane, London SW15 5LS (tel 020 8878 1187, fax 020 8487 9959, e-mail georgeperry2001@aol.com)

PERRY, Grayson; *b* 24 March 1960; *Career* artist; winner Turner Prize 2003; *Solo Exhibitions* James Birch Gallery London 1984 and 1985, The Minories Colchester 1986, Birch & Conran London 1986, 1987, 1988 and 1990, Garth Clark Gallery NY 1991, David Gill Gallery London 1991–92, Clara Scremini Gallery Paris 1994, Anthony d'Offay Gallery London 1994 and 1996–97, Laurent Delaye Gallery London 2000, fig-1 London 2000, Stedelijk Museum Amsterdam 2002, Guerrillla Tactics (Stedelijk Museum Amsterdam) 2002, Guerrilla Tactics (Barbican Art Centre) 2002; *Group Exhibitions* Young Contemporaries (ICA London) 1982, Ian Birkstead Gallery London 1983, Essex Artists (Epping Forest Museum and The Minories Colchester) 1985, Curious Christian Art (James Birch Gallery London) 1985, Gallozi e La Placa NY 1985, Mandelzoon Rome 1986, Read Stremmel Gallery San Antonio Texas 1988, Words and Volume (Garth Clark Gallery NY and Nishi Azabu Wall Tokyo) 1989, Essex Ware (Chelmsford and tour) 1991–92, Fine Cannibals (Oldham Art Gallery and tour) 1992, The Raw and the Cooked (Barbican Art Gallery London and tour) 1993–95, Indigo Gallery Boca Raton Florida 1995, Whitechapel Open (Whitechapel Gallery London) 1995, Philippe Rizzo Gallery Paris 1995, Hot Off the Press (Tullie House Glasgow, Norwich, Croydon Clock Tower and Crafts Cncl London) 1996–97, Objects of our Time (Crafts Cncl London, Edinburgh, Manchester, Belfast, Cardiff and American Crafts Museum NY) 1997–98, Craft (Richard Salmon Gallery London and Kettle's Yard Cambridge) 1997–98, Glazed Expressions (Orleans House London) 1998, Over the Top (Ikon Gallery Birmingham and tour) 1998, 250 Vases, Plates and Services (Stedelijk Museum Amsterdam) 1999, Decadence (Crafts Cncl London) 1999, Narrative (Garth Clark Gallery NY) 1999, A Sense of Occasion, mac (Birmingham and tour) 2000 and 2001, Protest and Survive (Whitechapel Art Gallery London) 2000, British Art Show 5 (tour) 2000–01, East Wing Collection No 5: Looking With/Out (Courtald Inst of Art London) 2001 and 2002, Carts and Rafts! (Camberwell Coll of Arts London) 2001, Invitation à...Laurent Delaye Gallery invitée par la galerie Anton Weller (Galerie Anton Weller Paris) 2001, New Labour (Saatchi Gallery London) 2001, The Other Britannia (Tecla Sala Barcelona and tour) 2001, Self Portrayal (Laurent Delaye Gallery London) 2001, The Galleries Show (Royal Acad) 2002, Liverpool Biennial 2002; *Work in Public Collections* Br Cncl, Crafts Cncl of Eng, Stedelijk Museum Amsterdam, Shigarake Ceramic Cultural Park Japan, Syracuse Museum NY State, Hydra Fndn Greece, Pottery Museum Stoke-on-Trent, MOMA Glasgow, Fondation Musée d'Art Moderne Grand-Duc Jean Luxembourg, Saatchi Collection London; *Style*— Grayson Perry, Esq; ✉ c/o Victoria Miro Gallery, 16 Wharf Road, London N1 7RW (tel 020 7336 8106, e-mail info@victoria-miro.com)

PERRY, Dr Ian Charles; s of Capt Sidney Charles Perry (d 1984), of Bush Hill Park, Middx, and Marjorie Ellen, *née* Elliott; *b* 18 April 1939; *Educ* Highgate Sch, Guy's Hosp London (MB BS), RAF Inst of Aviation Med (Dip Aviation Med); *m* 27 July 1963, Janet Patricia, da of Maj Albert Edward Watson, of Burton Bradstock, Dorset; 2 da (Johanna Elizabeth b 18 Oct 1964, Helen b 7 July 1967); *Career* Lt RAMC 1963, Capt 2 i/c 24 Field Ambulance Aden 1965 and 1967 (SMO Aden Bde 1966), SMO (specialist in aviation med) Army Air Corps Centre 1967–68, 200 Army Pilots Course 1968–69, Maj SMO Conslt Aviation Med Army Air Corps Centre 1969, chm NATO (AG ARD) Aircrew Fatigue Panel 1969–72, ret 1973, RARO 1973–, TA (AAC) 1989–94; princ aviation and occupational med practice 1973–; conslt in occupational med Winchester and Eversleigh NHS Tst; sr conslt Avimed Ltd; conslt: IAOPA, Br Helicopter Advsy Bd, Jt Aviation Authy Med Gp; memb: Int Acad of Aviation and Space Med, US/AOPA Bd of Aviation Med Advsrs; author of papers on aviation med; conslt: The HSA; former chm: Br Assoc of Aviation Conslts, Grateley PC, Grateley PTA; tstee: Army Air Corps Museum, Preservation of Rural Eng; sec Nurdling Assoc of England; Freeman City of London 1973, Liveryman Worshipful Co of Gunmakers, Master Guild of Air Pilots and Navigators 1996; MBAC, MFOM, FRAeS, FAMA, FCMI (FIMgt 1998), FIOSH 1988; *Recreations* orchids, golf, shooting; *Clubs* Cavalry and Guards', Tidworth Golf; *Style*— Dr Ian Perry; ✉ The Old Farm House, Grateley, Hampshire SP11 8JR (tel 01264 889659/639, fax 01264 889639, mobile 07836 664670, e-mail ian@ianperry.com, websites www.ianperry.com); 19 Cliveden Place, London SW1W 8HD (tel 020 7730 8045/9328, fax 020 7730 1985); The Lister Hospital, Chelsea Bridge Road, London SW1W 8RH (tel 020 7730 1985/9328)

PERRY, Dr J David; *b* 21 April 1946; *Educ* Bristol GS, Middx Hosp Med Sch (MB), Univ of London (BSc, MB BS); *Career* house physician Oldchurch Hosp Romford then house surgn Middx Hosp 1971, casualty MO Middx Hosp and SHO in gen and chest med The London Hosp 1972–74, registrar in gen and chest med The London Hosp 1975–76 (SHO and registrar Dept of Rheumatology 1974–75), sr registrar in rheumatology The London Hosp and Prince of Wales Hosp Tottenham 1976–77, sr registrar in rheumatology Colchester and The London Hosp 1977–79, conslt rheumatologist The London Hosp (now Royal Hosps Tst) 1979–, clinical dir Musculoskeletal Directorate Royal Hosps Tst; univ teacher Univ of London; hon sr lectr Bart's London Hosp Med Coll and Queen Mary Westfield Coll, MO BAAB, med dir Crystal Palace Nat Sports Centre, co-organiser and treas Therapy Pool Appeal The London Hosp (pool opened by HRH The Princess Royal), memb Hispanic Soc Goldsmiths' Coll, former sec NE Thames Regnl Advsy Sub-ctee on Rheumatology and Rehabilitation, sec RSM Sports Med Section, hon sec Jt Med Cncl Royal Hosps NHS Tst, regnl advsr NE Thames RCP 2003; FRCP 1986; *Books* Hutchison's Clinical Methods (contrib chapter The Locomotor System, 18 edn, 1984 and 1995), Rheumatology Examination and Injection Techniques (jtly, 1992, 2 edn 1999); chapters in: Sports Medicine (ed J B King, 1992), Rheumatology (eds Klippel & Dieppe, 1994, 2 edn 1998); *Style*— Dr J David Perry; ✉ The Royal London Hospital, Mile End, London E1 1BB (tel 020 7377 7859, fax 020 7377 7807); London Independent Hospital (tel and fax 020 7791 1688)

PERRY, Jane; da of Evan Morgan Perry (d 1989), of Brighton, E Sussex, of Hilda Ellen, *née* Webb; *b* 28 September 1948; *Educ* Brighton and Hove HS for Girls GPDST, Univ of Exeter (BA); *m* 4 Nov 1972 (sep 1983), Derek John Brandon; 2 s (James Martin b 24 Dec 1977, Thomas Henry b 21 April 1980); *Career* advtg exec; research exec BMRB 1969–71, research assoc J Walter Thompson NY 1971–72, research mangr Manchester Evening News 1972–77, UK mangr IMS London 1977–82, media research mangr Davidson Pearce (now BMP) 1982–87: Young & Rubicam: media research mangr 1987–89, Euro media research dir 1989–2000; res dir The Media Edge EMEA 2000, chm EAAA Media Res Gp 1996–2000, media ed of Admap 2000–; FIPA 1995; *Books* European Marketing and Media Pocket-Book (annually 1991–2001), European Media Cost Comparison (1991, 1993, 1995–97), European Media Overspill (1992), Global Media Cost Comparison (1998, 2000–01), Asia-Pacific Marketing & Media pocket-book (2000), Americas Marketing & Media pocket-book (2000); *Style*— Ms Jane Perry; ✉ Admap, World Advertising Research Centre, Farm Road, Henley-on-Thames, Oxfordshire RG9 1EJ (tel 01491 411000, fax 01491 418600, e-mail jane2perry@hotmail.com)

PERRY, Prof John Grenville; s of Frederick Perry (d 1974), of Stoke-on-Trent, and Elsie, *née* Till (d 1998); *b* 21 May 1945; *Educ* Longton HS Stoke-on-Trent, Univ of Liverpool (BEng, MEng), Univ of Manchester (PhD); *m* 20 April 1968, Ruth Katharine, da of Eric Stanley Forrester (d 1989), of Fulford, Staffs; 2 s (Jonathan b 17 Nov 1970, Timothy b 10 June 1972); *Career* engr Costain Ltd 1967–70, project engr ICI Ltd 1970–74, sr lectr UMIST 1984–88 (lectr 1974–84); Univ of Birmingham: Beale prof 1988–, head Sch of Civil Engrg 1988–2000, dep dean Faculty of Engrg 1995–97; former chm local branch Lib Pty; non-exec dir Heartlands and Solihull NHS Tst 1998–; govr Bromsgrove Sch 1998–; MAPM 1988, FICE 1993 (MICE 1975); *Publications* co-author of the New Engineering Contract; author of over 70 pubns; *Recreations* ornithology, swimming, fell walking; *Style*— Prof John Perry; ✉ School of Civil Engineering, The University of Birmingham, Edgbaston, Birmingham B15 2TT (tel 0121 4145048)

PERRY, John William; s of John Perry, and Cecilia Perry; *b* 23 September 1938; *Educ* Wallington GS, Brasenose Coll Oxford (MA); *m* 4 Feb 1961, Gillian Margaret; 2 da (Jane (Mrs Wernette) b 1963, Sarah b 1965); *Career* Burroughs: dir of mktg Burroughs Machines Ltd 1967–71, dir of mktg Europe & Africa Div 1977–78, gp dir int mktg 1978–80, vice-pres strategic planning 1981–83, vice-pres Fin Systems Gp 1983–85, vice-pres Central USA 1985–86, md UK 1986; chm and md Unisys Ltd 1987–94 (corp offr Unisys Corporation 1990, pres fin line of business (worldwide) Unisys Corp 1993); chm Trace Computers 1996–; memb: Nat Enterprise Team CBI, Bd of Govrs Poly of E London 1989–91; involved with Business in the Community; *Recreations* reading, gardening, golf, music; *Style*— John Perry, Esq; ✉ c/o Trace Computers plc, 224–232 St John Street, London EC1V 4PH

PERRY, Jonathan Peter Langman; s of Thomas Charles Perry, and Kathleen Mary Perry; *b* 6 September 1939; *Educ* Peter Symonds Coll Winchester; *Career* chartered accountant; articled Butler, Viney & Childs 1956–62, Coopers & Lybrand 1962–66; Morgan Grenfell Group plc: joined 1966, dir Morgan Grenfell & Co Limited 1973, jtly i/c banking 1973–77, i/c New York office 1977–80, i/c banking and capital markets 1980–87, i/c overseas offices 1987–88, dir Morgan Grenfell Holdings 1987; fin advsr and proprietor Perry & Associates 1988–90, chm and chief exec Ogilvy Adams & Rinehart Ltd 1990–92, exec chm National Home Loans Holdings plc (Paragon Group of Companies plc) 1992–2007 (non-exec dir 1991–92), vice-chm HSBC Investment Banking Div 1997–99; non-exec dir Comcast UK Cable Partners Ltd 1994–98; memb Cncl of Int Stock Exchange 1986–88; yachtsman, memb Br Team Int 14s 1973, 1977 and 1983 (capt 1983), team capt Br Americas Cup Team 1986; FCA; *Recreations* sports (yacht racing, tennis, golf), music, painting, writing; *Clubs* Brooks's, Itchenor Sailing, Sussex Golf, Royal Yacht Squadron; *Style*— Jonathan Perry, Esq

PERRY, Mark (né Philip Perry); *Educ* Univ of Leicester (BA, MA); *Career* actor and impressionist; involved with Nat Children's Homes and Comic Heritage Charity; *Theatre* incl: Deathtrap (nat tour), No Man's Land (nat tour), Can't Pay Won't Pay (Hong Kong Arts Centre), Dangerous Corner (nat tour), seasons at Leicester Haymarket and Salisbury Playhouse; musicals incl: Gigi, Godspell, Joseph and the Technicolor Dreamcoat; *Television* for BBC: Mr Charity, Double Take, Celeb, Dead Ringers, Arena; Believe Nothing (ITV), 2DTV (ITV), Bremner, Bird and Fortune (Channel 4); *Radio* The Archers, Elephants and Eels, The Attractive Young Rabbi, Stephen Appleby's Life, Dead Ringers, regular news contrib Radio 3 Hong Kong; *Awards* for Dead Ringers: Sony Radio Award 2000, ITV Comedy Award 2001, Spoken Word Award 2001, Comedy Heritage Award 2002; BAFTA for Double Take, Golden Rose of Montreux for 2DTV 2001; *Recreations* 1960s Br progressive music, tennis, singing, spiritual atheism; *Style*— Mark Perry, Esq

PERRY, Sir Michael Sydney; GBE (2002, CBE 1990, OBE 1973), kt (1994); s of Lt Cdr Sydney Albert Perry, RNVR (d 1979), of Douglas, IOM, and Jessie Kate, *née* Brooker; *b* 26 February 1934; *Educ* King William's Coll IOM, St John's Coll Oxford (MA); *m* 18 Oct 1958, Joan Mary, da of Francis William Stallard (d 1948), of Worcester; 2 da (Carolyn b 1962, Deborah b 1963), 1 s (Andrew b 1967); *Career* Nat Serv RN 1952–54; Unilever plc: joined 1957, dir 1985–96, vice-chm 1991–92, chm and chief exec 1992–96; chm Centrica plc 1997–2004 (sometime dep chm predecessor companies, joined Bd as non-exec dir 1994), dep chm Bass plc 1996–2001; non-exec chm Dunlop Slazenger Group Ltd

P

1996–2002; non-exec dir: Br Gas 1994–97, Marks and Spencer plc 1996–2001; chm Chairmen's Counsel Ltd 2006–; vice-pres Liverpool Sch of Tropical Med; pres The Mktg Cncl 2000–04, vice-pres Chartered Inst of Mktg; chm Shakespeare Globe Tst 1993–96; tstee: Leverhulme Tst 1992–, Glyndebourne Arts Tst 1998–2005, Dyson Perrins Museum Tst 2000–; *Recreations* music (choral), golf; *Clubs* Oriental; *Style—* Sir Michael Perry, GBE; ✉ Bridges Stone Mill, Alfrick, Worcestershire WR6 5HR (tel 01886 833290)

PERRY, Dr Nicholas Mark; s of (Sidney) Arthur Perry, of London, and Constance Frances, *née* Sheere; *b* 23 October 1950; *Educ* Westminster, Bart's Med Sch (MB BS); *m* 12 May 1979, Angela Judith, da of Anthony Hillier Poil; 1 s (Alexander William Mark b 10 Oct 1983), 1 da (Francesca Elizabeth Sarah b 21 Feb 1987); *Career* house surgn Bart's 1975, house physician St Leonard's Hosp Hoxton 1976, SHO A/E Bart's 1976–78, SHO Hackney Hosp 1978–79, SHO in urology Bart's 1979–80; registrar in diagnostic radiology: St Thomas' Hosp 1980–82, Bart's 1982–83; sr registrar Bart's, Chase Farm Hosp and N Middx Hosp 1983–85, sr registrar Bart's, Great Ormond Street, Hackney and Homerton Hosps 1985–88; conslt radiologist: Bart's 1988–, King Edward VII Hosp Sister Agnes, 108 Harley St Breast Clinic, Princess Grace Hosp; conslt in breast screening Europe Against Cancer Euro Cmmn 1991–2000; chm: Advsy Ctee Euro Network of Reference Assessment Centres (EUREF) 1996–, Detection and Diagnosis Section Euro Soc of Mastology (EUSOMA); quality assurance dir London Region Breast Screening Prog 1988–2002, clinical dir Central and E London Breast Screening Serv 1990–; Nat Breast Screening Prog: chm Quality Assurance Mangrs Gp 1989–98, chm Equipment Ctee 1989–95; memb: Euro Gp for Breast Cancer Screening, BMA, British Assoc of Surgical Oncology, Euro Soc of Mastology; FRCS 1980, FRCR 1984; *Books* Radiological Casebook (1988), European Guidelines for Quality Assurance in Mammography Screening (2001), European Guidelines for Quality Assurance in Breast Cancer Screening and Diagnosis (2006); *Recreations* antiquarian books, lawn tennis (capt English Public Schs 1967, British Univs' Doubles champion 1974, vice-pres United Hosps Lawn Tennis Club, pres Bart's and Royal London Hosps Lawn Tennis Club 2000–05), lawn tennis memorabilia; *Clubs* Queen's, Hurlingham, All England Lawn Tennis; *Style—* Dr Nicholas Perry; ✉ 10 Cloncurry Street, London SW6 6DS; Breast Assessment Centre, St Bartholomew's Hospital, London EC1A 7BE (tel 020 7601 8841)

PERRY, Nick; *b* 1961; *Educ* Univ of Hull, Nat Film and TV Sch; *Career* playwright; TV dramas and stage plays incl: Arrivederci Millwall (prod 1985, jt winner of Samuel Beckett Award 1986), Smallholdings (performed Kings Head, 1986), Rockliffe's Babies (contrib to BBC series), Tales of Sherwood Forest (for Central TV), Clubland (BBC), The Vinegar Fly (Lyric Theatre Belfast, 1994), Near Cricket St Thomas, 1919 (McCarthy Theatre Scarborough, 1997), Steal Away (Sky films, 1999), The Escapist (Sky films, 2001), Superbomb (BBC, 2006); *Style—* Nick Perry, Esq; ✉ c/o Rochelle Stevens & Co, 2 Terretts Place, Upper Street, London N1 1QZ (tel 020 7359 3900, fax 020 7354 5729)

PERRY, Dr Norman Henry; s of Charles Perry (d 1984), of London, and Josephine, *née* Ehrlich (d 1986); *b* 5 March 1944; *Educ* Quintin Sch London, UCL (BA, PhD); *m* 7 Aug 1970, Barbara Ann, da of James Harold Marsden, and Margaret, *née* Lütkemeyer, of Sheffield; 2 s (Ben b 1974, Tom b 1977); *Career* lectr in geography UCL 1965–69, sr res offr GLC 1969–73, sr res fell Social Sci Res Cncl Survey Unit 1973–75; DOE: princ London & Birmingham 1975–79, princ London 1979–80, asst sec W Midlands 1980–86; Grade 4 head of Inner Cities Unit Dept of Employment and DTI 1986–88, Grade 3 regnl dir DTI W Midlands 1988–90; chief exec: Wolverhampton MBC 1990–96, Solihull MBC 1996–2000, The Housing Corp 2000–04; memb Bd English Partnerships 2002–04, dir The Housing Finance Corp 2003–04; non-exec dir Merlion Gp plc 2004–07, chm Public Servs Gp HBJ Gateley Wareing LLP 2007–; memb Advsy Gp The Almshouse Assoc 2005–; chm Assoc of Local Authy Chief Execs 1995–97, vice-pres Nat Fedn of Enterprise Agencies 1997–2000; dir: Wolverhampton Trg and Enterprise Cncl Ltd 1990–96, co sec Solihull Business Partnership 1996–2000; govr Univ of Wolverhampton 1993–96; hon sec Soc of Metropolitan Chief Executives 1997–2000; *Books* Vols in European Glossary of Legal and Administrative Terminology: German/English, Vol 18 Regional Policy (1974), Demands for Social Knowledge (with Elisabeth Crawford, 1976), Vol 29 Environmental Policy (1979), Public Enterprise (1989); *Recreations* reading history; *Style—* Dr Norman Perry

PERRY, Robert; s of Robert Perry (d 1999), of Glasgow, and Margaret, *née* Wright; *b* 2 June 1964; *Educ* Cranhill Secdy Sch, Glasgow Coll of Bldg and Printing (HND in Photography); *m* 23 Feb 1990, Margaret, da of Joseph Gilligan (d 1977); 3 s (Robert Eugene b 16 Feb 1996, Euan Joseph b 13 Oct 1997, Joseph Vincent b 16 Sept 2004), 1 da (Monica Frances b 11 April 1999); *Career* freelance press photographer (mainly The Independent) 1992, staff photographer Scotland on Sunday 1994–; Nikon Regnl Photographer of the Year 1993, Scottish Press Photographer of the Year 1996, Guinness Picture of the Year (Regnl) 1996, runner up Scottish Sports Photographer of the Year 1998, Royal Photographer of the Year 2001, runner up Nikon Fashion Photographer of the Year 2001; memb NUJ; *Style—* Robert Perry, Esq

PERRY, Dr Robert Henry; s of Frank Perry (d 1992), of Sileby, Loughborough, Leics, and Lois Ellen, *née* Harriman (d 2004); *b* 20 August 1944; *Educ* Loughborough GS, Univ of St Andrews (MB ChB), Univ of Newcastle upon Tyne (DSc); *m* 5 June 1971, Elaine King, da of James Cyril King Miller, WS (d 1979), of Colinton, Edinburgh; 1 s (Jonathan b 1972), 1 da (Nicolette b 1973); *Career* Newcastle Gen Hosp: sr registrar in neuropathology 1975–79, clinical scientist MRC Neuroendocrinology Unit, conslt neuropathologist 1980–; Univ of Newcastle: sr lectr in neuropathology 1986–91, reader in neurochemical pathology 1991–99, prof in neuropathology 1999–; author of res pubns on neuropathological correlations of dementia, dementia with Lewy bodies, Alzheimer's disease, Parkinson's disease and related topics; memb Br Neuropathological Soc; FRCP, FRCPath; *Recreations* sailing, skiing, salads, croquet; *Style—* Dr Robert Perry; ✉ Dilston Mill House, Corbridge, Northumberland NE45 5QZ (tel 01434 632083); Neuropatholgy Department, Newcastle General Hospital, Westgate Road, Newcastle upon Tyne NE4 6BE (tel 0191 256 3688, fax 0191 250 3196, e-mail robert.perry@ncl.ac.uk)

PERRY, Rodney Charles Langman (Rod); s of Thomas Charles Perry, of Felpham, W Sussex, and Kathleen Mary, *née* Moojen; *b* 23 July 1941; *Educ* Peter Symonds Coll Winchester; *m* 5 March 1965, Susan Geraldine, da of John Reginald Quertier, of East Boldre, Hants; 1 da (Sarah De Moulpied b 23 Feb 1967), 1 s (James Quertier b 20 Sept 1968); *Career* CA; articles Charles Comins & Co 1960–65, Coopers & Lybrand Zimbabwe 1965–69, ptnr PricewaterhouseCoopers (formerly Coopers & Lybrand before merger) 1976–99; ICAEW: memb Cncl 1984–86, chm Technology Gp 1984–86; FCA 1975; *Books* An Audit Approach To Computers (1986); *Recreations* tennis, golf, boating, painting; *Clubs* Royal Lymington Yacht, Brokenhurst Manor Golf; *Style—* Rod Perry, Esq; ✉ East Boldre House, East Boldre, Brockenhurst, Hampshire SO42 7WR (tel 01590 612407, fax 01590 612427, e-mail rodperry@dsl.pipex.com)

PERRY, Rupert; CBE (1997); s of Graham Perry (d 1968), and Ms Leece (d 1984); *b* 14 January 1948; *Educ* Gresham's; *Children* 1 da (Perignon b 3 Nov 1974), 1 s (Manhattan Graham b 22 Nov 1979); *Career* Campbell Connelly Music Publishers 1967–69, professional mangr Radio Luxembourg Music Publishers 1969–71, PA to gp dir Records EMI Ltd 1971–72; Capitol Records LA: dir Int Artists' Repertoire 1972–76, vice-pres A&R 1976–82; pres EMI America Records LA 1982–84, exec asst to chm of EMI Music Worldwide LA 1984–85, md EMI Australia 1985–86, pres and ceo Records UK & Eire 1986–95, pres and ceo Europe 1995–99, chm Records Group UK & Eire 1995–99; chm BPI 1993–95 (vice-chm 1990–93); sr vice-pres EMI Recorded Music 1999–2002; Int Fedn of the Phonographic Industry: chm European Regional Bd 1998–2002 (memb 1994–2002), memb Main Bd 1998–2002; memb: Music Sound Fndn, Nat Acad of Recording Arts & Sciences Inc (NARAS), Country Music Assoc (CMA), Bd Music for Youth Fndn Inc N America, Bd Rightsline 2003; *Recreations* the countryside, wine, music, soccer; *Clubs* Reform, Groucho, Bibury Tennis, Home House; *Style—* Rupert Perry, Esq, CBE; ✉ 8 Clifton Villas, London W9 2PH (tel 020 7266 1553, fax 020 7266 2338, mobile 07747 665976, e-mail rupertperry@hotmail.com)

PERRY, Stephen Lawrence Andrew; s of Jack Perry (d 1996), of London, and Doris-Kate Perry (d 1985); *b* 12 September 1948; *Educ* UCL (LLB); *m* 24 Dec 1980 (m dis 1998), Wendy, da of Joseph Bond (d 1957), and Lillian Bond; 1 da (Jodie b 1981), 1 s (Jack b 1984); *Career* md London Export Corporation Ltd; vice-chm China-Br Business Cncl, chm 48 Group Club; dir Somerstown Community Sports Centre; fell UCL; *Recreations* football, tai-chi; *Clubs* RAC, Hendon Golf; *Style—* Stephen Perry, Esq; ✉ London Export Corporation Limited, 3 Cambridge Terrace Mews, London NW1 4JJ (tel 020 7493 4009, fax 020 7491 7420, e-mail stephen@lexcorltd.com)

PERRY, Dr Wayne; s of William Perry (d 1947), of Hayes, Middlesex, and Margery Rideley, *née* Wilson; *b* 30 June 1944; *Educ* Royal Hosp Sch Ipswich, Univ of Birmingham Med Sch (MB ChB, MRCP), Accreditation by Jt Ctee on Higher Med Trg (RCP) in Gen (Internal) Med with a special interest in Metabolic Med; *m* 1980, Siew Mui Lee; *Career* house physician Queen Elizabeth Hosp Birmingham 1968, house surgn Dudley Rd Hosp Birmingham 1969; SHO: Dept of Med Harari Hosp Univ of Salisbury Rhodesia 1969 (Dept of Paediatrics), Chest Diseases King Edward VII Hosp Warwick 1971; registrar in med The Med Professorial Unit KCH London 1972, sr med registrar Dept of Metabolic Med Royal Nat Orthopaedic Hosp Stanmore 1974, asst prof Dept of Internal Faisal Univ Saudi Arabia 1979 (conslt physician and endocrinologist King Fahad Univ Hosp, hon conslt endocrinologist King Fahad Univ Hosp, hon conslt endocrinologist King Abdul Aziz Airbase Hosp); conslt endocrinologist: Harley St 1983, Metabolism and Bone Disease The Endocrine and Dermatology Centre Harley St 1987; author numerous learned articles in med jls; Sir Herbert Seddon Gold Medal and prize for original res (Inst of Orthopaedics Univ of London and Royal Nat Orthopaedic Hosp); medals awarded at VI and VII Saudi Med Confs 1981, 1982, and for the first graduating students from King Faisal Fahad Univ Dammam Saudi Arabia; registered Med Practioner GMC; approved conslt for UK: BUPA, PPP; FRSM; memb: BMA, Med Defence Union; *Recreations* violoncello, poetry, arcadian landscapes, France; *Style—* Dr Wayne Perry; ✉ The Endocrine Centre, 59 Wimpole Street, London W1E 8AF (tel 020 7935 2440)

PERRY OF SOUTHWARK, Baroness (Life Peer UK 1991), of Charlbury in the County of Oxfordshire; Pauline Perry; da of John George Embleton Welch (d 1963), and Elizabeth, *née* Cowan (d 1982); *b* 15 October 1931; *Educ* Wolverhampton Girls' HS, Girton Coll Cambridge (MA); *m* 26 July 1952, George Walter Perry, s of Percy Walter Perry (d 1939); 3 s (Hon Christopher b 1953, Hon Timothy b 1962, Hon Simon b 1966), 1 da (Hon Hilary (Hon Mrs Winstone) b 1955); *Career* teacher various secdy schs UK, USA and Canada 1953–56 and 1959–61; lectr in philosophy: Univ of Manitoba 1956–59, Univ of Massachusetts 1961–62; pt/t lectr in educn: Univ of Exeter 1963–66, Univ of Oxford 1966–70; access course tutor 1966–70, HM Chief Inspr of Schs 1981–86 (inspr 1970–74, staff inspr 1975–81), vice-chllr South Bank Univ (formerly South Bank Poly) 1987–93, pres Lucy Cavendish Coll Cambridge 1994–2001, pro-chllr Univ of Surrey 2001–06; chair Cncl Roehampton Univ 2001–05; freelance journalist and broadcaster; author of various books, chapters in books and numerous published articles, various radio and TV appearances; memb Prime Minister's Advsy Panel for the Citizen's Charter 1993–97; memb: House of Lords Select Ctee on the Scrutiny of Delegated Powers 1994–98, House of Lords Select Ctee on Stem-Cell Research, House of Lords Select Ctee on Science and Technol, Jt Select Ctee on Human Rights; jt chm All-Pty Assoc Parly Univs Gp 1993–; chm: South Bank Univ Enterprise Ltd 1988–93, DTI Export Gp for Educn and Training Sector 1993–98, Friends of Southwark Cathedral 1996–2002, Judges Panel for Chartermark Award 1997–2002, Archbishop's Review of the Crown Appointments Cmmn 1999–2001, Nuffield Cncl on Bio-Ethics Inquiry into the Use of Animals in Sci Research 2003–, CGLI Ctee on Quality and Standards 2005–; non-exec dir Addenbrooke's NHS Tst 1998–2001; memb: Governing Body Inst of Devpt Studies 1987–95, British Cncl's Ctee on Int Co-operation in HE 1987–96, ESRC 1988–91, Cncl Fndn for Educn Business Partnerships 1990–91, Bd South Bank Centre 1992–95, Ct Univ of Bath 1992–98, Bd of Patrons of the Royal Soc 1996–2001, Bd ESU 1998–2003, QCA Advsy Ctee on Standards 2004–; rector's warden Southwark Cathedral 1990–94; patron: British Youth Opera 1993–, Alzheimer's Research Tst 1993–, British Friends of Neve-Shalom Wahat-al-Salaam 2003–; pres: Ctee for Independent Further Education (CIFE) 2001–, Fndn for HE 2002–06, City & Westminster Branch CMI; vice-pres: Soc for Res in HE 1993–99, CGLI 1994–99; govr Greshams Sch 2000–06; Freeman City of London 1992, Liveryman Worshipful Co of Bakers 1992, Hon Freeman Fishmongers Co 2006; hon fell Sunderland Poly 1990, hon fell Girton Coll Cambridge 1995, hon fell Lucy Cavendish Coll Cambridge 2001, hon fell Roehampton Univ; Hon LLD: Univ of Bath 1991, Univ of Aberdeen 1994, South Bank Univ 1994; Hon DLitt Univ of Sussex 1992, Hon DEd Univ of Wolverhampton 1994, Hon DUniv Surrey 1995, Hon DLitt City Univ 2000; Hon FCP 1987, Hon FRSA 1988, CCMI (CIMgt) 1993, hon fell C&G 2000; *Recreations* music, walking; *Clubs* IOD; *Style—* The Rt Hon Baroness Perry of Southwark; ✉ House of Lords, London SW1A 0PW (e-mail pp204@supanet.com)

PERSAUD, Prof Bishnodat; s of Dhwarka Persaud, and Dukhni, *née* Surujbali; *b* 22 September 1933, Guyana; *Educ* Univ of Reading (Postgrad Dip Agric Econs, PhD), Queen's Univ Belfast (BScEcon); *m* Aug 1962, Lakshmi; 3 c (Rajendra, *qv*, Avinash, Sharda); *Career* res fell Inst of Social and Econ Res Univ of the WI 1965–74; Cwlth Secretariat: chief econs offr Commodities Div 1974–76, asst dir Econ Affrs Div 1976–81, dir and head Economic Affrs Div 1981–92; Univ of the WI Jamaica: prof of sustainable devpt 1992–96, hon prof 1996–; co-leader IDB Team on Socio-Economic Reform in Guyana 1994, chief tech co-ordinator Int Negotiations Caribbean Community 1996, sr assoc Caribbean Regnl Negotiating Machinery 2002–, advsr to Cwlth Secretariat and World Bank on small states 2005–06; memb: Bd of Dirs Central Bank Barbados 1973–74, Bd Cwlth Equity Fund 1989–93, Univ of Guyana Review Cmmn 1991 and 1996, Bd of Tstees Guyana Rainforest Programme 1992–2002, UN Ctee for Devpt Policy 1995–2000, Cmmn on Cwlth Studies 1995–96, Jamaica Conservation Tst 1995–99, Worldaware (UK) 1996–2006, Cwlth Partnership for Technol Mgmnt (UK) 1997–2001; served on many cmmns of enquiry and on int expert gps; numerous speeches and lectures incl address to Euro Foreign and Security Policies Conf of the Euro Movement 1991, numerous radio broadcasts and TV appearances in Cwlth countries, author of two books on econ devpt and contrib articles to professional and learned jls; memb Chatham House; FRSA; *Books* Developing with Foreign Investment (jtly, 1987), Economic Policy and the Environment (jtly, 1995); *Clubs* RAC; *Style—* Prof Bishnodat Persaud

PERSAUD, Dr Rajendra Dhwarka; s of Prof Bishnodat Persaud, *qv*, and Lakshmi, *née* Seeteram; *Educ* Haberdashers' Aske's, UCL (BSc, MB BS), Inst of Psychiatry London (MPhil, MSc), DHMSA, Dip Phil, Dip Health Econ; *Career* SHO and registrar Maudsley Hosp London 1987–92, clinical lectr Inst of Psychiatry London 1992–94 (hon sr lectr 1999–), conslt psychiatrist Maudsley Hosp London 1994–, Gresham prof for public understanding of psychiatry; research fell Johns Hopkins Univ USA 1990; Denis Hill Prize Maudsley Hosp 1992, Osler Medal Soc of Apothecaries 1992, RCPsych research prize and medal 1993; Florence Nightingale Annual Lecture 2002; in top ten list of Br psychiatrists nominated by RCPsych Independent on Sunday 2002; broadcaster on radio and TV, presenter All in the Mind (BBC Radio 4), regular contrib to progs incl Newsnight, Question Time, Tomorrow's World, Horizon and This Morning; patron of various charities incl: Psychiatry Research Tst, Nat Phobic Soc, Depression Alliance; memb Assoc of Br Sci Writers 2000; memb Inst of Journalists 1995; memb BMA 1994–; pres Alumni Soc UCL, fell UCL; FRCPsych 2005 (MFRCPsych 1992, Morris Marlowe Prize 2005), FRSA, FRSM; *Publications* Staying Sane (1999), The Grandeur of Delusion (2002); numerous articles in academic jls incl: British Jl of Psychiatry, BMJ, The Lancet, Psychological Medicine; *Recreations* tennis, theatre, poker; *Clubs* Reform, RAC, Queen's, IOD, Embassy, Wellington; *Style—* Dr Rajendra Persaud

PERSEY, Lionel Edward; QC (1997); s of Dr Paul Ronald Persey (d 1996), of London, and Irene, *née* Levinson; *b* 19 January 1958; *Educ* Haberdashers' Aske's, Univ of Birmingham (Holdsworth Prize, LLB), Université de Limoges, Inns of Court Sch of Law; *m* 1984, Lynn, da of Gordon Mear; 1 s (b 1999); *Career* called to the Bar Gray's Inn 1981 (Lord Justice Holker sr Award, Band Commercial Prize); in commercial and maritime practice 1982–, recorder 2002–; memb: Supplementary Panel of Treasury Counsel 1992–97, Commercial Bar Assoc, London Common Law and Commercial Bar Assoc; *Recreations* classical music, opera, reading, gardening; *Clubs* Reform; *Style—* Lionel Persey, QC; ✉ Quadrant Chambers, Quadrant House, 10 Fleet Street, London EC4Y 1AU (tel 020 7583 4444, fax 020 7583 4455, e-mail lionel.persey@quadrantchambers.com)

PERT, Prof Geoffrey James (Geoff); s of Norman James Pert (d 1984), of Norwich, Norfolk, and Grace Winifred, *née* Barnes; *b* 15 August 1941; *Educ* Norwich Sch, Imperial Coll London (BSc, PhD, Rowing purple); *m* 16 Sept 1967, Janice Ann, *née* Alexander; 1 da (Erin Mary b 3 Dec 1968); *Career* asst prof Univ of Alberta 1967–70, successively lectr, sr lectr, reader and prof Univ of Hull 1970–87, prof of physics Univ of York 1987–; author of numerous scientific pubns; FInstP 1978, FRS 1995; *Recreations* hill walking, gardening; *Clubs* Arctic; *Style—* Prof Geoff Pert; ✉ Department of Physics, University of York, Heslington, York YO10 5DD (tel 01904 432250, fax 01904 432214, e-mail gjp1@york.ac.uk)

PERT, His Hon Judge Michael; QC (1992); s of Lt Henry McKay Pert, RN (ret), and Noreen Margaret Mary, *née* Murphy; *b* 17 May 1947; *Educ* St Boniface's Coll Plymouth, Univ of Manchester (LLB); *m* 29 July 1971, Vivienne Victoria, da of Ernest George Braithwaite; 2 da (Lucy Claire b 27 Aug 1975, Katherine Olivia b 10 Feb 1979), 1 s (Benjamin McKay b 4 March 1977); *Career* called to the Bar Gray's Inn 1970; recorder 1988–2004 (asst recorder 1984–88), circuit judge (Midland Circuit) 2004–; *Recreations* bee keeping, sailing; *Style—* His Hon Judge Pert, QC

PERTH, 18 Earl of (S 1605); John Eric Drummond; s of 17 Earl (d 2002); *b* 7 July 1935; *Educ* Trinity Coll Cambridge (BA), Harvard Univ (MBA); *m* 1, 1963 (m dis 1972), Margaret Ann, da of Robert Gordon; 2 s (James, Viscount Strathallan b 24 Oct 1965, Hon Robert b 7 May 1967); m 2, 1988, Mrs Marion Elliot; *Heir* s, Viscount Strathallan; *Clubs* Boodle's; *Style—* The Rt Hon the Earl of Perth

PERTWEE, Christopher Ferens; DL (Essex 1996); s of Norman Pertwee, and Eileen Pertwee; *b* 25 November 1936; *Educ* Tonbridge; *m* 1960, Carole, da of A G Drayson, of Sutton Valence, Kent; 3 s (Mark, Julian, Nicholas); *Career* chm Pertwee Holdings Ltd 1970–; pres UK Agric Supply Trade Assoc 1982–83; pro-chllr Univ of Essex 1998–2006 (memb Cncl 1990–96); pres: Essex Agric Soc 2003–04, Colchester Catalyst Charity 2004– (chm 1993–2004); dir Essex Community Fndn 1996–2000; tstee St Helena Hospice 2007–; hon fell Univ of Essex 1996; High Sheriff Essex 1995–96; Master Worshipful Co of Farmers 1998–99; *Recreations* sport, gardening, antiques; *Clubs* Farmers'; *Style—* Christopher Pertwee, Esq, DL; ✉ The Bishops House, Frating, Colchester, Essex CO7 7HQ

PERTWEE, Richard James Charles Drury; s of Capt James Waddon Martyn Pertwee, CBE (d 2000), of Winchester, Hants, and Margaret Alison, *née* Elliott; *b* 2 May 1955; *Educ* Sherborne, Worcester Coll Oxford (BA); *m* 15 Aug 1981, Gail, da of Wilfred McBrien Swain, OBE (d 1983); 2 da (Laetitia b 1984, Sophie b 1987); *Career* joined RNR 1978, Sub Lt 1980, res 1982; Richards Butler & Co: articled clerk 1978–80, slr 1980–82; asst then ptnr: Trevor Robinson & Co 1982–85, Joynson-Hicks 1985–89; ptnr Taylor Wessing (formerly Taylor Joynson Garrett) 1989–2006 (managing ptnr 1993–95, conslt 2006–); magistrate SE Hants 2006–; *Recreations* tennis, cricket; *Clubs* Sherborne Pilgrims, Vincent's (Oxford), MCC, Sloane; *Style—* Richard Pertwee, Esq; ✉ Taylor Wessing, Carmelite, 50 Victoria Embankment, Blackfriars, London EC4Y 0DX (tel 020 7300 7000, fax 020 7300 7100)

PESARAN, Prof (Mohammad) Hashem; s of Jamal Pesaran (d 1973), and Effat Pesaran; *b* 30 March 1946; *Educ* Univ of Salford (BSc, Athletics colours), Harvard Univ, Univ of Cambridge (PhD, Basketball half-blue); *m* 1969, Marian Fay, *née* Swainston; 3 s (Bijan b 12 Oct 1973, Jamal b 5 Jan 1975, Hassan Ali b 30 Dec 1992), 2 da (Eva-Leila b 24 Sept 1978, Natasha-Guiti b 19 March 1990); *Career* 1 Lt Farahabad Barracks Tehran 1976; jr res offr Dept of Applied Economics Univ of Cambridge and lektor Trinity Coll Cambridge 1971–73, head Econ Res Dept Central Bank of Iran 1974–76 (asst to Vice-Govr 1973–74), under sec Miny of Educn Iran 1977–78; Univ of Cambridge: teaching fell and dir of studies in economics Trinity Coll 1979–88, lectr in economics 1979–85, reader in economics 1985–88, prof of economics and professorial fell Trinity Coll 1988–; prof of economics and dir Prog in Applied Econometrics UCLA 1989–93, res fell Inst for Study of Labor (IZA) Bonn 1999–, res fell CESifo Research Network Munich 2000–; visiting lectr Harvard 1982, visiting fell ANU 1984 and 1988; visiting prof: Univ of Rome 1986, UCLA 1987–88, Inst of Advanced Studies Vienna 1991, Univ of Pennsylvania 1993, Univ of Southern Calif 1995, 1997 and 1999; dir: Camfit Data Ltd 1986–, Acorn Investment Trust 1987–89 and 1991–93, Cambridge Econometrics 1985, 1988–89 and 1992–96 (hon pres 1996–); non-exec dir Chiltern Gp 1999–; memb: HM Treasy Academic Panel 1993–, Advsy Ctee UK Meteorological Office 1994–97, Bd of Tstees Economic Research Forum of Arab Countries, Iran and Turkey 1996–, Cncl of Advsrs for the MENA region World Bank 1996–2000, Bd of Tstees Br Iranian Tst 1997–, Academic Econometric Panel Office for Nat Statistics 1997–, Cncl Royal Economic Soc 2007–; charter memb Oliver Wyman Inst 1997–2000; memb Editorial Bd: Cambridge Jl of Economics 1981–89, Econometric Theory 1984–87, Cyprus Jl of Economics 1990–, Hellenic Review 1993–, Net Exposure: The Electronic Jl of Fin Risk 1996–2001; assoc ed: Econometrica 1984–85, Jl of Economic Dynamics and Control 1995–; fndr ed Jl of Applied Econometrics 1986–; memb Advsy Bd Jl of Economic Surveys 1995–, George Sell Prize Inst of Petroleum 1990, Royal Econ Soc Prize for 1990–91 1992, Best Paper Award Econometric Reviews 2002–04; Hon DLitt Salford 1993; fell: Econometric Soc 1989, Jl of Econometrics 1990; FBA 1998; *Books* World Economic Prospects and the Iranian Economy - a Short Term View (1974), Dynamic Regression - Theory and Algorithms (jtly, 1980), Keynes' Economics - Methodological Issues (jt ed, 1985), The Limits to Rational Expectations (1987), Data-FIT - an Interactive Software Econometric Package (jtly, 1987), Disaggregation in Economic Modelling (jt ed, 1990), Microfit 3.0 - an Interactive Software Econometric Package (jtly, 1991), Non-Linear Dynamics, Chaos and Econometrics (jt ed, 1993), Handbook of Applied Econometrics Vol 1 (jt ed, 1995), Working with Microfit 4.0 - Interactive Econometric Analysis (jtly, 1997), Handbook of Applied Econometrics Vol II (jt ed, 1997), Energy Demand in Asian Developing Economies (jtly, 1998), Analysis of Panels and Limited Dependent Variables (jt ed, 1999), Global and National Macroeconometric Modelling: A Long-Run Structural Approach (jtly, 2006), Explaining Growth in the Middle East (jt ed, 2007); *Recreations* basketball, swimming, squash, jogging; *Style—* Prof Hashem Pesaran, FBA; ✉ Trinity College, Cambridge CB2 1TQ (tel 01223 338403, fax 01223 335471, e-mail hashem.pesaran@econ.cam.ac.uk, website www.econ.cam.ac.uk/faculty/pesaran)

PESCHARDT, Michael Mogens; s of Mogens Jan Hagbarth Peschardt, and Betty Joyce, *née* Foster; *b* 17 November 1957; *Educ* Merchant Taylors', Univ of Sussex; *m* 9 July 1977, Sarah Louise, da of Tom James Vaughan; 3 s (Joseph Mogens b 1980, Jack Oliver b 1982, Samuel Thaddeus b 1984), 1 da (Lily Mae b 1993); *Career* news prodr BBC Radio Manchester 1980–82, chief parly journalist BBC Regnl Broadcasting until 1986, sports reporter BBC TV News, currently Australia corr BBC TV; *Recreations* surfing, football; *Style—* Michael Peschardt, Esq

PESCOD, District Judge Peter Richard; s of Philip Pescod (d 1965), of Darlington, Co Durham, and Elsie, *née* Parnaby; *b* 29 June 1951; *Educ* Queen Elizabeth GS Darlington, Univ of Newcastle upon Tyne (LLB); *m* 15 April 1978, Barbara Jane, da of John Magoveny King, of Morpeth, Northumberland; 1 da (Jennifer b 21 May 1981), 1 s (Henry b 12 April 1983); *Career* admitted slr 1975; ptnr Hay and Kilner 1976–2002; dist judge (NE Circuit) 2002–; memb Northumberland CC 1989–93; Parly candidate (Cons) Blaydon 1987 and 1992; vice-pres Forum of Insurance Lawyers 1993–95; memb: Northumberland FPC 1985–90 (chm Med Serv Ctee 1988–96), Family Health Services Appeal Authy 1996–2002, Nat Tst, Eng Heritage, Law Soc; chm of govrs Ovingham Middle Sch 1993–96, chm Ovington Parish Cncl 2007–; *Recreations* drama, auction sales, building, landscape gardening, architecture; *Clubs* Anglo Belgian, Newcastle upon Tyne Lit and Phil; *Style—* District Judge Pescod; ✉ The Law Courts, Quayside, Newcastle upon Tyne NE13 1LA (tel 0191 201 2000, fax 0191 201 2001)

PESCOD, Prof (Mainwaring Bainbridge) Warren; OBE (1977); s of Bainbridge Pescod (d 1979), and Elizabeth, *née* Brown (d 1973); *b* 6 January 1933; *Educ* Stanley GS Co Durham, King's Coll Durham (BSc), MIT (SM); *m* 16 Nov 1957, (Mary) Lorenza, da of John Francis Coyle (d 1970); 2 s (Duncan Warren b 1959, Douglas James b 1961); *Career* teaching and res assoc MIT 1954–56, res assoc Dept of Civil Engrg King's Coll Durham 1956–57, lectr and actg head Dept of Engrg Fourah Bay Coll, UC of Sierra Leone 1957–61, asst engr Babtie Shaw and Morton Glasgow 1961–64, prof and chm Environmental Engrg Div Asian Inst of Technol Bangkok 1964–76; Univ of Newcastle upon Tyne: Tyne & Wear prof of environmental control engrg 1976–98 (prof emeritus 1998–), head Dept of Civil Engrg 1983–98; memb Northumbrian Water Authy 1986–89, dir Northumbrian Water Group plc 1989–97; chm and md Environmental Technology Consultants Ltd 1988–99, chm and md Environmental Technology Consultants, Motherwell Bridge Group 1999–2003, chm MB Technology (Malaysia) Sdn Bhd 1996–2001, corp fell Safety and Ecology Corporation Ltd; CEng, FICE 1973, FCIWEM (formerly FIPHE) 1962, FCIWM 1985, MRSH 1964–98; *Books* Water Supply and Wastewater Disposal in Developing Countries (ed, 1971), Treatment and Use of Sewage Effluent for Irrigation (ed with A Arar, 1988); *Recreations* golf, reading; *Clubs* British and Royal Bangkok Sports (Bangkok); *Style—* Professor Warren Pescod, OBE; ✉ Tall Trees, High Horse Close Wood, Rowlands Gill, Tyne & Wear NE39 1AN (tel 01207 542104, fax 01207 545906, e-mail m.b.pescod@ncl.ac.uk); Safety and Ecology Corporation Ltd, Nautilus House, Redburn Court, Earl Grey Way, Royal Keys, North Shields, Newcastle upon Tyne NE29 6AR (tel 0191 296 2000, fax 0191 296 2029, e-mail wpescod@sec-uk.com)

PESEK, Libor; Hon KBE (1996); *b* 22 June 1933; *Career* fndr Prague Chamber Harmony 1958, chief conductor Slovak Philharmonic 1980–81, conductor-in-residence Czech Philharmonic Orch 1982–, music dir Royal Liverpool Philharmonic Orch 1987–97 (conductor laureate 1997–); hon fell Univ of Central Lancashire 1997; worked as guest conductor with orchs incl: London Symphony, The Philharmonia, Los Angeles Philharmonic and St Louis Symphony Orchs, Moscow and Japan Philharmonic Orchs, La Scala Milan, Oslo Philharmonic, Orchestre National de France, Orchestre de Paris, Berlin Symphony, Dresden Staatskapelle, Pittsburgh, Montreal, Indianapolis and Philadelphia Orchs; *Recordings* incl: Dvorák's Symphony Cycle, Britten's Sinfonia da Requiem, Peter Grimes and the Young Person's Guide to the Orchestra, Strauss' Ein Heldenleben, Berg's Chamber Concerto, Stravinsky's symphonies for wind instruments, Ravel's Daphnis and Chloë, Suk's Asrael Symphony, Suk's Summer's Tale, Suk's Ripening, Mahler's Symphonies 9 and 10, various works by Haydn, Mozart, Janácek and Martinu; *Recreations* physics, Eastern philosophy, literature (especially Kafka, Tolstoy and Dostoyevsky); *Style—* Libor Pesek, Esq, KBE; ✉ IMG Artists, Lovell House, 616 Chiswick High Road, London W4 5RX (tel 020 8233 5800, fax 020 8233 5801, e-mail artistseurope@imgworld.com)

PESKIN, Richard Martin; s of Leslie Peskin (d 1980), and Hazel Pauline Peskin (d 1980); *b* 21 May 1944; *Educ* Charterhouse, Queens' Coll Cambridge (MA, LLM); *m* 6 Feb 1979, Penelope Ann Elizabeth Howard, *née* Triebner; 1 s (Michael b 1966), 2 da (Elizabeth b 1969, Virginia b 1979); *Career* Great Portland Estates plc: dir 1968–, dep md 1972–85, md 1985–2000, chm 1986–; FRSA 1989, CIMgt 1989; *Recreations* crosswords, composing limericks, fine wine, golf; *Clubs* MCC, RAC, Mark's, Annabel's; *Style—* Richard Peskin, Esq; ✉ 41 Circus Road, London NW8 9JH (tel 020 7289 0492); Great Portland Estates plc, 33 Cavendish Square, London W1G 0PW (tel 020 7647 3000, fax 020 7016 5500)

PESTON, (Hon) Juliet Clare Elaine; da of Baron Peston (Life Peer), *qv*, and Helen, *née* Conen; *b* 5 August 1961; *Educ* Highgate Wood Comp, Creighton Comp, Trinity Coll Cambridge; *Career* chef: Alastair Little 1985–96, Lola's 1996–99; exec chef: The Cow 1999–2000, Alastair Little Restaurants 2002–, Coach & Horses London EC1 2003–04, Lola's 2004–05; Chef of the Year The Independent 1995, Best New Restaurant Time Out 1997, Best Brunch Time Out 1998, Best Gastropub Time Out 2004, Remy Martin Award 2004; *Clubs* Groucho, Colony, Jerry's; *Style—* Miss Juliet Peston; ✉ 24 Westminster Gardens, Marsham Street, London SW1P 4JD (tel 020 7828 3141, e-mail julietpeston@btopenworld.com)

PESTON, Baron (Life Peer UK 1987), of Mile End in Greater London; Maurice Harry Peston; s of Abraham Peston; *b* 19 March 1931; *Educ* Bellevue Bradford, Hackney Downs London, LSE (BScEcon), Princeton Univ USA; *m* 17 Nov 1958, Helen, da of Joseph Conroy; 2 s (Hon Robert James Kenneth b 1960, Hon Edmund Charles Richard b 1964), 1 da (Hon Juliet Claire Elaine, *qv* b 1961); *Career* prof of economics Queen Mary Univ of London; chm Econ Affairs Ctee House of Lords 2001; *Style—* The Rt Hon Lord Peston; ✉ House of Lords, London SW1A 0PW (e-mail pestonmh@parliament.uk)

PETCH, David; CBE (2000); s of Tom Petch (d 1978), of Halifax, W Yorks, and Mary, *née* Clarke (d 2002); *b* 9 January 1946, Halifax, W Yorks; *Educ* St Bedes GS Bradford, Univ of Keele (BA); *m* 3 Sept 1988, Jill Knight (d 2005); *Career* govt serv MOD, NI Office and Cabinet Office 1971–2001, memb Police Complaints Authy 2001–04, cmmr Ind Police Complaints Cmmn 2004–; patron Wigmore Hall, memb Royal Instn; *Recreations* swimming, walking, watching cricket and rugby league, reading history; *Clubs* Scarborough CC; *Style—* David Petch, Esq, CBE; ✉ The Independent Police Complaints Authority, 90 High Holborn, London WC1V 6BH (tel 020 7166 3092, fax 020 7166 3392, e-mail david.petch@ipcc.gsi.gov.uk)

PETCH, Howard Wesley; CBE (2003, OBE 1997), JP; s of Herbert Petch (d 1966), and Annie, *née* Hall (d 1972); *b* 14 December 1943, Guisborough, N Yorks; *Educ* Guisborough GS, Askham Bryan Coll, Lancs Coll of Agric (NDA); *m* 16 Aug 1973, Shirley Joyce, *née* Riding; 2 s (Craig Stuart b 1976, Gavin Roy b 1980), 1 da (Tracey Dawn b 1977); *Career* farming in family business 1960–65, VSO Zambia 1966–67, sr lectr/sr warden Myerscough Coll 1969–79, vice-princ Warwickshire Coll of Agric 1979–85, princ Bishop Burton Coll 1985–97, exec dir Napaeo (Assoc of Land Based Colleges) 1997–2006, chief exec Landex 2006–; memb: LSC, Bd Countryside Agency 2005–, Bd Cmmn for Rural

Communities 2006–; FRASE 2001; *Recreations* sport, gardening, walking; *Style*— Howard Petch, Esq, CBE, JP; ✉ Commission for Rural Communities, John Dower House, Crescent Place, Cheltenham, Gloucestershire GL50 3RA

PETCH, Dr Michael Charles; OBE (2001); s of Dr Charles Plowright Petch (d 1987), of Wolferton, Norfolk, and Edna Margaret, *née* Stirling; *b* 15 July 1941; *Educ* Gresham's, St John's Coll Cambridge, St Thomas' Hosp (MA, MD, MB BChir); *m* 19 April 1965, Fiona Jean Shepheard, da of Cdr David George Fraser Bird, of Nyewood, W Sussex; 2 s (Tom b 1966, Simon b 1968), 1 da (Amanda b 1971); *Career* sr registrar Nat Heart Hosp 1971–77, conslt cardiologist Papworth and Addenbrooke's Hosps 1977–, assoc lectr Univ of Cambridge; memb Cncl Br Cardiac Soc 1985–89; contrib: British Med Jl, Lancet, Heart; MRCP 1967, FRCP 1980, fell American Coll of Cardiology 1980, fell Euro Soc of Cardiology 1995; *Books* Heart Disease (1989); *Recreations* natural history, sailing, opera; *Style*— Dr Michael Petch, OBE; ✉ 20 Brookside, Cambridge CB2 1JQ (tel 01223 365226, fax 01223 302858); Papworth Hospital, Cambridge CB3 8RE (tel 01480 830541, fax 01480 831083)

PETER, John Anthony; s of Dr András Péter (d 1944), and Veronika, *née* Nagy (d 1977); *b* 24 August 1938; *Educ* various state schs in Hungary, Campion Hall Oxford (MA), Lincoln Coll Oxford (BLitt); *m* 1978, Linette Katharine, da of Rai Bahadur Amar Nath Purbi and Lilian Roberts; *Career* reporter and editorial asst Times Educational Supplement 1964–67; The Sunday Times: editorial staff 1967–79, dep arts ed 1979–84, chief drama critic 1984–2003, contributing drama critic 2003–; *Books* Vladimir's Carrot: Modern Drama and the Modern Imagination (1987); *Style*— John Peter, Esq; ✉ The Sunday Times, 1 Pennington Street, London E1 9XW (tel 020 7782 5000)

PETERBOROUGH, Bishop of 1996–; Rt Rev Ian Patrick Martyn Cundy; s of late Dr Henry Martyn Cundy, and Kathleen Ethel, *née* Hemmings; *b* 23 April 1945; *Educ* Monkton Combe Sch, Trinity Coll Cambridge (MA), Tyndale Hall Bristol; *m* 1969, Josephine Katherine, *née* Boyd; 2 s, 1 da; *Career* ordained: deacon 1969, priest 1970; curate Christ Church New Malden 1969–73, lectr in church history and Christian doctrine Oak Hill Coll 1973–77, team rector of Mortlake with East Sheen 1978–83, examining chaplain to Bishop of Southwark 1978–83, warden Cranmer Hall St John's Coll Durham 1983–92, bishop of Lewes 1992–96; church cmmr 2004–; chm Cncl of Christian Unity 1998–; memb: Anglican Old Catholic Int Theol Conf 1980–90, Faith and Order Advsy Gp 1981–96, Advsy Bd of Miny 1991–92, Ct Univ of Sussex 1992–96; memb House of Lords 2001–; pres St John's Coll Durham 1999–; govr: Monkton Combe Sch 1986–98, Eastbourne Coll 1993–96, Lancing Coll 1994–98, UC Northampton 1997–; tstee: Oakham Sch 1996–, Uppingham Sch 1996–; *Recreations* music, walking, photography; *Style*— The Rt Rev the Lord Bishop of Peterborough; ✉ Bishop's Lodging, The Palace, Peterborough PE1 1YA (tel 01733 562492, fax 01733 890077, e-mail bishop@peterborough-diocese.org.uk)

PETERKEN, Dr George Frederick; OBE (1994); s of Stanley Peterken (d 1982), and Norah, *née* Broomfield (d 1989); *b* 21 October 1940; *Educ* Haberdashers' Aske's Hampstead, KCL (BSc, AKC), UCL (PhD), Univ of London (DSc); *m* 1964, Susan, da of Alec Walker; 2 s (Andrew b 1967, Michael b 1969); *Career* res demonstrator Botany Dept UCW Aberystwyth 1964–65, scientific co-ordinator Nature Conservancy 1965–67; woodland ecologist 1969–92 with: Nature Conservancy, Nature Conservancy Cncl, Jt Nature Conservation Ctee; Bullard fell in forest res Harvard Univ 1989–90, Leverhulme res fell 1990; ind ecology conslt 1993–; pres Gwent Wildlife Tst, advsr Woodland Tst, memb Ctee Lower Wye Valley Soc, memb Jt Advsy Ctee Lower Wye Valley AONB, memb Br Ecological Soc 1962–, memb Inst of Chartered Foresters 1970–; *Publications* Guide to the Check Sheet for IBP Areas (1967), Woodland Conservation and Management (1981), Natural Woodland: Ecology and Conservation in Northern Temperate Regions (1996); also author of numerous book chapters, articles in specialist jls, book reviews, popular articles, and conference proceedings; *Recreations* bowling, golf, estate mgmnt, hill walking; *Style*— Dr George Peterken, OBE; ✉ Beechwood House, St Briavels Common, Lydney, Gloucestershire GL15 6SL (tel 01594 530452)

PETERS, Andi; *b* 29 July 1970; *Educ* Emanuel Sch; *Career* television presenter, prodr and dir, first LWT music exec prodr, commissioning ed for children and young people Channel Four Television Corp 1998–2002, exec ed of popular music BBC 2003–; *Television* presented for BBC: But First This (BFT) 1989, CBBC 2 1989, The Broom Cupboard 1990–92, Smash Hits Awards 1993, 1994 and 1995, Children In Need 1993 and 1994, The Ozone (also prodr/dir) 1993–96, Live and Kicking 1993–96, The Travel Quiz 1994, Take Two 1995, EEK 1995, Good Fortune 1995, Short Change 1996, City Hospital 2006; for ITV as presenter: Free Time 1988, The Noise 1996–97, The Weekend Show 1997, Celebrity 2000, Dancing on Ice Extra 2006, Sunday Feast 2006; regular presenter Andi Meets (Channel Four) 1999–; as prodr: Train 2 Win, The Ozone 1993–96, An Audience with The Spice Girls 1997; presenter for Channel Four: Miami Spice 1998; *Radio* Hit Music Sunday (Capital FM) 2002–03; *Awards* twice winner Top Personality on TV (voted by Newsround), three times winner Smash Hits Poll for Best TV Presenter; *Style*— Andi Peters, Esq; ✉ c/o James Grant Management, 94 Strand on the Green, London W4 3NN (tel 020 8742 1950, fax 020 8742 4951)

PETERS, Prof Andrew Raymond (Andy); s of Raymond Barlow Peters, of Shepshed, Leics, and Dorothy Ellen, *née* Sparrow; *b* 10 December 1949; *Educ* Ashby de la Zouch Boys' GS, RVC (BVetMed, MRCVS), Open Univ (BA), Univ of Nottingham (PhD), Univ of London (DVetMed, DSc); *m* Jean Elizabeth, *née* Pallett; 3 s (Daniel Joseph b 13 July 1980, Thomas Michael b 13 June 1982, Robert James b 1 Jan 1987); *Career* practising vet surgn 1972–74, demonstrator in animal physiology Univ of Nottingham 1974–79, sr vet offr Meat and Livestock Cmmn 1979–87, sr exec (pharmaceuticals) British Technology Group 1987–88, regulatory mangr Hoechst Animal Health 1989–93, prof of animal health and prodn RVC Univ of London 1993–98, sr dir (vaccine devpt) VMRD Pfizer Ltd 1998–2006; fndr Arpexas Ltd 2006–; conslt Genecom 2006–; memb RZS: Animal Welfare Ctee, UK Vet Products Ctee, UK Advsy Gp on Vet Residues; UK rep Standing Ctee Int Congress on Animal Reproduction; memb: Assoc of Vet Teachers and Research Workers, Br Soc of Animal Science, BVA, Br Cattle Vet Assoc, Pig Vet Soc; FRCVS 1982, FIBiol 1983; *Books* Reproduction in Cattle (1986), Vaccines for Veterinary Applications (1993); also author of approx 140 published papers in animal/vet science journals, reg contrib to scientific and industry confs; *Recreations* hill walking, running, swimming, DIY building; *Style*— Prof Andy Peters

PETERS, Frank David; s of Alfred George Charles Peters (d 1985), and Georgina, *née* Robins; *b* 7 January 1952; *Educ* Kings Heath Boys' Tech Sch, Birmingham Coll of Art & Design, Lanchester Poly (Cert in Design Visual Communication (3 Dimensions)); *Partner* Carmen Martinez-Lopez; 1 da (Christina Onesiresoan-Martinez b 15 Aug 1976); *Career* exhbn designer 1975–77, proprietor own co 1977–80 (sold to Badger Graphics), freelance designer 1980–84; fndr: Creative Facility Associates (gp mktg, PR & translation servs) 1984–, Sherborne Group (interior design & build contractors and exhbn contractors) 1994–, Mera Properties (residential and commercial property developers); currently involved in design mgmnt and mktg in leisure, entertainment and educn sectors (work incl Euro motor show stands for Land Rover/Rover motor show stand Geneva, etc); memb Policy Ctee Birmingham Design Initiative; co-creator Birmingham Contemporary Music Gp (under artistic direction of Sir Simon Rattle); exec dir CSD; memb Steering Ctee: West Midlands Creative Industries Forum, Centre Product Design Information; FRSA, MCSD; *Recreations* cooking, film, classical music; *Clubs* Edgbaston Priory; *Style*— Frank Peters, Esq; ✉ 29 Blenheim Road, Moseley, Birmingham B13 9TY; Creative Facility Associates Ltd, Number One, of Sherborne Gate, Sherborne Street Wharf, Birmingham B16 8DE (tel 0121 608 6000, fax 0121 608 2223)

PETERS, James; s of Joseph Peters (d 1997), and Mary, *née* Hunt; *b* 30 March 1958, Farnham, Surrey; *m* 29 July 1993, Penny, *née* Lennard; 1 s (Christopher b 3 Feb 1986), 1 da (Sarah b 13 July 1989); *Career* dir Powerline Electronics Ltd 1980–88, dep chm XP Power plc 1988–; *Style*— James Peters, Esq; ✉ XP Power plc, Horseshoe Park, Pangbourne, Berkshire RG8 7JW (tel 0118 976 5080, e-mail jpeters@xppower.com)

PETERS, Prof Sir (David) Keith; kt (1993); s of Herbert Lionel Peters, of Baglan, Port Talbot, and Olive Mainwaring, *née* Hare; *b* 26 July 1938; *Educ* Glanafan GS Port Talbot, Welsh Nat Sch of Med Univ of Wales (MB BCh); *m* 1, 1961 (m dis 1976), Jean Mair Garfield; 1 s (Andrew b 1961), 1 da (Katharine b 1969); m 2, 1979, Pamela, da of Norman Wilson Ewan, of Cambridge; 2 s (James b 1980, William b 1989), 1 da (Hannah b 1982); *Career* prof of med Royal Postgraduate Med Sch 1977–87 (lectr 1969–75, reader 1975–77), regius prof of physic Univ of Cambridge Sch of Clinical Med 1987–2005, fell Christ's Coll Cambridge 1987–2005 (hon fell 2005–); memb: MRC 1984–88, Advsy Cncl Sci and Technol 1987–90, Cncl of Deans of UK Med Schs and Faculties 1992– (chm 1996–97); chm: Nat Kidney Res Fund 1980–86, Nat Radiological Protection Bd 1994–98, Br Heart Fndn 1994–98; pres Acad of Med Sciences 2002–; chm Cncl Cardiff Univ 2004–; Hon MD Univs of: Wales 1986, Nottingham 1996, Birmingham 1998, Bristol 2005, St Andrews 2006; Hon DSc Univs of: Aberdeen 1994, Leicester 1999, Glasgow 2001, Sussex 2004, Keele 2006; Dr (hc) Univ of Paris 1996; hon fell: Imperial Coll Sch of Med 1999, Cardiff Univ 2001, Univ of Wales Swansea 2001; FRCP 1975, FRCPath 1991, FRCPEd 1995, FRS 1995, FMedSci 1998; *Books* Clinical Aspects of Immunology (jt ed, 1982 and 1993); *Recreations* tennis; *Clubs* Garrick; *Style*— Prof Sir Keith Peters; ✉ 7 Chaucer Road, Cambridge CB2 2EB (tel 01223 356117, e-mail dkp1000@medschl.cam.ac.uk)

PETERS, Dame Mary Elizabeth; DBE (2000, CBE 1990, MBE 1973), DL (2003); da of Arthur Henry Peters (d 1990), and Hilda Mary Ellison (d 1956); *b* 6 July 1939; *Educ* Ballymena Acad, Portadown Coll, Belfast Coll of Domestic Science; *Career* formerly home economics teacher Graymount Girls' Secdy Sch; int athlete 1961–74, represented N Ireland at every Cwlth Games 1958–74; achievements incl: fourth place pentathlon Olympic Games 1964, Silver medal shot Cwlth Games 1966, Gold medal pentathlon and shot Cwlth Games 1970, Gold medal pentathlon Olympic Games 1972 (world record), Gold medal pentathlon Cwlth Games 1974; team mangr Br Women's Athletics Team 1979–84 (incl Moscow and LA Olympic Teams); memb: NI Sports Cncl 1973–93 (vice-chm 1977–80), Sports Cncl (GB) 1974–77 (re-elected 1987–93), Sports Aid Fndn, London Marathon Charity Tst 1998–; pres British Athletics Fedn 1996–98, ambass Br Olympic Assoc 1996–; dep chm NI Tourist Bd 1996–2002; chm: NI Ctee of Sport for the Disabled 1984–91, Ulster Games Fndn 1990–93, Belfast 1991 Sports Ctee; past memb Women's Ctee Int Amateur Athletic Fedn, pres Ulster Sports & Recreation Tst, patron NI Amateur Athletic Fedn, formerly pres NI Women's AAA; md Mary Peters Sports Ltd, columnist Irish edn Daily Mail 1994–96; patron Intensive Care Unit Royal Victoria Hosp, patron Integrated Educn Cncl 1998–, memb; Hon DSc New Univ of Ulster 1974, Hon DUniv Queen's Univ Belfast 1998, Hon DLitt Loughborough Univ 1999; Freedom of Lisburn 1998, Hall of Fame Award Dublin and Belfast 1998; *Recreations* fitness training, patchwork; *Style*— Dame Mary E Peters, DBE, DL; ✉ Willowtree Cottage, River Road, Dunmurry, Belfast BT17 9DP (tel and fax 028 9061 8882)

PETERS, Prof (Adrien) Michael; s of Adrien John Peters, and Barbara Muriel Peters; *b* 17 May 1945, Lancaster; *Educ* Middlesbrough HS, Liverpool Inst HS, St Mary's Hosp Med Sch London (BSc), Univ of Liverpool (MB ChB, MD), Univ of London (MSc); *m* 1; 1 s; m 2, 1980, Rosemary Cox; 2 s, 1 da; *Career* house offr Victoria Central Hosp Wallasey 1970–71, house offr Queen Elizabeth Hosp Gateshead 1971–72, lectr in physiology Univ of Liverpool 1972–74, GP NSW 1974–78, GP Liverpool 1978–79, res fell Dept of Diagnostic Radiology Royal Postgrad Med Sch London and hon sr registrar Dept of Diagnostic Radiology Hammersmith Hosp 1979–82, res physician Glaxo Gp Res Ltd 1982–84 (concurrently hon pt/t conslt in med imaging Dept of Diagnostic Radiology Hammersmith Hosp), sr lectr in diagnostic radiology (nuclear med) Royal Postgrad Med Sch London 1984–89 (reader in nuclear med 1989–95), hon sr lectr in nephrology Inst of Child Health Univ of London 1984–93, hon conslt in diagnostic radiology Hammersmith Hosp 1984–99 (conslt-in-charge (nuclear med) Dept of Diagnostic Radiology 1991–99), hon conslt in paediatric radiology Hosp for Sick Children Gt Ormond St London 1988–94 and 1996–2001 (conslt 1984–88), prof of diagnostic radiology Royal Postgrad Med Sch London 1995–97 (memb Higher Degrees Ctee 1996–97), prof of diagnostic radiology Imperial Coll Sch of Med London 1997–99 (departmental rep Higher Degrees Ctee 1997–99, memb Safety Ctee 1996–98, chm Radiation Safety Ctee 1996–98), hon conslt in nuclear med Hammersmith Hosp 1999–2000, prof of nuclear med Univ of Cambridge and hon conslt in nuclear med Addenbrooke's Hosp Cambridge 1999–2004, professorial fell New Hall Cambridge 1999–2004, prof of applied physiology Brighton and Sussex Medical Sch 2004–; visiting fell Div of Nuclear Med Dept of Radiology Hosp for Sick Children Toronto 1985; regnl advsr in nuclear med E Anglia; memb: Panel on Radiolabelled Platelet Survival Studies Int Ctee for Standardisation in Haematology Radionuclide Panel 1988, Advsy Gp - Pharmacology Working Pty MRC Cyclotron Unit Hammersmith Hosp 1995, Standards of Care Ctee Br Thoracic Soc 1995, Advsy Gp - Radiochemistry Working Pty MRC Cyclotron Unit Hammersmith Hosp 1996, Int Consensus Ctee Quality Assurance of Quantitative Measurements of Renal Function from the Renogram 1996, Radiation Safety Ctee Hammersmith Hosps Tst 1997–98; memb Editorial Bd: Br Jl of Radiology 1989–95, Euro Jl of Nuclear Med 1990–, Nuclear Med Communications 1997–; memb: Br Nuclear Med Soc 1987– (memb Cncl 1989–92), BIR 1989– (memb Nuclear Med Sub-Ctee 1989–92), Soc of Nuclear Med 1992–; FRCR 1995, FRCPath 1996 (MRCPath 1984), FRCP 1997 (MRCP 1993), FMedSci 2002; *Publications* Physiological Measurements with Radionuclides in Clinical Practice (jtly, 1998), Nuclear Medicine in Radiological Diagnosis (ed, 2003); author of articles in learned jls; *Recreations* soccer, jazz, dogs, walking; *Style*— Prof Michael Peters

PETERS, Michael Harold Barry; OBE (1990); s of Hyman Peters (d 1986), of London, and Claire Peters (d 1998); *b* 12 February 1941; *Educ* Luton GS, London Coll of Printing (NDD), Yale Univ Sch of Architecture (Euro fell, MFA); *m* 1963, Josephine, da of Alfred and Rachel Levy; 1 s (Gary b 1964), 1 da (Sarah b 1967); *Career* graphic designer; CBS TV (New York) Cato Peters O'Brien 1965–66, Klein Peters 1966–68, Michael Peters & Partners (became Michael Peters Group plc 1983 then Michael Peters Ltd 1990) 1970–92, fndr chm and creative dir Identica (now The Identica Partnership) 1992–; life pres DBA (fndr 1986); lectr worldwide, author of numerous pubns; visiting prof Bezalel Sch of Art Jerusalem; memb Alliance Graphique Internationale 1985, fell Royal Charter of Designers 1986; *Projects* incl: identities for numerous govt depts, Conservative Pty identity, numerous other worldwide corp identity projects, packaging design projects and worldwide literature systems; *Awards* D&AD, Clio, NY Art Dirs' Club, Los Angeles Art Dirs' Club, Stock Exchange (for annual report design), numerous other graphic and typographic awards worldwide; *Recreations* walking, gardening, music, collector of contemporary British crafts; *Style*— Michael Peters, Esq, OBE; ✉ The Identica Partnership, Newcombe House, 45 Notting Hill Gate, London W11 3LQ

PETERS, Prof Nicholas Simon; s of Laurence Peters, of London, and Valerie, *née* Benjamin; *b* 18 February 1960; *Educ* Latymer Upper Sch, Royal Free Hosp Sch of Med London (MB BS), Univ of London (MD); *m* 18 June 1992, Charlotte, da of Geoffrey Darke; 2 s; *Career* postgrad med trg Bart's and St Thomas' Hosp 1986–88, cardiology trg Nat Heart and

Royal Brompton Hosps 1988–91, Br Heart Fndn jr res fell 1991–93, sr registrar (cardiology) Hammersmith Hosp 1993–95, sr lectr and conslt St Mary's Hosp Paddington 1995–98, prof of cardiology and conslt St Mary's Hosp Imperial Coll London 1998–; prof of pharmacology Coll of Physicians and Surgns Columbia Univ NY 1997–, dir of electrophysiology research American Cardiovascular Research Inst 2001–, Med Ctee ARA 1999–; ed European Heart Jl 1996–; FRCP 1998 (MRCP 1987), fell American Coll of Cardiology 2003; *Publications* more than 100 scientific papers, book chapters and reviews on cardiology and heart rhythm disturbances; *Recreations* rowing (several times nat champion 1976–78, represented England 1978), running, art, classic cars; *Clubs* Leander; *Style*— Prof Nicholas Peters; ✉ Department of Cardiology, St Mary's Hospital, Paddington, London W2 1NY (tel 020 7886 2468, fax 020 7886 1763, e-mail n.peters@imperial.ac.uk)

PETERS, Prof Timothy John; s of Stanley Frederick Peters (d 1993), of Uley, Dursley, Gloucester, and Paula, *née* March (d 1973); *b* 10 May 1939; *Educ* King's Sch Macclesfield Cheshire, Univ of St Andrews (MB ChB, MSc, DSc), Univ of London (PhD), The Rockefeller Univ NY; *m* 21 Sept 1965, Judith Mary, da of Dr William Basil Bacon (d 1983), of Manchester; 2 da (Carolyne b 1967, Sarah b 1969), 1 s (Christopher b 1983); *Career* successively lectr, sr lectr then reader Royal Postgrad Med Sch Univ of London 1972–79, head Div of Clinical Cell Biology Clinical Res Centre Harrow 1979–88, prof and head of Dept of Clinical Biochemistry GKT 1988–, dir of pathology King's Healthcare 1992–98, sub-dean for research and higher degrees King's Coll Sch of Med and Dentistry 1992–98, sub-dean for higher degrees and postgraduates King's Coll Sch of Med 1998–2000, assoc dean (flexible trg) Thames Postgraduate Med and Educn Dept Univ of London 2000–; Raine visiting prof 1994, Br Cncl visiting prof Dept of Biochemistry Univ of Western Australia 1995; ed Alcohol and Alcoholism 1991–94, ed-in-chief Addiction Biology 1995–; tstee and memb Cncl Sir Richard Stapley Educational Tst 1992–, tstee and chair Areca Concern 2001–; FRCP 1974, FRCPE 1981, FRCPath 1984, FRSA 1996; *Publications* International Handbook of Alcohol Dependence and Problems (ed jtly, 2001); *Recreations* baroque recorders, narrow boats; *Clubs* RSA; *Style*— Prof Timothy J Peters; ✉ Department of Clinical Biochemistry, GKT, Denmark Hill, London SE5 9PJ (tel 020 7346 3008, fax 020 7737 7434)

PETERSEN, Prof Ole Holger; s of Rear Adm Jorgen Petersen (d 1986), and Elisabeth, *née* Klein; *b* 3 March 1943; *Educ* Med Sch Copenhagen Univ (MB ChB, MD); *m* 1, 1968 (m dis 1995), Nina Bratting, da of Wilhelm Jensen, of Copenhagen, Denmark; 2 s (Jens b 26 May 1969, Carl b 25 Dec 1970); m 2, June 1995, Nina Burdakova, da of Nikolay Kolichev, of Grozny, Russia; *Career* Lt Royal Danish Army Med Corps 1970–71; sr lectr in physiology Univ of Copenhagen 1973–75 (lectr 1969–73), prof of physiology Univ of Dundee 1975–81, exec ed Pflügers Archiv (Euro jl of physiology) 1978–; Univ of Liverpool: George Holt prof of physiology 1981–; foreign sec Physiological Soc 1992–98, MRC research prof 1998–; memb Scientific Advsy Bd Max Planck Inst for Molecular Physiology Dortmund 1995–, fndn memb Academia Europaea (chair Physiology and Med Section 1996–, memb Cncl 1998–); memb: Royal Danish Acad of Sciences and Letters 1988, Int Faculty Danish Res Acad 1993, Acad of Medical Sciences 1998, Int Advsy Bd Inst Biomed Sci Univ of Chile 1998–; Jacobaeus Prize (Novo Nordic Fndn) 1994; FRS 2000, Hon FRCP 2001; *Books* The Electrophysiology of Gland Cells (1980); *Recreations* music; *Style*— Prof Ole Petersen; ✉ MRC Secretory Control Research Group, The Physiological Laboratory, University of Liverpool, Brownlow Hill, Liverpool L69 3BX (tel 0151 7945322, fax 0151 7945327, e-mail o.h.petersen@liverpool.ac.uk)

PETERSHAM, Viscount; Charles Henry Leicester Stanhope; s and h of 11 Earl of Harrington, *qv*, and Eileen, *née* Grey; *b* 20 July 1945; *Educ* Eton; *m* 1, 1966 (m dis), Virginia Alleyne Freeman, da of Capt Harry Freeman Jackson (d 1993), of Cool-na-Grena, Co Cork; 1 s (Hon William b 1967), 1 da (Hon Serena (Viscountess Linley) b 1970); m 2, 1984, Anita, formerly w of 21 Earl of Suffolk and Berkshire, and yr da of Robin Fuglesang (d 1991), of Lacock, Wilts; *Career* FRGS; *Recreations* shooting, sailing (circumnavigation 1983–85 SY Surama), hunting (Master of the Limerick Hounds 1974–77 and 1990–93), carriage driving (competed World Games Rome 1998), racing, fishing; *Style*— Viscount Petersham

PETERSON, Alan Edward; s of Edward Peterson, MBE (d 2005), of Cardiff, and Nell, *née* James; *b* 22 October 1947; *Educ* BTech; *m* 5 June 1971, Margaret Diane; 1 s (Hywel Rhys b 8 Feb 1978); *Career* gen mgmnt Alcan (UK) 1973–81, chm West & Welsh Holdings 1982–89, md ACI Rockware Gp 1990–95, chief exec Meyer International plc 1996–2000; chm: The Peterson Consultancy Ltd 2000–, Rubicon Retail Ltd 2001–05, Paperpak Holdings Ltd 2002–07, Refresco Holdings BV 2003–06, HSS Hire Service Holdings Ltd 2004–07; CCMI; *Recreations* opera, cricket, rugby, Nat Hunt race horse owner; *Clubs* Cardiff RFC, Cardiff and County, Surrey CCC; *Style*— Alan Peterson, Esq; ✉ 153 Cyncoed Road, Cyncoed, Cardiff CF23 6AG

PETERSON, Rev Prof David Gilbert; s of Gilbert Samuel Peterson (d 1995), of Sydney, Aust, and Marie Jean, *née* Roe (now Mrs Leggatt); *b* 29 October 1944; *Educ* Univ of Sydney (MA), Univ of London (BD), Univ of Manchester (PhD), Australian Coll of Theol (ThSchol); *m* 1970, Lesley Victoria, da of Kenneth John Stock; 3 s (Mark David b 1973, Christopher David b 1975, Daniel John b 1978); *Career* ordained deacon Anglican Church of Aust 1968, asst curate St Matthew's Manly NSW 1968–70, lectr Moore Theol Coll Sydney 1970–75, postgrad research Univ of Manchester and Sunday asst St Mary's Cheadle 1975–78, lectr Moore Theol Coll 1978–79, rector and sr canon St Michael's Cathedral Wollongong NSW 1980–84, head Dept of Ministry and lectr in New Testament Moore Theol Coll 1984–96, princ Oak Hill Coll London 1996–2007; visiting prof Middlesex Univ 2004–, research fell Moore Theological Coll Sydney 2007–; Tyndale fell; memb Soc of New Testament Studies; *Publications* Hebrews and Perfection (1982), Engaging with God: a Biblical Theology of Worship (1992), Possessed by God: a New Testament Theology of Holiness and Sanctification (1995), Witness to the Gospel: The Theology of Acts (ed with I H Marshall, 1997), Where Wrath and Mery Meet: proclaiming the atonement today (2001), The Word made Flesh: Evangelicals and the Incarnation (2003), Christ and his People: Proclaiming Christ from Isaiah (2003); *Recreations* golf, swimming, music; *Style*— The Rev Prof David Peterson; ✉ 9A Massey Street, Gladesville, NSW 2111, Australia (tel 00 61 2 9879 6550)

PETERSON, Gilles; MBE (2004); s of Armin Moehrle (d 2002), of Switzerland, and Michelle Fouquet; *b* 28 September 1964, Caen, France; *m* 22 Dec 1999, Atsuko Hirai; 2 s (Olivier b 9 Oct 1997, Luc b 21 Sept 2001); *Career* radio presenter and DJ; early DJ residencies incl: Electric Ballroom, Special Branch at The Royal Oak, Dingwalls Camden 1986–92, Heaven; fndr (with James Lavelle) That's How It Is (nightclub) 1993, currently plays regularly worldwide; fndr: Acid Jazz (record label), Talkin' Loud Records (Phonogram) 1989 (releases incl Roni Size's New Forms (winner Mercury Music Prize 1997)); DJ on pirate radio stations incl: Invicta, KJazz, Solar Radio, On Horizon; presenter: BBC Radio London, Jazz FM, Kiss FM 1990–98, Worldwide on BBC Radio 1 1998– (Best Specialist Radio Show Sony Awards 2000); *Albums* incl: Jazz Juice, compiled EMI Blue Note artists series, Gilles Peterson in Africa, Gilles Peterson in Brazil, Gilles Peterson: Worldwide, Vol 2, and Vol 3, Gilles Peterson: Worldwide/Programme 4, Desert Island Mix: Journeys By DJs, Impressed with Gilles Peterson Vol 1 and Vol 2; *Style*— Gilles Peterson, Esq, MBE; ✉ c/o John Slade, Elastic Artist Agency, Flat 5, 3 Newhams Row, London SE1 3UZ (tel 020 7367 6224, fax 020 7367 6206, e-mail john@elasticartists.net)

PETHICK, Jan Stephen; s of Maj Thomas Francis Henry Pethick (d 1981), of Ventnor, IOW, and Denise Joyce, *née* Clark (d 1994); *b* 16 September 1947; *Educ* Clifton Coll, Jesus Coll Oxford; *m* 20 Dec 1974, Belinda Patricia, da of Douglas Collins, of Hare Hatch, Berks; 2 da (Emily b 26 May 1975, Nancy b 15 April 1977), 1 s (Benjamin b 18 May 1981); *Career* stock jobber/trader Pinchin Denny & Co 1969–74, Midland Doherty Eurobond Trading 1975–77, exec dir Bonds Lehman Bros Kuhn Loeb 1977–84, md Shearson Lehman Hutton International Inc 1986–90, dir Luthy Baillie Dowsett Pethick & Co Ltd 1990–96 (also co-fndr), head of global debt origination Dresdner Kleinwort Benson 1996–2000; md and chm of debt capital markets Europe Merrill Lynch International 2000–; memb Bd London Sch of Hygiene and Tropical Medicine 2006; chm of tstees Childhood First; High Sheriff Gtr London 2007–08; *Recreations* golf, tennis; *Clubs* New Zealand Golf, Queen's, Turf, Swinley Forest Golf, Royal St George's Golf, Portland Bridge; *Style*— Jan Pethick, Esq; ✉ 71 Kew Green, Kew, Richmond, Surrey TW9 3AH (tel 020 8940 2426); Merrill Lynch International, 2 King Edward Street, London EC1A 1HQ (tel 020 7995 2638)

PETHIG, Prof Ronald (Ron); s of Charles Edward Pethig (d 1997), of Sanderstead, Surrey, and Edith Jane, *née* Jones; *b* 10 May 1942; *Educ* Purley GS, Univ of Southampton (BSc, PhD, DSc), Univ of Nottingham (PhD); *m* 10 Aug 1968, Angela Jane, da of John Stephen Sampson, of Tibshelf, Derbys (d 1973); 1 s (Richard John b 16 June 1971), 1 da (Helen Jane b 17 Jan 1976); *Career* ICI fell Univ of Nottingham 1968–71, corpn memb Marine Biological Laboratory Woods Hole USA 1982–, adjunct prof of physiology Med Univ S Carolina USA 1984–90; Univ of Wales: reader 1982–86, personal chair 1986–, dir Inst of Molecular and Biomolecular Electronics 1986–1998, dean Faculty of Sci 1991–93; dir P & B (Sciences) Ltd 1989–2000; vice-pres for research then pres and ceo Aura Biosystems Systems Inc 2000–03 (currently memb Bd); Marine Biological Lab Woods Hole: corporation memb 1982, adjunct sr scientist 2005, Eugene and Millicent Bell endowed fell in tissue engrg 2006–: memb: SERC Molecular Electronics Ctee 1991–94, Int Evaluation Ctee of Swedish Nat Bd for Industrial and Tech Devpt 1991–92, Exec Ctee Snowdonia National Park Soc 1991–94; Innovation Prize IEE/IMechE/Br Design Cncl 1988, Innovation Award Inst of Physical Sciences in Medicine 1994, Innovation Award Biological Engrg Soc 1994, first recipient of Herman P Schwan Award Oslo 2001; CEng 1975, FIEE 1986; *Books* Dielectric and Electronic Properties of Biological Materials (1979); *Recreations* mountain walking, restoring old scientific instruments, bird watching; *Style*— Prof Ron Pethig; ✉ School of Informatics, University of Wales, Bangor, Dean Street, Bangor, Gwynedd LL57 1UT

PETIT, Sir Dinshaw Manockjee; 5 Bt (UK 1890), of Petit Hall, Island of Bombay; né Jehangir Petit but obliged, under a trust created by Sir Dinshaw Manockjee Petit, 1 Bt, to adopt the name of the first Bt; s of Sir Dinshaw Manockjee Petit, 4 Bt (d 1998); *b* 21 January 1965; *Educ* Pierrepont Sch, New Hampshire Coll; *m* 1994, Laila, da of Homi F Commissariat; 1 s (Rehan b 4 May 1995), 1 da (Aisha b 30 Jan 1998); *Heir* s, Rehan Petit; *Career* pres: N M Petit Charities, Sir D M Petit Charities, F D Petit Sanatorium, Persian Zoroastrian Amelioration Fund, Petit Girls' Orphanage, D M Petit Gymnasium, J N Petit Inst, Bombay Native Dispensary; memb Mgmnt Ctee: B D Petit Parsi Gen Hosp, Garib Zarthostiona Rehethan Fund; tstee: Bai Sakarbai Dinshaw Petit Hosp for Animals, Concern India Fndn; *Style*— Sir Dinshaw Petit, Bt; ✉ Petit Hall, 66 Nepean Sea Road, Bombay 400 006, India (tel 00 91 22 2363 7333, fax 00 91 22 2264 4680, e-mail ljp@vsnl.com)

PETIT, Pascale; da of Michel Petit, and Muriel, *née* McCarthy; *Educ* Glos Coll of Art and Design (BA), RCA (MA); *Career* poet; poetry ed Poetry London 1989–2005, tutor The Poetry Sch 1997–2000 and 2007–08; shortlisted Forward Prize for Best Single Poem 2000, selected as a Next Generation Poet Arts Cncl/Poetry Book Soc 2004; FZS; *Books* Heart of a Deer (1998), Tying the Song (co-ed, 2000), The Zoo Father (2001, Arts Cncl of England Writers' Award 2001, New London Writers' Award 2001, Poetry Book Soc recommendation, shortlisted T S Eliot Prize 2002), El Padre Zoológico /The Zoo Father (2004, bilingual edn Mexico), The Huntress (2005, shortlisted T S Eliot Prize 2006), The Wounded Deer: Fourteen Poems after Frida Kahlo (2005), The Treekeeper's Tale (2008); *Recreations* travel, going to contemporary art exhibitions; *Style*— Pascale Petit; ✉ 26 Clacton Road, London E17 8AR (website www.pascalepetit.co.uk); Seren, 57 Nolton Street, Bridgend CF31 3AE (tel 01656 663018, fax 01656 649226, e-mail general@seren-books.com, website www.seren-books.com)

PETO, Sir Henry George Morton; 4 Bt (UK 1855); s of Cdr Sir Henry Francis Morton Peto, 3 Bt, RN (d 1978); *b* 29 April 1920; *Educ* Sherborne, CCC Cambridge; *m* 1947, Frances Jacqueline, JP, da of late Ralph Haldane Evers; 2 s; *Heir* s, Francis Peto; *Career* RA 1939–46; manufacturing industry 1946–80; *Style*— Sir Henry Peto, Bt; ✉ Stream House, Selborne, Alton, Hampshire GU34 3LE

PETO, Sir Michael Henry Basil; 4 Bt (UK 1927); s of Brig Sir Christopher Henry Maxwell Peto, 3 Bt, DSO (d 1980); *b* 6 April 1938; *Educ* Eton, ChCh Oxford (MA); *m* 1, 1963 (m dis 1970), Sarah Susan, da of Maj Sir Dennis Stucley, 5 Bt; 1 s, 2 da; m 2, 1971 (m dis 2001), Lucinda Mary, da of Maj Sir Charles Douglas Blackett, 9 Bt; 2 s; *Heir* s, Henry Peto; *Career* called to the Bar Inner Temple 1960; ret; *Style*— Sir Michael Peto, Bt; ✉ 12 St Helen's Terrace, Spittal, Berwick-upon-Tweed TD15 1RJ (tel 01289 306911)

PETO, Sir Richard; kt (1999); *b* 14 May 1943; *Educ* Univ of Cambridge (MA), Univ of London (MSc); *Career* research offr MRC Statistical Research Unit 1967–69; Dept of the Regius Prof of Med Univ of Oxford: research offr 1969–72, lectr 1972–75, reader 1975–79; Nuffield Dept of Clinical Med Univ of Oxford: univ reader in cancer studies 1979–92, prof of med statistics and epidemiology 1992–, co-dir (with Prof Rory Collins, *qv*) Clinical Trial Service Unit and Epidemiological Studies Unit (CTSU); fndn fell Green Coll Oxford 1979–; General Motors visiting prof Int Agency for Research on Cancer (IARC) Lyon 1992; hon prof Chinese Acad of Preventive Med 1989–, adjunct prof Cornell Univ 1990–, hon prof Peking Union Med Coll 1995–; Caradog Jones lectr RSS 1992, Rickman Godlee lectr UCL 1999; MA (by incorporation) Univ of Oxford 1974, Hon Dr Univ of Tampere 1992, Hon DSc Univ of London 1999, Hon DSc Univ of Southampton 2003; hon memb Swedish Soc of Internal Med 1988, academician Acad of Finland 2001, membre étranger Associé de l'Académie des Sciences France 2002; FRS 1989, Hon FFPHM 1992, fndr fell Acad of Med Sciences 1998, Hon FRCP 1999 (Hon MRCP 1987); Offr Cross of the Order of Merit (Poland) 2002; *Awards* Guy Silver Medal RSS 1986, Helmut Horten Fndn Award (jtly) 1989, Gairdner Fndn Award Canada 1992, Frohlich Award NY Acad of Sciences 1993, Donald Reid Medal London Sch of Hygiene 1993, Polish Cardiac Soc Medal of Merit 1993, La Médaille de la Ville de Paris (Échelon Vermeil) 1994, European Award for Excellence in Stroke Research (jtly) 1995, Oettlé Meml Medal SA 1996, Prix Raymond Bourgine for Achievement in Cancer Research (jtly) 1996, Gold Award Polish Health Promotion Fndn 1997, Prix Louis Jeantet for Med 1997, 10th World Conf on Tobacco or Health Award 1997, Fothergill Medal Med Soc of London (jtly) 1998, Leverhulme Prize Liverpool Sch of Tropical Med (jtly), 1998, Polish Presidential Public Health Award 2000, Int Aspirin Sr Award (jtly) 2000, Prince Mahidol Award for Public Health (jtly) Thailand 2000, Lynn Sage Distinguished Award in Breast Cancer Research 2001, King Olav V Prize Norwegian Cancer Soc (jtly) 2002, Mott Prize General Motors Cancer Research Fndn 2002, Royal Medal Royal Soc 2002; *Style*— Sir Richard Peto, FRS; ✉ Clinical Trial Service Unit and Epidemiological Studies Unit, Richard Doll Building, Old Road Campus, Oxford OX3 7LF

PETRE, 18 Baron (E 1603); John Patrick Lionel Petre; o s of 17 Baron Petre (d 1989), and Marguerite Eileen, *née* Hamilton; *b* 4 August 1942; *Educ* Eton, Trinity Coll Oxford (MA); *m* 16 Sept 1965, Marcia Gwendolyn, o da of Alfred Plumpton, of Portsmouth; 2 s (Hon Dominic William b 1966, Hon Mark Julian b 1969), 1 da (Hon Clare Helen b 1973); *Heir* s, Hon Dominic Petre; *Career* chm: Essex St John Ambulance 1992–2002, Essex Land and Business Assoc 1998–2001, Brentwood Theatre Tst 1998–2002; HM Lord-Lt Essex

P

2002– (DL 1991); *Style—* The Rt Hon the Lord Petre; ✉ Writtle Park, Highwood, Chelmsford, Essex

PETRIE, Sir Peter Charles; CMG (1980); 5 Bt (UK 1918); s of Sir Charles Petrie, 3 Bt (d 1977), and of Cecilia, Lady Petrie (d 1987); suc his half-bro, Sir Richard Petrie, 4 Bt 1988; *b* 7 March 1932; *Educ* Westminster, ChCh Oxford (MA); *m* 1958, Countess Lydwine Maria Fortunata, da of Count Charles Alphonse von Oberndorff, of The Hague and Paris; 2 s, 1 da; *Heir* s, Charles Petrie; *Career* 2 sec UK Delegation NATO Paris 1958–61, first sec New Delhi 1961–64, chargé d'affaires Katmandu 1963, Cabinet Office 1965–67, UK Mission to UN (NY) 1969–73, cnsllr (head of Chancery) Bonn 1973–76, head of Euro Integration Dept (Int) FCO 1976–79, min Paris 1979–85; ambass to Belgium 1985–89; advsr to govr Bank of England on Euro and Parly affairs 1989–2003; memb: Institut de l'Euro Lyon Conseil d'Administration 1995–99, Franco-British Cncl 1995–2003 (chm 1997–2002); corresponding memb Académie de Comptabilité Paris 1996–, memb Cncl City Univ 1997–2002; *Clubs* Brooks's, Beefsteak, Jockey (Paris); *Style—* Sir Peter Petrie, Bt, CMG; ✉ 16A Cambridge Street, London SW1V 4QH; 4 Hameau du Jardin, 50310 Lestre, Paris, France (e-mail lydwinep@aol.com)

PETROU, Prof Maria; da of Konstantinos Petrou (d 1971), and Dionisia, *née* Voziki; *b* 17 May 1953, Thessaloniki, Greece; *Educ* Aristotelian Univ of Thessaloniki (BSc), Univ of Cambridge (Zonta Int Award, Greek state scholarship, Alex Onassis scholarship, PhD); *m* 4 July 1981 (m dis 1996); 1 s (Costas Alexander Palmer b 15 June 1983); *Career* lectr in astronomy Maths Dept Kapodistrian Univ of Athens 1981–83, postdoctoral research asst Dept of Theoretical Physics Univ of Oxford 1983–86, postdoctoral research assoc NERC Unit for Thematic Info Systems (NUTIS) Dept of Geography Univ of Reading 1986–87, princ investigator Rutherford Appleton Lab 1987–88, lectr, sr lectr then reader Dept of Electronic and Electrical Engrg Univ of Surrey 1988–98, prof of image analysis (personal chair) Univ of Surrey 1998–2005, prof of signal processing Imperial Coll London 2005– (head Communications and Signal Processing Gp 2006–); theme ldr Data and Information Fusion Defence Technoly Centre (DIF-DTC); chm: Tech Ctee 7 for Remote Sensing Int Assoc for Pattern Recognition (IAPR) 1998–2002, British Machine Vision Assoc (BMVA) 1999–2002, Soc for Pattern Recognition 1999–2002; memb E Asia Panel Royal Soc; assoc ed IEEE Transactions on Image Processing 1994–98, newsletter ed IAPR 1994–98, currently hon ed IEE Electronics Letters; memb Editorial Bd: Electronic Letters on Computer Vision and Image Analysis, Pattern Recognition and Image Analysis, Applied Intelligence; author of more than 350 scientific papers; Metrology Award 1991; Sr MIEEE, FIEE 1998 (memb Cncl 2004–), CEng 1999, fell IAPR 2000 (treas 2002–), FREng 2004, distinguished fell BMVA 2006; *Books* Image Processing: The Fundamentals (jtly, 1999), Image Processing: Dealing with Texture (2006); *Recreations* theatre, travelling; *Style—* Prof Maria Petrou; ✉ Department of Electrical and Electronic Engineering, Imperial College, Exhibition Road, London SW7 2AZ

PETT, David John; *Educ* Wanstead HS, Lincoln Coll Oxford (exhibitioner, MA), Coll of Law Guildford; *Career* articled clerk Bond Pearce Plymouth 1978–80, asst slr (tax) Clifford-Turner 1980–83, slr Pinsent Masons (formerly Pinsent Curtis Biddle) 1983– (ptnr 1985–); Nat Practice Head of Tax and Pensions 1995–2000; memb Share Scheme Lawyers Gp 1993, memb Inland Revenue Advsy Gp on Employee Share Schemes, former memb Tport Users Consultative Ctee (Midlands Area), memb Network Rail 2002–; tstee Thinktank (Birmingham Museum of Science and Industry) 2002–; *Books* A Practical Guide to Employee Share Schemes (1989), ESOPs - The Use of Trusts with Employee Share Schemes (1991), Employee Share Schemes Handbook (1993), The New Employee Share Incentives: AESOPs and EMI (with David Cohen, 2001); Employee Share Schemes (2 vols, looseleaf, 1996–); *Recreations* orchestral timpanist; *Style—* David Pett, Esq; ✉ Pinsent Masons, 3 Colmore Circus, Birmingham B4 6BH (tel 0121 200 1050, fax 0121 626 1040, e-mail david.pett@pinsents.com)

PETTER, Hugh David Michael; s of Michael Gordon Petter, of Broxbourne, Herts, and Evelyn Mary, *née* Leakey (d 1997); *b* 5 September 1966; *Educ* Sheredes Sch Hoddesdon, Portsmouth Poly (BA, DipArch); *m* 20 May 1995, Chloë Susannah, da of Rory Forrester, and Antonia Forrester (d 1997); 1 s (Harry Alexander James b 9 July 1999), 1 da (Charlotte Antonia Evelyn b 19 Dec 2000); *Career* architect; dir Robert Adam Architects 1997– (assoc 1993–97); work exhibited at: Contrapunti Rome 1991, Millenovecentonovantadue Rome 1992, Architettura Contemporanea Rome 1992, Prince of Wales's Inst of Architecture 1993, The Other Modern Bologna 2000, A Decade of Art and Architecture 1992–2002 NY 2002, The Prince's Fndn 2003, The New English Country House London 2003 (also Bristol 2004), The Georgian Gp 2004, Traditional Architects Gp 2005, Big Brainstorm Exhibition London 2006; sr tutor Prince of Wales's Inst of Architecture 1992–98 (estab fndn course); memb: Traditional Architects Gp RIBA, Building Sub-Ctee Br Sch at Rome 1999–2003, Int Bilding Study Gp 2000–, Exec Ctee The Georgian Gp 2003–, Educn Working Gp The Georgian Gp 2004–, Devpt Advsy Gp Br Sch at Rome 2004–, London Branch Ctee Country Land and Business Assoc 2006–, Cncl of Advsrs Inst of Classical Architecture and Classical America 2007–; The Arts & Crafts Movement in Surrey; Building Magazine Diploma Prize 1990, Rome Scholarship in Architecture 1990–92, ARCUK William Kretchmer Award for Postgrad Research 1991, commendation Harrogate Dist Design Awards for Environmental Excellence 1998, highly commended Rochford Conservation Design and Heritage Award 2002, Palladio Award (for Millennium Gate Atlanta) 2006, winner RIBA competition for listed building work at Clapham London 2006; bro Art Workers' Guild 2002– (chm 2006–); bro Coll of Traditional Practitioners of the Int Network for Traditional Building, Architecture and Urbanism; memb: RIBA, ARB, Inst of Classical Architecture NY, Europa Nostra 2002–; FRSA; *Publications* Lutyens in Italy: the Building of the British School at Rome (1992); contrib: Annali Accademici Canadesi Vol VIII (1992), The Golden City: Essays on the Architecture and Imagination of Beresford Pite (1993), The Classicist Vol II (1995), Ancient Rome: the Archaeology of the Eternal City (2000); *Recreations* fly fishing, shooting, English watercolours and prints, architectural history, gardens, photography, Italy, my family; *Clubs* Black's; *Style—* Hugh Petter, Esq; ✉ Robert Adam Architects, Upper High Street, Winchester, Hamptonshire SO23 8UT (tel 01962 843843, fax 01962 843303, e-mail hugh.petter@robertadamarchitects.com)

PETTIFER, Brian Warren Bowers; s of Fred Tyler Pettifer (d 1965), of Grimsby, Lincs, and Chrystine, *née* Thompson; *b* 10 October 1935; *Educ* Oundle, Univ of Hull (BA), Open Univ (BSc); *m* 2 Oct 1965, Veronica Mary, da of Dr Georg Tugendhat (d 1973), of Essex; 3 s (Crispin b 1967, Adam b 1969, Daniel b 1970), 1 da (Teresa b 1974); *Career* served HAC 1963–66; admitted slr 1963; in own practice 1966–92, ptnr Rollit Farrell & Bladon 1992–98; underwriter Lloyd's 1977–98; pt/t lectr Univ of Hull 1994–; pres Cleethorpes Cons Assoc 1998–2001; cncllr: Lindsey CC 1970–74, Humberside CC 1974–77; chief whip Cons Pty and shadow chm for planning 1974–77; chm: Humberside Youth Assoc 1974–75, Barton-on-Humber Youth Centre Mgmnt Ctee 1974–88, Humberside European Conservative Cncl 1983–86; capt Law Soc Golf Club 1985–86, hon steward Wimbledon Tennis tournament 1989–; Liveryman Worshipful Co of Makers of Playing Cards 1991; NP, FCIArb, FHEA 2001; *Recreations* skiing, golf, tennis; *Clubs* Oriental, Ski Club of GB, Kandahar Ski; *Style—* Brian Pettifer, Esq; ✉ Cob Hall, Priestgate, Barton-on-Humber, North Lincolnshire DN18 5ET (tel 01652 632248, fax 01652 660077)

PETTIFER, Julian; s of Stephen Henry Pettifer (d 1980), of Malmesbury, Wilts, and Diana Mary, *née* Burton (d 2003); *b* 21 July 1935; *Educ* Marlborough, St John's Coll Cambridge (MA); *Career* television broadcaster and author; Nat Serv 1953–55, basic trg with Rifle Bde, cmmnd Northamptonshire Regt, served as 2 Lt in Korea and Hong Kong; TV series incl: BBC Tonight, Panorama, 24 Hours, Diamonds in the Sky, The Living Isles, Missionaries, Nature, Biteback, Assignment, British Steel Challenge, ITV's Nature Watch, Automania; radio series incl: Asia File, Crossing Continents, State of Africa, Conservation Pioneers, The Age of the Park; awarded BAFTA Reporter of the Year 1968–69, Royal Geographical Soc Cherry Kearton Award for Wildlife Films 1990, Mungo Park Award Royal Scottish Geographical Soc 1998; pres: Berks, Bucks and Oxon Wildlife Tst (BBOWT), Malmesbury Civic Tst, RSPB; vice-pres: Royal Soc for Nature Conservation, Br Naturalists' Assoc; *Books* Diamonds in the Sky (with Kenneth Hudson, 1979), Nature Watch (with Robin Brown, 1981), Automania (with Nigel Turner, 1984), The Nature Watchers (with Robin Brown, 1985), Missionaries (with Richard Bradley, 1990), Nature Watch (with Robin Brown, 1994); *Recreations* music, theatre, tennis, gardening, books; *Clubs* Queen's; *Style—* Julian Pettifer, Esq; ✉ c/o Curtis Brown, 28/29 Haymarket, London SW1Y 4SP

PETTIT, Sir Daniel Eric Arthur; kt (1974); s of Thomas Edgar Pettit (d 1940), of Liverpool, and Pauline Elizabeth, *née* Kerr (d 1957); *b* 19 February 1915; *Educ* Quarry Bank HS Liverpool, Fitzwilliam Coll Cambridge (MA); *m* 1940, Winifred (d 2004), da of William Standing Bibby, of Liverpool (d 1951); 2 s (Richard, Michael); *Career* Mil Serv 1940–46, Maj RA; serv: UK, Africa, India, Burma; TA Hon Col (movement); UK team Olympic Games 1936; sch master 1938–39 and 1946–47; Unilever MGT 1948–59; chm: SPD Ltd (Unilever) 1960–70, Nat Freight Corp 1970–78; dir: Bransford Farmers Ltd 1973–, Bransford Leisure Pursuits Ltd 1973–, Lloyds Bank Ltd 1977–78; chm Birmingham and W Midlands Lloyds Bank Ltd 1978–85, dir Lloyds Bank (UK) Ltd 1979–85, chm Post Office Staff Superannuation Fund 1979–83; pres and chm The Industry Cncl for Packaging and the Environment (Incpen) 1979–90, chm PosTel Investment Ltd 1982–83; dir: Black Horse Ltd 1984–85, Lloyds Bank Unit Tst 1984–85; chm RDC Properties Ltd 1987–2004; memb: Nat Ports Cncl 1971–80, Freight Integration Cncl 1971–78, Fndn of Mgmnt Educn 1973–78; chm Econ Devpt Ctee for Distributive Trades 1974–78; fell Huguenot Soc; Freeman City of London 1971, Liveryman Worshipful Co of Carmen 1971; hon fell Fitzwilliam Coll Cambridge 1985; CIMgt, FCIT (pres 1972), FIM, FRSA, FIP (vice-pres), MIPM; *Recreations* watching cricket and football, fishing, country pursuits, farm interests; *Clubs* Hawks' (Cambridge), MCC, Farmers'; *Style—* Sir Daniel Pettit; ✉ Bransford Court Farm, Worcester WR6 5JL (tel 01905 830098)

PETTIT, Rosemary; da of late G H N Pettit, and Ruby, *née* Garner; *b* 22 May 1944; *Educ* Bury St Edmunds GS, Bedford Coll London (BSc), Inst of Educn Univ of London (PGCE); *Career* primary sch teacher 1966–68, copy ed Penguin Books 1971–73, researcher LWT 1973–74, section ed Marshall Cavendish 1974–75, jt ed Traditional Acupuncture Jl 1982–90, jt ed Clarion (jl of Gladstone Club) 1982–86, prop Blenheim Books 1992–; sec: Ind Publishers' Guild 1979–89, Book Packagers' Assoc 1985–98, Directory & Database Publishers Assoc (DPA) 1989–2005; dir Paddington Industrial Association Ltd 1984–86, memb Mgmnt Ctee Paddington Law Centre 1984–86, traditional crafts organiser Art in Action 1984–89, judge DPA Awards 1993–2004, dir Digital Content Forum 1999–2005; memb: Publishing Assessment Section Nat Cncl for Vol Qualifications 1989, Books-across-the-Sea Ctee ESU 1989–2005, Cncl Advtg Standards Bd of Fin 1991–2005, Bd Liberal Democrat News 1993–96, PPA Parly and Legal Consultative Gp 1994–2005, Business Information Forum 1997–2005; dir Publishing Nat Trg Orgn 1990–2003; memb Liberal Party 1979, Westminster N Lib Democrat Assoc (sec, membership sec, vice-chm, chm) 1979–90; Social and Liberal Democrat candidate for By Election 1989 (Cncl elections 1982), chm Kensington Liberal Democrat Assoc 1993–95; membership sec Brackenbury Residents Assoc 2000–; *Books* The Craft Business (1975), Occupation Self Employed (2 edn, 1981), Five Go To Parliament (1992); *Style—* Ms Rosemary Pettit; ✉ 45 Bradmore Road, London W6 0DT (tel and fax 020 8846 9707, e-mail rosemarypettit@onetel.com)

PETTMAN, Prof Barrie Owen; Baron of Bombie (1999); s of Matthew Mark Pettman (d 1967), and Ivy, *née* Warcup (d 2001); *b* 22 February 1944; *Educ* Hull GS, Hull Tech Coll (BSc), City Univ Business Sch (MSc, PhD), International Mgmnt Centres (DLitt); *m* 1, 1970 (m dis 1986), Heather Richardson; m 2, 1987, Norma (d 1991); m 3, 1992, Maureen, da of George Crowther (d 1944); *Career* lectr Dept of Social Admin Univ of Hull 1970–82, dir Manpower Unit Univ of Rhodesia 1978–79, registrar Int Mgmnt Centres 1983–; dir: MCB Univ Press 1970–2004, Int Inst of Social Econ 1972–; ed: International Journal of Social Economics 1973–79, International Journal of Manpower 1980–84, Management Research News 1981–2005, Equal Opportunities International 1981–2005 (asst ed 1982–), International Journal of Manpower 1980–84, International Journal of Sociology & Social Policy 1984–2005, International Journal of New Ideas 1992–98; jt ed Managerial Law 1975–2005; asst ed: Employee Relations 1978–82, Archives of Economic History 1983–; visiting prof Canadian Sch of Mgmnt 1983–2003, Home Sec's rep Humberside Police Authy 1994–2000; hon vice-pres Br Soc of Commerce 1975–; chm: Inst of Sci Business 1972–79, Inst of Trg and Devpt Humberside Branch 1990–2000; pres Burke's Peerage & Gentry (UK) Ltd 2003–; memb: Manpower Soc 1977–91, Int Inst of Social Econs; FCI, FRGS, FRSA, FIMfgE, FIMS, FCIPD, FCMI, MIAM; *Books* Training and Retraining (1973), Labour Turnover and Retention (1975), Equal Pay (1975), Manpower Planning Workbook (1976, 1984), Industrial Democracy (1984), Discrimination in the Labour Market (1980), Management: A Selected Bibliography (1983), The New World Order (1996), Social Economies in Transition (1996), Self Development (1997), The Internationalisation of Franchising (1998), The Ultimate Wealth Book (1998), What Self-Made Millionniares Really Think, Know and Do (2002); *Recreations* golf, shooting; *Clubs* The Reform; *Style—* Prof Barrie Pettman, Baron of Bombie; ✉ Enholmes Hall, Patrington, Hull HU12 0PR (tel 01964 630033, fax 01964 631716); MCB University Press, 62 Toller Lane, Bradford, West Yorkshire BD8 9BY (tel 01274 777700, fax 01274 785200, e-mail barrie.o.pettman@barmarick.co.uk)

PETTY, Very Rev John Fitzmaurice; s of Dr Gerald Fitzmaurice Petty, TD, MRCS, LRCP, FRCGP (d 1986), and Edith Stuart, *née* Knox (d 1977); *b* 9 March 1935; *Educ* King's Sch Bruton, RMA Sandhurst, Trinity Hall Cambridge (MA), Cuddesdon Theol Coll; *m* 10 Aug 1963, Susan, da of Sir Geoffrey Peter Shakerley (d 1982); 1 da (Rachel b 1965), 3 s (Simon b 1967, Mark b 1969, Jeremy b 1972); *Career* cmmnd RE 1955, seconded Gurkha Engrs Malaya/Borneo 1959–62, resigned cmmn as Capt 1964; ordained Sheffield Cathedral: deacon 1966, priest 1967; curate St Cuthbert's Fir Vale Sheffield 1966–69, priest i/c Bishop Andrewes' Church Southwark 1969–75, area dean Ashton-under-Lyne 1983–87, vicar St John's Hurst Ashton-under-Lyne 1975–87, hon canon Manchester Cathedral 1986, provost of Coventry 1988–2000, dean of Coventry 2000, chaplain to Mount House Residential Home for the Elderly Shrewsbury 2001–07; hon chaplain RAPC (Offrs Accounts) Ashton-under-Lyne 1977–87; memb Ctee St Helier Artificial Kidney Fund (SHAK) 1967–69, chm Tameside Aids and Services for the Handicapped (TASH) 1981–87; co-ordinator: Ambulance for the Elderly 1976–87, Holidays for Belfast Families 1977–86, Home for Homeless Girls Tameside 1977–87; tstee The Simeon Tst 2003–; Hon DLitt Coventry Univ 1996; *Recreations* cycling, skiing; *Style—* The Very Rev John Petty; ✉ 4 Granville Street, Copthorne, Shrewsbury, Shropshire SY3 8NE (tel 01743 231513)

PEYTON, Kathleen Wendy; da of William Joseph Herald, and Ivy Kathleen, *née* Weston; *b* 2 August 1929; *Educ* Wimbledon HS, Manchester Sch of Art (ATD); *m* Sept 1950 Michael Peyton; 2 da (Hilary b 1956, Veronica b 1958); *Career* author; art teacher Northampton HS 1953–55; memb Soc of Authors; *Publications* incl: as Kathleen Herald Sabre the Horse from the Sea (1947), The Mandrake (1949), Crab the Roan (1953); as K M Peyton: Flambards (1967, Guardian award, televised 1977), The Edge of the Cloud (1969, Carnegie medal), Flambards in Summer (1969), Pennington's Seventeenth Summer

(1970), A Pattern of Roses (1972), Prove Yourself a Hero (1977), A Midsummer Night's Death (1978), Flambards Divided (1981), Dear Fred (1981), Who, Sir? Me, Sir? (1983), The Sound of Distant Cheering (1985), Darkling (1989), No Roses Round the Door (1990), Late to Smile (1992), The Wild Boy and Queen Moon (1993), Snowfall (1994), The Swallow Tale (1996), Swallow Summer (1997), Unquiet Spirits (1997), Firehead (1998), Blind Beauty (1999), Stealaway (2001), Small Gains (2003), Greater Gains (2005), Blue Skies and Gunfire (2006); *Recreations* walking, gardening, sailing; *Style—* Mrs Kathleen Peyton; ✉ Rookery Cottage, North Fambridge, Chelmsford, Essex CM3 6LP (tel 01621 828 545)

PEYTON, Ven Nigel; JP (Notts 1987); s of late Hubert Peyton, and Irene Louise, *née* Ellis; *b* 5 February 1951; *Educ* Latymer Upper Sch, Univ of Edinburgh (MA, BD), Edinburgh Theological Coll, Union Theological Seminary NY (Scottish fellowship, STM); *m* 1981, Anne Marie Therese Campbell, *née* McQuillan, wid of Colin Campbell; 3 c (Emily Anne b 1972, Jennifer Rose b 1977 d 1995, Mark Niall b 1982); *Career* ordained: deacon 1976, priest 1977; chaplain St Paul's Cathedral Dundee 1976–82, diocesan youth chaplain 1976–85, priest-in-charge All Souls Invergowrie 1979–85, chaplain Univ Hosp Dundee 1982–85, vicar All Saints Nottingham 1985–91, chaplain Nottingham Bluecoat Sch 1990–92, priest-in-charge Lambley 1991–99, diocesan miny devpt advsr 1991–99, archdeacon of Newark 1999–; bishops' selector 1992–2000, proctor in Convocation 1995–, sr selector 2001–; dir Ecclesiastical Insurance Gp 2005–; *Publications* Dual Role Ministry (1998); *Recreations* music, reading, gardening, walking, real ale; *Clubs* Nottingham Forest FC; *Style—* The Ven the Archdeacon of Newark; ✉ Dunham House, Westgate, Southwell, Nottinghamshire NG25 0JL (tel 01636 817206, fax 01636 815882, e-mail archdeacon-newark@southwell.anglican.org)

PEYTON-JONES, Julia; OBE (2003); da of Jeremy Norman Peyton-Jones (d 1985), and Rhona Gertrude Jean, *née* Wood (d 2005); *b* 18 February 1952; *Educ* Byam Shaw Sch of Drawing and Painting (London Weekend TV/Byam Shaw bursary 1973–75, dip, LCAD Distinct), RCA (MA, John Minton travelling scholar); *m* 1975 (m dis 1985), Prosper Riley-Smith; *Career* painter 1974–87; fndr cataloguer 20 Century Pictures Dept Phillips Auctioneers London 1974–75, lectr in painting and humanities Edinburgh Sch of Art 1978–79, curator Atlantis Gallery 1980–81, exhbn organiser Wapping Artists Open Studios Exhbn 1981–82, exhbn organiser Tolly Cobbold Eastern Arts 4th Nat Exhbn 1982–84, exhbn organiser Raoul Dufy 1877–1953 (Hayward Gallery) 1983–84, exhbns sponsorship offr Arts Cncl and S Bank Bd 1984–87, exhbn organiser Linbury Prize for Stage Design 1986–87, curator Hayward Gallery 1988–91, dir Serpentine Gallery 1991–; Arts Cncl: purchaser Arts Cncl Collection 1989–90, Visual Arts Projects Ctee 1991–93, Visual Arts, Photography and Architecture Panel 1994–96, Film and TV Panel 1996–97; tstee: PADT 1987–88, Chisenhale Tst 1987–89, New Contemporaries 1988–90, The Place 2002–03; memb Exec Ctee Linbury Prize for Stage Design 1988–96; judge: Citibank Private Banking Photography Prize 1997, BP Portrait Award Nat Portrait Gallery 1997, 1998 and 1999, Tate Gallery Turner Prize 2000; memb Ct of Govrs London Inst 1998–2002; Hon FRCA 1997, Hon FRIBA 2003; *Recreations* opera, theatre, cinema; *Style—* Ms Julia Peyton-Jones, OBE; ✉ Serpentine Gallery, Kensington Gardens, London W2 3XA (tel 020 7402 6075, fax 020 7402 4103)

PFEFFER, Dr Jeremy Michael; s of Maurice Leslie Pfeffer, of Manchester, and Hannah, *née* Posen; *b* 23 September 1946; *Educ* Manchester Grammar, UCH London (MB BS, BSc); *m* 5 Sept 1972, Vivian Barbara, da of Dr Eric Norman, of Liverpool; 2 s (James b 1978, Paul b 1979), 1 da (Kate b 1992); *Career* house surgn Professorial Surgical Unit UCH London 1972, house physician Newmarket Gen Hosp 1972–73, sr house offr and registrar chest med Papworth Hosp Cambridge 1973–74, sr house offr psychiatry Fulbourn Hosp Cambridge 1974–75, sr house offr and registrar psychiatry Bethlem Royal and Maudsley Hosp 1975–78, sr registrar psychiatry The London and Bethlem Royal and Maudsley Hosps 1978–80; conslt psychiatrist: The Royal London Hosp 1980–96, Royal Brompton Hosp 1994–; former hon sr lectr London Hosp Med Coll, hon sr lectr Nat Heart and Lung Inst ICSTM 1996–; former examiner RCPsych, variously offr and memb psychiatric ctees at local regnl and nat level; memb RSM, FRCPsych 1988 (MRCPsych 1977), FRCP 1990 (MRCP 1974); *Books* Medicine and Psychiatry: A Practical Approach (ed with Francis Creed, 1982), Psychiatric Differential Diagnosis (with Gillian Waldron, 1987); *Recreations* music, reading, food, football; *Style—* Dr Jeremy M Pfeffer; ✉ 97 Harley Street, London W1N 1DF (tel 020 7935 3878)

PHAM, Prof Duc-Truong; OBE (2003); s of Van-Xam Pham, of Ho Chi Minh City, Vietnam and ThiNinh, *née* Vu; *b* 16 February 1952; *Educ* Univ of Canterbury NZ (BEng, PhD, DEng); *m* 19 May 1979, Paulette Thi Nga, da of Pierre Laforet, of Lyon, France; 1 da (Kim-Anh b 1982); *Career* lectr Univ of Birmingham 1979–88, prof of engrg Univ of Wales 1988–; CEng, FIEE, FREng; *Books* Robot Grippers (ed with WB Heginbotham, 1986), Expert Systems in Engineering (ed, 1988), Artificial Intelligence in Design (ed, 1990), Neural Networks for Identification, Prediction and Control (with X Liu, 1995), Intelligent Quality Systems (with E Oztemel, 1996); *Style—* Prof Duc-Truong Pham, OBE; ✉ School of Engineering, Cardiff University, PO Box 925, Cardiff CF24 0YF (tel 029 2087 4429)

PHARAOH, Paul Grenville; s of late Morton Grenville Pharaoh, of Salt, Staffs, and Kathleen Jean, *née* Bishop; *b* 16 April 1947; *Educ* Chesterfield GS, Bishop Vesey's GS, Univ of Manchester (LLB), Liverpool Coll of Commerce; *m* 27 Oct 1969, Lynn Margaret, da of Alan Edward Francis; 1 da (Claire Rachael b 9 Oct 1973), 1 s (Richard Paul b 13 Jan 1976); *Career* admitted slr 1971; ptnr Bettinsons 1973–90 (asst slr 1971–73); Shakespeares: ptnr 1990–96, memb Mgmnt Bd 1990–93, head of practice devpt 1990–93, head of Commercial Dept and Quality Team 1992–96; ptnr Educn Dept Martineau Johnson 1996–; Law Soc: memb Cncl 1990–2002, chm Entry Casework Ctee 1992–94, vice-chm Trg Ctee 1992–94, chm Legal Practice Course Bd 1993–95, memb Strategy Ctee 1993–96, chm Conf Ctee 1994–95, chm Adjudication & Appeals Ctee 1995–96, chm Compliance & Supervision Ctee 1996–98, memb Policy Ctee 1998, memb Professional Standards Appeals Panel 1998–, memb Cncl Conduct Ctee 2003–; Birmingham Law Soc: chm Young Slrs' Gp 1978–82, memb Cncl 1981–, jt hon sec 1983–88; hon sec W Midland Assoc of Law Socs 1988–90; hon sec Birmingham Settlement 1986–90 (hon treas 1973–86), chm Advsy Ctee Ind Inquiry into W Midlands Police Serious Crime Squad 1989–91; memb: Ct Univ of Birmingham 1980–90, Cncl Birmingham Medico-Legal Soc 1989–91, Competences in Undergraduate Law Courses Advsy Ctee CNAA 1990–93, Membership Ctee City 2000 1992–94, Lottery Working Gp Birmingham Repertory Theatre 1996–98, School Appeals Ctee for Cumbria 1999–2000, Corp of Lakes Coll W Cumbria 1999– (chm Audit Ctee 2000–), Irton PCC 2002–; author of various articles in legal jls; memb Law Soc 1971; FRSA; *Recreations* theatre, reading, hill walking, tennis; *Style—* Paul Pharaoh, Esq; ✉ 45 Pilkington Avenue, Sutton Coldfield, West Midlands B72 1LA (tel and fax 0121 354 4099); Martineau Johnson, No 1 Colmore Square, Birmingham B4 6AA (tel 0870 763 1314, fax 0870 763 1714, e-mail paul.pharaoh@martjohn.com)

PHARO-TOMLIN, Col John Axel; s of Axel Christian Pharo-Tomlin (d 1965), of Dane Court, St Peter's-in-Thanet, Kent, and Edith Madelaine Quayle, *née* Tomlin (d 1974); *b* 8 April 1934; *Educ* Radley, RMA Sandhurst; *m* 1, 19 Dec 1964, Joanna Marguerite Kate (d 1991), da of Lt-Col John Boileau Pemberton (d 1974), of Axminster, Devon; 1 s (Edward b 1968), 2 da (Sally (Mrs Thomas Gandon) b 1965, Alice (Mrs Stephen Reid) b 1975); m 2, 22 June 2002, Dr Christine Elizabeth Keown, da of Donald Keown, of Eastbourne, E Sussex; *Career* cmmnd 14/20 King's Hussars 1954, Adj 1961, instr RMA Sandhurst 1963, RNSC 1966, Sqdn Ldr 14/20 King's Hussars 1967, GSO 2 Singapore Dist 1968, Second-in-Cmd Duke of Lancaster's Own Yeo 1971, Bde Major 11 Armoured Bde 1972, GSO 1 Operational Requirements MOD 1975, CO 14/20 King's Hussars 1977 (despatches 1979), Col AG 16/17/18 MOD 1980, Col M1 (A) MOD 1984, ret 1986; mangr Banque Paribas London 1986–92; memb Mole Valley DC 1992–99; pres Leigh and District Cottage Garden Soc 1999; Freeman City of London 1987; FIMgt 1984–99; *Books* The Ramnuggur Boys (2002); *Recreations* country pursuits, politics, music; *Clubs* Cavalry and Guards'; *Style—* Col John Pharo-Tomlin; ✉ Peverel, Leigh, Reigate, Surrey RH2 8NX (tel and fax 01306 611247, e-mail johnpt@btinternet.com)

PHAROAH, Prof Peter Oswald Derrick; s of Oswald Higgins Pharoah (d 1941), and Phylis Christine, *née* Gahan (d 1991); *b* 19 May 1934; *Educ* Lawrence Meml Royal Mil Sch Lovedale India, Palmer's Sch Grays, Univ of London (MD, MSc); *m* 17 May 1960, Margaret Rose, da of James McMinn (d 1978); 1 da (Fiona b 1961), 3 s (Paul b 1962, Mark b 1966, Timothy b 1975); *Career* MO Dept of Public Health Papua New Guinea 1963–74, sr lectr London Sch of Hygiene and Tropical Med 1974–79, prof of public health Univ of Liverpool 1979–98 (prof emeritus 1998–); FFPHM 1980, FRCP 1997, FRCPCH 1997; *Recreations* philately, walking; *Style—* Prof Peter Pharoah; ✉ 11 Fawley Road, Liverpool L18 9TE (tel 0151 724 4896); Department of Public Health, University of Liverpool, Liverpool L69 3GB (tel 0151 794 5577)

PHELAN, Dr Martin Kennedy; s of John Lazarian Phelan (d 1986), of Ballymullen, Abbeyleix, Ireland, and Mary Prisca, *née* Kennedy (d 1964); *b* 24 October 1938; *Educ* Finchley Catholic GS, UCH London (BDS, LDSRCS, DOrth, FDSRCS, capt and colours for football), Clare Coll and Addenbrooke's Hosp Cambridge (LMSSA, MB BChir), London Coll of Osteopathic Med (MLCOM); *m* 10 June 1967, Almut Brigitte, da of Johannes Karl Wünsche; 3 s (Sean b 22 May 1968, Timothy b 11 Nov 1970, Patrick b 24 July 1976), 2 da (Marianne b 8 Sept 1969, Annette b 13 Jan 1981); *Career* formerly: various hosp jobs London and Univ of Cambridge, asst surgn Queen Elizabeth II Hosp Welwyn Garden City 1970, orthopaedic physician UCH and Middlesex Hosp 1988–90, orthopaedic physician Royal London Homoeopathic Hosp, tutor London College of Osteopathic Medicine; currently: private practitioner in orthopaedic and sports med Harley St, med offr Newmarket Race Course, lectr in psychosomatic med and history of med; sr memb list Clare Coll Cambridge, medico-legal expert witness listed in FT Law & Tax; former memb Cncl Inst of Orthopaedic Med; sec then vice-pres Anglo American Med Soc; memb: Ctee Byron Soc, Euro Atlantic Gp, Cambridge Philosophical Soc, Cambridge Univ Heraldic & Genealogical Soc; Freeman City of London 1979; FRSM; KM; *Recreations* horse riding, skiing, tennis, fishing, farming, country sports; *Style—* Dr Martin Kennedy Phelan; ✉ 148 Harley Street, London W1G 7LG (tel 020 7935 3356, fax 020 7224 0557)

PHELPS, Prof Alan David Reginald; s of (Joseph John) Reginald Phelps (d 1984); *b* 2 June 1944; *Educ* King's Coll Cambridge (MA), UC Oxford (DPhil, MA); *m* 1970, Susan Helen, *née* Marshall; 1 da (Katherine Lucy Helen b 1988); *Career* postgrad asst CERN Geneva 1966, postgrad research Univ of Oxford 1966–69, research assoc UKAEA Culham 1969; postdoctoral research fell: Univ of Oxford 1970, Imperial Coll London 1970–72; Nat Acad of Scis research assoc AFCRL USA 1972–73, research offr Univ of Oxford 1973–78; Univ of Strathclyde: lectr in physics 1978–89, sr lectr 1989–92, reader 1993, prof of plasma physics 1993–, head Dept of Physics and Applied Physics 1998–2001 (dep head 1993–98 and 2004–07); memb: Physics Coll EPSRC 1995–2007, American Physical Soc, IEEE; CPhys, FInstP (chm Plasma Physics Gp 1995–97), FRSE 1997; *Publications* author of over 200 research papers in jls, conference proceedings and reports 1966–; *Style—* Prof Alan Phelps, FRSE; ✉ Department of Physics, University of Strathclyde, John Anderson Building, Glasgow G4 0NG (tel 0141 548 3166, fax 0141 552 2891, e-mail a.d.r.phelps@strath.ac.uk)

PHELPS, Humphrey; s of Albert Phelps (d 1975), and Elsie Elizabeth, *née* Price (d 1990); *b* 5 May 1927, Glos; *m* 5 April 1951, Pauline, *née* Charlton; 4 s (Nicholas b 1952, Simon b 1955, Adrian b 1958 d 1968, Rupert b 1960); *Career* writer and farmer; memb Soc of Authors 1977; FRSL; *Publications* incl: Just Across The Fields (1976), Just Over Yonder (1977), Just Where We Belong (1978), The Forest of Dean (1982), Uncle George & Company (1984), Country Anecdotes (1990), Forest Voices (1996); *Recreations* reading, gardening, gossiping; *Style—* Humphrey Phelps, Esq

PHELPS, John Christopher; s of Anthony John Phelps, CB, of London, and Sheila Nan, *née* Rait (d 1967); *b* 25 May 1954; *Educ* Whitgift Sch S Croydon, Univ of Liverpool (LLB); *m* 13 April 1985 (m dis 1997), Isabelle Michele Jeanine, da of Maurice Albert Haumesser (d 1987), of Nancy, France; 1 s (Christopher b 1988), 1 da (Jessica b 1991); m 2, 5 April 2002 (m dis 2007), Sarah Katharine, da of Charles Reginald Pressley, of Goring-by-Sea, West Sussex; 1 da (Hannah Lily b 23 Aug 2003); *Career* admitted slr 1978; ptnr Beachcroft LLP 1986–; Freeman City of Oxford; *Books* VAT for Solicitors (with Julian Gizzi, 1993, 3 edn 2002); *Recreations* football, rugby and cricket spectator, squash and reading; *Clubs* MCC; *Style—* John Phelps, Esq; ✉ Beachcroft LLP, 100 Fetter Lane, London EC4A 1BN (tel 020 7242 1011, fax 020 7894 6660, e-mail jphelps@beachcroft.co.uk)

PHELPS, Maurice; s of Harry Thomas Phelps (d 1973), and Lilian Carter; *b* 17 May 1935; *Educ* Wandsworth Sch, CCC Oxford (BA); *m* 1960, Elizabeth Anne Hurley; 2 s, 1 da; *Career* personnel dir Heavy Vehicle Div Leyland Vehicles 1977–80, Bd memb personnel British Shipbuilders 1980–87, Br Ferries Ltd 1987–89, managing ptnr Emslie Phelps Associates and Value Through People Ltd, chm EP-Saratoga (Europe) Ltd; Freeman City of London, Freeman Worshipful Co of Watermen and Lightermen; *Publications* The People Policies Audit (1999), Measuring the People Contribution (2000), Human Resources Benchmarking (2002), A Thameside Family (2007), The Adventures of Mr Golly (2007); *Recreations* surfing, sailing, squash; *Style—* Maurice Phelps, Esq; ✉ Abbotsfield, Goring Heath, Oxfordshire RG8 7SA (tel 01491 681916); Maurice Phelps Associates (e-mail mail@mauricephelps.com)

PHILIP, Rt Hon Lord; Alexander Morrison Philip; PC (2005); s of Alexander Philip, OBE (d 1979), and Isobel Thomson Morrison; *b* 3 August 1942; *Educ* HS of Glasgow, Univ of St Andrews (MA), Univ of Glasgow (LLB); *m* 9 Oct 1971, Shona Mary, da of Kenneth Macrae, of St Andrews; 3 s (Jamie b 24 Oct 1977, Colin b 8 June 1979, Tom b 25 June 1983); *Career* slr 1967–72, admitted Faculty of Advocates 1973, QC (Scot) 1984, advocate depute 1982–85, chm Med Appeal Tbnls 1987–92, chm Scottish Land Court and pres Lands Tbnl for Scotland 1993–96, Senator Coll of Justice in Scotland (Lord of Session) 1996–2007; contrib Oxford DNB; *Recreations* piping, golf; *Clubs* Royal Scottish Pipers' Soc (Edinburgh), Hon Co of Edinburgh Golfers, Western (Glasgow); *Style—* The Rt Hon Lord Philip; ✉ Parliament House, Edinburgh EH1 1RQ (tel 0131 225 2595)

PHILIP, Prof George David Edge; s of David Philip (d 1957), and Elsie, *née* Edge (d 1995); *b* 29 October 1951, London; *Educ* Christ's Hosp, Oriel Coll Oxford (BA), Nuffield Coll Oxford (DPhil); *m* 14 Aug 1974, Carol, *née* Egan; *Career* research fell Inst of Latin American Studies London 1975–76, LSE: lectr in Latin American politics 1976–86, reader in comparative and Latin American politics 1986–2001, prof of comparative and Latin American politics 2001–, head Dept of Govt 2004–; chm Third World Politics Gp European Consortium for Political Research 1999–2003; editorial advsr Political Economy in Latin America series 2000–02; *Publications* The Rise and Fall of the Peruvian Miltary Radicals 1968–76 (1978), Oil and Politics in Latin America: Nationalist Movements and State Companies (1982), The Military in South American Politics (1985), Politics in Mexico (ed, 1985), Political Dilemmas of Military Regimes (co-ed, 1986), The Mexican

P

Economy (ed, 1988), The Presidency in Mexican Politics (1992), The Political Economy of International Oil (1994), Democracy in Latin America: Surviving conflict and crisis? (2003), Britain and Latin America (co-ed); author of jl articles and chapters; *Recreations* following political events and occasionally writing about them; *Clubs* Oxford and Cambridge; *Style—* Prof George Philip; ✉ London School of Economics, Houghton Street, London WC2A 2AE (tel 020 7955 7191, e-mail g.philip@lse.ac.uk)

PHILIP-SØRENSEN, (Nils) Jørgen; CBE; s of Erik Philip-Sørensen (d 2001), of Lillon, Skane, Sweden, and Brita Hjordis Bendix, *née* Lundgren (d 1984); *b* 23 September 1938; *Educ* Herlufsholm Kostskole Naestved Denmark, Niels Brock Commercial Sch (CPH); *m* 1, 1962 (m dis 1992), Ingrid, da of Eigil Baltzer-Andersen (d 1965); 3 da (Annette b 1963, Christina b 1965, Louisa b 1968), 1 s (Mark b 1973); m 2, 1997, Elise, da of Elias Olrik (d 1975); *Career* estab modern security industry in Europe; fndr Group 4 Securitas cos, chm Group4Securicor plc, ret 2006; pres Ligue Internationale des Societes de Surveillance; hon memb Cncl Br Security Industry Assoc; owner and chm Ecover Gp (sponsors of winning show garden Chelsea Flower Show 2005); owner: Dormy House Hotel Broadway, Strandhotellet and Ruth's Hotel Skagen Denmark; sponsoring chm: yacht Group 4 (British Steel Challenge 1992/93, Global Challenge 1994/95, BT Challenge 1996/97), yacht Team Group 4 (Around Alone Race 1998/99, Europe 1 New Man Star 2000, Vendee Globe 2000/01), yacht Ecover (EDS Atlantic Challenge 2001, Transat Jacques Vabre 2001, Route du Rhum 2002, Rolex Fastnet 2003, Transat Jacques Vabre 2003, Defi Atlantique 2003, The Transat 2004, Vendee Globe 2004, Calais 1000 Mile Race 2004, Round Britain and Ireland 2005, Fastnet 2005, Transat Jacques Vabre 2005, Velux 5 Oceans 2006); sponsor Br Team Admirals Cup 1995; Soldier of the Year award Sweden; hon citizen of Cork 1985, ambass of Skagen Denmark 1994; *Recreations* sailing (fishing vessel 'Oke'), photography, travelling, book collecting; *Clubs* Hurlingham, Reform, Mosimann's; *Style—* Jørgen Philip-Sørensen, Esq, CBE; ✉ Farncombe House, Broadway, Worcestershire WR12 7LJ (tel 01386 854252, fax 01386 858833)

PHILIPPS, Hon Roland Alexander; s of 3 Baron Milford (d 1999), of Llanstephan, Powys, and Viscountess Norwich, *née* Mary Makins, of London; *b* 20 September 1962; *Educ* Eton, Trinity Coll Cambridge (MA); *m* 1991, Felicity Kate Rubinstein, *qv*, da of Hilary Rubinstein, *qv*; 1 s (Nathaniel Alexander b 19 Dec 1996); *Career* publishing dir: Macmillan London 1989–94, Hodder and Stoughton 1994–2002; md John Murray (Publishers) 2002–, dir Hodder Headline Ltd 2003–; *Recreations* reading, food and drink; *Style—* The Hon Roland Philipps; ✉ 231 Westbourne Park Road, London W11 1EB

PHILIPS, District Judge; Justin Robin Drew; s of Albert Lewis Philips (d 1978), of Pinner, London, and Henrietta, *née* Woolfson; *b* 18 July 1948; *Educ* John Lyon Sch Harrow, Coll of Law London; *Career* called to the Bar Gray's Inn 1969; in practice Criminal Bar 1970–89, met stipendiary magistrate 1989–2000, district judge (Magistrates' Court) 2000–, chm Inner London Youth Courts 1992–2001, asst recorder of the Crown Court 1994–99, recorder 1999–2006, lead judge London's first Dedicated Drugs Court 2005–; hon sec Hendon Reform Synagogue 1990–94, tstee Tzedek Charity; memb Br Acad of Forensic Sciences; *Recreations* music, Judaic studies, attempting to keep fit; *Style—* District Judge Justin Philips; ✉ West London Magistrates Court, 181 Talgarth Road, London W6 8DN (tel 0845 600 8889)

PHILIPSON, Maj Christopher Roland; s of Major Thirlwell Philipson, MC (d 1952), of Fordham Abbey, Cambs, and Daphne, *née* Gladstone (d 1971); *b* 4 March 1929; *Educ* Eton, Sandhurst; *m* 1 Jan 1958, Mary, da of Sir Reginald MacDonald-Buchanan, KCVO, MC (d 1981), of Cottesbrooke Hall, Northampton; 2 da (Caroline b 1959, Joanna b 1961); *Career* Maj Life Gds, served in Germany, Cyprus, Egypt, Aden 1947–61; chm British Bloodstock Agency plc 1992– (md 1980–92); *Recreations* shooting, gardening; *Clubs* Turf; *Style—* Maj Christopher Philipson; ✉ Queensberry House, Newmarket, Suffolk (tel 01638 665021)

PHILIPSON-STOW, Robert Nicholas; DL (Greater London 1999); o s of Guyon Philipson Philipson-Stow (d 1983; 6 and yst s of Sir Frederick Samuel Philipson Stow, 1 Bt), and Alice Mary, *née* Fagge (d 1989); *b* 2 April 1937; *Educ* Winchester; *m* 25 Sept 1963, Nicolette Leila, er da of Hon Philip Leyland Kindersley; 2 s (Robert Rowland b 23 Sept 1970, Edward Miles b 30 April 1972), 1 da (Georgina Mary b 26 Oct 1976); *Career* Nat Serv 2 Lt RHG 1955–57; co sec Miles Druce & Co Ltd 1966–68; ptnr: George Henderson & Co stockbrokers 1970–74, Henderson Crosthwaite & Co stockbrokers 1974–86; chief ops offr Guinness Mahon Holdings plc 1986–99; chm: Thames Tube Ltd 1999–2000, Line Management Ltd 1999–2006; chm Crown and Manor Boys' Club Hoxton, govr Malvern Girls' Coll 1993–2002; FCA 1963; *Clubs* White's; *Style—* Robert Philipson-Stow, Esq, DL; ✉ Priors Court, Long Green, Gloucester GL19 4QL (tel 01684 883221)

PHILLIMORE, 5 Baron (UK 1918); Sir Francis Stephen Phillimore; 6 Bt (UK 1881); o s of 4 Baron Phillimore (d 1994), and Anne Elizabeth, *née* Smith-Dorrien-Smith (d 1995); *b* 25 November 1944; *Educ* Eton, Trinity Coll Cambridge; *m* 1971, Nathalie, da of late Michel Anthony Pequin, of Paris, France; 1 da (Hon Arabella Maroussia b 22 Feb 1975), 2 s (Hon Tristan Anthony Stephen b 18 Aug 1977, Hon Julian Michel Claud b 3 Nov 1981); *Heir* s, Hon Tristan Phillimore; *Career* called to the Bar Middle Temple 1972; steward Hurlingham Polo Assoc, pres Binfield Heath Polo Club, vice-pres Henley Soc, tstee Venice in Peril Fund; memb: Shiplake Parish Cncl, Eye and Dunsden Parish Cncl; Liveryman Worshipful Co of Fishmongers (memb Ct of Assts); Commendatore dell'Ordine della Stella della Solidarieta' Italiana; *Recreations* the arts, polo, real tennis, sailing, shooting, Venetian rowing; *Clubs* Royal Yacht Sqdn, Brooks's, Pratt's, City Barge; *Style—* The Rt Hon the Lord Phillimore; ✉ Coppid Hall, Binfield Heath, Oxfordshire RG9 4JR

PHILLIP, Brig (Roger) Martyn Hill; s of Idris Phillips (d 1985), and Bessie, *née* Hill (d 2001); *b* 16 March 1945; *Educ* Neath GS for Boys, Guy's Hosp Dental Sch (BDS), Eastman Dental Inst London (MSc); *m* 15 April 1968, Valerie, *née* Jones; 1 s (Rhodri David b 14 June 1972), 1 da (Rachel Alexandra b 30 July 1974); *Career* cmmnd RADC 1967, served UK, Germany, NI and Hong Kong, cmd consIt in oral and maxillofacial surgery Germany 1990–94, consIt advsr oral and maxillofacial surgery Army 1996–98, defence consIt advsr oral and maxillofacial surgery 1998–; defence consIt advsr on numerous ctees; memb: Central Ctee for Hosp Dental Servs, RSM, Br Orthodontic Assoc; Army Med Servs Rugby 1972, Army Med Servs Tennis 1975–95 (chm 1994–2001); GSM NI, Queen's Golden Jubilee Medal; LDSRCS 1968, DOrthRCS 1984; FDSRCPS 1981, fell Br Assoc of Oral and Maxillofacial Surgns; *Recreations* skiing, tennis, travel, pottering in the garden; *Style—* Brig Martyn Phillip; ✉ Maxillofacial Unit, Royal Hospital Haslar, Gosport, Hampshire PO12 2AA (tel 023 9276 2927, fax 023 9276 2929, e-mail martphil@dsca.mod.uk)

PHILLIPS, Prof Adrian Alexander Christian; CBE (1998); s of Eric Lawrance Phillips, CMG, of London, and Phyllis Mary, *née* Bray (d 1991); *b* 11 January 1940; *Educ* The Hall Sch, Westminster, ChCh Oxford (MA), UCL (DipTP); *m* 16 Feb 1963, Cassandra Frances Elais, da of late David Francis Hubback, CB, of London; 2 s (Oliver b 1965, Barnaby b 1968); *Career* Planning Serv Miny of Housing 1962–68, sr res offr then asst dir Countryside Cmmn 1968–74, asst to Exec Dir then head of Programme Co-ordination Unit UN Environment Programme Nairobi 1974–78, programme dir Int Union for Conservation of Nature & Natural Resources Switzerland 1978–81, dir gen Countryside Cmmn 1981–92, prof of countryside and environmental planning Univ of Wales Cardiff 1992–2001; chm: World Cmmn on Protected Areas 1994–2000, Wales Ctee RSPB 1992–98, Policy Ctee CPRE 2001–06; advsr National Heritage Meml Fund 1995–99, tstee: WWF/UK 1997–2003, The Nat Tst 2005–; hon fell Landscape Inst; MRTPI 1966, RSA 1982, FRGS 1983; *Recreations* walking, stroking the cats; *Clubs* Royal Over-Seas League; *Style—* Prof Adrian Phillips, CBE; ✉ 2 The Old Rectory, Dumbleton, Evesham, Worcestershire WR11 7TG (tel and fax 01386 882094, e-mail adrianp@wcpa.demon.co.uk)

PHILLIPS, Alice; da of David Alban, of Sedbergh, Cumbria, and Lesley Alban; *b* 1 August 1960; *Educ* Kendal HS for Girls, Newnham Coll Cambridge (MA); *m* 9 Aug 1986, Simon Phillips; 1 da (Joanna Ruth b 22 April 1999); *Career* teacher of English rising to head of English Royal Masonic Sch Rickmansworth 1983–93, dep headmistress Tormead Sch Guildford 1993–99, headmistress St Catherine's Sch Bramley 2000–; memb GSA 2000–; memb Guildford Chamber Choir; FRSA; *Recreations* singing, gardening, cookery, drum playing; *Clubs* Univ Women's; *Style—* Mrs Alice Phillips; ✉ St Catherine's School, Station Road, Bramley, Guildford, Surrey GU5 0DF (tel 01483 899605, fax 01483 899606, e-mail headmistress@stcatherines.info)

PHILLIPS, Andrew Bassett; s of William George Phillips (d 1972), and Doreen May, *née* Harris (d 1983); *b* 26 September 1945; *Educ* Newport HS, Univ of Reading (BA, MCLIP); *m* 1976, Valerie Christine, da of Alexander Cuthbert; 2 s (Edward b 1978, Simon b 1983), 1 da (Jocelyn b 1980); *Career* British National Bibliography Ltd 1969–70, National Libraries ADP Study 1970–71, Nat Cncl for Educnl Technol 1971–73; pt/t lectr West London Coll 1972–75; British Library: various positions in bibliographic servs and reference divs 1973–90, dir Humanities and Social Sciences 1990–96, head of Br Library's Review of Legal Deposit 1996–99; dir: Cedar Audio Ltd 1992–94, Saga Continuation Ltd 1993–99; memb: Governing Body City Literary Inst 1982–87, Cncl of Friends of the British Library 1990–2002 and 2004–06 (sec 2004–06), St Bart's Hosp Archives Ctee 2000–; Shakespeare's Birthplace: tstee 1991–2003, hon fell 2003–; advsr Br Univs Film and Video Cncl 2000–06; tstee Black Country Museum Devpt Tst 2004–; *Publications* The People's Heritage (ed, 2000), Inventing the 20th Century (contrib, 2000); author of various reviews and articles; *Clubs* London Press; *Style—* Andrew Phillips, Esq; ✉ 23 Meynell Road, London E9 7AP (tel 020 8985 7413, fax 020 8985 1698)

PHILLIPS, (William) Bernard; s of Stanley George Phillips (d 1968), of Sutton Coldfield, and Enid Effie, *née* Eades (d 1998); *b* 26 April 1944; *Educ* Bishop Vesey GS Sutton Coldfield, Hertford Coll Oxford (MA); *m* 1, 13 May 1967 (m dis 1986), Christine Elizabeth, da of Arthur Charles Wilkinson, of Maidstone; 3 s (Andrew b 1968, Simon b 1972, William b 1974); m 2, 1 Aug 1987, Deborah Grace, da of Ellis Green (d 1975), of Sheffield; *Career* schoolmaster 1966–67, lectr 1967–70; called to the Bar Inner Temple 1970, in practice NE Circuit 1971–, recorder 1989– (asst recorder 1984–89); legal assessor: GMC 2002–, Royal Pharmaceutical Soc 2006–; memb Inner Temple 1964; *Recreations* cookery, gardening, collecting books; *Style—* Bernard Phillips, Esq; ✉ 26 Paradise Square, Sheffield S1 2DE (tel 0114 273 8951, fax 0114 276 0848)

PHILLIPS, Caryl; *b* 13 March 1958; *Educ* The Queen's Coll Oxford (BA); *Career* author and stage/screen writer; author of articles in various jls; writing instructor Arvon Fndn 1983–; writer in residence: The Factory Arts Centre 1980–82, Literary Criterion Centre Univ of Mysore 1987, Univ of Stockholm 1989, Amherst Coll MA 1992–98 (also co-dir Creative Writing Center, visiting writer 1990–92, prof of English 1994–98, Hon AM 1995), Nat Inst of Educn Singapore 1994; Barnard Coll Columbia Univ NY: prof of English and Henry R Luce prof of migration and social order 1998–2005, dir Barnard Forum on Migration 1998–2005, dir of initiatives in the humanities 2003–05; prof of English Yale Univ; visiting lectr: Univ of Ghana 1990, Univ of Poznan 1991; visiting prof of English NYU 1993, visiting prof in Humanities Univ of West Indies 1999; visiting writer Humber Coll Toronto 1992 and 1993; consIt ed Faber Inc 1992–94, contrib ed Bomb Magazine 1993, series ed Faber & Faber 1996–, co-prodr The Final Passage (Channel 4) 1996; memb: Drama Panel Arts Cncl 1982–85, Prodn Bd BFI 1985–88, Bd Bush Theatre 1985–89, Bd The Caribbean Writer 1989; hon sr memb Univ of Kent 1988, Hon DUniv Leeds Metropolitan 1997; Br Cncl Fiftieth Anniversary fell 1984, Guggenheim Fndn fell 1992; FRSL 2000; *Awards* Arts Cncl Bursary in Drama 1984, BBC Giles Cooper Award (for The Wasted Years) 1984, Malcolm X Prize for Literature (for The Final Passage) 1985, Martin Luther King Meml Prize (for The European Tribe) 1987, Sunday Times Young Writer of the Year (for Cambridge) 1992, Rockefeller Fndn Bellagio Residency 1994, James Tait Black Meml Prize (for Crossing the River) 1994, Lannan Literary Award 1994, Nat Book Critics Circle finalist in fiction (for A Distant Shore) 2004, Cwlth Writers Prize Best Book (Eurasia) (for A Distant Shore) 2004; *Television and Radio Dramas* Lost in Music (BBC) 1984, The Hope and the Glory (BBC) 1984, The Record (Channel 4) 1985, Crossing the River (Radio 3) 1987, Writing Fiction (Radio 4) 1991, The Final Passage (Channel 4) 1996, A Kind of Home: James Baldwin in Paris (Radio 4) 2004, Hole Cristobel (Radio 3) 2005; *Television and Radio Documentaries* Welcome to Birmingham USA (Central) 1983, Black on Black (LWT) 1983, St Kitt's Independence (Radio 4) 1983, Bookmark (BBC) 1984, Sport and the Black Community (Radio 4) 1984, No Complaints - James Baldwin at 60 (Radio 4) 1985, Darker Than Blue: Curtis Mayfield (BBC) 1995, The Spirit of America (Radio 4) 1995, These Islands Now: Transformations in British Culture (Radio 3) 1995, Extravagant Strangers (Radio 3) 1997, Fifty Years of West Indian Migration (Radio 4) 1998, Martin Luther King: 'I Have a Dream' Speech (Radio 4) 2003, I Too Am America: Slavery in New York City (Radio 4) 2004; *Film* Playing Away 1987, The Mystic Masseur 2001; *Fiction* The Final Passage (1985), A State of Independence (1986), Higher Ground (1989), Cambridge (1991), Crossing the River (1993), The Nature of Blood (1997), A Distant Shore (2003), Dancing in the Dark (2005); *Non-Fiction* The European Tribe (1987), Extravagant Strangers: A Literature of Belonging (ed, 1997), The Right Set: An Anthology of Tennis Writing (ed, 1999), The Atlantic Sound (2000), A New World Order (2001); *Plays* Strange Fruit (1980), Where There is Darkness (1982), The Shelter (1983), The Wasted Years (radio play, 1985), The Prince of Africa (radio play, 1987); *Recreations* running, golf; *Style—* Caryl Phillips, Esq; ✉ c/o Georgia Garrett, A P Watt, 20 John Street, London WC1N 2DR (tel 020 7282 3106, fax 020 7282 3142)

PHILLIPS, Dr Celia Mary; er da of Percival Edmund Phillips (d 1989), and Marjorie, *née* Hughes; *b* 16 December 1942; *Educ* Dunfermline HS, Windsor Sch Hamm, High Wycombe HS, LSE (BSc, PhD); *m* 23 June 1973, Rev Preb Ronald Frederick Swan, *qv*, o s of Frederick William Swan (d 1975), of Southampton; 1 da (Elly b Dec 1974), 1 s (Toby b May 1978); *Career* LSE: lectr 1967–99, dean of undergraduate studies 1986–89, sr tutor Interdisciplinary Inst of Mgmnt 1994–99, sr fell in social statistics 1999–, assoc dean (gen course) 2004–; memb Educn Ctee ILEA 1975–78, tstee St Catherine's Cumberland Lodge Windsor 1987–2007; govr: Sir John Cass's Fndn and Red Coat C of E Secdy Sch 1997– (chm of govrs 2000–), London Guildhall Univ 2002–; bishops' selector 2003–; hon citizen Tralee 1991; FRSS; *Books* Changes in Subject Choice at School and University (1969), Statistical Sources in Civil Aviation (1979), The Risks in Going to Work (with J Stockdale, 1989), Violence at Work (with J Stockdale, 1991), The Management of a Local and an International Shopping Centre (in Cases in Marketing, ed Hanne Hartvig Larsen, 1997), Understanding Marketing: A European Casebook (ed jtly, 2000); *Recreations* choral singing (Chelsea Opera Group and others), boating, walking, reading; *Clubs* Lymington Town Sailing, Royal Lymington Yacht; *Style—* Dr Celia Phillips; ✉ Statistics Department, London School of Economics and Political Science, Houghton Street, London WC2A 2AE (tel 020 7955 7644, fax 020 7790 2518, e-mail c.phillips@lse.ac.uk)

PHILLIPS, Prof David; OBE (1999); s of Stanley Phillips (d 1979), of South Shields, Tyne & Wear, and Daphne Ivy, *née* Harris (d 2004); *b* 3 December 1939; *Educ* South Shields Grammar Tech Sch, Univ of Birmingham (BSc, PhD); *m* 21 Dec 1970, (Lucy) Caroline, da of Clifford John Scoble, of Plymouth, Devon; 1 da (Sarah Elizabeth b 1975); *Career* Fulbright fell Univ of Texas Austin USA 1964–66, exchange fell Royal Soc/Acad of Sciences USSR 1966–67; Univ of Southampton: lectr 1967–73, sr lectr 1973–76, reader

1976–80; The Royal Inst of GB: Wolfson prof of natural philosophy 1980–89, dep dir 1986–89; Imperial Coll London: prof of physical chemistry 1989–, head of dept 1992–2002, Hofmann prof of chemistry 1999–, dean Faculties of Life Sciences and Physical Sciences 2002–05, sr dean 2005–06, professor emeritus 2006–; res scientist in applications of lasers in chemistry biology and med, author of 570 scientific papers reviews and books in this field, various appearances on BBC TV and Radio incl Royal Inst Christmas Lectures for Young People with JM Thomas 1987; vice-pres and gen sec Br Assoc for the Advancement of Science 1988–89; RSC Nyholm lectr 1994, Michael Faraday Award Royal Soc 1997; FRSC 1976; *Books* Time-correlated Single-photon Counting (with D V O'Connor), Time-resolved Vibrational Spectroscopy (with G H Atkinson), Jet-Spectroscopy and Molecular Dynamics (with J M Hollas); *Recreations* music, theatre, popularisation of science; *Clubs* Athenaeum; *Style—* Prof David Phillips, OBE; ✉ 195 Barnett Wood Lane, Ashtead, Surrey KT21 2LP (tel 01372 274385); Department of Chemistry, Imperial College London, Exhibition Road, London SW7 2AZ (tel 020 7594 5716, fax 020 7594 5812, e-mail d.phillips@imperial.ac.uk)

PHILLIPS, Sir (John) David; kt (2000), QPM (1994); s of late Percy Phillips, and Alfreda, *née* Crane; *b* 1944; *Educ* Univ of Manchester (BA); *m* Nancy Wynn, da of late Eric Rothwell; 1 s (John M b 1977); *Career* Asst Chief Constable Gtr Manchester Police 1983–88, Dep Chief Constable Devon and Cornwall Constabulary 1988–93, Chief Constable Kent Constabulary 1993–2003, dir Nat Centre for Policing Excellence 2003–; pres ACPO 2001–03; hon fell Christchurch Coll Canterbury; CCMI; *Recreations* golf, cricket, walking, reading; *Style—* Sir David Phillips, QPM

PHILLIPS, David Anthony; OBE (1994); s of Garfield Phillips (d 1981), and Elvira, *née* Roberts (d 1981); *b* 27 April 1943; *Educ* Cardiff HS, Univ of Bristol Dental Sch (BDS, Paediatric Dentistry prize, Prosthetics prize, American Soc of Paedodontics award); *m* 1968, Anne, *née* Llewellyn Evans; 1 da (Rachel b 1971); *Career* house offr (oral surgery) Bristol Royal Infirmary 1965–66, dental practitioner 1966–81; Med Protection Soc: dental sec 1981–85, dep sec Dental Div 1985–89, sec Bd of Dental Protection 1989–98, dental dir Dental Protection 1989–98; int consult Dental Protection Ltd 1998–99; non-exec dir Herts NHS Tst 1994–95, chm Wellhouse NHS Tst 1995–99; chm: DenCare Ltd 1999–2003 (non-exec dir 1997–99), Denplan Ltd 2000– (memb Advsy Bd 1988–), Two-Ten Health Ltd 2000–, Oasis Dental Care Ltd 2003–; dir W E H Oakley Ltd 1996–2003; non-exec dir Oasis Healthcare plc 2004–; specialist advsr House of Commons Select Ctee on Health 1992–94; pres Metropolitan Branch BDA 1991–92; lay memb General Osteopathic Cncl 1997–2003 (chm Professional Conduct Ctee 1998–2003, treas 2001–03); memb Advsy Bd Nat Soc of Dental Practitioners USA 1988–, supporting memb FDI, fndr memb Cwlth Dental Assoc; dir George Warman Pubns 1991–; chm: CandoCo Dance Co 2000–, Cordent Tst 2002– (memb Bd 1989–); memb Bd and tstee Different Strokes Charity 2000–; elected memb GDC 2002; FRSM, fell Int Coll of Dentists, FDSRCS 2001; *Recreations* golf, gardening, oil painting, sculpture; *Clubs* East India; *Style—* David Phillips, Esq, OBE; ✉ Eaglewood, Sheethanger Lane, Felden, Hertfordshire HD3 0BG (tel 01442 252348, fax 01442 404197, mobile 07980 037272, e-mail david.aphillips@dtn.ntl.com)

PHILLIPS, Prof David George; s of George Phillips, and Doris Phillips; *b* 15 December 1944, London; *Educ* Sir Walter St John's Sch London, St Edmund Hall Oxford (DipEd, MA, DPhil); *m* 6 April 1968, Valerie Mary, *née* Bache; 2 da (Rebecca Jane b 19 May 1970, Janet Catherine b 13 May 1972); *Career* teacher: Huntingdon GS 1967–69, Chipping Norton Sch 1969–75; Univ of Oxford: tutor then lectr in educnl studies 1975–96, reader in comparative educn 1996–2000, prof of comparative educn 2000–; fell St Edmund Hall Oxford 1984–; ed: Oxford Review of Educn 1984–2003, Research in Comparative and Int Educn 2006–; series ed Oxford Studies in Compatative Educn 1992–; memb: Teacher Educn Cmmn Wissenschaftsrat 1990–91, Cncl German Inst for Int Educnl Research 1992–94 (memb Scientific Ctee 1992–98), Educnl Science Cmmn Miny of Science, Research and the Arts Germany 2003–04; chm Br Assoc for Int and Comparative Educn 1998–2000; FRSA 1987, AcSS 2002, FRHistS 2002; *Publications* incl: Zur Universitätsreform in der Britischen Besatzungszone 1945–1948 (1983), The Second Foreign Language: Past Development, Current Trends and Future Prospects (jtly, 1983), Diversification in Modern Language Teaching: Choice and the National Curriculum (jtly, 1993), Pragmatismus und Idealismus: Das 'Blaue Gutachten' und die Britische Hochschulpolitik in Deutschland 1948 (1995), Education in Germany: Tradition and Reform in Historical Context (ed, 1995), Education in Eastern Germany Since Unification (ed, 2000), Implementing European Union Education and Training Policy: A Comparative Study of Issues in Four Member States (jt ed, 2003), Educational Policy Borrowing: Historical Perspectives (jt ed, 2004), Comparative and International Education: An Introduction to Theory, Method and Practice (jtly, 2006); subject of Cross-national Attraction in Education: Accounts from England and Germany - A Festschrift for David Phillips (2006); author of numerous jl articles; *Recreations* travel, walking, art history, old books; *Style—* Prof David Phillips; ✉ St Edmund Hall, Oxford OX1 4AR; Department of Education, 15 Norham Gardens, Oxford OX2 6PY (tel 01865 274024, fax 01865 274027)

PHILLIPS, David John; QC (1997); s of Sir Raymond Phillips (d 1982), of Teddington, and Lady Phillips, *née* Evans; *b* 4 May 1953; *Educ* Rugby, Univ of Aix-en-Provence, Balliol Coll Oxford (MA); *m* Ann Nicola, da of Ronald Beckett (d 1971); 1 da (Meredith Rose b 1990), 1 s (Edward Raymond b 1993); *Career* called to the Bar Gray's Inn 1976, Wales & Chester Circuit 1977 (Arden, Atkin, Mould & Reid Prize 1977), recorder of the Crown Court 1998– (asst recorder 1994–98), head of chambers 199 Strand London 2000–06, dep High Court judge 2002–; dir Disability Law Service; legal chm FAPL Tbnl, legal chm Sports Dispute Resolution Panel, judicial chm Nat Greyhound Racing Club Appeal Tbnl; admitted to the Bar of Gibraltar 2004, memb of the Bar of the Eastern Carribean 2005; memb Ctee Barristers' Benevolent Assoc 1993– (jt hon treas 1999–); *Recreations* hill walking, cinema; *Style—* David Phillips, QC; ✉ Wilberforce Chambers, 8 New Square, Lincoln's Inn, London WC2A 3QP (tel 020 7306 0102, fax 020 7306 0095, e-mail dphillips@wilberforce.co.uk)

PHILLIPS, Sir Fred Albert; kt (1967), CVO (1966), QC; s of Wilbert A Phillips, of Brighton, St Vincent; *b* 14 May 1918; *Educ* Univ of London (LLB), Univ of Toronto, McGill Univ Montreal (MCL); *Career* called to the Bar Middle Temple; cabinet sec West Indies Fedn 1960–62, govr St Kitts, Nevis and Anguilla 1967–69; Cable and Wireless plc: sr legal advsr 1969–91, sr govt relations conslt 1992–97; chm: Grenada Telecommunications Ltd, Telecoms of Dominica until 1997, Agricultural Venture Tst; dir: Barbados External Telecommunications (former), Barbados Telephone Co, St Kitts and Nevis Telecommunications Ltd until 1997; Hon LLD Univ of the W Indies; KStJ 1968; *Recreations* writing; *Style—* Sir Fred Phillips, CVO, QC; ✉ PO Box 3298, St John's, Antigua (tel 268 461 3683, fax 268 463 0350, e-mail fredp@candw.ag)

PHILLIPS, Graham D; *Educ* Univ of Liverpool (BArch); *Career* architect; Arup Associates 1971–75; Foster & Partners: joined 1975, resident dir Hong Kong 1979–86, md Hong Kong 1985–86, ptnr 1991–, md 1993–; memb HKIA, RIBA; *Projects* incl: offices for IBM at Greenford, HongKong Bank, Sainsbury building Univ of East Anglia, Chek Lap Kok Airport Hong Kong; *Style—* Graham D Phillips, Esq; ✉ Foster & Partners, Riverside 3, 22 Hester Road, London SW11 4AN

PHILLIPS, Sir (Gerald) Hayden; GCB (2002, KCB 1998, CB 1989); s of Gerald Phillips (d 1995), of Tunbridge Wells, and Dorothy Florence, *née* Joyner (d 1992); *b* 9 February 1943; *Educ* Cambridgeshire HS, Clare Coll Cambridge (MA), Yale Univ (MA); *m* 1, 23 Sept 1967, Dr Ann Watkins, da of Prof S B Watkins (d 1966); 1 s (Alexander b 1970); 1 da (Rachel b 1974); m 2, 11 July 1980, Hon Laura Grenfell, da of 2 Baron St Just (d 1984); 1 s (Thomas Peter b 1987), 2 da (Florence b 1981, Louisa Henrietta b 1984); *Career* princ private sec to Home Sec 1974–76, dep chef de cabinet to Pres the Euro Communities 1977–79, asst sec Home Office 1979–81, under sec of state Home Office 1981–86, dep under sec of state Cabinet Office 1986–88, dep sec HM Treasy 1988–92, perm sec Dept for Culture, Media & Sport (formerly Dept of National Heritage) 1992–98, perm sec Lord Chllr's Dept and clerk of the Crown in Chancery 1998–; dir St Just Farms Ltd; sr advsr to bd Hanson Capital 2005–; memb: Inst Advanced Legal Studies, Ct of Govrs Henley Management Coll, Cncl Marlborough Coll, Fitzwilliam Museum Tst, Cncl Salisbury Cathederal; hon bencher Inner Temple 1998; *Clubs* Brooks's, Pratt's; *Style—* Sir Hayden Phillips, GCB; ✉ House of Lords, London SW1A 0PW (tel 020 7219 3246)

PHILLIPS, Prof Ian; s of Stanley Phillips (d 1942), of Whitworth, Lancs, and Emma, *née* Price (d 1960); *b* 10 April 1936; *Educ* Bacup and Rawtenstall GS, St John's Coll Cambridge (MA, MD), St Thomas' Hosp Med Sch London; *Career* emeritus prof of med microbiology and former clinical dean UMDS London, emeritus hon consult microbiologist Guy's and St Thomas' Hosp Tst; civil consult microbiology RAF 1979–2000; memb Cncl RCPath 1974–76 and 1987–90, chm Dist Med Team St Thomas' Hosp London 1978–79, chm Br Soc for Antimicrobial Chemotherapy 1979–82, memb Vet Products Ctee 1981–85, chm Assoc of Med Microbiologists 1990–91, pres European Soc of Clinical Microbiology and Infectious Disease 1995–96; memb Botanical Soc of the British Isles; Freeman City of London 1975, Liveryman Worshipful Soc of Apothecaries; hon memb Croatian Acad of Med Scis 1997; FFPHM, FRCP, FRCPath; *Books* Laboratory Methods in Antimicrobial Chemotherapy (ed with D S Reeves, J D Williams and R Wise, 1978), Microbial Disease (with D A J Tyrell, GS Goodwin and R Blowers, 1979); *Clubs* Athenaeum, RSM; *Style—* Prof Ian Phillips; ✉ Department of Microbiology, St Thomas' Hospital, Lambeth Palace Road, London SE1 7EH

PHILLIPS, Prof John Hartley; s of Frederick Hartley Phillips (d 1999), of Dorking, Surrey, and Winifred Joan, *née* Francis (d 1972); *b* 19 February 1941; *Educ* Leighton Park Sch Reading, Christ's Coll Cambridge (Darwin Prize, MA, PhD); *m* 1965, Kerstin Birgitta, da of Nils Bruno Halling; 2 da (Ingrid Kristina b 24 June 1968, Karin Anne b 8 April 1970); *Career* lectr in biochemistry Makerere Univ Kampala Uganda 1967–69, on MRC scientific staff Laboratory for Molecular Biology Cambridge 1969–74; Univ of Edinburgh: lectr in biochemistry 1974–92, prof of biology teaching 1992–, head Dept of Biochemistry and head of Biomedical Scis 1993–96, vice-provost Faculty Gp of Medicine and Veterinary Medicine 1996–2001; chair Couple Counselling Scotland 2001–07; *Style—* Prof John Phillips; ✉ 46 Granby Road, Edinburgh EH16 5NW (tel 0131 667 5322, e-mail john.h.phillips@blueyonder.co.uk)

PHILLIPS, Jonathan; s of Gilbert Reginald Phillips, of Walsall, W Midlands, and Ruby May, *née* Hughes; *b* 21 May 1952; *Educ* Queen Mary's GS Walsall, St John's Coll Cambridge (MA, PhD), Inst of Educn Univ of London (PGCE); *m* 31 Aug 1974, Amanda Rosemary, da of Ivor William Broomhead; 2 s (Ian Benjamin b 25 Oct 1980, Alexander Thomas b 22 May 1982); *Career* DTI: joined 1977, seconded to Economics Directorate CBI 1982–83, seconded as sec to Ctee of Inquiry into Regulatory Arrangements at Lloyd's 1986–87, asst sec DTI 1987–93; under sec and head Exec Agencies Directorate Dept of Transport 1993–96, dir of investigations and enforcement DTI 1996–98, dir of fin and resource mgmnt DTI 1998–2000, DG resources and services DTI 2000–02, seconded as operating strategy dir Sea Systems BAE Systems 2002, political dir NI Office 2002–05, perm sec NI Office 2005–; *Style—* Mr Jonathan Phillips; ✉ Northern Ireland Office, 11 Millbank, London SW1P 4PN (tel 020 7210 6456, e-mail jonathan.phillips@nio.x.gsi.gov.uk)

PHILLIPS, Leslie Samuel; OBE (1998); s of Frederick Arthur Phillips (d 1934), and Cecelia Margaret, *née* Newlove (d 1984); *b* 20 April 1924; *Educ* Chingford Sch, Italia Conti; *m* 1 (m dis), Penelope Noel, da of Richard Thorpe Bartley (d 1963); 2 da (Caroline Elizabeth b 30 Oct 1949, Claudia Mary b 4 Oct 1951), 2 s (Andrew Richard Bartley b 21 Nov 1954, Roger Quention b 16 Nov 1959); m 2, Angela Margaret, da of Lt-Col Alexander Scoular (d 1978); 1 step s (Daniel Alexander Scoular b 6 Sept 1970); *Career* actor, director and producer; Mil Serv DLI; vice-pres Royal Theatrical Fund, fndr memb Theatre of Comedy; began acting 1935, numerous comedy and serious roles; vice-pres Disabled Living Fndn 2002–; Evening Standard Special Award for life-long contribution to British cinema 1997, Dilys Powell Award for lifetime achievement London Critics Circle 2007; Comic Icon Loaded Magazine Awards 2003, Greatest Living Engllishman Loaded Magazine Awards 2006, Best Trouper Oldie Magazine Awards 2007; *Theatre* incl: Dear Octopus, On Monday Next, For Better For Worse, The Man Most Likely To..., Chapter 17, Pride and Prejudice, The Merry Wives of Windsor, Camino Real, Love for Love, The Cherry Orchard, Passion Play, Painting Churches, August, Woof, RSC 1996–98, On the Whole its Been Jolly Good, Naked Justice; *Television* incl: Our Man At St Mark's, Summer's Lease, Chancer, Life After Life, Who Bombed Birmingham?, Rumpole, Mr Palfrey, Thacker, The Oz Trial, Lovejoy, The Changeling, Bermuda Grace, Royal Celebration, Vanity Dies Hard, Love on a Branch Line, Honey for Tea, 2 Golden Balls, The Pale Horse, The Canterville Ghost, Edgar Wallace (series, Germany), Tales of the Crypt, L for Liverpool, Dalziel and Pascoe, One Foot in the Past, The Best of British, The Sword of Honour, Take A Girl Like You, It's Only TV But I Like It, Legends, Into The Void, Holby City, Jonathan Ross Show, Midsomer Murders, Where The Heart Is, Revolver, Unto the Wicked 2002, The Last Detective 2007; *Radio* incl: The Navy Lark, Round the World in 80 Days, Wind in the Willows, Philip and Rowena, England Their England, Great Pleasure, Maclean - The Memorex Years, Coward Centenary, Me and Little Boots, Cousin Bette, Bristow (Coward Centenary), Queen Mother 100th Birthday, Backbencher, Les Misèrables, Democracy and Language, Tales from the Backbench, Professor Branestorm, Queen Mother Memoriam, Ghosts of Albion, Cads, Dr Who, The Hitch Hiker's Guide to the the Galaxy, Princess Seraphina; *Film* over 100 films incl: Ferdinando, Les Girls, Carry On Nurse, Doctor in Love, The Longest Day, Out Of Africa, Empire of the Sun, Scandal, King Ralph, August, Day of the Jackal, Saving Grace, Cinderella, Harry Potter and the Philosopher's Stone, Tomb Raider, Thunderpants, Three Guesses, Harry Potter and the Chamber of Secrets, Carry on Columbus, Churchill - The Hollywood Years, Colour Me Kubrick, Millions, Venus (Best Supporting Actor Br Ind Film Awards 2006, nominated Best Supporting Actor BAFTA Awards 2007); *Books* Hello (autobiography, 2006); *Style—* Leslie Phillips, Esq, OBE; ✉ c/o ICM, 76 Oxford Street, London W1D 1BS (tel020 7636 6565); c/o Curtis Brown, 29 Haymarket, London SW1Y 4SP

PHILLIPS, Malcolm John; s of Thomas John Phillips (d 1978), of Pembroke Dock, Dyfed, and Hilda Mary, *née* Morse (d 1978); *b* 18 January 1945; *Educ* Pembroke GS, Univ Coll of Wales Aberystwyth (BSc), Univ of Salford (PhD); *m* 1970, Ena Christine; 1 da (Ceri b 4 June 1981); *Career* product devpt mangr Van Den Bergh & Jurgens plc 1969–71 (brand mgmnt 1971–74), mktg mangr New Product Devpt Cadbury plc 1974–78, Crookes Healthcare Ltd 1978–93 (mktg mangr Cosmetics and Toiletries then all brands, head of mktg Healthcare, dir sales and mktg), mktg dir Pfizer Consumer Healthcare 1994–2000, dir Rx to OTC Switches Europe 2000–; memb Economic Affairs Ctee The Euro Proprietary Assoc; memb Mktg Soc; *Recreations* food, wine, relaxation; *Style—* Malcolm Phillips; ✉ Rx to OTC Switches Europe, Pfizer Consumer Healthcare, IPC IS, Walton Oaks, Dorking Road, Walton-on-the-Hill, Surrey KT20 7NS (tel 01737 331561, e-mail malcolm.phillips@pfizer.com)

PHILLIPS, Capt Mark Anthony Peter; CVO (1974), ADC(P); s of Maj Peter William Garside Phillips, MC (d 1998), late 1 King's Dragoon Gds, and Anne Patricia, *née* Tiarks (d 1988); *b* 22 September 1948; *Educ* Marlborough, RMA Sandhurst; *m* 1, 1973 (m dis 1992), HRH

The Princess Royal (*see* Royal Family section); 1 s (Peter b 15 Nov 1977), 1 da (Zara b 15 May 1981); m 2, 1997, Sandy, da of James Pflueger, and Nancy Pflueger, of Honolulu, Hawaii, and former w of Stephen Clarke; 1 da (Stephanie Noelani Sanford 2 Oct 1997); *Career* 1 The Queen's Dragoon Gds 1969, Regtl Duty 1969–74, co instr RMA Sandhurst 1974–77, Army Trg Directorate MOD 1977–78, ret; student RAC Cirencester 1978–79; personal ADC to HM The Queen 1974–; memb GB three day event teams: World Championships 1970, European Championships 1971, Olympic Games Munich 1972 (team Gold medal), Olympic Games Mexico 1968 (reserve), Olympic Games Montreal 1976 (reserve), Olympic Games Seoul 1988 (team Silver medal); winner Badminton Horse Trials 1971, 1972, 1974 and 1981 (second person ever to win event four times); dir: Gleneagles Mark Phillips Equestrian Centre 1988–92, Gloucestershire TEC 1991–97, Equiland Ltd; govr Hartpury Coll until 2000; memb Royal Caledonian Hunt; patron Young Glos; int trainer and course designer; chm: British Equestrian Olympic Fund 1989–96, Br Equestrian Fedn Fund 1997–; chef d'équipe and coach US Equestrian Team 1993–; farmer; Liveryman Worshipful Cos of: Farriers, Saddlers, Loriners; Hon Liveryman Worshipful Co of Farmers; Freeman: Worshipful Co of Carmen, City of London; hon fell Br Horse Soc 2005; *Clubs* Buck's (hon memb); *Style*— Captain Mark Phillips, CVO, ADC(P); ✉ Aston Farm, Cherington, Tetbury, Gloucestershire GL8 8SW

PHILLIPS, Mark Daniel; s of Gerald Phillips, of Manchester, and Barbara, *née* Cohen; *b* 3 April 1961, Manchester; *Educ* Manchester Grammar, University Coll London (LLB), Coll of Law; *m* Jane Burns; 2 da (Hannah b 27 Sept 1996, Eve b 13 June 1998); *Career* admitted slr 1986; slr specialising in new media, video and computer games, interactive entertainment and publishing; Clifford Turner (latterly Clifford Chance) 1984–88, (also Van Dourne & Sjollema Amsterdam 1985), Harbottle and Lewis 1988– (ptnr 1990–, jt head eCommerce and Technol Gp); tstee and dir Performing Arts Labs Ltd, memb Exec Ctee Edinburgh Interactive Entertainment Festival; memb: Law Soc 1986, Soc for Computers and Law; *Recreations* family, sport, the arts; *Style*— Mark Phillips Esq

PHILLIPS, Mark Paul; QC (1999); s of Norman John Phillips, and Wendy Sharron, *née* Cashman; *b* 28 December 1959; *Educ* The John Hampden Sch High Wycombe, Univ of Bristol (LLB, LLM); *m* 11 Aug 1984, Deborah Elizabeth, da of Norman Fisher, of Castleton, Derbys; 2 da (Kathryn Mary b 22 Oct 1990, Sarah Olivia Enid b 4 Aug 1993), 1 s (Jack Nathan Robert b 7 April 1996); *Career* called to the Bar Inner Temple 1984; practising commercial law and specialising in insolvency, city and football work at the 3–4 South Square chambers 1986–, recorder 2000– (asst recorder 1998–2000); memb Cncl: Insolvency Lawyers Assoc 1999–2005 (vice-pres 2001–02, pres 2002–03), Assoc of Business Recorvery Professionals 2004– (fell 2004); memb Int Insolvency Inst 2007–; memb: Nat Youth Theatre of GB 1977–82, Br Debating Team to USA Speaking Union 1983; *Books* Byles on Bills of Exchange (contrib, 1988), Paget's Law of Banking (contrib, 1989, 1996, 2003 and 2007), Butterworth's Insolvency Law Handbook (co-ed, 1990, 1994, 1997, 1999, 2003, 2005 and 2006); *Style*— Mark Phillips, Esq, QC; ✉ 3/4 South Square, Gray's Inn, London WC1R 5HP (tel 020 7696 9900, fax 020 7696 9911, e-mail markphillips@southsquare.com or markphillipsqc@btinternet.com)

PHILLIPS, Michael David; s of Frank Phillips, and Cynthia Margaret, *née* Bond; *b* 22 June 1955; *Educ* Rickmansworth GS, Univ of Bath (BSc), PCL (DipArch); *m* 23 Aug 1986, Jane Louise, *née* Hamon; 2 s (James b 28 April 1988, Harry b 9 May 1991), 1 da (Sarah b 6 April 1995); *Career* architect; DeVerre Urban Design prize PCL 1981; Casson Conder 1974, Ralph Erskine 1975, Moxley Jenner 1978, Powell Moya 1978–79, Hutchison Locke & Monk 1981–85; ptnr Michael Phillips Assocs 1985–; prizewinner: IBA Int Soc Housing Competition Berlin, Edinburgh Royal Mall urban regeneration competition, Arndale Centre redevelopment competition; RIBA; *Style*— Michael Phillips, Esq

PHILLIPS, Mike; OBE (2007); s of George Milton Phillips (d 1972), and Marjorie Phillips, of New York; *Educ* Highbury Sch London, Univ of London (BA), Univ of Essex (MA), Goldsmiths Coll London (PGCE); *partner* Dr J Owen; 2 s (Akwesi George b 17 Oct 1974, Ivan Akojo Romario b 12 July 1994); *Career* writer; teacher and community worker, ed Westindian World, educn offr BBC 1977–79, tv prodr Diverse Productions, sr lectr in media studies Univ of Westminster 1983–93, writer in residence Royal Festival Hall South Bank Centre 1996–97; freelance journalist and broadcaster BBC World Service, Radio Four, Guardian, Sunday Times, Observer; winner Silver Dagger The Crime Writers Assoc 1990, Arts Fndn Thriller Writing Fellowship 1997–98; govr Middlesex Univ 2002–; tstee Nat Heritage Meml Fund 2002–; Hon DUniv Middlesex 2001; FRSA, FRSL; *Books* Community Work and Racism (1982), Smell of the Coast (short stories, 1987), Blood Rights (1989), The Late Candidate (1990), Boyz N The Hood (1991), Notting Hill in the Sixties (1991), Whose Cities? (contrib, 1991), Shelter Anniversary Book (contrib, 1991), Point of Darkness (1994), An Image to Die For (1995), The Dancing Face (1997); as Joe Canzius: Fast Road To Nowhere (1996), A Shadow of Myself (2000), London Crossings (2001); screenplays: Bloodrights (BBC Television, 1990), The Late Candidate, Yardie (BBC), Expendable Man; *Recreations* gardening, reading, contemporary music; *Style*— Dr Mike Phillips, OBE, FRSL; ✉ c/o Harper Collins UK, 77–85 Fulham Palace Road, London W6 8JB (tel 020 8741 7070)

PHILLIPS, (David) Nicholas; s of (David) Cecil Phillips (d 1988), of Sandwich, Kent, and Megan, *née* Davey (d 2000); *b* 13 January 1953; *Educ* Dover Coll; *m* 13 Sept 1980 (m dis 2000), Anne Rosemary, da of Ernest Frank Robert Cross (d 1980), of Salfords, Surrey; 1 s (Oliver Nicholas b 1984), 2 da (Lucy Vanessa b 1987, Amelia Fleur b 1991); m 2, 9 April 2002, Angelica Anatolyevna Osipova, da of Anatoly Osipov (d 2003); *Career* admitted slr 1977; ptnr: Stephenson Harwood 1987–2003, Hill Dickinson 2003–; memb Law Soc 1977; Freeman Worshipful Co of Slrs 1980; Liveryman Worshipful Co of Shipwrights 2000; *Recreations* sailing, scuba diving, shooting; *Style*— Nicholas Phillips, Esq; ✉ 303 Cardamom Building, 31 Shad Thames, London SE1 2YR (tel 020 7407 0914); Hill Dickinson LLP, Irongate House, Duke's Place, London EC3A 7HX (tel 020 7280 9102, fax 020 7283 1144)

PHILLIPS, Nicolas Hood (Nick); s of John Henry Hood Phillips (d 1977), and Winifred Marion, *née* Shovelton (d 1994); *b* 7 August 1941; *Educ* St Paul's, St John's Coll Oxford (MA); *m* June 1969, Katherine, da of late Robert Kirk; 1 da (Clare b Dec 1971), 2 s (Christopher b June 1973, Benedict b June 1976); *Career* early posts in mktg and res (Fisons Ltd, S H Benson, AGB Research and EMI Ltd) 1962–67, res controller Granada Television 1967–73, head of res COI 1973–78, mktg servs dir Beecham Products 1978–84, dir Granada Television 1984–89, DG IPA 1989–2001, dir Hood Phillips Conslts Ltd 2002–; chm Broadcasters Audience Research Bd 2000–02; tstee Carers UK 2002–06 (vice-chm 2004–06), tstee Charities Evaluation Services 2007–; FRSA 1992, FIPA 2001, FCAM 2003; *Recreations* travel, opera, bridge, family; *Style*— Nick Phillips, Esq; ✉ 83 Elm Bank Gardens, Barnes, London SW13 0NX (tel 020 8408 0133, e-mail hoodphillips@blueyonder.co.uk)

PHILLIPS, (Jeremy) Patrick Manfred; QC (1980); s of Manfred Henry Phillips (d 1963), and Irene Margaret, *née* Symondson (d 1970); *b* 27 February 1941; *Educ* Charterhouse; *m* 1970, Virginia Gwendolyn Dwyer; 2 s (Rufus b 1969, d 1989, Marcus b 1970); m 2, 1976, Judith Gaskell Hetherington; 2 s (Tobias b 1982, Seamus b 1985), 2 da (Rebekah b 1979, Natasha b 1980); *Career* articled clerk Thomson McLintock & Co CAs 1958–61; called to the Bar Gray's Inn 1964, pracisting barr 1964–2003; head of chambers: 2 Temple Gardens 1991–98, New Court Chambers 2000–03; DTI inspr into affairs of Queens Moat House plc 1993; landowner (900 acres); owner and dir of ops of Kentwell Hall 1971–, deviser and originator of Kentwell Hall's annual re-creation of Tudor domestic life 1978–; sometime contrib to successive ed of Cooper's Manual of Auditing and Cooper's Students' Manual of Auditing; dir Care International UK 1986–98; *Books* author of various articles and pamphlets on Kentwell Hall, Tudor domestic life and heritage educn; *Recreations* Kentwell Hall, Tudor buildings, Tudor domestic life; *Style*— Patrick Phillips, Esq, QC

PHILLIPS, (Ian) Peter; OBE (2004), JP (Inner London); s of Bernard Phillips (d 1996), of Ferring-on-Sea, W Sussex, and Constance Mary Clayton (d 1984); *b* 13 October 1944; *Educ* Highgate Sch, Sorbonne; *m* 2 May 1970, Wendy, da of Maurice Samuel Berne, of London NW11; 1 s (Leo b 1972), 1 da (Kira b 1974); *Career* ptnr Bernard Phillips & Co London 1968–82, ptnr and UK head of corporate recovery services Arthur Andersen 1982–88, jt admin Br and Cwlth Holdings 1990, ct receiver estate of Robert Maxwell 1991; chm Buchler Phillips 1988–99, chm Buchler Phillips Lindquist Avey Ltd 1997–99, dir Kroll Buchler Phillips Ltd 1999–2005; dir Joint Insolvency Monitoring Unit Ltd 1997–98; treas North Kensington Neighbourhood Law Centre 1972, dir Hampstead Theatre 1991–2004 (chm 1997–2001); pres Insolvency Practitioners Assoc 1988–89; memb Lord Chancellor's Advsy Ctee on Justice of the Peace for Cities of London and Westminster, memb Br Acad of Experts; accredited Relate counsellor 2006; tstee Restorative Justice Consortium 2006–; FCA 1968, FIPA 1981, FCCA 1983; *Recreations* riding, skiing, modern jazz, baroque music, coastal path walking, photography, theatre, close-up magic; *Style*— Peter Phillips, Esq, OBE; ✉ 5 Turner Drive, London NW11 6TX (tel 07836 572277)

PHILLIPS, Peter; *Educ* Univ of Oxford (organ scholar); *m* 1997, Caroline; 1 s (Edmund b April 1997); *Career* fndr dir The Tallis Scholars (choral gp specialising in Renaissance sacred music) 1973–, co-fndr and dir Gimell Records Ltd 1981– (affiliated to Philips Classics 1996–2000); co fndr and artistic dir Tallis Scholars Summer Schs: Oakham 2000–, Seattle 2005–, Sydney 2007–; music columnist The Spectator 1983– (cricket corr 1989); contrib: Musical Times (proprietor 1995–), Early Music, New Republic, Guardian, Music and Letters, Music and Musicians, The Listener, RA Magazine, Evening Standard, BBC Music Magazine; numerous TV and radio broadcasts on progs incl Music Weekly (BBC Radio 3 and World Service) and Kaleidoscope and Today (Radio 4), Tallis Scholars and Gimell Records subject of South Bank Show documentary (LWT) 1990 and cover feature Gramophone magazine 1994; live broadcasts from BBC Proms 1988, 2001, 2003 and 2007, Edinburgh Festival 2007, Aldeburgh, Bath and Cheltenham Festivals, regular tours of Europe, US and Far East, around eighty concerts a year, broadcast from Sistine Chapel featured on Japanese and Italian TV to mark cleaning of Michelangelo's Last Judgement, collaboration with BBC 4 on Life and Music of William Byrd 2003; conducted: Dutch Chamber Choir, Collegium Vocale Gent, BBC Singers, Finnish Radio Choir, Taipei Chamber Singers, Vox of NY, Woodley Ensemble, Markell's Voices Novosibirsk, Tudor Choir Seattle; Chevalier de l'Ordre des Arts et des Lettres (France) 2005; *Recordings* incl: Josquin des Près' Missa Pange lingua and Missa La sol fa re mi (Gramophone Magazine Record of the Year 1987), Palestrina's Missa Assumpta est Maria and Missa Sicut lilium (Gramophone Early Music Award 1991), Josquin's L'Homme armé Masses (Prix Diapason d'Or 1989, International Record Critics' Award 1990), Lassus' Missa Osculetur me (Prix Diapason d'Or 1989), Victoria Requiem (Ritmo Early Music Award Spain, 1988), Rore's Missa Praeter rerum seriem (Gramophone Early Music Award and Classic FM People's Choice 1994), Tallis' Christmas Mass (1998), Live in Oxford (1998), Morales Missa Si Bona Suscepimus (2001), Gombert Magnificats (2002), John Browne: Music for the Eton Choirbook (2005, Gramophone Early Music Award 2005); *Books* English Sacred Music 1549–1649 (1991), Companion to Medieval and Renaissance Music (contrib, 1992), What We Really Do (2003); *Recreations* cooking, black and white photography, cricket, Arabia; *Clubs* Chelsea Arts, MCC; *Style*— Peter Phillips, Esq; ✉ 22 Gibson Square, London N1 0RD (tel 020 7354 0627, e-mail gibsonsq@gmail.com); 48 rue des Francs-Bourgeois, 75003 Paris, France

PHILLIPS, Richard A R; s of Sir Raymond Phillips, and Hazel, *née* Evans; *b* 26 April 1955, Teddington, Middx; *Educ* Rugby, Balliol Coll Oxford (BA, Elton Shakespeare prize); *Family* 1 s (Alexander b 1991), 3 da (Meriel b 1997, Branwen b 1997, Anna b 2004); *Career* slr specialising in railways, privatisations, public/private partnerships and project finance; ptnr Freshfields Bruckhaus Deringer 1989–; memb Law Soc; FRSA; *Style*— Richard Phillips, Esq; ✉ Freshfields Bruckhaus Deringer, 65 Fleet Street, London EC4Y 1HS (tel 020 7832 7136, e-mail richard.phillips@freshfields.com)

PHILLIPS, Richard Charles Jonathan; QC (1990); s of Air Cdre M N Phillips (d 1986), and Dorothy Ellen, *née* Green (d 1987); *b* 8 August 1947; *Educ* King's Sch Ely (King's scholar), Sidney Sussex Coll Cambridge (exhibitioner); *m* 9 Sept 1978, Alison, OBE, da of David Arthur Francis; 1 da (Ella Rose b 31 March 1995); *Career* called to the Bar 1970, specialises in town and country planning and local govt; asst Parly boundary cmmr for England; govr King's Sch Ely; *Recreations* natural history, travel, photography; *Style*— Richard Phillips, Esq, QC; ✉ Francis Taylor Building, Temple, London EC4Y 7BY (e-mail clerks@ftb.eu.com)

PHILLIPS, Prof Richard Thomas; s of Thomas Phillips (d 1983), and Connie, *née* Checketts (d 2001); *b* 13 April 1956, Dudley; *Educ* Dudley GS, Clare Coll Cambridge (MA, PhD); *m* 17 Sept 1982, Catherine Lynette, *née* MacKenzie; 1 da (Corinne Anita b 6 Dec 1993); *Career* lectr Univ of Exeter 1983–91, Univ of Cambridge 1992–, fell Clare Coll Cambridge 1992–; memb Editorial Bd Solid State Communications 1992–; author of papers in learned jls; memb: Inst of Physics 1974–, American Physical Soc 1990–; *Style*— Prof Richard Phillips; ✉ Cavendish Laboratory, J J Thomson Avenue, Cambridge CB3 0HE (tel and fax 01223 337342, e-mail rtp1@cam.ac.uk); Clare College, Cambridge CB2 1TL

PHILLIPS, Rear Adm Richard Thomas Ryder; CB (1998); s of Brig T H Phillips (d 1979), and Arabella Phillips (d 1989); *b* 1 February 1947; *Educ* Wrekin Coll, BRNC Dartmouth, RNC Greenwich; *m* 1, Sue Elizabeth, *née* Groves (d 1996); 1 da (Sara Arabella); m 2, Belinda. *née* Round Turner; 1 step s (Richard), 1 step da (Emma); *Career* joined RN 1965; served with: HMS Penelope, HMS Glamorgan; CO HMS Scimitar 1974–76; warfare offr HMS Naiad 1976–78, Lt Cdr (CO) HMS Hubberston 1978–80, exec offr HMS Apollo 1980, Cdr 1981, Cdr (Training) HMS Raleigh 1982, Directorate of Naval Plans MOD 1982–85; CO: HMS Charybdis 1985, HMS Scylla 1986; Capt 1986, asst dir of defence operational requirements MOD 1987, CO HMS Cornwall 1988–90, Capt of Royal Naval Presentation Team 1991–92, Cmdr 1992, COS Surface Flotilla 1993, CO HMS Illustrious 1993, ADC to HM The Queen 1993–95, Rear Adm 1996, ACDS Operational Requirements (Sea) MOD 1996–99, ret; dir Future Systems Marconi Naval System 1999–2000, dir BAE Systems Ops Gp 2000–02, dir BAE Sea Systems 2002–04, clerk and ceo Worshipful Co of Haberdashers 2004–; Younger Bro Trinity House 1984–; Freeman: City of London, New Orleans, Fort Lauderdale; FNI 1998; *Recreations* sailing, shooting, tennis; *Clubs* Royal Yacht Squadron, Cargreen Sailing; *Style*— Rear Adm Richard Phillips, CB, FNI

PHILLIPS, Robert; s of John Anthony Phillips (d 1985), of London, and Susan Ryka Phillips; *b* 17 March 1964; *Educ* Charterhouse, Balliol Coll Oxford, Univ of London (BA); *m* 1991, Venetia Rose, da of 2 Baron Freyberg, OBE, MC (d 1993); 2 s (Gabriel Joseph b 8 April 1995, Gideon Dylan b 20 March 1997); *Career* fndr ptnr and md Jackie Cooper PR (independent consumer PR consultancy) 1988–; clients incl: Coca Cola GB, Scottish Courage, Guinness/UDV, Oz, Procter & Gamble; awards won for products/clients incl: Wondebra, Daewoo, PlayStation 2; frequent lectr on integrated mktg communications; memb Policy Ctee Britain-Israel Public Affrs Ctee; *Recreations* football, politics and cooking; *Clubs* MCC; *Style*— Robert Phillips, Esq

PHILLIPS, Robert Sneddon (Robbie); s of William James Phillips (d 1982), and Mary Jane Sneddon (d 1983); *b* 15 September 1932; *Educ* George Heriot's Sch Edinburgh, Univ of Edinburgh (MB ChB); *m* 2 Oct 1957, Isabella Newlands (Ella), da of George Forrest (d

1969); 1 da (Gillian Moir b 16 March 1961), 1 s (Graeme Robert b 2 Nov 1964); *Career* Surgn Lt RNVR 1957–59; conslt orthopaedic surgn 1967–; contrib to numerous pubns on orthopaedic matters; memb Methodist Church; public speaker on works of Robert Burns; FBOA, FRCSEd, FRCS; *Recreations* golf (pres Cheshire Union of Golf Clubs 2005–06); *Clubs* Stockport Cricket, Hazel Grove Golf, Forty, MCC, Rotary; *Style*— Robbie Phillips, Esq; ✉ 3 Milverton Drive, Bramhall, Stockport SK7 1EY (tel 0161 440 8037)

PHILLIPS, Sir Robin Francis; 3 Bt (UK 1912); s of Sir Lionel Francis Phillips, 2 Bt (d 1944); *b* 29 July 1940; *Educ* Aiglon Coll Switzerland; *Heir* none; *Career* owner of Ravenscourt Theatre Sch Ltd Hammersmith London; *Style*— Sir Robin Phillips, Bt; ✉ 12 Manson Mews, Queen's Gate, London SW7 5AF (e-mail robin@robin39.fsnet.co.uk, website www.dramaschoollondon.com)

PHILLIPS, Prof Robin Kenneth Stewart; s of John Fleetwood Stewart Phillips, and Mary Gordon, *née* Shaw; *Educ* Royal Free Hosp (MB BS), St Mary's Hosp London (MS); *m* 14 June 1975, Janina, da of Jan and Elizabeth Nowak; 1 da (Eva b 1982), 1 s (Henry b 1984); *Career* conslt surgn St Mark's Hosp 1987– (clinical dir 2004–), sr lectr Bart's 1987–90, conslt surgn Homerton Hosp 1990–93, dean St Mark's Academic Inst 1997–2002, hon prof of colorectal surgery Imperial Coll 2000–; pres Br Colostomy Assoc 2000–05, vice-pres Section of Coloproctology RSM 2000 (pres 2006–07), dir Polyposis Registry Cancer Research UK (CRUK)1993–, hon admin dir INSIGHT (Int Soc for the Investigation of Gastrointestinal Hereditary Tumours); FRCS 1979, FRCSEd (ad eundem) 2002, FRCPSGlas 2003; *Publications* author of over 200 reviewed pubns on colorectal disorders; *Recreations* fly fishing, being walked by the dog, wine, family; *Style*— Prof Robin Phillips; ✉ St Mark's Academic Institute, St Mark's Hospital, Harrow, Middlesex HA1 3UJ (tel 020 8235 4251, fax 020 8235 4277, e-mail marie.gun@cancer.org.uk)

PHILLIPS, Siân; CBE (2000); da of David Phillips (d 1961), and Sally, *née* Thomas (d 1985); *Educ* Pontardawe GS, Cardiff Coll Univ of Wales (BA), RADA (Meggie Albanesi scholarship, Bancroft Gold medal); *m* 1, 1956 (m dis 1959), Dr D Roy; m 2, 1959 (m dis 1979), Peter O'Toole, *qv*; 2 da (Kate b 1961, Pat b 1964); m 3, 1979 (m dis 1992), Robin David Sachs, s of Leonard Sachs (d 1990); *Career* actress; former BBC News reader/announcer Wales; dir Film Wales, vice-pres Royal Welsh Coll of Music and Drama, vice-pres Actors Benevolent Fund; memb: Gorsedd of Bards 1960, Drama Ctee Arts Cncl 1970–75, Arts Cncl Touring Co Wales; govr Welsh Coll of Music and Drama, former govr St David's Theatre Tst; fell Welsh Coll of Music and Drama 1991; delivered RTE annual (Huw Wheldon) lecture on BBC TV 1993; Special Award BAFTA Wales 2000; Hon DLitt Univ of Wales 1983; hon fell: Cardiff Coll Univ of Wales 1980, Polytechnic of Wales 1988, Trinity Coll Carmarthen 1998, Swansea Coll Univ of Wales 1998; FRSA 2002; *Theatre* London prodns incl: Hedda Gabler 1959, Ondine, Duchess of Malfi 1961, Lizard on the Rock 1961, Gentle Jack 1963, Maxibules 1964, Night of the Iguana 1964 (best actress nomination), Ride a Cock Horse 1965, Man and Superman (best actress nomination), Man of Destiny 1966, The Burglar 1967, Epitaph for George Dillon 1972, A Nightingale in Bloomsbury Square 1973, The Gay Lord Quex 1975, Spinechiller 1978, You Never Can Tell 1979, Pal Joey 1979–81 (best actress in a musical nomination), Dear Liar 1982, Major Barbara (NT) 1983, Peg 1984, Gigi 1985, Thursday's Ladies 1987, Brel 1988, Paris Match 1989, Vanilla 1990, The Manchurian Candidate 1991, Painting Churches (Playhouse), Ghosts 1993 (nomination Artist of the Year, Wales), Marlene (RNT Studio) 1994, An Inspector Calls (Royale Broadway) 1995, A Little Night Music (RNT, Olivier Award nomination for Best Supporting Performance in a Musical 1996) 1995–96, Marlene (nat tour, nomination Olivier Best Actress in a Musical Award) 1996, Marlene (int tour) 1998, Marlene (Broadway, DramaDesk and Tony nominations for Best Actress in a Musical) 1999, Lettice and Lovage (UK tour) 2001, My Old Lady (Dolittle, LA) 2001–02, My Old Lady (NY) 2002, The Old Ladies 2003, The Dark (Donmar) 2004, The Unexpected Man (UK tour) 2005; *Television* drama series incl: Shoulder to Shoulder, How Green was my Valley (BAFTA Best Actress Award), Crime and Punishment, Tinker Tailor Soldier Spy, Barriers, The Oresteia of Aeschylus, I Claudius (BAFTA Best Actress Award and Best Performance Royal TV Soc), Vanity Fair, Shadow of the Noose, Snow Spider (BAFTA nomination), Emlyns Moon (1990, BAFTA Best Actress nomination), Perfect Scoundrels 1991, The Chestnut Soldier 1991 (BAFTA nomination), The Borrowers 1992, host BAFTA Wales Award Ceremony, Scolds Bridle, The Aristocrats 1999, The Magician's House (2 series) 1999 and 2000, Nikita 1999, The Last Detective, Murder Room; *Film* incl: Becket 1963, Goodbye Mr Chips 1968 (Best Supporting Actress awards), Murphy's War 1970, Under Milk Wood 1971, Dune (dir David Lynch) 1984, Valmont (dir Milos Forman) 1989, Dark River, A Painful Case (RTE), Age of Innocence (dir Martin Scorsese) 1992, Heidi (Disney), House of America (dir Marc Evans) 1997, Alice Through the Looking Glass 1998, Coming and Going 2000; *Radio* incl: Bequest to a Nation, Antony and Cleopatra, Henry VIII, All's Well That Ends Well, Oedipus, Phaedra, The Maids, A Leopard in Autumn; *Records* Pal Joey, Gigi, Peg, Bewitched Bothered and Bewildered (single), I Remember Mama, A Little Night Music, Desirée 1900, Mme Armfeldt 1996, Marlene 1997, And So It Goes (solo) 2002; *Other* Falling in Love Again (concert tour Israel and UK, cabaret engagement Fire Bird Cafe NYC) 1999 and 2000, Almost like being in Love (cabaret, RNT) 2001, Falling in Love Again (cabaret season) 2001, Divas at the Donmar 2001, Falling in Love Again (cabaret tour) 2003; *Books* Sian Phillips' Needlepoint (1987), Private Faces (autobiography, 1999), Public Places (autobiography vol II, 2001), Public Places (2003); *Recreations* gardening, drawing, needlepoint; *Style*— Miss Sîan Phillips, CBE; ✉ c/o Simon Beresford, Dalzell & Beresford, 26 Astwood Mews, London SW7 4DE

PHILLIPS, Stephen Paul; s of Alfred Phillips, and Flora, *née* Kelvin; *b* 26 November 1959, Glasgow; *Educ* Hutchesons' GS Glasgow, Univ of Glasgow (LLB); *m* 1 May 1987, Rona Cameron; 2 da (Catriona b 17 Feb 1994, Lucy b 8 March 1997); *Career* admitted slr 1982; slr specialising the public and wider not-for-profit sector; ptnr: Alexander Stone & Co 1987, Burness LLP (following merger) 1998–; dir Four Acres Charitable Tst; memb Law Soc of Scotland 1982; *Publications* incl SCVO Guide to Constitutions and Charitable Status (2006); *Recreations* skiing, hill walking, DIY, photography, piano; *Style*— Stephen Phillips, Esq; ✉ e-mail stephillips1@btinternet.com; Burness LLP, 242 West George Street, Glasgow G2 4QY (tel 0141 248 4933, fax 0141 204 1601, e-mail stephen.phillips@burness.co.uk)

PHILLIPS, Thomas Bernard Hudson (Tom); s of late Prof Arthur Phillips OBE, and Kathleen, *née* Hudson; *b* 12 August 1938; *Educ* King's Sch Canterbury; *m* 14 July 1979, Rosemary Eleanor, da of Maj R A D Sinclair (ret), of Burnham-on-Crouch, Essex; 1 s (Roland b 12 Dec 1980), 1 da (Laura b 9 May 1982); *Career* slr; State Counsel Kenya 1967–70; Herbert Smith: joined 1970, ptnr 1977–96, conslt 1996–; memb Law Soc; *Recreations* sailing, skiing, golf; *Style*— Tom Phillips, Esq; ✉ c/o Herbert Smith, Exchange House, Primrose Street, London EC2A 2HS (tel 020 7374 8000)

PHILLIPS, (Mark) Trevor; OBE (1999); s of George Milton Phillips (d 1972), of Georgetown, Guyana, and Marjorie Eileen, *née* Canzius; *b* 31 December 1953, London; *Educ* Wood Green Sch, Queen's Coll Georgetown, Imperial Coll London (BSc); *m* 25 July 1981, Asha Aline Francine, da of Padmashree Jehangir Bhownagary, of Bombay and Paris; 2 da (Sushila b 11 July 1984, Holly b 7 Jan 1988); *Career* pres NUS 1978–80; LWT: researcher (Skin, The London Programme) 1980–82, prodr (Black on Black, Club Mix, The Making of Britain, Devil's Advocate) 1982–86; reporter This Week Thames TV 1986–87; LWT: ed and presenter The London Programme 1987–99, presenter Nation 1992–93, head of current affairs 1993–94, exec prodr factual progs 1995–98; md Pepper Productions 1994–2000; memb London Assembly (Lab) London 2000–03, chair London Assembly 2000–03; chm: Cmmn for Racial Equality 2003–06, Cmmn for Equality and Human Rights 2006–; chm: London Arts Bd, Runnymede Tst 1993–98, Hampstead Theatre 1994–98, London Tourist Bd 2001, Cncl RTS 2001–, Cncl Liberty 2002–; memb Arts Cncl of England 1997–98; presenter: The Midnight Hour (BBC) 1994–97, In Living Colour (BBC) 1996–98, Crosstalk (LNN) 1996–99, The Material World 1998–99; US Prized Pieces Winner (public affrs/news) 1985, RICS Journalist and Broadcasters Award 1988, Royal Television Soc Awards 1988, 1993 and 1998; Hon MA; Hon DLitt: Westminster Univ, South Bank Univ, City Univ; memb RTS 1990; ARCS, FRSA; Chevalier de la Lègion d'Honneur 2007; *Books* Partners In One Nation (1986), Windrush: The Irresistible Rise of Multicultural Britain (co-author), Britain's Slave Trade (introduction); *Recreations* music, crosswords, America, running; *Clubs* The Groucho, Home House; *Style*— Trevor Phillips, Esq, OBE

PHILLIPS, Trevor Thomas (Tom); CBE; s of David John Phillips, and Margaret Agnes, *née* Arnold; *b* 24 May 1937; *Educ* Henry Thornton GS, St Catherine's Coll Oxford (MA), Camberwell Sch of Arts and Crafts (NDD); *m* 1, 12 Aug 1961 (m dis 1988), Jill Purdy; 1 da ((Eleanor) Ruth b 21 Jan 1964), 1 s (Conrad Leofric (Leo) b 26 Jan 1965); m 2, 26 Oct 1995, Fiona Maddocks, *qv*; *Career* artist; visiting artist and Josep Lluis Sert practitioner in the arts Carpenter Center Harvard 1993; composer of the opera IRMA (recorded twice by Obscure Records 1977 and Matchless Recordings 1988, performed at Bordeaux Festival, Istanbul Festival and ICA); writer and critic for TLS and RA Magazine; translated, illustrated, printed and published Dante's Inferno 1983, TV dir of A TV Dante for Channel 4 with Peter Greenaway (first prize Montreal Festival 1990, Prix Italia 1991); chm Royal Acad Library 1989–94, currently chm of exhbs Royal Acad; visitor Inst for Advanced Study Princeton 2005, Slade Prof of Art History Univ of Oxford 2005–06; vice-chm copyright Cncls 1984–88, hon pres S London Art Soc 1988–, pres Heatherley's Sch of Art 2004; tstee: Nat Portrait Gallery 1998, Br Museum 1999; fell London Inst 1999; hon fell: St Catherine's Coll Oxford 1992, Bretton Hall Univ of Leeds 1994; hon memb RSPP 1999; RE 1987, RA 1989 (ARA 1984) *Work in Collections* Tate Gallery, V&A, Br Museum, Nat Portrait Gallery, Br Cncl, MOMA NY, Philadelphia Museum, Library of Congress, Bibliothèque Nationale Paris, Aust Nat Gallery Canberra, Museum of Fine Arts Budapest; *Exhibitions* worldwide since 1969 incl: retrospective exhibition (Kunsthalle Basel, Germeente Museum The Hague, Serpentine Gallery London) 1974–75, portrait retrospective (Nat Portrait Gallery) 1989, N Carolina Museum 1990, retrospective (Royal Academy) 1992, new works (V&A) 1992, retrospective (Yale Center for British Art) 1993, Univ of Penn 1993, South London Gallery 1997, Dulwich Picture Gallery 1997, Modern Art Museum Fort Worth 2001; curator: Africa - The Art of a Continent (Royal Acad) 1993–95, We Are The People National Portrait Gallery 2004, Flowers Gallery London 2004, Flowers Gallery NY 2005; *Designed Tapestries* St Catherine's Coll Oxford, HQ Channel 4, Morgan Grenfell Office; *Other Work Incl* paintings, sculpture and glass screen The Ivy Restaurant, designer The Winter's Tale (Globe Theatre) 1997, translator and designer Otello (ENO, 1998), designer The Entertainer (Derby Playhouse) 2003; *Books* Trailer (1971), Works and Texts to 1974 (1975), A Humument (1980, revised edns 1987, 1997 and 2005), Heart of a Humument (1985), Where Are They Now - The Class of '47 (1990), Works and Texts Vol II (1992), A Humument - Variants and Variations (1992), Merely Connect (with Salman Rushdie, 1994), Aspects of Art (1997), Music in Art (1997), The Postcard Century (2000), Waiting For Godot (2000), We Are The People (2004), Merry Meetings (2005); *Recreations* watching cricket, collecting postcards, playing ping pong; *Clubs* Chelsea Arts, Groucho, SCCC; *Style*— Tom Phillips, Esq, CBE, RA; ✉ 57 Talfourd Road, London SE15 (tel 020 7701 3978, fax 020 7703 2800, e-mail tom@tomphillips.co.uk, website www.humument.com and www.tomphillips.co.uk)

PHILLIPS OF SUDBURY, Baron (Life Peer UK 1998), of Sudbury in the County of Suffolk; Andrew Wyndham Phillips; OBE (1996); *b* 15 March 1939; *Educ* Uppingham, Trinity Hall Cambridge (BA); *m* 1968, Penelope Ann, *née* Bennett; 2 da (Hon Caitlin, Hon Alice), 1 s (Hon Oliver); *Career* admitted slr 1964, fndr Bates, Wells & Braithwaite London 1970–; fndr Parlex Group (trans Euro lawyers' gp) 1971; fndr chm Legal Action Gp 1971, fndr and chm Citizenship Fndn 1989– (currently pres); fndr Lawyers in the Community 1987, co-fndr Solicitors Pro Bono Gp (currently pres); dir Faraday Underwriting Ltd; freelance journalist and broadcaster, "legal eagle" on BBC Radio 2 Jimmy Young Show 1975–2001; fndr memb Nat Lottery Charities Bd 1994–96; memb Bd Public Interest Research Centre, Social Audit; memb Cncl Charter 88 until 1994; memb Parly Jt Ctee on the Consolidation of Bills; memb Scott Tst 1991–2001; chllr Univ of Essex; tstee (inter alia): Gainsborough's House, Phillips Fund; patron of several charities; *Publications* The Living Law, Charitable Status - A Practical Handbook (1980, 5 edn 2003), Charity Investment - Law & Practice (jtly); *Recreations* local history, architecture and the Arts, theatre, assorted sports, books, walking; *Style*— The Rt Hon the Lord Phillips of Sudbury, OBE; ✉ River House, The Croft, Sudbury, Suffolk CO10 1HW (tel 01787 882151, fax 01787 376096); Bates, Wells & Braithwaite, 2 Cannon Street, London EC4M 6YH (tel 020 7551 7777, fax 020 7551 7800, e-mail a.phillips@bateswells.co.uk)

PHILLIPS OF WORTH MATRAVERS, Baron (Life Peer UK 1999), of Belsize Park in the London Borough of Camden; Sir Nicholas Addison Phillips; kt (1987), PC (1995); *b* 21 January 1938; *Educ* Bryanston, King's Coll Cambridge; *m* 1972, Christylle Marie-Thérèse Rouffiac, *née* Doreau; 2 da, 1 step s, 1 step da; *Career* RNVR 1956–58; called to the Bar Middle Temple 1962; jr counsel to MOD and to Treasy in Admty matters 1973–78, QC 1978, recorder of the Crown Court 1982, judge of the High Court of Justice (Queen's Bench Div) 1987–95, a Lord Justice of Appeal 1995–99, a Lord of Appeal in Ordinary 1999–2000, Master of the Rolls 2000–05, Lord Chief Justice 2005–; chm: BSE Inquiry 1998–2000, Lord Chllrs' Advsy Ctee on Public Records 2000–; vice-pres Br Maritime Law Assoc 1993–; chm: Law Advsy Ctee Br Cncl 1991–97, Cncl of Legal Educn 1992–97; memb: Advsy Cncl Inst of European and Comparative Law 1999–, Cncl of Mgmnt Br Inst of Int and Comparative Law 1999–, Advsy Cncl Inst of Global Law 2000–; visitor: Nuffield Coll Oxford 2000–05, UCL 2000–05, Darwin Coll 2005–; govr Bryanston Sch 1975– (chm of govrs 1981–); hon fell: King's Coll Cambridge 2003, Univ of London 2006; Hon LLD Univ of Exeter 1998, Hon DCL City Univ 2003, Hon LLD Univ of Birmingham 2003; hon fell Soc for Advanced Legal Studies 1999; *Style*— The Rt Hon Lord Phillips of Worth Matravers, PC; ✉ Royal Courts of Justice, London WC2A 2LL

PHILLIPSON, Brian; s of Robert Phillipson, of Yateley, Hants, and Elizabeth, *née* Conway; *b* 18 April 1953, Tynemouth, Tyne & Wear; *Educ* CCC Cambridge (MA), Open Univ (Cert); *m* 5 April 1975, Denise; 1 da (Janet Margaret b 10 Feb 1978), 3 s (Andrew Christian b 13 Sept 1979, Jonathan Joseph b 15 Aug 1988, James Richard Alexander b 20 March 1990); *Career* apprentice then various posts in technical depts BAC Warton 1971–81, posts in prodn control and manufacturing systems rising to head of dept British Aircraft Corp Preston 1981–87, head of project then project dir European Fighter Aircraft BAe Warton 1987–90, dir of projects BAe Military Aircraft Div Warton 1990–93, RCDS 1994, dir of strategy and planning British Aerospace plc 1995–96, md Eurofighter GmbH 1997–99; BAE Systems plc: md Type 45 Destroyer 2000–01, gp md Sea Systems 2002–03, gp md Major Prog Assurance 2003–04; prog mgmnt dir Eurofighter GmbH 2004–07, chief operating offr Eurofighter GmbH 2007–; memb Cncl RINA 2002–04; N E Rowe Medal RAeS 1975, BAC Portal Gold Award 1976, Katie Wingfield Award ABARC/RAeS 1979; Liveryman Worshipful Co of Engrs 2002, Freeman City of London 2002; CEng, FRAeS 1994, FRINA 2002, FREng 2004; *Recreations* garden, skiing, hiking, theatre, music; *Style*— Brian Phillipson, Esq; ✉ Eurofighter GmbH, Am Soeldnermoos 17,

P

D-85399 Hallbergmoos, Germany (tel 00 49 811 801 897, fax 00 49 811 801 552, e-mail brian.phillipson@eurofighter.com)

PHILLIPSON, Prof David Walter; s of Herbert Phillipson (d 1992), of Castle Bytham, Lincs, and Mildred, *née* Atkinson (d 1995); *b* 17 October 1942; *Educ* Merchant Taylors', Gonville & Caius Coll Cambridge (MA, PhD, LittD); *m* 1967, Laurel, *née* Lofgren; 1 s (Arthur Veric b 1970), 1 da (Tacye Elizabeth b 1978); *Career* sec/inspr Nat Monuments Cmmn Northern Rhodesia and Zambia 1964–73, asst dir Br Inst in Eastern Africa 1973–78 (pres 1994–2005), keeper of archaeology, ethnography and history Glasgow Museums 1979–81; Univ of Cambridge: dir Univ Museum of Archaeology and Anthropology 1981–2006, fell Gonville & Caius Coll 1988–2006 (emeritus fell 2006–), reader in African prehistory 1991–2001, prof of African archaeology 2001–2006; ed African Archaeological Review 1987–94; Reckitt Archaeological Lecture Br Acad 2000; FSA 1979 (treas 1987–93), FBA 2002; *Books* Mosi-oa-Tunya: a handbook to the Victoria Falls Region (ed, 1975), Prehistory of Eastern Zambia (1976), Later Prehistory of Eastern and Southern Africa (1977), African Archaeology (1985, 2 edn 1993), The Monuments of Aksum (1997), Ancient Ethiopia (1998), Archaeology at Aksum, Ethiopia, 1993–7 (2000); numerous contribs to edited vols and learned jls; *Clubs* Oxford and Cambridge; *Style*— Prof David Phillipson; ✉ 11 Brooklyn Terrace, Threshfield, Skipton BD23 5ER

PHILLIPSON, Peter; *b* 6 March 1954; *Educ* Newcastle Poly; *Career* Gillette Co: salesman/area sales mangr UK 1978–1983, brand mangr deodorants UK 1983–85, brand supervisor UK 1985–86, mktg mangr Europe 1986–88, new business devpt dir North Atlantic 1988–89, mktg dir Europe 1989–90; United Distillers (Guinness plc): mktg dir UK 1990–92, mktg dir Int 1992–94; md First Choice Holidays and exec dir First Choice Holidays and Flights plc 1994–96, Diageo plc 1996–99 (md United Distillers UK, memb bd United Distillers Ltd, memb bd Dillon's Ireland); chief exec: Eldridge Pope & Co plc 1999–2001, Tussauds Gp 2001–; non-exec dir Saga Gp Ltd; *Style*— Peter Phillipson, Esq; ✉ The Tussauds Group, Silverglade, Leatherhead Road, Chessington, Surrey KT9 2QL

PHILLIS, Sir Robert Weston; kt (2004); s of Francis William Phillis (d 2000), and Gertrude Grace, *née* Pitman (d 1999); *b* 3 December 1945; *Educ* John Ruskin GS, Univ of Nottingham (BA); *m* 16 July 1966, Jean, da of Herbert William Derham; 3 s (Martin b 1971, Benjamin b 1974, Timothy b 1974); *Career* with: Thomson Regional Newspapers Ltd 1968–69, British Printing Corp 1969–71; lectr in industrial rels Univ of Edinburgh and Scottish Business Sch 1971–75; personnel dir and subsequently md Sun Printers Ltd 1976–79; md: Independent Television Publications Ltd 1979–82 (dir 1979–87), Central Independent Television plc 1981–87 (non-exec dir 1987–91); gp md Carlton Communications 1987–91, chief exec ITN Ltd 1991–93 (dir 1982–87 and 1991–93); BBC: md World Service 1993–94, chm BBC Enterprises Ltd 1993–94, dep DG BBC 1993–97, chief exec BBC Worldwide 1994–97; chief exec Guardian Media Group plc 1997–2006 (non-exec dir 2006–), chm Guardian Newspapers Ltd 1997–2006; chm: Zenith Productions 1984–91, Trader Media Gp 1997–2006, GMG Endemol Entertainment 1997–2000, All3Media Gp Ltd 2004–; dir: PPA 1979–82, ITV Cos Assoc 1981–87, International Cncl Nat Acad of TV Arts & Sciences 1985– (vice-chm 1994–97, life fell 1998), Worldwide Television Ltd 1991–93, Jazz FM Ltd 1999–2006, Radio Investments Ltd 1999–2004, Artsworld Channels Ltd 2000–02, ITV plc 2005–; vice-pres EBU 1996–97, dir and tstee Television Tst for the Environment 1985–2006; chm: Expert Panel ITC Prog Supply Review 2002, Ind Review of Govt Cmmns 2004; RTS: memb 1988–, chm 1989–92, vice-pres 1994–2004, pres 2004–; Hon DLitt: Univ of Salford 1999, City Univ 2000, Hon DLett Univ of Nottingham 2003; hon prof Univ of Stirling 1997, hon fell Univ of the Arts London 2006, fell Hughes Hall Univ of Cambridge 2002–06; MA Cambridge 2006; FRSA 1984, FRTS 1988; *Recreations* golf, skiing, military and political history; *Clubs* Garrick, Reform, Groucho; *Style*— Sir Robert Phillis; ✉ e-mail robert.phillis@btconnect.com

PHILP, Prof Ian; s of Thomas Philp (d 1995), of Edinburgh, and Agnes, *née* Yule; *b* 14 November 1958; *Educ* George Watson's Coll, Univ of Edinburgh; *m* 1984, Anne, *née* Boyd; 2 da (Hannah Louise b 24 July 1985, Emily Kathryn b 18 Jan 1987), 1 s (Alexander Thomas b 6 April 1992); *Career* postgrad trg in geriatric med, internal med, gen practice, rehabilitation med and public health in England, Scotland and USA 1981–90; hon conslt geriatric med Univ of Southampton 1990–94, hon conslt and prof of geriatric med Univ of Sheffield 1994–; nat dir for older people Dept of Health 2000–; Nuffield fell Br Geriatrics Soc 1989; presenter How to Live Longer (BBC 1) 2006; David Wallace Medal Aust Gerontological Soc 1991, UK Hosp Dr Team of the Year (Care of the Elderly) 1998, Queen's Anniversary Prize for HE 2002; FRCPEd 1993, FRCP 1995; *Publications* Assessing Elderly People (ed, 1994), Outcomes Assessment in Elderly People (ed, 1997), Family Care of Older People in Europe (ed, 2001); *Recreations* international cinema, independent travel; *Clubs* Sheffield United FC; *Style*— Prof Ian Philp; ✉ tel 0114 222 6270, fax 0114 222 6230, e-mail i.philp@sheffield.ac.uk

PHILP, Dr Mark François Edward; s of Albert Frederic Philp, of Cumbria, and Myriam, *née* Coulon; *b* 17 May 1952, Liverpool; *Educ* Chislehurst and Sidcup GS, Univ of Bradford (BA, CQSW), Univ of Leeds (MSc), Univ of Oxford (MPhil, DPhil); *m* 9 Feb 2004, Sarah Catherine Turvey, da of Charles Robert Turvey; 1 s (Joseph b 31 July 1985), 2 da (Ruth b 5 Dec 1988, Hannah b 3 June 1993); *Career* jr research fell Jesus Coll Oxford 1980–83, fell and tutor Oriel Coll Oxford 1983–, head Dept of Politics and Int Relations Univ of Oxford 2000–; memb Advsy Bd to Wicks Ctee 2002–; memb: Political Studies Assoc 1983, American Political Science Assoc 2001; FRHistS 1998; *Books* Godwin's Political Justice (1986), Paine (1989), The French Revolution and British Popular Politics (ed, 1991), Political and Philosophical Writings of William Godwin (7 vols, ed, 1992), Napoleon and the Invasion of Britain (with A Franklin, 2003), Resisting Napoleon (2006), Political Conduct (2007); *Recreations* music, swimming, literature; *Style*— Dr Mark Philp; ✉ Oriel College, Oxford OX1 4EW (tel 01865 276595, fax 01865 278725, e-mail mark.philp@politics.ox.ac.uk)

PHILPOT, Elizabeth; da of William Edmund Devereux Massey, CBE (d 1991), of Dorking, Surrey, and Ingrid, *née* Glad-Block (d 2003); *b* 8 April 1943; *Educ* Heathfield Sch Ascot, Courtauld Inst Univ of London (BA), Univ of Glasgow (MLitt), Johann Wolfgang Goethe-Universität Frankfurt am Main (Dip); *m* 10 Sept 1977, Timothy Stephen Burnett Philpot, s of Christopher Burnett Philpot (d 1971), of Pickering, N Yorks; *Career* local govt offr LCC (later GLC and ILEA) 1962–65, asst keeper of the muniments Westminster Abbey 1968–69, admin asst Bedford Coll London 1969–70; HM Dip Serv 1970–82: third sec Brasilia Embassy, info attaché Paris Embassy; freelance lectr and art historian 1982–, lectr in history of art Univ of Surrey 1990–2003, lectr Assoc for Cultural Exchange Study Tours Cambridge 1993–94, artistic dir Musée de Faykod France 1999–; chm Reigate Branch Nat Cncl of Women of GB 1990–93, memb Nat Cncl of Women of GB Health Ctee 1988–94; Freeman City of London 1975, Liveryman Worshipful Co of Clockmakers 1983 (Steward 1989); *Publications* Judith and Holofernes: Changing Images in the History of Art (essay included in Translating Religious Texts, 1993), Mary Magdalene - Saint or Sinner? The Visual Image, and also The Triumph of Judith - Power and Display in Art (two papers in Talking it Over: Perspectives on Women and Religion 1993–95, ed jtly), The Fourth-Century Mosaics of the Roman Villa at Lullingstone in Kent (essay in KAIROS Studies in Art History and Lit in honour of Prof Gunilla Åkerström-Hougen, 1998), Susanna: Indecent Attraction/Fatal Exposure (essay in Believing in the Text, 2004), Film and Apocryphal Imitation of the Feminine: Judith of Bethulia (essay in Theology and Literature: Rethinking Reader Responsibility, ed jtly, 2006); *Recreations* art history, travel, photography, horology, theatre, music, swimming, sailing; *Style*— Mrs Timothy Philpot; ✉ Ivinghoe, 9 Croft Avenue, Dorking, Surrey RH4 1LN (tel and fax 01306 882739, e-mail elizabethphilpot@aol.com)

PHILPOTTS, Paul; s of Raymond Dennis Philpotts (d 1987), and Ruby Elizabeth May, *née* Richards (d 1973); *b* 22 July 1957; *Educ* Eton, Univ of Durham (BSc); *m* 22 May 1982, Joanna Stephanie, da of Gerald Hearley; 1 da (Alexandra Lucy b 29 Oct 1987); *Career* asst ed: Control & Instrumentation 1979–81, Computer Systems 1981–82; ed Food Processing 1983; mktg mangr Techpress Publishing 1983–85, account gp dir Hill & Knowlton 1986–88, sr conslt Shandwick Consultants 1988–89, mktg dir IML Group 1989–92, dir Shandwick Consultants 1992–94, divnl md Burson-Marsteller 1994–96, md Burson-Marsteller UK 1996–98, dir Burson-Marsteller Europe 1996–98, Euro pres Ogilvy PR Worldwide 1998–2000, jt chief exec Square Mile Communications 2000–01, dir BSMG Worldwide 2001, gp chief exec IC2 Gp 2001–02, chief exec Kinross & Render 2003–04, chief operating offr DDA Gp 2004–; *Recreations* cinema, motor racing, travel; *Style*— Paul Philpotts, Esq; ✉ Grey Cedars, Station Road, Woldingham, Surrey CR3 7DD (tel 01883 653559, fax 01883 653203); DDA Group 192–198 Vauxhall Bridge Road, London SW1V 1DX (tel 020 7932 9800)

PHIN, Dr Nicholas Fulton (Nick); *b* 5 May 1958; *Educ* Kilmarnock Acad, Univ of Glasgow (MB ChB), Univ of Wales Cardiff (LLB (Legal Aspects of Med)); *Career* dir of public health: Grimsby HA 1991–92, Scunthorpe and Grimsby 1992–96, Dyfed Powys HA 1996, Telford and Wrekin Primary Care Tst, Shropshire Co; currently conslt in health protection Cheshire & Merseyside Health Protection Unit Health Protection Agency; FFPHM 1998 (MFPHM 1991); *Style*— Dr Nick Phin

PHIPPARD, Sonia Clare; da of Brig Roy Gordon Phippard, and Gillian Anne, *née* Menzies; *Educ* Wadhurst Coll, Somerville Coll Oxford; *Career* joined civil service 1981; Cabinet Office (MPO) 1981–87, Dept of Educn and Science 1987–89, princ private sec to Cabinet Sec 1989–92, project dir Next Steps 1992–94, seconded Coopers & Lybrand 1995–97, dir Central Secretariat Cabinet Office 2000–01 (dep dir 1997–99), dir of sustainable agriculture and livestock products DEFRA 2001–06, dir food and farming (EU and analysis) DEFRA 2006–; *Recreations* amateur dramatics, food, time with friends; *Style*— Miss Sonia Phippard; ✉ c/o Nobel House, 17 Smith Square, London SW1P 3JR

PHIPPEN, Peter S; s of Dennis Phippen, of Worthing, W Sussex, and Margaret, *née* Sangster; *b* 9 February 1960; *Educ* Reading Sch, Churston GS, Fitzwilliam Coll Cambridge (MA); *m* 1983, Liz, *née* Walden; 4 c (Ben b 1988, Jessie b 1991, Harriet b 1993, Sam b 2000); *Career* IPC Magazines: grad trainee 1982–83, asst publisher 1983–84, assoc publisher 1984–86, mktg mangr 1986–87; BBC Magazines: mktg mangr 1987–88, mktg dir 1988–90, publishing dir (Radio Times and others) 1990–93, md 1993–97; md BBC Worldwide (UK) 1997–98; chief exec BBC Worldwide Americas 1998–2001, md BBC Magazines 2001–; chm: Frontline Ltd, BBC Haymarket Exhibitions Ltd, Galleon Ltd, Origin Publishing Ltd; *Recreations* squash, triathlons, history, playing jazz piano, walking; *Clubs* Soho House; *Style*— Peter Phippen, Esq

PHIPPS, Dr Colin Barry; s of Edgar Reeves Phipps; *b* 23 July 1934; *Educ* Acton Co Sch, Swansea GS, UCL, Univ of Birmingham; *m* 1956, Marion May, da of Clifford Harry Lawrey; 2 s, 2 da; *Career* dep chm and chief exec Clyde Petroleum Ltd 1979–83; chm: Clyde 1983–94, Greenwich Resources plc 1989–2002, Universal Ceramic Materials plc 1993–97, Recycling Services Group plc 1996–2004, Desire Petroleum Ltd 1996–, Lawrence Industries Ltd 2002–04; MP (Lab) Dudley W 1974–79; memb: Cncl of Europe 1976–79, Western Euro Union 1976–79; chm Falkland Islands Fndn 1990–92; FGS 1956, FInstPet 1972, MIGeol 1978, CGeol 1992, FEI 2004, CSci 2005; *Clubs* Reform, Chelsea Arts; *Style*— Dr Colin Phipps; ✉ Mathon Court, Mathon, Malvern, Worcestershire WR13 5NZ (tel 01684 892267)

PHIPPS, Matthew Llewelyn; s of Michael Phipps, of Bridgend, S Wales, and Sian, *née* Morgan; *b* 9 October 1966, Cardiff; *Educ* Cheltenham Coll, Univ of Reading, Univ of Westminster, Inns of Court Sch of Law; *m* 3 April 1999, Caroline, *née* Evans; 1 da (Caitlin b 17 May 2001), 1 s (Iolo b 31 Dec 2002); *Career* admitted slr 1999; slr specialising in liquor, public entertainment, gaming and new establishment licensing; Eversheds 1995–2001, assoc Osborne Clark 2001–04, ptnr TLT Slrs 2004–; memb Law Soc 1999; *Recreations* rugby, wine, cooking; *Clubs* Cardiff and County, Newport Boat; *Style*— Matthew Phipps, Esq; ✉ TLT Solicitors, One Redcliff Street, Bristol BS1 6TP (tel 0117 917 8020, e-mail mphipps@tltsolicitors.com)

PHIPPS, Robin; *Career* Legal & General Group plc: joined 1982, IT dir 1985, memb Bd 1996–2007, gp dir sales and mktg 1996–99 gp dir retail business 1999–2001, gp dir UK ops 2001–06, gp exec dir UK 2006–07; memb Bd ABI (currently dep chm and chm Life Insurance Cncl); *Style*— Robin Phipps, Esq

PIA, Paul Dominic; WS (1971); s of Joseph Pia (d 2001), and Louise, *née* Lombardi (d 1979); *b* 29 March 1947, Edinburgh; *Educ* Holy Cross Acad Edinburgh, Univ of Edinburgh (LLB), Univ of Perugia (Dip); *m* 9 July 1977, Anne Christine, *née* Argent; 3 da (Camilla Francis b 16 Sept 1980, Roberta Anne b 19 July 1985, Sophie-Louise b 24 April 1988); *Career* slr; trainee Lindsays WS 1968–70; ptnr Burness LLP (previously W & J Burness WS) 1974– (joined 1970); memb Scottish Cons and Unionist Assoc 1969–74, chm Edinburgh S Young Cons 1969–71; dir: Imaginate (Scottish int children's festival) 1989–94, Dewar Arts Awards 2002–; memb Bd Japan Soc of Scotland 1990– (chm 1996–2000), tstee Big Issue Fndn Scotland 1998– (chm 2003–), fndr memb Scottish N American Business Cncl (dir 2000–04), tstee Baxters Fndn/Gordon & Ena Baxter Fndn 2002–, memb Corp Governance Unit IOD 2003–04, ind memb Nominations Ctee Scottish Enterprise Edinburgh & Lothian 2005–, assoc memb Scottish Fedn of Housing Assocs; chm project to create Edinburgh-Kyoto Friendship Garden at Lauriston Castle Edinburgh 2000; memb Law Soc of Scotland 1971, NP 1971; FInstD 1980; *Publications* Care, Diligence and Skill: a corporate governance handbook for arts organisations (co-author, 1990, 5 edn 2002); *Recreations* hill walking, travel, languages, oriental culture; *Style*— Paul Pia, Esq, WS; ✉ 67 Woodfield Park, Edinburgh EH13 0RA (tel 0131 441 7057); Burness LLP, 50 Lothian Road, Festival Square, Edinburgh EH3 9WJ (tel 0131 473 6106, fax 0131 473 6006, e-mail paul.pia@burness.co.uk)

PIATKUS, Judith (Judy); da of Raphael Emmanuel Assersohn (d 1988), and Estelle Freda, *née* Richenberg (d 1993); *b* 16 October 1949; *Educ* South Hampstead HS; *m* 1, 5 Dec 1971 (m dis 1985), Brian John Piatkus; 1 s, 2 da; *m* 2, 30 Dec 1990, Cyril Bernard Ashberg; 1 step da; *Career* md and publisher Piatkus Books 1979–; *Publications* Little Book of Women's Wisdom by Judy Ashberg (2001), Lovers Wisdom (2004); *Recreations* reading; *Style*— Ms Judy Piatkus; ✉ Piatkus Books, 5 Windmill Street, London W1T 2JA (020 7631 0710, fax 020 7436 7137, e-mail info@piatkus.co.uk)

PIATT, Andrew; s of Kenneth Piatt, and Edna, *née* Williams; *b* 6 June 1964, Culcheth, Cheshire; *Educ* Culcheth HS, Univ of Southampton (LLB); *m* 17 April 1993, Keren, *née* Williams; 2 s (Adam b 25 March 1996, Gareth b 13 Feb 2000); *Career* called to the Bar 1987, admitted slr 1997; non-practising barr: South Ribble BC 1987–88, St Helens BC 1988–96; ptnr DLA Slrs 1996–2003, ptnr and head of planning law Halliwells Slrs LLP 2003–; author of articles on planning law in Estates Gazette, Jl of Planning and Environmental Law; church warden Christ Church Croft; *Recreations* gardening, gym; *Style*— Andrew Piatt, Esq; ✉ Halliwells LLP, St James's Court, Brown Street, Manchester M2 2JF (tel 0161 831 2740, fax 0870 365 8024, e-mail andrew.piatt@halliwells.com)

PICARDA, Hubert Alistair Paul; QC (1992); s of Pierre Adrien Picarda (d 1985), and Winifred Laura, *née* Kemp (d 1988); *b* 4 March 1936; *Educ* Westminster, Magdalen Coll Oxford (MA, BCL, open exhibitioner), UCL (Bunnell Lewis prize for Latin verse); *m* 1, 4 March

1976 (m dis 1995), Ann Hulse, da of Stanley Stone; 1 s (Dominic Nicholas Piers b 7 March 1977), 1 da (Claudia Caroline Holly b 19 Feb 1979); m 2, 26 April 2000, Sarah Elizabeth, da of His Hon Judge Goss (d 1963); *Career* called to the Bar Inner Temple 1962, Profumo scholar 1963, admitted ad eundem Lincoln's Inn and Gray's Inn 1965, night lawyer with Daily Express and Sunday Express (Beaverbrook Newspapers) 1964–72, in practice Chancery Bar 1964–; memb Senate of Inns of Ct and Bar Cncl 1978–81; managing ed: Charity Law and Practice Review 1992–, Receivers Administrators and Liquidators Quarterly 1993–; memb Editorial Bd: Butterworths Jl of Int Banking and Fin Law, Tst Law Int, Jl of Business Law; visiting lectr in receivership law Malaysian Bar Cncl, Sabah Law Assoc and Law Socs of Singapore and Hong Kong 1994, visiting lectr in banking and derivative trading law Malaysian Bar Cncl and Advocates Assoc of Sarawak 1995, Law Soc of Singapore and Malaysian Bar Cncl 1996, visiting lectr Singapore Legal Acad 2000–01; W A Lee Equity Lecture Queensland Univ of Technol Aust 2001; hon pres Charity Law Assoc 1992–; memb: Insolvency Lawyers' Assoc, Chancery Bar Assoc, Inst of Conveyancers (pres 2000); *Books* Picarda Law and Practice Relating to Charities (1977, 3 edn 1999), Picarda Law Relating to Receivers Managers and Administrators (1984, 3 edn 2000); *Recreations* Andalusian baroque, Latin, Spain in WWII, Early Romantic music, conversation; *Clubs* Turf, Beefsteak, Pratt's, White's, Bembridge Sailing; *Style*— Hubert Picarda, Esq, QC

PICK, Prof John Morley; s of John Mawson Pick, of Ripon, N Yorks, and Edith Mary, *née* Morley; *b* 12 October 1936; *Educ* King Edward VI Sch Retford, Univ of Leeds (BA, PGCE), Univ of Birmingham (MA), City Univ (PhD); *m* 19 April 1960, Ann Clodagh, da of Sydney Simmons Johnson (d 1983), of Eastbourne, E Sussex; 1 s (Martyn b 1963), 1 da (Catherine b 1965); *Career* dir Dillington House Coll of Adult Educn and Arts Centre 1973–76, head of arts policy and mgmnt studies City Univ 1976–90, Gresham prof of rhetoric Gresham Coll City Univ 1983–88, prof of arts mgmnt City Univ 1985–91 (prof emeritus 1991–); visiting prof in arts mgmnt South Bank Univ 1997–2001, distinguished visiting scholar Univ at Buffalo NY 2006–; *Books* Arts Administration (1980), The State of The Arts (1981), The West End: Mismanagement And Snobbery (1983), The Theatre Industry (1984), The Modern Newspeak (1985), Managing The Arts? (1987), Arts in a State (1988), Vile Jelly (1991), Arts Administration: Politics, Bureaucracy and Management in the Arts (1995), Building Jerusalem: The Arts, Industry and the British Millennium (1999), Managing Britannia (2002), Mr Phipps' Theatre (2006); *Recreations* theatre, writing, comedy; *Style*— Prof John Pick; ✉ 97A South Street, Eastbourne, East Sussex BN21 4LR

PICK, Robert David Arthur; s of Werner Rolf Theodor Pick, of Claygate, Surrey, and Margaret Hermine, *née* Fischer; *b* 13 June 1942; *Educ* Charterhouse, Pembroke Coll Oxford (Holford scholar, MA); *m* 1969, Christine Elizabeth, da of John Hardy Layton Royle; 2 da (Isabel b 1972, Rebecca b 1976), 1 s (Rupert b 1974); *Career* admitted slr 1969; asst slr Macfarlanes London 1969–72; Baker & McKenzie: asst slr London 1972–74, Hong Kong 1974–76, ptnr Hong Kong 1976–81, Singapore 1981–83, London 1983–2002; memb Bar: Hong Kong 1974, Brunei 1981, Victoria Aust 1983; NP Hong Kong 1977–81; memb DTI SE Asia Trade Advsy Gp 1988–91, DTI Korea Trade Action Ctee 1999–2000; memb Bd of Govrs: Kellett Sch Hong Kong 1978–81, Tanglin Sch Singapore 1981–83, SOAS Univ of London 1993–2007 (hon treas 1996–2004); memb Cncl Percival David Fndn of Chinese Art 2004–07; Liveryman Worshipful Co of Tallow Chandlers 1992; memb Law Soc; *Recreations* gardening, music, golf; *Clubs* Oxford and Cambridge, Woking Golf, Hong Kong, Shek-O (Hong Kong), MCC (assoc memb); *Style*— Robert Pick, Esq; ✉ The Old Vicarage, Shamley Green, Guildford, Surrey GU5 0UD (tel 01483 892071, e-mail robert@pickmail.net)

PICKARD, David Keith; s of Roger Willows Pickard, and June Mary, *née* Golby; *b* 8 April 1960; *Educ* King's Sch Ely, St Albans Sch, Corpus Christi Coll Cambridge (choral scholar, MA); *m* Elizabeth, *née* Finney; 2 s (Adam b 16 Feb 1994, Oliver b 22 Feb 1996); *Career* co mangr ROH 1984–87, administrator New Shakespeare Co 1987–89, md Kent Opera 1989–90, asst dir Japan Festival 1991 1990–92, artistic administrator European Arts Festival 1992–93, chief exec Orchestra of the Age of Enlightenment 1993–2001, gen dir Glyndebourne Festival Opera 2001–; tstee Shakespeare Globe Tst 2005–; *Recreations* playing piano duets, cooking; *Style*— David Pickard, Esq; ✉ Glyndebourne Festival Opera, Glyndebourne, Lewes, East Sussex BN8 5UU (tel 01273 812321, fax 01273 814088, e-mail david.pickard@glyndebourne.com)

PICKARD, J Nigel; s of Ralph Pickard, and Jane, *née* Potts; *b* 10 March 1952, Worthing, West Sussex; *Educ* Truro Sch, Gregg Sch Southampton, Southampton Coll of Art (Dip); *m* 9 March 1974, Hazel; 2 s (Daniel b 5 Jan 1980, Matthew b 5 May 1982), 1 da (Rebecca (twin) b 5 May 1982); *Career* film ed 1972–77, floor mangr and asst dir 1977–79, prog dir 1979–83, exec prodr 1983–85, controller of children's progs TVS 1986–89, controller entertainment and drama features Scottish TV 1989–91, dir of progs Family Channel 1992–96, vice-pres prodns Flextech and gen mangr Challenge TV and Maidstone Studios 1997–98, controller CITV 1998–2000, controller CBBC 2000–02, dir of progs ITV 2002–06, dir of family and children's RDF Television 2006–; memb: BAFTA, RTS; Special Award Children's BAFTA Awards 2006; *Recreations* golf, walking, sailing, shooting; *Style*— Nigel Pickard, Esq; ✉ RDF Television, The Gloucester Building, Kensington Village, London W14 8RF (tel 020 7013 4440, e-mail nigel.pickard@rdfmedia.com)

PICKARD, Dr John; *b* 11 September 1963; *Educ* Univ of Wales at Bangor (BMus, PhD), Royal Conservatory The Hague (Dutch govt scholarship); *Career* composer; studied with William Mathias then Louis Andriessen; sr lectr Univ of Wales Bangor 1989–93, sr lectr Univ of Bristol 1993–; compositions incl: 4 symphonies (No 3 cmmnd by BBC 1996), Piano Sonata, The Flight of Icarus (cmmnd by BBC 1991, London première BBC Proms 1996), Channel Firing (premièred BBC Nat Orch of Wales) 1993, String Quartets Nos 1 and 3 (cmmnd by Britten Quartet), String Quartet No 2 (cmmnd by Allegri Quartet), String Quartet No 4 (cmmnd by Sorrel Quartet), Piano Concerto (cmmnd by Dresdner Sinfoniker) 2000, various orchestral, brass band and chamber works; *Recordings* Piano Sonata, A Starlit Dome, String Quartets Nos 2–4; *Recreations* astronomy, gardening, swimming; *Style*— Dr John Pickard; ✉ c/o Bardic Edition, 6 Fairfax Crescent, Aylesbury, Buckinghamshire HP20 2ES (tel and fax 01296 428609, website www.johnpickard.co.uk)

PICKARD, Sir (John) Michael; kt (1997); s of John Stanley Pickard (d 1979), of Epsom, Surrey, and Winifred Joan Pickard; *b* 29 July 1932; *Educ* Oundle; *m* 1959, Penelope Jane, da of Christopher Catterall; 3 s, 1 da; *Career* fin dir Br Printing Corp Ltd 1965–68, md: Trust Houses Ltd, Trust House Forte 1968–71; chm: Happy Eater Ltd (fndr) 1972–86, Grattan plc 1978–84, Courage Ltd and Imperial Brewing & Leisure Ltd 1981–86; dep chief exec Imperial Group plc 1985–86, chief exec Sears plc 1988–92 (dep chief exec 1986–88); chm: Freemans plc 1988–92, London Docklands Development Corporation 1992–98, London First Centre 1998–2001, National House-Building Cncl 1998–2002, The Housing Forum 1999–2002, Freeport plc 2001–03; non-exec dir: Brown Shipley Holdings Ltd 1986–93, Electra Investment Trust 1989–2002, Nationwide Building Society 1991–94, The Pinnacle Clubs Ltd 1992–99, Bentalls plc 1993–2001, Docklands Light Railway Ltd 1994–98, London First 1992–2002, Bullough plc 1995–2002 (chm 1996–2002), Servus Holdings Ltd (chm) 1997–2001, United Racecourses (Holdings) Ltd 1995–2003; dep chm Epsom Racecourse 2003–06; memb Ctee AA 1994–99; chm Cncl Roedean Sch 1981–90, chm Governing Body Oundle Sch 2004– (govr 1987–2000); Hon LLD Univ of East London 1997; Master Worshipful Co of Grocers 1995–96; FCA; *Recreations* sport, education; *Clubs* Walton Heath, MCC, Pilgrims', Boodle's; *Style*— Sir Michael Pickard

PICKARD, Paul Ian; s of Ivan Pickard, of Doxey, Staffs, and Mary, *née* Sutcliffe; *b* 10 August 1958; *Educ* King Edward VI GS Stafford, Stradbroke Coll Sheffield (NCTJ Cert Photography, winner NCTJ Student of the Year Award); *Career* Stafford Newsletter 1980–84, sr photographer Derby Evening Telegraph and Coventry Evening Telegraph 1984, with Wolverhampton Express & Star 1984–98, currently freelance editorial and PR photographer; staged reportage exhibition of photography Shire Hall Gallery Stafford 1998; *Awards* Kodak Royal Picture of the Year 1984, Canon/UK Press Gazette Sports Picture of the Year 1986, News Picture of the Year Ilford Photographic Awards 1989, Feature Picture of the Year Ilford Photographic Awards 1990, highly commended various awards 1991, runner up Press Photographer of the Year Ilford Photographic Awards 1991, highly commended Nat Sports Photographer of the Year 2003; *Style*— Paul Pickard, Esq; ✉ tel 01785 282637, mobile 07720 238997

PICKEN, Ralph Alistair; yr s of late Dr David Kennedy Watt Picken, TD, JP, DL, of Cardiff, and late Liselotte Lore Inge, *née* Regensteiner; *b* 23 May 1955; *Educ* Shrewsbury, Univ of Birmingham (LLB); *Career* admitted slr 1980; Trowers & Hamlins London: joined 1981, resident Muscat 1981–86, ptnr 1984–, managing ptnr 1996–99; memb: Law Soc, Int Bar Assoc, Anglo-Omani Soc, City of London Solicitors Co; *Recreations* theatre, opera, travel, wine; *Clubs* MCC, Cardiff and County, Chatham Dining; *Style*— Ralph Picken, Esq; ✉ 15 Jeffreys Street, London NW1 9PS (tel 020 7485 5121); Trowers & Hamlins, Sceptre Court, 40 Tower Hill, London EC3N 4DX (tel 020 7423 8000, fax 020 7423 8001, e-mail rpicken@trowers.com)

PICKERING, Alan Michael; CBE (2004); s of Frank Pickering, and Betty Pickering; *Educ* Exhall Grange Sch Coventry, Univ of Newcastle upon Tyne (BA); *Career* clerical offr British Railways 1967–69, head of membership servs EETPU 1972–92, ptnr Watson Wyatt 1992–; chm: Nat Assoc of Pension Funds 1999–2001, European Fedn for Retirement Provision 2001–04, Plumbing Industry Pension Scheme 2001–, Life Acad 2006–; memb Occupational Pensions Bd 1992–97 (vice-chm 1995), non-exec dir Pensions Regulator 2005–; frequent contrib to numerous periodicals; assoc Pension Mgmnt Inst 1982; *Publications* A Simpler Way to Better Pensions (2002); *Recreations* long-distance running as a participant, horse racing as a spectator, travelling at home and abroad; *Clubs* Blackheath Harriers (pres 1992–93); *Style*— Alan Pickering, Esq, CBE; ✉ Watson Wyatt Limited, 21 Tothill Street, London SW1H 9LL (tel 020 7222 8033, fax 020 7222 9182, e-mail alan.pickering@eu.watsonwyatt.com)

PICKERING, Donald Ellis; s of John Joseph Pickering (d 1978), of Newcastle upon Tyne, and Edith, *née* Ellis (d 1983); *b* 15 November 1933; *Educ* privately; *Career* actor; trained Old Vic Theatre Sch under Michel St Denis 1950–52, Old Vic Co 1952, Stratford 1954, Bristol Old Vic 1957–59, RNT 1987–90 and 1995; *Theatre* West End incl: Poor Bitos, School for Scandal (and NY), Case in Question, Conduct Unbecoming (nominated Tony Award), Male of the Species, Hay Fever; RNT credits incl: The Magistrate, Le Misanthrope, Mother Courage; *Television* incl: The Pallisers, Private Lives, Irish RM, Yes Prime Minister, Return to Treasure Island; *Films* incl: Nothing but the Best, Thirty Nine Steps, Half Moon Street, The Man Who Knew Too Little, Monk Dawson, Paradise; *Recreations* gardening, riding, tennis; *Style*— Donald Pickering, Esq; ✉ Back Court, Manor House, Eastleach Turville, Cirencester, Gloucestershire GL7 3NQ; (tel 01367 850 476)

PICKERING, John; s of Leslie Pickering (d 1982), and Audrey Margaret, *née* Green; *b* 23 July 1955, Rotherham, S Yorks; *Educ* Oakwood Comp Sch Rotherham, Thomas Rotherham Sixth Form Coll Rotherham, Univ of Manchester (LLB), Coll of Law Chester; *m* 20 Nov 1981, Julie; 1 da (Lauren Sarah b 26 Aug 1984), 1 s (Joseph John b 2 Feb 1989); *Career* admitted slr 1979; slr specialising in personal injury particularly clinical negligence and catastrophic injury cases; ptnr Irwin Mitchell 1990– (joined as articled clerk, currently nat head Personal Injury Dept); slr rep CMO's Advsy Gp on reform of the law on clinical negligence; pres Pan European Orgn of Personal Injury Lawyers (PEOPIL), sr fell Assoc of Personal Injury Lawyers (formerly Coll of Personal Injury Law), govr Assoc of Trial Lawyers of America, tstee Neurocare; memb: Aust Lawyers Alliance, SA Assoc of Personal Injury Lawyers; author of various articles for legal jls, co-ed Jordans Civil Court Service; memb: Law Soc (memb and assessor for Personal Injury Panel, memb Clinical Negligence Panel), Action against Medical Accidents (AvMA, memb Clinical Negligence Panel); *Recreations* theatre, music, squash, motor sports, golf; *Style*— John Pickering, Esq; ✉ Irwin Mitchell, Riverside East, 2 Millsands, Sheffield S3 8DT (tel 0870 1500 100, e-mail john.pickering@irwinmitchell.com)

PICKERING, Prof John Frederick; s of William Frederick Pickering (d 1973), of Slough, Berks, and Jean Mary, *née* Clarke (d 2005); *b* 26 December 1939; *Educ* Slough GS, UCL (BSc, PhD, DSc); *m* 25 March 1967, Jane Rosamund, da of Victor William George Day (d 1993), of Bristol; 2 da (Rachel b 1970, Catherine b 1974); *Career* industrial market research exec 1961–62; lectr: Univ of Durham 1964–66, Univ of Sussex 1966–73; sr directing staff Admin Staff Coll Henley 1974–75; UMIST: prof of industrial economics 1975–88, vice-princ 1983–85, dean 1985–87; Univ of Portsmouth (formerly Portsmouth Poly): vice-pres 1988–90, actg pres 1990–91, dep pres 1991–92, dep vice-chllr 1992–94; conslt economist 1994–; prof of business strategy Univ of Bath 1997–2000; visiting prof: Univ of Durham Business Sch 1995–98, Univ of Southampton Sch of Mgmnt 2001–04; memb: Retail Prices Index Advsy Ctee 1974–95, MMC 1990–99, Competition Cmmn Appeal Tbnl 2000–03, Competition Appeal Tbnl 2003–; memb Gen Synod C of E 1980–90, church cmmr 1983–90; pres BCMS-Crosslinks 1986–92; non-exec dir Staniland Hall Ltd 1987–94; tstee and chm VTCT 2004–06; memb Royal Economic Soc 1973, MInstD; FIMgt 1987, FRSA 1998; *Books* Resale Price Maintenance in Practice (1967), The Small Firm in the Hotel and Catering Industry (jtly, 1971), Industrial Structure and Market Conduct (1974), The Acquisition of Consumer Durables (1977), The Economic Management of the Firm (jt ed, 1984); *Recreations* cricket, classical music, theatre; *Clubs* Royal Cwlth Soc; *Style*— Prof J F Pickering; ✉ 1 The Fairway, Rowlands Castle, Hampshire PO9 6AQ (tel 023 9241 2007, fax 023 9241 3385)

PICKERING, John Michael; s of late John Dennis Pickering, of Rough Hill, Lache, Chester, and Margaret, *née* Owen; *b* 25 January 1941; *Educ* Rossall Sch Fleetwood; *m* 20 Sept 1947, Elizabeth Josephine, *née* Tatton; 1 s (John Alexander b 3 Nov 1970), 1 da (Christine Elizabeth b 10 July 1972); *Career* farmer (900 acres with 800 cows Cheshire, 1500 acres Anglesey), dairy food processor and property developer; High Sheriff Cheshire 1995–96; memb Worshipful Co of Farmers; *Recreations* rugby, shooting, skiing and all country sports; *Style*— John Pickering, Esq; ✉ Rough Hill, Lache, Chester, Cheshire CH4 9JS (tel 01244 671011)

PICKERING, Paul Granville; s of Arthur Samuel Pickering (d 1962), of Rotherham, S Yorks, and Lorna Cynthia, *née* Groocock; *b* 9 May 1952; *Educ* Royal Masonic Schs Bushey, Univ of Leicester (BA, Sports colours); *m* 11 Dec 1983, Alison, da of Albert Leslie Beckett; 1 da (Persephone Alyce b 1 Feb 1993); *Career* Thomson Graduate Trg Scheme, Latin America corr Now! magazine, columnist The Times, Sunday Times and Punch 1981–84, novelist 1984–; Br Cncl reading tour of France 1995; included in Best of Young British Novelists (WH Smith Top 10) 1989; memb Soc of Authors; FRGS; *Novels* Wild About Harry (1985), Perfect English (1986), The Blue Gate of Babylon (1989, New York Times Notable Book of the Year), Charlie Peace (1991); *Anthologies* Winter's Tales (short story, 1989), Hakakawa Japan (short story, 1993) Oldie Magazine (short stories, 1999); *Plays* After Hamlet (New Grove Theatre, 1994), Beach (1998), Walk Her Home (Louvre Paris, 1999); *Recreations* scuba diving, bird-watching; *Clubs* Holland Park Lawn Tennis; *Style*—

Paul Pickering, Esq; ✉ c/o Caroline Wood, Felicity Bryan Agency, 2A North Parade, Banbury Road, Oxford OX2 6LX (tel 01865 513816, e-mail caroline@felicitybryan.com)

PICKERING, Robert Mark; s of Richard Bray Pickering, and Lorna Gwendolyne, *née* Browne; *b* 30 November 1959; *Educ* Westminster, Lincoln Coll Oxford (MA); *Career* admitted slr 1984; asst slr Allen & Overy 1982–85, with Cazenove & Co 1985–2001 (ptnr 1993), chief exec Cazenove Group plc 2002–, chief exec JP Morgan Cazenove and Cazenove Group Ltd 2005–; *Recreations* fishing, art, wine; *Clubs* Vincent's (Oxford), Flyfishers', Links (NY); *Style*— Robert Pickering, Esq; ✉ JP Morgan Cazenove Ltd, 20 Moorgate, London EC2R 6DA (tel 020 7588 2828)

PICKERING OF KINTRADWELL, Ralph Bernard; s of George Cecil Pickering (d 2007), of Lockerbie, Dumfriesshire, and Janet, *née* McEachern; *b* 21 February 1958; *Educ* Dumfries Acad, Napier Univ (BA); *m* 26 April 1986 (m dis 2006), Fiona Margaret, da of Dr John Richard Campion Stubbs, of Arncliffe, Dumfries; 1 s (Lewis John Fitzyork b 28 Oct 1990), 1 da (Ellen Mary Elizabeth b 5 May 1993); *Career* land manager and accountant; 5th laird of Kintradwell 1986–; land mangr Smiths Gore 1979–85, sr ptnr Pickering Gordon & Co 1985–91, with Norwich Union 1991–93, with Sony IT Europe 2001–; prop Fitzyork Estates 1986–, Decor 8 Interior Design Belgium 2003–05; dir: Nith Tyne Developments Ltd 1988–91, Harp Art Records USA 1996–2002; chm: Friends of Conheath Chapel Ltd 2002–; dir Tradewinds Africa Ltd 2002–07, chm Pickering Mensah a Amoah (Ghana) Ltd; elder Kirkbean Church 1990– (memb Congregational Bd 1987–2001, property convenor 1995–2001), elder St Andrews Church Brussels 2001– (property convenor 2003–05); treas Kirkbean Sch Bd 1996–2000, chm Kirkbean Hall and Amenity Ctee 1993–97 and 1999–2000, chm Dumfries and Galloway Branch Architectural Heritage Soc of Scotland 2000–02 (memb Ctee 1998–); memb: Dumfries and Lockerbie Agric Soc 1978–2000, Scottish Landowners' Fedn 1987–2001, Kirkbean Community Cncl 1988–2000, Huddersfield and Dist Family History Soc 1989–; author of various articles on architecture; *Recreations* painting, fishing, gardening, domestic architecture, travel; *Style*— Ralph Pickering of Kintradwell; ✉ Broomhill, Lockerbie, Dumfriesshire DG11 1LT (tel 01387 811600, e-mail ralph_pickering@hotmail.com); Kintradwell, Brora, Sutherland; Monrovia Estate, Korforidua, Ghana; Rue du Bailli 38, 1050 Brussels, Belgium

PICKERSGILL, Dr David Eric; s of Douglas Pickersgill (d 1990), and Vera, *née* Firth; *b* 13 October 1946, Bradford; *Educ* Burnley GS, Univ of Bristol (MB, ChB); *m* 8 Oct 1967, Hilary, *née* Jones; 2 s (Nicolas b 7 Jan 1969, Dominic b 4 April 1971); *Career* house offr Southmead Hosp Bristol 1969–70, SHO and registrar Worcester Royal Infirmary 1970–72, GP North Walsham (Norfolk) 1973–2002; chm: Norfolk Local Medical Ctee 1986–92, Medical Advsy Ctee NHS Appeal Authy 1996–2006; BMA: memb 1969–, memb Cncl 1989–, treas 2002–, tstee BMA Pension Scheme, tsee BMA Charities; tsee Medical Fndn for AIDS and Sexual Health; *Publications* General Practice and the Law (1993), Private Medical Practice (1993), GP's Guide to Private and Professional Work (1994), Dispensing and General Practice (1995); *Recreations* golf, bird watching, travel, cookery, music; *Clubs* Sheringham Golf, Hunstanton Golf, Rosapenna Golf; *Style*— Dr David Pickersgill; ✉ 18 Uplands Park, Sheringham, Norfolk NR26 8NE (tel 01263 822010)

PICKETT, Prof John Anthony; CBE (2004); s of Samuel Victor Pickett (d 1983), of Glenfield, Leicester, and Lilian Frances, *née* Hoar; *b* 21 April 1945; *Educ* King Edward VII GS, Univ of Surrey (BSc, PhD); *m* 11 July 1970, Ulla Birgitta, da of John Skålén; 1 da (Hilda Amelia b 14 Nov 1975), 1 s (Erik Jarl b 30 Jan 1981); *Career* postdoctoral fell UMIST 1970–72, sr scientist Chem Dept Brewing Res Fndn 1972–76, princ scientific offr Dept of Insecticides and Fungicides Rothamsted Experimental Station 1976–83, head Biological and Ecological Chem Dept Rothamsted Research 1984–, scientific dir Rothamsted Centre for Sustainable Pest and Disease Mgmnt 2007–; special prof Univ of Nottingham 1991–; chm Advsy Ctee Sch of Applied Chem Univ of N London 1993–95, hon memb Academic Staff Univ of Reading 1995–, external examiner Imperial Coll London and Univ of Sussex, cncllr Int Soc of Chemical Ecology 1991–2000 (vice-pres 1994, pres 1995), scientific advsr Int Fndn for Sci Stockholm 1996–; chm Working Gp on the Future of Sites of Special Sci Interest (SSSIs) Royal Soc 2000–01; memb: Visiting Gp IPO-DLO Netherlands 1993, Conference Grants Ctee Royal Soc 1997–99, Sectional Ctee Royal Soc 1997–2000 and 2007–, Deutsche Akademie der Naturforscher Leopoldina 2001, Governing Cncl Int Centre of Insect Physiology and Ecology (ICIPE) Nairobi 2005, Dorothy Hodgkin Fellowship Selection Panel Royal Soc 2006–08, chm Royal Soc Working Gp on Devpt for Biofuels 2006–; guest ed The Biochemist 1998; memb Editorial Bd: Jl of Chemical Ecology 1991–, Int Jl of Tropical Insect Sci 2006–; The Rank Prize Nutrition and Crop Husbandry 1995, Int Soc of Chemical Ecology Silver Medal 2002; Hon DSc Univ of Nottingham; hon life memb Assoc of Applied Biologists (AAB) 2004, foreign memb Royal Swedish Acad of Agric and Forestry 2005; CChem 1975; FRSC 1982, FRES, MACS 1993, FRS 1996 (memb Cncl 2000–02), MRI 1997; *Publications* over 300 incl patents; *Recreations* jazz trumpet playing; *Style*— Prof John Pickett, CBE, FRS; ✉ Department of Biological Chemistry, Rothamsted Research, Harpenden, Hertfordshire AL5 2JQ (tel 01582 763133 ext 2321, fax 01582 762595, e-mail john.pickett@bbsrc.ac.uk)

PICKFORD, David Michael; s of Aston Charles Corpe Pickford (d 1945), of London, and Gladys Ethel, *née* May (d 1981); *b* 25 August 1926; *Educ* Emanuel Sch London, Coll of Estate Mgmnt; *m* 1956, Elizabeth Gwendoline (d 2005), da of John Hooson (d 1972), of Denbigh; 2 da (Penelope Anne b 1952, Elizabeth Jane b 1957), 1 s (Charles John Norcliffe b 1960); *Career* chartered surveyor; chm: Haslemere Estates plc 1983–86 (md until 1983), Lilliput Property Unit Trust 1984–97, Compco Holdings plc 1986–2002, Gulliver Developments Property Unit Trust 1989–99, Wigmore Property Investment Trust plc 1993–96, Swift Balanced Property Unit Trust 1993–97, Lionbrook Property Fund 1997–2002; dir: London and Nationwide Missions Ltd 1980–, Youth With A Mission 1987–99, Care Campaigns Ltd 1988–, Louth Estates Ltd 1990–2000, and many others; chm: Mission to London 1981–2001, Prison Fellowship England and Wales 1989–93; hon life pres The Boys' Bde London, vice-pres London City YMCA 1993–98, patron Christians In Property, organizer of Residential Christian Conference Centre for 15–25 year-olds (1000 visitors each year), dir Billy Graham Evangelistic Association Ltd 1987–2000; FRICS; *Recreations* sheep farming, youth work; *Style*— David Pickford, Esq; ✉ Elm Tree Farm, Mersham, Ashford, Kent TN25 7HS (tel 01233 720200, fax 01233 720522)

PICKFORD, Robert William Granville; s of late Col Richard Ellis Pickford, TD, DL, of Hathersage, Derbys, and late Mary Avice, *née* Glossop; *b* 26 November 1941; *Educ* Rugby, Univ of Sheffield (LLB); *m* 11 Oct 1980, Heather Elizabeth, da of Francis Ernest Woodings, of Chesterfield, Derbys; 1 da (Olivia b 21 Dec 1981), 1 s (Bartholomew b 9 Sept 1985); *Career* admitted slr 1966, NP 1966; ptnr W & A Glossop Sheffield, former conslt Keeble Hawson Sheffield, currently notary Graysons Sheffield; dir The Notaries Guarantee Ltd 1979–; memb Law Soc; *Style*— Robert Pickford, Esq; ✉ 4–12 Paradise Square, Sheffield S1 1TB (tel 0114 272 9184)

PICKLES, Eric; MP; *b* 20 April 1952; *Educ* Greenhead GS, Leeds Poly; *m* Sept 1976, Irene; *Career* cncllr Bradford Met DC 1979–91 (chm Social Servs Ctee 1982–84, chm Educn Ctee 1984–86, ldr Cons Gp 1987–91, ldr of the Cncl 1988–90), MP (Cons) Brentwood and Ongar 1992–; PPS to Min for Industry DTI 1993, vice-chm Cons Pty 1993–97, opposition frontbench spokesman on social security 1998–2001, shadow min for tport and for London 2001–02, shadow sec of state for local govt 2002–07, dep chm Cons Pty 2005–, shadow sec of state for communities and local govt 2007–; memb Select Ctee: Environment 1992–93, Tport 1996–97, Environment, Tport and Regions 1997–; chm All Pty Film Industry Gp 1997–2002; memb Cons Pty Nat Union Exec Ctee 1975–91, nat chm Young Conservatives 1980–81; dep ldr Cons Gp on the Assoc of Met Authorities 1989–91, chm Cons Pty Nat Local Govt Advsy Ctee 1992– (memb 1985–); memb Cncl of Europe 1997–98; local govt ed Conservative Newsline 1990–; memb Yorks RHA 1982–90; *Recreations* films, opera, golf; *Style*— Eric Pickles, Esq, MP; ✉ House of Commons, London SW1A 0AA

PICKSTOCK, Samuel Frank (Sam); CBE (1989); s of Francis John Pickstock (d 1981), of Stafford, and Hilda Jane, *née* Billington; *b* 10 August 1934; *Educ* King Edward VI GS Stafford; *m* 1957, Edith, da of Joseph Lawton (d 1980), of Hanley; *Career* dir: John McLean & Sons Ltd and its subsids 1976–94, Tarmac Properties Ltd and its subsids 1977–91, Tarmac plc 1984–94, Tarmac Atlantic Wharf Developments Ltd 1985–94; chief exec John McLean & Sons Ltd (chm subsids) 1981–94; dir: Countryside Properties plc 1994–2003, Eco Energy Controls Ltd 1995–, Stonepine Management Services Ltd 1996–; CCMI, FInstLEx, FInstD; *Recreations* weeding and thinking about both the energy efficiency of central heating systems and the politics of housing from 1918 to the present day; *Style*— Sam Pickstock, Esq, CBE; ✉ The Crows Nest Holding, Coton End, Gnosall, Stafford (tel 01785 822755); The Lodge at Crows Nest, Coton End, Gnosall, Stafford (tel 01785 823173)

PICKTHORN, Sir James Francis; 3 Bt (UK 1959), of Orford, Co Suffolk; s of Sir Charles William Richards Pickthorn, 2 Bt (d 1995), and Helen Antonia, *née* Mann; *b* 18 February 1955; *Educ* Eton; *m* 17 Jan 1998, Clare, da of Brian Craig-McFeely; 2 s (William Edward Craig b 1998, George Arthur Henry b 2001); *Heir* s, William Pickthorn; *Career* chartered surveyor; ptnr Kinney & Green 1991–94, fndr Pickthorn estate agent and chartered surveyor 1994–; memb HAC; Liveryman Worshipful Co of Bowyers; *Style*— Sir James Pickthorn, Bt; ✉ 45 Ringmer Avenue, London SW6 5LP; Pickthorn (tel 020 7621 1380, e-mail james.pickthorn@pickthorn.co.uk)

PICKUP, Col Christopher John; LVO (2007), OBE (1984); s of Wing Cdr K H Pickup, and Vera, *née* Halliwell (d 1943); *b* 26 August 1942; *Educ* Abingdon Sch, RMA Sandhurst; *m* 1, 16 Dec 1967 (m dis 2002), Elizabeth Anne, da of Robert Geoffrey Spencer (d 1971); 1 s (Charles b 1970), 1 da (Lucy b 1971); m 2, 3 July 2004, Deborah, da of Maj Ian Eldridge; *Career* cmmnd RA 1962, transferred Army Air Corps 1972, Army Staff Coll 1972–74; various cmd and staff appts UK, Borneo, Germany incl COS and Regtl Col Army Air Corps 1990–92, ret 1994; sec The Royal Warrant Holders Assoc 1996–2007; *Recreations* walking, fishing; *Clubs* Army and Navy; *Style*— Col Christopher Pickup, LVO, OBE; ✉ Voelas, Doctors Commons Road, Berkhamsted, Hertfordshire HP4 3DR (tel 07811 111270)

PICKUP, David Francis William; CB (2002); s of Joseph Pickup, of Wells, Somerset, and Murial, *née* Clarke; *b* 28 May 1953; *Educ* Poole GS, Central London Poly, Inns of Court Sch of Law; *m* 1975, Anne Elizabeth Round; *Career* called to the bar 1976, called to the bar Gibraltar 1988; HM Treasy Slrs Dept: legal asst Litigation Div 1978–81, sr legal asst Energy Dept 1981–87, head Judicial Review Section Litigation Div 1987–88, princ establishment fin and security offr 1988–90, head Chancery Litigation Div 1990–91, head MOD Advsy Div 1991–95; the slr HM Customs & Excise 1995–2004, DG HM Revenue and Customs 2006–07, Attorney-Gen of the Falkland Islands 2007–; *Recreations* cricket, skiing, music, food and wine, travel; *Clubs* Pyrford Cricket, Herefordshire Golf; *Style*— David Pickup, Esq, CB; ✉ Attorney General's Chambers, Cable Cottage, Stanley, Falkland Islands (tel 00 500 27273, e-mail dpickup@sec.gov.uk)

PICKUP, Ronald Alfred; s of Eric Pickup (d 1981), of Chester, and Daisy, *née* Williams; *b* 7 July 1940; *Educ* King's Sch Chester, Univ of Leeds (BA), RADA; *m* 9 Aug 1964, Lans Talbot, da of Claude Traverse, of Encino, CA, USA; 1 s (Simon b 1971), 1 da (Rachel b 1973); *Career* actor; in rep Leicester 1964, first title role Shelley (Royal Court) 1965, Nat Theatre Co 1966–72; memb Global Co-operative for a Better World; *Theatre* roles incl: Rosalind in all-male As You Like It (NT), Long Day's Journey Into Night (NT), Richard II (NT), The Cherry Orchard (West End), Amy's View (RNT) 1997 and (Broadway) 1999, Romeo and Juliet (NT) 2001, Peer Gynt (NT) 2001, Proof (Donmar Warehouse) 2002; *Television* incl: Jennie, Orwell, Fortunes of War, Behaving Badly 1988, Not with a Bang 1988, Time to Dance 1991, The Riff-Raff Element (BBC) 1992–93, The Rector's Wife (film for TV) 1993, The Cold Light of Day (Screen 2, BBC) 1994, Message for Posterity (BBC revival of Dennis Potter's work), Ruth Rendell's Case of Coincidence 1994, The Dying Day 1995, title role in Henry IV (adapted by John Caird for BBC) 1995, Hornblower 1998, Hetty Wainthropp Investigates, Casualty, Ivanhoe (6 part series), Dalziell & Pascoe (BBC), The Bill (ITV), Inspector Lynley Mysteries (BBC), Waking the Dead (BBC), Midsomer Murders (ITV), The Last Detective (ITV), Featherboy (BBC), Cambridge Spies (BBC); *Films* incl: Day of the Jackal, The Thirty Nine Steps, Never Say Never Again, The Mission, The Fourth Protocol, Eleni, My Friend Walter, Bring Me The Head of Mavis Davis, Breathtaking, The Secret Passage, Tulse Luper Suitcase, Evilenko; *Recreations* walking, reading, listening to music; *Clubs* BAFTA; *Style*— Ronald Pickup, Esq

PICKWOAD, Michael Mervyn; s of William Mervyn Pickwoad (d 1976), of Windsor and Ludham, and Anne Margaret, *née* Payne Cook (d 1992); *b* 11 July 1945; *Educ* St George's Sch Windsor Castle, Charterhouse, Univ of Southampton (BSc Eng); *m* 27 Oct 1973, Vanessa Rosemary, da of Leslie William Orriss, of Cookham, Berks; 3 da (Zoë b 1975, Katharine b 1977, Amy b 1979); *Career* film production designer; architectural models for Nat Tst 1972, series of four architectural drawings for Hugh Evelyn Prints 1973, exhibition design Treasures of the Mind (TCD Quatercentenary Exhibition) 1992, exhibitor Directors Eye (MOMA Oxford) 1996, gallery design for eastern art collection Ashmolean Museum Oxford 1997; memb: Georgian Gp, BAFTA, GBFD; *Television* incl: Ex 1991, Murder Most Horrid 1991, Running Late 1992, Class Act 1993, The Dying of the Light (YTV) 1994, Cruel Train (Screen 2) 1994, Witness Against Hitler (Screen 2) 1995, Kavanagh QC 1995, Element of Doubt (Carlton) 1996, Kavanagh QC 1997, Cider With Rosie (Carlton) 1998, A Rather English Marriage (Screen 2) 1998, David Copperfield (TNT Network) 1998, The Last of the Blonde Bombshells (BBC) 1999, The Sleeper (TV Film, BBC) 2000, Hans Christian Andersen, My Life as a Fairytale (Hallmark) 2001, Wild West (BBC) 2002, Death in Holy Orders (BBC) 2002, The Deal (Channel 4) 2003, Sad Cypress (LWT) 2003, The Hollow (LWT) 2003, Death on the Nile (LWT) 2003, Frances Tuesday (ITV Network) 2004, Archangel (BBC) 2004, Margaret (Channel 4) 2005, Sweeney Todd (BBC) 2005, Longford (Channel 4) 2006 (nomination BAFTA Awards), Towards Zero (ITV) 2006, Nemesis (ITV) 2006, Bertrams Hotel (ITV) 2006, Ordeal by Innocence (ITV) 2007, The Old Curiosity Shop (ITV) 2007; *Film* incl: Comrades 1985, Withnail and I 1986, The Lonely Passion of Judith Hearne 1987, How to Get Ahead in Advertising 1988, The Krays 1989, Let Him Have It 1990, Century 1992, Food of Love 1996, Honest 1999, High Heels, Low Lifes 2000; *Music Videos* incl: I'll Save the World (Eurythmics) 1999, 17 Again (Eurythmics) 1999; *Recreations* architectural history, drawing, photography, sailing, history of transport; *Style*— Michael Pickwoad, Esq; ✉ 3 Warnborough Road, Oxford OX2 6HZ (tel 01865 511106, fax 01865 556563); Casarotto Marsh Ltd, National House, 60–66 Wardour Street, London W1V 4ND (tel 020 7287 4450)

PICOT, Derek A; s of Lesley Picot (d 2002), of Jersey, and Dorothy, *née* Johnson; *b* 11 March 1952, Jersey; *Educ* Queen's Coll Taunton, Ealing Hotel Sch (Dip); *m* 11 Dec 1981, Joanna, *née* Boursin; 1 da (Dominique b 30 April 1984), 1 s (Stefan b 18 Feb 1986); *Career* Savoy Hotel Gp 1972–80, exec asst mangr Hilton Int 1980–84, resident mangr Mandarin Oriental 1984–86, gen mangr Sheraton London 1986–95, regnl dir Meridien Canada 1995–98, vice-pres Meridien London 1999–2001, regnl dir Meridien Aust 2002, regnl gen mangr Jumeirah London 2003–; chair Knightsbridge Business Gp, memb Regnl Ctee Br

Hospitality Assoc; tstee Sidney Lawton Music Tst; Master Innholder; Freeman City of London; fell Inst of Hospitality; *Publications* Hotel Reservations (1994); *Recreations* tennis, cycling, travel; *Clubs* Lord's Taverners; *Style*— Derek Picot, Esq, FHI, MI; ✉ Jumeirah Carlton Tower, Cadogan Place, London SW1X 9PY (tel 020 7235 1234)

PICTON-TURBERVILL, Geoffrey; s of Wilfrid Picton-Turbervill (d 2002), and Shirley, *née* Masser; *b* 11 May 1959; *Educ* Marlborough, ChCh Oxford (MA), Guildford Coll of Law; *m* 27 June 1987, Mary Teresa, da of David Mowbray Balme; 2 s (Harry David b 23 Oct 1990, Thomas Joshua b 11 Nov 1995), 2 da (Lucy Charlotte b 19 Sept 1992, Isabel Cara b 27 April 1997); *Career* trainee slr Farrer & Co 1983–85; Ashurst 1986–: asst slr 1986–90, assoc ptnr 1990–94, ptnr 1994– (currently head of global energy specialising in oil and gas, electricity and other infrastructure projects and related fin transactions), resident ptnr New Delhi Office 1994–95; memb: Law Soc, Int Bar Assoc, Inst of Petroleum, Assoc of Int Petroleum Negotiators, RIIA; *Recreations* family, music, sport; *Clubs* MCC, Vincent's (Oxford); *Style*— Geoffrey Picton-Turbervill, Esq

PIDD, Prof Michael; s of Ernest Pidd, of Sheffield, and Marion, *née* Clark; *b* 3 August 1948; *Educ* High Storrs GS Sheffield, Brunel Univ (BTech), Univ of Birmingham (MSc); *m* 2 Jan 1971, Sally Anne, da of Eric Victor Nutt, of London; 2 da (Karen b 18 Aug 1977, Helen b 22 Jan 1981); *Career* team leader operational res Cadbury Schweppes Ltd 1971–75, lectr in operational res Aston Univ 1975–79; Lancaster Univ: lectr then sr lectr in operational res 1979–92, prof of mgmnt studies 1992–96, prof of mgmnt science 1996–, head of Dept of Mgmnt Science 1997–2000; pres Operational Res Soc 2000–01; winner President's medal OR Soc; memb: St Thomas Church Lancaster, INFORMS; *Books* Computer Simulation in Management Science (1984, 1988, 1992, 1997 and 2004), Computer Modelling for Discrete Simulation (1989), Tools for Thinking: Modelling in Management Science (1996 and 2003), System Modelling: Theory and Practice (2004); *Recreations* fell-walking, church activities; *Style*— Prof Michael Pidd; ✉ Department of Management Science, The Management School, Lancaster University, Bailrigg, Lancaster LA1 4YX (tel 01524 593870, fax 01524 844885, e-mail m.pidd@lancaster.ac.uk)

PIERCE, Rt Rev Anthony Edward; *see:* Swansea and Brecon, Bishop of

PIERCE, David Glyn; s of Gwilym John Pierce, of London, and Hilda Alice Pierce; *b* 1942; *Educ* Stationers' Co Sch London, Univ of Exeter (BA); *m* 1, 1963, Anne Valerie Sherwood; 1 s (Adam b 1967), 1 da (Rebecca b 1970); m 2, 9 Feb 1991, Victoria Isobel, da of Samuel Seymour, of Seattle, Washington, USA; 1 da (Alexandra b 1988), 1 s (Marcus b 1992); *Career* TV time buyer Garland Compton 1964–68 (media trainee 1963), head of Media Gp Foote Cone & Belding 1968–77, head of TV buying Everetts 1977–82; Media Campaign Services: joined 1982, assoc dir responsible for planning and research 1987–; MCAM 1981; *Recreations* competitive cycling, memb Velo Club des Londres; *Style*— David Pierce, Esq; ✉ Media Campaign Limited, 20 Orange Street, London WC2H 7ED (tel 020 7389 0800, fax 020 7839 6997)

PIERCY, 3 Baron (UK 1945); James William Piercy; s of 2 Baron Piercy (d 1981), and Oonagh Lavinia, JP (d 1990), da of Maj Edward John Lake Baylay, DSO; *b* 19 January 1946; *Educ* Shrewsbury, Univ of Edinburgh (BSc); *Heir* bro, Hon Mark Piercy; *Career* AMIEE, FCCA; *Style*— The Rt Hon the Lord Piercy; ✉ 36 Richford Street, London W6 7HP

PIERCY, Prof Nigel Francis; s of Gilbert Piercy (d 1984), of Cambridge, and Helena Gladys, *née* Sargent (d 2001); *Educ* Cambridge GS for Boys, Heriot-Watt Univ (BA, DLitt), Univ of Durham (MA), Univ of Wales (PhD); *m* 1 (m dis), (Patricia) Jean; 1 s (Niall Christopher b 1979); m 2, Stephanie Monica, da of Eric James Oscar Burges (d 1991); m 3, Nikala; *Career* planner Amersham International 1974–77; sr lectr Newcastle Poly 1977–81 (lectr 1972–74); Univ of Wales: lectr 1981–83, sr lectr 1983–86, reader 1986–88, prof of mktg and strategy Cardiff Business Sch 1988–96, Sir Julian Hodge chair in mktg and strategy Cardiff Business Sch 1996–2001, prof of strategic mktg and dir strategic sales res consortium Cranfield Univ 2002–03 (head Mktg Gp 2003); Univ of Warwick prof of mktg 2003–, chair of Sales and Account Mgmnt Research Unit, chair of Sales and Strategic Customer Mgmnt Network; visiting prof: Neeley Sch of Business Texas Christian Univ 1993–94, Haas Sch of Business Univ of Calif Berkeley 1994, Fuqua Sch of Business Duke Univ NC 1999, Univ of Vienna 2003; Author of the Year UK Inst of Mktg 1980–82; FCIM 1988; *Books* Export Strategy (1982), Managing Marketing Information (with M Evans, 1983), The Management Implications of New Information Technology (ed, 1984), Marketing Organisation (1985), Management Information Systems (ed, 1986), Marketing Budgeting (1986), Preparing Marketing for the New Millenium (ed, 1991), Market-Led Strategic Change (1991, 3 edn 2002), Marketing Stategy and Competitive Positioning (jt author, 1998, 3 edn 2003), Strategic Management: Strategizing Your Way to the Future (1999), Tales From the Marketplace: Stories of Revolution, Reinvention and Renewal (1999), Strategic Marketing (with D Cravens, 8 edn 2005), Total Integrated Marketing (jt author, 2003); *Style*— Prof Nigel Piercy; ✉ Warwick Business School, The University of Warwick, Coventry CV4 7AL (tel 024 7652 3911, fax 024 7652 4628, mobile 07747 617725, e-mail nigel.piercy@wbs.ac.uk)

PIERRE, Antony David (Tony); s of Jean Pierre, of Chislehurst, Kent, and Sara Fajga, *née* Libchaber; *b* 25 February 1956; *Educ* Alleyn's Sch Dulwich, City Univ Business Sch (BSc); *m* 27 May 1990, Michelle Linda, da of late Bernard Langdon; 1 da (Klara Sophie b 2 Aug 1991), 1 s (Magnus George b 11 May 1995); *Career* CA 1981, currently ptnr Baker Tilly Corp Finance; FCA 1992 (ACA 1982); FRSA; *Recreations* skiing, squash, tennis, theatre, opera; *Clubs* RAC; *Style*— Tony Pierre, Esq; ✉ Baker Tilly, 2 Bloomsbury Street, London WC1B 3ST (tel 020 7413 5100, fax 020 7413 5101, e-mail tony.pierre@bakertilly.co.uk)

PIERS, Sir James Desmond; 11 Bt (I 1661); s of Sir Charles Robert Fitzmaurice Piers, 10 Bt (d 1996); *b* 24 July 1947; *m* 1975, Sandra Mae Dixon; 1 da (Christine Sarah b 1976), 1 s (Stephen James b 1979); *Heir* s, Stephen Piers; *Career* barr and slr; ptnr Fasken, Martineau & DuMoulin; *Style*— Sir James Piers, Bt; ✉ Fasken, Martineau & DuMoulin, 2100–1075 West Georgia Street, Vancouver, BC, Canada V6E 3G2 (tel 00 1 604 631 4769, fax 00 1 604 631 3232, e-mail jpiers@van.fasken.com)

PIERS, Martin James; s of Karl Piers, of Ewell, Surrey, and Meryl Menzies; *b* 12 September 1954; *Educ* Hertford GS, Univ of Southampton (LLB); *m* 26 Feb 1993, Ana Maria, da of Raphael Ortega, of Malaga, Spain; *Career* admitted slr 1979; Gouldens (merged with Jones Day 2003): ptnr 1983–2007, head Europe Employment Law Gp; lectr on dir personal liability and employment law; contrib business law section Financial Times; memb: Employment Lawyers Assoc, European Employment Lawyers Assoc; *Books* Guide to Directors and Officers Liability and Loss Prevention (1989); *Recreations* theatre, tennis, walking; *Clubs* RAC; *Style*— Martin Piers, Esq

PIETERSEN, Kevin Peter; MBE (2006); s of Jannie Pietersen, and Penny Pietersen; *b* 27 June 1980, Pietermaritzburg, South Africa; *Educ* Maritzburg Coll, Univ of South Africa; *Career* cricketer; clubs: KwaZulu-Natal 1998–2000, Nottinghamshire CCC 2001–04, Hampshire CCC 2005–; England: 30 Test caps, 61 one day appearances, 6 Twenty20 appearances, one day debut v Zimbabwe 2004, Test debut v Australia 2005 (memb Ashes winning team), memb squad World Cup WI 2007, memb squad Twenty20 World Cup 2007; Emerging Player of the Year and One-Day Player of the Year Int Cricket Cncl Awards 2005; *Publications* Crossing the Boundary (2006); *Style*— Mr Kevin Pietersen, MBE; ✉ c/o Hampshire County Cricket Club, The Rose Bowl, Botley Road, West End, Southampton SO30 3XH (tel 01652 688900, fax 01652 688900, e-mail info@missionsportsmanagement.com, website www.missionsportsmanagement.com); website www.kevinpietersen.com

PIGGOTT, Harold Ebenezer; s of Percy Henry Heath Piggott (d 1979), and Mary Gertrude, *née* Saunders (d 1962); *b* 14 April 1937; *Educ* Worthing HS for Boys, Brighton Tech Coll (City & Guilds); *m* 5 Sept 1959, Barbara Ethel, da of William John Tunbridge, of Cornwall; 3 da (Susan b 17 July 1960, Clare b 8 Aug 1965, Amanda b 29 April 1968); *Career* fndr Harold E Piggott Ltd 1962; chm and sec ASS (radio, TV and electrical retailers, Sussex) 1969–76; Hearts of Oak Friendly Society Ltd: dir 1977–, vice-chm 1986, 1991 and 1994, chm 1991–93 and 1998–2005; chm: Hearts of Oak Insurance Group Staff Pension Scheme 1987–88, 1995–96 and 1998–99, Hearts of Oak Trustees Ltd 1991–93 and 1998–2000, London Aberdeen & Northern Mutual Assurance Society Ltd 1997–2005 (vice-chm 1995–97), FS Mgmnt Ltd 1998–2005, Legislation Sub-Ctee Friendly Association Soc, WBC Radio for Worthing Ltd 2002–03; fndr chm Harold E Piggott Ltd 1962–; pres Association of Friendly Societies Ltd 1996–97 (vice-pres 1995–96); memb DHSS Appeals Tbnl 1975–87; cncllr W Sussex CC 1974–85 (chm of catering County Hall 1980–85); Worthing Borough Cncl: cncllr Heene Ward 1974–95, mayor 1982–83, ldr of Cncl 1989–94 (dep ldr 1982–89), exec accountant Worthing Borough Sussex Police Consultative Ctee 1989–92, chm Worthing Centenary Ctee 1990, hon alderman of Worthing 1995–; chm W Sussex Branch Assoc of Dist Cncls 1992–93 (vice-chm 1991–92); Lord of the Manor of Netherhall Old Newton Suffolk; pres Worthing Hard of Hearing Club, past chm and vice-pres Sussex Parkinson's Disease Soc; govr C of E Sch 1974–93; Liveryman: City of London 1977– (Freeman 1972), Worshipful Co of Basketmakers (Steward 1988); fndr chm City of London Freeman Assoc of Sussex; life memb: Guild of Freeman of City of London, Nat Tst, Worthing Civic Soc, Sussex Mayors' Assoc; fell American Biographical Inst 1995; FInstD 1965, FIMgt 1983, FCEA 1983, FFA 1987, FRSA 1988, MCII 1990, Fell Assocs of Int Accountants 2005; *Books* Beauty & History in the South East (article in Hearts of Oak Magazine, 1978), Why Friendly Societies Will Continue to Play a Key Role (article in Association of Friendly Societies Year Book 1997/98); *Recreations* swimming, chess, snooker, golf, reading; *Clubs* The Manorial Soc of GB, The United Wards Club of City of London, Offington Park; *Style*— Harold Piggott, Esq; ✉ The White House, Mill Lane, Ashington, Pulborough, West Sussex RH20 3BX (tel 01903 893644, fax 01903 891372, e-mail haroldpiggott@aol.com); Apartment at Playa Sol, 11–15 Avenida Gola D'estany, Santa Margarita, Rosas, Spain; Hearts of Oak Friendly Society Ltd, Hearts of Oak Insurance Group, Registered Office, 9 Princess Road West, Leicester LE1 6TH (tel 0116 254 9010, fax 0116 255 1147)

PIGOT, Sir George Hugh; 8 Bt (GB 1764), of Patshull, Staffs; s of Maj-Gen Sir Robert Anthony Pigot, 7 Bt, CB, OBE (d 1986), and his 1 w, Honor, *née* Gibbon (d 1964); *b* 28 November 1946; *Educ* Stowe; *m* 1, 2 Dec 1967 (m dis 1973), Judith Sandeman, er da of late Maj John Hele Sandeman Allen, RA; 1 da (Melanie Barbara b 4 Dec 1969); m 2, 2 Feb 1980 (m dis 1993), Lucinda Jane, yr da of Donald Charles Spandler; 2 s ((George) Douglas Hugh b 17 Sept 1982, (Robert) Edward Richard b 26 Sept 1984); m 3, 5 April 2006, Odette Kruger, yr da of Walter Stanley, of Port Elizabeth, South Africa; *Heir* s, Douglas Pigot; *Career* with Coutts & Co 1965–67, Hogg Robinson & Gardner Mountain 1967–69; freelance photographer 1970–77, founded Padworth Fisheries (trout farm) 1977, chm and md Padworth Fisheries Ltd 1981–95, mgmnt conslt Positive Response 1995–; dir Southern Trout Ltd 1993–95 (md 1994–95), md Custom Metalcraft Ltd 1998–; memb Cncl British Trout Assoc 1986–93 (hon treas 1990–92); sec-gen Residential Sprinkler Assoc 1998–2003, chief exec Fire Sprinkler Assoc 2003–2007; *Recreations* trout, classic cars, golf; *Style*— Sir George Pigot, Bt; ✉ Mill House, Mill Lane, Padworth, Berkshire RG7 4JX (tel 0118 971 2322, fax 0118 971 3015)

PIGOTT, Sir (Berkeley) Henry Sebastian; 5 Bt (UK 1808), of Knapton, Queen's County; s of Maj Sir Berkeley Charles Pigott, 4 Bt (d 1982), and Christabel, *née* Bowden-Smith (d 1974); *b* 24 June 1925; *Educ* Ampleforth; *m* 4 Sept 1954, (Olive) Jean, o da of John William Balls (d 1975), of Surlingham, Norfolk; 2 s (David John Berkeley b 1955, Antony Charles Philip b 1960), 1 da (Sarah Jane Mary b 1964); *Heir* s, David Pigott; *Career* served WWII RM 1944–45; farmer; Freeman of City of Baltimore USA; *Recreations* sailing (in Guinness Book of Records (1988 edn) for smallest single-handed circumnavigation); *Style*— Sir Henry Pigott, Bt; ✉ Brook Farm, Shobley, Ringwood, Hampshire BH24 3HT (e-mail henry@shobley.freeserve.co.uk)

PIGOTT-SMITH, Timothy Peter (Tim); s of Harry Thomas Pigott-Smith (d 2005), of Stratford-upon-Avon, and Margaret Muriel, *née* Goodman; *b* 13 May 1946; *Educ* Wyggeston Boys GS Leicester, King Edward VI GS Stratford-upon-Avon, Univ of Bristol (BA), Bristol Old Vic Theatre Sch; *m* 1972, Pamela, da of Alfred Miles; 1 s (Tom Edward b 1976); *Career* actor and director; Hon DLitt Univ of Leicester; *Theatre* numerous tours and rep incl: Birmingham, Cambridge, Nottingham and Bristol; Bristol Old Vic 1969 incl: Major Barbara, As You Like It; Prospect Theatre 1970–71 incl: Much Ado About Nothing, Boswell's Johnson, Hamlet (tour and West End); RSC 1972–75 incl: Roman Plays, Cymbeline, Dr Watson in Sherlock Holmes (London and Broadway); RNT 1987–88 incl: Coming into Land, Octavius Caesar in Antony & Cleopatra, Henry Moule in Entertaining Strangers, Winter's Tale, Cymbeline, Tempest; other credits incl: Traps (Royal Court) 1977, Benefactors (Vaudeville) 1984, Bengal Lancer (Leicester Haymarket and Lyric Hammersmith) 1985, Old Times 1993, Mr Rochester in Jane Eyre (Playhouse) 1993–94, Robert Ross in The Picture of Dorian Gray (Lyric Hammersmith) 1994, Retreat (Orange Tree) 1995, The Letter (Lyric Hammersmith) 1995, The Alchemist, Mary Stuart (RNT) 1996, Heritage (Hampstead Theatre Club) 1997, The Iceman Cometh (Almeida, Old Vic and Broadway) 1998–99, Five Kinds of Silence (Lyric Hammersmith) 2000, Julius Caesar (Barbican) 2002, Christmas Carol (Lyric Hammersmith) 2002, Mourning Becomes Electra (RNT) 2003, Hecuba (Donmar Warehouse) 2004, Women Beware Women (RSC) 2006, See How They Run (Duchess) 2006; Compass Theatre (artistic dir 1989–92) incl: Julius Caesar, Amadeus, Royal Hunt of the Sun (dir) 1989, Playing the Wife (dir); also dir Company by Samuel Beckett (Edinburgh, Fringe First Award) 1987, Hamlet (Regent's Park) 1994, The Real Thing (nat tour); *Television* incl: The Glittering Prizes, Wings, Eustace and Hilda, The Lost Boys, Henry IV (part 1), Measure for Measure, Fame is the Spur, School Play, Francis Crick in Life Story, The True Adventures of Christopher Columbus, The Bullion Boys, The Shadowy Third, No Mama No, I Remember Nelson, The Traitor, Struggle, Wilderness Years, Ronald Merrick in Jewel in the Crown (BAFTA, TV Times, Broadcasting Press Guild Best Actor Awards), The Chief, Calcutta Chronicles (documentary), Innocents, The Vice, Pompeii, Eroica, North and South, Taken at the Flood; *Film* incl: Aces High, Joseph Andrews, Sweet William, The Hunchback of Notre Dame, The Day Christ Died, Richard's Things, Clash of the Titans, Escape to Victory, State of Emergency, Remains of the Day, Bloody Sunday, Laissez Passer, Gangs of New York, The Four Feathers, Alexander, Entente Cordiale, V for Vendetta, Fly Boys; *Recreations* music, reading; *Style*— Tim Pigott-Smith, Esq

PIKE, Dr Douglas Charles McDonald; s of Douglas William Pike (d 1974), and Rachel Brunton, *née* McDonald (d 1979); *b* 25 August 1938; *Educ* City of London Sch, Univ of Bristol (BDS); *m* 1965, Julia Margaret, *née* Summers; 2 da (Rebecca b 1966, Amelia b 1968), 1 s (Mathew b 1972); *Career* gen dental practitioner Sudbury Suffolk; chm Green Light Tst; visiting lectr Univ of Stellenbosch SA; memb: BDA, Gen Dental Practitioners Assoc; hon sec SAAD; *Recreations* walking, sailing, gardening; *Style*— Dr Douglas Pike; ✉ Scotland Place, Stoke by Nayland, Colchester, Essex CO6 4QG (tel 01206 262098, fax 01206 263339); The Dental Practice, 5 Bank Buildings, Sudbury, Suffolk CO10 6SX (tel 01787 881100)

PIKE, Prof Edward Roy; s of Anthony Pike (d 1968), of Abercarn, Monmouth, and Rosalind, *née* Davies (d 1982); *b* 4 December 1929; *Educ* Southfield Sch Oxford, UC Cardiff (BSc,

PhD); *m* 1955, Pamela, da of William Henry Spearing Sawtell (d 1978); 1 s, 2 da; *Career* served RCS (SHAPE HQ France) 1948–50; Fulbright scholar Faculty of Physics MIT 1958–60, chief scientific offr Scientific Civil Serv 1960–91, visiting prof of mathematics Imperial Coll London 1984–86, Clerk Maxwell prof of theoretical physics KCL 1986–, head Sch of Physical Sciences and Engrg KCL 1991–94; dir: Stilo Technol Ltd 2002–04 (chm 1996–2002), Stilo International plc 2002–04 (chm 2000–02), Phonologica Ltd 2004–05; chm Adam Hilger Ltd 1981–85, dir Richard Clay plc 1985–86; vice-pres Inst of Physics 1981–85; fell UC Cardiff 1981, FKC 1993; FInstP, CPhys, FIMA, CMath, FRS; *Publications* Photon Correlation and Light Beating Spectroscopy (jt ed, 1974), High Power Gas Lasers (ed, 1975), Photon Correlation Spectroscopy and Velocimetry (jt ed, 1977), Frontiers in Quantum Optics (jt ed, 1986), Fractals, Noise and Chaos (jt ed, 1987), Quantum Measurement and Chaos (jt ed, 1987), Squeezed and Non-classical Light (jt ed, 1988), Photons and Quantum Fluctuations (jt ed, 1988), Inverse Problems in Scattering and Imaging (jt ed, 1991), Photon Correlation and Light Scattering Spectroscopy (jt ed, 1997), The Quantum Theory of Radiation (jtly, 1995), Scattering (jt ed, 2002); numerous papers in scientific jls; *Recreations* languages, music; *Style*— Prof E R Pike, FRS; ✉ 8 Bredon Grove, Malvern, Worcestershire WR14 3JR (tel 01684 574910); King's College London, Strand, London WC2R 2LS (tel 020 7848 2043, e-mail roy.pike@kcl.ac.uk)

PIKE, Francis Bruce; s of Esmund Francis Victor Wallace Pike, of Old Brow, Bimport, Shaftesbury, Dorset, and Elizabeth Rosemary, *née* Dun; *b* 13 February 1954; *Educ* Uppingham, Univ of Paris, Selwyn Coll Cambridge (MA); *m* 7 Oct 1993, India-Jane Romaine, da of Marcus Oswald Hornby Lecky Birley, and Lady Annabel Goldsmith; *Career* INVESCO (then AMVESCAP plc): joined Samuel Montagu Investment Management 1979, md Tokyo 1983–87, dir INVESCO MIM Management Ltd 1987–90, pres INVESCO MIM Asset Management (Japan) Ltd 1990–92, chm INVESCO MIM Investment Trust Management Ltd 1992–93, latterly ceo INVESCO Asia Pacific; NM Rothschild & Sons Ltd: joined 1998, dir of continuation investments, chm Rothschild Ventures, chm Rothschild Japan; dir: Outblaze Ltd, Scottish Investment Ltd; *Recreations* reading; *Style*— Francis Pike, Esq

PIKE, John Douglas; s of Rev Horace Douglas Pike, of Rufforth, N Yorks, and Phyllis Joyce, *née* Langdon; *b* 4 October 1947; *Educ* Queen Elizabeth GS Wakefield, Keighley Sch, Jesus Coll Cambridge (MA), De Montfort Univ (MA); *m* 11 Oct 1975, Rosemary Elizabeth, da of Archibald Richard Harlow (d 1985), of Wetherby, W Yorks; 1 da (Alison b 23 July 1981), 2 s (Richard b 28 April 1983, Stephen b 18 July 1985); *Career* Booth and Co: articled clerk 1969–71, slr 1972–76, ptnr 1976–97, head Commercial Property Dept 1991–97, mktg ptnr 1993–94, head Environmental Unit 1992–97; ptnr and head Property Gp Addleshaw Booth & Co (following merger) 1997–2003, ptnr Addleshaw Goddard (following merger) 2003–; NP; memb: Law Soc, Slrs Benevolent Assoc; dir Urban Mines; chm of govrs St Peter's Sch York; *Recreations* outdoor sports, gardening; *Style*— John Pike, Esq; ✉ Addleshaw Goddard, Sovereign House, Sovereign Street, Leeds LS1 1HQ (tel 0113 209 2000, fax 0113 209 2060, mobile 07775 586357)

PIKE, Malcolm J; *Career* admitted slr 1984; slr specialising in employment law; ptnr Addleshaw Goddard 1992– (managing ptnr Contentious and Commercial Div); chm Rugby Football League Contract Disputes Panel; memb: Int Bar Assoc, Employment Lawyers Assoc, Industrial Law Soc; *Publications* Butterworth's Encyclopaedia of Forms and Precedents (advsy ed and contrib), Essential Facts Employment (legal ed), The Lawyers Factbook (ed and contrib), Jordan's IPD Employment Law Service (contrib); *Style*— Malcolm Pike, Esq; ✉ Addleshaw Goddard, 100 Barbirolli Square, Manchester M2 3AB (tel 020 7788 5566, fax 0161 934 6060, e-mail malcolm.pike@addleshawgoddard.com)

PIKE, Dr Richard Andrew; s of Tudor Morgan Pike, of Gosport, Hants, and Eileen Mary, *née* Oxley; *b* 2 April 1950; *Educ* Gosport County GS, Downing Coll Cambridge (scholar, pres Anglo-Japanese Soc, MA, PhD); *m* 26 April 1986, Fiona Elizabeth, da of Murdoch MacLean Henry; 2 da (Emma Elizabeth b 1 Sept 1987, Claire Fiona b 10 March 1990), 1 s (Stuart Richard b 13 Dec 1993); *Career* British Petroleum 1975–93: devpt engr Engrg Dept London 1975–80, area commissioning engr Shetland 1980–82, business devpt co-ordinator Joint Ventures London 1982–83, devpt superintendent Pipelines and Facilities Div Aberdeen 1984–85, offshore prodn engr North Sea 1985–86, mangr Sullom Voe Terminal (tech) Shetland 1986–88, mangr Joint Venture Japan 1988–89, gen mangr (chemicals) Tokyo 1989–93, dir Samsung-BP Chemicals S Korea 1989–91, pres BP Chemicals Japan 1991–93; DG Inst of Mechanical Engineers 1993–98, exec vice-chm Professional Engineering Publishing Ltd 1993–98, ops mangr Cambridge Mgmnt Consulting 1998–2000, sr assoc Gaffney Cline & Assocs 2000–06, chief exec Royal Soc of Chemistry 2006–; Award to Excellence Inst of Plant Engineers 1991; Freeman City of London; FIMechE 1988, FIChemE 1991, FInstPet 1992, FIEE 1996, FRSC 2006; *Recreations* reading, swimming (swam from Yell to Unst and Mainland to Yell Shetland Islands 1980); *Style*— Dr Richard Pike; ✉ Royal Society of Chemistry, Burlington House, Piccadilly, London W1J 0BA (tel 020 7440 3301, fax 020 7440 3331)

PIKE, Rosamund; *Career* actress; *Theatre* Hitchcock Blonde (Royal Court and Lyric Theatre), Summer & Smoke (Nottingham Playhouse, Apollo Theatre London), Gaslight (Old Vic Theatre); *Television* Wives and Daughters, Trial & Retribution IV, Love in a Cold Climate, Foyle's War; *Film* A Rather English Marriage, Die Another Day, Promised Land Hotel, The Libertine (Best Supporting Actress Br Ind Film Awards 2005), Pride and Prejudice, Doom, Devil You Know, Fracture, Fugitive Pieces; *Style*— Ms Rosamund Pike; ✉ c/o PFD, Drury House, 34–43 Russell Street, London WC2B 5HA (tel 020 7344 1010, fax 020 7836 9544)

PIKE, Air Vice Marshal Warwick John; s of Capt Thomas Pike, of Grantham, Lincs, and Molly, *née* Buckley (d 1996); *Educ* Sir John Port Sch, Guy's Hosp London (MSc, MB BS); *m* 28 Feb 1968, Susan; 2 s (Jonathan b 13 July 1969, Alister b 15 Feb 1971), 2 da (Lucy b 19 Oct 1977, Sophie b 29 Nov 1979); *Career* cmmnd RAF 1970, served UK, Singapore, Hong Kong and Germany, CO Princess Mary's RAF Hosp Cyprus 1990–92, dir Med Personnel (RAF) 1992–94, served MOD 1994–96, dir Primary Health Servs (RAF) 1996–99, COS later chief exec Defence Secdy Care Agency 1999–2002, DG Med Servs (RAF) 2002–04; QHP 1997–2004; professional advsr to RAFA; DRCOG, DAvMed, MFOM, FRSM 2002; *Recreations* walking, theatre, history; *Clubs* RAF; *Style*— Air Vice Marshal Warwick Pike; ✉ 23 High Street, Alconbury, Huntingdon PE28 4DS (tel 01480 890178, e-mail warwick.pike@virgin.net)

PIKETT, Christopher; s of late Maj Cecil Charles Pikett, and Joan Madeleine Pikett; *b* 15 October 1952; *Educ* West Bridgford GS Nottingham, Univ of Southampton (LLB); *m* 18 Sept 1976, Geraldine Barbara, da of Derek Alan Stopps; 2 s (Oliver James b 1980, Edward Guy b 1983); *Career* called to the Bar Middle Temple 1976, legal advsr in indust 1976–82; dir of legal servs and co sec Varity Holdings and subsidiaries 1987–89; 3M United Kingdom plc: co sec and gen mangr legal affrs 1989–2007, dir legal affrs 2007–; memb Hon Soc of Middle Temple; *Style*— Christopher Pikett, Esq; ✉ 3M United Kingdon plc, 3M Centre, Cain Road, Bracknell, Berkshire RG12 8HT (tel 01344 858565, fax 01344 858553, e-mail cpikett1@mmm.com)

PILCHER, David Richard; s of Archibald Bertram Pilcher (d 1996), and Sylvia, *née* Adlard (d 1995); *b* 26 March 1937; *Educ* Aldenham; *m* 4 April 1970, Veronica Betty, da of George Brown (d 1983), of Wimborne; 1 da (Sarah Elizabeth b 26 Feb 1972), 1 s (Jonathan David b 21 July 1973); *Career* CA with Pridie Brewster & Gold 1957–67; The Royal Opera House: chief accountant 1968–95, head of fin 1995–96; project accountant RNT 1996–2001, sec Royal Opera House Benevolent Fund 2000–; ATII 1966, FCA 1977 (ACA 1966); *Recreations* music, theatre, amateur dramatics; *Style*— David Pilcher, Esq; ✉ The Manor House, 87 Manor Road, Barton-le-Clay, Bedfordshire MK45 4NR (tel 01582 883842, e-mail dpilcher@fish.co.uk); Royal Opera House, Covent Garden, London WC2E 9DD (tel 020 7212 9128)

PILCHER, Rosamunde; OBE (2002); *Career* writer; *Books* incl: A Secret to Tell (1955), April (1957), The Day of the Storm (1960), On my Own (1965), Sleeping Tiger (1967), Another View (1969), The End of Summer (1971), Snow in April (1972), The Empty House (1973), Under Gemini (1977), Wild Mountain Thyme (1980), The Carousel (1983), Voices in Summer (1985), The Shell Seekers (1988), The Blue Bedroom and Other Stories (1990), September (1990), Another View (1990), Flowers in the Rain and Other Stories (1991), Coming Home (1995), The Key (1996), Winter Solstice (2000); *Style*— Ms Rosamunde Pilcher, OBE

PILDITCH, Sir Richard Edward; 4 Bt (UK 1929); s of late Sir Philip Harold Pilditch, 2 Bt, and bro of Sir Philip John Frederick Pilditch, 3 Bt (d 1954); *b* 8 September 1926; *Educ* Charterhouse; *m* 7 Oct 1950, Pauline Elizabeth Smith; 1 s, 1 da; *Heir* s, John Pilditch; *Career* serv: WWII 1939–45, RNVR and RN 1944–46 (incl serv in India and Ceylon); *Style*— Sir Richard Pilditch, Bt

PILE, Col Sir Frederick Devereux; 3 Bt (UK 1900), of Kenilworth House, Rathgar, Co Dublin; MC (1945); s of Gen Sir Frederick Alfred Pile, 2 Bt, GCB, DSO, MC (d 1976), and his 1 w Vera, da of Brig-Gen Frederick Lloyd, CB; *b* 10 December 1915; *Educ* Weymouth Coll, RMC Sandhurst; *m* 1, 1940, Pamela (d 1983), da of late Philip Henstock; 2 da; *m* 2, 1984, Violet Josephine Andrews, da of Alfred Denys Cowper; *Heir* n, Anthony Pile; *Career* served WWII 1939–45, Col Royal Tank Regt, Korea 1953, Suez Expedition 1956; Br Jt Servs Mission Washington DC 1957–60, Cmdt RAC Driving and Maintenance Sch 1960–62, distribution mangr Vaux and Associated Breweries 1963–65, gen sec Royal Soldiers Daughters Sch 1965–72; *Books* Better Than Riches; *Recreations* fishing, cricket, travelling; *Clubs* MCC; *Style*— Col Sir Frederick Pile, Bt, MC; ✉ Beadles, Cowbeech, Hailsham, East Sussex BN27 4JJ

PILGER, John Richard; s of Claude Harold Pilger (d 1989), and Elsie, *née* Marheine (d 1989), of Sydney; *b* Sydney; *Educ* Sydney HS; *Children* 1 s (Sam b 1973), 1 da (Zoe b 1984); *Career* journalist, film-maker and author; trained with Sydney Daily Telegraph and Sunday Telegraph; formerly with: Reuter London, Daily Mirror, World in Action (Granada TV), ATV/Central TV; has written for: Daily Mirror, New Statesman, New York Times, Los Angeles Times, The Nation, Guardian, Independent, The Age, Aftonbladet, Il Manifesto; war corr: Vietnam, Cambodia, Indo-Pakistan, Biafra, Middle East; has made 57 documentary TV films, many with late David Munro, notably Year Zero - The Silent Death of Cambodia (1979), Death of a Nation, the Timor Conspiracy (1994), Inside Burma: Land of Fear (1996) and The War on Democracy (2007); Edward Wilson fell Deakin Univ Aust 1995, visiting prof Cornell Univ NY; awards incl: Descriptive Writer of the Year 1966, Reporter of the Year 1967, Journalist of the Year 1967, International Reporter of the Year 1970, News Reporter of the Year 1974, Campaigning Journalist of the Year 1977, Journalist of the Year 1979, Reporter Sans Frontières 1980, UN Media Peace prize 1980, UN Media Gold Medal 1981, George Foster Peabody Award (US) 1990, Richard Dimbleby Award (BAFTA) 1991, American Acad Award (Emmy) 1991, Sophie Prize for Human Rights (Norway) 2003, RTS Award 2005; Hon DLitt: Staffordshire Univ 1994, Kingston Univ 1999; Hon DPhil Dublin City Univ 1995, Hon Dr Arts Oxford Brookes Univ 1997, Hon DLaws Univ of St Andrews 1999, Hon DUniv Open Univ 2001; memb NUJ; *Books* The Last Day (1975), Aftermath: the Struggle of Cambodia and Vietnam (1983), The Outsiders (1984), Heroes (1986), A Secret Country (1989), Distant Voices (1992), Hidden Agendas (1998), The New Rulers of the World (2002), Tell Me No Lies: Investigative Journalism and its Triumphs (ed, 2004), Freedom Next Time (2006–07); *Recreations* swimming, sunning, mulling; *Style*— John Pilger, Esq; ✉ 57 Hambalt Road, London SW4 9EQ (tel 020 8673 2848, fax 020 8772 0235, e-mail jpmarheine@hotmail.com, website www.johnpilger.com)

PILKINGTON, (Richard) Godfrey; s of Col Guy Reginald Pilkington, DSO, TD (d 1970), of St Helens, Merseyside, and Margery, *née* Frost (d 1973); *b* 8 November 1918; *Educ* Clifton, Trinity Coll Cambridge (MA); *m* 14 Oct 1950, Evelyn Edith (Eve), da of Philip Robert Stanley Vincent (d 1933), of Gerrards Cross, Bucks; 2 s (Andrew b 1955, Matthew b 1964), 2 da (Penny b 1956, Clarissa b 1958); *Career* WWII Lt (Temp Actg Capt) Anti-Tank and Medium Gunners RA, served BNAF I Army and CMF Italy 1940–46; art dealer Frost and Reed Ltd 1947–53, fndr and ptnr Piccadilly Gallery London 1953–, ed Pictures and Prints 1951–60; Master Fine Art Trade Guild 1964–66, chm Soc of London Art Dealers 1974–77; govr Wimbledon Sch of Art 1990–2000; *Recreations* walking, gardening, tennis, golf, boating; *Clubs* Athenaeum, Garrick, Hurlingham; *Style*— Godfrey Pilkington, Esq; ✉ 45 Barons Court Road, London W14 9DZ (tel 020 7385 8278); The Old Vicarage, Lamb Lane, Buckland, Faringdon, Oxfordshire; Piccadilly Gallery, 43 Dover Street, London W1X 3RE (tel 020 7629 2875, fax 020 7499 0431)

PILKINGTON, Lionel Alexander (Leo); s of Arthur Henry Lionel Alexander Pilkington, and Pauline Eva, *née* Cox; *b* 5 August 1947; *Educ* Stowe, Keele Univ (BA); *Partner* Alison Clarke; *Career* called to the Bar Inner Temple 1974; in practice 1974–80, ed Euro Law Centre 1980–85, info offr Clifford Chance 1985–90, sr crown prosecutor 1990–2001 and 2004–, Crown Advocate 2005–; memb Police Complaints Authy 2001–04; *Recreations* squash, tennis, opera, other (classical) music, photography, reading (novels, philosophy, poetry); *Clubs* RAC; *Style*— Leo Pilkington, Esq; ✉ 37 Albert Square, London SW8 1BY (tel 020 7582 3196, fax 020 7273 6401, mobile 07720 061894, e-mail leo.pilkington@albertsquare.demon.co.uk)

PILKINGTON, Stephen Charles (Steve); CBE (2005), QPM (1998); s of Charles Leonard Pilkington, of Hampshire, and Joan, *née* Herd; *Educ* Andover GS, Queen Elizabeth Coll London (BSc, PhD); *m* Anne; 3 s; *Career* Met Police: joined 1972, sergeant 1976–78, inspr 1978–82, i/c unit HQ East Dulwich 1982–84, promoted to chief inspr 1984–87, (seconded to Police Exec Research Forum Washington DC 1984), superintendent 1987–89, divnl superintendent then chief superintendent 1989–94, cdr 1994–96, dep to asst cmmr for central London 1996–98; chief constable Avon and Somerset Constabulary 1998–; *Recreations* walking, canoeing, gardening, ornithology; *Style*— Steve Pilkington, Esq, CBE, QPM; ✉ Avon and Somerset Constabulary, Police Headquarters, PO Box 37, Valley Road, Portishead, Bristol BS20 8QJ (tel 01275 816000, e-mail chief.constable@avsom.police.uk)

PILKINGTON OF OXENFORD, Baron (Life Peer UK 1995), of West Dowlish in the County of Somerset; Rev Canon Peter Pilkington; s of Frank Pilkington (d 1977), of Newcastle upon Tyne, and Doris Pilkington (d 1985); *b* 5 September 1933; *Educ* Dame Allan's Sch Newcastle upon Tyne, Jesus Coll Cambridge (BA, MA); *m* 1966, Helen (d 1997), da of Charles Wilson, of Riseholme, Lincoln and Elleron Lodge, N Yorks; 2 da (Hon Celia b 1970, Hon Sarah b 1972); *Career* schoolmaster St Joseph's Coll Chidya Tanganyika 1955–58, ordained 1959, curate of Bakewell Derbys 1959–62, schoolmaster Eton Coll 1965–75, headmaster King's Sch Canterbury 1975–86, high master St Paul's Sch London 1986–92; hon canon of Canterbury Cathedral 1975–90, canon emeritus 1990–; memb Parole Bd 1990–95; chm Broadcasting Complaints Cmmn 1992–96; sits as Cons House of Lords, oppn spokesman on educn and employment 1997–98; *Clubs* Garrick, Beefsteak; *Style*— The Rev Canon the Lord Pilkington of Oxenford; ✉ Oxenford House, Ilminster, Somerset TA19 0PP

PILL, Rt Hon Lord Justice; Rt Hon Sir Malcolm Thomas; kt (1988), PC (1995); s of Reginald Thomas Pill, MBE (d 1987), and Anne Elizabeth, *née* Wright (d 1982); *b* 11 March 1938;

Educ Whitchurch GS, Trinity Coll Cambridge (MA, LLM), Hague Acad of Int Law (Dip); *m* 19 March 1966, Prof Roisin Mary Pill, DL, da of Dr Thomas Prior Riordan, of Swansea; 2 s (John b 1967, Hugh b 1968), 1 da (Madeleine b 1971); *Career* serv RA 1956–58, Glamorgan Yeo (TA) 1958–67; called to the Bar Gray's Inn 1962 (bencher 1987); third sec FO 1963–64 (Delgns to UN Gen Assembly, ECOSOC and Human Rights Cmmn), recorder of the Crown Court 1976–87, QC 1978, judge of the High Court of Justice (Queen's Bench Div) 1988–95 (presiding judge Wales & Chester Circuit 1989–93), a Lord Justice of Appeal 1995–; judge of the Employment Appeal Tbnl 1992–95; chm Euro Parly Constituency Ctee for Wales 1993, dep chm Parly Boundary Cmmn for Wales 1993–95; chm: UNA (Welsh Centre) Tst 1969–77 and 1980–87, Welsh Centre for Int Affairs 1973–76, UK Ctee Freedom from Hunger Campaign 1978–87; tstee Dominic Barker Tst 1997–; Hon LLD Univ of Glamorgan 1998; hon fell Univ of Cardiff 1998; *Publications* A Cardiff Family in the Forties (1999); *Clubs* Army and Navy, Cardiff and Co; *Style*— The Rt Hon Lord Justice Pill; ✉ Royal Courts of Justice, Strand, London WC2A 2LL

PILLEY, John Cyril Dorland; s of Capt Eric Charles Pilley, and Elsa Celeste, *née* Henderson; *b* 25 January 1935; *Educ* Charterhouse, ChCh Oxford; *m* 1 Feb 1985, Caroline Yvonne, da of Ian Gillett Gilbert; *Career* ADC to CINC Far East 1960–61, ADC to CIGS 1961–62, Adj 1 Bn Coldstream Guards 1964–66, ret as Capt; dir: Henderson Unit Trust Management 1982, Henderson Administration Ltd 1987; chm Russell Wood Ltd 1989; *Recreations* tennis, fishing, riding; *Clubs* Boodle's, City of London; *Style*— John Pilley, Esq; ✉ Trotton Old Rectory, Hampshire (tel 01730 813612); Russell Wood Ltd, 19 Berkeley Street, London W1J 8ED (tel 020 7495 7666)

PILLING, Christopher Robert; s of Robert Granville Pilling (d 1992), of Applethwaite, Cumbria, and Florence Mary, *née* Pollard (d 1966); *b* 20 April 1936; *Educ* King Edward's Sch Birmingham, Univ of Leeds (BA), Loughborough Coll (CertEd); *m* 6 Aug 1960, Sylvia, da of Willam Edward Hill, and Gladys Hill; 1 s (Mark Christopher b 24 Dec 1961), 2 da (Zoë Rachel b 2 Sept 1963, Ceri Susannah b 23 April 1966); *Career* writer and teacher; asst d'Anglais École Normale d'Instituteurs Moulins 1957–58; asst teacher of French and PE: Wirral GS 1959–61, King Edward's Sch for Boys Camp Hill Birmingham 1961–62, Ackworth Sch Pontefract 1962–73 (house master); head of modern languages and house master Knottingley HS 1973–78, tutor in literature Dept of Adult Educn Univ of Newcastle upon Tyne 1978–80, head of French, teacher of German, Latin, Italian and gen studies Keswick Sch 1980–88; reviewer TLS 1973–74; numerous broadcasts BBC Radio 3; memb: Cumbrian Poets, Soc of Authors, Translators Assoc, Cercle Edouard et Tristan Corbière, North Cumbria Playwrights; rep Cumbria vintage squash team 1990–, SRA county grade referee 1995, Cumbria county badge 1997; *Awards* Arts Cncl Grant 1971, Arts Cncl Translator's Grant 1977, Northern Playwrights' Kate Collingwood Award (for Torquemada) 1983, Northern Arts Writers' Award 1985, prizewinner Concours Européen de Création Littéraire Centre Culturel du Brabant Wallon 1992, Tyrone Guthrie Centre Residency (awarded by Northern Arts) 1993, Euro Poetry Translation Network Residencies (awarded by Northern Arts) 1995 and 1997, Bourse des Communautés Européennes 1996, Hawthornden fell 1998, Translator Residency Br Centre for Literary Translation UEA 2000; *Poetry* Snakes & Girls (1970, New Poets Award), Fifteen Poems (1970, New Poets Award), In All the Spaces on All the Lines (1971), Wren & Owl (1971), Andrée's Bloom and the Anemones (1973), Light Leaves (1975), War Photographer from the Age of 14 (1983), Foreign Bodies (1992), Cross your Legs and Wish (1994), These Jaundiced Loves: A Translation of Tristan Corbière's Les Amours Jaunes (1995), The Lobster Can Wait (1998), In the Pink, Poems on Paintings by Matisse (1999), The Press (trans with D Kennedy of La Presse by Max Jacob, 2000), The Dice Cup (trans with D Kennedy of Le Cornet à Dès by Max Jacob, 2000), Tree Time (2003), Love at the Full: A Translation of Lucien Becker's Plein Amour (2004), Alive in Cumbria (with photographer Stuart Holmes, 2005); anthologies incl: PEN New Poems 1, 2 (1971, 1972), Four Poetry & Audience Poets (1971), VER Anthologies (1974, 1981, 1990), 21 Years of Poetry & Audience (1975), Arts Cncl New Poetry 1, 2, 3, 4, 9 (1975–78, 1983), A Mandeville Fifteen (1976), Peterloo Poems for Christmas (1981), Adam's Dream: Poems from Cumbria and Lakeland (1981), The Oxford Book of Christmas Poems (1983), Cloud Station (1983), Lancaster Literature Festival Anthologies (1983, 1984, 1986, 1990, 1992, 1993), Between Comets: for Norman Nicholson at 70 (1984), Speak to the Hills (1985), Voices of Cumbria (1987), PEN New Poetry II (1988), New Christian Poetry (1990), The New Lake Poets (1991), Northern Poetry Two (1991), The Poetry Book Society Anthology 3 (1992), The Forward Book of Poetry (1994), A Squillet of Wise Fool's Gold (Nat Autistic Soc, 1994), Swarthmoor Anthology (1995), Glitter When You Jump (1996), Robinson (Figures Mythiques) (1996), National Poetry Competition Winning Poems (2001), LAMDA XVI Anthology of Verse and Prose (2003), Paging Doctor Jazz (2004), Cat Kist (2004), The Ticking Crocodile (2004), Life Classes (in Take Five 04, 2004); translations incl in: Peterloo Anthology 1 (1979), The Oxford Book of Verse in English Translation (1980), Modern Poetry in Translation 8, 9, 16 (1995, 1996 and 2000), Arsenal (Littératures) (1999); co-translations of collections incl: Water Music from the Turkish of Lale Müldür (1998), Twelfth Song from the Turkish of Hulki Aktunç, The Swimmers from the Hebrew of Agi Mishol, Miracle from the Hebrew of Amir Or (1998), The Dice Cup (translation with David Kennedy, of Le Cornet à Dès I by Max Jacob, 2000), Tratti Moby Dick (Faenza Italy, 2003); poems published in: The Spectator, The Observer, The New Statesman, TLS, Poetry Review, The London Magazine, Encounter, Critical Quarterly, Ambit, Lettres d'Europe, The Critical Survey, The North, Poetry Wales, Outposts, Blade, Metre, Brando's Hat, Stand, The New Welsh Review, The New Review, Pitch, The Independent, Poetry & Audience, Max Jacob à la Confluence, Arsenal, Other Poetry, Quadrant, Cloud Station, Pennine Platform, Write Away, and others *Plays* Torquemada (1983), The Ghosts of Greta Hall (with Colin Fleming, 2000), Emperor on a Lady's Bicycle (2001); *Articles* Max (Jacob) and the Onion (in London Magazine, 1995), Le Quatrième Tristan et l'Aile de Marcelle and Dialogue Imaginaire (in Tristan Corbière en 1995, 1996), Traduire Le Cornet à dés en anglais (in Max Jacob à la Confluence, 2000), On the Nature of Inspiration (in Pitch, 2001), Ask a Question or Two (in Seize the Day, 2001), Over The Top (in In Other Words, 2001); *Recreations* playing squash (sec and match sec Keswick Squash Club), listening to classical music and jazz, going to the theatre, reading poetry, fiction and philosophy, looking at wildlife and art; *Style*— Christopher Pilling; ✉ 25 High Hill, Keswick, Cumbria CA12 5NY (tel 017687 73814)

PILLING, John R; s of Arthur Maurice Pilling (d 1986), and Hope Elizabeth Clarke Pilling, *née* Brinton (d 1992); *b* 11 October 1944, London; *Educ* Shrewsbury, Bromsgrove and Worcester Coll of FE (ONC, HNC); *m* July 1970, Clare Patricia, *née* North; 2 da (Serena Hope (MrsWhite) b 12 Oct 1972, Vicky Blanche b 14 Feb 1975); *Career* Brintons Ltd carpet mfrs: apprentice and mgmnt trainee 1963–67, asst prodn engr 1967–70, prodn engr 1970–80, engrg divnl mangr 1980–88, engrg dir (main bd) 1988–92, mfrg dir (main Bd) 1992–98, gp mfrg dir 1998–2002, gp md 2002–04, exec vice-chm 2004; supporter No Euro campaign; Freeman City of London, Liveryman Worshipful Co of Weavers; MIMechE 1971, FIMechT 2002, FREng 2003; *Recreations* travelling and understanding cultural diversity, the Peninsular Wars and historical perspective around the Duke of Wellington, gardening (especially trees and shrubs), shooting, dogs and dog handling, trout fishing, tennis, garden, estate and home improvements; *Style*— John R Pilling, Esq; ✉ Redmarley, Great Witley, Worcestershire WR6 6JS (tel 01299 896214, e-mail j.pilling@virgin.net)

PILLINGER, Prof Colin Trevor; CBE (2003); s of Alfred Pillinger (d 1985), and Florence, *née* Honour (d 2001); *b* 9 May 1943; *Educ* Kingswood GS, Univ of Wales (BSc, PhD), Univ of Bristol (DSc); *m* Judith Mary, da of late (Gordon) Jack Hay; 1 da (Shusanah Jane b 30 Jan 1976), 1 s (Nicolas Joseph b 11 Aug 1977); *Career* res assoc Dept of Chemistry Univ of Bristol 1972–76 (postdoctoral res asst 1968–72), sr res assoc Dept of Earth Sciences Univ of Cambridge 1978–84 (res assoc 1976–78, at Trinity Hall 1981–84); Open Univ: sr res fell 1984–90, personal chair in planetary sciences Dept of Earth Sciences Open Univ 1990–97, Gresham prof of astronomy 1996–2000, prof of planetary science 1997–, head Planetary Space Sciences Research Inst 1997–2005; princ investigator ESA Int Rosetta Cometary Mission 1994–2000, Co-I status 2000–, lead scientist BEAGLE 2 project for ESA Mars Express Mission 1997–; author of more than 1000 refereed papers, conference procedings, abstract reports, scientific journalism and three books; numerous contributions on radio, television, newspapers and magazines; Asteroid 15614 named Pillinger; SERC Special Replacement Award 1984–89, Wolfson Research Award 1990–93, Aston Medal British Mass Spectrometry Soc 2003, A C Clarke Award 2005, BIS Space Achievement Medal 2005, Reginald Mitchell Medal 2006; fell Univ Coll Swansea 2003; memb: British Mass Spectrometry Soc 1981, Int Astronomical Union 1991; fell British Steel Corporation 1972–74, fell Meteoritical Soc 1986 (memb 1972), FRAS 1981, FRS 1993, FRGS 1993; *Recreations* farming, soccer, animals; *Style*— Prof Colin Pillinger, CBE, FRS; ✉ Planetary and Space Sciences Research Institute, The Open University, Walton Hall, Milton Keynes MK7 6AA (tel 01908 652119, fax 01908 655910, e-mail psrg@open.ac.uk)

PILSWORTH, Michael John (Mick); s of Alwyne Pilsworth, of Retford, Notts, and Catherine, *née* Silverwood; *b* 1 April 1951; *Educ* King Edward VI GS Retford, Univ of Manchester (BA, MA); *m* 7 Oct 1972 (m dis 2004), Stella Frances, da of Donald Lionel Hore, of Bristol; 1 da (Rosa Grace b 8 March 1977), 1 s (Thomas James b 18 Dec 1984); m 2, 22 Aug 2004, Deborah Anne-Marie, da of Sylvester Marlin, of Dublin; *Career* research asst Inst of Advanced Studies Manchester Poly 1972–73, lectr in adult educn Univ of Manchester 1976–78 (research fell 1973–75), research assoc Centre for TV Research Univ of Leeds 1979, prog devpt exec London Weekend TV 1983–84 (researcher 1979–82), gp devpt controller TVS Entertainment plc 1987–88 (head of prog planning and devpt 1985–86), chief exec MGMM Communications Ltd 1988–89, md Alomo Productions Ltd 1990–93, md SelecTV plc 1993 (dir 1990–93), chief exec Chrysalis TV Gp and dir Chrysalis plc 1993–2002, md Martini Media Ltd 2002–, chm Motive TV 2005–; memb RTS; *Books* Broadcasting in The Third World (1977); *Recreations* swimming, tennis, cinema, reading; *Style*— Mick Pilsworth, Esq; ✉ 16 Castleknock Green, Castleknock, Dublin 15, Ireland (tel 00 353 822 3248)

PILTON, Patrick William; s of William Alfred Pilton (d 1982), and Ethel Violet Pilton (d 1988); *b* 24 October 1938; *Educ* Raines Fndn GS Whitechapel; *m* 1963 (m dis), Mellanie Harrington; 1 s (Simon Mark b 4 Nov 1963), 1 da (Trudi b 1 Jan 1969); *Career* journalist; trainee reporter Pontypridd Observer 1960–61, reporter East London News Agency 1961–62; sub-ed: Western Mail & Echo Cardiff 1964–65 (reporter 1962–64), Evening Post Reading 1965–67; sub-ed Daily Mirror 1968–69, chief sub-ed Evening Post Hemel Hempstead 1969–71 (dep chief sub 1967–68), asst ed (night) The Journal Newcastle upon Tyne 1971–73; The Sun: asst night ed 1973–76, dep night ed 1976–79, assoc features ed 1979; ed Sunday Sun Newcastle upon Tyne 1980–81, night ed Daily Express 1983–85 (dep night ed 1981–83), exec ed (prodn) Today 1985–86, dep ed London Daily News 1986–87, leader Publishers Planning Team Mirror Group Newspapers 1987, asst ed Today 1989–91 (night ed 1987–89), ed South Wales Echo Cardiff 1991–93, gp managing ed Mirror Group Newspapers 1993–2001, dir editorial operations Press Assoc 2001–; *Books* Every Night at the London Palladium (1976), Page Three: Story of the Sun's Page Three Girls (1978); *Recreations* cricket, watching rugby, walking, theatre; *Clubs* Surrey CCC; *Style*— Patrick Pilton, Esq; ✉ Press Association, PA News Centre, 292 Vauxhall Bridge Road, London SW1V 1AE

PIMBLEY, Stephen John; s of John Pimbley, of Cardiff, S Glamorgan, and Marjorie, *née* James; *b* 18 January 1959; *Educ* Stanwell Sch Penarth S Glamorgan, Middx Poly (BA), Royal Coll of Art (MA); *m* 30 April 1994, Katherine, da of Dennis Lannon; 1 s (Sydney b 16 Jan 1996); *Career* successively: architect Richard Rogers Partnership, architect/dir Troughton McAslan Ltd; currently architect/dir SMC Alsop (formerly Alsop & Störmer, Alsop Architects then Alsop and Ptnrs); ARCUK 1987, RIBA 1988; *Style*— Stephen Pimbley, Esq

PIMLOTT, Graham; *Career* admitted slr 1976, later ptnr Lovell White Durrant slrs, sec Takeover Panel 1981–83, corp fin dir Kleinwort Benson 1986–89, head of corp fin then chief exec Merchant Banking Div Barclays de Zoete Wedd 1989–96, dir of planning, ops and technol Barclays plc 1997–99; chm Tilney Gp Holdings Ltd; non-exec dir: Tesco plc 1993–2005, Hammerson plc 1993–2005 (dep chm), Provident Financial plc 2003–07; chm Export Credit Guarantee Dept 2004–, memb Auditing Practices Bd; *Style*— Graham Pimlott, Esq

PINCHER, (Henry) Chapman; s of Maj Richard Chapman Pincher (d 1964), and Helen, *née* Foster (d 1960); *b* 29 March 1914; *Educ* Darlington GS, KCL (BSc, Carter medallist), Inst of Educn Univ of London; *m* 16 Nov 1965, Constance Sylvia Wolstenholme; 1 da (Patricia b 1947), 1 s (Michael b 1949); *Career* RAC 1940, Mil Coll of Sci 1942, Tech SO Rocket Div Min of Supply 1943–46; staff Liverpool Inst 1936–40, defence sci and medical ed Daily Express 1946–73 (Journalist of the Year 1964, Reporter of the Decade 1966), asst ed Daily Express and chief def corr Beaverbrook Newspapers 1973–79, freelance writer and business conslt 1979–, regular corr Field magazine; Hon DLitt Univ of Newcastle; FKC 1979; academician Russian Acad for the Problems of Defence, Security and Internal Affrs 2005; Order of the Great Victory (Russia) 2006; *Books* Breeding of Farm Animals (1946), A Study of Fishes (1947), Into the Atomic Age (1947), Spotlight on Animals (1950), Evolution (1950), It's Fun Finding Out (with Bernard Wicksteed, 1950), Sleep and How to Get More of It (1954), Not with a Bang (1965), The Giantkiller (1967), The Penthouse Conspirators (1970), Sex in our Time (1973), The Skeleton at the Villa Wolkonsky (1975), The Eye of the Tornado (1976), The Four Horses (1978), Inside Story (1978), Dirty Tricks (1980), Their Trade is Treachery (1981), The Private World of St John Terrapin (1982), Too Secret Too Long (1984), The Secret Offensive (1985), Traitors (1987), A Web of Deception (1987), Contamination (1989), The Truth About Dirty Tricks (1990), One Dog and Her Man (1991), A Box of Chocolates (1993), Pastoral Symphony (1993), Life's a Bitch! (1996), Tight Lines (1997); *Recreations* fishing, natural history, music; *Style*— Chapman Pincher, Esq; ✉ The Church House, 16 Church Street, Kintbury, Hungerford, Berkshire RG17 9TR (tel 01488 658397)

PINCHES, Rosemary Vivian; da of Lt-Col Harold Francis Bidder, DSO, JP (d 1971), formerly of Ravensbury Manor, Morden, Surrey, and Lilias Mary Vivian, *née* Rush (d 1973); ggf was George Parker Bidder 'The Calculating Boy', illustrious engineer with Robert Stephenson and others, pres Inst of Civil Engineers, etc; *b* 19 January 1929; *Educ* Glendower Sch London, Westonbirt Sch Glos; *m* 26 July 1952, John Harvey Pinches, MC, s of John Robert Pinches (d 1968), of Holland Park Ave, London; 2 da (Joanna Harriet (Mrs Charles Hansard) b 1954, Sarah Carolan Rosemary b 1956); *Career* personal asst to Sir John Heaton-Armstrong Chester Herald Coll of Arms 1948–52; heraldic publisher and author, genealogist, proprietor of Heraldry Today (publishing house and bookshop specialising in heraldry and genealogy) 1954–; memb: Heraldry Soc, AGRA, Soc of Genealogists, Wilts Archaeological Inst, Wilts Family History Soc; *Books* Elvin's Mottoes Revised (1971), A European Armorial (with Anthony Wood, 1971), The Royal Heraldry of England (with John H Pinches, 1974), A Bibliography of Burke's 1876–1976 (1976);

P

Recreations horse-racing, browsing in old bookshops, playing bridge; *Style*— Mrs John Pinches; ✉ Parliament Piece, Ramsbury, Marlborough, Wiltshire SN8 2QH (tel 01672 520613/520617, fax 01672 520183, e-mail heraldry@heraldrytoday.co.uk, website www.heraldrytoday.co.uk)

PINCHES, Stuart John Allison; s of George Arthur Pinches (d 1993), and Marjorie Allison; *b* 2 April 1947; *Educ* Friern Barnet GS, Poly of Central London (Dip Photography & Film); *m* 18 Dec 1970 (m dis 1991), (Brigid) Imelda, da of Patrick Behan (d 1969), of Edenderry, Co Offaly, Eire; m 2, 21 June 1994, Sandie, da of Stanley Montague, of London; *Career* gen mgmnt exec United Artists Corporation Ltd 1968–70, project mangr Organon International BV Holland 1971–73, md Viscom Ireland Ltd Dublin 1974–77, assoc dir Purchasepoint Group London 1978–79, divnl md Viscom Group London 1979–81, head of Programme Servs TVS plc 1981–85, md AKA Ltd London 1986–87, jt md Roach and Partners Ltd 1989–93, fndr SP Management Consulting (UK) 1993, pres and ceo Pinches Management Consulting USA Inc 1995–2000; exec mgmnt and consulting assignments for: MTV Networks Europe, Village Roadshow/Austereo/Optus, Pittard Sullivan, Emap plc, Pacific Investments, Media Advisors Int, Capital Media Gp plc, Sportsworld Media Gp plc, Ascent Media Gp Inc, BBC Broadcast Ltd; *Recreations* personal development and fitness, collecting music, motor sport, photography; *Style*— Stuart Pinches, Esq; ✉ 53 Pier House, Cheyne Walk, London SW3 5HG (tel 020 7349 0391, e-mail stuart@wiseones.demon.co.uk)

PINCKNEY, David Charles; s of Dr Charles Percy Pinckney (d 1982), of Ascot, Berks, and Norah Manisty, *née* Boucher (d 1988); *b* 13 September 1940; *Educ* Winchester, New Coll Oxford (MA); *m* 25 May 1974, Susan Audrey, da of Col Austin Richards (d 1974), of Writtle, Essex; 2 da (Katherine b 1974, Caroline b 1976), 1 s (Charles b 1977); *Career* sr audit ptnr Peat Marwick Mitchell CAs France 1977–83 (London 1963–67, Paris and Lyons 1968–83), md Wrightson Wood Financial Services Ltd 1984–86, gp fin dir Thornton and Co Ltd 1987–97, vice-chm AXA Investment Managers 1998–2003; chm: Ventus VCT plc 2005–, Syndicate Asset Mgmnt plc 2005–, Rutley European Property Ltd 2005–; dir East Hampshire Housing Assoc 1995–99; govr Br Sch Paris 1981–83; memb Ctee of Mgmnt Inst of Child Health 1992–96; FCA (ACA 1966); *Recreations* skiing, tennis, classic cars, opera; *Clubs* Brooks's (chm 1999–2002), Hurlingham, Vincent's (Oxford); *Style*— David Pinckney, Esq; ✉ Southcot House, Chapmanslade, Westbury, Wiltshire BA13 4AU (tel 01373 832568)

PINCUS, George Bernard; s of Dr Joseph Victor Pincus (d 1946), of Brighton, and Ruth, *née* Burns (d 2003); *b* 13 November 1942; *Educ* Epsom Coll; *m* 1, 21 May 1965 (m dis); 2 s (Benjamin b 1969, Damian b 1970); m 2, 20 Dec 1986, Carolyn, *née* Shaljean; *Career* md: PVAF 1974–84, BBDO Ltd 1984–90, Interpartners 1990–; dir Retail Marketing Partnership 1990–, chm The Works London Ltd 1998–; chm Cncl Epsom Coll 2003– (memb 1965–, vice-chm 1995–2003); *Recreations* visual arts, theatre, history, travel; *Style*— George B Pincus, Esq; ✉ Willoughbys West, Wrens Hill, Oxshott, Surrey KT22 0HN; office (tel 01372 844406)

PINDAR, George Thomas Ventress (Tom); OBE (1986), DL; s of George Kyte Grice Pindar (d 1959), and Mary Ann, *née* Ventress (d 1973); *b* 30 January 1928; *Educ* Scarborough HS, Leeds Coll of Technol, Georgia State Coll (MBA); *m* 22 May 1953, Margery Joyce Pointer; 1 da (Margaret Ann b 17 Nov 1954), 1 s (George Andrew b 27 Oct 1957); *Career* pres G A Pindar & Son Ltd (holding co for printing, software and franchise business interests); chm Scarborough Renaissance Town Team; memb Co of Merchant Adventurers of the City of York, Liveryman Worshipful Co of Stationers and Newspaper Makers; *Recreations* theatre, music, swimming, hill walking, gardening; *Style*— Tom Pindar, Esq, OBE, DL; ✉ Court Close, 10 High Street, Scalby, Scarborough, North Yorkshire YO13 0PT (tel 01723 372414); G A Pindar & Son Ltd, Thornburgh Road, Eastfield, Scarborough, North Yorkshire YO11 3UY (tel 01723 581581, fax 01723 502335, website www.pindar.com)

PINDER, Dr Jennifer Marion; da of John Raymond Pinder (d 1988), of Doncaster, S Yorks, and Elizabeth Ross, *née* Ward (d 1991); *b* 15 December 1947; *Educ* Queen Ethelburga's Sch Harrogate, Doncaster Tech Coll, Univ of Sheffield (BDS), RCS England (MGDS), Birkbeck Coll London (BSc); *Partner* Ross Henderson; *Career* in gen dental practice in various locations incl City of London 1971–75, Sunnybrook Hosp Univ of Toronto 1976–78, assoc in gen dental practice City of London 1978–88, in own practice 1988–2002; chm and pres Gen Dental Practitioners Assoc 1983–87, fndr chm Women in Dentistry 1985–87 (hon pres 1997–2000), pres Metropolitan Branch BDA 1990–91 (sec 1987–94); memb: GDC 1984–2001, Standing Dental Advsy Ctee 1990–93, Standing Ctee on Dental and Surgical Materials 1992–94, Bd Faculty of Gen Dental Practitioners 1992–98 (vice-dean 1995–96), Stakeholder Bd Southern Trains 2006; govr Eastman Dental Hosp 1986–91; FFGDP (UK) RCS 2006; *Recreations* Burmese cats, IT, genealogy, embroidery; *Style*— Dr Jennifer Pinder; ✉ 16 Chelsfield Gardens, London SE26 4DJ (tel 020 8291 0063, e-mail jenniferpinder1@btinternet.com); Jennifer Pinder, BUPA Wellness Dental Centre, 36–38 Cornhill, London EC3V 3ND (tel 020 7200 5800, www.dentistforphobics.co.uk)

PINE, Courtney; OBE (2000); *b* 18 March 1964; *Career* jazz musician (saxophonist, also plays clarinet, flute and keyboards); fndr memb: Jazz Warriors 1985, The Abiba Jazz Arts 1985; presenter: Millennium Jazz (BBC Radio 2) 1999, Global Jazz Tour (BBC World Service) 2000–01, Courtney Pine's Jazz Crusade (BBC Radio 2) 2001–, UK Black (BBC Radio 2) 2003, Jazz Makers (BBC Radio 2) 2004; musical dir BBC Windrush Gala Concert; MOBO Award for Best Jazz Act 1996 and 1997 (nominated 2001), Best Live Band BBC Jazz Awards 2002, Gold Badge Award Br Acad of Composers and Songwriters; fell Leeds Coll of Music 2002, Hon DMus Univ of Westminster; *Albums* Journey To The Urge Within 1986 (Silver Award), Out Of Many One People (with Jazz Warriors) 1987, Destiny's Song & The Image Of Pursuance 1988, The Vision's Tale 1989, Closer To Home 1990, Within the Realm of Our Dreams 1991, To the Eyes of Creation 1993, Modern Day Jazz Stories 1996 (nominated Mercury Music Prize 1996), Underground 1997, Another Story (remixes) 1998, Back in the Day 2000, Devotion 2003; *Soundtracks* History is Made at Night 1999, It Was an Accident 2000 (nominated Best Ind Film Score Award), Mandela: A Living Legend (BBC 1) 2002; *Style*— Courtney Pine, Esq, OBE; ✉ c/o Free Trade Agency, Free Trade House, 9 Chapel Place, Rivington Street, London EC2A 3DQ

PINHORN, Margaret (Maggie) (Mrs Martin Dyke-Coomes); da of George Herbert Pinhorn (d 1996), and Mary Elizabeth Suther (d 1963); *b* 1 November 1943; *Educ* Walthamstow Hall Sch for Girls Sevenoaks, Central Sch of Art and Design London; *m* 24 June 1978, Martin Dyke-Coomes, *qv*, s of Ernest Thomas Dyke-Coomes, of Crawley, W Sussex; 1 s (Ned Alexander b 1981), 1 da (Amy Elizabeth b 1983), 2 adopted s (Anthony b 1967, Claude b 1973); *Career* artist, dir, designer, prodr; fndr of Alternative Arts 1971– and dir: Covent Garden St Theatre 1975–88, Soho Street Theatre 1988–93; started career in films in 1965 at Pinewood Studios in Art Dept of James Bond movie; worked on Br feature films incl: Chitty Chitty Bang Bang, Otley, Till Death Us Do Part; ind film maker, made Dynamo (1970), and Tunde's Film (1973); started Basement Community Arts Workshop in Cable Street 1972; made one of the first 'Open Door' progs for BBC TV and went on to res and present the first BBC TV series 'Grapevine' for Community Programmes Unit; nat co-ordinator of the Assoc of Community Artists 1974–79; vice-chm Tower Hamlets Arts Ctee 1975–79; memb: Arts Cncl Community Art Ctee 1975–79, Gtr London Arts Community Arts Ctee 1979–81; dir: Circus UK 1985–, Alternative Art Galleries 1991–95, Spitalfields Arts Devpt Prog 1993–, Cityside Regeneration Raising the Profile prog 1998–2002; *Recreations* being with my children, creative cooking, collecting wines, travel, philosophy, the arts; *Clubs* West Ham Football, Soho Society; *Style*— Ms Maggie Pinhorn; ✉ Alternative Arts, Top Studio, Montefiore Centre, Hanbury Street, London E1 5HZ (tel 020 7375 0441, fax 020 7375 0484, e-mail info@alternativearts.co.uk)

PINKER, Prof Robert Arthur; CBE (2005); s of Joseph Pinker (d 1976), and Dora Elizabeth, *née* Winyard (d 1987); *b* 27 May 1931; *Educ* Holloway Co Sch, LSE (Cert Soc Sc), Univ of London (BSc, MSc); *m* 24 June 1955, Jennifer Farrington (1994), da of Fred Boulton (d 1941); 2 da (Catherine b 1963, Lucy b 1965); *Career* Nat Serv, 2 Lt Royal Ulster Rifles 1951–52; TA, Lt London Irish Rifles 1952–54; head of Sociology Dept Goldsmiths Coll London 1964–72, Lewisham prof of social admin Goldsmiths and Bedford Colls London 1972–74, prof of social studies Chelsea Coll London 1974–78; LSE: prof of social work studies 1978–93, prof of social admin 1993–96 (prof emeritus 1996–), pro-dir 1985–88; pro-vice-chllr for social sci Univ of London 1988–90; chm: Social Admin Assoc 1974–77, Advsy Cncl Centre for Policy on Ageing 1971–81 (chm of govrs 1981–94), Jl of Social Policy 1981–86 (ed 1977–81), Editorial Bd Ageing and Soc 1981–91; scientific advsr Nursing Res DHSS 1974–79 and 1980–82; memb: Social Sci Res Cncl 1972–76, Working Pty on Role and Tasks of Social Workers Barclay Ctee 1981–82, Cncl Advertising Standards Authy 1988–96, Cncl Direct Mail Accreditation and Recognition Centre 1995–96; govr Goldsmiths Coll London 2001–07; Press Complaints Cmmn: memb 1991–2003, actg chm 2002–03, int conslt 2003–; chm Deptford Challenge Tst 2006–; hon fell Goldsmiths Coll London 1999; fell Soc of Eds 2004; *Recreations* reading, writing, travel, unskilled gardening; *Style*— Prof Robert Pinker, CBE; ✉ 76 Coleraine Road, Blackheath, London SE3 7PE (tel 020 8858 5320, fax 020 8293 4770, e-mail rpinker@freenetname.co.uk); London School of Economics and Political Science, Houghton Street, London WC2A 2AE (tel 020 7405 7686)

PINNELL, Raoul Michael; s of late David Andrew Pinnell, OBE, and Madeleine Laura, *née* Farrell; *b* 13 June 1951; *Educ* Bradfield Coll, Ealing Sch of Mgmnt (HND Business Studies), PCL (Dip Mktg), Imede Switzerland (PED); *m* 31 Aug 1976, Judith Jane, da of John Goslett, MBE; 2 s (Henry b 19 May 1983, Philip b 8 July 1985); *Career* salesman H J Heinz 1971–72, product mangr Findus 1972–75, gp product mangr Table Top South Africa 1975–77; Nestlé (Findus): regnl sales mangr 1977–79, gp product mangr new product devpt 1979–80, mktg mangr new product devpt 1981–83, mktg mangr existing brands 1983–85, gen mktg mangr 1985–89; The Prudential Assurance Co Ltd: nat mktg mangr 1989–90, mktg dir 1991–94; dir of mktg National Westminster Bank plc 1994–96, vice-pres branding and marketing communications Shell International Petroleum Co Ltd 1996–2003, chm Shell Brands Int AG 2004–; FCIM; *Clubs* IOD; *Style*— Raoul Pinnell, Esq; ✉ Shell Brands International AG, Baarermatte, CH-6340 Baar, Switzerland (tel 00 41 41 769 4251)

PINNINGTON, Christopher John; s of William F Pinnington, of Cheshire, and Dorothy Joan Pinnington (d 1970); *b* 22 August 1956; *Educ* Stonyhurst, Univ of Bristol (BSc); *m* 1986, Fiona Mary, da of D N A McLure; 2 s (James Oliver b 8 March 1989, Benjamin William b 13 Feb 1995), 1 da (Harriet Anna b 31 May 1991); *Career* graduate trainee rising to assoc dir D'Arcy Masius Benton & Bowles 1978–82, dir Wight Collins Rutherford Scott 1982–88, managing ptnr Ball WCRS Sydney 1988–90, managing ptnr FCO Ltd 1990–93, ceo Euro RSCG Wnek Gosper 1993–2004, global chief exec Euro RSCG Worldwide UK 2004–06, chief operating offr Euro RSCG Worldwide 2006–; MIPA; *Recreations* sailing, tennis, advertising; *Clubs* Hurlingham, RAC; *Style*— Christopher Pinnington, Esq; ✉ Euro RSCG Worldwide, Cupola House, 15 Alfred Place, London WC1 (tel 020 7240 4111)

PINNINGTON, Roger Adrian; TD; s of William Austin Pinnington (d 1979), of Alderley Edge, Cheshire, and Elsie Amy Pinnington (d 1983); *b* 27 August 1932; *Educ* Rydal Sch Colwyn Bay, Lincoln Coll Oxford (MA); *m* (Marjorie) Ann, da of George Alan Livingstone Russell, of Beverley, E Yorks; 3 da (Suzanne b 1963, Sally-Ann b 1964, Nikki b 1975), 1 s (Andrew b 1967); *Career* 2 Lt RA 1952, Maj Royal Mil Police 1960; dir: William E Cary Ltd 1964–74, Jonas Woodhead & Sons plc 1968–74; md TRW Cam Gears Ltd 1974–82, vice-pres TRW Europe Inc 1980–82, dep chm and chief exec UBM Group plc 1982–85, dir Norcros plc 1985–86; dir and chief exec: Royal Ordnance plc 1986–87, Pilgrim House Group 1987–89; chm: Blackwood Hodge plc 1988–90, Petrocon Group plc 1989–91, Aqualisa Products Ltd 1991–93, Jenbacher Holdings (UK) plc 1991–95, Toleman Holdings Co Ltd 1992–94, Lynx Group plc 1992–98, Cortworth plc 1994–97, Huntingdon Life Sciences Group plc 1994–99, BWA Group plc 1994–2000, DF Group Ltd 1998–2000; dir Swithland plc 1993–94; currently chm: Armour Trust plc, Harford Consultancy Services Ltd, Montanaro Holdings Ltd; Freeman City of London, Liveryman Worshipful Co of Glaziers 1977; CIMgt 1988, FRSA 1983; *Recreations* gardening, collecting silver sauce bottle labels; *Clubs* Vincent's (Oxford), RAC; *Style*— Roger A Pinnington, Esq, TD

PINNOCK, Trevor David; CBE (1992); s of Kenneth Alfred Thomas Pinnock, of Canterbury, Kent, and Joyce Edith, *née* Muggleton; *b* 16 December 1946; *Educ* Canterbury Cathedral Choir Sch, Simon Langton GS Canterbury, Royal Coll of Music (winner maj performance prizes organ and harpsichord); *Career* harpsichordist and conductor; London debut with Galliard Harpsichord Trio (jt fndr) 1966, solo debut Purcell Room London 1968, NY debut Metropolitan Opera conducting Giulio Cesare 1988; formed The English Concert 1972 (dir 1973–2002), London debut of the English Concert English Bach Festival 1973; artistic dir and princ conductor Nat Arts Centre Orchestra Ottawa 1991–96; conductor The English Concert BBC Proms; tours of Europe, USA, Canada, Japan, South America (solo, with The English Concert, and as orchestral conductor); memb European Brandenburg Ensemble (tours of UK and Far East) 2006–; Baroque Instrumental Section Gramophone Award 2001 (for recording of Bach Partitas); Hon Dr Univ of Kent, Hon PhD Univ of Ottawa 1993; Hon RAM; Officier de l'Ordre des Arts et des Lettres (France) 1998; *Recordings* extensive discography incl solo, concerto and chamber work; *Style*— Trevor Pinnock, Esq, CBE; ✉ c/o Askonas Holt Ltd, 27 Chancery Lane, London WC2A 1PF (tel 020 7400 1751, fax 020 7400 1799, e-mail info@askonasholt.co.uk)

PINSENT, Sir Matthew Clive; kt (2005), CBE (2001, MBE 1993); s of Rev Ewen Macpherson Pinsent, of Child Okeford, Dorset, and Jean Grizel, *née* McMicking; *b* 10 October 1970; *Educ* Eton, St Catherine's Coll Oxford (BA); *Career* amateur rower; memb Leander Club 1989–, sr int debut 1989 (jr debut 1987), ret from int competition 2004; honours incl: Gold medal coxless pairs World Jr Championships 1988, Bronze medal coxed fours World Championships 1989, Gold medal coxless pairs World Championships 1991 (new world record 6 mins 21 secs), 1993, 1994 (new world record 6 mins 18 secs), 1995, 2001 and 2002 (new world record 6 mins 14 secs), Gold medal coxless pairs Olympic Games Barcelona 1992 (new Olympic record 6 mins 27 secs), Gold medal coxless pairs Olympic Games Atlanta 1996, Gold medal coxless fours World Championships 1997, 1998 and 1999, Gold medal coxless fours Olympic Games Sydney 2000, Gold medal coxed pairs World Championships 2001, Gold medal coxless fours Olympic Games Athens 2004; flagbearer Olympic Games Sydney 2000; memb IOC 2002–04; pres OUBC 1992–93 (twice univ boat race winner); winner Team of the Year BBC Sports Personality of the Year Awards 1996 (with Steve Redgrave) and 2004 (with James Cracknell, Ed Coode and Steve Williams), Thomas Keller medal FISA 2005; *Recreations* golf; *Style*— Sir Matthew Pinsent, CBE; ✉ c/o Leander Club, Henley-on-Thames, Oxfordshire RG9 2LP (tel 01491 575782)

PINTER, Harold; CH (2002), CBE (1966); s of Jack Pinter (d 1997), and Frances Pinter; *b* 10 October 1930; *Educ* Hackney Downs GS; *m* 1, 1956 (m dis 1980), Vivien Thompson (Vivien Merchant) (d 1982); 1 s; m 2, 1980, Lady Antonia Fraser, *qv*; *Career* playwright, director, actor; Cwlth Award 1981, David Cohen Prize for Lifetime Achievement in

Literature 1995, Laurence Olivier Special Award 1996, Molière d'Honneur 1997, Sunday Times Award for Literary Excellence 1997, Critics' Circle Award 2000, Brianza Poetry Prize 2000, South Bank Show Award 2001, Golden Pen Award 2001, Hermann Keston Medallion 2001, World Leaders' Award 2001, Premio Fiesole ai Maestri del Cinema 2001, Critics' Circle Special 50th Year Award 2004, Nobel Prize for Literature 2005, Wilfred Owen Poetry Prize 2005, Franz Kafka Prize 2005, European Theatre Prize 2006; Hon DLitt: Univ of Reading 1970, Univ of Birmingham 1971, Univ of Glasgow 1974, UEA 1974, Univ of Stirling 1979, Brown Univ RI 1982, Univ of Hull 1986, Univ of Sussex 1990, Univ of East London 1994, Univ of Sofia 1995, Univ of Bristol 1998, Univ of London 1999, Univ of Aristotle Thessaloniki 2000, Univ of Florence 2001, Univ of Turin 2002, Dublin Univ 2004, Univ of Leeds 2007; hon memb: American Acad and Inst of Arts & Letters 1984, American Acad of Arts and Sciences 1985; hon fell: Modern Language Assoc, Queen Mary Coll London 1987; CLit 1998 (FRSL), fell BAFTA 1997; Legion d'Honneur (France) 2007; *Directing* The Collection (Aldwych) 1962, The Lover and The Dwarfs (Arts) 1963, The Birthday Party (Aldwych) 1964, The Man in the Glass Booth (London) 1967 (NY 1968), Exiles (Mermaid) 1970, Butley (Criterion, film 1973) 1971, Next of Kin (NT) 1974, Otherwise Engaged (Queen's) 1975 (NY 1977), The Innocents (NY) 1977, Blithe Spirit (NT) 1977, The Rear Column (Globe) 1978, Close of Play (NT) 1979, The Hothouse (Hampstead) 1980, Quartermaine's Terms (Queen's) 1981, Incident at Tulse Hill (Hampstead) 1982, The Trojan War Will Not Take Place (NT) 1983, The Common Pursuit (Lyric Hammersmith) 1984, One for the Road (Lyric Studio) 1984, Sweet Bird of Youth (Haymarket) 1985, Circe and Bravo (Hampstead, Wyndham's) 1986, Mountain Language (NT) 1988 (televised), Vanilla (Lyric) 1990, The New World Order (Royal Court) 1991, The Caretaker (Comedy) 1991, Party Time (Almeida, televised 1992) 1991, Oleanna (Royal Court and Duke of York's) 1993, Landscape (Gate Dublin, RNT, televised 1995) 1994, Taking Sides (Chichester Festival and Criterion) 1995, Twelve Angry Men (Comedy) 1996, Life Support 1997, Ashes to Ashes (Royal Court, Italy and France) 1997–98, The Late Middle Classes 1999, Celebration and The Room 2000, No Man's Land (RNT) 2001, The Old Masters (Comedy) 2004; *Acting* Anew McMaster Co (Ireland) 1951–53, Donald Wolfit Company 1953, rep at Chesterfield, Whitby, Huddersfield, Colchester, Bournemouth, Torquay, Birmingham, Palmers Green, Worthing and Richmond 1953–59, Mick in The Caretaker (London) 1960, Lenny in The Homecoming (Watford) 1969, Deeley in Old Times (Los Angeles) 1985, Hirst in No Man's Land (London) 1992–93, Roote in The Hothouse (Chichester, London) 1995, Look Europe! (Almeida) 1997, Mojo (film) 1997, The Collection (Gate Dublin) 1997 (Donmar Warehouse 1998), Mansfield Park (film) 1998, The Tailor of Panama (film) 2000, One for the Road (New Ambassadors and Lincoln Center Festival NY) 2001, Sketch: Press Conference (RNT) 2002, Krapp's Last Tape (Royal Court) 2006; *Plays* The Room (1957), The Birthday Party (1957), The Dumb Waiter (1957), The Hothouse (1958), A Slight Ache (1958), A Night Out (1959), The Caretaker (1959), Night School (1960), The Dwarfs (1960), The Collection (1961), The Lover (1962), Tea Party (1964), The Homecoming (1964), The Basement (1966), Landscape (1967), Silence (1968), Night (1969), Old Times (1970), Monologue (1972), No Man's Land (1974), Betrayal (1978), Family Voices (1980), Victoria Station (1982), A Kind of Alaska (1982), One For the Road (1984), Mountain Language (1988), The New World Order (1991), Party Time (1991), Moonlight (1993), Ashes to Ashes (1996), Celebration (1999); *Screenplays* The Caretaker (1962), The Servant (1962), The Pumpkin Eater (1963), The Quiller Memorandum (1965), Accident (1966), The Birthday Party (1967), The Homecoming (1969), The Go-Between (1969), Langrishe Go Down (1970), A la Recherche du Temps Perdu (1972), The Last Tycoon (1974), The French Lieutenant's Woman (1980), Betrayal (1981), Victory (1982), Turtle Diary (1984), The Handmaid's Tale (1987), Reunion, The Heat of the Day (1988), The Comfort of Strangers (1989), The Trial (1989), Sleuth (2007); *Poetry* War (2003); *Style*— Harold Pinter, Esq, CH, CBE, CLit; ✉ c/o Judy Daish Associates, 2 St Charles Place, London W10 6EG (tel 020 8964 8811, fax 020 8964 8966, website www.haroldpinter.org)

PINTUS, Matthew; s of Ronald Pintus, of Surrey, and Carmel, *née* Corcoran; *b* 14 September 1956; *Educ* Ampleforth, Univ of Warwick, Guildford Coll of Law; *Career* Russell Cooke Potter and Chapman 1981–85, Macfarlanes 1985– (currently ptnr i/c of probate); memb Soc of Tst and Estate Practitioners; *Publications* Butterworths Wills Probate and Administration (ed Contentious Matters section), Butterworths Encyclopaedia of Forms and Precedents (ed Insolvent Estates section); *Recreations* bridge, opera, sailing; *Clubs* Garrick; *Style*— Matthew Pintus, Esq; ✉ Macfarlanes, 10 Norwich Street, London EC4A 1BD (tel 020 7831 9222, fax 020 7831 5607)

PIPE, Martin Charles; CBE (2000); s of D A C Pipe, of Somerset, and B A Pipe; *b* 29 May 1945; *Educ* Queen's Coll Taunton; *m* Mary Caroline, 1 s (David Edward b 7 Feb 1973); *Career* racehorse trainer; major wins incl: Champion Hurdle (twice), Grand National, Welsh National, Irish National, Scottish National, Midlands National, Hennessy Gold Cup, Mackeson Gold Cup; trained 4 winners at Royal Ascot; only trainer to train over 200 winners in a season, trained 28 winners at Cheltenham Festival, only trainer to train 4 winners at Cheltenham Festival in consecutive years; champion trainer Nat Hunt 15 times; Hon DSc Univ of Liverpool 2007; *Books* subject of Martin Pipe - The Champion Trainer's Story; *Style*— Martin Pipe, Esq, CBE; ✉ Pond House, Nicholashayne, Wellington, Somerset TA21 9QY (tel 01884 840715, fax 01884 841343, e-mail martin@martinpipe.co.uk, website www.martinpipe.co.uk)

PIPER, Geoffrey Steuart Fairfax; DL (Merseyside 1993); s of Sqdn Ldr Donald Steuart Piper (d 1972), of Bakewell, Derbys, and Nancy Fairfax, *née* Robson (d 1990); *b* 8 June 1943; *Educ* Repton, Pembroke Coll Cambridge (MA); *m* 29 July 1967, Susan Elizabeth, da of Roswell Douglas Arnold; 3 da (Jennifer (Mrs William Simms) b 1968, Angela (Mrs Simon Golton) b 1970, Caroline (Mrs Hugh Strickland) b 1973), 1 s (Charles b 1980); *Career* ptnr i/c Deloitte Haskins & Sells: CI 1980–86, Liverpool 1986–90; pres Jersey Soc of Chartered and Certified Accountants 1983–85, pres Liverpool Soc of Chartered Accountants 1999–2000; chm Business Opportunities on Merseyside 1987–93, dep chm LSC Gtr Merseyside 2001–03; dir: Mersey Partnership 1993–, Coral Products plc 1995–; chief exec NW Business Leadership Team 1990–, memb NW Regnl Assembly 1998–, chm NW Regnl Review Bd 2003–, chm London 2012 NW Business Forum; FCA 1973; *Recreations* sport, poetry, choral music; *Clubs* Royal & Ancient, MCC, Lincoln City FC; *Style*— Geoffrey Piper, Esq, DL; ✉ Smithy House, Handley, Cheshire CH3 9DT (tel 01829 770825); North West Business Leadership Team, Daresbury Laboratories, Keckwick Lane, Daresbury, Warrington, Cheshire WA4 4AD (tel 01925 212078, fax 01925 212095, e-mail geoffrey.piper@nwblt.co.uk)

PIPPARD, Prof Martin John; s of Dr John Sutton Pippard, of Woodford Green, Essex, and Kathleen Marjorie, *née* Fox; *b* 16 January 1948; *Educ* Buckhurst Hill Co HS Univ of Birmingham (BSc, MB ChB); *m* 15 May 1976, Grace Elizabeth, da of Wallace Swift, of Barnsley, S Yorks; 1 da (Helen b 1977), 2 s (Timothy b 1980, Benjamin b 1983); *Career* conslt haematologist MRC Clinical Res Centre Harrow 1983–88, prof of haematology Univ of Dundee 1989–, dean Univ of Dundee Med Sch 2007– (undergrad teaching dean 2001–06); memb: Br Soc for Haematology, American Soc of Hematology, Assoc of Clinical Pathologists, assoc ed British Jl of Haematology; FRCPath 1994 (MRCPath 1982), FRCP 1988, FRCPEd 1998; *Publications* author of scientific papers on iron metabolism and its disorders; *Recreations* hill walking, gardening; *Style*— Prof Martin Pippard; ✉ Medical School, University of Dundee, Dundee DD1 9SY (tel 01382 660111, e-mail m.j.pippard@dundee.ac.uk)

PIRIE, David Alan Tarbat; s of Maj Halyburton Berkeley Pirie, MC, TD, DM (d 1984), and Joyce Elaine, *née* Tarbat; *b* 4 December 1946; *Educ* Trinity Coll Glenalmond, Univ of York (BA); *m* 21 June 1983, Judith Leslie, da of Maj William Leslie Harris (d 1985); 1 da (Alice b 1984), 1 s (Jack b 1987); *Career* writer, film and TV critic; Time Out: TV critic 1970–74, film critic 1974–80, film ed 1981–84; film critic 1976–: Kaleidoscope (BBC Radio 4), BBC World Service, Capital Radio; contrib 1976–: The Times, Sunday Times, The Media Show, Did You See?, The South Bank Show, Sight and Sound, Movie Magazine; film columnist Options Magazine 1981–92, literary ed Event Magazine 1980–81; film and TV screenwriter 1984–; works incl: Rainy Day Women 1984 (winner Drama Prize NY Film and TV Festival), Total Eclipse of the Heart (screenplay), Mystery Story (screenplay from own novel), Wild Things (BBC TV film) 1989, Never Come Back (winner Best Mini-series prize Chicago Film Festival) 1990, Ashenden (TV series) 1991, Natural Lies (TV series) 1992, Black Easter (winner Best TV Feature Prize Chicago Film Festival), The Element of Doubt (TV film) 1996, Breaking the Waves (collaboration on Lars von Trier's award-winning feature film), The Woman in White (BAFTA nominated TV serial, winner Drama Prize Houston Int TV & Film Festival 1998), Murder Rooms: The Dark Beginnings of Sherlock Holmes (Edgar nominated TV series), The Wyvern Mystery (TV film) 1999, The Safe House (TV series), Murder Rooms (TV series) 2001 (winner Best TV Detective Series Crimescene/Sherlock Holmes Magazine/NFT Awards 2002), Night Gallery (US TV) 2002, Sad Cypress (TV film) 2003, The Strange Case of Arthur Conan Doyle (TV film) 2004; sr tutor Br Film and TV Prodrs Assoc Advanced Screenwriting Course 1990–; *Books* Heritage of Horror (1973), Mystery Story (1980), Anatomy of the Movies (1981), The Patient's Eyes (2001), The Night Calls (2002), The Dark Water (2004), A New Heritage of Horror (2007); *Recreations* running; *Clubs* Soho House; *Style*— David Pirie, Esq; ✉ c/o Stephen Durbridge, The Agency (London) Ltd, 24 Pottery Lane, London W11 4LZ (tel 020 7727 1346, fax 020 7727 9037, e-mail info@theagency.co.uk)

PIRIE, Dr (Duncan) Madsen; s of Douglas Gordon Pirie, and Eva, *née* Madsen; *b* 24 August 1940; *Educ* Univ of Edinburgh (MA), Univ of St Andrews (PhD), Univ of Cambridge (MPhil); *Career* prof of philosophy and logic Hillsdale Michigan USA 1975–78, pres Adam Smith Institute 1978–, memb PM's Citizen's Charter Panel 1991–95; *Books* Trial and Error & The Idea of Progress (1978), Test Your IQ (with Eamonn Butler, 1983), Book of the Fallacy (1985), Micropolitics (1988), Privatization (1988), Boost Your IQ (with Eamonn Butler, 1991), Blueprint for a Revolution (1992), The Sherlock Holmes IQ Book (with Eamonn Butler, 1995); *Recreations* films; *Style*— Dr Madsen Pirie; ✉ Adam Smith Institute, 23 Great Smith Street, London SW1P 3BL (tel 020 7222 4995, fax 020 7222 7544)

PIRRET, David John; s of George Riddle Pirret, of Edinburgh, and Marion, *née* Taylor Maxwell; *b* 29 December 1952; *Educ* Eastwood HS Glasgow, Univ of Strathclyde (BA); *m* 1 March 1980, Patricia Zoe Frances, da of Maj Patrick Dennis Warren; 1 da (Heather Marion Joy b 30 Nov 1981), 2 s (Andrew George Nigel, James Patrick Gordon (twins) b 5 Jan 1985); *Career* various posts in Royal Dutch/Shell Gp 1974–79, divnl mangr Shell Chemicals UK Ltd 1987–89, lubricants dir Shell UK Ltd 1989–92, retail dir Shell UK Ltd 1992–96, head of mktg Shell Int Petroleum Co Ltd 1996–97, pres and co chm Shell Brasil SA 1997–2001, exec vice-pres global businesses Shell Int Petroleum Co Ltd 2001–02, ceo and pres Pennzoil Quaker State Co USA 2002–03, ceo Shell Lubricants 2003–; *Recreations* golf, sailing; *Clubs* RAC; *Style*— David Pirret, Esq; ✉ Shell International Petroleum Co Ltd, Shell Centre, London SE1 7NA (tel 020 7934 5747, fax 020 7934 6938)

PISSARIDES, Prof Christopher Antoniou; s of Antonios Pissarides, of Cyprus, and Eudokia, *née* Georgiades; *b* 20 February 1948; *Educ* Pancyprian Gymnasium Nicosia, Univ of Essex (BA, MA), LSE (PhD); *m* 24 July 1986, Francesca Michela, da of Antonio Cassano, of Rome; 1 s (Antony b 1987), 1 da (Miranda b 1988); *Career* LSE: lectr 1976–82, reader 1982–86, prof 1986–, convener Economics Dept 1996–99, dir Macroeconomics Research Prog 1990–, dir Int Summer Sch in Economics 1993–96 and 2001–03; research fell: Centre for Economic Policy Research 1994–, Inst for the Study of Labor (IZA) Bonn 2001–; visiting prof: Harvard Univ 1979–80, Princeton Univ 1984, European Univ Inst 1989, Univ of Calif Berkeley 1989–90; Houblon-Norman fell Bank of England 1994; memb Bd Review of Economic Studies 1983–92; bd chm Economica 2007– (ed 1980–83, assoc ed 1996–), assoc ed Economic Jl 2000–05; conslt: World Bank, EU, OECD; expert Treasy Ctee House of Commons 2001–05, memb Cyprus Monetary Policy Ctee 2000–, non-national sr assoc Forum for Economic Research in the Arab Countries, Iran and Turkey 2002–, memb Employment Taskforce EC 2003–04; memb Interim Governing Bd Univ of Cyprus 1989–95; jt winner IZA Prize in Labor Economics 2005; memb: Royal Economic Soc (memb Cncl 1996–2001), European Economic Assoc (memb Cncl 2005–); fell Econometric Soc (memb Cncl 2005–), FBA 2002; *Books* Labour Market Adjustment (1976), Equilibrium Unemployment Theory (1990, 2 edn 2000); also author of articles in professional jls; *Recreations* gardening, cooking; *Style*— Prof Christopher Pissarides; ✉ London School of Economics and Political Science, Houghton Street, London WC2A 2AE (tel 020 7955 7513, fax 020 7831 1840, e-mail c.pissarides@lse.ac.uk)

PITCHER, Sir Desmond Henry; kt (1992); s of George Charles Pitcher (d 1968), of Liverpool, and Alice Marion, *née* Osborne (d 1985); *b* 23 March 1935; *Educ* Liverpool Coll of Technol; *m* 1, 1961 (m dis 1973), Patricia, *née* Ainsworth; 2 da (Stephanie, Samantha (twins) b 18 May 1965); m 2, 1978 (m dis 1984), Carol Ann, *née* Rose; 2 s (George b 1 Oct 1978, Andrew b 1 March 1981); m 3, 1991, Norma Barbara, *née* Niven; *Career* devpt engr A V Roe & Co 1957–58, systems engr Automatic Telephone & Electrical Co 1958–60, nat mangr engrg Sperry Univac Ltd 1961–69; md: MDS (Data Processing) Ltd 1966–71, Sperry Univac Ltd 1971–73; dep chm Sperry Rand Ltd 1973–76 (dir 1971–73), vice-pres Int Div Sperry Univac Corp 1973–76; md: Truck and Bus Div BL Ltd 1976–78, Plessey Telecommunications and Office Systems 1978–83; dir Plessey Co 1979–83, non-exec vice-chm The Littlewoods Organisation 1993–95 (chief exec 1983–93), chm and dir Sign Brick 1999–; dir: United Utilities plc (formerly North West Water Gp plc) 1990– (dep chm 1991–93, chm 1993–98), Steeltower 2001–05, Knowledgebutton Ltd 2002–05; non-exec dir: NatWest Bank (Northern Advsy Bd) 1989–92, National Westminster Bank plc 1994–98; dep chm Everton FC Ltd 1990–98 (dir 1987–98), chm Merseyside Devpt Corp 1991–98; chm and tstee: Rocking Horse Appeal, Royal Liverpool Childrens Hosp 1997–2003 (vice-pres 2004–); tstee Outward Bound; Faraday lectr 1973–74; visiting prof of business policy Univ of Manchester 1993–98, hon fell Liverpool John Moores Univ 1993; DL Merseyside 1993–99; Freeman: City of London 1987, Worshipful Co of Info Technologists 1987; CEng, FIEE 1968, FBCS 1975, Hon FIDE 1977, CIMgt 1985, FRSA 1987; *Publications* Water Under the Bridge - 30 Years of Industrial Management (2003); *Recreations* football, opera, golf; *Clubs* Brooks's, Royal Birkdale Golf, RAC, Royal Liverpool Golf, Lancashire CC; *Style*— Sir Desmond Pitcher; ✉ Folly Farm, Sulhamstead, Berkshire RG7 4DF (tel 01189 302 326)

PITCHFORD, Hon Mr Justice; Sir Christopher John Pitchford; kt (2001); *b* 28 March 1947; *Educ* Dyffryn Comp Newport, Queen's Coll Taunton, QMC (LLB); *Career* called to the Bar Middle Temple 1969; recorder 1987, QC 1987, dep judge of the High Court 1995–2000, leader Wales & Chester Circuit 1999–2000, judge of the High Court (Queen's Bench Div) 2000–, a presiding judge of the Wales & Chester Circuit 2002–; arbitrator Motor Insurers' Bureau 1994–2000; *Style*— The Hon Mr Justice Pitchford

PITFIELD, Michael; s of Edward George Pitfield (d 1976), and Robina Heslop (d 1996); *b* 22 May 1945; *Educ* Univ of London (BSc), Univ of Reading (MA); *m* 12 Aug 1972 (m dis 2004), Angela May, da of Albert Victor McCallin (d 1969); 2 s (Alexander b 1975, Alastair b 1982), 1 da (Anna b 1979); *Career* asst dir Inst of Personnel Mgmnt 1978–89 (special

P

advsr 1989–), dir Thames Valley Business Sch 1989–90, dir of int business Henley Mgmnt Coll 1990–2006 (visiting exec fell 2006–); regular contrib to newspapers, magazines and journals, frequent speaker at int conferences and seminars; memb: European Business Govt Rels Cncl 1993–, Bd of Tstees IPRF 1995, Bd Henley-Nederland, Bd Henley in Denmark, Bd Club 7 Pinewood Studios 2002–, Bd Enless PErception Ltd 2006–; chm Advsy Bd Cygnus Devpt Inc (USA) 2000–; emeritus memb Bd UNICON (USA) 1994– (chm 1997); chartered marketer 1999; Chartered FCIPD (FIPD 1980), FRSA 1992, MIPRA 1994, FCIM 1998; *Books* How To Take Exams (1980), Developing International Managers (1996), IPD Guide to International Management Development (1997); *Recreations* writing, genealogy, history, cinema, travel; *Style—* Michael Pitfield, Esq; ✉ Henley Management College, Greenlands, Henley-on-Thames, Oxfordshire RG9 3AU

PITHER, Dr Charles Edward Pither; s of David E Pither, of Garston, Herts, and June, *née* Cadisch; *b* 21 July 1953; *Educ* Aldenham, St Thomas' Hosp Med Sch London (MB BS); *m* 22 Sept 1979, Jane Patricia Anne, da of Cdr David Roberts, MBE, RN; 3 da (Claire Elizabeth Wensley b 12 July 1982, Kate Victoria b 14 Nov 1984, Stephanie Jane Eleanor b 22 Dec 1986); *Career* instr in anaesthesia Univ of Cincinnati Med Center Ohio 1984 (fell in pain control and regnl anaesthesia 1983–84); St Thomas' Hosp: lectr and hon sr registrar 1984–85, conslt pain specialist 1986–2004, med dir INPUT Pain Mgmnt Unit 1989–2004; currently: med dir (pain servs) Powys Health Care Tst, med dir The Realhealth Inst; past sec Soc for Back Pain Research; winner Sci art 2001; co-winner: King's Fund maj grant 1987, Evian Health Award 1993; FRCA 1982; *Recreations* gardening, country sports, vintage motor cars, travel; *Style—* Dr Charles Pither; ✉ 3 Richmond Mansions, Denton Road, Twickenham, Surrey TW1 2HH (tel 020 8241 2420); The Realhealth Institute, 23–31 Beavor Lane, London W6 9AR (tel 020 8846 3714, fax 020 8563 8778, e-mail cpither@doctors.org.uk)

PITHER, Jon Peter; s of Philip John Pither (d 1965), and Vera, *née* Roth (d 1980); *b* 15 June 1934; *Educ* Dauntsey's Sch West Lavington, Queens' Coll Cambridge (MA); *m* 1961, Karin Jutta, da of Werner Gropp; 1 s (Michael Gordon Carsten b 1963), 1 da (Brigitte Clare b 1965); *Career* cmmnd Royal Sussex Regt 1969; dir: Surrey Management Services Ltd 1991–, Alumasc Group plc 1992–, Active Capital Tst plc 1996–, SOC Gp plc 1997–, Jourdan plc 1997–, Premier Direct Group plc 1997–, Metnor Group plc 1998–, The AIM VCT plc 1998–, Ultimate Leisure plc 1999–, Gold Mines of Sardinia 2001–, St Helen's Capital 2004–; Liveryman Worshipful Co of Fanmakers; *Recreations* golf; *Clubs* Athenaeum, Wisley Golf, NZ Golf, St George's Hill Golf; *Style—* Jon P Pither, Esq; ✉ Surrey Management Services, Mulberry House, 6 Clare Hill, Esher, Surrey (tel 01372 470279, fax 01372 470541)

PITKEATHLEY, Baroness (Life Peer UK 1997), of Caversham in the Royal County of Berkshire; Jill Elizabeth Pitkeathley; OBE (1993); da of Roland Wilfred Bisson (d 1980), of St Sampson's, Guernsey, and Edith May *née* Muston (d 2001); *b* 4 January 1940, Guernsey, CI; *Educ* Ladies' Coll Guernsey, Univ of Bristol (BA); *m* 1961 (m dis 1978), William Pitkeathley, s of Joseph Pitkeathley; 1 s (Hon Simon William b 9 May 1964), 1 da (Hon Rachel b 2 Aug 1966); partner, David Emerson; *Career* social worker Manchester and Essex 1961–67, voluntary servs co-ordinator NHS 1970–82, Nat Consumer Cncl 1983–86, chief exec Carers UK (formerly Nat Cncl for Carers) 1986–98; chair: New Opportunities Fund 1998–2004, Children and Families Ct Advsy and Support Service (CAFCASS) 2004–; pres: Community Cncl for Berks, Volunteering England; chair Future Builders Advsy Panel 2005–; Hon Dr: Univ of Bristol, London Met Univ; *Publications* It's My Duty Isn't It? (1989), Only Child: How to Survive Being One (1994), Cassandra and Jane (2004); *Recreations* walking, theatre, grandchildren, gardening; *Style—* The Rt Hon the Lady Pitkeathley, OBE; ✉ House of Lords, London SW1A 0PW (tel 020 7219 0358, e-mail pitkeathleyj@parliament.uk)

PITMAN, Sir Brian Ivor; kt (1994); s of Ronald Ivor Pitman, and Doris Ivy, *née* Short; *b* 13 December 1931; *Educ* Cheltenham GS; *m* 1954, Barbara Mildred Ann; 2 s (Mark, David), 1 da (Sally); *Career* chief exec and dir Lloyds Bank plc 1983–97 (dep chief exec 1982–83), chm Lloyds TSB Group plc 1997–2001 (gp chief exec 1996–97), currently sr advsr Morgan Stanley & Co Int; dir: Lloyds Bank California 1982–86, The National Bank of New Zealand 1982–97, Lloyds Bank International Ltd 1985–87 (dep chief exec 1978–81), Lloyds Merchant Bank Holdings Ltd 1985–88, NBNZ Holdings Ltd 1990–97; non-exec chm Next plc 1998–2002, chm Acturis Ltd 2000–; non-exec dir: Carlton Communications 1998–2003, Tomkins plc 2000–, The Carphone Warehouse Gp plc 2001–, Singapore Airlines Ltd 2003–, ITV plc 2003– (interim non-exec chm 2004); pres: British Bankers' Assoc 1996–97, Chartered Inst of Bankers 1997–98; govr Ashridge Mgmnt Coll 1997–; Master Guild of Int Bankers 2002–03; Hon DSc: City Univ 1996, UMIST 2000; *Recreations* golf, cricket, music; *Style—* Sir Brian Pitman

PITMAN, Giles William; s of Capt John Pitman (ka 1943), and Elizabeth Cattanach Pitman (d 1997); *b* 5 September 1938; *Educ* Eton, ChCh Oxford (MA); *m* 1961, Jane, da of Maj George De Pree; 2 s, 1 da; *Career* jt gp md Pitman plc 1981–85, fin dir Really Useful Group plc 1988–89, chief exec Summer International plc 1989–91, chm Spectral Technology Group Ltd 1991–96, ops dir The Financial Training Company 1993–94; non-exec dir: Marine & General Mutual Life Assurance Society 1976–96, Oxford House Group plc 1991–92, Hambro Insurance Services Group plc 1993–98, BFSS Investments Ltd 1993–2003, Market Link Publishing 1996–97, Sandford Ellis Ltd 1996–97, Close Brothers Protected VCT plc 1997–, Baltic Media Group Ltd 1999–2000; chm: Chant Group plc 1995–97, View Inn plc 1997–98, Peartree Foods Ltd 2001–04, High Birch Property Ltd 2001–04, W B Bawn 2002–04; hon treas: BFSS 1992–96; FCA, ACMA; *Recreations* country sports; *Clubs* Cavalry and Guards'; *Style—* Giles Pitman, Esq; ✉ Penny Cottage, Albury, Ware, Hertfordshire SG11 2LX (tel 01279 771293, fax 01279 771820)

PITMAN, Jennifer Susan (Jenny); OBE (1998); da of George Harvey, and Mary Harvey; *b* 11 June 1946; *Educ* Sarson Secdy Girls' Sch; *m* 1, 1965 (m dis), Richard Pitman; 2 s (Paul Richard, Mark Andrew Pitman, *qv*); m 2, 1997, D Stait; *Career* national hunt racehorse trainer 1975–99; dir Jenny Pitman Racing Ltd 1975–, ptnr DJS Racing 1996–, author; major races won incl: Midlands National 1977 (Watafella), Massey Ferguson Gold Cup 1980 (Bueche Giorod), Welsh National 1982 (Corbiere), 1983 (Burrough Hill Lad) and 1986 (Stears By), Grand National 1983 (Corbiere) and 1995 (Royal Athlete), King George VI Gold Cup 1984 (Burrough Hill Lad), Hennessy Gold Cup 1984 (Burrough Hill Lad), Cheltenham Gold Cup 1984 (Burrough Hill Lad) and 1991 (Garrison Savannah), Whitbread Trophy 1985 (Smith's Man), Ritz Club National Hunt Handicap 1987 (Gainsay), Sporting Life Weekend Chase 1987 (Gainsay), Philip Cornes Saddle of Gold Final 1988 (Crumpet Delite), Welsh Champion Hurdle 1991 (Wonderman) and 1992 (Don Valentino), Scottish Grand National 1995 (Willsford), Sun Alliance Chase 1996 (Nathen Lad), Supreme Novice Hurdle 1996 (Indefence), Ladbroke Hurdle Leopardstown 1997 (Master Tribe), Racing Post Chase Kempton 1997 (Mudahim), Irish National Fairyhouse 1997 (Mudahim), Stayers Hurdle Cheltenham (Princeful) 1998; first woman to train Grand National and Gold Cup winners, trainer of Esha Ness (winner of the aborted Grand National 1993); awards incl: Golden Spurs Racing Personality of the Year 1983, Cwlth Sports Awards 1983 and 1984, Piper Heidsieck Trainer of the Year 1983–84 and 1989–90, Variety Club of GB Sportswoman of the Year 1984, Golden Spurs Best National Hunt Trainer 1984; *Books* Glorious Uncertainty (autobiography, 1984), Jenny Pitman The Autobiography (1998); novels: On the Edge (2002), Double Deal (2002), The Dilemma (2003), The Vendetta (2004), The Inheritance (2005); *Style—* Mrs Jenny Pitman, OBE; ✉ Owls Barn, Kintbury, Hungerford, Berkshire RG17 9SX (tel 01488 669191, fax 01488 668999)

PITMAN, Mark Andrew; s of Richard Thomas Pitman, and Jennifer Susan (Jenny) Pitman, OBE, *qv*; *b* 1 August 1966; *Educ* Wycliffe Coll; *m* 1995, Natasha Susan Cowen; 2 da (Darcy Rose b 11 Oct 1996, Tahlia b 6 Jan 2001); *Career* national hunt jockey; debut 1983, professional 1984; trainer 1997–; second yst jockey to complete the National Course 1984, second place Conditional Jockey Championship 1986–87; asst trainer to Mrs Jenny Pitman 1993– (retained jockey 1988–93); career best of 57 winners in a season 1989–90 (incl second place in Cheltenham Gold Cup and won Ritz Club Jockey of the Meeting Aintree), second in Grand National Aintree 1991; maj races won incl: Tote Cheltenham Gold Cup 1991, Welsh Champion Hurdle 1991, The Martell Cup Steeple Chase, The Mumm Club Novices Steeple Chase, The Larchlap Chase, The Midlands Grand National, The EBF Hurdle Final, The Charterhouse Mercantile Chase, The Swish Hurdle, The John Bull Chase, The Sporting Life Weekender HCP Chase, The Old Road Securities Novice Chase, The Souter of Stirling Novices Chase; trainer 1997–2006; trained winners incl: Royal & Sun Alliance Novice Hurdle, Weatherbys Champion Bumper, Hennessy Gold Cup, Charisma Gold Cup, Tolwirth Hurdle, 2nd in Martell Grand National; bloodstock agent 2006–; television and radio presenter 2006–; *Style—* Mark Pitman, Esq; ✉ Owl's Barn, Kintbury, Hungerford, Berkshire RG17 9SX (tel 07836 792771, e-mail mark@markpitmanracing.co.uk, website www.markpitmanracing.co.uk)

PITT, Hon Bruce Michael David; o s of Baron Pitt of Hampstead (Life Peer, d 1994), and Dorothy Elaine, *née* Alleyne; *b* 18 June 1945; *Educ* King Alfred Sch Hampstead, UCL (LLB); *Career* called to the Bar Gray's Inn 1970; memb: Sub-Ctee Criminal Bar Assoc Advsy Body to Law Cmmn on Special Defence - Duress and Entrapment Coercion 1974, Bar Cncl Young Barristers' Ctee 1974–75, Senate Inns of Court and Bar Cncl 1975–76, Attorney-Gen's List of Counsel 1981–, Race Rels Ctee Bar Cncl 1990–93; recorder SE Circuit 1993–, head of chambers 1995–; dir Camden Training Centre 1996–2001; jt pres Br Caribbean Assoc 1995–; memb: Hampstead Lab Pty 1960–, Campaign Against Racial Discrimination 1964–67; memb Bars of Jamaica, Trinidad and Tobago, Barbados, and West Indies Associated States; *Recreations* swimming, arts, watching cricket; *Clubs* MCC; *Style—* The Hon Bruce Pitt; ✉ Phoenix Chambers, First Floor, Gray's Inn Chambers, Gray's Inn, London WC1R 5JA (tel 020 7404 7888, fax 020 7404 7897, e-mail clerks@phoenix-chambers.co.uk)

PITT, Nicholas John; s of George Stanhope Pitt (d 1983), of E Horsley, Surrey, and Lesley Henrietta, *née* Bayley; *b* 21 October 1950; *Educ* Aldenham, Lancaster Univ; *Partner* Alison Lang; *Career* sub ed Stratford Express 1977–79, sports writer The Sunday Times 1979–87, chief sports writer London Daily News 1987; The Sunday Times: dep sports ed 1988–94, sports ed 1994–96, sports writer 1996–; ed Close Up magazine 2006–; special award Br Sports Journalism Awards 1985; *Books* The Paddy and The Prince (1998); *Recreations* golf, tennis; *Clubs* Wimbledon Park Golf, Priory Park Tennis; *Style—* Nicholas Pitt, Esq; ✉ The Sunday Times, 1 Pennington Street, London E1 9XW (tel 020 7782 5714, fax 020 7782 5720, e-mail pittnj@globalnet.co.uk)

PITT, Ruth Angela; da of Graham James Tyrrell Pitt, of Bristol, and Jean, *née* Patterson; *b* 14 August 1952; *Educ* Chew Valley Sch, Weston-super-Mare Tech Coll, Univ of York (BA); *Partner* Ali Rashid; 1 da (Rebecca), 2 s (Josef, Thomas); *Career* trainee feature writer and sub ed IPC Magazines 1977–80; freelance writer and broadcaster for various women's magazines, newspapers, Radio Tees and BBC Radio 4 1973–80, creative writing teacher Ryedale Evening Inst 1973–80, reporter and prodr Radio Tees and Radio Aire 1980–82, sr reporter and presenter Yorkshire TV 1982–88, fndr and md Real Life Productions 1988–96, guest presenter Woman's Hour (BBC Radio 4) 1993–96, head of documentaries, religion and schools Granada TV 1996–99, ed Everyman series (BBC 1) April 1999–, creative dir documentaries BBC 2000–; advsy chair Guardian Edinburgh International TV Festival 1998, judge Sony Radio Awards 2004; formerly: memb and advsr Yorks and Humberside Arts Bd, memb North British Housing Assoc; memb: RTS 1993, BAFTA 1996; *Awards* Best Regnl Current Affrs Series RTS 1993, runner-up Options Business Woman of the Year 1995, NW Best Documentary Prize RTS 1998, Brian Redhead Special Award RTS 1998, Best Documentary Broadcast Production Awards 1998, Int Emmy 1998, NY Festival World Medal 1998, Sandford St Martin Premier Award 2003; *Recreations* running, walking, skiing, cooking, yoga, reading, family life; *Style—* Ms Ruth Pitt; ✉ c/o BBC Religion, New Broadcast House, Oxford Road, Manchester M60 1SJ (tel 0161 200 2020)

PITT FORD, Prof Tom; *Educ* Univ of London (BDS, PhD); *Career* reader UMDS London 1995–98 (sr lectr 1982–95); Dental Inst KCL: prof of endontology and hon conslt in restorative dentistry 1998–, vice-dean and dir of educn; memb: BDA, British Endodontic Soc, British Soc for Restorative Dentistry, European Soc of Endodontology, Int Assoc of Dental Research, American Assoc of Endodontists, Int Assoc of Dental Traumatology; ILTM, LDSRCS 1971, FDSRCPS 1975; *Style—* Prof Tom Pitt Ford; ✉ Dental Institute, Guy's Tower, King's College London, Guy's Hospital, London SE1 9RT

PITT-KETHLEY, (Helen) Fiona; da of Rupert Singleton Pitt-Kethley (d 1975), and Olive, *née* Banfield; *b* 21 November 1954; *Educ* Haberdashers' Aske's Girls' Sch, Chelsea Sch of Art (BA, Biddulph painting prize); *m* 1995, James Plaskett; 1 s (Alexander Michael b 15 Sept 1996); *Career* poet, travel writer, novelist and journalist; *Books* poetry collections: Sky Ray Lolly (1986), Private Parts (1987), The Perfect Man (1989), Dogs (1993), Double Act (1996), Memo from a Muse (1997); others: Journeys to the Underworld (travel book, 1988), The Misfortunes of Nigel (novel, 1991), The Literary Companion to Sex (anthology, 1992), The Maiden's Progress (novella, 1992), Too Hot to Handle (essays and letters, 1992), The Pan Principle (travel book, 1993), The Literary Companion to Low Life (anthology, 1995), Red Light Districts of the World (essays, 2000), Baker's Dozen (novel, 2000), My Schooling (autobiography, 2000); *Recreations* karate, rock-hunting, snorkelling, adopting feral cats; *Style—* Ms Fiona Pitt-Kethley

PITTAWAY, David Michael; QC (2000); s of Michael Pittaway, JP, MRCVS, of Coventry, and Heather Yvette, *née* Scott; *b* 29 June 1955; *Educ* Uppingham, Sidney Sussex Coll Cambridge (exhibitioner, MA); *m* 26 March 1983, Jill Suzanne, da of Dr Ian Douglas Bertie Newsam, MRCVS, of Cambridge; 2 s (James Frederick Henry b 9 July 1986, Charles Edward Benet b 22 July 1989); *Career* called to the Bar Inner Temple 1977 (bencher 1998); recorder Midland & Oxford Circuit 2000– (asst recorder 1998–2000); chllr Dio of Peterborough 2006; legal memb Mental Health Review Tbnl 2002–, legal assessor GMC 2002–04, legal assessor RCVS 2004–; chm Professional Negligence Bar Assoc 2005–07, memb Bar Cncl 1999–2005; FCIArb 1986; *Publications* Pittaway & Hammerton Professional Negligence Cases (1998), Atkin's Court Forms (vols 8, 28 and 29 (2)); *Recreations* gardening, music, travel; *Clubs* Garrick, RAC, Redclyffe Yacht, Wareham; *Style—* David Pittaway, Esq, QC; ✉ Hailsham Chambers, 4 Paper Buildings, Temple, London EC4Y 7EX (tel 020 7643 5000, e-mail david.pittaway@hailshamchambers.com)

PITTEWAY, Prof Michael Lloyd Victor; s of Lloyd Sydney Pitteway (d 1990), and Elsie Maud, *née* Hall (d 1947); *b* 10 February 1934; *Educ* Felsted, Queens' Coll Cambridge (MA, PhD, ScD); *m* 2 April 1956, Cynthia Ethel Patricia, da of Percival Henry Wilkins (d 1955), of Leicester; *Career* Harkness fell USA 1959–61, sr res fell Radio and Space Res Lab Slough 1961–63, computer dir Univ of Nottingham 1963–67, emeritus prof Brunel Univ 1985– (head of Computer Sci Dept 1967–85); assoc conslt Quanti Sci Information Technologies 1991–; FBCS 1968, FIMA 1972, FInstP 1978, FRSA; *Recreations* music, duplicate bridge, golf; *Clubs* Castle Royle Golf and Country; *Style—* Prof Michael Pitteway; ✉ Hedgerows, Star Lane, Knowl Hill, Berkshire RG10 9XY; Department of

Information Systems and Computing, Brunel University, Uxbridge UB8 3PH (tel 01895 203397 ext 2233, fax 01895 251686, e-mail mike.pitteway@brunel.ac.uk)

PITTILO, Prof (Robert) Michael; s of Robert Dawson Pittilo, and Betsy Brown, *née* Baird; *b* 7 October 1954, Edinburgh; *Educ* Kelvinside Acad Glasgow, Univ of Strathclyde (BSc), NE London Poly CNAA (PhD); *m* 1 Aug 1987, Dr Carol Margaret Blow; *Career* electron microscopist Glasgow Royal Infirmary and Univ of Strathclyde 1976–78, research asst NE London Poly 1978–80, post doctoral research asst Dept of Histopathology Middx Hosp Medical Sch 1981–85, hon research assoc Dept of Histopathology Univ Coll and Middx Sch of Medicine 1985–94, lectr, sr lectr and reader in biomedical sciences Kingston Univ 1985–91, prof of biomedical sciences and head of life sciences Kingston Univ 1992–94, dean Faculty of Health and Social Care Sciences Kingston Univ and St George's Hosp Medical Sch 1995–2001, pro-vice-chllr Univ of Herts 2001–05, princ and vice-chllr Robert Gordon Univ 2005–; chm UH Health 2003–05, dir UH ventures 2001–05, dir Univation Ltd 2005–07; memb numerous NHS and Dept of Health ctees and panels incl: chair Regulatory Working Gp on Herbal Medicine 2002–03, memb Modernising Healthcare Sciences Prog Bd 2005–, chair Working Gp to support the statutory regulation of acupuncture, herbal medicine and traditional Chinese medicine 2006–; non-exec dir and HE rep NHS Beds and Herts SHA 2002–05; memb Quality Assurance Agency for HE (QAA) and HEQC gps and working parties incl chair Nat Benchmarking Steering Gp for Health Professions 2003–06; memb ctees Cncl for Professions Supplementary to Medicine and Health Professions Cncl; memb: Cncl Section of Pathology RSM 1993–97, degree accreditation panels Inst of Biomedical Science 1995–, Working Gp on Educn and Trg for Complementary and Alternative Medicine BMA 1996, Educn Ctee Chartered Soc of Physiotherapy 2002–, Univs UK 2005–, Exec Ctee Univs Scotland 2006– (convenor Learning and Teaching Ctee 2006–); tstee Prince's Fndn for Integrated Health 2003–, memb NE Ctee Scottish Cncl for Devpt and Industry 2005–, memb Aberdeen City and Shire Economic Forum 2005–, non exec dir Scottish Enterprise Grampian 2006–; memb Bd QAA and QAA (Scot) 2006–; memb: Br Soc for Parasitology, Br Soc for Thrombosis and Haemostasis, Research Defence Soc, Royal Soc of Medicine; fell Royal Microscopical Soc, fell Linnean Soc, FRSM, FZS, FRSTMH, FRSH 1993, CBiol 1994 FIBiol 1994, FIBMS 1997, FRSA 2001; *Recreations* photography, hill walking, motocycling, cinema, music, clay pigeon shooting; *Clubs* Royal Northern and Univ; *Style—* Prof Michael Pittilo; ✉ The Robert Gordon University, Schoolhill, Aberdeen AB10 1FR (tel 01224 262001, fax 01224 262626, e-mail r.m.pittilo@rgu.ac.uk)

PITTOCK, Prof Murray; s of Dr Malcolm Pittock, and Dr Joan, *née* Mould; *b* 5 January 1962; *Educ* Aberdeen GS, Univ of Glasgow (Bradley Medal, Buchanan Prize, Fotheringham Bursary, MA), Balliol Coll Oxford (Snell exhibitioner, ESU scholar, Nat Speech Communication Assoc of America visiting scholar, DPhil); *m* 15 April 1989, Dr Anne Pittock; 2 da (Alexandra b 31 Jan 1990, Davidona b 7 June 1994); *Career* various posts incl lectr Pembroke Coll Oxford, jr research fell Linacre Coll Oxford and Br Acad postdoctoral fell Univ of Aberdeen until 1989, lectr then reader in English lit Univ of Edinburgh 1989–96, prof in lit Univ of Strathclyde 1996–2003 (head of English studies 1997–2000, memb Ct 1998–2000, founding dir Glasgow-Strathclyde Sch of Scottish Studies 1999–2002), prof of Scottish and Romantic lit Univ of Manchester 2003– (head of English and American studies 2003–04, dep head Arts Histories and Cultures 2004–06); Thomas Reid Inst fell Univ of Aberdeen 1994, sr Warnock fell Yale Univ 1998 and 2000–01, visiting fell in advanced Welsh and Celtic studies Univ of Wales 2002; ed Scottish Literary Jl 1995–2000, assoc ed Oxford DNB 1998–, jt founding ed Scottish Studies Review 2000–07; pres Scottish Ctee of Profs of English 2001–03; memb: Cncl Assoc for Scottish Literary Studies 1990–, Fellowship Ctee Lit, Language and History Section RSE 2004–, Humanities Research Ctee RSE 2006–, AHRC English Postgraduate Panel 2006–; memb: HE Acad, Int Assoc of Univ Profs of English; BP Humanities Research Prize 1992–93, Chatterton lectr in poetry Br Acad 2002, various invited lectureships; pres: Boswell Soc 2001–02, Edmund Burke Soc; tstee Jacobite Studies Tst 2003–; FRHistS 1992, FSA Scot 1995, fell English Assoc (FEA) 2001, FRSA 2002, FRSE 2004; *Books* The Invention of Scotland (1991), Spectrum of Decadence: The Literature of the 1890s (1993), Poetry and Jacobite Politics in Eighteenth-Century Britain and Ireland (1994), The Myth of the Jacobite Clans (1995), Inventing and Resisting Britain (1997), Jacobitism (1998), Celtic Identity and the British Image (1999), Scottish Nationality (2001), A New History of Scotland (2003, called for Wolfson Prize for the Public Understanding of History), The Edinburgh History of Scottish Literature (co-ed, 2006), The Reception of Sir Walter Scott in Europe (ed, 2007); *Recreations* walking, debating (memb Br Isles debating team 1984, former Oxford Union debating champion, convenor of debates and dep speaker for life Glasgow Univ Union), chess; *Style—* Prof Murray Pittock, FRSE; ✉ School of Arts, Histories and Cultures, Arts Building, University of Manchester, Manchester M13 9PL (tel 0161 275 3143, e-mail m.pittock@manchester.ac.uk)

PITTS, His Hon Judge Anthony Brian; s of Sir Cyril Pitts, and Barbara, *née* Sell; *b* 18 May 1946; *Educ* Cranleigh Sch, Pembroke Coll Oxford; *m* 21 June 1980, Sally-Jane, *née* Spencer; 1 s, 1 da; *Career* called to the Bar 1975; recorder of the Crown Court 1997, circuit judge (SE Circuit) 2002–; *Style—* His Hon Judge Pitts

PIZZEY, Erin Patria Margaret; da of Cyril Carney, MBE (d 1980), and Ruth Patricia Last; *b* 19 February 1939; *Educ* Leweston Manor Sherborne; *m* 1, 1961 (m dis 1979), John Leo Pizzey; 1 s (Amos b 1967), 1 da (Cleo b 1961); *Career* author, journalist and social reformer; fndr of the Int Shelter Movement for Battered Men, Women and Children; memb: Royal Soc of Literature, Soc of Authors; Int Order of Volunteers for Peace Diploma of Honour 1981, Nancy Astor Award for Journalism 1983, Distinguished Leadership Award (World Congress of Victimology) 1987, Valentino Palm d'Oro Award for Literature 1994; hon citizen of San Ginani D'Asso Italy 1993; patron: Care and Comfort Romania 1998, Mankind 2004, Derwent Domestic Violence Forum 2005; opened refuge for victims of domestic violence Bahrain (the first in the Arab world) 2007; has contributed to many leading newspapers and journals; author of articles: Choosing a Non-Violent Relationship, Sexual Abuse Within the Family; TV documentaries incl: Scream Quietly 1975, Chiswick Women's Aid 1977, That Awful Woman 1987, Cutting Edge: Sanctuary 1991, Who's Failing the Family 1999; *Non-Fiction* Scream Quietly or the Neighbours Will Hear (1974), Infernal Child (1978), The Sluts Cookbook (1981), Erin Pizzey Collects (1983), Prone To Violence (1982), All In The Name of Love, Wild Child (autobiography, 1995), Grandmothers of the Revolution (2000), Women on Men - Who are the Victims (2000); *Fiction* The Watershed, In the Shadow of the Castle, The Pleasure Palace, First Lady, The Consul General's Daughter (1988), The Snow Leopard of Shanghai (1989), Other Lovers (1991), Morningstar (1992), Swimming With Dolphins (1993), For the Love of a Stranger (1994), Kisses (1995), The Wicked World of Women (1996), The Fame Game (2000); *Short Stories* The Man in the Blue Van, The Frangipani Tree, Addiction, Dancing; *Recreations* reading, cooking, antiques, violin, wine, travel; *Style—* Erin Pizzey; ✉ Flat 5, 29 Lebanon Park, Twickenham TW1 3DH (tel 020 8241 6541, e-mail pizzey@blueyonder.co.uk)

PLAISTOWE, (William) Ian David; s of David William Plaistowe (d 1975), and Julia, *née* Ross Smith (d 1998); *b* 18 November 1942; *Educ* Marlborough, Queens' Coll Cambridge; *m* 1968, Carolyn Anne Noble, da of Tom Kenneth Noble Wilson; 2 s (Richard William Ian b 1969, Peter David Alexander b 1972), 1 da (Nicola Louise b 1977); *Career* Arthur Andersen: joined 1964, ptnr 1976, head of Accounting & Audit Practice London 1984–87, managing practice dir Audit and Business Advsy Practice Europe, Middle East, Africa and India 1992–2002; pres ICAEW 1992–93, chm London Soc of Chartered Accountants 1981–82, chm Auditing Practices Bd 1994–2002, memb Int Auditing and Assurance Standards Bd 2002–04; memb Cncl Univ of Buckingham 2003–; Master Worshipful Co of CAs 2002–03; FCA; *Recreations* golf, tennis, squash, skiing, gardening; *Clubs* Carlton, Moor Park Golf; *Style—* Ian Plaistowe, Esq; ✉ Heybote, Ellesborough, Aylesbury, Buckinghamshire HP17 0XF (tel 01296 622758, e-mail ianplaistowe@aol.com)

PLANER, Nigel George; s of George Victor Planer, and (Margaret) Lesley, *née* Weeden (d 2000); *b* 22 February 1953; *Educ* Westminster, Univ of Sussex, LAMDA; *m* 1, 19 Aug 1989 (m dis 1994), Anna, da of Michael Lea; 1 s (Stanley b 5 Sept 1988); m 2, 3 April 1999 (m dis 2003), Frankie, da of Gerald Park; 1 s (Harvey b 3 Aug 1999); *Career* actor; memb: Equity 1977, Writers' Guild 1987; *Theatre* incl: Leeds Playhouse, Young Vic, Oxford Playhouse, Hampstead Theatre, Regent's Park; memb original cast Evita, Man of the Moment, Angry Old Men, Chicago, Feel Good, High Life, We Will Rock You, Wicked; plays incl On the Ceiling (Birmingham Rep and Garrick Theatre London) 2005; *Television* leading roles incl: Shine on Harvey Moon, Rollover Beethoven, King and Castle, The Young Ones, Filthy Rich and Catflap, Number Twenty Seven, Blackeyes, Frankenstein's Baby, The Comic Strip Presents, The Naked Actor, Bonjour La Classe, Wake Up With, The Magic Roundabout, Cuts, The Grimleys, The Flood, Hogfather; *Films* incl: The Supergrass, Brazil, Yellowbeard, More Bad News, The Strike, Land Girls, Bright Young Things, Virgin Territory; *Scripts* incl: Radio 4 sketches, Not the Nine O'Clock News, Funseekers (Channel 4 film), King and Castle (Thames); *Live appearances* incl: fndr memb Comic Strip, Comedy Store, Edinburgh Festival, MTV NY, Adelaide Festival (Aust), Hammersmith Odeon; *Awards* winner BPI Award Best Comedy Record 1984; *Books* Neil's Book of the Dead (1983), I, An Actor (1987), A Good Enough Dad (1992), Let's Get Divorced (1994), Therapy and How to Avoid It (1996), Unlike the Buddha (1997), The Right Man (1998), Faking It (2001), On the Ceiling (2005); *Style—* Nigel Planer, Esq; ✉ c/o PFD, Drury House, 34–43 Russell Street, London WC2B 5HA (tel 020 7344 1010, fax 020 7352 7356)

PLANT, Charles William; s of James Plant, and Nancy, *née* Webb (d 2003); *b* 28 October 1944, Neyland, Pembrokeshire; *Educ* Newcastle-under-Lyme HS, St John's Coll Cambridge (McMahon law scholar), Coll of Law; *m* 28 Sept 1968, Anne, *née* Jacobsen; 1 s (Nicholas), 2 da (Justine, Georgina); *Career* admitted slr 1969; Herbert Smith LLP: articled clerk 1967–69, asst Litigation Dept 1967–76, ptnr 1976–2005, conslt 2005–; ed-in-chief Blackstone's Civil Practice; chm of govrs Coll of Law; memb: Lord Chllr's Advsy Ctee on Legal Educn and Conduct 1994–2000, Legal Servs Consultative Panel 2000–03, Law Soc; *Recreations* golf, art, French Riviera; *Clubs* Athenaeum; *Style—* Charles Plant, Esq; ✉ Herbert Smith LLP, Exchange House, Primrose Street, London EC2A 2HS (tel 020 7374 8000, e-mail charles.plant@herbertsmith.com)

PLANT, Dr Gordon Terence; s of Thomas Edmund Plant (d 1998), and Sheila May, *née* Atkinson; *b* 4 July 1952; *Educ* Woking Co GS for Boys, Downing Coll Cambridge (scholar, MA, MD), St Thomas' Hosp Med Sch London (exhibitioner, MB BChir); *m* 29 April 1978, Dr Marilyn Jane Plant, *née* Dirkin; 3 da (Eleanor Margaret, Emma Louise, Katharine Elizabeth); *Career* house physician St Thomas' Hosp London 1977–78, SHO Westminster Hosp 1978–80, registrar Addenbrooke's Hosp Cambridge 1980–82, Wellcome Tst research assoc Physiological Lab Univ of Cambridge 1982–86, registrar and sr registrar Nat Hosp for Neurology and Neurosurgery London 1986–89, research fell Smith-Kettlewell Research Inst Univ of Calif San Francisco 1989–90, conslt neurologist Nat Hosp for Neurology and Neurosurgery London, Moorfields Eye Hosp and Med Eye Unit St Thomas' Hosp London 1991–, service dir neuro-ophthalmology Moorfields Eye Hosp 1994–, hon conslt St Luke's Hosp for the Clergy; hon sr lectr: UCL 1991–, GKT (formerly UMDS) 1991–; visiting prof City Univ 2006–; assoc ed Opthalmologica 2001–, memb Editorial Bd Neuro-opthalmology 2003–; vice-pres Section of Ophthalmology RSM 2001–04; memb: BMA, Assoc for Research in Vision and Opthalmology 1986, European Brain and Behaviour Soc 1990, Br Isles Neuro-ophthalmology Club 1991, American Acad of Sciences 1993, European Neuro-ophthalmology Soc 1994, Ophthalmic Club 1994; MRC Travelling Fellowship 1989–90; FRSM 1993, FRCP 1994, FRCOphth 2005; *Publications* Optic Neuritis (ed, 1986); numerous pubns concerning neurology, neuro-ophthalmology and visual science in academic jls; *Recreations* music, painting; *Style—* Dr Gordon T Plant; ✉ The National Hospital for Neurology and Neurosurgery, Queen Square, London WC1N 3BG (tel 020 7391 8956, fax 020 7391 8994, e-mail gordon.plant@uclh.org)

PLANT OF HIGHFIELD, Baron (Life Peer UK 1992), of Weelsby in the County of Humberside; Prof Raymond Plant; s of Stanley Plant (d 1983), and Marjorie Plant; *b* 19 March 1945; *Educ* Havelock Sch Grimsby, King's Coll London (BA), Univ of Hull (PhD); *m* 27 July 1967, Katherine Sylvia, da of Jack Dixon (d 1989); 3 s (Hon Nicholas b 1969, Hon Matthew b 1971, Hon Richard b 1976); *Career* sr lectr in philosophy Univ of Manchester 1967–69, prof of politics Univ of Southampton 1979–94, master St Catherine's Coll Oxford 1994–99; Univ of Southampton: pro-chllr 1996–99, prof of European political thought 2000–; prof of jurisprudence and political philosophy KCL 2002–; lectures: Stevenson (Univ of Glasgow) 1981, Agnes Cumming (UC Dublin) 1988, Stanton (Univ of Cambridge) 1989–90 and 1990–91, Sarum (Univ of Oxford) 1991, Ferguson (Univ of Manchester) 1995, Gore (Westminster Abbey) 1996, Scott Holland (Manchester Cathedral) 1996, J P MacIntosh Meml (Univ of Edinburgh) 1996, Eleanor Rathbone (Univ of Bristol) 1997, G Ganz Univ of Southampton 2005, Boutwood Univ of Cambridge 2006, Bampton Univ of Oxford 2007; chm: Lab Pty Cmmn on Electoral Systems 1991–93, Fabian Soc Cmmn on Citizenship and Taxation 1998–2000; author and contrib to New Statesman and Society, The Independent, The Times, etc; pres Acad of Learned Societies in the Social Sciences 1999–2001, pres NCVO; memb: Fabian Soc, Political Studies Assoc UK; fell Univ of Cardiff 1999, visiting fell CCC Cambridge 2006; hon fell: St Catherines's Coll Oxford 2000, Harris Manchester Coll Oxford 2000; Hon DLitt: Univ of Hull, London Guildhall Univ; FRSA 1992; *Books* Social and Moral Theory in Social Work (1970), Hegel: An Introduction (1973), Community and Ideology (1974), Political Philosophy And Social Welfare (1981), Philosophy Politics and Citizenship (1984), Equality Markets And the State (1984), Conservative Capitalism in Britain And The United States: A Critical Appraisal (1988), Citizenship Rights and Socialism (1989), Modern Political Thought (1991), Hegel on Philosophy and Religion (1997), Politics, Theology and History (2001); *Recreations* ornithology, opera, Bach, Mozart; *Style—* Prof the Rt Hon Lord Plant of Highfield; ✉ 6 Woodview Close, Bassett, Southampton SO2 3P2 (tel 023 8076 9529, e-mail raymond.plant@kcl.ac.uk)

PLANTE, Prof David; *b* 4 March 1940; *Educ* l'Université de Louvain Belgium, Boston Coll (BA); *Career* instr of English English Sch Rome 1961–62, instr of English Boston Sch of Modern Languages MA 1964–65, instr of French St John's Prep Sch Devon MA 1965–66, writing workshop City Literary Inst London 1970–74, bursary Arts Cncl 1977; writer in residence: UEA 1977–78 (Henfield fell 1977), Tulsa Univ OK 1980–82, King's Coll Cambridge 1985–86, Adelphi Univ Garden City NY 1988, Université du Québec Montréal 1990; Guggenheim fell 1982; lectr Gorky Inst of Literature Moscow 1990; Columbia Univ NY: prof of writing 1998–, dir Fiction Concentration Writing Div 2000–, memb Ctee on Instruction Sch of the Arts; sr memb King's Coll Cambridge 1997; FRSL 2002; *Awards* Pushcart Prize (for profile Jean Rhys: A Remembrance) 1982, O Henry Prize (for short story Work) 1983, Prize for Artistic Merit American Acad and Inst of Arts and Letters 1983, Award of Excellence Boston Coll 2000, Pushcart Prize (for essay Returning to Providence) 2001; *Publications* novels: The Ghost of Henry James (1970), Slides (1971), Relatives (1972), The Darkness of the Body (1974), Figures in Bright Air (1976), The Family (1978, nominated US Nat Book Award 1978), The Country (1981, reissued 1983), The Woods (1982), The Francoeur Novels: The Family, The Woods, The Country (1984), The Foreigner (1984), The Catholic (1986, reissued 1987), The Native (1991), The Accident (1991), Annunciation (1994), The Age of Terror (1999, reissued 2000); other work: Difficult Women: Portraits of Jean Rhys, Sonia Orwell, Germaine Greer (non-fiction, 1983, reissued 1986), The Mystery of Our Suffering (play, 2000), American Ghosts, a Memoir (2005), ABC (2007); author of numerous short stories, profiles, essays, articles and reviews; *Style*— Prof David Plante

PLANTEROSE, Rowan Michael; s of Anthony Ernest Charles Planterose, of Chedworth, Glos, and Jean D'Arcy, *née* Palmer; *b* 19 February 1954; *Educ* Eastbourne Coll, Downing Coll Cambridge (MA, LLB); *m* 23 Oct 1999, Elizabeth Zoe Claire, *née* Dawson; 1 da (Abigail d'Arcy b 24 Feb 2001); *Career* called to the Bar 1978; chartered arbitrator 2002; slr, ptnr Davies Arnold Cooper 2004– (managing ptnr 2007–); FCIArb 1989 (memb Cncl 1991–2000); *Publications* Bernstein: Dispute Resolution Handbook (co-author, 4 edn 2003), The Arbitration Act 1996: A Commentary (4 edn, 2007); *Recreations* squash, skiing, gliding; *Style*— Rowan Planterose, Esq; ✉ Davies Arnold Cooper, 6–8 Bouverie Street, London EC4Y 8DD (tel 020 7293 4216, fax 020 7936 2020, e-mail rplanterose@dac.co.uk)

PLANTIN, Marcus; *Career* various positions rising to exec prodr light entertainment BBC TV until 1985; London Weekend Television: controller of entertainment 1985–91, dir of progs and md LWT Progs 1991–92; network dir ITV Network Centre 1992–97; dir of progs LWT Productions 1998–2000, dir of progs LWT and United Productions 2000–, dir Int Entertainment Production and Formats Granada Media 2000–; memb: Cncl and Television Ctee BAFTA 1998–2000; FRTS; *Style*— Marcus Plantin, Esq; ✉ London Weekend Television Ltd, The London Studios, Upper Ground, London SE1 9LT (tel 020 7620 1620)

PLASCOW, Ronald; s of Oscar Plascow, and Liese Plascow (d 2004); *b* 22 October 1956, London; *Educ* Latymer Upper Sch, Univ of Bordeaux, Univ of Sheffield (LLB); *m* June 1984, Joanna Plascow; 2 da (Clare b 2 May 1986, Harriet b 16 Jan 1989); *Career* slr; Franks Charlesly & Co: articled clerk 1979–81, asst slr 1981–82; slr and divnl legal advsr Trafalgar House plc 1982–84, sr slr Lovell White Durrant 1984–89; Mills & Reeve: slr 1989–91, ptnr 1991–, head Construction and Engrg Team; memb: Law Soc 1981, CIArb 1990 (memb Ctee and former sec E Anglia Branch); *Publications* Tolley's Guide to Construction Contracts (1999); *Recreations* reading, walking dogs, films, music (jazz), theatre, art; *Style*— Ronald Plascow, Esq; ✉ Mills & Reeve, 112 Hills Road, Cambridge CB2 1PH (tel 01223 222261, fax 01223 222221, e-mail ron.plascow@mills-reeve.com)

PLASKETT, Maj-Gen Frederick Joseph; CB (1980), MBE (1966); s of Frederick Joseph Plaskett (d 1982), and Grace Mary Plaskett (d 1988); *b* 23 October 1926; *Educ* Wallasey GS, Chelsea Poly; *m* 1, 9 Sept 1950, Heather (d 1982), da of Maurice William Kington (d 1976), of Salisbury, Wilts; 4 da (Helen b 1951, Wendy b 1954, Kate b 1960, Lucy b 1965); m 2, 1984, Mrs Patricia Joan Healy, da of Richard Upton, of Wimborne, Dorset; *Career* RN (Fleet Air Arm) 1944–45, Army 1945–81 (cmmnd India 1945); regtl and staff appts: India, Korea, Japan, Malaya, W Africa, Germany, UK; ret as Maj-Gen; dir gen Tport and Movements (Army) 1981; Col Cmdt RCT 1981–91; cmmr Royal Hosp Chelsea 1985–88; dir gen Road Haulage Assoc Ltd 1981–88; dir: Paccar UK (Foden Trucks) 1981–97, Road Haulage Insurance Services 1983–88, Br Road Fedn 1982–88, BR London Midland Regn 1986–92 (chm 1989–92); Freeman City of London 1979, Liveryman Worshipful Co of Carmen 1979; FCIT; *Recreations* sailing, fishing, gardening; *Clubs* Army and Navy; *Style*— Maj-Gen Frederick Plaskett, CB, MBE; ✉ c/o National Westminster Bank plc, The Commons, Shaftesbury, Dorset SP7 8JY

PLASKITT, James Andrew; MP; s of Ronald Plaskitt (d 1996), and Phyllis, *née* Euston; *b* 23 June 1954; *Educ* Pilgrim Sch Bedford, UC Oxford (MA, MPhil); *Career* lectr in politics UC Oxford 1977–79, lectr in govt Brunel Univ 1979–84, lectr in politics ChCh Oxford 1984–86, with Oxford Analytica Ltd 1984–97 (dir of consultancy 1995–97); MP (Lab) Warwick and Leamington 1997–, Parly under sec of state DWP 2005–, memb Treasy Select Ctee 1999–2005; ldr Oxfordshire CC 1990–96 (cncllr 1985–97); memb: MSF, Charter 88, Liberty, Lab campaign for electoral reform; *Style*— James Plaskitt, MP; ✉ House of Commons, London SW1A 0AA (tel 020 7219 6207)

PLATA, Rick; *b* 12 May 1958; *Educ* Haliford GS, Kingston Coll Surrey; *m* 20 Sept 1987, Robin Beth, da of Joseph Moskowitz, of NY; 1 s (Matthew b 14 June 1992), 1 da (Alexandra b 25 March 1995); *Career* sr planner/buyer Foote Cone and Belding 1980–82 (asst media planner/media planner 1979–80), media mangr The Leagas Delaney Partnership 1982–84; Laing Henry Advertising: dir of media planning 1984–86, media/bd dir (concurrently md Communique Media ind media co within agency) 1986–89; sr vice-pres/dir of business devpt Hill Holliday Connors Cosmopolus Advertising Inc NY 1992–93 (sr vice-pres/media dir 1989–92), media dir/Euro media co-ordinator Burkitt Weinreich Bryant Clients and Co Ltd 1993–95; head of sales NBC Europe 1996–98 (head of strategic planning NBC Super Channel 1995–96), dir of advertising and sales Fox Kids Europe 1998–; sometime memb: Educn Ctee IPA, Media Ctee American Assoc of Advtg Agencies, Editorial Bd Agency Magazine; recipient: Media Week award, recognition and distinction for work performed on behalf of NYC (given by Mayor David Dinkins) 1991; memb: NY Advtg Club, Soc of Advtg Media Professionals, D&AD; *Recreations* tennis, golf, theatre, music; *Clubs* Groucho, Blue Bird, RAC; *Style*— Rick Plata, Esq

PLATELL, Amanda Jane; da of Francis Ernest Platell, and Norma June, *née* Malland; *b* 12 November 1957; *Educ* Penrhos Methodist Ladies Coll, Univ of Western Aust (BA); *Career* reporter Perth Daily News 1978–81, Sydney Bureau chief Perth Daily News 1983; sub ed: Sydney Sun 1984, Harpers Bazaar 1985, Today Newspaper 1986; metro dep ed London Daily News 1987, dep ed Today 1987–92 (features prodn ed 1987), gp managing ed Mirror Group Newspapers 1993, also dir of marketing MGN 1993, mktg dir Independent 1993–95, md Independent and Independent on Sunday 1995–96, ed Sunday Mirror 1996–97, ed Sunday Express 1998–99, head of media Conservative Party 1999–2001; columnist: New Statesman, Daily Mail; presenter Morgan and Platell (Channel 4) 2004–; *Books* Scandal (1999); *Recreations* cars, eating out, travelling; *Style*— Miss Amanda Platell

PLATER, Alan Frederick; CBE (2005); s of Herbert Richard Plater, and Isabella Scott Plater; *b* 15 April 1935; *Educ* Kingston HS Hull, King's Coll Newcastle upon Tyne; *m* 1, 1958 (m dis 1985), Shirley Johnson; 2 s, 1 da; m 2, 1986, Shirley Rubinstein; 3 step s; *Career* architect until 1961, writer 1961–; pres Writers' Guild of GB 1991–95 (co chm 1986–87), writer in residence Aust Film Television & Radio Sch Sydney 1988; hon fell Humberside Coll of FE 1983, Hon DLitt Univ of Hull 1985, Hon DCL Univ of Northumbria 1997, Hon DUniv Open Univ 2004, Hon DLitt Univ of Newcastle 2005; FRSL 1985, FRSA 1990; *Theatre* A Smashing Day, Close the Coalhouse Door, And a Little Love Besides, Swallows on the Water, Trinity Tales, The Fosdyke Saga, Fosdyke Two, On Your Way, Riley!, Skyhooks, A Foot on the Earth, Prez, In Blackberry Time, Rent Party, Sweet Sorrow, Going Home, I Thought I Heard A Rustling, Shooting the Legend, All Credit to the Lads, Peggy for You, Tales from Backyard, Only a Matter of Time, Barriers, The Last Days of the Empire, Charlie's Trousers, Blonde Bombshells of 1943, Confessions of a City Supporter, Sweet William, Tales from the Golden Slipper; *Television* plays: So Long Charlie, See the Pretty Lights, To See How Far It Is (trilogy), Land of Green Ginger, Willow Cabins, The Party of the First Part, The Blacktoft Diaries, Thank You Mrs Clinkscales, Misterioso, Doggin' Around, The Last of the Blonde Bombshells, Belonging, The Last Will and Testament of Billy Two-Sheds; biographies: The Crystal Spirit, Pride of our Alley, Edward Lear - On the Edge of the Sand, Coming Through, Selected Exits; series and serials: Z Cars, Softly Softly, Shoulder to Shoulder, Trinity Tales, The Good Companions, The Consultant, Barchester Chronicles, The Beiderbecke Affair, The Fortunes of War, The Beiderbecke Tapes, A Very British Coup, The Beiderbecke Connection, Oliver's Travels, Dalziel & Pascoe, Lewis; *Radio* The Journal of Vasilije Bogdanovic, All Things Betray Thee, The Lower Depths, Only a Matter of Time, Time Added on for Injuries, The Devil's Music, Abandoned Projects, Stories for Another Day; *Films* The Virgin & the Gypsy, It Shouldn't Happen to a Vet, Priest of Love, Keep the Aspidistra Flying; *Awards* Writer's Guild Radio Award 1972, Sony Radio Award 1983, RTS Writer's Award 1984/5, Broadcasting Press Guild Award 1987 and 1988, BAFTA Writer's Award 1988, Banff Television Festival Grand Prix 1989, RTS Regional Award 1994, BAFTA Cymru Writers Award 1994, Biarritz Festival Writer's Award 2005, Dennis Potter BAFTA Award 2005; *Books* The Beiderbecke Affair (1985), The Beiderbecke Tapes (1986), Misterioso (1987), The Beiderbecke Connection (1992), Oliver's Travels (1994), Doggin' Around (2006); plays and short pieces in various anthologies, contrib The Guardian, New Statesman and others; *Recreations* reading, theatre, jazz, snooker, talking, listening; *Clubs* Dramatists'; *Style*— Alan Plater, Esq, CBE

PLATFORD, Richard John; s of Eric Roy Platford, of Great Warley, Essex, and Joan Mary, *née* Willis; *b* 20 January 1945; *Educ* Felsted, Trinity Hall Cambridge (MA), London Business Sch (MBA); *m* 29 Dec 1973 (m dis), Marie Renee, da of Rene Louis de Peyrecave; 4 s (James Alexander b 11 July 1976, Giles Richard b 26 April 1978, Edward William, Thomas Henry (twins) b 14 April 1983); *Career* mgmnt trainee Rolls Royce Aero Engines 1963–64, systems implementation offr Rolls Royce 1967–69, trainee Paris then prodn controller/materials mangr Milan Otis Elevator 1971–75, dir of materials Clark Equipment 1976–78; PricewaterhouseCoopers (formerly Coopers & Lybrand before merger): conslt 1978–79, ptnr Manufacturing Europe 1983–87 (mangr 1979–83), ptnr Manufacturing UK 1987–91, chm Int Pharmaceutical Sector Programme 1991–98, global ldr Pharmaceutical Gp 1998–2000, ptnr Pharmaceutical Gp 2000–02; ptnr IBM Business Consulting Services 2002–05, pres and ceo CellVir 2006–; Freeman City of London, Liveryman Worshipful Co of Needlemakers; CEng, MIEE 1978, fell British Prodn and Inventory Control Soc 1978, MIMgt 1979, MIMC 1985; *Recreations* golf, tennis, skiing, opera, music; *Style*— Richard Platford, Esq; ✉ 15 Rue Georges Pitard, Paris 75015, France; Flat 1, Admirals Court, Horselydown Lane, London SE1 2LJ

PLATT, Adrian; s of Clifford Lowe Platt, OBE (d 1982), of Chislehurst, Kent, and Katharine Eileen, *née* Everington (d 1975); *b* 28 November 1935; *Educ* Marlborough, Univ of Lyons; *m* 24 Sept 1960, Valerie, da of Richard Bois (d 1956); 2 da (Emma (Mrs Stephen Howard) b 1965, Katie (Mrs Giles Lawton) b 1967); *Career* Nat Serv 4 RHA 1954–56, TA HAC 1956–62; dir Sedgwick Collins Ltd 1964–; chm: Sedgwick Forbes Marine Ltd 1968–69, Sedgwick Forbes Bland Payne Marine Ltd 1969–; dir: Sedgwick Group plc 1981–93 (md special projects 1991–93), Sedgwick Group Development Ltd 1993–99; chm: Sedgwick Marine and Aviation Group 1986–88, Sedgwick Ltd Development Group 1988–93, Sedgwick James Overseas Cos Ltd 1990–91; dir Cncl for Music in Hosps; govr Corp of the Sons of the Clergy; Past Master Worshipful Co of Vintners (Liveryman 1956), Freeman Worshipful Co of Shipwrights 1988; *Recreations* tennis, golf, shooting, music, walking, reading; *Clubs* HAC, IOD, Sloane, Marks; *Style*— Adrian Platt, Esq; ✉ Hatchfield Cottage, Butlers Hill, West Horsley, Surrey KT24 6AZ (tel 014865 4729, e-mail adrian.platt@virgin.net)

PLATT, Anthony Michael Westlake; CBE (1991); s of James Westlake Platt, CBE (d 1972), and Veronica Norma Hope, *née* Arnold (d 1987); *b* 28 September 1928; *Educ* St George's Coll and Belgrano Day Sch Buenos Aires, Stowe, Institut auf dem Rosenberg St Gallen, Balliol Coll Oxford (BA); *m* 1, 12 April 1952 (m dis 1982), (Jennifer) Susan, *née* Scott-Fox; 3 s (Michael b 1953, Timothy b 1961, Robin b 1962); m 2, 14 April 1984, Heather Mary (formerly Mrs Stubbs), *née* McCracken (d 1986); 1 step s (Rupert Stubbs b 1960), 1 step da (Imogen Stubbs b 1961); m 3, 18 Dec 1987, Sarah Elizabeth, *née* Russell; *Career* 2 Lt RA 1947–49, pilot offr RAFVR 1949–51; FO 1951–56: Br Embassy Prague 1953–54, Perm Delgn to UN 1955–56; various positions Shell Group (UK and abroad) 1956–84; chief exec London C of C and Industry 1984–91, advsr to Cncl Br C of C in Continental Europe 1992–95; Freeman City of London 1991; *Books* Parallel 40 North to Eureka (2000), Belovedest: A Marriage of Opposites (2006); *Recreations* walking, opera, languages; *Style*— Anthony Platt, Esq, CBE; ✉ 17 Westgate Street, Bury St Edmunds, Suffolk IP33 1QG

PLATT, Prof Colin Peter Sherard; s of James Westlake Platt, CBE (d 1972), of Jersey, and Veronica Norma Hope, *née* Arnold (d 1987); *b* 11 November 1934; *Educ* Collyers Sch Horsham, Balliol Coll Oxford (MA), Univ of Leeds (PhD); *m* 1, 8 Feb 1963 (m dis), Valerie, da of Thomas Ashforth (d 1976), of Cannock, Staffs; 2 da (Emma b 17 July 1963, Tabitha b 3 Jan 1967), 2 s (Miles b 9 April 1965, Theo b 20 Dec 1971); m 2, 14 June 1996, Claire, da of Hugh Donovan (d 2005); *Career* Nat Serv RN Leading Coder Special 1953–54; lectr in medieval archaeology Univ of Leeds 1962–64; Dept of History Univ of Southampton: lectr 1964–74, sr lectr 1974–79, reader 1979–83, prof of history 1983–99, ret; Wolfson History Prize 1990; FSA 1968, FRHistS 1971; *Books* The Monastic Grange in Medieval England (1969), Medieval Southampton: The Port and Trading Community, AD 1000–1600 (1973), Excavations in Medieval Southampton 1953–1969 (1975), The English Medieval Town (1976), Medieval England: A Social History and Archaeology from the Conquest to 1600 AD (1978), The Atlas of Medieval Man (1979), The Parish Churches of Medieval England (1981), The Castle in Medieval England and Wales (1982), The Abbeys and Priories of Medieval England (1984), Medieval Britain from the Air (1984), The Traveller's Guide to Medieval England (1985), The National Trust Guide to Late Medieval and Renaissance Britain (1986), The Architecture of Medieval Britain: A Social History (1990), The Great Rebuildings of Tudor and Stuart England (1994), King Death: The Black Death and its Aftermath in Late-Medieval England (1996), Marks of Opulence: The Why, When and Where of Western Art 1000–1914 (2004); *Recreations* reading fiction, visiting antiquities, entertaining friends; *Style*— Prof Colin Platt, FSA; ✉ The Old Rectory, Littlehempston, Totnes, Devon TQ9 6LY (tel 01803 862598)

PLATT, David Andrew; s of Frank Platt, and Jean, *née* Jackson; *b* 10 June 1966; *Educ* South Chadderton Comp Sch; *m* 1992, Rachel Vaughan; *Career* professional footballer; Manchester United 1983–85 (no appearances), Crewe Alexandra 1985–88 (145 appearances, 60 goals), transferred for £200,000 to Aston Villa 1988–91 (over 125 appearances, over 60 goals), transferred for £5.5m to Bari Italy 1991–92 (35 appearances, 16 goals), transferred for £6.5m to Juventus Italy 1992–93 (22 appearances, 4 goals, winners UEFA Cup 1993), transferred to Sampdoria Italy for £5.2m 1993–95 (61 appearances, 20 goals, winners Italian Cup 1994), transferred to Arsenal for £4.75m 1995–98 (108 appearances, 15 goals, winner League Championship and FA Cup double 1998); England: 62 caps (15 as capt 1994–96), 27 goals, played in World Cup Italy 1990 (scoring 3 goals), played in European Championship Sweden 1992 (scoring 1 goal) and England 1996; coach Sampdoria Italy 1998–99, mangr Nottingham Forest FC 1999–2001, coach England under-21s 2001–04; PFA Player of the Year 1990; *Books* David Platt: Achieving the Goal (1995); *Recreations* horse racing, golf, tennis; *Style*— David Platt, Esq; ✉ c/o PO Box 257, Alderley Edge SK9 7WP

PLATT, David Wallace; s of Christopher Platt, of Knock, Ulster, and Susan Harriette La Nauze, *née* Wallace; *b* 13 September 1964; *Educ* Campbell Coll, Trinity Hall Cambridge (MA); *Career* called to the Bar Middle Temple 1987; TV presenter BBC NI, freelance broadcaster and media trainer; Parly candidate (Cons) Cambridge 1997; chm Cambridge Univ Cons Assoc 1986, formerly political research asst and aide House of Commons and Cons Central Office; former London memb Exec CPRE; govr: Churchill Gardens Primary

Sch, Pimlico Sch; *Books* Educating Our Future (1986), Blue Tomorrow (2001); *Recreations* politics, football, architecture, conservation, Greek history; *Style*— David Platt, Esq; ✉ Crown Office Chambers, 2 Crown Office Row, Temple, London EC4Y 7HJ (tel 020 7583 1227, e-mail platt@crownofficechambers.com)

PLATT, Dame Denise; DBE (2004, CBE 1996); da of Victor Platt (d 1980), of Cheshire, and May, *née* Keeling (d 1996); *b* 21 February 1945; *Educ* Congleton GS for Girls, UC Cardiff (BSc(Econ)); *Career* social worker Middx Hosp 1968–73, sr social worker Guy's Hosp 1973–76, gp ldr Southwark Social Servs 1976–78, princ social worker Hammersmith Hosp 1978–83, dir of Social Serv London Borough Hammersmith and Fulham 1986–94 (asst dir 1983–86), under sec social servs Assoc of Metropolitan Authorities (AMA) 1994–97, head of social servs Local Government Assoc 1997–98, chief inspr Soc Servs Inspectorate Dept of Health 1998–2004, chair Cmmn for Social Care Inspection 2004–; pres Assoc of Dirs of Social Servs 1993–94; chair Nat Inst for Social Work 1997–98; vice-chair Nat Cncl for Domiciliary Care Servs until 1995, memb Advsy Gp Policy Studies Inst until 1994, memb Academic Cncl Royal Postgrad Med Sch until 1994, tstee and vice-chm Nat AIDS Tst until 1998; memb: Ministerial Action Gp on AIDS 1991–93, Dept of Health Steering Gp Community Care Devpt Prog (formerly Dept of Health Caring for People Advsy Group), Cncl Central Cncl for Educn and Trg in Social Work (CCETSW), Home Sec's Task Force on Youth Justice 1997–98, Disability Rights Task Force 1997–98, Ind Reference Gp on Mental Health 1997–98, Strategic Review of London's Health Servs 1997–98, Ind Review Bd Cheshire Fire & Rescue Serv 2007–; tstee and dir Family Planning Assoc 2005–, chair Nat AIDS Ts 2006–, tstee NSPCC 2006–; govr Univ of Bedfordshire 2006–; Hon DSocSci Brunel Univ 1998; AIMSW 1968, FRSA 2002; *Recreations* music, watercolours, walking; *Clubs* Reform; *Style*— Dame Denise Platt, DBE; ✉ Commission for Social Care Inspection, 33 Greycoat Street, London SW1P 2QF (tel 020 7979 2000, e-mail denise.platt@csci.gsi.gov.uk)

PLATT, Eleanor Frances; QC (1982); er da of Dr Maurice Leon Platt (d 1966), of Sussex, and Sara, *née* Stein (d 1983); *b* 6 May 1938; *Educ* Univ of London (LLB); *m* 1963, Frederick Malcolm Lind; 1 da (Amanda b 1965), 1 s (Jonathan b 1969); *Career* called to the Bar Gray's Inn 1960; jt head of specialist family law chambers 1990–2007, recorder SE circuit 1982–2004, dep judge (Family Div) High Court of Justice 1987–2004; memb: Matrimonial Causes Rule Ctee 1986–90, Gene Therapy Advsy Ctee 1993–98; treas Family Law Bar Assoc 1990–95 (acting chm 1995), dep chm NHS Tbnl 1995–2002, legal assessor GMC and Gen Dental Cncl 1995–; vice-pres Bd of Deputies of British Jews 2003–06 (chm Law Parly and General Purposes Ctee 1988–94); chm New London Synagogue 1994–99, pres Jewish Family Mediation Register 1998–; pres Medico-Legal Soc 2002–04; memb Family Mediators Assoc 1997; *Recreations* the arts, travel, family; *Style*— Miss Eleanor Platt, QC; ✉ One Garden Court, Temple, London EC4Y 9BJ (tel 020 7797 7900, fax 020 7797 7929, e-mail platt@1gc.com)

PLATT, Jane Christine; da of George Platt, of Gayton, Wirral, and Miriam Platt; *b* 8 January 1957, Liverpool; *Educ* St Catherine's Coll Oxford (MA); *m* 1980, David Bill; *Career* chief exec Barclays Stockbrokers and Barclays Bank Tst Co 1996–2001, pres asset mgmnt Reuters 2001–03, chief operating offr Reuters Business Divs 2003–04, chief exec NS&I 2006–; dir: Edinburgh UK Tracker Tst plc 2004–06, Witan plc 2005; tstee Reuters Pension Fund 2004; memb: Securities Inst 1996, Guild of Int Bankers 2003; *Recreations* theatre, opera; *Clubs* Cornhill; *Style*— Ms Jane Platt; ✉ 375 Kensington High Street, London W14 8SD

PLATT, Sir Martin Philip; 3 Bt (UK 1959); s of Hon Prof Sir Peter Platt, 2 Bt (d 2000); *b* 9 March 1952; *m* 1971, Frances Corinne Moanna, da of Trevor Samuel Conley; 3 s, 2 da; *Style*— Sir Martin Platt, Bt; ✉ RDI, Outram, South Island, New Zealand

PLATT, Richard Andrew; *b* 1947; *Educ* Samuel Pepys Secdy Modern Sch Brockley; *m* Jocelyn; 3 s (Stephen b 28 Aug 1977, James b 1 April 1980, Nicholas b 6 Oct 1983), 2 da (Rebecca b 29 May 1988, Georgin b 6 Jan 1994); *Career* media buyer Masius Wynne Williams 1970–76, dep md Tape Consultancy 1976–82, asst programmer Network 10 Sydney 1982–84, head of programming Sky Channel 1984–88, dir of progs Maxwell Entertainment 1988–89, controller of progs Scansat 1989–91; dir of broadcasting: Meridian Television 1995– (controller of programming 1991–95), MAI Media 1995–, United Broadcasting and Entertainment 1997–; dir of broadcasting and channel devpt United Broadcasting and Entertainment 1998–2000; dir: Rap Consultancy 1991–, ITFC Ltd 1995–2000, United Interactive 1998–99, Rapture 1998–2000, TSMSI 1998–2000, Wapbeats International Ltd 2001–02, the24 Ltd 2003–; *Recreations* soccer, photography, cinema, theatre; *Style*— Richard Platt, Esq; ✉ Rap Consultancy Ltd, Beech Cottage, North Common Lane, Landford, Wiltshire SP5 2EL (tel 01794 390869, mobile 07940 527561, e-mail platfull@lineone.net)

PLATT, Stephen; s of Kenneth Norman Platt, of Stoke-on-Trent, and Joyce, *née* Pritchard; *b* 29 September 1954; *Educ* Longton HS Stoke-on-Trent, Wade Deacon Sch Widnes, LSE (BSc); *Children* 1 da (Rachel Louise b 22 Sept 1977); *Career* teacher Moss Brook Special Sch 1972–73, dir Self Help Housing Resource Library 1977–79, co-ordinator Islington Community Housing 1979–83, ed Roof 1986, news ed New Society 1986–87 (actg ed 1987–88); ed: Midweek 1988–89, Enjoying the Countryside 1989–90, New Statesman 1990–96; currently journalist and writer incl editorial conslt Channel 4 1996–; website and conrib ed Time Team 1999–, website ed Dispatches 1999–2005, contrib Red Pepper 2005–; co-ordinator Maasai Culture and History Project 2003–05; *Recreations* archaeology, amphibians, bears (real and fictional), countryside, football, growing things, mountains, music, running; *Clubs* Red Rose, Port Vale; *Style*— Stephen Platt, Esq; ✉ 46 Tufnell Park Road, London N7 0DT (tel 020 7263 4185, e-mail mail@steveplatt.net)

PLATT OF WRITTLE, Baroness (Life Peer UK 1981), of Writtle in the County of Essex; Beryl Catherine Platt; CBE (1978), DL (Essex 1983); da of Ernest Myatt (d 1950); *b* 18 April 1923; *Educ* Westcliff HS for Girls, Girton Coll Cambridge (MA); *m* 1949, Stewart Sydney Platt (d 2003), s of Sydney Rowland Platt (d 1946); 1 s (Hon Roland Francis b 1951), 1 da (Hon Victoria Catherine (Hon Mrs Davies) b 1953); *Career* tech asst Hawker Aircraft Ltd 1943–46, BEA 1946–49; memb Chelmsford RDC 1958–73; Essex CC: elected 1965, alderman 1969–74, vice-chm 1980–83, hon alderman 2005, chm Educn Ctee 1971–80, chm Further Educn Sub-Ctee 1969–71, memb Advsy Ctee on Women's Employment 1984–88; chm Equal Opportunities Cmmn 1983–88; memb House of Lords Select Ctee: on Murder and Life Imprisonment 1988–89, on Sci and Technol 1982–85, 1990–94, 1997–2001 and 2003–; vice-pres Parly Sci Ctee 1996–2000 (memb Cncl 2000–03); memb Ct: Univ of Essex 1968–99, City Univ 1968–78, Brunel Univ 1985–92, Cranfield Univ 1989–2003, Middx Univ 2000–; memb: Cncl City and Guilds of London Inst 1974–95, Univ of Cambridge Appts Bd 1975–79; vice-pres UMIST 1985–92, chllr Univ of Middx 1993–2000; memb: Engrg Cncl 1982–90, Cncl RSA 1983–88, Cncl Careers Research and Advsy Ctee 1983–93, Engrg Trg Authy 1990–92, Ctee on the Public Understanding of Sci 1990–93, Cncl Fndn for Sci and Technol 1991–98, Meteorological Advsy Ctee 1992–2000 (chm 1995–2000); pres: Nat Soc for Clean Air and Environmental Protection 1991–93, Pipeline Industries Guild 1994; vice-pres Assoc of CCs 1992–97; non-exec dir British Gas plc (now BG plc) 1988–94, dir Smallpiece Tst 1989–94 (fell 1988); Freeman City of London 1988, Liveryman Worshipful Co of Engrs 1988 (emeritus memb Ct of Assts 2002–); hon fell: Women's Engrg Soc 1988, Girton Coll Cambridge, Univ of Glamorgan (formerly Poly of Wales), Manchester Metropolitan Univ (formerly Poly of Manchester), UMIST 1992; Hon Insignia Award City and Guilds London Inst 1988; Hon LLD Univ of Cambridge 1988, Hon DTech Loughborough Univ; Hon DSc: Cranfield Inst, City Univ, Nottingham Trent Univ, Univ of Westminster, Univ of Sheffield; Hon DUniv: Salford, Open Univ, Bradford (Eng), Essex, Brunel (Tech), Middlesex 1993, Sheffield Hallam 2001; Eur Ing, FEANI 1988, FREng 1987, Hon FIStructE 1991, Hon FICE 1991, Hon FRAeS 1994 (FRAeS 1986), FRSA, FITD, FIGasE, Hon FCGI Hon FCP, Hon FIMechE; *Recreations* reading, swimming for pleasure; *Clubs* Oxford and Cambridge; *Style*— The Rt Hon the Baroness Platt of Writtle, CBE, DL, FREng; ✉ House of Lords, London SW1A 0PW

PLATTEN, Rt Rev Stephen George; *see:* Wakefield, Bishop of

PLATTS, Graham John; s of Joseph Henry Platts (d 1992), and Lois, *née* Brown; *b* 1 June 1950; *Educ* Christ's Coll Finchley, Portsmouth Poly (BSc); *m* 13 Sept 1975, Sandra Doreen, da of Kenneth Sidney Dark; 1 da (Deborah Suzanne b 16 Nov 1979), 1 s (Christopher David b 25 March 1981); *Career* supervisor Farrow Middleton & Co CAs 1977–78 (trainee 1971–75); Dearden Farrow (following merger): mangr 1979–81, sr mangr 1981–85, managing ptnr Poole office 1986–87 (ptnr 1985); BDO Stoy Hayward (following merger): managing ptnr Poole office 1987–90, regnl managing ptnr 1990–; memb: Dorset C of C and Indust, CBI; FCA 1980, MAE 1995; *Recreations* most sports especially tennis, theatre, films, cycling, reading; *Style*— Graham Platts, Esq; ✉ 17 Heath Road, St Leonards, Ringwood, Hampshire BH24 2PZ (tel 01425 475355); BDO Stoy Hayward, Old Orchard, 39–61 High Street, Poole, Dorset BH15 1AE (tel 01202 681221, fax 01202 687211, mobile 078 6074 7087, e-mail graham_j_platts@bdo.co.uk)

PLATTS, Nigel Landsbrough; s of Francis Arthur Platts, and Mabel Landsbrough, *née* Williams; *b* 20 October 1945; *Educ* Whitgift Sch, Oriel Coll Oxford (MA); *m* 26 July 1969, Anne Christine, da of Samuel Walker; 1 s (Thomas b 22 May 1978), 2 da (Philippa b 8 Feb 1972, Hannah b 8 April 1980); *Career* CA 1970; KPMG (formerly Peat Marwick Mitchell & Co then KPMG Peat Marwick): successively articled clerk, sr mangr, ptnr (managing ptnr Int Markets 1992–95 and KLegal 1999–2001), ret 2001; dir Crown Agenst for Overseas Govt and Administration, sr advsr KPMG LLP; FCA; *Recreations* collecting books, playing golf, watching rugby and cricket; *Clubs* MCC, Tonbridge Golf; *Style*— Nigel Platts, Esq; ✉ 2 Briton Crescent, South Croydon CR2 0JE

PLATTS-MILLS, Jonathan Lewis (Jo); s of John Faithful Fortescue Platts-Mills (d 2001), and Janet Katherine, *née* Cree (d 1992); bro of Mark Platts-Mills, QC, *qv*; *b* 11 March 1939; *Educ* Bryanston (capt rowing 1st eight), Balliol Coll Oxford (MA, head of Torpids); *m* 1, 1966 (m dis 1998); 1 s (Thomas Tiberius b 17 March 1968), 1 da (Ioana Patricia b 19 Nov 1970); m 2, 1999, Else, *née* Trad; *Career* grad apprentice Davy United Sheffield 1960–62, plate mill project engr Romania 1965–67, cold rolling mill project mangr Algeria 1969–73, project mangr Humphreys and Glasgow London 1973–76; Lonrho plc gp: various appts incl sr exec project mangr Volkswagen UK HQ, sugar mills in Benin, re-estab Lonrho ops in Tanzania, started Lonrho business in USSR 1989, assoc dir 1990–91, main bd dir i/c new projects CIS, Zaïre, Angola and Belgium 1991–97; currently developing a project to convert disused oil rigs into refuges for big fish; Yeoman Worshipful Co of Ironmongers; FIMechE 1992; *Recreations* hill walking, occasional rowing and sailing; *Clubs* Athenaeum, Leander; *Style*— Jo Platts-Mills, Esq; ✉ Rue Gaston Imbert, 04280 Cereste, France (tel 00 33 4 92 79 01 02, e-mail jo.platts-mills@wanadoo.fr)

PLATTS-MILLS, Mark Fortescue; QC (1995); s of John Faithful Fortescue Platts-Mills (d 2001), and Janet Katherine, *née* Cree (d 1992); bro of Jonathan (Jo) Platts-Mills, *qv*; *b* 17 January 1951; *Educ* Bryanston, Balliol Coll Oxford (BA); *m* 1982, Dr Juliet Anne Britton; 1 s (John b 1988); *Career* called to the Bar Inner Temple 1974; memb Inner Temple and Lincoln's Inn; *Recreations* sailing, hockey, gardening; *Style*— Mark Platts-Mills, Esq, QC; ✉ 8 New Square, Lincoln's Inn, London WC2A 3QP (tel 020 7405 4321)

PLAUT, (Eur Ing) Rudolf (Rudi); CBE (1998, OBE 1993); *b* 19 February 1932; *Educ* Whitgift Sch, City Univ (BSc, pres Students' Union); *m* 1960, Margaret Gray; 1 s, 2 da; *Career* Nat Serv 1956–58; asst departmental mangr Steel Co of Wales Ltd 1958–61, dir Moplant Ltd 1961–72; chm: Northmace & Hendon Ltd 1973–, Techniquest Enterprises Ltd 1986–2002, NCF Asset Finance Ltd 1992–2002, Greyfriars Capital Ltd 2003–; chm Advsy Bd Xenos Wales Business Angels Network 1996–2001; founding chm Techniquest (Science Centre) 1986–2002; CBI: chm SE Wales Area 1987–91, chm Wales Economic Trends Panel 1998–, memb Wales Regnl Cncl 1990–97 and 1998–, memb Educn and Trg Affrs Ctee (UK) 1996–2006; chm and pro-chllr Univ of Glamorgan 1991–96, chm HE Engrg Panel Welsh Jt Educn Ctee 1985–88, chm Qualifications, Curriculum and Assessment Authy for Wales 1993–98; memb: Wales Advsy Bd for Local Authy HE 1987–90, Gen Teaching Cncl for England 2000–01 (chm Registration Ctee), Br Cncl Ctee for Wales 2000–06, Wales and W Regnl Ctee RSA 2002–04; assessor for public appts Wales and NI, tstee Darwin Centre for Biology and Med 1993–2003; hon treas South Wales Baptist Coll 1980–2000, tstee S Wales Baptist Assoc 2003– (moderator 2005–); vice-pres Mid Glamorgan Scout Assoc (formerly co cmmr) 1978–; Liveryman Welsh Livery Guild 1993; Hon Dr Univ of Glamorgan 1997; CEng, CCMI, Eur Ing, FRSA, FIMechE; *Publications* author of several articles in various learned jls and various appearances on TV news and current affrs progs; *Recreations* walking, swimming, family; *Style*— Rudi Plaut, Esq, CBE; ✉ Northmace & Hendon Ltd, Northmace House, Taffs Well, Cardiff CF15 9XF (tel 029 2081 5204, fax 029 2081 3959, e-mail rplaut@northmace.com)

PLAYFORD, His Hon Jonathan Richard; QC (1982); s of Maj Cecil Roche Bullen Playford (d 1977), of London, and Euphrasia Joan, *née* Cox; *b* 6 August 1940; *Educ* Eton, Univ of London (LLB); *m* 1978, Jill Margaret, da of William Herbert Dunlop, MBE (d 1982), of Doonside, Ayr; 1 s (Nicholas b 1981), 1 da (Fiona b 1985); *Career* called to the Bar Inner Temple 1962 (bencher 1991); recorder of the Crown Court 1985–98, circuit judge (SE Circuit) 1998–2006; memb Criminal Injuries Compensation Bd 1995–98; *Recreations* music, country pursuits, horology; *Clubs* Garrick; *Style*— His Hon Jonathan Playford, QC

PLAZAS, Mary; da of Francisco Plazas, and Albertina, *née* de Oliveira; *b* 9 September 1966; *Educ* Didcot Girls' Sch, RNCM (Dip Professional Performance, GMus, Alexander Young Award, Curtis Gold Medal, Claire Croiza Prize for French Song), Nat Opera Studio (Peter Moores Fndn Award); *Career* soprano; studied with Ava June RNCM, Eric Tappy Geneva 1994; operatic debut ENO 1992; co princ ENO 1995–98; pres Bicester Choral and Operatic Soc, patron Opera Anywhere; *Performances* solo recitals incl: Wigmore Hall, Purcell Room, Birmingham Town Hall, The Royal Exchange Theatre Manchester, Herbert von Karajan Centre Vienna; festivals incl: Cheltenham Festival, Aldeburgh Festival, Chester Festival 1995, Bath Festival, Bregenz Festival; roles incl: The Voice from Heaven in Verdi's Don Carlos (ENO 1992, Royal Opera BBC Proms 1996), title role in The Cunning Little Vixen (ENO), Susanna in Le Nozze di Figaro (Opera North), Elisetta in Il Matrimonio Segreto (Opera North), Adina (English Touring Opera), Anne Truelove (Opera Factory, London and Lisbon 1994, New Israeli Opera 1999), Poulenc's La Voix Humaine (Aix-en-Provence, RNCM), Madame Silvaklang in Die Schauspieldirektor (Garsington Opera), Marzelline in Fidelio (ENO), Mimi in La Bohème (ENO, Opera North and Royal Albert Hall), Leila in The Pearl Fishers (ENO), Frasquita and Michaela in Carmen (ENO), Oscar (ENO), Nanetta in Falstaff (ENO), Adina (ENO), Dorabella (ENO), Fiordiligi (ENO), Elvira (ENO, Glyndebourne Touring Opera and Valladolid), Salud La Vida Breve (Opera North), second angel in Pfitzner's Palestrina (Royal Opera House and New York), Tina in Flight by Jonathan Dove - World Premiere (Glyndebourne Touring Opera & Festival), Duchess in Powder Her Face (Thomas Adès, Aldeburgh, Almeida) 1999 and (LSO) 2006, Mimi in La Bohème (Bregenz Festival 2001 and 2002), Mum in Greek (London Sinfonietta 2003), Mrs Coyle in Owen Wingrave (Concertgebouw Amsterdam 2003), Anne Truelove (Bavarian State Opera Munich 2003); concerts incl: Haydn's Creation (conducted by Sir David Willcocks, Royal Albert Hall), Tippett's A

P

Child of our Time (Royal Festival Hall and St Petersburg), Mahler 8 (conducted by Sinopoli, Royal Albert Hall), Brahms Requiem (with CBSO, Sakari Oramo), Shostakovich 14 (with Irish Chamber Orch), Karin in world premiere of Gerald Barry's The Bitter Tears of Petra Van Kant (with Dublin Symphony Orch); performances with: LSO, BBC National Orch of Wales and Hallé Orch under Kent Nagano and Mark Elder, BBC Philharmonic under Giannandrea Noseda; *Television* First Enchantress in Dido and Aeneas (conducted by Richard Hickox, BBC Television, also recorded for Chandos) Powder Her Face (Channel 4), Flight (Glyndebourne, Channel 4); *Recordings* Mercadante's Emma d'Antiocchia (A Hundred Years of Italian Opera/Opera Rara), Pacini's Maria d'Ingilterra (Opera Rara with Philharmonia under David Parry), L'Enfant et Les Sortilèges (LSO under Previn), Marguerite in Faust (Chandos/Parry/Philharmonia), Adina in L'Elisir (Chandos/Parry/Philharmonia), Micaela in Carmen (Chandos/Parry/Philharmonia), Liu in Turandot (Chandos/Parry/Philharmonia), Zerlina in Don Giovanni (Chandos/Parry/Philharmonia), Fauré's La Naissance de Vênus (BBC Philharmonic under Yan Pascal Tortelier); *Awards* winner Nat Fedn Music Socs/Esso Award for Young Singers 1989, Isobel Baille Performance Award 1990, Kathleen Ferrier Memorial Scholarship 1991; *Recreations* cinema, tap dancing, cross stitch, listening to the radio, meeting friends, godchildren; *Style*— Ms Mary Plazas; ✉ c/o Owen/White Management, 59 Lansdowne Place, Hove, East Sussex BN3 1FL (tel 01273 727127, fax 01273 328128, e-mail owenwhite@compuserve.com)

PLEMING, Nigel Peter; QC (1992); s of Rev Percy Francis Pleming (d 1978), of Lincs, and Cynthia Myra, *née* Cope, later Mrs Tuxworth (d 2001); *b* 13 March 1946; *Educ* Tupton Hall GS Derby, King Edward VI GS Spilsby, Liverpool Coll of Commerce, Kingston Poly (LLB), UCL (LLM); *m* 22 Sept 1979, Evelyn Carol Joan, *née* Hoffmann; 2 da (Joanna b 10 April 1985, Katherine b 11 Jan 1989), 1 s (William b 29 Oct 1986); *Career* lectr in law 1969–73; called to the Bar Inner Temple 1971, in practice 1973–; Hon LLD Kingston Univ 1999; *Recreations* cricket, chess, guitar; *Clubs* RAC, Garrick; *Style*— Nigel Pleming, Esq, QC; ✉ 39 Essex Street, London WC2R 3AT (tel 020 7832 1111, fax 020 7353 3978)

PLENDER, (William) John Turner; s of William Plender (d 1977), of Wiltshire, and Averil Maud, *née* Turnbull; m, 2, Stephanie, *née* Harris; 2 s; *b* 9 May 1945; *Educ* Downside, Oriel Coll Oxford; *m* (m dis 1989), Sophia Mary, *née* Crombie; 1 s, 2 da; m 2, Stephanie, *née* Harris; 2 s; *Career* CA and writer; Deloitte Plender Griffiths & Co 1967–70, Investors' Chronicle 1970–71, The Times 1972–74, fin ed The Economist 1974–79, FCO 1980–81, freelance journalist, publisher and broadcaster 1982–, currently columnist FT; chm Pensions Investment Research Consultants Ltd (PIRC) 1992–2002, dir Quintain plc 2002– (chm 2007–); chm Advsy Cncl Centre for the Study of Financial Innovation 1997–; memb: London Stock Exchange Quality of Markets Advsy Ctee 1992–95, DTI Co Law Review Steering Gp 1998–2001, Advsy Bd Assoc of Corp Treasurers 2002–, World Bank OECD Private Sector Advsy Gp on Corp Governance 2002–; FCA 1970; *Books* That's The Way The Money Goes (1981), The Square Mile (with Paul Wallace, 1985), A Stake In The Future (1997), Going Off the Rails (2003), Ethics and Finance (jtly, 2007); *Clubs* Travellers; *Style*— John Plender, Esq; ✉ Financial Times, 1 Southwark Bridge, London SE1 9HL (tel 020 7873 3000, fax 020 7873 3748, e-mail john.plender@ft.com)

PLENDER, Richard Owen; QC (1989); s of George Plender, and Louise Mary, *née* Savage; *b* 9 October 1945; *Educ* Dulwich Coll, Queens' Coll Cambridge (BA, LLB, LLD, Rebecca Squire Prize), Univ of Sheffield (PhD), Univ of Illinois (LLM, JSD, Coll of Law Prize); *m* 16 Dec 1978, Patricia Clare, da of Wing Cdr John Lawson Ward (d 1974); 2 da (Sophie Clare b 31 Aug 1986, Amy Louise b 30 May 1991); *Career* called to the Bar Inner Temple 1972 (Berridale Keith prize, bencher 1996); recorder of the Crown Court 1998–, judge Employment Appeal Tbnl 2003–; legal advsr UN High Cmmn for Refugees 1976–78, referendaire European Court 1980–83; dir Centre of European Law Kings Coll London 1988–90, prof assoc Univ of Paris II; hon sr memb Robinson Coll Cambridge, hon visiting prof City Univ; *Books* International Migration Law (1972, 2 edn 1988), Fundamental Rights (1973), Cases and Materials on the Law of the European Communities (1980, 3 edn 1993), A Practical Introduction to European Community Law (1980), Introduccion al Derecho Comunitario (1985), Basic Documents on International Migration Law (1988, 2 edn 1996), Legal History and Comparative Law (1990), The European Contracts Convention - The Rome Convention on the Choice of Law for Contracts (1991, 2 edn 2001), The European Courts Practice and Precedents (gen ed and contrib, 1997), European Courts Procedure (looseleaf edn, 2001–); *Recreations* classical music, writing light verse; *Style*— Richard Plender, Esq, QC; ✉ 20 Essex Street, London WC2R 3AL (tel 020 7842 1200, fax 020 7842 1207, telex 893468 SXCORT G)

PLENDERLEITH, Ian; CBE (2002); s of Raymond William Plenderleith, and Louise Helen, *née* Martin; *b* 27 September 1943; *Educ* King Edward's Sch Birmingham, ChCh Oxford (MA), Columbia Business Sch NY (MBA, Beta Gamma Sigma medal); *m* 1 April 1967, Kristina Mary, da of John Hardy Bentley, OBE (d 1980); 2 da (Melanie b 1969, Cressida b 1976), 1 s (Giles b 1972); *Career* Bank of England 1965–2002: seconded as tech asst to UK Exec Dir International Monetary Fund Washington DC 1972–74, private sec to Govr 1976–79, alternate dir Euro Investment Bank 1980–86, head Gilt Edged Div 1982–90, govt broker 1989–2002, assoc dir i/c market operations 1990–94, exec dir i/c fin market ops 1994–2002, alternate dir Bank for International Settlements Basel 1994–2002, dir Bank of England Nominees Ltd 1994–2002, memb Monetary Policy Ctee 1997–2002; dep govr and memb Monetry Policy Ctee South African Reserve Bank 2003–; dir London Stock Exchange 1989–2001 (dep chm 1996); chm: Stock Borrowing and Lending Ctee 1990–95, G-10 Governors Gold and Foreign Exchange Ctee 1995–2001, Sterling Money Markets Liaison Gp 1999–2002, Co-op for Public Deposits 2003–, South African Money Markets Liasion Gp 2004–; co-chm Government Borrowers Forum 1991–94; memb: Editorial Bd OECD Study on Debt Mgmnt 1990–93, G-10 Ctee on Global Financial System 1994–2002; hon sec Tillington CC 1983–2003; memb: Advsy Bd Inst of Archaeology Devpt Tst UCL 1987–96, Bd of Overseers Columbia Business Sch 1991–, Legal Risk Review Ctee 1991–92, Fin Law Panel 1992–94, Fundraising Planning Gp St Bartholomew's Hosp 1992–94, Cncl Br Museum Friends 1993–99 and 2000–03, Bd of City Arts Tst 1997–2003, Fundraising Planning Ctee Bart's and London Hosps 1998–2003, External Advsy Panel Oxford Mathematical Inst 2000–03, Advsy Bd Oxford Business Alumni 2002–03, Br Museum Townley Steering Gp 2002–03, Christ Church Campaign Bd 2002– (memb Fin Ctee 1998–2003), Advsy Bd Global Borrowers and Investors Forum 2003–, Assoc of Black Securities and Investment Professionals 2005–; vice-pres London Old Edwardians Assoc Ctee 2004– (memb 1996–); memb: Advsy Bd The Actors Centre 2002–, Cncl Shakespeare's Globe 2002–; MSI 1991; Liveryman Worshipful Co of Innholders 1977; FACT 1989; *Recreations* archaeology, theatre, cricket, skiing, long-distance walking; *Clubs* Tillington CC, Bankers', MCC, London Capital (memb Advsy Bd 2002–); *Style*— Ian Plenderleith, Esq, CBE; ✉ South African Reserve Bank, PO Box 427, Pretoria 0001, South Africa

PLEWES, Jeremy John Lawrence; s of Lawrence William Plewes, CBE, of Kensworth, Beds, and Faith Sybil Etrenne, *née* Downing; *b* 5 September 1940; *Educ* Marlborough, ChCh Oxford (MA, BM BCh); *m* 12 Feb 1966, Jenna Rose, da of Lt Cdr Vernon Judge Glassborow (d 1971), of Yelverton, Devon; 1 da (Caryl Robin b 1969), 1 s (Andrew Burns b 1970); *Career* conslt orthopaedic surgn Royal Orthopaedic Hosp Birmingham 1982–, sr clinical lectr in surgery Univ of Birmingham 1982–; FRCS; *Recreations* photography, oenology, sailing; *Style*— Jeremy Plewes, Esq; ✉ Selvas Cottage, Withybed Green, Alvechurch, Worcestershire B48 7PR (tel 0121 445 1624); 81 Harborne Road, Edgbaston, Birmingham B15 3HG; Royal Orthopaedic Hospital, Birmingham B31 2AP (tel 0121 627 1627)

PLEYDELL-BOUVERIE, Hon Peter John; 2 s of 8 Earl of Radnor, *qv*, of Longford Castle, Salisbury, and his 1 w Anne, *née* Seth-Smith; *b* 14 January 1958, London; *Educ* Harrow, Trinity Coll Cambridge; *m* 14 June 1986, Hon Jane Victoria, da of Baron Gilmour of Craigmillar, PC (Life Peer), *qv*; 2 s (Timothy b 12 June 1987, Jamie b 23 July 1989), 2 da (Lara b 20 Dec 1993, Clare (twin) b 20 Dec 1993); *Career* assoc dir Kleinwort Grieveson Investment Mgmnt Co and fund mangr Grieveson Grant & Co 1980–86, investment dir Fidelity Int and Fidelity Investment Services Ltd 1986–96; currently dir: Ebble Devpts, Longford Farms Ltd; tstee Harnham Water Meadows Tst, jt chm Avon and Stour Rivers Assoc, memb Ctee Prince's Tst Salisbury, patron Salisbury Samaritans, patron Downton Heritage Trail; High Sheriff Wilts 2007–08 (Under-Sheriff 2005–06); *Recreations* fishing, countryside, opera, ballet; *Clubs* Pratt's; *Style*— The Hon Peter Pleydell-Bouverie; ✉ Newcourt, Downton, Salisbury, Wiltshire SP5 3JF (tel 01722 410495, e-mail peter.pb@virgin.net)

PLOTKIN, Prof Henry Charles; s of Bernard Solomon Plotkin (d 1985), of Johannesburg, South Africa, and Edythe, *née* Poplak (d 1987); *b* 11 December 1940; *Educ* Highlands North HS Johannesburg, Univ of the Witwatersrand (BSc), Univ of London (PhD); *m* 1975, Victoria Mary, *née* Welch; 1 da (Jessica b 12 Dec 1976), 1 s (Jocelin b 29 Jan 1980); *Career* MRC scientist 1965–72 (MRC travelling fell 1970–72, postdoctoral fell Stanford Univ 1971–72); UCL: lectr 1972–88, reader 1988–93, prof 1993–, head Dept of Psychology 1993–98; memb: Experimental Psychology Soc 1968, Assoc for Study of Animal Behaviour 1972; *Books* The Nature of Knowledge (1994), Evolution in Mind (1997), The Imagined World Made Real (2002), Evolutionary Thought in Psychology: A Brief History (2004); also 3 edited and co-edited anthologies, approximately 100 scientific papers; *Recreations* music, house in France, family, 'Spurs supporter; *Style*— Prof Henry Plotkin; ✉ Department of Psychology, University College London, Gower Street, London WC1E 6BT (tel 020 7679 7573, fax 020 7436 4276, e-mail h.plotkin@ucl.ac.uk)

PLOUVIEZ, Peter William; s of Charles Plouviez; *b* 30 July 1931; *Educ* Sir George Monoux GS, Hasting GS; *m* 1978, Alison Dorothy Macrae; 2 da (by former m); *Career* gen sec Br Actors' Equity Assoc 1974–91; chm: Radio and TV Safeguards Ctee 1974–91, Festival of Br Theatre 1983–91; cncllr St Pancras 1962–65, Parly candidate (Lab) St Marylebone By-Election 1963; vice-chm Confedn of Entertainment Unions 1974–91, vice-pres Int Fedn of Actors 1989–92, treas Entertainment Charities Fund, memb Theatres Tst (dep chm 1992–); chm: Fedn of Entertainment Unions 1991, Nat Cncl for Drama Training 1991–, Equity Tst Fund 1991–, Dancers Resettlement Tst; *Style*— Peter Plouviez, Esq

PLOWMAN, John Patrick; s of late Robert Gilbee Plowman, of Bolter End, Bucks, and Ruth Wynn, *née* Dutton; *b* 20 March 1944; *Educ* St Edward's Sch Oxford, Univ of Grenoble, Univ of Durham (BA); *m* 8 Sept 1973, Daphne Margaret, da of Dr Alexander Kennett (d 1984), of Swanage, Dorset; 1 da (Katherine b 1974), 2 s (Hugo b 1977, William b 1981); *Career* Lt Royal Marines Res 1967–70; MOD: joined 1967, Private Office Ministers of State for Def 1969–71; on secondment: Civil Service Selection Bd 1975, Cabinet Office 1976–78; MOD and UK delgn to UN Law of Sea Conf 1979–81, memb Bd of Property Servs Agency (Supplies) 1982–84, DOE 1984–87 and 1990–93, UK permanent rep to the European Communities 1987–90, head of environmental protection (Europe) 1990–93, NW regnl dir Depts of Environment and Tport 1993–94, dir Wildlife and Countryside DOE 1994–98, dir Road Safety and Environment DETR 1998–2001, chm Driver and Vehicle Operator Gp DTLR 2001–02 (gp modernisation dir 2003); dir John Plowman Associates Ltd 2003–; tstee Parly Advsy Cncl for Tport Safety 2004–, memb Bd Roadsafe 2006–; memb London Advsy Cncl Univ of Durham, govr Charlotte Sharman Sch 2002; FIMgt 1984; *Recreations* tennis, fishing, music, building restoration, book collecting; *Clubs* Royal Over-Seas League; *Style*— John Plowman

PLOWMAN, Jon; s of C Plowman, and F J Plowman; *Educ* Stanborough Sch Welwyn Garden City, UC Oxford; *Career* former asst dir Royal Court Theatre, then freelance theatre dir and prodr Granada TV; currently head of comedy entertainment BBC; work incl: French and Saunders (BAFTA Award), Murder Most Horrid, Absolutely Fabulous (3 series, Int Emmy for Best Popular Arts Prog 1993 and 1994, and 2 BAFTA Awards), A Bit of Fry & Laurie (4th series), Smith & Jones (2 series), The Vicar of Dibley, Ted & Alice, The Office (2 Golden Globe Awards); exec prodr: Shooting Stars, Gimme, Gimme, Gimme, In The Red, Comedy Nation, Goodness Gracious Me, League of Gentlemen, Comic Relief, Little Britain; 3 BAFTA nominations, 1 Int Emmy; FRTS, FRSA; *Clubs* National Liberal; *Style*— Jon Plowman; ✉ c/o BBC TV Entertainment Group, Television Centre, Wood Lane, London W12 7RJ (tel 020 8743 8000)

PLOWRIGHT, Joan Ann; (Lady Olivier), DBE (2004, CBE 1970); da of William Ernest Plowright; *b* 28 October 1929; *Educ* Scunthorpe GS, Laban Art of Movement Studio, Old Vic Theatre Sch; *m* 1, 1953 (m dis), Roger Gage; m 2, 1961, Sir Laurence Olivier, later Baron Olivier (Life Peer, d 1989); 1 s, 2 da; *Career* leading actress stage, film and television; memb Cncl RADA, vice-pres English Stage Co; Int Award 18th Annual Crystal Awards Women in Film USA 1994; DLitt Univ of Hull 2001; *Theatre* first stage appearance If Four Walls Told (Croydon Rep Theatre) 1948, with Bristol Old Vic and Old Vic Co South Africa Tour 1952, first London stage appearance in The Duenna (Westminster) 1954, Moby Dick (Duke of York's) 1955, with Nottingham Playhouse 1955–56, with English Stage Co (Royal Court) 1956, The Crucible, Don Juan, The Death of Satan, Cards of Identity, The Good Woman of Setzuan, The Country Wife (transferred to Adelphi 1957), The Chairs, The Making of Moo (Royal Court) 1957, The Entertainer (Palace) 1957, The Chairs, The Lesson (Phoenix NY) 1958, The Entertainer (Royale NY) 1958, The Chairs, The Lesson, Major Barbara (Royal Court) 1958, Hook Line and Sinker (Piccadilly) 1958, Roots (Royal Court and Duke of York's) 1959, Rhinoceros (Royal Court) 1960, A Taste of Honey (Lyceum NY) 1960 (Tony Award for Best Actress); leading actress with NT 1963–74; opening season 1963: St Joan, Uncle Vanya, Hobson's Choice; The Master Builder 1964, Much Ado About Nothing 1967 and 1968, Three Sisters 1967 and 1968, The Advertisement 1968, Love's Labour's Lost 1968, The Merchant of Venice 1979, A Woman Killed With Kindness 1971, The Rules of the Game 1971, Eden End 1974; Rosmersholm (Greenwich) 1973, Saturday, Sunday, Monday (Queen's) 1974–75, The Sea Gull (Lyric) 1975, The Bed Before Yesterday (Lyric) 1975 (Variety Club of GB Award 1977), Filumena (Lyric) 1977 (SWET Award 1978), Enjoy (Vaudeville) 1980, The Cherry Orchard (Haymarket) 1983, The House of Bernarda Alba (Globe) 1986; Chichester Festival: Uncle Vanya, The Chances 1962, St Joan (Evening Standard Award for Best Actress), Uncle Vanya 1963, The Doctor's Dilemma, The Taming of the Shrew 1972, Cavell 1982, The Way of the World 1984, If we are Women (Greenwich Theatre) 1995, Absolutely! (perhaps) (Wyndhams Theatre) 2003; directed: A Prayer for Wings 1985, Married Love 1988, Time and The Conways 1990/91; *Films* The Entertainer 1960, Equus, Britannia Hospital 1962, Three Sisters 1970, Wagner, Revolution 1985, Drowning by Numbers 1988, The Dressmaker 1988, I Love You to Death 1989, Avalon 1989, Denis, Last Action Hero 1992, Driving Miss Daisy 1992, A Place for Annie 1993, Widows Peak 1993, A Pin for the Butterfly 1993, On Promised Land 1994, Hotel Sorrento 1994, A Pyromaniacs Love Story 1994, The Scarlet Letter 1994, Jane Eyre 1995, Mr Wrong 1995, 101 Dalmatians 1996, The Assistant 1997, Dance With Me, Tea With Mussolini, Tom's Midnight Garden, Dinosaur (voice), Callas Forever, George and the Dragon, Bringing Down the House, I am David, Mrs Palfrey at the Claremont 2007–08; films for TV incl: The Merchant of Venice, Brimstone and Treacle, A Dedicated Man, House of Bernada Alba (1991), Stalin (Best Supporting TV actress Golden Globe 1993), Enchanted April

(BBC Screen Two, Best Supporting Film Actress Golden Globe 1993, Best Supporting Film Actress Oscar Nomination 1993) 1992, Clothes in The Wardrobe 1992, Return of the Native 1994; *Books* And That's Not All (autobiography, 2001); *Recreations* reading, music, entertaining; *Style*— Dame Joan Plowright, DBE; ✉ c/o ICM Ltd, Oxford House, 76 Oxford Street, London W1N 0AX (tel 020 7636 6565, fax 020 7323 0101)

PLOWRIGHT, Rosalind Anne; da of Robert Arthur Plowright, and Celia Adelaide Plowright; *b* 21 May 1949; *Educ* Notre Dame HS Wigan, Royal Northern Coll of Music Manchester; *m* 1984, James Anthony Kaye; 1 s (Daniel Robert), 1 da (Katherine Anne); *Career* soprano; London Opera Centre 1974–75, debut as Agathe in Der Freischütz (Glyndebourne Chorus and Touring Co) 1975, with ENO, WNO and Kent Opera 1975–78, Miss Jessel in Turn of the Screw (ENO) 1979, Ortlinde in Die Walküre (Royal Opera House debut) 1980; 1980–81: Bern Opera (Adriadne, Alceste), Frankfurt Opera (Ariadne, Aida, Il Trovatore), Munich Opera (Ariadne); debuts: USA, Paris, Madrid and Hamburg 1982, La Scala, Milan, Edinburgh Festival, San Francisco and Carnegie Hall NY 1983, Berlin, Houston, Pittsburgh, San Diego and Verona 1985, Rome, Florence and Holland 1986, Tulsa, NY Philharmonic, Buenos Aires, Santiago, Chile, Israel, Paris Opera and Bonn 1987, Lausanne, Geneva, Oviedo and Bilbao 1988, Zurich, Copenhagen and Lisbon 1989, Vienna, Torre del Lago and Bregenz 1990, Athens 1995, Scotland 1999; *Roles* principal roles incl: Amelia in Un Ballo in Maschera, Amneris in Aida, Desdemona in Otello, Elisabetta in Don Carlos, title role in Norma, Leonora in La Forza del Destino, title role in Tosca, title role in Medea, Lady Macbeth in Macbeth, title role in Ariadne auf Naxos, Abigaille in Nabucco, Giorgetta in Il Tabarro, title role in La Giaconda (Opera North) 1993; *Recordings* for EMI: Mary Stuart, Otello, Les Côntes d'Hoffman; for Deutsche Grammophon: Il Trovatore, La Forza del Destino, Mahler Resurrection Symphony; La Vestale for Orfeo Records, Elijah for Chandos Records; *Awards* incl: First Prize Int Competition for Opera Singers (Sofia 1979), Prix Fndn Fanny Heldy (Nat Acad du Disque Lyrique 1985); *Recreations* fell walking; *Style*— Miss Rosalind Plowright; ✉ c/o Victoria Smith Management, 2 Police Cottages, North End Lane, Droxford, Hampshire S032 3QN (tel 01489 878787)

PLUMB, Baron (Life Peer UK 1987), of Coleshill in the County of Warwickshire; (Charles) Henry Plumb; kt (1973), DL (Warks 1977); s of Charles Plumb, of Ansley, Warks, and Louise, *née* Fisher; *b* 27 March 1925; *Educ* King Edward VI Sch Nuneaton; *m* 1947, Marjorie Dorothy, da of Thomas Victor Dunn, of Bentley, Warks; 1 s (Hon John Henry), 2 da (Hon Mrs Holman, Hon Mrs Mayo); *Career* MEP (Cons) The Cotswolds 1979–99, chm Agric Ctee Euro Parl 1979–82, ldr (Cons) EDG Euro Parl 1982–87, pres Euro Parl 1987–89; pres NFU 1970–79 (dep pres 1966–69, vice-pres 1964–66, memb Cncl 1959–), chm Br Agric Cncl 1975–79; pres Warks County Fedn of Young Farmers' Clubs 1974–, pres Nat Fedn 1976–86; memb Cncl: CBI, Animal Health Tst; pres: COPA 1975–77, RASE 1977 (dep pres 1978), Int Fedn of Agric Prodrs 1979–; chllr Coventry Univ 1995–; hon pres Ayrshire Cattle Soc; chm Int Policy Cncl on Agric, Food and Trade; pres: Conservative Countryside Forum 1998, Campden and Chorleywood Food Research Assoc 1998; govr City Technol Coll Kingshurst 1988–2002; Hon Liveryman Worshipful Co of Fruiterers 1991, memb Ct of Assts Worshipful Co of Farmers (Master 2006–); hon fell Wye Coll London; Hon DSc Cranfield 1983; FRSA 1970, FRAgS 1974; Order of Merit (Fed Repub of Germany) 1976, Grand Cross Order of Merit (Portugal) 1987, Order of Merit (Luxembourg) 1988, Grand Cross Order of Civil Merit (Spain) 1989, Knight Cdr Cross of the Order of Merit (Fed Repub of Germany) 1990; *Publications* The Plumb Line - A Journey Through Agriculture and Politics (2001), Modern Agriculture in Africa; *Clubs* Farmers', St Stephen's, Coleshill Rotary (hon memb); *Style*— The Lord Plumb, DL; ✉ Maxstoke, Coleshill, Warwickshire B46 2QJ (tel and fax 01675 464156); House of Lords, London SW1A 0PW (fax 020 7219 1649, e-mail plumbh@parliament.uk)

PLUMBLY, HE Sir Derek John; KCMG (2001, CMG 1991); s of John Cecil Plumbly (d 1987), and Jean Elizabeth, *née* Baker; *b* 15 May 1948; *Educ* Brockenhurst GS, Magdalen Coll Oxford (BA); *m* 10 Nov 1979, Nadia, da of Youssef Gohar, of Cairo, Egypt; 1 da (Sara b 1983), 2 s (Samuel b 1985, Joseph b 1987); *Career* VSO Pakistan 1970–71, FCO 1972, Middle East Centre for Arab Studies (MECAS) Lebanon 1973, second sec Jedda 1975, first sec Cairo 1977, FCO 1980, first sec Washington DC 1984, cnsllr and dep head of mission Riyadh 1988–92, counsellor and head of Chancery UKMIS NY 1992–96, sr int drugs co-ordinator and dir Drugs and Int Crime FCO 1996–97, dir Middle East and N Africa 1997–2000, ambass to Saudi Arabia 2000–03, ambass to Egypt 2003–; *Clubs* Travellers; *Style*— HE Sir Derek Plumbly, KCMG; ✉ c/o Foreign & Commonwealth Office (Cairo), King Charles Street, London SW1A 2AH

PLUMMER OF ST MARYLEBONE, Baron (Life Peer UK 1981), of St Marylebone in the City of Westminster; Sir (Arthur) Desmond Herne Plummer; kt (1971), TD (1950), JP (London 1958), DL (Greater London 1970); s of late Arthur Herne Plummer, and late Janet McCormick; *b* 25 May 1914; *Educ* Hurstpierpoint Coll, Coll of Estate Mgmnt; *m* 1941, Ella Margaret (Pat) (d 1998), da of Albert Holloway, of Epping, Essex; 1 da (Hon Sally Jane); *Career* sits as Cons peer in House of Lords; memb: St Marylebone BC 1952–65 (mayor 1958–59), LCC St Marylebone 1960–65, ILEA 1964–76; GLC: memb for Cities of London and Westminster 1964–73, memb for St Marylebone 1973–76, ldr of oppn 1966–67 and 1973–74, ldr GLC 1967–73; chm: National Employers' Life Assurance Co 1983–89, Portman Building Society 1983–90 (pres 1990–), Horserace Betting Levy Bd 1974–82, Epsom and Walton Downs Trg Grounds Mgmnt Bd 1974–82, Nat Stud 1975–82; pres: Met Assoc of Bldg Socs 1983–89, London Anglers' Assoc 1976–; memb Ct Univ of London 1967–77; fndr memb Order of St John Cncl for London 1971–94; FAI 1948, Hon FASI 1966, FRICS 1970, FRSA 1974; KStJ 1986; *Clubs* Carlton, RAC, MCC; *Style*— The Rt Hon the Lord Plummer of St Marylebone, TD, DL; ✉ 4 The Lane, Marlborough Place, St Johns Wood, London NW8 0PN

PLUNKET, 8 Baron (UK 1827); Robin Rathmore Plunket; s of 6 Baron Plunket (d 1938), and bro of 7 Baron (d 1975); *b* 3 December 1925; *Educ* Eton; *m* 1951, Jennifer, da of late Bailey Southwell, of South Africa; *Heir* bro, Hon Shaun Plunket; *Career* formerly Capt Rifle Bde; forester; *Recreations* fishing; *Clubs* Boodle's; *Style*— The Rt Hon the Lord Plunket; ✉ Rathmore, Chimanimani, Zimbabwe (tel 00 263 262281); 39 Lansdowne Gardens, London SW8 2EL (tel 020 7622 6049)

PLYMOUTH, Bishop of (RC) 1986–; Rt Rev (Hugh) Christopher Budd; s of John Alfred Budd (d 1993), and Phyllis Mary, *née* Pearson (d 1978); *b* 27 May 1937; *Educ* Salesian Coll Chertsey, Cotton Coll, Ven English Coll Rome, Pontifical Univ Gregoriana Rome (PhL, STL, STD); *Career* tutor in theol Rome 1965–71, lectr in theol Newman Coll Birmingham and asst priest St Brigid's Northfield 1971–76, head of trg Catholic Marriage Advsy Cncl 1976–79, rector St John's Seminary Wonersh Guildford 1979–85, admin Brentwood Cathedral 1985–86; ecumenical canon Truro Cathedral (Anglican) 1999–; hon life fell Newman Coll of HE 2001–; *Recreations* walking, watching cricket; *Style*— The Rt Rev the Bishop of Plymouth; ✉ Bishop's House, 31 Wyndham Street West, Plymouth, Devon PL1 5RZ (tel 01752 224414, fax 01752 223750, e-mail bishop@plymouth-diocese.org.uk)

PLYMOUTH, 3 Earl of (UK 1905); Other Robert Ivor Windsor-Clive; DL (Salop 1961); Viscount Windsor (UK 1905), Baron Windsor (E 1529); s of 2 Earl of Plymouth, DL, PC (d 1943), and Lady Irene Corona, *née* Charteris (d 1989), da of 11 Earl of Wemyss; *b* 9 October 1923; *Educ* Eton; *m* 1950, Caroline Helen, da of Edward Rice, of Dane Court, Eastry, Kent; 3 s, 1 da; *Heir* s, Viscount Windsor; *Career* late Coldstream Gds; memb Standing Cmmn on Museums and Galleries 1972–82, chm Reviewing Ctee on Export of Works of Art 1982–85; FRSA; KStJ; *Style*— The Rt Hon the Earl of Plymouth, DL; ✉ The Stables, Oakly Park, Ludlow, Shropshire SY8 2JW

POBERESKIN, Louis Howard; *b* 16 August 1948; *Educ* Case Western Reserv Univ (BS, MD); *m* 1, 28 Nov 1980; 2 da (Sarah b 1983, Lisa b 1983); m 2, 21 April 2005, Caroline; *Career* sr registrar in neurosurgery Addenbrooke's Hosp Cambridge 1981–85, conslt neurosurgeon Derriford Hosp 1985–; FRCSEd 1987; *Style*— Louis Pobereskin, Esq; ✉ Department of Neurosurgery, Derriford Hospital, Plymouth (tel 01752 792539, fax 01752 763395, e-mail louis.pobereskin@phnt.swest.nhs.uk)

POCOCK, HE Dr Andrew John; s of John Francis Pocock, of Maraval, Trinidad, and Vida Erica, *née* Duruty; *b* 23 August 1955, Port of Spain, Trinidad; *Educ* St Mary's Coll Port of Spain (Island schol), Queen Mary Coll Univ of London (BA, MA), Peterhouse Cambridge (PhD); *m* 4 Nov 1995, Julie, *née* Mason; *Career* joined UN Dept FCO 1981, second then first sec Br High Cmmn Lagos 1983–86, first sec: Southern African Dept FCO 1986–88, Br Embassy Washington USA 1988–92, Personnel Mgmnt Dept FCO 1992–94; asst head S Asia Dept FCO 1994–96, cnsllr seconded to RCDS 1996, dep high cmmr Canberra 1997–2001, head Southern African Dept FCO 2001–03, high cmmr to Tanzania 2003–06, ambass to Zimbabwe 2006–; *Recreations* reading, walking, tennis, cricket; *Style*— HE Dr Andrew Pocock; ✉ c/o Foreign & Commonwealth Office (Harare), King Charles Street, London SW1A 2AH (tel 00 263 4 752275, e-mail andrew.pocock@fco.gov.uk)

PODGER, Geoffrey John Freeman; CB (2003); s of late Leonard Podger, and late Beryl Enid, *née* Freeman; *b* 3 August 1952; *Educ* Worthing HS for Boys, Pembroke Coll Oxford (open scholar, MA); *Career* MOD: admin trainee 1974–77, seconded to Int Staff NATO HQ Brussels 1977–79, princ 1979–82; DHSS 1982–88, on loan as sec to Port Stanley Hosp Fire Inquiry Falkland Islands 1985; Dept of Health: private sec to Chm NHS Management Bd 1985–87, asst sec 1987, princ private sec to sec of state for Social Servs 1987–88, project mangr NHS Review 1988–92, head International Relations Unit 1992–93, under-sec for Health Promotion 1993–96; under-sec (Food Safety and Science Group) MAFF 1996–97, under-sec (Jt Food Safety and Standards Gp) Dept of Health and MAFF 1997–99, chief exec Food Standards Agency 2000–03, exec dir European Food Safety Authy (EFSA) 2003–05, chief exec HSE 2005–; *Clubs* Athenaeum; *Style*— Geoffrey Podger, Esq, CB

PODMORE, John; s of Alfred Eric Podmore (d 1998), of Stockport, and Alice, *née* Pearson; *b* 29 August 1954, Stockport; *Educ* Stockport Sch, City London Poly (BSc), Goldsmith's Coll London (PGCE); *m* 1978 (m dis 2002), Susan, *née* Pressley; 2 da (Gemma Louise b 17 Feb 1982, Rachel Helen b 2 July 1984); *Career* dep govr then governing govr HMP Belmarsh 1994–98, govr HMP Swaleside 1998–2001, team ldr HM Inspectorate of Prisons 2001–03, govr HMP Brixton 2003–06, operational advsr Dept for Offender Health 2006–; chair Release, dir Rugby House; Marjory Fry special commendation Howard League for Penal Reform, Butler Tst Award; *Recreations* motorcycling, travel, cooking; *Style*— John Podmore, Esq; ✉ Offender Health - Department of Health, 133–135 Waterloo Road, London SE1 8UG (tel 07968 908369, e-mail john.podmore@dh.gsi.gov.uk)

POET, Bruno; s of Robert Poet, of Wolverhampton, and Margarete Poet; *b* 2 July 1972; *Educ* Oundle, Mansfield Coll Oxford (BA); *m* Annabel; 1 da (Emilia); *Career* lighting designer; memb Assoc of Lighting Designers 1996–; *Theatre* credits incl: The Enchantment, Aristocrats (Nat Theatre), Midnight's Children (RSC at the Barbican, NY), King Lear (ETT, Old Vic), All About My Mother (Old Vic), Antarctica, Tess (West End), Phaedra (Donmar Warehouse), Dumb Show (Royal Ct), Tobias and the Angel, The Skin of our Teeth (Young Vic), Ubu The King (Barbican, Tron, Dundee Rep), The Schuman Plan (Hampstead), Don Juan, Hansel and Gretal (Lyric Hammersmith), Things You Shouldn't Say Past Midnight (Soho), A Soldier's Tale (QEH) and The Three Musketeers, The Importance of Being Earnest, The Lemon Princess, Alice in Wonderland, Volpone, Major Barbara, Playboy of the Western World, The Homecoming, The Seagull, The Birthday Party, The Glass Menagerie, The Cherry Orchard, Sexual Perversity in Chicago (regnl theatres); *Opera* prodns incl work for the int opera houses in Sydney, Barcelona, Bologna, Ancona, Porto, Geneva, Granada and Antwerp, and in the UK for Garsington Opera (ten consecutive seasons), ENO, Scottish Opera, Royal Opera House and Opera North; Helpmann Award (nomination, for Rusalka) 2007, CATS Award (for Midsummer Night's Dream and Dundee Rep) 2007; *Recreations* sailing, skiing, travel; *Style*— Bruno Poet, Esq; ✉ 22 St Andrew's Street, Millbrook, Cornwall PL10 1BE (tel 01752 822983, mobile 07973 600987, e-mail bruno@brunopoet.co.uk, website www.brunopoet.co.uk); c/o Clare Vidal Hall, 57 Carthew Road, London W6 0DU (tel 020 8741 7647, fax 020 8741 9459)

POGGE von STRANDMANN, Prof Hartmut Johann Otto; s of Dr Johann Leopold Pogge (d 1945), and Erica, *née* von Strandmann (d 1995); *Educ* J H Voss-Gymnasium Eutin, Bonn Univ, Berlin Univ, Hamburg Univ, Univ of Oxford (DPhil); *m* 1970, Hilary M Bennett; 1 s, 1 da; *Career* sr scholar St Antony's Coll Oxford 1962–66, research fell and jr dean Balliol Coll Oxford 1966–70, lectr in modern European history Univ of Sussex 1970–77, official fell and praelector in modern history UC Oxford and univ lectr Univ of Oxford 1977–2005 (emeritus fell 2005–), curator UC Oxford 1985–2006, prof of modern history Univ of Oxford 1996–, dir Modern European History Research Centre Univ of Oxford 1998–2002; visiting prof: S Carolina, Rostock Univ, Washington and Lee Univ VA, Namibia Research Centre for Social Sciences Berlin; lectured widely in Britain, Germany, USA, Australia and Russia; Studienstiftung des Deutschen Volkes 1964–66, Akademiestipendium 1974–76, Br Acad Res Readership 1986–88; Arbeitskreis Deutscher England Forschung 1984–, Freundes Kreis des German Historical Insts London 1985–95, memb Deutscher Historiker Verband; univ chm Gibbs Tst Fund 2001–06; memb Nat Tst, friend of the Ashmolean Museum; FRHistS 1985; *Books* Die Erforderlichkeit des Unmoeglichen (1965), Unternehmens Politik und Unternehmens Fuehrung (1978), Walther Rathenau: Industrialist, Banker, Intellectual and Politician. Notes and Diaries (1985), The Coming of the First World War (1988), The Revolutions in Europe 1848–1849: From Reform to Reaction (2000), Ins tiefste Afrika. Paul Pogge und seine präkolonialen Reisen ins sdliche Kongobecken (2004); *Recreations* tennis, walking, swimming, skiing, music, theatre, art; *Style*— Prof Hartmut Pogge von Strandmann; ✉ University College, Oxford OX1 4BH (tel 01865 276602)

POGMORE, John Richard; s of Edward Richard Fry Pogmore, MBE (d 1986), and Edith Mary, *née* Trevitt (d 1997); *b* 12 June 1942; *Educ* Southwell Minster GS, Univ of London (MB BS); *m* 18 June 1966, Trina Ann Leigh, da of Frederick Waterman (d 2000); 2 s (Simon b 1970, James b 1972); *Career* cmmnd RAF 1963, ret 1980 with rank of Wing Cdr; former conslt obstetrician and gynaecologist Birmingham Women's Hosp, former conslt gynaecologist Priory Hosp Edgbaston; former chm Hosp Recognition Ctee RCOG; pres: Birmingham Medicolegal Soc 2005–, Birmingham and Midland Obstetrician and Gynaecological Soc 2005–; FRCOG 1988; *Recreations* cartography, wine, golf; *Clubs* RAF; *Style*— Mr John Pogmore; ✉ Priory Hospital, Priory Road, Edgbaston, Birmingham B5 7UG (tel 0121 440 2323, fax 0121 446 5686, e-mail jpog@doctors.org.uk)

POLAK, Prof Dame Julia Margaret; DBE (2003); da of Carlos Polak, and Rebeca, *née* Mactas; *b* 29 June 1939; *Educ* Univ of Buenos Aires (MD, Dip Histopathology), Univ of London (DSc); *m* 1961, Daniel Catovsky, s of Felix Catovsky; 1 da (Marina b 1963), 2 s (Elliot Sebastian b 1973, Michael David b 1976); *Career* Buenos Aires: demonstrator 1961–62, SHO in surgery and med 1962, registrar and sr registrar 1963–67; Royal Postgrad Med Sch (Imperial Coll Sch of Med at Hammersmith Hosp following merger 1997): res asst Dept of Histochemistry 1968–69, asst lectr 1970–73, lectr 1973–79, sr lectr 1979–82, reader 1982–84; Dept of Histopathology Hammersmith Hosp: hon conslt 1979–, prof of endocrine pathology 1984–, dep dir 1988–91, head Dept of Histochemistry 1991–; ed of numerous med jls and organiser of int and nat med meetings; external ctees incl:

P

chm Immunocytochemistry Club, chm Br Endocrine Pathologists Club, memb Exec Ctee Cncl Circulation of American Heart Assoc, memb Cncl Histochemical Soc of GB 1984–86, memb Bd of Studies on Pathology; memb learned socs incl: American Thoracic Soc, Br Cardiac Soc, Br Neuroendocrine Gp, Cwlth Assoc for Devpt, IBRO, NY Acad of Sciences; memb: BMA, RSM, American Assoc of Pathologists; FRCPath 1986 (memb 1974); Benito de Udaondo Cardiology prize 1967; *Books* incl: Gut Hormones (with S R Bloom, 1981), Basic Science in Gastroenterology, Vol I: Structure of the Gut (jtly, 1982), The Systematic Role of Regulatory Peptides (with S R Bloom and E Lindenlaub, 1983), Immunolabelling for Electron Microscopy (with I M Varndell, 1984), Endocrine Tumours - The Pathobiology of Regulatory Peptide-producing Tumours (with S R Bloom, 1985), Regulatory Peptides (1989), In Situ Hybridization: Principles and Practice (with J O D McGee, 1990), Electron Microscopic Immunocytochemistry: Principles and Practice (with J V Priestley, 1992), Diagnostic Histopathology of Neuroendocrine Tumours (1993), Clinical Gene Analysis and Manipulation - Tools, Techniques and Troubleshooting (with J A Z Jankowski and Sir David Weatherall, 1996), Future Strategies for Tissue and Organ Replacement (with Larry L Hench and P Kemp, 2002); *Style*— Prof Dame Julia Polak, DBE; ✉ Tissue Engineering and Regenerative Medicine Centre, Faculty of Medicine, Imperial College, 3rd Floor, Chelsea and Westminster Hospital, 369 Fulham Road, London SW10 9NH (e-mail julia.polak@imperial.ac.uk)

POLAND, Michael Desmond; s of Kenneth Gordon Poland (d 1970), of Liphook, Hants, and Hester Mary Beatrice, *née* Chichele-Plowden (d 1993); *b* 9 August 1937; *Educ* Downside; *m* 1 (m dis 1981), Elizabeth, da of late Philip Asprey; 4 da (Lara (Mrs William Sussmann) b 1969, Emma (Mrs Stefan Oberholzer) b 1970, Lisa (Mrs Miles Heathfield) b 1973, Anna b 1974); m 2, 20 Feb 1981, Carolyn Mary, da of late Wing Cdr William James Maitland Longmore, CBE (d 1988), of Bishop's Waltham, Hants; *Career* dir: Ajax Insurance Holdings Ltd (formerly The Ajax Insurance Association Ltd) 1964–91, John Poland & Co Ltd 1968–89 and 1991–2003, Stackhouse Poland Ltd (formerly Cannon Rogers Ltd then Poland Insurance Brokers Ltd) 1974–2001 (chm 1974–97), Barker Poland Financial Management Ltd (formerly Stackhouse Poland Financial Management Ltd) 1978–2006, The Ajax Insurance Association Ltd 1980–91; chief exec HP Motor Policies at Lloyd's 1974–82; chm: Radio Victory Ltd 1984–85 (dir 1982–85), Beechbourne Ltd 1989–2006; dir A H Worth Ltd 1990–98; Master IOW Foxhounds 1983–95, chm IOW Woodland Forum 1997–; *Recreations* foxhunting, thoroughbred horse breeding, conservation, sailing; *Style*— Michael Poland; ✉ Lower Preshaw House, Upham, Southampton SO32 1HP (tel 01489 892652, fax 01489 891331, e-mail michael.poland@virgin.net)

POLE, *see also:* Carew Pole

POLE, Sir Peter Van Notten; 5 Bt (GB 1791); s of late Arthur Chandos Pole and kinsman of Sir Cecil Pery Van Notten-Pole, 4 Bt (d 1948); *b* 6 November 1921; *Educ* Guildford GS; *m* 1949, Jean Emily, da of late Charles Douglas Stone; 1 s, 1 da; *Heir* s, Peter Pole; *Career* 1939–45 war as Flt Sgt, pilot RAAF; accountant, ret; FASA, ACIS; *Style*— Sir Peter Pole, Bt; ✉ 249 Dartnell Parade, Cambrai Village, 85 Hester Avenue, Merriwa, Western Australia 6030, Australia

POLGLASE, Timothy; s of Frank Polglase, of Fowey, Cornwall, and Betty, *née* Skinner (d 2002); *b* 15 January 1962, Newton Abbot, Devon; *Educ* Fowey Sch, St Austell Sixth Form Coll, St John's Coll Oxford (MA), Coll of Law Guildford; *m* 9 Aug 1991, Laura Elizabeth, *née* Duncan; 2 da (Katherine Isobel b 22 Jan 1994, Amy Elizabeth b 14 Oct 1996); *Career* Norton Rose: articled 1984–86, slr 1986–94 (secondments to Milbank, Tweed, Hadley & McCloy NY 1988–89 and Bank of England 1990–91), ptnr 1994–2002; ptnr Allen & Overy LLP 2002–; author of articles in professional pubns; memb City of London Slrs Co 1994; *Recreations* sailing, skiing; *Clubs* Royal Ocean Racing, Royal Fowey Yacht, Hayling Island Sailing; *Style*— Timothy Polglase, Esq; ✉ Allen & Overy LLP, One New Change, London EC4M 9QQ (tel 020 7330 3000, fax 020 7330 9999, e-mail tim.polglase@allenovery.com)

POLIAKOFF, Stephen; CBE (2007); s of Alexander Poliakoff (d 1996), and Ina, *née* Montagu (d 1992); *b* 1 December 1952; *Educ* Westminster, Univ of Cambridge; *m* 5 Oct 1983, Sandy Welch; 1 da (Laura b 4 March 1985), 1 s (Alexander b 22 Jan 1991); *Career* playwright and screenwriter; FRSL; *Theatre* Clever Soldiers (Hampstead Theatre) 1974, The Carnation Gang (Bush Theatre) 1974, Hitting Town (Bush Theare) 1975, City Sugar (Comedy Theatre) 1975 (Evening Standard Award for Most Promising Playwright), Heroes (Royal Court Theatre) 1975, Strawberry Fields (NT) 1977, Shout Across the River (RSC) 1978, American Days (ICA) 1979, Summer Party (Crucible Theatre Sheffield) 1980, Favourite Nights (Lyric Theatre Hammersmith) 1981, Breaking The Silence (RSC) 1984, Coming in to Land (Nat Theatre) 1987, Playing with Trains (RSC) 1989, Sienna Red (Peter Hall Co) 1992, Sweet Panic (Hampstead Theatre) 1996, Blinded By The Sun (NT) 1996 (Critics Circle Award for Best Play), Talk of the City (RSC) 1998, Remember This (NT) 1999; *Television* Stronger Than The Sun (BBC) 1977, Caught on a Train (BBC) 1980 (BAFTA Award for Best Single Play), Soft Targets (BBC) 1982, She's Been Away (BBC) 1989 (Venice Film Festival Award), The Tribe (BBC) 1997, Shooting the Past (BBC) 1999 (RTS Award for Best Drama, Prix Italia), Perfect Strangers (BBC) 2001 (RTS Awards for Best Writer and Best Drama, BAFTA Dennis Potter Award 2002, Peabody Award), The Lost Prince (BBC) 2003 (3 Emmy Awards), Friends and Crocodiles (BBC) 2006, Gideon's Daughter (BBC) 2006; *Film* Bloody Kids 1980, Runners 1983, Hidden City 1988, Close My Eyes 1991 (Evening Standard Award for Best British Film 1992), Century 1994, Food of Love 1998; *Publications* Stephen Poliakoff Plays: One (Clever Soldiers, Hitting Town, City Sugar, Shout Across the River, American Days, Strawberry Fields), Two (Breaking the Silence, Playing with Trains, She's Been Away, Century), Three (Caught on a Train, Coming in to Land, Close My Eyes); Perfect Strangers (screenplay), Remember This, Shooting the Past (screenplay), Sienna Red, Sweet Panic/Blinded by the Sun, Talk of the City, The Lost Prince (screenplay), Friends & Crocodiles/Gideon's Daughter (screenplays); *Recreations* cinema, cricket; *Style*— Stephen Poliakoff, Esq, CBE, FRSL

POLIZZI DI SORRENTINO, (Hon) Olga; CBE (1990); eldest da of Baron Forte (Life Peer); *b* 1947; *Educ* St Mary's Sch Ascot; *m* 1, Sept 1966, Marchese Alessandro Polizzi di Sorrentino (decd), s of Gen Polizzi di Sorrentino (d 1980); 2 da (Alexandra b 28 Aug 1971, Charlotte b 9 April 1974); m 2, Oct 1993, (Hon) William Hartley Hume Shawcross, *qv*, s of Baron Shawcross, GBE, PC, QC (Life Peer, d 2003); *Career* exec dir Forte plc until 1996; dir Rocco Forte Hotels Ltd, md Hotel Tresanton Ltd, dir Millers Bespoke Bakery; elected to Westminster City Cncl 1989–94; tstee: St Mary's Sch Ascot, Italian Hosp Fund; vice-chm KCL; *Style*— Mrs Olga Polizzi, CBE; ✉ Rocco Forte Hotels Ltd, Savannah House, 11 Charles II Street, London SW1Y 4QU (tel 020 7321 2626)

POLKINGHORNE, Rev Dr John Charlton; KBE (1997); s of George Baulkwill Polkinghorne (d 1981), and Dorothy Evelyn, *née* Charlton (d 1983); *b* 16 October 1930; *Educ* Elmhurst GS Street, Perse Sch Cambridge, Trinity Coll Cambridge (BA, PhD, MA, ScD), Westcott House Cambridge; *m* 26 March 1955, Ruth Isobel (d 2006), da of Hedley Gifford Martin (d 1979); 2 s (Peter b 1957, Michael b 1963), 1 da (Isobel Morland b 1959); *Career* Nat Serv RAEC 1948–49; fell Trinity Coll Cambridge 1954–86; lectr: Univ of Edinburgh 1956–58, Univ of Cambridge 1958–65 (reader 1965–68, prof of mathematical physics 1968–79); ordained: deacon 1981, priest 1982; curate: Cambridge 1981–82, Bristol 1982–84; vicar Blean Kent 1984–86, fell, dean and chaplain Trinity Hall Cambridge 1986–89 (hon fell 1989), pres Queens' Coll Cambridge 1989–96 (fell 1996–, hon fell 1996), Proctor in Convocation 1990–2000, hon fell St Edmund's Coll Cambridge 2002; chm: Ctee on Use of Foetal Material 1988–89, Nuclear Physics Bd 1978–79, Task Force to Review Servs for Drug Misusers 1994–96, Advsy Ctee on Genetic Testing 1996–99; memb: SRC 1975–79, Doctrine Cmmn 1989–96, Human Genetics Advsy Cmmn 1996–99, Human Genetics Cmmn 2000–02; chm govrs Perse Sch 1972–81; Templeton Prize 2002; Hon DD: Univ of Kent 1994, Univ of Durham 1999; Hon DSc: Univ of Exeter 1994, Univ of Leicester 1995, Marquette Univ 2003; Hon DHum Hong Kong Baptist Univ 2006; FRS 1974; *Books* The Analytic S-Matrix (1966), The Particle Play (1979), Models of High Energy Processes (1980), The Way the World Is (1983), The Quantum World (1984), One World (1986), Science and Creation (1988), Science and Providence (1989), Rochester Roundabout (1989), Reason and Reality (1991), Science and Christian Belief (1994), Serious Talk (1995), Scientists as Theologians (1996), Beyond Science (1996), Searching for Truth (1996), Belief in God on an Age of Science (1998), Science and Theology (1998), Faith, Science and Understanding (2000), Faith in the Living God (2001), The God of Hope and the End of the World (2002), Quantum Theory (2002), Living with Hope (2003), Science and the Trinity (2004), Exploring Reality (2005), Quantum Physics and Theology (2007); *Recreations* gardening; *Style*— The Rev Dr John Polkinghorne, KBE, FRS; ✉ 74 Hurst Park Avenue, Cambridge CB4 2AF (tel 01223 360743, fax 01223 360743)

POLL, Prof (David) Ian Alistair; OBE (2002); s of Ralph Poll, of Great Yarmouth, Norfolk, and Mary, *née* Hall; *b* 1 October 1950; *Educ* Heckmondwike GS, Imperial Coll London (BSc), Cranfield Inst of Technol (PhD); *m* 31 May 1975, Elizabeth Mary, da of Ewart John Read (d 1968), of Painswick, Glos; 2 s (Edward b 1977, Robert b 1980), 1 da (Helen b 1984); *Career* Future Projects Dept Hawker Siddeley Aviation 1972–75, sr lectr in aerodynamics Cranfield Inst of Tech 1985–87 (res asst 1975–78, lectr 1978–85); Univ of Manchester: prof of aeronautical engrg and dir Goldstein Laboratory 1987–95, head Engrg Dept 1991–94, head Aerospace Div 1994–95; fndr and md Flow Science Ltd 1990–95; Cranfield Univ: head Coll of Aeronautics 1995–2000, dir Coll of Aeronautics 2001–04, prof of aerospace engrg 2004–; Cranfield Aerospace Ltd: fndr and md 1996–99, tech dir 1999–2004, business devpt and tech dir 2004–; visiting scientist: DFVLR Göttingen W Germany 1983, NASA Langley Res Centre VA 1983, 1989 and 1990, NASA Ames Research Centre CA 1995 and 1998, Stanford Univ 1998; memb: Fluid Dynamics Panel NATO Advsy Gp for Aerospace R&D 1991–97, Aerospace Ctee DTI 1999–2004, Aerospace Technol Steering Gp 2004–, CAA Uninhabited Air Vehicle Steering Ctee 2006–; RAeS: memb Cncl 1996–, vice-pres 1998–2000, pres 2001, chm Learned Soc Bd 1997–2000, chm Cranfield Univ Branch 1997–, chm Strategic Review Bd 2000, chair Uninhabited Air Vehicle Ctee 2005–, Hodgson Prize 2001, Wilbur and Orville Wright lectr 2002; Int Cncl of the Aeronautical Scis (ICAS): memb Gen Assembly 1997–, chair Prog Ctee 2006– (memb 1997–), pres Int Cncl 2008–; memb Cncl Air League 1997–; vice-pres (technical progs) Confedn of Euro Aerospace Socs (CEAS) 2003–04, sr vice-pres City and Guilds Coll Assoc 2004–; memb Cncl Royal Acad of Engrg 2004–; author of over 100 papers on aerodynamics; Liveryman Worshipful Co of Coachmakers and Coach Harness Makers; ACGI 1972; memb RUSI 2005–; CEng 1978, FRAeS 1987, FREng 1996, FAIAA 2000, FCGI 2004; *Recreations* golf, political debate; *Clubs* Athenaeum, RAF; *Style*— Prof Ian Poll, OBE, FREng; ✉ Cranfield Aerospace Limited, Cranfield, Bedfordshire MK43 0AL (tel 01234 754743, fax 01234 751181, e-mail d.i.a.poll@cranfield.ac.uk)

POLLACK, Anita Jean; da of John Samuel Pollack (decd), of Sydney, Aust, and Kathleen, *née* Emerson (decd); *b* 3 June 1946; *Educ* Sydney Tech Coll (Dip Advertising), City of London Poly (BA), Birkbeck Coll London (MSc); *m* Philip Stephen Bradbury; 1 da (Katherine Louise Pollack Bradbury b 4 Sept 1986); *Career* former advtg copywriter Aust, book ed London 1970–74, res asst to late Rt Hon Barbara Castle 1981–89, MEP (Lab) London SW 1989–99, head of European policy English Heritage 2000–2006, European conslt 2006–; *Recreations* family; *Style*— Ms Anita Pollack; ✉ 139 Windsor Road, London E7 0RA (tel 020 8471 1637)

POLLARD, Sir Charles; kt (2001), QPM (1990); s of Humphrey Charles Pollard (d 1990), and Margaret Isobel, *née* Philpott (d 1986); *b* 4 February 1945; *Educ* Oundle, Univ of Bristol (LLB); *m* 13 July 1972, Erica Jane Allison, da of Gordon Daniel Jack; 2 s (Jonathan, Christopher), 1 da (Rosemary); *Career* Met Police 1964–66, travelled abroad 1967, Met Police 1968–80 (latterly Chief Inspr); Sussex Police: Supt Eastbourne Sub-Div 1980–84, Chief Supt Operational Support Dept HQ Lewes 1984–85; asst Chief Constable Thames Valley Police 1985–88, dep asst cmmr i/c Plus Programme and later SW Area Met Police 1988–91, Chief Constable Thames Valley Police 1991–2002; chm Justice Research Consortium 2002–, reader in criminology Univ of Pennsylvania 2002–; chm Oxford Common Purpose 1996–98, vice-chm Thames Valley Partnership 1991–2002; visiting fell Nuffield Coll Oxford 1993–2001; memb Youth Justice Bd for England and Wales 1998– (acting chm 2003–04), memb Bd Centre for Mgmnt and Policy Studies 2000–02; memb ACPO (chm Quality Serv Ctee 1991–94, chm No 5 (S East) Region 1996–99); contributes to nat media and learned journals on policing, criminal justice and restorative justice; Dr of Laws (hc): Univ of Buckingham 2001, Univ of Bristol 2003; *Recreations* walking, bridge, tennis, family pursuits; *Clubs* Royal Over-Seas League; *Style*— Sir Charles Pollard, QPM, LLB; ✉ Youth Justice Board for England and Wales, 11 Carteret Street, London SW1H 9DL (tel 020 7271 3057, fax 020 7271 3030)

POLLARD, David Nigel; s of John Stuart Pollard (d 2001), and Ruth, *née* Rath; *b* 30 August 1956, Leeds, Yorks; *Educ* Cranbrook Sch, St John's Coll Cambridge, Coll of Law Chester; *m* 15 June 1991, Louise Elizabeth, *née* O'Hara; 2 da (Jessica b 9 May 1994, Elizabeth b 4 March 1996), 1 s (Andrew b 14 Feb 1998); *Career* admitted slr: Eng and Wales 1980, Hong Kong 1986; slr specialising in pensions and employment law; articled clerk then slr Lewis Lewis & Co 1978–82; Freshfields: slr London and Singapore offices 1982–90, ptnr 1990–; co-ed Trust Law Int jl; Wallace Medal Assoc of Pension Lawyers 1998; chm Assoc of Pension Lawyers 2001–03, former vice-chair Industrial Law Soc, memb Law Soc; *Publications* Guide to the Pensions Act 1995 (ed, 1995), Corporate Insolvency: Employment and Pension Rights (3 edn 2007); *Recreations* Cwlth pensions cases; *Clubs* Singapore Cricket; *Style*— David Pollard, Esq; ✉ 55 Colebrooke Row, Islington, London N1 8AF (tel 020 7359 4215, e-mail teampollard@yahoo.co.uk); Freshfields Bruckhaus Deringer, 65 Fleet Street, London EC4Y 1HS (tel 020 7832 7060, fax 020 7832 7001, e-mail david.pollard@freshfields.com)

POLLARD, Eve (Lady Lloyd); da of Ivor Pollard, and Mimi Pollard; *m* 1, 8 Dec 1968 (m dis), Barry Winkleman; 1 da (Claudia b 15 Jan 1972); m 2, 23 May 1979, Sir Nicholas Lloyd, *qv*; 1 s (Oliver b 6 Aug 1980); *Career* fashion ed: Honey 1967–68, Daily Mirror Magazine 1968–69; reporter Daily Mirror 1969–70; women's ed: Observer Magazine 1970–71, Sunday Mirror 1971–81; asst ed Sunday People 1981–83, features ed and presenter TV-am 1983–85; ed: Elle (launch, USA) 1985–86, Sunday Magazine (News of the World) 1986, You Magazine (Mail on Sunday) 1986–87, Sunday Mirror and Sunday Mirror Magazine 1988–91, Sunday Express and Sunday Express magazine 1991–94; devised two series Frocks on the Box for ITV 1985; hon pres Women in Journalism 1999– (chair 1995–99), Editor of the Year Newspaper Focus Awards 1990; memb: English Tourist Bd 1993–2000, Newspaper Panel Competition Cmmn 1999–; visiting fell Bournemouth Univ; vice-chm Wellbeing charity; *Books* Jackie (1971), Splash (jtly Val Corbett and Joyce Hopkirk, 1995), Best of Enemies (1996), Double Trouble (1997), Unfinished Business (1998), Jack's Widow (2006); *Style*— Miss Eve Pollard; ✉ c/o Noel Gay, 19 Denmark Street, London WC2H 8NA

POLLARD, (Andrew) Garth; s of late Rev George Pollard, and Elizabeth Beatrice, *née* Briggs; *b* 25 April 1945; *Educ* Queen's Coll Taunton, King's Coll London (LLB); *m* 26 May 1973, Lucy Petica, da of the late Prof Charles Martin Robertson, of Cambridge; 3 s

(Finn b 1978, Tam b 1980, Liam b 1982); *Career* admitted slr 1969; Clifford-Turner: slr 1969–75, ptnr 1975–87; Clifford Chance: ptnr 1987–2002, exec ptnr 1991–99, chief operating offr 2000–01; chm of govrs St Christopher Sch, govr Birkbeck Coll London; chm Suffolk Heritage Housing Assoc; AKC; *Recreations* music, walking, motorcycling; *Style*— Garth Pollard, Esq; ✉ Clifford Chance, 10 Upper Bank Street, London E14 5JJ (tel 020 7006 1000, fax 020 7006 5555)

POLLARD, Ian Douglas; s of Douglas Pollard, DFC (ka 1945), and Peggy, *née* Murfitt (d 1989); *b* 9 June 1945; *Educ* Perse Sch Cambridge; *m* 25 July 1964, Dianna, da of Prof Alexander Deer, of Cambridge; 3 da (Juliette b 1964, Samantha b 1966, Arushka b 1987), 2 s (Rufus b 1992, Kian b 1995); *Career* chm and md Flaxyard plc 1972–; architectural designer of: Marcopolo (Observers Bldg) 1987, Sainsbury's Homebase Kensington 1988, Martin Ryan Inst for Marine Scis Galway 1991; designer and creator of gardens at Hazelbury Manor Wilts and Abbey House Gardens Malmesbury Wilts; featured as 'naked gardener' in Going to Work Naked (ITV) 2005; ARICS; *Recreations* gardening, cycling, diving; *Style*— Ian Pollard, Esq; ✉ The Abbey House, Market Cross, Malmesbury, Wiltshire SN16 9AS (tel 01666 827650, fax 01666 822782, e-mail info@abbeyhousegardens.co.uk)

POLLARD, John Stanley; s of Prof Arthur Pollard (d 2002), of North Cave, Humberside, and Ursula Ann Egerton, *née* Jackson (d 1970); *b* 4 January 1952; *Educ* King's Sch Macclesfield, Hymers Coll Hull, Univ of Leeds (LLB); *m* 14 Sept 1974, Clare Judith, da of Arnold Walter George Boulton (d 1992), of Cookham Dean, Berks; 3 s (Samuel John b 1979, Joseph William b 1981, Edward George b 1984); *Career* admitted slr 1977; HM asst dep coroner Cheshire, HM coroner Manchester S District, HM asst dep coroner Manchester W District; memb Congleton Town Cncl 1983–2007; Parly candidate (SDP) Crewe and Nantwich 1983; chm LRC (4 x 4) Ltd 1999–, chm Dane Housing Ltd 1999–, dir Dane Housing Ltd, dir and tstee Astbury Mere Tst; memb: Law Soc, Coroners Soc of England and Wales (memb Nat Cncl); *Recreations* football, sport, gardening, politics; *Style*— John Pollard, Esq; ✉ Greenways, Sprink Lane, Key Green, Congleton, Cheshire CW12 3PF; HM Coroner, 10 Greek Street, Stockport SK3 8AB (tel 0161 476 0971, fax 0161 476 0972, e-mail john.pollard@stockport.gov.uk)

POLLARD, Prof (Alan) Mark; s of Alan Pollard (d 1985), and Elizabeth Pollard (d 1998); *b* 5 July 1954, Auckland, NZ; *Educ* Heckmondwyke GS, Sowerby Bridge GS, Univ of York (BA, DPhil); *m* 1992, Dr Rebecca Nicholson; 2 da (Sarah Elizabeth b 8 May 1993, Louise Etta b 22 April 1997); *Career* analytical research offr Research Lab for Archaeology Univ of Oxford 1978–84, lectr in inorganic chemistry UC Cardiff 1984–90, prof of archaeological sciences Univ of Bradford 1990–2004 (head of dept 1990–99, pro-vice-chllr (research) 2001–04), Edward Hall prof of archaeological science Univ of Oxford 2004–; nat co-ordinator for science-based archaeology 1987–90; MRSC 1990, FSA 1993; *Publications* author of 191 pubns incl: Archaeological Chemistry (jtly, 1996), Handbook of Archaeological Science (jt ed, 2001); *Recreations* cycling, morris dancing and playing, stamps; *Style*— Prof Mark Pollard; ✉ Research Laboratory for Archaeology and the History of Art, University of Oxford, Dyson Perrins Building, South Parks Road, Oxford OX1 2QY (tel 01865 285228)

POLLARD, Stephen John; s of Ronald Arthur Pollard, and Elsie, *née* Raw; *Educ* Dulwich Coll, ChCh Oxford (MA), Kingston Poly (MPhil); *m* 1973, Judith Ann, *née* Lacy; 1 s, 3 da; *Career* civil servant; MOD: joined 1975, sr civil service 1989, dir (fin and secretariat) Avionics, Weapons and Info Systems 1989–93, head mgmnt services (organisation) 1993–96, dir mgmnt and consultancy services 1996–97, dir Central and Eastern Europe 1997–2000, head Overseas Secretariat 2000–; chm London Oriana Choir 1986–93, govr St James's Sch Tunbridge Wells 1992–; *Recreations* music (especially choral singing), mountain walking, current affairs, cookery, holidays in France; *Style*— Stephen Pollard, Esq; ✉ Ministry of Defence, Room 332, Metropole Building, Northumberland Avenue, London WC2N 5BP (tel 020 7218 6144, fax 020 7218 1242, e-mail registry@seco.fsnet.co.uk)

POLLER, Prof Leon; s of Nathan Kristian Poller (d 1975), of Southport, Lancs, and Helena, *née* Minshull (d 1987); *b* 15 April 1927; *Educ* Univ of Manchester (MB ChB, DSc, MD); *m* 9 July 1955, Jean Mavis, da of James Albert Dier, MBE (d 1989), of Bolton, Lancs; 2 s (David b 1962, John b 1965); *Career* Lt, Capt, Maj RAMC 1953–55, CDEE Porton Down Miny of Supply; jr hosp appts Manchester 1957–61, conslt haematologist and dir UK Ref Lab for Anticoagulant Reagents and Control Collaborating Centre WHO 1961–92, fndr organiser UK Nat External Quality Assessment Scheme on blood coagulation 1969–90, fndr organiser WHO External Quality Assessment Scheme in blood coagulation (WHO IEQAS) 1970–90, princ investigator WHO Biological Standards 1972–76; over 300 published papers, books and reviews on blood coagulation and thrombosis; chm: Int Ctee Standardization in Haematology Task Force Blood Coagulation 1972–96, ICSH Task Force on Quality Control in Blood Coagulation 1980–2000, WHO IEQAS in Blood Coagulation Advsy Group, Nat and Int Med Scientific Ctees; co-chm ISHT Sub-Ctee on Anticoagulant Control 1980–2002; project ldr: Euro Community Concerted Action on Anticoagulation 1994–2002, Euro Community Action on Anticoagulation 2002–; sec Manchester Thrombosis Res Fndn 1988–; chm Manchester and Dist Home for Lost Dogs; hon prof Univ of Manchester 1990; MRCS, LRCP, FRCPath 1968; *Books* Theory and Practice of Anticoagulant Treatment (1962), Recent Advances in Blood Coagulation 1–7 (ed, 1968–96), Recent Advances in Thrombosis (ed, 1972), Thrombosis and its Management (ed, 1993), Procduction of Basic Diagnostic Laboratory Reagents (ed, 1995), The Activated Partial Thromboplastin Time and the Prothrombin Time (1998), Oral Anticoagulants (ed, 1996); *Recreations* forestry, cricket (playing), music (listening); *Clubs* Athenaeum; *Style*— Prof Leon Poller; ✉ Department of Life Sciences, University of Manchester 3.239 Stopford Building, Oxford Road, Manchester M13 9PT (tel and fax 0161 275 5424, e-mail ecaa@man.ac.uk or leon.poller@man.ac.uk)

POLLINS, Martin; s of Harry Pollins (d 1969), of London, and Hetty Pollins (d 1991); *b* 11 December 1938; *Educ* Brighton Tech Sch; MBA 1999; *m* 1, March 1963 (m dis 1980); m 2, Dec 1980, Susan Elizabeth, da of Arthur Edwin Hines, of Brighton; 4 s (Andrew, Richard, Nicholas, Matthew), 1 da (Anna); *Career* chartered accountant; ptnr PRB Martin Pollins 1968–2005; chm: Professional Enterprise Gp plc 1986–97, Britton Price Ltd 1996–, Bizezia Ltd 2001–; dir: Network Technology plc 1995–2006, Movision Entertainment Ltd 2002–; memb Cncl ICAEW 1987–96; FCA 1964, ATII 1964; *Recreations* spectator of sport; *Style*— Martin Pollins, Esq; ✉ 3 North Lodge, High Street, Newick, East Sussex BN8 3LY; Bizezia Limited, Kingfisher House, Hurstwood Grange, Hurstwood Lane, Haywards Heath, West Sussex RH17 7QX (tel 01444 220920, fax 01444 220930, e-mail mpollins@bizezia.com)

POLLITT, Prof Christopher John; s of Almora John Pollitt, and Freda Hebbert, *née* Ashcroft; *b* 7 February 1946; *Educ* Oriel Coll Oxford (MA), LSE (PhD); *Partner* Hilkka Helena Summa; 2 s from prev m (Thomas John b 22 April 1971, Jack Christopher b 12 Aug 1972); *Career* asst princ then princ Home Civil Serv (MOD, Miny of Technol, DTI) 1967–73, sr lectr Middx Poly 1973–75, lectr then sr lectr in govt Open Univ 1975–90; Brunel Univ: prof of govt and co-dir Centre for the Evaluation of Public Policy and Practice 1990–98, dean Faculty of Social Scis 1994–97, prof of public mgmnt Erasmus Univ Rotterdam 1999–2006, prof of public mgmnt Univ of Leuven 2006–; hon jt ed Public Admin 1980–88, non-exec dir Hillingdon Hosp Tst 1995–97; numerous research grants and consultancies with public and govt bodies incl: ESRC, EC, HM Treasy, OECD, World Bank; memb Cncl RIPA 1990–92, pres Euro Evaluation Soc 1996–98; *Books* incl: Managerialism and the Public Services (1990, 2 edn 1993), The Essential Public Manager (2003), Public Management Reform: a Comparative Analysis (with Geert Bouckaert, 2004); *Recreations* squash, walking, owl-watching; *Style*— Prof Christopher Pollitt; ✉ Instituut voor de overheid, Van Evenstraat 2A, BE-3000 Leuven, Belgium (e-mail pollitt@fsw.eur.nl)

POLLOCK, *see also:* Montagu-Pollock

POLLOCK, Sheriff Alexander; s of late Robert Faulds Pollock, OBE, and late Margaret Findlay Pollock, *née* Aitken; *b* 21 July 1944; *Educ* Rutherglen Acad, Glasgow Acad, BNC Oxford (Domus exhibitioner, MA), Univ of Edinburgh (LLB), Perugia Univ (for foreigners); *m* 1975, Verena Francesca Gertraud Alice Ursula, da of late J Reginald Critchley, of Ware, Herts; 1 da (Francesca b 1976), 1 s (Andrew b 1979); *Career* slr 1970–73, advocate Scottish Bar 1973–91; MP (Cons): Moray and Nairn 1979–83, Moray 1983–87; memb Commons Select Ctee on Scottish Affrs 1979–82; PPS to George Younger: as Sec of State for Scotland 1982–86, as Sec of State for Def 1986–87; sec Br Austrian Parly Gp 1979–87, Advocate Depute 1990–91; Floating Sheriff of Tayside, Central and Fife at Stirling 1991–93, Sheriff of Grampian, Highland and Islands at Aberdeen and Stonehaven 1993–2001, at Inverness and Portree 2001–05, at Inverness 2005–; memb Queen's Body Guard for Scotland (Royal Co of Archers) 1984–; *Clubs* New (Edinburgh), Highland (Inverness); *Style*— Sheriff Alexander Pollock; ✉ Drumdarrach, Forres, Moray IV36 1DW

POLLOCK, Prof Christopher John; CBE (2002); *b* 28 March 1947; *Educ* Solihull Sch, Trinity Hall Cambridge (MA), Univ of Birmingham (PhD, DSc); 2 c; *Career* Broodbank fell Univ of Cambridge Botany Sch 1971–74; Welsh Plant Breeding Station: higher scientific offr 1974–76, sr scientific offr 1976–82, principal scientific offr/UG7 1982–89, head of Enviromental Adaption Gp 1985–93; sr Fulbright fell Dept of Biochemistry Univ of Calif Davis 1979–80, sr reasearch fell Dept of Agronomy Purdue Univ IN 1987–92; research dir IGER 1993–2007; hon prof: Inst of Biological Science Univ of Wales Aberystwyth 1993–, Sch of Agric Univ of Nottingham; ed advsr The New Phytologist; chair: Advsy Ctee for Releases into the Environment 2003–, Research Priority Gp for Sustainable Farming and Food 2003–07; memb: Cncl Soc for Experimental Biology 1990–93 (memb Ctee Plant Science 1987–90), Stapeldon Tst 1993–, Cncl Univ of Wales Aberystwyth Coll 1994–, Climate Changes Impacts Review Gp 1995–96; FRAgS, FIBiol; *Recreations* golf, woodwork, hill walking, reading, music; *Style*— Prof Christopher Pollock, CBE; ✉ Institute of Rural Sciences, University of Wales, Aberystwyth SY23 3AL (tel 01970 624471, fax 01970 611264, e-mail cip@aber.ac.uk)

POLLOCK, David (Charles) Treherne; s of Brian Treherne Pollock (d 1994), and Helen Evelyn (d 1995), da of Brig-Gen Sir Eric Holt-Wilson, CMG, DSO; *b* 7 April 1938; *Educ* St Andrew's Pangbourne, Nowton Court, The Hill Sch, St Lawrence Coll; *m* 1961, Lisbeth Jane, *née* Scratchley; 2 s (Piers, Blair), 1 da (Sophie-Jane (Mrs Richard Johnson)); *Career* cmmnd The Gordon Highlanders 1956–59; The Economist 1961–68; dir: Mathers & Streets Ltd 1968–69, Charles Barker (City) Ltd 1969–70, Dewe Rogerson Ltd 1970–88, Dewe Rogerson Group Ltd 1975–88, Maxwell Stamp plc 1988–2002; chm: Bloxham Group Holdings Ltd 1992–2000, Sponsorship Research Co Ltd 1995–99, Netpoll Ltd 1997–2002; tstee Restoration of Appearance and Function Tst (RAFT) 1994– (chm 2000–); *Clubs* Brooks's, City of London; *Style*— David Treherne Pollock, Esq; ✉ 9 The Chase, London SW4 0NP (tel 020 7622 1535, fax 020 7498 6400, e-mail david@trehernepollock.com); France tel 00 33 55 96 61 408

POLLOCK, David Raymond John; s of Eric John Frank Pollock (d 1992), of Dulwich, and Beryl Olive, *née* Newens (d 1982); *b* 22 October 1949; *Educ* Dulwich Coll, Keele Univ (BA); *m* 30 July 1975, Barbara Ann (d 2005), da of Henry Chambré, MBE, of Hendon; 1 da (Sarah Charlotte Chambré b 23 Aug 1980), 1 s (Thomas Hugo John b 19 March 1984); *Career* MOD: admin trainee 1972, higher exec offr 1975 (private sec to Chief Sci Advsr), princ 1978; asst dir Primary Markets Div Int Stock Exchange 1989–91 (head of Industry Policy Unit 1986, head of Business Devpt Primary Mkts Div 1988), dir Newspaper Publishers Assoc 1992–97 (dir designate 1991), dir Electrical Contractors' Assoc 1997–; memb: Cncl until 1998 and Fin Ctee Royal Instn of GB, Asia House (lectured on Lao textiles 2004), Soc of Archer Antiquaries, S American Explorers' Club Lima Peru; Liveryman Worshipful Company of Stationers and Newspaper Makers; FRSA; *Recreations* country pursuits, travel, tribal textiles, drawing and painting, books, conviviality; *Style*— David Pollock, Esq; ✉ 46 Dacres Road, London SE23 2NR (tel 020 8699 3883); The Electrical Contractors' Association, 34 Palace Court, London W2 4HY (tel 020 7313 4803, fax 020 7221 7344)

POLLOCK, Sir George Frederick; 5 Bt (UK 1866), of Hatton, Middx; s of Sir (Frederick) John Pollock, 4 Bt (d 1963); *b* 13 August 1928; *Educ* Eton, Trinity Coll Cambridge (MA); *m* 1951, Doreen Mumford, da of Norman Ernest Keown Nash, CMG (d 1966); 2 da (Charlotte Anne b 1952, Catherine Frances Jill b 1955), 1 s (David Frederick b 1959); *Heir* s, David Pollock; *Career* 2 Lt 17/21 Lancers 1948–49; admitted slr 1956; artist-photographer and audio-visual creator 1963–2000, ret; hon vice-pres: Disabled Photographers' Soc, Croydon Camera Club; Hon FRPS (pres 1978), Hon PAGB, FRSA, EFIAP; *Clubs* DHO; *Style*— Sir George F Pollock, Bt; ✉ 83 Minster Way, Bath BA2 6RL (tel 01225 464692)

POLLOCK, Prof Griselda Frances Sinclair; da of Alan Winton Seton Pollock (d 1986), and Kathleen Alexandra, *née* Sinclair (d 1964); *b* 11 March 1949; *Educ* Queen's Coll London, Lady Margaret Hall Oxford (MA), Courtauld Inst of Art (MA, PhD); *m* 30 Oct 1981, Prof Antony Bryant, s of Paul and Leonie Bryant, of London; 1 s (Benjamin b 22 March 1983), 1 da (Hester b 7 Feb 1986); *Career* lectr in art history Univ of Manchester 1974–77; Univ of Leeds: lectr in art history and film 1977–85, sr lectr 1985–90, prof of social and critical histories of art 1990–, dir Centre for Cultural Studies 1987–2000, exec Centre for Jewish Studies 1995–, dir Centre for Cultural, Analysis Theory and History 2001–; author of numerous articles in jls; Tate Gallery Liverpool Advsy Bd 1988–94; FRSA 1996; *Books* Millet (1977), Vincent Van Gogh (1978), Mary Cassatt (1980), Old Mistresses Women Art and Ideology (1981), The Journals of Marie Bashkirtseff (1985), Framing Feminism: Art and the Women's Movement (1987), Vision and Difference: Feminism, Femininity and the Histories of Art (1988), Dealing with Degas (co-ed with R Kendall, 1992), Avant-Garde Gambits 1888–1893: Gender and the Colour of Art History (1992, Walter Neurath Meml Lecture), Generations and Geographies in the Visual Arts (1996), Avant-Gardes and Partisans Reviewed (with Fred Orton, 1996), Mary Cassatt (1998), Differencing The Canon (1999), Looking Back to the Future (2000), Encountering Eva Hesse (with Vanessa Corby, 2006), Psychoanalysis and the Image (2006), Museums after Modernism (2007), Encounters in the Virtual Feminist Museum (2007), Conceptual Odysseys (2007); *Recreations* running, cinema; *Style*— Prof Griselda Pollock; ✉ CentreCATH, Old Mining Building, University of Leeds, Leeds LS2 9JT (e-mail g.f.s.pollock@leeds.ac.uk)

POLLOCK, John C; s of Alfred Kenneth Pollock (d 1994), of Bexhill, E Sussex, and Ruby Nora Kathleen, *née* Briggs (d 2003); *b* 4 June 1940; *Educ* Dulwich Coll; *m* 3 March 1972, Renee Mary Desborough; 1 s (James Martin b 2 June 1978); *Career* sr Layton Bennett Billingham & Co chartered accountants 1963–64 (articled clerk 1958–63), chartered accountant Ernst & Whinney The Hague 1965–66 (London 1966–67), Litton Industries Zurich 1968–70, md MCA/Universal Pictures Amsterdam 1970–74, estab Netherlands office Josolyne Layton-Bennett & Co 1974–82 (ptnr UK firm), following merger estab Leeds office Arthur Young 1982–85 (returned as UK desk ptnr in the Netherlands 1985–89), equity ptnr Ernst & Young Netherlands 1990–2000 (following merger with Ernst & Whinney 1989), ed Ernst & Young's Netherlands Briefing (English language bulletin); supervisory dir Eurocommercial Properties NV 2006–; former chair CCAB The

Netherlands, treas Br Business Assoc (Netherlands), former memb Assoc of Br Sch in The Netherlands; numerous articles published and lectures given; MBCS (fndr memb), FCA, RA (NL); *Recreations* skiing, walking, photography, travel, gardening, formerly a keen alpinist; *Style*— John C Pollock, Esq; ✉ tel 00 31 70 511 7153, e-mail john.pollock@wanadoo.nl

POLLOCK, Peter Glen; s of Jack Campbell Pollock (d 1953), and Rebecca Shields Marshall, *née* Clarke (d 1985); *b* 6 September 1946; *Educ* Nautical Coll Pangbourne, Univ of St Andrews (MA); *m* 3 Sept 1977, Nicola Sara, da of Derek William Bernard Clements, of Cirencester, Glos; 2 s (Jonathan William Campbell b 1982, Matthew Charles Simon b 1984), 1 da (Antonia Rebecca b 1991); *Career* fin dir: Hawker Siddeley Power Transformers Ltd 1978–83, Fisher Controls Ltd 1983–85; gp chief exec ML Holdings plc 1985–92, mgmnt conslt Peter Pollock & Co 1992–94; dir: Faversham Oyster Fishery Co 1993–94, Menvier Swain Group plc 1993–97, Mentmore Abbey plc (formerly Platignum plc) 1994–99; chm: Valetmatic Holdings Ltd 1994–97, Second Phase Industries Ltd 1994–, Lionheart plc 1997–2004 (dir 1996–2004); chief exec LPA Group plc 1997–; memb: Ctee RUKBA 1985–98, Cncl SBAC 1989–92; memb Fin Ctee Railway Industry Assoc 2000–; FCA (admitted assoc 1973); *Recreations* music, tennis, country pursuits, skiing, golf; *Clubs* Knole, Knole Park Golf; *Style*— Peter Pollock, Esq; ✉ Platt Common House, St Mary's Platt, Sevenoaks, Kent TN15 8JX (mobile 07881 626123, e-mail ppollock@lpa-group.com)

POLLOCK-HILL, Stephen David; s of Malcolm William Lyttleton Pollock-Hill (d 1995), of Malaga, Spain, and Jeanne, *née* Beale (d 2005); *b* 22 March 1948; *Educ* Harrow, Sorbonne, Univ de Madrid, Univ de Vienna, Hatfield Poly (HND); *m* 18 June 1983, Samantha Ann Maria Russell, da of Sir (William) Russell Lawrence, QC (d 1976); 1 s (Robert b 1977), 1 da (Talitha Louise b 1985); *Career* documentalist Mead Carney France (mgmnt conslts) 1970–71; Nazeing Glass Works: sales liaison offr 1972, sales rep 1973, sales mangr 1975, export mangr 1976, sales dir 1980–91, jt md 1990–98, chm 1992–; chm and md Nazeing Glass Investments 1990–, chm Globe Trotter Suitcase Co Ltd 2003–05; memb Euro Domestic Glass Ctee 1978–, chm Sci Museum Glass Gallery Ctee 1978–90, memb Cncl Glass Mfrs' Cncl 1980–88, chm GMF Domestic and Handmade Glass Ctee 1980–88, chm Br Glass Educnl Tst 2000–, Euro domestic glass advsr EEC-CPIV Ctee Brussels 1985–90; chm: CPRE Herts 1993–96 (vice-pres 1998–), Herts Business Link Lea Valley Branch 1998–2002, IOD Herts Branch 2000–03; dir Bd Herts Business Link 2000–03; memb Fin and Gen Purposes Ctee Tree Cncl; memb Devpt Ctee Univ of Hertfordshire 1995–99, memb Advsy Ctee Univ of Hertfordshire Business Sch, memb Advsy Ctee European Business Sch London (memb Academic Bd 1998–2005); co-fndr CASE (Campaign Against Stevenage Expansion), ctee memb and tstee The Friends of Forster Country; memb E of Eng Sustainable Devpt Round Table; life memb: Nat Tst, Int Wine & Food Soc; Freeman City of London, Liveryman Worshipful Co of Glass Sellers; *Recreations* conservation, lawn tennis, real tennis, gardening, trees, fine wine, writing; *Clubs* Hatfield House Real Tennis, The October (hon sec); *Style*— Stephen Pollock-Hill, Esq; ✉ Nazeing Glass Investments Ltd, Broxbourne, Hertfordshire EN10 6SU (tel 01992 464485, fax 01992 450966, e-mail s.pollock-hill@nazeing-glass.com)

POLTIMORE, 7 Baron (UK 1831); Sir Mark Coplestone Bampfylde; 12 Bt (E 1641); s of Capt the Hon Anthony Gerard Hugh Bampfylde (d 1969), and Brita Yvonne (now Mrs Guy Elmes), *née* Baroness Cederström; suc gf, 6 Baron, 1978; *b* 8 June 1957; *Educ* Radley; *m* 12 June 1982, Sally Anne, da of Dr Norman Miles, of Upton, Hants; 2 s (Hon Henry Anthony Warwick b 3 June 1985, Hon Oliver Hugh Coplestone b 15 April 1987), 1 da (Hon Lara Fiona Brita b 14 May 1990); *Heir* s, Hon Henry Bampfylde; *Career* Christie's: assoc dir Picture Dept 1984, dir and head of 19th Century Picture Dept 1987–97, chm Christie's Australia plc 1997–2000, dep chm Christie's Europe 1998–2000; md e-auction room 2000–02; Sotheby's: sr dir 2002, chm 19th and 20th century pictures 2004–06, chm Sotheby's UK 2006–; former chm UK Friends of Bundanon; *Books* Popular 19th Century Painting, A Dictionary of European Genre Painters (with Philip Hook, 1986); *Clubs* White's; *Style*— The Rt Hon the Lord Poltimore; ✉ North Hidden Farm, Hungerford, Berkshire RG17 0PY

POMEROY, Brian Walter; CBE (2006); *b* 26 June 1944; *Educ* The King's Sch Canterbury, Magdalene Coll Cambridge (MA); *m* 7 Aug 1974, Hilary Susan; 2 da (Gabriela b 1975, Alisa b 1977); *Career* ptnr Touche Ross mgmnt conslts (now Deloitte Consulting): ptnr 1975, seconded as under sec in DTI 1981–83, sr ptnr Deloitte Consulting 1995–99 (md 1987–95); non-exec dir Rover Gp plc 1985–88; memb Ctee of Enquiry into Regulatory Arrangements at Lloyd's 1986, ind memb Cncl Lloyd's 1996–2004, dep chm Lloyd's Regulatory Bd 1996–2002; dep chm: Limit Underwriting Ltd 2006–, QBE Insurance Europe Ltd 2006–; chm: AIDS Awareness Tst 1993–96, Centrepoint 1993–2001, European Public Health Fndn 1997–2004, The King's Consort 2000–05, Homeless Link 2001–05, Raleigh Int 2005–07, Financial Inclusion Taskforce HM Treasy 2005–, Payments Cncl 2007–; memb: Cncl Mgmnt Conslts Assoc 1996–99, Disability Rights Task Force 1997–99, Fabian Soc Cmmn on Citizenship and Taxation 1998–2000, Nat Lottery Cmmn 1999–2008 (chm 1999–2000 and 2002–03), Bd Social Market Fndn 2000–, Pensions Protection and Investments Accreditation Bd 2000–05, Audit Cmmn 2003–, Ind Inquiry into Drug Testing at Work 2003–04, Financial Reporting Review Panel 2004–; tstee: Money Advice Tst 1999–, Space Studios 2004–05, Children's Express 2004–07, Lloyd's Charitable Tst 2004–, Photographers' Gallery 2006–; Master Co of Mgmnt Conslts 2000–01; FCA 1978, FRSA 1994; *Publications* articles on public finance, regulation and public-private partnership; *Recreations* photography, tennis, cycling; *Style*— Brian Pomeroy, CBE; ✉ 7 Ferncroft Avenue, London NW3 7PG (tel 020 7435 2584, fax 020 7794 0765, e-mail pomeroybw@aol.com)

POMFRET, Christopher Charles (Chris); s of Jack Gregson Pomfret (d 1987), and Eileen Norah Pomfret, of Canterbury, Kent; *b* 15 November 1949, Liverpool; *Educ* Simon Langton GS for Boys Canterbury, Univ of Southampton (BSc); *m* 1975, Jaqueline Ruth; 2 da (Helen Victoria b 1976, Suzanne Mary b 1979), 1 s (David Charles b 1982); *Career* Unilever: trainee Van den Berg and Jurgens Ltd 1971–73, public affrs mangr Unilever Ltd 1973–76, sales rep rising to sr brand mangr Walls Ice Cream 1976–80, mktg controller Gelato Brazil 1980–82, gen mktg mangr Birds Eye Walls 1983–90, mtkg dir Cogesal Paris 1990–92, sr mktg memb global ice cream strategy Rotterdam 1992–94, sr vice-pres European ice cream strategy Rotterdam 1994–97, business dir frozen foods Birds Eye Walls Ltd 1997–2003, mktg and sustainability co-ordinator Unilever plc 2003–04; dir Mktg and Sustainability Consultancy Ltd 2005–; memb: Cncl ISBA until 2003 (also dir), Bd Food Standards Agency 2005– (actg chm Welsh Advsy Ctee 2006), Govt Round Table on Sustainable Consumption until 2006, Customer Ctee on Life and Pensions ABI 2005–; memb Corporate Advsy Bd and sr assoc Prog for Industry Univ of Cambridge 2003–; tstee CHASE 2004–; FRSA; *Publications* Can Sustainability Sell? (2002), I Will If You Will (co-author, 2006); *Recreations* music, golf, travel, gardening; *Clubs* St Enodoc Golf, Highpost Golf; *Style*— Chris Pomfret, Esq

POMMIER, Pascal; s of Jean-Jacques Marcel Pommier, of Paray-le-Monial, France, and Yvette Renee Monique, *née* Gonnin; *b* 15 December 1964; *Educ* Ces Cours Jean Jeaures (DEFO Dip), CFA Mercurey Coll (CAP); *m* 24 Sept 1999, Joanna Moussa; 1 da (Marnia Georgia b 14 Oct 2006); *Career* chef; apprenticeship Hotel Moderne Charolles France 1980–82, Hotel Belvedere du Pelvoux Pelvoux France 1982–83, Mil Serv Macon France 1983–84, Restaurant Alain Raye Albertville France 1985–86, The Mill House Hotel Kingham Oxon 1986–88, The Normandie Hotel Bury Lancs 1988–96 (Lancashire Life Restaurant of the Year 1988, Ackerman Clover Award annually 1989–96, 3 AA Rosettes annually 1990–96, County Restaurant of the Year Good Food Guide 1993 and 1994, Egon Ronay Star annually 1990–96, Michelin Star 1995 and 1996), The Captain's Table Woodbridge Suffolk 1998– (2 AA Rosettes annually 1999–2002 and 2006– (1 AA Rosette annually 2003–05), Michelin Bib Gourmand annually 1999–, Good Food Guide annually 1999–, 1 Star Harden Guide 2007); *Recreations* rugby, football, travel; *Style*— Pascal Pommier, Esq; ✉ The Captain's Table, 3 Quay Street, Woodbridge, Suffolk IP12 1BX (tel 01394 383145, fax 01394 388508, website www.captainstable.co.uk)

POMPA, Prof Leonardo (Leon); s of Dominic Albert Pompa (d 1976), of Edinburgh, and Maria Annunziata Pompa (d 1956); *b* 22 February 1933; *Educ* Bournemouth Sch, Univ of Edinburgh (MA, PhD); *m* 9 Aug 1962, (Juliet) Caroline, da of Sir Rupert Leigh Sich, CB (d 1995); 1 s (Nicholas b 1963), 1 da (Antonia b 1965); *Career* lectr in philosophy Univ of Edinburgh 1961–77; Univ of Birmingham: prof of philosophy 1977–97, dean of arts 1984–87 and 1989–92, head Sch of Philosophy and Theol 1993–94, emeritus prof 1997–; memb Cncl Hegel Soc of GB (former pres), former memb Cncl Nat Ctee for Philosophy; chm Philosphy Panel HEFCE Research Assessment Exercise 1995–96; memb Editorial Bd: New Vico Studies 1981–, Collingwood Studies 1994–, Cuadernos sobre Vico 1996–, History of European Ideas 1996–, Storia, antrpologia e scienze del linguaggio 1996–; memb: Br Soc for History of Philosophy (former memb Mgmnt Ctee), Aristotelian Soc 1964–, Business Ctee of the General Cncl of Univ of Edinburgh 2001–03; fell Inst for Cultural Research 1980–; *Books* Vico: A Study of the New Science (1975, 2 edn 1990), Substance and Form in History (ed with W H Dray, 1982), Vico: Selected Writings (trans and ed, 1982), Human Nature and Historical Knowledge: Hume Hegel Vico (1990, paperback 2002), Vico: The First New Science (ed and trans, 2002); *Recreations* music, sport, literature, foreign travel, wine; *Clubs* Murrayfield Golf; *Style*— Prof Leon Pompa; ✉ 32 Dublin Street, Edinburgh EH3 6NN (tel 0131 556 7264, e-mail leonpompa@hotmail.com)

PONCIA, Dr John; s of Anthony Edward Poncia (d 1982), of Warks, and Mary Winifred, *née* Tams (d 1997); *b* 15 April 1935; *Educ* Ratcliffe Coll, Univ of Edinburgh Med Sch (MB ChB), DPM; *m* 1, 1959, Elizabeth Madaleine (d 1972), da of late Alexander Birrell Grosset, of Fife; 4 s (Jonathan b 1960 d 1995, Gavin b 1962, Fergus b 1964, Hugo b 1970); m 2, 1994, Rosamond, MBE, Dame SMO Malta, da of late Brig Charles Wynn-Pope, OBE; *Career* house offr Royal Infirmary Edinburgh, registrar St George's Hosp London, sr registrar Westminster Hosp, conslt psychotherapist Broadmoor Hosp 1974–95; Freeman City of London, Liveryman Worshipful Soc of Apothecaries; MRCPsych; *Recreations* yachting, shooting; *Clubs* Royal Thames Yacht, Bembridge Sailing; *Style*— Dr John Poncia; ✉ 26 Eccleston Street, London SW1W 9PY (tel 020 7730 2828)

POND, Christopher Richard (Chris); s of late Charles Richard Pond (d 1986), and late Doris Violet, *née* Cox (d 1998); *b* 25 September 1952; *Educ* Minchenden Sch Southgate, Univ of Sussex (BA); *m* 1, 28 Dec 1990 (m dis 1999), Carole Tongue, *qv*, da of Archer Tongue; 1 da; m 2, 21 March 2003, Lorraine, da of Roualeyn Melvin; 1 da; *Career* research asst Birkbeck Coll London 1974–75, research offr Low Pay Unit 1975–79, lectr in econs Civil Serv Coll 1979–80, dir Low Pay Unit 1980–97; MP (Lab) Gravesham 1997–2005, PPS to Rt Hon Dawn Primarolo, MP, *qv*, as Paymaster Gen 1999–2003, Parly under sec of State Dept of Work and Pensions 2003–05; chair Capacity Builders 2005–; visiting lectr in econs Univ of Kent 1981–82, visiting prof/research fell Univ of Surrey 1984–86, conslt Open Univ 1987–88 and 1991–92; conslt on Social Policy to Euro Cmmn 1996, memb Select Ctee on Social Security 1997–99, chair Low Pay Unit 1998–; former memb Mgmnt Cttes of Unemployment Unit and Child Poverty Action GP; memb: TGWU, Editorial Bd Charity Magazine, Royal Acad; hon visiting prof Middx Univ 1995–; *Books* Inflation and Low Incomes (1975), Trade Unions and Taxation (1976),To Him Who Hath (1977), The Povery Trap: a study in statistical sources (1978), Taxing Wealth Inequalities (1980) Taxation and Social Policy (1981), Low Pay: Labour's Response (1983), The Changing Distribution of Income, Wealth and Poverty, in Restructuring Britain (1989), A New Social Policy For The Active Society (chapter in Old and New Poverty, 1995), Beyond 2002 - Long Term Policies for Labour (jtly, 1999); *Recreations* running, reading; *Clubs* Gravesend Road Runners and Athletics (18 marathons completed); *Style*— Chris Pond, Esq

PONDER, Prof Bruce Anthony John; s of late Anthony West Ponder, and Dorothy Mary, *née* Peachey; *b* 25 April 1944; *Educ* Charterhouse, Jesus Coll Cambridge (open scholar, MA), St Thomas' Hosp Med Sch (open scholar, MB BChir), UCL (PhD); *m* 2 Aug 1969, Margaret Ann, da of John Eliot Hickinbotham; 3 da (Jane b 2 March 1971, Katherine b 20 March 1973, Rosamund b 10 Sept 1975), 1 s (William b 5 June 1976); *Career* house physician St Thomas' Hosp 1968, house surgn Kent and Canterbury Hosp 1969, house physician Brompton Hosp 1969, SHO Lambeth and St Thomas' Hosp 1969, med registrar St Thomas' and Worthing Hosps 1970–73, clinical res fell ICRF 1973–77, Hamilton Fairley fell Cancer Research Campaign (CRC) Harvard Med Sch 1977–78, clinical scientific offr ICRF Bart's 1978–80, CRC fell and sr lectr in med Inst of Cancer Research and Royal Marsden Hosp 1980–86, head of human cancer genetics Inst of Cancer Research 1987–89, reader in cancer genetics and hon conslt physician Royal Marsden, St George's and Guy's Hosps 1987–89, hon conslt physician Addenbrooke's and Royal Marsden Hosps 1989–; Univ of Cambridge: dir CRC Human Cancer Genetics Group 1989–, CRC prof of human cancer genetics 1992–96, prof of clinical oncology 1996–2006, Li Ka Shing prof of oncology 2006–; co-dir: Strangeways Research Laboratories Cambridge 1996–, Hutchison/MRC Research Centre 2000–; dir Cancer Research UK Cambridge Research Inst 2005–, chm Scientific Cncl of WHO Int Agency for Cancer Research Lyon 2006–; Gibb fell CRC 1990, fell Jesus Coll Cambridge 1992; Croonian lectr RCP 1997; treas Br Assoc for Cancer Research 1983–86; Int Public Service Award Nat Neurofibromatosis Fndn 1991, Merck Prize European Thyroid Assoc 1996, Hamilton-Fairley Award European Soc for Medical Oncology 2004, Bertner Award M D Anderson Hosp 2007; FRCP 1988 (MRCP 1970), FMedSci 1998, FRCPath 2001, FRS 2001; *Books* Cancer Biology and Medicine (series ed with M J Waring, 1989–96); *Recreations* gardening, golf, travel, wine; *Clubs* Royal West Norfolk Golf; *Style*— Prof Bruce Ponder; ✉ CR UK Research Institute, Robinson Way, Cambridge CB2 0RE (tel 01223 404124, e-mail bruce.ponder@cancer.org.uk)

PONNAPPA, Shoba; OBE (2000); da of K V Sreenivasan (d 1992), and Bharathi Sreenivasan (d 1990); *b* 19 January 1949; *Educ* Walsingham House Sch Mumbai, Kirtland HS OH, Elphinstone Coll Mumbai (Wordsworth scholar, BA), Univ of Mumbai (MA); *m* 1976, Reginald K M Ponnappa; 1 c (Kaveri-Priya b 1982); *Career* lectr Evelyn Hone Coll Lusaka 1970–71 and 1974–77, mangr Danai Bookshop 1973; served British Cncl: London 1977–89, Zimbabwe 1989–93, Zambia 1994–97, Mauritius (Madagascar and Seychelles) 1997–2001; dir British Cncl Repub of Korea 2002–05, dir British Cncl South Africa 2005–; *Recreations* theatre, reading, learning Korean; *Clubs* Mauritius Gymkhana; *Style*— Mrs Shoba Ponnappa, OBE; ✉ c/o British Council, 10 Spring Gardens, London SW1A 2BN; British Council, Ground Floor, Forum 1, Braampark, 22 Hoofd Street, Braamfontein, Johannesburg 2001, South Africa (tel 00 27 11 718 4300, fax 00 27 11 718 4400, e-mail shoba.ponnappa@britishcouncil.org.za)

PONSONBY, Sir Ashley Charles Gibbs; 2 Bt (UK 1956), of Wootton, Co Oxford; KCVO (1993), MC (1945); s of Col Sir Charles Edward Ponsonby, 1 Bt, TD, DL (d 1976), and Hon Winifred Gibbs, da of 1 Baron Hunsdon (d 1935); *b* 21 February 1921; *Educ* Eton, Balliol Coll Oxford; *m* 14 Sept 1950, Lady Martha, *née* Butler, da of 6 Marquess of Ormonde, CVO, MC (d 1971); 4 s (Charles Ashley b 1951, Rupert Spencer b 1953, Luke Arthur b 1957, John Piers b 1962); *Heir* s, Charles Ponsonby; *Career* Schroder Wagg &

Co Ltd (dir 1962–80); dir: Equitable Life Assurance Soc 1969–86, Rowntree Mackintosh Ltd 1974–86, Schroder Global Tst plc 1963–89 (chm 1964–87); church cmmr 1963–80; memb Cncl Duchy of Lancaster 1979–93; HM Lord-Lt Oxon 1980–96; Liveryman Worshipful Co of Grocers; KStJ 1989; *Clubs* Pratt's; *Style—* Sir Ashley Ponsonby, Bt, KCVO, MC; ✉ Grim's Dyke Farm, Woodstock, Oxfordshire OX20 1HJ (tel 01993 811422, fax 01993 813139)

PONSONBY, Thomas Charles George; s of George Thomas Ponsonby (d 1984), of Thurles, Co Tipperary, and Elizabeth Penelope Melville, *née* Wills; *b* 23 August 1950; *Educ* Eton, Trinity Coll of Music, Eurocentre Neuchâtel, Br Inst Florence; *m* 1980 (m dis 1985), Elisabeth Marie Philippine, da of Jean Masurel, of Paris; 1 s (Sebastian Jean b 1983); *Career* asst Foreign Tours Dept Ibbs & Tillett 1974–78, asst to Victor Hochhauser 1978–81, tour mangr Euro Community Youth Orch and Chamber Orch of Europe 1982–83, Music Dept Br Cncl 1983–89, exec dir Br Assoc of Concert Agents 1989–94, Business Relations Dept British Cncl 1995–96, project asst IMG Artists 1997, mangr public relations Van Walsum Management Ltd 1997–2000, administrative dir Jerwood Charitable Fndn 2000–; memb: King Edward VII British-German Fndn, Stefan Zweig Ctee Br Library; tstee Colin Keer Tst; *Recreations* mountains, food, architecture; *Style—* Thomas Ponsonby, Esq; ✉ 28 Brook Green, London W6 7BL; The Jerwood Charitable Foundation, 22 Fitzroy Square, London W1T 6EN (tel 020 7388 6287, e-mail thomas.ponsonby@jerwood.org)

PONSONBY OF SHULBREDE, 4 Baron (UK 1930), of Shulbrede, Sussex; Frederick Matthew Thomas Ponsonby; JP (Westminster 2006); also Baron Ponsonby of Roehampton (Life Peer UK 2000), of Shulbrede in the County of West Sussex; sits as Baron Ponsonby of Roehampton; o s of 3 Baron Ponsonby of Shulbrede (d 1990), and his 1 w, Ursula Mary, *née* Fox-Pitt; *b* 27 October 1958; *Educ* Holland Park Comprehensive Sch, UC Cardiff, Imperial Coll London; *Heir* none; *Career* cncllr London Borough of Wandsworth 1990–94; Lab Pty educn spokesman House of Lords 1992–97, memb European Sub-Ctee C 1997–98, memb Science and Technol Select Ctee 1998–99, memb Constitution Select Ctee 2000–01; delg to: Cncl of Europe 1997–2001 (chm UK 50th Anniversary Ctee), WEU 1997–2001, OSCE 2001–; FIMMM (FIMM 1996); *Style—* The Rt Hon Lord Ponsonby of Shulbrede, JP; ✉ House of Lords, London SW1A 0PW

PONTEFRACT, Bishop of 2002–; Rt Rev Anthony William (Tony) Robinson; *b* 25 April 1956; *Educ* Bedford Modern Sch, Salisbury and Wells Theol Coll; *Career* asst curate St Paul Tottenham 1982–85, team rector Resurrection Leicester 1989–97 (team vicar 1985–89), rural dean Christianity North Leicester 1992–97, hon canon Leicester Cathedral 1994–97, archdeacon of Pontefract 1997–2003, bishop of Pontefract 2002–; *Style—* The Rt Rev the Bishop of Pontefract; ✉ Pontefract House, 181a Manygates Lane, Sandal, Wakefield, WF2 7DR (tel 01924 250781, fax 01924 240490, e-mail bishop.pontefract@wakefield.anglican.org)

PONTER, Prof Alan Robert Sage; s of Arthur Tennyson Ponter (d 1964), of Bath, and Margaret Agatha Ponter (d 1974); *b* 13 February 1940; *Educ* King Henry VIII GS Abergavenny, Imperial Coll London (BSc, ARCS, PhD), Univ of Cambridge (MA); *m* 1, 12 Sept 1962, Sonia (d 1999), da of Robert Hutchinson Valentine (d 1997), of Workington, Cumbria; 1 s (David Robert Arthur b 1964 d 1986), 3 da (Ruth Virginia b 1964, Kathryn Emma b 1968, Alexandra Margaret Valentine b 1980); m 2, 15 April 2006, Rosemary Fiona, da of Rhys Albert Davies (d 1980), of Llansadwrn, Carmarthenshire; *Career* visiting lectr Iowa Univ 1964, res fell Brown Univ RI 1964–65, lectr Univ of Glasgow 1965–66, sr asst researcher Engrg Dept Univ of Cambridge 1966–69, fell Pembroke Coll Cambridge 1967–69, prof of engrg Brown Univ USA 1976–78; Univ of Leicester: lectr 1969–74, reader 1974–76, prof of engrg 1978–, pro-vice-chllr 1987–91 and 1993–96; visiting prof Univ of Calif Santa Barbara 1991–92, consIt prof Univ of Chongqinq People's Repub of China 1991–; memb several SERC and EPSRC ctees and working parties on mechanical engrg, conslt to EEC and others on structural integrity of structures particularly at high temperatures; *Publications* Creep of Structures (1982), about 150 articles in applied mathematics and engrg literature; *Recreations* reading, music and walking; *Style—* Prof Alan Ponter; ✉ Peakes Lodge, 50 Main Street, Burrough-on-the-Hill, Leicestershire LE14 2JQ; University of Leicester, University Road, Leicester LE1 7RH (tel 01664 454675, fax 0116 252 2525, e-mail asp@le.ac.uk)

PONTIUS, His Hon Judge Timothy Gordon; s of Gordon Stuart Malzard Pontius (d 1993), and Elizabeth Mary, *née* Donaldson (d 1996); *b* 5 September 1948; *Educ* Boroughmuir Sr Secdy Sch Edinburgh, Univ of London (LLB, external); *Career* called to the Bar Middle Temple 1972, in practice at Criminal Bar 1972–88, judge advocate 1988, asst judge-advocate gen HM Forces 1991, recorder 1993–95, circuit judge (SE Circuit) 1995–; *Recreations* music, swimming, travel; *Style—* His Hon Judge Pontius; ✉ The Crown Court, 1 Pocock Street, London SE1 0BT (tel 020 7922 5800)

PONTON, Prof John Wylie (Jack); s of late John Ronald Ponton, of Berwickshire, and late Nancy, *née* Wylie; *b* 2 May 1943; *Educ* Melville Coll Edinburgh, Univ of Edinburgh (BSc, PhD); *m* 1973, Katherine Jane Victoria, da of Jack Eachus; *Career* Univ of Edinburgh 1967– (successively lectr, sr lectr, ICI prof of chemical engrg), res fell McMaster Univ Canada 1969–70, NATO fell and assoc prof Case Western Reserve Univ 1975, process engr ICI Mond Div 1979; contribs to jls of chemical, mech, electrical and info engrg; foreign fell Russian Acad of Technological Scis 1992; FIChemE, FREng 1991, FRSA 1993; *Recreations* music, gardening, cycling, amateur radio (GM0RWU); *Style—* Prof Jack Ponton, FREng; ✉ Legerwood, Earlston, Berwickshire TD4 6AS; Department of Chemical Engineering, University of Edinburgh, King's Buildings, Edinburgh EH9 3JL (tel 0131 650 4858, fax 0131 650 6551, e-mail jack@ecosse.org)

PONTON, Michael Thomas John; s of Thomas Bevan Ponton (d 1991), and Zena May, *née* Bennett; *b* 11 July 1946; *Educ* Canton HS for Boys Cardiff, Inst of Health Servs Mgmnt (Dip), Inst of Health Record Info and Mgmnt (Dip), Harvard Grad Business Sch (Alumna); *m* 1; 2 da (Lisa Meirwen b 13 April 1972, Karen Jane b 16 Oct 1975); m 2, 26 Feb 1983, Patricia Ann, da of Richard James Taylor; 2 s (Richard Michael Thomas b 25 Jan 1984, David Michael James b 17 Feb 1987); *Career* clerk: Ely Hosp Cardiff 1962–63, United Cardiff Hosps 1963–65, Cardiff Royal Infirmary 1965–68; admin asst St Mary's Hosp London 1968–72, dep hosp sec Leicester Gen Hosp 1972–74, sector admin Swansea N Hosps 1974–77; asst gen mangr W Glamorgan HA 1982–85 (area planning offr 1977–82), unit gen mangr Swansea N Unit 1988–90, asst dist gen mangr E Dyfed HA 1990–92, jt md E Dyfed and Pembrokeshire HAs 1992–95, md Dyfed HA 1995–96, chief exec Health Promotion Wales 1996–99 head Health Promotion Div Welsh Office 1999–; FHSM; *Recreations* reading, walking, music, gardening, rugby football; *Style—* Michael Ponton, Esq; ✉ Health and Well-Being Strategy and Planning Team, National Assembly for Wales, Cathays Park, Cardiff CF10 3NQ (tel 029 2082 6533)

POOLE, Anthony; s of Gregory Bordinal Poole, of Stamford, and Anne, *née* Beveridge (d 1974); *b* 14 February 1960; *Educ* Ermysted's GS Skipton, Univ of Leeds (BSc), Leeds Sch of Architecture (BA Arch, DipArch); *m* Margaret, *née* McManus; 1 da (Hannah Isabel 12 June 1996), 1 s (Matthew Alexander 3 Jan 2000); *Career* architect; Jack Whittle & Partners Chester 1984–85, McCormick Associates Chester 1985, Martin Joyce & Associates Leeds 1987–88; Sheppard Robson (architects, planners and interior designers) London: joined 1988, assoc 1996–98, ptnr 1998–; Wellcome Tst Genome Campus Cambridge 1993–96, Edward Jenner Inst for Vaccine Research Compton 1996–98, Dept of Epidemiology Univ of Oxford 1996–98, Imperial Coll-Royal Sch of Mines 1999, Dept of Biomedical Sci Univ of Manchester 1999, Chemistry Dept Queen Mary & Westfield Coll London 2000, Napp Pharmaceuticals 2001, Dept of Biological Anthropology Univ of Cambridge 2001, Dept of Experimental Physics Queen's Univ Belfast 2001; RIBA; *Recreations* cricket, sailing, ski-ing; *Style—* Anthony Poole, Esq; ✉ Sheppard Robson, 77 Parkway, London NW1 7PU (tel 020 7504 1700, fax 020 7504 1701, e-mail tony.poole@sheppardrobson.com)

POOLE, (Richard) Bruce; s of David Poole, and Iris Poole; *Educ* Charterhouse, Univ of Exeter, Westminster Coll; *Career* chef; trainee mangr Stakis Hotel plc, commis chef Bibendum 1990–92, chef de partie The Square 1992–93, head chef Chez Max 1993–94, head chef/dir Chez Bruce 1994– (One Michelin Star 1999, Carlton London Best Br Restaurant 1999, 3 AA Rosettes, 6/10 Good Food Guide); active participant Leuka 2000 (charity dinners, guest appearances and cookery demonstrations); *Recreations* cycling, football, wine; *Style—* Bruce Poole, Esq; ✉ Chez Bruce, 2 Bellevue Road, Wandsworth Common, London SW17 7EG (tel 020 8672 0114, fax 020 8767 6648)

POOLE, 2 Baron (UK 1958); David Charles Poole; s of 1 Baron Poole, PC, CBE, TD (d 1993), and his 1 w, Betty Margaret, *née* Gilkison (d 1988); *b* 6 January 1945; *Educ* Gordonstoun, ChCh Oxford, INSEAD Fontainebleau; *m* 1, 21 Sept 1967 (m dis), Fiona, da of John Donald; 1 s (Hon Oliver John b 30 May 1972); m 2, 1975, Philippa, da of late Mark Reeve, of Lower Brook House, King's Somborne, Hants; m 3, 6 Jan 1995, Mrs Lucinda Edsell; *Heir* s, Hon Oliver Poole; *Career* Samuel Montagu & Co 1967–74, Bland Payne & Co 1974–78, Capel-Cure Myers 1978–87, Bonomi Gp 1987–90, James Capel 1990–94 (chm James Capel Corporate Finance Ltd, exec dir James Capel & Co Ltd), seconded as memb Policy Unit Prime Minister's Office 1992–94, ceo Ockham Holdings plc 1994–2002; non-exec dir Financial News 1999–; *Clubs* Brooks's, Royal Yacht Squadron, City; *Style—* The Rt Hon the Lord Poole

POOLE, David James; s of Thomas Herbert Poole (d 1978), and Catherine, *née* Lord (d 1980); *b* 5 June 1931; *Educ* RCA; *m* 5 April 1958, Iris Mary, da of Francis Thomas Toomer (d 1968); 3 s (Edward b 1959, Vincent b 1960, Bruce b 1964); *Career* served RE 1949–51; sr lectr in painting and drawing Wimbledon Sch of Art 1961–77; featured in series Portrait (BBC TV) 1976, featured in magazine Frankfurter Allgemeine 1986; pres Royal Soc of Portrait Painters 1983–91; ARCA 1954, RP 1968; cmmnd by the City of London Corp to paint the official portrait group of the Royal Family to commemorate HM Queen Elizabeth II Silver Jubilee Luncheon; *Portraits* incl: HM The Queen, HRH Prince Philip, HM Queen Elizabeth the Queen Mother, HRH The Princess Royal, HRH The Prince of Wales, HRH The Duke of York, HRH Prince Edward, Earl Mountbatten, Sir Alan Lascelles, Lord Charteris, Sir Michael Adeane, Sir Philip Moore, Sir William Heseltine, Sir Robert Fellowes, distinguished membs of govt, HM Forces, industry, commerce, medical, the academic and legal professions; *Solo Exhibitions* London 1978, Zürich 1980; *Work in Private Collections* HM The Queen, Australia, Bermuda, Canada, France, Germany, Italy, South Africa, Saudia Arabia, Switzerland, USA; *Recreations* travel, being in the country; *Style—* David J Poole, Esq, PPRP, ARCA; ✉ Trinity Flint Barn, Weston Lane, Weston, Petersfield, Hampshire GU32 3NN (01730 265075)

POOLE, (Francis) Henry Michael; s of Charles Frederick John Kaitting Poole (d 1976), of Lanteglos-by-Fowey, Cornwall, and Stella Mary Grant, *née* Morris; *b* 23 September 1949; *Educ* Eton, Trinity Hall Cambridge; *m* 20 Sept 1975, Diana Mary Olga, da of Eric Arthur Parker (d 1983), of Headcorn, Kent; 2 da (Angelica Lucy Daphne b 1978, Stella Antonia Felicity b 1980), 1 s (Frederick Henry Eric b 1983); *Career* Credit Lyonnais Securities (formerly Laing and Cruickshank Institutional Equities): joined 1971, ptnr 1979, dir 1985–, consIt 2003–04; estab Henry Poole Consulting 2004–; non-exec dir Rockware Gp 1986–87; FSI (memb London Stock Exchange 1979); *Books* European Paper Directory (1988), Knowing When to Stop (2001); *Recreations* bridge, history, riding, mountain walking; *Style—* Henry Poole, Esq; ✉ 74 Hornton Street, London W8 4NU; Gibbet Oast, Leigh Green, Tenterden, Kent TN30 7DH

POOLE, Sheriff Isobel Anne; da of John Cecil Findlay Poole (d 1985), and Constance Mary, *née* Gilkes (d 1992); *b* 9 December 1941; *Educ* Oxford HS for Girls, Univ of Edinburgh (LLB); *Career* advocate 1964, former standing jr counsel to the Registrar Gen for Scot; Sheriff of: Lothian and Borders 1979–, Edinburgh 1986–2007 (pt/t sheriff 2007–); external examiner Comparative Criminal Procedure Univ of Edinburgh 2001–02; chair Sir Walter Scott Club Edinburgh 2004–; memb: Sheriffs' Cncl 1980–85, Scot Lawyers' Euro Gp; *Publications* contrib Dictionary of National Biography; *Recreations* country, the arts, houses, gardens, friends; *Clubs* Scottish Arts, New (Edinburgh); *Style—* Sheriff Isobel Anne Poole; ✉ Sheriffs' Chambers, Sheriff Court House, 27 Chambers Street, Edinburgh EH1 1LB

POOLE, James; *Educ* Univ of Cambridge (BA); *m* Jenny, *née* White; 2 c; *Career* journalist and ed (10 yrs at Sunday Times and dep city ed and foreign ed Business News and ed Multinational Business), subsequently head of corp affrs Barclays, vice-chm Shandwick Consultants Ltd until 1999, investor rels and corp communications dir Old Mutual plc 1999–; advsr to: Dept of Tport (on privatisation of BR), British Gas (on demerger plans), Marks & Spencer and Shell (on critical issues); judge Financial Journal's Fin Journalist and Young Fin Journalist of the Year 1993, 1994 and 1995; memb: Euro Public Affrs Forum, Spokesman Gp IIMR; MIPR; *Style—* James Poole, Esq

POOLE, (Jeremy) Quentin Simon; s of Graham Poole, of Kingswear, S Devon, and Dr Jill Poole, *née* Prichards; *b* 7 January 1955; *Educ* Epsom Coll, Univ of Warwick (LLB); *Career* admitted slr 1981; sr ptnr Wragge & Co 2003– (ptnr 1985–, managing ptnr 1995–2003); memb: Birmingham Law Soc 1981, Law Soc 1981; *Recreations* cricket; *Style—* Quentin Poole, Esq; ✉ Wragge & Co, 55 Colmore Row, Birmingham B3 2AS (tel 0121 233 1000, fax 0121 214 1099, telex 338728 WRAGGE G)

POOLE-WILSON, Prof Philip Alexander; s of Denis Smith Poole-Wilson, CBE (d 1998), and Monique Michelle, *née* Goss (d 1985); *b* 26 April 1943; *Educ* Marlborough, Trinity Coll Cambridge (MA, MB BChir, MD), St Thomas' Hosp Med Sch; *m* 25 Oct 1969, Mary Elizabeth, da of Dr William Horrocks Tattersall (d 1999); 2 s (William, Michael), 1 da (Oenone); *Career* hon conslt physician Royal Brompton Nat Heart & Lung Hosp 1976–; Nat Heart and Lung Inst Faculty of Med Imperial Coll London: sr lectr and reader 1976–84, vice-dean 1981–84, prof of cardiology 1984–88, Simon Marks Br Heart Fndn prof of cardiology 1988–, head of div Nat Heart and Lung Inst Imperial Coll Sch of Med 1997–2000; visiting prof Charing Cross and Westminster Med Sch 1988–97; memb Cncl Br Heart Fndn 1985–98, pres Euro Soc of Cardiology 1994–96 (sec 1990–92), pres World Heart Fndn 2003–04; FESC, FACC, FRCP 1978, FMedSci 1998; *Recreations* opera, gardening, countryside; *Style—* Prof Philip Poole-Wilson; ✉ 174 Burbage Road, London SE21 7AG (tel 020 7274 6742); National Heart and Lung Institute, Imperial College London, Dovehouse Street, London SW3 6LY (tel 020 7351 8179, fax 020 7351 8113, e-mail p.poole-wilson@imperial.ac.uk)

POOLER, Amanda Elizabeth (Mandy); da of Kenneth Hindley Pooler, of Bolton, Lancs, and Adrianne, *née* Sherlock; *b* 23 May 1959; *Educ* Bolton Sch, Jesus Coll Oxford (MA); *m* Paul Andrew Eden; 2 c (Max, Eleanor (twins) b 18 June 1990); *Career* grad recruit (mktg) Thomson Organisation 1980–82; Ogilvy & Mather advtg agency: joined 1982, bd dir 1989, media dir 1990–98; UK md then chief exec MindShare 1998–2001; WPP: ceo The Channel 2002–06, dir Kantar UK 2006–; chair AGB Nielsen Media Research UK; Advertising Woman of the Year (Adwomen) 1994; memb Mktg Soc; FIPA; *Style—* Ms Mandy Pooler; ✉ Kantar Group, 6 More London Place, Tooley Street, London SE1 2QY

POOLES, Michael Philip Holmes; QC (1998); s of Dennis John Pooles (d 1999), and Joan Ellen, *née* Holmes; *b* 14 December 1955, Burgh Apton, Norfolk; *Educ* Perse Sch Cambridge, QMC London (LLB); *m* 17 April 1984, Fiona, *née* Chalmers; 2 s (Alexander David Grant b 21 Oct 1985, Guy Philip Grant b 16 June 1988); *Career* called to the Bar Inner Temple 1978 (Scarman scholar, Treas's prize); practising barr Hailsham Chambers

P

1980– (head of chambers 2004–), recorder Crown Ct 2000–; memb: Professional Conduct and Complaints Ctee Bar Cncl 1997–2000, Legal Servs Ctee Bar Cncl 2000–05, Bar Standards Bd 2006–; govr Perse Sch Cambridge; *Recreations* reading, gardening; *Clubs* RAC; *Style*— Michael Pooles, Esq, QC; ✉ Hailsham Chambers, 4 Paper Buildings, Temple, London EC4Y 7EX (tel 020 7643 5000, e-mail michael.pooles@hailshamchambers.com)

POOLEY, Dr Derek; CBE (1995); s of Richard Pike Pooley (d 1988), of Port Isaac, Cornwall, and Evelyn, *née* Lee (d 1985); *b* 28 October 1937; *Educ* Sir James Smith's Sch Camelford, Univ of Birmingham (BSc, PhD); *m* 1961, Jennifer Mary, da of William Arthur Charles Davey (d 1980), of Birmingham; 2 s (Michael Bruce b 1967, Benjamin John b 1969), 1 da (Miriam Jane b 1973); *Career* head Materials Devpt Div Harwell 1976–81, dir energy research Harwell 1981–83, chief scientist Dept of Energy 1983–86, dir Winfrith Technology Centre 1989–90, md AEA Nuclear Business Group 1991–94, chief exec UKAEA 1996–98, ind conslt 1998–, chm Waste Mgmnt Technology Ltd 2006–; *Recreations* travel, walking, history, gardening; *Style*— Dr Derek Pooley, CBE; ✉ 11 Halls Close, Drayton, Abingdon, Oxfordshire OX14 4LU (tel and fax 01235 537507)

POOLEY, Prof Frederick David; s of Frederick Pooley (d 1964), and Ellen, *née* Dix (d 1996); *b* 3 February 1939; *Educ* Univ of Wales Coll of Cardiff (BSc, MSc, PhD); *m* 18 Aug 1962, Patricia Mary, da of John Boyt Williams (d 1992), of Abergavenny, Gwent; 2 s (Anthony John b 1964, Andrew David b 1966), 1 da (Susan Elizabeth b 1968); *Career* res fell MRC 1966–69; Univ of Wales Coll of Cardiff: lectr in minerals engrg Dept of Mineral Exploitation 1969–76, sr lectr 1976–77, reader 1977–87, prof Sch of Engrg 1987–2006; research prof Cardiff Medical Sch 2006–; author of numerous papers and articles on dust disease, res and biological treatment of minerals; fell Minerals Engrg Soc 1986; CEng 1977, MAIME 1979, FIMM 1994, MCIWEM 1995; *Recreations* sailing; *Clubs* PH Yacht; *Style*— Prof Frederick Pooley; ✉ Medical Microscopy Sciences Medical School, Cardiff University, Heath Park, Cardiff CF14 4XN (tel 029 2077 7963, fax 029 2079 8216)

POOLEY, Graham Howard John; s of John Henry William Pooley (d 2004), and Joan Margaret, *née* Price (d 1983); *b* 11 March 1949; *Educ* Brentwood Sch, Oriel Coll Oxford (MA); *m* 8 May 1971 (m dis 1993); 1 s (Oliver Edward b 1973), 1 da (Laura Kathleen May b 1976); *Career* dir Barclays de Zoete Wedd Ltd 1986–89, md Chase Investment Bank 1989–92, in own consultancy co 1993–; Chelmsford borough cncllr 1995–2003; memb Lib Dem Pty; *Recreations* music, bridge, Essex past and present, family friends and good conversation; *Style*— Graham Pooley; ✉ 49 Lockside Marina, Hill Road South, Chelmsford, Essex CM2 6HF (tel 01245 351633)

POOLEY, Joseph; s of Arthur Edward Pooley, of Richmond, N Yorks, and Marjorie, *née* Lister; *b* 8 December 1946; *Educ* Barnard Castle Sch, Univ of Newcastle upon Tyne (MB BS, MD); *m* 2 July 1977, Jane Elizabeth, da of Ronald George Mills; 1 s (Nicholas James b 21 Sept 1985), 1 da (Victoria Jane b 15 Aug 1988); *Career* house surgn and house physician Royal Victoria Infirmary Newcastle upon Tyne 1971–72, demonstrator in anatomy Med Sch Univ of Newcastle 1972–73, sr surgical house offr Royal Victoria Infirmary 1973–74, registrar in surgery Newcastle Surgical Rotation 1974–77, orthopaedic surgical registrar Royal Victoria Infirmary 1978, res assoc Dept of Surgical Science Univ of Newcastle 1978–80, sr registrar in orthopaedic surgery Northern Region 1980–83, sr lectr in orthopaedics Univ of Newcastle 1985–97 (lectr 1983–85); conslt orthopaedic surgn: Royal Victoria Infirmary and Freeman Hosp 1985–97, Queen Elizabeth Hosp Gateshead 1997–; British Orthopaedic Research Soc: President's medal 1978–80, travelling fell 1983; British Orthopaedic Assoc: Robert Jones Gold medal and prize 1983, Euro travelling scholar 1984; memb: BMA 1972, British Orthopaedic Research Soc 1980, British Orthopaedic Oncology Soc 1988; FRCS (MRCS 1977); *Recreations* tennis, walking, music; *Style*— Joseph Pooley, Esq; ✉ Department of Orthopaedic Surgery, Queen Elizabeth Hospital, Gateshead, Tyne & Wear NE9 6SX (tel 0191 487 8989)

POOLEY, Moira Helen; da of Roger Francis Lewis (d 1978), of Chadwell Heath, Essex, and Kathleen, *née* Kingseller; *b* 17 June 1950; *Educ* Ursuline Convent Brentwood, QMC London (LLB); *m* 1, May 1971 (m dis); 1 s (Oliver Edward b 24 March 1973), 1 da (Laura Kathleen May b 10 Nov 1976); m 2, 16 April 1993, Anthony Goldstaub, QC; 1 da (Harriet Helena b 8 May 1996); *Career* called to the Bar Middle Temple 1974; memb local govt and planning bar assocs; vice-chm: Little Baddow Parish Cncl 1981–84, Barnston Parish Cncl 1988–92; chm: Social Security Appeal Tbnl 1986–, Nat Insurance Tbnl 1986–; *Recreations* poultry keeping, archaeology, cookery; *Style*— Mrs Moira Pooley; ✉ 4 King's Bench Walk, Temple, London EC4Y 9DL (tel 020 7353 3581)

POOLEY, Robert John; s of Sydney John Pooley (d 1972), and Hilda Vera, *née* Salmon (d 1990); *b* 9 February 1935; *Educ* Medburn Sch; *m* 1, 24 Feb 1962 (m dis 1973), Yvonne Margaret, da of William Pereira (d 1976), of Hatfield, Herts; 1 s (Julian David John b 26 Feb 1964 d 1994), 1 da (Katharine Yvonne 12 March 1966); m 2, 5 July 1974 (m dis 2001), Carolyn, da of Dr J Alfred Lee (d 1998); 1 da (Samantha Carolyn Merlyn b 30 July 1974), 1 s (Sebastian Robert John b 3 May 1979); m 3, 21 May 2003, Dorothy Jane, da of Philip Saul; *Career* RAF SAC 4 Sqdn 1953–57; De Havilland Aircraft Co 1957–61; chm: Pooley Flight Equipment Ltd (dir devpt), Robert Pooley Ltd, Pooley Aviation Ltd, Air Pilot Publishing Ltd, Technical Aviation Publications Ltd, Pooley Sword Ltd; ed and publisher Pooley Flight Guides 1961; tstee Museum of Army Flying Devpt Tst; dir Middle Wallop Int Air Show (AAC); pres: 1187 Sqdn ATC, 1372 Sqdn ATC; vice-pres: Helicopter Club of GB, Guild of Aviation Artists, Br Precision Pilots' Assoc; chm: Professional Flying Instrs Assoc, The Balloon Club, Central Flying Intrs Sch Ltd; chm Soc of the St John Ophthalmic Hosp Jerusalem 1987–91, memb Cncl Herts Order of St John 1986; pres St John Ambulance Bde Hemel Hempstead; Freeman City of London 1971, Liveryman Guild of Air Pilots and Air Navigators 1971 (Master 1987–88), Liveryman Worshipful Co of Stationers and Newspaper Makers; FRIN 1979, FRAeS 1981; CStJ 1992 (OStJ 1987); *Books* Pooley's Flight Guides (1962–2008), Pilots Information Guide (1982 and 1986); *Recreations* flying, ballooning, riding, sub-aqua, Cresta; *Clubs* Royal Aero, Tiger; *Style*— Robert Pooley, Esq; ✉ Forter Castle, Glenisla, Angus PH11 8QW; Collingwood Court, Shoreham-by-Sea, West Sussex BN43 5SB (tel 01234 750677)

POON, Prof Wilson Che Kei; s of C P Poon, and K Y Poon; *b* 26 September 1962; *Educ* St Paul's Co-Educnl Sch Hong Kong, Rugby, Peterhouse Cambridge, St John's Coll Cambridge (PhD); *m* 13 Aug 1988, Heidi; 1 da (Rebecca b 16 Aug 1998), 1 s (Aidan b 2 Sept 2000); *Career* research fell St Edmund's Coll Cambridge 1987–88, lectr Portsmouth Poly 1989; Sch of Physics Univ of Edinburgh: lectr 1990–97, sr lectr 1997–99, prof 1999–; author of more than 100 papers in learned jls; memb Doctrine Ctee Scottish Episcopal Church; FInstP, FRSE 2004; *Recreations* piano, violin, painting; *Style*— Prof Wilson Poon; ✉ School of Physics, The University of Edinburgh, The Kings Buildings, Mayfield Road, Edinburgh EH9 3JZ (tel 0131 650 5297, e-mail w.poon@ed.ac.uk)

POPAT, Surendra (Andrew); CBE (1997); s of Dhirajlal Kurji Popat (d 1989), of Putney, London, and Kashiben, *née* Chitalia (d 1963); *b* 31 December 1943; *Educ* Govt Secdy Sch Dar Es Salaam Tanzania, Univ of London (LLB), Univ of Calif (LLM); *m* 4 Feb 1995, Suzanne Joy, da of Edward James Wayman (d 1976); 1 s (Chetan Andrew b 10 May 1999); *Career* called to the Bar Lincoln's Inn 1969, apptd list of the dir of public prosecutions by the then attorney gen Sir Michael Havers 1984, admitted memb Inner Temple 1985, recorder of the Crown Ct 1998– (asst recorder 1992–98); legal memb Criminal Injuries Compensation Appeals Panel 2000–; contested (Cons) Palewell Ward E Sheen 1978, Parly candidate (Cons) Durham NE gen election 1983, Parly candidate (Cons) Bradford S 1992 gen election, treas Surbition Cons Assoc 1985, dir John Patten's election campaign 1987, contested (Cons) European Parliament Election London Regn 1999; chm Disraeli Club (Cons Pty orgn to promote intellectual dialogue) 1993–; memb Professional Conduct Ctee GMC 2000–; memb Professional Performance Ctee GMC 2002–; tstee Brooke Hosp for Animals 1998–2000; Freeman City of London 1987, Liveryman Worshipful Co of Plaisterers 1987 (memb Ct of Assts 2001–); *Recreations* travel, theatre, cricket, tennis, reading historical biographies; *Clubs* Carlton, MCC; *Style*— Andrew Popat, Esq, CBE; ✉ 9 King's Bench Walk, Temple, London EC4Y 7DX (tel 020 7353 7202, fax 020 7583 2030)

POPE, Cathryn Mary; *b* 6 July 1957; *Educ* RCM, Nat Opera Studio; *Career* soprano; debut Sophie in Werther (ENO) 1982, int debut Gretel in Hänsel and Gretel (Netherlands Opera Amsterdam); *Roles* with ENO incl: Gretel in Hänsel and Gretel 1987 and 1990, Despina in Cosi fan Tutte 1988, Oksana in Christmas Eve 1988, Leila in The Pearl Fishers 1988, Mélisande in Pelléas and Mélisande 1990, Pamina in The Magic Flute 1990, Donna Elvira in Don Giovanni 1991, Susanna in The Marriage of Figaro 1991 and 1993, Goosegirl in Königskinder 1992, Tatyana in Eugene Onegin 1994; other performances incl: Marguerite in Faust (New Sussex Opera) 1989, Nedda in Pagliacci, Emma in Khovanshchina, Micaela in Carmen, Giorgetta in Il Tabarro; *Recordings* incl Anne Truelove in The Rake's Progress (Decca); *Style*— Miss Cathryn Pope; ✉ tel and fax 01932 248518

POPE, Gregory (Greg); MP; s of late Samuel Pope, and Sheila Pope; *b* 29 August 1960; *Educ* St Mary's Coll RC GS Blackburn, Univ of Hull (BA); *m* 2 Aug 1985, Catherine, *née* Fallon; 2 s, 1 da; *Career* cncllr: Hyndburn BC 1984–88, Blackburn BC 1989–91; MP (Lab) Hyndburn 1992– (Parly candidate (Lab) Ribble Valley 1987), oppn whip 1995–97, asst Govt whip 1997–2001; *Recreations* walking, chess, music; *Style*— Greg Pope, Esq, MP; ✉ House of Commons, London SW1A 0AA

POPE, Jeremy James Richard; OBE (1985); s of Philip William Rolph Pope (d 1996), of Dorchester, Dorset, and Joyce Winifred Harcourt, *née* Slade; *b* 15 July 1943; *Educ* Charterhouse, Trinity Coll Cambridge (MA); *m* 1969, Hon Jacqueline Dorothy Mametz Best, da of Lt-Col 8 Baron Wynford, MBE, DL, of Dorchester, Dorset (d 2002); 3 s (Rory b 1970, Rupert b 1973, Toby b 1977); *Career* admitted slr 1969; dir: Eldridge Pope & Co plc 1969–99 (md 1988, dep chm 1987–99), Winterbourne Hosp plc 1981–89 (fndr chm), JB Reynier Ltd 1984–99; chm: Realstream Ltd 1987–92, Highcliff Hotel (Bournemouth) Ltd 1988–99, EP Fine Wines Ltd 1999–2001, Chilworth Science Park Ltd 2001–04, Milk Link Ltd 2001–05, Exeter Investment Gp plc 2002 (dir 1999–2004), Chilworth Manor Ltd; fndr chm English Farming & Food Partnerships 2003–; chm Smaller Firms' Cncl CBI 1981–84; memb: Dept of Trade Advsy Panel on Co Law 1980–81, NEDC 1981–85, Royal Cmmn on Environmental Pollution 1984–92, Exec Ctee Food and Drinks Fedn (dep pres 1987–90), Top Salary Review Body 1986–93, Bd SW England RDA 1998–2004 (dep chm 1999–2004); chm: Wessex Medical Tst 1992–98 (tstee 1991–97), Mgmnt Ctee Devonshire and Dorset Regimental Museum 1995–2000, Dorset Area Economic Partnership, Bournemouth, Dorset and Poole Economic Partnership 1998–2000, SW Chamber of Rural Enterprise (CORE) 2001–03; dir Dorset TEC 1998–2000, memb Bd Bournemouth, Dorset and Poole LSC 2000–03, memb Wessex Regnl Ctee Nat Tst 2007–; tstee: Devonshire and Dorset Regiment's Regimental Charities 1995–2000, Tank Museum 2000–, Jurassic Coast Tst (formerly World Heritage Coast Tst) 2004–; dir Weymouth and Portland Nat Sailing Acad 2004–; memb Exec Ctee Brewers' Soc 1977–88; govr Forres Sch Swanage 1983–92; memb Law Soc; Liveryman: Worshipful Co of Innholders (Renter Warden 2005, Upper Warden 2007), Worshipful Co of Gunmakers; Hon DLitt Bournemouth Univ; FRSA 1989, ARAgS 2003; *Recreations* gardening, field sports, cooking, beekeeping; *Style*— Jeremy Pope, Esq, OBE; ✉ Field Cottage, West Compton, Dorchester, Dorset DT2 0EY (tel and fax 01300 321104, e-mail jeremy.pope@wdi.co.uk)

POPE, Martin John; s of Anthony Peter Pope, and Patricia, *née* Servant; *b* 8 August 1963; *Educ* Dame Alice Owen Sch Potters Bar, Barnet Art Coll, Stradbroke Coll Sheffield (NCTJ); *Family* 1 da (Isabella b 25 Aug 2003); *Career* chief photographer: The Hendon Times 1987–90, Katz Pictures 1990–2006, K2 @ Katz Pictures 2002–06, syndication @ Camera Press 2005–; features photographer Daily Telegraph 1995–; assignments incl: Romania 1990 and 1991, Albanian elections 1992, Somalia famine 1992, Iraqi Kurdistan 1993, gold panning/AIDS Zimbabwe 1993, South Africa in transition 1993–94, life after the Zapatista rebellion Chiapas Mexico 1995, rural Uganda 1999, rebuilding communities Rwanda 1999, living with Islam Beirut, Damascus and Cairo 2002, America's War on Terrorism Djibouti 2004; work included in World Press Exhbn 1994; Fuji Feature Award 1992, Canon Press Photo of the Year 1992, Kodak Portfolio Award 1993; *Style*— Martin Pope, Esq; ✉ tel and fax 01945 860244, mobile 07850 656962, e-mail martin.pope@telegraph.co.uk

POPE, Timothy Patrick; s of Bryan George Patrick Pope, of Walton-on-Thames, Surrey, and Mary Margaret Pope; *b* 23 March 1948; *Educ* Glynn GS; *m* Dec 1980, Gerda Hendrika Maria, da of L T M Rokebrand; 3 s (Alexander b Sept 1983, Michael b Aug 1985, William b Feb 1988); *Career* ptnr Deloitte Haskins & Sells 1979 (articled clerk 1966–70), currently risk mgmnt ptnr for PricewaterhouseCoopers in the UK (formerly Coopers & Lybrand before merger); FCA (ACA 1970); *Recreations* golf, photography, shooting; *Clubs* Brooks's, RAC, St George's Hill Lawn Tennis, The Wisley Golf; *Style*— Timothy Pope, Esq; ✉ PricewaterhouseCoopers, 1 Embankment Place, London WC2N 6RH (tel 020 7583 5000)

POPESCU, Mark Cannan; s of Julian John Hunter Popescu, of Mellis, Suffolk, and Christine Pullein-Thompson (d 2005); *b* 9 September 1960; *Educ* King James Coll Henley, Univ of Exeter (BA); *Partner*, Lesley Pauline Tring; 2 s (Oliver Jack b 2 April 1989, Daniel Edward b 3 Jan 1991), 1 da (Anna Helen b 9 July 1997); *Career* reporter Devonair Radio Exeter 1983–84, news ed GWR Radio Swindon 1984–86, prodr BBC Radio News London 1986–87; ITN: prodr News at One 1987–88, home news ed 1988–89, ed Forward Planning 1989–91, political news ed Westminster 1991–94, ed The Lunchtime News 1994–96, ed News at Ten and head of Special Progs ITN for ITV 1996–98; ed BBC Six O'Clock News 1999–2001, ed BBC Ten O'Clock News 2001–03, editorial dir BBC News 24 2004– (sr ed 1998); maj assignments incl: Romanian Revolution 1990 (sr prodr), Kuwait City 1991 (sr prodr), General Election 1992 (campaign news ed), Party Confs 1991, 1992 and 1993 (ed); *Recreations* kite flying, cooking and oneirology; *Style*— Mark Popescu, Esq; ✉ BBC News, Room 4600, TV Centre, Wood Lane, London W12 7RJ (tel 020 8624 9999)

POPHAM, Stuart Godfrey; s of George Popham (d 1986), and Ena, *née* Davison (d 1999); *b* 20 July 1954; *Educ* Reed's Sch Cobham, Univ of Southampton (LLB); *m* 1978, Carolyn, da of John Dawe; 2 da (Laura b 1983, Emma b 1990), 1 s (Ben b 1984); *Career* admitted slr 1978; sr ptnr Clifford Chance 2003– (joined 1976, ptnr 1984); memb Cncl RIIA 2005; memb Law Soc 1978; *Recreations* sailing, water sports, theatre, ballet; *Clubs* Hayling Island Sailing, Royal Thames Yacht; *Style*— Stuart Popham, Esq; ✉ Clifford Chance, 10 Upper Bank Street, London E14 5JJ (tel 020 7006 1000, fax 020 7006 5555, e-mail stuart.popham@cliffordchance.com)

POPLE, Andrew Howard; *Educ* BA, MPhil, MBA; *Career* with Bank of England 1983–88; Abbey National plc: regnl dir 1992–94, dir Life Assurance Div and chief exec subsid Scottish Mutual 1994–96, md Retail Banking 1996–2002; ceo and vice-chm Kessler Financial Services International 2003–; *Style*— Andrew Pople, Esq; ✉ Kessler Financial Services International, 102 Jermyn Street, London SW1Y 6EE (tel 020 7451 7080)

POPPLEWELL, Andrew John; QC (1997); s of Sir Oliver Popplewell, and Catherine Margaret, *née* Storey; *b* 14 January 1959; *Educ* Radley, Downing Coll Cambridge (MA); *Career* called to the Bar Inner Temple 1981; *Recreations* opera, wine, golf; *Clubs* Hawks' (Cambridge); *Style*— Andrew Popplewell, Esq, QC; ✉ Brick Court Chambers, 7–8 Essex Street, London WC2R 3LD (tel 020 7379 3550, fax 020 7379 3558)

POPPLEWELL, Richard John; LVO (2000, MVO 1990); s of Norman Stanley Popplewell (d 1941), and Eileen Mary Louise, *née* Jagger (d 1975); *b* 18 October 1935; *Educ* King's Coll Cambridge (chorister, organ scholar), Clifton (organ scholar, Sawyer prize, ARCO), RCM (organ scholar, ARCM); *m* 1963, Margaret, da of Frank Lawrence Conway; 1 s (James David b 1970); *Career* asst organist St Paul's Cathedral 1958–66, dir of music St Michael's Cornhill 1966–79, organist, choirmaster and composer HM Chapels Royal St James's Palace 1979–2000, prof of organ RCM 1962–2000; accompanist and asst conductor The Bach Choir 1966–79; soloist Proms 1965; special cmmr RSCM; memb: Assoc of Cathedral Organists, ISM, RSM; FRCM, FRCO; *Compositions* published choral works incl: There Is No Rose 1974, The National Anthem (dedicated by Gracious Permission to HM Queen Elizabeth II) 1984, Two Final Amens 1989, O How Amiable 1992, A Vast Cloud of Love 1996, I Will Lift Up Mine Eyes 1998, various anthems for royal baptisms; published organ works incl: Suite for Organ 1974, Puck's Shadow 1976, Easter Hymn 1977, Chants d'oiseaux, des poules, des moutons et des vaches 1977, Elegy 1980, Concerto in D 1981, Prelude on Down Ampney 1982, Romance 1986, Triumphal March 1993; *Recreations* swimming, reading; *Style*— Richard Popplewell, Esq, LVO; ✉ 71 Browning Road, Ledbury, Herefordshire HR8 2GA (tel 01531 634967)

PORRITT, (Hon Sir) Jonathon Espie; 2 Bt (UK 1963), of Hampstead, Co London; does not use title; er s of Baron Porritt, GCMG, GCVO, CBE (Life Peer and 1 Bt; d 1994), and his 2 w, Kathleen Mary, *née* Peck (d 1998); *b* 6 July 1950; *Educ* Eton, Magdalen Coll Oxford; *m* 1986, Sarah, da of Malcolm Staniforth, of Malvern, Worcs; 2 da (Eleanor Mary b 1988, Rebecca Elizabeth b 1991); *Heir* bro, Hon Jeremy Porritt; *Career* dir Friends of the Earth 1984–90; dir Forum for the Future, co fndr Real World, co-dir Prince of Wales's Business and Environment Prog; chm UK Sustainable Devpt Cmmn 2000–; author and broadcaster; writer and presenter: Where On Earth Are We Going? (BBC) 1991, How To Save The World (Channel 4) 1992; *Books* Seeing Green: the Politics of Ecology Explained, The Friends of the Earth Handbook, The Coming of the Greens, Where On Earth Are We Going?, Save the Earth, Captain Eco, Playing Safe: Science and the Environment, Capitalism as if the World Matters; *Style*— Jonathon Porritt; ✉ 9 Lypiatt Terrace, Cheltenham, Gloucestershire GL50 2SX

PORTAL, Sir Jonathan Francis; 6 Bt (UK 1901), of Malshanger, Church Oakley, Co Southampton; s of Sir Francis Spencer Portal, 5 Bt (d 1984), and his 2 w, Jane Mary, da of late Albert Henry Williams, OBE; *b* 13 January 1953; *Educ* Marlborough, Univ of Edinburgh (BCom); *m* 9 Oct 1982, Louisa Caroline, er da of Sir John Hervey-Bathurst, Bt, *qv*; 3 s (William Jonathan Francis b 1987, Robert Jonathan b 1989, John Arthur Jonathan b 1993); *Heir* s, William Portal; *Career* chartered accountant; chief accountant Seymour Int Press Distributors 1986–89, gp fin controller Henderson Admin Gp plc 1989–91, fin dir Grosvenor Venture Managers Ltd 1992–93, mangr int 3i Group plc 1995–97, self employed fin dir 1993–; govr Old Malthouse School Swanage; Liveryman Clothworkers' Co; FCA 1977; *Recreations* travel, music, country sports; *Style*— Sir Jonathan Portal, Bt; ✉ Burley Wood Ashe, Basingstoke, Hampshire RG25 3AG (tel 01256 770269, e-mail jonathanp@jpdirectors.com)

PORTARLINGTON, 7 Earl of (I 1785); George Lionel Yuill Seymour Dawson-Damer; Baron Dawson (I 1770), Viscount Carlow (I 1776); s of Air Cdre Viscount Carlow (k on active serv 1944) and gs of 6 Earl of Portarlington (d 1959); *b* 10 August 1938; *Educ* Eton; *m* 26 July 1961, Davina, eld da of late Sir Edward Henry Windley, KCMG, KCVO; 3 s (Charles George Yuill Seymour, Viscount Carlow b 1965, Hon Edward Lionel Seymour b 1967, Hon Henry Lionel Seymour b 1971), 1 da (Lady Marina Davina b 1969); *Heir* s, Viscount Carlow; *Career* Page of Honour to HM The Queen 1953–55; dir: G S Yuill & Co Pty Ltd Sydney; *Recreations* skiing, fishing; *Clubs* Union (Sydney); *Style*— The Rt Hon the Earl of Portarlington; ✉ 118 Wolseley Road, Point Piper, NSW 2027, Australia (tel 00 612 9363 9725, fax 00 612 327 4691); Gledswood, Melrose, Roxburghshire TD6 9DN (tel 01896 822558, fax 01896 823324)

PORTAS, Mary; da of Samuel Edward Newton (d 1980), of Watford, Herts, and Mary Theresa, *née* Flynn (d 1977); *b* 28 May 1960; *Educ* Watford Coll of Art (HND in visual merchandising); *m* 5 Sept 1987, Graham Charles Portas; 1 s (Mylo b 19 Jan 1994), 1 da (Verity b 23 Nov 1995); *Career* leading retail marketeer and window designer; visual merchandiser Harrods dept store until 1984, visual mangr Top Shop (150 stores) 1984–91; Harvey Nichols: head of marketing 1989–91, mktg dir 1991–97 (most notable window designs for Harvey Nichols incl Financial Times newspaper sculptures and empty charity Christmas windows); fndr Yellow Door consultancy 1997–; columnist Saturday Telegraph Magazine; recipient various awards for best window design, int lectr on the art of visual mktg; MInstD 1994; memb: RSA 1994, Mktg Gp of GB 1995; *Books* Windows: The Art of Retail Display (2000); *Recreations* keen dramatist and set designer for The Abbey Theatre (The Company of Ten) and The Pump House Theatre; *Style*— Mrs Mary Portas; ✉ Yellow Door Creative Marketing Ltd, The Heals Building, 22–24 Torrington Place, London WC1E 7HD (tel 020 7580 0707, fax 020 7290 0505)

PORTEN, Anthony Ralph; QC (1988); s of Ralph Charles Porten (d 1976), and Joan, *née* Edden; *b* 1 March 1947; *Educ* Epsom Coll, Emmanuel Coll Cambridge (BA); *m* 17 Oct 1970, Kathryn Mary, da of John Rees Edwards, JP (d 1988); 2 da (Lucinda b 1973, Deborah b 1976); *Career* called to the Bar Inner Temple 1969 (bencher 2002); recorder of the Crown Court 1993–2001, head of chambers 2–3 Gray's Inn Square 2001–; asst cmmr Boundary Cmmn for England; fell Soc for Advanced Legal Studies; *Recreations* family, walking, motoring; *Clubs* RAC; *Style*— Anthony Porten, Esq, QC; ✉ 2–3 Gray's Inn Square, London WC1R 5JH (tel 020 7242 4986, fax 020 7405 1166, e-mail aporten@2-3graysinnsquare.co.uk)

PORTER, *see also:* Horsbrugh-Porter

PORTER, Dr Angus; *b* 9 June 1957; *Educ* Univ of Cambridge (BA, PhD); *m*; 3 c; *Career* formerly with Mars Confectionery (sometime UK sales dir and UK mktg dir), md Consumer Div BT plc 2000–03 (previously UK consumer mktg dir), customer dir and memb Bd Abbey National plc 2003–05; non-exec dir MyTravel Gp plc 2002–; *Style*— Dr Angus Porter; ✉ The Nineteenth, Treadaway Hill, Flackwellheath, Buckinghamshire HP10 9PD (tel 01628 530059, e-mail angus.porter@btopenworld.com)

PORTER, Colin Grant; s of William Graham Porter (d 1973), and Edna May, *née* Wilson; *b* 18 March 1951; *Educ* Syon Sch Isleworth, Harrow Sch of Art, Wolverhampton Sch of Art (BA); *m* 15 July 1972, Janice Ann, da of Albert Edward Manning; 4 s (Joel Edward William b 26 Oct 1976, James Henry b 30 Aug 1978, William Alexander b 11 Feb 1982, Theo Hugh b 2 April 1989); *Career* jr graphic designer Fitch & Company 1977, graphic designer Murdoch Design Associates 1973–74, assoc dir Fitch & Company 1978–79 (sr designer 1974–79), founding ptnr Coley Porter Bell 1979–99 (chm 1994–99), co-fndr and chm Corpbrand Identity 1999–; regular tutor and speaker on design and design management for various orgns incl Design Cncl and Market Res Soc; awarded: 3 Clios (US) 1989, 1 Clio (US) 1990, 3 Clios (US) 1991, Design Business Assoc Design Effectiveness Award 1990, various D & AD Awards; one-man painting exhibition (Smith's Gallery Covent Garden) 1991; fndr memb and bd dir Design Business Assoc (chm 1997–99); memb: D & AD 1975, FCSD 1986; *Recreations* painting, collecting paintings and ephemera; *Style*— Colin Porter, Esq

PORTER, David Andrew; s of Michael Robert Porter, OBE (d 2003), of Hereford, and Cecile Jane Graeme, *née* Stuart (d 1988); *b* 22 April 1960; *Educ* Dulwich Coll, Open Univ; *Career* media exec Garrott Westbourne Ltd 1977–78, media mangr Woolward Royds (Edinburgh) Ltd 1980–82, co dir Yellowhammer Advertising Co 1986–89 (media exec 1978–80, dep md 1982–89), md Axle Media Ltd 1989–90; media dir: Generator Advertising and Marketing Ltd 1989–90, The Leisure Process Ltd 1990; subsequently assoc dir Media Campaign Services, media dir Lansdown Conquest 1994–95; co dir: The Media Business 1995–99, co dir MediaCom 1999–; MIPA 1987; *Style*— David Porter, Esq; ✉ MediaCom, 180 North Gower Street, London NW1 2NB (tel 020 7874 5500)

PORTER, David John; s of George Edward Porter (d 1964), of Lowestoft, and Margaret Elizabeth, *née* Robinson; *b* 16 April 1948; *Educ* Lowestoft GS, New Coll of Speech and Drama London; *m* 25 March 1978, Sarah Jane, da of Rev Peter Shaw (d 1979); 2 s (Thomas Edward b 1982, Samuel George b 1986), 2 da (Victoria Louise b 1979, Alice Elizabeth b 1988); *Career* teacher London 1970–72, dir and co-fndr Vivid Children's Theatre 1972–78; head of drama: Benjamin Britten HS Lowestoft 1978–81, Kirkley HS Lowestoft 1998– (co-ordinator of performing arts 2003–); Cons party agent: Eltham 1982–83, Norwich North 1983–84, Waveney 1985–87; MP (Cons) Waveney 1987–97; memb Select Ctee: on Social Security 1991–92, on Educn 1992–96, on Educn and Employment 1996–97; cncllr Waveney DC; PR conslt David Porter Freelance Communications 1997–2005; *Recreations* writing, Waveney past present and future, family; *Style*— David Porter, Esq; ✉ 11 Irex Road, Pakefield, Lowestoft NR33 7BU (tel 01502 516195, e-mail david@davidporter.co.uk)

PORTER, Henry Christopher Mansel; s of Maj Harry Robert Mansel Porter, MBE, of Pershore, Worcs, and Anne Victoria, *née* Seymour; *b* 23 March 1953; *Educ* Wellington, Univ of Manchester (BA), Perugia Univ Italy; *m* Elizabeth Mary Elliot; 2 da (Miranda Victoria Elliot b 30 Oct 1985, Charlotte Mary Clementine Elliot b 22 Oct 1988); *Career* journalist; Evening Standard 1979–81, feature writer Sunday Times 1981–83 (columnist 1983–87); ed: Illustrated London News 1987–89, Sunday Correspondent Magazine 1989–90; exec ed Independent on Sunday 1990–91, currently London ed Vanity Fair; *Books* Lies, Damned Lies and Some Exclusives (1984), Remembrance Day (1999), A Spy's Life (2001), Empire State (2003), Brandenberg (2005); *Recreations* walking, painting, art galleries, reading; *Style*— Henry Porter, Esq; ✉ Vanity Fair, Condé Nast Publications Ltd, 1 Hanover Square, London W1R 0AD (tel 020 7499 9080)

PORTER, James Forrest; CBE (1991); s of Ernest Porter, and Mary Violetta Porter; *b* 2 October 1928; *Educ* Salford GS, Dudley Trg Coll, LSE, Inst of Educn Univ of London; *m* 1952, Dymphna (d 2006), da of Leo Francis Powell; 2 da (Louise, Alison); *Career* princ Bulmershe Coll of Higher Educn 1967–78, dir gen Cwlth Inst 1978–91; Univ of London Inst of Educn: visiting fell Dept of Int & Comparative Educn 1991–92, Nuffield res fell 1992–, head of int affrs 1993, actg dean 1994–95; conslt UN 1975–; Cwlth fell Aust 1977, chm World Educn Fellowship 1979–; memb: UGC 1970–76, James Ctee on Teacher Educn 1972–, IBA 1973–80, BBC Educn Cncl 1987–92; chm Newsconcern International 1983–91 and 1994–, memb Bd Round Table Magazine 1986–; Hon FCP; *Clubs* Phyllis Court; *Style*— James Porter, Esq, CBE; ✉ The Garden Flat, 4 The Hermitage, 29 Vicarage Road, Henley on Thames RG9 1HT (tel 01491 413797, e-mail porterforr@aol.com)

PORTER, Marguerite Ann (Mrs Henson); da of William Albert Porter, and Mary Maughan; *b* 30 November 1948; *m* 1, 1970 (m dis 1978), Carl Myers; m 2, 1 Aug 1986, Nicholas Victor Leslie Henson, *qv*, s of Leslie Henson; 1 s (Keaton Leslie b 24 March 1988); *Career* Royal Ballet Co: joined 1966, soloist 1973, princ 1978–85, guest artist 1985–, currently govr; danced The Queen in Matthew Bourne's Swan Lake (Broadway) 1998; choreographer: Dancing at Lughnasa (Royal Lyceum Edinburgh), Private Lives (RNT); dir Yorkshire Ballet Seminars; *Publications* Ballerina - A Dancer's Life (1989); Marguerite Porter's Balletcise (video, 1992); *Recreations* motherhood, reading, friends, theatre, choreography; *Style*— Ms Marguerite Porter

PORTER, Mark Edward; s of Robert George Porter, of Oxted, Surrey, and Sybil Elizabeth, *née* Brebner (d 1998); *b* 15 March 1960, Aberdeen; *Educ* Trinity Sch of John Whitgift Surrey, Trinity Coll Oxford (MA); *m* June 2001, Elizabeth, *née* Hubbard; 2 s (Alexander George b 2003, Finlay John b 2007); *Career* art dir several magazines 1986–93, freelance art dir and design conslt 1993–95; The Guardian: assoc art dir 1995–98, art dir 1998–2000, creative ed 2000–; contrib to many books and jls on magazine and newspaper design; memb Alliance Graphique Internationale 2004; Gold medal D&AD 2006 (Silver medal 1996, 2004 and 2006), Gold and Silver medals Soc of Pubn Designers NY 2003; *Recreations* family, food and cooking, hispanophilia; *Style*— Mark Porter, Esq; ✉ The Guardian, 119 Farringdon Road, London EC1R 3ER (tel 020 7713 4576, e-mail mark.porter@guardian.co.uk)

PORTER, Michael James Robert; *b* 18 January 1945; *Educ* Marlborough; *m*; 2 c; *Career* audit clerk Arthur Young & Co Paris 1963, audit sr Peat Marwick Mitchell & Co 1968–71 (articled clerk 1963–68), Main Bd dir and gp co sec Allied Polymer Group Ltd 1976–78 (gp co sec 1972–76); BTR plc: admin dir Miles Redfern-Dunstable 1978–81, admin mangr 1981–83, mangr Special Projects 1983, md BTR Insurance Services 1983–86; gp co sec Stone International plc 1986–87, gp co sec FKI plc 1987– (asst co sec 1987–89); *Recreations* stamp collecting, music, theatre; *Style*— Michael Porter, Esq; ✉ FKI plc, c/o Woodfield House, Halifax Road, Hipperholme, Halifax, West Yorkshire HX3 8HD (fax 01422 205530)

PORTER, Peter Neville Frederick; s of William Ronald Porter (d 1982), of Brisbane, Aust, and Marion, *née* Main (d 1938); *b* 16 February 1929; *Educ* C of E GS Brisbane, Toowoomba GS; *m* 1, 24 March 1961, Shirley Jannice (d 1974), da of Dr Richard Nichol Henry; 2 da (Katherine Sybilla Marion b 1962, Clarissa Jane b 1965); m 2, 2 Nov 1991, Christine Berg, da of John Donovan; *Career* poet; journalist Brisbane 1947–48, warehouseman Brisbane until 1951, clerk London 1951–53 and 1955–56, bookseller London 1956–59, advertising copywriter 1959–68, freelance writer 1968–; former memb Literature Panel Arts Cncl; Hon DLitt: Univ of Melbourne 1985, Loughborough Univ 1986, Univ of Sydney 1999, Queensland Univ 2001; FRSL 1983; *Awards* London Magazine Poetry Prize 1962, Australian Literature Gold Medal 1990, Age Poetry Book of the Year 1997, Philip Hodgins Meml Prize 2000, Queen's Gold Medal for Poetry 2002, CLitt 2007; *Books* Collected Poems (1983, contents of 9 previously published volumes, Duff Cooper Meml Prize 1984), Fast Forward (1984), The Automatic Oracle (1987, Whitbread Poetry Award 1988), Possible Worlds (1989), The Chair of Babel (1992), Millennial Fables (1994), Book of Modern Australian Verse (ed, 1996), Dragons in Their Pleasant Palaces (1997), Collected Poems (vol 2, 1999), Max is Missing (2001, Forward Poetry Prize 2002), Afterburner (2004, shortlisted T S Eliot Prize 2004), 18 Poems (2006); *Recreations* music, Italy; *Style*— Peter Porter, Esq, FRSL; ✉ Flat 3, 42 Cleveland Square, London W2 6DA (tel 020 7262 4289)

PORTER, Richard Bruce; s of Maynard Eustace Prettyman Porter (d 1984), and Irene Marjorie, *née* Turner (d 1994); *b* 20 January 1942; *Educ* St Joseph's Coll Ipswich, City of London Coll (BSc Econ); *m* 1965, Susan Mary, da of Philip Early; 2 da (Anna Lucie b 10 Feb 1970, Kitty b 10 Jan 1972); *Career* market researcher: A C Nielsen 1965–70, Brooke Bond Oxo 1970–75; mgmnt conslt Peat Marwick 1975–81 (incl postings as project dir and devpt economist India and SE Asia), environmental conslt Africa and Far East Environmental Resources Ltd 1981–84, ptnr Strategy Consltg Unit KPMG 1984–94, exec dir Sight Savers (charity) 1994–2005, dep dir Int Agency for the Prevention of Blindness (IAPB) 2005–; *Books* jt author: Energy from Waste, Science Parks and the Growth of High Technology Firms; *Recreations* cinema, theatre, tennis, reading, bridge; *Style*— Richard Porter, Esq; ✉ 15 Park Road, Burgess Hill, West Sussex RH15 8EU (tel 01444 232602); International Agency for the Prevention of Blindness, London School of Hygiene and Tropical Medicine, Keppel Street, London WC1E 7HT (tel 020 7958 8325, fax 020 7958 7325, e-mail rporter@v2020.org)

P

PORTER, Richard James; s of Capt James Graham Porter, of Conwy, Gwynedd, and Ann, *née* Wharry; *b* 28 November 1951; *Educ* Eton, UC Oxford (MA, MSc, BM BCh); *m* 26 July 1974, Diana Isabel, da of Douglas James Roper Austin (d 1979); 2 da (Charlotte b 1977, Alice b 1980); *Career* sr registrar in obstetrics and gynaecology St Mary's Hosp London and Addenbrooke's Hosp Cambridge 1984–88, conslt in obstetrics and gynaecology Bath Royal United Hospital NHS Tst 1989–, dir Maternity Services Wilts Health Care 1992–, obstetric advsr WHO (Europe, Central Asia and Russia) 1995–; chm Assoc for Community Based Maternity Care 2000–; FRCOG 1998 (memb 1982); *Recreations* wine, theatre; *Style*— Richard Porter, Esq; ✉ Weston Lea, Weston Park, Bath BA1 4AL (tel 01225 425618); Bath Clinic, Claverton Down Road, Bath BA2 7BR (tel 01225 835555)

PORTER, Richard William; s of Dr W A Porter, of Hove, E Sussex, and Phyllis May, *née* Richardson; *b* 25 March 1946; *Educ* Brighton Coll; *m* 1 Oct 1988, Tracy Jane Vallis-Porter, da of Stanley Vallis; 1 da (Emily Louise b 17 Jan 1994); *Career* insurance broker: Halford Shead Lloyd's Broker 1965–71, G P Turner 1971–73; Alexander and Alexander Ltd (formerly Alexander Stenhouse UK Ltd): joined 1973, mangr Reading Branch 1974–78, unit dir City Branch 1978–81, exec dir mktg London and Lloyd's 1981–82, devpt dir City Branch 1983–86, divnl dir Central Insurance 1987–88, exec dir 1989–94, ceo Alexander and Alexander Europe Ltd 1995–98; dir EMANI 2000–; memb: RIIA, Inst of Risk Mgmnt 1997; FCII 1971, MIMgt 1984; *Recreations* squash, rugby; *Style*— Richard Porter, Esq; ✉ Holmgarth, Betchworth Avenue, Earley, Berkshire RG6 7RJ (tel 0118 926 5637, e-mail rporter@holmgarth100.fsnet.co.uk)

PORTER, Rt Hon Sir Robert Wilson; kt (1971), PC (NI 1969), QC (NI 1965); s of late Joseph Wilson Porter; *b* 23 December 1923; *Educ* Model Sch, Foyle Coll Londonderry, Queen's Univ Belfast (LLB); *m* 1953, Margaret Adelaide, da of late F W Lynas; 1 s, 1 da (and 1 da decd); *Career* RAFVR 1942–46, RA (TA) 1950–56; fndn scholar Queen's Univ Belfast 1947–48; called to the Bar: NI 1950, Repub of Ireland 1975, Middle Temple 1988; counsel to Attorney-Gen for NI 1963–64 and 1965; min of health and social servs NI 1969, Parly sec 1969 and min of home affrs NI 1969–70; chm War Pensions Appeal Tbnl for NI 1961–66 (vice-chm 1959–61); MP (U): Queen's Univ Belfast 1966–69, Lagan Valley 1969–73; county court judge NI 1978–95; recorder: Londonderry 1979–81, Belfast 1993–95; *Clubs* RAF; *Style*— The Rt Hon Sir Robert Porter, QC; ✉ Larch Hill, Church Close, Ballylesson, Belfast BT8 8JX

PORTER, Robin Anthony; s of Maurice Malcolm Porter (d 1986), and Danuta, *née* Monitz; *b* 15 September 1945; *Educ* Highgate Sch, Univ of Leeds (LLB); *m* 14 Sept 1974 (d 1992), Monica Jolan, da of Péter Dénes Halász, of Munich, Germany; 2 s (Adam b 1978, Nicholas b 1983); *Career* articled clerk Titmuss Sainer & Webb 1968–70; admitted slr 1971; asst slr: Commercial Property Dept Clifford-Turner & Co 1971–72, Company and Commercial Dept McKenna & Co 1972–73, Company and Commercial Dept Penningtons 1974; Wilde Sapte: asst slr Commercial Property Dept 1974–75 ptnr Commercial Property Dept 1975–84 and 1987–91 (ptnr i/c New York Office 1984–87); ptnr Banking Group Waltons & Morse 1991–95; projects dir The International Tax and Investment Centre 1996 (conslt central and eastern Europe 1996–99); sr lectr The Coll of Law 2001– (lectr 1999–2001); Freeman City of London 1987, Liveryman Worshipful Company of Musicians 1990; memb Law Soc 1971; Fell HE Acad 2007 (registered practitioner 2001); *Recreations* music, theatre, tennis, skiing, cycling; *Style*— Robin Porter, Esq; ✉ Flat 117, Clifford's Inn, Fetter Lane, London EC4A 1BX

PORTER, Ronald Frank; yst s of Frank Porter, and Mary, *née* MacRae (of the Clan MacRae, of Eilean Donan Castle); *b* 25 September 1949; *Educ* KCL (LLB); *Career* freelance journalist 1971–; ed Euro News 1991–; memb: Br Assoc of Journalists 1992–, London Press Club 1994–, Royal Soc of St George (City of London branch), Victorian Soc, Cons Policy Forum, 1912 Club, Irish Peers Assoc; patron Nat Art Collections Fund; cncllr Sevenoaks (Dunton Green) 1986–90, sch govr 1986–92; Brother Justicia Lodge; Freeman of City of London 1995; Knight Cdr of the Order of Stanislas 1997, Chevalier Knight Templars 1996; *Publications* contrib to various jls and magazines mainly on food, wine and politics for magazines such as What's On, Aspire and New World; book reviewer Political Quarterly 1980–; *Recreations* wining and dining, reading political biographies, having a good time in general; *Clubs* Nat Liberal, Farmers', Ritz Casino, IOD, Naval, Royal Cwlth, ESU; *Style*— Ronald Porter; ✉ c/o Child & Co, 1 Fleet Street, London EC4Y 1BD (e-mail ronald@porter6677.fsnet.co.uk)

PORTES, Prof Richard David; CBE (2003); s of Herbert Portes; *b* 10 December 1941; *Educ* Yale Univ, Balliol Coll and Nuffield Coll Oxford (Rhodes scholar); *m* 1, 1963 (m dis), Barbara Frank; m 2, 2006, Hélène Rey; *Career* fell Balliol Coll Oxford 1965–69; prof of economics: Princeton Univ 1969–72, Univ of London 1972–94, London Business Sch 1995–; dir d'études EHESS Paris 1978–, pres Centre for Econ Policy Research 1983–, sec-gen Royal Economic Soc 1992–; memb Cncl on Foreign Relations; fell Econometric Soc 1983, FBA 2004; *Books* Planning and Market Relations (1971), Deficits and Detente (1983), Threats to International Financial Stability (1987), Global Macroeconomics (1987), Blueprints for Exchange Rate Management (1989), External Constraints on Macroeconomic Policy (1991), Economic Transformation of Central Europe (1993), European Union Trade with Eastern Europe (1995), Crisis? What Crisis? Orderly Workouts for Sovereign Debtors (1995); *Recreations* swimming; *Style*— Prof Richard Portes, CBE; ✉ Department of Economics, London Business School, Regent's Park, London NW1 4SA (tel 020 7000 8424, fax 020 7000 8401, e-mail rportes@london.edu)

PORTILLO, Rt Hon Michael Denzil Xavier; PC (1992); yst s of Luis Gabriel Portillo (d 1993), and Cora Waldegrave, *née* Blyth; *b* 26 May 1953; *Educ* Harrow Co Sch for Boys, Peterhouse Cambridge (MA); *m* 12 Feb 1982, Carolyn Claire, da of Alastair G Eadie; *Career* Ocean Transport and Trading Co 1975–76, Cons Res Dept 1976–79, special advsr to Sec of State for Energy 1979–81, Kerr McGee Oil (UK) Ltd 1981–83, special advsr to sec of state for Trade and Industry 1983, special advsr to Chllr of the Exchequer 1983–84; MP (Cons): Enfield Southgate 1984–97, Kensington and Chelsea 1999–2005 (Parly candidate Birmingham Perry Barr 1983); asst Govt whip 1986–87, Parly under sec of state for Social Security 1987–88, min of state for Tport 1988–90, min for Local Govt and Inner Cities 1990–92, chief sec to the Treasy 1992–94, sec of state for Employment 1994–95, sec of state for Defence 1995–97; shadow Chllr of the Exchequer 2000–01; memb Int Cmmn on Missing Persons in the former Yugoslavia; non-exec dir BAE Systems 2002–06; television credits: Portillo's Progress (Channel 4) 1998, Great Railway Journeys: Granada to Salamanca (BBC TV) 1999, The Legacy of Division (BBC Radio) 2000, Barca and the General (BBC Radio) 2002, Art that Shook the World: Richard Wagner's Ring (BBC TV) 2002, Portillo in Euroland (BBC TV) 2002, Elizabeth I (BBC TV) 2002, When Michael Portillo became a Single Mum (BBC TV) 2003; columnist Sunday Times 2004–; *Clubs* Chelsea Arts; *Style*— The Rt Hon Michael Portillo; ✉ Suite 99, 34 Buckingham Palace Road, London SW1W 0RH

PORTLAND, 12 Earl of (GB 1689); Timothy Charles Robert Noel Bentinck; also Viscount Woodstock, Baron Cirencester (both GB 1689), and Count Bentinck (Holy Roman Empire); o s of 11 Earl of Portland (d 1997), and his 1 w, Pauline (d 1967), da of late Frederick William Mellowes; *b* 1 June 1953; *Educ* Harrow, UEA (BA); *m* 1979, Judith Ann, da of John Robert Emerson, of Cheadle, Staffs; 2 s (William Jack Henry, Viscount Woodstock b 19 May 1984, Hon Jasper James Mellowes b 12 June 1988); *Heir* s, Viscount Woodstock; *Career* actor as Timothy Bentinck; *Style*— The Earl of Portland

PORTMAN, 10 Viscount (UK 1873); Christopher Edward Berkeley Portman; s of 9 Viscount Portman (d 1999); *b* 30 July 1958; *m* 1, 30 July 1983, Caroline, da of Terence Ivan Steenson, of Caversham, Berks; 1 s (Hon Luke Oliver Berkeley b 31 Aug 1984); m 2, 7 Dec 1987, Patricia Martins, da of Bernardino Pim, of Rio de Janeiro, Brazil; 2 s (Hon Matthew Bernardo Berkeley b 24 Sept 1990, Hon Daniel Edward Berkeley b 27 July 1995); *Heir* s, Hon Luke Portman; *Career* chm Portman Settled Estates Ltd, dir Brickleton Integrated Technologies; *Recreations* computer science, molecular nanotechnology (8th colleague of The Foresight Inst for Molecular Nanotechnology Palo Alto CA), paragliding, scuba diving; *Style*— The Viscount Portman; ✉ The Portman Estate, 38 Seymour Street, London W1H 7BP (tel 020 7563 1400)

PORTMAN, Rachel Mary Berkeley; da of Berkeley Charles Portman, and Penelope, *née* Mowat; *b* 11 December 1960; *Educ* Charterhouse, Worcester Coll Oxford (exhibitioner); *m* 25 Feb 1995, Count Uberto Pasolini Dall'Onda; 3 da (Anna Gwendolen b 27 Sept 1995, Giulia Ginevra b 20 March 1998, Niky Joan Pasolini b 19 Aug 1999); *Career* composer; *Film* Experience Preferred but not Essential (Channel 4), Reflections (Court House Films), Sharma and Beyond (Enigma/Goldcrest), Antonia and Jane (BBC Films), Rebecca's Daughters, Life is Sweet (Thin Man Films), Where Angels Fear to Tread (Stagescreen), Used People (20th Century Fox), Benny and Joon (MGM), Friends (Working Title), Great Moments in Aviation (Miramax), The Joy Luck Club (Disney), Sirens (Miramax), War of the Buttons (Warner Bros), The Road to Wellville (Columbia), Only You (Tri-Star/Columbia), Smoke (Miramax), A Pyromaniac's Love Story (Hollywood), To Wong Foo (Universal), Palookaville (Samuel Goldwyn Co), Adventures of Pinocchio (New Line/Savoy Pictures), Emma (Miramax), Marvin's Room (Miramax), Addicted to Love (Warner Bros), Beauty and the Beast II (Disney), Home Fries (Warner Bros), Beloved (Disney), The Other Sister (Disney), Ratcatcher (Pathe Films), The Cider House Rules (Miramax) 1999, The Closer you Get (Fox Searchlight Pictures) 1999, The Legend of Bagger Vance (DreamWorks), Chocolat (Miramax) 2000; *Television* incl: Last Day of Summer (Moving Picture Co), Reflections (Channel 4), Four Days in July (BBC TV), Good as Gold (BBC TV), The Little Princess (LWT), 1914 All Out (Yorkshire TV), Falklands War: Untold Story (Yorkshire TV), Short and Curlies (Portman/British Screen/Channel 4), 90 Degrees South (John Gau Prodns), Cariani and The Courtesans (BBC TV), Storyteller (Henson Orgn), Loving Hazel (BBC TV), Sometime in August (BBC TV), Charlie the Kid (Thames TV), Living with Dinosaurs (Henson Orgn), Oranges Are Not the Only Fruit (BBC TV), Nice Work (BBC TV), The Woman in Black (Central Films), Widowmaker (Central Films), Shoot to Kill (Zenith/Yorkshire TV), Mr Wakefield's Crusade (BBC Wales), Think of England (BBC TV), Twice Through the Heart (BBC TV), The Cloning of Joanna May (Granada TV), Flea Bites (BBC TV), Elizabeth R (BBC TV); *Other* trailer for Mike Leigh (London Film Festival), Ourselves Alone (Royal Court Theatre), Fantasy for Cello and Piano (Salisbury Festival); *Awards* BFI Young Composer of the Year 1988, Tric Celebrity Awards Schneider Trophy for Theme Music of the Year (for Precious Bane) 1989, Bafta Award Nominations for Best Score (for Oranges Are Not the Only Fruit 1989 and The Woman in Black), Women in Film/Rank Films Laboratories Award for Creative Originality 1996, Academy Award for Best Original Musical or Comedy Score (for Emma) 1996, Int Prize for Film and Media Music 1997, Academy Award nomination for Best Original Score (for The Cider House Rules) 1999, Flanders International Film Festival Award (Ratcatcher) 1999, Academy Award nomination for Best Original Score (for Chocolat) 2000, Grammy nomination for Best Score Soundtrack (for The Cider House Rules) 2000, Muse Award New York Women in Film and Television 2000, Women in Music Touchstone Award 2001; *Style*— Ms Rachel Portman; ✉ c/o Blue Focus Management LLC, 9200 Sunset Boulevard, Suite 231, Los Angeles, CA 90069, USA

PORTMANN, Prof Bernard Claude; s of late Henry Paul Portmann, and Emilie Emma, *née* Jaques; *b* 6 February 1940; *Educ* Calvin Coll Geneva, Geneva Univ (MB, Swiss Med Dip, MD); *m* 1, 1963 (m dis 1969); m 2, 1970, Hermine Elisabeth, da of Leo Bertholdt Neumann; 2 c (Barbara b 8 Feb 1971, Jan b 26 Oct 1972); *Career* lectr in pathology Univ Hosp Geneva 1968–72 (house offr 1966–67); KCH London: research fell Liver Unit 1973–75, res histopathologist 1975–78, conslt 1978–, prof of hepatopathology 1997–; hon sr lectr Univ of London 1978–97; assoc ed Jl of Hepatology 1995–99, special section ed Liver Transplant 2002–04; travelling fellowship Mount Sinai Med Center NY 1982; memb: Pathology Soc of GB and I, Assoc of Clinical Pathology, Br Soc Gastroenterology, European Soc Pathology, Int Acad of Pathology, American Assoc for the Study of Liver Diseases; former memb Ctee Br Assoc for Study of the Liver; FRCPath 1989 (MRCPath 1977); *Books* Pathology of the Liver (jtly, 1994, 5 edn 2007), The Practice of Liver Transplantation (jtly, 1995); *Recreations* DIY, reading, art exhibitions; *Style*— Prof Bernard Portmann; ✉ 20 Ewelme Road, Forest Hill, London SE23 3BH (tel 020 8699 6717, fax 020 8291 4006); Institute of Liver Studies, King's College Hospital, Denmark Hill, London SE5 9RS (tel 020 3299 3734, fax 020 3299 3125, e-mail bernard.portmann@kcl.ac.uk)

PORTNO, Dr Antony David (Tony); CBE (1998); *b* 30 May 1938; *Educ* Accrington GS, Univ of London (BSc, PhD); *Career* Bass 1961–64, Brewing Research Fndn 1964–69, devpt mangr Pfizer 1969–71; Bass plc 1971–98: rejoined as quality control mangr Bass Production Ltd Burton on Trent 1971, princ scientist Bass Brewers Runcorn 1975, gp research scientist Bass plc Burton on Trent 1975, dir of research Bass plc 1976, dir Britannia Soft Drinks 1983, main bd dir Bass plc 1985–98 (memb Exec Ctee 1989–98), dir Bass UK Ltd 1988–93, chm Britvic Soft Drinks 1990–96, chm Bass Brewers Ltd 1991–98, chm Bass Leisure 1996–98; chm Evans Halshaw Holdings plc 1998–; non-exec dir Gallaher Ltd; Liveryman Worshipful Co of Brewers; FIBrew; *Recreations* fishing, antiquarian book collecting, gardening; *Style*— Dr Tony Portno, CBE

PORTNOY, Leslie Reuben; s of Israel Portnoy, and Miriam Portnoy; *b* 27 May 1939; *Educ* Manchester Grammar, Univ of Manchester (LLB); *m* 7 March 1961, Stephanie, da of Nathan Swift; 1 s (Jonathan b 10 May 1966), 1 da (Naomi b 25 Oct 1969); *Career* called to the Bar Gray's Inn 1961; dep circuit judge 1978, memb Panel under Jewish Tbnl (Shops Act) 1980, asst recorder 1981, recorder 1988; *Style*— Leslie Portnoy, Esq; ✉ 95 Cavendish Road, Salford, Manchester M7 4NB (tel 0161 740 2286); 9 St John Street, Manchester M3 4DN (tel 0161 955 9000, fax 0161 955 9001)

PORTSDOWN, Archdeacon of; *see:* Lowson, Ven Christopher

PORTSMOUTH, Bishop of (RC) 1988–; Rt Rev (Roger Francis) Crispian Hollis; s of (Maurice) Christopher Hollis (d 1977), of Mells, Somerset, and Margaret Madelaine, *née* King (d 1984); *b* 17 November 1936; *Educ* Stonyhurst, Balliol Coll Oxford, Pontifical Gregorian Univ Rome; *Career* Nat Serv 2 Lt Somerset LI 1954–56; ordained priest 1965, asst priest Amesbury Wilts 1966–67, asst RC chaplain Oxford Univ 1967–70 (sr RC chaplain 1970–77), RC asst to Head of Religious Broadcasting BBC 1977–81, admin Clifton Cathedral and vicar-gen Clifton Diocese 1981–87, auxiliary bishop Archdiocese of Birmingham 1987–88; *Recreations* golf, cricket watching; *Style*— The Rt Rev the Bishop of Portsmouth; ✉ Bishops House, Edinburgh Road, Portsmouth PO1 3HG (tel 023 9282 0894, fax 023 9286 3086, e-mail bishop@portsmouth-dio.org.uk)

PORTSMOUTH, Dr (Owen Henry) Donald; s of Oliver Spencer Portsmouth (d 1970), of Swansea, and Gwendolen Anne, *née* Trevor Owen (d 1991); *b* 24 May 1929; *Educ* Blundell's, St Thomas' Hosp Med Sch London (MB BS, DTM and H), Keele Univ (MA); *m* 1, 18 Sept 1954, Moira Heloise (d 1979), da of Alan John Sinclair (d 1967), of Kenya; 3 s (Charles b 1956, Richard b 1958, Andrew b 1961), 1 da (Helen b 1964); m 2, 3 Jan 1981, Glennis Cook, *née* Weddle; 1 step da (Esther b 1975); *Career* jr hosp appointments 1953–56, med serv Kenya Govt 1956–66 (med specialist 1960–66), conslt physician in geriatric med E Birmingham Hosp 1966–94, sr clinical lectr in biomedical ethics Univ of

Birmingham 1994–2005; visiting sr lectr Univ of Malawi 1997; pres W Midlands Inst of Geriatric Med (dir 1975–93), chm Medical Ethics Special Interest Gp Br Geriatrics Soc 1995–2001, vice-chm Solihull HA 1984–90, chm of tstees Rayner House and Yew Trees, Dawson meml lectr Queens Univ Kingston Ontario 1984, Kirk Meml lectr Birmingham Heartlands Hosp 1996, memb Midlands Multi-Centre Res Ethics Ctee 1997–2001, President's Medal Br Geriatrics Soc 1996; FRCPEd 1971, FRCP 1977; *Recreations* heraldry, architecture, history, foreign travel; *Style*— Dr Donald Portsmouth; ✉ Oakfield, 12 Paddock Drive, Dorridge, Solihull, West Midlands B93 8BZ (tel and fax 01564 775032, e-mail dportsmout@aol.com)

PORTSMOUTH, Bishop of 1995–; Rt Rev Dr Kenneth William Stevenson; s of Frederik Robert Stevenson (d 1993), of East Linton, East Lothian, and Margrete, *née* Hoffmeyer; *b* 9 November 1949; *Educ* Edinburgh Acad, Univ of Edinburgh (MA), Salisbury/Wells Theol Coll, Univ of Southampton (PhD), Univ of Manchester (DD); *m* 1970, Sarah Julia Mary, da of John Morton Glover; 3 da (Elisabeth Helen *b* 29 Nov 1971, Katharine Anne *b* 30 April 1974, Alexandra Margrete *b* 25 Jan 1984), 1 s (James Christian William *b* 6 July 1979); *Career* curate Grantham 1973–76, sr curate Boston 1976–80, pt/t tutor Lincoln Theol Coll 1975–80, chaplain and lectr Univ of Manchester 1980–86, visiting prof Univ of Notre Dame IN 1983, rector Holy Trinity and St Mary Guildford 1986–95; chm: Anglo-Nordic-Baltic Theological Conf 1997– (sec 1985–97), Porvoo Panel 2005– (vice-chm 1999–2005), Educn Div C of E, Nat Soc; memb C of E: Liturgical Cmmn 1986–96, Faith and Order Advsy Gp 1991–96, Doctrine Cmmn 1996–2004; memb House of Lords 1999–; Hon LLD Univ of Portsmouth 2007; FRHistS 1990; Knight Cdr of Danneborg (Denmark) 2006; *Books* Nuptial Blessing: a Study of Christian Marriage Rites (1982), Eucharist and Offering (1986), Jerusalem Revisited (1988), The First Rites (1989), Covenant of Grace Renewed: a vision of the Eucharist in the 17th Century (1994), Handing On: Borderlands of Worship and Tradition (1996), The Mystery of Baptism in the Anglican Tradition (1998), All the Company of Heaven (1998), Abba Father: Using and Interpreting the Lord's Prayer (2000), Love's Redeeming Work: The Anglican Quest for Holiness (ed, 2001), Do This: The Shape, Style and Meaning of the Eucharist (2002), The Lord's Prayer: A Text in Tradition (2004), Rooted in Detachment: Living the Transfiguration (2007), Waiting and Watching: The Riddle of Advent (2007); *Recreations* music (piano), historical biographies, thrillers, Denmark; *Clubs* Farmers', Nikaean, Nobody's Friends, Royal Yacht Squadron, Royal Naval Portsmouth; *Style*— The Rt Rev the Lord Bishop of Portsmouth; ✉ Bishopsgrove, Osborn Road, Fareham, Hampshire PO16 7DQ (tel 01329 280247, fax 01329 231538, e-mail bishports@portsmouth.anglican.org)

PORTSMOUTH, 10 Earl of (GB 1743); Quentin Gerard Carew Wallop; DL (Hants 2004); also Baron Wallop (GB 1720), Viscount Lymington (GB 1720); Hereditary Bailiff of Burley in the New Forest; s of Viscount Lymington (d 1984) and his 2 w Ruth Violet, née Sladen (d 1978); suc gf 9 Earl (d 1984); *b* 25 July 1954; *Educ* Eton, Millfield; *m* 1, 1981 (m dis 1985), Candia Frances Juliet, only da of Colin McWilliam, and Margaret, *née* Henderson; 1 s (Oliver Henry Rufus, Viscount Lymington *b* 22 Dec 1981), 1 da (Lady Clementine Violet Rohais *b* 20 Nov 1983); *m* 2, 1990, Annabel, eldest da of Dr Ian Fergusson, and Rosemary, *née* Howard; 1 da (Lady Rose Hermione Annabel *b* 23 Oct 1990); *Heir* s, Viscount Lymington; *Career* non-exec dir Grainger Trust plc 1987–2002; pres Basingstoke Cons Assoc; patron Hampshire Branch Br Red Cross; churchwarden St Andrew's Church Farleigh Wallop; Liveryman Worshipful Co of Fishmongers (memb Ct of Assts 2006); *Recreations* shooting, travel, wine, food, promoting access to justice; *Clubs* Buck's, White's, Int Assoc of Cape Horners; *Style*— The Rt Hon the Earl of Portsmouth, DL; ✉ Farleigh House, Farleigh Wallop, Basingstoke, Hampshire RG25 2HT (tel 01256 321026)

PORTWIN, Guy Lyster; s of Edwin Thomas Portwin, of Herts, and Elizabeth Emily Louise, *née* Gadd; *b* 28 December 1949; *Educ* Merchant Taylors'; *Family* 4 c (Liza, Emma, Guy, John); *m* 2001, Polly Jane, *née* Hance; *Career* dir: Comprint Ltd 1972–86, Wheatland Journals Ltd 1973–90, Turret Press (Holdings) Ltd 1979–84; md Turret-Wheatland Ltd 1984–88; chm: Turret Group plc 1988–90, Hill Media Ltd 1991–, Trophex Ltd 1991–, Hill Communications Ltd 1992–, Toy News Ltd 1992–95; dir: European Toy Fair Ltd, Millhouse Publishing International Ltd 1992–94, Association Publishing Ltd 1995–; MFH: Jt Master Bicester Hunt with Whaddon Chase 1996–99, Jt Master Vale of Aylesbury Hunt 2000–02, Jt Master Vale of Aylesbury with Garth and S Berks Hunt 2003–05 (dep chm 2007–); FInstD 1985; *Recreations* riding, reading; *Clubs* Durrants; *Style*— Guy Portwin, Esq; ✉ Round Hill, Kimblewick, Aylesbury, Buckinghamshire HP17 8TB (e-mail guyportwin@yahoo.co.uk); Hill Media Ltd, Marash House, 2/5 Brook Street, Berkhamsted, Hertfordshire HP23 5ED (tel 01442 826826, fax 01442 823400)

POSNANSKY, Jeremy Ross Leon; QC (1994); s of Anthony Victor Posnansky, of London, and late Evelyn Davis, JP, *née* Leon (previously Posnansky); *b* 8 March 1951; *Educ* St Paul's, Coll of Law London; *m* 31 Dec 1974, Julia Mary, da of Richard Sadler, MBE (d 1967), of Bournemouth; 2 da (Charlotte *b* 1976, Zoë *b* 1979); *Career* called to the Bar Gray's Inn 1972 (bencher 2003), admitted to the Bar of Antigua and Barbuda; in ind practice at the Bar 1972–2007, with Farrer & Co, Slrs 2007–; asst recorder 1995–98, recorder 1998–2002; currently dep judge of the High Court (Family Div); memb Inner London Family Courts Servs and Business Ctees 1991–94; memb Hon Soc of Gray's Inn; fell Int Acad of Matrimonial Lawyers; *Recreations* scuba diving, travel, computers; *Style*— Jeremy Posnansky, Esq, QC; ✉ Farrer & Co, 66 Lincoln's Inn Fields, London WC2A 3LH (tel 020 7242 2022)

POSNER, Lindsay Steven; s of Dennis Posner, and Pauline Posner; *b* 6 June 1959; *Educ* Latymer GS, Univ of Exeter (BA), RADA; *Partner* Megan Wheldon; 2 da (Merle, Maud), 1 s (Nat); *Career* assoc dir Royal Court Theatre 1986–92; plays directed: The Treatment, Death and the Maiden (Best Play Olivier Awards), American Bagpipes, Colquhoun and MacBryde, Blood, Downfall, Ambulance, Ficky Stingers, The Doctor of Honour, Cheek By Jowl (Sheffield), Leonce and Lena, American Buffalo (Young Vic), The Misanthrope (Young Vic), The Provok'd Wife (Old Vic), Handel's Giulo Cesare (Royal Opera), After Darwin (Hampstead), Volpone (RSC Swan), Taming of the Shrew (RSC tour), The Rivals (RSC Swan), Twelfth Night (Royal Shakespeare Theatre), A Life in the Theatre (Apollo), The Hypochondriac (Almeida), Power (RNT), Oleana (Garrick), The Birthday Party (Duchess), Fool for Love (Apollo), Sexual Perversity in Chiago (Comedy), Tartuffe (RNT), Guilo Cesare (ROH), Love Counts (Almeida), Tom & Viv (Almeida); dir of The Maitlands (BBC), dir of Jenufa; *Style*— Lindsay Posner

POSNER, Prof Rebecca; da of William Reynolds (d 1958), and Rebecca, *née* Stephenson (d 1988); *b* 17 August 1929; *Educ* Nuneaton HS for Girls, Somerville Coll Oxford (BA, DPhil); *m* 5 Aug 1953, Michael Vivian Posner, CBE (d 2006), s of Jack Posner (d 1978); 1 s (Christopher Nicholas *b* 14 Sept 1965), 1 da (Barbara Virginia *b* 7 July 1968); *Career* res fell Girton Coll Cambridge 1960–63, prof of French studies and head of Dept of Modern Languages Univ of Ghana 1963–65, reader in linguistics Univ of York 1965–78, professorial fell St Hugh's Coll Oxford 1978–96 (hon fell 1996–), prof of the romance languages Univ of Oxford 1978–96 (emeritus prof 1996–), research assoc Oxford Univ Centre for Linguistics & Philology 1996–, Leverhulme emeritus fell 1997; pres Philological Soc 1996–2000 (vice-pres 2000–); memb: Linguistic Soc of America, Société de Linguistique Romane, Linguistics Assoc of GB, Modern Humanities Res Assoc, Soc for French Studies, Assoc for French Language Studies; *Books* Consonantal Dissimilation in the Romance Languages (1960), The Romance Languages (1966), Introduction to Romance Linguistics (1970), Trends in Romance Linguistics and Philology (with J N Green, 1980–93), The Romance Languages (Cambridge Language Survey, 1996),

Linguistic Change in French (1997), Las Lenguas romances (1998); *Recreations* gardening, walking, music, travel; *Style*— Prof Rebecca Posner; ✉ Rushwood, Jack Straw's Lane, Oxford (tel 01865 763578, e-mail rebecca.posner@st-hughs.ox.ac.uk)

POST, Herschel; s of Herschel E Post (d 1973), and Marie, *née* Connelly (d 1997); *b* 9 October 1939; *Educ* Yale Univ (AB), New Coll Oxford (MA), Harvard Law Sch (LLB); *m* 24 Aug 1963, Peggy, da of Charles H Mayne (d 1963); 1 s (Herschel Day *b* 1969), 3 da (Clarissa *b* 1975, Eliza *b* 1977, Olivia *b* 1982); *Career* dep admin Parks Recreation and Cultural Affrs Admin City of NY 1972–73, vice-pres Morgan Guaranty Trust Co Brussels and London 1974–84, pres and dir Posthorn Global Asset Management and Shearson Lehman Global Asset Management 1984–90, chief operating offr Lehman Bros and Lehman Bros Securities 1990–95, chief exec and dep chm Coutts & Co 1995–2000 (chief operating offr Coutts Gp 1995), int md (business devpt) Christie's Int plc 2000–; dir: Investors Capital Tst plc 1999–, Ahli United Bank (UK) plc 2001–, Ahli United Bank BSC 2002–; dep chm: London Stock Exchange 1989–95, EFG Private Bank Ltd 2002–, CRESTCO Ltd 2002–; dir Notting Hill Housing Gp 2002–, chm Woodcock Fndn (US) 2000–, treas You Can Do IT 2002–; *Clubs* Athenaeum, Queen's; *Style*— Herschel Post, Esq; ✉ tel 020 7389 2295, fax 020 7389 2009

POST, Martin Richard; s of Kenneth Richard Post (d 1973), and Barbara Ruby, *née* Arnell; *b* 3 September 1958; *Educ* Watford GS for Boys (head prefect), Univ of York (BA), Darwin Coll Cambridge (PGCE), Open Univ (MA); *m* 23 Dec 1999, Kathryn Jane, da of William Watts; 1 s (Benjamin Richard *b* 27 Jan 2003); *Career* teacher: Kings Sch Rochester 1982–84, Mill Hill Co HS 1985–89, Richard Hale Sch Hertford 1989–95; headmaster Watford GS for Boys 2000– (dep head 1995–2000); pres Old Fullerians Assoc; *Recreations* sports of all types, reading, my family; *Clubs* Mill Hill Co HS Old Boys' FC; *Style*— Martin Post, Esq; ✉ Watford Grammar School for Boys, Rickmansworth Road, Watford, Hertfordshire WD18 7JF (tel 01923 208900, fax 01923 208901, e-mail head.watfordboys@thegrid.org.uk)

POSTE, Dr George H; CBE (1999); *Educ* Univ of Bristol (BVSc, PhD); *Career* SmithKline Beecham plc: joined Smith Kline & French Laboratories 1980, various sr R&D appts, chm research and devpt 1992–97, main bd dir 1992–, chief science and technol offr 1997–99; ceo Health Technology Networks 1999–; chm: diaDexus, Structural GenomiX; memb Bd: AdvancePCS, Monsanto; Pitt fell Pembroke Coll Cambridge 1996–, pres Arizona Biodesign Inst Arizona State Univ 2003–; co-ed Cancer and Metastasis Reviews, co-ed Advanced Drug Delivery Reviews, former chm Editorial Bd Bio/Technology, memb editorial bds of various other jls; memb UK Human Genetics Advsy Ctee, memb US Defense Science Bd Dept of Defense, memb Cncl on Foreign Rels; former memb US Govt Ctees on: Nat Insts of Health, NASA, Office of Technol Assessment, State Dept, Commerce Dept, Defense Dept; former chm: R&D Steering Ctee Pharmaceutical Mfrs' Assoc Washington DC, Scientific Ctee Assoc of the British Pharmaceutical Industry; sometime memb governing body: Gordon Research Confs, Nat Fndn for Biomedical Research, Life Sciences Research Fndn, Center for Molecular Genetics and Med Stanford Univ, Philadelphia Coll of Pharmacy and Science, Alliance for Ageing, Keystone Center, Royal Soc of Med Fndn, US Nat Center for Genome Resources; Hon DSc: Univ of Bristol 1987, Univ of Sussex 2000; Hon LLD: Univ of Bristol 1995, Univ of Dundee 1998; distinguished fell Hoover Inst Stanford Univ; FRCVS 1987, FRCPath 1989, Hon FRCP 1993, FRS 1997, FMedSci 1997; *Recreations* military history, photography, motor racing; *Style*— Dr George Poste, CBE, FRS; ✉ Health Technology Networks, PO Box 647, Gilbertsville, PA 19525, USA (tel 610 705 0828, fax 610 705 0810, e-mail gposte@healthtechnetwork.com)

POSTGATE, Prof (John) Nicholas; s of Ormond Oliver Postgate (d 1989), of Winchester, Hants, and Patricia Mary, *née* Peet; *b* 5 November 1945; *Educ* Winchester, Trinity Coll Cambridge (BA); *m* 1, 1968 (m dis 1999), Carolyn June, da of Dr Donald Arthur Prater; 1 s (Richard Laurence *b* 30 March 1973), 1 da (Elizabeth Anne *b* 14 July 1975); *m* 2, Sarah Helen, da of Ronald Blakeney; 1 s (Louis Alexander Ormond *b* 13 Dec 2000), 1 da (Jessica Laura *b* 28 March 2002); *Career* asst lectr in Akkadian SOAS Univ of London 1967–71; fell Trinity Coll Cambridge 1970–74; dir British Sch of Archaeology in Iraq 1975–81 (asst dir 1972–75); Univ of Cambridge: lectr in history and archaeology of the ancient Near East 1982–85, reader in Mesopotamian studies 1985–94, prof of Assyriology 1994–; dir of excavations: Abu Salabikh Iraq 1975–89, Kilise Tepe Turkey 1994–98; FBA 1993; *Books* Early Mesopotamia: Society and Economy at the Dawn of History (1992); *Style*— Prof Nicholas Postgate, FBA; ✉ Trinity College, Cambridge CB2 1TQ (tel 01223 338443); Faculty of Oriental Studies, University of Cambridge, Sidgwick Avenue, Cambridge CB3 9DA (tel 01223 335120)

POSTLETHWAITE, Peter (Pete); OBE (2004); *b* 16 February 1945, Warrington, Cheshire; *Career* actor; *Television* incl: Going Straight 1978, Doris And Doreen 1978, Afternoon Off 1979, Minder 1982 and 1993, Cyrano de Bergerac 1985, Casualty 1986, Coast to Coast 1987, Tumbledown 1989, Treasure Island 1990, Needle 1990, Boon 1990, A Child from the South 1991, Between the Lines 1992, Lovejoy 1993, Sharpe 1994, Martin Chuzzlewit 1994, Lost for Words 1998, Alice in Wonderland 1998, Butterfly Collectors 1999, Animal Farm 1999, The Sins 2000, Shattered City: The Halifax Explosion 2003; *Films* incl: The Duellists 1977, A Private Function 1985, To Kill a Priest 1988, Number 27 1988, The Dressmaker 1988, Distant Voices Still Lives 1988, They Never Slept 1990, Hamlet 1990, The Grass Arena 1991, Alien III 1992, The Last of the Mohicans 1992, Waterland 1992, Split Second 1992, In the Name of the Father 1993 (Oscar nomination), Anchoress 1993, The Usual Suspects 1995, Suite 16 1995, When Saturday Comes 1996, James and the Giant Peach 1996, Dragonheart 1996, William Shakespeare's Romeo and Juliet 1996, Brassed Off 1996, Crimetime 1996, The Serpent's Kiss 1997, The Lost World: Jurassic Park 1997, Bandyta 1997, Amistad 1997, Among Giants 1998, Wayward Son 1999, The Divine Ryans 1999, When the Sky Falls 2000, Rat 2000, Ring of Fire 2001, The Shipping News 2001, Triggermen 2002, Between Strangers 2002, The Limit 2003, Strange Bedfellows 2004; *Style*— Pete Postlethwaite, Esq, OBE

POTTER, see also: Lee-Potter

POTTER, Christopher John; s of Frank Potter (d 1995), and Catherine, *née* Kerr; *b* 1 April 1959; *Educ* King's Coll London (BSc, AKC, MSc), London Coll of Music (ALCM); *Career* publisher and md Fourth Estate 2000–03, ed-in-chief Harper Press 2003–; titles commissioned incl: The Stone Diaries by Carol Shields (winner Pulitzer Prize 1994), The Shipping News by E Annie Proulx (winner Pulitzer Prize 1995), Longitude by Dava Sobel (Book of the Year 1996), Fermat's Last Theorem by Simon Singh (1997), The Hours by Michael Cunningham (winner Pulitzer Prize 1999), The Amazing Adventures of Kavalier and Clay by Michael Chabon (winner Pulitzer Prize 2001), Bel Canto by Ann Patchett (winner Orange Prize 2002); Ed of the Year (NIBBIES) 1994; *Style*— Christopher Potter, Esq; ✉ 30 Rhondda Grove, London E3 5AP (tel and fax 020 8980 7301); Fourth Estate Ltd, 77–85 Fulham Palace Road, London W6 8JB (tel 020 8741 4414, e-mail christopherpotter@4thestate.co.uk)

POTTER, David Roger William; s of late William Edward Potter, and Joan Louise, *née* Frost; *b* 27 July 1944; *Educ* Bryanston, UC Oxford (MA); *m* 1, 1966 (m dis 1984), Joanna Trollope, *qv*; 2 da (Louise (Mrs Paul Ansdell) *b* 1969, Antonia (Mrs Jon Prentice) *b* 1971); *m* 3, 1991, Jill, da of James Benson; 1 da (Harriet *b* 1993); *Career* National Discount Co 1964–69; md: Credit Suisse First Boston 1969–81, Samuel Montagu and various subsidiaries 1981–87, Midland Montagu Corporate Banking 1987–89, David Potter Consultants 1989–90; chm and chief exec Guinness Mahon & Co Ltd 1990–98, gp chief exec Guinness Mahon Holdings 1990–98; dep chm Investec Bank UK 1998–99; chm

P

Camco Int 2006–; dir: Thomas Cook Group 1989–91, The Rose Partnership 2000, Noble Gp 2000–, Infocandy 2000–, WMC Communications 2001–03, New Media Spark 2002–Numerica Gp plc 2003–05, Solar Integrated Technologies 2004–, Deltron Electronics 2005–06, Guinness Flight Venture Capital Tst 2005–, Quercus plc 2006–, Vycon Inc 2007–; former chm Bd London Film Cmmn; memb: Bd of Advsrs The Capital Club of London, Cncl Centre for the Study of Financial Innovation; govr and hon treas KCL, govr Bryanston Sch, chm Nat Film & TV Sch Fndn; tstee: Worldwide Volunteering, Nelson Mandela Childrens Fndn; memb Guild of Int Bankers; FKC 2006; *Recreations* shooting, golf, gardening; *Clubs* Vincent's (Oxford), London Capital; *Style*— David R W Potter, Esq; ✉ 6 Norland Square, London W11 4PX (e-mail david@davidpotter.org)

POTTER, Edward; s of Flt Lt Edward Josef Data (d 1974), of Krakow, Poland, and Eleanor, *née* Bolton (d 1976); *b* 15 September 1941; *Educ* Bolton Tech Sch, Manchester Regnl Coll of Art, Oxford Sch of Architecture (DiplArch); *Career* architect; ptnr Edward Potter Assocs (chartered architects in gen practice and specialists in restoration of historic buildings); chm: S London Soc of Architects 1993–95, Wandsworth Soc Open Spaces Ctee 1993–2005; dir Sculpture House Kingston upon Thames 1995–; RIBA rep Wandsworth Conservation Advsy Ctee 1995–; RIBA Thesis Prize 1968; RIBA, FIAS, FCIOB; *Recreations* railways; *Clubs* Chelsea Arts; *Style*— Edward Potter, Esq; ✉ 59 Westover Road, London SW18 2RF (tel 020 8870 7595, fax 020 8870 8683)

POTTER, Jon Nicholas; s of Robert Edward Potter, and June, *née* Rosemayer; *b* 19 November 1963; *Educ* Burnham GS, Univ of Southampton (BA), Aston Business Sch (MBA); *m* Tracy Clare, *née* Holland; 2 s (Max Frederick b 4 April 1997, Hugo Nicholas b 24 March 1999), 2 da (Sophie Ann, Lucy Thérèse (twins) b 31 May 2002); *Career* hockey player; memb Hounslow Hockey Club (capt Nat League winners 1990 and 1992); Bronze medal Olympic Games LA 1984, Silver medal World Cup London 1986, Silver medal Euro Cup Moscow 1987, Gold medal Olympic Games Seoul 1988, Gold medal Euro Cup Winners Cup 1990, Bronze medal Euro Cup 1991, 6th Olympic Games Barcelona 1992; 234 int caps; England capt World Cup 1994; most capped male GB player; Hockey Player of the Year 1987–88; mktg mangr: KP Foods 1988–92, Nestlé Rowntree 1992–95; mktg dir Čokoládovny (Nestle Prague) 1995–97; Guinness Ltd: Euro mktg dir 1997–99, global brands dir 2000; global brand dir Guinness Diageo 2000–04, gen mangr Diageo venture Africa 2005–07, pres Diageo vodka and rum mktg portfolio 2007–; dir GAPL Ltd Singapore, non-exec dir England Hockey Ltd; *Recreations* skiing, tennis, travel, music; *Clubs* Ladykillers; *Style*— Jon Potter, Esq; ✉ 279 Old Stamford Road, New Canaan, CT 06840, USA (e-mail jon.potter@diageo.com)

POTTER, Rt Hon Lord Justice; Rt Hon Sir Mark Howard; PC (1996), kt (1988); s of Prof Harold Potter (d 1951), and Beatrice Spencer, *née* Crowder (d 1978); *b* 27 August 1937; *Educ* Perse Sch Cambridge, Gonville & Caius Coll Cambridge (MA); *m* 1962, Undine Amanda Fay, da of Maj James Eric Miller (Rajputana Rifles); 2 s (Nicholas b 6 Sept 1969, Charles b 27 Dec 1978); *Career* cmmnd 15 Medium Regt RA 1958, 289 Light Para Regt RHA (TA) 1960–65; asst supervisor legal studies Univ of Cambridge (Gonville & Caius, Queen's, Sydney Sussex, Girton) 1961–68; called to the Bar Gray's Inn 1961 (bencher 1987), practised Fountain Court, QC 1980, judge of the High Court of Justice (Queen's Bench Div) 1988–96, presiding judge Northern Circuit 1991–94, judge in charge Commercial Ct 1994–95, a Lord Justice of Appeal 1996–, pres Family Div and head of family justice 2005–; chm: Bar Public Affrs Ctee 1987, Lord Chancellor's Advsy Ctee on Legal Educn and Conduct 1998–99, Legal Services Consultancy Panel 2000–05; vice-chm: Cncl of Legal Educn 1989–91, Advsy Ctee Lord Chllr's Civil Justice Review 1985–88; hon fell: Gonville & Caius Coll Cambridge 1998–, KCL 2005–; tstee Somerset House Tst; *Recreations* family, sporting; *Clubs* Garrick, Saintsbury, St Enedoc Golf; *Style*— The Rt Hon Sir Mark Potter; ✉ Royal Courts of Justice, Strand, London WC2 (tel 020 7947 6084)

POTTER, Michael Nicholas; s of Alan Edward Potter, of Reigate, Surrey, and Evelyn, *née* Leigh; *b* 17 October 1949; *Educ* Royal GS Guildford, Univ of London (BSc); *m* 1973, Janet Nyasa, da of late Jeffrey Arthur Griffiths; 1 s (Tom b 1977), 2 da (Lillie b 1979, Chloe b 1981); *Career* joined Haymarket Publishing 1971–83 (publishing dir Campaign and Marketing), fndr and chief exec Redwood Publishing 1983–2003; launched over 40 magazines incl: BBC Top Gear, M & S Magazine, BBC Good Food, Boots Health and Beauty; fndr and exec chm Seven Publishing 2003– (publisher of delicious and Sainsbury's Magazine) and Seven Squared 2007–; non-exec dir 4imprint 2001–03; past chm and Cncl memb Mktg Gp of GB; fndr memb and past chm Assoc of Publishing Agencies, dir Periodicals Publishers Assoc 1995–2004; memb: Devpt Bd Prince's Tst 2003–05, Business Advsy Gp Surrey CCC, Prince's Tst Trading Bd 1999–2007, Devpt Bd Nat Portrait Gall 1999–2007, Devpt Bd Royal Court Theatre 1999–2007, Fundraising and Marketing Ctee Cancer Res UK 2007–; grad memb CIM; FRSA; *Awards* Publishing Company of the Year 1990, Magazine of the Year PPA Awards 1994, 1996, 1997 and 1998, Marcus Morris Award for Outstanding Contrib to Magazine Industry 1998; *Recreations* motor sport, cars (new and old), opera, cricket, travel, theatre; *Clubs* Groucho, Bentley Drivers, Porsche (GB); *Style*— Michael Potter, Esq; ✉ Seven Publishing, Sea Containers House, 20 Upper Ground, London SE1 9PD (tel 020 7775 7775, fax 020 7401 9423, e-mail mpotter@7publishing.co.uk)

POTTERTON, Homan; s of Thomas Edward Potterton (d 1960), and Eileen, *née* Tong (d 1990); *b* 9 May 1946; *Educ* Kilkenny Coll, Trinity Coll Dublin (BA, MA), Univ of Edinburgh (Dip History of Art); *Career* cataloguer Nat Gallery of Ireland 1971–73, asst keeper Nat Gallery London 1974–80, dir Nat Gallery of Ireland 1980–88, ed Irish Arts Review 1993–2001 (publisher 2000–01); contrib: Burlington Magazine, Apollo, Connoisseur, Country Life, Financial Times; FSA, HRHA; *Books* Irish Church Monuments 1570–1880 (1975), A Guide to the National Gallery (1976), The National Gallery, London (1977), Reynolds and Gainsborough - Themes and Painters in the National Gallery (1976), Pageant and Panorama - The Elegant World of Canaletto (1978), Irish Art and Architecture (with Peter Harbison and Jeanne Sheehy, 1978, reissued 1993), Venetian Seventeenth Century Painting (1979), Dutch Seventeenth and Eighteenth Century Paintings in the National Gallery of Ireland - a complete catalogue (1986) The Golden Age of Dutch Paintings from the National Gallery of Ireland (exhibition catalogue, 1986), Rathcormick: A Childhood Recalled (2001), Potterton People and Places: Three Centuries of an Irish Family (2006); *Clubs* St Stephens's Green (Dublin), Royal Over-Seas League; *Style*— Homan Potterton, Esq; ✉ e-mail hpotterton@free.fr; Colombel Bas, 81140 Castelnau-de-Montmiral, France (tel and fax 00 33 5 63 40 53 52, website www.potterton.ie)

POTTINGER, Frank; *b* 1932; *Educ* Edinburgh Coll of Art (DA); *Career* artist and sculptor; engrg apprenticeship 1948–53; art teacher 1965–73, lectr in art Aberdeen Coll of Educn 1973–85, visiting lectr Aberdeen, Dundee, Glasgow and Edinburgh Colls of Art 1982–90, pt/t lectr Edinburgh Coll of Art 1990–93; chm Scottish Sculpture Workshop 1980–90; RSA 1991; *Exhibitions* 57 Gallery 1965, Richard Demarco Gallery 1971, Peterloo Gallery 1975, Compass Gallery 1976, Yorkshire Sculpture Park 1979 and 1984, Scottish Sculpture Workshop 1981, 1983, 1987, 1991 and 1993, Scottish Sculpture Trust 1982, Fruitmarket Gallery 1983, Aberdeen Art Gallery 1983, Camden Arts Centre 1983, Pier Art Centre 1984, Hands Off (Crawford Arts Centre) 1985, Sculptors' Drawings (Scottish Arts Cncl) 1985, Peacock Ten 1985, Landscapes (Open Eye Gallery) 1987, Kingfisher Gallery 1988, Twin City (Aberdeen and Regensburg) 1988, Waverley Taylor Gallery 1989, Decorated Ceramics (Open Eye Gallery) 1989, Inverclyde Print Biennial 1989, Scottish Sculpture Now (Aberdeen Art Gallery) 1989, 21 Years of Contemporary Art (Compass Gallery) 1990, Ceramic Sculpture (Open Eye Gallery) 1990, Haldane Connections (Glasgow Sch of Art) 1990, Scottish Art in the 20th Century (Royal West of England Acad) 1991, Shoebox Sculpture Exhbn (Univ of Hawaii) 1993, The Rock Drill and Beyond 1999, Harlech Print Open 2000, RSA William Gillies Travel Award Lithuania 2002, Glasgow Art Fair 2003; *Work in Collections* Hunterian Gallery, Univ of Dundee, Paisley Museum Gallery, Scottish Arts Cncl, IBM, Leeds Educn Authy, Royal Mail, Heriot-Watt Univ, LASMO plc, The Woodland Tst, Western Isles Health Bd, Scottish Parliament; *Awards* Scottish Arts Cncl 1978, William J Macaulay Prize RSA 1979, SAC Sculpture Conf Oakland CA 1982, IBM Award Soc of Scottish Artists 1986, Mobil North Sea Award Scottish Sculpture Workshop 1991, William Gillies Travel Award 2002; *Style*— Frank Pottinger, Esq, RSA; ✉ 30/5 Elbe Street, Edinburgh EH6 7HW (tel 0131 553 5082)

POTTS, David Tom; s of Tom Potts (d 1989), and Enid Elizabeth Potts (d 1964); *b* 18 March 1957, Manchester; *Educ* Hartshead Co Secdy Sch Ashton-under-Lyne; *m* Rosanne, da of George Hunt, and Lorna Hunt; 2 s (Daniel Edward Tom b 20 May 1986, George David b 4 July 1989); *Career* Tesco plc: joined as gen asst Manchester 1973, store mangr Ryde IOW 1981, dir London 1989, ceo NI and I 1994, plc bd dir 1998–, dir i/c UK ops 2000–; visiting prof Univ of Ulster; *Recreations* golf, football, squash; *Clubs* Hanbury Manor Golf, Manchester City FC, Seaviews Port, Royal Acad; *Style*— David Potts, Esq; ✉ Tesco plc, Tesco House, Delamare Road, Cheshunt, Hertfordshire EN8 9BA (tel 01992 646495, fax 01992 644651, e-mail david.potts@tesco.com)

POTTS, James Richardson; OBE (1998); s of James Kenneth Potts (d 1973), of Somerset, and Nina Kathleen, *née* Hayman; *b* 13 November 1944; *Educ* King's Sch Bruton, Wadham Coll Oxford (MA), Univ of London (PGCE), Univ of Bristol (postgrad cert in film and drama); *m* 13 Aug 1969, Maria, *née* Strani; 1 da (Nina-Maria Penelope b 30 Sept 1972), 1 s (Alexander James Kenneth b 11 June 1976); *Career* British Council: English language teacher and educnl TV and radio prodr 1969–71, TV prodr Addis Ababa 1971–75, TV and film prodr Nairobi 1975–77, educnl TV/technol conslt London 1977–80, regnl dir N Greece 1980–85, cultural attaché Prague 1986–89, head East and Central Europe Dept and dep dir Europe Div London 1990–92, dir Aust 1993–; *Recreations* film-making, poetry, blues guitar, walking and watersports, foreign cultures and literatures; *Style*— James Potts, Esq, OBE

POTTS, James Richardson (Jim); OBE (1998); s of James Kenneth Potts (d 1973), and Nina Kathleen, *née* Hayman (d 2001); *b* 13 November 1944; *Educ* King's Sch Bruton, Wadham Coll Oxford (MA), Inst of Educn Univ of London (PGCE), Univ of Bristol (Postgrad Cert); *m* Aug 1969, Maria, *née* Strani; 1 s (Alexander James Kenneth), 1 da (Nina-Maria (Mrs David Rennie)); *Career* Br Cncl: film and TV prodr Ethiopia 1971–75, film and TV prodr Kenya 1975–77, media conslt and ed Educnl Broadcasting Int 1977–80, regnl dir Northern Greece 1980–85, dir Czechoslovakia 1986–89 (concurrently cultural attaché), head E and Central Europe Dept London 1990–93, dir Aust 1993–99, dir Sweden 2000–04 (concurrently cultural attaché); co-fndr Living Arts Exchange; cultural relations advsr and arts project mangr 2004–; academic dir Durrell Sch of Corfu 2007–; 3 documentary films, many educnl films overseas and 2 Blues CDs; *Publications* Literary Links, Australia and Britain (preface, 1997), Swedish Reflections, From Beowulf to Bergman (co-ed, 2003), Corfu Blues (2006); numerous jl and magazine articles on poetry, media and film; *Recreations* Greek islands and walking in Epirus, blues music, poetry, visual arts and photography; *Clubs* Royal Over-Seas League, Corfu Reading Soc, Friends of Mt Athos, William Barnes Soc; *Style*— Jim Potts, Esq, OBE; ✉ PO Box 380, Corfu 49100, Greece (tel 00 30 26610 22939, e-mail jimipotts@hotmail.com)

POTTS, Michael Stuart; DL (Merseyside 2000); s of late Thomas Edmund Potts, ERD, of Bray on Thames, Berks, and late Phyllis Margaret, *née* Gebbie; *b* 2 September 1938; *Educ* Hilton Coll South Africa, Repton; *m* 23 May 1964, Virginia May Lindsay, da of late Gp Capt Hugh Whittall Marlow, OBE, AFC, of Cape Town, South Africa; 3 s (Andrew b 1966, Alexander b 1968, Rupert b 1970); *Career* chartered accountant; ptnr Coopers & Lybrand: Ireland 1968–70, UK 1970–92 (sr ptnr Liverpool Office 1971–92); dir: H J Uren & Sons Ltd 1993–2003, W O & J Wilson Ltd 1994–; pres North West Cancer Research Fund 2002– (chm 1993–2002); dir: Mersey Regnl Ambulance Service (NHS Tst) 1993–99, Grosvenor Grain & Feed Co Ltd 1999–2004, Universities Superannuation Scheme Ltd 1999–2007; pres Liverpool Soc of Chartered Accountants 1982–83; memb Cncl: Merseyside C of C and Industry 1974–92 (hon treas 1974–82), Univ of Liverpool 1979–89 and 1993–2006 (dep treas 1986–89, hon treas 1993–99, pres 1999–2004, pro-chllr 2004–06), ICAEW 1988–92; High Sheriff of Merseyside 2006; Liveryman: Worshipful Co of Clockmakers, Worshipful Co of Chartered Accountants; FRSA 2001, FCA; *Publications* Potts of Leeds: Five Generations of Clockmakers (2006); *Recreations* sailing, golf, motoring, horology; *Clubs* Dee Sailing (Cdre 1979–80), Royal Liverpool Golf (treas 1992–96), Aston Martin Owners', Antiquarian Horological Soc; *Style*— Michael Potts, Esq, DL; ✉ Brooke House, The Parade, Parkgate, South Wirral, Cheshire CH64 6RN (tel 0151 336 1494, office tel and fax 0151 353 0701, e-mail mspotts@pottsclocks.co.uk)

POTTS, Paul John; s of Michael Henry Potts (d 1960), of Sheffield, and Sylvia Brenda Potts; *b* 21 January 1950; *Educ* Worksop Coll; *m* 1, 1976 (m dis 1994), Gabrielle Jane Fagan; 1 s, 2 da; m 2, 1994, Judith Anne Fielding; *Career* gen reporter Sheffield Star 1968–74, lobby corr Yorkshire Post 1974–78; gen reporter: Daily Telegraph 1978–81, Mail on Sunday 1981–82; political ed News of the World 1982–86, dep ed The Express 1988–95 (political then asst ed 1986–88), chief exec Press Association 2000– (ed-in-chief 1995–); chm Bd of Dirs Canada Newswire 2003–, memb Nominations Ctee Reuters Founders Share Co Ltd; Hon DLitt Univ of Sheffield 2002; *Recreations* all sports, horse racing; *Style*— Paul Potts, Esq; ✉ The Press Association, 292 Vauxhall Bridge Road, London SW1V 1AE (tel 020 7963 7000)

POTTS, Robin; QC (1982); s of Flt Lt William Potts (d 1971), and Elaine Muriel, *née* Winkle (d 1958); *b* 2 July 1944; *Educ* Wolstanton GS, Magdalen Coll Oxford (BA, BCL); *m* 1 (m dis 1982), Eva Rebeca, *née* Giwercer; 1 s (James Rupert b 1970); m 2, 8 March 1985, Helen Elizabeth, da of Neville Duncan Sharp, of IOW; 2 s (Timothy Edward b 1986, Christopher William b 1988), 1 da (Emma Clare b 1990); *Career* called to the Bar Gray's Inn 1968 (bencher 1993); conslt ed Gore-Browne on Cos; *Recreations* gardening, reading, wine; *Style*— Robin Potts, Esq, QC; ✉ The Grange, Church Lane, Pinner, Middlesex HA5 3AB

POULTER, John; *Educ* Berkhamsted Sch, Queen's Coll Oxford (open scholar, MA); *Career* sales mangr Telsec Instruments 1965–67, sales mangr Cambridge Instruments 1967–72, industrial exec Wm Brandts 1972–73, mktg and sales dir Cambridge Instruments 1973–77, gen mangr Robinsons 1977–81, md Vokes Ltd 1981–88; Spectris plc (formerly Fairey Gp plc): chief exec 1988–2001, non-exec chm 2001–; non-exec chm: Kymata Ltd 1998–2001, Wyko Gp Ltd 2001–04, Snell and Wilcox Ltd 2002–, Filtronic plc 2006–; non-exec dir: Crest Packaging plc 1993–96, BTP plc 1996–2000, Lloyds Smaller Companies Investment Tst plc 1992–2002, Kidde plc 2000–05 (chair Remuneration Ctee), Smaller Companies Value Tst plc 2002–, RAC plc 2002–05 (chair Remuneration Ctee), London Metal Exchange Ltd 2002–05, Macquarie European Infrastructure plc 2003–05, Suffolk Life plc 2006–; *Style*— John Poulter, Esq; ✉ Spectris plc, Station Road, Egham, Surrey TW20 9NP

POULTER, Prof Leonard William (Len); s of Leonard Frederick George Poulter (d 1986), and Florence May, *née* Brown; *b* 26 February 1944; *Educ* Tottenham GS, Univ of London (MPhil, PhD, DSc); *m* Jean Margaret, *née* Carr; 2 da (Lara Ann b 6 July 1969, Shelley Jane b 26 May 1972); *Career* research asst Inst of Basic Med Sci London 1970–76, asst prof Trudeau Inst Saranac Lake NY 1976–81; Royal Free Hosp Sch of Med: lectr 1981–84, sr lectr 1984–90, reader 1991–95, prof and chm of div 1996–, head Dept of Immunology 1997–2003; Connolly Hosp Dublin: scientific dir Asthma Research Centre 1991–2003, prog dir Dept of Respiratory Medicine 2004–; dir Biomedical Consultancy Co 2003–; memb: Br Soc of Immunology, Br Thoracic Soc, Euro Respiratory Soc; FRCPath 1992 (MRCPath 1980), FRCPI 1996; *Publications* author of over 200 publications on immunology of inflammatory disease with special emphasis on chronic infection and lung disease, particularly asthma; *Recreations* playing guitar, photography, enjoying my grandchildren; *Style*— Prof Len Poulter; ✉ LWP Research Associates, Saranac Lodge, Morris Walk, Wyboston, Bedfordshire MA44 3AU (tel 01480 211470, e-mail consults@lwpresearch.com)

POUND, Sir John David; 5 Bt (UK 1905), of Stanmore, Co Middlesex; s of Sir Derek Allen Pound, 4 Bt (d 1980); Sir John Pound, 1 Bt, was head of the firm John Pound & Co, Portmanteau Manufacturers, and Lord Mayor of London 1904–05; *b* 1 November 1946; *Educ* Burebank Sch Aylsham; *m* 1, 20 July 1968 (m dis 1978), Heather Frances O'Brien, o da of Harry Jackson Dean (d 2001); 1 s (Robert John b 1973); m 2, 1978, Penelope Ann, da of Grahame Arthur Rayden (d 1997); 2 s (Christopher James b 1982, Nicholas Edward b 1986); *Heir* s, Robert Pound; *Career* account dir Computer Software; *Style*— Sir John Pound, Bt; ✉ 5 The Croft Way, West Pennant Hills, NWA 2125, Australia

POUND, Stephen Pelham; MP; s of Pelham Pound, and Dominica, *née* James; *b* 3 July 1948; *Educ* Hertford GS, LSE (Dip Industrial Relations, BSc, pres Union); *m* 1976, Maggie, da of Lyndon Griffiths; 1 da (Emily Frances b 1988), 1 s (Pelham Joseph b 1990); *Career* seaman 1965–66, bus conductor 1966–68, bookseller's clerk 1969–70, hospital porter 1971–79, student LSE 1979–84, housing offr 1984–97; MP (Lab) Ealing N 1997–; cncllr Ealing 1982–, mayor of Ealing 1995–96; *Recreations* watching football, playing cricket, collecting comics and listening to jazz; *Clubs* St Joseph's Catholic Social, Fulham FC Supporters'; *Style*— Stephen Pound, Esq, MP; ✉ House of Commons, London SW1A 0AA (tel 020 7219 1140, fax 020 7219 5982, e-mail stevepoundmp@parliament.uk)

POUNDER, Prof Derrick John; s of Wilfred Pounder, of Pen-y-coedcae, Mid Glamorgan, and Lilian, *née* Jones; *b* 25 February 1949; *Educ* Pontypridd Boys GS, Univ of Birmingham (MB, ChB); *m* 28 Nov 1975, Georgina, da of Patrick Kelly, of Tullamore, Co Offaly; 2 da (Sibéal b 30 March 1985, Sinéad b 9 Sept 1991), 1 s (Emlyn b 18 May 1989); *Career* lectr then sr lectr in forensic pathology Univ of Adelaide, dep chief med examiner Edmonton Alberta and assoc prof Univs of Alberta and Calgary 1985–87, prof of forensic med Univ of Dundee 1987–; consltg expert to UN, OSCE and Cncl of Europe; memb SNP; past chm Physicians for Human Rights, memb Bd of Govrs UN Vol Fund for Victims of Torture; Freeman Llantrisant; FRCPA, FFPathRCPI, FCAP, FRCPath, FHKCPath, FFFLM (RCP); *Recreations* photography, medieval architecture, almost-lost causes; *Style*— Prof Derrick Pounder; ✉ Centre for Forensic and Legal Medicine, University of Dundee, Dundee DD1 4HN (tel 01382 388020, fax 01382 348021, e-mail d.j.pounder@dundee.ac.uk)

POUNDER, Prof Robert Edward (Roy); *b* 31 May 1944; *Educ* Eltham Coll, Peterhouse Cambridge (state scholar, exhibitioner, sr scholar, MA, Prize in Natural Sciences (twice), Prize in Med (twice)), Guy's Hosp Med Sch London (clinical entrance scholar), Univ of Cambridge (BChir, MB, MD), Univ of London (DSc); *m* Prof Christine A Lee, *qv*; 2 s (Jeremy, Tom); *Career* house physician Guy's Hosp London 1969–70, house surgn Addenbrooke's Hosp Cambridge 1970, SHO (med) Hammersmith Hosp London 1971, SHO (cardiology) Brompton Hosp London 1971–72, registrar then sr registrar (gen med, gastroenterology and diabetes) Central Middx Hosp 1972–76, sr registrar (gen med) St Thomas' Hosp London 1976–80 (locum conslt physician 1977–78), hon conslt physician Royal Free Hosp London 1980–2005; Royal Free Hosp Sch of Med (later Royal Free and UC Med Sch UCL): sr lectr in med 1980–85, reader in med 1985–92, clinical sub-dean 1986–88, prof of med 1992–2005, dir Centre for Gastroenterology (jtly with Dept of Med UCL Med Sch) 1994–2002, vice-head Dept of Med 1995–2005, pres SCR 1996–2002; assoc med dir Gray's Inn Div Royal Free Hampstead NHS Tst 1992–96, memb Exec Ctee Royal Free Hampstead NHS Tst 1994–96, non-exec memb Bd Camden and Islington HA 1996–2002; scientific sec VIII European Helicobacter pylori Study Gp Meeting Edinburgh 1993–95; delivered numerous invited and plenary lectures in UK and overseas; clinical vice-pres RCP 2002–04 (memb Cncl 1987–89 and 1997–2000, assoc int dir for Australasia and Far East 2004–), chm of tstees Alimentary Pharmacology and Therapeutics Tst 1988–99; memb Cncl Br Digestive Fndn 1987–98 (chm Bd of Tstees 1997–98); founding ed Alimentary Pharmacology and Therapeutics 1987–, founding ed-in-chief GastroHep.com 2000–, int advsr Chinese Jl of Gastroenterology, scientific reviewer for learned jls, memb Ctee Med Writers Gp Soc of Authors 1998–2002, memb European Assoc of Science Eds; sec Prout Club; memb: Friends of Peterhouse (sometime chm Cncl), 1942 Club, Wilks XV, Sir Arthur Hurst Dining Club; govr St Paul's Sch 2001– (dep chm 2007–); fell: Fellowship of Postgrad Med, Med Soc of London, American Coll of Gastroenterology (memb Int Ctee); memb: BMA, Br Soc of Gastroenterology (hon sec 1982–86, memb Cncl 1996–99), American Gastroenterological Assoc, European Assoc for Gastroenterology and Endoscopy; FRCP 1984 (MRCP 1971); *Books* Long Cases in General Medicine (ed, 1983, 2 edn 1988), Doctor, There's Something Wrong with my Guts (ed, 1983), Recent Advances in Gastroenterology (ed vols 6–10, 1986–94, biennial), Diseases of the Gut and Pancreas (jt ed, 1987, 2 edn 1994), Advanced Medicine 23 (jt ed, 1987), The British Society of Gastroenterology 1937–1987: A Collection of Scientific Papers (ed, 1987), Classic Papers in Peptic Ulcer (conslt ed, 1988), A Colour Atlas of the Digestive System (jtly, 1989), Landmark Papers: The Histamine H2-Receptor Antagonists (ed, 1990), European Word Book of Gastroenterology (jt ed, 1994), Bockus Gastroenterology (section ed, 1994), Current Diagnosis and Treatment (jt ed, 1996), Inflammatory Bowel Disease (jtly, 1998); *Clubs* Garrick; *Style*— Prof Roy Pounder; ✉ Centre for Gastroenterology, Department of Medicine, Royal Free and University College Medical School, Rowland Hill Street, London NW3 2PF (tel 020 7830 2243, fax 01285 644126, e-mail roy.pounder@rcplondon.ac.uk)

POUNDS, Prof Kenneth Alwyne (Ken); CBE (1984); s of Harry Pounds (d 1976), and Dorothy Louise, *née* Hunt (d 1981); *b* 17 November 1934; *Educ* Salt Sch Shipley, UCL (BSc, PhD); *m* 1, 29 Dec 1961, Margaret Mary (d 1976), da of Patrick O'Connell (d 1969); 2 s (David Edwin b 12 May 1963, John Michael b 13 April 1966), 1 da (Jillian Barbara b 12 June 1964); m 2, 10 Dec 1982, Joan Mary, da of Samuel Millit (d 1983); 1 s (Michael Andrew b 5 Aug 1983), 1 da (Jennifer Anne b 22 Feb 1987); *Career* Univ of Leicester: asst lectr 1960, lectr 1962, dir X-Ray Astronomy Gp 1969–94, reader in physics 1971, prof of space physics 1973–, head of physics 1986–93 and 1998–2002; chief exec Particle Physics and Astronomy Res Cncl 1994–98; author of over 250 publications worldwide; playing memb Kibworth CC; fndr memb BNSC Mgmnt Bd; memb Cncl: SERC (chm Astronomy, Space and Radio Bd 1980–84), Royal Soc 1986–87; pres Royal Astronomical Soc 1990–92; Hon DUniv York 1984; Hon DSc: Loughborough Univ 1992, Sheffield Hallam Univ 1997, Univ of Warwick 2001, Univ of Leicester 2005; FRS 1981; *Recreations* cricket, football, music; *Style*— Prof Ken Pounds, CBE, FRS; ✉ 12 Swale Close, Oadby, Leicestershire (tel 0116 271 9370); University of Leicester, Leicester LE1 7RH (tel 0116 252 3509, fax 0116 252 3311, e-mail kap@star.le.ac.uk)

POUNTAIN, Christopher Charles; s of Charles Alfred Pountain, of Edinburgh, and Jean Mary, *née* Stanfield; *b* 4 May 1953; *Educ* Royal High Sch Edinburgh, Univ of St Andrews (BSc); *m* 29 July 1988, Joyce Margaret, da of William Thomson, of Balrownie, nr Brechin; 2 s (Andrew William, David Charles); *Career* actuary student Scottish Widows Fund 1975–79, insurance analyst Wood Mackenzie 1979 (dir 1985, merger with County NatWest 1988), London Office County NatWest 1988, Morgan Stanley International 1989, corp fin and planning mangr rising to general mangr international CGU plc 1992–; FFA 1978; *Recreations* hill walking, skiing, cinema going, reading; *Style*— Christopher Pountain, Esq; ✉ CGU plc, St Helen's, 1 Undershaft, London EC3P 3DQ (tel 020 7662 2006)

POUNTNEY, David Willoughby; CBE (1994); s of Edward Willoughby Pountney (d 1997), and Dorothy Lucy, *née* Byrt (d 1984); *b* 10 September 1947; *Educ* St John's Coll Choir Sch Cambridge, Radley, St John's Coll Cambridge (MA); *m* 23 Feb 1980, Jane Rosemary, da of Maj James Emrys Williams (d 1978); 1 da (Emilia b 1981), 1 s (James b 1984); *Career* dir of productions: Scottish Opera 1976–80, ENO 1983–93; dir of operas in: Ireland, Holland, Germany, Italy, Aust and USA, all maj Br cos; princ productions incl: Janácek cycle (Scot Opera, WNO), Bussoni's Dr Faust (ENO, Deutsche Oper), The Lady Macbeth of Mtensk (ENO), Hänsel and Gretel (ENO, Evening Standard Award), Wozzeck, Pelleas et Mélisande, world première of Philip Glass' The Voyage (Met Opera NY) 1992, Moses und Aron (Bayerische Staatsoper) 2006, Die Soldaten (Ruhr Triennale) 2006, Khovanschina (WNO) 2007, La Juive (Zurich) 2007, La Forza del Destino (Vienna Staatsoper) 2008; translated numerous operas from Czech, Russian, German and Italian and original libretti for Steven Oliver, Sir Peter Maxwell Davies and John Harle; dir for Nottingham Playhouse: Twelfth Night, As You Like It; Intendant Bregenzer Festspiele 2003–; Chevalier de l'Ordre des Arts et des Lettres (France); *Recreations* croquet, cooking, gardening; *Clubs* Garrick; *Style*— David Pountney, Esq, CBE

POVEY, Sir Keith; kt (2001), QPM (1991); s of Trevor Roberts Povey (d 1983), and Dorothy, *née* Parsonnage (d 1965); *b* 30 April 1943; *Educ* Abbeydale GS Sheffield, Univ of Sheffield (Bramshill scholar, BA); *m* 1964, Carol Ann, da of late Albert Harvey; 2 da (Allyson Patricia b 11 Sept 1965, Louise Ann b 23 Feb 1970); *Career* Sheffield City Police 1961–84; posts incl: cadet 1961, constable 1962, chief inspr HM Inspector of Constabulary NE Region 1981–82 (memb Secretariat Home Office Enquiry into Yorkshire Ripper case), FBI Academy USA 1982, supt and sub-divnl cdr Sheffield City Centre 1982–84 (ground cdr for policing during miners' dispute at Orgreave Coking Plant); staff offr HM Chief Inspector of Constabulary Home Office 1984–86 (reported on Zimbabwe Republic Police 1984), asst chief constable Humberside 1986–90, deputy chief constable Northants 1990–93, chief constable Leicestershire Constabulary 1993–97, HM Inspector of Constabulary 1997–2001, HM Chief Inspector of Constabulary 2002–05; ACPO: chm General Purposes Ctee, chm Crime Prevention Sub-Ctee, head Working Gp on Police Patrol, rep Home Office Working Party on Special Constabulary; *Recreations* jogging, flying; *Style*— Sir Keith Povey, QPM

POVEY, Robert Frederick Donald; s of Donald James Frederick Povey (d 1987), and Ellen Lillian, *née* Nye (d 1987); *b* 8 July 1944; *Educ* Strand GS, Brixton Sch of Bldg; *m* 1, 23 March 1966 (m dis 1970), Pauline, da of Ernest John Wise; m 2, 22 June 1974 (m dis 1996), Karen Moira, da of late Arthur Reginald Whitfield; m 3, 16 Nov 1996, Lynda, da of late Lester Harvey; *Career* engr; conslt Mitchell McFarlane and Ptnrs; formerly chm Surrey Branch of Inst of Structural Engrs, memb ctees of SCI producing pubns for structural engrs; FIStructE; *Recreations* bowls, IT; *Style*— Robert Povey, Esq

POWELL, Anthony; s of Arthur Lawrence Powell (d 1939), of Manchester, and Alice, *née* Woodhead; *b* 2 June 1935; *Educ* William Hulmes GS Manchester, St Andrew's Coll Dublin, Central Sch of Arts and Crafts London; *Career* costume and set designer for theatre and film; served Royal Corps of Signals (Br Army occupation of the Rhine) 1953–55; asst to Sir Cecil Beaton and Oliver Messel; lectr in theatre design Central Sch of Art and Design 1958–71, RSA scholar 1958, freelance design conslt Sabre Sportwear and Jantzen Swimwear 1960–69, Br Colour Cncl 1965–67, numerous building interior designs incl Sutton Place 1981–83; Agatha Christie and Archeology Exhbn (Essen, Vienna, Basle, Berlin and Br Museum London) 2001–02; numerous books written about him and his work; RDI 1999; Hon FRCA 1997, hon fell London Inst (now Univ of the Arts London) 2002; Hon DDes Univ of Greenwich 2003; *Theatre* Women Beware Women (RSC) 1961, School for Scandal (Haymarket and NY) 1961, Comedy of Errors (RSC and world tour) 1963, The Rivals (Haymarket) 1966, Fish Out of Water (London) 1971, Private Lives (London, NY, USA tour) 1972, Ring Round the Moon (Ahmanson Theatre LA) 1975, Amadeus (Paris) 1981, Lettice and Lovage (costumes for Maggie Smith, NY) 1990, Hay Fever (London and provincial tour) 1992, Trelawny of the Wells (RNT) 1992, Sunset Boulevard (London/LA 1993, Broadway 1994, Frankfurt/Toronto 1995, Aust and US tour 1996), Tom Sawyer (musical, Broadway) 2001, Cole Porter's Anything Goes (RNT and Theatre Royal) 2002–03, Hedda Gabler (Théâtre Marigny Paris) 2003; *Opera* Rinaldo (Sadlers Wells Opera and Komische Oper Berlin) 1960, La Belle Hélène (Sadlers Wells Opera) 1962, Il Seraglio (Sadlers Wells Opera) 1962, Capriccio (Glyndebourne Festival Opera) 1965, Martins Lie (for US TV) 1965, Capriccio (Paris Opera) 2004; *Films* Royal Hunt of the Sun 1968, Joe Egg 1969, A Town Called Bastard 1970, Nicholas and Alexandra 1971, Travels with my Aunt 1972, Papillon 1973, That Lucky Touch 1974, Buffalo Bill and the Indians 1975, Sorcerer 1976, Death on the Nile 1977, Tess 1978–79, Priest of Love 1980, Evil Under the Sun 1981, Indiana Jones and the Temple of Doom 1983, Pirates 1984–85, Ishtar 1985–86, Nostromo (preparation) 1986–87 and 1989, Frantic 1987, Indiana Jones and the Last Crusade 1988, Hook 1990–91, Walt Disney's 101 Dalmatians (costumes for Glenn Close) 1996, The Avengers 1997, The Ninth Gate 1998, Walt Disney's 102 Dalmations 1999; *Awards* for Best Costume Design incl: Tony Award for School for Scandal 1963, US Academy Award for Travels with my Aunt 1973, LA Drama Critics' Circle Awards (sets and costumes) for Ring Around the Moon 1975, Br and US Academy Awards for Death on the Nile 1979, US Academy Award for Tess 1981, César Award (France) for Pirates 1987, Drama-logue Critics Award and LA Drama Critics' Circle Award for Sunset Boulevard 1993; US Academy Award nominations for: Pirates 1987, Hook 1992, 102 Dalmations 2001; Career Achievement Award (Costume Designers' Guild Hollywood) 2000, Irene Sharaff Lifetime Achievement Award (Theatre Devpt Fund NY) 2004; *Recreations* music, gardening, collecting, laughing; *Style*— Anthony Powell, Esq; ✉ c/o Andrew S P Glynne, Glynnes Solicitors, Empire House, 175 Piccadilly, London W1V 9DB (tel 020 7486 3166, fax 020 7486 2164, e-mail solicitors@glynnes.co.uk)

POWELL, Ashley Craig; s of Anthony and Sandra Powell; *b* 13 February 1962; *Educ* Whitefield Comp; *m* 15 June 1997 Marcia Estelle, da of Gerald Altman (d 1999); *Career* professional toastmaster; sr dep pres Guild of Int Professional Toastmasters; vice-chm Br Professional Toastmasters Authy, vice-chm Toastmasters for Royal Occasions; dep princ: Ivor Spencer Sch for Professional Toastmasters, Ivor Spencer Int Sch for Butler Administrators/Personal Assistants; sr conslt Guild of Professional After Dinner Speakers; assoc Guild of Int Butler Administrators/Personal Assistants, assoc LAMDA; memb Guild of Int Professional Toastmasters 1990– (Toastmaster of Year 2001); *Recreations* after dinner speaking, organising special events; *Style*— Ashley Powell, Esq; ✉ 9 Lancaster House, Park Lane, Stanmore, Middlesex HA7 3HD (tel 020 8385 7644, mobile 07956 214631)

POWELL, (John) Christopher; s of Air Vice-Marshal John Frederick Powell, OBE, AE, and Geraldine Ysolda, *née* Moylan; bro of Baron Powell of Bayswater, KCMG (Life Peer), and Jonathan Nicholas Powell, *qqv*; *b* 4 October 1943; *Educ* Canterbury Cathedral Choir Sch, St Peter's Sch York, LSE (BSc); *m* 1973, Rosemary Jeanne, da of Ralph Symmons; 2 s (Ben b 1974, Jamie b 1977), 1 da (Lucy b 1980); *Career* account mgmnt trainee Hobson Bates 1965–67, account mangr Wasey's 1967–69; BMP DDB: joined as ptnr and shareholder 1969, jt md 1975–86, chief exec 1986–98, chm 1999–2003; non-exec dir:

P

Riverside Studios 1989–, United News and Media plc 1995–2006, Britain in Europe 2005–, Dr Foster LLP 2006–; memb Corporate Finance Advsy Bd PricewaterhouseCoopers 2005–; pres IPA 1993–95; chm: IPPR 2001– (tstee 1999–), NESTA 2003–; dep chm Public Diplomacy Bd 2006–; dep chm Riverside Community NHS Tst 1994–2000, chm Ealing and Hounslow HA 2000–02; tstee Divert 2000–02; hon advsr Bd of Int Family Health 1997–2004; *Recreations* riding, tennis, gardening, theatre; *Style*— Christopher Powell, Esq

POWELL, David Beynon; s of David Eynon Powell (d 1942), and Catherine Ada, *née* Beynon (d 1997); *b* 9 February 1934; *Educ* Gowerton GS, Christ's Coll Cambridge (MA, LLB), Yale Law Sch (LLM), Harvard Business Sch (SMP18); *m* 1, 1973 (m dis), Pamela Turnbull; *m* 2, 1997, Eeva Coombs; *Career* Nat Serv Flying Offr RAF 1952–54; slr Supreme Court, dep legal advsr BLMC Ltd 1970–73, dir of gp legal servs BL Ltd (British Leyland) 1974–83, gp legal dir Midland Bank plc (now part of HSBC Bank Group plc) 1984–91, dir of gp legal servs Guinness plc (now part of Diageo Group plc) 1992–94, legal advsr PA Consulting Group 1994–96, legal advsr Domino Printing Sciences plc 1996–2000, legal advsr Oxford Professional Training Ltd and dir and legal advsr Oxford Gp Services Ltd 2000–; non-exec dir Ross Gp plc 1995–2000; memb Air Tport Users Cncl 1997–2000; memb Ctee Oxfordshire Branch Cambridge Soc 2004–; *Recreations* reading, music, tennis, travel; *Style*— David Powell, Esq; ✉ 4 The Covert, Woodstock, Oxfordshire OX20 1UU (tel 01993 811567, e-mail david.b.powell@btinternet.com)

POWELL, David (Dick); s of Arthur Barrington Powell, CMG, of Pwllmeyni, Gwent, and Jane, *née* Weir; *Educ* Ampleforth, Manchester Poly (DipAD), RCA (MDesRCA, Burton award 1975 and 1976); *m* (Jennifer) Lucy, da of Peter Talbot Willcox; 1 da (Jemma b 25 July 1980), 3 s (Oscar b 1 Sept 1983, Freddie b 24 Feb 1985, Gus b 5 Dec 1992); *Career* product designer; co-fndr CAPA Partnership 1976–79, freelance designer 1980–83, fndr (with Prof Richard Seymour, *qv*) Seymour-Powell 1984– (clients incl Nokia, Ford, Aqualisa); memb Design Cncl 1996–, pres elect D&AD 2005; Hon Dr of Fine Arts Center of Creative Studies Detroit 2002; FRSA 1993, FCSD 1993; *Television* contrib BBC Design Classics, Designs on Britain and LWT Design Education series 1986, subject of Channel 4 Designs on Your... series 1998, Better By Design (six part Channel 4 series) 2000, BBC Innovation Nation 2000; *Awards* Best Overall Design and Product Design (for Norton F1 motorcycle) Design Week Awards 1990, D&AD Silver Award (for Technophone Cellular Telephone) 1991, ID Award and D&AD Silver Award (for MuZ Skorpian motorcycle) 1993, winner Product Design category BBC Design Awards 1994, CSD Minerva Award (for MuZ Skorpian) 1994, ID Award (for Sun Voyager) 1994, D&AD President's Award (for outstanding contribution to design) 1995, DBA Design Effectiveness Award 1995, 2002 and 2003, Special Commendation Prince Philip Designers' Prize 1997 (shortlisted 2003), Janus France 1998, Starpack Award 2003, corp film for Samsung European Premium Design 2003, Gerald Frewer Meml Trophy Inst of Engrg Designers 2003; *Books* Presentation Techniques (1985, revised edn 1988, translations in Dutch and Spanish); *Recreations* motorcycles; *Style*— Dick Powell, Esq; ✉ Seymour Powell, 327 Lillie Road, London SW6 7NR (tel 020 7381 6433, fax 020 7381 9081, e-mail design@seymourpowell.com, website www.seymourpowell.com)

POWELL, Gregory; *b* 21 January 1948, Edgware, Middx; *Educ* Birkbeck Coll London (BSc), LSE (LLB); *Career* admitted slr; trainee slr W H Thompson, investigating offr Local Govt Ombudsman, founding ptnr Powell Spencer & Ptnrs Slrs; pres London Criminal Courts Slrs Assoc; Criminal Legal Aid Lawyer of the Year 2004–05; *Style*— Gregory Powell, Esq; ✉ Powell Spencer & Partners, 290 Kilburn High Road, London NW6 2DD (e-mail gregpowell@psplaw.co.uk)

POWELL, (Richard) Guy; s of Richard Albert Brakell Powell (d 1957), and Stella Float, *née* Young (d 1990); *b* 28 April 1927; *Educ* King's Sch Canterbury, Hertford Coll Oxford (MA); *Career* admitted slr 1953; ptnr: Rooper & Whately 1960–70, Lee & Pembertons 1970–92 (conslt 1992–96); in private practice 1996–; clerk Prowdes Educnl Fndn 1974–94 (tstee 1994–, administrative tstee 1994–2007); memb Cncl Private Libraries Assoc 1963–; Freeman City of London 1948, Liveryman Worshipful Co of Drapers 1952; FRSA 1957; memb Vereinigung der Freunde Antiker Kunst (Switzerland) 1960; *Recreations* book collecting, Anglican church music; *Clubs* Oxford and Cambridge, Royal Over-Seas League; *Style*— R Guy Powell, Esq; ✉ Broad Eaves, Hawks Hill Close, Leatherhead, Surrey KT22 9DL (tel 01372 374561)

POWELL, Jeffrey Richard (Jeff); s of Alfred William John Powell, of Canvey Island, Essex, and late Dorothy Faith, *née* Parkin; *b* 21 February 1942; *Educ* Buckhurst Hill Co HS, Regent St Poly; *m* 1 (m dis); 2 da (Natalie Jane b 22 May 1972, Natasha Dawn b 14 April 1974); *m* 2, 20 Feb 1987, Maria del Consuelo Ortiz de Powell, da of Gen Jose Ortiz Avila; 1 s (Jeffrey Jose b 17 March 1988); *Career* Walthamstow Guardian 1959–66 (jr reporter, sports ed); Daily Mail: sports sub ed 1966–69, football reporter 1969–71, chief soccer corr 1971–89, chief sports feature writer 1989–; British Sports Reporter of the Year 1978, 1983 and 1985, British Sports Journalist of the Year 1985, British Sports Feature Writer of the Year 1995, Sports Reporter of the Year British Press Awards 2005, Variety Club Award for Lifetime Achievement in Sports Journalism 2005; memb: Football Writers' Assoc 1969 (chm 1982–83 and 1989–90), Sportswriters' Assoc 1969, Boxing Writers' Club 1999; *Books* Bobby Moore, The Authorised Biography; *Recreations* golf, tennis, theatre, opera, chess; *Clubs* RAC, Tramp, Harris Golf; *Style*— Jeff Powell, Esq; ✉ Daily Mail, Northcliffe House, 2 Derry Street, Kensington, London W8 5TT (tel 020 7938 6229, fax 020 7938 4053, e-mail jeff.powell@dailymail.co.uk)

POWELL, John Lewis; QC (1990); s of Gwyn Powell (d 1981), of Ammanford, Carmarthenshire, and Lilian Mary, *née* Griffiths; *b* 14 September 1950; *Educ* Christ Coll Brecon, Amman Valley GS, Trinity Hall Cambridge (MA, LLB); *m* 1 Sept 1973, Eva Zofia Lomnicka, *qv*, 3 c (Sophie Anna b 14 Feb 1980, Catrin Eva (Katie) b 3 Jan 1982, David John b 3 Feb 1985); *Career* called to the Bar Middle Temple (Harmsworth scholar) 1974, bencher 1998; head of chambers 1997–2000; recorder and dep high ct judge; currently memb chambers 4 New Square 2000–; Parly candidate (Lab) Cardigan 1979; pres Soc of Construction Law 1991–93, chm Law Reform Ctee General Cncl of the Bar 1997–98; memb Chancery Bar Assoc; PNBA; *Books* Encyclopedia of Financial Services Law (with Prof Eva Lomnicka), Professional Negligence (with R Jackson), Palmer's Company Law (jt ed, 25 edn 1991), Issues and Offers of Company Securities: The New Regimes; *Recreations* travel, sheep farming, walking, international politics; *Style*— John L Powell, Esq, QC

POWELL, Jonathan Leslie; s of James Dawson Powell, and Phyllis Nora, *née* Sylvester; *b* 25 April 1947; *Educ* Sherborne, UEA; *m* 29 Dec 1990, Sally Brampton; *Career* script ed then prodr Granada TV 1969–77; BBC TV: prodr 1977–84 (prodr of classic serials incl The Mayor of Casterbridge, Tinker Tailor Soldier Spy, Testament of Youth, The Barchester Chronicles and The Old Men at the Zoo), head of drama series and serials 1984–87, head Drama Group 1987, controller of BBC1 1988–92; dir of drama and international devpt Carlton Television 1993–; memb Cncl BAFTA 1998–2000; *Recreations* fishing; *Style*— Jonathan Powell, Esq; ✉ Carlton Television, 35–38 Portman Square, London W1H 6NU (tel 020 7486 6688)

POWELL, Jonathan Nicholas; s of Air Vice-Marshal John Frederick Powell, OBE, AE, and Geraldine Ysolda, *née* Moylan; bro of Baron Powell of Bayswater, KCMG (Life Peer), and (John) Christopher Powell, *qqv*; *b* 14 August 1956; *Educ* Univ Coll Oxford (MA), Univ of Pennsylvania (MA); *m* Karen Drayne (m dis 1997); 2 s (John b 10 Sept 1982, Charles b 14 Aug 1985); another 2 da (Jessica Sophie b 25 Oct 1997, Rosamund Ysolda b 31 March 1999); *Career* with: BBC 1978, Granada TV Manchester 1978–79; FCO 1979–81, second sec Br Embassy Lisbon 1981–83; first sec: FCO London 1983–85, CDE Stockholm

1985, CSCE Vienna 1985–89; FCO London 1989–91, first sec Br Embassy Washington 1991–95; COS to Rt Hon Tony Blair, MP: as Ldr of Oppn 1995–97, as PM 1997–2007; *Style*— Jonathan Powell, Esq; ✉ c/o 10 Downing Street, London SW1A 2AA

POWELL, (Geoffrey) Mark; s of Francis Turner Powell, MBE, of East Horsley, Surrey, and Joan Audrey, *née* Bartlett (d 2003); *b* 14 January 1946; *Educ* Tonbridge, St Chad's Coll Durham (BA); *m* 24 July 1971, Veronica Joan, da of Paul Frank Rowland (d 1993), of Clymping, W Sussex; 2 da (Jessica (Mrs James Cobb) b 1973, Catriona b 1976); *Career* L Powell Sons & Co 1968–72, ptnr Powell Popham Dawes & Co 1972–77, dir Laing & Cruickshank 1977–86; chief exec: CL-Alexanders Laing & Cruickshank Holdings Ltd 1987–89 (dir 1986–89), Laurence Keen 1989–95; chm: Rathbone Brothers plc 2003– (gp md 1995–2003), SVM UK Active Fund plc 2006 (dir 2004–); dir Assoc of Private Client Investment Managers and Stockbrokers 1994– (chm 2000–06), memb Takeover Panel 2001–; memb Cncl REACH 1996–2001, dep chm Fight for Sight 1999–; Freeman City of London 1967, memb Ct of Assts Worshipful Co of Haberdashers 1989–; FSI (memb London Stock Exchange 1971), FRSA; *Clubs* MCC, City of London, Boodle's; *Style*— Mark Powell, Esq; ✉ Creedhole Farm, High Button, Thursley, Surrey GU8 6NR (tel 01428 683163); Rathbone Brothers plc, 159 New Bond Street, London W1S 2UD (tel 020 7399 0000, fax 020 7399 0061)

POWELL, Michael Peter; s of Arthur Owen Powell (d 1967), of Oxford, and Jane, *née* Mustard; *b* 24 July 1950; *Educ* Wellington, New Coll Oxford (MA), Middx Hosp Med Sch (MB BS); *m* 13 Jan 1979, Dr Jennifer Shields, da of (Leslie) Stuart Shields, QC; 3 da (Ruth b 29 May 1981, Alice b 27 Sept 1983, Penny b 13 Sept 1986); *Career* registrar and research registrar Neurosurgery Dept Frenchay Hosp Bristol 1980–83; currently neurosurgn: The Nat Hosp for Neurology and Neurosurgery (sr registrar 1983–85), UCH, RNOH London; hon conslt: Whittingdon Hosp, St Thomas' Hosp, St Luke's Hosp for the Clergy, King Edward VII Hosp for Offrs; civilian advsr in neurosurgery to the RAF; FRCS; *Style*— Michael Powell, Esq; ✉ The National Hospital, Queen Square, London WC1N 3BG (tel 020 7837 3611 ext 3176)

POWELL, Neil Ashton; s of late Ian Otho James Powell, of Orford, Suffolk, and Dulcie Delia, *née* Lloyd; *b* 11 February 1948; *Educ* Sevenoaks Sch, Univ of Warwick (BA, MPhil); *Career* ed Tracks 1967–70, English teacher Kimbolton Sch Huntingdon 1971–74, head of English St Christopher Sch Letchworth 1978–86 (English teacher 1974–78), owner The Baldock Bookshop 1986–90; writer in residence Samuel Whitbread Sch Shefford 1988, resident tutor Arvon Fndn Totleigh Barton 1989, tutor Bd of Extra Mural Studies Univ of Cambridge 1991, tutor WEA Eastern Region 1994–, visiting tutor Norwich Sch of Art 1995–97; contrib poetry, fiction, essays and reviews to: Critical Quarterly, Encounter, The Guardian, The Independent, The Listener, London Magazine, New Statesman, PN Review, Poetry Review, Sunday Telegraph, Times Literary Supplement, various anthologies, BBC Radio 3 and Radio 4; Soc of Authors Gregory Award 1969; memb Soc of Authors 1974; *Books* Suffolk Poems (1975), At the Edge (1977), Carpenters of Light (1979), Out of Time (1979), A Season of Calm Weather (1982), Selected Poems of Fulke Greville (ed, 1990), True Colours: New and Selected Poems (1991), Unreal City (1992), The Stones on Thorpeness Beach (1994), Roy Fuller: Writer and Society (1995), Gay Love Poetry (ed, 1997), The Language of Jazz (1997), Selected Poems (1998), Collected Poems of Donald Davie (ed and introduced, 2002), Collected Poems of Adam Johnson (ed and introduced, 2003), George Crabbe: An English Life (2004), A Halfway House (2004), Amis and Son: Two Literary Generations (2008); *Style*— Neil Powell, Esq; ✉ c/o A P Watt Limited, 20 John Street, London WC1N 2DR

POWELL, Sir Nicholas Folliott Douglas; 4 Bt (UK 1897); s of Sir Richard George Douglas Powell, MC, 3 Bt (d 1980); descends from Walter Powell (d 1567), descendant of Rhys ap Tewdwr Mawr, King of South Wales; *b* 17 July 1935; *Educ* Gordonstoun; *m* 1, 26 May 1960 (m dis 1987), Daphne Jean, yr da of Maj George Henry Errington, MC; 1 da (Catherine Mary b 1961), 1 s (James Richard Douglas b 17 Oct 1962); *m* 2, 10 July 1987, Davina Hyacinth Berners, er twin da of Michael Allsopp, *qv*; 2 s (Benjamin Ranulph Berners b 5 Jan 1989, Oliver Michael Folliott b 4 Nov 1990), 1 da (Mamie Josephine Berners b 21 April 1992); *Heir* s, James Powell; *Career* Lt Welsh Gds 1953–57; co dir; *Style*— Sir Nicholas Powell, Bt

POWELL, Peter James; s of James Powell Moore Montague (d 1981), and Margaret, *née* Jones; *b* 24 March 1951; *Educ* Uppingham; *m* 31 Jan 1990 (m dis), Anthea Turner, da of Brian Turner; *Career* presenter BBC Radio Birmingham 1970–77, disc jockey BBC Radio 1 1977–89 (UK's Top Live Disc Jockey Carl Alan Awards 1980); fndr (with Russ Lindsay, *qv*) James Grant Media Ltd 1984, ptnr and dir James Grant Media Group Ltd; mangr: Phillip Schofield 1985–, Andi Peters 1993–, Margherita Taylor 1997–, Ben Shepherd 1998–, Jenni Falconer 1998–, Ant and Dec 1999–, Anna Walker, Fearne Cotton, Holly Willoughby, Jayne Middlemiss, Jonathan Wilkes, Kerry Katona, Reggie Yates, Simon Cowell, Stephen Mulhern, Richard and Judy; hon vice-pres Nat Assoc of Youth Clubs, assoc dir main bd Radio Lollipop UK; *Recreations* sailing, skiing; *Clubs* RORC, RYA, RAC; *Style*— Peter Powell, Esq; ✉ James Grant Media Group Ltd, 94 Strand on the Green, Chiswick, London W4 3NN (tel 020 8742 4950, fax 020 8742 4951)

POWELL, Philip B; s of Frank James Powell (d 1987), and Elizabeth Anne, *née* Hamel (d 1977); *b* 3 November 1954; *Educ* Highbury Co GS, LSE, UEA (BA); *m* 1, 10 March 1978 (m dis 1998), Jacqueline Anne, da of Frank Lloyd; 2 s (Matthew Frank b 16 Jan 1982, Christopher James b 22 May 1984), 1 da (Joanne Alice b 4 Jan 1988); *m* 2, 7 Sept 2007, Catherine Harding, da of John Mayes; *Career* Unilever plc: grad mgmnt trainee Walls Ice Cream 1974–76, sr product mangr Walls Ice Cream 1976–80, gp product mangr Iglo Ola Netherlands 1980–81, sr brand mangr Lever Brothers 1982–83; mktg mangr Colmans of Norwich Reckitt & Colman plc 1983–86, fndr The Marketing House Norwich 1986–88, dir of mktg Goodman Fielder Wattie NZ 1989–91, business devpt mangr Cow & Gate Nutricia 1991–93, mktg dir Office for National Statistics 1994–99, account dir TSO Ltd 2000–03, mktg controller Iceland Foods plc 2003–04, dir Heawood Research Ltd 2004–06, Nutricia Ltd 2006–; fndr chm Canned Food Info Serv NZ 1990–91; memb: Infant & Diabetic Food Assoc 1991–92, Dissemination Ctee Govt Statistical Serv, EC Statistical Dissemination Working Pty; led EU mission on collaborative dissemination to Ottowa Canada 1996; MCIM; *Publications* Effective Presentation via User Consultation ISI Istanbul 1997, The Dynamics of the Information Market ISI Helsinki 1999; *Recreations* carpentry, history, books, squash, cinema, travelling, cooking; *Style*— Philip B Powell, Esq; ✉ 14 Westfield Close, Bath BA2 2EA (tel 01225 344369, mobile 07785 957768, e-mail philip.powell@blueyonder.co.uk)

POWELL, Polly Augusta Marchant (Mrs Vaughan Grylls); da of Geoffry Powell (d 1999), and Philippa, *née* Cooper; *b* 1 August 1959; *Educ* Francis Holland Sch London, Univ of Manchester (BA); *m* 1994, Prof Vaughan Grylls, *qv*; 1 da (Hattie b 13 Aug 1992), 1 s (George 2 Oct 1994); *Career* founding publishing dir HarperCollins Illustrated 1998; publishing dir: Cassell Illustrated 2002, Chrysalis Books 2004; dir Anova Books Co Ltd 2005–; *Recreations* tennis; *Style*— Ms Polly Powell; ✉ Anova Books Company Ltd, 151 Freston Road, London W10 6TH (tel 020 7314 1400)

POWELL, Robert; *b* 1 June 1944; *Career* actor; *Theatre* incl: repertory Stoke-on-Trent 1964–65, Hamlet (Leeds) 1971, Travesties (RSC) 1975, Terra Nova (Watford) 1982, Private Dick 1982–83, Tovarich (Chichester Festival Theatre, nat tour then Piccadilly Theatre) 1991, Sherlock Holmes - The Musical (Bristol Old Vic and nat tour) 1993, Kind Hearts and Coronets (nat tour) 1998, Single Spies (nat tour) 2002, The Picture of Dorian Gray (nat tour) 2003; *Television* incl: Doomwatch 1969–70, title role in Shelley (BBC film) 1971, Jude the Obscure (BBC series) 1971, Mrs Warren's Profession 1972, Mr Rolls and Mr

Royce 1972, Looking for Clancy (serial) 1975, title role in Zeffirelli's Jesus of Nazareth 1976 (Best Actor TV Times and Italian TV Times Awards, Int Arts Prize Fiuggi Film Festival, Grand Prize St Vincent Film Festival Italy), You Never Can Tell (BBC) 1977, The Four Feathers (NBC) 1978, Pygmalion 1981, The Hunchback of Notre Dame (CBS) 1982, Frankenstein (Yorkshire) 1984, Shaka Zulu (series) 1985, Richard Hannay in Hannay (Thames, 2 series) 1987–88, Ambrosius in Merlin and the Crystal Cave (Noel Gay/BBC) 1991, Cortez in The Golden Years (Brook/Channel Four) 1992, DC Dave Briggs in 5 series of The Detectives (BBC series) 1992–97, Mark Williams in Holby City (BBC series); *Films* incl: Secrets 1971, Running Scared 1972, The Asphyx 1972, Asylum 1972, title role in Ken Russell's Mahler 1974, Capt Walker in Ken Russell's Tommy 1975, Beyond Good and Evil 1977, The Thirty-Nine Steps 1978, Harlequin 1980 (Best Actor Paris Film Festival), Jane Austen in Manhattan 1980, The Survivor 1980, Imperative 1981 (Best Actor Venice Film Festival 1982), The Jigsaw Man 1982, What Waits Below 1983, D'Annunzio and I 1986, Down There in the Jungle (Venezuela) 1987, The Sign of Command 1989, The Long Conversation with a Bird 1990, The First Circle 1990, Once on Chunuk Bair 1991, The Mystery of Edwin Drood 1992, Colour Me Kubrick 2004; *Style*— Robert Powell, Esq; ✉ c/o Diamond Management, 31 Percy Street, London W1T 2DD (tel 020 7631 0400, fax 020 7631 0500)

POWELL, Stephen Joseph; s of Joseph Thomas Powell (d 1958), of Goffs Oak, Herts, and Dorothy May, *née* Welch (d 2000); *b* 26 May 1943; *Educ* Cheshunt GS, The Royal Dental Hosp of London Sch of Dental Surgery (BDS, FDS RCS, MOrth RCS); *m* 6 July 1968, Yvonne Heather, da of Sydney Frederick Williams, of Pucklechurch, Avon; 2 da (Rebecca b 1986, Charlotte b 1991); *Career* sr registrar in orthodontics Hosp for Sick Children Gt Ormond St and The Royal Dental Hosp London 1972–74; conslt in orthodontics: St George's Hosp London 1975–, King's Coll Hosp GKT Sch of Med and Dentistry London 1986–; dir: PP Business Conferences Ltd, Othodontic Independent Practitioners Ltd; memb: Cncl Soc of St Augustine of Canterbury, BDA, Br Orthodontic Soc, European Orthodontic Soc, American Assoc of Orthodontists; *Publications* 3 Dimensional Facial Imaging at the Clinical Interface (1999); numerous other papers on therapeutic facial change and measurement; *Recreations* tennis, swimming, music, theatre, French culture; *Clubs* Athenaeum; *Style*— Stephen Powell, Esq; ✉ 5 Hood Road, Wimbledon, London SW20 0SR (tel 020 8946 3401); Le Milord, Appt 51, 7 Rue Marius Maiffret, 06310 Beaulieu-sur-Mer, France (tel 00 33 4 93 01 41 93); 2A Barham Road, Wimbledon, London SW20 0EU (tel 020 8946 3064, mobile 07747 865563, e-mail stephenjpowelll@msn.com); St George's Hospital, Blackshaw Road, Tooting, London SW17 0LT

POWELL, Timothy Martin (Minnow); s of Arthur Barrington Powell CMG, and Jane, *née* Weir; *b* 17 September 1954; *Educ* Ampleforth, Jesus Coll Oxford (BA); *m* Victoria Elizabeth, da of Peter Geoffrey Holmes; 2 s (Alexander James Barrington b 26 June 1987, Toby Peter Johnathan b 3 Aug 1990); *Career* Touche Ross (now Deloitte & Touche): joined 1976, CA 1979, ptnr 1985–; FCA; *Recreations* golf; *Clubs* Northern Counties, Woking Golf, Royal Porthcawl Golf, Rye Golf, Royal St Georges Golf, R&A, Royal West Norfolk, Northumberland Golf; *Style*— Minnow Powell, Esq; ✉ Deloitte & Touche, Hill House, 1 Little New Street, London EC4A 3TR (tel 020 7936 3000, fax 020 7583 8517)

POWELL OF BAYSWATER, Baron (Life Peer UK 2000), of Canterbury in the County of Kent; Sir Charles David; KCMG (1990), kt (1990); s of Air Vice-Marshal John Frederick Powell, OBE, RAF, and Geraldine Ysolda, *née* Moylan; bro of Jonathan Nicholas Powell, and (John) Christopher Powell, *qqv*; *b* 6 July 1941; *Educ* King's Sch Canterbury, New Coll Oxford (BA); *m* 24 Oct 1964, Carla, da of Domingo Bonardi, of Italy; 2 s (Hugh b 1967, Nicholas b 1968); *Career* memb HM Dip Serv, Helsinki, Washington, Bonn and EEC Brussels 1963–83, private sec and advsr on foreign affrs and defence to PM 1983–91 (under-sec 1987); dir: Jardine Matheson (and associates) 1991–2000, National Westminster Bank plc 1991–2000 (chm International Advsy Bd), Arjo Wiggins Appleton plc 1992–2000, J Rothschild Name Co 1992–2002, Louis Vuitton-Moet Hennessy SA 1994– (chm LVMH UK 2001–), Br Mediterranean Airways 1997–2007, Textron Inc 2001–, Caterpillar Inc 2001–, Yell Gp Ltd 2002–, Schindler Holdings 2003–; chm: Sagitta Asset Mgmnt 2001–05, Safinvest 2006–, Magna Holdings 2006–; dep chm: Trafalgar House plc 1994–1996, Said Holdings 1994–2000, Northern Trust Global Services 2004–; chm Int Advsy Bd Rolls-Royce 2006–; memb Int Advsy Bd: Textron Corp, ACE Insurance, Barrick Gold; chm Atlantic Partnership; pres China-Britain Business Cncl 1998–; chm of tstees Oxford Business Sch, tstee Aspen Inst USA, tstee British Museum; *Recreations* walking; *Style*— The Rt Hon the Lord Powell of Bayswater, KCMG; ✉ 24 Queen Anne's Gate, London SW1H 9AA

POWELL-SMITH, Christopher Brian; s of Edgar Powell-Smith (d 1970), and Theodora Kirkham Baker (d 1984); *b* 3 October 1936; *Educ* City of London Sch, Law Soc's Sch of Law (Travers-Smith scholar, Clements Inn Prize); *m* 1964, Jenny, da of Douglas Goslett; 2 da (Amanda b 1968, Emily b 1972), 2 s (Giles b 1970, Edward b 1975); *Career* Cameron McKenna (formerly McKenna & Co): ptnr 1964–98, managing ptnr 1984–88, head Corp Dept 1988–92, sr ptnr 1992–97; non-exec chm Black & Decker Group Inc 1988– (non-exec dir 1970–), KBC Advanced Technology plc 2004– (non-exec dir 1997–); non-exec dir: Carlsberg Brewery Ltd 1987–92, Martins Printing Gp Ltd 1998–; memb Ctee of Mgmnt Thames Valley Housing Assoc 1995–; TA: cmdg offr HAC 1976–78, regtl Col and master gunner HM Tower of London 1978–80; tstee Richmond Parish Lands Charity 1997–; memb: Law Soc 1959, Int Bar Assoc 1975, City of London Slrs' Co 1987; *Recreations* golf, choral singing, walking; *Clubs* City of London, Brooks's, Royal Mid-Surrey Golf; *Style*— Christopher Powell-Smith, Esq, TD

POWELL-TUCK, Prof Jeremy; s of late Dr Geoffrey Alan Powell-Tuck, and Catherine Gwendoline, *née* Kirby, of Cleeve Hill, Glos; *b* 20 May 1948; *Educ* Epsom Coll, Univ of Birmingham (MB ChB, MD); *m* Fiona Caroline, da of Charles William Sandison Crabbe (d 1969); 1 s (Thomas b 1984), 2 da (Amy b 1987, Rosie b 1988); *Career* research fell St Mark's Hosp 1974–80, research fell Dept of Nutrition London Sch of Hygiene and Tropical Med 1980–81, sr registrar of med and gastroenterology Charing Cross, W Middx and Westminster Hosps 1981–88, head Human Nutrition Unit St Bartholomew's and the Royal London Hosp Sch of Medicine and Dentistry 1988–, conslt physician Bart's and The Royal London Hosp 1988–; contrib chapters on nutritional therapy and gastro-intestinal disease; memb Cncl Br Assoc for Parenteral and Enteral Nutrition; FRSM 1976, FRCP 1992 (MRCP 1973); *Recreations* choral music, tennis, sailing; *Style*— Prof Jeremy Powell-Tuck; ✉ 9 Horbury Crescent, London W11 3NF (tel 020 7727 2528); Centre for Adult and Paediatric Gastroenterology, St Bartholomew's and the Royal London School of Medicine and Dentistry (tel 020 7882 2631)

POWER, Sir Alastair John Cecil; 4 Bt (UK 1924), of Newlands Manor, Milford, Southampton; s of Sir John Patrick McLannahan Power, 3 Bt (d 1984), and Melanie, adopted da of Hon Alastair Erskine (s of 6 Baron Erskine; d 1987); *b* 15 August 1958; *m* 19 Sept 1981, Virginia Newton; 2 da (Melanie-Anne Louise b 15 July 1984, Amanda Jane b 15 Oct 1986), 1 s (Mark Alastair John b 15 Oct 1989); *Heir* s, Mark Power; *Style*— Sir Alastair Power, Bt

POWER, Prof Anne; CBE (2000, MBE); *Career* Martin Luther King Southern Christian Leadership Conference 1966, warden Africa Centre London 1966–67, co-ordinator Friends Neighbourhood House 1967–72, co-ordinator North Islington Housing Rights Project 1972–79, nat conslt DOE Priority Estates Project 1979–87, advsr Welsh Office and Rhondda BC 1989–93; LSE: successively academic visitor, visiting research assoc Dept of Social Policy 1981–88, currently professor in social policy; fndr dir Nat Tenants Resource Centre; dep dir Centre for Analysis of Social Exclusion; advsy memb panel of experts to EC on urban problems and social segregation in cities, memb Urban Task Force, cmmr Sustainable Devpt Cmmn, memb Govt Urban and Housing Sounding Bds; *Publications* Property Before People: The Management of Twentieth Century Council Housing (1987), Housing Management - A Guide to Quality and Creativity (1991), Hovels to High-rise - State Housing in Europe since 1850 (1993), Swimming Against the Tide: Polarisation or Progress on 20 Unpopular Council Estates 1980–95 (jtly, 1995), Dangerous Disorder: Riots and Violent Disturbances in Thirteen Areas of Britain 1991–92 (jtly, 1997), Estates on the Edge - The Social Consequences of Mass Housing in Northern Europe (1997), The Slow Death of Great Cities? Urban abandonment or urban renaissance (jtly, 1999), Cities for a Small Country (jtly, 2000), Boom or Abandonment (jtly, 2003), East Enders: Family and community in East London (jtly, 2003), Sustainable Communities and Sustainable Development: A Review of the Sustainable Communities Plan (2004), Jigsaw Cities: Big Places, Small Spaces (jtly, 2004); also author of numerous governmental reports and articles in the press on social policy and housing issues incl One Size Doesn't Fit All (chair of ind cmmn of inquiry into the future of cncl housing in Birmingham); *Style*— Prof Anne Power, CBE; ✉ Department of Social Policy, London School of Economics and Political Science, Houghton Street, London WC2A 2AE (tel 020 7955 6330, fax 020 7955 6571, e-mail anne.power@lse.ac.uk)

POWER, Jonathan Richard Adrian; s of Patrick Power (d 1994), of Boars Hill, Oxford, and Dorothy Power (d 1984); *b* 4 June 1941; *Educ* Liverpool Inst HS, Univ of Manchester (BA), Univ of Wisconsin (MA); *m* 1 (m dis 1988), Anne Elizabeth, da of Dennis Hayward, of Southampton; 3 da (Carmen b 18 Jan 1966, Miriam b 23 May 1968, Lucy b 24 Nov 1978); m 2, Jean-Christine, da of Arvid Eklund, of Gothenburg, Sweden; 1 da (Jenny b 25 June 1990); *Career* foreign affrs columnist International Herald Tribune 1974–91, independent foreign affrs columnist 1991– (column syndicated to 16 princ US, Canadian and European papers and 31 African, Asian, Latin American and Australasian papers), commentator on foreign affrs Int Herald Tribune 2003–; memb Int Inst for Strategic Studies 1980–, memb Common Room Queen Elizabeth House Univ of Oxford 1996–; *Film* It's Ours Whatever They Say (Silver Medal Venice Film Festival 1972); *Books* Development Economics, World of Hunger, The New Proletariat, Against Oblivion, Vision of Hope - 50 Years of the United Nations, Like Water on Stone (2001), Conundrums of Humanity (2006); *Recreations* walking, cycling, opera; *Style*— Jonathan Power, Esq; ✉ Adelgatan 6, Lund, Sweden (tel 00 44 7785 351172, e-mail jonatpower@aol.com)

POWER, Richard; s of Frank Power, and Emily, *née* Williams; *b* 29 October 1953, Dudley, W Midlands; *Educ* Dudley GS, Wednesbury Photographic Coll; *m* Marie, *née* Doherty; *Career* photographer's asst Frank Power Photography 1971–74, various positions Dept of Employment Merseyside and Whitehall 1974–1984 (latterly private sec to Norman Tebbit and Sir Peter Morrison), various positions rising to communications dir Forte Plc 1984–1996; various positions rising to md Rocco Forte Hotels 1996–; formerly: dir London Tourist Bd, dir Whitehall and Industry Gp, memb Mgmnt Bd Br Hospitality Assoc; MCIPR 1988, FHCIMA 1990; *Recreations* sport, music, gardening; *Style*— Richard Power, Esq; ✉ Rocco Forte Hotels, Savannah House, 11 Charles II Street, London SW1Y 4QU (tel 020 7766 3106, fax 020 7321 2424, e-mail rpower@roccofortehotels.com)

POWER, Vince; Hon CBE (2006); s of John Power (d 1972), and Brigid Power (d 1986); *b* 29 April 1947, Kilmacthomas, Co Waterford, Ireland; *Educ* Dungarvan Vocational Coll; *m* 1967 (m dis 1979); 3 c; 2 c from 1 ptnr; 3 c from current ptnr; *Career* early career as Woolworths, labourer and demolition worker, owner chain furniture shops N London 1964–82; opened The Mean Fiddler Harlesden 1982, Mean Fiddler Orgn became Mean Fiddler Music Gp plc 2001, chm until 2004, non-exec dir until 2005, sold Mean Fiddler Gp 2005; prop Vince Power Music Gp 2005–; also fndr: Subterania 1989, The Grand Clapham 1991, The Jazz Cafe 1992, The Forum 1993, The Garage 1993, Upstairs at the Garage 1994, The Crossbar 1995, The Mean Fiddler Dublin 1995, The Palace Luton 1995, The Powerhaus 1996, The Complex 1996, The Cube 1996, Power' Bar 1996, ZD 1996, Bartok 1998, Ion Restaurant & Bar 1998, Point 101 1998, London Astoria 2000, Mean Fiddler 2000, One Seven Nine 2001, G-A-Y 2002, Union-Undeb 2003, Berkeley Square Cafe 2003; promoter: Reading Festival 1989–2004, London Fleadh 1990–2005, Phoenix Festival 1993–97, Tribal Gathering 1995–97, Fleadh New York 1997, Madstock 1992, 1994, 1996 and 1998, Neil Young 1993, Paul Weller 1996, The Sex Pistols 1996 (first UK performance for 20 years), Big Love 1996, Mount Universe 1996, Jamiroquai 1997, Fleadh Chicago 1998–, Fleadh San Francisco 1998–, Temptation 1998, Cream Fields 1998, Pulp 1998, Fleadh Boston 1999–, Homelands 1999–, Homelands Scotland 1999, Homelands Ireland 1999, Leeds 1999–, Glasgow Green 2000–, National Adventure Sports Weekender 2001–, Doctor Music 2003; operational mangr Glastonbury Festival 2002–05; patron Nat Depression Campaign; involved with Cradle (Bosnian children's charity); Irish Post Award 1995; *Style*— Vince Power, Esq, CBE; ✉ website www.vpmg.net

POWERS, Anthony Jonathan William; s of Michael Powers (d 1994), and Frances, *née* Wilson; *b* 13 March 1953; *Educ* Marlborough, The Queen's Coll Oxford (BA), Univ of York (DPhil), private study with Nadia Boulanger; *m* 1984, Helen Frances, da of late Dr C Priday; 1 s (Richard b 1991), 1 da (Camilla b 1993); *Career* lectr in music Dartington Coll of Arts 1978–80, composer in res Southern Arts 1980–82, tutor in composition Univ of Exeter and Dartington Coll of Arts 1983–86, composer in res Univ of Wales Cardiff 1989–; chm Assoc of Professional Composers 1995–97 (memb 1985); *Compositions* incl: Stone, Water, Stars (BBC Symphony Orch) 1987, Horn Concerto (Royal Liverpool Philharmonic Orch) 1990, Cello Concerto (Kings Lynn Festival) 1990, Terrain (BBC Nat Orch of Wales) 1993, Symphony (BBC Nat Orch of Wales, premièred BBC Proms) 1996, Symphony No 2 (BBC Symphony Orch) 1999, A Picture of the World (BBC Singers) 2001, Air and Angels (Three Choirs Festival) 2003; *Style*— Mr Anthony Powers; ✉ c/o Music Department, Oxford University Press, 70 Baker Street, London W1U 7DN (tel 020 7616 5900, fax 020 7616 5901)

POWERS, Dr Michael John; QC (1995); s of late Reginald Frederick Powers, of Parkstone, Dorset, and late Kathleen Ruby, *née* Whitmarsh; *b* 9 February 1947; *Educ* Poole GS, Middx Hosp Med Sch London (BSc, MB BS, DA), Poly of Central London (Dip Law); *m* 1, 16 Nov 1968 (sep 1989), Meryl Julia, da of late Frank Edward Hall, of Bournemouth, Dorset; 1 da (Julia b 1972), 1 s (Andrew b 1982); m 2, 22 June 2001, Pamela Jean, da of late Ronald Barnes, of Manchester; *Career* registered med practitioner 1972–, house surgn Middx Hosp 1972–73, house physician Royal S Hants Hosp 1973–74, SHO Royal United Hosp Bath 1974–75, registrar (anaesthetics) Northwick Park Hosp Harrow 1975–77; called to the Bar Lincoln's Inn 1979 (bencher 1998); practising at Common Law Bar specialising in med and pharmaceutical law, HM asst dep coroner Westminster 1981–87; pres SE England Coroners Soc 1987–88; students' cnsllr to Hon Soc of Lincoln's Inn 1983–90; memb: Soc of Doctors in Law, Medico-Legal Soc; fell Faculty of Forensic and Legal Medicine 2007; *Books* The Law and Practice on Coroners (with Paul Knapman 1985), Casebook on Coroners (with Paul Knapman, 1989), Medical Negligence (with Nigel Harris, 1990 and 1994), Sources of Coroners' Law (with Paul Knapman, 1999), Clinical Negligence (with Nigel Harris, 2000 and 2007); *Recreations* helicopter pilot, music; *Clubs* RSM (fell); *Style*— Dr Michael Powers, QC; ✉ Clerksroom, Equity House, Blackbrook Park Avenue, Taunton TA1 2PX (tel 0845 083 3000, fax 0845 083 3001, e-mail powersqc@medneg.co.uk, website www.medneg.co.uk)

POWERS, William; MBE (1982), JP, DL (Beds 1989); s of Capt John Powers (d 1974), and Doris Gladys, *née* Rickard; *b* 2 September 1924; *m* 27 June 1953, Janet Elsie Elisabeth, da of Archibald Fletcher; 2 da (Lynda Elisabeth b 1954, Jane Alison b 1957); *Career* Beds & Herts Regt 1941, 9 Commando 2 Special Serv Bde 1942–45 (despatches 1943),

P

Mounted Police Palestine 1945–47, appointed Dist Supt 1947, Trans-Jordan Frontier Force 1947–49, seconded Maj; chief exec Shaw & Kilburn Luton 1968–86, chm S Beds Health Care Tst 1990–; pres: Luton and Dist Royal Br Legion, Luton and Dunstable Operatic Soc; vice-pres Luton Household Div Assoc, patron Luton and Dunstable Burma Star Assoc; dir Norfolk and Breckland Tattoo 1998; High Sheriff Beds 1987; memb The Lord Chancellor's Advsy Ctee, JP and dep chm Luton Magistrates' Court, chm S Beds Cmmrs of Taxes; FIMI 1965; *Clubs* The Household Div Luton; *Style—* William Powers, Esq, MBE, DL; ✉ The Old Vicarage, Norwich Road, Ludham, Great Yarmouth, Norfolk NR29 5QA

POWERS-FREELING, Laurel Claire; da of Lloyd Marion Powers, of Bloomfield Hills, Michigan, and Catharine Joyce, *née* Berry (d 1992); *b* 16 May 1957; *Educ* Bloomfield Andover HS Michigan, Barnard Coll Columbia Univ NY (AB), Alfred P Sloan Sch MIT (MS); *m* 28 Jan 1989, Dr Anthony Nigel Stanley Freeling, s of Prof Paul Freeling, OBE; 1 s (Matthew Charles Powers-Freeling b 26 Dec 1991), 1 da (Catharine Grace Powers-Freeling b 1 March 1994); *Career* sr conslt Price Waterhouse Boston and NY 1983–85 (conslt 1980–85), mangr McKinsey & Co Inc London and NY 1987–89 (conslt 1985–87), corp fin offr Morgan Stanley International London 1989–91; Prudential Corporation plc: dir of corp strategy 1991–93, dir of private financial planning servs 1993–94; gp fin dir Lloyds Abbey Life plc 1994–96, md Savings & Investments Lloyds TSB Gp plc 1997–98, dir retail devpt and fin UK Retail Bank Lloyds TSB Gp plc 1998–99, md Wealth Mgmnt Div Lloyds TSB Gp plc 2000–01, chief exec Marks and Spencer Money 2001–05 (bd memb Marks and Spencer plc 2001–04), sr vice-pres and UK country mangr American Express 2005–; non-exec dir: Bank of England 2002–05, Environmental Resources Mgmnt Ltd 2005–; chm Montisi Harpsichord Performance Center (Tuscany) 2006–; *Recreations* classical music, needlework, cookery; *Clubs* Riverside; *Style—* Mrs Laurel Powers-Freeling

POWERSCOURT, 10 Viscount (I 1743); Mervyn Niall Wingfield; also Baron Wingfield (I 1743), and Baron Powerscourt (UK 1885, title in House of Lords); s of 9 Viscount Powerscourt (d 1973), and Sheila Claude, *née* Beddington (d 1992); *b* 3 September 1935; *Educ* Stowe; *m* 1, 1962 (m dis 1974), Wendy Ann Pauline, da of Ralph C G Slazenger; 1 s, 1 da; m 2, 1979 (m dis 1995), Pauline, da of W P Van, of San Francisco, CA; *Heir* s, Hon Mervyn Wingfield; *Style—* The Rt Hon the Viscount Powerscourt

POWIS, 8 Earl of (UK 1804); Dr John George Herbert; also Baron Powis, of Powis Castle, Co Montgomery, Baron Herbert of Chirbury, Co Salop, and Viscount Clive, of Ludlow, Co Salop (all UK 1804), Baron Clive, of Walcot, Co Salop (GB 1794), and Baron Clive of Plassey, Co Limerick (I 1762); eldest s of 7 Earl of Powis (d 1993), and Hon Katharine Odeyne de Grey, yst da of 8 Baron Walsingham, DSO, OBE (d 1965); *b* 19 May 1952; *Educ* Wellington, McMaster Univ Ontario (MA, PhD); *m* 1977, Marijke Sophia, eldest da of Maarten N Guther, of Ancaster, Ontario, Canada; 2 s (Jonathan Nicholas William, Viscount Clive b 1979, Hon Alexander Sebastian George b 1994), 2 da (Lady Stephanie Moira Christina b 1982, Lady Samantha Julie Esther b 1988); *Heir* s, Viscount Clive; *Career* asst prof of English lit Redeemer Coll Ancaster Ontario 1989–92; *Style—* The Rt Hon the Earl of Powis; ✉ Powis Castle, Welshpool, Powys

POWIS, Russell John; s of George Henry Powis, of Birmingham, and Nellie, *née* Croft; *b* 6 August 1947; *Educ* Yardley GS; *m* 30 May 1970, Susan Mary, da of Ernest John Cotterill; 3 s (Richard James Andrew b 27 Feb 1973, David Russell James b 1 Oct 1974, Stephen Robert Edward b 1 Jan 1983); *Career* articled clerk Russell Durie Kerr Watson and Co 1965–70; PricewaterhouseCoopers (formerly Coopers & Lybrand before merger): joined 1976 (Birmingham), tax ptnr (Cardiff) 1982, ptnr i/c tax practice 1990; currently conslt dir Quantum Advisory Ltd; FCA (ACA 1970); *Recreations* spectator sports, golf; *Clubs* Cardiff and County; *Style—* Russell Powis, Esq

POWLES, Prof Raymond Leonard; CBE (2003); s of Leonard William David Powles (d 1989), and Florence Irene, *née* Conolly; *b* 9 March 1938; *Educ* Eltham Coll, Bart's Med Sch London (BSc, MB BS, MD); *m* 1980, Louise Jane, da of Roy Frederick Richmond; 3 s (Sam Tristan Richmond, Luke Alexander Richmond (twins) b 2 Feb 1982, Max Ashley Richmond b 30 May 1989), 1 da (Gabriella Louise b 12 April 1985); *Career* house physician Bart's London 1965–66, resident med offr Royal Marsden Hosp London 1967–68, Leukaemia Fund fell to Prof George Mathe Ville Juif Paris 1968, Tata Meml Fund leukaemia fell Royal Marsden Hosp and Inst of Cancer Res Sutton Surrey 1969–72, ICRF sr scientific offr Bart's 1972–74, conslt and head Leukaemia and Myeloma Units Royal Marsden Hosp 1974–2003; recognised teacher Univ of London 1977–, clinical tutor RCP 1990–, currently head Leukaemia and Myeloma Unit Parkside Cancer Clinic Wimbledon and Univ of London emeritus prof of haematological oncology ICR; invited lectures throughout world on leukaemia res and treatment, author of over 1200 scientific papers and book chapters on leukaemia; lifetime achievement award CPAA, India; chm Nuclear Accident Sub-Ctee EBMT, chm Scientific Ctee on Haemoporotic Growth Factors American Soc of Haematology; dir: Biopartners GmbH, Myogenic Biotech Ltd; variously memb: Cancer Patient Aid Assoc, Royal Marsden Special HA, MRC Working Pty on Leukaemia, UK Cancer Co-Ordinating Sub-Ctee on Leukaemia and Bone Marrow Transplantation (UKCCCR), Dept of Health Standing Med Advsy Sub-Ctee on Cancer, Br Assoc for Cancer Res, American Cancer Soc Sci Writers' Alumni, Euro Bone Marrow Transplantation Soc Working Pty for Leukaemia, Int Bone Marrow Transplant Registry Advsy Ctee, WHO Ctee Int Prog of Leukaemia Effects of the Chernobyl Accident, EORTC Anti-Fungal Ctee, SW Thames Regional Negotiating Team (Drugs and Supplies), London Bone Marrow Transplant Gp, Bd New Health Network (also tstee), Dept of Health Ind Reconfiguration Panel, Dept of Health Perceptions of the NHS Panel (also co-ordinator), Healthcare Inspections Advsy Team Cabinet Office Public Sector Team; sometime hon conslt CEGB; med advsr: The Bud Flanagan Leukaemia Fund, Leukaemia Soc of Ireland; specialist leukaemia advsr to BACUP; variously memb Editorial Bd: Leukaemia Research, Bone Marrow Transplantation, Indian Jl of Cancer Chemotherapy, Indian Jl of Med and Paediatric Oncology, Experimental Haematology; memb Int Advsy Panel: for virus infections Wellcome Ltd, on fungus infections Pfizer Ltd, on leukaemia Pharmitalia Carlo Erba Ltd; memb: Bd Euro Soc for Med Oncology, Euro Bone Marrow Transplantation Soc, Int Soc for Experimental Haematology, Int Transplantation Soc, American Soc of Haematology, Int Immunocompromised Host Soc, Euro Haematology Assoc, Br Soc of Haematology, Br Transplantation Soc, Assoc of Cancer Physicians, Br Soc of Pharmaceutical Med, Br Acad of Forensic Scis, BMA; FRCP 1980, FRCPath 1993; *Recreations* sport, cinema, cooking; *Style—* Prof Raymond Powles, CBE; ✉ Little Garratts, 19 Garratts Lane, Banstead, Surrey SM7 2EA (tel 01737 353632); Parkside Cancer Clinic, 49 Parkside, Wimbledon SW19 5NB (tel 020 8944 7979, fax 020 8605 9103, e-mail myeloma@clara.co.uk)

POWLES, His Hon Judge Stephen Robert; QC (1995); s of Andrew Frederick Arthur Powles, and Nora, *née* Bristol; *b* 7 June 1948; *Educ* Westminster, UC Oxford (MA); *m* 12 April 1975, Geraldine Patricia Hilda, da of Dr Campbell Millar Taggart Adamson; 1 s (Henry b 1979), 1 da (Olivia b 1981); *Career* called to the Bar: Middle Temple 1972 (Harmsworth maj exhibitioner, Astbury law scholar), Lincoln's Inn 1976; recorder of the Crown Court 1994–2005, circuit judge (SE Circuit) 2005–; memb Panel of Tbnl Membs Accountancy Investigation and Discipline Bd 2004–; registered mediator CEDR, ACI, ADR Chambers (alternative dispute resolution gp), Railway Industry Dispute Resolution (RIDR), ResoLex; CIMechE; *Recreations* sailing, hill walking, joinery, my border terrier; *Clubs* Royal Solent Yacht; *Style—* His Hon Judge Powles, QC; ✉ Henderson Chambers, 2 Harcourt Buildings, Middle Temple Lane, Temple, London EC4Y 9DB (tel 020 7583 9020, fax 020 7583 2686, e-mail spowles@hendersonchambers.co.uk)

POWLES, Prof Trevor James; CBE (2003); s of Leonard William David Powles (d 1989), and Florence Irene, *née* Conolly; *b* 8 March 1938; *Educ* Eltham Coll, Bart's Med Coll (BSc, MB BS, MRCP, PhD); *m* Penelope Margaret, da of Walter and Doreen Meyers, of Durban, South Africa; 2 s (James Watson b 19 Dec 1969, Thomas Bartholomew b 10 April 1971), 1 da (Lucy Alexandra b 31 Jan 1975); *Career* house physician and registrar Royal Postgrad Med Sch Hammersmith Hosp 1967–68, med registrar Bart's 1969–70, MRC clinical res fell Inst of Cancer Res London 1971–73; Royal Marsden Hosp London and Sutton: sr registrar and lectr 1974, sr lectr 1974–78, conslt physician 1978–2003, head Breast Cancer Unit 1994–2003, med dir Common Tumours Div 2000–2003; prof of breast oncolgy Inst of Cancer Research London 1998–2003 (emeritus prof 2003–); conslt med oncologist (breast cancer): Parkside Hosp Wimbledon 2003–, Lister Hosp London 2003–, St Anthony's Hosp Cheam 2003–, Harley St Clinic London 2005–; visiting prof: MD Anderson Cancer Centre Houston USA 1993, Dana Faber Cancer Center Harvard 1996, Tom Baker Cancer Centre Calgary Canada 1998; invited lectures throughout world on various aspects of breast cancer biology, diagnosis and treatment; tstee Breast Cancer Res Tst; memb: Br Breast Gp, Assoc of Cancer Physicians, Int Soc for Cancer Chemoprevention (vice-pres), Euro Soc for Med Oncology, American Soc of Clinical Oncology, Br Assoc of Cancer Research; patron Breast Cancer Care; FRCP 1983; *Books* Breast Cancer Management (jtly, 1981), Prostaglandins and Cancer (jtly, 1982), Medical Management of Breast Cancer (jtly, 1991); *Recreations* horse riding, skiing, reading; *Clubs* RAC; *Style—* Prof Trevor Powles, CBE; ✉ Parkside Oncology Clinic, 49 Parkside, Wimbledon, London SW19 5NB (tel 020 8247 3384)

POWNALL, David; *b* Liverpool; *Educ* Keele Univ; *Career* playwright and novelist; worked in motor industry and Zambian copper mining industry; former dramatist in residence: Century Theatre, Duke's Playhouse Lancaster; co-fndr Paines Plough Theatre Co; Hon DLitt Keele Univ 2000; FRSL 1976; *Awards* incl: John Whiting Prize (for Beef), Best Foreign Play on Broadway New York Theatre Yearbook, LS Directors' Award (for Livingstone and Sechele), nomination Best Play Plays and Players 1984, LA Drama Desk Awards 1988 (for Master Class), Giles Cooper Award for Radio Drama (twice), Sony Award (gold award, two silver awards); *Stage Plays* incl: Richard III, Motocar, Music to Murder By, An Audience Called Edouard, Beef, Livingstone and Sechele, Master Class, Elgar's Rondo, Getting the Picture, Death of a Faun; *Radio Plays* incl: Butterfingers, Flos, Pound on Mr Greenhill, Elgar's Third; *Publications* The Composer Plays: Master Class, Elgar's Rondo, Elgar's Third, Music to Murder By (collection, 1996); author of ten novels and a collection of short stories; *Style—* David Pownall, Esq, FRSL

POWNALL, Michael Graham; s of Raymond Pownall (d 1984), and Elizabeth Mary, *née* Robinson; *b* 11 October 1949; *Educ* Repton, Univ of Exeter (BA); *m* 14 Sept 1974, Deborah Ann, da of Thomas Hugh McQueen; 2 da (Sarah Elizabeth b 20 Aug 1978, Rebecca Claire b 19 May 1980); *Career* Parliament Office House of Lords: joined 1971, seconded as private sec to Ldr of House of Lords and Govt Chief Whip 1980–83, establishment offr and sec to Chm of Ctees 1983–88, princ clerk of private bills 1988–90, princ clerk of ctees 1991–95, clerk of jls and info office 1995–97, reading clerk 1997–2003, clerk asst 2003–; *Recreations* birdwatching; *Style—* Michael Pownall, Esq; ✉ 13 Flanders Road, London W4 1NQ (tel 020 8994 0797); House of Lords, London SW1A 0PW (tel 020 7219 3171, e-mail pownallmg@parliament.uk)

POWNER, Prof Edwin Thomas (Eddie); s of Thomas Powner (d 1989), of Stoke on Trent, and Evelyn, *née* King; *b* 22 April 1938; *Educ* Univ of Durham (BSc), Univ of Manchester (MSc, PhD); *m* 8 Sept 1962, Barbara, da of William Henry Turner (d 1963), of Stoke on Trent; 2 s (Stephen John b 25 Dec 1966 d 13 March 1987, Peter David b 30 May 1972), 1 da (Suzanne b 18 March 1969); *Career* UMIST: electronics engr 1960–63, lectr 1963–74, sr lectr 1974–79, reader 1979–80, prof of electronic engrg 1980–92, vice-princ and pro-vice-chllr 1986–88, dean of technol 1989–92; Univ of Sussex: prof of electronic engrg 1992–, dean of engrg 1996–99, head of electronics, communication and electrical engrg; author of numerous tech pubns; Inst of Nat Electrical Engrs: past memb Cncl, chm Library Ctee, memb Professional Bd, memb Qualifications Bd, memb Accreditation Bd, local chm NW Centre 1988–89, memb Scholarships and Prizes Ctee; memb PHEE (Profs and Heads of Electrical Engrg Sectoral Gp Engrg Cncl); CEng, FIEE 1987 (MIEE 1965); *Books* Digital Simulation (jtly), Digital Signal Processing (jtly); *Recreations* photography, mechanisms and clocks, railways; *Style—* Prof Eddie Powner; ✉ School of Engineering and Design, University of Sussex, Falmer, Brighton BN1 9QT (tel 01273 678586, fax 01273 678399, e-mail e.t.powner@sussex.ac.uk)

POWNER, John; s of John Reginald Powner, of London, and Jean, *née* McLeish; *b* 18 May 1962; *Educ* The Campion GS Hornchurch, Southend Coll of Technol, Brighton Poly (BA); *Career* graphic designer: Mitchell Beazley Publishing, Pentagram Design; fndr Atelier Works 1991; *Clubs* D&AD, VMCC; *Style—* John Powner, Esq; ✉ Atelier Works, The Old Piano Factory, 5 Charlton King's Road, London NW5 2SB (tel 020 7284 2215, fax 020 7284 2242, website www.atelierworks.co.uk)

POYNTER, Kieran Charles; s of Kenneth Reginald Poynter, of Sanderstead, Surrey, and Catherine Elizabeth, *née* Reilley; *b* 20 August 1950; *Educ* Salesian Coll, Imperial Coll London (BSc, ARCS); *m* 20 Aug 1977, Marylyn, da of Cmdt Thomas Melvin (d 1969), of Athlone, Ireland; 3 s (Dominic b 1979, Benedict b 1980, Andrew b 1983), 1 da (Louise b 1981); *Career* CA 1974; PricewaterhouseCoopers LLP (formerly Price Waterhouse before merger): joined 1971, ptnr 1982, responsible for servs to insurance sector in UK 1983–94 and in Europe 1989–94, sr client ptnr 1993–98, memb Price Waterhouse World Firm Insurance Group 1986–94, memb Euro Supervisory Bd 1993–98, memb Exec 1994–98, managing ptnr 1996–2000, memb Global Bd 1997–98, memb UK Mgmnt Bd 1998–, chm and sr ptnr 2000–; memb: Insurance Ctee ICAEW 1983–95, Standing Inter-Professional Liaison Gp Accounting and Actuarial Professions 1987–97, Accounting and Auditing Standards Ctee Lloyd's of London 1988–90, Life Insurance Accounting Ctee ABI 1992–94, HM Govt Task Force on Deregulation of Fin Servs Sector 1993–94, Solvency and Reporting Ctee at Lloyd's 1994–96, Disputes Resolution Panel at Lloyd's 1996–98, Cncl for Industry and HE 1998–, PricewaterhouseCoopers Global Supervisory Bd 1998–2000, PricewaterhouseCoopers Global Leadership Team 2000–, Steering Ctee Heart of the City 2000–, President's Ctee CBI 2001–, Cncl Prince of Wales Int Business Leaders Forum 2001–, Transatlantic Cncl British American Business Inc 2001–, Cncl NIESR 2004–, IPPR Task Force on Ethnic Diversity in the Private Sector 2004, President's Ctee London First 2006–, Pres's Gp Employers' Forum on Disability 2006; chm Gooda Walker Loss Review Ctee at Lloyd's 1991–92, chm Syndicate 387 Loss Review at Lloyd's 1992–93; dir Royal Automobile Club Ltd 2007–; tstee: Industry in Educn 1999–, Royal Anniversary Tst 2007–; FCA 1979, FRSA 1994, KHS 1999; *Recreations* golf, shooting; *Clubs* RAC; *Style—* Kieran Poynter, Esq; ✉ 15 Montpelier Mews, London SW7 1HB (e-mail kieranp@aol.com); PricewaterhouseCoopers LLP, 1 Embankment Place, London WC2N 6RH (tel 020 7583 5000, fax 020 7804 2989, e-mail kieran.poynter@uk.pwc.com)

POYNTON, Malcolm; s of Norman Albert Pointon, and Jocelyn Margaret, *née* MacDonald; *b* 25 December 1966, NZ; *Educ* Auckland Univ; *m* 6 May 1998, Lisa, *née* Harriden; 1 da (Eden Odile b 1 Sept 2003); *Career* jr creative: Gurney Nagle Advtg Auckland 1985, HKM Advtg Auckland 1986, BBDO London 1989; writer HKM/Rialto Auckland 1989, art dir Omon Sydney 1990, founding ptnr and creative dir Green Girl Publishing Sydney 1993, sr creative The Campaign Palace Sydney, Melbourne and Auckland 1993, dep creative dir M&C Saatchi London 1995, exec creative dir Saatchi & Saatchi Sydney 2000, exec creative dir Ogilvy London 2003; more than 40 int advtg awards incl Gold award Cannes 1999, 2000, 2001, 2005 and 2007 (Silver 2000, 2001, 2005, 2006 and 2007, Bronze 1991, 1998, 2000, 2001, 2004, 2005, 2006 and 2007); memb D&AD; patron CALM (Campaign Against Living Miserably) UK; memb NZ yachting team 1984–85, memb Aust yachting team 1991, hon coach NZ Yachting Fedn; *Recreations* yachting, snowboarding, flyfishing, outdoor pursuits; *Clubs* Soho House, Union; *Style—* Malcolm Poynton, Esq; ✉ Ogilvy London, 10 Cabot Square, Canary Wharf, London E14 4QB (tel 020 7345 3000, e-mail malc@ogilvy.com)

POYSER, Dr Norman Leslie; s of George Clifford Poyser (d 1987), and Marjorie Ellis, *née* Knight (d 1982); *b* 9 August 1947; *Educ* High Pavement GS Nottingham, Sch of Pharmacy Univ of London (BPharm), Univ of Edinburgh (PhD, DSc, Sandoz prize); *m* 1, 1976, Valerie Lesley (d 1985), da of Dr James Rennie Whitehead; 1 s (Timothy James), 1 da (Natalie Claire); m 2, 1990, Moira Anderson Scott; 2 step da (Carolyn Scott, Beverley Begley); *Career* Univ of Edinburgh: ICI research fell 1971–73, MRC research fell 1973–75, lectr 1975–87, sr lectr 1987–, head Dept of Pharmacology 1995–98; memb: Soc for Endocrinology 1972, Br Pharmacological Soc 1974, Soc for Reproduction and Fertility 1975; *Publications* Prostaglandins in Reproduction (1981); numerous pubns incl original articles, contribs to books and review articles; *Recreations* tennis, bridge, golf, theatre-going, concert-going, watching sport on TV; *Clubs* Colinton Lawn Tennis (Edinburgh), Merchants of Edinburgh Golf; *Style—* Dr Norman Poyser; ✉ University of Edinburgh, Hugh Robson Building, George Square, Edinburgh EH8 9XD (tel 0131 651 1692, fax 0131 650 3711, mobile 07726 889885, e-mail norman.poyser@ed.ac.uk)

PRAG, Derek Nathan; s of late Abraham J Prag, and Edith Prag (d 1992); *b* 6 August 1923; *Educ* Bolton Sch, Emmanuel Coll Cambridge (MA); *m* 1948, Dora Weiner; 3 s; *Career* Br Army 1942–47; econ journalist Reuters 1950–55, freelance ed Financial Times Business Letter from Europe 1975–77, i/c Anglo-American Section of Info Serv of High Authy of the Euro Coal and Steel Community 1955–59, head Pubns Div Jt Info Serv of Euro Communities 1959–67, dir London Press and Info Office of Euro Communities 1965–73, ran own consultancy on rels with EEC 1973–79; MEP (EDG 1979–92, EPP 1992–94) Hertfordshire 1979–94; Cons spokesman Constitutional Ctee 1982–84 and 1987–94 (first vice-chm 1987–94 (elected chm 1993 but stood down)), Cons spokesman Political Affrs Ctee 1984–87, sr vice-chm Ctee of Enquiry into Fascism and Racism 1986, sr vice-chm Euro Parl ASEAN Delgn 1979–87; memb: Tport Ctee 1991–94, Euro Parl Israel Delgn 1991–94, Security Sub-Ctee 1984–94; vice-pres Israel-Euro Parly Intergroup 1987–94; memb or alternate memb Foreign Affrs and Security Ctee 1979–94; rapporteur: on EU's ext relations for draft treaty on Euro Union adopted 1984, on Seat of the EC Insts and working-place of the Euro Parl (Prag Report, adopted 1989 by 223 votes to 173, decided on gradual concentration of Euro Parl's work and staff in Brussels); pres: London Europe Soc 2000– (chm 1973–2000), Herts Assoc of Local Cncls 2003–; chm: Euro Parl's All-Pty Gp on Disablement 1980–94, Welwyn Hatfield Access Gp 1995–2002; fndr memb Cons Gp for Europe (dep chm 1974–77 and 1991–93, pres Herts Branch 1995–); Cdr Order of Leopold II (Belgium) 1996; hon dir EEC Cmmn 1974, Silver Medal of Euro Merit 1974, Hon DLitt Herts 1993, Hon MEP 1994; *Publications* Businessman's Guide to the Common Market (with late E D Nicholson, 1973); many booklets and articles on Euro subjects; *Recreations* listening to music, reading, swimming, gardening, languages (speaks seven); *Clubs* Royal Over-Seas League, Anglo-Belgian, RAC (Brussels); *Style—* Mr Derek Prag; ✉ Pine Hill, 47 New Road, Digswell, Hertfordshire AL6 0AQ (tel 01438 715686, e-mail derekprag@aol.com)

PRAG, Prof (Andrew) John Nicholas Warburg; s of Adolf Prag (d 2004), and Dr Frede Charlotte Prag, *née* Warburg (d 2004); *b* 28 August 1941; *Educ* Westminster, BNC Oxford (Domus exhibitioner, hon scholar, MA, Dip Classical Archaeology, sr Hulme scholar, DPhil); *m* 6 July 1969, Dr Kay Prag, da of Douglas James Wright (d 1979), of Sydney, NSW; 1 s (Jonathan Ralph Warburg b 1975), 1 da (Kate Susannah b 1977); *Career* temp asst keeper Dept of Antiquities Ashmolean Museum Oxford 1966–67; Univ of Manchester: keeper of archaeology Manchester Museum 1969–, sr lectr 1977, hon lectr Dept of History 1977–83, hon lectr in archaeology 1984–, hon res fell Sch of History and Classics 2002, reader in classics and ancient history 2002–04, prof of archaeological studies 2004–05, emeritus prof of classics 2005–; hon prof Manchester Museum 2005–; visiting prof Dept of Classics McMaster Univ Hamilton Ontario 1978; ed Archaeological Reports 1975–87, memb Cncl British Sch at Athens (visiting fell 1994); family rep Advsy Bd Warburg Inst Univ of London; FSA 1977; *Books* The Oresteia: Iconographic & Narrative Tradition (1985), Making Faces Using Forensic and Archaeological Evidence (with Richard Neave, 1997, 2 edn 1999), Periplous: Papers on Classical Art and Archaeology Presented to Sir John Boardman (ed with G R Tsetskhladze and A M Snodgrass, 2000), Seianti Hanunia Tlesnasa: The Story of an Etruscan Noblewoman (with J Swaddling, 2002), The Archaeology of Alderley Edge (with Simon Timberlake, 2005); *Recreations* music, cooking, travel; *Style—* Prof A J N W Prag, FSA; ✉ The Manchester Museum, The University of Manchester, Manchester M13 9PL (tel 0161 275 2665, fax 0161 275 2676, e-mail john.prag@manchester.ac.uk)

PRAG, Thomas Gregory Andrew; s of Adolf Prag, of Oxford, and Frede Charlotte, *née* Warburg; *b* 2 January 1947; *Educ* Westminster, BNC Oxford (MA); *m* 4 April 1971, Angela Mary, da of late Leslie Hughes; 3 s (Benjamin David b 18 Nov 1972, Henry John b 17 Feb 1975, Nicholas Timothy b 18 Nov 1977); *Career* studio mangr BBC Radio Bush House 1968–70, BBC Radio Oxford 1970–78, prog organiser BBC Highland Inverness 1978–81, md and prog controller Moray Firth Radio 1981–2001 (chm 2000–01), memb for Scot Radio Authy 2001–03, chm Media Support Solutions 2001–; memb Highland Cncl 2007–, former pres Inverness C of C, former chm Highland Festival, sec Moray Firth Radio Charity Tst, memb Bd of Govrs UHI Millennium Inst, memb Bd Inverness Harbour Tst, memb Bd of Govrs Eden Court Theatre 2007–; FIMgt, fell Radio Academy 1998; *Recreations* home and family, elderly Daimler convertible, novice golfer, gentle sculling and coxing, gardening to feed marauding deer; *Clubs* Inverness Rotary; *Style—* Thomas Prag, Esq; ✉ Windrush, Easter Muckovie, Inverness IV2 5BN (tel 01463 791697, e-mail prag@ecosse.net)

PRAGNELL, Michael; *b* 1946; *Educ* Douai Sch, St John's Coll Oxford (BA), INSEAD Fontainebleau (MBA); *Career* Courtaulds Ltd London and USA 1968–74, First National Bank of Chicago 1974–75; Courtaulds plc 1975–95: ceo Courtaulds Coatings, sometime chief fin offr, exec dir 1990–95; ceo Zeneca Agrochemicals 1995–2000, exec dir Zeneca Group plc (later AstraZeneca plc) 1997–2000, fndr ceo Syngenta AG 2000–; pres Crop Life International 2003–05, memb Supervisory Bd Advanta BV 1996–2000, non-exec dir David S Smith (Holdings) 1996–2000; *Style—* Michael Pragnell, Esq; ✉ Syngenta AG, Schwarzwaldallee 215, PO Box, CH-4002 Basel, Switzerland

PRAIN, Philip James Murray; s of (John) Murray Prain, DSO, OBE, TD, DL (d 1985), and (Lorina) Helen Elspeth, *née* Skene (d 1993); *b* 14 November 1936; *Educ* Eton, Clare Coll Cambridge (MA); *m* 28 Sept 1972, Susan Ferrier, da of Andrew Munro Marr (d 1955); 1 da (Philippa Victoria b 1975); *Career* 2 Lt Black Watch 1955–57, Lt TARO, memb Queen's Body Guard for Scotland (Royal Co of Archers) 1966; called to the Bar Inner Temple 1963; with Kleinwort Benson Ltd 1962–2000, dir Kleinwort Benson (Hong Kong) Ltd 1979–83; chm Manor Gardens Enterprise Centre Islington 1987–95; memb: Cncl United World Coll of the Atlantic S Wales 1992–2000, Fin Ctee Br Red Cross 1992–2001; dir E London Small Business Centre 1996–2006, dir E London Small Business Charity 1996–2006; tstee: Westminster Amalgamated Charity 1983– (chm Bd of Tstees 1995–2002), All Saints Fndn Margaret Street 1988–94, St Clement Dane's Holborn Estate Charity 1989–, Nat Canine Defence League (now Dogs Tst) 1989– (chm Cncl 1996–2002, vice-pres 2002–); underwriting memb Lloyds 1978–98; Freeman City of London 1978, Liveryman Worshipful Co of Founders 1978 (memb Ct of Assts 2000, Master 2005–06); *Recreations* travel, photography; *Clubs* Beefsteak, MCC, Hurlingham, Royal and Ancient Golf, Downhill Only (Wengen), Leander (Assoc), Hong Kong, Hong Kong Jockey; *Style—* Philip Prain, Esq; ✉ 73 Woodsford Square, London W14 8DS (tel 020 7603 7767, fax 020 7602 9609)

PRAIS, Prof Sigbert Jon; s of Samuel Prais, and Bertha Prais; *b* 19 December 1928; *Educ* King Edward's Sch Birmingham, Univ of Birmingham (MCom), Univ of Cambridge (PhD, ScD); *m* 1971, Vivien Hennessy; 1 s, 3 da; *Career* post-doctoral fell Univ of Chicago, Dept of Applied Economics Univ of Cambridge 1950–57, research offr NIESR 1953–59, UN Tech Assistance Orgn 1959–60, IMF Washington 1960–61, fin dir Elbief Co 1961–70, sr research fell NIESR 1970–, visiting prof of economics City Univ 1975–95; memb: Cncl Royal Econ Soc 1979–83, Cncl City Univ 1990–93, Mathematics Ctee Schs Examination and Assessment Cncl 1991–93; Hon DLitt City Univ 1989, Hon DSc Birmingham Univ 2006; FBA 1985; *Books* Analysis of Family Budgets (co-author, 1955), Evolution of Giant Firms in Britain (1976), Productivity and Industrial Structure (1981), Productivity, Education and Training (1995), From School to Productive Work (1997), Social Disparities and the Teaching of Literacy (2001); articles in economic and statistical jls, esp on influence of educn and training on economic growth; *Style—* Prof Sigbert Prais, FBA; ✉ 83 West Heath Road, London NW3 (tel 020 8458 4428); office (tel 020 7654 1939)

PRANCE, Prof Sir Ghillean (Iain) Tolmie; kt (1995); s of Basil Camden Prance, CIE, OBE (d 1947), and Margaret Hope, *née* Tolmie (d 1970); *b* 13 July 1937; *Educ* Malvern Coll, Univ of Oxford (MA, DPhil); *m* 13 July 1961, Anne Elizabeth, da of Rev Archibald MacAlister Hay (d 1980); 2 da (Rachel b 1963, Sarah b 1966); *Career* NY Botanical Gardens: res asst 1963–68, BA Krukoff curator Amazonian Botany 1968–75, dir res 1975–81, vice-pres 1977–81, sr vice-pres 1981–88, dir Inst Econ Botany 1981–88; adjunct prof City Univ NY 1968–99; ldr Amazonian Exploration Prog 1965–88; dir Royal Botanic Gardens Kew 1988–99, dir of science The Eden Project 1998–; visiting prof: tropical studies Yale Univ 1983–88, Univ of Reading 1988–; McBryde prof US Nat Tropical Botanical Garden Hawaii 2000–02; author of numerous papers and books; memb Bd of Dirs: Margaret Mee Amazon Tst 1988–98, Lovaine Tst 1989–99, Royal Botanic Gardens Kew Fndn 1990–99; exec dir Orgn Flora Neotropica (UNESCO) 1975–88, memb Mayor's Cmmn on Cable TV White Plains NY 1981–88; tstee: Au Sable Inst of Environmental Studies 1984–, WWF 1989–93, Horniman Museum 1990–99, World Humanities Action Tst 1994–99, New Island Tst 1995–, Global Diversity Fndn (chm), Brazilian Atlantic Rainforest Tst (chm); patron: Bioregional Devpt Gp 1995–, Sheffield Botanic Gardens Tst 1997–, Serra do Mar Reserva Ecologica (now Reserva Ecologica Guapi-açú) Brazil 1997–, Soc of Botanical Artists 1997–; International Cosmos prize 1993, Asa Gray Award American Soc of Plant Taxonomists 1998, Lifetime of Discovery Award RGS 1999, Fairchild Medal for Plant Exploration 2000, Distinguished Economic Botanist Award of Soc Econ Botany 2002, Allerton Award US Nat Tropical Botanical Garden 2005; Dr (hc) Göteborgs Univ 1983; DSc (hc): Univ of Kent 1994, Portsmouth Univ 1994, Kingston Univ 1994, Univ of St Andrews 1995, Bergen Univ Norway 1996, Sheffield Univ 1997, Florida Int Univ 1997, Lehman Coll City Univ NY 1998, Univ of Liverpool 1998, Glasgow Univ 1999, Univ of Plymouth 1999, Keele Univ 2000, Univ of Exeter 2000; hon fell Royal Botanic Garden Edinburgh 1995, hon research fell Royal Botanic Gardens Kew 1999; Patrons Medal RGS 1994; FLS 1963, FRGS 1989, FRS 1993; fell AAAS 1990; VMH, RHS 1999; foreign memb Royal Danish Acad Scis and Letters 1988, corr memb Brazilian Acad of Scis 1976, foreign memb Royal Swedish Acad Sci 1989; *Books* Arvores De Manaus (1975), Extinction Is Forever (1977), Biological Diversification in the Tropics (1981), Leaves (1986), Amazonia (1985), Wild Flowers for all Seasons (1988), White Gold (1989), Out of the Amazon (1992), Bark (1993), The Earth Under Threat (1996), Rainforests of the World (1998); *Recreations* music; *Clubs* Explorers' (fell 1978); *Style—* Prof Sir Ghillean Prance, FRS; ✉ The Old Vicarage, Silver Street, Lyme Regis, Dorset DT7 3HS (tel 01297 444991, fax 01279 444955, e-mail gtolmiep@aol.com)

PRASAD, Alfred Patrick; *Educ* Inst of Hotel Mgmnt Madras; *Career* chef; advanced chef training Maurya Sheraton Delhi, trained at Bukhara Delhi and Dum-Pukht Delhi, chef Dakshin ITC Sheraton Hotel Madras 1996–99, sous chef Veeraswamy London 1999–2001, exec chef Tamarind London 2002– (joined 2001, Michelin Star 2001–05); *Style—* Alfred Patrick Prasad, Esq; ✉ Tamarind, 20 Queen Street, Mayfair, London W1J 5PR

P

PRASHAR, Baroness (Life Peer UK 1999), of Runnymede in the County of Surrey; Usha Prashar; CBE (1995); *b* 29 June 1948; *Educ* Wakefield Girls' HS, Univ of Leeds (BA), Univ of Glasgow (Dip Social Admin); *m* 21 July 1973, Vijay Sharma; *Career* conciliation offr Race Rels Bd 1971–76, dir Runnymede Tst 1976–84, research fell Policy Studies Inst 1984–86, dir Nat Cncl for Voluntary Orgn 1986–91, chm The Parole Bd 1997–2000, First Civil Serv Cmmr 2000–05 (pt/t Civil Serv cmmr 1990–96), chair Judicial Appts Cmmn 2005–; non-exec dir: Channel Four Television Corporation 1992–99, Unite Gp plc 2001–04, ITV plc 2005–; visiting prof Univ of Exeter; memb: Arts Cncl of GB 1979–81 and 1994–97, Study Cmmn on the Family 1980–83, Social Security Advsy Ctee 1980–83, Exec Ctee Child Poverty Action Gp 1984–85, Gtr London Arts Assoc 1984–86, London Food Cmmn 1984–90, BBC Educnl Broadcasting Cncl 1987–88, Advsy Cncl Open Coll 1987–88, Elfrida Rathbone Soc 1988–91, Slrs' Complaints Bureau 1989–91, Lord Chllr's Advsy Ctee on Legal Educn 1991–97, Royal Cmmn on Criminal Justice 1991–93, Bd Energy Saving Tst 1992–97, Ealing Hounslow and Hammersmith HA 1993–96, Bd Salzburg Seminar 2000–04, House of Lords and House of Commons Jt Ctee on Human Rights 2001–04; vice-pres Cncl for Overseas Student Affrs 1986–91, vice-chm Br Refugee Cncl 1987–90, chm English Advsy Ctee Nat AIDS Tst 1988–89, vice-pres Patients' Assoc 1990–91, chm Nat Literacy Tst 2000–05 (dep chm 1992–2000); patron: Sickle Cell Soc 1986–, Tara Arts, Wise Thoughts; tstee: Thames Help Tst 1984–86, Charities Aid Fndn 1986–91, Independent Broadcasting Telethon Tst 1987–93, Camelot Fndn 1996–2001, BBC World Service Tst 2001–05, Miriam Rothschild and John Foster 2007, Cumberland Lodge 2007; hon assoc Nat Cncl of Women of GB 1989–; memb Cncl Royal Holloway Coll London 1992–97, chllr De Montfort Univ 2000–06 (govr 1996–2006); hon fell Goldsmiths Coll London 1992; Hon LLD: De Montfort Univ, South Bank Univ, Univ of Greenwich 1998, Leeds Metropolitan Univ 1999; FRSA 1989; *Books* contrib to: Britain's Black Population (1980), The System - A Study of Lambeth Borough Council's Race Relations Unit (1981), Scarman and After (1984), Sickle Cell Anaemia Who Cares? A Survey of Screening Counselling Training and Educational Facilities in England (1985), Routes or Road Blocks - A Study of Consultation Arrangements Between Local Authorities and Local Communities (1985), Acheson and After - Primary Health Care in the Inner City (1986); *Recreations* country walks, golf, music; *Clubs* Reform, Royal Cwlth Soc; *Style—* The Baroness Usha Prashar, CBE; ✉ Judicial Appointments Commission, Steel House, 11 Tothill Street, London SW1H 9LH

PRATCHETT, Terence David John (Terry); OBE (1998); s of David and Eileen Pratchett, of Hay-on-Wye; *b* 28 April 1948; *Educ* High Wycombe Tech HS, Beaconsfield Public Library; *m* Lyn Marian, da of Jean and Richard Purves; 1 da (Rhianna Katie b 1976); *Career* writer; various regnl journalism 1965–80, press offr Central Electricity Generating Bd 1980–87, full time writer 1987–; memb Soc of Authors (memb and former chm Mgmnt Ctee); Hon DLitt Univ of Warwick 1999; Carnegie Medal 2002; *Books* The Carpet People (1971), The Dark Side of the Sun (1976), Strata (1981), The Colour of Magic (1983), The

Light Fantastic (1986), Equal Rites (1987), Mort (1987), Sourcery (1988), Wyrd Sisters (1988), Pyramids (1989), Truckers (1989), Guards! Guards! (1989), The Unadulterated Cat (illustrated by Gray Jolliffe, 1989), Eric (illustrated by Josh Kirby, 1989), Good Omens (with Neil Gaiman, *qv*, 1990), Moving Pictures (1990), Diggers (1990), Wings (1990), Reaper Man (1991), Witches Abroad (1991), Small Gods (1992), Only You Can Save Mankind (1992), Lords and Ladies (1992), Johnny and the Dead (1993), Men at Arms (1993), Soul Music (1994), Interesting Times (1994), The Discworld Companion (with S Briggs, 1994), Maskerade (1995), Johnny and the Bomb (1996), Feet of Clay (1996), Hogfather (1996), Jingo (1997), The Last Continent (1998), Carpe Jugulum (1998), The Science of Discworld (with Ian Stewart, *qv*, and Jack Cohen, 1999), The Fifth Elephant (1999), The Truth (2000), Last Hero (2001), Night Watch (2002), Monstrous Regiment (2003); *Recreations* writing, walking, computers, life; *Style—* Terry Pratchett, Esq, OBE; ✉ c/o Colin Smythe, PO Box 6, Gerrards Cross, Buckinghamshire SL9 8XA (tel 01753 886000, fax 01753 886469, e-mail cpsmythe@aol.com)

PRATLEY, Alan Sawyer; s of Frederick Pratley (d 1970), and Hannah, *née* Sawyer (d 1981); *b* 25 November 1933; *Educ* Latymer Upper Sch, Sidney Sussex Coll Cambridge (BA); *m* 1, 29 Aug 1960 (m dis 1979), Dorothea, da of Walter Rohland; 2 da (Christiane b 14 Nov 1961, Alexa b 5 Jan 1963); m 2, 22 Dec 1979, Josette Kairis; 1 da (Fiona b 3 Feb 1981); m 3, 7 Feb 1996; *Career* head of German Dept Stratford GS 1958–60, asst dir examinations Civil Service Cmmn 1960–68, asst sec Home Office 1971–73 (princ 1968–71); Cmmn of the European Communities: head of Individual Rights Div 1973–79, dep head of cabinet to Christopher Tugendhat as UK EEC cmmr 1979–80, advsr to Michael O'Kennedy as EEC cmmr for Republic of Ireland 1981, dir-gen admin 1981–86, dep fin controller 1990– (dir fin control 1986–90); *Recreations* tennis; *Clubs* Travellers; *Style—* Alan Pratley, Esq; ✉ Commission of the European Communities, CSM2, 8th floor, Bureau no 100, Avenue de Tervuren, 1049 Brussels, Belgium (tel 00 32 2 295 2686, fax 00 32 2 295 0141)

PRATLEY, David Illingworth; s of Arthur George Pratley, of Dorset, and Olive Constance, *née* Illingworth; *b* 24 December 1948; *Educ* Westminster, Univ of Bristol (LLB); *m* 1996, Caryn Lois Faure Walker (d 2004); *Career* PR offr Thorndike Theatre Leatherhead 1970–71, press and publicity offr Queen's Univ Belfast 1971–72, dep dir Merseyside Arts Assoc 1972–76, dir Gtr London Arts Assoc 1976–81, regnl dir Arts Cncl of GB 1981–86, chm Dance Umbrella Ltd 1986–92, chief exec Royal Liverpool Philharmonic Soc 1987–88, md Trinity Coll of Music 1988–91, chm Nat Campaign for the Arts 1988–92, dir of leisure, tourism and economic devpt Bath City Cncl 1992–96, lottery policy advsr Arts Cncl of England 1996–; ptnr: David Pratley Associates 1996–; *Books* Culture for All (1981), The Pursuit of Competence - the Arts and the European Community (1987), Musicians Go To School (1993); *Recreations* arts, travel, gardens, countryside; *Clubs* Athenaeum; *Style—* David Pratley, Esq; ✉ 54 Walnut Tree Walk, London SE11 6DN (tel 020 7582 9266, e-mail davidpratley@aol.com)

PRATT, (Richard) Camden; QC (1992); s of late Richard Sheldon Pratt, of Grantham, Lincs, and late Irene Gladys, *née* Whalley; *b* 14 December 1947; *Educ* Boston GS, Westcliff HS, Lincoln Coll Oxford (MA, Hanbury law scholar); *m* 4 Aug 1973, (Dorothy Jane) Marchia, da of late Capt William Paul Allsebrook, of Athens; *Career* called to the Bar Gray's Inn 1970 (bencher 2001); recorder of the Crown Court 1993–, dep judge of the High Court (Family Div) 1994–; chm: Sussex Courts Liaison Ctee 1993–, Sussex Sessions Bar Mess 1995–2006; *Recreations* people; *Style—* Camden Pratt, Esq, QC; ✉ 1 King's Bench Walk, Temple, London EC4Y 7DB (tel 020 7936 1500, fax 020 7936 1590)

PRATT, (Edmund) John; s of Edmund Addison Pratt (d 1970), and Ruth Marie Erneste, *née* Wilkinson; *b* 14 October 1944; *Educ* Warwick Sch, Imperial Coll London (BSc(Eng) Civil Engrg, MSc(Eng) Tport); *m* 21 Dec 1968, Jennifer Grace, *née* Reynolds; 2 da (Polly Louise b 22 Nov 1972, Sophie Alice b 2 May 1974); *Career* engr Sir William Halcrow & Partners 1966–70, civil engr The Costain Group 1970–73, conslt P-E Consulting Group 1973–76, dir and gen mangr George Longden Construction Ltd (subsid of Whitecroft plc) 1976–79, northern UK gen mangr Damp Proofing Div Rentokil plc 1979–81, sales and mktg dir Steetley Brick Ltd 1981–85, gp mktg dir David Webster Ltd 1986–88, chm Leading Edge Management Consultancy Ltd 1994– (sr ptnr 1988–94); dir CIM Holdings Ltd 1996–2002, dir CAM Fndn Ltd 2000–02, Marketing Developments Ltd 2001–; non-exec dir First Whitehall Properties Ltd 1998–; chm CIM 2000–01, non-exec dir Marketing Cncl 2000–02; Liveryman Worshipful Co of Marketors 2001–; FCIM, MIMC, MICE, CEng, CMC; *Recreations* classic cars, family history, cycling; *Style—* John Pratt, Esq; ✉ Leading Edge Management Consultancy Ltd, Bancroft House, 34 Bancroft, Hitchin, Hertfordshire SG5 1LA (tel 01462 440345, fax 01462 420345, e-mail john.pratt@lead-edge.co.uk)

PRATT, Roger James Edward; s of Francis William Pratt, and Phillis May, *née* Swift; *Educ* Loughborough GS, Univ of Durham (BA), London Film Sch (Dip); *Career* cinematographer; memb: BAFTA 1993–, Acad of Motion Picture Arts and Sciences 1995–, BSC; Tech Achievement Award RTS; *Films* asst cameraman Bleak Moments, second asst Monty Python and the Holy Grail; dir of photography: Brazil 1985, Mona Lisa 1986, Scoop 1987 (TV movie), Consuming Passions 1988, Batman 1989, The Fisher King 1991, Shadowlands 1993, The Line, the Cross and the Curve 1993, Frankenstein 1994 (nomination Best Cinematography BSC), Twelve Monkeys 1995, In Love and War 1996, The Avengers 1998, Grey Owl 1999, The End of the Affair 1999 (nomination Best Cinematography: BAFTA Awards, Oscars), 102 Dalmatians 2000, Chocolat 2000 (nomination Best Cinematography BAFTA Awards), Iris 2001, Harry Potter and the Chamber of Secrets 2002, Troy 2004, Harry Potter and the Goblet of Fire 2005; *Recreations* opera; *Clubs* Groucho; *Style—* Roger Pratt, Esq

PRATT, Sandy Robert Gammack; s of Alexander Robert Pratt (d 1976), of Elgin, Scotland, and Daphne Lesley Crofton, *née* McCann; *b* 25 December 1951; *Educ* Blairmore Sch Aberdeenshire, Fettes, Christ's Coll Cambridge (MA, LLM); *m* 8 Jan 1977, Helen, da of Joseph Aubrey Pritchard (d 1963), of Chester; 1 da (Samantha b 13 June 1980), 1 s (James b 21 Oct 1983); *Career* admitted slr Supreme Court 1978; authorised insolvency practitioner 1987–, ptnr Corporate and Financial Dept Norton Rose 1988– (trainee slr 1976–78, asst slr 1978–88); Freeman: City of London, Worshipful Co of Slrs; memb: Law Soc, City of London Law Soc, Insolvency Practitioners' Assoc, Soc of Practitioners' of Insolvency, Insolvency Lawyers' Assoc, Int Bar Assoc, Assoc Européenne des Praticiens des Procédures Collectives; *Books* Norton Rose "Corporate Insolvency Law and Practice" booklet (ed, 3 edn, 1993); *Recreations* rugby (Cambridge blues 1973 and 1974), genealogy, golf, shooting, fishing, woodturning; *Clubs* London Scottish FC, The Whale, Hawks' (Cambridge), Denham Golf; *Style—* Sandy Pratt, Esq; ✉ 21 Mooreland Road, Bromley, Kent BR1 3RD (tel 020 8464 9385); Norton Rose, Kempson House, Camomile Street, London EC3A 7AN (tel 020 7283 6000, fax 020 7283 6500)

PREBBLE, Stuart Colin; s of Dennis Stanley (d 2000), and Jean Margaret, *née* McIntosh (d 1981); *b* 15 April 1951; *Educ* Beckenham & Penge GS, Univ of Newcastle upon Tyne (BA); *m* 25 Aug 1978, Marilyn Anne, da of George Charlton, of Newcastle upon Tyne; 2 da (Alexandra Juliette b 1979, Claire Samantha b 1982 d 1996); *Career* reporter BBC TV 1973–79; Granada TV: ed World in Action 1986–89 (prodr 1981–86), head of regnl progs 1989–92; controller of network factual programmes ITV Network Centre 1992–96, chief exec Granada Sky Broadcasting 1996–98; Granada Media Gp: dir of channels 1998–, md channels and interactive media 1999–; ceo ONdigital 1999–2001, chief exec ITV 2001–03, co-fndr Liberty Bell Productions 2003–; fndr Campaign for Quality TV, advsr Victim Support; *Books* A Power in the Land (1988), The Lazarus File (1989), The Grumpy Old Men Handbook (2004), Grumpy Old Men: The Secret Diary (2005), Grumpy Old Christmas (2006); *Recreations* music, writing, travel; *Style—* Stuart Prebble, Esq; ✉ Liberty Bell Productions, 4A Exmoor Street, London W10 6BD

PREDDY, Clifford Stanley Frank (Cliff); s of Stanley Preddy (d 1988), and Kathleen, *née* Turner; *b* 30 April 1947, Croydon; *Educ* John Newnham Sch Croydon, John Ruskin GS Croydon, Univ of Bristol (BSc, MSc); *m* 11 Aug 1970, Jill Mary; 1 da (Heloise Amber b 9 Jan 1972), 1 s (Daniel Seth b 21 May 1974); *Career* Logica: joined as mathematician/programmer 1969, conslt and project mangr 1972–79, various line mangr roles 1979–87, exec dir Logica plc 1987–96, md Logica UK 1990–96; fndr and md Charteris 1996–2000, non-exec dir Charteris plc (following floatation on Stock Exchange) 2000–; chm CODASciSys plc (formerly Science Systems plc) 1997–2003 (non-exec dir 2003–06), non-exec dir CODA plc (following demerger) 2006–07; non-exec dir Computacenter plc 2002–; FBCS 1995; *Style—* Cliff Preddy, Esq; ✉ c/o Charteris plc, Charteris House, 39–40 Bartholomew Close, London EC1A 7JN

PREECE, Andrew Douglas; s of Bernard Charles Preece, of Walton on the Hill, Stafford, and Joyce Mary, *née* Clayton; *b* 28 September 1944; *Educ* King Edward V1 GS Stafford, Selwyn Coll Cambridge (MA); *m* 5 Oct 1968, Caroline Jane, da of Edmund Arthur Bland (d 1988); 2 da (Victoria Jane b 31 March 1972, Joanna Mary b 19 Jan 1981), 1 s (James Douglas b 4 Aug 1976); *Career* articled clerk asst slr Hall Collins 1968–71; Herbert Smith: asst slr 1971–74, assoc ptnr 1974–77, ptnr 1977–2005, conslt 2005–; memb UK Energy Lawyers Gp; Freeman Worshipful Co of Slrs; memb Law Soc; *Recreations* sailing, golf; *Clubs* Moor Park Golf, RAF Yacht; *Style—* Andrew Preece, Esq; ✉ Hyde Farm, Hyde Lane, Great Missenden, Buckinghamshire HP16 0RF; Flat 12, President's Quay House, 72 St Katherine's Way, London E1; Herbert Smith, Exchange House, Primrose Street, London EC2A 2HS (tel 020 7374 8000, fax 020 7374 0888)

PREECE, Ralph Stephen; s of John Raymond Preece, of 1 Ashgrove, Dinas Powis, South Glamorgan, and Doris, *née* Derrick; *b* 14 May 1946; *Educ* KCS, Cathays HS Cardiff; *m* 27 Dec 1969, Marilyn Preece, JP, da of Edwin Ralph Gardener Thomas; 2 da (Justine Claire b 28 Sept 1973, Natalie Jane b 27 Feb 1976); *Career* articled clerk Richard Davies & Co Cardiff 1965–70, qualified chartered accountant 1970, Coopers & Lybrand 1970–76 (Johannesburg, London, Cardiff), insolvency specialist Mann Judd Cardiff 1976–79; Deloitte & Touche (formerly Touche Ross): moved to Birmingham Office 1979, ptnr 1983, moved to Leeds Office, ptnr i/c Corp Special Servs (now Corp Recovery) 1983–, ptnr i/c London Office 1994–; memb Transvaal Soc of CAs 1972, FCA 1979 (ACA 1970), MICM 1986, MIPA 1988 (memb Cncl 1997–), memb Assoc Européenne des Practiciens des Procedures Collectives 1988, MSPI 1990 (memb Cncl 1996–); *Recreations* gardening, golf; *Clubs* Leeds; *Style—* Ralph Preece, Esq; ✉ Deloitte & Touche, PO Box 810, Stonecutter Court, 1 Stonecutter Street, London EC4A 4TR (tel 020 7936 3000, fax 020 7583 1198)

PREISKEL, Prof Harold Wilfred; s of David Preiskel (d 1983), of London, and Lili, *née* Wick; *b* 1 June 1939; *Educ* St Paul's, Guy's Med and Dental Sch (LDSRCS, BDS, FDSRCS, MDS), Ohio State Univ (MSc); *m* 22 Aug 1962, Nira, da of Joshua Orenstein (d 1977), of Tel Aviv; 3 s (Daniel b 1965, Ronald b 1969, Alon b 1976), 1 da (Daphne b 1979); *Career* house surgn 1962, lectr in restorative dentistry Royal Dental Hosp Sch of Surgery 1966–69, hon conslt Guy's Hosp 1971, chm London Dental Study Club 1971, examiner in dental prosthetics RCS 1972, staff examiner in prosthetic dentistry Univ of London 1974 (examiner 1969), pt/t conslt in prosthetic dentistry Guy's Hosp Dental Sch 1974 (sr lectr 1969, lectr 1962–66); prof KCL; chm Editorial Bd of Int Jl of Prosthodontists 1988 (a founding ed), memb Editorial Bd Jl of Dentistry 1972–; Thomas Hinman award Atlanta Georgia 1975, Int Circuit Course award of the American Coll of Prosthodontists 1988; pres: Int Coll of Prosthodontists 1987–91 (first pres), American Dental Soc of London, BDA metropolitan branch 1981–82, American Prosthodontic Assoc 2006 (first non-American pres); chm of tstees Alpha Omega Charitable Tst; memb: Br Soc for Restorative Dentistry, Br Soc for Study of Prosthetic Dentistry, European Prosthodontic Assoc, European Dental Soc, American Dental Soc of London, American Dental Soc of Europe, Carl O Boucher Prosthodontic Soc, American Acad Esthetic Dentistry (fndr), American Equilibration Soc, Fédération Dentaire Internationale, Int Coll of Prosthodontists (fndr); fell Int Coll of Dentists; hon citizen of New Orleans 1978; *Books* author of textbooks that have become standard works incl: Precision Attachments in Dentistry (1968, 1973, 1979), Precision Attachments in Prosthodontics Vol 1 & 2 (1985, trans in six languages), Overdentures Made Easy (printed in English, German, Spanish and Japanese); *Recreations* classical music, aviation; *Style—* Prof Harold Preiskel; ✉ 25 Upper Wimpole Street, London W1G 6NF (tel 020 7935 4525, fax 020 7486 8337, e-mail harold.preiskel@lineone.net)

PRENDERGAST, Sir (Walter) Kieran; KCVO (1991), CMG (1990); s of Lt Cdr Joseph Henry Prendergast (d 1989), and Mai, *née* Hennessy (d 1988); *b* 2 July 1942; *Educ* St Patrick's Coll Sydney, Salesian Coll Chertsey, St Edmund Hall Oxford; *m* 10 June 1967, Joan, da of Patrick Reynolds (d 1974); 2 s (Damian b 1968, Daniel b 1976), 2 da (Siobhain b 1971, Brigid b 1973); *Career* HM Dip Serv (ret); Istanbul 1964, Ankara 1965, FO 1967, Nicosia 1969, FCO 1972, The Hague 1973, asst private sec to two foreign secs (Rt Hon Anthony Crosland and Rt Hon Dr David Owen) 1976, UK Mission to UN New York 1979, Tel Aviv 1982, head of Southern African Dept FCO 1986–89; high cmmr: Zimbabwe 1989–92, Kenya 1992–95; ambass to Turkey 1995–97, under sec-gen Political Affrs UN NY 1997–2005; dir: Blue Hackle, Hakluyt, The Ind Diplomat; sr advsr BHP Billiton; *Recreations* family, walking, reading, shooting, wine; *Clubs* Beefsteak, Garrick, Muthaiga (Nairobi); *Style—* Sir Kieran Prendergast, KCVO, CMG; ✉ 26 Beckwith Road, London SE24 9LG; Bonneval, La Chapelle-aux-Saints, 19120, France

PRENDERGAST, His Hon Robert James Christie Vereker; s of Capt Richard Henry Prendergast (d 1965), of Roehampton, London, and Jean, *née* Christie (d 1988); *b* 21 October 1941; *Educ* Downside, Trinity Coll Cambridge (MA); *m* 16 April 1971, Berit, da of Wilburg Thauland (d 1982), of Oslo, Norway; 1 da (Victoria b 1973); *Career* called to the Bar Middle Temple 1964; recorder (SE Circuit) 1987–89, circuit judge (SE Circuit) 1989–2006; pres St Gregory's Soc (Downside Old Boys) 1999–2002; *Recreations* most gentle pursuits; *Style—* His Hon Robert Prendergast; ✉ 5 King's Bench Walk, Temple, London EC4Y 7DN

PRENTER, Patrick Robert; CBE (1995), JP (1980); s of Robert Gibson Prenter, OBE (d 1991), of Loanhead, Midlothian, and Katherine Emily, *née* Scott; *b* 9 September 1939, Edinburgh; *Educ* Loretto Sch Musselburgh, Trinity Hall Cambridge (MA); *m* 8 Dec 1962, Susan, *née* Patrick; 2 s (Richard Gibson Scott b 7 July 1963, Michael Hugh Patrick b 18 March 1970), 2 da (Lucinda Emily b 6 April 1967, Melinda Louise b 13 Oct 1978); *Career* md MacTaggart Scott 1967–99; Castle Rock Housing Assoc: memb Bd 1975–2005, chm 1995–2000; dir Forth Ports Authy 1984–91, pres Scot Engrg Employers' Assoc 1985–86, tax cmmr 1988–2003; dir Scot Chamber Orch 1995–; govr Loretto Sch 1982–89; Lord-Lt Midlothian 2003–; *Recreations* music, opera, reading, gardening, golf, tennis, skiing; *Clubs* RAC, New (Edinburgh), Free Foresters, Hon Co of Edinburgh Golfers; *Style—* Patrick Prenter, Esq, CBE, JP

PRENTICE, Bridget; JP (1985), MP; da of late James Corr, and Bridget Corr; *b* 28 December 1952; *Educ* Our Lady and St Francis Sch Glasgow, Univ of Glasgow (MA), Univ of London (PGCE), South Bank Univ (LLB); *m* 20 Dec 1975 (m dis), Gordon Prentice, MP, *qv*; *Career* rector's assessor Univ of Glasgow 1972–73, teacher London Oratory Sch 1974–86 (head of careers 1984–86), head of careers John Archer Sch 1986–88; London Borough of Hammersmith and Fulham: cncllr 1986–92, chm Lab Gp 1986–90, chm Public Servs Ctee 1987–90; MP (Lab) Lewisham E 1992–; memb Select Ctee on Parly Admin (ombudsman) 1992–95, oppn whip 1995–97, asst govt whip 1997–98, PPS to Brian

Wilson, MP as Min for Trade 1998–99, PPS to Lord Chancellor 1999–2001, asst govt whip 2003–05, Parly sec DCA 2005–; memb Home Affairs Select Ctee House of Commons 2001–03; memb GMB; *Recreations* football, reading, music, crosswords, gardening, badminton (qualified coach), my cats; *Style*— Bridget Prentice, MP; ✉ House of Commons, London SW1A 0AA (tel 020 7219 3503, fax 020 7219 5581)

PRENTICE, Christopher Norman Russell; s of Ronald Prentice (d 1984), and Sonia, *née* Bowring; *b* 5 September 1954, London; *Educ* Shrewsbury, ChCh Oxford (BA); *m* 24 June 1978, Nina, *née* King; 2 s (Andrew b 26 Jan 1981, Robert b 27 Sept 1988), 2 da (Helen b 14 July 1982, Alessandra (Muffie) b 27 Nov 1985); *Career* diplomat; entered HM Dip Serv 1977, desk offr Near East and North Africa Dept FCO 1977–78, trg MECAS (Middle Eastern Centre of Arabic Studies) Lebanon and London 1978–79, third then second sec Kuwait 1980–83, Middle East analyst Assessments Staff Cabinet Office 1983–85, first sec (Near East and South Asia) Washington DC 1985–89, asst head European Community Dept (External) FCO 1989–90, asst private sec to Foreign Sec 1990–93, dep head of mission Budapest 1994–98, head Near East and North Africa Dept FCO 1998–2002, ambass to Jordan 2002–06; *Recreations* photography, walking, cricket, mountains, golf; *Clubs* Athenaeum, MCC and other cricket clubs; *Style*— Christopher Prentice, Esq; ✉ c/o Foreign & Commonwealth Office, King Charles Street, London SW1A 2AH

PRENTICE, Gordon; MP; s of late William Prentice, and Esther Prentice; *b* 28 January 1951; *Educ* George Heriot's Sch Edinburgh, Univ of Glasgow (MA); *m* 20 Dec 1975, Bridget Prentice, *qv*, MP for Lewisham East, da of late James Corr; *Career* with Lab Pty Policy Directorate 1982–92, Lab Pty local govt offr 1985–92, MP (Lab) Pendle 1992–; London Borough of Hammersmith and Fulham: cncllr 1982–90, ldr Lab Gp 1984–88 (dep ldr 1982–84), ldr of Cncl 1986–88; *Style*— Gordon Prentice, Esq, MP; ✉ House of Commons, London SW1A 0AA

PRENTICE, Graham Noel; *b* 1955; *Educ* Peter Symonds Coll Winchester, Churchill Coll Cambridge (BA); *m* 1975, Beverley Annette Prentice; 2 da (Katy b 1987, Alice b 1989); *Career* admitted slr 1980; articled clerk Wragge & Co 1978–80, ptnr Freshfields 1986– (joined 1981); *Publications* Irregular Resolution of Unincorporated Association May Not be a Nullity (1980), The Enforcement of Outsider Rights (1980), Protected Shorthold Tenancies: Traps for the Unwary (I, II, III, 1982), Remedies of Building Sub-Contractors against Employers (1983); *Recreations* photography, skiing; *Style*— Graham Prentice, Esq; ✉ Freshfields, 65 Fleet Street, London EC4Y 1HS (tel 020 7936 4000, fax 020 7832 7001)

PRENTICE, Prof (Hugh) Grant; s of Dr Hugh Prentice (d 1982), and Jean Waddell, *née* Morton (d 1997); *b* 18 March 1944; *Educ* Clayesmore Sch Dorset, KCL, St George's Hosp Sch of Med London (MB BS, Brackenbury prize in surgery, clinical class prize); *m* (m dis); 1 da (Lucy Victoria b 24 Sept 1971), 2 s (Matthew Grant b 15 Oct 1974, Thomas Morton b 2 June 1976); *Career* sr registrar in haematology St George's Hosp London and Royal Marsden Hosp Surrey 1974–77; Royal Free Hosp/Royal Free and Univ Coll Med Sch: sr lectr/hon conslt haematologist 1978–92, prof of haematological oncology 1992–2002 (prof emeritus 2002–), head Dept of Haematology 1996–2002; dir Bone Marrow Transplant Prog and conslt haematologist The London Clinic 2002–; currently chief scientific advsr Pharmion Corp Boulder CO and Cambridge; author of pubns on leukaemia treatment, bone marrow transplantation and infection in the immune compromised host; tstee Children's Leukaemia Tst, memb Exec Ctee Int Bone Marrow Transplant Registry (IBMTR) 1995–98 and 2000–; FRCP, FRCPath; *Recreations* snow skiing, dinghy sailing; *Style*— Prof Grant Prentice; ✉ Haematology Department, The London Clinic, 20 Devonshire Place, London W1G 6BW (tel 020 7535 5503, fax 020 7535 5502, e-mail g.prentice@rfc.ucl.ac.uk)

PRENTICE, Nicholas John (Nick); s of late Norman Frank Prentice; *b* 14 February 1956; *Educ* Mount Grace Sch Potters Bar, Queens' Coll Cambridge (MA); *m* 28 Dec 1978, Jane Patricia; 2 da (Philippa Mary b 3 Dec 1981, Kate Victoria b 22 June 1983); *Career* Arthur Andersen: joined 1978, CA 1981, ptnr 1988–, managing ptnr South Practice 1991–97, UK managing ptnr Tax and Legal 1995–98, managing ptnr Tax & Legal Europe, Middle East, India and Africa 1998–2001, managing pntr Ptnr Matters 2001–02; ptnr Ernst & Young 2002–; memb Ethics Ctee ICAEW 1984–87; FCA 1981, ATII 1981, memb Int Fiscal Assoc 1986; *Recreations* ornithology, bridge, theatre, travel, genealogy; *Style*— Nick Prentice, Esq; ✉ Ernst & Young, Becket House, 1 Lambeth Palace Road, London SE1 7EU (tel 020 7980 0802)

PRESCOTT, Jeremy Malcolm; s of Rev Malcolm Crosby Prescott, CF, QHC, and Mary, *née* Webber (d 1974); *b* 26 March 1949; *Educ* Ampleforth, Fitzwilliam Coll Cambridge, Cass Business Sch; *m* 20 March 1982, Jacqueline Mary Elizabeth, *née* Kirk; 1 s (John Edmund Philip), 1 da (Katherine Mary); *Career* CA; with Peat Marwick Mitchell & Co 1970–76, joined Samuel Montagu & Co Ltd 1976, dir of corp fin HSBC Samuel Montagu 1987–97, md corp fin HSBC Investment Bank plc 1997–2002; FCA 1979; *Books* How to Survive the Recession (1982); *Style*— J M Prescott, Esq; ✉ 142 Court Lane, London SE21 7EB (tel 020 8693 3173, e-mail jeremymprescott@aol.com)

PRESCOTT, Prof John Herbert Dudley; s of Herbert Prescott (d 1959), of Barrow-on-Humber, Lincs, and Edith Vera, *née* Crowder (d 1993); *b* 21 February 1937; *Educ* Haileybury, Univ of Nottingham (BSc, PhD); *m* 23 July 1960, Diana Margaret, da of Frank Mullock, of Poulton Hall, Chester; 2 s (Ian b 26 May 1961, Tony b 22 Aug 1962), 2 da (Joanna b 8 July 1965, Sarah-Vivien b 24 April 1968); *Career* dir H Prescott (Goxhill) Ltd 1959–78 (chm 1970–78), demonstrator in agric Univ of Nottingham 1960–63, lectr in animal prodn Univ of Newcastle upon Tyne 1963–74, animal prodn offr FAO UN (Argentina) 1972–74, head of animal prodn and devpt East of Scotland Coll of Agric 1974–78, prof of animal prodn Univ of Edinburgh 1978–84, dir Grassland Res Inst Hurley 1984–86, dir Animal and Grassland Res Inst 1986, dir of res Grassland and Animal Prodn 1986–88, princ Wye Coll London 1988–2000; dir Natural Resources Int Ltd 1997–2000 (chm and acting chief exec 1996); Meat and Livestock Cmmn: memb Beef Improvement Ctee 1984–90, memb Res Ctee 1988–90, memb Beef R&D Ctee 1990–94; chair: Tech Ctee on Response to Nutrients AFRC 1988–94, Nat Resources Int Fndn 1998–2004; pres: Br Soc of Animal Prodn 1988, Agric and Forestry Section BAAS 1994–95, chair Conf of Agric Profs 1989; memb: Cncl Br Grassland Soc 1984–87, Nat Agric Awards Ctee Nuffield and RASE 1997–2003; tstee East Malling Tst for Horticultural Res 1998–; Br Cncl: memb Ctee for Int Co-operation in HE (S America 1989–94, Southern Africa 1994–2000, Slovakia (mission) 1997, Southern Africa (mission) 1999), memb Agric and Vet Advsy Ctee 1988–96, chair Natural Resources Advsy Ctee 1997, vice-chair Sci Engrg and Environment Advsy Ctee 1997–2001, UK chair Treaty of Windsor with Portuguese Univs 1998–; Macaulay Land Use Res Inst: Sci Advsy Ctee 1990–92, Governing Body 1992–97; memb: Governing Body and Corp Hadlow Coll 1988–98, Cncl RVC 1988–98 and 2001–04, Cncl Univ of Kent at Canterbury 1988–2000; chm Sir George Stapledon Meml Tst 1992–2004; Liveryman Worshipful Co of Farmers 2000–; hon fell: Inst for Grassland and Environmental Res 1989, Wye Coll London 2000, ICSTM London 2001; FIBiol 1983, FRAgS 1986, FRSA 1999; *Recreations* walking, wildlife, country pursuits; *Clubs* Farmers'; *Style*— Prof John Prescott

PRESCOTT, Rt Hon John Leslie; PC (1994), MP; s of late John Herbert Prescott, JP, of Chester, and late Phyllis Prescott; *b* 31 May 1938; *Educ* Ellesmere Port Secdy Modern Sch, Ruskin Coll Oxford, Univ of Hull (BSc); *m* 1961, Pauline, da of Ernest Tilston, of Chester; 2 s; *Career* joined Lab Pty 1956; former trainee chef & merchant seaman (NUS official 1968–70); Parly candidate (Lab) Southport 1966, MP (Lab) Kingston upon Hull E 1970–, delegate Cncl of Europe 1973–75, PPS to sec of state for Trade 1974–76, ldr Lab Pty Delegn European Parl 1976–79 (memb 1975–79); oppn spokesman on: Tport 1979–81, Regnl Affrs 1981–Nov 1983; memb Shadow Cabinet 1983–97; oppn front bench spokesman on: Tport Nov 1983–84 and 1988–93, Employment 1984–87, Energy 1987–88, Employment 1993–94; dep ldr Lab Pty 1994–2007 (candidate Lab Pty dep leadership election 1988 and 1992, candidate leadership election 1994); dep PM 1997–2007, sec of state for the Environment, Tport and the Regions 1997–2001, First Sec of State 2001–07 (with responsibility for Local Govt and the Regions 2002–06); *Publications* Alternative Regional Strategy: A Framework for Discussion (1982), Planning for Full Employment (1985), Real Needs - Local Jobs (1987), Moving Britain into the 1990s (1989), Moving Britain into Europe (1991), Full Steam Ahead (1993), Financing Infrastructure Investment (1993), Jobs and Social Justice (1993); *Style*— The Rt Hon John Prescott, MP; ✉ House of Commons, London SW1A 0AA (tel 020 7219 3000)

PRESCOTT, Sir Mark; 3 Bt (UK 1938), of Godmanchester, Co Huntingdon; s of Maj (William Robert) Stanley Prescott (d 1962, yr s of Col Sir William Prescott, 1 Bt), by his 1 w (Hylda) Gwendolen, *née* Aldridge (d 1992), and n of Sir Richard Stanley Prescott, 2 Bt (d 1965); *b* 3 March 1948; *Educ* Harrow; *Heir* none; *Career* racehorse trainer; *Style*— Sir Mark Prescott, Bt; ✉ Heath House, Moulton Road, Newmarket, Suffolk CB8 8DU (tel 01638 662117, fax 01638 666572)

PRESCOTT, Michael; s of Wilfred Prasad Prescott (d 1984), of London, and Gretel, *née* Kunzli, of London; *b* 21 November 1961; *Educ* Christ's Coll Finchley, St Catherine's Coll Oxford (BA), UC Cardiff (Dip Journalism); *m* 1990, Rachel, *née* Storm; 2 s, 1 da; *Career* reporter Coventry Evening Telegraph 1984–86, political corr Press Assoc 1986–89, political corr Sunday Correspondent 1989–90, political corr BBC Radio 1990–92; Sunday Times: political corr 1992–93, chief political corr 1993–99, political ed 1999–2001; head corp communications and vice-chm Public Affrs Weber Shandwick 2001–; *Style*— Michael Prescott, Esq

PRESCOTT, Peter Richard Kyle; QC (1990); s of Capt Richard Stanley Prescott (d 1987), of Cordoba, Argentina, and Sarah Aitchison, *née* Shand; *b* 23 January 1943; *Educ* St George's Coll Argentina, Dulwich Coll, UCL (BSc), QMC (MSc); *m* 23 Sept 1967, Frances Rosemary, da of Wing Cdr Eric Henry Bland (d 1980), of Tonge Corner, Sittingbourne; 1 da (Miranda Katherine b 1971), 2 s (Richard Julyan Kyle b 1973, Thomas Alexander Kyle b 1975); *Career* called to the Bar Lincoln's Inn 1970 (bencher 2001); *Books* The Modern Law of Copyright (with Hugh Laddie and Mary Vitoria, *qv*, 1980, 3 edn 2000); *Recreations* flying, music, cooking, reading; *Style*— Peter Prescott, Esq, QC; ✉ 8 New Square, Lincoln's Inn, London WC2A 3QP (tel 020 7405 4321, fax 020 7405 9955)

PRESCOTT, Richard; *b* 15 March 1962; *Educ* Calthorpe Park Comp Sch Fleet, W London Inst of HE (BA); *m*; 1 c; *Career* PR dept Sealink Br Ferries 1985–88, Attenborough Assocs PR 1988–90, PR mangr Mercury Communications 1990–93 (memb team which launched Mercury Music Prize 1992), corp PR mangr Whitbread plc 1993–97, dir of communications RFU 1997– (England media mangr during Rugby World Cup 2003); sometime freelance broadcaster, contrib BBC Radio Five Live 1992–94, sports commentator BBC GLR 1994–97; *Style*— Richard Prescott, Esq; ✉ Rugby Football Union, Rugby House, Rugby Road, Twickenham, Middlesex TW1 1DS

PRESCOTT THOMAS, John Desmond; RD* (1977, clasp 1987), DL (Co and City of Bristol 2005); s of William Prescott Thomas (d 1973), and Beatrice Isobel, *née* Jones (d 2000); *b* 28 May 1942; *Educ* Rhyl GS, Whitchurch GS, Jesus Coll Oxford (MA); *m* 1, 7 Oct 1967 (m dis 1993), Bridget Margaret, da of Rev Canon Adrian Denys Somerset-Ward (d 1976); 2 da (Viveka Ruth b 1969, Bronwen Jane b 1971); m 2, 14 Oct 1994, Dr Heather Elizabeth Graham; *Career* BBC: grad trainee 1963–65, asst prodr sch TV 1965–68, prodr 1968–76, sr prodr modern languages and European studies 1976–81, head of schs broadcasting TV 1981–84, head Bristol network prodn centre 1984–86, head of broadcasting South and West 1986–91; md Westcountry Television Ltd 1991–95; md JPT Media Assocs Ltd 1995–; wrote and produced: radiovision prog on Stanley Spencer's Burghclere paintings (Japan Prize nomination 1965), TV adaptation of Peter Carter's The Black Lamp, 12 Euro documentary and language series, two interactive trg resources, 28 int media consultancy projects; three BAFTA/RTS award nominations; visiting prof Faculty of Art Media and Design UWE (dep chm Bd of Govrs); Bolland Lecture Bristol Poly 1984, Arts Lecture Univ of Bath 2000, Keynote Lecture Košice Television Festival 2000; articles in pubns incl: TES, Br Language Teaching Jl, Le Français dans le Monde; dir: @t Bristol, Harbourside Fndn, The Exploratory; former: chm SW Arts, dep chm The Harbourside Centre, vice-chm Channel West, dir SW Media Devpt Agency, dir Exeter and Devon Arts Centre, dir Watershed Arts Tst, memb Euro Bd CIRCOM Regional; former tstee: Bath Int Festival, TV Tst for the Environment, Bristol Cathedral Tst, St George's Music Tst; RNR: cmmnd 1963, qualified ocean cmd 1974, Cdr 1978, exec offr London Div 1983–84, Severn Div 1984–92; Dr of Arts (hc) UWE 2002; FRTS 1995; commandeur Commanderie de Bordeaux 1999; *Books* Two EFL stories for children, Encounter: France (1980), Dès le Début, Dicho y Hecho, Alles Klar (1983), The Media in Governance (co-author, 1998), The UNESCO Media Management Manual (2006); *Recreations* languages, sailing, flying, photography, restoring a Citroën traction-avant, playing the alto saxophone; *Style*— John Prescott Thomas, Esq, DL; ✉ 30 Royal York Crescent, Clifton, Bristol BS8 4JX (tel and fax 0117 907 7573, e-mail jptmedia@compuserve.com)

PRESLAND, Frank George; *b* 27 February 1944; *Educ* Univ of London (Fairbridge Cwlth scholar, BSc), Univ Coll of Rhodesia and Nyasaland; *Career* admitted slr 1973; Frere Cholmeley Bischoff: joined 1973, ptnr 1976–98, chm 1992–98; jt chm Eversheds (following merger) 1998–99; co-fndr and chief exec Twenty-First Artists (co-prop until 2005), chief exec Sanctuary Gp plc 2006–; *Recreations* yachting; *Style*— Frank Presland, Esq

PRESLEY, Prof John Ralph; s of Ralph Presley, of Dinnington, S Yorks, and Doris, *née* Edson; *b* 17 September 1945; *Educ* Woodhouse GS Sheffield, Lancaster Univ (BA), Loughborough Univ (PhD); *m* 15 July 1967, Barbara, da of Kenneth Mallinson, of Kegworth, Derby; 2 da (Joanne Marie b 29 July 1968, Catherine Jane b 2 Sept 1972), 1 s (John Robert Ralph b 9 June 1981); *Career* Loughborough Univ: lectr 1969–76, sr lectr 1976–81, reader 1981–84, prof of economics 1984–, dir Banking Centre 1985–89, head Dept of Economics 1991–96; sr economic advsr Miny of Planning Saudi Arabia 1979–80, chief economic advsr Saudi Br Bank 1979–2006, visiting scholar Harvard Univ 1982, visiting professorial fell Univ of Nottingham 1989–90; DTI: memb Ctee for ME Trade 1992–2000, chm Area Action Ctee for Gulf Cooperation Cncl Countries and Yemen 1993–98; assoc dir Maxwell Stamp plc 1981–; memb Exec Ctee Saudi-British Soc, memb Omani-British Friendship Assoc, chm Forward Planning Ctee Arab Gulf 1994–98; Islamic Devpt Bank Prize for Islamic Banking and Fin 2002; *Books* European Monetary Integration (with P Coffey, 1971), Currency Areas: Theory and Practice (with G E J Dennis, 1976), Robertsonian Economics (1978), Pioneers of Modern Economics Vol 1 (ed with D O'Brien, 1983), Directory of Islamic Financial Institutions (1988), Pioneers of Modern Economics Vol 2 (ed with D Greenaway, 1989), A Guide to the Saudi Arabian Economy (with A J Westaway, 1983, 2 edn 1989), Banking in the Arab Gulf (with R Wilson, 1991), Essays on Robertsonian Economics (ed, 1992), Robertson on Economic Policy (ed with S R Dennison, 1992), Islamic Finance (with P Mills, 1999); *Recreations* gardening, reading, music, travel, conservation; *Style*— Prof John Presley; ✉ Station Farm, Station Road, Melbourne, Derbyshire DE73 8BQ (tel 01332 865380, e-mail stationfarm2@yahoo.co.uk)

PRESS, Dr (Christopher) Martin; s of Gp Capt Charles Henry Press, of Great Gormellick, Cornwall, and Christina, *née* Hindshaw; *b* 24 January 1944; *Educ* Bedales, King's Coll

P

Cambridge (BA), UCH (MB BChir, MA), Chelsea Coll London (MSc); *m* 10 June 1967, Angela Margaret, da of Charles Douglas Lewis, of Dibden, Hants; 5 s (Matthew b 1970, Joseph b 1972, Samuel b 1974, Benjamin b 1980, Daniel b 1984); *Career* med registrar Royal Post Grad Med Sch Hammersmith Hosp 1971–73, MRC research fell Univ of Calif 1973–75, asst prof of med and paediatrics Yale Univ Sch of Med 1981–87, currently conslt physician and hon sr lectr Royal Free Hosp Med Sch and dir Pancreatic Islet Transplantation Unit Royal Free Hosp; hon sec Transplantation Section RSM; memb: BMA, Br Diabetic Assoc, American Diabetic Assoc; *Recreations* orienteering, bell ringing, canal cruising; *Style—* Dr Martin Press; ✉ 99 Highfield Lane, Southampton SO17 1NN (tel 023 8055 1617); Department of Endocrinology, Royal Free Hospital, London NW3 3QG (tel 020 7830 2171)

PREST, Nicholas Martin; CBE (2001); s of Prof Alan Richmond Prest (d 1984), of Wimbledon, and Pauline Chasey, *née* Noble; *b* 3 April 1953; *Educ* Manchester Grammar, ChCh Oxford (MA); *m* 1985, Anthea Joy Elisabeth, da of Stuart John Guthrie Neal, of Wales; 2 da (Clementine Joy Chasey b 1987, Tabitha Rose Florence b 1992), 1 s (Frederick George Alan b 1989); *Career* entered civil serv MOD 1974 admin trainee, princ offr 1979; joined United Scientific Hldgs plc (later Alvis plc) 1982; Alvis plc: dir 1985–2004, chief exec 1989–2004, chm and chief exec 1996–2004; chm: Aveva 2006–, Cohort plc 2006–; chm Defence Manufacturers Assoc 2001–04, vice-chm Defence Industries Cncl 2004; *Recreations* walking, music, shooting; *Clubs* MCC, Cavalry and Guards; *Style—* Nicholas Prest, Esq, CBE; ✉ 85 Elgin Crescent, London W11 2JF (tel 020 7792 4821)

PRESTON, John Anthony Russell; s of late Dennis Anthony Gurney Preston, and Margaretta Constance, *née* Higson; *b* 9 September 1953; *Educ* Marlborough; *m* 23 Nov 1991, Maria, *née* Djurkovic; *Career* stage mangr Open Space Theatre 1973, asst film ed 1974–78, freelance journalist 1981–83, TV ed Time Out 1983–86, ed Arts Section Evening Standard 1986–90, arts ed The Sunday Telegraph 1990–99, television critic The Sunday Telegraph 1997–; *Books* Touching the Moon (1990), Ghosting (1996), Ink (1999); *Style—* John Preston, Esq; ✉ c/o PFD, Drury House, 34–43 Russell Street, London WC2B 5HA (tel 020 7344 1000)

PRESTON, Michael David; s of Richard Preston, and Yetta, *née* Young (d 1958); *b* 12 December 1945; *Educ* St Paul's, Exeter Coll Oxford (sr open scholar, MA); *m* 1, 13 April 1969 (m dis 1994), Stephanie Ann, *née* Levy; 2 s (Matthew b 1972, Robert b 1975); *m* 2, 10 Jan 1998, Sherri Remmell, *née* Becker; 1 da (Hanna b 2000), 1 s (Samuel b 2002); *Career* articled clerk Price Waterhouse London; fndr shareholder and dir Sterling Publishing Group plc until 1995 (dep chm 1990–94), former dir Debrett's Peerage Ltd, ptnr Alberdale & Co, ceo Image Innovations Holdings Inc; dir: Phosphagenics Ltd, Edentify Inc; FCA 1971; *Recreations* music, painting, wine; *Clubs* MCC; *Style—* Michael Preston, Esq; ✉ Alberdale & Co, 12 Curzon Street, London W1J 5HL (tel 020 7647 9900, fax 020 7647 9911, e-mail mdp@alberdale.com)

PRESTON, (Christopher) Miles Cary; s of Alan Tomlinson Preston, TD, and Audrey Anne Flint, *née* Wood, of Shrewsbury, Salop; *b* 12 April 1950; *Educ* Shrewsbury; *m* 5 June 1974, Jane Mowbray, da of Norman Seddon Harrison (d 1988), and Jeanne, *née* Peirce, of Blackheath, London; 2 da (Caroline Mowbray b 28 Dec 1978, Georgina Clare b 20 Nov 1986); *Career* admitted slr 1974; ptnr Radcliffes & Co 1980–94, sr ptnr Miles Preston & Co 1994–; served on Sir Gervais Sheldon's Family Law Liaison Ctee 1982; Slrs' Family Law Assoc: fndr memb 1982, memb Main Ctee 1982–88, chm Working Pty on Procedure 1982–88; Int Acad of Matrimonial Lawyers: fndr memb 1986, govr 1986–92, pres English Chapter 1989, pres Euro Chapter 1989–92, parliamentarian to Main Ctee 1989–92, pres Main Acad 1994–96 (pres-elect 1992), counsel to Acad 2000–02; chm: Old Salopian Ctee 1992–94, Osteopathic Educnl Fndn 1994–; memb The President's Int Family Law Ctee 1994–; *Recreations* food, travel and classic cars; *Clubs* Turf, Leander; *Style—* Miles Preston, Esq; ✉ Miles Preston & Co, 10 Bolt Court, London EC4A 3DQ (tel 020 7583 0583, fax 020 7583 0128, e-mail miles.preston@milespreston.co.uk)

PRESTON, (Bryan) Nicholas; OBE (1985); s of Bryan Wentworth Preston, MBE (d 1965), and Jean Brownlie, *née* Reid (d 1991); *b* 6 February 1933; *Educ* Eton, RAC Cirencester; *m* 1955, Elsbeth, *née* Hostettler; 1 s, 2 da; *Career* farmer; dir Stone Manganese Marine Ltd 1963–99, chm Br Marine Equipment Cncl 1966–68 and 1976–78; chm Tetbury Hosp Tst Ltd 2000–05 (tstee 1992–2006), memb Bd Princes' Tst - Business for Gloucestershire 1996–2001; memb: BOTB E Euro Trade Cncl 1979–82, BOTB Euro Trade Ctee 1972–89; Liveryman Worshipful Co of Shipwrights; *Recreations* field sports, skiing; *Clubs* Boodle's; *Style—* Nicholas Preston, Esq, OBE; ✉ Park Farm, Beverston, Gloucestershire GL8 8TT (tel and fax 01666 502435)

PRESTON, Prof Paul; CBE (2000); s of Charles Ronald Preston (d 1973), and Alice, *née* Hoskisson (d 1956); *b* 21 July 1946; *Educ* St Edward's Coll Liverpool, Oriel Coll of Oxford (BA, DPhil), Univ of Reading (MA); *m* 24 March 1983, Gabrielle, da of William Anthony Ashford-Hodges; 2 s (James Mark William b 20 Jan 1987, Christopher Charles Thomas b 2 April 1989); *Career* lectr in history Univ of Reading 1974–75; Queen Mary Coll: lectr 1975–79, reader 1979–85, prof 1985–91; LSE: prof of international history 1991–94, Principe de Asturias prof 1994–; Marcel Proust chair European Acad of Yuste 2006; Comendador de la Orden de Mérito Civil 1987; Ramon Llull Int Prize 2005; FRHistS 1982, FBA 1994; Gran Cruz de la Órder de Isabel la Católica 2006; *Books* The Coming of the Spanish Civil War (1978), The Triumph of Democracy in Spain (1986), The Spanish Civil War (1986), The Politics of Revenge (1990), Franco: A Biography (Yorkshire Post Book of the Year, 1993), Comrades: Portraits from the Spanish Civil War (1999), Doves of War: Four Women of Spain (2002), Juan Carlos: A People's King (2004); *Recreations* opera, classical music, modern fiction, wine, supporting Everton FC; *Style—* Prof Paul Preston, CBE, FBA; ✉ Department of International History, London School of Economics and Political Science, Houghton Street, London WC2A 2AE (tel 020 7955 7107, fax 020 7955 6757, e-mail p.preston@lse.ac.uk)

PRESTON, Peter John; s of John Whittle Preston; *b* 23 May 1938; *Educ* Loughborough GS, St John's Coll Oxford; *m* 1962, Jean Mary Burrell; 2 s, 2 da; *Career* ed The Guardian 1975–95, ed-in-chief Guardian and Observer 1995–96, editorial dir Guardian Media Gp 1996–98; contrib: The Guardian, The Observer; memb PCC until 1994, chm Assoc of Br Eds 1996–99; govr Br Assoc for Central and Eastern Europe 2000–; *Style—* Peter Preston, Esq; ✉ c/o The Guardian, 119 Farringdon Road, London EC1R 3ER (e-mail p.preston@guardian.co.uk)

PRESTRIDGE, Jeffrey John; s of Stanley Prestridge, of Sutton Coldfield, W Midlands, and Helen Joyce, *née* Carpenter; *b* 8 April 1959; *Educ* Bishop Vesey GS, Loughborough Univ (BSc); *m* 10 Sept 1983, Susan, *née* Dove; 3 s (Matthew Stanley George b 25 March 1991, Mark Christopher Jeffrey b 21 Sept 1992, James David Luke b 11 Feb 1994); *Career* articled clerk Price Waterhouse Chartered Accountants 1980–82, res asst Debenham Tewson Chinnocks 1982–84, self-employed 1984–86, dep ed World Investor 1986–87, economist Bristol & West Building Society 1987, dep ed Money Management Magazine 1987–90; family fin ed: The Sunday Telegraph 1990–94, The Mail on Sunday 1994–; winner of several awards for personal fin journalism; Financial Planning Certificate 2000; *Books* Jeff's Lunchbox (1992), Complete Personal Finance Guide (2001); *Recreations* swimming, running, photography, squash, WBA FC; *Style—* Jeffrey Prestridge, Esq; ✉ 10 Upper Hitch, Carpenders Park, Hertfordshire WD1 5AW (tel 020 8428 5190); The Mail on Sunday, Northcliffe House, 2 Derry Street, London W8 5TS (tel 020 7938 6000, e-mail jeff.prestridge@mailonsunday.co.uk)

PRESTWICH, Prof Michael Charles; s of John Oswald Prestwich (d 2003), of Oxford, and Menna, *née* Roberts (d 1990); *b* 30 January 1943; *Educ* Charterhouse, Magdalen Coll Oxford, ChCh Oxford (MA, DPhil); *m* 11 May 1973, Margaret Joan, da of Herbert Daniel (d 1980), of Glossop; 2 s (Robin b 1974, Christopher b 1976), 1 da (Kate b 1980); *Career* res lectr ChCh Oxford 1965–69, lectr in medieval history Univ of St Andrews 1969–79; Univ of Durham: reader in medieval history 1979–86, prof of history 1986–, pro-vice-chllr 1992–99; FRHistS 1972, FSA 1980; *Books* War, Politics and Finance under Edward I (1972), The Three Edwards: War and State in England 1272–1377 (1980), Documents Illustrating the Crisis of 1297–8 in England (1980), Edward I (1988), English Politics in the Thirteenth Century (1990), Armies and Warfare in the Middle Ages: The English Experience (1996), Plantagenet England (2005); *Recreations* skiing; *Style—* Prof Michael Prestwich, FSA; ✉ 46 Albert Street, Western Hill, Durham DH1 4RJ (tel 0191 386 2539); Department of History, 43 North Bailey, Durham DH1 3EX (e-mail m.c.prestwich@durham.ac.uk)

PRETTY, Dr Katharine Bridget (Kate); da of Maurice Walter Hughes (d 1975), of Birmingham, and Bridget Elizabeth Whibley, *née* Marples; *b* 18 October 1945; *Educ* King Edward VI HS for Girls Birmingham, New Hall Cambridge (scholar, MA, PhD); *m* 1, 1967 (m dis), Graeme Lloyd Pretty; *m* 2, 1988, Prof Tjeerd Hendrik van Andel, *qv*; *Career* Univ of Cambridge: fell and lectr in archaeology New Hall 1972, admissions tutor New Hall 1979–82, sr tutor New Hall 1985–91 (emeritus fell 1995–), princ Homerton Coll 1991–, memb Univ Fin Bd 1986–96, chm Faculty Bd of Archaeology and Anthropology 1991–2004, memb Univ Gen Bd 1997, chm Cncl Sch of Humanities and Social Sciences 1997–2003, pro-vice-chllr 2004–; sec Cambs Archaeological Ctee 1974–79; chm: RESCUE Br Archaeological Tst 1978–83, OCR (Oxford, Cambridge and RSA Examinations Bd) 1998–2004; vice-pres RSA 1998–2004, vice-pres Cncl for Br Archaeology 2004–, tstee Prince's Teaching Inst 2007–; FSA 2000; *Recreations* archaeology in the Arctic, botany and gardening; *Style—* Dr Kate Pretty; ✉ Homerton College, Hills Road, Cambridge CB2 2PH (tel 01223 507131, fax 01223 507130, e-mail kp10002@cam.ac.uk)

PREVETT, Geoffrey James (Geoff); s of James William Prevett, of Ewell, Surrey, and Helen Lillian, *née* Luckett; *b* 30 November 1944; *Educ* Westminster; *m* 25 June 1966, Joan, da of Thomas Bevan, of Maesteg, S Wales; 1 da (Melanie b 6 Feb 1973), 1 s (Christopher b 31 Jan 1980); *Career* admitted slr 1978; Travers Smith Braithwaite 1963–79, Lewis Lewis and Co 1979–82 (ptnr 1981), ptnr Eversheds (Jaques and Lewis before merger) 1982–; memb Law Soc; chartered arbitrator 2000; DipICArb, FCIArb; *Recreations* music, theatre, reading, cricket; *Style—* Geoff Prevett, Esq; ✉ 22 Northcliffe Close, Worcester Park, Surrey KT4 7DS (tel 020 8337 3377); Eversheds, Senator House, 85 Queen Victoria Street, London EC4V 4JL (tel 020 7919 4500, fax 020 7919 4919)

PREVEZER, Susan; (QC); da of Prof Sydney Prevezer (d 1997), and Enid Margaret, *née* Austin; *b* 25 March 1959; *m* 26 June 1994, Benjamin Matthew Freedman, s of Bill Freedman; 2 da (Edie b 30 April 1996, Toby b 5 Jan 1998); *Career* called to the Bar 1983; memb: Commercial Bar Assoc, Chancery Bar Assoc; *Style—* Ms Susan Prevezer, QC; ✉ Essex Court Chambers, 24 Lincoln's Inn Fields, London WC2A 3ED

PREVOST, Sir Christopher Gerald; 6 Bt (UK 1805); s of Sir George James Augustine Prevost, 5 Bt (d 1985), and Muriel Emily, *née* Oram (d 1939); *b* 25 July 1935; *Educ* Cranleigh; *m* 1964, Dolores Nelly, o da of Dezo Hoffmann; 1 s, 1 da; *Heir* s, Nicholas Prevost; *Career* late 95 Regt; fndr Mailtronic Ltd manufacturers and suppliers of mailroom equipment (chm and md 1977–91); past memb Exec Cncl Huguenot Soc; *Recreations* gardening; *Style—* Sir Christopher Prevost, Bt; ✉ 33 La Providence, Rochester, Kent ME1 1NB

PRICE, Adam; MP; *b* 23 September 1968; *Educ* Amman Valley Comp Sch, Univ of Wales Cardiff, Saarland Univ; *Career* res assoc Dept of City and Regnl Planning Univ of Wales Cardiff 1991–93; Menter a Busnes: project mangr 1993–95, exec mangr 1995–96, exec dir 1996–98; md Newidiem Econ Devpt Consultancy 1998–2001; MP (Plaid Cymru) Carmarthen E and Dinefwr 2001–; Parly candidate (Plaid Cymru) Gower 1992; vice-chair All-Pty Steel Gp; memb: All-Pty Sci Ctee, All-Pty Parly Cricket Gp, All-Pty Arts and Heritage Gp, All-Pty Football Gp, Inter Parly Union; *Publications* The Collective Entrepreneur (1992), The Welsh Renaissance: The Innovation and Inward Investment in Wales (1992), Rebuilding Our Communities: A New Agenda for the Valleys (1993), Quiet Revolution? Language, Culture and Economy in the Nineties (1994), The Diversity Dividend (1996), The Other Wales: The Case for Objective 1 Funding Post 1999 (1998); *Recreations* contemporary culture, good friends, good food, travel; *Clubs* Ammanford Workingman's Social; *Style—* Adam Price, Esq, MP; ✉ House of Commons, London SW1A 0AA; Constituency Office, 37 Wind Street, Ammanford, Carmarthenshire SA18 3DN (tel 01269 597677, fax 01269 591334, e-mail pricea@parliament.uk)

PRICE, Barrie; s of Albert Price (d 1978), and Mary, *née* Melvin (d 1982); *b* 13 August 1937; *Educ* St Bede's GS Bradford; *m* 15 April 1963, Elizabeth, da of William Murphy (d 1979), and Jane, *née* Hurley (d 1994); 4 s (Nicholas Becket b 1963, Joseph b 1965, Gerard b 1968, Mark b 1974), 1 da (Catherine b 1966); *Career* trainee accountant 1953–58, sr ptnr Lishman Sidwell Campbell and Price 1974– (ptnr 1962–), chm and md Lishman Sidwell Campbell & Price Ltd (formerly Slouand Ltd) 1968–; sr ptnr: LSCP LLP 2003–, Administrative Business Solutions LLP 2004–, Eura Audit UK 2005–; vice-pres Eura Audit Int 2006– (memb Bd 2001–); dir: Lishman Sidwell Campbell and Price Tstees Ltd, Lishman Sidwell Campbell and Price Financial Services Ltd, Tywest Investments Ltd, Slouand Ltd, Yorks Accountants Ltd, Yorks Consultants Ltd, Yorks Accountants and Auditors Ltd, Financial Centres Ltd, A1 Accountants Ltd, Ripon Accountants Ltd, Ripon Improvement Tst Ltd, Lyons St John Ltd, LSCP Ltd, Yorks Image Ltd, LSCP Properties Ltd, LSCP Nominees Ltd, SAP Infotech Pvt India 2005–; accountant UK On Line Ltd and A2Z Financial Services Ltd; various appointments: AUKOL Ltd, Development Sharing (High Skellgate) Ltd, Gibsons Hotel (Harrogate) Ltd, Online Administrator Ltd; cncllr: Ripon City Cncl 1968–91 (mayor 1980–81, dep mayor 1974–75, 1982–83 and 1987–88), Harrogate Borough DC 1974–91 (dep leader 1987–88 and 1990–91, chm Econ Devpt Ctee); chm: Ripon Life Care and Housing Tst, Ripon City and Dist Devpt Assoc 1969–90, Harrogate Theatre Appeal 2001–06; pres: Ripon City Cons Assoc 1995– (formerly sec and treas), Ripon Civic Soc 2004–; tstee: City of Ripon Festival (chm 1981–), Yorks Film Archive (chm 1981–91), Ripon Cathedral Appeal 1994–97, Ripon Museum Tst Appeal (chm 1998–2000); memb: Ripon Chamber of Trade and Commerce 1962–83 (pres 1975–77, life memb 1983–), RC Diocese of Leeds Finance Ctee and Bd 1989–94, Ripon Tennis Centre, RSC, Yorkshire Agric Soc (life), Nat Tst (life), Skipton and Ripon Cons Assoc; govr St Wilfrid's RC Sch Ripon 1970–91; Freeman City of London 2005–, Liveryman Worshipful Co of CAs 2005–; FCA 1968 (ACA 1959), FCCA; *Recreations* opera, football, racing, farm animals, gardening; *Clubs* Opera North, Ripon Race Course Members, Bradford City AFC, Royal Over-Seas League, sLOANE; *Style—* Barrie Price, Esq; ✉ Prospect House, 54 Palace Road, Ripon, North Yorkshire HG4 1HA (tel 01765 602058); Eura Audit UK, Eva Lett House, 1 South Crescent, Ripon, North Yorkshire HG4 1SN (tel 01765 690890, fax 01765 690296, e-mail b.price@lscp.com)

PRICE, Caroline Sarah; da of Geoffrey Ball (d 2003), of Guildford, Surrey, and Mary, *née* Goodwin (d 2002); *b* 18 September 1948; *Educ* Tormead Sch Guildford, KCL (LLB); *m* 11 Sept 1971 (m dis 2007), Richard Mervyn Price, OBE, QC, *qv*; 1 s (Timothy b 13 Jan 1975), 2 da (Kathryn b 3 Dec 1977, Emma b 28 July 1983); *Career* called to the Bar Gray's Inn 1970; legal asst Home Office 1971–74; Legal Advsr's Branch Home Office: lawyer (grade 7) 1985–89, lawyer (grade 6) 1989–95, asst legal advsr 1995–2004; asst dir Govt Lawyers Trg Nat Sch of Govt Cabinet Office 2004–; co sec and dir Mason & Ball Investments Ltd 1974–; *Recreations* singing, theatre and opera, walking; *Style—* Mrs Caroline Price; ✉ National School of Government, Sunningdale Park, Larch Avenue, Ascot, Berkshire SL5 0QE

PRICE, Charles Beaufort; s of Mervyn Beaufort Price, and Jessie Price; *b* 7 November 1945; *Educ* King's Coll Taunton, QMC (BA); *m* 29 May 1971, Patricia Ann; 1 s (Gareth Charles b 29 March 1978), 1 da (Isabelle Louise b 8 Sept 1981); *Career* md N M Rothschild & Sons (Singapore) Limited 1976–79, dir N M Rothschild & Sons Limited 1985–96 (chm Wales 1992–96); head of banking and treasury Singer & Friedlander Ltd 1997–; AIB; *Recreations* gardening, rugby, opera; *Style*— Charles Price, Esq; ✉ Singer & Friedlander Ltd, 21 New Street, Bishopsgate, London EC2M 4HR

PRICE, Prof Christopher Philip; s of Philip Bright Price (d 1955), and Frances Gwendoline Price (d 1986); *b* 28 February 1945; *Educ* Univ of London (BSc), Univ of Birmingham (PhD), Univ of Cambridge (MA); *m* 1968, Elizabeth Ann, da of late Frederick Dix; 2 da (Carolyn Sarah b 2 Jan 1974, Emma Jane b 21 Nov 1975); *Career* biochemist; basic grade biochemist Coventry & Warwick Hosp 1967–72, sr grade then princ grade biochemist E Birmingham Hosp 1972–76; conslt biochemist: Southampton Gen Hosp 1976–80, Addenbrooke's Hosp Cambridge 1980–88; prof of clinical biochemistry St Bartholomew's & The Royal London Sch of Med & Dentistry (formerly London Hosp Med Coll) 1988–2001; Barts and the London NHS Tst: clinical dir for biochemistry 1988–98, clinical dir for pathology 1998–2001; vice-pres of outcomes research Diagnostics Div Bayer Health Care 2002–05; visiting prof in chemical biochemistry Univ of Oxford 2006–; memb: Assoc for Clinical Biochemistry (chm 1991–94, pres 2003–06), American Assoc for Clinical Chemistry (memb Bd of Dirs 2000–03), Int Soc for Clinical Enzymology; Hon DSc De Montfort Univ 1998; CChem, CSci, EurClinChem, FRSC, FRCPath (memb Cncl 1996–99), FACB; *Publications* ed 8 books incl Principles & Practice of Immunoassay (2 edn), Point of Care Testing (2 edn), Evidence-Based Laboratory Medicine (2 edn); over 300 research papers and reviews; *Recreations* walking, gardening, reading; *Style*— Prof Christopher Price

PRICE, Clair Jennifer (Jennie); da of Cliff Price, of Newport, Salop, and Beryl, *née* Agates; *b* 7 February 1960; *Educ* KCL (LLB); *m* 7 Oct 1988, Michael Storey Hall, FRICS; *Career* legal advsr Heating and Ventilation Contractors Assoc 1983–88, litigation lawyer Bristows 1989–90, head of legal and public affrs Building Employers Confedn 1990–96, dir Major Contractors Gp 1996–99, chief exec Construction Confedn 1999–2000, chief exec Waste and Resources Action Prog (WRAP) 2000–; visiting fell Cranfield Sch of Mgmnt 2004; fndr memb Construction Industry Bd DETR, memb Environment Innovations Advsy Gp DTI; Hon MRICS 2000, FRSA 2002; *Recreations* horse racing; *Style*— Ms Jennie Price; ✉ WRAP, The Old Academy, 21 Horse Fair, Banbury, Oxfordshire OX16 0AH (tel 01295 819903, fax 01295 819911, e-mail jennie.price@wrap.org.uk)

PRICE, Prof Sir Curtis Alexander; KBE (2006 (honorary award made substantive on taking British citizenship), Hon KBE 2005); s of Dalias Price, and Lillian, *née* Alexander; *b* 7 September 1945; *Educ* Univ of Southern Illinois (BMus), Harvard Univ (AM, PhD); *m* 1981, Rhian, *née* Samuel; 1 step s; *Career* prof of music Washington Univ St Louis USA 1974–81; KCL: lectr in music 1981–84, reader in music 1984–88, King Edward prof 1988–95; principal RAM 1995–; pres Royal Musical Assoc; sec Purcell Soc; tstee: Handel Inst, Wigmore Hall, Assoc Bd Royal School of Music, Amadeus Fndn, London String Quartet Competition, Mendelssohn Scholarship Fund, Purcell Sch; Knox travelling fell 1970, Guggenheim fell 1981; hon memb RAM 1993, FKC 1995, FRNCM 2001, FRCM 2002; *Awards*: Rockefeller Award 1973, Alfred Einstein Award American Musicological Soc 1977, Dent Medal Royal Musical Assoc 1985; *Books* Henry Purcell and the London Stage (1984), Music in the Early Baroque Era (1994), Italian Opera in Late Eighteenth Century London (1995); *Style*— Prof Sir Curtis Price, KBE; ✉ Royal Academy of Music, Marylebone Road, London NW1 5HT (tel 020 7873 7377, fax 020 7873 7314)

PRICE, His Hon Judge David; s of Bevan Glyn Price (d 2003), and Nora, *née* Amos; *b* 27 September 1943, Nottingham; *Educ* Kind Edward VI Sch Stratford upon Avon, Univ of Leeds (LLB); *m* 31 July 1971, Jennifer, *née* Newton; 2 s (Timothy Rupert David b 14 July 1974, Robert Edward James b 23 Dec 1975); *Career* called to the Bar Inner Temple 1968; practising barr Midland Circuit 1968–93, recorder of the Crown Court 1992–2004, circuit judge 2004–; asst Parly boundary cmmr 1992; chm: Employment Tbnls 1993–2004, Reinstatement Ctee for Reserved Forces 1996–2004; *Clubs* Market Harborough Golf, United Services, The BBs; *Style*— His Hon Judge David Price; ✉ Derby Crown Court, The Morledge, Derby DE1 2XE (tel 01332 622600, fax 01332 622543, e-mail hhjudgedavid.price@judiciary.gsi.gov.uk)

PRICE, David William James; s of Richard J E Price (d 1983), of Quinta da Romeira, Bucelas, Portugal, and Miriam Joan, *née* Dunsford; *b* 11 June 1947; *Educ* Ampleforth, CCC Oxford (MA); *m* 1971, Shervie Ann Lander, da of Sir James Whitaker, 3 Bt (d 1999); 1 da (Hesther b 1971), 1 s (William b 1973); *Career* farmer and merchant banker; dir: Warburg Investment Management Ltd 1978, S G Warburg & Co Ltd 1982–87; chm Mercury Asset Management plc 1983–97, dep chm Mercury Asset Management Group plc 1987–97; chm: Aberdeen All Asia Tst 1997–, F & C Management 1999–2004, Heritage Lincs 1997–, Scottish American Investment Co 1997–, Big Food Gp 2000–04, Melchior Japan Investment Tst 2006–; chm: Orders of St John Care Tst, Cncl RCL; cncllr London Borough of Lambeth 1979–82; *Clubs* Brooks's, Lincolnshire; *Style*— David Price, Esq; ✉ Harrington Hall, Spilsby, Lincolnshire PE23 4NH

PRICE, Eric Hardiman Mockford; s of Frederick Hardiman Price, and Florence Nellie Hannah; *b* 14 November 1931; *Educ* St Marylebone GS, Christ's Coll Cambridge (BA, MA); *m* 3 Feb 1963, Diana Teresa Anne Mary Stanley, da of Stanley Joseph Leckie Robinson (d 1962), of Harbury Hall, Warwicks; 3 da (Caroline b 29 Jan 1964, Nichola b 28 March 1966, Ashling b 6 July 1970), 1 s (Julian b 27 Feb 1969); *Career* Nat Serv Army 1950–52, HAC 1952–57; economist: Central Electricity Authy Electricity Cncl 1957–58, Br Iron and Steel Fedn 1958–62; chief economist Port of London Authy 1962–67; Miny of Tport: sr econ advsr 1966–69, chief econ advsr 1967–71, dir of econs 1971–75; DOE: under sec econs 1972–76, dir of econs and statistics 1975–76; under sec econs and statistics: Depts of Trade Indust and Consumer Protection 1977–80; under sec and chief economic advsr: Dept of Energy 1980–92, DTI 1992–93; special conslt National Economic Research Associates 1993–2000; dir Robinson Bros (Ryders Green) Ltd 1985–; prop The Energy Economics Consultancy 1995–2000; Br Inst of Energy Econs: memb Cncl 1980–2006, vice-chm 1981–82 and 1988–89, chm 1982–85, hon memb 2006–; FREconS, FRSS, FInstD, MInstPet; *Recreations* tennis, history, horseracing; *Clubs* Moor Park Golf (hon memb), Batchworth Park Golf, Riverside, Health & Leisure; *Style*— Eric Price, Esq; ✉ Batchworth House, Batchworth Heath Farm, London Road, Rickmansworth, Hertfordshire WD3 1QB (tel 01923 824471, fax 01923 828895, e-mail eric.price@lineone.net)

PRICE, Sir Francis Caradoc Rose; 7 Bt (UK 1815), QC (1992); s of Sir Rose Francis Price, 6 Bt (d 1979), and Kathleen June, yr da of Norman William Hutchinson, of Melbourne, Aust; *b* 9 September 1950; *Educ* Eton, Trinity Coll Univ of Melbourne, Univ of Alberta; *m* 1975, (Hon Madam Justice) Marguerite Jean, da of Roy Samuel Trussler, of Victoria, BC; 3 da (Adrienne Calantha Rose b 1976, Megan Kathleen Rose b 1977, Glynis Nicola Rose b 1982); *Heir* bro, Norman Price; *Career* barr and slr Canada, ptnr Reynolds Mirth Richards & Farmer; chartered arbitrator; *Books* Pipelines in Western Canada (1975), Mortgage Actions in Alberta (1985), Conducting a Foreclosure Action (1996); *Recreations* cricket, theatre, opera; *Clubs* Faculty; *Style*— Sir Francis Price, Bt, QC; ✉ 9626 95 Avenue, Edmonton, Alberta T6C 2A4, Canada (tel home 00 1 780 469 9555, work 00 1 780 497 3388, fax 00 1 780 429 3044, e-mail fprice@rmrf.com)

PRICE, Frank Christopher (Chris); s of Geoffrey Arthur Price, of Wilmslow, Cheshire, and Celia Price; *b* 1946; *Educ* Uppingham, Univ of Nottingham (industry scholar, BSc), Leicester Poly (DMS); *m* 1, 1970 (m dis 1992), Catherine; 1 s (Geoffrey Michael b 19 Sept 1974), 1 da (Anne Elisabeth b 17 Dec 1976); m 2, 1995, Sylvia; *Career* British Shoe Machinery Ltd: grad apprentice, mangr Machinery R&D Dept, memb Bd of Mgmnt 1981–85; engrg dir Rearsby Automotive Ltd Leicester 1985–87; USM TEXON Ltd (formerly United Machinery Gp Ltd): dir R&D 1987–93, dir Product and Process Devpt 1993–96; Rolls-Royce plc: engrg and technol dir Energy Businesses 1997–2001, engrg and technol dir Operations 2001–03, exec vice pres Engrg and Techol - Purchasing 2004–; named inventor on 20 patents; hon sr industry fell and hon visiting prof de Montfort Univ 1992–, special prof Univ of Nottingham 1996–; IMechE: chm E Midlands Branch 1986–88, vice-pres 1991–93, dep pres 1993–94, pres 1995–96; memb Senate Engrg Cncl; Freeman City of London 1995, memb Ct of Assts Worshipful Co of Engrs 2002 (Liveryman 1995, Middle Warden 2007); FIMechE 1985 (MIMechE 1976), FREng 1993 (hon treas 2003–), FIEE 1995; *Recreations* skiing, theatre, walking, gardening, golf; *Style*— Chris Price, Esq, FREng; ✉ Rolls-Royce plc, PO Box 31, Derby DE24 8BJ (tel 01332 249228, e-mail chris.price@rolls-royce.com)

PRICE, Sir Frank Leslie; kt (1966), DL; s of George Frederick Price (d 1978), and Lucy Price (d 1978); *b* 26 July 1922; *Educ* St Mathias Sch Birmingham, Vittoria St Arts Sch; *m* 1, 1944 (m dis 1976), Maisie Edna, da of Albert Davis; 1 s (Noel Bayley); m 2, 1983 (m dis 1984), Veronica, da of Zubadri Singh; m 3, Daphne, da of John Ling (d 1947); *Career* md Murrayfield Real Estate Co Ltd 1958–68; chm: Midlands Arts Centre for Young People 1960–66 (fndr), Birmingham and Midlands Investments Ltd 1967–74, Telford New Town Corp 1968–72, Br Waterways Bd 1968–84, Wharf Holdings 1968–72, M L Alkan Ltd 1972–75, Price Brown Partnership (formerly Sir Frank Price and Compania Sociedad Colectiva) 1985–2006; dir: Comp Devpts Assoc 1968–80, National Exhibition Centre Ltd 1970–76, Butlers and Colonial Wharfs Ltd 1971–76; cncllr and alderman Birmingham City Cncl 1949–75, Lord Mayor of Birmingham 1964–65; DL: Warks 1970–82, W Midlands 1974–82, Hereford & Worcs 1973–82; memb: Cncl Town and Country Planning Assoc 1954–74, Lord Chllr's Advsy Ctee 1967–72, Nat Water Cncl 1975–79, English Tourist Bd 1975–82; pres Br Assoc of Industrial Eds 1979–83; Freeman City of London; FSVA, FCIT, FRICS; *Publications* One Man's View (series of articles), Being There (autobiography); *Clubs* Reform; *Style*— Sir Frank Price, DL; ✉ Casa Noel, 42 Los Limoneros los Galardos, Almeria 04630, Spain (tel 00 34 950 617586, e-mail pongoprice@hotmail.com)

PRICE, His Hon Judge Gerald Alexander Lewin; QC (1992); s of Denis Lewin Price, of Cowbridge, S Glamorgan, and Patricia Rosemary, *née* Metcalfe; *b* 13 September 1948; *Educ* Haileybury, Coll of Law, Inns of Court Sch of Law; *m* 28 Dec 1974, Theresa Elizabeth, da of Hilary Baldwin Iremonger-Watts; 2 s (Alexander Baldwin Lewin b 27 Feb 1981, Lawrence Christopher b 3 Dec 1983); *Career* called to the Bar Middle Temple 1969, private practice at Bar Cardiff 1969–77, resident magistrate Bermuda 1977–81, chm Price Control Cmmn 1979, registrar of Supreme Court Bermuda 1980, chief magistrate Bermuda, sr coroner, chm Land Valuation Appeals Tbnl, chm Liquor Licensing Bd and chm Jury Revising Ctee 1981–84, private practice at Bar Cardiff 1984–2000, recorder 1990–2000, circuit judge (Wales & Chester Circuit) 2000–; Parly candidate (Cons): Newport Gwent Feb and Oct 1974, Gower 1987; Anglican lay preacher 1969–; *Recreations* travel, motorboats, Menorca, sunshine, tennis, classical music, comedy; *Clubs* RYA, Royal Commonwealth Soc, Glamorgan Lawn Tennis & Croquet; *Style*— His Hon Judge Gerald Price, QC

PRICE, James Richard Kenrick; QC (1995); s of Lt-Col Kenrick Jack Price, DSO, MC (d 1982), and Juliet Hermione, *née* Slessor (now Mrs de Laszlo, wid of John de Laszlo); *b* 14 September 1948; *Educ* Eton, St Edmund Hall Oxford (BA); *m* 1983, Hon Virginia Yvonne, da of 5 Baron Mostyn, MC (d 2000); *Career* called to the Bar Inner Temple 1974; *Recreations* gardening, skiing, hill walking, fine and decorative arts, dogs; *Clubs* Brooks's, Beefsteak; *Style*— James Price, Esq, QC; ✉ 26 Seymour Walk, London SW10 9NF (tel 020 7352 8973); Pettifers, Lower Wardington, Banbury, Oxfordshire OX17 1RU (tel 01295 750232); 5 Raymond Buildings, Gray's Inn, London WC1R 5BP (tel 020 7242 2902, e-mail jamesprice@5rb.com)

PRICE, John Alan (Jack); QC (1980); s of Frederick Leslie Price (d 1976); *b* 11 September 1938; *Educ* Stretford GS, Univ of Manchester (LLB); *m* 1, 1964 (m dis 1982), Elizabeth Myra, da of Stanley Priest; 1 s, 1 da; m 2, 1984, Alison Elizabeth, da of Stanley Ward; *Career* called to the Bar Gray's Inn 1961, in practice on Northern Circuit, dep circuit judge 1975–, recorder Crown Court 1980–; *Recreations* tennis, golf; *Style*— Jack Price, Esq, QC; ✉ 25 Byrom Street, Manchester M3 4PF (tel 0161 834 5238)

PRICE, John Philip; s of late Eifion Wyn Price, of Rhayader, Powys, and Kathleen, *née* Woodfield; *b* 11 December 1949; *Educ* Monmouth, CCC Oxford (MA, BPhil); *Partner* Diana Elizabeth Chrouch; 1 da (Natasha Maya Celine); *Career* called to the Bar Inner Temple 1974; DG Dairy Industry Fedn (formerly Dairy Trade Fedn) 1986–98, co sec Express Dairies plc 1998–2003, dir of corporate affrs Arla Foods UK plc 2003–07; *Books* The English Legal System (1979); *Style*— John Price, Esq; ✉ 20 Rossmore Court, Park Road, London NW1 6XX (tel 020 7723 9485)

PRICE, Air Vice Marshal John Walter; CBE (1979, OBE 1973); s of Henry Walter Price, MM (d 1984), and Myrza, *née* Griffiths (d 1958); *b* 26 January 1930; *Educ* Solihull Sch, RAF Coll Cranwell; *m* 1, 1956, Margaret Sinclair (d 1989), da of John McIntyre, of Sydney, Aust; m 2, 2004, Ilse Gertrud Burrows, *née* Koepke, of Papenburg, Germany; *Career* cmmnd from RAF Coll Cranwell 1950; Sqdn flying appts: Vampires and Venoms Germany, Meteors with 77 Sqdn RAAF Korea (despatches 1953), Vampires and Meteors Aust; staff appts in Air Miny 1961–64, cmd No 110 Sqdn Sycamores and Whirlwinds Malaya and Borneo 1964–66, DS RAF Staff Coll 1967, PSO to CAS 1968–70, cmd No 72 Sqdn Wessex 1970–72, dep dir Ops MOD Air 1973–75, cmd RAF Laarbruch (Buccaneers and Jaguars) Germany 1976–78, Gp Capt Ops HQ Strike Cmd 1979, dir Ops Strike MOD Air 1980–82, ACAS Ops 1982–84, ret as Air Vice Marshal 1984; Clyde Petroleum plc 1984–95, currently oil and gas exploration and prodn conslt and UK mangr Courage Energy; DL Hereford & Worcs 1995–2005; memb Bd of Govrs Solihull Sch 1979–2005 (chm 1982–2005); Freeman City of London 2001, Liveryman Worshipful Co of Fuellers 2001 (memb Ct of Assts 2003–, Jr Warden 2005); MRAeS, MEI, CCMI; *Recreations* travel, spending time with wife and family; *Clubs* Army and Navy, RAF; *Style*— Air Vice Marshal John Price, CBE, DL; ✉ 2 Palace Yard, Hereford HR4 9BJ (tel and fax 01432 272292)

PRICE, (Arthur) Leolin; CBE (1996), QC (1968, Bahamas 1969, NSW 1987); s of Evan Price (d 1959), and Ceridwen Price (d 1974); *b* 11 May 1924; *Educ* Judd Sch Tonbridge, Keble Coll Oxford (scholar, MA); *m* 1963, Hon Rosalind (Lindy) (d 1999), da of 1 and last Baron Brecon, PC (d 1976); 2 s, 2 da; *Career* called to the Bar Middle Temple 1949 (bencher 1970, treas 1990), ad eundem Lincoln's Inn 1959; head of chambers; barr: Br Virgin Islands 1994, Gibraltar 1996; vice-chm Soc of Cons Lawyers 1987–96; dir: Marine Adventure Sailing Trust plc 1982–89, Thornton Asian Emerging Markets Investment Trust plc 1989–95; pres SR Pan-European Investment Trust (formerly Child Health Res Investment Trust plc) 1999–2001 (chm 1987–99, dir 1980–2001, hon pres 2001–); chm Inst of Child Health 1976–2007; govr and tstee Great Ormond St Hosp for Sick Children 1972–2007; govr: Br Postgraduate Med Fedn 1976–96, Christ Coll Brecon 1977–; chllr Diocese of Swansea and Brecon 1982–99, memb Provincial Ct Church in Wales 1996–; hon fell UCL 2001; fell Inst of Child Health 1996; *Clubs* Carlton, Garrick; *Style*— Leolin

P

Price, Esq, CBE, QC; ✉ 32 Hampstead Grove, London NW3 6SR (tel 020 7435 9843); 10 Old Square, Lincoln's Inn, London WC2A 3SU (tel 020 7405 0758, fax 020 7831 8237, e-mail leolinprice@tenoldsquare.com); Moor Park, Llanbedr, Crickhowell, Powys NP8 1SS (tel 01873 810443, fax 01873 810659); Selborne Chambers, 174 Phillip Street, Sydney 2000, Australia (tel 00 61 2 233 5188, fax 00 61 2 9233 1137)

PRICE, Lionel Dennis Dixon; s of Harold Price (d 1988), of Birkenhead, and Florence Mitchley, *née* Thompson (d 1996); *b* 2 February 1946; *Educ* Bolton Sch, CCC Cambridge (MA); *m* 19 Oct 1968, Sara Angela, da of Ronald William Holt (d 1991), of Gerrards Cross; 3 s (Matthew b 1972, Edward b and d 1974, James b 1975); *Career* Bank of England 1967–79, alternate exec dir IMF 1979–81; Bank of England: head Info Div 1981–84, head Int Div 1985–90, head Economics Div 1990–94, dir of Central Banking Studies 1994–97; md sovereign ratings Fitch IBCA Ltd 1997–2001, chief economist Fitch Ratings 2001–06; dir Rocol Ltd 1991–93; treas Policy Studies Inst 1993–97; *Recreations* genealogy, walking; *Style*— Lionel Price, Esq; ✉ 102 Clarence Road, St Albans, Hertfordshire AL1 4NQ

PRICE, Dame Margaret Berenice; DBE (1993, CBE 1982); da of late Thomas Glyn Price; *b* 13 April 1941; *Educ* Pontllanfraith Secondary Sch, Trinity Coll of Music London (hon fellow); *Career* opera singer; debut with Welsh Nat Opera 1962; has appeared in all major opera houses incl: La Scala, Vienna State, Munich, Paris, Hamburg, San Francisco, Met Opera NY, Chicago Lyric Opera; also concert and Lieder career, renowned for her interpretation of Mozart, performed first recital in re-opened Wigmore Hall 1992; winner Elizabeth Schumann Prize for Lieder, Ricordi Prize for Opera, Silver Medal Worshipful Co of Musicians, Bayerische Kammersängerin 1979; Hon DMus Univ of Wales 1983, hon fell UCW Aberystwyth 1991, Hon RAM; *Style*— Dame Margaret Price, DBE

PRICE, Michael Anthony; LVO (1991); s of Francis George Price (d 1964), of Reading, Berks, and Lena Beatrice, *née* Tombs (d 2006); *b* 13 August 1944; *Educ* Forest GS Winnersh, JSDC Greenwich; *m* Elizabeth Anne, da of late Alfred John Cook; 1 da (Victoria Jane b 18 Jan 1972), 1 s (Nicholas David James b 20 Nov 1974); *Career* diplomat (ret); economic attaché New Delhi 1969–72, second sec (political) Freetown 1973–74, FCO 1974–75, first sec Paris 1975–78, consul Montreal 1978–83, dep press sec to foreign sec 1983–88, press sec Washington DC 1988–92, consul-gen Tokyo 1992–94, cnsllr 10 Downing St 1994–95, cnsllr Paris 1995–99, high cmmr to Fiji 2000–03 (concurrently high cmmr to Kiribati, Tuvalu and Nauru); *Recreations* cricket, cooking, Gilbert and Sullivan; *Style*— Michael Price, Esq, LVO; ✉ Kasauli, Church Field, Monks Eleigh, Suffolk IP7 7JH

PRICE, His Hon Judge Nicholas Peter Lees; QC (1992); s of Frank Henry Edmund Price, MBE (Mil) (d 1991), and Agnes Lees, *née* Brittlebank; *b* 29 September 1944; *Educ* Prince of Wales Sch Nairobi, Univ of Edinburgh; *m* 4 Jan 1969, Wilma Ann Alison, *née* Steel; 1 s (James Alexander Lees b 9 March 1971), 1 da (Nicola Catherine Lees b 3 Nov 1973); *Career* called to the Bar Gray's Inn 1968 (bencher 2000), ad eundem memb Middle Temple; asst recorder 1983, recorder 1987–2006, circuit judge (SE Circuit) 2006–; Bar Cncl: memb 1993–95, vice-chm Legal Servs Ctee 1993, vice-chm Public Affrs Ctee 1995, vice-chm Professional Conduct and Complaints Ctee 2005; memb: Continuing Educn Ctee Gray's Inn 1998–2002 (chm 2001–02), Inns Advocacy Trg Ctee (IATC) 2001–, Bar Professional Standards Ctee 2002–04; *Style*— His Hon Judge Price, QC; ✉ The Crown Court at Kingston upon Thames, 6–8 Penrhyn Road, Kingston upon Thames, Surrey KT1 2BB (tel 020 8240 2500)

PRICE, Prof Patricia M; da of Michael Hogan, of Coventry, Warks, and Jane, *née* Quill; *b* 13 August 1957; *Educ* Newnham Coll Cambridge (MA), King's Coll Hosp Med Sch (MB BChir, MRCP), Univ of Cambridge (MD, Lionel Whitby medal); *m* 1, 1984 (m dis), Dr C G A Price; 2 s (Oliver b 8 Oct 1986, Rory b 24 Sept 1988); m 2, 1994, Prof Terry Jones; *Career* oncology training Radiotherapy and Oncology Unit Royal Marsden Hosp 1988–89 (registrar 1984–88), CRC clinical scientist Inst of Cancer Research 1988–89, reader in clinical oncology Imperial Coll Sch of Med at Hammersmith Hosp (Royal Postgrad Med Sch until merger 1997) and hon conslt oncologist Hammersmith Hosp and Ealing Hosp 1989–2000, head MRL and CRC PET Oncology Gp MRC Cyclotron Unit Hammersmith Hosp Clinical Scis Centre; currently: Ralston Paterson prof of radiation oncology Christie Hosp Manchester, princ clinical scientist Univ of Manchester Wolfson Molecular Imaging Centre, chm UK Academic Clinical Oncology and Radiology Research Network; memb various UK, European and American oncology advsy ctees; Varian Clinical Research Award Euro Soc for Therapeutic Radiology and Oncology 1985, Sterling Oncology Award 1989; memb: BMA 1981, Br Oncological Assoc 1987 (sec 1991–93, pres 2002–04); FRCR 1987, FRCP 1995; *Publications* Treatment of Cancer (4 edn, 2002); over 100 pubns in the field of oncology; *Style*— Prof Pat Price; ✉ Academic Department of Radiation Oncology, Christie Hospital, Wilmslow Road, Manchester M20 4BX (tel 0161 446 8003, fax 0161 448 8111)

PRICE, Dr Paul Anthony; s of Wolf Price, of London, and Dinah, *née* Shafar; *b* 15 May 1949; *Educ* Christ's Coll GS Finchley, UCL (BSc), UCH Med Sch (MB BS); *m* 15 March 1985, Sandra Margaret, *née* Miller; *Career* sr house offr physician: Brompton Hosp, Enfield Dist Gen Hosp 1973–75; hon registrar and Parkinson's Disease Soc res fell KCH 1977–78, registrar UCH 1978–79, hon sr registrar Bart's 1979–83, sr registrar St George's Hosp Gp London 1983–85, conslt physiotherapist and endocrinologist Great Western Hospital Swindon 1985–; cncl memb Section of Endocrinology RSM; FRCP, FRSM, memb BMA; *Books* chapters in books on neurology and endocrinology; *Recreations* music, playing the bassoon; *Style*— Dr Paul Price; ✉ Department of Medicine, Great Western Hospital, Marlborough Road, Swindon SN3 6DD (tel 01793 604315, fax 01793 604501)

PRICE, Rt Rev Peter Bryan; *see:* Bath and Wells, Bishop of

PRICE, His Hon Judge Philip John; QC (1989); s of Ernest Price, and Sarah Eunice, *née* Morgan; *b* 16 May 1943; *Educ* Cardiff HS, Pembroke Coll Oxford; *m* 27 March 1967, Mari Josephine, da of Thomas Stanley Davies; 2 da (Alexandra Ruth b 1973, Harriet Angharad b 1975), 1 s (Matthew Huw Caradog b 1978); *Career* lectr in law Univ of Leeds 1966–70, called to the Bar Gray's Inn 1969, practising on Wales & Chester Circuit 1971–93, Temple 1991–93; circuit judge (Wales & Chester Circuit) 1993–; memb Mental Health Review Tbnl 1995–, ctee memb Cncl of Circuit Judges 1998– (sr vice-pres 2007); chllr Diocese of Monmouth 1992–; Church in Wales: memb Governing Body 1992–, pres Disciplinary Tbnl 2001–05, chm Standing Ctee 2005–; tstee LATCH (Welsh children's cancer charity) 1996– (chm 2006–); *Recreations* books, buildings, cricket; *Clubs* Cardiff and County; *Style*— His Hon Judge Philip Price, QC; ✉ 2nd Floor, Churchill House, Churchill Way, Cardiff CF1 4HH (tel 029 2041 5500)

PRICE, Richard Lloyd Duffield; s of David Henderson Price, and Janet Helen, *née* Duffield; *b* 13 April 1949; *Educ* Royal GS Newcastle upon Tyne, Magdalen Coll Oxford (BA), Univ of London (Postgrad Dip Applied Social Studies); *m* 1981, Joanna Mary, da of William Murray; 2 s (Gregory Richard Murray b 10 Sept 1982, Alastair Joseph Murray b 4 Oct 1985); *Career* probation offr Inner London Probation Serv 1973–77, info offr Personal Social Serv Cncl 1977–78, dep dir Int Year of the Child (UK) 1978–80, communications mangr Nexos Office Systems Ltd 1980–83, md The EuroPR Gp Ltd 1984–; MIPR 1984, memb PRCA 1985; *Recreations* singing, cricket, family activities; *Clubs* Oxford and Cambridge; *Style*— Richard Price, Esq; ✉ The EuroPR Group, 5th Floor, The Courtyard, 7 Francis Grove, Wimbledon, London SW19 4DW (tel 020 8971 6420, fax 020 8971 6401, e-mail rprice@europrgroup.com)

PRICE, Richard Mervyn; OBE (1995), QC (1996); s of William James Price (d 1987), of S Yorks, and Josephine May, *née* Preston (d 2000); *b* 15 May 1948; *Educ* King Edward VII Sch Sheffield, King's Coll London (LLB); *m* 1971 (m dis 2007), Caroline Sarah Price, *qv*, da of Geoffrey Ball, and Mary Ball, of Surrey; 1 s (Timothy George b 13 Jan 1975), 2 da (Kathryn Sara b 3 Dec 1977, Emma Charlotte Louisa b 28 July 1983); *Career* called to the Bar Gray's Inn 1969 (bencher 2002); standing counsel on election law Cons Central Office 1986–, recorder 2004–; chm Conduct Ctee Bar Cncl, memb Bar Standards Bd; *Recreations* politics, theatre, films, music, walking, cycling; *Clubs* RAC, St Stephen's; *Style*— Richard Price, Esq, OBE, QC; ✉ Littleton Chambers, 3 King's Bench Walk North, Temple, London EC4Y 7HR (tel 020 7797 8600, fax 020 7797 8699)

PRICE, His Hon Judge Richard Neville Meredith; s of Christopher Price (d 1980), and Valerie Ruby, *née* Greenham (d 1992); *b* 30 May 1945; *Educ* Marsh Court Stockbridge, Sutton Valence, Coll of Law Guildford; *m* Oct 1971, Avril Judith, da of Edward Purser Lancaster (d 1954), and Dorothy Margaret, *née* Collins; 3 s (Andrew b 10 Nov 1974, Simon b 24 Sept 1979, David b 10 June 1986); *Career* slr 1970–90, called to the Bar Middle Temple 1990, recorder 1990–96 (asst recorder 1986–90), circuit judge 1996–, resident judge Portsmouth and IOW; hon recorder City of Portsmouth 2006; *Recreations* choral singing, sailing, reading, listening to music; *Clubs* Seaview Yacht, Royal London Yacht; *Style*— His Hon Judge Richard Price; ✉ Portsmouth Combined Court Centre, Courts of Justice, Winston Churchill Avenue, Portsmouth, Hampshire

PRICE, Richard Shirvell; MBE; *b* 1933; *Educ* Milton Acad Mass, Leeds GS, Liverpool Inst Sch, Univ of Leeds; *m* 1963, Joan, *née* Silk; 1 s, 1 da; *Career* served RNVR and RNR 1951–64; Nat Serv Supply Offr RN 1955–57; PRO Benger Laboratories Ltd 1957–59, freelance journalist 1957–59, sr PRO PIDA (Agricultural Authy) 1959, PRO, orgn mangr then sales controller Bayer (UK) 1960–62, fndr and ed PULSE (the GP newspaper, now published by Morgan Grampian) 1960–62, md Pharmacia (UK) Ltd 1962–65, sales dir Granada Television (Overseas) Ltd 1965–67, former chm Primetime plc gp (included Primetime Television largest ind UK prog distributor) founded 1968, dir Digital Classics plc (former chm); chm: RPTA Ltd, Watermill Theatre Newbury; jt chm The Performance Co; BAFTA: memb Cncl 1982–97, hon treas 1984–91, chm and tstee 1991–93, dep chm 1993–95; local cncllr Paddington 1963–65, Parly candidate (Cons) N Paddington 1969 and 1970; chm CPC study gps on Traffic and Broadcasting 1965–68; chm local MENCAP Soc 1980–86; govr: Parkwood Hall Sch 1986–2000 (chm of govrs 1990–94), Home Farm Tst for Learning Difficulties 1993– (chm 2000–04); chm LSE Media Advsy Gp 1995–97, memb Fulbright Advsy Ctee 1995–2001, vice-chm Charities Tax Reform Gp 2003–; tstee TAPS; FRTS 1985 (memb Cncl 1975–83); *Style*— Richard Price, Esq; ✉ RPTA Ltd, Queen's Wharf, Queen Caroline Street, London W6 9RJ (tel 020 8600 2660, e-mail richardprice@rpta.co.uk)

PRICE, Richard Stephen; s of Dr David Brian Price, OBE, of Bridgend, Mid Glamorgan, and Menna Myles, *née* Jones (d 1988); *b* 27 May 1953; *Educ* Cowbridge GS, Univ of Leeds; *m* 3 May 1980, Nicola Mary, da of Philip Griffin, of Henstridge, Somerset; 2 da (Roseanna b 4 Dec 1986, Susannah Kate Rhiannon b 1 Feb 1993), 1 s (Nicholas b 13 Sept 1988); *Career* admitted slr 1977, sr ptnr CMS Cameron McKenna (formerly McKenna & Co) 1984– (i/c ME practice 1984–88); memb City of London Slrs' Co, memb Law Soc; *Recreations* golf; *Style*— Richard Price, Esq; ✉ CMS Cameron McKenna, Mitre House, 160 Aldersgate Street, London EC1A 4DD (tel 020 7367 3000, fax 020 7367 2000)

PRICE, Robin Mark Dodgson; s of Wilfred Barrie Price, of Knowle, West Midlands, and Jocelyn Mary, *née* Berry; *b* 30 April 1956; *Educ* The Leys Sch Cambridge, Univ of Bristol (LLB); *m* 27 Sept 1986, Jane, da of Vyvian Hugh Reginald Rawson; 1 s (Joe Gulliver b 19 Nov 1990), 1 da (Eleanor Alice b 22 Sept 1992); *Career* chartered accountant Arthur Young McClelland Moores 1978–82, md Frontline Video Ltd 1983–87, ptnr HHCL and Partners 1987–97, dir Chime Communications plc 1997–2002, chief operating offr McCann Erickson UK and Ireland and vice-pres operations McCann Erickson EMEA 2003–; ACA, FIPA; *Recreations* tennis, golf, cricket, ballet and modern dance; *Clubs* Roehampton; *Style*— Robin Price, Esq; ✉ McCann Erickson Advertising Ltd, 7–11 Herbrand Street, London WC1N 1EX (tel 020 7961 2305, fax 020 7961 2874, e-mail robin.price@europe.mccann.com)

PRICE, Roland John Stuart; s of Philip Stuart Price, of Tamworth, and Rowena Mary, *née* Jones; *b* 29 July 1961; *Educ* Sydney GS Aust, Royal Ballet Sch London; *Career* ballet dancer (ret); Gold Medal Adeline Genée Award 1978; princ dancer: Sadler's Wells Royal Ballet (now Birmingham Royal Ballet) 1984– (joined 1979), Boston Ballet USA 1990–94, freelance 1995–; princ roles incl: The Two Pigeons, La Fille Mal Gardée, Coppélia, Giselle, Romeo and Juliet, Swan Lake, The Sleeping Beauty, The Snow Queen, Abdallah, The Nutcracker, Études, many one act ballets incl creations by Macmillan and Bintley; Lawrence Olivier Award nominee 1980 and 1985; freelance dance teacher and coach 1999–; *Recreations* opera; *Style*— Roland Price, Esq

PRICE, Sean; QPM (2005); *Educ* QMC (BSc), Univ of Cambridge (MSt); *m* Jacqueline; 1 s (Harry James b 23 July 2004); *Career* joined Merseyside Police 1979, Asst Chief Constable then Dep Chief Constable Nottinghamshire Police 1998–2003, Chief Constable Cleveland Police 2003–; *Recreations* cycling, cooking, reading, playing musical instruments (badly); *Style*— Sean Price, Esq, QPM; ✉ Cleveland Police, PO Box 70, Ladgate Lane, Middlesbrough TS8 9EH

PRICE, Vivian William Cecil; QC (1972); s of late Evan Price; *b* 14 April 1926; *Educ* Judd Sch Tonbridge, Trinity Coll Cambridge, Balliol Coll Oxford; *m* 1961, Elizabeth Anne, da of late Arthur Rawlins; 3 s, 2 da; *Career* RN 1946–49; called to the Bar: Middle Temple 1954 (bencher 1979), Hong Kong 1975, Singapore 1979; dep judge of the High Court (Chancery Div) 1975–85; *Clubs* Travellers; *Style*— Vivian Price, Esq, QC; ✉ Redwall Farmhouse, Linton, Kent ME17 4AX (tel 01622 743682)

PRICHARD, Prof Brian Norman Christopher; CBE (1996); s of Sir Norman George Mollett Prichard (d 1972), of London, and Winifred, *née* Just (d 1989); *b* 7 November 1932; *Educ* Merton House Sch, Battersea GS, St George's Hosp Univ of London (BSc, MSc, MB BS); *m* 8 Sept 1956, Denise Margaret, da of Edward Stoneham (d 1982), of Ewell; 2 s (Andrew J N Prichard, FRCS, Rev Ian E B Prichard), 2 da (Ruth (Mrs Bowers), Catherine (Mrs Bonnington)); *Career* SHO in surgery Dorking Gen Hosp 1958–59, registrar St George's Hosp 1959–61 (house offr posts 1957–58); Royal Free and Univ Coll Med Sch (formerly UCH Med Sch): research asst 1961–62, lectr in clinical pharmacology 1962–68, sr lectr 1968–75, reader 1975–80, prof 1980–, conslt physician 1973–; author of about 200 reviews and papers; Astra Award Int Soc of Hypertension (for the introduction of beta adrenergic blocking drugs into the treatment of hypertension) 1979; vice-pres Cons Med Soc (past chm), cncllr London Borough of Wandsworth (chm Standards and Ethics Ctee); chm: Inst of Alcohol Studies, Action on Drinking and Driving, SACRE Wandsworth; non-exec dir Richmond Pharmacology Ltd St George's Hosp; past pres Int Soc of Cardiovascular Therapy; memb: American Heart Assoc, Br Cardiac Soc, Br Pharmacological Soc, Assoc of Physicans, Br Soc of Hypertension, Int Soc of Hypertension; hon memb European Soc of Hypertension; FRCP 1977, FFPM 1989, FESC 1996, FACC 1997, fell Br Pharmacological Soc 2004, FRSM; *Books* Biological Effects of Drugs in Relation to their Plasma Concentration (ed with D S Davies, 1973), Prescribing - What, When, Why? (with J Fry and M Godfrey, 1986), Beta Blockers in Clinical Practice (with J M Cruickshank, 2 edn 1994); *Recreations* photography, walking; *Clubs* RAC; *Style*— Prof B N C Prichard, CBE; ✉ 108 Chapelier House, Eastfields Avenue, Putney, London SW18 3LR (tel 020 8870 3066); Centre for Clinical Pharmacology, Royal Free and University College Medical School, University College London, 5 University Street, London WC1E 6JJ (tel 07918 176285, fax 020 7679 6211)

PRICHARD, David; s of late Richard Evan Prichard, of Exmouth, Devon, and late Phyllis, *née* Hiscock; *b* 23 September 1948; *Educ* Kingston GS, Bartlett Sch of Architecture (BSc,

DipArch, Sir Andrew Taylor Prize); *m* 23 Sept 1988, Catherine Jamison, da of Ian McCarter; 1 da (Isobel b 13 Nov 1984), 2 s (Charlie b 28 Feb 1986, George b 16 Dec 1988); *Career* architect; ptnr MacCormac Jamieson Prichard Architects 1979–2005, co-fndr (with Neil Deely) Metropolitan Workshop LLP 2005; buildings and masterplans at: Milton Keynes Devpt Corp, Warrington Devpt Corp, Queen Mary Univ of London, Spitalfields Market, LDDC, offices in Havant Hants CC, Bow HAT, Cable and Wireless Coll Coventry 1990–94 (Building of the Year Award 1994), Imperial Coll London, Gala Theatre Durham, Durham Clayport Library, Ballymun Regeneration Dublin, Meadowbank Club, Jersey Archive, City of Durham, Poplar, Adamstown Dist Centre, Dublin Docks, Oslo City Cncl; visiting lectr: Univ of Brighton. Univ of Cambridge; RIBA external examiner 1981–2003: Univ of Kent, UCL, Univ of North London, Edinburgh Coll of Art; Civic Tst: regnl and nat assessor 1990–2003, chm Nat Awards Panel 2004–, tstee 2004–; several RIBA Awards and Civic Tst Awards, RTPI of Ireland Planning Achievement Award 1999; RIBA 1974, FRSA, FICPD; *Recreations* family, walking, gardening; *Style*— David Prichard, Esq; ✉ Wilmot Cottage, Mote Road, Ivy Hatch, Sevenoaks, Kent TN15 0NT (tel 01732 810063); Metropolitan Workshop LLP, 14–16 Cowcross Street, Farringdon, London EC1M 6DG (tel 020 7566 0450, e-mail david.prichard@metwork.co.uk, website www.metwork.co.uk)

PRICHARD, Desmond George Michael (Des); QFSM (2006); s of Aubrey Veron Prichard, of Milton Keynes, Bucks, and Ellen, *née* Grosse; *b* 9 December 1953, London; *Educ* Bletchley GS, Putteridgebury Coll (Dip), Henley Mgmnt Coll (MBA); *m* 25 July 1987, Ruth Ann, *née* Stanton; 1 s (Benjamin Thomas Stanton b 17 Jan 1991); *Career* joined Fire and Rescue Serv 1976; served in Beds and Bucks, lectr in command leadership and mgmnt Fire and Rescue Serv Coll 1991–94; E Sussex Fire Serv: asst chief fire offr 1995–96, dep chief fire offr 1996–2001; chief exec and chief fire offr E Sussex and Brighton & Hove 2001–; chm Assoc of Princ Fire Offrs, bd dir for HR Chief Fire Offrs Assoc; Long Service and Conduct Medal 1996; memb Inst of Fire Engrs 1984, MCIPD 1994; *Recreations* rugby, skiing, theatre, watching Chelsea FC; *Clubs* Bletchley RUFC (vice-pres); *Style*— Des Prichard, Esq, QFSM; ✉ East Sussex Fire & Rescue Service Headquarters, 20 Upperton Road, Eastbourne, East Sussex BN21 1EU (tel 01323 462060, e-mail des.prichard@esfrs.org)

PRICHARD, Mathew Caradoc Thomas; CBE (1992), DL (1994); s of Maj Hubert de Burgh Prichard, of Pwllywrach, Cowbridge (ka 1944), and Rosalind Margaret Clarissa Hicks, *née* Christie; *b* 21 September 1943; *Educ* Eton, New Coll Oxford (BA); *m* 1, 20 May 1967, Angela Caroline (d 2004), *née* Maples; 2 da (Alexandra b 1968, Joanna b 1972), 1 s (James b 1970); m 2, 10 Feb 2007, Lucinda Mary, *née* Oliver; *Career* chm Agatha Christie Ltd 1977–; chm Welsh Arts Cncl 1986–94, memb Arts Cncl GB 1983–94, pres Nat Museum of Wales 1997–2002 (vice-pres 1992–96), memb Bd WNO Ltd; High Sheriff Co of Glam 1973–74; *Recreations* golf, cricket, bridge; *Clubs* Boodle's, Cardiff and County, R&A, Royal Porthcawl Golf, MCC; *Style*— Mathew Prichard, Esq, CBE, DL

PRICHARD JONES, Kenneth Victor; s of John Victor Jones, MBE (d 1981), and Eunice Aldwyn Marie, *née* Prichard (d 1976); *b* 12 September 1946; *Educ* Clifton, Univ of Kent at Canterbury (BA); *m* 26 Sept 1967, Dagmar Eva, da of Col Pavel Svoboda (d 1993), of Putney, London; 3 s (Sebastian b 1973, Piers b 1975, Christian b 1980), 1 da (Lucy b 1978); *Career* admitted slr 1972; memb Law Soc; friend of Keats-Shelley Meml Assoc; Medal of Honour for Conservation Europa Nostra 1994; breeder Dreadnought herd of white park cattle; *Books* F is for Franchising (2 edn, 1983), Encyclopaedia of Forms and Precedents (Agency Documents vol, 1984, revised edn 1992), Merchandising (contrib, 1987), Commercial Hiring and Leasing (contrib, 1989), Encyclopaedia of Forms and Precedents (Food vol, 1995), The Law and Practice of Franchising (with Prof John Adams, 5 edn 2006); *Recreations* swimming, motor racing; *Clubs* Brooklands, Bluecoats, Veteran Car, Vintage Sports Car; *Style*— Kenneth Prichard Jones, Esq; ✉ Field Place, Warnham, West Sussex RH12 3PB (tel 01403 265004, mobile 07836 768596, e-mail westwind@whiteparks.com)

PRICKETT, Prof (Alexander Thomas) Stephen; s of Rev William Ewart Prickett (d 1975), of Canterbury, Kent, and Barbara Browning, *née* Lyne; *b* 4 June 1939; *Educ* Kent Coll Canterbury, Trinity Hall Cambridge (scholar, MA, PhD, T H prize for English, Edward George Harwood prize for English, Cambridge Univ membs' prize), UC Oxford (DipEd); *m* 1, 1966 (m dis 1981), Diana Joan, da of George Mabbutt; 1 da (Ruth Charlotte b 1970), 1 s (Mark Thomas b 1974); m 2, 1984 (m dis 2001), Maria Angelica Alvarez; m 3, 2001, Patricia Erskine-Hill; *Career* teacher of English: Methodist Coll Uzuakoli E Nigeria 1962–64, Univ of Sussex 1967–82, Aust Nat Univ Canberra Australia 1983–89; regius prof of English language and literature Univ of Glasgow 1990–, prof of English Duke Univ N Carolina USA 2001–; govr Bishop Otter Coll of Educn 1974–77, tstee Fernley Hartley Tst 1978–83; chm: Higher Educn Gp 1971–82, Higher Educn Fndn 1991–95; pres George MacDonald Soc 1995–; fell Australian Acad of Humanities 1986; *Books* Do It Yourself Doom (1962), Coleridge and Wordsworth: The Poetry of Growth (1970), Romanticism and Religion (1976), Victorian Fantasy (1979), Words and the Word (1986), The Bible (1991), Origins of Narrative (1996), World's Classics Bible (ed, 1997), The Bible and Literature: A Reader (ed, 1999), Literature, Science and Religion: Fundamentalism vs Irony 1700–1999 (2002), Education! Education! Education! Managerial Ethics and the Law of Unintended Consequences (ed, 2002); *Recreations* walking, skiing, tennis, attending conferences; *Style*— Prof Stephen Prickett; ✉ Department of English Literature, University of Glasgow, Glasgow G12 8QQ (tel 0141 339 8855, fax 0141 330 4601)

PRIDAY, Charles Nicholas Bruton; s of Christopher Bruton Priday, QC (d 1992), and Jill Holroyd, *née* Sergeant; *b* 17 July 1959; *Educ* Radley, UC Oxford, City Univ London; *m* 17 July 1982, Helen Elizabeth, da of M M Jones; 2 da (Elizabeth b 1987, Emma b 1989); *Career* called to the Bar Middle Temple 1982; *Recreations* escaping to the Cotswolds, golf, tennis; *Clubs* Oxford Unicorns Real Tennis, Moreton Morrell Real Tennis; *Style*— Charles Priday, Esq; ✉ 7 King's Bench Walk, Temple, London EC4Y 7DS (tel 020 7583 0404, fax 020 7583 0950, telex 887491 KBLAW)

PRIDAY, Helen Elizabeth; da of Michael Montague Jones (d 1995), of Radley, Oxon, and Alison Priscilla, *née* Shepherd (d 1993); *b* 24 September 1957; *Educ* Dragon Sch Oxford, Radley; *m* 17 July 1982, Charles Nicholas Bruton Priday, *qv*, s of Christopher Bruton Priday, QC (d 1992), of London; 2 da (Elizabeth b 1987, Emma b 1989); *Career* publicity and promotions mangr W H Freeman & Co Oxford 1978–82, ed Pitkin Pictorials London 1982–83, mktg and publicity dir Times Books Angus and Robertson London 1983–, promotions dir The Times Supplements 1990–97 (The Times Literary Supplement, The Times Educational Supplement, The Times Higher Education Supplement), fndr HP: M (Helen Priday Marketing) 1997–, dir Equus Event Ltd 2001–03; conslt: Daily Telegraph/House & Garden Fair 1999–, The Spirit of Christmas 2001–; MIDM, FRSA; *Recreations* walking in the Cotswolds, tennis, golf, good food and wine, travelling in France, Ile de Ré, gardening, theatre, opera; *Clubs* St Enodoc Golf, Great Rissington, Vauban Societé; *Style*— Mrs Helen Priday; ✉ HP: M, 13 St Peter's Street, Islington, London N1 8JD (tel 020 7359 4337, fax 020 7354 3502, e-mail h.priday@btinternet.com)

PRIDDIS, Rt Rev Anthony Martin; *see:* Hereford, Bishop of

PRIDE, Prof Stephen James; s of George William Pride (d 1989), of NSW, Aust, and Winifred Agnes Mary, *née* Whittaker (2006); *b* 8 January 1949; *Educ* Hampton HS Melbourne, Monash Univ (BSc), Aust Nat Univ (PhD, Peter Stroud prize); *Career* res fell Open Univ 1974–78, lectr in mathematics KCL 1978–79, prof of mathematics Univ of Glasgow 1992– (lectr 1979–87, reader 1987–92); memb: Australian Mathematical Soc 1971, London Mathematical Soc 1975 (memb Ed Bd 1989–99), Edinburgh Mathematical Soc 1979 (memb ctee 2001–03), Mathematics Coll EPSRC 1997–2000, Cwlth Scholarship Cmmn Panel of Advsrs 2000–06, Editorial Bd Semigroup Forum 2004–, Editorial Bd Int Electronic Jl of Algebra 2006–; author of over 77 articles on group and semigroup theory and some aspects of theoretical computer science; FRSE 1992; *Recreations* outdoor activities (especially cycling), gardening, travelling, songwriting and music production; *Style*— Prof Stephen Pride, FRSE; ✉ Department of Mathematics, University of Glasgow G12 8QW (tel 0141 330 6528, fax 0141 330 4111, e-mail sjp@maths.gla.ac.uk)

PRIDEAUX, Sir Humphrey Povah Treverbian; kt (1971), OBE (1945), DL (Hants 1983); s of Walter Treverbian Prideaux (d 1958), of Ockley, Surrey, and Marion Fenn, *née* Arbuthnot (d 1958); bro of Sir John Francis Prideaux, OBE, DL (d 1993) and Walter Arbuthnot Prideaux, CBE, MC, TD (d 1995); *b* 13 December 1915; *Educ* St Aubyn's Rottingdean, Eton, Trinity Coll Oxford; *m* 1939, Cynthia, da of late Lt-Col H Birch Reynardson, CMG; 4 s; *Career* Jt Planning Staff War Office 1945, Naval Staff Coll 1948, Cmdt Sch of Admin 1948, Chiefs of Staff Secretariat 1950–53, ret; dir: NAAFI 1956–73 (chm 1963–73), The London Life Assoc Ltd 1964–88 (vice-pres 1965–72, pres 1973–88), Brooke Bond Liebig Ltd 1968–81 (chm 1972–81), W H Smith & Son Ltd 1969–81 (vice-chm 1977–81), Morland & Co 1981–93 (chm 1983–93), Grindlays Bank 1982–85; chm Lord Wandsworth Fndn 1966–92; Liveryman Worshipful Co of Goldsmiths; *Clubs* Cavalry and Guards'; *Style*— Sir Humphrey Prideaux, OBE, DL; ✉ Kings Cottage, Buryfields, Odiham, Hampshire RG29 1NE (tel 01256 703658, e-mail hptprideaux@aol.com)

PRIDEAUX, Julian Humphrey; OBE (1995); s of Sir Humphrey Povah Treverbian Prideaux, OBE, DL, *qv*, and Cynthia, *née* Birch-Reynardson; *b* 19 June 1942; *Educ* St Aubyn's Rottingdean, Eton, RAC Cirencester (Dip); *m* 5 Aug 1967, Rosamund Jill, da of Richard Patrick Roney-Dougal (d 1993), of Bridgnorth, Shropshire; 2 s (Adam b 1968, Nigel b 1971); *Career* land agent; Burd and Evans Chartered Surveyors Shrewsbury 1964–67; Col the Hon GC Cubitt and Others 1967–69; The National Trust: land agent Cornwall Region 1969–77, dir Thames and Chilterns Region 1978–86, chief agent 1987–97, dep DG and sec 1997–2002; tstee: Rural Housing Tst 2001–, Nat Gardens Scheme 2003–05 (memb Cncl 1987–); memb Cncl Chelsea Physic Garden 2003– (chm Exec Ctee); FRICS 1974; *Recreations* walking; *Clubs* Farmers'; *Style*— Julian Prideaux, Esq, OBE; ✉ Bellbrook, Donhead St Mary, Shaftesbury, Dorset SP7 9DL (tel 01747 828125)

PRIDEAUX, Michael Charles Terrell; s of Sir John Francis Prideaux, OBE, DL (d 1993), and Joan Terrell, *née* Pigott-Brown; *b* 23 October 1950; *Educ* Eton, Trinity Coll Cambridge (MA); *m* 1975, Susan Henriette, da of Charles Peto Bennett (d 1977); 1 da (Laura (Mrs Guy Sanderson) b 1976), 1 s (John b 1979); *Career* fin advertisement mangr Financial Times 1979–80 (UK advertisement dir 1980–83), chief exec Charles Barker City 1983–89; dir: Charles Barker Gp 1983–89, Charles Barker plc 1987–89; dir of gp public affrs BAT Industries plc 1989–98, corp and regulatory affrs dir British American Tobacco plc 1998–; *Recreations* gardening, opera; *Clubs* Brooks's, Sussex; *Style*— Michael Prideaux Esq; ✉ Selehurst, Lower Beeding, Horsham, West Sussex RH13 6PR (tel 01403 891501); British American Tobacco plc, Globe House, 4 Temple Place, London WC2R 2PG (tel 020 7845 1000)

PRIEST, Christopher McKenzie; JP (East Sussex 1996); s of Walter Mackenzie Priest, and Millicent Alice, *née* Haslock; *b* 14 July 1943; *Educ* Cheadle Hulme Sch; *m* Laura Lee, *née* McClure; 2 c (Simon Walter, (Elizabeth Millicent (twins) b 23 Oct 1989); *Career* writer; tstee Hastings and Rother CAB 2000–, memb Soc of Authors; *Awards*: James Tait Black Memorial Prize for Fiction 1995, World Fantasy Award 1996, Arthur C Clarke Award 2002; *Books* Indoctrinaire (1970), Real-Time World (short stories, 1974), Fugue for a Darkening Island (1972), Inverted World (1974), The Space Machine (1976), A Dream of Wessex (1977), An Infinite Summer (short stories, 1979), The Affirmation (1981), The Glamour (1984), The Quiet Woman (1990), The Book on the Edge of Forever (non-fiction, 1994), The Prestige (1995), The Extremes (1998), The Dream Archipelago (short stories, 1999), The Separation (2002); *Style*— Christopher Priest; ✉ c/o PFD, Drury House, 34–43 Russell Street, London WC2B 5HA (tel 020 7344 1000, fax 020 7836 9539)

PRIEST, David James; s of James George Priest (d 1945), and Phoebe Young, *née* Logan (d 2000); *b* 20 June 1937; *Educ* Kingston Coll; *m* 23 May 1959, Carol-Ann, da of Arthur Basham (d 1994), of Westcliff-on-Sea, Essex; 1 s (Christopher David b 1961), 1 da (Melanie Jayne b 1966); *Career* engr: Vicker Armstrongs Aircraft Ltd Weybridge 1954–61, Br United Airways 1961–65; various positions Standard Telephones and Cables Ltd (subsid of ITT) 1965–75; md: Barking-Grohe Ltd (ITT) 1975–79, ITT Jabsco Ltd 1979–83, Woods Air Movement Ltd 1983–2001; past chm GEC Int Assoc; past pres: Fedn of Environmental Trade Assocs, Heating and Ventilation Mfrs Assoc; chm and memb Bd Colchester Institute Corp; memb Ct Univ of Essex, memb Bd Anglia Ruskin Univ 2003–06; tstee Winsley's Charity (Alms Houses); memb Rotary Int; hon fell London South Bank Univ; CEng, FIMechE; *Recreations* swimming, tennis; *Clubs* Colchester Engrg Soc, The Mayflower (vice-pres); *Style*— David Priest, Esq; ✉ 44 Lexden Road, Colchester, Essex CO3 3RF (tel 01206 513042, e-mail priest.family@ntlworld.com)

PRIEST, Prof Eric Ronald; s of Ronald Priest, of Halesowen, Worcs, and Olive Vera, *née* Dolan; *b* 7 November 1943; *Educ* King Edward VI Birmingham, Univ of Nottingham (BSc), Univ of Leeds (MSc, PhD); *m* 25 July 1970, Clare Margaret, da of Rev William Henry Wilson, of St Andrews, Fife; 3 s (Andrew Nicholas b 1973, David Mark b 1978, Matthew Aidan b 1978), 1 da (Naomi Clare b 1982); *Career* Univ of St Andrews: prof of theoretical solar physics 1983, lectr in applied mathematics 1969, reader 1977, James Gregory prof of mathematics 1997, Wardlaw prof of mathematics 2002–; memb Norwegian Acad of Scis and Letters 1994; FRSE 1985, FRS 2002; *Books* Solar Flare Magnetohydrodynamics (1981), Solar Magnetohydrodynamics (1982), Solar System Magnetic Fields (1985), Dynamics and Structure of Solar Prominences (1989), Magnetic Flux Ropes (1990), Basic Plasma Processes on the Sun (1990), Advances in Solar System MHD (1991), Mechanisms of Chromospheric and Coronal Heating (1991), Dynamics of Solar Flares (1991), Magnetic Reconnection (2000); *Recreations* bridge, singing, hill walking, aerobics, children; *Style*— Prof Eric Priest, FRSE, FRS; ✉ Mathematical Institute, University of St Andrews University, St Andrews, Fife KY16 9SS (tel 01334 463709, fax 01334 463748, e-mail eric@mcs.st-and.ac.uk)

PRIEST, Keith; s of William John Priest, of Sunderland, and Christina, *née* Black; *b* 26 April 1950; *Educ* Bede Sch Sunderland, AA Sch of Architecture (AADipl); *m* 2 Aug 1979, Ann, *née* Buckley; 1 da (Lucy Eleanor b 17 April 1980); *Career* architect; Sir Denys Lasdun & Partners until 1973, design dir Wolff Olins design consltts 1975–78, fndr ptnr Fletcher Priest Architects 1978–; princ projects: Vodafone World HQ, IBM UK Laboratories, Stratford City, Science Museum IMAX, London Planetarium, Sony Computer Entertainment, AMVBBDO, Peoplebuilding Hemel; memb: Design Advsy Bd NHS London 2001, Cncl AA 2002, Urban Gp Br Cncl of Offices; memb D&AD, memb AA; RIBA, FRSA; *Recreations* family and friends, reading, Italian rural pursuits; *Style*— Keith Priest, Esq; ✉ Fletcher Priest Architects, 34/42 Cleveland Street, London W1T 4JE (tel 020 7034 2200, fax 020 7637 5347, e-mail k.priest@fletcherpriest.com, website www.fletcherpriest.com); Fletcher Priest Bösl, Marsilusstrasse 20 50937, Köln, Germany (tel 00 49 221 941 050, fax 00 49 221 941 0510, e-mail 100257.3443@compuserve.com)

PRIEST, Larry; *Educ* Univ of Birmingham (BA), Dip Arch (Birm), RIBA; *Career* architect; Aldington Craig + Collinge, Associated Architects, Mark Humphries Architects, ptnr Bryant Priest Newman; visiting tutor Univ of Central England, assessor RIBA design awards; *Style*— Larry Priest, Esq; ✉ Bryant Priest Newman, 43 Three Shires Road, Bearwood, West Midland B67 5BS (tel 0121 429 9049, fax 0121 429 1815)

P

PRIEST, Margaret Diane (Mrs Tony Scherman); da of Arthur Edmund Priest (d 1995), and Gertrude, *née* Tommason (d 2007); *b* 15 February 1944; *Educ* Dagenham Co HS Essex, SW Essex Tech Coll and Sch of Art Walthamstow, Maidstone Coll of Art (DipAD), RCA (John Minton scholar, MA, Silver medallist); *m* 1 Sept 1972, Tony Scherman, s of Paul Scherman (d 1996); 1 s (Leo b 2 April 1975), 2 da (Georgia Donna b 13 Jan 1978, Claudia Eve b 3 April 1980); *Career* artist; educator: Harrow Sch of Art 1970–74, St Martin's Sch of Art London 1972–76, Univ of Waterloo Sch of Architecture Ontario 1982–83, Univ of Toronto Sch of Architecture 1983–95; prof of fine art Univ of Guelph Ontario 1983–2000 (prof emeritus 2000–), visiting critic to schs of art and architecture UK, USA and Canada; work in numerous public and private collections; public art projects incl: The Monument to Construction Workers (Cloud Park Toronto) 1993; memb Bd: Ontario Coll of Art and Design 2005–; *Exhibitions* major solo exhibitions incl: Arnolfini Gallery Bristol 1970 and 1974, Garage Art Limited London 1974, Felicity Samuel Gallery London 1976, Theo Waddington Gallery London, Toronto, New York and Montreal 1980–83, Marianne Friedland Gallery Toronto 1985 and 1987, Albemarle Gallery London 1989, To View from Here Gallery Hamilton and Macdonald Stewart Art Centre Guelph 1996, Kelowna Art Gallery Br Colombia 2000; numerous gp exhibitions since 1969 in Eng, Scot, Yugoslavia, Switzerland, Belgium, Canada, USA, Australia, Germany and Italy; *Awards* Arts Cncl of GB 1969, Internationale Jugendtriennale Drawing Award 1979, Ontario Arts Cncl Drawing Award 1981, Governor Gen's Award for Architecture 1994, Ontario Confederation of Univ Faculty Assocs Teaching Award 1996; *Style*— Ms Margaret Priest; ✉ 38 Dunvegan Road, Toronto, Ontario M4V 2P6, Canada (tel 00 1 416 922 9699, fax 416 944 0814, e-mail info@margaretpriest.com)

PRIESTLEY, Clive; CB (1983); s of Albert Ernest Priestley (d 1985), of Bournemouth, Dorset, and Annie May Priestley (d 1974); *b* 12 July 1935; *Educ* Loughborough GS, Univ of Nottingham (BA, MA), Harvard Univ; *m* 1, 1961 (m dis 1984), Barbara Anne, *née* Wells; 2 da (Rebecca, Alison); m 2, 1985, Daphne June Challis Loasby, OBE, JP, DL, da of Walter Challis Franks, JP (d 1969); *Career* Nat Serv (Army) 1958–60; civil serv 1960–83 (under sec PM's office 1979–83), divnl dir BT plc 1983–88, conslt on orgn and mgmnt 1988–94, Millennial Serv Office St Paul's Cathedral 1998–2000; govr: RSC 1984–2004, City Literary Inst 1994–96; memb: Cncl Bart's Med Coll 1990–95 (vice-pres 1993–95, acting pres 1995), Arts Cncl of GB 1991–95, Cncl Queen Mary & Westfield Coll London 1995–2002, Arts Cncl of England 1996–97, Bd Trinity Coll of Music 1997–2005, Br Soc of Gastroenterology 2000–05, The Thiepval Project 2000–05; chm: London Arts Bd 1991–97, Trafalgar Square 2000 1996–98, Cncl of Dance Educn and Trg 1997–2000, Bart's Med Coll Tst 1997–; govr Shalbourne C of E Sch 2004–; Freeman City of London 1989, Liveryman Worshipful Co of Glaziers 1989–2002; hon perpetual student Bart's Med Coll; Hon FTCL; *Clubs* Army and Navy; *Style*— Clive Priestley, Esq, CB; ✉ Field House, Ham, Wiltshire SN8 3QR (tel and fax 01488 669094, e-mail clivprs@aol.com)

PRIESTLEY, Hugh Michael; s of James Frederick Priestley, MC, of Headbourne Worthy House, Hants, and Honor Purefoy, *née* Pollock; *b* 22 August 1942; *Educ* Winchester, Worcester Coll Oxford (MA); *m* 9 July 1968, Caroline Clarissa Duncan, da of Brig John Hume Prendergast, DSO, MC, of Amesbury Abbey, Wilts; 2 da (Alexandra b 1971, Susannah b 1974); *Career* The Times Newspaper 1964–66, Henderson Administration 1972–93, dir Rathbone Investment Mgmnt (formerly Laurence Keen) 1993–2005; dir of three quoted investment tst companies; tstee Independent Age (formerly RUKBA) 2005– (also chm Investment Sub-Gp); hon fell UCL (treas 1981–98); *Recreations* shooting, skiing, fishing; *Clubs* City of London, Boodle's, MCC; *Style*— Hugh Priestley, Esq; ✉ 52 Chelsea Gate Apartments, 93 Ebury Bridge Road, London SW1W 8RB

PRIESTLEY, Leslie William; TD (1974); s of George Priestley (d 1947), and Winifred, *née* Young (d 1994); *b* 22 September 1933; *Educ* Shooters Hill GS; *m* 8 Oct 1960, Audrey Elizabeth, da of Sidney Humber (d 1978); 1 s (Ian b 1967), 1 da (Jane b 1970); *Career* head of mktg Barclaycard 1966–73, local dir Barclays Bank 1978–79 (asst gen mangr 1974–77), sec gen Ctee of London Clearing Bankers 1979–83, dir Banker's Automated Clearing Servs Co 1979–83, md Barclays Insurance Services 1983–84, regnl gen mangr Barclays Bank 1984–85, chief exec TSB England & Wales plc 1985–89 (also dir TSB Group and Trustcard Ltd 1985–89); chm: Hill House Hammond Ltd 1988–89, Mortgage Express 1988–89, Caviapen Investments Ltd 1993–2003, Civil Aviation Authy Pension Scheme 1993–2003, Caviapen Trustees Ltd 1993–2003, Financial Telemarketing Services plc 1995–2003, Tenax Capital Ltd 2005–, Generali Pan Europe Ltd 2006–; dir: London Electricity plc (formerly LEB) 1984–96, Pearce Signs Group Ltd 1989–2003, Pinnacle Insurance plc 1990–2003, Omnia ICL Ltd 1992–94, Prudential Banking plc 1996–2006, Egg plc 2000–06, Currencies Direct Ltd 2005–; banking advsr Touche Ross & Co 1990–96, vice-chm Guernsey Fin Services Cmmn 1999–2005, advsr financial servs Satyam Computer Servs Ltd 2005–; memb: Monopolies & Mergers Commission 1990–96, London C of C and Industry 1992–96; visiting fell UCNW 1989–95, conslt ed Bankers Magazine 1972–81; dir Civil Aviation Authy 1990–96; FCIB, CCMI, FCIM, FRSA; *Recreations* reading, gardening, golf, theatre; *Clubs* RAC, Sundridge Park Golf, Chislehurst Golf; *Style*— Leslie Priestley, Esq, TD; ✉ c/o Tenax Capital Ltd, Dominican House, 4 Priory Court, Pilgrim Street, London EC4V 6DE (tel 020 7003 8700, fax 020 7003 8701)

PRIESTLEY, Philip John; CBE; s of Frederick Priestley (d 1963), and Caroline, *née* Rolfe (d 1982); *b* 29 August 1946; *Educ* Boston GS, UEA (BA); *m* 14 Nov 1972, Christine, da of Mrs M Sanders (d 1987); 1 da (Maya b 30 March 1976), 1 s (Max b 1 Nov 1978); *Career* FCO 1969–71, third sec Sofia 1971–73, third later second sec Kinshasa 1973–76, first sec FCO 1976–79, head of Chancery Wellington 1979–83, first sec FCO 1984–87, commercial cnsllr/dep head of mission Manila 1987–90, ambass to Gabon 1990–91, fell Center for International Affairs Harvard Univ 1991–92, consul-gen Geneva 1992–95, head N America Dept FCO 1996–2000, high cmmr to Belize 2001–04; Blue Diamond Ventures 2006–; FRSA; *Recreations* golf, theatre; *Style*— Philip Priestley, Esq, CBE; ✉ c/o Foreign & Commonwealth Office, King Charles Street, London SW1A 2AH

PRIESTLEY, Dr Robert Henry; s of Henry Benjamin Priestley, of Nantwich, Cheshire, and Margaret Alice, *née* Lambert; *b* 19 March 1946; *Educ* Brunts GS Mansfield, Univ of Southampton (BSc), Univ of Exeter (PhD); *m* 1970, Penelope Ann, da of Sydney Fox; 2 da (Rosalind Jane b 8 Sept 1975, Jessica Mary b 28 May 1978); *Career* plant pathologist Lord Rank Res Centre Rank Hovis McDougall Research Ltd 1970–73; National Institute of Agricultural Botany: cereal pathologist 1973–78, head Cereal Pathology Section 1978–82, head Plant Pathology Dept 1982–88; gen sec Institute of Biology 1989–97; mgmnt conslt HQ Strike CMD 1998–2002, princ conslt and lectr Centre for Mgmnt and Policy Studies Sunningdale Park 2002–06; memb: Cncl Fedn of British Plant Pathologists 1980–81, British Nat Ctee for Microbiology 1982–89, Ctee of Mgmnt Biological Cncl 1989–91, Parly and Scientific Ctee 1989–97, Bd Cncl for Science and Technology Insts 1989–97, Nominations Ctee Int Union of Biological Sciences 1994–97; sec UK Cereal Pathogen Virulence Survey 1974–82, chm EC Biologists' Assoc 1992–96, memb Br Soc for Plant Pathology 1980 (treas 1981–87, UK rep 1988–92); owner Ro-Po Publishing; CBiol, FIBiol, FIMgt; *Books* Identification and Control of Diseases (1982), Diseases of Oilseed Rape and Fodder Brassicas (1985), Diseases of Grasses and Herbage Legumes (1988), Football League Programmes of the Late 1940s; author of consultancy reports and numerous scientific papers on crop diseases; *Recreations* music, art, architecture, football; *Style*— Dr Robert Priestley; ✉ 17 Wallingford Gardens, Daws Hill Lane, High Wycombe HP11 1QS (tel 01494 446660)

PRIESTMAN, Dr Jane; OBE (1991); da of Reuben Stanley Herbert (d 1986), and Mary Elizabeth, *née* Ramply (d 1957); *b* 7 April 1930; *Educ* Northwood Coll, Liverpool Coll of Art (NDD, ATD); *m* 1954 (m dis), Arthur Martin Priestman; 2 s (Matthew Temple b March 1958, Paul Dominic b June 1961); *Career* designer; design practice 1954–75, design mangr BAA 1975–86, dir of architecture and design British Railways Board 1986–91, design mgmnt conslt 1991–; visiting prof in int design De Montfort Univ; memb Design Cncl 1996–99, enabler CABE, chm RIBA Awards Gp; memb: NHS London Design Advsy Gp, NHS Design Brief Working Gp; dir London Open House; govr: Cwlth Inst, Kingston Univ; Hon DDes: De Montfort Univ 1994, Sheffield Hallam Univ 1998; Hon FRIBA, FCSD; *Recreations* opera, city architecture, textiles, travel; *Clubs* Architecture; *Style*— Dr Jane Priestman, OBE; ✉ 30 Duncan Terrace, London N1 8BS (tel 020 7837 4525, fax 020 7837 4525, e-mail jane.priestman@virgin.net)

PRIESTMAN, Paul Dominic; s of Martin Priestman (d 2003), of Bourne, Cambs, and Jane, *née* Herbert; *b* 8 June 1961; *Educ* St Christopher's Sch Letchworth, Central St Martin's (BA, RSA Student Design Award), RCA (MDes, RSA Student Design Award, DIA Mellchet Meml Award); *m* 18 Aug 1990, Hon Tessa Mitford, da of 5 Baron Redesdale (d 1991); *Career* designer; fndr Priestman Associates (now Priestman Goode Ltd) 1987; exhbns incl: Making Their Mark London 1987, Design Advantage (Design Cncl London) 1992, Best of British Design Hong Kong 1993, Design of the Times London 1995, Product of Desire Glasgow 1996, Design Cncl's 20 Designers Paris 1997, perm display Philadelphia MOMA 1998, Industry of One (Craft Cncl) 2001, Lateral Design (Glynn Vivian Art Gallery) 2001, Communicating Change Design Museum 2001, Joined Up Design for Schools (V&A) 2005; lectures incl: RSA, Design Cncl, Br Cncl, DTI, Bangkok, Johannesburg, New Delhi, São Paulo, ICA London, Tokyo, Aust, China; chair Design Business Assoc 2001–03; chair Design Sector Skills Panel 2005–, memb Design Cncl 2005–, memb Exec D&AD 2005–; FRSA; *Awards* Second Int Design Comp Japan 1986, Best Foreign Product Award Japan 1989, Design Cncl Opportunity Ulster Award 1990, G Mark Award Japan 1991, Design Week Award Best Product 1991, 1993 and 2003 (highly commended 1994), Mother and Baby Award for Excellence 1994, ID Annual Design Review 1996, 1997 and 2000, finalist BBC Design Awards 1996, IF German Industrial Design Award 1998, Millennium Product Award 1999 (three) and 2000, Gold IDEA US Industrial Design Excellence Awards 2000 and 2001, Int Design Effectiveness Award 2002, winner of German IF Award for Priestman Goode website 2003, Design Week Awards for Best Consumer Product and Best Hospitality Environment 2005; *Recreations* sailing, skiing, drawing; *Style*— Paul Priestman, Esq; ✉ c/o Kirsty Dias, Priestman Goode, 110 Crawford Street, London W1H 2JD (tel 020 7935 6665, fax 020 7935 0668)

PRIESTMAN, Dr Terrence James; s of Francis Dennis Priestman (d 1980), of Bournemouth, and Vera Mercy, *née* Jackman (d 1962); *b* 1 January 1945; *Educ* King Henry VIII Sch Coventry, King's Coll London, Westminster Med Sch London (MB BS, Frederick Bird prize); *Career* house offr: in radiotherapy and oncology Westminster Hosp London 1968, in gen surgery Bolingbroke Hosp London 1968–69; SHO: in gen med Willesden Gen Hosp 1969–70, in cardiology London Chest Hosp 1970, in radiotherapy and oncology Westminster Hosp 1970–71; sr registrar Christie Hosp and Holt Radium Inst Manchester 1973–74, conslt in radiotherapy and oncology Velindre Hosp Cardiff 1974–77, med advsr in oncology Wellcome Research Labs and hon conslt in radiotherapy and oncology Westminster Hosp 1977–81, conslt Queen Elizabeth and Dudley Road Hosps Birmingham 1981–89 (chm Div of Radiotherapy and conslt in administrative charge Dept of Radiotherapy and Oncology Queen Elizabeth Hosp 1982–87), conslt clinical oncologist Royal Hosp Wolverhampton 1989–2000, clinical dir of oncology and haematology New Cross Hosp Wolverhampton 2005–; memb Med Exec Ctee Central Birmingham HA 1984–87; W Midlands RHA: memb Regnl Scientific Ctee 1986–91, chm Regnl Advsy Ctee on Radiotherapy and Oncology 1990–94; Royal Coll of Radiologists: memb Faculty Bd (Radiotherapy and Oncology) 1984–87 (elected) and 1987– (ex-officio), memb Cncl 1987–89, rep Br Assoc for Radiation Protection 1989–93 (chm 1990–91), rep Standing Intercollegiate Ctee on Nuclear Med 1989–94, registrar Faculty of Clinical Oncology 1994–96, dean Faculty of Clinical Oncology 1996–98, vice-pres 1997–98, chair The X-Appeal 2003–; series ed CancerBACKUP pubns 1999–2002 (medical reviewer 2004–); memb: Cncl Section of Oncology RSM 1986–87, Nat Ctee Br Assoc of Surgical Oncology 1981–84; Twining Medal for Research Royal Coll of Radiologists; MRCP 1971 DMRT 1972, FRCR (FFR) 1973, MD 1981, FRCP 1984; *Books* Cancer Chemotherapy: an introduction (3 edn, 1989), Coping With Chemotherapy (2005), Coping With Breast Cancer (2006); author of various book chapters and numerous original articles; ed Clinical Oncology 1989–94 (dep ed 1987–89); *Recreations* watercolour painting; *Style*— Dr Terrence Priestman; ✉ 25 White Horse Lane, Stepney, London E1 3NE (tel 020 7790 5121, e-mail terryp.doc@btopenworld.com)

PRIMAROLO, Rt Hon Dawn; PC (2002), MP; *b* 2 May 1954; *Educ* Thomas Bennett Comp Sch Crawley, Bristol Poly (BA), Univ of Bristol; *m* 7 Oct 1972 (m dis), Michael Primarolo; 1 s (Luke b 24 Jan 1978); m 2, 29 Nov 1990, Ian Ducat; *Career* former legal sec and advice worker 1972–75; cncllr Avon CC 1985–87; MP (Lab) Bristol S 1987–, memb Select Ctee on Members' Interests 1990–92, shadow min for health 1992–94, shadow spokesperson for treasy 1994–97, fin sec to the Treasy 1997–99, paymaster gen 1999–; *Style*— The Rt Hon Dawn Primarolo, MP; ✉ PO Box 1002, Bristol BS99 1WH (tel 0117 909 0063); House of Commons, London SW1A 0AA (tel 020 7219 3000)

PRIMOST, Norman Basil; s of Sydney Simon Primost (d 1976), of London, and Regina, *née* Bader (d 1991); *b* 25 June 1933; *Educ* St Paul's, LSE (LLB), Trinity Hall Cambridge; *m* 30 Aug 1965, Debbie Doris, da of Chaim Ferster; 1 da (Belinda Rosemary (Mrs Mindell) b 10 April 1967), 3 s (Mark Stephen Adam b 12 July 1969, David Jonathan Andrew b 23 Jan 1975, Simon Henry William b 29 Sept 1977); *Career* Nat Serv censoring mail RASC Military Corrective Estab Colchester 1954–56; called to the Bar Middle Temple 1954; pupillage with Montague Waters QC 1956–57, gen common law practice specialising in property law, with particular emphasis on landlord and tenant law 1957–, head of chambers 1 Temple Gardens 1986–94; legal corr Stock Exchange Jl 1967–69, ed Restrictive Practices Reports 1969–71; pres B'nai B'rith First Lodge of England 2005–; *Recreations* theatre, chess, modern literature, classical music; *Clubs* Wig & Pen, King's Head Theatre; *Style*— Norman Primost, Esq; ✉ Grande Vue, 98 West Heath Road, Hampstead, London NW3 7TU (tel 020 8458 9757); 39 Crag Head, Manor Road, Bournemouth, Dorset; 5 Pump Court, Temple, London EC4Y 7AP (tel 020 7353 2532, fax 020 7353 5321)

PRIMROSE, Andrew Hardie; s of Kenneth Alexander (d 1939), of Glasgow, and Mary Dougall, *née* Campbell (later Mrs Primrose; d 2003); *b* 25 September 1939; *Educ* Glenalmond, UC Oxford (open scholar, BA), Univ of Glasgow (Cunninghame bursary in Scots law, LLB); *m* 1, Helen Mary (d 1986), da of David Clark Banks; 1 s (David Alexander b 1965), 1 da (Alison Clare b 1968); m 2, Margaret (Meg) (d 1997), da of John Royston Laidlaw; m 3, Fiona Jane, da of Alexander Young Garvie; *Career* Maclay Murray & Spens: admitted slr in Scot 1964, ptnr 1966–2002, managing ptnr 1978–85, moved to open first London office 1989, chm Environmental Law Unit 1990–2000, returned to Glasgow 1995; external examiner in conveyancing and clerk to Gen Cncl Univ of Glasgow 1984–88; Int Bar Assoc: chm Real Estate Ctee 1988–92, chair Legal Practice Section 2000–02, chm Educnl Tst 2002–04, hon life memb 2005; chm Glasgow Jr C of C 1971–72 (senator Jr Chamber Int), Rotary Fndn Exchange scholar to Indiana 1974, memb Bd Scottish Industrial Estates Corp 1973–75, tstee West of Scotland TSB (then TSB

Scotland), dir Glasgow C of C 1987–89, fndr chm Glasgow City Ctee Macmillan Cancer Relief, chm Old Glenalmond Club 1997–2000, chm Univ of Glasgow Tst 2005–, co-chm Glasgow Royal Infirmary Appeals Tst 1999–2003; memb Ctee of Cncl Glenalmond Coll 1999–; chm Hamilton Bequest 1998–; memb: Royal Faculty of Procurators in Glasgow 1966–2002, UK Environmental Law Assoc 1991–2002, Law Soc of England 1994–2005; dir Merchants House of Glasgow 1996–2002, Lord Dean of Guild Merchants House 2003–05; memb Incorporation of Hammermen in Glasgow (deacon 1985–86), Liveryman City of London Slrs' Co 1995; *Books* Drafting and Negotiating Commercial Leases in Scotland (co-author, 1985, 2 edn 1993), Butterworths Environmental Regulation (co-author, 1997); *Recreations* playing and watching sport, active sports: golf, curling, walking, history; *Clubs* Western Gailes Golf (Ayrshire), Vincent's (Oxford), Western (Glasgow); *Style—* Andrew Primrose, Esq; ✉ 2 Grange Road, Bearsden, Glasgow G61 3PL (tel 0141 943 1371, e-mail andrew.primrose@btopenworld.com)

PRIMROSE, Sir John Ure; 5 Bt (UK 1903), of Redholme, Dumbreck, Co of City of Glasgow; s of Sir (Alasdair) Neil Primrose, 4 Bt (d 1986), and (Elaine) Noreen, o da of Edmund Cecil Lowndes, of Buenos Aires, Argentina; *b* 1960; *m* 1983 (m dis 1987), Marion Cecilia, da of Hans Otto Altgelt, of Buenos Aires, Argentina; 2 da (Christine Anne b 1984, Jennifer Diana b 1986); *Heir* bro, Andrew Primrose; *Style—* Sir John Primrose, Bt; ✉ Puerto Victoria, Alto Parana Misiones, Argentina

PRINCE, Dr John Anthony; s of Flt Lt Allan Leslie Prince (ka 1944), and Mary Pamela, *née* Paul; *b* 5 November 1941; *Educ* Giggleswick Sch, ChCh Oxford (MA, BM BCh, DIH, MRCGP, MFOM); *Career* conslt occupational physician: Occidental Oil Inc 1977–83, Tower Hamlets HA London Hosp 1983, London Borough of Tower Hamlets 1983–, News International 1985–86; memb Tower Hamlets DHA, former sr ptnr Tower Med Centre, special advsr on disablement to DSS; memb: BMA, Soc of Occupational Med; FRSM; *Recreations* literature, history, antiquarianism, natural history, walking; *Style—* Dr John Prince; ✉ The Old Rectory, Sutton Mandeville, Salisbury, Wiltshire SP3 5NA

PRINCE-SMITH, Sir (William) Richard; 4 Bt (UK 1911), of Hillbrook, Keighley, W Riding of Yorks; s of Sir William Prince-Smith, 3 Bt, OBE, MC (d 1964), and Marian Marjorie (d 1970); *b* 27 December 1928; *Educ* Charterhouse, Clare Coll Cambridge (MA); *m* 1, 1955, Margaret Ann, o da of late Dr John Carter, of Loughton, Essex; 1 s (James William (decd)), 1 da (Elizabeth Ann (Mrs Colin Earl) b 1957); m 2, 1975, Ann Christina, da of late Andrew Faulds, OBE, of Colchester, Essex; *Career* former farmer and agric landowner, ret; *Clubs* The Springs (Rancho Mirage); *Style—* Sir Richard Prince-Smith, Bt; ✉ 40–735 Paxton Drive, Rancho Mirage, CA 92270–3516, USA (tel (760) 321–1975)

PRINGLE, Alexandra Jane Reina; da of Alexander James Sommerville Pringle, and Natalie May, *née* Afriat; sis of John Richard Pringle, *qv*; *b* 13 March 1953; *Educ* Kensington HS, Putney HS, Cambs Coll of Arts & Technol (BA), UCL (post grad res); *Children* 1 s (Daniel Hilton b 30 April 1986); *Career* editorial asst Art Monthly 1976–78; editorial dir: Virago Press 1978–90 (dir 1984–), Hamish Hamilton 1990–94; dir Toby Eady Associates (literary agency) 1994–99, ed-in-chief Bloomsbury Publishing 1999–; *Clubs* Chelsea Arts, Groucho; *Style—* Ms Alexandra Pringle; ✉ Bloomsbury Publishing, 36 Soho Square, London W1D 3QY (tel 020 7494 2111, fax 020 7434 0151)

PRINGLE, Anne Fyfe; CMG (2004); da of George Grant Pringle, of Glasgow, and Margaret Fyfe, *née* Cameron; *b* 13 January 1955; *Educ* Glasgow HS for Girls, Univ of St Andrews (MA); *m* 20 April 1987, Bleddyn Glynne Leyshon Phillips; *Career* joined FCO 1977, third sec Moscow 1980–83, vice-consul (commercial) San Francisco 1983–85, UK rep Brussels 1986–87, first sec FCO 1987–91, UK rep Brussels 1991–94 (on loan to European Political Co-operation Secretariat); FCO: African (Equatorial), Security Co-ordination Dept 1994–96, head Common Foreign and Security Policy Dept 1996–98, head Eastern Dept 1998–2001; ambass Czech Repub 2001–04, dir strategy and info FCO 2004–; memb Bd VSO 1996–97, memb Czech/Slovak Assoc; FRSA 2001; *Recreations* walking, skiing, music; *Style—* Anne Pringle, CMG; ✉ c/o Foreign & Commonwealth Office, King Charles Street, London SW1A 2AH

PRINGLE, Air Marshal Sir Charles Norman Seton; KBE (1973, CBE 1967); s of Seton Pringle, OBE (d 1955), of Dublin, and Ethel Louisa, *née* McMunn (d 1938); *b* 6 June 1919; *Educ* Repton, St John's Coll Cambridge (MA); *m* 1946, Margaret Elisabeth, da of Bertie Sharp (d 1956), of Baildon, W Yorks; 1 s (Andrew Charles Seton b 30 April 1949 d 2006); *Career* RAF: joined 1941, dir gen of engrg RAF 1969–70, AO Engrg Strike Cmd 1970–73, DG of engrg 1973, controller of engrg and supply and chief engr 1973–76; sr exec Rolls Royce Ltd 1976–78, dir Hunting Engrg 1976–78, dir and chief exec Soc of Br Aerospace Cos 1979–85; dir: FR Gp plc 1985–89, Aeronautical Tsts 1987–96; Cncl memb: RAeS 1968–87 (pres 1975–76), Air League 1976–92, CBI 1978–84, RSA 1978–83 and 1986–92; sec Def Industries Cncl 1978–84, pres Inst of Mechanical & Gen Tech Engrs 1979–82, pres Smeatonian Soc of Civil Engrs 2006; chm: CEI 1977–78 (treas 1980–83), Governing Body Repton Sch 1987–92 (memb 1985–92); Liveryman Worshipful Co of Coachmakers & Coach Harness Makers; CCMI, FREng 1977, Hon FRAeS 1989; *Recreations* photography, ornithology; *Clubs* RAF; *Style—* Air Marshal Sir Charles Pringle, KBE, FREng, Hon FRAeS; ✉ Appleyards, Fordingbridge, Hampshire SP6 3BP; K 9 Sloane Avenue Mansions, London SW3 3JP (e-mail charles.pringle@btinternet.com)

PRINGLE, Hamish Patrick; s of Robert Henry Pringle (d 1990), of Nassau, Bahamas, and Pamela Ann, *née* Molloy; *b* 17 July 1951; *Educ* Trinity Coll Glenalmond, Trinity Coll Oxford (BA); *m* 24 July 1977, Vivienne Elizabeth, da of Dr H Michael Lloyd (d 1976), of Ripley, Surrey; 3 s (Sebastian b 1983, Benedict b 1985, Tristan b 1989), 1 da (Arabella Elizabeth Lloyd b 1993); *Career* grad trainee Ogilvy & Mather advtg 1973–74, account exec McCormick Richards 1974–75, account dir Boase Massimi Pollitt 1975–79, new business dir Publicis 1979–82, dir Abbott Mead Vickers/SMS 1982–86, md Madell Wilmot Pringle 1986–90, dir Leagas Delaney Partnership 1990–92; K Advertising (formerly KHBB): new business dir 1992–93, gp account dir 1993, jt md 1993–97, chm and ceo 1994–97; vice-chm and mktg dir Saatchi & Saatchi 1997–99 Brand Beliefs Ltd 1999–; IPA: memb Cncl 1985–86 and 1992–, chm Advertising Effectiveness Awards Ctee 1994–96; chm NABS Gen Mgmnt Ctee 1996–98; MIPA 1985; *Recreations* sport, gardening, property development, art, family; *Style—* Hamish Pringle, Esq

PRINGLE, Jack Brown; s of John Pringle, of Nottingham, and Grace Mason, *née* Cowler; *b* 13 March 1952; *Educ* Nottingham HS for Boys, Univ of Bristol (BA, DipArch, professors' prize, travelling scholarship for architecture); *m* 1992 (m dis 2002), Claire; 2 da (Maxine, Francesca); *Career* architect; Powell Moya and Partners 1973 and 1975–82; ptnr: Jack Pringle Architects 1982–85, Pringle Brandon Architects 1985–; RIBA: memb Cncl 1981–87 and 2002–, vice-pres 1982–83 and 2002–04, pres 2005–07, rep Br Cncl visit to Romania 1982, memb Educn Visiting Bd to Schs of Arch 1985–, memb visiting gp to China 1992 and 1993, chm Visiting Bd Sri Lanka Sch of Architects 1995, chair Professional Services Bd 2003–; memb CNAA Architecture Bd 1986–87; RIBA 1975, FRSA 1981; *Recreations* flying, sailing; *Style—* Jack Pringle, Esq; ✉ Pringle Brandon Architects, 10 Bonhill Street, London EC2A 4QJ (tel 020 7466 1000, e-mail jack-pringle@pringle-brandon.co.uk)

PRINGLE, John Richard; s of Alexander James Sommerville Pringle, of London, and Natalie May, *née* Afriat; bro of Alexandra Pringle, *qv*; gs of W M R Pringle, MP; *b* 30 May 1951; *Educ* Shrewsbury, AA Sch of Architecture (AADipl); *m* 1975, Penny Richards, *qv*, da of Denis George Richards, OBE; 1 s (Patrick b 1982), 1 da (Georgina b 1984); *Career* architect; Mario Pérez De Arce L Santiago de Chile 1972–73, Pascall & Watson London 1976–77, Scott Brownrigg & Turner Guildford 1977–78, ptnr Michael Hopkins & Partners 1981–96 (joined 1978), fndr ptnr Pringle Richards Sharratt 1996–; work incl: Sheffield Gallery and Winter Garden 1996–2002, Shrewsbury Music Sch 1999–2001, Oldham Cultural Quarter 1999–2001, Herbert Art Gallery & Museum Coventry 2002–; lectr: Europe 1987–, N America 1995–; RIBA external examiner Univ of N London 1991–94, external examiner Univ of Nottingham 2003–06; AA: memb 1969, memb Cncl 1987–97, hon treas 1991–93, pres 1993–95; memb Project Enabling Panel CABE, memb ARB/RIBA Validation Panel; tstee Michael Ventris Meml Fund 2003–; memb Bd Architectural Educn ARCUK 1986–93, chair Sheffield Urban Design Review Panel 2006–, RIBA 1983 (memb Cncl 2002–06, hon treas 2002–05); *Recreations* travel, Italian, pinball machines; *Style—* John Pringle, Esq; ✉ Pringle Richards Sharratt, Studio 11, Canterbury Court, Kennington Park, 1 Brixton Road, London SW9 6DE (tel 020 7793 2828, e-mail john.pringle@prsarchitects.com)

PRINGLE, Margaret Douglas (Maggie); da of John Douglas Pringle, of Sydney, Aust, and Celia, *née* Carroll; *Educ* Convent of the Holy Child London, Convent of the Sacred Heart Sydney, Lady Margaret Hall Oxford (MA); *Career* journalist; former asst on: diary Evening Standard, Pendennis column The Observer; former fiction ed: Nova, Woman; London ed Doubleday 1979–81, sr ed John Murray 1981–82, commissioning ed Michael Joseph 1983–97, literary ed Today 1987–92, books conslt Sunday Express 1992–93, books ed Daily Mirror 1993–95, books ed The Sun 1995–96, books conslt Daily Telegraph and Punch 1996, asst ed books and comment The Express 1996–98 (literary ed 1998–2001); *Books* Dance Little Ladies (1977); *Recreations* reading, travel; *Style—* Ms Maggie Pringle; ✉ 16 Meadow Road, London SW8 1QB (tel 020 7735 3171, e-mail maggie.pringle2@btinternet.com)

PRINGLE, Mike; MSP; s of Robert Pringle, and Pauline Pringle; *b* 25 December 1945, Zambia; *Educ* Edinburgh Acad, Napier Coll Edinburgh; *m* 16 Oct 1971, Maggie, *née* Birkett; 2 s (Iain, Kevin); *Career* Royal Bank of Scotland 1966–72, prop TMM Ltd 1974–89; city cncllr 1992–94, regnl cncllr Lothian 1994–95, cncllr City of Edinburgh 1995–2003; MSP (SDP) Edinburgh South 2003– (candidate UK Gen Election 1997, Scot Parl 1999); memb SDP 1982, equal opportunities spokesperson 2003–04, dep justice spokesperson 2005–; Free Tibet Campaign; memb SERVAS; *Recreations* football (Heart of Midlothian FC), rugby, cinema, theatre, holidaying in Scotland, collecting wine; *Style—* Mike Pringle, Esq, MSP; ✉ The Scottish Parliament, Edinburgh EH99 1SP (tel 0131 348 5788, fax 0131 348 6489, e-mail mike.pringle.msp@scottish.parliament.uk)

PRINGLE, Lt Gen Sir Steuart Robert; 10 Bt (NS 1683), KCB (1982); o s of Sir Norman Hamilton Pringle, 9 Bt (d 1961), and Winifred Olive, *née* Curran; *b* 21 July 1928; *Educ* Sherborne; *m* 5 Sept 1953, Jacqueline Marie, o da of late Wilfrid Hubert Gladwell; 2 s (one of whom d 2006), 2 da; *Heir* s, Simon Pringle; *Career* RM 1946, Lt 1949, Capt 1957, Maj 1964, Lt-Col 1971, Col 1975, Maj-Gen RM Commando Forces 1978–79, COS to Cmdt Gen RM 1979–81, Cmdt Gen RM 1981–84, Col Cmdt RM 1989–90, Rep Col Cmdt RM 1991–92; chm and chief exec Chatham Historic Dockyard Tst 1984–91; pres: St Loyes Fndn Exeter 1984–2000, City of London Branch RM Assoc 1984–2004; vice-pres Royal Naval Benevolent Tst 1984–, dir Medway Enterprise Agency 1986–89; memb Ct of Assts Worshipful Co of Plaisterers; Hon DSc City Univ 1982, Hon LLD Exeter Univ 1994; Man of the Year Award 1982; CIMgt 1984; *Clubs* Royal Thames Yacht, Army and Navy; *Style—* Lt-Gen Sir Steuart Pringle, Bt, KCB; ✉ 76 South Croxted Road, Dulwich, London SE21 8BD

PRIOR, Hon David Gifford Leathes; eld s of Baron Prior, PC (Life Peer), *qv*; *b* 1954; *m* 1987, Caroline, da of Peter Holmes, of Shotesham, Norfolk; 2 c (Nicholas James Peter, Helena Caitlin Elizabeth (twins) b 1988); *Career* barr; formerly with: Lehman Brothers, Lazards, British Steel (latterly commercial dir); MP (Cons) Norfolk N 1997–2001, dep chm and ceo Cons Pty 1998–2001; chm: Brownsword Ltd, IPS Gp, Norfolk and Norwich Univ Hosp NHS Tst 2002–; *Style—* David Prior, Esq

PRIOR, Baron (Life Peer UK 1987), of Brampton in the County of Suffolk; James Michael Leathes Prior; PC (1970); 2 s of Charles Bolingbroke Leathes Prior (d 1964), of Norwich; *b* 11 October 1927; *Educ* Charterhouse, Pembroke Coll Cambridge; *m* 30 Jan 1954, Jane Primrose Gifford, 2 da of Air Vice-Marshal Oswin Gifford Lywood, CB, CBE (d 1957); 3 s (Hon David, Hon Simon, Hon Jeremy), 1 da (Hon Mrs Roper); *Career* farmer and land agent in Norfolk and Suffolk; MP (Cons): Lowestoft 1959–83, Waveney 1983–87; PPS to: pres of BOT 1963, min of Power 1963–64, Rt Hon Edward Heath (leader of the oppn) 1965–70; min of Agric Fisheries and Food 1970–72, a dep chm Cons Pty 1972–74 (vice-chm 1965), lord pres of Cncl and ldr of House of Commons 1972–74, oppn front bench spokesman on employment 1974–79; sec of state: Employment 1979–81, NI 1981–84; chm: Industry and Parl Tst 1990–93, Rural Housing Tst, Great Ormond Street Hosp Special Tstees until 1994, Royal Vet Coll until 1994–98; memb: Tenneco Euro Advsy Cncl until 1997, American Int Gp Advsy Bd 1988–2006; non-exec chm Allders Ltd until 1994; chm: GEC plc 1984–98, African Cargo Handling Ltd 1998–2001, Ascot Underwriting 2001–06; dep chm Celtel (formerly MSI Cellular Investment BV) 2000–05; non-exec dir: United Biscuits (Holdings) plc until 1994, J Sainsbury 1984–96, Barclays plc 1984–88; chllr Anglia Poly Univ 1994–99; chm Arab-British C of C 1996–2003; *Books* A Balance of Power; *Recreations* cricket, gardening, philately, field sports, golf; *Style—* The Rt Hon Lord Prior, PC; ✉ House of Lords, London SW1A 0PW

PRIOR-PALMER, Simon Erroll; s of Maj-Gen George Erroll Prior-Palmer, CB, DSO (d 1977), by his 2 w, Lady Doreen, *née* Hope (d 1998); bro of Lucinda Green, *qv*; *Educ* Eton, ChCh Oxford (MA); *m* 1984, Lady Julia Lloyd George, da of 3 Earl Lloyd George of Dwyfor, DL, *qv*; 3 s (George b 1988, Arthur b 1991, Harold b 1998), 1 da (Lara b 1994); *Career* J P Morgan London and NY 1973–82 (dir Morgan Guaranty Ltd 1982); Credit Suisse First Boston: dir Investment Banking 1982, co-head Canadian Investment Banking 1982–84, md 1986, head UK Investment Banking 1987–98, sr advsr 2004–05; cmmr Postal Servs Cmmn (Postcomm) 2006, dir Inter Lotto (UK) Ltd 2006; tstee Macmillan Cancer Support 2000–; FRSA 1989 (memb Cncl 2006); *Recreations* tennis, golf, skiing; *Clubs* White's; *Style—* Simon Prior-Palmer

PRISK, Mark; MP; *b* 12 June 1962; *Educ* Truro Sch, Univ of Reading; *m* 1989, Lesley; *Career* chartered surveyor; self-employed businessman and dir 1991–, writer for property and business media, regular speaker at business confs; Parly candidate (Cons): Newham NW 1992, Wansdyke 1997; MP (Cons) Hertford and Stortford 2001–, shadow fin sec to the Treasy, shadow paymaster gen 2002–04, opposition whip 2004–05, shadow min Businiess and Enterprise 2005–; memb Welsh Affrs Select Ctee 2001–05, Parly chm First Defence 2001–04; Cons Pty: chm Cornwall Young Conservatives 1978–80, chm Univ of Reading Cons Assoc 1980–82, vice-chm Nat Campaigns Fedn of Cons Students 1982–83, sec Environment Ctee Bow Gp 1984–86, vice-chm Campaigns Westminster N 1986, 1989 and 1990–91, chm Bushey Heath Conservatives 1998–2000; tstee Industry and Parly Tst 2007–, memb Parly choir 2002–; memb Nat Ctee Peace Through NATO 1983–85; mentor and memb Bd The Prince's Youth Business Tst Herts and Beds 1995–2000; chm Sch Technol Centre Appeal Fund, chm of govrs Stratford GM Sch 1993–95; *Recreations* Saracens RFC, playing the piano; *Style—* Mark Prisk, Esq, MP; ✉ House of Commons, London SW1A 0AA (tel 020 7219 6358, website www.markprisk.com)

PRITCHARD, Prof Colin; s of Sydney William Pritchard (d 1986), and Doris (d 1947); *b* 24 February 1936; *Educ* Univ of Manchester (Postgrad Cert), Univ of Bradford (MA), Univ of Southampton (PhD); *m* 15 Sept 1962, Beryl, da of Ivor William Harrison (d 1968); 2 da (Rebecca Anne Harrison b 26 Feb 1967, Claire Elizabeth b 23 Dec 1968); *Career* RAF 1954–56, serv in Cyprus and Suez 1956; lectr Dept of Psychiatry Univ of Leeds 1970–76, dir of social work Univ of Bath 1976–80, fndn prof of social work Univ of Southampton 1980–; memb: Central Cncl Educn and Training in Social Work 1974–81, Southampton

Health Authy 1981–86; advsr (mental health) UN PREDEP Macedonia 1996; memb: Assoc of Child Psychiatry and Psychology 1965, Br Assoc of Social work 1970, American Assoc of Suicidology 1988, Int Assoc of Social Work (BR rep and bd memb 1988–); FRSA 1994; *Books* Social Work Reform or Revolution? (with R K S Taylor, 1978), The Protest Makers: The British Anti-Nuclear Movement Twenty Years On (with R K S Taylor, 1980), Social Work with Adolescents (with R Jones, 1980), Social Work with the Mentally Ill (with A J W Butler, 1986), Maintaining Staff Morale (1987), Suicide the Ultimate Rejection: A Psycho-Social Study (1995), King David: War and Ecstasy; contrib to comparisons of: Suicide and Violent Death in the Western World 1964–86, Suicide and Unemployment in UK and EEC, Elderly Suicide: Salutary or Disregarded Neglect 1964–90; *Recreations* family, friends, fell walking, squash, mourning Yorkshire and English Cricket; *Clubs* Hemsworth Miners Welfare, Fitzwilliam (hon life memb); *Style*— Prof Colin Pritchard; ✉ 33 Bassett Avenue, Bassett, Southampton SO1 7DP (tel 023 8076 9169); School of Medicine, Mental Health Group, University of Southampton, Southampton SO14 0YG (tel 023 8059 4000, fax 023 80593 939, telex 47661, e-mail cpl@soton.ac.uk)

PRITCHARD, David Peter; s of late Norman Pritchard, and Peggy, *née* Fotherby; *b* 20 July 1944; *Educ* Read GS, Univ of Southampton (BSc); *m* 1 (m dis); 1 da (Louisa b 1971), 1 s (James b 1978); m 2, 5 May 1993, Elizabeth, *née* Cresswell; *Career* Hawker Siddeley Aviation 1966–71, William Brandt's Sons & Co 1971–72, Edward Bates & Sons Ltd 1972–78, md Citicorp Investment Bank Ltd 1978–86, sr vice-pres and gen mangr Europe Royal Bank of Canada 1986–95, gp treas and md TSB Hill Samuel Markets 1995–96; with SIB 1996–98, gp treas and gp dir Lloyds TSB Gp 1998–2003, dep chm Lloyds TSB Gp 2003–05, non-exec chm Cheltenham & Gloucester 2005, chm Songbird Estates 2005–; dir: LCH.Clearnet Group Ltd, Scottish Widows plc, Motability Tenth Anniversary Tst; *Recreations* bicycle racing, cross country skiing, photography; *Style*— David Pritchard, Esq

PRITCHARD, (Iorwerth) Gwynn; s of Rev Robert Islwyn Pritchard (d 1988), and Megan Mair, *née* Lloyd (d 2001); *b* 1 February 1946; *Educ* schs in England and Wales, King's Coll Cambridge (MA); *m* 1, 17 Oct 1970, Marilyn, née Bartholomew (d 1994); 2 s (Matthew Osian b 1975, Dafydd Islwyn b 1989), 1 da (Nia Siân b 1977); m 2, 18 Dec 1998, Althea Sharp; *Career* prodr and dir BBC OU Productions 1970–77; prodr: BBC Wales 1977–82, HTV Wales 1982–85; Channel 4 TV: commissioning ed 1985–88, sr commissioning ed educn 1989–92; BBC Wales: head of progs 1992–97, head of Welsh broadcasting 1997–2001; sec gen INPUT 2001–05, ind prodr 2005–; tstee: Welsh Writers Trust, Coleg Harlech 1992–2000; memb Bd Welsh Int Film Festival 1994–98; Winston Churchill Meml Fellowship 1973, Sir Huw Weldon Broadcasting Fellowship 1990; Chevalier de l'Ordre des Arts et des Lettres (France) 1990; *Publications* Dal Pen Rheswm (contrib ed, 1999); *Recreations* reading, swimming, walking; *Style*— Gwynn Pritchard, Esq; ✉ 25 Westbourne Road, Penarth, Vale of Glamorgan CF64 3HA (tel 029 2070 3608, e-mail gwynnpritchard@hotmail.com)

PRITCHARD, Rt Rev John Lawrence; *see:* Oxford, Bishop of

PRITCHARD, Mark Andrew; MP; s of Frank Pritchard (d 1983), and Romona, *née* Davies; *b* 22 November 1966, Manchester; *Educ* London Guildhall Univ (MA), CIM (DipM), Elim Coll (Cert); *m* 20 May 1997, Sondra Janae; *Career* chief researcher Into the Voids (book on homelessness) 1992, asst ed Return Ticket (book on long-term unemployment) 1994, fndr own mktg communications co, co dir 1998–; MP (Cons) The Wrekin 2005– (Parly candidate (Cons) Warley 2001); memb Environmental Select Ctee 2005–, vice-chm All Pty Parly Gp on Social Care 2005–, vice-chm All Pty Parly Gp on Argentina 2005–, sec Cons Parly Def Ctee, sec Cons Foreign Affrs Gp; memb Steering Gp to establish Habitat for Humanity 1994; MCIM, MCIPR, MCIJ, assoc memb Market Research Soc; *Recreations* skiing, walking miniature schnauzers, writing; *Style*— Mark Pritchard, Esq, MP; ✉ House of Commons, London SW1A 0AA (tel 020 7219 8494, e-mail pritchardm@parliament.uk); Constituency Office, 25 Church Street, Wellington, Shropshire TF1 1DG (tel 01952 256080)

PRITCHETT, Matthew (Matt); MBE (2002); s of Oliver Pritchett, feature writer, and Joan, *née* Hill, of London; gs of Sir Victor Sawdon Pritchett, CH, CBE (d 1997); *b* 14 July 1964; *Educ* Addey & Stanhope GS, St Martin's Sch of Art (graphics degree); *m* 12 Dec 1992, Pascale Charlotte Marie Smets; 3 da (Edith b 13 April 1994, Mary b 29 Jan 1996, Dorothy b 8 Oct 2001), 1 s (Henry b 26 Nov 1997); *Career* freelance cartoonist for New Statesman, Punch, Daily Telegraph and Spectator, front page cartoonist Daily Telegraph 1989–; Cartoonist of the Year What the Papers Say 1992 and 2004, Cartoon Arts Tst Award 1995, 1996 and 1999, Cartoonist of the Year UK Press Awards 1996, 1998, 2000 and 2005; *Books* Best of Matt (annually, 1991–); *Style*— Matt Pritchett, Esq, MBE

PROBERT, David Henry; CBE (1996); s of William David Thomas Probert (d 1994), of Birmingham, and Doris Mabel, *née* Mayell (d 1987); *b* 11 April 1938; *Educ* Bromsgrove HS; *m* 14 June 1968, Sandra Mary, da of John Howard Prince (d 1988); 1 da (Jane b 1974), 1 s (Russell b 1979); *Career* various posts: ICI Metals Div 1960–66, Coopers & Lybrand 1966–71; gp fin dir: BSA Ltd 1971–73, Mills & Allen International Ltd 1974–75; W Canning plc: gp fin dir 1976–, chief exec 1979–85, chm and chief exec 1986–98; non-exec chm Ash & Lacy plc 1998–2000; non-exec dir: Linread plc 1983–90, ASD plc 1984–90, Sandvik Ltd 1986–90, Beatson Clark plc 1987–88, Rockwool Ltd 1988–90 and 1992–95, William Siinclair Holdings plc 1994–2001, Saville Gordon Estates plc 1998– (chm); chm: PPP Healthcare Group plc 1996–98 (dir 1988–98), Leigh Interests plc 1996–97 (dir 1995–97); chm Crown Agents 1990–98 (crown agent 1981–, dep chm 1985–90); memb: W Midlands Regnl Cncl CBI 1978–84 and 1988–90, Br Hallmarking Cncl 1983–90, Cncl Birmingham C-of-C 1990–98 (vice-pres 1991–94, pres 1994–95); chm W Midlands Lord's Taverners 1996–98 (memb Ctee 1985–99); Freeman: City of London, Worshipful Co of Secs and Administrators, Worshipful Co of Founders; CIMgt, FCMA, FCCA, FCIS; *Recreations* reading, music, theatre; *Clubs* RAC; *Style*— David Probert, Esq, CBE

PROBERT, Lt-Col Richard Harlackenden Carwardine; OBE (mil 1959), DL (Suffolk 1983); s of Col (Geoffrey) Oliver Carwardine Probert, CBE (d 1987), of Great Bevills, Suffolk, and Ruby Margaret Alexandra, *née* Marc (d 1992), with collateral family links with Bures and Earls Colne dating back to 14 century (*see* Burke's Landed Gentry 18 edn, Vol I, 1965); *b* 19 April 1922; *Educ* Eton, RMCS Shrivenham; *m* 25 April 1945, Elisabeth Margaret, da of Donald Boase Sinclair, OBE, WS, (d 1972), of Edinburgh; 2 da (Camilla (m Tim Melville-Ross, *qv*) b 1946, Anne (Mrs Edward Tozer) b 1948), 1 s (Geoffrey b 1953); *Career* served WWII RHA 1940–45, Normandy and NW Europe 1944–45, instr in gunnery 1945–46, RMCS Shrivenham 1946–48, graduated ptsc 1948, Royal Armament Res and Design Estab 1948–51 (Tripartite Conf Washington 1951), 3 RHA BAOR 1951–54, staff Dir-Gen of Artillery 1954–56, Br Nuclear Def Trials Aust 1957; Dir Staff Lt-Col RMCS 1956–59; Bexford Ltd Brantham Suffolk (makers of photographic film base taken by the astronauts on the 1 moon walk 1969): md 1962–76 (Queen's Award to Industry 1966, 1969, 1971 and 1973); farmer; High Sheriff Suffolk 1980–81; memb: PCC 1962–97, Diocesan Synod 1976–79, Deanery Synod 1976–97; hon lay canon St Edmundsbury Cathedral 1984–91; memb: Ct Univ of Essex 1966–, Suffolk Ctee TAVR & ACF 1980–2000, Suffolk Ctee CLA 1981–94 (pres 1991–94), W Suffolk branch ESU (pres 1981–86); branch pres: Royal Br Legion 1977–, Scouts 1977–91; First Prize Conservation Cup W Suffolk Farming and Wildlife Advsy Gp 1981, Hon Lay Canon Emeritus Medal 2006; Freeman City of London 1956, Liveryman Worshipful Co of Ironmongers 1965– (Master 1977–78); FRSA 1964; *Recreations* countryside, conservation, walking, travel; *Clubs* Army and Navy; *Style*— Lt-Col Richard Probert, OBE, DL; ✉ Chapel Barn Cottage, Bevills Farm, Bures, Suffolk CO8 5LD

PROBY, Sir William Henry; 3 Bt (UK 1952) of Elton Hall, Peterborough, Cambs; DL (Cambs 1995); s of Sir Peter Proby, 2 Bt (d 2002), and Blanche Cripps, da of Col Henry Harrison Cripps; *b* 13 June 1949; *Educ* Eton, Lincoln Coll Oxford (MA), Brooksby Coll of Agric; *m* 1974, Meredyth Anne, da of Timothy David Brentnall, of Preston, Rutland; 4 da (Alexandra b 1980, Alice b 1982, Frances Rose b 1986, Isabella b 1991); *Career* farmer and fin advsr; asst dir Morgan Grenfell 1980–82; dir: M M & K Ltd 1986–98, Ellis & Everard plc 1988–99, Booker Countryside Ltd 1994–96; chair Keygate Property Investments Ltd 1999–, dir MGM Assurance Ltd 2006–; chair Nat Tst 2003– (memb Fin and Investment Ctee 2002–), pres Historic Houses Assoc 1993–98, memb Cncl Tate Britain 1999–; High Sheriff Cambs 2001–02; FCA 1975; *Recreations* skiing, shooting, music; *Clubs* Brooks's, Boodle's; *Style*— Sir William Proby, Bt, DL; ✉ Elton Hall, Peterborough PE8 6SH (tel 01832 280223, fax 01832 280584, e-mail whp@eltonhall.com); 8 Ormonde Place, London SW1W 8HX (tel 020 7730 6360)

PROCHASKA, Dr Alice Marjorie Sheila; da of John Harold Barwell (d 1983), of Cambridge, and Hon Sheila Margaret Ramsay, *née* McNair (d 2000); *b* 12 July 1947; *Educ* Perse Sch for Girls Cambridge, Somerville Coll Oxford (MA, DPhil); *m* 25 June 1971, Franklyn Kimmel Prochaska, s of Franklin Anton Prochaska (d 1952), of Cleveland, USA; 1 da (Elizabeth b 1980), 1 s (William b 1982); *Career* asst keeper: London Museum 1971–73, Public Record Office 1975–84; sec and librarian Inst of Historical Res Univ of London 1984–92, dir of special collections British Library 1992–2001; univ librarian Yale Univ 2001–; cmmr Royal Cmmn on Historical Manuscripts 1998–2001; author of numerous articles on archives and various aspects of Br history ca 1800 to present; organiser of special expos incl: London in the Thirties 1973, Young Writers of the Thirties 1976; memb: Nat Cncl on Archives (chm 1991–95), Steering Gp History at the Univs Def Gp 1987–92, Nat Curriculum History Working Gp Dept of Educn and Sci 1989–90, Heritage Educn Tst, Bd of Govrs London Guildhall Univ 1995–2001, Academic Cncl Fathom.com 2000–01, Sir Winston Churchill Archive Tst 1995–2001, Steering Gp Digital Library Fedn 2001–, Assoc of Res Libraries 2001– (chair Ctee on Access and Collections 2003–05), Center for Research Libraries Bd 2003– (vice-chair 2003–04), Advsy Cncl Yale Center for British Art 2002–, Section on Rare Books and Manuscripts Int Fedn of Library Assocs (chair 1999–2003); chm Lewis Walpole Library Tstees 2001–; hon fell: Inst of Historical Res 2001, Royal Holloway Univ of London 2002; FRHistS 1987 (memb Cncl 1991–95, vice-pres 1995–99); *Books* London in the Thirties (1973), History of the General Federation of Trade Unions, 1899–1980 (1982), Irish History from 1700 - A Guide to Sources in the Public Record Office (1986), Margaretta Acworth's Georgian Cookery Book (ed with Frank Prochaska, 1987); *Recreations* family life, travel, reading; *Style*— Dr Alice Prochaska; ✉ Sterling Memorial Library, Yale University, PO Box 208240, New Haven, CT 06520–8240, USA (e-mail alice.prochaska@yale.edu)

PROCTOR, Michael Richard Edward; s of Edward Francis Proctor, and Stella Mary Major, *née* Jones; *Educ* Shrewsbury (entrance scholar), Trinity Coll Cambridge (scholar, MA, PhD, ScD); *Career* Univ of Cambridge: res fell Trinity Coll 1974–77, asst lectr 1977–82, lectr 1982–93, reader 1993–2000, prof of astrophysical fluid dynamics 2000–, vice-master Trinity Coll 2006–; instr and asst prof MIT 1975–77; author of over 125 papers in various jls; tstee: Gladstone Memorial Tst, First and Third Trinity Boat Club; govr Mill Hill Sch; FRAS 1977, memb IAU 2000; FRS 2006; *Recreations* gardening, travelling; *Style*— Prof Michael Proctor, FRS; ✉ Trinity College, Cambridge CB2 1TQ (tel 01223 338407, fax 01223 765900, e-mail mrep@damtp.cam.ac.uk)

PROCTOR, Nigel Colin; s of Norman Henry Proctor, of Plymouth, Devon, and Edith Joyce, *née* Webb; *b* 20 May 1956, Gloucester; *Educ* Plymstock Sch Plymouth, Univ of Southampton (BSc), Coll of Law London; *m* 22 Aug 1981, Susan, *née* Lampard; 2 s (Nicholas James b 28 Nov 1988, Matthew Ross b 8 Aug 1992); *Career* admitted slr 1990; civil engr: D Balfour & Sons 1977–81, C H Dobbie & Ptnrs 1981–84; slr McKenna & Co 1984–95 (incl period as engrg asst and articled clerk); ptnr: Davies Arnold Cooper 1997–99 (slr 1995–97), Hammonds 1999–2005, Addleshaw Goddard 2005–; memb Law Soc; CEng 1983, MICE 1983 (chm Manchester branch 2003–04), FCIArb 2000; *Style*— Nigel Proctor, Esq; ✉ Addleshaw Goddard, 100 Barbirolli Square, Manchester M2 3AB (tel 0161 934 6320, fax 0161 934 6060, e-mail nigel.proctor@addleshawgoddard.com)

PROCTOR, Timothy D (Tim); *Educ* Univ of Wisconsin Madison, Univ of Chicago (JD, MBA); *Career* called to the Bar: NY, NJ, PA; attorney Union Carbide Corporation 1975–80; Merck & Co Inc: sr attorney 1980–83, sec New Products Ctee 1984–85, European counsel 1985–88, US div counsel 1988–91, vice-pres and assoc gen counsel 1991–92; gen counsel and sec Glaxo Wellcome Inc 1992–98 (vice-pres 1992–94, sr vice-pres 1994–96, sr vice-pres HR 1996–98), dir worldwide HR GlaxoSmithKline plc 1998–99, gen counsel and memb Exec Ctee Diageo plc 2000–; former memb Bd: Northwestern Mutual Life Insurance Co, CARE USA, Duke Univ Law Sch; memb Bd Wachovia Corp 2006–; memb: American Bar Assoc, Assoc of Corporate Counsel (former memb Bd), Int Bar Assoc; *Style*— Mr Timothy D Proctor; ✉ Diageo plc, 8 Henrietta Place, London W1G 0NB (tel 020 7927 4902, fax 020 7927 5099)

PROCTOR-BEAUCHAMP, Sir Christopher Radstock; 9 Bt (GB 1745), of Langley Park, Norfolk; s of Rev Sir Ivor Cuthbert Proctor-Beauchamp, 8 Bt (d 1971); *b* 30 January 1935; *Educ* Rugby, Trinity Coll Cambridge (MA); *m* 1965, Rosalind Emily Margot, da of Gerald Percival Wainwright, of St Leonards-on-Sea; 1 da (Rosalind Caroline b 1967), 2 s (Charles Barclay b 1969, Robert Ivor b 1971); *Heir* s, Charles Proctor-Beauchamp; *Career* slr with Gilbert Stephens Exeter until 1997, ret; *Style*— Sir Christopher Proctor-Beauchamp, Bt; ✉ The Coach House, Balfour Mews, Sidmouth EX10 8XL

PROES, Capt Richard Geoffrey; s of Maj Geoffrey Ernest Sullivan Proes (ka 1941), and Nancy Madeleine, *née* Churcher (d 1983); *b* 18 August 1937; *Educ* Wellington, RMA Sandhurst; *m* 28 May 1970, Victoria Margaret, da of Maj Arthur Michael Temple Trubshawe (d 1985); *Career* Capt Grenadier Gds 1957–68; salmon farmer; dir: Kyles of Bute Salmon Ltd 1981–, Scottish Salmon Growers Assoc 1983–98, Scottish Salmon Bd 1990–98; *Recreations* motor cruising, shooting, fishing; *Clubs* Army and Navy; *Style*— Capt Richard Proes; ✉ West Glen Caladh, Tighnabruaich, Argyll PA21 2EH (tel 01700 811224)

PROESCH, Gilbert; *b* 1943, Dolomites; *Educ* Wolkenstein Sch of Art, Hallein Sch of Art, Munich Acad of Art, St Martin's Sch of Art; *Career* artist, in partnership with George Passmore, *qv* since 1967; shortlisted Turner Prize 1984, Turner Prize 1986; Living Sculpture incl: The Red Sculpture, 3 Living Pieces, Underneath the Arches, Our New Sculpture, Reading from a Stick; *Selected Two Person Exhibitions* Snow Show (St Martins Sch of Art London) 1968, Shit and Cunt (Robert Fraser Gallery London) 1969, The Paintings (Whitechapel Art Gallery London, Kunstverein Dusseldorf, Koninklijk Museum voor Schone Kunsten Antwerp) 1971–72, Dusty Corners (Art Agency Tokyo) 1975, Photo-Pieces 1971–1980 (Stedelijk van Abbemuseum Eindhoven, Georges Pompidou Centre Paris, Kunsthalle Bern, Whitechapel Art Gallery London) 1980–81, Gilbert & George (touring, galleries incl: Contemporary Arts Museum Houston, The Solomon R Guggenheim Museum NY, Milwaukee Art Museum Milwaukee) 1984–85, Pictures 1982 to 85 (Hayward Gallery London, Lenbachaus Munich, Palacio de Velazquez Madrid) 1987, For AIDS Exhibition (Anthony d'Offay Gallery London) 1989, The Cosmological Pictures (touring, galleries incl: Palazzo delle Esposizioni Rome, Fundació Joan Miró Barcelona, Irish MOMA Dublin, Kunsthalle Zürich, Wiener Secession Vienna, Tate Gallery Liverpool) 1991–93, Gilbert & George China Exhibition (The Art Museum Shanghai, Nat

Art Gallery Beijing) 1993, Shitty Naked Human World (Wolfsburg Kunstmuseum Germany) 1994, The Naked Shit Pictures (South London Art Gallery) 1995, New Testamental Pictures (Museo do Capodimonte Naples) 1998, Black White and Red 1971 to 1980 (James Cohan Gallery New York) 1998, The Rudimentary Pictures (inaugural exhibition, Milton Keynes Gallery) 1999, Nineteen Ninety Nine (Kunstmuseum Bohn, Museum of Contemporary Art Chicago, Museum Moderner Kunst Vienna) 1999–2001, Enclosed and Enchanted (MOMA Oxford) 2000, New Horny Pictures (White Cube London) 2001, Gilbert & George: A Retrospective (Sch of Fine Art Athens, Kunsthaus Bregenz) 2002, The Dirty Words Pictures (Serpentine Gallery London) 2002, Thirteen Hooligan Pictures (Bernier/ Eliades Athens) 2004, 20 London E1 Pictures (Modern Art Museum St Etienne, Kestner Gesellschaft Hannover) 2004–05, Gilbert & George (British Pavilion Venice Biennale) 2005; *Work in Collections* incl: Arario Gallery Chungnam, Astrup Fearnley Museet fur Moderne Kunst Oslo, Denver Art Museum, Nat Portrait Gallery London, San Francisco MOMA, Tate Modern London; *Style—* Gilbert Proesch; ✉ White Cube, 48 Hoxton Square, London N1 6PB (tel 020 7930 5373, fax 020 7749 7480)

PROFFITT, Stuart Graham; s of Geoffrey Arnold Proffitt, and Sheila Patricia, *née* Whitehurst; *Educ* Uppingham, Worcester Coll Oxford; *Career* editorial asst rising to non-fiction publishing dir Collins Publishers 1983–92, publisher HarperCollins Trade Div 1992–98, publishing dir Penguin Press 1998–; chm Samuel Johnson Prize for non-fiction 1998–; *Recreations* walking, reading, music; *Clubs* Brooks's; *Style—* Stuart Proffitt, Esq; ✉ Penguin Books, 80 Strand, London WC2 (tel 020 7010 3000, fax 020 7010 6703)

PROFUMO, David John; s of John Dennis Profumo, CBE (d 2006), of London, and Valerie Babette Louise, *née* Hobson (d 1997); *b* 30 October 1955, London; *Educ* Eton (scholar), Magdalen Coll Oxford (Demy, MA); *m* 22 March 1980, Helen Ann, *née* Fraser; 2 s (Alexander James b 25 Sept 1983, Thomas David b 6 June 1986), 1 da (Laura Ann Louise b 24 Feb 1992); *Career* asst master Eton Coll 1978, asst master Shrewsbury Sch 1979, researcher English Dept KCL 1979–81, dep ed The Fiction Magazine 1982, columnist Daily Telegraph 1987–95; judge Booker Prize 1989; Geoffrey Faber Meml Prize 1989; memb Soc of Authors; FRSL 1997; *Publications* The Magic Wheel (co-ed with Graham Swift, *qv*, 1985), Sea Music (1988), In Praise of Trout (1989), The Weather in Iceland (1993), Bringing the House Down (2006); *Recreations* fishing, shooting, shopping; *Clubs* Flyfishers', Bundha; *Style—* David Profumo, Esq; ✉ c/o Gillon Aitken Associates Ltd, 18–21 Cavaye Place, London SW10 9PT (tel 020 7373 8672, fax 020 7373 6002)

PROSSER, Sir David John; kt (2005); s of Ronald Thomas Prosser, and Dorothy, *née* Denham; *b* 26 March 1944; *Educ* Ogmore GS, UCW Aberystwyth; *m* Nov 1971, Rosemary Margaret, da of Alan Snuggs; 2 da; *Career* Sun Alliance Group 1965–69, Hoare Govett 1969–73, CIN Management 1973–88; Legal & General Group plc: investment dir 1988–91, chief exec 1991–2006; memb Bd: ABI 1995–2004, Intercontinental Hotel Gp plc 2003–, Investec 2006–; FIA 1971; *Recreations* golf, family activities; *Clubs* RAC (memb Bd); *Style—* Sir David Prosser; ✉ 206 Gilbert House, The Barbican, London EC2Y 8BD

PROSSER, Gwyn; MP; *Career* MP (Lab) Dover 1997–; *Style—* Gwyn Prosser, Esq, MP; ✉ House of Commons, London SW1A 0AA (tel 020 7219 3000)

PROSSER, Sir Ian Maurice Gray; kt (1995); s of Maurice Clifford Prosser (d 1992), and Freda Prosser; *b* 5 July 1943; *Educ* King Edward's Sch Bath, Watford GS, Univ of Birmingham (BComm); *m* 1964 (m dis 2003), Elizabeth Herman; 2 da (Sarah, Joanna); m 2, 2003, Hilary Prewer; *Career* Coopers and Lybrand (accountants) 1964–69; InterContinental Hotel Gp plc (formerly Bass plc): joined Bass Charrington Ltd 1969, memb Main Bd 1978, vice-chm 1982–87, gp md 1984–87, chm and chief exec 1987–2000, chm 2000–03; non-exec dir: Brewers & Licensed Retailers Assoc (formerly Brewers' Soc) 1983–2000 (chm 1992–94), The Boots Co plc 1984–96, Lloyds TSB Group plc 1988–99, BP plc 1997– (dep chm 1999–), Glaxo Smithkline (formerly Smithkline Beecham) 1999– (sr ind non-exec dir), Sara Lee Corp 2004–; chm World Travel & Tourism Cncl 2000–03; Hon DUniv Birmingham; Liveryman Worshipful Co of Brewers; FCA; *Recreations* bridge, golf, gardening; *Style—* Sir Ian Prosser

PROSSER, Prof James Anthony William (Tony); s of James Allan Prosser (d 1968), and Flora Gertrude, *née* Evans; *b* 3 May 1954; *Educ* Ludlow GS, Univ of Liverpool (LLB); *m* 1998, Charlotte Louise, *née* Villiers; 1 da (Amelia Marisa Villiers b 2001), 1 s (Laurence Edward Villiers b 2002); *Career* res asst in law Univ of Southampton 1974–76; lectr in law: Univ of Hull 1976–79, Univ of Sheffield 1980–89; sr lectr in law Univ of Sheffield 1989–92, John Millar prof of law Univ of Glasgow 1992–2002, prof of public law Univ of Bristol 2002–; visiting prof: European Univ Inst 1990 (Jean Monnet fell 1987–88), Univ of Rome 1992, 1996 and 2003; memb: Soc of Public Teachers of Law 1976, Socio-Legal Studies Assoc 1990; *Books* Test Cases for the Poor (1983), Nationalised Industries and Public Control (1986), Waiving the Rules (with C Graham, 1988), Privatizing Public Enterprises (with C Graham, 1991), Privatisation and Regulatory Change in Europe (with M Moran, 1994), Law and the Regulators (1997), Regulating the Changing Media (jtly, 1998), Regulation and Markets Beyond 2000 (jtly, 2000), The Limits of Competition Law (2005); *Recreations* walking, listening to jazz, travel; *Style—* Prof Tony Prosser; ✉ Department of Law, Wills Memorial Building, The University of Bristol, Queens Road, Bristol BS8 1RJ

PROSSER, Baroness (Life Peer UK 2004), of Battersea in the London Borough of Wandsworth; Margaret Theresa Prosser; OBE (1997); da of Frederick James (d 1973), of London, and Lilian Mary, *née* Barry (d 1983); *b* 22 August 1937; *Educ* St Philomena's Convent Carshalton, NE London Poly; *m* 15 Feb 1957 (m dis); 1 s (Hon Jeffrey Jonathan b 1958), 2 da (Hon Carol Ann b 1960, Hon Stella Jane b 1963); *Career* advice centre organiser Home Office Funded Community Devpt Project 1974–77, law centre advsr 1977–83; TGWU: dist organiser 1983–84, nat women's sec 1984–92, nat organiser 1992–98, dep gen sec 1998–2002; pres TUC 1995–96 (memb Gen Cncl 1985–96), treas Lab Pty 1996–2001; chair Women's Nat Cmmn 2002–07, dep chair Cmmn for Equality and Human Rights (CEHR) 2006–; memb: Employment Appeal Tbnl 1995–2007, Central Arbitration Ctee 2000–02, Low Pay Cmmn 2000–05; non-exec dir Royal Mail 2004–; assoc memb Inst of Legal Execs 1981–83; *Recreations* walking, cooking; *Style—* The Rt Hon the Lady Prosser, OBE; ✉ Flat 34, 4 Grand Avenue, Hove, East Sussex BN3 2LE (tel 01273 723859, e-mail mprosser@onetel.com)

PROSSER, Rt Hon Lord; William David Prosser; PC (2000); s of David G Prosser, MC, WS, of Edinburgh; *b* 23 November 1934; *Educ* Edinburgh Acad, CCC Oxford (MA), Univ of Edinburgh (LLB); *m* 1964, Vanessa, da of Sir William O'Brien Lindsay, KBE; 2 s, 2 da; *Career* passed advocate 1962, QC (Scot) 1974, dean Faculty of Advocates 1983–86 (vice-dean 1979–83), senator Coll of Justice in Scotland (a Lord of Session) 1986–2001; chm: Royal Lyceum Theatre Co Edinburgh 1987–92, Scottish Historic Bldgs Tst 1988–98, Royal Fine Art Cmmn for Scotland 1990–95, Chamber Gp of Scotland 1993–98, Scottish Architectural Educn Tst 1994–2007; pres Franco-Br Lawyers Soc 1999–2002, memb Franco-Br Cncl 1997–; Hon FRIAS 1995; *Clubs* New (Edinburgh), Scottish Arts; *Style—* The Rt Hon Lord Prosser; ✉ 7 Randolph Crescent, Edinburgh EH3 7TH (tel 0131 225 2709); 6 Cité Pigalle, 75009 Paris (tel 0033 1 40 23 04 33)

PROTHEROE, Col Alan Hackford; CBE (1991, MBE 1980), TD (and Bar), DL (Bucks 1993); s of Rev B P Protheroe (d 1971); *b* 10 January 1934; *Educ* Maesteg GS; *m* 1, 1956, Anne Miller (d 1999), da of H M Watkins (d 1984); 2 s; m 2, 2004, Rosemary Margaret Louise Tucker, da of J L Wells (d 1993); *Career* Nat Serv 2 Lt Welch Regt 1954–56, Col TA; reporter: Glamorgan Gazette 1951–53, BBC Wales 1957–70; industrial corr Wales BBC 1959–64, ed Wales News and Current Affrs 1964–70; BBC TV News: asst ed 1970–72, dep ed 1972–77, ed 1977–80, asst dir BBC News and Current Affrs 1980, asst DG 1982–87; dir: Visnews Ltd 1982–87, Defence Public Affairs Consultants Ltd 1988–, Europac Gp 1989– (chm 1991–2000), TRBL Training Company; md The Services Sound and Vision Corp 1988–94; memb Cncl RUSI 1984–87, fndr memb Assoc of Br Eds (chm 1987), chm Eastern Wessex Reserve Forces Assoc 1991–99; lectr and contrib to jls on def and media affrs; memb Mgmt Bd Royal British Legion; Hon Col Pool of Army Info Offrs 1991–96; MIPR, FCMI; *Recreations* wine, photography; *Clubs* Army and Navy; *Style—* Col Alan Protheroe, CBE, TD, DL; ✉ Amberleigh House, 60 Chapman Lane, Flackwell Heath, Buckinghamshire HP10 9BD (tel and fax 01628 528492)

PROUD, George; s of Albert Proud (d 1972), of Durham, and Frances, *née* Sigworth; *b* 23 August 1943; *Educ* Royal GS Newcastle upon Tyne, Univ of Durham (BDS), Univ of Newcastle upon Tyne (MB BS, MD); *m* 25 July 1970, Janet Mary, da of Joseph Davies (d 1978), of Worthing; 1 da (Kathryn Siân b 8 Sept 1973), 1 s (Stuart James b 1 April 1976); *Career* conslt surgn Royal Victoria Infirmary Newcastle upon Tyne 1981–2000, former gen sec Br Transplantation Soc; past chm MRCS Clinical Examination Gp RCS; memb: Assoc of Surgns of GB and I, Vascular Surgical Soc; Trg Bd RCS 1997–2000, Higher Surgical Training Ctee RCS 1996–98, regnl advsr RCS, regnl speciality advsr Gen Surgery RCS, i/c Northern Office RCS 1996–2000; advsr on hand-arm vibration disease HSE and Faculty of Occupational Health RCP; memb: Vibration White Finger Med Reference Panel DTI, Hosp Recognition Ctee RCS, Devpt Ctee Nat Guidelines on Mgmnt of Thyroid Cancer; fndr memb: Weardale Ski Club, NE Ski Assoc; former pres Heaton on Tyne Rotary Club; Hunterian prof of surgery RCS 1979; Jacksonian Prize for Surgery RCS 1981; memb BMA, FRCS; *Publications* many papers on surgical topics; *Recreations* skiing, fell walking, photography; *Clubs* North of England Surgical Soc (former pres); *Style—* George Proud, Esq; ✉ Cartref, Marchburn Lane, Riding Mill, Northumberland NE44 6DN (tel 01434 682393, fax 01434 682781, mobile 07990 970202, e-mail george@g-proud-frcs.demon.co.uk)

PROUDMAN, Sonia Rosemary Susan; QC (1994); da of Kenneth Oliphant Proudman, of London, and Sati, *née* Hekimian; *b* 30 July 1949; *Educ* St Paul's Girls' Sch, Lady Margaret Hall Oxford (MA); *m* 19 Dec 1987, David Crispian Himley Cartwright, s of Himley Cartwright, of Henley-on-Thames; 1 da; *Career* called to the Bar Lincoln's Inn 1972 (bencher 1996), in practice at the Chancery Bar 1972–, asst recorder 1997–2000, recorder 2000–; memb Univ of Oxford Law Faculty Advsy Bd 2000; dep judge of the High Ct 2001–, memb QC Selection Panel 2005; *Clubs* Hurlingham, CWIL; *Style—* Miss Sonia Proudman, QC; ✉ 11 New Square, Lincoln's Inn, London WC2A 3QB (tel 020 7831 0081, fax 020 7405 2560/0798)

PROUT, David John; s of late Donald Cornell Prout, of Budleigh Salterton, Devon, and Kathleen Susan Constance, *née* Miller; *b* 13 November 1947; *Educ* Rugby, Hatfield Coll Durham, Univ of Reading (BA); *m* 17 July 1971, Amanda Jane, da of late Clifford Sherwood Nell; 2 s (Oliver Samuel b 13 June 1981, Jonathan Benedict b 9 Dec 1984); *Career* photographer; trained at GEC 1965, started Creed Lane Studio 1975; clients incl: William Collins, Grant Thornton, Schlumberger, Arthur Andersen, Vauxhall Motors, BT, Esso, CEPEC, Rank Xerox, Dept of Health, Amersham International; closed down Creed Lane after 25 years and founded the London office of ICRNetwork an Internet and e-business solutions provider with offices in Milan, Barcelona, New York and Monaco; dir corporate communications ICRNetwork BV; work published in Graphis; former teacher Canterbury Coll of Art; memb Graphics Gp and various ctees Chartered Soc of Designers 1976–94; FCSD 1985 (MCSD 1976), FRSA 1994; *Recreations* restoring pre-war cars, skiing, building and flying model aircraft with sons; *Clubs* MG Car, Octagon Car; *Style—* David Prout, Esq; ✉ e-mail david@icrnetwork.com, website www.icrnetwork.com

PROVAN, James Lyal Clark; s of John Provan, and Jean, *née* Clark; *b* 19 December 1936; *Educ* Oundle, RAC Cirencester; *m* 1960, Roweena Adele, da of Andrew H S Lewis; 1 da (Pepita Clare b 1961), 2 s ((John) Lyal, Andrew James (twins) b 1963); *Career* cncllr Tayside 1978–82, MEP NE Scot 1979–89, chm McIntosh Donald 1989–94, exec dir Scot Financial Enterprise 1990–92, chm McIntosh of Dyce 1991–94; MEP (Cons): S Downs W 1994–99, SE England 1999–2004; vice-pres Euro Parly 1999; currently non-exec dir CNH Global NV; chm Rowett Research Inst 1992–99; memb AFRC 1990–94, memb Lloyds; FAAV, FRSA, FRAgS; *Publications* Europe's Freedom to Farm (1995), Europe's Freedom to Farm II: Rejuvenating the Rural Economy (1998), Europe's Fishing Blues (1998), Keep the £ or Join the Euro? (2002); *Recreations* country pursuits, flying, sailing, music; *Clubs* Royal Perth, Farmers', East India; *Style—* James Provan, Esq; ✉ Summerfield, Glenfarg, Perth PH2 9QD (tel 01577 830714, fax 01574 830733)

P

PROWSE, Dr Keith; s of Valentine Prowse (d 2002), of Rugby, Warks, and Irene Ellen, *née* Rogers (d 1989); *b* 23 December 1937; *Educ* Lawrence Sheriff GS Rugby, Univ of Birmingham (BSc, MB ChB, MD); *m* 22 Sept 1962, Hilary Ann, da of Reginald Varley (d 1971), of Sutton Coldfield, W Midlands; 1 da (Carolyn b 1972), 1 s (Robert b 1975); *Career* lectr in med Univ of Birmingham 1968–71, Inserm res fell unité 14 Centre Hospitalier Universitaire Nancy 1971–72, conslt physician N Staffs Hosp 1972–2002, sr clinical lectr in respiratory med Dept of Postgrad Med Keele Univ 1986–2002, med dir N Staffs Hosp NHS Tst 1993–2001; pres Br Thoracic Soc 1996–97 (chm 1992–96), chm Br Lung Fndn 2005– (fndr memb Cncl), UK rep and hon sec Euro Bd Pneumology 1992–97 (pres 1997–2002); Hans Sloane fell and dir Int Office RCP 1999–2004; FRCP 1977; *Recreations* castles, owls, walking, music, travel; *Clubs* Y; *Style—* Dr Keith Prowse; ✉ Kyriole, Pinewood Road, Ashley Heath, Shropshire TF9 4PP (tel 01630 672879); 540 Etruria Road, Basford, Newcastle, Staffordshire ST5 0SX (tel 01782 630270)

PROWSE, Philip; s of late Alan William Auger Prowse, and Violet Beatrice, *née* Williamson; *b* 29 December 1937; *Educ* King's Sch Worcester, Malvern Coll of Art, Slade Sch of Fine Art; *Career* director and designer for opera, ballet and theatre; head Theatre Design Dept Slade Sch 1995–2003, prof UCL 1999–2003 (emeritus prof 2003–); professional debut with Royal Ballet's Diversions (ROH) 1961; worked with numerous cos incl: Glasgow Citizens' Theatre (dir 1970–2004), RNT, RSC, Old Vic, Royal Opera, Royal Ballet, ENO, Sadler's Wells Royal Ballet, WNO, Scottish Opera, Opera North, English Nat Ballet (Festival Ballet), Scottish Ballet; worked extensively in Europe and USA; *Theatre* prodns as dir incl: Chinchilla (NY), Phedra (with Glenda Jackson, Old Vic and Aldwych), The Duchess of Malfi (with Ian McKellen, *qv*, RNT and Chicago); for Greenwich Theatre incl: The White Devil, The Seagull, The Orphan; works for Citizens' Theatre Glasgow: The Picture of Dorian Gray, Private Lives, The Milk Train Doesn't Stop Here Anymore, The Soldiers, Don Carlos (both at Edinburgh Int Festival); other recent prodns incl: A Woman of No Importance (RSC), The White Devil (RNT), Lady Windermere's Fan (Albery and tour), The Vortex (also designer, Garrick, with Rupert Everett); *Opera* prodns as dir incl: La Gioconda (Opera North), Giovanna D'Arco (ROH), Tamburlaine (WNO), The Pearl Fishers (ENO); for Opera North: Orpheus, The Threepenny Opera, Aida, Daphne; *Ballet* as designer incl: The Sleeping Beauty (Dutch Nat Ballet/Vienna State Opera), Swan Lake (Munich); for Royal Ballet: The Sleeping Beauty, Swan Lake, Carmina Burana; *Style—* Philip Prowse, Esq; ✉ c/o Cruickshank Cazenove, 97 Old South Lambeth Road, London SW8 1XU (tel 020 7735 2933, fax 020 7820 1081)

PROWTING, Peter Brian; s of Arthur Edwin Alfred Prowting (d 1977), of Littlehampton, and Edith Kate, *née* Jones (d 1987); *b* 19 December 1924; *Educ* Ickenham HS, Frays Coll Uxbridge; *m* 1, 22 Oct 1948 (m dis 1965), Phyllis; 1 da (Wendy b 9 Sept 1956); m 2, 24 Nov 1966, Elizabeth Anne (Liz), da of Wing Cdr Leslie George Mobsby, RAF (d 1967), of Chenies, Bucks; *Career* Prowting plc: dir 1948–2000, chm 1955–2000; chm Prowting

Investments plc 1958–; Estates & General plc: dir 1974–2000, chm 1982–2000, non-exec dir 2000–04; *Recreations* gardening, golf, jazz; *Style—* Peter Prowting, Esq; ✉ The Old Bank House, High Street, Chalfont St Giles, Buckinghamshire HP8 4QA (tel 01494 876729, fax 01494 876727, e-mail pfc@ohf.uk.net)

PRYCE, Jonathan; s of Isaac Price (d 1976), of N Wales, and Margaret Ellen, *née* Williams (d 1986); *b* 1 June 1947; *Educ* Holywell GS, Sch of Art Kelsterton, Edge Hill Coll of Educn, RADA; *Career* actor; patron: Friends United Network, Saving Faces; fell Welsh Coll of Music and Drama; Hon Dr Univ of Liverpool 2006; *Theatre* Everyman Theatre Liverpool 1972, Nottingham Playhouse 1974, RSC 1979 and 1986, Royal Court 1980, NT 1981, Lyric Hammersmith, Queens Theatre, Vaudeville Theatre, Drury Lane Theatre Royal 1989–90, Music Box and Belasco NY, Broadway Theatre NY; roles incl: Richard III, Hamlet, Macbeth, Petruchio, Angelo, Octavius Caesar, Mick in the Caretaker, Gethin Price in Comedians, Tallys Folly, Trigorin, Astrov, Engineer in Miss Saigon, Fagin in Oliver! (London Palladium) 1994–95, Prof Higgins in My Fair Lady (Nat Theatre and Theatre Royal) 2001; other credits incl: A Reckoning (Soho Theatre), The Goat or Who is Sylvia? (Almeida and Apollo) 2004, Dirty Rotten Scoundrels (NY) 2006; *Television* incl: Daft as a Brush, Playthings, Glad Day, Roger Doesn't Live Here Anymore, The Caretaker, Comedians, Timon of Athens, Martin Luther Heretic, Praying Mantis, Two Weeks in Winter, The Man from the Pru, Selling Hitler, Mr Wroe's Virgins, Thicker than Water, David, HR 2007, The Baker Street Irregulars 2007; *Film* incl: Voyage of the Damned, Breaking Glass, Loophole, Ploughmans Lunch, Something Wicked This Way Comes, Brazil, Man on Fire, Jumpin' Jack Flash, Doctor and the Devils, Haunted Honeymoon, Consuming Passions, The Adventures of Baron Munchausen, The Rachel Papers, Glengarry Glen Ross, The Age of Innocence, Barbarians at the Gate, Great Moments in Aviation, A Business Affair, Deadly Advice, Shopping, Carrington, Evita, Regeneration, Tomorrow Never Dies, Ronin, Stigmata, Very Annie Mary, What a Girl Wants, Pirates of the Caribbean: The Curse of the Black Pearl 2003, Just One of Those Things, Brothers Grimm, Pirates of the Caribbean: Dead Man's Chest 2006, Pirates of the Caribbean: At World's End 2007, Leatherheads 2007; *Awards* Tony Award and Theatre World Award (for Comedians) 1977, SWET/Olivier Award (for Hamlet) 1980, Olivier Award (for Miss Saigon) 1990, Variety Club of GB Stage Actor of 1990, Tony Award for Best Actor in a Musical 1991, Drama Desk Award, Cannes Film Festival Award for Best Actor (for Carrington) 1995, Evening Standard Award for Best Actor (for Carrington) 1995, Special Award BAFTA Cymru 2001; *Style—* Jonathan Pryce, Esq; ✉ c/o Julian Belfrage Associates, 46 Albemarle Street, London W1S 4DF (tel 020 7491 4400, fax 020 7493 5460)

PRYCE, (George) Terry; CBE (1994); s of Edwin Pryce (d 1951), and Hilda, *née* Price (d 2004); *b* 26 March 1934; *Educ* Welshpool GS, Nat Coll of Food Technol; *m* 1957, Thurza Elizabeth, da of Arthur Denis Tatham (d 1942); 2 s (Simon Charles Conrad b 1961, Timothy John Robert b 1965), 1 da (Sarah Jane b 1970); *Career* Dalgety plc: dir 1972, md 1978–81, chief exec 1981–89; chm: Solway Foods Ltd 1990–94, Jas Bowman & Sons Ltd 1991–, York House Gp Ltd 1996–2003; dir HP Bulmer Holdings plc 1984–94; former chm Bd for Food Sci and Technol Univ of Reading, chm Horticultural Research Int 1991–1997; memb: Cncl AFRC 1986–94, Advsy Bd Inst of Food Research 1988–94; MFC, CCMI, FIFST; *Recreations* sport (golf), reading; *Clubs* Athenaeum, MCC; *Style—* G Terry Pryce, Esq, CBE

PRYCE, Vicky; da of Nicholas Courmouzis (d 1987); *b* Athens, Greece; *Educ* LSE (BSc, MSc); *m* 19 May 1984, Christopher Murray Paul Huhne, MP, *qv*, s of Peter Ivor Paul Huhne; 3 da, 2 s; *Career* economist then chief economist Williams & Glyn's Bank 1973–83, corporate economist Esso Europe 1983–86, chief economist then ptnr KPMG 1986–2001, ptnr London Economics 2001–02, chm Good Corporation 2001–02, chief economic advsr and DG DTI 2002–, dep head Govt Economics Office 2004–07, jt head Govt Economic Serv 2007–; visiting prof Cass Business Sch 2001–06; memb: Bd of Tstees RSA 2006–, Advsy Bd Centre for Int Business and Mgmnt Judge Business Sch Univ of Cambridge 1999–, Cncl Royal Economics Soc 2002–07, Cncl Univ of Kent 2005–, Int Advsy Bd British American Business Inc; Fourth Warden Worshipful Co of Mgmnt Conslts 2006; fell Soc of Business Economists; *Recreations* movies, theatre, Chelsea FC; *Clubs* Reform; *Style—* Mrs Vicky Pryce; ✉ Department for Business, Enterprise and Regulatory Reform, 1 Victoria Street, London SW1H 0ET (tel 020 7215 6059, fax 020 7215 6910, e-mail vicky.pryce@dti.gsi.gov.uk)

PRYCE-JONES, David Eugene Henry; s of Alan Pryce-Jones (d 2001), of Newport, RI, and Thérèse Fould-Springer (d 1953); *b* 15 February 1936, Vienna; *Educ* Eton, Magdalen Coll Oxford (MA); *m* 29 July 1959, Clarissa, *née* Caccia; 2 da (Jessica b 1961, Candida b 1963), 1 s (Adam b 1973); *Career* literary ed Spectator 1963–64, visiting lectr Univ of Iowa 1964–65, special corr Daily Telegraph 1966–82, visiting prof California State Coll Hayward 1968 and 1970, visiting prof California State Univ Berkeley 1972, sr ed National Review NY 1999; HH Wingate Prize 1986, Sunlight Fndn Prize 1989; FRSL 1975; *Publications* fiction: Owls and Satyrs (1961), The Sands of Summer (1963), Quondam (1965), The Stranger's View (1967), Running Away (1971), The England Commune (1975), Shirley's Guild (1979), The Afternoon Sun (1986), Inheritance (1992), Safe Houses (2007); non-fiction: Graham Greene (1963), Next Generation: Travels in Israel (1965), The Hungarian Revolution (1969), The Face of Defeat (1972), Evelyn Waugh and his World (ed, 1973), Unity Mitford (1976), Vienna (1978), Paris in the Third Reich (1981), Cyril Connolly: Journal and Memoir (1983), The Closed Circle (1989), You Can't Be Too Careful (1992), The War That Never Was (1995), Betrayal: France, The Arabs and The Jews (2006); *Recreations* travel, music; *Clubs* Beefsteak, Garrick; *Style—* David Pryce-Jones, Esq; ✉ c/o Christopher Sinclair-Stevenson, 3 South Terrace, London SW7 2TB (tel 020 7581 2550)

PRYDE, Roderick Stokes; OBE (1999); s of William Gerard Pryde (d 1955), and Patricia Mary, *née* Stokes (d 1959); *b* 26 January 1953; *Educ* George Watson's Coll Edinburgh, Univ of Sussex (BA), UCNW (PGCE, TEFL); *m* 1, 16 July 1976 (m dis), Dominique, *née* Cavalier; 1 da (Claire Patricia b 12 Sept 1979); m 2, 25 March 1989, Susanne Mona Graham, da of George Hamilton; 2 da (Beatrice Grace Hamilton b 14 Oct 1989, Madeleine Eve Hamilton b 20 July 1993), 1 s (Frederick William Hamilton b 1 June 1991); *Career* lectr Univ of Dijon 1975–76, mgmnt trainee and English language co-ordinator Societé Française des Pneumatiques Michelin 1977–81; British Council: asst regnl language offr 1981–83, dir of studies Milan 1983–87, regnl dir Seville 1987–88, regnl dir Bilbao 1988–89, Japanese language trg SOAS 1989–90, dir Kyoto 1990–92, dir Western Japan 1992–94, dir English Language Centre Hong Kong 1994–98, dir Portugal 1998–2000, dir Educnl Enterprises 2000–02, asst DG 2002–, regnl dir India and Sri Lanka 2005–; *Recreations* reading, walking, swimming; *Clubs* Watsonian (Edinburgh), Commonwealth, Caledonian Soc of Delhi; *Style—* Roderick Pryde, Esq, OBE

PRYKE, Sir Christopher Dudley; 4 Bt (UK 1926); s of William Dudley Pryke (d 1994), suc uncle Sir David Dudley Pryke, 3 Bt (d 1998); *b* 17 April 1946; *Educ* Hurstpierpoint Coll; *m* 1, 1973 (m dis 1986), Angela Gay (d 1995), da of late Harold Noel Meek; 1 s (James Dudley b 29 Dec 1977); m 2, 21 Nov 1999, Marilyn Wright, da of Gerald William Henry Williamson (d 2007); *Heir* s, James Pryke; *Career* chartered surveyor, Liveryman Worshipful Co of Tallow Chandlers; *Clubs* Buck's, Hadley Wood Golf; *Style—* Sir Christopher Pryke, Bt; ✉ 23 Wavendon Avenue, Chiswick, London W4 4NP (tel 020 8747 1559, e-mail prykes@blueyonder.co.uk)

PRYNNE, Andrew Geoffrey Lockyer; QC (1995); s of Maj-Gen Michael Whitworth Prynne, CB, CBE (d 1977), and Jean Violet, *née* Stewart (d 1977); *b* 28 May 1953; *Educ* Marlborough, Univ of Southampton (LLB); *m* 30 July 1977, Catriona Mary, da of Maj Henry Gordon Brougham (d 1958); 3 da (Jessica Jean, Miranda Wendy, Natasha Sally); *Career* called to the Bar Middle Temple 1975; CEDR accredited mediator 2000; asst Boundary Cmmr 1999; *Recreations* sailing, fishing, shooting, theatre, music; *Clubs* Royal Yacht Sqdn, Royal Solent Yacht, Island Sailing; *Style—* Andrew Prynne, Esq, QC; ✉ Mount Le Hoe, Benenden, Kent TN17 4BW; House Boat Periwinkle, Old Ferry Wharf, 106 Cheyne Walk, London SW10 0DG; 2 Harcourt Buildings, Middle Temple Lane, Temple, London EC4Y 9DB

PRYOR, Dr Arthur John; CB (1997); s of late Quinton Arthur Pryor, of Budleigh Salterton, Devon, and late Elsie Margaret, *née* Luscombe; *b* 7 March 1939; *Educ* Harrow Co GS, Downing Coll Cambridge (MA, PhD); *m* 1964, Marilyn Kay, da of late Sidney Petley; 1 da (Clare Marianne b 1969), 1 s (Mark John b 1973); *Career* asst lectr then lectr in Spanish and Portuguese UC Cardiff 1963–66, asst princ then princ DTI 1966–73, first sec Civil Aviation and Shipping British Embassy Washington DC 1973–75; DTI: princ Commercial Rels and Exports Div 1975–77, asst sec (Shipping Policy, Air Div, Int Trade Policy) 1977–85, regnl dir W Midlands 1985–88; DG Br Nat Space Centre 1988–93, under sec Competition Policy Div DTI 1993–96; competition conslt 1996–; memb: Inter-Agency Ctee on Global Environmental Change 1990–93, Reporting Panel of Competition Cmmn 1998–2003, Competition Appeal Tbnl (formerly Appeal Panel of Competition Cmmn) 2000–; contrib to modern languages and space pubns; *Recreations* tennis, golf, book collecting; *Style—* Dr Arthur Pryor, CB; ✉ c/o Competition Appeal Tribunal, Victoria House, Bloomsbury Place, London WC1A 2EB

PRYOR, John Pembro; s of (William) Benjamin Pryor, and Kathleen Martha Amelia, *née* Pembro (d 1959); *b* 25 August 1937; *Educ* Reading Sch, KCL, KCH Medical Sch (MS); *m* 25 July 1959, Marion, da of Illtyd Thomas Hopkins; 4 s (Andrew b 1962, Damian b 1964, Justin b 1966, Marcellus b 1968); *Career* Hunterian prof RCS 1971–72 and 1994–95, conslt urological surgn with special interest in andrology King's Coll Hosp and St Peter's Hosp 1974–94; Inst of Urology London Univ: dean 1978–85, sr surgn 1992–98; first chm Br Andrology Soc 1978–85, memb Ctee British Assoc of Urological Surgeons 1979–82 (St Peter's Medal 1995), chm European Assoc of Gen Microsurgeons 1992–96; pres Euro Soc for Impotence Research 1999–2001 (lifetime achievement award 2002), chm Impotence Assoc 1999–2001, chm European Sexual Dysfunction Alliance 1999–2004; treas Br Jl of Urology 1991–99, chair European Acad for Sexual Medicine 2004–; Liveryman Worshipful Soc of Apothecaries; FRCS; *Books* Andrology (1987), Urological Prostheses, Appliances and Catheters (1992), Impotence: An Integrated Approach to Clinical Practice (1993); *Style—* John Pryor, Esq; ✉ The Lister Hospital, Chelsea Bridge Road, London SW1W 8RH (tel 01424 814949, fax 01424 814945)

PRYOR, Nicholas David; s of (Richard) Vivian Pryor, of Newquay, Cornwall, and Ruth Gibson, *née* Budd; *b* 13 October 1946, London; *Educ* Whitgift Sch Croydon (Victoria Schol, Lewis Prizeman), Univ of Bristol (LLB), Coll of Law, LSE (Dip, MSc); *m* 1, (m dis); m 2, 13 Oct 2004, Lesley, *née* Stockwell; *Career* called to the Bar Middle Temple 1970 (Blackstone scholar, Churchill Prize), admitted slr 1981; asst litigation slr Rowe & Maw 1981–83, sr asst litigation slr Coward Chance (later Clifford Chance) 1983–90, litigation ptnr Manches & Co 1990–95, co slr and head UK Legal Dept Kwelm Insurance Services Ltd 1995–97, ind commercial mediator and conslt 1997–; non-exec dir CEDR 1995–98 (fndr memb Trg Faculty 1991); memb Mediation Panel: Ct of Appeal, London Ct of Int Arbitration, CIArb; fndr memb: Panel of Ind Mediators, Lamport Hall Gp; memb Lloyd's/Int Underwriting Assoc Mediation Steering Gp; dir Bluebell Railway plc; accredited mediator: CEDR 1992, ADR; MCIArb 2001, memb CPR Inst of Dispute Resolution NY; *Publications* Mediators on Mediation (contrib, 2005); *Recreations* opera, walking, historic motorsport; *Style—* Nicholas Pryor, Esq; ✉ c/o David Douglas, Independent Mediation Chambers (tel 020 7127 9223, e-mail admin@independentmediators.co.uk)

PRYS-DAVIES, Baron (Life Peer UK 1983), of Llanegryn in the County of Gwynedd; Gwilym Prys Prys-Davies; s of William and Mary Matilda Davies; assumed by deed poll 1982 the surname Prys-Davies in lieu of his patronymic; *b* 8 December 1923; *Educ* Towyn Sch, Univ Coll of Wales Aberystwyth; *m* 1951, Llinos, da of Abram Evans; 3 da (Hon Catrin Prys (Hon Mrs Waugh) b 1957, Hon Ann Prys b 1959, Hon Elin Prys b 1963); *Career* RN 1942–46; slr 1956, ptnr Morgan Bruce and Nicholas slrs 1957–87 (conslt 1987–93), special advsr to Sec of State for Wales 1974–78; chm Welsh Hosp Bd 1968–74; memb: Welsh Cncl 1967–69, Econ and Social Ctee EEC 1978–82; oppn front bench spokesman on: NI 1982–93, Welsh affrs 1987–95; pres Univ of Wales Swansea 1997–2001; chm NPFA (Cymru) 1998–2000; memb Br-Irish Parly Body 1989–95; hon fell: Univ of Wales Aberystwyth, Univ of Wales Swansea, Trin Coll Carmarthen, Univ of Wales Inst Cardiff; Hon LLD Wales; OStJ; *Publications* A Central Welsh Council 1963, Y Ffermwr a'r Gyfraith (1967); *Style—* The Rt Hon the Lord Prys-Davies; ✉ Lluest, 78 Church Road, Tonteg, Pontypridd, Rhondda-Cynon-Taf; House of Lords, London SW1A 0PW

PRYS-ROBERTS, Prof Cedric; s of William Prys Roberts (d 1992), of Exeter, and Winifred, *née* Osborne Jones (d 1990); *b* 8 August 1935; *Educ* Dulwich Coll, Bart's Med Sch (MB BS), Univ of Oxford (MA, DM), Univ of Leeds (PhD); *m* 1961, Linda Joyce, da of Tom Bickerstaff; 2 da (Kathryn Rachel b 1 May 1962, Lesley Elaine b 17 July 1965), 2 s (Simon Alastair b 25 March 1964, Dr Curig Owen Prys-Roberts b 25 Sept 1968); *Career* SHO/registrar Middx Hosp London and research fell Univ of Leeds 1964–67, clinical reader in anaesthetics Univ of Oxford 1967–76, hon conslt anaesthetist Radcliffe Infirmary Oxford 1967–76, fell Worcester Coll Oxford 1970–76; prof of anaesthesia: Univ of Calif San Diego 1973–74, Univ of Bristol 1976–99 (emeritus 2000–); hon conslt anaesthetist Bristol Royal Infirmary and Bristol Royal Hosp for Sick Children 1976–99; pres Royal Coll of Anaesthetists 1994–97; Hunterian prof Royal Coll of Surgns of England 1978; senator Euro Acad of Anaesthesiology 1984–92, pres Soc of Anaesthetists of the SW Regn 1992, fell (by election) Aust and NZ Coll of Anaesthetists 1986; hon fell: South African Coll of Med 1996, Coll of Anaesthetists RCSI 1997; memb d'honneur Collège Français des Anesthésistes-Réanimateurs; founding ed Current Opinion in Anaesthesiology 1988–95, author of numerous articles in learned jls on physiology and pharmacology related to anaesthesia and intensive therapy; FRCA, FANZCA; *Books* The Circulation in Anaesthesia (ed, 1980), Pharmacokinetics of Anaesthesia (ed, 1984), Monitoring in Anaesthesia and Intensive Care (ed, 1994), International Practice of Anaesthesia (ed, 2 vols, 1996); *Recreations* mountaineering, skiing, philately and postal history, music (playing trumpet); *Style—* Prof Cedric Prys-Roberts; ✉ Foxes Mead, Cleeve Hill Road, Cleeve, Bristol BS49 4PG (e-mail cedricpr@tiscali.co.uk)

PRZYBYLSKI, Steve; s of Jerzy Przybylski (d 1962), and Mary Elisabeth, *née* Godfrey (d 2003); *b* 31 March 1950; *Educ* Lawrence Sheriff Sch Rugby, Weymouth GS; *m* 15 June 1981, Ellen, *née* Parkin; 2 da (Sarah Ellen b 18 June 1982, Rebecca Jane b 16 Jan 1986); *Career* DHSS 1970–79, Lord Chllr's Dept 1979–86; with CPS 1986–, head of resources and performance 1999–; govr Chelmsford County HS for Girls; *Recreations* sailing, rugby; *Clubs* Maldon Yacht, Gateshead Fell RFC; *Style—* Steve Przybylski, Esq; ✉ Crown Prosecution Service, 50 Ludgate Hill, London EC4M 7EX (tel 020 7796 8072, fax 020 7796 8368, e-mail steve.przybylski@cps.gsi.gov.uk)

PUCKRIN, Arthur William; s of Thomas William Puckrin (d 1977), of Middlesbrough, and Eleanor Mary, *née* Cumiskey; *b* 5 May 1938; *Educ* Middlesbrough HS, Univ of London (LLB, BL); Outward Bound Mountain Sch Ullswater; *m* 2 April 1966 (m dis 1994), Patricia Ann, da of Charles Henry Dixon (d 1972), of Middlesbrough; 2 s (Geoffrey Arthur b 1984, James William b 1986); *Career* called to the Bar 1966; legal advsr Dorman Long

Steel Ltd 1966–71, Parly advsr to City of London Corp 1971; memb Bar Assoc for Commerce Fin and Industry 1967–; athlete, long distance runner and long distance swimmer; record holder for: Pennine Way 250 miles, Southern Highlands of Scotland 170 miles, Welsh 14 Peaks over 3000 feet, N Yorks Moors 80 miles, Lyke Walk N Yorks Moors 120 miles; defeated 50 horses over 44 miles at Wolsingham Horse Trials, record holder for 110 mile walk Middlesbrough to York and back in 23 hours 40 mins; Ironman Triathlete 1997, Br Ironman (Age Gp) champion 1998, 1999, 2000, 2001, 2002, 2004, 2005 and 2006, Scottish Ironman Triathlon Champion 2000; represented GB World Triathlon Championships Nice 1997, Sweden 1999 (finished fifth place) and Ibiza 2003 (3 mile swim, 75 mile cycle and 20 mile run); bronze medallist Euro Sprint Quadrathon Championship 1998, Euro Quadrathon Champion Cyprus 1999, GB Quadrathon Champion 1999 (1.5 mile swim, 6 mile canoe, 40 mile cycle, and 6 mile run); bronze medallist World Quadrathon Championships Czech Republic 2000, World Quadrathlon Champion Montreal 2001; Double Ironman (5 mile swim, 224 mile cycle and 52 mile run): Age Gp Champion Canada 2001, 2002, 2003 and 2004, World Champion Mexico 2001, S American Champion Ecuador 2002, World Champion Quebec 2002; second place USA Triple Ironman Championships VA 2002 and fifth place 2004 (8 mile swim, 336 mile cycle and 80 mile run, oldest person ever to complete this distance); World Deca-Biathlon Champion Mexico 2002 (1,120 mile cycle and 262 mile run, first ever Br winner, world record time), competed World Deca-Triathlon Championship Hawaii 2004 (24 mile swim, 1,120 mile cycle and 262 mile run, world record time), South American 24 Hour Cycling Champion Mexico 2005 (world record distance), Deca-Triathlon Championship France 2006 (world record), World Cup Triple Ironman Championship Virginia 2006 (world record), Deca World Challenge Mexico 2006 (world record); represented GB playing bridge on 8 occasions incl 2 World Championships and four Euro Championships; life memb: Fell Runners' Assoc, Darlington HF Walking Club, Br Long Distance Swimming Assoc; life master English Bridge Union; Queen's Scout; FCIS 1977, MIMgt 1980; *Clubs* Hartlepool Bridge, Middlesbrough and Cleveland Harriers, Lyke Wake, Cleveland Triathlon, Road Runners, Cleveland Wheelers, Long Distance Walkers Assoc; *Style*— Arthur W Puckrin, Esq; ✉ 3 Romanby Gardens, Middlesbrough, Cleveland TS5 8BW (tel 01642 593807); 257 Acklam Road, Middlesbrough TS5 8BW (tel 01642 534841)

PUDDEPHATT, Andrew Charles; OBE (2003); s of Andrew Ross Puddephatt, and Margaret, *née* Deboo; *b* 2 April 1950; *Educ* Kingsbury Sch Dunstable, Sidney Sussex Coll Cambridge (BA), Architectural Assoc (dip); *Children* 2 da (Leni Joanne Wild, Kelly Wild); *Career* teacher ILEA 1979, computer programmer CAP/CPP 1979–81, researcher Jt Action Docklands Gp 1985–89, gen sec Liberty/The Nat Cncl for Civil Liberties 1989–95, dir Charter 88 1995–99, dir Article XIX 1999–2004; currently dir Global Ptnrs & Associates Ltd; chair Audit Ctee Parly Ombudsman; chair Coordinated Action Against Domestic Abuse (CAADA); *Recreations* music, literature; *Style*— Andrew Puddephatt, OBE

PUGH, Prof Alan; s of Albert Pugh (d 1989), and Stella, *née* Gough (d 1991); *b* 7 March 1936; *Educ* Whitchurch GS, UC of S Wales and Monmouthshire (BSc, Page Prize in Engrg), Univ of Nottingham (PhD); *m* Alison Jean (d 1995), da of Robert Lindsay; 1 da (Judith Caroline (Mrs Watson) b 30 Oct 1961), 1 s (Simon David b 7 Nov 1962); m 2, 1997, Dr Elizabeth Anne, da of Paul Bowler (d 2003); *Career* postgrad apprenticeship BBC 1957–59, design engr on Br nuclear submarine prog Rolls Royce 1959–61, lectr then sr lectr in electrical engrg Univ of Nottingham 1961–78 (J Langham-Thompson Premium 1968); Univ of Hull: prof of electronic engrg 1978–96, head of dept 1978–90, dean 1987–90, pro-vice-chllr 1990–93, emeritus prof 1996–; vice-pres IEE 1997–2000; memb NATO Collaborative Research Grant Ctee 1995–98, chm Permanent Steering Ctee European Standing Observatory on the Engrg Profession and Educn (ESOEPE) 2002–06, chm Accreditation of European Engrg Progs and Grads (EUR-ACE) Project Bd 2004–05; FIEE 1979 (MIEE 1964), FRSA 1982, FREng 1992; *Books* Robot Vision (1983), Robot Sensors (Vol 1 - Vision, Vol 2 - Tactile and Non-Vision, 1986), Machine Intelligence and Knowledge Engineering for Robotic Applications (with A K C Wong, 1987); *Recreations* hill walking, flying, pottering around the house and garden; *Style*— Prof Alan Pugh, FREng; ✉ Cherry Tree Cottage, Wateringdike Lane, Goodmanham, York YO43 3JD (tel 01430 871225)

PUGH, Alun John; s of Maurice Thomas Pugh, and Violet Jane Pugh; *b* 9 June 1955; *Educ* Tonypandy GS, Polytechnic of Wales, Univ Coll Cardiff; *m* 1978 (m dis 2002), Janet; 1 s, 1 da; *Career* lectr Brigend Coll 1983, sr lectr Newcastle Coll 1987, head of sch Llandrillo Coll 1992, asst princ West Cheshire Coll 1996; memb Nat Assembly for Wales (Lab) Clwyd West 1999–2007; currently min for culture, Welsh language and sport; *Recreations* mountaineering; *Clubs* Oesterreichische Alpenverein (Innsbruck), Colwyn Bay British Legion; *Style*— Mr Alun Pugh, Esq

PUGH, Andrew Cartwright; QC; s of Lewis Gordon Pugh (d 1989), and Erica, *née* Cartwright (d 1997); *b* 6 June 1937; *Educ* Tonbridge, New Coll Oxford (MA); *m* 28 April 1984, Chantal Helene, da of Andre Langevin (d 1987); 2 da (Alexandra b 21 Nov 1985, Sophie b 16 Sept 1987); *Career* Nat Serv Royal Sussex Regt 1955–57; Bigelow fell Univ of Chicago 1959–60; called to the Bar Inner Temple 1961; SE Circuit: bencher 1989, recorder 1990–2003; legal assessor: GMC, GDC; Liveryman Worshipful Co of Skinners; *Recreations* tennis, gardening, reading; *Clubs* Oxford and Cambridge; *Style*— Andrew Pugh, Esq, QC; ✉ Blackstone Chambers, Blackstone House, Temple, London EC4 9BW (tel 020 7583 1770, fax 020 7822 7222, e-mail clerks@blackstonechambers.com)

PUGH, Dr John; MP; s of James Pugh, of Nottingham, and Patricia, *née* Caig; *b* 28 June 1948, Liverpool; *Educ* Univ of Durham (BA), Univ of Liverpool (MA), Victoria Univ of Manchester (PhD); *m* 24 Aug 1971, Annette, *née* Sangar; 1 s (David b 21 Oct 1977), 3 da (Nicola b 12 Nov 1979, Christina b 31 March 1981, Sarah b 5 Oct 1982); *Career* head of philosophy and religious studies Merchant Taylors' Sch Crosby 1985–2001; MP (Lib Dem) Southport 2001–; memb Tport, Local Govt and Regions Select Ctee 2001–05, Lib Dem spokesperson for educn 2002–05, Lib Dem spokesperson for tport 2005–, vice-chair All Pty Gp on Burma; cncllr Sefton MBC 1987–2002 (ldr Lib Dem Gp 1992–2001, cncl ldr 2000–01); former memb Merseyside Police Authy; memb CAMRA Campaign for Real Ale; *Publications* Christian Understanding of God; *Recreations* weightlifting, cycling; *Style*— Dr John Pugh, MP; ✉ 27 The Walk, Birkdale, Southport, Merseyside PR8 4BG (tel 01704 569025); 35 Shakespeare Street, Southport, Merseyside PR8 5AB (tel 01704 533555, fax 01704 884160); House of Commons, London SW1A 0AA

PUGH, Jonathan Mervyn Sebastian; s of John Mervyn Cullwick Pugh, of Upton upon Severn, Worcs, and Kay Sanderson, *née* Fitzmaurice; *b* 17 February 1962; *Educ* Downside, Oxford Poly (BA); *m* 15 May 1992, Anna, *née* Forsyth; 1 s (Thomas b 3 May 1995), 1 da (Phoebe b 23 March 1998); *Career* freelance cartoonist and illustrator; regular contrib: Punch 1989–92, The Independent 1992–94; The Times: Diary cartoonist 1995, main pocket cartoonist 1996–; Cartoon Art Tst Pocket Cartoonist of the Year 1998, 2000 and 2001, Press Gazette Cartoonist of the Year 2001 (finalist 1999, 2000 and 2003); *Clubs* Chelsea Arts; *Style*— Jonathan Pugh, Esq; ✉ The Times, 1 Pennington Street, London E98 1TT

PUGH, Richard Henry Crommelin; DL (Hereford and Worcester 1991); s of John James Edgar Pugh (d 1944), of Buxton, Derbys, and Charlotte Winifred Crommelin, *née* Sadler (d 1977); *b* 9 September 1927; *Educ* Buxton Coll, Univ of London (LLB); *m* 15 Aug 1953, Ann, da of Roy Waddington Swales (d 1979), of Fernilee, Derbys; 1 da (Helen b 1956), 1 s (Stephen b 1958); *Career* Nat Serv RAF 1947–49; qualified CA; Grattan Warehouses Ltd 1951–56; chm Kay & Co Ltd (Home Shopping Div of Great Universal Stores) 1968–96, dep chm The Great Universal Stores plc 1990–96; chm Whiteaway Laidlaw Bank 1990–96; chm: Worcester Cathedral Appeal and Tstees 1982–2002, Worcester Royal Infirmary NI Tst 1993–95; tstee Charles Hasting Educn Centre 1999–2003; Freeman City of London 1984, Liveryman Worshipful Co of Chartered Secretaries 1984 (memb Ct of Assts 1994); fell Worcester Coll of Further Educn; FCA 1951, ACIS 1951, ACMA 1959, FRGS; OStJ (co-chm Order of St John 1994–98, memb Chapter Gen Order of St John 1996–98, memb Cncl Worcester Order of St John); *Recreations* travel, swimming, genealogy; *Style*— Richard Pugh, Esq, DL; ✉ 6 Swinton House, 85 Gloucester Terrace, London W2 3HB (tel 020 7262 4252, e-mail rpugh2@hotmail.com)

PUGHE, Brig Neville Morris; s of Maj Morris George Pughe (d 1951), and Dorothy Edith, *née* Goss; *b* 10 January 1936; *Educ* Exeter Sch, RMA Sandhurst, RMCS Shrivenham, RAF Staff Coll Bracknell; *m* 19 Jan 1963, Linda Jane, da of Denis Carr Chetwood (d 1974); 3 s (David Michael Stephen b 9 Jan 1964, Richard Neville Iain b 31 July 1965, Jonathan Owen b 7 Feb 1967); *Career* cmmnd RA 1955, Bde Maj 16 Parachute Bde 1972–74, instr Staff Coll Camberley 1974–76, CO 26 Field Regt RA 1976–78, Col GS MOD 1980–82, AMA Washington 1983–85, def attaché Bonn 1986–88, dep cdr SW Dist 1988–89; ADC to HM The Queen 1988–90; chief exec: Surrey Heath BC 1990–97, Royal Coll of Organists 2005–; pres Age Concern N Dorset, patron Help the Aged Dorset, govr RNLI; FCMI (FIMgt 1988), FIPD 1996; Officer's Cross Order of Merit of Federal Republic of Germany 1993; *Publications* Ulster Snapshot (1989), Elusive Glory (2006); *Recreations* gardening, music, writing, British-German relations; *Style*— Brig Neville Pughe; ✉ Glebe Cottage, Donhead St Mary, Shaftesbury, Dorset SP7 9DQ (tel 01747 828084, fax 01747 828246, e-mail neville.pughe@btinternet.com)

PUGSLEY, His Hon Judge David Philip; s of Rev Clement Harry Howell Pugsley (d 1967), and Edith Alsop, *née* Schofield (d 1956); *b* 11 December 1944; *Educ* Shebbear Coll, St Catharine's Coll Cambridge (MA), Univ of Birmingham (MPhil 1995); *m* 31 Dec 1966, Judith Mary, da of John S Mappin, 2 da (Joanna Hazel b 28 March 1972, Alison Jane b 12 Feb 1974); *Career* called to the Bar Middle Temple 1968; chm Birmingham Region Industrial Tbnls 1985–, recorder Midland & Oxford Circuit 1991–92 (practised until 1985), circuit judge (Midland & Oxford Circuit) 1992–; memb Parole Bd 1998–; *Books* Industrial Tribunals - Compensation for Loss of Pension Rights (jtly, 1990), Contract of Employment (jtly, 1997), Butterworth Employment Compensation Calculator (jtly, 1999); ed panel The Civil Court Practice (The Green Book); *Recreations* fishing, golf, walking; *Clubs* Lansdowne; *Style*— His Hon Judge Pugsley; ✉ 3 Fountain Court, Steelhouse Lane, Birmingham B4 6DR (tel 0121 236 5854)

PULESTON JONES, Haydn; s of Iago Oliver Puleston Jones (d 1971), and Elizabeth Ann, *née* Morris; *b* 16 September 1948; *Educ* Welshpool HS, KCL (LLB, AKC); *m* 9 June 1973, Susan Elizabeth, da of Lt Cdr George Karn (d 1969); 2 s (Simon b 1975, Nicholas b 1978); *Career* Linklaters (formerly Linklaters & Alliance): joined 1971, ptnr 1979–2003, head of banking 1995–99, head of banking mgmnt team 1998–2003; chm Banking Law Sub-Ctee City of London Law Soc 1994–98 (memb Sub-Ctee 1980–98); pres Montgomeryshire Soc 2000–01 (memb Ctee 1974–91, vice-pres 1993–2000); tstee Montgomeryshire Soc Charitable Tsts 1983–; memb: Law Soc 1973–2003, City of London Slrs' Co 1980–2003, Fin Law Panel's Single Currency Liaison Gp 1996–98; Loan Market Assoc: memb Working Pty on Primary Documentation in the Syndicated Loans Market 1998–2001, memb Documentation Ctee 2001–03; memb Ctee Plaxtol Local History Gp 2003–; *Recreations* gardening, classical music, genealogy; *Style*— Haydn Puleston Jones, Esq; ✉ Ducks Farm, Dux Lane, Plaxtol, Sevenoaks, Kent TN15 0RB

PULFORD, John; MBE; s of George Pulford, of Manchester (d 1980), and Mary Beatrice, *née* Beigel (d 2004); *b* 3 July 1943, Macclesfield; *Educ* Cranfield Sch of Mgmnt (MBA); *m* 8 July 1972, Ann, *née* Baker; 2 s (Thomas George b 2 Jan 1979, Jonathan Henry b 17 Aug 1985), 1 da (Louise Elisabeth b 5 June 1983); *Career* mgmnt conslt Arthur Andersen 1969–82, dir Nesco Investments plc 1982–84, chief exec Colmore Investments Ltd 1984–92, mgmnt conslt 1992–96, chief exec Direct Image Systems and Communications 1996–2004, chief exec Hendi Group Ltd 2004–; chm Govt and Industry Ctee BPIF; chm: Community Serv Vols, ACT (Arts Centre Tst) Cornwall, Ex Cathedra; memb Worshipful Co of Mgmnt Conslts 2003; *Recreations* voluntary sector, music; *Style*— John Pulford, Esq, MBE; ✉ Scawswater Mill, Idless, Truro, Cornwall TR4 9QR (tel 01872 273734); Community Service Volunteers, 237 Pentonville Road, London N1 9NJ; Hendi Group, 10 East Road, London N1 6AD (tel 07771 905300, e-mail john.pulford@hendi.net)

PULLEN, Dr Roderick Allen (Rod); *b* 11 April 1949; *m* 1971, Karen Lesley, *née* Sketchley; 4 s, 1 da; *Career* diplomat; with MOD 1975, second sec Brussels 1978, MOD 1980, first sec Madrid 1981, dep high cmmr Suva 1984–88, first sec FCO 1988–90, cnsllr (technol) Paris 1990–94, dep high cmmr Nairobi 1994–97, dep high cmmr Lagos 1997–2000, high cmmr to Ghana 2000–04, ambass to Zimbabwe 2004–06, UK special rep to the Sudan/Darfur Peace Process 2006, fell Trinity Coll Cambridge 2006–; *Style*— Dr Rod Pullen; ✉ Trinity College, Cambridge CB2 1TQ

PULLINGER, Anthony Giles Broadbent; s of Sir Alan Pullinger, CBE (d 2002), of Herts, and his 1 w, Felicity Charmian Gotch, *née* Hobson (d 1964); *b* 24 May 1955; *Educ* Marlborough, Balliol Coll Oxford; *m* 2 Oct 1982, Henrietta Mary Conyngham, da of Maj Richard Conyngham Corfield (d 1997), of Warks; 1 s (Jack b 1985), 2 da (Rosanna b 1988, Isla b 1992); *Career* stockbroker Laing & Cruickshank 1978–90, seconded to Panel on Takeovers and Mergers 1982–84, ptnr Laing & Cruickshank 1984–87, dir Alexanders Laing & Cruickshank 1985–89, dep DG Panel on Takeovers and Mergers 1990–; Freeman: City of London 1986, Worshipful Co of Grocers 1986; *Recreations* fishing, riding, mountaineering, music, travel, natural history; *Clubs* City of London; *Style*— Anthony Pullinger, Esq; ✉ The Panel on Takeovers and Mergers, 10 Paternoster Square, London EC4M 7DY (tel 020 7382 9026, fax 020 7638 1554, e-mail tonypullinger@aol.com)

PULLMAN, Bruce John; s of Bernard John Pullman, of Brockenhurst, Hants, and Dorothy Jean, *née* Hayes; *b* 4 April 1957; *Educ* Canford Sch, Merton Coll Oxford (BA); *m* 14 July 1979, Joanna Alexis Hamilton, da of John Edward Hamilton Davies, of Whitby, N Yorks; 2 da (Rebecca b 1984, Abigail b 1985), 1 s (Joshua b 1989); *Career* NM Rothschild & Sons Ltd 1979–81, dir County NatWest Investment Management 1987–93 (joined 1981, responsible for quantitative investment research and product devpt), md Hill Samuel Investment Management 1993, dir QUANTEC Ltd (investment consultancy) 1993–94, head of fin engrg Smith New Court 1995, head of asset mgmnt consulting Merrill Lynch 1995–96, head of strategy Gartmore Investment Management 1997–98, md Astute Computers 1999–2001; exec dir: Choice Matching Ltd 2001–04, Harrier Music Ltd 2004–06, Osprey Music Ltd 2004–06, Prime Ribs Ltd 2006–07, Colour Envelopes Ltd 2007–; chair Sch Ctee US Business Sch in Prague; MSI 1993; *Books* Portfolio Insurance (contrib, ed Donald L Luskin, 1988); *Recreations* Evangelical church, humanitarian aid to Eastern Europe and the former Soviet Union, int youth music festivals, rigid inflatable boats (RIBs); *Style*— Bruce Pullman, Esq; ✉ 3 Wellington Place, Captains Row, Lymington, Hampshire SO41 9RS (tel 07734 889987, e-mail bp@pobox.com)

PULLMAN, Philip; CBE (2004); s of Alfred Pullman (d 1953), and Audrey, *née* Merrifield (d 1990); *b* 19 October 1946; *Educ* Ysgol Ardudwy Harlech, Univ of Oxford (MA), Weymouth Coll of Educn (PGCE); *m* 1970, Judith; 2 s (James b 1971, Thomas b 1981); *Career* author; teacher middle sch Oxford 1972–86, pt/t sr lectr Westminster Coll Oxford 1986–96; Astrid Lindgren Memorial Award for Literature 2005; patron Centre for the Children's Book Newcastle upon Tyne; hon fell: Westminster Coll Oxford 1999, Univ of Wales Bangor 2003; Hon DLitt: Oxford Brookes Univ 2002, UEA 2003; Hon DUniv:

P

Surrey 2003, UCE 2003; Freeman City of London 2007; FRSL 2001; *Publications* incl: Galatea (novel, 1978); children's books: The Ruby in the Smoke (1985, Int Reading Assoc Children's Book Award 1988), The Firework-Maker's Daughter (1995, Smarties Gold Award 1996), Clockwork, or All Wound Up (1996, shortlisted for Whitbread Children's Book of the Year 1997, shortlisted for Carnegie Medal 1997); novels for teenagers: The White Mercedes (1992), Northern Lights (1995, Guardian Children's Fiction Award 1996, Carnegie Medal 1996, Br Book Awards Children's Book of theYear 1996), The Subtle Knife (1997), Mossycoat (1998), I Was a Rat! (1999), Puss in Boots (2000), The Amber Spyglass (2000, Br Book Awards Children's Book of the Year 2001, Whitbread Book of the Year 2001, His Dark Materials trilogy adapted for stage 2003), Lyra's Oxford (2003), The Scarecrow and his Servant (2004); plays: Frankenstein (1992), Puss in Boots (produced 1997); author various short stories and articles; *Recreations* drawing; *Style—* Philip Pullman, Esq, CBE, FRSL; ✉ c/o A P Watt Ltd, 20 John Street, London WC1N 2DR

PULVERMACHER, (Francis) Michael; s of Francis Howard Pulvermacher (d 1978), of Pentyrch, Glamorgan, and Marjorie Constance Denman, *née* Wheatley (d 2005); *b* 26 July 1938; *Educ* Framlingham, Univ of London (LLB, LLM); *m* 17 Sept 1966, Diana, da of Lt-Col James William Randall Penrose (d 1966), of Shernal Green, Worcs; 3 da (Joanna b 1968, Isobel b 1969, Helen b 1971), 1 s (Francis b 1975); *Career* admitted slr 1961; ptnr Alms and Young 1968–93, conslt Risdon Hosegood 1994–; hon sec Somerset Law Soc 1971–84; NP 1961; pres: Assoc of SW Law Socs 1977–78, Somerset Law Soc 1998–99, Notaries Soc 2003–05 (lectr 1983–, vice-pres 2001–03, memb Cncl); licensed reader Quantock Towers Benefice Bath & Wells Dio 2005; memb: Law Soc 1961, Lord Chllr's Legal Aid Advsy Ctee 1986–93, Bd of Mgmnt Nationwide Ind Slrs' Gp 1989–93, Notaries Qualification and Advsy Bd 1999–; vice-chm Exmoor Nat Park Access Forum 2003–06, tstee St James' Pool Taunton Charity; *Recreations* hill walking, sailing, bee keeping, campanology; *Style—* Michael Pulvermacher, Esq; ✉ 6 Higher Vexford, Lydeard Saint Lawrence, Taunton, Somerset TA4 3QF

PUNTER, Prof David Godfrey; s of Douglas Herbert Punter (d 1958), of London, and Hilda Mary, *née* Manning (d 1996); *b* 19 November 1949; *Educ* Fitzwilliam Coll Cambridge (MA, PhD); *m* 1 (m dis 1988), Jenny Jane, *née* Roberts; 1 s (Joshua Anthony Kemble b 22 June 1982), 1 da (Miranda Catherine Amani b 30 Dec 1982); m 2, Caroline Mary, *née* Case; 1 da (Isobel Maeve b 16 Dec 1988); *Career* lectr UEA 1973–84 (sr lectr 1984–86), prof and head of dept Chinese Univ of Hong Kong 1986–88, prof of English studies Univ of Stirling 1988–2000 (head of dept 1988–94 and 1996), currently prof of English and grad dean of arts Univ of Bristol; visiting prof Fudan Univ Shanghai 1983; dep dir ILEA courses on sixth-form practical criticism teaching 1978 and 1980, dir Devpt of Univ English Teaching Project (DUET) 1985–86, judge Br Cncl Creative Writing Award in English Hong Kong 1987, memb Bd of Advsy Eds Text and Context 1987–93; conslt: Sch of Humanities and Arts Hampshire Coll MA 1983, curriculum devpt Univ of Hamburg 1989; co-organiser American Vision, Visions of America: New Directions in Culture and Literature conf Hong Kong, memb Bd of Dirs Edinburgh Book Festival 1992–98, pres Br Assoc for Romantic Studies 1993–95, specialist subject assessor Quality Assessment Exercise HEFCE 1994–95, advsr Romanticism Section ESSE Conf Glasgow 1995, co-organiser Second Conf Int Gothic Assoc Glasgow 1995, vice-chm Scottish Ctee of Professors of English 1995–2000, specialist subject assessor and team ldr Quality Assessment Exercise SHEFC 1996–98; sec: Cncl for Univ English 1993–95, Cncl for Coll and Univ English 1994–95 (chm 1995–97); chm: Editorial Advsy Bd Gothic Studies 1995–, Exec Ctee Int Gothic Assoc 1995–; memb Editorial Bd: Stirling Edition of James Hogg 1991–94, Romanticism in Context 1995–, La Questione Romantica 1997–; memb of numerous academic ctees; fell Centre for European Romanticism Univ of Glasgow 1998–; DLitt Univ of Stirling 2000; FRSA 1998, FSA Scot 1999; *Books* The Literature of Terror: A History of Gothic Fictions from 1765 to the Present Day (1980, trans Italian 1985), Romanticism and Ideology: Studies in English Writing 1765–1830 (with David Aers and Jonathan Cook, 1981), Blake, Hegel and Dialectic (1982), The Hidden Script: Writing and Unconscious (1985), Introduction to Contemporary Cultural Studies (1986), William Blake: Selected Poetry and Prose (1988), The Romantic Unconscious: A Study in Narcissism and Patriarchy (1989), Notes on Selected Poems of Philip Larkin (1991, reprinted 1995), The Gothic Tradition: Vol I of The Literature of Terror (new edn, 1996), The Modern Gothic: Vol II of The Literature of Terror (new edn, 1996), William Blake: The New Casebook (ed, 1996), Romanticism: Vol 36 of Annotated Bibliography of English Studies (ed, 1997), Notes on William Blake's 'Songs of Innocence and Experience' (1998), Gothic Pathologies: The Text, the Body and the Law (1998), Spectral Readings (ed, 1999), Companion to the Gothic (ed, 1999), Writing the Passions (2000), Postcolonial Imaginings (2000); also author of 40 jl articles and 53 book chapters; *Poetry* China and Glass, Lost in the Supermarket, Asleep at the Wheel, Selected Short Stories; *Recreations* walking, throwing parties, travel; *Clubs* Oxford and Cambridge, Arts, Authors; *Style—* Prof David Punter; ✉ Department of English, University of Bristol, Bristol BS8 1TB (e-mail david.punter@bristol.ac.uk)

PURCELL, Michael Thomas; s of Thomas Bernard Purcell, and Edna Shelia, *née* Bache; *b* 26 November 1948, Birmingham; *Educ* Halesown Coll, Univ of Birmingham (LLB), Guildford Coll of Law; *m* 22 Sept 1979, Deborah Claire, *née* Lawrence; 2 s (Matthew John b 21 Aug 1982, Edward Thomas b 6 Feb 1986), 1 da (Claire Eleanor b 1 March 1990); *Career* admitted slr 1975, slr-advocate (Higher Courts) 2006; research asst to Dr John Pitcher New Coll Oxford 1973, asst slr Wallace Robinson & Morgan 1975, head Criminal Dept Derek T Prescott & Co 1978, fndr Purcell Parker & Co (formerly Michael T Purcell) 1979; memb: Birmingham Duty Slr Ctee 1990 (chm 1995), Appeals Ctee Legal Servs Cmmn 1998 (also memb Billing Appeals Ctee), Criminal Ctee Birmingham Law Soc 1999, Law Soc; church warden Hampton Arden Church 1985–95; friend: Royal Shakespeare Theatre, Birmingham Royal Ballet, Barber Inst of Fine Art Birmingham; *Recreations* collection of medieval manuscripts and bi-folum, chess, motor sport, theatre; *Style—* Michael Purcell, Esq; ✉ Hampton House, Bellemere Road, Hampton in Arden, Solihull, West Midlands B92 (tel 0121 236 9781, e-mail allistrue@btinternet.com); Purcell Parker, 204–206 Corporation Street, Birmingham B4 6QB

PURCELL, Roger Bernard Allan; s of Bernard George Purcell (d 1982), of Leatherhead, and Hazel Cecily, *née* Roseberry; *b* 27 April 1945; *Educ* Shrewsbury, Pembroke Coll Cambridge (MA); *Career* chartered accountant; Binder Hamlyn 1966–72, First Investors and Savers 1972–74, Save & Prosper Gp 1974–86, County Securities 1986–87, FSA (formerly Securities and Investments Bd) 1987–2002, chartered accountant in practice 2002–; FCA 1969; *Recreations* walking, choral singing; *Style—* Roger Purcell, Esq; ✉ 202 Old Brompton Road, London SW5 0BU (tel 020 7370 3028)

PURCHAS, Christopher Patrick Brooks; QC (1990); s of late The Rt Hon Sir Francis Purchas, and late Patricia Mona Kathleen, *née* Milburn; bro of Robin Purchas, QC, *qv*; *b* 20 June 1943; *Educ* Marlborough, Trinity Coll Cambridge; *m* 1, 7 Dec 1974 (m dis 1995), Bronwen Victoria Mary; 2 da (Léonie Melissa b 2 Aug 1978, Domino Octavia b 5 April 1983); m 2, 27 May 1998, Diana Hatrick, wid of Dr Ian Hatrick; *Career* called to the Bar Inner Temple 1966 (bencher 1995); recorder of the Crown Court 1986–, dep High Court judge 1999–; accredited ADR mediator 2004–; *Recreations* golf, tennis, shooting; *Style—* Christopher Purchas, Esq, QC; ✉ Crown Office Chambers, Temple, London EC4Y 7HJ (tel 020 7797 8100, fax 020 7797 8101, e-mail purchas@crownofficechambers.com)

PURCHAS, Robin Michael; QC (1987); s of late Rt Hon Sir Francis Purchas, and Patricia Mona Kathleen, *née* Milburn; bro of Christopher Purchas, QC, *qv*; *b* 12 June 1946; *Educ* Marlborough, Trinity Coll Cambridge (MA); *m* 3 Sept 1970, (Denise) Anne Kerr, da of Capt David Finlay, RN; 1 s (James Alexander Francis b 27 Sept 1973), 1 da (Charlotte Robin b 3 Nov 1975); *Career* called to the Bar Inner Temple 1968 (bencher 1996); recorder of the Crown Court 1989–, dep High Court judge 1994–; memb Bar Cncl 2000–02; *Recreations* tennis, golf, fishing, skiing, opera, theatre; *Clubs* Queen's, Lansdowne, Boodle's; *Style—* Robin Purchas, Esq, QC; ✉ Francis Taylor Building, Temple, London EC4Y 7BY (tel 020 7353 8415, fax 020 7353 7622)

PURCHASE, Kenneth; MP; s of late Albert Purchase, and late Rebecca Purchase; *b* 8 January 1939; *Educ* Springfield Secdy Modern, Wolverhampton Poly (BA); *m* 1960, Brenda, *née* Sanders; *Career* apprentice toolmaker foundry industry 1956–60, experimental component engr aerospace industry 1960–68, toolroom machinist British Leyland 1968–76, in Property Div Telford Devpt Corp 1977–80, housing mangr Housing Dept Walsall MBC 1981–82, business devpt advsr Black Country Devpt Agency 1982–92; MP (Lab, Co-op Pty sponsored) Wolverhampton NE 1992– (also contested 1987); PPS to Rt Hon Robin Cook, MP 1997–2003; memb: Trade and Industry Select Ctee 1995–97, Foreign Affrs Select Ctee 2005–; chm PLP Backbench Trade and Industry Ctee 1993–97; jt chm Commons Export Gp; cncllr: Wolverhampton Co BC 1970–74, Wolverhampton MBC 1973–90; memb: Wolverhampton DHA 1985–87 and 1988–90, Wolverhampton Community Health Cncl 1990–96, DSS Benefits Tbnl, Wolverhampton and Dist Manpower Bd; *Recreations* jazz; *Style—* Ken Purchase, Esq, MP; ✉ House of Commons, London SW1A 0AA (tel 020 7219 3602, fax 020 7219 2110); Constituency Office (tel 01902 397698, fax 01902 397538, e-mail ken.purchase@cwcom.net)

PURDIE, Prof David Wilkie; s of Robert Wilkie Purdie (d 1990), and Jean Wilson Purdie (d 2000); *b* 13 August 1946; *Educ* Ayr Acad, Univ of Glasgow (MB ChB); *m* 24 June 1983, Dr Katharine Ann, da of Maj Thomas Arklay Guthrie; 1 s (Arklay Robert Wilkie b 1984), 2 da (Catriona Jean Chalmers b 1986, Mhairi-Rose Wilson b 1988); *Career* ship's surgn SS Canberra P&O Lines Ltd London 1970–72, MRC res registrar Univ of Glasgow 1973–75, registrar Queen Mother's Hosp and Western Infirmary Glasgow 1975–78, lectr Univ of Dundee 1978–83, sr lectr Univ of Leeds 1983–89, prof and dir of postgrad med educn Univ of Hull 1989–94, hon conslt gynaecologist Royal Hull Hosps Tst 1989–2003, fndn dean Postgrad Med Sch Univ of Hull 1994–95, head of clinical res Centre for Metabolic Bone Disease Hull Royal Infirmary/Univ of Hull 1995–2003, conslt Edinburgh Osteoporosis Centre 2003–06; hon fell Sch of Clincal Sciences Univ of Edinburgh 2004–; chm Br Menopause Soc 1997–99, memb Scientific Advsy Gp Nat Osteoporosis Soc; author of scientific articles on osteoporosis, oestrogen, oestrogen receptor modulation, and related subjects; author and freelance journalist, articles in The Scotsman and Sunday Times, columnist Golf Int; memb Cncl: Saltire Soc, Old Edinburgh Club; chm Sir Walter Scott Soc 2007–, past pres Boswell Soc; MD (commendation) 1990; FSA Scot 1981, FRCOG 1988, FRCPEd 1997; *Recreations* classical rhetoric, golf, Scottish Enlightenment studies, life and works of Robert Burns; *Clubs* New (Edinburgh), Scottish Arts, Lord's Taverners, Sunningdale Golf, Pine Valley Golf (USA); *Style—* Prof David W Purdie; ✉ Duncan's Land, 4 India Place, Edinburgh EH3 6EH (tel 0131 225 1199, e-mail dwpurdie@ednet.co.uk)

PURDON, Maj-Gen Corran William Brooke; CBE (Mil 1970), MC (1945), CPM (1982); s of Maj-Gen (William) Brooke Purdon, DSO, OBE, MC, and Dorothy Myrtle, *née* Coates; *b* 4 May 1921; *Educ* Rokeby Sch Wimbledon, Campbell Coll Belfast, RMC Sandhurst; *m* 28 July 1945, (Maureen) Patricia, da of Maj James Francis Petrie (d 1952), and Betty, *née* Dundas (d 1984); 2 s (Patrick b 1947 d 2005, Timothy b 1949), 1 da (Angela (Mme Zerrouck) b 1959); *Career* cmmnd Royal Ulster Rifles 1939, Army Commandos, France and Germany 1940–45 (wounded, MC), Palestine Emergency 1945–46, Egypt 1949–51, Malayan Emergency 1956–58, Cyprus Emergency 1958; CO 1 Bn Royal Ulster Rifles, BAOR and Borneo Confrontation 1962–65, GSO1 and chief instr Sch of Inf Warminster 1965–67, Cdr Sultan's Armed Forces Sultanate of Oman and Dir of Ops Dhofar War 1967–70, Cmdt Sch of Inf Warminster 1970–72; GOC: NW Dist 1972–74, Near East Land Forces 1974–76, ret as Maj-Gen; dep cmmr Royal Hong Kong Police 1978–81; currently freelance mil advsr; dir: Falconstar Ltd (Mil Trg Teams) 1983–85, Defence Systems Ltd 1985–89; govr Royal Humane Soc 1984–2006, Hon Col Queen's Univ Belfast OTC 1975–78, pres Army Gymnastic Union 1973–76, patron Small Arms Sch Corps Old Comrades Assoc 1985–90; St John Ambulance: cdr Wiltshire 1981–83, memb Cncl 1981–86, pres Devizes Div 1993–99; Hon Col D Co (London Irish Rifles) The London Regt 1986–93; pres: London Irish Rifles Regtl Assoc 1993–, Royal Ulster Rifles Regtl Assoc 1993–; MIMgt; Bravery Medal (Oman) 1968, Distinguished Service Medal (Oman) 1969, Commendation Medal (Oman) 1970, Service Medal Order of St John 1999, Médaille d'Honneure de St Nazaire 2000; KStJ 1983; Chevalier Légion d'Honneur (France) 2005; Pingat Jasa Malaysia 2006; *Publications* List the Bugle - Reminiscences of an Irish Soldier (1993); *Recreations* physical fitness, writing, St Nazaire Soc, English bull terriers and German shepherd dogs; *Clubs* Army and Navy, Hong Kong; *Style—* Maj-Gen Corran Purdon, CBE, MC, CPM; ✉ Old Park House, Devizes, Wiltshire SN10 5JR (tel 01380 724876)

PURDUM, Richard Curtis; s of Rufus Purdum (d 1970), of Blawenberg, New Jersey, USA, and Mary Louise, *née* Reed (d 1970); *b* 26 February 1943; *Educ* Princeton HS Princeton New Jersey, Chouinard Art Inst Los Angeles; *m* 6 Dec 1976, Jill, da of Ralph Thomas; *Career* served US Navy 1965–69; MGM Animation/Chuck Jones Enterprises 1965, dir and animator Richard Williams Animation London 1969–79, fndr Richard Purdum Productions 1980 (studio produces traditional character animation primarily for advertising and title sequences); awards for animated commercials incl: Grand Prix Cinema 24 Int Advertising Festival 1977, Clio Award for Craftsmanship in Animation 1977, Gold award Int Film and TV Festival of New York 1984, Br Animation Awards for best design in animation and best advertising concept in animation 1988, Br Animation Award best animated commercial 1990; *Recreations* cats; *Style—* Richard Purdum, Esq; ✉ Richard Purdum Productions, Kings Court, 2–16 Goodge Street, London W1P 1FF (tel 020 7636 5162, fax 020 7436 5628)

PURDY, Dr Martin Terence; s of Gordon Purdy, OBE (d 1976), and Margaret Mary Purdy (d 1950); *b* 22 February 1939; *Educ* Oakham Sch, Lancing, Poly of Central London, Univ of York (MA), Univ of Birmingham (PhD); *Career* ptnr APEC Architects 1969–; formerly teaching and res positions at Birmingham Sch of Architecture and Aston Univ; foremost designs incl: Community Resources Centre Sheffield Cathedral, Ecumenical Centre Skelmersdale, St Bartholomew's Church and Centre East Ham, Froud Centre Manor Park; currently architect to: Sheffield Cathedral, Birmingham Parish Church; memb RIBA; *Publications* Housing on Sloping Sites (with Barry Simpson, 1984), Churches and Chapels - a design and development guide (1991), author of numerous articles on church architecture; *Style—* Dr Martin Purdy; ✉ APEC Architects, 413 The Custard Factory, Gibb Street, Digbeth, Birmingham B9 4AA (tel 0121 683 7771, fax 0121 683 7779)

PURDY, District Judge; Quentin Alexander Purdy; s of Gordon Purdy, OBE, FRCS (d 1976), and Margaret Dorothy Annie, *née* Stokes; *b* 23 August 1960; *Educ* Gresham's, Leicester Poly (BA), UCL (LLM), Inns of Court Sch of Law (Bar exams); *m* 3 Sept 1988, Elizabeth Audrey, da of William Alfred Hazelwood, of Paddock Wood, Kent; 2 da (Anna Elizabeth b 10 Oct 1992, Helen Sophie b 4 Oct 1994); *Career* called to the Bar Gray's Inn 1983 (A Band Tst Award); practising in Common Law Chambers London and on SE Circuit, cmmr for oaths; actg metropolitan stipendary magistrate 1998–2000, dep dist judge 2000–03, dist judge (Magistrates' Courts) 2003–; memb Cwlth Magistrates' and Judges' Assoc; deacon Dormansland Baptist Church 2001–; *Recreations* reading, foreign travel, walking, sailing, dog walking, cycling; *Style*— District Judge Purdy; ✉ City of Westminster Magistrates' Court, 70 Horseferry Road, London SW1P 2AX

PURI, Om; s of Tek Chand Puri (d 1990), and Tara Devi Puri (d 1967); *b* 18 October 1950; *Educ* Khalsa Coll Patiala India, Nat Sch of Drama Delhi (Dip), Film and TV Inst Pune India (Dip); *m* 1 May 1993, Nandita Chaudhuri; 1 s (Ishaan b 2 July 1997); *Career* actor; teacher of movement and speech Actor's Studio Mumbai 1977; *Television* incl: Sadgati (Deliverance) 1982, White Teeth 2002, Second Generation 2003, The Sea Captain's Tale (for the BBC's adaptation of Chaucer's Canterbury Tales) 2003; *Films* incl: City of Joy 1991, Wolf 1993, My Son the Fanatic 1997, East is East 1998, The Parole Officer 2000, Dev 2004, Lakshya 2004; *Awards* Nat Award India 1982 and 1984, Soviet Land Nehru Award USSR 1987, Padmashree India 1990; *Recreations* gardening, travel, reading; *Style*— Om Puri, Esq; ✉ c/o Conway Van Gelder Ltd, 3rd Floor, 18–21 Jermyn Street, London SW1Y 6HP (tel 020 7287 0077, fax 020 7494 3324)

PURKIS, Dr Andrew James; OBE (2002); s of Clifford Henry Purkis, OBE (d 1994), of Trevone, N Cornwall, and Mildred Jeannie, *née* Crane (d 1993); *b* 24 January 1949; *Educ* Highgate Sch, CCC Oxford (BA), St Antonys Coll Oxford (DPhil); *m* 18 July 1980, Jennifer Harwood, da of Francis Harwood Smith, of Willaston, Cheshire; 1 da (Joanna b 1980), 1 s (Henry b 1982); *Career* princ NI Office 1977–80 (admin trainee 1973–76, private sec 1976– 1977), asst dir Nat Cncl for Voluntary Orgns 1986–87 (head of policy analysis 1980–84, head of policy planning 1984–86); dir Cncl for the Protection of Rural England 1987–91, public affrs sec to the Archbishop of Canterbury 1992–98, chief exec Diana Princess of Wales Memorial Fund 1998–2005, chief exec Tropical Health and Educn Tst 2005–; chair Empty Homes Agency 2004–. chm Pedestrians Assoc, dir Green Alliance; FRSA 1989; *Books* Housing and Community Care (jtly, 1982), Health in the Round (jtly, 1984); *Recreations* walking, birdwatching, surf riding, travel, theatre, music; *Style*— Dr Andrew Purkis, OBE; ✉ 38 Endlesham Road, Balham, London SW12 8JL (tel 020 8675 2439); Tropical Health and Education Trust (tel 020 7679 8207)

PURLE, His Hon Judge Charles Lambert; QC (1989); s of Robert Herbert Purle (d 1982), and Doreen Florence, *née* Button; *b* 9 February 1947; *Educ* King Edward VI GS Retford, Univ of Nottingham (LLB), Worcester Coll Oxford (BCL); *m* 1, 1969 (m dis 1990), Lorna Barbara, da of Roy Sinclair Brown; 1 da (Sally b 12 Sept 1972), 1 s (William b 5 March 1977); m 2, 1991, Virginia Dabney Hopkins, da of Charles Peter Rylatt; 2 s (Charles Carter Lee b 19 June 1992, Harry George Hopkins b 13 Sept 1993), 2 da (Nancy Elizabeth Lambert b 5 Oct 1995, Helena Mary Rose b 22 Sept 1997); *Career* called to the Bar Gray's Inn 1970, in practice 1974–2007, specialist chancery circuit judge Birmingham Civil Justice Centre 2007–; *Recreations* opera, music, my children, horse racing; *Style*— His Hon Judge Purle, QC; ✉ Birmingham Civil Justice Centre, 33 Bull Street, Birmingham B4 6DS

PURNELL, Rt Hon James; PC (2007), MP; s of John Purnell, and Janet Purnell; *b* 2 March 1970, London; *Educ* Balliol Coll Oxford (BA); *Career* researcher to Rt Hon Tony Blair, *qv*, 1989–92, strategy conslt Hydra Assocs 1992–94, research fell IPPR 1994–95, head of corp planning BBC 1995–97, special advsr to Rt Hon Tony Blair 1997–2001, MP (Lab) Stalybridge and Hyde 2001–, PPS to Ruth Kelly, MP, *qv*, as fin sec to HM Treasy; memb Work and Pensions Select Ctee House of Commons 2001–03, min for broadcasting and tourism 2005–06, min of state Dept for Work and Pensions 2006–07, sec of state for Culture, Media and Sport 2007–; former cncllr London Borough of Islington (chair Early Years Ctee, chair Housing Ctee); *Recreations* football, films, theatre, music; *Clubs* Stalybridge Labour; *Style*— The Rt Hon James Purnell, MP; ✉ House of Commons, London SW1A 0AA

PURNELL, Nicholas Robert; QC (1985); *b* 29 January 1944; *Educ* Oratory Sch, King's Coll Cambridge (open exhibitioner, MA); *Career* called to the Bar Middle Temple 1968 (bencher 1990); practising barr specialising in commercial fraud cases, currently head Cloth Fair Chambers; recorder 1986–; jr counsel to Inland Revenue 1977–79, jr Treasy counsel 1979–85; memb: Gen Bar Cncl 1974–92, Lord Chllr's Advsy Ctee on Legal Educn and Conduct 1991–97, Criminal Ctee Judicial Studies Bd; chm Criminal Bar Assoc 1990–91; govr Oratory Sch; fell Soc of Advanced Legal Studies, FICPD; *Style*— Nicholas Purnell, Esq, QC; ✉ Cloth Fair Chambers, 39–40 Cloth Fair, London EC1A 7NR

PURNELL, Paul Oliver; QC (1982); s of Oliver Cuthbert Purnell (d 1948), and Pauline Purnell; *b* 13 July 1936; *Educ* Oratory Sch, Jesus Coll Oxford (MA); *m* 1966, Celia Consuelo Ocampo; 3 c (Elizabeth b 1968, Richard b 1971, Catherine b 1974); *Career* called to the Bar Inner Temple 1963 (bencher 1992), treasy counsel Central Criminal Court 1976–82, recorder 1984–; *Recreations* motorcycles, gardening; *Clubs* Cavalry, Hurlingham; *Style*— Paul Purnell, Esq, QC

PURSLOW, Christopher George (Chris); s of George Ellis Purslow (d 1985), and Lillian Rose, *née* Embrey; *b* 27 March 1946; *Educ* The High Sch Newcastle under Lyme, Univ of Bristol (BA, BArch); *m* 12 Aug 1970 (m dis 1977), (Sally) Louise, da of Dr Carl Basch, of South Orange, New Jersey; *Career* architect; Courtaulds Ltd Coventry 1967–68, Tarmac Ltd Wolverhampton 1968–69, Philip Johnson (Architect) NY 1969–72, Rice/Roberts (Architects) London 1972–74, London Borough of Islington 1974–88 (borough architect 1983–88), dir of architecture Glasgow 1988–96, dir Glasgow Print Studio, dir Architects in Housing; RIBA, RIAS; *Recreations* theatre, music, architecture, skiing and making waves; *Style*— Chris Purslow, Esq; ✉ Rosslyn House, 1a Victoria Circus, Glasgow G12 9LH (tel 0141 334 8162); Kilmory Ross, Tayvallich, Argyll PA31 8PQ (e-mail chrispurslow@macunlimited.net)

PURTON, Peter John; OBE (2000); *b* 18 July 1933; *Educ* Aldwickbury, Aldenham; *m* 6 Sept 1958, Mary, *née* Fone, of Chipperfield, Herts; 1 da (Catherine b 1960), 2 s (William b 1962, Thomas b 1965); *Career* 3 Regt RHA 1951–53, 290 (City of London) Field Regt RATA 1953–60; admitted slr 1958; Norton Rose 1953–94; memb Cncl Law Soc 1969–86, dep pres Family Welfare Assoc 1990– (chm 1983–90); memb Bd of Govrs Aldenham Sch 1981–94; chm Wine Standards Bd of Vinters Co 1993–99; Master: Worshipful Co of Slrs 1983–84, Worshipful Co of Tallow Chandlers 2002–03; memb Anglo-American Real Property Inst; FRSA, LMRTPI; *Books* The Organisation and Management of a Solicitors Practice (gen ed, 1979), Butterworths Planning Law and Practice (jt gen ed, 1990), Cordery on Solicitors (conslt ed, 1995); *Recreations* swimming, shooting, stalking, walking, heritage, jigsaw puzzles and family; *Clubs* Union Soc of Westminster; *Style*— Peter Purton, Esq, OBE; ✉ Park Farmhouse, Sandford St Martin, Chipping Norton, Oxfordshire OX7 7AH (tel 01608 683652, fax 01608 683173, e-mail purton@tiscali.co.uk)

PURVES, Elizabeth Mary (Libby); OBE (1999); da of James Grant Purves, CMG (d 1984), of Suffolk, and Mary, *née* Tinsley; *b* 2 February 1950; *Educ* Sacred Heart Tunbridge Wells, St Anne's Coll Oxford; *m* 1980, Paul Heiney, the broadcaster, s of Norbert Wisniewski (d 1970), of Sheffield; 1 s (Nicholas b 1982 d 2006), 1 da (Rose b 1984); *Career* journalist and broadcaster; presenter: Radio 4 Today, Midweek, The Learning Curve; radio documentaries incl: Street Gospel, Holy Bones, Mysterious Ways; tstee Nat Maritime Museum 1996–; *Books* Britain at Play (1982), Adventures Under Sail (1982), Sailing Weekend Book (with Paul Heiney, 1985), How Not To Be A Perfect Mother (1986), One Summer's Grace (1989), How Not to Raise a Perfect Child (1991), How Not To Be The Perfect Family (1994), Holy Smoke (1998), Radio (2002); Novels: Casting Off (1995), A Long Walk in Wintertime (1996), Home Leave (1997), More Lives Than One (1998), Regatta (1999), Passing Go (2000), A Free Woman (2001), Mother Country (2002), Radio: A True Love Story (2002), Continental Drift (2003), Acting Up (2004), Love Songs and Lies (2006); *Recreations* yachting, walking, writing; *Clubs* Ocean Cruising, Royal Cruising; *Style*— Ms Libby Purves, OBE; ✉ c/o David Miller, RCW, 20 Powis Mews, London W11 1JN

PURVES, (Andrew) Geoffrey; s of Maj Andrew Purves (d 1967), of High Heaton, Newcastle upon Tyne, and Blanche, *née* Lawson; *b* 12 June 1944; *Educ* Heaton GS, Univ of Durham (BA), Univ of Newcastle upon Tyne (BArch); *m* 12 Oct 1968, (Elizabeth) Ann, da of James Campbell Finlay, of Newcastle upon Tyne; *Career* chartered architect; sr ptnr Geoffrey Purves Partnership (multi-disciplinary practice: architecture, planning, project mgmnt, econ and devpt consultancy, planning supervision) 1977–2003, dir Purves Ash LLP 2003, dir Purves Ash Mgmnt Services Ltd 2004; dir: Newcastle Arch Workshop Ltd 1985–98, RIBA Enterprises Ltd 1996–2002, Saunders and Purves Ltd, Purves Ltd, Clayton Development Ltd, Br Architectural Library Property Tst; chm Northern Architecture Centre 1995–98; lectr (pt/t design tutor) Dept of Architecture Univ of Newcastle upon Tyne 1983–84, visiting research fell Centre for Arts and Humanities in Health and Med Univ of Durham 2001; RIBA: chm Northumbria Branch 1981–83, chm Northern Region 1988–89, memb Nat Cncl 1991–97, hon treas 1995–97; memb: English Partnership Northern Regnl Design Panel 1994–98, Architects Registration Bd Investigation Panel; memb Cncl ARCUK 1991–97; tstee Br Architectural Library Tst 1995–97; Architects Benevolent Soc: memb Cncl 2000, hon treas 2002–; memb Ctee CIArb (Northumbria Branch) 2000–04; professional advsr Millennium Cmmn 1997–2002; chm Newcastle Diocesan Advsy Ctee 2000, govr Heaton Manor Sch 2001–03; Freeman City of London 1992, memb Worshipful Co of Chartered Architects 1992 (memb Ct of Assts 1999); RIBA, FRIAS, FRSA, MCIArb, MAE, FInstD; *Publications* Healthy Living Centres (2002), Churches of Newcastle and Northumberland (2006); author of various articles in professional and tech jls; *Recreations* sailing, flying; *Clubs* Athenaeum, Clyde Cruising, Royal Northumberland Yacht, Northern Counties; *Style*— Geoffrey Purves, Esq; ✉ Hawthorn House, Kirkwhelpington, Northumberland NE19 2RT (tel 01830 540376, fax 01830 540377, e-mail a.g.purves@btinternet.com); Purves Ash LLP, 8 North Terrace, Newcastle upon Tyne NE2 4AD (tel 0191 232 0424, fax 0191 244 6400, e-mail geoffrey.purves@purvesash.com, website www.purvesash.com)

PURVES, Peter John; s of (John) Kenneth Purves (d 1987), of Preston, Lancs, and Florence, *née* Patton (d 1976); *b* 10 February 1939; *Educ* Arnold Sch Blackpool, Alsager Teachers Training Coll (DipEd); *m* 1, 29 Sept 1962 (m dis 1981), Gillian Diane Emmett; 1 s (Matthew b 1963), 1 adopted da (Lisa b 1963); m 2, 5 Feb 1982, Kathryn Lesley Evans; *Career* producer, writer, director, actor and presenter; began in repertory theatre Barrow in Furness 1961–63, London Theatre and TV 1963–65; md Purves Wickes Video Projects Ltd 1984–; specialist presenters trainer BBC Elstree 1993–, princ tutor London Acad of Radio, Film and TV 2004; pres: Rugby Animal Tst, Radio Nene Valley 1996, Canine Supporters Charity 1997–; memb bd New Wolsey Theatre Company Ipswich 2000–, princ Expertise (speaker/presentation consult), vice-patron Dog for the Disabled; *Theatre* incl: various pantomimes 1978–, Once in a Lifetime (Blackpool) 1981, prodr Bobby Davro's Not in Front of the Children 1993; *Television* BBC incl: Dr Who 1965–66, Blue Peter 1967–78, Special Assignments 1976–79, Crufts Dog Show 1976–, We're Going Places 1978–80, Stopwatch 1978–81, Kickstart 1978–92, darts presenter 1979–84, Ten Glorious Years 1989, Superdogs 1990–93, Crimewatch Midlands 1989–91, Blue Peter Theme Night 1998, The Office 2001, Fun at the Funeral Parlour 2001, Children in Need 2001, This is Dom Jolly 2003, The Way We Travelled 2003, Britain on the Box 2003, Inside Out 2003; other credits incl: Makers (HTV) 1983–84, Work Out (HTV) 1985, Babble (Channel 4) 1985–87, Pets Go Public (Channel 5) 1998–, Breed All About It (Discovery Channel) 1998–, Wild At Heart (Anglia) 2002, Kitchen Confidential (Anglia) 2002, The All New Harry Hill Show (ITV) 2003, RI:SE (C4) 2003, Pet Rescue (C4) 2003, The Doctor Who Story (BBC) 2004, TV's Greatest Moments (Five) 2004, The Evel Knievel Story (Five) 2004; *Radio* presenter BBC Radio Northampton 1995–97; narrator BBC audio CD: Dr Who - The Massacre, Dr Who - The Myth Makers, Dr Who - The Celestrial Toymaker, Dr Who - The Dalek Masterplan, Dr Who - The Savages; official commentator: The Royal Show Stoneleigh 1993–2004, The Royal Bath and West of England Show Shepton Mallet 1997–2004, The Great Yorkshire Show Harrogate 2000, All About Dogs Brentwood 2001–03; *Publications* Tess, The Story of a Guide Dog (1980); ed Peter Purves' Mad About Dogs (monthly, 1997–99); *Clubs* Vaudeville Golf Soc, Seckford Golf; *Style*— Peter Purves, Esq; ✉ c/o Wendy Downes, Downes Presenters, 96 Broadway, Bexleyheath, Kent DA6 7DE (tel 020 8304 0541, fax 020 8301 5591); personal e-mail (peter.purves@btinternet.com)

PURVES, Thomas Finlayson Grant (Tom); s of Thomas Finlayson Purves (d 1968), and Christine Home Grant (d 1983); *b* 25 November 1948; *Educ* Daniel Stewart's Coll Edinburgh; *m* 10 July 1976, Hilde, da of Ornulf Boye Hansen, of Oslo, Norway; 1 s (Thomas Alexander), 1 da (Christina Ragnhild); *Career* Rolls Royce: student engrg apprentice (Car Div Crewe) 1967–70, various positions Rolls Royce Motors at home and later export sales, joined Euro Distribution Office Lausanne 1979, Kuwait Office 1979 (area mangr ME and Africa), returned to Lausanne 1981 (sales mangr Europe, ME and Africa), returned to UK as dir sales ops 1983; md BMW (GB) Ltd 1990–96 (joined as sales dir UK 1985), md Sales and Mktg Rover Group Ltd 1996–99, chm and ceo BMW (US) Holding Corp 1999–; *Recreations* golf, music, family, motorcycling; *Clubs* RAC, Ridgewood Country; *Style*— Tom Purves, Esq; ✉ BMW (US) Holding Corp, 300 Chestnut Ridge Road, Woodcliff Lake, New Jersey 07677, USA (tel 201 307 3500, fax 201 307 3515, e-mail tom.purves@bmwna.com)

PURVES, Sir William; kt (1993), CBE (1988), DSO (1951); s of Andrew Purves (d 1945), and Ida Purves (d 1996); *b* 27 December 1931; *Educ* Kelso HS; *m* 1958 (m dis 1988), Diana Troutbeck, da of Nicholas Gosselin Pepp Richardson (d 1944); 2 s, 2 da; m 2, 9 Feb 1989, Rebecca Jane, *née* Lewellen; *Career* served Cwlth Division Korea; formerly with National Bank of Scotland (now Royal Bank of Scotland); Hongkong and Shanghai Bank: early appts Japan (mangr) and Hong Kong (chief accountant), gen mangr international 1979–82, exec dir Banking 1982–84, dep chm 1984–86, dep chm and chief exec 1986, chm The Hongkong and Shanghai Banking Corporation Ltd 1986–92, chm HSBC Holdings plc 1990–98 (concurrently chief exec 1990–92), chm Midland Bank plc 1993–98 (dir 1987–93); chm The British Bank of the Middle East 1979–98, dir Marine Midland Bank 1979–98; chm Hakluyt & Co Ltd 1999–; dep chm: Alstom SA 1998–2003, Aquarius Platinum 2004–; non-exec dir: Shell Transport and Trading Co plc 1993–2002, East Asiatic Company Ltd A/S 1995–99, Reuters Founders Share Company Ltd 1998–2007, Trident Safeguards 1999–2003, Scottish Medicine 1999–2003; memb: Int Cncl Textron Inc 1998–2002, Hong Kong Chief Exec's Cncl of Int Advsrs 1998–2002; pres Int Monetary Conf Toronto 1992; memb Gen Ctee Scottish Rugby Union 1997–99; Master Guild of Int Bankers 2004–05; Hon DUniv: Stirling, Sheffield, Strathclyde, Nottingham, Napier, Hong Kong; Dr (hc): Hong Kong Open, UMIST; FCIB, FCIB (Scotland); Grand Bauhina Medal (Hong Kong) 2001; *Recreations* golf; *Clubs* Hong Kong, Hong Kong Jockey (hon steward), Hong Kong Golf, Caledonian (London), RAC; *Style*— Sir William Purves, CBE, DSO; ✉ 100 Ebury Mews, London SW1W 9NX (tel 020 7823 6775, fax 020 7824 8351)

PURVIS, Christopher Thomas Bremner; CBE (2002); s of Dr Victor Bremner Purvis (d 1995), and Joanna Isabel, *née* Gibbs (d 1995); *b* 15 April 1951; *Educ* Bradfield Coll, Keble Coll Oxford (MA); *m* 21 June 1986, Phillida Anne, *née* Seaward; 3 da (Kerensa Toura Isabel b 26 March 1988, Xenobe Eva Wendela b 8 March 1990, Eila Blanche Honor b 27 Aug 1993), 1 s (Lucian Annesley Bremner b 31 May 1992); *Career* UBS Investment Bank (and predecessor firms): joined S G Warburg & Co Ltd 1974, dir Warburg Investment Management International Ltd 1980, dir S G Warburg & Co Ltd 1983, mangr Tokyo office 1982–87 and 1989–92, md SBC Warburg 1995–97, advsr SBC Warburg (now UBS Investment Bank) 1997–; dir: F&C Pacific Investment Tst plc (now Witan Pacific Investment Tst plc) 1997–2006 (chm 2000–06), Fleming Japanese Smaller Companies Investment Tst plc 2000–03, Martin Currie Japan Investment Tst plc 2001–05, Japan 21 2002–, Tribune UK Tracker Tst plc 2004–, IntoUniversity 2006–; chief exec Japan 2001 Ltd 1999–2003; memb Ctee Tokyo Stock Exchange Membership 1990–92; pres Handel House Tst Ltd (chm and project dir 1997–2007); chm: The Acad of Ancient Music 2000–, Japan Arena 2004–, Japan Soc 2006–; tstee: Sir Siegmund Warburg's Vol Sett 1997–, J Paul Getty Jr Charitable Tst 2004–, Winston Churchill Meml Tst 2007–; govr Royal Acad of Music 2004–07; *Recreations* music, wine, reading; *Style*— Christopher Purvis, Esq, CBE; ✉ 19 Norland Square, London W11 4PU (tel 020 7221 6985, e-mail christopher@purvis.co.uk)

PURVIS, Jeremy; MSP; s of George Purvis, of Berwick-upon-Tweed, and Eileen Purvis; *b* 15 January 1974, Berwick-upon-Tweed; *Educ* Berwick-upon-Tweed HS, Brunel Univ (BSc); *Career* research asst to Rt Hon Sir David Steel, KBE, PC, DL (now Baron Steel of Aikwood (Life Peer)), *qv* 1993, Parly asst Liberal Int 1994, Parly asst ELDR (European Lib Dem and Reform Pty) Gp European Parliament 1995, PA to Rt Hon Lord Steel of Aikwood, KBE, PC, DL 1996–98, with GJW Scotland (Parly affrs co) 1998–2001, dir McEwan Purvis (strategic communications consultancy) 2001–03, MSP (Lib Dem) Tweeddale, Ettrick and Lauderdale 2003–; Lib Dem finance spokesman 2003–05, Lib Dem justice and home affrs spokesman 2005–; *Style*— Jeremy Purvis, Esq, MSP; ✉ The Scottish Parliament, Edinburgh EH99 1SP (tel 0131 348 5801, fax 0131 348 6488, e-mail jeremy.purvis.msp@scottish.parliament.uk, website www.jeremypurvis.org)

PURVIS, John Robert; CBE (1990), MEP (Cons) Scotland; s of Lt-Col Robert William Berry Purvis, MC; *b* 6 July 1938; *Educ* Cargilfield Barnton Edinburgh, Glenalmond Coll, St Salvator's Coll, Univ of St Andrews; *m* 1962, Louise S Durham; 1 s, 2 da; *Career* md Gilmerton Mgmnt Servs Ltd 1973–92, managing ptnr Purvis & Co 1986–; dir: James River (UK) Holdings Ltd 1988–95, Edgar Astaire & Co Ltd 1993–94, Jamont NV 1994–95, European Utilities Trust plc 1994–, Crown Vantage Ltd 1995–2001, Curtis Fine Papers Ltd 1995–2001; chm: Kingdom FM Radio Ltd 1997–, Belgrave Capital Mgmnt Ltd 1999–; MEP (EDG) Mid Scotland and Fife 1979–84, MEP (EPP/ED Cons) Scotland 1999–; vice-chm Economic and Monetary Affairs Ctee 2002–; memb: Scottish Landowners' Fedn Taxation Ctee 1978–99, IBA London (chm for Scotland) 1985–89, Scottish Advsy Ctee on Telecommunications 1990–97; chm SCUA Econ Ctee 1986–97, vice-pres Scottish Cons & Unionist Assoc 1987–89; FInstD; *Clubs* Cavalry and Guards', Farmers', New (Edinburgh), Royal and Ancient (St Andrews); *Style*— John Purvis, Esq, CBE, MEP; ✉ PO Box 29222, St Andrews, Fife KY16 8WL (tel 01334 475830, fax 01334 477754, e-mail purvisco@jpurvis.co.uk or jpurvis@europarl.eu.int)

PURVIS, (Prof) Stewart Peter; CBE (1999); s of Peter Purvis (d 1998), and Lydia, *née* Stewart (d 1997); *b* 28 October 1947; *Educ* Dulwich Coll, Univ of Exeter (BA); *m* 2 Sept 1972 (m dis 1993), Mary, da of Arthur Presnail; 1 da (Helen b 1974); partner, Jacqui Marson; 1 s (Tom b 1994), 1 da (Jess b 1999); *Career* formerly presenter Harlech TV, news trainee BBC 1969; ITN: journalist 1972, prog ed News at Ten 1980–83, ed Channel Four News 1983, dep ed 1983–89, ed 1989–91, ed-in-chief 1991–95, chief exec 1995–2003; prof of TV journalism City Univ London 2003–; former pres EuroNews; dir Royal Marsden NHS Tst 1999–, former dep chm Kings Cross Partnership; RTS awards for: The Pope in Poland 1979, Return of the Canberra 1982; Broadcasting Press Guild Award for Best News or Current Events Prog (Channel Four News) 1984, BAFTA award for Best News or Outside Broadcast (Channel Four News) 1987 and 1988; FRTS; *Style*— Stewart Purvis, Esq, CBE

PUSINELLI, David Charles; s of Lt-Col Charles Cecil Lennox Pusinelli (d 1996), and Margaret, *née* Smith; *b* 4 September 1956, Barnard Castle, Co Durham; *Educ* Bradfield Coll Berks, BNC Oxford (open scholar, BA); *m* 17 April 1995, Frances Evelyn, *née* van der Byl; 1 s (Piers John Lennox b 15 May 1997), 1 da (Tara Frances b 3 Sept 1999); *Career* CA 1980; Coopers & Lybrand 1977–86 (sr mangr 1984–86), dir Close Brothers Corporate Finance 1986–2002, dir corporate devpt Close Brothers Gp plc 2002–; *Recreations* skiing; *Style*— David Pusinelli, Esq; ✉ Close Brothers Group plc, 10 Crown Place, London EC2A 4FT (tel 020 7655 3379, fax 020 7247 1203)

PUTROV, Ivan; s of Oleksandr Ivanovich Putrov, of Kyiv, Ukraine, and Natalia Vasilievna Berezina; *b* 8 March 1980, Kyiv, Ukraine; *Educ* Kyiv State Choreographic Inst 1990–97, Royal Ballet Sch 1997–98; *Career* ballet dancer; Royal Ballet: joined 1998, princ dancer 2002– (currently Royal Ballet's youngest male princ); memb jury Serge Lifar Int Ballet Competition 2004; collaborated with many artists incl Jay Joplin, *qv*, Mario Testino, The Pet Shop Boys, Johnnie Shand Kydd, Mary Macartney Donald and Sam Taylor-Wood, *qv* (incl Strings); *Performances* with Royal Ballet incl: Albrecht in Giselle, Basilio in Don Quixote, Solor in La Bayadère, Boy with Matted Hair in Shadowplay, Prince Siegfried in Swan Lake, Jean de Brienne in Raymonda, Lensky in Onegin, Prince Desire in Sleeping Beauty, Franz in Coppélia, Prince and Hans-Peter in The Nutcracker (televised BBC), Le Spectre de la Rose, lead in Symphony in C, lead in The Four Temperaments, title role in The Prodigal Son, lead in Scènes de ballet, Beliaev in A Month in the Country, Prince Florimund in Awakening pas de deux (performed for 101st birthday of HRH the late Queen Elizabeth the Queen Mother); lead roles with ballet cos of nat theatres of Hungary and Ukraine incl: La Sylphide (broadcast to 85 countries on World Service), Le Spectre de la rose, Giselle, Carmen, Onegin; *Awards* Premier Prix Prix de Lausanne 1996, Gold Medal Serge Lifar Int Ballet Competition 1996, Gold Medal Nijinsky Festival 2001, Outstanding Young Male Dancer Critics' Circle Dance Awards 2002, Medal for Work and Achievement (awarded by pres of Ukraine) 2004; *Style*— Ivan Putrov, Esq; ✉ The Royal Ballet, Royal Opera House, Covent Garden, London WC2E 9DD (tel 020 7212 9165, e-mail janine.limberg@roh.org.uk)

PUTTERGILL, Graham Fraser; s of Henry William Puttergill (d 1984), of Gonubie, South Africa, and Elizabeth Blanche, *née* McClelland (d 1991); *b* 20 March 1949; *Educ* St Patrick's Coll Port Elizabeth; *m* 7 Aug 1976, Susan Jennifer, da of Victor James Wilkinson, of Dorchester, Dorset; 2 s (Miles b 1982, David b 1987), 2 da (Robyn b 1985, Lucy b 1989); *Career* 1 Lt Cape Town Highlanders 1967–68; chm HSBC Benefit Consultants Ltd 1982–2000 (md 1977–82), exec chm HSBC Insurance Brokers Ltd 1985–2000, dep chm HSBC Insurance Holdings Ltd 1993–2000; vice-chm and ceo Premium Credit Ltd 2004–05 (chm 2000–04); chm of govrs Caldicott Sch 2004– (govr 2000–); ACII 1973, FPMI 1983; *Recreations* family, golf, tennis; *Clubs* City, Beaconsfield Golf, Pearl Valley; *Style*— Graham Puttergill, Esq; ✉ The Redwood, Long Grove, Seer Green, Buckinghamshire HP9 2QH (e-mail graham.puttergill@pcl.co.uk)

PUTTNAM, Baron (Life Peer UK 1997), of Queensgate in the Royal Borough of Kensington and Chelsea; Sir David Terence Puttnam; kt (1995), CBE (1983); s of Capt Leonard Arthur Puttnam, RA (d 1981), of Winchmore Hill, and Marie Beatrice, *née* Goldman; *b* 25 February 1941; *Educ* Minchenden GS London; *m* 22 Sept 1961, Patricia Mary, da of Maj John Frederick Jones, of Folkestone, Kent; 1 s (Hon Alexander David b 5 April 1966), 1 da (Hon Deborah Jane (m Loyd Grossman, *qv*) b 25 Jan 1962); *Career* film prodr; chm Enigma Productions Ltd 1978–, chm and ceo Columbia Pictures 1986–88; chm: Nat Film & TV Sch Ltd 1987–96, Nat Endowment for Science, Technology and the Arts (NESTA) 1998–2003, General Teaching Cncl 2000–02, Nat Museum of Photography Film and Television; dep chm Channel 4 2006–; dir: Anglia TV Group plc, Chrysalis Group until 1996; dep chm Channel 4 2006–; pres Cncl for Protection of Rural England 1985–92; advsr Dept of Educn and Skills 1997–; memb Educn Standards Task Force 1997–2001; chair of tstees Nat Teaching Awards 1998–; pres UNICEF UK 2002–; tstee: Tate Gallery 1985–92, Landscape Fndn, Science Museum, Royal Acad of Arts; vice-pres BAFTA 1994–2004; govr LSE 1997–2002; chllr: Univ of Sunderland 1997–, OU 2007–; Hon LLD Bristol 1983, Hon LittD Leeds 1992; Hon DLitt: Leicester 1986, Univ of Bradford 1993, Humberside 1996, Sunderland 1996, Univ of Westminster 1997, Univ of Kent at Canterbury 1998; Hon DMus RSAMD 1998; hon fell: Univ of Manchester, Cheltenham and Gloucester Coll of HE 1998, London Guildhall Univ 1999, Imperial Coll London 1999; visiting prof Film Dept Univ of Bristol 1985–98; fell BAFTA 2006; FRGS, FRSA, FRPS, FCGI 1999; Chevalier de l'Ordre des Arts et des Lettres (France) 2006 (Officier 1991); *Awards* Special Jury Prize (Cannes) for The Duellists 1977, two Academy Awards and four Br Academy Awards for Midnight Express 1978, four Academy Awards (incl Best Film) and three Br Academy Awards (incl Best Film) for Chariots of Fire 1981, three Academy Awards and eight Br Academy Awards (incl Best Film) for The Killing Fields 1985, Palme D'Or for The Mission 1986, Michael Balcon Award for outstanding contrib to the Br film industry Br Academy Awards 1982; *Books* The Third Age of Broadcasting (co-author, 1982), Rural England (co-author, 1988), The Undeclared War: The Struggle for Control of the World's Film Industry (1997); *Recreations* reading; *Clubs* Athenaeum, MCC, Chelsea Arts; *Style*— The Rt Hon Lord Puttnam, CBE; ✉ c/o House of Lords, Westminster, London SW1A 0PW

PUXLEY, James Henry Lavallin; DL (Berks 2005); s of John Philip Lavallin Puxley, of Wickham Heath, Newbury, and Aline Carlos *née* Wilson; *b* 23 October 1948; *Educ* Eton, Univ of Bristol (BA), RAC Cirencester (Dip Rural Estate Mgmnt); *m* 26 April 1991, Deborah Anne, da of Col Iain Ferguson; 1 da (Felicia Margaret Lavallin b 19 January 1996); *Career* self employed mangr family estate; High Sheriff Berks 2000–2001; ARICS 1976, MRAC 1974; *Recreations* country sports, travel; *Clubs* Farmers'; *Style*— James Puxley, Esq, DL; ✉ Welford Park, Welford, Newbury, Berkshire RG20 8HU (tel 01488 608691, fax 01488 657896, e-mail jpuxley@welfordpark.co.uk)

PUXON, Dr (Christine) Margaret; QC (1982); da of Reginald Wood Hale (d 1960), of Bournemouth, and Clara Lilian, *née* Poulton (d 1947); *b* 25 July 1915; *Educ* Abbey Sch Malvern Wells, Univ of Birmingham (MRCS, LRCP, MB ChB), MD(Obst); *m* 1, Sept 1937, Ralph Weddell; 1 da (Imogen Margaret b 1 Dec 1938), 1 s (Adrian John Goldsbrough b 8 Nov 1941); m 2, 1945, Francis Edward Mortimer Puxon; 1 s (Paul b 23 Dec 1948); m 3, 15 Sept 1955, Frederick Morris Williams (d 6 Feb 1986); *Career* house surgn appts 1941–42, gynaecological registrar Queen Elizabeth Hosp Birmingham 1942–43, conslt to Essex CC 1945–48; called to the Bar Inner Temple 1954, practised in criminal, family and civil work SE Circuit, head of East Anglian Chambers 1978–85, recorder 1983–89, dep circuit judge 1970–89; currently non-practising barr actg as medical legal conslt; memb Genetic Manipulation Advsy Gp, Privy Cncl appointed memb of Cncl of Royal Pharmaceutical Soc 1975–89, memb Clinical Res Ethics Ctee RCGP 1985–90, chm Ethics Ctee Lister Fertility Clinic Lister Hosp 1987–, chm Soc of Doctors in Law; Liveryman Worshipful Soc of Apothecaries; hon memb Royal Pharmaceutical Soc; FRSM, FRCOG 1976; *Books* The Family and the Law (1972), numerous contribs to medical jls and text books, consulting ed Medical Law Reports (1993–99); *Recreations* opera, travel; *Style*— Dr Margaret Puxon, QC; ✉ 19 Clarence Gate Gardens, Glentworth Street, London NW1 6AY (tel 020 7723 7922, e-mail margaretpuxon@aol.com)

PYANT, Paul; s of Leonard Vincent Pyant (d 1976), of Croydon, Surrey, and Jean Pheobe, *née* Frampton; *b* 22 July 1953; *Educ* Haling Manor Croydon, RADA (1973 Charles Killick Award); *Career* lighting designer; prodn electrics and asst lighting mangr Glyndebourne Opera 1974–87, freelance 1988–; memb: Labour Party, CND, Nat Tst, Woodland Tst, Assoc of Lighting Designers, United Artists 829 (USA) 1994; *Theatre* RNT (dir Nicholas Hytner, *qv*) incl: Wind in the Willows 1990, The Madness of George III 1991, Carousel 1992; RNT (dir Trevor Nunn, *qv*): Arcadia 1993, Troilus & Cressida 1999, Candide 1999, Relapse 2001, A Streetcar Named Desire 2003; Donmar Warehouse (dir Sam Mendes, *qv*) incl: Assassins 1992, Cabaret 1993, Company 1995; Donmar Warehouse (dir David Leveaux, *qv*) Nine 1997, Electra 1998; other credits incl: Orpheus Descending (dir Sir Peter Hall, *qv*, London and New York (Broadway debut)) 1988, The Tempest (RSC) 1993, Talking Heads (dir Alan Bennett, *qv*, Comedy Theatre London and tour) 1997, Alarms and Excursions 1998, Long Days Journey into Night 2000, Humble Boy (RNT and West End) 2003, All's Well that Ends Well (RSC) 2003–04, The Woman in White 2004, Hamlet (Old Vic) 2004, Home Place (Gate Dublin) 2005, Whose Life is it Anyway? (London); *Opera* incl: King Priam (Kent Opera) 1984, Xerxes (ENO) 1985, Lady Macbeth of Mtsensk (ENO) 1987, Death in Venice (Glyndebourne) 1990, Le Nozze Di Figaro (Wien Festival) 1991, Gawain (ROH) 1991, Fedora (Wien Staatsoper debut) 1994, Stiffelio (La Scala debut) 1995, Pique Dame (Metropolitan Opera debut) 1995, Don Giovanni (Kirov Opera debut) 2000, Boulevard Solitude (ROH) 2001, Vanessa (Opera de Monte Carlo debut) 2001, Boulevard Solitude (ROH), Die Fledermaus (Glyndebourne) 2003, The 10 Passion (Aldeburgh, Almeida, Bregenz Festival) 2004, Peter Grimes (Salzburg Festival debut) 2005; *Ballet* for English Nat Ballet incl: Sleeping Beauty 1993, Giselle 1994, Cinderella 1996, Nutcracker 1997 (also Boston Ballet 1997); for Northern Ballet Theatre incl: Romeo and Juliet 1991, Christmas Carol 1992, Swan Lake 1992, Cinderella 1993, Dracula 1996, Hunchback of Notre Dame 1998; *Awards* Olivier Award nomination for Wind in the Willows 1990, Hamlet 2001 and A Streetcar Names Desire 2003, Tony nominations for Orpheus Descending 1989 and for Arcadia 1993/94, Drama Desk nomination for Carousel 1993/94, winner New York Critics' Award for Carousel 1994, Green Room Aust nomination for Xerxes 1997; *Recreations* steam locomotives, gardening, walking; *Style*— Paul Pyant, Esq; ✉ c/o Jeffrey Cambell Management (tel 01323 411444, fax 01323 411373, e-mail cambell@theatricaldesigners.co.uk)

PYE, Chris; s of Thomas Pye, of Lancaster, and Margaret, *née* Kirkwood (d 1994); *b* 21 March 1947; *Educ* Lancaster Royal GS, UC Oxford (open exhibitioner), Hatfield Coll Durham (BA); *m* 1, 1974, Valerie Pownall; 1 da (Holly b 1974); m 2, 1986, Frances Hambidge; *Career* prodr, exec prodr then head of dept Granada TV Manchester 1969–79, prodr, exec prodr and writer for NBC, ABC and CBS TV Los Angeles 1979–93, head of factual entertainment Scottish Television Enterprises 1993, chief exec Anglia Television Enterprises 1993–94; BBC TV: head of independent cmmns 1994, head of Entertainment Gp 1995–96, head of commercial and business affrs BBC Prodn 1996–2000; commercial dir Granada Creative 2000–03, vice-pres of worldwide formats Sony Pictures Television International 2003–; *Recreations* music, bridge; *Style*— Chris Pye, Esq

PYE, Brig Hugh William Kellow; OBE (2003); s of Brig Randall Thomas Kellow Pye, DSO, OBE (d 2002), of Lindfield, W Sussex, and Peggy Muriel, *née* Sagar-Musgrave-Brooksbank (d 1999); *b* 23 May 1938; *Educ* Wellington, RMA Sandhurst; *m* 8 June 1968, Mary Ann, da of Cdr the Hon David Edwardes, DSC, RN (d 1983), of Wincanton, Somerset; 1 s (Robert Alec Kellow b 1970), 1 da (Victoria Ann (Mrs Colin Elwell) b 1973); *Career* cmmnd 12 Royal Lancers (POW) 1958, Cdr Berlin Armd Sqdn 1968, Staff Coll Camberley 1971, GSO2 INT JSIS Hong Kong 1972, Armed Forces Staff Coll Norfolk Virginia USA 1976, cmdg 9/12 Royal Lancers (POW) 1977–79 (despatches), AMS MS 4 1979–82, dep Chief of Staff (DCOS) and Cdr Br Contingent UNFICYP 1982–84, Col Co-ordination Staff Coll Camberley 1984–85, project mangr, Dep Cdr and advsr Oman Cmd and Staff Coll 1986–89, Dep Cdr SW Dist and Cdr Br Element AMF (L) 1990–92, ret; Hon Col: Leics and Derbys Yeo (PAO) TA 1992–2003, 9/12 Royal Lancers (POW) 1995–2003, City and Co of Bristol ACF 2000–04; treas Soc of Merchant Venturers Bristol 1992–2003; govr: Colston's Collegiate Sch 1992–2003 (chm 1994–2003), Colston's Girls' Sch 1992–2003; tstee: Gtr Bristol Fndn 1993–99, Cancer and Leukaemia in Childhood

(CLIC) 1996–2004 (chm 1996–2004), Southwest Fndn 2000– (vice-chm 2001–03, chm 2003–), CLIC Sargent 2005–06 (jt chm 2005–06), Bristol Cathedral Tst 2005– (vice-chm 2005–07, chm 2007–, chm Cathedral Appeal 2005–), Somerset Community Fndn 2007–; patron: Bristol Foyer 2000–03, Fast Track 2000–03; Hon LLD Univ of Bristol 2003; FRSA 2001; Sultan of Oman's Commendation Medal 1989; *Recreations* shooting, fishing, gardening; *Clubs* Cavalry and Guards'; *Style*— Brigadier Hugh Pye, OBE; ✉ Tuxwell Farm, Spaxton, Bridgwater, Somerset TA5 1DF (tel 01278 671833, fax 01278 671803, e-mail hughpye@btopenworld.com)

PYE, Nigel Lindsay; s of Herbert Francis Pye, Cuckfield, W Sussex, and Doreen Mary, *née* Starr; *b* 1 May 1945; *Educ* Whitgift Sch; *m* 1, 1972 (m dis 1985), Frances Jean Fermor; 1 s (Matthew Francis b 1976), 1 da (Alexandra Claire b 1978); m 2, 1988, Hilary, da of John Thomas Carroll; *Career* articled clerk James Edwards Dangerfield & Co London 1964–69, assigned to Alexander Grant & Co Chicago 1970–71, London office Tansley Witt & Co (successor firm of James Edwards Dangerfield & Co) 1971–79 (ptnr 1976); Arthur Andersen: ptnr London office 1979–85, managing ptnr Cambridge office 1985–91, managing ptnr Manchester office 1991–96, ptnr St Albans office 1996–98, sr ptnr Cambridge office 1998–2001, ret; chm Croydon Soc of Chartered Accountants 1984–85; dir: S Cambridge Training and Enterprise Cncl 1989–91, Cambridge Arts Theatre 1991, Cambridge Network Ltd 2000–01; memb: Cncl CBI 1989–91, E of England Cncl CBI 1998–2001, Devpt Ctee The Prince's Tst in Cambridgeshire 1999–2005; govr Long Road Sixth Form Coll Cambridge 1999–2003; tstee: Mary Wallace Fndn 2003–06, Cambridge Fndn 2003–; FCA 1979 (ACA 1969), FRSA 2000; *Recreations* sailing, walking, travel, theatre; *Clubs* Naval and Military; *Style*— Nigel Pye, Esq; ✉ 9 Brookside, Cambridge CB2 1JE (tel 01223 368002, fax 01223 513409, e-mail nigelpye@ntlworld.com)

PYE, Tom; *Educ* Lincoln Coll of Art (BTEC Dip), Wimbledon Sch of Art (BA); *Career* theatre, set and costume designer; *Theatre* prodns incl: The Angel Project (13 Spaces/towerblocks accross the city, dir Deborah Warner, *qv*, Perth Int Arts Festival Aust), The Euston Project (dir Deborah Warner, The Euston Tower (LIFT), Diary of One Who Vanished (dir Deborah Warner, ENO/NT tour, London, Paris, Dublin, Amsterdam, NY and Munich), Turn of the Screw (dir Deborah Warner, ROH, Barbican and Bobigny Paris), Don Giovanni (Aix-en-Provence Festival and world tour), Jeanne D'Arc au Bucher (dir Deborah Warner, BBC Proms Royal Albert Hall), Fiddler on the Roof (Broadway), The Rape of Lucreita (Bayerische Opera), St John Passion (dir Deborah Warner, ENO), Medea (dir Deborah Warner, Queen's Theatre London and Abbey Theatre Dublin), The Power Book (NT), The Diary of One Who Vanished (ENO, RNT), Near Life Experience, The Magic Flute (Opera North); *Television* art director Just William (series II, Talisman Films/BBC); prodn designer: Medea, King Lear and Measure for Measure (BBC Open Univ, dir Fiona Shaw, *qv*), Twelfth Night (Channel 4), Helen West (ITV), The Late Michael Clark (BBC), Movie Talk and Preview (SKY TV), ITV Sports Awards (live from Wembley), pop promotions incl New Order, commercials incl Persil, Ford Fiesta, Zoom; scenic artist Comic Strip Presents (two series); *Films* prodn designer: Helen West (3 films for TV, Deep Sleep, Shadow Play, A Clear Conscience), Gloriana (dir Phyllida Lloyd, *qv*, film for TV), Maua King and Emperor (feature film), The Late Michael Clark (film for TV); art dir: Christie Malry's Own Double Entry (feature film), Richard II (dir Deborah Warner, film for TV), A Feast at Midnight (feature film); wardrobe asst Robin Hood Prince of Thieves (feature film); other prodn design incl: studio shows, award ceremonies and live specials for MTV Europe and VH1; *Clubs* Century; *Style*— Tom Pye, Esq; ✉ c/o Douglas & Kopelman Artists Inc, 393 West 49th Street, Suite 5G, New York NY 10019

PYE, William Burns; s of Sir David Pye, CB, FRS (d 1959), of Elstead, Surrey, and Virginia Frances, *née* Kennedy; *b* 16 July 1938; *Educ* Charterhouse, Wimbledon Sch of Art, Sch of Sculpture RCA; *m* 1963, Susan Marsh; 1 s (Tristram b 18 March 1966), 2 da (Rebecca Jane b 2 June 1968, Alexandra Virginia b 4 Aug 1973); *Career* sculptor; visiting prof Calif State Univ 1975–76; made films Reflections 1971, From Scrap to Sculpture 1971; elected pres Hampshire Sculpture Tst 2002; FRBS, Hon FRIBA, *Commissions and Sculptures on Public Sites* Zemran (South Bank London), King's Cross House Cmmn (Pentonville Rd London), water sculpture (Aston Univ Campus), mural at Vauxhall railway stn, Slipstream and Jetstream water sculptures (Gatwick North Terminal), Curlicue (Greenland Dock London Docklands), Alpheus (Gatwick Forte Crest Hotel), Chalice (Fountain Square, 123 Buckingham Palace Rd), Orchid (The Peacocks Woking), Aventino (Mercury House London), Cristos (St Christopher's Place London), Flyover (M25 Clacket Lane Service Station), Downpour (Br Embassy Muskat Oman), Derby Cascade (Market Square Derby), Cader Idris (Central Square Cardiff), Aquarena (Millennium Square Bristol), Wilton House (Wilts), Nat Botanic Garden of Wales, Jubilee Fountain (Lincoln's Inn London), eight features for water gardens Alnwick Castle, Colisée Pyramid (Le Colisée St Ouen Paris), Jefferson (Louisville Kentucky), Mesa (Phoenix Arizona), Eastgate (Cincinnati Ohio), Regency (Racine Wisconsin), San-Mateo (California), Kagoshima City (Japan), Hong Kong Int Airport; *Work in Public Collections* incl: Arts Cncl of GB, MOMA NY, Contemporary Art Soc, Royal Albert Museum Exeter, Birmingham City Art Gallery, Szepmuveszeti Museum Budapest, Graves Art Gallery Sheffield, National Museum of Wales, Utsukushi-ga-hara Open Air Museum Japan, Nat Portrait Gallery; *Solo Exhibitions* incl: Redfern Gallery London 1966, 1969, 1973 and 1975, Bertha Schaefer Gallery NY 1970, Bear Lane Gallery Oxford 1972, Ikon Gallery Birmingham 1975, Morgan Thomas Gallery LA 1976, Yorkshire Sculpture Park 1978, Winchester Great Hall 1979, Welsh Touring Exhbn 1980, London Business Sch 1986, The Rotunda One Exchange Square Hong Kong 1987, New Art Centre Roche Ct 2004; *Group Exhibitions* incl: Towards Art II (Arts Cncl Gallery), Internationale der Zeichnung (Darmstadt), Middleheim 10th Biennale of Sculpture (Antwerp), British Sculptors '72 (RA), British Painting and Sculpture Today (Indianapolis Museum of Art), Royal Jubilee Exhbn of Contemporary British Sculpture (London), Budapest Int Exhbn of Small Sculpture (Prix de Sculpture), British Sculpture in the 20th Century (Whitechapel Art Gallery), Welsh Sculpture Tst Inaugural Exhbn (Margam Park, Port Talbot), 6th Henry Moore Grand Prize Exhbn (Br nomination, Utsukushi-ga-hara Museum Japan), Chelsea Harbour Sculpture '93, sculpture at Schönthal Switzerland, Tate Britain 2004; *Awards* Prix de Sculpture Budapest In Sculpture Exhbn 1981, Vauxhall Mural Competition 1983, Peace Sculpture Competition (for Ackers Park Small Heath Birmingham) 1984, Art at Work Award Wapping Arts Tst (for Sculpture at Gatwick Airport) 1988, Assoc of Business Sponsorship of the Arts Award 1988, Royal UENO Award Japan 1989; *Recreations* playing the flute; *Style*— William Pye; ✉ 43 Hambalt Road, Clapham, London SW4 9EQ (tel 020 8673 2318, office tel 020 8682 2727, office fax 020 8682 3218)

PYLE, Michael John Findlay; s of Gordon Findlay Pyle (d 1962), of Loughton, Essex, and Mabel Ellen, *née* Stallwood (now Mrs Mossman); *b* 16 August 1942; *Educ* Woodbridge Sch, Northern Poly Sch of Architecture London (DipArch), Sch of Planning and Landscape Architecture Birmingham (DipLA); *Family* 2 da (Charlotte Emma Pyle b 25 May 1972, Katie Louise Pyle b 3 March 1975); m, 24 March 2001, Tracy Baulcombe; *Career* jr architect engaged on educnl bldgs Herts CC 1965–68, sr architect involved with health and social servs bldgs City of Birmingham Architects' Dept 1968–72; Mason Richards Partnership: joined 1972, assoc 1973–82, ptnr responsible for various industrial, commercial and retail projects UK and Europe 1982–85, founding sr ptnr Birmingham Office 1985–2004; ind conslt architect 2004–; conslt Church Lukas Architecture and Design 2004–06, ops dir Birmingham Architectural Div Capita Percy Thomas 2006–; memb: Ctee Wolverhampton Soc of Architects 1973–85 (chm 1980), W Midlands Regnl Cncl RIBA 1980–82; currently memb: Faculty of Bldg, RHS, Nat Tst, English Heritage; RIBA 1967; racehorse owner and breeder (Goldeva - winner Sefton Plate Chester 2001, Shergar Cup Ascot 2002, Cammidge Trophy Doncaster and Flying Fillies Pontefract 2004); *Recreations* horse racing, travel, walking, reading; *Style*— Michael J F Pyle, Esq; ✉ Capita Percy Thomas, 1st Floor, York House, 38 Great Charles Street, Birmingham B3 3JY (tel 0121 212 3525, fax 0121 212 3545, email mike.pyle@capita.co.uk)

PYM, Baron (Life Peer UK 1987), of Sandy in the County of Bedfordshire; Francis Leslie Pym; PC (1970), MC (1945), DL (Cambs 1973); o s of Leslie Ruthven Pym, JP, DL (d 1945), sometime MP for Monmouth and Lord Cmmr of the Treasy, and Iris Rosalind (d 1982), da of Charles Somerville Orde; *b* 13 February 1922; *Educ* Eton, Magdalene Coll Cambridge (hon fell); *m* 25 June 1949, Valerie Fortune, er da of Francis John Heaton Daglish; 2 s (Hon (Francis) Jonathan Pym, Hon Andrew Leslie), 2 da (Hon Charlotte Hazell (Hon Mrs Lightbody), Hon Sarah Lucy (Hon Mrs Birchall)); *Career* served WWII 9 Queen's Royal Lancers (despatches twice), Capt; served in African and Italian campaigns; memb Herefordshire CC 1958–62; contested (Cons) Rhondda 1959, MP (Cons) Cambs 1961–83 and SE Cambs 1983–87; Parly sec to the Treasy and Govt chief whip 1970–73, sec of state for NI 1973–74; oppn spokesman on: agric 1974–76, House of Commons affrs and devolution 1976–78, foreign and cwlth affrs 1978–79; sec of state for defence 1979–81; chllr of the Duchy of Lancaster, paymaster gen and ldr House of Commons 1981, lord pres of the Cncl and ldr House of Commons 1981–82, foreign and cwlth sec 1982–83; pres Atlantic Treaty Assoc 1985–88, chm ESU 1987–92; memb Cncl Univ of Liverpool 1949–53; *Books* The Politics of Consent (1984), Sentimental Journey: Tracing an Outline of Family History (1998); *Style*— The Rt Hon the Lord Pym; ✉ Everton Park, Sandy, Bedfordshire SG19 2DE

PYMAN, Avril; *see:* Sokolov, Dr Avril

PYMONT, Christopher Howard; QC (1996); s of late John Pymont, of Penn, Bucks, and Joan, *née* Marmoy; *b* 16 March 1956; *Educ* Marlborough (scholar), Christ Church Oxford (scholar, MA); *m* 1996, Meriel Rosalind, da of Roger Lester and late Ann Lester of Pinner Hill; 1 da (Harriet Ann Eloise b 5 Feb 1998), 2 s (Nicholas John Frederick b 28 April 2000, Benedict Anthony Edmund b 26 Feb 2003); *Career* called to the Bar Gray's Inn 1979; specialist in chancery and commercial law, recorder 2004–; *Style*— Christopher Pymont, Esq, QC; ✉ Maitland Chambers, 7 Stone Buildings, Lincoln's Inn, London WC2A 3SZ

PYPER, Mark Christopher Spring-Rice; s of Arthur Spring-Rice Pyper (d 1994), of Seaford, E Sussex, and Rosemary Isobel, *née* Ferguson; *b* 13 August 1947; *Educ* Winchester, Balliol Coll Oxford, Univ of London (BA); *m* 7 April 1979, Jennifer Lindsay, da of Raymond James Gilderson (d 1975), of Seaford; 1 s (Robin Spring-Rice b 1983), 2 da (Sarah Katharine b 1986, Alice Rosemary b 1989); *Career* asst headmaster St Wilfrid's Prep Sch Seaford Sussex 1977–79 (asst master 1972–77), dep headmaster Sevenoaks Sch Kent 1988–90 (asst master then registrar 1979–88), headmaster Gordonstoun Sch 1990–, princ the Gordonstoun Schools 1999–; dir Sevenoaks Summer Festival 1979–90; *Clubs* MCC; *Style*— Mark Pyper, Esq; ✉ Gordonstoun School, Elgin, Moray IV30 5RF (tel 01343 837837)

PYSDEN, Edward Scott; *Educ* Dulwich Coll, King's Sch Macclesfield, Univ of Manchester (LLB); *Career* slr; Eversheds: articled clerk 1970–72, slr 1972–74, ptnr 1974–; John Peacock Prize Law Soc finals 1970; memb Law Soc 1972; dir Marketing Manchester, chm Hallé Concert Soc, dir Hallogen, past chm Pro Manchester, memb Inst of Fiscal Studies; *Recreations* classical music, golf, good food and wine; *Clubs* Prestbury Golf; *Style*— Edward Pysden, Esq; ✉ Eversheds, 70 Great Bridgewater Street, Manchester M1 5ES (tel 0161 831 8000, fax 0161 831 8888, e-mail edwardpysden@eversheds.com)

PYTEL, Walenty; s of Wladislaw Pytel, of Bath, and Jadwiga Pytel; *b* 10 February 1941; *Educ* Leominster Minster Sch, Hereford Coll of Art (NDD); *m* 7 Oct 1963, Janet Mary, da of William Sidney Spencer (d 1973), of Westington Court; 1 s (Jeremy Walenty Spencer b 1964), 1 da (Victoria Catharine Mary b 1968); *Career* sculptor in steel and bronze; works incl: mural Lord Montague Beaulieu 1972, Chanel Perfume Paris 1975, sculpture cmmnd by MPs to commemorate Queen's Silver Jubilee New Palace Yard Westminster 1977, unicorn from HRH Princess Anne to Portuguese Govt 1979, Cwlth beasts for Sir Edward du Cann MP, Sir John Hall MP and Patrick Cooke, Take Off Birmingham Int Airport 1985, unicorn representing coat of arms for Lord and Lady Leigh Stoneleigh Abbey 1989, 5 vikings for Anders Wilhelmsen & Co 1996,17 ft war meml in bronze cmmnd by Ludlow Branch Royal Br Legion 2000, 3 25ft riverside sculptures cmmd by S Herefords DC 2000, 25ft dragonfly and butterfly cmmd by S Glos Cncl 2000, 10 Millennium Planet Walk sculptures cmmd by Tamworth BC 2000, 2 15ft cranes for Mazak Europe Machine Tools, Colin Grazier war meml Tamworth; exhibitions: Marbella 1985, New Jersey 1987, San Diego 1987, Mitukoshi Gallery Tokyo 1987, Soc of Wildlife Artists Mall Galleries 1988 (award winner), Essen Germany 1989, Couvert de Recollets Cognac France 1992, Belvoir Castle 2002, Artparks 2003, Nature in Art Twigworth 2003, Santa YNez Valley Classic Art Show USA, Cornes Japan, Art & Gems, Dubai; work in various private collections; Coventry Design Award 2001 (for Wings over Water conservation area bridge); memb Soc of Br Sculptors; ARBS; *Recreations* salmon fishing, game shooting, sailing; *Style*— Walenty Pytel, Esq; ✉ Hartleton, Bromsash, Ross-on-Wye HR9 7SB (tel and fax 01989 780536); Wyebridge 2, 26 High Street, Ledbury HR8 1DS (tel 01531 634102, e-mail info@wyebridge.com, website www.wyebridge.com)

P

Q

QUAH, Prof Danny; s of Chong-eng Quah, of Penang, Malaysia, and Phaik-im, *née* Goh; *b* 26 July 1958, Penang, Malaysia; *Educ* Princeton Univ (AB), Harvard Univ (PhD); *children* 2 s (Carter Tyson b 13 Aug 1994, Mason Tyson b 8 Nov 1996); *Career* asst prof of econs MIT 1986–91; LSE: lectr then reader in econs 1991–96, prof of econs 1996–, dir Andrew Mellon Prog for the Study of IT and the Weightless Economy 1998–2002, head Dept of Econs 2006–; visiting asst prof Harvard Univ; conslt: Bank of Eng, World Bank, Monetary Authy of Singapore; memb Prog Ctee: Econometric Soc 1991, 1997, 1999, 2000 and 2003, European Econ Assoc 1995–96, Royal Econ Soc 1997–98; exec dir Nat Econ Performance Prog Centre for Econ Performance LSE 1994–99; prog chair European Econ Assoc 2000; assoc ed Jl of Econ Growth 1996–, res reader Br Acad 1996–98; one of ten ESRC Heroes of Dissemination 2001; govr NIESR 2002–; *Recreations* taekwon-do (black belt, England Patterns Champion and sparring runner-up 2005, Britain sparring runner-up 2005); *Style*— Prof Danny Quah; ✉ Department of Economics, LSE, Houghton Street, London WC2A 2AE (tel 020 7955 7535, fax 020 7955 6592, e-mail dq@econ.lse.ac.uk)

QUALLINGTON, (Herbert) Timothy; s of Herbert Edward Quallington (d 1959), and Dorothy, *née* Smith (d 1971); *b* 2 November 1935; *Educ* Kent Coll Canterbury (BA), Brunel Univ (MA); *m* 16 Sept 1961, Jean Frances, da of Frank Loudonsack Barker (d 1992); 1 s ((Herbert) Philip b 20 Sept 1962), 2 da ((Brenda) Elizabeth 4 Jan 1965, Rachel Mary b 16 March 1966); *Career* Nat Serv Armament Fitter RAF 1954–57; photographer Jack Harley Ltd Cranleigh 1961–62, photographer Central Electricity Res Laboratories Leatherhead 1962–63, sr photographer and studio mangr Cncl of Industrial Design (now Design Cncl) 1964–88 (photographer 1963–64), self employed commercial social and editorial photographer 1988–, lectr in photography Farnborough Coll of Technol 1988–2000, lectr in photography Univ of the Third Age 2000–; work published in various local and nat newspapers and magazines incl Design Magazine and Engineering Magazine, paper on The Photography of Lighting Installation presented to Illuminating Engrg Soc 1971; former external course and student assessor SIAD and external assessor for BIPP at W Surrey Coll of Art Farnham; asst Scout master and asst Rover Scout ldr 1st Oxshott Scout Gp 1957–60; FRSA 1969, FBIPP 1970, FRPS 1971, FCSD 1974; *Recreations* family, local church, interior design, gardening, caravanning and photography; *Clubs* Rotary Int (past pres local Rotary); *Style*— Timothy Quallington, Esq; ✉ 2 Woodland Grange, Cranleigh, Surrey GU6 7HY (tel 01483 273361)

QUANT, Mary (Mrs A Plunket Greene); OBE (1966); da of Jack Quant, and Mildred Quant; *b* 11 February 1934; *Educ* Goldsmiths' Coll of Art London; *m* 1957, Alexander Plunket Greene; 1 s (Orlando Plunket Greene); *Career* fashion designer; estab Mary Quant Gp of Cos 1955, Mary Quant cosmetics launched 1966, fndr Mary Quant Ltd (co-chm until 2000); non-exec dir House of Fraser plc 1997–; memb: Design Cncl 1971, Br and USA Bicentennial Liaison Ctee 1973, Advsy Cncl V&A 1976–78; winner: Maison Blanche Rex Award 1964, Sunday Times Int Award 1964, Piavola d'Oro Award 1966, Annual Design Medal Inst of Industrial Artists and Designers 1966, Hall of Fame Award Br Fashion Cncl 1990; sr fell RCA 1991, hon fell RSA 1993; hon fell Goldsmiths Coll London 1993; Hon BA Winchester Sch of Art 2000, Hon DUniv Wales 2001; FSIA 1967, RDI 1969, FRSA 1995; *Publications* Quant by Quant, Colour by Quant, Quant on Make-Up, Mary Quant Classic Make-Up & Beauty Book; *Style*— Miss Mary Quant, OBE; ✉ Mary Quant Limited, 1st Floor, Lynton House, 7–12 Tavistock Square, London WC1H 9LT

QUANTRILL, Prof Malcolm William Francis; s of Arthur William Quantrill (d 1976), of Norwich, and Alice May, *née* Newstead (d 1979); *b* 25 May 1931; *Educ* City of Norwich Sch, Univ of Liverpool (BArch), Univ of Pennsylvania (MArch), Tech Univ of Wroclaw (DScEng); *m* 1 (m dis 1965), Arja Irmeli Nenonen; m 2, 18 Dec 1971, Esther Maeve, da of James Brignell Dand (d 1982), of Chester; 2 s (Christopher b 1961, Jan b 1962), 2 da (Francesca b 1974, Alexandra b 1978); *Career* dir Architectural Assoc London 1967–69, dean Sch of Architecture North London Poly 1973–80, prof of architecture Univ of Jordan Amman 1980–83, distinguished prof of architecture Texas A&M Univ 1986–; dep ed Art International Lugano 1978–83, ed-in-chief Studies in Architecture and Culture (CASA) 1988–; fndr memb The Thomas Cubitt Tst London (tstee 1977, sec 1977–80); ASCA (Assoc of Collegiate Schs of Architecture) distinguished prof 1990, Thomas Cubitt lectr 1993, Kivett lectr 1994; Assoc of Architecture Research Cncls Consortium of N America (ARCC) Haecker Award for leadership in architectural research 2002–03; RIBA 1961; Knight Cdr of the Order of the Finnish Lion 1988; *Books* Gotobed Dawn (1962), Gotobedlam (1964), John Gotobed Alone (1965), Ritual and Response in Architecture (1974), Monuments of Another Age (with Esther Quantrill, 1976), On the Home Front (novel, 1977), Alvar Aalto: A Critical Study (1983), Reima Pietilä: Architecture, Context and Modernism (1985), The Environmental Memory (1987), Reima Pietilä: One Man's Odyssey in Search of Finnish Architecture (1988), Constancy and Change in Architecture (1991), Urban Forms, Suburban Dreams (1993), Finnish Architecture and the Modernist Tradition (1995), The Culture of Silence: Architecture's Fifth Dimension (1998), The Norman Foster Studio: Consistency Through Diversity (1999), Latin American Architecture: Six Voices (2000), Juha Leiviskä and the Continuity of Finnish Modern Architecture (2001), The Architectural Project (with Alfonso Corona-Martinez, 2003), Plain Modern: the architecture of Brian Mackay-Lyons (2005); *Recreations* photography, travel, tennis, broadcasting; *Clubs* Garrick; *Style*— Prof Malcolm Quantrill; ✉ 1200 Langford Street, College Station, TX11840–4343, USA (tel 00 1 979 693 9840, e-mail mquantrill@archmail.tamu.edu)

QUARANTO, Leonard Anthony; s of Angelo V Quaranto, of Warwick, RI, and Vincenza, *née* Rizzo (d 2003); *b* 11 June 1947, Providence, RI; *Educ* L'Université d'Orléans-Tours, Georgetown Univ Washington DC (BS), George Washington Univ Washington DC (JD); *m* 15 Sept 1973, Nancy Kathleen, *née* Burns; 1 s (Paul Anthony b 3 Oct 1990); *Career* memb DC Bar 1978; asst int counsel: Ralston Purina Co 1978–80, Chrysler Corp 1980–84; gen counsel Boles World Trade Corp 1984, chief counsel EMEA Kimberly-Clark Corp 1985–2001, gen counsel and co sec Allied Domecq plc 2001–05, private investor 2006–, gen counsel EFAD Hldg Co KSCC Kuwait 2007; memb American Bar Assoc 1978–; *Recreations* hunting (N Cotswolds), shooting, skiing, travel, theatre, wines and dining; *Clubs* National Liberal; *Style*— Leonard Quaranto, Esq; ✉ Glebe House, Naunton, nr Cheltenham, Gloucestershire GL54 3AT (tel 01451 850679, e-mail leonard@quaranto.fsworld.co.uk)

QUARMBY, Dr Arthur; s of Harold Quarmby (d 1981), of Lane House, Holmfirth, and Lucy May, *née* Barrow; *b* 18 March 1934; *Educ* Pocklington Sch, Leeds Sch of Architecture and Town Planning (DipArch); *m* 13 Aug 1957, Jean Valerie, da of Herbert Mitchell, of Hebble Drive Holmfirth; 1 s (Jonathan Hugh, b 1961), 1 da (Rachel Jane b 1964); *Career* architect; plastics structures in Europe and the Antarctica, world's largest transparent inflated dome (for 20th Century Fox), assault craft for Rotork Marine, conslt on structural plastics, world authy on earth-sheltered architecture, architectural journalist; chief constable of the Graveship of Holme; memb: Huddersfield Choral Soc, Colne Valley Male Voice Choir; Hon DSc 1996; RIBA 1959, FRIBA 1985, FRSA; *Books* The Plastics Architect (1974); *Recreations* music, archaeology, watersports, hill walking; *Clubs* Inigo Jones; *Style*— Dr Arthur Quarmby; ✉ Underhill, Holme, West Yorkshire (tel 01484 682372)

QUARMBY, Dr David Anthony; CBE (2003); s of Frank Reginald Quarmby (d 1983); *b* 22 July 1941; *Educ* Shrewsbury, King's Coll Cambridge (MA), Univ of Leeds (PhD, Dip Industrial Mgmnt); *m* 1968, Hilmary, da of Denis Hilton Hunter; 4 da; *Career* md London Tport Exec Buses 1978–84 (memb 1975–84), jt md J Sainsbury plc 1988–96 (dir 1984–96); chm: British Tourist Authy 1996–2003, English Tourist Bd 1996–99, Docklands Light Railway 1999–2001 (dir 1998), SeaBritain 2005 2003–05, Strategic Rail Authy (SRA) 2004–06 (shadow SRA 1999–2001, memb 2001–06, dep chm 2002–04), Transport Research Inst Napier Univ 2006–, dir NedRailways 2007–; dep chm S London Econ Devpt Alliance 1999–2003, dep chm and sometime chm New Millennium Experience Co 1997–2001; non-exec dir: Bd DETR 1996–98, Greenwich Millennium Tst 1998–2000, London First 1998–2002; memb Transport for London 2000–04, memb Bd Elderhostel Inc 2006–, conslt in transport and tourism 2006–; pres Inst of Logistics 1996–99; chm: Retail Action Gp for Crime Prevention 1995–96, James Allen's Girls' Sch Dulwich 1995–98 (govr 1987–98, dep chm 1992–95), S London Business Leadership 1996–99; dir Blackheath Concert Halls 1990–94, tstee St Paul's Cathedral Fndn 2005–; memb: Sch Curriculum and Assessment Authy 1993–95, Crime Prevention Agency Bd 1995–97, Panel 2000; memb Ct Univ of Greenwich 1999–; tstee Nat Maritime Museum 2005–; Hon DSc Univ of Huddersfield 1999; FCILT, CIMgt, CORS; *Recreations* music, singing, photography, walking, family life; *Style*— Dr David Quarmby, CBE; ✉ 13 Shooters Hill Road, Blackheath, London SE3 7AR (tel 020 7654 6015, e-mail david@quarmby.org.uk)

QUAST, Philip; s of Colin Philip Quast, and Lorraine, *née* Elphick; *b* 30 July 1957; *Educ* Nat Inst of Dramatic Art Sydney (BA); *m* 3 Jan 1981, Carol, *née* Tart; 3 s (Edwin b 28 March 1990, Harrison b 1 Dec 1991, Toby b 18 May 1995); *Career* actor; performed with Sydney, Melbourne and Nimrod Theatre Cos Aust; *Theatre* Aust theatre credits incl: Javert in Les Misérables (original Aust prodn, Sydney Critics Award, Mo Award 1987), Adam in The Mystery Plays of Wakefield, The Narrator in The Threepenny Opera, Jack in A Hard God, Orlando in As You Like It, Gower in Pericles, Flysche in Song of the Selchies, Henry/Laertes in The Marriage/Hamlet, Aufidius in Coriolanus, Wolf/Cinderella's Prince in Into The Woods, Dr Neville Craven in The Secret Garden (Sydney Critics Award, 2 Mo Awards), Captain Hook in Pan, Francisco in The White Devil, On the Wallaby, No End of Blame, A Month in the Country, Candide, Shark Infested Waters, Carmen - Another Perspective, Martin in The Goat or Who is Sylvia? (MTC) 2003, Willy Brandt in Democracy (STC) 2005, Lopakhin in The Cherry Orchard (STC) 2006; London credits incl: Javert in Les Misérables, George in Sunday in the Park with George (NT, Olivier Award 1990), The Hunting of the Snark, Saint Joan, The Fix (musical, Olivier Award 1997), Emile DeBeque in South Pacific (NT, Olivier Award 2001); RSC: Fred/Chorus in A Christmas Carol, King of Navarre in Love's Labour's Lost, Lodovico in The White Devil, Banquo in Macbeth, Achilles in Troilus and Cressida, Archibald Craven in The Secret Garden, Antonio in The Merchant of Venice, Trigorin in The Seagull, Miles Glorious in A Funny Thing Happened on the Way to the Forum (NT), George Tenet in Stuff Happens (NT), Peron in Evita (West End, Olivier Award nomination 2007) 2006; *Concerts* Javert in Les Misérables: 10th Anniversary Concert (Royal Albert Hall) 1995, Hey, Mr Producer! 1998 (concert in honour of Sir Cameron Mackintosh); The Stars Come Out, Night of 1000 Voices (Royal Albert Hall), Domar Diva (season) 2002, A Little Night Music (Comedy Theatre London) 2006, Follies Concert (London) 2007; *Television* General Cornelius in Cleopatra (US mini-series), The Minister in The Damnation of Harvey McHugh, Once in a Blue Moon, Playschool, Colour in the Creek, Flight into Hell, Cassidy, Fields of Fire, Brides of Christ, Police Rescue, Patrol Boat, All Good Friends, The Governor (series two), Ultraviolet, Corridors of Power; *Films* Emoh Ruo, Around the World in 80 Ways, To Market, To Market, Napoleon; TV films: Army Wives, The First Kangaroos, Me & Mrs Jones, The Caterpillar Wish 2006, Clubland 2006; *Recordings* South Pacific, The Secret Garden (RSC cast recording and Australian highlights CD), The Fix, Les Misérables (complete symphonic recording and 10th anniversary concert CD), Paris, Great Moments in Australian Musical Theatre, Once in a Blue Moon, Lift Off Live!, Play School, Napoleon, Philip Quast Live at the Donmar, Evita (London cast) 2006; *Style*— Philip Quast, Esq; ✉ c/o Conway van Gelder Ltd, 18–21 Jermyn Street, London SW1Y 6HP (tel 020 7287 0077, fax 020 7287 1940)

QUASTEL, Dr Anthony Stephen; s of Gerald Quastel, of London, and late Rita Joy Leonora Quastel; *b* 14 November 1955; *Educ* St Dunstan's Coll Catford, Middx Hosp Med Sch Univ of London (MB BS); *Career* princ in gen practice 1984; res appts in med and surgery 1980–81, SHO in psychiatry Middx Hosp 1982, currently princ in gen practice; memb Obesity Mgmnt Assoc (chair Ethics Ctee); FRSM; *Recreations* gardening, politics, talking; *Style*— Dr Anthony Quastel; ✉ Rome Cottage, 7 Rome Road, New Romney, Kent TN28 8DN (tel 01797 362493); 204 High Street, Bromley, Kent (tel 020 8464 4599, fax 020 8464 3471); 25 Rue de L'Abbaye, St Georges, France 62770 (tel 00 33 3 21 03 71 87)

QUAYLE, John Bryant; s of late George Quayle, and Christina, *née* Lonsdale (d 1994); *b* 13 October 1945; *Educ* Llandovery Coll, Fitzwilliam Coll Cambridge (MA, MB BChir), St George's Hosp Med Sch London (MChir); *m* 4 March 1972, Prudence Margaret, da of (John) Denis Smith; 3 da (Tamsin Elinor b 4 Jan 1975, Ruth Elizabeth b 26 Oct 1976, Anna Margaret 27 March 1979); *Career* sr surgical registrar (rotation) St George's Hosp London 1978–82 (house physician 1970), conslt surgn Royal Shrewsbury Hosp and Princess Royal Hosp Telford 1982–; memb Cncl Surgical Section RSM 1980–, memb Assoc for Coloproctology of GB and Ireland; memb Worshipful Soc of Apothecaries 1974; FRCS 1974; *Recreations* riding, sailing, music, walking; *Clubs* RSM; *Style*— John Quayle, Esq; ✉ Shropshire Nuffield Hospital (tel 01743 282500); Royal Shrewsbury Hospital, Shrewsbury; Princess Royal Hospital, Telford

QUAYLE, Quinton; *b* 5 June 1955; *Educ* Univ of Bristol, Ecole Nationale d'Administration Paris; *m* 1979, Alison, *née* Marshall; 2 s; *Career* joined HM Dip Serv 1977, third later second sec Bangkok 1979–83, served FCO 1983–86, first sec Paris 1987–91, FCO EU Dept 1991–93, on secondment Price Waterhouse Mgmnt Consultants 1993–94, dir Jt Export Promotion Directorate FCO 1994–96, cnsllr, consul-gen and dep head of mission Jakarta 1996–99, int dir Br Trade International 1999–2002, ambass to Romania 2002–06, ambass to Thailand 2007–; *Recreations* book collecting; *Style*— Quinton Quayle, Esq

QUAYLE, Robert Brisco MacGregor; s of John Pattinson Quayle, of South Petherton, Somerset, and Doreen Helen MacGregor, *née* MacMullen; *b* 6 April 1950; *Educ* Monkton Combe Sch, Selwyn Coll Cambridge (MA); *m* 30 Sept 1972, (Deborah) Clare, da of Sir (Francis) Alan Pullinger, CBE, of Bovingdon, Herts; 2 da (Hannah b 1976, Eily b 1978), 3 s (Jonathan b 1981, William b 1985, Thomas b 1988); *Career* admitted slr 1974; Linklaters & Paines 1974–76, clerk of Tynwald and sec House of Keys 1976–87, ptnr Travers Smith Braithwaite 1987–90 (conslt 1990–98); chm: Total (IOM) Ltd, Neville James Int Funds PCC plc, Communicator Insurance Co Ltd; dir: Bradford & Bingley Int Ltd, AXA Isle of Man Ltd; memb Supervisory Bd Isle of Man Steam Packet Co; cmmr Northern Lighthouse Bd; govr Monkton Combe Sch; author of various articles on Parly affrs and history of IOM; *Recreations* family, church (licensed lay reader); *Style*— Robert Quayle, Esq; ✉ Mullen Beg, Patrick, Isle of Man (tel 01624 842912, fax 01624 843356, e-mail rqmann@manx.net)

QUEENSBERRY, 12 Marquess of (S 1682); Sir David Harrington Angus Douglas; 11 Bt (S 1668); also Viscount Drumlanrig, Lord Douglas of Hawick and Tibbers (both S 1628), and Earl of Queensberry (S 1633); s of 11 Marquess (d 1954), by his 2 w Cathleen, *née* Mann (d 1959); *b* 19 December 1929; *Educ* Eton; *m* 1, 1956 (m dis 1969), Ann, da of Maurice Sinnett Jones and formerly w of George Arthur Radford; 2 da (Lady Emma Cathleen b 1956, Lady Alice (Lady Alice Melia) b 1965); 1 s (Ambrose Carey b 1961, with Anne Carey); m 2, 1969 (m dis 1986), Alexandra Mary Clare Wyndham, da of Guy Wyndham Sich; 3 s (Sholto Francis Guy, Viscount Drumlanrig b 1967, Lord Milo Douglas b 1975, Lord Torquil Douglas b 1978), 1 da (Lady Kate Douglas b 1969); m 3, 3 July 2000, Hsueh-Chun Liao; 1 da (Beth Shan Ling b 1999); *Heir* s, Viscount Drumlanrig; *Career* late 2 Lt RHG; prof of ceramics RCA 1959–83; pres Design and Industries Assoc 1976–78; ptnr Queensberry Hunt design group; dir Highland Stoneware; tstee: Laura Ashley Fndn, Paolozzi Fndn; sr fell RCA, Hon Dr Staffordshire Univ; *Style*— The Most Hon the Marquess of Queensberry; ✉ 63 Penfold Street, London NW8 8PQ (tel 020 7535 7120, fax 020 7535 7101, e-mail partners@queensberryhunt.com)

QUELCH, Prof John Anthony; s of Norman Quelch (d 2006), of Stratford St Mary, Suffolk, and Laura Sally, *née* Jones (d 1997); *b* 8 August 1951; *Educ* King Edward VI Sch Norwich, Exeter Coll Oxford (BA), Univ of Pennsylvania (MBA), Harvard Univ (MS, DBA); *m* 17 June 1978, Joyce Ann, da of Harold Loring Huntley; *Career* asst prof Univ of Western Ontario 1977–79; Harvard Business Sch: asst prof 1979–84, assoc prof 1984–88, prof of business admin 1988–93, Sebastian S Kresge prof of mktg 1993–98, sr assoc dean 2001–, Lincoln Filene prof of business admin 2001–; dean London Business Sch 1998–2001; dir: Reebok Int Ltd 1984–96, WPP Group plc 1985–, US Office Products Co 1994–97, Cncl of Better Business Bureaux 1996–98, Pentland Group plc 1997–99, Graduate Mgmnt Admission Cncl 1998–2001, Blue Circle Industries plc 2000–01, easyJet plc 2000–03, Accion Int 2002–06, Inverness Medical Innovations Inc 2003–, Pepsi Bottling Group 2004–, Gentiva Health Services 2005–, ViTrue 2006–, Epiphany Biosciences 2007–; chm Massachusetts Port Authy 2002–; hon consul-gen Kingdom of Morocco 2004–; *Books* Advertising and Promotion Management (1987), Multinational Marketing Management (1988), Sales Promotion Management (1989), How to Market to Consumers (1989), The Marketing Challenge of Europe 1992 (1991), Ethics in Marketing (1992), Marketing Management (1993), Cases in European Marketing Management (1994), Cases in Product Management (1995), Cases in Marketing Management and Strategy: An Asia Pacific Perspective (1996), Global Marketing Management (1999), Cases in Strategic Marketing Management: Business Strategies in Latin America (2001), Cases in Strategic Marketing Management: Business Strategies in Muslim Countries (2001), Problems and Cases in Health Care Marketing (2004), Marketing Management (2004), The Global Market (2004), The New Global Brands (2005), Business Solutions for the Global Poor (2007); *Recreations* tennis, squash; *Clubs* Harvard (Boston), Brooks's; *Style*— Prof John Quelch; ✉ Harvard Business School, Morgan Hall 185, Soldiers Field, Boston, Massachusetts 02163, USA (tel 00 1 617 495 6325, fax 00 1 617 496 5637, e-mail jquelch@hbs.edu)

QUENBY, John Richard; s of Richard Quenby (d 1942), of Bedford, and Margaret, *née* Wyse (d 1991); *b* 30 October 1941; *Educ* Bedford Modern Sch, Open Univ (BA); *m* 1, (m dis 1997), Sandra, da of Col Noel Frederick Charles King (d 1974), of Sydney, Aust; 2 da (Georgia Margaret b 1970, Fiona Elizabeth b 1971); m 2, Frances, da of late Harvey Maynard (d 1997); *Career* dir Granada Computer Servs Ltd 1983–85, md Granada Overseas Hldgs Ltd 1985–89, dir and chm of various subsidiaries and assoc companies; chm CBQC Ltd 2002–04, non-exec dir Beds and Shires Health and Care NHS Tst 1992–97 (chm 1994–97); chief exec and dir RAC Motor Sports Assoc 1990–2001; dir: Trireme Tst 1994–97 (chm 1995–97 and 2006–), Auto Cycle Union 1995–98, Speedway Control Bd 1995–2002 (chm 1998–2002), Motorcycle Circuit Racing Control Bd 1995–2000 (chm 1995–2000), branch chm Royal Br Legion 2005–06 and 2007–; *Recreations* cricket, historic motor racing; *Clubs* Bedford Rowing, MCC, RAC, MG Car; *Style*— John Quenby, Esq; ✉ Royal Automobile Club, Pall Mall, London SW1Y 5HS

QUENTIN, Caroline; *b* 1961; *Career* actress; *Theatre* Roots (RNT), Our Country's Good (Garrick), Low Level Panic (Royal Court), Sugar and Spice (Royal Court), Les Miserables (Palace Theatre), Mirandolina (Lyric Hammersmith), The Live Bed Show (Garrick), The London Cuckolds (RNT); *Television* appearances incl: All or Nothing at All, Men Behaving Badly (six series and Christmas special) 1992–99, An Evening with Gary Lineker 1994, Jonathan Creek 1996–99 (three series), Kiss Me Kate 1998–2000 (three series), The Innocent (Granada) 2000, Hot Money (Granada) 2001, Goodbye Mr Steadman (Alibi) 2001, Blood Strangers (Granada) 2002, Blue Murder (Granada) 2003, Life Begins 2002, Von Trapped 2004, Blue Murder II 2004; Best Comedy Actress Comedy Awards 1995; *Style*— Ms Caroline Quentin; ✉ c/o Amanda Howard Associates, 21 Berwick Street, London W1F 0PZ (tel 020 7287 9277)

QUICKE, Sir John Godolphin; kt (1988), CBE (1978), DL (Devon 1985); s of Capt Noel Arthur Godolphin Quicke (d 1943), and Constance May Quicke; *b* 20 April 1922; *Educ* Eton, New Coll Oxford; *m* 1953, Prudence Tinné, da of Rear Adm Charles Pierre Berthon, CBE (d 1965); 3 s, 3 da; *Career* farmer and landowner; chm SW Regnl Panel Miny of Agric 1972–75, pres CLA 1975–77; memb SW Regnl Bd Natwest Bank 1973–92, chm Exeter Local Bd Commercial Union Assurance Co 1980–92; memb: Consultative Bd Jt Consultative Orgn for R&D, Food and Agric 1980–84, Countryside Cmmn 1981–88, Properties Ctee Nat Tst 1984–97; vice-chm N Devon Meat Ltd 1982–86; chm: Agric EDC, NEDO 1983–88, Soc for the Responsible Use of Resources in Agric and on the Land 1983–96, Estates Panel Nat Tst 1984–92, Agric Sector Gp NEDO 1988–90; memb Bd Univ of Plymouth (formerly Poly of the South West) 1989–93; pres Royal Bath and West of England Soc 1989–90; RASE Bledisloe Gold Medal 1985; Hon DSc: Univ of Exeter 1989, Univ of Plymouth 1991; Hon FRASE 1989; *Recreations* music, gardening; *Style*— Sir John Quicke, CBE, DL; ✉ Sherwood, Newton St Cyres, Exeter, Devon EX5 5BT (tel 01392 851216)

QUIGLEY, Sir (William) George Henry; kt (1993), CB (1982); s of William George Cunningham Quigley (d 1969), and Sarah, *née* Martin (d 1987); *b* 26 November 1929; *Educ* Ballymena Acad, Queen's Univ Belfast (fndn scholar, BA, PhD); *m* 5 May 1971, Moyra Alice, da of Frank Munn (d 1970); *Career* NI Civil Serv: joined 1955, perm sec Dept of Manpower Servs 1974–76, perm sec Dept of Commerce 1976–79, perm sec Dept of Fin 1979–82, perm sec Dept of Fin and Personnel 1982–88; chm Ulster Bank Ltd 1989–2001 (dep chm 1988–89); dir: Short Brothers plc 1989– (chm 1999–), National Westminster Bank plc 1990–99, NatWest Pension Tstees 1992–2002 (chm 1997–2002), Independent News and Media (UK) 2001–; professorial fell Queen's Univ Belfast 1988–92; memb: Fair Employment Cmmn for NI 1989–93, Cncl NI C of C and Industry 1989–92, Cncl CBI (NI div) 1990–94, Nat Ctee of Inquiry into HE 1996–97, Qualifications and Curriculum Authy 1997–99; chm: IOD (NI div) 1990–94, Royal Hosps Gp NHS Tst 1992–95, NI Econ Cncl 1994–98, Co-Operation North 1994–96, NI Centre in Europe 1997–99, Scottish Fee Support Review 1998–2000, Lothbury Property Tst 2000–, Review of Parades Cmmn of NI 2001–02, Bd Inst of Br-Irish Studies UC Dublin 2005–; pres: Economic and Social Research Inst Dublin 1999–2002, Inst of Int Trade of Ireland 1999–2001; Hon LLD Queen's Univ Belfast, Hon DUniv Ulster, Hon DUniv Open Univ 2005; CIMgt 1977, Hon FIMgtI; *Books* Registrum Johannis Mey (co-author with Dr E F D Roberts, 1972); *Recreations* historical research, reading, music, gardening; *Style*— Sir George Quigley, CB

QUIGLEY, Ian Spiers; s of John Spiers Quigley, of Inverness, and Celia, *née* Bennett; *b* 29 November 1946; *Educ* Aberdeen GS, Oban HS, Univ of Glasgow (LLB); *m* 6 July 1973, Elizabeth Ann, da of Tom Rutherford Lindsay; 2 da (Claire Lee b 8 March 1975, Victoria Lindsay b 24 June 1977); *Career* apprentice Wright Johnston & MacKenzie Glasgow; Maclay Murray & Spens: joined 1975, seconded to Linklaters & Paines London 1976, ptnr Maclay Murray & Spens 1977–; memb: Law Soc of Scotland, Soc of HM Writers to the Signet; NP; *Recreations* hill walking, cross-country skiing, cycling, gardening; *Clubs* New (Edinburgh); *Style*— Ian Quigley, Esq; ✉ Pomathorn Cottage, Howgate, Midlothian EH26 8PJ (tel 01968 672334); Maclay Murray & Spens, 3 Glenfinlas Street, Edinburgh EH3 6AQ (tel 0131 226 5196, fax 0131 226 3174)

QUIGLY, Isabel Madeleine; da of Richard Quigly (d 1971), and Clarice, *née* Ford (d 1977); *Educ* Godolphin Sch Salisbury, Newnham Coll Cambridge (5 scholarships, BA); *Career* editorial asst Penguin Books 1949–52, freelance writer 1952–, tri-lingual job at League of Red Cross Societies Geneva 1954, lit ed The Tablet 1985–97, pt/t archivist RSL 1997–99; film critic The Spectator 1956–66; sometime lectr City Literary Inst and other freelance lecturing; translator of more than 100 books from Italian, Spanish and French; contrib numerous jls and newspapers; judge: Booker Prize, Guardian Children's Books Prize, Heinemann Award, Betty Trask Award, Winifred Holtby Prize, Valle Inclán Prize, Wingate Awards, Somerset Maugham Award, Margaret Rhondda Award, Time Life Award; appeared on television and radio progs incl: Kaleidoscope (BBC Radio 4), Woman's Hour (BBC Radio 4), numerous World Service broadcasts; memb Cncl Soc of Authors; past memb: Cncl RSL, Mgmnt Ctee Soc of Authors, Lit Panel Arts Cncl, Lit Panel SE Arts, Ctee of Mgmnt PEN; memb Cncl Ctee Translators Assoc; tstee: PEN Lit Fndn (until 2003), Pension Fund Ctee Soc of Authors, Almedingen House RSL; involved with: local charities, work for prisoners, children in hosp; memb: Soc of Authors 1955, PEN 1955; FRSL 1989; *Awards* John Florio Prize (for best trans from Italian with Silvano Ceccherini's The Transfer) 1966, runner-up for trans of Giorgio Bassani's The Garden of the Finzi-Continis; *Books* The Eye of Heaven (1955, pub in USA as The Exchange of Joy), Charlie Chaplin, Early Comedies (1968), The Heirs of Tom Brown: the English School Story (1982, 2nd edn 1982); ed: Shelley (1956, reprinted 1985), Stalky & Co (1987, reprinted 1999), The Royal Society of Literature, a portrait (2000); *Style*— Isabel Quigly, FRSL; ✉ c/o RSL, Somerset House, Strand, London WC2R 1LA

QUILTER, Jeffrey Derek (Jeff); s of Alfred Stanley Quilter (d 1984), and Dorothy Lillian, *née* Rainbird (d 1976); *b* 7 September 1950; *Educ* St Martin's Sch for Boys; *m* 4 Aug 1984, Alison Judith, da of John Stout; 3 s (James b 30 Aug 1970, Joel b 24 June 1994, Finn b 3 Aug 1996), 1 da (Nicola b 22 Aug 1974); *Career* Doyle Dane Bernbach advtg agency 1970–74, French Gold Abbott 1974–78, Grey Advertising 1978–82, Publicis 1982–86, Ted Bates Advertising 1986–88; ops dir: Simons Palmer Clemmow Johnson 1988–97, TBWA Simons Palmer (following merger) 1997–98, TBWA GGT Simons Palmer (following merger) 1998–; MIPA 1985, memb Cartophillic Soc 1985; *Recreations* golf, cartophilly, cricket; *Clubs* Lancashire CCC; *Style*— Jeff Quilter, Esq; ✉ The Old Plough House, Plough Lane, Belsize, Sarratt, Hertfordshire WD3 4NN; TBWA GGT Simons Palmer, 76–80 Whitfield Street, London W1 (tel 020 7573 6666, fax 020 7573 6667)

QUIN, Baroness (Life Peer 2006), of Gateshead in the County of Tyne and Wear; Joyce Gwendolen Quin; PC (1998); *b* 1944; *Career* MEP (Lab) Tyne & Wear 1979–89; MP (Lab): Gateshead E 1987–97, Gateshead E and Washington W 1997–2005; memb Select Ctee on Treasy and the Civil Serv 1987–89; oppn spokesperson: on trade and indust 1989–92, on employment 1992–97, on Europe 1993–97; min of state: Home Office 1997–98, FCO 1998–99, MAFF 1999–2001; visiting prof Centre for Urban and Regnl Devpt Studies Univ of Newcastle 2003, hon lectr Univ of Durham 2003; memb Cncl RCVS 1992–96; hon fell Univ of Sunderland 1986, hon fell St Mary's Coll Durham 1993; *Style*— The Rt Hon the Lady Quin, PC

QUINLAN, Chris Charles; s of Edward Charles Quinlan, of Betchworth, Surrey, and June, *née* Richiardi; *b* 21 December 1954; *Educ* Alleyn's Sch Dulwich, Univ of Sheffield (LLB); *m* 4 April 1987 (m dis 1994); *Career* slr Wilkinson Kimbers 1981–83, advtg control offr IBA 1983–84, asst sec Beecham Gp plc 1984–85, controller of advtg The Cable Authy 1985–90, mktg dir Carlton Cabletime Ltd (subsid of Carlton Communications plc) 1990–92, dir Media Matrix Ltd 1992–; memb: Jt Industry Ctee for Cable Audience Res, Cable TV Assoc Mktg Gp, Bd of Mgmnt Gp 64 Theatre London; memb: Law Soc 1981, Mktg Soc 1992; chm Kingston and Surbiton Cons Assoc 2006; *Books* Making Sense of Computers in General Practice (jtly, 1995); *Recreations* ballooning, directing plays, inventing games; *Style*— Chris Quinlan, Esq; ✉ The Media Matrix Partnership, Lutidine House, Newark Lane, Ripley, Surrey GU23 6BS (tel 01483 270480, e-mail cq.media@matrix-group.co.uk)

QUINLAN, Sir Michael Edward; GCB (1991, KCB 1985, CB 1980); s of late Gerald Andrew Quinlan, of Hassocks, W Sussex, and late Roseanne Quinlan; *b* 11 August 1930; *Educ* Wimbledon Coll, Merton Coll Oxford; *m* 1965, (Margaret) Mary, *née* Finlay; 2 s, 2 da; *Career* RAF 1952–54; civil servant 1954–92: def cnsllr UK delgn to NATO 1970–73, under sec Cabinet Office 1974–77, dep under sec of State (policy and programmes) MOD 1977–81, dep sec (industry) Treasy 1981–82, perm sec Dept of Employment 1983–88, MOD 1988–92; dir: Lloyds Bank plc 1992–95, Pilkington plc 1992–99, Ditchley Fndn 1992–99, Lloyds TSB Group plc 1995–98; tstee Science Museum 1992–2001, chm Tablet Tst 2001–; visiting prof KCL 1992–95 and 2002–, public policy scholar Woodrow Wilson Center Washington DC 2000, consulting sr fell IISS 2004–; hon fell Merton Coll Oxford 1989; *Publications* Thinking About Nuclear Weapons (1997), European Defense Cooperation (2001); also author of various articles on defence and public service; *Recreations* golf, watching cricket, listening to music; *Clubs* RAF, MCC, Chipping Norton GC; *Style*— Sir Michael Quinlan, GCB; ✉ 3 Adderbury Park, West Adderbury, Oxfordshire OX17 3EN

QUINN, (James Steven) Brian; s of James Joseph Quinn (d 1977), of Lancs, and Elizabeth, *née* Thomas; *b* 16 June 1936; *Educ* Waterpark S Ireland, UCD, King's Inn Dublin (LLB, BCL); *m* 1, 1963 (m dis 1998), Blanche Cecilia, da of Richard Francis James (d 1986), of Spain; 2 s (James b 1963, Alexander b 1969), 1 da (Susannah b 1965); m 2, 2004, Catherine; *Career* head Industrial Activities Prices and Incomes Bd 1969–71, dir M L H Conslts

1971–79, corporate devpt advsr Midland Bank Int 1977–80, chief industrial advsr Price Cmmn 1977–78; chm: Brightstar Communications 1983–85, BAJ Holdings 1985–87, Harmer Holbrook 1987–88, Bliss Mill Mgmnt 1997–98, Signet Online 1997–99; chm and chief exec Digital Computer Services 1989–96 (dir 1985–96), chm Loan Line 1998–2000, dir QM Security Ltd 2002–05, DG IIC 2003– (tstee 1982–97, chm Exec Ctee 1984–87, pres 1988–91), chm Central Equipment Holdings Ltd 2003–04; memb Exec Ctee Inst of Euro Trade and Technol 1983–98, chm Gtr London Regnl Cncl Inst of Mgmnt (formerly BIM) 1990–93, tstee Int Communications Centre San Diego State Univ 1990–, chm Editorial Bd The Professional Manager 1991–98; *Recreations* golf, reading, poetry, veteran vehicles; *Clubs* Athenaeum; *Style—* Brian Quinn, Esq; ✉ 29 Bliss Mill, Chipping Norton, Oxfordshire OX7 5JR

QUINN, Brian; CBE (1996); s of Thomas Quinn, and Margaret, *née* Cairns; *b* 18 November 1936; *Educ* Univ of Glasgow (MA), Univ of Manchester (MA(Econ)), Cornell Univ (PhD); *m* 1961, Mary, *née* Bradley; 2 s (Aidan Thomas b 1962, David Bradley b 1969), 1 da (Fiona Anne b 1965); *Career* economist African Dept IMF 1964–70, IMF rep Sierra Leone 1966–68; Bank of England: Economics Div 1970–74, Chief Cashier's Dept 1974–77, head of Info Div 1977–82, asst dir Banking Supervision Div 1982–84, asst dir and head Banking Supervision Div 1984, asst dir and head of banking supervision 1986, exec dir i/c banking supervision and banking ops 1988–96, actg dep govr 1995, ret 1996; md Brian Quinn Consultancy Ltd 1996–; non-exec chm: Nomura Bank International plc 1996–99, Celtic plc 2000– (non-exec dir 1996–); non-exec dir: Bankgesellschaft Berlin (UK) plc 1996–2000, Britannia Asset Mgmnt Ltd 1998–2002, Genworth Financial Mortgage Insurance Ltd 2004–, Qatar Financial Centre Regulatory Authy 2006–; memb Toronto Centre Advsy Bd 1997–; conslt: IMF 1997–, Singapore Govt 1997–2002, McKinsey & Co 1998–, Sumitomo-Mitsui Banking Corp 2000–01, World Bank; chm Steering Ctee Fin Markets Gp LSE 1996–2001; hon prof of economics and finance Univ of Glasgow 2006–; FIBScot; *Recreations* watching football, fishing, golf, listening to music; *Style—* Brian Quinn, CBE; ✉ Celtic Football Club, Celtic Park, Glasgow G40 3RE

QUINN, James Stephen Christopher (Jim); s of James Quinn (d 1988), of Stourbridge, W Midlands, and Kathleen, *née* Kearns (d 1989); *b* 11 July 1939, Wolverhampton; *Educ* Cotton Coll, Univ of Birmingham (LLB); *m* 5 Sept 1964, Patricia Anne, *née* George; 2 s (Adrian James b 3 July 1969, Simon Paul b 23 March 1971), 1 da (Anna Kathryn b 25 May 1973); *Career* admitted slr 1964; ptnr MFG Slrs (formerly Norton Fisher) 1965–; dep registrar Co Court Midlands Circuit 1969–81; memb Lord Chllr's Advsy Panel 1990–99; memb: Law Soc, Common Law Bar Assoc, Inst for Continuing Educn; dir: Holy Trinity Convent Sch Ltd 1986–91, Wolverley NHS Tst 1991–95; chm Father Hudson's Soc, dir Catenian Assoc; Order of the Holy Sepulchre of Jerusalem; *Recreations* golf, caravanning, singing; *Style—* Jim Quinn, Esq; ✉ MFG Solicitors LLP, 20–21 The Tything, Worcester WR1 1HD (tel 01905 610410, fax 01905 610191, e-mail jim.quinn@mfgsolicitors.com)

QUINN, Marc; *b* 1964, London; *Educ* Millfield, Univ of Cambridge; *Career* artist; marble sculpture Alison Lapper Pregnant installed Trafalgar Square 2005; *Selected Solo Exhibitions* Bronze Sculpture (Jay Jopling/Otis Gallery London) 1988, Bread Sculpture (Galerie Marquardt and Middendorf Gallery Washington, DC) 1990, Out of Time (Jay Jopling/Grob Gallery London) 1991, Marc Quinn (Galerie Jean Bernier Athens) 1993, Marc Quinn (Jay Jopling/Art Hotel Amsterdam) 1994, The Blind Leading the Blind (Jay Jopling/White Cube London) 1995, Art Now. Emotional Detox: The Seven Deadly Sins (Tate Gallery London) 1995, Marc Quinn (South London Gallery London) 1998, Incarnate (Gagosian Gallery New York) 1998, Kunstverein Hanover 1999, Fondazione Prada Milan 2000, Groniger Museum 2000, Still Life (White Cube 2 London) 2000, A Genomic Portrait. John Sulston by Marc Quinn (Nat Portrait Gallery London) 2001, Tate Liverpool 2002, Behind the Mask: Portraits (Hatton Gallery Newcastle) 2002, The Overwhelming World of Desire (Paphiopedilum Winston Churchill Hybrid) (Goodwood Sculpture Park W Sussex) 2003, The Overwhelming World of Desire (Phragmipedium Sedenii) (Peggy Guggenheim Collection Venice) 2003, Flesh (Irish MOMA Dublin) 2004, The Incredible World of Desire (IBM Building NY) 2004, Meat Sculptures (Mary Boone Gallery NY) 2005, Chemical Life Support (White Cube London) 2005, Recent Sculptures (Groninger Museum) 2006, MACRO Rome 2006, Mary Boone Gallery NY 2007; *Selected Group Exhibitions* Group Show (Grob Gallery London) 1990, Modern Masters (Grob Gallery London) 1991, Sydney Biennial (Sydney) 1992, British Art (Barbara Gladstone Gallery New York) 1992, Strange Developments (Anthony d'Offay Gallery London) 1992, London Portfolio (Karsten Schubert Ltd London) 1992, Restaurant (Marc Jancou Paris) 1993, Real (Vienna Secession Vienna) 1993, Art Cologne (Saatchi Collection Cologne) 1993, Sonsbeek '93 (Arnhem) 1993, Prospect '93 (Frankfurt) 1993, Young British Artists II (Saatchi Collection London) 1993, Time Machine (British Museum London) 1994, Life is too Much (Galerie des Archives Paris) 1994, Ripple Across the Water (Minato Prefecture and Shibuya Prefecture Tokyo) 1995, Contemporary British Art in Print (Scottish Museum of Modern Art Edinburgh) 1995, Faith, Hope, Charity (Kunsthalle Vienna) 1995, Time Machine (Musée Egizio Turin) 1995, Happy End (Kunsthalle Dusseldorf) 1996, Works on Paper (Irish Museum of Modern Art Dublin) 1996, Feed and Greed (MAK Vienna) 1996, Hybrid (De Appel Foundation Amsterdam) 1996, Thinking Print. Books to Billboards 1980–95 (Museum of Modern Art New York) 1996, A Ilha do Tesouro (Funda ao Calouste Gulbenkian Lisbon) 1997, The Body (Art Gallery of New South Wales Australia) 1997, Sensation (Royal Academy of Arts London) 1997, Follow Me (Kunstverein Kehdingen Freiburg) 1997, The Quick and the Dead: Artists and Anatomy (Royal College of Art London) 1997, Inner Self (Mitchell-Innes & Nash New York (1998), The Colony Room 50th Anniversary Art Exhibition (A22 Projects London) 1998, Group Exhibition (Galleri Faurschou Copenhagen (1998), A Portrait of Our Times: An Introduction to the Logan Collection (San Francisco Museum of Modern Art San Francisco) 1998, Physical Evidence (Kettle's Yard Cambridge) 1998, Presence (Tate Gallery Liverpool) 1999, Now it's my Turn to Scream (Haines Gallery San Francisco) 1999, Officina Europa (Galleria d'Arte Moderna di Bologna) 1999, Something Warm and Fuzzy (Demoines Art Centre) 1999, Out There (White Cube 2 London) 2000, Psycho (Anne Faggionato London) 2000, Conversation (Milton Keynes Gallery) 2000, Wellcome Wing (The Science Museum London) 2000, Heads and Hands (Decatur House Museum Washington) 2001, In the Freud Museum (Freud Museum London) 2002, Thinking Big: Concepts for 21st Century British Sculpture (Peggy Guggenheim Collection Venice) 2002, Rapture: Art's Seduction by Fashion Since 1970 (Barbican Gallery London) 2002, Statements 7 (50th Venice Biennale) 2003, FRESH: Contemporary British Artists in Print (Edinburgh Printmakers) 2003, Fourth Plinth Proposal (Nat Gallery London) 2003, Garden of Eden (Helsinki City Art Museum) 2004, The Body: Art & Science (Nat Museum Stockholm) 2005, Summer Exhibition (Royal Acad of Art London) 2005, Art Out of Place (Norwich Castle and Museum Art Gallery) 2005, Egomania (Museum of Contemporary Art Modena) 2006, Aftershock: Contemporary British Art 1990–2006 (Guangdong Museum of Art and Capital Museum Beijing) 2006–07, La Triennale di Milano 2007, A Matter of Life and Death (Holburne Museum Bath) 2007, Genesis (Centraal Museum Utrecht) 2007; work in private collections incl: British Museum London, Deutsche Bank London, Saatchi Collection London, Stedlijk Museum Amsterdam, Tate Gallery London, Museum of Modern Art New York; *Style—* Marc Quinn, Esq

QUINN, Prof Niall Patrick; *b* 24 August 1948; *Educ* Downside, Gonville & Caius Coll Cambridge (BChir, MA, MD); *m* 1, 23 March 1974, Sheherazade Tafazzoli; m 2, 28 June 1985, Julie Brandler; *Career* méd res étranger Hôpital de la Salpêtrière Paris 1978–79, SHO Nat Hosp London 1979–80, research fell, hon lectr and lectr Maudsley and King's Coll Hosps and Inst of Psychiatry and KCH Med Sch 1980–88; Inst of Neurology UCL: lectr rising to reader 1988–97, clinical sub dean 1995–2004, prof 1997–2007, emeritus prof 2007–; hon conslt neurologist Nat Hosp for Neurology and Neurosurgery 1990–; memb Editorial Bd Lancet Neurology 2004–; memb Assoc of Br Neurologists, memb Irish Neurological Assoc, corresponding fell American Acad of Neurology, corresponding memb American Neurological Assoc, hon foreign memb Société Française de Neurologie, hon memb Int Movement Disorder Soc 2006 (sec 2001–02, chair European section 2005–06); FRCP 1994; *Books* Disorders of Movement: Clinical, pharmacological and physiological aspects (jtly, 1989), Parkinsonism (jtly, 1997); author of 300 original papers on movement disorders in peer review jls; *Recreations* Argentine tango, skiing; *Clubs* Athenaeum, Hawks' (Cambridge); *Style—* Prof Niall Quinn; ✉ Private Consulting Rooms, National Hospital for Neurology and Neurosurgery, Queen Square, London WC1N 3BG (e-mail n.quinn@ion.ucl.ac.uk)

QUINN, (Thomas) Richard; s of Thomas Quinn (d 1994), and Helen, *née* McDonald; *b* 2 December 1961; *Educ* Bannockburn HS; *m* 17 Feb 1990 (m dis 1993), Fiona Christine, da of Frank David Johnson; 1 s (Joshua Burns b 18 Nov 1990), 1 da (Robyn Helen b 12 Sept 1989); *Career* jockey; vice-pres Jockey's Assoc 1992–; first ride 1978, first winner Kempton 1981, Euro champion apprentice 1983, Br champion apprentice 1984, most winners 149 in 1996 (second in Jockeys' Table); 25 major races won (all Group One) incl: Irish Oaks, French 1,000 guineas, Spanish 1,000 guineas, Kenya 2,000 guineas, Gran Premio d'Italio, Prix de la Forêt 1986, Derby Italiano 1987 (second 1994), Yorkshire Oaks 1988, R & V Europe Preis 1989, Cheiveley Park Stakes 1989 Dewhurst Stakes 1990, Irish St Léger 1990 and 1995, Grosser Preis der Berliner Bank 1990, 214th St Leger 1990, Irish Oaks 1990, Gran Premio de Milano 1987, 1991 and 1996, Faith Sultan Mehmet II Trophy 1991, Brent Walker Fillies Mile 1991, Ciga Prix Marcel Boussac 1991, Rothmans Int (Canada) 1992, Prix Royal Oak (French Leger) 1992, Dubia Poule d'essai des Poulices 1992, Gran Criterium 1993, Italian Derby 1994, Juddmonte Lockinge Stakes 1996, Prix Vermeille 1998; ridden winners in 25 countries incl: GB, France, Ireland, Italy, Germany, USA, Canada, Aust, South Africa, Denmark, Holland, Sweden, Spain, Turkey, Belgium, Kenya, Saudi Arabia and Hong Kong; *Recreations* gardening, skiing; *Style—* Richard Quinn, Esq

QUINN, Terry; *b* 17 November 1951; *Educ* St Aloysius Coll Glasgow, Langside Coll; *m* Pat; 1 s, 1 da; *Career* ed-in-chief M Publications Scotland 1975–79, asst ed Buckinghamshire Advertiser 1979–81; ed: Bedfordshire Times & Herts Express Series and N Herts Gazette & Express Series 1982–84, Telegraph & Argus 1984–89, Evening News Edinburgh 1989–92; editorial dir Thomson Regional Newspapers 1994 (dep editorial dir 1992–94), ed Scottish Daily Record 1994–98, sr vice-pres for readership Thomson Newspapers USA and Canada, publisher Fairfax Sunday Newspapers NZ 2002–04, gp editorial devpt mangr Fairfax NZ 2003–04, editor-in-chief APN Regnl Papers 2004–; *Recreations* newspapers, books, music, football, tennis, travel; *Style—* Terry Quinn, Esq

QUINT, (Joan) Francesca Rae; da of Dr George Gomez (d 2004), of London, and Dr Joan Gomez, of Surrey; *b* 1 October 1947; *Educ* St Paul's Girls' Sch, KCL (LLB, AKC, Leathes Prize); *m* 1, 14 June 1980, Dr Lancelot Lionel Ware, OBE (d 2000); m 2, 17 Sept 2006, (Charles) Edward Hoskins; *Career* called to the Bar Gray's Inn 1970 (Francis Bacon scholar 1969), ad eundem Lincoln's Inn 1980; with Charity Cmmn 1972–89 (asst cmmr 1974, dep cmmr 1984); ind practice: Castle Chambers Exeter 1990–96, 11 Old Sq (East) 1990–2001, 11 Old Sq (West) 2001–06, Radcliffe Chambers 2006–; memb Exec Ctee Charity Law Assoc 1995–, tstee Statute Law Soc 1987–, memb Chancery Bar Assoc 1990–; memb Exec Ctee Assoc of Charitable Fndns 1990–94, memb Advsy Bd Almshouse Assoc 1990–; tstee: Bishopsgate Fndn 1991–94, St Peter's Convent Woking 1994–2004, Elizabeth Finn Care 1994–; govr Dulwich Coll 2004–, memb Mensa 1974–; *Books* Butterworth's Encyclopaedia of Forms and Precedents (contrib Charities, 1987, 1996 and 2002), Running a Charity (1993, 2 edn 1997), Charity Law Association Model Governing Instruments (1996, 2 edn 2003), Charities: The law and practice (looseleaf, jtly); *Recreations* walking, classical music, theatre, art; *Style—* Ms Francesca Quint; ✉ Radcliffe Chambers, 11 New Square, Lincoln's Inn, London WC2A 3TS (tel 020 7831 0081, fax 020 7405 2560, e-mail f.quint@radcliffechambers.com)

QUINTON, Baron (Life Peer UK 1983), of Holywell in the City of Oxford and County of Oxfordshire; Anthony Meredith Quinton; s of Surgn Capt Richard Frith Quinton, RN (d 1935), and Gwenllyan Letitia Quinton; *b* 25 March 1925; *Educ* Stowe, ChCh Oxford (MA); *m* 1952, Marcelle, da of late Maurice Wegier, of New York; 1 s, 1 da; *Career* served WWII RAF; fell All Souls Coll Oxford 1949–55, fell New Coll Oxford 1955–78, pres Trinity Coll Oxford 1978–87; pres Royal Inst of Philosophy 1991–2004; memb Arts Cncl of GB 1979–82, chm Br Library Bd 1985–90; FBA (vice-pres 1985–86); *Books* Political Philosophy (ed, 1967), The Nature of Things (1973), Utilitarian Ethics (1973), The Politics of Imperfection (1978), Francis Bacon (1980), Thoughts and Thinkers (1982), From Wodehouse to Wittgenstein (1998), Hume (1998); *Clubs* Garrick, Beefsteak; *Style—* The Rt Hon the Lord Quinton, FBA; ✉ A11 Albany, Piccadilly, London W1J 0AL (tel 020 7287 8686, fax 020 7287 9525)

QUIRICI, Daniel; s of Ernest Quirici, of Paris, and Candide, *née* Postai; *b* 8 June 1948; *Educ* Ecole des Hautes Etudes Commerciales Paris (MBA), Stanford Univ (PhD); *m* 1 Sept 1972, Margaret, da of Donald Wright Mann, of NY; 2 s (Alexandre b 15 Aug 1973, Francois b 23 May 1979), 1 da (Florence b 14 Feb 1978); *Career* assoc prof HEC 1970–76, assoc Arthur D Little 1976–82, sr vice-pres Credit Commercial de France (CCF) Paris 1983–91, md CCF Holdings Ltd 1986–91, chief exec Deloitte & Touche (D & T) Corporate Finance Europe Ltd 1991–97, md Citigroup 1999–2003, ptnr Echo Capital Ltd 2003–; *Recreations* tennis, golf; *Clubs* RAC, Hurlingham; *Style—* Daniel Quirici, Esq; ✉ 8 Montpelier Square, London SW7 1JU (work e-mail daniel.quirici@echo-capital.com)

QUIRK, Hon Eric Randolph; s of Baron Quirk, CBE, FBA (Life Peer), *qv*, and Jean, *née* Williams (d 1995); *b* 30 December 1951; *Educ* Highgate Sch, UCL (LLB); *m* 1, 30 July 1977 (m dis 1995), Patricia Anne, da of Stanley Lawrence Hemsworth; 2 da (Catharine b 25 May 1979, Sara b 14 Nov 1980), 1 s (Richard b 2 April 1983); m 2, 17 June 2006, Sheila Basford, da of Gerald Mann; *Career* admitted slr 1975; asst slr: Slaughter & May 1973–77, Alexander Tatham & Co 1978–81; ptnr: Alsop Wilkinson Manchester (formerly Lee Lane-Smith) 1981–93 (trg ptnr 1982–92), Laytons 1993–98, Fox Brooks Marshall 1998–2003, Cobbetts 2003–; memb: Legal Resources Gp Educn Ctee 1988–93, UCL Alumnus Soc, Law Soc; friend Hallé Orchestra, friend Opera North; *Recreations* violin, string quartets, rugby and cricket spectator (season ticket holder Sale Sharks RUFC), language, fell walking, opera, 20th century theatre, European architecture, political banter, finding humour in life; *Clubs* Middlewich Concert Orchestra, Lymm RUFC; *Style—* The Hon Eric Quirk; ✉ The Elms, Trouthall Lane, Plumley, Knutsford, Cheshire WA16 9RY (tel 0845 165 5230, fax 0845 404 2414)

QUIRK, Baron (Life Peer UK 1994), of Bloomsbury in the London Borough of Camden; Sir (Charles) Randolph Quirk; kt (1985), CBE (1976); s of late Thomas Quirk, and Amy Randolph Quirk; *b* 12 July 1920; *Educ* Cronk y Voddy Sch, Douglas HS IOM, UCL (MA, PhD, DLitt), Yale Univ; *m* 1, 1946 (m dis 1979), Jean (d 1995), da of Ellis Gauntlett Williams; 2 s (Hon Eric Randolph Quirk, *qv*, Hon Robin Antony b 1955); m 2, 1984, Gabriele, da of Judge Helmut Stein; *Career* prof of English language: Univ of Durham 1958–60, Univ of London 1960–68, Quain prof of English language and literature UCL 1968–81, vice-chllr Univ of London 1981–85; memb: Bd Br Cncl 1983–91, Cncl RADA

1985–2004, House of Lords Select Ctee 1997–2002; govr English Speaking Union 1980–85; pres: Inst of Linguists 1983–86, Br Acad 1985–89, Coll of Speech and Language Therapists 1987–91; chm: Hornby Educnl Tst 1979–93, Br Library Advsy Ctee 1984–96; tstee Wolfson Fndn 1987–; Hon DUniv: Lund, Uppsala, Paris, Liège, Nijmegen, Salford, Reading, Leicester, Newcastle, Durham, Bath, Open, Essex, Bar Ilan, Southern Calif, Westminster, Brunel, Sheffield, Glasgow, Prague, London, Poznan, Aston, Richmond, Copenhagen, Bucharest, Queen Margaret; foreign fell: Royal Belgian Acad of Sci, Royal Swedish Acad, Finnish Acad of Sci, American Acad of Arts and Sci; fell and res fell UCL; hon master of the Bench Gray's Inn; FBA, fell Academia Europaea; *Books* A University Grammar of English (1973), Style and Communication in the English Language (1982), English in the World (1985), A Comprehensive Grammar of the English Language (1985), Words at Work (1986), English in Use (1990), A Student's Grammar of the English Language (1990), An Introduction to Standard English (1993), Grammatical and Lexical Variance in English (1995); ed English Language Series (Longman); *Clubs* Athenaeum; *Style—* The Rt Hon the Lord Quirk, CBE, FBA; ⊠ University College London, Gower Street, London WC1E 6BT (tel 020 7219 2226)

QUIRKE, Pauline; *b* 8 July 1959; *m* Steve; 1 s (Charlie), 1 da (Emily); *Career* actress; trained at Anna Scher Theatre; *Theatre* A Tale of Two Cities (Royal Court) 1979, Dick Whittington (Hackney Empire) 1990–91 *Television* incl: Dixon of Dock Green 1968, Eleanor 1973, Pauline's Quirkes 1975, Angels 1976, Pauline's People 1977, Shine on Harvey Moon 1982, Girls on Top 1985, Rockliffe's Babies 1987, Casualty 1986, Birds of a Feather (8 series) 1989–94, Jobs for the Girls 1993, The Sculptress 1995, First Sign of Madness 1996, Double Nougat 1996, Deadly Summer 1997, Real Women 1997–99, Maisie Raine 1998–99, David Copperfield 1999, Office Gossip 2000, Down to Earth 2000–02 (three series), Randall & Hopkirk 2001, Murder in Mind 2001, Being April 2002, Carrie's War 2003; *Film* Little Dorrit 1986, The Elephant Man 1987, Getting it Right 1988, The Return of the Soldiers 1988, Still Lives-Distant Voices 1989, Our Boy (BBC Screen One) 1997, The Canterville Ghost (Carlton film) 1997, Check-Out Girl 1998, Arthur's Dyke 2000, Redemption RD 2001, Waiting for Giro 2003; *Awards* Best Comedy Newcomer 1991, British Comedy Actress Award 1993, Variety Club of GB BBC TV Personality of the Year 1994, TV Quick Awards Best Drama Actress 1998; nominated: BAFTA Best Actress Award 1997, Royal Television Soc Best Actress Award 1997, Nat Television Awards Most Popular Comedy Performer 1997; *Style—* Ms Pauline Quirke; ⊠ c/o DB Management, Pinewood Studios, Iver, Buckinghamshire SL0 0NH (tel 01753 654400, fax 01753 655701, e-mail aewen@dbman.co.uk)

QURESHI, Ashar; s of Azhar Naseem Qureshi (d 2001), and Faiza, *née* Feroze (d 1999); *b* 21 January 1965, Lahore, Pakistan; *Educ* Harvard Coll (BA), Harvard Univ (JD); *m* 15 Jan 1995, Mahkeen, *née* Malik; 2 da (Raniyah b 11 Oct 1995, Aidah b 9 May 2001), 1 s (Ahad Abbas b 24 March 1999); *Career* admitted NY Bar 1990; slr specialising in int corporate

finance and M&A; ptnr Cleary Gottlieb Steen & Hamilton LLP 1999– (joined 1990); memb Advsy Bd Practising Law Inst; author of numerous pubns; tstee Graham Layton Tst; *Recreations* riding, polo, theatre; *Style—* Ashar Qureshi, Esq; ⊠ Cleary Gottlieb Steen & Hamilton LLP, City Place House, 55 Basinghall Street, London EC2V 5EH (tel 020 7614 2226)

QURESHI, Murad; AM; s of Mushtaq Qureshi, and Khalida Qureshi; *b* 27 May 1965; *Educ* UEA (BA), UCL (MSc); *Career* worked in housing, devpt and regeneration until 2004; cncllr Church St City of Westminster 1998–2006; GLA: memb London Assembly (Lab) London (list) 2004–, dep chair Environment Ctee, memb Tport Ctee and London Fire and Emergency Planning Authy; memb: Socialist Environment and Resources Assoc (SERA); *Recreations* cricket, football; *Clubs* MCC; *Style—* Murad Qureshi, Esq, AM; ⊠ Greater London Authority, City Hall, The Queen's Walk, London SE1 2AA (tel 020 7983 4400, fax 020 7983 5679, e-mail murad.qureshi@london.gov.uk)

QURESHI, Dr Shakeel Ahmed; s of Mohammed Aslam Qureshi, of Luton, Beds, and Sara Begum Qureshi; *b* 20 March 1952; *Educ* Thomas Rotherham Coll, Rotherham GS, Univ of Manchester Med Sch (MB ChB); *m* 29 Dec 1968, Azra Siddique, da of Mohammed Siddique Qureshi, of Rawalpindi, Pakistan; 1 da (Noreen b 14 April 1971), 3 s (Sajid Shakeel b 21 May 1977, Abid Shakeel b 14 Feb 1980, Imran Shakeel b 29 July 1982); *Career* house physician Luton and Dunstable Hosp Luton 1976–77, house surgn Manchester Royal Infirmary 1977, sr house physician Joyce Green Hosp Dartford 1977–79, med registrar Barnet Gen Hosp 1979–80, cardiology res registrar Harefield Hosp 1980–83; conslt paediatric cardiologist: Rawalpindi Pakistan 1983–85, Royal Liverpool Children's Hosp 1987–88 (sr registrar paediatric cardiology 1986), Guy's Hosp 1988–; memb: BMA 1976, Br Cardiac Soc, Br Paediatric Cardiac Assoc, Assoc of European Paediatric Cardiologists; FRCP 1994 (MRCP 1979); *Recreations* cricket; *Style—* Dr Shakeel Qureshi; ⊠ Department of Paediatric Cardiology, Evelina Children's Hospital, Guy's and St Thomas's Trust, Lambeth Palace Road, London SE1 7EH (tel 020 7188 4547, fax 020 7188 4556)

QUYSNER, David William; s of late Charles William Quysner, of Mildenhall, Suffolk, and Marjorie Alice, *née* Partington; *b* 26 December 1946; *Educ* Bolton Sch, Selwyn Coll Cambridge (MA), London Business Sch; *m* 11 Sept 1971, Lindsay Jean Parris, da of Sir Norman Biggs; of Hurstpierpoint, W Sussex; 2 da (Sarah Louise b 1976, Deborah Helen b 1977), 1 s (Simon James b 1980); *Career* Investors in Industry plc (now 3i plc) 1968–82, dir Abingworth plc 1986–99; chm: Comino Gp plc 1999–2006, Quester VCT3 plc 2000–05, Br Venture Capital Assoc 1996–97, RCM Technol Tst 2003–, Capital for Enterprise Advsy Bd DTI 2005–; *Recreations* opera, golf; *Style—* David Quysner, Esq; ⊠ Abingworth Management Ltd, 38 Jermyn Street, London SW1Y 6DN (tel 020 7534 1500, fax 020 7287 0480)

Q

R

RABAGLIATI, Duncan Charles Pringle; s of Brig (Charles) Ian Evershed Rabagliati (d 1991), of Menston, W Yorks, and Joan, *née* Pringle; *b* 3 January 1945; *Educ* Sedbergh; *m* Mair Alethea, da of (Christopher) Ivor Williams; 2 s (Alastair James b 15 Jan 1974, Jonathan Stuart b 5 Oct 1975), 1 da (Sarah Louise b 9 June 1980); *Career* articled clerk Booth & Co Leeds 1964–69; McKenna & Co London: asst slr 1969–73, ptnr 1973–91, conslt 1991–94; ptnr: Payne Hicks Beach 1991–92 (conslt 1992), Wedlake Bell 1992–2002 (conslt 2002–05); conslt Gregsons 2005–; hon legal advsr Fedn of Br Historic Vehicle Clubs 1995–98, legal advsr International Historic Vehicle Orgn 1997–2005; chm Formula Jr Historic Racing Assoc 1993–, historian 500 Owners Assoc Ltd (chm 2003–05); UK rep Historic Cmmn FIA 2002–; winner 4 FIA Lurani Trophies (1 as organiser, 3 as class winner); *Books* The Formula One Record Book (jtly, 1971), A Record of Grand Prix and Voiturette Racing (13 vols, jtly, 1985–2002), The Asian Buyers' Guide to UK Property (contrib, 1996); contrib to numerous motoring books and magazines; *Recreations* motoring history, historic motor racing, genealogy, skiing; *Style—* Duncan C P Rabagliati, Esq

RABAN, Jonathan; s of Rev Peter J C P Raban, and Monica, *née* Sandison; *b* 14 June 1942; *Educ* Univ of Hull (BA); *m* 1985 (m dis 1992), Caroline Cuthbert; m 2, 1992, Jean Lenihan; 1 da (b 1992); *Career* lectr in Eng and American Lit UCW 1965–67, UEA 1967–69, professional writer 1969–; FRSL; *Books* The Technique of Modern Fiction (1969), Mark Twain: Huckleberry Finn (1969), The Society of the Poem (1971), Soft City (1973), Arabia Through The Looking Glass (1979), Old Glory (1981, Heinemann award RSL 1982, Thomas Cook award 1982), Foreign Land (1985), Coasting (1986), For Love and Money (1987), God, Man and Mrs Thatcher (1989), Hunting Mister Heartbreak (1990, Thomas Cook Award 1991), The Oxford Book of the Sea (ed, 1992), Bad Land: An American Romance (1996, Nat Book Critics' Circle Award 1997), Passage to Juneau: A Sea and its Meanings (1999), Surveillance (2006); *Recreations* sailing; *Clubs* Groucho, Cruising Assoc; *Style—* Jonathan Raban, Esq, FRSL

RABIN, Prof Brian Robert; s of Emanuel Rabin (d 1973), and Sophia, *née* Neshaver (d 1982); *b* 4 November 1927; *Educ* Latymer's, UCL (BSc, MSc, PhD); *m* 29 Aug 1954, Sheila Patricia, da of Charles Patrick George (d 1972); 1 s (Paul Robert b 27 Jan 1958), 1 da (Carol (Mrs Costa) b 23 Sept 1959); *Career* UCL 1954–: asst lectr then lectr 1954–63, reader in biochemistry 1963–67, prof of enzymology 1967–70, head of Biochemistry Dept 1970–88, fell UCL 1984, prof of biochemistry 1988–94 (prof emeritus 1994); fndr dir London Biotechnology Ltd 1985–, dir Cogent Ltd and Cogents Holdings Ltd 1986–89; inventions covered by issued patents: ultra sensitive prosthetogen-based assays, licensed and employed on Dade-Behring analysers for assaying TSH and troponin levels in human blood, completely novel cancer treatment involving humanised antibodies and a mutated (reverse polarity) human enzyme (in course of development by LBL); FZS 1972, FIBiol 1972, EMBO 1980, memb Académie Für Umuweltfragen 1987; *Recreations* travel, carpentry; *Clubs* Athenaeum; *Style—* Prof Brian Rabin; ✉ 22 Leaf House, Catherine Place, Harrow HA1 2JW (tel 020 8861 5278)

RABINOWITZ, Harry; MBE (1978); s of Israel Rabinowitz (d 1960), and Eva, *née* Kirkel (d 1971); *b* 26 March 1916; *Educ* Athlone HS, Univ of the Witwatersrand, London Guildhall Sch of Music; *m* 1, 15 Dec 1944 (m dis 2000), Lorna Thurlow, da of Cecil Redvers Anderson (d 1970); 2 da (Karen Lesley b 1947, Lisa Gabrielle b 1960), 1 s (Simon Oliver b 1951); m 2, 18 March 2001, Mary C Scott; *Career* Corpl SA Forces 1942–43; conductor BBC Radio 1953–60; head of music: BBC TV Light Entertainment 1960–68, LWT 1968–77; currently freelance conductor/composer; conductor: Hollywood Bowl 1983–84, Boston Pops 1985–92, London Symphony Orchestra, Royal Philharmonic Orchestra, Carnegie Hall 1996, Merchant Ivory 35th Anniversary Celebration; conductor for films: Chariots of Fire, Manhattan Project, Heat & Dust, The Bostonians, Maurice, Time Bandits, Return to Oz, L'Argent, Camille Claudel, Ballad of the Sad Cafe, J'Embrasse Pas, La Voix, Pour Sacha, Les Carnassiers, Howard's End, The Ark and the Flood, Tractions, The Remains of the Day, Shirley Valentine, Business Affair, Grosse Fatigue, Le Petit Garçon, The Flemish Board, Mantegna et Fils, La Fille de d'Artagnan, Death and the Maiden, Jefferson in Paris, Nelly and Mr Arnold, The Secret Agent, The Stupids, The Proprietor, Star Command, La Belle Verte, Surviving Picasso, The English Patient, Tonka, Amour Sorcier, My Story So Far, City of Angels, Place Vendôme, A Soldier's Daughter Never Cries, Message in a Bottle, Cotton Mary, The Talented Mr Ripley, The Golden Bowl, Possession, The Music Box, Le Divorce, Bon Voyage, Cold Mountain; TV: New Faces 1987–88, Paul Nicholas Special 1987–88, Julia MacKenzie Special 1986, Nicholas Nickleby, Drummonds, The Insurance Man, Absent Friends, Simon Wiesenthal Story, Marti Caine Special, Alien Empire, Battle of the Sexes; composer TV: Agatha Christie Hour, Reilly Ace of Spies, The Great Depression, Memento Mori, DW Griffiths Father of Film; conductor theatre: World Premieres of 'Cats' and 'Song and Dance'; Discs: Michael Crawford, Sarah Brightman, The Music of Duke Ellington (with Johnny Mathis), The Music of George Gershwin (with Jack Jones), Radio City Christmas Album, 11 Japanese song hits (with RPO), Phil Woods: I Remember; awards: Br Acad of Songwriters, Composers and Authors (BASCA) Gold award 1986, Radio and TV Industries award 1984, Allmusic Lifetime Contrib Gold award 1990, Freeman City of London 1996; *Recreations* wine tasting, gathering edible fungi; *Style—* Harry Rabinowitz, Esq, MBE; ✉ 7 East View Cottages, Pleaslake, Surrey GU5 9RG (tel 01306 730674, e-mail mitziscott@aol.com)

RABINOWITZ, Laurence; QC (2002); s of Joseph Rabinowitz (d 1992), of SA, and Mary, *née* Alexander; *b* 3 May 1960; *m* 16 July 1989, Suzanne Jacqueline, da of Dr Alan Benster; 2 s (Samuel, Jacob), 1 da (Josephine); *Career* jr counsel for the Crown (Chancery) 1995; memb Middle Temple; *Style—* Laurence Rabinowitz, Esq, QC; ✉ 1 Essex Court, Temple, London EC4Y 9AR (e-mail lrabinowitz@oeclaw.co.uk)

RACE, Russell John; JP, DL; s of Russell Edgar Race (d 1982), and Winifred Olive, *née* Clissold (d 1996); *b* 28 May 1946; *Educ* Sir Joseph Williamson's Mathematical Sch Rochester, Univ of Liverpool (BA); *Career* economist White Fish Authy 1967–70, dir ABN AMRO Hoare Govett 1985–97 (investment analyst 1970–76, corp fin 1976–97); dir: Goldshield Group plc 1998–2004, T Clarke plc 1998–, Neutec Pharma plc 2002–06; chm Chatham Maritime Tst, memb Ct of Assts Rochester Bridge Tst; memb Ct of Assts Worshipful Co of Glaziers & Painters of Glass; FRSA; *Recreations* music, sport, freemasonry; *Clubs* Naval and Military, London Capital, Castle (Rochester); *Style—* Russell Race, Esq, JP, DL; ✉ 3 Copse Close, Pattens Lane, Rochester, Kent ME1 2RS (tel 01634 406347)

RACKHAM, Oliver; OBE (1998); s of Geoffrey Herbert Rackham (d 1981), of Norwich, and Norah Kathleen, *née* Wilson (d 1953); *b* 17 October 1939; *Educ* King Edward VI Sch Norwich, Norwich City Coll, CCC Cambridge (BA, Parker Exhibitioner, fndn scholar, PhD); *Career* research worker in Plant Breeding Inst Cambridge 1968–72; fell and later praelector CCC Cambridge 1964–; Univ of Cambridge: research worker in Dept of Botany 1964–68 and 1972–90, research worker Dept of Geography 1988–2000, jr proctor 1996–97, hon prof of historical ecology 2006–; lectr for Field Studies Cncl and Kingcombe Tst; Hon DUniv Essex 2000; hon fell Br Naturalists' Accoc 2007–; FBA 2002; *Books* Hayley Wood: its history and ecology (1975), Trees and Woodland in the British Landscape (1976, 2 edn 1990), Ancient Woodland: its history, vegetation and uses in England (1980, 2 edn 2003), History of the Countryside (winner of Angel Literary Award, 1986), The Last Forest: the history of Hatfield Forest (1989), The Illustrated History of the Countryside (winner of Sir Peter Kent Conservation Award and Natural World Book Prize, 1994), The Making of the Cretan Landscape (with J A Moody, 1996), The Nature of Southern Europe (with A T Grove, 2001), Woodlands (New Naturalist volume 100, 2006); author of over 40 articles concerning fieldwork in Greece, Crete and S Europe and historical ecology in Britain; winner Peter Scott Memorial Award 2001; *Recreations* study of timber framed buildings; *Style—* Dr Oliver Rackham, OBE, FBA; ✉ Corpus Christi College, Cambridge CB2 1RH (tel 01223 360144, fax 01223 339041, e-mail or10001@cam.ac.uk)

RADCLIFFE, David Andrew; s of Clinton Bower Radcliffe, and Margaret Radcliffe; *b* 13 June 1942; *Educ* The Leys Sch Cambridge, Univ of Cambridge (MA); *m* 22 May 1971, Elisabeth Mary, da of David Scotson Bramley (d 2003); 2 s (James b 11 Nov 1975, Matthew b 5 Jan 1981), 1 da (Emily b 7 Feb 1978); *Career* cmmnd RM Reserve 1967, ret 1971; called to the Bar Inner Temple 1966; recorder of the Crown Court 1987–, immigration and asylum adjudicator 1998–2005, immigration judge 2005–; memb Asylum and Immigration Tbnl 2005–; vice-pres Putney Soc 1987– (chm 1983–85); *Recreations* golf, tennis, swimming, walking; *Clubs* Roehampton; *Style—* David Radcliffe, Esq; ✉ 18 Red Lion Court, off Fleet Street, London EC4A 3EB (fax 020 7520 6248/9, DX 478 LDE)

RADCLIFFE, John Peter; s of John Maurice Radcliffe (d 1949), of Bristol, and Margery Bloomfield Lumsden (d 1974); *b* 9 January 1935; *Educ* Cheltenham Coll (open scholar), Clare Coll Cambridge (exhibitioner, MA); *m* 1, 5 Sept 1959, Bridget Jane, da of Dr William Leslie Cuthbert (d 1999), of Stirling; 2 da (Virginia Frances b 10 Oct 1961, Polly Clare b 10 Dec 1965), 1 s (Jonathan James b 31 July 1963); m 2, 21 May 2001, Sheila Mary, da of Patrick Butler, of Hatfield; *Career* asst to commercial mangr (economics) UKAEA Industrial Group 1960–61; BBC: prodr World Service Current Affairs 1961–64, prodr responsible for history BBC Schools Television 1965–70, sr prodr responsible for social sciences BBC Open Univ Prodns 1970–72, exec prodr BBC Continuing Educn Television 1972–84, exec prodr BBC Computer Literacy Project 1980–83, head of BBC Open Univ Prodn Centre 1984–89, md BBC Subscription Television 1990–93; exec prodr The MultiMedia Corp 1994–97, md Fast Media 1997–; *Recreations* hill walking, photography, literature, computing, conversation; *Style—* John Radcliffe, Esq; ✉ 106 Richmond Avenue, Islington, London N1 0LS (tel 020 7837 5039, e-mail johnradcliffe@blueyonder.co.uk)

RADCLIFFE, Julian Guy Yonge; OBE (2000), QVRM (2004), TD; s of Maj Guy Lushington Yonge Radcliffe, MBE, and Anne Marigold, *née* Leyland; *b* 29 August 1948; *Educ* Eton, New Coll Oxford; *m* Frances Harriet Thompson; 2 s, 1 da; *Career* Lloyd's broker and underwriting memb of Lloyd's; md: Investment Insurance Int 1973–81, Control Risks Ltd 1976–81; dir: Credit Insurance Assoc Ltd 1975–83, Hogg Group plc 1986–94, Aon Risk Services (UK) Ltd (formerly Bain Hogg International) 1994–, Loss Management Group 1994–; chm International Art and Antique Loss Register Ltd 1991–; cmmnd Royal Yeo 1971 (Lt-Col 1993), cmmnd Dorset Yeo 1997–99, Col MOD 2000; Upper Bailiff Worshipful Co of Weavers 1995–96; *Recreations* farming, shooting, military and strategic studies; *Clubs* City of London, Cavalry and Guards'; *Style—* Julian Radcliffe, Esq, OBE, QVRM, TD; ✉ 32 Brynmaer Road, London SW11 4EW; Art Loss Register, 63–66 Hatton Garden, London EC1N 8LE (e-mail julian.radcliffe@artloss.com)

RADCLIFFE, Mark; s of Philip Radcliffe, and Doreen, *née* Goad; *Educ* Bolton Sch, Univ of Manchester (BA); *Career* lavatory attendant Piccadilly Radio 1979–83, prodr Radio 1 1983–85, head of music Piccadilly Radio 1985–86, prodr rising to sr prodr BBC Manchester 1986–, presenter (with Marc Riley, *qv*) BBC Radio 1 1991–2004, currently presenter Radio 2 (also sometime presenter Radio 4 and 5 Live, BBC TV); dir M And TV prodns; co-fndr Halon Music Prize 2002; Sony Gold Awards 1992, 1998, 1999, 2001 and 2007 (Best Music Prog), NME Best DJ in the World Today 1997 and 1998; *Records* The Worst Album in the World (1999), Songs of the Back Bar (1999), Our Kid Eh (2001), On The Razzle (2002), Mahone Brew (2006); *Books* Show Business: Diary of a Rock & Roll Nobody (1999), Northern Sky (2005); *Recreations* just music and kids and Manchester City FC; *Style—* Mark Radcliffe, Esq; ✉ c/o PBJ Management, 7 Soho Street, London W1D 3DQ (tel 020 7287 1112)

RADCLIFFE, Mark Hugh Joseph; DL (Hants 1997); s of Hugh John Reginald Joseph Radcliffe, MBE (d 1993), and Marie-Thérèse (Mariquita), *née* Pereira; cous and hp of Sir Sebastian Everard Radcliffe, 7 Bt, *qv*; *Educ* Downside; *m* 20 Feb 1963, Anne, da of Maj-Gen Arthur Evers Brocklehurst, CB, DSO; 3 da (Lucinda b 1964, Emily Marie Louise (Mrs Alex Rogers) b 1968, Camilla Mary b 1971); *Career* 2 Lt Coldstream Gds 1956–58; mktg mangr Cape Asbestos Ltd 1958–68, chief exec Lancer Boss Group Ltd 1968–74, md Triang Pedigree Ltd 1974–78, dir TI Group plc 1978–92, chm Upton Management Services Ltd 1992–2006; CBI: dep DG 1991–93, estab National Manufacturing Cncl 1991, advsr on industrial affrs 1991–94; non-exec chm: Metsec plc 1993–98, IE Gp plc 1997–2000; non-exec dir: London Stock Exchange 1993–98, William Jacks plc 1994–99, Reliance Security Group plc 1995–2005; ind dir Securities and Futures Authy Ltd 1993–2001; patron Meridian Tst 1996–, chm Hants Youth Options 1997–; High Sheriff Hants 1996–97, vice-pres Countess of Brecknock Hospice 1998–, govr Southampton Inst 1999–2000; FInstD; *Recreations* shooting, golf, tennis, fishing, gardening; *Clubs* Cavalry and Guards', Pratt's, MCC; *Style—* Mark Radcliffe, Esq, DL; ✉ The Malt House, Upton, Andover, Hampshire SP11 0JS (tel 01264 736266)

RADCLIFFE, Paula Jane; MBE (2002); da of Peter Radcliffe, and Patricia Radcliffe, of Beds; *b* 17 December 1973; *Educ* Loughborough Univ (BA); *m* Gary Lough; 1 da (Isla Olivia b 17 Jan 2007); *Career* athlete; World Junior Cross Country champion 1992, Br champion 5000m 1995, 1996 and 1997, winner European Cross Country Championship 1998 and 2003, Silver medal 10000m World Championships 1999, winner Great North Run 2000 and 2003, World Half Marathon champion 2000, 2001 and 2003, fourth place 10000m Olympic Games 2000 (fifth place 5000m 1996), winner (long course) World Cross Country Championships 2001 and 2002 (second place 1997 and 1998, third place 1999, second place (short course) 2001), winner London Marathon 2002, 2003 (women's world record, 2 hours 15 mins 25 secs) and 2005 (women only world record 2 hours 17 mins and 42 seconds), Gold medal 5000m Cwlth Games 2002, Gold medal 10000m European Championships 2002, winner Chicago Marathon 2002, winner NY Marathon 2004, Gold medal marathon World Championships 2005; twice winner NYC Road Mile, world best over 5 miles, 8 km and 10 km; UK and Cwlth record holder: 3000m (8 mins 22.20 secs), 5000m (14 mins 29.11 secs); UK, Cwlth and European record holder 10000m (30 mins 1.09 secs); European best over half marathon 66 mins 47 secs; Br Athletics Team Womens Capt 1998, 1999, 2000, 2001 and 2002; Junior Athlete of the Year 1992, Br Athletic Fedn Athlete of the Year 1997, Br Sports Writers Reebok Trophy 1997, Sunday Times Sportswoman of the Year 1999, Br Athletic Fedn and Sports Writers Female Athlete of the Year 1999 and 2001, Women of the Year Outstanding Achievement Award 2002, Int Assoc of Athletics Fedns World Female Athlete of the Year 2002, BBC Sports Personality of the Year 2002, Br Athletics Writers' Assoc Female Athlete of the Year 2002, 2003 and 2005, Walpole Sporting Award 2003; *Recreations* athletics, most sports, reading, relaxing; *Clubs* Bedford & County Athletics, British Milers, Loughborough Students Athletic; *Style—* Ms Paula Radcliffe, MBE; ✉ c/o Abigail Tordoff, Octagon, 81/83 Fulham High Street, London SW6 3TW (tel 020 7862 0039, e-mail abigail.tordoff@octagon.com)

RADCLIFFE, Sir Sebastian Everard; 7 Bt (UK 1813), of Milnesbridge House, Yorks; s of Capt Sir (Joseph Benedict) Everard Henry Radcliffe, 6 Bt, MC (d 1975), and Marcia Helen, *née* Turville-Constable-Maxwell (now Mrs Howard M S Tanner); *b* 8 June 1972; *Heir* cous, Mark Radcliffe, DL, *qv*; *Style—* Sir Sebastian Radcliffe, Bt

RADCLYFFE, Sarah; da of Capt Charles Raymond Radclyffe, of Lew, Oxon, and Helen Viola Egerton, *née* Cotton; *b* 14 November 1950; *Educ* Heathfield Sch Ascot; *m* 29 June 1996, William Penton Godfrey; 2 s (Sam Charles Radclyffe b 30 March 1989, Callum Penton Radclyffe Godfrey b 7 Feb 1995); *Career* film prodr 1978–; films incl: The Tempest 1979, My Beautiful Laundrette 1985, Caravaggio 1985, Wish You Were Here 1986, Sammy and Rosie Get Laid 1987, A World Apart 1988, Paperhouse 1989, Fools of Fortune 1990, Edward II 1991, Robin Hood 1991, Dakota Road 1992, Sirens 1993, Second Best 1993, Bent 1996, Cousin Bette 1997, Les Miserables 1998, The War Zone 1999, Ratcatcher 1999, There's Only One Jimmy Grimble 2000, Love's Brother 2003, Tara Road 2004, Free Jimmy 2006, How About You 2007, The Edge of Love 2007; dir: Channel 4 1995–99, Film Cncl 1999–2004; govr BFI 1996–99; *Style—* Miss Sarah Radclyffe; ✉ Sarah Radclyffe Productions Ltd, 10–11 St George's Mews, London NW1 8XE (tel 020 7483 3556, fax 020 7586 8063, e-mail sarah@srpltd.co.uk)

RADDA, Prof Sir George Karoly; kt (2000), CBE (1993); *b* 9 June 1936, Gyor, Hungary; *Educ* Pannonhalma Hungary, Eotvos Univ Budapest, Merton Coll Oxford (MA, DPhil); *m*; 3 c (from previous m); *Career* research assoc Univ of Calif Berkeley 1962–63; Univ of Oxford: jr res fell Merton Coll 1961–64, lectr in organic chemistry St John's Coll 1963–64, departmental demonstrator in biochemistry 1964–66, fell and tutor in organic chemistry Merton Coll 1964–84, univ lectr in biochemistry 1966–84, dir Br Heart Fndn NMR Res Gp 1983–2003, Br Heart Fndn prof of molecular cardiology 1984–2003, professorial fell Merton Coll 1984–2003 (emeritus fell 2003–), hon dir MRC Biochemical and Clinical Magnetic Resonance Unit 1988–96, head Dept of Biochemistry 1991–96; chief exec MRC 1996–2003, chm Nat Cancer Res Inst 2001–03; memb: various panels SRC, various panels and sub-ctees MRC (memb Cncl and Strategy Ctee 1988–92, memb Cell Bd 1982–87, chm Cell and Disorders Bd 1988–92, chm Human Genome Mapping Directed Prog Ctee 1993–96, chm Human Genome Mapping Coordinating Ctee 1994–96); memb Cncl: Royal Soc 1990–92, ICRF 1991–96 (chm Scientific Advsy Ctee 1994–96); pres Soc of Magnetic Resonance in Med 1985–86; memb: Fachbeirat Max-Planck-Institut für Systemphysiologie Dortmund 1987–92, Int Advsy Bd Euro Soc for Magnetic Resonance in Med and Biology (ESMRMB) 1994–96, Int Advsy Cncl Biomedical Research Cncl Singapore 2003–; consltt: ICI Pharmaceuticals 1978–95, Oxford Magnet Technology 1985–87, CIBA Geigy UK Ltd 1985–90, Otsuka Electronics 1987–88; non-exec dir BTG plc 1999–; memb Academia Europena 1999; tstee Cancer Research UK 2003–; author of over 700 pubns in reviewed scientific and med jls worldwide, ed Clinical Cardiology 1994–; memb Ed Bd Jl of Royal Soc Interface 2004–; Colworth Medal 1969, Feldberg Fndn Prize 1981, Br Heart Fndn Gold Medal and Prize for Cardiovascular Research 1982, CIBA Medal and Prize Biochemical Soc 1983, Gold Medal Soc of Magnetic Resonance in Med 1984, Buchanan Medal Royal Soc 1987, Skinner Lecture Medal RCR 1989, Rank Prize in Nutrition 1991; numerous named lectures incl: Welbeck Meml Lecture Coll of Radiographers London 1990, ICI Canada Distinguished Lectureship Ottawa 1992, Louise Bertram Abraham Lecture RCP London 1993, Linacre Lecture St John's Coll Cambridge 1994, Paul Lauterbur Lectr 2001; Hon DM Bern Univ 1985, Hon DSc (Med) Univ of London 1991; Hon DSc: Univ of Stirling 1997, Univ of Sheffield 1999, Debrecen Univ Hungary 2001, Univ of Birmingham 2003, Universitéde la Mediterranèe 2003; Hon DMed Heinrich Heine Univ of Düsseldorf, Hon DSc Univ of Aberdeen 2004; memb: Chemical Soc 1961–79, Biochemical Soc 1964, Br Photobiology Soc 1964–76, Br Biophysical Soc 1967–78; Hon FRCR 1985, Hon FRCP 1997, hon fell American Heart Assoc (Citation for Int Achievement) 1987; FRS 1980, fell Soc of Magnetic Resonance 1994, founding fell Acad of Med Sci 1998, founding fell Int Soc of Heart Research 2000, fell Int Acad of Cardiovascular Sci 2001; *Style—* Prof Sir George K Radda, CBE, FRS; ✉ University Laboratory of Physiology, Parks Road, Oxford OX1 3PT; Merton College, Oxford OX1 4JD

RADFORD, Prof Colin Buchanan; OBE (1994); s of Walter Buchan Radford (d 1995), of London, and Elizabeth Robertson, *née* Collie (d 1990); *b* 28 May 1931; *Educ* Ashby-de-la-Zouch Boys' GS, RMA Sandhurst, Univ of Nottingham (BA, MA, PhD); *m* 5 April 1958, Ingeborg Sara (Inge), da of Chaim Frenkel (d 1938), of Vienna; 1 da (Katy b 24 April 1961), 1 s (Tim b 23 Feb 1963); *Career* cmmnd RA 1952, served until 1957; asst head of recruitment for employee rels Esso Petroleum 1961–62, head of modern languages Up Holland GS 1962–66; Queen's Univ Belfast: prof of French 1975–93 (prof emeritus 1994), dir Sch of Modern and Medieval Languages 1987–92; author of books incl four on French lit; chm: Arts Cncl of NI 1991–94, Alliance Française de Belfast 1991–2001; memb Bd Br Inst in Paris 1988–92, memb and hon treas Soc of French Studies 1972–92; tstee: Grand Opera House Belfast 1993–2000, UDR Benevolent Fund 1986–2001; Commandeur dans l'Ordre des Palmes Académiques France 1989 (Officier 1986); *Recreations* theatre, gardener's mate; *Style—* Prof Colin Radford, OBE; ✉ The Hill, Woburn Road, Millisle, Co Down BT22 2HY (tel 028 9186 1361)

RADFORD, His Hon Judge David Wyn; s of late Robert Edwin Radford, CB, of Guildford, Surrey, and Eleanor Margaret, *née* Jones; *b* 3 January 1947; *Educ* Cranleigh Sch, Selwyn Coll Cambridge (MA, LLM); *m* 23 Sept 1972, Nadine, da of Joseph Poggioli, of London; 2 da (Carina b 1975, Lauren b 1986), 2 s (Simon b 1982, Peter b 1983); *Career* called to the Bar Gray's Inn 1969; recorder 1993–96 (asst recorder 1988–93), circuit judge (SE Circuit) 1996–2002, sr circuit judge 2002–; Lib Parly candidate Hampstead 1975–83; *Recreations* spending time with family, visiting areas and places of natural and historical heritage, following soccer, reading widely; *Style—* His Hon Judge Radford; ✉ Snaresbrook Crown Court, Hollybush Hill, Snaresbrook, London E11 1QW

RADFORD, Jonathan Vaughan; s of Patrick Vaughan Radford, CBE, MC, TD, DL, of Langford Hall, Newark, Notts, and Evelyn, *née* Wilkinson; *b* 11 June 1959; *Educ* Eton, Univ of Bristol (BA); *m* 10 Dec 1999, Caroline, née Higgins; 1 da (Freya Chiara b 6 Jan 2002), 1 s (Enzo Vaughan b 8 Feb 2005); *Career* accountant; Peat Marwick Mitchell and Co London 1981–86, fin dir Stag Furniture Holdings plc 1992–95 (various mgmnt positions 1986–92), chief exec Elit Group Ltd 1996–2001; chm and non-exec dir various private cos; Freeman City of London 1987, Liveryman Worshipful Co of Furniture Makers 1987; ACIS 1990, FCA 1994 (ACA 1984); *Recreations* Venice and art; *Clubs* Annabel's; *Style—* Jonathan Radford, Esq; ✉ Oasby House, Oasby, Grantham, Lincolnshire NG32 3NA (tel 01529 455415, e-mail jonathan@oasbyhouse.co.uk)

RADFORD, Matthew; *b* 1953; *Educ* Camberwell Sch of Art (BA); *Career* artist; teacher: Camberwell Sch of Art 1981–84, Drawing Center NY 1985–86, NY Studio Sch 1989–93; visiting lectr Slade Sch of Art 2000; *Solo Exhibitions* Letchworth Museum and Art Gallery 1980, Kettle's Yard 1984, Chuck Levitan NY 1985, Donald Wren Gallery NY 1987, Frank Bernarducci Gallery NY 1988 and 1990, CVII NY 1989, Tatistcheff Gallery Los Angeles 1993 (NY 1991), Grace Borgenicht Gallery NY 1993 and 1994, Houldsworth Fine Art London 1994 and 1997–2004 (annually), Newsreel: new etchings (Alan Cristea Gallery) 2003, Works on Paper (Advanced Graphics London) 2005, Paintings and Prints (Glasgow Print Studio) 2005, Farbe + Figur (Städtische Galerie Villingen-Schwenningen) 2005, The Space Between: New Paintings (SW1 Galleries London) 2006, Milton Gallery (St. Paul's School London) 2006, Random Empires (Chelsea Art Gallery Silicon Valley) 2006; *Group Exhibitions* Royal Festival Hall 1980, 1981 and 1983, RA Diploma Galleries 1980, Stock Exchange Gallery 1981, British Drawing (Hayward Gallery) 1982, The Drawing Center 1985 and 1993, Donald Wren Gallery 1987, New York Observed (Frank Bernarducci Gallery) 1988, Downtown Perspectives (Adelphi Univ NY) 1988, New York Art Now (Helander Gallery Palm Beach) 1989, Visions and Visionaries (Tavelli Gallery Aspen) 1989, Quest (NY Studio Sch) 1989, Social Studies (Lintas Worldwide NY) 1989, Art and Law (Minnesota Museum of Art and tour) 1990, New York at Night (Helander Gallery) 1990, Four Artists (Houldsworth Fine Art) 1990, New Faces, New Work (Tatistcheff & Co NY) 1991, On the Move (Champion Gallery Stamford) 1991, ICAF91, Houldsworth Fine Art 1991, 1992, 1993 and 1994, City (Martin County Cncl of the Arts Florida) 1992, Mall Galleries 1992, People (Gallery Three Zero NY) 1992, Art92, Isolation (Tatistcheff Gallery) 1992, Art93, Mostyn Open Exhibition 1993, Art94, Lew Allen Horwich Gallery Santa Fe 1994 and 1995, Grace Borgenicht Gallery 1994 and 1995, East Wing Exhibition Contemporary Art at the Courtauld 1996, A Selection of Post-War International Painting and Sculpture (Martin Browne Fine Art Sydney) 1997, Etchings from Hope Sufferance Press (Marlborough Fine Art London) 1998, Art Auction for Children of the Sudan (Bernard Jacobsen Gallery London) 1998, Artaid 98 (City Art Centre Edinburgh) 1998, New Showing (Houldsworth Fine Art London) 1999, Free Lemonade (Robert Miller Gallery NY) 2002, Advanced Graphics London 2003, Face Value (Chelsea Art Gallery Silicon Valley) 2005; *Work in Collections* incl: British Land Co, Champion Int Corporate, Credit Suisse, Deutsche Bank AG, Fidelity Insurance Co, Hiscox Holdings Ltd, McDonald's Corporation, Met Museum of Art NY, NY Public Library, Reader's Digest Collection, Yale Center for British Art; *Awards* Jeffrey Archer Prize 1981, GLC Award 1982, Eastern Arts Major Award 1983, Honarium-Drawing Center 1985, ED Fndn 1989, Platinum Disc five times (for Beautiful South's Carry On Up The Charts); *Recreations* cricket, literature and old films; *Style—* Matthew Radford, Esq

RADFORD, (Oswald) Michael James; s of Oswald Charles Radford, of Haslemere, Surrey, and Ruth, *née* Presser; *b* 24 February 1946; *Educ* Bedford Sch, Worcester Coll Oxford (BA), Nat Film and TV Sch; *m* 4 Aug 1990 (m dis 1997), Iseult Joanna, *née* St Aubin de Teran; 1 s (Felix Louis b 6 March 1991), 1 da (Amaryllis James b 23 Feb 2005); *Career* director; freelance film dir 1979–; govr Nat Film and TV Sch 1982–90; memb: DGA, American Acad; *Television* documentary films for BBC incl: The Madonna and The Volcano (Grand Prix Nyon Documentary Film Festival 1979), The Last Stronghold of the Pure Gospel, La Belle Isobel, The White Bird Passes (Scot Acad Award 1980); *Films* Another Time, Another Place 1983 (Best Film Award Cannes Film Festival, Special Jury Prize Celtic Film Festival, George Sadoul Prize Paris for Best Foreign Film), Nineteen Eighty Four 1984 (Standard Best Film of the Year Award), White Mischief 1988, Il Postino 1994 (David Lean Award for Best Direction, nominated for 5 Oscars incl Best Director and Best Screenwriter), B Monkey 1997, Dancing at the Blue Iguana 2000, The Letters 2002, The Merchant of Venice 2004, Flawless 2006; *Recreations* fishing, skiing, snooker; *Clubs* Groucho; *Style—* Michael Radford, Esq

RADFORD, Prof Peter Frank; s of Frank Radford (d 1994), and Lilian, *née* Marks (d 1981); *b* 20 September 1939; *Educ* Tettenhall Coll, Cardiff Coll of Educn, Purdue Univ USA, Univ of Glasgow (Dip PE, MSc, PhD); *m* 1961, Margaret, da of Richard Beard; 1 da (Elizabeth Anne b 18 Dec 1967); *Career* lectr and asst prof McMaster Univ Canada 1967–75; Univ of Glasgow: dir and head Dept of Physical Educn and Recreation 1976–87, prof and head Dept of Physical Educn and Sports Science 1987–94; Br Athletic Fedn: vice-chm 1992–93, chm 1993–94, exec chm 1994–97; Brunel Univ: prof of sport sciences 1997–2004, head Dept of Sport Sciences 1997–2000, dir of research 2000–04, hon prof and assoc 2007; chm: Scottish Consultative Gp on Sports Med and Sports Science 1984–90, Sports Cncl Drug Advsy Gp 1991–95 (memb 1988–91), Sport Cncl's Review of Coaching in Sport (Coaching Matters) 1991–93, Cncl of Europe's Int Anti-Doping Convention 1990 (memb Monitoring Gp 1990–95, vice-chm 1992–94, chm 1994–98); memb: Scottish Sports Cncl 1983–90, Int Working Gp on Anti-Doping in Sport 1991–93, Mgmnt Ctee Nat Sports Med Inst 1991–94; Hon DSc Univ of Wolverhampton 2006; *Athletics achievements* memb GB athletics teams 1958–64, winner bronze medal 100m and 4 x 100m Olympic Games Rome 1960; former world record holder: 200m/220yds 1960, 4 x 110yds relay 1963, indoor 50m 1959, junior 100m and 200m 1958; Br 100m record set in Paris 1958 remained unbroken for 20 years; *Publications* The Celebrated Captain Barclay (2001); also contrib to various jls, conf proceedings and books on sport educn, sports science, sports history and doping control; *Recreations* sports history 1650–1850, 18th and 19th century sporting art, gardening; *Style—* Prof Peter Radford; ✉ Bank House, 8 Sheep Street, Burford, Oxfordshire OX18 4LT (tel 01993 824836, e-mail peter.radford@dsl.pipex.com)

RADFORD, Roger George; OBE (2005); s of Ernest Reginald Radford (d 1977), and Evelyn, *née* Lamont (d 1985); *b* 17 March 1944; *Educ* City of London Sch; *m* 29 May 1971, Susan, da of Geoffrey Mitchell; 2 s (Andrew b 15 July 1974, James b 20 August 1980), 1 da (Juliette b 27 May 1977); *Career* Clerical Medical & General Life Assurance Soc 1963–84, sec C of E Pensions Bd 1984–2004; govr St Nicholas Sch Elstree 1985–2006 (chm 1994–97); chm St Nicholas Elstree Church Cncl 2003–05 (hon treas 1997–), hon treas Elstree and Borehamwood PCC 2005–, chm Aldenham Deanery Pastoral Ctee 2005–; AIA 1975; *Recreations* cricket, golf, gardening, reading; *Clubs* John Carpenter, Jesters, Mill Hill Golf; *Style—* Roger Radford, Esq, OBE; ✉ 22 Bishops Avenue, Elstree, Hertfordshire WD6 3LZ

RADICE, Baron (Life Peer UK 2001), of Chester-le-Street in the County of Durham; Giles Heneage Radice; PC (1999); s of Lawrence Wallace Radice (d 1996; himself s of Evasio Radice) and Patricia, eldest da of Sir Arthur Pelham Heneage, DSO, JP, DL, sometime

R

MP for Louth; *b* 4 October 1936; *Educ* Winchester, Magdalen Coll Oxford; *m* 1, 1959 (m dis 1969), Penelope, er da of late Robert Angus, JP, DL, of Ladykirk, Ayrshire, by his w (subsequently Lady Moore); 2 da (Adele b 1961, Sophia b 1964); *m* 2, 1971, Lisanne, *née* Koch; *Career* former head Res Dept GMWU; MP (Lab): Chester-le-Street 1973–83, Durham N 1983–2001; chm Manifesto Gp in Labour Party 1980–83, oppn front bench spokesman on employment 1981–83, shadow educn sec 1983–87, memb Select Ctee on Treasy (chm 1997–2001), chm Select Ctee on Public Service 1996–97, chm European Econ Sub-Ctee House of Lords 2002–06; memb Cncl Policy Studies Institute 1978–82, chm European Movement 1995–2001, chm Br Assoc for Central and Eastern Europe 1997–, chm French-Br Cncl 2003–; *Style* — The Rt Hon the Lord Radice, PC

RADICE, Thomas Evasio; s of Italo de Lisle Radice, CB (d 2000), and Betty, *née* Dawson (d 1985); *b* 1 November 1940; *Educ* Westminster (Queen's scholar), Magdalen Coll Oxford (Demy, BA); *m* 22 April 1972, Jennifer, da of Sir John Blagden, OBE, TD (d 1985); 2 s (Mark John de Lisle b 21 July 1973, Simon Dominic b 20 Sept 1976), 1 da (Louisa Catherine b 21 Feb 1975); *Career* civil servant; HM inspr of taxes Inland Revenue 1962–66, asst princ then princ Miny of Public Building and Works 1966–70, princ Lord Chllr's Dept 1970–71, princ Property Services Agency DOE 1971–74, asst sec to Bd (sr princ) Nat Enterprise Bd 1974–78, head Highways Services Div Dept of Tport 1978–81, sec to Cmmn Royal Cmmn on Environmental Pollution 1981–86, head Heritage Div DOE 1986–91; SE Regnl Office DOE: jt regnl controller (planning) Kent, Sussex and Surrey 1991–93 (Kent 1994), regnl controller (housing) 1993–94; dir regeneration, housing and environment Govt Office for the SE 1994–95, sr clerk House of Lords 1996–2003, ret; life memb: Friends of the Lake District, Friends of Nat Parks; memb: Oxford and Cambridge Musical Club, Nat Tst, Ramblers' Assoc, London Cycling Campaign, Friends of the Earth, Sustrans; vice-chm Hendon Music Soc; memb Ctee Proms at St Jude's Hampstead Garden Suburb; *Recreations* hill walking, cycling, conservation, music, travel; *Style* — Thomas Radice, Esq; ✉ 10 Middleton Road, London NW11 7NS (tel 020 8455 1025); 2 Gale Crescent, Lower Gale, Ambleside, Cumbria LA22 0BD

RADLEY, Gordon Charles; s of late Ronald Neterfield Radley, and late Diana, *née* Nairn; *b* 26 March 1953; *Educ* Bromley GS, Stockwell Coll of Educn, Highbury Coll; *m* 4 May 1985, Joan Elizabeth, da of late Keith Smith, of Polegate, E Sussex; *Career* promotion prodr HTV 1974–76, promotion prodr Anglia TV 1977–78; presenter: Grampian TV 1979, Points West BBC TV West 1979–81, TVS 1981–85; presenter and reporter South Today BBC TV South, presenter, newsreader and reporter Anglia News Anglia TV 1988–90, anchor and interviewer Sky News 1995–; freelance presenter, reporter, prodr and dir satellite TV, BBC and ITV; media and PR conslt; dir Radley Corporation Ltd; *Recreations* country pursuits, cycling, keeping fit; *Style* — Gordon Radley, Esq; ✉ Wellington House, Tilford, Surrey GU10 2EH (tel and fax 01252 794642)

RADNOR, 8 Earl of (GB 1765); Sir Jacob Pleydell-Bouverie; 11 Bt (GB 1714); also Viscount Folkestone, Baron Longford (both GB 1747), and Baron Pleydell-Bouverie (GB 1765); patron of two livings; s of 7 Earl of Radnor, KG, KCVO (d 1968), and his 1 w, Helena Olivia (who m 2, 1943, Brig Montacute William Worrell Selby-Lowndes, and d 1985), da of late Charles Adeane, CB (whose w Madeline, CBE, JP, was gda of 1 Baron Leconfield); *b* 10 November 1927; *Educ* Harrow, Trinity Coll Cambridge; *m* 1, 1953 (m dis 1962), Anne, da of Donald Seth-Smith, MC; 2 s (one of whom, Hon Peter John Pleydell-Bouverie, *qv*); *m* 2, 1963 (m dis 1985), Margaret, da of Robin Fleming, of Catter House, Drymen; 4 da; *m* 3, 1986, Mary Jillean Gwenellan Pettit (d 2004), da of William Edward Montague Eddy, DSO, DFC; *Heir* s, Viscount Folkestone; *Career* landowner, farmer, fish farmer and fish trader; chm Longford Farms Ltd; pres Dyslexia Inst 1972–94, chm Br Dyslexia Assoc 1971–76, govr French Hospital (La Providence) 1971–, memb House of Lords Select Ctee (agriculture, food and consumer affrs) 1985–90 and 1991–93, co-opted House of Lords Sub-Ctee (science and technology - 'Sustainable Fisheries') 1995; *Recreations* field sports, fly-tying, fishing, bird-watching, painting, drawing, looking at pictures; *Clubs* Farmers'; *Style* — The Rt Hon the Earl of Radnor; ✉ Longford Castle, Salisbury, Wiltshire SP5 4EF

RAE, Barbara Davis; CBE (1999); da of James Rae, Provost (d 1982), of Crieff, Perthshire, and Mary, *née* Young; *b* 1943; *Educ* Morrisons Acad Crieff, Edinburgh Coll of Art, Moray House Coll of Educn; *Career* artist; art teacher: Ainslie Park Comp Edinburgh 1968–69, Portobello Secdy Sch Edinburgh 1969–72; lectr in drawing painting and printmaking Aberdeen Coll of Educn 1972–74, lectr in drawing and painting Glasgow Sch of Art 1975–96, exchange teacher Fine Art Dept Univ of Maryland 1984; memb: Art Panel CNAA 1986–, Cncl RSW 1986–90 (vice-pres for East 1992–), Royal Fine Art Cmmn for Scotland 1995–2000; pres Soc of Scottish Artists 1982–84; tstee Arts Educn Tst 1986–90; memb: RSA, RSW, RGI; DLitt Univ of Aberdeen 2003; Hon Dr of Art Napier Univ 1999, Hon DLitt Univ of Aberdeen 2003; RA 1996, FRCA 2003; *Exhibitions* New '57 Gallery Edinburgh 1967 and 1971, Univ of York 1969, Univ of Aberdeen and Aberdeen Art Gallery 1974, Peterloo Gallery Manchester 1975, Stirling Gallery Stirling 1976, Greenock Arts Guild 1976, Gilbert Parr Gallery London 1977, Univ of Edinburgh 1978 and 1979, The Scottish Gallery Edinburgh 1979, 1983, 1987, 1988, 1990, 1995 1998, Wright Gallery Dallas TX 1985, Leinster Fine Art London 1986, Glasgow Print Studio 1987 and 1997, The Scottish Gallery London and Edinburgh 1989–90, Earth Pattern (William Jackson Gallery London) 1992, Altandhu to Atejate (Glasgow Print Studio 1992, Hunt/Jennings Gallery London 1993, Jorgensen Fine Art Dublin 1993), The Reconstructed Landscape (Highland regn touring exhbn Scotland) 1993, Art First (Cork Street Gallery) 1994, 1996, 1997 and 1999, Jorgensen Fine Art Dublin 1995 and 2005, Graphics Studio Dublin 1997, Glasgow Print Studio Scotland 1997, Art First London 1997, The Scottish Gallery Edinburgh 1998, Gallery Galtung Oslo 1998, Art First London 1999, Edinburgh Int Festival (The Scottish Gallery) 2000, Beach (Art First London) 2001, Irish Paintings (Art First London) 2002, Travelog (Glasgow Print Studio) 2003, The Walled Garden (Castlegate Gallery Cockermouth Cumbria) 2003, Prints (Graphic Studio Gallery Dublin) 2003, An Tlarthar - The West (Scottish Gallery Edinburgh) 2003, Tom Caldwell Gallery Belfast 2004 and 2006, Northouse Gallery Manningtree 2004, Royal Hibernian Acad Dublin 2004 and 2005 (invited artist), The Adam Gallery Bath 2005, Barbara Rae - Monotypes (Scottish Gallery Edinburgh) 2005, Edinburgh Festival Exhbn (Scottish Gallery Edinburgh) 2006, North House Gallery Manningtree 2006, Graphic Studio Gallery Dublin 2007; *Collections* work in numerous private and public collections incl: Bank of England, HRH Prince Philip, Br Museum, Royal Bank of Scotland, Nat Gall of Modern Art Edinburgh; tapestry cmmn for Edinburgh Festival Theatre 1994, carpet cmmn for the Bute Room in the Royal Museum of Scotland; *Awards* Arts Cncl Award 1968, maj Arts Cncl Award 1975–81, Guthrie Medal RSA 1977, May Marshall Brown Award (RSW Centenary Exhibition) 1979, RSA Sir William Gillies Prize 1983, Calouste Gulbenkian Printmaking Award 1983, Alexander Graham Munro Award RSW 1989, Hunting Gp Prize 1990, Scottish PO Bd Award RSA 1990, Scottish Amicable Award RGI 1990, W J Burness Award RSA 1990; *Style* — Dr Barbara Rae, CBE, RA

RAE, Fiona; *b* 10 October 1963, Hong Kong; *Educ* Croydon Coll of Art (Fndn Course), Goldsmiths' Coll of Art London (BA); *Career* artist; shortlisted Turner Prize 1991, shortlisted Eliette Von Karajan Prize for Young Painters (Austria) 1993; tstee Tate Gallery 2005–; *Solo Exhibitions* Third Eye Centre Glasgow 1990, Pierre Bernard Gallery Nice 1990, Waddington Galleries London 1991, Kunsthalle Basel 1992, ICA London 1993–94, John Good Gallery NY 1994, Galerie Nathalie Obadia Paris 1994, Waddington Galleries London 1995, Contemporary Fine Arts Berlin 1996, Saatchi Gallery London (with Gary Hume) 1997, The British School at Rome 1997, Luhring Augustine NY 1997,

Kotyi Ogura Gallery Nagoya 1999, Luhring Augustine New York 1999; *Group Exhibitions* incl: Freeze (Surrey Docks London) 1988, Anderson O'Day Gallery London 1989, Promises promises (Serpentine Gallery London and École de Nîmes) 1989, Br Art Show (McLellan Galleries Glasgow, Leeds City Art Gallery, Hayward Gallery London) 1990, Aperto (Venice Biennale) 1990, Witte de With Center for Contemporary Art Rotterdam 1990, Anthony Reynolds Gallery London 1990, Who Framed Modern Art or The Quantitative Life of Roger Rabbit (Sidney Janis Gallery NY) 1991, Br Art from 1930 (Waddington Galleries London) 1991, A View of London (Salzburger Kunstverein) 1991, John Moores Liverpool Exhbn XVII (Walker Art Gallery) 1991, La Metafisica della Luce (John Good Gallery NY) 1991, Abstraction (Waddington Galleries) 1991, Turner Prize Exhbn (Tate Gallery London) 1991, The Contemporary Art Society: 80 Years of Collecting (Hayward Gallery and UK tour) 1991–92, Play between Fear and Desire (Germans van Eck Gallery NY) 1992, New Voices: Recent Paintings from the British Council Collection (Euro tour) 1992–95, A Decade of Collecting: Patrons of New Art Gifts 1983–93 (Tate Gallery) 1993–94, Moving into View: Recent British Painting (Arts Cncl Collection, Royal Festival Hall and UK tour) 1993–95, Unbound: Possibilities in Painting (Hayward Gallery) 1994, Chance, Choice and Irony (Todd Gallery London and John Hansard Gallery Univ of Southampton) 1994, Here and Now (Serpentine Gallery) 1994, Repicturing Abstraction (Marsh Art Gallery Univ of Virginia Richmond Va) 1995, From Here (Waddington Galleries and Karsten Schubert London) 1995, Malerei: Sechs Bilder, Sechs Positionen (Galerie Bugdahn und Kaimer Düsseldorf) 1995, Des limites du tableau: les possibles de la peinture (Musée Départemental de Rochechouart Haute-Vienne) 1995, Nuevas Abstracciones (Museo Nacional Centro de Arte Reina Sofia Madrid and also touring) 1996, About Vision: New British Painting in the 1990s (MOMA Oxford and UK tour) 1996–98, Treasure Island (Calouste Gulbenkian Fndn Lisbon) 1997, Ian Davenport, Michael Craig-Martin, Zebedee Jones, Michael Landy and Fiona Rae (Waddington Galleries London) 1997, Paintings and Sculpture (Luhring Augustine NY) 1997, Sensation: Young British Artists from The Saatchi Collection (Royal Acad) 1997, ACE! 1998, Axis 1998, UK Maximum Diversity 1998, Sensation: Young British artists from the Saatchi Collection (Museum für Gegenwart Berlin) 1998–99; *Collections* work in public collections incl: Arts Cncl of GB, Br Cncl, Contemporary Art Soc, Fonds National d'Art Contemporain (FNAC) Paris, Fonds Régional d'Art Contemporain d'Ile de France, Hamburger Bahnhof - Museum für Gegenwart Berlin SMPK Marx Collection, Musée Départemental de Rochechouart Haute-Vienne, Sintra MOMA Portugal - Berardo Collection, Tate Gallery, Walker Art Gallery Liverpool, Astrup Fearnley MOMA Oslo, Calouste Gulbenkian Foundation Lisbon, Fundación 'la Caixa' Barcelona, Government Art Collection, Southampton City Art Gallery; *Style* — Ms Fiona Rae; ✉ c/o Luhring Augustine Gallery New York, 531 West 24th Street, New York, NY 10011 (tel 001 212 206 9100, fax 001 212 206 9055)

RAE, Sheriff Rita Emilia Anna; QC (Scot 1992); da of Alexander Smith Cowie Rae (d 1993), and Bianca Angela Carmela Ermanna, *née* Bruno; *b* 20 June 1950; *Educ* St Patrick's HS Coatbridge, Univ of Edinburgh (LLB); *Career* apprentice Biggart Lumsden & Co Glasgow (slrs) 1972–74, asst slr Biggart Baillie & Gifford Glasgow 1974–76, asst then ptnr Ross Harper & Murphy Glasgow 1976–81, admitted to Faculty of Advocates 1982, temp sheriff 1988–97, sheriff of Glasgow and Strathkelvin 1997–; temp Judge of the High Ct 2004; memb: Parole Bd for Scotland 2001– (vice-chair 2005–), Sentencing Cmmn for Scotland 2004–; sec Glasgow Bar Assoc until 1981, tutor in advocacy and pleading Univ of Strathclyde until 1982; memb: Scot Assoc for Study of Delinquency, SACRO; *Recreations* walking, music, opera, theatre, reading, travelling to Italy, gardening, piano; *Style* — Sheriff Rita E A Rae, QC; ✉ Glasgow Sheriff Court, Sheriff's Chambers, 1 Carlton Place, Glasgow G5 9DA (tel 0141 429 8888)

RAE, Ronald; *b* 27 September 1946; *Educ* Ayr GS, Edinburgh Coll of Art; *Partner* Pauline MacDonald; *Career* sculptor, granite carver, painter and graphic artist; projects incl: granite sculptures - The Tragic Sacrifice of Christ 1978, Abraham 1981, Return of the Prodigal 1983, O Wert Thou in the Cauld Blast 1984, Man of Sorrows, John the Baptist, Famine, Cutty Stool 1985, The Good Samaritan 1997, St Kilda Wake 1989, Wounded Elephant 1990, Mother and Child 1991, Widow Woman, Insect and Celtic Cross 1992, Sacred Cow, Boy with Calf 1993, Elephant and Rhino, Flight into Egypt, Lazarus 1995, Fallen Christ, Christ the Healer, War Veteran 1997, Dung Beetle, Animals in War Meml, Bear 1998, Elephant and Calf, Tyger Tyger 1999, Wild Boar, Vulture and Carcass, Fish, Bison 2000, Pisces, Ox 2001, Baby Elephant with a Broken Trunk, The Lion of Scotland 2003, Heavy Horse and Foal 2007; FRBS 1998 (memb RBS 1996); *Selected Exhibitions* Maclaurin Art Gall Ayr 1977, Compass Gall Glasgow and 369 Gall Edinburgh 1980, City Art Centre Edinburgh 1982, Open Eye Gall 1986, Glasgow Garden Festival 1988, St John's Church Edinburgh 1989, Nunnery Square Sheffield 1994, Milton Keynes 1995–99, Royal Museum of Scotland 1996, Regent's Park London 1999–2002, The Jerwood Sculpture Park Witley Court 2000–, The Natural History Museum 2001, Sculpture Exhibiton Yorkshire Sculpture Park 2002–06, Compass Gall 2004, Scottish Churches House 2004–05, The Balmaha Bibles 2004–08, Sculpture Exhibition Holyrood Park 2006–07; *Books* Ronald Rae Sculpture (1994 and 2002), Ronald Rae at Holyrood Park (2007); *Recreations* writing poetry and philosophy, listening to classical music (guest speaker on BBC Radio 3); *Style* — Ronald Rae, Esq; ✉ mobile 07773 482336, e-mail pauline@ronaldrae.co.uk, website www.ronaldrae.co.uk

RAEBURN, James Blair (Jim); s of James Raeburn (d 2002), of Jedburgh, and Martha, *née* Blair (d 1988); *b* 18 March 1947; *Educ* Hawick HS; *m* 22 June 1974, Rosemary, da of late Robert Bisset; 2 da (Nicola b 3 March 1976, Jill b 12 Nov 1977); *Career* dir: Scot Print Employers Fedn 1984–2007, Scot Newspaper Publishers Assoc 1984–2007, Press Standards Bd of Finance Ltd 1990–, Nat Cncl for the Trg of Journalists Ltd 1993–2006, Scot Daily Newspaper Soc 1996–, Publishing Nat Trg Orgn 2000–02; memb Soc of High Constables of Edinburgh; FCIS; *Clubs* Gullane Golf, Rotary of Portobello (Edinburgh); *Style* — Jim Raeburn, Esq; ✉ 21 Lansdowne Crescent, Edinburgh EH12 5EH (tel 0131 535 1064, e-mail info@sdns.org.uk)

RAEBURN, Prof John Alexander (Sandy); TD (1978); s of Lt-Col Hugh Adair Raeburn, RAMC (d 1975), and Christine Constance, *née* Forbes (d 2000); *b* 25 June 1941; *Educ* Loretto, Univ of Edinburgh (MB ChB, PhD); *m* 1, 12 Aug 1967 (m dis 1980); 2 da (Morag Elspeth Jean b 1969, Alison Forbes b 1971), 1 s (Hugh Alasdair b 1974); *m* 2, 17 May 1980, Arlene Rose, da of George Conway, MBE, of Edinburgh; 2 step s (Kenneth Robert Aitchison b 1970, Ian George Aitchison b 1972); *Career* Maj TA&VR RAMC; sr res fell Univ of Leiden 1972–73, sr lectr in human genetics Univ of Edinburgh 1973–89, prof of clinical genetics Univ of Nottingham 1990–2003, prof of genetics Sultan Qaboos Univ Sultanate of Oman 2003–; former pt/t genetic advsr to Assoc of Br Insurers, former med advsr to Adult Cystic Fibrosis Assoc (ACFA); former chm: Scottish Downs Syndrome Assoc, Scottish Cncl Cystic Fibrosis Res Tst; FRCPEd 1976, FRCPI 1998; *Recreations* Scottish literature, fishing; *Style* — Prof Sandy Raeburn, TD

RAEBURN, (Sir) Michael Edward Norman; (4 Bt, UK 1923, but does not use his title); s of Sir Edward Alfred Raeburn, 3 Bt (d 1977), and Joan, da of Frederick Hill, of Boston, USA; *b* 12 November 1954; *m* 1979 (m dis 1994), Penelope Henrietta Theodora, da of Alfred Louis Penn (d 1963), of London; 2 s, 3 da; *Heir* s, Christopher Raeburn; *Career* legal registration offr with civil service; *Style* — Michael Raeburn, Esq; ✉ HM Land Registry, Forest House, Forest Road, Hawkenbury, Tunbridge Wells, Kent TN2 5AQ

RAEBURN, Sheriff Susan Adiel Ogilvie; QC (Scot 1991); da of George Ferguson Raeburn (d 1993), of Aberdeenshire, and Rose Anne Bainbridge, *née* Morison (d 2006); *b* 23 April

1954; *Educ* St Margaret's Sch for Girls Aberdeen, Univ of Edinburgh (LLB); *Career* apprentice Messrs Fyfe Ireland 1974–76, admitted Faculty of Advocates 1977, sheriff of Glasgow and Strathkelvin 1993– (temp sheriff 1988–93); pt/t chm: Social Security Appeal Tbnls 1985–92, Medical Appeal Tbnls 1992–93; *Recreations* the arts, travel; *Style—* Sheriff S A O Raeburn, QC; ✉ Sheriffs Chambers, Sheriff Court of Glasgow and Strathkelvin, 1 Carlton Place, Glasgow (tel 0141 429 8888)

RAFFAELLI, Surgn Rear Adm Philip Iain; s of Nello Raffaelli (d 1984), and Margaret, *née* Anderson (d 1995); *b* 24 November 1955, Kirkcaldy, Fife; *Educ* Univ of Edinburgh (BSc, MB ChB), LSHTM Univ of London (MSc), JSDC, RCDS; *m* 18 Nov 2006, Fiona Ivy Edwards; 1 s (Paul b 29 June 1978), 1 da (Jenny b 21 Jan 1980); *Career* prof of naval occupational medicine Faculty of Occupational Medicine/Royal Naval Medical Serv 1997–99, dir of health RN 1999–2002, medical OIC Inst for Naval Medicine 2003–04, chief exec Def Medical Educn and Trg Agency 2004–06; MOD: DG Medical Operational Capability 2006–, Medical DG (Naval) 2007–; chm AFOM Mgmnt Bd 1999–2002, chief examiner Faculty of Occupational Medicine 2002–05; Eroll-Eldridge Prize 1990; MRCGP 1984, FFOM 1997 (MFOM 1989); *Recreations* squash, golf, guitar; *Style—* Surgn Rear Adm Philip Raffaelli; ✉ Defence Medical Services Department, Ministry of Defence, Floor 7, Zone F, Main Building, Horseguards Avenue, Lonodn SW1A 2HB (tel 020 7218 4457, fax 020 7807 8805, e-mail philip.raffaelli894@mod.uk)

RAFFAN, Keith William Twort; MSP; s of Alfred William Raffan, TD, and Jean Crampton, *née* Twort; *b* 21 June 1949; *Educ* Robert Gordon's Coll Aberdeen, Trinity Coll Glenalmond, Corpus Christi Coll Cambridge (MA); *Career* Diary columnist Sunday Express 1976–79, Parly corr Daily Express 1981–83 (editorial writer 1979–81); Parly candidate (Cons): Dulwich Feb 1974, E Aberdeenshire Oct 1974; MP (Cons) Delyn 1983–92; MSP (Lib Dem) Scotland Mid and Fife 1999–; memb Select Ctee on Welsh Affrs 1983–92, introduced Controlled Drugs (Penalties) Act 1985; pres: Wales Young Cons 1987–90, Wales Cons Trade Unionists 1984–87; memb NUJ; *Clubs* Carlton, RAC, Chelsea Arts, Flint Cons, Prestatyn Cons; *Style—* Keith Raffan, Esq, MSP; ✉ The Scottish Parliament, Edinburgh EH99 1SP (tel 0845 278 1999)

RAFFAN, Mark Thomas; s of Albert Smith Raffan, of Langley, Kent, and Joan, *née* Martin; *b* 18 May 1963; *Educ* Knoll Sch for Boys Hove, Brighton Tech Coll (City & Guilds); *m* 1993, Paula Georgia, da of George Kyriacou, of Limassol, Cyprus; 1 da (Georgia Naomi b 1993), 2 s (Charlie Laithe b 1995, Harry Thomas b 1997); *Career* trainee The Eaton Restaurant Hove 1978–81, chef de partie Gravetye Manor Hotel & Country Club 1984–85 (commis chef 1981–83), chef tournant Walper Terrace Hotel Kitchener Ontario Feb-June 1985, chef tournant Le Gavroche London 1985–86, chef Gravetye Manor Hotel 1988–91 (jr sous chef 1986–87, sous chef 1987–88), exec chef The Royal Palaces of HM King Hussein of Jordan 1991–95, head chef and co-prop Gravetye Manor Hotel 1999– (head chef 1995–); memb Acorn Club 1995–96; *Awards* Cookery and Food Assoc Gold Medal, Acorn Award 1990, Egon Ronay 1 star, Michelin star 1998; *Recreations* shooting, the countryside; *Style—* Mark Raffan, Esq; ✉ Gravetye Manor Hotel, Vowels Lane, East Grinstead, West Sussex RH19 4LJ (tel 01342 810496, fax 01342 810080)

RAFFE, Prof David James; s of John Neish Raffe (d 1992), of Norwich, and Elizabeth Constance, *née* Kendrew; *b* 5 May 1951; *Educ* The Leys Sch Cambridge, New Coll Oxford (BA), Nuffield Coll Oxford (BPhil); *m* 1979, Shirley Sandra, *née* Paine; 1 s (Alasdair b 1982), 1 da (Sonia b 1984); *Career* Univ of Edinburgh: prof of sociology of educn 1992– (lectr in educn 1979–85, reader 1985–92), dir Centre for Educnl Sociology 1995–2001 (research fell 1975–79, dep dir 1979–87, co-dir 1987–95), dir of research Sch of Educn 2002–; dir: Inst for the Study of Educn and Society 1996–98, Scottish Executive School-College Working Gp on Qualifications 2004–05; memb: Tomlinson Working Group on 14–19 Reform 2003–04, Scottish Executive Curriculum Review Prog 2004–; occasional conslt OECD and Euro Cmmn; chm Euro Sci Fndn Network on Transitions in Youth 1993–97; Scot Educnl Res Assoc (SERA) Medal for educnl research 1984; memb: Br Sociological Assoc, BERA, RSA, SERA; *Books* Reconstructions of Secondary Education (co-author, 1983), Fourteen to Eighteen (1984), Education and the Youth Labour Market (1988), A British Baccalaureat (co-author, 1990), Part-Time Higher Education (co-author, 1998), Policy Making and Policy Learning in 14–19 Education (co-author, 2007); *Style—* Prof David Raffe; ✉ 128 Comiston Drive, Edinburgh EH10 5QX (tel 0131 447 2844)

RAFFERTY, Hon Mrs Justice; Dame Anne Judith; DBE (2000); da of John Rafferty (d 1953), of Lancashire, and Helena, *née* Marchant (d 1987), of Lancashire; *Educ* Wolverhampton Girls' HS, Univ of Sheffield (LLB), Inns of Court Sch of Law; *m* 1977, Brian Barker (His Hon Judge Barker, QC), *qv*, eld s of William Barker; 4 da (Anne Camilla Frances b 11 April 1980, Helen Davina Gillow b 31 Aug 1981 d 5 July 1983, Edwina Mary Gillian b 6 Oct 1983, Felicity Abigail Clare b 5 June 1985); *Career* called to the Bar Gray's Inn 1973, pupillage with late Simon Evans (His Hon Judge Evans) at 4 Brick Court 1974, QC 1990, recorder SE Circuit 1991–, dep High Court judge 1996–, head of chambers 4 Brick Court (now 9 Bedford Row) 1993–2000, judge of the High Court of Justice (Queen's Bench Div) 2000–, presiding judge SE Circuit 2003–06; Criminal Bar Assoc: sec 1989–91, vice-chm 1993–95, chm 1995–97; memb: Pigot Ctee 1988–89, Royal Cmmn on Criminal Justice 1991–93; govr Expert Witness Inst 1996–98; govr St Andrews Prep Sch Eastbourne 1990–2006 (chm 2001–03), memb Cncl Eastbourne Coll 1994–2006, memb Appeal Ct Univ of Oxford 2003–; *Style—* The Hon Mrs Justice Rafferty, DBE; ✉ Royal Courts of Justice, Strand, London WC2A 2LL (tel 020 7947 6761, fax 020 7947 6650, e-mail mrsjustice.rafferty@judiciary.gsi.gov.uk)

RAFFERTY, John Campbell; *b* 30 June 1951; *Educ* Edinburgh Acad, Univ of Edinburgh (LLB); *Career* Burness Solicitors (formerly W & J Burness): trainee slr 1973–75, asst slr 1975–77, ptnr 1977–; tutor in taxation Univ of Edinburgh 1973–77; dir F&C Private Equity Tst plc; memb Soc of HM Writers to the Signet 1979, FSI 1994, MInstD; hon consul for Canada; *Recreations* hill walking, skiing, gardening; *Clubs* New (Edinburgh); *Style—* John Rafferty, Esq; ✉ Burness Solicitors, 50 Lothian Road, Festival Square, Edinburgh EH3 9WJ (tel 0131 473 6000, fax 0131 473 6006, mobile 07770 236 430)

RAFTERY, Andrew Thomas; s of Andrew Raftery (d 1987), of York, and Nora Maria, *née* Kelly; *b* 29 June 1943; *Educ* St Michael's Jesuit Coll, Univ of Leeds Sch of Med (BSc, MB ChB, MD); *m* 6 Aug 1980, Anne Christine, da of Norman Turnock, of Buxton, Derbys; 1 da (Catherine b 1981), 2 s (Andrew b 1985, Dominic b 1989); *Career* lectr in anatomy Univ of Leeds 1970–73, surgical registrar Yorkshire HA 1974–75, lectr in surgery Univ of Manchester 1976–80, lectr in surgery and hon conslt Univ of Cambridge 1980–83, consIt surgn (gen surgery and transplantation) Sheffield HA 1983–; external examiner in surgery Univ of Cambridge 1983–; examiner Primary FRCS: England 1985–91, Glasgow 1989–; memb Ct of Examiners RCS 1991– (chm Ct of Examiners 1994–97), pres Br Assoc of Clinical Anatomists 1996–2000; RCS: invited memb Cncl 1994–97, memb Cncl 2001, chm Med Students Liaison Ctee 2004–, vice-chm Patient Liaison Gp 2004–; numerous contribs to books and jls; MIBiol, FRCS; *Recreations* horse racing, theatre, watercolour painting; *Style—* Andrew Raftery, Esq; ✉ Renal Unit, Northern General Hospital, Herries Road, Sheffield S5 7AU (tel 0114 243 4343)

RAGGATT, Timothy Walter Harold; QC (1993); s of Walter George Raggatt (d 1976), and Norah Margaret Raggatt (d 1987), of Redditch, Hereford and Worcester; *b* 13 April 1950; *Educ* Redditch Co HS, King's Coll London (LLB); *m* 1991, Carol Marion, da of Wilfred Carl Overton; *Career* called to the Bar Inner Temple 1972 (bencher 1999); tutor Inns of Court Sch of Law 1972–73, pupillage 3 Fountain Court Birmingham 1973–74, recorder of the Crown Court 1994– (asst recorder 1991); memb Midland & Oxford Circuit 1974–; *Recreations* golf, bridge, scuba diving; *Clubs* Athenaeum, RAC, Blackwell Golf; *Style—* Timothy Raggatt, Esq, QC; ✉ 4 King's Bench Walk, Temple, London EC4Y 7DL (tel 020 7353 3581, fax 020 7583 2257)

RAGLAN, 5 Baron (UK 1852); FitzRoy John Somerset; JP (Monmouthshire, now Gwent, 1958), DL (1971); s of 4 Baron Raglan, JP (d 1964, who was descended from 5 Duke of Beaufort), and Hon Julia Hamilton, da of 11 Lord Belhaven and Stenton; *b* 8 November 1927; *Educ* Westminster, Magdalen Coll Oxford, RAC Cirencester; *m* 1973 (m dis), Alice, yr da of Peter Baily, of Great Whittington, Northumberland; *Heir* bro, Hon Geoffrey Somerset; *Career* sits as ind peer in House of Lords; Capt Welsh Gds; chm: Cwmbran New Town Devpt Corpn 1970–83, Courtyard Arts Tst 1974–83, Bath Preservation Trust 1975–77, Bath Soc 1977–, Bugatti Owners' Club 1988–; pres: Bath Centre Nat Tst, UK Housing Trust 1982– (chm S Wales Region 1976–89), Usk Civic Soc; memb Sub-Ctee D (Food and Agric) of House of Lords Ctee on European Communities 1974–85 and 1987–92 (chm 1976–78); patron: Usk Farmers' Club, Raglan Baroque Players; memb UK Housing Assoc (later Tst) 1974–90 (pres 1982–89, chm Welsh Region 1975–89), chm United Welsh Housing Assoc 1989–91 (pres 1991–); *Style—* The Rt Hon the Lord Raglan, DL; ✉ Cefntilla Court, Usk, Gwent (tel 01291 672050)

RAI, Dr Gurcharan Singh; s of Gurdev Singh Rai, of London, and Kartar Kaur Rai; *b* 30 July 1947; *Educ* Tollington GS London, Univ of Newcastle upon Tyne (MB BS, MD), Univ of London (MSc); *m* 8 Nov 1977, Harsha, da of Shri Lal Bhatia (d 1980), of India; 2 s (Sandeep b 30 Sept 1978, Gurdeep b 18 Nov 1981); *Career* house offr Nottingham Gen Hosp 1971–72, registrar in med Newcastle Univ Hosp 1974–76 (SHO 1972–73), sr res assoc Univ of Newcastle upon Tyne 1976–78, sr registrar in geriatric med Chesterton Hosp Cambridge 1978–80; conslt physician: Whittington Hosp 1980–, Royal Northern Hosp 1980–; sr lectr UC Med Sch 1980–; prof in geriatric med Univ of Nijmegen The Netherlands 1991–92; chm Regnl Advsy Cmmn Geriatric Med NE Thames Region; fell American Geriatrics Soc, memb Br Geriatrics Soc; FRSM (pres Section of Geriatrics and Gerontology 2006), FRCP 1988; *Books* Databook on Geriatrics (1980), Case Presentations in Clinical Geriatric Medicine (1987), Manual of Geriatric Medicine (1991), Multimedia Postgraduate Medicine (1998, 2 edn 2000), Medical Ethics and the Elderly (1999, 2 edn 2004), Elderly Care Medicine (2000), Elderly Medicine - A Training Guide (2002), Revision for MRCP Part 2: Clinical Long Cases (2003), Revision for MRCP Part 2: Data Interpretation (2003), Managing Cardiovascular Disease in the Elderly (2003), Essential Facts in Geriatric Medicine (2005), Shared Care of Older People (2006); *Recreations* chess, stamp collecting; *Style—* Dr Gurcharan Rai; ✉ Care of Older People, Whittington Hospital, Highgate Hill, London N19 5NF (tel 020 7288 5326)

RAIKES, Vice Adm Sir Iwan Geoffrey; KCB (1976), CBE (1967), DSC (1943), DL (Powys 1983); s of Adm Sir Robert Henry Taunton Raikes, KCB, CVO, DSO and bar (d 1953), and Ida Guinevere (Queenie), *née* Evans (d 1983); *b* 21 April 1921; *Educ* RNC Dartmouth; *m* 1947, Cecilia Primrose, da of Philip Gerald Benedict Hunt (d 1958), of Woodhayes, Woodlands, Southampton; 1 s, 1 da; *Career* RN 1935, HMS Sussex 1939–40, HMS Repulse 1940, HMS Beagle Atlantic convoys 1941, submarines Atlantic, Mediterranean and North Sea 1942–45, HM Submarine Sealion 1941–42, HM Submarine Saracen 1942–43; cmd HM Submarines: H43 1943–44, Varne 1944–45, Virtue 1945–46, Talent 1948–49, Aeneas 1951–52; Cdr 1952, staff of C-in-C Allied Forces Mediterranean 1953–55, exec offr HMS Newcastle (Far East) 1955–57, JSSC 1957, commander S/M Third Submarine Sqdn 1958–60, Capt 1960, cmd HMS Loch Insh (Persian Gulf) 1961–62, dep dir Undersurface Warfare MOD 1962–64, dir plans and Operations (Singapore) on staff of C-in-C Far East 1965–66, IDC 1967, cmd HMS Kent 1968–69, ADC to HM The Queen 1969–70, Rear Adm 1970, naval sec MOD 1970–72, flag offr First Flotilla 1973–74, flag offr Submarines and cdr Submarines Eastern Atlantic 1974–76, Vice Adm 1973, ret 1977; chm United Usk Fishermen's Assoc 1978–92, memb Governing Body and Representative Body Church in Wales 1980–93; *Recreations* fishing, shooting, gardening; *Clubs* Naval and Military; *Style—* Vice Adm Sir Iwan Raikes, KCB, CBE, DSC, DL; ✉ Aberyscir Court, Brecon, Powys LD3 9NW

RAILTON, David; QC (1996); s of Andrew Scott Railton, and Margaret Elizabeth, *née* Armit; *b* 5 June 1957; *Educ* Balliol Coll Oxford; *m* 1996, Sinéad Major; 1 s (b 12 Nov 1998), 1 da (b 24 Jan 2002); *Career* called to the Bar Gray's Inn 1979 (bencher 2005), recorder 2000; *Recreations* cricket, golf; *Style—* David Railton, Esq, QC; ✉ Fountain Court Chambers, Temple, London EC4Y 9DH (tel 020 7583 3335)

RAINE, Craig Anthony; s of Norman Edward Raine, and Olive Marie Raine, *née* Cheesbrough; *b* 3 December 1944; *Educ* Barnard Castle Sch, Exeter Coll Oxford; *m* 1972, Elisabeth Ann Isabel, da of Dr Eliot Slater, OBE (d 1982); 1 da (Nina b 1975), 3 s (Isaac b 1979, Moses b 1984, Vaska b 1987); *Career* poet; fell New Coll Oxford, ed Areté magazine; FRSL 1984; *Publications* The Onion Memory (1978), A Martian Sends A Postcard Home (1979), Rich (1984), The Electrification of the Soviet Union (1986), A Choice of Kipling's Prose (ed, 1987), '1953' (1990, staged at Citizens' Theatre Glasgow 1992 and Almeida Theatre 1996), Haydn and the Valve Trumpet (1990), Rudyard Kipling: Selected Poetry (ed, 1992), History: The Home Movie (1994), Clay. Whereabouts Unknown (1996), A la recherche du temps perdu (2000), In Defence of T S Eliot (2000), Collected Poems 1978–1999 (2000), T S Eliot (2006); *Recreations* music, skiing; *Style—* Craig Raine, Esq, FRSL; ✉ New College, Oxford OX1 3BN

RAINE, George Edward Thompson; s of Reginald Thompson Raine, MC (d 1960), of Stocksfield, Northumberland, and Mary Dorothy, *née* Tomlinson (d 1976); *b* 1 August 1934; *Educ* Rugby, Emmanuel Coll Cambridge (MA), St Thomas' Hosp Med Sch (MB BChir); *m* 11 June 1960, Ena Josephine, da of Joseph Noble; 1 da (Meriel b 1965); *Career* sr conslt orthopaedic surgn W Middlesex Univ Hosp 1974–96; orthopaedic surgn Royal Masonic Hosp London 1987–97, orthopaedic surgn to Brunel Univ Coll Sports and Dance Injuries Clinic; orthopaedic surgn to: Brentford FC 1987–97, Crystal Palace FC, various sporting bodies; formerly sr orthopaedic registrar: St George's Hosp London, Rowley Bristow Orthopaedic Hosp Pyrford Surrey, Centre for Hip Surgery Wrightington; former govr The Lady Eleanor Holles' Sch Hampton; vice-pres BackCare (formerly the Nat Back Pain Assoc) memb: Br Orthopaedic Sports Trauma Assoc, Expert Witness Inst; Freeman City of London 1987; fell British Orthopaedic Assoc, FRCS, FRSM; *Recreations* English Lake District, foreign travel; *Clubs* Whitefriars, Athenaeum, St George's Hill Lawn Tennis; *Style—* George E T Raine, Esq; ✉ Pelham's View, 32 Pelhams Walk, Esher, Surrey KT10 8QD (tel 01372 466656, fax 01372 470265, e-mail georgeraine@paedic.demon.co.uk)

RAINE, Dr June Munro; da of David Harris, of Saffron Walden, Essex, and Isobel *née* Munro; *b* 20 June 1952; *Educ* Herts and Essex HS Bishop's Stortford (Ashdown scholarship), Somerville Coll Oxford (Alice Horsman travelling fellowship, BA, MSc), Univ of Oxford Medical Sch (MRC postgraduate scholarship, BM BCh); *m* 18 Oct 1975, Anthony Evan Gerald (d 1995), s of John Wellesley Evan Raine, OBE; 1 s (Charles b 1984), 1 da (Juliet b 1986); *Career* sr med offr Medicines Div Dept of Health 1985–89; gp mngr Medicines Control Agency 1989–98; dir Post-Licensing Div Medicines Control Agency 1998–; princ assessor Medicines Cmmn 1992–; memb DTI Foresight Healthcare Task Force (Public and Patients) 1999–2000, memb various working gps of EC on aspects of pharmaceutical regulation; author various publications on pharmacology, adverse drug effects and regulation of medicines; FRSM, FRCPEd 1995, MRCP, MRCGP, MFPHM; *Recreations* music, opera, travel, skiing; *Style—* Dr June Raine; ✉ Medicines Control Agency, Market Towers, 1 Nine Elms Lane, London SW8 5NQ (tel 020 7273 0400, fax 020 7273 0675, e-mail june.raine@mca.gov.uk)

R

RAINE, Sandra Margaret; da of Charles Kitchener Lovell (d 1976), and Mary Rosamund, *née* O'Hare; *b* 7 March 1958; *Educ* Convent of the Sacred Heart Hammersmith, Univ of Newcastle upon Tyne (BA); *m* 9 Aug 1980, Ian Henry Raine, s of Joseph Raine; *Career* pensions asst Dunlop Ltd 1980, admin offr NE Cncl on Alcoholism 1980–82, sr admin asst Newcastle Poly 1982–85, urban prog asst Gateshead MBC 1985–86, asst divnl dir admin, finance and personnel Royal Co of Berks 1986–90, asst co sec AA 1990–91, benevolent fund sec Chartered Inst of Building 1992–94, sec and chief exec Inst of Gas Engrs 1994–99, co sec and corp servs mangr PCHA 1999–2004, exec dir Int Headache Soc 2004–05, private conslt 2006–; ind tstee Inst of Plumbing and Heating Engrg 2005–; ACIS; *Recreations* gymnasium, swimming; *Clubs* Nirvana Sport and Leisure; *Style—* Mrs Sandra Raine

RAINGOLD, Gerald Barry; s of Henry Raingold (d 1979), of London, and Frances Raingold (d 1992); *b* 25 March 1943; *Educ* St Paul's, Inst of Chartered Accountants, London Grad Sch of Business Studies (MBA); *m* 12 July 1978, Aviva, da of Henry Petrie (d 1962), of London; 2 da (Nina b 2 Aug 1979, Karen b 23 July 1983), 1 s (Andrew b 18 Sept 1981); *Career* articled clerk then chartered accountant Cole Dickin & Hills 1963–68, Cooper Bros 1968–72 (mangr 1972), sr mangr corporate fin Wallace Brothers Bank 1972–76, sr conslt Midland Montagu Gp 1976–78, dep md Banque Paribas London 1978–95 (formerly mangr, sr mangr, asst gen mangr), chm Dawnay Day Corporate Finance Ltd 1995–, dir Dawnay Day & Co Ltd 1995–; non-exec dir: Pinnacle Insurance Gp plc, Simmons Bedding Gp plc, I Point Media plc, Hartfield Securities plc; memb: London Business Sch Alumni, City Ctee Inst of Mgmnt 1980–83, IOD City Branch, RIIA, Bus Graduates Assoc; Sloan fell MSc Prog London Business Sch; Freeman City of London 1987; FCA 1968, FInstD 1987, FRSA 1993; *Recreations* opera, ballet, tennis, reading; *Clubs* MCC, Naval; *Style—* Gerald Raingold, Esq; ✉ 12 Marston Close, London NW6 4EU (tel 020 7328 5800, fax 020 7328 0286); Dawnay Day & Co Ltd, 10 Grosvenor Gardens, London SW1W 0DH (tel 020 7509 4570, fax 020 7509 4575, car 07798 915511, e-mail gerald.raingold@dawnay-day.co.uk)

RAJ, Prof Mahendra; s of G Mahendra, of Kerala, India, and P Valsala; *b* India; *Educ* Kerala Univ India (BSc), Baylor Univ USA (MBA), Univ of Arizona (MS, PhD); *m* Nandini Raj; 1 da (Trishna); *Career* lectr Univ of Arizona 1989–92, sr lectr Univ of Waikato 1993–96, prof of finance Robert Gordon Univ 1996–; memb: Accounts Cmmn for Scotland 2001–, Reporting Panel Competition Cmmn 2005–, Scottish Legal Aid Bd 2006–; ed Studies in Economics and Finance 2001–, author of articles in professional pubns and learned jls; conslt Cwlth of Nations; fell American Soc for Business and Behavioural Sciences (winner Outstanding Service Award); FHEA; *Recreations* magic, tennis, chess; *Style—* Prof Mahendra Raj; ✉ 5 Earlswells Drive, Cults, Aberdeen AB15 9NW (tel 01224 861448, e-mail mahend_raj@yahoo.com); Aberdeen Business School, Robert Gordon University, Garthdee, Aberdeen AB10 7QG (tel 01224 263103, fax 01224 263143, e-mail m.raj@rgu.ac.uk)

RAJA RAYAN, Raj Kumar; OBE (1999); s of Ramanathan Chelvarayan Raja Rayan, of Ceylon, and Lingamani, da of Prof C Suntharalingam; *b* 6 April 1953; *Educ* Harrow, Guy's Hosp Dental Sch (BDS), Eastman Dental Hosp (MSc); *m* Ahila, da of Sanmugam Arumugam, of Ceylon; 1 da (Dipa Lakshmi b 3 Nov 1980), 2 s (Darshan Kumar b 3 Aug 1982, Ravi Kumar b 11 Dec 1987); *Career* currently: dean Faculty of Gen Dental Practitioners UK, dean Royal Coll of Surgeons of England, practice Harley St, dir of primary dental care Eastman Dental Inst of Oral Health Scis (former dir Bd of Mgmnt); former assoc advsr Br Postgrad Med Fndn, accredited teacher Univ of London; emeritus examiner RCS for memb in Gen Dental Surgery; former examiner RCS for Diploma in Gen Dental Practice, fellowship examiner Examining Bd for Dental Surgery Assts; past pres Br Soc for General Dental Surgery; former chm Inst of Transcultural Oral Health, former chm of examinations Faculty of Gen Dental Practitioners UK (also former vice-dean); elected memb Gen Dental Cncl; former memb Conf of UK Advsrs NW Thames, past pres Anglo Asian Odontological Gp, fndr Central London MGDS Study Gp; Cottrell Award 1990, Ahmed Oration Indian Dental Assoc 1991, various nat and int lectures; life memb: Nat Autistic Soc, Music Acad of India, Int Inst of Tamil Studies, Judicial Appointments Ctee, Exec Ctee of Dentists Provident Soc (Friendly Soc); hon life memb: General Dental Practitioners Assoc, Anglo-Asian Odontological Gp, Indian Dental Assoc, Sri Lanka Dental Assoc; former memb: Lord Chllr's Advsy Ctee on JPs, Standing Advsy Ctee to Sec of State for Health; hon fell: Int Coll of Dentists, Pierre Fanchard Acad (former UK chm), FFGDP (UK), FDS RCS, LDS RCS, MGDS RCS, MRD RCS, RCPS, DRD RCS; *Books* Self Assessment Manual and Standards (manual of clinical standards in dental practice, contrib 1991), Path Ways in Practice (distance learning manual in dental practice, contrib 1993), Dentists Patients & Minorities - Towards the new Millennium (co-ed); Selection Criteria for Dental Radiography (RCS publication), Practical Dentistry - Dentistry Jl (ed-in-chief), MGDS Compendium; contributions to numerous learned jls (specialist in Restorative Dentistry); *Recreations* cricket, chess, bridge, golf; *Clubs* MCC, Magpies Cricket; *Style—* Raj K Raja Rayan, Esq, OBE; ✉ 46 Harley Street, London W1N 1AD (tel and fax 020 7631 5213)

RAJAGOPAL, Dr Krishnamurthy (Raj); *Educ* IIT Madras (BTech), UMIST (MSc), Univ of Manchester (PhD); *m*; 2 c; *Career* BOC Group plc: various ops positions Edwards 1981–93, md Edwards Vacuum Equipment 1993–95, md Vacuum Technology Div 1995–97, chief exec BOC Edwards 1997–, exec dir BOC Group plc 2000–; non-exec dir FSI Int; IEE Gold Medal 2003; CEng, FIMechE, FIEE, FCMI; *Recreations* squash, golf; *Style—* Dr K Rajagopal; ✉ BOC Edwards, Manor Royal, Crawley, West Sussex RH10 2LW

RAJANI, Shashi Haridas; s of Haridas Savji Rajani (d 1989), and Gomtiben, *née* Suchak; *b* 24 May 1934; *Educ* HR Meml Central Sch Tabora Tanzania, Govt Secdy Sch Dar es Salaam Tanzania; *m* Chandrika (Sandra), da of Gordhandas Tulshidas Modi; 3 da (Rita b 24 June 1961, Priya b 13 March 1967, Nina Karen b 18 April 1973); *Career* called to the Bar Lincoln's Inn 1955, admitted slr 1975; advocate Tanzania 1956–70: in private practice 1956–64, asst then sr asst administrator-gen (incl official receiver in bankruptcies and company liquidations and several other statutory positions) Govt of Tanzania 1964–70, public prosecutor for bankruptcy offences 1964–70, public prosecutor for company law offences 1965–70, state attorney (criminal prosecutions and appeals) 1967–70, legal conslt Nat Bank of Commerce 1968–70; mangr Insolvency Dept Coopers & Lybrand CAs London 1970–76, sr asst slr Linklaters & Paines London 1977–88, sr asst slr Cameron Markby London 1988, ptnr Cameron Markby Hewitt 1989–93, ptnr and head Corp Rescue and Insolvency Gp Nicholson Graham & Jones 1994–2002, ptnr and head Business Recovery Gp Davies Arnold Cooper 2002–04, ptnr Moon Beever 2005–06, conslt Africa Legal Network 2007–; licensed insolvency practitioner 1986; memb: Tanzania Law Soc 1956–70 (memb Cncl 1963–64), Law Soc 1976– (chief insolvency assessor 2000–05, insolvency assessor 2006–), City of London Law Soc 1984–2006 (memb Insolvency Law Sub-Ctee 1991–2006, dep chm 1995–98), INSOL Europe (formerly Euro Assoc of Insolvency Practitioners) 1980–2006, Insol Int 1980–, Insolvency Lawyers' Assoc 1990–99 (memb Cncl 1992–97), Soc of Practitioners in Insolvency (now Assoc of Business Recovery Professionals R3) 1991– (memb Membership Ctee 1997–2003), Soc of English and American Lawyers 1992–95, Candlewick Ward Club 1998–2002, Admission, Licensing and Disciplinary and Appeal Ctees Assoc of Chartered Certified Accountants 2000–02 (memb Panel of Assessors 2003–), Soc of Asian Lawyers 2002– (chm Advsy Bd 2004–); visiting prof London Guildhall Univ 1992–; Freeman City of London 1984; Freeman City of London Solicitors' Co 1984; *Publications* Tolley's Corporate Insolvency Handbook (1991), Tolley's Company Law (contrib insolvency and other chapters, 1983–), Insolvency Law & Practice (jl, chief ed 1989–), Tolley's Corporate Insolvency (1994), Tolley's Insolvency Law (looseleaf jt conslt ed 1996–), Tolley's Insolvency Costs & Fees (compiler, 1996–); *Recreations* tennis, table tennis, badminton, chess, music (electronic organ), snooker; *Style—* Shashi Rajani, Esq; ✉ Tudor Heights, Mill Lane, Broxborough, Hertfordshire EN10 7AZ (tel 01992 466806, fax 01992 460707, mobile 07890 607577, e-mail shashirajani@hotmail.com); PKJ French Solicitors, 2nd Floor, Queens House, Kymberley Road, Harrow, Middlesex HA1 1VS (tel 020 8861 8833, fax 020 8861 8823, e-mail shashi@pkpfrench.com)

RAKE, Sir Michael Derek Vaughan; kt (2007); s of Derek Shannon Vaughan Rake, and Rosamund, *née* Barrett; *b* 17 January 1948; *Educ* Wellington; *m* 1 (m dis), Julia, *née* Cook; 3 s (Matthew b 5 Dec 1972, Jamie b 12 March 1974, Piers b 19 Dec 1976); m 2, Caroline, *née* Thomas; 1 s (Ashley b 1 July 1985); *Career* Turquands Barton Mayhew London and Brussels 1968–74; KPMG: joined Brussels 1974, made ptnr 1979, ptnr i/c audit Belgium and Luxembourg 1983–86, resident sr ptnr Middle East 1986–89, ptnr London 1989–2007, memb UK Bd 1991–2006 (chm 1998–2006), regnl mangr ptnr SE reg 1992–94, chief exec London and SE reg 1994–96, chief operating offr UK 1996–98, sr ptnr KPMG UK 1998–2006, chm KPMG Europe 1999–2002, chm KPMG Int 2002–07; chm BT Gp plc 2007–; chm BitC (Business in the Community) 2004– (dep chm 1998–2004); memb: Bd Prince of Wales Int Business Leaders Forum 1999–, Bd IFSL 2001–06, President's Ctee CBI 2001–06, Advsy Bd Cambridge Judge Inst 2002–, Bd Transatlantic Business Dialogue 2004–, Int Advsy Ctee CBI 2005–, Bd Business for New Europe 2006–, London Financial High Level Stakeholder Gp 2006–, Int Business Cncl of World Economic Forum 2006–, DTI Task Force on US/UK Regulation 2006–; vice-pres RNIB 2003–, memb Bd Guards Polo Club 2005–, patron Head Teachers Initiative 2006–; Reviseur D'Entreprise (Luxembourg); ICAEW, FCA 1970, MCMI 2006; *Recreations* polo, skiing; *Style—* Sir Michael Rake

RALLI, Sir Godfrey Victor; 3 Bt (UK 1912), of Park Street, City of Westminster; TD; s of Sir Strati Ralli, 2 Bt, MC (d 1964); *b* 9 September 1915; *Educ* Eton; *m* 1, 24 June 1937 (m dis 1947), Nora Margaret (d 1990), o da of late Charles Forman, of Lodden Court, Spencers Wood, nr Reading; 1 s, 2 da; m 2, 24 March 1949, Jean (d 1998), da of late Keith Barlow; *Heir* s, David Ralli; *Career* Ralli Brothers Ltd 1936–62 (apart from Army Serv 1939–45); chm: G & L Ralli Investment & Tstee Co Ltd 1962–75, Greater London Fund for the Blind 1962–82; *Recreations* golf, fishing, gardening; *Clubs* Naval and Military; *Style—* Sir Godfrey Ralli, Bt, TD; ✉ Panworth Hall, Ashill, Thetford IP25 7BB

RALLS, Keith John; s of Bernard Joseph Ralls (d 1983), of Wylye, Wilts, and Annie Ellen, *née* Bennett (d 2002); *b* 29 September 1938; *Educ* Bishops Wordsworth's Sch Salisbury, Bournemouth Tech Coll, Univ of Southampton (BSc), E Midlands Mgmnt Centre Derby (Sr Exec Prog); *m* 1, 19 May 1962 (m dis 2001), Patricia Maureen, *née* Webb; 4 c; m 2, 8 March 2002, Gillian June, *née* Barratt; *Career* engrg apprentice De Havilland Aircraft Co Christchurch 1956–60, graduate trainee rising to sr analytical engr English Electric Co 1963–70; GEC: asst sales mangr Power Transmission Div 1970–74, commercial dir Power Transformer Co 1974–77; gen mangr Herbert Morris Heavy Crane and Conveyor Div Davy Corporation Loughborough (also memb Commercial Exec Ctee Davy Corporation) 1977–79, gen mangr Adamson Butterley Crane Div Norcross Telford 1979–80; GEC: project dir Power Transmission Div 1981–85, mktg dir Transmission & Distribution Projects Ltd 1986; GEC Alsthom: md T & D Power Electronic Systems Ltd 1986–98, md GEC Alsthom T & D Systems Group 1995–98, also dir various GEC Alsthom subsids UK and Europe; Alstom: sr vice-pres T & D System Business 1998–99, md T & D Power Electronic Systems 1998–99, country dir T & D UK 1999, chm T & D Ltd 1999–2001, memb Bd Alstom UK Ltd 1999–2002; pres BEAMA Ltd 2000–02; non-exec dir Dynex Semiconductors Ltd 2001–; IEE: memb Bd Power Div 1987–90 and 1991–97 (chm 1994–95), memb Learned Soc Bd 1993–95, memb Cncl 1993–96; Royal Acad of Engrg: memb Awards Ctee 1997–2000, memb Fin and Audit Ctee 2000–03 (memb Membership Ctee 2003–06); pres Electrical and Electronic Industries Benevolent Assoc (EEIBA) 2002–04; memb Bd of Govrs Univ of Staffordshire 1999–2006; memb Rotary Club of Stafford 2005; pres Old Wordsworthian's Assoc 2006–; FIEE 1986, FREng 1996; *Recreations* badminton, golf, grandchildren; *Style—* Keith Ralls, Esq, FREng; ✉ Long Compton Farm, Sandyford, Stone, Staffordshire ST15 0QB (tel 01782 796223, e-mail keithralls@swynnerton.freeserve.co.uk)

RALLS, Peter John Henry; QC (1997); s of Ivan Jack Douglas Ralls, and Sybil Gladys White, *née* Child; *b* 18 July 1947; *Educ* Royal Russell Sch Surrey, UCL; *m* 1, 1978 (m dis), Anne Elizabeth, *née* Marriott; m 2, 1997, Tonia Anne, *née* Clarke; 1 da (Emily Catherine Louise b 1997), 2 s (Jonathan Jack Edward b 1998, Thomas William Randolph b 2001); *Career* VSO Swaziland 1965; called to the Bar Middle Temple 1972, head of chambers 29 Bedford Row 1997–, asst recorder 1998–2000, recorder 2000–; *Recreations* yacht racing, cricket (chm Lower Combined Clubs); *Clubs* MCC, Royal London Yacht (Cowes, Cdre 1998), Royal Yacht Sqdn, Brooks's; *Style—* Peter Ralls, QC; ✉ Outer Temple Chamber, 222 Strand, London WC2R 1BA (tel 020 7353 6381, fax 020 7583 1786, e-mail peter.rallsqc@outertemple.com)

RALPH, Prof Brian; s of Reginald James (d 1960), and Gwenthellian Anne, *née* Thomas (d 1990); *b* 4 August 1939; *Educ* City of Norwich Sch, Jesus Coll Cambridge (BA, MA, PhD, ScD); *m* 22 June 1961, Anne Mary, da of Leslie Ernest Perry, of Bath; 1 da (Zoanna); *Career* lectr Dept of Metallurgy and Material Sci Univ of Cambridge 1966–83 (demonstrator 1964–66, fell and tutor Jesus Coll 1964–83); prof and head Dept of Metallurgy and Material Sci Univ Coll Cardiff 1984–87, prof and head Dept of Materials Technol Brunel Univ 1987–93 (dean of technol 1991–96); hon prof Warsaw Univ of Technol 1994; co-ed over forty res monographs in the field of microscopy and physical metallurgy; Hon DEng Hanyang Univ S Korea 2006; FIM, FInstP, Hon FRMS, CEng, CSci, CPhys, Eur Ing; *Recreations* sailing, woodwork, music; *Clubs* Cardiff and County; *Style—* Prof Brian Ralph; ✉ Ty Carrog, St Brides-Super-Ely, Cardiff CF5 6EY (tel 01446 760469); School of Engineering and Design, Brunel, The University of West London, Uxbridge, Middlesex UB8 3HP (tel 01895 274000, fax 01985 203205, e-mail brian.ralph@brunel.ac.uk)

RALPH, Philip Pyman; s of Leslie Philip Ralph, VRD (d 1994), of Hatch Beauchamp, Somerset, and (Christian) Doreen, *née* Pyman (d 1973); *b* 4 August 1931; *Educ* Fettes, Clare Coll Cambridge (BA); *m* 20 Aug 1960, Joan Frances (Jill), da of Dr John Scott Brown; 2 s (Charles Philip b 1962, Nicholas John b 1963); *Career* Nat Serv 1950–52; articled clerk Albert Goodman & Company 1955–58, accountant Peat Marwick Mitchell & Company 1958–62, exec Corp Fin Dept Hill Samuel & Company Ltd 1962–71 (dir 1968–71), jt md Spey Investments Ltd 1971–76; dir and head Corp Fin Dept: William Brandt & Company Ltd 1973–76, Charterhouse Japhet Ltd 1976–81; dir corp fin The General Electric Company plc 1981–88, vice-chm The Summit Group plc 1988–99; non-exec dir: Chamberlin & Hill plc 1971–97, Olim Convertible Trust plc 1989–99, Northgate Information Solutions plc 1996–2000; memb Cncl GDST 1997–2001; FCA 1969; *Style—* Philip Ralph, Esq; ✉ Oak Tree House, Warboys Road, Kingston Hill, Surrey KT2 7LS (tel 020 8546 6903)

RALPH, Richard Peter; CMG (1997), CVO (1992); s of Mr Peter Ralph, of Walmer, Kent, and late Evelyn Marion, *née* Horsley; *b* 27 April 1946; *Educ* King's Sch Canterbury, Univ of Edinburgh (MSc); *m* 1, 1969 (m dis 2001); 1 s (James Patrick Eveleigh b 14 Aug 1970), 1 da (Lucy Katharine b 4 Jan 1974); m 2, 2002, Jemma Victoria Elizabeth; *Career* HM Dip Serv: third sec FCO 1969, Vientiane 1970–73, Lisbon 1974–77, FCO 1977–81, Harare

1981–84, FCO 1984–89, Washington DC 1989–93, ambass to Latvia 1993–95, govr of the Falkland Is (concurrently cmmr of South Georgia and the South Sandwich Is) 1996–99, ambass to Romania 1999–2002, ambass to Peru 2003–06; *Style*— Richard Ralph, Esq, CMG, CVO

RALSTON, Stuart Hamilton; *b* 24 October 1955; *Educ* Allan Glen's Sch Glasgow, Univ of Glasgow (MB ChB, MD); *Career* jr house offr Glasgow Royal Infirmary 1978–79, SHO Falkirk and Dist Royal Infirmary 1979–80, SHO Aberdeen Teaching Hosps 1980–81, registrar in gen med Glasgow Royal Infirmary 1981–84 (sr registrar 1984–86), sr registrar in gen med and rheumatology Southern Gen Hosp 1986–87, sr registrar in rheumatology Centre for Rheumatic Disease Glasgow Royal Infirmary 1987–89, locum conslt physician Stobhill Hosp Glasgow 1989, Wellcome sr research fell in clinical science and hon conslt physician Molecular Immunology Gp Rheumatic Diseases Unit Northern Gen Hosp Edinburgh then transferred to Univ Dept of Orthopaedic Surgery Western Infirmary Glasgow 1989–91, currently dir Inst of Med Sciences Univ of Aberdeen, prof of med and bone metabolism Dept of Med and Therapeutics Univ of Aberdeen Med Sch and hon conslt physician Aberdeen Royal Hosps NHS Tst (sr lectr and hon conslt physician 1991–94, reader 1994–); sec Area Ctee of Physicians Aberdeen Hosps 1997–99 (asst sec 1995–97), memb Med Receiving Unit Planning Gp Aberdeen Royal Hosps NHS Tst 1997–99; memb: Hip Fracture Working Pty RCPEd 1990–91, Oliver Bird Ctee for Research into Rheumatism Nuffield Fndn 1992–97, Research Sub-Ctee Arthritis Research Campaign 1995–99 and 2003–, Heberden Ctee Br Soc of Rheumatology 1997–2001, Older People's Research Grants Ctee PPP Healthcare Med Tst 1999–2002, Bd Int Bone and Mineral Soc 2001–, Ctee for Safety of Meds 2002– (memb Biologicals Sub-Ctee 1998–2002), Physiology and Pharmacology Panel Wellcome Tst 2002–, MRC: memb Molecular and Cellular Med Bd Grants Ctee A 1995–97, memb Molecular and Cellular Med Bd 1998–99, memb Physiological Med and Infections Bd 1999–2002; scientific advsr: Nat Assoc for Relief of Paget's Disease 1997–, Nat Osteoporosis Soc 1997–; examiner RCPEd 1996–; chm of organising ctees of various int confs and symposia; ed-in-chief Calcified Tissue Int 2000–, section ed European Jl of Endocrinology 1998–; Prix Osteofluor European 1986, Fitzgerald-Peel Prize Scottish Soc of Physicians 1986, Alexander Fletcher Prize and lectr RCPGlas 1987, Michael Mason Prize Br Soc of Rheumatology 1997, Paget Fndn Research Award 1999, Boy Frame Meml lectr Henry Ford Hosp Detroit 2002, Goodall Meml lectr RCPGlas 2002; pres: European Calcified Tissues Soc 1997–, UK Bone and Tooth Soc 1998–99 (memb Ctee 1992–94); memb: Royal Medico-Chirurgical Soc of Glasgow 1979–, Scottish Soc for Experimental Med 1982–, Br Soc for Rheumatology 1989–, Scottish Soc of Physicians 1990–, Soc for Endocrinology 1994–, Assoc of Physicians 1996–; MRCP 1980, FRCPGlas 1991, FRCPEd 1994, FMedSci 1999, FRSE 2005; *Style*— Stuart Ralston, Esq; ✉ Rheumatic Diseases Unit, University of Edinburgh, Western General Hospital, Edinburgh EH4 2XU (tel 0131 537 1088)

RAMMELL, Bill; MP; *b* 1959; *Educ* Burnt Hill Comp, UC Cardiff (BA, pres Students' Union); *m* Beryl; 2 c; *Career* successively: mgmnt trainee British Rail, regnl offr NUS, head Youth Servs Basildon Cncl, gen mangr Univ of London Union; MP (Lab) Harlow 1997–; former PPS to Rt Hon Tessa Jowell, MP, *qv*; Parly under sec of state FCO 2002–05, min of state for universities DfES 2005–; memb: Select Ctee on Euro Legislation, Euro Standing Ctee B, Dep Leader Lab Campaign Team; chm Lab Movement for Europe, hon pres South East Economic Devpt Strategy (SEEDS), treas Future of Europe Tst; led campaign against Univ top-up fees; cncllr Harlow Cncl 1985–97 (sr cncllr and chm ruling Lab Gp); memb Lab Campaign for Electoral Reform; *Recreations* football, cricket and travel; *Style*— Bill Rammell, Esq, MP

RAMOS, Yosvani; s of Juan Ramos, of Camagüey, Cuba, and Gisela Fonte; *b* 23 June 1979, Camagüey, Cuba; *Educ* Nat Ballet School of Cuba; *Career* ballet dancer; soloist: Jeune Ballet de France 1997–99, Ballet de l'Opéra Nat de Paris 1999; English Nat Ballet: joined 1999, sr soloist 2000, princ dancer 2003; prodns incl: Coppélia, Swan Lake, Giselle, Cinderella, Romeo & Juliet, Nutcracker and Sleeping Beauty; int competitions incl: Grand Prix Havana 1995, Silver Medal and Best Couple Varna 1996, Silver Medal Jackson MS 1998, Gold Medal Paris 1998, Silver Medal Nagoya 1999; *Style*— Yosvani Ramos, Esq; ✉ c/o English National Ballet, Markova House, 39 Jay Mews, London SW7 2ES

RAMPLING, Charlotte Tessa; OBE (2001); *b* 5 February 1946, Sturmer; *Career* actress; Hon Cesar for Career 2001; Chevalier de l'Ordre des Arts et des Lettres (France) 1990, Chevalier de la Legion d'Honneur 2002; *Films* incl: Rotten to the Core 1965, Georgy Girl 1966, The Long Duel 1967, The Damned 1969, Three 1969, How to Make it 1969, Tis Pity She's a Whore 1971, The Ski Bum 1971, Corky 1972, Asylum 1972, Henry VIII and his Six Wives 1973, Giordano Bruno 1973, Caravan to Vaccares 1974, Zardoz 1974, The Night Porter 1974, Flesh And The Orchard 1974, Yuppi Du 1975, Foxtrot 1975, Farewell my Lovely 1975, Sherlock Holmes in New York 1976, Orca the Killer Whale 1977, The Purple Taxi 1977, Stardust Memories 1980, The Verdict 1982, Infidelities 1983, Viva La Vie! 1984, He Died with his Eyes Open 1985, Sadness and Beauty 1985, Max my Love 1986, Mascara 1987, Angel Heart 1987, DOA 1988, Paris By Night 1988, Frames From the Edge 1989, Rebus 1989, Hammers Over the Anvil 1991, La Femme Abandonnée 1992, The Radetsky March 1993, Time is Money 1994, Murder in Mind 1994, Samson Le Magnifique 1995, Asphalt Tango 1996, Invasion of Privacy 1996, La Denière Fete 1996, The Wings of the Dove 1997, Great Expectations 1999, The Cherry Orchard 1999, Signs and Wonders 2000, Aberdeen 2000, Under the Sand 2000, The Fourth Angel 2001, Superstition 2001, Spy Game 2001, Summer Things 2003, I'll Sleep When I'm Dead 2003, Swimming Pool 2003, The Statement 2003, Immortal (Ad Vitam) 2004, Jerusalemski sindrom 2004, Le Chiavi di casa 2004, Vers le sud 2004; *Style*— Ms Charlotte Rampling, OBE

RAMPLING, Prof Roy Peter; s of Alan William Rampling (d 1984), and Lorenza, *née* Camilleri (d 1966); *b* 13 September 1946; *Educ* Clacton Co HS, Imperial Coll (BSc, PhD, DIC), Chelsea Coll (MSc), UCL (MB BS); *m* 27 Dec 1975, Susan Mary, da of Richard Erskine Bonham-Carter, of Knebworth; 1 da (Laura Elizabeth b 1977), 2 s (Thomas William b 1979, Jack Richard b 1984); *Career* currently prof of neuro-oncology Dept of Radiation Oncology Univ of Glasgow; ARCS, memb Inst of Physics 1972, FRCR 1984, FRCPGlas 1992, FRCP 2003 (MRCP 1981); *Style*— Prof Roy Rampling; ✉ Beatson West of Scotland Cancer Centre, 1053 Great Western Road, Glasgow G12 0YH (tel 0141 211 2000, e-mail r.rampling@udcf.gla.ac.uk)

RAMPTON, (Anthony) James Matthew; s of John Richard Anthony Rampton, QC, of London, and Carolyn Mary, *née* Clarke; *b* 22 May 1964; *Educ* St Paul's, Davidson Coll NC (scholar), Exeter Coll Oxford (BA); *m* 1992, Mary Anne Howlett Jones; 3 da (Helen Catherine, Emma Sarah, Catherine Rachel); *Career* dep film ed (listings) The Independent 1988–89, TV writer The Independent on Sunday 1990–93, contributing features ed The Independent 1993–95, freelance feature writer 1995–; *Recreations* rugby, cricket; *Style*— James Rampton, Esq; ✉ c/o The Independent (tel 020 7005 2000)

RAMSAY, Sir Alexander William Burnett; 7 Bt (UK 1806), of Balmain, Kincardineshire; s of late Sir Alexander Burnett Ramsay, 6 Bt (d 1965); is the presumed heir to the Baronetcy of Burnett of Leys (cr 1626); *b* 4 August 1938; *m* 1963, Neryl Eileen, da of J C Smith Thornton, of Trangie, NSW; 3 s (Alexander David b 1966, Ian John b 1968, David Burnett b 1971); *Heir* s, Alexander Ramsay; *Style*— Sir Alexander Ramsay, Bt

RAMSAY, Andrew; CB (2007); s of Norman Bruce Ramsay, and Marysha Octavia Ramsay; *b* 30 May 1951; *Educ* Winchester, Univ of London (BA); *m* 1983, Katharine Celia Marsh; 2 da; *Career* civil servant; various posts Depts of Tport and Environment 1974–93; DCMS: head of arts, sport and lottery 1993–96, head of corp servs 1996–2000, dir of creative industries and broadcasting 2000–01, dir of creative industries, broadcasting, gambling and lottery 2001–04, DG economic impact 2004–06, DG culture, creativity and economy 2006–; *Recreations* gardening, opera, birds; *Style*— Andrew Ramsay, Esq, CB; ✉ Department for Culture, Media and Sport, 2–4 Cockspur Street, London SW1Y 5DH (tel 020 7211 6410, fax 020 7211 6460, e-mail andrew.ramsay@culture.gsi.gov.uk)

RAMSAY, Andrew Charles Bruce; CB (2007); s of Norman Bruce Ramsay (d 1952), and Marysha Octavia, *née* Skrynska (d 1960); *b* 30 May 1951; *Educ* Winchester, Univ of London (BA); *m* 9 July 1983, Katharine Celia, da of David Marsh; 2 da (Isobel Daisy b 22 Dec 1985, Octavia Beatrice b 5 July 1988); *Career* HM Civil Service: joined DOE and Dept of Tport 1974, private sec to jr min for Tport 1978–80, princ DOE and Dept of Tport 1980–85, asst sec DOE 1986–93, under sec and head Arts, Sport and Lottery Gp Dept of National Heritage 1993–96, head Corporate Services Gp 1996–2000, DG Creative Industries Broadcasting, Gambling and Lottery Gp DCMS (formerly Dept of National Heritage) 2000–06, DG Culture, Creativity and Economy Gp DCMS 2006–; *Recreations* gardening, opera, birds; *Style*— Andrew Ramsay, Esq, CB; ✉ Department for Culture, Media & Sport, 2–4 Cockspur Street, London SW1Y 5DH (tel 020 7211 6000, fax 020 7211 6460)

RAMSAY, Andrew Vernon; s of Douglas Charles Ramsay, of Glos, and Dorothy Isobel, *née* Shankland; *b* 7 July 1948; *Educ* Chosen Hill Sch, Churchill Coll Cambridge (MA); *m* 3 July 1971, Ruth Irene, da of Francis James Mullen; 1 s (William James b 27 Oct 1975), 1 da (Elizabeth Jean b 9 Jan 1978); *Career* apprentice AEI Rugby 1966–70, contract engr GEC Electrical Projects 1970–72; CEGB: exec offr Legal and Insurance Dept 1972–74, princ Engrg Servs Dept 1974–79; sec Chartered Instn of Bldg Servs Engrs (CIBSE) 1985–97 (dep sec 1979–84), DG Engrg Cncl 2001–02 (dir for engrs' regulation 1997–2001), exec dir Engrg Cncl UK 2002–; memb Bd Quality Assurance Agency (QAA) 2005–; FIEE 2001 (MIEE 1980), FCIS 1985; *Recreations* opera, cycling; *Clubs* Rumford; *Style*— Andrew Ramsay, Esq; ✉ Engineering Council (UK), 10 Maltravers Street, London WC2R 3ER (tel 020 7240 7891)

RAMSAY, Maj-Gen Charles Alexander; CB (1989), OBE (1979); s of Adm Sir Bertram Home Ramsay, KCB, KBE, MVO (Allied Naval C in C Invasion of Europe 1944, kas 1945), and Helen Margaret Menzies (d 1993); descended from Sir Alexander Ramsay, 2 Bt of Balmain, Kincardineshire; *b* 12 October 1936; *Educ* Eton, Sandhurst; *m* 1967, Hon Mary, da of 1 Baron MacAndrew, TD, PC (d 1979); 2 s, 2 da; *Career* cmmnd Royal Scots Greys 1956, Staff Coll, Canada 1967–68, cmd Royal Scots Dragoon Gds 1977–79, Cdr 12 Armd Bde and Osnabruck Garrison 1980–82, dep DMO MOD 1983–84, GOC Eastern Dist 1984–87; dir gen TA and Army Orgn 1987–89, resigned from Army 1989; chm: Eagle Enterprises Ltd (Bermuda) 1990–95, The Wine Co (Scotland) Ltd 1991–93, Cockburns of Leith Ltd 1993–2004; dir: John Menzies plc 1990–2004, Potomac Holdings Inc (USA) 1990–2005, Edinburgh Military Tattoo Ltd 1991–2007, Grey Horse Properties Ltd 1991–, Morningside Management llc (USA) 1993–2004; farmer and landowner; Col The Royal Scots Dragoon Gds 1992–98; memb Queen's Body Guard for Scotland (Royal Co of Archers); *Recreations* field sports, horse racing, country affrs, travel; *Clubs* Boodle's, Cavalry and Guards', New (Edinburgh), Pratt's; *Style*— Maj-Gen C A Ramsay, CB, OBE; ✉ Bughtrig, Coldstream, Berwickshire TD12 4JP

RAMSAY, Gordon James; OBE (2006); *b* 8 November 1966, Glasgow; *Educ* Oxford Tech Coll; *m* Cayetana Elizabeth (Tana), da of Chris Hutcheson; 4 c (Megan, Jack (twin), Holly (twin), Matilda); *Career* apprentice footballer Glasgow Rangers FC until 1983; hotel and catering mgmnt course Oxford Tech Coll 1983–85; chef: Mayfair Intercontinental Hotel (under Michael Coker) 1985, Harvey's Restaurant London (under Marco Pierre White) 1985–87, Le Gavroche Restaurant London 1987–89, Hotel Diva Isola 2000 South of France (under Albert Roux) 1989–91, kitchens of Guy Savoy Paris 1991–93, Le Jamin Restaurant Paris (under Joel Robuchon) 1993, chef/proprietor Aubergine Restaurant Chelsea 1993–98 (1 Michelin star 1995, 2 Michelin stars 1997), chef and jt prop Gordon Ramsay Holdings Ltd 1997– (restaurants incl: Gordon Ramsay 1998– (2 Michelin stars 1999, 3 Michelin stars 2001), Pétrus 1999– (1 Michelin star 1999, 2 Michelin stars 2007), Gordon Ramsay at Claridge's 2001– (1 Michelin star 2003), Verre at Hilton Dubai Creek 2001–, Angela Hartnett at the Connaught 2002– (1 Michelin star 2004), The Savoy Grill 2003– (1 Michelin star 2004), Banquette 2003–, Boxwood Café 2004–, Maze 2005–, Gordon Ramsay at The Conrad Tokyo 2005–, La Noisette 2006– (1 Michelin star 2007), Gordon Ramsay at The London NY 2006–); Chef of the Year Catey Awards 2000 and 2006 (Newcomer of the Year 1995), numerous other awards, restaurants awarded top ratings in pubns incl Zagat, Harden's Guide and Good Food Guide; *Television* Ramsay's Kitchen Nightmares (Channel 4) 2004 (BAFTA Award), 2005 and 2006, Hell's Kitchen (ITV) 2004 and (Fox US) 2005 and 2006, The F-Word (Channel 4) 2005 and 2006; *Books* Passion for Flavour (1996), Passion for Seafood (1999), A Chef for all Seasons (2000), Just Desserts (2001), Secrets (2003), Gordon Ramsay Kitchen Heaven (2004), Gordon Ramsay Makes it Easy (2005), Gordon Ramsay's Sunday Lunch and Other Recipes from the F-Word (2006), Humble Pie (autobiography, 2006); *Style*— Gordon Ramsay, Esq, OBE; ✉ Gordon Ramsay, 1 Catherine Place, London SW1E 6DX (tel 020 7592 1370)

RAMSAY, Prof Lawrence Eccles; s of William Ramsay (d 1970), of Ayrshire, Scotland, and Margaret Cables, *née* Eccles (d 1989); *b* 11 June 1943; *Educ* Cumnock Acad, Univ of Glasgow (MB ChB); *m* 17 Sept 1965, Mary Helen, da of Harry Hynd (d 1971), of Lanark, Scotland; 1 da (Helen b 1970), 3 s (William b 1972, Alan b 1974, Iain b 1983); *Career* Surgn Lt RN 1968–73, HMS Osprey 1968–69, HMS Jufair 1969–70, Admty Med Bd 1970–71, RNH Haslar 1971–73; lectr in medicine Univ of Glasgow 1977–78, conslt physician Royal Hallamshire Hosp 1978–, prof of clinical pharmacology and therapeutics Univ of Sheffield 1991– (reader in clinical pharmacology 1985–91); ed British Journal of Clinical Pharmacology 1988–94; visiting memb to Australasia for Br Pharmacological Soc 1989; memb: Cncl World Hypertension League 1989, Br Pharmacopoeia Cmmn 1980–98, Ctee on Review of Medicines 1982–91, Sub Ctee on Pharmacovigilance CSM 1992–98, Assoc of Physicians 1987; pres Br Hypertension Soc 1997–99 (sec 1985–89, vice-pres 1995–97); FRCP 1985 (memb 1970); *Recreations* soccer, golf, travel; *Style*— Prof Lawrence Ramsay; ✉ 85 Redmires Road, Lodge Moor, Sheffield S10 4LB (tel 0114 276 6222)

RAMSAY, Louise; MBE (2000); da of Andrew Ramsay, and Jennifer, née Symons; *b* 9 August 1968; *Educ* Queen Anne's Sch Caversham; *Family* Patrick Rogers; 1 da (Isabel); *Career* dir of games services BOA 1991–2000 (attended 5 Olympic and Olympic Winter Games, dep chef de mission Sydney 2000), team mangr England rugby team 2001– (winners Six Nations Championship 2001 and 2003 (Grand Slam 2003), ranked no 1 in world for first time 2003, winners World Cup Aust 2003), team mangr Br and Irish Lions tour to NZ 2005; *Recreations* travel, photography; *Style*— Ms Louise Ramsay, MBE; ✉ Rugby Football Union, Rugby House, Rugby Road, Twickenham, Middlesex TW1 1DS

RAMSAY, Richard Alexander McGregor; s of Alexander John McGregor Ramsay (d 1986), and Beatrice Kent, *née* De La Nauze; *b* 27 December 1949; *Educ* Trinity Coll Glenalmond, Univ of Aberdeen (MA); *m* 19 July 1975, Elizabeth Catherine Margaret, da of Robert Cecil Blackwood (d 1969); 1 da (Catherine Anne Blackwood b 1 Feb 1981), 1 s (Alistair Robert Blackwood b 19 Feb 1983); *Career* chartered accountant; articled clerk Price Waterhouse 1972–75, Grindlay Brandts Ltd 1975–78, Hill Samuel and Co Ltd 1979–88 (dir 1984–88, seconded as dir Industrial Devpt Unit DTI 1984–86), dir Barclays de Zoete Wedd Ltd 1988–93 (md Corp Fin Div 1990–93), dir Ivory & Sime Investment Management 1993–96, fin dir Aberdeen FC 1997–2000, md Regulation and Fin Affrs Ofgem 2001–03, vice-chm

R

Intelli Corp Fin Ltd 2003–06 (non-exec dir 2007–); non-exec dir Artemis AiM VCT plc 2001– (chm 2001–03); FCA; *Recreations* skiing, mountain walking, gardening, historic and classic cars; *Clubs* City of London; *Style—* Richard Ramsay, Esq; ✉ The Little Priory, Sandy Lane, South Nutfield, Surrey RH1 4EJ (tel 01737 822329)

RAMSBOTHAM, Baron (Life Peer UK 2005), of Kensington in the Royal Borough of Kensington and Chelsea; Gen Sir David John Ramsbotham; GCB (1993, KCB 1987), CBE (1980, OBE 1974); s of Rt Rev Bishop John Alexander Ramsbotham (d 1989), of Hexham, Northumberland, and Eirian Morgan, *née* Morgan Owen (d 1988); *b* 6 November 1934; *Educ* Haileybury, CCC Cambridge (MA); *m* 26 Sept 1958, Susan Caroline, da of Robert Joicey Dickinson, of Corbridge, Northumberland (d 1980); 2 s (Hon James David Alexander b 30 Aug 1959, Hon Richard Henry b 8 June 1962); *Career* cmmnd Rifle Bde 1958, Royal Green Jackets CO 2 RGJ 1974–76, Cdr 39 Inf Bde 1978–80, RCDS 1981, dir PR (Army) 1982–84; Cdr: 3 Armd Div 1984–87, UK Field Army 1987–90; inspr gen TA 1987–90, Adj Gen 1990–93, ADC Gen 1990–93; HM Chief Inspr of Prisons for England and Wales 1995–2001; memb Cncl IISS 1996–2002; hon bencher Gray's Inn 2001; hon fell CCC Cambridge 2001; Hon DCL 1999; CIMgt 1993; FRSA 1999, FCGI 1999; *Recreations* sailing, art and art history, penal reform; *Clubs* MCC, Beefsteak; *Style—* Gen the Lord Ramsbotham, GCB, CBE; ✉ House of Lords, London SW1A 0PW

RAMSDALE, Dr David; s of William Ramsdale (d 1985), and Winifred, *née* Horne (d 2002); *b* 3 December 1950; *Educ* St Mary's Coll Blackburn, Univ of Manchester Med Sch (BSc, MB ChB, MD); *m* 6 March 1976, Bernadette; 2 s (Christopher b 17 Feb 1978, Mark b 10 June 1980), 1 da (Kathryn b 30 March 1982); *Career* research fell Dept of Cardiology Wythenshawe Hosp 1979–81, sr registrar in cardiology Sefton Gen Hosp, Broadgreen Hosp and Regnl Cardiothoracic Centre Liverpool 1981–87, conslt cardiologist The Cardiothoracic Centre Liverpool 1987–; memb: Br Pacing and EP Gp 1981, Br Cardiac Soc 1983, Br Cardiovascular Intervention Soc (former memb Cncl); chm Cardiothoracic Centre Heart Appeal; FRCP 1992 (MRCP 1978); *Publications* Practical Interventional Cardiology 1 and 2, Illustrated Coronary Intervention, Color Atlas of Infective Endocarditis; numerous book chapters and more than 150 pubns on a wide variety of cardiovascular topics; *Recreations* golf; *Clubs* Formby Golf; *Style—* Dr David Ramsdale; ✉ The Cardiothoracic Centre, Liverpool NHS Trust, Thomas Drive, Liverpool L14 3PE (tel 0151 228 1616, fax 0151 220 8573, e-mail david.ramsdale@ctc.nhs.uk)

RAMSDALE, Prof Peter Alan; *Educ* UMIST (BSc), Univ of Birmingham (PhD); *Career* engr Plessey West Leigh, lectr in electronics Lanchester Poly Coventry 1970–74, sr lectr then princ lectr RMCS Shrivenham 1974–83, mangr Radio Lab rising to chief res fell and mangr Radio Dept STC Technology Ltd (STL) 1983–90, tech dir Unitel 1990–92, chief engr One2One (formerly Mercury Personal Communications and Unitel) 1992–2001 (also head Technol and Architecture Dept), prop Peter Ramsdale Ltd 2001–, fndr Spectrum Trading Associates 2004, dir Safe Haven Technologies Ltd 2004–06; responsible for major devpts in cellular radio and personal communications; memb: DTI/SERC/Industry LINK Personal Communications Mgmnt Ctee 1988–1991, EPSRC Communications Coll 1994–, Technology Foresight Prog Communications Panel Office of Sci and Technol 1994–98, Radiocoms Agency Radio Res Advsy Ctee 2000–2004; visiting prof: Centre for Satellite Engrg Res Univ of Surrey 1993–96, Centre for Communications Systems Engrg Res Univ of Surrey 1996–2004, Centre for Telecoms Res KCL 2004–; visiting lectr UCL 1996–2001 (memb Postgrad Courses Mgmnt Ctee); memb Cncl ERA Technology Ltd 1994–2000; IET (formerly IEE): chm Professional Gp E8 (Radiocommunication Systems) Ctee 1992–98, chm Communication Networks and Services TPN Exec Team 2004– (memb 2000–03), memb Electronics Divnl Bd; sometime memb Bd of Graduateship Examiners Inst of Physics; author of over 50 papers and nine patents, co-author of four books; CEng, FIET, FREng 1999; *Style—* Prof Peter Ramsdale; ✉ Peter Ramsdale Ltd, Bishops Cottage, Widdington, Saffron Walden, Essex CB11 3SQ (tel 01799 540412, e-mail peter.ramsdale@btinternet.com)

RAMSDEN, (HE) Sir John Charles Josslyn; 9 Bt (E 1689), of Byram, Yorks; o s of Sir Caryl Oliver Imbert Ramsden, 8 Bt, CMG, CVO (d 1987), and Anne, Lady Ramsden; *b* 19 August 1950; *Educ* Eton, Trinity Coll Cambridge (MA); *m* 14 Dec 1985, (Jennifer) Jane, da of Rear Adm Christopher Martin Bevan, CB; 2 da (Isobel Lucy b 27 April 1987, Stella Evelyn b 4 Aug 1989); *Heir* undetermined; *Career* Dawnay Day & Co Ltd (merchant bankers) 1972–74; HM Dip Serv: entered 1975, second sec Dakar 1976–78, first sec Delgn to MBFR Talks Vienna 1979, head of Chancery and consul Hanoi 1980–82, FCO (successively Econ Rels Dept, Perm Under Sec's Dept, EC Dept and Western European Dept) 1982–90, cnsllr and dep head of mission Embassy to GDR 1990, cnsllr and dep head Berlin Office 1990–93, head Information Dept FCO 1993–96, dep perm rep UK Mission to UN Geneva 1996–98, head Central and NW Europe Dept FCO 1999–2003, ambass to Croatia 2004–; *Recreations* painting; *Clubs* Beefsteak; *Style—* Sir John Ramsden, Bt; ✉ c/o Foreign & Commonwealth Office (Zagreb), King Charles Street, London SW1A 2AH

RAMSDEN, Prof Richard Thomas; s of late Thomas William Ramsden, of Balmerino, Fife, and late Elaine Napier, *née* Meikle; *b* 30 December 1944; *Educ* Madras Coll St Andrews, Univ of St Andrews (MB ChB); *m* 1, 1968 (m dis 1984), Wendy Margaret, *née* Johnson; 2 da (Helen b 1972, Fiona b 1977), 1 s (Alistair b 1974); m 2, 1985, (Eileen) Gillian, da of late Clifford Whitehurst, and late Anne Whitehurst; *Career* conslt otolaryngologist and hon prof in otolaryngology Manchester Royal Infirmary; hon lectr: Dept of Surgery Univ of Manchester, Dept of Audiology Speech Pathology and Educn of the Deaf Univ of Manchester 1977; author of chapters and articles on aspects of ear surgery; asst ed Jl of Laryngology and Otology; memb Editorial Bd: Otology and Neurology, Revue de Laryngologie Otologie Rhinologie, ENT Jl; memb Nat Ctee of Enquiry into Perioperative Deaths; memb Cncl Section of Otology RSM 1990–95 (sec, treas, vice-pres, pres 1994–95), co-fndr Euro Acad for Otology and Neuro-otology, examiner and memb Bd Intercollegiate Bd in Otolaryngology 1992–99, memb Ct of Examiners RCPSGlas 1987–2003, memb SAC in Otolaryngology 1998–2004; chm Br Cochlear Implant Gp 1989–96, memb Collegium Oto-Rhino-Laryngologicum Amicitiae Sacrum, memb UK Cncl on Deafness, corresponding memb Deutsche Gesellschaft für Hals-Nase-und Ohrenheilkunde; hon memb: Danish ENT Soc, Irish ENT Soc, American Otological Soc, Slovac Soc; pres Br Assoc of Otolaryngologists - Head and Neck Surgeons 2005–, pres North of Eng Otolaryngological Soc 2000–01; patron Nat Assoc for Deafened People; med advsr Neurofibromatosis Assoc, advsr on otolaryngology Nat Inst for Clinical Excellence; Leon Goldmann prof lectr Univ of Cape Town 1998, Yearsley lectr 2001; winner Dalby Prize Royal Soc of Med 1992, Wilde Medal 1994, VS Subramaniam lectr and Gold Medal 1995, winner WJ Harrison Prize for Otology 1999, Jobson Horne Prize BMA 2001, Smyth Lecture and Medal Br Assoc of Otolaryngologists - Head and Neck Surgeons 2003; memb BMA 1977, FRCS 1973, FRCSEd (ad hominem) 2000; *Recreations* golf, otology; *Clubs* St Andrews New, St Andrews Soc of Manchester (pres), Wilmslow Golf; *Style—* Prof Richard Ramsden; ✉ Brick Bank, Brick Bank Lane, Allostock, Knutsford, Cheshire WA16 9LY (tel 01477 544838); 23 Anson Road, Manchester M14 5BZ (tel 0161 225 0041); Manchester Royal Infirmary, Oxford Road, Manchester M13 9WL (tel 0161 276 4639, fax 0161 276 8511, e-mail richard.ramsden@man.ac.uk)

RAMSDEN, Stephen; *b* 2 March 1957; *Educ* Smithills Moor GS Bolton; *Career* trainee NW RHA 1975–83 (IHA 1981), dep unit gen mangr Oldchurch Hosp Romford Essex 1983–88; chief exec: Mount Vernon Hosp NHS Tst 1991–93 (unit gen mangr 1988–91), Mount Vernon & Watford Hosps NHS Tst 1994–98 (project offr 1993–94), Luton & Dunstable Hosp NHS Tst 1998–; memb King's Fund Organisational Audit Cncl (now HQS); MHSM; *Style—* Stephen Ramsden, Esq; ✉ Luton & Dunstable Hospital NHS Trust, Lewsey Road, Luton, Bedfordshire LU4 0DZ (tel 01582 497001)

RAMSEY, Hon Mr Justice; Sir Vivian Arthur; kt (2005); s of Rt Rev Ian Thomas Ramsey (d 1972 former Bishop of Durham), and Margaret (Margretta), *née* McKay (d 1997); *b* 24 May 1950; *Educ* Abingdon Sch, Harley Sch Rochester NY USA, Oriel Coll Oxford (MA), City Univ (Dip Law); *m* 14 Aug 1974, Barbara, da of Lt-Col Gerard Majella Walker, of Hitchin, Herts; 2 da (Helen b 1980, Katharine b 1984), 2 s (Nicholas b 1981, James b 1986); *Career* grad engr Ove Arup & Ptnrs 1972–77, called to the Bar Middle Temple 1979 (bencher 2002); practising barr 1981–2005, arbitrator (incl ICC arbitration) 1988–2005 (mediator 1991–2005), QC 1992, asst recorder 1998–2000, recorder 2000–05, head of chambers Keating Chambers 2002–05, judge of the High Court of Justice (Queen's Bench Div) 2005–, judge in charge Technol and Construction Court 2007–; special prof Dept of Civil Engrg Univ of Nottingham 1990–, visiting prof Centre of Construction Law KCL 2007–; ctee official referee Bar Assoc 1986–91; treas: St Swithuns Hither Green 1977–84, Swanley Village Sports and Social Club 1986–2005 (chm 1990–98); chm Swanley Action Gp 1990–2005; MICE 1977; *Publications* Keating on Building Contracts (7 edn, 2000, supplement 2004, 8 edn 2006); also ed Construction Law Jl 1984–2005 (conslt ed 2005–); *Recreations* building renovation, vineyards; *Style—* The Hon Mr Justice Ramsey; ✉ Royal Courts of Justice, Strand, London WC2A 2LL

RAMSHAW, Prof Colin; *b* 12 October 1936; *Educ* Univ of Newcastle upon Tyne (BSc, PhD); *Career* sr scientific offr Miny of Aviation 1962–66, scientific offr Central Instrument Res Laboratories ICI plc 1966–74, sr staff and section mangr ICI Corporate Laboratory 1974– (res assoc, memb Fluid Separation Panel); fndr jt research scheme Univ of Newcastle upon Tyne (with John Porter) 1981, jt fndr ICI/ETSU project Heriot-Watt Univ (with Prof K Cornwell), conslt EEC Joule 1 programme on energy conservation 1990–, jt fndr Protensive Ltd 1999 (currently tech dir); prof of chem engrg Univ of Newcastle upon Tyne 1991–2002 (visiting prof 1989–91, emeritus prof 2002–), EPSRC chair of Responsive Processing Univ of Newcastle upon Tyne 1996–2002; visiting prof Cranfield Univ 2003; author of various papers in learned journals; memb Inst of Chemical Engrs Res Ctee 1984–86; FREng 1989; *Style—* Prof Colin Ramshaw, FREng; ✉ 20 High View, Ponteland, Newcastle upon Tyne NE20 9ET (tel 01661 872436, office 0191 242 2006, e-mail colinramshaw@onetel.com)

RAMSHAW, Wendy Anne Jopling; CBE (2003, OBE 1993); da of Angus Ramshaw (d 1989), and Flora, *née* Hollingshead (d 1982); *b* 26 May 1939; *Educ* Sunderland Girls HS, Saint Mary's Convent Berwick-upon-Tweed, Coll of Art and Industrial Design Newcastle upon Tyne (NDD), Univ of Reading (ATD), Central Sch London; *m* David John Watkins, s of Jack Watkins; 1 da (Miranda Abigail Watkins b 22 April 1967), 1 s (Richard Mark Watkins b 11 July 1974); *Career* artist and designer; artist in residence Western Inst Aust 1978–79, visiting artist in collaboration Wedgwood 1981–82, visiting artist Glass Dept RCA 1985, artist in residence Printmakers Workshop Inverness 1996, artists in residence (with Miranda Watkins) Pallant House Chichester 1999; visiting prof: San Diego State Univ 1984, Bezalel Acad Jerusalem 1984, RCA London 1998–2001; site specific public artworks situated in the UK 1993–2003; govr London Inst 2000, patron Contemporary Applied Arts London; on Crafts Cncl Index; patron Bristol Cancer Help Centre; Lady Liveryman Worshipful Co of Goldsmiths 1986; hon fell London Inst 1999; FCSD 1972, FRSA 1972; RDI 1999; *Exhibitions* incl: Wendy Ramshaw - David Watkins (Goldsmiths Hall London) 1973, Nat Gallery of Victoria Aust 1978, V&A 1982, Bristol City Museum and Art Gallery (retrospective) 1983, Wendy Ramshaw/David Watkins (Schmuckmuseum Pforzheim) 1987, Jewellery Strategies/Jewellery Variations (Mikimoto Tokyo) 1993, Picasso's Ladies (V&A, American Craft Museum NY and Inst Mathildenhöhne Darmstadt) 1998–2001, Millennium Exhibition (Contemporary Applied Arts London) 2000, Room of Dreams (Scottish Gallery Edinburgh) 2002, Prospero's Table (Sofa Chicago) 2004, Wendy Ramshaw - Jewellery (Blackwell The Arts and Crafts House) 2004, Collect (V&A) 2005; *Selected Large-Scale Commissions* garden gate Fellows' Garden St John's Coll Oxford 1993, Double Screen EH9681 V&A 1996, moving gate Mowbray Park Sunderland 1998–2001, Millennium Medal for HM The Queen 1999–2000, The Prince of Wales Medal (for Classic Design Awards Homes & Gardens in assoc with V&A) 2000, glass door panels and bronze door handles Millennium Building Southwark Cathedral 2000, circular gates in aluminium Sculpture at Goodwood 2001; *Work in Public Collections* incl: Br Museum, Musée des Arts Décoratifs Paris, MOMA Kyoto, Philadelphia Museum of Art, Schmuckmuseum Pforzheim, Stedelijk Museum Amsterdam, Cooper-Hewitt Museum Smithsonian Inst NY, V&A, Aust Nat Gallery Canberra, Kunstindustrimuseet Oslo, Royal Museum of Scotland Edinburgh, Science Museum London, Powerhouse Sydney; *Awards* Cncl of Industrial Design Award 1972, De Beers Diamond Int Award 1975, Art in Architecture RSA 1993; *Publications* Wendy Ramshaw (exhbn catalogue), From Paper to Gold (exhbn catalogue), Jewel Drawings and Projects - Contemporary Jewellery Issues, Picasso's Ladies - Jewellery by Wendy Ramshaw, The Big Works - Wendy Ramshaw, Wendy Ramshaw - Jewellery (exhbn catalogue); *Recreations* visiting museums and art galleries, travelling, reading; *Style—* Miss Wendy Ramshaw, CBE, RDI; ✉ c/o Faculty of RDIs, Royal Society of Arts, 8 John Adam Street, London WC2N 6EZ

RANA, Baron (Life Peer UK 2004), of Malone in the County of Antrim; Dijit Singh Rana; MBE (1996), JP (1986); s of late Paras Ram Rana; *b* 20 September 1938; *Educ* Punjab Univ; *m* 1966, Uma, da of Kishore Lal Passi, of Phillaur, India; 2 c (Hon Rajesh b 1968, Hon Ramesh b 1970); *Career* pres: Belfast Chamber of Trade and Commerce 1991–92, NI C of C and Industry 2004–05; fndr: India Business Forum 1985, Rana Charitable Tst 1996; vice-pres UNICEF 2004–, chm Thanksgiving Sq 2002–; govr Lagan Coll 1990–94; hon consul for India in NI 2004–; Hon Dr: Univ of Ulster 1999, Queen's Univ Belfast 2004; Pravasi Bharatiya Samman Award (India) 2007; *Style—* The Rt Hon the Lord Rana, MBE

RANA, HE Prabal Shumshere Jung Bahadur; CVO (1980); s of Rt Hon Gen Kiran Shumshere Jung Bahadur Rana (d 1983), and Rani Yubarajya Laxmi, *née* Shah (d 2003); *b* 16 February 1939, Kathmandu, Nepal; *Educ* Bishop Cotton Sch Shimla, St Stephen's Coll Delhi (BA), UCL (BA); *m* 27 April 1963, Shanti, da of Sahebju Banendra Bikram Shah; 2 c (Prashant b 12 May 1965, Prabir b 5 May 1967); *Career* Nepalese diplomat; entered Nepalese Foreign Serv 1964, posted Rome 1965–67, posted Islamabad 1969–73, first sec and consul-gen NY 1977–79, cnsllr London 1982–87, dir S Asia Assoc for Regnl Co-operation (SAARC) Secretariat Kathmandu 1992–96, ambass to the Ct of St James's 2003– (concurrently accredited to Denmark, Norway, Sweden, Finland, Iceland and Ireland); charter pres Rotary Club of Kantipur Kathmandu 2001–03; *Recreations* bridge, photography, painting; *Style—* HE Mr Prabal Rana, CVO; ✉ Shanti Sadan, Siddhartha Colony, Budanilkantha, Kathmandu, Nepal; The Royal Nepalese Embassy, 12A Kensington Palace Gardens, London W8 4QU (tel 020 7229 1594, fax 020 7792 9861, e-mail melondon@btconnect.com)

RAND, Gerald Frederick; s of William Frederick Rand (d 1960), of Herts, and Elsie Mary White (d 1926); *b* 10 November 1926; *Educ* Merchant Taylors'; *m* 1, 13 July 1949, Eileen Margaret, da of William Alexanda Winson (d 1975), of Herts; 1 s (Stephen b 1953); m 2, 1 Nov 1972, Clarissa Elizabeth (d 2003), da of Thomas William Barker (d 1956), of Hull; *Career* ret master builder; chm Rand Contractors Ltd 1952–68, md Power Plant Int 1962–71, chm Manor Minerals (UK) Ltd 1985–; landowner; memb CLA; elected to Société Jersiaise 1967; memb Governing Cncl The Manorial Soc of GB 1985–, regnl chm Domesday Nat Ctee 1986–; Lord of the Manor of: Lynford, Mundford, Cranwich Norfolk;

Freeman City of London 1986; FSA Scot 1993; *Recreations* shooting, hunting, studies in medieval history, historic buildings; *Style*— Gerald F Rand, Esq; ✉ The Dhoon Maughold, Isle of Man IM7 1HL (tel 01624 862328, fax 01624 816635)

RANDALL, Adrian John Laurence; s of Robert Bennet Randall (d 1950), of London, and Ivy Ellen, *née* French (d 1986); *b* 4 December 1944; *Educ* Harrison Coll Barbados, Univ of Hull (BSc); *m* 1, 5 Sept 1970 (m dis 1990), Suzanne, da of William Marshall, of Morpeth, Northumberland; 2 da (Nicola Jane b 6 Oct 1973, Emma Louise b 3 June 1976); m 2, 18 March 1995, Jennifer LeSbirel, da of Cecil Henry Sturgess; *Career* articled clerk Harper Smith Bennett & Co Norwich 1964–68; Tate & Lyle plc: accountant Zambia Sugar Co Ltd 1971–76, accountant Tate & Lyle plc 1976–78, fin controller Tate & Lyle Agribusiness Ltd 1978–79, fin dir Unalco Div 1980–84; Hays Group: chief exec Anti-Pollution Chemicals Ltd 1984–85, gen mangr Gen Chemicals Div London 1986–87 (fin mangr 1985–86); dir of fin and resources Cancer Research Campaign 1987–94, ptnr (charities) BDO Stoy Hayward (formerly Moores Rowland) 1994–2000, charities mgmnt conslt 2000–04; exec dir Charities Consortium 2000–04, charity finance head conslt Charity and Fundraising Appointments 2000–04, charities conslt Goldwins 2002–04, ceo Heart & Stroke Fndn of Barbados 2004–; pres Essex Soc of Chartered Accountants 1988–89, co-fndr and past chm The Charity Fin Dirs Gp 1988–92, chm The Charities Tax Reform Gp 1992–94, visiting prof to the chair of charity fin South Bank Univ 1992–2003; memb: Bd Chartered Accountants in Business 1988–92, Cncl Assoc of Charity Ind Examiners (ACIE) 2002–04, Charity Cmmn Ctee to review Charities SORP; ICAEW: chm Career Devpt Gp 1988–92, chm Charity Accounts Working Pty, memb Carniovascular Disease Task Force Barbados 2006–07, memb Nat Chronic Non-Communicable Diseases Cmmn Barbados 2007–; fell ACIE 2006 (memb 2001); FCA 1979 (ACA 1968); *Books* Managing Your Solvency (1994), Charities and Taxation (1995), A Practical Guide to SORP and the Regulations (1997), Preparing Charity Accounts (1999, 2 edn 2001, 3 edn 2005), Charity Taxation (2001), The ICSA Guide to Charity Accounting (2001), Financial Management in the Voluntary Sector (2001); *Recreations* swimming, watching cricket, reading, theatre, music, charity activities; *Clubs* Norfolk CCC, Rotary, Barbados Cricket Assoc, Empire Cricket, Old Harrisonian Soc, Barbados Nat Tst, Barbados Museum and Historical Soc; *Style*— Adrian Randall, Esq; ✉ Apartment 4C, Hastings Towers, Hastings, Christ Church, Barbados, West Indies (tel 00 246 228 2757, e-mail hfobceo@sunbeach.net)

RANDALL, Gwendolen Mary; da of Albert Joseph Benjamin and Emily Amelia Triggs; *b* 30 December 1950; *Educ* Mary Datchelor Girls' Sch Camberwell, Univ of Bristol (open scholar, Clothworkers' Co exhbn, BA); *m* 7 July 1973, David John Randall, s of Eric Frank Randall, MBE; 1 da (Katherine b 3 Nov 1979); *Career* teacher of French Ridgeway Sch Wroughton 1973–74, head of Modern Languages St Mary's Sch Calne Wilts 1974–76, teacher of French and English Gymnasium Andreanum Hildesheim Germany 1977–79, teacher of French and head of Drama St Mary's Sch Calne 1980–85, dep head Dauntsey's Sch W Lavington Devizes Wilts 1985–94, head Framlingham Coll and jr section Brandeston Hall 1994–; FRSA; *Recreations* sailing, drama, tennis, piano, debating, keen interest in equestrian pursuits; *Style*— Mrs Gwendolen Randall, FRSA; ✉ Framlingham College, Framlingham, Suffolk IP13 9EY (tel 01728 723789, fax 01728 724546)

RANDALL, Helen; da of Dennis Randall, of Oxon, and Monica, *née* Wilson; *b* May 1962, London; *Educ* Tunbridge Wells GS for Girls, Kent Coll for Girls, RSA (TEFL), Univ of Manchester (BA); *Partner* Azucena Tejada; *Career* admitted slr 1991; articled clerk then slr Lovells 1988–95, slr London Borough of Camden 1995–97, ptnr Nabarro Nathanson 2001–04 (slr 1997–2001), ptnr and head of public sector commercial dept Trowers & Hamlins 2004–; chm New Local Govt Network (NGLN) 2004– (dir 2001–04); memb Sir Ian Byatt's Procurement Task Force; *Publications* Butterworth's Local Government Act (1999), Tottel's Local Government Contracts and Procurement (2006), PFI Encyclopaedia (contrib); author of numerous NLGN pubns; *Recreations* herding cats and nailing jellies to walls; *Style*— Ms Helen Randall; ✉ Trowers & Hamlins, Sceptre Court, 40 Tower Hill, London EC3N 4DX (tel 020 7423 8436, fax 020 7423 8001, e-mail hrandall@trowers.com)

RANDALL, Jeff William; s of Jeffrey Charles Randall, and Grace Annie Randall; *b* 3 October 1954; *Educ* Royal Liberty GS Romford, Univ of Nottingham (BA), Univ of Florida; *m* 8 Feb 1986, Susan Diane, da of H W Fidler; 1 da (Lucy Susan b 10 Jan 1989); *Career* research economist Wolverhampton Poly 1980–82, Hawkins Publishers 1982–85, asst ed Financial Weekly 1985–86, city corr Sunday Telegraph 1986–88, city ed Sunday Times 1989–95 (joined 1988), dir Times Newspapers 1994–95, jt dep chm Financial Dynamics 1995–96, asst ed Sunday Times 1996, sports ed Sunday Times 1996–97, ed Sunday Business 1997–2001, business ed BBC 2001–05, ed-at-large Daily Telegraph 2005–; columnist Sunday Telegraph 2001–04; presenter BBC Radio Five Live 2004–; FT Analysis Financial Journalist of the Year 1991, London Press Club Business Journalist of the Year 2001, Best Broadcast and Decade of Excellence Prizes Business Journalism Awards 2003, PR Week Communicator of the Year 2004, Harold Wincott Award for Best Business Broadcaster 2004; Hon Dr: Anglia Poly Univ 2001, Univ of Nottingham 2006; *Recreations* golf, horse racing, football; *Clubs* Brooks's, Wentworth, Stock Brook Manor Golf, Langland Bay Golf; *Style*— Jeff Randall, Esq

RANDALL, (Alexander) John; MP; s of Alec Randall (d 1996), and Joyce, *née* Gore; *b* 5 August 1955; *Educ* Merchant Taylors' Northwood, SSEES Univ of London (BA); *m* 1986, Katherine, da of John Gray; 2 s (Peter b Oct 1989, David b Nov 1993), 1 da (Elizabeth b Dec 1995); *Career* md Randalls of Uxbridge Ltd 1986–97; MP (Cons) Uxbridge (by-election) 1997–; oppn whip 2000–; chm Uxbridge Cons Assoc 1994–97; tour ldr: Birdquest Holidays 1988–94, Limosa Holidays 1994–97; *Recreations* ornithology, opera, travel, rugby, cricket; *Clubs* Uxbridge Conservative, Saracens RFC, Middlesex CCC; *Style*— John Randall, Esq, MP; ✉ House of Commons, London SW1A 0AA (tel 020 7219 6885)

RANDALL, John Yeoman; QC (1995); s of Dr Richard Francis Yeoman Randall, of Birmingham, and Jean Evelyn, *née* Child; *b* 26 April 1956; *Educ* Rugby, Loomis Inst Connecticut, Jesus Coll Cambridge (MA); *m* 1982, Christine, da of late (Gordon) Keith Robinson, and late Shirley Grace, *née* Temple, of Sydney, Aust; 1 s (Oliver Yeoman b 1985), 1 da (Sally Jenine b 1988); *Career* called to the Bar Lincoln's Inn 1978 (bencher 2003), called to the Bar NSW 1979; asst recorder of the Crown Court 1995–99, recorder of the Crown Court 1999–, dep judge of the High Court 2000–; head of chambers 2001–04 (dep head 1998–2001), barr and slr WA 2001; chm Midland Chancery and Commercial Bar Assoc 1996–2001, memb Legal Services Consultative Panel 2000–; visiting fell Univ of NSW 2004–; *Recreations* travel, sports, music; *Style*— John Randall, Esq, QC; ✉ St Philip's Chambers, 55 Temple Row, Birmingham B2 5LS (tel 0121 246 7000, fax 0121 246 7001, e-mail clerks@st-philips.co.uk)

RANDALL, Nicholas Justin Lee (Nik); s of William Randall, of Sevenoaks, and May; *b* 24 November 1958; *Educ* Sevenoaks Sch, Univ of Liverpool Sch of Architecture (Reilly Medal); *Partner* Susan Mary Corio; 1 s (Louis Homer Corio); *Career* architect; ptnr Alan Brookes Associates 1988 (became Brookes Stacey Randall Fursdon 1993 and Brookes Stacey Randall 1997); winners of 15 major design awards for projects incl: RIBA Awards 1992, 1995 and 1997, Civic Tst Awards 1993 and 1996, Royal Fine Art Cmmn, Sunday Times Building of the Year, Jeux d'Esprit Award 1995, Int Interchange of the Year 2003; work in permanent collection of the V&A Museum London; projects incl: East Croydon Station, The Lowe Flat and The Lowe House London, Thames Water Tower, The Churchill Centre Rotterdam, Transport Interchange Enschede, bridges at Cardiff Bay, The Art House London, The Boating Pavilion Streatley, Wembley Park 2000 (phase one), de Maere Textile Inst Enschede, Pet Shop Boys studio London; founding dir and chm Space Craft Architects 2003–; projects incl: Harrietsham CEP Sch, Longlands for Urban Splash, Bridgwell Island Bristol, New South Central London, The Pod House; *Recreations* family, friends, football, skiing, travelling, cinema; *Style*— Mr Nik Randall, RIBA; ✉ Space Craft Architects, 16 Winchester Walk, London SE1 9AQ (tel 020 7407 9394, fax 020 7407 9395, e-mail nik.randall@spacecraft-architects.com)

RANDALL, Paul Nicholas; s of Jack Sidney Randall, of Sunbury-on-Thames, Middx, and Grace Ruth, *née* Fletcher; *b* 26 January 1960; *Educ* City of London Sch, KCL (LLB, AKC), Coll of Law; *m* 27 April 1985, Anamaria Dans Randall, da of William Enrique Dans Coath; 2 s (James William Alexander b 6 Oct 1987, William Henry Charles b 7 Nov 1990); *Career* Wedlake Bell 1982–87, Ashurst 1987–; *Style*— Paul Randall, Esq; ✉ Ashurst, Broadwalk House, 5 Appold Street, London EC2A 2HA (tel 020 7638 1111)

RANDALL OF ST BUDEAUX, Baron (Life Peer UK 1997), of St Budeaux in the County of Devon; Stuart Jeffrey Randall; *b* 22 June 1938; *Educ* Univ of Wales (BSc); *m* 1963, Gillian Michael; 3 da (Hon Jennifer, Hon Joanna, Hon Emma); *Career* MP (Lab) Hull West 1983–97, PPS to Rt Hon Roy Hattersley as dep ldr of the Lab Pty and shadow Chllr of the Exchequer 1984–85; front bench spokesman: on agric, fisheries and food 1985–87, on home affairs 1987–92; chm ACWI Ltd, chm The Genesis Initiative; *Style*— The Rt Hon Lord Randall of St Budeaux; ✉ House of Lords, London SW1A 0PW

RANDALL-PAGE, Peter; s of Charles Randall-Page, and Joan Mary, *née* Teale; *b* 2 July 1954; *Educ* Eastbourne Coll, Bath Acad of Art (BA); *m* 10 March 1984, Charlotte Eve, da of Philip Harry Hartley; 1 s (Thomas Charles b 16 Sept 1984), 1 da (Florence Ruth b 7 Aug 1987); *Career* sculptor; solo exhibitions incl: Sculpture & Drawings 1980–1992 (Leeds City Art Galleries, Yorkshire Sculpture Park, Royal Botanic Garden Edinburgh and Arnolfini Gallery Bristol, organised by Henry Moore Centre Leeds), Boulders and Banners (Wenlock Priory, Shropshire and Reed's Wharf Gallery London) 1994, In Mind of Botany (Royal Botanic Gardens Kew) 1996, Whistling in the Dark (Ljubljana Slovenia, and Gouda The Netherlands) 1998, Nature of the Beast (Djanogly Gallery Nottingham, Graves Gallery Sheffield and Towner Gallery Eastbourne) 2001, Sculpture and Drawings (Natueal History Museum London) 2003, Lyveden New Bield (sculpture) with accompanying works on paper (Fermynwoods Contemporary Art Northants) 2006; commissions incl: National Trust Derwentwater 1995, LDDC Butlers Wharf London 1996, Manchester City Cncl St Ann's Square 1996, Lothian Regional Cncl and others Hunters Square Edinburgh 1996, BUPA House London 1996, Nuffield Coll Oxford 1999, Royal Botanic Gardens Kew, Millennium Seed Bank Wakehurst Place Sussex 2000, Sculpture at Goodwood 2000 and 2003; work in collections incl Tate Gallery and British Museum; res fell visual and performance arts Dartington Coll of Arts 1999–2000 and 2002–05; memb Design Team Educn Resource Centre (ERC) Eden Project 2002–05; invited artist Gwangju Biennale South Korea 2004; Hon DArts Univ of Plymouth 1999; FRSA, memb RBS, memb RWA; *Style*— Peter Randall-Page, Esq; ✉ PO Box 5, Drewsteignton, Exeter, Devon EX6 6YG (tel and fax 01647 281270, e-mail contact@peterrandall-page.com, website www.peterrandall-page.com)

RANDERSON, Jennifer Elizabeth (Jenny); JP (1982), AM; *b* 26 May 1948; *Educ* Wimbledon HS, Bedford Coll London (BA), Inst of Educn Univ of London (PGCE); *m* 1970, Dr Peter Frederick Randerson; 1 s (James b 1976), 1 da (Eleri b 1979); *Career* teacher: Sydenham HS 1970–72, Spalding HS 1972–74, Llanishen HS 1974–76; lectr Coleg Glan Hafren Cardiff 1976–99; memb Nat Assembly for Wales (Lib Dem) Cardiff Central 1999–; cncllr: Cardiff City Cncl 1983–96, Cardiff City and County Cncl 1995–2000 (ldr of the oppn 1995–99); Nat Assembly for Wales 2000–: min for culture, sport and the Welsh language 2000–03, spokesperson on health and social servs and finance 2003–07, chm Assembly Business Ctee 2003–07, memb Equal Opportunities Ctee 2003–07; memb Lib Dem Pty 1979– (chair Welsh Exec 1988–90, parly candidate 1987, 1992 and 1997); memb: Charter 88, Friends of the Earth, Friends of Nant Fawr; *Recreations* travel, theatre and concert-going, gardening; *Style*— Mrs Jenny Randerson, AM; ✉ National Assembly for Wales, Cardiff Bay, Cardiff CF99 1NA (tel 029 2089 8355, fax 029 2089 8356, e-mail jenny.randerson@wales.gov.uk)

RANDLE, Prof James Neville; s of James Randle (d 1989), and Florence, *née* Wilkins (d 1980); *b* 24 April 1938; *Educ* Waverley GS Birmingham, Aston Tech Coll Birmingham; *m* 1963, Jean Violet (d 2006), da of Alfred Robert Allen; 1 s (Steven James b 1966), 1 da (Sally Joanne b 1968); *Career* Rover Co Ltd: apprentice 1954–61, tech asst 1961–63, project engr 1963–65; Jaguar Cars Ltd: project engr 1965–72, chief vehicle res engr 1972–78, dir of vehicle engrg 1978–80, dir of product engrg 1980–90, dir of vehicle and concept engrg 1990–91, leader of team that produced Jaguar XJ40 (winner Top Car award 1986) and Jaguar XJ220 (winner Turin and Horner prize 1988); ind engrg conslt 1991–; chm and chief exec Randle Engineering and Design 1994–, ceo Lea Francis Ltd 2000–, tech dir Gibbs Technologies 2003–05; dir: Automotive Engineering Centre Univ of Birmingham 1992–2006, Lea Francis Ltd 1997–; hon prof of automobile engrg Univ of Birmingham 1992–2006, visiting prof of engrg design Royal Acad of Engrg, visiting prof of mfrg engrg De Montfort Univ; non-exec dir United Turbine UK Ltd 1992–97, chm Coventry Autoplane Club 2007–; former memb Cncl IMechE (chm Automobile Div 1987–88), fndr memb Autotech, memb Prince Philip Design Award Ctee 1992–2002; Crompton Lanchester Medal 1986, James Clayton Prize 1986, Sir William Lyons International Award 1987, Prince Philip Design Awards Ctee 1992–2002; FREng 1988, FIMechE, FInstD, FRSA, RDI 1994, Hon FCSD 2000; *Recreations* flying, sailing, skiing, hill walking; *Style*— James Randle, RDI, FREng; ✉ Pear Tree House, High Street, Welford-on-Avon, Warwickshire CV37 8EF (e-mail j.n.randle@btinternet.com); University tel 0121 414 4162, fax 0121 414 3688; Company tel 01789 751139, fax 01789 751140

RANDLE, Thomas John; s of Norvell Lee Randle (d 1989), and Mary Sylvia O'Connell (d 1999); *b* 21 December 1958; *Educ* Orange Coast Coll, Chapman Coll, Univ of Southern Calif; *Children* 1 da (Bella Sidney Randle Racklin b 14 July 1992); *Career* tenor; solo concert debut Bach Weinachtsoratorium (Leipzig Rundfunksinfonie) 1987, operatic debut as Tamino in The Magic Flute (ENO) 1988, Molgui in The Death of Klinghoffer (feature film, Channel 4); *Performances* incl: Tippett Songs for Dov (LA Philharmonic) 1985, Rossini Stabat Mater (London Philharmonic) 1988, Tamino in the Magic Flute (ENO 1988, 1989 and 1990, Glyndebourne Opera 1991), Handel Messiah (Royal Philharmonic) 1989, 1990 and 1991, Borodin La Mer (LSO) 1989, Haydn Die Jahreszeiten (Boston Symphony Orch) 1989, Beethoven Ninth Symphony (Scottish Chamber Orch 1989, Bergen Philharmonic Orch 1991, Prague Spring Festival 1996), Pelleas in Pelleas et Melisande (ENO) 1989, title role in Oedipus Rex (Madrid Opera) 1989, title role in L'Orfeo (Valencia 1989, Oviedo Opera Festival 1990), Haydn Die Schöpfung (Tivoli Festival Copenhagen 1990), Liszt Faust Symphony (BBC Scottish Symphony Orch (1990), Tippett The Ice Break (London Sinfonietta) Proms 1990, Ferrando in Cosi fan Tutte (Scottish Opera and Brussels Opera 1990, Geneva Opera 1992), Purcell Fairy Queen (Aix-en-Provence) 1989, Mozart Requiem (Acad of London) 1991, Paul McCartney Liverpool Oratorio 1992 (Ravinia Festival Chicago Aug, Helsinki Festival Finland Sept, Munich Symphony Orch Oct), Ferrando in Cosi fan Tutte (Geneva Opera) 1992, Pelleas in Pelleas et Melisande (with Peter Brook) Theatre Les Bouffes du Nord Paris (and Euro tour) 1992/93, Mozart Die Zauberflöte (Schleswig-Holstein Festival Hamburg 1993/94, Deutsche Oper Berlin 1996), Magic Flute (Auckland Opera NZ) 1993/94, Britten Gloriana, Earl of Essex (Opera North and Royal Opera House Covent Garden) 1993/94, Peter Schat World Premiere Opera Symposion (Netherlands Opera) 1993/94, Haydn L'Incontro

R

Improviso (Garsington Opera Festival) 1993/94, Taverners' Apocalypse (world premiere, London Proms) 1993/94, Mozart Don Giovanni (Los Angeles Music Center Opera 1993/94, Munich Staatsoper 1995), Achilles in King Priam (ENO) 1995, Tippett The Mask of Time (LSO under Sir Colin Davis) 1995, Mendelssohn Elijah (Radio Orch France under Richard Hickox) 1995, Don Ramiro in La Cenerentola (Garsington Opera) 1995, Britten War Requiem (with BBC Scottish Symphony under Martyn Brabbins) 1995, title role in Handel Samson (with The Sixteen under Harry Christophers, Spanish tour) 1995, Mozart Requiem and Nono Canti di Vita e d'amore (concert tour with Bundesjugendorchester for Int Physicians for the Prevention of Nuclear War on 50th anniversary of Hiroshima bombing) 1995, Requiem der Versöhnung/Requiem of Reconciliation (world premiere with Israel Philharmonic under Helmuth Rilling) 1995, Mahler Das Klagende Lied (BBC Symphony under Alexander Lazarev, BBC Proms) 1995, Oberon in The Fairy Queen (ENO new prodn) 1995/96, Paris in La Belle Hélène (ENO new prodn) 1995/96, Gerald in Lakmé (Victoria State Opera Australia) 1996, title role in Idomeneo (Scottish Opera) 1996, The Country of the Blind (by Mark-Anthony Turnage, ENO/Aldeburgh Festival) 1997, Paul Bunyan (by Britten, Royal Opera House debut) 1997, title role in Solimano (by Hasse, Innstruck Festival and Deutsche Oper Berlin) 1997, Poisoned Kiss and A Cotswold Romance (concerts with LSO, under Richard Hickox, by R Vaughan-Williams) 1997, Tom Rakewell in The Rake's Progress (by Stravinsky, Netherlands Opera and Lausanne Opera) 1998–99, Gloriana (by Britten, BBC TV and Opera North) 1999, title role in Lucio Silla (Garsington Opera) 1998, Gawain (by Harrison Birtwhistle, ROH) 2000, The Last Supper (by Harrison Birtwhistle, world premiere, Statsoper Berlin with Daniel Barenboim) 2000, Tom Rakewell in Rake's Progress (Theâtre Champs Elysèes) 2000/01, Loge in Das Rheingold (ENO) 2002, Benedict in Beatrice et Benedict (WNO) 2002, Bajazet in Tamerlano (Paris, London and Halle) 2002, Der Maler in Lulu (Netherlands Opera) 2002, Das Lied von der Erde (with Royal Opera Orch Covent Garden) 2002; *Recordings* incl: set of a cappella choral settings of sacred texts (Pater Noster, Stabat Mater, Vinea Mea, Electa, Benediction Amen, Ave Maria, Ave Verum Corpus) 1981–83, Purcell Fairy Queen (with Les Arts Florrissante under William Christie, from the Aix-en-Provence Festival) 1989, Tippett The Ice Break (with London Sinfonietta under David Atherton) 1990, complete Handel Messiah (with RPO under Owain Arwel Hughes), Handel Esther (with The Sixteen under Harry Christophers) 1995, Britten War Requiem (with BBC Scottish Symphony under Martyn Brabbins) 1995, Non Canti di Vita e d'amore (with Bamberg Symphony under Ingo Metzmacher) 1995, Handel Samson (with Harry Christopher and The Sixteen), A Cotswold Romance (with LSO, under Richard Hickox) 1997, Handel Tamerlano (with Trevor Pinnock and the English Concert) 2001; *Film* Molgi in The Death of Klinghoffer 2003, The Magic Flute 2006; *Recreations* motorsports (especially Formula One); *Style*— Thomas Randle, Esq; ✉ c/o IMG Artists, Lovell House, 616 Chiswick High Road, London W4 5RX (tel 020 8747 9977, fax 020 8747 9131)

RANDOLPH, Prof Sarah Elizabeth; da of John Hervey Randolph (d 1975), of Sherborne, Dorset, and Dorothy Elizabeth, *née* Eyre; *b* 21 March 1949, Sherborne, Dorset; *Educ* St Anne's Coll Oxford (BA), KCL (PhD); *m* 27 March 1976, David John Rogers; 2 da (Emily Sarah b 9 July 1979, Thea Jane b 12 May 1982), 1 s (Jack David b 20 July 1984); *Career* Jubilee postdoctoral research fell Royal Holloway Univ of London 1973–74; Univ of Oxford: departmental demonstrator in vertebrate zoology Dept of Zoology 1974–80, lectr in zoology St Anne's Coll 1977–78, lectr in zoology New Coll 1979–80, Leverhulme Tst research fell Dept of Zoology 1980–85, Royal Soc univ research fell Dept of Zoology 1985–95, lectr in zoology Pembroke Coll 1988–91, extraordinary lectr in zoology New Coll 1991–95, Isobel Laing tutorial fell in med biology Oriel Coll 1994–99, Wellcome Tst sr research fell in basic biomedical sci Dept of Zoology 1995–2000, univ research lectr 1996–99, reader in parasite ecology 1999–2002, supernumerary fell Oriel Coll 1999–2001, NERC sr research fell Dept of Zoology 2000–05, prof of parasite ecology 2002–, tutorial fell in biological sciences ChCh 2002–, sr research fell EU Framework 6 EDEN project Dept of Zoology 2005–; *Publications* Remote Sensing and Geographical Information Systems in Epidemiology (ed with S I Hay and D J Rogers, 2000); numerous jl articles, conf papers and book contribs; *Recreations* gardening, tennis, cycling, textiles; *Style*— Prof Sarah Randolph; ✉ Department of Zoology, University of Oxford, South Parks Road, Oxford OX1 3PS (tel 01865 271241, fax 01865 271240)

RANFURLY, 7 Earl of (I 1831); Gerald François Needham Knox; also Baron Welles (I 1781), Viscount Northland (I 1791), and Baron Ranfurly (UK 1826); er s of Capt John Needham Knox, RN (d 1967, ggs of Hon John Knox, 3 s of 1 Earl of Ranfurly), and Monica, *née* Kitson (d 1975); suc kinsman, 6 Earl of Ranfurly, KCMG 1988; *b* 4 January 1929; *Educ* Wellington; *m* 22 Jan 1955, Rosemary Beatrice Vesey, o da of Air Vice-Marshal Felton Vesey Holt, CMG, DSO (d 1931); 2 s (Edward John, Viscount Northland b 21 May 1957, Hon Rupert Stephen b 5 Nov 1963), 2 da (Lady Elizabeth Marianne (Mrs Empson) b 24 Feb 1959, Lady Frances Christina (Mrs Gordon-Jones) b 13 Feb 1961); *Heir* s, Viscount Northland; *Career* former Lt Cdr RN; memb London Stock Exchange 1963–94; *Style*— The Rt Hon the Earl of Ranfurly; ✉ Maltings Chase, Nayland, Colchester, Essex (tel 01206 262224)

RANG, Dr Humphrey Peter; *b* 13 June 1936; *Educ* Univ Coll Sch Hampstead, UCL (BSc, MSc), UCH Med Sch (MB BS), Balliol Coll Oxford (DPhil, MA); *Career* Univ of Oxford: J H Burn research fell Dept of Pharmacology 1961–64, research asst Dept of Pharmacology 1964–65, lectr 1965–72, fell and tutor in physiology Lincoln Coll 1967–72; prof of Pharmacology Univ of Southampton 1972–74; prof and head Dept of Pharmacology: St George's Hosp Med Sch London 1974–79, UCL 1979–83; dir Novartis Inst for Med Sciences (formerly Sandoz Inst for Med Research) 1983–97, head Scientific Advsy Bd Biofrontera AG 1997–2004; prof of pharmacology UCL 1995–2001, prof emeritus 2001–; visiting research assoc Dept of Pharmacology Albert Einstein Coll of Med NY USA 1966–67; organizing sec Symposia on Drug Action Biological Cncl 1979–84; conslt Sandoz Ltd Basle 1981–83; ed-in-chief Br Jl of Pharmacology 2005– (memb Editorial Bd 1968–74); memb Editorial Advsy Bd: Molecular Pharmacology 1975–90, Archives of Pharmacology 1977–95; memb: Neurosciences Bd MRC 1974–77, Ctee Br Pharmacological Soc 1977–80, Govt Grant Bd Royal Soc 1980–, Exec Ctee Int Congress of Pharmacology 1981–84, Senate Univ of London 1981–83, Wellcome Tst Neurosciences Panel 1988–90; Poulsson Medal Norwegian Pharmacological Soc 1994, Gaddum Medal Br Pharmacological Soc 1972; memb Academia Europaea 1991, hon memb Hungarian Pharmacological Soc 2006; FRS 1980, FMedSci 1997; *Style*— Dr Humphrey Rang, FRS

RANK, John Rowland; s of Capt Rowland Rank, RFA (d 1939), of Aldwick Place, W Sussex, and Margaret, *née* McArthur (d 1988); n of late J Arthur Rank (Baron Rank, d 1972), fndr of Rank Orgn, and gs of late Joseph Rank, fndr of Rank Flour Milling; *b* 13 January 1930; *Educ* Stowe; *Career* property owner; Lord of the Manor of Saham Toney Norfolk; Rank Ltd 1948–50; patron Wessex Cancer Help Centre; tstee Chichester Centre of Arts (former chm); former tstee: Stansted Park Fndn, Ian Askew Charitable Tst; hon patron Chichester Festival Theatre; former memb Cncl: Sussex Diocese, Friends of Chichester Cathedral, Funtington Parish; sometime memb Ct of Corp of Sons of Clergy; memb and hon sec Sennicotts Church Advsy Cncl; former memb Pagham PCC; hon pres Bognor Regis Drama Club, vice-pres Chichester Fencing Club; Freeman City of London 1989; *Recreations* theatre, architectural, gardening, travelling, art exhibitions; *Clubs* Georgian Gp, Regency Soc of Brighton and Hove, Sloane; *Style*— John Rank, Esq; ✉ Riverside, Old Bosham, Chichester, West Sussex PO18 8HP

RÁNKI, Dezsö; *b* 1951; *Educ* Franz Liszt Acad; *Career* pianist; appeared with numerous major orchs incl: Berlin Philharmonic, London Philharmonic, Concertgebouw Amsterdam, Eng Chamber Orch, Orchestre National de France, NHK Tokyo; worked with numerous leading conductors incl: Zubin Mehta, Kurt Sanderling, Sir Georg Solti, Vaclav Neumann, Kyrill Kondrashin, Jeffrey Tate; appeared at venues incl: London, Paris, Amsterdam, Berlin, Vienna and Milan; festivals: Lucerne, Vienna, Prague Spring, Berlin, Helsinki, Bath, BBC Proms; various recordings on Hungaraton, Teldec and Quint Records; first prize Robert Schumann Competition Zwickau 1969, first prizec Int Liszt Competition Budapest 1973, Kossuth Prize Hungary 1978, Grand Prix de l'Académie Charles-Cros; *Style*— Dezsö Ránki, Esq

RANKIN, Alastair John; s of William Brian Rankin (d 1976), and Margaret Christine, *née* Crawford (d 1983); *b* 5 September 1951, Belfast; *Educ* Royal Belfast Academical Instn, TCD (BA); *m* 26 Oct 1979, Gillian Elizabeth Susanne, *née* Dorrity; 2 s (Maurice John b 6 Aug 1982, Timothy Brian b 18 July 1985); *Career* apprentice slr 1974–77; Cleaver Fulton Rankin: asst slr 1977–80, ptnr 1980–, managing ptnr 2003–05, sr ptnr 2005–; slr General Assembly Presbyterian Church in Ireland, memb UK Delgn CCBE 1999– (head 2005–06); Law Soc of NI: memb Cncl 1985–, treas 1992–95, jr vice-pres 1995–96, pres 1996–97, sr vice-pres 1997–98; hon sec Ulster Architectural Heritage Soc 1985–95; memb: Law Soc of NI 1977, Law Soc of Ireland 1997, Soc of Tst and Estate Practitioners; *Recreations* choral singing; *Clubs* Ulster Reform, Bushfoot Golf; *Style*— Alastair J Rankin, Esq; ✉ Cleaver Fulton Rankin, 50 Bedford Street, Belfast BT2 7FW (tel 028 9024 3141, fax 028 9024 9096, e-mail a.rankin@cfrlaw.co.uk)

RANKIN, Ian James; OBE (2002); s of James Rankin (d 1990), and Isobel, *née* Vickers (d 1979); *b* 28 April 1960; *Educ* Univ of Edinburgh (MA); *m* 5 July 1986, Miranda, *née* Harvey; 2 s (Jack b 18 Feb 1992, Kit b 15 July 1994); *Career* writer and radio dramatist; presenter Ian Rankin's Evil Thoughts (Channel 4), reviewer Newsnight Review (BBC); books trans into 23 languages; memb: Crime Writers Assoc 1987– (pres 1999–2000), Soc of Authors; Gold Dagger Award 1997, Grand Prix du Roman Noir 2003; Hon Degrees: Univ of Abertay Dundee, Univ of St Andrews, Univ of Edinburgh; *Books* Inspector Rebus novels incl: Knots and Crosses, Hide and Seek, Tooth and Nail, A Good Hanging and Other Stories, Strip Jack, The Black Book, Mortal Causes, Let It Bleed, Black and Blue, The Hanging Garden, Dead Souls, Set In Darkness, The Falls, Resurrection Men, A Question of Blood, Fleshmarket Close (Crime Thriller of the Year Br Book Awards 2005), The Naming of the Dead; Jack Harvey novels incl: Blood Hunt, Bleeding Hearts, Witch Hunt; other pubns incl: Beggars Banquet (short stories), Watchman (novel); *Recreations* Times crossword, rock music, seedy bars; *Style*— Ian Rankin, Esq, OBE; ✉ c/o Curtis Brown Ltd, Haymarket House, 28–29 Haymarket, London SW1Y 4SP

RANKIN, Sir Ian Niall; 4 Bt (UK 1898), of Bryngwyn, Much Dewchurch, Co Hereford; s of late Lt-Col (Arthur) Niall Talbot Rankin, yr s of 2 Bt; s unc, Sir Hugh Rankin, 3 Bt 1988; *b* 19 December 1932; *Educ* Eton, ChCh Oxford (MA); *m* 1, 1959 (m dis 1967), Alexandra, da of Adm Sir Laurence George Durlacher, KCB, OBE, DSC; 1 da (Zara Sophia (Hon Mrs Humphrey Drummond) b 1960), 1 s (Gavin Niall b 1962); *m* 2, 1980 (m dis 1998), June, er da of late Capt Thomas Marsham-Townshend; 1 s (Lachlan John b 1980); *Heir* s, Gavin Rankin; *Career* Lt Scots Gds (Res); dir of industrial cos: New Arcadia Explorations Ltd, Slumberfleece Ltd, I N Rankin Oil Ltd; patron The Samaritans, govr Moorfields Eye Hosp; FRGS; *Recreations* shooting, yachting; *Clubs* Royal Yacht Sqdn, Pratt's, Car Clamp Recovery, White's; *Style*— Sir Ian Rankin, Bt; ✉ 97 Elgin Avenue, London W9 2DA (tel office 020 7286 0251, home 020 7286 5117)

RANKIN, James Deans (Hamish); s of James Deans Rankin (d 1963), of Barnoldswick, Lancs, and Florence Elizabeth, *née* Wight; *b* 17 February 1943; *Educ* Merchiston Castle Sch Edinburgh, Gonville & Caius Coll Cambridge (MA); *m* 6 Oct 1973, Susan Margaret, da of Francis Eric Adams; 1 s (Andrew Deans b 15 May 1975), 1 da (Sally Margaret b 5 May 1977); *Career* Agric Div ICI: res 1965–68, projects and engineering 1968–71, plant commissioning and management Ammonia Works 1971–77, res management 1977–83; process technol gp mangr ICI New Science Gp 1983–88, R&D mangr ICI Films 1988–93, ICI Engineering 1993–94, ICI sr science and technol assoc 1994; visiting prof Dept of Engrg Science Univ of Oxford 1997–2003, visiting prof Dept of Chem Engrg UMIST (now Univ of Manchester) 2000–; FREng 1987, FIChE 1987; *Recreations* domestic engineering, motoring, church bell ringing, photography; *Style*— Hamish Rankin, Esq, FREng; ✉ Department of Chemical Engineering, University of Manchester, Sackville Street, Manchester M60 1QD (tel 0161 306 3982)

RANKIN, James Rowland Evelyn; s of Charles Winton Browne Rankin (d 1977), of London, and Marina, *née* de Borchgrave d'Altena; *b* 21 January 1959, London; *Educ* Eton, Univ of Buckingham (LLB); *m* 15 March 1997, Jane, *née* Clarke; 2 da (Charlotte b 16 July 1998, Millie b 8 Aug 2002); *Career* called to the Bar 1983; practising barr specialising in licensing law; involved with Theatre in Tst; *Recreations* shooting; *Clubs* Brooks's, Garrick, Annabel's; *Style*— James Rankin, Esq; ✉ 5 Marville Road, London SW6 7BB (tel 020 7371 9996, fax 0870 140 0319); Francis Taylor Building, Inner Temple, London EC4Y 7BY (tel 020 7400 6454, fax 020 7400 6464, e-mail james.rankin@ftb.eu.co.uk)

RANKIN, (Christopher) Paul; s of Hugh Rankin, of Bangor, Co Down, and Iris, *née* Gracey; *b* 1 October 1959; *Educ* Royal Belfast Academical Instn, Hutchesons' GS Glasgow, Queen's Univ Belfast; *m* 22 March 1984, Jeanne Marie, da of Prof Richard Allen Lebrun, of Winnipeg, Canada; 2 da (Claire Nasya b 19 Aug 1986, Emily Paige b 25 March 1989); *Career* worked as waiter while travelling world 1981–83; chef: Le Gavroche 1984–86, Club 19 Saskatchewan 1986, (tournant) Four Seasons Hotel Vancouver 1987, Mount View Hotel Calistoga Napa Valley CA 1988; chef/prop Roscoff restaurant Belfast 1989–99; prop: Cafe Paul Rankin 1995–, Cayenne 1999–, Rain City 2002–, Roscoff Brasserie 2004–; awards for Roscoff: Michelin star 1991, Caterer and Hotelkeeper Newcomer of the Year 1991, included in Gault Milau 300 best restaurants in Europe, Britain's Best Restaurant Courvoisier's Book of the Best 1994, and Great British Chefs II 1995, 4/5 Good Food Guide 1996 and 1997; TV appearances on Hot Chefs 1991 and Gourmet Ireland (BBC) 1993, Ready Steady Cook (BBC) 1994–95; memb Académie Culinaire de Grande Bretagne; *Books* Hot Chefs (1991), Gourmet Ireland (1993), Hot Food, Cool Jazz (1994), Goumet Ireland II (1995), Ideal Home Cooking (1998), New Irish Cookery (2003); *Recreations* yoga, cycling, playing with the kids; *Style*— Paul Rankin, Esq; ✉ The Paul Rankin Group, 2 Beechill Industrial Park, 96 Beechill Road, Belfast BT8 7QN (tel 028 9049 2727)

RANKIN-HUNT, Maj David; LVO (2005, MVO 1993), MBE (2000), TD (1990); s of James Rankin-Hunt, of Wales, and Edwina Anne, *née* Blakeman; *b* 26 August 1956; *Educ* Christ Coll Brecon, St Martin's Sch; *Career* Lt Scots Gds, Maj The London Scottish Regt (51 Highland Vol) 1989– (a regimental tstee), Regtl Col The London Scottish Regt 2007–; Lord Chamberlain's Office 1981–: registrar 1987–89, employed in The Royal Collection 1989– (administrator 1993–); Norfolk Herald of Arms Extraordinary 1994–, dep inspr of Regtl Colours 1995–, dep inspr of RAF Badges 1996–; pres Berks, Bucks and Oxon branch Scots Guards Assoc 2007–; county pres Berks St John Ambulance 1994–99, dir of ceremonies Priory for Wales Order of St John 1995–2004; lay steward St George's Chapel Windsor Castle; curatorial advsr Berkshire Yeomanry Museum, tstee Guards' Museum 2003–; KStJ; genealogist Antigua and Barbuda Orders of Chivalry, grand offr Order of Merit Antigua; *Recreations* military history, conservation issues, dogs, music, books; *Clubs* Army and Navy; *Style*— Maj David Rankin-Hunt, LVO, MBE, TD; ✉ 7 Cumberland Lodge Mews, The Great Park, Windsor, Berkshire SL4 2JD (tel 01784 437269); The Royal Collection, St James's Palace, London SW1A 1BQ (tel 020 7930 4832)

RANSLEY, Philip Goddard; *b* 17 August 1942; *Educ* Northgate GS Ipswich, Gonville & Caius Coll Cambridge (MA, annual prize), Guy's Hosp Med Sch London (MB BChir, Treas's medal and prize in clinical surgery); *Career* conslt urological surgn: Gt Ormond St Hosp for Sick Children 1977–, Guy's Hosp 1998–, The St Peter's Hosps 1977–98; sr lectr in paediatric urology Inst of Child Health and hon sr lectr in paediatric urology Inst of Urology London 1977–; pres Euro Soc for Paediatric Urology 1994–99; FRCS 1971; *Awards* Registrar's Prize NE Metropolitan Region Surgical Soc 1972, Simpla Prize for Research Br Assoc of Urological Surgns 1975, John Latimer Lecture American Urological Assoc 1982, Inaugural Nils Ericsson Meml Lecture 1984, Dantec Prize Br Assoc of Urological Surgns 1985, distinguished overseas guest Section of Surgery and hon fell American Acad of Pediatrics 1989, Dantec Prize Br Assoc of Urological Surgns 1991, St Peter's Medal Br Assoc of Urological Surgns 1999, Paediatric Urology Medal American Acad of Paediatrics 2001; *Publications* author of numerous pubns in learned jls; *Style*— Philip Ransley, Esq; ✉ 234 Great Portland Street, London W1W 5QT (tel 020 7390 8323, fax 020 7390 8324, e-mail pgr2@doctors.org.uk)

RANSON, Dr Rosalind; *b* 15 January 1965; *Educ* King Edward VII Upper Sch Melton Mowbray, St George's Hosp Med Sch London (MB BS), King's Coll London (MA); *Career* GP London 1993–, deanery tutor for sessional GPs London Deanery 2001–; memb GMC 1999– (memb Standards and Ethics Ctee); author of contribs to learned jls; memb Medico-Legal Soc; MRCGP 1994; *Recreations* violin (quartet playing), skiing; *Style*— Dr Rosalind Ranson; ✉ Woodside Health Centre, 3 Enmore Road, London SE25 5NT

RANTZEN, Esther Louise (Mrs Desmond Wilcox); CBE (2006, OBE 1991); da of Henry Barnato (Harry) Rantzen (d 1992), of London, and Katherine, *née* Leverson (d 2005); *b* 22 June 1940; *Educ* N London Collegiate Sch, Somerville Coll Oxford (MA); *m* 22 Dec 1977, Desmond Wilcox (d 2000); 2 da (Emily b 1978, Rebecca b 1980), 1 s (Joshua b 1981); *Career* television prodr and presenter; studio mangr BBC Radio 1963; BBC TV: researcher 1965, dir 1967, researcher and reporter Braden's Week 1968, presenter and prodr That's Life 1973–94, prodr documentary series The Big Time 1976; presenter: That's Family Life, Hearts of Gold 1988–94, Drugwatch, Childwatch, Esther 1994–2002, That's Esther; pres: Meet-a-Mum Assoc, Assoc of Youth with ME (AYME), ChildLine, anti-Bullying Alliance; vice-pres ASBAH; tstee NSPCC 2006 (hon memb 1989); memb: Consumer Cncl 1981–90, Health Educn Authy 1989–95, Health Visitors Assoc, Contact-a-Family (families of disabled children), DEMAND (furniture for the disabled), Downs Children Assoc; patron: Addenbrooke's Kidney Patients Assoc, Hillingdon Manor Sch for Autistic Children, Princess Diana's Sch, The New Sch at West Heath; tstee Ben Hardwick Meml Fund, champion Community Legal Service 2000; Hon DLitt: South Bank Univ 2000, Southampton Inst, Univ of Portsmouth 2003; *Awards* Special Judges' Award RTS 1974, BBC Personality of 1975 Variety Club of GB, Euro Soc for Organ Transplant Award 1985, Special Judges' Award for Journalism RTS 1986, Richard Dimbleby Award BAFTA 1988, RTS Hall of Fame 1997, Lifetime Achievement Award Women in Film and TV; *Books* Kill the Chocolate Biscuit (with Desmond Wilcox, 1981), Baby Love (with Desmond Wilcox, 1985), Ben - The Story of Ben Hardwick (with Shaun Woodward, 1985), Esther - The Autobiography (2001), A Secret Life (2003); *Recreations* growing old disgracefully; *Style*— Ms Esther Rantzen, CBE; ✉ ChildLine, London E1 6GL; c/o Billy Marsh Associates, 76a Grove End Road, London NW8 9ND (tel 020 7449 6930)

RAPHAEL, Adam Eliot Geoffrey; s of Geoffrey George Raphael (d 1969), of London, and Nancy May, *née* Rose; *b* 22 April 1938; *Educ* Charterhouse, Oriel Coll Oxford (MA); *m* 16 May 1970, Caroline Rayner, da of George Ellis (d 1954), of Cape Town, South Africa; 1 s (Thomas Geoffrey b 1971), 1 da (Anna Nancy b 1974); *Career* 2 Lt RA 1956–58; political corr The Guardian 1974–76 (foreign corr Washington 1969–73 and South Africa 1973), exec ed The Observer 1988–93 (political corr 1976–81, political ed 1981–87), presenter Newsnight BBC TV 1987–88, writer on home affairs The Economist 1994–2004, ed The Good Hotel Guide 2004–; Investigative Reporter of the Year Granada 1973, Journalist of the Year British Press Awards 1973; *Books* My Learned Friends (1990), Grotesque Libels (1993), Ultimate Risk (1994); *Recreations* tennis, skiing, reading; *Clubs* Garrick, RAC, Hurlingham, SCGB; *Style*— Adam Raphael, Esq; ✉ 50 Addison Avenue, London W11 4QP (tel 020 7603 9133)

RAPHAEL, Frederic Michael; s of Cedric Michael Raphael, TD (d 1979), and Irene Rose, *née* Mauser; *b* 14 August 1931; *Educ* Charterhouse, St John's Coll Cambridge (MA); *m* 17 Jan 1955, Sylvia Betty, da of Hyman Glatt; 2 s (Paul b 1958, Stephen b 1967), 1 da (Sarah b 1960 d 2001); *Career* author; FRSL 1964; *Books* Obbligato (1956), The Earlsdon Way (1958), The Limits of Love (1960), A Wild Surmise (1961), The Graduate Wife (1962), The Trouble with England (1962), Lindmann (1963), Darling (1966), Orchestra and Beginners (1967), Like Men Betrayed (1970), Who Were You With Last Night? (1971), April, June and November (1972), Richard's Things (1973, screenplay 1981), California Time (1975), The Glittering Prizes (1976, TV plays 1976, Writer of the Year Award), Heaven and Earth (1985), After The War (1988), The Hidden I (1990), Of Gods and Men (1992), A Double Life (1993), Old Scores (1995), Coast to Coast (1998); short stories: Sleeps Six (1979), Oxbridge Blues (1980, TV plays 1984), Think of England (1986), The Latin Lover (1994), All His Sons (1999), Fame and Fortune (The Glittering Prizes II) (2007); screenplays: Nothing but the Best (1964), Darling (Acad Award, 1965), Two for the Road (1967), Far From the Madding Crowd (1967), A Severed Head (1972), Daisy Miller (1974), Rogue Male (1976), Something's Wrong (dir, 1978), School Play (1979), The Best of Friends (1979), Richard's Things (1980), Oxbridge Blues (1984), After the War (1989), The Man In The Brooks Brothers Shirt (dir 1990, ACE Award), Armed Response (1995), Eyes Wide Shut (1999), Coast to Coast (2002); biography: Somerset Maugham and his World (1977), Byron (1982); essays: Bookmarks (ed, 1975), Cracks in the Ice (1979), The Necessity of Anti-Semitism (1997), The Great Philosophers (ed with Ray Monk, 2000), Personal Terms (2001), The Benefits of Doubt (2003), Autobiography: A Spoilt Boy (2003); From the Greek (play, 1979), Karl Popper: Historicism and Its Poverty (1998), Eyes Wide Open (1999), The Benefits of Doubt (2001), Rough Copy (2004), Some Talk of Alexander (2006), Cuts and Bruises (2006); Petronius' Satyrica (solo trans, 2003); translations (with Kenneth McLeish): Poems of Catullus (1976), The Oresteia (1978, televised as The Serpent Son BBC 1979), Complete plays of Aeschylus (1991), Euripides' Medea (1994), Euripides' Hippolytos (1997); Sophokles' Aias (1998); *Recreations* tennis, bridge; *Clubs* Savile; *Style*— Frederic Raphael, Esq, FRSL; ✉ c/o Ed Victor Ltd, 6 Bayley Street, London WC1B

RAPLEY, Prof Christopher Graham (Chris); CBE (2003); s of Ronald Rapley, of Bath, and Barbara Helen, *née* Stubbs; *b* 8 April 1947; *Educ* King Edward's Sch Bath, Jesus Coll Oxford (MA), Victoria Univ of Manchester Jodrell Bank (MSc), Univ of London (PhD); *m* 13 June 1970, Norma, da of Y Khan, of Georgetown, Guyana; 2 da (Emma Jane, Charlotte Anne (twins) b 1971); *Career* UCL Dept of Space and Climate Physics: lectr 1981–87, reader 1988–91, prof of remote sensing science 1991–97; fell St Edmund's Coll Cambridge 1999–; MSSL: head Remote Sensing Gp 1982–94, assoc dir 1990–94; exec dir Int Cncl of Scientific Unions Int Geosphere-Biosphere Prog Royal Swedish Acad of Sciences Stockholm Sept 1994–97, chair UK Nat Ctee Int Geosphere-Biosphere Prog 1998–2000, dir Br Antarctic Survey 1998–2007; sr visiting scientist NASA Jet Propulsion Lab 2005–; pres Scientific Ctee on Antarctic Research 2006–; chair Int Polar Year 2007–2008 Planning Gp Int Cncl of Science 2003–04, memb Int Polar Year 2007–2008 Jt Ctee 2005–; author of over 150 research pubns on space astronomy and earth observation; memb: Remote Sensing Soc, American Geophysical Union; hon prof: UCL 1998–, UEA 1998–; *Recreations* jogging, photography; *Style*— Prof Chris Rapley, CBE; ✉ British Antarctic Survey, High Cross, Madingley Road, Cambridge CB3 0ET (e-mail christopher.rapley@mac.com)

RAPLEY, Jane Margaret; OBE (2001); da of John Edward Robert Rapley, of Wisborough Green, W Sussex, and Ella Mary, *née* Jones (d 1970); *b* 10 July 1946; *Educ* Ickenham HS, Ealing Sch of Art, Nottingham Coll of Art (DipAD), RCA (MA); *partner* since 1977, Peter David Towse; 1 da ((Crystal) Bella Towse b 31 Oct 1984); *Career* design mangr (men's knitwear) Sabre International Textiles 1971–76, design and design mgmnt conslt Chateau Stores of Canada 1977–78, dir (men's casualwear) J R Associates 1977–81, retail dir South Molton Clothing Depot 1981–83, dir (men's retail and design collections) Burrows & Hare 1984–87, dir Peter Towse Design Servs 1983–; lectr on design history, design mgmnt, knitwear and menswear 1970–80: Middlesex, Brighton, Kingston, Trent and Lancashire Polys, Textile Inst, Costume Soc; lectr on: knitwear Central Sch of Art & Design 1977–81, menswear RCA 1981–84; Central Saint Martins Coll of Art & Design (formerly Central Sch of Art & Design): head Textile Dept 1987–89, dean Sch of Fashion & Textiles 1989–2005, head 2006–; ACSD 1977–; FRSA 2002; *Books* The Art of Knitting, Shimi Jimi; *Recreations* reading the early works of Sergei Kaplovitch, collecting back copies of School Friend; *Clubs* Kit Kat (St Petersburg), The Union (London); *Style*— Ms Jane Rapley, OBE; ✉ Central Saint Martins College of Art & Design, Southampton Row, London WC1B 4AP (tel 020 7514 7000, fax 020 7514 7152, e-mail j.rapley@csm.arts.ac.uk)

RAPPORT, Prof Nigel Julian; s of Anthony David Rapport, of Cardiff, and Anita, *née* Glaser; *b* 8 November 1956, Cardiff; *Educ* Clifton, Gonville & Caius Coll Cambridge (scholar, MA), Univ of Manchester (PhD); *m* 3 May 1996, Elizabeth, da of Kenneth Munro; 1 s (Callum b 13 Sept 1987), 1 da (Emilie b 3 Jan 1999); *Career* chair of anthropological and philosophical studies Univ of St Andrews 1996–2004, sr Canada research chair in globalization, citizenship and justice Concordia Univ Montreal 2005; visiting prof Univ of Copenhagen 2000, external prof Norwegian Univ of Science and Technol Trondheim 2002–; pres Anthropology and Archaeology Section BAAS 2001, sec Assoc of Social Anthropologists of the Cwlth 1994–98; Curl Essay Prize Royal Anthropological Inst 1996, BP Prize Lectureship RSE 1996; founding fell Inst of Contemporary Scotland 2000, FRSA 2002, FRSE 2003; *Books* incl: Talking Violence (1987), Diverse World Views in an English Village (1993), The Prose and the Passion (1994), Transcendent Individual (1997), Key Concepts in Social and Cultural Anthropology (2000), The Trouble with Community (2002), I am Dynamite: An Alternative Anthropology of Power (2003); *Recreations* appreciating art and literature, travel, sport; *Style*— Prof Nigel Rapport

RAPSON, Sydney Norman John (Syd); BEM (1984); s of Sidney Rapson (d 1942), and Doris, *née* Fisher; *b* 17 April 1942; *Educ* Southsea and Paulsgrove Secdy Modern Schs, Portsmouth Dockyard Coll, Nat Cncl of Labour Colls; *m* 17 March 1967, Phyllis, da of Frank Williams; 1 da (Sydna b 6 March 1973), 1 s (John b 26 July 1975); *Career* MOD 1958–97 (joined as apprentice aircraft fitter, ret as industrial technician (aircraft)), MP (Lab) Portsmouth N 1997–2005; PPS to MOD 2003, memb Defence Select Ctee, memb Accommodation and Works Ctee; cncllr: Portsmouth City Cncl 1971–77 and 1979–99 (dep ldr 1995–96), Hampshire CC 1973–77; Lord Mayor City of Portsmouth 1990–91, Hon Alderman City of Portsmouth 1999; Freeman City of London 1991; ISM 1998; *Recreations* swimming, gardening, politics; *Style*— Syd Rapson, Esq, BEM

RASCH, Sir Simon Anthony Carne; 4 Bt (UK 1903), of Woodhill, Danbury, Essex; s of Sir Richard Guy Carne Rasch, 3 Bt (d 1996), and his 1 w, Anne Mary, *née* Dent-Brocklehurst (d 1989); *b* 26 February 1948; *Educ* Eton, RAC Cirencester; *m* 31 Oct 1987, Julia, er da of Maj Michael Godwin Plantagenet Stourton and Lady Joanna Stourton, *née* Lambart, da of Field Marshal 10 Earl of Cavan; 1 da (Molly Clare Anne b 10 Sept 1990), 1 s (Toby Richard Carne b 28 Sept 1994); *Heir* s, Toby Rasch; *Career* page of honour to HM 1962–64; chartered surveyor; Liveryman Worshipful Co of Grocers; *Clubs* Pratt's; *Style*— Sir Simon Rasch, Bt

RASHID, Dr Abutaleb Muhammed Fazlur (Faz); s of Dr A M M A Rouf (d 1972), of Barisal, Bangladesh, and Shamse Ara, *née* Ahmed (d 1995); *b* 29 December 1937; *Educ* Univ of Dhaka (MB BS, MSc); *m* 9 June 1968, Faozia Sultana, da of M Habibullah (d 1987), of Chandpur, Bangladesh; 2 da (Tina Farzana b 1971, Samantha Fahima b 1972); *Career* various trg posts in pathology Dhaka Med Coll and Hosp 1962–70, asst prof of pathology Inst of Post Grad Med and Res Dhaka 1970–74, asst in pathology Inst of Pathology Free Univ of Berlin 1974–75, registrar in pathology Royal Sussex Co Hosp 1975–78, sr registrar in pathology Southampton Gen Hosp and Poole Gen Hosp 1978–80, conslt pathologist Darent Valley Hosp (formerly Joyce Green Hosp) 1980–2006, clinical dir pathology servs Dartford & Gravesham NHS Trust 1992–97, ret; coll tutor RCPath 1990–2002; past pres Dartford Bengali Assoc, past chm and treas London and SE Branch and former memb Central Exec Ctee Bangladesh Med Assoc in UK, chm Friends of Bangladesh UK 2001–02, chm (London SE) Bangladesh Welfare Assoc 2001–02; former chm Regnl Exec Ctee BMA Dartford and Medway; memb: ACP, BSCC, ODA; FRCPath; *Recreations* swimming, jogging, snooker, gardening, DIY, computers; *Style*— Dr Faz Rashid; ✉ tel 020 8306 0580

RASHID, Prof Aly; *b* 14 October 1958; *Educ* Burnage HS Manchester, Univ of Manchester (MB ChB, DRCOG, MD); *m* Claire; 2 da (Eleanor, Rosalind), 1 s (Theo); *Career* house dr positions N Manchester Gen Hosp and Royal Preston Hosp 1982–83, vocational trg scheme in gen practice Hope Hosp Salford 1983, SHO 1984–85, trainee GP Swinton 1985–86; princ in gen practice: St Matthews Med Centre Leicester 1986–92, Countesthorpe Health Centre Leicester 1992–; formerly RCGP research fell in gen practice Dept of Community Health and clinical tutor in gen practice Med Sch Univ of Leicester; prof of primary health care De Montfort Univ 1998– (currently head Div of Primary Care); RCGP: memb Faculty Bd 1987–, memb Nat Cncl 1991–, memb Exec Ctee 1993–, nat chm of educn 1993–, RCGP observer Assoc of Univ Depts of Gen Practice 1993–, dir Nat Leadership Prog 2002–; performance assessor GMC 2000–; memb: Conf of Postgrad Advsrs in Gen Practice Univs of the UK 1993–, Jt Ctee on Postgrad Trg for Gen Practice (JCPTGP) 1996–, Advsy Gp on Med Educn and Trg in Gen Practice Dept of Health 1996–, Med Audit Advsy Gp (MAAG) 1996–; med writer Leicester Mercury 1989–92, also author of numerous pubns in academic jls; FRCGP 1991 (MRCGP 1986); *Recreations* tennis, cricket (former rep Manchester and Lancashire Colleges and capt Manchester Med Sch Cricket Team, currently player for village team Willoughby Waterleys); *Clubs* Carisbrooke Lawn Tennis (Leicester); *Style*— Prof Aly Rashid

RASHLEIGH, Jonathan Michael Vernon; s of Nicholas Vernon Rashleigh, of Norton Lindsey, Warks, and Rosalie Mary, *née* Matthews; *b* 29 September 1950; *Educ* Bryanston; *m* 5 April 1975, Sarah, da of John Norwood, of Knowle, W Midlands; 3 s (Charles b 1979, Hugh b 1986, Philip b 1988), 1 da (Julia b 1982); *Career* Ernst and Whinney 1968–76, 3i Group 1976–90 (dir 3i plc 1986–90); dir: Legal & General Investment Management Ltd 1991–93, National Australia Group 1993–95, Henderson Crosthwaite Ltd 1995–99, Investec UK Ltd 1999–2000; Freeman City of London, Liveryman Worshipful Co of Tobacco Pipe Makers and Tobacco Blenders 1972; MSI 1993; FCA 1979 (ACA 1974), FRSA 1995; *Recreations* chess, theatre, cricket, golf; *Style*— Jonathan Rashleigh, Esq; ✉ Longeaves, Norton Lindsey, Warwickshire CV35 8JL (tel 01926 842523, e-mail jonathan@jrashleigh.freeserve.co.uk)

RASHLEIGH, Sir Richard Harry; 6 Bt (UK 1831), of Prideaux, Cornwall; s of Sir Harry Evelyn Battie Rashleigh, 5 Bt (d 1984), and Honora Elizabeth, *née* Sneyd; *b* 8 July 1958; *Educ* All Hallows Sch Dorset; *m* 3 Feb 1996, Emma F C, eldest da of John McGougan; 1 s (David William Augustine b 1 April 1997), 1 da (Ruth Honora b 1 June 1999); *Heir* s, David Rashleigh; *Career* mgmnt accountant; with Arthur Guinness Son & Co plc

R

1980–82, Dexion-Comino International Ltd 1982–84, United Biscuits plc 1985–88, Wessex Housing 1988–90, self-employed 1990–; ACMA; *Recreations* sailing, tennis, shooting; *Clubs* Royal Fowey Yacht; *Style*— Sir Richard Rashleigh, Bt; ✉ Menabilly, Par, Cornwall PL24 2TN

RATCLIFF, Rev Canon David William; s of George and Dorothy Ratcliff, of Canterbury, Kent; *b* 3 November 1937; *Educ* Canterbury Cathedral Choir Sch, St Michael's Sch Ingoldisthorpe, KCL, Edinburgh Theol Coll; *m* 1962, Gillian Mary, da of Frederick and Dorothy Price; 3 s (Andrew b 1964, James b 1966, Timothy b 1970); *Career* asst curate Croydon 1962–69, vicar St Mary's Sittingbourne 1969–75, advsr in adult educn Dio of Canterbury 1975–91, chaplain-rector Anglican (Ecusa) Church Frankfurt-am-Main 1991–98, archdeacon of Germany and Northern Europe 1996–2005, canon of Gibraltar Cathedral 1996–2005, chaplain Anglican Church Stockholm 1998–2002; hon minor canon Canterbury Cathedral 1975–91 and 2003–, hon chaplain Br Embassy Stockholm 1998–2002; hon pres Euro Assoc for Ecumenical Adult Educn 1982–88; founding memb Cncl of Anglican-Episcopal Churches in Germany, Br rep German EV Kirchentag Ecumenical Ctee 1978–97, previous memb European Movement of Christian Assoc for Europe; asst dir Telephone Samaritans 1966–75; *Recreations* music, singing; *Style*— The Rev Canon David W Ratcliff; ✉ 9 The Orchards, Elham, Canterbury, Kent CT4 6TR (tel 01303 840624)

RATCLIFFE, Anne Kirkpatrick; da of Dr John Kirkpatrick Ratcliffe (d 1997), and Alice Margaret, *née* Vaughan-Jones; *b* 19 April 1956; *Educ* Cheltenham Ladies' Coll, Univ of Southampton (BSc), City Univ (Dip Law); *Career* called to the Bar Inner Temple 1981; in practice SE Circuit 1981–; memb Family Law Bar Assoc, memb Soc of Cons Lawyers; *Recreations* collecting modern art, gardening; *Style*— Miss Anne Ratcliffe; ✉ 5 Pump Court, Temple, London EC4Y 7AP (tel 020 7353 2532, fax 020 7353 5321)

RATCLIFFE, Prof (Richard) George; s of Dr Frederick William Ratcliffe, and Joyce Ratcliffe; *b* 3 April 1953; *Educ* Royal GS Newcastle upon Tyne, Manchester Grammar, Merton Coll Oxford (MA, DPhil); *m* 17 April 1982, Susan Margaret Hazelden; 1 s, 1 da; *Career* jr res fell Merton Coll Oxford 1978–81, higher scientific offr ARC Food Res Inst 1982–84; Univ of Oxford: lectr 1984–96, sr res fell New Coll 1984–89, fell and tutor in biological sci New Coll 1989–, reader 1996–2000, prof of plant scis 2000–; memb Advsy Bd Jl of Experimental Botany 1994–, memb Int Advsy Ctee Wageningen NMR Centre 1994–; visiting prof Université de Picardie Amiens 2001–04; *Publications* Regulation of Primary Metabolic Pathways in Plants (ed with N J Kruger and S A Hill, 1999), Principles and Problems in Physical Chemistry for Biochemists (with N C Price, R A Dwek and M R Wormald, 2001); author of papers in scientific jls; *Recreations* book collecting, gardening, hill walking; *Style*— Prof R G Ratcliffe; ✉ New College, Oxford OX1 3BN; Department of Plant Sciences, University of Oxford, South Parks Road, Oxford OX1 3RB (tel 01865 275000, e-mail george.ratcliffe@plants.ox.ac.uk)

RATCLIFFE, (James) Terence; MBE (1987), JP (1972); s of John Ratcliffe (d 1995), of Bury, and Alice, *née* Bennet (d 1981); *Educ* Bury HS, Univ of Manchester (DipArch); *m* 8 Sept 1956, Mary Grundy (Molly), da of Reginald Victor Adlem (d 1990), of Bury; 3 s (Mark b 1961, Jonathon b 1964, Nicholas b 1965), 1 da (Elisabeth (twin) b 1965); *Career* architect, chm R G Partnership Ltd; ARIBA; *Recreations* athletics, YMCA; *Style*— Terence Ratcliffe, Esq, MBE; ✉ Ivy House, Bolton Road, West, Holcombe Brook, Bury, Lancashire; Ratcliffe Groves Partnership, 105 Manchester Road, Bury, Lancashire (tel 0161 797 6000); Ratcliffe Groves Partnership, 83–84 Long Acre, Covent Garden, London (tel 020 7240 9827)

RATHBONE, Julian Christopher; s of Christopher Fairrie Rathbone (d 1960), and Decima Doreen, *née* Frost (d 1984); *b* 10 February 1935; *Educ* Clayesmore Sch Dorset, Magdalene Coll Cambridge (BA); *Career* author; English teacher: Ankara Coll and Univ of Ankara 1959–62, various schs UK 1962–73 (head English Dept Bognor Regis Comp Sch 1970–73); full time author 1973–; contrib: The Guardian, New Statesman, Literary Review, The Independent, The Independent on Sunday, The Sunday Telegraph; Southern Arts bursary 1977, literary advsr Royal Berks Library Servs 1983–84; Deutsches Krimi Preis (Grünfinger) 1989, Crime Writers' Assoc Best Short Story Award 1993, Swanage Int Poetry Competition First Prize 1994; memb Soc of Authors; *Books* incl: Diamonds Bid (1967), Trip Trap (1971), Bloody Marvellous (1975), King Fisher Lives (1976, nominated Booker Prize for Fiction), A Raving Monarchist (1977), Joseph (1979, nominated Booker Prize for Fiction), A Last Resort (1980), A Spy of the Old School (1982), Wellington's War (1984), Lying in State (1985), ZDT (1986), The Crystal Contract (1988), The Pandora Option (1990), Dangerous Games (1991, TVM screenplay 1994), Sand Blind (1993), Intimacy (1995), Accidents Will Happen (1995), Blame Hitler (1997), The Last English King (1997), Trajectories (1998), Kings of Albion (2000), Homage (2001), A Very English Agent (2002), As Bad as it Gets (2003), The Indispensable Julian Rathbone (2003), Birth of a Nation (2004), The Mutiny (novel, 2007); *Radio Play* Albert and the Truth About Rats (Suddeutscher Rundfunk 1990); *Screenplays* Dangerous Games (1993), President Mega (1996), Skiller (2001); *Recreations* painting, music; *Style*— Julian Rathbone; ✉ Sea View, School Road, Thorney Hill, Christchurch, Dorset BH23 8DS (tel and fax 01425 673313, e-mail julian.rathbone@btinternet.com)

RATHBONE, William; s of William Rathbone (d 1992), of Charlbury, Oxon, and Margaret Hester (Peggie), *née* Lubbock (d 1986); *b* 5 June 1936; *Educ* Radley, ChCh Oxford (MA), IMEDE Lausanne (Dip Business Studies); *m* 1960, Sarah Kynaston, da of Brig Hugh S K Mainwaring, CB, CBE, DSO, TD (d 2006); 1 da (Lucy Elena b 17 April 1970), 1 s (William b 19 July 1974); *Career* Nat Serv cmmnd 2 Lt Royal Artillery 1954–56 (served Malaya 1955–56); The Ocean Group plc 1959–88: Elder Dempster Lines 1959–69 (based Nigeria and Ghana for 4 years), started up tanker and bulk carrier div 1969–71, IMEDE Lausanne 1972, dir Wm Cory & Sons Ltd 1973–74, gen mangr Ocean Inchcape Ltd 1974–79, exec dir Gastranco Ltd 1979–88; dir and chief exec Royal United Kingdom Beneficent Assoc and Universal Beneficent Soc 1988–2001; non-exec dir Rathbone Brothers plc (fund mgmnt and banking gp) 1994–2003; tstee: Queen's Nursing Inst, Honeywood Tst, North Waltham Village Tst, Eleanor Rathbone Charitable Tst, Hadfield Tst, Southwark Cathedral Millennium Tst, Br Museum Friends; memb: Ct New England Co, Cncl St Peter's Convent Woking; vice-pres Christ Church (Oxford) United Clubs; Freeman City of London, Liveryman Worshipful Co of Skinners; *Recreations* the arts, opera, theatre, fishing, shooting, rowing, friends; *Clubs* Brooks's, Leander; *Style*— William Rathbone, Esq; ✉ 7 Brynmaer Road, London SW11 4EN (tel 020 7978 1935, fax 020 7978 1938)

RATHCAVAN, 3 Baron (UK 1953); Hugh Detmar Torrens O'Neill; 3 Bt (UK 1929); o s of 2 Baron Rathcavan, PC (d 1994), and his 1 w, Clare Désirée, *née* Blow (d 1956); *b* 14 June 1939; *Educ* Eton; *m* 1983, Sylvie Marie-Thérèse, da of late Georges Wichard du Perron, of Provence, France; 1 s (Hon François Hugh Nial b 26 June 1984); *Heir* s, Hon François O'Neill; *Career* Capt Irish Gds; journalist: Irish Times, Observer, Financial Times; chm: St Quentin Restaurants 1980–89, Brasserie St Quentin 2002–; dir: Savoy Hotel Management and Savoy Restaurants 1989–94, Northern Bank Ltd 1990–97, The Old Bushmills Distillery Co Ltd 1990–99; chm: NI Airports 1986–92, NI Tourist Bd 1988–96; memb Br Tourist Authy 1988–96; memb: House of Lords Euro Select Ctee D, Br-Irish Interparliamentary Body until 1999; *Recreations* food, travel; *Clubs* Beefsteak, Pratt's; *Style*— The Lord Rathcavan; ✉ 14 Thurloe Place, London SW7 2RZ (tel 020 7584 5293, fax 020 7823 8846); Cleggan Lodge, Ballymena, Co Antrim BT43 7JW (tel 028 2568 4209, fax 028 2568 4552, e-mail lordrathcavan@btopenworld.com)

RATHCREEDAN, 3 Baron (UK 1916), of Bellehatch Park, Oxon; Christopher John Norton; s and h of 2 Baron Rathcreedan, TD (d 1990), and Ann Pauline, *née* Bastian; *b* 3 June 1949; *Educ* Wellington, RAC Cirencester; *m* 1978, Lavinia Anne Ross, da of Alan George Ross Ormiston (d 1996), of Arlington, Glos; 2 da (Hon Jessica Charlotte b 13 Nov 1983, Hon Serena Clare b 12 Aug 1987; *Heir* bro, Hon Adam Norton; *Career* pedigree livestock auctioneer; chm KVN Stockdale Ltd, dir Norton & Brooksbank Ltd; Liveryman Worshipful Co of Founders; *Recreations* horse racing, gardening; *Clubs* Turf; *Style*— The Rt Hon Lord Rathcreedan; ✉ Stoke Common House, Purton Stoke, Swindon, Wiltshire SN5 4LL (tel 01793 772492, fax 01793 772806, e-mail rathcreedan@dial.pipex.com)

RATHDONNELL, 5 Baron (I 1868); Thomas Benjamin McClintock-Bunbury; s of 4 Baron Rathdonnell (d 1959); *b* 17 September 1938; *Educ* Charterhouse, RNC Dartmouth; *m* 2 Oct 1965, Jessica Harriet, o da of George Gilbert Butler (eighth in descent from 2 Baron Dunboyne) and Norah Pomeroy Colley, gggda of 4 Viscount Harberton; 3 s (Hon William b 6 July 1966, Hon George b 26 July 1968, Hon James b 21 Feb 1972), 1 da (Hon Sasha b 10 Feb 1976); *Heir* s, Hon William McClintock-Bunbury; *Style*— The Rt Hon the Lord Rathdonnell; ✉ Lisnavagh, Rathvilly, Co Carlow, Republic of Ireland (tel 00 353 5991 61104, website www.lisnavagh.com)

RATLEDGE, Prof Colin; s of Fred Ratledge (d 1975), of Preston, Lancs, and Freda Smith Proudlock (d 1986); *b* 9 October 1936; *Educ* Bury HS, Univ of Manchester (BSc, PhD); *m* 25 March 1961, Janet Vivien, da of Albert Cyril Bottomley (d 1977), of Preston, Lancs; 2 da (Alison b 7 July 1964, Jane b 15 July 1971), 1 s (Stuart b 15 March 1968); *Career* research fellowship MRC Ireland 1960–64, research scientist Unilever plc 1964–67; Univ of Hull: lectr 1967–73, sr lectr 1973–77, reader 1977–83, personal chair 1983, head Dept of Biochemistry 1986–88, prof of microbial biochemistry 1988–2004 (emeritus prof 2004–); memb Euro Fedn of Biotechnol (Sci Advsy Ctee 1984–90), vice-pres Soc of Chem Industry 1993–96; chm: Soc of Chemical Industry 1989–91, Br Co-ordinating Ctee for Biotechnol 1989–91, Food Research Grant Bd and memb Food Research Ctee AFRC 1989–92, Inst of Biology Biotechnol Gps 1989–2001, Inst of Biology Industrial Biology Ctee 1993–96; memb: Int Union of Biochemistry Biotechnol Ctee 1984–96, Int Cncl of Scientific Unions Press Ctee 1994–97; sec Int Ctee of Environmental and Applied Microbiology 1990–94; Kathleen Barton-Wright Meml lectr (Soc for Gen Microbiology and Inst of Biology) 1994, Australian Soc of Microbiology visiting lectr 1986, NZ Soc of Microbiology visiting lectr 1986; memb: Soc for Gen Microbiology, Soc of Chem Industry, Biochemical Soc, American Oil Chemists Soc; ed-in-chief World Journal of Microbiology and Biotechnology 1986–2005, exec ed Biotechnology Letters; FRSC 1970, FIBiol 1983, FRSA 1987, fell Int Inst of Biotechnology 1993; *Books* The Mycobacteria (1977), Microbial Technology: Current State, Future Prospects (1979), The Biology of the Mycobacteria (vol 1 1982, vol 2 1983, vol 3 1989), Biotechnology for the Oils and Fats Industry (1984), Microbial Technology in the Developing World (1987), Microbial Lipids (vol 1 1988, vol 2 1989), Microbial Physiology and Manufacturing Industry (1988), Biotechnology: Economic and Social Aspects (1992), Industrial Applications of Single Cell Oils (1992), Biochemistry of Microbial Degradation (1993), Mycobacteria: Molecular Biology and Virulence (1999), Basic Biotechnology (2001, 3 edn 2006), Single Cell Oils (2005); *Recreations* enjoying my grandchildren, hill walking, bonsai gardening, chess; *Style*— Prof Colin Ratledge; ✉ 49 Church Drive, Leven, Beverley, East Yorkshire HU17 5LH (tel 01964 542690); Department of Biological Sciences, University of Hull, Hull HU6 7RX (tel 01482 465243, fax 01482 465458, e-mail c.ratledge@hull.ac.uk)

RATLIFF, John Harrison; s of Anthony Hugh Cyril Ratliff, and Jean, *née* Harrison; *b* 13 January 1957; *Educ* Clifton, UC Oxford (BA), Univ of Amsterdam (DIEI); *m* 27 July 1985, Pascale, da of Pierre Bourgeon; *Career* called to the Bar Middle Temple 1980; winner of Hon Sir Peter Bristow Award 1981, young lawyers prog Germany 1981–82, J C Goldsmith and Assoc Paris 1983–84, ptnr Stanbrook and Hooper Brussels 1987–99, ptnr Wilmer Cutler Pickering Hale and Dorr LLP 1999– (currently co-chair European Antitrust and Competition Dept); memb: Int Bar Assoc, Anglo Germany Lawyers Assoc, Rheinischer Internationaler Juristen Verein; *Recreations* music, travel, sport; *Clubs* Reform; *Style*— John Ratliff, Esq; ✉ Wilmer Cutler Pickering Hale and Dorr LLP, Bastion Tower, Place du Champ de Mars / Marsveldplein 5, BE 1050, Brussels, Belgium

RATNER, Richard Anthony; TD (1981); s of Jack Louis Ratner (d 1970), of Bryanston Court, London, and Vivienne, *née* Salbstein (d 1976); *b* 21 September 1949; *Educ* Epsom Coll, Univ of Leeds (LLB); *m* 27 July 1974, (Silvia) Jane, da of Maj A C Hammond, TD (d 1990); 2 s (James Anthony Mark b 1975, Christopher Piers Alexander b 1980), 1 da (Katie Emma Jayne b 1979); *Career* textile industry (latterly chm U U Textiles plc) 1972–81, dir institutional sales and ptnr Kitcat & Aitken & Co 1981–91, dir and head of institutional sales Carr Kitcat & Aitken Ltd 1991–93, sr vice-pres Williams de Broë 1993–96, dir Mees Pierson Securities 1996–97, dir and head of res Seymour Pierce 1997–; conslt: Owen & Robinson plc 1986–95, Seasons Garden Centres 1988–92; ptnr West St Antiques Dorking 1990–; Maj The Queen's Own Hussars (TA) 1968–85; memb Court of Common Cncl for the Ward of Broad St 1981–91; former chm: Broad St Ward Club, Soc of Young Freeman, Bd of Govrs City of London Sch; former govr: Bridewell Royal Hosp, Christ's Hosp, Abinger Hammer Village Sch; chm Mitchell City of London Charity; former memb: City Branch TA & VRA, HAC; Freeman City of London 1976, Liveryman Worshipful Co of Gunmakers 1979; memb: Lloyd's 1975–84, Stock Exchange 1984, FSI 1992; *Books* The English Civil War (contrib, 1971); *Recreations* antique firearms, antiques, model railways; *Clubs* Cavalry and Guards'; *Style*— Richard Ratner, Esq, TD; ✉ Hill House, Hammerfield, Abinger Hammer, Dorking, Surrey (tel 01306 730182); Seymour Pierce, 29–30 Cornhill, London EC3 (tel 020 7648 8700)

RATSEY, Dr David Hugh Kerr; s of Capt Franklin Ratsey, and Mary Gwendoline Lucy, *née* Walduck; *b* 7 June 1944; *Educ* Sherborne, St Bartholomew's Hosp (MB BS, MRCS, LRCP); *m* 6 Sept 1969, Christine, da of Arthur William Tutt-Harris; 3 s (Matthew David, Timothy James, Nicholas Paul), 1 da (Anna Mary); *Career* pre-registration post Prince of Wales Hosp Tottenham then house surgn Whipps Cross Hosp Leytonstone 1968–69, sr house offr in anaesthesia St Bartholomew's Hosp 1970–71, Alwyn bursar and res registrar in anaesthesia St Bartholomew's Hosp 1971–72, anaesthetic registrar St George's Hosp 1973–75, trainee then princ Gen Practice 1975–80, pt/t clinical asst Royal Homeopathic Hosp 1975–82 and 1986–92, consltg Homeopathic practice 1980–; locum conslt homeopathic physician Kent and Sussex Weald NHS Tst 1994–96 (substantive 1996–); Faculty of Homeopathy: elected Cncl 1983, offr 1984, external examiner 1984, founder memb official Ct of Examiners 1987, vice-pres 1987 and 1988, pres 1992–95; *Recreations* sailing; *Clubs* Medical Soc of London; *Style*— Dr David Ratsey

RATTLE, Sir Simon Denis; kt (1994), CBE (1987); *b* 19 January 1955; Liverpool; *Educ* Royal Acad of Music; *m* 1, Elise Ross; 2 s; *m* 2, Candace Allen; partner, Magdalena Kozena; 1 s; *Career* conductor; played percussion with the Royal Liverpool Philharmonic Orch aged 15, asst conductor Bournemouth Symphony Orch and Sinfonietta 1974–76, assoc conductor Royal Liverpool Philharmonic and BBC Scottish Symphony Orchs 1977–80; City of Birmingham Symphony Orch: princ conductor and artistic advsr 1980–98, music dir 1990–98; chief conductor and artistic dir Berlin Philharmonic Orch 2002–; princ guest conductor LA Philharmonic 1979–94; princ guest conductor: Rotterdam Philharmonic 1981–84, Orch of the Age of Enlightenment 1992–; artistic advsr Birmingham Contemporary Music Gp 1992–; artistic dir South Bank Summer Music Festival 1981–83; worked with various other major orchs incl: London Sinfonietta, The Philharmonia, London Philharmonic, Berlin Philharmonic, Rotterdam Philharmonic, Stockholm Philharmonic, Philadelphia Orch, Chicago, San Francisco, Toronto, Cleveland and Boston

Symphony Orchs; Festival Hall debut 1976, Glyndebourne debut 1977, US debut 1979, NY debut 1985, Concertgebouw Amsterdam debut 1986, US operatic debut 1988, Royal Opera House Covent Garden debut 1990, Vienna Philharmonic debut 1993; Hon DMus: Univ of Birmingham, Univ of Leeds, Univ of Liverpool, Univ of Oxford, Birmingham Conservatoire; Hon Senator Hanns Eisler Acad for Music Berlin 2005; Officier de l'Ordre des Arts et des Lettres (France) 1995; *Operas* conducted incl: The Cunning Little Vixen (Glyndebourne 1977 and Covent Garden 1990), Ariadne auf Naxos (Glyndebourne, 1981), Der Rosenkavalier (Glyndebourne, 1982), The Love for Three Oranges (Glyndebourne, 1983), Idomeneo (Glyndebourne, 1985), Katya Kabanova (ENO, 1985), Porgy and Bess (Glyndebourne, 1986), L'heure escagnole and L'enfant et les sortilèges (Glyndebourne, 1987), The Marriage of Figaro (Glyndebourne, 1989), Cosi fan Tutte (Glyndebourne, 1991), Pelléas et Mélisande (Netherlands Opera, 1993), Don Giovanni (Glyndebourne, 1994), Parsifal (Netherlands Opera, 1997 and ROH, 2001); *Recordings* over 60 for EMI incl: Mahler's 2nd (with CBSO, 1987, Gramophone Record of the Year and Best Orchestral Recording 1988), Turanglila Symphony (with CBSO, 1987, winner Grand Prix du Disque and Grand Prix Caecilia 1988), Porgy and Bess (with London Philharmonic, 1988, winner Gramophone Opera Award 1989, Int Record Critics' Award 1990, Grand Prix in Honorem de l'Académie Charles Cros 1990, Prix Caecilia, Br Phonographic Industry Classical Award, Edison Award), Szymanowski Litany for the Virgin Mary (Germany's Echo Award for best symphonic recording 1994), Schoenberg Chamber Symphony No 1 and Variations and Erwartung (with Birmingham Contemporary Music Gp and CBSO, Gramophone Best Orchestral Recording Award 1995), Szymanowski Stabat Mater (with City of Birmingham Symphony Chorus and CBSO, Gramophone Best Choral Award and Best Engrg Award 1995), Szymanowski Violin Concertos Nos 1 and 2 (with CBSO, Gramophone Best Concerto Award 1997); *Awards* Choc d'Anné for Brahms Piano Concerto Op 15 1990, Gramophone Artist of the Year 1993, Mountblanc de la Culture Award (for private vision) 1993, Toepfer Fndn of Hamburg Shakespeare Prize 1996, BBC Music Magazine Outstanding Achievement Award 1997, RSA Albert Medal 1997, Outstanding Achievement Award South Bank Show Awards 1999 (in honour of 18 years work with Birmingham Symphony Orch), Diapson Recording of the Year Award for Beethoven Piano Concertos 1999, Gramophone Best Opera Recording (for Szymanowski King Roger with CBSO) 2000; for recording of Mahler 10 with Berlin Philharmonic: Gramophone Best Orchestral Recording 2000, Gramophone Record of the Year 2000, Grammy Award for Best Orchestral Performance 2001; *Style*— Sir Simon Rattle, CBE; ✉ c/o Askonas Holt, Lonsdale Chambers, 27 Chancery Lane, London WC2A 1PF

RATTUE, Andrew; s of Maurice Rattue (d 1985), and Elenar, *née* Goodfellow (d 1997); *b* 10 December 1960, Salisbury, Wilts; *Educ* Bishop Wordsworth's Sch Salisbury, BNC Oxford (BA), Birkbeck Coll London (MA), KCL (PGCE); *m* 22 Oct 1988, Jacqueline, *née* Roynon; 1 da (Polly b 29 July 1993), 3 s (Ben b 30 March 1995, Joe b 26 Dec 1997, Sam b 19 June 2001); *Career* Mill Hill Sch 1985–88, Haberdashers' Aske's Sch Elstree 1988–93, Fulbright teaching exchange Greenhill Sch Dallas TX 1990–91, head of English Highgate Sch 1993–96, dep head Royal GS Guildford 1996–2005, headmaster Royal GS Worcester 2005–; memb: Assoc of Sch and Coll Leaders 1996, HMC 2005; *Recreations* drama, American culture, the Victorians, sport, cooking; *Clubs* East India; *Style*— Andrew Rattue, Esq; ✉ Royal Grammar School, Upper Tything, Worcester WR1 1HP (tel 01905 613391, fax 01905 726892, e-mail office@rgsw.org.uk)

RAUSING, Kirsten; da of Gad Rausing (d 2000), and Birgit, *née* Mayne; *b* 6 June 1952, Lund, Sweden; *Career* moved to UK 1980; non-exec dir Tetra Pak International (now Tetra Laval Gp) 1983–; prop: Lanwades and St Simon Studs (both Newmarket), Staffordstown Stud (Co Meath); memb Cncl and vice-chm Thoroughbred Breeders' Assoc 1985–89 and 1991–95, dir British Bloodstock Agency plc 1994–2001, dir Jockey Club Estates 1994–, dir National Stud 1998–2003; memb: Bd Fedn Europeenne des Assocs d'Eleveurs de Pur Sang Anglais 1994–2005 (chm 2002–05), Selbourne Ctee of Enquiry into Veterinary Research 1996–97, Faculty of Veterinary Science External Advsy Gp Univ of Liverpool 2007–; *Publications* Statistical Overview of the Thoroughbred Breeding Industry in Europe (2004); *Clubs* Jockey; *Style*— Ms Kirsten Rausing; ✉ Tetra Laval Group, PO Box 430, CH-1009 Pully, Switzerland

RAUSING, (Dr) Sigrid Maria Elisabet; da of Hans Anders Rausing, and Märit Margareta Elisabet, *née* Norrby; *b* 29 January 1962, Lund, Sweden; *Educ* Univ of York (BA), UCL (MSc, PhD); *m* 1, 12 Dec 1996, Dennis Hotz; 1 s (Daniel b 27 Oct 1997); m 2, 14 Feb 2003, Eric Abraham; 1 step s (Alexis b 28 Feb 1981), 1 step da (Natalia b 16 Nov 1988); *Career* chair Sigrid Rausing Tst 1995–; publisher: Granta 2006–, Portobello Books 2006–; memb Bd Atlantic Books UK 2006–; memb Bd Human Rights Watch NYC; govr Sevenoaks Sch; hon fell Anthropology Dept UCL 1997–98; Int Service Human Rights Award (Global Human Rights Defender, jtly) 2004, Beacon Special Award for Philanthropy 2005, Changing Face of Philantropy Award Women's Funding Network 2006; *Publications* History, Memory and Identity in Post-Soviet Estonia: The end of a collective farm (2004); author of articles in jls and chapters in books; *Recreations* riding, walking, conservation; *Clubs* Campden Hill Tennis; *Style*— Ms Sigrid Rausing; ✉ Sigrid Rausing Trust, Eardley House, 4 Uxbridge Street, London W8 7SY (tel 020 7908 9890, fax 020 7908 9899)

RAVEN, Hugh Jonathan Earle; s of John Earle Raven (d 1980), of Cambridge, and Constance Faith Alethea, *née* Hugh Smith; *b* 20 April 1961, London; *Educ* King's Coll Choir Sch, Marlborough Coll, Friend's Sch Saffron Walden, Cambridge Coll of Arts & Technol, Harper Adams Agricultural Coll, Univ of Kent at Canterbury; *m* 18 July 1992, Jane Stuart-Smith; 2 da (Kitty Sarah Faith b 8 Aug 1995, Madeline Emma Beatrix b 2 June 1997); *Career* researcher to Chris Smith MP (shadow economic sec to HM Treasy) 1987–88, researcher to Ron Davies MP (shadow min of state for food and agriculture) 1988–91, co-ordinator Sustainable Agriculture Food and Environment (SAFE) Alliance 1991–95, policy strategist Br Overseas Aid Gp 1996, convenor Govt's Green Globe Task Force 1997–99, advsr on rural policy to Michael Meacher MP (environment min) 1999–2000, project dir Organic Scotland 2000–01, environment advsr Esmee Fairbairn Fndn 2000–, dir Soil Assoc Scotland 2006–; memb: Rural and Agricultural Affrs Advsy Ctee BBC 1994–97, Bd Scottish Natural Heritage 2004–07, UK Sustainable Devpt Cmmn 2004–; dir: Ardtornish Estate Co 1996–, The Big Box Network 2004–, Morvern Community Devpt Co 2005–07; cncllr (Lab) Royal Borough of Kensington and Chelsea 1990–94 (chair and dep ldr of oppn 1992–94), Parly candidate (Lab) Argyll and Bute 1999, 2001 and 2003, expert advsr Lab Party Environmental Policy Cmmn 1992–97, chair SERA (Lab Party environmental affiliate) 1997–99; memb UK Exec Ctee Br American Project 1996–98; tstee: Soil Assoc 1991–99, Lochaber and Dist Fisheries Tst 1995– (chm 1995–2002), RSPB 1997–2002; *Publications* Off our Trolleys: Food retailing and the hypermarket economy (co-author, 1994), Modernising UK Food Policy: the case for reforming MAFF (co-author, 1996), Essential Scotland (contrib, 1998), Town and Country (contrib, 1998), Environment Scotland: Prospects for Sustainabaility (contrib, 1999), The Meat Business (contrib, 1999), Community and Environment (contrib, 1999); *Recreations* reading, theatre, sailing, walking, fishing; *Clubs* Soho House, Farmers'; *Style*— Hugh Raven, Esq; ✉ Kinlochaline, Morvern, by Oban, Argyll PA34 5UZ (tel 01967 421394, e-mail hugh@morvern.demon.co.uk); Soil Association, Tower Mains, 16 Liberton Brae, Edinburgh EH16 6EA (tel 0131 666 2474, e-mail hraven@soilassociation.org)

RAVEN, James (Jim); s of Patrick Raven, and Irene, *née* Cosson; *b* 23 June 1953; *Educ* William Penn Secdy Sch London; *m* 15 June 1975, Wendy Margaret; 3 da (Lyanne b 21 Sept 1976, Ellie b 17 Aug 1979, Jodie b 1 Nov 1985); *Career* trainee reporter Press Association 1969–70; reporter: SE London Mercury 1970–73, freelance 1973–75, Fleet St News Agency 1975, The Sun and freelance 1975–77, Sevenoaks Chronicle 1977–78, Kent Evening Post 1978–81; TVS Television: joined as scriptwriter 1981, later prodr, ed Coast to Coast (regnl news magazine prog) 1989–92 (formerly dep ed); Meridian Broadcasting: controller of news, sport and current affrs 1992–96, dir of news, sport and current affrs 1996–97, dir of news and sport 1997–98; dir of news strategy United Broadcasting and Entertainment 1997–99 (dir of news 1999–), md United Sport 1999–2000, md Granada Sport 2000–; London Young Journalist of the Year 1972; *Books* Pinnacle of Ice, The Triad Consignment, When Strangers Came, The Venice Ultimatum; *Recreations* painting, travelling, reading, writing; *Style*— Jim Raven, Esq

RAVENS, Jan; *b* 14 May 1958, Clatterbridge; *Educ* Homerton Coll Cambridge (pres Footlights); *m* Max Hole, *qv*; 1 s (Louis); 2 s from prev m (Alfie, Lenny); *Career* actress and comedienne; *Theatre* incl: The Sloane Ranger Revue (Duchess Theatre), The End of the World Show (Chichester Studio), Loitering Within Tent (Chichester Studio), Ha Bloody Ha (Gate Theatre and Edinburgh), The Relapse (Chichester), Tom Jones (Watford), Twelfth Night (Birmingham Rep), After Easter (RSC), Pentecost (RSC, Best Play Evening Standard Awards 1995); *Television* appearances incl: Carrott's Lib (BBC), Spitting Image (Central), Luv (BBC), Alexei Sayle's Stuff (BBC), No Frills (BBC), An Actors Life For Me (BBC), Harry Enfield and Chums (BBC), One Foot In The Grave (BBC), The Final Frame (Channel 4), Duck Patrol (LWT), The Grimleys (series 1–3, Granada), Kiss Me Kate (BBC), Doctors (BBC), 2DTV (2 series, ITV), Bremner, Bird and Fortune (Channel 4), Alistair McGowan's Big Impression (3 series, BBC 1), Dead Ringers (5 series, BBC), Alter Ego (Ronin Entertainment), Midsomer Murders: Death and Dreams (ITV); *Radio* incl: Brunch (Capital), Hanna, I'll Find You (BBC Radio 4), The Treacle Well (BBC Radio 4), Life, Death and Sex With Mike and Sue (BBC Radio 4), Dead Ringers (10 series, BBC Radio 4), Revolting People (BBC Radio 4), Oxygen (BBC World Service); *Film* La Passione (Heathtour Films); *Style*— Ms Jan Ravens; ✉ c/o Amanda Howard Associates, 21 Berwick Street, London W1F 0PZ (tel 020 7287 9277, fax 020 7287 7785, e-mail mail@amandahowardassociates.co.uk)

RAVENSDALE, 3 Baron (UK 1911); Sir Nicholas Mosley; 7 Bt (GB 1781), of Ancoats, Lancashire, and of Rolleston, Staffordshire, MC (1944); s of Sir Oswald Mosley, 6 Bt (d 1980), and (first w) Lady Cynthia Blanche, *née* Curzon (d 1933), da of 1 Marquess of Curzon Kedleston and 1 Baron Ravensdale; suc aunt, Baroness Ravensdale (who was also cr a Life Peer as Baroness Ravensdale of Kedleston 1958) 1966; suc father as 7 Bt 1980; *b* 25 June 1923; *Educ* Eton, Balliol Coll Oxford; *m* 1, 1947 (m dis 1974), Rosemary Laura (d 1991), da of late Marshal of the RAF Sir John Maitland Salmond, GCB, CMG, CVO, DSO, by his 2 w, Hon Monica Grenfell; 3 s (Hon Shaun Nicholas b 1949, Hon Ivo Adam Rex b 1951, Hon Robert b 1955), 1 da (Hon Clare Imogen b 1959); m 2, 1974, Verity Elizabeth, 2 da of late N J B (Jack) Raymond, of Basingstoke, and former w of (John) Adrian Bailey; 1 s (Hon Marius b 1976); *Heir* s, Hon Shaun Mosley; *Career* Capt Rifle Bde WW II; author (as Nicholas Mosley); FRSL 1980; *Novels* Meeting Place (1962), Accident (1966, filmed by Joseph Losey), Assassins (1967), Impossible Object (1968), Natalie Natalia (1971), The Assassination of Trotsky (1972), Catastrophe Practice (1979), Imago Bird (1980), Serpent (1981), Judith (1986), Hopeful Monsters (1990, Whitbread Book of the Year), Children of Darkness and Light (1996), The Hesperides Tree (2001), Inventing God (2003), Look at the Dark (2005); *Non-Fiction* incl: Julian Grenfell (1976), Rules of the Game: Sir Oswald and Lady Cynthia Mosley 1896–1933 (1982), Beyond the Pale, Sir Oswald Mosley 1933–80 (1983), Efforts at Truth (autobiography, 1994), The Uses of Slime Mould: Essays of Four Decades (2004); *Recreations* gardening; *Style*— The Rt Hon the Lord Ravensdale, MC; ✉ 2 Gloucester Crescent, London NW1 7DS (tel 020 7485 4514); c/o PFD, Drury House, 34–43 Russell Street, London WC2B 5HA

RAVENSWORTH, 9 Baron (UK 1821); Sir Thomas Arthur Hamish Liddell; 14 Bt (E 1642); s of 8 Baron Ravensworth (d 2004); *b* 27 October 1954; *Educ* Gordonstoun, RAC Cirencester; *m* 18 June 1983, Linda, da of Henry Thompson (d 1986), of Gosforth, Newcastle upon Tyne; 1 da (Hon Alice Lorina b 24 April 1986), 1 s (Hon Henry Arthur Thomas b 27 Nov 1987); *Heir* s, Hon Henry Liddell; *Career* branch chm local NFU and other ctees Northumberland NFU 1989–90; memb Ctee Northumberland CLA 1990–; *Recreations* shooting; *Style*— The Rt Hon the Lord Ravensworth; ✉ Eslington Park, Whittingham, Alnwick, Northumberland NE66 4UR (tel 01665 574653, car 079 7167 5757)

RAVERA, John Eli; s of Eli Vardo (d 1978), and Louesa, *née* Avogadari (d 1960); *b* 27 February 1941, Surrey; *Educ* Camberwell Jr Sch of Art, Camberwell Sch of Art (studied under C Vogal); *m* Daphne Mary (d 2002), da of William Olive Stanley Williams; 1 s (Marcus Jonathan b 25 Jan 1973); *Career* sculptor in clay for bronzes; memb Art Workers Guild; past pres RSBS; ARBS (pres 2987–90), FRSA; *Exhibitions* Walberswick 1960, 1961 and 1962, Ealing Abbey 1970, Guildhall (City) 1970, Richmond Park 1970, Whitegift Gall 1920, York Open Air Show 1971, Rye 1971, Augustine Gall 1971 and 1972, Hounslow Festival Sculpture 1972, RA 1975 and 1976, Alwin Gall 1977, Woodlands 1977, Bexleyheath 1985, Haywards Heath 1985, London, South Africa; *Major Commissioned Works* Acad of Arts Hong Kong 1982, Morgan's Walk London 1983, Lagos, Colgrave's Banbury, Tibb's The Builders Oxon, Norwich, Midland Bank, The Diners' Club 1986, Archimede's Award for Engrg, London Fashion Award, Bexleyheath, Haywards Heath, London Dockland Devpt 1987, Kensal Green Cemetery, Bayswater 1989, Elstree Tower, Ipswich 1990, Barbican Centre, Oxford, Bracknell Town Centre, Hemel Hempstead 1992, Chatham Town Centre 1993, Tokyo 1994, Reading 1996, Maidenhead 1996, Bexleyheath 1997, St Mary St Josph Sch Sidcup 1998, Bracknell Town Centre 2003, Staines FC 2003, Geronimo (Life and 1/4) Bronze Dorsington Stratford-upon-Avon, Albert Einstein (Life and 1/4) Bronze Stratford-upon-Avon 2004; *Style*— John Ravera, PPRBS, FRSA

RAWCLIFFE, Roger Capron; s of Brig James Maudsley Rawcliffe, OBE, MC, TD (d 1965), and Margaret Duff Capron (d 1982); *b* 2 August 1934; *Educ* Rossall Sch, Trinity Coll Cambridge (open exhibitioner, Henry Arthur Thomas travelling scholarship, MA); *m* 1960, Mary Elizabeth White, da of Maurice White; 1 s (James Maurice b 1966); *Career* Nat Serv 1952 Grenadier Gds and E Lancs Regt, 2 Lt 1953, Lt 1954, Capt Stowe CCF 1963, Maj 1964, OC 1966, Hon Col IOM ACF 1987 (Gen Serv Medal, Cadet Forces Medal and Bar); articled to Sir Thomas Robson at Price Waterhouse; Stowe Sch: asst master 1960–80, head of dept 1967, housemaster 1969; lectr School of Extension Studies Univ of Liverpool 1981–; lectr Centre for Manx Studies 1997–; guest lectr Swan Hellenic Cruises 1967–2004; ptnr Pannell Kerr Forster 1982–91; dir: Rothschild Asset Management (Isle of Man) 1987–91, Isle of Man Breweries Ltd (now Heron and Brearley Ltd) 1992–, Singer & Friedlander (Isle of Man) 1992–2005; chm IOM Soc of Chartered Accountants 1993–94; govr Rossall Sch 1980–2001; tstee: King William's Coll 1987–94, Manx National Heritage 1991–; memb: HAC 1960, Soc of Tst and Estate Practitioners 1990; FCA 1970 (ACA 1960); *Books* A Time of Manx Cheer: A History of the Licensed Trade in the Isle of Man (co-author, 2002), No Man Is an Island: A History of the Finance Sector in the Isle of Man (2007); *Style*— Roger Rawcliffe, Esq; ✉ The Malt House, Bridge Street, Castletown, Isle of Man IM9 1ET (tel 01624 825667, fax 01624 827218)

RAWLINGS, Keith John; s of Jack Frederick Rawlings (d 1985), and Eva, *née* Mullis (d 1996); *b* 24 April 1940; *Educ* Kent Coll Canterbury; *m* 21 Dec 1963, Susan Mary, da of Thomas Johnson (d 1967); 1 s (Jonathan James Ashley b 27 March 1965), 1 da (Sarah Louise (Mrs Watson) b 15 Feb 1967); *Career* insurance broker and ind fin advsr; chm Burlington Insurance Group 1969–91, dir London & Edinburgh Trust plc 1986–87, dir Rutland Trust plc 1987–91, gp business devpt dir Bain Hogg Ltd 1991–95, dir Aurora Financial Group 1995–2004, dep chm Bishops plc 1995–2004, chm Premier Health Mgmnt

R

Group 2004–, chm Creative Action Group Europe Ltd 2004–; FCII; *Recreations* golf, tennis, skiing, sailing, bridge, travel; *Clubs* St James's, Carnegie; *Style*— Keith Rawlings, Esq; ✉ Summerhayes, Cliff Road, Hythe, Kent CT21 5XQ (tel 01303 267014, e-mail keithrawlings@ukonline.co.uk); Premier Occupational Healthcare Limited, Premier House, Shearway Business Park, Pent Road, Folkestone, Kent CT19 4RG (tel 01303 298100)

RAWLINGS, Baroness (Life Peer UK 1994), of Burnham Westgate in the County of Norfolk; Patricia Elizabeth Rawlings; da of late Louis Rawlings, and Mary, *née* Boas de Winter; *b* 27 January 1939; *Educ* Oak Hall Surrey, Le Manoir Lausanne, Univ of Florence, UCL (BA), LSE (Dip Int Rels); *m* 1962 (m dis 1967), David Wolfson (later Baron Wolfson of Sunningdale, *qv*); *Career* Parly candidate (Cons): Sheffield 1983, Doncaster 1987; special advsr to Min on Inner Cities DOE 1987–88; MEP (Cons) Essex SW 1989–94; memb Euro Parl Ctee on: Youth, Educn, Culture, Media, Sport, Foreign Affrs; vice-chm Euro Parl's Delgn to Romania, Bulgaria, and Albania; House of Lords: oppn whip 1997–98, oppn min for Foreign Affrs 1997–, oppn min for Int Devpt 1998–; chm Cncl KCL 1998–2007; BRCS: memb 1964–, chm Appeals London Branch 1964–88, Nat Badge of Hon 1981, hon vice-pres 1988–, patron London Branch 1997; pres: NCVO 2002–07, BADA 2005–; memb: Children's Care Ctee LCC 1959–61, WMHNR Nursing Westminster Hosp to 1968, Br Bd of Video Classification, Cncl Peace Through NATO, IISS, Euro Union Women, Bd Br Assoc for Central & Eastern Europe 1994–2001, RIIA 1996–, Br Cncl 1997–2000; vice-pres EU Youth Orch 1992–, dir Eng Chamber Orchestra and Music Soc; tstee Chevening Estate 2002–; Hon DLitt Univ of Buckingham; hon fell: KCL 2003, UCL 2005; Bulgarian Order of the Rose Silver Class 1991, Grand Official Order of the Southern Cross Brazil 1997; *Recreations* music, art, architecture, golf, skiing, travel, gardening; *Clubs* Queen's, Grillions (hon sec), Royal West Norfolk; *Style*— The Baroness Rawlings

RAWLINS, Brig Gordon John; OBE (1986); s of Arthur James Rawlins, of New Milton, Hants, and Joyce Rosemary, *née* Smith; *b* 22 April 1944; *Educ* Welbeck Coll, RMA Sandhurst, RMCS (BSc); *m* 1, 28 Aug 1965, Ann Rose (d 1986), da of Alfred George Beard (d 1981); 1 s (Richard James b 1968); m 2, 25 Oct 1986, Margaret Anne (Meg), da of James Martin Edward Ravenscroft; 1 step s (Hamish Richmond Haddow b 1970), 1 step da (Islay Elizabeth Haddow b 1972); *Career* cmmnd REME 1964; Staff Coll (Maj) 1977–78, Maj GSO2 ASD 1 MOD 1978–80, Maj 21C 5 Armd Workshop 1981–82, Lt-Col CO 7 Armd Workshop 1982–84, Lt-Col Mil Asst to MGO MOD 1984–86, Col PB21 MOD 1986, Col Sec to COS Ctee MOD 1987, Brig Cmd Maint 1 (BR) Corps 1988; served Aden, Oman, Jordan, UK, Hong Kong and BAOR, ret as Brig 1989; sec Inst of Mfrg Engineers and chief exec Instn of Industrial Mangrs (now Inst of Mgmnt) 1988–91, dep sec Instn of Electrical Engrs 1991–2000 (dir of memb servs 2000–02), sec National Electronics Cncl 1991; Liveryman Worshipful Co of Turners 1991; CEng 1982, FIEE 1991; *Recreations* rugby, cricket, music; *Clubs* Army and Navy; *Style*— Brig G J Rawlins, OBE

RAWLINS, Prof Sir Michael David; kt (1999), DL (Tyne & Wear 1999); s of Rev Jack Rawlins (d 1946), of Kingswinford, Staffs, and Evelyn Daphne, *née* Douglas-Hamilton; *b* 28 March 1941; *Educ* Hawtreys, Uppingham, St Thomas' Hosp Med Sch London (BSc, MB BS, MD); *m* 3 Aug 1963, Elizabeth Cadbury Rawlins, JP, da of Edmund Hambly (d 1985), of Seer Green, Bucks; 3 da (Vicky b 1964, Lucy b 1965, Suzannah b 1972); *Career* lectr in med St Thomas' Hosp Med Sch London 1968–71, sr registrar Hammersmith Hosp London 1971–73, MRC visiting res fell Karolinska Inst Stockholm 1972–73, Ruth and Lionel Jacobson prof of clinical pharmacology Univ of Newcastle upon Tyne 1973– (public orator 1990–93); visiting prof Royal Perth Hosp WA 1980, Ruitinga van Sweiten prof Academic Med Centre Amsterdam 1998; author of papers on clinical pharmacology and therapeutics; memb: Nat Ctee Pharmacology 1977–83, Cncl St Oswalds Hospice 1977–98 (vice-pres 1998–), Ctee on Toxicity of Chemicals in Food Consumer Prods and Environment 1989–92; chm: Sub-Ctee Safety Efficacy and Adverse Reactions 1987–92, Ctee Safety of Meds 1993–98 (memb 1980–98), Advsy Cncl on the Misuse of Drugs 1998–, Nat Inst for Clinical Excellence 1999–; vice-chm Northern Regnl HA 1990–94, pres NE Cncl on Addictions 1990–; Bradshaw lectr RCP London 1987, William Withering lectr RCP London 1994, Wellcome lectr and medallist Soc of Apothecaries 1996, Sidney Watson Smith lectr RCPEd 1999, Wallace Hemingway lectr Univ of Bradford 2000, Nye Bevan lectr Br Oncology Assoc 2000, Bradlow Oration RCS 2002; Dixon Medal Ulster Med Soc 1994, Hutchinson Medal RSM 2003; FRCP 1977 (MRCP 1968), FRCPE 1987, FFPM 1989, FRSM, FMedSci, Hon FRCA 2000; *Books* Variability in Human Drug Response (with S E Smith, 1973); *Recreations* music; *Clubs* Northern Counties; *Style*— Prof Sir Michael Rawlins, DL; ✉ 29 The Grove, Gosforth, Newcastle upon Tyne NE3 1NE; Shoreston House, Shoreston, Seahouses, Northumberland; University of Newcastle upon Tyne, Wolfson Unit of Clinical Pharmacology, Newcastle upon Tyne NE2 4HH (tel 0191 222 8041, fax 0191 232 3613, e-mail m.d.rawlins@ncl.ac.uk)

RAWLINS, Prof (John) Nicholas Pepys; s of Surgn Vice Adm Sir John Rawlins, KBE; *Educ* Winchester (rowing: winner Coxed Pairs Nat Youth Championships 1967, fourth place Coxed Pairs World Youth Championships 1967), UC Oxford (BA, DPhil, rowed Isis III 1969); *Career* University Coll Oxford: Weir jr res fell 1978–80, sr res fell 1982, tutorial fell 1983–2005, professorial fell 2005–07; Fogarty res fell Johns Hopkins Univ 1979–80, Royal Soc Henry Head res fell in neurology 1981–83; Univ of Oxford: lectr 1983, prof of behavioural neuroscience 1998–2005, Watts prof of psychology 2005–; professorial fell Wolfson Coll Oxford 2008–; author of over 190 professional articles published since 1976; co-chm Wellcome Tst Neuroscience Panel 2004–07 (memb 1996–2000, chm Cognitive and Higher Systems Sub-panel); memb: Nuffield Fndn Bioethics Panel, Wellcome Tst Basic Science Interest Gp 2000–04, Wellcome Tst Neuroscience Strategy Ctee 2004–; tstee Schizophrenia Tst; memb Experimental Psychology Soc; *Recreations* walking, wine, snorkelling, skiing, period architecture, wildlife, food, gardens, my children; *Style*— Prof Nicholas Rawlins; ✉ Wolfson College, Oxford OX2 6UD (tel 01865 271424)

RAWLINS, Peter Jonathan; *b* 30 April 1951; *Educ* St Edward's Sch Oxford, Keble Coll Oxford (MA); *m* 1, 1973 (dis 1999), Louise, *née* Langton; 1 da (Juliette b 2 Sept 1978), 1 s (Oliver b 19 Feb 1981); m 2, 2000, Christina *née* Conway; 1 da (Georgia b 3 June 2000), 3 s (Sam b 20 Oct 2001, Kit b 18 April 2004, Joe b 7 Sept 2006); *Career* with Arthur Andersen 1972–85 (seconded as PA to dep chm and chief exec Lloyd's of London 1983–84), md R W Sturge & Co and dir Sturge Holdings plc (and subsids) 1985–89, chief exec London Stock Exchange 1989–93, md (Europe, Middle E and Africa) Siegel & Gale Ltd 1996–97; ind conslt 1993–; dir: Scala Business Solutions NV 1998–2000, Logistics Resources Ltd 1999–2002, Oyster Partners Ltd 2001–02; chm Higham Group plc 2004–05, non-exec dir Royal Bournemouth and Christchurch Hosps NHS Fndn Tst 2005–07; chm Assoc for Research into Stammering in Children; chm Spitalfields Festival, dir Covent Garden Festival Ltd; memb: RNT Devpt Cncl, Advsy Cncl Keble Coll Oxford; FCA, FRSA; *Recreations* tennis, shooting, travelling; *Clubs* MCC; *Style*— Peter Rawlins, Esq; ✉ Ramley House, Ramley Road, Lymington, Hampshire SO41 8LH (tel 01590 689661, fax 01590 689662, e-mail peter@rawlinsp.fsnet.co.uk)

RAWLINSON, Sir Anthony Henry John; 5 Bt (UK 1891); s of Sir (Alfred) Frederick Rawlinson, 4 Bt (d 1969), and Bess, *née* Emmatt (d 1996); *b* 1 May 1936; *Educ* Millfield; *m* 1, 1960 (m dis 1967), Penelope Byng, da of Rear Adm Gambier John Byng Noel, CB; 1 s, 1 da; m 2, 1967 (m dis 1976), Pauline Strickland, da of John Holt Hardy; 1 s; m 3, 1977 (m dis 1997), Helen Leone, da of Thomas Miller Kennedy; 1 s; *Heir* s, Alexander Rawlinson; *Career* fashion photographer (portraits); *Recreations* tennis, cricket, fishing; *Style*— Sir Anthony Rawlinson, Bt

RAWLINSON, David Ian (Iain); s of (James) Keith McClure Rawlinson, and Griselda Maxwell, *née* Carlisle; *b* 18 September 1958, Liverpool; *Educ* Birkenhead Sch, Jesus Coll Cambridge (MA), Inns of Court Sch of Law; *m* 1, 1991 (m dis 1995); m 2, 1997, Fiona Charlotte, *née* Stubbs; 1 s (Thomas Carlisle b 21 April 1999), 1 da (Kitty May Ogilvie b 24 Jan 2003); *Career* called to the Bar Lincoln's Inn 1981; corporate fin roles: Lazard Bros & Co Ltd 1986–94, Robert Fleming London 1994–95, Robert Fleming Johannesburg 1995–2000; head of corporate fin Robert Fleming South Africa (later Fleming Martin) 1997–2000, dir South Africa Holding Bd RF Holdings SA Ltd 2000, chief operating offr Fleming Family & Partners Ltd (FF&P) 2000–02, chief exec FF&P Advsy Ltd 2000–04, sr advsr FF&P 2004–05, chief exec The Highland Star Gp 2004–05, dir strategy and memb Advsy Cncl G3 (The Good Governance Gp) 2004–; non-exec dir: Dana Petroleum plc, Sindicatum Carbon Capital Ltd, Global Philanthorpic Ltd, Edgo Energy Ltd; chm Tusk Tst 2005–; *Recreations* writing, military history, flying, music, country and water sports, Africa; *Style*— Iain Rawlinson, Esq; ✉ tel 07799 882382, e-mail iain@rawlinsonpartners.com

RAWLINSON, Dr John Robert; s of Douglas Robert Rawlinson, of Radley, Oxon, and June Frances, *née* Vincent; *b* 26 November 1953, Brighton; *Educ* Henley GS, Abingdon Sch, ChCh Oxford (MA, BM, BCh); *m* 17 Nov 1979, Mary Helen, *née* Norwood; 1 da (Nichola Jane Bushell b 26 July 1982), 2 s (Peter John b 18 Sept 1983, James Edward b 19 Feb 1986); *Career* house offr in surgery Churchill Hosp Oxford 1979–80, house offr in med then SHO in A&E Gloucester Royal Hosp 1980–81, gen practice trg scheme Cirencester 1981–84, SHO in obstetrics and gynaecology Swindon 1984, princ GP Ascot 1984–; memb Cncl BMA 2004–06; memb Synod All Saints Church Wokingham Deanery 1996–99; MRCGP 2007; *Publications* PCG Development Guide (chapter on Implications for Primary Care, 1999); *Recreations* photography, gardening, swimming, reading; *Style*— Dr John Rawlinson; ✉ Radnor House Surgery, 25 London Road, Ascot, Berkshire SL5 7EN (tel 01344 874011, fax 01344 628868)

RAWNSLEY, Andrew Nicholas James; s of Eric Rawnsley, of Leeds, Yorks, and Barbara, *née* Butler; *b* 5 January 1962, Leeds, Yorks; *Educ* Rugby, Sidney Sussex Coll Cambridge (scholar, MA); *Career* writer and broadcaster; BBC 1983–85, The Guardian 1985–93 (political columnist 1987–93), assoc ed and chief political columnist The Observer 1993–; presenter: A Week in Politics (Channel 4) 1989–97, The Agenda (ITV) 1996, Bye Bye Blues (Channel 4) 1997, Blair's Year (Channel 4) 1998, Westminster Hour (Radio 4) 1998–2006, The Unauthorised Biography of the United Kingdom (Radio 4) 1999, The Sunday Edition (ITV) 2006–, The Rise and Fall of Tony Blair (Channel 4) 2007; Student Journalist of the Year 1983, Young Journalist of the Year 1987, What the Papers Say Columnist of the Year 2000, Channel 4/House Magazine Political Awards Book of the Year 2001, Channel 4 Political Awards Journalist of the Year 2003, Public Affairs Award Political Journalist of the Year 2006; FRSA; *Publications* Servants of the People: The Inside Story of New Labour (2000); *Recreations* books, movies, wine, Mah Jong, scuba diving, skiing; *Style*— Andrew Rawnsley, Esq; ✉ The Observer, 119 Farringdon Road, London EC1R 3ER (tel 020 7278 2332, fax 020 7837 2114, telex 8811746 GUARDN G, e-mail a.rawnsley@observer.co.uk)

RAWSON, Prof Dame Jessica Mary; DBE (2002, CBE 1994); da of Roger Nathaniel Quirk, CB (d 1964), and Paula, *née* Weber; *b* 1 January 1943; *Educ* St Paul's Girls' Sch, New Hall Cambridge (MA, LittD), SOAS Univ of London (BA); *m* May 1968, John Graham Rawson, s of Graham Stanhope Rawson (d 1953); 1 da (Josephine b 1972); *Career* asst princ Miny of Health 1965–67; Dept of Oriental Antiquities Br Museum: asst keeper II 1967–71, asst keeper I 1971–76, dep keeper 1976–87, keeper 1987–94; warden Merton Coll Oxford 1994–, pro-vice-chllr Univ of Oxford 2005–; guest prof Heidelberg Univ Kunst Historiches Institut 1989, visiting prof Dept of Art Univ of Chicago 1994; vice-chm GB China Centre 1985–87, chm Oriental Ceramic Soc 1993–97, govr SOAS Univ of London 1998–2003 (vice-chm 1999–2003); memb: Br Library Bd 1999–2003, Nuffield Languages Enquiry 1998–99; advsr: Centre of Ancient Civilisation, Inst of Archaeology, Chinese Acad of Social Sciences 2002–; Barlow Lecture Univ of Sussex 1979 and 1994, Levintritt Meml Lecture Harvard Univ 1989, Albert Reckitt Archaeological Lecture Br Acad 1989, A J Pope Meml Lecture Smithsonian Inst Washington 1991, Harvey Buchanan Lecture Cleveland Museum of Art 1993, Peter Murray Meml Lecture Birkbeck 1998, Spring Lecture Pratt Inst USA 1998, Sammy Yu-Kuen Lee Lecture Centre for Pacific Rim Studies UCLA Getty Museum 1998, KSLo Memorial Lecture Hong Kong 1998, Beatrice Blackwood Lecture Oxford 1999, Creighton Lecture Univ of London 2000, Zeitlyn Lecture Br Acad 2001; Hon DLitt: Royal Holloway Coll London 1998, Univ of Sussex 1998, Univ of Newcastle upon Tyne 1999; FBA 1990; *Books* Animals in Art (1977), Ancient China, Art and Archaeology (1980), Chinese Ornament, the Lotus and the Dragon (1984), Chinese Bronzes, Art and Ritual (1987), Ancient Chinese Bronzes in the Collection of Bella and PP Chiu (1988), Western Zhou Bronzes from the Arthur M Sackler Collections (1990), Ancient Chinese and Ordos Bronzes (with Emma Bunker, 1990), British Museum Book of Chinese Art (ed, 1992), Chinese Jade from the Neolithic to the Qing (1995), Mysteries of Ancient China: New Discoveries from the Early Dynasties (1996), China, The Three Emperors (ed with Evelyn Rawski, 2005); *Style*— Prof Dame Jessica Rawson, DBE, FBA; ✉ Merton College, Oxford OX1 4JD (tel 01865 276351, fax 01865 276282, e-mail wardensoffice@admin.merton.ox.ac.uk)

RAWSTHORN, Alice; da of Peter Rawsthorn, and Joan, *née* Schofield; *b* 15 November 1958; *Educ* Shevington Comp Wigan, Ramsey Comp Halstead, Clare Coll Cambridge (MA); *Career* grad trainee journalist International Thomson Orgn 1980–82, media ed Campaign magazine 1983–85, FT 1985–2001 (design corr, Paris corr, entertainment industry corr, architecture and design critic), dir Design Museum 2001–06 (tstee 1992–2001, dep chm 2000–01); chair Design Advsy Gp Br Cncl 2003–06, lead advsr on visual arts Arts Cncl 2004–07; design critic Int Herald Tribune 2006–, columnist NY Times 2006–; memb: BBC Charter Review Panel 2004–06, Nat Cncl Arts Cncl of England 2007–; tstee Whitechapel Art Gallery 1994–; *Books* Yves Saint Laurent (1996), Marc Newson (1999); *Style*— Ms Alice Rawsthorn

RAWSTHORNE, Anthony Robert; s of Frederic Leslie Rawsthorne (d 1991), and Nora, *née* Yates, of Blundellsands, nr Liverpool; *b* 25 January 1943; *Educ* Ampleforth, Wadham Coll Oxford (MA); *m* 18 Dec 1967, Beverley Jean, da of Richard Osborne, and Jean; 1 s (Richard Anthony b 1968), 2 da (Josephine Alice b 1969, Mary-Anne b 1969); *Career* Home Office 1966–97: various positions incl Prison Dept, Race Relations Div, Criminal Dept 1966–77, head Crime Policy Planning Unit 1977–79, head Personnel Div 1979–82, sec Falkland Islands Review Ctee 1982, princ private sec to Home Sec 1983, head of div Immigration and Nationality Dept 1983–86, head Establishment Dept 1986–91, head Equal Opportunities and General Dept 1991, under sec/dep DG Policy and Nationality Immigration and Nationality Dept 1991–97, dir Customs Policy HM Customs & Excise 1997–2000, sr clerk House of Lords 2001–05, memb Professional Conduct Ctee and Fitness to Practise Panel GMC 2001–; *Recreations* bridge, squash, art exhibitions; *Style*— Anthony Rawsthorne, Esq

RAY, Dr Christopher; s of Harold Ray (d 1977), and Margaret, *née* Noble; *b* 10 December 1951, Rochdale, Lancs; *Educ* Rochdale GS, UCL (BA), Churchill Coll Cambridge (PhD), Balliol Coll Oxford; *m* 20 March 1976, Carol Elizabeth, *née* Morrison; *Career* Bank of England 1976–78, Oxford Univ Press 1984–88, Nat Univ of Singapore 1988–89, Portland State Univ 1989–91, KCS Wimbledon 1996–2001, John Lyon Sch Harrow 2001–04, high master Manchester GS 2004–; MInstP 1996, FRSA 2004; *Books* The Evolution of Relativity (1987), Time, Space and Philosophy (1991), A Companion to the Philosophy of Science (contrib, 2000); *Recreations* chess, opera, fell walking; *Clubs* East India; *Style*— Dr Christopher Ray; ✉ High Master's Office, The Manchester Grammar School, Old Hall Lane, Manchester M13 0XT (tel 0161 224 7201, e-mail highmaster@mgs.org)

RAY, Prof John David; s of Albert Ray (d 1961), and Edith, *née* Millward; *b* 22 December 1945, London; *Educ* Latymer Upper Sch, Trinity Hall Cambridge (MA, Thomas Young Medal); *m* 1997, Sonia Falaschi-Ray; *Career* research asst British Museum 1970, lectr in Egyptology Univ of Birmingham 1970–77, Herbert Thompson prof of Egyptology Univ of Cambridge 2005– (reader 1977–2005), fell Selwyn Coll Cambridge 1979–; memb Ctee Egypt Exploration Soc 1976–99; assessor Parly Review Ctee on Export of Works of Art 2004–; reviewer: The Times, TLS, Times Higher Educn Supplement; FSA 2000, FBA 2004; *Books* The Archive of Hor (1976), Reflections of Osiris: Lives from Ancient Egypt (2001), Demotic Papyri and Ostraca from Qasr Ibrim (2005); *Recreations* listening to Beethoven, being walked by a golden retriever; *Style*— Prof John Ray; ✉ Selwyn College, Cambridge CB3 9DQ (tel 01223 335854, fax 01223 335837, e-mail jdr1000@cam.ac.uk)

RAY, Peggy Ruth; da of Robert Sayers Ray, of North Carolina, USA, and Marguerite, *née* McEachern; *b* 13 May 1954, Lima, Peru; *Educ* Int Sch of Geneva, Univ of Sussex (BA, LLB); *Career* admitted slr 1980; town planning offr Lincolnshire CC 1974–76; Donne Mileham & Haddock Slrs Brighton: trainee slr 1977–80, asst slr 1980–81; asst slr Wiseman Lee Slrs London 1981–85, co-fndr and ptnr Goodman Ray 1985–; estab: www.carelaw.org.uk, Slrs Family Law Assoc Guide to Good Practice for Slrs Representing Children; memb: Resolution (formerly Slrs Family Law Assoc) 1985– (past roles incl memb Nat Ctee and chair Children's Ctee), Assoc of Lawyers for Children, Legal Aid Funding Review Panel; Unicef Child Rights Lawyer of the Year 2001, Legal Aid Lawyer (Family) of the Year 2005; memb Law Soc 1980 (past memb Family Law Ctee and Children Sub-Ctee); *Publications* incl: Know-How for Family Lawyers (1993), Grandparents and the Law (2001); *Recreations* travel, walking, reading; *Style*— Ms Peggy Ray; ✉ Goodman Ray, 450 Kingsland Road, Dalston, London E8 4AE (tel 020 7254 8855, fax 020 7923 4345, e-mail peggyray@goodmanray.com)

RAY, Robert John; *Educ* Hatfield Poly; *Career* SCC & B Lintas 1983–86, Davidson Pearce 1986–87, DMB & B then The Media Centre 1987–97, fndr memb and jt md MediaVest 1997–2000, md Starcom Worldwide (P&G GBU EMEA) 2000–03, Robert Ray Associates 2003–05, mktg dir Newspaper Soc 2005–; memb Mktg Soc 2000; *Recreations* snowboarding, mountain boarding, motorcycle trials riding, cross-country running; *Style*— Robert Ray, Esq; ✉ Newspaper Society, St Andrew's House, 18–20 St Andrew's Street, London EC4A 3AY

RAY, Sidney; *b* 5 October 1939; *Educ* Owen's Sch London, North London Poly (BSc), Regent St Poly, City Univ (MSc); *m*; 2 s; *Career* cadet instr and RAF civilian instr ATC 1956–68; photographer and lectr in photography; asst chemist Research Laboratories Gas Cncl 1959–60, photographic chemist Johnsons of Hendon Ltd 1960–66, pt/t lectr 1962–66, lectr Univ of Westminster (formerly Poly of Central London) 1966–, examiner various colls and courses 1972–, organiser of confs 1978–, conslt for govt depts, industry, publishers and others; regular contributor Br Jl of Photography, contributing ed Photoresearcher magazine; regular book reviewer: British Book News, The Photographer, The Photogrammetric Record, Jl of Photographic Science, Photoresearcher, Professional Photographer; numerous articles in photographic jls, many hundreds of photographs published, author of 14 photographic textbooks and contributor to 8 others; accredited sr imaging scientist 1994; memb: NATFHE, Photogrammetric Soc, Euro Soc for the History of Photography, The Steroscopic Soc, Cinema Theatre Assoc, Greater London Industrial Archaeology Soc, Assoc of Historical and Fine Art Photographers; fell Master Photographers Assoc 1986, fell Royal Microscopical Soc 1992, Hon FRPS 2001 (FRPS 1972), Hon FBIPP 2001 (FBIPP 1974); *Style*— Sidney Ray, Esq; ✉ University of Westminster, Faculty of Communication, Watford Road, Northwick Park, Harrow HA1 3TP (tel 020 7911 5000 ext 4531, fax 020 7911 5943, website www.leonardo.itrg.wmin.ac.uk/rays/home.htm)

RAYBAN, Chloë; *see:* Bear, Carolyn Ann

RAYLEIGH, 6 Baron (UK 1821) John Gerald Strutt; s of Hon Charles Richard Strutt (d 1981; s of 4 Baron Rayleigh), and Hon Mrs (Jean Elizabeth) Strutt, *née* Davidson, da of 1 Viscount Davidson; suc uncle 5 Baron Rayleigh 1988; *b* 4 June 1960; *Educ* Eton, RAC Cirencester; *m* 2 May 1991, Annabel Kate, yst da of Maj William Garry Patterson, Life Guards, and Hon Sandra Debonnaire, *née* Monson, da of 10 Baron Monson; 4 s (Hon John Frederick b 29 March 1993, Hon William Hedley Charles b 11 Nov 1994, Hon Hugo Richard b 12 Feb 1998, Hon Theodore James b 16 Sept 2000); *Heir* s, Hon John Strutt; *Career* Lt Welsh Guards (ret); chm: Lord Rayleigh's Farms Ltd, Eastern Data Processing Ltd; Liveryman: Worshipful Co of Grocers, Worshipful Co of Farmers; *Style*— The Rt Hon the Lord Rayleigh

RAYMOND, Paul; *b* 15 November 1925; *Educ* St Francis Xaviers Coll Liverpool, Glossop GS Derbys; *Children* 1 da (Deborah b 28 Jan 1956 d 1992), 1 s (Howard b 23 Nov 1959); *Career* RAF 1944–47; musician, music hall artiste, impresario, night club proprietor, publisher, West End property owner; memb Grand Order of Water Rats; *Style*— Paul Raymond, Esq; ✉ Paul Raymond Organisation Ltd, 2 Archer Street, London W1V 7HF (tel 020 7292 8000, fax 020 7287 8965)

RAYMOND, Peter James; s of George Arthur Raymond (d 1986), of Tunbridge Wells, Kent, and Joyce, *née* Goodwin (d 1999); *b* 16 February 1947; *Educ* Tonbridge; *m* 1, (m dis); 1 s (Tom b 26 June 1974), 1 da (Anna b 16 Feb 1978); m 2, 11 April 1998, Lesley, *née* Keen; *Career* Cripps Harries Hall: joined 1967, admitted slr 1969, ptnr 1972–, head Private Client Dept 1990–96; Law Soc: memb Cncl 1996–2000, chm Probate Section 1997–99, currently memb Exec Probate Section; pres Tunbridge Wells Tonbridge and Dist Law Soc 1989 (former sec), hon slr Crowborough Citizens' Advice Bureau 1983–2003; vice-pres League of Friends Pembury Hosp (former chm), memb Cncl South of England Agric Soc 1971–86, memb Tunbridge Wells AHA 1987–89; *Style*— Peter Raymond, Esq; ✉ Cripps Harries Hall LLP, Wallside House, 12 Mount Ephraim Road, Tunbridge Wells, Kent TN1 1EG (tel 01892 506346, fax 01892 506366, e-mail peter.raymond@crippslaw.com)

RAYNE, Hon Robert Anthony; s of Baron Rayne (Life Peer, d 2003), by his 1 w, Margaret (decd); *b* 1949; *m* Jane, da of late Robert Blackburn, the aviation pioneer; 1 s; *Career* ceo London Merchant Securities plc 1983–2007, non-exec chm Derwent London plc 2007–; dir: Weatherford Int Inc 1987, Westpool Investment Trust plc 1984–, Inflexion plc 2004–06; chm and tstee The Rayne Fndn, chm and tstee The Rayne Tst, tstee The Place to Be; *Recreations* art, cycling; *Style*— The Hon Robert A Rayne; ✉ Derwent London plc, 25 Savile Row, London W1S 2ER

RAYNER, Colin Robert; s of Charles Wilfred Rayner, of Brighton, E Sussex, and Helen Patricia, *née* Rollins; *b* 28 October 1938; *Educ* St George's Coll Weybridge, Middx Hosp Univ of London (MB BS, MS); *m* 1, 1 Jan 1966 (m dis), Margaret Mary, da of Harold Salt (d 1973), of Cheltenham, Glos; 2 da (Clare Rachel b 9 Nov 1967, Suzannah Louise b 15 March 1971), 1 s (Dominic James b 5 Feb 1969); m 2, 1998, R Lester; 1 s (Matthew b 1993); *Career* Ethicon res fell 1974, John Lawson fell Westminster Hosp 1975, conslt plastic surgn Aberdeen Royal Infirmary and Royal Aberdeen Children's Hosp 1978–91; dir of clinical burns res and conslt plastic surgeon Birmingham Accident Hosp and Selly Oak Hosp Birmingham 1991–1992, dir of burns and plastic surgery S Birmingham HA 1992–95, dir of plastic surgery Univ Hosp Birmingham 1995–98, med dir Birmingham Day Surgery Clinic Ltd 1997, currently conslt plastic surgeon BUPA Hosp Solihull and BUPA Hosp Worcester; chm Ethical Ctee and memb Nat Disaster Planning Ctee Br Assoc of Plastic Surgns, advsr to Soviet Govt at time of train disaster 1989; visiting prof Chelyabinsk, Urals, Russia for first Russia - GB advanced surgical trg course; memb Br Assoc Plastic Surgns; author of over 40 scientific pubns; Pulvertaft Prize (hand surgery) 1976, Assoc of Surgns Special Educnl Award 1981; FRCS 1969, FRCSEd 1980; *Recreations* skiing, opera, developing international medical relationships; *Style*— Colin Rayner, Esq; ✉ 64 Wellington Road, Edgbaston, Birmingham B15 2ET

RAYNER, Patrick Brear; s of Wing Cdr M O Rayner, OBE (d 2000), of Skipton, N Yorks, and Kathleen, *née* Brear (d 1998); *b* 11 November 1951; *Educ* Woolverstone Hall, Univ of St Andrews (Harkness scholar, MA); *m* 1, 29 Dec 1976 (m dis 1986), Susan Mary, *née* Gill; m 2, 30 April 1987, Stella Joanna, *née* Forge; 2 s (Edward b 24 April 1988, Frederick b 29 June 1992), 1 da (Margot b 30 Jan 1990); *Career* research asst BBC Scot 1975–76, research fell Univ of St Andrews 1976–77, freelance presenter and reporter 1977–78; BBC Scotland: features prodr 1978–82, radio drama prodr 1982–95, ed radio drama 1995–98, head of radio drama 1998–; *Awards* Pye Award for Best Prodn 1981, Sony Gold Awards 1986, 1993 and 1998, Sony Silver Awards 1987 and 1988, Sony Bronze 1994; *Publications* Handlist for the Study of Crime in Early Modern Scotland (1982); *Recreations* golf, cricket, theatre, carpentry; *Clubs* MCC, North Berwick Golf; *Style*— Patrick Rayner, Esq; ✉ BBC, 40 Pacific Quay, Glasgow G51 1DA (tel 0141 422 6000, e-mail patrick.rayner@bbc.co.uk)

RAYNER, Paul; *m*; 3 s, 1 da; *Career* early career with General Electric, Rank Industries and Elders IXL Gp, joined Rothmans Holdings Ltd 1991, chief operating offr British American Tobacco Australasia Ltd 1999–2001, finance dir British American Tobacco plc 2002–; non-exec dir Centrica 2004–; *Recreations* tennis, swimming, golf, cycling; *Style*— Mr Paul Rayner; ✉ British American Tobacco plc, Globe House, 4 Temple Place, London WC2R 2PG

RAYNER, Maj Ranulf Courtauld; s of Brig Sir Ralph Herbert Rayner, MBE (d 1977), of Ashcombe Tower, nr Dawlish, S Devon, and (Edith) Elizabeth, *née* Courtauld (d 1992); *b* 25 February 1935; *Educ* Eton, RMA; *m* 2 July 1970, Annette Mary, da of Brig Angus Binny, CBE, MICE, of Skilgate, Somerset; 2 s (Ralph b 8 Sept 1971, Giles b 25 June 1975); *Career* cmmnd 9 Queen's Royal Lancers 1955, instr RMA Sandhurst 1962, Army Flying Sch 1964, Royal Horse Gds 1965, cmd Ind Sqdn Cyprus 1967, ret 1969; local steward Devon and Exeter Steeplechases; represented Army at: Polo, Skiing, Cresta run (capt Cresta Team 1959–69); High Sheriff Devon 2000; *Books* The Story of Yachting (1988), The Story of Skiing (1989), The Story of the Sporting Gun (1991), The Story of the America's Cup (2000); *Recreations* yachting, shooting, fishing, riding, flying, skiing, water sculpture; *Style*— Maj Ranulf Rayner; ✉ Ashcombe Tower, Dawlish, Devon EX7 0PY (tel 01626 863 178, office 01626 862 484, fax 01626 867 011)

RAYNER, Prof Steve; s of Lt-Col Harry Rayner (d 1991), of Littlehampton, W Sussex, and Esmé Rayner; *b* 22 May 1953, Bristol; *Educ* Dorking Co GS, Univ of Kent at Canterbury (BA), UCL (PhD); *m* 2004, Heather Katz; 1 da (Jessica); *Career* lectr in social anthropology Extra-Mural Studies Dept Univ of London 1977–78; research assoc: Centre for Occupational and Community Research London 1979–83, Russell Sage Fndn NY 1980–81, Dept of Computer Sci Columbia Univ 1982–83 (visiting scholar 1981 and 1982); research assoc rising to sr research staff Energy Div Oak Ridge Nat Lab Tennessee 1983–91 (dep dir Center for Global Environmental Studies 1990–91), chief scientist Pacific Northwest Nat Lab 1996–99 (sr prog mangr Global Environmental Mgmnt Studies and mangr Global Change Gp 1991–96), chief social scientist Int Research Inst for Climate Prediction 1999–2002, prof of environmental and public affrs Sch of Int and Public Affrs Columbia Univ 1999–2002, dir James Martin Inst and James Martin prof of sci and civilization Saïd Business Sch Univ of Oxford 2002–, professorial fell Keble Coll Oxford 2002–; visiting scholar Boston Univ Sch of Public Health 1982, adjunct asst prof of sociology Univ of Tennessee 1986, adjunct faculty US Govt Exec Seminar Center Oak Ridge Tennessee 1988–91, visiting assoc prof Prog in Science, Technol and Soc Cornell Univ 1990, adjunct assoc prof Science, Technol and Soc Grad Prog Virginia Poly Inst 1997–98; memb Editorial Bd: Environment, Integrated Assessment, Environmental Science and Policy, Global Environmental Change, Population and Environment; memb: Royal Cmmn on Environmental Pollution, Advsy Ctee UK Climate Impacts Prog, Bd of Advsrs Nanotechnology Policy Fndn, Sciencewise Steering Gp and Review Panel OST; former memb: Advsy Bd ESRC Genomics Survey, Oxford Cmmn on Sustainable Consumption, Int Advsy Bd Encyclopedia of Global Environmental Change; past pres Sociology and Social Policy Section BAAS, lead author Working Gp III Intergovernmental Panel on Climate Change; Martin-Marietta Energy Systems Significant Event Award 1988 and 1989, Dir's Award for Scientific and Engrg Excellence Pacific Northwest Lab 1993, Homer M Calver Award Environment Section American Public Health Assoc 1994; memb: Assoc of Social Anthropologists of the Cwlth 1980, Soc for Risk Analysis 1984, Sigma Xi 1989, BAAS 2002, European Assoc for the Study of Sci and Technol 2002, Soc for the Social Study of Sci 2002; FRAI 1976, fell Soc for Applied Anthropology 1984, FRSA 2004, fell AAAS 2004; *Publications* Measuring Culture: A Paradigm for the Analysis of Social Organization (jtly, 1985), Rules, Decisions and Inequality in Egalitarian Societies (jt ed, 1988), Making Markets: An Interdisciplinary Perspective on Economic Exchange (jtly, 1992), Human Choice and Climate Change: An International Assessment (4 vols, jt ed, 1998), Markets, Distribution, and Exchange after Societal Cataclysm (jtly, 2000); author of over 100 articles in books and jls; *Recreations* building, gardening, boating; *Clubs* Cosmos (Washington DC); *Style*— Prof Steve Rayner; ✉ James Martin Institute, Saïd Business School, Park End Street, Oxford OX1 1HP (tel 01865 288938, e-mail steve.rayner@sbs.ox.ac.uk)

RAYNER, Timothy Michael; s of Peter Michael Rayner, of Norwich, and Valerie, *née* Bostock; *b* 4 August 1960, Blackpool; *Educ* Rossall Sch Fleetwood, KCL (LLB), College of Law Chester; *m* 5 Oct 2000, Elizabeth Ann, *née* Blease; *Career* admitted slr 1985; trainee slr Eversheds 1983–85, Addleshaw Sons & Latham 1986–95 (ptnr 1993–95); United Utilities plc: gp legal mangr 1995–98, gen counsel and co sec 1998–2007; co sec Rolls-Royce plc 2007–; memb Law Soc 1985; *Recreations* spectating motor sport, riding own showhunter; *Style*— Timothy Rayner, Esq; ✉ Rolls-Royce plc, 65 Buckingham Gate, London SW1E 6AT

RAYNER JAMES, Jonathan Elwyn; QC (1988); s of Basil James, and Moira Holding, *née* Rayner; *b* 26 July 1950; *Educ* KCS Wimbledon, Christ's Coll Cambridge (MA, LLM), Univ of Brussels (grad course Licencié Spécial en Droit Européen); *m* 3 Jan 1981, Anne, da of Henry McRae (d 1984); 1 s (Daniel Charles Rayner b 23 Dec 1981); *Career* called to the Bar Lincoln's Inn 1971 (Hardwick entrance scholar, Eastham (Maj) scholar, bencher 1994); in practice specialising in intellectual property Chancery Bar 1975–, recorder of the Crown Court 1998–2004 (asst recorder 1994–98); memb Editorial Bd Entertainment Law Review 1990–; memb: Chancery Bar Assoc 1975, Patent Bar Assoc; *Books* EEC Anti-Trust Law (co-author, 1975), Executors and Administrators, Halsbury Laws (co-ed 4 edn vol 17, 1976), Copinger and Skone James on Copyright (co-ed 12 edn, 1980 and 13 edn, 1991, 14 edn, 1998), The Encyclopaedia of Forms and Precedents (jt consltg ed for Intellectual Property matters vol 15, 1989); *Recreations* France; *Clubs* RAC; *Style*— Jonathan Rayner James, Esq, QC; ✉ Hogarth Chambers, 5 New Square, Lincoln's Inn, London WC2A 3RJ (tel 020 7404 0404)

RAYNES, Prof (Edward) Peter; s of Edward Gordon Raynes (d 1995), and Ethel Mary, *née* Wood (d 1994); *b* 4 July 1945; *Educ* St Peter's York, Gonville & Caius Coll Cambridge (MA, PhD); *m* 19 Sept 1970, Madeline, da of Cecil Ord (d 1967); 2 s (Michael b 1974, Andrew b 1977); *Career* dep chief scientific offr Royal Signals and Radar Establishment

Malvern until 1992 (joined 1971), dir of research Sharp Laboratories of Europe Ltd 1995–98 (chief scientist 1992–95); prof of optoelectronic engrg Univ of Oxford 1998–; FRS 1987, FInstP; *Books* Liquid Crystals: Their Physics, Chemistry and Applications (with C Hilsum 1983); *Recreations* choral and solo singing; *Style*— Prof Peter Raynes, FRS; ✉ 23 Leadon Road, Malvern, Worcestershire WR14 2XF (tel 01684 565497); Department of Engineering Science, University of Oxford, Parks Road, Oxford OX1 3PJ (tel 01865 273024, fax 01865 273905, e-mail peter.raynes@eng.ox.ac.uk)

RAYNOR, His Hon Judge Philip; QC (1994); s of Wilfred Raynor, and Sheila Raynor, of Leeds; *b* 20 January 1950; *Educ* Roundhay Sch Leeds, Christ's Coll Cambridge (scholar, MA); *m* 20 Oct 1974, Judith; 1 da (Michelle b 10 Jan 1979), 1 s (Jonathan b 12 Jan 1984); *Career* lectr in law Univ of Manchester 1971–74, called to the Bar Inner Temple 1973, in practice Northern Circuit, recorder of the Crown Court 1993– (asst recorder 1988–93), head of chambers 40 King Street 1996–2001, dep judge of the High Court 2000–, circuit judge 2001–, specialist circuit judge Technol and Construction Court 2006–; *Recreations* travel, music, dining out; *Style*— His Hon Judge Raynor, QC; ✉ Courts of Justice, Crown Square, Manchester M3 3FL (tel 0161 954 1800)

RAYNSFORD, Hon Mrs (Joan Rosemary); *née* Wakefield; OBE (1981); eldest da of 1 and last Baron Wakefield of Kendal (d 1983), and Rowena Doris, *née* Lewis (d 1981); the Wakefield family can trace its lineage to Roger Wakefield, of Challon Hall, nr Kendal, Westmorland, *temp* Elizabeth I. The family is recorded in the first generation of Kendal money men and was contemporary with London Bankers listed in the first London Directory of 1677. Wakefield's Bank was established in 1788 in the Old House, Kendal and subsequently became the Kendal Bank. This was taken over by the Bank of Liverpool in 1893 which amalgamated with Martins Bank in 1918 and is now Barclays Bank; *b* 18 November 1920; *Educ* Francis Holland Sch, Downe House, Univ of Berlin; *m* 18 March 1944, Capt Antony Edward Montague Raynsford, DL, RN (ret) (d 1993, sr descendant of Henry Rainsford, of Rainford Hall, Lancs, and of the Manor of Great Tew, Oxon (d ca 1430)), er s of Lt-Col Richard M Raynsford, DSO, JP, DL (d 1965); 1 s (Richard), 1 da (Julia (Lady Boyd)); *Career* chm: Shapland & Petter Holdings Ltd 1983–92, Battlefields (Holdings) Ltd, Lake District Estates Co Ltd, Ullswater Navigation & Transit Co Ltd, Ravenglass & Eskdale Railway Co Ltd; vice-chm Cons Nat Women's Ctee 1971–72 (chm Gtr London Women's Ctee 1968–71), memb Int Exec Ctee European Union of Women 1979–81; vice-pres British Ski Fedn 1966–69; *Recreations* skiing, walking in mountains; *Clubs* Lansdowne, Ski Club of GB (chm 1972–75, pres 1981–91), Kandahar Ski (chm 1977–82); *Style*— The Hon Mrs Raynsford, OBE; ✉ Milton Malsor Manor, Northampton NN7 3AR; The Old House, Kendal, Cumbria LA9 4QG

RAYNSFORD, Rt Hon Wyvill Richard Nicolls (Nick); PC (2001), MP; s of Wyvill John Macdonald Raynsford (Capt Northants Yeo, ka 1944), and Patricia Howell, *née* Dunn (d 1956); *b* 28 January 1945; *Educ* Repton, Sidney Sussex Coll Cambridge (MA), Chelsea Sch of Art (Dip Art and Design); *m* 30 Aug 1968, Anne Elizabeth, da of late Col Marcus Jelley, of Northampton; 3 da; *Career* market res A C Neilsen Co Ltd 1966–68, Student Co-operative Dwellings 1972–73, SHAC (London Housing Aid Centre) 1973–86 (dir 1976–86), dir Raynsford Dallison Associates Ltd (housing conslts) 1987–93; cncllr London Borough of Hammersmith and Fulham 1971–75; MP (Lab): Fulham 1986–87, Greenwich 1992–97, Greenwich and Woolwich 1997–; front bench spokesman for London 1993–94, shadow housing and construction min and spokesman for London 1994–97, Parly under-sec of state for London and construction 1997–99, min of state for housing, planning and London Jul-Oct 1999, min of state for Housing and Planning 1999–2001, min of state for Local Govt and the Regions 2001–05; chm: Fire Protection Assoc Cncl 2005, Construction Industry Cncl 2006, NHBC Fndn 2006; memb Inst of Housing 1978; Hon FICE 2003, Hon FRTPI 2005, Hon FRIBA 2007; *Books* A Guide to Housing Benefit (1982); *Style*— The Rt Hon Nick Raynsford, MP; ✉ House of Commons, London SW1A 0AA (tel 020 7219 2773, fax 020 7219 2619)

RAZ, Prof Joseph; s of Shmuel and Sonya Zaltsman; *b* 21 March 1939; *Educ* Hebrew Univ of Jerusalem (MJuris), Univ of Oxford (DPhil); *m* 8 Sept 1963 (m dis 1979), Yael; 1 s (Noam b 1969); *Career* lectr then sr lectr in Hebrew Univ of Jerusalem 1967–72; Balliol Coll Oxford: fell and tutor in jurisprudence 1972–85, prof of philosophy of law 1985–2006; research prof Univ of Oxford 2006–; prof Columbia Univ NY 2002– (visiting prof 1995–2002); hon foreign memb American Acad of Arts and Sciences 1992; Hon Dr Catholic Univ Brussels 1993; FBA 1987; *Books* The Concept of a Legal System (1970, 2 edn 1980), Practical Reason and Norms (1975, 2 edn 1990), The Authority of Law (1979), The Morality of Freedom (1986), Ethics in the Public Domain (1994), Engaging Reason (2000), Value, Respect and Attachment (2001), The Practice of Value (2003); *Style*— Prof Joseph Raz, FBA; ✉ Balliol College, Oxford OX1 3BJ (tel 01865 277721, fax 01865 277803)

RAZZALL, Baron (Life Peer UK 1997), of Mortlake in the London Borough of Richmond upon Thames; (Edward) Timothy Razzall; CBE (1993); s of Leonard Humphrey Razzall, of Barnes, London, a Master of the Supreme Court 1954–81, and Muriel, *née* Knowles (d 1968); *b* 12 June 1943; *Educ* St Paul's, Worcester Coll Oxford (BA); *m* 1 (m dis); 1 da (Hon Katharine Mary b 31 Oct 1970), 1 s (Hon James Timothy b 8 Nov 1972); m 2 (m dis), Deirdre Bourke, da of Duncan Taylor-Smith; *Career* admitted slr 1969; ptnr Frere Cholmeley Bischoff 1973–95; ptnr Argonaut Associates 1995–; London Borough of Richmond upon Thames: cncllr 1974–98, chm Policy and Resources Ctee and dep ldr 1983–96; treas: Lib Pty 1987–88, Lib Dems 1988–2000; DTI spokesman for Lib Dems in House of Lords 1998–2000, chm Lib Dems Gen Election Campaign 1999–; *Recreations* all sports; *Clubs* Nat Lib, MCC; *Style*— The Rt Hon Lord Razzall, CBE

REA, Christopher William Wallace (Chris); s of William Wallace Rea, TD, DL, of Meigle Perthshire, and Helen Chalmers, *née* Bissett; *Educ* HS of Dundee, Univ of St Andrews (MA); *m* 18 Sept 1974, Daphne Theresa (Terri), da of George James Manning (d 1973); 1 da (Alison Jane b 2 July 1981); *Career* rugby union footballer and broadcaster; 13 caps for Scotland 1968–71; memb: Br Lions tour party to NZ 1971, 4 major overseas tours; played for Barbarians RFC; MCC: asst sec 1995–, head of mktg and public affrs 1995–; communications mangr Int Rugby Bd 2000–; BBC: joined admin 1970, rugby corr Radio Sports Dept 1972, presenter TV's Rugby Special 1988–94, radio golf commentator 1985; rugby and golf corr The Scotsman, ed Rugby News, rugby corr Independent on Sunday 1990–2000; *Books* Illustrated History of Rugby Union (1977), Injured Pride (1980), Scotland's Grand Slam (1984); *Recreations* golf, walking; *Style*— Chris Rea, Esq

REA, Rev Ernest; s of Ernest Rea (d 1975), of Belfast, and Mary Wylie, *née* Blue (d 1973); *b* 6 September 1945; *Educ* Methodist Coll Belfast, Queen's Univ Belfast (BA, BD), Union Theol Coll Belfast; *m* 1, 13 Sept 1973 (m dis 1994), Kathleen (Kay), da of Robert Kilpatrick (d 1987), of Belfast; 2 s (Stephen Ernest b 28 April 1975, Jonathan Robert b 17 April 1978); m 2, 1 July 1995, Gaynor Vaughan, da of David and Leah Jones, of Tamworth, Staffs; *Career* asst minister Woodvale Park Presbyterian Church Belfast 1971–74, minister Bannside Presbyterian Church Banbridge Co Down 1974–79; prodr religious progs BBC NI 1979–84, sr prodr religious progs BBC South and West 1984–88, editor Network Radio 1988–89, head of religious broadcasting BBC 1989–2001; presenter Beyond Belief (BBC Radio 4); *Recreations* theatre, reading, playing tennis and golf, music, good company; *Style*— The Rev Ernest Rea

REA, 3 Baron (UK 1937); Sir (John) Nicolas Rea; 3 Bt (UK 1935); s of Hon James Rea (d 1954; 2 s of 1 Baron Rea), by his 1 w, Betty, *née* Bevan (d 1965); suc unc, 2 Baron, 1981; *b* 6 June 1928; *Educ* Dartington Hall, Belmont Hall Sch MA, Dauntsey's Sch West Lavington, Christ's Coll Cambridge (MA, MD), UCH Med Sch London; *m* 1, 1951 (m dis 1991), Elizabeth Anne, da of William Hensman Robinson (d 1944), of Woking, Surrey; 4 s (Hon Matthew, Hon Daniel, Hon Quentin, Hon Nathaniel), 2 da (Hon Bess, Hon Rosy); m 2, 1991, Judith Mary, da of Norman Powell (d 1989), of Lytham St Annes, Lancs; *Heir* s, Hon Matthew Rea; *Career* Nat Serv Actg Sergeant Suffolk Regt; sits as Labour peer in House of Lords, spokesman on health and overseas devpt 1992–97; med practitioner in NHS general practice Kentish Town Health Centre 1957–62 and 1968–1993, ret; research fell Paediatrics Ibadan Univ Nigeria 1962–65, lectr in social med St Thomas' Hosp Med Sch London 1966–68; vice-chm Nat Heart Forum 1985–95; chm: Appropriate Health Resources and Technology Action Gp (AHRTAG) 1992–97, All-Pty Food and Health Forum 1992–; memb Cncl Outward Bound Tst 1988–95; DPH, DCH, DObst; FRSM (pres Section of Gen Practice 1985–86); FRCGP; *Recreations* music (bassoon), travel, outdoor activities; *Style*— The Rt Hon the Lord Rea; ✉ House of Lords, London SW1A 0PW (tel 020 7607 0546, fax 020 7687 1219, e-mail reajn@parliament.uk)

READ, Prof Andrew Fraser; s of Ronald Read, of Cambridge, NZ, and Sophie, *née* Carruthers; *b* 12 September 1962, Hawera, NZ; *Educ* Univ of Otago (BSc), Univ of Oxford (Cwlth scholar, DPhil); *m* 19 June 1992, Dr Victoria Braithwaite, da of Alan Braithwaite; 2 s (James Alan b 8 April 1995, Matthew Ronald b 9 June 1997); *Career* jr research fell ChCh Oxford 1988–92, lectr in zoology St Catherine's Coll Oxford 1989–90, Lloyds of London tercentenary fell Univ of Oxford 1991–92; Univ of Edinburgh: BBSRC advanced research fell 1993–97 (granted second fellowship 1998 but resigned), prof of natural history 1998–; adjunct prof Univ of Tromsø Norway 1992–97; Thomas Henry Huxley Award Zoological Soc of London 1991, Young Investigator Award American Soc of Naturalists 1991, Scientific Medal Zoological Soc of London 1999; FRSE 2003; *Books* The Evolutionary Biology of Parasitism (ed with A E Keymer, 1990), Parasite Variation: Ecological and Immunological Consequences (ed with M E Viney, 2002); *Recreations* barbeques; *Style*— Prof Andrew Read; ✉ University of Edinburgh, School of Biological Sciences, King's Buildings, Ashworth Laboratories, West Mains Road, Edinburgh EH9 3JT (tel 0131 650 5506, fax 0131 650 5456, e-mail a.read@ed.ac.uk)

READ, Prof Frank Henry; s of Frank Charles Read (d 1976), and Florence Louisa, *née* Wright (d 1996); *b* 6 October 1934; *Educ* Haberdashers' Aske's, Univ of London (ARCS, BSc), Univ of Manchester (PhD, DSc); *m* 16 Dec 1961, Anne Stuart, da of Neil Stuart Wallace; 2 da (Kirsten Victoria b 17 Oct 1962, Nichola Anne b 12 Feb 1964), 2 s (Jonathon Hugh Tobias b 16 June 1965, Sebastian Timothy James b 18 Aug 1970); *Career* Univ of Manchester: lectr 1959–68, sr lectr 1968–74, reader 1974–75, prof of physics 1975–98, res dean of Faculty of Science 1993–95, Langworthy chair of physics 1998–2002, emeritus prof 2002–; vice-pres Inst of Physics 1984–89; conslt in charged particle optics 1976–; memb: Cncl of Royal Soc 1987–89, Sci Bd SERC 1987–90; FRS 1984, FInstP 1973, FIEE 1998, SMIEEE 2002; *Books* Electrostatic Lenses (1976), Electromagnetic Radiation (1980); *Recreations* stone-masonry, landscaping, riding; *Style*— Prof Frank Read, FRS; ✉ Hardingland Farm, Macclesfield Forest, Cheshire SK11 0ND (tel 01625 425759); School of Physics and Astronomy, University of Manchester, Manchester M13 9PL (e-mail frank.read@physics.org)

READ, Dr Graham; *b* 16 January 1947; *Educ* Queen Elizabeth's GS Barnet, Fitzwilliam Coll Cambridge (open exhibitioner in natural scis, MA, MB BChir, coll prize, MRCP), Univ of Manchester Med Sch (surgical prize); *m* 13 April 1974, Joan Elizabeth, *née* Hughes; 2 s (Philip Alexander b 17 March 1976, Stuart Noel b 17 April 1979), 1 da (Helena Magdalen b 1 Aug 1977); *Career* jr posts in med Manchester Royal Infirmary and Crumpsall Hosp Manchester, registrar then sr registrar in radiotherapy Christie Hosp Manchester; currently: conslt in radiotherapy and oncology Christie Hosp Manchester and hon assoc lectr in radiotherapy Univ of Manchester, dir of cancer servs Royal Preston Hosp; head clinician Lancs and S Cumbria Cancer Network; memb: MRC Working Pty on Testicular Tumours 1979–, Cancer Statistics Gp Cancer Research Campaign 1982, MRC Working Pty on Advanced Bladder Cancer 1983–, NW Regnl Med Ctee 1988–92, Clinical Oncology Casemix Gps Devpt Project, Integrated Clinical Workstation Project, Cncl RCR (memb Faculty Bd of Clinical Oncology 1988–94); chm Clinical Oncology Speciality Working Gp NHSME Clinical Terms Project; memb: Br Assoc for Cancer Research, Br Inst of Radiology, Br Oncological Assoc, American Soc of Clinical Oncology; FRCR 1978, FRCP 2001; *Publications* author of numerous articles in the fields of testicular and bladder cancer and gen oncology, also author of book chapers; *Style*— Dr Graham Read; ✉ Director of Cancer Services, Royal Preston Hospital, Sharoe Green Lane North, Fulwood, Preston PR2 9HT (tel 01772 716565, fax 01772 710089)

READ, Keith Frank; CBE (1997); s of Alan George Read, OBE (d 2007), of Walmer, Kent, and Dorothy Maud, *née* Richardson (d 1988); *b* 25 April 1944, Hounslow, Middx; *Educ* King's Sch Bruton, Britannia RNC Dartmouth (scholar), RN Engrg Coll Dartmouth; *m* 2 April 1966, Sheila, *née* Roberts; 2 da (Rebecca b 6 Jan 1967, Anna b 24 Dec 1970), 1 s (Peter b 27 Sept 1968); *Career* RN: Midshipman 1963–64, HM Submarine Ocelot 1968–69, HM Submarine Sovereign 1970–73, sr engr HM Submarine Repulse 1974–76, Cdr 1980, Cdr HMS Collingwood 1980, exec offr Clyde Submarine Base 1984–88, Capt 1988, dep dir Naval Logistics Plans 1989, RCDS 1990, naval attaché Rome and def attaché Albania 1992–96, ret RN 1996; mangr Southern Europe Ganley Int 1997–98, chief exec Inst of Marine Engrg, Science and Technol 1999–; memb Advsy Bd Greenwich Maritime Inst 1999–, dir Shadow Engrg and Technol Bd 2001–02, memb Tech Ctee RNLI 2002–, memb Sci Cncl Bd 2003–, chair Chief Execs Ctee Engrg Instns 2004–; CEng 1972, FIEE 1988, FIMarEST 1999, FRSA 2000; *Recreations* music, theatre, sailing, family; *Clubs* Quart, Woodroffe's; *Style*— Keith Read, Esq, CBE; ✉ Institute of Marine Engineering, Science and Technology, 80 Coleman Street, London EC2R 5BJ (tel 020 7382 2660, e-mail keith.read@imarest.org)

READ, Martin; s of Charles Enderby Read (d 1993), of Ulceby, Lincs, and Lillian Clara, *née* Chambers (d 1999); *b* 24 July 1938; *Educ* Queen Elizabeth's GS Alford, Wadham Coll Oxford (MA); *m* 27 April 1963, Laurette, da of J T Goldsmith (d 1960), of Hendon, London; 2 da (Robyn Lisa b 7 Sept 1966, Abigail Kim b 14 May 1970); *Career* articled clerk Hammond Suddards Bradford 1959–62; Slaughter and May: asst slr 1963–70, ptnr 1971–95, conslt 1995–99; past vice-chm Law Soc Standing Ctee on Company Law, past chm Company Law Sub-Ctee City of London Law Soc; memb Law Soc 1963; *Recreations* theatre, opera, literature, golf, cricket; *Clubs* MCC, Royal St George's; *Style*— Martin Read, Esq; ✉ Michaelmas House, Bois Avenue, Chesham Bois, Amersham, Buckinghamshire HP6 5NS (tel 01494 725121)

READ, Dr Martin Peter; s of late Peter Denis Read, and Dorothy Ruby Read; *b* 16 February 1950; *Educ* Queen Mary's GS Basingstoke, Peterhouse Cambridge (BA), Merton Coll Oxford (DPhil); *m* 1974, Marian Eleanor, *née* Gilbart; 1 s (Laurence), 1 da (Eleanor); *Career* various posts in mktg, fin, ops, systems devpt Overseas Containers Ltd 1974–81, joined International Paint (Courtalds) 1981, corp commercial dir Marine Coatings 1981–84 and gen mangr Europe 1984–85; joined GEC Marconi 1985, gen mangr Marconi Secure Radio 1986–87, dir Marconi Defence Systems Ltd 1987–89, md Marconi Command and Control Systems 1989–91, gp md Marconi Radar and Control Systems Gp 1991–93; gp chief exec LogicaCMG plc (formerly Logica plc) 1993–2007; non-exec dir: Asda plc 1996–99, The Boots Gp plc 1999–2006, Southampton Innovations Ltd 1999–2003, British Airways plc 2000–; memb: Cncl for Industry and HE 2000–, President's Ctee CBI 2004–, DTI Strategy Bd 2005–06; tstee Hampshire Technol Centre 1990–, tstee Southern Focus (formerly Portsmouth Housing) Tst 1992–2000, dir Portsmouth Housing Assoc 1993–2007, govr Highbury Coll Portsmouth 1989–99, memb Cncl Univ of Southampton 1999–, tstee Shelter 2004– (memb Fin Ctee 2000–04); Hon DTech Loughborough Univ

2000; CDipAF 1976, MInstD 1991, CIMgt 1994, fell IET 2005; *Publications* article in Jl of Applied Physics; *Recreations* French and German novels, drama, military history, travel, gardening; *Style*— Dr Martin Read

READ, District Judge Maureen Antonia; da of Marcel Meisl (d 1991), of Senica, Slovakia, and Gertrude, *née* Schwarz (d 1955), of Vienna, Austria; *b* 19 June 1945; *Educ* Queenswood Sch, Kingston Poly (BA); *m* 29 June 1968, Derek Alan Read; 1 da (Charlotte Helen b 23 May 1970), 1 s (Marcel James b 6 July 1971); *Career* justice clerks asst Malden and Surbiton Magistrates Court 1967–70, articles 1976–79, admitted slr 1979, dep co court and district registrar Western Circuit 1988–92; district judge: Bow Co Court 1992–97, Bromley Co Court 1997–2005, Barnstaple and Exeter Co Courts 2005–; asst recorder 1996–2000, recorder 2000–; memb Law Soc; *Recreations* theatre, swimming, adult literacy, grandchildren; *Style*— District Judge Maureen Read; ✉ Barnstaple County Court, Civic Centre, Barnstaple, Devon EX31 1DY (e-mail mread@lix.compulink.co.uk)

READ, Prof Nicholas Wallace (Nick); s of Wallace Frederick Read, of Blagdon Hill, Somerset, and Doris Vera, *née* Scriven; *b* 7 July 1945; *m* (m dis); 4 da (Esther b 1973, Katherine b 1978, Emily b 1982, Diane b 1986), 1 s (Alexander b 1980); *Career* conslt physician Northern General Hospital and Community Health Sheffield Trusts 1981–2002, conslt physician and psychotherapist Claremont Hosp Sheffield 2001–; prof of gastrointestinal physiology and nutrition Univ of Sheffield 1988–98 (prof of integrated med 2000–01); dir Centre for Human Nutrition 1988–98; psychoanalytical psychotherapist 1997–; memb: Br Soc of Gastroenterology 1974, Nutrition Soc 1986; FRCP 1987, UKCP 1998; *Books* Irritable Bowel Syndrome (1984, 2 edn 1990), BDS Textbook of Physiology (1988), Gastrointestinal Motility, Which Test (1989), Food and Nutritional Supplements (2001), Sick and Tired: Healing the Diseases Doctors Cannot Cure (2005), Irritable Bowel Syndrome Self-Management Programme (website, 2006); *Recreations* hill walking, running, birdwatching, writing; *Style*— Prof Nick Read; ✉ 35 Lister Street, Ilkley, West Yorkshire LS29 9ET (e-mail nickwread@blueyonder.co.uk, website www.nickread.co.uk)

READ, (Charles) Patrick Wilson; s of Sir Charles David Read (d 1957), of London, and Frances Edna, *née* Wilson; *b* 17 March 1942; *Educ* Harrow; *m* 1966, Susan Viner, da of Brian Viner Edsall, of Wisborough Green, W Sussex; 1 s (Jason b 1968); *Career* chief exec Young & Co's Brewery plc 1997– (md 1976–97); Liveryman Worshipful Co of Brewers; *Recreations* shooting, fishing; *Style*— Patrick Read, Esq; ✉ Young & Co's Brewery plc, Ram Brewery, Wandsworth, London SW18 (tel 020 8875 7000, fax 020 8870 9444, telex 8814530, e-mail hq@youngs.co.uk)

READ, Peter Graham; s of Edward Arthur Anthony Read, of Westcliff-on-Sea, Essex, and Madge Patricia, *née* Harwood; *b* 5 June 1956, Rochford, Essex; *Educ* Westcliff HS for Boys, Univ of Southampton; *m* 28 June 1980, Jennifer Margaret, *née* Monnickendam; 1 s (Jonathan Henry b 7 Jan 1983); *Career* CA 1979; Peat Marwick Mitchell & Co (now KPMG): joined 1976, sr mangr 1986, ptnr 1990–, head of transaction services for ICE market 1998, head of market 2002–; memb Audit Ctee ECB; schoolboy memb England trampoline team; *Clubs* RAC, Professional Cricketers Assoc; *Style*— Peter Read, Esq; ✉ KPMG LLP, 1 Puddle Dock, Blackfriars, London EC4V 3PD (tel 020 7311 3246, fax 020 7311 2965, e-mail peter.read@kpmg.co.uk)

READ, Prof Peter Leonard; s of Leonard Frederick Read, of Dunstable, Beds, and Dorothy Helen, *née* Moore; *b* 18 October 1953, Hampstead, London; *Educ* Univ of Birmingham (BSc), Univ of Cambridge (PhD); *m* 28 July 1979, Janette Dorothy Ann, *née* Kenny; 1 da (Elizabeth Helen Mary b 14 July 1985), 1 s (Nicholas Peter Robert b 23 April 1987); *Career* Met Office 1979–91; Univ of Oxford: fell by special election St Cross Coll 1989–91, MA (by incorporation) 1990, fell and tutor in physics Trinity Coll 1991–, lectr 1991–, titular reader 1999–2002, titular prof of physics 2002–, head Geophysical and Planetary Fluid Dynamics Research Gp Atmospheric, Oceanic and Planetary Physics Sub-Dept; visiting prof Université d'Aix-Marseille 2003; co-investigator: Composite Infrared Spectrometer Team NASA/European Space Agency Cassini Orbiter Mission (launched 1997), Pressure Modulator Infrared Radiometer Team NASA Mars Climate Orbiter Mission (launched 1998), Mars Climate Sounder Team NASA Mars Reconnaissance Orbiter Mission (launched 2005); memb Editorial Bd: Physics and Chemistry of the Earth 1996–2000, Surveys in Geophysics 1996–2006, Quarterly Jl RMS 2000–; memb Royal College of Organists; memb European Geophysical Soc 1980– (Golden Badge Award 2000, chair Nonlinear Processes in Geophysics Working Gp); FRAS 1979, FRMetS 1980 (memb Cncl 2000–02); *Books* The Martian Climate Revisited: Atmosphere and Environment of a Desert Planet (with S R Lewis, 2004); *Recreations* singing, organist, walking, cycling; *Style*— Prof Peter Read; ✉ Atmospheric, Oceanic and Planetary Physics, Clarendon Laboratory, Parks Road, Oxford OX1 3PU (tel 01865 272082, fax 01865 272923, e-mail p.read1@physics.ox.ac.uk)

READ, Dr Peter Robert; CBE (2000); s of Frederick John Read (d 1966), and Winifred Harriet, *née* Gregory; *b* 18 January 1939; *Educ* Purley Co GS, Charing Cross Hosp Med Sch; *m* 11 Oct 1965, Norma, *née* Rowlands; 1 da (Josephine Lisa b 24 April 1970), 1 s (Simon Jonathan b 10 June 1971); *Career* Hoechst Gp of Companies 1971–99 (ret as chm); non-exec dir: Vernalis plc, SSL Int plc, Innogenetics; former non-exec dir Celltech Gp plc; past pres Assoc of Br Pharmaceutical Assoc, past chm Centre for Medicines Research, past chm Research Defence Soc; former memb Bd SE of England Devpt Agency (SEEDA); Freeman City of London, Liveryman Worshipful Soc of Apothecaries; Hon DSc De Montfort Univ; FFPM 1989, FRCP 1996; *Recreations* music, opera, garden, rugby; *Style*— Dr Peter Read, CBE; ✉ c/o SSL International plc, 35 New Bridge Street, London EC4B 6BW

READ, Piers Paul; s of Sir Herbert Edward Read, DSO, MC (d 1968), and Margaret, *née* Ludwig (d 1996); *b* 7 March 1941; *Educ* Ampleforth, St John's Coll Cambridge (BA, MA); *m* 29 July 1967, Emily Albertine, da of (Evelyn) Basil Boothby, CMG, of London; 2 s (Albert b 1970, William b 1978), 2 da (Martha b 1972, Beatrice b 1981); *Career* author; artist in residence Ford Fndn Berlin 1963–64, sub ed Times Literary Supplement London 1965, Harkness fell Cwlth Fund NY 1967–68, adjunct prof of writing Univ of Columbia 1980; memb: Ctee of Mgmnt Soc of Authors 1973–76, Literature Panel Arts Cncl London 1975–77, Cncl RSL 2002–07; chm Catholic Writers' Guild 1992–97, govr Cardinal Manning Boys' Sch London 1985–90, bd memb Aid to the Church in Need 1988–; FRSL 1972; *Books* Games in Heaven with Tussy Marx (1966), The Junkers (1968), Monk Dawson (1969), The Professor's Daughter (1971), The Upstart (1973), Alive: the story of the Andes Survivors (1974), Polonaise (1976), The Train Robbers (1978), A Married Man (1979), The Villa Golitsyn (1981), The Free Frenchman (1986), A Season in The West (1988), On the Third Day (1990), Ablaze, The Story of Chernobyl (1993), A Patriot in Berlin (1995), Knights of the Cross (1997), The Templars (1999), Alice in Exile (2001), Alec Guinness: The Authorised Biography (2003), Hell and Other Destinations (2006); *Style*— Piers Paul Read, Esq, FRSL; ✉ 23 Ashchurch Park Villas, London W12 9SP (tel 020 7727 5719, office 020 7460 2499, e-mail piersread@dial.pipex.com)

READ, Richard Michael Hodgson; s of Lt Richard Hodgson Read (d 1936), of Eastbrook Hall, Dinas Powis, and Dorothy Jessie, *née* Penwarden (d 1985); *b* 24 December 1936; *Educ* Clifton, St James' Sch Maryland, Univ of London (BSc); *m* 1, 21 July 1964 (m dis 1969), Jennifer Diane, da of Marcus Leaver (d 1966), of Mill Hill; *m* 2, 29 Oct 1993 (m dis 2005), Susan Anne Icke; *Career* CA; R H March Son & Co and Mann Judd & Co 1962–79, ptnr Touche Ross & Co 1979–81, dir various cos affiliated to Lloyd's 1981–90; chm: D G Durham Group plc 1988–93, Culver Holdings plc 1991–; underwriting memb Lloyd's; memb CBI: Smaller Firms Cncl 1973–79, Cncl 1978–79, Welsh Cncl; FCA; *Recreations* skiing, golf, swimming; *Clubs* Cardiff & County, Royal Porthcawl Golf; *Style*— Richard Read, Esq; ✉ Llanmaes, St Fagans, Cardiff CF5 6DU (tel 029 2067 5100)

READ, Thomas Bonamy; s of Sir Herbert Edward Read, DSO, MC (d 1968), and Margaret, *née* Ludwig (d 1996); *b* 21 December 1937; *Educ* Ampleforth, Univ of Leeds (BA); *m* Celia Mary, da of Charles Guy Vaughan-Lee, DSC (d 1984); 3 s (Alexander Paul b 26 April 1968, James Herbert b 6 Dec 1969, Matthew Charles b 16 April 1974); *Career* reporter and educn correspondent Daily Mirror 1962–67, BBC Radio 1967–; prodr Reith Lectures 1981, ed Analysis Radio 4 1982–84; World Serv 1984–96: head of Central Talks and Features 1987, acting ed World Serv in English 1989, dir BBC Monitoring 1991–96; winner Sony Award for best documentary 1984; project mangr Nat Recording Project Public Monuments and Sculpture Assoc 1997–2002; tstee The Bleddfa Trust 1996–; chm Bd of Govrs More House Sch 1996–2005; *Recreations* travel; *Style*— Thomas Read, Esq; ✉ 31 St Albans Road, London NW5 1RG (tel and fax 020 7485 0256)

READE, Rt Rev Nicholas Stewart; *see:* Blackburn, Bishop of

READER, HE David George; s of Stanley Reader (d 2000), and Annie Reader; *b* 1 October 1947; *Educ* Barrow GS; *m* 1969, Elaine, da of John Oswald McKnight; 1 s (Andrew b 1975), 1 da (Clare b 1980); *Career* joined FO 1964, high cmmr to Swaziland 2001–04, ambass to Cambodia 2005–; *Clubs* Royal Over-Seas League; *Style*— HE Mr David Reader; ✉ c/o Foreign & Commonwealth Office (Phnom Penh), King Charles Street, London SW1A 2AH

READING, Anthony John; MBE (1978); *b* 8 August 1943; *Educ* Brighton Coll; *m* 1966; 1 s; *Career* articled clerk Spain Bros Dalling and Co Brighton 1962–66, audit sr and asst mangr Whinney Murray Ernst and Ernst Brussels 1966–70, md Donaldson Europe Belgium 1978–80 (dir of fin 1970–76, dir of mfrg 1976–77), gp exec Thomas Tilling plc London 1980–83, divnl gp chief exec BTR plc 1983–87, gp md Polly Peck International plc 1987–89, gp md Pepe Group plc 1989–90; Tomkins plc: divnl dir 1990–92, chief operating offr North America 1992–95, jt md Operations 1995–96, chm Tomkins Corp USA 1996–2003; non-exec dir: Spectris 2004–, e2v Technologies plc 2004–, The Laird Group plc 2004–, George Wimpey plc 2005–; chm Organization for Int Investment 2002–03; FCA 1966; *Recreations* family, music, golf, bridge, watersports; *Clubs* Naval and Mil, Lambourne; *Style*— Anthony Reading, Esq, MBE; ✉ c/o Spectris plc, Station Road, Egham, Surrey TW20 9NP

READING, Peter; s of Wilfred Gray Reading, of Liverpool, and Ethel Mary, *née* Catt; *b* 27 July 1946; *Educ* Liverpool Coll of Art (BA); *m* 1, 5 Oct 1968 (m dis 1996), Diana Joy, da of Edward Thomas Gilbert; 1 da (Angela b 14 April 1977); m 2, 24 Dec 1996, Deborah Joyce Jackson; m 3, 17 April 2002, Penelope Anne Hamblen; *Career* poet; schoolteacher 1967–68, lectr in art history Liverpool Coll of Art 1968–70; writer in residence Sunderland Poly 1980–82; writing fell UEA 1997, Lannan literary resident Marfa Texas 1998–99; Cholmondeley Award for Poetry 1978, Dylan Thomas Award 1983, Whitbread Award (Poetry Category) 1986, literary fellowship award Lannan Fndn USA 1990 and 2004; FRSL 1988; *Poetry* incl: Water and Waste (1970), For the Municipality's Elderly (1974), The Prison Cell & Barrel Mystery (1976), Nothing for Anyone (1977), Fiction (1979), Tom O'Bedlam's Beauties (1981), Diplopic (1983), 5 x 5 x 5 x 5 x 5 (1983), C (1984), Ukulele Music (1985), Stet (1986), Essential Reading (1986), Final Demands (1988), Perduta Gente (1989), Shitheads (1989), Evagatory (1992), 3 in 1 (1992), Last Poems (1994), Collected Poems (2 Vols, 1995 and 1996), Work in Regress (1997), Chinoiserie (1997), Ob (1999), Apopthegmatic (1999), Repetitious (1999), Marfan (2000), untitled (2001), Faunal (2002), Collected Poems (Vol 3, 2003), -273.15 (2005); *Style*— Peter Reading; ✉ c/o Bloodaxe Books, Highgreen, Tarset, Northumberland NE48 1RP

READING, Dr Peter Richard; s of Dr Harold Garnar Reading, and Barbara Mary, *née* Hancock; *b* 1 May 1956; *Educ* St Edward's Sch Oxford, Gonville & Caius Coll Cambridge (entrance and sr exhibitioner, MA), Moscow State Univ (Br Cncl research scholar), Univ of Birmingham (PhD); *m* Dr Catherine Austin, *née* Fountain; 1 s, 2 da, 2 step da; *Career* various appts as Health Serv mangr 1984–94; chief exec: Lewisham and Guy's Mental Health NHS Tst 1994–98, UCL Hosps NHS Tst 1998–2000, Univ Hosps of Leicester NHS Tst 2000–; CCMI 2007; *Recreations* children, cats, dogs, Oxford United, Russian history; *Style*— Dr Peter Reading; ✉ University Hospitals of Leicester NHS Trust, Trust Headquarters, Gwendolen House, Gwendolen Road, Leicester LE5 4QF (tel 0116 258 8563, e-mail peter.reading@uhl-tr.nhs.uk)

READING, 4 Marquess of (UK 1926); Simon Charles Henry Rufus Isaacs; also Baron Reading (UK 1914), Viscount Reading (UK 1916), Earl of Reading and Viscount Erleigh (both UK 1917); s of 3 Marquess of Reading, MBE, MC (d 1980); *b* 18 May 1942; *Educ* Eton, Univ of Tours; *m* 1979, Melinda, yr da of Richard Dewar; 2 da (Lady Sybilla b 3 Nov 1980, Lady Natasha b 24 April 1983), 1 s (Julian Michael Rufus, Viscount Erleigh b 26 May 1986); *Heir* s, Viscount Erleigh; *Career* Lt 1st Queen's Dragoon Gds 1961–64; stockbroker 1964–74, memb London Stock Exchange 1970–74; mktg dir: Brahmaco Int 1975–80, Ralph Lauren Cosmetics 1979–83, Abbey Lubbock 1984–92, Abbey Sports and Events 1984–92; chm: Lands End and John O'Groats 1992–96, Anglo Russian JVC 1992–2002, Cure Int (UK) 2004–, KICC; dir: Nelson Recovery Tst, Flying Hosp Inc 1998–, Westminster Oil 2005–; pres: Dean Close Sch 1990–2000, Stoke Park Club 2005–; memb Cncl: The Garden Tomb in Jerusalem, Anglo-Israel Assoc; patron Barnabas Fund 1998–; *Clubs* Cavalry and Guards', MCC, All England Lawn Tennis, White's, Stoke Park (pres 2005–); *Style*— The Most Hon the Marquess of Reading; ✉ 7 Cecily Hill, Cirencester GL7 2EF

READY, Nigel Peter; s of Colin Peter Ready (d 1986), and Monica Isabel Elms, *née* Tapper (d 2007); *b* 13 July 1952; *Educ* Wycliffe Coll, Jesus Coll Cambridge (MA); *m* 29 Dec 1973, Marisa, da of Germano Brignolo, of Asti, Italy; 1 da (Natasha Isabella b 1975), 2 s (Oliver James b 1976, Thomas Nigel b 1985); *Career* Notary Public 1980; ptnr Cheeswrights 1981– (managing ptnr 1990–); hon sec Soc of Public Notaries of London 1988–2000, vice-pres Fédération des Associations de Notaires Européens 1991–, chm Soc of Scrivener Notaries of London 2000–03; dep cmmr of maritime affrs Republic of Vanuatu 1995–; Freeman City of London, memb Ct of Assts Worshipful Co of Scriveners (chm Notarial Ctee 1997–, Renter Warden 2000–01, Upper Warden 2001–02, Master 2002–03), Liveryman Worshipful Co of Shipwrights; LRPS; *Books* The Greek Code of Private Maritime Law (jtly, 1982), Brooke's Notary (10 edn, 1988, Supplement 1991, 12 edn 2002, Hong Kong Supplement 2005), Ship Registration (1991, 3 edn 1998), Ship Registration Law and Practice (consulting ed, 2002); *Recreations* wine, opera, photography, travel; *Style*— Nigel Ready, Esq; ✉ c/o Cheeswrights, 10 Philpot Lane, London EC3M 8BR (tel 020 7623 9477, fax 020 7623 5428)

REAMSBOTTOM, Barry Arthur; s of Agnes Mulholland; *b* 4 April 1949; *Educ* St Peter's RC Secdy Sch Aberdeen, Aberdeen Acad; *Career* trade union leader; scientific asst Isaac Spencer & Co Aberdeen 1966–69, social security offr DHSS Aberdeen 1969–76, area offr NUPE Edinburgh 1976–79; Civil and Public Servs Assoc: head of Educn Dept 1979–87, ed Red Tape (CPSA official jl) and press offr 1987–92, gen sec 1992–98; gen sec Public and Commercial Services Union 2001–02 (jt gen sec 1998–2001), researcher to Speaker of House of Commons; vice-pres Trade Union Committee for Transatlantic and European Undersranding; memb NUJ 1987–; fell Centre for American Studies Salzburg; *Recreations* golf, books, music, art appreciation, laughter and the love of friends; *Style*— Barry Reamsbottom, Esq; ✉ 156 Bedford Hill, London SW12 9HW (tel 020 8675 4894, e-mail reamsy156@lycos.co.uk)

REARDON SMITH, Sir William Antony John; 4 Bt (UK 1920), of Appledore, Co Devon; s of Sir William Reardon Reardon Smith, 3 Bt (d 1995), and his 1 w, Nesta, *née* Phillips (d

R

1959); *b* 20 June 1937; *Educ* Wycliffe Coll; *m* 1962, Susan Wight, da of Henry Wight Gibson, of Cardiff; 3 s ((William) Nicolas Henry b 1963, Giles Antony James b 1968, Harry Alexander b 1979), 1 da (Henrietta Nesta b 1965); *Heir* s, Nicolas Reardon Smith; *Career* dir Reardon Smith Line plc 1959–85, dir World Trade Centre 1986–87, tstee and chm Joseph Strong Frazer Trust; tstee Royal Merchant Navy Sch Fndn until 2004, govr Bearwood Coll until 2004; memb Milford Haven Port Authy to 1999, dir Milford Dock Co and Marine and Port Services to 1999; Liveryman Worshipful Co of Shipwrights, Liveryman Worshipful Co of World Traders, Freeman Worshipful Co of Poulters, Clerk Worshipful Co of Fuellers; Knight Grand Cross of the Military and Hospitaler Order of St Lazarus of Jerusalem (Bailiff 2002); *Recreations* golf, shooting, walking; *Clubs* Royal Porthcawl, Cardiff & County; *Style*— Sir William Reardon Smith, Bt; ✉ 26 Merrick Square, London SE1 4JB (tel 020 7403 5723)

REASON, (Bruce) John; s of Claude Leon Reason (d 1980), of Dunstable, Beds, and Gladys May Reason (d 1976); *Educ* Dunstable GS, Univ of London; *m* Joan, da of William Wordsworth (d 1938), of Penistone, S Yorks; 3 s (Ross George b 1961, Mark John b 1962, William b 1968 d 1974); *Career* journalist, author and publisher; News Chronicle Manchester and News of the World Manchester 1953, The Recorder Fleet St 1953–54, sports news ed News of the World London 1955–63 (asst sports ed Manchester 1954–55), prodn ed The Cricketer magazine 1966–76; rugby corr: The Daily Telegraph 1964–79, The Sunday Telegraph 1979–; memb: NUJ, Inst of Journalists; political work for Cons Pty until 1990; *Books* The 1968 Lions (1968), The Victorious Lions (1971), The Lions Speak (1972), The Unbeaten Lions (1974), Lions Down Under (1977), The World of Rugby (1978), Backs to the Wall (1980); *Recreations* golf, gardening, property devpt; *Clubs* MCC, Royal Mid-Surrey Golf; *Style*— John Reason, Esq; ✉ The Sunday Telegraph, 1 Canada Square, Canary Wharf, London E14 5DT (tel 020 7538 5000)

REAVILLE, Richard Maxwell; s of late Jack Reaville, and late Pauline Elizabeth, *née* Sharp; *b* 4 June 1954; *Educ* Claremont Sch Nottingham, Clarendon Coll of FE, RNCM; *Career* tenor; business career 1975–82, studied at RNCM with John Cameron 1982–86; professional debut as Don Jose in Carmen (WNO) 1985, solo debut in L'Incoronazione di Poppea (Glyndebourne) 1986; *Performances* operas incl: Billy Budd (ENO), Tamino in The Magic Flute (London Chamber Opera), Ferrando in Cosi fan Tutte (Holland Park Festival), Lord Puff in The English Cat (Henze Biennial Festival Gütersloh and Berlin) 1989, Ernesto in Don Pasquale (tour), Simon Boccanegra (concert performance at Tivoli Festival Copenhagen) 1992, Eisenstein in Die Fledermaus (Mid Wales Opera) 1992, Hoffmann in Les Côntes d'Hoffman (Bristol) 1993, Don José in Carmen (European Chamber Opera) 1996; concert and recital performances incl: Mendelssohn Paulus (Staatskapelle Weimar), Verdi Requiem (with Orchestre Philharmonique de Loraine), Beethoven Ninth Symphony (with Odense Symphony Orch Denmark 1990, also Brussels, Namur and Dinant 1992, Brugge, Antwerp and Ninove with Belgium Nat Orch 1995), Mozart Requiem and Bach Johannes Passion (with Århus Chamber Orch Denmark, Randers Byorkester) Messiah, Dvorák Stabat Mater and Johannspassion (with Esbjerg Chamber Orch in tour of Denmark), Ligeti Grand Macabre (Odense Symphony Orch Denmark), J S Mayr Requiem (UK première at St John's Smith Square) 1992, Verdi Requiem (Köln, Düsseldorf and St Malo) 1993, Mozart Requiem (with Orchestre de Chambre de Wallonie at Knokke-Heist), Concert Rossini Petite Messe Solonelle (with Copenhagen Boys' Choir), Bach St John Passion arias (with Sönerjuland Orch Denmark under Nicholas Cleobury) 1995, Rossini Stabat Mater (Finland) 1995, Bach St Matthew Passion (with Jyvaskyla Orch Finland) 1996, Mahler Das Lieb Von Der Erde (with Örebro Chamber Orch Sweden and Randers Byorkester) 1997, The Last Temptations (Nilsia Festival Finland) 1999; various other concert engagements with orchs incl BBC Philharmonic and English String Orch; solo contract with Scot Opera in Param Vir's Broken Strings, concert engagements in Finland, France, Belgium and UK; radio broadcast with Norwegian Radio of Britten's Serenade for Tenor, Horn and Strings 2001; *Recordings* incl: Billy Budd (ENO), The Love for Three Oranges (with Lyon Opera Orch, finest classical music recording award 1989), Puccini's Messe di Gloria (with Ostrava Choir and Orch of Czech Republic) 1995; *Recreations* politics, golf; *Style*— Richard Reaville, Esq; ✉ c/o Nicholson Proud Limited, PO Box 53911, London SW15 2UX (tel 020 8788 4745, e-mail info@nicholsonproud.com); e-mail rcreaville@hotmail.com, website www.nicholsonproud.com

REAY, Master of; Hon Aeneas Simon Mackay; also Baron Aeneas Mackay; s and h of 14 Lord Reay (and h to S Btcy, Netherland Baronies and Jonkheership), and his 1 w, Hon Annabel Thérèse Fraser, da of 15 Lord Lovat, DSO, MC, TD (d 1995); *b* 20 March 1965; *Educ* Westminster, Brown Univ USA; *Style*— The Master of Reay

REAY, 14 Lord (S 1628); Sir Hugh William Mackay; 14 Bt (NS 1627); also Chief of Clan Mackay, Jonkheer Mackay (Netherlands 1816), Baron Mackay van Ophemert (Netherlands 1822), and Baron Mackay (Netherlands 1858); s of 13 Lord Reay (d 1963, having been naturalised a British subject 1938), by Charlotte, da of William Younger (bro of 1 Viscount Younger of Leckie); *b* 19 July 1937; *Educ* Eton, ChCh Oxford; *m* 1, 1964 (m dis 1978), Hon Annabel Térèse Fraser, da of 15 Lord Lovat, DSO, MC, TD (d 1995); 2 s (Hon Aeneas Simon, Master of Reay b 1965, Hon Edward Andrew b 1974), 1 da (Hon Laura Elizabeth b 1966); m 2, 1980, Hon Victoria Isabella Anne, *née* Warrender, da of 1 Baron Bruntisfield, MC (d 1993); 2 da (Hon Antonia Alexandra b 1981, Hon Isabel Violet Grace b 1985); *Heir* s, Master of Reay; *Career* MEP 1973–79, vice-chm Cons Gp European Parl, delg to Cncl of Europe and WEU 1979–85; sits as Conservative in House of Lords, a Lord in Waiting 1989–91, Parly under-sec of state DTI 1991–92; *Clubs* Pratt's, White's; *Style*— The Rt Hon the Lord Reay

REBUCK, Gail Ruth; CBE (2000); da of Gordon Woolfe Rebuck, and Mavis, *née* Joseph; *b* 10 February 1952; *Educ* Lycée Français de Londres, Univ of Sussex (BA); *m* 1 April 1985, Philip Gould (now Baron Gould of Brookwood (Life Peer)), *qv*; 2 da (Hon Georgia Anne Rebuck Gould 18 May 1986, Hon Grace Atalanta Rebuck Gould b 6 June 1989); *Career* prodn asst Grisewood & Dempsey 1975, ed then publisher Robert Nicholson Pubns 1976–79, publisher Hamlyn Paperbacks 1979–82, fndr ptnr and publishing dir non-fiction Century Publishing Co Ltd 1982–85, publisher Century Hutchinson 1985–89, chm Random House Div Random Century (Century Hutchinson bought by Random House Inc) 1989–91, chm and chief exec Random House Gp Ltd 1999– (publisher of over 40 imprints incl: Jonathan Cape, Chatto & Windus, Century, William Heinemann, Hutchinson, Ebury, Bantam, Doubleday, Vintage, Arrow, Corgi, Black Swan, Harvill Secker, BBC Books and Virgin Books); non-exec dir: The Work Fndn 2001–, BSkyB 2002–; tstee IPPR 1993–2003, memb Creative Industries Task Force 1997–2000; memb Cncl RCA 1999–; FRSA 1989; *Recreations* reading, travel; *Style*— Ms Gail Rebuck; ✉ The Random House Group Ltd, 20 Vauxhall Bridge Road, London SW1V 2SA (tel 020 7840 8882, fax 020 7233 6120)

RECORD, Norman John Ronald; s of George Ronald Record (d 1967), of Newton Abbot, Devon, and Dorothy Millie Rowland (d 1996); *b* 19 May 1934; *Educ* Wembley Co GS, UCL (BSc); *m* 1 April 1961, Susan Mary, da of Ernest Samuel Weatherhead (d 1969), of Paignton, Devon; 2 s (Guy b 1964, Justin b 1966); *Career* 2 Lt RAOC 1955–57; economist; formerly held planning and mktg posts in C & J Clark Ltd from 1964, and Perkins Engines Ltd 1957–64, corp planning dir C & J Clark Ltd 1980–91, sr ptnr Business Economics Management Consultants 1991–; memb Cncl CBI 1982–93; memb Fabian Soc; author of papers on Macro-Economics; originator of The Theory of The Output Gap in the Control of The Economy; fell Soc Business Economists, FIMgt; *Recreations* current affrs, theatre, local history, swimming; *Clubs* Royal Over-Seas League; *Style*— Norman Record, Esq; ✉ 30 St Medard Road, Wedmore, Somerset BS28 4AY (tel and fax 01934 712 326, e-mail n.record@talk21.com)

REDDAWAY, HE David Norman; CMG (1993), MBE (1980); s of late (George Frank) Norman Reddaway, CBE (d 1999), and Jean Muriel, *née* Brett, OBE; *b* 26 April 1953; *Educ* King's Coll Sch Cambridge, Oundle, Fitzwilliam Coll Cambridge (exhibitioner, MA); *m* 1981, Roshan Taliyeh, da of late Narcy Mirza Firouz, and Louise Laylin Firouz; 2 s (Alexander Bahram b 1983, Milo Firouz b 1996), 1 da (Touran b 1987); *Career* joined FCO 1975, language trg SOAS 1976, language trg Iran 1977, third then second sec (commercial) Tehran 1978–79, second then first sec (Chancery) Tehran 1979–80, first sec Madrid 1980–84, first sec FCO 1985–86, private sec to Min of State FCO 1986–88, first sec (external political) New Delhi 1988–90, chargé d'affaires Tehran 1990–93 (cnsllr 1991), minister Buenos Aires 1993–97, head of Southern European Dept FCO 1997–99, dir Public Services FCO 1999–2001, UK special rep for Afghanistan (with personal rank of ambass) 2002, visiting fell Harvard Univ 2002–03, high cmmr to Canada 2003–06, ambass to Ireland 2006–; hon vice-pres Raleigh Int 1998–; *Recreations* skiing, tennis, Persian carpets and art; *Clubs* Hawks' (Cambridge); *Style*— HE Mr David Reddaway, CMG, MBE

REDDIHOUGH, His Hon Judge John Hargreaves; s of Frank Hargreaves Reddihough, of Manchester, and Mabel Grace, *née* Warner; *b* 6 December 1947; *Educ* Manchester Grammar, Univ of Birmingham (LLB); *m* 26 June 1981, Sally Margaret, da of Bert Fryer, of Crawley, 1 da (Gayle b 1981), 1 s (Alex b 1984); *Career* called to the Bar Gray's Inn 1969; recorder 1994; circuit judge: Midland & Oxford Circuit 2000–01, NE Circuit 2001–; resident judge Grimsby Combined Court 2001–; *Recreations* skiing, travel, gardening, music, reading; *Style*— His Hon Judge John Reddihough; ✉ Grimsby Combined Court, Town Hall Square, Grimsby, South Humberside DN31 1HX (tel 01472 265250)

REDDISH, John Wilson; s of Frank Reddish, of Middleton, Gtr Manchester, and Elizabeth, *née* Hall; *b* 19 January 1950; *Educ* Manchester Grammar, Lincoln Coll Oxford (MA); *m* 20 May 1978, Dawn Marian, da of Edward Henry John McKenzie Russell (d 1963); 1 da (Helena b 1987); *Career* teaching assoc Northwestern Sch of Law Chicago 1971–72, called to the Bar Middle Temple 1973, in practice 1974–; pt/t chm Special Educnl Needs Tbnl 1994–, pt/t chm Protection of Children Act Tbnl 2000–02 (temp pres 2001), pt/t chm Care Standards Tbnl 2002–; memb Family Law Bar Assoc; *Recreations* cricket, croquet; *Clubs* Dulwich Sports; *Style*— John Reddish, Esq; ✉ 1 King's Bench Walk, Temple, London EC4Y 7DB (tel 020 7936 1500, fax 020 7936 1590, e-mail jreddish@btinternet.com)

REDDY, Thomas; s of Thomas Reddy (d 1973), of Poulton-le-Fylde, and Charlotte Winifred Teresa, *née* Hickey (d 1987); *b* 6 December 1941; *Educ* Baines's Sch Poulton; *m* 30 Aug 1969, Phyllis Wendy, da of Stanley Smith (d 1969), of Manchester and Lytham St Anne's; 1 da (Verity b 1971), 1 s (Christian b 1973); *Career* journalist 1968–70, dir and exec creative dir Royds McCann 1970–87, chief exec Tom Reddy Advertising 1987–; broadcaster on advertising TV and radio; guest lectr in advertising UMIST and Lancaster Univ; *Recreations* book collecting; *Clubs* Manchester Tennis and Racquets; *Style*— Thomas Reddy, Esq; ✉ Tom Reddy Advertising (tel 0870 122 0161, e-mail ads@tra.co.uk)

REDER, Dr Peter; s of late Jack Mannie Reder, of London, and Beatrice, *née* Kantor; *b* 29 June 1946; *Educ* Kilburn GS, Univ of Birmingham Med Sch (MB, ChB); *m* 15 Aug 1979, Dr Geraldine Sarah Mary, *née* Fitzpatrick; 1 s (Nicholas b 17 Jan 1984); *Career* conslt child psychiatrist Wolverton Gdns Child and Family Consultation Centre W London Mental Health Tst 1985–2003; hon sr lectr Imperial Coll Sch of Med (formerly Charing Cross and Westminster Med Sch) 1990–2003, dir Wolverton Gdns Centre for Relationship Studies 1993–2003; DPM, DCH, DObstRCOG, FRCPsych 1993 (MRCPsych 1975); *Books* Beyond Blame: Child Abuse Tragedies Revisited (jtly, 1993), Assessment of Parenting (jtly, 1995), Lost Innocents: A Follow-Up Study of Fatal Child Abuse (jtly, 1999), Family Matters: Interfaces Between Child and Adult Mental Health (jtly, 2000), Studies in the Assessment of Parenting (jtly, 2003); author of pubns on psychotherapy, family therapy, child psychiatry, child abuse, parenting breakdown and training; *Clubs* Roehampton, Ashley Wood Golf; *Style*— Dr Peter Reder

REDESDALE, 6 Baron (UK 1902), of Redesdale, Co Northumberland, also cr Baron Mitford, of Redesdale in the County of Northumberland (Life Baron) 2000, and sits as such in the House of Lords; Rupert Bertram Mitford; o s of 5 Baron Redesdale (d 1991), and Sarah Georgina Cranstoun, *née* Todd; *b* 18 July 1967; *Educ* Milton Abbey, Highgate Sch, Univ of Newcastle upon Tyne (BA); *m* 1998, Helen, da of D H Shipsey; 1 s (Hon Bertram David b 2000), 2 da (Clementine Ann b 2001, Amelia Sarah b 2003); *Heir* s, Hon Bertram Mitford; *Career* overseas devpt spokesman for Liberal Democrats 1993–; memb Cncl Inst Advanced Motorists; *Style*— The Rt Hon Lord Redesdale; ✉ The School House, Rochester, Newcastle upon Tyne NE19 1RH; 2 St Mark's Square, London NW1 7TP

REDFARN, Stephen Charles; s of Dr Cyril Aubrey Redfarn (d 1988), of London, and Isabel Mary, *née* Williams (d 1987); *b* 7 May 1943; *Educ* Westminster, King's Coll London (BSc), London Mgmnt Centre (Dip Business Admin); *m* 1990, Frances Yin Hong; 1 s (James Yin Aubrey b 26 Oct 1995); *Career* with Hill Samuel & Co Ltd 1966–68, dir Dawnay Day & Co Ltd investment bankers 1968–78, head of corp fin Henry Ansbacher & Co 1978–83, conslt Touche Ross 1983–87, head of capital markets AIB London 1987–90, chief exec Westcountry Television Ltd 1990–97; currently chm Media Equity Associates Ltd; non-exec dir Kitley House Hotel Ltd; external examiner in accounting CNAA 1986; chm Business Graduates Assoc 1981; Freeman City of London, Liveryman Worshipful Co of Tallow Chandlers; *Recreations* fly fishing, collecting 18th century glass, exploring China; *Clubs* Reform, Royal Anglo Belgian; *Style*— Stephen Redfarn, Esq

REDFERN, (David) Alan; s of Thomas Leonard Redfern (d 1991), and Gladys, *née* George (d 1974); *b* 23 November 1932; *Educ* Wyggeston Sch Leicester, Sidney Sussex Coll Cambridge (exhibitioner, MA); *m* 1, 1958, Edith Marie Allamand (d 1980); 1 s (Charles b Feb 1964), 1 da (Isabelle b Sept 1961); m 2, 1983, Marie-Louise Montmasson; 1 s (Alexander b Dec 1980), 1 da (Céline b Aug 1984); *Career* admitted slr 1958; ptnr specialising in int commercial arbitration and construction law Freshfields 1963–95; called to the Bar Middle Temple 1995; memb Chambers at 1 Essex Court Temple 1995–; arbitrator in int commercial disputes; vice-chm Int Court of Arbitration ICC, memb Int Panel American Arbitration Assoc, former vice-pres Middle East Assoc, past chm Int Arbitration Club; memb Int Bar Assoc; FCIArb; *Books* Law & Practice of International Commercial Arbitration (2 edn, 1991); *Recreations* literature, art, windsurfing, walking; *Clubs* Royal Thames Yacht, Roehampton; *Style*— Alan Redfern, Esq; ✉ One Essex Court, London EC4Y 9AR

REDFERN, Rt Rev Alastair Llewellyn John; *see:* Derby, Bishop of

REDFERN, (Margaret) June; da of John Towers Redfern, of West Ferry, Dundee, and Margaret, *née* Campbell (d 1979); *b* 16 June 1951; *Educ* Edinburgh Coll of Art; *Career* artist; pt/t tutor (fine art) Preston Poly 1982–83, jr fell (fine art) Cardiff Coll of Art 1983, artist in residence Nat Gallery London 1985; guest artist: Univ of Minnesota 1986, Kunstacademie I Trondheim 1992; Andrew Grant scholarship 1972–73, First Prize Scottish Young Contemporaries 1972, Scottish Arts Cncl Award 1982; patron Child Pyschotherapy Tst Scotland 1992–; *Solo Exhibitions* Scottish Arts Cncl Edinburgh 1976, Third Eye Centre Glasgow 1977, Leeds Educn Authy 1977, Women's Arts Alliance London 1978, Henderson Gallery Edinburgh 1978 (drawings 1980), 369 Gallery Edinburgh 1981, Air Gallery London 1984, Third Eye Centre Glasgow 1985, Marianne Deson Gallery Chicago 1985, Nat Gallery London 1986, Mercury Gallery Edinburgh 1987, Bradford Art Galleries and Museums 1987, Aberdeen Art Galleries and Museums 1988,

Towner Art Gallery Eastbourne 1988, Mercury Gallery London 1988, Trinity Gallery London 1990, Compass Gallery Glasgow 1991, Bohun Gallery Henley 1992, 1994 and 1997, Wrexham Arts Centre 1992, Maclaurin Art Gallery Ayr 1992, Wrexham Library Arts Centre 1992 (touring Maclaurin Art Gallery and Museum Ayr 1992), MAC Birmingham 1993, Portal Gallery Bremen 1994, Scottish Gallery 1996, 1999 and 2001, Boundary Gallery London 1996, 1999 and 2001, Bohun Gallery 1998, Oilon Canvas Boundary Gallery 1998, Open Eye Gallery Edinburgh 2003, Caledonian Girls (Nicholas Hagen Fine Art London) 2004–05; *Invited Artist* Éiese, Carlow, Ireland; *Public Collections* incl: Nat Gallery London, BBC TV, Robert Fleming plc, Hiscox Holdings, Charlotte Englehart Fndn Boston, Texaco, Albertina Museum Vienna, Procter & Gamble, Glasgow Art Galleries and Museums, Lillie Art Gallery Glasgow, Lithoprint UK, 3i, Scottish Equitable Standard Life, New Hall Cambridge, DOC TV Canada, British Trade Commission NY, Scottish Life, and also paintings in various hospitals; *Television* incl: The Bigger Picture (BBC 2) 1994, Edinburgh Nights (The Late Show, BBC 2) 1994, Weathering the Storm (BBC Scotland and BBC 2), Oil on Canvas (BBC 2), Bonnard Omnibus (BBC2); *Style*— Ms June Redfern; ✉ 12 Lawley Street, London E5 0RJ (tel 020 8985 1426, fax 020 8986 3621, website www.juneredfern.com)

REDFERN, Prof Walter David; s of Walter Barton Redfern (d 1968), of Liverpool, and Charlotte, *née* Jones (d 1986); *b* 22 February 1936; *Educ* Bootle GS, Univ of Cambridge (MA, PhD); *m* 30 March 1963, Angela, da of John Robert Kirkup (d 1978), of Chester-Le-Street, Co Durham; 1 da (Kate b 20 Sept 1968), 1 s (Sam b 9 Dec 1970); *Career* prof of French Univ of Reading 1980–2001 (lectr 1963, reader 1972, now emeritus); visiting prof Univ of Illinois 1981–82; memb Soc For French Studies; *Books* Private World of Jean Giono (1968), Paul Nizan (1972), Queneau: Zazie Dans le Métro (1980), Puns (1984), Georges Darien (1985), A Calm Estate (1986), Clichés and Coinages (1989), Feet First: Jules Vallès (1992), Michel Tournier (1996), Louis Guilloux (1998), All Puns Intended: Jean-Pierre Brisset (2001), Writing on the Move: Albert Londres and Investigative Journalism (2004); *Recreations* jazz, cinema, writing; *Style*— Prof Walter Redfern; ✉ 8 Northcourt Avenue, Reading RG2 7HA (tel 0118 987 1083); French Department, University of Reading, Whiteknights, Reading RG6 6AA (tel 01183 788322 ext 8322, fax 0118 931 8122, e-mail lfsrdfen@reading.ac.uk)

REDGRAVE, Adrian Robert Frank; QC (1992); s of late Cecil Frank Redgrave, and Doris Edith Redgrave; *b* 1 September 1944; *Educ* Abingdon Sch, Univ of Exeter (LLB); *m* 7 Oct 1967, Ann, da of late Jack Bryan Cooper; 2 s (William Alexander Frank b 6 April 1971, Matthew Robert Charles b 23 May 1977), 1 da (Lucy Rebecca Jane b 28 Sept 1972); *Career* called to the Bar Inner Temple 1968, recorder 1985–; *Recreations* tennis, wine, garden, France, Bangalore Phall; *Style*— Adrian Redgrave, Esq, QC; ✉ 1 Chancery Lane, London WC2A 1LF (tel 0845 634 6666)

REDGRAVE, Corin William; s of Sir Michael Redgrave (d 1985), and Lady Redgrave (Rachel Kempson); bro of Vanessa Redgrave, *qv*, and Lynn Redgrave, *qv*; *b* 16 July 1939; *Educ* Westminster, King's Coll Cambridge; *m* 2; Kika Markham, the actress; 4 c; *Career* actor and director; fndr and artistic dir Moving Theatre; *Theatre* credits for Young Vic incl: The Crucible, Some Kind of Hero, Julius Caesar, Measure for Measure, Coriolanus, Rosmersholm; other credits incl: Chips With Everything (London/New York), The Right Honourable Gentleman (Her Majesty's), Lady Windermere's Fan (Phoenix), Abelard and Heloise (Wyndham's), The Romans (RSC), The Norman Conquests (Library, Manchester), The Case of David Anderson (Travers and Lyric Studio), Some Kind of Hero (Croydon Warehouse), The Flag (Bridge Lane), Casement (Bridge Lane), Julius Caesar (Alley Theatre, Texas), The Country Girl (Greenwich), Some Sunny Day (Hampstead), General From America (RSC), Marat Sade (RNT), HRH (tour and West End), Gross Indecency (Plymouth Theatre Royal) 1998, Not About Nightingales (RNT 1998 and (NY) 1999, In Extremis/De Profundis (RNT) 2000, The Cherry Orchard (RNT) 2000, Song At Twilight (Gielgud Theatre) 2000, No Man's Land (RNT) 2001, The Browning Version (Derby Playhouse) 2002, Blunt Speaking (Chichester) 2002, The General From America (Alley Theatre Houston and NY) 2002, Honour (RNT) 2003, The Recruiting Officer (Garrick Theatre Lichfield) 2003, Resurrection (Garrick Theatre Lichfield) 2003, The Entertainer (Liverpool Playhouse) 2003, King Lear (RSC) 2004, Tynan (RSC) 2004; as dir incl: Romeo and Juliet (Moscow), Lillian (Lyric Shaftesbury and Fortune), Real Writing (Moving Theatre at Riverside Studios), Ousama (USA); *Television* for BBC incl: Hassan, In Good King Charles' Golden Days, The Tenant of Wildfell Hall, The Fall of Kevin Walker, Measure for Measure, Persuasion, Henry IV, Dangerfield, presenter of Omnibus -Voyage Round Michael Redgrave, DCI Walsh in The Ice House; other credits incl: Antony and Cleopatra (ATV), I Berlioz (South Bank Show, LWT), Circle of Deceit (YTV), Throwaways (Zenith North), Trial & Retribution (La Plante Prodns), The Women in White (ITV), Ultraviolet, Trial and Retribution; *Films* credits incl: The Deadly Affair, A Man For all Seasons, Charge of the Light Brigade, The Magus, When Eight Bells Toll, David Copperfield, Oh! What a Lovely War, The Girl with a Pistol, The Red Baron, Between Wars, Serail, The Governor, Excalibur, Wagner, Eureka, The Fool, In The Name of the Father, Four Weddings and a Funeral, The Opium War, The Man Who Drove with Mandela; *Publications* Michael Redgrave, My Father (1st ed, Richard Cohen Books, 1995); *Recreations* playing the piano; *Style*— Corin Redgrave, Esq

REDGRAVE, Lynn Rachel; OBE (2002); da of Sir Michael Redgrave (d 1985), and Lady Redgrave (Rachel Kempson); sis of Vanessa Redgrave, *qv*, and Corin Redgrave, *qv*; *b* 8 March 1943; *Educ* Queensgate Sch, Central Sch of Speech and Drama; *m* 2 April 1967, John Clark; 1 s (Benjamin b 7 May 1968), 2 da (Kelly b 26 Feb 1970, Annabel b 5 July 1981); *Career* actress and playwright; *Theatre* professional debut in A Midsummer Night's Dream (Royal Court) 1962; Nat Theatre 1963–66 (fndr memb): Hamlet, The Recruiting Officer, Much Ado About Nothing, Hay Fever, Andorra, Mother Courage, Love for Love (tour Moscow and Berlin); West End roles 1968–71 incl: The Tulip Tree, Slag, Born Yesterday, The Two of Us; A Better Place (Gate Theatre Dublin) 1972; Broadway roles incl: debut Black Comedy 1967, My Fat Friend, Knock Knock, Mrs Warren's Profession (Tony nomination), Saint Joan, Sister Mary Ignatius Explains It All For You, Aren't We All? (Drama Desk nomination) 1985–86, Sweet Sue 1987, Love Letters 1989, Shakespeare For My Father (Tony nomination) 1993, The Master Builder 1993, Moon Over Buffalo 1996; US tours 1976–77: California Suite, The Two of Us, Saint Joan, Thursday's Girls, Hellzapoppin; other plays: Misalliance (Chicago, Sarah Siddons and Jefferson Awards), Twelfth Night (American Shakespeare Festival Conn) 1978, The King and I (tour) 1982, Les Liaisons Dangereuses (Ahmanson Theatre LA) 1988–89, The Cherry Orchard (La Jolla Playhouse San Diego) 1990, Three Sisters (London) 1990, Don Juan in Hell (Hollywood) 1991, The Notebook of Trigorin 1996, Moon Over Buffalo 1996, Strike Up the Band 1998, The Mandrake Root 2001, Noises Off 2001, Talking Heads 2003, The Exonerated 2004; *Television* in UK: A Midsummer Night's Dream, Pygmalion, Vienna 1900, Egg on the Face of the Tiger, Pretty Polly, A Woman Alone (BBC) 1988, Death of a Son (Best TV Actress) 1989, Fighting Back 1992, Calling the Shots 1994, Varian's War; in US: Love Boat, Fantasy Island, Hotel, House Calls (CBS, Golden Globe nomination), Teachers Only (NBC), Chicken Soup (ABC), Gauguin the Savage (CBS), Rehearsal for Murder (CBS), The Shooting (CBS, Emmy nomination), The Bad Seed (ABC), Walking on Air (PBS), The Old Reliable (PBS) 1988, Jury Duty (ABC) 1990, Whatever Happened to Baby Jane (ABC) 1991; host: Not for Women Only, AM America, The Weight Watchers Magazine Show, One Second Before Sunrise, In Performance at the White House (PBS) 1989, Rude Awakening (Showtime) 1998–99, A Season for Miracles (Hallmark) 1999, Hall of Fame (CBS) 1999, Different Lifetime 1999; *Radio* As

You Like It (BBC), Three Sisters (BBC), Vile Bodies (BBC), Artist Descending a Staircase (Irish Radio), Tales for Halloween (US); *Films incl* Tom Jones, Girl With Green Eyes, Georgy Girl (Best Actress NY Film Critics, Golden Globe Award, Academy nomination Best Actress 1967), The Deadly Affair, Smashing Time, The Virgin Soldiers, The Last of the Mobile Hotshots, Don't Turn the Other Cheek, The National Health, Every Little Crook and Nanny, Everything You Always Wanted to Know About Sex, The Happy Hooker, The Big Bus, Sunday Lovers, Morgan Stewart's Coming Home, Getting It Right 1989, Midnight 1990, Shine 1996, Gods and Monsters 1998 (Best Supporting Actress Golden Globe Awards 1999, Oscar nomination for Best Supporting Actress 1999), Touched 1999, The Annihilation of Fish 1999, The Simian Line 1999, The Next Best Thing 1999, How to Kill Your Neighbor's Dog 2000, Venus and Mars 2000, The Simian Line 2001, The Annihilation Of Fish 2001, My Kingdom 2001, Anita and Me 2002, Spider 2003, Peter Pan 2003, Kinsey 2004; *Books* This is Living (1991), Named President of the Players (1994); *Recreations* cooking, gardening, horse riding; *Style*— Ms Lynn Redgrave, OBE

REDGRAVE, Sir Steven Geoffrey (Steve); kt (2001), CBE (1997, MBE 1986); s of Geoffrey Edward Redgrave, of Marlow Bottom, Bucks, and Sheila Marion, *née* Stevenson; *b* 23 March 1962; *Educ* Marlow C of E First Sch, Holy Trinity Sch Marlow, Burford Sch Marlow Bottom, Great Marlow Sch; *m* 12 March 1988, (Elizabeth) Ann, da of Brian John Callaway, of Cyprus; 2 da (Natalie b 1991, Sophie b 1994), 1 s (Zak b 16 Feb 1998); *Career* sports conslt; notable achievements incl: runner-up double sculls World Jr Championships 1980, 20 wins Henley Royal Regatta 1981–2001, Gold medal coxed fours Olympic Games Los Angeles 1984, Wingfield Sculls champion 1985–89, Gold medal coxless pairs World Championships 1986 and 1987 (Silver medal coxed pairs 1987), 3 Gold medals Cwlth Games 1986 (single sculls, coxed fours, coxless pairs), Gold medal coxless pairs Olympic Games Seoul 1988 (Bronze medal coxed pairs), indoor world rowing champion 1991, world champion coxless pairs 1991, Gold medal coxless pairs Olympic Games Barcelona 1992, world champion coxless pairs 1993, 1994 and 1995, world record holder coxless pairs 1994, Gold medal coxless pairs Olympic Games Atlanta 1996, world champion coxless fours 1997, 1998 and 1999, Gold medal coxless fours Olympic Games Sydney 2000; flagbearer Olympic Games 1992 and 1996; winner Team of the Year (with M Pinsent) BBC Sports Personality of the Year Awards 1992 and 1996, BBC Sports Personality of the Year 2000, Golden Personality BBC Sports Personality of the Year Awards 2003; pres Amateur Rowing Assoc (ARA), dir Five Gold (www.fivegold.co.uk), hon vice-pres Diabetes UK; Hon DTech Loughborough Univ 2001; Hon DUniv: Buckingham, Nottingham, Durham, Hull, Buckinghamshire Chilterns UC, Reading, Heriot-Watt, Open Univ, Oxford Brookes, Aberdeen Univ; *Publications* A Golden Age (autobiography, with Nick Townsend), Steve Redgrave's Complete Book of Rowing, You Can Win at Life (with Nick Townsend); *Clubs* Marlow Rowing, Leander; *Style*— Sir Steve Redgrave, CBE; ✉ c/o PO Box 3400, Marlow, Buckinghamshire SL7 3WX (tel 01627 483021, e-mail melanie@casitas.tv, website www.ssrct.co.uk and www.steveredgrave.com)

REDGRAVE, Vanessa; CBE (1967); da of Sir Michael Redgrave (d 1985), and Lady Redgrave (Rachel Kempson); sis of Corin Redgrave, *qv*, and Lynn Redgrave, *qv*; *b* 30 January 1937; *Educ* Queensgate Sch, Ballet Rambert, Central Sch of Speech and Drama; *m* 1962 (m dis 1967), Tony Richardson (d 1991), s of Clarence Albert Richardson (d 1969); 2 da (Natasha Richardson, Joely Richardson, the actresses); *Career* actress, numerous stage and film performances; *Theatre* Touch of the Sun (Saville) 1958, A Midsummer Night's Dream (Stratford) 1959, Look on Tempests 1960, The Tiger and the Horse 1960, Lady from the Sea 1960; with Royal Shakespeare Theatre Co: As You Like It 1961, Taming of the Shrew 1961, Cymbeline 1962; The Seagull 1964, The Prime of Miss Jean Brodie (Wyndham's) 1966, Daniel Deronda 1969, Cato Street 1971, The Threepenny Opera (Prince of Wales) 1972, Twelfth Night (Shaw Theatre) 1972, Antony and Cleopatra (Bankside Globe) 1973, Design for Living (Phoenix) 1973, Macbeth (LA) 1974, Lady from the Sea (NY) 1976, Roundhouse 1979, The Aspern Papers (Haymarket) 1984, The Seagull (Queen's) 1985, Chekov's Women (Lyric) 1985, The Taming of the Shrew and Antony and Cleopatra (Haymarket) 1986, Ghosts (Young Vic, transferred to Wyndham's) 1986, Touch of the Poet (Young Vic, transferred to Comedy) 1988, Orpheus Descending (Haymarket) 1988 and (NY) 1989, A Madhouse in Goa (Lyric Hammersmith) 1989, When She Danced (Globe, Best Actress Evening Standard Drama Awards) 1991, Heartbreak House (Yvonne Arnaud Guildford and Haymarket) 1992, Maybe (Royal Exchange) 1993, John Gabriel Borkman (RNT) 1996, Lady Windermere's Fan (Haymarket) 2002, The Hollow Crown (Princess of Wales Theatre Toronto) 2004; theatrical debut as director: Antony and Cleopatra (Riverside Studios) 1995; *Films* A Suitable Case for Treatment 1966 (Cannes Festival Best Actress Award 1966), The Sailor from Gibraltar 1967, Blow-Up 1967, Camelot 1967, Red White and Zero 1967, Charge of the Light Brigade 1968, Isadora 1968, A Quiet Place in the Country 1968, The Seagull 1969, Drop-Out 1970, La Vacanza 1970, The Trojan Women 1971, The Devils 1971, Mary Queen of Scots 1972, Murder on the Orient Express 1974, Out of Season 1975, Seven Per Cent Solution 1975, Julia 1976 (Academy Award 1977, Golden Globe Award), Agatha 1978, Yanks 1978, Bear Island 1978, Playing for Time 1980, My Body My Child 1981, Wagner 1983, The Bostonians 1984, Wetherby 1985, Steaming 1985, Comrades 1987, Prick Up Yours Ears 1987, Consuming Passions 1988, A Man for All Seasons 1988, Orpheus Descending 1990, Young Catherine 1990, Howards End 1992 (best supporting actress Oscar nomination 1993), The Wall 1992, Great Moments in Aviation 1993, Mother's Boy 1993, The House of the Spirits 1993, Crime & Punishment 1993, They 1993, Little Odessa 1994, A Month by the Lake 1996, Déjà Vu 1996, Wilde 1997, Smilla's Feeling for Snow 1997, Mrs Dalloway 1997, Deep Impact 1997, Cradle Will Rock 1998, Mirka 1998, Uninvited 1998, Girl Interrupted 1999, A Rumour of Angels 2000, Crime and Punishment 2000, If These Walls Could Talk II 2000 (best actress Screen Actors Guild Awards 2001), The Fever 2002, The Keeper 2003, Venus 2006; *Publications* Pussies and Tigers (1963), Vanessa - An Autobiography (1992); *Style*— Miss Vanessa Redgrave, CBE

REDHEAD, Prof Michael Logan Gonne; s of Robert Arthur Redhead (d 1992), and Christabel Lucy Gonne, *née* Browning (d 1966); *b* 30 December 1929; *Educ* Westminster, UCL (BSc, PhD); *m* 3 Oct 1964, Jennifer Anne, da of Montague Arthur Hill; 3 s (Alexander b 1965, Julian b 1968, Roland b 1974); *Career* dir Redhead Properties Ltd 1962, ptnr Galveston Estates 1970; prof: philosophy of physics Chelsea Coll London 1984–85, philosophy of physics KCL 1985–87, history and philosophy of sci Univ of Cambridge 1987–97; co-dir Centre for Philosophy of Natural and Social Science LSE 1998–, centennial prof of philosophy LSE 1999–2002; vice-pres Wolfson Coll Cambridge 1992–96 (fell 1988), Tarner lectr Trinity Coll Cambridge 1991; visiting fell All Souls Coll Oxford 1995, FKC 2000; pres Br Soc for the Philosophy of Sci 1989; Lakatos award 1988; FInstP, FBA; *Books* Incompleteness Nonlocality and Realism (1987), From Physics to Metaphysics (1995), Objectivity Invariance and Convention (with T Debs, 2007); *Recreations* tennis, music, poetry; *Clubs* Athenaeum, Hurlingham, Queen's; *Style*— Prof Michael Redhead, FBA; ✉ 119 Rivermead Court, Hurlingham, London SW6 3TA (tel 020 7736 6767)

REDMAN, Prof Christopher Willard George; s of Prof Roderick Oliver Redman (d 1975), and (Annie) Kathleen Redman (d 1996); *b* 30 November 1941; *Educ* Perse Sch Cambridge, Univ of Cambridge (MA, MB BChir); *m* 8 Aug 1964, Corinna Susan, da of Prof Sir Denys Lionel Page, KBE (d 1978); 4 s (Paul b 1967, Andrew b 1969, George b 1972, Oliver b 1982), 1 da (Sophie b 1972); *Career* intern and resident dept of pathology Johns Hopkins Hosp Baltimore USA 1967, house offr Children's Hosp Sheffield 1969, sr house offr Jessop

R

Hosp Sheffield 1969, lectr regius Dept of Med Radcliffe Infirmary Oxford 1970 (house offr 1968), prof Nuffield Dept of Obstetrics John Radcliffe Hosp Oxford 1993– (univ lectr 1976, clinical reader 1988, clinical prof 1992); FRCP 1982, FRCOG as eundum 1993; *Recreations* walking; *Style*— Prof Christopher Redman; ✉ Nuffield Department of Obstetrics and Gynaecology, John Radcliffe Hospital, Oxford OX3 9DU (tel 01865 221009)

REDMAN-BROWN, Geoffrey Michael; s of Arthur Henry Brown (d 1999), of Newport, Gwent, and Marjorie Frances Joan, *née* Redman (d 1969); assumed by Deed Poll the additional surname of Redman before his patronymic 1960; *b* 30 March 1937; *Educ* Newport HS, Balliol Coll Oxford (MA); *m* 23 Feb 1988, Mrs Jean Wadlow; *Career* Nat Serv RAF 1956–58; Phillips & Drew (subsequently UBS Ltd): joined 1961, ptnr 1970–86, dir 1986–90, ret 1990; dir Jean Wadlow Associates Ltd 1991– (chm 1994–); endowment fund tstee Balliol Coll Oxford 1988–, chm Balliol Coll Old Membs' Ctee 1991–2001; Prov Grand Master for Oxfordshire: United Grand Lodge of England 1985–2001, Grand Lodge of Mark Master Masons 1994–2004; Prov Grand Master for London and Metropolitan Counties Royal Order of Scotland 1996–; tstee New Masonic Samaritan Fund 1991–2001; chm The League of Remembrance 2005– (hon treas 1990–05); Freeman City of London, Liveryman Worshipful Co of Broderers 1977; MSI (memb Stock Exchange 1967), AIIMR (AMSIA 1972); *Recreations* swimming, gardening, travel, opera and the arts; *Clubs* Garrick, Savile, City of London, RAC, United and Cecil; *Style*— Geoffrey Redman-Brown, Esq; ✉ 5 Three Kings Yard, Davies Street, Mayfair, London W1K 4JR (tel 020 7629 2638, mobile 07866 425975, e-mail grb@jeanwadlow.co.uk)

REDMAYNE, Hon Sir Nicholas John; 2 Bt (UK 1964), of Rushcliffe, Nottingham; s of Baron Redmayne, DSO, TD, PC, DL (Life Peer and 1 Bt, d 1983); *b* 1 February 1938; *Educ* Radley, RMA Sandhurst; *m* 1, 7 Sept 1963 (m dis 1976), Ann (d 1985), da of Frank Birch Saunders, of Kineton, Warks; 1 s, 1 da; m 2, 1978, Mrs Christine Diane Wood Hewitt, da of late Thomas Wood Fazakerley; 2 step s; *Heir* s, Giles Redmayne; *Career* cmmnd Grenadier Gds 1958–62; with Grieveson Grant & Co 1963–86, chm Kleinwort Benson Securities 1991–96, chief exec Kleinwort Benson Ltd 1994–95, dep chm Kleinwort Benson Gp 1995–96; *Recreations* shooting, tennis, skiing, gardening; *Style*— The Hon Sir Nicholas Redmayne, Bt; ✉ Walcote Lodge, Walcote, Lutterworth, Leicestershire LE17 4JR (tel 01455 552637, e-mail redmayne@walcotelodge.co.uk)

REDMON, Anne Bryan; da of Bryan Collins Redmon (d 1981), and Elizabeth Howe Redmon (d 2003); *b* 13 December 1943, Stamford, CT; *Educ* Shipley Sch Bryn Mawr PA, Univ of Pennsylvania; *m* 8 Aug 1964, Benedict Nightingale; 2 s (Christopher b 13 March 1966, Piers b 1 June 1973) 1 da (Magdalen b 19 Dec 1969); *Career* writer; fiction reviewer The Sunday Times 1979–81; freelance work incl: BBC Kaleidoscope, Books and Bookmen, London Magazine; visiting assoc prof of creative writing Univ of Michigan Ann Arbor MI; writer in residence HMP Wandsworth London 1992–2003, NUJ Access to Journalism co-ordinator Writers in Prison Network 2003–05; speaker USIS American Conf Budapest 1980, speaker Univ of Kentucky Women's Writers Conf 1991; judge The Faber Prize 1980; Best First Work Award Yorkshire Post 1974, Soc of Authors Travel Grant 1993; memb St Thomas of Canterbury Catholic Church Fulham; memb: PEN 1980, Soc of Authors 2003, NUJ 2004; FRSL 1979; *Publications* Emily Stone (1974), Music and Silence (1979), Second Sight (1987), The Genius of the Sea (1992), The Judgement of Solomon (1995), The Head of Dionysos (1997), In Denial (2003); *Recreations* travel, swimming, needlework; *Clubs* Hurlingham; *Style*— Anne Redmon, FRSL; ✉ c/o PFD, Drury House, 34–43 Russell Street, London WC2B 5HA (tel 020 7344 1000, fax 020 7836 9539, website www. pfd.co.uk)

REDMOND, Prof Anthony Damien; OBE (1994); s of Gerard Redmond (d 1976), and Kathleen, *née* Bates (d 1997); *b* 18 November 1951; *Educ* Cardinal Langley Sch, Univ of Manchester (MB ChB, MD); *m* 22 Dec 1972, Caroline Ann, da of Dr John Arthur Howarth, of Devon; 3 da (Katherine Mary b 12 Dec 1978, Sarah Michelle b 15 Sept 1980, Helen Margaret b 24 April 1982); *Career* dir S Manchester Accident Rescue Team 1987–92 (attended Armenian Earthquake 1988, Lockerbie Air Crash 1988, Iranian Earthquake 1990, Kurdish refugees 1991, Ex-Yugoslavia 1992), conslt in emergency med N Staffs Trauma Centre 1991–99, prof of emergency med Keele Univ 1995–99 (sr lectr 1992–95, now emeritus prof); chief exec UK-Med 1993–; dir Operation Phoenix Sarajevo 1994–96 (ldr ODA med team Sarajevo 1993); WHO conslt Ex-Yugoslavia 1992–93, memb UN Disaster Assessment and Co-ordination Team; fndr ed Archives of Emergency Med 1984–93; med advsr Staffs Ambulance Service 1999–, med dir Univ Clinical Centre Pristina Kosovo 1999–2000, conslt Humanitarian Affairs Dept for Int Devpt 2000–; assoc med dir BUPA 2001–, sr memb Med Appeals Tbnl 2001–, non-exec dir Casualty Plus 2004–, chm Manchester Medicolegal Services Ltd 1997–, pres Casualties Union 1998–2006, dean Hope Hosp Univ of Manchester 2006–; memb: Resuscitation Cncl UK, Fontmell Gp for Disaster Relief; Soviet Order for Personal Courage 1989 (for work in Armenian Earthquake); Mancunian of the Year 1992; DMCC (Dip Med Care of Catastrophes Soc of Apothecaries of London) 2003; FRSM, MRCP UK 1981, FRCSEd 1982, MIMgt 1985, FFAEM 1995, FRCPGlas 1991, FFIMC, RCSEd 2002; *Books* Lecture Notes on Accident and Emergency Medicine (1984), Accident and Emergency Medicine (jtly 1989), The Management of Major Trauma (1991), The ABC of Conflict and Disaster (2005); *Recreations* music; *Style*— Prof Anthony D Redmond, OBE; ✉ 27 Byrom Street, Manchester M3 4PF (tel 0161 832 9935, fax 0161 833 0643, e-mail profadr@aol.com)

REDMOND, Anthony Gerard (Tony); s of Alfonso Redmond (d 2002), of Liverpool, and Margaret Florence, *née* Judge (d 1984); *b* 18 May 1945; *Educ* St Mary's Coll Crosby; *m* 24 May 1973, Christine Mary, da of Edmund Pinnington; 2 s (Dominic b 10 Aug 1976, Mark b 12 May 1980), 2 da (Emily b 9 July 1978, Sarah-Kate b 14 Aug 1984); *Career* chief accountant Liverpool City Cncl 1975–78, dep fin dir Wigan MBC 1978–82, treas and dep chief exec Knowsley MBC 1982–87, treas Merseyside Police Authy 1986–87, chief exec and fin dir London Borough of Harrow 1987–2001, chm and chief exec Cmmn for Local Admin and Local Govt Ombudsman 2001–; Freeman City of London; memb CIPFA 1969 (memb Inst Cncl), FRSA 1996, FCPA (Aust) 2005; *Recreations* football, rugby, cricket, tennis, theatre, cinema, passionate interest in ballet; *Clubs* Waterloo, Wasps and Lancashire Rugby, Cricketers'; *Style*— Tony Redmond, Esq; ✉ Commission for Local Administration, Millbank Tower, Millbank, London SW1P 4QP (tel 020 7217 4692, fax 020 7217 4621, e-mail t.redmond@lgo.org.uk)

REDMOND, John Vincent; s of Maj Robert Spencer Redmond, TD, of Knutsford, Cheshire, and Marjorie Helen, *née* Heyes; *b* 10 April 1952; *Educ* Wrekin Coll, Western Reserve Acad Ohio, Univ of Kent at Canterbury (BA); *m* 21 May 1977, Tryphena Lloyd (Nina), da of Jenkin John Lloyd Powell, of Carmarthen, Dyfed; 2 s (William b 1981, Samuel b 1985); *Career* admitted slr 1976; Cobbetts Manchester 1974–75, Clyde & Co Guildford and London 1975–78, Laytons Bristol and London 1978–2000, Osborne Clarke 2000– (ptnr and head of construction law); chm Soc of Construction Law 1996–98; chartered arbitrator and adjudicator; hon sec Soc of Construction Arbitrators; memb Law Soc 1976, FCIArb; *Recreations* mountains, sailing, real tennis; *Style*— John Redmond, Esq; ✉ Osborne Clarke, 2 Temple Back East, Temple Quay, Bristol BS1 6EG (tel 0117 917 3458, fax 0117 917 3459, e-mail john.redmond@osborneclarke.com)

REDMOND, Stephen John; s of Thomas Redmond, and late Mary Redmond; *b* 15 November 1955; *Educ* IPD (grad); *m* 1, 1978, Hazel (d 2004); 1 s (Matthew b 28 Oct 1982), 1 da (Hayley b 9 Feb 1985); m 2, 2005, Estelle; *Career* HR conslt; British Coal plc: asst head of industry trg Western Area 1983–86, dep head of staff admin NE Area 1986–88; dir Personnel N Devon HA 1988–90, dir Personnel and Support Services Weston Area Health Tst 1990–95, dir HR Plymouth Hosp NHS Tst 1995–97, head of personnel Dept of Health 1997–99, nat dir HR NHS Wales Nat Assembly for Wales 1999–2006, chair Doctors and Dentists Disciplinary Appeal Panels, memb GLG Healthcare Cncl; *Recreations* collector of antique and old cuff links (2000 pairs in the collection); *Style*— Stephen Redmond, Esq; ✉ >e-mail< stephen@mainepartnership.com

REDSHAW, HE Tina Susan; da of Trevor Redshaw (d 2004), and Doreen Cooper, *née* Langley; *b* 25 January 1961, Eastbourne, E Sussex; *Educ* Univ of York (BA), Open Univ (MSc); *m* 15 June 2001, Phongphun Khogapun; 1 da (Alisha Eve Redshaw b 25 Oct 2001); *Career* diplomat; dir Soc for Anglo-Chinese Understanding 1985–89; VSO: country prog dir China and Mongolia 1990–94, regnl prog dir SE Asia 1994–98, regnl funding mangr SE Asia (based Bangkok) 1998–99; entered HM Dip Serv 1999, first sec (political) Beijing 2000, ambass to East Timor 2003–; *Recreations* swimming, watching performing arts, listening to jazz, walking; *Style*— HE Ms Tina Redshaw; ✉ c/o Foreign & Commonwealth Office (Dili), King Charles Street, London SW1A 2AH (tel 00 670 331 2652)

REDWOOD, Dr David Robert; s of Edward James Redwood (d 1967), and Florence Maude Elizabeth, *née* Harper; *b* 4 November 1935; *Educ* King's Sch Worcester, Jesus Coll Cambridge (MA, MB BChir); *m* 1, 1960, Mehranguise (d 1980); 3 s (Michael b 1961, Simon b 1963, David b 1970); m 2, 1 May 1982, Janet Elizabeth (d 2000), da of George Young, CBE; 1 da (Katherine b 1984), 1 s (Jamie b 1987); *Career* head of cardiovascular diagnosis Nat Inst of Health Bethesda Maryland USA 1973–76 (visiting scientist 1968–76), head of cardiology Cedars of Lebanon Hosp Miami Florida USA 1976–77; conslt cardiologist: St George's Hosp London 1977–96, St Anthony's Hosp Cheam Surrey 1977–; author of chapters in cardiology textbooks and numerous papers in scientific jls; FRCP; *Recreations* sailing, walking, photography, golf; *Style*— Dr David Redwood; ✉ St Anthony's Hospital, London Road, Cheam, Surrey SM3 9DW (tel 020 8337 6691)

REDWOOD, Rt Hon John Alan; PC (1993), MP; s of William Charles Redwood, of Kent, and Amy Emma, *née* Champion; *b* 15 June 1951; *Educ* Kent Coll Canterbury, Magdalen Coll Oxford (BA), St Antony's Coll Oxford (DPhil, MA); *m* 1974 (m dis 2004), Gail Felicity, da of Robert Stanley Chippington; 1 da (Catherine b 1978), 1 s (Richard b 1982); *Career* fell All Souls Coll Oxford 1972–86 and 2003–; investment analyst Robert Fleming & Co 1974–77, clerk, mangr then dir NM Rothschild Asset Mgmnt 1977–83, advsr to Treasy and Civil Service Select Ctee 1981, head Prime Minister's Policy Unit 1983–85, dir (Overseas Corporate Finance) NM Rothschilds 1986–87; non-exec dir: Norcros plc 1986–89 (chm 1987–89), BNB Resources plc 2000–; chm and non-exec dir: Mabey Securities Ltd 1999–, Concentric plc 2003–; MP (Cons) Wokingham 1987–; Parly under sec of state for corporate affrs DTI 1989–90, min of state for corporate affairs, fin servs and telecommunications 1990–92, min of state for local govt and inner cities DOE 1992–93, sec of state for Wales 1993–95 (resigned to contest Cons leadership), shadow trade and industry sec 1997–99, shadow sec for environment, tport and the regions 1999–2000, shadow deregulation sec 2004–05, chm Cons Party Economic Policy Review 2005–; Cons Pty leadership candidate 1995 and 1997; cncllr Oxfordshire CC 1973–77; assoc prof Middx Univ Business Sch 2000–; *Books* Reason, Ridicule and Religion: The Age of Enlightenment in England 1660–1750 (first published 1976, reissued 1996), Popular Capitalism (1987), The Global Marketplace (1994), Our Currency, Our Country (1997), The Death of Britain? (1999), Stars and Strife (2001), Just Say No (2001), Third Way Which Way (2002), Singing the Blues (2005), Superpower Struggles (2005), I Want to Make a Difference (2006); *Recreations* village cricket, water sports; *Style*— The Rt Hon John Redwood, MP; ✉ House of Commons, London SW1A 0AA (tel 020 7219 4205)

REDWOOD, Sir Peter Boverton; 3 Bt (UK 1911), of Avenue Road, St Marylebone; s of Sir Thomas Boverton Redwood, 2 Bt (d 1974), and his 1 w, Ruth Mary, *née* Creighton (d 1989); *b* 1 December 1937; *Educ* Gordonstoun; *m* 22 Aug 1964, Gilian Waddington, o da of John Lee Waddington Wood, of Limuru, Kenya; 3 da (Anna Kathryn (Mrs Patrick Thomson) b 1967, Colina Margaret Charlotte b 1969, Gaynor Elizabeth (Mrs Richard French) b 1972); *Heir* half-bro, Robert Redwood; *Career* Nat Serv 1956–58, cmmnd Seaforth Highlanders (Reg Cmmn) 1959, KOSB served in UK (despatches), BAOR, Netherlands, ME, Africa and Far East, Staff Coll Camberley 1970, Nat Def Coll Latimer 1978–79, Col, ret 1987; memb Queen's Body Guard for Scotland (Royal Co of Archers); Liveryman Worshipful Co of Goldsmiths; *Recreations* shooting, silversmithing; *Clubs* New (Edinburgh), Puffins; *Style*— Sir Peter Redwood, Bt; ✉ c/o Royal Bank of Scotland, 8–9 Quiet Street, Bath BA1 2JN

REED, Alec Edward; CBE (1994); s of Leonard Reed (d 1953), of London, and Anne, *née* Underwood (d 1983); *b* 16 February 1934; *m* 16 Sept 1961, Adrianne Mary, da of Harry Eyre (d 1943); 2 s (James b 12 April 1963, Richard b 27 March 1965), 1 da (Alexandra b 22 Jan 1971); *Career* fndr chm: Reed Executive plc 1960–2000, Inter-Co Comparisons Ltd 1969–70, Reed Business Sch 1971, Medicare Ltd 1975–86; hon chm and chief exec Andrews and Ptnrs Ltd 1985–89; pres: Inst of Employment Conslts 1974–78, Int Confedn of Private Employment Agencies Assoc 1978–81; chm Employment Think Tank 1979; memb: Helpage Exec Ctee 1983–88, Oxfam Fundraising Ctee 1989–92, Cncl CIMA 1991–95; fndr: Womankind Worldwide 1988, Ethiopiaid 1989–, Women@Risk, Acad of Enterprise 2000–; prof of enterprise and innovation Royal Holloway Univ of London 1993–2003, visiting prof London Guildhall Univ 1999–2006; elected hon fell Royal Holloway 1988, Hon PhD London Guildhall Univ; FCMA, FIPD; *Books* Returning to Work (1989), Reed My Lips (1990), Innovation in Human Resource Management (2001), Capitalism is Dead: Peoplism Rules (2003); *Recreations* portrait painting, family, theatre, cinema, tennis, riding; *Style*— Alec Reed, Esq, CBE

REED, Andrew (Andy); MP; s of James and Margaret Reed; *b* 17 September 1964; *Educ* Stonehill HS Birstall, Longslade Community Coll Birstall, De Montfort Univ (BA); *m* 29 Aug 1992, Sarah Elisabeth, da of Mike Chester; *Career* Euro affrs advsr Leicestershire CC 1994–96 (formerly employment offr), MP (Lab/Co-op) Loughborough 1997– (contested seat 1992); PPS to: Kate Hoey, MP 2000–01, Rt Hon Margaret Beckett, MP 2001–03, Paymaster General 2005–; memb All-Pty Parly: Manufacturing Gp, Univs Gp, Adult Educn Gp, Rugby Union Gp, Pharmaceutical Gp, Retail Gp, Indian Gp; memb PLP: Educn & Employment Ctee, Environment & Tport Ctee, Trade & Industry Ctee; Charnwood BC: cncllr 1995–97, chm Econ Devpt Ctee 1995–97, memb Policy & Fin Ctee 1995–97; govr: Stonehill HS 1990–94, Sileby Highgate Sch 1994–; *Recreations* rugby, tennis; *Style*— Andy Reed, MP; ✉ House of Commons, London SW1A 0AA (tel 020 7219 3000, website www.andyreedmp.org.uk)

REED, Crispin Grant John; s of Michael Reed, and Shelagh, *née* Jameson; *b* 30 July 1962; *Educ* Buckhurst Hill Co HS, Univ of Dundee (BA), CIM (DipM), C&G (Photography); *Partner* Jacqueline McMenemy; 1 s (Cameron John Adam Reed b 28 Nov 2002); *Career* advtg exec: grad trainee Struthers Glasgow 1984–85; account exec Chetwynd Haddons 1985–86; Leo Burnett London: account mangr to account dir 1986–92; regnl account dir Leo Burnett Singapore 1992–95; bd dir and head account mangr Leo Burnett London 1995–99; dir in charge Collett Dickenson Pearce 1999–2000; former md Springer & Jacoby International (UK), former gp md Springer & Jacoby Gp UK; assoc memb D&AD, memb External Advsy Ctee, Euro Business Sch; MInstD; *Recreations* photography, golf, football, skiing; *Style*— Crispin Reed, Esq; ✉ crispin_reed@hotmail.com

REED, Gavin Barras; s of Lt-Col Edward Reed (d 1953), and Greta Milburn, *née* Pybus (d 1964); *b* 13 November 1934; *Educ* Eton, Trinity Coll Cambridge (BA); *m* 28 June 1957, Muriel Joyce, da of Humphrey Vaughan Rowlands (d 1985), and Edna Muriel, *née* Foster (d 1990); 3 da (Fiona b 1958, Joanna b 1960, Lucinda b 1962), 1 s (Christopher b 1964); *Career* Nat Serv Pilot Fleet Air Arm; joined The Newcastle Breweries Ltd 1958, ret as vice-chm Scottish & Newcastle plc 1994; ret as chm John Menzies plc 2002; current directorships incl: Hamilton & Inches Ltd (chm), Maclay Gp plc (chm); Liveryman Worshipful Co of Brewers; *Recreations* shooting; *Clubs* New (Edinburgh); *Style—* Gavin Reed, Esq; ✉ Broadgate, West Woodburn, Northumberland NE48 2RN

REED, Jamie; MP; *b* 4 August 1973; *Educ* Whitehaven Sch, Manchester Met Univ, Univ of Leicester; *Career* MP (Lab) Copeland 2005–; *Style—* Jamie Reed, MP; ✉ House of Commons, London SW1A 0AA

REED, Jane Barbara; CBE (2000); da of William Charles Reed, and Gwendoline Laura Reed; *b* 31 March 1940; *Educ* Royal Masonic Sch for Girls; *Career* ed Woman's Own 1969–79, publisher Quality Monthly Gp IPC 1979–81, ed-in-chief Woman 1981–83, md Holborn Publishing Gp IPC 1983–85, managing ed News UK Ltd 1986–89, dir of corp affrs News International 1989–2000 (conslt 2000–), dir Times Newspapers Holdings Ltd 2002–; dir Nat Acad of Writing 2001–; non-exec dir The Media Tst; chm Media Soc 1995–97; memb Cncl Nat Literacy Tst; tstee St Katharine and Shadwell Tst; *Books* Girl about Town (1964), Kitchen Sink or Swim (with Deirdre Saunders, 1981); *Recreations* music, writing, work, family, painting; *Clubs* Groucho; *Style—* Ms Jane Reed, CBE; ✉ News International, 1 Virginia Street, London E98 1EX

REED, Ven John Peter Cyril; s of Cyril Gordon Reed (d 1992), and Madeleine Joan, *née* Stenning (d 1990); *b* 21 May 1951; *Educ* Monkton Combe Sch, KCL (BD), Ripon Coll Oxford (CertTheol); *m* 21 July 1979, Gillian Mary, da of Kenneth Frederick Coles (d 2001); 1 da (Jennie Elizabeth Antoinette b 21 July 1985), 1 s (Simon John Gordon b 7 Oct 1987); *Career* prod gp devpt Imperial Gp 1969–73, ops mangr Res & Mktg Wales Ltd 1973–75; curate Croydon Parish Church 1979–82, precentor Cathedral & Abbey Church of St Alban 1982–86, rector Timsbury and Priston Parishes 1986–93, team rector Ilminster & Dist Team Miny 1993–99, archdeacon of Taunton 1999–; chaplain RAFA, chaplain Air Cadets, memb Bd Folk South West; *Recreations* cricket, fly fishing, real ale, surfing, gardening, music; *Clubs* Bath & Wells Clergy CC; *Style—* The Ven the Archdeacon of Taunton; ✉ Diocese of Bath and Wells, 4 Westerkirk Gate, Staplegrove, Taunton, Somerset TA2 6BQ (tel 01823 323838, fax 01823 325420, e-mail adtaunton@bathwells.anglican.org)

REED, Sub Lt Peter Kirby; s of Leo Reed, of Nailsworth, Glos, and Susan, *née* Hollingsworth; *b* 27 July 1981, Seattle, USA; *Educ* Cirencester Deer Park Comp and Coll, Britannia RNC, UWE (BEng), Univ of Oxford (Rowing blue); *Career* rower; offr rising to Sub Lt RN 1999–2001, appointed acting higher rank of Lt 2007; memb OUBC (incl varsity boat races 2004 and 2005 (winner)), memb Leander Club; achievements incl: champion coxless fours World Cup 2005 and 2006, Gold medal coxless four World Championships 2005 and 2006, winner Stewards Cup Henley Royal Regatta 2005, winner Nat Trials 2005, 2006 and 2007; memb Henley Royal Regatta Stewards; Combined Servs Sportsman of the Year 2005; largest recorded lung capacity in Britain (9.38 litres); *Recreations* playing guitar and piano, hiking, music, travelling, cinema; *Clubs* Vincent's (Oxford); *Style—* Sub Lieutenant Peter Reed; ✉ Sesame House, Watledge, Nailsworth, Gloucestershire GL6 0AU (e-mail peterkreed@hotmail.com); c/o Chris Evans-Pollard, The Professional Sports Group, The Town House, 63 High Street, Cobham, Surrey GU24 8AF (tel 01276 858930, fax 01276 856974, e-mail chris@profsports.com)

REED, Hon Lord; Robert John Reed; *b* 7 September 1956; *Educ* George Watson's Coll, Univ of Edinburgh (LLB), Balliol Coll Oxford (DPhil); *m* 1988, Jane, *née* Mylne; 2 da; *Career* admitted Faculty of Advocates 1983, called to the Bar Inner Temple 1991; standing jr counsel: Scottish Educn Dept 1988–1989, Scottish Office Home and Health Dept 1989–1995, QC 1995, advocate depute 1996–98, a senator Coll of Justice 1998–, ad hoc judge European Court of Human Rights 1999, princ commercial judge 2006–; memb Advsy Bd Br Inst of Int and Comparative Law 2001–06; expert advsr EC/Cncl of Europe Jt Initiative on Turkey 2002–04, chm Franco-Br Judicial Co-operation Ctee 2005–, pres EU Forum of Judges for the Environment 2006–; memb UN Task Forces on Aarhus Convention 2006–, convenor Children in Scotland 2006–; hon prof: Glasgow Caledonian Univ 2005–, Glasgow Univ 2006–; *Publications* European Law Reports 1997– (Scottish ed), A Guide to Human Rights in Scotland (with J L Murdoch, 2001); contrib to various books on constitutional and European law; *Style—* The Hon Lord Reed; ✉ Court of Session, Parliament House, Edinburgh EH1 1RQ (tel 0131 225 2595, fax 0131 240 6711)

REEDIE, Sir Craig Collins; kt (2006), CBE (1999); s of Robert Lindsay Reedie (d 1993), of Stirling, Scotland, and Anne, *née* Smith (d 1993); *b* 6 May 1941, Stirling, Scotland; *Educ* HS of Stirling, Univ of Glasgow (MA, LLB); *m* 9 Sept 1967, Rosemary Jane, *née* Biggart; 1 s (Colin John b 13 Sept 1968), 1 da (Catriona Jane b 16 May 1972); *Career* Scottish Badminton Union: sec 1964–71, treas 1965–74, vice-pres 1974–77, pres 1977–79; Int Badminton Fedn: memb Cncl 1970–77, vice-pres 1977–81, chm Cncl 1979–84, pres 1981–84, chm Business Ctee 1984–92, tech delg Olympic Games Barcelona 1992; chm BOA 1992–2005, dep chm UK Sport 1998–2002 (memb Cncl 1996–2002), memb Cncl Gen Assoc of Int Sports Fedns 1984–92 (treas 1988–92); IOC: appointed 1994, memb Marketing Cmmn 1995–, memb IOC Cmmn 2000, co-ordination Athens 2004, evaluation Games of 2008, co-ordination Beijing 2008, memb Prog Cmmn 2006–; dir: Manchester Cwlth Games Ltd, Manchester 2002 Ltd; dir: London 2012 Ltd 2003–05, LOCOG 2005– (memb Audit and Renumeration Ctees); World Anti-Doping Agency: memb Fndn Bd 2000–, chm Fin and Admin Co 2000–, memb Exec Ctee 2003–; memb Cncl European Olympic Ctees 2001–; Messrs Tindal, Oatts & Rodger Slrs 1964–66, DL Bloomer & Ptnrs Fin Advsrs 1966–2002 (sr ptnr 1985–2002); Univ of Glasgow: memb Ct 2000–, chm Pension Scheme Tstees 2000–, chm Investment Ctee 2000–; memb NHS in Scotland Resource Allocation Steering Gp 1998–99; Hon DUniv Glasgow 2002, Hon LLD Univ of St Andrews 2005; *Clubs* Ranfurly Castle Golf (capt 1989), Western Gailes Golf, Royal and Ancient, East India; *Style—* Sir Craig Reedie, CBE; ✉ Senara, Hazelwood Road, Bridge of Weir, Renfrewshire PA11 3DB (tel 01505 613434, fax 01505 615295, mobile 07768 502971)

REEKIE, Jonathan; s of Dr Andrew Reekie, of Marlborough, Wilts, and Virginia, *née* Cadbury; *b* 2 September 1964; *Educ* Marlborough, Bristol Business Sch; *m* 18 June 1993, Caroline, *née* Gibbs; 2 da (Honor b 25 May 1994, Rose b 17 Sept 1995); *Career* co mangr Musica Nel Chiostro Batignano Italy 1984–88 (dir 1989–), co co-ordinator Glyndebourne Festival Opera 1987–91, dir Almeida Opera 1991–2002 (gen mangr Almeida Theatre 1991–97), chief exec Aldeburgh Music 1997–; *Style—* Jonathan Reekie, Esq; ✉ Snape Maltings Concert Hall, Snape, Suffolk IP17 1SP (tel 01728 687100, fax 01728 687120)

REEN, Rob; s of William John Reen, of Swansea, and Olwen Beryl, *née* Kimmings; *b* 31 July 1951; *Educ* Penlan Sch Swansea, Cheltenham Coll of HE (BA), Univ of Wales Cardiff (PGCE); *m* Joan, da of Bob Kerfoot; 1 step s (Christopher), 1 step da (Kirsty); *Career* hotelier and painter; teacher in art and design Mayfield GS 1974–76, head Art and Design Sir Henry Floyd GS 1976–89; proprietor Ynyshir Hall 1989–; numerous exhbns and one-man shows, work in int collections; memb Welsh Rarebits consortium; *Awards* Welsh Tourist Bd 5 Star 2001, RAC Gold Ribbon Award 1993–96, AA Courtesy and Care Award 1994, AA 3 Red Star Status 1995–96; *Recreations* golf; *Clubs* Aberdovey Golf; *Style—* Rob Reen, Esq; ✉ Ynyshir Hall, Eglwysfach, Machynlleth, Powys SY20 8TA (tel 01654 781209, fax 01654 781366)

REES, Allen Brynmor; s of Allen Brynmor Rees (d 1941), of Penarth, S Glamorgan, and Elsie Louise, *née* Hitchcock (d 1958); *b* 11 May 1936; *Educ* Monmouth, Univ of Wales Aberystwyth (LLB); *m* 26 Aug 1961, Nerys Eleanor, da of Wynne Evans (d 1977), of Meifod, Powys; 2 da (Meriel Anne Brynmor b 7 Oct 1968, Eleanor Haf Brynmor b 22 Aug 1975); *Career* former sr ptnr Rees Page Slrs (incorporating Darbey-Scott-Rees, Pages and Skidmore Hares & Co); chm W Midlands Rent Assessment Panel 1968–93, princ slr to Birmingham Midshires Building Society 1976–92; pt/t chm Social Security Tbnls 1980–92, regnl chm Employment Tbnls 1993–2004; memb Legal Aid Bd Ctee 1975–92, Negligence Panel rep for Wolverhampton Area of Law Soc 1982–92; author The Solicitors Notebook for Solicitors Jl 1968–91, ed Handbook for Employment Tribunal Chairmen 1999–2006; chm Bilston Round Table 1974 (memb 1966–77), pres Bilston Rotary Club 1984 and 1985 (memb 1974–93); pres Exec Ctee Old Monmothians 1977 (memb 1966–92); memb Law Soc 1962; *Recreations* watching rugby, shooting, skiing, gardening; *Style—* Allen Rees, Esq; ✉ Rossleigh, Shaw Lane, Albrighton, Wolverhampton WV7 3DS; Yr Hen Ystabl, Meifod, Powys (tel 01902 372423)

REES, Angharad Mary; da of Prof Linford Rees, CBE (d 2004), and Catherine Magdalen, *née* Thomas (d 1993); *b* 16 July 1949; *Educ* Commonwealth Lodge Surrey, Sorbonne Paris, Rose Bruford Drama Coll, Univ of Madrid; *m* 1, 12 Sept 1973 (m dis 1993); 2 s (Linford James de Lerrison b 20 July 1974, Rhys William de Lerrison b 12 Dec 1976); *m* 2, 29 April 2005, Hon David Malcolm McAlpine, s of Baron McAlpine of Moffat (Life Peer, d 1990); *Career* actress; jewellry designer Angharads Shop; *Theatre* incl: A Winter's Tale (Young Vic), Gulliver's Travels (Mermaid), It's a Two Foot Six Inch Above the Ground Word (Wyndhams), John Osborne's A Picture of Dorian Gray (Greenwich), The Millionairess (Haymarket), A Handful of Dust (Lyric Hammersmith), Romeo and Juliet (Watford), Hamlet (Welsh Nat Theatre), Richard II (Redgrave Theatre), An Ideal Husband (Peter Hall Prodn); *Television* for BBC incl: As You Like It, Dennis Potter's Joe's Ark, Dear Brutus, Gathering Storm, Anthony Trollope's The Way We Live Now (series), Poldark (series), Brian Moore's The Temptation of Eileen Hughes, Trainer (series); other credits incl: The Piano Player (YTV), Forgotten Story (series, HTV), Master of the Game (CBS), Close to Home (2 series, LWT); *Film* incl: Under Milk Wood, Moments, the Girl in Blue Velvet, The Love Bug; *Awards* nominated Best Newcomer Award for Moments, nominated Best Actress (Radio) Award 1985; *Style—* The Hon Mrs David McAlpine; ✉ c/o Chatto & Linnit, 123A Kings Road, London SW3 4DL (tel 020 7352 7722); Angharad's Shop, 14 Bulstrode Street, London W1U 2JG

REES, Christopher Wyn; *b* 1955, Wales; *Educ* Christ's Coll Cambridge (MA); *Career* slr specialising in IT law; ptnr Herbert Smith LLP; Herbert Ruse Prizeman 1978; *Publications* Database Law (1998); *Recreations* tennis, skiing, singing; *Clubs* Hurlingham, MCC; ✉ Herbert Smith LLP, Exchange House, Primrose Street, London EC2A 2HS (tel 020 7374 8000)

REES, Sir David Allan (Dai); kt (1993); *b* 28 April 1936, Silloth, Cumbria; *Educ* UCNW Bangor (BSc, PhD), Univ of Edinburgh (DSc), Sloan Sch of Industrial Mgmnt (Sr Execs Prog); *m* 1959, Myfanwy Margaret, *née* Parry Owen; 2 s, 1 da; *Career* lectr in chemistry Univ of Edinburgh 1960–70, visiting prof of biochemistry Univ of Wales Cardiff 1972–77, various positions rising to princ scientist and sci policy exec Unilever Research Colworth Lab Sharnbrook Bedford 1970–82, pt/t dir MRC Cell Biophysics Unit KCL 1980–82, dir Nat Inst for Med Res 1982–87, chief exec MRC 1987–96 (memb Cncl 1983–96, fndr dir MRC Collaborative Centre Mill Hill 1983–86); memb: LINK Steering Gp 1987–89, Advsy Bd for Res Cncls 1987–93, Ctee for the Euro Devpt of Sci and Technol (CODEST) 1991–94, Advsy Bd Forensic Scis Serv Agency 1992–, Euro Sci and Technol Assembly (ESTA) and Bureau 1994–; chm Euro Med Res Cncls 1990–94, vice-pres Fondation Louis Jeantet de Medicine 1991–1996, pres Euro Sci Fndn 1994–1999; Carbohydrate Chemistry Award Chemical Soc 1970, Colworth Medal Biochemical Soc 1970; Hon DSc: Edinburgh 1989, Wales 1991, Stirling Univ 1995, Leicester 1997; Hon DUniv York 2007; FRSC 1975, FRS 1981 (Philips lecture 1984, memb Cncl 1985–87), FIBiol 1983; Hon FRCP 1986, hon fell UCNW 1988, FKC 1989, FRCPEd 1998; *Publications* numerous res pubns in learned jls on polysaccharide biochemistry and biophysics, cell surface interactions and on sci policy; *Style—* Sir Dai Rees, FRS; ✉ Ford Cottage, 1 High Street, Denford, Kettering, Northamptonshire NN14 4EQ (tel 01832 733502, e-mail drees@nimr.mrc.ac.uk)

REES, Edward Parry; QC (1998); s of Edward Howell Rees (d 1962), and Margaret Rees Rees, *née* Parry; *b* 18 June 1949; *Educ* Howardian HS Cardiff, Cowbridge GS, UCW Aberystwyth (LLB); *m* Kathleen, da of Stanley Wiltshire; 2 c; *Career* called to the Bar 1973; fndr memb Lawyers for Liberty, fndr memb and co-sec Lawyers for Nuclear Disarmament, memb Gen Cncl of the Bar (representative of the Criminal Bar Assoc) 1997–2000; hon fell in Criminal Process Sch of Law Kent Univ; *Publications* Blackstone's Guide to the Proceeds of Crime Act (2002); *Recreations* family and garden; *Style—* Edward Rees, Esq, QC; ✉ Doughty Street Chambers, 11 Doughty Street, London WC1N 2PG (tel 020 7404 1313, fax 020 7404 2283)

REES, Her Hon Judge Eleri Mair; da of Ieuan Morgan (d 1990), and Sarah Alice, *née* James; *b* 7 July 1953; *Educ* Ardwyn GS Aberystwyth, Univ of Liverpool (LLB); *m* 9 Aug 1975, Dr Alan Rees; *Career* called to the Bar Gray's Inn 1975; clerk to the Justices Bexley Magistrates' Court 1983–94, metropolitan stipendary magistrate (subsequently dist judge (Magistrates' Court)) 1994–2002, recorder 1997–2002, circuit judge (Wales & Chester Circuit) 2002–; ed Family Court Reporter 1992–94; memb Cncl Univ of Wales Cardiff 2002–; *Recreations* travel, cookery, skiing; *Style—* Her Hon Judge Rees; ✉ c/o Wales and Chester Circuit Office, 2nd Floor, Churchill House, Churchill Way, Cardiff CF10 2HH

REES, Gareth Mervyn; s of Joseph Rees (d 1981), of Llangadog, Wales, and Gwen Rees (d 1988); *b* 30 September 1935; *Educ* Llandovery HS, St Mary's Hosp Univ of London (MB BS, MS); *m* 1, 1962 (m dis 1968), Anne Frisby Richards; 1 s (Philip b 1964); *m* 2, 1969, Prof Dame Lesley Rees, DBE, *qv*, da of Howard Leslie Davis (d 1942); *Career* house surgn and house physician St Mary's Hosp 1960, int res fell Dept of Heart Surgery Univ of Oregon Portland 1970; St Bartholomew's Hosp London: conslt heart surgn 1973–2000, conslt i/c Dept of Cardio-thoracic Surgery 1984–2000, sr surgeon St Bartholomew's Hosp 1996–2000, emeritus cardio-thoracic surgeon 2000–; conslt cardiac surgeon Harley Street Clinic; memb: Cardiac Soc, Int Coll of Surgns, Assoc of Thoracic Surgns UK; author of numerous scientific papers on subjects related to heart and lung surgery in specialist jls; FRCS 1966, FRCP 1983; *Recreations* fishing, skiing, rugby football; *Clubs* Garrick, Llandovery RFC; *Style—* Gareth Rees, Esq; ✉ 23 Church Row, Hampstead, London NW3 6UP; Loc Ceppatelli, Via Ceppatelli 51, Orbicciano, Camaiore 55041, Lucca, Italy

REES, Geoffrey; CBE (2003); s of Sidney Rees (d 1996), of Neath, W Glamorgan, and Mary, *née* Thomas (d 1981); *b* 28 February 1946; *Educ* Neath Boys' GS, St Luke's Coll Univ of Exeter (RFC, Devon RFC, Neath RFC), Emmanuel Coll Cambridge (Rugby blue, capt CURUFC, London Welsh RFC, Middx RFC); *m* June 1974, Diana Jane, da of Peter Wride; 1 da (Rebecca Jane b Aug 1976), 1 s (Gareth Thomas b Jan 1978); *Career* asst history master Shene Boys' Sch Richmond 1969–71, history master and house tutor Eastbourne Coll 1974–76, head of humanities and head of sixth form Billericay Sch 1976–79, dir of studies Coombe Dean Sch Plymouth 1979–82, dep princ Bideford Community Coll 1982–85, headmaster Burrington Sch Plymouth 1985–87, princ Ivybridge Sports and Community Coll (formerly Ivybridge Community Coll) 1987–; chm Devon Science and Technol Regnl Orgn 1988–90; educn liaison offr IOD 1991–97; chm Devon Assoc of Secdy Heads 1992–94, vice-chm Devon Educn Business Partnership Cncl 1992–93; memb: Devon and Cornwall TEC Strategic Educn Forum 1993–95, SW Regl Cncl FEFC 1998–2000, Bd of Devon and Cornwall LSC 2001–; govr: Coll of St Mark and St John Plymouth 1998–2006, Univ of Plymouth 1999–2006; memb NAHT 1988–; FRSA 1994; *Recreations* rugby, sailing, surfing, theatre, travel; *Clubs* Welsh Academicals RFC, London Welsh RFC, Hawks' (Cambridge); *Style—* Geoffrey Rees, Esq, CBE; ✉ Ivybridge Sports and Community College, Harford Road, Ivybridge, Devon PL21 0JA (tel 01752 691000/896662, fax 01752 691247, e-mail grees@ivybridge.devon.sch.uk)

R

REES, Dr Helene Ceredwyn; da of Delwyn Garland Rees, of South Yarra, Victoria, Aust, and Jean Helene, *née* Höette; *b* 8 April 1948; *Educ* Presbyterian Ladies Coll Melbourne Aust, Univ of Melbourne (MB BS), LLB 1996; *m* 1, 17 Dec 1971 (m dis 1984), David Alan McDonald, s of Alan McDonald; 2 s (Lachlan James b 11 March 1974, Alexander Rhys b 25 April 1980), 1 da (Kate Helene b 17 July 1975); m 2, 4 May 1991, Dr Christopher Daking Macfarlane Drew, s of late Sir Robert Drew, KCB, CBE; *Career* annual appts in gen med and surgery in maj teaching hosps in Melbourne 1972–73, in trg in pathology Melbourne Aust 1973–81 (The Royal Children's Hosp, Fairfield Infectious Diseases Hosp, Alfred Hosp, Prince Henry's Hosp), sr registrar in histopathology Hammersmith Hosp 1984–86 (registrar 1981–84), sr lectr and hon conslt in histopathology St Bartholomew's Hosp Med Coll 1986–94, pathologist Farrer-Brown Histopathology 1994–99, conslt histopathologist Hammersmith Hosps NHS Tst 1999–2003, conslt anatomical pathologist Royal Hobart Hosp 2004–; memb: Kew Soc, Hunterian Soc 1984, Graduate Union of Univ of Melbourne 1980, Soc of Doctors in Law 1993; vice-pres Med Soc of London 1990–91 (fell 1984); Freeman City of London 1986, Liveryman Worshipful Soc of Apothecaries 1989 (Yeoman 1985); FRCPA (Aust) 1980, FRCPath 1996 (MRCPath 1984); *Recreations* gymnastics, golf, classical music; *Clubs* Hogarth, Overstone Golf; *Style—* Dr Helene Rees; ✉ c/o Department of Anatomical Pathology, Royal Hobart Hospital, Liverpool Street, Hobart 7001, Tasmania

REES, John Charles; QC (1991); s of Ronald Leslie Rees (d 1985), of Cardiff, and Martha Terese, *née* Poole; *b* 22 May 1949; *Educ* St Joseph's Sch Cardiff, St Illtyd's Coll Cardiff, Jesus Coll Cambridge (McNair Scholar, MA, LLM, Russell Vick prize, Boxing blue); *m* 30 July 1970, Dianne Elizabeth, da of William Kirby, of Cardiff; 3 s (Christopher Lloyd b 26 Nov 1973, Jonathan Elystan b 27 Feb 1977, William Ronald b 7 Nov 1987), 1 da (Felicity Ann Rose b 21 Aug 1980); *Career* called to the Bar Lincoln's Inn 1972; steward Br Boxing Bd of Control (chm Welsh Area Cncl); tstee and govr St John's Coll Cardiff; *Recreations* reading, music, sport (especially football and boxing); *Clubs* Hawks' (Cambridge); *Style—* John Rees, Esq, QC; ✉ Marleigh Lodge, Druidstone Road, Old St Mellons, Cardiff, South Glamorgan CF3 9XD (tel 029 2079 4918); 33 Park Place, Cardiff, South Glamorgan CF1 3BA (tel 029 2023 3313)

REES, Canon (Vivian) John Howard; s of Herbert John Rees, and Beryl, *née* Thomas; *b* 21 April 1951, Eastbourne, Sussex; *Educ* Skinners' Sch Tunbridge Wells, Univ of Southampton (LLB), Coll of Law London, Wycliffe Hall Oxford (MA), Univ of Leeds (MPhil); *m* 17 May 1980, Dianne Elizabeth, *née* Hamilton; 2 da (Katherine Elizabeth b 20 May 1987, Rebecca Frances Anne b 29 Oct 1989); *Career* admitted slr 1975; Cooke Matheson & Co 1975–76; ordained deacon Ripon Dio 1979, priest 1980; curate Moor Allerton Team Miny 1979–82, chaplain and tutor Sierra Leone Theological Hall Freetown 1983–85; slr and ptnr Winckworth Sherwood 1986–; registrar: Oxford Dio 1988–, Province of Canterbury 2000–, Clergy Discipline Tbnl 2006–; treas Ecclesiastical Law Soc 1995–, legal advsr Anglican Consultative Cncl 1998–, vice-chair Legal Advsy Cmmn C of E 2001–; provincial canon Canterbury Cathedral 2001–; memb Law Soc 1975; *Recreations* walking, second-hand bookshops; *Style—* Canon John Rees; ✉ 36 Cumnor Hill, Oxford OX2 9HB (tel 01865 865875, e-mail vjhrees@btinternet.com); Winckworth Sherwood, 16 Beaumont Street, Oxford OX1 2LZ (tel 01865 297214, fax 01865 726274, e-mail jrees@winckworths.co.uk)

REES, Jonathan Nigel; s of Arthur Ernest Rees (d 1990), and Thelma Maureen, *née* Scott; *b* 29 September 1955; *Educ* Jesus Coll Oxford (MA); *m* 1 Sept 1996, Kathryn Jayne, da of Wilfred Taylor; 1 da (Elizabeth Margaret b 2000), 1 s (Nicholas John b 2002); *Career* with DTI 1977–81, private sec to min for Trade 1981–84, with EC 1984–86, with DTI 1986–89, industry cnsllr UK rep to the EU 1989–94, with DTI 1994, memb PM's Policy Unit 1994–97, dir Citizen's Charter Unit Cabinet Office 1997–2000, dir consumer and competition policy DTI 2000–04, dep ceo (policy) HSE 2004–; *Recreations* sport, travel, theatre; *Clubs* MCC; *Style—* Jonathan Rees, Esq

REES, Laurence Mark; s of Alan Rees (d 1973), and Julia, *née* Mark (d 1977); *b* 19 January 1957; *Educ* Solihull Sch, Worcester Coll Oxford (BA); *m* 1987, Helena, *née* Brewer; 3 c; *Career* BBC TV: research trainee 1978–79, researcher 1979–81, dir and prodr 1982–92, ed Timewatch 1992–2003 (winner of 3 Emmy Awards as exec prodr for various historical documentaries 1993–95), creative dir BBC TV History progs 2000–; researcher Man Alive and That's Life 1979–81, dir Holiday 1982, writer and prodr 40 Minutes 1984–88, prodr and dir Clive James 1988–90, writer and prodr A British Betrayal 1990, writer and prodr History of Propaganda - We Have Ways of Making You Think 1992, exec prodr Remember Season on Anniversary Liberation of Auschwitz 1995, writer, dir and prodr The Nazis - A Warning From History 1997 (Broadcast Critics Award 1997, Broadcast Magazine Award 1997, George Foster Peabody Award 1997, Best Factual Series BAFTA 1997), writer and prodr War of the Century 1999, writer and prodr Horror in the East 2000, writer and prodr Auschwitz: the Nazis and the Final Solution 2005; Hon DLitt Univ of Sheffield 2005; *Books* Electric Beach (1990), Selling Politics (1992), The Nazis - A Warning From History (1997), War of the Century (1999), Horror in the East (2001), Auschwitz: the Nazis and the Final Solution (2005); *Recreations* my three children; *Style—* Laurence Rees, Esq

REES, Prof Dame Lesley Howard; DBE (2001); da of Howard Leslie Davis (d 1942), and Charlotte Patricia Siegrid, *née* Young (d 1960); *b* 17 November 1942; *Educ* Pate's Girls' GS Cheltenham, Malvern Girls' Coll, Bart's Med Coll (MB BS, MD, DSc); *m* 21 Dec 1969, Gareth Mervyn Rees, *qv*, s of Joseph Philip Rees; *Career* ed Clinical Endocrinology 1979–84, public orator Univ of London 1984–86, sub dean Bart's Med Coll 1983–87, chm Soc for Endocrinology 1984–87, sec gen Int Soc for Endocrinology 1984–, prof of chem endocrinology Bart's Med Coll, dean Bart's Med Coll 1989–95; dir Int Office and dir of educn Royal Coll of Physicians (London) 1997–2001; Hon DSc: Univ of Ulster, City Univ; FRCP 1979, FRCPath 1988; *Books* author numerous papers on endocrinology; *Recreations* reading, music, art, skiing, cooking; *Style—* Prof Dame Lesley Rees, DBE; ✉ 23 Church Row, Hampstead, London NW3 6UP (tel and fax 020 7794 4936, e-mail lesleyrees@waitrose.com)

REES, Prof Michael Ralph; *b* 19 April 1950; *Educ* Shene GS, UEA (BSc), Univ of Sheffield (MB ChB, Herbert Price Prize (jtly)), DMRD; *m* Ann; 2 da (Joanna, Jennifer); *Career* jr hosp appts Royal Infirmary and Royal Hallamshire and Northern Gen Hosps Sheffield 1976–79, sr registrar in radiology Sheffield Area and Trent Regnl Trg Scheme 1981–83 (registrar 1979–81), sr registrar in cardiac radiology Northern Gen Hosp Sheffield 1983–84, consIt cardiac radiologist Killingbeck Regnl Cario-thoracic Unit and St James Univ Hosp Leeds 1984–93, prof of radiological science Keele Univ Sch of Postgrad Med and conslt in cardiovascular intervention N Staffordshire Hosp Stoke-on-Trent 1993–95, prof of clinical radiology Univ of Bristol 1995–2005, prof of vascular studies Univ of Wales Bangor 2005–, head of Sch of Medical Sciences Univ of Wales Bangor 2007; res fell/assoc Dept of Radiology and Cardiology Univ of Iowa 1984–85, res assoc in cardiac imaging Deborah Heart & Lung Centre NJ 1985, prof of radiology and med (cardiology) Stanford Univ 1992–93; visiting prof Univ of Ioannina 1996–; chm: Nat Hosp Jr Staff Ctee 1979–84, Jr Membs Forum BMA 1982–83, Non Trust Hosps Gp Med Ctee 1991–93; elected memb GMC 1984–89; BMA: memb 1976, memb Cncl 1979–84 and 2003–, memb Leeds Exec Ctee 1986–88, memb Med Academic Staff Ctee 1995– (also chm), memb Central Conslts Staff Ctee 1996–, memb Negotiating Sub-Ctee 1996–, chm Med Academic Staff Ctee 2000–; memb: American Med Assoc 1985–86, Radiological Soc of N America 1985, Br Cardiac Soc 1986, Br Cardiovascular Intervention Soc 1987 (memb Cncl 1992–), Br Interventional Radiology Soc 1988, Cardiovascular Cncl American Heart Assoc 1988, Br Med Laser Assoc 1989 (memb Cncl 1990–), Cardiovascular and Interventional Radiology Soc of Europe 1990 (memb Membership Ctee 1993–99), European Med Laser Assoc 1992, Int Soc of Endovascular Surgery 1993, RSM 1993, Forum on Angiology 1993, BMA Bd of Science 1999–2003, Jt Conslts Ctee 2003–06, Nat Inst for Health Faculty Implementation Gp 2006; vice-pres European Soc Cardiac Radiology 2005– (sec 1999–2005), chm Cardiac Ctee European Soc of Radiology 2007; PhD (hc) Univ of Ioannina (Greece) 2006 fell: Int Coll of Angiology 1988, American Coll of Angiology 1992; FRCPEd, FRCR; *Publications* author of various book chapters and numerous articles in academic jls; *Style—* Prof Michael Rees; ✉ Room 184, Brigantia Building, Clinical School, Penrallt Road, Bangor, Gwynedd LL57 2AS (e-mail m.rees@bangor.ac.uk)

REES, Morgan Alexander; s of Richard Rees, and Guity Saadat; *b* 8 November 1974, Southampton, Hants; *Educ* Cleeve Sch Cheltenham, Cardiff Univ; *Career* magazine ed; editorial asst Loaded 1994–97, commissioning ed GQ 1997–2000, assoc ed Jack 2000–01, dep ed Maxim 2001–03, ed/ed-in-chief Men's Health 2003–; New Ed of the Year BSME 2004, Ed of the Year Rodale Pubns 2005 and 2006, Men's Magazine's Ed of the Year BSME 2006, Ed of the Year PPA 2007, Rodale Pubns Edition of the Year 2007; memb BSME; *Recreations* surfing, kickboxing, Asain cinema, contemporary US literary fiction, architecture; *Style—* Morgan Rees, Esq; ✉ The National Magazine Company, 33 Broadwick Street, London W1F 0DQ (tel 020 7339 4400, e-mail morgan.rees@natmag-rodale.co.uk)

REES, Nigel Thomas; s of (John Cedric) Stewart Rees (d 1989), and Frances Adeline, *née* Gleave (d 1982); *b* 5 June 1944; *Educ* Merchant Taylors' Crosby, New Coll Oxford (Trevelyan scholar, MA); *m* 6 May 1978, Susan Mary, da of Jack Bates (d 1962); *Career* radio and TV presenter, author, actor, guest speaker, lectr; BBC Radio 4: Today 1976–78, The Burkiss Way 1976–80, Quote...Unquote 1976–, Stop Press 1984–86; ITV: Amoebas to Zebras 1985–87, Challenge of the South 1987–88; pres Johnson Soc 2006–07; *Books* Quote...Unquote (3 vols 1978–83), Graffiti (5 vols 1978–86), Why do We Say...? (1987), The Newsmakers (1987), Talent (1988), A Family Matter (1989), Dictionary of Popular Phrases (1990), Dictionary of Phrase and Allusion (1991), Best Behaviour (1992), Politically Correct Phrasebook (1993), Epitaphs (1993), As We Say In Our House (1994), Phrases and Sayings (1995), Cassell Dictionary of Clichés (1996), Dictionary of Slogans (1997), Cassell Companion to Quotations (1997), Cassell Dictionary of Anecdotes (1999), Cassell's Movie Quotations (2000), Cassell's Humorous Quotations (2001), A Word in Your Shell-like (2004), Cassell's Dictionary of Catchphrases (2005), Brewer's Famous Quotations (2006), A Man About a Dog (2006), All Gong and No Dinner (2007); *Recreations* listening to music, swimming; *Style—* Nigel Rees, Esq; ✉ 7 Hillgate Place, London W8 7SL (e-mail nigel.rees@btinternet.com)

REES, Owen; CB (1991); s of John Trevor Rees (d 1970), and Esther (d 1977), *née* Phillips; *b* 26 December 1934; *Educ* Llanelli GS, Univ of Manchester (BA); *m* 17 May 1958, Elizabeth (d 1991), da of Harold Frank Gosby (d 1955); 1 s (David), 2 da (Philippa, Helen); *Career* HM Civil Serv (ret); Bd of Trade 1959–69, Cabinet Office 1969–71; Welsh Office 1971–94: head Euro Div Welsh Office 1972–75, sec for Welsh Educn 1977–78, head Educn Dept 1978–80, dir Indust Dept 1980–85, head Econ and Regnl Policy Gp 1985–90, head Agriculture Dept 1990–94; dep chm Qualifications, Curriculum and Assessment Authy for Wales 1997–2006; *Style—* Owen Rees, Esq, CB; ✉ 4 Llandennis Green, Cyncoed, Cardiff CF23 6JX

REES, Paul; s of David Rees, of Wombourne, W Midlands, and Pauline, *née* Young; *b* 14 November 1967, West Bromwich; *Educ* Ounsdale HS Wombourne, Crewe and Alsager Coll (BA); *m* 14 Dec 2002, Denise Jeffrey; 1 s (Tom b 4 Jan 2005); *Career* journalist; Brumbeat 1991–92, Raw 1992–94; ed: Kerrang! 1999–2002 (joined 1995), Q 2002–; Specialist Consumer Magazine of the Year PPA Awards 2001; *Style—* Paul Rees, Esq; ✉ Q, Mappin House, 4 Winsley Street, London W1W 8HF (tel 020 7182 8000, fax 020 7182 8547, e-mail paul.rees@emap.com)

REES, Peter John; s of Leslie Marchant Rees, of St Florence, Dyfed, and Betty, *née* Bass; *b* 21 April 1957; *Educ* Baines Sch Poulton-le-Fylde, Downing Coll Cambridge (MA), Nottingham Trent Univ (MBA); *m* 20 August 1999, Nicola Jane, da of Dr John P Mumford, of Staverton, Northants; 1 da from previous m (Megan b 7 May 1988); *Career* admitted slr 1981; ptnr Norton Rose 1987–2006, ptnr Debevoise & Plimpton LLP 2006–; memb IBA (former chm Int Construction Projects Ctee), former chm Technology and Construction Slrs Assoc, dep sec-gen IBA UK and Ireland; Freeman Worshipful Co of Slrs; memb: RHS, Law Soc; hon memb: Assoc of Fells and Legal Scholars Center, Bd of Advsrs for Int Legal Studies; chartered arbitrator, ADR accredited mediator, TeCSA accredited adjudicator; FCIArb (chm Practice and Standards Ctee, memb Bd of Mgmnt); *Books* Jurisdiction and Judgments (1993, 4 edn 2005); *Recreations* association football, golf, scuba diving, theatre, gardening; *Clubs* Hawks' (Cambridge), Staverton Park Golf; *Style—* Peter J Rees, Esq; ✉ Debevoise & Plimpton LLP, Tower 42, Old Broad Street, London EC2N 1HQ (tel 020 7786 9000, fax 020 7588 4180)

REES, Baron (Life Peer UK 1987), of Goytre in the County of Gwent; Peter Wynford Innes Rees; PC (1983), QC (1969); s of Maj-Gen Thomas Wynford Rees, CB, CIE, DSO, MC, Indian Army (d 1959), of Goytre Hall, Abergavenny, and Rosalie, da of Sir Charles Alexander Innes, KCSI, CIE (d 1966); *b* 9 December 1926; *Educ* Stowe, ChCh Oxford; *m* 1969, Mrs Anthea Peronelle Wendell, da of late Maj Hugh John Maxwell Hyslop, Argyll & Sutherland Highlanders; *Career* served Scots Gds 1945–48; called to the Bar Inner Temple 1953, bencher; practised Oxford circuit; contested (Cons): Abertillery 1964 and 1965, Liverpool, West Derby, 1966; MP (Cons): Dover 1970–74, Dover and Deal 1974–83, Dover 1983–87; PPS to Solicitor-Gen 1972, min of state HM Treasury 1979–81, min for Trade 1981–83, chief sec to Treasury and memb Cabinet 1983–85; former memb: Ct and Cncl Museum of Wales, Museum and Galleries Cmmn; former chm CLM plc and dir various other companies; Liveryman Worshipful Co of Clockmakers; *Clubs* Boodle's, Beefsteak, White's, Pratt's; *Style—* The Rt Hon the Lord Rees, PC, QC; ✉ Goytre Hall, Abergavenny, Monmouthshire NP7 9DL; 39 Headfort Place, London SW1X 7DE

REES, Peter Wynne; s of Gwynne Rees, of Virginia Water, Surrey, and late Elizabeth Rodda, *née* Hynam; *b* 26 September 1948; *Educ* Pontardawe GS, Whitchurch GS, Bartlett Sch of Architecture, UCL (BSc), Welsh Sch of Architecture, Univ of Wales (BArch), Poly of the South Bank (BTP); *Career* architectural asst Historic Buildings Div GLC 1971–72, asst to Gordon Cullen CBE 1973–75, architect Historic Areas Conservation Div DOE 1975–79, asst chief planning offr Borough of Lambeth 1979–85; Corp of London: controller of planning 1985–87, city planning offr 1987–; tstee Bldg Conservation Tst 1987–91, fndr memb and dir Br Cncl for Offices; life memb: SPAB, Nat Tst; President's Award Br Cncl for Offices 2003, Barbara Miller Award Faculty of Building 2004; Freeman City of London 1985; memb: RIBA 1975, FRTPI 1982, FRSA 1988; *Publications* City of London Unitary Development Plan; author of various technical planning pubns and contribs to professional jls; *Recreations* swimming, Nordic skiing, playing the viola, music, tidying; *Style—* Peter Wynne Rees, Esq; ✉ City Planning Officer, Corporation of London, PO Box 270, Guildhall, London EC2P 2EJ (tel 020 7332 1700, fax 020 7332 1806)

REES, Philip; s of John Trevor Rees, of Ebbw Vale, Gwent, and Olwen Muriel, *née* Jones (d 1982); *b* 1 December 1941; *Educ* Monmouth, Univ of Bristol (LLB); *m* 6 Aug 1969, Catherine, da of Joseph Stephen Good, of Cardiff; 1 s (David Stephen b 27 Aug 1970), 1 da (Siân Catrin b 1 Oct 1973); *Career* called to the Bar 1965, recorder of the Crown Court 1983–; asst boundary cmmr; *Recreations* music, sport; *Clubs* Cardiff and County; *Style—* Philip Rees, Esq; ✉ 35 South Rise, Llanishen, Cardiff CF10 5RF (tel 029 2075 4364); 9 Park Place, Cardiff CF1 3DP (tel 029 2038 2731, fax 029 2022 542)

REES, Prof Philip Howell; CBE (2004); s of Foster Rees (d 2004), and Mona, *née* Howell (d 1995); *b* 17 September 1944; *Educ* King Edward's Sch Birmingham, St Catharine's Coll Cambridge (MA), Univ of Chicago (MA, PhD); *m* 1968, Laura, da of Edward C Campbell; 1 s (Gareth David b 19 June 1971), 1 da (Chloe b 16 March 1974); *Career* Univ of Leeds: lectr 1970–80, reader 1980–90, prof 1990–; Hofstee visiting fell NIDI The Hague 1995, distinguished visiting fell Univ of Adelaide 1996; co-ordinator ESRC/JISC Census Prog 1992–97 and 1998–2002; Gill Meml Award RGS 1996; FRGS 1970; FBA 1998; *Books* Spatial Population Analysis (1977), Residential Patterns in American Cities (1979), Population Structures and Models (1985), Migration Processes & Patterns (vol 2, 1992), Population Migration in the European Union (1996), The Determinants of Migration Flows in England (1998), Internal Migration and Regional Population Dynamics in Europe (1999), The Census Data System (2002); *Recreations* walking; *Style*— Prof Philip Rees, CBE, FBA; ✉ 8 Moseley Wood Gardens, Cookridge, Leeds LS16 7HR (tel 0113 267 6968); School of Geography, University of Leeds, Leeds LS2 9JT (tel 0113 343 3341, fax 0113 343 3308, e-mail p.h.rees@leeds.ac.uk)

REES, Robert (Rob); MBE (2006); s of Stephen Rees, and Gillian, *née* Chambers; *b* 28 June 1968, Ilford, Essex; *Educ* Forest Sch, Westminster Coll (Dip Catering); *m* 6 Dec 2002, Renata, *née* Petruv; 1 s (Jack William b 9 Dec 2005), 1 da (Madeleine Rose b 30 April 2007); *Career* chef; various positions 1987–: Le Gavroche, Bath Spa Hotel, Royal Crescent Hotel, Hyatt Grand Cayman, Circus, Splinter; dir: Country Elephant Ltd 1994–2007, Taste of West 2004–06, Rob Rees Ltd, The Cotswold Chef Ltd; chief exec Wiggly Worm Ltd; dir Stroud Mid Glos Educn Business Partnership, gen govr British Nutrition Fndn 2002–, chm Kraft Cares Health 4 Schools 2004–; food conslt and ambass Glos Food Vision; memb Bd: Food Standards Agency 2000–04, Meat Hygiene Ctee 2000–04, Sch Food Tst 2005–, England Mktng Advsy Bd; memb: Cotswold Area of Outstanding Natural Beauty (AONB) Conservation Bd 2004–06; freelance journalist for pubns incl: Cotswold Life, Citizen, BBC Gloucestershire; tstee Glos Co Assoc Blind 2004–06; supporter Sense; *Awards* Egon Ronay Star 1989, 2 AA Rosettes 1995–99, Michelin Bibendum 1999; *Recreations* watching Arsenal FC, music, travel, food; *Style*— Rob Rees, Esq, MBE; ✉ Rob Rees Ltd, Osborne Cottage, Far Oakridge, Gloucestershire GL6 7PF (tel 01285 760170, mobile 07767 842568, e-mail info@robrees.com)

REES, Simon John; s of Dan Rees, of Epsom, Surrey, and Margaret May Rose, *née* Stephenson; *b* 7 July 1960; *Educ* Kingston GS; *m* 18 Aug 1984, Gillian Gaye, da of Kenneth Horne; 1 s (Jonathan Charles b 24 Nov 1987), 1 da (Charlotte Emma b 2 Oct 1989); *Career* media asst rising to TV buyer D'Arcy McManus & Masius 1978–81, sr planner/buyer Colman and Partners 1982–86 (TV buyer 1981–82); TMD Carat Advertising: sr TV buyer 1986–88, TV mangr then assoc dir 1988, broadcast dir and memb Bd 1989, head of Carat TV (UK) 1990–98, dep md 1995–98; MindShare (WPP jt media op of O&M and J Walter Thompson): UK md 1998–2001, ceo 2001–02; ceo Simon Rees Consultancy Ltd 2003–, ceo FiftyLessons 2004, ptnr ReInventive LLP, fndr dir Digital Planet Ltd 2006; tstee Basic Needs 2006; fell: Acad of Chief Execs, Leaders Quest India and South Africa; MIPA, FRGS, FRSA; *Sporting Achievements* schoolboy hockey int (England) 1976–78, 96 full int caps hockey (indoor and field) Wales 1979–90; *Recreations* running, cycling, swimming, mountaineering, walking, golf, hockey (also hockey coach); *Clubs* Southgate Hockey (various League and Cup Winner medals), Berkshire Triathlon Squad; *Style*— Simon Rees, Esq

REES-MOGG, Baron (Life Peer UK 1988), of Hinton Blewitt in the County of Avon; William Rees-Mogg; kt (1981); s of late Edmund Fletcher Rees-Mogg, JP, of Cholwell House, Somerset, and Beatrice, da of Daniel Warren, of New York State, USA; *b* 14 July 1928; *Educ* Charterhouse, Balliol Coll Oxford (MA, pres Oxford Union); *m* 1962, Gillian Shakespeare, yr da of Thomas Richard Morris, JP, Mayor of St Pancras 1962; 3 da (Hon Emma Beatrice b 1962, Hon Charlotte Louise b 1964, Hon Annunziata Mary b 1979), 2 s (Hon Thomas Fletcher b 1966, Hon Jacob William b 1969); *Career* Financial Times: joined 1952, chief ldr writer 1955–60, asst ed 1957–60; Sunday Times: city ed 1960–61, political and economic ed 1961–63, dep ed 1964–67; ed The Times 1967–81, memb Exec Bd Times Newspapers Ltd 1968–81, dir The Times 1968–81, dir Times Newspapers Ltd 1978–81; columnist: The Times 1992–, Mail on Sunday 2004–; chm: Pickering & Chatto (Publishers) Ltd 1983–, Sidgwick & Jackson 1985–88, Sinclair-Stevenson Ltd 1989–92, IBC Group plc 1993–98, Fleet Street Publications Ltd 1995–; dir: GEC plc 1981–97, M&G Group 1987–94, The Private Bank and Trust Co (now EFG Private Bank Ltd) 1993–2005, Value Realisation Trust plc 1996–99; vice-chm Bd of Govrs BBC 1981–86; chm: Arts Cncl of GB 1982–88, Broadcasting Standards Cncl 1988–93; pres: Inst of Journalists 1963–64, English Assoc 1983–84, Thorney Island Soc 1992–; High Sheriff Somerset 1978; *Books* An Humbler Heaven (1977), The Reigning Error: The Crisis of World Inflation (1974), Blood in the Streets (with Jim Davidson, 1987), The Great Reckoning (with Jim Davidson, 1991), Picnics on Vesuvius (1992), The Sovereign Individual (with Jim Davidson, 1997); *Clubs* Garrick; *Style*— The Rt Hon Lord Rees-Mogg; ✉ 17 Pall Mall, London SW1Y 5LU (tel 020 7242 2241, fax 020 7405 6216)

REES OF LUDLOW, Baron (Life Peer UK 2005), of Ludlow in the County of Shropshire; Prof Sir Martin John Rees; OM (2007), kt (1992); s of Reginald Jackson Rees (d 1994), and (Harriette) Joan, *née* Bett (d 1985); *b* 23 June 1942; *Educ* Shrewsbury, Trinity Coll Cambridge (MA, PhD); *Career* prof Univ of Sussex 1972–73, Plumian prof of astronomy and experimental philosophy Univ of Cambridge 1973–91, dir Cambridge Inst of Astronomy 1977–91, Royal Soc research prof 1992–2003, master Trinity Coll Cambridge 2004–; Astronomer Royal 1995–2005; pres: Royal Astronomical Soc 1992–94, BAAS 1994–95, Royal Soc 2005–; Regents fell Smithsonian Inst Washington 1984–88, visiting prof Harvard Univ, visiting prof Univ of Leicester 2001–; tstee: British Museum 1996–2002, Nat Endowment for Science, Technology and the Arts (NESTA) 1998–2001, Inst for Advanced Study Princeton 1998–, Kennedy Meml Tst 1999–2004, IPPR 2001–, Nat Museums for Science and Industry 2003–; foreign hon memb American Acad of Arts and Scis, memb Pontifical Acad of Scis, memb Academia Europaea; foreign memb: Royal Swedish Acad of Science, Accademia Lincei (Rome), Norwegian Acad of Sciences, Netherlands Acad of Arts & Sciences, Finnish Acad of Arts and Sciences 2003–; Balzan International Prize 1989, Bower Prize for Science Franklin Institute 1998, Gruber Cosmology Prize 2001, Einstein Award for Science 2003, Crafoord Prize Royal Swedish Acad of Science 2005; Hon Freeman Worshipful Co of Clockmakers; Hon DSc: Univ of Sussex, Univ of Uppsala, Keele Univ, Univ of Leicester, Univ of Newcastle, Univ of Copenhagen, Univ of Toronto, Univ of Durham, Univ of Oxford; hon memb: American Philosophical Soc, Russian Acad of Science, US Nat Acad of Scis; fell King's Coll Cambridge 1969–2003, hon prof Imperial Coll London 2001–; hon fell: Indian Acad of Scis 1990–, Trinity Coll Cambridge 1995–, Jesus Coll Cambridge 1996–; FRS, Hon FInstP; Officier de l'Ordre des Arts et des Lettres (France) 1991; *Publications* Gravity's Fatal Attraction (1996), Before the Beginning (1997), Just Six Numbers (1999), New Perspectives in Astrophysical Cosmology (2000), Our Cosmic Habitat (2001), Our Final Century (2003); author of many scientific and general articles; *Recreations* rural pursuits; *Style*— The Rt Hon the Lord Rees, OM, FRS; ✉ c/o Trinity College, Cambridge CB2 1TQ

REES ROBERTS, Tristan William Otway; s of Peter William Rees Roberts (d 1998), of Hants, and Ursula Vivien, *née* McCannell; *b* 11 April 1948; *Educ* Frensham Heights, Farnham GS, Trinity Hall Cambridge (MA, BArch, DipArch); *m* 21 March 1970, Anna Ingelin, da of Edmund George Noel Greaves, of Cambridge; 2 da (Saria Mona Natascha b 1973, Ariana Lucia Katrina b 1979), 1 s (Marcus Lucien Branch b 1975); *Career* architect in private practice with Henry Freeland and Jeremy Lander 1980–; most important cmmns: new court Magdalene Coll Cambridge, library Pembroke Coll Cambridge, library Trinity Hall Cambridge, cmmns at other Cambridge Colls, Glaziers Hall London, Emmaus UK, Temple Bar, Thorpe Hall, Univ of Cambridge; Freeman City of London 1986; *Recreations* painting, massage therapist, hill walking; *Style*— Tristan Rees Roberts, Esq; ✉ 13 Caius Terrace, Glisson Road, Cambridge CB1 2HJ (tel 01223 368101); Freeland Rees Roberts Architects, 25 City Road, Cambridge (tel 01223 366555)

REESE, Dr Alan John Morris; TD (1958, clasps 1964, 1970 and 1976), JP (Middx 1974); s of Joseph Reese (d 1968), of Plymouth, Devon, and Emily, *née* Brand (d 1984); *b* 26 August 1920; *Educ* Plymouth Coll, Bart's Med Coll London (MB BS, MD); *m* 24 Jan 1959, Margaret Denise, da of Ernest George Turner (d 1969), of Battersea, London; 1 da (Victoria (Mrs Crispin Morton) b 1960), 1 s (Charles b 1962); *Career* emergency cmmn RAMC 1945; served: Egypt, Palestine, Cyrenaica, Malta; war substantive Capt 1946, released 1948; TA: Capt 1948, Maj 1953, Lt-Col 1966; T&AVR 1967, Lt-Col RARO; sr registrar in pathology St George's Hosp London 1950–54, lectr in pathology Univ of Bristol 1954–56, sr lectr in pathology Inst of Basic Med Scis Univ of London RCS 1956–82, WHO prof of pathology Univ of Mandalay Burma 1963–64, hon conslt in morbid anatomy Whittington Hosp 1966–82; examiner in pathology: RCS 1973–79, RCSEd 1978–92; called to the Bar Middle Temple 1955; memb Islington Cons Assoc 1960–, contested seats on Islington Borough Cncl, vice-pres Islington S and Finsbury Cons Assoc 1987–2005, contested Lewisham W on ILEA 1986, Cons cncllr and chm Health Ctee Met Borough of St Pancras 1959–62; memb Senate Univ of London 1974–83; govr Godolphin & Latymer Sch 1976–85; Freeman City of London 1943, Liveryman Worshipful Soc of Apothecaries 1948 (Yeoman 1943–48); LMSSA 1943, FRCPath 1968 (MRCPath 1963); OStJ 1974; *Books* The Principles of Pathology (2 edn, 1981); *Recreations* fishing; *Clubs* Army and Navy; *Style*— Dr Alan Reese, TD, JP; ✉ 9 Hopping Lane, Canonbury, London N1 2NU (tel 020 7226 2088)

REESE, Prof Colin Bernard; s of Joseph Reese (d 1968), and Emily Reese (d 1984); *b* 29 July 1930; *Educ* Dartington Hall Sch, Clare Coll Cambridge (BA, PhD, MA, ScD); *m* 29 June 1968, Susanne Leslie, da of Joseph Charles Henry Bird (d 1985); 1 da (Lucy b 13 Aug 1970), 1 s (William Thomas b 11 July 1972); *Career* res fell Harvard Univ 1957–58; Univ of Cambridge: res fell Clare Coll 1956–59, univ demonstrator in chemistry 1959–63, official fell and dir of studies in chemistry Clare Coll 1959–73, asst dir of res 1963–64, lectr in chemistry 1964–73; King's Coll London: Daniell prof of chemistry 1973–98, prof emeritus; FRS 1981, FKC 1989; *Style*— Prof Colin Reese, FRS; ✉ 21 Rozel Road, London SW4 0EY (tel 020 7498 0230, e-mail colin.reese@kcl.ac.uk)

REEVE, Dermot Alexander; OBE (1996); s of Alexander James Reeve, and Monica, *née* Reagan; *b* 2 April 1963; *Educ* King George V Sch Kowloon Hong Kong; *m* 1, 20 Dec 1986 (m dis 1992), Julie Lynne, da of Keith Chester; 1 da (Emily Kaye b 14 Sept 1988); *m* 2, 18 July 2002, Fiona, *née* Parkes; *Career* former professional cricketer; TV cricket commentator and analyst Channel 4 1999–; Sussex CCC 1983–87 (awarded county cap 1986); Warks CCC: joined 1988, awarded county cap 1989, vice-capt 1990, capt 1993–96; best bowling 7–37 v Lancs 1987, best batting 202 not out v Northants 1990; played 9 off-seasons in Perth WA; England: memb tour NZ 1992, memb World Cup squad Aust 1992, memb tour to India and Sri Lanka 1992/93, one day ints debut v West Indies 1991, memb squad 7 match one-day int series South Africa 1996; coach Somerset CCC 1997–2000; honours: Hong Kong Cricketer of the Year 1980, Hong Kong Sports Personality of the Year 1980, NatWest Trophy winners Sussex 1986 (Man of the Match award) and Warks 1990 (Man of the Match award, only player to achieve award for different counties in finals), twice W Australian Pennent Cricketer of the Year, League Premiers with Mount Lawley CC 1987 and Claremont Nedlands CC 1990, Benson & Hedges Cup winners Warwickshire 1994 and 1995, Britannic Assurance County Championship winners Warks 1994 and 1995, winners NatWest Trophy Warwickshire 1995 (runners-up 1994), Axa Equity & Law League Champions Warwickshire 1994, awarded Man of the Match Award in 3 Natwest Trophy finals, Wisden Cricketer of the Year 1995, Midlands Sportsman of the Year 1995; Hon DSc Univ of Birmingham 1996; *Recreations* after-dinner speaking, boxing, guitar, golfing holidays, skiing, swimming; *Style*— Dermot Reeve, Esq, OBE; ✉ e-mail dermotreeve@hotmail.com

REEVE, John; s of Clifford Alfred Reeve, and Irene Mary Turnidge Osborne; *b* 13 July 1944; *Educ* Westcliff HS Essex; *m* 2, 21 Dec 1974, Sally Diane, da of Eric Welton; 1 da (Emily Virginia Welton b 27 Jan 1979); *Career* Corporation of Lloyd's 1960–62, Selby Smith & Earle 1962–67, Peat Marwick Mitchell & Co 1967–68, Roneo Vickers Office Equipment Group 1968–76, Wilkinson Match Ltd 1976–77, Amalgamated Metal Corporation Ltd 1977–80, dir of fin British Aluminium Co plc 1980–83, dir of fin Mercantile House Holdings plc 1983–87; Sun Life Corporation plc: joined as dep gp md Sun Life Assurance Society plc 1988, gp md 1989–95, non-exec dir 1995–96; exec chm Willis Group Ltd 1995–2000; currently chm: Temple Bar Investment Trust plc (dir 1992–), ALEA Gp Holdings (Bermuda) Ltd; chm The English Concert 1987–; non-exec dir: HMC Group plc 1988–94, PEC Concerts Ltd, Invest in Thames Gateway London Ltd, Lamarsh Services Ltd, Autologus Transfusion Ltd; govr Research into Ageing 1991–96; pres Inst of Business Ethics 1997–2000 (dep pres 1991–96); chm: East London Partnership 1996– (memb Bd 1991–96), East London Business Alliance 2000–; memb: Cncl Business in the Community, Life Insurance Cncl 1991–94 (memb Bd 1994–95), Bd Assoc of Br Insurers 1993–95, Exec Ctee Int Insurance Soc 1996–2001 (memb Bd 1993–2001), Int Advsy Bd British American Business Cncl 2000–; dir London First 1998–; govr NIESR; FCA 1977 (ACA 1967), CIMgt 1990, FRSA 1999; *Recreations* yachting, music, theatre; *Clubs* Athenaeum, Essex Yacht; *Style*— John Reeve, Esq

REEVE, Michael Arthur Ferard; s of Maj Wilfrid Norman Reeve, OBE, MC (d 1976), of London, and Agnes Bourdon, *née* Ferard; *b* 7 January 1937; *Educ* Eton, UC Oxford (MA); *m* 30 Dec 1970, Charmian Gay, da of David Royden Rooper, of London; 2 s (Hugo b 10 Dec 1973, Luke b 15 Sept 1977); *Career* dir: Elliott Group of Peterborough 1969–83, Charterhouse Bank 1965–74, Copleys Bank 1974–80, Rea Bros 1977–80, Greyhound Bank 1981–87, Collins Collins & Rawlence (Hamptons estate agents) 1982–85, The Tregeare Company Ltd 1981–, Finsbury Growth Trust plc 1991– (chm), Nettleton & Co Ltd 2001–; chm: Close Brothers AIM VCT plc 1998–, Saddleback Corp Ltd 2005–, Silk Road Oil and Gas Ltd 2006–; treas BSES Expeditions Ltd 2003–; chm Airborne Forces Charities 2005; memb: RIIA, The Pilgrims; FCA 1964; *Recreations* gardening, reading; *Clubs* Boodle's; *Style*— Michael Reeve, Esq; ✉ 138 Oakwood Court, London W14 8JS (tel 020 7602 2624)

REEVE, Prof Michael David; s of Arthur Reeve (d 1973), and Edith Mary, *née* Barrett (d 2001); *b* 11 January 1943; *Educ* King Edward's Sch Birmingham, Balliol Coll Oxford (Domus Scholar, Craven Scholar, Hertford Scholar, Ireland Scholar, Gaisford Prize for Greek Verse, Derby Scholar, MA); *m* 4 July 1970 (m dis 1999), Elizabeth Klingaman; 2 s (William Frederick b 23 Sept 1972, Edward Arthur b 19 Jan 1979), 1 da (Hilda Katharine (Mrs A Palmer) b 9 Feb 1976); *Career* Harmsworth sr scholar Merton Coll Oxford 1964–65, Woodhouse research fell St John's Coll Oxford 1965–66, gasthörer Free Univ Berlin 1965–66, fell and lectr in classics Exeter Coll Oxford and CUF lectr in classics Univ of Oxford 1966–84, emeritus fell Exeter Coll Oxford 1984–, Kennedy prof of Latin Univ of Cambridge 1984–2006 (dir of research 2006–07), fell Pembroke Coll Cambridge 1984–; gastprofessor Univ of Hamburg 1976, visiting lectr McMaster Univ 1979, visiting prof Univ of Toronto 1982–83; memb Ed Bd: Materiali e Discussioni 1992–, Revue d'Histoire des Textes 1994–; winner Premio Capitolino Rome 1991; corresponding memb Akademie der Wissenschaften Göttingen 1990–, foreign memb Istituto Lombardo Milan 1993–; FBA 1984; *Publications* Classical Quarterly (jt ed, 1981–86), Cambridge Classical

R

Texts and Commentaries (ed, 1984–), Cambridge Classical Studies (jt ed, 1984–), Pembroke College Gazette (ed, 1992–97); Daphnis & Chloe (ed, 1982), Pro Quinctio (ed, 1992), Vegetius (ed, 2004), Geoffrey of Monmouth (ed, 2007); *Style*— Prof M D Reeve, FBA; ✉ Pembroke College, Cambridge CB2 1RF (tel 01223 338106)

REEVE, Nigel John; s of George Edward Reeve, of Bramford, Suffolk, and Edna May, *née* Chennary; *b* 19 August 1952; *Educ* Everton House Sch Ipswich; *m* 1, 1982 (m dis 1988), Maritje Geertruida, *née* Lamberts, of Haarlem, Holland; m 2, 7 Oct 1988, Lindsay Marion, da of Capt Trevor Maldwyn Jones (d 1973); *Career* admin Eastern Counties Newspapers 1969–76, sales Radio Orwell Ipswich 1976–81, sales mangr Two Counties Radio Bournemouth 1981–83, sales dir County Sound Guildford 1983–85; Invicta Sound: sales dir 1985–87, dep md 1985–88, md 1988–91; conslt Essex Radio 1991–92, sales dir Classic FM 1992–96, md London New Radio (LBC/News Direct) 1996–2000, fndr and chief exec Fusion Radio Hldgs Ltd 2000–; dir: Mellow 1557 Ltd Colchester until 1991, Invicta Continental SARL France until 1991, Radio Advertising Bureau 1994–96, Fusion 107.3FM 2000–, Kestrel FM Ltd 2002–, Kick FM Ltd 2002–, Rugby FM 2002–, Fusion Radio Slaes Ltd; chm: Commercial Radio Creative Awards until 1994, Ind Radio Conf Ctee until 1994, Millenium FM Ltd 2001–, Fusion 107.9FM Ltd 2002–; memb: The Marketing Soc 1994–, Ctee The Radio Festival 1995–96; dir and tstee Invicta Charity for the Disabled of Kent until 1991; *Recreations* golf, soccer (Ipswich Town FC); *Clubs* Chart Hills Golf, Carnegie, Solus; *Style*— Nigel Reeve, Esq

REEVE, Roy Stephen; CMG (1998); s of Ernest Arthur Reeve, of London, and Joan, *née* Thomas; *b* 20 August 1941; *Educ* Dulwich Coll, LSE (BScEcon, MScEcon), Chartered Inst of Secs (postgrad scholar); *m* 6 June 1964, Gill, da of Leslie Lee (d 1993); 2 da (Kirsti Jane b 3 March 1969, Sally Elizabeth b 1 Aug 1971); *Career* HM Customs and Excise 1961–62; HM Dip Serv: joined FCO 1966, third sec Moscow 1968–71, first sec FCO 1973–78, first sec (commercial) Moscow 1978–80, FCO 1980–83, cnsllr on loan to Home Civil Serv 1983–85, dep consul-gen Johannesburg 1985–88, head of Commercial Mgmnt and Export Dept FCO 1988–91, consul-gen Sydney 1991–95, HM ambass Ukraine 1995–1999, ret; head of Mission to Armenia OSCE 1999–2003, ambass and head of OSCE Mission to Georgia 2003–; hon sr res fell Centre for Russian and East European Studies Univ of Birmingham; *Recreations* motorcycling, scuba diving; *Clubs* Union (Sydney); *Style*— Mr Roy Reeve, CMG; ✉ c/o Foreign & Commonwealth Office, King Charles Street, London SW1A 2AH (e-mail roy.reeve@osce.org)

REEVES, Anthony Alan; s of Allen Joseph Reeves, MBE (d 1976), and Alice Turner, *née* Pointon (d 1966); *b* 5 March 1943; *Educ* Hanley HS, Coll of Law; *m* 19 Aug 1967 (m dis 2003), Jane, da of William Thowless (d 1942); 2 da (Rachel b 1969, Ruth b 1974), 1 s (Max b 1972); *Career* admitted slr 1965, sr ptnr KJD (formerly Kent Jones and Done Slrs) 1978–; chm: The Byatt Gp Ltd 1974–79, The CAS Group plc 1985–90, Gresley Brownhills Ltd (formerly Daniel Platt Ltd) 1992–, Domain Dynamics (Holdings) Ltd 2001–03, Epichem Gp Ltd 2005–07 (non-exec); non-exec dir: Steelite International plc 1983–2002, Stoke City FC 1984–85, Bullers plc 1984–86, Butler Woodhouse Ltd 1987–94, David Lean Films Ltd 1997–, John Charcol Holdings Ltd 2006–; sec Waterford Wedgwood Holdings plc 1986; chm of tstees: The Beth Johnson Fndn 1973–, The David Lean Fndn 1997–; chm: Law Soc Sub-Ctee on Coal Mining Subsidence 1985–2005 (memb Law Soc), Keele Univ Devpt Tst 1993–2004; hon legal advsr Br Ceramic Confedn 2000–; memb: Nat Exec Cncl Age Concern 1976–78, N Staffs Med Inst Cncl 1979–82, Cncl Keele Univ 1999–2003; hon life memb BAFTA 2002–; *Recreations* family, field sports, art, ballet, opera, gardening; *Style*— Anthony Reeves, Esq; ✉ KJD, Churchill House, 47 Regent Road, Hanley, Stoke-on-Trent ST1 3RQ

REEVES, Anthony Henry; s of Herbert Henry Reeves (d 1999), and Kathleen Norah Reeves (d 1963); *b* 8 September 1940; *Educ* Sir Walter St Johns; *m* 1972, Jacqueline, da of Herbert Mitchell Newton-Clare, of Edgeworth, Glos; 4 s, 2 da; *Career* former dir Alfred Marks Bureau Ltd, chm and chief exec Lifetime Corp USA (acquired HCC 1986) 1986–93, chm Medic International 1993–96; chief exec Delphi Group Ltd (formerly Computer People Group plc) 1994–2001; chm and ceo: The Hot Gp plc 2001–05, Spur Lodge Ltd 2006–; chm Paystream Accounting Services Ltd 2006–, co-chm Berkeley Scott Gp 2007–; *Recreations* golf, running, cycling; *Clubs* RAC, Royal Wimbledon Golf, Reform, Royal Mid-Surrey Golf; *Style*— Anthony H Reeves, Esq; ✉ Spur Lodge, 142 Upper Richmond Road West, London SW14 8DS (tel 020 8878 4738, e-mail tony.reeves@spurlodgelimited.com)

REEVES, Christopher Reginald; s of Reginald Raymond Reeves (d 1989), and Dora Grace, *née* Tucker (d 1962); *b* 14 January 1936; *Educ* Malvern Coll; *m* June 1965, Stella Jane, da of Cdr Patrick Whinney, of Guernsey; 3 s; *Career* Nat Serv cmmnd Rifle Bde (served Kenya and Malaya) 1955–58; merchant banker; Bank of England 1958–63, Hill Samuel Ltd 1963–67; Morgan Grenfell & Co Ltd: joined 1968, dir 1970, head Banking Div 1972, dep chm and dep chief exec 1975, gp chief exec 1980, jt chm 1984; dep chm and gp chief exec Morgan Grenfell Group plc (formerly Morgan Grenfell Holdings Ltd) 1985–87; Merrill Lynch: sr advsr to pres of Merrill Lynch Capital Markets 1988, vice-chm Merrill Lynch International Ltd 1989–93, chm Merrill Lynch Europe/ME 1993–98, dep chm Merrill Lynch International 1998–99, sr advsr Merrill Lynch Holdings Ltd 1999–; chm MGM Assurance 1999–; dir: Latin America Capital Partners Ltd 1995–2005, India Fund 1998–, India Growth Fund 1998–2003; non-exec dir: Balfour Beatty plc 1982–2003, Allianz Cornhill Insurance Co Ltd 1983–, Oman International Bank 1984–2001, EIH (Oberoi Hotels) 2002–; govr Dulwich Coll Prep Sch until 1999, memb Cncl City Univ 1992–2004 (treas); Hon DSc City Univ; CIMgt; *Recreations* sailing, country sports, skiing; *Clubs* Boodle's, Royal Yacht Sqdn, Royal Southern Yacht, Itchenor Sailing; *Style*— Christopher Reeves, Esq; ✉ 2 King Edward Street, London EC1A 1HQ

REEVES, Colin Leslie; CBE (1999); s of Leslie Reeves, of Warks, and Isabelle; *b* 4 April 1949; *Educ* Birkenhead Sch, Clare Coll Cambridge (MA), Univ of Wales Bangor (MSc, PhD), Liverpool John Moores Univ (CPFA), Cornell Univ (DipBA); *m* Christine, *née* Lloyd; 2 da (Helen Madeleine b 12 Aug 1981, Caroline Georgina b 11 Jan 1984); *Career* lectr Univ of Wales Bangor 1971–73, accountancy and audit asst Warrington Co Borough 1973–75, asst treas Ellesmere Port and Neston Borough Cncl 1975–80, dep dir of fin Stratford-upon-Avon DC 1980–84, dep dir of fin NW Thames RHA 1984–85, dir of fin Paddington and N Kensington DHA 1985–86, regnl dir of fin NW Thames RHA 1986–94, national dir of fin and performance NHS Exec 1994–2001, dir Accountancy Fndn Review Bd 2001–2003, self-employed healthcare conslt 2003–; memb: Advsy Ctee on Mentally Disordered Offenders Dept of Health/Home Office 1993–94, Nat Steering Gp on Capitation 1993–94, Nat Steering Gp on Capital 1993–94, Culyer Ctee on R&D 1993–94, Chllr of Exchequer's Private Finance Panel 1994–95, Butler Ctee on the Review of the Audit Cmmn 1995, Chief Medical Offr's Nat Screening Ctee 1996–2001, Review of the Office of Nat Statistics reporting to HM Treasy 1999, Bd Accountancy Nat Trg Orgn 1999–2001, Co-ordinating Gp on Audit and Accounting Issues DTI/HM Treasy 2002, Consultative Ctee on Review of the Listing Regime FSA 2002; non-exec dir and chm Audit Ctee Oxford Radcliffe Hosps NHS Tst 2005–; hon treas Headway 2002–; *Publications* The Applicability of the Monetary Base Hypothesis to the UK, the USA, France and West Germany (1974), Feasibility Study into the Implementation of a Capital Charges System in Chile (ODA, 1997); regular contrib to various professional jls; *Recreations* sport (especially cricket and golf), history of test match cricket, former regnl int and county hockey player; *Clubs* MCC, RAC, Goring and Streatley Golf, Henley Hawks Rugby Football, Flying Ferrets Golf Soc; *Style*— Dr Colin L Reeves, CBE

REEVES, Rev Donald St John; s of Henry St John Reeves (d 1984), and Barbara Eugn, *née* Rusbridger (d 1967); *b* 18 May 1934; *Educ* Sherborne, Queens' Coll Cambridge (MA); *Career* lectr British Cncl 1957–60, curate All Saints Maidstone 1963–65, domestic chaplain to Bishop of Southwark 1965–68, vicar St Peter's St Helier 1968–80, rector St James's Piccadilly 1980–98, dir The Soul of Europe 1998–; MLitt Univ of Oxford 2003; *Books* Church and State (ed, 1984), For God's Sake (1988), Making Sense of Religion (1989), Down to Earth (1996); *Recreations* playing the organ, gardening, bee-keeping, watching TV soap operas; *Clubs* Athenaeum, Royal Over-Seas League; *Style*— The Rev Donald Reeves; ✉ The Coach House, Church Street, Crediton, Devon EX14 2AQ (tel 01363 775100)

REEVES, Dame Helen May; DBE (1999, OBE 1986); da of Leslie Percival William Reeves (d 1967), and Helen Edith, *née* Brown; *b* 22 August 1945; *Educ* Dartford Girls' GS, Univ of Nottingham; *Career* probation offr then sr probation offr Inner London Probation Serv 1967–79, chief exec Victims Support 1980–2005; vice-pres World Soc of Victimology 1994–2006; chair: European Forum for Victim Servs 1999–2005, Expert Ctee on Victims of Crime and Terrorism Cncl of Europe 2005–; cmmr RSA Risk Cmmn 2006–; Hon MA Univ of Nottingham 1998, Hon LLD Univ of Warwick 2001; FRSA 1991; *Recreations* gardening, food, architecture; *Style*— Dame Helen Reeves, DBE; ✉ e-mail h.reeves@virgin.net

REEVES, Prof Nigel Barrie Reginald; OBE (1987); s of Capt Reginald Arthur Reeves (d 1994), of Battle, E Sussex, and Marjorie Joyce, *née* Pettifer (d 1993); *b* 9 November 1939; *Educ* Merchant Taylors', Worcester Coll Oxford (BA), St John's Coll Oxford (DPhil); *m* 1, 1964 (m dis 1976), Ingrid, *née* Söderberg; 1 s (Dominic Hans Adam b 1968), 1 da (Anna b 1973); m 2, 3 April 1982, Minou, da of Sadegh Samimi (d 1978); *Career* lectr in English Univ of Lund 1964–66, lectr in German Univ of Reading 1968–74, Alexander von Humboldt fell Univ of Tübingen 1974–75, Univ of Hamburg 1986; Univ of Surrey: prof of German 1975–90, head Linguistic and Int Studies Dept 1979–89, dean Faculty of Human Studies 1986–90, dir Surrey Euro Mgmnt Sch 1989–90; Aston Univ: prof of German and head of Languages and Euro Studies Dept 1990–96, pro-vice-chllr 1996–2007; visiting prof and memb Cncl Euro Business Sch London 1983–90; chm Inst of Linguists 1985–88 (vice-pres 1989–); pres: Nat Assoc of Language Advsrs 1986–90, Assoc of Teachers of German 1987–89; vice-pres Conference of Univ Teachers of German 1995–97 (exec vice-pres 1988–91), chm Nat Congress on Languages in Educn 1986–90; memb: Governing Bd Inst of Germanic Studies Univ of London 1989–94, Academic Advsy Cncl Linguaphone Inst 1989–2005, Steering Ctee Centre for Modern Languages Open Univ 1991–95, Academic Advsy Cncl Univ of Buckingham 1991–2002, Educn Ctee London C of C and Industry Examinations Bd 1993–2006, Bd of British Training International 1998–2000, Advsy Cncl Scot Higher Educn Funding Cncl (SHEFC) Scotlang Project 2000–02, Irish Research Cncl for the Humanities and Social Sciences 2001, Univ Cncl for Modern Languages 2002–07; chm Academic Advsy Bd Br Inst of Traffic Educn Res 2001–02; tstee London C of C Industry Educn Tst 2001–; chm of govrs: Matthew Boulton Higher and Further Educn Corp Birmingham 1999–2002 (govr 2002–), Quality Assurance Agency Benchmarking Steering Ctee 2003–07, Languages Ladder Working Gp DfES 2004–06; medal Euro Fndn for Quality Mgmnt 1996; hon fell Hong Kong Translation Soc 2006, FIL 1981, FRSA 1986, CIEX 1986; Goethe Medaille (Goethe Inst Munich) 1989, Officer's Cross of the Order of Merit (Germany) 1999; *Books* Heinrich Heine, Poetry and Politics (1974, 2 edn 1994), Friedrich Schiller, Medicine, Psychology and Literature (with K Dewhurst, 1978), The Marquise of O and Other Short Stories by Heinr Kleist (with F D Luke, 1978), Business Studies, Languages and Overseas Trade (with D Liston, 1985), The Invisible Economy, A Profile of Britain's Invisible Exports (with D Liston, 1988), Making Your Mark, Effective Business Communication in Germany (with D Liston, M Howarth and M Woodhall, 1988), Franc Exchange, Effective Business Communication in France (with C Sanders, Y Gladkow and C Gordon, 1991), Spanish Venture. Basic Business Communication in Spanish (with B Gould, L Nogueira-Pache and K Bruton, 1992), Linguistic Auditing: A Guide to Identifying Foreign Language Communication Needs in Corporations (with C Wright, 1996), The European Business Environment: Germany (ed with Helen Kelly-Holmes, 1997), Pathways to Proficiency: The Alignment of Language Proficiency Scales for Assessing Competence in English Language (with Richard West, 2003); *Recreations* gardening, walking; *Style*— Prof Nigel Reeves, OBE; ✉ Pro-Vice-Chancellor's Office, Aston University, Birmingham B4 7ET (tel 0121 359 3611 ext 4214, fax 0121 359 2792, e-mail n.b.r.reeves@aston.ac.uk)

REEVES, Philip Thomas Langford; s of Herbert John Reeves (d 1983), of Cheltenham, Glos, and Lilian, *née* Langford (d 1963); *b* 7 July 1931; *Educ* Naunton Park Secdy, Cheltenham Sch of Art, RCA; *m* 1961, Christina Donaldina, *née* MacLaren (d 1994); 1 da; *Career* artist; head of printmaking Glasgow Sch of Art 1972–91 (lectr in graphic design 1954–70); fndr memb: Edinburgh Printmaker's Workshop 1963, Glasgow Print Studio 1972; winner Glasgow Herald Art Exhbn 1980; memb: SSA 1965, Royal Glasgow Inst of the Fine Arts 1981; fell Royal Soc of Painter Etchers 1963; RSW 1959 (pres 1998), RSA 1976 (ARSA 1972); *Exhibitions* Compass Gall 1974, 1977 and 1990, Edinburgh Printmaker's Workshop (retrospective) 1981, New 57 Gall (retrospective) 1982, Mercury Gall 1987, Cyril Gerber Fine Art 1993, Paintings and Prints 1983–93 (Lillie Art Gall) 1993, Fine Art Soc 1994, Dick Inst 1994; *Recreations* table tennis, snooker; *Style*— Philip Reeves, Esq, RSA

REEVES, Vic; *né* (Roderick) James (Jim) Moir; *b* 24 January 1959; *Career* comedian, part of comedy duo with Bob Mortimer, *qv*; *Television* incl: Vic Reeves Big Night Out (Channel 4) 1990 & 1991, Weekenders (Channel 4) 1992, The Smell of Reeves and Mortimer (3 series, BBC) 1993, 1995 and 1998, A Night in with Vic and Bob (Boxing Day special) 1993, A Nose Through Nature (BBC) 1995, Shooting Stars (BBC) 1995, 1996, 1998, 2002 and 2003, It's Ulrika (BBC) 1997, Families at War (BBC) 1998–99, Bang Bang, It's Reeves and Mortimer (BBC) 1999, Randall and Hopkirk (Deceased) (2 series, BBC) 2000–02, On Set With Randall and Hopkirk (Deceased) (BBC) 2000, We Know Where You Live (Channel 4) 2001, contestant Celebrity Mastermind (BBC) 2002, Eluard in Surrealissimo - The Trial of Dali (BBC) 2002, Catterick (BBC 3) 2004, All Star Comedy Show (ITV) 2004; *Film* Churchill: The Hollywood Years 2003; *Tours* Vic Reeves Big Night Out 1990 and 1991, The Smell of Reeves and Mortimer 1994 and The Weathercock Tour 1995, Shooting Stars (nat tour) 1996, Shooting Stars/Fast Show Live (Labatt's Apollo) 1998; *Video* incl: Shooting Stars - Unviewed & Nude 1996, Shooting Stars - Unpicked and Plucked 1997; *Recordings* Dizzy (single, UK no 1), I Will Cure You (album), I'm A Believer (EMF) 1995; *Exhibitions* Sunboiled Onions (Percy Miller Gallery London) 2000; *Awards* BAFTA Award for Originality 1991, Best Live Performance British Comedy Awards 1992, Best Comedy Series British Comedy Awards 1993, BAFTA Award for Best Light Entertainment 1997; *Books* Big Night In (1991), Smell of Reeves and Mortimer (1993), Shooting Stars (1996), Sunboiled Onions (1999), Me: Moir: Volume One, 0–20 (2006); *Style*— Vic Reeves; ✉ c/o PBJ Management Ltd, 7 Soho Street, London W1D 3DQ (tel 020 7287 1112, fax 020 7287 1191, e-mail general@pbjmgt.co.uk, website www.pbjmgt.co.uk)

REGAN, Carolyn; *Educ* Lycée Français de Londres, Somerville Coll Oxford (BA); *Career* early career as European tour guide American Inst for Foreign Studies and PR offr New Shakespeare Theatre Co London; nat admin trainee NHS 1981–83, asst admin Middx Hosp London 1983–85, dir Services for People with Learning Disabilities Riverside HA 1985–89; Ealing HA: co-ordinator Services for Elderly People 1989–90, dir of purchasing 1990–92, acting chief exec 1992–93; dir of acute commissioning Ealing, Hammersmith & Hounslow Health Agency 1993–1996, chief exec W Herts HA 1996–1999, chief exec

E London & The City HA 1999–; chair HIV & AIDS Consortium Burns Review; business in the arts advsr Bromley by Bow Ltd Action Space; *Recreations* aerobics, swimming, cooking, writing poetry, gardening, theatre; *Style*— Ms Carolyn Regan; ✉ North East London Strategic Health Authority, 81 Commercial Road, London E1 1RD (tel 020 7655 6601, fax 020 7655 6621)

REGAN, Rt Rev Edwin; *see:* Wrexham, Bishop of (RC)

REGAN, Prof Lesley; da of John Regan, of London, and Dorothy, *née* Thorne; *b* 8 March 1956; *Educ* Lady Eleanor Holles Sch, Royal Free Hosp Sch of Med (MB BS, MD); *m* 1990, Prof John Summerfield, s of Sir John Crampton Summerfield, CBE, QC (d 1997); 2 da (Jenny, Clare (twins) b 11 Dec 1992); 2 step da (Nuala, Jessica), 2 step s (Oliver, James); *Career* sr registrar in obstetrics and gynaecology Addenbrooke's Hosp Cambridge 1986–90; Univ of Cambridge: sr research assoc MRC Embryo and Genetic Research Gp 1986–88, dir of med studies Girton Coll 1986–90; sr lectr and conslt in obstetrics and gynaecology St Mary's Hosp London 1990–96, dir Subspecialty Trg Prog (RCOG) in Reproductive Med Imperial Coll Sch of Med Hammersmith and St Mary's Hosps London 1995–, prof and head Dept of Obstetrics and Gynaecology Imperial Coll at St Mary's Campus London 1996–; Aleck Bourne lectr 1990, Rosenfelder lectr 1999, Wim Shelleken lectr 2000, Alexander Gordon lectr 2003, Lettsomian lectr 2004, Green Armytage lectr (RCOG) 2006, Victor Bamey lectr 2007; visiting prof Harvard Center of Excellence for Women's Health 2000, visiting prof and examiner University of Hong Kong 2003, visiting prof in obstetrics and gynaecology to South Africa 2004; recipient research grant awards from: MRC 1992 and 2000, Arthritis and Rheumatism Cncl 1993, Wellbeing 1996, 2005 and 2006, Br Heart Fndn 1997, Save the Baby Charity 1990, 1996, 1998, 2001, 2003–06 (annually), Wellcome Tst 1999 and 2001, Royal Soc 2001, Health, Technology and Assessment UK 2003; tstee Inst of Obstetrics and Gynacology, tstee and memb Steering Ctee Save the Baby Charity, professional advsr to Miscarriage Assoc, pres UK Assoc of Early Pregnancy Units 2005–, memb Cncl RCOG (elected memb for Int Representation 2006); memb: Cncl Br Fertility Soc 1992–95, Euro Soc of Human and Reproduction and Embryology 1986, Fedn of Gynaecologists and Obstetricians 1997 (expert advsr in reproductive med); memb Editorial Bd: Human Fertility, Jl of Reproductive Immunology; contrib to TV documentaries: Staying Alive (Channel 4), Horizon - Waiting For A Heartbeat (BBC2) 2006; Woman of Achievement Award 2005 (for services to med, particularly recurrent miscarriage and infertility); FRCOG 1998 (MRCOG 1985); *Publications* Miscarriage - What Every Woman Needs to Know (1997, republished 2001), Your Pregnancy Week By Week (2005); also author of articles on reproductive med incl the causes and treatment of infertility and recurrent miscarriage, also on minimally invasive treatment for uterine fibroids; *Recreations* writing and broadcasting for lay public on medical health issues, enjoying our family home in Provençe; *Style*— Prof Lesley Regan; ✉ Department of Obstetrics and Gynaecology, Imperial College at St Mary's, Mint Wing, South Wharf Road, London W2 1NY (tel 020 7886 1798, fax 020 7886 6054, e-mail l.regan@imperial.ac.uk)

REGAN, Mark Peter; MBE (2004); *b* 28 January 1972, Bristol; *Career* rugby union player (hooker); clubs: Bristol RUFC (120 appearances), Bath RUFC 1997–2002 (125 appearances), Leeds Tykes RUFC 2002–05, Bristol Rugby 2005–; England: 39 caps, debut v South Africa 1995, winners Five Nations Championship 1996, winners Six Nations Championship 2001 and 2003 (Grand Slam 2003), ranked no 1 team in world 2003, winners World Cup Aust 2003, memb squad World Cup France 2007; memb squad Br Lions tour to South Africa 1997, memb World XV 1998; *Recreations* spending time with family, golf (4 handicap); *Style*— Mark Regan, Esq, MBE

REGAN, Michael Denis; s of Denis Charles Regan (d 1965), of Westcliff-on-Sea, Essex, and Selina, *née* Webb; *b* 4 October 1955; *Educ* Westcliff HS for Boys, Pembroke Coll Oxford (MA); *m* 20 Feb 1987, Henrietta, da of Henry George Richard Falconar (d 1981), of Horsham, W Sussex; 1 s (George b 1987), 1 da (Grace b 1990); *Career* admitted slr 1980; Rowe and Maw (now Mayer Brown Rowe & Maw): articled clerk 1978–80, asst slr 1980–85, ptnr 1985–, ptnr i/c Lloyd's office 1988–92; ACIArb 1984; *Books* JCT Management Contract (jtly); *Recreations* watching cricket; *Style*— Michael Regan, Esq; ✉ Mayer Brown Rowe & Maw LLP, 11 Pilgrim Street, London EC4V 6RW

REGESTER, Michael; s of Hugh Adair Regester (d 1994), of Royston, Herts, and Monique, *née* Levrey; *b* 8 April 1947; *Educ* St Peter's Sch Guildford Surrey, Newport GS Newport Essex; *m* 1 (m dis 1993), Christine Mary, da of Denis Harrison; 2 da (Lucinda Jane b 12 April 1971, Alice Mary b 8 Aug 1975); m 2, Leanne Tara, da of Margaret Moscardi; 1 s (Daniel b 13 Feb 1995), 1 da (Kimberley (twin) b 13 Feb 1995); *Career* mangr of public affrs (Euro, W Africa, ME) Gulf Oil Corporation 1975–80, jt md Traverse-Healy & Regester Ltd 1980–87, dir Charles Barker Public Relations 1987–90, md Regester plc 1990–94, ptnr Regester Larkin Ltd 1994–; memb Bd Int PR Assoc 1988, FIPR 1990, MInstPet 1990; *Books* Crisis Management (1987), Investor Relations (with Neil Ryder, 1990), Risk Issues and Crisis Management (with Judy Larkin, 1997); *Recreations* sailing, opera, cooking; *Clubs* Wig and Pen; *Style*— Michael Regester, Esq; ✉ Regester Larkin Ltd,16 Doughty Street, London WC1N 2PL (tel 020 7831 3839, fax 020 7831 3632, e-mail mregester@regesterlarkin.com)

REGO, Paula; da of José Fernandes Figueiroa Rego (d 1966), of Portugal, and Maria De São José Paiva; *b* 26 January 1935; *Educ* St Julian's Sch Carcavelos Portugal, Slade Sch of Fine Art; *m* 1959, Victor Willing, s of George Willing; 2 da (Caroline b 1956, Victoria Camilla b 1959), 1 s (Nicholas Juvenal b 1961); *Career* artist; pt/t lectr Slade Sch of Fine Art 1983–90, assoc artist Nat Gallery London 1990, Gulbenkian Fndn bursary 1962–63; sr fell RCA; subject of book Paula Rego (by John McEwen, 1992); Hon DUniv: St Andrews 1999, UEA 1999; Hon Dr: Rhode Island Sch of Design 2000, UCL 2004, Univ of Roehampton 2005; Hon DLitt Univ of Oxford 2005; *Solo Exhibitions* SNBA Lisbon 1965, Galeria S Mamede Lisbon 1971, Galeria da Emenda Lisbon 1974, Galeria Modulo Oporto 1977, Galeria III Lisbon 1978, Air Gallery London 1981, Edward Totah Gallery London 1982, 1984, 1985 and 1987, Arnolfini Bristol 1983, Gallery Espace Amsterdam 1983, Midland Group 1984, The Art Palace NY 1985, Travelling Show 1987, Retrospective Exhibition (Gulbenkian Fndn Lisbon and Serpentine Gallery London) 1988, Nursery Rhymes (Marlborough Graphics, travelling exhbn Plymouth, Manchester and elsewhere, Nat Gallery 1991, South Bank Centre) 1991–96, Peter Pan and Other Stories (Marlborough Fine Art) 1992, Peter Scott Gallery Lancaster Univ 1993, Dog Woman (Marlborough Fine Art) 1994, Marlborough Fine Art NY 1996, retrospective exhibition (Tate Gallery Liverpool and Centro Cultural de Belem Lisbon Portugal) 1997, Dulwich Picture Gallery 1998, Marlborough Fine Art Madrid 1999, Gulbenkian Fndn Lisbon 1999, Abbot Hall Kendal 2001, Yale Center for Br Art 2002, Museu Serralves Porto 2004–05, Tate Britain 2005, print retrospective touring exhbn (Talbot Rice Gallery Edinburgh, Brighton Museum and others) 2005–07, Marlborough Fine Art 2006; *Group Exhibitions* incl: S Paulo Biennale 1969 and 1985, Br Art Show 1985, Cries and Whispers (Br Cncl) 1988, Br Art (Japan) 1990, Innocence and Experience (Manchester City Art Gallery and touring) 1992, British Figurative Art in the 20th Century (British Arts Cncl and the Israel Museum Jerusalem) 1993, Unbound (Hayward Gallery) 1994, Saatchi Gallery 1994, Spellbound: Art and Film (Hayward Gallery) 1996, British Art Show (Hayward Gallery) 2000, Encounters (Nat Gallery) 2000, Jane Eyre and Other Stories (Marlborough Fine Art) 2003; *Books* Peter Pan, Nursery Rhymes, Pendle Witches, The Children's Crusade; subject of: Paula Rego by John McEwen (1992, 1997 and 2006), Paula Rego by Fiona Bradley (2002), Complete Graphic Work by Tom Rosenthal (2003), Paula Rego's Map of Memory (by Dr Maria Manuel Lisboa); *Style*— Ms Paula Rego; ✉ Marlborough Fine Art, 6 Albemarle Street, London W1X 4BY (tel 020 7629 5161, fax 020 7629 6338)

REICH, Steve; s of Leonard J Reich (d 1991), of New York, and June, *née* Sillman, of Los Angeles; *b* 3 October 1936; *Educ* Cornell Univ, Juilliard Sch of Music, Mills Coll (MA); *m* 30 June 1976, Beryl, *née* Korot; 1 s (Ezra b 13 Aug 1978); *Career* composer; studied under Darius Milhaud and Luciano Berio; fndr Steve Reich and Musicians 1966; works incl: It's Gonna Rain 1965, Come Out 1966, Piano Phase 1967, Violin Phase 1967, Pendulum Music 1968, Four Organs 1970, Phase Patterns (for four electric organs) 1970, Drumming 1971, Clapping Music 1972, Music for Mallet Instrument, Voices and Organ 1973, Six Pianos 1973, Music for Eighteen Musicians 1976 (new recording 1999, Grammy Award for Best Recording by Small Ensemble 1999), Variations for Winds, Strings, and Keyboards 1979, Tehillim 1981, Vermont Counterpoint 1982, Eight Lines 1983, The Desert Music 1984, New York Counterpoint 1985, Six Marimbas 1986, The Four Sections 1987, Electric Counterpoint 1987, Different Trains 1988 (winner Grammy Award for Best Contemporary Composition 1990), Typing Music 1 (from The Cave) 1989, The Cave 1993, Nagoya Marimbas 1994, Duet 1994, City Life 1995 (premiered at Queen Elizabeth Hall), Proverb 1995 (cmmnd for BBC Proms), Triple Quartet 1999, Know What is Above You 1999, Three Tales 2002, Cello Counterpoint 2003, You Are (variations) 2004, Variations for Vibes, Pianos and Strings 2005, Daniel Variations 2006; dance music: Fase 1983, Falling Angels, Eight Lines, Sextet, Impact (winner of Bessie Award 1986); all major works recorded on: Nonesuch label, RCA Victor, ECM, Deutsche Grammophon, Angel, Disques Shandar, Columbia, CBS Odyssey; cmmns for: Holland Festival, San Francisco Symphony Orch, Rothko Chapel, Ransom Wilson, Brooklyn Academy of Music (for Pat Metheny), WDR Cologne, Saint Louis Symphony Orch, Kronos Quartet, London Sinfonietta, South Bank Centre/Serious Speakout; study grants incl: Univ of Ghana, American Soc for Eastern Arts California, NY State Cncl on the Arts 1974, DAAD Artists in Residence Award Berlin 1974, Rockefeller Fndn grants 1975, 1978, 1981 and 1990, National Endowment for the Arts grants 1974 and 1976, Guggenheim fell 1978, Koussevitzky Fndn Award 1981, Shuman Award Columbia Univ 2000, Praemium Imperiale 2006, Polar Music Prize 2007; Chubb fell Yale Univ 2007; elected memb: American Acad of Arts and Letters 1994, Bavarian Academy of Arts, Commandeur de l'Ordre des Arts et des Lettres (France) 1999, Franz Liszt Acad 2006, American Acad of Arts and Sciences 2007; *Style*— Steve Reich, Esq; ✉ c/o Andrew Rosner, Allied Artists Agency, 42 Montpelier Square, London SW7 1JZ (tel 020 7589 6243, fax 020 7581 5269)

REICHMANN, Paul; s of Samuel Reichmann, and Renee Reichmann; *b* 1930, Vienna; *Career* co-fndr Olympia & York Developments Ltd; projects incl: First Canadian Place Toronto (offices) 1975, World Financial Center NY 1986, concept and realisation Canary Wharf project London 1987; exec chm Canary Wharf Group plc until 2003, chief exec Reichmann Group of Companies (incl International Property Corp); tstee and jt unitholder: Retirement Residences Real Estate Investment Tst, CPL Long Term Care Real Estate Investment Tst, IPC US Income Commercial Real Estate Investment Tst; *Style*— Paul Reichmann, Esq

REID, Sir (Philip) Alan; KCVO (2007); s of Philip Reid (d 1981), of Glasgow, and Margaret, *née* McKerracher (d 1976); *b* 18 January 1947; *Educ* Fettes, Univ of St Andrews (LLB); *m* 14 July 1971, Maureen Anne Reid, da of Alexander Petrie, of Cupar, Fife, Scotland; 1 da (Caroline b 1981), 1 s (Richard b 1984); *Career* exec chm KPMG Management Consultancy Europe, head UK Management Consultancy KPMG 1994–98 and international chm KPMG Management Consulting 1996–98; chief fin offr: KPMG UK 1998–2001, KPMG Europe 1999–2001, KPMG Int 1999–2001; chief operating offr KPMG 2001–02; Keeper of the Privy Purse and Treas to HM The Queen 2002–, Receiver Gen to Duchy of Lancaster 2002–; pres Management Consultancies Assoc 1997; tstee: Royal Collection Tst 2002, Historic Royal Palaces Tst 2002 (dep chm 2007–); memb Cncl Kings Fund; govr Edward VII Hospital (Sister Agnes) 2004; CA 1973, FTII 1981, FRSA 1993; *Recreations* family, Arsenal FC, films, golf, skiing; *Clubs* MCC; *Style*— Sir Alan Reid, KCVO; ✉ Buckingham Palace, London SW1A 1AA (tel 020 7930 4832)

REID, Alan; MP; *b* 7 August 1954; *Educ* Ayr Acad, Univ of Strathclyde; *Career* cncllr (Lib Dem) Renfrew DC 1988–96; Parly candidate (Lib Dem): Paisley and Renfrewshire S 1992, Dunbartonshire W 1997; MP (Lib Dem) Argyll and Bute 2001–; jr Lib Dem whip 2001–05, memb Broadcasting Select Ctee 2001–05; memb Scottish Lib Dem Pty Exec until 2003, spokesperson Scottish Lib Dem Common Fisheries Policy Reform 2001–05; memb AUT; *Style*— Alan Reid, Esq, MP; ✉ House of Commons, London SW1A 0AA

REID, Sir Alexander James; 3 Bt (UK 1897), of Ellon, Aberdeenshire; JP (Cambs and Isle of Ely 1971), DL (1973); s of Sir Edward James Reid, 2 Bt, KBE (d 1972), and Tatiana (Tania), *née* Fenoult (d 1992); *b* 6 December 1932; *Educ* Eton, Magdalene Coll Cambridge; *m* 1955, Michaela Ann, da of late Olaf Kier, CBE, of Royston, Herts; 1 s (Charles Edward James b 1956), 3 da (Christina b 1958, Jennifer (Mrs Rory Collins) b 1959, Alexandra Catherine (Mrs Charles Lloyd) b 1965); *Heir* s, Charles Reid; *Career* 2 Lt 1 Bn Gordon Highlanders 1951, served Malaya; Capt 3 Bn Gordon Highlanders TA, ret 1964; chm: Ellon Castle Estates Co Ltd 1965–96, Cristina Securities Ltd 1970–, Cytozyme (UK) Ltd 1985–92; hon pres Clan Donnachaidh Soc (chm 1994–2003), govr Heath Mount Prep Sch 1970–92 (chm 1976–92); High Sheriff Cambridge 1987–88; Liveryman Worshipful Co of Farmers; *Recreations* shooting, all country pursuits; *Clubs* Caledonian; *Style*— Sir Alexander Reid, Bt, DL; ✉ Lanton Tower, Jedburgh, Roxburghshire TD8 6SU (tel 01835 863443, fax 01835 864636)

REID, Dr Allan William; s of William Reid, and Abigail Simpson Reid; *Educ* Glasgow Acad, Univ of Glasgow (MB ChB); *Career* Glasgow Royal Infirmary: conslt radiologist 1989–, clinical dir (imaging) 1996–2000, head Dept of Radiology 2000–; conslt radiologist Ross Hall Hosp 1991–; memb Editorial Bd Jl of Endovascular Therapy; William Hunter Medal 1979; memb Int Soc for Endovascular Specialists 1996; FRCR 1986 (MRCR 1983), FRCP 2002; *Recreations* photography, travel, golf, swimming; *Clubs* Royal Scottish Automobile, Glasgow Golf; *Style*— Dr Allan Reid; ✉ Glasgow Royal Infirmary, Glasgow G31 2ER (tel 0141 211 4783, fax 0141 211 4781, e-mail awr@northglasgow.scot.nhs.uk); Ross Hall Hospital, Glasgow G52 3NQ

REID, Derek D; *Educ* Inverurie Acad, Univ of Aberdeen, Robert Gordon Univ; *m*; 2 c; *Career* Cadbury-Schweppes: joined 1968, variously dir foods business then tea business until 1986; involved with MBO of Cadbury-Schweppes to form Premier Brands plc 1986, left following takeover by Hillsdown Holdings plc 1990; dir various small cos; chief exec Scottish Tourist Bd 1994–96; chm Harris Tweed Textiles Ltd; visiting prof of tourism Univ of Abertay Dundee; govr Pitlochry Theatre; Hon DBA Robert Gordon Univ 1995; *Recreations* Scottish contemporary art, classical music, cricket, golf, fishing; *Style*— Derek Reid, Esq; ✉ Broom Hill, Kinclaven, Stanley, Perthshire PH1 4QL (tel and fax 01250 883209, e-mail dd.reid@ukonline.co.uk)

REID, (John) Dominic; OBE (2002); s of John Reid, OBE, RIBA, DL (d 1992), and Sylvia Mary, *née* Payne; *b* 24 September 1961; *Educ* Oundle (music scholar), Downing Coll Cambridge (MA), UCL (DipArch); *m* 18 May 1991, Suzanne Antoinette, da of Leon Schultz (d 1967); 1 da (Grace Danousha b 22 Nov 2001); *Career* 2 Lt RA 1981; architect: Doshi-Raje 1984–85, Austin-Smith: Lord 1986–89, Richard Horden Assoc Ltd 1989–90; ptnr John & Sylvia Reid 1990–92, princ Reid & Reid 1992–, dir Designers Collaborative Ltd 1996–2000, chief exec London Film Cmmn 1999–2000; memb Cultural Strategy Partnership for London 1999–2000; pageantmaster Lord Mayor's Show 1992–, prodr Tribute & Promise Parade (VJ Day) 1995, conslt Flora London Marathon 1996–2000, prodr Reopening Canada House by HM The Queen 1998, prodr Reserve Forces

R

Experience 1998, exec dir Oxford and Cambridge Boat Race 2000–04, prodr San Carlos Falklands 25 2007, dir 2010 Anniversary Prog Royal Soc 2007–; conslt: The Queen's Golden Jubilee 2002, Olympic Parade of Heroes 2004, Virgin Atlantic Nassau and Cuba Inaugural Flight 2005; Trooper rising to Capt TA 1990–2000; Liveryman Worshipful Co of Grocers; RIBA, FRSA; OStJ; *Recreations* telemarking, sailing, cycling; *Clubs* HAC, Leander; *Style*— Dominic Reid, Esq, OBE; ✉ Reid & Reid, The Barge, Hindringham Road, Great Walsingham, Norfolk NR22 6DR (tel 01328 824420, fax 01328 824422, e-mail dominic@reidandreid.com)

REID, Gavin Donald; s of Donald Reid (d 2006), and Elizabeth, *née* Pittilo; *b* 9 June 1966, Edinburgh; *Educ* Daniel Stewart's and Melville Coll Edinburgh, Napier Coll Edinburgh, RNCM (GMus, PPRNCM, Hiles Medal), Guildhall Sch of Music and Drama; *Partner* Lucy Rimmer; 2 s (James b 5 Aug 2004, Jack b 19 June 2006); *Career* freelance musician (trumpet), teacher and administrator 1989–2001, educn co-ordinator Bridgewater Hall Manchester 2001–02, gen mangr Manchester Camerata 2003–06 (educn co-ordinator 1996–2003), dir BBC Scottish Symphony Orch 2006–; fell Clore Leadership Prog 2004–05; *Recreations* family; *Style*— Gavin Reid, Esq; ✉ BBC Scottish Symphony Orchestra, City Hall, Candleriggs, Glasgow G1 1NQ (tel 0141 338 2142, e-mail gavin.reid@bbc.co.uk)

REID, Rt Hon George Newlands; PC (2003); s of George Reid (d 1978), and Margaret Forsyth (d 1969); *b* 4 June 1939; *Educ* Dollar Acad, Univ of St Andrews (MA, Gold Medal in history, pres Students' Rep Cncl), Union Coll USA (Dip Int Rels); *m* 1, 11 April 1964 (m dis), Catherine Stott; 1 da (Caroline Lucinda); m 2, 4 July 1968, Daphne Ann, da of Calum MacColl; 1 da (Morag Marsaili); *Career* reporter Daily Express 1961–62, political corr Scottish TV 1962–64, prodr Granada TV 1964–68, head of news and current affrs Scottish TV 1968–74, MP (SNP) Clackmannan and E Stirlingshire 1974–79 (Parly candidate (SNP) Ochil 1997), freelance broadcaster and journalist BBC TV and Radio and various newspapers 1979–84, dir Public Affrs League of Red Cross and Red Crescent Socs Geneva 1985–90 (head of information 1984–90), dir Int Red Cross Promotion Bureau 1990–92, int conslt 1992–98; MSP (SNP): Mid Scotland and Fife 1999–2003, Ochil 2003–07; Scottish Parl: presiding offr 2003–07 (dep presiding offr 1999–2003), convener Scottish Parly Bureau and Corp Body, convener Parly Conveners 1999–2003; vice-convener SNP 1997–99, memb Conslt Steering Gp for Scottish Parly 1998–99; dir Scottish Cncl Research Inst 1978–81; visiting prof Univ of Glasgow 2006–; memb: Assembly of Cncl of Europe 1976–79, Assembly of WEU 1976–79; Scottish Politician of the Year, Herald Awards 2003 and 2005; Hon LLD Univ of St Andrews 2005, Hon DUniv Queen Margaret 2006; Pirogov Gold medal (for work as chief Red Cross delg in Armenian Earthquake) USSR 1989, Medal of Foreign Min of Russian Fedn 2007; *Books* Red Cross, Red Crescent (ed, 1989), Casualties of Conflict (ed, 1990); *Recreations* gardening, cross-country skiing; *Style*— The Rt Hon George Reid; ✉ Coneyhill House, 28 Kenilworth Road, Bridge of Allan, Stirling FK9 4DU

REID, (James) Gordon; QC (Scot 1993); s of James Rae Reid (d 1977), of Edinburgh, and Constance May, *née* Lawrie; *b* 24 July 1952; *Educ* Melville Coll Edinburgh, Univ of Edinburgh (LLB); *m* 12 Sept 1984, Hannah Hogg, da of William Hopkins; 3 s (William Lawrie b 21 July 1987, James Hogg (twin), Jonathon Rae b 10 Dec 1989), 1 da (Joanna Margaret Grant b 26 Oct 1991); *Career* slr in Scot 1976–80 (apprentice slr 1974–76), admitted Faculty of Advocates 1980, standing jr counsel to Scot Office Environment Dept 1986–93, temp judge Court of Session 2002–; called to the Bar Inner Temple 1991; pt/t VAT chm 1997–, special cmmnr for income tax 1997–; memb: Soc of Construction Law 1990, Agric Law Assoc 1990–2003; FCIArb 1994; *Recreations* tennis, general fitness; *Style*— J Gordon Reid, Esq, QC; ✉ Blebo House, By St Andrews, Fife KY15 5TZ; Advocates' Library, Parliament House, Edinburgh EH1 1RF (clerk tel 0131 226 5071, fax 0131 225 3662); Atkin Chambers, 1 Atkin Building, Gray's Inn, London WC1R 5BQ (tel 020 7404 0102)

REID, Ven (William) Gordon; s of William Albert Reid (d 1987), and Elizabeth Jean, *née* Inglis (d 1990); *b* 28 January 1943; *Educ* Galashiels Acad, Univ of Edinburgh (MA), Keble Coll Oxford (MA), Cuddesdon Theol Coll; *Career* curate St Salvador's Edinburgh 1967–69, chaplain and tutor Salisbury Theol Coll 1969–72, rector St Michael and All Saints Edinburgh 1972–84, provost Inverness Cathedral 1984–88, chaplain St Nicholas' Ankara Turkey 1988–89, chaplain St Peter and St Sigfrid Stockholm Sweden 1989–92, vicar-gen Dio in Europe 1992–, canon of Gibraltar Cathedral 1992–98, archdeacon in Europe 1996–98, priest i/c St Michael's Cornhill 1997–98, dean of Gibraltar 1998–2000, chaplain All Saints Milan 2000–, archdeacon Italy and Malta 2000–; cncllr: Corp of City of Edinburgh 1972–74, Lothian Regnl Cncl 1974–84; chm Lothian and Borders Police Bd 1982–84; Freeman City of London 1997; *Books* The Wind from the Stars (1992), Every Comfort at Golgotha (1999); *Recreations* reading, languages; *Clubs* New (Edinburgh); *Style*— The Ven Gordon Reid, Archdeacon of Italy and Malta; ✉ Via Solferino 17, Milan 20121, Italy (tel and fax 00 39 02 655 2258)

REID, Prof Gordon McGregor; *b* 9 February 1948; *Educ* Univ of Glasgow (Tech Cert Lab Sci), Univ of Wales Cardiff (BSc), Queen Elizabeth Coll London/British Museum of Natural History (PhD); *m*; 1 c; *Career* animal research technician Zoological Dept Univ of Glasgow 1966–68; VSO field biologist: Botswana 1968–69, Nigeria 1969–70; pt/t demonstrator in zoology Univ of London Colls and Examinations Lab 1974–78, lectr in biology Univ of Sokoto Nigeria 1979–81, conservation offr (natural history) Liverpool Museum 1982–84, keeper of natural history (conservation) Nat Museums on Merseyside Liverpool 1984–85, keeper of natural history Horniman Museum London 1985–91, dir and chief exec North of England Zoological Soc at Chester Zoo 1995– (curator-in-chief 1992–95); visiting research fell/guest lectr Nat Museum of Natural History Smithsonian Instn Washington and Nat Zoological Soc of Mexico, visiting prof Univ of Liverpool Dept of Veterinary Clinical Sci and Animal Husbandry 1999–; an inspector of zoos (Govt appt) and conslt biologist to various WWF projects, Br Exec Serv Overseas inspr of Hungarian zoos 1998; memb: Cncl World Assoc of Zoos and Aquariums (chm Aquarium Ctee 2002–06), Cncl European Assoc of Zoos and Aquariums 2001– (co-chm Research Ctee), Cncl Assoc of Leading Visitor Attractions, Editorial Advsy Bd Int Zoo Yearbook 2000–, WWF Progs Ctee 2003–; pres Linnean Soc of London 2003–06; memb: World Conservation Union (IUCN) (memb Conservation Breeding Specialist and Asian Elephant Specialist Gps), European Union of Aquarium Curators (memb Exec Ctee 1999–), Bd cultural consortium englandsnorthwest (chair Gardens Strategy); tstee Nat Museums Liverpool 2001– (memb HR Ctee and Human Remains Working Gp), global chair IUCN/Species Survival Cmmn (SSC)/Wetlands Int (WI) Freshwater Fish Specialist Gp, served on South African Agency for Science and Technology Advancement (SAASTA) strategic and operational review panel, pres elect World Assoc of Zoos and Aquariums (WAZA); two new species of fish Labeo reidi and Nannocharax reidi named in honour; Hon fell Liverpool John Moore's Univ 2006, Hon Dr of Science Univ of Chester 2006; CBiol 1994, FIBiol 1994; Huesped de Honor of Bolivia 2004; *Publications* author of over 100 published works incl books, peer reviewed scientific papers and popular articles; *Style*— Prof Gordon McGregor Reid; ✉ North of England Zoological Society, Zoological Gardens, Upton, Cheshire CH2 1LH (tel 01244 650201, fax 01244 380405, e-mail gordonr@chesterzoo.co.uk)

REID, Graham Charles; s of Charles Anderson Reid (d 1984), of Stoke D'Abernon, Surrey, and Mona Ethel, *née* Hinton (d 1993); *b* 29 August 1945; *Educ* KCS Wimbledon (scholarship), King's Coll London; *m* 22 Aug 1970, Gaye, da of Leonard Frank Peskett; 1 s (Stephen James b 27 May 1974); *Career* articled clerk Legg London & Co 1965–68; Grant Thornton (formerly Thornton Baker): rose to mangr London office 1969–77, estab Ipswich office 1977, ptnr 1979–2002, sr ptnr 1995–2002; princ Robertson Reid 2002–; treas Suffolk Branch IOD 1990–; memb Area Bd for Prince's Tst Business Div (Suffolk)1991–2002 (vice-chm 1993–95, chm 1995–2002), chm Prince's Tst Bd for Suffolk 2000–06, memb Prince's Tst Regnl Cncl for East of England 2000–06; FCA 1979 (ACA 1970); *Recreations* music, wine, sport, narrow boating; *Style*— Graham Reid, Esq; ✉ Mitchery Farmhouse, Rattlesden, Bury St Edmunds, Suffolk IP30 0SS (tel 01449 737661, e-mail grahamcreid@msn.com)

REID, Harry; *b* Scotland; *m*; 2 s; *Career* Ogilvy & Mather advtg: joined early '70s, regional dir Asia (Hong Kong) 1986–91, chm and regional dir for Europe and ME (London) 1991–94, chief operating offr worldwide 1994–95; pres FCB International 1995–; *Recreations* cricket, Asian antiques, recently golf; *Style*— Harry Reid, Esq; ✉ FCB International, 55 Newman Street, London W1T 3EB (tel 020 7947 8002)

REID, Harry William; s of William Reid (d 1989), and Catherine Robertson Craighead, *née* MacLean; *b* 23 September 1947; *Educ* Aberdeen GS, Fettes, Worcester Coll Oxford (BA); *m* 24 May 1980, Julie Wilson, da of late Henry Davidson; 1 da (Catherine MacGregor b 22 October 1983); *Career* The Scotsman: sometime sportswriter and feature writer, leader writer 1970–73, educn corr 1973–77, features ed 1977–81; sport and leisure ed Sunday Standard 1981–82; The Herald: exec ed 1982–83, dep ed 1983–97, ed 1997–2000; special advsr to SMG plc 2000–01, commissioning conslt St Andrew Press 2002–; visiting fell New Coll Univ of Edinburgh 2001; cmmnd by Church of Scotland to write special report on its situation, structure and prospects 2001, memb Church and Soc Cncl Church of Scotland 2005–06; govr Fettes Coll 2002–; Hon DUniv Glasgow 2001, Dr (hc) Univ of Edinburgh 2001; *Publications* Dear Country: A Quest for England (1992), Outside Verdict: An Old Kirk in a New Scotland (2002), The Final Whistle? Scottish Football: The Best and Worst of Times (2005), Deadline: The Story of the Scottish Press (2006); *Recreations* exploring Scotland and European cities, hill walking, supporting Aberdeen FC; *Style*— Harry Reid, Esq; ✉ 12 Comely Bank, Edinburgh EH4 1AN (tel 0131 332 6690)

REID, Hubert Valentine; s of Robert Valentine Reid (d 1949), of Hove, E Sussex, and Doris, *née* Marchant (d 1997); *b* 24 November 1940; *Educ* Harrow; *m* 9 May 1964, Margaret; 3 s (Robert b 1966, Simon b 1968, Oliver b 1974); *Career* exec dir Hugh Baird & Sons Ltd 1971–77; Boddingtons Gp plc: exec dir 1977, asst md 1980, md 1984, chief exec 1985, chm 1995; chm: Enterprise Inns plc 1997–, Ibstock plc 1998–99 (non-exec dir 1995–99), Royal London Mutual Insurance Soc Ltd 1999–2005 (non-exec dir 1996–2005), Midas Income and Growth Tst plc (formerly Taverners Tst plc) 2004– (non-exec dir 1996–); dep chm Majedie Investments plc 2000– (dir 1999–); non-exec dir: Bryants Gp plc 1993– (chm 2000–01), Greenalls Gp plc 1996–97, Michael Page Int plc 2003–; govr Harrow Sch 1993–2001, tstee John Lyons Charity 1993–2001; FInstD; *Recreations* golf, tennis; *Clubs* Naval and Military; *Style*— Hubert Reid, Esq; ✉ Enterprise Inns plc, 3 Monkspath Hall Road, Solihull, West Midlands B90 4SJ (tel 0121 733 7700, fax 0121 733 1748)

REID, Sir Hugh; 3 Bt (UK 1922), of Springburn, Co of City of Glasgow, and of Kilmaurs, Co Ayr; s of Sir Douglas Neilson Reid, 2 Bt (d 1971), and Margaret Brighton Young, *née* Maxtone (d 1992); *b* 27 November 1933; *Educ* Loretto; *Heir* none; *Career* RAF 1952–56, served Egypt and Cyprus, RAF (VRT) 1963–75, Flying Offr; self-employed travel conslt 1961–; *Recreations* travel, skiing, aviation, cooking; *Style*— Sir Hugh Reid, Bt; ✉ Caheronaun Park, Loughrea, Co Galway, Ireland; 4772 Vouni Village, Limassol District, Republic of Cyprus

REID, Rt Hon Dr John; PC (1998), MP; *b* 8 May 1947; *m* 1, Cathie (d 1998); 2 s (Kevin, Mark); m 2, Carine Alder, 2002; *Career* res Lab Pty in Scot 1979–83, advsr to Rt Hon Neil Kinnock MP 1983–85, Scot organiser Trade Unionists for Labour 1986–87; MP (Lab): Motherwell N 1987–97, Hamilton N and Bellshill 1997–2005, Airdrie and Shotts 2005–; oppn front bench dep spokesman on children 1988–89, oppn front bench spokesman on Armed Forces 1990–97, min of state (armed forces) MOD 1997–98, min for tport 1998–99, sec of state for Scotland 1999–2001, sec of state for NI 2001–02, min without portfolio and chm Lab Pty 2002–03, Ldr of the House of Commons and Pres of the Cncl 2003, sec of state for health 2003–05, sec of state for defence 2005–06, sec of state Home Office 2006–07; memb Lab Pty NEC 2001–03; fell Armed Forces Parly Scheme; *Recreations* crosswords and watching football; *Style*— The Rt Hon Dr John Reid, MP; ✉ House of Commons, London SW1A 0AA (tel 020 7219 3000, e-mail reidj@parliament.uk); constituency office: 115 Graham Street, Airdrie ML6 6DE (tel 01236 748777, fax 01236 748666)

REID, Prof John Low; OBE (2001); s of James Reid (d 1961), of Glasgow, and Irene Margaret; *b* 1 October 1943; *Educ* Kelvinside Acad Glasgow, Fettes, Univ of Oxford (MA, BM BCh, DM); *m* 2 May 1964, Randa, da of Naguib Aref Pharaon (d 1987), of London; 1 s (James b 1965), 1 da (Rebecca b 1967); *Career* house offr Radcliffe Infirmary Oxford and Brompton Hosp London 1968–70, res fell, sr lectr then reader Royal Postgrad Med Sch London 1970–78, visiting scientist Nat Inst of Health Bethesda Maryland USA 1973–75; Univ of Glasgow: regius prof materia medica 1978–89, regius prof of med and therapeutics 1989–; ed: Clinical Science 1982–84, Journal of Hypertension 1987–94; FRCPGlas 1979, FRCP 1987, FRSE 1995, FRCPI 1997, FMedSci 1998; *Books* Handbook of Hypertension (23 vols since 1981), Lecture Notes on Clinical Pharmacology (7 edns since 1981); *Recreations* gardening, books, outdoors; *Style*— Prof John Reid, OBE; ✉ Dhubaniel, Gartocharn, Dunbartonshire G83 8NJ (tel 01389 830315); Western Infirmary, Glasgow (tel 0141 211 2884, fax 0141 211 2895)

REID, Dr Mark McClean; s of E Mayne Reid, CBE (d 1985), and Meta, *née* Hopkins (d 1990); *b* 27 December 1937; *Educ* Bangor GS, Queen's Univ Belfast (MB BChir); *m* 10 July 1964, Barbara, da of James Cupples (d 1986); 1 s (Alistair b 18 Aug 1966), 2 da (Fiona b 1 Nov 1968, Claire b 20 July 1973); *Career* conslt paediatrician with special interest in new-born Royal Maternity Hosp Belfast 1978–2005, ret; pres: Irish Perinatal Soc 1979–80, Ulster Paediatric Soc 1987–88; chm: NI Postgrad Paediatric Cmmn 1985–, Royal Maternity Hosp and Royal Belfast Hosp for Sick Children 1996–98; memb: BMA, Br Paediatric Assoc (memb Cncl 1981–84), Ulster Med Soc, Ulster Paediatric Soc, Irish Perinatal Soc, Ulster Obstetric and Gynaecological Soc, Cncl RCPI 1994–99; FRCPGlas, FRCPI, FRCPEd; *Books* Handbook Neonatal Intensive Care (jtly, 1 and 2 edns), various pubns on perinatal or neonatal field in Br Euro and N American jls 1967–; *Recreations* mountain climbing, travel, cycling, gardening, photography; *Style*— Dr Mark Reid; ✉ 10 Kensington Gardens, Hillsborough, Co Down BT26 6HP (tel 02892 682267)

REID, Michael William Peter Cameron; s of late William Arthur Reid, colonial offr, and Judy, *née* McNally, civil servant; *b* 25 April 1946; *Educ* Gordonstoun, City of London Coll; *m* 1, 22 April 1970, Margaret Wendy, *née* Aikman (d 1999); 2 s (James Cameron b 24 Sept 1973, Alexander Cameron b 21 July 1978), 1 da (Victoria Sarah Cameron b 21 Feb 1975); m 2, 21 June 2001, Janet, *née* Russell; 1 step da (Alexandra Joanne b 16 Aug 1975); *Career* chief exec Titmuss Sainer Dechert Slrs 1987–95, chief exec Watson, Farley and Williams Slrs 1995–2002, commercial dir Northamptonshire CC 2003–; FCCA 1980 (ACCA 1973); *Recreations* travelling, mountain walking; *Style*— Michael Reid; ✉ Biggin Lodge, Yardley Hastings, Northamptonshire NN7 1HN

REID, His Hon Judge (James) Robert; QC (1980); s of His Hon Judge John Alexander Reid, MC (d 1969), and Jean Ethel, *née* Ashworth (d 1991); *b* 23 January 1943; *Educ* Marlborough, New Coll Oxford, (MA); *m* 25 May 1974 (m dis 2002), Anne Prudence, da of John Arkell Wakefield; 2 s (Edward b 1976, David b 1978), 1 da (Sarah b 1980); *Career* called to the Bar Lincoln's Inn 1965 (bencher 1988); recorder of the Crown Court 1985–99, head of chambers, circuit judge (SE Circuit) 1999–; memb Court of Arbitration on Sport

1999–; chm Barristers' Benevolent Assoc 1995–99; FCIArb; *Style*— His Hon Judge Reid, QC; ✉ c/o Treasury Office, Lincoln's Inn, London WC2A 3TL

REID, Sir Robert Paul (Bob); kt (1990); *b* 1 May 1934; *Educ* Univ of St Andrews (MA); *m* 1958, Joan Mary; 3 s (Douglas, William, Robert); *Career* Shell International Petroleum Co Ltd: joined 1956, posted overseas (Brunei, Nigeria, Thailand and Australia), dir 1984–90; chm and chief exec Shell UK Ltd 1985–90; chm: British Rail 1990–95, London Electricity plc 1994–97, Sears plc 1995–99, British Borneo Oil & Gas plc 1995–2000, ICE Futures 1999–; dep govr Bank of Scotland 1997–2004; non-exec dir: Merchants Trust 1995–, Sun Life Financial Services of Canada 1997–2004, Avis Europe plc 1997–2004 (chm 2002–04), Siemens 1998–2006, Intercontinental Exchange Inc 2001, HBOS plc 2001–04, CHC Helicopter Corporation 2004; chm: Conservatoire for Dance and Drama, Edinburgh Business Sch, Fndn for Young Musicians, Learning Through Landscapes; memb Cncl for Industry and HE; tstee: Sci Museum 1987–92, Fndn for Young Musicians, Civic Tst, IPE Charitable Tst; chllr Robert Gordon Univ 1993–2004; companion Inst of Mgmnt; Hon LLD: Univ of St Andrews 1987, Univ of Aberdeen 1988; Hon DSc Univ of Salford 1990; Hon Dr: South Bank Univ 1995, Sheffield Hallam Univ 1995; Hon FCGI, FRSE; *Recreations* golf; *Clubs* MCC, R&A, Royal Melbourne (Melbourne), Royal Mid-Surrey, Frilford Heath Golf; *Style*— Sir Bob Reid; ✉ 24 Ashley Gardens, London SW1P 1QD (tel 020 7233 6349, e-mail bobreid@theice.com)

REID, Robert Rickman; s of Robert John Reid, and Kathleen Mary, *née* Cowley; *b* 20 August 1966; *Educ* Treverton Coll Mooi River, Silwood Kitchen Private Cooking Coll Cape Town; *Career* chef; Carlton Hotel Johannesburg 1988–89, Roger Verge's Moulin de Mougins (3 Michelin stars) 1989–91, Cordile Restaurant Strasbourg (3 Michelin stars) 1991, Joel Roubishon Restaurant (3 Michelin stars) 1991–93, head chef Marco Pierre White Hyde Park Hotel London (3 Michelin stars) 1993–2001, head chef The Oak Room Marco Pierre White Le Meridian Hotel London 2001–03, White's 2003–; won numerous South African nat competitions, South African Young Chef of the Year Award 1988; *Recreations* fishing, shooting, travelling, sailing; *Style*— Robert Reid, Esq

REID, Seona Elizabeth; da of George Robert Hall Reid (d 1981), of Glasgow, and Isobel Margaret, *née* Sewell; *b* 21 January 1950; *Educ* Park Sch Glasgow, Univ of Strathclyde (BA), Univ of Liverpool (DBA); *Career* business mangr Theatre Royal Lincoln 1972–73, PR offr Northern Dance Theatre 1973–76, PR offr Ballet Rambert 1976–79, freelance 1979–80, dir Shape London 1980–87, asst dir Strategy and Regnl Devpt Gtr London Arts 1987–90, dir Scottish Arts Cncl 1990–99, dir Glasgow Sch of Art 1999–; vice-chair: Lighthouse Centre for Architecture, Design and the City; memb Bd: Suspect Culture, Out of the Box at Cove Park; memb: Scottish Advsy Ctee Br Cncl, Knowledge and Evaluation Ctee AHRC; Hon DArts Robert Gordon Univ, Hon DLitt Univ of Glasgow, Hon DLitt Glasgow Caledonian Univ, hon prof Univ of Glasgow; FRSA; *Recreations* walking, food, the Arts, travel; *Style*— Ms Seona Reid; ✉ The Glasgow School of Art, 167 Renfrew Street, Glasgow G3 6RQ (tel 0141 353 4500, e-mail s.reid@gsa.ac.uk)

REID, Prof Stephen Robert; s of Stephen Robert Reid (d 1978), of Manchester, and Mary, *née* Beresford (d 1976); *b* 13 May 1945; *Educ* Chorlton GS Manchester, Victoria Univ of Manchester (BSc, PhD), Univ of Cambridge (MA, ScD); *m* 30 Aug 1969, Susan, da of Geoffrey Bottomley; 3 s (Andrew b 25 June 1971, David b 24 April 1974, Alistair 10 Oct 1980); *Career* research offr CEGB 1969–70; lectr: Dept of Engrg UMIST 1970–76, Dept of Engrg Univ of Cambridge 1976–80; Jackson prof of engrg sci Univ of Aberdeen 1980–84, Conoco prof of mech engrg UMIST (now Univ of Manchester) 1985–2004 (pro-vice-chllr for academic devpt 1992–95, pro-vice-chllr for research 2001–04), 6th century research prof of dynamic structural mechanics Univ of Aberdeen 2006–; ed-in-chief Int Jl of Mechanical Sciences 1987–; pres IMA 2000–01; author of over 200 tech papers; Safety Award in Mech Engrg IMechE; fell Clare Coll Cambridge 1977–80; FIMA 1982, FIMechE 1984, FASME 1992, FREng 1993; *Style*— Prof Stephen Reid, FREng; ✉ 2 Waters Reach, Poynton, Stockport, Cheshire SK12 1XT (tel 01625 872842); Department of Engineering, University of Aberdeen, Fraser Noble Building, King's College, Aberdeen AB24 3UE (e-mail steve.reid@abdn.ac.uk)

REID BANKS, Lynne; da of Dr James Reid-Banks (d 1953), and Muriel Alexandra Marsh (d 1982, actress, stage name Muriel Alexander); *b* 31 July 1929; *Educ* various schs in England and Canada, Italia Conti Stage Sch, RADA; *m* Chaim Stephenson, sculptor; 3 s (Adiel b 1965, Gillon b 1967, Omri b 1968); *Career* actress 1949–54, reporter ITN 1955–62, teacher of English Israel 1963–71; full time writer and lectr 1971–; visiting teacher and lectr to international schs: Tanzania 1988, Israel (Arab Sector) 1989, Nepal 1990, US (incl Navajo Reservation) 1991, India 1991 and 1997, Germany 1996, Canary Islands 1999, Bulgaria 1999, Paris 2000 and 2002, Trieste 2000, Budapest 2000, Geneva 2001 and 2004, Zimbabwe 2001, Australia 2001, South Africa 2004, Tobago 2005, Palestine 2005, Japan 2006; involved in video conferencing worldwide through Pulycom/AT&T; author of several plays for stage, TV and radio, numerous articles in The Observer, The Guardian, TES, The Times, The Telegraph, Sunday Telegraph, The Independent and various magazines; memb: Soc of Authors, Equity, PEN; *Plays* It Never Rains (BBC TV, 1954), Already It's Tomorrow (BBC TV, 1955), All in a Row (1956), The Killer Dies Twice (1956), The Gift (1969, ITV 1975), The Stowaway (BBC Radio, 1970), The Eye of the Beholder (1975), A Question of Principle (Radio 4, 1987), Travels of Yoshi and the Tea-Kettle (for children, Polka Theatre 1991–92, Fringe Award); *Fiction* The L-Shaped Room (1960, film 1962, 10 translations, several radio versions), An End to Running (1962), Children at the Gate (1968), The Backward Shadow (1970, serialised BBC Radio 4 2005), Two is Lonely (1974), Defy the Wilderness (1981), The Warning Bell (1984), Casualties (1987), Fair Exchange (1998); *Biographical novels* Dark Quartet - the story of the Brontës (1976, Yorks Arts Literary Award), Path to the Silent Country (sequel, 1977); *For young adults* One More River (1973, rewritten and reissued 1992), Sarah and After (1975), My Darling Villain (1977), The Writing on the Wall (1981), Melusine - a Mystery (1988), Broken Bridge (sequel to One More River, 1995); *Children's* The Adventures of King Midas (1977, rewritten and reissued 1993), The Farthest-Away Mountain (1977), I, Houdini (1978), The Indian in the Cupboard (1980, also film, Pacific NW Choice Award 1984, Calif Young Readers' Medal 1984, Virginia Children's Choice 1988, Massachusetts Children's Choice 1988, Rebecca Caudill Award 1988, Arizona Children's Choice 1989 and others), Maura's Angel (1984), The Fairy Rebel (1985), Return of the Indian (1986, Indian Paintbrush Award Wyoming 1989), Secret of the Indian (1989, Great Stone Face Children's Book Award Vermont 1991), The Magic Hare (1991), The Mystery of the Cupboard (1993, West Virginia Children's Book Award, 1995), Harry the Poisonous Centipede (1996, Smarties Silver Medal 1997, Nevada Children's Choice Award 2001), Angela and Diabola (1997), The Key to the Indian (1998), Moses in Egypt (1998), Alice-by-Accident (2000), Harry the Poisonous Centipede's Big Adventure (2000), The Dungeon (2002), Stealing Stacey (2004), Tiger, Tiger (2004), Harry the Poisonous Centipede Goes to Sea (2005); *History* Letters to My Israeli Sons (1979), Torn Country: An Oral History of Israel's War of Independence (1982); *Recreations* theatre, travel, gardening, talking; *Style*— Ms Lynne Reid Banks; ✉ c/o Watson Little Ltd, 48–56 Bayham Place, London NW1 0EU (tel 020 7388 7529, fax 020 7388 8501, website www.lynnereidbanks.com)

REID ENTWISTLE, Dr Ian; s of John Morton Entwistle, and Mary, *née* Reid; *b* 29 September 1931; *Educ* Rivington and Blackrod Sch, Univ of Liverpool Med Sch (MB ChB, FRCGP, FFOM (I), FFOM, DFFP, Cert GAM); *m* 15 May 1969, Anthea Margaret (d 1979), da of Kenneth Evans, of West Kirby, Wirral; 2 s (John b 1972, Alexander b 1973); *Career* Surgn Lt HMS Eaglet RNR 1962–65; specialist (EU accredited) in occupational med RCP; princ med offr RMS Queen Mary, Queen Elizabeth and Queen Elizabeth II 1961–; casualty offr David Lewis Northern Hosp Liverpool 1957, house physician to prof of child health Royal Liverpool Children's Hosp 1957, princ in private and NHS practice 1958–2001, med supt Cunard plc 1966–96, med conslt Br Eagle Int Airlines 1966–68, sr gp med conslt United Gas Industries 1971–80, conslt in occupational med to Nuffield Hosps 1993–95, med dir Berkeley St Travel Clinic 1996–2002, conslt occupational physician Previa UK Ltd 1996–2003, National Medical 1998–2003, BMI 1998–, med examiner Linpac Plastics Ltd 1998–; sr med conslt until 2001: BHS plc, Mothercare; ptnr Lawwise Medico-legal Consultants; pt/t med conslt: American Colloid Co 1989–95, Bass Taverns 1993–95, Spillers Foods Ltd 1996–97; pt/t authorised assessor and examiner: Civil Aviation Authy 1966–, Maritime and Coastguard Agency 1966–; examiner to Med Servs DWP 1995–2004; accredited specialist in occupational medicine; appointed selected medical practitioner in compliance with Home Office police pension regulations 2003–; conslt Pre-Retirement Assoc; chm Brewing Industry Med Advsrs 1987–97; treas and sec Merseyside and N Wales RCGP 1973–80 (bd memb 1963–89), jt treas and sec Soc of Occupational Med (Merseyside) 1961–67, memb Cncl Birkenhead Med Soc 1995– (pres 1998–99); memb: Aerospace Physiology and Med Working Pty Cncl of Europe 1974–, NASA 1969–; med advsr West Kirby Swimming Club for Disabled; underwriting memb Lloyd's 1978–99; memb Assurance Med Assoc, FRAeS, assoc fell Aerospace Med Assoc USA 1973, FCIM 1988; *Books* Exacta Mecanix (5 edn 1988), Exacta Paediatrica (3 edn 2003), Exacta Medica (4 edn 2003); *Recreations* motor racing, horticulture, horology, photography, railway modelling; *Clubs* Cheshire Pitt, Manchester Naval Offrs Assoc; *Style*— Dr Ian Reid Entwistle; ✉ Knollwood, 42 Well Lane, Gayton, Wirral CH60 8NG (tel 0151 342 2332, mobile 07795 096270); consultation suite: 42 Well Lane, Gayton, Wirral CH60 8NG (tel 07050 261 980, fax 0151 342 5135, e-mail ianreidentwistle@tiscali.co.uk)

REID SCOTT, David Alexander Carroll; s of Maj Alexander Reid Scott, MC (d 1960), and Ann, *née* Mitchell (d 1953); *b* 5 June 1947; *Educ* Eton, Lincoln Coll Oxford (MA); *m* 1, 23 April 1972, Anne (d 1988), da of Phillipe Clouet des Pesruches (d 1977); 3 da (Iona b 1975, Camilla b 1976, Serena b 1979); m 2, 7 July 1990 (m dis 1997), Elizabeth, da of John Latshaw; m 3, 25 Sept 1997, Clare, da of Maj Ivan Straker; 1 s (Nico b 2001); *Career* 1 vice-pres White Weld & Co 1969–77, seconded sr advsr Saudi Arabian Monetary Agency 1978–83, md Merrill Lynch & Co 1983–84, md DLJ Phoenix Securities Ltd 1984–98, vice-chm Donaldson Lufkin & Jenrette 1998–2000, vice-chm CSFB 2000–01, chm Hawkpoint Partners 2001–; *Recreations* Irish country life, field sports, arts, antiques; *Clubs* Turf, Kildare St, Whites; *Style*— David A C Reid Scott, Esq; ✉ 2 Cottesmore Gardens, London W8 5PR (tel 020 7938 1831); Ballynure, Grange Con, Co Wicklow, Ireland (tel 00 353 45 403162, fax 00 353 45 403329)

REIDY, Dr John Francis; s of Frederick Cyril Reidy (d 1957), and Marie Isobel, *née* Smith (d 2002); *b* 25 August 1944; *Educ* Stonyhurst, St George's Hosp Med Sch and King's Coll London (MB BS, MRCS); *m* 25 Nov 1978, Dianne Patricia, da of Gerald Eugene Murphy, of Launceston, Tasmania; 1 s (Thomas Edward b 19 Nov 1980), 1 da (Laura Eugenie b 1 June 1982); *Career* conslt radiologist Guy's and St Thomas' Hosp 1980–, hon conslt radiologist Gt Ormond St Children's Hosp 1997–; Liveryman Worshipful Soc of Apothecaries; fell Cardiovascular and Interventional Soc of Europe, FRCR 1975, FRCP 1988 (LRCP 1967, MRCP 1970); *Books* numerous pubns on cardiovascular and interventional radiology; *Style*— Dr John Reidy; ✉ 19 Cumberland Street, London SW1V 4LS (tel 020 7834 3021); Radiology Department, Guy's Hospital, London SE1 9RT (tel 020 7188 5565, fax 020 7188 5523, e-mail john.reidy@gstt.nhs.uk)

REIF, Prof Stefan Clive; s of Peter Reif (d 1989), and Annie, *née* Rapstoff (d 2002); *b* 21 January 1944; *Educ* Boroughmuir Sch Edinburgh, Univ of London (BA, William Lincoln Shelley studentship, PhD), Univ of Cambridge (MA, LittD); *m* 1967, Shulamit, da of Edmund (d 1995) and Ella Stekel (d 1992); 1 da (Tanya b 25 Dec 1968), 1 s (Aryeh b 30 Jan 1970); *Career* lectr in Hebrew and Semitic languages Univ of Glasgow 1968–72, asst prof of Hebrew language and literature Dropsie Coll Philadelphia 1972–73; Univ of Cambridge: dir Genizah Res Unit 1973–2006, head Oriental Div Univ Library 1983–2006, prof of medieval Hebrew studies 1998–2006, fell St John's Coll 1998–; visiting prof: Hebrew Univ of Jerusalem 1989 and 1996–97, Univ of Pennsylvania 2001; memb Int Advsy Panel Int Soc for the Study of Deuterocanonical and Cognate Literature; memb: Br Assoc for Jewish Studies (pres 1992), Jewish Historical Soc of England (pres 1991–92), Cambridge Theological Soc (pres 2002–04); hon fell Mekize Nirdamim Soc Jerusalem; FRAS 1980; *Books* Shabbethai Sofer and his Prayer-Book (1979), Interpreting the Hebrew Bible (1982), Published Material from the Cambridge Genizah Collections (1988), Genizah Research After Ninety Years (1992), Judaism and Hebrew Prayer (1993), Hebrew Manuscripts at Cambridge University Library (1997), A Jewish Archive from Old Cairo (2000), Why Medieval Hebrew Studies? (2001), The Cambridge Genizah Collections: Their Contents and Significance (2002), Problems with Prayers (2006); *Recreations* squash, cricket and football; *Style*— Prof Stefan Reif; ✉ Genizah Research Unit, Cambridge University Library, West Road, Cambridge CB3 9DR (tel 01223 766370, fax 01223 333160, e-mail scr3@cam.ac.uk)

REILLY, Mary Margaret; da of John Patrick Reilly (d 1987), and Helena; *b* 22 May 1953; *Educ* Notre Dame, UCL (BA); *m* 17 March 1979, Mark Richard Charles Corby, s of Peter John Siddons Corby; 1 da (b 1981), 1 s (b 1986); *Career* ptnr Deloitte & Touche 1987–; chm: London Devpt Agency 2004–, London regnl cncl CBI 2004–06; FCA 1989 (ACA 1978), FRSA 1989; *Recreations* country pursuits, skiing, opera, theatre; *Style*— Ms Mary Reilly; ✉ Deloitte & Touche LLP, Hill House, 1 Little New Street, London EC4A 3TR (tel 020 7007 2994, fax 020 7007 2173, e-mail mmreilly@deloitte.co.uk)

REILLY, (David) Nicholas (Nick); CBE; s of John Reilly (d 1981), of Anglesey, and Mona, *née* Glynne Jones; *b* 17 December 1949; *Educ* Harrow, St Catharine's Coll Cambridge (MA); *m* Susan, *née* Haig; 2 da (Natasha b 1978, Jessica b 1981), 1 s (George b 1979); *Career* investment analyst 1971–74; General Motors: joined 1974, finance dir Moto Diesel Mexicana Mexico 1980–83, supply dir Vauxhall Motors 1984–87, vice-pres IBC 1987–90, mfrg dir Vauxhall Ellesmere Port 1990–94, vice-pres Quality General Motors Europe 1994–96, chm and md Vauxhall Motors 1996–2002, vice-pres General Motors Corp 1997–, pres and ceo GM Daewoo (Korea) 2001–; chm IBC Vehicles 1996–2002, memb Bd Saab GB 1996–2002; chm: Trg Standards Cncl 1997–2001, CBI Econ Affairs Ctee 1999–2001, Chester, Ellesmere, Wirral TEC (CEWTEC) 1990–94, Oundle Sch Fndn 1997–2001, Adult Learning Inspectorate (ALI) 2000–02; memb Cmmn for Integrated Tport 1998–2001; FIMI 1990 (vice-pres 1996); *Recreations* tennis, swimming, sailing, golf, skiing, watching rugby and other sports, music, opera, theatre; *Clubs* RAC, Oundle Rugby (founding memb), Luton Rugby, Leicester Rugby; *Style*— Nick Reilly, Esq, CBE

REINTON, Sigurd E; s of Dr Lars Reinton (d 1987), and Ingrid, *née* Evang (d 1984); *b* 9 November 1941; *Educ* Univ of Oslo, Univ of Lund (MBA); *m* 19 Nov 1966, Arlette, da of Roger Dufresne; 2 da (Sandra b 27 Oct 1967, Karine 15 May 1971); *Career* Nat Serv 1960–61; co-fndr Audio Nike Lund 1964–66, account planner then account supr Young & Rubicam Stockholm/Copenhagen 1966–68; McKinsey & Co London: joined 1968, ptnr 1976–81, dir 1981–88; chm Express Aviation Services London 1988–91; dir: Aubin Holdings 1988–98, Freewheel Film Finance Ltd 2000–03, NATS Holdings Ltd 2007–; chm Mayday Healthcare NHS Tst 1997–99, chm London Ambulance Service NHS Tst 1999–; memb Nat Cncl NHS Confedn 1998–; Ambulance Servs Assoc: memb Nat Cncl 2001–, dir 2005–; memb Advsy Bd The Foundation 2005–; author of various articles on corp strategy (FT, McKinsey Quarterly); *Recreations* political and economic history, theatre, flying (PPL/IR); *Clubs* RAC; *Style*— Sigurd E Reinton, Esq; ✉ London

Ambulance Service NHS Trust, 220 Waterloo Road, London SE1 8SD (tel 020 7921 5185, fax 020 7921 5127)

REISS, Charles Alexander; s of Dr J C Reiss (d 1979), of London; *b* 23 March 1942; *Educ* Bryanston; *m* 1978, Susan, da of Sir John Newson-Smith; 3 da (Rowan b 10 Sept 1978, Holly b 1 Sept 1980, Bryony b 22 Aug 1986); *Career* political corr and leader writer Evening News 1975–80, political editor Evening Standard 1985– (political corr and leader writer 1980–85); *Clubs* RAC; *Style*— Charles Reiss, Esq; ✉ Evening Standard, Northcliffe House, 2 Derry Street, London W8 5EE

REISS, Canon Robert Paul; s of Paul Reiss (d 1986), and Beryl Reiss (d 1995); *b* 20 January 1943; *Educ* Haberdashers' Aske's Sch Hampstead, Trinity Coll Cambridge (MA), Westcott House Cambridge; *m* 7 Nov 1985, Dixie, *née* Nichols; 1 da (Anya b 27 Nov 1991); *Career* ordained deacon 1969, priest 1970; curate St John's Wood Dio of London 1969–73, asst missioner Rajshahi Mission Dio of Dacca Bangladesh May-Sept 1973, chaplain Trinity Coll Cambridge 1973–78, selection sec Advsy Cncl for the Church's Miny 1978–85 (sr selection sec 1983–85), team rector Grantham Dio of Lincoln 1986–96, archdeacon of Surrey 1996–2005, canon of Westminster 2005–; memb Gen Synod 1990–2005; tstee Churches Conservation Tst 2002–; *Publications* Say One For Me (contrib, 1992); *Recreations* cricket, golf; *Clubs* Oxford and Cambridge, MCC, Worplesdon Golf; *Style*— Canon Robert Reiss; ✉ 1 Little Cloister, Westminster, London SW1P 3PL (tel 020 7654 4804, e-mail robert.reiss@westminster-abbey.org)

REITH, Gen Sir John George; KCB (2003, CB 2000), CBE (1991, OBE 1989); s of John Archibald Frederick Reith, and Jean Hope, *née* Cameron; *Educ* Eliots Green Sch, RMA Sandhurst, Army Staff Coll; *Career* MA to GOC Northern Ireland 1984–86 (mentioned in despatches 1985, 1986); CO 1 Bn Parachute Regt 1986–88, COS 1 Armed Div Germany 1988–90, COS 1 (UK) Div Gulf 1990–91, cmd 4 Armed Bde Germany 1992–93, cmd UN Sector SW Bosnia 1994, dir Int Organisations MOD 1994–95, dir Mil Ops MOD 1995–97, cmd Ace Mobile Force (Land) NATO 1997–99, cmd Albania Force NATO 1999, Asst Chief of Defence Staff (Policy) MOD 2000–01, Chief of Jt Ops 2001–04, DSACEUR NATO 2004; GSM 1962 (with NI Bar 1971), Queen's Jubilee Medal 1977, Gulf Medal with Rosette (combat zone) 1991, Liberation Medal (Class 2, Kuwait) 1991, Victory Medal 1991 (Saudi Arabia), Queen's Commendation for Valuable Service 1994, UNPROFOR Medal 1994, Kosovo Medal 1999, Queen's Golden Jubilee Medal 2002; Freeman City of London; Cross of Merit (Class 2, Czech Republic) 1999, Order of the Golden Eagle (Albania) 1999; *Recreations* walking, gardening, cooking; *Clubs* Army and Navy; *Style*— Gen Sir John Reith, KCB, CBE; ✉ DSACEUR, SHAPE, BFPO 26 (tel 00 326 544 4949, fax 00 326 544 4205)

REITH, Dr William (Bill); s of Andrew Christie Millar Reith, of North Berwick, and Catherine Mathieson, *née* Wishart; *b* 17 August 1950; *Educ* North Berwick HS, Univ of Edinburgh (BSc, MB ChB, Judo blue); *m* Gillian, da of John Brown; 2 da (Jane Susan b 27 March 1980, Sally Fiona b 7 May 1982); *Career* trainee Aberdeen Vocational Trg Scheme for General Practice 1975–78, princ in general practice Westburn Medical Gp Foresterhill Health Centre Aberdeen 1978–; regnl advsr in general practice Grampian Health Bd 1986–96 (assoc advsr 1983–86), special advsr in primary care Scottish Cncl for Postgrad Med and Dental Educn 1997–98; RCGP: chm NE Scotland Faculty Bd 1986–89, memb UK Cncl 1990–2003, chm UK Educn Network 1993–94, hon sec UK Cncl 1994–99, chm Scottish Cncl 2000–03, chm Postgrad Training Ctee 2005–; memb: Jt Ctee on Postgrad Trg for General Practice 1992–99, Clinical Res and Audit Gp Health Dept Scottish Office 1993–98, Scottish Acad of Med Royal Colls and Faculties 2000–, Advsy Panel NHS Scotland Review of Mgmnt 2002–03; hon sr lectr Dept of General Practice Univ of Aberdeen 1993–98 (hon clinical lectr 1983–93); FRCGP 1991 (MRCGP 1978), FRCPEd 1994, FRSA 1998, founding fell Inst of Contemporary Scotland (FFCS) 2001; *Recreations* food and wine, hill walking; *Style*— Dr Bill Reith; ✉ 54 Gray Street, Aberdeen AB10 6JE (tel 01224 326380, e-mail bill.reith@btinternet.com)

RELPH, Simon George Michael; CBE (2004); s of Michael George Leighton Relph (d 2004), the film writer, director and producer, and Doris, *née* Ringwood (d 1978); *b* 13 April 1940; *Educ* Bryanston, King's Coll Cambridge (MA); *m* 14 Dec 1963, Amanda Jane, da of Col Anthony Grinling, MC (d 1981), of Dyrham Park, Wilts; 1 s (Alexander James b 16 June 1967), 1 da (Arabella Kate b 17 Sept 1975); *Career* film producer; asst dir feature films 1961–73, prodn admin Nat Theatre 1974–78, prodn supervisor Yanks 1978, exec prodr Reds 1979–80, prodr and co-prodr 1981–85 (The Return of the Soldier, Privates on Parade, The Ploughman's Lunch, Secret Places, Wetherby, Comrades), chief exec Br Screen Finance Ltd 1986–90, exec prodr Enchanted April 1991, co-prodr Damage 1992; prodr: Secret Rapture 1992, Camilla 1993, Look me in the Eye 1994, Blue Juice 1994, Slab Boys 1996, Land Girls 1997; exec prodr: Hideous Kinky 1998–99, Bugs (Imax 3D film); chm Children's Film and TV Fndn 1999–2005, chm BAFTA 2000–02, dir Bristol Old Vic 2000–, dir South West Screen 2001–; industry prof of film Univ of Bristol 2001–; memb Cncl RCA 1989–99, govr BFI 1991–97, govr Nat Film and TV Sch 2002–; Hon FRCA; Chevalier de l'Ordre des Arts et des Lettres (France); *Recreations* golf, photography, fishing; *Style*— Simon Relph, Esq, CBE

REMFRY, David Rupert; MBE (2001); s of Geoffrey Rupert Remfry, of Worthing, W Sussex, and Barbara, *née* Ede; *b* 30 July 1942; *Educ* Hull Coll of Art; *m* 1, 1963 (m dis 1971), Jacqueline Wayne Alwyn; 2 s (Jacob Rupert b 1967, Samuel b 1968); *m* 2, 1976 (m dis 1994), Jacqueline Ruby Crisp; 1 s (Gideon Jethro b 1970), 1 step s (Joe b 1966); *Career* artist; elected memb: Royal Watercolour Soc 1987, Royal Acad of Art 2006; *Solo Exhibitions* incl: New Grafton Gallery 1973, Editions Graphiques 1974, Ferens Gallery Hull 1975, Folkestone Art Gallery 1976, Mercury Gallery London (biennially) 1978–94 and 1997, Bohun Gallery Henley-on-Thames 1978, 1981, 1983, 1985, 1987, 1991, 1993 and 1996, Galerie de Beerenburght Holland 1979, 1980, 1982 and 1983, Ankrum Gallery Los Angeles 1980, 1983, 1985 and 1987, Middlesbrough Art Gallery 1981, Zack Schuster Gallery Boca Raton 1986, 1988 and 1990, Margaret Lipworth Fine Art Boca Raton 1992, 1994 and 1997, Nat Portrait Gallery 1992, Portal Gallery Bremen Germany 1993 and 1995, Tatistcheff Gallery NY 1996, Elaine Baker Gallery Boca Raton 1999, 2002, 2003 and 2007, Boca Raton Museum of Art 1999 and 2002, Neuhoff Gallery NY 1999, 2001 and 2004, PSI Contemporary Art Gallery NY (MOMA affiliate) 2001–02, V&A London 2003, Butler Inst of American Art OH 2004, Ferens Gallery Hull 2005, Fitzwilliam Museum Cambridge 2005; *Work in Collections* Boca Raton Museum of Art, Royal Collection, Nat Portrait Gallery, V&A Museum, Middlesbrough Art Gallery, Swathmore Coll Pa, Museo Rayo Columbia, Minnesota Museum of American Art, Butler Inst of Art OH USA, Br Museum London, Fitzwilliam Museum Cambridge, Orlando Museum of Art FL, New Orleans Museum of Art USA, Bass Museum of Art Miami USA, Contemporary Art Soc London; *Recreations* opera and music generally, theatre, reading, dancing; *Clubs* Chelsea, Colony, Groucho, Soho House NY, Century Assoc, Arts; *Style*— David Remfry, Esq, MBE, RA; ✉ 19 Palace Gate, London W8 5LS (e-mail david@davidremfry.com)

REMINGTON, (James) Stephen Steel; s of Douglas Gordon Remington (d 1983), and Marjorie, *née* Steel (d 1983); *b* 19 March 1947; *Educ* Wellington, Trinity Coll Dublin (BA); *Career* theatre mangr Nottingham Playhouse 1971–72, drama offr Eastern Arts Association 1972–74, dir The Playhouse Harlow 1974–79, chief exec Sadler's Wells London 1979–94 (joined as dir), chief exec Action for Blind People 1994–; chair Vision 2020 UK 2002–; Princ/Dir of the Year UK Charity Awards 2000; Liveryman Worshipful Co of Spectacle Makers 2007; Chevalier de l'Ordre des Arts et des Lettres (France) 1991; *Recreations* gym, walking; *Clubs* Garrick; *Style*— Stephen Remington; ✉ Action for Blind People, 14–16 Verney Road, London SE16 3DZ (tel 020 7635 4800, fax 020 7635 4900, e-mail stephen.remington@actionforblindpeople.org.uk)

REMNANT, 3 Baron (UK 1928); Sir James Wogan Remnant; 3 Bt (UK 1917), CVO (1979); o s of 2 Baron Remnant, MBE (d 1967), and Norah Susan, *née* Wogan-Browne (d 1990); *b* 23 October 1930; *Educ* Eton; *m* 24 June 1953, Serena Jane, o da of Cdr Sir Clive Loehnis, KCMG, RN (ret), and his w, Rosemary Beryl, o da of Maj Hon Robert Dudley Ryder, 4 s of 4 Earl of Harrowby; 3 s, 1 da; *Heir* s, Hon Philip Remnant, *qv*; *Career* Nat Serv Lt Coldstream Guards 1948–50; ptnr Touche Ross & Co 1958–70; dir: Australian Mercantile Land and Finance 1957–69, Australia & NZ Banking Group 1965–81, Union Discount Co of London 1969–92 (dep chm 1970–86), Ultramar plc 1970–91 (dep chm 1981–91); Touche Remnant & Co: md 1970–80, chm 1980–89; chm: TR City of London Trust 1978–90 (dir 1973–90), TR Pacific Investment Trust 1987–94, National Provident Institution 1990–95 (dir 1963–95); dir: TR Technology 1988–98, Bank of Scotland 1989–96 (chm London Bd 1979–91), London Merchant Securities 1994–2002, various other cos; chm Assoc of Investment Tst Cos 1977–79; pres: YMCA England 1983–96 (previously govr and pres London Central YMCA), Florence Nightingale Fndn 1987–2004; chm Learning Through Landscapes Trust 1989–2000, tstee The Royal Jubilee Trusts 1989–99 (chm 1980–88, hon treas 1972–80); church cmmr 1976–84; Liveryman: Worshipful Co of Salters (Master 1995–96), Worshipful Co of Chartered Accountants; FCA; GCStJ (Bailiff of Egle OStJ 1993–99); *Style*— The Rt Hon the Lord Remnant, CVO; ✉ Bear Ash, Hare Hatch, Reading, Berkshire RG10 9XR

REMNANT, Hon Philip John; s and h of 3 Baron Remnant, CVO, *qv*; *b* 20 December 1954; *Educ* Eton, New Coll Oxford (MA); *m* 1977, Caroline, da of Capt Godfrey Cavendish; 1 s (Edward b 1981), 2 da (Eleanor b 1983, Sophie b 1986); *Career* Peat Marwick Mitchell and Co 1976–82, Kleinwort Benson Limited 1982–90 (dir 1988–90); Barclays de Zoete Wedd Ltd: dir 1990, md corp fin 1992, jt head UK corp fin 1993–94, head UK corp fin 1994–95, dep chief exec corp fin 1995–97, co-head M&A (advsy) 1997; dep head UK investment banking Credit Suisse First Boston 1998–2001, DG The Takeover Panel 2001–03, vice-chm and head UK investment banking Credit Suisse First Boston 2003–05, sr advsr Credit Suisse 2006–; ACA, MSI; *Style*— The Hon Philip Remnant; ✉ Credit Suisse, One Cabot Square, London E14 4QJ (tel 020 7888 8888)

RENALS, Sir Stanley; 4 Bt (UK 1895); s of Sir James Herbert Renals, 2 Bt (d 1927), and Susan Emma, *née* Crafter (d 1957); suc bro, Sir Herbert Renals, 3 Bt (d 1961); *b* 20 May 1923; *Educ* City of London Freemen's Sch; *m* 2 Jan 1957, Maria Dolores Rodriguez Pinto, da of José Rodriguez Ruiz (d 1948); 1 s; *Heir* s, Stanley Renals; *Career* serv Merchant Navy 1939–62, entered as apprentice and ret with Master Mariner (FG) Certificate World Wide; *Style*— Sir Stanley Renals, Bt; ✉ 52 North Lane, Portslade, East Sussex BN4 2HG

RENCHER, Derek; s of Walter Samuel Rencher (d 1974), of Birmingham, and Alice Gertrude, *née* Houlton (d 1960); *b* 6 June 1932; *Educ* Handsworth GS, Janet Cranmore Sch of Ballet Birmingham, Bournville Sch of Arts and Crafts Birmingham, RCA, Barbara Vernon Sch of Russian Ballet, Royal Ballet Sch; *Career* Royal Ballet performances: King of the East and Pas de Six in Prince of the Pagodas, Orion in Sylvia, Demophoon in Persephone, Haeman in Antigone, Grey Prince in Lady and the Fool, Lysander in A Midsummer Night's Dream, White Boy in Patineurs, Paris and Lord Capulet in Romeo and Juliet, Elgar in Enigma Variations, Czar Nicholas in Anastasia, Rothbart in Swan Lake, Duke in Giselle, Prince and King in Beauty, Paris Singer in Isadora, Rakitin in Month in the Country, Ancestor in Shadow Play, Emperor Franz Josef in Mayerling, Mons G M in Manon, Zeus in Creatures of Prometheus, Brahmin in La Bayadère, Doctor in Winter Dreams, Don Quixote in Don Quixote, Carrabosse in Sleeping Beauty; designer of: Swanlake Act III (Philadelphia Ballet), One in Five (Canadian National and Australian Ballet), Lament of the Waves and Siesta (Royal Opera House); *Recreations* gardening, painting, needlework, cooking, swimming, walking, book illustration; *Style*— Derek Rencher, Esq; ✉ The Royal Opera House, Covent Garden, London WC2 (tel 020 7240 1200)

RENDEL, Christopher; s of Peter Leland Fitzgerald Rendel, of Hourne Farm, Crowborough, E Sussex, and Mona Catherine, *née* Milligan, of Hammersmith, London; *b* 1 February 1955; *Educ* Bryanston, Univ of Bristol; *m* Patricia Mary; 2 s (George Oliver b 1983, Charles William b 1988); *Career* advtg exec; account mangr Mathers & Bensons 1974–80, account dir Abbott Mead Vickers 1981–87, dir FCO 1987–90, gp dir Ogilvy & Mather 1990–95, md Foote Cone & Belding 1995–98, Windmill Partnership 1999–; dir Ambache Chamber Orch 1994–; MIPA; *Recreations* music, antiques, classic cars, tennis and (watching) football; *Style*— Christopher Rendel, Esq

RENDEL, David; *b* 15 April 1949; *Educ* Eton, Univ of Oxford (BA, Rowing blue); *m*; 3 s; *Career* vol teacher VSO Cameroon and Uganda, computing and fin mgmnt with Shell International, British Gas and Esso until 1990; Parly candidate (Lib Dem): Fulham 1979 and 1983, Newbury 1987 and 1992; MP (Lib Dem) Newbury 1993–2005, spokesman (Lib Dem) on: local govt 1993–97, social security and welfare 1997–99, higher educn 2001–05; cncllr Newbury DC 1987–95 (chm Fin Sub-Ctee 1991–92, chm Recreation Ctee 1992–93); memb Public Accounts Ctee 1999–2003, memb Procedure Ctee 2001–02; *Recreations* sport, travel, walking; *Style*— David Rendel, Esq

RENDELL OF BABERGH, Baroness (Life Peer UK 1997), of Aldeburgh in the County of Suffolk; Ruth Barbara Rendell; CBE (1996); da of Arthur Grasemann (d 1973), and Ebba Elise Grasemann, *née* Kruse (d 1963); *b* 17 February 1930; *m* 1950 (re-married 1977), Donald John Rendell (d 1999); 1 s (Simon b 1953); *Career* writer; FRSL; *Awards* incl: Arts Cncl Nat Book Award Genre Fiction 1981, CWA 4 Gold Dagger Awards 1976, 1987, 1988 and 1990, 1 Silver Dagger 1984, Mystery Writers of America 3 Edgar Allen Poe Awards 1974, 1984 and 1987, Sunday Times Award for Literary Excellence 1990, Cartier-CWA Diamond Dagger Award 1991; *Books* From Doon with Death (1964), The Face of Trespass (1971), A Judgement in Stone (1976), Master of the Moor (1982), The Killing Doll (1984), An Unkindness of Ravens (1985), The New Girlfriend (1985), Live Flesh (1986), Talking to Strange Men (1987), The Veiled One (1988), The Bridesmaid (1989), Going Wrong (1990), Kissing the Gunner's Daughter (Hutchinson, 1991), The Crocodile Bird (1993), Simisola (1994), Blood Lines (1995), The Keys to the Street (1996), Road Rage (1997), A Sight for Sore Eyes (1998), Harm Done (1999), Piranha to Scurfy (2000), The Babes in the Wood (2002); under pseudonym Barbara Vine: A Dark-Adapted Eye (1986), A Fatal Inversion (1987), House of Stairs (1989), Gallowglass (1990), King Solomon's Carpet (1991), Asta's Book (1992), No Night Is Too Long (1994), The Brimstone Wedding (1996), The Chimney Sweeper's Boy (1998), Grasshopper (2000), The Minotaur (2005), End in Tears (2005); *Recreations* reading, walking, opera; *Clubs* Groucho, Detection; *Style*— The Rt Hon Baroness Rendell of Babergh, CBE; ✉ 11 Maida Avenue, Little Venice, London W2 1SR; Cherry Tree Cottage, Groton, Suffolk

RENDER, Phillip Stanley; s of Stanley Render, of Bransholme, Hull, and Bessie, *née* Bestwick; *b* 15 January 1944; *Educ* Malet Lambet HS Hull; *m* 21 Oct 1967, Patricia Mary, da of Alfred Bernard Rooms, of Hull; 2 s (Adrian b 1973, Andrew b 1978), 1 da (Suzanne b 1982); *Career* chartered surveyor in sole practice 1982–, dir Beverley Building Society 1986–; surveyor to Tstees Beverley Consolidated Charity 1973–2006; memb: Sub-Ctee Northern Assoc of Surveyors 1988–, Exec Ctee E Yorks Branch Salmon and Trout Assoc; FRICS 1968; *Recreations* salmon and trout fishing, badminton; *Clubs* Hull and E Riding Sports, S Hunsley Fly Fishing; *Style*— Phillip Render, Esq; ✉ Virginia House, 245 Northgate, Cottingham, North Humberside (tel 01482 848327)

RENFREW OF KAIMSTHORN, Baron (Life Peer UK 1991), of Hurlet in the District of Renfrew; (Andrew) Colin Renfrew; s of Archibald Renfrew (d 1978), of Giffnock, Glasgow, and Helena Douglas, *née* Savage (d 1994); *b* 25 July 1937; *Educ* St Albans Sch, St John's Coll Cambridge (BA, PhD, ScD); *m* 21 April 1965, Jane Margaret, da of Ven Walter Frederick Ewbank, Archdeacon Emeritus and Canon Emeritus of Carlisle Cathedral; 1 da (Hon Helena (Hon Mrs Renfrew-Knight) b 23 Feb 1968), 2 s (Hon Alban b 24 June 1970, Hon Magnus b 5 Nov 1975); *Career* Nat Serv Flying Offr (Signals) RAF 1956–58; reader in prehistory and archaeology Univ of Sheffield 1965–72 (formerly lectr and sr lectr), res fell St John's Coll Cambridge 1965–68, Bulgarian Govt scholarship 1966, visiting lectr UCLA 1967, prof of archaeology and head of dept Univ of Southampton 1972–81, Disney prof of archaeology Univ of Cambridge 1981–2004 (head of dept 1981–92), dir McDonald Inst for Archaeological Res 1992–2004 (fell 2004–); fell St John's Coll Cambridge 1981–86, master Jesus Coll Cambridge 1986–97 (fell 1986–); memb: Royal Cmmn for Historic Monuments of England 1977–87, Ancient Monuments Advsy Bd 1983–2002, Historic Bldgs and Monuments Cmmn 1984–86 (chm Sci Panel 1983–89); chm Nat Curriculum Art Working Gp 1990–91; tstee Br Museum 1990–2000; European Science Fndn Latsis Prize 2003, Balzan Prize 2004; Freeman City of London, Hon Citizen Deme of Sitagroi (Greece) 2000; Hon DLitt: Univ of Sheffield 1987, Univ of Southampton 1995, Univ of Liverpool 2004, Univ of Edinburgh 2004, Univ of St Andrews 2006; Dr (hc) Athens Univ 1991; hon prof Univ of Science and Technol Beijing 2005; hon fell: St John's Coll Cambridge 2005, Jesus Coll Cambridge 2005; FSA 1968, FSA Scot 1970, FBA 1980, Hon FRSE 2001; *Books* The Explanation of Culture Change: Models in Prehistory (ed, 1973), British Prehistory, a New Outline (ed, 1977), Problems in European Prehistory (1979), Approaches to Social Archaeology (1984), The Archaeology of Cult: The Sanctuary at Phylakopi (1985), Archaeology and Language: The Puzzle of Indo-European Origins (1987), The Cycladic Spirit (1991), Loot Legitimacy and Ownership: the Ethical Crisis in Archaeology (2000), Figuring It Out (2003); *Recreations* modern art, travel; *Clubs* Athenaeum, Oxford and Cambridge; *Style—* Lord Renfrew of Kaimsthorn, FBA, FSA; ✉ McDonald Institute for Archaeological Research, Downing Street, Cambridge CB2 3ER (tel 01223 333521); University of Cambridge, Department of Archaeology, Downing Street, Cambridge CB2 3DZ (tel 01223 333 521, fax 01223 333506))

RENNARD, Baron (Life Peer UK 1999), of Wavertree in the County of Merseyside; Christopher John Rennard; MBE; s of late Cecil Rennard, and Jean Rennard; *b* 8 July 1960, Liverpool; *Educ* Liverpool Blue Coat Sch, Univ of Liverpool (BA); *m* 1989, Ann, *née* McTegart; *Career* E Midlands regnl agent Lib Pty 1984–88 (election agent Mossley Hill Liverpool 1982–84), election co-ordinator Social and Lib Dems 1988–89, dir of campaigns and elections Lib Dems 1989–2003, chief exec Lib Dems 2003–; *Style—* The Rt Hon the Lord Rennard, MBE; ✉ 4 Cowley Street, London SW1P 3NB (tel 020 7222 7999, fax 020 7233 3140, e-mail chris.rennard@libdems.org.uk)

RENNERT, Jonathan; s of Sidney Rennert, of London, and Patricia, *née* Clack; *b* 17 March 1952; *Educ* St Paul's, Royal Coll of Music (fndn scholar), St John's Coll Cambridge (organ scholar, MA); *m* 10 April 1992, Sheralyn, *née* Ivil; 1 da (Imogen b 7 Jan 1996); *Career* organ recitalist, choral conductor and writer; dir of music: St Jude's Church London SW5 1975–76, St Matthew's Ottawa 1976–78, St Michael's Cornhill City of London 1979–, St Mary-at-Hill City of London 1996–; conductor: Cambridge Opera 1972–74, St Michael's Singers 1979–, The Elizabethan Singers 1983–88, St Mary-at-Hill Baroque Chamber Orch & Soloists 1996–; musical dir London Motet and Madrigal Club 1995–, master of choristers St Mary's Reigate Boys' Choir 1997–2000; many concert and recital tours on four continents; CD and LP recordings, radio and TV broadcasts as conductor, solo organist, organ accompanist, harpsichord continuo player; musician-in-residence Grace Cathedral San Francisco 1982; fndr and dir Cornhill Festival of Br Music; moderating and trg examiner Assoc Bd of the Royal Schs of Music, examiner Royal Coll of Organists; course dir and chm Central London District Ctee Royal Sch of Church Music; hon sec to the tstees Sir George Thalben-Ball Meml Tst; past pres The Organ Club, past memb Cncl Royal Coll of Organists, current memb Cncl Organists' Benevolent League; hon fell Royal Canadian Coll of Organists 1987; Master Worshipful Co of Musicians 2003–04, Warden Performers' and Composers' Section Incorporated Soc of Musicians 2002–03; ARCM 1970, LRAM 1970, FRCO 1970; *Books* William Crotch 1775–1847 Composer Artist Teacher (1975), George Thalben-Ball (1979); *Style—* Jonathan Rennert, Esq; ✉ 46 Doods Road, Reigate, Surrey RH2 0NL (tel and fax 01737 244604, mobile 07799 641699, e-mail jonathanrennert@hotmail.com)

RENNIE, Allan; *b* 5 July 1960, Stirling; *Educ* Kilsyth Acad; *Career* sub ed The Sun 1987, chief sub ed Sunday Scot 1990, asst features ed Evening News 1991, successively asst features ed, dep sports ed, features ed and asst ed Daily Record 1993, ed Sunday Mail 2000–; chm: Scottish Daily Newspaper Soc, Newspaper Press Fund Glasgow; *Recreations* golf, running; *Clubs* Hallion; *Style—* Allan Rennie, Esq; ✉ The Sunday Mail, One Central Quay, Glasgow G3 8DA (tel 0141 309 3403, e-mail arennie@sundaymail.co.uk)

RENNIE, Prof Ian George; s of Peter Bruce Rennie, of Whirlowdale, S Yorks, and Vera Margaret, *née* Haworth (d 2003); *b* 10 November 1952; *Educ* Prescott GS, Univ of Sheffield (MB ChB); *m* 1, 28 Aug 1976 (m dis 1986), Janet Mary Rennie; m 2, 19 July 1986, Sharon, da of Stanley Herbert Markland, of Waterloo, Liverpool; 1 s (James Peter b 1987), 1 da (Rachel Anne b 1988); *Career* lectr Dept of Ophthalmology Univ of Liverpool 1982–85, prof Dept of Ophthalmology and Orthoptics Univ of Sheffield 1995– (sr lectr 1985–95); non-exec dir Central Sheffield Univ Hosps Tst 1991–97; hon conslt ophthalmic surgn Royal Hallamshire Hosp 1985–; ed Eye 1995–; master Oxford Congress 2006–; Ashton Medal 1995, Duke Elder Medal 2001, Percival J Hay Medal 2004, Owen Aves Medal 2004; dip opthalmology European Cncl of Opthalmology 2003; memb RSM; FRCSEd 1981, FRCOphth 1989 (memb Cncl 1995–99, vice-pres 1999–2000, sr vice-pres 2000–03); *Recreations* astronomy, windsurfing; *Style—* Prof Ian Rennie; ✉ Church Lane House, Litton, Buxton, Derbyshire SK17 8QU (tel 01298 871586); Department of Ophthalmology and Orthoptics, University of Sheffield, Royal Hallamshire Hospital, Sheffield (tel 0114 276 2902, fax 0114 276 6381, e-mail i.g.rennie@sheffield.ac.uk)

RENNIE, Dr James Stark; s of Gavin Gordon Rennie (d 1988), of Elie, Fife, and Euphemia Mourning, *née* Agnew (d 1985); *b* 22 May 1949; *Educ* Coatbridge HS, Univ of Glasgow (BDS, PhD); *m* 1976, Ann Maris, da of Dr Douglas Campbell; 2 s (Gavin Alistair Gordon b 23 Jan 1979, David Anthony Cameron b 26 Aug 1980); *Career* house offr Glasgow Dental Hosp 1973–74, MRC research fell Glasgow Dental Hosp and Dept of Pathology Glasgow Royal Infirmary 1974–77, research fell Dept of Dental Med and Surgery Univ of Melbourne 1980–82, hon conslt in oral pathology Gtr Glasgow Health Bd 1983–; Univ of Glasgow: lectr Dept of Oral Med and Pathology 1977–84, sr lectr Dept of Oral Scis 1984–, memb Faculty of Med 1984–87, memb Senate 1985–88; W of Scotland postgrad advsr in dentistry 1990–94, dir of postgrad dental educn Scottish Cncl for Postgrad Med and Dental Educn 1994–, postgrad dental dean for Scotland 1998–; exec offr: Dental Ctee Scottish Cncl for Postgrad Med and Dental Educn 1993–, Scottish Dental Vocational Trg Ctee 1993–; memb: Chief Med Offr's Advsy Gp on Postgrad Med and Dental Educn 1990–91, Exec Ctee Conf of UK Postgrad Dental Deans 1991–, GDC 1994–99; Royal Coll of Physicians and Surgeons Glasgow: memb Dental Cncl 1990–94, sec Dental Cncl 1992–94; author of numerous scientific pubns in academic jls; tstee: Yorkhill Children's Tst 1988–90; deacon Incorporation of Skinners and Glovers of Glasgow 1986–87; FDS RCPSGlas, FDSRCSE, FFGDP, FRCPath, FRCPEd; *Recreations* golf, salmon fishing; *Style—* Dr James Rennie; ✉ NHS Education for Scotland, 2nd Floor, Hanover Buildings, 66 Rose Street, Edinburgh EH2 2NN (tel 0131 220 8607, fax 0131 225 5891)

RENNIE, Dr Janet Mary; da of Arthur Ball (d 1965), of Liverpool, and Marjorie Kennerley, *née* Jones; *b* 2 December 1954; *Educ* Belvedere Sch GPDST Liverpool, Univ of Sheffield (MB ChB, MD), Univ of London (DCH); *m* 1, 28 Aug 1976 (m dis 1986), Ian George Rennie, s of Peter Bruce Rennie; m 2, 28 Aug 1992, Ian Roscoe Watts, s of William Watts; *Career* jr hosp posts 1978–85, sr res asst Univ of Liverpool 1983–85, lectr in paediatrics Univ of Cambridge 1985–88, conslt neonatal med Rosie Maternity Hosp Cambridge 1988–95, conslt and sr lectr in neonatal med KCH London 1995–2004, conslt and sr lectr in neonatal med UCL Hosps 2004–; dir of med studies Girton Coll Cambridge 1991–95; assoc ed Archives of Disease in Childhood 1992–2001; memb: Ctee Neonatal Soc 1991–95, Ctee Br Assoc of Perinatal Medicine 1991–2001, Specialist Advsy Ctee Training Neonatal Med RCPCH 1998–2005 (chair 2001–05), Academic Bd RCPCH 1998–2001; Hon MA Univ of Cambridge; memb: RSM, Paediatric Res Assoc, Expert Witness Inst, Acad of Experts; FRCP, FRCPCH; *Books* Neonatal Cerebral Investigation, Neonatal Cranial Ultrasound, Textbook of Neonatology, Manual of Neonatal Intensive Care; numerous chapters in books on neonatal medicine; *Recreations* gym, piano, cooking; *Style—* Dr Janet Rennie; ✉ Elizabeth Garrett Anderson Obstetric Hosp, UCL Hospital, Huntley Street, London WC1E 6DH (tel 0845 155 5000 ext 8692, fax 020 7582 8353, e-mail janetmrennie@btinternet.com)

RENNIE, John Aubery; s of James Rennie (d 1987), and Ethel May, *née* Byford; *b* 19 January 1947; *Educ* KCS Wimbledon, Bart's Med Sch London; *m* 12 Aug 1972, Sheelagh Ruth, da of John Robert Winter, of White Cottage, Harmans Cross, Dorset; 3 da (Natasha Louise b 1973, Sara Rosalind b 1976, Rachel Suzannah b 1979), 1 s (Alexander John b 1982); *Career* lectr in surgery Charing Cross Hosp London, resident surgical offr St Mark's Hosp London, sr lectr and conslt King's Coll Hosp London (formerly sr registrar); fndr memb Bureau of Overseas Med Servs; FRSM, FRCS; *Style—* John Rennie, Esq; ✉ Church Farm House, Batcombe, Dorset DT2 7BG (tel 01935 83698); Department of Surgery, King's College Hospital, London SE5 (tel 020 7346 3017, fax 020 7346 3438)

RENOU, Janet (Jan); da of Eric Jones (d 2002), and Norma, *née* Lynas; *b* 16 January 1956; *Educ* Cleveland GS for Girls, Loughborough Coll of Arts Design (BA), Leicester Poly (PGCE), Teacher Trg Agency (NPQH); *Children* 2 da (Amy Ellen b 13 Dec 1982, Sophie Elizabeth b 12 April 1988); *Career* teacher Rawlins Community Coll Loughborough 1979–89 (pastoral head years 10 and 11), post 16 co-ordinator and head of art and design Djanogly City Technol Coll Nottingham 1989–91, dir of studies rising to vice-princ Landau Forte Coll Derby 1991–2002, headteacher Skipton Girls' HS 2002–; memb SHA 1991–, tstee Craven Mechanics Inst; *Recreations* hill walking, drawing and painting, swimming, travel, theatre, reading, music; *Style—* Mrs Jan Renou; ✉ Skipton Girls' High School, Gargrave Road, Skipton, North Yorkshire BD23 1QL (tel 01756 707600, fax 01756 701068, e-mail renouj@sghs.org.uk)

RENSHALL, (James) Michael; CBE (1991, OBE 1977); s of Arthur Renshall (d 1973), and Ethel, *née* Gardner (d 1970); *b* 27 July 1930; *Educ* Rydal Sch, Clare Coll Cambridge (MA); *m* Aug 1960, Kathleen Valerie, da of Harold Tyson, of Liverpool; 1 da (Susan b 1961); *Career* chartered accountant; ptnr KPMG Peat Marwick 1977–92; ICAEW: tech dir 1970–77, memb Cncl 1986–90, chm Accounting Standards Ctee 1986–90, dep chm Fin Reporting Review Panel 1991–96; dir Centre for Dispute Resolution 1990–2000, govr, vice-chm and treas Expert Witness Inst 1996–2007; hon treas CGLI 2000–03 (memb Cncl 2000–); dir KC3.net, chm C&G Pension Scheme 2004–; Master Worshipful Co of Chartered Accountants 1995–96; FCA, Hon FCGI 2005; *Recreations* theatre, art, economic and military history, gardens; *Clubs* Oxford and Cambridge; *Style—* Michael Renshall, Esq, CBE; ✉ New House, Staunton-on-Wye, Herefordshire HR4 7LW (tel and fax 01981 500624, e-mail mrenshall@aol.com)

RENSHAW, Sir (John) David; 4 Bt (UK 1903), of Coldharbour, Wivelsfield, Sussex; s of Sir (Charles) Maurice Bine Renshaw, 3 Bt (d 2002), and Isabel Bassett Popkin (later Mrs L E S Cox; decd); *b* 9 October 1945; *Educ* Ashmole Sch Southgate; *m* 1970 (m dis 1988), Jennifer, da of late Gp Capt Fredrick Murray, RAF; 2 da (Joanna b 1973, Catherine b 1978), 1 s (Thomas b 1976); *Heir* s, Thomas Renshaw; *Career* served Army 1960–69, Corpl; fatstock offr Meat and Livestock Cmmn 1974–88, self-employed furniture maker; chm Cambridge Scottish Soc 1999–2002 (ret); *Recreations* skiing, narrowboating, Scottish country dancing; *Style—* Sir David Renshaw, Bt; ✉ c/o 8 Graham House, Birdcage Walk, Newmarket, Suffolk CB8 0NE (tel 01638 603294); Chalet Stephen L'Epervier No 1, La Nouy, Thollon-les-Memises 74500, France (tel 00 33 4 50 70 05 31)

RENSHAW, Peter Bernard Appleton; s of Bernard Artoune Renshaw (d 1991), of Sale, Cheshire, and Elsie Renshaw, *née* Appleton (d 1954); *b* 23 July 1954; *Educ* Charterhouse, Selwyn Coll Cambridge; *m* 16 Oct 1982, Patricia Ann, da of Robert Vernon Caffrey, of Sale, Cheshire; 1 s (Thomas Peter b 1987); *Career* ptnr: Slater Heelis Slrs Manchester 1982–98 (articled clerk 1977–79, slr 1979–82), Addleshaw Booth & Co 1998–2002; chm Boutinot Ltd 2002–, non-exec dir W R Swann & Co Ltd 1998–; NP 1988; memb Law Soc; *Recreations* walking, gardening, skiing; *Style—* Peter Renshaw, Esq; ✉ Boutinot Ltd, Brook House, Northenden Road, Gatley, Cheshire SK8 4DN (tel 0161 908 1312, fax 0161 908 1345, e-mail peterr@boutinot.com)

RENTON, Dr Andrew; s of Michael Paul Renton, of London, and Yvonne Renee, *née* Labaton; *b* 8 February 1963; *Educ* Manchester Grammar, Univ of Nottingham (BA), Univ of Reading (PhD); *Career* fndr and artistic dir Quiet Theatre 1985–88, fndr memb Thin Men Performance Ensemble 1985–89, art critic Blitz magazine 1988–91, Br corr Flash Art magazine 1989–95, dir Cleveland (project space and imprint) London 1996–97, curator The Cranford Collection London 1999–, Slade curator Slade Sch of Fine Art London 2001–02 (lectr in theoretical studies 1997–2001), art columnist Evening Standard 2002–, dir of curating Goldsmiths Coll London 2003–; exhibitions curated: The Times London's Young Artists (Olympia London) 1991, Show Hide Show (Anderson O'Day London) 1991, Confrontaciones (Palacio di Velázquez Madrid) 1991–92, Molteplici Culture (Museo del Folklore Rome) 1992, Barcelona Abroad (Euro Visual Arts Centre Ipswich) 1992, Nothing is Hidden (London) 1992, Walter Benjamin's Briefcase (Oporto) 1993, Manifesta I (Rotterdam) 1996, Browser (Vancouver) 1997, Bankside Browser (Tate Modern) 1999, Total Object Complete with Missing Pots (Tramway Glasgow) 2001, Shumakom (Artists House Jerusalem) 2002; *Books* Technique Anglaise: current trends in British art (ed jtly, 1991); *Recreations* sleep; *Style—* Dr Andrew Renton; ✉ 5A Plympton Street, London NW8 8AB (tel 020 7724 2988, fax 020 7724 2989, e-mail ar@ar001.co.uk)

RENTON, Prof Peter Brian; s of Percy Renton (d 1974), and Margaret Adela, *née* Costain (d 1999); *b* 21 June 1944, Colby, IOM; *Educ* Castle Rushen HS IOM (Noble scholar), Univ of Liverpool (BSc, PhD); *m* June 1973, Diana Bronwen, *née* Kruger; *Career* fell then staff physicist CERN Geneva 1969–72, research physicist Vrije Universiteit Brussel 1972–76, prof of physics Univ of Oxford 1976–; ctee memb PPARC, memb Users' Advsy Ctee CERN Geneva; CPhys, FInstP 1984; *Publications* Electroweak Interactions (1990); contrib to Particle Physics; *Recreations* walking, birds and wildlife, running, theatre; *Style—* Prof Peter Renton

RENTON OF MOUNT HARRY, Baron (Life Peer UK 1997), of Offham in the County of East Sussex; Ronald Timothy (Tim) Renton; PC (1989), DL (E Sussex 2004); yr s of Ronald Kenneth Duncan Renton, CBE (d 1980), by his 2 w Eileen, MBE, yst da of Herbert James Torr, of Morton Hall, Lincs, and gda of John Torr, MP for Liverpool 1873–80; *b* 28 May 1932; *Educ* Eton, Magdalen Coll Oxford (MA); *m* 1960, Alice Blanche Helen, da of Sir James Fergusson of Kilkerran, 8 Bt (d 1973); 2 s (Hon Alexander James Torre b 1961, Hon Daniel Charles Antony (twin) b 1965), 3 da (Hon Christian Louise b 1963, Hon

R

(Katherine) Chelsea (twin) b 1965, Hon Penelope Sally Rosita b 1970); *Career* dir: Silvermines Ltd 1967–84, ANZ Banking Gp 1968–75; former md Tennant Trading; Parly candidate (Cons) Sheffield Park 1970, MP (Cons) Sussex Mid 1974–97, chm Cons Employment Ctee, PPS to John Biffen (as chief sec to Treasy) 1979–81, pres Cons Trade Unionists 1980–84 (vice-pres 1978–80), PPS to Sir Geoffrey Howe (as chllr and foreign sec) 1983–84, Parly under sec FCO 1984, min of state FCO 1984–87, min of state Home Office 1987–89, govt chief whip 1989–90, min for the Arts 1990–92, memb Select Ctee on Nat Heritage 1995–97, chm Sub-Ctee House of Lords Select Ctee on Europe 2002–06 (memb 1997–2001), chm House of Lords Info Ctee 2007–; chm Br Hong Kong Parly Gp 1992–97, memb Advsy Bd Know-How Fund for Central and Eastern Europe FCO (assistance to Russia, Central and Eastern Europe) 1992–2000, vice-chm Br Cncl 1992–98; Parly consltt to Robert Fleming & Co 1992–97, chm Fleming Continental Euro Investment Trust plc 1999–2003 (dir 1992–99); fndr pres (with Mick Jagger) Nat Music Day 1992; memb: Advsy Cncl BBC 1982–84, Governing Cncl Roedean Sch 1982–97 (pres 1998–2005), Devpt Cncl Parnham Tst 1992–2000, Criterion Theatre Tst 1992–2001, Advsy Cncl Br Consltts Bureau 1997–2002, Cncl Univ of Sussex 2000–; pres Cncl Brighton Coll 2007–; chm Cons Foreign and Cwlth Cncl 1983–84; tstee Mental Health Fndn 1985–89; chm Sussex Downs Conservation Bd 1997–2005, chm South Downs Jt Ctee 2005–; *Publications* The Dangerous Edge (1994), Hostage to Fortune (1997), Chief Whip (2004); *Recreations* writing, cultivating a vineyard, mucking about in boats, opera; *Clubs* Garrick; *Style—* The Rt Hon Lord Renton of Mount Harry, PC, DL; ✉ House of Lords, London SW1A 0PW

RENTOUL, (James) Alexander (Alex); s of Francis Rentoul, of Chiswick, London, and Sylvia Christian Rentoul; *b* 23 June 1952; *Educ* Westminster, Worcester Coll Oxford (MA); *m* 25 June 1983, Tessa Caroline Anna, da of Jeremy Stuart Latham; 3 da (Rebecca Katherine b 20 March 1990, Olivia Caroline Anna b 7 Dec 1991, Hannah Clementine Poppy b 6 March 1995); *Career* chartered accountant: KPMG Peat Marwick London 1975–79, Arthur D Little Inc London 1980–84, assoc dir corp devpt Martin Bierbaum plc 1984–85; sr planning mangr Imperial Group plc 1985, princ Fin Servs & Strategy Practice Booz Allen & Hamilton Inc London 1985–87, dir Sandler Rentoul Associates Ltd 1987–93, gp commercial dir Nurdin & Peacock plc 1993–96, sr consltt Garner International 1998, chief exec Upton & Southern Holdings plc 1998–99 (following acquisition of Garner International); dir House Schools Gp 2002–; govr: Bassett House Sch, Orchard House Sch, Prospect House Sch; ACA 1979; *Style—* Alex Rentoul, Esq; ✉ 42 Hartington Road, London W4 3TX (tel 020 8987 9777, fax 020 8987 9747, e-mail alex@rentoul.com)

RENWICK, David; *Career* comedy screenwriter; Writers' Guild Award for Best Comedy Writer 1992, Writer's Award Broadcasting Press Guild 1997, BAFTA Dennis Potter Award 1999; *Work* with Andrew Marshall, *qv*, for LWT: End of Part One (Harlequin Award), Whoops Apocalypse (NY International Film and TV Festival Award, RTS Award 1981), Hot Metal (Emmy nomination); for BBC TV: Alexei Sayle's Stuff 1989–91 (International Emmy, BPG Award, RTS Award), If You See God, Tell Him 1993; others incl: The Burkiss Way (BBC Radio 4), The Steam Video Company (Thames), Whoops Apocalypse (film, ITC), Wilt (film, Rank/LWT); as solo writer: One Foot in the Grave (BBC 1) 1989–2000 (Br Comedy Award 1991, 1992, 1993, 1995, 1996, 1997 and 2001, RTS Awards 1992, 1993 and 1994, Br Academy Award 1992, TV and Radio Club Industries Award 1995), four episodes of Agatha Christie's Poirot (LWT) 1990–91, Angry Old Men (stage play and Radio 4) 1996, Jonathan Creek (BBC) 1997 (Br Academy Award 1997, RTS Award, Nat Television Award 1998, Broadcast Productions Award 1999); *Style—* David Renwick, Esq; ✉ c/o Roger Hancock Ltd, 4 Water Lane, London NW1 8NZ (tel 020 7267 4418)

RENWICK, George Frederick; s of George Russell Renwick (d 1984), of Sidlesham, W Sussex, and Isabella Alice, *née* Watkins (d 2002); *b* 27 July 1938; *Educ* Charterhouse, New Coll Oxford (MA); *m* 16 March 1974, Elizabeth Zoe, da of Strathearn Gordon, CBE (d 1983); 1 da (Helen b 1978); *Career* Nat Serv Lt RA 1957–59; teaching assoc Northwestern Univ Sch of Law Chicago 1962–63; admitted slr 1966; ptnr Slaughter and May 1970–96 (joined 1963), chm Railway Industry Dispute Resolution Ctee 1996–, vice-chm Access Disputes Ctee 2005–; CEDR accredited mediator 2000; slr Worshipful Co of Fishmongers 1986–96; memb: Addington Soc (chm 1990–91), Law Soc; govr Marchant-Holliday Sch 2001–; *Clubs* Athenaeum, MCC; *Style—* George Renwick, Esq; ✉ 33 Dovehouse Street, London SW3 6JY (tel 020 7352 7895)

RENWICK, 2 Baron (UK 1964), of Coombe, Co Surrey; Sir Harry Andrew Renwick; 3 Bt (UK 1927); s of 1 Baron Renwick, KBE (d 1973), by his 1 w, Dorothy, *née* Parkes; *b* 10 October 1935; *Educ* Eton; *m* 1, 1965 (m dis 1989), Susan, da of Capt Kenneth Lucking (decd), and Mrs M Stormonth Darling (decd); 2 s (Hon Robert b 19 Aug 1966, Hon Michael b 26 July 1968); m 2, 1989, Mrs Homayoun Mazandi, da of late Col Mahmoud Yasdanparst (Pakzad); *Heir* s, Hon Robert Renwick; *Career* dir Gen Technology Systems 1975–93; ptnr W Greenwell and Co 1963–80; pres EURIM (European Informatics Market) 2000– (chm 1993–2000); memb Cncl Nat Cncl of Educnl Technol 1994–97; memb House of Lords Select Ctee: on the Euro Communities 1988–92 and of Sub-Ctee B (energy tport and technol) 1987–92, on Sci and Technol 1992–96; vice-pres Parly IT Ctee 2006– (vice-pres 1992–2000), hon sec Parly Space Ctee 1997–2000; vice-pres Br Dyslexia Assoc 1982– (chm 1977–82), chm Dyslexia Educnl Tst 1986–2002; *Clubs* White's, Turf, Carlton; *Style—* The Rt Hon Lord Renwick; ✉ 38 Cadogan Square, London SW1X 0JL (tel 020 7584 9777, fax 020 7581 9777, e-mail renwickha@ukonline.co.uk)

RENWICK, Iain William; *b* 29 August 1958, s of Robert Coates Renwick (d 1987), and Ann Buchanan, *née* Dodds; *Educ* Univ of Glasgow; *m* 5 May 2006 (civil partnership), Christopher James O'Hare; *Career* ceo Liberty plc 2003–07; chm Crusaid; FRSA 2005; *Recreations* gardening, keep-fit, golf, tennis, diving; *Clubs* Soho House; *Style—* Iain Renwick, Esq

RENWICK, Sir Richard Eustace; 4 Bt (UK 1921), of Newminster Abbey, Morpeth, Northumberland; s of Sir Eustace Deuchar Renwick, 3 Bt (d 1973), and late Diana Mary, da of Col Bernard Cruddas, DSO; *b* 13 January 1938; *Educ* Eton; *m* 1966, Caroline Anne, da of late Maj Rupert Leonard Eversley Milburn, JP (2 s of Sir Leonard Milburn, 3 Bt, JP), and late Anne, da of Maj Austin Scott Murray, MC; 3 s (Charles Richard b 1967, Harry Timothy b 1968, Rory Eustace Deuchar b 1975); *Heir* s, Charles Renwick; *Career* late Capt Northumberland Hussars; *Recreations* hunting, racing, point-to-pointing; *Clubs* Northern Counties (Newcastle); *Style—* Sir Richard Renwick, Bt; ✉ Whalton House, Whalton, Morpeth, Northumberland NE61 3UZ (tel 01670 775383)

RENWICK OF CLIFTON, Baron (Life Peer UK 1997), of Chelsea in the Royal Borough of Kensington and Chelsea; Sir Robin William Renwick; KCMG (1989, CMG 1980); s of late Richard Renwick, of Edinburgh, and late Clarice, *née* Henderson; *b* 13 December 1937; *Educ* St Paul's, Jesus Coll Cambridge, Univ of Paris (Sorbonne); *m* 1965, Annie Colette, *née* Giudicelli; 1 s (John), 1 da (Marie-France); *Career* Nat Serv Army 1956–58; entered Foreign Service 1963, Dakar 1963–64, FO 1964–66, New Delhi 1966–69, private sec to Min of State FCO 1970–72, first sec Paris 1972–76, cnsllr Cabinet Office 1976–78, head Rhodesia Dept FCO 1978–80, political advsr to Lord Soames as Govr of Rhodesia 1980, visiting fellow Center for Int Affairs Harvard Univ 1980–81, head of Chancery Washington 1981–84, asst under sec of state FCO 1984–87; HM ambass: to South Africa 1987–91, to Washington 1991–95, ret; chm Fluor Ltd (UK) 1996–; dep chm: Robert Fleming (Holdings) Ltd 1999–2000, Canal Plus 1997–99, BHP Billiton 1997–2005, Fluor Corporation 1997–, SABMiller (formerly South African Breweries) 1999–; vice-chm: Investment Banking JP Morgan (Europe) 2001–, JP Morgan Cazenove 2005–; dir: Richemont 1995–, British Airways 1996–2005; tstee The Economist; Hon LLD Univ of the Witwatersrand, Hon DLitt Coll of William and Mary Williamsburg VA; hon fell Jesus Coll Cambridge 1992; FRSA; *Books* Economic Sanctions (1981), Fighting with Allies (1996), Unconventional Diplomacy (1997); *Recreations* tennis, trout fishing; *Clubs* Hurlingham, Travellers, Brooks's, Pilgrims; *Style—* The Rt Hon Lord Renwick of Clifton, KCMG; ✉ JP Morgan plc, 10 Aldermanbury, London EC2V 7RF

REPIN, Vadim Victorovich; s of Victor Repin, of Novosibirsk, Russia, and Galina Karpova Repin; *b* 31 August 1971; *Educ* Novosibirsk Conservatory; *m* Caroline Diemuntsch; *Career* violinist; first prize Wieniawski Int Competition (aged eleven), winner Reine Elisabeth Concours; appeared with numerous orchs incl: Concertgebouw Orch, Berlin Symphony, NHK of Japan, Kirov Orch, San Francisco Symphony Orch, RPO, Chicago Symphony Orch, Montreal Symphony Orch, Orchestre de la Suisse Romande, Detroit Symphony, Tonhalle Zürich Orch, New York Philharmonic, Los Angeles Philharmonic, Orchestre National de France; recitals incl: La Scala, Carnegie Hall, Vienna Musikverein, Suntory Hall, Tokyo; *Recordings* on Erato Disques: Shostakovich Violin Concerto Op 99 No 1 and Prokofiev Violin Concerto Op 63 No 2 (with Hallé Orch under Kent Nagano) 1995, Prokofiev Violin Sonata Op 80 No 1 and Op 94 No 2 (with pianist Boris Beresovsky) 1995, Tchaikovsky Violin Concerto and Sibelius Violin Concerto (with LSO under Emmanuel Krivine) 1996, Ravel Sonata & Medtner Sonata (with pianist Boris Beresovsky) 1997, Mozart Violin Concerti 2, 3 and 5 (with Vienna Chamber Orchestra under Yehudi Menuhin), Tutta Bravura 1999, Live at the Louvre 1999, Strauss Sonata Op, Stravinsky Divertimento, Bartok Rumanian Folkdances (with Boris Beresovsky) 2001; on Philips: Tchaikovsky & Miaskovsky Violin Concerti (with Mariinsky Orch under Valery Gergiev) 2003; *Recreations* motoring; *Style—* Vadim Repin, Esq; ✉ c/o Eleanor Hope, Schönburgstrasse 4, A-1040 Vienna, Austria (tel 00 43 1 585 3980, fax 00 43 1 585 3981)

RETALLACK, James Keith; s of Charles Keith Retallack (d 1975), of Birmingham, and Betty Margery, *née* Heaps (d 1978); *b* 8 July 1957; *Educ* Malvern, Univ of Manchester (LLB); *Career* articled clerk Lee Crowder & Co 1979–81, admitted slr 1981; Edge & Ellison: asst slr 1981–84, assoc 1984–88, ptnr 1988–, head Employment Unit 1990–, sr ptnr 1998–2000; Hammond Suddards Edge: ptnr 2000–01, head of Birmingham office 2000–01; gp resources dir Aggregate Industries plc 2001–; *Recreations* music, reading, gardening, skiing, travel, shooting; *Style—* James Retallack, Esq; ✉ Aggregate Industries plc, Bardon Hall, Copt Oak Road, Markfield, Leicestershire (tel 01530 816600)

REUBEN, David; s of David Sassoon Reuben (d 1961), and Nancy, *née* Nissan-Jiddah; bro of Simon David Reuben, *qv*; *b* 14 September 1938; *Educ* Sir Jacob Sassoon HS Bombay, Sir John Cass Coll London; *m* 1976, Debra; 1 da (Jordana), 2 s (David, Jamie); *Career* dir Mount Star Metals until 1972, dir Metal Traders Gp 1974–77, chm Transworld Metal Group 1977–2000, jt ceo Reuben Brothers Ltd 1988–, co-fndr and tstee Reuben Brothers Fndn 2002–; Entrepreneur of the Year Variety Club Annual Property Awards 2005; *Recreations* painting, writing, golf, other sports; *Clubs* Coombe Hill Golf, Annabel's, Hurlingham, Wentworth; *Style—* David Reuben, Esq; ✉ Motcomb Estates Limited, 42–43 Upper Berkeley Street, London W1H 5QJ (tel 020 7972 0094, fax 020 7972 0097, e-mail rstone@motcomb.co.uk)

REUBEN, Simon David; s of David Sassoon Reuben (d 1961), and Nancy, *née* Nissan-Jiddah; bro of David Reuben, *qv*; *Educ* Sir Jacob Sassoon HS Bombay, Sir John Cass Coll London; *m* Aug 1973, Joyce, *née* Nounou; 1 da (Lisa-Dana-Renee b 20 Jan 1978); *Career* md J Holdsworth & Co Ltd 1965–77, md Devereux Gp of Cos 1970–77, dir and jt princ Trans World Metals Gp 1977–2000, jt ceo Reuben Brothers Ltd 1988–, co-fndr and tstee Reuben Brothers Fndn 2002–; Entrepreneur of the Year Variety Club Annual Property Awards 2005; *Recreations* film, history, avoiding cocktail parties; *Clubs* Yacht Club de Monaco, Monte Carlo Tennis, Hurlingham, Wentworth; *Style—* Simon Reuben, Esq; ✉ Reuben Brothers SA, 9 Place du Molard, 1204 Geneva, Switzerland (tel 0041 22 787 5021, fax 0041 22 787 5029, e-mail rb@reubros.com, lkeane@reubros.com or rstone@motcomb.co.uk)

REUPKE, Michael; s of Dr Willm Reupke (d 1968), and Frances Graham, *née* Kinnear; *b* 20 November 1936; *Educ* Latymer Upper Sch, Jesus Coll Cambridge (MA), Coll of Europe Bruges (Dip Euro Studies); *m* (Helen) Elizabeth, da of Edward Restrick (d 1988); 1 s (Peter b 1965), 2 da (Alison b 1968, Rachel b 1971); *Career* Reuters 1962–89: trainee journalist 1962, journalist (Geneva, London, Conakry, Paris, Bonn) 1962–69, Euro mgmnt 1970–73, chief rep W Germany 1973–74, mangr Latin America 1975–77, ed-in-chief 1978–89, gen mangr 1989; consltt 1990–; dir: Visnews Ltd 1985–89, Compex Ltd 1992–, Radio Authy 1994–99; tstee Reuter Fndn 1984–89; memb: Int Inst of Communications, Media Law Gp, Int Press Inst; *Recreations* walking, cooking, wine; *Clubs* Leander, RAC; *Style—* Michael Reupke; ✉ 27A Upper High Street, Thame, Oxfordshire OX9 3EX

REVELL, John; s of Edward Revell (d 1973), and Sithy, *née* Walton (d 1969); *b* 13 November 1947; *Educ* Wycliffe Coll, Univ of Exeter (BA), Coll of Law Guildford; *m* 26 June 1971, Yvonne, da of Edward Smith, and Mary Smith; 1 s (Neil b 28 July 1973), 1 da (Sally b 12 Oct 1976); *Career* admitted slr 1973; with Pepler and Jenkins Slrs Bath 1970–74, County Prosecuting Slrs' Office Exeter 1974–84, area prosecuting slr Plymouth 1985–86; Crown Prosecution Serv: branch crown prosecutor Plymouth 1986–93, branch crown prosecutor Bournemouth 1994–99, chief crown prosecutor Dorset 1999–; chair Dorset Criminal Justice Bd 2002–04; involved with: Victim Support Dorset, Witness Service Dorset, Dorset Race Equality Cncl; *Recreations* walking, swimming, gardening, reading, theatre; *Style—* John Revell, Esq; ✉ Crown Prosecution Service Dorset, Oxford House, Oxford Road, Bournemouth, Dorset BH8 8HA (tel 01202 498700, fax 01202 498860)

REVELL, Prof Peter Allen; s of William Allen Revell, of Leicester, and Edith Emma, *née* Pitts; *b* 28 January 1943; *Educ* Wyggeston GS Leicester, Univ of London (BSc, MB BS, PhD); *m* 11 Nov 1967, Margaret Ruth, da of John Sharples (d 1982), of Exeter; 2 s (Matthew Peter b 14 Jan 1969, David John b 25 Sept 1977), 1 da (Elizabeth Ruth b 23 March 1971); *Career* res fell MRC; presently prof, consltt pathologist and head Dept of Histopathology Royal Free and Univ Coll Sch of Med; formerly lectr, sr lectr then reader Inst of Pathology The London Hosp Med Coll; visiting prof Queen's Univ Kingston Ontario; memb: Int Skeletal Soc, Euro Soc of Biomaterials, various scientific socs in pathology and orthopaedics; FRCPath 1988 (MRCPath 1976); *Books* Pathology of Bone (1986), contrib chapters in various other books, many papers in med jls; *Recreations* choral singing and music, walking, swimming, photography; *Style—* Prof Peter Revell; ✉ The Royal Free and University College School of Medicine, Royal Free Campus, Rowland Hill Street, London NW3 2PF (tel 020 7794 0500)

REVELL, Stephen Michael; s of Alfred Vincent Revell (d 2000), and Doris, *née* Peaty (d 1985); *b* 20 December 1956; *Educ* St Mary Coll Blackburn, Christ's Coll Cambridge (MA); *m* 10 Nov 1979, Anne Marie, da of Brian Higgins; *Career* ptnr Freshfields (now Freshfields Bruckhaus Deringer) 1987– (asst slr 1979–87, US managing ptnr 1998–2002); memb: Int Bar Assoc, American Bar Assoc, Law Soc; Freeman: Worshipful Co of Slrs 1988, City of London 1995; *Recreations* skiing, fell walking, sugar lump collecting, travelling; *Style—* Stephen Revell, Esq; ✉ 42 Canonbury Park South, London N1; Freshfields Bruckhaus Deringer, Whitefriars, 65 Fleet Street, London EC4Y 1HS (tel 020 7936 4000, fax 020 7832 7001, telex 889292, e-mail stephen.revell@freshfields.com)

REWSE-DAVIES, Jeremy Vyvyan; *b* 24 November 1939; *m* 1, 1961 (m dis) Teri Donn; 1 s (Jason Saul b 1968), 1 da (Jessica Lucy b 1968); m 2, 1975 (m dis), Kezia de Winne; m 3, 1983, Iga Przedrzymirska; 1 s (Alexander Henry Thomas b 1985); *Career* prodn designer BBC TV 1964–74 (jtly designed Dr Who Daleks), freelance interior and TV designer

1974–76; Office Planning Consultants: sr designer 1976–79, design dir 1979–81, md 1981–86; design dir and dep chm Business Design Group 1986–88, dir of design London Transport 1988–99; dir: 4IV Design Consultants 1999–2003, Rewse Davies Assoc 1999–, The Arts Club (London) Ltd 2001–; pres Chartered Soc of Designers 1992–93; FCSD 1978 (MCSD 1964), FRSA 1980; *Books* Designed for London (jtly, 1995), Modern Britain 1932–39 (jtly); *Recreations* birdwatching, gardening and trips to Africa; *Clubs* The Arts; *Style*— Jeremy Rewse-Davies, Esq; ✉ La Vigerie 82330, St Vincent de Varren, France (e-mail jrewsedavies@hotmail.com)

REYNARD, Dr Adrian John; s of Gordon Reynard, of W Sussex, and Daphne, *née* Rogers; *b* 23 March 1951; *Educ* Alleynes GS, Oxford Poly (HND Mech Eng, fndr pres Oxford Poly Automobile Club); *m* Gill; 4 c; *Career* project engr Br Leyland 1974–75, chief designer Hawke Racing Cars 1976–77, ceo Sabre Automotive Ltd/Reynard Racing Cars Ltd 1977–89, fndr chm and ceo Reynard Composites Ltd 1989, fndr chm and ceo Reynard Special Vehicle Projects and Reynard Aviation Ltd 1996; visiting prof of engrg and applied sci Cranfield Univ, visiting prof in motorsport design Oxford Brookes Univ 2000; Design Cncl Award 1990, Queen's Award for Export 1990 and 1996, Sir Henry Royce Gold Medal for Excellence 1992, Castrol Inst of Motor Industry Gold Medal for contributions to the motor industry 1995, Crompton Lanchester Medal IMechE 2001, MIA Outstanding Contribution Award 2001; numerous motor racing trophies and championships; Hon DEng Oxford Brookes Univ 1994; FRSA 1991, FIMechE 1993, CRAeS 1997, FREng 1999; *Recreations* flying (private pilots licence), power boating, water skiing, scuba diving, clay pigeon shooting, model aircraft radio control flying, occasional karting; *Style*— Dr Adrian Reynard; ✉ website www.adrianreynard.com

REYNOLDS, Prof Alan James; s of Russell Hogarth Reynolds (d 1972), of Toronto, Canada, and Edith Emily, *née* Brownlow; *b* 8 September 1934; *Educ* Univ of Toronto (BASc), Univ of London (PhD); *m* 31 July 1962, Caroline Mary, da of Albert William Edwin Bury (d 1985), of Billericay, Essex; 2 s (Andrew Hogarth b 1963, James Haldane b 1967); *Career* research fell Cavendish Laboratory Univ of Cambridge 1960–62, assoc prof Dept of Civil Engrg and Applied Mechanics McGill Univ Montreal 1962–66; Brunel Univ: reader 1966–82, prof 1982–97, head Dept of Mechanical Engrg 1983–94, pro-vice-chllr 1991–96, prof emeritus 1997–; dir of research Buckinghamshire Coll 1995–99 (visiting prof 1999–2006), visiting prof London Inst 2000–04; memb CVCP Academic Audit Unit 1992–96, memb Cncl IMechE (chm Gtr London Branch) 1990–92 and 2001–05; MASCE 1963, FIMechE 1980, FRSA 1983; *Books* Thermofluid Dynamics (1970), Turbulent Flows in Engineering (1974, Russian edn 1976, Romanian edn 1980), The Finances of Engineering Companies (1992); *Style*— Prof Alan Reynolds; ✉ 30 Boileau Road, London W5 3AH (tel 020 8248 7641); Higher Nanterrow Farm, Nanterrow Lane, Connor Downs, Hayle, Cornwall TR27 5BP (tel 01209 715433)

REYNOLDS, Alan Munro; *b* 27 April 1926; *Educ* Woolwich Poly Sch of Art, RCA; *m* 1951, Vona; *Career* teacher Central Sch of Arts and Crafts London 1954–61, sr lectr St Martin's Sch of Art London 1985– (teacher 1954–85); *Solo Exhibitions* Redfern Gallery London 1952, 1960 and 1972, Durlacher Gallery New York 1954, Leicester Galleries London 1958, Annely Juda Fine Art London 1978, Gallerie Rénee Ziegler Zurich 1980 (with Malcolm Hughes and Peter Lowe), Juda Rowan Gallery London 1982 and 1986, Galerie Wack Kaiserslautern 1986 and 1990, Repères A la Galerie Lahumière Paris; *Group Exhibitions* incl: London Gp Exhibition 1950, British Contemporary Painting (British Cncl Exhibition Olso and Copenhagen) 1955, British Painting 1952–77 (Royal Acad London) 1977, Creation Modern Art and Nature (Scottish National Gallery of Modern Art Edinburgh) 1984, Systematic Constructive Drawings (Univ of York) 1986, Non-Objective World Revisited (Annely Juda Fine Art London) 1988, 1959–1989 30 years (Galerie Renée Ziegler Zurich) 1989; One Man Exhibition Annely Juda Fine Art London 1991, One Man Exhibition Galerie Art Nürnberg 1992; *Selected Public Collections* Walker Art Gallery Liverpool, Tate Gallery London, Victoria and Albert Museum London, Nat Gallery of Victoria Melbourne, Cincinnati Art Museum Ohio, Nat Gallery of Canada Ottawa, Bibliothèque Paris; Arts Cncl Purchase Award 1967; *Style*— Alan Reynolds, Esq

REYNOLDS, Antony James (Tony); s of C V Reynolds, of Hertford, Herts, and Mildred Vera Reynolds; *b* 21 April 1936; *Educ* Westminster; *m* 14 June 1955, Grace; 2 da (Kim Laura b 1959, Briony Jane b 1963), 1 s (Kevin Antony b 1961); *Career* Procter & Gamble 1960–65, vice-pres sales and mktg Tenco Div Coca Cola Foods 1965–83, fndr own business (UB Group) 1983–95; currently chm: Boston Foods Ltd, Reynolds Management Services, Lasting Impressions Ltd; lectr on franchising; FCIM; *Recreations* water skiing, windsurfing, swimming; *Clubs* Rotary; *Style*— Tony Reynolds, Esq; ✉ Reynolds Management Services, Shardeloes House, The Thatchway, Angmering,West Sussex BN16 4HY (tel 01903 784030, fax 01903 859237)

REYNOLDS, Dr (Eva Mary) Barbara; da of Alfred Charles Reynolds (d 1969), and Barbara, *née* Florac (d 1977); *b* 13 June 1914; *Educ* St Paul's Girls' Sch, UCL (BA, PhD); *m* 1, 5 Sept 1939, Lewis Guy Melville Thorpe (d 1977); 1 s (Adrian Charles b 1942), 1 da (Kerstin b 1949); m 2, 30 Oct 1982, Kenneth Robert Imeson (d 1994); *Career* asst lectr in Italian LSE 1937–40, lectr in Italian Univ of Cambridge 1940–62, reader in Italian Univ of Nottingham 1966–78 (warden of Willoughby Hall 1963–69); visiting prof in Italian: Univ of Calif Berkeley 1974–75, Wheaton Coll Illinois 1977–78, Trinity Coll Dublin 1980 and 1981, Hope Coll Michigan 1982; hon reader Univ of Warwick 1975–80; managing ed Seven (an Anglo-American literary review) 1980–88 and 1993–; chm: Univ Women's Club 1988–90, Dorothy L Sayers Soc 1983–94 (pres 1994–); Hon DLitt: Wheaton Coll Illinois 1979, Hope Coll Michigan 1982, Univ of Durham 1995; Silver medal for servs to Italian culture 1964, Silver medal for servs to Anglo-Veneto cultural rels 1971, Cavaliere Ufficiale al Merito della Repubblica Italiana 1978; *Books* The Linguistic Writings of Alessandro Manzoni (1952), The Cambridge Italian Dictionary (gen ed Vol I 1962, Vol II 1981), Dante: Paradise (trans with Dorothy L Sayers, 1962), Guido Farina, Painter of Verona (with Lewis Thorpe, 1967), Dante: Poems of Youth (trans, 1969), Concise Cambridge Italian Dictionary (1975), Ariosto: Orlando Furioso (trans Vol I 1975, Vol II 1977), Dizionario Italiano-Inglese, Inglese-Italiano (Signorelli-CUP, 1985), The Translator's Art (ed with William Radice, 1987), The Passionate Intellect: Dorothy L Sayers' Encounter with Dante (1989), Dorothy L Sayers: Her Life and Soul (1993), The Letters of Dorothy L Sayers: 1899–1936, The Making of a Detective Novelist (ed, 1995), The Letters of Dorothy L Sayers: 1937–1943 - From Novelist to Playwright (ed, 1997), The Letters of Dorothy L Sayers: 1944–1950 - A Noble Daring (ed, 1999), The Letters of Dorothy L Sayers: 1951–1957 - In the Midst of Life (ed, 2000), Dorothy L Sayers: Child and Woman of Her Time (ed, 2002), Dante: the Poet, the Political Thinker, the Man (2006); *Clubs* Univ Women's, RAF; *Style*— Dr Barbara Reynolds; ✉ 220 Milton Road, Cambridge CB4 1LQ (tel 01223 565380, fax 01223 424894, e-mail reynolds@miltonroad.demon.co.uk)

REYNOLDS, Brian James; s of late Thomas Reynolds, and late Beatrice, *née* Rutherford; *b* 22 April 1938; *Educ* Downhills Sch Tottenham; *m* 1, 19 Sept 1959 (m dis 1977), Janet, *née* Gallagher; 1 s (Andrew), 1 da (Suzanne); m 2, 1982, Patricia Ann, da of George McIntyre; *Career* slr's clerk and litigation clerk 1953–59, fin journalist, dir and co sec Financial Information Co 1959–81, Daily Express 1981–85; dir: Money Marketing (Design) Public Relations Ltd 1985–86, Streets Communications Ltd 1986–92, Paternoster Partnership Ltd 1992–99, Reywood Communications Ltd, Newsquoter Ltd; *Recreations* lifetime supporter Tottenham Hotspur FC; *Style*— Brian Reynolds, Esq; ✉ Reywood Communications, 1st Floor, 19 Earl Street, London EC2A 2AL (tel 020 7456 9503, fax 020 8357 7599, mobile 07946 532491, e-mail brian@reywood.com)

REYNOLDS, David Geoffrey; OBE (1997); s of William Oliver Reynolds, OBE, of Follifoot, nr Harrogate, and Eleanor, *née* Gill; *b* 11 June 1948; *Educ* Bedford Sch, LAMDA; *m* 5 Sept 1970, Valerie, *née* Wells; 2 da (Emma b 5 Oct 1973, Tessa b 7 July 1976); *Career* dep stage mangr Spa Theatre Whitby 1967, stage mangr Sheffield Playhouse 1967–68, dir Yorkshire Television 1973–79 (floor mangr 1968–73), freelance dir 1979–86, controller of entertainment Yorkshire Television 1993–95 (dep controller of entertainment 1986–92), gp controller of entertainment Yorkshire Tyne-Tees Television plc 1995–98, controller comedy drama and drama features Yorkshire Tyne-Tees Television 1998–; TV work incl: Emmerdale, Hadleigh, The Sandbaggers, The Onedin Line, When The Boat Comes In, Juliet Bravo, Give Us a Break, Big Deal, Bergerac, Lovejoy, The Beiderbecke Affair, Room At The Bottom (Int Emmy nomination and Best Comedy award Banff Festival), prodr The New Statesman (Int Emmy winner, BAFTA award), prodr and dir Home to Roost (Int Emmy nomination), prodr and co-dir A Bit of a Do (Broadcasting Press Guild award for Best Entertainment Series, RTS award Best Drama Series and Br Comedy awards Best ITV and Channel 4 Sitcom and Best Br TV Comedy), prodr and dir Stay Lucky, dir A Touch of Frost, prodr Life and Crimes of William Palmer, dir David Jason in his Element, exec prodr Fat Friends, exec prodr My Uncle Silas; *Recreations* boating, theatre, photography, films, travel; *Style*— David Reynolds, Esq, OBE; ✉ Pencob House, Scotton, Knaresborough, North Yorkshire HG5 9HZ (tel 01423 862854); Yorkshire-Tyne Tees Television, The Television Centre, Leeds LS3 1JS (tel 0113 243 8283, fax 0113 234 3645)

REYNOLDS, Sir David James; 3 Bt (UK 1923), of Woolton, Co Lancaster; s of Lt-Col Sir John Francis Roskell Reynolds, 2 Bt, MBE (d 1956), and Millicent Orr-Ewing (d 1932); gda of 7 Duke of Roxburgh, and ggda of 7 Duke of Marlborough; *b* 26 January 1924; *Educ* Downside; *m* 1966, Charlotte Baumgartner; 2 da (Lara Mary b 1 March 1967, Sofie Josefine b 5 May 1968), 1 s (James Francis b 10 July 1971); *Heir* s, James Reynolds; *Career* serv WWII in North Africa, Italy, Austria, Palestine, Capt 15/19 Hussars on demobilisation; *Style*— Sir David Reynolds, Bt

REYNOLDS, Prof David James; s of Leslie Reynolds (decd), and Marian, *née* Kay; *b* 17 February 1952; *Educ* Dulwich Coll, Gonville & Caius Coll Cambridge (MA, PhD); *m* 1977, Margaret Philpott Ray; 1 s; *Career* Harvard Univ: Choate fell 1973–74, Warren fell 1980–81; Univ of Cambridge: res fell Gonville & Caius Coll 1978–80 and 1981–83, asst history lectr 1984–88, lectr 1988–97, reader in int history 1997–2002, prof of int history 2002–; FBA 2005; *Books* The Creation of the Anglo-American Alliance 1937–41 (1981, Bernath Prize Soc for Historians of American Foreign Relations 1982), An Ocean Apart: The Relationship between Britain and America in the 20th Century (jtly, 1988), Britannia Overruled: British policy and World Power in the 20th Century (1991), Allies at War: The Soviet, American, and British Experience 1939–45 (jt ed, 1994), The Origins of the Cold War in Europe (ed, 1994), Rich Relations: The American Occupation of Britain 1942–45 (1995, Soc for Military History Distinguished Book Award 1996), One World Divisible: A Global History since 1945 (2000), From Munich to Pearl Harbor: Roosevelt's America and the origins of the Second World War (2001), In Command of History: Churchill Fighting and Writing the Second World War (2004, Wolfson History Prize 2004), From World War to Cold War: Churchill, Roosevelt and the International History of the 1940s (2006), Summits: Six Meetings that Shaped the Twentieth Century (2007); *Style*— Prof David Reynolds; ✉ Christ's College, Cambridge CB2 3BU (tel 01223 334900)

REYNOLDS, Dr Edward Henry; s of William Henry Reynolds (d 1999), of Broad Towers, Caerleon, Gwent, and (Mary) Angela, *née* Keane (d 1989); *b* 13 October 1935; *Educ* The Oratory, WNSM Cardiff (MB BCh, MD); *m* 20 July 1968, Angela Pauline, da of John Martin Anthony Sheehan (d 1960), of 28 Manor Rd, Cheam, Surrey; 1 da (Catherine b 1974); *Career* visiting asst prof of neurology Yale Univ Med Sch 1970, conslt neurologist Maudsley and King's Coll Hosps London 1974–98; chm: The Fund for Epilepsy 1993–2004, The Centre for Epilepsy King's Coll Hosp 1993–98; dir Inst of Epileptology King's Coll 1994–2000, hon sr lectr Dept of Clinical Neuroscience King's Coll Sch of Medicine 2004–; sec MRC Coordinating Gp for Epilepsy 1978–83, memb Ctee Br Neuropsychiatry Assoc 1987–93, pres Int League Against Epilepsy 1993–97 (pres Br branch 1993–96 (sec 1979–84), vice-pres 1989–93), chm ILAE/IBE/WHO Global Campaign Against Epilepsy 1997–2001; memb BMA, FRCP 1980, FRCPsych 1985; *Books* incl: Folic Acid in Neurology, Psychiatry and Internal Medicine (ed with M I Botez, 1979), Epilepsy and Psychiatry (ed with M R Trimble, 1981), Paediatric Perspectives on Epilepsy (ed with E Ross, 1985), The Bridge Between Neurology and Psychiatry (ed with M R Trimble, 1989); *Recreations* golf, tennis; *Clubs* RAC; *Style*— Dr Edward Reynolds; ✉ Buckles, Yew Tree Bottom Road, Epsom Downs, Surrey KT17 3NQ (tel 01737 360867, fax 01737 363415, e-mail reynolds@buckles.u-net.com)

REYNOLDS, Fiona Claire; CBE (1998); da of Dr Jeffrey Alan Reynolds, and Margaret Mary, *née* Watson; *b* 29 March 1958; *Educ* Rugby HS for Girls, Newnham Coll Cambridge (MA, MPhil); *m* 23 May 1981, Robert William Tinsley Merrill; 3 da (Alice Kezia b 12 Nov 1990, Margaret Rose b 28 March 1992, Olivia Jane b 13 June 1995); *Career* sec Council for National Parks 1980–87; dir: Council for the Protection of Rural England 1992–98 (asst dir (policy) 1987–92), Women's Unit Cabinet Office 1998–2000; DG National Trust 2001–; Global 500 UN Environment Prog Award 1990; *Recreations* walking, cycling, reading, classical music; *Style*— Ms Fiona Reynolds, CBE; ✉ The National Trust, 36 Queen Anne's Gate, London SW1H 9AS

REYNOLDS, Prof Francis Martin Baillie; Hon QC (1993); s of Eustace Baillie Reynolds (d 1948), and Emma Margaret Hanby, *née* Holmes (d 1933); *b* 11 November 1932; *Educ* Winchester, Worcester Coll Oxford (scholar, MA, DCL); *m* 1965, Susan Claire, da of Hugh William Shillito; 2 s (Barnabas William Baillie b 1967, Martin Alexander Baillie b 1969), 1 da (Sophie Francesca b 1973); *Career* Bigelow teaching fell Univ of Chicago 1957–58, fell Worcester Coll Oxford 1960–2000 (emeritus fell 2001); called to the Bar Inner Temple 1961, hon bencher 1979; prof of law Univ of Oxford 1992–2000, emeritus prof 2001– (reader 1977–92); visiting lectr Univ of Auckland 1971 and 1977; Arthur Robinson & Hedderwicks visiting fell: Univ of Melbourne, Monash Univ 1989; Ebsworth & Ebsworth visiting prof Univ of Sydney 1993, Simpson Grierson visiting prof Univ of Auckland 1995, Koo & Partners visiting prof Univ of Hong Kong 2002; visiting prof Nat Univ of Singapore 1984, 1986, 1988, 1990–92, 1994, 1996, 1997 (David Marshall visiting prof) and 2000–01, 2003, 2005 and 2007; visiting prof: UCL 1986–89, Univ of Otago 1993, Int Maritime Law Inst IMO Malta 1996–2007; ed: Lloyd's Maritime and Commercial Law Quarterly 1983–87, The Law Quarterly Review 1987–; FBA 1988; *Books* Bowstead and Reynolds On Agency (co-ed 13 and 14 edns, ed 15, 16, 17 and 18 edns), Chitty On Contract (co-ed 24–29 edns), Benjamin's Sale of Goods (co-ed 1–7 edns), English Private Law (co-ed, 2000), Carver on Bills of Lading (with Sir Guenter Treitel, 2001, 2 edn 2005); *Recreations* music, walking, travel; *Style*— Prof Francis Reynolds, QC, FBA; ✉ 61 Charlbury Road, Oxford OX2 6UX (tel 01865 559323, fax 01865 511894, e-mail francis.reynolds@law.ox.ac.uk)

REYNOLDS, Gillian; MBE (1999); da of Charles Beresford Morton (d 1970), of Liverpool, and Ada Kelly (d 1962); *b* 15 November 1935; *Educ* Liverpool Inst HS for Girls, St Anne's Coll Oxford (MA), Mount Holyoke Coll; *m* 23 Sept 1958 (m dis 1983), Stanley Ambrose Reynolds, s of Ambrose Harrington Reynolds (d 1970), of Holyoke, USA; 3 s (Ambrose Kelly b 12 June 1960, Alexander Charles b 3 Jan 1970, Abel Stanley b 5 Sept 1971); *Career* TV and radio broadcaster 1964–; radio critic: The Guardian 1967–74, The Daily Telegraph 1975–; prog controller Radio City Liverpool 1974–75; Media Soc Award for Distinguished Journalism 1999; pres Assoc of Sr Members St Anne's Coll Oxford 1994–97 (hon fell); memb: Mount Holyoke Coll Alumnae Assoc, Cncl Soc of Authors 2000; tstee Nat Museums and Galleries Merseyside 2001; visiting fell Bournemouth Univ 2003; hon fell Liverpool John Moores Univ 2004; first fell Radio Acad 1990, FRSA, FRTS; *Recreations* listening to the radio, the company of friends; *Clubs* Royal Society of Arts; *Style*— Ms Gillian Reynolds, MBE; ✉ Flat 3, 1 Linden Gardens, London W2 4HA (tel 020 7229 1893, fax 020 7243 2621, e-mail ycf79@dial.pipex.com)

REYNOLDS, Ian Tewson; s of Eric Tewson Reynolds (d 1968), of Radlett, Herts, and Joyce, *née* Holt (d 1997); *b* 3 December 1943; *Educ* Watford GS, LSE (BSc Econ); *m* 20 Dec 1980, Gillian, da of Thomas Noel Castree Prosser DFM (d 1994); 2 da (Christina Louise b 12 Oct 1982, Frances Emilie b 3 Feb 1986); *Career* sales rep Shell Mex and BP 1965–67, sales exec Haymarket Press 1967–68; IBM UK Ltd: various sales and mktg positions 1968–87, dir of mktg and servs Basingstoke 1987–90, vice-pres of communications Paris 1991–92, dir of personnel and corp affrs Portsmouth 1992–94; chief exec ABTA Ltd 1994–2005, chm Citybond Holdings plc 2006–; non-exec dir: General Industries plc 1997–, NTP Ltd 2003–; non-exec dir St Mary's NHS Tst 1995–2003, chm Wandsworth PCT 2007–; tstee: Family Holiday Assoc 1995– (chm 2006–), The Travel Fndn 2003–, St Mary's Paddington Charitable Tst 2004–; fell Industry and Parliament Tst 1993; MBCS 1973, FInstD 1992, FRSA 1992, CCMI (CIMgt 1990); *Recreations* golf, tennis, skiing, sailing; *Clubs* Hurlingham; *Style*— Ian Reynolds, Esq; ✉ Murray Cross, 4 Murray Road, Wimbledon, London SW19 4PB (tel 020 8946 7978, e-mail ian.reynolds@blueyonder.co.uk)

REYNOLDS, Jane Caroline Margaret; JP (1991); da of Maj Thomas Reynolds, MC (d 1981), of Richmond, N Yorks, and Cynthia Myrtle Margaret, *née* Eden (later Mrs Witt, d 1982); *b* 4 March 1953; *Educ* Winchester Co HS for Girls, Brighton Poly, Lincoln Meml Clinic for Psychotherapy; *Career* student teacher St Mary's Wrestwood Educnl Tst Ltd 1970–72, offr i/c Gary Richard Homes Ltd 1972–76, matron Alison House (St John's Wood) Ltd 1976–81, dir The Westminster Soc for Mentally Handicapped Children and Adults 1983–87 (devpt offr 1981–83), hosp mangr Leavesden Hosp 1987–91, chief exec Royal Masonic Benevolent Instn 1991–2000, sec The Masonic Fndn for the Aged and the Sick 1992–2000; NHS Gen Mgmnt Training Scheme III, Cabinet Office Top Mgmnt Prog 1999; chair Continuing Care Review Panel: NE London SHA 2003–06, SE London SHA 2004–06, NHS London 2006–; memb: Registered Homes Act (1984) Tbnl Panel 1990–98, Criminal Injuries Compensation Appeals Panel 2000–, Gtr London Magistrates' Courts' Authy 2003–05, Postgrad Med Educn and Trg Bd 2003–; chm Life Opportunities Tst 1990–; Freeman City of London 1993, Liveryman Worshipful Co of Glass-sellers 1994; FIMgt 1988 (MBIM 1977); *Recreations* travelling, the arts, seizing opportunities; *Style*— Miss Jane Reynolds, DMS, FCMI; ✉ 33 Carlton Mansions, Randolph Avenue, London W9 1NP

REYNOLDS, John Nigel; s of Hugh Robert Anthony Reynolds, of Thurlestone, Devon, and Judith, *née* Gabriel; *b* 8 September 1966, Harlow, Essex; *Educ* CCC Cambridge (MA); *m* 10 Aug 1991, Karen, *née* Randall; 4 c (Adam, Mary, Hannah (triplets) b 24 Feb 1997, Katie b 9 Nov 1999); *Career* md corp finance and advsy HSBC 1992–99, md Credit Suisse First Boston 1999–2001, ceo Houlihan Lokey Howard & Zukin (Europe) Ltd 2002–06, ceo Nikko Energy Ltd 2006–07, chm and chief exec Reynolds Ptnrs Ltd 2007–; chm C of E Ethical Investment Advsy Gp 2006–; vice-pres Save the Children, tstee and treas Radicle; FIEE 1999, FEI 2000; *Recreations* weightlifting, rock climbing, moral philosophy; *Clubs* Athenaeum; *Style*— John Reynolds, Esq; ✉ Reynolds Partners Limited, 1 Northumberland Avenue, London WC2N 5BW (tel 020 7872 5797)

REYNOLDS, (James) Kirk; QC (1993); s of Hon Mr Justice James Reynolds, of Helen's Bay, Co Down, and Alexandra Mary Erskine, *née* Strain; *b* 24 March 1951; *Educ* Campbell Coll Belfast, Peterhouse Cambridge (MA); *Career* called to the Bar Middle Temple 1974, bencher 2000; Hon RICS 1997; *Books* Handbook of Rent Review (1981), Dilapidations: the Modern Law and Practice (1994, 3 edn 2004), Essentials of Rent Review (1995), Renewal of Business Tenancies (1997, new edn 2002); *Style*— Kirk Reynolds, Esq, QC; ✉ Falcon Chambers, Falcon Court, London EC4Y 1AA

REYNOLDS, His Hon Martin Paul; s of Cedric Hinton Fleetwood Reynolds (d 1993), of London, and Doris Margaret, *née* Bryan (d 1982); *b* 25 December 1936; *Educ* Univ Coll Sch, St Edmund Hall Oxford (MA); *m* 17 June 1961, Gaynor Margaret, da of Stuart Morgan Phillips (d 1957); 3 s (Simon Stuart Hinton b 1964, Peter Bryan b 1966, Thomas Edward Barnsbury b 1969); *Career* qualified teacher 1961; called to the Bar Inner Temple 1962; recorder of the Crown Court 1993–95, circuit judge (SE Circuit) 1995–2006; cncllr London Borough of Islington 1968–71 and 1973–82; pres Mental Health Review Tbnl 1997–, memb Parole Bd 2006–; Parly candidate Harrow W Oct 1974; ACIArb 1985; *Books* Negotiable Instruments for Students (1964); *Recreations* sailing, travel in France, music; *Clubs* Savage, Bar Yacht, Dutch Barge Assoc; *Style*— His Hon Martin Reynolds

REYNOLDS, Michael Arthur; s of William Arthur Reynolds (d 1981), of Hakin, Dyfed, and Violet Elsie, *née* Giddings (d 1978); *b* 28 August 1943; *Educ* Milford Haven GS, Cardiff Coll of Art (DipAD); *m* 1 (m dis 1971), Patricia; 1 s (Joseph Michael b 1970); m 2 (m dis 1974), Judith; m 3 (m dis 1995), Jill Caroline; m 4, 22 Feb 2003, Gill Patricia; 2 s (Joseph Louis b 1987, Oliver James b 1992); *Career* creative dir KPS Ltd Nairobi 1968, copywriter J Walter Thompson 1971, gp head Benton & Bowles 1973; creative dir: ABM 1975, McCann Erickson 1979, Interlink 1981, MWK (and shareholder) 1983, Pearson Partnership 1987; film dir Good Film Co 1991–; gp creative dir Osprey Communications plc; dir and creative dir Beeholm Ltd 2002–; MIPA; *Recreations* gardening, rare books, classic motorcars; *Clubs* Chelsea Arts; *Style*— Michael Reynolds, Esq; ✉ e-mail crazed@mikebeeholm.demon.co.uk

REYNOLDS, Michael John; s of William James Reynolds (d 1981), and Audrey, *née* Turpitt; *b* 8 October 1950; *Educ* Felsted, Keele Univ, Strasbourg Univ (Droit Comparé); *Career* Allen & Overy: articled clerk 1974–76, asst slr 1976–81, seconded to EC 1978, ptnr and head EC Law Dept 1981–; visiting prof of Euro competition law Univ of Durham; chm Anti Trust Ctee Int Bar Assoc; memb Euro Ctee British Invisibles, Cncl Int Bar Assoc; *Recreations* boats, learning languages, travel; *Clubs* Travellers, Cercle Gaulois (Brussels), Warande (Brussels); *Style*— Michael Reynolds, Esq; ✉ Allen & Overy, One New Change, London EC4 (tel 020 7330 3000, fax 020 7330 9999)

REYNOLDS, Dr Paul Joseph; s of Patrick Reynolds, and Catherine, *née* Miller; *b* 5 March 1957; *Educ* Univ of Strathclyde (BA), Univ of London (PhD, RSGS Scot Univs Medal); *m* 1984, Karen Solveig, *née* Eide; 1 s, 2 da; *Career* BT: joined 1983, various mgmnt roles 1983–89, sr mangr Int Voice Products 1989–91, dir Office of the Chm 1991–93, prog dir Info Communication and Entertainment 1993–94, gen mangr Scot 1994–97, dir Strategy 1997–98, dir networkBT 1998–99, md Networks and Info Services 1999–2000, chief exec BT Wholesale 2000–, exec dir BT plc 2001–; *Recreations* walking, skiing, guitar, photography; *Style*— Dr Paul Reynolds; ✉ BT plc, BT Centre, 81 Newgate Street, London EC1A 7AJ

REYNOLDS, (Christopher) Paul Michel; s of Christopher John Loughborough Reynolds, of Lymington, Hants, and Elisabeth, *née* Ewart-James; *b* 23 February 1946; *Educ* Ardingly, Worcester Coll Oxford (BA); *m* 25 July 1950, Louise, da of Bishop Eric William Bradley Cordingly (d 1976); 1 s (James Edward b 1974), 1 da (Alice Elizabeth b 1976); *Career* joined BBC Norwich 1968, BBC Radio 1970–78; BBC corr: NY 1978–82, Brussels 1982–85, Jerusalem 1985–87; diplomatic and court corr BBC News & Current Affrs Radio 1987–98, Washington corr BBC 1998–2001, world affrs corr BBC News Online 2001–; *Recreations* birdwatching; *Style*— Paul Reynolds, Esq; ✉ BBC News Online, 7540 Television Centre, London W14 7RG (tel 020 7576 4909)

REYNOLDS, Sir Peter William John; kt (1985), CBE; s of late Harry Reynolds, of Amersham, and Gladys Victoria French; *b* 10 September 1929; *Educ* Haileybury; *m* 1955, Barbara Anne, da of Vincent Kenneth Johnson, OBE; 2 s (Mark, Adam); *Career* Nat Serv 2 Lt RA 1948–50; Unilever Ltd 1950–70 (trainee, md then chm Walls (Meat & Handy Foods) Ltd); Rank Hovis McDougall plc: asst gp md 1971, gp md 1972–81, chm 1981–89, dep chm 1989–93; chm Pioneer Concrete (Holdings) plc 1992–; dir 1981–93: Ranks Pension Ltd, RHM Overseas Ltd, RHM Research Ltd, RHM Overseas Finance BV (Holland), RHM International Finance NV, RHM Holdings (USA) Inc, Purchase Finance Co Ltd, RHM Operatives Pensions Ltd; dir: Avis Europe Ltd, Cilva Holdings plc, Guardian Royal Exchange plc, The Boots Co plc 1986–; dir Nationwide Anglia Building Society 1990–92; memb Consultative Bd for Resources Devpt in Agric 1982–84, chm Resources Ctee Food and Drink Fedn 1983–86 (fndr memb of Ctee 1974–), memb EDC for Food and Drink Mfrg Industry 1982–87, memb Covent Garden Market Authy; dir Industrial Devpt Bd for NI 1982–89, memb Peacock Ctee on Financing the BBC 1985–86; govr Berkhamsted Schs 1985–, life govr Haileybury Coll 1985–; dir Fremantle Housing Tst 1992–; High Sheriff Bucks 1990–91; *Recreations* travel, reading, gardening; *Style*— Sir Peter Reynolds, CBE

REYNOLDS, Richard Christopher; s of Stanley Reynolds (d 1960), and Christine, *née* Barrow; *b* 2 June 1945; *Educ* Peter Symonds Winchester, Croydon Tech Sch, Croydon Tech Coll; *m* 2 March 1968, Sharon, da of Peter Bragg, of Great Bookham, Surrey; 1 s (Paul), 1 da (Julia); *Career* md Barratt East London 1983–, dir Barratt Southern 1983–, md Barratt Thames Gateway 2005; tstee Stratford Devpt Partnership 1993–; patron Discover (The Children's Discovery Centre) 1998; memb Br Inst of Architectural Technicians, MCIAT, MRICS, MAPM; FCIM, FCIH, FCIOB, FCMI, FASI, FInstD; *Recreations* clay pigeon shooting, scuba diving, cycling; *Style*— Richard Reynolds, Esq; ✉ Barratt East London, Central House, 32–66 High Street, Stratford, London E15 2PF (tel 020 8522 5500, fax 020 8519 5536, DX 5408)

REYNOLDS, Roger; s of Arthur Wesley Reynolds, and Bernice Eileen Marcia, *née* Newman; *b* 25 January 1950, Romsey, Hants; *Educ* Romsey Secdy Modern; *m* 22 July 1972, Rosemary Eva; 1 da (Catherine Marie b 22 Dec 1976), 1 s (Paul Robert b 16 Sept 1979); *Career* Met Police: joined 1967, cadet corp 1967–69, constable 1969–76, sergeant 1976–99, ops head Traffic Cameras Unit 1992–99; RPS: memb 1984–, memb Cncl 1993–, pres 2003–; memb Surrey Photographic Assoc 1989–; Meritorious Service Award Photographic Alliance of GB (PAGB) 1996, Fenton Medal RPS 2002; fell British Photographic Exhbns, FRPS 1996 and 2000 (Hon FRPS 2003), fell British Professional Photographers' Assoc 2004; *Recreations* travel, photography; *Style*— Roger Reynolds, Esq; ✉ The Royal Photographic Society, Fenton House, 122 Wells Road, Bath BA2 3AH (tel 01225 462841, e-mail president@rps.org)

REYNOLDS, Simon Anthony; s of Maj James Reynolds (d 1982), of Leighton Hall, Carnforth, Lancs, and Helen Reynolds (d 1977); *b* 20 January 1939; *Educ* Ampleforth, Heidelberg Univ; *m* 1970, Beata Cornelia, da of late Baron Siegfried von Heyl zu Herrnsheim (d 1982), of Schlosschen, Worms, Germany; 2 s, 2 da; *Career* dealer in fine art; co-curator Kingdom of the Soul exhbn on German Symbolism (Birmingham Museum & Art Gallery) 2000; *Books* The Vision of Simeon Solomon (1984), Hymns to Night...and the Poets of Pessimism (1994), Sir William Blake Richmond RA (biography, 1995); *Recreations* writing, collecting fine art, travelling; *Style*— Simon Reynolds, Esq; ✉ 64 Lonsdale Road, Barnes, London SW13 9JS (tel 020 8748 3506, fax 020 8741 5923)

REYNTIENS, (Nicholas) Patrick; OBE (1976); s of Nicholas Serge Reyntiens, OBE (d 1951), and Janet Isabel, *née* MacRae (d 1975); *b* 11 December 1925; *Educ* Ampleforth, Regent St Poly, Edinburgh Coll of Art (DA); *m* 8 Sept 1953, Anne Mary, da of Brig-Gen Ian Bruce, DSO, MBE (d 1956); 2 s (Dominick Ian, John Patrick), 2 da (Edith Mary, Lucy Anne); *Career* WWII Lt 2 Bn Scots Guards 1943–47; artist specialising in stained glass; work includes: Coventry Cathedral, Liverpool Met Cathedral, Derby Cathedral, Eton Chapel, Great Hall Christ Church Oxford, Washington DC Episcopalian Cathedral; other works included in private collections; co-fndr Burleighfield and Reyntiens Trust 1967–76; lectured worldwide incl: Canada, USA, Mexico, Paris, Ghent, Calcutta, Delhi, Bombay; Toronto (retrospective exhbn) Chartres Boston 1991; designed and painted the great west window of Southwell Minster 1996, designed windows of the South Transept and the Lady Chapel of Ampleforth Abbey 2002; art critic The Tablet 1973–97, art corr The Oldie 1994–, art critic Catholic Herald 1997–; written for jls incl: Arts International Review, Spectator, Arts News Review and Modern Painters; memb Panel of Architectural Advsrs to: Westminster Abbey until 1996, Westminster Cathedral, Brompton Oratory; fell Br Soc of Master Glass Painters; *Books* The Beauty of Stained Glass (1990), The Technique of Stained Glass (1967, 4 edn 1991); *Style*— Patrick Reyntiens, Esq, OBE; ✉ Winterbourne Lodge, Ilford Bridges Farm, close Stocklinch, Ilminster, Somerset TA19 9HZ (tel and fax 01460 52241)

RHEAD, David Michael; s of late Harry Bernard Rhead, JP; *b* 12 February 1936; *Educ* St Philip's GS Edgbaston; *m* 1958, Rosaleen Loretto, *née* Finnegan; 4 da; *Career* chm: LCP Holdings plc 1965–87 (fin dir 1968, dep chm 1973), Capital Industries plc 1991–99, Energy Technique plc (formerly Benson Group plc) 1995–99; non-exec dir Brintons Ltd 1995–2002; Freeman City of London; CCMI; FCA; *Recreations* fishing, golf; *Style*— David Rhead, Esq; ✉ 20 Buckton Close, Sutton Coldfield, West Midlands B75 5TF (tel 0121 308 4762)

RHIND, Prof David William; CBE (2001); s of William Rhind (d 1976), and Christina, *née* Abercombie; *b* 29 November 1943; *Educ* Berwick GS, Univ of Bristol (BSc), Univ of Edinburgh (PhD), Univ of London (DSc); *m* 27 Aug 1966, Christine, da of William Frank Young, of Berwick-upon-Tweed; 1 s (Jonathan b 1969), 2 da (Samantha b 1972, Zoe b 1979); *Career* res offr Univ of Edinburgh 1968–69, res fell RCA 1969–73, reader (former lectr) Univ of Durham 1973–81, prof of geography Birkbeck Coll London 1982–91, DG and chief exec Ordnance Survey 1992–98; vice-chllr City Univ 1998–2007; visiting fell: Int Trg Centre Netherlands 1975, ANU 1979; author of over 100 tech papers; chm: Cmmn on the Social Sciences of the Acad of Learned Socs for the Social Sciences 2000–03, London HE Consortium 2000–03, HE Staff Devpt Agency 2002–04, Statistics Cmmn 2003– (memb 2000–03), Islington Improvement Bd 2003–04, Business and Industry Strategy Gp Univs UK 2005–, Mgmnt Bd London Science Hub 2006–; memb Cncl ESRC 1996–2000; non-exec dir Bank of England 2006–; advsr House of Lords Select Ctee Sci of Technol 1984–85, memb Govt Ctee of Enquiry on Handling of Geographic Info 1985–87; hon sec RGS 1988–91, vice-pres Int Cartographic Assoc 1984–91; govr: Bournemouth Univ 1995–98, Ashridge Mgmnt Coll 1999–2004; winner UK Assoc for Geographic Information Decadel Award 1997; Hon DSc: Univ of Bristol 1993, Loughborough Univ 1996, Univ of Southampton 1998, Kingston Univ 1999, Univ of Durham 2001, London Metropolitan Univ 2003, Royal Holloway Univ of London 2004, St Petersburg State Poly Univ 2007; hon fell: Birkbeck Coll London 2000, Queen Mary Univ of London 2007; FRGS 1970 (Patron's Medal 1997), FRICS 1991, CIMgt 1998, FRS 2002, FBA 2002, FRSS 2003; *Books* Land Use (with R Hudson, 1980), A Census User's Handbook (1983), An Atlas of EEC Affairs (with R Hudson and H Mounsey, 1984), Geographical Information Systems (ed, with D Maguire and M Goodchild, 1991, 2 edn with P Longley, M Goodchild and D Maguire, 1999), The New Geography (with J Raper and J Shepherd, 1992), Framework for the World (1997), Geographical Information Systems and Science (with P Longley, M Goodchild and D Maguire 2001, 2 edn 2005); *Style*— Prof David Rhind, CBE; ✉ 1 Cold Harbour Close, Wickham, Hampshire PO17 5PT (tel 01329 834743, e-mail d.rhind@city.ac.uk)

RHODES, Anthony John David; s of John Percy Rhodes (d 1985), of Leigh-on-Sea, Essex, and Eileen Daisy, *née* Frith (d 1984); *b* 22 February 1948; *Educ* Westcliff GS, CCC Cambridge (MA); *m* 14 Dec 1974, Elisabeth Marie Agnes Raymonde, da of Lt-Col Pierre Fronteau (d 2006), of Lisieux, France; 1 s (Christophe b 1978), 1 da (Sophie b 1984); *Career* Shell International Petroleum Co 1969–73, Ocean Transport & Trading Ltd 1975–80, Bank of America International Ltd 1980–95, Credit Suisse 1995–97, conslt in fin services 1997–98, HSBC 1998–2004, ind conslt 2004–; *Books* Syndicated Lending - Practice and Documentation (author and gen ed, 2004), Euromoney Encyclopaedia of Debt Finance (gen ed, 2006); *Recreations* opera, classical music, golf, hill walking, oil painting; *Style*— Anthony Rhodes, Esq; ✉ tel 020 7359 0067, e-mail ajdrhodes@hotmail.com

RHODES, Benjamin; s of Dr Brian William Rhodes (d 1994), and Joan, *née* Martin (d 1972); *b* 12 November 1952; *Educ* Oundle, Univ of Manchester; *m* 1977 (m dis 1998), Carol Kroch (decd); 2 s; *Career* opened Benjamin Rhodes Gallery (in partnership with Carol Kroch) July 1985–Aug 1994, opened Jason & Rhodes (with Gillian Jason) 1994–99, opened Rhodes + Mann with Fred Mann; *Style*— Benjamin Rhodes, Esq

RHODES, Prof (John) David; CBE (2000, OBE 1992); son of Jack Rhodes, and Florence Rhodes; *b* 9 October 1943; *Educ* Univ of Leeds (BSc, PhD, DSc), Univ of Bradford (DEng); *m* 1965, Barbara Margaret Pearce; 1 s, 1 da; *Career* research fell Univ of Leeds 1966–67 (research asst 1964–66), sr research engr Microwave Devpt Labs USA 1967–69; Dept of Electrical and Electronic Engrg Univ of Leeds: lectr 1969–72, reader 1972–75, prof 1975–81, industrial prof 1981–; fndr, chm and tech dir Filtronic Components Ltd 1977–2006, chm Filtronic plc (formerly Filtronic Comtek plc) 1994–Jan 2006 (ceo Jan-Sept 2006, conslt Sept 2006–); awards incl: Microwave Prize (USA) 1969, Browder J Thompson Award (USA) 1970, Queen's Award for Technological Achievement 1985, Queen's Award for Export Achievement 1988, Price Phillip Medal Royal Acad of Engrg 2003; Hon DEng Univ of Bradford 1988, Hon DSc Napier Univ 1995; FIEEE 1980, FIET (FIEE 1984), FREng (FEng 1987), FRS 1993; *Publications* Theory of Electrical Filters (1976), author of numerous technical papers; *Style*— Prof J David Rhodes, CBE, FREng; ✉ Department of Electrical and Electronic Engineering, University of Leeds, Leeds LS2 9JT; Filtronic plc, The Waterfront, Salts Mill Road, Shipley, West Yorkshire BD18 3TT

RHODES, Gary; OBE (2006); step s of John Smellie, of London, and Jean, *née* Ferris; *b* 22 April 1960; *Educ* Howard Sch Gillingham, Thanet Tech Coll (City and Guilds, Chef of the Year, Student of the Year); *m* 7 January 1989, Yolanda Jennifer, da of Harvey Charles Adkins; 2 s (Samuel James b 24 Sept 1988, George Adam b 17 May 1990); *Career* Amsterdam Hilton Hotel 1979–81 (commis de cuisine, chef de partie), sous chef Reform Club Pall Mall 1982–83, head chef Winstons Eating House Feb-Oct 1983, sr sous chef Capital Hotel Knightsbridge 1983–85; head chef: Whitehall Restaurant Essex 1985–86, Castle Hotel Taunton 1986–90 (Michelin star 1986), Greenhouse Restaurant Mayfair 1990–96 (Michelin star 1996); city rhodes 1997–2003 (Michelin star 1997), Rhodes in the Square 1998–2003 (Michelin star 2000), Rhodes & Co Edinburgh 1999–2002 (Bib Gourmand award 2001), Rhodes & Co Manchester 1999–2003 (Bib Gourmand award 2002), Rhodes & Co W Sussex 2001–2002, Rhodes Twenty Four London 2003– (Michelin star 2005), Rhodes at the Calabash Hotel Grenada W Indies 2003–, Rhodes W1 at the Cumberland Hotel 2005–, Arcadian Rhodes (with P&O cruises) 2005–, Rhodes D7 Dublin 2006–; TV series (with accompanying books): Rhodes Around Britain (BBC) 1994, More Rhodes Around Britain (BBC) 1995, Open Rhodes Around Britain (BBC) 1996, Fabulous Food (BBC) 1997, New British Classics 1999, At the Table (BBC) 2000–01, Spring into Summer (BBC) 2002, Autumn into Winter (BBC) 2002, Hell's Kitchen 2005; Special Catey Award 1996; hon prof Thames Valley Univ 2003; FCGI 2005; *Books* Short Cut Rhodes (1997), Sweet Dreams (1998), The Cook Pack (2000), Gary Rhodes Step by Step Cooking (2001), The Complete Rhodes Around Britain (2001), Gary Rhodes Great Fast Food (2001), Food with Friends (2002), The Complete Cookery Year (2003), Keeping It Simple (2005); *Style*— Gary Rhodes, Esq, OBE; ✉ website www.garyrhodes.com

RHODES, Sir John Christopher Douglas; 4 Bt (UK 1919), of Hollingworth, Co Palatine of Chester; s of Lt-Col Sir Christopher George Rhodes, 3 Bt (d 1964); *b* 24 May 1946; *Heir* bro, Michael Rhodes; *Style*— Sir John Rhodes, Bt

RHODES, John Guy; s of Canon Cecil Rhodes, of Bury St Edmunds, and Gladys, *née* Farlie; *b* 16 February 1945; *Educ* King Edward VI Birmingham, Jesus Coll Cambridge (MA); *m* 11 June 1977, Christine Joan, da of Peter Dorrington Batt, MC, of Bury St Edmunds; 2 s (Alexander Luke b 1979, Nicholas Hugh b 1981); *Career* articled clerk Macfarlanes 1968; admitted slr 1970, slr specialising in trusts and tax for UK and int private clients, ptnr Macfarlanes 1975–2006 (sr advsr 2006–); *Recreations* woodlands, tennis, skiing; *Style*— John Rhodes, Esq; ✉ Macfarlanes, 10 Norwich Street, London EC4A 1BD (tel 020 7831 9222, fax 020 7831 9607, e-mail jgr@macfarlanes.com)

RHODES, Prof Peter John; s of George Thomas Rhodes (d 1969), and Elsie Leonora, *née* Pugh (d 1998); *b* 10 August 1940; *Educ* Queen Elizabeth's GS Barnet, Wadham Coll Oxford (minor scholar, MA), Merton Coll Oxford (Harmsworth sr scholar, Craven fell, DPhil); *m* 1971, (m dis 2001) Jan Teresa, da of John Mervyn Adamson; *Career* Univ of Durham: lectr in classics and ancient history 1965–77, sr lectr 1977–83, prof of ancient history 1983–2005, hon prof 2005–; jr fell Center for Hellenic Studies Washington DC 1978–79, visiting fell Wolfson Coll Oxford 1984, visiting research fell Univ of New England NSW Australia 1988, memb Inst for Advanced Study Princeton NJ 1988–89; visiting fell Corpus Christi Coll Oxford 1993, Leverhulme research fell 1994–95, visiting fell All Souls Coll Oxford 1998, Langford Family eminent scholar Florida State Univ 2002; foreign memb Royal Danish Acad 2005; FBA 1987; *Books* The Athenian Boule (1972), Commentary on the Aristotelian Athenaion Politeia (1981), Aristotle: The Athenian Constitution (1984), The Greek City States (1986, 2 edn 2007), Thucydides II (1988), Thucydides III (1994), The Development of the Polis in Archaic Greece (ed with L G Mitchell, 1997), The Decrees of the Greek States (with D M Lewis, 1997), Thucydides IV.1–V.24 (1999), Ancient Democracy and Modern Ideology (2003), Greek Historical Inscriptions 404–323 BC (with R G Osborne, 2003), Athenian Democracy (ed, 2004), A History of the Classical Greek World 478–323 BC (2005); also author of various articles and reviews in learned jls; *Recreations* music, travel, typography; *Style*— Prof P J Rhodes; ✉ Department of Classics, University of Durham, 38 North Bailey, Durham DH1 3EU (tel 0191 334 1670, fax 0191 334 1671)

RHODES, Robert Elliott; QC (1989); s of Gilbert Gedalia Rhodes (d 1970), of London, and Elly Brook; *b* 2 August 1945; *Educ* St Paul's, Pembroke Coll Oxford (MA); *m* 16 March 1971 (m dis 1996), Georgina Caroline, da of Jack Gerald Clarfelt, of Timsbury, Hants; 2 s (Matthew b 1973, James b 1975), 1 da (Emily b 1983); *Career* called to the Bar Inner Temple 1968; first prosecuting counsel to Inland Revenue at Central Criminal Court and Inner London Crown Courts 1981–89 (second prosecuting counsel 1979), recorder of the Crown Court 1987, head of chambers 1998–2003; dep chm IMRO Membership Tbnl Panel 1992–2001, memb Appeal Panel ICAEW 1998–2004, chm AIDB Disciplinary Tbnls 2004; *Recreations* reading, listening to opera, watching cricket, playing real tennis, theatre, ballet, art; *Clubs* MCC, Épée, Annabel's, Garrick; *Style*— Robert Rhodes, Esq, QC; ✉ Outer Temple, 222–225 Strand, London WC2R 1BA

RHODES, Prof Roderick Arthur William; s of Keith Firth Rhodes, and Irene, *née* Clegg; *b* 15 August 1944; *Educ* Fulneck Boys' Sch, Univ of Bradford (BSc), St Catherine's Coll Oxford (BLitt), Univ of Essex (PhD); *Children* 1 s (Edward Roderick b 25 June 1979), 1 da (Bethan Margaret b 30 Oct 1981); *Career* Univ of Birmingham 1970–76, Univ of Strathclyde 1976–79, Univ of Essex 1979–89, prof of politics and head of Dept Univ of York 1989–94, prof of politics Univ of Newcastle upon Tyne 1994–2002, distinguished prof of political science and dir Research Sch of Social Sciences ANU 2003–; adjungeret prof Institut for Statskundskab, Kobenhans Universitet 1998–2003, visiting research prof of politics and public policy Griffith Univ Brisbane; chm Public Admin Ctee Jt Univ Cncl for Social and Public Admin 1996–99; pres Political Studies Assoc 2002–05 (chm 1999–2002); research dir ESRC Whitehall Research Prog 1984–99, chair Local Governance Steering Ctee of ESRC 1992–98; ed Public Admin 1986–; fell Aust Acad of Social Sci 2004–; *Books* Control and Power in Central-Local Government Relations (1981, 2 edn 1999), The National World of Local Government (1986), Beyond Westminster and Whitehall (1988), Policy Networks in British Government (ed, 1992), Prime Minister, Cabinet and Core Executive (jt ed, 1995), Understanding Governance (1997), United Kingdom (ed, 2 vols, 2000), Transforming British Government (ed 2 vols, 2000), Interpreting British Governance (jtly, 2003), Governance Stories (jtly, 2006); *Style*— Prof Roderick Rhodes; ✉ Research School of Social Sciences, Australian National University, Canberra, ACT 0200, Australia (tel 00 61 (0)2 6125 1991, fax 00 61 (0)2 6125 3051, e-mail roderick.rhodes@anu.edu.au)

RHODES, Zandra Lindsey; CBE (1997); da of Albert James Rhodes (d 1988), of Chatham, Kent, and Beatrice Ellen, *née* Twigg (d 1968), fitter at Worth, Paris; *b* 19 September 1940; *Educ* Medway Technical Sch for Girls Chatham, Medway Coll of Art Rochester, Royal Coll of Art (DesRCA); *Career* started career as textile designer 1964, set up print factory and studio with Alexander McIntyre 1965, sold designs (and converted them into clothes) to Foale and Tuffin and Roger Nelson, transferred to fashion industry 1966, partnership with Sylvia Ayton producing dresses using own prints, opened Fulham Rd clothes shop (fndr ptnr and designer) 1967–68, first solo collection US 1969 (met with phenomenal response from Vogue and Women's Wear Daily), thereafter established as foremost influential designer (developed unique use of printed fabrics and treatment of jersey), prodr annual spectacular fantasy shows USA; fndr (with Anne Knight and Ronnie Stirling): Zandra Rhodes (UK) Ltd, Zandra Rhodes Shops 1975–86; md: Zandra Rhodes (UK) Ltd 1975–, ZLR Ltd (formerly Zandra Rhodes Shops); first shop London 1975 (others opened in Bloomingdales NY, Marshall Field Chicago, Seibu Tokyo and Harrods London), shops and licencees now worldwide; Zandra Rhodes designs currently incl: interior furnishing, wallpaper, scarves, hosiery, mens' ties, sheets and pillowcases, saris, jewellery, rugs, kitchen accessories, fine china figurines; launched fine arts and prints collections Dyanssen Galleries USA 1989, fur collection for Pologeorgis Furs 1995–; solo exhibitions incl: Texas Gallery Houston 1981, La Jolla Museum of Contemporary Art San Diego 1982, Barbican Centre 1982, Parson's Sch of Design NY 1982, Art Museum of Santa Cruz 1983, The Surface and Beyond Phoenix Art Museum 1997; work represented in numerous permanent costume collections incl: V&A, City Museum & Art Gallery Stoke-on-Trent, Royal Pavilion Brighton Museum, City Art Gallery Leeds, Met Museum NY, Museum of Applied Arts & Sciences Sydney, Nat Museum of Victoria Melbourne; fndr Zandra Rhodes Fndn 1997–; notable licences incl: Eva Stillman Lingeria (USA) 1977, Wamsutta sheets and pillow cases (USA) 1976, CVP Designs interior fabrics and settings (UK) 1977, Philip Hockey Decorative Furs (UK) 1986, Zandra Rhodes Saris (India) 1987, Littlewoods Catalogues (UK) for printed t-shirt and Intasia sweaters 1988, Hilmet silk scarves and men's ties (UK) 1989, Bonnay perfumes 1993, Coats Patons needlepoint (UK) 1998, Pologeorgis Furs (USA) 1995, Zandra Rhodes II hand painted ready to wear collection (Hong Kong) 1995, Grattan Catalogue sheets and duvets (UK); set and costume designer Aida (ENO) 2007; acknowledged spokeswoman and personality of 60s and 70s (famous for green and later pink coloured hair), frequent speaker on fashion and design; subject of numerous documentaries and films incl: This is Your Life 1985, Classmates 1989, Colour Eye 1991; Designer of the Year English Fashion Trade UK 1972, Emmy Award for Best Costume Design Romeo and Juliet on Ice CBS TV 1984, Best Show of the Year New Orleans 1985, Woman of Distinction Award Northwood Inst Dallas Texas 1986, Lifetime Achievement Award (Hall of Fame) Br Fashion Awards 1995; key to Cities of: Miami, Hollywood, Philadelphia; hon fell Kent Inst of Art and Design 1992; Hon DFA Int Fine Arts Coll Miami, Hon Dr RCA, Hon DD CNAA 1987, Hon DLitt Univ of Westminster 2000; RDI 1977, FSIAD 1982; *Books* The Art of Zandra Rhodes (1984, US edn 1985, republished 1995); *Recreations* gardening, travelling, drawing, watercolours; *Style*— Miss Zandra Rhodes, CBE; ✉ The Zandra Rhodes Foundation, 79–85 Bermondsey Street, London SE1 3XF (tel 020 7403 0222, fax 020 7403 0555), Zandra Rhodes Publications, 444 South Cedros, Studio 160, Solana Beach, CA 92075, USA (tel 00 1 619 792 1814)

RHYS, Prof (David) Garel; CBE (2007, OBE 1989); s of Emyr Lewys Rhys, and Edith Phyllis, *née* Williams; *b* 28 February 1940; *Educ* Ystalyfera GS, Univ of Swansea (BA), Univ of Birmingham (MCom); *m* (Charlotte) Mavis, da of Edward Colston Walters; 1 s (Jeremy Charles), 2 da (Angela Jayne, Gillian Mary); *Career* lectr Univ of Hull 1967–70 (asst lectr 1965–67); Univ Coll Cardiff 1970–87: lectr, sr lectr, prof; prof Cardiff Business Sch Univ of Wales 1987–2005, dir Centre for Automotive Industry Res Cardiff Business Sch Cardiff Univ (part of the Univ of Wales until 2005) 1991–2005, emeritus prof Univ of Cardiff 2005–; advsr to: Select Ctees House of Commons and House of Lords, Nat Audit Office; conslt to govt depts, lead conslt to UNIDO 1995–96; chm: Welsh Automotive Forum 2001–, Economic Res Advsy Panel Nat Assembly for Wales 2002–; pres Inst of the Motor Industry 2004–; memb: bd Welsh Devpt Agency 1994–98, UK Round Table on Sustainable Devpt 1996–2000, HE Funding Cncl for Wales 2003–; Freeman City of London 2000, Liveryman Worshipful Co of Carmen 2000; FITA 1987, FIMI 1989, FRSA; *Books* The Motor Industry: An Economic Survey (1971), The Motor Industry in the European Community (1989); *Recreations* walking, gardening, amusing my grandchildren; *Clubs* RAC; *Style*— Prof Garel Rhys, CBE; ✉ Cardiff University, Aberconway Building, Colum Drive, Cardiff CF10 3EU (tel 029 2087 4281, fax 029 2087 4419, e-mail rhysg@cf.ac.uk)

RHYS, Matthew (*né* Matthew Evans); s of Glyn Evans, and Helen Evans; *b* 1974, Cardiff; *Educ* Ysgol Gyfun Gymraeg Glantaf, RADA; *Career* actor; Patricia Rothermere Scholarship 1993, Welsh BAFTA Best Actor 1998 *Theatre* The Graduate 2000, Romeo and Juliet (RSC) 2004–05; *Films* House of America 1996, Titus 1998; *Recreations* shooting; *Style*— Matthew Rhys, Esq; ✉ c/o Dallas Smith, PFD, Drury House, Drury Lane, London WC2B 5HA (tel 020 7344 1010)

RHYS, (William Joseph) St Ervyl-Glyndwr; s of Edward John Rhys (d 1955), and Rachel, *née* Thomas (d 1986); *b* 6 July 1924; *Educ* Newport HS Gwent, Univ of Wales, Guy's Hosp Med Sch London, St John's Coll Cambridge (MA, MB BS); *m* 1961, Dr Ann Rees (High Sheriff Co of Dyfed 2006–07); 6 da (Dr Rhian b 1962, Dr Catrin b 1964, Dr Mared b 1966, Ceril (Dr Rhys-Dillon) b 1969, Ffion b 1973, Dr Mirain b 1980), 1 s (Rob b 1981); *Career* Nat Serv Sqdn Ldr RAF Inst Aviation Med and Empire Test Pilot Sch; house surgn, registrar and radium registrar appts: Guy's Hosp 1948, Addenbrooke's Hosp 1949, Royal Postgrad Med Sch Univ of London 1953, Univ of Wales Coll of Med 1956; conslt gynaecologist Welsh Hosp Bd 1962, MOH Cardiganshire 1966–74, conslt physician in community med Dyfed 1974–82, hon med advsr Welsh Nat Water Devpt Authy 1966–82, hon chm of med servs Royal Nat Eisteddfod of Wales 1976, 1984 and 1992, Univ of Cambridge rep on Cncl and Ct of Govrs UC Wales 1979–86, chm of tstees St John's Coll Dyfed 1987–96 (memb 1979–); High Sheriff Co of Dyfed 1979–80; cmmr St John Ambulance Bde Ceredigion 1982–89, pres Scout Assoc Ceredigion 1983–2003, chm Hospitallers' Club Dyfed 1983–; memb: Exec Ctee Assoc of Friends of Nat Library of Wales 1984–, Welsh Scout Cncl 1984–, Governing Body Ceredigion Schs 1985–96 and 1998–2002 (chm 1987–91); pres Mid Wales BMA 1999–2001, pres History of Medicine

R

Soc of Wales 2007– (vice-pres 2005–06); memb Hon Soc of Cymmrodorion 2005–, hon memb (White Robe) Gorsedd of Bards of Wales; Lord of the Barony of Llawhaden, Freeholder of Llawhaden Castle, Lord of the Manor of Llanfynydd (Celtic, pre-Norman), Freeman City of London, Liveryman Worshipful Soc of Apothecaries; MRCOG, MFCM; CStJ; *Publications* Leopold Kohr at 80 (1990), Proceedings 34th International Congress History of Medicine (contrib, 1994), Seen Across the Atlantic (2001), Llandeilo and Llandilo (2001), Tician y Fro Dal yn Sain Ffagan (2002), Edward Richard of Ystrad Meurig (contrib, 2002), Were Those The Days? Events a Surgeon Can't Forget (2003), Lost Head in Cors Caron (2007); *Recreations* medical history, genealogical research, local history, musing in churchyards; *Clubs* RAF; *Style*— St Ervyl-Glyndwr Rhys, Esq; ✉ Plas Bronmeurig, Ystrad Meurig, Ceredigion, SY25 6AA (tel 01974 831650)

RHYS EVANS, Peter Howell; s of Gwilym Rhys Evans, MC, of Rickledown, Durham, and Jean Marjorie, *née* Foord; *b* 17 May 1948; *Educ* Ampleforth, Bart's (MB BS, Cricket and Rugby colours), Univ of Paris, Gustave-Roussy Inst (DCC); *m* 1, 6 Jan 1973 (m dis), Irene Mossop; 2 s (Matthew b 1 Feb 1976, Marc b 2 May 1980), 1 da (Melissa b 2 March 1984); m 2, 30 Sept 1994, Frances Knight; 2 da (Olivia Frances b 5 April 1996, Sophie Katherine b 25 June 1998), 1 s (James Peter (twin) b 25 June 1998); *Career* qualified Bart's 1971, conslt and sr lectr ENT surgery Univ of Birmingham 1981–86, conslt ENT and head neck surgn The Royal Marsden Hosp 1986–; hon civilian conslt ENT surgn to the RN 1991–; visiting conslt ENT surgn St Bernard's Hosp Gibraltar; examiner RCS 1986–94, fndr memb Euro Acad of Facial Surgeons 1978 (vice-pres 1987), memb Nat Cncl Otolaryngological Res Soc 1984–88, memb Cncl RSM 1991–97; asst ed Jl of Laryngology & Otology 1986–96; Freeman City of London 1990, Freeman Worshipful Soc of Apothecaries; hon ENT surgn: St Mary's Hosp, King Edward VII Hosp for Officers; hon sr lectr Univ of London; memb BMA, MRCS 1971, LRCP, FRSM, FRCS 1978; *Publications* Cancer of Head and Neck (ed, 1983), Face and Neck Surgical Techniques - Problems and Limitations (ed, 1983), Facial Plastic Surgery - Otoplasty (guest ed, 1985), Principles and Practice of Head and Neck Oncology (ed, 2002), contrib to med jls and books on head and neck cancer and aquatic ape theory; *Recreations* skiing, golf, tennis, anthropology; *Style*— Peter Rhys Evans, Esq; ✉ The Halt, Smugglers Way, The Sands, Farnham, Surrey GU10 1NB; 106 Harley Street, London W1N 1AF; The Royal Marsden Hospital, Fulham Road, London SW3 6JJ (tel 020 7935 3525, 020 7352 8171 ext 2730 and 2731, fax 020 7351 3785)

RHYS JONES, Griffith (Griff); s of Elwyn Rhys Jones, and Gwyneth Margaret Jones; *b* 16 November 1953; *Educ* Brentwood Sch, Emmanuel Coll Cambridge (MA); *m* 21 Nov 1981, Joanna Frances, da of Alexander James Harris; 1 s (George Alexander b 1985), 1 da (Catherine Louisa b 1987); *Career* actor and writer; BBC radio prodr 1976–79; dir Talkback; chm Hackney Empire Appeal Ctee; FWCMD, FRSA; *Theatre* Charley's Aunt 1983, Trumpets and Raspberries 1985, The Alchemist 1986, Arturo Ui 1987, Thark 1989–90, Wind in the Willows 1990–91, The Revengers' Comedies 1991, An Absolute Turkey 1994, Plunder (Savoy) 1997, The Front Page 1998; dir Twelfth Night RSC 1989; *Opera* Die Fledermaus 1989; *Radio* Do Go On (Radio 4), The Griff Rhys Jones Show (Radio 2); *Television* comedy series incl: Not The Nine O'Clock News 1979–82, Alas Smith and Jones 1984, The World According to Smith and Jones 1986–87, Small Doses 1989, Smith and Jones 1991; co-presenter Comic Relief (BBC); presenter: Bookworm; plays incl: A View of Harry Clarke 1989, Ex (Screen One) 1991, Demob 1993; Restoration 2003–04, Mine All Mine 2004; *Film* Morons From Outer Space 1985, Wilt 1989, Up N Under 1997, Puckoon; *Records* Bitter & Twisted, Scratch 'n' sniff, Alas Smith & Jones, Not the Nine O'Clock News; *Awards* Emmy Award for Alas Smith & Jones, Br Comedy Top Entertainment Series Award for Smith & Jones 1991, Br Comedy Top Entertainment Performer (with Mel Smith) for Smith & Jones 1991; Olivier Award for Best Comedy Performance for Charley's Aunt and Absolute Turkey, Sony Silver Award for Do Go On 2000, Mont Blanc Award for Arts Patronage 2003 (fundraising chm for Hackney Empire); *Books* The Lavishly Tooled Smith and Jones (1986), Janet Lives with Mel and Griff (1988), Smith and Jones Head to Head (1992), The Nation's Favourite Poems (ed, 1996), The Nation's Favourite Comic Poems (ed, 1998), The Nation's Favourite Twentieth Century Poems (ed, 1999), To the Baltic with Bob (2003); *Clubs* Groucho; *Style*— Griff Rhys Jones, Esq; ✉ Talkback Management, 20–21 Newman Street, London W1T 1PG (tel 020 7861 8000, fax 020 7861 8001)

RHYS WILLIAMS, Sir (Arthur) Gareth Ludovic Emrys; 3 Bt (UK 1918), of Miskin, Parish of Llantrisant, Co Glamorgan; s of Sir Brandon Rhys Williams, 2 Bt, MP (d 1988), and Caroline Susan, eldest da of Ludovic Anthony Foster (d 1990), of Greatham Manor, Pulborough, W Sussex; *b* 9 November 1961; *Educ* Eton, Univ of Durham, INSEAD; *m* 14 Sept 1996, Harriet, da of Maj Tom Codnor, of Glos; 2 s (Ludo Dhaulagiri b 12 Oct 2001, Hugo Thomas Casmir b 6 July 2003), 1 da (Tacita Clementine b 17 May 2006); *Heir* s, Ludo Rhys Williams; *Career* md: NFI Electronics 1990–93, Rexam Custom Europe 1993–96, BPB plc; dir Central Europe 1996–2000, ceo Vitec Gp plc 2001–; CEng, MIET, MIMechE, CCMI; *Recreations* conjuring, travel; *Clubs* Garrick; *Style*— Sir Gareth Rhys Williams, Bt

RIBBANDS, Mark Jonathan; s of Henry Stephen Ribbands (d 2001), and Christina Ivy, *née* Saggers (d 1984); *b* 6 January 1959; *Educ* Forest Sch (expelled for making bombs), NE London Poly (BSc); *m* 30 May 1987 (m dis 1998), Maya, da of Flt Offr Wassoudeve Goriah, DFC (d 1969); 2 s (Adam b 27 Sept 1993, James Ming b 26 July 2004); *Career* md Ribbands Explosives Ltd 1982–; involved with: explosives disposal, demolition, dealing in firearms, ammunition and explosives; video presenter: The Power of Explosives 1998, It Didn't Look Like a Bomb 2001, Power and Precision: An Introduction to Explosives 2003; memb Cncl Inst of Explosives Engrs 1988 and 1992–; FGS 1983, FRGS 1983, MIExpE 1985; *Recreations* scuba diving, flying helicopters, motorcycling, driving fast cars, shooting, playing with fire, building things, growing things, the company of intelligent women, hedonistic excess; *Clubs* Milk & Honey, Kingly; *Style*— Mark Ribbands, Esq; ✉ Dyson's Farm, Long Row, Tibenham, Norfolk NR16 1PD (tel 01379 674444, fax 020 7681 2197, e-mail ribbands@ribbands.co.uk, website www.ribbands.co.uk); 59 Greencoat Place, London SW1P 1DS

RIBBANS, William; s of Maurice Arthur Ribbans, MBE, of Ilmington, Warks, and Sheila Beryl, *née* Brightwell; *b* 28 November 1954; *Educ* Northampton GS for Boys, Royal Free Hosp Sch of Med London (BSc, MB BS), Univ of Liverpool (MChOrth), Univ of Glamorgan (PhD); *m* 10 Sept 1983, Siân Elizabeth, da of Phillip Noel Williams; 3 da (Rebecca Elizabeth b 3 Feb 1985, Hannah Alexandra b 31 Dec 1988, Abigail Victoria b 4 May 1992); *Career* house surgn and physician Royal Free Hosp London 1980–81; SHO: in orthopaedics and casualty Luton and Dunstable Hosp 1981–82, in gen surgery Northwick Park Hosp Harrow 1982–84; radiology registrar St Mary's Paddington 1984–85; orthopaedic registrar: Wexham Park Slough 1985–86, Northwick Park Hosp Harrow 1986–87; orthopaedic clinical fell Harvard Univ 1987–88; orthopaedic sr registrar: Central Middx Hosp 1988–89, Middx Hosp and UCH 1989–90; orthopaedic fell Sheffield Children's Hosp 1990, conslt in orthopaedic surgery (with special interests in sports injuries, post-traumatic limb reconstruction, foot and ankle, and surgery for the haemophilic patient) Royal Free Hosp 1991–95, hon sr lectr Royal Free Hosp Sch of Med 1991–2001; reader in surgery: Univ of London 1991–95, Northampton Gen Hosp 1996–; memb Ct of Examiners RCS 2003– (tutor 1998–2001); hon orthopaedic surgn: Northampton Saints RFC 1996–, Northampton Town FC 1999–, English Nat Ballet; visiting prof Univ of Northampton 2005–; FRCSEd 1985, FRCSOrth 1990, MChOrth 1990, FBOA 1991, FRCS Eng 2001, FFSEM 2006; *Recreations* sports (especially rugby and athletics), antiques, philately; *Clubs* Old Northamptonians RFC; *Style*— William J Ribbans, Esq; ✉ Chartlands, Cherry Tree Lane, Great Houghton, Northamptonshire NN4 7AT; Department of Orthopaedic Surgery, Northampton General Hospital, Cliftonville, Northampton NN1 5BD (tel 01604 885019, e-mail wjribbans@uk-consultants.co.uk, website www.billribbans.com)

RIBEIRO, Bernard Francisco; CBE (2004); s of Miguel Augustus Ribeiro (d 1995), and Matilda, *née* Ampiah (d 2000); *b* 20 January 1944, Achimota, Ghana; *Educ* Dean Close Sch Cheltenham, Middx Hosp Medical Sch; *m* 8 June 1968, Elisabeth Jean, *née* Orr; 1 s (Richard Francisco b 19 April 1973), 3 da (Nicola Helen b 22 July 1975, Joanna Charlotte, Tessa Elisabeth (twins) b 10 Nov 1978); *Career* registrar in surgery Orsett Hosp Essex 1970–72, registrar then sr registrar in surgery Middx Hosp London 1972–78, lectr in urology Accra 1974–75, conslt gen surgn Basildon Univ NHS Tst 1979–; surgical advsr to Expert Advsy Gp on AIDS and to UK Advsy Panel on Blood-Born Viruses 1994–2003; pres: RCS 2005– (memb Cncl 1998–2005), Assoc of Surgns of GB and I 1999–2000 (hon sec 1991–96); medical vice-chm E of Eng Advsy Ctee on Clinical Excellence 2002–05; memb Bd of Visitors HMP Chelmsford 1982–92; govr Dean Close Sch 2006–; memb Test and Itchen Assoc; memb Ct of Assts Worshipful Co of Barbers; memb Assoc of Surgns of GB and I, FRCS 1972, FRCP 2006, hon fell Coll of Physicians and Surgeons of Ghana (FCPSG) 2006, fell Acad of Medicine of Malaysia (FAMM) 2006; *Publications* Concise Surgery (contrib, 1998), Surgery in the United Kingdom (2001), Emergency Surgery: Principles and Practice (contrib, 2006); *Recreations* field sports (shooting and fishing); *Clubs* Flyfishers', Surgical 60 Travellers; *Style*— Bernard Ribeiro, Esq, CBE; ✉ The Royal College of Surgeons, 35–43 Lincoln's Inn Fields, London WC2A 3PE (tel 020 7869 6009, fax 020 7869 6005, e-mail president@rcseng.ac.uk)

RICE, Prof (Charles) Duncan; s of James Inglis Rice, and Jane Meauras Findlay, *née* Scroggie; *b* 20 October 1942; *Educ* Univ of Aberdeen (MA), Univ of Edinburgh (PhD); *m* 1967, Susan, *née* Wunsch; 3 c (James b 1976, Sam b 1984, Jane b 1989); *Career* lectr Univ of Aberdeen 1966–69, assoc prof of history Yale Univ 1975–79 (asst prof of history 1970–75), prof of history and dean of Coll Hamilton Coll 1979–85, vice-chllr NYU 1985–96, princ and vice-chllr Univ of Aberdeen 1996–; memb of Bd: Scottish Enterprise Grampian, Nat Tst for Scotland, Rowett Research Inst, Univs and Colls Employers Assoc (UCEA) until 2006, Scottish Ballet until 2004, Scottish Opera until 2005; chm UK Socrates-Erasmus Cncl until 2007; memb Heritage Lottery Fund Ctee for Scotland; Burgess of Guild of the City of Aberdeen; FRSE 1998, FRSA, FRHistS; *Books* The Rise and Fall of Black Slavery (1975), The Scots Abolitionists 1831–1961 (1982); *Recreations* hill walking, contemporary Scottish literature, studio ceramics; *Clubs* Royal Northern & Univ (Aberdeen); *Style*— Prof C Duncan Rice, FRSE; ✉ University of Aberdeen, King's College, Aberdeen AB24 3FX (tel 01224 272134/5, fax 01224 488605, e-mail lois.brown@abdn.ac.uk)

RICE, Janet; da of George Robert Whinham (d 1992), of Amble, Northumberland, and Ella, *née* Grey (d 1972); *b* 14 December 1949; *Educ* Duchess's County GS for Girls Alnwick, City of Leeds & Carnegie Coll of Educn (Cert Ed); *m* 7 Aug 1971, Martin Graham Rice, s of Alfred Victor Rice; *Career* pensions asst Clarke Chapman-John Thompson Ltd 1972–74, clerical offr DHSS 1974; British Gas plc (now BG Gp plc): pensions asst northern region 1974–78, pensions offr HQ 1978–85, asst pensions admin mangr 1985–86, pensions admin mangr 1986–89, mangr Pensions and Int Benefits 1989–96, gp head of pensions 1996–2001; dir ICL Pensions Tst Co 2002–; memb Advsy Cncl OPDU Ltd 1999–2005; memb Soc of Antiquaries of Newcastle upon Tyne 2000–; FPMI 1993 (assoc 1979, memb Cnl 1998–2001); *Recreations* walking, gardening, reading, family and local history; *Style*— Mrs Janet Rice; ✉ 17 Springfield Road, Pamber Heath, Tadley, Hampshire RG26 3DL

RICE, Ladislas Oscar; *b* 20 January 1926; *Educ* Reading Sch, LSE (BSc), Harvard Grad Sch of Business Admin (MBA); *Children* 1 s (Sebastian b 1970), 1 da (Valentina b 1973); *Career* W H Smith & Son Ltd 1951–53, sr ptnr Urwick Orr & Partners 1953–66, md Minerals Separation 1966–69, chm Burton Group plc 1969–80 (dep chm 1980–93); current directorships incl: Sovereign High Yield Investment Co Ltd, Scudder New Europe Fund Inc; memb Cncl: CBI 1972–79, RSA 1977–82; memb Fin Ctee Nat Tst 1980–88; vice-chm E Anglian RHA 1987–93, dir Whittington Hosp NHS Tst 1994–99; CIMgt, FIMC; *Recreations* travel, books, pictures; *Clubs* Brooks's, Harvard (NYC); *Style*— Ladislas Rice, Esq; ✉ 19 Redington Road, London NW3 7QX (tel 020 7435 8095); La Casa di Cacchiano, Monti in Chianti, Siena, Italy

RICE, Michael Penarthur Merrick; CMG (2002); s of Arthur Vincent Rice (d 1969), of Penarth, Glam, and Dora Kathleen, *née* Blacklock (d 1980); *b* 21 May 1928; *Educ* Challoner Sch; *Career* Nat Serv 1946–48; chm Michael Rice Group Ltd 1955–2004, dir Eastern England TV Ltd 1969–83; advsr The Bahrain-Br Fndn 1990–2004; conslt: Govts of Egypt, Jamaica, and Oman, and also Carreras-Rothmans Ltd 1956–75, Govt of Bahrain 1963–, Saudi Arabia 1974–; chm: The PR Consultants' Assoc 1978–81 (co-fndr, hon memb 1985), The Bahrain Soc 1998–2007; memb Int Soc of Egyptologists; museum planning and design for: Qatar Nat Museum, The Museum of Archaeology and Ethnography Riyadh Saudi Arabia, 6 prov museums in Saudi Arabia, Oman Nat Museum, The Museum of the Sultan's Armed Forces Oman, Qasr al-Masmak Riyadh Saudi Arabia; The Aga Khan Award for Architecture 1980; tstee: Soc for Arabian Studies, Elene Nakou Fndn; FCIPR (FIPR 1975); Order of Bahrain (first class) 2003; *Books* The Temple Complex at Barbar Bahrain (1983), Dilmun Discovered The First Hundred Years of the Archaeology of Bahrain (1984), Search for the Paradise Land: the Archaeology of Bahrain and the Arabian Gulf (1985), Bahrain Through the Ages: The Archaeology (ed, 1985), The Excavations at Al-Hajjar Bahrain (1988), Egypt's Making (1990, revised edn 2004), The Archaeology of the Arabian Gulf (1993), Bahrain Through The Ages: The History (ed, 1993), False Inheritance - Israel in Palestine (1994), The Power of the Bull (1997), Egypt's Legacy - The Archetypes of Western Civilisation (1997), Who's Who in Ancient Egypt (1999), Consuming Ancient Egypt (jt ed, 2003), Swifter than the Arrow: The Golden Hunting Hounds of Ancient Egypt (2006); *Recreations* collecting English watercolours, antiquarian books, embellishing a garden, the opera and listening to music; *Clubs* Athenaeum; *Style*— Michael Rice, Esq, CMG; ✉ Odsey House, Odsey, Baldock, Hertfordshire SG7 6SD (tel 01462 742706, fax 01462 742395, e-mail michaelricecmg@mac.com)

RICE, Olwen Mary; da of James Anthony Rice, of Rugeley, Staffs, and Mary, *née* Wood; *b* 2 August 1960; *Educ* Hagley Park Sch Rugeley, London Coll of Printing (HND, NCTJDip); *m* 16 Nov 1990, Andrew Tilley, s of Raymond Tilley, of Tettenhall, Wolverhampton; 1 da (Grace b 27 June 1995); *Career* rep Oxford Mail 1980–84, news ed Fitness Magazine 1984–85, health and beauty ed Chat Magazine 1985–87, dep ed Best Magazine 1987–88, ed Living Magazine 1988–93, ed Woman's Weekly 1993–; *Recreations* sport, reading, writing; *Style*— Ms Olwen Rice; ✉ Woman's Weekly, Kings Reach Tower, Stamford Street, London SE1

RICE, Peter Anthony; s of John Daniel Rice (d 1981), of Newry, Co Down, and Brigid Tina, *née* McVerry (d 1990); *b* 25 June 1950; *Educ* Abbey GS Newry, Lancaster Univ (BA), Univ of Buckingham (MA); *Career* Duncan C Fraser & Co 1971–74, Wood Mackenzie & Co 1974–88 (ptnr 1981), dir Hill Samuel & Co 1986–87, gp corp fin and planning mangr Commercial Union Assurance plc 1988–92, UK divnl dir Commercial Union 1993–98, dir Morley Fund Management 1998–2000; non-exec dir: Lloyd Thompson plc 1990–94, Gartmore Smaller Companies Investment Tst 2000–, Rostrum Gp Ltd 2000–05; chm Edinburgh Central Cons Assoc 1977–79, fndr chm Scot Bow Group 1980–82; FIA 1974, memb Stock Exchange 1981; *Clubs* Athenaeum; *Style*— Peter Rice, Esq; ✉ The Old Rectory, 6 Redington Road, Hampstead, London NW3 7RG (tel 020 7431 3176)

RICE, Susan Ilene; CBE (2005); da of Samuel Wunsch (d 1982), and Etta Waldman Wunsch (d 1992); *b* 7 March 1946; *Educ* Wellesley Coll Mass (BA), Univ of Aberdeen (MLitt); *m* 3 July 1967, Prof C Duncan Rice, s of Dr James Inglis Rice; 2 s (James b 10 Oct 1976, Sam b 3 May 1984), 1 da (Jane (Beady) b 24 Nov 1989); *Career* med researcher Yale Univ Med Sch 1970–73, dean Saybrook Coll Yale Univ 1973–79, staff aide to Pres Hamilton Coll 1980–81, dean of students Colgate Univ 1981–86; sr vice-pres and div head Nat Westminster Bancorp 1986–96; Bank of Scotland: dir of business projects 1997–98, head of branch banking 1998–99, md Personal Banking 1999–2000; chief exec Lloyds TSB Scotland plc 2000–; non-exec dir: Scottish and Southern Energy plc 2003–, Bank of England 2007–; chair: Ctee of Scottish Clearing Bankers, Edinburgh Int Book Festival 2001–, Adsvy Ctee Scottish Centre for Research on Social Justice, Consumer Affrs and Community Re-investment Ctee NY State Bankers Assoc; dir: Scottish Business in the Community 2001–, UK Charity Bank 2001–, Scotland Futures Forum 2005–, Gtr Jamaica Devpt Corp, Neighborhood Housing Services of NYC, NY Community Investment Co, S Bronx Overall Economic Devpt Corp; tstee David Hume Inst; advsr: Community Re-investment Inst, Seton Hall Center for Public Service, Women's World Banking in N America; memb: HM Treasy Policy Action Team on Access to Fin Services, Foresight Sub-Ctee on Retail Fin Services, BP Scottish Advsy Bd, HM Treasy Financial Inclusion Taskforce 2005–, Business Advsy Forum Oxford Univ Saïd Business Sch 2006–, Cncl Chartered Inst of Bankers Scot, Scottish Advsy Task Force on The New Deal, Aberdeen Common Purpose Advsy Bd, New Jersey Legislature Housing Advsy and Steering Ctees; HRH The Prince of Wales ambass for Scot for corporate responsibility 2005–06; pres Community Devpt Finance Assoc; memb Nat Panel of Judges Bruner Fndn Rudy Bruner Award 1997; induction American Acad of Women Achievers 1994, Business Person of Year Sunday Independent Award Ireland 1999, Corp Elite Business Award - Business Woman Business Insider 2002, Spirit of Scotland Annual Business Award 2002, Lifetime Achievement Award Women in Banking and Finance 2005; Burgess of Guild City of Aberdeen 1999; Hon DBA Robert Gordon Univ 2001, Dr (hc) Univ of Edinburgh 2003, Hon DLitt Heriot-Watt Univ 2004, Hon DUniv Paisley 2005, Hon DUniv Glasgow 2007; FCIBS 1998, FRSE 2002, CCMI 2003, FRSA 2004; *Recreations* hill walking, opera, modern art, reading; *Style*— Ms Susan Rice, CBE; ✉ Lloyds TSB, Henry Duncan House, 120 George Street, Edinburgh EH2 4TS (tel 0131 260 0401, fax 0131 260 0922, e-mail susan.rice@lloydstsb.co.uk)

RICE, Sir Timothy Miles Bindon (Tim); kt (1994); s of Hugh Gordon Rice (d 1988), and Joan Odette, *née* Bawden; *b* 10 November 1944; *Educ* Lancing, La Sorbonne; *m* 1974, Jane, da of Col A H McIntosh, OBE (d 1979); 1 da (Eva Jane Florence b 1975), 1 s (Donald Alexander Hugh b 1977); 1 da (Zoe Joan Eleanor b 1998, with Nell Sully); *Career* writer and broadcaster; lyricist for stage shows: Joseph and the Amazing Technicolour Dreamcoat (music by Andrew Lloyd Webber) 1968, Jesus Christ Superstar (music by Andrew Lloyd Webber) 1970, Evita (music by ALW) 1976, Blondel (music by Stephen Oliver) 1983, Chess (music by Bjorn Ulvaeus and Benny Andersson) 1984, Cricket (music by Andrew Lloyd Webber) 1986, Starmania/Tycoon (music by Michel Berger) 1991, some lyrics for Beauty and the Beast (music by Alan Menken) 1994, Heathcliff (music by John Farrar) 1996, King David (music by Alan Menken) 1997, The Lion King (music by Elton John) 1997, Aida (music by Elton John) 1998; lyrics for animated film musicals: Aladdin (music by Alan Menken) 1992, The Lion King (music by Elton John) 1994, The Road to El Dorado (music by Elton John) 2000; major songs incl: Don't Cry For Me Argentina, A Whole New World, The World is Stone, One Night in Bangkok, I Know Him So Well, Superstar, Any Dream Will Do, I Don't Know How To Love Him, Can You Feel The Love Tonight?, Circle of Life, All Time High, You Must Love Me, Hakuna Matata; co-fndr: Pavilion Books, GRRR Books; chm Stars Organisation for Spastics 1983–85, pres Lord's Taverners 1988–90 and 2000, chm Fndn for Sport and the Arts 1991–, chm Richmond Park Cons Assoc 1996–2003; Cameron Macintosh prof of contemporary theatre St Catherine's Coll Oxford 2003; memb Soc of Distinguished Songwriters (SODS), elected to Songwriters Hall of Fame US 1999; numerous gold and platinum discs, 12 Ivor Novello awards, 3 Tony awards, 6 Grammys, 3 Oscars, 3 Golden Globes; *Publications* incl: Guinness Book of British Hit Singles (10 vols) and many related books, Evita (1978), Treasures of Lord's (1989), Oh What a Circus (memoirs, 1999), Debrett's People of Today 2007 (contrib article on Paul McCartney, 2006); *Recreations* cricket, history of popular music, chickens; *Clubs* MCC (pres 2002–03), Garrick, Saints & Sinners (chm 1990–91), Groucho, Chelsea Arts, Dramatists', Cricketers of New South Wales, Athanaeum; *Style*— Sir Tim Rice

RICE EDWARDS, (John) Martin; s of James Trevor Rice Edwards (d 1984), and Edith Anne, *née* Gower (d 1990); *b* 25 February 1934; *Educ* Charterhouse, Wadham Coll Oxford (MA), Radcliffe Infirmary Oxford (BM BCh); *m* Minette, da of Reginald Harding; 3 s (Sam b 1975, Sebastian b 1977, Hallam b 1981); *Career* Radcliffe Infirmary Oxford: house surgn and house physician 1960, sr house offr then registrar Dept of Neurosurgery 1965; sr registrar in neurosurgery Nat Hosp for Nervous Diseases currently conslt neurosurgeon Chelsea and Westminster Hosp and NW Thames Regnl Neurosciences Centre Charing Cross Hosp London; memb Cncl Soc of Br Neurosurgeons; memb: Royal Med Soc, Georgian Gp; FRCS; *Books* Topical Reviews in Neurosurgery (1985); *Recreations* architecture, fine arts, opera; *Style*— Martin Rice Edwards, Esq; ✉ Ham House Stables, Ham, Richmond, Surrey TW10 7RS (tel 020 8940 6605); Regional Neurosciences Centre, Charing Cross Hospital, Fulham Palace Road, London W6 8RF (tel 020 8846 1182, fax 020 8846 1195)

RICH, Allan Jeffrey; s of Norman Rich, and Tessa, *née* Sawyer; *b* 9 October 1942; *m* 5 June 1966, Vivienne, da of Fred Ostro; 1 s (Jason b 8 May 1970), 2 da (Michaela b 6 May 1968, Natalie b 13 May 1972); *Career* TV buyer Masius Wynne Williams 1959–65, co fndr and media dir Davidson Pearce Berry & Spottiswoode 1965–74, fndr, chm and chief exec The Media Business (now The Media Business Group plc) 1975–, gp chm Mediacom TMB 1999, gp chm and vice-chm Europe Mediacom 2001–02; non-exec chm: Sports Revolution 2005–, Esprit 2006–; non-exec dir: Cello 2004–, Media Meterica 2005–; MAA 1966, MIPA 1966; *Recreations* tennis, football, cricket, golf; *Style*— Allan Rich, Esq

RICH, Josef Lionel (Joe); OBE (1997); s of Morris Rich (d 1990), of Manchester, and Sarah, *née* Cohen (d 1995); *b* 13 August 1938; *Educ* Stand GS for Boys, Univ of Edinburgh (BDS), Faculty of General Dental Practitioners RCS England (DGDP UK); *m* 1, 1962 (m dis 1980), Jennifer, da of George Brown; 2 da (Deborah b 1968, Katherine b 1973), 1 s (Daniel b 1969); m 2, 1984, Jacqueline, da of Edward Tawil; 1 da (Sylvia b 1985), 1 s (Charles b 1986); *Career* assoc gen dental practitioner 1962–65, in own dental practice Eccles Manchester 1966–; pt/t gen dental surgn Hope Hosp Salford 1968–74, pt/t lectr Oral Surgery Dept Dental Sch Univ of Manchester 1976–81; postgraduate dental tutor Salford and Trafford HAs, dental practice advsr Manchester FHSA 1988–91, hon clinical asst Dept Restorative Dentistry Univ Dental Hosp of Manchester; elected memb GDC 1996–; BDA: chair Gen Dental Servs Ctee 1991–97, memb Representative Bd 1996–, tstee Tst Fund 1998, memb Representative Body 1999–, memb Exec Bd 2000–, pres 2007–08; chm: Salford Local Dental Ctee 1977–87, Fedn of NW Local Dental Ctees 1980–87, Central Assessment Panel (Peer Review) 1991–95, Central Audit and Peer Review Panel 1995–; memb Bd of Mgmnt Br Dental Guild 1989–97, chair Bd of Mgmnt Manchester Dental Educn Centre 2000–, memb Manchester Dental Educn Tst 2000–; assoc dir Altrincham AFC 1999–; past pres Manchester Edinburgh Univ Club, pres Odontology Section Manchester Med Soc 1979; tstee Mandent Tst 1998–; fndr, past warden and life memb Cncl Hale and Dist Hebrew Congregation; memb: RSM, Br Endodontic Soc, Edinburgh Dental Alumni Soc, Faculty of Gen Dental Practitioners RCS; FDSRCSE 2003; *Recreations* salmon fishing (memb Salmon and Trout Assoc), bridge, food and wine, watching Manchester City FC; *Style*— Joe Rich, Esq, OBE; ✉ 1 Stanhope Road, Bowdon, Altrincham, Cheshire WA14 3LB (tel 0161 926 8115); (tel 0161 788 9815, mobile 0777 5633112, e-mail joerichbds@aol.com)

RICH, His Hon Michael Samuel; QC (1980); s of Sidney Frank Rich, OBE, JP (d 1985), of Streatham, London, and Erna Babette, *née* Schlesinger (d 1988); *b* 18 August 1933; *Educ* Dulwich Coll, Wadham Coll Oxford (MA); *m* 1 Aug 1963, Janice Sarita, da of Henry Jules Benedictus; 1 da (Sara b 1964), 3 s (Benedict b 1966, Jonathan b 1969, Edmund b 1970); *Career* Lt RASC 1954; called to the Bar Middle Temple 1959 (bencher 1985, reader 2006); recorder 1986–91, circuit judge (SE Circuit) 1991–2005; pt/t memb Lands Tbnl 1993–; memb Hong Kong Bar; pres Dulwich Soc, tstee S London Liberal Synagogue; *Books* Hills Law of Town and Country Planning (1968); *Clubs* Garrick; *Style*— His Hon Michael Rich, QC; ✉ 18 Dulwich Village, London SE21 7AL (tel 020 8693 1957)

RICH, Nigel Mervyn Sutherland; CBE (1995); s of Charles Rich, and Mina Rich; *Educ* Sedbergh, New Coll Oxford (MA); *Career* articled clerk Deloitte Plender Griffiths 1967–71, accountant DH & S NY 1971–73, Jardine Matheson Hong Kong, Manila and South Africa 1974–94, md Hong Kong Land 1986–88, md Jardine Matheson 1988–94, ceo Trafalgar House 1994–96; chm: Exel 2002–05, Slough Estates Int 2006–; dep chm Xchanging 2006–; dir: KGR, John Armit Wines, Matheson & Co, Pacific Assets; dep chm Asia House; co-chm Philippine British Business Cncl; chm of govrs Downe House Sch; Freeman City of London, Renter Warden Worshipful Co of Tobacco Pipemakers and Tobacco Blenders; FCA 1971; *Recreations* golf, windsurfing, horseracing; *Clubs* Boodle's, Turf, MCC, R&A, Hurlingham, Denham Golf, NZ Golf; *Style*— Nigel Rich, Esq, CBE

RICHARD, Prof Alison Fettes; DL; da of Gavin Richard, and Joyce Richard; *b* 1 March 1948; *Educ* Queenswood Sch, Newnham Coll Cambridge (MA), Queen Elizabeth Coll Univ of London (PhD); *m* 1976, Robert E Dewar; 2 da, 1 s (decd); *Career* Yale Univ: asst prof 1972–80, assoc prof 1980–86, prof of anthropology 1986–2003, chair Dept of Anthropology 1986–90, dir Yale Peabody Museum of Natural History 1991–94, provost 1994–2002, Franklin Muzzy Crosby prof of the human environment 1998–2003, emeritus prof 2003–; vice-chllr Univ of Cambridge 2003–, fell Newnham Coll Cambridge 2003–; pres Cambridge Network 2003–; memb Editorial Bd: Folia Primatologica 1982–95, American Jl of Primatology 1988–97; author of numerous scientific articles on primate evolution, ecology and social behaviour in academic jls; co-dir Program of Conservation and Devpt in Southern Madagascar 1977–2003, conslt Species Survival Cmmn Int Union for the Conservation of Nature 1982–90, conslt Canadian Broadcasting Corporation 1982 and 1988, research fell Japan Soc for the Promotion of Science 1987; memb: External Advsy Ctee Duke Univ Primate Center 1980–94, Anthropology Visiting Ctee Harvard Bd of Overseers 1984–86, Int Advsy Gp of Scientists to Govt of Madagascar 1983–86, External Review Ctee for Anthropology Stanford Univ 1986, Duke Univ 1988 and State Univ of NY Stony Brook 1989, Scientific Advsy Cncl L B S Leakey Fndn 1986–96, Physical Anthropology Research Panel Nat Science Fndn 1988–91, Scientific Advsy Cncl Wenner-Gren Fndn for Anthropological Research 1991–94, Bd Liz Claiborne/Art Ortenberg Fndn 1998–, ESRC 2004–; memb Bd WWF-US 1995–2004 (memb Nat Cncl 1992–95), tstee WWF-Int Bd 2007–; hon fell Wolfson Coll Cambridge 2003–; hon degrees: Univ of Peking 2004, Univ of Antananarivo Madagascar 2005, York Univ Canada 2006, Univ of Edinburgh 2006; Officier de l'Ordre National (Madagascar) 2005; *Publications* Behavioral Variation: case study of a Malagassy lemur (1978), Primates in Nature (1985); *Recreations* opera, gardening, cooking; *Clubs* Athenaeum; *Style*— Prof Alison Richard, DL; ✉ Office of the Vice-Chancellor, The Old Schools, Trinity Lane, Cambridge CB2 1TN

RICHARD, Sir Cliff, *né* Harry Rodger Webb; kt (1995), OBE (1980); s of Rodger Oscar Webb (d 1961), and Dorothy Marie Bodkin (formerly Webb), *née* Beazley; *b* 14 October 1940; *Educ* Riversmead Sch Cheshunt; *Career* singer and actor; first hit record Move It 1958, own series on BBC and ITV, various repertory and variety seasons; 14 gold records, 35 silver records; films: Serious Charge 1959, Expresso Bongo 1960, The Young Ones 1961, Summer Holiday 1962, Wonderful Life 1964, Finders Keepers 1966, Two a Penny 1968, His Land 1970, Take Me High 1973; musicals: Time 1986, Heathcliff (title role) 1996; vice-pres: PHAB, Tear Fund, Princess Alice Hospice Tst, Roy Castle Lung Cancer Fndn, various other charitable orgns; Bernard Delfont Award for outstanding contribution to showbusiness 1995, South Bank Show's Outstanding Achievement Award 2000; *Books* Which One's Cliff (1977), Happy Christmas from Cliff (1980), You, Me and Jesus (1983), Jesus, Me and You (1985), Single-Minded (1988); *Recreations* tennis, wine-making (own vineyards in Portugal); *Style*— Sir Cliff Richard, OBE; ✉ c/o PO Box 46C, Esher, Surrey KT10 0RB (tel 01372 467752, fax 01372 462352, website www.cliffrichard.org)

RICHARD, Baron (Life Peer UK 1990), of Ammanford in the County of Dyfed; Ivor Seward Richard; PC (1993), QC (1971); s of Seward Thomas Richard, of Cardiff, and Isabella Irene Richard; *b* 30 May 1932; *Educ* St Michael's Sch Llanelly, Cheltenham Coll, Pembroke Coll Oxford (MA); *m* 1, 1956 (m dis 1962), Geraldine Maude, da of Alfred Moore, of Hartlepool, Co Durham; 1 s (Hon David Seward b 1959); m 2, 1962 (m dis 1985), Alison Mary, da of Joseph Imrie, of Alverstoke, Hants; 1 s (Hon Alun Seward b 1963), 1 da (Hon Isabel Margaret Katherine b 1966); m 3, 1989, Janet, da of John Jones, of Oxford; 1 s (Hon William John b 1990); *Career* called to the Bar Inner Temple 1955, Parly candidate (Lab) S Kensington Gen Election 1959 and LCC Election 1961, MP (Lab) Barons Court 1964–74, PPS to Sec of State for Def 1966–69, Parly under-sec of state for Def (Army) 1969–70, oppn spokesman Posts and Telecommunications 1970–71, dep oppn spokesman for Foreign Affrs 1971–74, UK perm rep at the UN 1974–79, chm Rhodesia Conf Geneva 1976; UK cmmr to the Cmmn of the European Communities 1981–85 responsible for: employment, social affrs, educn and vocational trg; Ldr of the Oppn in House of Lords 1992–97, Lord Privy Seal and ldr of the House of Lords 1997–98; chm Cmmn on the Powers and Electoral System of the Nat Assembly of Wales 2002–04; memb: Fabian Soc, Lab Lawyers; *Style*— The Rt Hon Lord Richard, PC, QC; ✉ 2 Paper Buildings, Temple, London EC4; House of Lords, London SW1A 0PW (tel 020 7219 3000)

RICHARD, Wendy; MBE (2000); da of Henry William Emerton (d 1954), of St Albans, and Beatrice Reay, *née* Cutter (d 1972); *Educ* Royal Masonic Sch Rickmansworth, Italia Conti Drama Sch; *m* 17 March 1990, Paul Peter Anthony Glorney; *Career* actress; Northern TV Personality of the Year 1989; patron Cairn Terrier Relief Assoc, vice-patron Dogs for the Disabled; *Theatre* incl: Blithe Spirit, Cinderella, No Sex Please We're British, Are You Being Served?, Let's Go Camping; *Television* roles and appearances incl: Harpers West One, Arthur Haynes Show, Dixon of Dock Green, Dad's Army, Z Cars, West Country Tales, various TV plays, Are You Being Served?, Eastenders, Grace and Favour, Up Pompeii, Spooner's Patch, Little and Large, Blankety Blank, Punchlines, Pyramid Game, Not on Your Nellie, On the Buses, Fenn Street Gang, Please Sir, Hugh and I, Hogg's Back, Rainbow, No Hiding Place, Both Ends Meet, Newcomers, Give us a Clue, Celebrity Squares, We Love TV, All Star Secrets, Crackerjack, Secrets Out, Music Game, Zodiac Game, Wogan, 3-2-1, TV-am, Breakfast TV, Nationwide, Thank Your Lucky Stars, Dad You're A Square, Vintage Quiz, Kelly Monteith, Dick Emery, Telly Addicts, Danger Man; *Radio* incl: Just a Minute, Film Quiz, The Law Game; *Film* incl: Bless This House, No Blade of Grass, Carry on Matron, Carry on Girls, Are You Being Served?, Gumshoe, Don't I Look Like the Lord's Son, Doctor in Clover; *Books* Wendy Richard...no

R

"S": My Life Story (2000); *Recreations* embroidery work, gardening, cooking; *Clubs* Lady Taverners; *Style*— Ms Wendy Richard, MBE; ✉ Angel Francis Ltd, 12 D'Arblay Street, London W1F 8DU

RICHARDS, (William Samuel) Clive; OBE (2000), DL (Herefordshire 2006); *b* 1 September 1937; *Educ* Bishop Vesey GS Sutton Coldfield; *m*; 3 c; *Career* articled clerk Peat Marwick Mitchell & Co Birmingham Office 1959–60, investment analyst rising to managing ptnr Wedd Durlacher & Co 1960–70, chief exec Rothschild Investment Tst 1970–75, gp fin dir N M Rothschild & Sons Ltd 1974–76, fndr Clive Richards & Co (investment and fin servs co, specialising in venture capital) 1976–; fndr and former chm Micro Business Systems plc 1978; former chm: Steel Burrill Jones Gp plc, Telephone Information Services plc, Security Archives plc; chm: Intelligent Environments Gp plc, ESG Herefordshire Ltd; non-exec dir: Minerva plc, Xpertise Gp plc, Corin Gp plc, various other private cos; commercial farm owner (2,300 acres); pres Hereford Fedn of Young Farmers' Clubs; memb Cncl (representing Hereford) RASE 1995–; fndr Clive Richards Charity 1987, vice-pres Shaw Tst, memb Ctee Lord Mayor of London's Charity 1996–97; govr Bishop Vesey GS; chm Malvern Festival Theatre Tst; former treas and memb Ctee London Welsh RFC, patron and chm Bromyard Sports Assoc; High Sheriff Gtr London 1991–92; memb: Ct of Assts Worshipful Co of Chartered Accountants (Master 1996–97), Ct of Assts Worshipful Co of Gunmakers, Worshipful Co of Bowyers, Worshipful Co of Information Technologists; FIMgt, FCMA 1960, FCA 1960; *Recreations* rugby, cricket, shooting, gardening, art, Nelsonia, breeding Hereford cattle and Black Labrador dogs; *Clubs* Reform, RAC; *Style*— Clive Richards, Esq, OBE, DL; ✉ Clive Richards & Co, Lower Hope, Ullingswick, Hereford HR1 3JF (tel 01432 820557, fax 01432 820515, e-mail cr@crco.co.uk)

RICHARDS, Hon Mr Justice; Sir David Anthony Stewart; kt (2003); s of late Kenneth Richards, of Heswall, Wirral, and late Winifred Edith, *née* Purdoe; *b* 9 June 1951; *Educ* Oundle, Trinity Coll Cambridge (MA); *m* 28 April 1979, Gilliam Moira, da of late Lt-Col W A Taylor; 1 s (Mark b 16 Oct 1981), 2 da (Sarah b 13 Jan 1985, Charlotte b 13 Jan 1985); *Career* called to the Bar Inner Temple 1974, jr counsel (Chancery) to DTI 1989–92, QC 1992, bencher Lincoln's Inn 2000, judge of the High Court of Justice (Chancery Div) 2003–; *Clubs* Garrick; *Style*— The Hon Mr Justice David Richards; ✉ Royal Courts of Justice, Strand, London WC2A 2LL

RICHARDS, Lt-Gen David Julian; CBE (2000), DSO (2001); s of Col John Downie Richards, and Pamela Mary Richards; *Educ* Eastbourne Coll (head boy, rugby capt), UC Cardiff (BA); *m* Caroline; 2 da (Joanna, Philippa); *Career* cmmnd RA 1971; regtl duty and staff 11 Armd Bde 1974–83, Staff Coll Camberley 1984, Cdr Field Battery 47 Field Regt 11 Armd Bde, COS Berlin Inf Bde 1986–88, instr Staff Coll 1988–91, CO 3 Regt RHA 1991–94, Col Army Plans MOD 1994–96, Higher Command and Staff Course 1996, Cdr 4 Armd Bde Germany 1996–98, Chief Jt Force Ops Permanent Jt HQ 1998–2001, Cdr UK Task Force East Timor 1999, Cdr UK Jt Task Force Sierra Leone 2000 (twice), Maj-Gen COS NATO ACE Rapid Reaction Corps Germany 2001–02, Asst Chief of the Gen Staff (ACGS) 2002–05, Lt-Gen Cdr Allied Rapid Reaction Corps Germany 2005–08, Cdr NATO/ISAF Afghanistan 2006–07; *Recreations* military history, fast cars, opera, riding, wine, offshore sailing; *Clubs* Royal Cruising, RA Yacht, Army Sailing Assoc (Cdre), British Kiel Yacht (Adm), Army and Navy; *Style*— Lt-Gen David Richards, CBE, DSO; ✉ c/o Military Secretary, Army Personnel Centre, Kentigern House, 65 Brown Street, Glasgow G2 8EX (tel 0141 224 2546)

RICHARDS, David Thomas; s of Ralph Henry Richards (d 1990), of Cardiff, and Brenda Mary, *née* Brobin (d 2003); *b* 30 November 1954; *Educ* Whitchurch HS Cardiff, New Univ of Ulster Coleraine (BA); *m* 10 Aug 1979, Veryan Cumming, *née* Black, da of Griffith Black; 1 s (Adair b 19 June 1982), 2 da (Morna b 19 Aug 1984, Fiona b 6 Dec 1989); *Career* exec offr DTI 1978–79; Welsh Office: admin trainee 1979, various positions rising to princ 1983, with Housing Policy Div 1983–86, with Local Govt Fin Div 1986–90, head Econ and Regnl Policy Div 1990–92, head Industry and Regnl Policy Div 1992–94, head Fin Progs Div 1994–97, princ fin offr 1997–99; fin dir Nat Assembly for Wales 1999–2006, dir NHS Governance Project 2006–; chair Patent Office Steering Bd 2002–; *Recreations* books, playing the harp; *Style*— David Richards, Esq; ✉ National Assembly for Wales, Cathays Park, Cardiff CF1 3NQ (tel 029 2082 5177, e-mail david.richards@wales.gsi.gov.uk)

RICHARDS, Dean; MBE (1996); s of Brian Richards, of Hinckley, Leics, and Marion, *née* Green; *b* 11 July 1963; *Educ* St Martins HS, John Cleveland Coll; *m* 2 Aug 1986, Nicola Anne, da of Kenneth Milbank Stephenson; 1 da (Jessica b 6 April 1993), 3 s (Joseph and William (twins) b 20 Nov 1997, Charles b 2000); *Career* rugby union player and coach; formerly with Roanne club France; Leicester RFC 1982–2004 (over 300 appearances as player, dir of rugby 1998–2004, winners Courage Clubs' Championship 1995, Zurich Premiership 2000, 2001 and 2002, Zurich Championship 2001 and Heineken Cup 2001 and 2002), coach FC Grenoble Rugby (France) 2004–05, dir of rugby Harlequins RFC 2005–; England: former schs and under 21 rep, full debut v Ireland 1986 (scoring 2 tries), 48 full caps, memb World Cup squads 1987, 1991 (runners-up) and 1995 (4th place), memb Grand Slam winning squads 1991, 1992 and 1995; memb Br Lions tour Aust 1989 (3 test appearances) and NZ 1993 (3 test appearances); also rep Leics and Midlands Div; Whitbread/Rugby World Player of the Year 1991; constable Leics Constabulary 1982–95; *Recreations* shooting, anything sport related except ultra distance running; *Style*— Dean Richards, Esq, MBE; ✉ Harlequins Rugby Football Club, Stoop Memorial Ground, Langhorn Drive, Twickenham, Middlesex TW2 7SX

RICHARDS, Derek William; s of William Albert Richards (d 1985), of Croydon, Surrey, and Mary Ann Ruby, *née* Bissell (d 1985); *b* 6 December 1943; *Educ* Wandsworth GS, Regent Street Poly Sch of Photography (Kodak scholarship, Dip Advtg Photography); *m* 10 June 1972, Rosemary Pauline, da of Reginald Arthur Sturman; *Career* photographer (specialising in people, travel and locations); initially asst to David Swann and Norman Parkinson, freelance advtg photographer 1967–, fndr Derek Richard Studios Ltd 1972, San Francisco 1982–84; numerous assignments for leading UK and USA based advtg agencies and design gps; memb Assoc of Photographers 1972 (memb Ctee 1973–75), fndr memb British Decoy and Wildfowl Carvers' Assoc (award winner 1989–2004); elected to Somerset Guild of Craftsmen 2006 (memb Gallery Ctee); *Recreations* restoring and 'trialing' vintage sports cars, decoy carving, film, theatre, walking, bird watching; *Clubs* Vintage Sports Car; *Style*— Derek Richards, Esq; ✉ Penn House, Hardington Mandeville, Somerset BA22 9PL (tel 01935 862958, e-mail info@derekrichards.co.uk)

RICHARDS, Sir Francis Neville; KCMG (2002, CMG 1994), CVO (1991); o s of Sir (Francis) Brooks Richards, KCMG, DSC (d 2002); *b* 18 November 1945; *Educ* Eton, King's Coll Cambridge (MA); *m* 16 Jan 1971, Gillian Bruce, da of I S Nevill, MC (d 1948); 1 s (James b 1975), 1 da (Joanna b 1977); *Career* Royal Green Jackets 1967–69; HM Dip Serv: third sec to second sec Moscow 1971–73, second sec to first sec UK Delgn to MBFR talks Vienna 1973–76, FCO 1976–85, asst private sec to sec of state 1980–82, cnsllr (econ and commercial) New Delhi 1985–88, head of S Asian Dept FCO 1988–90, high cmmr to Namibia 1990–92, min Moscow 1992–95, asst under sec of state Central and Eastern Europe FCO 1995–96, dir Europe FCO 1996–97, dep under sec of state FCO 1998; dir GCHQ 1998–2003, govr and C-in-C Gibraltar 2003–06; dir Centre for Studies in Security and Diplomacy Univ of Birmingham 2007–, chm Nat Security Inspectorate 2007–; chm Bletchley Park Tst 2007–, tstee Imperial War Museum 2007–; KStJ 2003; *Recreations* riding, walking, travel; *Clubs* Brooks's, Special Forces; *Style*— Sir Francis Richards, KCMG, CVO; ✉ King's Mill House, Painswick, Gloucestershire GL6 6RT

RICHARDS, Gillian (Gill); da of S Goy (d 2004) and E Goy, *née* Twitchett; *b* 16 March 1951, Gateshead, Newcastle-upon-Tyne; *Educ* Loughborough HS for Girls, Univ of Wales Bangor (BA, MEd), Univ of Reading (PGCE); *m* 1976, Peter John Richards; 1 s (William James Strode b 23 Aug 1979), 1 da (Philippa Kate Strode b 16 Nov 1982); *Career* The Sir John Hunt Sch Telford 1973–74, Queen's Park HS Chester 1974–92, sr teacher Rhyl HS 1992–96, headmistress The Belvedere Sch GDST Liverpool 1997–2005 (dep head 1996–97), headmistress Bolton Sch Girls' Div 2005–; tstee P H Holt Liverpool; memb: ASCL 1996, GSA 1997; *Recreations* skiing, cooking, reading, walking, travel; *Style*— Mrs Gill Richards; ✉ Bolton School Girls' Division, Chorley New Road, Bolton BL1 4PB (tel 01204 840201, fax 01204 434710, e-mail hm@girls.bolton.sch.uk)

RICHARDS, Prof (William) Graham; CBE (2001); s of Percy Richards, and Julia, *née* Evans; *Educ* Birkenhead Sch, BNC Oxford (MA, DPhil, DSc); *Career* jr res fell Balliol Coll Oxford 1964–66, CNRS Paris 1965–66; Univ of Oxford: lectr 1966–94, reader 1994–96, prof 1996–, chm of chemistry 1997–; Fulbright fell Stanford Univ 1975–76; dir: Isis Innovation Ltd, IP2IPO Gp plc, Inhibox Ltd; founding scientist Oxford Molecular Gp plc; ed Jl of Molecular Graphics 1984–96; Lloyd of Kilgerran Prize 1996, Mullard Award of Royal Soc 1998, Italgas Prize 2001, ACS Award for Computers in Chemical and Pharmaceutical Research 2004; memb American Chemistry Soc 1980; FRSC 1966, fell AAAS 1998; *Publications* over 350 scientific papers, 15 books; *Recreations* sport; *Clubs* Vincent's (Oxford); *Style*— Prof Graham Richards, CBE; ✉ Brasenose College, Oxford OX1 4AJ (tel 01865 275908, fax 01865 275905, e-mail graham.richards@chem.ox.ac.uk)

RICHARDS, Prof Ivor James; s of Philip James Richards (d 1981), of Newmarket, Suffolk, and Ivy Gwenllian, *née* Kimber (d 1995); *b* 1 May 1943; *Educ* Newmarket GS, Univ of Wales (MA); *m* 5 June 1976 (m dis 1995), Anne Rostas; 1 da (Sarah Elizabeth b 13 March 1983), 1 s (Owen James b 30 Dec 1984); *Career* assoc architect Sir Leslie Martin Architects Cambridge 1969–87; works incl: Faculty of Music Univ of Cambridge 1975–85, Royal Concert Hall Glasgow 1978–90, Centro de Arte Moderna Gulbenkian Fndn Lisbon 1980–84, Royal Scottish Acad of Music and Drama Glasgow 1988, Ecumenical Church Cambridge 1991–, Masters' Houses Stowe Sch Buckingham 1993–, Orientation Centre Hadrian's Wall Steelrigg Northumberland National Park 1998–; prof of architecture Sch of Architecture: Univ of Wales Cardiff 1986–95, Univ of Newcastle upon Tyne 1995–2004; emeritus prof of architecture Univ of Newcastle upon Tyne 2004–; external examiner: Sch of Architecture Univ of Newcastle upon Tyne, Sch of Architecture Univ of Nottingham, Sch of Architecture Univ of Central England, Sch of Architecture Univ of Singapore 1997–98; advsr Northumberland National Park 1998–2002; memb Advsy Bd Sch of Architecture Carnegie Mellon Univ Pittsburgh PA USA 1997–; memb ARB, chartered memb ARIBA; *Publications* Manhattan Lofts (2000), Ecology of the Sky (2001), Groundscrapers and Subscrapers (2001); *Recreations* writing, walking, cities and architecture; *Style*— Prof Ivor Richards

RICHARDS, Dr (Shirley) Jane; OBE (1997); da of (Francis) David Murley Richards (d 1979), and Elisabeth Mortimer, *née* Beck (d 1995); *b* 28 June 1933, Bournemouth; *Educ* Crediton HS for Girls, UCL (MB BS, F T Roberts Prize for Obstetrics); *Career* jr house posts Freedom Fields Hospital Plymouth 1958–61, asst GP Marshfield Glos 1961–64, GP princ Exeter 1965–96, chm Rep Body BMA 1995–98; Cwlth Med Assoc: pres 1998–2001, sec 2001–03;); memb: BMA, RSM; LRCP, MRCS, DObstRCOG, DCH, FRCGP (MRCGP 1969); *Style*— Dr Jane Richards, OBE; ✉ Quarryfield House, Whitestone, Exeter EX4 2JS (tel 01392 811492, e-mail sjaner@tiscali.co.uk)

RICHARDS, John Parry; s of Ellis Parry Richards (d 1985), of Rhiwbina, Cardiff, and Gwyneth, *née* Prosser (d 1998); *b* 16 August 1947; *Educ* Highgate Sch; *m* 1, 31 Dec 1976, Elizabeth Wendy Strachan (d 1995), da of James Douglas Moore Mather; m 2, 1 July 1999, Gillian Susan, da of Dr Geoffrey Hirst (d 2005); 2 s (Robert James b 1 Nov 1978, Alastair John b 16 Sept 1981), 1 step s (Henry Alexander Leon b 30 July 1983); *Career* articled clerk Barton Mayhew & Co (now part of Ernst & Young) 1967; specialist in insolvency and restructuring work 1975–; ptnr Deloitte 1983– (joined 1979), liquidator Bank of Credit and Commerce International SA 1992–; FCA 1979 (ACA 1971), FIPA 1986 (MIPA 1982), FABRP 1986; *Recreations* golf, classic cars, sailing, watching cricket and rugby, theatre, opera and ballet, walking; *Clubs* Old Cholmeleian Soc, Hever Golf; *Style*— John Richards, Esq; ✉ Deloitte, PO Box 810, 66 Shoe Lane, London EC4A 3WA (tel 020 7404 0110, fax 020 7404 0112, e-mail jrichards@deloitte.co.uk)

RICHARDS, Keith; *b* 18 December 1943; *Educ* Sidcup Art Sch; *Partner* (sep) Anita Pallenberg; 2 s (Marlon b 10 Aug 1969, Tara b 26 March 1976 d 4 June 1976), 1 da (Dandelion b 17 April 1972); m 1, 18 Dec 1983, Patti, *née* Hansen; 2 da (Theodora b 18 March 1985, Alexandra b 28 July 1986); *Career* guitarist and songwriter; Rolling Stones formed London 1962; signed recording contracts with: Impact Records/Decca 1963, London Records/Decca 1965, CBS 1983, Virgin 1992; has worked with Chuck Berry, Buddy Guy, Muddy Waters, Eric Clapton, Johnnie Johnson, John Lee Hooker and others; albums with Rolling Stones: The Rolling Stones (1964, reached UK no 1), The Rolling Stones No 2 (1965, UK no 1), Out Of Our Heads (1965, UK no 2), Aftermath (1966, UK no 1), Big Hits: High Tide and Green Grass (compilation, 1966, UK no 4), got LIVE if you want it! (live, 1967), Between The Buttons (1967, UK no 3), Flowers (US compilation, 1967, US no 3), Their Satanic Majesties Request (1967, UK no 3), Beggars Banquet (1968, UK no 3), Through The Past Darkly: Big Hits Vol 2 (compilation, 1969, UK no 2), Let It Bleed (1969, UK no 1), Get Yer Ya-Ya's Out! (live, 1970, UK no 1), Stone Age (compilation, 1971, UK no 4), Sticky Fingers (1971, UK no 1), Hot Rocks 1964–71 (US compilation, 1972, US no 4), Exile On Main Street (1972, UK no 1), More Hot Rocks (US compilation, 1973, US no 9), Goat's Head Soup (1973, UK no 1), It's Only Rock'n'Roll (1974, UK no 2), Made In The Shade (compilation, 1975, UK no 14), Rolled Gold - The Very Best of The Rolling Stones (compilation, 1975, UK no 7), Black and Blue (1976, UK no 2), Love You Live (live, 1977, UK no 3), Some Girls (1978, UK no 2), Emotional Rescue (1980, UK no 1), Tattoo You (1981, UK no 2), Still Life: American Concert 1981 (live, 1981, UK no 4), Undercover (1983, UK no 3), Rewind 1971–1984 (compilation, 1984, UK no 23), Dirty Work (1986, UK no 4), Steel Wheels (1989, UK no 2), Flashpoint (live, 1991, UK no 6), Voodoo Lounge (1994, UK no 1), Bridges to Babylon (1997, UK no 6), Forty Licks (2002); solo albums: Talk Is Cheap (1988, UK no 37), Live at the Hollywood Palladium December 15 1988 (1991), Main Offender (1992), Wingless Angels (1996); concert films: Sympathy For The Devil (dir Jean Luc Godard) 1969, Gimme Shelter 1970, Ladies and Gentlemen, The Rolling Stones 1977, Let's Spend The Night Together (dir Hal Ashby) 1983, Hail, Hail, Rock'n'Roll (with Chuck Berry) 1986, Flashpoint (film of 1990 Steel Wheels World Tour) 1991, Live at the Hollywood Palladium December 15 1988 (DVD, 2002); feature film: Michael Kohlhgaas 1969; *Style*— Keith Richards, Esq; ✉ c/o Munro Sounds, 5 Church Row, Wandsworth Plain, London SW18 1ES

RICHARDS, Prof Keith Sheldon; s of Maurice Richards (d 1973), of Cornwall, and Jean, *née* Young; *b* 25 May 1949; *Educ* Falmouth GS, Jesus Coll Cambridge (MA, PhD); *m* 18 August 1973, Susan Mary, da of Frederick Brooks; *Career* lectr in geography Coventry Poly 1972–77 (sr lectr 1977), lectr Dept of Geography Univ of Hull 1978–84 (sr lectr 1984); Univ of Cambridge: lectr Dept of Geography 1984–, reader in physical geography 1995, prof of geography 1995–, head Dept of Geography 1994–99, exec sec Ctee for Interdisciplinary Environmental Studies 1995–99, dir Scott Polar Research Inst 1997–2002; Emmanuel Coll Cambridge: fell 1984, dir of studies in geography 1984–96, asst bursar 1986–94 (dep bursar 1989); Br Geomorphological Research Gp: Ctee memb 1978–80, hon sec 1980–83, jr vice-chm 1992, vice-chm 1993–94, chm 1994–95; vice-pres (research) RGS/IBG 2004–07 (hon sec 2003–04), pres Geography Section BAAS 2005–06;

memb: Br Hydrological Soc, Quaternary Research Assoc; NERC: memb Aquatic and Atmospheric Physical Sciences Ctee 1990–93, memb Steering Ctees 1995–97, memb Peer Review Coll 2004–; BGRG ed 1984–89, memb ed bd and book review ed Earth Surface Processes and Landforms 1990–98; HEFCE: memb Geography Panel Research Assessment Panel (RAE) 2001, chair Geography and Environmental Studies Sub-Panel RAE 2008; assessor for Environment and Climate Prog DGXII EC 1996–; Cuthbert Peek Award RGS 1983, Leverhulme research fell 1985; CGeog 2002; *Books* Stochastic Processes in One-Dimensional Series: An Introduction (1979), Geomorphological Techniques (ed with A S Goudie and others, 1982), Rivers: Form and Process in Alluvial Channels (1982), Geomorphology and Soils (ed with R R Arnett and S Ellis, 1985), River Channels: Environment and Process (ed, 1987), Slope Stability: Geotechnical Engineering and Geomorphology (ed with M Anderson, 1987), Landform Monitoring, Modelling and Analysis (ed with S Lane and J Chandler, 1998), Glacier Hydrology and Hydrochemistry (ed with M Sharp and M Tranter, 1998); author of over 150 papers on geomorphology, hydrology, river and slope processes in various academic jls; *Recreations* reading, travel, opera; *Style*— Prof Keith Richards; ✉ Department of Geography, University of Cambridge, Cambridge CB2 3EN (tel 01223 333393, e-mail ksr10@cam.ac.uk)

RICHARDS, Martin Barnabas; s of William Antony Richards (d 2004), and Betty, *née* Barlow; *b* 13 August 1959; *Educ* Warwick Sch, Univ of Bristol (LLB), Univ of Cambridge (MSt); *m* 3 Aug 2001, Judith, *née* Ackers; 2 s (Charlie b 8 May 1992, Hugh b 24 June 1994), 2 step s (Robert, Marcus (twins) b 2 Jan 1987); *Career* Constable rising to Supt Warks Police 1982, Asst Chief Constable then Dep Chief Constable Avon and Somerset Police 1998, Chief Constable Wilts Police 2004–; memb: Wilts Strategic Bd, Wilts Criminal Justice Bd; tstee Police Dependents Tst; hon fell Inst of Transport Admin; *Recreations* all forms of sport, especially football, cricket and rugby, incurable Wolverhampton Wanderers fan, passion for and encyclopaedic knowledge of chocolate bars and sweets; *Clubs* Wilts and Bath Advanced Motorcyclists (pres); *Style*— Martin Richards, Esq; ✉ Wiltshire Police, Police Headquarters, London Road, Devizes, Wiltshire SN10 2DN (tel 01380 734035, fax 01380 734176, e-mail martin.richards@wiltshire.pnn.police.uk)

RICHARDS, Martin Edgar; s of Edgar Lynton (Tony) Richards, CBE, MC, TD (d 1983), and Barbara, *née* Lebus (d 1993); *b* 27 February 1943; *Educ* Harrow; *m* 30 Jan 1969, Caroline, da of Edwin Billing Lewis (d 1948), and Kay, *née* Gilbert (d 1990); 1 da (Catherine b 1972), 1 s (Charles b 1975); *Career* admitted slr 1968; ptnr Clifford Chance LLP 1973–; tstee: Int Lawyers Project, Thames Community Fndn; *Style*— Martin E Richards, Esq; ✉ Clifford Chance, 10 Upper Bank Street, London E14 5JJ (tel 020 7006 1000, fax 020 7006 5555)

RICHARDS, Prof Martin Paul Meredith; s of Paul Westmacott Richards, and Sarah Anne, *née* Hotham; *b* 26 January 1940; *Educ* Westminster, Trinity Coll Cambridge (MA, PhD, ScD); *m* 1, 1961 (m dis 1966), Evelyn Cowdy; m 2, 1999, Sarah, *née* Smalley; *Career* SRC post-doctoral fell 1965–67; Univ of Cambridge: research fell Trinity Coll 1965–69, head Centre for Family Research 1967–2005, lectr in social psychology 1970–89, reader in human devpt 1989–97, head of dept Social and Political Scis Faculty 1996–99, prof of family research 1997–2005, emeritus prof 2005–; visiting fell Dept of Biology Princeton Univ 1966–67, visitor Center for Cognitive Studies Harvard Univ 1967 and 1968, Mental Health Research Fund fell 1970, Wineguard visiting prof Univ of Guelph 1987, visiting lectr NZ Fedn of Parents Centres 1984 and 1987, hon visiting prof Dept of Soc Scis City Univ 1992–94, de Lissa fell Univ of S Australia 1993, Williams Evans visiting fell Univ of Otago 1997; *Books* Race, Culture, and Intelligence (ed jtly, 1972), The Integration of a Child into a Social World (ed, 1974), Benefits and Hazards of the New Obstetrics (ed jtly, 1977), Separation and Special Care Baby Units (jtly, 1978), Infancy: the World of the Newborn (1980), Parent-Baby Attachment in Premature Infants (ed jtly, 1983), Children in Social Worlds: Development in a Social Context (ed with Paul Light, 1986), Divorce Matters (jtly, 1987), Family Life (ed jtly), The Politics of Maternity Care (ed jtly, 1990), Sexual Arrangements: Marriage and Affairs (with J Reibstein, 1992), Obstetrics in the 1990s: Current Controversies (ed jtly, 1992), The Troubled Helix: Social and Psychological Implications of the New Human Genetics (ed jtly, 1996), What is a Parent? (ed with A Bainham and S Day Sclater, 1999), Body Lore and Laws (ed jtly, 2002), Children and their Families: Contact, Rights and Welfare (ed jtly, 2003), Blackwell Companion to the Sociology of Families (ed jtly, 2003), Supporting Children Through Family Change (jtly, 2003), Kinship Matters (ed jtly), Death Rites and Rights (ed jtly, 2007); also author of numerous reviews and papers in learned jls; *Recreations* listening to country music, bird-watching, alpine gardening; *Style*— Prof Martin Richards; ✉ Centre for Family Research, University of Cambridge, Free School Lane, Cambridge CB2 3RF (tel 01223 334510, e-mail mpmr@cam.ac.uk)

RICHARDS, Menna; da of Penri Richards, of Maesteg, Mid Glamorgan, and Dilys, *née* Watkins; *b* 27 February 1953; *Educ* Maesteg GS, UCW Aberystwyth (BA); *m* 1985, Patrick Hannan; *Career* radio & TV journalist BBC Wales 1976–83; HTV Wales: journalist 1983–99, head of factual progs 1991, dir of progs 1993, md 1997–2000; controller BBC Wales 2000–; *Recreations* music, friends, family; *Style*— Ms Menna Richards; ✉ BBC Wales, Broadcasting House, Llandaf, Cardiff CF5 2YQ (tel 029 2032 2001, fax 029 2055 5286)

RICHARDS, Prof Michael Adrian; CBE (2001); s of Donald Richards (d 1994), and Peronelle, *née* Armitage-Smith; *b* 14 July 1951; *Educ* Radley, Trinity Coll Cambridge (MA), Bart's Med Coll London; *Career* ICRF research fell in med oncology Bart's London 1982–86, hon conslt in med oncology Guy's Hosp London 1986–95 (ICRF sr lectr 1986–91, ICRF reader 1991–95), clinical dir Cancer Services Guy's and St Thomas' Hosp London 1991–99, Sainsbury prof of palliative med St Thomas' Hosp London 1995–, head Academic Div of Oncology KCL 1998–99, nat cancer dir Dept of Health 1999–, chair Nat Cancer Research Inst 2006–; former tstee: Science Museum, Marie Curie Cancer Care; FRCP 1993, Hon FRCR 2000, FFPHM 2002; *Publications* over 150 papers related to cancer and cancer services; *Recreations* hill walking, classical music; *Style*— Prof Michael Richards, CBE; ✉ Department of Health, Richmond House, Whitehall, London SW1A 2NS (tel 020 7188 7432, fax 020 7188 4727, e-mail mike.richards@gstt.sthames.nhs.uk)

RICHARDS, Maj Gen Nigel William Fairbairn; CB (1998), OBE (1987); s of Lt-Col William Fairbairn Richards, TD (d 1987), of Eastbourne, E Sussex, and Marjorie May, *née* Salter; *b* 15 August 1945; *Educ* Eastbourne Coll, Peterhouse Cambridge; *m* 27 July 1968, Christine Anne Helen, da of Maj-Gen Charles William Woods, CB, MBE, MC (d 1996); 1 da (Helen b 1971), 2 s (Charles b 1972, Peter b 1976); *Career* cmmnd RA 1965, RN Staff Coll 1976, CO 7 Regt RHA 1983–86, cmd 5 Airborne Bde 1989–90, RCDS 1991, Dir Army Staff Duties MOD 1991–93, chief of Combat Support HQ ACE Rapid Reaction Corps 1994–96, GOC 4 Div 1996–98, Hon Regtl Col 7 Parachute Regt RHA 1999–2005; Col Cmdt RA 2001–06; chm Confedn of Br Serv and Ex-Serv Organisations 1999–2002; chm The Peterhouse Soc 2001–04; pres: Br Scouts in Western Europe 1994–96, Army boxing and hockey 1996–98; *Recreations* cricket, fishing, skiing, golf; *Clubs* Army and Navy; *Style*— Maj Gen Nigel Richards, CB, OBE; ✉ 14 Berkeley Place, Wimbledon, London SW19 4NN

RICHARDS, Penny; da of Denis Richards, of London, and Barbara, *née* Smethurst; *b* 6 November 1950; *Educ* N London Collegiate Sch, AA Sch of Architecture (AADipl); *m* 28 June 1975, John Pringle, *qv*, s of Alexander (Sandy) Pringle; 1 s (Patrick b 24 Sept 1982), 1 da (Georgina b 28 Dec 1984); *Career* architect; with Rick Mather Architects 1977–81, ptnr Pringle + Richards Architects 1981–96, dir Pringle Richards Sharratt Architects 1996–; projects incl: Shrewsbury music sch and auditorium (RIBA Award 2001), Gallery Oldham (RIBA Award 2002), Sheffield Millennium Gallery and Winter Garden (Civic Tst Award and RIBA Award 2003); first year tutor AA Sch of Architecture 1979–80, first year tutor (architecture) Oxford Poly 1990–91; external examiner: South Bank Univ 1990–94, Westminster Univ 1996–99, Bartlett Sch of Architecture UCL 2003–; visiting prof Grad Sch of Architecture Univ of Pennsylvania 2000–01; vice-pres AA 2002–03 (memb Cncl 1998–2003), assessor Civic Tst 2000–, reader Queen's Anniversary Prizes 2002, memb RIBA Educn Ctee 1999–, memb RIBA Educn Tst Fund Ctee 1999–; RIBA 2000; *Recreations* everything to do with Italy: being there, speaking Italian, cooking Italian; growing English plants in Italy and Italian plants in England; *Style*— Ms Penny Richards; ✉ 29 Tadema Road, London SW10 0PZ (tel and fax 020 7351 4770); Pringle Richards Sharratt Architects, Studio 11, Canterbury Court, Kennington Park, 1 Brixton Road, London SW9 6DE (tel 020 7793 2828, fax 020 7793 2829, e-mail penny.richards@prsarchitects.com)

RICHARDS, Peter; s of Alfred James Clifford Richards (d 1969), of Stoke-sub-Hamdon, Somerset, and Eileen Mary Richards (d 2002); *b* 10 December 1954; *Educ* Yeovil GS, Plymouth Poly, Canterbury Sch of Architecture (DipArch), Univ of Reading (MSc); *m* 1, 1983 (m dis 1986), Elizabeth, *née* Wilmott; m 2, 1988, Isabel, *née* Miles; *Career* DOE PSA 1980–83; HOK Cecil Denny Highton: project architect 1983–88, assoc 1988–90, ptnr 1990–95, dir (i/c incl museums, further educn, higher educn and urban regeneration projects) 1996–2004; princ own architecture practice 2004–; Conservation Award for works to the Alfred Waterhouse bldg Royal Borough of Kensington and Chelsea; RIBA, memb Assoc of Project Mangrs (MAPM), MInstD; *Recreations* conservation of historic buildings; *Style*— Peter Richards, Esq; ✉ Grove Lodge, 11 Lambridge, Bath BA1 6BJ (tel 01225 310860, fax 01225 429630, e-mail pr@lrm-architects.co.uk)

RICHARDS, Prof Peter; s of Dr William Richards (d 1981), and Barbara Ashton, *née* Taylor (d 1971); *b* 25 May 1936; *Educ* Monkton Comb Sch, Emmanuel Coll Cambridge (MA, MB BCh, MD), St George's Hosp Med Sch, RPMS London (PhD); *m* 1, 6 July 1959 (m dis 1986), Anne Marie, da of Svend Larsen (d 1964), of Odense, Denmark; 1 s (Alan), 3 da (Marianne, Annette, Christina); m 2, 26 July 1987, Dr Carol Anne, da of Dr Raymond Seymour, of Wendlebury; *Career* hon sr lectr St Mary's Hosp Med Sch (lectr in med 1967–70) and conslt physician St Peter's Hosp Chertsey 1970–73, sr lectr and conslt physician St George's Hosp and Med Sch 1973–79, dean, prof of med and hon conslt physician St Mary's Hosp Med Sch 1979–95, fndr pro-rector med educn Imperial Coll of Sci Technol and Med 1988–95, med dir and conslt physician Northwick Park Hosp 1995–98; pres Hughes Hall Cambrige 1998–2006, chm Cncl of Deans of UK Medical Schs and Faculties 1994–95; elected memb GMC 1994–2003; chm: GMC Performance Procedures Evaluation Gp 1996–2000, chm Professional Conduct Ctee 2002–03 (dep chm 1999–2002); med advsr Parly Health Service Ombudsman 1999–2001; non-exec dir West Suffolk Hospitals NHS Tst 2001–06; RCP: Fitzpatrick lectr 1989, chm Educn Ctee 1992–95, memb Cncl 1994–97; memb Cncl Anglo-Finnish Soc 1984–; Freeman City of London 1985, Liveryman Worshipful Soc of Apothecaries 1984; Septemviri Univ of Cambridge 2000–05; hon fell: Emmanuel Coll Cambridge 2002, Hughes Hall Cambridge 2006 (past pres); fndr FMedSci 1998, FRCP 1976; Knight Order of the White Rose (Finland) 2001; *Books* The Medieval Leper and His Northern Heirs (1977), Understanding Water, Electrolyte and Acid Base Metabolism (jtly, 1983), Wasser-und Elektrolythaushalt: Diagnostik und Therapie (jtly, 1985), Living Medicine (1990), Entry to Medicine (1996, 2 edn 1997), The New Learning Medicine (jtly, 1997, Soc Authors Prize for Best General Medical Book 1998), Learning Medicine (17 edn, 2006); *Recreations* social history, walking, listening to music, Finland; *Clubs* Garrick, Hawks' (Cambridge); *Style*— Prof Peter Richards; ✉ Barefords, 78 Commercial End, Swaffham Bulbeck, Cambridge CB5 0NE (tel 01223 812007, e-mail pr229@cam.ac.uk)

RICHARDS, His Hon Judge Philip Brian; s of Glyn Bevan Richards (d 1976), of Ynysybwl, and Nancy Gwenhwyfar, *née* Evans (d 1992), of Bargoed; *b* 3 August 1946; *Educ* Cardiff HS, Univ of Bristol (LLB); *m* 1, 17 July 1971 (m dis 1988), Dorothy Louise, da of Victor George (d 2003), of Ystrad Mynach; 2 da (Rhuanedd b 1974, Lowri b 1978); m 2, 26 March 1994, Julia, da of Roy Jones (d 2002), of Tylorstown; 1 da (Megan b 1995), 1 step s (David b 1980); *Career* called to the Bar Inner Temple 1969; in practice 1969–2001, circuit jr Wales & Chester Circuit 1994, head of chambers 30 Park Place Cardiff 1994–99, recorder of the Crown Court 2000–01 (asst recorder 1995–99), circuit judge (Wales & Chester Circuit) 2001–; Parly candidate (Plaid Cymru) 1974 and 1979; chm Parliament for Wales Campaign 1996–98, candidate Nat Assembly of Wales 1999; chm Judicial Welsh Language Trg Sub-Ctee of Lord Chllr's Standing Ctee on Welsh Language 2001–03 and 2005–; vice-pres: Mountain Ash RFC (also patron), Neyland RFC; tstee Welsh Writers' Tst, chm Bd of Govrs Ysgol Gyfun Rhydfelen 1988–95, govr Ysgol Gynradd Gymraeg Abercynon 1999–2006; *Recreations* music, sport, literature, walking; *Clubs* Cardiff and County; *Style*— His Hon Judge Philip Richards; ✉ Cardiff Crown Court, The Law Courts, Cathays Park, Cardiff CF10 3PG

RICHARDS, Rt Hon Lord Justice; Rt Hon Sir Stephen Price Richards; kt (1997), PC (2005); s of Richard Alun Richards, of Llandre, Dyfed, and late Ann Elonwy Mary, *née* Price; *b* 8 December 1950; *Educ* KCS Wimbledon, St John's Coll Oxford (MA); *m* 29 May 1976, Lucy Elizabeth, da of Dr Frank Henry Stubbings, of Cambridge; 2 s (Matthew b 1979, Thomas b 1981), 1 da (Emily b 1984); *Career* called to the Bar Gray's Inn 1975 (bencher 1992); standing counsel to Dir Gen of Fair Trading 1989–91 (second jr counsel to DG 1987–89), a jr counsel to The Crown common law 1990–91, first jr Treasy counsel common law 1992–97; recorder of the Crown Court 1996–97, judge of the High Court of Justice (Queen's Bench Div) 1997–2005, presiding judge of the Wales & Chester Circuit 2000–03, a Lord Justice of Appeal 2005–; dep chm Boundary Cmmn for Wales 2001–05; govr KCS Wimbledon 1998–2007 (chm Governing Body 2004–07); Hon LLD Univ of Glamorgan 2004; *Books* Chitty on Contracts (co ed 25 and 26 edns); *Recreations* the Welsh hills; *Style*— The Rt Hon Lord Justice Richards; ✉ Royal Courts of Justice, Strand, London WC2A 2LL

RICHARDS, His Hon Judge (David) Wyn; s of Evan Gwylfa Richards (d 1987), of Llanelli, and Florence Margretta, *née* Evans (d 1988); *b* 22 September 1943; *Educ* Gwendraeth GS, Llanelli GS, Trinity Hall Cambridge; *m* 23 Dec 1972, Thelma Frances, *née* Hall; 5 s (Mark b 1974, Cennydd b 1976, Hywel b 1977, Daniel Owen b 1981, Aled Wyn b 1988); *Career* called to the Bar Inner Temple 1968; recorder of the Crown Court 1985, circuit judge (Wales & Chester Circuit) 1998–, asst cmmr Boundary Cmmn Wales 1982 and 1994; *Style*— His Hon Judge Wyn Richards; ✉ Civil Justice Centre, Caravella House, Quay West, Quay Parade, Swansea SA1 1SP (tel 01792 510350, fax 01792 473520)

RICHARDSON, Sir Anthony Lewis; 3 Bt (UK 1924), of Yellow Woods, Province of Cape of Good Hope, South Africa; s of Sir Leslie Lewis Richardson, 2 Bt (d 1985), of Cape Town, South Africa, and Joy Patricia, *née* Rillstone; *b* 5 August 1950; *Educ* Diocesan Coll Cape Town; *m* 1985, (Honor) Gillian, da of Robert Anthony Dauney, of Paddington, Sydney, Aust; 1 da ((Honor) Olivia Phoebe b 9 Sept 1990), 1 s (William Lewis b 15 Oct 1992); *Heir* s, William Richardson; *Career* stockbroker L Messel & Co London 1973–75, insurance broker C T Bowring London and Johannesburg 1975–76; stockbroker: Fergusson Bros Hall Stewart & Co Johannesburg and Cape Town 1976–78, W Greenwell & Co London 1979–81; dir S G Warburg Securities London 1986–95 (joined 1981), exec dir SBC Warburg Dillon Read London (now Warburg Dillon Read) 1995–; seconded to: S G Warburg Securities/Potter Partners Aust 1986–89, SBC Warburg SA 1996–; memb London Stock Exchange; *Recreations* various sports, photography; *Clubs* Boodle's,

R

Hurlingham, Annabel's; *Style*— Sir Anthony Richardson, Bt; ✉ 128 Trafalgar Place, Sandhurst 2196, Johannesburg, South Africa; SBC Warburg, PO Box 61028, Marshaltown 2107, South Africa (tel 00 27 11 836 2601, fax 00 27 11 836 2609)

RICHARDSON, Prof Brian Frederick; s of Ronald Frederick Richardson, CBE (d 1991), of London, and Anne Elizabeth, *née* McArdle (d 2005); *b* 6 December 1946, Woodford; *Educ* Ampleforth, Lincoln Coll Oxford, Bedford Coll London; *m* 31 March 1973, Catherine, da of Paul Normand; 3 da (Sophie b 24 Aug 1975, Alice b 23 Feb 1979, Laura b 25 Nov 1983); *Career* lectr in Italian: Univ of Strathclyde 1970–72, Univ of Aberdeen 1972–76, Univ of Leeds 1977–96; prof of Italian language Univ of Leeds 1996–; FBA 2003; *Style*— Prof Brian Richardson; ✉ Department of Italian, School of Modern Languages and Cultures, University of Leeds, Leeds LS2 9JT

RICHARDSON, His Hon Judge David John; s of Abraham Eric Richardson (d 1991), and Gwendoline, *née* Ballard (d 1982); *b* 23 June 1950; *Educ* John Ruskin GS Croydon, Trinity Hall Cambridge (MA, LLB); *m* 1980, Jennifer Margaret, da of Sidney Cooke (d 1998); 1 s (Samuel James b 19 Sept 1982), 1 da (Rosemary Anne b 5 May 1985); *Career* called to the Bar 1973; recorder 1997, circuit judge (SE Circuit) 2000–; C of E: ordained deacon 1985, ordained priest 1986, hon curate Emanuel Church S Croydon 1985–; *Style*— His Hon Judge Richardson; ✉ c/o The Court Service, New Cavendish House, 18 Maltravers Street, London WC2R 3EU

RICHARDSON, Frank Anthony; s of Albert Edward Richardson, and Eileen, *née* Roberts; *b* 20 March 1933; *Educ* Leeds Central HS; *m* 6 Sept 1958, Patricia Elsie, da of Robert Stevenson Taylor; *Career* agent and organiser Cons Party 1956–73, sec Nat Union of Cons Agents 1971–73; assoc dir: John Addey Assocs 1973–77, Charles Barker Watney & Powell 1978–83; dir: Charles Barker Watney & Powell 1983, Shandwick Public Affairs 1990–94; sr ptnr Richardson Consultants 1994–; admin sec: Parly Info Tech Ctee 1985–2004, Parly Space Ctee 1989–2006, Parly Road Tport Study Gp 1987–99; jt sec Euro Inter-Parly Space Conference 2002; vice-pres Cons Group for Europe 1992–95; Freeman City of London 1993; memb Yorks Athletics Team 1958; *Recreations* tennis, swimming, travel; *Style*— Frank Richardson, Esq; ✉ 22 Gloucester Place Mews, London W1U 8BA (tel 020 7487 4872)

RICHARDSON, Prof Genevra; CBE (2007); da of John Richardson (d 2002), of Broadshaw, W Lothian, and Josephine, *née* Henderson; *b* 1 September 1948; *Educ* KCL (LLB, LLM); *m* 12 April 1977, Sir Oliver Thorold, 16 Bt, *qv*, s of Sir Anthony Henry Thorold, 15 Bt (d 1999); 1 s, 1 da; *Career* lectr in law UEA 1979–87; Queen Mary Univ of London: lectr 1987–89, reader 1989–94, prof of public law 1994–2005, dean Faculty of Law 1996–99; prof of law King's Coll London 2005–; chair: Mgmnt Ctee Prisoners' Advice Service 1994–2003, Ind Enquiry into Care and Treatment of Darren Carr 1996–97, Expert Ctee advising Mins on Reform of Mental Health Legislation 1999; memb: Mental Health Act Cmmn 1987–92, Mgmnt Ctee Public Law Project 1991–2001, Animal Procedures Ctee 1998–, Cncl on Tribunals 2001–, Cncl MRC 2001–; author of books and jl articles in public law, criminal justice and mental health and the law; tstee: Med Coll of St Barts Hosp Tst 1999–2004, Nuffield Fndn 2002–; Hon FRCPsych 2004; *Style*— Prof Genevra Richardson, CBE; ✉ School of Law, King's College, Strand, London WC2R 2LS

RICHARDSON, Jeremy William; QC (2000); s of Thomas William Sydney Raymond Richardson (d 2000), of Retford, Notts, and Jean Mary, *née* Revill; *b* 3 April 1958; *Educ* Forest Sch, QMC London (LLB); *Partner* David Carruthers (civil partnership 2006); *Career* called to the Bar Inner Temple 1980; memb NE Circuit 1982– (sec 1991–96), recorder 2000– (asst recorder 1998–2000), dep High Court judge (Family Div) 2004–; memb Gen Cncl of the Bar 1992–94; *Clubs* Athenaeum; *Style*— Jeremy Richardson, QC; ✉ 3 Park Court, Park Cross Street, Leeds LS1 2QH (tel 0113 297 1200, fax 0113 297 1201, e-mail clerks@11kbw.co.uk)

RICHARDSON, Dr Joanna; da of Capt Frederick Richardson, Intelligence Corps (d 1978), and Charlotte Elsa, *née* Benjamin (d 1978); *Educ* The Downs Sch Seaford, St Anne's Coll Oxford (MA, DLitt); *Career* author; FRSL 1959 (memb Cncl 1961–86); Chevalier de l'Ordre des Arts et des Lettres (France) 1987; *Books* Fanny Brawne: A Biography (1952), Théophile Gautier: His Life and Times (1958), Edward FitzGerald (1960), FitzGerald: Selected Works (ed, 1962), The Pre-Eminent Victorian: A Study of Tennyson (1962), The Everlasting Spell: A Study of Keats and His Friends (1963), Essays by Divers Hands (ed, 1963), Edward Lear (1965), George IV: A Portrait (1966), Creevey and Greville (1967), Princess Mathilde (1969), Verlaine (1971), Enid Starkie (1973), Verlaine, Poems (ed and translator, 1974), Stendhal: A Critical Biography (1974), Baudelaire, Poems (ed and translator, 1975), Victor Hugo (1976), Zola (1978), Keats and His Circle: An Album of Portraits (1980), Gautier, Mademoiselle de Maupin (translator, 1981), The Life and Letters of John Keats (1981), Letters from Lambeth: the Correspondence of the Reynolds Family with John Freeman Milward Dovaston 1808–1815 (1981), Colette (1983), Judith Gautier (1986, French edn 1989, awarded Prix Goncourt de la biographie, first time to a non-French writer), Portrait of a Bonaparte: the Life and Times of Joseph-Napoléon Primoli 1851–1927 (1987), Baudelaire (1994); *Style*— Dr Joanna Richardson; ✉ c/o Curtis Brown Ltd, 4th Floor, Haymarket House, 28–29 Haymarket, London SW1Y 4SP (tel 020 7396 6600)

RICHARDSON, John Stephen; s of Rev James H Richardson, of Settle, N Yorks, and Rachel, *née* Varley; *b* 2 December 1953, Oldham; *Educ* Rossall Sch, Selwyn Coll Cambridge (ICI industrial scholar, MA, PGCE); *m* 25 Oct 1989, Ruth W, *née* Vardy; 2 s (Matthew b 21 Aug 1990, Peter b 19 July 1991), 1 da (Sarah b 20 Dec 1994); *Career* mathematics teacher, housemaster and curriculum dir Dean Close Sch Cheltenham 1977–84 (also CO CCF/RAF section), mathematics teacher Eton Coll 1984–92 (also house list chapel steward, master i/c under 16 rowing, CO CCF/RAF section and treas Eton Action), headmaster Culford Sch Bury St Edmunds 1992–2004, headmaster Cheltenham Coll 2004–; inspr Ind Schs Inspectorate, vice-chm Curriculum, Evaluation and Mgmnt Centre Univ of Durham; memb: Ctee HMC (chm East Div 2000–02), NAHT; memb Cncl of Reference Cheltenham Youth for Christ, tstee TISCA (The Ind Schs Christian Alliance); fndn fell Univ of Gloucester; FRSA; *Recreations* reading, sailing, mountaineering; *Clubs* East India; *Style*— John Richardson, Esq; ✉ College House, Thirlestaine Road, Cheltenham, Gloucestershire GL53 7AA (tel 01242 705597, e-mail richardson.john@cheltcoll.gloucs.sch.uk); Cheltenham College, Bath Road, Cheltenham, Gloucestershire GL53 7LD (tel 01242 265600, fax 01242 265630, e-mail info@cheltcoll.gloucs.sch.uk)

RICHARDSON, Very Rev John Stephen; s of James Geoffrey Richardson, of Rossendale, Lancs, and Myra, *née* Greenwood; *b* 2 April 1950; *Educ* Haslingden GS, Univ of Southampton (BA), St John's Coll Nottingham; *m* 29 July 1972, Elizabeth Susan (Sue), da of James Anness Wiltshire (d 1986), of Calne, Wilts; 2 da (Sarah Elizabeth b 1975, Ruth Mary b 1977), 2 s (Benjamin Stephen b and d 1981, Thomas Samuel John b 1982); *Career* various appts Cadbury Schweppes Bristol; asst curate St Michael and All Angels Bramcote Nottingham 1974–77, priest-in-charge Emmanuel Church Southill and curate Radipole and Melcombe Regis Team Miny 1977–80, asst missioner and lay trg advsr Dio of Salisbury and priest-in-charge Winterborne Monkton with Winterborne Came and Whitcombe with Stinsford 1980–83, vicar Christ Church Nailsea 1983–90, advsr in evangelism Dio of Bath and Wells 1986–90, provost and vicar of the Cathedral Church of St Peter Bradford 1990–2000, dean after the cathedral's measure 2000–01, vicar Wye, Brook and Hastingleigh 2001– (and Eastwell with Boughton Aluph 2004–), chaplain Imperial Coll London (Wye Campus) 2001–, area dean West Bridge Dio of Canterbury 2003–, priest i/c Petham, Waltham and Elmsted 2006–; vice-pres Cncl Church's Ministry to the Jews 1994–; memb: Cncl St John's Theological Coll Nottingham 1988–94, Gen Synod 1993–2001 (memb Bd of Mission 1995–2000), Cncl Evangelical Alliance 1994–2000, Archbishop's Cncl and Bd of Fin Dio of Canterbury 2004–; govr: Bradford GS 1990–2001, Giggleswick Sch 1993–2002, Bolling Community Coll 1995–2001; tstee and vice-chm Acorn Christian Healing Tst 1990–2007, tstee Spennithorne House of Healing 1990–97; involved with local radio stations 1985–, memb Radio Leeds Local Broadcasting Cncl 1991–95; dir: Bradford Breakthrough 1992–2001, Spring Harvest 1998–2003 and 2007–, Mildmay Mission Hosp 2004– (chm 2007–), Kent Community Housing Tst 2005–; chm Spring Harvest Charitable Tst 2003–; MInstD 1994; *Books* Ten Rural Churches (1988); *Recreations* football, cricket, spotting 1950's and 1960's municipal bus fleets; *Clubs* Kent and Canterbury, Farmers'; *Style*— The Very Rev John Richardson; ✉ The Vicarage, Cherry Garden Crescent, Wye, Ashford, Kent TN25 5AS (tel 01233 812450, e-mail johnrichardson@imperial.ac.uk and john.richardson@wyechurch.co.uk)

RICHARDSON, Keith William; s of Robert John David Richardson (d 1975), and Esmé Audrey, *née* Haynes (d 1990); *b* 1 November 1942; *Educ* Kelvinside Acad Glasgow, RSAMD Glasgow; *Children* 1 da (Taransay Jo Chisholm b 19 Nov 1972); *Career* television producer; stage mangr: Glasgow Citizens Theatre 1961–62, Pitlochry Festival Theatre 1963; theatrical agency dir SCOTTS 1963–69, asst stage mangr, stage mangr, floor mangr and production mangr Yorkshire Television 1969–77, prodr Tyne Tees Television 1977–78 (incl Paper Lads), prodr Yorkshire Television 1978–82 (incl Thundercloud, Second Chance, Horace, Harry's Game), head of drama Tyne Tees Television 1983–84 (exec prodr: Operation Julie, 4 Dramaramas; prodr: The Wedding, Supergran), dep controller of drama Yorkshire Television 1988–95 (exec prodr: Scab, May We Borrow Your Husband, Cloud Waltzer, 1914, All Out, Flying Lady Series I, Flying Lady Series II, Comeback, Mohicans, Climbing Out, Home Movies, The Contract, A Place of Safety, A Dinner of Herbs, Tears in the Rain, Magic Moments, The Beiderbecke Connection, Till We Meet Again, Talking Takes Two, Yellowthread Street, Missing Persons, Shoot to Kill, The World of Eddie Weary, Guests of the Emperor, Death Train, Mission Top Secret, Heartbeat I, Heartbeat II, III and IV, 15: The Life & Death of Philip Knight, The Wanderer, A Pinch of Snuff, The Dwelling Place, The Cinder Path, Firm Friend Series II, Ellington, Finney, Paparazzo; prodr A Day in Summer, original script cmmn Blood and Peaches), gp controller of drama Yorkshire Tyne Tees Television 1995–2004 (exec prodr: Heartbeat V, VI, VIII, IX, X, XI, XII and XIII, Ellington Series, Strike Force, Respect, The Governor II, Stiff Upper Lips, The Rag Nymph, The Moth, Supply and Demand, Trial and Retribution I, Black Velvet Band, Dingles Down Under, Changing Places, The Inspector Pitt Mysteries - The Cater Street Hangman, Lost for Words, Trial & Retribution II, Emmerdale - Revenge, Maisie Raine II, Fit, Fresh & Funky, Don't Look Now - The Dingles in Venice, The Secret, Emmerdale, Shipman, The Royal I, II and III), controller of drama Granada Yorkshire 2004– (exec prodr: Heartbeat XIV, XV, XVI and XVII, The Royal IV, V and VI, Steel River Blues, The Marchioness Disaster, Falling); writer and dir Heartbeat: The Musical Celebration; chm TAPS 2007–; former memb Bd Scottish Film Production Fund and Glasgow Film Fund; Int Emmy award for Supergran, BAFTA award for Emmerdale; for Lost for Words: Int Emmy, BAFTA award, Peabody award; Outstanding Contribution to FRTS Yorkshire 2005; FRTS 2004; *Recreations* reading, whisky (collecting and drinking!); *Style*— Keith Richardson, Esq; ✉ ITV Yorkshire, Television Centre, Kirkstall Road, Leeds LS3 1JS (tel 0113 222 8400, fax 0113 243 4387, e-mail keith.richardson@itv.com)

RICHARDSON, (William) Kenneth; s of James McNaughton Richardson, of Stirling, and Jane Ann McKay, *née* Monteith; *b* 16 November 1956; *Educ* HS of Stirling, Univ of St Andrews (MA); *Career* planning asst Scot Opera 1983–87; Royal Opera: co-mangr 1987–90, gen mangr 1990–94, admin Royal Opera House Garden Venture 1987–91; artistic dir Dublin Grand Opera Soc 1990–91; arts dir Barbican Centre 1994, dir Covent Garden Festival 1996–2001, arts dir Chicago Humanities Festival 2002, assoc dir Greenwich Theatre 2002–05, dir 2008 Temple Festival 2006–; ind opera and music theatre dir and conslt 1995–; tstee: Tête à Tête Opera 2003–, Streetwise Opera 2004–; FRSA 2005; *Style*— Kenneth Richardson, Esq; ✉ tel 07713 487205, e-mail kenneth@kennethrichardson.co.uk, website www.kennethrichardson.co.uk

RICHARDSON, Mark Rushcliffe; s of late Brig Charles Walter Philipps Richardson, DSO, and late Hon Averil Diana Richardson; *b* 17 September 1947; *Educ* Wellington, ChCh Oxford (MA); *m* 1, 29 Sept 1973 (m dis 2001), Cherry Victoria, da of late Sidney Wallace Smart; 2 da (Melanie b 13 Nov 1974 d 1994, Davina b 19 Jan 1976), 1 s (Hugo b 24 Nov 1981); m 2, 8 April 2003, Caroline Eden Kaye, da of Air Vice Marshal Peter Williamson, CBE, DFC; *Career* dir Lazard Bros & Co Ltd 1986–90, chief investment offr Chase Manhattan Private Bank 1992–95, ceo and chief investment offr Chase Asset Management 1996–99, ptnr Robert Kimbell Assocs 2000–02, md Atlantic Wealth Management Ltd 2002–05; *Recreations* country pursuits, skiing, modern British art; *Clubs* Pratt's, Boodle's; *Style*— Mark Richardson, Esq; ✉ Marston Hill Farm, Greatworth, Banbury, Oxfordshire OX17 2HF (tel 01295 760639)

RICHARDSON, Michael Norman; s of Norman Richardson (d 1965), and Ethel, *née* Spittle (d 1978); *b* 23 February 1935; *Educ* Dulwich Coll; *m* 13 April 1976, Rosemarie Christina, da of Emmerich von Moers (d 1946); 4 da (Penelope, Theresa, Christina, Alexandra); *Career* RAF 1958–60; admitted slr 1958; Lawrence Graham (specialising Int Corporate Fin) 1985–2000; chm Quadrant Associates Ltd 2000–07; dep chm Henry Ansbacher & Co Ltd 1970–77; memb Law Soc 1958, FInstD 1987; *Recreations* all sports, gardening, art; *Clubs* Oriental, MCC; *Style*— Michael Richardson, Esq; ✉ The Coach House, Midgham Park, Midgham, Berkshire RG7 5UG (tel 0118 971 0016)

RICHARDSON, Miranda; *b* 3 March 1958; *Career* actress; *Theatre* incl: All My Sons (Derby Place), Educating Rita (Leicester Haymarket), The Designated Mourner (RNT), Insignificance (Bristol Old Vic), The Maids (Bristol Old Vic), Who's Afraid of Virginia Woolf? (Bristol Old Vic), Aunt Dan and Lemon (Almeida), Edmond (Royal Court), A Lie of the Mind (Royal Court), Etta Jenks (Royal Court); *Television* Agony 1979, The Comic Strip Presents 1982, A Woman of Substance 1983, Alas Smith and Jones 1984, The Death of the Heart 1985, Blackadder II 1986, The Storyteller 1987, Blackadder III 1987, Blackadder's Christmas Carol 1988, Blackadder Goes Forth 1989, Die Kinder 1990, Old Times 1991, Mr Wakefield's Crusade 1991, Absolutely Fabulous 1992, A Dance to the Music of Time 1997, Ted and Ralph 1998, Blackadder Back and Forth 1999, The Lost Prince (TV film for BBC) 2002, Merlin's Apprentice 2004, Gideon's Daughter 2005; *Film* Underworld 1985, The Innocent 1985, Dance with a Stranger 1985, Sweet as You Are 1987, Empire of the Sun 1987, Eat the Rich 1987, After Pilkington 1987, Ball-Trap on the Cote Sauvage 1989, The Fool 1990, Twisted Obsession 1990, The Bachelor 1991, Enchanted April 1991, The Crying Game 1992, Damage 1993, The Line, the Cross and the Curve 1993, Century 1993, The Night and the Moment 1994, Tom and Viv 1994, Fatherland 1994, Swann 1996, The Evening Star 1996, Kansas City 1996, Saint-Ex 1997, The Apostle 1997, The Designated Mourner 1997, St Ives 1998, The Scold's Bridle 1998, Merlin 1998, Jacob Two Two Meets the Hooded Fang 1999, Alice in Wonderland 1999, The King and I 1999, Sleepy Hollow 1999, Chicken Run 2000, Get Carter 2000, Snow White 2000, The Hours 2001, Spider 2002, The Rage in Lake Placid 2002, The Actors 2002, The Lost Prince 2002, Falling Angels 2003, The Hollywood Years 2003, The Prince and Me 2003, The Phantom of the Opera 2003, Wah-Wah 2004, Spinning Into Butter 2004, Harry Potter and the Goblet of Fire 2004, Southland Tales 2005, Paris, Je T'aime 2005, Provok'd 2005, Puffball 2006, Fred Claus 2006; *Style*— Ms Miranda Richardson; ✉ c/o Paul Lyon Maris, ICM Ltd, Oxford House, 76 Oxford Street, London W1D 1BS (tel 020 7636 6565, fax 020 7323 0101)

RICHARDSON, Natasha Jane; da of Tony Richardson (d 1991), and Vanessa Redgrave, *qv*; *b* 11 May 1963; *Educ* Central Sch of Speech and Drama; *m* 1, 1990 (m dis), Robert Michael John Fox, *qv*; m 2, 1994, Liam Neeson; *Career* actress; *Theatre* season at Leeds Playhouse, A Midsummer Night's Dream (New Shakespeare Co), Hamlet (Young Vic), The Seagull (Lyric Hammersmith, tour and Queen's Theatre) 1985, China (Bush Theatre), High Society (Haymarket and Victoria Palace) 1987, Anna Christie (Young Vic) 1992 (London Theatre Critics) and (Broadway) 1993 (Tony Award nomination, Outer Critics' Circle Award for Best Actress, Drama Desk Award for Best Actress, Theatre World Award for Outstanding Debut), Cabaret (Donmar Warehouse) 1994 and (Broadway) 1997 (Best Actress (Musical) Tony Awards, Outer Critics' Circle Award, Drama Desk Award), Closer (Music Box Theater NYC) 1999, Lady from the Sea (Almeida) 2003, A Streetcar Named Desire (Roundabout Theatre and Studio 54) 2005; *Television* In A Secret State (BBC) 1985, Ghosts (BBC) 1986, Hostages (Granada) 1992, Suddenly Last Summer (BBC) 1993, Zelda (TNT) 1993, Haven (CBS Mini-Series) 2001, The Man Who Came to Dinner 2000; *Films* Every Picture Tells A Story 1985, Gothic 1987, A Month In The Country 1987, Patty Hearst 1988, Fat Man and Little Boy 1989, The Handmaid's Tale 1990, The Comfort of Strangers 1990, The Favor, the Watch and the Very Big Fish 1991, Past Midnight 1991, Sins of the Flesh 1992, Widow's Peak 1994, Nell 1994, The Parent Trap 1998, Wakin' Up In Reno 2000, Blowdry 2001, Chelsea Walls 2002, Waking Up in Reno 2002, Maid in Manhattan 2003, Asylum 2005, The White Countess 2005; *Awards* Most Promising Newcomer Plays and Players 1986; Best Actress: Plays and Players 1990, Evening Standard Film Awards 1990 and 2006, Prague Film Festival 1994; *Style*— Miss Natasha Richardson

RICHARDSON, Dr Nicholas James; s of John William Richardson (d 1987), and Eileen, *née* Allan (d 1954); *b* 4 February 1940, Winchester, Hants; *Educ* Winchester (scholar), Magdalen Coll Oxford (Roberts Gawen scholar, BA, BPhil, DPhil, hon mention Conington Prize 1971); *m* 14 Dec 1968, Catherine Eugenie, *née* Vafopoulou; 2 s (Alexander William b 18 May 1969, Andrew John Nicholas b 28 July 1974), 2 da (Penelope Iona b 4 Feb 1973, Catherine Maria Elly b 22 Nov 1984); *Career* lectr in classics Pembroke Coll Oxford 1964–65, lectr in classics Trinity Coll Oxford 1965–66, HM Treasy 1967–68, fell and tutor in classics Merton Coll Oxford 1968–2004 (emeritus fell 2004–), warden Greyfriars Hall Oxford 2004–; visiting fell: Center for Hellenic Studies Washington DC 1980–82, Princeton Univ 1989, Stanford Univ 2003; govr Plater Coll Oxford 1993–99, tstee Newman Tst Oxford 1997–, memb Oxford and Cambridge Catholic Educn Bd 1992– (sec 1996–2000); FSA 1985; *Books* The Homeric Hymn to Demeter (1974), The Iliad: A Commentary, Vol VI Books 21–24 (1993), The Homeric Hymns (contrib, 2003); *Recreations* real tennis, skiing, walking; *Clubs* Oxford and Cambridge, Sloane, Oxford Antiquaries; *Style*— Dr Nicholas Richardson; ✉ Greyfriars Hall, Iffley Road, Oxford OX4 1SB (tel 01865 256763, e-mail nicholas.richardson@greyfriars.ox.ac.uk)

RICHARDSON, Dr Nigel Peter Vincent; s of Vincent Boys Richardson (d 1965), of Barnet, Herts, and Jean Frances, *née* Wrangles; *b* 29 June 1948; *Educ* Highgate Sch, Trinity Hall Cambridge (MA), Univ of Bristol (PGCE), UCL (PhD); *m* 25 Aug 1979, (Averon) Joy, da of Rev Peter H James; 2 s (Matthew James b 11 Oct 1982, Thomas Stephen b 18 Oct 1984); *Career* Uppingham Sch: memb History Dept 1971–89, sixth form tutor 1977–83, second master 1983–89; headmaster Dragon Sch Oxford 1989–92, dep headmaster and dir of studies King's Sch Macclesfield 1992–94, headmaster The Perse Sch Cambridge 1994–2008; course dir Summer Language Sch Sweden and Bell Sch Cambridge 1972–82; chm HMC 2007; ed Conference and Common Room 1999–2002; govr: Greycotes Sch Oxford 1989–92, King's Coll Sch Cambridge 1998–2004; BBC Radio 4: jt question compiler Top of the Form 1982–87, contrib Thought for the Day 1982–; Walter Hines Page ESU scholar 2003; *Publications* The Effective Use of Time (1984, 2 edn 1989), First Steps in Leadership (1987); author of various histories and biographies for school use; contrib: TES, The Times, Daily Telegraph; *Recreations* music, writing, sport, gardening, travel; *Style*— Dr Nigel Richardson; ✉ The Perse School, Hills Road, Cambridge CB2 2QF (tel 01223 568300, fax 01223 568293, e-mail office@perse.co.uk)

RICHARDSON, (William) Norman Ballantyne; DL (Greater London 1985); s of Robert Richardson (d 1974), of Wishaw, Lanarkshire, and Sarah Maddick, *née* Shields; *b* 8 October 1947; *Educ* King Edward VI GS Birmingham (now King Edward VI Aston Sch), Goldsmiths Coll London; *Career* asst master Rosary RC Sch London 1970–78, dep head Emmanuel C of E Sch London 1979–81; headmaster: All Saints' C of E Sch London 1981–85, Christ Church C of E Sch London 1985–92, St Michael's C of E Sch London 1992–96; educn/headteacher conslt 1997–; chm: ILEA Divnl Consultative Ctee of Headteachers 1985–86 and 1989–90 (memb 1981–90), Local Advsy Ctee on Primary/Secdy Transfer 1987–88, ILEA Central Consultative Ctee of Headteachers 1989–90 (memb 1982–90), Consultative Ctee of Heads and Deputies in the Royal Borough of Kensington and Chelsea 1989–90, London Headteachers' Assoc (Kensington and Chelsea) 1990–91, London Diocesan Headteachers' Cncl 1991–92, 1993–94 and 1995–96 (memb 1984–96); memb: Colne/East Gade Advsy Ctee on Educn 1977–81, ILEA Standing Advsy Cncl on Religious Educn 1985–90, Royal Borough of Kensington and Chelsea Standing Advsy Cncl on Religions Educn 1989–92, London Borough of Haringey Standing Advsy Cncl on Religious Educn 1992–94; govr: Leavesden Green Infant Sch 1977–81, Leavesden Green Junior Sch 1977–81; chm London (South) Ctee: Royal Jubilee and Prince's Tsts 1984–90, The Prince's Tst 1990–95; sec: London Youth Involvement Ctee Queen's Silver Jubilee Tst 1981–83, Greater London Ctee Royal Jubilee and Prince's Tsts 1983–84; govr RNLI 1998–; life memb: Friends of St Columba's Church of Scotland, Friends of St George's Chapel Windsor, Friends of St Paul's Cathedral, Friends of Royal Free Hosp, Friends of York Minster; memb: RSL, Constitutional Monarchy Assoc, Monarchist League, European Atlantic Gp, Friends of the Prince's Tst, Friends of the Royal Acad, The Pilgrims, Queen's English Soc, St James's Branch Royal Br Legion; featured in: The Observer Guide to Chelsea 1987, Good Schools Guide 1991; FRGS 1969, FRSA 1974 (life fell 2005), MBIM (later MIMgt, now MCMI) 1986, FCollP 1989 (MCollP 1985), MInstAM 1990, MIIM 1990, MISM (now MInstLM) 1990, MInstFM 1990; *Recreations* reading biographies, genealogy and travel; *Clubs* Royal Commonwealth Soc, Royal Over-Seas League, RSA, Manchester Literary and Philosophical Soc; *Style*— W N B Richardson, Esq, DL; ✉ 16 Registry Close, Kingsmead, Davenham, Northwich, Cheshire CW9 8UZ (e-mail wnbrichardson@hotmail.com)

RICHARDSON, Peter Edward Hugh; s of late Edward William Moreton Richardson, of Malvern, Worcs, and Pamela Merle, *née* Case-Morris; *b* 12 April 1955; *Educ* Malvern Coll, The Queen's Coll Oxford (MA); *m* 22 Sept 1984, Miriam Elizabeth, da of Dennis Brian Chance, of Chesham, Bucks; 1 s (Michael William b 1 Nov 1987), 1 da (Heather Caroline b 9 April 1990); *Career* trainee CA Price Waterhouse & Co 1976–77; Butterworth & Co (Publishers) Ltd: commissioning ed 1977–82, sr commissioning ed 1982–84, managing ed 1984–85; Churchill Livingstone (medical div of Pearson Professional): publisher 1985–87, publishing mangr 1987–90, publishing dir 1990–94, dir healthcare info and mgmnt 1994–97; md Royal Society of Medicine Press Ltd 1997–; chm Exec Medical Gp of the Publishers Assoc 1993–97; *Publications* E-Biomed and PubMed Central - a publisher's view (1999), How to Get Your Medical Book Published (2001), A Guide to Medical Publishing and Writing (2002); *Recreations* music, France; *Style*— Peter Richardson, Esq; ✉ 3 Butlers Close, Amersham, Buckinghamshire HP6 5PY (tel 01494 722017); Royal Society of Medicine, 1 Wimpole Street, London W1G 0AE (tel 020 7290 2920, fax 020 7290 2929, e-mail peter.richardson@rsm.ac.uk)

RICHARDSON, Philip Edward; s of Wilfrid Laurence Richardson (d 1983), of Solihull, and Nellie Elizabeth, *née* Hands (d 1966); *b* 6 October 1945; *Educ* Tudor Grange GS Solihull, Coll of Law; *m* 26 May 1969, Corrinne Mary, da of John Woodall (d 1983), of Flyford Flavell; 2 s (Toby b 1972, Tom b 1977), 2 da (Polly b 1975, Prue b 1980); *Career* slr; ptnr Dawkins and Grey 1971–2000; memb: Law Soc 1970, Birmingham Law Soc 1970 (jt hon sec 1980–89, PR offr 1987, vice-pres 1989–90, pres 1990–91); dir English String Orch Ltd 1984–2003; hon consul: Netherlands 1982–2001, Belgium 1984–2002; pres Birmingham Consular Assoc 1987–89; chm Birmingham City Cncl Standards Ctee 1998–, vice-chm Hill and Moor PC 1987–89, tstee The Housing Assoc Charitable Tst 1995–2001; chm of govrs Pershore HS 1988–2005; Chevalier of the Order of Orange Nassau (Netherlands), Knight Order of Leopold (Belgium); *Recreations* music, railways; *Clubs* The Birmingham; *Style*— Philip Richardson, Esq; ✉ Bluebell Cottage, Hill, Pershore, Worcestershire WR10 2PP (tel and fax 01386 860664, e-mail richardsonathill@aol.com)

RICHARDSON, Ray; *b* 3 November 1964; *Educ* Roan Sch, St Martin's Sch of Art, Goldsmiths Coll London; *m* 1989; 2 s; *Career* artist; memb Assoc of Royal Engravers 2005; *Collections* Nat Portrait Gallery, De Beers London, J P Morgan London, Anglo American, Kasen-Summer Collection NYC, Tama Art Univ Tokyo, Ralph Lauren London and NY, V&A, RCA; *Selected Shows* Boycott Gallery Brussels 1989, 1992, 1995, 1998, 2000, 2001, 2003, 2004 and 2005, Galerie 31 Lille 1990, Galerie Alain Blondel Paris 1994, 1996, 1998, 2000 and 2003, Glasgow Print Studio 1992 and 1998, Beaux Arts London 1994, 1996 and 1999, Mendenhall Gallery LA 1998, Gallery Aoyama Tokyo 1999, Gallery Aoyama Tokyo 2002, Advanced Graphics London 2002 and 2004, Fabien Fryns Fine Art Puerto Banus 2002 and 2004, New Arts Gallery Litchfield Hills CT 2005, Mendenhall-Sobieski Gallery Pasadena CA 2005, Boycott Gallery 2006, Advanced Graphics 2006, Eleven Fine Art London 2006, Advanced Graphics London 2007 and Boycott Gallery Brussels 2008; *Television and Radio* Oil on Canvas (BBC 2) 1997 and 1999, Fresh (LWT) 1998, Sampled (Channel 4) 1998, Grand Designs (Channel 4) 2004, Artists' Music (BBC Radio 3) 2006, Oil on Canvas (BBC 2) 2006, Artists and their Music (Radio 3) 2006; *Awards* BP Portrait Award 1990, Br Cncl Award 1989 and 1999, commemorative sculpture for Sir Matt Busby Scotland 1997; *Books* One Man on a Trip (1996), Oil on Canvas (1997), British Figurative Painting (1997), British Sporting Heroes (1998); *Recreations* football; *Clubs* King Vic Football, The Royal Brussels British Football, Old Roan FC, Old Tennisonians FC; *Style*— Ray Richardson, Esq; ✉ c/o Advanced Graphics, 32 Long Lane, London SE1 4AY

RICHARDSON, Robert Oliver; s of Robert Frederick Oliver (d 1987), and Marie, *née* Richardson (d 2001); *b* 26 September 1940; *Educ* Stretford GS; *m* 1, 1968 (m dis), Gwyneth Marilyn, *née* Hunt; m 2, 24 Aug 1974, Sheila Muriel Boustead, da of Cecil John Norman Miller, MBE; 1 s (James Malcolm b 8 April 1977), 1 step s (Michael John b 6 Oct 1961); *Career* journalist Daily Mail 1965–67 and 1968–72, ed Welwyn and Hatfield Times 1973–81, ed Herts Advertiser 1981–87, freelance journalist 1987–92 (contracted to The Independent 1990–92), staff journalist The Independent 1992–94, freelance journalist 1994–98, staff journalist Sunday Business 1998–2001, freelance journalist 2002–04 and 2005–, staff journalist The Observer 2004–05; memb Crime Writers' Assoc 1985– (vice-chm 1992–93 and 2005–06, chm 1993–94 and 2006–07); *Books* The Book of Hatfield (1977), The Latimer Mercy (1985, John Creasey Meml Award for best first crime novel), Bellringer Street (1988), The Book of the Dead (1989), The Dying of the Light (1990), Sleeping in the Blood (1991), The Lazarus Tree (1992), The Hand of Strange Children (1993), Significant Others (1995), Victims (1997); *Recreations* reading, walking, history, crosswords; *Style*— Robert Richardson, Esq; ✉ c/o Gregory and Company, 3 Barb Mews, London W6 7PA (tel 020 7610 4676, fax 020 7610 4686)

RICHARDSON, Roger Hart; RD (1965); s of Justin Richardson (d 1975), of Headley, Surrey, and Margery, *née* Wolfe (d 1996); *b* 13 August 1931; *Educ* Rugby, Christ's Coll Cambridge (MA); *m* 25 Oct 1967, Evelyn Louise, da of Dr Paul Kane, MD (d 1993); 1 s (Matthew b 1969), 1 da (Lydia b 1970); *Career* Lt Cdr RNR 1949–70; chm and md Beaver & Tapley Ltd (furniture mfrs) Southall 1975–98; Master Worshipful Co of Furniture Makers 1988 (Liveryman 1961, memb Ct of Assts 1974, Jr Warden 1987, Sr Warden 1987); FRSA 1992; *Recreations* sailing, travel, music, bird watching, wine; *Clubs* RNSA; *Style*— Roger Richardson, Esq, RD; ✉ 11 Broom Water, Teddington, Middlesex TW11 9QJ (tel 020 8977 7921, fax 020 8255 6494, e-mail richardson@blueyonder.co.uk)

RICHARDSON, Stephen Laurence; s of Laurence Richardson, of St Davids, Dyfed, and Rosalae, *née* Reilly; *b* 20 June 1959; *Educ* Maghull GS Liverpool, Ysgol Dewi Sant St David's, Faculty of Music Univ of Manchester, RNCM (Countess of Munster Award, Moores Fndn Award, Kay Opera Prize); *m* 19 July 1986, Colleen Delores, *née* Barsley; 2 da (Elise Delores b 3 Dec 1990, Abigail Rosina b 27 Sept 1992); *Career* bass; performed with orchs incl: LSO, City of Birmingham Symphony, Montreal Philharmonic, London Philharmonic, Hallé, Scottish National, London Sinfonietta, LSO, English String Orch, BBC Philharmonic, English Concert, Prague Symphony, BBC National Orch of Wales; worked with conductors incl: Sir John Pritchard, Neeme Järvi, Oliver Knussen, Trevor Pinnock, Sir Simon Rattle, Andrew Parrott, Jiri Belohlavec, Richard Hickox; appeared at festivals incl: Aldeburgh, Edinburgh, Frankfurt, Singapore, Brussels, Turin, Boston, Tanglewood, Hong Kong; *Performances* over 70 operatic roles incl: The King in Aida (ENO, Opera North), Colline in La Boheme (WNO), Priam in The Trojans (WNO), Da Silva in Ernani (WNO), Don Ferrando in Il Trovatore (Scottish Opera), Private Willis in Iolanthe (Scottish Opera), Ratcliffe in Billy Budd (Scottish Opera), Johann in Werther (Scottish Opera), Sarastro in The Magic Flute (Opera North), He-Ancient in A Midsummer Marriage (Opera North), Father in The Jewel Box (Opera North), Mongolian Soldier in Judith Weir's A Night at the Chinese Opera (Kent Opera), 150 anniversary performance of Mendelssohn's Elijah (BBC Proms) 1996; world premieres incl: Sir Joshua Cramer in Gerald Barry's The Intelligence Park, Where the Wild Things Are (Glyndebourne Festival Opera), Higglety Pigglety Pop (Glyndebourne Festival Opera), John Taverner's Eis Thanaton and Resurrection, Benedict Mason's Music for Three Charlie Chaplin Films; given recitals in Wigmore Hall London, Frankfurt, Prague, Berlin and Cologne; *Recordings* incl: Where the Wild Things Are, Goehr's The Death of Moses, Purcell's Ode for the Birthday of Queen Mary 1694, Mozart's Requiem, Macmillan's Vistitatio Sepulchri; *Recreations* sailing, fishing, painting, family life; *Style*— Stephen Richardson, Esq; ✉ Harrison/Parrott Ltd, 12 Penzance Place, London W11 4PA (tel 020 7228 9166, fax 020 7221 5042)

RICHARDSON, Prof Stephen Michael; s of David Richardson, of Carshalton, Surrey, and Frances Joan, *née* Pring; *b* 8 December 1951; *Educ* Wimbledon Coll, Imperial Coll London (BSc(Eng), PhD, Hinchley Medal IChemE); *m* 5 June 1976, Hilary Joy, da of Malcolm Graham Burgess; 2 da (Helen Alice b 23 Feb 1979, Susan Margaret Clare b 7 June 1984), 1 s (Martin David b 4 Oct 1980); *Career* Univ of Cambridge: Rolls-Royce research asst 1975–76, 1851 research fell 1976–77; Dept of Chemical Engrg Imperial Coll London: lectr 1978–87, Nuffield research fell 1984–85, sr lectr 1987–92, reader 1992–94, prof 1994–, head of dept 2001–; visiting prof Loughborough Univ 1995–98; CEng 1988, FIChemE 1990 (MIChemE 1988), FREng 1996, FCGI 1999; *Publications* incl: Fluid Mechanics (Hemisphere NY, 1989), Blowdown of Pressure Vessels (Trans IChemE, 1992), Piper Alpha (Loss Prevention Bulletin, 1995); *Recreations* music, gardening, walking; *Style*— Prof Stephen Richardson, FREng; ✉ Department of Chemical Engineering, Imperial College, London SW7 2AZ (tel and fax 020 7594 5589, e-mail s.m.richardson@imperial.ac.uk)

R

RICHARDSON, Vicky; da of Anthony Richardson, and Margaret, *née* Ballard; *b* 16 October 1968, London; *Educ* N London Collegiate Sch, Central Sch of Art and Design, Chelsea Sch of Art, Univ of Westminster (BA), Napier Univ (NCTJ Cert); *m* 6 Feb 1999, Adrian Friend; 3 da (Agnes b 4 March 2000, May b 3 Feb 2002, Eliza b 7 April 2007); *Career* asst ed Public Sector Building 1995–96, ed Public Service and Local Govt 1996–97, sr reporter RIBA Jl 1997–2000, dep ed RIBA Jl 2000–02, ed Blueprint 2004–; memb Photostore Panel Crafts Cncl 2005–; tstee Campaign for Drawing 2006–; Highly Commended PPA Editor of the Year 2007; *Publications* In Defence of the Dome (jtly, 1998), New Vernacular Architecture (2001); *Style*— Ms Vicky Richardson; ✉ Blueprint, 6 - 14 Underwood Street, London N1 7JQ (tel 020 7549 2542, e-mail vrichardson@wilmington.co.uk)

RICHARDSON-BUNBURY, Lt Cdr Sir (Richard David) Michael; 5 Bt (I 1787), of Augher, Co Tyrone; eldest s of Richard Richardson-Bunbury (d 1951; ggs of Sir James Richardson-Bunbury, 2 Bt), and Florence Margaret Gordon (d 1993), da of Col Roger Gordon Thomson; suc kinsman, Sir Mervyn Richardson-Bunbury, 4 Bt (d 1953); *b* 27 October 1927; *Educ* RNC Dartmouth; *m* 15 July 1961, Jane Louise, da of Col Alfred William Pulverman, IA (d 1938); 2 s (Roger Michael b 1962 d 1994, Thomas William b 1965); *Heir* s, Thomas Richardson-Bunbury; *Career* Midshipman (S) RN 1945, Sub Lt (S) 1947, Lt (S) 1948, Lt Cdr 1956, sec to Head of UK Serv Liaison Staff Australia 1956–58, RN Staff Coll, Greenwich 1960–61, Capt's sec HMS Ark Royal 1961–64, sec to Flag Offr Naval Flying Trg 1964–67, ret 1967; entered computer services industry 1967, ret 1987; dir Sandy Laird Ltd 1988–96; pres HMS Sussex Assoc 1991–2002; *Publications* A Short History of Crowcombe (1999); *Recreations* woodwork, gardening, reading, travel; *Style*— Lt Cdr Sir Michael Richardson-Bunbury, Bt, RN; ✉ Upper House, Crowcombe, Taunton, Somerset TA4 4AG (tel 01984 618223)

RICHARDSON OF CALOW, Baroness (Life Peer UK 1998), of Calow in the County of Derbyshire; Rev Kathleen Margaret Richardson; OBE (1996); da of Francis William Fountain (d 1986), and Margaret, *née* Heron (d 1991); *b* 24 February 1938; *Educ* St Helena Sch Chesterfield, Stockwell Coll (teacher's cert), Wesley House Cambridge (theol trg); *m* 1964, Ian David Godfrey Richardson; 3 da (Hon Kathryn Jane b 1966, Hon Claire Margaret b 1968, Hon Anne Elizabeth b 1970); *Career* teacher Hollingwood Sec Sch Chesterfield 1958–61, Wesley deaconess Methodist Church 1961–64, pastoral worker Methodist/C of E Stevenage 1973–77, Methodist min W Yorks 1979–86, chm W Yorks District Methodist Church 1987–95, pres Methodist Conf 1992–93, co-ordinating sec Methodist Church 1995–99, moderator Free Churches Cncl and pres Churches Together in England 1995–99; Hon DLitt Univ of Bradford, Hon LLD Univ of Liverpool, Hon DD Univ of Birmingham 2000; *Recreations* reading, needlework; *Style*— The Rt Hon the Rev Baroness Richardson of Calow, OBE; ✉ House of Lords, London SW1A 0PW (tel 020 7219 0314)

RICHARDSON OF DUNTISBOURNE, Baron (Life Peer UK 1983), of Duntisbourne in the County of Gloucestershire; Gordon William Humphreys Richardson; KG (1983), MBE (1944), TD (1979), PC (1976); s of John Robert and Nellie Richardson; *b* 25 November 1915; *Educ* Nottingham HS, Gonville & Caius Coll Cambridge (MA, LLB); *m* 1941, Margaret Alison, er da of late Very Rev Hugh Richard Lawrie Sheppard, Canon and Precentor of St Paul's Cathedral; 1 da (Hon Sarah (Hon Lady Riddell) b 1942), 1 s (Hon Simon Bruce Sheppard b 1944); *Career* govr Bank of England 1973–83 (memb Ct 1967–83), serv WWII S Notts Hussars Yeo, Staff Coll Camberley and War Office; barr 1946–55, memb Bar Cncl 1951–55, hon bencher Gray's Inn 1973–; with ICFC 1955–57; former chm: J Henry Schroder Wagg, Schroders Ltd, Schroders Inc; former chm Industrial Devpt Advsy Bd, former chm Ctee on Turnover Taxation 1963–64; memb: NEDC 1980–83 (and 1971–73), Co Law Amendment Ctee (Jenkins Ctee) 1959–62; one of HM Lts City of London 1974–; former memb Ct Univ of London, former tstee Nat Gallery, dep high steward Univ of Cambridge 1982–; dir: Glyndebourne Arts Tst 1980–88, Royal Opera House 1983–88; Hon DSc: City Univ 1976, Aston Univ 1979; Hon LLD Univ of Cambridge 1979, Hon DCL UEA 1984; Liveryman Worshipful Co of Mercers; *Clubs* Brooks's, Pratt's; *Style*— The Rt Hon the Lord Richardson of Duntisbourne, KG, MBE, TD, PC; ✉ tel 020 7629 4448

RICHENS, Melanie; da of Gordon William Richens, of Swindon, Wilts, and Mavis Estelle, *née* Andrews; *b* 21 August 1969, Swindon, Wilts; *Educ* Kingsdown Sch Swindon, NEW Coll Swindon, Poly of Wales (LLB), Coll of Law Guildford; *Career* admitted slr 1993; slr specialising in product liability and regulatory law (formerly specialising in personal injury); Thring Townsend (formerly Townsends): joined 1991, slr 1993, ptnr 2000–; noteworthy Ct of Appeal and House of Lords cases incl: Carroll and CRS v Dunlopard ORS, Goodes v ESCC; author of numerous legal articles; memb: Wessex C of C, Thames Valley C of C; dir and tstee Headway (Swindon & District), former memb Mgmnt Ctee Headway (Bath & District); *Recreations* arts and crafts, driving, personal development especially NLP, coaching and hypnotherapy; *Style*— Miss Melanie Richens; ✉ Thring Townsend, 6 Drakes Meadow, Penny Lane, Swindon SN1 3LL (tel 01793 410800, fax 01793 412510, e-mail mrichens@ttuk.com)

RICHER, Julian; LVO (2007); s of Percy Isaac Richer, and Ursula Marion Haller; *b* 9 March 1959, London; *Educ* Clifton; *m* 15 Oct 1982, Rosemary Louise, *née* Hamlet; *Career* salesman HiFi Markets Ltd 1977; fndr and chm: Richer Sounds 1978–, JR Properties 1989–, Audio Partnership plc 1994–, The Richer Partnership 1997–, JR Publishing 1998–; dir Duchy Orginal 1998–2006; vice-pres RSPCA 2003–; fndr and chm Persula Fndn 1994–; patron: Irwell Valley Housing Assoc 2003–; ambass Centrepoint 2000–; Hon DBA: Bournemouth Univ, Kingston Univ; *Publications* The Richer Way (1995, 4 edn 2001), Richer on Leadership (1999); *Recreations* radio-controlled models, drumming, reading, walking, travel; *Style*— Julian Richer, Esq, LVO; ✉ Richer Sounds plc, Richer House, Hankey Place, London SE1 4BB (tel 020 7403 1310, fax 020 7827 9003, e-mail julian.richer@richersounds.com)

RICHMOND, Barbara Mary; da of James Wallace Duff; *b* 28 July 1960; *Educ* St Aelred's RC HS, UMIST (BSc); *m* 25 Feb 1982, Alexander James Richmond; *Career* Arthur Andersen & Co Manchester 1981–87; GEC Alsthom: fin controller (Distribution Switchgear) 1987, fin controller (Transmission Switchgear) 1988, fin dir (Electrical Distribution Gp) 1989–92; gp fin dir: Whessoe plc 1994–97 (gp fin controller 1992–93), Croda International plc 1997–2006, Inchcape plc 2006–; non-exec dir: Carclo plc 2000–06, Scarborough Building Soc 2005–; FCA 1984; *Recreations* walking, gardening, travel, motor sport; *Style*— Mrs Barbara Richmond

RICHMOND, Dr David John Hamilton; s of Dr Jack Hamilton Richmond (Maj RAMC, d 1969), and Gwendoline Mabel, *née* Thompson (d 1999); *b* 18 October 1936; *Educ* Leighton Park Sch Reading, Pembroke Coll Cambridge, Guy's Hosp (MA, MB BChir, DObst RCOG, FRCA); *m* 14 Feb 1975, Susan Elizabeth Helen, da of Charles W Malcolm, of Auckland, NZ; 2 da (Felicity b 4 Oct 1977, Amanda b 11 Feb 1982), 1 s (William b 11 March 1979); *Career* Nat Serv, PO navigator RAF 1955–57; formerly: registrar St George's Hosp, registrar Bart's, sr registrar Queen Elizabeth Hosp Birmingham; conslt anaesthetist Royal Wolverhampton Hosps NHS Trust 1971–; memb: Obstetric Anaesthetist Assoc, Assoc of Anaesthetists of GB; *Recreations* golf, tennis, bridge; *Clubs* South Staffordshire Golf, Wolverhampton Lawn Tennis & Squash; *Style*— Dr David Richmond; ✉ Greenways, Stockwell End, Tettenhall, Wolverhampton WV6 9PH (tel 01902 751448); New Cross Hospital, Wolverhampton WV10 0QP (tel 01902 307999)

RICHMOND, John; *b* 1960; *Educ* Kingston Poly (BA); *m* Angie Hill; *Career* fashion designer; began career in own co producing John Richmond collection, simultaneously worked freelance for Emporio Armani, Fiorucci, Joseph Tricot and 'Pin-Up' for Deni Cler, ptnr with Maria Cornejo producing Richmond/Cornejo label 1984–87 (shops in London and 16 in Japan), solo 1987–; int catwalk shows from 1991: The International Palace of Destroy, Dinner with Dali March 1992; estab diffusion range 'Destroy', clients incl Elton John, George Michael, Madonna and Prince; *Style*— John Richmond, Esq; ✉ 54 Conduit Street, London W1S 2YY

RICHMOND, Jon; s of David Richmond, of Glasgow, and Josephine, *née* Thompson; *b* 8 March 1953; *Educ* Westwood Sch Glasgow, Univ of Edinburgh (BSc, MB ChB); *m* 4 July 1974, Anne Emily, *née* Cullen; 2 da (Karen Anne b 10 June 1981, Susan Emily b 13 May 1987); *Career* various jr med posts Lothian Health Bd and Univ of Edinburgh 1977–84, sr registrar (plastic and reconstructive surgery) Royal Prince Alfred Hosp Sydney 1984–85, visiting fell Mayo Clinic and Louisville Hand Surgery Assoc USA 1985; Animals (Scientific Procedures) Inspectorate (ASPI) Home Office: inspr then superintending inspr Home Office 1986–96, chief inspr 1996–2003; head Animals (Scientific Procedures) Div (ASPD) Home Office 2003–; author of various scientific and govt pubns; FRCSEd 1981, FRSM 2001; *Recreations* family, golf, land yachting, reading; *Style*— Jon Richmond, Esq; ✉ Home Office, PO Box 6779, Dundee DD1 9WN (tel 01382 223189, e-mail jon.richmond@homeoffice.gsi.gov.uk)

RICHMOND, Kevin Charles; s of Eric Charles Richmond, of Nottingham, and Loraine Christine, *née* Turner; *Educ* Padstow Comp, Nottingham Acad of Speech Dance and Drama; *Career* ballet dancer/teacher; child actor Nottingham Playhouse Rep 1971 (also appeared in film The Ragman's Daughter), with touring co Dance for Everyone (Theatre in Education) 1976–77, with London Festival Ballet/English Nat Ballet 1977–; *Roles* danced in all Christopher Bruce prodns for English Nat Ballet incl: The Dream is Over, The World Again (cr role), Land (cr role), Cruel Garden, Symphony in Three Movements (cr role), Swansong (SWET Award nomination 1988, also produced for TV); other Eng Nat Ballet 1977–99 roles incl: Furbo in Tetley's Pulcinella, Jester and an Ugly Sister in Stevenson's Cinderella, Hilarion in Skeaping's Giselle, Headmistress in Lichine's Graduation Ball (also produced for TV), Dr Coppélius in Hynd's Coppélia, Tybalt in Sir Frederick Ashton's Romeo and Juliet, Lead Bandit in Petit's Carmen, Lead Boy in Ailey's Night Creature, Chief Eunuch in Schéhérazade, Tchaikovsky/Drosselmeyer in Schaufuss' The Nutcracker, Hortensio in John Cranko's The Taming of the Shrew, The Gopak and Chinese Dance in Ben Stevenson's The Nutcracker, Fate in Robert North's A Stranger I Came (cr role), Young Man in Brandstrup's White Nights (cr role); teacher training course Royal Acad of Dancing; also appeared in film Nijinsky; title role in Christopher Hampson's A Christmas Carol; currently ballet master Ballett Basel; *Recreations* archery; *Style*— Kevin Richmond; ✉ e-mail ucantalk2me@aol.com

RICHMOND, Sir Mark Henry; kt (1986); s of Harold Sylvestor Richmond (d 1952), and Dorothy Plaistowe (d 1976); *b* 1 February 1931; *Educ* Epsom Coll, Clare Coll Cambridge (BA, PhD, ScD); *m* 1958, Shirley Jean, da of Dr Vincent Townrow (d 1982); 1 s (Paul b 1964), 2 da (Clare b 1959, Jane b 1962, d 1987); *Career* scientific staff Med Res Cncl 1958–65; reader in molecular biology Univ of Edinburgh 1965–68, prof of bacteriology Univ of Bristol 1968–81, vice-chllr Univ of Manchester 1981–90, chm SERC 1990–94, gp head of research Glaxo 1993–95; pres Epsom Coll 1992–2001; currently with Sch of Public Policy UCL; chm Ctee of Vice-Chllrs and Princs 1987–89; tstee: Nat Gallery 1993–2001, Tate Gallery 1995–99; hon fell Pembroke Coll Cambridge 2004; FRS 1980; *Recreations* walking, gardening; *Clubs* Athenaeum; *Style*— Sir Mark Richmond, FRS

RICHMOND, LENNOX AND GORDON, 10 (and 5 respectively) Duke of (E 1675, UK 1876); Charles Henry Gordon Lennox; also Earl of March, Baron Settrington (both E 1675), Earl of Darnley, Lord Torbolton (all S 1675), Duc d'Aubigny (Fr 1684), Earl of Kinrara (UK 1876), and Hereditary Constable of Inverness Castle; s of 9 Duke of Richmond and (4 of) Gordon (d 1989), and Elizabeth Grace, *née* Hudson (d 1992); descended from King Charles II and Louise Renée de Penançoët de Kérouaille, who was cr Baroness Petersfield, Countess of Fareham and Duchess of Portsmouth for life by King Charles II and Duchesse d'Aubigny by King Louis XIV of France; *b* 19 September 1929; *Educ* Eton, William Temple Coll Rugby; *m* 26 May 1951, Susan Monica, o da of Col Cecil Everard Grenville-Grey, CBE, of Hall Barn, Blewbury, Berks, by his w, Louise Monica, eldest da of Lt-Col Ernest Fitzroy Morrison-Bell, OBE, JP, DL; 2 da (Lady Ellinor Caroline b 1952, Lady Louisa Elizabeth (Lady Louisa Collings) b 1967), 1 s (Charles Henry, Earl of March and Kinrara b 1955), and 2 adopted da (Maria b 1959, Naomi (Mrs Burke) b 1962); *Heir* s, Earl of March and Kinrara; *Career* late 2 Lt KRRC; FCA 1956–; chm: Dexam Int (Holdings) Ltd 1956–, Goodwood Gp of Cos 1969–; chm John Wiley & Sons Ltd 1991–98 (previosly vice-chm and dir); dir: Industrial Studies William Temple Coll 1962–67, Country Gentlemen's Assoc Ltd 1975–89; memb: House of Laity Gen Synod 1960–80, Central and Exec Ctee World Cncl Churches 1968–75; church cmmr 1962–75; chm: Bd for Mission and Unity Gen Synod 1968–77, House of Laity Chichester Dio 1976–79, Chichester Cathedral Tst 1985–91; vice-chm Archbishops' Cmmn on Church and State 1966–70; memb: W Midlands Regnl Econ Planning Cncl 1965–68, W Sussex Economic Partnership Steering Ctee 1997–; pres: Sussex Rural Community Cncl (latterly Action in rural Sussex) 1973–2006 (chm Rural Housing Advsy Ctee 1996–2006), Chichester Festivities 1977–, S of England Agric Soc 1981–82, Br Horse Soc 1976–78, Sussex Enterprise (formerly Sussex C of C) 1980–, Planning for Economic Prosperity in Chichester and Arun Dists 1989– (chm 1985–89), SE England Tourist Bd 1990–2003 (vice-pres 1974–90), AMREF (African Medical and Research Fndn) 2000–; chm: Rugby Cncl of Social Serv 1961–68, Dunford Coll (YMCA) 1969–82, Christian Orgns Res and Advsy Tst (CORAT) 1970–87, Tstees Sussex Heritage Tst 1978–2000, Assoc of Int Dressage Event Organisers 1987–94, Bognor Regis Regeneration and Vision Gp 2001–07, Sussex Community Fndn 2006–; Chllr Univ of Sussex 1985–98 (treas 1979–82); Lord-Lt of West Sussex 1990–94 (DL 1975–90); hon treas and dep pres Historic Houses Assoc 1975–86; patron Sussex CCC 1991–; Hon LLD Univ of Sussex 1987; Medal of Honour Br Equestrian Fedn 1983; CIMgt 1982; *Style*— His Grace the Duke of Richmond, Lennox and Gordon; ✉ Molecomb, Goodwood, Chichester, West Sussex PO18 0PZ (tel 01243 527861); office: 01243 755000, fax 01243 755005, e-mail richmond@goodwood.co.uk)

RICHMOND-WATSON, Anthony Euan; s of Euan Owens Richmond-Watson (d 1954), and Hon Gladys Gordon, *née* Catto (d 1967); *b* 8 April 1941; *Educ* Westminster, Univ of Edinburgh (BCom); *m* 1, 1966, Angela, da of John Broadley, of Somerset (d 1979); 1 da (Tamsin b 1967), 1 s (Luke b 1971); m 2, 1976, Geraldine Ruth Helen, da of Charles Barrington, of Cornwall (d 1966); 1 da (Alice b 1976); *Career* merchant banker; dir Morgan Grenfell & Co Ltd 1975–96 (joined 1968), dir and dep chm Deutsche Morgan Grenfell Gp plc (formerly Morgan Grenfell Gp plc) 1989–96; dep chm: Melrose Resources plc 1999–, Gazelle Corp Finance Ltd 2003–; chm Yule Catto & Co plc 2000– (dir 1978–), chm Norfolk Capital Gp plc 1986–90 (dir 1985–90); MICAS; *Style*— Anthony Richmond-Watson, Esq

RICKARD, Dr John Hellyar; s of Peter John Rickard (d 1999), of Devon, and Irene Eleanor, *née* Hales (d 2004); *b* 27 January 1940; *Educ* Ilford Co HS, Univ of Oxford (MA, DPhil), Aston Univ (MSc); *m* 6 April 1963, Christine Dorothy, da of Claude Hudson (d 1963), of Essex; 2 da (Rosemary b 1964, Wendy b 1967), 1 s (Robin b 1965); *Career* former res fell Univ of Oxford; sr econ advsr: Dept of Prices and Consumer Protection 1976–78, central policy review staff Cabinet Office 1978–82, HM Treasy 1982–84; the econ advsr State of Bahrain 1984–87, chief econ advsr Dept of Tport 1987–91, under sec economics HM Treasy 1991–94, chief econ advsr Dept of Tport 1994, IMF fiscal advsr Miny of Finance Moldova 1995, conslt economist 1995–2003; non-exec dir Isle of Wight

Healthcare NHS Tst 2003–06, tstee Earl Mountbatten Hospice 2003–; MCIT; *Books* Macro-Economics (with D Aston, 1970); *Recreations* sailing, music; *Clubs* Island Sailing; *Style—* Dr John Rickard; ✉ Bay House, Lanes End, Totland Bay, Isle of Wight PO39 0BE (tel and fax 01983 754669, e-mail jrickard@btinternet.com)

RICKARDS, Prof (Richard) Barrie; s of Robert Rickards (d 1999), and Eva, *née* Sudborough (d 1995); *b* 12 June 1938, Leeds; *Educ* Goole GS, Univ of Hull (Reckitt scholar, BSc, PhD, DSc), Univ of Cambridge (MA, ScD); *Career* curator Dept of Geology UCL 1963, asst-in-research Univ of Cambridge 1964–66, sr scientific offr Br Museum of Nat History 1966, lectr in geology TCD 1967–69, curator Sedgwick Museum of Geology Univ of Cambridge 1969–2006; Dept of Earth Sciences Univ of Cambridge: lectr 1969–90, reader 1991–99, prof of palaeontology and biostratigraphy 1999–2005, emeritus prof 2005–; dir of studies Christ's Coll Cambridge 1969–2001 and 2002–06, currently life fell Emmanuel Coll Cambridge; proctor Univ of Cambridge 1983–85; sec Br and Irish Graptolite Gp (BIG G); memb organising ctees of various int confs and symposia; past ed: Palaeontological Assoc Newsletter, Ludlow Research Gp Bulletin; memb Editorial Bd Lethaia; awards incl: John Phillips Medal Yorks Geological Soc 1988, Lyell Medal Geological Soc 1997; CGeol, FGS; *Publications* Fishers on the Green Roads (novel, 2002); numerous papers in learned jls; *Recreations* angling, long-distance running; *Style—* Prof Barrie Rickards; ✉ Emmanuel College, Cambridge CB2 3AP; Department of Earth Sciences, University of Cambridge, Downing Street, Cambridge CB2 3EQ (tel 01223 333437, e-mail wagreen@esc.cam.ac.uk)

RICKELL, Andrew David Rickell (Andy); s of David Rickell, and June Rickell; *b* 9 May 1963, York; *Educ* Huntington Sch York, Selwyn Coll Cambridge (BA), Univ of Southampton (Cert); *m* 26 Oct 1998, Ruth; 1 s (Mark); *Career* community devpt 1994–99, co-ordinator Disability Action Cheltenham 1999–2001, chief exec Br Cncl of Disabled People 2001–04, exec dir and disability cmmr Scope 2004–; Methodist church local preacher; Young Business Person of the Year 1986; memb Chartered Inst of Taxation 1989; *Style—* Andy Rickell, Esq; ✉ Scope, 6 Market Road, London N7 9PW (tel 020 7619 7100, e-mail andy.rickell@scope.org.uk)

RICKETT, Brig Johnny Francis; CBE (1990, OBE 1982, MBE 1967); s of Francis William Rickett (d 1981), and Lettice Anne, *née* Elliot (d 1985); *b* 7 September 1939; *Educ* Eton, RMCS, Def Servs Staff Coll India, RCDS; *m* June 1964, Frances (Fanny) Seton, da of Charles Francis Seton de Winton, CBE (d 2001); 2 da (Sophy Frances b 1965 d 1970, Emily Frances b 1974), 1 s (Charles Edward Francis (Charlie) b 1975); *Career* Welsh Guards, seconded for loan serv Fed Reg Army S Arab Emirates 1963–65; served: Aden, India, Hong Kong, Kenya, Germany, USA, NI, Falkland Islands; CO 1WG 1980–82; Cdr 19 Inf Brigade and Colchester Garrison 1984–86, Dep Cdr and COS HQ SE Dist Aldershot 1987–90, Mil Attaché Paris 1991–94, Regtl Lt-Col Welsh Guards 1988–94; ADC to HM The Queen 1993–95; Comptroller Union Jack Club 1995–; pres Ex-Service Fellowship Centres; tstee: Colonie Franco-Britannique, Old Etonian Tst, Airborne Assault Normandy Tst; dep chm of govrs Penhurst Sch Chipping Norton, govr Moreton Hall Prep Sch; chm Barton PC; Queen's Commendation for Brave Conduct 1964, mentioned in despatches 1974; FInstD 2000 (MInstD 1996); Knight of Magistral Grace SMOM, Chevalier of the Order of Danneborg (Denmark) 1975, Cdr Order of Merit (France) 1992; *Recreations* falconry, shooting, fishing, gardening, opera; *Clubs* Institute of Directors; *Style—* Brig Johnny Rickett, CBE; ✉ Union Jack Club, Sandell Street, Waterloo, London SE1 8UJ (tel 020 7928 6401, fax 020 7902 6060, e-mail brigadier@ujclub.co.uk)

RICKETT, William Francis Sebastian (Willy); s of Sir Denis Hubert Fletcher Rickett, KCMG, CB (d 1997), of Salisbury, and Ruth Pauline, *née* Armstrong (d 2003); *b* 23 February 1953; *Educ* Eton (Oppidan scholar), Trinity Coll Cambridge (MA); *m* 16 June 1979, Lucy Caroline, da of J H Clark (d 1997); 1 s ((Oliver Patrick) Oscar b 20 June 1983), 1 da (Rosanna Madeleine b 14 March 1986); *Career* Dept of Energy: joined 1975, private sec to perm sec 1977–78, princ 1978–81, private sec to Prime Minister 1981–83, seconded to Kleinwort Benson Ltd 1983–85, asst sec Electricity Privatisation 1987–90 (Oil Div 1985–87), under sec Energy Efficiency Office 1990–93; dir of fin DOE 1993–97, dir town & country planning DETR 1997–98, dep sec and head of econ and domestic affairs Secretariat Cabinet Office 1998–2000, head integrated tport taskforce DETR 2000, DG tport strategy and planning DETR 2000–01, DG transport strategy, roads, local and maritime transport DTLR 2001–02, DG strategy, fin and delivery Dept for Tport 2003–04, seconded to Ernst & Young 2004–06, DG energy DTI 2006–; non-exec dir Redland Roof Tiles 1994–97; FRSA, FIHT; *Recreations* children, painting, sports; *Style—* Willy Rickett, Esq; ✉ Department of Trade and Industry, 1 Victoria Street, London SW1H 0ET

RICKETTS, Prof Martin John; s of Leonard Alfred Ricketts (d 2000), and Gertrude Dorothy, *née* Elgar (d 1997); *b* 10 May 1948; *Educ* City of Bath Boys' Sch, Univ of Newcastle upon Tyne (BA), Univ of York (DPhil); *m* 1975, Diana Barbara, *née* Greenwood; 1 s, 1 da; *Career* econ asst Industrial Policy Gp 1970–72, research fell Inst of Econ and Social Research Univ of York 1975–77; Univ of Buckingham (formerly UC at Buckingham): lectr in econs 1977–82, sr lectr 1982–85, reader 1985–87, prof of econ orgn 1987–, dean Sch of Business 1993–97, pro-vice-chllr 1993, dean Sch of Humanities 2002–; econ dir NEDO 1991–92; visiting prof Virginia Poly, Inst and State Univ 1984; tstee Inst of Econ Affrs 1992–, hon prof Heriot-Watt Univ 1996–; memb Royal Econ Soc, Scottish Econ Soc, American Econ Soc; FRSA; *Books* The Economics of Energy (with M G Webb, 1980), The Economics of Business Enterprise (1987, 3 edn 2002), The Many Ways of Governance (1999); also author of numerous papers on public finance, public choice, housing economics and economic organisation; *Recreations* music (especially playing piano and oboe); *Style—* Prof Martin Ricketts; ✉ Department of International Studies, University of Buckingham, Hunter Street, Buckingham MK18 1EG (tel 01280 814080, fax 01280 822245, e-mail martin.ricketts@buck.ac.uk)

RICKETTS, Sir Peter Forbes; KCMG (2003, CMG 1999); s of late Maurice Alan Ricketts, of Lechlade, and Dilys, *née* Davies; *b* 30 September 1952; *Educ* Bishop Vesey's GS Sutton Coldfield, Pembroke Coll Oxford (BA); *m* 13 Sept 1980, Suzanne Julia, da of Ivor Horlington; 1 s (Edward b 1982), 1 da (Caroline b 1987); *Career* FCO: joined UK Mission to the UN 1974, third sec Singapore 1975–78, second sec UK Delgn to NATO 1978–81, first sec 1981–83, asst private sec to Foreign Sec 1983–85, first sec Washington 1986–89, dep head of Security Policy Dept 1989–91, head of Hong Kong Dept 1991–94, cnsllr (Financial and Euro Affairs) Paris 1994–97, dep political dir 1997–99, dir int security 1999–2000, chm Jt Intelligence Ctee Cabinet Office 2000–01, political dir FCO 2001–06, UK rep NATO 2003–06, perm under sec of state and head of the diplomatic serv FCO 2006–; *Recreations* Victorian art, Chinese porcelain, restoring Normandy farmhouse; *Style—* Sir Peter Ricketts, KCMG; ✉ Foreign & Commonwealth Office, King Charles Street, London SW1A 2AH

RICKETTS, Robert Anthony; s of Robert Harold Ricketts (d 2003), and Mavis, *née* Harrington; *b* 5 September 1962, London; *Educ* Emerson Park Sch, UCL (LLB), Law Soc Coll of Law; *m* 26 Aug 1990, Carole, *née* Pottinger; 1 s (Alexander b 22 March 1995), 1 da (Katherine b 15 Jan 1998); *Career* admitted slr 1987; Norton Rose 1985–89, Aviation Gp Frere Cholmeley 1989–95, founding ptnr Clark Ricketts 1995–; memb Br Helicopter Advsy Bd, memb Br Business Gen Aviation Assoc; memb Law Soc 1987; *Publications* Butterworth's Encyclopaedia of Forms and Precedents (Civil Aviation Section, 1993 and 2006); *Recreations* travel, cricket; *Style—* Robert Ricketts, Esq; ✉ Clark Ricketts LLP Solicitors, Waterman House, 41 Kingsway, London WC2B 6TP (tel 020 7240 6767, fax 020 7836 0699, e-mail robertricketts@clarkricketts.com)

RICKETTS, Sir (Robert) Tristram; 8 Bt (UK 1828), of The Elms, Gloucestershire, and Beaumont Leys, Leicestershire; s of Sir Robert Ricketts, 7 Bt (d 2005), of Minchinhampton, Glos, and Anne Theresa, *née* Cripps (d 1998); *b* 17 April 1946; *Educ* Winchester, Magdalene Coll Cambridge (MA); *m* 1969, Ann, yr da of Eric William Charles Lewis, CB (d 1981), of London; 1 s (Stephen Tristram b 1974), 1 da (Clare Jessica b 1977); *Heir* s, Stephen Ricketts; *Career* with DG's Dept GLC 1968–74; Horserace Betting Levy Bd: asst princ offr 1974–79, chief exec 1980–93, memb 1993–98 and 2000–05, chief exec 2005–; British Horseracing Bd: chief exec 1993–2000, sec gen 2000–05; chm Independent Betting Adjudication Service Ltd 2005–; dir: Racecourse Technical Services Ltd 1980–93 and 1994–98, Horseracing Forensic Laboratory Ltd 1986–93 and 2005–07, British Horse Industry Confederation Ltd 2000–05 (chm 2002–05); chm European Pattern Ctee 1993–2005, memb Exec Cncl Int Fedn of Horseracing Authorities 2001–05; *Clubs* Athenaeum; *Style—* Sir Tristram Ricketts, Bt; ✉ 47 Lancaster Avenue, London SE27 9EL (tel 020 8670 8422); office: 52 Grosvenor Gardens, London SW1W 0AU (tel 020 7333 0043, fax 020 7333 0041, e-mail tristram.ricketts@hblb.org.uk)

RICKFORD, Jonathan Braithwaite Keevil; CBE (2001); s of Richard Braithwaite Keevil Rickford (d 1990), and Dorothy Margaret, *née* Latham; *b* 7 December 1944; *Educ* Sherborne, Magdalen Coll Oxford (MA, BCL, Gibbs prize in law); *m* 20 July 1968, Dora Rose, da of Rt Rev Norman Sargant (d 1985); 1 s (Richard b 7 July 1971), 2 da (Margaret b 10 Dec 1973, Alice b 24 March 1975); *Career* barr 1970–85, slr 1985–; teaching assoc in law Univ of Calif Sch of Law 1968–69, lectr in law LSE 1969–72, sr legal asst Dept of Trade 1974 (asst 1972), Law Offrs Dept AG's Chambers 1976–79; DTI (formerly Dept of Trade): asst slr (co law) 1979–82, under sec (legal) 1982–84, the Slr 1984–87; British Telecommunications plc: slr and chief legal offr 1987–89, dir of govt rels 1989–93, dir of corp strategy 1993–96; sr fell Br Inst of Int and Comparative Law 1996–97, sr assoc European Public Policy Advisers (EPPA) 1997–98, project dir The Co Law Review 1998–2001, dir Co Law Centre 2003–06 (professorial fell 2006–); The Competition Cmmn (formerly Monopolies and Mergers Cmmn) 1997–2004; visiting prof in int corp law Leiden Univ The Netherlands 2002, visiting prof LSE 2003–; FRSA 1991; *Recreations* sailing; *Clubs* Bosham Sailing; *Style—* Jonathan Rickford, Esq, CBE; ✉ e-mail jrickford@aol.com

RICKFORD, Dr William Jeremy Keevil; s of Richard Braithwaite Keevil Rickford (d 1990), of Dartmouth, Devon, and Dorothy Margaret Hart, *née* Latham; *b* 4 December 1949; *Educ* Sherborne, St Thomas' Hosp Med Sch London (MB BS); *m* 9 Oct 1982, Jacqueline Ann, da of Kenneth Cooke Burrow, MBE, of Sandgate, Folkestone, Kent; 1 da (Emma b 15 Dec 1983), 1 s (Thomas b 7 Jan 1986); *Career* asst prof Dept of Anaesthesiology Univ of Maryland Baltimore USA 1986–88, conslt anaesthetist E & N Hertfordshire NHS Health Tst 1988–; FRCA, FFARCSI; *Recreations* skiing, sailing; *Clubs* Royal Dart Yacht; *Style—* Dr W J K Rickford; ✉ Department of Anaesthetics, Lister Hospital, Corey's Mill, Stevenage, Hertfordshire SG1 4AB (tel 01438 314333 and 01438 781086, e-mail rickfordwjk@aol.com)

RICKMAN, Alan; *Educ* Latymer Upper Sch, Chelsea Sch of Art, RCA, RADA; *Career* actor and director; seasons at Library Theatre Manchester, Haymarket and Phoenix Theatre Leicester, Crucible Theatre Sheffield, Birmingham Rep Theatre and Bristol Old Vic; *Theatre* incl: The Devil is an Ass and Measure for Measure (Birmingham, Edinburgh Festival and NT) 1976–77, The Tempest, Captain Swing, Love's Labour's Lost and Antony and Cleopatra (RSC) 1978–79, Antonio (Nottingham Playhouse) 1979, Fears and Miseries of the Third Reich (Glasgow Citizens' Theatre) 1979–80, The Summer Party (Crucible Sheffield) 1980, The Devil Himself (Lyric Studio) 1980, Commitments (Bush Theatre) 1980, Philadelphia Story (Oxford Playhouse) 1981, The Seagull (Royal Court) 1981, Brothers Karamazov (Edinburgh Festival and USSR) 1981, The Last Elephant (Bush Theatre) 1981, Bad Language (Hampstead Theatre Club) 1983, The Grass Widow (Royal Court) 1983, The Lucky Chance (Royal Court) 1984, As You Like It, Troilus and Cressida, Les Liaisons Dangereuses and Mephisto (RSC) 1985–86, Les Liaisons Dangereuses (West End and Broadway) 1986–87, Tango at the End of Winter (Edinburgh and West End) 1991, Hamlet (Riverside Studios and Br tour) 1992, Antony & Cleopatra (NT) 1998, Private Lives (Albery Theatre (Olivier Award nomination Best Actor 2002)) 2001 and (Richard Rogers Theatre NY (Tony nomination for Best Actor)) 2002, My Name is Rachel Corrie (Royal Court, Galway Festival, Edinburgh Festival and NY) 2005–06; as dir prodns incl: Desperately Yours (New York) 1980, Other Worlds (asst dir, Royal Court) 1983, Live Wax (Edinburgh Festival) 1986, Wax Acts (West End and tour) 1992, The Winter Guest (Yorkshire Playhouse and Almeida) 1995; *Television* incl: Romeo and Juliet 1978, Therese Raquin 1979, Barchester Chronicles 1982, Busted 1982, Pity in History 1984, Benefactors 1989, Revolutionary Witness 1989, Spirit of Man 1989; *Radio* incl: The Dutch Courtesan, Polly, Rope, Manchester Enthusiasts, Gridlock, Trick to Catch the Old One, A Good Man in Africa, That Man Bracken, Blood Wedding, The Seagull, The Magic of my Youth; *Films* incl: Die Hard 1988, The January Man 1989, Quigley Down Under 1990, Truly, Madly, Deeply 1991, Closetland 1991, Close My Eyes 1991, Robin Hood, Prince of Thieves 1991, Bob Roberts 1992, Fallen Angels 1993, Mesmer 1993, An Awfully Big Adventure 1994, Sense and Sensibility 1995, Michael Collins 1995, Rasputin 1995, Dark Harbour 1997, Judas Kiss 1997, Dogma 1998, Galaxy Quest 1999, Blow Dry 1999, Play 2000, The Search for John Gissing 2000, Harry Potter and the Philosopher's Stone 2001, Harry Potter and the Chamber of Secrets 2002, Love Actually 2002, Harry Potter and the Prisoner of Azkaban 2003, Something the Lord Made 2004, Harry Potter and the Goblet of Fire 2005, Snow Cake 2006, Perfume: The Story of a Murderer 2006, Nobel Son 2007, Harry Potter and the Order of the Phoenix 2007; as dir The Winter Guest 1997; *Awards* Bancroft Gold Medal RADA 1974, Tony Nomination for Les Liaisons Dangereuses 1988, Time Out Award for Tango at the End of Winter 1992, Best Actor Evening Standard Film Awards for Robin Hood, Prince of Thieves, Close My Eyes and Truly, Madly, Deeply 1991, Best Supporting Actor BAFTA Film Awards for Robin Hood, Prince of Thieves 1992, Best Actor for Mesmer Montreal Film Festival 1994, Emmy Award for Rasputin 1996, BAFTA nomination for Sense and Sensibility 1996, Golden Globe Award and SAG Award for Best Actor for Rasputin 1997, Best Film for The Winter Guest Chicago Film Festival 1997, OCIC Award and Best First Feature Film Award Venice Film Festival 1997; *Style—* Alan Rickman; ✉ c/o ICM Ltd, Oxford House, 76 Oxford Street, London W1D 1BS (tel 020 7636 6565, fax 020 7323 0101)

RICKMAN, Prof Geoffrey Edwin; *b* 9 October 1932; *Educ* Peter Symonds Sch Winchester, BNC Oxford (MA, DPhil); *m* 18 April 1959, Anna Rosemary, *née* Wilson; 1 da (Elizabeth Jane b 1962), 1 s (David Edwin b 1964); *Career* jr res fell The Queen's Coll Oxford 1959–62; Univ of St Andrews: lectr in ancient history 1962–, sr lectr 1968–, prof 1981–97, master United Coll of St Salvator and St Leonard 1992–96, pro-vice-chllr 1996–97, emeritus prof 1997; memb IAS Princeton 1998; hon fell Br Sch at Rome 2002 (chm Cncl 1997–2002); FSA 1963, FBA 1989, FRSE 2001; *Books* Roman Granaries and Storebuildings (1971), The Corn Supply of Ancient Rome (1980); *Recreations* swimming, listening to opera; *Style—* Prof Geoffrey Rickman, FSA, FBA, FRSE; ✉ 56 Hepburn Gardens, St Andrews, Fife KY16 9DG (tel 01334 472063); School of Classics, St Salvator's College, The University, St Andrews, Fife (tel 01334 476161)

RICKS, Catherine Louise (Katy); da of Paul Koralek, CBE, of London, and Jenny, *née* Chadwick; *b* 16 March 1961; *Educ* Camden Sch for Girls, Balliol Coll Oxford (MA); *m* 1983, David Ricks; *Career* asst teacher: St Paul's Girls' Sch 1985–87, King Edward's Sch Edgbaston 1987–90, Latymer Upper Sch 1990–92; head of English St Edward's Sch Oxford 1992–97, dep head Highgate Sch 1997–2002, head Sevenoaks Sch 2002–; *Style—*

Mrs Katy Ricks; ✉ Sevenoaks School, Sevenoaks, Kent TN13 1HU (tel 01732 467702, e-mail hm@sevenoaksschool.org)

RICKSON, Ian; s of Richard Rickson, and Eileen, *née* Frost; *b* 8 November 1963; *Educ* Univ of Essex (BA), Goldsmiths Coll London (PGTC); *Partner* Polly Teale; 2 c (Jack Gould b 6 Nov 1985, Eden Rickson b 2 Aug 2000); *Career* artistic dir Royal Court Theatre 1998–2006; prodns for the Royal Court incl: The Winterling, Alice Trilogy, The Sweetest Swing in Baseball, Fallout, The Night Heron, Boy Gets Girl, Mouth to Mouth (and Albery), Dublin Carol, The Weir (Duke of Yorks and Broadway), The Lights, Pale Horse, Mojo (and Steppenwolf Theatre Chicago), Ashes and Sand, Some Voices, Killers, 1992 Young Writers' Festival, Wildfire; other prodns incl: The Day I Stood Still (RNT), The House of Yes (The Gate), Me and My Friend (Chichester Festival Theatre), Queer Fish (BAC), First Strike (Soho Poly), La Serva Padrona (opera, Broomhill), The Seagull, Krapp's Last Tape; hon fell Goldsmiths Coll London; *Clubs* Black's, The Hospital; *Style—* Ian Rickson; ✉ Royal Court Theatre, Sloane Square, London SW1W 8AS (tel 020 7565 5050)

RIDDELL, Alan Gordon; s of George Riddell (d 1989), and Elizabeth, *née* Mellin (d 1981); *Educ* Greenock Acad, Univ of Glasgow (MA), Jordanhill Coll of Educn (CertEd); *m* Barbara, *née* Kelly; 2 da (Catriona b 1981, Rowena b 1983); *Career* teacher of history and economics Greenock Acad 1971–74, princ teacher of history Eyemouth HS 1974–75; DOE: joined 1975, various positions in planning, local govt fin and ports div 1975–81, asst private sec to Min of Housing 1981–83, head of fin branch Inner Cities Directorate 1983–86, Deregulation of Rents 1986–87, private sec to Min of State (Local Govt Water and Planning) 1987–90, head Private Rental Sector Div 1990–92, princ private sec to Sec of State for the Environment 1992–94, sec Ctee of Standards in Public Life (The Nolan Ctee) 1994–97, head of Regeneration Policy Div 1997–98, regnl dir Govt Office for East of England 1998–2002, dep head Neighbourhood Renewal Unit 2002–07, ret; chair Standards Ctee Sevenoaks DC; memb Ctee Empty Homes Agency; *Style—* Alan Riddell, Esq

RIDDELL, Dr (John) Alistair; OBE (1988); s of Alexander Riddell (d 1954), and Mary McFarlane, *née* Mackintosh (d 1946); *b* 11 February 1930; *Educ* Glasgow Acad, Univ of Glasgow (MB ChB); *m* 1, 23 March 1956 (sep 1997), Elizabeth Park McDonald (d 1999), da of Alexander Davidson; 1 s (Alexander Davidson b 10 June 1957), 3 da (Frances Anne Mackintosh b 23 Jan 1960, Aileen McDonald b 7 May 1962, Valerie Elizabeth b 21 April 1968); m 2, 3 Sept 1999, Dr Susan Anne Fraser, da of Dr Thomas N Fraser; *Career* house offr (med and surgery) Hairmyres Hosp Lanarkshire 1953–54, SHO (obstetrics) Bellshill Hosp Lanarkshire 1954–55, trainee GP Glasgow 1955, princ in gen practice East End Glasgow 1956–95, estab gp practice Easterhouse Glasgow 1958, pt/t clinical asst (geriatrics) Lightburn Hosp 1968–78; memb: Glasgow Local Med Ctee 1964–95 (treas 1972–78, sec 1978–91), Glasgow Area Med Ctee 1974–94, Bd of Gen Practice Fin Corp 1975–90 (vice-chm 1989–90), Bd CAB Easterhouse 1978–82; BMA: memb Gen Med Servs Ctee 1972–96 (negotiator 1982–87, vice-chm 1984–87), memb Scottish Gen Med Servs Ctee 1972–97 (chm 1984–87), memb Cncl 1983–98 and 2001– (treas 1987–96), memb Bd BMA Services Ltd 1987–97, chm Community Care Ctee 1991–94, BMA Professional Services 1996–97, chm BMA Charities 2001–; treas Cwlth Med Assoc 1989–2001, chm Jt Professional Bd of Mgmnt Healthcall 1994–96, memb GMC 1994–99 (chm Assessment Referral Ctee); dir Silver Birch 1996–2007 (chm 1997–2003); assessor Scottish Community Fund 1996–, adviser Princess Royal Trust for Carers (Scotland); elder Church of Scotland; Gold Medallist BMA 1997; memb: Grand Antiquity 1967, N Parish Washing Green Soc 1967; Freeman Citizen of Glasgow 1961, memb Incorporation of Bonnetmakers and Dyers 1961; FRCGP 1983 (MRCGP 1966), FRCPGlas 1996; *Recreations* golf, gardening, hill walking; *Clubs* RSM; *Style—* Dr Alistair Riddell, OBE; ✉ 27 Upper Glenburn Road, Bearsden, Glasgow G61 4BN (tel 0141 942 0235, e-mail ajriddellsafraser@btinternet.com)

RIDDELL, Sir John Charles Buchanan; 13 Bt (NS 1628), of Riddell, Roxburghshire, CVO (1990), DL (Northumberland 1990); s of Sir Walter Riddell, 12 Bt (d 1934), and Hon Rachel Lyttelton, JP (d 1965) (yst da of 8 Viscount Cobham, JP, DL, and Hon Mary Cavendish, da of 2 Baron Chesham); *b* 3 January 1934; *Educ* Eton, ChCh Oxford (MA); *m* 1969, Hon Sarah, LVO (1993), da of Baron Richardson of Duntisbourne, KG, MBE, TD, PC (Life Peer), *qv*, sometime govr of Bank of England; 3 s (Walter John b 1974, Hugh Gordon b 1976, Robert Henry b 1982); *Heir* s, Walter Riddell; *Career* 2 Lt 2 KRRC; chartered accountant; banker; contested (Cons): Durham NW Feb 1974, Sunderland S Oct 1974; dir: UK Provident 1975–85, First Boston (Europe) Ltd 1975–78, Northumbrian Water Group plc 1992–97; chm: Govett Investment Trust 1995–2004, Northern Rock plc (formerly Northern Rock Building Soc) 2000–04 (dep chm 1992–99, dir 1981–85 and 1990–2004); dep chm: IBA 1981–85, Credit Suisse First Boston 1990–95 (dir 1978–85), Alpha Bank London Ltd 1995–2004; dir: MC BBL Securities Ltd 1995–99; sr advsr ING Barings; private sec and treas to TRH The Prince and Princess of Wales 1985–90, memb Prince's Cncl 1985–90; chm Northumbria Ctee National Trust 1995–2003; tstee: Guinness Tst Gp 1998–2000, Winston Churchill Meml Tst 1998–2007; HM Lord-Lt Northumberland 2000–; FRSA 1989; *Clubs* Garrick, Northern Countries; *Style—* Sir John Riddell, Bt, CVO, DL; ✉ Hepple, Morpeth, Northumberland

RIDDELL, Norman Malcolm Marshall; *b* 30 June 1947; *m*; 3 s; *Career* Royal Bank of Scotland plc: commercial banking 1965–69, investment mgmnt 1969–79; chief investment dir then md Britannia Gp of Investment Companies 1979–86, dir Charterhouse plc 1986–89, chief exec Capital House Investment Management Ltd 1986–93, dir INVESCO plc 1993–96; chm: United Overseas Gp plc 1997–99, Savoy Asset Management plc 1997–2000, Norman Riddell & Associates Ltd 1997–, IRML 2003–; dir: Life Assurance Holdings Corporation Ltd 1995–2004, AMIC Securities Ltd 1997–2005, Improvement Pathway 1999–2002, Clubhaus plc 1999–2004, Progressive Value Management Ltd 2000–, Progressive Special Situations Ltd 2000–, Pathway One VCT plc 2001–; MCIBS, AIIMR (AMSIA 1974); *Recreations* sports (spectator), travel, gardening, plate collecting, music, wine; *Clubs* Capital; *Style—* Norman Riddell, Esq; ✉ 68 King William Street, London EC4N 7DZ

RIDDELL, Peter John Robert; s of Kenneth Robert Riddell (d 1964), and Freda Riddell (d 2006); *b* 14 October 1948; *Educ* Dulwich Coll, Sidney Sussex Coll Cambridge (MA); *m* 23 July 1994, Avril, da of late Richard Hillier Walker; 1 da (Emily b 16 July 1996); *Career* FT: city staff 1970–72, property corr 1972–74, Lex columnist 1975–76, econ corr 1976–81, political ed 1981–88, US ed 1989–91; The Times: political columnist and commentator 1991–, political ed 1992–93, asst ed (politics) 1993–; regular appearances on radio and TV current affairs progs such as Week in Westminster; visiting prof of political history Queen Mary & Westfield Coll London 2000–03; chm Cncl Hansard Soc for Parly Govt 2007–, memb Bd Centre Contemporary Br History; Econ and Fin Journalist of the Year Wincott Awards 1981, Political Journalist of the Year 1985, Political Studies Assoc Political Columnist of the Year 2005; Hon DLitt Univ of Greenwich 2001; hon fell Sidney Sussex Coll Cambridge 2005, hon fell Political Studies Assoc 2007; FRHistS 1998; *Books* The Thatcher Government (1983, 2 edn 1985), The Thatcher Decade (1989, 2 edn as The Thatcher Era and Its Legacy, 1991), Honest Opportunism - the rise of the career politician (1993, 2 edn 1996), Parliament Under Pressure (1998, 2 edn as Parliament Under Blair 2000), Hug Them Close (2003, Channel 4 Political Book of the Year), The Unfulfilled Prime Minister (2005, 2 edn 2006); *Recreations* opera, theatre, watching cricket and baseball, reading; *Clubs* Garrick, Surrey CC, MCC; *Style—* Peter Riddell, Esq; ✉ The Times, 1 Pennington Street, London E1 9XN (tel 020 7782 5578, e-mail peter.riddell@the-times.co.uk)

RIDDICK, Graham Edward Galloway; s of John Julian Riddick (d 1997), and late Cecilia Margaret (d 1991), da of Sir Edward Ruggles-Brise, 1 Bt, MC, TD, MP for Maldon (Essex) 1922–42 (d 1942); *b* 26 August 1955; *Educ* Stowe, Univ of Warwick; *m* 1988, Sarah Northcroft; 1 s (George John Galloway b 5 Jan 1991), 2 da (Rosannah Cecilia Mary b 10 April 1993, Charlotte Louise b 3 Jan 1996); *Career* MP (Cons) Colne Valley 1987–97, PPS to Hon Francis Maude as Fin Sec to the Treasy 1990–92, PPS to John MacGregor as Sec of State for Tport 1992–94; memb: Educn Select Ctee 1994–95, Deregulation Select Ctee 1995–97, Educn and Employment Select Ctee 1996–97; former vice-chm Cons Back Bench Employment Ctee; former sec: All-Pty Wool Textile Parly Gp, Cons Back Bench Trade and Industry Ctee; memb CBI London Regnl Cncl 1999–2005; gp marketing and communications dir Onyx Environmental Gp plc 1997–2000, business devpt dir DeHavilland Info Services plc 2000–05, commercial dir Adfero Ltd 2005–; former memb Freedom Assoc Nat Cncl, former pres Yorks Cons Political Centre (CPC); *Recreations* shooting, fishing, tennis, squash, bridge, photography; *Style—* Graham Riddick, Esq; ✉ Adfero Ltd, 183 Marsh Wall, South Quay Plaza 2, London E14 9SH

RIDDING, Caroline; da of Graham Ridding, of Bolton, and Carol Ann, *née* Power; *b* 6 August 1970, Bolton; *Educ* Canon Slade Sch Bolton, Univ of Westminster (HND), Univ of Plymouth (BSc); *m* 31 Dec 2001, Matthew Lamprell; *Career* book buying mangr Tesco Stores Ltd 1999–2006, md Avon Books Harper Collins Publishers 2006–; *Style—* Miss Caroline Ridding; ✉ HarperCollins Publishers, 77–85 Fulham Palace Road, London W6 8JB (tel 020 8307 4659, e-mail caroline.ridding@harpercollins.co.uk)

RIDDING, John Joseph; *b* 25 June 1965; *Educ* Bedales, UC Oxford (BA); *m*; 1 c; *Career* journalist; Asia Pacific desk head Oxford Analytica 1996–97; Financial Times: Korea corr 1989–91, dep features ed 1991–93, Paris corr 1993–96, Hong Kong Bureau chief 1996–98, dep managing ed 1998–99, managing ed 1999–; *Style—* John Ridding, Esq; ✉ Financial Times, 1 Southwark Bridge, London SE1 9HL

RIDDLE, District Judge Howard Charles Frazer; s of Cecil Riddle (d 1987), of Sevenoaks, Kent, and Eithne, *née* McKenna (d 1997); *b* 13 August 1947; *Educ* Judd Sch Tonbridge, LSE (LLB); *m* 31 Aug 1974, (Susan) Hilary, da of Dr André Hurst (d 1992), of Ottawa, Canada; 2 da (Stephanie b 1979, Poppy b 1984); *Career* SSRC Canada 1971–76, sr ptnr Edward Fail Bradshaw & Waterson 1985–95; met stipendiary magistrate 1995–2000 (acting met stipendiary magistrate 1993–95), district judge (magistrates' court) 2000–, memb Sentencing Advsy Panel 2004–; vice-chm London Area Ctee Legal Aid Bd 1993–95; memb Law Soc 1969; *Recreations* rugby football, walking, tennis, cycling; *Clubs* Druidstone; *Style—* District Judge Riddle; ✉ Greenwich Magistrates Court, 9 Blackheath Road, London SE18 8PG (tel 020 8694 0033)

RIDDLE, Philip; s of Clifford Stanley Frederick Riddle, of Dunfermline, and Anne Munro, *née* Black; *b* 6 May 1952; *Educ* Dunfermline HS, Univ of Cambridge (MA), Univ of Edinburgh (MBA); *m* 10 Sept 1977, Catherine, da of Douglas Adams; 3 s (Cameron Alexander b 25 Jan 1983, Christopher David b 1 Oct 1984, Douglas Philip b 19 Dec 1988); *Career* mktg Shell UK 1977–80, oil products trader Shell Int 1980–82, head of oil and gas trading Brunei Shell 1982–85, business devpt mangr Shell Int 1985–88, area co-ordination Shell Int 1988–91, md Shell Namibia 1991–94, regnl devpt dir Shell South Africa 1994–95, vice-pres Shell LPG Europe 1995–99, chm Maximedia Ltd 2000–01, chief exec VisitScotland 2001–; former hon consul for The Netherlands Namibia; *Recreations* skiing, walking, reading, enjoying Scotland!; *Style—* Philip Riddle, Esq; ✉ VisitScotland, Ocean Point One, 94 Ocean Drive, Edinburgh EH6 6JH (tel 0131 472 2201, fax 0131 332 4441, e-mail philip.riddle@visitscotland.com)

RIDEL, David William; s of Maurice William Ridel, of Bournemouth, Dorset, and Violet Georgina, *née* Tull (d 1983); *b* 20 December 1947; *Educ* Forest GS Wokingham, Univ of Bristol (BA, BArch); *m* 23 Oct 1971, Felicity Laura, da of Rev Thomas Herbert Lewis; 2 s (Thomas William b 6 Jan 1976, Jack William b 7 Feb 1983), 1 da (Gemma Laura b 31 July 1977); *Career* architectural asst Marshall Macklin Monaghan Toronto Canada 1969–70, assoc architect Richard Lee Architect Bristol 1972–75, chief architect Community Housing Architects Team London 1975–79, chief exec Community Housing Assoc London 1979, sr architect YRM Architects London 1979–86, ptnr Building Design Partnership 1986–92, princ memb LSI architects LLP Norwich 1992–; corp memb RIBA 1974; govr Norwich Sch of Art & Design 1993–; *Recreations* skiing, ballet, opera, theatre; *Style—* David Ridel, Esq; ✉ LSI Architects, The Old Drill Hall, 23A Cattle Market Street, Norwich NR1 3DY (tel 01603 660711, fax 01603 623213, e-mail david.ridel@lsiarchitects.co.uk)

RIDEOUT, Prof Roger William; s of Sidney Rideout (d 1949), of Bromham, Beds, and Hilda Rose, *née* Davies (d 1985); *b* 9 January 1935; *Educ* UCL (LLB, PhD); *m* 1, 30 July 1960 (m dis 1976), Marjorie Roberts, da of Albert Roberts, of Bedford; 1 da (Tania Mary b 1965); m 2, 24 Aug 1977, Gillian Margaret, *née* Cooper (d 2005); *Career* Nat Serv Lt RAEC 1958–60; lectr: Univ of Sheffield 1960–63, Univ of Bristol 1963–64; called to the Bar Gray's Inn 1964; UCL: sr lectr 1964–65, reader in Eng law 1965–73, prof of labour law 1973–2000, dean of faculty 1975–77, vice-dean and dep head Dept of Law 1982–89, dir of res studies 1993–99, fell 1997; memb Phelps-Brown Ctee 1967–68, chm Industrial Law Soc 1977–80 (vice-pres 1983–), pt/t chm Employment Tbnls 1983–2003 (salaried 2003–07), dep chm Central Arbitration Ctee 1978–2003; ILO Missions to: Gambia 1981–83, Somalia 1990–91, Egypt 1992–94; fell Soc for Advanced Legal Studies (FSALS); *Books* Trade Unions and the Law (1973), Industrial Tribunal Law (1980), Principles of Labour Law (5 edn, 1989), Bromham in Bedfordshire: A History (2003); *Recreations* local history; *Style—* Prof Roger Rideout; ✉ 255 Chipstead Way, Woodmansterne, Surrey SM7 3JW (tel 01737 213489, fax 01737 219350, e-mail rw.rideout@ntlworld.com)

RIDER, Prof Barry Alexander Kenneth; s of Kenneth Leopold Rider, of Cambridge, and Alexina Elsie, *née* Bremner; *b* 30 May 1952; *Educ* Bexleyheath Boys' Secdy Modern Sch, Univ of London (LLB, PhD), Univ of Cambridge (MA, PhD); *m* 1 Aug 1976, Normalita Furto, da of Don Isidro Rosales; 1 da (Mei Ling Antionette b 14 Dec 1979); *Career* called to the Bar Inner Temple 1977; fell (now fell commoner) Jesus Coll Cambridge 1976–, lectr in law Univ of Cambridge 1978–96, prof of law Univ of London 1996–2004, dir Inst of Advanced Legal Studies Univ of London 1996–2004, prof of mercantile law Univ of the Free State South Africa 1998–, hon sr research fell Inst of Advanced Legal Studies Univ of London 2004–; conslt Beechcroft LLP 2004–06; head Commercial Crime Unit Cwlth Secretariat 1981–89, specialist advsr Trade and Industry Select Ctee House of Cmmns 1989–93; conslt to Islamic Financial Services Bd and former conslt to UN, UNDP, UNCTAD, WHO, IMF, World Bank, EU and CFTC; secondments to govts incl: Hong Kong, Singapore, Malaysia, Philippines, Barbados, Trinidad, South Africa, Zimbabwe, Mozambique, Zambia, India; visiting appts: Univ of Florida, Supreme People's Procuratorate Univ China, Univ of Hong Kong, Univ of Palermo; pres Br Inst of Securities Laws, exec dir Centre for Int Documentation on Organised and Economic Crime; int advsr: Centre for Criminology Univ of Hong Kong, Centre for Int Law and Policy New England Sch of Law, Faculty of Law Univ of Cyprus, Inst of Criminal Justice Beijing; chm: Hamlyn Tst 2001–04, Exec Ctee Soc of Advanced Legal Studies; gen ed of various jls incl: The Company Lawyer, Amicus Curiae, Jl of Financial Crime, International Jl of Disclosure and Governance, International and Comparative Corporate Law Jl; author, co-author and contrib to numerous books and works; Freeman City of London, memb Ct of Assts Worshipful Co of Pattenmakers (Warden 2005–07, Master 2007–); hon prof of laws Beijing Normal Univ 2006–, visiting prof Renmin Univ of China 2006–; Hon LLD: Penn State Univ, Univ of the Free State South Africa; hon fell Soc of Advanced Legal Studies; FRSA, FIPI; *Recreations* riding, historic buildings, war games, paranormal;

Clubs Oxford and Cambridge, Athenaeum, Civil Service; *Style—* Prof Barry Rider; ✉ Jesus College, Cambridge CB5 8BL (e-mail b.rider@jesus.cam.ac.uk)

RIDER, Steve; *Career* formerly: reporter and features writer Hayters, sports presenter and reporter LBC/IRM, sports ed Anglia TV, presenter and reporter Thames TV; presenter: Sportsnight (BBC) 1985–91, Grandstand (BBC) 1991–; current chief golf presenter BBC TV; presenter: Cwlth Games 1986, New Zealand 1990, Canada 1994 and Malaysia 1998 (BBC), Winter Olympics Calgary, Albertville, Lillehammer and Nagano (BBC), Olympic Games Moscow (ITV) 1980, Barcelona 1992 (BBC, Olympic Ctee Golden Rings Award, Sports Award RTS), Atlanta 1996 and Sydney 2000, Whitbread Round the World Race (BBC) 1997/98, Cricket World Cup (BBC) England 1999; presenter of several corp videos; host of several award ceremonies and press conferences; Sports Presenter of the Year TV and Radio Industries Club 1994, Sports Presenter of the Year RTS 1996; *Style—* Steve Rider, Esq; ✉ c/o Blackburn Sachs Associates, 2–4 Noel Street, London W1F 8GB (tel 020 7292 7555)

RIDGE, Rupert Leander Pattle; s of Maj Robert Vaughan Ridge (d 1987), of Brockley and Lacock, and Marian Ivy Edith, *née* Pattle (d 1977); *b* 18 May 1947; *Educ* King's Coll Taunton; *m* 1971, Mary Blanche, da of Maj Martin Gibbs (d 1994), of Chippenham, and Elsie Margaret Mary, *née* Hamilton Dalrymple; 4 c (Thomas Leander Pattle b 1972, Marian Sophia b 1973, Edward Francis b 1976, Adeline Dyce Albinia Rose b 1979); *Career* offr Light Infantry 1968–73, with British Aerospace Defence (formerly British Aircraft Corporation) 1973–94 (numerous roles mostly as commercial exec), int dir Leonard Cheshire International 1994–2004, advsr Motivation Charitable Tst 2004–; tstee Action around Bethlehem Children with Disability (ABCD) 1994–2005 (chm 1998–2005), tstee Wellspring Counselling 2004– (chm 2006–); former chm St Michael's Cheshire Home Axbridge; *Recreations* gardening and smallholding mgmnt; *Style—* Rupert Ridge, Esq; ✉ Motivation Charitable Trust, Brockley Academy, Brockley Lane, Backwell, Bristol BS48 4AQ (tel 01275 464012, fax 01275 464019, e-mail ridge@motivation.org.uk)

RIDGWAY, George; s of John George Ridgway (d 1988), of Leicester, and Constance Winifred, *née* Bruce (d 1980); *b* 16 October 1945; *Educ* Wyggeston Sch, Leicester Poly; *m* 20 June 1970, Mary, da of John Chamberlain; 2 c (Imogen Kate b 6 Nov 1973, Julian George b 14 March 1978); *Career* chartered accountant; fin dir Ridgway & Co (Leicester) Ltd (machine tool manufacturers) 1980–98, sr ptnr Pole Arnold Leics 1986–2002, md HLB AV Audit plc 2002–05, ptnr Numerica LLP 2002–05, client ptnr Vantis plc; pres Leics and Northants Soc of CAs 1990–91, memb Cncl ICAEW 1994–2002, chair Business Law Ctee ICAEW; chair Leicester Coll; chair Leics Wooden Spoon Soc; dir Leicester Comedy Festival; FCA, ACiM; *Style—* George Ridgway, Esq; ✉ Alma House, Station Road, Attleborough, Norfolk NR17 2AS (e-mail georgeridgeway@btinternet.com)

RIDGWAY, Judith Anne (Judy); da of Dr Leslie Randal Ridgway, of Eastbourne, E Sussex, and Lavinia, *née* Bottomley; *Educ* St Christopher Sch Letchworth, Keele Univ; *Career* former assoc dir Welbeck PR; cookery ed Woman's World Magazine 1984–90; freelance writer on: food, wine, cookery, catering, travel; int olive oil expert (author of EU papers on taste and flavour in olive oil 1993 and 2002); memb: Guild of Food Writers, Soc of Authors; Companion Guilde de Fromagers, Confrèrie de St Uguzon 1990, Judges Panel Leone d'Oro Awards Verona 1996, 1998, 1999, 2000 and 2002; *Books* The Vegetarian Gourmet (1979), Salad Days (1979), Home Preserving (1980), The Seafood Kitchen (1980), The Colour Book of Chocolate Cookery (1981), Mixer, Blender, Processor Cookery (1981), The Breville Book of Toasted Sandwiches (1982), Waitrose Book of Pasta, Rice and Pulses (1982), Making the Most of: Rice, Pasta, Potatoes, Bread, Cheese, Eggs (1983), The Little Lemon Book, The Little Rice Book, The Little Bean Book (1983), Barbecues (1983), Cooking with German Food (1983), Frying Tonight (1984), Sprouting Beans and Seeds (1984), Man in the Kitchen (jtly, 1984), Nuts and Cereals (1985), The Vegetable Year (1985), Wining and Dining at Home (1985), Wheat and Gluten-Free Cookery (1986), Vegetarian Wok Cookery (1986), Cheese and Cheese Cookery (1986), 101 Ways with Chicken Pieces (1987), Pocket Book of Oils, Vinegars and Seasonings (jtly, 1989), Carr's Connoisseurs Cheese Guide (1989), The Vitamin and Mineral Diet Cookbook (1990), Catering for a Wedding (1991), The Vegetarian Delights (1992), The Quick After Work Pasta Cookbook (1993), Food for Sport (1994), Quick After-Work Vegetarian Cookbook (1994), The Noodle Cookbook (1994), Clearly Delicious (jtly, 1994), Quick After Work Winter Vegetarian Cookbook (1996), The Olive Oil Companion (1997), The Cheese Companion (1999), Optimum Nutrition Cookbook (jtly, 1999), French Traditional Cheeses (2001), Judy Ridgway's Best Olive Oil Buys Round the World (2002 and 2005); wine: The Wine Lover's Record Book (1988), The Little Red Wine Book (1989), The Little White Wine Book (1989), Best Wine Buys in the High Street (1996), The Wine Tasting Class (1996), Best Wine Buys (1997); children's cookery: 101 Fun Foods to Make (1982), Cooking Round the World (1983), Festive Occasions (1986), Food and Cooking Round the World (jtly, 1986), Healthy Eating (jtly, 1990); how to books: Home Cooking for Money (1983), Running Your Own Wine Bar (1984), Successful Media Relations (1984), Running Your Own Catering Business (1993), Catering Management Handbook (jtly, 1994); *Recreations* opera, bridge, boating, cycling; *Style—* Ms Judy Ridgway; ✉ 5E Sussex Heights, St Margaret's Place, Brighton BN1 2FQ (tel 01273 733122, fax 01273 774177, e-mail jridgway@oliveoil.org.uk, website www.oliveoil.org.uk)

RIDING, Joanna; da of Alan Riding, of Longridge, Lancs, and Glenys Pauline, *née* Duxbury; *b* 9 November 1967; *Educ* Penwortham Girls HS, Blackpool & Fylde Coll of FE, Bristol Old Vic Theatre Sch; *Career* actress; spent three years whilst a student as solo and band vocalist; *Theatre* for Chichester incl: Dorothy in The Wizard of Oz, Anne in The Merry Wives of Windsor, Rosie in My Mother Said I Never Should; for RNT incl: Julie Jordan in Carousel, Anne Egerman in A Little Night Music, Sarah Brown in Guys and Dolls, Oh What a Lovely War; other credits incl: Happy as a Sandbag (Swan Worcester), Around the World in Eighty Days (Liverpool), Sally in Me and My Girl (Adelphi), Susie in Lady Be Good (Regents Park), The Picture of Dorian Day (Lyric Hammersmith and tour), Sarah Stone in No Way to Treat a Lady (Arts Theatre), Hey Mr Producer (Lyceum), Bertrande in Martin Guerre (Nat tour), Jane Smart in The Witches of Eastwick (Theatre Royal and Prince of Wales), Eliza Doolittle in My Fair Lady (Theatre Royal), Maggie Hobson in Hobson's Choice (Manchester Royal Exchange), Miss Gossage in The Happiest Days of our Life (Manchester Royal Exchange), Ruth in Blithe Spirit (Theatre Royal Bath and The Savoy London), Fenela in Playing for Time (Salisbury Playhouse); guest singer Jason Robert Brown concert (Players Theatre), own cabaret performance (Delfont Rooms and Prince of Wales), several musical workshops for new writers; cast album recordings of several shows; *Television* incl: Sean's Show (Channel X), The Brian Conley Show (LWT), Casualty (BBC), Strike Command (YTV), Wing and a Prayer (Thames), Holby City (BBC), The Royal (BBC), Midsomer Murders (ITV), Heart Beat (YTV), Terri in Where the Heart Is (YTV); *Radio* incl The Ruby in the Smoke (BBC7), The Shadow in the North (BBC7), Between Friends (BBC4), We (BBC4); *Awards* Olivier Award for Best Actress in a Musical for Carousel 1993, Olivier Award for Best Actress in a Musical for My Fair Lady 2003; nominated: Olivier Award for Best Actress in a Musical for Guys and Dolls 1997, Olivier Award for Best Actress in a Musical for The Witches of Eastwick 2001, Manchester Evening Standard Award for Best Actress, What's On Stage Award nomination for Best Actress for Blithe Spirit; *Recreations* music, reading, crosswords, keep fit; *Style—* Ms Joanna Riding

RIDING, (Frederick) Michael Peter; s of Frederick N Riding (d 2001), of Alton, Hants, and Elizabeth, *née* Lockwood (d 1999); *Educ* Barnard Castle Sch, Univ of Leeds (BA); *m* 31 May 2003, Ellie; 1 da, 2 s from previous m (Victoria b 10 Jan 1970, George b 20 Dec 1971, Samuel b 21 Feb 1973); *Career* sr vice-pres Asia Chemical Bank NY 1980–83; Lloyds Bank plc: princ mangr Far E Div Lloyds Bank International Ltd 1984–85, gen mangr Asia 1985–87, gen mangr trade finance 1987–89, gen mangr UK retail banking 1989–91, gen mangr commercial banking 1991–95, dir of commercial banking 1996–97, md Commercial Financial Servs 1997–99, md Corp Banking 2000–03, md Wholesale Banking 2004–; dir: Home Entertainment Corp plc 2004–, N Bristol NHS Tst 2004–; FCIB 1991; *Recreations* golf, theatre, art, opera; *Clubs* RAC, Royal Lytham St Anne's Golf, Weston-super-Mare Golf; *Style—* Michael Riding, Esq; ✉ Lloyds TSB Group plc, 25 Gresham Street, London EC2V 7HN (tel 020 7356 2218)

RIDING, Robert Furniss; s of William Furniss Riding, FCA (d 1985), of Manchester, and Winifred, *née* Coupe (d 1993); *b* 5 May 1940; *Educ* Stockport GS, ChCh Oxford (MA); *Career* dir and later chm Nat Commercial Devpt Capital Ltd 1980–85, gen mangr Williams & Glyn's Bank plc 1982–85, treas and gen mangr The Royal Bank of Scotland plc 1985–86, dep chm and chief exec RoyScot Finance Gp plc 1986–90; chm: RoyScot Tst plc 1984–90, Royal Bank Leasing Ltd 1986–90, RoyScot Vehicle Contracts Ltd 1986–90, RoyScot Factors Ltd 1986–90, RoyScot Finance Services Ltd 1988–90, Conister Tst plc (IOM) 1992–2002 (dir 1991–2002), IOM Int Broadcasting plc 2004–05; non-exec dir: Int Commodities Clearing House Ltd 1985–86, Royal Bank of Scotland AG (Switzerland) 1985–86, Direct Line Insurance plc 1986–88, Royal Bank Gp Services Ltd 1987–90, A T Mays Gp plc 1988–90, Commercial Finance Ltd (IOM) 1992–2002, Rycroft Finance & Leasing Ltd (IOM) 1996–2001, The With Profits Plus Fund plc (IOM) 1996–, IOM Int Business Sch 2000–; memb: Exec Ctee Assoc of Manx Bankers 1993–99 (pres 1997–99), Exec Ctee IOM Centre IOD 1994–2003 (chm 1999–2003), Cncl IOD 1999–2003; tstee Seamanship Fndn 1990–96, tstee Island Tst 2000–, tstee and former chm Assoc of Sea Trg Orgns 1981–; hon life memb RYA (memb Cncl 1983–99, chm of trg 1984–89, hon treas 1994–99); memb Sodor and Man Diocesan Synod 1997–2003 and 2005–07; chm Friends of St German's Cathedral 1996–2006; FCIB 1976; *Recreations* sailing, motoring; *Clubs* Island Cruising (vice-pres, cdre 1988–90), Manx Motor Racing (chm 1999–), Manx Classic Car (pres 2005–), Rolls-Royce Enthusiasts', Bentley Drivers', Westfield Sports Car; *Style—* Robert Riding, Esq; ✉ Ballakeil House, Smeale, Isle of Man IM7 3EQ (tel 01624 880151, fax 01624 880834); Ashley House, Derbyhaven, Isle of Man IM9 1TZ (tel 01624 822587); Middlewood, Old Banwell Road, Locking, North Somerset BS24 8BT (tel 01934 822587)

RIDLEY, Sir Adam Nicholas; kt (1985); s of Jasper Ridley (s of Maj Hon Sir Jasper Ridley, KCVO, OBE, 2 s of 1 Viscount Ridley, by the Maj's w Countess Nathalie, da of Count Benckendorff, sometime Russian ambass in London) and Cressida Bonham Carter (d 1998) (da of Baroness Asquith of Yarnbury and gda of H H Asquith the Lib PM); nephew by marriage of Baron Grimond, TD, PC, of Firth, Co Orkney; *b* 14 May 1942; *Educ* Eton, Balliol Coll Oxford, Univ of Calif Berkeley; *m* 1, 1970 (m dis), Lady Katharine Rose Celestine Asquith, 2 da of 2 Earl of Oxford and Asquith; m 2, 1981, Margaret Anne (Biddy), da of Frederic Passmore, of Virginia Water, Surrey; 3 s (Jasper, Luke (twins) b 29 May 1987, Jo b 16 Aug 1988); *Career* Dept of Economic Affairs 1965–69, HM Treasy 1970–71, Central Policy Review Staff 1971–74; former econ advsr and asst dir CRD, dir CRD 1979 election campaign; special advsr: to the Chllr of the Exchequer 1979–84, to Chllr of the Duchy of Lancaster; min in charge of the Office of Arts and Libraries (also mangr Personnel Office) 1985; memb EC Expert Gp on Economic and Social Concepts in the Community 1976–79; exec dir Hambros Bank Ltd and Hambros plc 1985–97, chm of tstees Equitas Gp of Cos 1996–; DG London Investment Banking Assoc 2000–05; Lloyd's of London: chm Names Ctee 1994–95, dep chm Assoc of Lloyd's Membs 1995– (memb Bd 1990–), memb Cncl Lloyd's and memb Lloyd's Regulatory Bd 1997–99; memb Bd: Sunday Newspaper Publishing plc 1989, Leopold Joseph plc 1998–2004; dep chm Nat Lottery Charities Bd 1995–99, non-exec dir Morgan Stanley Bank Int Ltd 2006–; tstee St Christopher's Hospice 1987–; *Style—* Sir Adam Ridley; ✉ c/o Equitas Trust, 8th Floor Peninsular House, 36 Monument Street, London EC3R 8LJ

RIDLEY, Prof Brian Kidd; s of Oliver Archbold Ridley (d 1990), and Lillian Beatrice, *née* Dunn (d 1965); *b* 2 March 1931; *Educ* Yorebridge GS, Gateshead GS, Univ of Durham (BSc, PhD); *m* 16 May 1959, Sylvia Jean, da of Walter Reginald Nicholls; 1 s (Aaron Max b 31 July 1962), 1 da (Melissa Sophie b 3 Sept 1965); *Career* research appt Mullard Research Lab Redhill 1956–64; Dept of Physics Univ of Essex: lectr 1964–67, sr lectr 1967–71, reader 1971–84, prof 1984–90, research prof 1990–; visiting appt RRE Malvern 1966; distinguished visiting prof Cornell Univ 1967; visiting prof: Stanford Univ 1967, Danish Tech Univ 1969, Princeton Univ 1973, Cornell Univ 1976 and 1990–, Univ of Lund 1977, Univ of Santa Barbara 1981, Eindoven Tech Univ 1983; memb Exec Bd of Jl of Physics: Condensed Matter 2000–03; various consultancy appts; awarded Paul Dirac Medal and Prize Inst of Physics 2001; memb American Physical Soc 1992; FInstP 1972, FRS 1994; *Books* Time, Space and Things (1976, 3 edn, 1995), The Physical Environment (1979), Quantum Processes in Semiconductors (1982, 4 edn, 1999), Electrons and Phonons in Semiconductor Multilayers (1997), On Science (2001); *Recreations* piano, tennis; *Style—* Prof Brian Ridley, FRS; ✉ Department of Electronic Systems Engineering, University of Essex, Colchester, Essex CO4 3SQ (tel 01206 873333)

RIDLEY, Prof Frederick Fernand; OBE (1978); *b* 11 August 1928; *Educ* The Hall Hampstead, Highgate Sch, LSE (BSc, PhD), Univ of Paris, Univ of Berlin; *m* 1967, Paula Frances Cooper Ridley, OBE, DL, *qv*; 2 s, 1 da; *Career* Univ of Liverpool: lectr 1958–65, prof of political theory and instns 1965–95, sr fell Inst of Public Admin & Mgmnt 1995–2006; visiting prof: Graduate Sch of Public Affairs Univ of Pittsburgh 1968, Coll of Europe Bruges 1975–83; chm: Job Creation Prog Manpower Servs Cmmn Merseyside 1975–77, Area Manpower Bd 1987–88 (vice-chm 1978–87); memb: Jt Univ Cncl for Social and Public Admin 1964– (chm 1972–74), Exec Political Studies Assoc 1967–75 (hon vice-pres 1995–), Cncl Hansard Soc 1970–94, Political Sci Ctee SSRC 1972–76, Ctee Euro Gp on Public Admin 1973–92, Public and Social Admin Bd CNAA 1975–82, Res Advsy Gp Arts Cncl 1979–82, Exec Merseyside Arts (Regnl Arts Assoc) 1979–84, Social Studies Res Ctee CNAA 1980–83 (chm), Advsy Cncl Granada Fndn 1984–98; vice-pres: Rencontres Européennes des Fonctions Publiques 1990–94, Acad Cncl Forschungsinst für Verwaltungswissenschaft Speyer 1992–2005, Entretiens pour l'Admin Publique en Europe 1994–2000; tstee Friends of Merseyside Museums and Galleries 1977–85; hon pres Politics Assoc 1976–81 (hon fell 1995–); ed: Political Studies 1969–75, Parliamentary Affairs 1975–2004; *Publications* numerous books and articles on political science and public admin; *Style—* Prof Frederick Ridley; ✉ 24 North Road, Grassendale Park, Liverpool L19 0LR (tel 0151 427 1630, fax 0151 494 1828)

RIDLEY, Ian Robert; s of Robert Edwin Ridley, of Weymouth, Dorset, and Barbara, *née* Fullbrook; *b* 23 January 1955; *Educ* Hardye's Sch Dorchester Dorset, Bedford Coll London (BA); *m* 22 Oct 1977, Josephine Anne, da of Gerald Leighton; 1 s (Jack William b 6 April 1990), 1 da (Alexandra Judith b 12 Feb 1986); *Career* editorial asst Building Magazine 1976, sports ed Worksop Guardian 1977–79, sports sub ed and reporter Evening Post Echo Hemel Hempstead 1979–80; The Guardian: sports sub ed 1980–85, asst sports ed 1985–87, dep sports ed 1987–88, sports writer 1988–90; sports feature writer The Daily Telegraph 1990–93, freelance writer and journalist 1993–94, football corr The Independent on Sunday 1994–98, football columnist The Observer 1998–; memb: NUJ, Football Writers' Assoc, SWA, Assoc Internationale de Presse Sportive; *Books* Season in the Cold: A journey through English football, Cantona: The Red and the Black, Tales from the Boot Camps (with Steve Claridge), Addicted (with Tony Adams, 1998), Hero and Villain (with Paul Merson, 1999), Floodlit Dreams: How to Save a Football Club (2006); *Style*— Ian Ridley, Esq

RIDLEY, Malcolm James; s of Eric Malcolm Thomas Ridley (d 1972), and Pauline Esther (d 1972); *b* 10 March 1941; *Educ* Trinity Sch Croydon, Univ of Bristol (LLB); *m* 1, 14 July 1962 (m dis 1976), Joan Margaret, da of Stanley Charles Martin (d 2001); 2 da (Camilla b 1970, Estelle b 1972); m 2, 9 April 1977, Bridget Mina, da of Dr Charles Edward O'Keeffe (d 1963); 1 da (Susannah b 1977), 1 s (John b 1979); *Career* chartered accountant; Price Waterhouse Vancouver 1962–68, Price Waterhouse London 1974–79, ptnr Coopers & Lybrand London 1981–96 (joined 1979), sole practitioner 1996–; CA Canada 1966, FCA 1980, ATII 1974; *Recreations* cricket, golf, tennis, bridge, theatre, opera; *Clubs* MCC, Walton Heath Golf; *Style*— Malcolm Ridley, Esq; ✉ Moor Lodge, Horsham Road, Holmwood, Dorking, Surrey RH5 4NA (tel 01306 889594); office (tel 01306 741457, fax 01306 741458, e-mail mjr@moorlodge10.freeserve.co.uk)

RIDLEY, Dr Matthew White (Matt); s and h of 4 Viscount Ridley, KG, GCVO, TD , *qv*; *b* 7 February 1958; *Educ* Eton, Magdalen Coll Oxford (DPhil); *m* 16 Dec 1989, Dr Anya Christine Hurlbert, da of Dr Robert Hurlbert, of Houston, TX; 1 s (Matthew White b 27 Sept 1993), 1 da (Iris Livia b 16 June 1997); *Career* author and businessman; The Economist: sci ed 1984–87, Washington corr 1987–89, American ed 1990–92; chm: Int Centre for Life 1996–2003, Northern 2 Venture Capital Tst 1999–, Northern Rock plc 2004–; dir: Northern Investors plc, P A Holdings; FRSL, FMedSci; *Books* Warts and All (1989), The Red Queen (1993), The Origins of Virtue (1996), Genome (1999), Nature via Nurture (2003), Francis Crick (2006); *Style*— Dr Matt Ridley; ✉ Blagdon, Seaton Burn, Newcastle upon Tyne NE13 6DD

RIDLEY, 4 Viscount (UK 1900); Sir Matthew White Ridley; 8 Bt (GB 1756), KG (1992), GCVO (1994), TD, JP (1957); also Baron Wensleydale (UK 1900); s of 3 Viscount Ridley, CBE (d 1964), and Ursula, OBE, 2 da of Sir Edwin Lutyens, OM, KCIE, the architect, by Sir Edwin's w Lady Emily Lytton (da of 1 Earl of Lytton, GCB, GCSI, CIE, PC, sometime Viceroy of India and s of the novelist Bulwer Lytton, cr Baron Lytton); *b* 29 July 1925; *Educ* Eton, Balliol Coll Oxford (BA); *m* 3 Jan 1953, Lady Anne Katherine Lumley, da of 11 Earl of Scarbrough, KG, GCSI, GCIE, GCVO, PC; 1 s, 3 da; *Heir* s, (Hon) Dr Matt Ridley, *qv*; *Career* served Coldstream Gds (NW Europe) 1943–46, served Northumberland Hussars 1947–64, Lt-Col TA, Bt-Col, Hon Col Northumberland Hussars Sqdn Queen's Own Yeo RAC TA, Col Cmdt Yeo RAC TA 1982–86; chm Northumberland CC 1967–79, pres Assoc of CCs 1979–84, chllr Univ of Newcastle upon Tyne 1989–99; Lord Steward of HM's Household 1989–2001; chm Northern Rock Building Soc 1988–93; memb Layfield Ctee 1974–76; HM Lord-Lt Northumberland 1984–2000 (DL 1968); chm N of England TA&VRA 1980–84; pres Cncl of TAVRAS 1984–89; Hon DCL Univ of Newcastle upon Tyne 1989; hon fell: ARICS, Newcastle Poly; Order of Merit (W Germany), KStJ 1984; *Recreations* dendrology, fishing; *Clubs* Boodle's, Pratt's; *Style*— Col the Rt Hon the Viscount Ridley, KG, GCVO, TD; ✉ Boston House, Blagdon, Seaton Burn, Newcastle upon Tyne NE13 6DB

RIDLEY, (Robert) Michael; s of M R Ridley (d 1969), and J E L, *née* Carlisle (d 2000); *b* 8 January 1947; *Educ* Clifton, St Edmund Hall Oxford (MA, CertEd, Cricket blue); *m* 28 Dec 1985, Jennifer M, *née* Pearson; 2 da (Katie b 4 June 1989, Vickie b 14 Nov 1990); *Career* teacher and housemaster Wellington Coll 1970–82, teacher (on exchange) Sydney C of E GS 1974, head of English Merchiston Castle Sch Edinburgh 1982–86, headmaster Denstone Coll 1986–90, princ Royal Belfast Academical Instn 1990–2006; HMC: memb 1986, chm Irish Div 2001, memb Membership Ctee 2001–06; played cricket for Ireland 1968, vice-capt Oxford Univ Cricket Club 1970; *Recreations* golf, walking, theatre, reading; *Clubs* Royal Co Down Golf, Boat of Garten Golf, Ulster Reform; *Style*— Michael Ridley, Esq; ✉ 2 Shelling Ridge, Ravarnet, Lisburn BT27 5DW (tel 028 9266 2048)

RIDLEY, Michael Kershaw; KCVO (2000, CVO, 1992); s of late George K and Mary Ridley, of Eccleston, Chester; *b* 7 December 1937; *Educ* Stowe, Magdalene Coll Cambridge (MA); *m* 1968, Diana Loraine, da of Roy A McLernon, of Knowlton, Quebec; *Career* Grosvenor Estate: Canada and US 1965–68, London 1969–72; property mangr British and Commonwealth Shipping Co 1972–81, clerk of the Cncl Duchy of Lancaster 1981–2000; memb Advsy Panel Greenwich Hosp 1978–2002; memb Ct Lancaster Univ 1981–2000; pres Assoc of Lancastrians in London 2000–01; chm Royal Borough of Kensington and Chelsea Standards Ctee 2001–06; tstee Feathers Clubs Assoc; FRICS; *Recreations* reading, golf, walking; *Clubs* Brooks's, Garrick, Royal Mid-Surrey (Golf); *Style*— Sir Michael K Ridley, KCVO; ✉ 37 Chester Row, London SW1W 9JE

RIDLEY, Paula Frances Cooper; OBE (1996), JP (Liverpool City 1977), DL (Merseyside 1989); da of Ondrej Clyne, and Ellen, *née* Cooper; *b* 27 September 1944; *Educ* Greenhead HS Huddersfield, Kendal HS Westmorland, Univ of Liverpool (MA); *m* 21 Jan 1967, Prof Frederick Fernand Ridley, OBE, *qv*; 2 s (Joseph Francis b 12 July 1970, Dominic Andrew b 29 Sept 1974), 1 da (Caroline Rachel b 3 April 1976); *Career* lectr in politics and public admin Liverpool Poly 1966–72; project coordinator Regeneration Projects Ltd 1981–84, conslt BAT Industries Small Business 1983–95, dir Community Initiatives Res Tst 1983–90, memb Bd Brunswick Small Business Centre Ltd 1984–95, assoc CEI Consultants 1984–88, presenter and assoc ed Helpful Productions ind TV prodn co 1989–92; chm: Liverpool Housing Action Tst 1992–2007, V&A 1998–; dir Calouste Gulbenkian Fndn (UK branch) 1999–2007; memb: Bd Merseyside Development Corp 1991–98, IBA 1982–88, Royal Cmmn on Long Term Care of the Elderly 1998–99; tstee: Tate Gallery 1988–98 (chm Tate Gallery Liverpool 1988–98), Granada Telethon Tst 1988–94, National Gallery 1995–98; memb Ct Univ of Liverpool 1972– (memb Cncl 1998–), chm Merseyside Civic Soc 1986–91, life govr Liverpool and Huyton Colls 1979–94; hon fell Liverpool John Moores Univ 2002, Hon LLD Univ of Liverpool 2003; FRSA, Hon FRIBA 2005; *Publications* author of articles in various professional jls; *Recreations* art, architecture and heritage; *Style*— Mrs Paula Ridley, OBE, DL; ✉ 24 North Road, Grassendale Park, Liverpool L19 0LR (tel 0151 427 1630); 69 Thomas More House, Barbican, London EC2Y 8BT

RIDLEY, Prof Tony Melville; CBE (1986); s of John Edward Ridley (d 1982), and Olive, *née* Armstrong (d 1997); *b* 10 November 1933; *Educ* Durham Sch, King's Coll Durham (BSc), Northwestern Univ Illinois (MS), Univ of Calif Berkeley (PhD); *m* 20 June 1959, Jane, da of John William Dickinson (d 1984); 1 da (Sarah b 1962), 2 s (Jonathan b 1963, Michael b 1966); *Career* Nuclear Power Gp 1957–62, GLC 1965–69, DG Tyne & Wear Passenger Tport Exec 1969–75, md Hong Kong Mass Transit Railway Corp 1975–80, memb Bd London Regnl Tport (formerly London Tport Exec) 1980–88 (md Railways 1980–85), chm London Underground Ltd 1985–88; dir: Docklands Light Railway 1982–88 (chm 1987–88), London Tport International 1981–88 (chm 1982–87); md Eurotunnel 1989–90 (non-exec dir 1987–90); Imperial College London: prof of tport engrg 1991–99, head of Dept of Civil and Environmental Engrg 1997–99, emeritus prof of tport engrg 1999–; dir Univ of London Centre for Tport Studies 1994–95, sr tport advsr London 2012 Olympic Bid 2004–05; pres Light Rail Transit Assoc 1974–92; memb: Senate Engrg Cncl 1997–2000 (chm Bd for Engrg Profession 1997–99), Taskforce 10 (Science Technol and Innovation) UN Millennium Project 2002–05; pres: Assoc for Project Mgmnt 1999–2003, Commonwealth Engineers Cncl 2000–, Exec Cncl World Fedn of Engrg Orgns 2000–; int pres CILT 1999–2001; tstee RAC Fndn for Motoring 1999– (memb Public Policy Ctee 1997–); chm Building Schs for the Future Investments LLP (BSFI) 2007–; first recipient Highways Award of Inst of Highways and Transportation 1988, first recipient Herbert Crow Award Worshipful Co of Carmen 2001, President's Award Engrg Cncl 2002; Freeman City of London 1982, Liveryman Worshipful Co of Carmen 1982; Hon DTech Napier Univ 1996, Hon DEng Univ of Newcastle upon Tyne 1997; hon fell Worshipful Co of Paviors 2006–; FICE (pres 1995–96, memb Cncl 1990–97), FCILT, FIHT, fell Hong Kong Inst of Engineers, fell Inst of Transportation Engrs, FRSA, FREng 1992, FCGI 1995, FAPM 1996, Hon FIA 1999; *Publications* articles in transport, engineering and other journals; *Recreations* theatre, music, international affairs; *Clubs* RAC, Hong Kong, Hong Kong Jockey; *Style*— Prof Tony M Ridley, CBE, FREng; ✉ Orchard Lodge, Stichens Green, Streatley, Berkshire RG8 9SU (tel 01491 871075)

RIDLEY-THOMAS, Roger; s of John Montague Ridley-Thomas (d 1973), of Norwich, and Christina Anne, *née* Seex (d 1976); *b* 14 July 1939; *Educ* Gresham's; *m* 1962, Sandra Grace McBeth, da of William Morrison Young, OBE; 2 s (Christopher b 1964, Simon b 1966), 2 da (Philippa b 1970, Sarah b 1972); *Career* Royal Norfolk Regt 1958–60; newspaper publishing; Eastern Counties Newspapers Ltd 1960–65; advertisement mgmnt: Middlesbrough Evening Gazette 1965–67, Western Mail and Echo Ltd 1968–70, Newcastle Chronicle and Journal Ltd 1970–72; asst md The Scotsman Publications Ltd 1972–80; md: Aberdeen Journals Ltd 1980–84, The Scotsman Publications Ltd 1984–89, Thomson Regnl Newspapers Ltd 1989–94; chm and dir Thomson Free Newspapers Ltd 1989–94; dir: Radio Forth Ltd 1978–81, Aberdeen Journals Ltd 1980–84 and 1990–94, Aberdeen C of C 1981–84, Scottish Business in the Community 1984–90, The Scotsman Publications Ltd 1984–94, The Scotsman Communications Ltd 1984–94, Thomson Regional Newspapers Ltd 1985–94, Scottish Business Achievement Award Tst Ltd 1985–2003, Edinburgh C of C and Mfrs 1985–88, Regnl Daily Advertising Cncl 1989–93, Belfast Telegraph Newspapers Ltd 1990–94, Western Mail & Echo Ltd 1990–94, Chester Chronicle Ltd 1990–94, Newcastle Chronicle & Journal Ltd 1990–94, Thames Valley Newspapers Ltd 1990–94, Cardrona Ltd 1995–, Milex Ltd 1996–; chm: Anglia FM Ltd 1996–98, The Adscene Group plc 1996–99, Norcor Holdings plc 1996–2000, Roys (Wroxham) Ltd 1997–, Norfolk Christmas Trees Ltd 2000–; pres Scottish Daily Newspaper Soc 1983–85; cncl memb: CBI 1983–86, Scottish Wildlife Appeal Ctee 1985–88; *Recreations* vegetable growing, shooting, fishing, golf, tennis, travel; *Clubs* New (Edinburgh); *Style*— Roger Ridley-Thomas, Esq

RIDPATH, Michael William Gerrans; s of Andrew Ridpath (d 2005), of Bircham, Norfolk, and Elizabeth, *née* Hinds Howell (d 1999); *b* 7 March 1961; *Educ* Millfield, Merton Coll Oxford (exhibitioner, BA); *m* 1, 1985, Candy Ann Helman (d 1992); 2 da (Julia b 17 Feb 1990, Laura b 30 Dec 1992); m 2, 1994, Barbara Ann, da of James P Nunemaker (d 1999); 1 s (Nicholas b 19 May 1997); *Career* writer; trader Saudi Int Bank 1982–91, venture capitalist Apax Partners & Co 1991–94; author 1994–; treas Royal Literary Fund 1999; memb: Soc of Authors 1995, Crime Writers' Assoc 1995; *Books* Free to Trade (1995), Trading Reality (1996), The Marketmaker (1998), Final Venture (2000), The Predator (2001), Fatal Error (2003), On the Edge (2005), See No Evil (2006); *Style*— Michael Ridpath, Esq; ✉ c/o Carole Blake, Blake Friedman Literary Agency Ltd, 122 Arlington Road, London NW1 7HP (tel 020 7284 0408, e-mail mail@michaelridpath.com, website www.michaelridpath.com)

RIDSDALE, (Robert) Peter; s of Arthur Ridsdale (d 1985), and Audrey Gwendoline, *née* Oakley (d 1974); *b* 11 March 1952; *Educ* Leeds Modern GS; *m* 1 (m dis), Shirley Ruth; 2 s (Simon Nicholas b 5 Sept 1976, Paul Anthony b 30 Jan 1979); m 2 (m dis), Jacqueline; 2 s (Matthew Peter b 30 Jan 1985, Joseph Michael b 23 May 1988); m 3, 22 April 1995, Sophie Victoria, *née* Hobhouse; 2 da (Charlotte Louise b 13 May 1996, Olivia Rose b 26 Dec 1997); *Career* personnel offr Appleyard of Leeds 1969–72, personnel mangr Baker Perkins 1972–78, industrial rels mangr ICL 1978–81, vice-pres HR International Div Schering Plough Corp 1981–85, md Top Man then md Evans Ltd Burton Group plc 1985–91, jt chief operating offr Alexon Group plc 1991–93, chief exec QVC - The Shopping Channel 1993–94, gp md then chief exec The Tulchan Group Ltd 1994–2000; chm: Leeds United FC 1997–2003 (former dir), Leeds United plc (parent co of Leeds United FC) 1998–2003, Education Leeds 2001–04, NSC Technology Group plc 2001–03, Motor Solutions Ltd 2001–03, Cardiff City Football Club Holdings 2005–, Cardiff City Football Club Ltd 2005–; non-exec dir: Fii plc 1997–2003, Ideal Shopping Direct plc 2000–01, Sports Card plc 2000–01; FInstD, memb Mktg Soc; *Style*— Peter Ridsdale, Esq

RIEDL, Martin Paul; s of Kurt Riedl, and Ruth, *née* Schechner; *b* 12 September 1949; *Educ* Sutton Valence, Ealing Sch of Photography (Dip Photography); *m* 1, 18 April 1980 (m dis 1990), Patricia Kilbourn, *née* Dumond; 2 s (Alexander David b 17 Nov 1981, Arthur Jonathan b 15 June 1983); m 2, 7 June 2002, Annie Bronwen, da of Edward Augustus Williams; 1 s (Harry Edward b 11 Sept 1990); *Career* photographer; asst to: Robert Dowling 1973–75, Derek Coutts 1975–77; freelance photographer 1978–, opened own studio 1979–; fndr Film in Educn film prodn co 2004; Chalk and Water (photography exhbn, Chichester Festival Theatre) 2006; awarded two merits and two silvers Assoc of Photographers, D & AD silver nomination, second place Polaroid European Final Art Awards, prizewinner London Photographic Awards; memb Assoc of Photographers 1976; *Recreations* sculpture, skiing, badminton, tennis; *Clubs* Chelsea Arts, Cobden; *Style*— Martin Riedl, Esq; ✉ Martin Riedl Photography, 3 Water Lane, London NW1 8NZ (tel 020 7428 9262, fax 020 7482 1822, e-mail mriedl@easynet.co.uk, website www.martinriedl.co.uk); Film in Education (e-mail info@filmineducation.com, website www.filmineducation.com)

RIFFAT, Prof Saffa; *Educ* Univ of Oxford (DPhil, DSc); *m*; *Career* sr research fell Univ of Westminster 1986–88, lectr and reader Loughborough Univ of Technol 1988–92; Univ of Nottingham: British Gas prof of architectural technol and energy 1992–97, head Sch of the Built Environment 1996–, ICI prof of refrigeration technol 1998–2002, Baxi prof of sustainable energy systems 2002–, dir Inst of Bldg Technol, dir Inst of Sustainable Energy Technol (ISET); hon prof: Chongqing Univ, Dalian Univ of Technol; delivered keynote speeches at confs worldwide, author of over 350 papers for refereed jls and int confs; over 20 inventions related to heating, ventilation, power generation, lighting, heat recovery, refrigeration, air conditioning and renewable energy, currently desiging and raising funds for Nottingham Eco-Village (world's first eco-village driven by hydrogen); awarded Technol Transfer Fellowship; fndr memb Midlands Renewable Energy Technol Transfer (MRETT); memb Advsy Bd: Baxi Technologies, Premas International, MRETT, David Wilson Homes; CEng, FIMechE, FCIBSE, FInstE; *Style*— Prof Saffa Riffat; ✉ School of the Built Environment, University of Nottingham, Nottingham NG7 2RD

RIFKIND, Rt Hon Sir Malcolm Leslie; KCMG (1997), PC (1986), QC (Scot 1985), MP; s of Elijah Rifkind, of Edinburgh; *b* 21 June 1946; *Educ* George Watson's Coll Edinburgh, Univ of Edinburgh (LLB, MSc); *m* 1970, Edith Amalia, *née* Steinberg; 1 s, 1 da; *Career* advocate, called to the Bar Edinburgh 1970; MP (Cons): Edinburgh Pentlands Feb 1974–97, Kensington and Chelsea 2005– (Parly candidate Edinburgh Central 1970); memb Select Ctee Euro Secdy Legislation 1975–76, oppn front bench spokesman on Scottish affrs 1975–76, jt sec Cons Foreign and Cwlth Affrs Ctee 1978, memb Select Ctee on Overseas Devpt 1978–79, Parly under sec of state Scottish Office 1979–82, Parly under sec of state FCO 1982–83, min of state FCO 1983–86, sec of state for Scotland 1986–90, sec of state for transport 1990–92, sec of state for defence 1992–95, sec of state for foreign and Cwlth affrs 1995–97, shadow sec of state for work and pensions 2005; non-exec chm Armourgroup Int plc 2004–, non-exec dir Aberdeen Asset Mgmnt plc 2000–, conslt BHP Billiton Petroleum; memb Queen's Body Guard for Scotland (Royal Co of Archers) 1993–; Hon Col: 162 Movement Control Regt Royal Logistics Corps 1996–2005, City of Edinburgh Univs OTC; *Recreations* walking, reading, field sports; *Style*— The Rt Hon Sir Malcolm Rifkind, KCMG, QC, MP; ✉ House of Commons, London SW1A 0AA

RIGBY, Alfred; s of Robert Marsden Rigby (d 1984), of Freckleton, Lancs, and Betsy Alice, *née* Bownass (d 1980); *b* 18 June 1934; *Educ* Kirkham GS, Univ of Manchester (BA, MA), Univ of London (DipTP), British Sch Rome (RS); *m* 1, 1958, Ann Patricia (d 1998), da of Maj George Flynn, MBE, MC (d 1978), of Bucks; 1 s (Christopher Simon b 1961), 1 da (Susan Elizabeth b 1964); m 2, 1999, Shirley Anne, da of Thomas Harvey Simpson (d 1985), of Cheshire; *Career* dep regnl architect NW Metropolitan RHB 1960–64, chief architect City of Westminster 1964–73 (2 Civic Tst awards), dir of architecture London Borough of Camden 1973–79 (3 Civic Tst awards), sr ptnr John R Harris Partnership (conversion of Dorchester Hotel, rehabilitation of HM Prison Strangeways) 1986–93, Rigby Culpin Partnership 1993–98; patron Bath FC (RFU); memb Cons Pty; FRIBA, FIMgt, FRSA, RTPI; *Books* Sir Banister Fletcher: A History of Architecture on the Comparative Method (contrib 1963 edn); *Recreations* painting, cricket, rugby, opera, theatre; *Clubs* MCC, Athenaeum; *Style*— Alfred Rigby, Esq; ✉ 5 Clattergrove, Painswick, Gloucestershire GL6 6ST

RIGBY, Sir Anthony John; 3 Bt (UK 1929), of Long Durford, Rogate, Co Sussex; s of Sir John Rigby, 2 Bt, ERD (d 1999); *b* 3 October 1946; *Educ* Rugby; *m* 1978, Mary, da of Robert Oliver, of Cheshire; 3 s, 1 da; *Career* sch teacher; *Style*— Sir Anthony Rigby, Bt

RIGBY, Jean Prescott; da of Thomas Boulton Rigby (d 1987), and Margaret Annie, *née* Whiteside; *Educ* Elmslie Girls' Sch Blackpool, Birmingham Sch of Music, RAM (Principal's prize), RSA (Peter Stuyvesant scholarships), Nat Opera Studio (Leverhulme & Munster scholar); *m* 21 Nov 1987, Jamie Hayes; 3 s (Daniel Thomas b 7 March 1989, Oliver James b 27 Nov 1990, Matthew Peter b 25 Sept 1992); *Career* opera singer (mezzo soprano); princ mezzo soprano ENO 1982–90; Royal Opera House debut 1983, Glyndebourne debut 1984; roles incl: title role in Carmen, Octavian in Der Rosenkavalier, Lucretia in The Rape of Lucretia, Penelope in Il Ritorno d'Ulisse in Patria, Magdalena in Die Meistersinger, Maddalena in Rigoletto, Dorabella in Cosi fan Tutte, Jocasta in Oedipus Rex, Nicklaus in Les Côntes d'Hoffman, Isabella in L'Italiana in Algeri, Charlotte in Werther, Helen in King Priam, Rosina in The Barber of Seville, Angelina in La Cenerentola, Idamante in Idomeneo, Irene in Theodora, 150 anniversary performance of Mendelssohn's Elijah (BBC Proms) 1996; numerous TV appearances and recordings; winner: bursary ROH, Royal Overseas League competition, ENO Young Artists competition, Silver medal Worshipful Co of Musicians; hon fell Birmingham Conservatoire; Hon ARAM 1984, Hon FRAM 1989, ARCM, ABSM; *Recreations* theatre, sport, cooking, British heritage; *Style*— Ms Jean Rigby; ✉ c/o Askonas Holt, Lonsdale Chambers, 27 Chancery Lane, London WC2A 1PF

RIGBY, Dr Michael Laurence; s of Thomas Rigby, of Burnley, and Kathleen, *née* Barker; *b* 19 March 1947; *Educ* Colne GS, Univ of Leeds Med Sch (MB ChB, MD); *Children* 3 da (Jessica Clair Louise b 27 March 1981, Olivia Jane b 22 Oct 1982, Claudia Anne b 16 April 1985); *Career* registrar Gen Infirmary Leeds 1974–75, res registrar Children's Hosp Birmingham 1975–77, Canadian Heart Fndn fell Hosp for Sick Children Toronto 1978–79, conslt paediatric cardiologist Brompton Hosp London 1983– (sr registrar 1979–83), dir of paediatrics and conslt paediatric cardiologist Royal Brompton Hosp London 1990–, sr lectr in paediatrics Nat Heart and Lung Inst London 1990–; memb: Br Cardiac Soc 1990, Argentian Soc of Cardiology, Brazilian Soc of Cardiology, Assoc for Euro Paediatric Cardiology; FRCP, FRCPCH; *Books* The Morphology of Congenital Heart Disease (1983), The Diagnosis of Congenital Heart Disease (1986), Paediatric Cardiology (2002); *Recreations* athletics, piano, the study of terrapins; *Style*— Dr Michael Rigby; ✉ Royal Brompton Hospital, Sydney Street, London SW3 6NP (tel 020 7351 8542, fax 020 7351 8547, e-mail m.rigby@rbht.nhs.uk)

RIGBY, Sir Peter; kt (2002), DL (2000); s of John Yates Rigby (d 1972), of Liverpool, and Phyllis, *née* Newman (d 2001); *b* 29 September 1943, Liverpool; *Educ* Waterloo GS Liverpool; *m* (m dis); 2 s (James Peter b 6 March 1971, Steven Paul b 6 Dec 1972); *Career* fndr, chm and ceo Specialist Computer Holdings plc 1975–, pres SCH International plc 2000–; chm: Mallory Ct Hotel 1997–, Patriot Aviation Ltd 2002–; tstee: Rigby Fndn 1995–, RAF Museum 2006–; chm Millennium Point Tst 1996–2003, patron Acorns Children's Hospice; Hon DUniv Central England 2000, Hon DSc Aston Univ 2003; *Recreations* flying (helicopter and fixed wing), sailing, classical music; *Style*— Sir Peter Rigby, DL; ✉ Specialist Computer Holdings plc, James House, Warwick Road, Birmingham B11 2LE

RIGBY, Peter Stephen; *b* 30 July 1955; *Educ* King George V GS Southport, Univ of Manchester (BA); *m* 1, 25 Aug 1979, Stasia Teresa; 1 s (Nicholas Ian b 1981); m 2; 2 da; *Career* asst factory accountant Metal Box 1978–80 (trainee accountant 1976–78), fin accountant Book Club Associates 1980–83, gp accountant Stonehart Publications 1983–86, chief exec International Business Communications (Holdings) plc 1989–98 (fin dir 1987, dep chief exec 1988), chm Informa 1998–2004, chief exec T&F Informa plc 2004–07, chm Informa plc 2007–; numerous co directorships; ACMA 1980; *Recreations* golfing, jogging, squash, weight training, soccer, rugby, reading, theatre, music; *Style*— Peter Rigby, Esq

RIGG, Prof Jonathan Digby; s of Nigel Rigg, of Tunbridge Wells, Kent, and Kathleen, *née* Foster; *b* 25 November 1959, Calcutta, India; *Educ* SOAS Univ of London (BA, PhD); *m* 1985, Janie, *née* Bickersteth; 2 s (Joshua Eliot b 1990, Samuel Morris b 2001), 2 da (Eleanor Grace b 1992, Francesca Poppy b 1998); *Career* SOAS Univ of London: British Acad research fell 1986–89, lectr in SE Asian geography 1989–93; Dept of Geography Univ of Durham: lectr 1993–95, reader 1995–2003, prof 2003–; FRGS; *Books* Southeast Asia: A Region in Transition - A Thematic Human Geography of the Asean Region (1991), More than the Soil: Rural Change in Southeast Asia (2001), Southeast Asia: The Human Landscape of Modernization and Development (2003), Living with Transition in Laos: Market Integration in Southeast Asia (2005); *Style*— Prof Jonathan Rigg; ✉ Department of Geography, University of Durham, South Road, Durham DH1 3LE (tel 0191 334 1925, e-mail j.d.rigg@durham.ac.uk)

RIGHTON, Caroline Anne; da of Patrick Cornelius Donovan, and Maureen, *née* Doyle; *b* 26 February 1958; *Educ* La Retraite HS, Univ of Cardiff; *m* 1978, Mark; 2 s (Ben b 1981, James b 1989); *Career* journalist: rep Falmouth Packet 1977–79, chef The Seafood Restaurant Falmouth 1979–81, proprietor/publisher Carrick and West Cornwall Review 1980–82, sr prodr BBC Radio Cornwall 1982–84; presenter of various TV programmes 1982–98 incl: Matrix 1982–84, Good Morning Britain 1985–87, BBC Breakfast Time 1988, newsreader BBC News 1989, Good Health 1990, Business Daily (Channel 4)1991–93, various programmes for UK Living 1994, Good Morning with Anne and Nick (BBC1) 1995, Check it Out 1996, After Hours (Radio 5) 1997; md Visage TV 1998, controller of features and prog devpt Carlton Television 1999–2003, media mgmnt conslt 2004–; ind prodr for Really Vital Television Ltd; journalist: The Times, The Guardian, Woman and Home; columnist and assoc ed Popular Craft 1997–98, columnist Family Circle Magazine 1997; *Publications* The Life Audit (2005); *Recreations* cooking, walking, reading; *Style*— Ms Caroline Righton; ✉ e-mail caroline@carolinerighton.com

RILEY, Prof Alan John; s of Arthur Joseph Riley (d 1993), of Chestfield, Kent, and Edith Ada, *née* Rashbrook (d 1998); *b* 16 July 1943; *Educ* Bexley GS, Univ of London, Charing Cross Hosp Med Sch Univ of London (MB BS), Univ of Manchester (MSc); *m* 1, 14 Nov 1964 (m dis 1976), Pamela Margaret, da of Leonard George Allum, of London; 1 da (Veronica b 1968), 1 s (John b 1971); 2 adopted s (Grant b 1968, Robert b 1970); m 2, 11 Dec 1976, Elizabeth Jane, da of Capt Arthur Norman Robertson (d 1959); *Career* GP Bideford 1970–76, specialist in sexual med 1972–; sr lectr and hon conslt in human sexuality St George's Hosp Med Sch 1995–98, prof of sexual med Lancs Postgrad Sch of Med and Health Univ of Central Lancashire 1998–; dir: MAP Publishing Ltd 1991–95, Sexual Problems Services St George's Hosp London 1995–98; ptnr: SMC Developments 1986–, SMC Research 1985–; ed: British Jl of Sexual Med 1983–91, Sexual and Marital Therapy 1986–, The Jl of Sexual Health 1991–96; ed advsr Jl of Sex and Marital Therapy 1998–; author of over 100 pubns on aspects of sexual and reproductive med; dep co surgn St John Ambulance Bde (ret 1988); pres Br Soc for Sexual Impotence Research 2002; memb: Assoc of Sexual and Marital Therapists 1979, Royal Soc of Med, BMA; LRCP 1967, MRCS 1967, DObstRCOG 1969, FZS 1977, FFPM RCP 1992 (MFPM RCP 1989); OStJ 1983; *Recreations* woodwork, photography, boating, natural history; *Style*— Prof Alan Riley; ✉ Kings Park, Cwmann, Lampeter, Ceridigion SA48 8HQ (tel 01570 421264, e-mail alanriley@doctors.org.uk)

RILEY, Bridget; CH (1999), CBE (1974); da of John Fisher Riley (d 1991), of Cornwall and, Bessie Louise, *née* Gladstone (d 1975); *b* 24 April 1931; *Educ* Cheltenham Ladies' Coll, Goldsmiths Coll of Art, RCA; *Career* artist; AICA critics' prize 1963, John Moores Exhibition prize Liverpool 1963, Peter Stuyvesant Fndn travel bursary to USA 1964, int prize XXXIV Venice Biennale 1968, int prize Ohara Museum 8 Int Print Biennale Tokyo 1972, Praemium Imperiale Award for Painting 2003; colour projects for: Royal Liverpool Hosp 1980–83, St Mary's Hosp Paddington 1986–87; designed Colour Moves (Ballet Rambert) 1983; tstee Nat Gallery 1981–88, represented in major museums and art collections worldwide; Hon DLitt: Univ of Manchester 1976, Univ of Ulster 1986, Univ of Oxford 1994, Univ of Cambridge 1995, Univ of Exeter 1997, Univ of London 2005; Hon DA De Montfort Univ 1996; memb American Acad of Arts and Sciences 2006; *Exhibitions* Gallery One London 1962–63, Bridget Riley, Drawings (MOMA NY) 1966–67, Br Pavilion XXXIV Biennale Venice 1968, European Retrospective (Br Cncl touring exhbn Hanover, Berne, Dusseldorf, Turin and Prague) 1970–72, Retrospective Exhbn (Br Cncl touring US< Aust and Japan) 1978–80, Working with Colour (Arts Cncl of GB touring exhbn) 1984–85, According to Sensation 1982–1992 (Arts Cncl of GB touring exhbn Kunsthalle Nüberg, Quadrat Bottrop, Joseph Albers Museum and Hayward Gallery) 1992, Bridget Riley: Paintings from the 60s and 70s (Serpentine Gallery London) 2000, Bridget Riley: Paintings 1982–2000 and Early Works on Paper (PaceWildenstein NY) 2000, Bridget Riley: Reconnaissance (DIA Center for the Arts NY) 2001, Bridget Riley: Retrospective (Tate Britian) 2003, Bridget Riley: New Work (Museum Haus Esters and Kaiser Wilhelm Museum Krefeld) 2004, Bridget Riley (Museum of Contemporary Art Sydney) 2004–05; *Style*— Miss Bridget Riley, CH, CBE; ✉ c/o Karsten Schubert, 47 Lexington Street, London W1R 3LG (tel 020 7734 9002, fax 020 7734 9008)

RILEY, Christopher John (Chris); s of Bernard Francis Riley (d 1981), of Nottingham, and Phyllis Wigley (d 1954); *b* 20 January 1947; *Educ* Ratcliffe Coll, Wadham Coll Oxford (MA), UEA (MA); *m* 24 Sept 1982, Helen Marion, da of Ernest Amos Arthur Mynett, of Sidcup, Kent; 2 s (Timothy James b 1983, Mark Edward b 1985); *Career* HM Treasy: econ asst 1969–72, sr econ asst 1972–74, econ advsr 1974–79, sr econ advsr 1979–88, under sec 1988–95; chief economist: DOE 1995–97, DETR 1997–2001, DTLR 2001–02, Dept for Tport 2002–05; assoc Oxera Consulting Ltd 2005–; Gwilym Gibbon research fell Nuffield Coll Oxford 1977–78; *Recreations* music, especially choral singing; *Style*— Chris Riley

RILEY, Maj-Gen Jonathon Peter; DSO (1996); s of John S Riley, and Joyce, *née* Outen; *Educ* Kingston GS, UCL (BA), Univ of Leeds (MA), Cranfield Univ (PhD), RMA Sandhurst; *Career* cmmnd Queen's Royal Regt, served: 1 Bn 1974–76 and 1979–83, 3 Bn 1983–84, 1 Bn 1988–89; transferred Royal Welch Fusiliers 1990, served 1 Bn 1994–96, instr RMA Sandhurst 1984–86, student Staff Coll 1987 (instr 1993), COS 6 Armd Bde 1990–92, COS 1 Armd Div 1996–98, Cmd 1 Mechanized Bde 1998–2000, Jt Task Force Cdr Sierra Leone 2000–01, Asst Cmdt (Land) JSSC 2001–03, Dep Cmdg Gen CMATT (Iraq) and New Iraqi Army 2003, Cmdg Gen Multinational Div (SE) and GOC Br Forces Iraq 2004–05, sr Br mil advsr US Central Cmd 2005–07; service in UK, Germany, NI (six tours), Central America, USA, Denmark, Sierra Leone, former Yugoslavia (five tours) and Iraq (two tours); memb: Catholic Record Soc 1988, Army Records Soc 2003, RCDS, Countryside Alliance, Crisis; Offr Legion of Merit (USA) 2005; memb Cncl: Centre for Defence & International Security Studies (CDISS), RUSI; visiting fell Dept of Modern History Univ of Birmingham; *Books* History of the Queen's Royal Regiment (1985), From Pole to Pole (1988, 2 edn 1999), Soldiers of the Queen (1992), White Dragon (1995), Napoleon and the World War, 1813 (2000), Regimental Records of the RWF Vols VI and VII (2001), The Life of General Hughie Stockwell (2006), Napoleon as a General (2007), That Astonishing Infantry (ed, 2007); *Recreations* field sports, rowing, walking, running, writing; *Clubs* Naval and Military; *Style*— Maj-Gen Jonathon Riley, DSO

RILEY, Very Rev Kenneth Joseph; OBE (2003); s of Arthur Riley (d 1954), of Flint, and Mary Josephine, *née* Birks (d 1975); *b* 25 June 1940; *Educ* Holywell GS, UCW Aberystwyth (Robert Bryan music scholar, BA), Linacre House Oxford (MA), Wycliffe Hall Oxford; *m* 4 Jan 1968, Margaret, da of Aubrey Deninson; 2 da (Jane b 27 Jan 1969, Kay b 17 May 1972); *Career* ordained: deacon 1964, priest 1965; asst curate Emmanuel Fazakerley Liverpool 1964–66; chaplain: Brasted Place Coll 1966–69, Oundle Sch 1969–75, Univ of Liverpool 1975–83; vicar Mossley Hill Liverpool 1975–83, warden of readers Liverpool 1979–83, rural dean Childwall 1982–83, canon residentiary Liverpool Cathedral 1983–93, dean of Manchester 1993–2005, dean emeritus 2005–; *Books* Liverpool Cathedral (1987); *Recreations* music, drama, films; *Style*— The Very Rev K J Riley, OBE; ✉ 145 Turning Lane, Southport PR8 5HZ

RILEY, Marc; s of Albert Riley, and Josephine Riley; *Educ* St Gregory's GS Manchester; *Career* musician: The Fall 1978–83, The Creepers 1983–86; mangr In-Tape record label 1983–86, cartoonist Oink (children's comic) 1986–89, record promoter (incl Factory Records, 4AD, Circa) 1990–92; broadcaster BBC: Radio 1 (with Mark Radcliffe, *qv*) 1992–2004, Radio 5 1992–, 6 Music 2004–; *Awards* Sony Gold award (daytime) 1998, Sony Gold award (daytime music) 1999, Sony Gold award (daily sequences) 2001, Sony Silver award, Sony Bronze award; *Recreations* listening to/playing music, squash, five-a-side football, watching Manchester City FC; *Style*— Marc Riley, Esq; ✉ c/o PBJ Management, Soho Square, London (tel 020 7434 6700, e-mail marc.riley@bbc.co.uk)

RILEY, Prof Norman; s of late Willie Riley, of Hebden Bridge, West Yorks, and Minnie, *née* Parker; *Educ* Calder HS, Univ of Manchester (BSc, PhD); *m* 5 Sept 1959, Mary Ann, da of late Michael Mansfield; 1 s (Stephen b 1961), 1 da (Susan b 1964); *Career* asst lectr in mathematics Univ of Manchester 1959–60, lectr in mathematics Univ of Durham 1960–64; UEA: sr lectr in mathematics 1964–66, reader in mathematics 1966–71, prof of applied mathematics 1971–99, now emeritus; FIMA 1964; *Recreations* music, photography, travel; *Style*— Prof Norman Riley; ✉ School of Mathematics, University of East Anglia, Norwich NR4 7TJ (tel 01603 592586)

RILEY, Prof Patrick Anthony; s of Bertram Hurrell Riley (d 1961), and Olive, *née* Stephenson (d 1987); *b* 22 March 1935; *Educ* Manegg Sch Zurich, King Edward VII Sch King's Lynn, UCL, UCH Med Sch London (MB BS, PhD, DSc); *m* 5 July 1958, Christine Elizabeth, da of Dr Islwyn Morris (d 1972), of Treorchy, Glamorgan; 2 da (Sian b 12 Feb 1962, Caroline b 25 June 1963), 1 s (Benjamin b 20 Feb 1968); *Career* Rockefeller res scholar 1962–63, MRC jr clinical res fell 1963–66, Beit meml res fell 1966–68, Wellcome res fell 1968–70, sr lectr in biochemical pathology UCH Med Sch 1974–76 (lectr 1970–73), prof of cell pathology UCL 1984–2000 (reader 1976–84), emeritus prof of cell pathology Univ of London 2000–, dir Totteridge Inst for Advanced Studies 2001–; exec ed Melanoma Research 1990–2006; FIBiol 1976, FRCPath 1985; *Publications* Faber Pocket Medical Dictionary (with P J Cunningham, 1 edn 1966), Hydroxyanisole: Recent Advances in

R

Anti-Melanoma Therapy (1984); over 200 scientific papers on free radical pathology, cancer and pigmentation; *Recreations* music, painting, astronomy, photography; *Clubs* Athenaeum, Linnean; *Style—* Prof Patrick Riley; ✉ 2 The Grange, Grange Avenue, London N20 8AB (tel 020 8445 5687); Gray Cancer Institute, Box 100, Mount Vernon Hospital, Northwood, Middlesex HA6 2JR

RILEY, Phil; *Educ* Columbia Business Sch (MBA); *m*; 3 c; *Career* grad trainee BRMB FM 1980; Chrysalis: md and launch dir 100.7 Heart FM W Midlands and Heart 106.2 FM London 1994, chief exec 1999–2007; chm MXR consortium; memb: Bd Digital Radio Devpt Bureau (DRDB), Radio Centre, RAJAR; *Recreations* keeping fit (completed a number of triathlons); *Style—* Phil Riley, Esq

RILEY, Simon James Blair; s of James Riley (d 1985), and Joanna, *née* Walker; *b* 27 February 1946; *Educ* Gordonstoun; *m* 1, 7 April 1973 (m dis 1984), Jacqueline Lila (Jackie), da of Col Henry Lancelot (Harry) Gullidge, of Taunton, Somerset; 2 da (Claire-Louise b 6 Sept 1975, Victoria b 19 Aug 1980); m 2, 29 Oct 1988, Estaire Joyce Danielle, da of Prof Johan De Vree; m 3, 9 June 1999, June Marion, da of Michael Farrell, of Arthurstown, Co Wexford; 2 c (Alexander Robert James, Jessica Joanna Margot (twins) b 14 June 2000); *Career* surveyor; Kirk & Kirk 1964–67, Grant Wilkinson & Co 1967–73 (dir 1970), dir James Riley & Associates 1973–83, conslt in Spain 1983–88, property developer 1988–; memb Ctee Br Automobile Racing Club; MNAEA 1965; *Recreations* racing motor cars, reading, collecting; *Clubs* Lighthouse, British Automobile Racing, Jaguar Drivers'; *Style—* Simon Riley, Esq; ✉ 23 Rossetti Garden Mansions, Flood Street, Chelsea, London SW3 5QX (tel 020 7351 0248, fax 020 7622 7207, mobile 07974 669357)

RILEY-SMITH, Prof Jonathan Simon Christopher; s of Maj (William Henry) Douglas Riley-Smith (d 1981), of Tadcaster, N Yorks and Brewhurst, Loxwood, W Sussex, and Elspeth Agnes Mary, *née* Craik Henderson (d 1990); *b* 27 June 1938; *Educ* Eton, Trinity Coll Cambridge (BA, MA, PhD, DLitt); *m* 27 July 1968, Marie-Louise Jeannetta, da of Wilfred John Sutcliffe Field, of Norwich, Norfolk; 1 s (Tobias Augustine William b 19 Oct 1969), 2 da (Tamsin Elspeth Hermione b 10 Sept 1971, Hippolyta Clemency Magdalen b 10 Nov 1975); *Career* lectr in medieval history Univ of St Andrews 1966–72 (asst lectr 1964–65); Univ of Cambridge: asst lectr 1972–75, lectr 1975–78, fell Queens' Coll 1972–78, dir of studies in history 1972–78, praelector 1973–75, librarian 1973 and 1977–78; prof of history Royal Holloway and Bedford New Coll London 1978–94 (head Dept of History 1984–90), Dixie prof of ecclesiastical history Univ of Cambridge 1994–2005 (Dixie prof emeritus 2005–), fell Emmanuel Coll Cambridge 1994–2005, chm Bd of Faculty Univ of Cambridge 1997–99; librarian Priory of Scotland Most Ven Order of St John 1966–78, Grand Priory 1982–; hon fell Inst of Historical Res 1997–; corresponding fell Medieval Acad of America 2006; FRHistS 1971; KStJ 1969 (CStJ 1966), Knight of Grace and Devotion SMOM 2002 (Knight of Magistral Grace SMOM 1971, Officer of Merit Pro Merito Melitensi 1985); *Books* The Knights of St John in Jerusalem and Cyprus (1967), Ayyubids, Mamlukes and Crusaders (with U and M C Lyons, 1971), The Feudal Nobility and The Kingdom of Jerusalem (1973), What Were The Crusades? (1977, 3rd ed 2002), The Crusades Idea and Reality (with L Riley-Smith, 1981), The First Crusade and The Idea of Crusading (1986), The Crusades: A Short History (1987, 2 edn 2005), Les Croisades (translation, 1990), Breve storia della Crociate (trans, 1994), The Atlas of the Crusades (ed, 1991), Grosser Bildatlas der Kreuzzüge (trans, 1992), The Oxford Illustrated History of the Crusades (ed, 1995), Cyprus and the Crusades (ed with N Coureas, 1995), Atlas des Croisades (trans, 1996), Montjoie. Studies in Crusade History in Honour of Hans Eberhard Mayer (ed jtly, 1997), The First Crusaders (1997), Hospitallers: The History of the Order of St John (1999), Al Seguito delle Crociate (trans, 2000), Dei Gesta per Francos, Etudes sur les croisades dédieés à Jean Richard (ed jtly, 2001); *Recreations* the past and present of own family; *Style—* Prof Jonathan Riley-Smith; ✉ Emmanuel College, Cambridge CB2 3AP (tel 01223 334200)

RIMER, Hon Mr Justice; Sir Colin Percy Farquharson Rimer; kt (1994); s of late Kenneth Rowland Rimer, of Beckenham, Kent, and late Maria Eugenia, *née* Farquharson; *b* 30 January 1944; *Educ* Dulwich Coll, Trinity Hall Cambridge (MA, LLB); *m* 3 Jan 1970, Penelope Ann, da of late Alfred William Gibbs; 1 da (Catherine b 1971), 2 s (David b 1972, Michael b 1974); *Career* res asst Inst of Comparative Law Paris 1967–68; called to the Bar Lincoln's Inn 1968 (bencher 1994); in practice 1969–94, QC 1988, judge of the High Court of Justice (Chancery Div) 1994–; *Recreations* music, novels, walking; *Style—* The Hon Mr Justice Rimer; ✉ Royal Courts of Justice, Strand, London WC2A 2LL

RIMINGTON, Dame Stella; DCB (1996); da of David Whitehouse, of Newstead; *b* 1935; *Educ* Nottingham HS for Girls, Univ of Edinburgh (MA); *Children* 2 da; *Career* DG Security Service 1992–96 (joined 1969); non-exec dir: Whitehead Mann GKR (formerly GKR Group) 1997–2001, Marks & Spencer plc 1997–2004, BG Group plc 1997–2005, Royal Marsden NHS Tst 1998–2001; chm Inst of Cancer Research 1997–2001; tstee RAF Museum 1998–2001; Hon Air Cdre 7006 (VR) Intelligence Squadron RAuxAF 1997–2001; Hon LLD: Univ of Nottingham 1995, Univ of Exeter 1996, London Metropolitan Univ 2004, Univ of Liverpool 2005; *Books* Open Secret (autobiography, 2001), At Risk (2004), Secret Asset (2006); *Style—* Dame Stella Rimington, DCB

RING, Malcolm Spencer Humbert; TD; s of Gp Capt Spencer Leonard Ring, CBE, DFC (d 1980), and Jessie Margaret Ring; *b* 25 February 1944; *Educ* Haileybury; *m* 17 Aug 1978, Elizabeth Anne, da of Michael Henman; 3 s (Jonathan b 1980, Charles b 1982, Thomas b 1985), 1 da (Emma b 1987); *Career* Regtl Col TA HAC 1989–90 (joined 1969, CO Lt-Col 1986–88); admitted slr 1969; ptnr: Taylor & Humbert 1973–82, Taylor Garrett (now Taylor Wessing) 1982– (managing ptnr 1989–90); memb Law Soc; *Recreations* fishing, cricket, hockey, gardening; *Clubs* Oriental, HAC; *Style—* Malcolm Ring, Esq, TD; ✉ Taylor Wessing, Carmelite, 50 Victoria Embankment, Blackfriars, London EC4Y 0DX (tel 020 7300 7000, fax 020 7300 7100, telex 268014)

RINGROSE, Ven Hedley Sidney; s of Sidney Ringrose (d 1964), of Oxford, and Clara, *née* Strong (d 1967); *b* 29 June 1942; *Educ* West Oxfordshire Coll, Salisbury Theol Coll, Open Univ (BA); *m* 1969, Rosemary Anne, da of Reginald William Palmer; 1 s (Christopher Jude b 18 Nov 1970), 2 da (Emma Jane b 24 Dec 1972, Louise Clare b 21 Oct 1976); *Career* ordained: deacon 1968, priest 1969; asst curate: Bishopston Bristol 1968–71, Easthampstead 1971–75; vicar St George Gloucester with Whaddon 1975–88, rural dean Gloucester City 1983–88, vicar of Cirencester 1988–98, rural dean of Cirencester 1989–97, archdeacon of Cheltenham 1998–, reserved canon Gloucester Cathedral 1998– (hon canon 1986–98); memb Gen Synod C of E 1990–2005; chm Diocesan: Bd of Patronage 1990–98, House of Clergy 1994–98, Bd of Educn 1998–; tstee: Glenfell House 1998–, St Matthias Fndn 1999– (chm 2005–), Sylvanus Lysons Tst 2000–; memb: Cirencester Soc in London 1989–, Ecclesiastical Law Soc 2000–; *Recreations* travel, cycling, driving; *Style—* The Ven the Archdeacon of Cheltenham; ✉ The Sanderlings, Thorncliffe Drive, Cheltenham, Gloucestershire GL51 6PY (tel 01242 522923, fax 01242 235925, e-mail archdchelt@star.co.uk)

RINGROSE, Dr Peter Stuart; s of Arthur Ringrose, of Colchester, Essex, and Roma Margaret, *née* Roberts; *b* 9 October 1945, Leicester; *Educ* Alderman Newton Boys' GS Leicester, CCC Cambridge (Francis Bacon scholar, MA, MPhil, PhD); *m* 11 March 1966, Nancy Elaine; 2 s (Simon Andrew b 16 Sept 1966, Timothy John b 6 Dec 1967), 1 da (Lucy Victoria b 3 April 1977); *Career* dept head Roche Pharmaceuticals 1970–79, div dir of chemotherapy, infectious diseases and molecular sciences Sandoz Forschungsinstitut Vienna 1979–82, sr vice-pres Worldwide Drug Discovery and Medicinal R&D Europe Pfizer Inc 1982–96, chief scientific offr Bristol-Myers Squibb and pres Pharmaceutical Research Inst Princeton 1997–2002, chm BBSRC 2003–; non-exec dir: Cambridge Antibody Technology 2003–06, Astex Therapeutics 2005–, Rigel Pharmaceuticals 2005–; memb Scientific Advsy Bd: Accenture Life Sciences 2003–, Merlin Biosciences 2003–05, Cempra Pharmaceuticals 2006–, Schering-Plough Inc 2007–; William Pitt fell Pembroke Coll Cambridge 1998–2006 (hon fell 2006, chair Coll Corporate Devpt Ctee), memb Chemistry Advsy Bd Univ of Cambridge; chm Hever Gp of Pharmaceutical R&D Heads 1999–2002; memb: Governing Cncl NY Acad of Sciences 2001–05, Cncl Fndn for Science and Technology; former memb: Policy Advsy Bd Centre for Medicines Research International, Science and Regulatory Exec Pharmaceutical Research and Manufacturers of America, Center for Advanced Biotechnology and Medicine NJ, Scientific Ctee Assoc of Br Pharmaceutical Industries; memb Chllr's Ct of Benefactors Univ of Oxford 1998–; *Recreations* drawing, painting, 18th century history, scuba diving, renovating old houses; *Clubs* Athenaeum; *Style—* Dr Peter Ringrose; ✉ Biotechnology and Biological Sciences Research Council, Polaris House, North Star Avenue, Swindon SN2 1UH (tel 01793 413223, e-mail peter.ringrose@bbsrc.ac.uk)

RINK, John Stuart; s of Paul Lothar Max Rink (d 1977), and Mary Ida McCall, *née* Moore; *b* 25 October 1946; *Educ* Sedbergh, Univ of London (LLB); *m* 22 May 1971, Elizabeth Mary, da of Thomas Edgar Pitkethly; 1 s (Max Edgar b 2 Feb 1973), 1 da (Lucinda Mary b 1 Jan 1975); *Career* Allen & Overy: trainee slr 1970–72, asst slr 1972–77, ptnr 1977–, managing ptnr Litigation Dept 1989, managing ptnr 1994–2003, memb Bd 2003–04; legal dir British Aerospace plc 1994–95; dir Brixton plc 2003–06; memb Bd Eversheds 2004, Robson Rhodes 2004–06; memb Law Soc; *Recreations* golf, rugby, walking, opera; *Clubs* City Law, Royal Wimbledon Golf, Royal West Norfolk Golf, Windermere Motor Boat Racing, MCC; *Style—* John Rink, Esq; ✉ 2 Camp View, Wimbledon, London SW19 4UL (tel 020 8947 4800)

RINTOUL, Dr Gordon Charles; s of Henry Rintoul, and Janet, *née* Brown; *b* 29 May 1955; *Educ* Allan Glen's Sch Glasgow, Univ of Edinburgh (BSc), Univ of Manchester (MSc, PhD); *m* 1997, Stephanie Jane, *née* Budden; 1 s (Cameron Henry); *Career* res supervisor Chemical Museum Devpt Project 1982–84, conslt and tutor Open Univ 1984, curator Colour Museum 1984–87, dir Catalyst: The Museum of the Chemical Industry 1987–98, chief exec Sheffield Galleries and Museums Tst 1998–2002, dir Nat Museums of Scotland 2002–; pres (NW region) Assoc for Science Educn 1995–98, treas Assoc of Ind Museums 1991–97 (memb Cncl 1989–2002); memb: Registration Ctee Resource: The Cncl for Museums, Archives and Libraries 1995–2002, Cncl Museums Assoc 1998–2002, Bd SCRAN (Scottish Cultural Resources Access Network) 2002–06; dip Museum Assoc; *Recreations* travel, reading, cooking; *Style—* Dr Gordon Rintoul; ✉ National Museums of Scotland, Chambers Street, Edinburgh EH1 1JF (tel 0131 247 4260, fax 0131 247 4308, e-mail g.rintoul@nms.ac.uk)

RIORDAN, Linda; MP; *b* 31 May 1953; *Educ* Univ of Bradford; *Career* private sec to Alice Mahon MP, cncllr Calderdale BC; MP (Lab/Co-op) Halifax 2005–; non-exec dir Calderdale and Huddersfield NHS Tst, chair Ovenden Initiative, memb Bd Pennine Housing 2000–; *Style—* Ms Linda Riordan, MP; ✉ House of Commons, London SW1A 0AA

RIORDAN, Stephen Vaughan; QC (1992); s of Charles Maurice Riordan, and Betty Morfydd, *née* Harries (d 1983); *b* 18 February 1950; *Educ* Wimbledon Coll, Univ of Liverpool (LLB); *m* 19 Feb 1983, Jane Elizabeth, da of Ernest Victor Thomas; 2 da (Alexandra Jane b 24 Aug 1983, Charlotte Ann b 2 March 1985); *Career* called to the Bar Inner Temple 1972, recorder of the Crown Court 1990– (asst recorder 1986–90), head of chambers; *Recreations* singing; *Style—* Stephen Riordan, Esq, QC; ✉ 19 Gwydrin Road, Liverpool L18 3HA (tel 0151 722 1726); 1st Floor, 25 Castle Street, Liverpool, Merseyside L2 4TA

RIPLEY, Prof Brian David; s of Eric Lewis Ripley, of Farnborough, Hants, and Sylvia May, *née* Gould; *b* 29 April 1952; *Educ* Farnborough GS, Churchill Coll Cambridge (MA, Smith's Prize, PhD); *m* 1973, Ruth Mary, *née* Appleton; *Career* Univ of London: lectr in statistics Imperial Coll 1976–80, reader in statistics 1980–83; prof of statistics Univ of Strathclyde 1983–90, prof of applied statistics Univ of Oxford 1990–, professorial fell St Peter's Coll Oxford 1990–; Adams Prize Univ of Cambridge 1987; memb Int Statistical Inst 1982, fell Inst of Mathematical Statistics 1987, FRSE 1990; *Books* Spatial Statistics (1981), Stochastic Simulation (1987), Statistical Inference for Spatial Processes (1988), Modern Applied Statistics with S-Plus (with W N Venables, 1994 and 1997), Pattern Recognition and Neural Networks (1996), S Programming (with W N Venables, 2000); *Recreations* natural history; *Style—* Prof Brian Ripley, FRSE; ✉ Department of Statistics, University of Oxford, 1 South Parks Road, Oxford OX1 3TG (tel 01865 272861, fax 01865 272595, e-mail ripley@stats.ox.ac.uk)

RIPON AND LEEDS, Bishop of 2000–; Rt Rev John Richard Packer; s of Rev Canon John William Packer, of Bridge, Kent, and Hilda Muriel, *née* Hatch; *b* 10 October 1946; *Educ* Manchester Grammar, Keble Coll Oxford (BA Modern History, BA Theol, MA), Univ of York (Dip); *m* 30 Dec 1971, Barbara Priscilla Deborah, da of late Donald Fingland Jack, of Scarborough, N Yorks; 1 da (Catherine Ruth b 1976), 2 s (Richard James b 1978, Timothy Stephen b 1980); *Career* curate St Peter's St Helier Morden 1970–73, dir of pastoral studies Ripon Hall 1973–75, Ripon Coll Cuddesdon 1975–77, chaplain St Nicolas' Abingdon 1973–77, vicar Wath upon Dearne with Adwick upon Dearne 1977–86, rural dean Wath 1983–86, rector Sheffield Manor 1986–91, rural dean Attercliffe 1990–91, archdeacon of W Cumberland 1991–96, priest i/c Bridekirk 1995–96, bishop of Warrington 1996–2000; memb Gen Synod C of E 1985–91, 1992–96, 2000–; *Recreations* history, walking; *Style—* The Rt Rev the Bishop of Ripon and Leeds; ✉ Bishop Mount, Hutton Bank, Ripon, North Yorkshire HG4 5DP (tel 01765 602045)

RIPPON, Angela; OBE (2004); da of John and Edna Rippon; *b* 12 October 1944; *Career* journalist and television broadcaster; formerly with BBC Plymouth and Westward Television, joined BBC 1973, first woman journalist newsreader 1975, fndr memb TV-am 1982, with Channel 7 (USA) 1984, worked on BBC and ITV programmes, joined LBC Radio 1990, currently with BBC TV and ITV news; vice-pres: Br Red Cross, NCH Action for Children, Riding for the Disabled Assoc; vice-pres Eng Nat Ballet, patron Support Dogs; Barker Variety Club of GB; Hon Dr of Humanities American Int Univ 1994; *Television* BBC credits incl: Come Dancing, The Antiques Roadshow, Top Gear, Angela Rippon Meets..., The Morecambe and Wise Christmas Show, Eurovision Song Contest, 1979 General Election, Olivier Awards, Masterteam, Matchpoint, Angela Rippon's Summer Journey, In the Country, BBC Television News, The Wedding of HRH Prince Charles and Lady Diana Spencer, Crufts, Watchdog Healthcheck, The Holiday Programme, Sun Sea and Bargain-Spotting (BBC2) 2005–06; ITV and Channel 4 credits incl: What's My Line, A Game of War, The Windsors - sale of a lifetime, Open House, The Big Breakfast, Hidden Talents of the Rich and Famous, Live with Angela Roppon (ITV News Channel) 2003–05; overseas credits: The Nobel Prize (CNN - Turner Network), Those Were the Days (Sky), The Key to the White House (American Educnl TV), Simply Money, arts and entertainment corr CBS Boston, Channel 9 Aust; *Radio* credits incl: Breakfast with Angela Rippon (LBC), Angela Rippon's Drive Time (LBC), The Health Show (Radio 4), Friday Night with Angela Rippon (Radio 2), Friday Night is Music Night, numerous Radio 2 documentaries, compere Radio 2 music compilation progs and live transmissions with BBC Concert Orch; *Awards* New York Film Festival Silver Medal 1972, TV and Radio Industries Club Newsreader of the Year 1976, 1977 and 1987, TV Personality of the Year 1977, Emmy Award 1984 (for Channel 7 Boston), Entertainment Reporter of the Year 1984 (Boston), Sony Radio Award 1990, New York Radio Silver Medal 1992, Radio Personality of the Year 1993, RTS Roll of Honour 1997, European Woman of Achievement 2002; *Books* Riding (1980), In the Country (1980), Mark Phillips - The Man and his Horses (1982), Angela Rippon's Westcountry (1982), Victoria Plum (eight children's books, 1983), Badminton - a celebration (1983), Fabulous at 50 and Beyond (2003); *Style*— Ms Angela Rippon, OBE

RISDON, Prof (Rupert) Anthony; s of Capt Dennis Stanley Risdon (d 1986), and Olga Caris Argent, *née* Davis; *b* 5 March 1939; *Educ* Charing Cross Hosp Med Sch (MB BS, MD); *m* 15 April 1961, Phyllis Mary, da of Frederick Hough, of IOM; 2 s (James) Mark b 1964, Simon Paul b 1967); *Career* lectr in histopathology Charing Cross Hosp Med Sch 1966–68, conslt pathologist Addenbrooke's Hosp Cambridge 1975–76, reader in morbid anatomy London Hosp Med Coll 1976–85, head Histopathology Dept Great Ormond St Hosp for Sick Children 1985–; memb: Pathology Soc of GB and I, Int Acad Pathology, Assoc of Clinical Pathologists; FRCPath; *Recreations* walking, swimming; *Style*— Prof Anthony Risdon; ✉ The Hospital for Sick Children, Department of Histopathology, Great Ormond Street, London WC1N 3JH (tel 020 7405 9200)

RISHTON, John; *Career* with Ford of Europe 1979–94; British Airways plc: financial controller USA 1994–96, sales controller 1996–98, ops controller 1998–99, commercial controller 1999–2001, chief financial offr 2001–05, memb Exec Bd 2001–05; finance dir Ahold 2006–; non-exec dir: Allied Domecq plc 2003–, Rolls-Royce plc 2007–; *Style*— John Rishton, Esq; ✉ Ahold, Albert Heijnweg 1, 1507 EH Zaandam, The Netherlands

RITBLAT, Lady; Jillian Rosemary (Jill) Ritblat; da of Max Leonard Slotover, FRCS, of Monte Carlo, Monaco, and Peggy Cherna, *née* Cohen; *b* 14 December 1942; *Educ* Newcastle upon Tyne Church HS, Roedean, Westfield Coll London (BA); *m* 1, 21 April 1966 (m dis 1981), Elie Zilkha; 1 s, 1 da; m 2, 27 Feb 1986, Sir John Ritblat, *qv*; *Career* called to the Bar Gray's Inn 1964; pupillage to Robin Simpson, QC, Victor Durand & Jeremy Hutchinson's Chambers 1964–65; alternate delegate for Int Cncl of Jewish Women UN Geneva 1977–79; Patrons of New Art Tate Gallery: events organiser 1984–87, chm 1987–90, memb Acquisitions Sub-Ctee 1992–93; memb Int Cncl Tate Gallery 1995– (vice-chm 1996–2001); co-curator: The Curator's Egg (Anthony Reynolds Gallery) 1994, One Woman's Wardrobe (V&A, Catalogue Design and Art Direction (D&AD) Silver Award for Graphic Design 1999) 1998–99; exec prodr Normal Conservative Rebels: Gilbert & George in China (Edinburgh Film Festival 1996, Gold Medal Chicago Film Festival 1996); memb: Assoc of MOMA Oxford (now Modern Art Oxford) 1986– (memb Cncl 1993–), Int Cncl Jerusalem Museum 1987–, Advsy Cncl Friends of the Tate Gallery 1990–, Nat Art Collections Fund Special Events Ctee 1991–92, William Townsend Meml Lectureship Ctee 1991–, Bd New Contemporaries 1991– (vice-chm 1992–), Bd Jerusalem Music Centre 1991–, Arts Cncl Appraisal for W Midlands Arts 1994, Royal Acad of Music Devpt Ctee 2002–; patron Nat Alliance for Art, Architecture and Design 1994–, design tstee Public Art Cmmrs Agency 1996–99, tstee RIBA Tst 2006–; memb Jury: Painting in the Eighties 1987, Turner Prize 1988, British Airways New Artist Award 1990, Swiss Bank Corporation Euro Art Competition 1994 and 1995, NatWest 90's Prize for Art 1994 and 1995, Financial Times Arts and Business Awards 2000 and 2001, Building Cmmn RIBA Regnl Award 2001; RIBA; *Recreations* art, opera, travelling, skiing, food, people; *Style*— Lady Ritblat; ✉ Lansdowne House, Berkeley Square, London W1J 6ER

RITBLAT, Sir John Henry; kt (2006); s of Montie Ritblat (d 1984), and Muriel, *née* Glaskie; *b* 3 October 1935; *Educ* Dulwich Coll, Univ of London, Coll of Estate Mgmnt; *m* 1, 1960, Isabel Paja Steinberg (d 1979); 2 s (Nicholas b 19 Aug 1961, James b 18 Feb 1967), 1 da (Suzanne b 15 Sept 1962); m 2, 27 Feb 1986, Jill Ritblat, *qv*, *née* Slotover; *Career* articles West End firm of surveyors and valuers 1952–58, fndr ptnr and chm Conrad Ritblat and Co (conslt surveyors and valuers) 1958, md Union Property Holdings (London) Ltd 1969, chm The British Land Company plc 1970–2006 (md 1970–2004, hon pres 2007–), chm Milner Estates plc 1997–; cmmr Crown Estate Paving Cmmn 1969, memb Bd of Govrs The Weizmann Inst 1991, sole sponsor British Nat Ski Championships 1978–2001, hon surveyor King George's Fund for Sailors 1979, memb Cncl RGS 1984 (life memb 1982), pres British Ski Fedn 1994– (vice-pres 1984–89), dep chm and govr RAM; memb: Prince of Wales' Royal Parks Tree Appeal Ctee, Fin Devpt Bd NSPCC, British Library Bd 1995, Governing Body RAM 1998; dep chm and govr Hall Sch, govr London Business Sch (chm 2006–); hon life FRSA, life fell Royal Instn 2001 (memb Cncl 2002–); FSVA 1968, CIMgt, Hon RA; *Recreations* antiquarian books, old buildings, galleries, golf, skiing, real tennis; *Clubs* RAC, MCC, Carlton, Cresta (St Moritz), Queen's; *Style*— Sir John Ritblat

RITCHIE, Alasdair William; s of James Martin Ritchie (d 1993), of Beaconsfield, and Noreen Mary Louise, *née* Johnston; bro of Hamish Martin Johnston Ritchie, *qv*; *b* 10 March 1946; *Educ* Loretto; *m* 4 April 1970 (m dis), Fiona Margaret, da of James Barr Richardson; 1 da (Sally Ann b 2 June 1973), 1 s (Cameron Glen b 28 April 1976); *Career* trainee Trumans Brewery 1964–66, mktg exec Scott Paper USA 1966–68, dir Lonsdale Crowther UK 1971–73 (dep md 1973–76), dir Grey Advertising UK 1976–79, fndr Holmes Knight Ritchie (md 1979–90); TBWA: UK chm 1990–96, UK chief exec 1990–97, pres Europe 1996–98; pres and ceo TBWA International 1997–98, sr vice-pres (ops) TBWA Worldwide (following merger with Omnicom's BDDP Worldwide gp) 1998; pres (worldwide) Octagon (sports mktg arm of Interpublic Group) 1998–2003; ptnr Tangerine consultancy NY 2003–; MIPA; *Recreations* shooting, fishing, golf; *Clubs* Denham Golf,Branton Woods; *Style*— Alasdair Ritchie, Esq; ✉ 230 Pea Pond Road, Katonah, NY10536, USA

RITCHIE, Maj-Gen Andrew Stephenson; CBE (1999); s of Rev Canon David Caldwell Ritchie (d 2000), and Dilys, *née* Stephenson; *b* 30 July 1953, London; *Educ* Harrow Co Boys' Sch, RMA Sandhurst, Univ of Durham (BA); *m* 16 Dec 1981, Camilla, *née* Trollope; 2 da (Annabel b 3 Dec 1986, Charlotte b 30 Apr 1992), 1 s (Alexander b 12 Nov 1988); *Career* cmd RA 1973, regtl serv UK, Belize, Rhodesia and Germany 1974–84, Staff Coll 1985, SO Second Dir of Mil Ops MOD 1986–87, 3 RHA Germany, Cyprus and UK 1988–90, SO First Dir of Army Plans MOD 1990–92, CO 1 RHA UK 1992–95, COS 3 (UK) Div/Multinational Div SW Bosnia 1995–96, Higher Cmd and Staff Course 1997, Cdr RA 3 (UK) Div 1997–98, Dir Personal Servs (Army) 1998–2000, RCDS 2001, Dir Corporate Communications (Army) MOD 2001–02, GOC 4 Div 2002–03, Cmdt RMA Sandhurst 2003–06; dir Goodenough Coll 2006–; pres RA Hunt 2006–; tstee Br Forces Fndn 2003–; memb Cncl Marlborough Coll 2006–, govr Princess Helena Coll 2006–; Hon Col 100 (Yeo) Regt RA(V) 2000–, Col Cmdt RA 2005–; *Recreations* hunting, opera, tennis, golf; *Clubs* Boodle's; *Style*— Maj-Gen Andrew Ritchie, CBE; ✉ Goodenough College, Mecklenburgh Square, London WC1N 2AB (tel 020 7753 0574, e-mail director@goodenough.ac.uk)

RITCHIE, Prof Donald Andrew; CBE (2005), DL (Merseyside 2002); s of Andrew Ritchie (d 1985), of Falkirk, and Winifred Laura, *née* Parkinson (d 1998); *b* 9 July 1938; *Educ* Latymer's Sch London, Univ of Leicester (BSc), Postgrad Med Sch Univ of London (PhD); *m* 22 Aug 1962, (Margaret) Jeanne, da of Henry Eden Collister, of Port St Mary, IOM; 1 da (Sarah b 1967), 1 s (Charles b 1969); *Career* research assoc Biophysics Dept Johns Hopkins Univ 1964–66, sr lectr Dept of Virology Univ of Glasgow 1972–78 (lectr 1966–72); Univ of Liverpool: prof of genetics 1978–2003, pro-vice-chllr 1992–95; Royal Soc Leverhulme Tst sr research fell 1991–92; Royal Acad of Engrg visiting prof Univ of Liverpool 2004–06; SERC: chm Molecular Biology and Genetics Ctee 1985–88, memb Science Bd 1988–91, chm Educn and Trg Panel 1988–91; NERC: memb Cncl 1990–95, chm Terrestrial and Freshwater Sciences Ctee 1992–95, chm Marine and Freshwater Microbial Biodiversity Steering Ctee 1999–2005; professional affrs offr Soc for Gen Microbiology 1998–2001; memb: DTI Biotechnol Jt Advsy Bd 1991–94, Food Res Ctee AFRC 1991–94, Cncl Marine Biological Assoc 1991–94, Fin and Environment Ctees Inst of Biology 1996–2002; Bd of Environment Agency: memb Bd 1998–2005, dep chm 2001–05; chm: Merseyside Nat Art Collections Fund 1996–2000, Liverpool Scottish Museum Tst 1999–, Cncl of Military Educn Ctees, King's Regt Museum Tst 2006–; memb Cncl Liverpool Sch of Tropical Med 1993–98; memb: RFCA NW England and IOM 1995–, SaBRE Merseyside 2003–06; govr: IOM Int Business Sch 2000–, Shrewsbury Sch 2003– (dep chm 2006–); Hon Col Univ of Liverpool OTC 2001–07; FIBiol 1978, FRSE 1979, CBiol 1985; *Books* Molecular Virology (with T H Pennington, 1975), Introduction to Virology (with K M Smith FRS, 1980); *Recreations* painting, gardening, walking; *Clubs* Athenaeum (Liverpool), Army and Navy; *Style*— Prof Donald Ritchie, CBE, DL, FRSE; ✉ Glenfinnan, 19 Bertram Drive, Meols, Wirral CH47 0LG (tel 0151 632 1985, e-mail d.a.ritchie@liverpool.ac.uk)

RITCHIE, Hamish Martin Johnston; s of James Martin Ritchie (d 1993), of Beaconsfield, Bucks, and Noreen Mary Louise, *née* Johnston; bro of Alasdair William Ritchie, *qv*; *b* 22 February 1942; *Educ* Loretto, ChCh Oxford (MA); *m* 20 Sept 1967, (Judith) Carol, da of Frank Knight Young (d 1992), of Bearsden, Scotland; 1 s (Stuart b 1970), 1 da (Susan b 1972); *Career* md Hogg Robinson UK Ltd 1980–81 (dir 1974–80); chm: Marsh & McLennan Companies UK Ltd 1983–2004, dir Marsh Ltd 1997–2004; dir Br Insurance Brokers Assoc 2002–04; chm R&A Pension Fund; tstee: Eng Nat Ballet 2000–05, Princess Royal Tst for Carers 2000–05, Tower Hill Tst; *Recreations* music and all sport (especially golf); *Clubs* MCC, RAC (dir 1990–99), Royal & Ancient, Denham Golf; *Style*— Hamish Ritchie, Esq; ✉ Oldhurst, Bulstrode Way, Gerrards Cross, Bucks SL9 7QT (tel 01753 883262)

RITCHIE, Ian Carl; CBE (2000); s of Christopher Charles Ritchie (d 1959), and Mabel Berenice, *née* Long (d 1981); *b* 24 June 1947, Hove, Sussex; *Educ* Varndean GS Brighton, Liverpool Sch of Architecture, Central London Poly (DipArch); *m* Jocelyne Van den Bossche; 1 s (Inti Timote Hugo b 1983); *Career* architect; ptnr Chrysalis Architects 1979–81, princ Ian Ritchie Architects 1981–, co-fndr and dir Rice Francis Ritchie (RFR) Paris (engrg design) 1981–88; projects incl: Fluy House Picardy 1976–77, Eagle Rock House Sussex 1980–82, La Villette Science City (with A Fainsilber) Paris 1981–86, The Louvre (sculpture courts and pyramids with I M Pei) Paris 1985–93, Roy Square Housing Limehouse 1986–88, Ecology Gallery at Natural History Museum 1989–90, Reina Sofia CARS Madrid (with Castro and Onzono) 1989–91, offices at Stockley Park London 1989–91, Albert Cultural Centre Somme 1991–93, Terrasson Cultural Greenhouse 1992–94, Leipzig Messe Central Glass Hall (with V Marg) 1992–96, HV Pylons for Electricité de France 1995, London Regatta Centre 1995–97, Crystal Palace Concert Platform 1997, Scotland's Home of Tomorrow Glasgow 1997, The Spire (Dublin's 21st century nat monument) 1998, ARTE TV HQ Strasbourg 1998, White City Redevelopment 1998–, Milan's Light Monument, Plymouth Theatre Royal Prodn Centre 1999–2002, RSC Courtyard Theatre 2005, Jubilee Line Extension Bermondsey Station, L'Arche Cloud Paris; cmmr: Royal Fine Art Cmmn (RFAC) 1995–99, CABE 1999–2001 (now cmmr emeritus); advsr Nat History Museum 1991–95, advsr to the Lord Chllr 1999–2004, advsr Arup Fndn 2003–, masterplanner to British Museum 2004–06, govr and architectural advsr RSC 2001– (memb Int Cncl 2006–); designs exhibited and published worldwide; special prof Sch of Civil Engrg Univ of Leeds 2001–04, prof of architecture Royal Acad of Arts 2004–; visiting prof: Moscow Univ 1991, TU Vienna 1994–95; has taught at: Oita Univ Japan 1970, Planning Sch PCL 1972, Architectural Assoc 1979–82; DTI IBIS Project gatekeeper 1996–2001, chm Europan UK 1997–2003; memb: Urban Design Advsy Gp LDDC 1990–97, Cncl UK Steel Construction Inst 1994–97, Editorial Bd CITY jl 1994–99, Research Advsy Ctee Nat Maritime Museum 1995–97, UK Govt Foresight Construction Panel 1996–98, Spatial Devpt Strategy Policy Cmmn GLA 2000–01, Advsy Ctee Interdisciplinary Design for the Built Environment (IDBE) Univ of Cambridge 2001–04, European Construction Technol Platform High Level Gp 2005–, Mayor of London's Design Panel 2007–, UK Nat Construction Technol Platform, Built Environment Panel and Design Panel ctees Royal Cmmn for the Exhbn of 1851; RIBA: external examiner 1983–95 and 2000–04, Pres's Medal assessor 1987, nat chm of awards 1988, Civic Tst assessor, chair RIBA Stirling Awards 2006; Royal Acad of Arts: memb Cncl, chm Arts Collections and Library Ctee 2000–, memb Mgmnt Ctee 2001–04, memb Magazine Editorial Bd; memb: IABSE, Scientists for Global Responsibility; registered ARB 1979, registered German architect 1993, Tableau de L'Ordre des Architectes Français 1982; Hon DLitt Univ of Westminster 2000; RIBA 1979, FRSA 1981, RA 1998; *Awards* Silver Medal Architectural Design 1982, Plus Beaux Ouvrages de Construction Metallique France 1986 and 1988, IRITECNA Prize for Europe 1991, Eric Lyons Meml Award for Euro Housing 1992, Robert Matthew Award for innovation and advancement of architecture Commonwealth Assoc of Architects 1994, RFAC Tst Arts Building of the Year 1998, Stephen Lawrence Award 1998, RIBA Awards 1998, 2000, 2003 and 2004, shortlisted Stirling Prize 1998, 2003 and 2004, Civic Tst Award 1998 and 2002, AIA Award London 1998 and 2003, RFAC Tst Sports Building of the Year 2000, Silver Medal Académie d'Architecture France 2000, 2 Design Cncl Millennium Product Awards 2000, Regeneration of Scotland Supreme Award 2000, IABSE Int Outstanding Structure Award 2000, Copper Building of the Year 2000, Innovation in Copper Award 2000 and 2003, RFAC Tst Building of the Year 2003, Abercrombie Architectural Design Award 2005, West Midlands Architect of the Year 2006; *Publications* (Well) Connected Architecture (1994), Architektur mit (Guten) Verbindungen (1994), The Biggest Glass Palace in the World (1997), subject of Ian Ritchie Tecnoecologia (A Rocca, 1998, in Italian, trans into English as Ian Ritchie Technoecology, 1998), Plymouth Theatre Royal Production Centre (2003), The Spire (2004), RSC Courtyrard Theatre (2006), Leipzig Glass Hall (2007); *Recreations* art, swimming, reading, writing; *Clubs* Arts; *Style*— Ian C Ritchie, Esq, CBE, RA; ✉ c/o Ian Ritchie Architects Limited, 110 Three Colt Street, London E14 8AZ (tel 020 7338 1100, fax 020 7338 1199, e-mail iritchie@ianritchiearchitects.co.uk, website www.ianritchiearchitects.co.uk)

RITCHIE, Ian Russell; s of Hugh Russell Ritchie (d 1985), of Leeds, and Sheelah, *née* Mathews; *b* 27 November 1953; *Educ* Leeds GS, Trinity Coll Oxford (MA); *m* 10 June 1982, Jill Evelyn, da of Douglas Middleton-Walker, of Boston Spa, W Yorks; 2 s (Andrew Russell b 13 Jan 1987, Bruce Douglas b 6 March 1990); *Career* called to the Bar Middle Temple 1976 (Astbury law scholar), in practice 1976–78; industrial rels advsr Engrg Employers' Assoc Yorks 1978–80, various posts rising to head of prodn servs Granada Television Manchester 1980–88; Tyne Tees Television: dir of resources 1988–91, md 1991–93, gp dep chief exec Yorkshire Tyne Tees Television Holdings plc (following merger) 1992–93 (resigned); md The Television House 1993–94, md London News Network 1994–95, chief exec Channel 5 Broadcasting 1996–97, md Russell Reynolds Assocs exec search conslts 1997–98, chief exec Middle East Broadcasting Centre 1998–2000; Associated Press: ceo Television News 2000–, vice-pres Global Business 2002–, md AP Int 2002–; formerly: chm Newcastle Common Purpose, dir The Wearside Opportunity, dir West Ham United plc, govr Univ of Northumbria at Newcastle (formerly Newcastle Poly); FRSA; *Recreations* golf, tennis, theatre; *Clubs* Vincent's (Oxford); *Style*— Ian Ritchie, Esq

RITCHIE, Jean Harris; QC (1992); da of Walter Weir Ritchie (d 1979), and Lily, *née* Goodwin; *b* 6 April 1947; *Educ* St Martin's Sch Solihull (scholar), King's Coll London (LLB, AKC), McGill Univ Montreal (LLM); *m* Guy Thomas Knowles Boney, QC, *qv*, s of Dr Knowles Boney, MD; 2 s (R Oliver C b 21 Jan 1979, Christian V K b 29 March 1981); *Career* called to the Bar Gray's Inn 1970 (Churchill scholarship, Lord Justice Holker sr exhbn, bencher 2000); recorder W Circuit 1993–, head of chambers 2000–04; memb: Supreme Ct Rule Ctee 1993–97, Bd and Civil Ctee Judicial Studies Bd 1996–2001, QC Selection Panel 2006–; chm of the inquiry into the care and treatment of Christopher Clunis 1993–94, chm Ritchie Inquiry into Quality and Practice within the NHS arising from the actions of Rodney Ledward 1999–2000; memb Medical Ethics Ctee King Edward Hosp London 2003–, memb City Panel Treloar Tst 2005–; chm of govrs Norman Court Prep Sch 1996–2000; *Recreations* family; *Style*— Miss Jean Ritchie, QC; ✉ King's Head House, Stockbridge, Hampshire SO20 6EU

RITCHIE, Prof Lewis Duthie; OBE (2001); s of Lewis Duthie Ritchie, of Fraserburgh, and Sheila Gladys, *née* Noble; *b* 26 June 1952; *Educ* Fraserburgh Acad, Univ of Aberdeen (Collie bursar, BSc, MB ChB, MD, John Watt prize, Smith Davidson Prize, Munday and Venn prize, RCGP Aberdeen and Kincardine prize), Univ of Edinburgh (MSc); *m* 8 July 1978, Heather, da of Arthur William Skelton; *Career* MO Aberdeen Hosps 1978–81, trainee in community med 1981–84, princ GP Peterhead Health Centre 1984–, hon conslt in public health med Grampian Health Bd 1993– (conslt in public health med 1987–92), Sir James Mackenzie prof of gen practice Univ of Aberdeen 1993– (lectr in gen practice 1984–92, head Dept of Gen Practice and Primary Care 1993–); John Perry Prize (Primary Health Care Gp Br Computer Soc) 1991, Ian Stokoe Meml Award (RCGP) 1992, Blackwell Prize (Univ of Aberdeen) 1995, Eric Elder Medal (Royal NZ Coll of GPs); MBCS 1985, chartered computer engr 1993, chartered IT professional 2004; FRSM 1985, FFPHM 1993 (MFPHM 1983), FRCGP 1994 (MRCGP 1982), FRCPEd 1995, FRSA 2001, FBCS 2004; *Books* Computers in Primary Care (1984, 2 edn 1986, Spanish edn 1991); author of pubns on cardiovascular disease, community hospitals, computers, immunisation, oncology; *Recreations* church, dog walking, swimming, reading military history and biography, classical music, art appreciation; *Clubs* Deir; *Style*— Prof Lewis Ritchie, OBE; ✉ Cramond, 79 Strichen Road, Fraserburgh, Aberdeenshire AB43 9QJ (tel 01346 510191, fax 01346 515598); Department of General Practice and Primary Care, University of Aberdeen, Foresterhill Health Centre, Westburn Road, Aberdeen AB25 2AY (tel 01224 553066, fax 01224 550683, e-mail l.d.ritchie@abdn.ac.uk)

RITCHIE, Richard Bulkeley; s of W Ritchie (d 1984), of Dublin, and Ruth Mary, *née* Bulkeley; *b* 6 September 1952; *Educ* Shrewsbury, St Catherine's Coll Oxford (BA); *m* 28 Sept 1985, Dr Susan Rosemary Foister, da of Philip Foister, Hastings; 2 s (Felix b 1986, Joshua b 1992), 1 da (Isabella b 1988); *Career* called to the Bar Middle Temple 1978, standing counsel to the DTI in insolvency matters 1989, jr cncl to the Crown (Chancery A Panel) 1994–2004; *Style*— Richard Ritchie, Esq; ✉ 24 Old Buildings, Lincoln's Inn, London WC2A 3UJ (tel 020 7404 0946, fax 020 7405 1360)

RITCHIE, Prof William; OBE (1994); s of Alexander Ritchie, and Rebecca Smith, *née* Caldwell; *b* 22 March 1940; *Educ* Wishaw High Sr Secdy Sch, Univ of Glasgow (BSc, PhD); *m* 29 March 1965, Elizabeth Armstrong Bell; 2 s (Derek Alexander b 26 June 1967, Craig William b 11 Dec 1968), 1 da (Lynne Elspeth b 10 Feb 1978); *Career* res asst Univ of Glasgow 1963; Univ of Aberdeen: asst lectr 1964–66, lectr 1966–72, sr lectr 1972–79, prof 1979–95, dean of Faculty of Arts and Social Sciences 1988–89, vice-princ 1990–95; vice-chllr Lancaster Univ 1995–2002; dir Aberdeen Inst for Coastal Science and Mgmnt 2002–, Macaulay Land Use Research Inst 2006; adjunct prof World Maritime Univ Malmo 2002–; former hon prof Louisiana State Univ; hon ed Jl of Coastal Conservation; ind chm Scottish Aquaculture Research Forum 2004–, chm Monitoring Ctee Shetland Oil Terminal Environmental Advsy Gp, memb Bd of Tstees Nat Maritime Museum 2000–05; nat chm Royal Scottish Geographical Soc 2005– (former chm Aberdeen Branch); sometime memb: Scot Examination Bd, Scot Univs Cncl of Entrance, Nature Conservancy Cncl (Scot); formerly: recorder and pres Section E BAAS, chm Scottish Office Ecological Steering Gps for the oil spill in Shetland, chm Sec of State for Scotland's Advsy Ctee on Sustainable Devpt, chm Sec of State for Scotland's Ctee on SSSIs, vice-chm Sullom Voe Oil Terminal Environmental Advsy Gp, chm St Fergus Dunes Tech Mgmnt Ctee, convenor SCOVACT, memb Fulbright Cmmn; memb Cncl RSE; Hon DUniv Stirling, Hon DSc Lancaster Univ; FRSGS 1980, FRSE 1982, FRICS 1989; *Books* Mapping for Field Scientists (1977), Beaches of Highlands and Islands of Scotland (1978), Beaches of Scotland (1984), Surveying and Mapping for Field Scientists (1988), The Coastal Sand Dunes of Louisiana (Volume 1 Isles Dernieres (1989), Volume 2 Plaquemines (1990), Volume 3 Chandeleurs (1992), Volume 4 Bayou Lafourche Coastline (1995); *Style*— Prof William Ritchie, OBE, FRSE; ✉ AICSM, School of Geosciences, King's College, Aberdeen AB24 3UE (tel 01224 273856, fax 01224 272497)

RITCHIE OF DUNDEE, 5 Baron (UK 1905); (Harold) Malcolm Ritchie; s of 2 Baron Ritchie of Dundee (d 1948), and Sarah Ruth, da of Louis Jennings, MP; suc bro, 4 Baron, 1978; *b* 29 August 1919; *Educ* Stowe, Trinity Coll Oxford (MA); *m* 1948, Anne, da of Col Charles G Johnstone, MC, of Durban, South Africa; 1 da (Hon Philippa Jane b 1954), 1 s (Hon (Charles) Rupert Rendall b 1958); *Heir* s, Hon Rupert Ritchie; *Career* Capt KRRC WWII, served ME, Greece and Italy; headmaster Brickwall House Sch 1965–72 (asst headmaster 1952–65), English and drama teacher Bedgebury Sch until 1984; Lib Dem educn spokesman House of Lords 1985–93; pres Rye Memorial Care Centre 1999–, pres Arts Dyslexia Tst 1999–; *Recreations* the arts; *Style*— The Rt Hon Lord Ritchie of Dundee; ✉ The Roundel, Springsteps, Winchelsea, East Sussex TN36 4EH (tel 01797 226440)

RITCHLEY, Martin Howard; s of Robert William Ritchley (d 1964), of Orpington, Kent, and Bertha Amy, *née* Jones (d 1999); *b* 1 July 1946; *Educ* City of London Sch; *m* 3 July 1970, (Mary) Elizabeth, da of Albert William Burns (d 1969), of Stevenage, Herts; 2 da (Catherine b 1971, Anna b 1980), 1 s (David b 1975); *Career* articled to Barton Mayhew & Co Chartered Accountants 1964–70; Coventry Economic Building Society: chief accountant 1970–76, sec 1976–83; Coventry Building Society: sec 1983–89, dir 1985–2006, dep chief exec 1989–90, chief exec 1990–2006; chm CV One Ltd 2002–06; non-exec dir NFU Mutual Insurance Soc 2003–; chm Building Socs Assoc 2001–02 (memb Cncl 1996–2006, dep chm 2000–01), memb FSA Practitioner Panel 1998–2001, memb Exec Ctee Cncl of Mortgage Lenders 2001–02; govr Coventry Univ 1993–2001; Hon DBA Coventry Univ 2002; FCA 1979 (ACA 1969), FCIB 2002; *Recreations* golf; *Clubs* Coventry Golf, Saunton Golf; *Style*— Martin Ritchley, Esq

RITSON, Dr (Edward) Bruce; s of Maj Harold Ritson (d 1979), of Edinburgh, and Ivy, *née* Catherall (d 1972); *b* 20 March 1937; *Educ* Edinburgh Acad, Univ of Edinburgh, Harvard Univ (MD, MB ChB, DPM); *m* 25 Sept 1965, Eileen Teresa, da of Leonard Carey, of Dublin; 1 da (Fenella b 1968), 1 s (Gavin b 1970); *Career* dir Sheffield Region Addiction Unit 1968–71, conslt and clinical dir Royal Edinburgh Hosp 1971–2002, sr lectr in psychiatry Univ of Edinburgh 1971–; advsr WHO 1977–, conslt W Australia Alcohol and Drug Authy 1983; vice-pres: Med Cncl on Alcohol, Substance Misuse Faculty RCPsych; chm: Howard League (Scotland) until 2006, DVLA Drug and Alcohol Advsy Ctee, Art in Healthcare, Scottish Health Action on Alcohol Problems; FRCPsych 1979, FRCP (Edinburgh) 1987; *Books* The Management of Alcoholism (with C Hassall, 1970), Alcohol: The Prevention Debate (with M Grant, 1983), Alcohol Our Favourite Drug (1986), Tackling Alcohol Together (1999); *Recreations* theatre, travel, squash; *Style*— Dr Bruce Ritson; ✉ 4 McLaren Road, Edinburgh EH9 2BH (tel 0131 667 1735); Royal Edinburgh Hospital, Morningside Park, Edinburgh EH10 5DX (tel 0131 537 6000, e-mail drbruceritson@zoom.co.uk)

RITTER, Prof Mary Alice; *Educ* Berkhamsted Sch for Girls, St Hilda's Coll Oxford (MA, Dip), Wolfson Coll Oxford (DPhil); *Family*; 3 s; *Career* research assoc Univ of Connecticut 1976–78, research fell ICRF London 1978–84; Imperial College London (formerly Royal Postgrad Med Sch London): lectr 1982–86, sr lectr1986–88, reader in immunology 1988–91, prof of immunology 1991–, vice-dean (educn) 1992–97, asst vice-princ (postgrad med) 1998–2000, dir Grad Sch of Life Scis and Med 2000–06, pro-rector (postgraduate and int affrs) 2004–; memb Cncl and chm Scientific Advsy Panel Action Research 1997–2000 (vice-chm Scientific Advsy Panel 1994–96); chm Nat Steering Ctee Research Cncls UK GRAD Prog 2005– (memb 2004–05); memb: Research Advsy Ctee Research into Ageing 2000–05, New Route PhD Consortium Nat Steering Ctee 2001–, Prog Review Ctee Cambridge-MIT Inst 2004–, Non-Clinical Trg and Career Devpt Panel MRC 2005–, Academic Careers Ctee (Non-Clinical) Acad of Medical Sciences 2006–, PM's Initative 2 Ctee 2006–, Govt UKIERI Evaluation Panel 2006–, German Excellence Initiative (Third Stream) 2006 and 2007; FHEA (FILT 2001), FRSA 2004, FCGI 2006, FRCPath 2006; *Publications* The Thymus (jtly, 1992); more than 100 research articles in scientific learned jls; *Recreations* travelling, gardening, cycling, biography, baroque music, ballet, opera; *Style*— Prof Mary Ritter; ✉ Imperial College London, Level 4, Faculty Building, South Kensington Campus, Exhibition Road, London SW7 2AZ (tel 020 7594 1412, fax 020 7594 8802)

RITTERMAN, Dame Janet Elizabeth; DBE (2002); da of Charles Eric Palmer, of Sydney, Australia, and Laurie Helen, *née* Fuller; *b* 1 December 1941; *Educ* N Sydney Girls' HS, NSW State Conservatorium of Music (Frank Shirley Prize, Shadforth Hooper Prize, DSCM), Sydney Teachers' Coll Univ of Sydney, Univ of Durham (BMus), Univ of London (Hilda Margaret Watts Prize for Musicology, MMus, PhD); *m* 19 Dec 1970, Gerrard Peter Ritterman; *Career* teacher: Strathfield Girls' HS Sydney 1963–66, Swaffield Jr Mixed Infants Sch London 1967–68, Cheltenham Girls' HS Sydney 1968–69, Watford GS for Girls 1969–74; sr lectr in music: Middx Poly 1975–79, Goldsmiths Coll London 1980–87; Dartington Coll of Arts: head of music 1987–90, dean 1988–90, princ 1990–93; dir Royal Coll of Music 1993–2005 (vice-pres 2005–); visiting prof in music educn Univ of Plymouth 1993–2005; external examiner: BA Kingston Poly 1987–90, Univ of Glasgow 1991–95, KCL 1995–99; chief external examiner: PGCE Bradford and Ilkley Community Coll 1987–91, Welsh Coll of Music and Drama 1990–93, Manchester Metropolitan Univ 1991–93; chair: Arts Cncl Review of Training of Opera Singers 1992–93, ABRSM (Publishing) Ltd 1993–2005, Arts Cncl of England and BBC Nat Review of Orchestral Provision 1994–95, Subject Panel in Music Univ of London 1994–2000, The Mendelssohn and Boise Fndns 1996–98 and 2002–04, Advsy Cncl Arts Research Ltd 1997–2005, Fedn of Br Conservatoires 1998–2003, Postgrad Ctee AHRB 2002–04; memb: Music Ctee Schs Examination and Assessment Cncl 1989–92, Exec Bd SW Arts 1991–93, Music Panel Arts Cncl of GB 1992–98, RMA Cncl 1994–2004, Exec Ctee ISM 1996–99, Bd ENO 1996–2004, Postgrad Panel AHRB 1998–2002, Euro Sci Fndn Humanities Programme 1999–2002, Steering Ctee London HE Consortium 1999–2005, Arts Cncl of England 2000–02, DfES Advsy Ctee Music and Dance Scheme 2001–05, Br Acad Review 'Creativity and the Economy' 2002–03, Wissenschaftsrat Bundesministerium für Bildung Wissenschaft und Kultur Austria 2003–, Nominating Ctee AHRC 2005–, Educn Advsy Ctee Nuffield Fndn 2007–; tstee: The Countess of Munster Musical Tst 1993–2005, Plymouth Chamber Music Tst; conslt Govrs' Music Ctee Bd of Govrs of Wells Cathedral Sch 1993–2000; govr: Purcell Sch 1996–2000, Heythrop Coll London 1996–2006, Goldsmiths Coll London 2002–; fell Heythrop Coll Univ of London 2007; memb: ISM, RMA, RSM, Soc for Research in the Psychology of Music and Music Educn; Hon DUniv Univ of Central England Birmingham 1996, Hon DLitt Univ of Ulster 2004, Hon DUniv Middlesex 2005; fell: UC Northampton 1997, Dartington Coll of Arts 1997, RCA 2004; Hon RAM 1995, Hon GSMD 2000; FRSA, FRNCM 1996, FHEA 2007; *Conference papers* incl: A Nineteenth Century Phoenix: the Concert Spirituel in Paris 1800–1830 (1986), Educating Tomorrow's Musicians (1988), Music History: its role in Higher Education Music (1989), Principle and Practice: the future of higher education in music (1991), First Impressions, Second Thoughts: Composers and their Reworkings (1993), Tradition and the individual talent: a musical perspective (1993), The Conservatoire within the Community: Challenging the Values (1994), Music Education National Debate 'Performing Music, Knowing Music' (1995), Learning What it is to Perform: A Key to Peer Learning for Musicians (1998), Teaching How to Learn, Learning How to Teach: Educating Musicians for the Twenty-first Century (1999), Grove as Director (2000), Making Music Work (2000); *Publications* Training the Specialist Class Music Teacher of the Future (Music for a Small Planet, Int Soc for Music Educn Yearbook, 1984), Les concerts spirituels à Paris au début du XIXe siècle (Revue internationale de musique française 1985), Questions unanswered or unasked?: Thoughts on teacher-student interaction in music education (Int Jl of Music Educn, 1987), Music plus?: a recipe for success (Music Teacher, 1989), Music History - on the decline? (Br Jl of Music Educn, 1990), Piano Music and the Public Concert (Chopin Studies, ed J Samson 1992), Craft for Art's Sake: Variations on a Traditional Theme (1995), 'Gegensätze, Ecken und scharfe Kanten': Clara Schumanns Besuche in England, 1856–1888 (1996), On Teaching Performance (Musical Performance: A Guide to Understanding, ed J Rink, 2002), Grove as First Director of the RCM (George Grove: Music and Victorian Culture, ed M Musgrave, 2003), The Royal College of Music, 1883–1899: pianists and their contribution to the forming of a national conservatoire (Musical Life in Europe (1770–1914): Compositional, Institutional, and Political Challenges, ed M Fend and M Noiray, 2005); *Reports* National Review of Opera Training (Arts Cncl of GB 1993), ACE and BBC Review of National Orchestral Provision - Consultation Document (Arts Cncl 1995), The Conservatories of Finland (National Bd of Educn Finland) 1997, Learning What it is to Perform: a Key to Peer Learning for Musicians (2000); *Recreations* theatre, reading, country walking; *Style*— Dame Janet Ritterman, DBE; ✉ e-mail jritterman@blueyonder.co.uk

RITTNER, Luke Philip Hardwick; *b* 24 May 1947; *Educ* Blackfriars Sch, City of Bath Tech Coll, Dartington Coll of Arts, LAMDA; *m* 1974, Corinna Frances Edholm; 1 da; *Career* asst admin Bath Festival 1968, admin dir Bath Festival 1974–76, dir and fndr Assoc for Business Sponsorship of the Arts (now Arts and Business) 1976–83, sec-gen Arts Cncl of GB 1983–90, British cultural dir Expo '92 Seville 1990–92, dir of communications and public affrs Sotheby's 1992–99; currently chief exec Royal Acad of Dance; non-exec dir Carlton Television 1990–93; judge Theatre Panel Olivier Awards 1992–94, jury memb Shakespeare Prize 2000–06, judge Dance Panel Olivier Awards 2003–04, judge Theatre Panel Olivier Awards 2007–; chm: English Shakespeare Co 1990–94, Exec Bd LAMDA 1994–, London Chorus (formerly London Choral Soc) 1994–2005; memb: Cncl Almeida Theatre 2000–02, Bd The Actors Centre 2000–02; patron: New London Orch 1998–2003, Dartington Coll of Arts Appeal 2002–; tstee: Victoria and Albert Museum 1980–83, The Hanover Band 1998–2002; Hon Doctor of Arts Univ of Bath 2004, Hon DCL Univ of Durham 2006; *Clubs* Garrick; *Style*— Luke Rittner, Esq; ✉ Royal Academy of Dance, 36 Battersea Square, London SW11 3RA

RIVERDALE, 3 Baron (UK 1935); Sir Anthony Robert Balfour; 3 Bt (UK 1929); s of Hon Mark Robin Balfour (d 1995) and Susan Ann, *née* Phillips (d 1996), suc grandfather 2 Baron Riverdale, DL (d 1998); *b* 23 November 1960; *Heir* cous, Arthur Michael Balfour b 24 Nov 1938; *Style*— The Rt Hon the Lord Riverdale

RIVERS, Prof Isabel; da of Anthony Haigh (d 1989), and Pippa, *née* Dodd (d 1976); *b* 9 May 1944; *Educ* St Helen's Sch Northwood, Girton Coll Cambridge (BA), Columbia Univ NY (MA, PhD); *m* 15 June 1963, Thomas Max Rivers, s of Erwin Rothbarth (d 1944), and Myfanwy, *née* Charles (d 2000); 1 s (Oliver Max 29 Nov 1966), 1 da (Frances Lucy b 28 Feb 1971); *Career* asst lectr Sch of English and American Studies UEA 1969–70, Ottilie Hancock research fell Girton Coll Cambridge 1970–73, lectr Dept of English Univ of Leicester 1973–84 (reader 1984–85), tutorial fell in English St Hugh's Coll Oxford 1985–2004; Univ of Oxford: lectr in English 1985–2004, titular reader 1996–2000, titular prof of English language and literature 2000–04; prof of eighteenth-century english literature and culture Queen Mary Univ of London 2004–, co-dir Dr Williams's Centre for Dissenting Studies 2004–; Leverhulme major research fell 2000–03; memb Int Assoc of Univ Professors of English 2004, fell of the English Assoc 2004; *Books* The Poetry of Conservatism, 1600–1745: A Study of Poets and Public Affairs from Jonson to Pope (1973), Classical and Christian Ideas in English Renaissance Poetry: A Students' Guide (1979, 2 edn 1994), Books and their Readers in Eighteenth-Century England (ed, 1982), Reason, Grace and Sentiment: A Study of the Language of Religion and Ethics in England, 1660–1780 (2 vols, 1991–2000), Books and their Readers in Eighteenth-Century England: New Essays (ed, 2001); *Recreations* opera, theatre, art galleries, looking at churches and houses, gardening; *Style*— Prof Isabel Rivers; ✉ School of English and Drama, Queen Mary, University of London, Mile End Road, London E1 4NS (e-mail i.rivers@qmul.ac.uk)

RIVETT-CARNAC, Cdr Miles James; 9 Bt (UK 1836), of Derby; DL (Hants 1996); s of Vice Adm James Rivett-Carnac (d 1970), and Isla Nesta, *née* Blackwood (d 1973); suc bro, Rev Canon Sir (Thomas) Nicholas Rivett-Carnac, 8 Bt (d 2004); *b* 7 February 1933; *Educ* RNC Dartmouth; *m* 11 Oct 1958, April Sally, da of Maj Arthur Andrew Sidney Villar (d 1966), of London; 1 da (Lucinda Jane (Lulu Guinness, *qv*) b 1960), 2 s (Jonathan James b 1962, Simon Miles b 1966); *Heir* s, Jonathan Rivett-Carnac; *Career* Cdr RN 1965, cmd HMS Woolaston 1963–65 (despatches), Armed Forces Staff Coll Norfolk Virginia USA 1965, cmd HMS Dainty 1966–68, MOD 1968–70, ret 1970; joined Baring Bros & Co Ltd 1970 (dir 1975), md Outwich Ltd Johannesburg 1976–78, pres Baring Bros Inc 1978–81; memb Exec Ctee Baring Bros & Co 1981, dir Barings plc 1986–94, chief exec Baring Asset Management Ltd 1986–92, chm Baring Securities 1993–94; chm Tribune Investment Trust 1985–; dir: London Stock Exchange 1992–95, Allied Domecq plc (Allied-Lyons plc until 1994) 1992–97, Guinness Flight Hambro Asset Management Ltd; chm Hampshire and IOW Boys' Clubs, memb Exec Ctee King Edward VII Hosp, memb Cncl King George V Fund for Sailors; High Sheriff Hants 1995; Elder Brother Trinity House 1992; Vice-Lord Lt Hants 1999–; *Recreations* golf, tennis, stamps, racing; *Clubs* White's, Links (NY); *Style*— Cdr Sir Miles Rivett-Carnac, Bt, RN, DL; ✉ Martyr Worthy Manor, Winchester, Hampshire SO21 1DY (tel 01962 779 311)

RIVIERE, William D'Oyly; s of late Michael Valentine Briton Rivière, and Bridget D'Oyly, *née* D'Oyly-Hughes; *b* 15 May 1954; *Educ* Bradfield Coll, King's Coll Cambridge (MA); *m* 29 Aug 1992, Isabelle Sarah, *née* Corbett; 2 da (Camilla Isa b 4 May 1999, Miranda Josephine b 6 Aug 2002), 1 s from previous partner (Leo Forte b 27 June 1975); *Career* lectr: Univ of Verona 1980–84, Osaka Gakuin Univ 1985–89, Univ of Urbino 1990–; prof of modern English literature Univ of Urbino 1999–; author; memb Royal Soc of Asian Affairs 1990–; runner-up Trask Awards RSL 1989; Freeman Worshipful Co of Goldsmiths 1990; FRSL 2000; *Books* Watercolour Sky (1990), A Venetian Theory of Heaven (1992), Eros and Psyche (1994), Borneo Fire (1995), Echoes of War (1997), Kate Caterina (2001), By the Grand Canal (2004); *Recreations* travelling, sailing and planting trees; *Clubs* Travellers; *Style*— William Rivière, Esq

RIVINGTON, James Maitland Hansard; s of Herbert Lawrence Rivington, of London, and Catherine Sybil, *née* Cooke; *b* 21 October 1959; *Educ* St Paul's Sch London (Fndn Scholar), Magdalen Coll Oxford (exhibitioner, BA), Oxford Poly; *Career* Blackwell Scientific Publications London and Oxford 1982–86, publications offr The British Academy 1986–; Liveryman Worshipful Co of Stationers & Newspaper Makers 1984; Freeman City of London 1982; *Recreations* playing cricket in the summer, supporting Brentford FC in the winter; *Style*— James Rivington, Esq; ✉ 7 Julien Road, Ealing, London W5 4XA (tel 020 8579 4816); The British Academy, 10 Carlton House Terrace, London SW1Y 5AH (tel 020 7969 5200)

RIVLIN, His Hon Judge Geoffrey; QC (1979); s of Allenby Rivlin (d 1973), and May Rivlin (d 1980); *b* 28 November 1940; *Educ* Bootham Sch York, Univ of Leeds (LLB); *m* 1974, Maureen Smith, Hon ARAM, prof of violin RCM; 2 da (Emma b 30 Aug 1977, Sophie b 29 Nov 1981); *Career* called to the Bar Middle Temple 1963 (Colombus Prize in Int Law, bencher 1987); in practice NE Circuit 1963–89, jr of NE Circuit 1967–78, recorder of the Crown Court 1978–89, circuit judge (SE Circuit) 1989–2004, sr circuit judge 2004–; chm Advsy Bd Computer Related Crime Research Centre Queen Mary & Westfield Coll London 1996–2003; govr: St Christopher's Sch Hampstead 1990–98, N London Collegiate Sch 1992–2002; *Books* Understanding the Law (3rd edn, 2004); *Style*— His Hon Judge Rivlin, QC; ✉ Southwark Crown Court, 1 English Grounds, off Battlebridge Lane, London SE1 2HU

RIX, Rt Hon Lord Justice; Hon Sir Bernard Anthony Rix; kt (1993), PC (2000); s of Otto Rix (d 1982), of London, and Sadie, *née* Silverberg (d 1996); *b* 8 December 1944; *Educ* St Paul's, New Coll Oxford (MA), Harvard Law Sch (Kennedy scholar, LLM); *m* 1983, Hon Karen Debra Young, er da of Baron Young of Graffham, PC, *qv*; 3 s (Jacob, Gideon, Jonathan), 2 da (Hannah, Rachel); *Career* called to the Bar Inner Temple 1970 (bencher 1990, reader 2004, treas 2005); QC 1981, memb Senate of the Inns of Court and Bar 1981–83, recorder of the Crown Court 1990–93, judge of the High Court of Justice (Queen's Bench Div) 1993–2000, judge i/c Commercial List 1998–99; chm Advsy Cncl Centre of Commercial Law Studies Queen Mary Univ of London 2003–, tstee and dir Br Inst of Int and Comparative Law 2003–; chm Commercial Bar Assoc 1992–93, vice-pres Br Insur Law Assoc 2006–; pres Harvard Law Sch Assoc of the UK 2002–, vice-pres British Friends of Bar Ilan Univ 1999– (chm 1987–99), memb Bd of Tstees of Bar Ilan Univ 1988–99; vice-chm Central Cncl for Jewish Community Servs 1993–96; dir: London Philharmonic Orch 1986–, The Spiro Inst 1995–99; patron Wiener Library 2006–; FCIArb 1999; *Publications* author report on Jewish Youth Services and Organisations 1994; *Recreations* music, opera, Italy; *Style*— The Rt Hon Lord Justice Rix; ✉ Royal Courts of Justice, Strand, London WC2R 2LL (tel 020 7947 6000)

RIX, Baron (Life Peer UK 1992), of Whitehall in the City of Westminster and of Hornsea in Yorkshire; Sir Brian Norman Roger Rix; kt (1986), CBE (1977), DL (Greater London 1987); s of Herbert Dobson Rix (d 1966), of E Yorks, and Fanny, *née* Nicholson (d 1976); *b* 27 January 1924; *Educ* Bootham Sch York; *m* 1949, Elspet Jeans (the actress Elspet Gray), da of James MacGregor-Gray (d 1954), of Surrey; 2 da (Hon (Elspet) Shelley b 1951 d 2005, Hon Louisa b 1955), 2 s (Hon Jamie MacGregor b 1958, Hon Jonathan Robert MacGregor b 1960); *Career* WWII RAF and Bevin Boy; professional actor 1942, with White Rose Players Harrogate 1943, actor-manager 1948–77; ran repertory cos at Ilkley, Bridlington and Margate 1948–50, toured Reluctant Heroes and brought to Whitehall Theatre 1950–54, Dry Rot 1954–58, Simple Spymen 1958–61, One for the Pot 1961–64, Chase Me Comrade 1964–66, Stand By Your Bedouin, Uproar in the House and Let Sleeping Wives Lie Garrick Theatre 1967–69, She's Done It Again 1969–70, Don't Just Lie There, Say Something! 1971–73 (filmed 1973), Robinson Crusoe 1973, A Bit Between the Teeth 1974–75, Fringe Benefits 1976–77; entered films 1951 and subsequently made 13 films incl Reluctant Heroes 1951 and Dry Rot 1956; BBC TV contract to present farces on TV 1956–72, first ITV series Men of Affairs 1973, A Roof Over My Head (BBC) 1977; presenter: Let's Go (BBC TV series, first ever for people with a learning disability) 1978–83, BBC Radio 2 Series 1978–80; dir and theatre controller Cooney-Marsh Group 1977–80, chm Playhouse (Whitehall) Ltd 1992–93; memb Arts Cncl 1986–93 (chm Drama Panel, chm Arts and Disability Monitoring Ctee 1986–93); pres MENCAP 1998– (sec gen 1980–87, chm 1988–98); chm: Ind Devpt Cncl for People with Mental Handicap 1981–88, Libertas 1987–2006; tstee Theatre of Comedy 1983–93; pres Friends of Normansfield (chm 1976–2003), hon vice-pres Radio Soc of GB; Vice Lord-Lt Greater London 1988–97; chllr Univ of E London 1997–; fell Humberside Univ 1984; Hon MA: Univ of Hull 1981, Open Univ 1983; Hon DUniv Essex 1984, Hon DSc Univ of Nottingham 1987, Hon Dr Univ of Bradford 2000; Hon LLD: Univ of Manchester 1986, Univ of Dundee 1994, Univ of Exeter 1997; Hon FRSM 1998, Hon FRCPsych 1999 *Awards* Evian Health Award 1988, RNID Communicator of the year Award 1990, Spectator Campaigner of the Year Award 1999, Yorkshireman of the Year Lifelong Achievement Award 1999, Br Neuroscience Assoc Award for Public Service 2001, Lifetime Achievment Award UK Charity Awards 2001, ePolitix Charity Champions Lifetime Achievement Award 2004; *Books* My Farce from My Elbow (autobiography, 1975), Farce about Face - A Further Autobiography (1989), Tour de Farce (Touring Theatres and Strolling Players, 1992), Life in the Farce Lane (1995), History of Farce, Gullible's Travails (ed and contrib, 1996), All About Us! (2006); *Recreations* cricket, gardening, amateur radio; *Clubs* Garrick, MCC, Lord's Taverners (pres 1969–70); *Style*— The Rt Hon Lord Rix, CBE, DL; ✉ House of Lords, London SW1A 0PW

RIX, Gerald George; TD (and Clasp); s of Frederick Thomas Rix, DFC (d 1996), of Herts, and Olive Louise, *née* Sharp (d 1999); *b* 19 November 1934; *Educ* East Barnet GS, Univ of Dundee (MA), DipCAM; *m* 1, Nov 1957 (m dis 1973), Patricia Dyer; 1 da (Charlotte Emma b 1960), 2 s (Jonathan b 1961, Matthew Gerald b 1963); m 2, Dec 1975, Isla, da of Thomas McLauchlan (d 1967), of Clunes, Perthshire; *Career* RAF 1953–55; TA 1959–86, various Logistic, Engr and Reconnaissance Units, UK and NATO staff appts, Maj 1976; PR Div and Marine Fuel Mktg Div Shell Int Petroleum Co Ltd 1955–61; Foote, Cone & Belding Gp: joined PR Div 1961, fndr dir Welbeck PR 1967 (later concurrently md Welbeck City); Carl Byoir & Assocs: dep chm 1984–86, chm 1986–87; Hill and Knowlton London: gp md 1986, gp dep chm 1987; fndr Minerva Communications Services 1987–92, dir Hallmark Mktg Communications Winchester 1987–92; memb Educn Ctee IPR 1972 and 1978, diploma examiner, chief examiner and moderator CAM Fndn 1974–79 (visiting lectr to Athens 1976), memb Nat Speakers' Panel Advertising Assoc 1976–93, educn convenor Int PR Assoc World Congress London 1979, PR moderator Centre for Business Studies 1981–85, memb Mgmnt Ctee Assoc for Business Sponsorship of the Arts 1983–85, chm Diploma Working Party IPR 1985–86, memb Consultancy Mgmnt Ctee PRCA 1987–88; personal tutor Univ of Stirling 1990–94; double Abertay Soc prizewinner 1993; MIPA 1971, memb Int PR Assoc 1979, FIPR 1987 (MIPR 1962); *Recreations* fly fishing, shooting, archaeology; *Clubs* Special Forces; *Style*— Gerald Rix, Esq, TD; ✉ Main Street, Port Charlotte, Isle of Islay, Argyll PA48 7TX (tel and fax 01496 850595)

RIX, Dr Keith John Barkclay; s of Sgt Kenneth Benjamin Rix (d 2000), of Wisbech, Cambs, and Phyllis Irene, *née* Cousins (d 1984); *b* 21 April 1950; *Educ* Wisbech GS, Univ of Aberdeen (BMedBiol, MB ChB, MD), Univ of Edinburgh (MPhil); *m* 31 Jan 1976, Elizabeth Murray, da of Robert Lumsden (d 1993), of Tullibody, Clackmannanshire; 3 da (Virginia b 1977, Marianne b 1981, Rowena b 1982); *Career* visiting res scientist Res Inst on Alcoholism NY State Dept of Mental Hygiene 1973, res fell Dept of Physiology Univ of Aberdeen 1975–76, registrar in psychiatry Royal Edinburgh Hosp 1976–79, lectr in psychiatry Univ of Manchester 1979–83, visiting lectr Alcohol Studies Centre Univ of Paisley 1979–2000, unit med advsr and consIt psychiatrist St James's Univ Hosp Leeds 1983–94, sr lectr in psychiatry Univ of Leeds 1983–2000, visiting consIt psychiatrist HMP Leeds 1983–; consIt forensic psychiatrist: Leeds Community and Mental Health Servs Teaching NHS Tst 1994–2000, The Grange 2000–, Cygnet Hosp Wyke 2006–; fndr Aberdeen Cncl on Alcohol Problems, fndr memb Scottish Cncl on Alcohol Problems; past chm Ctee of Leeds ConsIt Psychiatrists; RCPsych: former chm MCQ Clinical Topics Panel, memb Panel of Observers; memb British Acad of Forensic Sciences; past pres Leeds and W Riding Medico-Legal Soc; assoc memb GMC (memb Fitness to Practise Panel); MIBiol, CBiol 1985, FRCPsych 1992 (MRCPsych 1979), MAE 1995, FEWI 2002 (MEWI 1997); *Books* Alcohol and Alcoholism (1977), Alcohol Problems (with Elizabeth Lumsden Rix, 1983), A Handbook for Trainee Psychiatrists (1987); *Recreations* bird watching, jazz, theatre, opera; *Clubs* Ronnie Scott's, RSM; *Style*— Dr Keith Rix; ✉ The Grange, 92 Whitcliffe Road, Cleckheaton, West Yorkshire BD19 3DR (tel 01274 878604, fax 01274 869898, e-mail drrix@the-grange.org.uk, website www.drkeithrix.co.uk)

RIX, Timothy John; CBE (1997); s of Howard Terrell Rix (d 1979), and Marguerite Selman, *née* Helps (d 1996); *b* 4 January 1934; *Career* Sub Lt RNVR 1952–54; Mellon fell Yale Univ 1957–58; Longmans Green & Co Ltd: joined 1958, overseas educnl publisher 1958–61, publishing mangr Far E and SE Asia 1961–63, head of English language teaching publishing 1964–68, divnl md 1968–72, jt md 1972–76, chief exec 1976, chm 1984; chm and chief exec: Longman Group Ltd 1984–90, Addison-Wesley-Longman Group Ltd 1988–89; dir: Pearson Longman Ltd 1979–83, Goldcrest TV 1982–83, Yale Univ Press 1984–, ECIC (Management) Ltd 1990–92, Blackie and Son Ltd 1990–95, Blackwell Ltd 1991–95, Meditech Media Ltd 1997–2003, Frances Lincoln Publishers Ltd 1997–, Jessica Kingsley Publishers Ltd 1997–, Scottish Book Source Ltd 1999–; chm Book Marketing Ltd 1990–2003, sr consIt The Pofcher Co and van Tulleken Co 1990–2006; pres Publishers Assoc 1982–84, dep chm Nat Book League 1985–86; chm: Book Tst 1986–88, Book House Training Centre 1986–89, Br Library Centre for the Book 1990–95, Soc of Bookmen 1990–92, British Library Publishing 1991–2003, Bell Educnl Tst 1994–2001 (govr 1990–2004), Book Aid Int 1994–2007, Nat Book Ctee 1996–2003, Edinburgh Univ Press 2001–07; memb: Br Cncl Publisher Advsy Ctee 1978–98 (chm 1993–98), Br Cncl Bd 1988–97, Arts Cncl Literature Panel 1983–87, Br Library Advsy Cncl 1982–86, Br Library Bd 1986–96, Devpt Ctee Oxford Poly (now Oxford Brookes Univ) 1991–97, Cncl Ranfurly Library Servs 1991–94, Fin Ctee of Delegacy OUP 1992–2002, Health Educn Authy Bd 1995–99; hon pres Ind Publishers Guild 1993–2008; Liveryman Worshipful Co of Stationers & Newspaper Makers; CCMI (CIMgt), FInstD, FRSA; *Recreations* reading, landscape, wine; *Clubs* Garrick; *Style*— Timothy Rix, Esq, CBE; ✉ 27 Wolseley Road, London N8 8RS (tel 020 8341 4160, e-mail tim@rixpublishing.co.uk)

RIZA, Alper; QC (1991); s of Ali Riza (d 1985), and Elli, *née* Liasides; *b* 16 March 1948; *Educ* American Acad Larnaca Cyprus, English Sch Nicosia Cyprus; *m* 14 Aug 1981, Vanessa, da of Dr Patrick Hall-Smith, of Brighton; 2 da (Lily b 27 Dec 1981, Isabella b 20 July 1989); *Career* called to the Bar Gray's Inn 1973, appeals lawyer Jt Cncl for Welfare of Immigrants 1977–82, barr in private practice 1982–, recorder 2000– (asst recorder 1992–2000); *Recreations* music, chess; *Style*— Alper Riza, Esq, QC

RIZZI, Carlo; *Educ* Milan Conservatoire (studied with Maestro Rosada), Bologna (studied with Vladimir Delman), Academia Chigiana (studied with Franco Ferrara, awarded Dip of Merit); *Career* conductor; currently music dir Welsh Nat Opera; debut 1982 conducting Donizetti's L'Ajo nell'imbarrazzo (Angelicum, Milan); conducted for Welsh National Opera: Il Barbiere di Siviglia, Count Ory, Rigoletto, Elektra, Tosca, La Favorite, Eugene Onegin, Turandot, Nabucco, Cavalleria Rusticana, I Pagliacci, Don Giovanni, Simon Boccanegra, Fidelio, Boris Godunov, Fidelio, Un Ballo in Maschera, La Boheme, La Traviata, Le Nozze di Figaro, The Rake's Progress, Carmen, Der Rosenkavalier, Peter Grimes, Tristan and Isolde, Der Rosenkavalier, Katya Kabanova; other works conducted incl: Tancredi (Rossini), Torquato Tasso (Donizetti), Beatrice di Tenda (Bellini), La Voix Humaine (Poulenc), L'Italiana in Algeri, Falstaff (Salieri's as well as Verdi's), L'Occasione fa il Ladro, La Scala di Seta, Madama Butterfly, Otello, La Cenerentola, L'Ellisir d'Amore, Norma, Lucia di Lammermoor, Macbeth, Il Trovatore, La pietra del paragone; has worked with orchs in Milan, Bologna, Rome, Berlin, London, Tel Aviv, Paris, Chicago, Munich, Cologne, New York, Los Angeles, San Francisco and at the Ravinia and Edinburgh Festivals; debuts: Britain at Buxton Festival 1988 (Torquato Tasso), Australian Opera Co in Sydney 1989 (Il Barbiere di Siviglia), Netherlands Opera

R

Amsterdam 1989 (Don Pasquale), Royal Opera House Covent Garden 1990 (La Cenerentola), Berlin 1992 (L'Italiana in Algeri), Cologne 1992 (La Scala di Seta and l'Occasione fa il ladro), with Israel Philharmonic 1993 (Rossini's Mosé), Metropolitan Opera NY 1993 (La Boheme and Il Barbiere di Siviglia); *Recordings* incl: L'Italiana in Londra (Cimarosa), Il Furioso sull'Isola di San Domingo (Donizetti), Ciro in Babilonia (Rossini), La Scuffiara (Paisiello), La Pescatrice (Piccinni), La Traviata (Verdi), Faust (Gounod), Rigoletto (operatic arias with Thomas Hampson and Jerry Hadley), Verdi Choruses with the Accademia of Santa Cecilia, Resphighi Tone Poems with the London Philharmonic, Un Ballo in Maschera, L'Arlesienne (Bizet); *Awards* second prize Besançon Conductor's Competition 1983, first prize Toscanini Conductors' Competition in Parma 1985, Italian Critics' Prize (for L'Italiana in Londra); *Style*— Carlo Rizzi, Esq; ✉ c/o Allied Artists Agency, 42 Montpelier Square, London SW7 1JZ (tel 020 7589 6243, fax 020 7581 5269)

ROACH, Prof Gary Francis; s of John Francis Roach (d 1982), and Bertha Mary Ann, *née* Walters (d 1975); *b* 8 October 1933; *Educ* UC S Wales and Monmouthshire (BSc), Univ of London (MSc), Univ of Manchester (PhD, DSc), Technical Univ of Lodz (ScD); *m* 3 Sept 1960, Isabella Grace Willins Nicol; *Career* Flying Offr Educn Branch RAF 1955–58; res mathematician BP 1958–61, lectr UMIST 1961–66, visiting prof Univ of Br Columbia 1966–67; Univ of Strathclyde: lectr 1967–70, sr lectr 1970–71, reader 1971–79, prof 1979–96 (emeritus prof 1996–), dean Faculty of Sci 1982–85; memb Incorporation of Bonnetmakers & Dyers Glasgow 1981 (Deacon 1997–98); FRAS 1964, FIMA 1967, FRSE 1975, FRSA 1991; OStJ 1992; *Books* Green's Functions (2 edn, 1982), Introduction to Linear and Nonlinear Scattering Theory (1995); *Recreations* mountaineering, photography, philately, gardening, music; *Style*— Prof Gary Roach, FRSE; ✉ 11 Menzies Avenue, Fintry, Glasgow G63 0YE (tel 01360 860335); Department of Mathematics, University of Strathclyde, Livingstone Tower, 26 Richmond Street, Glasgow G1 1XH (tel 0141 552 4400, ext 3804)

ROACH, (Charles) Graham; s of Norman Charles Roach (d 1974), and Hazel, *née* Pascoe (d 1996); *b* 26 August 1947, Exeter, Devon; *m* 8 June 2005, Valerie Jane, *née* Smith; 1 s (Shaun Charles b 21 April 1971), 2 da (Tanya Jane b 10 March 1972, Louise Ann b 5 June 1976); *Career* joined family business 1962 (dir 1968–), fndr and ceo Flagship Foods 1999–2004, currently vice-chm Tulip Ltd; *Recreations* horse racing, shooting; *Style*— Graham Roach, Esq; ✉ Tulip Ltd, Newtons Margate, Bodmin, Cornwall PL31 1HF (tel 01208 262612, fax 01208 262672, e-mail cgroach@roachfoods.co.uk)

ROACHE, Brig Andrew Hugh; *Educ* Bablake Sch Coventry, Univ of Bristol (BVSc); *Career* civilian vet practice Dyfed, Derbyshire, Devon 1972–80; RAVC 1980–2002, Regtl VO Household Cavalry Mounted Regt 1989–91, Cmdt Defence Animal Centre 1994–97, dir Army Vet and Remount Services 1997–2002; memb Farriers' Registration Cncl 2002–; Liveryman Worshipful Co of Farriers 1994; MRCVS 1972; *Style*— Brig Andrew Roache

ROACHE, Linus William; s of William Patrick (Bill) Roache, *qv*, of Manchester, and Anna, *née* Cropper (d 2007); *b* 1 February 1964; *Educ* Bishop Luffa Comp Sch Chichester, Rydal Sch N Wales, Central Sch of Speech and Drama; *Career* actor; *Theatre* RSC Stratford/Barbican season 1987–88: Titus Andronicus, Indigo, A Question of Geography, Julius Caesar; RSC season 1990–91: Richard II, King Lear, The Last Days of Don Juan; Royal Manchester Exchange: The Glass Menagerie (Manchester Evening News Awards nomination for Best Actor), Love's Labour's Lost 1992, Richard II 1993; other credits incl: Five Finger Exercise (Cambridge Theatre Co), The Mother (Contact Theatre Manchester, Manchester Evening News Awards nomination for Best Supporting Actor), Colder Climate (Royal Court), A Taste of Honey (Theatre Royal Nottingham), Keeping Tom Nice (Almeida Theatre), Divine Gossip, Juno and the Paycock (RNT), Deep Blue Sea (Almeida and West End), The Book of Spencer (The Odeon Paris), This is a Chair (Royal Court), Uncle Vanya (RSC Young Vic), Richard II (Almeida); *Television* incl: A Sort of Innocence (BBC) 1986, Saracen (Central) 1989, Vincent Van Gogh (Omnibus, BBC) 1990, Keeping Tom Nice (BBC) 1990, Black and Blue (BBC) 1992, Seaforth (BBC) 1994, The Gathering Storm 2002, RFK 2002; *Films* Priest 1994, The Wings of The Dove 1997, The Venice Project 1999, Siam Sunset 1999, Best 2000, Pandaemonium 2000, Hart's War 2002, Blind Flight 2003, Beyond Borders 2003, The Chronicles of Riddick 2004, The Forgotten 2004; *Recreations* golf, walking and exploring Great Britain; *Style*— Linus Roache, Esq

ROACHE, William Patrick; MBE (2001); s of Dr William Vincent Roache (d 1982), and Hester Vera, *née* Waddicor; *b* 25 April 1932; *Educ* Rydal Sch Colwyn Bay; *m* 1978, Sara McEwen, da of Sidney Mottram; 2 s (Linus William Roache, *qv*, William James), 1 da (Verity Elizabeth); *Career* army serv: joined RWF 1951, cmmnd 1952, served W Indies and Germany, seconded Trucial Oman Scouts, Capt Gulf 1955–56; actor in repertory film and TV; role of Ken Barlow in Coronation Street 1960–; vice-pres E Cheshire Hospice; Hon MA Univ of Derby 2003, Hon DLitt Chester Univ 2007; *Recreations* golf, tennis; *Clubs* Wilmslow Golf; *Style*— William Roache, Esq, MBE; ✉ c/o Sara Roache Management (tel 01625 582364)

ROADS, Dr Christopher Herbert; s of Herbert Clifford Roads (d 1963), of Kneesworth, Cambs, and Vera Iris, *née* Clark (d 1986); *b* 3 January 1934; *Educ* Cambridge & County Sch, Trinity Hall Cambridge (open scholar, MA, PhD); *m* 24 April 1976 (m dis 1996), Charlotte Alicia Dorothy Mary, da of Neil Lothian (d 1996), of Minterne Magna, Dorset; 1 da (Cecilia Iris Muriel Lothian b 1981); *Career* Lt RA Egypt 1952–54; advsr to War Office on Disposal of Amnesty Arms 1961–62, keeper Dept of Records Imperial War Museum (IWM) 1962–70 (dep DG 1964–79); fndr and dir: Cambridge Coral Starfish Res Gp 1968–, Duxford Aviation Museum (IWM) 1971–79; tstee later dir HMS Belfast Pool of London 1970–79; UNESCO conslt in design and operation of audiovisual archives and museums in general 1976–; dir: Nat Sound Archive 1983–92, Historic Cable Ship John W Mackay 1986–; dir: Museums and Archives Development Associates Ltd 1977–85, Cedar Audio Ltd 1986–92, AVT Communications Ltd 1986–92, National Discography Ltd 1986–92, Symcom Ltd 1994–95; founding md and acting chm Historic Arms Exhibitions and Forts LLC (Oman) 2001–; assoc dir (consultancy) R&D Dept British Library 1992–94, advsr and dir-elect Jet Heritage Museum Hurn 1995–, dir-elect Historic Arms Heritage Museum of Oman 2000–; hon pres World Expeditionary Assoc 1971–; pres: Cambridge Numismatic Soc 1964–66, Archive and Cataloguing Commission of Int Film and TV Cncl (UNESCO category A) 1970–, Int Film and TV Cncl 1990–92; vice-pres: Duxford Aviation Soc 1974–, English Eight 1980–; memb Cncl of Scientific Exploration Soc 1971–82; life pres Historical Breech Loading Small Arms Assoc 1973–, chm Heritage Arms Rescue 1996–; hon sec Cambridge Univ Long Range Rifle Club 1979–, vice-pres Cambridge Univ Rifle Assoc 1987– (memb Cncl 1955–87); Churchill fellowship 1971, visiting fell Centre of Int Studies Univ of Cambridge 1983–84; Silver Jubilee Medal 1977; Freeman City of London 1996, Liveryman Worshipful Co of Gunmakers 1996; FRGS; Order of Independence 2 Class (Jordan) 1977; *Recreations* rifle shooting (winner of various competitions incl Nat Match Rifle Championship Hopton 5 times), flying, marine and submarine exploration, wind surfing, cine and still photography; *Clubs* Hawks' (Cambridge), Oxford and Cambridge; *Style*— Dr Christopher Roads; ✉ The White House, 90 High Street, Melbourn, Royston, Hertfordshire SG8 6AL (tel 01763 260866, fax 01763 262521); DX 12, Bahia Dorada, 29693 Estepona, Malaga, Spain (tel and fax 00 34 952 76 9407, mobile 07803 129220); Historic Arms, Exhibitions and Forts LLC, PO Box 3726, Post Code 112 Ruwi, Muscat, Sultanate of Oman (office tel 00 968 24501218, residence tel and fax 00 968 24596603, office fax 00 968 24795056, mobile 00 968 99797326)

ROADS, Elizabeth Ann; MVO (1990); da of Lt-Col James Bruce, MC (d 1973), and Mary Hope, *née* Sinclair (d 1993); *b* 5 July 1951; *Educ* Lansdowne House Edinburgh, Cambs Coll of Technol, Study Centre for Fine Art London; *m* 23 April 1983, Christopher George William Roads, s of Dr Peter George Roads; 2 s (Timothy George Sinclair b 7 Sept 1986, William Peter Alexander b 22 Sept 1988), 1 da (Emily Ann Hope Clara b 3 Oct 1994); *Career* Inst of Educn Univ of London 1970, Christie's London 1970–74, Ct of The Lord Lyon 1975–, Lyon Clerk and Keeper of the Records 1986–, temp Linlithgow Pursuivant of Arms Extraordinary 1987, Carrick Pursuivant of Arms 1992–; articles in heraldic and genealogical jls; hon treas Scottish Record Soc; Queen's Silver Jubilee Medal 1977, Queen's Golden Jubilee Medal 2002; fell: Heraldry Soc of Scotland (memb 1977, chm 1997–2000), Royal Heraldry Soc of Canada 2004; FSA Scot 1986; OStJ 1999; *Recreations* history, reading, country pursuits, the family; *Style*— Mrs C G W Roads, MVO; ✉ 9 Denham Green Place, Edinburgh EH5 3PA; Court of The Lord Lyon, HM New Register House, Edinburgh EH1 3YT (tel 0131 556 7255, fax 0131 557 2148)

ROBARDS, Prof Anthony William; OBE (2002); s of Albert Charles Robards, of Lamberhurst, Kent, and Kathleen Emily Robards; *b* 9 April 1940; *Educ* The Skinners' Sch, UCL (BSc, PhD, DSc); *m* 1, 1962 (m dis 1985), Ruth, *née* Bulpett; 1 s (Martin David b 1967), 1 da (Helene Elizabeth b 1970); m 2, 1987, Eva Christina, da of Bo Knutson-Ek, of Lidingo, Sweden; *Career* currently HSBC Prof of Innovation Univ of York; visiting res fell: ANU 1975, Univ of Stockholm 1986; chm York Science Park Ltd; pres: Royal Microscopical Soc 1982–84, York & N Yorks C of C 1996–97; dir N Yorks Business Link 1995–2004, non-exec chm York Test Gp Ltd 1999–; dep govr Co of Merchant Adventurers of the City of York; tstee: Yorks Cancer Research 2006–, Capt James Cook Tst Whitby 2006–; FIBiol, DipRMS; *Books* Low Temperature Methods in Biological Electron Microscopy (with U B Sleytr, 1985); *Recreations* horse riding, horology, sailing; *Style*— Prof Anthony Robards, OBE; ✉ Shrubbery Cottage, Nun Monkton, North Yorkshire YO26 8EW (tel 01423 331023); The Innovation Centre, York Science Park, York YO10 5DG (tel 01904 435105, e-mail awr1@york.ac.uk)

ROBARTS, (Anthony) Julian; s of Lt-Col Anthony Vere Cyprian Robarts (d 1982); *b* 6 May 1937; *Educ* Eton; *m* 1961, Edwina Beryl, da of Rt Hon Sir John Gardiner Sumner Hobson, OBE, TD, QC, MP (d 1967); 2 s, 1 da; *Career* banker; dir then md Coutts & Co 1963–91, dir Coutts Fin Co 1967–91, regnl dir NatWest Bank 1971–92; dir: The Int Fund for Insts Inc (USA) 1983–92, The F Bolton Group Ltd 1970–, Hill Martin 1992–2003 (chm 1993–2003), Wild Rose Holdings Ltd 2001–; chief exec The Iveagh Trustees Ltd 1993–98; tstee: Beit Med Meml Fellowships 1992–2001, Sargent Cancer Care 1997–2000; hon treas Union Jack Club 1970– (also vice-pres); *Recreations* shooting, gardening, opera; *Clubs* Pratt's, MCC, Brooks's; *Style*— Julian Robarts, Esq; ✉ Bromley Hall, Standon, Ware, Hertfordshire SG11 1NY (tel 01279 842422)

ROBATHAN, Andrew Robert George; MP; s of late Douglas Robathan, and Sheena, *née* Gimson; *b* 17 July 1951; *Educ* Merchant Taylors' Sch Northwood, Oriel Coll Oxford; *m* 20 Dec 1991, Rachael, *née* Maunder; 1 s (Christopher Nicholas Andrew b 6 Dec 1996), 1 da (Camilla Mary Lavinia b 23 July 1999); *Career* offr Coldstream Gds and SAS 1974–89, rejoined for Gulf War 1991; cncllr London Borough of Hammersmith and Fulham 1990–92, MP (Cons) Blaby 1992–, PPS to Iain Sproat as min of state Dept of Nat Heritage 1995–97, shadow min for trade and industry 2002–03, int devpt 2003, shadow def min 2004–05, dep chief whip Cons Pty 2005–; chm Cons Backbench Defence Ctee 1994–95; vice-chm: Cons Backbench NI Ctee 1994–95 and 1997–2001, Cons Defence Ctee 1997–2001, Cons Backbench Policy Gp on Int Affrs and Defence 2001–02, All-Pty Cycling Gp (formerly chm), Parly Renewable and Sustainable Energy Gp; chm Halo Tst 2003–06; *Recreations* mountain walking, tennis, skiing, wildlife, shooting; *Style*— Andrew Robathan, Esq, MP; ✉ House of Commons, London SW1A 0AA

ROBB, Prof Alan Macfarlane; s of Alexander Robb (d 1982), of Aberdeen, and Jane Margaret Robb; *b* 24 February 1946; *Educ* Robert Gordon's Coll Aberdeen, Gray's Sch of Art, RCA (MA); *m* 1969, Cynthia Jane, da of John Neilson, of Glasgow; 1 s (Daniel Alexander John b 1971), 1 da (Annabel Ellen Jane b 1974); *Career* artist and teacher; art master Oundle Sch Peterborough 1972–75; Crawford Sch of Art Cork Ireland: lectr in painting 1975–78, head of painting 1978–80, head of fine art 1980–82; head Sch of Fine Art Duncan Jordanstone Coll of Art Dundee 1983–2003 (prof 1990–); speaker Context and Collaboration Int Public Art Symposium Birmingham 1990; specialist advsr in fine art CNAA 1987– (memb Fine Art Bd); chief examiner in fine art NCEA Ireland, external examiner in painting and printmaking Sheffield Poly 1987–90; memb: Steering Gp Nat Assoc for Fine Art Educn 1988–, Chief Exec's Res Advsy Gp Ctee Scottish Higher Educn Funding Cncl 1994–98; lead assessor (quality assessment) in fine art SHEFC; dir: Art in Partnership 1986–91, Workshop and Studio Provision for Artists Scotland (WASPS) 1984–94, Br Health Care Arts 1989–93, advsr Cwlth Cmmn 1998–2004; *Public Collections*: Aberdeen Art Gallery, Dundee Art Gallery, Crawford Gallery Cork, Fleming-Wyfold Art Fndn, Huntarian Glasgow Univ, Montgomery Securities New York, HRH Duke of Edinburgh - Arts Cncls of Ireland and Northern Ireland, Royal Coll of Art, Robert Gordon Univ, Univ of Dundee; *Exhibitions* regularly exhbns since 1968 at: Aberdeen Artists, Scot Soc of Artists, Royal Scot Acad, Royal Glasgow Inst, Royal Scottish Soc Watercolourists; solo incl: The New 57 Gallery Edinburgh 1972, Cork Art Soc 1976, Scot Arts Cncl touring exhibition 1978–79, Triskel Art Centre Cork 1979, Gallery 22 Cupar 1986, Francis Cooper Gallery Ducan Jordanstone Coll of Art Dundee 1991, Seagate Gallery 1996, EastWest Gallery London 1997 and 1999, The House of Miracles (EastWest Gallery London) 2005, Ayermanana/Yestermorrow (Fundacion Antonio Saura, Cuenca, Spain) 2006; group incl: Scot Young Contemporaries 1967–68, Univ of York 1970, RCA 1971, Architectural Assoc 1971, Napier Ct Trinity Coll Cambridge 1971, Eduardo Paolozzi's choice of the London postgrad sch shows 1972, Royal Acad 1972, E Midlands Arts 1973, EVA Limerick 1977–81, Clare Morris Open 1980 and 1982, Cork Art Soc 1978 and 1980, Peacock Printmakers touring exhibition The Art of Thinking 1985, 'Allegories of Desire' Small Mansion House London 1992, 'Five Scottish Artists' Centre D'Art En l'Ile Geneva 1994, Allan Stone Gallery NY 1996, Bruton St Gallery London 1996, 'I Live Now' Howard/Guild, Academie Gallery Utrecht 1999; *Awards* (painting) Arbroath Open 1968, (painting) Irish Open Exhibition of Visual Art Limerick 1977, (painting) Clare Morris Open 1982, Aberdeen Artists 1989, William J Macaulay RSA 2000; *Publications* Irish Contemporary Art (1982), In the Mind's Eye (1996), The House of Miracles (2005); *Style*— Prof Alan Robb; ✉ School of Fine Art, Duncan of Jordanstone College of Art, University of Dundee, Perth Road, Dundee (tel 01382 345226, fax 01382 200983)

ROBB, Andrew MacKenzie; s of William MacKenzie Robb (d 1983), and Kathleen Rhona Harvey, *née* Gibbs (d 1990); *b* 2 September 1942; *Educ* Rugby; *Children* 2 da (Fiona b 1967, Erica b 1969); *Career* T Wall & Sons Ltd 1961–69, Hoskyns Gp Ltd 1969–71, gp finance dir P&O 1983–89 (finance controller Bulk Shipping Div 1971–75, finance controller 1975–83), exec dir Pilkington plc 1989–2003 (gp finance dir 1989–2001); non-exec dir: Alfred McAlpine plc 1993–2003, KESA Electricals 2003–, Corus plc 2003–, Laird Gp 2004–; memb Urgent Issues Task Force Accounting Standards Bd 1992–97; Freeman City of London, Liveryman Worshipful Co of Glaziers; JDipMA 1973; FCMA 1968, FCT 1992; *Recreations* fly fishing, golf; *Clubs* In & Out; *Style*— Andrew Robb, Esq

ROBB, George Alan; WS (1968); s of George Robb (d 1969), of Inverdee, Cults, Aberdeen, and Phyllis Mary, *née* Allan (d 1966); *b* 20 May 1942; *Educ* Aberdeen GS 1946–60, Univ of Aberdeen (MA), Univ of Edinburgh (LLB); *m* 3 Aug 1973, Moira Ann, da of Sidney Milne Clark, of Bieldside, Aberdeen; 3 s (Andrew George b 19 Oct 1976, Michael Nicholas b 22 Dec 1984, Jonathan Alexander b 17 March 1991), 1 da (Judith Olivia b 30 May 1978); *Career* law apprentice Davidson and Syme WS Edinburgh 1966–68; asst: Davidson and Syme WS 1968–69, Edmonds and Ledingham Aberdeen 1969–71, Brander and Cruickshank Advocates Aberdeen 1971–73 (ptnr 1973–83); dir: Aberdeen Trust plc (now Aberdeen Asset Management plc) 1983–91 (chm 1991–92), Aberdeen Petroleum plc 1982 (chm 1992–93), Aberdeen Devpt Capital plc 1986–2004, Aberdeen European Investment Trust plc 1990–98, Asset Management Investment Company plc 1994 (md), Goshawk Insurance Holdings plc 1997–2004, Britannic Global Income Tst plc 2000–04; chm: Media and Income Trust plc 2000 (dir 1989), Premier Recovery Trust plc 2001; govr Edgeborough Prep Sch Frensham; memb: Law Soc of Scot 1966, WS Soc 1968, IOD 1984 (memb Aberdeen Ctee 1984–88); FInstPet 1983; *Recreations* shooting, gardening, family; *Clubs* Brooks's; *Style*— George A Robb, Esq, WS

ROBB, Sir John Weddell; kt; *Career* chm: British Energy plc 1995–, Hewden-Stuart plc 1999–; non-exec dir Unigate plc 1996–; dep chm Horserace Betting Levy Bd 1993–; tstee Royal Botanic Garden Edinburgh 1997–; *Style*— Sir John Robb

ROBBÉ, Dr Iain J; s of Jack Robert Robbé, and (Annette) Yvonne, *née* Conners; *b* 3 November 1955; *Educ* Charterhouse, KCL (BSc), Westminster Med Sch (MB BS, MRCS, LRCP), Univ of London (MSc), Univ of Wales (MSc); *m* 1984, Gillian Nancy, da of Brig P Douglas Wickenden, RAMC (ret); *Career* jr hosp doctor 1980–84, specialist trg in public health med 1984–88, dir of public health and planning Worthing Health Authy 1988–91, dir of public health med Gwent Health Authy 1991–93, sr lectr in public health med Univ of Wales Coll of Med 1993–; FFPHM 1995 (MFPHM 1987); *Recreations* wildlife and environmental protection, wine tasting, gardening; *Style*— Dr Iain J Robbé; ✉ Whips Cottage, Dawn of Day, Grosmont, Abergavenny, Gwent NP7 8LT; Centre for Applied Public Health Medicine, School of Medicine, Cardiff University, Temple of Peace and Health, Cathays Park, Cardiff CF10 3NW (tel 029 2040 2480, fax 029 2040 2504, e-mail robbe@cardiff.ac.uk)

ROBBIE, David Andrew; s of Frank Robbie, of Greenmount, Lancs, and Dorothy, *née* Holt; *b* 20 June 1963, Lancs; *Educ* Univ of St Andrews (MA); *Career* finance dir: CMG plc (now Logica CMG) 2000–03, Royal P&O Nedlloyd NV 2004–05, Rexam plc 2005–; non-exec dir BBC 2007–; tstee Almeida Theatre; ACA; *Recreations* theatre, travel; *Clubs* RAC; *Style*— David Robbie, Esq; ✉ Rexam plc, 4 Millbank, London SW1P 3XR (tel 020 7227 4155, e-mail david.robbie@rexam.com)

ROBBIE, Victor Allan Cumming; s of W Allan Robbie (d 1995), of Aberdeen, and Mae, *née* Milne; *b* 22 March 1945; *Educ* Dumbarton Acad, Shawlands Acad; *m* 20 Jan 1968, Christine Elizabeth, da of Harold Featherby Jaggard (d 1987); 2 da (Gabrielle Sara b 3 Sept 1971, Kirsten Nicola b 7 May 74), 1 s (Nicholas Allan Graham b 13 June 1978); *Career* Sunday Post and Weekly News 1963–65, Scottish Daily Mail 1965–66, Daily Telegraph 1967–68, Daily and Sunday Telegraph (Sydney) 1969–71, Evening Standard 1971–73, athletics corr Daily Mirror 1980–86 (joined 1973), The Independent 1986–87, sports ed Scotland on Sunday 1988–89, sports ed The Independent 1989–91, asst ed and head of sport Daily Mail 1991–97; publisher: Golf Travel Magazine, PGA Yearbook; dir VR Assocs, fndr Scotlands-golf-Courses.com; *Books* Athletics Yearbook (1987), Scotland's Golf Courses: The Complete Guide (1997, revised edn, 2001), Tennis 98 (ed, 1998), Ireland's Golf Courses: The Complete Guide (2001, revised edn 2006); *Recreations* archaeology, travel, golf, watching my wife garden, Usquebaugh; *Clubs* Harris Golf, North Hants Golf; *Style*— Victor Robbie, Esq; ✉ e-mail vic@vrassociates.co.uk

ROBBINS, Christopher; s of William Henry Robbins (d 1959), and Marion Elizabeth Millington, *née* Rees (d 1982); *b* 16 June 1946; *Educ* The Skinners' Sch Tunbridge Wells, Univ of Sussex (BA), Warburg Inst Univ of London (MPhil); *Career* lectr Dept of Philosophy Univ of York 1969–75, princ Welsh Office Cardiff 1975–77, admin Cncl of Euro Strasbourg 1977–84; HM Dip Service: Euro Community Dept 1984–87, first sec New Delhi 1987–90, asst head Central and South African Dept 1990–91, head of Project and Export Policy Div DTI (on loan) 1991–94, commercial cnsllr The Hague 1994–98 and concurrently consul gen Amsterdam 1996–98, ambass to Lithuania 1998–2001, min-cnsllr and dep head of mission Seoul 2001–05; *Books* Sartre & The Moral Life, Philosophy (1976), La Santé Rationnée (contrib, 1981), The End of An Illusion (contrib, 1984); *Recreations* the arts; *Style*— Christopher Robbins, Esq; ✉ c/o Foreign & Commonwealth Office, King Charles Street, London SW1A 2AH

ROBBINS, James; s of (Richard) Michael Robbins (d 2002), of London, and Elspeth, *née* Bannatyne (d 1993); *b* 19 January 1954; *Educ* Westminster, ChCh Oxford (BA, ed Isis); *m* 30 Oct 1981, Gillian Elizabeth Cameron, da of Dr Brian C Gee, of Portadown; 1 da (Emily Maeve Cameron b 23 March 1991); *Career* BBC: news trainee 1977, Belfast newsroom 1979–83, reporter TV news (based London) 1983–87, Southern Africa corr (based Johannesburg) 1987–91, Europe corr (based Brussels) 1992–98, diplomatic corr (based London) 1998–; major assignments incl: hunger strikes Maze Prison, UK miners' strike, resignation of Pres P W Botha, rise of F W De Klerk, release of Nelson Mandela, political reforms and violence South Africa, aftermath of Maastricht Summit, future of the European Union, attacks on USA Sept 11 2001, war in Afghanistan and Iraq, crises at UN NY, Middle East peace process and Iran, series on India and China (Race to the Top of the World); *Recreations* family, reading, walking, music, cooking and eating, tennis, looking out of train windows; *Style*— James Robbins; ✉ Room 2505, BBC Television Centre, Wood Lane, London W12 7RJ (tel 020 8624 8550)

ROBBINS, Prof Keith Gilbert; s of Gilbert Henry John Robbins, and Edith Mary, *née* Carpenter; *b* 9 April 1940; *Educ* Bristol GS, Magdalen Coll and St Antony's Coll Oxford (MA, DPhil), Univ of Glasgow (DLitt); *m* 24 Aug 1963, Janet Carey, da of John Thomson, of Fulbrook, Oxon; 3 s (Paul b 1965, Daniel b 1967, Adam b 1972), 1 da (Lucy b 1970); *Career* lectr Univ of York 1963–71, dean of Faculty of Arts UCNW Bangor 1977–79 (prof of history 1971–79), prof of modern history Univ of Glasgow 1980–91, vice-chllr Univ of Wales Lampeter 1992–2003, sr vice-chllr Univ of Wales 1995–2001; vice-pres RHS 1984–88; pres: Historical Assoc 1988–91, Ecclesiastical History Soc 1980–81; Raleigh lectr Br Acad 1984, Ford lectr Oxford 1987, Winston Churchill travelling fell 1990; memb Humanities Research Bd Br Acad 1994–97 (memb Arts and Humanities Research Bd 1998–2003); ed History 1977–86; Hon DLitt: UWE, Univ of Wales; FRHistS 1970; FRSE 1991; *Books* Munich 1938 (1968), Sir Edward Grey (1971), The Abolition of War (1976), John Bright (1979), The Eclipse of a Great Power: Modern Britain 1870–1975 ((1983), 2 edn 1870–1992 (1994)), The First World War (1984), Nineteenth Century Britain: Integration and Diversity (1988), Appeasement (1988, 2 edn 1997), Churchill (1992), History, Religion and Identity in Modern Britain (1993), Politicians, Diplomacy and War in Modern British History (1994), Bibliography of British History 1914–89 (1996), Great Britain: Identities, Institutions and the Idea of Britishness (1997), The World since 1945: A Concise History (1998), The British Isles 1901–1951 (2002), Britain and Europe 1789–2005 (2005); *Recreations* music; *Style*— Prof Keith Robbins, FRSE; ✉ Rhydyfran, Cribyn, Lampeter, Ceredigion SA48 7NH (tel 01570 470349, e-mail profkgr@clara.co.uk)

ROBBINS, Prof Peter Alistair; s of Michael John Robbins, and Shirley Dean, *née* Swift; *Educ* Univ of Oxford (BA, DPhil, BM BCh), Open Univ (BA); *Career* house surgn Gloucester Royal Hosp 1984–85, house physician John Radcliffe Hosp Oxford 1985; Univ of Oxford: lectr (physiology) 1985–96, reader 1996–98, prof of physiology 1998–, fell and med tutor The Queen's Coll 1985–; memb: Physiological Soc 1985, American Physiological Soc 1992; *Publications* contrib to scientific jls incl: Jl of Physiology, Jl of Applied Physiology, Respiration Physiology, Experimental Physiology, Circulation, American Jl of Cardiology; *Recreations* walking, fishing, piano, bridge, sailing; *Style*— Prof Peter Robbins; ✉ Department of Physiology, Anatomy and Genetics, Oxford University, Parks Road, Oxford OX1 3PT (tel 01865 272490, fax 01865 282486, e-mail peter.robbins@dpag.ox.ac.uk)

ROBBINS, His Hon Judge Stephen Dennis; s of Lt-Col J Dennis Robbins, OBE, TD (d 1986), of Essex, and Joan, *née* Mason; *b* 11 January 1948; *Educ* Marlborough, Coll of Europe Bruges; *m* 28 Sept 1974, Amanda Robbins, JP, da of J Michael Smith, of Cheshire; 3 da (Harriet b 1976, Victoria, Camilla (twins) b 1979); *Career* called to the Bar Gray's Inn 1969; in practice SE Circuit 1972–94, recorder Crown Court 1987–94, circuit judge (SE Circuit) 1994– (sitting Southwark, Maidstone and Central Criminal Court); London Common Law Bar Assoc and Senate Overseas Rels; chm: Disciplinary Ctee Potato Mktg Bd 1988–94, Mental Health Review Tbnls 1994–; memb Parole Bd 2001–; *Recreations* walking, swimming, shooting, music, collecting ephemera; *Style*— His Hon Judge Robbins; ✉ Hillcrest Farm, Sevington, Ashford, Kent TN24 0LJ (tel 01233 502732); 2 The Studios, Edge Street, London W8 7PN (tel 020 7727 7216)

ROBERSON, Sidney (Sid); s of Percy Harold Roberson, of Worthing, and Ivy Ethel Hannah, *née* Holliwell (d 1970); *b* 15 March 1937; *Educ* Enfield GS; *m* 1, 1961, Brenda, da of Harold Milverton; 1 da (Hannah b 1967); m 2, 1990, Suzi Staniland; 2 s (Charlie b 1984, Nathaniel b 1991), 1 da (Florence Ivy b 1988); *Career* began career as runner in art studio, resident in USA 1961–64, subsequently art dir then copywriter various advtg agencies; int photographer 1968–, commercial dir 1971– (own co 1973–92, Roberson films 1996–); freelance dir; progs incl: The Sweeney, Robin of Sherwood, Lab Pty Political Broadcasts 1988 and 1989, Harry (BBC1), Hamish Macbeth (BBC1), Fast Show (BBC2); *Awards* over fifty int awards for commercials incl: two Gold Lions at Cannes, two Gold Arrows Br TV Advtg awards, Silver award D & AD; The Fast Show: BAFTA nomination, RTS Best Comedy Award, 1st Prize TV Comedy Awards; 3rd place Mr Universe; *Recreations* gym, tennis, children, travel; *Style*— Sid Roberson, Esq

ROBERTS, Prof Sir (Edward) Adam; KCMG (2002); s of Michael Roberts (d 1948), of London, and Janet, *née* Adam-Smith (d 1999); *b* 29 August 1940; *Educ* Westminster, Magdalen Coll Oxford (BA); *m* 16 Sept 1966, Frances Primrose, da of Raymond Horace Albany Dunn (d 1951), of Ludham, Norfolk; 1 da (Hannah b 1970), 1 s (Bayard b 1972); *Career* asst ed Peace News 1962–65, lectr int rels LSE 1968–81 (Noel Buxton student 1965–68); Univ of Oxford: Alastair Buchan reader in int rels 1981–86, professorial fell St Antony's Coll 1981–86, Montague Burton prof of int rels 1986–2007, fell Balliol Coll 1986–; chm of govrs William Tyndale Sch 1976–78; Leverhulme major res fell 2000–03; govr Ditchley Fndn 2001–; memb: Cncl Int Inst for Strategic Studies 2002–, Advsy Bd UK Defence Acad 2003–; hon fell: LSE 1997, St Antony's Coll Oxford 2006; FBA 1990; *Books* The Strategy of Civilian Defence: Non-violent Resistance to Aggression (ed, 1967), Nations in Arms: The Theory and Practice of Territorial Defence (1976, 2 edn, 1986), Documents on the Laws of War (with Richard Guelff, 1982, 3 edn 2000), United Nations, Divided World: The UN's Roles in International Relations (ed with Benedict Kingsbury, 1988, 2 edn 1993), Hugo Grotius and International Relations (ed with Hedley Bull and Benedict Kingsbury, 1990), Humanitarian Action in War (1996); *Recreations* rock-climbing, mountaineering; *Clubs* Alpine; *Style*— Prof Sir Adam Roberts, KCMG, FBA; ✉ Balliol College, Oxford OX1 3BJ (tel 01865 277777, fax 01865 277803, e-mail adam.roberts@balliol.oxford.ac.uk)

ROBERTS, Col Alan Clive; OBE (2001, MBE 1982), TD (1969), JP (1977), DL (W Yorks 1982); s of late Maj William Roberts, MBE, RA, and Kathleen Roberts; *b* 28 April 1934; *Educ* Askham House Sch Taunton, Rutherford Coll Newcastle, Manchester Poly (MPhil), Univ of Bradford (PhD); *m* 1956, Margaret Mary, *née* Shaw; 2 s; *Career* Nat Serv 1954–56; TA: Lt 269 (W Riding) Field Regt RA 1956, Capt 1962, Maj 1968, Lt-Col cmdg Univ of Leeds OTC 1972–79, Col and Dep Cdr TA NE Dist 1980–, TA advsr to GOC NE Dist 1980–, Regtl Col Univ of Leeds OTC 1980–90 and 2000–; ADC 1980–84; Hon Col: Univ of Leeds OTC 1990–2000, Yorks ACF (N & W) 1993–, 269 (W Riding) Battery 106 (Yeomanry) Regt RA(V) 2000–; Hon Col Commandant RA 1996–2001; head of Biomaterials Lab Dept of Plastic and Maxillo-Facial Surgery St Lukes Hosp Bradford 1960–; Bradford Hosps NHS Tst and predecessors: conslt clinical scientist 1970–, dir of R&D 1992–2002; Univ of Leeds: Crown rep Cncl 1985, pro-chllr 1986–2000, chm Ct and Cncl 1986–2000, dir Univ of Leeds Fndn 1986–89, chm Advsy Bd Inst of Nursing 1994–96, convocation lectr 2000; Univ of Bradford: visiting sr research fell Plastic and Burns Research Unit 1988–, dir Biomaterials Research Unit 1990–, memb Advsy Ctee Dept of Biomedical Sciences 1992–, hon prof 2000–, clinical dir Prosthetic Solutions Ltd 2005; Cncl of Europe fell Univs of Gothenburg, Malmö and Stockholm 1968, prof of biomaterials in surgery Academic Surgical Unit Univ of Hull 1994–; visiting prof/lectr: Univ of Indiana 1968, Univ of Texas 1968, 1974 and 1985, Dept of Polymer Technol Manchester Poly 1970–80, Stomatology Inst Univ of Bordeaux 1971, Plastic Surgery Inst Univ of Utrecht 1972, Univ of Pennsylvania 1975, Twente Univ of Technol Netherlands 1976, Univ of São Paulo 1976, Univ of Jakarta 1986, Trinity Coll Dublin 1987, Univ of Tokyo 1987, Univ of Moscow 1987, Univ of Malaysia 1988; guest lectr: Faculty of Dental Surgery RCS England 1969 and 1980, Faculty of Plastic Surgery RCS England 1976; dean's research lectr RMCS 1977; numerous research and consultancy appts in the field of biomaterials and adhesives for plastic/reconstructive surgery; lead researcher/inventor Indermil tissue adhesive 1993 and Zeflosil prosthetic adhesive 2007; vice-pres RSM 2007 (hon treas 2003–07); memb Br Standards Ctees on Cardio-Vascular Materials and Toxicology of Med Polymers; vice-chm Co of W Yorks Jt Emergency Exec Ctee 1983–88, chm Quality of Life Gp and memb Head and Neck Working Gp Yorks Regnl Cancer Orgn 1993–98, vice-chm Expert Working Gp Regnl R&D Ctee Yorks RHA 1994–95, memb Health Servs Res Gp Northern and Yorks RHA 1995–97, memb Research Advsy Ctee NHS Exec Northern and Yorks R&D Directorate 1998–, chm Bradford Research Ethics Ctee 2003–; ed Jl of the Inst of Br Surgical Technol 1965–69, assessor Jl of Biomedical Engrg 1979; CGLI: chief examiner in maxillo-facial technol 1968–98, hon life memb 1978, vice-chm Sr Awards Ctee 1991–, pres CGLI Assoc (CGA) 1997–2003; moderator BTech higher technol courses 1985–97, examiner Univ of Sheffield Sch of Clinical Dentistry 1995–; chm Cncl of Mil Educn Ctees UK Univs 1990–96, dep chm Ctee of Chairmen of Univ Cncls 1993–97, memb Int Advsy Bd Med Sch Universiti Malaysia Sarawak 1993–; vice-pres Leeds Boys' Bde 1972–, chm of tstees W Riding Artillery Tst 1983–; pres: Br Red Cross Soc W Yorks 1983–, W Yorks SSAFA - Forces Help 1998–, NSPCC Leeds 2001–; vice-chm Yorks and Humberside TAVRA 1987–89 and 1993–; dir Weetwood Hall Ltd 1992–; govr: Gateways Sch 1992–2007, Pocklington Sch 2000–07; tstee: Edward Boyle Meml Tst 1986–98, W Yorks Sculpture Park 1995–; patron: Crime Stoppers 1995–, Age Concern 1995–; memb Cncl Br Red Cross Soc 1995–96; Denney Award for Innovation in Surgical Technol Inst of Surgical Technol 1960, Insignia Award in Technol CGLI 1969 and 1976, Prince Philip Medal for Outstanding Achievements in Science and Technol 1970, Merit and Achievement Award for Medical Materials Devpt Inst of Science and Technol 1972, Red Cross Badge of Honour 1992; hon sec Fellowship of Prince Philip Medallists 1993–, hon sub dean N Yorks RSM 2001–03; pres: Bradford Medico-Chirurgical Soc 1997–98, Br Inst of Surgical Technologists 1998–; hon life memb US Army Med Research Soc 1971; memb: Med Protection Soc, Biological Engrg Soc (also memb Artificial Organs Gp), Assoc of Clinical Biochemists, W Riding Medico Legal Soc; non-regtl memb HAC 2000–; chm Cncl Order of St John S and W Yorks 2004–; Hon Liveryman Worshipful Co of Clothworkers 2000; Hon LLD Univ of Leeds 2000, Hon DSc Univ of London 2005, Hon DSc Univ of Bradford 2007, Hon DTech Brunel Univ 2007; AIMechE 1967, CBiol 1971, FIBiol 1987 (MIBiol 1970), memb NY Acad of Sciences 1987,

R

FCGI 1990, FRSM 1993, CIMechE 1996, FLS 1999; CStJ 2001 (OStJ 1994), Companion Order of the League of Mercy 2002; *Books* Obturators and Prosthesis for Cleft Palate (1965), Facial Prosthesis: The Restoration of Facial Defects by Prosthetic Means (1972), Maxillo-Facial Prosthetics: A Multidisciplinary Practice (jtly, 1972), Adhesives in Surgery: How it Works Encyclopaedia (jtly, 1988); also author of numerous papers in med and scientific jls; *Recreations* silver, sculpture, music; *Clubs* Army and Navy; *Style*— Col Alan Roberts, OBE, TD, DL; ✉ The Grange, Rein Road, Morley, Leeds LS27 0HZ; St Luke's Hospital, Bradford BD5 0NA (tel 01274 365158, fax 01274 365552)

ROBERTS, Dr Alan Frederick; CBE (1996); s of Harry Frederick Roberts (d 1982), of Sussex, and Edith Clara, *née* Reid; *b* 13 October 1935; *Educ* Whitgift Sch Croydon, Imperial Coll London (BSc, PhD, DSc, ACGI, DIC); *m* 12 March 1960, Kathleen Joan, da of Owen Leonard Wallis; 2 s (David Alan b 1963, Patrick James b 1965); *Career* post-doctoral fell Imperial Coll 1959–60; Safety in Mines Research Estab: jr research fell 1960–62, sr sci offr 1962–67, princ sci offr 1967–75; HSE: head Research Planning Gp 1975–77, dep dir Safety Engrg Lab 1977–78, dir Explosion and Flame Lab 1981–89 (dep dir 1978–81), dir Nuclear Safety Research Mgmnt Unit 1989–92, dir Research and Lab Servs Div 1992–94, chief exec Health and Safety Laboratory 1994–95, conslt 1995–; FIChemE 1978, FREng 1993 (CEng 1967); *Books* The Coal Mines of Buxton (1985), Turnpike Roads around Buxton (1993); *Recreations* walking, local history; *Style*— Dr Alan Roberts, CBE, FREng; ✉ 18 Dovedale Crescent, Buxton, Derbyshire SK17 9BJ (tel 01298 24952)

ROBERTS, Allan Deverell; s of Irfon Roberts, of Priory Wall House, Lewes, E Sussex, and Patricia Mary, *née* Allan; *b* 14 July 1950; *Educ* Eton, Magdalen Coll Oxford (MA); *m* 7 Dec 1991, Dr Irene Anne Graham Reilly; 3 s (Hugh b 14 Feb 1993 (d 21 May 1995), Duncan b 26 April 1995, Ewan b 26 April 1997); *Career* slr in private practice 1974–76; Govt Legal Serv: legal asst 1976–78, sr legal asst 1978–84, asst slr DHSS 1984–89, under sec DSS/Dept of Health 1989–96; dir legal environment, countryside and planning DoE 1996–97, dir legal environment, housing and local Govt DETR 1998–99, dir Legal Legislation Unit DTLR (formerly DETR) 1999–2002, counsel to the Chm of Ctees House of Lords 2002–; memb Law Soc; *Recreations* walking, music, football; *Style*— Allan Roberts, Esq; ✉ Legislation Office, 1st Floor, West Front, House of Lords, London SW1A 0PW

ROBERTS, Amy Scarlett; da of Jonathan Roberts, of Beaminster, Dorset, and Anne Scarlett, *née* Streatfeild; *b* 5 June 1970; *Educ* Queen Margaret's Sch York, Newcastle Coll of Art and Technol, UWE (BA), Central St Martins (MA); *Career* fashion designer; studio asst fashion houses incl Givenchy 1995–96, deuxième dessinatrice (asst) fashion houses incl Christian Dior 1996–2000, with John Galliano , *qv*, 1995–2000, head designer Ghost 2000–; *Recreations* drama, riding, clubs, music, photography; *Style*— Miss Amy Roberts; ✉ Ghost, The Chapel, 263 Kensal Road, London W10 5DB (tel 020 8962 3762)

ROBERTS, Andrew; s of Simon Roberts, of Cobham, Surrey, and Katie Roberts; *b* 13 January 1963, London; *Educ* Gonville & Caius Coll Cambridge (exhibitioner, hon sr scholar, BA); *m* 1, (m dis); 1 s (Henry b 2 June 1997), 1 da (Cassia b 3 June 1999); m 2, 2007, Susan Gilchrist; *Career* author; Wolfson Prize for History 1999, James Stern Silver Pen Award 1999; Hon DHL Westminster Coll MO; FRSL 2000, FRSA 2003; *Books* The Holy Fox (1991), Eminent Churchillians (1994), Salisbury: Victorian Titan (1999), Napoleon and Wellington (2001), Hitler and Churchill: Secrets of Leadership (2003), What Might Have Been (ed, 2004), Waterloo: Napoleon's Last Gamble (2005), A History of the English-Speaking Peoples Since 1900 (2006), The Correspondence Between Mr Disraeli and Mrs Sarah Brydges Willyams (2007); *Clubs* Beefsteak, Brooks's, Garrick, Aspinall's, Annabel's, Mark's, George Bar, Saintsbury, Pilgrims, Univ Pitt (Cambridge), Walbrook (hon memb), Other Other (Wisconsin, hon memb), Chaos (NY, hon memb); *Style*— Andrew Roberts, Esq; ✉ 22 South Eaton PLace, London SW1W 9TA (tel 020 7730 3091, e-mail andrew@roberts-london.com, website www.andrew-roberts.net)

ROBERTS, Anne Clark; da of William Cunningham (d 1972), of Scotland, and Ann Simpson Lyon, *née* Clark; *b* 11 January 1961; *Educ* Larbert HS, Univ of Aberdeen (MA); *m* 13 Aug 1988, Thomas John Blackburn Roberts, s of Thomas Blackburn Roberts, CBE, TD, DL (d 1979); 1 da (Verity Anne b 15 Jan 1992), 1 s (William John Blackburn b 1 March 1995); *Career* with Next plc 1984–88, md The National Trust (Enterprises) Ltd 1988–94; non-exec dir: Remploy Ltd 1993–97, Samuel Courtauld Tst Enterprises 1996–99; dir Country Manor Devpts Ltd 1996–2006; memb Inland Waterways Amenity Advsy Cncl 1993–95; winner: Nat Training Award 1987, Cosmopolitan Woman of Tomorrow Award (Industry and Commerce) 1989; *Recreations* family pursuits, conservation; *Style*— Mrs Anne C Roberts; ✉ Manor Farmhouse, Wootton Fitzpaine, West Dorset DT6 6NQ

ROBERTS, Anthony Howard Norman; s of Kenneth Arthur Norman Roberts (d 1982), and Ivy Beatrice Maude Roberts (d 1970); *b* 15 November 1938; *Educ* Bancroft's Sch, Univ of Leeds (BSc), St Catharine's Coll Cambridge (MA), Worcester Coll Oxford (BM BCh, MA); *m* 24 March 1972, Dr (Fiona Edith) Vivian, da of Prof Richard Broxton Onians (d 1986), and Rosalind Lathbury Onians; 2 da (Clare b 1974, Natasha b 1976); *Career* lectr in chemical engrg Univ of Surrey 1961–64; conslt plastic and hand surgn Stoke Mandeville Hosp and dir Oxford Region Burn Unit 1985–2001 (emeritus conslt 2001–), surgical tutor 1989–94, regnl advsr in plastic surgery 1996–99 (chm Specialist Trg Ctee Oxford and Wessex), med advsr St John Ambulance Nat HQ 2003–04; chm of tstees and dir of research Restore - Burn and Wound Research (formerly Stoke Mandeville Burns and Reconstructive Surgery Research Tst), civilian conslt advsr to the RAF 1998–2001 (hon civilian conslt in surgery 2002–); hon sr lectr in surgery UCL 1999–; visiting prof: Chinese Univ of Hong Kong 1990– (C C Wu prof 1996), Dhaka Univ 2005–; visiting lectr/prof: Southern Africa 1988 and 1995, Australia 1990 and 1993, India 1990, 1993, 1999 and 2001, Israel 1992, Papua New Guinea 1993, Bosnia 1994, 1996, 2001 and 2003, Egypt 1995, 1997 and 1999–2005, Russia 1997, China 1998, Botswana 1998, Azerbaijan 1998, 1999 and 2000, Philippines 1999, Kosovo 2001, Romania 2004, Bangladesh 2005; examiner general surgery RCPSGlas 1997–2004, intercollegiate examiner MRCS 2004–; author of articles in med, surgical and ornithological jls; second in command surgical team the Bradford disaster 1985; ldr disaster relief team: Athens Refinery Fire 1992, Operation Phoenix Bosnia 1994–96; memb Cncl St John Ambulance IOW 2002– (dep county surgn 2003–); memb: Br Burn Assoc 1976– (co-opted memb Ctee 1998–2002, chm Burn Prevention Ctee 1999–2002), Br Assoc of Plastic Surgns 1986–, Br Soc for Surgery of the Hand 1986– (memb Cncl 1996–2000), Int Soc for Burn Injuries 1990– (memb Disaster Planning Ctee), Int Soc of Surgery of the Hand (memb War Injuries Ctee); memb Ringing and Migration Ctee Br Tst for Ornithology 2006–; Freeman City of London 2007; FRCS 1976, FRCSGlas 2004; *Books* contrib: Bander's Aid (A Guide to the Australian Bird in the Hand) (3 edn, 1994), Paediatric Care in Developing Countries (2002); *Recreations* ornithology, sport, travel; *Clubs* Hawks' (Cambridge), British Ornithological Union, Cambridge Univ Cruising, Seaview Yacht, RAF; *Style*— Mr Anthony Roberts, FRCS; ✉ Haseley Manor, Arreton, Isle of Wight PO30 3AN (tel and fax 01983 865420)

ROBERTS, Antony Mabon (Tony); s of Lt Hylton Mabon Roberts (d 1987), and Phyllis Mary, *née* Dickinson; *b* 9 July 1939; *Educ* Birkenhead Sch, Univ of Hamburg, Univ of Cambridge (MA), Yale Univ (MA); *m* 7 Aug 1965, Angela Dale, da of Maj Eric William Huggins, of Southwold, Suffolk; 1 s (Benjamin Mabon b 1969), 1 da (Clare Joy b 1972); *Career* sr prodr BBC TV 1976–; prodns incl: English Law 1968, Avventura 1971, Ensemble 1975, The Living City 1977, Wainwright's Law 1980, Whatever Happened to Britain 1982, Honourable Members 1983, Politics of Pressure 1985, Téléjournal 1983, Heute Direkt 1984, Issues of Law 1986, Person to Person 1988, Give and Take 1989, When In Germany 1991; ptnr Gratus and Roberts Productions 1991–; addiction treatment cnsllr Priory Hosp Roehampton; accredited cnsllr; *Recreations* cricket, tennis, golf; *Clubs* MCC; *Style*— Tony Roberts, Esq; ✉ 59 Breamwater Gardens, Ham, Richmond, Surrey TW10 7SG (tel 020 8940 9631)

ROBERTS, Prof Bernard; s of John William Roberts (d 1985), and Annie Margaret, *née* Leahy (d 1996); *b* 19 February 1946, Ireland; *Educ* Bletchley Road Sch, Bletchley GS, Univ of Hull (univ prize in applied maths, BSc), Univ of Sheffield (PhD); *m* 2 Oct 1971, Margaret Patricia, da of Ernest Cartlidge; 4 s (Alastair b 1977, James b 1979, Michael b 1981, Richard b 1986); *Career* jr research fell in applied mathematics Univ of Sheffield 1967–71; Univ of St Andrews: temp lectr applied mathematics 1971–73, lectr applied mathematics 1973–87, reader in applied mathematics 1987–94, prof of solar magnetohydrodynamics 1994–, head of applied mathematics 1997–98; one year leave of absence Enrico Fermi Inst Univ of Chicago 1974–75; conslt in coronal physics American Science and Engineering Mass 1977; visiting prof: Observatoire de Paris 1981, Space Science Center Univ of New Hampshire 1985–86, Univ of Leuven 1988–89, Univ of New Hampshire 1990 and 2002, Universitat de les Balears de Mallorca 1993; visiting scientist: Space Science Center Univ of New Hampshire 1980–81, Institut für Astronomie Zürich 1982, National Center for Atmospheric Research Colorado 1989; memb: NASA Skylab Workshop on Active Regions Colorado 1978–81, USA Global Oscillation Network Group 1987, Theory Research Assessment Panel PPARC 1998–2001; guest investigator USA Solar Maximum Mission 1980, 1984–86 and 1987–89; NASA res scientist Dept of Physics and Astronomy Univ of Iowa 1985–86; chm UK Solar Physics Community 1992–98, memb Solar System Advsy Panel PPARC 2001–03; Saltire Award For Distinguished Contributions to the Physical Sciences 1998; FRAS 1994, FRSE 1997; *Publications* numerous learned lectrs, reviews and articles in scientific jls, incl chapter 3 in Solar System Magnetic Fields (1985), chapter 6 in Advances in Solar System Magnetohydrodynamics (1991), articles in Encyclopedia of Astronomy and Astrophysics (2001); *Recreations* hill walking; *Style*— Prof Bernard Roberts, FRSE; ✉ School of Mathematics and Statistics, University of St Andrews, St Andrews, Fife KY16 9SS (tel 01334 463716, fax 01334 463748)

ROBERTS, Christopher Keepfer; s of John Anthony Roberts, and Pauline Isobel, *née* Keepfer; *b* 26 March 1956; *Educ* Denbigh HS, Jesus Coll Cambridge (MA); *Career* ptnr Allen & Overy 1985– (asst 1978–85); memb Law Soc; *Recreations* sailing, squash; *Clubs* Reform, RAC, Little Ship; *Style*— Christopher K Roberts, Esq

ROBERTS, Dr Clive John Charlton; s of Capt John Charlton Roberts (d 1982), of Taunton, and Monica, *née* Cousins; *b* 27 May 1946; *Educ* Taunton Sch, King's Coll Med Sch London (MB BS), Univ of Bristol (MD); *m* 1 (m dis 1998), 6 April 1968, Ruth Diane, da of Charles Henry Sandham, of Wigan; 2 da (Sally Kathryn b 1973, Rebecca b and d 1972), 2 s (Daniel John Charlton b 1975, Samuel James b 1982); m 2, 29 July 2000, Joanna Clare, da of Laurence Daniel McGeer, of Dublin; 2 s (Ambrose Jacob McGeer Roberts b 1998, Stanley Abram McGeer Roberts b 2003), 1 da (Olivia Marie McGeer Roberts b 1999); *Career* registrar in med Plymouth Gen Hosp 1972–74, conslt sr lectr in clinical pharmacology and med Bristol Royal Infirmary and Univ of Bristol 1981–, chm Div of Med Bristol Royal Infirmary 1993–95, clinical dean Faculty of Med Univ of Bristol 1997–2006; chief med offr AxaSunLife Assurance Society plc 1993–; author of papers and ed of books on clinical pharmacology; regnl advsr Royal Coll of Physicians 1994–96 (memb Acad Med Gp and chm Standing Ctee Membs); vice-chm Backwell PC 1987–95, chm Backwell Residents' Assoc 1990–95; memb Br Pharmacological Soc; FRCP 1987, FHEA 2007; *Books* Treatment in Clinical Medicine, Gastro Intestinal Disease (1983); *Recreations* local and family history, cycling, running; *Style*— Dr Clive Roberts; ✉ Clapton Wick Farm, Clevedon Lane, Clapton in Gordano, North Somerset BS21 7AG; Clinical Dean's Office, Centre for Medical Education, 39–41 St Michael's Hill, Bristol BS2 8DZ (tel 0117 954 6513, fax 0117 954 6514, e-mail c.j.c.roberts@bris.ac.uk)

ROBERTS, Prof (Victor) Colin; s of Ernest Roberts (d 1993), and Marjorie Frances, *née* Edwards (d 1987); *b* 11 February 1943; *Educ* Christ's Hosp, KCL (BSc(Eng), AKC), Univ of Surrey (MSc, PhD); *m* 27 July 1968, Christine Joan, da of Walter Clifford Lake; 2 da (Tara Jane b 27 June 1972, Catherine Elizabeth b 30 Nov 1973); *Career* apprentice Associated Electrical Industries Rugby 1961, engr Associated Electrical Industries Manchester then Compagnie Française Thomson-Houston Paris until 1967; KCH Med Sch London: research asst 1967–71, lectr in biomedical engrg 1971–75, sr lectr 1975–83, prof of biomedical engrg 1983–90; fndn prof of med engrg and physics King's Coll Sch of Med and Dentistry London 1990–2003 (now emeritus), dir of med engrg KCH NHS Tst 1990–2003, dir Nat Centre of Rehabilitation Engrg 1991–2003, dir Cornwall Mobility Centre 2004–, chm Royal Cornwall Hosps NHS Tst 2005–07 (non-exec dir 2003–05), chm Cornwall Medi-Park Ltd 2005–, non-exec dir NHS Innovations SW Ltd 2007–; visiting prof: Univ of Plovdiv Bulgaria 1997–, Peninsula Med Sch 2004–; ed: Med and Biological Engineering and Computing 1985–92, Med Engrg and Physics 1993–98 (hon ed 1999–2006); memb: Bd of Surgical Specialties RCS 1977–82, Admin Cncl Int Fedn for Med and Biological Engrg 1991–97, Med Engrg Coll EPSRC 1995–97 and 2000–06; chm: Professional Ctee on Med Electronics IEE 1976–77, Br Design Awards Panel for Med Equipment Design Cncl 1979–81, Working Gp on Clinical Engrg Int Fedn for Med and Biological Engrg 1982–85; ptnr Health Professions Cncl 2004–06; Pres's Prize Biological Engrg Soc 1980, distinguished overseas lectr Instn of Engrs Aust 1987, Nightingale Prize Inst of Physics and Engrg in Med 1996, 25th Jubilee Medal Bulgarian Soc of Med Physics and Biomedical Engrg 1997, Leonardo da Vinci Award 2004; govr James Allen's Girls' Sch 1998–2004; hon memb: Instn of Biomedical Engrs of Aust 1987, Romanian Soc for Clinical Engrg 1991; Hon MD Med Univ of Plovdiv 1998; FRSM 1973, FIEE 1981, FInstP 1981, FSIAD 1981, fell Biological Engrg Soc 1993 (pres 1976–78), founder fell Inst of Physics and Engrg in Med 1995, fell Int Acad of Med and Biological Engrg 2002; *Books* Blood Flow Measurement (1972), Doulton Ink Wares (1993), Amputee Management (1995), Medical Radiation Physics (1995); *Recreations* classical music, opera, antique restoration; *Style*— Prof Colin Roberts; ✉ The Old Rectory, St Buryan, Cornwall TR19 6BB (e-mail stburyan@netscape.net)

ROBERTS, Prof Colin; s of Theophilus Roberts (d 1991), of Wrexham, and Daisy, *née* Roberts (d 1989); *b* 25 January 1937; *Educ* Univ of Liverpool (med students undergrad scholar, BSc, MB ChB, MD), Victoria Univ of Manchester (DipBact); *m* 8 July 1961, Marjorie Frances, da of James Conway; 2 s (David Colin b 15 Oct 1962, Philip John b 10 Oct 1967); *Career* registrar in pathology Sefton Gen Hosp Liverpool 1964–66 (house physician and house surgn 1963–64), hon sr registrar United Liverpool Hosps 1966–70, lectr in med microbiology Univ of Liverpool 1969–70 (lectr in pathology 1966–69); Regnl Public Health Lab Fazakerley Hosp Liverpool: asst microbiologist (sr registrar) 1970–73, sr microbiologist 1973–75, conslt med microbiologist 1975–87, dep dir 1977–87; Public Health Lab Serv: dep dir 1987–93, conslt med microbiologist 1987–99, med and scientific postgrad dean 1993–99; John Radcliffe Hosp Oxford: locum conslt microbiologist 2000–07, hon conslt 2007–08; hon conslt med microbiologist Mersey RHA 1975–87; Univ of Liverpool: hon lectr in infectious diseases 1975–87, hon lectr Sch of Tropical Med and Infectious Diseases 1985–87; hon prof LSHTM 1997–2008, memb Cncl: Assoc of Clinical Pathologists (asst sec 1990–92), Assoc of Med Microbiologists (pres 1994–95), RCPath (asst registrar 1990–92, registrar 1992–96, vice-pres 1996–99), Pathology Section RSM 1999– (hon treas 2003–05, pres elect 2007–09); chm Med Microbiology Scientific Advsy Ctee Clinical Pathology Accreditation (UK) 1996–2000; sec Assoc of Academic Clinical Bacteriologists and Virologists 2000–07, study module tutor LSHTM distance learning in hosp infection 2004–; asst ed Jl of Hosp Infection 2004–, memb Editorial Bd Int Jl of

Environmental Health Research; hon life memb Central Sterilising Club 1996 (chm 1992–96); hon fell Liverpool John Moores Univ 2001; memb numerous professional socs incl: Br Soc for the Study of Infection, Pathological Soc of GB and I; Hon DipHic 1999; FRCPath 1986, FRIPHH 1992, Hon FRCPCH 1996, Hon FFPH 1997, FMedSci 1998, FRCP 1999, FFPathRCPI 2000; *Publications* contrib chapters/ed various books and proceedings incl: Infectious and Communicable Diseases in England and Wales (contrib, 1990), Quality Control: Principles and Practice in the Microbiology Laboratory (jt ed, 1991, 2 edn 1999), A Supervisor's Handbook of Food Hygiene and Safety (1995); also author of numerous pubns in academic jls; *Recreations* theatre, music, art, literature, sport (rep Wales at schoolboy and youth level in soccer); *Clubs* Savage, RSM; *Style*— Dr Colin Roberts; ✉ Level 6, Microbiology Department, The John Radcliffe, Headington, Oxford OX3 9DU (tel 01865 220886, fax 01865 220890, e-mail colin.roberts@orh.nhs.uk)

ROBERTS, HE Colin; CVO (2006); *b* 31 July 1959; *Educ* King's Coll Cambridge (MA), Courtauld Inst of Art London (MPhil); *m* 2000, Camilla Frances Mary, *née* Blair; 2 s; *Career* diplomat; lectr Ritsumeikan Univ Kyoto 1983–84; called to the Bar 1986, in private practice 1986–89; entered HM Dip Serv 1989, Repub of Ireland Dept 1989–90, second sec FCO 1990, second sec (economic) then first sec (political) Tokyo 1990–94, EU Dept (Internal) FCO 1995–96, first sec (political/military) Paris 1997–98, head Common Foreign and Security Policy Dept FCO 1998–2000, cnsllr (political) Tokyo 2001–04, ambass to Lithuania 2004–; *Recreations* mountain sports, natural history, tennis, reading; *Style*— HE Mr Colin Roberts, CVO; ✉ c/o Foreign & Commonwealth Office (Vilnius), King Charles Street, London SW1A 2AH

ROBERTS, Dr Dafydd Llewellyn Lloyd; s of Capt William Jones Roberts (d 1981), of Holyhead, Gwynedd, and Kate, *née* Griffiths (d 1991); *b* 6 January 1949; *Educ* Holyhead Comp Sch, Univ of London (MB BS); *m* Mary Josephine, da of Richard Joseph Farrell; 1 da (Catherine Mary Lloyd b 17 Sept 1977), 1 s (Daniel William Lloyd b 12 Dec 1984); *Career* jr hosp appointments Royal London Hosp, Harold Wood Hosp Essex, Chase Farm Hosp Middx and Univ Hosp of Wales Cardiff 1972–75, med offr and GP 1975, dermatology trg posts Univ Hosp of Wales and N Staffs Hosps 1976–81, conslt dermatologist West Glamorgan Health Authy 1981, currently conslt dermatologist Swansea NHS Tst, current chm UK Skin Cancer Working Pty; former: sec Med Staff Ctee Swansea Hosps, memb W Glamorgan District Med Ctee, memb Welsh Med Ctee, chm Welsh Sub-Ctee of Dermatology, chm Welsh Audit Gp (Dermatology); author of various pubns relating to clinical dermatology especially on malignant melanoma and skin cancers; memb: BMA, Br Assoc of Dermatologists (former hon treas); fell American Acad of Dermatology, FRSM, FRCP 1994 (MRCP 1975); *Style*— Dr Dafydd Roberts; ✉ 49 Higher Lane, Langland, Swansea SA3 4NT (tel 01792 369919); Singleton Hospital, Sketty, Swansea SA22 8QA (tel and fax 01792 285324)

ROBERTS, David; s of Lewis Roberts, of Verwood, Dorset, and Edna, *née* Boley; *b* 4 March 1954; *m* (m dis 2007), Mary, *née* Stansfield; 1 s (Tom b 1980, Joe b 1983); *Career* design dir Guinness Publishing 1989–96, assoc dir Guinness Publishing 1992–, ed Guinness Rockopedia 1997–99, ed Guinness World Records Book of British Hit Singles 1999–2007, pop music and book publishing conslt 2007–; British Book Design and Production Award for the Guinness Encyclopedia; *Recreations* supplying radio commentaries for Watford FC, walking, painting, natural history; *Style*— David Roberts, Esq; ✉ Poppublishing, 25 Chelsea Gardens, Church Langley, Essex CM17 9RX (tel 01279 861802, e-mail poppublishing@googlemail.com)

ROBERTS, David John Marling; MC (1965); s of John Edmund Marling Roberts (d 1980), of Checkendon, Oxon, and Jean, *née* Wheelock (d 1988); *b* 6 February 1943; *Educ* Marlborough, RMA Sandhurst, Manchester Business Sch; *m* 16 Dec 1967, Nicola Chamberlin; 2 da (Kate (Mrs Harries), Harriet d 1996), 1 s (Mark); *Career* served Army (Green Jackets) 1961–71 (ret as Capt); W H Smith plc 1971–96: md Wholesale Div 1980–85, md Retail 1985–91 (Main Bd 1988), dep gp md 1991–94, gp md 1994–96; non-exec chm NAAFI 1996–2001 (dir 1993–2001); non-exec dir: NPI 1993–99 (dep chm 1998–99), Martin Currie Enhanced Income Tst plc 1999–2005; chm Tomorrow's Net Ltd 2000–; memb: Br Retailers' Assoc 1986–91, Exec Cncl Army Benevolent Fund 1988–; JP Berks 1978–87, High Sheriff Berks 2001–02; CIMgt; *Recreations* country activities, tennis, golf, restoring old houses; *Clubs* Army and Navy, MCC; *Style*— David Roberts, Esq, MC; ✉ e-mail roberts.sanham@lineone.net

ROBERTS, Dennis Laurie Harold; s of William Harold Roberts, of Meopham, Kent, and Gwendoline Vera, *née* Edwards; *b* 24 January 1949; *Educ* Univ of Sheffield (BA, MSc); *m* 1980, Anne Mary, *née* Hillhouse; 1 s (Edward William b 31 Dec 1985); *Career* civil servant; CSO 1972–76, DOE 1976–83, MOD 1983–85; DOE: head Local Govt Fin Div 1985–89, head Water Environment Div 1989–92, head Fin Div 1992–94; dir of statistics Office of Population Censuses and Surveys 1994–96, gp dir Socio-Economic Statistics Office for Nat Statistics 1996–98, gp dir Fin and Corp Services Office for NAT Statistics 1998–2000, dir Roads and Traffic Directorate 2000–; memb RSS 1975; *Recreations* walking, reading, watching football; *Style*— Dennis Roberts, Esq

ROBERTS, Sir Denys Tudor Emil; KBE (1975, CBE 1970, OBE 1960); s of William David Roberts (d 1954), of St Albans; *b* 19 January 1923; *Educ* Aldenham, Wadham Coll Oxford (MA, BCL); *m* 1, 1949 (m dis 1973), Brenda Dorothy, da of L Marsh; 1 s, 1 da; *m* 2, 1985, Anna Fiona Dollar, da of N G A Alexander; 1 s; *Career* WWII serv RA; called to the Bar Lincoln's Inn 1950; barr London 1950–53, crown counsel Nyasaland 1953–59; Gibraltar: QC 1960, attorney-gen 1960–62; Hong Kong: slr-gen 1962–66, QC 1964, attorney-gen 1966–73, chief sec 1973–78, chief justice 1979–88; chief justice Brunei 1979–2001, memb and pres Court of Appeal for Bermuda 1988–94, memb Hong Kong Court of Final Appeal 1997–2003, pres Brunei Court of Appeal 2002–2003; hon bencher Lincoln's Inn 1978, hon fell Wadham Coll Oxford 1984; SPMB (Brunei) 1984; *Books* Smuggler's Circuit (1954), Beds and Roses (1956), The Elwood Wager (1958), The Bones of the Wajingas (1960), How to Dispense with Lawyers (1964), I'll Do Better Next Time (1995), Yes Sir, But (2000), Another Disaster (2006); *Recreations* cricket, tennis, writing, walking; *Clubs* MCC (pres 1989–90), Hong Kong, Royal Commonwealth Soc; *Style*— Sir Denys Roberts, KBE; ✉ The Grange, North Green Road, Pulham St Mary, Norfolk IP21 4PZ

ROBERTS, Derek Franklyn; s of Frank Roberts, MBE (d 1981), of Wirral, Cheshire, and May Evelyn Roberts (d 1991); *b* 16 October 1942; *Educ* Park High GS Birkenhead, Liverpool Coll of Commerce, Harvard Business Sch (AMP); *m* 6 Sept 1969, Jacqueline, da of Sylvio Velho; 2 s (Maxwell Franklyn b 9 March 1971, Daniel Downes b 29 Dec 1972), 1 da (Katie Jane b 3 Sept 1976); *Career* Royal Insurance Co Ltd 1961–72; Huddersfield Building Society: insurance servs mangr 1972, business devpt mangr 1975, devpt mangr 1979, asst gen mangr (mktg) upon formation of Yorkshire Building Society 1982; Yorkshire Building Society: dir and chief exec 1987–96, chm 1997–2000; non-exec BWD Securities plc 1988–92; sr non-exec dir Kelda plc 1996–2005; FCII, FCIB, CIMgt; *Recreations* golf, gardening, skiing; *Clubs* Royal Liverpool Golf, Huddersfield Golf, Huddersfield RUFC, Woodsome Hall Golf; *Style*— Derek Roberts, Esq

ROBERTS, Dr Dewi Wyn; s of Capt John Roberts (d 1964), of Caernarvonshire, and Janet, *née* Griffith (d 1947); *b* 6 March 1939, Edern, Caernarvonshire; *Educ* David Hughes GS Anglesey, Downing Coll Cambridge (MA, MB, BChir, Athletics blue), Westminster Hosp Univ of London; *m* 10 Aug 1962, Dr Sheila Mary, *née* Benson; 1 s (John Griffith), 1 da (Catrin Ann Griffith Macey); *Career* house surgn and house physician Addenbrooke Hosp Cambridge; family doctor Daventry 1966–96; dir Community Justice Intevention Wales; High Sheriff Gwynedd 2007–08; former athlete (rep Wales), team mangr

Oxford/Cambridge Athletics 1990–2005, chm Pwllheli Sports Club, fndr memb Daventry rugby, squash and athletics clubs; MRCS, LRCP; *Clubs* Hawks' (Cambridge), Achilles (chm), RSM; *Style*— Dr Dewi Roberts; ✉ Derwen Deg, Hwfa Road, Bangor, Gwynedd LL57 2BN (tel 01248 354415)

ROBERTS, Dr Dorothy Elizabeth (Mrs Glen-Doepel); da of Noel Lee Roberts (d 1967), of Sydney, and Myrtle Winifred, *née* Reid (d 1967); *Educ* Methodist Ladies Coll Sydney, Sydney Conservatorium of Music; *m* 1957 (m dis 1969), William Glen-Doepel, s of Otto Glen-Doepel; 1 s (Peter Lee John b 1969); *Career* concert pianist; appeared at venues incl Royal Albert Hall, worked with orchs incl Hallé and London Symphony Orch, Northern Sinfonia, and London Bach players; given recitals in London and provinces, Australia, Amsterdam, Paris, Schloss Leitheim Concert Series Germany; known as performer of Clara Schumann tradition; protegée of Adelina de Lara, OBE; pupil of Clara Schumann; lectr in Clara Schumann tradition and technique, and the great pianists of the 19/20 century; abstract painter (as Dorothy Lee Roberts), exhibited works in London, NY and provincial galleries; memb: Friends of Lincoln museums and Art Gallery, Nat Art Collections Fund, Lincs Old Churches Tst; Hon AMusA 1945, Hon LMus 1947; Hon DLitt Univ of Bradford 1995; *Recreations* travel, reading; *Clubs* The Arts; *Style*— Dr Dorothy Roberts; ✉ Alveley House, 17 Lindum Road, Lincoln LN2 1NS (tel 01522 520942)

ROBERTS, Elizabeth Jane (Liz); da of Martin Gwylfa Roberts, of Timperly, Cheshire, and Hilda Elizabeth, *née* Gilbert; *b* 10 June 1960; *Educ* Sale GS for Girls, Univ of Sussex; *Children* 1 da (Eve b Nov 1992); *Career* editorial asst Phaidon Press 1982–83, sub ed then chief sub ed Building Magazine 1984–86; Media Week: broadcast reporter 1986–87, broadcast ed 1987–88, news ed 1988–89, dep ed 1989–90, ed 1990–92; freelance journalist 1993–96: The Guardian, Sunday Telegraph, Esquire, She; ed Nursery World 1997– (features ed 1996–97); *Recreations* music, walking, travel, food, literature; *Style*— Ms Liz Roberts

ROBERTS, Sir Gilbert Howland Rookehurst; 7 Bt (UK 1809), of Glassenbury, Kent, of Brightfieldstown, Co Cork and of the City of Cork; s of Col Sir Thomas Langdon Howland Roberts, CBE, 6 Bt (d 1979), and (Evelyn) Margaret, *née* Fielding-Hall (d 1992); *b* 31 May 1934; *Educ* Rugby, Gonville & Caius Coll Cambridge (BA); *m* 1958, Ines Eleonore, o da of late Alfons Leo Labunski, of Danzig; 1 s, 1 da; *Heir* s, Howland Roberts; *Career* serv Kenya with RE (E African GS medal); MIMechE; *Style*— Sir Gilbert Roberts, Bt; ✉ 3340 Cliff Drive, Santa Barbara, CA 93109–1079, USA

ROBERTS, (David Edward) Glyn; s of David Emlyn Roberts (d 1975), and Henrietta Liston, *née* Griffiths (d 1990); *b* 29 February 1932; *Educ* Calday Grange GS; *m* 1, 13 Oct 1955, Beryl Sheila Price (d 1968); 3 da (Deborah Mary, Angela Margeret, Ruth Alexandra); *m* 2, 11 Aug 1972, Elizabeth Mary, *née* Grimwade; 2 step s (Adrian Edward Ainsworth Thorn, Richard Charles Ainsworth Thorn), 1 step da (Patricia Lewis); *Career* Nat Serv 2 Lt RA 1955–57; actuary Royal Insurance Co 1949–61; stockbroker: Tilney and Co 1961–74, Roberts and Huish 1974–85, Ashton Tod McLaren 1985–88; md Quilter Goodison 1988–92 (dep chm 1992–96); FIA 1955, FCII 1959, memb Stock Exchange; *Style*— Glyn Roberts, Esq; ✉ No 2 Briery Close, Holbeck Lane, Windermere, Cumbria LA23 1NB (tel 01539 432047)

ROBERTS, Dr (James) Graeme; s of Rev Alexander Roberts (d 1993), of Dunblane, and Winifred, *née* Jack (d 1993); *b* 7 November 1942; *Educ* Hutchesons' Boys' GS Glasgow, Univ of St Andrews (King James VI Prize, Sr Hons Class Medal, MA), Univ of Aberdeen (PhD); *m* 1965, Elizabeth Watson Milo, *née* Tucker; 2 s (Neil John b 1967, Euan James b 1976), 2 da (Claire Elizabeth b 1971, Susanna Judith b 1973); *Career* Univ of Aberdeen: asst lectr in English 1964–68, lectr in English 1968–85, memb Ct 1981–89 and 1995–2005, sr lectr in English 1985–2005, head Dept of English 1993–96, vice-princ and dean Faculty of Arts and Divinity 1996–2001, vice-princ 2001–05; chair Scottish Museums Cncl; chair Aberdeen Performing Arts; elder Ferryhill Parish Church Aberdeen; FRSA 1996; *Recreations* swimming, walking, music; *Clubs* Royal Scots; *Style*— Dr Graeme Roberts; ✉ 17 Devanha Gardens, Aberdeen AB11 7UU; University Office, University of Aberdeen, King's College, Aberdeen AB24 3FX (tel 01224 272017, fax 01224 272082, e-mail j.g.roberts@abdn.ac.uk)

ROBERTS, (David) Gwilym Morris; CBE (1987); s of Edward Humphrey Roberts (d 1949), of Crosby, Merseyside, and Edith, *née* Roberts (d 1983); *b* 24 July 1925; *Educ* Merchant Taylors' Crosby, Sidney Sussex Coll Cambridge (MA); *m* 1, 16 Oct 1960, Rosemary Elizabeth Emily (d 1973), da of John Edmund Giles (d 1971), of Tavistock, Devon; 1 s ((Edward) Matthew Giles b 1963), 1 da (Annabel Elizabeth Giles b 1967); *m* 2, 14 Oct 1978, Wendy Ann, da of Dr John King Moore (d 1975), of Beckenham, Kent; *Career* Lt Cdr RNR, ret 1961; chartered civil engr; sr ptnr John Taylor and Sons 1981–90 (ptnr 1956–90), dir Thomas Telford Ltd 1983–89; chm: Acer Group Ltd 1987–92, Prog Bd BGS 1989–93, Football Stadia Advsy Design Cncl 1990–93, Westmeston Parish Cncl 1990–98 (memb 1983–99), Second Severn Crossing Tech Adjudication Panel 1992–97; visiting prof Loughborough Univ of Technol 1991–95; hon fell Sidney Sussex Coll Cambridge 1994, pres ICE 1986–87; memb Cncl: NERC 1987–93, Brighton Poly 1983–86; govr: Chailey Sch 1987–92, Roedean Sch 1987–93; Liveryman: Worshipful Co of Engrs, Worshipful Co of Constructors, Worshipful Co of Water Conservators; Freeman City of London; FREng 1986; *Publications* Chelsea to Cairo (2006); *Recreations* tennis, golf, local history; *Clubs* Oxford and Cambridge, Piltdown Golf; *Style*— Gwilym Roberts, Esq, CBE, FREng; ✉ c/o Upper Walland Farm, Wadhurst TN5 6NE

ROBERTS, Dr Howard Frederick; s of William Frederick John Roberts (d 1985), of Wallington, Surrey, and Hilda Gertrude, *née* Ward; *b* 7 January 1937; *Educ* Univ of London (MB BS, MPhil, MRCP); *m* 22 Aug 1981, Judith Margaret, da of William Bertram Wilson (d 1994), of Rowledge, Surrey; 3 da (Henrietta b 1983, Lucinda b 1985, Georgina b 1987); *Career* conslt child and adolescent psychiatrist S London and Maudsley Tst; assoc memb Br Psycho Analytical Soc 1985; MRCPsych 1974; *Style*— Dr Howard Roberts; ✉ 73 Onslow Gardens, London N10 3JY (tel 020 8883 7473)

ROBERTS, Sir Hugh Ashley; KCVO (2001, CVO 1998, LVO 1995); s of Rt Rev Dr Edward Roberts (d 2001), and Dorothy Frances, *née* Bowser (d 1982); *b* 20 April 1948; *Educ* Winchester, CCC Cambridge (MA); *m* 13 Dec 1975, Hon (Priscilla) Jane Stephanie Low (Hon Lady Roberts, CVO, *qv*, er da of late 1 Baron Aldington, KCMG, CBE, DSO, TD, PC, DL; 2 da (Sophie b 1978, Amelia b 1982); *Career* Christie Manson & Woods Ltd 1970–87 (dir 1978–87); Dep Surveyor of The Queen's Works of Art 1988–96, Dir of The Royal Collection and Surveyor of The Queen's Works of Art 1996–; FSA; *Recreations* gardening; *Style*— Sir Hugh Roberts, KCVO, FSA; ✉ The Royal Collection, St James's Palace, London SW1A 1BQ (tel 020 7930 4832)

ROBERTS, Humphrey Richard Medwyn; s of Hugh Medwyn Roberts (d 1961), of Southport, Lancs, and Enid Marjorie, *née* Pochin (d 1987); *b* 29 May 1931; *Educ* Leas Sch Hoylake, Aldenham, King's Coll Cambridge (MA), Westminster Med Sch (MB BChir, Bulkeley medal, Arthur Evans prize); *m* 21 March 1964, Pamela Ruth, da of Robert Barker; 2 da (Caroline Jane Medwyn b 1 Aug 1965, Katharine Lucy Medwyn b 29 June 1967), 1 s (James Hugh Medwyn b 28 June 1969); *Career* SHO Chelsea Hosp for Women 1963–64, res obstetrician Queen Charlotte's Hosp 1966–67, conslt obstetrician and gynaecologist Queen Mary's Hosp Roehampton 1968–79; Westminster Hosp: house surgn 1957–58, res obstetric asst 1958, registrar in obstetrics and gynaecology 1964–66, conslt obstetrician and gynaecologist 1968–91; hon conslt gynaecologist: Hosp of St John and Elizabeth 1971–80, St Luke's Hosp for the Clergy 1986–96; examiner: obstetrics and gynaecology Univs of Cambridge and London, diploma and membership RCOG, Central Midwives Bd; memb: BMA 1957, Medical Def Union 1957, Hospital Conslt and Staff Assoc 1982,

Chelsea Clinical Soc 1979 (pres 1993–94, sr tstee 1995–2002); FRCS 1961, FRCOG 1978 (MRCOG 1965); *Recreations* Sherlock Holmes, bird watching, gardening; *Style—* Humphrey Roberts, Esq; ✉ 64 Chartfield Avenue, London SW15 6HQ (tel 020 8789 1758)

ROBERTS, (Thomas) Ian; s of Thomas Ormerod Roberts, of Settle, N Yorks, and Joan, *née* Bilsborough; *b* 8 November 1956; *Educ* Giggleswick Sch, The Queen's Coll Oxford (MA); *Career* admitted slr 1982; ptnr: Booth & Co 1988–92 (joined 1982, assoc 1986), Irwin Mitchell 1992–; dir Kaye & Co (Huddersfield) Ltd 1989–2001; sec Yorkshire Young Slrs Gp 1982–88 (memb Ctee 1985–88); memb: Law Soc, Sheffield Law Soc; Law Soc nominee Records Preservation Ctee Br Records Assoc 2005–; N area rep Legal Educn and Trg Gp 1993–95, business govr The Sheffield Coll 1993–2001, memb Ct Univ of Bradford 1998–2004; sec Yorkshire Glass Manufacturers' Assoc 1983–88; memb: Yorkshire Archaeological Soc, Soc of Genealogists; pres Old Giggleswickian Club 2005–06 (hon sec 1995–98, chm 1998–2001); life memb: Nat Tst, English Heritage; memb N Craven Heritage Tst, tstee: Sheffield Gen Cemetery Tst 2005–, Rugby Fives Assoc; *Books* A Walk Round Stackhouse (1979); *Recreations* genealogy, local history, long case clocks, fives; *Clubs* Jesters, Rugby Fives Assoc; *Style—* Ian Roberts, Esq; ✉ Irwin Mitchell, Riverside East, 2 Millsands, Sheffield S3 8DT (tel 0870 1500 100, e-mail ian.roberts@irwinmitchell.com)

ROBERTS, Prof Ian Gareth; s of Idris Michael Roberts (d 1971), and Dorothy Sybil, *née* Moody (d 1997); *b* 23 October 1957; *Educ* Univ of Wales Bangor (BA), Univ of Southern Calif (PhD), Univ of Cambridge (DLitt); *m* 10 July 1993, Lucia, da of Luigi Cavalli; 1 s (Julian Maxwell b 11 June 1996), 1 da (Lydia Iona b 14 March 2001); *Career* asst de linguistique Anglaise Département de Langue et Littérature Anglaises Université de Genève 1985–86, maître-asst Département de Linguistique Générale Université de Genève 1986–91, prof and head of linguistics Univ of Wales Bangor 1991–96, prof and head of English linguistics Universität Stuttgart 1996–2000, prof of linguistics Univ of Cambridge 2000–, head of linguistics Univ of Cambridge 2000–05, professorial fell Downing Coll Cambridge 2000–; jt ed Jl of Linguistics 1994–2000 (asst ed 1996–2000); Prix Latsis de l'Université de Genève 1989; memb: Linguistic Soc of America 1982, Generative Linguistics in the Old World 1983, Linguistics Assoc of GB 1991, Fndn for Endangered Languages 1992, Philological Soc 2001; *Books* The Representation of Implicit and Dethematized Subjects (1987), Viagem Diacrônica pelas Fases do Português Brasileiro: Homagem a Fernando Tarallo (jt ed, 1993), Verbs and Diachronic Syntax: A Comparative History of English and French (1993), Clause Structure and Language Change (jt ed, 1994), Comparative Syntax (1996), The Syntax of the Celtic Languages (jt ed, 1996), Beyond Principles and Parameters: Essays in Memory of Osvaldo Jaeggli (jt ed, 1999), Syntactic Change: A Minimalist Approach to Grammaticalisation (jtly, 2003), Principles and Parameters in a VSO Language: A Case Study in Welsh (2005), Diachronic Syntax (2007), Comparative Grammar (ed, 6 vols, 2007); *Recreations* novels, music, fine wine; *Style—* Prof Ian Roberts; ✉ 4 Chancellor's Walk, Cambridge CB4 3JG (tel and fax 01223 356931, mobile 07775 514668); Department of Linguistics, University of Cambridge, Sidgwick Avenue, Cambridge CB3 9DA (tel 01223 331733, fax 01223 335053, e-mail igr20@cam.ac.uk)

ROBERTS, Sir Ivor Anthony; KCMG; s of Leonard Moore Roberts (d 1981), and Rosa Maria, *née* Fusco (d 1999); *b* 24 September 1946; *Educ* St Mary's Coll Crosby, Keble Coll Oxford (Gomm scholar, MA); *m* 4 May 1974, Elizabeth Bray, da of Norman Douglas Bernard Smith; 2 s (Huw Benedict Bernard b 1976, David Daniel Rowland b 1979), 1 da (Hannah Rebecca Louise b 1982); *Career* HM Dip Serv: joined 1968, ME Centre for Arabic Studies 1969, third then second sec Paris 1970–73, second then first sec FCO 1973–78, first sec Canberra 1978–82, dep head News Dept FCO 1982–86, cnsllr FCO 1986–88, min Madrid 1989–93, ambass to Yugoslavia 1996–97 (chargé d'affaires 1994–96), seconded as sr assoc memb St Antony's Coll Oxford 1998–99, ambass to Repub of Ireland 1999–2003, ambass to Italy 2003–06 (concurrently non-resident ambass to San Marino); pres Trinity Coll Oxford 2006–; patron Venice in Peril Fund; chm Cncl of the Br Sch in Rome; hon fell Keble Coll Oxford 2001; FCIL; *Recreations* opera, skiing, golf; *Clubs* Oxford and Cambridge, Downhill Only (Wengen); *Style—* Sir Ivor Roberts, KCMG; ✉ President's Lodgings, Trinity College, Oxford OX1 3BH (tel 01865 279900, fax 01865 279874, e-mail ivor.roberts@trinity.ox.ac.uk)

ROBERTS, His Hon Judge Jeremy Michael Graham; QC (1982); s of Lt-Col John Michael Harold Roberts (d 1954), and Eileen Dora, *née* Chaplin (d 2006); *b* 26 April 1941; *Educ* Winchester, BNC Oxford (BA); *m* 25 July 1964, Sally Priscilla, da of Col Frederick Peter Johnson, OBE, of Hants; *Career* called to the Bar Inner Temple 1965 (bencher 1992); recorder of the Crown Court 1981–2000, judge Central Criminal Court 2000–; *Recreations* theatre, opera, reading, horse and dog racing, canals; *Style—* His Hon Judge Jeremy Roberts, QC; ✉ Central Criminal Court, London EC4M 7EH (tel 020 7248 3277)

ROBERTS, John Anthony; s of John Owen Roberts (d 1985), and Elsie Edna May, *née* Leese (d 1994); *b* 12 February 1941; *Educ* Avondale Secdy Sch Stockport, Stockport Jr Commercial Sch; *m* 2 Sept 1967, Philomena Mary Therese, da of Christopher Thomas Coyne; 2 s (Christopher b 26 Oct 1971, Gerard b 30 Aug 1978), 1 da (Leanne b 5 Sept 1974); *Career* reporter Stockport Express 1958–62 (sports ed 1960–62); sports reporter: Daily Express Manchester 1965–78 (sports sub-ed 1962–65, NI sports corr 1965–68), The Guardian 1978–80; sports feature writer Daily Mail 1981–86, tennis corr and dep chief sports writer The Independent 1986–2006 (football corr 1991); NW Sports Journalist of the Year 1987; memb: Football Writers' Assoc, Lawn Tennis Writers' Assoc (chm 2001–03), Sports Journalists' Assoc of GB, Int Sports Press Assoc (AIPS); *Books* George Best - Fall of a Superstar (1973), The Team That Wouldn't Die (The Story of the Busby Babes) (1975), Official Centenary History of Everton (1978); ghosted autobiographies: Bill Shankly (1976), Kevin Keegan (1977); *Style—* John Roberts, Esq; ✉ 1 Bath Crescent, Cheadle Hulme, Stockport, Cheshire SK8 7QU (fax 0161 439 3097); The Independent, Independent House, 191 Marsh Wall, London E14 9RS (tel 020 7293 2847, fax 020 7293 2894)

ROBERTS, John Charles Quentin; s of late Hubert C Roberts, of Binsted, W Sussex; *b* 4 April 1933; *Educ* King's Coll Taunton, Univ of London (CSC Interpretership), Merton Coll Oxford (MA); *m* 1, 1959 (m dis 1979), Dinah, da of late Maj Trevor Webster-Williams, TD (d 1987), of Cheltenham; 1 da (Gwen b 1960), 1 s (Stephen b 1963); m 2, 1982 (m dis 2005), Elizabeth, *née* Gough-Cooper; *Career* Nat Serv Intelligence Offr RAF 1951–53; Shell International Petroleum Co (various mgmnt posts in Europe and Africa) 1956–61, asst master Marlborough 1963–73, dir The Britain-Russia Centre (formerly The Great Britain-USSR Assoc) 1974–93; chm Int Advsy Bd All-Russia State Library for Foreign Lit Moscow 1994–; memb: Cncl SSEES Univ of London 1981–92, Editorial Bd Herald of Europe Moscow 2000–; tstee: Sergei Rachmaninoff Fndn 2001–06, Keston Inst Oxford 2003–07; hon life memb London-Russia Soc 2002; *Books* Speak Clearly into the Chandelier: Cultural Politics Between Britain and Russia 1973–2000 (2000, Znamya Globus Award for Russian language edn 2001); *Recreations* music, family; *Clubs* Athenaeum; *Style—* John C Q Roberts, Esq

ROBERTS, John Edward; CBE (2004); s of Arthur Roberts (d 1976), and Dora, *née* Watkin (d 1987); *b* 2 March 1946; *Educ* Oldershaw GS Wallasey, Univ of Liverpool (BEng), St Helens Mgmnt Coll (DMS); *m* 20 June 1970, Pamela, da of William Baxter; 1 s (Richard b 1980), 1 da (Gemma b 1982); *Career* Manweb: fin dir 1984–91, md 1991–92, chief exec 1992–95; chief exec: S Wales Electricity 1996–97, Hyder Utilities 1997–99, United Utilities 1999–2006; non-exec dir: Royal Bank of Canada (Europe) Ltd 2005–, International Power plc 2006–; fell Liverpool John Moores Univ 2004, Hon DEng Univ of Liverpool 2004; FACCA 1983, FIEE 1992, FREng 2002; *Recreations* scuba diving, watching cricket, listening to opera; *Style—* Dr John Roberts, CBE

ROBERTS, John Frederick; *b* 30 March 1946; *Educ* Bristol GS, Univ of Bristol (BDS), Eastman Dental Center Rochester NY (Cert Paedodontics); *m* Gabriele Elizabeth; 2 s (Alexander John b 14 Oct 1979, Sebastian Frederick b 24 March 1983); *Career* house offr Bristol Dental Hosp 1971, assoc in gen dental practice Bristol 1972–74, princ in gen dental practice Johannesburg 1974–76, sr ptnr private paediatric dental practice London, sr demonstrator Dept of Orthodontics and Dentistry for Children UMDS Guy's Hosp 1978–1998; recognised teacher status in paediatrics Univ of London Faculty of Med and Dentistry 1990–; numerous invited lectures and courses UK and abroad; memb: BDA, Br Soc of Paediatric Dentistry, American Acad of Paedodontics, American Soc of Dentistry for Children, American Dental Soc of London, American Bd of Paedodontics, Euro Acad of Paediatric Dentistry; Specialist in Paediatric Dentistry 1998; *Publications* Kennedy's Paediatric Dentistry (co-author); author of various articles in Br Dental Jl; *Style—* John Roberts, Esq; ✉ 74 Bois Lane, Amersham, Buckinghamshire HP6 6BX (tel 01494 725685); 33 Weymouth Street, London W1G 7BY (tel 020 7580 5370, fax 020 7636 3094, e-mail john@paediatric-dentistry.co.uk, website www.paediatric-dentistry.co.uk)

ROBERTS, His Hon Judge John Houghton; s of John Noel Roberts, and Ida, *née* Houghton; *b* 14 December 1947; *Educ* Calday Grange GS, Trinity Hall Cambridge (MA); *m* 1, 1972 (m dis 1990), Anna Elizabeth, da of Peter Tooke Sheppard, of Essex; 3 s (James b 1974, Edward b 1976, William b 1978); m 2, 20 April 1991, Janice Mary, da of Frederic Wilkinson, of Merseyside; *Career* called to the Bar Middle Temple 1970; recorder of the Crown Court 1988–93, circuit judge (Northern Circuit) 1993–, resident judge Bolton Crown Court 1997–2001, circuit judge Liverpool Crown Court 2002–; *Recreations* golf, rugby football, music; *Clubs* Athenaeum (Liverpool), Heswall Golf, Waterloo FC, Nefyn Golf; *Style—* His Hon Judge John Roberts; ✉ Liverpool Crown Court, Queen Elizabeth II Law Courts, Derby Square, Liverpool

ROBERTS, Dr John Maxwell; *b* 4 April 1948; *Educ* Henbury Sch Bristol, Univ of Sheffield (BEng, PhD, Mappin Medal and Premium 1969, Br Iron and Steel Inst Prize 1969); *m* 1969, Angela, *née* Willis; 3 s (Ben Matthew b 1976, David Maxwell b 1979, Thomas Edmund b 1984); *Career* site engr Sir Alfred McAlpine & Sons Ltd 1972–74, engr and assoc Bertram Done & Partners 1974–81, dir Allott & Lomax (later Babtie Gp, now Jacobs) 1985– (engr 1981–85); projects incl: Battersea Power Station redevelopment, Pepsi Max Big One Rollercoaster, Br Airways London Eye wheel; James Forrest Medal and Premium ICE 1971–72, Lancashire and Cheshire Branch Prize IStructE 1984–85 and 1988–89, Sir Arnold Water Medal IStructE 1984–85, Gold Medal IStructE 2005; FICE, FIStructE (pres 1999–2000), FREng 1995; *Recreations* walking, gardening; *Clubs* Royal Anglesey Yacht; *Style—* Dr John Roberts, FREng; ✉ Jacobs, Fairbairn House, Ashton Lane, Sale, Manchester M33 6WP (tel 0161 962 1214, fax 0161 962 9462, e-mail johnm.roberts@jacobs.com)

ROBERTS, Keith; s of Cliff Roberts, andn Averay, *née* Collins; *Educ* Carshalton HS for Boys, Camberwell Sch of Art, Newcastle upon Tyne Poly (BA), RCA (MA); *Career* artist; commissions incl: Tindall, Riley & Co 1993, Br Airports Authy 1994, Defence of Britain Project Imperial War Museum London 1997, Egon Zhender Mgmnt Conslts 1998, AMBAC 1999, Crown Estates 2000; work in collections: Unilever, AMBAC, Pearsons, Tindall-Riley; memb: Parachute Regt Assoc, Flamenco Housing Co-op (chair 1997–2001); *Selected Solo Exhibitions* New Academy Gallery London 1993, 1996 and 1998, Blue Gallery London 1997, New Paintings (Curwen Gallery London) 1999, Adore the City (SM Gallery London) 2000, Keith Roberts (Boycott Gallery Brussels) 2000, Boycott Gallery Brussels 2002; *Selected Group Exhibitions* NEAC Annual (Mall Galleries London) 1990, Northern Graduates (New Academy Gallery London) 1990, Salon der Debutanten Holland 1991, Art London '91 (Olympia London) 1991, Discerning Eye (Mall Galleries London) 1991 and 1992, Contemporaries I (Eagle Gallery London) 1993, The Bridge Show (Lannan Gallery NY) 1994, What Happened Next? (Lannan Gallery NY) 1994, The Whitechapel Open (Whitechapel Gallery London) 1994, Making Marks (Mall Gallery London) 1994, 7th Oriel Mostyn Open (Mostyn Art Gallery Llandudno), Art '95 (London), Bureau de Change (Rustin Fndn Antwerp) 1996, 9th Oriel Mostyn Open (Mostyn Art Gallery Llandudno) 1997, Changing London (Eagle Gallery London) 1998, Bankside Browser (Tate Modern London) 1999, Art '99 (London Contemporary Art Fair) 1999, Crosscurrents (Lloyds Insurance Building London) 1999, Cheltenham & Gloucester Drawing Open (UK and Berlin) 1999–2000, The Crown Estates Projects London 2000, Holy Cow! (Clapham Art Gallery London) 2000, The Hunting Prize London 2000, Doughty & Sons London 2001, Urban Rhythms (SM Gallery London) 2001, Adapt Now (Art Gallery and Museum Glasgow) 2002, Headline (SM Gallery London) 2002, In Your Time (Percy Miller Gallery London) 2002; *Awards* Br Alcan Prize 1989, Marks & Spencer Prize NEAC 1990, Richard Ford Awards 1990, prizewinner Discerning Eye Mall Galleries London 1991, Barcelona Travel Award 1991, Delfina Studios Tst Scholarship 1992, Oppenheim-John Downes Meml Tst 1995, Triangle Artists Workshop Scholarship 1997; *Recreations* cycling; *Clubs* Surrey Road Cycling; *Style—* Keith Roberts, Esq; ✉ Flat B, 13 Waller Road, London SE14 5LE

ROBERTS, Prof Kenneth; s of Ernest William Roberts, and Nancy, *née* Williams; *b* 24 September 1940; *Educ* Stockport Sch, LSE (BSc, MSc); *m* 8 Aug 1964, Patricia, da of Frank Newton, of Macclesfield; 1 s (Gavin Paul b 19 Feb 1968), 2 da (Susan Alexis b 18 Dec 1970, Vanessa Jane (twin) b 19 Dec 1970); *Career* successively asst lectr, sr lectr, reader then prof Univ of Liverpool 1966–; memb: Br Sociological Assoc, Int Sociological Assoc, Euro Sociological Assoc, Leisure Studies Assoc, Inst of Career Guidance; *Books* Youth and Leisure (1983), The Changing Structure of Youth Labour Markets (1987), Leisure and Lifestyle (1989), Youth and Work (1991), Careers and Identities (1992), Youth and Employment in Modern Britain (1995), Poland's First Post-Communist Generation (1995), Leisure in Contemporary Society (1999), Surviving Post-Communism (2000), Class in Modern Britain (2001), The Leisure Industries (2004); *Style—* Prof Kenneth Roberts; ✉ 2 County Road, Ormskirk, Lancashire L39 1QQ (tel 01695 574962); Sociology Department, University of Liverpool, PO Box 147, Liverpool L79 3BX (tel 0151 794 2971, e-mail d.m.oconnor@liverpool.ac.uk)

ROBERTS, Malcolm John Binyon; s of Sqdn Ldr Kenneth Arthur Norman Roberts (d 1973), and Greta Kathleen, *née* Cooper; *b* 3 July 1951; *Educ* St Edmund's Sch Canterbury; *m* 28 April 1984, Caroline Mary, da of John Harry Scrutton; 2 s (Frederick, Charles), 1 da (Iona); *Career* ptnr Montagu Loebl Stanley 1979–86, dir Fleming Private Asset Management 1986–2000, JP Morgan Private Bank 2000–02, exec dir Rothschild Private Management 2002–; memb Stock Exchange Examination Ctee (Taxation) 1985–87; govr and tstee Granville Sch Sevenoaks 1986–, special tstee Moorfields Eye Hosp 1996– (chm 2005–), tstee Household Cavalry Museum Tst 2007–; Liveryman Worshipful Co of Barbers; FSI 2000 (memb Stock Exchange 1978), FRSA 2006; *Recreations* tennis, planting trees, shooting; *Clubs* City, Knowle, 1900; *Style—* Malcolm Roberts, Esq; ✉ Hillsmead, Godden Green, Sevenoaks, Kent TN15 0JR; Rothschild Private Management Ltd, 1 King William Street, London EC4N 7AR

ROBERTS, Martin Charles; s of Denis Walter Wakem Roberts (d 1988), of Epsom, Surrey, and Joan Mary, *née* Saunders; *b* 11 April 1955; *Educ* City of London Freemen's Sch, Univ of Kingston upon Thames (BA), Guildford Law Sch; *m* 3 Sept 1988, Jane Rosalind, da of John Henderson; 1 s (James William b 27 Sept 1992), 1 da (Georgina Rosalind b 5 Sept 1994); *Career* Pinsent Masons: articled clerk 1977–79, asst slr 1979–83, ptnr 1983–, memb Partnership Bd 1992–98, dep head Construction and Engrg Law Dept 1994–97, head of Power and Energy Sector 1997–2000, managing ptnr Construction and Engrg Sector 2000–03, head London office 2004–; CEDR accredited mediator 1997; Freeman City of London 1975, Liveryman City of London Slrs' Co 1985 (memb Ct 1999–, steward 2004–07); memb: Law Soc 1977, City of London Law Soc 1985 (memb Ctee 1997–, memb Ctee Litigation Sub Ctee 1991–2003); *Recreations* tennis, swimming, music, theatre, cinema; *Clubs* RAC; *Style*— Martin Roberts, Esq; ✉ Pinsent Masons, 30 Aylesbury Street, London EC1R 0ER (tel 020 7490 4000, fax 020 7490 2545, e-mail martin.roberts@pinsentmasons.com)

ROBERTS, Martin John Dickin; s of John Kenneth Dickin Roberts (d 1990), of Chester, and Iris Ruth, *née* Bond (d 1970); *Educ* Shrewsbury, Trinity Hall Cambridge (MA); *m* 26 Sept 1970, Ruth, da of Frank Packard (d 1982); 3 da (Anne b 1972, Sarah b 1975, Catheryn b 1985); *Career* admitted slr 1969; ptnr Slaughter and May 1975–2002; non-exec dir SOCO International plc 2004–; Freeman Worshipful Co of Slrs; memb Law Soc; *Recreations* spectator sports, boating, golf, reading; *Clubs* RAC; *Style*— Martin Roberts, Esq

ROBERTS, His Hon Judge (John) Mervyn; s of Mervyn Roberts (d 1991), and Catherine, *née* Thomas (d 2005); *b* 19 February 1941; *Educ* Hereford Cathedral Sch, KCL (LLB); *m* 30 Dec 1972, Phillippa Ann, *née* Critien; 1 da (Victoria Louise b 27 Feb 1975); *Career* called to the Bar 1963; recorder 1994–99 (asst recorder 1990–94), circuit judge (SE Circuit) 1999–; memb Criminal Injuries Compensation Bd 1998–99, memb Parole Bd 2002–; *Recreations* music, theatre, travelling, occasional golf; *Style*— His Hon Judge Mervyn Roberts; ✉ Inner London Crown Court, Sessions House, Newington Couseway, London SE1 6AZ (tel 020 7234 3100, fax 020 7234 3203)

ROBERTS, Michael Andrew; s of Michael Francis Roberts, and Georgina Sara Olmos Adriazola; *b* 14 May 1966; *Educ* Prior Park Coll Bath, St Benet's Hall Oxford (MA); *m* Michelle Cora Farrell; *Career* account mangr Decision Makers Ltd 1989–91; CBI 1991– (dir Business Environment 2000–); non-exec dir The Carbon Tst 2001–; memb: Standing Advsy Ctee on Trunk Road Assessment 1996–99, Dep PM's Panel on Transport White Paper 1997–98, Cmmn for Integrated Transport 2000–; memb: Green Alliance, National Tst; *Recreations* football, running (London marathon 1999, 2001 and 2003), skiing, cinema, music; *Clubs* Molesey Boat; *Style*— Michael Roberts, Esq; ✉ CBI, Centre Point, 103 New Oxford Street, London WC1A 1DU (tel 020 7379 7400)

ROBERTS, Michael Symmons; s of David Symmons Roberts, and Iris, *née* Corcoran; *b* 13 October 1963; *Educ* St Bartholomew's Sch Newbury, Univ of Oxford; *m* 1992, Ruth Humphreys; 3 s (Joseph, Patrick, Griffith); *Career* poet and dramatist; prodr and dir of numerous documentaries for radio and TV; Gregory Award for Br poets under 30 Soc of Authors 1988, Whitbread Poetry Award (for Corpus) 2004; shortlisted: T S Eliot Prize 2004, Forward Prize for Best Poerty Collection 2004, Griffin Int Poetry Prize 2005; *Radio* The Real Thing (BBC Radio 3, Sony Award), A Damn Good Lie (BBC Radio 1, Sandford St Martin Award), Anno Domini (BBC Radio 2) 1999, A Fearful Symmetry (BBC Radio 4 and World Serv) 2000 (Sandford St Martin Premier Award), Behold the Man (BBC Radio 2) 2000, Brimstone (BBC Radio 4) 2000, The Wounds (BBC Radio 4) 2001, The Hurricane (BBC Radio 4) 2002, A Higher Place (BBC Radio 4) 2002, Last Words (BBC Radio 4) 2002; *Libretti* in collaboration with James MacMillan: Raising Sparks (song cycle, Royal Festival Hall and BBC Radio 3) 1997, Quickening (choral oratorio, Royal Albert Hall and BBC Radio 3) 1999, Parthenogenesis (chamber opera, Edinburgh Festival and BBC Radio 3) 2000, The Birds of Rhiannon (choral, Royal Albert Hall) 2001, The Sacrifice (opera) 2003, Zaide (re-translation and completion unfinished libretto for Mozart opera) 2003; *Poetry* Soft Keys (1993), Raising Sparks (1999), Burning Babylon (2001, shortlisted T S Eliot Prize), Corpus (2004, Whitbread Poetry Award); poems published in numerous jls and newspapers incl: The Observer, The Guardian, TLS, London Review of Books, The Independent, London Magazine; *Recreations* playing football and cricket with my sons; *Style*— Michael Symmons Roberts, Esq; ✉ c/o David Godwin Associates, 55 Monmouth Street, London WC2H 9DG (tel 020 7240 9992)

ROBERTS, Michael Victor; s of Ernest Alfred Roberts (d 1990), and Lilian May, *née* Piper (d 1979); *b* 23 September 1941; *Educ* Cheshunt GS, Clare Coll Cambridge (MA), Loughborough Tech Coll; *m* 6 July 1972, Jane Margaret (d 1991), da of Francis Huddleston (d 1986); 1 s (Alfred b 1973), 1 da (Mary b 1975); *Career* asst librarian Loughborough Tech Coll 1964–66, asst cataloguer Leeds City Libraries 1966–68, dep bibliographical servs librarian City of London Libraries 1968–70; Guildhall Library: princ cataloguer 1970–73, keeper of Enquiry Servs 1973–82; dep dir City of London Libraries and Art Galleries 1982–95; ed: Guildhall Studies in London History 1973–81, Jl of the Framlingham Historical Soc 1997–, Archives and the Metropolis 1998; Library Assoc Local Studies Gp London and Home Counties Branch; memb: Cncl Br Records Assoc, East of England Regnl Archives Cncl; chm Bishopsgate Fndn 2002–05 (dep chm 1999–2002 and 2005–07), chm Framlingham Lanman Museum, tstee Framlingham Local History and Preservation Soc, tstee Housing the Homeless, sec and PR offr High Suffolk RNLI; Freeman City of London 1983, Liveryman Worshipful Co of Fletchers 1984; ALA 1967, MCLIP 2002; *Recreations* fishing, walking, local history; *Clubs* Harwich and Dovercourt Sailing, Bishopsgate Ward; *Style*— Michael Roberts, Esq; ✉ 43 College Road, Framlingham, Suffolk IP13 9ER (tel and fax 01728 724324)

ROBERTS, Michèle Brigitte; da of Reginald George Roberts, of Felton, nr Bristol, and Monique Pauline Joseph, *née* Caulle; *b* 20 May 1949; *Educ* St Mary's Abbey London, St Michael's Convent London, Univ of Oxford (MA), UCL (ALA); *Career* author and poet; formerly: p/t journalist, p/t teacher, pregnancy tester, cnsllr, res asst, book reviewer; librarian British Council Bangkok (responsible for S Vietnam and Cambodia) 1972–73; poetry ed: Spare Rib 1974–76, City Limits 1981–83; various Arts Council fellowships; involved in Int Women's Liberation Movement 1970–; visiting fell Nottingham Trent 1995–96, visiting prof Nottingham Trent Univ 1996–; univ writer in residence: Univ of Essex 1987–88, UEA 1992; Gay News Literary Award 1978, Arts Council Grant 1978, W H Smith Literary Award 1993; FRSL; *Novels* A Piece of the Night (1978), The Visitation (1983), The Wild Girl (1984), The Book of Mrs Noah (1987), In The Red Kitchen (1990), Daughters of the House (1992, shortlisted Booker Prize 1992, W H Smith Literary Award 1993), Flesh and Blood (1994), Impossible Saints (1997); *Poetry* The Mirror of the Mother (1986), Psyche And the Hurricane (1991), All the Selves I Was (1995); *Short stories* During Mother's Absence (1993); *Other works* contrib numerous stories and essays to anthologies, co-author numerous books of poetry and short stories, première of play The Journeywoman Colchester 1988, film script The Heavenly Twins (French TV and Channel 4); *Recreations* food, sex, foreign travel, gardening, reading; *Style*— Ms Michèle Roberts; ✉ c/o Aitken & Stone Ltd, 29 Fernshaw Road, London SW10 0TG (tel 020 7351 7561, fax 020 7376 3594)

ROBERTS, (David) Paul; s of Percival Roberts, and Nancy, *née* Samuel (d 1991); *b* 6 September 1947, Epsom; *Educ* Univ of Bristol (BSc, CertEd), Cambridge Inst of Educn (Dip); *m* 1969, Helen Margaret, *née* Shone; 2 da (Clare b 1973, Alison b 1975); *Career* teacher Ipswich Sch 1970–74, head of mathematics then dep head Harlington Upper Sch 1974–83; Notts CC: gen inspr then sr div inspr 1983–88, princ educn offr then sr asst dir 1989–92, princ inspr then dep dir of educn 1992–97; dir of educn Nottingham City Cncl 1997–2001; Capita Strategic Educn Servs: dir of educn Haringey Cncl 2001–03, dir 2003–04; Improvement and Devpt Agency: strategic advsr educn and children's servs 2004–05, dir strategy info and devpt 2005–; memb DfES Children Act Stakeholder Gp 2004–; advsr on creativity in schools to Mins of State DCMS and DfES 2005– (also chair Creative and Cultural Educn Advsy Bd 2007–); NESTA: memb Fellowship Prog Ctee 2003–06, memb Innovation Ctee 2006–; author of reviews and articles in local govt, educn and mathematical jls 1978–, memb Editorial Panel Action Research Jl 1991–2002; memb Bd Guideline Careers Ltd 1997–2001, memb Bd Nottingham Playhouse 1997–2001; memb: Assoc of Chief Insprs and Advsrs 1992–97, Assoc of Chief Educn Offrs 1997–2003; FRSA 1999; *Recreations* arts, hill walking; *Style*— Paul Roberts, Esq; ✉ Improvement and Development Agency, Layden House, 76–86 Turnmill Street, London EC1M 5LG (tel 020 7296 6163, e-mail paul.roberts@idea.gov.uk)

ROBERTS, Prof Paul Harry; s of Percy Harry Roberts (d 1969), and Ethel Francis, *née* Mann (d 1992); *b* 13 September 1929; *Educ* Ardwyn Sch Aberystwyth, UCW Aberystwyth (David Davies scholar), Gonville & Caius Coll Cambridge (minor scholar, BA, MA, PhD, ScD, George Green student, Smith Prize); *m* 16 Dec 1989, Mary Francis, *née* Tabrett; *Career* res assoc Univ of Chicago 1954–55, scientific offr AWRE Aldermaston 1955–56; ICI fell Univ of Durham 1956–59, lectr in physics King's Coll Durham 1959–61, assoc prof Yerkes Observatory Univ of Chicago 1961–63, prof of applied mathematics Univ of Newcastle upon Tyne 1963–86, prof of mathematics and geophysical sciences UCLA 1986–; awarded John Adam Fleming Medal by American Geophysical Union for outstanding contrib to the description and understanding of electricity and magnetism of the earth and its atmosphere 1999; fell American Geophysical Union 1987, fell AAAS 2001; FRAS 1955, FRS 1979; *Recreations* chess, playing bassoon; *Style*— Prof Paul Roberts, FRS; ✉ Department of Mathematics, UCLA, Los Angeles, CA 90095, USA (tel 310 206 2707, fax 310 206 3051, e-mail roberts@math.ucla.edu)

ROBERTS, Peter David Thatcher; s of Leonard Charles Roberts (d 1978); *b* 1 March 1934; *Educ* Alleyn's Sch Dulwich, King Edward VII Nautical Coll; *m* 1959, Elizabeth June, da of Dr W A Dodds, of Johannesburg, South Africa; 2 da (Susannah b 1964, Angela b 1965), 1 s (James b 1969); *Career* MN 1951–59, Lt RNR; Leinster/Hispania Maritime Ltd: joined 1960, dir 1963, md 1965; Hays plc: joined 1969, dir 1983–93; former dir Shipowners P & I Assoc Ltd (chm 1993–97); Master Co of Watermen and Lightermen of the River Thames 1993–94, emeritus memb Ct of Assts Worshipful Co of Shipwrights; assoc Hon Co of Master Mariners; MICS 1962; *Recreations* offshore sailing, golf; *Clubs* Royal Ocean Racing, RAC, Wildernesse (capt 2000), Royal St George's Golf; *Style*— Peter Roberts, Esq; ✉ Callenders Cottage, Bidborough, Tunbridge Wells, Kent TN3 0XJ (tel 01892 529053, fax 01892 535339)

ROBERTS, Peter John; s of Reginald Sidney Roberts (d 1992), of Horsham, W Sussex, and Evelyn Isobel, *née* Turner (d 1998); *b* 27 November 1938; *Educ* St Dunstan's Coll, Trinity Coll Cambridge (MA); *m* 1, 9 July 1960, Ann Belinda Le Grys (d 1990), da of Albert Kenneth Rice (d 1969); 2 da (Rachel b 1961, Hannah b 1966), 2 s (Simon b 1963, Ben b 1965); m 2, 19 July 1991, Anne Veronica, da of Patrick Joseph Dillon (d 2000); *Career* C & J Clark Ltd 1960–93: md Neptune Shoes Ltd 1972–80, head of corp planning Clarks Shoes 1980–85, mktg and prodn servs dir Clarks Shoes 1985–86, md Torlink Ltd 1987–93, franchise dir C & J Clark Int 1992–93; chief exec DGAA Homelife (formerly Distressed Gentlefolks' Aid Assoc) 1993–98, chm and md Nutmeg UK Ltd 2000–, non-exec dir Somerset Partnership NHS & Social Care Tst 1999–2004 (vice-chair 2003–04); chm Somerset Relate Marriage Guidance 1979–82 and 1987–90, hon treas Mediation-UK 2002–03, memb Nat Cncl RELATE 1979–96, tstee Bishop Simeon Tst for Educn & Welfare of South African Students 1990–2003, chm VOICES (vol sector umbrella gp of charities in care of elderly) 1996–99, interim dir Nat Heart Forum 1999, govr Chartfield Delicate Sch 1997–2002, dir New Futures Project WRVS 2002–03; chm of govrs: Crispin Sch 1978–89, Strode Coll 1989–93; *Recreations* gardening, travel, music, skiing; *Clubs* Reform; *Style*— Peter Roberts, Esq; ✉ Nutmeg UK Ltd, 23A Hornton Street, London W8 7NR (tel 020 7376 1636, e-mail peter.roberts@nutmeg-uk.com)

ROBERTS, Peter John Martin; s of Alfred John Victor Roberts, and Pamela, *née* Dodd; *b* 31 May 1963; *Educ* Tiffin Boys' Sch Kingston-Upon-Thames, Merton Coll Oxford (MA), Inst of Educn London (PGCE); *m* 1990, Marie, *née* Toudic; 3 da (Camille b 1991, Sophie b 1993, Juliette b 1994); *Career* Winchester Coll: asst master 1986–90, head of history 1990–97, master in coll 1991–2003; headmaster Bradfield Coll 2003–; *Recreations* cricket, bookbinding, fell walking; *Style*— Peter Roberts, Esq; ✉ Bradfield College, Bradfield, Reading RG7 6AR (tel and fax 0118 964 4510, e-mail headmaster@bradfieldcollege.org.uk)

ROBERTS, Hon Lady (Priscilla Jane Stephanie); *née* Low; CVO (2004, LVO 1995, MVO 1985); da of 1 Baron Aldington, KCMG, CBE, DSO, TD, PC, DL (d 2000), and Araminta, *née* MacMichael; sis of 2 Baron Aldington, *qv*; *b* 4 September 1949; *Educ* Cranborne Chase Sch, Westfield Coll London, Courtauld Inst of Art London; *m* 1975, Sir Hugh Ashley Roberts, KCVO, FSA, *qv*, s of Rt Rev Dr Edward Roberts (d 2001), sometime Bishop of Ely; 2 da (Sophie Jane Cecilia b 28 March 1978, Amelia Frances Albinia b 8 Feb 1982); *Career* curator Print Room Royal Library Windsor Castle 1975–, librarian Windsor Castle 2002–; FSA; *Books* Holbein (1979), Royal Artists (1987), Royal Landscape (1997), Queen Elizabeth II: A Birthday Souvenir Album (2006), Five Gold Rings: A Royal Wedding Souvenir Album (2007); *Exhibition Catalogues* Master Drawings in the Royal Collection (1985), Leonardo Da Vinci (1989), A King's Purchase (1993), Holbein and the Court of Henry VIII (1993), Views of Windsor: Watercolours by Thomas and Paul Sandby (1995), The King's Head. Charles I: King and Martyr (1999), Ten Religious Masterpieces from the Royal Collection: A Millennium Celebration (1999), Royal Treasures (ed, 2002), George III and Queen Charlotte (ed, 2004), Unfolding Pictures: Fans in the Royal Collection (2005); *Recreations* piano playing, singing, sewing; *Style*— The Hon Lady Roberts, CVO; ✉ Royal Library, Windsor Castle, Windsor, Berkshire SL4 1NJ (tel 01753 868286, fax 01753 854910)

ROBERTS, Prof Richard Henry; *b* 6 March 1946; *Educ* William Hulme's GS Manchester, Lancaster Univ (BA), Univ of Cambridge (MA, BD), Univ of Edinburgh (PhD); *m* 7 Sept 1968, Audrey, *née* Butterfield; 1 s (Anthony James b 10 Aug 1982); *Career* temp lectr in theology and religious studies Univ of Leeds 1975–76, lectr in systematic theology Univ of Durham 1976–89, Maurice B Reckitt res fell Dept of Religious Studies Lancaster Univ 1988–91, prof of divinity Univ of St Andrews 1991–95, prof of religious studies Lancaster Univ 1995–2003, now emeritus; founding dir: Centre for the History of the Human Sciences Univ of Durham 1988–91, Inst for Religion and the Human Scis Univ of St Andrews 1991–95; sr hon res fell Dept of Religious Studies Lancaster Univ 1994–95; memb Sociology of Religion Advsy Bd Int Theological Jl Concilium 1992–; founding memb Scientific Ctee Assoc for Rhetoric and Communication in South Africa; rapporteur res projects in sociology of religion ESRC 1993–; memb Editorial Bd: Literature and Theology 1988–, Jl of Contemporary Religion 1994–: memb: Soc for the Study of Theology 1975–, Centre for the History of the Human Scis Univ of Durham 1985–, Br/Int Comparative Literature Assoc 1987–, Int Sociological Assoc 1995– (pres Research Ctee 22 1998); hon prof of religious studies Univ of Stirling 2002–; fell Centre for Human Ecology Edinburgh 2003; *Books* Hope and its Hieroglyph: a critical decipherment of Ernst Bloch's' Principle of Hope' (1990), A Theology on Its Way: Essays on Karl Barth (1992), The Recovery of Rhetoric: persuasive discourse and disciplinarity in the human sciences (co-ed with J M M Good, 1993), Religion and the Transformations of Capitalism: Comparative Approaches (1995), Nature Religion Today: Paganism in the Modern World (co-ed with Jo Pearson and Geoffrey Samuel (1998), Time and Value (co-ed with Scott Lash and Andrew Quick, 1998), Religion, Theology and the Human Sciences (2001); *Recreations* astanga yoga, hill walking, music; *Style*— Prof Richard H Roberts; ✉ Department of Religious Studies, Lancaster University, Lancaster LA1 4YG (tel 01524 592420, fax 01524 847039, e-mail r.roberts@lancaster.ac.uk)

R

ROBERTS, Dr Richard John; s of John Walter, and Edna Wilhelmina, Roberts, of Saltford, Bristol; *b* 6 September 1943, Derby; *Educ* City of Bath Boys' Sch, Univ of Sheffield (BSc, PhD); *m* 1, 1965, Elizabeth, *née* Dyson; 1 da (Alison Elizabeth b 11 April 1967), 1 s ((Richard) Andrew b 30 Oct 1968); m 2, 1986, Jean Elizabeth Tagliabue; 1 s (Christopher John b 25 Jan 1987), 1 da (Amanda Rae b 10 Aug 1989); *Career* res assoc in biochemistry Harvard Univ 1971–72 (res fell 1969–70), asst dir for res Cold Spring Harbor Lab 1986–92 (sr staff investigator 1972–86); New England Biolabs: res dir 1992–2005, chief scientific offr 2005–, conslt and chm Scientific Advsy Bd 1974–92; chm Nat Advsy Ctee BIONET 1987–90 (memb 1984–86), exec ed Nucleic Acids Res 1987–; chm Bd of Scientific Counsellors Nat Center for Biotechnology Information (NCBI) 1996–2000, chm Steering Ctee on Genetics and Biotechnology ICSU 1998–2001, advsr to dir NASA Astrobiology Prog 2000–; memb: Scientific Advsy Bd Genex Corp 1977–85, Editorial Bd Nucleic Acids Research 1977–87, Editorial Bd Jl of Biological Chemistry 1979–84, Nat Advsy Ctee GENBANK 1982–89, panel NIH Study Section in Biochemistry 1985–88, Editorial Bd CABIOS (Computer Applications in the Biosciences) 1985–2001, panel NCI Cancer Centers Support Grant Review Ctee 1990–92, panel NLM Study Section 1993–95, Editorial Bd Current Opinion in Chemical Biology 1997–2001, Bd Albert Schweitzer Acad of Med 1998–; chm Scientific Advsy Bd Celera Corp 1998–2002; memb: Sci Advsy Bd Molecular Tool 1994–2000, Sci Advsy Bd Oxford Molecular Gp 1996–99, Sci Advsy Bd Conservation Law Fndn 1998–, Sci Advsy Bd PubMed Central 2000–03, Sci Advsy Bd Orchid Biosciences 2000–; Sci Advsy Bd: Diversa Corp 2003–, PubChem 2004–, RainDance Technologies 2004–, ICGEB 2005–; visiting prof Univ of Bath 1996–98, Wei Lun visiting prof Chinese Univ Hong Kong 1996, hon prof 4th Mil Med Univ Xian 2002; vice-pres Albert Schweitzer Acad of Med 2003–; memb: American Soc for Microbiology; patron Oxford Int Biomedical Center 1994–; assoc memb EMBO 1995; Nobel Prize for Physiology or Med 1993; John Simon Guggenheim fell 1979–80, ASM Fndn lectr 1988–89, Miller prof Univ of Calif Berkeley 1991, Bourke lectr Boston Univ 1994, Dakin lectr Adelphi Univ 1994, Golden Plate Award American Acad of Achievement 1994, Faye Robiner Award Ross Univ 1994, Ada Doisy lectr Univ Illinois Urbana 1996, William Ferdinand lectr Purdue Univ 1997, Steinberg/Wylie lectr Univ of Maryland 1997, Knudson lectr Oregon State Univ 1997, Medicus Magnus of the Polish Acad of Med 1998, Robert Church lectr on biotechnology Univ of Calgary 1998, Albert Einstein meml lectr Princeton Univ 2000, Sutton Lecture Univ of Kansas Med Center 2002; Hon MD: Univ of Uppsala 1992, Univ of Bath 1994; Hon DSc: Univ of Sheffield 1994, Univ of Derby 1995; FRS 1995, fell American Acad of Microbiology 1997, FAAAS 1997; *Style*— Dr Richard Roberts; ✉ New England Biolabs, 240 County Road, Ipswich, MA 01938, USA (tel 00 1 978 380 7215, fax 00 1 978 380 7406, e-mail roberts@neb.com)

ROBERTS, Prof Ronald John; s of Ronald George Roberts, and Marjorie, *née* Kneale; *b* 28 March 1941; *Educ* The GS Campbeltown, Univ of Glasgow (BVMS, PhD); m; 2 s; *Career* lectr in veterinary pathology Univ of Glasgow 1966–71 (asst in microbiology 1964–66); Univ of Stirling: sr lectr in biology and dir Aquatic Pathobiology Unit 1972–76, reader in aquatic pathobiology 1976–79, prof and dir Inst of Aquaculture 1979–96, emeritus prof 1996–; Hagerman distinguished visiting prof Univ of Idaho 1996–; advsr on fish pathology: Miny of Overseas Devpt UK 1973–, FAO 1974–; dir: Bradan Ltd, Heron Associates, Landcatch Ltd, Heron Pisces Ltd; chm Campbeltown and Kintyre Enterprise 1996–; sec Lady Linda McCartney Meml Tst 2001–; dep chm European Food Safety Authy Vetinary Panel 1993–; memb: Animals Ctee AFRC 1989–92, Fisheries Strategy Advsy Ctee ODA 1989–96, Scientific Advsy Ctee Cabinet Office 1994–95; scientific advsr Lithgow Gp plc 1996–2006, Res Grants Ctee Scottish Higher Educn Funding Cncl 2001–; chm Argyll and Bute Countryside Tst 1996–2006; ed: Jl of Fish Diseases 1977–, Aquaculture Research 1985–2000; Buckland Gold Medal 1985, Crookes Veterinary Award for res BVA 1989, Dalrymple-Champneys Cup and Medal 1990; cdr Most Noble Order of the Crown (Thailand) 1992; FRSE 1978 (memb Cncl 1980–83), FIBiol 1980, FRCPath 1985 (MRCPath 1974), FRCVS 1991 (MRCVS 1964); *Books* Fish Pathology (1978, 3 edn, 2001); author of numerous scientific papers; *Style*— Prof Ronald J Roberts, FRSE; ✉ Carrick Point, Ardnacross, Campbeltown, Argyll PA28 6QR

ROBERTS, Sir Samuel; 4 Bt (UK 1919), of Ecclesall and Queen's Tower, City of Sheffield, and West Riding of Yorkshire; s of Sir Peter Roberts, 3 Bt (d 1985), and Judith Randall, *née* Hempson (d 1998); *b* 16 April 1948; *Educ* Harrow, Univ of Sheffield (LLB), Manchester Business Sch (MBA); *m* 1977, Georgina Ann, yr da of David Cory, of Peterston-super-Ely, S Glamorgan; 3 da (Eleanor Judith b 1979, Olivia b 1982, Amelia b 1985), 1 s (Samuel b 1989); *Heir* s, Samuel Roberts; *Career* called to the Bar Inner Temple 1972; chm: Curzon Steels Ltd 1980–84, Cleyfield Properties Ltd, Angerman Godard & Loyd Ltd, Wiltshire & Co Ltd (insurance brokers); *Style*— Sir Samuel Roberts, Bt; ✉ 6 Caversham Street, London SW3 4AH (tel 020 7351 5663)

ROBERTS, Stephen Cheveley; s of Dr David Cheveley Roberts (d 1993), of Mill Hill, London, and Elizabeth, *née* Thornborough (d 1990); *b* 23 August 1956; *Educ* Mill Hill Sch, Univ Coll Oxford (MA, PGCE); *m* March 1985, Joanna Meryl, da of John Andrew Cunnison; 2 s (Matthew Timothy b 6 March 1986, Douglas Mark b 27 Sept 1987); *Career* credit analyst Orion Bank 1980–81, asst master Christ's Hosp Sch Horsham 1981–85, head of physics and housemaster Oundle Sch 1985–93, headmaster Felsted Sch 1993–; memb: HMC 1993, Secdy Heads Assoc 1993; govr St Aubyns Sch Woodford Green; *Recreations* golf, walking, reading; *Clubs* Vincent's (Oxford); *Style*— Stephen Roberts, Esq; ✉ Headmaster's House, Felsted School, Felsted, Dunmow, Essex CM6 3LL (tel 01371 822600, fax 01371 822607, e-mail scr@felsted.org)

ROBERTS, Stephen Pritchard; s of Edward Henry Roberts (d 1987), and Violet, *née* Pritchard (d 1998); *b* 8 February 1949; *Educ* Royal Coll of Music (ARCM 1969, GRSM 1971); *Career* professional singer (concert, oratorio and opera), baritone; memb Vocal Faculty Royal Coll of Music; regular performances Europe, tours to Far East, USA, Canada, S America, BBC recordings for radio and TV (Prom appearances); commercial recordings incl: St Matthew Passion, Carmina Burana, Sea Symphony, Elgar's The Apostles, Penderecki's St Luke Passion, Canterbury Pilgrims, Serenade to Music; opera repertoire incl: Marriage of Figaro and Die Fledermaus (Opera North), Gluck's Armide, Ravel's L'Heure Espagnole; opera recordings incl: Tippett's King Priam, Birtwistle's Punch and Judy; *Style*— Stephen Roberts, Esq; ✉ 144 Gleneagle Road, London SW16 6BA (tel and fax 020 8516 8830, e-mail srobertsbaritone@aol.com, website www.stephenroberts.uk.com)

ROBERTS, Stewart Brian; s of Evan John Roberts (d 1971), of Cheshire, and Joyce, *née* Potter (d 1992); *b* 21 March 1952; *Educ* Birkenhead Sch, St Peter's Coll Oxford (MA, PGCE); *m* 27 July 1985, Anna Susan, da of John Norman; 1 s (Jonathan Edward b 26 Sept 1992), 1 da (Sally Eleanor Joyce b 28 Dec 1993); *Career* asst master Birkenhead Sch 1975–78, asst master Shrewsbury Sch 1978–93 (housemaster 1984–93), founding head Chand Bagh Sch Lahore 1994, head master Dauntsey's Sch 1997– (second master 1995–97); Freeman City of London 2000; *Clubs* East India; *Style*— Stewart Roberts, Esq; ✉ Dauntsey's School, West Lavington, Wiltshire SN10 4HE (tel 01380 814500, fax 01380 814501, e-mail headmaster@dauntseys.wilts.sch.uk)

ROBERTS, Trevor John; s of Howard William Roberts (d 1982), of Wolverhampton, and Melba Lewis, *née* Bushell (d 2002); *b* 22 April 1940; *Educ* King Edward GS Stafford, Wolverhampton Poly; *m* 30 March 1970, Judith, da of William Samuel Wiggin, of Cannock, Staffs; 1 da (Andrea b 1978), 1 s (James b 1980); *Career* mangr of manufacturing depts Charles Richards & Sons Ltd 1969–74, tech mktg mangr Charles Richards Fasteners Ltd 1978–80 (prodn mangr 1974–78); jt owner and md: Doran Engineering Co Ltd 1982–97 (manufacturing dir 1980–82), Doran Engineering Holdings Ltd 1983–97; dir: Village Engineering Co Ltd 1983–94, Petrospec Bolting Ltd 1990–97, Lydford Precision Engineering Ltd 1998–2001; engrg mgmnt conslt Roberts Consulting 1997–2005; Inst of Industrial Mangrs: former memb Nat Cncl, former memb Nat Membership Exec, former chm and pres Wolverhampton Branch; pres Willenhall Rotary Club 1991–92; CEng, FIEE, FIMgt 1987, FIIM 1987, FIProdE 1988; *Recreations* swimming, reading, photography; *Style*— Trevor Roberts, Esq; ✉ 65 Badgers Croft, Eccleshall, Stafford ST21 6DS (tel 01785 851634)

ROBERTS, Sir William James Denby; 3 Bt (UK 1909), of Milner Field, Bingley, W Riding of Yorkshire; s of Sir James Denby Roberts, OBE, 2 Bt (d 1973); *b* 10 August 1936; *Educ* Rugby, RAC Cirencester; *Heir* n, James Roberts-Buchanan; *Career* collector of vintage aircraft; fndr and former owner Strathallan Aircraft Collection; *Style*— Sir William Roberts, Bt; ✉ Strathallan Castle, Auchterarder, Perthshire; Combwell Priory, Flimwell, Wadhurst, East Sussex

ROBERTS, William Morys; s of Gwilym James Roberts, MD (Maj Royal Army Med Corps 1945–46, d 1990), of Penarth, Glamorgan, and Eileen Burford, *née* Chivers (d 1995); *b* 8 December 1934; *Educ* Kingswood Sch Bath, Gonville & Caius Coll Cambridge (MA); *m* 29 July 1967, Patricia Anne, da of John Stratford Bettinson, of Ickleton, Cambs; 2 da (Sarah b 1969, Alice (Mrs Christopher Faulkner) b 1974), 1 s (Simon b 1972); *Career* RA 1953–54, Intelligence Corps 1954–55, 2 Lt (later Lt RARO); Turquand, Youngs and Co 1958–61; Wm Brandt's Sons & Co Ltd 1961–73: chief accountant 1965, sec 1970, dir 1971–73; dir Edward Bates and Sons Ltd 1973–75; Ernst & Young: ptnr 1976–94, head of London Insolvency Servs 1987–89, head of Corp Advsy Servs London 1989–92 and National 1991–94; Soc of Practitioners of Insolvency: memb Tech Ctee 1990–2001 (chm 1995), sr tech advsr 1994–2001; memb: Insolvency Rules Advsy Ctee 1984–92, Insolvency Practitioners Tbnl 1996–; memb: Saffron Walden Deanery Synod 1996–2003, Chelmsford Diocesan Synod 1997–2003 (memb Fin Ctee 1998, vice-chm 2001–03), Long Melford Parochial Church Cncl 2005–; churchwarden All Saints Church Great Chesterford 1976–93; FCA 1971 (ACA 1961); *Books* Insolvency Law and Practice (with J S H Gillies, 1988), Great Chesterford: A Brief History (jtly, 2000); *Recreations* gardening, Suffolk local history; *Clubs* IOD, Sea View Yacht; *Style*— W M Roberts, Esq; ✉ Pound Hall, The Green, Long Melford, Sudbury, Suffolk CO10 9DX (tel and fax 01787 311670); Dulce Domum, Ryde Road, Seaview, Isle of Wight

ROBERTS, Prof (Meirion) Wyn; s of Tom Roberts, OBE (d 1979), of Ammaford, Dyfed, and Mary, *née* Williams (d 1968); *b* 1 February 1931; *Educ* Amman Valley GS Ammanford, Univ of Swansea, Univ of Wales (BSc, PhD, DSc); *m* 23 March 1957, Catherine Angharad, da of John Lewis, of Ammanford, Dyfed; 1 s (Mark b 6 March 1964), 1 da (Karen b 26 May 1961); *Career* Imperial Coll of Sci London 1955–57, sr scientific offr Nat Chem Laboratory 1957–59, lectr Queen's Univ of Belfast 1959–66, chair of physical chem Univ of Bradford 1966–79, head Dept of Physical Chem UC Cardiff 1979–88, dep princ Univ of Wales Coll of Cardiff 1989–92, head of Sch of Chemistry 1988–97, research prof 1998–; visiting prof: Univ of Xiamen China 1985–, Univ of Calif Berkeley 1984; centenary lectr Indian Acad of Sciences 1984; chm Tstees of the Wool Fndn 1981–; memb: SERC Chem Ctee 1972–78, Univ Grants Physical Sciences Ctee 1982–88, CNAA 1989; Tilden Medal and Prize Royal Soc of Chem 1976, Royal Soc of Chem Award in Surface Chem 1987, Br Vacuum Cncl Prize and John Yarwood Meml Medal 1999; memb Bd of Govrs: Monmouth Haberdashers' Schs 1996–, Univ of Wales Inst Cardiff 1996–2001; hon fell UC Swansea 1987; FRSC 1966; *Books* Reactivity of Solids (ed, 1972), The Chemical Physics of Solids and their Surfaces (Chemical Soc Reports, 1972–79), Chemistry of the Metal Gas Interface (jtly, 1978), Interfacial Science (ed, 1997); *Recreations* rugby football; *Style*— Prof Wyn Roberts; ✉ 37 Heol-Y-Delyn, Lisvane, Cardiff CF14 0SR (tel 029 2075 2452); University of Cardiff, Department of Chemistry, PO Box 912, Cardiff CF10 3TB (tel 029 2087 4076, fax 029 2087 4030, telex 498635, e-mail robertsmw@cf.ac.uk)

ROBERTS OF CONWY, Baron (Life Peer UK 1997), of Talyfan in the County of Gwynedd; Rt Hon Sir (Ieuan) Wyn Pritchard Roberts; kt (1990), PC (1991); s of Rev E P Roberts, of Anglesey; *b* 10 July 1930; *Educ* Harrow, UC Oxford; *m* 1956, Enid Grace, da of W Williams, of Anglesey; 3 s; *Career* formerly journalist with The Liverpool Post and news asst with the BBC, Welsh controller and exec prodr TWW 1959–68, programme exec Harlech TV 1969; MP (Cons) Conwy 1970–97; PPS to Sec of State for Wales 1970–74, oppn frontbench spokesman on Welsh affrs 1974–79, Parly under sec Welsh Office 1979–87, min of state for Wales 1987–94, oppn spokesman on constitutional affrs (Wales) House of Lords 1997–2001, oppn spokesman on Welsh affrs House of Lords 2001–; pres Univ of Wales Coll of Med 1997–2004, vice-pres Univ of Cardiff 2004–; memb Gorsedd Royal National Eisteddfod 1966; hon fell: Univ of Wales Bangor 1995, Univ of Wales Aberystwyth 1997; *Clubs* Savile, Cardiff and County; *Style*— The Rt Hon Lord Roberts of Conwy, PC; ✉ Tan y Gwalia, Conway, Gwynedd LL32 8TY

ROBERTS OF LLANDUDNO, Baron (Life Peer UK 2004), of Llandudno in the County of Gwynedd; Rev John Roger Roberts; s of late Thomas C Roberts; *b* 23 October 1935; *Educ* John Bright GS Llandudno, UCNW Bangor, Handsworth Methodist Coll Birmingham; *m* 1962, Eirlys Ann (d 1995); 1 s (Hon Gareth), 2 da (Hon Rhian, Hon Sian); *Career* ordained Methodist min 1962; supt min Llandudno 1982–2002, min Toronto 2003–04; memb Aberconway BC 1976–87, Parly candidate Conwy 1979, 1983, 1987, 1992 and 1997; pres Welsh Lib Dems 1990–96, memb European Lib, Democratic and Reform Pty (ELDR), ldr Welsh European list ELDR 1999; chair: Aberconwy Talking Newspaper, Welsh Water Lifeline; tstee Fund for Human Need; radio and TV broadcaster (Welsh and English); *Style*— The Rt Hon the Lord Roberts of Llandudno

ROBERTSHAW, His Hon Judge Patrick Edward; s of late George Edward Robertshaw, and late May, *née* Tallis; *b* 7 July 1945; *m* 1972, Sally Christine Greenburgh, *née* Searle; 2 s, 2 da; *Career* called to the Bar Inner Temple 1968; recorder Crown and County Courts 1989–94, circuit judge (NE Circuit) 1994–; *Publications* The Inglorious Twelfth; *Recreations* travel, reading, photography; *Style*— His Hon Judge Robertshaw; ✉ Sheffield Combined Court Centre, 50 West Bar, Sheffield S3 8PH (tel 0114 281 2400)

ROBERTSON, Anderson Bain; s of Mungo Manderson Robertson (d 1932), of Bristol, and Minnie McAllister Bain, *née* Anderson (d 1987); *b* 22 October 1929; *Educ* Ardrossan Acad, Gray's Sch of Art, Aberdeen and Glasgow Sch of Art (DA, BA); *m* 13 July 1955, Mary Margaret Moffat (d 2002), da of Alexander Stewart Christie (d 1979), of Wishaw; 2 s (Maxwell Stewart b 1959, Paul Noel b 1961); *Career* RAOC 1948–50; head Dept of Art Nicolson Inst Stornoway 1969–79, govr Aberdeen Coll of Educn 1974–78, convener Central Advsy Ctee of Art EIS 1977–81, assessor Certificate of Sixth Year Studies in Art and Design 1977–89; artist; exhibitions at: Royal Scot Acad, Royal Glasgow Inst of Fine Arts, Royal Scot Soc of Painters in Water Colours, Royal Soc of Portrait Painters, Visual Arts Scotland (VAS), Royal Inst of Painters in Water Colours; private collections in GB and USA; professional memb VAS 1996; *Recreations* sailing; *Clubs* Glasgow Art; *Style*— Anderson B Robertson, Esq; ✉ Window Rock, Innellan, Dunoon, Argyll PA23 7TR (tel 01369 830755)

ROBERTSON, Andrew James; QC (1996); s of Pearson Robertson (d 1958), and Zillah Robertson (d 1991); *b* 14 May 1953; *Educ* Bradford GS, Christ's Coll Cambridge (scholar, MA); *m* 1981 Gillian Amanda; 1 da (Rebecca Francesca b 1984), 2 s (Hamish Alexander b 1985, Joshua Edward Adam b 1994); *Career* called to the Bar Middle Temple 1975; currently head of chambers King's Bench Walk, assoc tenant 9 Gough Square London and St John's Buildings Manchester; memb: Criminal Bar Assoc, Personal Injuries Bar Assoc; *Recreations* hockey, walking, history; *Style*— Andrew Robertson, Esq, QC;

✉ King's Bench Walk, 3 Park Court, Leeds LS1 1QH (tel 0113 297 1200, fax 0113 297 1201, e-mail clerks@llkbw.co.uk)

ROBERTSON, Andrew John; s of John Hector Robertson, and Jennifer Mary, *née* Cullen; *b* 17 November 1960; *Educ* Michaelhouse Balgowan Natal, City of London Poly, City Univ (BSc); *m* 13 Feb 1987, Susan Louise, da of Michael John Bayliss; 2 da (Amy Louise b 13 Aug 1988, Louisa Jane b 25 July 1991); *Career* Ogilvy & Mather: trainee media planner 1982, account dir 1986, memb Bd of Dirs 1987, mgmnt supervisor and new business dir 1988–89; gp dir J Walter Thompson Co 1989, chief exec WCRS 1990–95, md Abbott Mead Vickers BBDO Ltd 1995–2001, BBDO: ceo and pres North America 2001–04, global CEO 2004–; FIPA 1987; *Recreations* tennis, squash, opera, ballet; *Style*— Andrew Robertson, Esq

ROBERTSON, Andrew Ogilvie; OBE (1994); s of Alexander McArthur Ogilvie Robertson (d 1971), and Charlotte Rachel, *née* Cuthbert (d 1989); *b* 30 June 1943; *Educ* Glasgow Acad, Sedbergh, Univ of Edinburgh (LLB); *m* 4 July 1974, Sheila, da of Philip Sturton; 2 s (James Mungo Ogilvie b 9 Nov 1975, Alexander Philip Ogilvie b 11 Aug 1977); *Career* ptnr T C Young 1968–2006; sec and treas Clydeside Fedn of Community Based Housing Assocs 1978–93, sec The Briggait Co Ltd 1983–88, founding sec and legal advsr The Princess Royal Tst for Carers 1990–2006 (tstee 2006–); chm: Post Office Users' Cncl for Scotland 1988–99, Scottish Housing Assocs Charitable Tst 1990–, Scottish Building Soc 2003–06; chm Gtr Glasgow Community & Mental Health Servs NHS Tst 1994–98, chm Glasgow Royal Infirmary Univ NHS Tst 1997–99, chm Gtr Glasgow Primary Care NHS Tst 1999–2005, non-exec dir Gtr Glasgow Health Bd 1999– (vice-chair 2004–06), vice-chm Erskine Hosp Bishopston 2006– (sec 1976–2002); dir: The Merchants House of Glasgow 1980–, Glasgow C of C 1981–94; govr Sedbergh Sch 2000–; *Recreations* mountaineering, sailing, swimming, reading; *Clubs* Western (Glasgow); *Style*— Andrew Robertson, Esq, OBE; ✉ T C Young, 7 West George Street, Glasgow G2 1BA (tel 0141 221 5562, fax 0141 221 5024, e-mail aor@tcyoung.co.uk)

ROBERTSON, Angus; MP; s of Struan Robertson, and Anna, *née* Haenlein; *b* 28 September 1969; *Educ* Broughton HS Edinburgh, Univ of Aberdeen (MA); *Career* news ed Austrian Broadcasting Corp (ORF) 1991–98, reporter BBC Vienna 1992–98, communications conslt Communications Skills Int (CSI) 1994–2001; contrib NPR USA, RTE Ireland and ABC Aust 1992–98; candidate (SNP) Midlothian Scot Parly elections 1999; MP (SNP) Moray 2001–; shadow Scot min for Defence and Foreign Affrs 2003– (memb Scot shadow Cabinet, shadow Scot min for Defence 2001–03); SNP Westminster spokesman on Europe and def 2001–; vice-chm All-Pty Whisky Industry Gp 2001–, vice-chm All-Pty Offshore Oil and Gas Gp, memb All-Pty Fishing Industry Gp 2001–; memb Nat Exec Young Scot Nationalists (YSN) 1986, jr vice-pres Univ of Aberdeen Students Rep Cncl 1987–88, nat organiser Fedn of Student Nationalists 1988; SNP: int press spokesman UK Parly election 1997 and Scot Parly election 1999, memb Int Bureau 1998–, advsr European and Int Affrs SNP Gp Scot Parl 1999–2001; memb NUJ; past memb: Works Cncl Austrian Broadcast Corp, UN Corrs Assoc Vienna, Austrian Guild of PR Conslts; *Recreations* football, rugby, skiing, playing golf badly, films, travel, books, socialising and whisky tasting in moderation; *Style*— Angus Robertson, Esq, MP; ✉ House of Commons, London SW1A 0AA (e-mail robertsona@parliament.uk); Constituency Office, 9 Wards Road, Elgin IV30 1NL (tel 01343 551111, website www.moraymp.org)

ROBERTSON, Angus Frederick; s of Eric Desmond Robertson, OBE (d 1987), and Aileen Margaret, *née* Broadhead; *b* 4 November 1954; *Educ* Westminster, Univ of Stirling (BA); *m* (m dis), Frances Ellen, da of Patrick Carroll Macnamara, of Ardgay, Sutherland; *Career* called to the Bar Middle Temple 1978; *Clubs* Naval and Military; *Style*— Angus Robertson, Esq; ✉ 44 Rawlings Street, London SW3 2LS (tel 020 7581 2719); 18 Carlton Crescent, Southampton SO15 2ET (tel 023 8063 9001, fax 023 8033 9625)

ROBERTSON, (Charles) Archibald (Archie); OBE (2002); s of Donald Robertson, and Isabella, *née* Duncan; *b* 26 December 1953, Perth, Scotland; *Educ* Dingwall Acad, Stirling HS, Univ of Stirling (BA); *m* 1977, Judith, *née* Cranston; 2 da (Iona b 1978, Katy b 1983), 1 s (Neil b 1981); *Career* BP Int 1976–96 (head of transport distribution BP Oil Europe 1994–96), dir of ops Environment Agency 1996–2003, chief exec Highways Agency 2003–; memb Bd Dept for Transport 2006–; memb Cmmn for Integrated Transport; memb Green Alliance; FIHT; *Recreations* sport, skiing, snowboarding, squash, hill walking, following rugby union, the natural environment; *Clubs* Little Ship, Ski Club of GB; *Style*— Archie Robertson, Esq, OBE; ✉ Highways Agency, 123 Buckingham Palace Road, London SW1W 9HA (tel 020 7153 4700, fax 020 7153 4786, e-mail archie.robertson@highways.gsi.gov.uk)

ROBERTSON, Rev Charles; LVO (2005); s of Thomas Robertson (d 1941), of Glasgow, and Elizabeth, *née* Halley (d 1942); *b* 22 October 1940; *Educ* Camphill Sch Paisley, Univ of Edinburgh, New Coll Edinburgh; *m* 30 July 1965, Alison Margaret, da of Rev John Strachan Malloch, MBE, of Aberdeen; 1 s (Duncan John b 6 June 1967), 2 da (Mary Blackadder b 29 Dec 1968, Margaret Isobel b 5 Feb 1976); *Career* asst minister N Morningside Church Edinburgh 1964–65; parish minister: Kiltearn Ross-shire 1965–78, Canongate Kirk (The Kirk of Holyroodhouse) Edinburgh 1978–2005, minister emeritus 2005–; chaplain to: HM The Queen in Scotland 1991–, the High Constables and Guard of Honour of Holyroodhouse 1993–, the Lord High Cmmr the Gen Assembly of the Church of Scotland 1990, 1991 and 1996 (HRH The Princess Royal); convenor Gen Assembly's Panel on Worship 1995–99 (sec 1982–95); Church of Scotland rep Jt Liturgical Gp 1984–99 (chm 1994–99), tstee Church Hymnary Tst 1987–, pres Church Service Soc 1988–91 (hon pres 1991–); chaplain to: Clan Donnachaidh Soc 1981–96, Elsie Inglis Maternity Hosp 1982–87, Moray House Coll of Educn 1986–98, New Club Edinburgh 1986–, No 2 (City of Edinburgh) Maritime HQ Unit RAAF 1987–99, Edinburgh Univ at Moray House 1998–2002, No 603 (City of Edinburgh) Squadron RAAF 1999–, Incorporation of Goldsmiths of the City of Edinburgh 2000–, Co of Merchants of the City of Edinburgh 2002–, Edinburgh and Lothians Scots Guard Assoc 2004; Convenery of Trades of Edinburgh 2005; JP City of Edinburgh 1980–2006; lectr in church praise St Colm's Coll Edinburgh 1980–93; tstee: Edinburgh Old Town Tst 1987–91, Edinburgh Old Town Charitable Tst 1991–, Carnegie Tst for the Univs of Scotland 2005–; govr St Columba's Hospice 1986–2006; chm: Queensbury House Hosp 1989–95 (dir 1978–, vice-chm 1985–89), Queensbury House Tst 1996; memb: Exec Ctee Scot Veterans' Residences 1978–, Broadcasting Standards Cncl 1988–94, Historic Bldgs Cncl for Scotland 1990–99; sec Ctee to Revise the Church Hymnary 1995–2004; tstee Edinburgh World Heritage Tst 1999–2000; *Books* Singing the Faith (ed, 1990), Common Order (ed, 1994), St Margaret Queen of Scotland and Her Chapel (ed, 1994); sec of Ctees which compiled: Hymns for a Day (1983), Songs of God's People (1988), Worshipping Together (1991), Clann ag Urnaigh (1991), Common Ground (1998), By Lamplight (compiled with Elizabeth, Duchess of Hamilton, 2000); *Recreations* Scottish and Edinburgh history, hymnody, collecting Canongate miscellanea; *Clubs* Athenaeum, Puffins, New (Edinburgh, hon memb), Royal Scots (Edinburgh, hon memb); *Style*— The Rev Charles Robertson, LVO; ✉ 3 Ross Gardens, Edinburgh EH9 3BS (tel 0131 662 9025, e-mail canongate1@aol.com)

ROBERTSON, Douglas Laurence; s of Ronald John Robertson, of Milton Keynes, Bucks, and Agnes McKay (Nanette), *née* Reid; *b* 12 June 1952; *Educ* Dalkeith HS, Langley Park Sch for Boys, St Edmund Hall Oxford (MA); *m* 1 Nov 1975, Susan Winifred, da of John St Clair (d 1989), of Marden, Herefords; 1 s (Iain b 1979), 1 da (Carolyn b 1982); *Career* admitted slr 1977; ptnr: Kenneth Brown Baker Baker 1981, Turner Kenneth Brown 1983, Memery Crystal 1992–2007; non-exec chm Redab Properties plc 2007–; Freeman City of London 1986; FRSA; *Recreations* rugby and football, church activities (ordinand C of E); *Clubs* Vincent's (Oxford); *Style*— Douglas L Robertson, Esq; ✉ 19 Old Barn Close, Kemsing, Sevenoaks, Kent TN15 6RZ

ROBERTSON, (James) Douglas Moir; CBE (1992), DL (Surrey 1988); s of George Robertson (d 1984), and Jessie Barrie, *née* Brough (d 1993); *b* 15 November 1938; *Educ* Trinity Acad Edinburgh, Heriot-Watt Coll; *m* 29 June 1963, Caroline Blanche, da of David Stephen Adams (d 1994), of Edinburgh; 2 s (Graham b 1965, Brian b 1977), 1 da (Alison b 1970); *Career* princ Surveyors Collaborative 1969–; dir: Building Cost Information Service Ltd RICS 1962–95, Bobbett and Robertson 1994–96, Research Park Developments Ltd, Surrey Social and Market Research Ltd, Surrey History Tst; chm: Airports Policy Consortium 1984–93, Building Data Banks Ltd 1985–95; ldr Surrey CC 1990–93 (chm 1987–90); chm Environment Ctee Assoc of CCs 1990–92; pro-chllr Univ of Surrey 1998–2007 (chm Cncl 1995–98, emeritus pro-chllr 2007–), chm Cncl Federal Univ of Surrey 2000–; chm: Bournewood NHS Tst 1997–2002, National Crimebeat 1998–2005, N Surrey PCT 2002–06, Surrey PCT 2006–; High Sheriff Surrey 1997–98; Hon LLD Univ of Roehampton 2006, Hon DUniv Surrey 2007; FRICS 1969, FCMI (FIMgt 1971), FRSA 1989; *Publications* Guide to House Rebuilding Costs, Maintenance Price Book, Property Occupancy Analysis; papers on economics of construction industry, cost indices and trends and regnl govts; *Recreations* golf; *Clubs* Burhill; *Style*— Douglas Robertson, Esq, CBE, DL; ✉ 16 Homewaters Avenue, Sunbury-on-Thames, Middlesex TW16 6NS (tel 01932 786624, fax 01932 786190)

ROBERTSON, Prof Edmund Frederick; s of Edmund Jozef Chojnacki (d 1998), and Dorothy Mabel, *née* Warnes (d 1994); *b* 1 June 1943; *Educ* Madras Coll St Andrews (Tullis Prize, Sir William Robertson Prize, Dux), Univ of St Andrews (Taylor Thompson Bursary, BSc), Univ of Warwick (MSc, PhD); *m* 16 July 1970, Helena Francesca, da of Tadeusz Slebarski (d 2003); 2 s (Colin Edmund b 16 Nov 1974, David Anthony b 26 Sept 1978); *Career* Univ of St Andrews: lectr in mathematics 1968–84, sr lectr 1984–95, head Pure Mathematics Div 1988–91 and 2004–, head Algebra Research Team 1988–, prof of mathematics 1995–, head Sch of Mathematical and Computational Sciences 1997–2000, chair Groups, Algorithms and Programming (GAP) Cncl 2003– (memb 1997–2003), head Sch of Mathematics and Statistics 2000–01, assoc dir Centre for Interdisciplinary Res in Computational Algebra (CIRCA) 2000–; chair Scientific Ctee BMC 2005– (memb 2003–05); memb: EPSRC Mathematics Coll 1997–2000, EPSRC Peer Review Coll 2000–02, 2003–05 and 2006–, Scottish Mathematical Cncl 1997–2004; ed Proceedings A Royal Soc of Edinburgh 2004–07; memb: Edinburgh Mathematical Soc 1969– (memb Ctee 1986–89, memb Policy Advsy Ctee 1996–99), London Mathematical Soc 1977–, European Mathematical Soc 2000–; Partnership Award (for innovation in mathematics teaching in higher educn) 1992, European Academic Software Award 1994, Undergraduate Computational Engrg and Science Award Dept of Energy USA 1995, Best Mathematics Website Award Scientific American 2002, Exemplary Online Resources Award Merlot 2002; vice-chair Madras Tst 1986–; govr Morrison's Acad 1999–2007; FRSE 1997; *Publications* author of over 140 papers and 25 books incl award-winning History of Mathematics; ed Hutchinson Encyclopedia of Mathematics; *Style*— Prof Edmund Robertson, FRSE; ✉ Mathematical Institute, University of St Andrews, North Haugh, St Andrews, Fife KY16 9SS (tel 01334 463743, fax 01334 463748, e-mail edmund@mcs.st-and.ac.uk, website www-history.mcs.st-and.ac.uk/history)

ROBERTSON, Dr Elizabeth Margaret; da of Alastair Robertson, of Aberdeen, and Dorothy Elizabeth, *née* Barron; *b* 7 October 1951; *Educ* St Margaret's Sch for Girls Aberdeen, Univ of Aberdeen (MB ChB, DMRD); *Career* clinical dir of radiology Aberdeen Royal Hosps NHS Tst 1996–99, assoc med dir Grampian Univ Hospitals Tst 1999– (dep med dir 2003–04), hon clinical sr lectr in radiology Univ of Aberdeen; pres Scottish Radiological Soc 2002–04; memb: BMA, RSM; FRCR; *Style*— Dr Elizabeth Robertson; ✉ 95 King's Gate, Aberdeen AB15 4EN (tel 01224 326831); In Patient X-Ray Department, Aberdeen Royal Infirmary, Foresterhill, Aberdeen (tel 01224 681818 ext 54514)

ROBERTSON, Geoffrey Ronald; QC (1988); s of Francis Albert Robertson, of Longueville, Sydney, Aust, and Bernice Joy, *née* Beattie; *b* 30 September 1946; *Educ* Epping Boys HS, Univ of Sydney (BA, LLB), Univ of Oxford (Rhodes scholar, BCL); *m* Kathy Lette; 1 s (Julius Blake), 1 da (Georgina Blaise); *Career* called to the Bar Middle Temple 1973 (bencher 1997), fndr and head Doughty St Chambers 1990–, recorder 1999– (asst recorder 1993–99); appeal judge UN Special Court for War Crimes Sierra Leone 2002–; visiting prof: Univ of NSW Aust 1977, Univ of Warwick 1980–81, Birkbeck Coll London 1998–, QMC 2003–; exec memb Freedom of Info Campaign, memb Cncl JUSTICE; tstee Capital Cases Tst; Hon LLD Univ of Sydney; *Books* Reluctant Judas (1976), Obscenity (1979), People Against the Press (1983), Media Law (1984, 5 edn 2007), Hypotheticals (1986), Does Dracula Have Aids? (1987), Freedom, The Individual and the Law (1989, 2 edn 1993), The Justice Game (1998), Crimes Against Humanity (1999, 3 edn 2006), The Tyrannicide Brief (2005); *Plays* The Trials of Oz (BBC TV, 1991); *Recreations* tennis, opera, fishing; *Style*— Geoffrey Robertson, Esq, QC; ✉ 11 Doughty Street, London WC1N 2PG (tel 020 7404 1313, fax 020 7404 2283, e-mail g.robertson@doughtystreet.co.uk)

ROBERTSON, Dr (Andrew) Gerard; s of Henry Robertson, OBE (d 1974), of Lagos, Nigeria and Edinburgh, and Helen, *née* Flynn; *b* 14 January 1945; *Educ* St Joseph's Coll Dumfries, Univ of Glasgow (BSc, PhD, MB ChB); *m* 2 April 1970, Margaret Mary Dorothy, da of John Joseph McKee, KSG, of Glasgow; 5 s (John b 1977, Andrew b 1980, Francis b 1984, Gregory b 1986, Bernard b 1986); *Career* sr registrar in radiotherapy and oncology Christie Hosp Manchester 1981, conslt in radiotherapy and oncology Glasgow hosps 1982–; treas Assoc of Head and Neck Oncologists of GB; memb Catholic Union of GB; FRCR 1980, FRCPG 1988; *Recreations* golf; *Clubs* East Renfrewshire Golf; *Style*— Dr Gerard Robertson

ROBERTSON, Grace; OBE (1999); da of James Fyfe Robertson (d 1987), and Elizabeth, *née* Muir (d 1973); *b* 13 July 1930; *Educ* Kendal HS for Girls, Eothen Sch Caterham, Maria Grey Teacher Trg Coll Twickenham; *m* 16 Dec 1954, (Godfrey) Thurston Hopkins, s of Robert Thurston Hopkins (d 1958); 1 da (Joanna b 15 Jan 1960), 1 s (Robert James b 27 Oct 1961); *Career* photographer, lectr and broadcaster; photojournalist Picture Post 1949–57, freelance 1957–60, teacher 1965–78; subject of Master Photographers (BBC Radio 3 series) 1991, pubn The Nineties (BBC 2 prodn) 1993; Hon DLitt Univ of Brighton 1995, Hon FRPS 1996; *Exhibitions* Nat Museum of Photography, Film and TV 1986, Photographers Gallery 1987, Zelda Cheatle Gallery London 1989, Nat Museum of Wales Cardiff 1989, Gardner Centre Univ of Sussex 1990, Cathleen Ewing Gallery Washington DC 1992, RNT (retrospective exhbn) 1993, Watershed Bristol 1993, Univ of Brighton Sussex 1994, Leaving Their Mark: Sixteen Achieving Women of Eastbourne (Towner Gallery) 1995, Leica Gallery NY 1998, A Sympathetic Eye (retrospective exhbn, Univ of Brighton) 2002, Aberdeen Art Gallery 2002, The Lowry 2003, Breaking the Frame: Pioneering Women in Photojournalism (Museum of Photographic Arts San Diego) 2006; *Photographic Work in Collections incl* V&A, Nat Museum of Photography, Film and TV Bradford, Helmut Gernsheim Collection Univ of Texas, Nat Gallery of Aust, Hulton Getty Collection London; subject of Channel 4 documentary 1986, monograph Grace Robertson, Photojournalist of the 50's (Virago pubn) 1989; *Awards* Distinguished Photographers' Award (American Women in Photography Int) 1992; *Publications* A Sympathetic Eye (2002), Breaking the Frame: Pioneering Women in Photojournalism (2006); *Recreations* painting, reading, walking, listening to music; *Style*— Ms Grace Robertson, OBE; ✉ c/o

R

The Photographers' Gallery, Halina House, 5 Great Newport Street, London WC2H 7HY (tel 020 7831 1772); c/o Peter Fetterman, Gallery A7, 2525 Michigan Avenue, Santa Monica, California 90404, USA (tel 00 131 04 536463)

ROBERTSON, Air Marshal Graeme Alan; CBE (1988, OBE 1985); s of Ronald James Harold Robertson, DFC (d 1999), and Constance Rosemary, *née* Freeman, of Walton on the Naze, Essex; *b* 22 February 1945; *Educ* Bancroft's Sch, RAF Coll Cranwell (Sir Philip Sassoon Meml Prize), Open Univ (BA); *m* Barbara Ellen, da of Frederick William Mardon (d 1975); 1 da (Nicole Jane b 17 Dec 1975); *Career* pilot No 8 Sqdn (Hunters) Bahrain 1968–69, pilot/weapons instr No 6 Sqdn RAF Coningsby (Phantoms) 1970–72, instr pilot 288 Operational Conversion Unit RAF Coningsby (Phantoms) 1972–73, instr pilot/Flt Cdr 550th Tactical Fighter Trg Sqdn Luke AFB Arizona (Phantoms) 1973–75, Flt Cdr No 56 Sqdn RAF Wattisham (Phantoms) 1975–77, RAF Staff Coll 1977–78, Operational Requirements/Plans Staff MOD 1978–82, CO No 92 Sqdn RAF Wildenrath Germany (Phantoms) 1982–84, CO No 23 Sqdn RAF Stanley Falkland Is (Phantoms) 1984–85, CO RAF Wattisham 1985–87, Dir of Air Staff Briefing and Co-ordination MOD 1987–88, RCDS 1989, Dir of Defence Progs MOD 1990–91, Dep Cdr RAF Germany 1991–93, AOC No 2 Group 1993–94, ACDS (Programmes) MOD 1994–96, COS and Dep C-in-C Strike Command 1996–98; def and air advsr Br Aerospace 1999–2000, sr military advsr BAE SYSTEMS 2000–03; Hon Col 77 Regiment (Vols) RE 1996–99; Hon ADC to HM the Queen 1986–87; QCVSA 1973; md Blackbourne Wells Ltd 2003–, co-ordinator Br-American Community Relations MOD 2004–; Freeman City of London; FRAeS, FRSA; *Recreations* shooting, golf, sailing, winter sports; *Clubs* MCC, RAF; *Style*— Air Marshal G A Robertson, CBE; ✉ c/o National Westminster Bank plc, 4 Northgate, Sleaford, Lincolnshire NG34 7BJ

ROBERTSON, (Maj) Hugh Michael; MP; s of George Robertson, of Canterbury, and June, *née* McBryde; *b* 9 October 1962; *Educ* King's Sch Canterbury, RMA Sandhurst, Univ of Reading (BSc); *m* 17 May 2002, Anna Copson; *Career* offr The Life Guards 1985–95; active serv: NI 1987, UN Cyprus 1988, Gulf War 1991, Bosnia 1994; commanded Household Cavalry: HM The Queen's Birthday Parade 1993, state opening of Parliament 1993, Silver Stick Adj 1994–95; Schroder Investment Mgmnt 1995–2001 (asst dir 1999–2001); MP (Cons) Faversham and Mid Kent 2001–, sec Parly Fruit Gp 2001–, Cons whip 2002–, shadow min for sport and Olympics 2005–, chair Parly UN Gp 2005–; govr Westminster Fndn for Democracy 2005–; Armourers and Brasiers Prize 1986; FRGS 1995; Sultan of Brunei's Personal Order of Merit 1992; *Recreations* cricket, skiing, hockey, country sports; *Clubs* Cavalry and Guards, MCC (playing member); *Style*— Hugh Robertson, Esq, MP; ✉ House of Commons, London SW1A 0AA (tel 020 7219 8230); Faversham and Mid Kent Conservative Association, 8 Faversham Road, Lenham, Kent ME17 2PN (tel 01622 851616)

ROBERTSON, Ian; s of James Love Robertson (d 1992), of Glasgow, and Mary Hughes Reid (d 1980); *b* 10 August 1947, Glasgow; *Educ* Queen's Park Secdy Sch Glasgow; *m* 6 May 2001, Fiona Ann, *née* Hervey; by earlier m, 1 da (Lorna b 3 Sept 1971), 2 s (Graeme, Douglas (twins) b 4 Aug 1977); *Career* dir J&A Ferguson 1976–81, factory chief accountant United Biscuits Glasgow 1982–84, financial controller Terrys of York 1984–87, finance dir Northern Dairies 1987–91, gp financial controller Northern Foods 1991–94; Wilson Bowden plc: finance dir 1994–2002, gp chief exec 2003–; memb Financial Reporting Cncl 2004–; memb Eastwood DC 1973–84 (provost 1980–84); MICAS 1969 (pres 2004–05); *Recreations* reading, music; *Style*— Ian Robertson, Esq; ✉ Wilson Bowden plc, Leicester Road, Ibstock, Leicestershire LE67 6WB (tel 01530 260777, fax 01530 451884, e-mail irobertson@wilsonbowden.plc.uk)

ROBERTSON, Dr James Andrew Stainton; s of James Robertson, and Margaret Elodie, *née* Stainton; *b* 23 April 1949; *Educ* Highgate Sch, Univ of Essex (BA), LSE (MSc (Econ), PhD); *m* 1979, Ann Elizabeth Leatherbarrow; 1 da (Elodie b 1982), 1 s (Andrew b 1987); *Career* civil servant; sr econ asst and econ advsr Dept of Employment 1975–82, econ advsr Dept of Energy 1982–86, sr econ advsr DTI 1986–89, Dept of Tport 1989–90, head Industrial and Regnl Economics DTI 1990–93, chief econ advsr Dept of Employment 1993–95, dir Nat Audit Office 1995–; contrib various learned jls; *Recreations* family, D-I-Y, gardening; *Style*— Dr James Robertson; ✉ National Audit Office, 157–197 Buckingham Palace Road, London SW1W 9SP

ROBERTSON, James Campbell; s of Surgn Lt James Robertson (ka 1942), of Edinburgh, and Mathilda Mary, *née* Campbell; *b* 15 October 1941; *Educ* Epsom Coll, Guy's Hosp, Univ of London (MB BS); *m* 2 May 1970, Dr Margaret Elizabeth Robertson, da of late Charles Edwin Kirkwood, of Salisbury, Wilts; 3 s (Charles James b 1971 d 1995, Andrew b 1973, Alistair b 1974); *Career* conslt physician in rheumatology and rehabilitation Salisbury and Southampton DHAs and Wessex Regnl Rehabilitation Unit 1974–2006, dir Wessex Regnl Rehabilitation Unit 1980–90, currently private and medico-legal practice; fndr ed Care Science and Practice (now Jl of Tissue Viability); author of papers on prevention of neck and back pain, osteoporosis, measurement of physical signs, patient support systems, bandaging and interface pressure mgmnt and burns scarring; former chm and fndr memb Soc for Tissue Viability, memb Wessex Rehabilitation Assoc, memb Cncl Bath Inst of Medical Engrg; memb: BMA, Br Soc of Rheumatology, Ergnomics Soc, Back Pain Soc, Soc for Res in Rehabilitation (former sec); LRCP, FRCP, MRCS; *Books* Blueprint for a Clinical Grip Strength Monitor and Limb Strength Measurement System (1986); *Recreations* sailing, DIY; *Clubs* S Wales and S W Wessex Rheumatology; *Style*— Dr James Robertson; ✉ Rheumatology Department, Salisbury District Hospital, Salisbury, Wiltshire (tel 01722 336262 ext 4218)

ROBERTSON, James D; *b* 1931; *Educ* Glasgow Sch of Art; *Career* artist; Glasgow Sch of Art: pt/t lectr 1959, lectr 1967, sr lectr in drawing and painting 1975–96, artist in residence 1996–98; visiting lectr: Michaelis Sch of Fine Art Cape Town 1970, Gray's Sch of Art 1986, Duncan of Jordanstone Coll of Art 1986, Newcastle Poly 1986, Millersville Univ 1987, Sorbonne Univ Paris 2007; memb RGI 1980; Hon DLitt Univ of Glasgow 2001, Dip Paisley Art Inst (PAI) 2003; RSW 1962, RSA 1989 (ARSA 1974); *Solo Exhibitions* Douglas & Foulis Gallery 1961, Forum Gallery 1963, Loomshop Gallery 1972, Art Space Gallery 1980, Gallery 10 1982, Christopher Hull Gallery 1984, 1987 and 1989, Washington Gallery 1986, Ganser Gallery 1987, Ancrum Gallery 1989, 1991 and 1992, Blythswood Gallery 1989 and 1993, Lynne Stern Gallery 1990, Glasgow Art Club 1990, Portland Gallery 1992, William Hardie Gallery 1993, Roger Billcliffe Gallery Glasgow 1995, Jorgensen Fine Art Dublin 1995, 2002 and 2005, Abstracted Landscapes Clayton Gallery Newcastle 1997, Glasgow Sch of Art 2000, Roger Billcliffe Gallery Glasgow 2000, Roger Billcliffe Fine Art 2000 and 2006, retrospective show Glasgow Sch of Art 2000; *Group Exhibitions* incl: Richard De Marco Gallery, Five Glasgow Artists (Edinburgh Arts Centre), Contemporary Art from Scotland (Scottish Arts Cncl tour), Fine Art Soc, Compass Gallery, J D Kelly Gallery, Parkin Gallery, Gallery 10 1986, Interior (Royal Acad) 1986, Nine Glasgow Painters (Washington Gallery) 1987, Chicago Art Fair 1987, Bath Festival 1987, Hambledon Gallery 1987, Mayfair Gallery 1990 and 1993, Beaux Arts Gallery 1990, Macaulay Gallery 1990, Lynne Stern Gallery 1991, RSA 1991, RSW 1991, New Acad Gallery 1991 and 1992, Blythswood Gallery 1993, Christopher Hull Gallery 1993, N S Gallery 1994, Rebecca Hossack Gallery London (mixed show) 1999, RSW show at Richmond Hill Gallery London 1999, RSA show at Albemarle Gallery London 1999, Open Eye Gallery Edinburgh (mixed show) 2003, Falle Fine Art Gallery Jersey (mixed show) 2003; *Work in Public Collections* Br Contemporary Arts Soc, Hunterian Museum, Scottish Arts Cncl, Glasgow Art Galleries and Museums, Roya Scottish Acad; *Awards* Cargill award RGI 1971 and 1982, May Marshall Brown award RSW 1976, Sir William Gillies award RSW 1981, Shell Expro award 1985, Graham Munro award RSW 1987, Scottish Amicable award 1989, Scottish Post Office award RSA 1993, RSW Cncl Award at annual show in Royal Scottish Acad 1999; *Style*— James D Robertson, Esq, RSA

ROBERTSON, John; MP; *Educ* Shawlands Acad Sr Secdy Sch, Langside Coll, Stow Coll; *m* Eleanor, *née* Wilkins Munro; *Career* BT: joined 1969, tech offr 1973–87, special faults investigation offr 1987–91, customer service mangr 1991–95, field mangr 1995–99, local customer mangr 1999–2000; MP (Lab): Glasgow Anniesland 2000–05 (by-election), Glasgow NW 2005–; PPS to Kim Howells, MP (as Min of State FCO); House of Commons: Scottish Affrs Select Ctee 2001–05, European Scrutiny Select Ctee 2003–05, chair All Pty Communications Gp, vice-chair All Pty Shipbuilding and Ship Repair Gp, treas All Pty Scottish Football Gp, hon sec Scottish Parly Lab Pty Gp, sec Smoking and Health All Pty Gp, chair All Pty Gp on Music 2005–, chair All Pty Gp on Nuclear Energy 2005–, chair All Pty Nigeria Gp 2005–, vice-chair All Pty New Media Gp; constituency positions incl: branch chm 1987–91, constituency vice-chm 1990–94, chm 1995–2000, campaign co-ordinator 1987–2000, election agent 1995–2000; Communication Workers' Union (CWU): memb Glasgow Branch Ctee 1983–91, political and educn offr Glasgow Branch 1985–89; Soc of Telecom Executives (Connect): memb W of Scotland Ctee 1994–2000, chm W of Scotland Branch 1997–2000, nat negotiator 1998–2000; memb Lab Pty 1985–; *Recreations* football, cricket, reading, music; *Clubs* Garrowhill Cricket, Cambus Athletic, Old Kilpatrick Bowling; *Style*— John Robertson, Esq, MP; ✉ Glasgow North West Parliamentary Office, 131 Dalsetter Avenue, Glasgow G15 8TE (tel 0141 944 7298, fax 0141 944 7121, e-mail robertsonjo@parliament.uk)

ROBERTSON, John Davie Manson; CBE (1993, OBE 1978), DL (Sutherland); s of John Robertson (d 1972), and Margaret Gibson Wright (d 1987); *b* 6 November 1929; *Educ* Kirkwall GS, Univ of Edinburgh (BL); *m* 25 Feb 1959, Elizabeth Amelia, da of Donald William Macpherson (d 1987); 2 da (Susan b 1959, Fiona b 1965), 2 s (John b 1961, Sinclair b 1967); *Career* Anglo Iranian Oil Co and BP UK and ME 1953–58, chm S & J D Robertson Group 1979– (joined 1958), dir Stanley Services Ltd Falklands 1987–; chm North of Scotland Water Authy 1995–98; memb Bd of Mgmnt Orkney Hosps 1970–74; chm Orkney Health Bd 1983–91 (memb 1974–79, vice-chm 1979–83), chm Highland Health Bd 1991–97; chm Scot Health Mgmnt Efficiency Gp (SCOTMEG) 1985–95, chm and vice-chm Scot Health Bds Chaimen's Gp 1995–97; memb: Highlands and Islands Devpt Consultative Cncl 1988–91, Bd Highlands and Islands Enterprise 1990–95, NHS Tbnl 1990–; chm Lloyds TSB Scotland Fndn 1997–99 (tstee 1989–97); chm: Children's Panel Orkney 1971–76 (chm Advsy Ctee 1977–82), Orkney Savings Ctee 1974–78, Highland and Islands Savings Ctee 1975–78; memb Nat Savings Ctee for Scot 1975–78; chm Orkney Today 2003–, chm Orkney Media Gp 2007–; hon vice-consul Denmark 1972–2004, hon consul Germany 1976–2007; Hon Sheriff Grampian Highland and Islands 1977–; FRSA 1993, Hon FCIWEM 1996, FRSE 2000; Royal Order of Knight of Dannebrog (Denmark) 1982, The Officer's Cross of the Order of Merit (Germany) 1999 (Cavalier's Cross 1986); *Books* Uppies & Doonies (1967), An Orkney Anthology (1991), The Kirkwau Ba' (2004), Spinningdale and its Mill 1791–2000 (2004); *Recreations* shooting, fishing, history, art; *Clubs* New (Edinburgh); *Style*— John D M Robertson, CBE, DL, FRSE; ✉ Spinningdale House, Sutherland IV24 3AD (tel 01862 881240); S & J D Robertson Group Ltd, Shore Street, Kirkwall, Orkney (tel 01856 872961, fax 01856 875043)

ROBERTSON, John Shaw; s of David Robertson (d 2005), of Glasgow, and Margaret Lightbody, *née* Shaw (d 1995); *b* 7 April 1950; *Educ* Jordanhill Coll Sch Glasgow, Univ of Glasgow (MA, DipEd); *m* 1 Sept 1973, Mary, da of John Roy; 1 da (Claire b 16 Feb 1979), 1 s (Adam b 11 March 1984); *Career* successively teacher, asst princ, housemaster, then asst headmaster Daniel Stewart's & Melville Coll 1973–87; Dollar Acad: dep rector 1987–93, rector 1994–; princ examiner Higher English 1991–94; HMC: memb 1994–, chm Scot Div 2000 (sec 1999); memb SCU; FFICS 1999; *Publications* Stewart's Melville: The First Ten Years (1984); various articles in educational pubns; *Recreations* cricket, music, literature, travel; *Clubs* Dollar Cricket, East India, Dollar Burns (pres 1994); *Style*— John Robertson, Esq; ✉ Dollar Academy, Dollar, Clackmannanshire FK14 7DU (tel 01259 742511, e-mail rector@dollaracademy.org.uk)

ROBERTSON, John William; s of Ian Middleton Strachen Robertson, of Broughty Ferry, Dundee, and Agnes Ramsey Seaton, *née* Findlay; *b* 27 August 1956; *Educ* The HS of Dundee, Univ of Dundee (BSc, Zinn Hunter Award, Henry Dickson Prize, Gordon Mathewson Award), Univ of Liverpool (BArch); *m* 27 July 1984, Judy Ann, da of Thomas Gordon John Peacock; 2 da (Charlotte Elizabeth b 21 April 1986, Georgina Emily b 10 Feb 1988); 1 s (Edward James b 4 June 1990); *Career* architect; Fitzroy Robinson Partnership: qualified architect 1980, assoc 1983, ptnr 1985; Hurley, Robertson & Associates 1993–2005, John Robertson Architects 2005–, currently specialises in interior architectural projects and the design and construction of well known architectural projects in the Cities of London and Westminster; Freeman City of London 1986; memb: City Architecture Forum, City Property Assoc, AA; RIBA 1981; *Awards* commendation for high standard of design achieved in the Structural Steel Awards for Aviation House Gatwick Airport 1989, Br Cncl for Offices Award for One Great St Helens London 2000; City Heritage Award 2001, Royal Fine Art Cmmn Tst Award 2001 and Civic Trust Award 2002 Commendation for restoration of Daily Express Building Fleet Street, Br Cncl for Offices Award 2006 for 10 Queen Street Place London; *Recreations* bagpiping, golf, sailing, skiing, scuba diving; *Clubs* Berkshire Golf (Ascot), RAC; *Style*— John Robertson, Esq; ✉ John Robertson Architects, 111 Southwark Street, London SE1 0JF (tel 020 7633 5102, website www.jra.co.uk)

ROBERTSON, John Windeler; s of Maj John Bruce Robertson (d 1973); *b* 9 May 1934; *Educ* Winchester; *m* 1, 1959 (m dis 1984), Jennifer-Ann, da of Gontran Gourdou, of Switzerland; 1 s, 1 da; m 2, 1987, Rosemary Helen Jane Banks; *Career* dep chm Stock Exchange 1976–79 (memb 1956–89, memb Cncl 1966–86), sr ptnr Wedd Durlacher Mordaunt & Co 1979–86, dep chm Barclays de Zoete Wedd Securities Ltd (BZW) 1986–88; dir The Securities Assoc 1986–88; chm Guide Dogs for the Blind Assoc 1993–2000 (memb Cncl 1989–2000); tstee Lloyds TSB Fndn for Eng and Wales 1991–98; *Recreations* walking, marine art, bell ringing; *Clubs* City of London; *Style*— John Robertson, Esq; ✉ Eckensfield Barn, Compton, Chichester, West Sussex PO18 9NT (tel 023 9263 1239)

ROBERTSON, Katharine Eleanor Hannah Maria (Kate); da of William Anthony Archibald Godfrey, of Hadleigh, Suffolk, and Eleanor Bedford, *née* Wilson; *b* 10 October 1955; *Educ* St John's Coll Houghton Johannesburg, Univ of Cape Town (BA, LLB); *m* 23 June 1990, Bruce Michael Edwin Granville Robertson, s of Kenneth Robertson; 1 da (Ella Katharine Marjorie b 27 Nov 1991); *Career* advtg exec; J Walter Thompson Johannesburg SA: account supr 1982–83, account dir 1983–84, client servs dir 1984–86; J Walter Thompson Europe: Euro account dir 1987–91, regional dir-in-charge 1992–94; dir and head of European new business Bates Europe 1995–97; fndr and chief exec London office Scholz & Friends 1997–2002; Euro RSCG Worldwide: joined as exec vice-pres Europe 2003–04, exec vice-pres global brands and global brand dir Reckitt Benckiser 2004–06, UK gp chm 2006– (incorporating Euro RSCG London, Euro RSCG Biss Lancaster, Euro RSCG KLP, Euro RSCG Skybridge, Euro RSCG Fuel, CGI Brand Sense, Maitland Consultancy, Conran Design Group and EHS Brann); judge Media and Mktg Europe Awards 2006; *Style*— Mrs Kate Robertson; ✉ Euro RSCG Worldwide, Cupola House, 15 Alfred Place, London WC1E 7EB

ROBERTSON, Dr Kevin William; s of James Alexander Robertson, of Thurso, Caithness, and Elizabeth Margaret, *née* Grant; *b* 22 August 1965; *Educ* Thurso HS, Univ of Glasgow

(MB ChB, Livingstone prize for physiology, MD); *Career* jr house offr Univ Dept of Surgery then Univ Dept of Med Glasgow Royal Infirmary 1988–89, SHO Western Infirmary surgical specialities rotation Glasgow 1989–91, SHO W of Scotland rotation in surgery in gen 1991–93, SHO Dept of Vascular Surgery Glasgow Royal Infirmary 1993–94, SHERT (Scottish Hosps Endowment Research Tst) research fell and lectr Univ Dept of Surgery Glasgow Royal Infirmary and Beatson Inst for Cancer Research 1994–96, W of Scotland Higher Surgical trainee 1996–2002, conslt surgn N Glasgow Hosps NHS Univ Hospitals 2003–; memb: Amnesty Int, Médècins sans Frontière; fell Upper Gastro-Intestinal Surgical Unit St George's Hosp Sydney 2002–03, FRCSGlas 1992 (memb Cncl and Jr Advsy Ctee 1993–97, convenor Jr Advsy Ctee 1997–99), FRCS 2000; *Recreations* Lister, football, travel; *Clubs* Western Baths Swimming; *Style—* Dr Kevin Robertson; ✉ University Department of Surgery, Queen Elizabeth Building, Glasgow Royal Infirmary, Glasgow G31 2ER (tel 0141 211 4000)

ROBERTSON, Laurence Anthony; MP; s of James Robertson, and Jean Christine, *née* Larkin; *b* 29 March 1958; *Educ* St James' CE Secdy Sch, Farnworth GS, Bolton Inst of HE; *m* 1989, Susan; 2 step da (Sarah b 1973, Jemma b 1981); *Career* industrial conslt 1982–92, charity fundraising conslt 1992–97, MP (Cons) Tewkesbury 1997–; oppn whip 2001–03, shadow min for business 2003–05, shadow min for NI 2005–; memb House of Commons Select Ctees on: Jt Consolidated Acts 1997–2001, Social Security 1999–2001, European Scrutiny 1999–2001; former jt vice-chm Cons Backbench Ctee on Euro and Foreign Affrs, jt sec Cons Backbench Ctee on the Constitution 1997–2001, former memb 1922 Exec Ctee; *Recreations* racing, golf, the countryside, reading; *Style—* Laurence Robertson, Esq, MP; ✉ House of Commons, London SW1A 0AA (tel 020 7219 4196)

ROBERTSON, Sir Lewis; kt (1991), CBE (1969); s of John Robertson (d 1976); *b* 28 November 1922; *Educ* Trinity Coll Glenalmond; *m* 1950, Elspeth (decd), *née* Badenoch; 2 s, 1 da (and 1 s decd); *Career* served RAF Intelligence (Bletchley Park); accountant, industrialist, administrator, corporate recovery specialist, textile industry; chief exec and chm Robertson Industrial Textiles Scott & Robertson; dep chm and chief exec: Grampian Holdings Ltd 1971–76, Scottish Devpt Agency 1976–81; chm: F H Lloyd Holdings 1982–87, Triplex Foundries Group 1983–90 (later Triplex Lloyd plc), Girobank Scotland 1984–90, Borthwicks 1985–89, Lilley plc 1986–93, Havelock Europa plc 1989–92, Stakis plc 1991–95, Postern Ltd 1991–96; dir: Scottish & Newcastle Breweries 1975–87, Whitman International SA Geneva 1987–90, Scottish Financial Enterprise 1990–93, Bank of Edinburgh plc 1990–94, EFM Income Trust 1991–99, The Berkeley Hotel Co 1995–97, Advanced Management Programme Scotland Ltd 1996–2003; chm: Scottish Arts Cncl 1970–71, Scottish Ctee Br Cncl 1978–87, Carnegie Tst for Univs of Scotland 1990–2003 (memb Exec Ctee 1963–2003, tstee 1963–); tstee: Scottish Cancer Fndn 2000–06, Fndn for Skin Research 2000–03; memb: Monopolies Cmmn 1969–76, Restrictive Practices Court 1983–96; Bicentenary Medal RSE 2001, Lifetime Achievement Award Soc of Turnaround Practitioners 2004; Hon LLD: Univ of Dundee 1971, Univ of Aberdeen 1999; Hon DBA Napier Univ 1992; Hon DUniv: Stirling 1993, Glasgow 2003; Hon FRCSE 1999; FRSE 1978 (memb Cncl 1992–2000, treas 1994–99); *Recreations* reading, classical music, things Italian, listmaking; *Clubs* Athenaeum, New (Edinburgh); *Style—* Sir Lewis Robertson, CBE, FRSE; ✉ 29/5 Inverleith Place, Edinburgh EH3 5QD (tel 0131 552 3045, e-mail lr32scp@talk21.com)

ROBERTSON, Liz; *m* Patrick Deuchar, *qv*; 1 da (Briony Elizabeth b 4 July 1991); *Career* actress, singer and dancer; professional debut with dance gp The Go-Jos, formerly lead singer and dancer The Young Generation; theatre incl: Side By Side By Sondheim (Toronto), I Love My Wife (West End) 1977–78, Eliza Doolittle in My Fair Lady (tour then West End, Most Promising Actress Variety Club, nomination Oliveir Award) 1979, Jessica Mitford in The Mitford Girls (Chichester Festival) 1981, one-woman show West End (later on TV), Dance A Little Closer (Broadway), Song and Dance (West End), Kern Goes to Hollywood (Donmar Warehouse then Broadway) 1985, Killing Jessica (Richmond then West End) 1986, Canaries Sometimes Sing (West End) 1987, A Touch of Danger (tour) 1988, Bella Moriarty in Sherlock Holmes - The Musical (Exeter then West End) 1988/89, Anna in The King and I (US tour, Best Actress Award Miami) 1989–90, Maria in The Sound of Music (tour then Sadler's Wells and continued tour) 1991–93, Lets Do It (musical revue, Oxford and Chichester) 1994, Anna in The King and I (Covent Garden Festival) 1995, Marion in The Music Man (Regents Park) 1995, Olivia in Twelfth Night (Holders Festival Barbados) 1996, Jessica Fauldegate in Beethoven's Tenth (Chichester) 1996, Mavis in Stepping Out (musical tour and West End) 1997, Eliza in Hey Mr Producer (Lyceum) 1998, Something Wonderful (tour) 2000, Madame Giry in Phantom of the Opera (Her Majesty's Theatre) 2002–03, Joanne in Company (Derby Playhouse) 2005, Phyllis in Follies (Palladium) 2007; appeared in 4 Royal Variety Performances, VE Day celebrations Hyde Park; Enchanted Evenings with Liz Robertson (Radio 2) 1995–96; recorded albums: Somebody's Girl 1984, The Sound of Music 1993, My Fair Lady 1993; TV appearances: Good Life 1976, Song by Song (series) 1980–81, Green Green Grass 2005; *Style—* Ms Liz Robertson; ✉ c/o Burnett Granger Associates Ltd, 3rd Floor, 3 Clifford Street, London W1S 2LF (tel 020 7437 8008, fax 020 7836 6066)

ROBERTSON, Nathan James; s of John Robertson, of Cotgrave, Notts, and June Robertson; *b* 30 May 1977, Nottingham; *Educ* Dayncourt Comp; *Children* 1 da (Neve b 23 Oct 1997); *Career* badminton player, turned professional aged 16; achievements incl: Bronze medal men's doubles World Championships 1999, reached quarter finals men's doubles Olympic Games Sydney 2000, winner mixed doubles Dutch Open 2001, winner mixed doubles Malaysia Open 2002, winner mixed doubles and runner-up men's doubles Thailand Open 2004, Gold medal mixed doubles and Silver medal men's doubles European Championships 2004, Silver medal mixed doubles Olympic Games Athens 2004, winner mixed doubles All-England Championships 2005, winner mixed doubles Swiss Open 2005, Gold medal mixed doubles Cwlth Games 2006; *Recreations* family, golf, poker; *Style—* Nathan Robertson, Esq; ✉ c/o Badminton England, National Badminton Centre, Bradwell Road, Loughton Lodge, Milton Keynes MK8 9LA

ROBERTSON, Dr Neil Patrick; s of Dennis Robertson, and Barbara Robertson; *Educ* Cranleigh Sch, St Thomas' Med Sch (MB BS), Kandy Hosp Sri Lanka, Univ of London (MD); *Career* registrar in neurology Bristol Royal Infirmary 1990–91; Addenbrooke's Hosp Cambridge: clinical res assoc and hon clinical registrar 1992–95 (also at Hitchingbrooke Hosp Huntingdon), hon sr registrar 1995–97, hon conslt 1998; Univ of Cambridge: res registrar in neurology 1991–95, clinical lectr in neurology 1995–98, sr lectr in neurology 1998–99; sr registrar Nat Hosp for Neurology and Neurosurgery London 1997–98, sr lectr in neurology and hon conslt Univ Hosp of Wales 1999–; hon conslt: Hitchingbrooke Hosp Huntingdon 1998, Peterborough Hosp 1998, E Glamorgan Hosp Llantrisant 1999, Heath Hosp Cardiff 1999–; Charles Symonds Prize 1995; memb Med Protection Soc, assoc memb Assoc of Br Neurologists; FRCP 2002 (MRCP 1992); *Publications* author of numerous editorials and chapters in books; *Recreations* skiing, rugby, art, horticulture; *Style—* Dr Neil Robertson

ROBERTSON, Prof Pamela Beaumont; da of Charles Ian Barclay Reekie (d 2006), and Constance Marion, *née* Clarke (d 1979); *Educ* St George's Sch for Girls Edinburgh, UCL, Univ of Manchester; *m* 7 April 1984, William Robertson; 1 s (James Scott b 1986), 1 da (Elizabeth Clarke b 1988); *Career* sr curator Hunterian Art Gallery Univ of Glasgow; curator Whistler 2003 festival 2000–03, guest co-curator Charles Rennie Mackintosh (Glasgow Museums) 1996–97; chair Charles Rennie Mackintosh Soc 2003–07; memb: Historic Buildings Cncl Scotland 1998–2002, Curatorial Ctee Nat Tst for Scotland 2001–, Export Review Ctee for Works of Art 2004–; govr Glasgow Sch of Art 2006–; first recipient Iris Fndn Award for Outstanding Contribution to the Decorative Arts Bard Grad Sch NY 1998; FRSE 2003, FRSA 2007; *Books* Charles Rennie Mackintosh: The Architectural Papers (ed, 1990), Charles Rennie Mackintosh: Art is the Flower (1994), The Mackintosh House (1998, Scottish Museum of the Year Award for Publications 1999), The Chronycle: The Letters of Charles Rennie Mackintosh to Margaret Macdonald Mackintosh, 1927 (2001), Beauty and the Butterfly: Whistler's Depictions of Women (2003), Doves and Dreams: The Art of Frances Macdonald and J Herbert McNair (2006); *Style—* Prof Pamela Robertson; ✉ Hunterian Art Gallery, University of Glasgow, 82 Hillhead Street, Glasgow G12 8QQ

ROBERTSON, Prof Paul; *Career* violinist; leader Medici String Quartet; Medici String Quartet: formed 1971, artists in residence and fells of Lancaster Univ, currently artists in residence Univ of Surrey, launched own record label Whitehall 1992; currently visiting prof: of music and psychiatry Kingston Univ, Bournemouth Univ; guest lectures incl: City Univ, Medical Soc of London, The Study Soc, Coll of Psychic Studies, Music and The Young Mind Conference New Coll Sch Oxford, Brain, Art, Mind, Music Conference Univ of Bath, Music, Brain Function, SEAL Conference Budapest, Brain Function and The Mind Conference (with concert by Medici Quartet) Geneva Cantonal Hosp, Holburne Museum (Bath Festival), The Art and Music of Business (with concert by Medici String Quartet) Roffey Park Mgmnt Ins, HM Whitemoor Prison, RSA, Acad Med Centre of Amsterdam Anatomy Lesson (with concert by Medici String Quartet); broadcasts incl: interview with Margaret Howard (Classic FM, nominated for Prix Italia 1993), The Mind of Music (series of six dialogues and concerts for Classic FM) 1995, Music & The Mind (Channel 4 Television) 1995; 1995–96 tours: Italy, Bulgaria, Germany, The Netherlands, Scandinavia, Spain; 1994–95 festival appearances incl: Bath, Lichfield, Salisbury, Three Choirs; BBC Lunchtime Recital St John's Smith Square, Glories of the String Quartet (series of 6 concerts) Braithwaite Hall Croydon Clocktower; *Recordings* with Medici String Quartet incl: Beethoven The Complete String Quartets Cycle, Alan Bush Dialectic Quartet Op 15, Elgar String Quartet, Franck Piano Quintet in F minor (with John Bingham), Janácek The Kreutzer Sonata and Intimate Letters, Mendelssohn String Quartet Op 13, Shostakovich Two Pieces for Octet (with Alberni String Quartet), Ravel String Quartet, Smetana From My Life, Vaughan Williams Phantasy Quintet (with Simon Rowland-Jones), Music and the Mind - Musical Illustrations from Channel 4 series, double CD of selected works for Koch International; recordings on own label incl: Brahms Piano Quintet in F minor Op 13 (with John Lill), Delius A Song before Sunrise, Haydn Six String Quartets Op 20, Mozart's Journey to Prague (with Dorothy Tutin and Richard McCabe), Mozart Clarinet Quintet in A major K 581 (with Jack Brymer), Schubert Death and the Maiden, Dvorák String Quartet in F major Op 96 American; *Style—* Prof Paul Robertson; ✉ c/o Georgina Ivor Associates, 28 Old Devonshire Road, London SW12 9RB (tel 020 8673 7179, fax 020 8675 8058, e-mail GIvor@aol.com)

ROBERTSON, Peter Duncan Neil; s of Laurence Neil Robertson, Flt Lt RAF (despatches, d 1961), and Edith Pamela, *née* Moorhouse; *b* 23 May 1940; *Educ* Sandroyd Sch, Harrow; *m* 13 July 1962, Diana Helen, da of Dr R C Barbor (d 1989), of Rosefield Peldon, Essex; 1 da (Tania Gay b 1967), 1 s (Toby Neil b 1970); *Career* trainee R C Greig and Co 1958–61, Philip Hill Higginson Private Client and Pension Fund Mgmnt 1961–64, M&G Group plc 1965–95 (Far East investment dir M&G Investment Mgmnt 1971–95), T T International 1996–2005; dir: Invesco Asia plc 1980–, China Assets (Hong Kong) Ltd 1991–, M G Capital plc 2000, Hindsight Investment Mgmnt Cayman Ltd; MSI; *Recreations* shooting, golf, falconry, cooking, racing; *Clubs* Turf; *Style—* Peter Robertson, Esq; ✉ Broomsgrove Lodge, New Mill, Pewsey, Wiltshire SN9 5LE (tel 01672 811535, fax 01672 810286, e-mail oldbeangbr@yahoo.co.uk)

ROBERTSON, Peter McKellar; OBE (1987), JP (Ayrshire 1976), DL (1960); s of John McKellar Robertson, CBE (d 1939); *b* 5 June 1923; *Educ* Marlborough, Royal Tech Coll Glasgow (BSc); *m* 1951, Elspeth Marion, da of late James Charles Hunter, of Kilbarchan, Renfrewshire; 1 s (John), 2 da (Jane (Mrs Christopher Evans), Angela (Mrs Bruce Walker)); *Career* RN VR 1944–46; landowner; memb Ayrshire CC 1949–75; pres Assoc of CCs in Scotland 1974–75, memb Local Authy Accounts Cmmn Scotland 1974–87 (vice-chm 1983–87); *Recreations* classical music; *Clubs* Western (Glasgow); *Style—* Peter M Robertson, Esq, OBE, DL; ✉ Noddsdale, Largs, Ayrshire KA30 8SL (tel 01475 672382)

ROBERTSON, (David) Ranald Craig; s of David Stanley Robertson (d 1989), and Olive Mary, *née* Svendsen; *b* 23 April 1948; *Educ* Pukekohe HS NZ, Univ of Auckland (LLB); *m* 10 Sept 1977, Gillian Susan, da of Reginald Berwick; 1 s (Andrew), 1 da (Rhiannon); *Career* Lt 4 Medium Battery Royal NZ Artillery 1971–76, attachment to 200 Sussex Yeomanry Medium Battery RA(V) 1974–76; admitted barr and slr of Supreme Court of NZ 1973; EMI Music London 1974–80: business affrs exec, business affrs mangr (also of Liberty United Records); legal servs mangr CAP Gp plc 1980–87, admitted slr of Supreme Court of England 1980; ptnr: Stephenson Harwood 1987–93, Field Fisher Waterhouse 1993–96, Taylor Joynson Garrett 1996–97; fndr and princ Robertson & Co 1997–; fndr chm Legal Affrs Gp Computing Servs Assoc 1982–87, chm Fedn Against Software Theft 1985–86 (fndr and dir); LiverymanWorshipful Co of Information Technologists; memb Law Soc; *Books* Legal Protection of Computer Software, Butterworths Encyclopaedia of Forms and Precedents (contrib), European Computer Law (contrib), Sweet & Maxwell Outsourcing Practice Manual (contrib); *Clubs* Hurlingham; *Style—* Ranald Robertson, Esq; ✉ Robertson & Co (tel 020 7731 4626, fax 020 7731 4598)

ROBERTSON, Shirley Ann; OBE (2005, MBE 2001); da of Iain Robertson, of Dundee, and Elizabeth Ann, *née* Burnett; *b* 15 July 1968; *Educ* Alva Acad, Moray House Coll of Educn (BA); *Career* yachtswoman; competitive laser sailing 1983–88; memb Scottish squads: second place European Championships 1986, third place European Championships 1988, eighth place World Championships 1988; transferred to Europe class 1988, winner Br Olympic Trials 1992, ninth place Olympic Games Barcelona 1992, second place World Championships 1993, ranked World and European number one 1993–, fourth place World Championships 1997, winner National Women's match racing, second place World Championships 1998, third place ISAF World Championships (keelboat team event), Gold medal Europe class sailing Olympic Games Sydney 2000, Gold medal Yngling class sailing Olympic Games Athens 2004; selected memb Br Olympic Team Atlanta 1996 (fourth place), memb Br Sailing Team 1986–; winner Skol sports awards 1986 and 1988, World Sailor of the Year 2000, Yachtsman of the Year (UK) 2000; runner-up: Sunday Times Sportswoman of the Year 1993, Yachtsman of the Year 1993; *Style—* Miss Shirley Robertson, OBE; ✉ 2 Langtry Place, Castle Road, Cowes PO31 7QQ (tel 01983 297141)

ROBERTSON, Brig Sidney Park; MBE (1962), TD (1967), JP (1968), DL (1968); s of John Davie Manson Robertson (d 1934), and Elizabeth Park, *née* Sinclair; *b* 12 March 1914; *Educ* Kirkwall GS, Univ of Edinburgh (BCom), MIBS; *m* 1940, Elsa Miller (d 1997), da of James Miller Croy (d 1943); 1 s (Robert Sinclair), 1 da (Eileen Mary); *Career* served WWII, cmmnd RA 1940 (despatches NW Europe 1945); Maj cmdg 861 (ind) Light Anti-Aircraft Battery RA (Orkney and Zetland) TA 1956–61, Lt-Col cmd Lovat Scouts TA 1962–65, Brig CRA 51 Highland Div TA 1966–67, Hon Col 102 (Ulster and Scot) Light Air Def Regt RA (TA) 1975–80, Hon Col Cmdt RA 1977–80; managerial posts: Anglo-Iranian Oil Co ME 1946–51, mangr ops/sales Southern Div Shell-Mex and BP 1951–54, fndr Robertson firm 1954; chm Orkney Hosps Bd of Mgmnt and Orkney Health Bd 1965–79, chm RA Cncl of Scotland 1980–84; Royal Br Legion Scotland: pres Kirkwall Branch, hon vice-pres Highlands and Islands Area; vice-pres: Nat Artillery Assoc 1977–, RNLI Inst 1985–; pres RNLI Kirkwall Station Ctee 1997– (chm 1972–97); hon pres: Orkney Bn Boys' Brigade, Soc of Friends of St Magnus Cathedral, Orkney Family

R

History Soc 1996–2005, Orkney Norway Friendship Assoc 1999–2005; hon life vice-pres Longhope Lifeboat Museum Tst 2002; patron North Ronaldsay Heritage Tst 1995; Hon Sheriff Grampian Highlands and Islands 1969–, Vice Lord-Lt for the Islands Area of Orkney 1987–90; Freedom of Orkney 1990; hon fell Univ of Edinburgh 1996, Hon DLitt Napier Univ 2002; *Recreations* travel, hill walking, angling; *Clubs* Caledonian, New (Edinburgh); *Style*— Brig Sidney Robertson, MBE, TD, DL; ✉ Daisybank, Kirkwall, Orkney KW15 1LX (tel 01856 872085)

ROBERTSON, Simon Manwaring; s of David Lars Manwaring Robertson (d 1999), of Newick, E Sussex, and Pamela Lauderdale Manwaring, *née* Meares; *b* 4 March 1941; *Educ* Cothill Sch, Eton; *m* 26 June 1965, Virginia Stewart, da of Mark Richard Norman (d 1994), of Much Hadham, Herts; 1 s (Edward Manwaring b 1968), 2 da (Selina Manwaring b 1969, Lorna Manwaring b 1973); *Career* dir: Kleinwort Benson Ltd 1977–97, Kleinwort Benson Group plc 1988–97 (dep chm 1991–96, chm 1996–97); pres Goldman Sachs Europe Ltd 1997–2005, md Goldman Sachs Int 1997–2005; fndr Simon Robertson Associates 2005–; non-exec chm Rolls Royce 2005–; non-exec dir: Berry Bros & Rudd Ltd 1998, HSBC plc 2006–; dir Royal Opera House Covent Garden Ltd 2002–; tstee: Eden Project 2000–, Royal Opera House Endowment Fund 2001–; chm Royal Acad Tst 2002–; *Recreations* being in the Prättigau, tennis; *Clubs* White's, Boodle's, Racquet (NY); *Style*— Simon Robertson, Esq

ROBERTSON, Stanley Stewart John; CBE (1998); s of Jock Stanley Robertson, and Florence Kathleen, *née* Carpenter; *b* 14 July 1938; *Educ* Wandsworth Tech Coll, Liverpool Poly (DipEE); *m* 1961, Valerie, *née* Housley; 2 s, 2 da; *Career* student engrg apprentice UKAEA 1956–62, asst electrical engr CEGB 1962–67, electrical engrg mangr Shell Chemicals UK 1967–74; Health and Safety Exec: sr electrical inspr 1974–77, superintending inspr 1980–91 (dep superintending inspr 1977–80), dep chief inspr and regnl dir 1991–93, chief inspecting offr Railways 1993–98, md Robertson Safety Engineering Servs Ltd 1998–, exec dir Metro Solutions Ltd 2005–; conslt on safety and engrg 1998–, health and safety conslt to Taiwan High Speed Rail Corp 1998–2006; non-exec dir NQA Ltd 1993–96; chm: HSE Technol Ctee investigating RF ignition hazards St Fergus Scot 1979, Railway Industry Advsy Ctee Health and Safety Cmmn 1993–98, Nat Inspection Cncl for Electrical Installation Contracting 1993–95, HSE Ctee investigating safety of Forth Rail Bridge 1995–96; memb HSE Tech Ctee investigating collapse of railway tunnels at Heathrow Airport and New Austrian Tunnelling Method 1994; author of various pubns and tech papers on electrical and railway safety matters; CEng 1973, FIEE 1987 (MIEE 1973), MCIT 1994, FCILT 1998; *Recreations* listening to music, gardening; *Style*— Stanley Robertson, Esq, CBE

ROBERTSON, Prof Stephen Edward; s of Prof Charles Martin Robertson (d 2004), and Theodosia Cecil, *née* Spring Rice (d 1984); *b* 4 April 1946; *Educ* Westminster, Trinity Coll Cambridge (MA), City Univ (MSc), UCL (PhD); *m* 25 June 1966, Judith Anne (d 2005), da of Edwin Donald Kirk (d 1943); 1 da (Magdalene b 1977), 1 s (Colin b 1979); *Career* Royal Soc Scientific Info res fell UCL 1973–78, Fulbright scholar Univ of Calif Berkeley 1981, prof of info systems City Univ 1988–, researcher Microsoft Research Ltd 1998–; memb Universities' Research Assessment Panel for Library and Information Management 1996 and 2001; Tony Kent Strix Award Inst of Information Scientists 1998, Gerard Salton Award Assoc for Computing Machinery 2000; fell Girton Coll Cambridge 2003; fell Chartered Inst of Library and Info Professionals, MBCS; *Style*— Prof Stephen Robertson; ✉ Microsoft Research Ltd, 7 JJ Thomson Avenue, Cambridge CB3 0FB (tel 01223 479774, fax 01223 479999, e-mail ser@microsoft.com)

ROBERTSON, Stephen Peter; *Educ* Shenfield Sch, Univ of Nottingham (BSc Chemistry); *Career* mktg asst Dunlop Consumer Products 1976–79, gp product mangr Ashe Consumer (now Sara Lee) 1979–81, sr brands mangr Brooke Bond Oxo Foods (Unilever) 1981–85, mktg devpt mangr Alberto-Culver Co Ltd 1985–86, Euro mktg mangr Mars Inc Drinks Gp Europe 1986–92, mktg dir UK and Ireland Mattel Toys Ltd 1992–93, mktg dir B & Q plc (subsid of Kingfisher plc) 1993–2000, md e-Kingfisher DIY Direct (subsid of Kingfisher plc) 2000–; Mktg Soc: memb 1991, memb Mgmnt Team and dir of Soc 1994, chm 1997–98; *Style*— Stephen Robertson, Esq; ✉ B & Q plc, Link House, 2 Stoneycroft Rise, Chandlers Ford, Hampshire SO53 3YU (tel 023 8062 5102, fax 023 8062 5198)

ROBERTSON-MACLEOD, (Roderick) James Andrew; s of Col Roderick Cameron Robertson-Macleod, DSO, MC (d 1989), and Daphne Mary, *née* Bick; *b* 5 March 1951; *Educ* St Aubyn's Rottingdean, Milton Abbey; *m* 1991, Karen Theodora, da of Petre Barclay; 2 da (Katrina Rose b 2 Jan 1992, Louisa Iona b 15 Dec 1995), 1 s (Jack Alexander b 30 Sept 1993); *Career* joined Royal Green Jackets HM Forces 1970, UN Forces Cyprus 1971, Regtl Serv 1971–74, served NI 1975–76, ADC to GOC NI 1976–78, Adj 4 Royal Green Jackets 1978–80, ADC to TSH Prince and Princess of Monaco 1980–83; dir sports sponsorship co (pt of Markham Gp) 1983–89, commercial dir Operation Raleigh 1990–92, chief exec Raleigh International 1992–2003, dir John D Wood 2004–05, dir Aegis Defence Services 2005–06, conslt Gp 4 Securicor 2006–; *Recreations* tennis, skiing, running, politics; *Style*— James Robertson-Macleod, Esq; ✉ Hill House, Coneyhurst, West Sussex RH14 9DL (tel 01403 786877, e-mail jrobmac@btinternet.com)

ROBERTSON OF OAKRIDGE, 2 Baron (UK 1961); Sir William Ronald Robertson; 3 Bt (UK 1919); s of Gen 1 Baron Robertson of Oakridge, GCB, GBE, KCMG, KCVO, DSO, MC (d 1974); *b* 8 December 1930; *Educ* Charterhouse; *m* 1972, Celia, da of William Elworthy; 1 s; *Heir* s, Hon William Robertson; *Career* sat as Independent in House of Lords 1974–99; memb London Stock Exchange 1973–95, late Maj Royal Scots Greys; involved in Christian-based project for HMP The Verne; memb Ct of Assts Worshipful Co of Salters until 2001 (Master 1985–86); *Style*— Lord Robertson of Oakridge

ROBERTSON OF PORT ELLEN, Baron (Life Peer UK 1999), of Islay in Argyll and Bute; Sir George Islay MacNeill Robertson; KT (2004), GCMG (2004), PC (1997); s of George P Robertson (d 2002), of Dunoon, Argyll, and Marion I, *née* MacNeill (d 1996); *b* 12 April 1946; *Educ* Dunoon GS, Univ of Dundee (MA); *m* 1 June 1970, Sandra, da of late James U Wallace, of Dundee; 2 s (Malcolm b 1972, Martin b 1975), 1 da (Rachael b 1980); *Career* research asst Econs Gp Tayside Study 1968–69, Scottish organiser GMWU (now GMB) 1969–78; MP (Lab): Hamilton 1978–97, Hamilton S 1997–99; PPS to sec of state for Social Servs 1979; oppn spokesman on: Scotland 1979–80, Defence 1980–81, Foreign and Cwlth Affrs 1981–93 (dep FCO spokesman 1983, princ spokesman on Europe 1984–93); chief oppn spokesman on Scotland 1993–97, sec of state for defence 1997–99; sec-gen NATO 1999–2003; exec dep chm Cable and Wireless plc 2004–06, chm Cable and Wireless Int 2006–; non-exec dir: Weir Gp plc 2003–, Smiths Gp plc 2004–06; chm Scottish Lab Pty 1977–78; vice-chm Bd Br Cncl 1985–94; tstee 21st Century Tst, govr Ditchley Fndn 1988–; chm John Smith Memorial Tst 2004–, jr pres RIIA 2002–, hon vice-pres Operation Raleigh, hon patron Glasgow-Islay Assoc 2000–, co-chm British Russia Round Table 2005–, chm Cmmn on Global Road Safety 2006–; Hon Col London Scottish (Vols) Regt 2000–; Hon Sr Fell Foreign Policy Assoc 2000 Golden Plate Award Int Acad of Achievement 2000, English Speaking Union Winston Churchill Medal of Honour 2003, Transatlantic Leadership Award European Inst Washington DC 2003, Award for Distinguished International Leadership Atlantic Cncl of USA 2003, Global Leadership Award Chicago Cncl on Foreign Relations 2004, The Hanno R Elenbogen Citizenship Award The Prague Soc; Elder Bro Trinity House 2002, Hon Guild Bro Guildry of Stirling 2004; DSc (hc) Cranfield Univ RCMS 2000; LLD (hc): Univ of Dundee 2000, Univ of Bradford 2000, Baku State Univ Azerbaijan 2001, Nat Acad of Sciences Kyrkyz Repub 2002, Romanian Sch of Political and Administrative Studies 2003, Univ of St Andrews 2003, French Univ Armenia, Nat Acad of Sciences Azerbaijan, Glasgow Caledonian 2004; FRSA 1999, Hon FRSE 2003; Grand Cross Order of the Star (Romania) 2000, Grand Cross Order of Orange-Nassau (Netherlands) 2003, Grand Cross Order of Jesus (Portugal) 2003, Grand Cross Order of Isabel the Catholic (Spain) 2003, Grand Cross Order of Merit (Poland, Luxembourg, Italy, Hungary) 2003, Grand Cross Order of the Stara Planina (Bulgaria) 2003, Grand Cross Order of Merit (Federal Republic of Germany) 2003 (Commander's Cross 1991), Presidential Medal of Freedom (USA) 2003, Grand Cordon Order of Leopold (Belgium) 2003, Grand Cross Order of Grand Duke Gedeminos (Lithuania) 2003, Grand Cross Order of King Petar Kresmir IV (Croatia) 2003, Distinguished Public Service Medal US Department of Defence 2003, First Class Order of the Cross of the Tarra Mariana (Estonia) 2004, Order of the White Two-Arm Cross First Class (Slovakia) 2004, Commander of the Grand Cross The Order of Three Stars (Latvia) 2004, Grand Cross Order of Yaroslav the Wise (Ukraine) 2005; *Publications* Islay and Jura (2006); *Recreations* photography, golf, family, reading; *Clubs* Army and Navy, Royal Cwlth, Islay Golf; *Style*— The Rt Hon Lord Robertson of Port Ellen, KT, GCMG, PC, Hon FRSE

ROBERTSON-PEARCE, Dr Anthony Brian (Tony); s of John Gilbert Robertson-Pearce (d 1967), of Testwood House, Lyndhurst, Hants, and Damaris Aubrey, *née* Wilce (d 1946); *b* 3 April 1932; *Educ* Chideock Manor Sch, Christ's Coll Cambridge (BA), Univ of Stockholm (Dip Archaeological Photography), Alliance Française Paris (Dip French); *m* 1, 18 May 1956 (m dis 1973), (Ingrid) Christina, da of Erik Nystrom (d 1957), of Stockholm, Sweden; 2 da (Pamela b 22 April 1957, Penelope b 3 Oct 1965), 1 s (Michael b 3 Aug 1960); *m* 2, 7 June 1974 (m dis 1980), Catharina Carlsdotter, da of Capt Soldan Carl Fredrik Henningsson Ridderstad (d 1973), of Linkoping, Sweden; *Career* supervisor and photographer excavations Motya Sicily 1965, Br Sch of Archaeology Baghdad 1966, supervisor and MO Tell-A-Rimah N Iraq 1967, photographer and MO Br Excavations Tawilan Jordan 1968; Central Bd of Nat Antiquities (Riksantikvarieambetet) Stockholm: field archaeological photographer 1969, joined Publishing Dept 1972, subsequently head of publishing; Swedish TV film debut The Inquiry 1990 as Cdre in Royal Swedish Navy; PRO Sollentuna Kommun Stockholm 1983–88; dep govr Bd of Govrs American Biographical Inst Research Assoc; Int Biographical Centre Cambridge: dep DG (Europe), awarded Int Order of Merit (IOM) 1990, vice-consul for Sweden 2003–, life memb World Peace and Diplomacy Forum 2004; memb Swedish Nat Ctee ICOMOS (Int Cncl on Monuments and Sites), dep memb Assembly (Region R33) UN Int Parliament for Safety and Peace 1991–; Hon DH London 1991; Duine Uasal of the Clan Dhonnachaidh (Scotland), Gentleman of the Bodyguard Balgonie Castle Fife Scotland 1997–, appointed lifetime Ambassador General of the United Cultural Convention (USA) 2006; KStJ 1997; FRAI, FIBA; *Books* Dr James Robertson 1566–1652 (1972), The Prehistoric Enclosure of Ekornavallen Sweden (1974), The Ruins of Kronoberg Castle (1974), Kaseberg Ship-setting (1975), The Battle of Rotebro 1497 (1986), Klasroskolan 1804–1881 (1987), Living Science Volume 001 (author of Introduction on Iraq, 2003); provided most of the illustrative material for Assyrian Ivories from Nimrud (by Prof Sir M E L Mallowan, 1968); author of numerous Swedish archaeological reports 1970–79; *Recreations* riding, heraldic artwork, painting watercolours; *Clubs* Naval, Sallskapet Stockholm; *Style*— Dr Anthony B Robertson-Pearce; ✉ Ambassador-General Robertson-Pearce, UCC, Nybrogatan 54, S-11440 Stockholm, Sweden (tel 00 46 8 661 02 68, fax 00 46 8 667 64 96)

ROBIN, Sister (Mary) Gabriel; da of Clement Ernest Robin (d 1992), and Agnes Gertrude, *née* Appleton, of Harborne, Birmingham; *b* 27 December 1935; *Educ* St Paul's GS Edgbaston, Girton Coll Cambridge (MA), Inst of Educn Univ of London (Dip Religious Educn); *Career* headmistress Les Oiseaux Sch Westgate on Sea 1965–72 (asst mistress 1957–65); memb Int Gen Cncl Canonesses of St Augustine Congregation of Our Lady 1972–81 and 1990–96, provincial superior Br Province 1981–90, gen sec Conf of Religious in England and Wales 1989–98; memb Guild of Analytical Psychology and Spirituality (London); practising Jungian Psychotherapist; *Style*— Sister Gabriel Robin, CSA; ✉ More House, 53 Cromwell Road, London SW7 2EH (tel and fax 020 7225 1088, e-mail mgabrielrobin@btinternet.com)

ROBINS, John Vernon Harry; s of Col W V H Robins, DSO (d 1990), and Charlotte Mary, *née* Grier (d 1979); *b* 21 February 1939; *Educ* Winchester, Stanford Univ (SEP); *m* 11 Aug 1962, Elizabeth Mary, da of Alex Banister, OBE, of Sussex; 2 s (Nicholas Vivian James b 1963, Michael Victor Andrew b 1973), 1 da (Tessa Vivienne Mary b 1965); *Career* Nat Serv 2 Lt 2/10 PMO Gurkha Rifles 1959–61; md SNS Communications Ltd 1971–74, chief exec Bally Group (UK) Ltd 1974–79, gp fin dir Fitch Lovell plc 1979–84, dir fin and mgmnt servs Willis Faber plc 1984–89, gp fin dir Willis Corroon Group plc 1990–94, gp chief exec Guardian Royal Exchange plc 1994–99, ret; chm: Lane, Clark and Peacock 2000–03, Xchanging plc 2000–, Austin Reed plc 2000–06; non-exec dir: Church & Co plc 1993–96, Yorkshire Electricity Group plc 1996–97, Hyder plc 1997–99 (non-exec chm 1998–99), Alexander Forbes 2002– (dep chm 2004); chm: Br Insurers Int Ctee 1997–99, Policy Holders Protection Bd 1998–99; formerly chm Assoc of Corporate Treasurers; memb Ctee Barbican Arts Centre 2003–; Past Warden Worshipful Co of Glovers; FCT 1979; *Recreations* clocks, music; *Clubs* Brooks's; *Style*— John Robins, Esq; ✉ Brooks's, St James's Street, London SW1A 1LN (tel 020 7493 4411)

ROBINS, William J P (Bill); CB (1998), OBE (1984, MBE 1979); *Educ* BSc(Eng), MPhil; *Career* cmmnd Royal Corps of Signals; Dir of Cmd Control Communications and Info Systems (Army) until 1993, Maj-Gen 1993, ACDS (CIS) 1993–95, DG Information and Communication Services 1995–98, ret as Maj-Gen 1998; Col Cmdt Royal Signals; chm Royal Signals Inst 1998–2003; dir advanced concepts C41SR Gp BAE Systems 2001–03; visiting prof Cranfield Univ 2003; Freeman Worshipful Co of Information Technologists; CEng, CITP, FIEE, FBCS; *Clubs* Special Forces, Army and Navy; *Style*— Bill Robins; ✉ c/o RHQ Royal Signals, Blandford Camp, Dorset DT11 8RH (e-mail billrobins@walnutyard.co.uk)

ROBINSON, *see also:* Lynch-Robinson

ROBINSON, (George) Adrian; s of Thomas Gerard Robinson, BEM (d 1994), of Preston, Lancs, and Elizabeth, *née* Gillow (d 1997); *b* 3 November 1949; *Educ* Preston Catholic Coll, Pembroke Coll Oxford (MA, Cricket blue); *m* 6 April 1974, Susan Margaret, da of James Hopwood Edmondson (d 1995), of Accrington, Lancs; 2 s (Philip Adrian b 9 Sept 1984, Andrew James b 3 May 1987); *Career* various appts Midland Bank Ltd 1971–80; Airbus Industrie: sales fin mangr 1980–82, dep sales fin dir 1982–84, sales fin dir 1984; corporate fin dir Midland Bank plc 1985; md special fin gp Chemical Bank 1987–89 (dir Aerospace 1986–87), dep gen mangr The Nippon Credit Bank 1990–92; aerospace conslt 1992–; dir: Aircraft Lease Portfolio Securitization 94–1 Ltd, ALPS 94–1 (France) SARL, ALPS 94–1 (Belgium) NV, Pergola Ltd, Aircraft Lease Portfolio Securitisation 92–1 Ltd, Carotene Ltd, ALPS 92–1 UK Ltd, AerCo Ltd (also chm), AerCo Ireland Ltd, AerCo Ireland II Ltd, AerFi (Belgium) NV, AerFi Sverige Leasing AB, Aircraft Lease Securitisation Ltd (also chm); ACIB 1973; *Recreations* golf, tennis, shooting; *Clubs* Oxford Univ Cricket, Bearsted Golf; *Style*— Adrian Robinson, Esq

ROBINSON, (Francis) Alastair Lavie; s of late Mr and Mrs Stephen Robinson; *b* 19 September 1937; *Educ* Eton; *m* 29 April 1961, Lavinia Elizabeth Napier, da of late Cdr Trevylyan Napier, DSC (d 1940), and Mrs T Napier; 2 da (Camilla (Mrs Adam Fox) b 1967, Zoe b 1970); *Career* 2 Lt 4/7 Royal Dragoon Guards 1956–68; dir Mercantile Credit Co Ltd 1978–81 (joined 1959, gen mangr 1971–78); Barclays plc: chief exec pres Barclays American Corpn NC USA 1981–84, regnl gen mangr Barclays Bank International

1984–87, dir personnel Barclays Bank plc 1987–90, exec dir Barclays plc 1990–96, vice-chm 1992–96, chm UK Banking Services Barclays plc 1994–96; non-exec dir: Portman Building Society, RMC Group plc, Marshall of Cambridge (Holdings) Ltd, St Nicholas' Hospice; *Recreations* music, fishing; *Style*— Alastair Robinson, Esq; ✉ 24 Clarendon Street, London SW1V 4RF

ROBINSON, (Richard) Andrew; OBE (2004); s of Raymond Thomas Robinson, of Taunton, Somerset, and Patricia Mary, *née* Beckett; *b* 3 April 1964; *Educ* Richard Huish Coll, Loughborough Univ; *m* Samantha Elizabeth, da of John Andrew Morrison; 3 s (Oliver James b 21 July 1991, Edward George b 1 Feb 1993, Henry John b 12 Aug 1995), 1 da (Charlotte Elizabeth b 6 Sept 1997); *Career* rugby union player (flanker) and coach; clubs: Taunton 1981–83, Loughborough Univ 1982–86 (capt 1986), Bath 1986–2000 (capt 1991–93, coach 1997–2000); honours with Bath: Courage League Champions 1996, winners Pilkington Cup 1996; England: 8 caps, debut v Aust 1988, five nations debut v Scotland 1989, Player of the Year Five Nations Championship 1989, formerly asst coach Under 21s, coach full team 2000–04 (winners World Cup Aust 2003), head coach 2004–06; Br and Irish Lions: 6 appearances tour Aust 1989, asst coach tour Aust 2001, coach tour NZ 2005; physical educn and maths teacher: Writhlington Sch 1986–89, King Edward Sch Bath 1989–94; sports dir Colstons Collegiate Sch 1994–96; *Recreations* all sports (especially golf and cricket), gambling; *Style*— Andrew Robinson, Esq, OBE

ROBINSON, Dr Ann; da of Edwin James and Dora, *née* Thorne; *b* 28 January 1937; *Educ* St Anne's Coll Oxford (MA), McGill Univ Montreal (MA, PhD); *m* 1961, Michael Robinson; 2 s; *Career* fin journalist Beaverbrook Newspapers 1959–61; sometime lectr at Univs of: Durham, Bristol, Bath, Univ of Wales Coll of Cardiff (sr lectr in politics 1987–89); head of Policy Unit IOD 1989–95, DG Nat Assoc of Pension Funds 1995–2000; memb: Cncl RIIA 1991–97, MMC 1993–97; dir: WNO 1993–94, Great Western Holdings Ltd 1996–98, Almedia Capital 2000–; European Parly candidate (Cons) SE Wales 1979; memb: Equal Opportunities Cmmn 1980–85, Economic and Social Ctee EC 1986–93 (chm Industry Section 1990–92), Welsh Arts Cncl 1991–93, HEFC for Wales 1993–97, Pensions Protection and Investments Accreditation Bd 2000–05, Bd Harwich Haven Authy 2000–06, London Pensions Fund Authy 2001–05; tstee Dixon's Retirement and Employee Security Scheme 2000–06; memb: Bd of Academic Govrs Richmond Coll London 1992–, Bd of Govrs Commonwealth Inst 1992–97, Cncl Clifton Coll 1998–2003 (dep chm); *Publications* Parliament and Public Spending (1978), Tax Policy Making in the UK (with Prof C T Sandford, 1984), also author of numerous articles and chapters on public expenditure, House of Commons select ctees, taxation policy and EC matters; IOD publications: Business Leaders' Manifesto for the European Election (1989 and 1994), European Political Union (1990), A Currency for the Single Market (1990), Continuing Tax Reform (1990), Forward to Prosperity: A Business Leaders' Manifesto for the Next Government (1992), A Constitution for Europe? (with Paul Robinson, 2002); *Style*— Dr Ann Robinson

ROBINSON, (Moureen) Ann; *b* Blackpool; *Educ* Harris Tech Coll Preston, LSE; *m* 4 Nov 1961, Peter Crawford Robinson; *Career* civil servant 1958–93 (latterly dep chief exec Benefits Agency), chief exec Scope (formerly Spastics Soc) 1993–95, assoc dir Computer Sciences Corporation 1995–96, DG Br Retail Consortium 1997–99, chair Energywatch (Gas and Electric Consumer Cncl) 1999–2003, ptnr Rush Consultancy Servs 2004–, consumer policy dir uSwitch; memb: GMC, Prison Serv Pay Review Body; tstee Fndn for Credit Counselling; *Recreations* bridge; *Style*— Mrs Ann Robinson; ✉ 706 Duncan House, Dolphin Square, London SW1V 3PP (tel 020 7798 6728, e-mail annrob@ntlworld.com)

ROBINSON, Anne; da of late Bernard Robinson, and late Anne, *née* Wilson; *b* 26 September 1944; *Educ* Farnborough Hill Convent, Les Ambassadrices Paris XVI; *m* 1, 1968 (m dis 1973), Charles Martin Wilson, *qv*; 1 da (Emma Alexandra Wilson b 18 July 1970); m 2, 1980, John Penrose; *Career* Daily Mail 1966–68, The Sunday Times 1968–77, asst ed Daily Mirror 1980–93 (columnist 1983–93); columnist: Today 1993–95, The Times 1993–95, The Sun 1995–97, The Express 1997–98, The Times 1998–2001, The Daily Telegraph 2003–; presenter: Anne Robinson Show (BBC Radio 2) 1988–93, Points of View (BBC TV) 1988–97, Watchdog (BBC TV) 1993–2001, Weekend Watchdog (BBC TV) 1997–2001, Going for a Song (BBC TV) 2000–, The Weakest Link (BBC TV) 2000–, The Weakest Link (NBC TV) 2001–03, Great Britons (BBC TV) 2002, Test The Nation (BBC TV) 2002–, Guess Who's Coming to Dinner (BBC TV) 2003, Out Take TV (BBC TV) 2004–, What's the Problem? with Anne Robinson (BBC TV) 2005; hon fell Liverpool John Moores Univ 1996; *Books* Memoirs of an Unfit Mother (2001); *Recreations* reading, television, dogs, having opinions, decently cooked food; *Clubs* Bibury Cricket (vice-pres), Bibury Tennis (pres); *Style*— Ms Anne Robinson; ✉ c/o Tracey Chapman, PO Box 50445, London W8 9BE (tel 020 8870 6303, e-mail tracechapman@btinternet.com)

ROBINSON, Rt Rev Anthony William (Tony); *see*: Pontefract, Bishop of

ROBINSON, Dr Bill; s of Harold Desmond Robinson (d 1988), and Joyce Grover, *née* Liddington; *b* 6 January 1943; *Educ* Bryanston, Univ of Oxford (BA), Univ of Sussex (DPhil), LSE (MSc); *m* 19 Aug 1966, Heather Mary (d 1995), da of James Albert Jackson; 2 s (Nicholas, Matthew), 1 da (Rosemary); m 2, 1997, Priscilla Elizabeth, da of Cedric Ernest Stille; *Career* systems analyst IBM 1968–69, econ asst Cabinet Office 1969–70, econ advsr HM Treasy 1971–74, head of div Euro Cmmn 1974–78, ed Econ Outlook London Business Sch 1978–86, dir Inst of Fiscal Studies 1986–91; advsr Treasy Ctee House of Commons 1981–86, memb Retail Prices Advsy Ctee 1988–90; econ columnist The Independent 1989–91 and Independent on Sunday 2000–, special advsr to Chllr of Exchequer 1991–93, dir London Economics 1993–99, head UK business economist corporate finance and recovery PricewaterhouseCoopers 1999–2007, head of economics Forensic Dept KPMG 2007–; *Books* Medium Term Exchange Rate Guidelines for Business Planning (1983), Britain's Borrowing Problem (1993); *Recreations* the bassoon, skiing, opera, bridge, windsurfing; *Clubs* Reform; *Style*— Dr Bill Robinson; ✉ KPMG, 20 Farringdon Street, London EC4A 4PP (tel 020 7311 3515, fax 020 7311 3630, mobile 07715 704743, e-mail bill.robinson@kpmg.co.uk)

ROBINSON, Maj (Alfred) Christopher; s of Col Annesley Robinson, DSO (d 1976), of Long Melford, Suffolk, and Doris Lilian, *née* Barrett (d 1988); *b* 18 November 1930; *Educ* Wellington, RMA Sandhurst; *m* 1, 17 Aug 1957 (m dis 1961), Caroline Stafford (d 1996), da of Maj Christopher Scott-Nicholson (ka 1945), of Ruthwell, Dumfriesshire; m 2, 31 March 1962 (m dis 1978), Amanda, da of Paul Boggis-Rolfe (d 1988), of Bampton, Oxon; 2 da (Nicola b 1963, Polly b 1964), 2 s (Charles b 1964, Barnaby b 1970); *Career* 16/5 The Queen's Royal Lancers 1951–65; Trade Indemnity Co Ltd 1966–70, Glanvill Enthoven & Co Ltd 1970–73, The Spastics Soc (now Scope) 1973–91; tstee: The Little Fndn (chm 1996–), The Mother and Child Fndn (chm 2001–); pres Ferriers Barn Disabled Centre; vice-chm Colne Stour Countryside Assoc; lay chm Sudbury Deanery Synod, memb St Edmundsbury and Ipswich Diocesan Synod; chm Bures & Dist Branch Royal Br Legion; MInstF (MCIFM 1986); *Recreations* country conservation, wine appreciation; *Clubs* Essex; *Style*— Maj Christopher Robinson; ✉ Water Lane Cottage, Bures, Suffolk CO8 5DE (tel 01787 227179)

ROBINSON, Christopher John; CVO (1992, LVO 1986), CBE (2004); s of Rev Preb John Robinson (d 1974), of W Malvern, and Esther Hilda, *née* Lane (d 1983); *b* 20 April 1936; *Educ* Rugby, ChCh Oxford (MA, BMus), Univ of Birmingham (CertEd); *m* 6 Aug 1962, Shirley Ann, da of Harry Frederick Churchman (d 1991); 1 da (Elizabeth b 26 Sept 1968), 1 s (Nicholas b 3 June 1970); *Career* asst organist: ChCh Oxford 1955–58, New Coll Oxford 1957–58; music master Oundle Sch 1959–62; organist: Worcester Cathedral 1963–74 (princ conductor Three Choirs Festivals 1966, 1969 and 1972), St George's Chapel Windsor Castle 1975–91; organist and dir of music St John's Coll Cambridge 1991–2003; conductor: City of Birmingham Choir 1964–2002, Leith Hill Festival 1977–80, Oxford Bach Choir 1977–97; pres RCO 1982–84, chm Elgar Soc 1988–92, chm Ouseley Tst 2002–, actg dir of music Clare Coll Cambridge 2005–06; pres Friends of Cathedral Music 2004–; Hon MMus Univ of Birmingham 1987, DMus Lambeth 2002; hon fell UCE 1990; FRCO 1954, Hon RAM 1980, FRSCM 2004; *Recreations* cricket, foreign travel; *Style*— Dr Christopher Robinson, CVO, CBE; ✉ Manor Farmhouse, 51 Church Road, Hauxton, Cambridgeshire CB22 5HS (tel 01223 871911)

ROBINSON, Sir Christopher Philipse; 8 Bt (UK 1854), of Toronto, Canada; s of Christopher Robinson, QC (d 1974); suc kinsman, Sir John Robinson, 7 Bt (d 1988); *b* 10 November 1938; *m* 1962, Barbara Judith, da of Richard Duncan, of Ottawa; 2 s (Peter Duncan b 1967, Jonathan Richard b 1969); *Heir* s, Peter Robinson; *Style*— Sir Christopher Robinson, Bt

ROBINSON, Clare Lois; da of (John) Aubrey Robinson, of Portrush, NI, and Shirley Joan, *née* Lynas; *b* 1 March 1963, Larne, NI; *Educ* Belfast HS, Belfast Royal Acad, Univ of Bristol (LLB), Chester Law Sch; *m* 14 May 1994, Patrick McDonnell; 2 s (William Patrick b 7 Dec 1996, James Aubrey b 12 Feb 1998), 1 da (Megan Shirley b 19 Jan 2001); *Career* Osborne Clarke: slr 1987–, ptnr 1992–, head Litigation Dept 1999–2004; ADR Gp accredited mediator 2005–; memb Law Soc 1987–; *Recreations* reading, sport; *Style*— Ms Clare Robinson; ✉ Osborne Clarke, 2 Temple Back East, Temple Quay, Bristol BS1 6EG (tel 0117 917 4022, fax 0117 917 4023, email clare.robinson@osborneclarke.com)

ROBINSON, Prof Colin; s of James Robinson (d 1937), of Stretford, Lancs, and Elsie, *née* Brownhill (d 1959); *b* 7 September 1932; *Educ* Stretford GS, Univ of Manchester (BA); *m* 1, 13 July 1957 (m dis 1983), Olga, da of Harry West; 2 s (Julian b 1961, Stewart b 1964); m 2, 18 June 1983, Eileen Catherine, *née* Marshall; 2 s (Richard b 1966, Christopher b 1971), 2 da (Louise b 1967, Elaine b 1969); *Career* RAF 1950–53; head Economics Div Corp Planning Dept Esso Petroleum 1960–66, econ advsr natural gas Esso Europe 1966–68, prof of economics Univ of Surrey 1968–; editorial dir Inst of Econ Affrs 1992–2002; Br Inst of Energy Economists' Economist of the Year 1992; tstee Wincott Fndn; Int Assoc of Energy Economics' Outstanding Contrib to the Profession Award 1998; FSS 1969, FInstPet 1979, fell Soc of Business Economists 2000; *Books* Business Forecasting (1970), North Sea Oil in the Future (1977), The Economics of Energy Self Sufficiency (1984), Can Coal Be Saved? (1985), Energy Policy: Errors, Illusions and Market Realities (1993); *Recreations* walking, music, home improvements; *Style*— Prof Colin Robinson; ✉ Department of Economics, University of Surrey, Guildford, Surrey GU2 5XH (tel 01483 259171, e-mail colin@gunnersbury.freeserve.co.uk)

ROBINSON, Prof Daniel Nicholas; s of Henry S Robinson (d 1962), and Margaret, *née* Peters (d 1956); *b* 9 March 1937, NY; *Educ* Colgate Univ (BA), Hofstra Univ (MA), City Univ of NY (PhD); *m* 18 Sept 1967, Francine, *née* Malasko; *Career* Columbia Univ: res psychologist 1960–65, asst dir Sci Honors Program 1964–68, sr res psychologist 1965–68, asst dir of life sciences 1967–68; Amherst Coll MA: asst prof of psychology 1968–70, assoc prof of psychology 1970–71; Univ of Georgetown: assoc prof of psychology 1971–74, chm Psychology Dept 1973–76 and 1985–91, prof of psychology 1974–97, dir Graduate Program in Psychology 1981–83, adjunct prof of philosophy 1996–98, distinguished res prof 1997–2001, distinguished res prof emeritus 2001–; Philosophy Faculty fell Univ of Oxford 2002–, fell Oriel Coll Oxford 2002; visiting lectr in psychology Princeton Univ 1965–68, visiting prof Folger Shakespeare Inst 1977, visiting sr memb Linacre Coll Oxford 1990–, visiting lectr in philosophy Univ of Oxford 1991–99, visiting prof of psychology Princeton Univ 2001–02, visiting prof of psychology Columbia Univ 2002–05; memb Bd of Consulting Scholars James Madison Program in American Ideals & Instns Princeton Univ 2001–; involvement with: Nat Sci Fndn 1965–75, Nat Insts of Health 1967–70, Public Broadcasting System (for The Brain series 1978–84 and PBS and BBC for The Mind series 1985–88), Attorney Gen's Task Force on Crime 1980, MacArthur Fndn 1985, Dept of Health and Human Services Special Panel on Fetal Tissue Transplant Research 1988, Dept of Health and Human Services Sec's Advistory Ctee on Genetic Testing 2002; conslt developmental psychology Nat Inst of Mental Health 1997–98; Pres's Medal Colgate Univ 1986, Public Service Award Gen Servs Administration 1986, Lifetime Achievement Award Div of the History of Psychology American Psychology Assoc 2001, Distinguished Contribution Award Div of Theoretical & Philosophical Psychology American Psychology Assoc 2001; memb: Br Philosophical Assoc, American Philosophical Assoc, Soc of Scholars; fell British Psychological Soc 1980–99, fell Divs 3, 24 and 26 American Psychological Assoc (pres: Div 26 (History of Psychology) 1984–85, Div 24 (Theoretical Psychology) 1989–90); *Publications* The Enlightened Machine: An Analytical Introduction to Neuropsychology (1973), An Intellectual History of Psychology (1976), Systems of Modern Psychology: A Critical Sketch (1979), Psychology and Law: Can Justice Survive the Social Sciences? (1980), Toward a Science of Human Nature: Essays on the Psychologies of Hegel, Mill, Wundt and James (1982), Foundations of Psychobiology jtly, 1983), The Wonder of Being Human: Our Mind and Our Brain (jtly, 1984), Philosophy of Psychology (1985), Aristotle's Psychology (1989), An Intellectual History of Psychology (1995), Wild Beasts and Idle Humours: The Insanity Defense from Antiquity to the Present (1996), Praise and Blame: Moral Realism and Its Applications (2002), Consciousness and Mental Life (2007); *Recreations* gardening, writing fiction; *Clubs* Cosmos (Washington DC); *Style*— Prof Daniel Robinson; ✉ 34 Thackley End, Oxford OX2 6LB (tel 01865 556776); Philosophy Centre, University of Oxford, 10 Merton Street, Oxford OX1 4JJ (e-mail dan.robinson@philosophy.ox.ac.uk)

ROBINSON, David Foster; s of Arthur Robinson (d 2000), and Ellen Robinson, *née* Jackson (d 1989); *b* 29 May 1936; *Educ* King's Sch Macclesfield, Univ of Manchester (BA); *m* 5 Nov 1966, Hannah, da of Roger Alan Watson (d 1979), of Edinburgh; 2 s (William b 1968, Edward b 1970), 1 da (Caroline b 1971); *Career* Nat Serv 2 Lt RAPC 1960–62; ptnr Spicer & Oppenheim (formerly Spicer & Pegler) 1974–90 (joined 1962); chm: M M & K Ltd 1991–94, Interscene Ltd 1991–95, Oldham Lighting Ltd 1993–2002, Business Sound Ltd 1997–2000; dir: Identica Ltd 1992–2003, The Ratcliff Group Ltd 1992–2006, Exxtor Group (Holdings) Ltd 1994–99; chm Langford & Ulting PC 1978–, chm Plume Housing Assoc 1994–2004, vice-chm Moat Housing Group 1996–2007; FCA, FCMC; *Books* Human Asset Accounting (1972), Key Definitions in Finance (1980), Managing People (1984), Getting the Best out of People (1988), The Naked Entrepreneur (1990), Business Etiquette (1994); *Recreations* gardening, walking, tennis; *Clubs* City of London, IOD; *Style*— David Robinson, Esq; ✉ Luards, Langford, Maldon, Essex CM9 6QB (tel and fax 01621 859707, e-mail davidrobinson44@btinternet.com)

ROBINSON, David James Roper; s of Andrew Thomas Roper Robinson (d 2006), of Dulwich, London, and Barbara Anne, *née* Black; *b* 19 July 1955; *Educ* Westminster (Queen's scholar), Pembroke Coll Cambridge (fndn exhibitioner, MA); *m* 15 June 1996, Jennifer Jane, da of Sir Alan McLintock (d 2007); 1 s, 2 da; *Career* articled Bennett Welch & Co 1979–81, asst slr Glover & Co 1981–85, ptnr Frere Cholmeley 1989–98 (joined 1985), head Private Client Dept Frere Cholmeley Bischoff 1994–98, fndr ptnr Forsters 1998–; *Recreations* music, art, collecting books, travel; *Style*— David Robinson, Esq; ✉ Forsters, 31 Hill Street, London W1J 5LS (tel 020 7863 8333, fax 020 7863 8444, e-mail djrrobinson@forsters.co.uk)

ROBINSON, (David) Duncan; DL (Cambs 2004); s of Tom Robinson (ka 1944), and Ann Elizabeth, *née* Clarke; *b* 27 June 1943; *Educ* King Edward VI Sch Macclesfield, Clare Coll

R

Cambridge (scholar, MA), Yale Univ (Mellon fellowship, MA); *m* 7 Jan 1967, Elizabeth Anne (Lisa), da of Frederick Totten Sutton (d 1979), of Fairfield, Conn, USA; 2 da (Amanda Jane b 1971, Charlotte Elizabeth b 1989), 1 s (Thomas Edward b 1975); *Career* keeper of paintings and drawings Fitzwilliam Museum Cambridge 1976–81 (asst keeper 1970–76), fell and coll lectr Clare Coll Cambridge 1975–81; dir of studies in history of art Univ of Cambridge until 1981: Churchill, Clare, Lucy Cavendish, Queens' and Sidney Sussex Colls and New Hall; dir Yale Center for British Art New Haven 1981–95, ceo Paul Mellon Centre for Studies in British Art London, adjunct prof of history of art Yale Univ 1981–95, fell Berkeley Coll Yale Univ 1981–95, fell Clare Coll Cambridge 1995–2002, dir Fitzwilliam Museum Cambridge 1995–2007, master Magdalene Coll Cambridge 2002–, dep vice-chllr Univ of Cambridge 2005–; memb: Ctee of Mgmnt Kettle's Yard Univ of Cambridge 1970–81 and 1995–, Ct RCA 1975–78 and 1996–, Art Advsy Panel Arts Council of GB 1978–81 (memb Exhibitions Sub Ctee 1978–79, memb Art Fin Ctee 1979–80, memb Cncl and vice-chm Art Panel 1981), Assoc of Art Museum Dirs 1983–88; elector to Slade Professorship of Fine Art Univ of Cambridge 1978–81 and 1997–, govr Yale Univ Press 1987–95; pres Friends of Stanley Spencer Gallery Cookham 1998–, vice-pres NADFAS 2000–06; memb: Art and Artefacts Indemnity Advsy Panel to Fed Cncl on the Arts and the Humanities 1991–94 (chm 1992–94), Museums and Collections Advsy Ctee English Heritage 1996–2002, Fitzwilliam Museum Tst 1995–2007, Bd of Govrs SE Museums Serv 1997–99, Gainsborough's House Soc 1997–2002, Advsy Cncl Paul Mellon Centre for Studies in Br Art London 1997–2002 and 2005–, AHRB 1998–2003, Wingfield Arts Tst 2001–03, NW Essex Collection Tst 2002–07 (chair 2002–03, hon treas 2003–07), Museum Serv East of England 2001–03, Burlington Magazine Tst 2003–, Royal Collection Tst 2006–; tstee: Yale Univ Press London 1990–, Charleston Tst (USA) 1990–92, American Friends of the Georgian Gp 1992–94, Henry Moore Fndn 2006– (chair 2008–), Prince's Drawing Sch 2007– (chair); public, visiting and pt/t lectr UK and USA; memb Conn Acad of Arts & Scis 1991; FRSA 1990, FSA 2006; *Publications* numerous catalogues, articles and reviews; author of: A Companion Volume to the Kelmscott Chaucer (1975, re-issued as Morris, Burne-Jones and the Kelmscott Chaucer, 1982), Stanley Spencer (1979, revised edn 1990), Man and Measure: the Paintings of Tom Wood (1996), The Yale Center for British Art: A Tribute to the Genius of Louis I Kahn (1997), The Fitzwilliam Museum Cambridge: One Hundred and Fifty Years of Collecting (1998); *Style*— Duncan Robinson, Esq, DL; ✉ The Master's Lodge, Magdalene College, Cambridge CB3 0AG (tel 01223 332144, fax 01223 365150); Hall's Farm, South Windham, Vermont 05359, USA

ROBINSON, Dr Geoffrey Walter; CBE (1998); s of George Robinson (d 1987), of Loughborough, Leics, and Edith Margaret, *née* Wilson (d 1988); *b* 9 November 1945; *Educ* Aireborough GS Leeds, Univ of Nottingham (BSc, PhD); *m* 12 Aug 1967, Edwina, da of Thomas Ernest Jones (d 2003); 1 s (Richard Antony b 13 Oct 1970), 1 da (Catherine Louise b 29 April 1972); *Career* IBM: UK Labs 1969–82, scientific centre mangr 1982–84, tech programmes mangr 1984–85, UK tech dir 1985–86, dir of software devpt 1986–88, dir Hursley Lab 1988–92 and 1994–96, dir of technol 1996–97; DG and chief exec Ordnance Survey 1998–99; chief advsr on science and technol DTI 1992–94, chm Br Geological Survey 2002–04 (memb Bd 2001–05); non-exec dir Pirelli Gen plc 2002–05, Pirelli UK Tyres Ltd 2002–05; memb: Centre for Exploitation of Science and Technol 1986–92, NERC 1992–94, SERC 1992–94, PPARC 1994–98, Cncl for the Central Lab of the Research Cncls 1995–98, Bd Quality Assurance Agency for Higher Educn 1997–2000; ESRC: chm Innovation Research Prog 1994–2000, chm Virtual Soc Research Prog 1996–2000; pres BCS 1995–96, vice-pres IEE 1998–2000, dep chm Fndn for Science & Technol 1998–2000; memb Worshipful Co of Info Technologists 1988, memb Worshipful Co of Scientific Instrument Makers 1996; Hon DTech King Alfred's Coll Winchester (CNAA) 1992, Hon DUniv Leeds Metropolitan Univ 1997; FRSA 1992, FIEE 1993, FREng 1994, FBCS 1994 (MBCS 1988), CIMgt 1999; *Style*— Dr Geoffrey Robinson, CBE, FREng; ✉ Fardale, Hookwood Lane, Ampfield, Romsey, Hampshire SO51 9BZ (tel 023 8025 1112, e-mail gwr@fardale.org)

ROBINSON, Sir Gerrard Jude (Gerry); kt (2004); s of Anthony Robinson (d 1990), and Elizabeth Ann, *née* Stuart; *b* 23 October 1948; *Educ* St Mary's Coll Castle Head; *m* 1, 1969 (m dis 1990), Maria Ann, *née* Borg; 1 da (Samantha Erica b 22 April 1975), 1 s (Richard Steven b 30 Dec 1977); m 2, 1990, Heather Peta, da of Kenneth Arthur Leaman; 1 da (April Heather b 4 May 1991), 1 s (Timothy Gerrard b 23 April 1994); *Career* works accountant Lesney Products Ltd 1965–74, fin controller Lex Industrial Distribution and Hire 1974–80; Coca-Cola: fin dir 1980–81, sales and mktg dir 1981–83, md 1983–84; md Grand Metropolitan Contract Services 1984–87, chief exec Compass Group plc (following buyout from GrandMet) 1987–91; Granada Compass plc (Granada Gp plc until merger with Compass Gp plc 2000): chief exec 1991–96, chm 1996–2001; following demerger non-exec dir Granada plc 2001–03; chm: BSkyB plc 1995–98, Allied Domecq plc 2002–05; fndr Raphoe Management Limited 2005; chm Arts Cncl England 1998–2004; FCMA; *Recreations* golf, opera, chess, skiing, reading, music; *Clubs* Wisley; *Style*— Sir Gerry Robinson

ROBINSON, Helen; OBE; da of Dr John Christopher Wharton (d 1997), and Gertrude Margaret, *née* Dingwall (d 1996); *Educ* Roedean; *m* 1 (m dis 1979), Philip Robinson; m 2, Desmond Preston (d 1995); 1 s (decd), 1 da; *Career* fashion asst, fashion ed and latterly exec ed Vogue Magazine London and New York 1960–75; Debenhams plc: joined 1975, dir Dept Store, mktg and design mgmnt dir (Main Bd) 1981–86; mktg dir Condé Nast Publications Ltd 1986–88, gp md Thomas Goode & Co Ltd 1988–93 (resigned upon sale of co), special projects and mktg full-time consultancy Asprey Gp 1996–98, business consultancy MIA Pty Aust 1998–2000, chief exec New West End Co Ltd 2000–04; non-exec dir: British Airports Authy 1978–84 (memb Chm's Design Ctee 1988–95), London Transport 1984–95, London Electricity 1989–94, Churchill China plc 1996–98; vice-chm Cncl and chm Staff Ctee RCA 1982–2000, tstee RCA Fndn 2000–; memb: Design Mgmnt Advsy Gp London Business Sch 1985–95, Cncl The Cottage Homes (retail trade charity) 1995–96; govr and tstee Cwlth Inst 1994– (memb Exec Ctee 1997–); WWF: tstee 1988–95, chm WWF UK Ltd 1988–95, memb Cncl of Ambassadors 1999–2006, fell 2006–; Sr FRCA, Hon FCSD, FRSA; *Style*— Mrs Helen Robinson, OBE; ✉ 18 Doria Road, London SW6 4UG (tel 020 7736 8814, fax 020 7731 2165)

ROBINSON, Prof Hilary Frances; da of Ivor Robinson, of Oxford, and Olive, *née* Trask; *b* 25 June 1956; *Educ* John Mason HS Abingdon, Univ of Newcastle upon Tyne (BA), RCA (MA, Allen Lane/Penguin Books award), Univ of Leeds (PhD); *m* 1995, Alastair MacLennan; *Career* painted and exhibited 1979–85; freelance writer; tutor Glasgow Sch of Art 1987–92, ed Alba (Scottish visual art magazine) 1990–92; Univ of Ulster at Belfast: lectr in fine art 1992–2002, prof of the politics of art 2002–05, head Sch of Art & Design 2002–05 (research co-ordinator 1999–2002); dean Coll of Fine Arts Carnegie Mellon Univ USA 2005–; author of numerous pubns on feminist art; memb: Assoc of Art Historians 1988, Coll Art Assoc USA 1993, Assoc Int des Critiques d'Art 1996; *Books* Visibly Female (ed, 1987), The Rough Guide to Venice (co-author, 1989, 2 edn 1993), Feminism-Art-Theory 1968–2000 (2001), Reading Art, Reading Irigaray: The politics of art by women (2006); *Style*— Prof Hilary Robinson; ✉ College of Fine Arts, Carnegie Mellon University, 5000 Forbes Avenue, Pittsburgh, PA 15213, USA (tel 00 1 412 726 2615, e-mail hr@cmu.edu)

ROBINSON, Sir Ian; kt (2000); s of Thomas Mottram Robinson (d 1972), and Eva Iris, *née* Bird (d 1984); *b* 3 May 1942; *Educ* Univ of Leeds (BSc), Harvard Univ (SMP); *m* 28 Oct 1967, Kathleen Crawford, da of James Leay, of Edinburgh; 1 s (Andrew John b 1977), 1 da (Caroline Anne b 1973); *Career* Ralph M Parsons Co Ltd: dir of ops 1979, vice-pres (USA) 1983, md 1985; md John Brown Engineering Constructors Ltd 1986–90, chief exec John Brown Engineers & Constructors 1990–92; chm and chief exec John Brown plc 1992–95, chm Engrg Div and main bd dir Trafalgar House plc 1992–95, chief exec Scottish Power plc 1995–2001; chm Scottish Enterprise 2001–03; non-exec chm: Amey plc 2001–03, Hilton Gp plc 2001–06, Ladbrokes plc 2006–; non-exec dir: RMC Gp plc 2000–01, Siemens plc 2003–, Scottish Newcastle plc 2004–, Compass Gp plc 2006–; FIChemE, FREng 1994, FRSE 2003; *Recreations* golf; *Clubs* RAC; *Style*— Sir Ian Robinson, FREng; ✉ Ladbrokes plc, Imperial Drive, Rayners Lane, Harrow HA2 7JW (tel 020 8515 5726)

ROBINSON, Iris; MP, MLA; da of Joseph Collins (d 1957), of Belfast, and Mary McCartney; *b* 6 September 1949; *Educ* Knockbreda Intermediate Sch, Cregagh Tech Coll; *m* 25 July 1970, Rt Hon Peter Robinson, MP, MLA, *qv*, s of late David Robinson; 2 s (Jonathan David Peter b 5 Jan 1973, Gareth Andrew James b 30 Dec 1979), 1 da (Rebekah Louise b 15 May 1982); *Career* cncllr Castlereagh BC 1989–, MLA 1998–, MP (DUP) Strangford 2001–; Mayor of Castlereagh 1992, 1995 and 2000; fundraiser for Multiple Sclerosis charities; *Recreations* interior design; *Style*— Mrs Iris Robinson, MP, MLA; ✉ 12 North Street, Newtownards BT23 4DE (tel 028 9182 7701, fax 028 9182 7703, e-mail iris.robinson@ukgateway.net); House of Commons, London SW1A 0AA; Northern Ireland Assembly, Parliament Buildings, Stormont Estate, Belfast BT4 3XX

ROBINSON, Jancis Mary (Mrs N L Lander); OBE (2003); da of Thomas Edward Robinson (d 2000), of Eden House, Kirkandrews-on-Eden, Cumbria, and Ann, *née* Conacher; *b* 22 April 1950; *Educ* Carlisle HS, St Anne's Coll Oxford (MA); *m* 22 Oct 1981, Nicholas Laurence Lander, s of Israel Lennard Lander; 2 da (Julia Margaux b 10 July 1982, Rose Ellen b 6 March 1991), 1 s (William Isaac b 5 Sept 1984); *Career* early career experience: mktg and producing skiing holidays for Thomson Holidays 1971–74, undertaking odd jobs while writing for Good Food Guide 1975; asst ed then ed Wine and Spirit 1975–80, fndr Drinker's Digest 1977 (became Which? Wine Monthly 1980), ed Which? Wine Monthly and Which? Wine Annual Guide 1980–82, Sunday Times 1980–86 (wine corr, food corr, gen features); wine corr: The Evening Standard 1987–88, Financial Times 1989–, www.jancisrobinson.com 2001–; presenter and writer The Wine Programme (1983, 1985 and 1987), presenter Jancis Robinson's Christmas Wine List 1985, presenter BBC Design Awards 1986–87, narrator Design Classics 1987; presenter and writer: Jancis Robinson Meets 1987, Matters of Taste 1989 and 1991, Vintners' Tales 1993 and 1998 (Glenfiddich Award), Grape Expectations (US) 1994 and 1995, Jancis Robinson's Wine Course 1995, The Food Chain 1996 and 1998, Taste 1999; dir Eden Productions Ltd; wine conslt British Airways; Glenfiddich Awards: Best Book on Wine (The Great Wine Book) 1983, Broadcaster of the Year and Glenfiddich Trophy 1984, Wine Writer 1986, Food Writer 1986, Best Book on Wine (The Oxford Companion to Wine) 1995, Drink Writer of the Year and Glenfiddich Trophy 1996, TV Personality of the Year 1999; winner: Marques de Caceres Award 1985, Wine Guild of UK Premier Award 1986 and 1996, André Simon Meml Award 1987 and 1995, Wine Guild Award for Reference Book 1987, Clicquot Book of the Year (Vines, Grapes and Wines) 1987 and (The Oxford Companion to Wine) 1995, Silver Medal German Academy of Gastronomy 1988 and Gold Medal 1996, Decanter Magazine's (Wo)man of the Year 1999; memb Inst of Masters of Wine 1984; Jurade de St Emilion, Commanderie de Bontemps de Médoc et Graves; Hon DUniv Open Univ 1997; *Books* The Wine Book (1979), The Great Wine Book (1982), Masterglass (1983), How to Choose and Enjoy Wine (1984), Vines, Grapes and Wines (1986), Jancis Robinson's Food and Wine Adventures (1987), Jancis Robinson on The Demon Drink (1988), Vintage Timecharts (1989), The Oxford Companion to Wine (ed, 1994, 1999 and 2006), Jancis Robinson's Wine Course (1995 and 2003), Jancis Robinson's Guide to Wine Grapes (1996), Confessions of a Wine Lover (1997), Jancis Robinson's Wine Tasting Workbook (2000), The Oxford Companion to the Wines of North America (conslt ed, 2000), Jancis Robinson's Concise Wine Companion (2001), The World Atlas of Wine (5 edn with Hugh Johnson, 2001, 6 edn 2007); *Style*— Ms Jancis Robinson, OBE; ✉ website www.jancisrobinson.com

ROBINSON, Prof (Jenifer Ann) Jane; da of Reginald Milton London (d 1964), of Birmingham, and Florence, *née* Troop (d 1946); *b* 6 November 1935; *Educ* King Edward VI HS for Girls, Keele Univ (RHV, MA, PhD), N Staffs Poly (CIPD), Wolverhampton Poly (CertEd HVT); *m* 6 Feb 1959, Anthony David Robinson (d 2003), s of Alfred Anthony Robinson; 3 da (Ann Louise (Mrs Sutcliffe) b 3 Dec 1959, Felicity Jane (Mrs Wood) b 26 March 1962, Kathryn Mary (Mrs Roodner) b 21 April 1964); *Career* nursing educn and trg: The Royal Orthopaedic Hosp Birmingham (ONC) and The Queen Elizabeth Hosp Birmingham (RGN) 1952–57, Southmead Hosp Bristol (CMB Part 1) 1958–59; theatre sister Winford Orthopaedic Hosp Bristol 1957–58; staff nurse: Bristol Homeopathic Hosp 1959, North Staffs Royal Infirmary 1968–69; health visitor/school nurse: Staffs CC 1970–74, Staffs Area HA 1977–80 (nursing offr 1974–77); lectr in health visiting Wolverhampton Poly 1980–81, res offr Med Dept Sandwell HA 1981–83, lectr in health visiting Wolverhampton Poly 1983–84, dir Nursing Policy Studies Centre Univ of Warwick 1985–89, prof and head Dept of Nursing and Midwifery Studies Univ of Nottingham 1989–97 (emeritus 1997–), ind health workforce conslt 1997–, short term conslt The World Bank 2000; Fulbright sr research scholarship 1996; advsr to WHO 1985–96; chair: Nursing Research Ctee Trent RHA 1989–92, Women's Issues Sub-Ctee RCN 1995–98 (memb Health and Social Policy Ctee 1991–92); appointed by Sec of State to UK Central Cncl for Nursing Midwifery and Health Visiting 1993–96; RCN rep: Women's Nat Cmmn 1995–98, Working Gp Euro Nurse Researchers 1997–98; memb Local Research Ethics Ctee N Staffs HA 2003–; ed: Jl of Advanced Nursing 1997–2002, Int Nursing Review 2003–; memb Sigma Theta Tan Int (USA Honor Soc in Nursing) 1997–2002; MCIPD 1988, FRCN 1994; *Publications* An Evaluation of Health Visiting (1982), The NHS Under New Management (1990), Policy Issues in Nursing (1992), Nursing Beyond 2000 (contrib, 1994), Nurses Manage (1995), Health Needs Assessment (1996), Interdisciplinary Perspectives on Health Policy and Practice (1999); ed-in-chief Jl of Advanced Nursing (JAN) 2001– (ed 1997–2001); author of numerous articles and chapters in medical books; *Recreations* family pursuits with seven grandchildren, travel, bridge; *Clubs* Univ Women's; *Style*— Prof Jane Robinson; ✉ 78A Dartmouth Avenue, Newcastle, Staffordshire ST5 3PA (tel 01782 611266, e-mail jane.engine@ntlworld.com)

ROBINSON, Jason; MBE (2004); *b* 30 July 1974, Leeds; *Educ* Matthew Murray HS Leeds; *Career* rugby league and rugby union player; *Rugby League* with Wigan Warriors RLFC until 2000; represented GB (12 caps, scored tries in six successive GB test matches (jt record holder)) and England (7 caps); scored 184 tries in 302 rugby league games; *Rugby Union* with Sale Sharks RUFC 2000–07 (sometime capt, winners European Challenge Cup 2005 and Premiership 2006); England: 47 caps, capt 2004–05, debut v Italy 2001, winners Six Nations Championship 2001 and 2003 (Grand Slam 2003), ranked no 1 team in world 2003, winners World Cup Aust 2003, memb squad World Cup 2007; memb squad Br & I Lions tour to Aust 2001 and NZ 2005; *Style*— Jason Robinson, Esq, MBE

ROBINSON, Prof John; s of William Clifford Robinson (d 1982), and Annie, *née* Banks; *b* 11 July 1933; *Educ* Little Lever Secondary Sch, Radcliffe Jr Tech Coll, Salford Univ (BSc), Cranfield Univ (MSc), Inst of Sound and Vibration Res Univ of Southampton (PhD), Faculty of Engrg Sci and Mathematics Univ of Southampton (DSc); *m* 1, 3 Aug 1957 (m dis 1980), Cynthia, da of late Eric Nicholls; 2 s (Gary Edward b 16 Aug 1958, Lee John b 16 May 1961); m 2, 12 Sept 1984, Shirley Ann (decd), da of Roland Walter Bradley, of Bidford-on-Avon, Warks; *Career* Br and USA Aerospace Industry 1949–71, head

Robinson and Associates 1971–1995; conslt organiser World Congress and Exhibition on Finite Element Methods 1975–1995 (ed and publisher World Congress Proceedings 1975–1995), ed and publisher Finite Element News 1976–1995, lectr of worldwide courses on Understanding Finite Element Stress Analysis 1980–1995, fndr and memb Steering Ctee Nat Agency for Finite Element Methods and Standards 1983–1995, dir Robinson FEMInst 1986–1995, industrial res prof Univ of Exeter 1986–1995; composer and lyricist; fndr GBM Prodns; prodr (own musicals): Lorna Doone 1992, Shipperbottom's Rocking Horses 1994, Behind the Iron Mask (Duchess Theatre London) 2005; prodr (own ballets, in Vienna): The World of Bidlake Wood 1998, Alice Through the Looking Glass 2001; MRAeS 1962, MIMechE 1964, CEng; *Books* Structural Matrix Analysis for the Engineer (1966), Integrated Theory of Finite Element Methods (1973), Understanding Finite Element Stress Analysis (1981), Early FEM Pioneers (1985), articles; *Style*— Prof John Robinson

ROBINSON, John Harris; *b* 22 December 1940; *Educ* Woodhouse Grove Sch, Univ of Birmingham (BSc); *m* 2 March 1963, Doreen Alice; 1 s (Mark John b 9 March 1965), 1 da (Karen Claire b 1 Nov 1968); *Career* ICI 1962–65, Fisons 1965–70, sr conslt PA Consulting Group 1970–75, chief exec Woodhouse & Rixon (Holdings) 1975–79; Smith & Nephew plc: md Smith & Nephew Medical 1979–85, gp dir UK and Europe 1985–90, gp chief exec 1990–97, chm 1997–2000; chm: Low & Bonar plc 1997–2001, UK Coal (formerly RJB Mining plc) 1997–2003, George Wimpey plc 1999–2007, Railtrack Gp plc 2001–02, Paragon Healthcare Gp Ltd 2002–06, Bespak plc 2004–, Affinity Healthcare Ltd 2005–; non-exec dir Delta plc 1993–2001, operating ptnr Duke Street Capital 2001–; pres: IChemE 1999–2000, Chartered Inst of Mgmnt 2002–03; memb Industrial Devpt Advsy Bd DTI 1998–2000; pro-chllr and chm Cncl Univ of Hull 1998–2006; govr: Hymers Coll Hull 1984–, Woodhouse Grove Sch 2004–; Hon DEng Univ of Birmingham 2000, Hon DUniv Bradford 2000, Hon DBA Univ of Lincoln 2002, Hon DSc Univ of Hull 2006; memb Ct of Assts Worshipful Co of Engrs 2006 (Jr Warden 2007); CEng, FIChemE, CIMgt, FREng 1998; *Recreations* golf, cricket, walking; *Clubs* Athenaeum; *Style*— John Robinson, Esq; ✉ 146 Artillary Mansions, Victoria Street, London SW1H 0HX

ROBINSON, Sir John James Michael Laud; 11 Bt (E 1660), of London, DL (Northants); s of Michael Frederick Laud Robinson (d 1971), and Elizabeth Bridge (d 1977); suc gf, Maj Sir Frederick Robinson, 10 Bt, MC (d 1975, descended from Sir John Robinson, 1 Bt, Lord Mayor of London 1662–63 and s of Ven William Robinson, sometime Archdeacon of Nottingham and half-bro of Archbishop Laud); *b* 19 January 1943; *Educ* Eton, TCD (MA); *m* 1968, (Kathryn) Gayle Elizabeth (High Sheriff Northants 2001), da of Stuart Nelson Keyes, of Orillia, Ontario; 2 s, 1 da; *Heir* s, Mark Robinson; *Career* chartered fin analyst; landowner; chm: St Andrew's Hosp Northampton 1982–93, Northampton Gen Hosp NHS Tst 1994–98; *Style*— Sir John Robinson, Bt, DL; ✉ Cranford Hall, Cranford, Kettering, Northamptonshire NN14 4AL

ROBINSON, Prof John Joseph; s of James Reid Robinson (d 1983), and Elizabeth Mary, *née* Ennis (d 1985); *b* 11 June 1940; *Educ* Down HS Downpatrick, Queen's Univ Belfast (BAgr, PhD); *m* 26 Sept 1967, Margaret, da of Samuel James Magill; 1 da (Lyn Elizabeth b 29 Dec 1972), 1 s (Andrew James b 11 July 1974); *Career* postdoctoral research fell Queen's Univ Belfast 1966–67, ARC postdoctoral researcher Wye Coll London 1967–68; Rowett Research Inst Bucksburn Aberdeen: sr scientific offr 1968–73, principal scientific offr 1973–83, sr principal scientific offr (individual merit) 1983–94; Scottish Agric Coll Aberdeen: sr scientist in animal reproduction 1994–98, prof of animal reproduction 1998–; pres British Soc of Animal Science 1993–94; Fish Meal Manufacturers' Annual Research Award 1979, Research Medal RASE 1982, Sir John Hammond Meml Prize British Soc of Animal Production 1984, Sir William Young Award Royal Highland Agric Soc of Scotland 1989, George Hedley Meml Award Nat Sheep Assoc 1991; FRSE 1996; *Publications* author and co-author of over 400 publications incl refereed scientific papers, invited scientific reviews, book chapters and technical bulletins; *Recreations* gardening, club rambling; *Style*— Prof John Robinson, FRSE; ✉ 4 Hopecroft Terrace, Bucksburn, Aberdeen AB21 9RL; Scottish Agricultural College, The Ferguson Building, Craibstone Estate, Bucksburn, Aberdeen AB21 9YA (tel 01224 711052, fax 01224 711292, e-mail john.robinson@sac.ac.uk)

ROBINSON, John Martin; s of John Cotton Robinson, and Ellen Anne Cecilia (d 2003), eld da of George Adams, of Cape Town, South Africa; *b* 10 September 1948; *Educ* Fort Augustus Abbey, St Andrews, Oriel Coll Oxford (MA, DPhil, DLitt); *Career* librarian to Duke of Norfolk 1978–; ptnr Historic Bldgs Conslts; architectural writer Country Life 1974–; vice-chm Georgian Gp; Maltravers Herald of Arms Extraordinary 1989–; heraldic advsr to Nat Tst; chm Ctee Art and Architecture Westminster Cathedral 1996–; tstee Abbot Hall Art Gallery 1993–; FSA; Knight SMOM; *Books* The Wyatts (1980), Dukes of Norfolk (1983, 2 edn 1995), Georgian Model Farms (1983), Latest Country Houses (1984), Cardinal Consalvi (1987), Oxford Guide to Heraldry (jtly with Thomas Woodcock, 1988, 3 edn 2001), Temples of Delight (1990), Country Houses of the North West (1991), Treasures of The English Churches (1995), Windsor Castle (1996), Francis Johnson Architect (jtly with David Neve, 2001), The Staffords (2002), The Regency Country House (2005), Grass Seed in June (2006); *Clubs* Travellers, Roxburghe, Pitt, XV, Beefsteak, Pratt's; *Style*— John Robinson, Esq, FSA, Maltravers Herald of Arms Extraordinary; ✉ Beckside House, Barbon, via Carnforth, Lancashire LA6 2LT (tel 01524 276300, office 020 7831 4398, fax 020 7831 8831, e-mail mentmore@historical-buildings.co.uk)

ROBINSON, Sir Kenneth (Ken); kt (2003); s of James Robinson (d 1977), of Liverpool, and Ethel, *née* Allen (d 2005); *b* 4 March 1950; *Educ* Liverpool Collegiate GS, Wade Deacon GS, Bretton Hall Coll, Univ of Leeds (BEd), Univ of London (PhD); *m* 30 Jan 1982, Marie-Thérèse, da of Frederick George Watts, of Liverpool; 1 s (James b 11 Oct 1984), 1 da (Katherine Marie b 4 May 1989); *Career* educationist; dir Nat Curriculum Cncl Arts in Schools project 1985–89, prof of arts educn Univ of Warwick 1989–2000 (prof emeritus 2001–); chm Nat Advsy Ctee on Creative and Cultural Educn 1998–99; dir Culture, Creativity and the Young Cncl of Europe project; sr advsr to the pres J Paul Getty Tst LA 2000–06; European Business Speaker of the Year 2000; FRSA; *Books* Learning Through Drama (1977), Exploring Theatre and Education (ed, 1980), The Arts in Schools (princ author, 1982), The Arts and Higher Education (ed, 1983), The Arts 5–16 (1990), Arts Education in Europe (1997), All Our Futures: Creativity, Culture and Education (1999), Out of Our Minds: Learning to Be Creative (2001); *Recreations* theatre, music, cinema; *Style*— Sir Ken Robinson; ✉ 2803 Colorado Avenue, Santa Monica, CA 90404, USA

ROBINSON, Mark Nicholas; s of late Eric Robinson, of Leigh on Sea, Essex, and Kate Emily Robinson; *b* 24 January 1952; *Educ* Westcliff GS for Boys, Univ of Dundee (MA, vice-pres Students' Union); *m* 4 June 1976, Patricia Margaret, da of John Malone; 2 s (Matthew John b 31 July 1981, Rory Patrick b 20 Aug 1985), 1 da (Chloe Elizabeth b 16 Nov 1983); *Career* salesman Thomson Regional Newspapers 1975–76, Allardyce Advertising 1976–77, account exec Manton Woodyer Ketley 1977–78, account dir CDP/Aspect Advertising 1981–85 (account mangr 1978–81), dir Ted Bates 1985–87; business devpt dir: Dorland Advertising 1987–88, Horner Collis & Kirvan 1988–92, GGK 1992–93, Publicis 1993–97; mktg dir J Walter Thompson 1997–2001, md Miracle Media Gp 2001–2002, ceo Beatwax Communications 2002–05, worldwide head of mktg Vizeum 2005–; fndr and dir Radio Feltham 1994–, dir Prison Radio Assoc 2006–; dir Devpt Bd Royal Court Theatre 2000–, head London Advsy Gp Common Purpose 2004–; IPA: chm IPA Soc 1987–88, memb various ctees incl Devpt and Trg Ctee; chm NABS 1998–2000; FIPA 1991; *Recreations* cycling, films (fndr memb St Margarets Film Club); *Style*— Mark Robinson, Esq

ROBINSON, Mark Noel Foster; s of John Foster Robinson, CBE, DL (d 1988), and Margaret Eva Hannah, *née* Paterson (d 1977); *b* 26 December 1946; *Educ* Harrow, ChCh Oxford (MA); *m* 1982, Vivien Radclyffe, da of Alan Roger Douglas Pilkington (d 1968); 1 s (James b 1986), 1 da (Alice b 1983); *Career* called to the Bar Middle Temple 1975; UN Office 1972–77, exec office of UN Sec Gen as second offr 1975–77, asst dir Dip Staff Cwlth Secretariat 1977–83; MP (Cons): Newport W 1983–87, Somerton and Frome 1992–97; PPS to Rt Hon Nicholas Edwards as Sec of State for Wales 1984–85, Parly under sec of state Welsh Office 1985–87, PPS to Rt Hon Baroness Chalker as Min for Overseas Devpt FCO and to Parly Under Sec of State FCO 1992–94, PPS to Rt Hon Douglas Hurd as Sec of State for Foreign and Commonwealth Affairs 1994–95, PPS to Rt Hon William Waldegrave as Chief Sec to the Treasy until 1997; exec chair Cncl for Educn in the Commonwealth 1999–; dir: Leopold Joseph & Sons Ltd 1988–91 (non-exec 1991–94), Leopold Joseph Holdings plc 1994–95; exec dir Cwlth Press Union 1997–; memb Bd Cwlth Devpt Corp 1988–92; fell Indust and Parl Tst; memb Cncl Winston Churchill Meml Tst 1993; memb: RIIA, RUSI; FIMgt, FRSA; *Recreations* fishing, country pursuits; *Clubs* Travellers, Pratt's, Brooks's; *Style*— Mark Robinson, Esq

ROBINSON, (Anthony) Martin; s of Bryan Robinson, of Leeds, and Vera, *née* Gill; *b* 28 June 1962, Bradford; *Educ* Keble Coll Oxford (MA); *m* 18 May 1991, Helen Claire, *née* Howes; 1 s (Sam b 15 May 1996), 1 da (Katie b 25 March 1999); *Career* trainee Reckitt & Colman 1984–86, sales and mktg mangr then gen mangr Sara Lee Corporation 1986–90, engagement mangr McKinsey & Co Inc 1990–94, commercial dir Scottish & Newcastle 1994–97; Center Parcs: md European business 1997–99, chm Bd of Mgmnt 1999–2001, led MBO 2001, chm Europe 2001–04, chm Center Parcs (UK) Gp plc 2001–; chm Holmes Place 2006–; non-exec dir Regus plc, memb Supervisory Bd Disneyland Paris; *Recreations* skiing, keep fit, music, cars; *Style*— Martin Robinson, Esq

ROBINSON, Neil; s of Arthur Robinson, of Liverpool, and Margery Robinson (d 1989); *b* 25 April 1958; *Educ* Anfield Comp Sch Liverpool; *m* 1988, Susan Elizabeth, da of late John Carr Campbell FRCS; 1 s (Struan Campbell b 3 Oct 1994); *Career* journalist: S Yorkshire Times 1976, Evening Chronicle Newcastle 1979, Border Television 1986; Border Television: head of news and current affairs 1989, controller of programmes 1991, dir of programmes 2000; dir Cumbria Inward Invest Agency Ltd 1997–; Euro bd memb Co-operative International de la Recherche et d'Actions en Metiere de Communication 1998–; memb: Northern Production Fund Panel Northern Arts 1993–, Television Soc 1988, BAFTA Scot Ctee 1998–; FRSA 1995; *Clubs* Groucho; *Style*— Neil Robinson, Esq; ✉ Fayrefield, High Bank Hill, Kirkoswald, Cumbria

ROBINSON, Nicholas; s of Samuel Robinson (d 1987), and Sarah, *née* McCloy; *b* 7 November 1948; *Educ* The HS Greenock, Univ of Glasgow; *m* 15 April 1971, Elizabeth, da of Donald Campbell Service; 3 s (Gary b 16 Sept 1971, Graeme Campbell b 21 March 1974, Gordon Douglas b 15 July 1976); *Career* apprentice CA Wylie & Bisset CA's 1967–73, accountant then fin dir TAB Ltd 1973–76, accountant Fleming & Wilson CA's 1976–78, British National Oil Corporation 1978–79, fndr own practice 1979 (merged with Kidsons Impey 1982, now HLB Kidsons), currently dir of business devpt and North region managing ptnr HLB Kidsons; regular contrib to Business Press; MICAS 1973; *Recreations* motor cruising, golf, music; *Clubs* St James' (Manchester); *Style*— Nicholas Robinson, Esq

ROBINSON, Nicholas Ridley; s of late Capt Leslie Jack Robinson, JP, and late Eileen Mary, *née* Phillips; *b* 2 September 1952; *Educ* Dulwich Coll; *m* 1, 26 May 1976 (m dis 1980), Vivienne; m 2, 13 Sept 1980, Joanna Mary, da of late Wilford Henry Gibson, CBE, of Sanderstead, Surrey; 2 s (Stuart Laurence Ridley b 9 May 1984, Duncan Henry b 18 Aug 1987), 1 da (Felicity Mary b 1 April 1990); *Career* admitted slr 1977; sr ptnr Sandom Robinson 1988– (ptnr 1978–); co sec The Isthmian Football League Ltd; vice-chair Br Home and Hosp for Incurables 1996–; Freeman: City of London, Worshipful Co of Slrs, Worshipful Co of Farriers; memb Law Soc 1977, FCIArb 1993, Kent Soc of RFU Referees 1997; *Recreations* horse racing, soccer and Rugby Union; *Clubs* RAC; *Style*— Nicholas Robinson, Esq; ✉ Triumph House, Station Approach, Sanderstead Road, South Croydon CR2 0PL (tel 020 8651 5053, fax 020 8651 7029); home fax 020 8409 1979, e-mail nickrob@clara.net

ROBINSON, Nick; s of John Robinson, and Barbara Robinson; *b* 7 April 1947; *Educ* Wadham Coll Oxford (open scholar, MA); *m* 1985, Janice; 1 da (Elisabeth b 23 Nov 1988); *Career* dir Hicks Oubridge Public Affairs Ltd 1970–72, PR mangr Cooperative Wholesale Society 1972–74, PR mangr Manpower Ltd 1974–79, chm Datanews Ltd 1979–90, hon chm The Marketing Guild 1990–; hon ed Strategic Marketing magazine, fndr faculty dir in PR Inst of Mktg 1982–84; memb Br Assoc of Industrial Editors 1976, MIPR 1984; *Books* The Marketing Toolkit (1988), Persuasive Business Presentations (1989), Strategic Customer Care (1991); *Style*— Nick Robinson, Esq

ROBINSON, Paul; s of Harold George Robert Robinson (d 1995), and Sonja Diana, *née* Lapthorn, of Camberley, Surrey; *b* 31 December 1956; *Educ* Camberley GS, Magdalene Coll Cambridge, Univ of Manchester (BSc), MBA (Bradford) 1996; *m* 11 June 1983, Gillian, *née* Whitton; 2 s (Mathew Joseph b 22 May 1987, Joshua James b 2 Jan 1995); *Career* presenter ILR 1970s, gp prog dir Chiltern Radio Network 1980s (successfully relaunched Galaxy as a dance station); BBC Radio 1991–96: managing ed (latterly md and dep controller) Radio 1 1991–95, head of strategy and devpt responsible for new product devpt of Radios 1, 2, 3, 4 and 5 Live 1995–96; md Talk Radio 1996–98; vice-pres and md Disney Channel UK 1998–2004, sr vice-pres and md Walt Disney TV Int/Disney ABC Cable Networks Gp 2001–04; pioneered introduction of the selector computer music scheduling system into the BBC; judge: Sony Awards, BAFTA Awards; vice-pres Macmillan Nurses, sch govr Kempston Rural; memb Radio Acad 1986; MIMgt 1985; *Recreations* swimming, walking, gardening; *Style*— Paul Robinson, Esq

ROBINSON, Paul; *b* 15 October 1979, Beverley, Yorks; *Career* professional footballer; clubs: Leeds United 1996–2004 (first team debut 1998), Tottenham Hotspur 2004–; England: 38 caps, debut v Australia 2003, memb squad European Championship 2004 and World Cup 2006; *Style*— Mr Paul Robinson; ✉ c/o Tottenham Hotspur Football Club, White Hart Lane, 748 High Road, London N17 0AP

ROBINSON, Air Vice Marshal Paul Anthony; OBE (1994); s of Sqdn Ldr Frank Anthony Robinson, DFC (d 1998), and Eira, *née* Buckland-Jones; *b* 8 August 1949; *Educ* Peter Symonds' Sch Winchester, RAF Coll Cranwell, RAF Staff Coll Bracknell; *m* Sept 1971, Sarah Elizabeth Wood; 1 s (Tom b 1973), 1 da (Mary b 1975); *Career* cmmnd 1970; pilot 4 Sqdn (Harrier) RAF Wildenrath/Gütersloh Germany 1973–76; RAF Valley: instr Pilot 4 Flying Trg Sch 1978–81, Sqdn Cdr 1981, dep chief instr 1982; Flight Cdr 4 Sqdn RAF Gütersloh Germany 1983–85, Staff Offr MOD OR(Air) London 1986–88, OC 233 OCU (Harrier) RAF Wittering 1989–92, Wing Cdr Offensive Support HQ 1 Gp RAF Upavon/Benson (dir AOCC Kiseljak Bosnia) 1992–94, Gp Capt Air HQ 2 Gp Rheindalen Germany (Cdr Br Forces Op JURAL Saudi Arabia) 1994–96, Station Cdr RAF Coll Cranwell 1996–98, COS HQ Br Forces Cyprus 1998–2000, Cmdt Central Flying Sch 2000–02, Dep Chief Jt Ops (Ops Support) 2002–04; dir Buckland Defence Servs 2004; qualified flying instr A2 category 1979; UN Bosnia Medal 1993, GSM (Air Ops Iraq) 1995; Liveryman Guild of Air Pilots and Air Navigators; FRAeS; *Recreations* dinghy sailing, fishing, shooting, golf, history and archaeology; *Clubs* RAF; *Style*— Air Vice Marshal P A Robinson, OBE, FRAeS, RAF; ✉ tel 01400 272403, e-mail ser.par@btinternet.com)

R

ROBINSON, Dr Paul Hyman; s of Maurice Isaac Robinson, of Finchley, London, and Stella Robinson, *née* Hymanson; *b* 14 February 1950; *Educ* Haberdashers' Aske's, UCH Med Sch London (BSc, MB BS), Univ of London (MD); *m* 1, 29 July 1974 (m dis 1992), Susan Deborah, da of Joseph Saffer, of Bournemouth, Dorset; 2 da (Jessica b 1979, Zoë b 1988), 2 s (Matthew b 1981, Daniel b 1986); m 2, 11 April 1998, Sonja, da of Liselotte Wilberg; *Career* jr hosp doctor UCH, Whittington Hosp and Nat Hosp Queen Sq 1975–80, trainee psychiatrist Bethlem Royal and Maudsley Hosps 1980–86, sr lectr and consIt psychiatrist KCH and Maudsley Hosp 1986–90, consIt psychiatrist Gordon and Westminster Hosps and head Eating Disorders Unit Gordon Hosp 1990–96; Royal Free Hosp: consIt psychiatrist 1997–, head Eating Disorders Service; hon sr lectr Royal Free and UC Sch of Med; numerous pubns on anorexia nervosa, bulimia nervosa, gastric function and biology of cholecystokinin; assoc memb Inst Family Therapy 1988; FRSM 1983, FRCPsych 1995 (MRCPsych 1982), FRCP 2001 (MRCP 1977); *Books* Community Treatment of Eating Disorders (2006); *Style*— Dr Paul Robinson; ✉ tel 020 7830 2295, fax 020 7830 2876, e-mail paulhrobinson@hotmail.com

ROBINSON, Prof (William) Peter; s of John Robinson (d 1955), of Chichester, W Sussex, and Winifred Jenny, *née* Napper (d 1975); *b* 8 May 1933; *Educ* Christ's Hosp, BNC Oxford (MA, DPhil); *m* 21 Sept 1973, Elizabeth Joan, da of Peter Peill (d 1973), of Duffield, Derbys; 2 da (Katherine b 1975, Clare b 1977); *Career* Intelligence Corps 1 Lt 1952–54; lectr in psychology Univ of Hull 1961–65, sr res offr Inst of Educn Univ of London 1965–66, reader in psychology Univ of Southampton 1966–73, prof of educn Macquarie Univ Aust 1974–77; Univ of Bristol: prof of educn, dir Overseas Studies Centre, and dean of faculty 1977–88, prof of social psychology 1988–98, sr res fell 1998–, Leverhulme sr res fell Univ of Bristol 1999–; pres Int Assoc of Language and Social Psychology 1997–2000; former memb: Econ and Social Res Cncl, Psychology Ctee Educn and Human Devpt Ctee; former tstee Coll of St Paul and St Mary Cheltenham, vice-chm Redmaids Sch Bristol, tstee Bristol Municipal Charities; hon prof Inst Superior de Psicologia Aplicada Lisbon; fell Aust Psychological Soc 1975–81; FBPsS 1972; *Books* Language and Social Behaviour (1972), A Question of Answers (1972), Language Management in Education (1978), Communication in Development (1981), Handbook of Language and Social Psychology (1990, revised edn 2001), Deception, Delusion and Detection (1996), Language in Social Worlds (2002), Arguing to Better Conclusions (2006); *Recreations* badminton, travel; *Style*— Prof Peter Robinson; ✉ Department of Psychology, University of Bristol, Bristol BS8 1TN (fax 0117 928 8588, e-mail p.robinson@bristol.ac.uk)

ROBINSON, Rt Hon Peter David; PC (2007), MP, MLA; s of David and Sheliah Robinson; *b* 29 December 1948; *Educ* Annadale GS, Castlereagh Coll of Further Educn; *m* 1970, Iris Robinson, *qv*, *née* Collins; 2 s, 1 da; *Career* MP (DUP) Belfast E 1979–, memb NI Assembly 1982–86; gen sec DUP 1975–79, dep ldr DUP 1980– (resigned 1987, re-elected 1988); memb: NI Forum 1996–98, NI Assembly 1998–; min for Regnl Devpt NI Assembly 2000–; alderman Castlereagh Boro Cncl 1977–; *Style*— The Rt Hon Peter Robinson, MP, MLA; ✉ 51 Gransha Road, Dundonald, Belfast BT16 2HB (tel 028 9047 3111)

ROBINSON, Peter James Edmund; s of Tom Robinson, of Blockley, Glos, and Doreen, *née* Clingan; *b* 18 November 1965, Mombasa, Kenya; *Educ* St Catharine's Coll Cambridge (MA); *Children* 1 da (Eva b 26 Aug 1993); *Career* literary agent; ed Michael Joseph 1986–89, literary agent Curtis Brown 1989–2005, fndr and md Robinson Literary Agency Ltd; FRSA; *Recreations* music; *Clubs* Century; *Style*— Peter Robinson, Esq; ✉ Robinson Literary Agency Limited, Block A511, The Jam Factory, 27 Green Walk, London SE1 4TT (tel 020 7096 1460, e-mail peter@rlabooks.co.uk)

ROBINSON, Prof Peter Michael; s of Maurice Allan Robinson, and Brenda Margaret, *née* Ponsford; *b* 20 April 1947; *Educ* Brockenhurst GS, UCL (BSc), LSE (MSc), Australian Nat Univ (PhD); *m* 27 Feb 1981, Wendy Rhea, da of Morris Brandmark; 1 da; *Career* lectr LSE 1969–70; assoc prof: Harvard Univ 1977–79 (asst prof 1973–77), Univ of Br Columbia 1979–80; prof Univ of Surrey 1980–84, prof of econometrics LSE 1984–95, Tooke prof of economic science and statistics LSE 1995–, Leverhulme Tst personal research prof 1998–2003; author of numerous articles in learned jls and books; co-ed: Econometric Theory 1989–91, Econometrica 1991–96, Jl of Econometrics 1997–; jt ed Time Series Analysis Vol II 1996, ed Long Memory Time Series 2003; memb Editorial Bd Annals of Statistics and of various other jls; dr (hc) Carlos III Univ Madrid 2000; fell Econometric Soc; FIMS, FBA 2000; *Recreations* walking; *Style*— Prof Peter M Robinson; ✉ London School of Economics and Political Science, Houghton Street, London WC2A 2AE

ROBINSON, Philip; s of Sydney Albert Robinson (d 1971), and Myra Isabel, *née* Kelly (d 1981); *b* 8 May 1954; *Educ* Hackney Downs GS; *m* 21 July 1984, Charman, da of Percival Leonard Davis; 1 da (Olivia b 19 Nov 1985), 1 s (James b 10 Oct 1987); *Career* sr Philips Petroleum Co Europe Africa 1972–76, John Burnett & Co, Saffery Champness Fraser Littlejohn 1976–83, Holco Trading Co Ltd commodities traders 1983–86, gen mangr London Metal Exchange International Commodities Clearing House 1986–87, fin dir Metallgesellschaft Ltd 1987–90, dir of fin Assoc of Futures Brokers and Dealers 1990–91, dir fin and admin Securities and Futures Authy 1991–93, chief operating offr Investment Mgmnt Regulatory Orgn (IMRO) 1993–98; FSA: dir of communications and corp affrs 1998–2001, dir Community Affairs 2001–04, dir Pensions Review 2001–02, dir Deposit Takers 2002–04, dir Regulatory Transactions and Financial Crime 2004–07, dir Financial Crime and Intelligence 2007–; tstee Geffrye Museum Tst 2003–; memb Cncl ACCA 1993–96; FCCA 1985 (ACCA 1981), MSI 1992; FRSA 1999; *Recreations* rugby, sailing, Christianity; *Clubs* National, Brading Haven Yacht; *Style*— Philip Robinson, Esq; ✉ Financial Services Authority, 25 The North Colonnade, Canary Wharf, London E14 5HS (tel 020 7066 3220, e-mail philip.robinson@fsa.gov.uk)

ROBINSON, Stephen Julian Roper; s of Andrew Thomas Roper Robinson, of London, and Barbara Anne, *née* Black; *b* 28 September 1961; *Educ* Westminster, The Queen's Coll Oxford (scholar, BA); *Career* reporter Natal Witness South Africa 1983–85, freelance writer Cape Town 1985–86; Daily Telegraph: joined 1986, Belfast corr 1987, Johannesburg corr 1987–90, Washington corr 1990–97, foreign ed 1997–2001, asst ed 2001–05, comment ed 2005–; contrib The Spectator 1985–; winner T E Utley Meml Prize 1990; *Recreations* tennis, reading; *Style*— Stephen Robinson, Esq; ✉ 2 Albert Terrace Mews, London NW1 7TA (tel 020 7722 3332); The Daily Telegraph, 1 Canada Square, Canary Wharf, London E14 5DT (tel 020 7538 5000, fax 020 7538 7270, e-mail stephen.robinson@telegraph.co.uk)

ROBINSON, Stuart Jackson; *b* 21 September 1948; *Educ* Monks Park Comp Sch Bristol, Univ of Newcastle upon Tyne (BA), Dept of Educn Univ of Bristol (PGCE); *Career* Colston's Sch Bristol: head Econ Dept 1971–79, asst housemaster 1972–75, sixth form housemaster (boarding) 1975–79; head of upper sch Cheadle Hulme HS 1979–82; Southway Sch Plymouth: dep head 1982–87, acting head teacher 1987; head teacher: The John Bentley Sch 1987–94, St Bartholomew's Sch 1994–; chair, dir and tstee: Assoc of Secdy Heads in Wilts 1991–92, treas Calne Project Devpt Ctee 1990–94; memb: Exec Bd Wilts Educn Business Partnership 1992–94, Sports Centre Mgmnt Ctee 1987–94, Calne Business Assoc, Mgmnt Ctee Further Educn Centre; contrib Wilts Govr Trg Prog; chair and dir West Berks Educn Business Partnership 1995–, chair West Berks Drugs Reference Gp 1999–2002, dir Berks Business Educn Alliance; MCC coach, Hockey Assoc coach; FRSA; *Recreations* squash, village cricket, staff soccer; *Style*— Stuart Robinson, Esq; ✉ St Bartholomew's School and Business Enterprise College, Andover Road, Newbury, Berkshire RG14 6JP (tel 01635 521255, fax 01635 516420)

ROBINSON, Tony; *Educ* Wanstead Co HS, Central Sch of Speech and Drama; *Children* 1 s (Luke), 1 da (Laura); *Career* actor and writer; vice-pres Br Actor's Equity 1996–2000; memb Lab Pty NEC 2000–04; currently pres Young Archaeologists Club; Hon MA: Univ of E London, Univ of Bristol; Hon Dr: Univ of Exeter, Oxford Brookes Univ, Open Univ; *Theatre* numerous appearances as child actor incl original version of stage musical Oliver!, several years in rep theatre, theatre dir for 2 years, then successively with Chichester Festival Theatre, RSC and NT; Tony Robinson's Cunning Night Out Tour 2005 and 2006; *Television* incl: Ernie Roberts in Horizon documentary Joey, Baldrick in Black Adder (4 series, BBC), Sheriff of Nottingham in Maid Marian and Her Merry Men (also writer, 4 series), Alan in My Wonderful Life (3 series, Granada); as presenter: Points of View, Stay Tooned, three African documentary features for Comic Relief, Time Team (archaeology series, Channel 4), Great Journey to the Caribbean, 2 series of Worst Jobs in History (Channel 4), The Real Da Vinci Code (Channel 4), Me and My Mum (Channel 4); as writer: Fat Tulip's Garden (30 episodes, Central), Odysseus - the Greatest Hero of Them All (13–part series, BBC), Blood and Honey (26 episodes, BBC); *Awards* for writing: 2 RTS, BAFTA, Int Prix Jeunesse; *Publications* Archaeology is Rubbish (with Prof Mick Aston, 2002), In Search of British Heroes (2003), The Worst Jobs in History (with David Wilcock, 2004), The Worst Children's Jobs in History (2005), also author of 17 children's books incl Tony Robinson's Kings & Queens (1999); *Style*— Tony Robinson, Esq; ✉ c/o JHA, 114–115 Tottenham Court Road, London W1T 5AH

ROBINSON, (Walter) Trevor; TD (1956); s of Joseph Robinson (d 1969), of Sheffield, and Nellie, *née* Briggs (d 1977); *b* 2 September 1925; *Educ* City GS Sheffield; *m* 6 Sept 1947, Olive, da of Frederick Richer (d 1942), of Sheffield; 2 s (Michael b 1950, Anthony b 1954); *Career* Capt York and Lancaster Regt 1943–47; gen mangr Nat West Bank (formerly Westminster Bank) 1969–73 (joined 1941), chief exec Texas Commerce Bank International 1973–75, gen mangr Midland and International Banks Ltd 1975–78, exec vice-pres Manufacturers Hanover Tst Co 1978–86, dir TSB Bank plc 1986–90, chm Five Oaks Investments plc 1987–95, gen mangr HSBC US London Branch (Republic Nat Bank of New York) 1986–2000, chm HSBC Republic Investments Ltd 1991–2004, chm Republic New York Holdings (UK) 2000–06, ceo HSBC Republic London 2001–02; banking assessor to the enquiry into the failure of the BCCI 1992; dir: National Grid Co plc 1989–95, National Grid Group plc 1995–97; Freeman City of London 1974; FCIB; *Recreations* reading; *Style*— Trevor Robinson, Esq, TD

ROBINSON, Victor Philip; s of Francis Herbert Robinson (d 1962), and Constance Harriet, *née* Phillips (d 1975); *b* 26 November 1943; *Educ* Cranleigh Sch, St Mary's Hosp Med Sch (MB BS); *m* 30 Oct 1965, Elizabeth Margaret, da of Lt Cdr Kenneth Thomas Basset (d 1989); 4 da ((Anne) Michelle b 30 Aug 1966, Louise Frances b 27 Aug 1969, Charlotte Faye b 31 Jan 1972, Victoria Jane b 29 Aug 1974); *Career* consIt obstetrician and gynaecologist: Queen Charlotte's Maternity Hosp, St George's Hosp Med Sch, Hillingdon and Mount Vernon Hosps, Hillingdon HA, Harefield Hosp 1982–; obstetrician reponsible for the care of first known pregnancies following heart and lung transplantations in UK (presentation to World Congress); memb Jubilee Sailing Tst; memb: RSM, BMA; FRCOG; *Style*— Victor Robinson, Esq; ✉ Hillingdon Hospital, Uxbridge, Middlesex UB8 3NN (e-mail drvicrobinson@aol.com)

ROBINSON, Vivian; QC (1986); s of William Robinson (d 1986), of Wakefield, and Ann, *née* Kidd (d 2000); *b* 29 July 1944; *Educ* Queen Elizabeth GS Wakefield, The Leys Sch Cambridge, Sidney Sussex Coll Cambridge (BA); *m* 19 April 1975, (Nora) Louise, da of Maj Peter Duncan Marriner, TD (d 1988), of Rayleigh; 2 da (Katherine Anne b 12 Sept 1977, Anna Ruth b 12 July 1981), 1 s (Edward Duncan b 30 Jan 1980); *Career* called to the Bar Inner Temple 1967 (bencher 1991); recorder of the Crown Court 1986–; Liveryman and memb Court of Assts Worshipful Co of Gardeners (Master 2000–01); *Recreations* gardening, reading; *Clubs* Garrick, RAC, MCC, Pilgrims; *Style*— Vivian Robinson, Esq, QC; ✉ Queen Elizabeth Building, Temple, London EC4Y 9BS (tel 020 7583 5766, fax 020 7353 0339)

ROBINSON, Sir Wilfred Henry Frederick; 3 Bt (UK 1908), of Hawthornden, Wynberg, Cape Province, S Africa, and Dudley House, City of Westminster; s of late Wilfred Henry Robinson (3 s of 1 Bt), and late Eileen, *née* St Leger; suc unc, Sir Joseph Benjamin Robinson 1954; *b* 24 December 1917; *Educ* Diocesan Coll Rondebosch, St John's Coll Cambridge; *m* 1946, Margaret Alison Kathleen, da of late Frank Mellish, MC, of Rondebosch, South Africa; 1 s, 2 da; *Heir* s, Peter Robinson; *Career* former Maj Para Regt; vice-princ Diocesan Coll Sch Rondebosch 1969–77; fin offr Soc of Genealogists 1980–92; *Style*— Sir Wilfred Robinson, Bt; ✉ 102 Riverview Gardens, Barnes, London SW13 8RA

ROBINSON, Winifred; da of John Robinson, of Liverpool, and Mary Bernadette, *née* Whitehill; *b* 7 December 1957; *Educ* Notre Dame Collegiate Liverpool, Univ of Liverpool; *m* March 1998, Roger Wilkes; 1 s (Anthony John Roger b 1999); *Career* broadcaster; reporter and presenter North West Tonight (BBC TV) 1987–90, reporter File on Four (BBC Radio 4) 1990–91, local govt corr (BBC North West) 1991–94, reporter Today Programme (BBC Radio) 1995–98; presenter (BBC Radio): Today Programme 1998–2001, The World Today 1998–2001, You and Yours 2000–; *Recreations* gardening, cooking, reading; *Style*— Ms Winifred Robinson; ✉ You and Yours, BBC, London W1A 1AA (tel 020 7580 4468); c/o Maggie Pearlstine Associates Ltd, 31 Ashley Gardens, Ambrosden Avenue, London SW1P 1QE (tel 020 7828 4212)

ROBISON, Shona; MSP; *Educ* Alva Acad, Univ of Glasgow (MA), Jordanhill Coll; *Career* homecare organiser Glasgow City Cncl; MSP (SNP): Scotland NE 1999–2003, Dundee E 2003–07; Scot Parl: min for public health; memb SNP; *Recreations* hill walking, cooking; *Style*— Ms Shona Robison, MSP; ✉ The Scottish Parliament, Edinburgh EH99 1SP (tel 0131 348 5707, fax 01382 903205, e-mail shona.robison.msp@scottish.parliament.uk)

ROBOROUGH, 3 Baron (UK 1938); Sir Henry Massey Lopes; 6 Bt (UK 1805); s of 2 Baron Roborough (d 1992), and Helen, *née* Dawson (d 1998); *b* 2 February 1940; *Educ* Eton; *m* 1, 1968 (m dis 1986), Robyn Zenda Carol, da of John Bromwich, of Point Lonsdale, Victoria, Aust; 2 s (Hon Massey John Henry b 1969, Hon Andrew James b 1971), 2 da (Hon Katie Victoria b 1976, Hon Melinda Claire b 1978); m 2, 1986, Sarah Anne Pipon, 2 da of Colin Baker, of Peter Tavy, Devon; 2 da (Hon Emily Jane b 1987, Hon Louisa Constance b 1989); *Heir* s, Hon Massey Lopes; *Career* late Lt Coldstream Guards; landowner; *Style*— The Rt Hon the Lord Roborough; ✉ Briscoe House, Ford Street, Wellington, Somerset TA21 9NY (tel 01823 660730); The Maristow Estate Office, Common Lane, Roborough, Plymouth, Devon PL6 7BN (01752 695945)

ROBOTHAM, (John) Michael; OBE (1997); s of Alpheus John Robotham, OBE, JP, DL (d 1994), of Quarndon, Derbys, and Gwendolyn Constance, *née* Bromet (d 1999); *b* 27 March 1933; *Educ* Clifton; *m* 29 June 1963 (m dis 1989), Diana Elizabeth, da of Alfred Thomas Webb (d 1967); 2 s (Guy Thomas Blews b 1967, Adam John Blews b 1971 d 1982); m 2, 1989 (m dis 2006), Victoria Mary Cronjé, da of Victor St Clair Yates; m 3, Celia Margaret Powiecki, da of Canon John Smyth; *Career* 2 Lt 12 Royal Lancers 1957–59; assoc J M Finn & Co (membs of FSA) 1980–; dir: Western Selection plc 1971–, London Finance & Investment Gp plc 1984–; chm Monteagle SA 1996–; vice-pres Inst of Advanced Motorists 2002; FCA, MSI (memb Stock Exchange 1963); *Recreations* shooting, travel, golf; *Clubs* Cavalry and Guards', HAC, City of London; *Style*— Michael Robotham, Esq; ✉ Brickwall Farm House, Clophill, Bedfordshire MK45 4DA (tel 01525 861333, fax 01525 862477); J M Finn & Co, 4 Coleman Street, London EC2R 5TA (tel 020 7600 1660, fax 020 7600 1661); City Group Ltd, 30 City Road, London EC1Y 2AG (tel 020 7448 8950, fax 020 7638 9426)

ROBOZ, Zsuzsi; da of Imre Roboz (d 1945), and Edith, *née* Grosz (d 1976); *b* 15 August 1939; *Educ* Royal Acad of Arts London, Pietro Annigoni Florence; *m* 22 Jan 1964, (Alfred) Teddy Smith; *Career* artist; solo exhibitions incl: Hong Kong Arts Festival 1976, Revudeville (V&A) 1978, Drawn to Ballet (Royal Festival Hall) 1983, Budapest Spring Festival 1985 and 1988, Music Makers (Royal Festival Hall) 1987, Lincoln Center New York 1989, British Art Now - a personal view (ART 93, Business Design Centre) 1993, The Creators (Roy Miles Gallery London) 1994, The Spirit of Nature (David Messum Fine Art London) 1995, New Drawings (David Messum Fine Art London) 1997, XXth Century Illusions (David Messum Fine Art London) 1999, Drawn to Music (David Messum Fine Art London) 2002, Messum's Cork Street 2005; portraits incl: Lord Olivier in the Theatre Museum, Dame Ninette de Valois in Nat Portrait Gallery, Sir George Solti, Sir John Gielgud, Prince William of Gloucester in Barnwell Church; work in public collections incl: Tate Gallery London, Theatre Museum, V&A, Museum of Fine Arts Budapest, Pablo Casals Museum Puerto Rico, St John's Coll Cambridge, Royal Festival Hall London; memb Pastel Soc, FRSA; *Books* Women & Men's Daughters (1970), Chichester Ten, Portrait of a Decade (1975), British Ballet To-day (1980), British Art Now: A personal view (text by Edward Lucie-Smith, 1993), Roboz: A painter's paradox (text by John Russell Taylor, 2006); *Recreations* music, swimming, reading; *Clubs* Chelsea Arts, Arts; *Style*— Ms Zsuzsi Roboz; ✉ The Studio, 76 Eccleston Square Mews, London SW1V 19N (tel 020 7834 4617, fax 020 7724 6844)

ROBSON, Alexandra; da of Sir John Robson, KCMG, and Lady Robson; *b* 5 December 1963; *Educ* Sherborne Sch for Girls, KCL (BA); *m* 24 April 1993, Simon Brocklebank-Fowler, *qv*, s of Christopher Brocklebank-Fowler; 1 da; *Career* Vogue 1985–86, GCI London 1988–91, head of PR Historic Royal Palaces 1991–95, md Aurelia PR 1999–2005, md APR Communications 2005–; *Recreations* gardening, cinema, my daughter and husband; *Style*— Ms Alexandra Robson; ✉ APR Communications, Victoria House, 1A Gertrude Street, London SW10 0JN (tel 020 7349 3801, fax 020 7376 5295, mobile 07768 992401, e-mail arobson@aprcommunications.com)

ROBSON, Prof Brian Turnbull; s of Oswell Robson (d 1973), and Doris Lowes, *née* Ayre (d 1984); *b* 23 February 1939; *Educ* Royal GS Newcastle, St Catharine's Coll Cambridge (MA, PhD); *m* 21 Dec 1973, Glenna, da of Jack Leslie Ransom, MBE, DCM, Croix de Guerre (d 1974); *Career* lectr UCW Aberystwyth 1964–67, Harkness fell Univ of Chicago 1967–68, lectr Univ of Cambridge 1968–77, fell Fitzwilliam Coll Cambridge 1968–77; Univ of Manchester: prof of geography 1977–, dean Faculty of Arts 1988–90, pro-vice-chllr 1993–97; dir Centre for Urban Policy Studies 1987–; pres Inst of Br Geographers 1992–93, pres Manchester Statistical Soc 1995–97; chm Manchester Cncl for Voluntary Servs 1983–91; Fndr's Medal RGS 2000; FRGS 1973, AcSS 2000, FRSA 2007; *Books* Urban Analysis (1969), Urban Growth (1973), Urban Social Areas (1975), Managing The City (1987), Those Inner Cities (1988), Assessing the Impact of Urban Policy (1994), Index of Local Conditions (1995), The Impact of Urban Development Corporations (1998), Regional Development Agencies and Local Area Regeneration (2000), The State of English Cities (2001); *Recreations* theatre, watercolour painting, gardening; *Style*— Prof Brian Robson; ✉ 32 Oaker Avenue, West Didsbury, Manchester M20 2XH (tel 0161 445 2036); Department of Geography, University of Manchester, Manchester M13 9PL (tel 0161 275 3639, fax 0161 275 7878, e-mail brian.robson@man.ac.uk)

ROBSON, Bryan; OBE; s of Brian Jackson Robson, of Chester-Le-Street, Co Durham, and Maureen, *née* Lowther; *b* 11 January 1957; *Educ* Birtley Lord Lawson Comp; *m* 2 June 1979, Denise Kathleen, da of George Brindley, of Great Barr, Birmingham; 2 da (Claire b 17 Sept 1980, Charlotte b 17 June 1982), 1 s (Ben b 2 Sept 1988); *Career* professional footballer and mangr; player: West Bromwich Albion 1974–81, Manchester United 1981–94 (359 appearances and 99 goals, capt until 1994, FA Cup 1983, 1985 and 1990, Charity Shield 1983 and 1992, 1993, European Cup Winners' Cup 1991, Rumbelows Cup 1992, FA Premier League 1993 and 1994); player/mangr Middlesbrough FC 1994–2001 (promotion to Premier League 1995, finalists FA Cup and League Cup 1997); mangr: Bradford City 2003–04, West Bromwich Albion 2004–06, Sheffield United 2007–; England: player 1980–92 (90 caps, 26 goals, appointed capt 1982), asst coach 1994; charity work incl: Wallness Hurdles and Adventure Farm, Bryan Robson Scanner Appeal; Hon MA: Univ of Manchester 1992, Univ of Salford 1992; *Books* United I Stand (1984), Robbo (autobiography, 2006); *Recreations* horse racing; *Style*— Bryan Robson, Esq, OBE

ROBSON, Christopher; s of John Thomas Robson, and Eva Elizabeth, *née* Leatham; *b* 9 December 1953; *Educ* Cambridge Coll of Arts & Technol, Trinity Coll of Music London; *m* 1974 (m dis 1983), Laura Carin, da of Leonard Snelling, of Blackheath; partner, since 1993, Samantha Lambourne; 1 s (Joel Robson-Lambourne b 9 Dec 1994); *Career* counter-tenor; studied with: Nigel Wickens, James Gaddarn, Paul Esswood, Helga Mott, Geoffrey Parsons, Sir Peter Pears, Laura Sarti, Thomas Helmsley, John Shirley Quirke; concert debut Queen Elizabeth Hall with London Orpheus Choir and Orch 1976, operatic debut as Argones in Sosarme with Barber Opera Birmingham 1979; memb: London Oratory Choir 1974–81, Monteverdi Choir 1974–85, King's Consort 1979–86, Westminster Cathedral Choir 1981–84, ENO 1981–, New London Consort 1985–; roles with ENO incl: Shepherd in Monteverdi's Orfeo (ENO debut) 1981, title role in Akhnaten (UK premiere), Edgar/Mad Tom in Lear (UK premiere), Arsamenes in Xerxes, title role in Julius Caesar, Polinesso in Ariodante 1993 and 1996, Oberon in Midsummer Night's Dream 1995; has also performed princ roles with opera cos incl: Royal Opera Co Covent Garden, Houston Grand Opera, NY City Opera, Northern Stage, Covent Garden Opera Festival, Opera Factory London, Opera Factory Zurich, Nancy Opera, Frankfurt Opera, Scottish Opera, Berlin Kammeroper, Bavarian State Opera, São Paulo Opera, Innsbruck Landestheater, Badisches Staatstheater Karlsruhe, Pfalzbautheater Ludwigshafen, Bayerisches Staatsoper Munich, Opera North, Chicago Lyric Opera, Flanders Opera, Glyndebourne Touring Opera, Glyndebourne Festival Opera (world premiere of Flight 1998), Lyric Theatre Hammersmith (world premiere of The Maids); has performed with orchs incl: Royal Philharmonic, English Chamber Orch, London Sinfonietta, London Bach Orch, BBC Philharmonic, Northern Sinfonia, Bournemouth Sinfonietta, London Baroque Orch, European Baroque Orch, Hanover Band, Concentus Musicus Vienna, Tonhalle Orch Zurich, Vienna Symphony, City of London Sinfonia, Rochester Symphony Orch, Sharoun Ensemble Berlin; worked with conductors incl: Sir Charles Mackerras, Walter Weller, Claudio Abbado, Gustav Leonhardt, Roy Goodman, Niklaus Harnoncourt, Richard Hickox, Mark Elder, Paul Daniel, Ton Koopman, Rene Jacobs, Howard Arman, David Atherton, Sir Neville Marriner, Noel Davies, Sir Peter Maxwell Davies, John de Main, Christopher Keene, Peter Neumann, Brenton Langbein, Zubin Mehta, Simone Young; performed at festivals incl: BBC Proms, Chichester, Three Choirs, Greenwich, Camden, Almeida (world premiere of Casken's Golem), Huddersfield Contemporary Music, Aix en Provence, Montpelier, Stuttgart, Den Haag, Bruges, Barcelona, San Sebastian, Zurich, Salzburg, Wiener Moderne, Warsaw; gala performances incl: Royal Opera House Covent Garden 1986, ENO 1987, Sadler's Wells 1991; *Recordings* Valls' Missa Scala Aretina (with Thames Chamber Orch), Vivaldi's Nisi Dominus (with Kings Consort), Biber's Marienvespers (with Salzburg Bachchor) and Requiem (with New London Consort), The Delights of Posilipo (with New London Consort), Monteverdi's 1610 Vespers (with New London Consort), Monteverdi's Orfeo (with New London Consort), Blow's Venus and Adonis (with New London Consort), Heinrich Schütz Auferstehungs and Weinacht Historias, Tippett's The Ice Break (with London Sinfonietta), Maxwell-Davies' Resurrection (with BBC Philharmonic), Handel's Messiah (with Collegium Musicum 90), Casken's Golem (with Music Projects London), Locke's Psyche and Bach Magnificat (with New London Consort), Purcell's Odes (with the Orch of the Age of Enlightenment), Handel's Xerxes (Bavarian State Opera), Arne's Artaxerxes (PArley of Instruments), Vivaldi's Canatatas (New London Consort); *TV/Video* Xerxes (ENO), Ariodante (ENO), Orontea (Innsbruck Festival), Hail Bright Cecilia (Norrington), My Night with HAndel (Channel 4), Hell for Leather (DRS Television); *Awards* finalist Kathleen Ferrier Award 1978, winner GLAA Young Musician Award 1979, winner Wroclawskiego Szermierza Statuette Wroclaw Int Music Festival 1991, Opernfestspiel Prize Munich 1997; *Recreations* films, theatre, food and wine, driving; *Clubs* Home House; *Style*— Christopher Robson, Esq; ✉ c/o Music International, 13 Ardilaun Road, London N5 2QR (tel 020 7359 5183, fax 020 7226 9792)

ROBSON, Christopher William; s of Leonard Robson (d 1970), of Egglescliffe, Co Durham, and Irene Beatrice, *née* Punch (d 1984); *b* 13 August 1936; *Educ* Rugby; *m* 17 July 1965, Susan Jane, da of Maj John Davey Cooke-Hurle (d 1979), of Co Durham; 2 da (Sarah Louise b 1966, Lydia Katharine b 1969), 1 s (Andrew Leonard Feilding b 1973); *Career* Nat Serv Lt RASC 1955–57; admitted slr 1962, sr ptnr Punch Robson (formerly JWR Punch and Robson) 1971–95; chm Richmond (Yorks) Cons Assoc 1999–2001; fell Woodard Schs (Northern Div) Ltd 1974–85; memb Br Astronomical Soc; FRAS; *Recreations* astronomy, skiing, shooting, walking; *Style*— Christopher Robson, Esq; ✉ Rudd Hall, East Appleton, Richmond, North Yorkshire DL10 7QD (tel 01748 811339, fax 0845 638 1182, e-mail robson.rudd@virgin.net)

ROBSON, (William) David; s of (William) Michael Robson (d 1998), and Audrey Isobel Wales, *née* Dick (d 1964); *b* 28 January 1944; *Educ* Eton; *m* 27 Sept 1975, (Anne) Helen, da of Cecil Henry Gosling (d 1974); 1 da (Emma Lucy b 1977), 1 s ((William) Henry b 1979); *Career* Lloyd's member agent; chm Anton Holdings 1991–; Freeman City of London, Liveryman Worshipful Co of Vintners; *Recreations* golf, opera; *Clubs* White's, Pratt's; *Style*— David Robson, Esq; ✉ The Woods, Hatfield Broad Oak, Bishop's Stortford, Hertfordshire CM22 7BU (tel 012797 18452)

ROBSON, David Ernest Henry; QC (1980); s of Joseph Robson (d 1979), and Caroline, *née* Bowmaker; *b* 1 March 1940; *Educ* Robert Richardson GS Ryhope, ChCh Oxford (MA); *Career* called to the Bar Inner Temple 1965, memb NE circuit 1965, recorder Crown Ct (NE circuit) 1979–, bencher Inner Temple 1988, head of chambers 1980–99; pres Herrington Burn (Sunderland) YMCA 1986–2001, artistic dir Royalty Studio Theatre Sunderland 1986–88; *Recreations* acting, Italy; *Clubs* County Durham; *Style*— David Robson, Esq, QC; ✉ 3 Broad Chare, Quayside, Newcastle upon Tyne NE1 3DQ (tel 0191 232 2392)

ROBSON, Dr David John; s of Alan Victor Robson, TD, LDS, RCS(Ed), and Joan Dales, *née* Hawkins; *b* 23 February 1944; *Educ* Repton, Middx Hosp Univ of London (MB BS); *Career* conslt physician Greenwich HA 1978–, dir Greenwich HA HISS Project 1990–93; dir Greenwich Healthcare (now Queen Elizabeth Hosp NHS Tst): med 1993–96, information 1996–2004, med dir 2004–; FRCP 1986; *Clubs* Savage; *Style*— Dr David Robson; ✉ Queen Elizabeth Hospital, Stadium Road, Woolwich, London SE18 4QH (tel 020 8836 4350)

ROBSON, Derek; *b* 17 June 1967, Marlborough, Wilts; *m* Sarnia; 2 da (Millie, Evie); *Career* grad trainee Ogilvy & Mather Direct; Bartle Bogle Hegarty (BBH): account planner 1992–99, bd planner 1999–, dep UK planning dir 1999–2004, global business dir (Levi's and Interbrew) 2003–, md BBH London 2004–; *Style*— Derek Robson, Esq; ✉ BBH London, 60 Kingly Street, London W1B 5DS (tel 020 7734 1677)

ROBSON, Euan; *Educ* Univ of Newcastle upon Tyne (BA), Univ of Strathclyde (MSc); *Career* Scottish mangr Gas Consumers Cncl 1986–99; MSP (Lib Dem) Roxburgh & Berwickshire 1999–2007; Scottish Parl: memb Audit Ctee 1999–2001, memb Justice and Home Affrs Ctee 1999–2001, Justice I and Justice II Ctees 2001, dep min for Parl (later Parly business) 2001–03, chief whip 2001–03, dep min for educn and young people 2003–; memb: River Tweed Cmmrs 1993–2001, Inst of Consumer Affairs; hon sec Kelso Angling Assoc; cncllr Northumberland CC 1981–89; writer of articles and books on Scottish art; *Style*— Euan Robson, Esq

ROBSON, Ian; s of Edward Robson, of Langport, Somerset, and Lucy, *née* Greatorex; *b* 21 July 1950; *Educ* Consett GS Co Durham, Bath Acad of Art (BA), Brighton Poly (Postgrad Dip), Univ of Westminster (MBA); *m* 1, 1974, Julia Mary, da of Thomas William Manning; 2 da (Sarah Rose b 4 June 1978, Tessa Imogen Eva b 10 April 1980); m 2, 1987, Ellen Alunwen Frances, da of Alun Williams; 3 da (Lois Amy b 2 Nov 1988, Miranda Lucy, Sophie Frances (twins) b 5 March 1991); *Career* princ Robson Dowry Associates (formerly Robson Design Associates) brand and communication design consultancy 1976–; pt/t lectr in printmaking Brighton Poly 1975, visiting lectr in graphic design Fndn Studies Dept Winchester Sch of Art 1975–79, pt/t lectr in graphic design Somerset Coll of Arts and Technol 1984–86, memb DBA Trg Task Gp 1988–89, advsy memb Yeovil Coll of Art Advsy Panel 1989, industry rep govr Somerset Coll of Arts and Technol (memb Art and Design Advsy and Liaison Ctees, chair Audit Ctee) 1990–2000; CSD: area rep and memb Cncl SW Region 1984–91, hon treas SW Region 1985–89, educn rep to Bath Coll of HE 1987–88, memb Cncl 1993–2000; memb DMI 1999; MInstD 1997, MSCD (MSIAD 1982); *Exhibitions and Awards* Gane meml travelling scholar (Italy, Germany and Switzerland) 1972, open field print exhbn (UK tour) 1974, print graphic exhbn (Thumb Gallery London) 1975, Bull meml scholar 1976, SW Arts Award for Photography 1979, design work selected for Graphics UK London 1983/for London and overseas 1984, report and accounts work selected for exhbn at World Trade Centre 1987 and 1988, finalist Rank Xerox DTP Document of the Year Award 1989, Creative Contact Award for Promotional Literature 1991, Popcomm Award for Best Annual Report (Public Sector) 2003; *Recreations* family and home, the development of the design industry (art, architecture and design generally), gardening (practical as well as the history of gardens), photography (particularly rural and urban landscape), travelling in the UK and overseas, walking rural and coastline areas (with a particular interest in islands), skiing, tennis (club member), films and reading; *Style*— Ian Robson, Esq; ✉ Robson Dowry Associates Ltd, 2 Queen's Avenue, Clifton, Bristol BS8 1SE (tel 0117 946 6669, fax 0117 946 6978)

ROBSON, John Malcolm; s of Edward Stephen Robson (d 1989), and Joan Barbara, *née* Burchett; *b* 16 March 1952; *Educ* KCS Wimbledon, Univ of London (LLB); *m* 30 Aug 1991, Jennifer Lillias, da of Bernard Seed, of Sutton, Surrey; 2 s (David, Aidan), 1 da (Lillias); *Career* called to the Bar Inner Temple 1974, pt/t chm Appeals Service; FCIArb; *Recreations* swimming, cinemas, wines; *Clubs* RAC; *Style*— John Robson, Esq; ✉ 265 Fir Tree Road, Epsom Downs, Surrey (tel 01737 210121); Arden Chambers, 27 John Street, London WC1N 2BL (tel 020 7242 4244, fax 020 7242 3224)

ROBSON, Michael Anthony; s of Thomas Chester Robson, MM, CDM (d 1984), of Sunderland, and Gertrude Edith, *née* Thomas (d 1975); *b* 29 November 1931; *Educ* West Hartlepool GS, St Edmund Hall Oxford (MA); *m* 1, 6 Dec 1952, Cicely, da of James Frederick Bray (d 1934), of Hull; 1 da (Zuleika b 1953), 1 s (Jake b 1957); m 2, 11 Feb 1977 (m dis 2001), Judith, da of James Francis Smithies (d 1979), of Woolpit, Suffolk; *Career* RAF 1950–51; teacher Norfolk 1954–63; writer and film dir: Anglia TV 1963–69, BBC2 1970; freelance; memb Broadcasting Ctee Soc of Authors 1991–94; memb: Royal Soc of St George, RSL; life memb John Buchan Soc; *Books* incl: The Beargarden (1958), Time After Rain (1962), On Giant's Shoulders (jtly, 1976), Opium: The Poisoned Poppy (1992), Theatre: Buy Your Clichés Here (1992), The Girl from Arles (1994); *Radio Plays* incl: Landscape with Lies (1974), Weekend at Montacute (1976), Welcome, These Pleasant

R

Days! (1981), Intent to Deceive (1988), A Cambridge Mystery (1992), Obsession (1993), Jack's Back! (1994), Full Fathom Five (1995), The Girl from Arles (1999); *TV Plays* incl: An Adventure in Bed (1975), No Name, No Packdrill (1977), Heart to Heart (1979), Swallows and Amazons Forever! (1984), This Lightning Strikes Twice (1985), Hannay (series 1988–89), Handles (1989), An Ideal Husband (1990), The House of Eliott (1991), The Letter Killeth (1995), William Tell (1997), Escape into Fear (1998), The Sorcerer's Apprentice (1998), Obsession in August (1998), Darkness Visible (1998), Incident at Whitewater (2002); *Feature Films* incl: Got it Made (jtly, 1974), The Water Babies (1978), Holocaust 2000 (jtly, 1978), The Thirty-Nine Steps (1979), The Ballad of the Lost Valley (1990), In Silver Mist (1991); *Recreations* riding, reading, music, politics; *Clubs* Oxford and Cambridge; *Style—* Michael Robson, Esq; ✉ 2 Whitehill, Hindon, Wiltshire SP3 6EH

ROBSON, Peter Gordon; s of Donald Robson (d 1981), and Lette, *née* Brewer (d 1996); *b* 5 November 1937; *Educ* Scarborough HS; *Career* asst master Marton Hall Bridlington 1962–70, head of maths Cundall Manor York 1972–89 (sr master 1973–76), fndr Newby Books (publishers) 1990; *Books* Between the Laughing Fields (poems, 1966), Maths Dictionary (1979), Maths for Practice and Revision (5 vols, 1982–90), Fountains Abbey - a Cistercian Monastery (1983), The Fishing Robsons (1991), Everyday Graphs (1993), Coordinate Graphs (1993), Science Dictionary (1994), Early Maths (4 vols, 1999–2006), Car Registrations in the British Isles (2003), Car Registration Guide (2007); *Recreations* music, genealogy, heraldry, photography; *Style—* Peter Robson, Esq; ✉ 31 Red Scar Lane, Scarborough, North Yorkshire YO12 5RH (e-mail petrov37@btinternet.com)

ROBSON, Air Vice Marshal Robert Michael (Bobby); OBE (1971); s of Dr John Alexander Robson (d 1988), and Edith, *née* Knape (d 1992); *b* 22 April 1935; *Educ* Sherborne, RMA Sandhurst; *m* 4 April 1959, Brenda Margaret, da of Leslie Clifford Croysdill, MBE (d 1970), of Dorset; *Career* cmmnd 1955, RAF Regt 1958, navigator trg 1959, strike sqdns 1965, sqdn cdr RAF Coll 1968, def advsr Br High Cmmn Sri Lanka 1972, Nat Def Coll 1973, CO 27 Sqdn 1974–75, staff duties MOD 1978, CO RAF Gatow 1978–80, RCDS 1981, dir of initial offr trg RAF Coll 1982–84, dir of PR (RAF) 1985–87, head of study into offrs' terms of service 1987; ADC to HM The Queen 1979–80; ret 1987; sheep farmer 1987–98; dir Advanced Technology Industries Ltd 1993–98; chm: Prince's Tst Lincs, Fuel Mechanics Ltd 1995–98, Turbo UK Ltd 1994–2000; govr Witham Hall Prep Sch 1987– (chm of govrs 1995); FIMgt 1983; *Recreations* reading, opera, fishing, golf; *Clubs* RAF; *Style—* Air Vice Marshal Bobby Robson, OBE; ✉ Long Row Cottage, North Rauceby, Sleaford, Lincolnshire NG34 8XR (tel 01529 488631)

ROBSON, Sir Robert William (Bobby); kt (2002), CBE (1991); s of Philip Robson, of Langley Park, Co Durham, and Lilian, *née* Watt; *b* 18 February 1933; *Educ* Waterhouses Secdy Modern Sch; *m* 25 June 1955, Elsie Mary, da of Jack Wilfred Gray (d 1980); 3 s (Paul Martin b 24 June 1957, Andrew Peter b 28 March 1959, Robert Mark b 9 April 1963); *Career* professional footballer: Fulham FC 1950–56, West Bromwich Albion FC 1956–62, Fulham FC 1962–67; England international 1957–62: 20 full caps, under 23 and B caps, appeared in World Cup Sweden (1958) and Chile (1962); mangr: Vancouver Royals 1967–68 (also coach), Fulham FC 1968, Ipswich Town FC 1969–82 (FA Cup winners 1978, UEFA Cup winners 1981), England nat team 1982–90 (fourth place World Cup Italy 1990), PSV Eindhoven 1990–92 (Dutch League winners 1991 and 1992) and 1998–99 (Dutch Super Cup winners 1998), Sporting Lisbon 1992–93; head coach FC Porto 1994–96 (Portuguese Cup winners 1993/94, Portuguese Super Cup winners 1993/94 and 1994/95, Portuguese League winners 1994/95 and 1995/96); Barcelona FC: head coach 1996–97 (Spanish Super Cup winners 1996, Copa del Rey winners 1997, European Cup Winners Cup winners 1997), technical dir of football 1997–98; mangr Newcastle United FC 1999–2004, conslt coach Ireland nat team 2006–; pres Middlesex Wanderers AFC; Hon MA UEA 1997, Hon DCL Univ of Newcastle upon Tyne; Freeman City of Newcastle 2005; *Books* Time on the Grass (autobiography, 1982), So Near Yet So Far: Bobby Robson World Cup Diary (with Bob Harris, 1986), Against the Odds (with Bob Harris, 1990), An Englishman Abroad (with Bob Harris, 1998), Farewell But Not Goodbye (2005); *Recreations* golf, gardening, skiing, reading, music; *Style—* Sir Bobby Robson, CBE

ROBSON, Sir Stephen Arthur; kt (2000), CB (1997); s of Arthur Cyril Robson, ISO (d 1996), and Lilian Marianne, *née* Peabody (d 1972); *b* 30 September 1943; *Educ* Pocklington Sch, St John's Coll Cambridge (MA, PhD), Stanford Univ (MA); *m* 14 Dec 1974, Meredith Hilary, da of Ernest Lancashire (d 1982); 2 s (David Robert b 1 March 1978, Andrew Luke b 8 Sept 1979); *Career* dep sec HM Treasy, dir Fin, Regulation and Industry Directorate HM Treasy, second perm sec 1997–2000; non-exec dir: Royal Bank of Scot, Xstrata, JPMorgan Cazenove and Partnerships UK 2001–; *Recreations* sailing; *Clubs* Bosham Sailing; *Style—* Sir Stephen Robson, CB; ✉ JPMorgan Cazenove plc, London EC2R 6DA

ROCHA, John; CBE (2002); *b* 23 August 1953, Hong Kong; *Educ* Croydon Art Coll; *m* 2, Odette Gleeson; 3 c; *Career* fashion designer; encouraged by Irish Trade Bd estab career in Dublin late 1970s, worked in Milan 1988–90, subsequently estab John Rocha/Chinatown, introduced first menswear collection Autumn 1991, currently showing biannually in London, launched John Rocha at Waterford Crystal 1997, opened shop at 60 Sloane Avenue in Nov 1998; British Fashion Designer of the Year 1993; *Style—* Mr John Rocha, CBE

ROCHDALE, 2 Viscount (UK 1960); St John Durival Kemp; also Baron Rochdale (UK 1913); s of 1 Viscount Rochdale, OBE, TD, DL (d 1993), and Elinor Dorothea, CBE, JP, *née* Pease (d 1997); *b* 15 January 1938; *Educ* Eton; *m* 1, 5 Jan 1960 (m dis 1974), Serena Jane, da of Michael Clark-Hall; 2 s (Hon Jonathan Hugo Durival b 1961, Hon Christopher George b 1969), 2 da (Hon Joanna Victoria b 1964, Hon Susanna Jane b 1965); m 2, 1976, Mrs Elizabeth Anderton, da of Robert Norman Rossiter Boldon; *Heir* s, Hon Jonathan Kemp; *Style—* The Rt Hon Viscount Rochdale

ROCHE, Anthony Douglas (Tony); *b* 12 August 1943; *Educ* Wolverhampton Poly (BSc); *m*; 2 s, 2 step da; *Career* BR: various prodn and engrg positions 1959–85, prodn servs dir 1986–91, chief exec BR Maintenance Ltd 1992–96, dep md Network South East 1992–93, md Eversholt Train Leasing Co 1994, gp md Central Servs BR Bd 1994–96, memb Engrg, Servs and Safety BR Bd 1996–98; princ A D Roche Associates 1999–, dir First Class Partnerships Ltd 2000; govr Imperial Coll London 1997–2006; Hon DTech Oxford Brookes Univ; Sr Warden Worshipful Co of Engrs (memb Ct of Assts 2000); FIMechE (pres 2001), FREng 1997; *Recreations* reading, popular classical music, golf; *Style—* Tony Roche, Esq, FREng; ✉ 98 High Street, Odell, Bedford MK43 7AS (tel 01234 720196, fax 01234 721516, e-mail adroche@bigfoot.com)

ROCHE, Rt Rev Arthur; *see:* Leeds, Bishop of (RC)

ROCHE, David; s of Lawrence Roche (d 1983), of London, and Jocelyn, *née* Baker; *b* 8 May 1961, London; *Educ* Worth Sch Sussex, Hatfield Coll Univ of Durham (BA); *m* 20 June 1987, Johanna, *née* Kari; 3 s (Daniel b 19 Nov 1988, Maximilian b 20 Feb 1991, Benjamin b 23 Dec 1994); *Career* production planner Burlington Klopmann plc 1984–86, stock control mangr Horne Brothers plc 1986–89, product dir HMV Europe Ltd 1989–2001, product dir Waterstone's UK Ltd 2002–06, ceo Borders UK & Ireland Ltd 2006–; memb Advsy Bd: London Book Fair, MA in Publishing Univ of Kingston; pres Booksellers Assoc 2005–; Retail Personality of the Year Bookseller Retail Awards 2005; *Recreations* golf, scuba diving, learning to fly, cooking; *Clubs* MCC, Royal Wimbledon Golf, Soho House (fndr memb); *Style—* David Roche, Esq; ✉ Broadway House, 156 Hare Lane, Claygate, Surrey KT10 0RD (tel 01372 469672, e-mail davidroche@hotmail.co.uk); Borders UK Ltd, Stillerman House, 120 Charing Cross Road, London WC2H 0JR (tel 020 7395 3426, e-mail droche@bordersgroupinc.com)

ROCHE, Sir David O'Grady; 5 Bt (UK 1838), of Carass, Limerick; s of Lt-Cdr Sir Standish O'Grady Roche, 4 Bt, DSO, RN (d 1977), and Evelyn Laura, only da of late Maj William Andon, of Jersey; *b* 21 September 1947; *Educ* Wellington, Trinity Coll Dublin; *m* 1971, Hon (Helen) Alexandra Briscoe Gully, JP, da of late 3 Viscount Selby (d 1959), and formerly w of Roger Moreton Frewen (d 1972); 2 s (David Alexander O'Grady b 1976, 1 s decd), 1 da (Cecilia Evelyn Jonnë b 1979); *Heir* s, David Roche; *Career* CA, formerly with Peat Marwick Mitchell & Co; mangr Samuel Montagu Ltd; chm: Carlton Real Estates plc 1978–82, Echo Hotel 1986–94, Plaza Holdings Ltd 2000–; cncllr London Borough of Hammersmith and Fulham 1978–82; memb Estonian Govt Tax Reform Cmmn 1993–94; Liveryman Worshipful Co of Saddlers; FCA; *Recreations* shooting, sailing, yacht (Aramis); *Clubs* Buck's, Kildare St and Univ (Dublin), Royal Yacht Squadron; *Style—* Sir David Roche, Bt

ROCHE, (William) Martin; s of Albert Charles Roche (d 1973), and Josephine Francis Clare (d 1973); *b* 19 June 1952; *Educ* James Watt Coll Greenock, Univ of Aberdeen (MA); *m* 2 May 1992, Fiona, da of John G Temple; 2 da (Josie Ishbel Temple b 24 March 1993, Anna Caitlin Temple b 18 June 1995), 1 s (Franklin Dominic Temple b 15 Feb 1999); *Career* with family business 1970–76, in higher educn 1976–82, property mangr Cornellis Property Mgmnt 1982–83, econ devpt offr Borders Regional Cncl 1983–84, dir London Office Scottish New Town Devpt Corp 1984–86, public affrs dir Ash Gupta Communications 1986–87, with Bell Pottinger Communications (formerly Lowe Bell Communications) 1987–2000; fndr Anchor Reputation Management 2001–; regular writer and lectr on place mktg, brand strategy and economic devpt; *Recreations* political biography and history, literature, cricket, travel; *Style—* Martin Roche, Esq; ✉ Anchor Reputation Management, Stuppington Court Farm, Merton Lane, Canterbury, Kent CT4 7BP (tel 01227 456676, e-mail info@anchorlondon.com)

ROCHE, Peter Charles Kenneth; s of Dr (George) Kenneth Trevor Roche (d 1989), and Margaret Bridget, *née* Tyrrell; *b* 27 January 1947; *Educ* Stonyhurst; *m* 24 April 1971, Gloria Evelyn Margarita, da of John Hugh Cogswell Hicks MBE; 2 s (Daniel Peter James b 19 May 1977, Simon Matthew John b 5 Nov 1981), 1 da (Lucy Georgina 16 Feb 1979); *Career* articled clerk then audit sr Barton Mayhew & Co 1965–71, audit supervisor Deloitte & Co Nairobi 1971–73, chief accountant then gen mangr East African Fine Spinners Nairobi 1973–75, fin dir then dep md Futura Publications Ltd London 1975–80, fin and admin dir MacDonald Futura Publishers Ltd 1980–81, fin dir MacDonald & Co 1981–82, co-fndr, fin dir and dep md Century Publishing Co Ltd 1982–85, fin dir and dep md Century Hutchinson Ltd 1985–89, fin dir then gp md Random Century Group Ltd (Century Hutchinson bought by Random House Inc) 1989–92; The Orion Publishing Group Ltd: co-fndr, gp md 1992–2003, chief exec 2003–; non-exec chm Boxtree Ltd 1989–96; FCA 1976 (ACA 1971); *Recreations* cricket, rugby, tennis, books and newspapers; *Clubs* RAC, Kongonis Cricket; *Style—* Peter Roche, Esq; ✉ Field House, 20 Leigh Hill Road, Cobham, Surrey KT11 2HX (tel 01932 862713); The Orion Publishing Group Ltd, Orion House, 5 Upper St Martin's Lane, London WC2H 9EA (tel 020 7240 3444, fax 020 7240 4822, e-mail pcr@orionbooks.co.uk)

ROCHESTER, David John; s of Edward Rochester (d 1983), and Anne Edna, *née* Raine; *b* 29 October 1939; *Educ* The GS Reigate, Sorbonne; *m* 1, 2 Sept 1961 (m dis 1977), Anne, da of Joseph Ganter, of Morden, Surrey; 2 da (Lisa b 1966, Susan b 1968); m 2, 31 Dec 1977, Shannon Marie, da of Joseph Clements, of Twin Falls, Idaho, USA; 2 da (Raine b 1981, Hailey b 1984); *Career* ptnr Cazenove & Co 1961–81, pres Wedd Durlacher Mordaunt Inc 1981–83, md Merrill Lynch Ltd 1983–89, dir Private Fund Managers Ltd 1990–, pres Private Fund Managers Inc 1992–94, sr vice-pres Brean Murray & Co Inc 1994–; *Recreations* shooting, tennis, fishing, golf; *Clubs* City of London, The Brook (NY), The Leask (NY), Union (Sydney), Royal Sydney Golf; *Style—* David Rochester, Esq; ✉ Brean Murray & Co Inc, 570 Lexington Avenue, New York, NY 10022, USA

ROCHESTER, 2 Baron (UK 1931); Foster Charles Lowry Lamb; s of 1 Baron Rochester, CMG, JP, sometime MP Rochester and paymaster-gen in 1931 Nat Govt (d 1955); *b* 7 June 1916; *Educ* Mill Hill, Jesus Coll Cambridge (MA); *m* 12 Dec 1942, Mary (d 2000), da of Thomas Benjamin Wheeler, CBE (d 1981); 2 s (Hon David Lamb, Hon Timothy Lamb, *qv*), 1 da (and 1 da decd); *Heir* s, Hon David Lamb; *Career* former Capt 23 Hussars WWII; personnel mangr Mond ICI 1964–72; pro-chllr Keele Univ 1976–86; DL (Cheshire) 1979; Hon DUniv Keele 1986; *Clubs* Reform; *Style—* The Lord Rochester; ✉ 337 Chester Road, Hartford, Cheshire (tel 01606 74733)

ROCHESTER, Bishop of 1994–; Rt Rev Dr Michael Nazir-Ali; *b* 19 August 1949; *Educ* Univ of Karachi (BA), Fitzwilliam Coll and Ridley Hall Cambridge (PGCTh, MLitt, Burney Award), St Edmund Hall Oxford (BLitt, MLitt, Oxford Graduate Soc award), Aust Coll of Theol Univ of NSW (ThD), Westminster Coll PA (DHLitt), Lambeth (DD); *m* 1972, Valerie Cree; 2 s (Shamaoun b 1975, Ross b 1979); *Career* ordained: deacon 1974, priest 1976; asst curate Holy Sepulchre Cambridge 1974–76, tutorial supervisor in theology Univ of Cambridge 1974–76 (Burney lectr in Islam 1973–74), tutor then sr tutor Karachi Theol Coll 1976–81, assoc priest Holy Trinity Cathedral Karachi 1976–79, priest-in-charge St Andrew's Akhtar Colony Karachi 1979–81, provost Lahore Cathedral 1981–84, bishop of Raiwind 1984–86, asst to Archbishop of Canterbury and dir-in-residence Oxford Centre for Mission Studies 1986–89, asst bishop and hon curate Limpsfield and Titsey Diocese of Southwark and gen sec Church Mission Soc 1989–94; sec Archbishop's Cmmn on Communion and Women in the Episcopate (Eames Cmmn) 1988–98, Archbishop's nominee Cncl of Churches for Britain and Ireland 1990–94; memb: Anglican-RC Int Cmmn 1991–2005, Int Anglican-RC Cmmn on Unity and Mission 2000–05; canon theologian Leicester Cathedral 1992–94; chm: C of E Mission Theological Advsy Gp 1992–2001, House of Bishops Theological Gp 2004–, Cncl Trinity Coll Bristol, Working Party on Women in the Episcopate; memb: C of E Bd of Mission 1991–2001, Archbishop's Cncl 2001–, House of Bishops Standing Ctee 2001–05; dir Christian Aid 1988–97, tstee Traidcraft 1987–89, memb HFEA 1998–2003 (chm Ethics and Law Ctee), memb Advsy Cncl Concordis Int, memb Advsy Cncl Cohesion Centre CIVITAS; visiting prof in theology and religious studies Univ of Greenwich; various lectureships in colleges and univs in GB, USA, Canada and NZ; memb House of Lords 1999–; Hon DLitt: Univ of Bath, Univ of Greenwich; Hon DD Univ of Kent; hon fell: St Edmund Hall Oxford 1998, Fitzwilliam Coll Cambridge 2006; Paul Harris Rotary fell 2005; *Publications* Islam - A Christian Perspective (1983), Frontiers in Christian-Muslim Encounter (1987), Martyrs and Magistrates: Toleration and Trial in Islam (1989), From Everywhere to Everywhere (1990), Mission and Dialogue (1995), The Mystery of Faith (1995), Citizens and Exiles (1998), Shapes of the Church to Come (2001), Understanding My Muslim Neighbour (2002), Conviction and Conflict (2006); author of numerous articles, ed various papers and reports incl Report of the Lambeth Conf 1988, chaired various cmmns which have produced reports; *Recreations* cricket, hockey, table tennis, scrabble, listening to music, reading fiction, humour and poetry, writing poetry; *Clubs* Nikaean, Kent Brothers; *Style—* The Rt Rev the Lord Bishop of Rochester; ✉ Bishopscourt, Rochester, Kent ME1 1TS (tel 01634 842721, fax 01634 831136, e-mail bishops.secretary@rochester.anglican.org)

ROCK, Angus James; s of Ian George Rock, and Anne Elizabeth, *née* Lyons; *b* 16 September 1964; *Educ* Cooper Sch Bicester, Gosford Hill Sch Kidlington; *Career* designer Cherwell Laboratories 1983–86, proprietor A J R Marketing (design and mktg an electronic instrumentation range for motorsport) 1986–88, sales and mktg mangr Stack Ltd 1988–91; ptnr: Design Graphique 1991–93, Head to Toe 1993–; Br Design Award 1990,

DTI Smart Award 2004; *Recreations* squash, tennis, skiing, music, golf, classic cars; *Style—* Angus J Rock, Esq; ✉ Head to Toe, 6/8 Cumnor Road, Wootton, Boars Hill, Oxford OX1 5JP (tel and fax 01865 326600)

ROCK, David Annison; s of Thomas Henry Rock (d 1964), of Sunderland, Co Durham, and Muriel, *née* Barton (d 1964); *b* 27 May 1929; *Educ* Bede GS Sunderland, Univ of Durham (BArch, Certificate in Town Planning); *m* 1, 18 Dec 1954 (m dis 1985), Daphne Elizabeth Richards; 2 da (Felicity b 1957, Alice b 1963), 3 s (Adam b 1960, Jacob b 1961, Mark b 1963); m 2, 27 Sept 1989, Lesley Patricia, *née* Murray; *Career* 2 Lt BAOR RE 1953–55; sr architect Sir Basil Spence 1952–53 and 1955–58, ptnr David Rock Architects 1958–59, ptnr and fndr London Group Building Design Partnership 1959–71, fndr ptnr and chm Rock Townsend 1971–92, co fndr Workspace Business Centre concept in UK 1971, fndr dir Barley Mow Workspace 1974–93, fndr chm Dryden Street Collective 1971–78, fndr ptnr Camp 5 1992–, fin dir Huguenot Ct Ltd 2003–05 and 2006–; head Lottery Architecture Unit Arts Cncl of England 1995–99, memb Sports Cncl Lottery Awards Panel 1995–97; Graham Willis visiting prof Univ of Sheffield 1990–92; pres: RIBA 1997–99 (memb Cncl 1970–76, 1986–88 and 1995–2001, vice-pres 1987–88 and 1995–97), pres Architects Benevolent Soc 1997–99 and 2003– (vice-pres 2000–2003); chm Soc of Architect Artists 1986–92; memb CNAA Architecture Bd 1973–77, specialist assessor Higher Educn Funding Cncl England 1993–95; tstee: Montgomery Sculpture Tst 2000–05, S Norfolk Buildings Preservation Tst 2003–05; personal awards: Soane Medallion, Owen Jones Studentship, H B Saint Award, RIBA Building Industry Tst Fellowship, Crown Prize, Glover Medal, AIA President's Medal 1998; FCSD 1963, FRIBA 1968 (ARIBA 1953), hon fell FAIA 2001 (hon assoc 1998); *Books* Vivat Ware! Strategies to Enhance an Historic Town (1974), The Grassroot Developers (1980); *Recreations* painting, illustration, work; *Style—* David Rock, Esq, PPRIBA, FCSD, Hon FAIA; ✉ The Beeches, 13 London Road, Harleston, Norfolk IP20 9BH; Camp 5 (tel and fax 01379 854897, e-mail david.rock1@btinternet.com)

ROCK, Prof Paul Elliot; s of Ashley Rock (d 2002), of London, and Charlotte, *née* Dickson (d 1969); *b* 4 August 1943; *Educ* William Ellis GS, LSE (BSc), Nuffield Coll Oxford (DPhil); *m* 25 Sept 1965, Barbara (d 1998), da of Hayman Ravid (d 1989); 2 s (Matthew Charles b 1970, Oliver James b 1974); *Career* visiting prof Princeton Univ USA 1974–75, visiting scholar Miny of the Slr Gen of Canada; LSE: asst lectr 1967–70, lectr 1970–76, prof of sociology 1986–95, prof of social instns 1995–; visiting prof Univ of Pennsylvania 2006–07; fell Center for Advanced Studies in Behavioral Sciences Stanford California 1996; dir The Mannheim Centre 1992–95; memb: Sociology and Social Admin Ctee SSRC 1976–80, Exec Ctee Br Sociological Assoc 1978–79, Parole Bd 1986–89; ed The British Journal of Sociology 1988–95; FRSA 1997, FBA 2000; *Books* Making People Pay (1973), The Making of Symbolic Interactionism (1979), Understanding Deviance (jtly, 1982–98), A View From The Shadows (1987), Helping Victims of Crime (1990), The Social World of an English Crown Court (1993), Reconstructing a Women's Prison (1996), After Homicide (1998), Constructing Victims' Rights (2004); *Style—* Prof Paul Rock; ✉ London School of Economics and Political Science, Houghton Street, Aldwych, London WC2A 2AE (tel 020 7955 7296, fax 020 7955 7405, e-mail p.rock@lse.ac.uk)

ROCK, Stuart Peter; s of Peter Illsley Rock, of 10 Marlborough Place, Wimborne Minster, Dorset, and Wendy Julie, *née* Ives; *b* 23 September 1960; *Educ* Malvern, Magdalen Coll Oxford (BA); *Career* ed Director Publications 1989–96 (joined 1987), editorial dir Caspian Publishing 1996–; winner of the BPC Publications Ed of the Year (Business) PPA Awards 1998; *Books* Family Firms (1991); *Recreations* architecture, photography, beer, reading; *Style—* Stuart Rock, Esq

ROCKER, David; s of Richard Frederick Rocker (d 1984), of Hatfield Peverel, Essex, and Elizabeth Ellen, *née* Lewis (d 2000); *b* 9 June 1944; *Educ* King Edward VI Sch Chelmsford; *m* 1972 (m dis 1992), Jacolyn Jane, da of John Geoffry Matthews, of Finchingfield, Essex; *Career* admitted slr; ptnr Leonard Gray & Co 1968–71; legal advsr: Hawker Siddeley Group Ltd 1971–73, Trident TV 1973–79; dir of legal affrs Guinness plc 1982–86, chm Guinness Superlatives Ltd 1984–85, Guinness Overseas Ltd 1985–86; sr ptnr David Rocker & Co 1986–; chm: Rocker Ltd 1989–2000, Scarab Property Ltd 1999–2000, Cousin Ltd 2005–, Mirabeau Ltd 2005–, Burton & Co (Thorney) Ltd 2003–; *Recreations* motor racing, riding, bridge; *Style—* David Rocker, Esq; ✉ The Maltings, 21 The Green, Writtle, Essex CM1 3DT (tel 01245 420141)

ROCKLEY, Edward George (Ted); s of George Alfred Rockley (d 1982), and Catherine Rockley (d 1998); *b* 27 April 1952; *Educ* Quintin Kynaston, Hornsey Sch of Art, Middlesex Poly (DipAD); *m* 1983, Lyn Michelle Joniel, da of Colin Wakeley; 2 da (Camilla b 14 Sept 1984, Roseanna b 26 Nov 1992), 1 s (Joshua b 17 March 1987); *Career* animator and designer BBC Adult Literacy Project 1974–77, freelance animator 1977–81, co-dir Klactoveesedstene Animations Ltd 1981–; *Style—* Ted Rockley, Esq; ✉ Oscar Grillo & Ted Rockley Animations, 11 Gordon Road, London W5 2AD (tel and fax 020 8991 6978, e-mail klacto@klacto.com)

ROCKLEY, 3 Baron (UK 1934); James Hugh Cecil; s of 2 Baron Rockley (d 1976, whose f, 1 Baron, was er s of Lord Eustace Cecil, 3 s of 2 Marquess of Salisbury by his 1 w, Frances, the Gascoyne heiress), and Anne, da of Adm Hon Sir Herbert Meade-Fetherstonhaugh, GCVO, CB, DSO, yr bro of 5 Earl of Clanwilliam; *b* 5 April 1934; *Educ* Eton, New Coll Oxford; *m* 1958, Lady Sarah Primrose Cadogan, eldest da of 7 Earl Cadogan, MC, DL; 1 s, 2 da; *Heir* s, Hon Anthony Cecil; *Career* dir: Kleinwort Benson Ltd 1970–96, Equity & Law plc 1980–91, Christies International plc 1989–98, Cobham plc 1989–2002, Abbey National plc 1990–99, The Foreign and Colonial Investment Trust plc 1991–2003, Cadogan Group Ltd 1996–; chm: Dartford River Crossing 1988–93, Kleinwort Development Fund plc 1990–93, Midland Expressway 1992–93, Kleinwort Benson Group plc 1993–96, Hall and Woodhouse Ltd 2001–; Lambert Energy Advsy 2001–; tstee Nat Portrait Gallery 1981–88; chm Issuing Houses Assoc 1987–89; chm of govrs Milton Abbey Sch 1999–2004; memb Design Cncl 1988–94; Liveryman Worshipful Co of Salters (Master 1998–99); *Style—* The Rt Hon the Lord Rockley; ✉ Lytchett Heath, Poole, Dorset BH16 6AE (tel 01202 622228); Cadogan Group Ltd, 18 Cadogan Gardens, London SW3 2RP (tel 020 7730 4567)

RODDA, James (Jim); s of Alfred George Rodda, and Constance Ruby, *née* Thompson; *b* 16 August 1945; *Educ* Maldon GS, Univ of Reading (BA), Univ of Leicester; *m* July 1967, Angela Faith Hopkinson; 2 da, 1 s; *Career* successive appts at: Chamberlain Turton & Dunn Nottingham, Coopers & Lybrand London & Brussels, Thomas Cook Peterborough and New York, Lonconex London, Dial Contracts London, London Commodity Exchange; formerly: dir of fin and admin House of Commons, fin dir National Film and TV Sch; currently vol treas NCCPG (nat plant and collection scheme); memb John Hampden Soc, memb ICAEW; *Recreations* gardening, rambling; *Style—* Jim Rodda, Esq; ✉ c/o ICAEW, Chartered Accountants' Hall, Moorgate Place, London EC2P 2BJ

RODDICK, (Thomas) Gordon; *Educ* RAC Cirencester; *m* 1970, Dame Anita Roddick, DBE (d 2007); 2 da (Justine b 1969, Samantha b 1971); *Career* co-fndr and chm The Body Shop International plc 1976–; co-fndr The Big Issue; *Style—* Gordon Roddick, Esq; ✉ The Body Shop International plc, Watersmead, Littlehampton, West Sussex BN17 6LS

RODDICK, (George) Winston; CB (2004), QC (1986); s of William Daniel Roddick (d 1977), of Caernarfon, and Aelwen, *née* Hughes (d 1992); *b* 2 October 1940, Caernarfon; *Educ* Ysgol Syr Huw Owen, Caernarfon GS, Tal-Handak Malta, UCL (pres Law Soc 1964–65); *m* 24 Sept 1966, Cennin, da of James Parry, BEM (d 1986), of Caernarfon; 1 s (Daniel b 1977), 1 da (Helen b 1979); *Career* called to the Bar Gray's Inn 1968 (bencher 1997); recorder 1986–; counsel gen Nat Assembly for Wales 1998–2003; hon recorder of Caernarfon 2001; memb: Gen Cncl of the Bar 1992–95, Professional Conduct Ctee of the Bar 1994–96, Lord Chancellor's Advsy Ctee on Statute Law 1999–2003, Standing Ctee on the Use of Welsh Language in Legal Proceedings 1999–, Employed Barristers Ctee Bar Cncl 2000–03; chm Bristol and Cardiff Chancery Bar Assoc 1996–98; memb Editorial Bd: Cambridge Jl of Financial Crime 1995–98, Wales Law Jl 2001–; memb: Welsh Language Bd 1986–92, ITC 1998, S4C Authority 2004–; patron Caernarfon RFC 1994–, hon life memb Caernarfon Town Football Supporters' Club, vice-pres Caernarfon Male Voice Choir 1994–, pres Cantorion Creigiau 2000–; govr Ysgol y Wern Cardiff 1991–99, vice-pres UCW Aberystwyth 2000 (hon fell 1999); *Recreations* fishing; *Clubs* Caernarfon Sailing, Caernarfon RFC; *Style—* Winston Roddick, Esq, CB, QC

RODDIE, Prof Ian Campbell; CBE (1987), TD (1967); s of Rev John Richard Wesley Roddie (d 1953), of Belfast, NI, and Mary Hill, *née* Wilson (d 1973); *b* 1 December 1928; *Educ* Methodist Coll Belfast, Queen's Univ Belfast (BSc, MB BCh, BAO, MD, DSc); *m* 1, 14 March 1958, Elizabeth (Betty) Ann Gillon (d 1974), da of Thomas Honeyman, of Cheltenham, Glos; 3 da (Mary b 1960, Catherine b 1962, Sarah b 1963), 1 s (Patrick b 1965); m 2, 29 Nov 1974 (m dis 1983), Katherine Anne, da of Edward O'Hara, of Belfast, NI; 1 da (Claire b 1975), 1 s (David b 1977); m 3, 14 Nov 1987, Janet Doreen, da of Thomas Russell Lennon (d 1978), of Larne, NI; *Career* RAMC and T & AVR 1951–68, Queen's Univ Belfast OC Med Sub-Unit, ret Maj 1968; res med offr Royal Victoria Hosp Belfast 1953–54; Queen's Univ Belfast: lectr, sr lectr and reader in physiology 1954–64, Dunville prof of physiology 1964–87, dean Faculty of Med 1976–81, pro-vice-chllr 1984–87, prof emeritus 1988–; Harkness fell Univ of Washington Seattle USA 1960–61; staff conslt: Asian Development Bank Manila 1978–88, International Finance Corporation/African Project Devpt Facility/World Bank Washington 1989–2003; visiting prof: Univ of NSW Sydney 1983–84, Shinshu Univ Matsumoto 1984, The Chinese Univ of Hong Kong 1988–90; conslt physiologist Eastern Health and Social Servs Bd NI 1957–88 (memb Bd 1976–81), dep med dir and dir of med educn King Khalid Nat Gd Hosp Jeddah 1990–94; pres: Belfast Assoc of Univ Teachers 1974–76, Ulster Biomedical Engrg Soc 1979–81, Belfast Med Students Assoc 1982–83; memb: Physiological Systems Bd MRC 1974–76, NI Postgrad Med Cncl 1976–81, Med Advsy Ctee CVCP 1976–81, Home Def Scientific Advsy Ctee (chief regnl scientific advsr) 1977–88, Gen Dental Cncl 1978–81, Royal Irish Acad 1978–, GMC 1979–81; pres Royal Acad of Medicine in Ireland 1985–87, chm Ctee The Physiological Soc (UK) 1986–88; memb Physiological Soc 1956 (hon memb 1988); FRCPI 1965 (MRCPI 1957), MRIA 1978, emeritus memb Int Soc of Lymphology 1995; *Books* Physiology for Practitioners (2 edn, 1975), The Physiology of Disease (1975), Multiple Choice Questions in Human Physiology (6 edn, 2004); *Recreations* reading, writing, travel; *Clubs* Reform; *Style—* Prof Ian Roddie, CBE, TD; ✉ 32A Hazlewell Road, Putney, London SW15 6LR (tel 020 8789 1848, e-mail ian.roddie@gmail.com)

RODEN, 10 Earl of (I 1771); Sir Robert John Jocelyn; 14 Bt (E 1665); also Baron Newport (I 1743) and Viscount Jocelyn (I 1755); s of 9 Earl of Roden (d 1993), and Clodagh Rose, *née* Kennedy (d 1989); *b* 25 August 1938; *Educ* Stowe; *m* 1, 1970 (m dis 1982), Sara Cecilia, da of late Brig Andrew Dunlop; 1 da (Lady Cecilia Rose b 1976); m 2, 13 Feb 1986, Ann Margareta Maria, da of late Dr Gunnar Henning (d 1948); 1 s (Shane Robert Henning, Viscount Jocelyn b 1989); *Heir* s, Viscount Jocelyn; *Style—* The Rt Hon the Earl of Roden

RODENBURG, Patsy; OBE (2005); da of Marius Rodenburg, of London, and Margaret Edna, *née* Moody; *b* 2 September 1953; *Educ* St Christopher's Sch Beckenham, Central Sch of Speech and Drama London; *Career* voice coach RSC 1981–90; formed The Voice and Speech Centre 1988; head of voice: Guildhall Sch of Music and Drama 1981–, RNT 1990–; LGSM (The City of London) 1982, distinguished visiting prof Southern Methodist Univ Dallas 1989, hon memb VASTA 1995; assoc: The Michael Howard Studios New York 1996, Royal Court Theatre London 1999; works extensively in theatre, film, TV and opera incl: Europe, USA, Canada, Asia and Aust; coached many leading theatre and opera cos incl: Stratford Festival Theatre Canada, Kabuki Theatre Japan, NT of Greece, Lithuania, Norway, NT Sch of India, The Market Theatre Johannesburg, Peking Opera, Ex Machina (Robert Lepage); for GB: Royal Opera, ENO, Opera North, English Shakespeare Co, Cheek by Jowl, Theatre de Complicité; RNT 1990–2006; *Publications* The Right to Speak (1992), The Need for Words (1993), A Voice of your Own (video, 1995), The Actor Speaks (1996), Speaking Shakespeare (2002), Presence (2007); *Recreations* reading, travelling; *Style—* Ms Patsy Rodenburg, OBE; ✉ c/o Royal National Theatre, Upper Ground, South Bank, London SE1 9PX (tel 020 7928 2033)

RODENHURST, John Emberton; s of Jeffrey Royle Rodenhurst (d 1964), of Ellesmere, Shropshire, and Margaret Elizabeth, *née* Emberton, of Cockshutt, Shrewsbury; *b* 9 August 1941; *Educ* Oswestry HS for Boys; *m* 26 April 1967, Rosemary Barbara, da of Horace Harrison, of Moreton Say, Market Drayton; 1 s (Simon John b 29 Dec 1967), 1 da (Penelope-Jane b 30 Jan 1970); *Career* hotelier; proprietor Soughton Hall Hotel 1986–; *Recreations* shooting and country pursuits, good food and wine, a little golf, widespread travel, horse racing; *Style—* John Rodenhurst, Esq; ✉ Soughton Hall, Northop, Mold, Clwyd CH7 6AB (tel 01352 840 811, fax 01352 840 382)

RODERICK, Edward Joseph; s of Edward Deakin Roderick (d 1995), and Joan Roderick; *b* 23 October 1952; *Educ* De La Salle GS Liverpool; *m* 1974, Denise Ann, *née* Rowan; 2 s (Mark b 30 Jan 1976, Simon b 7 March 1978); *Career* B & I Line 1972–87 (head UK Freight Ops 1984–87), md Alexandra Molyneux Transport 1987–88; BET plc: md IFF 1988–90, gp dir UTCH Ltd 1988–90, dir UTL Ltd 1988–90, dir Seawheel 1988–90; gen mangr UK & Iberia Bell Lines 1990–92, divnl md (network and distribution) Hays plc 1992–95; Christian Salvesen plc: md Industrial Div 1996, chief exec 1997–2004; non-exec chm Passim Int Ltd 2005–, Truck Protect Ltd 2005–; non-exec dir Heywood Williams Gp plc 2002–; dir: Road Haulage Assoc Ltd 1998–2000, Freight Tport Assoc 2000–; non-exec dir Northern Ballet Theatre 1997–2000; Hon LLD De Montfort Univ 2001; MInstD 1987, FILog 1992, CIMgt 2000; *Recreations* golf, opera, ballet, swimming, wife and family; *Style—* Dr Roderick; ✉ Campbell House, Northampton Road, Higham Ferrers, Northamptonshire NN10 6AL

RODFORD, Neil John; *Educ* Preston Comp Sch, CIM (DipM); *Career* W H Smith: magazine sales mangr 1989–91, magazine mangr 1991–93, ops mangr 1993–94, gen mangr 1994–96; Harrods Hldgs: gen mangr Harrods Knightsbridge 1996–97, md Fulham FC 1997–2000; ptnr and business devpt mangr Keegan Partnership 2000–01, chief exec Formation Group plc 2001–; *Recreations* soccer, squash, golf, horse racing; *Style—* Neil Rodford, Esq; ✉ Formation Group plc, 9–13 Manchester Road, Wilmslow, Cheshire SK9 1BQ (tel 01625 539832, fax 01625 536402, e-mail neilr@formationgroupplc.com)

RODGER, Nicholas Andrew Martin; s of Lt Cdr Ian Alexander Rodger, RN, of Arundel, W Sussex, and Sara Mary, *née* Perceval; *b* 12 November 1949; *Educ* Ampleforth, Univ Coll Oxford (MA, DPhil); *m* 28 Aug 1982, Susan Eleanor, da of Henry Meigs Farwell, of Ickenham, Middx; 1 da (Ellen b 1984), 3 s (Christopher b 1987, Alexander b 1989, Crispian b 1997); *Career* asst keeper of Public Records 1974–91; Anderson fell National Maritime Museum Greenwich 1992–99; Univ of Exeter: sr lectr in history 1999–2000, prof of naval history 2000–; hon sec Navy Records Soc 1976–90; FBA, FSA, FRHistS; *Books* The Admiralty (1979), The Wooden World, An Anatomy of the Georgian Navy (1986), The Insatiable Earl: A Life of John Montagu, Fourth Earl of Sandwich 1718–1792 (1993), The Safeguard of the Sea. A Naval History of Britain, Vol 1, 660–1649 (1997), The Command of the Ocean: A Naval History of Britain 1649–1815 (2004); *Recreations* hill walking, music; *Style—* N A M Rodger, Esq, FBA; ✉ Department of History, University of

Exeter, Amory Building, Rennes Drive, Exeter EX4 4RJ (e-mail n.a.m.rodger@exeter.ac.uk)

RODGER OF EARLSFERRY, Baron (Life Peer UK 1992), of Earlsferry in the District of North East Fife; Alan Ferguson Rodger; PC (1992); s of Prof Thomas Ferguson Rodger, CBE (d 1978), of Glasgow, and Jean Margaret Smith, *née* Chalmers (d 1981); *b* 18 September 1944; *Educ* Kelvinside Acad Glasgow, Univ of Glasgow (MA, LLB), New Coll Oxford (DCL, MA, DPhil); *Career* jr research fell Balliol Coll Oxford 1969–70, fell and tutor in law New Coll Oxford 1970–72, memb Faculty of Advocates 1974 (clerk 1976–79), standing jr counsel (Scotland) to Dept of Trade 1979, advocate depute 1985–88, QC (Scot) 1985, home advocate depute 1986–88, SG Scotland 1989–92, Lord Advocate 1992–95, judge of the Court of Session 1995–96, Lord Justice-Gen and Lord Pres of the Court of Session 1996–2001, Lord of Appeal in Ordinary 2001–; hon bencher: Lincoln's Inn 1992, Inn of Ct NI 1998; memb Mental Welfare Cmmn for Scotland 1982–85; Maccabaean lectr British Acad 1991; visitor St Hugh's Coll Oxford 2003–; pres Holdsworth Club 1998–99; hon memb Soc of Public Teachers of Law 1992, corresponding memb Bayerische Akademie der Wissenschaften 2001; hon fell Balliol Coll Oxford 1999; Hon LLD: Univ of Glasgow 1995, Univ of Aberdeen 2001; FBA 1991, FRSE 1992; *Books* Owners and Neighbours in Roman Law (1972), Gloag and Henderson's Introduction to the Law of Scotland (asst ed, 10 edn, 1995); *Recreations* writing, walking; *Clubs* Athenaeum, Caledonian; *Style—* The Rt Hon Lord Rodger of Earlsferry, PC, FBA, FRSE

RODGERS, Brid; da of Thomas Stratford (d 1947), of Co Donegal, and Josephine, *née* Coll (d 1996); *b* 20 February 1935; *Educ* St Louis Convent Monaghan, UC Dublin (BA, HDipEd); *m* 16 July 1960, Antoin Rodgers, s of James Rodgers; 3 da (Mary b 18 April 1961, Anne b 5 June 1962, Bríd b 2 May 1965), 3 s (Séamus b 25 Oct 1963, Tom b 2 March 1971, Antoin b 24 April 1973); *Career* teacher 1957–60 and 1988–92; chairperson SDLP 1978–80, gen sec SDLP 1981–83, memb Irish Senate 1983–97, memb Craigavon Cncl 1985–93, ldr SDLP Cncl Gp Craigavon BC 1985–93, memb SDLP Talks Team Brooke-Mayhew Talks 1991, SDLP delg Forum for Peace and Reconciliation (Dublin Castle) 1994–95, elected to NI Forum for Political Dialogue 1996, chairperson SDLP Talks Team Castle Buildings Talks 1996–98, formerly pty spokesperson on Women, Cultural Affairs and Parades, dep ldr SDLP 2001–03; MLA (SDLP) Upper Bann 1998–2003; min of Agric and Rural Devpt NI Exec 1999–2002; former memb: Southern Educn & Library Bd, Standing Advsy Cmmn on Human Rights; dir Bord Bia 2004–; Hon LLD NUI 2003; *Style—* Ms Bríd Rodgers; ✉ 34 Kilmore Road, Lurgan, Co Armagh BT67 9BP (e-mail b100rodgers@btinternet.com)

RODGERS, Ian Louis; s of Charles Augustus Rodgers (ka 1942), and Doris, *née* Hanneman; *b* 12 January 1943; *Educ* Christ's Hosp; *m* 3 June 1967, Susanna, da of Rev Stanley James Pert (d 1974); 2 s (Mark b 1969, Paul b 1971); *Career* with Laurence Keen & Gardner 1959–71, ptnr Laurence Prust 1977–86 (joined 1971); dir: Framlington Asset Management Ltd 1986–89, Framlington Investment Management Ltd 1986–89, Framlington Investment Trust Services 1986–89; partnership dir: Christ's Hosp 1989–91 (fndr The Christ's Hosp Partnership), donation govr Christ's Hosp 1987–, One ACT (consultancy) 1991–; dir and memb Gen Cncl South American Mission Soc 1986–2006 (treas 1994–2000); Freeman City of London 1978, Liveryman Worshipful Co of Poulters; govr Richard Reeve's Fndn 2003– (vice-chm 2006–); memb: Stock Exchange 1973–86, Amicable Soc of Blues 1996–; MInstD 1989–, MInstF 1989–, MSI 1993–; *Recreations* fly fishing, music, theatre, photography, computing and DTP; *Clubs* City Livery; *Style—* Ian Rodgers, Esq; ✉ tel 020 8460 4280, e-mail rodgersi@nildram.co.uk

RODGERS, Joan; CBE (2001); da of Thomas Rodgers (d 1971), and Julia Rodgers; *b* 4 November 1956; *Educ* Whitehaven GS, Univ of Liverpool (BA), RNCM Manchester; *m* 1988, Paul Daniel, CBE, *qv*; 2 da (Eleanor b 4 Sept 1990, Rose b 14 May 1993); *Career* soprano; debut as Pamina in Die Zauberflöte at the Aix-en-Provence Festival; major roles incl: Zerlina in Don Giovanni (Royal Opera House Covent Garden, Paris), Pamina (Covent Garden, ENO, Paris Opera), Gilda in Rigoletto (ENO), Nannetta (ENO), Countess Almaviva in The Marriage of Figaro/Le Nozze di Figaro (ENO, Netherlands Opera Amsterdam), Susanna in Le Nozze di Figaro (Glyndebourne, Paris, Florence), Cleopatra in Giulio Cesare (Scottish Opera), Yolande (Edinburgh Festival), Despina in Cosi fan Tutte (Paris, Florence), Br premiere of Chabrier's Briséis (Edinburgh Festival), Fiordiligi in Cosi fan Tutte (Theatre de la Monnaie Brussels), Donna Elvira in Don Giovanni (Scottish Opera 1995, Paris 1996), Pamina in Die Zauberflöte (Met Opera NY 1995, Berlin 1996), Ginevra in Ariodante (ENO) 1996, Hero in Beatrice et Benedict (Brussels Opera), Blanche in Les Dialogues des Carmelites (Amsterdam), Governess in Britten's Turn of the Screw (Royal Opera House), Anne Truelove in The Rake's Progress (BBC Symphony Orchestra) 1997, Marschallin in Der Rosenkavalier for Scottish Opera, Ginevra in Ariodante (Munich) 2000; appeared at other operatic venues incl: Opera Bastille Paris, Zurich, Munich; given concerts in: London, Vienna, Madrid, Copenhagen, Salzburg, Paris, Lisbon; ABC tour of Australia 1995, BBC Proms; worked with conductors incl: Sir Colin Davis, Sir Georg Solti, Andrew Davis, Daniel Barenboim, Jeffrey Tate, Sir Simon Rattle, Zubin Mehta; winner Kathleen Ferrier Meml Scholarship 1981; *Recordings* incl: solo recital of Tchaikovsky Songs, Mozart Mass in C (under Harnoncourt), Mozart Da Ponte Operas (with the Berlin Philharmonic under Barenboim), Vaughan Williams Sea Symphony (with the Royal Liverpool Philharmonic under Vernon Handley), Beethoven 9th Symphony (with the Royal Liverpool Philharmonic under Charles Mackerras), Handel Messiah, Delius Mass of Life and Howells Hymns Paradisi (under Richard Hickox), Creation (with Frans Brüggen), Rachmaninov Songs (with Howard Shelley); *Recreations* walking, cooking, playing with my children; *Style—* Ms Joan Rodgers, CBE

RODGERS, Worshipful (Doris) June (Mrs Roger Evans); da of James A Rodgers, JP, of Craigavad, Co Down, and Margaret Doris, *née* Press; *b* 10 June 1945; *Educ* Victoria Coll Belfast, Trinity Coll Dublin (MA), Lady Margaret Hall Oxford (MA); *m* 6 Oct 1973, Roger Kenneth Evans, *qv*, s of Gerald Raymond Evans of Mere, Wilts; 2 s (Edward Arthur b 13 May 1981, Henry William b 8 Feb 1983); *Career* called to the Bar Middle Temple 1971; recorder of the Crown Court 1993–; chllr of the Dio of Gloucester 1990–; memb Court of Common Cncl City of London Ward Farringdon Without 1975–96, former memb City and East London Area HA; Freeman City of London 1975; memb: Hon Soc of Middle Temple, Ecclesiastical Law Soc; *Recreations* architectural history, Anglo-Normandy; *Clubs* Oxford and Cambridge; *Style—* The Worshipful Miss June Rodgers; ✉ 2 Harcourt Buildings, The Temple, London EC4Y 9DB (tel 020 7353 6961, fax 020 7353 6968, e-mail jrodgers@harcourtchambers.law.co.uk)

RODGERS, Peter David; s of late Francis Norman Rodgers, and Margaret Elizabeth, *née* Harte; *b* 8 October 1943; *Educ* Finchley Catholic GS, Trinity Coll Cambridge (MA); *m* 14 Sept 1968, Christine Mary Agnes, da of late Dr Duncan Primrose Wilkie, OBE; 2 da (Susannah b 29 May 1974, Georgia b 17 Oct 1985), 2 s (Benedict b 4 Nov 1980, William b 18 Jan 1982); *Career* trainee Oxford Mail 1966–67, regions ed Industry Week 1967–69, industrial corr The Guardian 1973–76 (technol corr 1970–73), energy ed The Sunday Times 1976–81; The Guardian: fin corr 1981–84, city ed 1984–90; fin ed The Independent 1990–97; Bank of England: sec 1997–2003, dir of communications 2003–; *Books* The Work of Art (1989); *Recreations* offshore sailing, gardening, theatre, music; *Style—* Peter Rodgers, Esq; ✉ Bank of England, Threadneedle Street, London EC2R 8AH (tel 020 7601 4444, e-mail peter.rodgers@bankofengland.co.uk)

RODGERS, Sir (Andrew) Piers Wingate; 3 Bt (UK 1964), of Groombridge, Kent; yr s of Sir John Charles Rodgers, 1 Bt, DL (d 1993), and Betsy, *née* Aikin-Sneath (d 1998); suc bro, Sir Tobias Rodgers, 2 Bt (d 1997); *b* 24 October 1944; *Educ* Eton, Merton Coll Oxford (BA); *m* 1, 9 Sept 1979 (m dis 2000), Marie-Agathe, da of Charles-Albert Houette, Croix de Guerre (d 1989), of Bléneau, France; 2 s (Thomas b 1979, Augustus b 1983); m 2, Ilona, da of Col A Medvedev, and Prof Natalia Medvedeva; 2 da (Hermione b 2001, Anna Laetitia b 2006); *Heir* s, Thomas Rodgers; *Career* with J Henry Schroder Wagg & Co Ltd 1967–73 (PA to chm 1970–73), dir Int Cncl on Monuments & Sites (ICOMOS) Paris 1973–79 (sec UK Ctee 1981), UNESCO expert (Implementation of World Heritage Convention) 1979–80, sec of Royal Acad of Arts London (also sec of Chantrey Bequest and British Inst Fund) 1981–96, dir Burlington Gardens Project Royal Acad of Arts 1996–97; memb Bd Warburg Inst Univ of London 1993–99; tstee: The Type Museum 1992–2004 (dir 2001–04), Africa 95 1993–2001; Freeman City of London, hon memb Ct of Assts Worshipful Co of Masons; memb Co of Merchant Adventurers of City of York; FRSA; Chevalier de l'Ordre des Arts et des Lettres (France) 1987, Ordre National du Mérite (France) 1991, Cavaliere Ufficiale Ordine al Merito della Repubblica Italiana 1992; *Clubs* Brooks's, Pratt's; *Style—* Sir Piers Rodgers, Bt; ✉ Peverell, Bradford Peverell, Dorset DT2 9SE

RODGERS, Toni Louise; da of William Neville Rodgers, and Shauneen Anne Rodgers; *Educ* Manchester Poly (BA); *Career* writer Elle Magazine, features ed Sky Magazine, ed Just Seventeen, launch ed Minx Magazine, ed Elle Decoration; winner BSME Editor of the Year Women's Non-Monthly Magazine 1993; judge OXO/Peugeot Design Awards; *Recreations* accumulating mid-century Italian glass and Scandinavian ceramics, touring boot fairs of the South East; *Style—* Ms Toni Rodgers; ✉ Editor, Elle Decoration, Endeavour House, 189 Shaftesbury Avenue, London WC2H 8JG (tel 020 7208 3489, fax 020 7208 3587, e-mail toni-rodgers@emap.com)

RODGERS OF QUARRY BANK, Baron (Life Peer UK 1992), of Kentish Town in the London Borough of Camden; William Thomas Rodgers; PC (1975); s of William Arthur Rodgers and Gertrude Helen Rodgers; *b* 28 October 1928; *Educ* Quarry Bank HS Liverpool, Magdalen Coll Oxford; *m* 1955, Silvia, da of Hirsch Szulman; 3 da; *Career* MP (Lab until 1981, thereafter SDP) Teesside Stockton 1962–79, Stockton N 1979–83 (Parly candidate Bristol W March 1957); in Lab Govts: Parly under sec DEA 1964–67, FO 1967–68, min of state BOT 1968–69, min of state Treasy 1969–70, MOD 1974–76, tport sec 1976–79; Lib Dem ldr House of Lords 1997–2001; gen sec Fabian Soc 1953–60 (remained memb until 1981), ldr UK Delgn Cncl Europe & WEU 1967–68, chm Expenditure Ctee Trade & Industry 1971–74; dir gen RIBA 1987–94, chm Advertising Standards Authy 1995–2000; Hon FRIBA, Hon FIStructE; *Books* Hugh Gaitskell (1963), The People into Parliament (1966), The Politics of Change (1982), Government and Industry (1986), Fourth Among Equals (2000); *Style—* The Rt Hon Lord Rodgers of Quarry Bank, PC; ✉ 43 North Road, London N6 4BE

RODNEY, 10 Baron (GB 1782); Sir George Brydges Rodney; 10 Bt (GB 1764); s of 9 Baron Rodney (d 1992), and Régine Elisabeth Lucienne Thérèse Marie Ghislaine, *née* Pangaert d'Opdorp (d 2003); *b* 3 January 1953; *Educ* Eton; *m* 20 Aug 1996, Jane, da of Hamilton Rowan Blakeney, of Hatherop, Glos; *Heir* s, Hon John Rodney; *Style—* The Rt Hon the Lord Rodney

RODNEY BENNETT, *see:* Bennett

RODRIGUES, Christopher John; CBE (2007); s of late Alfred John Rodrigues, and Joyce Margaret, *née* Farron-Smith; *b* 24 October 1949; *Educ* Univ Coll Sch, Jesus Coll Cambridge (MA, Rowing blue, pres CUBC), Harvard Business Sch (Baker scholar, MBA); *m* Priscilla Purcell Young; 1 s, 1 da; *Career* with Spillers Foods London 1971–72, Foster, Turner & Benson London 1972–74, MBA Harvard 1974–76, McKinsey & Co London 1976–79, American Express NY and London 1979–88; Thomas Cook Group Ltd: chief operating offr 1988–90, gp md 1990–92, gp chief exec 1992–95; gp chief exec Bradford & Bingley plc 1996–2004, pres and ceo Visa International 2004–06, chm VisitBritain 2007–; dep chm Provident Finanical 2007– (also chm Int Div); non-exec dir: Energis 1997–2002, FSA 1997–2003, Ladbrokes plc 2003–; steward Henley Royal Regatta 1998–; FRSA; *Recreations* cooking, skiing, rowing, shooting, opera, ballet; *Clubs* Leander (past chm), Hawks' (Cambridge), Arts; *Style—* Christopher Rodrigues, Esq, CBE; ✉ VisitBritain, Thames Tower, Blacks Road, London W6 9EL

RODWELL, His Hon Daniel Alfred Hunter; QC (1982); s of Brig Reginald Mandeville Rodwell, AFC (d 1974), and Nellie Barbara, *née* D'Costa (d 1967); *b* 3 January 1936; *Educ* Munro Coll Jamaica, Worcester Coll Oxford (BA); *m* 1967, Veronica Frances Ann, da of late Robin Cecil, CMG, of Hants; 2 s (William b 1967, Thomas b 1970), 1 da (Lucy b 1974); *Career* Nat Serv in W Yorks Regt, 2 Lt, TA (Capt); barr, recorder Crown Ct 1980–86, circuit judge 1986–2002 (dep circuit judge 2002–05); *Recreations* hunting, sailing (Emrys), gardening; *Clubs* Pegasus, Bar Yacht; *Style—* His Hon Daniel Rodwell, QC; ✉ Roddimore House, Winslow Road, Great Horwood, Milton Keynes MK17 0NY (tel 01296 712536, e-mail dan.rodwell@btinternet.com)

RODWELL, Dennis Graham; s of Albert James Rodwell, MBE (d 1991), and Constance Edith, *née* Scaddan (d 1999); *b* 24 January 1948; *Educ* Kingswood Sch Bath, Clare Coll Cambridge (MA, DipArch), Open Univ (Dip French); *m* 10 May 1975 (m dis 2002), Rosemary Ann, *née* Rimmer; 2 s (Nicholas b 1978, Christopher b 1979), 1 da (Melanie b 1982); *Career* architect, author and lectr; in practice Dennis Rodwell Architects 1975–98; works incl: historic building restorations, urban conservation and regeneration, heritage presentation, rescue and restoration of Melrose Station and its mgmnt as a mixed use commercial devpt 1985–2003; recipient numerous awards and commendations; int conslt on building conservation, urban conservation and sustainable urban devpt to World Heritage Centre and Div of Cultural Heritage UNESCO, German Agency for Tech Co-operation (GTZ), World Bank and Br Cncl 1999–; conservation offr/urban design City of Derby 1999–2003; memb The Edinburgh New Town Conservation Ctee 1981–84 and 1987–90, tstee The Trimontium Tst 1988–2000 (chm 1988–90); served ctees: Scottish Georgian Soc, Cncls of the Royal Incorporation of Architects in Scotland, Edinburgh Architectural Assoc; lecturing incl European Urban Conservation course Univ of Dundee 1991–93, speaking incl at int conservation confs 1975–; RIBA 1973, FRIAS 1982, FSA Scot 1990, FRSA 1991, memb Inst of Historic Building Conservation (IHBC) 1998; *Publications* Conservation and Sustainability in Historic Cities (2007); articles in jls and books upon historical, architectural and urban conservation subjects incl: European Heritage (1975), Architectural Conservation in Europe (1975), Civilising the City (1991), Journal of Architectural Conservation (2002–), World Heritage (2002–); *Recreations* travel, modern languages, walking, reading, photography, gardening, music; *Style—* Dennis Rodwell, Esq; ✉ Greenside Park, St Boswells, Melrose, Roxburghshire TD6 0AH (tel 01835 824625, mobile 07740 871043, e-mail dennis@dennisrodwell.co.uk)

RODWELL, John Francis Meadows; s of Maj Percival Francis (Jim) Rodwell, MBE, TD, of Halesworth, Suffolk; *b* 11 July 1946; *m* 9 March 1974, Rosie, da of John Trevor Munden Brook (d 1981), of Meole Brace, Shrewsbury; *Career* joined Suffolk and Cambs Regt 1965, Mons OCS 1965, Grenadier Gds 1968, psc 1979, ret Army 1983; SG Warburg & Co Ltd: joined 1983, corp and community affrs dir Mercury Asset Mgmnt 1996–98 (admin dir 1989–96), corp and community affrs dir Merrill Lynch Mercury 1998–99; corp affrs conslt 1999–2002, dir Sponsorship Consulting Ltd 2002–; chm: Hedley Foundation 2002– (tstee and dir 1984–2002), Fairhood Properties Ltd 2003–, Holbeck Properties Ltd 2003–, Mountbarrow Properties Ltd 2003–, Merewood Properties Ltd 2003–, Middlerigg Servs Ltd 2003–; memb HM Body Guard Hon Corps of Gentlemen at Arms 1998–, Worshipful Co of Skinners; *Recreations* Frenc inland waterways, skiing, golf; *Clubs* Cavalry and Guards' (chm 1996–2002, tstee 2002–), City of London, Royal West Norfolk Golf, Hunstanton Golf; *Style—* John F M Rodwell, Esq; ✉ 1 Palmerston House, 60 Kensington

Place, London W8 7PU; Bunkles, Church Street, Thornham, Norfolk PE36 6NJ (e-mail jrodwell@hedleyfoundation.org.uk)

ROE, Prof Derek Arthur; s of Arthur William Roe (d 1980), and Marjorie Irene, *née* Barrow (d 1969); *b* 31 August 1937; *Educ* St Edward's Sch Oxford, Peterhouse Cambridge (MA, PhD), Univ of Oxford (MA, DLitt); *Career* served Royal Sussex Regt and Intelligence Corps 1956–58; Univ of Oxford: lectr in prehistoric archaeology 1965–2003, fell St Cross Coll 1970– (vice-master 1988–90), hon dir Donald Baden-Powell Quaternary Res Centre 1975–2003, dir of grad studies in archaeology 1995–97 and 1998–99, prof of palaeolithic archaeology 1997–2003; memb Editorial Bd: Review of Archaeology until 2005, World Archaeology until 2005, L'Anthropologie, Oxford Jl of Archaeology, Geoarchaeology (until 2001), Proceedings of the Prehistoric Soc (until 2004); archaeological corr The Times 1961–66; govr St Edward's Sch Oxford 1970–; Henry Stopes Medal Geologists Assoc of London 1985; FSA 1978–2004; *Books* A Gazetteer of British Lower and Middle Palaeolithic Sites (1968), Prehistory: an Introduction (1970), Field Guide to the Oxford Region (Quaternary Res Assoc handbook, ed, 1976), The Lower and Middle Palaeolithic Periods in Britain (1981), Adlun in the Stone Age: the excavations of D A E Garrod in the Lebanon, 1958–1963 (2 vols, ed, 1983), Studies in the Upper Palaeolithic of Northwest Europe (ed, 1986), The Late Glacial in north-west Europe: human adaptation and environmental change at the end of the Pleistocene (jt ed, 1991), Olduvai Gorge, vol 5: Excavations in Beds III, IV and the Masek Beds, 1968, 1971 (jt ed, 1994), The Year of the Ghost: an Olduvai Dairy (2002); author of numerous articles, book chapters and scholarly papers; *Recreations* cricket and golf (mainly as a spectator), fly fishing, reading, writing, photography; *Style*— Prof Derek Roe

ROE, Geoffrey Eric; s of Herbert William Roe, of Cowes, IOW, and Florence, *née* Gordon; *b* 20 July 1944; *Educ* Tottenham GS; *m* 4 Oct 1968, Elizabeth Anne, da of Alfred George Ponton; 1 da (Alison b 2 Dec 1981), 1 s (David b 28 July 1985); *Career* Miny of Aviation 1963–67, asst private sec to Sir Ronald Melville 1967–69, Exports and Int Div Miny of Technol 1969–74, Army Guided Weapons Contracts Branch 1974–76, seconded to British Aerospace 1976–78; MOD: sec Rocket Motor Executive 1978–81, asst dir Contracts (Air) 1981–86, dir Contracts (Underwater Weapons) 1986–89, head Material Co-ordination (Navy) 1989–90, princ dir Navy and Nuclear Contracts 1990–91, DG Def Contracts 1991–95, DG Aircraft Systems 2 1995–97, md FR Aviation Ltd 1997–2002; dir: Cobham plc 1997–2002, SBAC 1998, Air Tanker Ltd 2000–03 (chm 2002–03); MCIPS 1993, FRAeS 1997; *Recreations* skiing, sailing, fell-walking, private flying; *Clubs* Lymington Town Sailing; *Style*— Geoffrey Roe, Esq; ✉ Pond Barton, Chevers Lane, Norton St Philip, Bath BA2 7NE

ROE, James Kenneth; s of Kenneth Alfred Roe (d 1988), of Devon, and Zirphie Norah, *née* Luke (d 1940); *b* 28 February 1935; *Educ* King's Sch Bruton; *m* 15 March 1958, Dame Marion Audrey Roe, DBE, *qv*, da of William Keyte (d 1977), of Devon; 2 da (Philippa b 1962, Jane b 1965), 1 s (William b 1969); *Career* Nat Serv cmmnd RN; banker; dir: Tokyo Pacific Holdings NV 1969–92, NM Rothschild & Sons Ltd 1970–92, Rothschild Tst Corp 1970–95, Jupiter European Investment Tst plc 1990–2000, GAM Selection Inc 1992–2005, Microvitec plc 1993–97, Jupiter International Group plc 1993–2000, The Fleming Capital and Income Investment Tst plc 1995–2002, Whitehall Fund Managers Ltd 1998–2000, JP Morgan Fleming Income and Capital Investment Tst plc 2002–06, Principle Capital Investment Tst plc 2005–; chm: Equity Consort Investment Tst plc 1973–95 (dir 1967–95), China Investment Tst plc 1993–98, Ronson plc 1993–98, New Star Investment Tst plc 2005–; dep chm Innovations Group plc 1985–96, memb Monopolies and Mergers Cmmn 1993–99; FInstD, FRSA; *Clubs* Brooks's, MCC; *Style*— James Roe, Esq; ✉ c/o New Star Asset Management Ltd, 1 Knightsbridge Green, London SW1X 7NE (tel 020 7225 9200, fax 020 7225 9300)

ROE, Dame Marion Audrey; DBE (2004); da of William Keyte (d 1977), and Grace Mary, *née* Bocking (d 1983); *b* 15 July 1936; *Educ* Bromley HS, Croydon HS (both GPDST), English Sch of Languages Vevey Switzerland; *m* 1958, James Roe, *qv*, s of Kenneth Roe; 2 da (Philippa b 1962, Jane b 1965), 1 s (William b 1969); *Career* Parly candidate (Cons) Barking 1979, MP (Cons) Broxbourne 1983–2005; PPS to Rt Hon John Moore as Sec of State for Tport 1986–87 (PPS to jr tport mins 1985–86), Parly under sec of state Dept of the Environment 1987–88; memb Commons Select Ctees on: Agric 1983–85, Social Servs 1988–89, Commons Procedure 1990–92, Sittings of the House 1991–92, Commons Liaison 1992–2005, House of Commons Admin 1991–97 (chm 1997–2005), Health 2000–01 (chm 1992–97); memb Speaker's Panel of Chm 1997–2005; managing tstee Parly Contributory Pension Fund 1990–97; jt sec Cons Pty Orgn 1985, memb 1922 Ctee Exec 1992–94, vice-chm 1922 Ctee 2001–2005 (sec 1997–2001); chm Cons House of Commons Benevolent Fund 1998–99; chm Cons Pty Parly Ctees on: Horticulture and Markets 1989–97 (sec 1983–85), Social Security Ctee 1990–97 (vice-chm 1988–90); vice-chm Cons Pty Parly: Environment Ctee 1990–97, Health Ctee 1997–99; sec All-Pty Br-Canadian Parly Gp 1991–97 (vice-chm 1997–); chm All-Pty Hospices Gp 1992– (sec 1990–92), jt chm All-Pty Gp on Breast Cancer 1997–2005; vice-chm: All-Pty Fairs and Showgrounds Gp 1992–2005 (jt chm 1989–92), All-Pty Parly Garden Club 1995–2005, All-Pty Gp on Alcohol Misuse 1997–2005, All-Pty Parly Gp on Domestic Violence 1999–2005; memb Exec Ctee: UK Branch Cwlth Parly Assoc 1997–2005 (vice-chm 2003–04), Br Gp Inter-Parly Union 1997–98 and 2001–05 (vice-chm 1998–2001); memb Dept of the Environment Advsy Ctee on Women's Employment 1989–92, substitute memb UK Delgn to Cncl of Europe and WEU 1989–92, UK rep on Cwlth Observer Gp monitoring elections in the Seychelles 1992, rep UK Branch Cwlth Parly Assoc Int Women Parliamentarians Ctee 2003–05; successfully sponsored Prohibition of Female Circumcision Act 1985 (Private Member's Bill), memb six-memb Inter-Parly Union Int Panel on Prohibition of Female Genital Mutilation 2002–05; Parly conslt to Horticultural Trades Assoc 1990–95; cncllr: London Borough of Bromley 1975–78, GLC (Ilford North Div) 1977–86; GLC: vice-chm Historic Bldgs Ctee 1977–78, whip for Planning and Communications Gp 1977–78, Cons dep chief whip 1978–82, vice-chm Gen Mgmnt Ctee 1978–81, leading Cons spokesman Police Ctee 1982–83, memb Cons Ldr's Ctee 1982–83, memb various other GLC ctees 1978–82; GLC rep on Gen Servs Ctee of AMA 1978–81, UK rep Conf of Local and Regnl Authorities of Europe 1981; chm The Children's Health Gp 2001–; memb: Gen Advsy Cncl BBC 1986–87, International Women's Forum 1992–2005, Euro Research Gp 1994–2005, NHS Confedn Parly Panel 2000–05, UNICEF Parly Advsy Ctee 2002–05, UNICEF UK Key Parly Supporters Gp 2002–05; govr Research into Ageing Tst 1988–97, hon regnl vice-pres Eastern Region Housebuilders Fedn 1993–2005; pres: Broxbourne Orgn for the Disabled (co-pres) 1991–2005, Save Temple Bar Campaign 1991–93, Lea Valley Arthritis Care 1993–2005; vice-pres: Women's Nat Cancer Control Campaign 1985–87 and 1988–2001, Herts Chamber of Trade & Commerce 1983–87 and 1988–2005, E Herts Operatic Soc 1986–2005, Herts Alcohol Problems Advsy Serv 1991–2005, Herts Assoc of Local Cncls 1991–2005, Capel Manor Horticultural and Environmental Centre 1994– (chm Capel Manor Horticultural and Environmental Centre Tst Fund 1989–94), Assoc of Dist Cncls 1994–2005, Herts Cons Soc 1995–2005, Hoddesdon Soc 2005–; patron: Herts St John Ambulance Appeal 1989, E Herts Hospice Care Serv 1994–2005, Oxford Int Centre for Palliative Care 1994–2005, Herts Co Youth Orchestras and Choirs 1995–2005, MOVE IT 1997–2005, UK Nat Ctee UN Devpt Fund for Women 2004–, Int Centre for Child Studies, Hospices of Hope 2005–, Broxbourne Parly Cons Assoc 2006– (pres Women's Section 1983–); vice-patron The Chaucer Clinic Appeal 2001–05; tstee Nat Benevolent Fund for the Aged 1999–; life memb Showmen's Guild of GB 2005–, memb Cncl Wine Guild of UK 2007–; Freeman City of London 1981, Freeman Borough of Broxbourne 2005, Liveryman Worshipful Co of Gardeners 1993 (Freeman 1989); fell Industry and Parl Tst 1990, FRSA 1990, Hon MIHort 1993, Hon Fellowship of Professional Business and Tech Mgmnt 1995; *Publications* The Labour Left in London - A Blueprint for a Socialist Britain (CPC pamphlet, 1985); *Recreations* opera, ballet, theatre; *Style*— Dame Marion Roe, DBE

ROE, Sally Jean; da of Ashley Petts, of Horbury, W Yorks, and Audrey, *née* Ellis; *b* 4 September 1956; *Educ* Wakefield Girls HS, St Hilda's Coll Oxford (BA); *Career* admitted slr 1981; slr specialising in construction and engrg law; Dawson & Co: trainee 1979–81, asst slr 1981–85, ptnr Dispute Resolution Dept 1985–88; Freshfields Bruckhaus Deringer: joined dispute resolution practice as assoc slr 1988, ptnr 1990–; dir Major Projects Assoc 2005–; higher courts (civil proceedings) qualification 1995; memb Law Soc; *Publications* Partnering and Alliancing in Construction Projects (with Jane Jenkins, 2003); *Recreations* skiing, walking, theatre, opera; *Style*— Mrs Sally Roe; ✉ Oliver House, 53A Strand on the Green, Chiswick, London W4 3PD (tel 020 8747 3445, fax 020 8994 1124); Freshfields Bruckhaus Deringer, 65 Fleet Street, London EC4Y 1HS (tel 020 7832 7277, fax 020 7832 7381, e-mail sally.roe@freshfields.com)

ROEBUCK, John Stanley; *b* 26 February 1953; *Educ* Chetham's Hosp Sch Manchester, Manchester Poly (hotel and catering admin), Ashridge Mgmnt Coll (exec devpt prog); *m* Susan; 1 da; *Career* hotelier; Trust House Forte (now Forte plc): grad mgmnt trainee THF Leisure Ltd 1967–77, Trust House Forte 1977–78, area trg offr THF Popular Catering Ltd 1978, regnl mangr Little Chef 1979, dep regnl dir Little Chef North East 1979–81, regnl dir Little Chef North East 1981–83, gen mangr Little Chef North 1984, ops dir Little Chef THF Catering Div 1984–86, exec dir Happy Eater Restaurants THF Roadside Catering Div 1986–89; former md Etrop Grange Ltd and Etrop Restaurants Ltd (5 crowns classification English Tourist Bd, County Hotel of the Year Good Food Guide 1993); FHCIMA; *Style*— John Roebuck, FHCIMA

ROEDY, William H (Bill); *b* 13 June 1948; *Educ* West Point, Harvard Univ (MBA); *Career* served US Military 10 years (incl as pilot and as Cdr NATO Missile Base); sometime vice-pres Nat Accounts LA, joined Home Box Office Cable TV and Cinemax 1979, various mktg appts and mgmnt conslt for TV stations in Boston Mass 1979–89, md and chief exec MTV Europe 1989–94, pres MTV Networks International 1994–; memb CCTA; *Style*— Bill Roedy, Esq; ✉ MTV Networks International, 180 Oxford Street, London W1D 1DS

ROEG, Nicolas Jack; CBE (1996); s of Jack Nicolas Roeg (d 1952), and Mabel Gertrude Silk (d 1985); *b* 15 August 1928; *Educ* Mercers Sch; *m* 1, 1957, Susan Rennie, da of Maj F W Stephen MC; 4 s (Joscelin, Nicolas, Lucien, Sholto); m 2, 1986, Theresa Russell; 2 s (Statten Jack, Maxmilian Nicolas Sextus); *Career* film director; fell BFI; *Film* credits incl: Performance, Walkabout, Don't Look Now, The Man Who Fell to Earth, Bad Timing, Eureka, Insignificance, Castaway, Track 29, Sweet Bird of Youth, Without You I'm Nothing (exec prodr), Cold Heaven, Young Indy, The Witches, Heart of Darkness, Two Deaths, Full Body Massage, Hotel Paradise, Samson and Delilah, The Sound of Claudia Schiffer, Kiss of Life (screenplay), Night Train (screenplay), History Play (screenplay), Puffball; *Style*— Nicolas Roeg, Esq, CBE; ✉ c/o ICM Ltd, Oxford House, 76 Oxford Street, London W1D 1BS (tel 020 7636 6565, fax 020 7323 0101)

ROFE, Brian Henry; s of Henry Alexander Rofe (d 1979), and Marguerite, *née* Browne; *b* 7 January 1934; *Educ* Shrewsbury, St John's Coll Cambridge (MA); *m* 26 May 1962, (Margaret) Anne, da of Rev Phillip R Shepherd; 1 da (Katharine (Mrs Johns) b 1 July 1963), 2 s (Christopher Henry b 16 Jan 1965, Andrew John b 1 April 1968); *Career* Nat Serv RA 1952–54, 2 Lt 1953, Actg Lt TA 1955; chartered engr, asst civil engr John Laing Construction 1957–63, asst/sr engr Rofe and Raffety 1963–69, res engr Draycote Reservoir 1967–69, ptnr Rofe Kennard and Lapworth (consulting water engrs) 1970–97, conslt Arup Water 1998–; prof of engrg design Univ of Hertford 1995–2003; contracts incl: Thames Groundwater Scheme 1971–76, Iraq RWS and Basrah Barrage 1975–82, Malaysia Lower Perak Scheme 1979–85, Ashford Flood Alleviation Scheme 1985–91, Blashford and Testwood Lakes Schemes 1986–96, Port Moresby WS Papua New Guinea 1995–2006; All Reservoirs Panel engr 1985–; senator Engrg Cncl 1997–99; Freeman: City of London, Worshipful Co of Grocers; FCIWEM (pres 1990–91), FICE 1972 (memb Cncl 1993–96, memb Scoss Ctee 2003–06), MConsE 1972, FREng 1993; *Books* Kempe's Engineers Year Book (Water Supply Chapter 1970–), Civil Engineering Reference Book (Water Supply Section), Blue Patches and Clear Water; *Recreations* bridge, sailing, painting; *Clubs* Cambridge Univ Cruising; *Style*— Brian Rofe, Esq, FREng; ✉ Laleham Cottage, 40 Churchfield Road, Walton-on-Thames, Surrey KT12 2SY (tel 01932 223147, e-mail brian.rofe@talk21.com)

ROFFE, Clive Brian; JP (1987); s of Philip Roffe (d 1961); *b* 4 June 1935; *Educ* Montpelier Coll Brighton; *m* 1966 (m dis 1997), Jacqueline Carole, *née* Branston; 2 da (Danielle Philippa Geraldine b 1970, Natasha Nicole b 1974); m 2, 4 June 2000, Michelle Nadler; *Career* Lloyd's underwriter 1966, fin conslt; chm: Melbo Petroleum Ltd 1970, Edinburgh Insurance Services 1971, Offshore Investments Ltd 1968, Gemini Business Centre 1992; co dir; Freeman City of London, Liveryman Worshipful Co of Bakers, Liveryman Worshipful Co of Feltmakers, memb Ct of Assts and Master Worshipful Co of Upholders; *Recreations* organ, philately, jogging; *Clubs* RAC, Guards Polo, City Livery, Lloyd's Yacht, Ward of Cheap, Ward of Aldgate, Strangers Norwich; *Style*— Clive Roffe, Esq; ✉ Hill House, Reedham, Norfolk NR13 3TW (tel 01493 700205)

ROGAN, Baron (Life Peer UK 1999), of Lower Iveagh in the County of Down; Dennis Robert David Rogan; s of Robert Henderson Rogan, and Florence, *née* Arbuthnott; *b* 30 June 1942, Banbridge, Co Down; *Educ* Wallace HS Lisburn, Belfast Coll of Technol, Open Univ (BA), Kennedy Sch of Govt Harvard Univ; *m* 7 Aug 1968, Lorna Elizabeth, *née* Colgan; 2 s (Timothy Robert John, Damian Ardis); *Career* mgmnt trainee Moygashel Ltd 1960–69, mktg and sales William Ewart & Sons Ltd 1969–72; Lamont Holdings plc: mktg and sales 1972–76, gen sales mangr 1976–78; fndr and md Dennis Rogan & Associates 1978–, fndr and exec chm Associated Processors Ltd 1985–, dir chm Stake Holder Communication Gp, dep chm Belfast Telegraph Newspapers 2000–, dir International Advsy Bd Independent News & Media Gp 2001–; sits as cross-bench peer in House of Lords, pres UU Pty (former chm), ldr UU Pty House of Lords; memb: Inter Parly Union, Cwlth Parly Assoc, RFCA for NI; former chm: South Belfast UU Constituency Assoc, Ulster Young Unionist Cncl, Lisburn Unit of Mgmnt Eastern Health and Social Services Bd; govr Westminster Fndn for Democracy 2005–; patron The Somme Assoc 2000–; memb Textile Inst; MBIM; *Recreations* rugby, gardening, oriental carpets, shooting; *Clubs* Reform (Belfast), Army and Navy; *Style*— The Rt Hon the Lord Rogan; ✉ 31 Notting Hill, Malone Road, Belfast BT9 5NS (tel 028 9066 2468, fax 028 9066 3410); 13 Little College Street, London SW1P 3SH (tel 020 7219 8625, fax 020 7219 1657); House of Lords, London SW1A 0PW (fax 020 7219 5979)

ROGER, David Bernard; s of John Grant Roger, of Newstead, Scotland, and Margaret Jean, *née* Dymock; *b* 23 February 1951; *Educ* Melville Coll Edinburgh, Univ of Newcastle upon Tyne (BA), Univ of Bristol (MA), Univ of Paris (Scenographic Diploma), ENO theatre design course; *Career* theatre designer; designs incl: La Mort de Zarathustra (Lucernaire Paris) 1979–80, The Mission (Soho Poly) 1982, The Knot Garden (Opera Factory) 1984, Akhnaten (ENO) 1985, La Boheme (Opera North) 1986, Temptation (RSC The Other Place) 1987, Faust parts 1 and 2 (Lyric Hammersmith) 1988, Simplicius Simplicissimus 1989, Cosi Fan Tutte (TV version Channel 4) 1989, Figaro (Opera Factory Zurich) 1990, Morte d'Arthur (Lyric Hammersmith) 1990, Manon Lescaut (Opera Comique Paris) 1990, Don Giovanni (TV version Channel 4) 1990, The Fiery Angel (Kirov St Petersburg, Royal

R

Opera House and NY Met Opera) 1991–92, The Return of Ulysses (ENO) 1992, The Coronation of Poppea (Opera Factory) 1992, The Bacchae (Opera Factory) 1993, Plunder (Savoy) 1995, Mr Worldly Wise (Royal Ballet) 1995, Madam Butterfly, Tosca, Aida and Carmen (Royal Albert Hall) 1997/98, Carmen (Royal Albert Hall) 1997/2001, Heat of the Sun (Carlton TV), Births Marriages and Deaths (BBC 2), Last Christmas (BBC 1), The Sins (BBC 1), Swallow (BBC1), Early Doors (BBC 2), Eroica (BBC 2), Riot at the Rite (BBC 2), Low Winter Sun (Channel 4), Sherlock Holmes (BBC 1), Persuasion (ITV); memb Soc of Br Theatre Designers; *Clubs* 2 Brydges Place; *Style*— David Roger, Esq; ✉ 52B College Road, London NW10 5ER (tel 020 8969 8354)

ROGERS, Anthony Peter Vernon (Tony); OBE (1985); s of Kenneth David Rogers (d 1983), and Eileen, *née* Emmott (d 1997); *b* 10 July 1942; *Educ* Highgate Sch, Coll of Law, Univ of Liverpool (LLM); *m* 31 July 1965, Anne-Katrin Margarethe, da of Dr Ewald Lembke; 2 da (Denise Claudia b 25 Aug 1966, Julia Simone b 12 July 1969); *Career* articled clerk London 1959–64, admitted slr 1965; cmmnd Army Legal Servs 1968, Capt 1968–73, Maj 1973–81, Lt Col 1981–89, Col 1989–92, Brig 1992–94, Maj Gen 1994–97; hon pres Int Soc for Mil Law and the Law of War 1997– (memb 1979–, vice-pres 1994–97); memb: Law Soc 1965–2007, Int Inst of Humanitarian Law 1993–99 (chm Ctee for Mil Instruction 1993–97); memb Int Fact-finding Cmmn 2002–06 (vice-pres 2004–06); fell Lauterpacht Research Centre for Int Law Univ of Cambridge 1999– (sr fell 2006–), fell Human Rights Centre Univ of Essex 1999–2004 (visiting fell 2005–),Yorke distinguished visiting fell Faculty of Law Univ of Cambridge 2004; FRSA 1995; *Books* Law on the Battlefield (1996 and 2004), ICRC Model Manual on the Law of Armed Conflict (princ author, 1999), MOD Manual of the Law of Armed Conflict (ed, 2004); *Recreations* music and the Arts, playing the piano (especially as an accompanist) and bassoon, walking (preferably in mountains), cricket; *Style*— A P V Rogers, Esq, OBE

ROGERS, Prof Chris; *Career* teaching posts: Queen Mary & Westfield Coll London, Univ of Cambridge, UC Swansea, Univ of Warwick; prof of probability Univ of Bath, prof of statistical science Univ of Cambridge 2002–; *Books* Diffusions, Markov Processes, and Martingales (with David Williams); *Style*— Prof Chris Rogers; ✉ Statistical Laboratory, Centre for Mathematical Sciences, Wilberforce Road, Cambridge CB3 0WB

ROGERS, Prof Colin; s of William Joseph Rogers (d 1952), and Margaret Anne Gwendoline, *née* Goodgame (d 1971); *b* 1 December 1940; *Educ* Magdalen Coll Sch Oxford, Univ of Oxford (BA), Univ of Toronto (MEd), Univ of Nottingham (MSc, PhD, DSc); *Career* lectr Univ of Nottingham 1968–71; assoc prof: Old Dominion Univ Virginia USA 1973–74, Univ of W Ontario Canada 1974–78 (asst prof 1971–73); prof Univ of Waterloo Canada 1981–88 (assoc prof 1978–81), chair mathematical engrg Loughborough Univ of Technol 1988–92, prof of applied mathematics Univ of NSW Aust 1992– (head Dept of Applied Mathematics 1998–2006); visiting prof: Univ of Adelaide Aust 1975, Univ of Cambridge 2002, Univ of Rome 2005, Univ of Bologna 2006; sr visitor Dept of Applied Mathematics and Theoretical Physics Univ of Cambridge 1979, adjunct princ research scientist Georgia Inst Technol 1989– (visiting prof 1982 and 1984), membre associé Centre de Recherches Mathématiques Université de Montréal Canada 1998–; memb Editorial Bd: Jl of Mathematical Analysis and Applications, Int Jl of Nonlinear Mechanics, Studies in Applied Mathematics, Boundary Value Problems; Centenary Medal (Aust) 2003; FInstP, FAA; *Books* Bäcklund Transformations and Their Applications (with W F Shadwick, 1982), Wave Phenomena: Modern Theory and Applications (ed with T B Moodie, 1986), Nonlinear Boundary Value Problems in Science and Engineering (with W F Ames, 1989), Nonlinear Equations in the Applied Sciences (ed with W F Ames, 1991), Bäcklund and Darboux Transformations: Geometry and Modern Applications in Soliton Theory (with W K Shief, 2002); *Recreations* Argentinian dance (estilo milonguero), athletics (Canadian National Masters Cross Country and 10,000 metres champion 1981); *Style*— Prof Colin Rogers, FAA; ✉ 4B/8 Hampden Street, Paddington, Sydney 2021, NSW (tel 00 61 29 332 4137); School of Mathematics, University of New South Wales, Sydney 2052, NSW, Australia (e-mail c.rogers@unsw.edu.au)

ROGERS, Colin Stuart; s of George Stuart Rogers (d 1982), and Jean Ritchie Christian (d 2000), of Farningham, Kent; *b* 6 February 1947; *Educ* St Olave's GS London, Univ of Essex (BA, MA); *m* 24 Nov 1972, Deborah, *née* Mortimer; 2 s (Benedict Randall b 19 June 1973, Thomas Mortimer b 6 Feb 1977); *Career* with ATV Network then Central Independent Television 1972–80: variously head of scripts, prodr of children's drama, prodr of single plays, ATV rep on ITV Network Children's Prog Ctee and ITV Labour Rels Ctee, latterly prodr of drama series Central Television; freelance prodr 1980–85 (series incl Spyship and Anna of the Five Towns, films incl Three Minute Heroes, Atlantis and The Groundling and the Kite for Play for Today and Space Station Milton Keynes for Screen Two; dir three shorts for The Golden Oldie Picture Show); BBC TV: exec prodr 1986–90, dep head Drama Series and Serials Dept 1986–88, prodr of series incl All Passion Spent 1986 (nominated BAFTA Best Drama Series), A Perfect Spy 1987 (TRIC Best BBC TV Series Award 1988, nominated BAFTA Best Drama Series 1988 and Best Mini-series Emmy 1989), Summer's Lease 1989 (nominated BAFTA Best Drama Series 1990, John Gielgud awarded Best Actor Emmy 1990); exec prodr Thin Air 1987, Sophia and Constance 1988, Shadow of the Noose 1989, Portrait of a Marriage 1990 (Grand Prize Banff Festival 1991), Spender (created with Jimmy Nail and Ian la Frenais) 1991; estab independent film drama prodn co Deco Films and Television Ltd 1990 (prodns incl continuing series of Resnick drama serials for BBC 1992– (Bronze Medal NY Festival 1992)), concurrently controller of drama Meridian Broadcasting Ltd 1991–95; at Meridian exec prodr of: Harnessing Peacocks (Gold Nymph Award Best Film and Silver Nymph Award Best Screenplay Monte Carlo Festival 1994) 1993, Under the Hammer 1994, The Ruth Rendell Mysteries 1994 and 1995 (Master of the Moor Silver Medal NY Festival 1995), The Vacillations of Poppy Carew 1994, The English Wife 1995; chm and chief exec Deco Group of Companies 1995– (prodr film Peggy Su! 1997), dir Cornwall Film Fund 2001–03; exec prodr: The Way Things Work 2002, Jubilee Pool 2002, Birt Dyneley 2002, Cheap Rate Gravity 2002, Fishing Film 2003; country dir India BBC World Serv Tst 2003–05, exec dir Nat Assoc for Literature Devpt 2005–06, country dir Nigeria BBC World Serv Tst 2007–; exec prodr: Jasoos Vijay (Thriller Prog of the Year Indian TV Awards), Haath Se Haath Milaa (UNICEF/Cwlth Broadcasting Assoc Award 2003, Best Public Service Ad Campaign Indian TC Awards 2004); vice-chair Cornwall and Isles of Scilly NHS Primary Care Tst 2006–; visiting lectr UC Falmouth 2005–; memb: Nat Advsy Ctee Kent Literature Festival 1993–98, Cncl RTS 1995–99, Media Centre for Cornwall Steering Gp 1999–2001 (dir 2001–), Ctee W Cornwall Branch CPRE 1999–, Cornwall CC Cultural Industrial Task Force 2000–03, Bd of Tstees Cornwall Theatre Co Ltd 2005–, Bd of Tstees Mencap 2005–, Bd of Govrs Mencap Nat Coll 2006–; memb: BAFTA, PACT, BFI, CIA (Cormwall Ind Film Makers Assoc), DPN (Digital Peninsula Network); FRTS, FRSA; *Books* A Bunch of Fives (1977); *Clubs* Groucho; *Style*— Colin Rogers, Esq; ✉ e-mail chairman@decofilms.co.uk

ROGERS, Danny; s of Prof Alan Rogers, and Wendy, *née* Prince; *Educ* Lord Howard of Effingham Sch, Univ of Leicester (BA); *Career* journalist; PR conslt 1993–96, freelance journalist 1996–2001, assoc ed (news) Marketing 2001–04, dep ed Marketing 2004, ed PR Week 2004–; *Recreations* football, tennis; *Style*— Danny Rogers, Esq; ✉ PR Week, 174 Hammersmith Road, London W6 7JP

ROGERS, Jane Rosalind; da of Prof Andrew W Rogers (d 1989), and Margaret Kathleen, *née* Farmer; *b* 21 July 1952; *Educ* New Hall Cambridge (BA), Univ of Leicester (PGCE); *m* Michael L Harris; 1 da (Kate Lucy b 1981), 1 s (Laurence Jay b 1984); *Career* novelist and playwright; Arts Cncl writer in residence Northern Coll Barnsley 1985–86, writer in residence Sheffield Poly 1987, Judith E Wilson visiting writer/fell Univ of Cambridge 1991, prof of creative writing Sheffield Hallam Univ 1994–; memb Soc of Authors; FRSL 1994; *Books* Separate Tracks (1983), Her Living Image (1984, Somerset Maugham Award 1985), The Ice is Singing (1987), Mr Wroe's Virgins (1991), Promised Lands (1995, Writers' Guild Best Fiction Book Award), Island (1999), Good Fiction Guide (ed, 2001), The Voyage Home (2004); *Television and Radio Work* Dawn and the Candidate (Channel 4, Samuel Beckett Award 1990), Mr Wroe's Virgins (BBC adaptation); radio adaptations incl: Shirley, Island; *Recreations* walking, travel, reading; *Style*— Ms Jane Rogers, FRSL; ✉ c/o Pat Kavanagh, PFD, Drury House, 34–43 Russell Street, London WC2B 5HA (tel 020 7344 1000, fax 020 7352 7356, e-mail jane.rogers@btinternet.com, website www.janerogers.org)

ROGERS, His Hon Judge John Michael Thomas; QC (1979); s of Harold Stuart Rogers, and Sarah Joan Thomas, *née* Bibby; *b* 13 May 1938; *Educ* Rydal Sch, Birkenhead Sch, Fitzwilliam House Cambridge (MA, LLB); *m* 1, 1971, Jennifer Ruth; 1 da (Caitlin Sarah b 1981); m 2, Angela Victoria; 1 s (Benamin b 1978), 1 da (Joanna b 1980); *Career* called to the Bar Gray's Inn 1963 (bencher 1990); recorder of the Crown Court 1976, ldr Wales & Chester Circuit 1990–92, circuit judge (Wales & Chester Circuit) 1998–; *Clubs* Reform, Pragmatists, Barbarians RFC; *Style*— His Hon Judge John Rogers, QC

ROGERS, Juliet Mary; s of Edward Maxwell Rogers, of Christchurch, NZ (d 1997), and Lois Josephine, *née* Ablett; *b* 2 May 1957, NZ; *Educ* Univ of Canterbury Christchurch (BA, MA), Victoria Univ Wellington (DipBA); *m* 28 Aug 1982 (sep), Perry Laurence Lennon; 1 da (Sophie Anna b 29 Feb 1984), 1 s (Chrisopher James Edward b 17 Jan 1987); *Career* sales rep William Collins Publishers 1978–80, probation offr Dept of Justice 1980–84, mktg mangr MacDonald Publishers 1987–90; md: Random House NZ 1990–98, Random House Aust 1998–2001, Murdoch Books Aust and UK 2002–; pres Aust Publishers Assoc; *Recreations* reading, film, gardening; *Style*— Ms Juliet Rogers; ✉ Murdoch Books, Pier 8/9, 23 Hickson Road, Millers Point, NSW 2000, Australia (tel 00612 8220 2000, fax 00612 8220 2558, e-mail julietr@murdochbooks.com.au)

ROGERS, Kevin Peter James; OBE (2005); s of William Harry Rogers, and Eileen Mary, *née* McCarthy; *Career* RN apprentice (gained HNC); joined HM Prison Serv 1963, dep govr Preston Prison 1985–87, dep govr HMP Camp Hill 1987–91, head of custody HMP Parkhurst 1991–93, memb Premier Prison Service 1993–, dir HMP and YOI Doncaster 1994–2001, dir HMP Dovegate 2001–; memb: Common Purpose Tst, Panel Investors in People, The Royal Assoc for Disability and Rehabilitation (RADAR); hon memb Yorkshire Excellence; selected as one of the RADAR People of The Year 1995; fund raiser for charities incl: WWF, Wizz Kids, Cancer Research, Leukemia Research; *Recreations* environment and endangered species, travel, running marathons (incl London and Disney FL); *Style*— Kevin Rogers, Esq, OBE; ✉ Kantara, Denaby Lane, Old Denaby, Doncaster, South Yorkshire DN12 4JX (tel 01709 582858, fax 01709 585992, e-mail k@kevinandelicia.f9.co.uk); Premier Prison Services, Her Majesty's Prison Dovegate, Uttoxeter, Staffordshire ST14 8XR (tel 01283 829584, fax 01283 829486)

ROGERS, Malcolm Austin; CBE (2004); s of James Eric Rogers, and Frances Anne, *née* Elsey; *b* 3 October 1948; *Educ* Oakham Sch, Magdalen Coll Oxford, ChCh Oxford (MA, DPhil); *Career* Nat Portrait Gallery: asst keeper 1974–83, dep dir 1983–94, keeper 1985–94; dir Museum of Fine Arts Boston 1994–; Liveryman Worshipful Co of Girdlers; FSA 1986; Chevalier L'Ordre des Arts et des Lettres (France) 2007; *Books* Dictionary of British Portraiture 4 Vols (jt ed, 1979–81), Museums and Galleries of London Blue Guide (1983, 3 edn 1992), William Dobson (1983), John and John Baptist Closterman: A Catalogue of their Works (1983), Elizabeth II: Portraits of Sixty Years (1986), Camera Portraits (1989), Montacute House (1991), Companion Guide to London (ed with Sir David Piper, 1992), The English Face (ed with Sir David Piper, 1992), Boughton House: The English Versailles (contrib, 1992), Master Drawings from the National Portrait Gallery (1993), Van Dyck 1599–1641 (contrib, 1999); *Recreations* food, wine, music, travel; *Clubs* Beefsteak, Algonquin (Boston, hon memb), Wednesday Evening Club of 1777 (Boston), Club of Odd Volumes (Boston), Thursday Evening (Boston), Commercial Club of Boston; *Style*— Malcolm Rogers, Esq, CBE, FSA; ✉ 540 Chestnut Hill Avenue, Brookline, MA 02445, USA (tel 00 1 617 369 3200, e-mail mrogers@mfa.org); La Bastille, Royalston, MA 01368, USA

ROGERS, Martin John; s of Douglas John Rogers, of Bargoed, S Wales, and Mary, *née* Sayce; *b* 21 July 1955; *Educ* Bargoed GS, UC of Wales Aberystwyth (BSc); *m* 1977, Beth, da of Peter Jones (d 2000), and Amy Jones; 3 da (Lucy Elizabeth b 31 Jan 1981, Kate Elinore b 2 Feb 1983, Sophie Jane b 11 May 1987); *Career* Pannell Kerr Forster: joined Cardiff Office 1976, ptnr 1985, sr ptnr Derby 1989–96; sr ptnr PricewaterhouseCoopers Derby (formerly Coopers & Lybrand before merger) 1996–99, gp fin dir Ascot plc 1999–2001, non-exec dir Quizid Technologies Ltd 2002–, managing ptnr E Midlands Mazars LLP 2005–; govr Univ of Derby 2005–; MInstD, FCA 1979; *Recreations* country sports, sailing, skiing; *Clubs* RAC; *Style*— Martin Rogers, Esq; ✉ Mazars LLP, Cartwright House, Tottle Road, Nottingham NG2 1RT (tel 0115 943 5363)

ROGERS, Prof (John) Michael; s of John Patrick Rogers (d 1961), of Dalton-in-Furness, Lancs, and Constance Mary, *née* Fisher (d 1994); *b* 25 January 1935; *Educ* Ulverston GS, CCC Oxford (MA), Oriel Coll Oxford (BPhil), Pembroke Coll Oxford (DPhil); *Career* Nat Serv RA 1953–55, later Capt Intelligence Corps TA; res fell Oriel Coll Oxford 1958–61, philosophy tutor Pembroke and Wadham Coll Oxford 1961–65, asst then assoc prof American Univ in Cairo 1965–77, asst then dep keeper Dept of Oriental Antiquities Br Museum 1977–91, Slade prof Univ of Oxford 1991–92, Khalili prof of Islamic art and archaeology SOAS Univ of London 1991–2000, hon curator Khalili Collection of Islamic art 2001–; advsr NACF, memb Editorial Ctee Burlington Magazine, corr memb Deutsches Archäologisches Institut 1989; FSA 1974, FBA 1988; Order Egyptian Republic Class II 1969; *Books* The Spread of Islam (1976), Islamic Art and Design 1500–1700 (1983), Süleyman the Magnificent (with R M Ward, 1980), Mughal Painting (1993), The Uses of Anachronism on Methodological Diversity in the History of Islamic Art (1994), Empire of the Sultans: Ottoman art from the collection of Nasser D Khalili (Musée d'art et d'histoire Geneva, 1995), Sinan (2006), The Arts of Islam: Teasures from the Nasser D Khalili Collection (exhbn catalogue, Art Gallery of NSW Sydney, 2007); author of numerous articles on arts, architecture and economic and social history of Islam; *Recreations* music, mountains, botany; *Clubs* Beefsteak; *Style*— Prof Michael Rogers, FBA, FSA; ✉ The Nasser D Khalili Collection of Islamic Art, 27 Liddell Road, off Maygrove Road, London NW6 2EW (tel 020 7625 9082, fax 020 7372 1491, e-mail michael@nourhouse.com)

ROGERS, Nicholas Emerson (Nick); s of Reginald Emerson Rogers (d 1983), and Doreen, *née* Burbidge (d 1991); *b* 15 March 1946; *m* 26 Oct 1973 (m dis 1997), Linda Jane; *Career* photographer: Sunday Independent Plymouth 1968–70, Reading Evening Post 1970–72; staff photographer Daily Mail 1973–78; dep picture ed The Observer 1983–86; feature photographer: The Times 1986–90, The European 1990, Sunday Telegraph 1990–96; freelance 1996–; Kodak Industrial and Commercial Photographer of the Year 1987, Feature Photographer of the Year Br Press Awards 1988, commended Nikon Awards 1988; FRPS; *Recreations* photography, sailing, walking, travel, watercolour painting, building model boats; *Style*— Nick Rogers, Esq; ✉ 19 Passage Road, Noss Mayo, Devon PL8 1EW (tel 01752 872738, e-mail nick@nickrogers.demon.co.uk)

ROGERS, Nick; s of Jonathon Rogers, of Lymington, Hants, and Ann, *née* Edlin; *b* 4 March 1977; *Career* yachtsman; achievements in 470 class incl: fourth place Olympic Games Sydney 2000, Bronze medal European Championships 2000, Silver medal Pre-Olympics

Athens 2003, Silver medal Olympic Games Athens 2004, Gold medal European Championships 2004 and 2005; memb RYA; *Clubs* Royal Yacht Sqdn, Royal Lymington Yacht; *Style—* Nick Rogers, Esq; ✉ 9 Fairlea Road, Lymington, Hampshire SO41 9EF (tel 01590 673011, e-mail nick@rogersglanfield.com)

ROGERS, Nigel David; s of Thomas Rogers (d 1980), of Wellington, Salop, and Winifred May, *née* Roberts (d 1999); *b* 21 March 1935; *Educ* Wellington GS, King's Coll Cambridge (MA), Hochschule für Musik Munich; *m* 1, 14 Oct 1961, Frederica Bement (d 1992), da of Edmund Parker Lord (d 1985), of Framingham, MA; 1 da (Lucasta Julia Webster b 26 May 1970); m 2, 15 Oct 1999, Lina Zilinskyte; 1 da (Georgina Ieva b 4 May 2002); *Career* singer and conductor; debut Studio der Frühen Musik, Munich 1961, specialised as leading exponent of baroque style of singing 1964–; performances of baroque operas in England, Germany, Holland, Poland, Switzerland and Austria, world-wide concerts and recitals; numerous recordings incl: Monteverdi 1610 Vespers, Monteverdi Orfeo, songs of John Dowland, Schütz, Christmas Story; Schubert, Die Schöne Müllerin; 17 C Airs de Cour etc; fndr: Chiaroscuro Vocal Ensemble 1980, Chiaroscuro Baroque Orch 1987; conducted baroque orchs in Italy, Spain, Switzerland, Lithuania; teacher Schola Cantorum Basiliensis Basle 1972–, prof of singing Royal Coll of Music 1979–2000; Hon RCM 1981; *Books* Companion to Baroque Music (chapter on Voice, 1991); *Style—* Nigel Rogers, Esq; ✉ Royal College of Music, Prince Consort Road, London SW7 2BS (tel 020 7589 3643, fax 020 7589 7740)

ROGERS, Peter Standing; JP; s of Harold Rogers (d 1997), and Joan Thomas, *née* Bibby; *b* 2 January 1940; *Educ* Prenton Secdy Sch Birkenhead, Cheshire Sch of Agriculture; *m* 12 June 1973, Margaret, *née* Roberts; 2 s (Richard Sion b 9 May 1975, Simon b 6 Nov 1978); *Career* farm mangr, sales mangr CIBA Geigy UK Ltd, self-employed farmer; AM (Cons) Wales North 1999–2003; chm Family Bench, vice-chm Ynys Mon Cons Assoc; *Recreations* sport, rural activities; *Clubs* Old Birkonians, Pragmatists, Welsh Crawshays; *Style—* Peter Rogers, Esq, AM; ✉ Bodrida, Bryn Siencyn, Angelsey LL61 6NZ (tel 01248 430241)

ROGERS, Philip John; MBE (1990); s of John William Rogers (d 1990), and Lilian Fleet (d 1991); *b* 4 October 1942; *Educ* Poly of North London (HNC); *m* 24 Nov 1979, Wendy Joan, *née* Cross, da of Leonard George Cross and Joan Sylvester Romans; 2 da (Ffion Clare b 25 May 1982, Ceri Frances b 29 Sept 1983), 1 s (Trystan Philip b 16 April 1985); *Career* trainee and optical instrument designer Hilger and Watts London 1960–66; Pilkington Optronics (now Qioptiq Ltd) 1966–2005 (chief optical designer from 1969, chief engr Optics 1994–2000), fndr VNF Ltd 2006; visiting prof Cranfield Univ 2007–; Int Society for Optical Engrg (SPIE): memb Bd 1995–97, memb European Steering Ctee 1984–86, memb Strategic Planning Ctee 1999–2001, memb Nominating Ctee 1996, memb Awards Ctee 1996–2001; memb: UK Inst of Physics Optical Gp Ctee 1991–97, Thomson Collège Scientifique et Technique Paris 1992–98, Imperial Coll Optics Advisory Ctee 1995–2005, Welsh Opto-Electronics Forum Steering Ctee 1996–98, UK Consortium for Photonics and Optics Mgmnt Ctee 1997–2004; holder of numerous patents, presented numerous papers and lectures worldwide, presented Open Univ prog 1977; assessor: Engrg Leadership Awards Royal Acad of Engrg 2000, Queen's Anniversary Prizes for Higher and Further Educn 2000; fell: Int Soc for Optical Engrg USA (1991), Optical Soc of America (1998); FREng 1998, FInstP 1992; *Awards* Finalist UK Mfrg Industry Achievement Award, Design Innovation of the Year 1996, Finalist Royal Acad of Engrg MacRobert 1997; *Publications* author of numerous articles and contributions in professional jls and books; *Recreations* listening to classical music, astronomy, computing, family activities; *Style—* Philip Rogers, Esq, MBE, FREng; ✉ 24 Cilgant Eglwys Wen, Bodelwyddan, Denbighshire LL18 5US (tel 01745 582498, e-mail philjrog@aol.com)

ROGERS, Ray; s of Thomas Kenneth Rogers (d 1989), of Guildford, and Mary Esther, *née* Walsh; *b* 19 October 1940; *Educ* Univ of Birmingham (BSc); *m* 1964, Carmel Anne; 2 s (Richard Thomas b 1965, Gareth Cunningham b 1967), 1 da (Stephanie Carmel b 1970); *Career* med physicist Royal London Hosp and Westminster Hosp 1962–70; Dept of Health: princ sci offr, supt engr, dep dir rising to dir Med Devices Directorate 1970–86; exec dir NHS Exec Info Mgmnt Gp 1991–98 (dep dir 1986–91), md Dragon Health International (consultancy) 1998–2007, ret; author of numerous sci and technol articles; companion BCS, chartered physicist; FInstP, FRSA; *Recreations* mountain hiking, music, science, pursuit of peace; *Style—* Ray Rogers, Esq

ROGERS, Lady; Ruth; *b* 2 July 1948; *Educ* Colorado Rocky Mountain Sch, Bennington Coll Vermont, London Coll of Printing; *m* 1973, Baron Rogers of Riverside, *qv*; 2 s (Roo b 18 Jan 1975, Bo b 2 Dec 1983), 3 step s (Ben b 12 June 1963, Zad b 5 Nov 1965, Ab b 12 July 1968); *Career* Art Dept Penguin Books 1971–73, Richard Rogers Architects 1974–85, chef/owner (with Rose Gray, *qv*) River Cafe 1987–; Italian Restaurant of the Year The Times 1988, Best New Restaurant Courvoisier Best of Best Awards 1989, Eros Awards Evening Standard 1994 and 1995; memb Bd Royal Court Theatre; *Books* with Rose Gray: The River Cafe Cook Book (1995, Food Book of the Year Glenfiddich Awards 1996), River Cafe Cook Book 2 (1997), River Cafe Italian Kitchen (1998), River Cafe Cook Book Green (2000), River Cafe Cook Book Easy (2003), River Cafe Two Easy (2005), River Cafe Pocket Books (2006); *Style—* Lady Rogers; ✉ River Cafe, Thames Wharf, Rainville Road, London W6 9HA (tel 020 7386 4200, fax 020 7386 4201)

ROGERS OF RIVERSIDE, Baron (Life Peer UK 1996), of Chelsea in the London Borough of Kensington and Chelsea; Richard George Rogers; *b* 23 July 1933; *Educ* Architectural Assoc London (AA Dip), Yale Univ (MArch, Fulbright and Yale scholar); *m* 1, 1960, Su Brumwel; 3 s; m 2, 1973, Ruth Elias; 2 s; *Career* chm Richard Rogers Partnership Ltd; winner of int competition for Pompidou Centre Paris 1977, winner of Lloyd's int competition for Headquarters London 1978; projects incl: PA Technol Centre phases 1, 2, 3 Cambridge 1970–84, Music Res Centre for Pierre Boulez and Miny Cultural Affairs Paris 1977, Fleetguard Factory France 1980, Inmos Microprocessor Factory Newport 1982, PA Technol Science Lab Princeton USA 1984, London Docklands Devpt 1984, Billingsgate Market Conversion 1985, Lloyd's of London 1986, Thames Reach Housing 1987, Terminal 5 Heathrow Airport 1989–, Reuters Docklands 1992, Channel 4 Headquarters 1994, Strasbourg Courts of Human Rights 1995, Piano di Castello Florence 1995, Thames Valley Univ 1996, Madrid Barajas Airport 1997–, Bordeaux Law Courts 1999, Millennium Dome 1999, Daimler Chrysler Berlin 1999, L'Hospitalet Hotel and Conference Centre Barcelona 1999–, Nat Assembly for Wales Cardiff 1999–, 88 Wood Street London 2000, Ashford Retail Designer Outlet 2000, Lloyd's Register of Shipping 2000, Montevetro Battersea 2000, Barcelona Bullring 2000–, Canary Riverside South London 2001–, Chelmsford Univ Campus Essex 2001–, Arts Quarter Chelmsford 2001–, Convoys Wharf London 2001–, Maggie's Centre London 2001–, Birmingham City Library 2002–, Leadenhall Street London 2002–, Broadwick Street London 2002, Silvercup Studios NY 2002–, Minami Yamashiro Primary Sch Japan 2003, Paddington Basin Waterside (and Grand Union Tower London 1999) 2004, Mossbourne Community Academy Hackney London 2004, Chiswick Park London 2004, Antwerp Law Cts Belguim 2005; masterplans: London Docklands Devpt 1984, South Bank London 1986, Shanghai 1994, Dunkirk France 1998, Mallorca 1998, Greenwich Peninsular London 2000, Tate Modern Bankside 2000–, Wembley London 2000–, Almada Portugal 2002–; visiting lectr at UCLA Princeton Columbia, Harvard and Cornell Univs USA, Saarinen prof Yale Univ 1985; chief advsr to the Mayor of London on architecture and urbanism, advsr to the Mayor of Barcelona's Urban Strategies Cncl; chm: tstees Tate Gallery 1984, Urban Task Force 1998–2001; memb RIBA Cncl, UN Architects' Ctee; hon tstee MOMA NY; RIBA Hon Dr (RCA)S RA, Royal Acad London, Royal Acad of Art, The Hague; Royal Gold Medal, RIBA 1985, exhibition Royal Acad London 1986; Praemium Imperiale Award 2000; Hon FAIA 1986, Hon FREng 2005; Chevalier de l'Ordre National de la Legion d'Honneur 1986; *Publications* Architecture - A Modern Review (1990), Cities for a Small Planet (with Philip Gumuchdjian, 1997), Cities for a Small Country (with Anne Power, 2000); subject of: By Their Own Design (Abbey Suckle Granada, 1980), Nine Projects - Japan - Richard Rogers Partnership (Blueprint Extra 3, 1991), The Architecture of Richard Rogers (Deyan Sudjic, 1994), Richard Rogers (Kenneth Powell, 1994), Richard Rogers Partnership - Works and Projects (ed Richard Burdett, 1996), Richard Rogers: Complete Works vols 1–2 (Kenneth Powell, 2001/2002) vol 3 (2005); *Style—* The Rt Hon Lord Rogers of Riverside; ✉ Thames Wharf, Rainville Road, London W6 9HA (tel 020 7385 1235, e-mail enquiries@rrp.co.uk. website www.rrp.co.uk)

ROGERSON, Daniel John (Dan); MP; s of Stephen John Rogerson, of Bodmin, Cornwall, and Patricia Anne, *née* Jones; *b* 23 July 1975, St Austell, Cornwall; *Educ* Bodmin Coll, Univ of Wales Aberystwyth; *m* 21 Aug 1999, Heidi Lee, *née* Purser; 1 s (Mawgan John b 24 Nov 2004); *Career* co-cncllr Bedford 1999, dep ldr Lib Dem Cncl Gp; Parly candidate (Lib Dem) Bedfordshire NE 2001, MP (Lib Dem) Cornwall N 2005–; *Style—* Dan Rogerson, Esq, MP; ✉ House of Commons, London SW1A 0AA (tel 020 7219 4707, e-mail rogersond@parliament.uk)

ROGERSON, Michael Anthony; s of Peter Anthony Rogerson (d 1984), of Virginia Water, Surrey, and Yvonne Marie, *née* Kennedy; *b* 19 February 1941; *Educ* Harrow; *m* 27 Sept 1969, Margaret Jane, da of Keith Gordon Blake, CBE (d 1982), of Guildford, Surrey; 1 da (Belinda Jane b 1971), 1 s (Richard Pierce Gordon b 1974); *Career* Spicer and Pegler: UK 1960–65, Aust 1965–67; Ernst & Whinney 1967–73; Grant Thorton: ptnr 1973–2006, conslt 2006–, memb Policy Bd 1990–97, chm Professional Practices Gp 1993–2001; chm Not for Profit Gp and charities 2001–; past chm: London Region CBI, Marriage Care; tstee CARE Int; past memb: Devpt Cncl Univ of Durham, Advsy Bd Univ of Durham Business Sch; Liveryman Worshipful Co of Skinners 1971; FCA 1965, FRSA 1996; *Recreations* golf, bridge, gardening, racing; *Clubs* Boodle's, Worplesdon Golf; *Style—* Michael Rogerson, Esq; ✉ Plumtree Cottage, Newnham Road, Newnham, Hampshire RG27 9AE (tel 01256 767847, e-mail michael.rogerson1@btinternet.com); Grant Thornton, Grant Thornton House, Euston Square, London NW1 2EP (tel and fax 0870 991 2341, e-mail michael.a.rogerson@gtuk.com)

ROGERSON, Nicolas; s of Hugh Rogerson (d 1973), and Helen Olivia, *née* Worthington; *b* 21 May 1943; *Educ* Winchester, Magdalene Coll Cambridge (MA); *m* 5 May 1998, Hon Caroline Le Bas, da of Baron Gilbert, PC (Life Peer), *qv*; *Career* co-fndr Dewe Rogerson Ltd 1969; ptnr Concept 2 Profit; Freeman City of London, memb Worshipful Co of Merchant Taylors 1964; *Recreations* fly fishing, skiing, sailing; *Clubs* Turf, Beefsteak, Royal Yacht Sqdn; *Style—* Nicolas Rogerson, Esq; ✉ Old Parsonage, Newtown, Isle of Wight PO30 4PA (tel 01983 531250); 4 Redfield Lane, London SW5 0RG (tel 020 7373 7089, mobile 07802 254490)

ROGERSON, Philip Graham; s of Henry Rogerson, and Florence, *née* Dalton; *b* 1 January 1945; *Educ* William Hulme's GS Manchester; *m* 21 Dec 1968, Susan Janet, da of Jack Kershaw, of Cleveleys, Lancs; 2 da (Penelope Rose b 2 Dec 1971, Hannah Rosemary b 7 April 1988), 1 s (Simon Andrew b 19 July 1974); *Career* various appts with the ICI Gp 1978–92 (gen mangr fin ICI plc 1989–92); British Gas plc (now BG plc): exec dir 1992–98, dep chm 1996–98; non-exec chm: PII Gp Ltd 1998–2002, Bertram Gp Ltd 1999–2001, Viridian Gp 1999–2005, KBC Advanced Technologies plc 1999–2004, Project Telecom plc 2000–2003, Copper Eye Ltd 2001–03, Aggreko plc 2002– (dep chm 1997–2002), Thus Gp plc 2004–, Carillion plc 2005– (dep chm 2004–05), Northgate plc 2006– (non-exec dir 2003–); non-exec dep chm International Public Relations (formerly Shandwick International plc) 1997–98; non-exec dir: Halifax Building Society (now Halifax plc) 1995–98, LIMIT plc 1998–2000, Wates City of London Properties plc 1998–2000, British Biotech plc 1999–2003, Octopus Capital 2000–01, Celltech plc 2003–04, Davis Service Gp plc 2004–; FCA, FCT; *Recreations* golf, tennis, theatre; *Style—* Philip Rogerson, Esq; ✉ 1 Providence Tower, Bermondsey Wall West, London SE16 4US (tel 020 7237 8962)

ROGISTER, Prof John; s of J J A Rogister (d 1985), of Solihull, and A Rogister, *née* Smal (d 1992); *b* 26 March 1941; *Educ* Solihull Sch, Keble Coll Oxford (pres OU English Club), Univ of Birmingham (BA), Worcester Coll Oxford (DPhil); *m* 1972, Margaret Kathleen, da of late Harold Jury, of New Malden; *Career* sr lectr in modern history Univ of Durham 1982–2001 (lectr 1967–82); assoc prof of history Université de Paris X 1982–84; visiting prof: Collège de France Paris (Bronze Medal of the Collège) 1987, 1999 and 2006, Scuola Normale Superiore Pisa 1988, Università degli Studi di Roma La Sapienza 2003; assoc dir of studies École Pratique des Hautes Études (IV Section) Sorbonne Paris 1988–, assoc prof of history Université Paul Valéry Montpellier III 1989–90 (guest prof 1996, 1998 and 1999); guest prof of history Université Lumière Lyon 2 2000; pres Int Cmmn for the History of Representative and Parliamentary Insts 1990–99 (hon pres 1999–); memb: Jury for the Prize (lit and history) of the Assoc de la Noblesse de France 1993–, French Govt Cmmn d'études de la Reconstruction des Tuileries 2006–, Conseil d'Administration of the Comité pour la Langue du Droit Européen Inst de France 2006– (vice-pres 2007–), Br section Franco-Br Cncl 2007–; Hon Dip Institul de Istorie 'Nicolae Iorga' Romanian Acad 1998; memb: Société de l'Histoire de France 1985, Société Royale des Archives Verviétoises (Belgium) 1989; corresponding memb Académie des Sciences Morales et Politiques Inst de France 2003; FRHistS 1978, FSA 1997; Offr Order of the Palmes Académiques (for services to French culture) 1988, Commandeur de l'Ordre National du Mérite 2001, Accademico (hc) Accademia Siculo-Normanna di Palermo e Monreale (Italy) 2004; *Publications* Durham University Journal (ed, 1975–81), 1776 American Independence Bicentennial Exhibition Catalogue, National Maritime Museum Greenwich (leading contrib, 1976), Parliaments, Estates and Representation (fndr ed, 1981–90), 16th Biennale Exhibition Catalogue, 'Casa dell'Uomo' (Milan, 1986), Louis XV and the Parlement of Paris 1737–1755 (1994); leading contrib to GB Nini Exhibition Catalogues (Urbino and Blois, 2001); also ed of unpublished texts of George I Bratianu (1990 and 1997) and author of over 50 articles and reviews in pubns incl English Historical Review, History, History Today and TLS; *Recreations* travel, music; *Clubs* Travellers, Oxford and Cambridge, City Univ, Fondation Universitaire (Brussels); *Style—* Prof J Rogister, FSA; ✉ 4 The Peth, Durham DH1 4PZ (tel 0191 386 4299, fax 0191 334 1041, e-mail j.m.rogister@durham.ac.uk)

ROHATGI, Pradip Krishna (Roy); s of Binay Krishna Rohatgi (d 1961), of Calcutta, India, and Shakuntala Rohatgi; *b* 10 November 1939; *Educ* St Xavier's Coll Calcutta, Univ of Calcutta (BCom), Univ of London (BSc); *m* 13 July 1974, Pauline Mary, da of Mervyn Harrold; *Career* sr economist and statistician in industrial market research London 1963–66, articled Mann Judd & Co 1966–69; Arthur Andersen: joined 1970, mangr 1973, ptnr 1980, i/c accounting and audit Dubai Office 1980–84, estab and ran Indian firm as managing ptnr 1982–89, returned to London as sr ptnr/conslt 1989–94; int tax and strategy conslt 1991–; visiting prof in int taxation RAU Univ SA 1996, adjunct prof in int taxation Regent Univ VA 1998–2000, adjunct prof in int taxation St Thomas Univ Sch of Law Miami 2000–07, academic dir/prof in int taxation for dip course organised by Fin Services Promotion Agency Govt of Mauritus 2003–05; visiting prof Vienna Univ of Economics and Business Administration 2006–; speaker and writer of articles on various business and professional issues; specialist on India related issues; conf dir Int Tax Planning Conf Bombay 1995–, fndr and tstee Fndn for Int Taxation 2006–; chm: Econ Affrs Ctee Indo-American C of C 1986–89, Int Business Ctee Bombay Mgmnt Assoc 1997–98; conslt to Min of Econ Affairs Mauritius and Mauritius Offshore Business

R

Activities Authy 2000–01; memb: Direct and Indirect Tax Ctee Assoc of C of C in India 1987–89, Exec Ctee Bombay Mgmnt Assoc 1987–89, Main Bd Trade Advsy Ctee for S Asia (DTI) 1992–94, Cncl Rotary Club of London 1992–94, Strategic Planning Soc 1994–, Nat Exec Cncl Indo-American C of C 1984–89, Int Tax Planning Assoc 1996–, Int Fiscal Assoc 1997–, Editorial Advsy Bd Private Capital Jl 2003–; govr Int Students' House London 1991–, hon treas The Children's Med Charity 1992–96; ATII 1967, FCA 1969, MBCS 1976, fell Inst of CAs in India 1980, FRSA; *Publications* Basic International Taxation (2001, 2 edn 2005, Chinese edn 2006); *Recreations* classical guitar, music, fine arts, travel, golf, sailing; *Clubs* Oriental, IOD, Rotary, Royal Soc of Arts, Royal Bombay Yacht, Royal Palms Country; *Style*— Roy Rohatgi, Esq; ✉ 43 Great Brownings, College Road, London SE21 7HP (tel 020 8670 3512, fax 020 8670 3551, e-mail roy@itpa.org)

RÖHL, Prof John Charles Gerald; s of Dr Hans-Gerhard Röhl (d 1976), of Frankfurt-am-Main, Germany, and Freda Kingsford, *née* Woulfe-Brenan; *b* 31 May 1938; *Educ* Stretford GS, Corpus Christi Coll Cambridge (MA, PhD); *m* 7 Aug 1964, Rosemarie Elfriede, da of Johann Werner von Berg (d 1946), of Hamburg; 1 da (Stephanie Angela b 1965), 2 s (Nicholas John, Christoph Andreas (twins) b 1967); *Career* RAF 1956–58; prof of history Univ of Sussex 1979– (lectr 1964–73, reader 1973–79, dean Sch of Euro Studies 1982–85); visiting prof of history: Univ of Hamburg 1974, Univ of Freiburg 1977–78; fell: Alexander von Humboldt Fndn 1970–71, Historisches Kolleg Munich 1986–87, Woodrow Wilson Int Center for Scholars Washington DC 1989–90, Inst for Advanced Study Princeton NJ 1994, Moses Mendelssohn Zentrum Potsdam 1996, Nat Humanities Center NC 1997–98; *Books* Germany Without Bismarck: The Crisis of Government in the Second Reich 1890–1900 (1967), From Bismarck to Hitler: The Problem of Continuity in German History (1970), 1914 - Delusion or Design? The Testimony of Two German Diplomats (1973), Philipp Eulenburgs Politische Korrespondenz (3 vols, 1976–83), Kaiser Wilhelm II - New Interpretations (ed with N Sombart, 1982), Kaiser, Hof und Staat - Wilhelm II und die deutsche Politik (1987), Der Ort Kaiser Wilhelms II in der deutschen Geschichte (ed, 1991), Wilhelm II: Die Jugend des Kaisers 1859–1888 (1993), The Kaiser and his Court: Wilhelm II and the Government of Germany (1994, jt winner Wolfson History Prize 1994), Purple Secret: Genes, 'Madness' and the Royal Houses of Europe (with Martin Warren and David Hunt, 1998), Young Wilhelm: The Kaiser's Early Life 1859–1888 (1998), Wilhelm II: Der Aufbau der Persönlichen Monarchie 1888–1900 (2001, Gissings Prize 2003), Wilhelm II: The Kaiser's Personal Monarchy 1888–1900 (2004); *Recreations* jazz, classical music, walking, bird watching; *Style*— Prof John C G Röhl; ✉ 11 Monckton Way, Kingston, Lewes, East Sussex BN7 3LD (tel 01273 472778); School of European Studies, University of Sussex, Brighton BN1 9QN (tel 01273 678005, fax 01273 623246)

ROITT, Prof Ivan Maurice; *b* 30 September 1927; *Educ* King Edward's Sch Birmingham, Balliol Coll Oxford (Domus exhibitioner, BA, DPhil, DSc); *m*; 3 c; *Career* research asst Univ of Leeds 1949–50, postgrad research student Univ of Oxford 1950–52; Middx Hosp Med Sch (now UCL): research fell 1953–65, reader in immunopathology 1965–68, prof and head Dept of Immunology 1968–92, head Dept of Rheumatology Research 1973–92, emeritus prof 1992; currently co-dir Immunoprotein Engrg Gp UCL; head Immunopathology Research Gp Medical Research Cncl 1968; WHO: dir Autoimmune Disorders Reference Library, chm Steering Ctee on Immunological Control of Human Reproduction; FRCPath 1974 (MRCPath 1966), FRS 1983, Hon FRSM 1993, Hon FRCP 1995 (Hon MRCP 1985); *Awards* Van Meter Prize American Goitre Assoc 1957, Gairdner Award Toronto 1964, Medal for discovery of thyroid autoimmunity Pisa Univ 1986; *Books* Slide Atlas of Essential Immunology (1992), Medical Microbiology (1998), Encyclopedia of Immunology (2000), Essential Immunology (2001), Immunology (2001); author of over 260 pubns in jls; *Recreations* golf, tennis, music, disputation and satisfaction of the gastronomic senses; *Style*— Prof Ivan Roitt; ✉ Department of Immunology, UCL Medical School, Ground Floor, The Windeyer Building, Cleveland Street, London W1T 4JF (tel 020 7679 9360, fax 020 7679 9400, e-mail i.roitt@ucl.ac.uk)

ROJO, Tamara; da of Pablo Rojo, of Madrid, and Sara Diez; *b* 1974; *Educ* Centro de Danza da Victor Ullate; *Career* ballerina; Compañia de Danza Victor Ullate (Comunidad de Madrid) 1991–96, princ English Nat Ballet 1997–2000, princ Royal Ballet 2000–; guest dancer: Ballet Co Madrid Victor Ullate, Scottish Ballet, Ente Publico Arena de Verona, Ballet de la Opera de Niza, Deutche Oper Ballet Berlin, Ballet Nacional de Cuba; prodns incl: La Sylphide, Giselle, Swan Lake, Sleeping Beauty, Bayadere, Paquita, The Nutcracker, Onegin, Don Quixote, Three Corner Hat, Le Beau Danube, Romeo and Juliet, Theme and Variations, Allegro Brillante, Who Cares?, Etudes, Carmen, Shadowplay, Rite of Spring, Song of the Earth, Mayerling, Images of Love, Ondine, Cinderella, Three Preludes, Grossa Fuga, Adagio Hammerclavier, In the Future, Sphinx, Voluntaries, Leaders, Before Night Fall, Arragio, Volando hacia la luz, Simum, Concierto para Tres, Amor Brujo, Nascita di Orfeo, Country Garden; *Awards* Gold Medal and Critics' Award Paris Concours 1994, First Prize of Italian Critics 1996, Outstanding Achievements in Dance Barclays Theatre Award 2000, Best Female Dancer Critics Circle Dance Awards 2001, Spanish Royal Gold Medal of Fine Arts 2002; *Style*— Ms Tamara Rojo; ✉ c/o Royal Ballet Company, Royal Opera House, Covent Garden, London WC2E 9DD

ROLAND, Prof Martin; CBE (2003); s of Peter Ernest Roland, and Eileen Margaret, *née* Osborne; *b* 7 August 1951; *Educ* Rugby, Univ of Oxford (MA, BM BCh, DM); *m* 1, Gillian Rogers; 1 s (Christopher); m 2, Rosalind Jane, *née* Thorburn; 2 s (Duncan (decd), Jonathan), 1 da (Alison); *Career* house physician Radcliffe Infirmary Oxford 1975, house surgn Royal United Hosp Bath 1975–76, GP vocational scheme Cambridge 1976–79, lectr in gen practice St Thomas' Hosp Med Sch and princ in gen practice London 1979–83, princ in gen practice Cambridge 1983–93, dir of studies in gen practice Cambridge Univ Sch of Clinical Med 1987–93, prof of gen practice Univ of Manchester 1993–, dir Nat Primary Care R&D Centre 1999–, dir NIHR Sch for Primary Care Research 2006–; author of numerous pubns on hosp referrals, back pain, use of time and quality of care in gen practice; MFPHM 1987, FRCGP 1994, FMedSci 2000, FRCP 2001 (MRCP 1978); *Style*— Prof Martin Roland, CBE; ✉ National Primary Care Research and Development Centre, Williamson Building, University of Manchester, Oxford Road, Manchester M13 9PL (tel 0161 275 7663, fax 0161 275 7600, e-mail m.roland@man.ac.uk)

ROLES, William Richard; s of Anthony John Howard Roles, of London, and Vanessa Jane, *née* Baldwin; *b* 4 September 1969, Eastbourne, Sussex; *Educ* Ardingly Coll, Mander Portman Woodward Coll London, Univ of Reading (BA), Coll of Law London (Dip); *m* 23 Aug 1997, Victoria Anne, *née* Dennison; 1 s (Alexander Richard Howard b 22 Sept 2001), 1 da (Eleanor Isobel b 27 Oct 2004); *Career* admitted slr 1997; trainee slr Steggles Palmer 1995–97, slr Wilde & Ptnrs 1997–99, slr Eversheds 1999–2004, ptnr and head Banking Dept Mills & Reeve 2004–; memb Law Soc 1997; *Recreations* Chelsea FC, history, family; *Style*— William Roles, Esq; ✉ Mills & Reeve, Francis House, 112 Hills Road, Cambridge CB2 1PH (tel 01223 364422, fax 01223 324549, e-mail william.roles@mills-reeve.com)

ROLFE, Christopher John; s of Frank Vere Rolfe (d 2000), and Nesta Margaret, *née* Smith (d 1996); *b* 16 August 1937; *Educ* Truro Cathedral Sch, Humphry Davy Sch, Royal West of England Acad Sch of Architecture (DipArch), Univ of Edinburgh (DipTP); *m* 3 Oct 1964, Phyllis Roseline, da of Thomas Henry Harry (d 1972), of Newlyn; 2 da (Kerstin Jane (Mrs W D C Beney) b 17 Feb 1967, Kerry Anne (Mrs I W Torrens) b 15 May 1969), 1 s (David Jon Vere b 27 Nov 1971); *Career* architect (ret); sr ptnr Christopher Rolfe & Assoc 1964–85, ind chartered architect and planning conslt 1985–2002; architect and planning conslt to: Bolitho Estates & Trusts 1975–2001, Barclays Bank Trust Co 1990–95, National Trust 1991–98; dir Haselden Estates Ltd 1990–93; chm and area rep Penzance Round Table 1968–74, chm St Clare Assoc 1981–82, local advsr to the Royal Nat Mission of Deep Sea Fisherman 1984–2002 (chm Local Advsy Ctee 1994–2001), clerk to Madron Parish Cncl 1984–2002, advsr to and tstee Garlidna Almshouses 1986–2005, clerk to Sir William Matthews and the Thomas Hosking Tst 1991–98; chm Steering Gp The Newlyn Centre 1998–99; winner Penwith Design Award 1995; RIBA 1964–2007, FRSA 1995–2002; *Books* The Tourist & Leisure Industry (1966); illustrator The Owl and the Hedgehog series; *Recreations* water-colourist, gardening, photography, bowls; *Clubs* Penlee (Newlyn) Bowls (chm); *Style*— Christopher Rolfe, Esq; ✉ Polteggan Farm, Penzance, Cornwall (e-mail chris.rolfe@lineone.net)

ROLFE, David John; *b* 2 April 1939; *Educ* King Edward VII Sch Sheffield, Univ of Sheffield; *m*; 3 da; *Career* architect; jt fndr Rolfe Judd Group 1968; Freeman City of London, Liveryman Worshipful Co of Chartered Architects; RIBA 1965; *Recreations* vintage motor sport, travel, music; *Clubs* East India; *Style*— David Rolfe, Esq; ✉ Rolfe Judd Group, Old Church Court, Claylands Road, London SW8 1NZ (tel 020 7556 1500, fax 020 7556 1501)

ROLINGTON, Alfred; *b* 31 December 1950; *Educ* (BA); *Career* dir EMAP Business Publishing 1979–82, md Eastside Publishing 1982–84, chief exec Lloyd's of London Press Business Publishing 1984–92, group md Jane's Information Group 1992–; *Clubs* Ronnie Scott's; *Style*— Alfred Rolington, Esq; ✉ Jane's Information Group, Sentinel House, 163 Brighton Road, Coulsdon, Surrey CR5 2NH (tel 020 8700 3702, fax 020 8700 3999, e-mail alfred.rolington@janes.co.uk)

ROLL, Michael; *m* Juliana Markova, the pianist; 1 s (Maximilian); *Career* pianist; debut aged twelve Royal Festival Hall playing Schumann's Concerto under Sir Malcolm Sargent, winner Leeds Int Pianoforte competition aged seventeen, US debut with Boston Symphony Orchestra 1974 (with Sir Colin Davis); worked with numerous major conductors incl: Pierre Boulez, Erich Leinsdorf, Kurt Masur, André Previn, Kurt Sanderling; appeared at festivals incl: Aldeburgh, Bath, Edinburgh, Granada, Hong Kong, Vienna, BBC Proms; given recitals in numerous venues incl: NY, Milan, Berlin, Dresden, Leipzig, London; concerto appearances with: Kurt Masur in Leipzig and London, Valery Gergiev in Leningrad and UK, Sergei Comissiona in Helsinki; performed Beethoven Concerti with Swedish Radio Orch, Rotterdam Philharmonic and Monte-Carlo orchs 1995–96; *Recordings* complete cycle of Beethoven Concerti (with RPO and Howard Shelley, first CD voted one of top CD releases for 1996 by BBC Music Magazine); *Style*— Michael Roll, Esq

ROLLAND, Lawrence Anderson Lyon; s of Lawrence Anderson Rolland (d 1959), of Leven, and Winifred Anne, *née* Lyon (d 1978); *b* 6 November 1937; *Educ* George Watsons Coll Edinburgh, Duncan of Jordanstone Coll of Art Dundee (DipArch); *m* 30 April 1960, Mairi, da of John McIntyre Melville (d 1980), of Kirkcaldy; 2 da (Gillian b 1961, Katie b 1967), 2 s (Michael b 1963, Douglas b 1966); *Career* sole ptnr L A Rolland 1960, jt sr ptnr Robert Hurd 1965, ptnr L A Rolland & Partners 1965, sr ptnr Hurd Rolland Partnership 1985–97 (conslt 1997–); winner of more than 20 awards and commendations incl: Saltire Soc, Civic Tst, RIBA, Europa Nostra, Times Conservation, Stone Fedn; fndr chm Scottish Construction Industry Gp 1980, memb Bd and Cncl NTS 2005–; chm Ct Univ of Dundee 1998–2004 (memb 1993–97), chllr's assessor Univ Dundee 2004–; chm Bd of Govrs Duncan of Jordanstone Coll of Art 1993–94, convenor Advsy Ctee for Artistic Matters for Church of Scotland 1975–80, gen tstee Church of Scotland 1979–, memb Building EDC and NEDC 1982–88, chm Educn Tsts RIBA 1996–, memb Bd ARB 1997– (chm Educn and Practice Advsy Gp 1999–2003); hon fell Bulgarian Inst of Architects 1987, hon dr Univ of Dundee 2004; pres: RIAS 1979–81, RIBA 1985–87; FRSA 1988, FRSE 1983; *Projects* incl: Queen's Hall concert hall Edinburgh, restoration and redesign of Bank of Scotland Head Office (original architect Sibbald, Reid & Crighton 1805, and later Bryce 1870), housing in Fife's Royal Burghs, Br Golf Museum St Andrews, General Accident Life Assurance York, Arch Const Royal Soc of Edinburgh, redesign of GMC Cncl Chambers London; *Recreations* music, fishing and more architecture; *Clubs* Reform; *Style*— Dr Lawrence Rolland, PPRIBA, PPRIAS, FRSE, FRSA; ✉ School House, Newburn, Upper Largo, Fife KY8 6JE (tel 01333 360383, e-mail rolland@newburn.org.uk)

ROLLES, Keith; s of Trevor Rolles, of Port Talbot, W Glamorgan, and Betty, *née* Hopkin; *b* 25 October 1947; *Educ* Quakers Yard GS Mid Glamorgan, The Royal London Hosp Med Coll (BSc, MB BS, MS); *m* 22 Aug 1970, Sharon, da of Thomas McGrath (d 1979); 2 s (David b 1981, Thomas b 1986); *Career* lectr in surgery and hon conslt surgn Univ of Cambridge and Addenbrooke's Hosp 1984–88, conslt surgn and dir Liver Transplant Unit The Royal Free Hosp 1988–; Hon MA Univ of Cambridge 1983; Hon MS Univ of London 1985; FRCS 1976; *Recreations* squash, tennis, skiing; *Style*— Keith Rolles, Esq; ✉ Academic Department of Surgery, The Royal Free and University College Medical School, Royal Free Campus, Rowland Hill Street, Hampstead, London NW3 2PF (tel 020 7830 2198)

ROLLIN, Dr Anna-Maria; da of George Tihanyi (d 1997), and Irene, *née* Herskovits (d 1996); *b* 1 March 1946, Budapest, Hungary; *Educ* Northlea Sch Bulawayo Rhodesia, Guy's Hosp Med Sch London (MB BS); *m* 27 July 1973, Henry Rapoport Rollin; 1 s (Aron David Rapoport b 15 Jan 1976), 1 da (Rebecca Ilona b 21 May 1979); *Career* anaesthetist; pre-registration house physician St Helen's Hosp Hastings 1970, pre-registration house surgn Guy's Hosp London 1970–71; SHO: Mpilo Hosp Bulawayo 1971, Guy's Hosp London 1971–72, St Thomas' Hosp London 1972–73; registrar anaesthetics Guy's Hosp London and Queen Victoria Hosp E Grinstead 1973–75, sr registrar anaesthetics Guy's Hosp London and Lewisham Hosp London 1975–77, conslt anaesthetist Epsom Gen Hosp Surrey 1977–, visiting conslt anaesthetist Children's Tst Tadworth 1995–2006, hon conslt anaesthetist Royal Surrey Co Hosp 2001–; memb Cncl: RSM Section of Anaesthesia 1987–90 and 2000– (pres 2004–05), Assoc of Anaesthetists of GB and I 1990–96 (asst hon treas 1992–94, vice-pres 1994–96, chair Risk Mgmnt Working Party 1995–98), Royal Coll of Anaesthetists 2001– (sr vice-pres 2007–, faculty tutor 1980–87, ed Bulletin 2001–05, memb Editorial Bd Br Jl of Anaesthesia, chm Hosp Visits Ctee 2005–), Preoperative Assoc 2003–, Assoc of Paediatric Anaesthetists 2004–; lead assessor in anaethesia GMC 1998– (also Professional and Linguistic Assessments Bd (PLAB) examiner 2002–); memb Central Conslts and Specialists Ctee (CCSC) and chm Anaesthetic Sub-Ctee BMA 1993–96; Dept of Health: memb Bd New ways of working in anaesthesia 2003–, memb Working Gp on Paediatric Anaethesia and Emergency Care in the Dist Gen Hosp 2004–, memb Working Party on Choice for Children 2004–; pres Br Anaesthetic and Recovery Nurses Assoc 2003–05 (life memb 2005–); chm Southern Soc of Anaesthetists 1991–92; memb: Soc of Anaesthetists of the SW Region, History of Anaesthesia Soc, European Soc of Anaesthesiology 2005–; LRCP 1970, MRCS 1970, FFARCS 1975, FRCA 1996; *Publications* Raising the Standard (jt ed, 1999), Raising the Standard: Information for Patients (jt ed, 2003); author of chapters in books and numerous pubns in learned jls; *Style*— Dr Anna-Maria Rollin; ✉ Department of Anaesthesia, Epsom General Hospital, Dorking Road, Epsom, Surrey KT18 7EG (tel 01372 735270, fax 01372 735497, e-mail anna.rollin@epsom-sthelier.nhs.uk)

ROLLINSON, Timothy John Denis; s of William Edward Denis Rollinson (d 1963), and Ida Frances, *née* Marshall; *b* 6 November 1953, London; *Educ* Chigwell Sch, Univ of Edinburgh (BSc); *m* 1975, Dominique Christine, *née* Favardin; 2 da (Marie-Claire Julie b 2 Feb 1981, Fiona Sophie b 10 Feb 1984), 1 s (William Benoit b 28 April 1986); *Career* Forestry Cmmn: district offr Kent 1976–78, New Forest 1978–81, head of growth and yield studies 1981–88, land use planning 1988–90, Parly and policy 1990–93, sec 1994–97, chief conservator Eng 1997–2000, head of policy and practice 2000–03, dir Forestry Gp

2003–04, DG and dep chm 2004–; pres Inst of Chartered Foresters 2000–02, chair Global Partnership on Forest Landscape Restoration 2002–; FICFor 1978, FIAgrE 2004, chartered environmentalist 2005, CCMI 2006; *Recreations* golf, travel; *Clubs* Craigmillar Park Golf; *Style*— Timothy Rollinson, Esq; ✉ Forestry Commission, 231 Corstorphine Road, Edinburgh EH12 7AT (tel 0131 314 6424, fax 0131 316 4344, e-mail tim.rollinson@forestry.gsi.gov.uk)

ROLLO, 14 Lord (S 1651); David Eric Howard Rollo; also Baron Dunning (UK 1869); s of 13 Lord Rollo (d 1997), and Suzanne, da of W H B Hatton; *b* 31 March 1943; *Educ* Eton; *m* 1971, Felicity Anne Christian, da of Lt-Cdr John Bruce Lamb, DSC, RN; 3 s (Hon James David William, Master of Rollo b 1972, Hon Thomas Stapylton b 1975, Hon William Eric John b 1978); *Heir* s, Master of Rollo; *Career* late Capt Grenadier Guards; *Style*— The Rt Hon the Lord Rollo

ROLLS, Prof Edmund Thomson; s of Eric Fergus Rolls, and May Martin, *née* Thomson; *b* 4 June 1945; *Educ* Hardye's Sch Dorchester, Jesus Coll Cambridge (MA), The Queen's Coll Oxford (Thomas Hardy scholar), Univ of Oxford (DPhil, DSc); *m* 1969 (m dis 1983), Barbara Jean, *née* Simons; 2 da (Melissa May, Juliet Helen); *Career* Univ of Oxford: fell by examination Magdalen Coll 1969–73, fell and tutor in psychology CCC 1973–, lectr in experimental psychology 1973–, prof of experimental psychology 1996–; assoc dir MRC Oxford Interdisciplinary Research Centre for Cognitive Neuroscience 1990–2003; sec: European Brain and Behaviour Soc 1973–76, Cncl European Neuroscience Assoc 1985–88; Spearman Medal Br Psychological Soc 1977; Canadian Cwlth fell 1980–81; Hon DSc Toyama Medical Univ 2005; memb Academia Europaea, membre d'honneur Société Française de Neurologie 1994; *Books* The Brain and Reward (1975), Thirst (with B J Rolls, 1982), Neural Networks and Brain Function (with A Treves, 1998), Introduction to Connectionist Modelling of Cognitive Processes (with P McLeod and K Plunkett, 1998), The Brain and Emotion (1999), Computational Neuroscience of Vision (with G Deco, 2002), Emotion Explained (2005), Memory, Attention and Decision-Making (2008); *Style*— Prof Edmund Rolls; ✉ University of Oxford, Department of Experimental Psychology, South Parks Road, Oxford OX1 3UD (tel 01865 271348, fax 01865 271416, e-mail edmund.rolls@psy.ox.ac.uk)

ROLPH, Susan (Sue); da of Wilf Rolph, and Maureen, *née* Cooper; *b* 15 May 1978; *Educ* Walbottle Sch, Newcastle Coll; *Career* swimmer; 50m freestyle: personal best 25.57 secs 1998, Silver medal European Short Course Championships 1996, Gold medal Cwlth Games 1998, Bronze medal European Short Course Championships (Cwlth record) 1998; 100m freestyle: personal best 55.17 secs 1998, Bronze medal (relay) European Championships 1995, Gold medal Cwlth Games (Games record) 1998, Gold medal (relay) Cwlth Games 1994, Silver medal (relay) Cwlth Games 1998, Gold medal European Short Course (Cwlth record) 1998, Gold medal European Championships Istanbul 1999; personal best 100m butterfly 59.95 secs (first British woman to swim inside one minute); 100m individual medley: Gold medal European Short Course Championships 1996 (Bronze medal 1998); Bronze medal (relay) 100m medley Cwlth Games 1998; 200m individual medley: personal best 2 mins 15.39 secs 1998, Gold Medal European Shortcourse Championships 1996, Bronze medal World Short Course Championships 1998, Bronze medal Cwlth Games (British record) 1998, Bronze medal European Short Course Championships 1998; memb Olympic squad 1996 and 2000; memb Millennium Youth Games Project; hon ambass of Newcastle 1998; *Awards* Newcastle sports personality of the year 1998; *Recreations* spend a lot of time with my boyfriend; *Clubs* City of Cardiff Amateur Swimming; *Style*— Miss Sue Rolph

ROMAINE, Michèle; da of late Robert Henry Robinson-Romaine, and Hilda, *née* Arundale; *b* 15 July 1957; *Educ* Teesside HS for Girls, Hartlepool Coll of FE, Wharton Business Sch; *m* 1985, Cdr Michael Maltby, RN; 1 da (Harriet Katherine Maltby b December 1989); *Career* journalist; former reporter with: Radio Humberside, Radio Victory, BBC News, ITN News; ed BBC West News Bristol 1992–94, head of BBC South East 1994–97, head of prodn Continuous News BBC 1997–99 (responsibilities incl BBC World, Radio 5 Live and BBC News 24), dir BBC prodn 1999–2000, dir Prodn Modernisation BBC 2000–04; currently ind conslt in digital prodn; memb Broadcast Trg and Skills Regulator Ofcom 2005–; memb: RTS, Radio Academy, Industrial Soc; *Recreations* cross-country riding, gardening; *Style*— Ms Michèle Romaine

ROMAINE, Prof Suzanne; *Educ* Bryn Mawr Coll (AB), Univ of Edinburgh (MLitt), Univ of Birmingham (PhD); *Career* early career: sr research scientist in linguistic anthropology Max-Planck-Institut-fr-Psycholinguistik Nijmegen, lectr in linguistics Univ of Birmingham; Merton prof of English language Univ of Oxford 1984–; Kerstin Hesslegren prof Univ of Uppsala 1991–92, Rotary Int Fndn fell Univ of Edinburgh, Canada Cwlth scholar Ontario Inst for Studies in Educn Univ of Toronto; Hon Dr: Univ of Tromsø 1998, Univ of Uppsala 1999; *Books* Socio-historical Linguistics: Its Status and Methodology (1982), Sociolinguistic Variation in Speech Communities (ed, 1982), The Language of Children and Adolescents: The Acquisition of Communicative Competence (1984), Pidgin and Creole Languages (1988), Bilingualism (1989, 2 edn 1995), Language in Australia (ed, 1991), Language, Education and Development: Urban and Rural Tok Pisin in Papua New Guinea (1992), Language in Society: An Introduction to Sociolinguistics (1994, 2 edn 2000), Communicating Gender (1999), Creole Genesis, Attitudes and Discourse. Studies Celebrating Charlene J Sato (ed with John Rickford, 1999), Vanishing Voices: The Extinction of the World's Languages (with Daniel Nettle, 2000); *Style*— Prof Suzanne Romaine; ✉ Merton College, Oxford OX1 4JD

ROMANES, (Constance) Margaret; OBE (1981), JP (1965), DL (Dorset 1989); da of Claud Valentine Gee (d 1951), and Hilda, *née* Bentham (d 1968); *b* 9 August 1920; *Educ* St Leonard's Sch, Girton Coll Cambridge (MA); *m* 29 June 1943, Giles John Romanes, s of Capt Francis John Romanes (d 1944); 2 da (Jane b 1946, Rosalind b 1947), 1 s (Julian b 1951 d 1994); *Career* dep chm Magistrates' Assoc 1981–87 (vice-pres 1990–); chm: Dorset branch Magistrates' Assoc 1981–89 (pres 1990–98), Weymouth and Portland Bench 1985–91; contrib to various jls and reader of papers at various int confs; memb: James Ctee (an Interdepartmental Ctee on Distribution of Criminal Business), Portland Borstal Youth Custody Centre Bd of Visitors 1971–86 (chm 1976–81), Salisbury Diocesan Synod 1976–84, Local Parole Review Ctee 1984–86, Penal Affairs Consortium 1995–98, Mgmnt Ctee Dorset Victim Support 1998–2004, various govt working parties; Bishop's selector for ACCM 1976–83, chm Dorset Care Tst 1984–94 (vice-pres 1994–97), chm Nat Forum of Care Tsts 1993–95; Lord Chllr's nominee on Legal Aid Duty Slr Ctee 1986–91; *Recreations* music (active memb of orchestras and chamber groups), gardening; *Clubs* RSM; *Style*— Mrs Margaret Romanes, OBE, DL

ROME, Richard Allan; s of Sidney Herbert Rome (d 1986), and Elsie Mary, *née* Gosling (d 2004); *b* 8 January 1943; *Educ* St Albans GS, St Albans Sch of Art, Chelsea Sch of Art; *m* 1969 (m dis 1982), Sally, *née* Gollop; 1 s (William Henry b 17 March 1970); *Career* sculptor; tutor and lectr: sculpture at Brighton Poly, North East London Poly, Canterbury Coll of Art 1975–89, sr lectr Wimbledon Sch of Art 1989–91, sr lectr MA course RCA 1991–; visiting lectr: Univ of Reading, Leeds Poly, Bath Acad, Kingston Poly, Ravensbourne Sch of Art, West Surrey Coll of Art, Reinhart Sch of Sculpture Baltimore, Syracuse Univ NY, RCA, Winchester Sch of Art, Sch of Art Inst Chicago; FRCA 1996, FRBS 1996; *Solo Exhibitions* Serpentine Gall 1975, Univ of Kent 1977, The Vicarage Chatham Street London 1982, Gillian Jason Gall 1982; *Group Exhibitions* incl: Magdalen Coll Oxford 1966, Univ of Sussex 1969, Brighton Festival 1972, Yorkshire Sculpture Park 1978, 1985, 1989, 1990, 1991, 1996, 1998 and 1999, Hayward Gall London 1979, Royal Acad 1983, Warwick Arts Tst 1984, Hamilton Univ NY 1984, Bokhoven Gall Amsterdam 1988, Greenwich Studios London 1992, Riverdale Sculpture Park 1993, Sportsman Gall Chicago 1998, Museum of Science and Industry Manchester 1999, Tate Gall Bankside London 1999, Royal West of England Acad Triennial Exhibition 1999, Canterbury Cathedral Precinct 2003; work in public collections incl: Arts Cncl of GB, Yorkshire Sculpture Park, Ironbridge Open Air Museum of Steel Sculpture, Millfield Sch, Nat Lottery Charities Bd HQ; public cmmn 2000 Cannizaro Park Millennium Fountain Sculpture; *Awards* Arts Cncl Major Award 1976, South East Arts Awards 1977 and 1984; *Publications* Fine Art Metal Casting: An Illustrated Guide to Mouldmaking and Lost Wax Proceses (2003); *Recreations* walking, skiing, travel; *Clubs* Chelsea Arts; *Style*— Richard Rome, Esq; ✉ The Vicarage, 51 Chatham Street, London SE17 1PA (tel 020 7701 3287); Royal College of Art, Sculpture School, 15–25 Howie Street, London SW11 4AS (tel 020 7590 4444, fax 020 7590 4460, e-mail richard.rome@rca.ac.uk)

ROMER, Stephen Charles Mark; s of late Mark Lemon Robert Romer, of Clavering, Essex, and Philippa Maynard, *née* Tomson; *b* 20 August 1957, Herts; *Educ* King's Coll Sch Cambridge, Radley, Trinity Hall Cambridge (BA, PhD); *m* 17 July 1982 (sep), Bridget Julia, *Née* Strevens; 1 s (Thomas Mark Strevens b 19 June 1985); *Career* Henry fell Harvard Univ 1978–79, teacher British Inst Paris 1983–88 (postgrad scholar 1979–80), asst associé Univ of Paris X 1987–89, asst prof Univ of Łódź Poland (British Cncl post) 1989–90, maître de confs Univ of Tours 1990–; visiting prof in French Colgate Univ NY, visiting fell Sidney Sussex Coll Cambridge; Gregory Award for Young Poets 1985, Prudence Farmer Award New Statesman 1985; *Poetry* Islay and other poems (1978), Idols (1986, Poetry Book Soc recommendation), Plato's Ladder (1992, Poetry Book Soc choice), Selected Poems of Jacques Dupin (trans, 1992), The New Poetry (contrib to anthology, 1993), Traductions, Passages: Le Domaine Anglais (ed, 1993), Tribute (1998), Twentieth-Century French Poems (ed, 2002), Anthologie Bilingue de la Poésie Anglaise (contrib, 2005), Tribut (selected poems in French translation, 2007); *Style*— Stephen Romer, Esq

ROMER-LEE, Alexander Knyvett (Alex); s of Knyvett Romer-Lee, OBE (d 1996), of Hickling, Norfolk, and Jeanne Pamela, *née* Shaw (d 1982); *b* 18 August 1953; *Educ* Eton, Institut Universitaire de Technologie Dijon; *m* Janet Christine; 1 da (Katherine Pamela b 6 Jan 1985), 1 s (Jonathan Knyvett b 15 Oct 1987); *Career* PricewaterhouseCoopers (formerly Deloitte Haskins & Sells and then Coopers & Lybrand): chartered accountant 1980, ptnr Southampton 1988, ptnr London 1988–89, managing ptnr Budapest 1990–91, ptnr London 1992–2001, ldr Central and Eastern Europe Financial Services 1996–2001; dir: Hibtrade Holdings Ltd 2001–, Sonali Bank (UK) Ltd 2002–, FCE Bank plc 2006–; chm: AKRL Ltd 2001–, Morning Papers Ltd 2002–, AK Recreations & Leisure Ltd 2006–; prop Les Amis de Whiteparish 1987–; FCA 1991; *Recreations* Burgundy wine, cricket, fishing, sailing; *Clubs* MCC, East India; *Style*— A K Romer-Lee, Esq; ✉ Nunns Orchard, Whiteparish, Salisbury, Wiltshire SP5 2RJ (tel 01794 884255, fax 01794 884591, e-mail akromerlee@aol.com)

ROMER-LEE, Robin Knyvett; s of Knyvett Romer-Lee, OBE (d 1996), of Green Farm, Hickling, Norfolk, and Jeanne Pamela, *née* Shaw (d 1982); *b* 27 October 1942; *Educ* Eton; *m* 30 March 1968, Annette Millet, da of George Henry Brocklehurst (d 1972); 2 s (Benjamin b 1971, Edward b 1973); *Career* insurance broker; chm Price Forbes Ltd 1992, ret; *Recreations* sailing, fishing, gardening; *Style*— Robin Romer-Lee, Esq; ✉ Doe's Farm, Wallow Lane, Naughton, Suffolk IP7 7BZ (tel 01473 657653)

ROMERO, Rebecca; *b* 24 January 1980, Carshalton, Surrey; *Educ* Wallington HS for Girls, Richmond upon Thames Coll, St Mary's Coll Twickenham; *Career* amateur rower and cyclist; memb: Kingston Rowing Club, Leander Club; sr int debut 2001; achievements incl: Silver medal quadruple sculls Cwlth Games 1998, Gold medal coxless pairs World Under 23 Championships 2000, winner quadruple sculls World Cup 2004 and 2005, Silver medal quadruple sculls Olympic Games Athens 2004, Gold medal quadruple sculls World Championships 2005; amateur cyclist 2006–, Silver medal individual pursuit World Track Cycling Championships 2007; *Style*— Miss Rebecca Romero; ✉ 50 The Row, Lane End, Buckinghamshire HP14 3JS (mobile 07968 198447, e-mail rebecca@rebeccaromero.co.uk, website www.rebeccaromero.co.uk)

ROMNEY, 8 Earl of (UK 1801); Sir Julian Charles Marsham; 14 Bt (E 1663); also Baron of Romney (GB 1716) and Viscount Marsham (UK 1801); s of Col Peter Marsham, MBE (s of Hon Sydney Marsham, yst s of 4 Earl of Romney), and Hersey, da of Maj Hon Richard Coke (3 s of 2 Earl of Leicester, KG, JP, DL, by his 2 w, Hon Georgina Cavendish, da of 2 Baron Chesham); suc kinsman, 7 Earl of Romney 2004; *b* 28 March 1948; *Educ* Eton; *m* 1975, Catriona, da of Sir Robert Christie Stewart KCVO, CBE, TD; 2 s (David, Viscount Marsham b 1977, Hon Michael b 1979), 1 da (Lady Laura b 1984); *Heir* s, Viscount Marsham; *Career* land agent; farmer; High Sheriff Norfolk 2007–08; *Recreations* conservation, golf, field sports; *Style*— The Rt Hon the Earl of Romney; ✉ Gayton Hall, King's Lynn, Norfolk PE32 1PL (tel 01553 636259, estate office 01553 636292)

RONALDSON, Cheryl Anne; da of John Ronaldson, of Pipewell, Northants, and Jenny, *née* Simpson; *b* 2 July 1966, Leicester; *Educ* Leicester HS for Girls, KCL (LLB, AKC), Coll of Law London; *partner* Dr Peter Ostler; *Career* admitted slr 1990; trainee slr then asst slr Barlow Lyde & Gilbert 1988–94, asst slr Clifford Chance 1994–98, ptnr and memb corporate insurance team Norton Rose 1999–; memb Law Soc; *Publications* A Practitioner's Guide to the FSA Regulation of Lloyd's (ed and co-author, 2001, 2 edn 2004); *Style*— Miss Cheryl Ronaldson; ✉ Norton Rose, 3 More London Riverside, London SE1 2AQ (tel 020 7444 3323, e-mail cheryl.ronaldson@nortonrose.com)

RONDEL, Prof Richard Kavanagh; s of William Allen Thomas Rondel (d 1963), and Edna Phyllis, *née* Sayer (d 2000); *b* 29 October 1931; *Educ* King Edward VI Sch Chelmsford, King's College London (second MB BS), St George's Hosp Med Sch London (final MB BS), DipRCOG, DipPharmMed; *m* 1962 (m dis 1992); 1 da (Nicola Louise de Chastelai b 7 Dec 1962), 1 s (Mark Richard de Chastelai b 2 Nov 1963); *Career* house appts St George's Hosp London 1956–58; Nat Serv RAMC, jr specialist in pathology, served Cyprus and Gibraltar 1958–60; registrar and res MO St George's Hosp Tooting 1960–62, med advsr John Wyeth Taplow 1963–65, dir of clinical research (UK) CIBA Laboratories Horsham 1965–74, dir of clinical research (Europe, ME and Africa) Bristol Myers International Corp 1975–80, dep chm Iphar Inst for Med Research Munich 1981–83, fndr md Oxford Workshops (contract research and consultancy) 1983–96; dir Pharmakopius International plc 1996–98; pres: Br Assoc of Pharmaceutical Physicians 1972–74 (hon life memb 1981), Int Fedn of Assocs of Pharmaceutical Physicians 1978–81; memb Cncl RCP London 1992–96; med dir and post-grad clinical tutor HPRU Med Research Centre Univ of Surrey 1997–2001, visiting prof Postgrad Med Sch Univ of Surrey 2001–04; fndn fell Faculty of Pharmaceutical Med 1989 (faculty registrar 1989–95); FRCP 1992; *Books* Adverse Drug Reactions (1973), Clinical Data Management (2000); *Recreations* travel, flying in vintage aircraft, fly fishing; *Style*— Prof R K Rondel; ✉ 2 King George Square, Park Hill, Richmond-on-Thames, Surrey TW10 6LG (tel and fax 020 8940 7852, e-mail richrondel@aol.com)

RONE, Ven James (Jim); s of James Rone (d 1967), and Bessie Rone (d 1982); *b* 28 August 1935; *Educ* Skerry's Coll Liverpool, St Stephen's House Oxford; *m* 1, 1956, Ivy, *née* Whitby (d 1970); 1 s (William Geoffrey), 1 da (Ann Carol); m 2, 1976, Mary Elizabeth, da of William Isaac Bancroft Angove; *Career* accountant ICI Ltd 1958–64, co sec/dir Timperley Engineering Ltd and other subsids of Reed International 1965–71, gp chief accountant Leigh and Sillavan Group 1971–73, fin offr Dio of Oxford 1973–79, ordination trg St Stephen's House Oxford 1979–80, curate Stony Stratford Parish Church 1980–82, vicar and rector Fordham with Kennett (Dio of Ely) 1982–89, residentiary canon/canon

R

treas Ely Cathedral 1989–95, archdeacon of Wisbech 1995–2003; memb Gen Synod C of E 1995–; memb Ecclesiastical Law Soc; FSCA 1971; *Recreations* listening to classical music, theatre, rugby and cricket (former player, now spectator), good food and wine; *Clubs* Carlton, Royal Over-Seas League; *Style*— The Ven Jim Rone; ✉ 32 Lumley Close, Ely, Cambridgeshire CB7 4FG

RONSON, Dame Gail; DBE (2004); da of Joseph Cohen, and Marie Cohen; *b* 3 July 1946, London; *m* 10 Sept 1967, Gerald Maurice Ronson, *qv*; 4 da (Lisa Debra, Amanda Caroline (Mrs Ronson-Langer), Nicole Julia (Mrs Ronson-Allalouf), Hayley Victoria (Mrs Goldenberg)); *Career* early career with Norwood Orphanage and Stepney Jewish Meals on Wheels, later involved as fundraiser with Central Br Fund for Jewish Refugees and Jewish Welfare Bd (sometime memb Cncl), former chm Women's Div Jt Israel Appeal, jt chair Cncl for a Beautiful Israel 1987–94, memb Bd Jewish Care 1992– (appeals chm and capital gifts chm 1998–, dep chm 2002–); tstee: Ronson Fndns 1980–95, Winnington Charitable Fndn, Park Chase Charitable Fndn; dir ROH 2001–, tstee ROH Tst 1985–; co-chm St Mary's Hosp Save the Baby Fund 1985–96, vice-pres Assoc for Research into Stammering in Childhood 1991–, tstee Home Farm Devpt Tst 1991–94, fundraiser Roundhouse Tst; *Style*— Dame Gail Ronson, DBE; ✉ Heron House, 19 Marylebone Road, London NW1 5JL (tel 020 7935 8756, fax 020 7487 2970, e-mail gailronson@heron.co.uk)

RONSON, Gerald Maurice; *b* 27 May 1939; *m* 10 Sept 1967, Gail, *née* Cohen, *qv*; 4 da; *Career* chief exec: Heron Corporation plc 1976– (chm 1988–93), Heron International plc (chm 1983–93); chm and chief exec Snax 24 Corporation Ltd; ambass of Druse Community Mount Carmel; *Style*— Gerald M Ronson, Esq; ✉ c/o Heron International plc, Heron House, 19 Marylebone Road, London NW1 5JL (tel 020 7486 4477, fax 020 7487 2970)

ROOCROFT, Amanda Jane; da of Roger Roocroft, of Coppull, Lancs, and Valerie, *née* Metcalfe; *b* 9 February 1966; *Educ* Southlands HS, Runshaw Tertiary Coll, Royal Northern Coll of Music; *m* David Gowland; *Career* soprano; winner Decca-Kathleen Ferrier Meml Prize and Silver Medal Worshipful Co of Musicians 1988, Royal Philharmonic Soc/Charles Heidsieck Award for operatic debut 1990; currently studies with Barbara Robotham; fell: Univ of Central Lancashire, Royal Northern Coll of Music; Hon Dr Univ of Manchester 2003; *Opera Performances* ROH incl: Fiordiligi in Cosi fan tutte, Guilietta in I Capuleti e i Montecchi, Mimi in La Boheme, Pamina in The Magic Flute, Cleopatra in Giulio Cesare, title role Madam Butterfly, Katya Kabanova, Desdemona in Otello; Bavarian State Opera Munich: Fiordiligi, Amelia in Simon Boccanegra, Donna Elvira in Don Giovanni, Desdomona in Otello; Glyndebourne Festival: Fiordiligi, Donna Elvira and title role in Katya Kabanova, title role in Jenufa; other performances incl: Don Elvira (Metropolitan Opera NY), Tatiana in Eugene Onegin (WNO); *Concert Performances* incl: The Proms, London's South Bank, Edinburgh Int Festival, City of Birmingham Symphony Orchestra with Sir Simon Rattle; *Recitals* incl: Wigmore Hall London, Concertgebouw Amsterdam, Musikverein Vienna, La Monnaie Brussels, Lincoln Center NY; appearances throughout the rest of the UK, Europe and NY (incl NY Philharmonic); *Recordings* incl: Vaughan Williams' Serenade to Music (Hyperion), Cosi fan Tutte (with Baroque English Soloists under John Eliot Gardiner, Deutsche Grammophon 1992), solo album Amanda Roocroft (EMI 1994), Mozart and his contemporaries (with the Academy of St Martin in the Fields and Sir Neville Marriner, 1996); *Recreations* reading, cooking, sewing; *Style*— Miss Amanda Roocroft; ✉ Ingpen and Williams, 7 St George's Court, 131 Putney Bridge Road, London SW15 2PA

ROOK, His Hon Judge Peter Francis Grosvenor; QC (1991); s of Dr Arthur Rook (d 1991), of Cambridge, and Frances Jane Elizabeth, *née* Knott (d 1990); *b* 19 September 1949; *Educ* King's Coll Choir Sch Cambridge, Charterhouse, Trinity Coll Cambridge (open exhibitioner), Univ of Bristol; *m* 2 Sept 1978, Susanna Marian, da of Richard Roland Tewson, of Great Sampford, Essex; 2 da (Annabel b 1979, Sophie b 1981), 1 s (Joshua b 1983); *Career* called to the Bar Gray's Inn 1973 (bencher 2000); first standing counsel to Inland Revenue Central Criminal Court and Inner London Courts 1989–91 (second standing counsel 1981–89), standing counsel to HM Customs and Excise SE Circuit 1989–91, recorder 1995–2005, head of chambers 18 Red Lion Court London 2002–05, circuit judge (SE Circuit) 2005– (sitting at Central Criminal Court); chm Criminal Bar Assoc 2002–03; *Books* Rook and Ward on Sexual Offences (with Robert Ward, 1990, 3 edn 2004); *Recreations* travel, theatre, tennis, squash, ornithology, tropical plants; *Clubs* Coolhurst Lawn Tennis and Squash, Globe Lawn Tennis; *Style*— His Hon Judge Rook, QC

ROOKER, Baron (Life Peer UK 2001), of Perry Barr in the County of West Midlands; Jeffrey William Rooker; PC (1999); *b* 5 June 1941; *Educ* Handsworth Tech Sch, Handsworth Tech Coll, Univ of Warwick (MA), Aston Univ (BScEng); *m* 1972, Angela (decd 2003); *Career* prodn mangr Rola Celestion Ltd 1967–70; lectr Lanchester Poly Coventry 1972–74, memb Birmingham Educn Ctee 1972–74; MP (Lab) Birmingham Perry Barr Feb 1974–2001; PPS to the Govt Law Offrs 1977; oppn front bench spokesman on: social services 1979–80, social security 1981–83, Treasy and econ affrs 1983–84, environment 1984–88, community care and social services 1990–92, educn 1992–93, shadow dep ldr House of Commons 1994–97; min of state MAFF 1997–99, min of state DSS 1999–2001, min of state for Citizenship and Immigration 2001–02, min of state for Housing and Planning ODPM 2002–05, min of state NI Office 2005–06, dep ldr House of Lords 2005–, min of state DEFRA 2006–; memb Public Accounts Ctee 1989, chair Lab Campaign for Electoral Reform 1989–95; memb Cncl IProdE 1975–80; CEng; *Style*— The Rt Hon the Lord Rooker, PC

ROOKLEDGE, Gordon Charles; s of Charles Harcourt Rookledge Collett (d 1954), of Johannesburg, South Africa, and Elsie Alicia, *née* Goodwin (d 1976); *b* 3 December 1933; *Educ* Stanley Park Secdy Sch; *m* 1 April 1960, Jennifer Mary, da of Robert Dampier Lush, of Carshalton, Surrey; 2 da (Sarah Louise b 1962, Emma Constance b 1966), 1 s (Gavin Alistair b 1964); *Career* Nat Serv RA 1952–54; sales rep: Austin Miles Ltd 1954–58, Eros Engraving Ltd 1958–64; sales mangr Westerham Press 1964–68; chm and md: Gavin Martin Ltd 1968–91 (fndr 1968), Sarema Press (Publishers) Ltd 1973–2004 (fndr 1973), KGM (Offset) Ltd 1983–2004 (fndr 1983); pt/t tutor RCA 1974–84, visiting lectr E Ham Coll of Technol and Middx Poly; proprietor Design Brief magazine 1985–86, fndr jt ed de Worde (quarterly jl of the Wynkyn de Worde Soc) 1993–95; adjudicator: Francis Minns Best Designed Book of the Year Award (Wynkyn de Worde Soc) 1991–95, Best Designed Lunchtime Keepsakes Award by BA Students from Camberwell Coll of Art and St Martins Coll of Art (Wynkyn de Worde Soc) 1991–95; chm Carshalton Soc 1985–96; library offr Carshalton and District History and Archaelogy Soc 2007– (pres 2002–04); memb: Sutton Arts Cncl 1995–2007, Brighton and Hove Civic Soc 1998–2005, The Clapham Soc (London) 2002–, The Regency Soc of Brighton and Hove, Typographic Circle (London), Soc of Genealogists; fndr and chm Friends of Historic Street Furniture (Carshalton and its Environs) 2001–05; Freeman: City of London 1993, Worshipful Co of Stationers 1993; *Books* Rookledge's International Typefinder (ed, 1983), Rookledge's Handbook of Type Designers (A Biographical Directory from the 15th Century to the present, ed, 1990), Rookledge's Architectural Identifier of Conservation Areas (1999), The Book of Carshalton at the Source of the Wandle (jt ed, 2002), Rookledge's Classic International Typefinder (ed, 2004); *Recreations* film and video, collecting print ephemera, paintings, swimming; *Clubs* Groucho, Chelsea Arts, Wynkyn De Worde Soc (memb 1990–99, memb Ctee 1991–96); *Style*— Gordon Rookledge, Esq; ✉ 15 Beeches Walk, Carshalton Beeches, Surrey SM5 4JS (fax 020 8770 1957, e-mail sarema@gordonrookledge.demon.co.uk)

ROOLEY, Anthony; s of Henry Rooley, and Madge Rooley; *b* 10 June 1944; *Educ* Royal Acad of Music (LRAM); *m* 1967, Carla; 3 da, 1 s (by Emma Kirkby); *Career* lutenist; given concerts in: Europe, USA, ME, Japan, S America, NZ, Aust; numerous radio and TV broadcasts in UK and Europe, numerous recordings for Decca, DHM, Virgin Classics; music admin: Eng Summer Schs 1973–79, The Future of Early Music in Br Conf 1977; fndr Early Music Centre 1976; teacher: Royal Acad of Music 1968, Guildhall Sch of Music and Drama 1971–74, RNCM 1975–76, Univ of Leicester 1976–79, Early Music Centre 1976–80, Schola Cantorum Basel 1985–, Japanese gashkus 1986–, Dartington Int Summer Sch 1986–; visiting Orpheus scholar Florida State Univ Tallahassee 2003; music theatre: Cupid and Death 1984, The Marriage of Pantalone 1985, Cupid and Psyche 1987, Venus and Adonis 1988, The Revels of Siena 1988, The Judgement of Paris 1989, Monteverdi's Balli 1990, Monteverdi's Orfeo 1991, Eccle's Semele 1992, Stradella's L'Anime del Purgatorio 1993, Il Pastor Fido 1994, Don Quixote 1996, Albion & Albanius 1997; co-dir Banquet of the Senses (film) 1993; dir The Consort of Musicke 1969–, artistic dir Musica Oscura (record co), advsr to the York Early Music Festival; hon visiting prof Music Dept Univ of York 1997; FRAM (1990); *Recordings* with soprano Evelyn Tubb: Bewitching Bracegirdle (vols I and II), Elegies, A Many Coloured Coat; *Books* Penguin Book of Early Music (1982), Performance - Revealing the Orpheus within (1990), Routledge Compendium of Contemporary Musical Thought (contrib, 1989), Everyman Companion to Early Music (contrib, 1990); author of various articles for: Guitar Magazine 1976, Lute Soc Jls, Lute Soc Jl of America, Early Music Magazine, Temenos; *Recreations* food, wine, sculpture, gardening, philosophy; *Style*— Anthony Rooley, Esq; ✉ 13 Pages Lane, London N10 1PU (tel 020 8444 6565, fax 020 8444 1008, e-mail consort@easynet.co.uk)

ROOLEY, Richard Herbert; s of George Arthur Rooley, CBE (d 2001), of Stoke Poges, Bucks, and Valeria, *née* Green (d 1994); *b* 24 April 1940; *Educ* Glasgow Acad, Morrisons Acad, Trinity Coll Dublin (BA, BAI); *m* 25 July 1964, (Ismena) Ruth Rooley, da of George Young (d 1956), of Eire; 1 s (George b 1966), 1 da (Ismena b 1968); *Career* Donald Smith & Rooley conslt engrs: joined 1964, assoc 1968, ptnr 1971–91; sr ptnr Rooley Consultants 1991–; ptnr Project Management Partnership 1978–; memb Cncl CIBSE 1972–81 and 1989–92, chm Bldg Servs Res and Info Assoc 1984–86, chm Nat Jt Consultative Ctee 1993; churchwarden Stoke Poges 1980–86, lay chm Burnham Deanery Synod 1985–86, reader C of E; Liveryman Worshipful Co of Engrs (Master 1999–2000), Master Worshipful Co of Constructors 1992–93; MConsE; American Soc of Heating Refrigerating and Air Conditioning Engrs (ASHRAE): memb Bd of Dirs 1980–83, vice-pres 1997–2001, pres 2003–04; FREng 1989 (hon sec Civil Engrg 1992–95, memb Cncl 1992–95), FICE, FIMechE, FCIBSE; *Recreations* golf; *Style*— Richard Rooley, Esq, FREng; ✉ Greenways, Church Lane, Stoke Poges, Buckinghamshire SL2 4PB (tel 01753 648040, fax 01753 648048, e-mail richard@rooley.com)

ROOM, Adrian Richard West; s of Richard Geoffrey Room (d 2002), and Cynthia Ida, *née* West (d 1976); *b* 27 September 1933; *Educ* Dauntsey's Sch West Lavington, Exeter Coll Oxford (MA); *Career* teacher of English and modern languages 1958; lectr in: English and modern languages 1969, Russian 1974 (sr lectr 1980–84); full-time writer 1984–; memb: English Place-Name Soc 1980, American Name Soc 1976; FRGS 1976; *Books* Place-Names of the World (1974), Great Britain: A Background Studies Dictionary (English-Russian) (1978), Room's Dictionary of Confusibles (1979), Place-Name Changes Since 1900 (1980), Naming Names (1981), Room's Dictionary of Distinguishables (1981), Dictionary of Trade Name Origins (1982), Room's Classical Dictionary (1983), Dictionary of Cryptic Crossword Clues (1983), A Concise Dictionary of Modern Place-Names in Great Britain and Ireland (1983), Dictionary of Confusing Words and Meanings (1985), Dictionary of Translated Names and Titles (1985), Dictionary of Irish Place-Names (1986), Dictionary of Britain (1986), Dictionary of True Etymologies (1986), Dictionary of Changes in Meaning (1986), Dictionary of Coin Names (1987), Dictionary of Contrasting Pairs (1988), Dictionary of Astronomical Names (1988), Dictionary of Place-Names in the British Isles (1988), Dictionary of World Place-Names Derived from British Names (1989), A Dictionary of Pseudonyms and their Origins (1989), An A to Z of British Life (1990), Dictionary of Dedications (1990), A Name for Your Baby (1992), The Street Names of England (1992), Brewer's Dictionary of Names (1992), Corporate Eponymy (1992), Place-Name Changes 1900–1991 (1993), The Naming of Animals (1993), A Dictionary of First Names (1994), African Placenames (1994), Cassell Dictionary of Proper Names (1994), Cassell Dictionary of First Names (1995), Literally Entitled (1995), Brewer's Dictionary of Phrase and Fable (reviser and ed, 1995 and 1999), An Alphabetical Guide to the Language of Name Studies (1996), Placenames of Russia and the Former Soviet Union (1996), A Dictionary of Art Titles (2000), A Dictionary of Music Titles (2000), Encyclopedia of Corporate Names Worldwide (2002), Placenames of France (2004), Dictionary of Pseudonyms (2004), Placenames of the World (2006), Nicknames of Places (2006), The Pronunciation of Placenames (2007); *Style*— Adrian Room, Esq; ✉ 12 High Street, St Martin's, Stamford, Lincolnshire PE9 2LF (tel and fax 01780 752097, e-mail adrian.room@virgin.net)

ROOM, Prof Graham; *b* 17 March 1947; *Educ* Christ's Coll Cambridge (MA), Balliol Coll Oxford (BPhil), Nuffield Coll Oxford (DPhil); *m* 31 March 1979, Susan; *Career* Univ of Bath: lectr in sociology 1973–86 (leave of absence as research fell Univ of Kent 1979–80), reader in social policy 1986–92, prof of European social policy 1992–, head Sch of Social Sciences 1995–97; conslt to EC on social action progs 1979–85, coordinator Evaluation of the Second European Prog to Combat Poverty 1985–89, coordinator EU Observatory on National Policies to Combat Social Exclusion 1990–93, memb Cncl of Europe Steering Gp on Poverty and Marginalisation 1990–91, special advsr House of Lords Select Ctee on the European Communities 1994; govr Swindon FE Coll 2002–03; AcSS 2004; *Books* The Sociology of Welfare: Social Policy, Stratification and Political Order (1979), Europe Against Poverty: The European Poverty Programme 1975–80 (jtly, 1982), Health and Welfare States of Britain: An Inter-Country Comparison (jt ed, 1983), Cross-National Innovation in Social Policy: European Perspectives on the Evaluation of Action-Research (1986), New Poverty in the European Community (1990), Towards a European Welfare State? (ed, 1991), Anti-Poverty Action-Research in Europe (1993), Beyond the Threshold: The Measurement and Analysis of Social Exclusion (ed, 1995), Poverty and Social Exclusion in Europe (jtly, 2002), Insecurity and Welfare Regimes in Asia, Africa and Latin America: Social Policy in Development Contexts (jtly, 2004), The European Challenge: Innovation, Policy Learning and Social Cohesion in the New Knowledge Economy (2005); *Style*— Prof Graham Room; ✉ Department of Social and Policy Sciences, University of Bath, Bath BA2 7AY (tel 01225 386090)

ROONEY, Terence; MP; s of late Eric Rooney, and Frances Rooney; *b* 11 November 1950; *Educ* Buttershaw Comp Sch, Bradford Coll; *m* 1969, Susanne Chapman; 1 s, 2 da; *Career* MP (Lab) Bradford N 1990–; PPS to: Rt Hon Michael Meacher MP 1997–2002, Rt Hon Keith Hill MP 2003–05; memb: Broadcasting Select Ctee 1991–97, Jt Select Ctee on House of Lords Reform 2003–04; chair Work and Pensions Select Ctee 2005–; *Style*— Terence Rooney, Esq, MP; ✉ House of Commons, London SW1A 0AA (tel 020 7219 3000)

ROOT, Jane; *b* 1957; *Educ* London Coll of Printing, Univ of Sussex; *Career* freelance journalist and film critic; with Cinema of Women (film distribution co) 1981–83, press offr and catalogue author Edinburgh Film Festival 1981–84, with BFI 1982–83 (wrote for The Cinema Book, Women's Guide to Film, Hollywood Now), writer and researcher

Open the Box Beat Productions 1983, co-fndr Wall to Wall Productions 1987 (head of prog devpt and jt md until 1996), head Independent Commissioning Gp BBC 1997–98, controller BBC 2 1999–2004 (responsible for launching Great Britons initiative and series incl The Weakest Link and The Office); Discovery Channel USA: gen mangr 2004–, exec vice-pres 2004–06, pres 2006–; pres and gen mangr Science Channel USA 2006–; memb Exec Ctee Edinburgh Int TV Festival 2006 and 2007; *Style*— Ms Jane Root; ✉ Discovery Communications LLC, One Discovery Place, Silver Spring, MD 20910, USA

ROOT, Jonathan Mark; s of Harold Root (d 2000), and Joan Root; *b* 7 April 1959; *Educ* Oakham Sch; *Career* fine art portrait and advertising photographer; lectr: Glasgow Sch of Art, Kingston Univ; cmmns incl: 'Twins' Liberty, J&B Whisky, Tennents Lager, British Airways, Benson and Hedges, Body Shop, Mulberry, Harvey Nichols, Canon Printers, Sony Hi-Fi, Liverpool FC, BSkyB, Shakespeare's Globe, American Express; exhbns incl: John Kobal Photographic Portrait Awards 1995, 1996 and 2000, Lurzer's archive 1998 and 2000, American Photo 2000, Britart at Selfridges 2003, The Edwardian Drape Society (Tapestry Gallery) 2004, Lords and Ladies (Tapestry Gallery) 2004, Brit Art exhbn Selridges 2005; worked for numerous newspapers and magazines incl: The Independent, The Observer, Daily Telegraph, Financial Times, New Scientist, Sunday Times, Vanity Fair, Harpers & Queen, Tatler, Jack; Erotic Photographer of the Year 2005; memb Assoc of Photographers 1995–; *Awards* winner Assoc of Photographers Silver and Merit Awards 1996 and 1997, Communication Arts Award of Excellence 1997, The Scottish Advertising Awards 1998, highly commended London Photographic Awards (LPA4) 2000, merit London Photographic Awards (LPA5) 2001, European Design Annual Certificate of Excellence 2000, Sony Campaign Cannes 2000; *Publications* cover and article Br Jl of Photography no 7101 1996, article in Zoom International 2000, cover and article Br Jl of Photography no 7493 2004; *Recreations* restoring classic cars; *Clubs* Jupiter Owners Auto; *Style*— Jonathan Root, Esq; ✉ Jonathan Root Photography, 21 Ferdinand Street, Chalk Farm, London NW1 8EU (tel 020 7485 5522, website www.jonathanroot.co.uk)

ROOTES, 3 Baron (UK 1959); Nicholas Geoffrey Rootes; o s of 2 Baron Rootes (d 1992), and Marian, *née* Hayter; gf 1 Baron Rootes, GBE, founded Rootes Motors; *b* 12 July 1951; *Educ* Harrow; *m* 1976, Dorothy Anne, da of Cyril Walter James Wood (d 1979), of Swansea, and formerly wife of Jonathan Burn-Forti; 1 step da (Lucinda Burn-Forti b 1963), 1 step s (Dante Burn-Forti b 1965); *Heir* cous, William Rootes; *Career* journalist, author and copywriter; dir Nick Rootes Associates 1997–; tstee Lord Rootes Charity Tst 1992–; *Books* The Drinker's Companion (1987), Doing a Dyson (1995); *Recreations* fly fishing, skiing, tennis; *Style*— The Rt Hon the Lord Rootes; ✉ 2 Cedars Road, Barnes, London SW13 OHP

ROOTS, Guy Robert Godfrey; QC (1989); s of William Lloyd Roots, TD, QC, MP (d 1971) of London, and Elizabeth Colquhoun Gow, *née* Gray (d 2000); *b* 26 August 1946; *Educ* Winchester, BNC Oxford (MA); *m* 17 May 1975, Caroline, da of (Alfred Saxon) Godfrey Clarkson (d 1970), of Herts; 3 s (William b 1978, Hamish b 1979, Sam b 1986); *Career* called to the Bar Middle Temple 1969 (Harmsworth scholar 1969); chm Planning and Environment Bar Assoc 2000–04; Liveryman Worshipful Co of Drapers 1972; fell Soc of Advanced Legal Studies 1998; *Publications* Butterworths' Compulsory Purchase and Compensation Service (gen ed), Ryde on Rating and the Council Tax (gen ed); *Recreations* sailing, fishing, skiing, photography, woodworking; *Clubs* Itchenor Sailing; *Style*— Guy Roots, Esq, QC; ✉ Francis Taylor Building, Temple, London EC4Y 7BY (tel 020 7353 8415, fax 020 7353 7622, e-mail clerks@ftb.eu.com)

ROPER, Brian; *Educ* Univ of Wales (BSc), Univ of Manchester (MA); *Career* tutor in economics UWIST 1971–72, lectr in economics Teesside Poly 1973–75, sr lectr then princ lectr in economics Leicester Poly 1975–80; Newcastle upon Tyne Poly: head Sch of Economics 1980–85, actg head Faculty of Professional Studies 1985–87, head Dept of Economics and Govt 1987, dean Faculty of Social Sciences 1987–88 (actg dean 1987), actg asst dir (academic) 1988, asst dir (resources) 1988–90; dep vice-chllr (academic affrs) and dep chief exec Oxford Poly (later Oxford Brookes Univ) 1991–93, vice-chllr and chief exec Univ of North London 1994–2002; London Met Univ: chief exec 2002–04, vice-chllr and chief exec 2004–; *Publications* author of numerous conference papers, book chapters, and articles in learned jls; *Style*— Brian Roper, Esq; ✉ London Metropolitan University, 166–220 Holloway Road, London N7 8DB (tel 020 7753 5181, fax 020 7753 5049)

ROPER, Jeremy James; s of Robert Burnell Roper, CB, of Lindfield, W Sussex, and Mary, *née* Petyt; *b* 13 June 1954; *Educ* KCS Wimbledon, Univ of Birmingham (LLB); *m* 20 Sept 1980, Alison Mary, da of Bryan Peter Studwell Cleal, of Wotton-under-Edge, Glos; 2 da (Katharine Mary b 1984, Elizabeth Diana b 1992), 1 s (Richard James b 1987); *Career* admitted slr 1979; ptnr: Needham and James slrs 1983–93, Dibb Lupton Broomhead 1993–95, Wansbroughs Willey Hargrave (now Beachcroft LLP) 1995–; memb Law Soc 1977; *Recreations* sport, vegetable gardening, theatre; *Style*— Jeremy Roper, Esq

ROPER, Baron (Life Peer UK 2000), of Thorney Island in the City of Westminster; John Francis Hodgess Roper; PC (2005); s of Rev Frederick Mabor Hodgess Roper, by his w Ellen Frances, *née* Brockway; *b* 10 September 1935; *Educ* William Hulme's GS Manchester, Reading Sch, Magdalen Coll Oxford, Univ of Chicago; *m* 1959, Valerie (d 2003), da of Rt Hon John Edwards, OBE, sometime MP; 1 da; *Career* former economics lectr Manchester Univ; Royal Inst of International Affairs: ed International Affairs 1983–88, head Int Security Prog 1985–88 and 1989–90, dir of studies 1988–89; head WEU Inst for Security Studies Paris 1990–95; Parly candidate: (Lab) Derbyshire High Peak 1964, (SDP) Worsley 1983; MP (Lab and Co-op 1970–81, SDP 1981–83) Farnworth 1970–83; PPS to Min of State for Industry 1978–79, Lab oppn spokesman on Defence (front bench), SDP chief whip 1981–83; Lib Dem chief whip House of Lords 2001–05; vice-chm: Anglo-German Parly Gp 1974–83, Anglo-Benelux Parly Gp 1979–83; Cncl of Europe: conslt 1965–66, memb Consultative Assembly 1973–80, chm Ctee on Culture and Educn 1979–80, memb WEU 1973–80, chm Ctee on Defence Questions and Armaments WEU 1977–80; chm: Lab Ctee for Europe 1976–80, Cncl on Christian Approaches to Defence and Disarmament 1983–89, GB/East Europe Centre 1987–90; hon treas Fabian Soc 1976–81; memb: Gen Advsy Cncl IBA 1974–79, Cncl Inst of Fiscal Studies 1975–90; vice-pres Manchester Statistical Soc 1971–, tstee History of Parliament Tst 1974–84; *Books* Towards Regional Co-operatives (with Lloyd Harrison, 1967), The Teaching of Economics at University Level (1970), The Future of British Defence Policy (1985), British-German Defence Co-operation (ed with Karl Kaiser, 1988), Franco-British Defence Co-operation (ed with Yves Boyer, 1988), Western Europe and the Gulf (ed with Nicole Gnesotto), Towards a New Partnership: US European Relations in the Post-Cold War Era (ed with Nanette Gantz); *Style*— The Rt Hon the Lord Roper, PC

ROPER, Stephen John; s of Stanley Dunham Roper, of Stratford-on-Avon, Warks, and Kathleen Nora Theresa, *née* Barry; *b* 14 April 1943; *Educ* Wimbledon Coll, Univ of Durham (BA); *m* 24 May 1969, Sophie Jaqueline, da of Georges Alex, Cmdt (ret) French Army; 2 da (Stephanie b 1970, Joanna b 1971), 1 s (Tristan b 1977); *Career* CA; Pannell Fitzpatrick & Co Kingston Jamaica WI 1971–75, ptnr Eacotts Burnham 1975–2005; *Recreations* reading, golf, tennis, skiing; *Clubs* Royal Ascot Golf, Rotary (Wokingham); *Style*— Stephen Roper, Esq; ✉ Lavendale House, Broomfield Park, Sunningdale, Berkshire SL5 0JS (tel 01344 624032)

ROPNER, Sir John Bruce Woollacott; 2 Bt (UK 1952), of Thorp Perrow, N Riding of Yorks; s of Sir Leonard Ropner, 1 Bt, MC, TD (d 1977). Sir Leonard's f, William, was 3 s of Sir Robert Ropner, JP, DL, cr a Bt 1904 (*see* Ropner, Bt, Sir Robert); *b* 16 April 1937; *Educ* Eton, St Paul's Sch USA; *m* 1, 1961 (m dis 1970), Anne Melicent, da of late Sir Ralph

Delmé-Radcliffe; 2 da (Jenny (Mrs Graham Simpson) b 1963, Katherine (Hon Mrs Henry Holland-Hibbert) b 1964); *m* 2, 1970 (m dis 1993), Auriol Veronica, da of late Capt Graham Lawrie Mackeson-Sandbach, of Caerllo, Denbighshire; 2 da (Carolyn Esme b 1971, Annabel Mariella b 1974), 1 s (Henry John William b 1981); *m* 3, 6 April 1996, Mrs Niki Tippett, da of Peter Agnew; *Heir* s, Henry Ropner; *Career* dir Ropner plc; High Sheriff N Yorks 1991–92; *Style*— Sir John Ropner, Bt; ✉ Thorp Perrow, Bedale, North Yorkshire (tel 01677 422710)

ROQUES, (David) John Seymour; s of Frank Davy Seymour Roques (d 1970), and Marjorie Mabel Martina Roques; *b* 14 October 1938; *Educ* St Albans Sch; *m* 20 April 1963, (Elizabeth) Anne, da of William John Mallender (d 1999); 2 s (David William Seymour b 1966, Edward John Seymour b 1977), 1 da (Sarah Elizabeth b 1968); *Career* Deloitte & Touche (formerly Touche Ross & Co): joined 1957, ptnr 1967, sr ptnr and chief exec 1990–99; chm Portman Building Soc 1999–2006 (non-exec dir 1995–2006); non-exec dir: British Nuclear Fuels plc 1990–2000, BBA Aviation plc (formerly BBA Gp plc) 1998–, Premier Farnell plc 1999–, Chubb plc 2003, Henderson Gp plc (formerly HHG plc) 2004–; memb Financial Reporting Review Panel 1991–94, memb Financial Reporting Cncl 1996–2001; Liveryman Worshipful Co of Chartered Accountants; MICAS 1962, FRSA 1990; *Recreations* rugby football, racing, opera, gardening; *Clubs* MCC, Harewood Downs Golf, Brooks's; *Style*— John Roques, Esq

ROSCOE, (John) Gareth; s of late John Roscoe, and late Ann, *née* Jones; *b* 28 January 1948; *Educ* Manchester Warehouseman and Clerks Orphan Sch (now Cheadle Hulme Sch), Stretford Tech Coll, LSE (LLB), Univ of Leicester (LLM) 2003; *m* 1, 29 Aug 1970 (m dis 1979), Helen Jane, da of Geoffrey Duke Taylor, of Skipton, N Yorks; 1 da (Kate b 26 July 1974); *m* 2, 29 Aug 1980, Alexis Fayrer (Alex Brett-Holt, *qv*), da of late Raymond Arthur Brett-Holt, of Esher, Surrey; 1 da (Philippa Claire b 8 Feb 1982), 1 s (Jonathan Hugh b 1 Aug 1983); *Career* called to the Bar Gray's Inn 1972; in practice 1972–75, Law Offr's Dept Attorney Gen's Chambers 1979–83, dep slr DOE 1987–89 (legal asst 1975–79, sr legal asst 1979, asst slr 1983–87); legal advsr to: co sec BBC until 1998, co sec BBC Worldwide Ltd until 1998, dir BBC Worldwide Ltd 1989–96, dir Educational Recording Agency Limited until 1998; conslt advsr DTI 1999–2001, legal advsr Competition Cmmn 2001–04 and 2005–, legal advsr Dept for Work and Pensions 2004–05; non-exec memb: Optimum NHS Tst 1995–97, KCH NHS Tst 2001–04; memb: Bar Cncl 1987–90 (memb Race Relations and Law Reform Ctees), Advsy Ctee Centre for Communications and Law UCL; *Recreations* music, gardening, company of friends; *Clubs* Athenaeum, Range Offrs' Assoc; *Style*— Gareth Roscoe, Esq; ✉ Competition Commission, Victoria House, Southampton Row, London WC1B 4AD (tel 020 7271 0183, fax 020 7271 0367, e-mail gareth.roscoe@cc.gsi.gov.uk)

ROSCOE, Dr Ingrid Mary; da of Dr Arthur Allen, CBE (d 1956), and Else Margaretha, *née* Markenstam (d 1968); adopted da of late Brig Kenneth Hargreaves, CBE; *b* 27 May 1944, Rugby; *Educ* St Helen's Northwood, Univ of Leeds (BA, PhD); *m* 5 Oct 1963, J R Marshall Roscoe, DL; 1 s (Nicholas b 20 June 1964), 2 da (Emma b 8 May 1966, Katherine b 9 July 1970); *Career* lectr in sculpture history Univ of Leeds 1990–96, ed Church Monuments Jl 1993–2000, ed-in-chief and co-author A Biographical Dictionary of British Sculptors 1660–1851 2000–07; author of articles on British sculpture in: Apollo, Gazette des Beaux-Arts, Grove Dictionary of Art, Walpole Soc Jl, Oxford DNB; memb Exec Ctee Walpole Soc 2000–05; tstee: Martin House Children's Hospice 1989–98, York Minster 2005–, Yorkshire Sculpture Park 2006–, Hepworth Art Gallery 2006–; patron: Prince's Tst W Yorks, Nat Mining Museum, Yorks Historic Churches, Calderdale Community Fndn, Yorks Vols Regtl Assoc; co rep NACE 1972–84; high steward Selby Abbey 2000–; HM Lord-Lt W Yorks 2004– (DL 1994–99, Vice Lord-Lt 1999–2004); FSA 1998; CStJ 2006; *Books* The Royal Exchange (contrib, 1997); *Recreations* family, British cultural history, walking; *Style*— Dr Ingrid Roscoe; ✉ Church House, Nun Monkton, York YO26 8EW; West Yorkshire Lieutenancy Office, Bowcliffe Hall, Bramham, Wetherby LS23 6LP

ROSCOE, Robert Simon; *b* 14 April 1949; *Educ* Haberdashers' Aske's; *Career* admitted slr 1976; Victor Lissack Roscoe & Coleman: joined 1969, ptnr 1978–, sr ptnr 1981–; dep dist judge (Magistrates' Court) 1997–; memb: Law Society (memb Cncl 1992–2000, chm Criminal Law Ctee 1995–98), City of Westminster and Holborn Law Soc, London Criminal Courts Slrs' Assoc (pres 1996–97), Criminal Law Slrs' Assoc, Slr's Assoc of Higher Court Advocates; *Recreations* Bolton Wanderers FC, Lancashire CCC; *Style*— Robert Roscoe, Esq

ROSE, Anthea Lorrainne; da of Philip Brown (d 1987), of Edinburgh, and Muriel, *née* Seftor; *b* 2 December 1946; *Educ* Lansdowne House Sch Edinburgh (head of sch), St Hugh's Coll Oxford (MA, pres Oxford Univ Liberal Club); *m* Aug 1971, Hannan David Rose, s of late Basil Nathan Rose; *Career* admin Open Univ 1968–69, personnel offr Beecham Pharmaceuticals 1969–71, admin Univ of Kent 1971–76; Assoc of Chartered Certified Accountants (ACCA): joined 1976, under sec 1982–88, dep chief exec 1988–93, chief exec 1993–2003; ind conslt 2003–; visiting prof Oxford Brookes Univ 2002; lay memb Nursing and Midwifery Cncl 2006–; Hon DBA Kingston Univ; *Recreations* travel, wine, food; *Style*— Mrs Anthea Rose; ✉ ALR Associates Ltd, 11 Campden Hill Court, London W8 7HX (tel 020 7937 3527, fax 020 7937 4068, e-mail anthea@thelondonroses.com)

ROSE, Anthony John Wynyard; s of John Donald Rose, FRS (d 1976), and Yvonne Valerie, *née* Evans (d 1996); *b* 22 January 1946; *Educ* Oundle; *m* 1972 (m dis 1990), Angela Katherine, da of Wing Cdr Thomas Kenneth Waite (d 1987), of Cheltenham, Glos; 1 da (Katherine Lucy b 19 March 1980), 3 s (Dominic John Wynyard, Alexander Richard Thomas (twins) b 4 Nov 1984, Oliver Louis Christopher b 2 Dec 1986); *m* 2, 1996, Beverly Jane Murray; *Career* Hon Artillery Co 1970–75; admitted slr 1970; slr Slaughter & May 1970–72 and ICI Ltd 1972–77, ed Aerostat 1975–82, ptnr Charles Russell 1978–92, ptnr Barlow Lyde & Gilbert 1992–98, conslt to Vizards Tweedie; dir: Paper House Group plc, Corporate Due Diligence Ltd, Cobra London Markets Ltd; memb Competition Ctee ICC; hon legal advsr Nat Army Museum; author of various articles on Euro competition law and hot air ballooning, awarded Aerostat medal; Freeman City of London 1975, Freeman Worshipful Co of Salters 1975; memb: Law Soc, Int Bar Assoc; *Recreations* ballooning, shooting, fishing, reading, tennis, dogs; *Clubs* Hon Artillery Co; *Style*— Anthony Rose, Esq; ✉ Bonnett Farm, Rendcomb, Gloucestershire GL7 7ET (tel 01242 870016, mobile 07802 284297, e-mail anthonyrose@anthonyrose.co.uk)

ROSE, Barry Michael; *b* 10 March 1945; *Educ* Univ of Manchester (BSc); *Career* asst investment mangr Co-operative Insurance Society Ltd 1971–76, investment mangr Scottish Life Assurance Co 1976–88, gen mangr investment Scottish Provident Institution 1988–93 (dir 1998–), chief exec Scottish Provident UK 1993–2001; dir: Baillie Gifford Shin Nippon Investment Tst 1998–, Wolfson Microelectronics plc 2001–, Liverpool Victoria Friendly Soc; FIA 1970; *Style*— Barry Rose, Esq

ROSE, Rt Hon Sir Christopher Dudley Roger; kt (1985), PC (1992); s of Roger Rose (d 1987), of Morecambe, and Hilda, *née* Thickett (d 1986); *b* 10 February 1937; *Educ* Morecambe GS, Repton, Univ of Leeds (LLB), Wadham Coll Oxford (BCL); *m* 5 Aug 1964, Judith, *née* Brand; 1 s (Daniel b 1967), 1 da (Hilary b 1969); *Career* lectr in law Wadham Coll Oxford 1959–60 (hon fell 1993), Bigelow teaching fell Law Sch Univ of Chicago 1960–61, called to the Bar Middle Temple 1960 (bencher 1983, dep treas 2001, treas 2002), QC 1974, recorder of the Crown Court 1978–85, presiding judge Northern Circuit 1987–90 (practised 1961–85), judge of the High Court of Justice (Queen's Bench Div) 1985–92, a Lord Justice of Appeal 1992–2006; chief surveillance cmmr 2006–; chm Criminal Justice Consultative Cncl 1994–2000, vice-pres Co Appeal (Criminal Div) 1997–2006; memb Senate Inns of Court and Bar 1983–85; govr Pownall Hall Sch 1977–89, UK tstee Harold

G Fox Fndn 1995–2005; *Clubs* Garrick; *Style*— The Rt Hon Sir Christopher Rose; ✉ Offie of the Surveillance Commissioners, PO Box 29105, London SW1V 1ZU

ROSE, Dr (Frank) Clifford; s of James Rose (d 1958), and Clare Rose (d 1960); *b* 29 August 1926; *Educ* King's Coll London, Westminster Med Sch (MB BS); *m* 16 Sept 1963, Angela Juliet, da of Erik Halsted (d 1979); 3 s (Sebastian b 1964, Jolyon b 1966, Fabian b 1968); *Career* hon consl t neurologist Charing Cross Hosp 1965–91, physician i/c Dept of Neurology Regnl Neurosciences Centre 1978–91; founding dir: Academic Neuroscience Unit Charing Cross and Westminster Med Sch 1985–91, London Neurological Centre 1991–; fndr dir Princess Margaret Migraine Clinic 1973–91; prof assoc in human sciences Brunel Univ 1989–99; sec-treas gen World Fedn of Neurology (WFN) 1990–98, scientific advsr Motor Neurone Disease Assoc 1988–91; editor: World Neurology 1990–98, Journal of the History of the Neurosciences 1992–97; chm: Headache and Migraine Res Gp World Fedn of Neurology 1980–95, Migraine Tst 1987–95, Independent Doctors Forum 1995–96, Research Panel for History of Neurosciences European Fedn of Neurological Societies 1998–2000; pres Section of Neurology RSM 1990–91, former pres Med Soc of London; Liveryman Worshipful Soc of Apothecaries; hon memb: Neurological Soc of Thailand 1992, Austrian Soc of Neurology 1992, Mexican Assoc for the Study of Headache 1992; FRSM, FRCP; *Books* author and ed of over 75 books on neurology incl: Advances in Stroke Research (1985), James Parkinson: His Life and Times (1989), Advances in Headache Research (vol 4, 1994), Recent Advances in Tropical Neurology (1995), Towards Migraine 2000 (1996), A Short History of Neurology: The British Contribution 1660–1910 (1999), Multiple Sclerosis at your Fingertips (2000), Twentieth Century Neurology: The British Contribution (2001), Neurology of the Arts (2004), The Neurobiology of Painting (2006); *Recreations* wine, reading history; *Clubs* Savile; *Style*— Dr Clifford Rose; ✉ Flat 9, 7 Weymouth Mews, London W1G 7DZ (tel 020 7636 6141, e-mail frangierose@googlemail.co.uk)

ROSE, David Leslie Whitfield; s of Leslie Rose (d 1980), of Leeds, and Joyce, *née* Whitfield (d 1981); *b* 27 February 1954; *Educ* Roundhay Sch Leeds, Downing Coll Cambridge, Inns of Court Sch of Law (MA, LLB); *m* 14 April 1982, Genevieve Mary, da of Thomas Vernon Twigge, of Burley-in-Wharfedale, W Yorks; 1 s (Matthew b 1986), 1 da (Alice b 1989); *Career* called to the Bar 1977, memb NE Circuit and Northern Chancery Bar Assoc; memb: Professional Negligence Bar Assoc, Northern Mediators 2000; dir No 6 Ltd 1998–; tstee St John's Church Moor Allerton 2000–, vice-chair Leeds Youth Opera 2002–; memb Hon Soc of Middle Temple; *Recreations* philately, music, reading; *Style*— David Rose, Esq; ✉ Atlow, 5 Oaklands Drive, Leeds LS16 8NZ; 6 Park Square East, Leeds LS1 2LW (tel 0113 245 9763, fax 0113 242 4395, e-mail chambers@no6.co.uk)

ROSE, Dinah Gwen Lison; QC (2006); da of Michael Rose, and Susan, *née* Latham; *b* 16 July 1965, London; *Educ* City of London Sch for Girls, Magdalen Coll Oxford (BA), City Univ (Dip); *m* 10 Feb 1991, Peter Kessler; 2 da (Hannah b 21 April 1997, Katherine Lucy b 18 Dec 1999); *Career* called to the Bar Gray's Inn 1989 (Arden scholar 1988); barr Blackstone Chambers 1990–; *Style*— Miss Dinah Rose, QC; ✉ Blackstone Chambers, Blackstone House, Temple, London EC4Y 9BW

ROSE, Gregory; s of Bernard William George Rose, OBE (d 1996), and Molly Daphne Rose, OBE, JP, DL, *née* Marshall; *b* 18 April 1948; *Educ* Magdalen Coll Oxford (BA); *Career* conductor; prof of conducting Trinity Coll of Music; appts incl: princ conductor Jupiter Orch, Singcircle, Circle, Jupiter Singers, COMA London Ensemble; guest appts incl: London Philharmonic, Ulster Orch, BBC Concert Orch, BBC Singers, Estonian Philharmonic Chamber Choir, Netherland Radio Chamber Orch, Netherland Radio Choir, Nederland Kamerkoor, Groupe Vocal de France, Westdeutscher Rundfunk Chor, Steve Reich and Musicians, Netherlands Wind Ensemble, and also orchs in Denmark, Norway, Finland, Holland, Poland, Latvia, Estonia, Ireland, Russia, India and Sri Lanka; series dir Almeida Festival (Cage at 70 1982, Reich at 50 1986); festivals have included BBC Proms 1978 and 1989, many TV and radio recordings throughout Europe; many compositions published incl: Birthday Ode for Aaron Copland, Tapiola Sunrise, Thambapani, Missa Sancta Pauli Apostoli, Missa Sacra Coeur, 3 Sets of Evening Canticles; fndr ctee memb Assoc of Br Choral Dirs, memb SPNM; Br Composer Award (Liturgical Category) 2007; *Recreations* walking, listening to music; *Style*— Gregory Rose, Esq; ✉ 57 White Horse Road, London E1 0ND (tel 020 7790 5883, e-mail gr@gregoryrose.org)

ROSE, Guy Simon; s of Henry Rose (decd), and Georgina Clifford, *née* Elkan; *Educ* Royal GS Guildford, Michaelhouse Coll SA; *Career* arbitrageur Myers & Co (Stockbrokers) 1963–67, with 3M Co (UK) plc 1970–73, publisher with Exchange Telegraph Co 1974–79, md Bandwagon Music Ltd 1980–86, sr ptnr Futerman, Rose & Associates (Literary Agents) 1992–; memb: Equity 1975–, Assoc of Authors' Agents 1995–, BAFTA; *Recreations* jazz, a capella singing; *Style*— Guy Rose, Esq; ✉ Futerman, Rose & Associates, 17 Deanhill Road, London SW14 7DQ (tel 020 8255 7755, fax 020 8286 4860, e-mail guy@futermanrose.co.uk)

ROSE, Prof Hilary Ann; da of Arthur Farrow Channell (d 1963), of Orpington, and Sylvia Gladys, *née* Brackenbury; *b* 14 January 1935; *Educ* Bromley HS GPDST, LSE (BA), Univ of Bradford (PhD); *m* 1, 31 Dec 1954, John William Chantler (d 1958); 1 s (Simon John b 2 Dec 1955); m 2, 29 June 1961, Prof Steven Peter Russell Rose, *qv*; 1 s (Benjamin Jacob b 9 March 1963); *Career* res asst Inst of Psychiatry Maudsley Hosp 1963–64, res offr Miny of Housing and Local Govt 1964, asst lectr then lectr LSE 1964–75, prof of social policy Univ of Bradford 1975–; dir W Yorks Centre for Res on Women 1985–94; hon res fell Univ of Essex 1971–72, visiting scholar Bunting Inst Harvard 1979–80, Osher fell The Exploratorium San Francisco 1993, guest prof Univ of Vienna 1996, res prof in sociology City Univ 1998–, Gresham prof physic 1999–; fell: Swedish Collegium for the Advanced Studies of the Social Sciences 1990–91, Centre for the Study of Technol and Culture Univ of Oslo 1992; Hill prof Centre for Advanced Feminist Studies Univ of Minnesota 1992, prof of feminist studies Univ of Gothenburg 1995; memb: Br Sociological Assoc, Women's Study Network (UK); memb Ed Bd: Int Jl of Health Studies, Innovation, Signs - a Jl of Women in Culture and Society, NORA; chm Br Soc for Social Responsibility in Science 1969–71, pres (Sociology) Br Assoc for the Advancement of Science 1987; *Books* Science and Society (with Steven Rose, 1969), The Radicalisation of Science (with S Rose, 1976), The Political Economy of Science (with S Rose, 1976), Countermovements and the Sciences: Yearbook of the Sociology of the Sciences (with Helga Nowotny, 1979), Love Power and Knowledge: towards a feminist transformation of the sciences (1994); *Recreations* music, walking, gardening, talking with friends; *Style*— Prof Hilary Rose

ROSE, Sir (Arthur) James; kt (2007), CBE (1996); *b* 15 May 1939; *m* 1960, Pauline; *Career* HMI: joined 1975, chief inspr for primary educn 1985; dir of inspection OFSTED 1995–99; educn conslt 1999–; chair Review of Teaching of Early Reading DfES 2006; memb Bd Qualifications and Curriculum Authy; FRSA 1990; *Recreations* gardening, running; *Style*— Sir James Rose, CBE

ROSE, Joyce Dora Hester; CBE (1981), JP (Herts 1963), DL (Herts 1990); da of Abraham (Arthur) Woolf (d 1972), of Hampstead, London, and Rebecca, *née* Simpson (d 1985); *b* 14 August 1929; *Educ* King Alfred Sch London, Queen's Coll London; *m* 6 Oct 1953, Cyril Rose, s of Benjamin Rose (d 1971), of Bedford; 1 da (Gillian b 1955); 2 s (Stephen b 1957, Andrew b 1959); *Career* chm Watford Magistrates Court 1990–94 (chm Family Panel); memb Herts: Magistrates Courts Ctee until 1995, Probation Ctee until 1995; chm Cncl and Nat Exec Magistrates Assoc 1990–93 (chm Herts Branch 1985–90); dir: Apex Tst 1994–2004, Herts Care Tst 1995–99, Herts Family Mediation Serv 1996–2002, SW Herts Hospice Charitable Tst (The Peace Hospice) 1996–2003; memb Children Act Advsy Ctee 1991–93; Lib Pty: pres 1979–80, chm 1982–83, chm Women's Lib Fedn 1987–88 (pres 1972 and 1973); memb Lib Dem Fed Appeals Panel 1994–2005; pres Rickmansworth Lib Dem Pty 2001–; vice-pres: Herts Branch Magistrates Asooc 1991–, Magistrates Assoc 1993–; former memb: Women's Nat Cmmn, Nat Exec UK Ctee UNICEF (vice-chm 1968–70); Hon LLD Univ of Hertfordshire 1992; *Clubs* Nat Lib; *Style*— Mrs Joyce Rose, CBE, DL; ✉ 2 Oak House, 101 Ducks Hill Road, Northwood, Middlesex HA6 2WQ (tel 01923 821385, fax 01923 840515)

ROSE, Sir Julian Day; 4 Bt (UK 1909), of Hardwick House, Whitchurch, Oxon and 5 Bt (UK 1872), of Montreal, Dominion of Canada; s of Sir Charles Henry Rose, 3 Bt (d 1966), by his w, Hon Phoebe Margaret Dorothy Phillimore, da of 2 Baron Phillimore; also suc kinsman, Sir Francis Rose, 4 Bt 1979; *b* 3 March 1947; *Educ* Stanbridge Earls Sch Romsey, RADA; *m* 1976, Elizabeth Good, da of Derrol Johnson, of Columbus, Ohio; 1 da (Miriam Margaret b 1984), 1 s (Lawrence Michael b 6 Oct 1986); *Heir* s, Lawrence Rose; *Career* commenced conversion to organic farming enterprise Hardwick Estate 1975; co-fndr and asst dir Inst for Creative Devpt Antwerp 1975–82, co-fndr The Assoc of Unpasteurised Milk Producers and Consumers 1989; memb: Cncl Soil Assoc 1984–1998, Bd UK Register of Organic Food Standards, Rural and Agric Affrs Advsy Ctee BBC 1989–91, Cncl Schumacher Soc 1993–2000, Ctee CLA Agriculture and Rural Economy Gp 1999–2003; chm Assoc of Rural Businesses in Oxfordshire 1996–2000, advsr SE England RDA and Rural Economy 1999–, fndr Euro Alliance for Artisan and Traditional Raw Milk Products 1999–, co-dir The Int Coalition to Protect the Polish Countryside until 2000; agric correspondent Environment Now 1989; writer and broadcaster on socio-environmental issues; tstee Dartington Hall Tst 1995–2000; *Style*— Sir Julian Rose, Bt; ✉ Hardwick House, Whitchurch, Oxfordshire RG8 7RB (e-mail hardwickestate@btinternet.com)

ROSE, Justin; *b* 30 July 1980, Johannesburg, South Africa; *Career* golfer; as amateur: winner England U16 and U18 aged 14, memb GB & I team Walker Cup 1997 (youngest ever player), winner St Andrews Links Trophy 1998, 4th place 127th Open Golf Championship 1998 (winner Silver Medal for Lowest Amateur Score, equalled all-time amateur scoring record); turned professional 1998; tounaments won: Victor Chandler British Masters 2002, Chunichi Crowns Japan 2002, Nashua Masters Southern African Tour 2002, Dunhill Championship 2002; *Recreations* tennis, soccer, cricket; *Style*— Justin Rose, Esq; ✉ c/o Rob Alter, IMG Golf Client Division, McCormack House, Burlington Lane, London W4 2TH (tel 020 233 5300, website www.justinrose.co.uk)

ROSE, Kenneth Vivian; CBE (1997); s of Dr J Rose; *b* 15 November 1924; *Educ* Repton, New Coll Oxford (scholar, MA); *Career* served Welsh Guards 1943–46 (attached Phantom 1945); asst master Eton Coll 1948; memb editorial staff Daily Telegraph 1952–60, fndr and writer Albany column Sunday Telegraph 1961–97; FRSL; *Books* Superior Person: a portrait of Curzon and his circle in late Victorian England (1969), The Later Cecils (1975), William Harvey: a monograph (1978), King George V (1983, Wolfson Award for History 1983, Whitbread Award for Biography 1983, Yorkshire Post Biography of the Year Award 1984), Kings, Queens and Courtiers: intimate portraits of the Royal House of Windsor (1985), Founders and Followers: literary lectures on the London Library (contrib, 1992), Elusive Rothschild: the life of Victor, Third Baron (2003); also author of contribs to Oxford DNB; *Clubs* Beefsteak, Pratt's; *Style*— Kenneth Rose, Esq, CBE, FRSL; ✉ 38 Brunswick Gardens, London W8 4AL (tel 020 7221 4783)

ROSE, Kevin John; s of Thomas Rose, of Bletchley, Bucks, and Jeanette Iris, *née* Farman; *b* 10 July 1956; *Educ* Bletchley GS; *m* July 1979, Gillian, da of Thomas Lovett; 1 s (Alexander John b 20 Dec 1985); *Career* mktg offr BOC 1976–78 (sales offr 1974–76); VAG (UK) - Volkswagen/Audi: fin controller Sales & Mktg 1978–80, field support mangr 1980–81, fleet ops mangr 1981–84, fleet servs mangr 1984–88, distribution mangr 1988–90, customer servs mangr 1990–91, regnl mangr 1991–93, head of mktg 1993–95; dir Seat UK 1995–99, dir Audi UK 1999–; *Recreations* squash, tennis, soccer coaching; *Style*— Kevin Rose, Esq; ✉ Audi UK, Yeomans Drive, Blakelands, Milton Keynes MK14 5AN (tel 01908 601313, fax 01908 601040, e-mail kevin.rose@audi.co.uk)

ROSE, Martin John; s of John Ewert Rose, of Chandlers Ford, Hants, and Margaret Mary, *née* Eames; *b* 21 March 1956; *Educ* St Mary's Coll Southampton, Univ of Warwick (LLB); *m* 7 May 1988, Emma Margaret Havilland, da of Robert Bernard Hutchinson, of Wimborne, Dorset; 2 s (George Edward b 1993, Simon Elliot b 2000), 1 da (Harriet Victoria b 1996); *Career* called to the Bar Middle Temple 1979; practising barr Western circuit 1980–86, legal conslt The Stock Exchange 1986, sr legal advsr The Securities Assoc 1986–89, sr asst slr Linklaters and Paines 1990–92, gp legal and compliance dir Smith & Williamson 1992–; MSI; *Recreations* gardening, naval history; *Style*— Martin Rose, Esq; ✉ Smith & Williamson, 25 Moorgate, London EC2R 6AY (tel 020 7131 4000, e-mail mjr@smith.williamson.co.uk)

ROSE, Gen Sir (Hugh) Michael; KCB (1994), CBE (1986), DSO (1995), QGM (1981), DL (Somerset 2003); s of late Lt Col Hugh Vincent Rose, IA, and late Mrs Barbara Phoebe Masters, *née* Allcard; *b* 5 January 1940; *Educ* Cheltenham Coll, St Edmund Hall Oxford (MA), Staff Coll, RCDS; *m* 1968, Angela Raye Shaw; 2 s; *Career* cmmnd: Gloucestershire Regt TAVR 1959, RAFVR 1962, Coldstream Guards 1964; served: Germany, Aden, Malaysia, Gulf States, Dhofar, N Ireland (despatches), Falkland Is (despatches); BM 16 Para Bde 1973–75, CO 22 SAS Regt 1979–82, cmd 39 Infantry Bde 1983–85, Cmdt Sch of Infantry 1987–88, dir Special Forces 1988–89, GOC NE Dist and cmd 2nd Infantry Div 1989–91, Cmdt Staff Coll 1991–93, cmd UK Field Army and Inspr Gen of TA 1993–94, Commander UN Protection Force Bosnia-Herzegovina 1994–95, Dep C-in-C Land Cmd 1995, Adj-Gen 1995–97; 28 Col Coldstream Guards 1999–; Hon Col Oxford Univ OTC 1995–99; Freeman City of London 1998, Liveryman Worshipful Co of Drapers 1998; hon fell St Edmund Hall Oxford 1995; Hon DLitt Univ of Nottingham 1999; Commandeur de la Legion d'Honneur 1995; *Publications* Fighting for Peace (1998), Washington's War (2007); *Recreations* skiing, sailing; *Clubs* Pratt's; *Style*— Gen Sir Michael Rose, KCB, CBE, DSO, QGM, DL; ✉ c/o Regimental HQ Coldstream Guards, Wellington Barracks, Birdcage Walk, London SW1E 6HQ

ROSE, Norman Hunter; WS; s of Rev David Douglas Rose, and Catherine Drummond, *née* Pow; *b* 11 March 1949; *Educ* Royal HS Edinburgh, Univ of Edinburgh (LLB); *m* 18 Oct 1980, Kay, da of Gordon Murray Sanderson; *Career* articled clerk A & W M Urquhart WS Edinburgh 1970–72, asst slr Dunfermline Town Cncl 1972–74, dep sec Law Soc of Scotland 1977–85 (asst sec 1974–76), dep dir of company affrs CBI 1985–88, dir of European affrs Electronic Data Systems Corp 1989–91 (assoc int gen counsel 1988–89), govt affrs conslt 1992–94, sec Br Paediatric Assoc 1995–96, conslt Jackaman Smith & Mulley Slrs Ipswich 1995–2002, DG Business Servs Assoc 1996–; dir Fedn Against Software Theft 1986–90; chm Euro Business Services Round Table 2004–; memb: Bd American Electronics Assoc 1989–91, Nat Cncl CBI 1996–2002, CBI Trade Cncl Assoc 1997–2002, Bd SITPRO 1998– (vice-chm 2003–05, chm 2006–, chm Communications Strategy Gp 2000–), Best Value Review Gp ODPM 2001–02, NHS Social Partnership Forum 2002–, Bd Asset Skills 2005– (also dep chair Cncl), European Forum for Business-Related Services 2004–05, European Forum on Services in Internal Market 2006–, Workplace Advsy Gp DfES 2006–, Widening Participation in Learning Sub-Gp Dept of Health 2006–; vice-chair European Soc of Assoc Execs 2006–; memb Editorial Advsy Bd: The Facilities Business 1999–2001, Government Opportunities 2000–, UNECE PPP Alliance 2002–; dir: Nat Archives of Scotland 1981–88, Edinburgh Medical Missionary Soc 1981–90, Scottish Export Assoc 2000–02; pres Edinburgh Univ Club of

London 1999–2002; memb: Law Soc of Scotland 1972, Soc of Writers to HM Signet in Scotland 1972, Soc of Slrs to the Supreme Courts in Scotland 1977 (memb Cncl 1981–85 (fiscal 1982–85)); hon lay chaplain Felixstowe Coll 1992–94; memb: Freston Parish Cncl 1995–2002, St Edmundsbury & Ipswich Diocesan Synod 2000–05; Liveryman Worshipful Co of World Traders 2003, Freeman Guild of Educators 2006; FRSA 1997, FIAM 1998; memb Order of St Lazarus of Jerusalem 1983– (receiver gen Commandery of Lochore 1983–87, justiciar England 2001–); *Recreations* music, hill walking, cooking; *Clubs* Home House, New Cavendish, Law Soc, Western (Glasgow), Little Ship, City Livery Yacht; *Style—* Norman Rose, Esq, WS; ✉ Red Brick Cottage, The Street, Freston, Ipswich, Suffolk IP9 1AF (tel 01473 780030); Business Services Association, Warnford Court, 29 Throgmorton Street, London EC2N 2AT (tel 07740 403181, e-mail nh.rose@btinternet.com)

ROSE, Paul Bernard; s of Arthur Rose (d 1974), and Norah, *née* Helman; *b* 26 December 1935; *Educ* Bury GS, Univ of Manchester (LLB), Inst of Advanced Legal Studies, Sorbonne; *m* 13 Sept 1957, Eve Marie Thérèse, da of Jean Lapu, of Paris; 2 s (Howard Imre b 25 Jan 1961, Daniel Sean b 18 Oct 1970), 1 da (Michelle Alison b 11 Oct 1964); *Career* called to the Bar Gray's Inn 1958, practising barr 1962–88; legal advsr Cooperative Union Ltd 1958–61, lectr Univ of Salford 1961–63; MP (Lab) Manchester Blackley 1964–79, PPS to Min for Tport 1966–68, frontbencher (Employment), fndr memb SDP; HM coroner Gtr London Southern Dist 1988–2003 (asst recorder 1975–88); pt/t immigration adjudicator 1987–, pt/t special adjudicator 1993–; pres SE Coroners' Soc; chm NW Sports Cncl 1966–68, memb Cncl of Europe 1968–70; patron St Lucia Soc; assoc Inst of Linguists; memb: Coroners' Soc, Medico-Legal Soc; *Recreations* sport, the arts, computers, writing, travel; *Style—* Paul B Rose, Esq; ✉ Lynnden, 70 Amersham Road, Chalfont St Peter, Buckinghamshire SL9 0PB (tel 01494 872276, e-mail ari2612@aol.com)

ROSE, Prof Richard; s of late Charles Imse, and Mary Rose, of St Louis, MO; *b* 9 April 1933; *Educ* Clayton HS MO, Johns Hopkins Univ (BA), LSE, Univ of Oxford (DPhil); *m* 1956, Rosemary, da of late James Kenny, of Whitstable, Kent; 2 s, 1 da; *Career* political PR Mississippi River Road 1954–55, reporter St Louis Post - Dispatch 1955–57, lectr in govt Univ of Manchester 1961–66; Univ of Strathclyde: prof of politics 1966–75, dir Centre for the Study of Public Policy 1976–2005; prof and dir Centre for the Study of Public Policy Univ of Aberdeen 2005–; visiting fell European Univ Inst Florence 1976, 1977, 1993 and 2001; guest prof: Wissenschaftszentrum Berlin 1988–90 and 2006, Central Euro Univ Prague 1992–95; Ransone lectr Alabama 1990, sr fell Oxford Internet Inst 2003–05; fndr memb Exec Ctee Euro Consortium for Political Res 1970, US Ambassador's appointee US-UK Fulbright Educnl Cmmn 1970–75, sec Res Ctee on Political Sociology Int Political Sci Assoc and Int Sociological Assoc 1970–85, fndr memb Exec Ctee Br Politics Gp in the US 1974–95; memb: Steering Ctee Choice in Social Welfare Policy Cncl of Euro Studies 1974–77, Home Office Working Pty on the Electoral Register 1975–77; convenor Work Gp on UK Politics Political Studies Assoc 1976–88, conslt to Chm NI Constitutional Convention 1976, memb Cncl Int Political Sci Assoc 1976–82, co-dir 1982 World Congress Programme Rio de Janeiro; specialist advsr House of Commons Public Admin Ctee 2002–03; conslt: OECD 1980–, World Bank 1992–, Cncl of Europe 1999; UNDP conslt Pres of Colombia 1990, scientific advsr Paul Lazarsfeld Soc Vienna 1991–; ed Journal of Public Policy 1985– (chm Bd 1981–84); memb Cncl British Irish Studies Assoc 1987; founding fell Soc for the Advancement of Socio-Economics 1989; fell: American SSRC Stanford Univ 1967, Woodrow Wilson Int Centre Washington DC 1974; Guggenheim fellowship 1973–74, foreign memb Finnish Acad of Sci and Letters 1985, hon vice-pres UK Political Studies Assoc 1986; Lasswell Lifetime Achievement Award in Public Policy 1999, Lifetime Achievement Award UK Political Studies Assoc 2000; Hon Dr Örebro Univ 2005; FBA 1992; *Books* incl: Politics in England (1965, 5 edn, 1989), Governing without Consensus - an Irish Perspective (1971), Electoral Behavior (1974), International Almanac of Electoral History (jtly, 1974, 3 edn, 1991), Presidents and Prime Ministers (jt ed, 1980), Do Parties Make a Difference? (1980, 2 edn, 1984), Understanding Big Government (1984), The Postmodern President (1988, 2 edn, 1991), Ordinary People in Public Policy (1989), Loyalties of Voters (jtly, 1990), Lesson - Drawing in Public Policy (1993), Inheritance in Public Policy (jtly, 1994), What is Europe? (1996), How Russia Votes (jtly, 1997), Democracy and Its Alternatives (jtly, 1998), International Encyclopedia of Elections 2000, The Prime Minister in a Shrinking World (2001), Elections without Order (jtly, 2002), Elections and Parties in New European Democracies (jtly, 2003), Learning From Comparative Public Policy (2005), Russia transformed (jtly, 2006); books and articles translated into 18 languages; *Recreations* architecture, historical Britain and modern America, music, writing; *Clubs* Reform, Cosmos (Washington DC); *Style—* Prof Richard Rose, FBA; ✉ 1 East Abercromby Street, Helensburgh, Argyll G84 7SP (tel 01436 672164, fax 01436 673125)

ROSE, Dr Stephen John; s of Bernard Rose (d 1967), of London, and Grace Alberta, *née* Hefford; *b* 20 March 1951; *Educ* Highgate Sch, Univ of Cambridge, Guy's Hosp Med Sch London (BA, MA, MB BChir, MD); *m* 29 Jan 1983, Beatriz; 2 da (Sybilla Alessandra b 1985, Eilidh Veronica b 1986); *Career* jr doctor Guy's Hosp, registrar Westminster Hosp Med Sch London, lectr Univ of Aberdeen, currently conslt and hon sr lectr Dept of Child Health Univ of Birmingham; memb Nat Exec Jr Hosp Drs; FRCP, FRCPCH; *Books* Case Histories in Paediatrics (1984), Early Recognition of Child Abuse (1984), Textbook of Medicine for Medical Students (1986), Paediatrics (2002), Legally Important Clinical Mistakes (2006); *Recreations* squash, rowing; *Clubs* Cambridge Union, Stratford-upon-Avon Boat; *Style—* Dr Stephen Rose; ✉ University Department of Paediatrics, Birmingham Heartlands Hospital, Bordesley Green East, Birmingham B9 5SS (tel 0121 424 1687, fax 0121 773 6458, e-mail sbrose98@aol.com)

ROSE, Prof Steven Peter Russell; s of Lionel Sydney Rose (d 1959), and Ruth, *née* Waxman (d 1988); *b* 4 July 1938; *Educ* Haberdashers' Aske's, King's Coll Cambridge (state scholar, open scholar, BA), Maudsley Inst of Psychiatry London (MRC scholar, PhD); *m* Prof Hilary Ann Rose, *qv*; 2 s (Simon John Chantler b 2 Dec 1955, Benjamin Jacob b 9 March 1963); *Career* Beit meml fell and Guinness res fell Dept of Biochemistry and New Coll Oxford 1961–63, Nat Inst of Health postdoctoral fell Istituto Superiore di Sanita Rome 1963–64, MRC res staff Nat Inst for Med Res then MRC Metabolic Reactions Res Unit Dept of Biochemistry Imperial Coll London 1964–69, lectr Extramural Dept Univ of London 1965–69, prof of biology, chair Dept of Biology and dir Brain and Behaviour Res Gp Open Univ 1969–, Gresham prof of physic (jtly with Hilary Rose) 1999–2002; visiting appts: res fell Hirnforschungsinstitut Leipzig 1961, sr res fell Australian Nat Univ 1977, prof Univ of Queensland Inst for Med Res 1979, scholar Museum of Comparative Zoology Harvard Univ 1980, Hill visiting distinguished res prof Univ of Minnesota 1992, Osher fell The Exploratorium San Francisco 1993, prof UCL 1999–; scientific sec Science Res Cncl Neurobiology Panel 1968–69, memb Neurochemical Gp (Biochemical Soc) Ctee 1970–75, dir and scientific advsr Edinburgh Science Festival 1991–97; pres Biology Section Br Assoc for the Advancement of Science 1996; memb editorial bds of numerous pubns 1973–; medal of the Univ of Utrecht 1989, PK Anokhin medal Inst of Physiology Moscow 1990, Sechenov medal 1992, Ariens Kappers medal 1999, Biochemical Soc medal 2002, Edinburgh medal 2004; fndr memb: Brain Research Assoc (memb Ctee 1965–68, 1970–75 and 1988–90), Br Soc for Social Responsibility in Science (memb Ctee 1969–70 and 1974–76); memb: Biochemical Soc, Int Soc for Neurochemistry, Brain Res Assoc, European Brain and Behaviour Soc, European Neurosciences Assoc, European Soc for Neurochemistry, COPUS 1997–2000; FIBiol 1970, FRSA 1980; *Books* The Chemistry of Life (1966), Science and Society (with Hilary Rose, 1969), The Conscious Brain (1973), No Fire, No Thunder (with Sean Murphy and Alastair Hay, 1984), Not In Our Genes (with Richard Lewontin and Leo Kamin, 1984), Molecules and Minds - Essays on Biology and the Social Order (1988), The Making of Memory (1992, Science Book prize 1993, new edn 2003), Lifelines (1997), Brainbox (1997), Brains to Consciousness (1998), Alas, Poor Darwin (with Hilary Rose, 2000), The 21st Century Brain (2005); ed of numerous books, author of numerous res papers; *Style—* Emeritus Prof Steven Rose; ✉ Department of Biology, Open University, Milton Keynes MK7 6AA (tel 01908 652125, fax 01908 654167, e-mail s.p.r.rose@open.ac.uk)

ROSE, Stuart Alan Ransom; *b* 17 March 1949, Havant, Hants; *Educ* St Joseph's Convent Dar es Salaam, Bootham Sch York; *Career* Marks & Spencer plc 1971–89: store departmental mangr 1971–75, head office merchandiser and buyer rising to head of dept and gp commercial exec 1976–87, commercial exec Europe 1987–89; Burton Gp: bd dir Debenhams 1989–91, md Evans 1991–93, md Dorothy Perkins 1993–94, memb Gp plc Bd and chief exec Burton Menswear, Evans, Dorothy Perkins and Principles 1994–97; chief exec: Argos plc 1998, Booker plc 1998–2000, Arcadia Gp plc 2000–02, Marks & Spencer plc 2004–; non-exec dir Land Securities plc; chm Br Fashion Cncl; *Style—* Stuart Rose, Esq

ROSE, Susan; *Career* journalist; early career as newspaper journalist; former ed: Your Home, Perfect Home; ed Ideal Home 2003–; *Style—* Ms Susan Rose; ✉ Ideal Home, IPC Media Ltd, King's Reach Tower, Stamford Street, London SE1 9LS

ROSEBERY, 7 Earl of (S 1703); Sir Neil Archibald Primrose; 9 Bt (S 1651), DL (Midlothian 1960); also Viscount of Rosebery, Lord Primrose and Dalmeny (both S 1700), Viscount of Inverkeithing, Lord Dalmeny and Primrose (both S 1703), Baron Rosebery (UK 1828), Earl of Midlothian, Viscount Mentmore, and Baron Epsom (all UK 1911); s of 6 Earl of Rosebery, KT, DSO, MC, PC (d 1974, the celebrated race horse owner and s of the Lib PM and Hannah, da of Baron Meyer de Rothschild, through whom Mentmore came into the family), by his 2 w, Hon Dame Eva, *née* Bruce, DBE, JP (da of 2 Baron Aberdare and former w of 3 Baron Belper); *b* 11 February 1929; *Educ* Stowe, New Coll Oxford; *m* 1955, (Alison Mary) Deirdre, da of Ronald William Reid, MS, FRCS; 1 s, 4 da; *Heir* s, Lord Dalmeny; *Style—* The Rt Hon The Earl of Rosebery, DL; ✉ Dalmeny House, South Queensferry, West Lothian EH30 9TQ (tel 0131 331 1784, fax 0131 331 1788, e-mail rosebery@dalmeny.co.uk)

ROSEMONT, David John; s of Leslie Rosemont (d 1964), of Oxted, Surrey, and Elizabeth, *née* Williams (who m 2, 1974, Air Cdre Philip E Warcup, and d 1997); *Educ* Lancing, AA Sch of Architecture; *m* 1, 8 Aug 1975 (m dis 2000), Elizabeth Abbott (Abbey), da of Frederick Milne Booth Duncan (d 1995), of Ayr, Scotland; 2 s (Hugo David b 3 March 1979, Jonathan Duncan b 22 Dec 1980); m 2, 20 Dec 2002, Frances Margaret Steele, *née* Lowry (d 2007), da of Rev Richard Lowry (d 1960), of Funchal, Madeira; *Career* architect 1971; assoc: Fairhursts Manchester 1975–77, SKP Architects London 1977–81; private practice The Rosemont Gp 1981–2005, conslt Husband & Carpenter Ltd 2005–; winner design awards Bath, Kingston upon Thames, Lambeth and Richmond upon Thames, winner Services to Business Community Civic Award London Borough of Wandsworth 2003; chm Wandsworth Challenge Partnership 1994–2004; vice-chm Wandsworth C of C 1995–98 and 1999–2000, dir Business Link London South West 1995–98, memb Bd Wandsworth Strategic Local Partnership 2002–05; MAE 1988, memb AA, RIBA, ACA; *Recreations* opera, photography, gastronomy, classic cars, places; *Clubs* Carlton, Berkshire Automobile; *Style—* David Rosemont, Esq

ROSEN, Emanuel; s of Capt Lionel Rosen, OBE (d 1977), of Hull, and Leah, *née* Levy, of Hull; *b* 23 September 1936; *Educ* Hull GS, Univ of Manchester (MD, BSc); *m* 9 Sept 1962, Hon June, da of Baron Lever (Life Peer, d 1976); 2 s (William David, Edward Leon), 1 da (Caroline Alexandra); *Career* hon conslt surgn Manchester Royal Eye Hosp, lectr in ophthalmology Univ of Manchester, visiting prof Dept of Visual Science UMIST; dir Rosen Eye Surgery Centre Salford Quays Manchester; past pres: Int Intraocular Lens Implant Club, UK Intraocular Lens Implant Soc, Euro Soc of Cataract and Refractive Surgns; FRCOphth, FRCSEd, FRPS; *Books* Fluorescence Photography of the Eye (1969), Basic Ophthalmoscopy (1972), Intraocular Lens Implantation (1983), Hazards of Light (1986), Visco-elastic Materials (1988), Intercapsular Surgery (1989), Quality of Cataract Surgery (1990), Ophthalmology for Medico-Legal Practitioners (1997), Corneal Topography (co-ed, 2000), Neuro-Ophthalmology (sr ed, 2000); *Recreations* golf, photography; *Style—* Emanuel Rosen, Esq; ✉ 10 St John Street, Manchester M3 4DY (tel 0161 832 8778, fax 0161 832 1486)

ROSEN, Prof Michael; CBE (1989); s of Israel Rosen (d 1969), of Dundee, and Lily Rosen, *née* Hyman (d 1996); *b* 17 October 1927; *Educ* Dundee HS, Univ of St Andrews (MB ChB); *m* 17 Oct 1955, Sally Barbara, da of Leslie Israel Cohen (d 1960); 2 s (Timothy b 1956, Mark b 1962), 1 da (Amanda (Dr Kirby) b 1959); *Career* Nat Serv Capt RAMC, served UK, Egypt and Cyprus 1952–54; sr registrar Cardiff 1957, fell Case Western Reserve Univ Cleveland OH 1960–61, conslt anaesthetist Cardiff Teaching Hosp 1961–93, hon prof in anaesthetics Univ of Wales 1984–93; dean Faculty of Anaesthetists RCS 1988; pres: Assoc of Anaesthetists of GB and I 1986–88, Coll of Anaesthetists 1988–91; vice-pres World Fedn of Socs of Anaesthesiology 2000–04 (treas 1992–2000), chm World Fedn of Soc of Anaesthesiology Fndn 2001–04, chm Dyscovery Tst 2001–; Sir Ivan Magill Gold Medal 1993; Hon LLD Univ of Dundee 1996; hon memb: Aust Soc of Anaesthesiologists 1974, French Soc of Anaesthesiologists 1978, Japanese Soc of Anaesthesiologists 1989, Univ Anaesthetists (USA) 1989; memb Acad of Med Malaysia 1989; FRCOG 1989, Hon FFARCSI 1990, FRCS 1994; *Books* Handbook of Percutaneous Central Venous Catheterisation (with I P Latto and W S Ng, 1981, 2 edn 1992), Obstetric Anaesthesia and Analgesia: Safe Practice (contrib, 1982), Intubation: Practice and Problems (with I P Latto, K Murrin, W S Ng, R S Vaughan and W K Saunders, 1985), Difficulties in Tracheal Intubation (with I P Latto and B Tindall, 1985), Patient-Control Analgesia (with M Harmer and M D Vickers, 1985), Consciousness Awareness and Pain in General Anaesthesia (with J N Lunn, 1987); *Style—* Prof Michael Rosen, CBE; ✉ 45 Hollybush Road, Cardiff CF23 6TZ (tel and fax 029 2075 3893, e-mail rosen@mrosen.plus.com)

ROSEN, Michael Wayne; s of Harold Rosen, of London, and Connie Ruby, *née* Isakofsky (d 1976); *b* 7 May 1946; *Educ* Harrow Weald Co GS, Watford Boys' GS, Middlesex Hosp Med Sch London (MB), Wadham Coll Oxford (BA), Nat Film Sch, Univ of Reading (MA), Univ of N London (PhD); *m* 1, 1976 (m dis 1987), Susanna, da of William Steele; 2 s (Joseph Steele Rosen b 7 July 1976, Eddie Steele Rosen b 9 June 1980 d 27 April 1999); m 2, 1987 (m dis 1997), Geraldine Clark, da of Jack Dingley; 1 s (Isaac Louis Rosen b 15 June 1987); m 3, 8 March 2003, Emma-Louise, da of Frederick Williams; 1 da (Elsie Lavender Ruby Rosen b 10 March 2001), 1 s (Emile Frederick Harold Rosen b 23 December 2004); *Career* writer/broadcaster; presenter: Poems by Post and Meridian Books (BBC World Serv), Treasure Islands (BBC Radio 4), Best Words (BBC Radio 3), Word of Mouth (BBC Radio 4), Readabout (YTV), True Lives; writer/presenter: Everybody Here (Channel 4, 1982), Black and White and Read All Over (Channel 4, 1983); performances in schs, colls, libraries and theatres throughout UK 1976–; Children's Laureate 2007–; lectr in Singapore, Aust, USA and Canada; visiting prof: London Met Univ, Middlesex Univ; *Awards* Sunday Times Student Drama Award 1968, C Day Lewis fell 1976, Signal Poetry Award 1982, The Other Award 1982, Smarties Award 1990, Eleanor Farjeon Award 1997, Talkies Award 1998, Sony Radio Acad Award 2003; *Books* Mind Your Own Business (1974), You Can't Catch Me (1981), Quick Let's Get Out of Here (1983), Don't Put Mustard in the Custard (1985), Hairy Tales and Nursery Crimes

R

(1985), The Wicked Tricks of Till Owlyglass (1989), The Golem of Old Prague (1990), Goodies and Daddies (1991), You Wait Till I'm Older Than You (1996), Michael Rosen's Book of Nonsense (1997), Snore! (1998), Rover (1999), Centrally Heated Knickers (2000), Michael Rosen's Sad Book (2004), Totally Wonderful Miss Plumberry (2006); anthologies: The Kingfisher Book of Children's Poetry (ed, 1985), A Spider Bought a Bicycle (ed, 1986), The Kingfisher Book of Funny Stories (ed, 1988), Rude Rhymes (ed, 1989), A World of Poetry (ed, 1991), The Chatto Book of Dissent (ed with David Widgery, 1991), The Vintage Book of Dissent (ed with David Widgery, 1996), Carrying the Elephant: A Memoir of Love and Loss (2002), This is Not My Nose (2004), In the Clonie (2005); *Plays* Backbone (1969, performed Royal Court), Regis Debray (1971, performed BBC Radio 4), Pinocchio in the Park (2001, Unicorn Theatre, performed Regents Park Open Air Theatre); *Recreations* Arsenal FC supporter, reading, second-hand book collecting; *Style—* Michael Rosen, Esq; ✉ c/o Peters Fraser & Dunlop Ltd, Drury House, 34–43 Russell Street, London WC2B 5HA (tel 020 7344 1000)

ROSEN, Murray Hilary; QC (1993); s of Joseph Rosen, and Mercia, *née* Herman, of London; *b* 26 August 1953; *Educ* St Paul's, Trinity Coll Cambridge (MA), Brussels Free Univ (Dip); *m* 1975, Lesley, *née* Samuels; 3 da, 1 s; *Career* called to the Bar Inner Temple 1976 (bencher 2004) (ad eundem Lincoln's Inn); recorder 2000–; ptnr and head of Advocacy Unit Herbert Smith 2004–; chm: Bar Sports Law Gp 1997–2001, Br Assoc for Sport and the Law 2003–; FCIArb 1999; *Recreations* books, music, cricket, real tennis; *Style—* Murray Rosen, QC; ✉ Herbert Smith, Exchange House, Primrose Street, London EC2A 2HS (tel 020 7374 8000, e-mail murray.rosen@herbertsmith.com)

ROSENBERG, Jenifer Bernice; OBE (1989); da of Philip Levene (d 1966), of London, and Jane-Sarah, *née* Kent (d 1982); *b* 1 October 1942; *Educ* Our Lady of Zion GS; *m* 1, 1 Aug 1975, Jack Goldstein (d 1975); m 2, 8 Feb 1982, Ian David Rosenberg (d 2006), s of Alfred Rosenberg (d 1984), of London; *Career* sr buyer Marks & Spencer plc 1960–74, fndr and md J and J Fashions Ltd 1974–92 (sold to Claremont Garments plc 1992); govr London Inst, vice-pres Textile Inst, memb Br Fashion Cncl, tstee Elderly Accommodation Counsel; fndr dir CILNTEC; chm and tstee Heart Cells Fndn, involved with Open the Door Appeal YWCA, exec memb Jewish Care organising Woman of Distinction Luncheon and Annual Bridge Day; memb: Summer Exhibition Preview Party Ctee Royal Acad of Arts, Charity Gala Evening Ctee, Grosvenor House Art and Antique Fair; Veuve Clicquot/IOD Business Woman of the Year Award 1986, Award from Tyne & Wear Cncl for Industrial and Commercial Enterprise (twice); *Recreations* theatre, photography, music, travelling, bridge; *Style—* Mrs Jenifer Rosenberg, OBE; ✉ 48 Queen's Grove, St John's Wood, London NW8 6HH (e-mail jrosenb174@aol.com)

ROSENBLOOM, Prof Richard Selig; s of Irving J Rosenbloom (d 1980), and Lillian S Rosenbloom (d 1972); *b* 16 January 1933; *Educ* Harvard Univ (AB, MBA, DBA); *m* 14 Oct 1956, Ruth Miriam, *née* Friedlander; 2 s (Joshua b 13 Aug 1958, Daniel b 27 Oct 1963), 1 da (Rachel b 13 Aug 1968); *Career* prof of business admin Harvard Univ 1960–; former non-exec dir Lex Service plc; dir: Arrow Electronics Inc, Executone Information Systems Inc; *Style—* Prof Richard S Rosenbloom; ✉ Harvard Business School, Boston, Mass 02163, USA (tel 617 495 6295, e-mail rrosenbloom@hbs.edu)

ROSENBROCK, Prof Howard Harry; *b* 16 December 1920; *Educ* Tonman Moseley Sch Slough, Slough GS (co major scholar), UCL (Salomons scholar, BSc, PhD, DSc, Clinton Prize), Univ of Manchester (MSc); *m* 1950, Cathryn June, *née* Press; 1 s, 2 da; *Career* signals offr RAFVR 1941–46; Radio Transmitter Section GEC Research Lab 1947–48, asst master and mathematics and physics teacher London CC 1948–49, tech asst Electrical Research Assoc 1949–51, asst to engr conslt John Brown & Co Ltd 1951–54, research mangr Constructors John Brown Ltd 1957–62 (joined 1954), on staff Control Gp Univ of Cambridge 1962–66; UMIST: prof of control engrg 1966–87 (now emeritus), vice-princ 1977–78; fell UCL 1978; memb: Advsy Ctee for Chemical and Process Engrg Mintech 1969–73, Computer Bd DES 1972–76, Br Nat Ctee Int Inst of Applied Systems Analysis 1972–78, IFAC Ctee on Social Effects of Automation 1975–; convenor Working Pty Cncl for Science and Soc on New Technol 1979–81; pres Manchester Medical Engrg Club 1970–71; Inst of Measurement and Control: chm Control Section 1958–59, memb Cncl 1958–66 and 1970–74, memb Educn Ctee 1958–60, vice-pres 1971–72, pres 1972–73; IEE: memb Cncl 1966–70, chm Educn and Trg Ctee 1976–77, vice-pres 1976–78; SRC: memb Control Panel 1966–72, chm Engrg Computing Requirements Tech Gp 1975–76, memb Engrg Bd 1976–78, memb Special Project in Computing Panel 1978; W C Williams Lecture Univ of Sheffield 1980, Sir Harold Hartley Lecture 1981, Halliburton Distinguished Lecture Series Texas Tech Univ 1985, Cockroft Lecture Manchester Technol Assoc 1986; Moulton Medal IChemE 1957, Sir Harold Hartley Medal Inst of Measurement and Control 1970, Control Systems Science and Engrg Award IEEE 1982, Control Achievement Award IEE 1988, Rufus Oldenburger Medal ASME 1994, Nordic Process Control Award 1995, Sir George Thomson Gold Medal 1998; Hon DSc Univ of Salford 1987; FIEE, FIChemE, FRS 1976, FREng 1984, ARPS 1990, Hon FInstMC 1992; *Books* Computational Techniques for Chemical Engineers (with C Storey, 1966), Mathematics of Dynamical Systems (with C Storey, 1970), State-Space and Multivariable Theory (1970), Computer-Aided Control System Design (1974), New Technology: Society, Employment and Skill (1981), Designing Human-Centered Technology (1989), Machines with a Purpose (1990), author of numerous scientific pubns; *Style—* Prof Howard Rosenbrock, FREng, FRS; ✉ Linden, Walford Road, Ross-on-Wye, Herefordshire HR9 5PQ (tel 01989 565372)

ROSENCRANTZ, Claudia; da of Alfred Rosenkranz (d 1986), and Leonore, *née* Meyer; *b* 23 June 1959; *Educ* Queen's Coll London; *Career* picture ed/journalist The Telegraph Sunday Magazine, Sunday Magazine and Elle 1979–86; TV researcher: Aspel & Company, Sunday Sunday, The Trouble with Michael Caine, An Audience with Victoria Wood, Dame Edna Experience (LWT, 1986); prodr: The Dame Edna Experience (series 2) 1989 (nominated for Br Acad Award), Incredibly Strange Film Show, A Late Lunch with Les (Channel 4) 1990, An Audience with Jackie Mason, A Night on Mount Edna (LWT) 1991 (Golden Rose of Montreux), Dame Edna's Hollywood (NBC), Edna Time (Fox), Elton John - Tantrums and Tiaras; prodr/dir Two Rooms, creator/prodr Dame Edna's Neighbourhood Watch (LWT, 1992); exec prodr: Don't Forget Your Toothbrush (Channel 4) 1994, Features Dept BBC (responsible for Out of This World and Prisoners in Time) 1994–95; controller Network Entertainment ITV 1995–2006 (responsible for 600 progs a year incl: WWT BAM, Ant & Dec's Saturday Night Take-Away, Popstars (Silver Rose of Montreux 2001), Pop Idol (Best Entertainment Programme TRIC Awards 2002), I'm A Celebrity Get Me Out of Here (BAFTA Award 2003), Ant and Dec's Saturday Night Takeaway), dir of programming LIVING and LIVING2 2006; Woman of the Year 2003; FRTS 2004; *Style—* Miss Claudia Rosencrantz

ROSENTHAL, Dennis; s of Hermann Rosenthal, and Ilse, *née* Loebenstein; *b* 18 August 1944, Johannesburg, SA; *Educ* King Edward VII HS Johannesburg (Jan Hofmeyr scholar), Univ of the Witwatersrand (BA, LLB), Univ of SA (BA); *m* 21 Dec 1971, Nadine, *née* Gehler; 4 s, 1 da; *Career* admitted attorney SA 1968, admitted slr England Wales 1978; articled to Lubbers, Spitz, Block and Rubenstein, lectr in law Univ of the Witwatersrand, attorney Werksmans Johannesburg 1971–74, lawyer Nedbank Syfrets Johannesburg 1974; ptnr: Victor Mishcon & Co 1980–87 (joined 1975), Hill Bailey 1987–89, Saunders Sobell Leigh & Dobin (latterly Forsyte Saunders Kerman) 1989–98, Paisner & Co (latterly Berwin Leighton Paisner) 1998–; memb: Law Soc 1981, Int Bar Asscoc; former govr: Menorah Primary Sch, Kisharon Sch; *Books* Guide to Credit Law and Practice, Financial Advertising Law, Goode: Consumer Credit Law and Practice (co-ed), Goode: Consumer Credit Reports (co-ed), Halsbury's Laws of England (contrib, 4 edn), Encyclopaedia of Forms and Precedents (contrib, 5 edn); *Recreations* music, art, gardening, reading; *Style—* Dennis Rosenthal, Esq; ✉ 7 Leeside Crescent, London NW11 0DA; Berwin Leighton Paisner, Adelaide House, London Bridge, London EC4R 9HA (tel 020 7427 1113, e-mail dennis.rosenthal@blplaw.com)

ROSENTHAL, Jim; s of Albi Rosenthal, of Oxford; *b* 6 November 1947; *Educ* Magdalen Coll Sch Oxford; *m* Chrissy; 1 s (Tom b 14 Jan 1988); *Career* TV sports presenter; Oxford Mail and Times 1968–72, BBC Radio Birmingham 1972–76, BBC Radio Sports Unit 1976–80, with ITV Sport 1980–; Sports Presenter of the Year (RTS) 1997 and 1999, Sports Presenter of the Year (TRIC) 1990; *Style—* Jim Rosenthal, Esq; ✉ ITV Sport, 200 Gray's Inn Road, London WC1X 8HF (tel 020 7843 8116, fax 020 7843 8153)

ROSENTHAL, Sir Norman Leon; kt (2007); s of Paul Rosenthal, and Kate, *née* Zucker; *b* 8 November 1944; *Educ* Westminster City GS, Univ of Leicester (BA), Sch of Slavonic and E Euro Studies, Free Univ of Berlin (Kunsthistorisches Seminar); *m* 1989, Manuela Mena Marques; *Career* art exhibitions organiser; first exhibition Artists in Cornwall Leicester Museum and Art Gallery 1965, librarian and res Thomas S Agnew & Sons 1966–68, exhibition offr Brighton Museum and Art Gallery 1970–71 (organised Follies and Fantasies for Brighton Festival), organiser (with Vera Russell) Artists Market (non-profit making gallery Covent Garden) 1972–73, exhibition offr Inst of Contemporary Arts London 1973–76 (organised The German Month 1974, Art into Society - Society into Art, Seven German Artists, The Greek Month 1975), exhibitions sec Royal Acad of Arts 1977–; memb: Bd Palazzo Grassi Venice 1985, Opera Board Royal Opera House Covent Garden 1995–99, Bd of Tstees Baltic Centre for Contemporary Art Gateshead 2004–, Comité Scientifique Réunion des Musées Nationaux Paris 2005–; German Br Forum Award 2003; Hon DLitt: Univ of Southampton, Univ of Leicester 2006; hon fell Royal Coll of Art London 1987, Chevalier de l'Ordre des Arts et des Lettres (France) (Cavaliere Ufficiale) 1992, Cross of the Order of Merit of the FRG 1993, Officier de l'Ordre des Arts et Lettres 2003, Order of the Aguila Azteca (Mexico) 2006; *Royal Academy Exhibitions* curator of loan exhbns incl: Robert Motherwell 1978, Post-Impressionism 1979, Stanley Spencer 1980, A New Spirit in Painting 1981, Great Japan Exhibition 1981–82, Painting in Naples, Caravaggio to Giordano 1982, Murillo 1983, The Genius of Venice 1983–84, From Vermeer to De Hooch, Dutch Genre Painting 1984, Chagall 1985, Joshua Reynolds 1986, New Architecture: Foster, Roger, Stirling 1986, The Age of Chivalry 1987, The Early Cézanne 1988, Henry Moore 1988, The Art of Photography 1989, Frans Hals 1990; other exhbn work at the Royal Acad (with Christos M Joachimides): German Art in the Twentieth Century 1985 (also shown at the Staatsgalerie Stuttgart), British Art in the Twentieth Century 1987 (also shown at the Staatsgalerie Stuttgart), Italian Art in the Twentieth Century 1989 (version shown at Palazzo Grassi Venice), American Art in the Twentieth Century 1993 (at Martin-Gropius-Bau Berlin 1994), Sensation: Young British Artists from the Saatchi Collection 1997, Charlotte Salomon 1998, Apocalypse 2000, The Genuis of Rome 2001, Botticelli's Dante 2001, Frank Auerbach 2001, 195 Rembrandt's Women 2001, Paris: Capital of the Arts 1900–1968 2002, Return of the Buddha 2002, The Galleries Show 2002, The Aztecs 2002, Masterpieces from Dresden 2003, Kirchner 2004, Illuminating the Renaissance 2004, Philip Guston 2004, Turks 600–1600 2005, Edvard Munch by Himself 2005, China: The Three Emperors 1662–1795 2005, Jacob van Ruisdael: Master of Landscape 2006, Modigliani and his Models 2006, USA TODAY: New American Art from the Saatchi Gallery 2006, Georg Baselitz Retrospective 2007; *Other Exhibitions*: Zeitgeist (Martin Gropius-Bau Berlin) 1982, Metropolis (Martin Gropius-Bau Berlin) 1991, The Age of Modernism - Art in the 20th Century (Martin-Gropius-Bau Berlin) 1997; *Style—* Sir Norman Rosenthal; ✉ The Royal Academy of Arts, Burlington House, Piccadilly, London W1J 0BD (tel 020 7300 5742, fax 020 7300 5774)

ROSENTHAL, Thomas Gabriel (Tom); s of late Dr Erwin Isak Jacob Rosenthal, and Elizabeth Charlotte, *née* Marx (d 1996); *b* 16 July 1935; *Educ* Perse Sch Cambridge, Pembroke Coll Cambridge (MA, PhD); *m* Ann Judith Warnford-Davis; 2 s (Adam, Daniel); *Career* 2 Lt RA 1954–56, Lt Cambridgeshire Regt TA 1956–80; md: Thames and Hudson International 1966 (joined Thames and Hudson 1959), Martin Secker and Warburg Ltd 1971 (chm 1980); chm William Heinemann 1980–84, chm and md various subsid cos 1980–84, chm and md Andre Deutsch Ltd (joined 1984) until 1997; chm Soc of Young Publishers 1961–62; chm The Bridgewater Press 1997–; memb: Cambridge Univ Appts Bd 1967–71, Exec Ctee Nat Book League 1971–74, Ctee of Mgmnt and tstee Amateur Dramatic Club Cambridge, Cncl RCA 1982–87, Exec Cncl ICA 1987–2002 (chm 1996–2002); tstee Fitzwilliam Museum Cambridge 2003–; *Books* A Reader's Guide to Modern European Art History (1962), A Reader's Guide to Modern American Fiction (1963), Monograph on Ivon Hitchens (with Alan Bowness, 1973), Monograph on Arthur Boyd (with Ursula Hoff, 1986), The Art of Jack B Yeats (1993), Sidney Nolan (2002), Paula Rego: The Complete Graphic Works (2002), Josef Albers: Formulation: Articulation (2006); introductions to: The Financier, The Titan, Jennie Gerhardt (Theodore Dreiser); articles in: The Times, The Guardian, TLS, THES Opera Now Daily Telegraph, London Magazine, Encounter, New Statesman, Spectator, Jl of Br Assoc for American Studies, Studio International, Dictionary of National Biography, Nature, The Bookseller; *Recreations* bibliomania, opera, looking at pictures, reading other publishers' books, watching cricket; *Clubs* Garrick, MCC; *Style—* Tom Rosenthal, Esq; ✉ 7 Huguenot House, 19 Oxendon Street, London SW1Y 4EH (tel 020 7839 3589, fax 020 7839 0651)

ROSEWELL, Bridget; da of Geoffrey Noel Mills (d 1978), and Helen Handescombe, *née* Rodd; *b* 19 September 1951; *Educ* Wimbledon HS, St Hugh's Coll Oxford (BA, MPhil); *m* (m dis); 1 s (Christopher Edward b 30 July 1978), 1 da (Harriet Sarah Louise b 6 April 1980); *Career* economist; Univ of Oxford: lectr St Hilda's Coll 1976–78, res offr Inst of Economics & Statistics 1976–81, lectr Somerville Coll 1978–81, tutor in economics Oriel Coll 1981–84; head Economic Trends Dept and dep dir Economic Affrs CBI 1984–86, chief Euro economist Wefa Ltd 1986–88, chm Business Strategies Ltd 1988–2000, founding dir and chm Volterra Consulting Ltd 1999–; conslt chief economist GLA; visiting prof City Univ Business Sch; non-exec dir: Britannia Building Soc; memb Advsy Bd: NEXSUS Network on Complexity, CRIC Univ of Manchester; special advsr Treasy Select Ctee; sometime memb: Res Priorities Bd ESRC, Ind Panel of Forecasters HM Treasy; author of numerous articles in various pubns; frequent lectr, presenter and broadcaster; memb Bd of Govrs Wimbledon HS; *Style—* Ms Bridget Rosewell; ✉ Volterra Consulting Ltd, Sheen Elms, 135C Sheen Lane, London SW14 8AE (tel 020 8878 6333, fax 020 8878 6685, e-mail brosewell@volterra.co.uk)

ROSEWELL, Michael John (Mike); s of Frederick Jack Rosewell (d 1974), of Walton-on-Thames, Surrey, and Anne Emma, *née* Helps (d 1984); *b* 22 January 1937; *Educ* Woking GS, LSE (BSc), Westminster Coll (PGCE); *m* 1961, Jill Drusilla, da of Stanley William Orriss; 2 da (Anna-Marie b 1964, Michelle Jane b 1969), 1 s (Daniel James b 1966); *Career* economics master, rowing coach and journalist: Ealing GS 1959–64, St George's Coll Weybridge 1964–76, St Edward's Sch Oxford 1976–95 (visiting coach 1999–); rowing journalist and writer: Surrey Herald 1963–76, Surrey Comet 1967–76, Evening Mail 1968–77, Oxford Times 1976–; features writer Rowing Magazine 1968–97, rowing corr The Times 1989–, feature writer Thames User 1992, ed Friends of the Boat Race 1995–, dep ed Regatta Magazine 1996–2001 (features writer 1987–); memb Cncl ARA 1968–2000 (chm Publicity Ctee, chm Jr Rowing Ctee, asst ed Br Rowing Almanack, Eng Rowing Team mangr, memb Exec Ctee, GB Jr Team delegate, GB Jr Crew coach); chief coach: ChCh Oxford 1978–90, Oxford Women's Boat Race Crew

1979–87, Wadham Coll Oxford 1995–98, Trinity Coll Oxford 1996; vice-chm Oxford Branch Parkinson's Disease Soc 1993–96; memb: Sports Writers' Assoc of GB 1990, Br Assoc of Rowing Journalists 1990 (chm 2002–05, pres 2005–); ARA Medal of Honour 1997; *Books* Beginners Guide to Rowing (1970); *Recreations* boating, golf, angling, gardening; *Clubs* Walton Rowing, Leander; *Style*— Mike Rosewell, Esq; ✉ Hillview, Broad Street, Long Compton, Warwickshire CV36 5JH (tel and fax 01608 684709)

ROSIER, (Frederick) David Stewart; s of Air Chief Marshal Sir Frederick Rosier, GCB, CBE, DSO, (d 1998), and Hettie Denise, *née* Blackwell; *b* 10 April 1951; *Educ* Winchester, Keble Coll Oxford (MA), RMA Sandhurst; *m* 27 Sept 1975, Julia Elizabeth, da of David Leslie Gomme; 1 s (Charles Frederick James b 8 Dec 1990); *Career* cmmnd 1st The Queen's Dragoon Gds 1973–78; resigned Capt 1978; exec dir S G Warburg & Co Ltd 1984–87 (joined 1978); dir: Warburg Investment Management Ltd 1982–87, Mercury Asset Management Group plc 1987–98, Mercury Bank AG 1990–95; dep chm Mercury Asset Management plc 1991–98, chm Merrill Lynch Channel Islands Ltd 1992–2002, md Merrill Lynch Investment Managers 1998–2002, chm Thurleigh Investment Managers LLP 2003–; dir: Threadneedle Asset Management Ltd, Forces Pensions Soc Investment Co, Armed Forces Charities Advsy Co; cncllr Wandsworth BC 1982–86; tstee: Burma Star Assoc, Nuffield Tst for the Armed Forces, 1st The Queen's Dragoon Gds Regtl Museum, Winchester Coll 1945 War Meml Fund; Liveryman Worshipful Co of Coachmakers and Coach Harness Makers; MSI; *Recreations* golf, skiing, sailing; *Clubs* Cavalry and Guards' (chm 2007–), Boodle's, Hurlingham, Valderrama, Swinley Forest, Itchenor Sailing; *Style*— David Rosier, Esq; ✉ tel 020 7340 9556, e-mail david@davidrosier.com

ROSIN, (Richard) David; s of Isadore Rowland Rosin (d 1993), of Zimbabwe, and Muriel Ena, *née* Wolff; *b* 29 April 1942; *Educ* St George's Coll Salisbury S Rhodesia, KCL, Westminster Hosp Sch of Med (MB BS, MS, LRCP, MRCS, DOHM, Arthur Evans meml prize in surgery, Rogers prize); *m* Michele Shirley, da of Ivor Moreton (d 1984); 2 da (Natasha Jane b 25 May 1972, Katya Sarah b 4 May 1983), 1 s (Alexei John b 8 Aug 1973); *Career* house physician then house surgn Westminster Hosp 1966–67, ship's surgn P&O Lines 1967, SHO in clinical pathology Westminster Hosp 1968, SHO (latterly Burns Unit) Birmingham Accident Hosp 1969, SHO (rotation) Westminster Hosp 1969–71; registrar: Sutton Hosp Surgery 1971–73, St Helier's Hosp Carshalton 1973–74; clinical asst St Mark's Hosp London 1974–75; sr registrar: Kingston Hosp 1975–77, Westminster Hosp 1977–79 (visiting lectr Univ of Hong Kong Sept-Dec 1978); currently conslt in gen surgery and surgical oncology St Mary's Hosp, former conslt surgn King Edward VII's Hosp for Offrs; clinical dir of surgery St Charles' Hosp 1990–92, chm Div of Surgery St Mary's Hosp 1992–95; Runcorn travelling fell 1976, Arris and Gale lectr RCS 1976, Ethicon Fndn scholar 1976 and 1978, Br Jl of Surgery travelling fell 1983, Penrose-May tutor RCS 1985–90, Hunterian prof RCS 1987, Arnott lectr RCS 1991, Gordon Taylor lectr 2005; visiting fell Pearson Coll Yale Univ; regnl advsr NW Thames Region RCS(Ed), examiner (MB BS) London and (FRCS) RCS(Ed), intercollegiate specialist examiner in gen surgery; past memb Cncl The Marie Curie Fndn; chm ICBSE 2003–; memb: Soc of Minimally Invasive Gen Surgns (fndr and hon sec), Surgical Research Soc, Assoc of Surgns of GB and I (SMIGS rep on Surgical Gastroenterology Ctee), RSM (pres Clinical Section 1982–83, pres Section of Surgery 1992–93, memb Cncl 2003–05, memb Cncl Oncology Section), Br Soc of Gastroenterology, Br Assoc of Surgical Oncology (former hon sec, pres 2003–04), London Med Soc, Hunterian Soc, Melanoma Study Gp (first hon sec 1986–89, pres 1989–92), World Soc of Hepato-Biliary Surgery, Int Coll of Surgns, Euro Assoc of Endoscopic Surgns, Assoc of Endoscopic Surgns of GB and I (memb Cncl 1995–2001); Freeman: City of London 1972, Worshipful Soc of Apothecaries 1971, Worshipful Co of Barber Surgns 1978; fell Assoc Upper Gastro-Intestinal Surgeons of GB and I, fell Assoc of Surgns of GB and Ireland, first hon fell Caribbean Coll of Surgns, hon fell South Africa Soc of Endoscopic Surgns; FRCS 1971 (memb Cncl 1994–2006, vice-pres 2004–06), FRCSE 1971, hon fell SAGES 1996 (memb 1994), FICS; *Books* Cancer of the Bile Ducts and Pancreas (jt ed, 1989), Head and Neck Oncology for the General Surgeon (jt ed, 1991), Diagnosis and Management of Melanoma in Clinical Practice (jt ed, 1992), Minimal Access Medicine and Surgery - Principles and Practice (ed, 1993), Minimal Access General Surgery (ed, 1994), Minimal Access Surgical Oncology (ed, 1995), Minimal Access Thoracic Surgery (ed, 1998), and series ed Minimal Access textbooks; also author of various book chapters and published papers; *Recreations* particularly golf, opera, music and theatre, history of medicine and surgery, travelling; *Clubs* Garrick, NZ Golf, Roehampton, MCC; *Style*— R David Rosin, Esq; ✉ 4 Ledbury Mews North, London W11 2AF (tel 020 7727 6331); 80 Harley Street, London W1G 7HL (tel and fax 020 7087 4260, mobile 078 3165 5036, e-mail rdrosin@uk-consultants.co.uk)

ROSINDELL, Andrew Richard; MP; s of Frederick William Rosindell, and Eileen Rosina, *née* Clark; *b* 17 March 1966; *Educ* Marshalls Park Secdy Sch; *Career* researcher and freelance journalist 1986–97, res asst to Vivian Bendall, MP; European Fndn: dir 1997–99, int dir 1999–2001; MP (Cons) Romford 2001– (Parly candidate (Cons) Glasgow Provan 1992 and Thurrock 1997); a vice-chm Cons Pty 2004–05, HM Oppn whip 2005–; memb Deregulation and Regulatory Reform Select Ctee 2001–05, memb Jt Ctee on Statutory Instruments 2002–03, sec Cons 92 Gp 2003–06, memb Constitutional Affairs Select Ctee 2003–05; chm: All-Pty Parly Isle of Man Gp 2005–, All-Pty Parly Monseratt Gp 2005–, All-Pty Parly Greyhound Gp 2006–, All-Pty St George's Day Gp 2007–; vice-chm: All-Pty Parly Iceland Gp 2005–, All-Pty CI Gp 2006–, Tackling Terrorism Gp 2006–, All-Pty Madagascar Gp 2007–; jt treas All-Pty Parly Denmark Gp 2001–; sec: All-Pty Parly Australia and NZ Gp 2001–, All-Pty Parly Falkland Islands Gp 2001–, All-Pty Liechtenstein Gp 2004–, Br Virgin Islands Gp 2006–; presented to Parl: St George's Day Bill 2006, Traditional Counties Towns and Villages Bill 2007; Cons Pty: joined 1981, chm Romford Young Cons 1983–84, memb Nat Union Exec Ctee 1986–88 and 1992–94, chm Gtr London Young Cons 1987–88 (chm anti-CND campaign 1983–84), chm Chase Cross Ward Cons 1988–99, int sec UK Young Cons 1991–98, chm Nat Young Cons 1993–94, chm Euro Young Cons 1993–97, chm Romford Cons Assoc 1998–2001, pres Havering Park Ward Cons 2000–; chm Int Young Dem Union 1998–2002 (UK Young Cons rep 1991–98, exec sec 1994–98), exec memb Int Dem Union (IDU) 1998–2002; cncllr Havering BC 1990–2002; co-ordinator Freedom Trg Prog 1993–98; memb: Cons Christian Fellowship, Cwealth Party Assoc, Inter Parly Union; chm: N Romford Community Area Forum 1998–2002, Cons Friends of Gibraltar 2002–; pres Romford Sqdn Air Trg Corps; vice-pres: Romford and Dist Scout Assoc 1995–, Romford FC; memb: Standing Advsy Cncl for Religious Educn Havering 1990–2000, London Accident Prevention Cncl 1990–95, Hornchurch Theatre Tst 1990–2002, Royal Soc of St George, Church of St Edward the Confessor Romford, Friends of the UK Overseas Territories; patron: Constitutional Monarchy Assoc, Justice for Dogs, Remus Meml Horse Sanctuary; hon memb: Falkland Islands Assoc, Havering-atte-Bower CC, Romford Model Railway Soc, N Romford Community Assoc; govr Dame Tipping C of E Sch 1990–2002; Mayor's Award for Community Action 1978; Feeman City of London 2003; *Publications* Defending Our Great Heritage (co-author, 1993); *Recreations* cycling, travel, history; *Clubs* East Anglian Staffordshire Bull Terrier (hon memb), The Staffordshire Bull Terrier Soc (hon memb), Romford Conservative and Constitutional (hon memb), RAF Assoc, Royal British Legion (Romford), Romford Golf (hon memb); *Style*— Andrew Rosindell, Esq, MP; ✉ House of Commons, London SW1A 0AA (tel 020 7219 8475, fax 020 7219 1960); Constituency Office, 85 Western Road, Romford, Essex RM1 3LS (tel 01708 766700, e-mail andrew@rosindell.com, website www.andrew.rosindell.com); Home tel 01708 761186

ROSKILL, Hon Julian Wentworth; s of Baron Roskill, PC, DL (d 1996), and Elisabeth Wallace, *née* Jackson; *b* 22 July 1950; *Educ* Winchester; *m* 1975, Catherine Elizabeth, 2 da of Maj William Francis Garnett (d 2004), of Quernmore Park, Lancaster; 2 s (Matthew b 1979, Oliver b 1981); *Career* admitted slr 1974; ptnr Mayer, Brown, Rowe & Maw LLP 1988– (head Employment Gp); memb: Law Soc, City of London Slrs' Co (former chm Employment Sub-Ctee), Employment Lawyers Assoc; *Recreations* photography, music, theatre, tennis; *Style*— The Hon Julian W Roskill; ✉ Mayer, Brown, Rowe & Maw LLP, 11 Pilgrim Street, London EC4V 6RW (tel 020 7248 4282, fax 020 7782 8944, e-mail jroskill@mayerbrownrowe.com)

ROSLING, (Richard) Alan; OBE (1994); s of Derek Norman Rosling, of Bucklers Hard, and Joan Elizabeth, *née* Heseltine; *b* 16 August 1962; *Educ* Univ of Cambridge (Richmond exhibitioner, BA), Harvard Business Sch (Baker scholar, Harkness fell, MBA); *m* 1990, Sarmila, da of Dr S K Bose; 3 s (Aidan Samya b 2 June 1993, Kieran Shaurya b 19 Dec 1996, Euan Sharanya b 23 Aug 1999); *Career* investment banker S G Warburg & Co Ltd 1983–86, chief exec Piersons (part of Courtaulds Textiles plc) 1988–90, memb PM's Policy Unit 1991–93, strategy devpt dir United Distillers 1993–97, Jardine Matheson Ltd 1998–2003 (latterly chm India), exec dir Tata Sons Ltd 2004–; chm: Br Business Gp Mumbai, City of London Advsy Bd for India, Indo-Br Business Ctee Bombay C of C; *Recreations* South Asia, travel, sailing; *Clubs* Bengal; *Style*— Alan Rosling, Esq, OBE

ROSLING, Derek Norman; CBE (1988); s of Norman Rosling (d 1984), and Jean, *née* Allen (d 1957); *b* 21 November 1930; *Educ* Shrewsbury; *m* 1 (m dis); 1 da (Jean b 1961), 2 s (Alan b 1962, John b 1964); m 2, Nov 2000, Julia Catherine Crookston; 1 step s (James b 1970); *Career* Hanson plc: fndr dir 1965, dir 1965–94, vice-chm 1973–93, ret 1994; FCA, FRSA; *Recreations* sailing, golf, theatre; *Clubs* Royal Yacht Squadron, Royal Southampton Yacht, Brokenhurst Manor Golf; *Style*— Derek N Rosling, Esq, CBE; ✉ Little Salterns, Bucklers Hard, Beaulieu, Hampshire SO42 7XE (tel 01590 616307, fax 01590 616347)

ROSS, Dr Alastair Robertson; s of Alexander James Ross (d 1985), of Dunblane, Perthshire, and Margaret Elizabeth McInnes, *née* Robertson (d 1983); *b* 8 August 1941; *Educ* McLaren HS Callander, Duncan of Jordanstone Coll of Art Dundee (DA); *m* 12 April 1975, Kathryn Margaret Greig, da of late John Ferrier Greig Wilson, of Arbroath, Tayside; 1 da (Alexandra b 1981); *Career* artist; lectr Duncan of Jordanstone Coll Univ of Dundee 1969–2003 (pt/t 1966–69), tutor Sch of Scottish Artists in Malta 1991–93; works incl: bronze panel Royal Calcutta Golf Club, bronze for Blackness Devpt Project Dundee, portrait in bronze of Sir Iain Moncreiffe of that Ilk at HM New Register House Edinburgh 1988 (awarded Sir Otto Beit Medal of Royal Soc Br Sculptors 1988); cmmn of a twice life-size torso in bronze for new Rank Xerox HQ Marlow Bucks 1988–89, one-man touring exhbn (26 sculptures) UK and USA 1996–97, cmmnd by Scotland on Sunday in assoc with Glenfiddich to design and produce Spirit of Scotland Awards 1998, cmmnd by P&O Steam Navigation Co to create bronze sculpture for newly-built cruise liner Aurora 2000; invited guest artist Brechin Arts Festival 2006, visiting prof Univ of Texas 1996; work represented in public and private collections worldwide; accorded personal civic reception by City of Dundee 1999; awarded: Dickson Prize for Sculpture 1962, Holo-Krome (Dundee) Sculpture Prize and Cmmn 1962, Scottish Educn Dept Travelling Scholarship 1963, Royal Scottish Acad Chalmers Bursary 1964, Royal Scottish Acad Carnegie Travelling Scholarship 1965, Duncan of Drumfork Scholarship 1965, Post-Grad Scholarship Scottish Educn Dept 1965–66, award winner in sculpture Paris Salon Exhibition 1967, awarded Medailles de Bronze 1968 and d'Argent 1970 Société des Artistes Français (membre associé 1970), Sir William Gillies Bequest Fund Award RSA 1989, Paisley Art Inst Reid Kerr Coll Award for Sculpture 2006; memb: Exec Ctee Fife Branch St John Assoc 1979–, RSA Alexander Nasmyth Fund Ctee 1986–89, RSA Spalding Fund Ctee 1986–89, Cncl Br Sch at Rome 1990–96, Fife Order Ctee Order of St John 1991–, Bd of Dirs Workshop and Artists' Studio Provision Scotland Ltd 1997–2005, Dundee Inst of Architects Architectural Awards Adjudication Panel RIAS 1998–2000, Saltire Soc Arts and Crafts in Architecture Awards Adjudication Panel 2001–05, Bd of Tstees The St Andrews Fund for Scots Heraldry 2001–, (Royal Scot Acad representative) Bd of Tstees for St John's Kirk of Perth 2001–05, Cncl RSA 1999–2001, Sculpture Advsy Panel Montrose Heritage Tst 2005–06, RSA Gen Purposes Ctee 2005–, RSA Kinross Scholarship Ctee 2005–; external assessor J D Fergusson Art Awards Tst 2005–06; elected librarian Royal Scottish Acad 2005; patron Univ of Abertay Dundee Fndn 2006–; Freeman City of London 1989; Hon DArts Univ of Abertay Dundee 2003; hon life memb Perthshire Art Assoc 2005; memb Soc Portrait Sculptors 1966, FRSA 1966, ARBS 1968 (vice-pres 1988–90, Scottish rep on Cncl 1972–92), professional memb SSA 1969 (memb Cncl 1972–75), FSA Scot 1971, FRBS 1975, ARSA 1980, MBIM 1989, Hon FRIAS 1992, RGI 2004, RSA 2005; SBStJ 1979, OStJ 1984, CStJ 1997 (memb Priory Cncl Priory of Scotland 1996–2004); *Publications* Alastair Ross - Sculptures 1960–2000 (2001); *Recreations* heraldry, genealogy, Scottish history; *Clubs* St Johns House, Royal Perth, Puffin's (Edinburgh); *Style*— Dr Alastair Ross; ✉ Ravenscourt, 28 Albany Terrace, Dundee DD3 6HS (tel 01382 224 235)

ROSS, Alexander (Sandy); s of Alexander Coutts Ross (d 1978), and Charlotte Edwards, *née* Robertson (d 1978); *b* 17 April 1948; *Educ* Grangemouth HS, Univ of Edinburgh (LLB), Moray House Coll; *m* Alison Joyce, *née* Fraser; 3 c (Andrew b 1 Sept 1983, Francis b 29 May 1986, Thomas b 13 July 1992); *Career* articled then slr Edinburgh 1970–74, lectr Paisley Coll of Technol 1974–76, prodr Granada Television Manchester 1977–86, controller of arts and entertainment Scottish Television 1986–97, dep chief exec Scottish Television Enterprises 1997–98, controller of regnl prodn Scottish Media Gp 1999–2000, md Scottish Television 2000–04, md Int Devpt Scottish Television 2004–; cncllr: Edinburgh Town Cncl 1971–75, Edinburgh Dist Cncl 1974–78; chm BAFTA Scotland, memb BAFTA, chm Salford Conf on Television from the Nations and Regions; *Recreations* reading, golf, music, watching football; *Clubs* Glen Golf, Haunted Major Golf Soc (N Berwick), Rhodes Golf, Hallion, Prestonfield Golf, Edinburgh Corporation Golf; *Style*— Sandy Ross, Esq; ✉ 7 Murrayfield Avenue, Edinburgh EH12 6AU (tel 0131 539 1192); Scottish Media Group plc, Cowcaddens, Glasgow G2 3PR (tel 0141 300 3000, fax 0141 300 3519, mobile 07803 970107, e-mail sandy.ross@smg.plc.uk)

ROSS, Alistair Charles; s of Alan Alistair Ross, OBE (d 1984), and Marjorie Evelyn, *née* Catch; *b* 29 November 1951; *Educ* Westminster, Charing Cross Hosp Med Sch (MB BS); *m* 19 Nov 1977, Alexandra Jane Elaine, da of Samuel Philippe Alexandre Holland; 2 da (Katherine Alexandra MacKenzie b 1980, Victoria Isobel MacKenzie b 1982), 1 s (James Alistair George MacKenzie b 1984); *Career* surgical registrar The London Hosp 1979–82, sr orthopaedic registrar St Mary's Hosp London 1982–88, conslt orthopaedic surgn Royal United Hosp and Royal Nat Hosp for Rheumatic Diseases Bath 1988–, dir Bath and Wessex Orthopaedic Res Unit 1988–2005; Euro travelling scholar Br Orthopaedic Assoc 1987, hon sr lectr Sch of Postgrad Medicine Univ of Bath 1992–, John Charnley tutor in orthopaedics RCS 1999–2002; assoc ed Jl of Bone and Jt Surgery 2006–; examiner Intercollegiate FRCS 2007–; memb: Int Soc of Limb Salvage (ISOLS), European Spine Soc, Br Orthopaedic Oncology Soc, Br Hip Soc, Br Assoc of Spinal Surgns, Rheumatoid Arthritis Surgical Soc (pres 1994, treas 1995–98, hon sec 1998–99), Educn Ctee Br Orthopaedic Assoc 1995–2002, Bd of Specialist Socs Br Orthopaedic Assoc 1998–2002; Freeman City of London 1977, Liveryman Worshipful Soc of Apothecaries 1993; LRCP, FRCS 1980 (MRCS 1976), FBOA 1988; *Recreations* music; *Clubs* Leander; *Style*— Alistair Ross, Esq; ✉ The Bath Clinic, Claverton Down Road, Bath BA2 7BR (tel 01225 835555, fax 01225 840100)

ROSS, Amanda; *née* Stevens; *b* 4 August 1962, Rochford, Essex; *Educ* Furtherwick Park Sch Canvey Is, SE Essex Sixth Form Coll, Univ of Birmingham (BA); *m* 6 Oct 1990, Simon Ross; *Career* researcher Central TV 1984, lead singer with big band touring Germany 1985, prodr, dir and format creation for ITV cos, BBC and VH1 until 1994, fndr (with husband, Simon) and jt md Cactus TV 1994–, TV prodns incl Richard & Judy (Channel 4) 2001– (estab Richard & Judy Book Club) and Saturday Kitchen (BBC 1); British Book Trade Award for inspiring wider reading 2005, Bookseller Retail Award for expanding the market 2006, nominated 4 RTS awards; tstee Kidscape; memb: BAFTA, RTS; *Publications* Richard & Judy's Wine Guide (2005), Saturday Kitchen Cookbook (2007); *Recreations* renovating house in Italy, my dogs; *Style*— Ms Amanda Ross; ✉ Cactus TV, Cactus Studios, 373 Kennington Road, London SE11 4PS (tel 020 7091 4900, fax 020 7091 4902, e-mail amanda.ross@cactustv.co.uk)

ROSS, Anthony Lee (Tony); s of Eric Turle Lee Ross (d 1982), and Effie, *née* Griffiths (d 1981); *b* 10 August 1938; *Educ* Helsby Co GS, Liverpool Regnl Coll of Art (NND); *m* 1, 16 Sept 1961 (m dis 1971), Carole Dawn, *née* D'Arcy; m 2, 1971 (m dis 1976), Joan Lillian, *née* Allerton; 1 da (Alexandra Ruth b 10 Aug 1971); m 3, 30 June 1979, Zoë, da of Cyril Albert Goodwin, of Cuffley, Herts; 1 da (Katherine Lee b 12 April 1980); *Career* author and illustrator; drawings in magazines incl Punch, Time and Tide, Town 1962–75, sr lectr Manchester Poly 1965–86, first book published 1973; TV films incl: Towser 1983, Little Princess 2006; exhibitions: London, Holland, Germany, Japan, USA, France; patron: Malcolm Sargent Cancer Fund for Children Readathon, Chelsea Children's Hosp Sch, Assoc of Illustrators; *Awards* USA, Holland, Japan, Belgium, E Germany, W Germany; *Books* illustrator for over 700 children's books incl: The Reluctant Vampire (by Eric Morecambe, 1982), Limericks (by Michael Palin, 1985), Fantastic Mr Fox (by Roald Dahl, 1988), The Magic Finger (by Roald Dahl, 1989), Alice Through The Looking Glass (by Lewis Carroll, 1992), Meet Just William Series (by R Crompton, 1999), Susan Laughs (with Jeanne Willis, 1999), Pippi Longstocking (2000), Worzel Gummidge (2000), What did I look like when I was a baby? (with Jeanne Willis, 2000), I want to be a cowgirl (with Jeanne Willis, 2001), Horrid Henry series (by Francesca Simon); author of 90 children's books incl: I'm Coming to Get You (1984), I Want my Potty (1986), A Fairy Tale (1991); *Recreations* travel; *Clubs* Chelsea Arts; *Style*— Tony Ross, Esq; ✉ Andersen Press, 20 Vauxhall Bridge Road, London SW1V 2SA

ROSS, Charlotte Miranda; da of Nigel Ross, of Dunkeld, and Janice, *née* McEwen; *b* 19 October 1969; *Educ* Arran HS, Univ of Glasgow (MA); *Career* journalist; asst ed Sunday Herald 1998–2000, ed S2 2000–01; The Scotsman: asst ed 2001–02, exec ed Features 2002–03; *Style*— Ms Charlotte Ross

ROSS, Lt-Col (Charles) Christopher Gordon; s of Maj Charles Gordon Ross, MC (d 1964), of Moor Park, Herts, and Iris Jefford, *née* Fowler (d 1976); *b* 8 July 1931; *Educ* Marlborough, RMA Sandhurst; *m* 27 April 1963, Fiona Mary Ghislaine Ross, da of Gp Capt Albert Peter Vincent Daly, AFC (d 1985), of Dalysgrove, Co Galway; 1 s (Alastair Charles Gordon b 24 Jan 1964), 1 da (Geraldine Catherine Ghislaine (Mrs Philip Dodds) b 7 April 1965); *Career* cmmnd 14/20 King's Hussars 1951, Lt Col 1974, resigned 1979; 14/20 King's Hussars Regt Assoc: vice-chm 1982–85, chm 1986–91, vice-pres 1991–92; diocesan sec Salisbury Diocese 1979–96, memb Gen Synod Dioceses Cmmn 1991–96, lay canon Salisbury Cathedral 1995–2000 (emeritus 2000–); chm Sarum St Michael Educnl Charity 1993–99 (govr 1989–99); chm Close Landscape Ctee 1998–, chm St Nicholas Hosp Salisbury 1999– (tstee 1997–), chm Salisbury Dio Forces Welfare Tst 1999–2007, chm Mgmnt Ctee Southern Theol Educn & Trg Scheme 1998–2002 (govr 1998–2006), tstee 14/20 King's Hussars Museum 2005–; FCMI (FIMgt 1981); *Books* The Canons of Salisbury (2000); *Recreations* gardening, reading, research; *Clubs* Army and Navy; *Style*— Lt-Col Christopher Ross; ✉ The Old Schoolhouse, Quidhampton, Salisbury, Wiltshire SP2 9AT (tel 01722 743516, fax 01722 742916, e-mail christopher.c.g.ross@googlemail.com)

ROSS, David Craib Hinshaw; s of Douglas Hinshaw Ross (d 1977), of Glasgow, and Jean Mitchell, *née* Blyth (d 1999); *b* 14 January 1948, Glasgow; *Educ* Kelvinside Acad Glasgow, Trinity Coll Glenalmond, Univ of Glasgow (LLB); *m* 5 Jan 1974, Helen Elizabeth, *née* Clark; 2 s (Peter David Hinshaw, Andrew Douglas), 1 da (Frances Elizabeth); *Career* slr; slr Maclay Murray & Spens 1972–75 (apprentice 1970–72); Biggart Baillie (formerly Biggart Baillie & Gifford WS): slr 1975–77, ptnr 1977–, head of corporate 1997–2001, chm and sr ptnr 2001–; chm Scottish Chambers of Commerce, dir Br Chambers of Commerce, memb Scottish Euro Preparations Ctee, dir and memb Exec Ctee Scottish Cncl for Devpt and Industry; hon vice pres Euro-American Lawyers Gp (former chm); author of various articles on energy and corporate governance matters; sec Loganair Ltd; chm A Panel Prince's Scottish Youth Business Tst; memb Ct Univ of Glasgow; NP; memb Law Soc of Scotland 1973; *Recreations* rhododendrons, swimming; *Clubs* Western (Glasgow); *Style*— David Ross, Esq; ✉ Biggart Baillie, Dalmore House, 310 St Vincent Street, Glasgow G2 5QR (tel 0141 228 8000, fax 0141 228 8310, dross@biggartbaillie.co.uk)

ROSS, David Peter John; s of John Malcolm Thomas Ross, of Grimsby, Lincs, and Linda Susan, *née* Thomas; *b* 10 July 1965, Grimsby, Lincs; *Educ* Uppingham, Univ of Nottingham (BA); *Family* 1 s (Carl Cosmo Thomas b 16 Jan 2003); *Career* chartered accountant Arthur Andersen 1988–91; Carphone Warehouse: co-fndr 1991, finance dir 1991–96, chief operating offr 1996–2003, dep chm 2003–; chm: National Express Gp 2001–, Gondola Holdings 2005–06; non-exec dir: Big Yellow Storage plc 2000–, Wembley National Stadium Ltd 2002–, Trinity Mirror plc 2004–, Cosalt plc 2005–; co-fndr Kandahar Tst and Kandahar Gp; tstee Nat Portrait Gallery 2006–; Entrepreneur of the Year 1999; ACA 1991; *Recreations* opera (fndr Nevill Holt Opera Festival); *Clubs* RAC; *Style*— David Ross, Esq; ✉ 61A Cadogan Square, London SW1X 0HZ; The Carphone Warehouse Gp plc, 1 Portal Way, London W3 6RS (tel 020 8896 5000, fax 020 8896 5005, e-mail rossd@cpwplc.com); Kandahar Group, 3rd Floor, Nuffield House, 41–46 Piccadilly, London W1J 0DS (tel 020 7534 1547, fax 020 7534 1560)

ROSS, David Thomas Mcleod; s of David Ross, and Margaret, *née* Mcleod; *b* 3 June 1949; *Educ* Boroughmuir Secdy Sch Edinburgh; *m* 25 Aug 1973 (m dis), Margaret Gordon Sharpe Ross, da of Robert Charters Russell, of Loanhead; 3 da (Lindsay b 1976, Louise b 1978, Heather b 1984); *Career* CA 1976; md Ivory and Sime plc 1988–90 (joined 1968, dir 1982), ptnr Aberforth Partners 1990–; non-exec dir: Aberforth Smaller Companies Trust plc 1990–94, Aberforth Split Level Trust plc 1990–94, US Smaller Companies Investment Trust plc 1991–98; memb: Co of Merchants of the City of Edinburgh, High Constables and Guard of Honour Holyrood House; FCCA; *Recreations* skiing, golfing; *Style*— David Ross, Esq; ✉ 5 Belgrave Crescent, Edinburgh EH4 3AQ (tel 0131 447 332 2232); Aberforth Partners, 14 Melville Street, Edinburgh EH3 7NS (tel 0131 220 0733, fax 0131 220 0735, e-mail david.ross@aberforth.co.uk)

ROSS, Prof Euan Macdonald; s of Dr James Stirling Ross (d 1992), of Welwyn Garden City, Herts, and Frances, *née* Blaze (d 1999); *b* 13 December 1937; *Educ* Aldenham, Univ of Bristol (MD, DCH); *m* 11 June 1966, Dr Jean Mary Palmer, da of George Palmer (d 1984); 2 s (Rev Matthew b 1967, Dr James b 1972); *Career* house physician Bristol Royal Infirmary 1962–63, SHO Aberdeen and Dundee Teaching Hosps 1963–64, registrar in paediatrics Dundee Teaching Hosps 1964–69, lectr in paediatrics Univ of Bristol 1969–74, sr lectr Middx and St Mary's Med Schs Univ of London 1974–84, conslt paediatrician Central Middx Hosp London 1974–84 and Charing Cross Hosp London 1984–89, prof of community paediatrics KCL 1989–2000; co-dir Child Studies Unit KCL; paediatric adviser Mid-Western Health Bd Ireland 2002–04; visiting lectr: Boston Children's Hosp Med Sch, Zamboanga Philippines 2000, Tirana Albania 2001; memb: Ct Univ of Bristol, Br Paediatric Surveillance Unit (fndr memb), Exec Bd Whizz-Kidz charity; tstee and memb Steering Ctee King's Maudsley Inst of Epileptology; examiner Sheffield Hallam Univ; FRCP 1980, FRCPCH 1997, FFPH 1997, Hon FRCPH 2002; *Books* Paediatric Perspectives on Epilepsy (1985), Epilepsy in Young People (1987), Paediatric Epilepsy (1994), Management for Child Health Services (1998), Paediatrics and Child Health (2001); *Recreations* Scottish matters, design, art and photography; *Clubs* Athenaeum, Harvean; *Style*— Prof Euan Ross; ✉ Linklater House, Mount Park Road, Harrow Hill HA1 3JZ (tel and fax 020 8864 4746)

ROSS, Hugh Robert; s of Flt Lt Robert James Ross, RAF (d 1954), and Marion Bertha, *née* Maidment; *b* 21 April 1953; *Educ* Christ's Hosp (RAF Benevolent Fund scholar), Univ of Durham (Kitchener scholar, BA), London Business Sch (NHS scholar, MBA); *m* 7 Aug 1981, Margaret Catherine, da of Joseph Martin Hehir; 1 da (Kate Mairead Hehir b 6 March 1984), 1 s (Robert Joseph Hehir b 10 May 1987); *Career* nat admin trainee Wessex RHA 1976–78, asst sector admin Princess Margaret Hosp Swindon 1978–80, patient servs offr Westminster Hosp London 1981–83 (asst admin 1980–81), dir of operational servs Bart's London 1985–86 (dep unit admin 1983–85); unit gen mangr: City Unit Coventry HA 1986–90, Leicester Gen Hosp 1990–93; chief exec: Leicester Gen Hosp NHS Tst 1993–95, United Bristol Healthcare NHS Tst 1995–2002; prog dir Bristol Health Serv Plan 2002–04, chief exec Cardiff and Vale NHS Tst 2004–; *Recreations* golf, Southampton FC, real ale; *Style*— Hugh Ross, Esq; ✉ Cardiff and Vale NHS Trust, Cardigan House, University Hospital of Wales, Heath Park, Cardiff CF14 4XW (tel 029 2074 2150, fax 029 2074 2968)

ROSS, James Hood; *Educ* Univ of Oxford (BA), Manchester Business Sch (Dip Business Mgmnt); *m*; 3 c; *Career* served RN 1957–59; British Petroleum: joined 1959, worked variously in UK, France and Africa, involved in demerger Shell-Mex BP and creation of BP Oil Ltd, asst gen mangr BP Tanker Co, dep chm Stolt Tankers and Terminals USA, gen mangr corp planning BP Group, chief exec and md BP Oil International 1986–88, pres and chief exec BP America Inc and an md The British Petroleum Co plc 1988–92; chief exec Cable and Wireless plc 1992–95; chm The Littlewoods Organisation 1996–2002, non-exec chm National Grid 1999–2002 (dep chm March-July 1999), non-exec dep chm National Grid Transco plc (following merger) 2002–; non-exec dir: McGraw Hill Inc (USA), DataCard (USA), Groupe Schneider (France), Prudential plc 2004–; vice-chm N W Business Leadership Team, former chm Manchester Business Sch, memb Bd N W Devpt Agency, tsee Cleveland Orch; *Style*— James Ross, Esq

ROSS, Lt-Col Sir (Walter Hugh) Malcolm; GCVO (2005, KCVO 1999, CVO 1994), OBE (1988), JP (2006); s of Col Walter John Macdonald Ross, CB, OBE, MC, TD, JP, DL (d 1982), of Netherhall, Bridge-of-Dee, Castle-Douglas, Kirkcudbrightshire, and Josephine May, *née* Cross (d 1982); *b* 27 October 1943; *Educ* Eton, RMA Sandhurst; *m* 31 Jan 1969, Susan (Susie) Jane, da of Gen Sir Michael Gow, GCB, DL; 2 da (Tabitha b 1970, Flora b 1974), 1 s (Hector b 1983); *Career* Scots Gds 1964–87; mgmnt auditor The Royal Household 1987–89; sec Central Chancery of The Orders of Knighthood 1989–90, Comptroller Lord Chamberlain's Office 1991–2006 (Asst Comptroller 1987–90), Master of the Household to TRH The Prince of Wales and The Duchess of Cornwall 2006–; extra equerry to HM The Queen 1988–; HM Lord-Lt Stewartry of Kirkcudbright 2006– (DL 2003); Brig Queen's Body Guard for Scotland (Royal Co of Archers); Freeman City of London 1994; *Clubs* White's, Pratt's, New (Edinburgh); *Style*— Lt-Col Sir Malcolm Ross, GCVO, OBE, JP

ROSS, Michael David (Mike); CBE (2001); s of Patrick James Forrest Ross, and Janet Emily, *née* Forsyth; *b* 9 July 1946; *Educ* Daniel Stewart's Coll Edinburgh; *m* 18 Oct 1973, Pamela Marquis, *née* Speakman; *Career* Scottish Widows: jt asst actuary 1970–75, asst actuary 1975–81, jt actuary 1981–86, asst gen mangr 1986–88, gen mangr 1988–90, actuary to the Society 1988–92, dep md 1990–91, main bd dir 1990–2003, chief exec 1991–2003; dep gp chief exec Lloyds TSB Group plc 2000–03; chm Assoc of Br Insurers; FFA 1969, CIMgt 1991, FRSA; *Publications* various contribs to Transactions of Faculty of Actuaries; *Recreations* golf, curling, skiing, gardening; *Clubs* Caledonian, Mortonhall Golf; *Style*— Mike Ross, CBE

ROSS, Nicholas David (Nick); s of John Caryl Ross, of Surrey, and Joy Dorothy, MBE, *née* Richmond; paternal gf Pinhas Rosen was signatory to Israel's Declaration of Independence and first Min of Justice; *b* 7 August 1947; *Educ* Wallington Co GS, Queen's Univ Belfast (BA); *m* 1 March 1985, Sarah Patricia Ann, da of Dr Max Caplin, OBE, of London; 3 s (Adam Michael b 1985, Samuel Max b 1987, Jack Felix b 1988); *Career* BBC freelance reporter and presenter N Ireland 1971–72; presenter radio: Newsdesk, The World Tonight 1972–74, World at One 1972–75 and 1984, Call Nick Ross 1986–97, Radio 4 Gulf News FM 1991, The Commission 1998–; prodr and dir documentaries incl The Fix and The Biggest Epidemic of Our Times 1981; presenter TV: fndr presenter BBC Breakfast TV, Sixty Minutes 1983–84, Man Alive, Out of Court, Fair Comment 1975–83, Watchdog, Star Memories, Crimewatch UK 1984–2007, Drugwatch 1985–86, A Week in Politics (Channel 4) 1986–88, various debates (BBC, ITV and BskyB), Crime Limited (BBC) 1993–94, Westminster with Nick Ross 1994–97, BBC TV political party conference coverage 1995, We Shall Overcome 1998 and 1999, So You Think You're a Good Driver 1999–2002, Destination Nightmares 1999–2000, Nick Ross (debates) 1999; chm corp conferences; memb: Govt Ctee on Ethics of Gene Therapy 1990–93, Health of the Nation Working Gp 1991–98, Gene Therapy Advsy Ctee 1993–96, Nat Bd for Crime Prevention 1993–95, Crime Prevention Agency 1995–99, Property Crime Reduction Task Force 1999–2002, Ctee on the Public Understanding of Science, Med Audit Ctee RCP, Nuffield Cncl on Bioethics 1999–2006, NHS Nat Plan Action Team 2000, Medical Ethics Ctee RCP 2004–; chm Science Book Prize 1991 and 2006; memb Advisory Bd: Crime Concern, Victim Support; pres Healthwatch, SANEline, Tacade; ambass WWF; patron: Prisoners Abroad, Missing Persons Helpline, Patients Assoc, Kidney Research Aid Fund, Animal Care Tst, Apex Tst, Br Wireless for the Blind Fund, Jewish Assc for the Mentally Ill, NICHS, Resources for Action, Simon Community of NI, London Accident Prevention Cncl, Myasthenia Gravis Assoc, Tacade, Young At Heart; dir: Health Quality Serv, Crimestoppers, Inst of Advanced Motoring, UK Stem Cell Fndn; chm Jill Dando Inst of Crime Science UCL; Broadcasting Press Guild Radio Broadcaster of the Year 1997, Best Documentary Celtic Film Festival 1999; hon fell UCL; Hon Dr Queen's Univ Belfast; FRSA, FRSM; *Recreations* influencing public policy, good food, scuba diving, skiing; *Style*— Nick Ross, Esq; ✉ PO Box 999, London W2 4XT (e-mail nickross@lineone.net, website www.nickross.com)

ROSS, Peter Angus; *Educ* Glasgow Acad; *m* 16 Aug 1962, Elliot Wallace, da of James Allan Baillie Montgomery (d 1982), of Glasgow; *Career* Nat Serv RA 1955–57; chm: Burnthills Group Ltd and subsids (fndr dir Burnthills (Contractors) Ltd, first memb of the gp 1963), Bowfield Hotel and Country Club Ltd, Goldenbolt International Ltd and assoc cos, LA Bowl (Ayr) Ltd, Ross (Iona) Ltd, Holburn Hi-Fi Ltd, Glasgow Audio Ltd, Hebridean Island Cruises Ltd and subsids, Atlas (Scotland) Ltd; dep chm: Mull & West Highland Narrow Gauge Railway Co Ltd, Hebridean Int Cruises plc; farms as Ladyland Estates and Grangehill Estates; fndr memb and past pres Johnstone Rotary Club 1975; Aims of Industry Award for Scotland 1982; Paul Harris Fellowship (Rotary Award) 1997; FInstD, FSA Scot; *Clubs* Nat Serv RA 1955–57; chm: Burnthills Group Ltd and subsids (fndr dir Burnthills (Contractors) Ltd, first memb of the gp 1963), Bowfield Hotel and Country Club Ltd, Goldenbolt International Ltd and assoc cos, LA Bowl (Ayr) Ltd, Ross (Iona) Ltd, Holburn Hi-Fi Ltd, Glasgow Audio Ltd, Hebridean Island Cruises Ltd and subsids, Atlas (Scotland) Ltd; dep chm: Mull & West Highland Narrow Gauge Railway Co Ltd,

Hebridean Int Cruises plc, Beith Golf Club Ltd; farms as Ladyland Estates and Grangehill Estates; fndr memb and past pres Johnstone Rotary Club 1975; Aims of Industry Award for Scotland 1982; Paul Harris Fellowship (Rotary Award) 1997; FInstD, FSA Scot; *Style—* P A Ross, Esq; ✉ Castlehill, Howwood, Renfrewshire PA9 1LA (tel 01505 704000, fax 01505 703000)

ROSS, (Carl) Philip Hartley; s of John Carl Ross (fndr Ross Foods Ltd); *b* 3 May 1943; *Educ* Shrewsbury; *m* 1, 1968, Pamela Jean, *née* Dixon; 3 da (Rachel b 1969, Kathryn b 1971, Amanda b 1975); m 2, 1985 Joanna Louise, *née* Norton; 2 s (Thomas b 1989, Samuel b 1991); *Career* chartered accountant; Peat Marwick Mitchell & Co 1961–65, Forrester Boyd & Co 1965–68; dir Cosalt Ltd 1971–75, md Orbit Holdings Ltd 1972–75; chm: Bristol & West Cold Stores Ltd 1974–83, Philip Ross & Co Chartered Accountants 1982–, S Cartledge & Son Ltd 1995–; sec: The Grange and Links Hotel Ltd 2004–, Sandilands Golf Club Ltd 2004–; FCA; *Recreations* golf, football; *Style—* Philip Ross, Esq; ✉ Rossa Farm, Rossa Lane, Trusthorpe, Mablethorpe, Lincolnshire LN12 2QH (tel 01507 441811); Philip Ross & Co, 2A Knowle Street, Mablethorpe, Lincolnshire LN12 2QH (tel 01507 472727, fax 01507 479280, e-mail philipross.accountants@virgin.net)

ROSS, Senator Shane Peter Nathaniel; s of John Ross, of Knockmore, Enniskerry, and Ruth Isabel, *née* Cherrington; *b* 11 July 1949, Dublin; *Educ* Rugby, TCD, Univ of Geneva; *m* 20 April 1974, Ruth, *née* Buchanan; 1 s (Hugh), 1 da (Rebecca); *Career* memb Seanad Éireann (Ind) Univ of Dublin panel 1981–; ptnr Dillon & Waldren Stockbrokers 1980 (chair 1980–87), formerly stock exchange corr Irish Times, business ed Sunday Independent 1995–; chm: Kleinwort Benson European Privatisation Tst plc 1994–96, Close FTSE 100 Fund plc 1999–2004, SVM Global Tst plc 2005–; former memb Irish Stock Exchange; *Recreations* tennis, skiing; *Clubs* Kildare St and Univ (Dublin); *Style—* Senator Shane Ross; ✉ Glenbrook, Enniskerry, Co Wicklow, Ireland (tel 00 353 1 211 6692); Seanad Iireann, Leinster House, Dublin 2, Ireland (tel 00 353 1 6183014, fax 00 353 1 6184192, e-mail shane.ross@oireachtas.ie)

ROSS, Stephen Lawrence; s of Julian Ross (d 1988), of London, and Miriam, *née* Gimmack (d 1994); *b* 11 December 1950; *Educ* Woodhouse GS; *m* (m dis); 1 s (Daniel Paul b 20 Feb 1979), 1 da (Nicola Jane b 2 Oct 1981); *Career* CA 1974; audit mangr Deloitte Haskin & Sells (London) 1976, ptnr Keane Shaw & Co (London) 1978, sr ptnr Ross Bennet-Smith (London) 1983; dir: Coliseum plc 2001–05, Sports Café Holdings plc 2005–; tstee Teenage Cancer Tst 1998–; FCA; *Recreations* horse racing, music; *Style—* Stephen L Ross, Esq; ✉ Ross Bennet-Smith Chartered Accountants, 112 Jermyn Street, London SW1Y 6LS (tel 020 7930 6000, fax 020 7930 7070, e-mail stephenr@rossbennetsmith.com, website www.rossbennetsmith.com)

ROSS, Dr Sue; da of Roy Ingram Craddock, of St Monans, Fife, and Eileen, *née* Lee; *b* 4 July 1952; *Educ* Nottingham Bluecoat Sch, Univ of St Andrews, CCC Oxford, Keele Univ (PhD), Univ of Northumbria; *Children* 2 da (Emma b 17 July 1986, Anna b 3 Oct 1991); *Career* dir of social work E Renfrewshire Cncl 1995–2001, chief exec Selby & York PCT 2001–2003, md Sue Ross Consulting Ltd 2004–; *Books* Social Work Management and Practice-Systems Principles (jtly, 1989); *Style—* Dr Sue Ross; ✉ Honeysuckle Cottage, Main Street, Bilbrough, North Yorkshire YO23 3PH (tel 01937 832082, fax 01937 830579, mobile 07985 699824)

ROSS, Tessa; da of Len Ross, of London, and Shannie, *née* Kingsley; *Educ* Westminster, Univ of Oxford (MA); *m* Dec 1987, Mark Scantlebury, s of Lester Scantlebury; 2 s (Joseph b 3 Aug 1989, Louis b 1 Aug 1996), 1 da (Matilda b 8 Feb 1993); *Career* head of devpt Br Screen 1989–93, head ind commissioning Drama BBC 1993–2000, head of drama Channel 4 2000–03, head Film Four 2003–; *Style—* Ms Tessa Ross; ✉ Film Four, 124 Horseferry Road, London SW1P 2TX (020 7306 6455, fax 020 7306 8355, e-mail tross@channel4.co.uk)

ROSS, Thomas Mackenzie; OBE (1999); s of Duncan C Ross, of Muir of Ord, Ross-shire, Scotland, and Elsie, *née* Mackenzie; *b* 4 May 1944; *Educ* Dingwall Acad, Univ of Edinburgh (BSc); *m* Oct 1967, Margaret, da of Robert Dewar; 1 da (Elaine Caroline b 1968), 1 s (Steven Graeme b 1970); *Career* trainee actuary Scottish Life Assurance Co Edinburgh 1966–70, consulting actuary and later vice-pres Charles A Kench & Associates Vancouver Canada 1971–76, ptnr Clay & Partners Consulting Actuaries 1976–93, princ Aon Consulting 1993–2004; chm: Scottish Life Assurance Co 1999–2001, Profile Corporate Communications Ltd 1999–2003, Penta Capital Ptnrs (Holdings) 2000–, Edinburgh UK Tracker Trust 2002–, Pension Policy Inst 2001–; dir Royal London 2001–, pres Faculty of Actuaries 2002–04, Nat Assoc of Pension Funds 1989–99 (chm 1995–97); memb: CBI Pensions Panel 1983–95, Take-Over Panel Code Ctee 2002–, Bd for Actuarial Standards 2006–; chm Children's Liver Disease Fndn 2002–; fell: Faculty of Actuaries 1970, Canadian Inst of Actuaries 1971, Pensions Management Inst 1987; ASA 1971; *Recreations* horse racing, golf, gardening, hill walking; *Clubs* Naval, Racehorse Owners Assoc, Country Gentlemen's Assoc; *Style—* Thomas Ross, Esq, OBE; ✉ Beauchamp Barn, Drayton Beauchamp, Buckinghamshire HP22 5LS (tel 01296 632388, fax 01296 630098, e-mail tom@tomross.co.uk)

ROSS COLLINS, Michael Stewart; s of Leslie Ross Collins (d 1984), and Stella Mabel, *née* Stewart; *b* 21 June 1938; *Educ* Harrow; *m* 1972 (m dis 1976), Janette Mary, *née* Bryan; *Career* Lt 1 Bn Royal Fusiliers; chm Ross Collins Ltd Lloyd's insurance brokers 1969–81, dir Colne Valley Water Co plc 1975–90; Sedgwick Gp plc: chm and dir of various cos within Sedgwick Gp 1981–97, dep chm Sedgwick Group Devpt Ltd 1997–99, managing exec Sedgwick Europe Devpt Gp 1997–, managing exec Marsh European Devpt Gp 1999–2000; non-exec dir: cos within Racal Gp plc 1997–2000, Securicor Gp plc 1997–99, Bacardi Corp 1997–; dep chm Rickmansworth Water Co plc 1988–90 (dir 1976–90), dir Three Valleys Water plc 1990–, dir NGM Restaurants Ltd 1989–98; chm Totteridge branch NSPCC 1982–92; tstee Sir Halley Stewart Tst, tstee Sir Malcolm Stewart Tst (chm 1998); chm Fan Museum Tst 1999–; Freeman City of London 1961, Master Worshipful Co of Fanmakers 1985–86, Liveryman Worshipful Co of Insurers; FInstD; *Recreations* golf, food, wine, travel, gardening, antique furniture, fans; *Clubs* Royal & Ancient, Royal St George's, Hadley Wood Golf, Hatfield House Tennis, Moreton Morrell, City Livery; *Style—* Michael S Ross Collins, Esq; ✉ Wynches, Much Hadham, Hertfordshire SG10 6BA; Marsh Ltd, No 1 The Marsh Centre, London E1 8DX (tel 020 7481 5526, fax 020 7481 5149, telex 882131)

ROSS GOOBEY, Alastair; CBE (2000); s of late George Henry Ross Goobey, and Gladys, *née* Menzies; *b* 6 December 1945; *Educ* Marlborough, Trinity Coll Cambridge (MA); *m* 1969, Sarah Georgina Mary, da of Cedric Ernest Stille; 1 da (Charlotte Elizabeth Jane b 4 March 1978), 1 s (George Alastair b 26 Nov 1980); *Career* grad trainee Investment Dept Kleinwort Benson Ltd 1968–72, investment mangr Hume Holdings Ltd 1972–77, pensions fund investment mangr Courtaulds 1977–81, dir Geoffrey Morley and Partners Ltd 1981–85, chief investment strategist James Capel and Co 1986–93 (special advsr to the Chllr of the Exchequer HM Treasy 1986–87 and 1991–92), chief exec Hermes Pensions Management Ltd 1993–2001; govr The Wellcome Tst 2002–; sr advsr Morgan Stanley Europe 2002–; chm: Private Finance Panel Ltd 1996–97, John Wainwright & Co Ltd 1997–2007, Hermes Focus Asset Mgmnt Ltd 2002–, Invista REIM plc 2006–; dir Argent Group plc 1997–; non-exec dir: Scottish Life Assurance Co 1978–86, Cheltenham & Gloucester Building Society 1989–91 and 1992–97, TR Property Investment Tst plc 1994–2004 (chm 2002–04), GCap Media plc 2005– (previously dep chm GWR Gp plc before merger 2003–05); pres Investment Property Forum 1995–2005, chm Int Corporate Governance Network 2002–05; memb: Goode Ctee on Pensions Law Reform 1992–93, Advsy Ctee on Film Finance 1995–96, Cncl Lloyd's 1997–2003; chm: ROH Benevolent Fund 2001–, ROH Pension Fund 2006–, American Friends of the National Gallery London 2006–; dir Almeida Theatre Ltd 2002–; memb: Bd Royal Opera 1995–97, National Gallery Investment Ctee 1995–, Bd Mgmnt Nat Opera Studio 1998–; govr Royal Acad of Music 2002–; tstee Cancerbackup 1999–; Parly candidate (Cons) W Leicester 1979; Freeman City of London, Hon Freeman Worshipful Co of Tobacco Pipe Makers and Tobacco Blenders 2001, Liveryman Worshipful Co of Gold and Silver Wyre Drawers; FRSA, Hon RICS 1999, Hon FIA 2001, Hon FSI 2003, Hon FRAM 2004; *Books* The Money Moguls (1986), Bricks and Mortals (1992), Kluwer Handbook on Pensions (jt ed); *Recreations* music, clarinet, piano, cricket; *Clubs* MCC, Reform, Bottesford CC; *Style—* Alastair Ross Goobey, Esq, CBE; ✉ e-mail a.ross.goobey@hermes.co.uk

ROSS MARTYN, John Greaves; s of Dr William Ross Martyn (d 1996), of Wilmslow, Cheshire, and Ida Mary Martyn, *née* Greaves (d 1993); *b* 23 January 1944; *Educ* Repton, Univ of Cambridge (MA, LLM); *m* 1, 4 Aug 1973 (m dis 1996), Pauline, da of Ronald Jennings (d 1979), of Morley, W Yorks; 1 da (Elizabeth b 1975), 1 s (Philip b 1978); m 2, 10 Sept 2005, Beryl Maureen, da of Ronald William Cook (d 2004), of Beckenham, Kent; *Career* asst lectr Birmingham Coll of Commerce 1966–68; called to the Bar Middle Temple 1969; in practice at Chancery Bar 1970–, recorder SE Circuit 1993; bencher Lincoln's Inn 1999; memb: Chancery Bar Assoc, Soc of Trust and Estate Practitioners, Assoc of Contentious Tst and Probate Specialists; chartered arbitrator, mediator; *Books* Williams, Mortimer and Sunnucks on Executors, Administrators and Probate, Family Provision: Law and Practice (1985), Theobald on Wills; *Recreations* gardening, skiing, rotary club activities; *Style—* John Ross Martyn, Esq; ✉ Hogarth Chambers, 5 New Square, Lincoln's Inn, London WC2A 3RJ (tel 020 7404 0404, fax 020 7404 0505, e-mail jgrossmartyn@hogarthchambers.com)

ROSS-MUNRO, (William) Colin Gordon; QC (1972); s of late William Ross-Munro and Adela Chirgwin; *b* 12 February 1928; *Educ* Lycée Français de Londres, Harrow, King's Coll Cambridge (BA); *m* 22 Jan 1958, Janice Jill Pedrana, *née* Brown; 1 da (Victoria d 1974); *Career* served Army Educn Corp and Scots Gds 1946–48; called to the Bar Middle Temple 1951 (bencher 1983); *Recreations* tennis, travel; *Clubs* Hurlingham, Queen's; *Style—* Colin Ross-Munro, Esq, QC; ✉ Blackstone Chambers, Blackstone House, Middle Temple, London EC4Y 7BH (tel 020 7583 1770, fax 020 7822 7222)

ROSS RUSSELL, Graham; *b* 3 January 1933; *Educ* Loretto, Trinity Hall Cambridge, Harvard Business Sch; *m* 1963, Jean Margaret, da of late Col K M Symington; 4 c; *Career* Laurence Priest & Co Stockbrokers 1963–88, chm Laurence Priest & Co Ltd 1986–88; chm: EMAP plc 1990–94, Securities Inst 1992–2000, F&C PEP Investment Trust plc (now F&C Capital Income Trust plc) 1993–2005, Foresight Technol 3 VCT plc 1996–2004; dir Barloworld Ltd 2001–03; chm UK Business Incubation 1998–; tstee Nesta 2001–; Stock Exchange: memb 1965–91, memb Cncl 1973–91, dep chm 1984–88; chm and govr Sutton's Hosp Charterhouse 1997; cmmr Public Works Loan Bd 1981–95, dir Securities and Investments Bd 1989–93; hon fell Trinity Hall Cambridge 2000; *Style—* Graham Ross Russell, Esq; ✉ 30 Ladbroke Square, London W11 3NB

ROSSBERG, Sara Jutta Maria; da of Manfred Rossberg, of Darmstadt, Germany, and Josefine, *née* Kamps (d 1978); *b* 14 October 1952; *Educ* Viktoria Sch Darmstadt, Acad of Fine Art Frankfurt/Main, Camberwell Sch of Art and Crafts; *Career* painter (based London since 1976); travelling scholar: German Nat Fndn 1976–77, DAAD 1977–78; portraits incl Anita Roddick (cmmnd by Nat Portrait Gall 1995); *Solo Exhibitions* Acad of Fine Art Frankfurt/ Main 1973, Int Art Fair Basle 1986, Kunstkeller Bern 1987, Treadwell Gall 1987, Thumb Gall London 1988, Don't I Know You? retrospective museum touring show 1989, Rosenberg & Stiebel Inc NY 1990, Louis Newman Galleries LA 1990, Thumb Gall 1991, Stiebel Modern NY 1991, 1993 and 1994, Warrington Mus and Art Gall 1992, Turnpike Gall Leigh 1996, Julian Hartnoll Gall London 1997, Galerie Vielle du Temple Paris 2003, Newhall Cambridge 2005, Albemarle Gallery London 2007; *Group Exhibitions* incl: Summer Show Royal Acad 1978, Chelsea Art Soc 1978, Treadwell Gall 1982, various int art fairs UK and abroad 1982–, Art by Woman Wolverhampton Art Gall 1988, self-portrait touring show 1988, Nat Portrait Gall 1989, 1990 and 1993, John Moores 16 Liverpool 1989, Drawing Show Thumb Gall 1988, 1990 and 1995, European Artists Works on Paper Kunstkeller Bern 1990, Discerning Eye Mall Galleries, Portrait Now Nat Portrait Gall, Singer & Friedlander Watercolour touring exhibition 1995, Art 99 London 1999, Br Artists in Paris Galerie Vieille ou Temple 2000, Artists of the Ideal MOMA Verona Italy 2002, Espace Belleville Paris 2004, Chateauroux: George Sand: A Modern View, What is Realism? (Albemarle Gallery) 2005; *Awards* Crown Award 1978, prizewinner 16th John Moore's Liverpool Exhbn 1989, commendation BP Awards Nat Portrait Gall 1990; *Recreations* music, running; *Style—* Ms Sara Rossberg

ROSSDALE, Fleur Viola; da of John Spencer Rossdale, and Lucie Marcelle Louise, *née* Bourcier; *b* 20 March 1957; *Educ* Francis Holland Sch, Florence Univ (Dip); *m* 1, 1982, Fletcher Robinson (m dis 1996); 2 s (George b 1984, William b 1986); m 2, 2000, Peter Wadley, RIBA; *Career* originator of the British Interior Design Exhibition staging first show-house in UK 1982, subsequent series of purpose built interior design led exhbns at The Chelsea Town Hall during 1980's and 90's, estab The British Interior Design Exhibition at Cambridge Gate Regents Park showing work of 30 leading interior designers 1997; co-fndr The Interior Design House 2002 (now interior design arm of Peter Wadley Architects), estab (with husband) Cheerdawn Ltd 2003; *Books* Classic Meets Contemporary (1998); *Recreations* include walking, writing, painting, tennis, boating and reading; *Clubs* Hurlingham; *Style—* Miss Fleur Rossdale; ✉ The Interior Design House, The Courtyard, Evelyn Road, Chiswick, London W4 5JL (tel 020 8747 8833, fax 020 8747 8872, e-mail fleur@wadleyarchitects.com)

ROSSE, 7 Earl of (I 1806); Sir (William) Brendan Parsons; 10 Bt (I 1677); also Baron Ballybritt and Oxmantown (I 1795), Lord of the Manors of Womersley and Woodhall in England and of Parsonstown, Newtown and Roscomroe in Ireland; s of 6 Earl of Rosse, KBE (d 1979), and Anne, *née* Messel (d 1992); half-bro of 1 Earl of Snowdon, GCVO, *qv*; *b* 21 October 1936; *Educ* Aiglon Coll Switzerland, Grenoble Univ, ChCh Oxford (MA); *m* 1966, Alison, da of Maj John Cooke-Hurle, of Startforth Hall, Barnard Castle; 2 s ((Laurence) Patrick, Lord Oxmantown b 1969, Hon Michael b 1981), 1 da (Lady Alicia b 1971); *Heir* s, Lord Oxmantown; *Career* late 2 Lt Irish Gds; UN official: Ghana, Dahomey, Mid-W Africa, Iran, Bangladesh, Algeria 1963–80; dir: Historic Irish Houses and Gardens Assoc 1980–91, Agency for Personal Services Overseas 1981–89, Birr Scientific and Heritage Fndn 1985–, Lorne House Tst 1993–2001; memb Irish Govt Advsy Cncl on Devpt Co-operation 1983–88, fndr Ireland's Historic Science Centre; LLD (hc) Dublin; Hon FEI; *Style—* The Earl of Rosse; ✉ Birr Castle, Co Offaly, Republic of Ireland (tel 00 353 57 912 0023, fax 00 353 57 912 0425)

ROSSER, Bradley John (Brad); s of Thomas Rosser, and Valerie, *née* Tranter; *b* 21 October 1963, Aust; *Educ* Trinity Coll HS Perth, Univ of Western Australia (BComm, Hackett studentship, Cwlth scholar), Cornell Univ (MBA); *m* 7 Sept 2002, Kate, *née* Bone; 2 da (Grace Josephine b 18 Oct 2003, Madeleine Jade b 2 Nov 2006); *Career* exec asst Bond Corporation Holding Ltd: to Television Chief Exec 1987, to Bd of Dirs 1987–88, to MD 1988–90, to Chm 1991–92; mgmnt consulting McKinsey & Co Inc UK 1992–95 (mangr 1994–95), gp corporate devpt dir Virgin Gp 1995–98 (memb Bd, non-exec dir Virgin cos incl Victory Cooperation, Virgin Clothing, Virgin Vie, Virgin Exec Aviation and Virgin Bride), gp vice-chm Instant Access Gp of Cos 2003–; former vice-chm London Broncos Rugby League Club; *Recreations* tennis, golf, cricket, water sports, travel; *Style—* Brad Rosser, Esq; ✉ Inside Track Seminars Ltd, Surrey House, 34 Eden Street,

Kingston-upon-Thames, Surrey KT1 1ER (tel 020 7565 0982, e-mail bradrosser@insidetrack.eu.com)

ROSSER, Michael John (Mike); s of John Desmond Rosser (d 1992), of Enfield, Middx, and Joan, *née* Oakley (d 2006); *b* 15 November 1943; *Educ* Edmonton Co GS; *m* Jo Haigh; 1 da (Katherine Joan b 31 Aug 1980), 1 s (David John b 18 March 1987), 2 step da (Jessica Daisy b 14 May 1986, Pollyanna Rose b 29 Nov 1988); *Career* media dir Allen Brady & Marsh 1975–77, md J Walter Thompson, JWT Direct and Conquest Media Manchester 1987–91 (media dir J Walter Thompson 1977–86), md FDS Group 1994– (corp devpt and recovery trg conslt 1993–); dir The Network Ltd (Field Marketing) 2001–03; non-exec dir Cougar Industries Ltd Watford, Plant Glazing Services & Nationwide Plant Ltd Barnsley, R J Stokes & Sons Ltd (Paint Manufacturing Div) Sheffield 1996–2000, non-exec chm and dir English Rose Hotels, dir and sales and marketing director ACM Waste Mgmnt plc; FIPA 1988; *Recreations* watching soccer, cricket and squash; golf (playing and watching); *Style*— Mike Rosser, Esq; ✉ The Royds, 326 Wakefield Road, Denby Dale, Huddersfield HD8 8SD (home tel 01484 866731, office 01484 860501, mobile 07836 695613, fax 01484 861424, e-mail fds.group@btclick.com)

ROSSER, Baron (Life Peer UK 2004), of Ickenham in the London Borough of Hillingdon; Richard Andrew Rosser; JP (1978); s of Gordon William Rosser (d 1985), and Kathleen Mary, *née* Moon (d 1985); *b* 5 October 1944; *Educ* St Nicholas GS Northwood, Univ of London (BSc); *m* 17 Nov 1973, Sheena Margaret, da of Iain Denoon; 2 s (Hon Keith Malcolm b 1976, Hon Colin Michael b 1977), 1 da (Hon Rachel Anne b 1980); *Career* Transport Salaried Staffs' Assoc: res offr 1968–76, fin offr 1976–77, sec London Midland Regn 1977–82, asst gen sec 1982–89, gen sec 1989–2004; non-exec dir Nat Offender Mgmnt Bd 2000–, non-exec chm Prison Service Audit Ctee 2003–; cncllr London Borough of Hillingdon 1971–78 (chm Fin Ctee 1974–78), Parly candidate (Lab) Croydon Central Feb 1974, memb Lab Pty Nat Exec Ctee 1988–98 (chm 1997–98, vice-chm 1996–97); memb Gen Cncl TUC 2000–04; chm Uxbridge Bench 1996–2000; CMILT 1968; *Style*— The Lord Rosser; ✉ House of Lords, London SW1A 0PW (tel 020 7219 4589)

ROSSI, Francis Dominic Nicholas Michael; s of Dominic Rossi, of Kent, and Anne, *née* Traynor; *b* 29 May 1949; *Educ* Sedgehill Sch London; *m* 1, 12 June 1967, Jean, *née* Smith; 3 s (Simon b 1967, Nicholas b 1972, Kieran b 1979); 1 da (Bernadette b 1984, with Elizabeth Gernon); m 2, Eileen, da of Michael Quinn; 3 s (Patrick b 1989, Flynn b 1990, Fursey b 1996), 1 da (Keira Tallulah b 1993); *Career* Status Quo (orignally known as Spectres formed 1962): co-fndr 1967, continual world touring 1967–, Gold and Silver discs every year since 1971; played at: launch of Prince's Trust 1983, Live Aid 1985, Knebworth 1990, Prince's Trust and Help a London Child charity performance Royal Albert Hall 1994; solo career launched 1996, Give Myself to Love (debut single), King of the Doghouse (debut album); ltd edn character jugs issued by Royal Doulton 1993; *Awards* Silver Clef award 1981, Ivor Novello award (for outstanding servs to music indust) 1984, World Music award Monaco 1991, BRIT award (for outstanding servs to music) 1991; *Books* Just for the Record (autobiography, 1993), XS All Areas (autobiography, 2004); *Recreations* collecting Koi carp, clay pigeon shooting; *Style*— Francis Rossi, Esq; ✉ c/o Duroc Media Ltd, Riverside House, 10–12 Victoria Road, Uxbridge, Middlesex UB8 2TW (tel 01895 810831, fax 01895 231499)

ROSSI, Mario; s of Carlo Rossi, of Glasgow, and Vitoria, *née* Bertoncini; *b* 11 February 1958; *Educ* Glasgow Sch of Art (BA) Royal Coll of Art (MA); *Partner* Lindsay Alker; 2 da (Vita Rossi, Stella); *Career* artist; lectr Goldsmiths Coll London 1985–90, currently sr lectr in painting Central St Martin's Sch of Art; work in the collections of: Arts Cncl Collection England, BBC Scotland, Contemporary Arts Soc, V&A, Gallery of Modern Art Edinburgh, Cleveland Art Gallery Middlesbrough, Unilever, Nordstern Cologne, British Council, Glaxo-Wellcome, EMI Worldwide, Tetrapak, DTI; Gulbenkian Rome scholar Br Sch at Rome 1982–83, fellowship in creative arts Trinity Coll Cambridge 1987–89, Coopers & Lybrand under 35 award Whitechapel Open 1988, Fulbright fell in visual art 1993–94, Artist Professional Devpt Scheme 1998–2000; *Solo Exhibitions* incl: The Archaeologist (Demarco Gallery, City Arts Centre) 1984, Interim Art 1985, Cleveland Gallery Middlesbrough 1987, Atelier 1 Hamburg 1987, Anderson O'Day Gallery London 1988, 1990 and 1993, Ozones (Wren Library, Trinity Coll Cambridge) 1989, Spacex Gallery Exeter 1990, Peter Scott Gallery Lancaster Univ 1991, Oldham Gallery 1991, Angel Row Gallery Nottingham 1991, Anderson O'Day Gallery Economist Bldg St James's 1992, Northern Arts Sunderland 1995, De La Warr Pavilion E Sussex 1999 and 2000, Cornerhouse Manchester 2000, AKA London, Metropole Galleries Folkestone; *Group Exhibitions* incl: Cross Currents (Third Eye Centre Glasgow) 1979, Scottish Young Contemporaries (Travelling Exhibition) 1981, Expressive Images (New 57 Gallery Edinburgh) 1982, 12 Artisti Britannici A Roma (Palazzo Barberini Rome) 1983, Five Painter (Riverside Studios) 1985, New Image Glasgow (Third Eye Centre Glasgow) 1985, New Art-New World (Sothebys London and NY) 1986, Contemporary British Woodcuts (Worcester Museum) 1986, The Vigorous Imagination-New Scottish Art (Scottish Nat Gallery of Modern Art Edinburgh and touring) 1987, Glasgow Garden Festival 1988, Fire and Metal (Goldsmiths' Gallery) 1988, Whitechapel Open (Whitechapel Gallery) 1988, John Moores 16 (Walker Art Gallery Liverpool) 1989, Scottish Art Since 1900 (Scottish Nat Gallery of Modern Art Edinburgh and The Barbican) 1989–90, Real Life Stories - The Cleveland Collection (Spacex Gallery Exeter) 1990, Post Morality (Kettle's Yard Cambridge) 1990, Post-Modern Prints (V&A) 1991, John Moores 17 (Walker Art Gallery Liverpool) 1991, Cleveland Drawing Bienale Middlesbrough 1991, Cross Over (Anderson O'Day Gallery) 1992, The Return of the Cadaure Equis (Drawing Centre NY) 1993, A Cloud Burst of Material Possessions (Towner Art Gallery Eastbourne, Worcester City Art Gallery, Purdy Hicks Gallery London, Mead Gallery Coventry) 1997, The Word (Addison Wesley Longman Harlow) 1997, Times of Our Lives (Whitworth Gallery Manchester) 2000, Shot on the Coast (film festival, St Mary in the Castle, Hastings) 2000, Host (Hastings Museum and Art Gallery) 2001, The Most Dangerous Game (Rhodes and Mann Gall London) 2002, Sanctuary (Gallery of Modern Art Glasgow) 2003, Smog (London Sch of Hygiene and Tropical Med) 2003, Strangers to Ourselves (South East of England) 2004, Something Strange (Fine Art Museum, Torino, Finland) 2004; *Publications* The End (2000), Cinematic Decay and Architectural Dissolution (2000), Monsters, Ghettos and the Neo-Baroque (2000); *Clubs* Chelsea Arts; *Style*— Mario Rossi, Esq; ✉ Seaside, Cliff End, Pett Level, East Sussex TN35 4EE (tel and fax 01424 813291)

ROSSITER, Mark Francis; Mark Edward Rossiter, of Warrington, and Kathleen, *née* Concannon; *b* 19 June 1962; *Educ* Boteler GS Warrington; *m* Elizabeth, *née* Farrow; *Career* journalist; Altrincham & Sale Guardian 1988–90, ed Warrington Guardian 1992–95, gp ed Guardian Series Newspapers 1995–96, ed dir Newsquest (Cheshire) Ltd 1996–97, ed-in-chief Bolton Evening News, Bury Times Gp & Leigh Jl, currently ed-in-chief N Wales Newspapers; *Awards* winner North West Young Journalist of the Year Br Guild of Editors 1985, winner Journalist of the Year Br Press Awards 1993; memb Soc of Editors; chm Fundraising Ctee Marie Curie Cancer Care (Bolton/Bury area); *Style*— Mark Rossiter, Esq; ✉ North Wales Newspapers, Mold Business Park, Wrexham Road, Mold, North Wales (tel 01352 707721)

ROSSLYN, 7 Earl of (UK 1801); Sir Peter St Clair-Erskine; 10 Bt (S 1666); also Baron Loughborough (GB 1780); s of 6 Earl of Rosslyn (d 1977), and Comtesse Athenaïs de Rochechouart-Mortemart; *b* 31 March 1958; *Educ* Eton, Univ of Bristol, Univ of Cambridge; *m* 1982, Helen M, eld da of C R Watters, of Sussex; 2 s (Jamie William, Lord Loughborough b 28 May 1986, Hon Harry b 9 May 1995), 2 da (Lady Alice b 14 June 1988, Lady Lucia b 1993); *Heir* s, Lord Loughborough; *Career* Metropolitan Police 1980–94, Thames Valley Police 1994–2000, cdr Metropolitan Police 2000–; tstee Dunimarle Museum; *Clubs* White's; *Style*— The Rt Hon the Earl of Rosslyn

ROSSMORE, 7 Baron (I 1796 & UK 1838); William Warner Westenra; s of 6 Baron Rossmore (d 1958); *b* 14 February 1931; *Educ* Eton, Trinity Coll Cambridge; *m* 1982, Valerie Marion, da of Brian Tobin, of Riverstown, Birr, Ireland; 1 s, 1 step da; *Heir* s, Hon Benedict Westenra; *Career* 2 Lt Somerset LI; co-fndr Coolemine Therapeutic Community Dublin; *Recreations* drawing and painting; *Clubs* Kildare St & Univ (Dublin); *Style*— The Rt Hon Lord Rossmore

ROSSOR, Prof Martin Neil; s of Harry Bruce Rossor, of Thorpeness, Suffolk, and Eileen, *née* Curry; *b* 24 April 1950; *Educ* Watford GS, Jesus Coll Cambridge (MA, MD, Ralph Horton-Smith Prize), KCH Med Sch London (MB BChir); *m* 5 July 1973, Eve Beatrix, da of Prof Kurt Lipstein, of Cambridge; 2 s (Alexander b 28 Aug 1979, Thomas b 20 July 1981), 1 da (Charlotte b 31 July 1984); *Career* house offr in gen med KCH and house offr in gen surgery The Brook Hosp London 1974–75, SHO in gen med Bart's 1975–76, SHO in thoracic med The Brompton Hosp 1976–77, SHO in neurology Nat Hosp for Nervous Diseases London 1977–78, registrar in clinical pharmacology and gen med Royal Postgrad Med Sch and Hammersmith Hosp London 1978, clinical scientist MRC Neurochemical Pharmacology Unit and hon registrar in neurology Addenbrooke's Hosp Cambridge 1979–82, sr registrar in neurology Nat Hosp for Neurology and Neurosurgery London 1983–86 (registrar in neurology 1982–83), conslt neurologist to The Nat Hosps for Neurology and Neurosurgery, St Mary's Hosp and the Western Ophthalmic Hosp London 1986–, sr lectr Inst of Neurology London 1992–98, clinical dir for neurology Nat Hosp for Neurology and Neurosurgery 1993–98 (prof of clinical neurology 1998–), prof of clinical neurology Imperial Coll London 2000–; dir UK Clinical Research Network for Dementia and Neurodegenerative Diseases (DeNDRoN); memb Med Advsy Panel Alzheimer Disease Soc 1986–2000; ed Jl of Neurology, Neurosurgery and Psychiatry, Euro ed Alzheimer's Disease and Associated Orders 1992–2001, memb Editorial Bd Euro Jl of Neurology 1994–97; memb: Assoc of Br Neurologists (memb Cncl 1993–96), RCPsych (affiliate), RSM, World Fedn of Neurology Dementia (memb Exec Ctee), Dementia Panel Euro Fedn of Neurological Socs (chm 1994–2000); patron Dementia Relief Tst; vice-pres Alzheimer Soc 2001–; Freeman City of London, Liveryman Worshipful Soc of Apothecaries (memb Ct of Assts 1999–); FRCP 1990, FMedSci 2002; *Books* Unusual Dementias (ed, 1992), The Dementias (ed with Prof Growdon, 1998); also author of numerous book chapters and original papers on Alzheimer's disease and related dementias; *Recreations* English literature, sailing, equestrian sports; *Clubs* Athenaeum; *Style*— Prof Martin Rossor; ✉ National Hospital for Neurology and Neurosurgery, Queen Square, London WC1N 3BG (tel 020 7829 8773, fax 020 7209 0182, e-mail m.rossor@dementia.ion.ucl.ac.uk)

ROSTRON, Chad Kenneth; s of Kenneth William Briggs Rostron, and Rosemary, *née* Arkwright; *b* 6 May 1951; *Educ* Sherborne, Univ of Newcastle upon Tyne (MB BS); *Career* conslt ophthalmologist St George's Hosp 1988, hon sr lectr Univ of London 1988; author of pubns on corneal and kerato-refractive surgery; DO 1979; memb RSM; FRCS 1983, FRCOphth 1989; *Style*— Chad Rostron, Esq; ✉ 10 Harley Street, London W1G 9PF (tel 020 7483 4921, fax 020 7467 8312, e-mail rostron@sgul.ac.uk, website www.chadrostron.co.uk)

ROSTRON, Timothy Peter (Tim); s of Frank Rostron, of Newbury, Berks, and Mildred Joan, *née* Scull; *b* 1 October 1955; *Educ* St Bartholomew's GS Newbury, Winchester Sch of Art (BA); *m* 1987 (m dis), Elizabeth, da of Philip Arnold Draper; *Career* freelance textile designer 1978–79, counterhand ice cream parlour Harrods 1979–80, trainee Doctor newspaper 1980–83, chief sub ed She Magazine 1983–86, features ed Elle Magazine 1987–88; Daily Telegraph: contrib 1986–, asst arts ed 1988–90, ed Weekend section 1990–93, dep arts ed 1993–98; arts ed National Post Canada 1998–; *Recreations* the gym; *Style*— Tim Rostron, Esq; ✉ National Post, 300–1450 Don Mills Road, Ontario M3B 3R5, Canada (tel (416) 383 2393, fax (416) 383 2305)

ROSWALD, Ann-Louise; da of Björn Thomas Roswald, of Scarborough, N Yorks, and Judith Elizabeth Holt, *née* Gullen; *b* 26 May 1974; *Educ* Pindar Sch Scarborough, Scarborough Sixth Form Coll, York Coll of Further and Higher Educn, Central St Martins (BA, Grad Fashion Week Award 1997); *m* 19 June 1999, Nicholas Gerard Hartley, s of Keith Hartley; 1 s (Harry Fitz b 1 July 2007); *Career* fashion designer; dir and head designer Ann-Louise Roswald; exhibited London Fashion Week; catwalk shows: NY 2000, Korea 2001, Hong Kong 2002, Singapore 2003; featured in pubns incl: Vogue, Elle Decoration, Harpers & Queen; Marks and Spencer New Generation Award 1998 and 1999; Ann Louise Roswald Bridal Wear launched 2007; design collaborations incl: Love Rosa (with high street retailer Oasis) 2004–, Lou Lou and Law (with Natasha Law) 2006–, Ann Louise Roswald for Evans Swimwear and Resort collection, Lavender Tst Charity T-shirt design donation; supporter of numerous charities incl Gilda's Club and Breast Cancer Research; memb ctee My Favouritr Dress Ball; *Recreations* photography, painting, walking, cycling, skiing, fishing, theatre and cinema; *Style*— Ms Ann-Louise Roswald; ✉ The Toy Factory, 11–13 Corsham Street, London N1 6DP (e-mail info@annlouiseroswald.com)

ROTH, Andrew; s of Emil Roth (d 1963), and Bertha, *née* Rosenberg (d 1984); *b* 23 April 1919; *Educ* De Witt Clinton HS NY, Coll of City of New York (BSS), Columbia Univ (MA), Michigan Univ, Harvard Univ; *m* 1, 2 Nov 1941 (m dis 1949), Renee Louise, da of Otto Knitel (d 1962), of NY; m 2, 30 June 1949 (m dis 1984), Mathilda Anna, *née* Friederich; 1 s (Bradley Neil Adrian b 1950), 1 da (Susan Teresa (Terry) b 1953); m 3, 13 Nov 2004, Antoinette Putnam; *Career* USNR Intelligence 1941–45; sr Lt 1945; reader History Dept City Coll NY 1939–40, high school history teacher 1940–41; journalist, foreign corr, author 1945–; memb NUJ; Hon Dr Open Univ 1992; *Books* Japan Strikes South (1941), French Interests and Policies in the Far East (1942), Dilemma in Japan (1945), The Business Background of MPs (1959–70), MP's Chart (1967–87), Enoch Powell Tory Tribune (1970), Can Parliament Decide? (1971), Heath and the Heathmen (1972), Lord on the Board (1972), The Prime Ministers Vol II (1975), Sir Harold Wilson, Yorkshire Walter Mitty (1977), Parliamentary Profiles (1984–85, 1988, 6 edn 2001), New MP's of 1997 (1997), New MP's of 2001 (2001), New MP's of 2005 (2005); *Recreations* sketching, toin chasing; *Style*— Andrew Roth, Esq; ✉ 34 Somali Road, London NW2 3RL (tel 020 7435 6673); 25 rue des Sabotiers, Lanrivain, Côte d'Armour, France

ROTH, Prof Klaus Friedrich; s of Franz Roth (d 1937), and Mathilde Roth; *b* 29 October 1925; *Educ* St Paul's, Peterhouse Cambridge (BA), UCL (MSc, PhD); *m* 29 July 1955, Melek (d 2002), da of Mahmoud Khairy Pasha (d 1954), of Sultana Melek Palace, Heliopolis, Cairo, Egypt; *Career* past master Gordonstoun 1945–46, memb Dept of Mathematics UCL 1948–66, prof Univ of London 1961–88 (emeritus prof 1989), prof of pure mathematics Imperial Coll London 1966–88 (visiting prof 1988–96), hon research fell Dept of Mathematics UCL 1996–; visiting prof MIT 1965–66 (visiting lectr 1956–57); Fields medal Int Mathematical Union 1958, De Morgan medal London Math Soc 1983, Sylvester medal Royal Soc 1991; memb: London Math Soc 1951, American Math Soc 1956; hon memb American Acad of Arts and Sciences 1966; fell: UCL 1979, Imperial Coll London 1999; hon fell Peterhouse Cambridge 1989; FRS 1960, Hon FRSE 1993; *Books* Sequences (with H Halberstam, 2 edn 1983); *Recreations* chess, cinema, ballroom dancing; *Style*— Prof Klaus Roth, FRS; ✉ Colbost, 16A Drummond Road, Inverness IV2 4NB (tel 01463 712595)

ROTH, Martin Joseph; s of David Roth (d 1958), and Lily Margaret, *née* Watts-Platt (d 1972); *b* 11 May 1924; *Educ* St Paul's, Peter Symonds Winchester, New Coll Oxford (MA); *m* 1951, Jean Patricia, da of Harold Ravenhill Hart; 1 da (Elisabeth Jane b 1952), 2 s

(Jeremy David b 1955, Peter John b 1956); *Career* served WWII Queen's Royal Regt (UK) and The Buffs (FE) 1943–46 (scriptwriter Radio SEAC Ceylon 1945–46); called to the Bar Lincoln's Inn 1949, in practice Chancery Bar 1950–87, conveyancing counsel to the Court 1980–87, head chambers 7 New Square 1980–87, bencher Lincoln's Inn 1981, Master of Moots Lincoln's Inn 1984–92, counsel to Crown Estates Cmmrs in common land cases 1985–87; Commons cmmr 1987–92, chief Commons cmmr 1993–96; keeper and chm of tstees The Cranston Library, tstee The Holmesdale Museum, tstee Reigate Priory Museum; chm (S Surrey Area) Oxford Univ Soc; memb Inst of Conveyancers 1971 (supernumary 1987); *Recreations* travel, antiquities, numismatics, literature, gardening; *Style—* Martin Roth, Esq; ✉ Fairhall, Colley Lane, Reigate, Surrey RH2 9JA (tel 01737 244734)

ROTH, Peter Marcel; QC (1997); s of Dr Stephen J Roth (d 1995), and Eva Marta, *née* Gondos; *b* 19 December 1952; *Educ* St Paul's (head boy), New Coll Oxford (open scholar, MA), Univ of Pennsylvania Law Sch (Thouron fell, LLM); *Career* called to the Bar Middle Temple 1977 (Harmsworth scholar); recorder 2000; visiting assoc prof Univ of Pennsylvania Law Sch 1987, visiting prof KCL 2003–; vice-pres Pennsylvania Law European Soc 1995–2003; chair: Insurance Working Party, Competition Law Assoc 2003–; tstee Br Inst of Int and Comparative Law 2006–; chair Terrence Higgins Tst 1989–94; *Publications* Bellamy & Child's European Community Law of Competition (jt ed, 2007); numerous articles in legal pubns; *Recreations* travel, music; *Style—* P M Roth, Esq, QC; ✉ Monckton Chambers, 1 & 2 Raymond Buildings, Gray's Inn, London WC1R 5NR (tel 020 7405 7211, fax 020 7405 2084, e-mail proth@monckton.com)

ROTH, Tim Simon; s of Ernie Roth (*né* Smith), and Ann Roth; *b* 14 May 1961, London; *Educ* Dick Shepherd Comp Sch Tulse Hill, Strand Comp Sch Brixton, Camberwell Sch of Art; *Family* 1 s (Jack b 1985) with Lori Baker; m 1993, Nikki Butler; 2 s (Timothy Hunter b 1995, Michael Cormac b 1996); *Career* actor; *Television* incl: Meantime 1981, Made in Britain 1982, Metamorphosis 1987, Common Pursuit 1992, Murder in the Heartland 1993, Heart of Darkness 1994; *Film* incl: The Hit 1984 (BAFTA nomination, Evening Standard Best Newcomer), To Kill a Priest 1988, The Cook, The Thief, His Wife and Her Lover 1989, Vincent and Theo 1990, Rosencrantz and Guildenstern are Dead 1990, Reservoir Dogs 1992, The Perfect Husband 1993, Little Odessa 1994, Captives 1994, Pulp Fiction 1994, Four Rooms 1994, Rob Roy 1995 (Oscar nomination, BAFTA winner, Golden Globe nomination), Everyone Says I Love You 1996, Mocking the Cosmos 1996, Liar 1997, Animals 1997, No Way Home 1997, Gridlock'd 1997, Hoodlum 1997, The Legend of 1900 1998, The War Zone (dir) 1999, Vatel 2000, Lucky Numbers 2000, Invincible 2001, Planet of the Apes 2001, The Musketeer 2001, To Kill a King 2003, Silver City 2004, Nouvelle-France 2004, Don't Come Knocking 2005, Dark Water 2005, Funny Games 2007, Youth Without Youth 2007; *Style—* Tim Roth, Esq; ✉ c/o Markham & Froggatt Ltd, 4 Windmill Street, London W1T 2HZ (tel 020 7636 4412, fax 020 7637 5233)

ROTHENBERG, Robert Michael (Bob); MBE (2007); s of Helmut Rothenberg, OBE (d 2003), and Anna Amalia, *née* Hannes (d 1991); *b* 10 August 1950; *Educ* Highgate Sch, Univ of Exeter (BA); *m* 10 July 1981, Philippa Jane, da of Stephen Fraser White, of Great Doddington, Northants; 2 da (Katie b 1982, Joanna b 1987), 1 s (Simon b 1983); *Career* chartered accountant 1975–; ptnr Blick Rothenberg Chartered Accountants 1979– (sr ptnr 1997–), dir Gatton Consulting Group Ltd 1987–92, lectr to professional audiences on taxation and co law 1981–; dir Think London 1997–; tstee Prince's Fndn for the Built Environment 2004–; govr Highgate Sch 1998–; hon treas Camden CAB 1982–87; FCA, CTA, MAE; *Books* Mastering Business Information Technology (1989), Understanding Company Accounts (4 edn, 1995); *Recreations* travel, skiing, opera, theatre; *Clubs* Garrick, MCC; *Style—* Bob Rothenberg, Esq, MBE; ✉ 74 Hillway, Highgate, London N6 6DP (tel 020 8348 7771, fax 020 7916 2322, e-mail bob@rothenberg.co.uk); Blick Rothenberg, 12 York Gate, London NW1 4QS (tel 020 7486 0111, e-mail bob.rothenberg@blickrothenberg.com)

ROTHERHAM, Miles Edward; s of Leonard Rotherham, CBE, of Horningsham, Wilts, and Nora Mary, *née* Thompson (d 1991); *b* 23 November 1941; *Educ* Dulwich Coll, Christ's Coll Cambridge (BA, MA); *m* 8 April 1972, Anne Jennifer, da of Maj Alan Holier James, TD, DL (d 1983), of Northlands, Winterton, South Humberside; 1 s (James b 1976), 1 da (Joanna b 1978); *Career* tech offr Inco 1964–68, sales mangr Int Nickel 1968–78; dir: Amari World Metals 1978–, Br Petroleum Metals Marketing 1979–89, Olympic Dam Marketing 1989–93; chm Miles Metals Ltd 1993–; friend of Battersea Park; Freeman City London 1978, Liveryman Worshipful Co of Goldsmiths 1981; CEng 1979, FIM 1979; *Recreations* antique collecting, boules; *Clubs* Athenaeum; *Style—* Miles Rotherham, Esq; ✉ 13 Soudan Road, London SW11 4HH

ROTHERMERE, 4 Viscount (UK 1919) Jonathan Harold Esmond Vere Harmsworth; 4 Bt (UK 1910); also Baron Rothermere (UK 1914); patron of three livings; s of 3 Viscount Rothermere (d 1998), and his 1 wife, Patricia Evelyn Beverley, *née* Matthews (d 1992); *b* 3 December 1967; *m* 15 July 1993, Claudia C, da of T J and Patricia Clemence, of London; 1 s (Hon Vere Richard Jonathan Harold Harmsworth b 20 Oct 1994), 3 da (Hon Eleanor Patricia Margaret Harmsworth b 17 Oct 1996, Hon Theodora Mairi Ferne Harmsworth b 9 July 2001, Hon Iris Geraldine Lilian Harmsworth b 6 Jan 2004); *Career* md: Courier Printing and Publishing until 1997, Evening Standard 1997–98; chm Daily Mail and General Tst plc 1998–; *Style—* The Rt Hon the Viscount Rothermere; ✉ Daily Mail and General Trust plc, Northcliffe House, 2 Derry Street, London W8 5TT (tel 020 7938 6613, fax 020 7937 0043, e-mail chairman@chairman.dmgt.co.uk)

ROTHEROE, Dominic Peter Alford (Dom); s of John William Rotheroe, of Gubblecote, Herts, and Jacqueline Patricia *née* Fearn; *b* 24 April 1964; *Educ* Aylesbury GS, Harrow Coll of HE (BA); *m* 1, 1983 (m dis 1987), Nataša, *née* Lušetić; m 2, 1994 (m dis 1996), Maja *née* Bogojević; *Career* writer and film dir; *Documentaries* dir and ed A Sarajevo Diary 1993 (nomination BAFTA Flaherty Award, special commendation Prix Europa), cameraman and ed Shadows on the Street 1996, cameraman and shoot dir Blockade 1996, dir and cameraman We Can Rebuild You 2000, writer, dir and cameraman The Coconut Revolution 2000 (Grand Prize FICA Film Festival Brazil 2001, Richard Keefe Meml Award Br Environmental Media Awards 2001, Silver Kite and Grand Prix Mar Del Plata Film Festival Argentina 2001), dir various documentaries Al Jazeera Int 2006–07; *Films* writer and dir My Brother Tom 2001 (Golden Rose Sochi Int Film Festival 2001, Best Debut St Petersburg Film Festival 2001, Herald Angel Award Edinburgh Film Festival 2001, Studio Bruxelles Award Flanders Film Festival 2001, Prix du Public Angers Premiersplans Film Festival France 2002, Artistic Contrib and Youth Jury Award Verona Film Festival 2002, Jury Prize Chatenay-Malabry Festival 2002), writer and dir Exhibit A 2006; *Publications* London Inn Signs (author and photographer, 1987); author of articles in various publications; *Recreations* films, music, literature, travel; *Style—* Dom Rotheroe, Esq

ROTHERWICK, 3 Baron (UK 1939); Sir (Herbert) Robin Cayzer; 3 Bt (UK 1924); eld s of 2 Baron Rotherwick (d 1996), and Sarah Jane, *née* Slade (d 1978); *b* 12 March 1954; *Educ* Harrow, RMAS, RAC Cirencester; *m* 1, 1982 (m dis 1994), Sara Jane M, o da of Robert James McAlpine, of Tilstone Fearnall, Cheshire, and late Mrs J McAlpine; 1 da (Hon Harriette Jane b 1986), 2 s (Hon Herbert Robin b 1989, Hon Henry Alexander b 1991); m 2, 2000, Tania Jane, o da of Christopher Fox and Jenny Atkinson; 1 s (Hon August Inigo b 2000, Hon Tommy Christopher b and d 2003), 1 da (Hon Clementine Eleanor b 2006); *Heir* s, Hon Herbert Cayzer; *Career* late The Life Guards; elected memb House of Lords 1999–, oppn spokesperson and whip 2001–05; memb Cncl of Europe 2000–01; dir: Cayzer Continuation PCC Ltd, Air Touring Ltd, Cornbury Estates Co Ltd; pres Gen Aviation Awareness Cncl (GAAC), memb Exec Ctee Popular Flying Assoc (vice-chm 1999–2001); *Recreations* aviation, sub-aqua, conservation; *Clubs* White's; *Style—* The Lord Rotherwick; ✉ Cornbury Park, Charlbury, Oxfordshire OX7 3EH (e-mail rr@cpark.co.uk)

ROTHMAN, Prof Martin Terry; s of Harry Rothman (d 1971), of London, and June, *née* Simmons; *b* 25 May 1948; *Educ* Streatham GS, Strand GS, Univ of Manchester (MB ChB); *m* 13 Sept 1976, Florence, da of Albert Knox, of Warrington, Lancs; 1 s (Alexander Matthew b 31 Oct 1979), 1 da (Emma Rachel b 26 March 1981); *Career* travelling scholar of the MRC 1980–82, Fogarty int fell 1980–82; travelling fellowship: US Nat Inst of Health 1980–82, Faculty in Dept of Cardiology Stanford Univ 1980–82; former conslt cardiologist Royal Brompton Nat Heart and Lung Hosp, conslt cardiologist Royal Hosps NHS Tst (London Chest Hosp) 1982–, interventional cardiologist 1982–; former dir: Intravascular Res Ltd, Circulation Res Ltd; dir Cardiac Res and Devpt: London Chest Hosp, Bart's and the London NHS Tst; dir: Datacam Ltd, Site Specific Therapy Ltd, Lombard Medical Ltd; author of numerous articles and chapters; co-inventor of an intravascular ultrasound device; memb Br Cardiac Soc, former pres Br Cardiovascular Intervention Soc; FRCP 1991; *Recreations* sailing, scuba diving, walking; *Style—* Prof Martin T Rothman; ✉ London Chest Hospital, Bonner Road, London E2 9JQ (tel 020 8983 2216, fax 020 8983 2381, e-mail martin.rothman@bartsandthelondon.nhs.uk)

ROTHSCHILD, Hon Emma Georgina; CMG (2000); da of 3 Baron Rothschild, GBE, GM, FRS (d 1990), and his 2 w, Teresa Georgina, MBE, JP, *née* Mayor; *b* 16 May 1948; *Educ* Somerville Coll Oxford (MA), MIT; *m* 1991, Prof Amartya Kumar Sen; *Career* MIT: assoc prof of humanities 1978–80, assoc prof of science technol and society 1979–88; directeur de recherche invité École des Hautes Études en Sciences Sociales Paris 1981–82, sr res fell King's Coll Cambridge 1988–96, dir Centre for History and Economics and fell King's Coll Cambridge 1996–; memb OECD Gp of Experts on Science and Technology in the New Socio-Economic Context 1976–80, OECD sci examiner Australia 1984–85; chm: UN Res Inst for Social Devpt 1999–, Rothschild Archive Tst 1999–, Kennedy Memorial Tst 2000–; memb: Governing Bd Stockholm Int Peace Res Inst 1983–93, Bd Olof Palme Meml Fund Stockholm 1986–, Royal Cmmn on Environmental Pollution 1986–93, Bd British Council 1993–, Bd UN Fndn 1998–, Cncl for Sci and Technol 1998–2001; *Books* Paradise Lost: the Decline of the Auto-Industrial Age (1973), Economic Sentiments (2001); author of articles in jls; *Style—* The Hon Emma Rothschild, CMG; ✉ King's College, Cambridge CB2 1ST

ROTHSCHILD, 4 Baron (UK 1885) Nathaniel Charles Jacob Rothschild; 5 Bt (UK 1847), OM (2002), GBE (1998); s of 3 Baron Rothschild, GBE, GM, FRS (d 1990), and his 1 w, Barbara, o da of late St John Hutchinson, KC; *b* 29 April 1936; *Educ* Eton, ChCh Oxford (BA); *m* 1961, Serena Mary, da of Sir Philip Dunn, 2 Bt, and Lady Mary St Clair-Erskine, da of 5 Earl of Rosslyn; 3 da (Hon Hannah Mary b 1962, Hon Beth Matilda b 1964, Hon Emily Magda b 1967), 1 s (Hon Nathaniel Philip Victor James b 1971); *Heir* s, Hon Nathaniel Rothschild; *Career* chm: Five Arrows Ltd 1980–, RIT Capital Partners, J Rothschild & Co Ltd; non-exec dep chm British Sky Broadcasting Gp plc 2003–; chm Bd of Tstees: Nat Gallery 1985–91, National Heritage Meml Fund 1992–98, National Heritage Lottery Fund 1994–98, Gilbert Collection Tst 1998–2006, Hermitage Rooms at Somerset House 1999–2006; Hon DLitt Univ of Newcastle upon Tyne 1998, Hon LLD Univ of Exeter 1998, Hon Dr Univ of Keele 2000, Hon DCL Univ of Oxford 2002, Hon DLitt Univ of Warwick 2003, Hon DSc Univ of London 2004, hon student ChCh Oxford 2006; Hon FBA 1998, Hon FRIBA 1998, Hon FRAM 2002, FKC 2002; Cdr Order of Henry the Navigator (Portugal) 1985; hon fell City of Jerusalem 1992, PhD Hebrew Univ of Jerusalem of Jerusalem 1992, Weizmann Award for Humanities and Science 1997; fell Ashmoelan Museum Oxford 2006; *Style—* The Rt Hon the Lord Rothschild, OM, GBE; ✉ 14 St James's Place, London SW1A 1NP (tel 020 7493 8111); The Dairy Queen Street, Waddesdon, Aylesbury, Buckinghamshire HP18 0JW (tel 01296 653235)

ROTHWELL, Prof Dame Nancy Jane; DBE (2005); *Educ* Univ of London (BSc, PhD, DSc); *Career* Univ of Manchester: prof of physiology 1994, chm Div of Neuroscience 1998–2000, currently MRC research prof and vice-pres for research; pres British Neuroscience Assoc 2000–04, chair Research Defence Soc 2004–07, memb Cncl Acad of Med Sciences 2002–05; tstee: Cancer Research UK 2002–, NESTA 2002–05; non-exec dir AstraZeneca plc 2006–; columnist Times Higher Educn Supplement 2004–06; delivered Royal Instn Christmas Lectures 1998, Pfizer Award for Innovative Science 2003; FMedSci 2000, FRS 2004; *Style—* Prof Dame Nancy Rothwell, DBE; ✉ The University of Manchester, Oxford Road, Manchester M13 9PL

ROTHWELL, Peter Francis; s of Prof William Rothwell, and Margaret, *née* Meehan; *b* 13 September 1959; *Educ* Manchester Grammar, St Edmund Hall Oxford (MA); *m* Sara Anne, da of Prof G Randell; 1 da (Emily Laura b 1 Jan 1985); *Career* Thomson Holidays 1982–88 (joined as grad trainee, successively mktg asst, mktg exec, product mangr, mktg mangr), dir for Europe Jetset International 1988, gen mangr Thomson Worldwide and Citibreaks April-Aug 1989, mktg dir Lunn Poly Ltd Aug 1989–93, purchasing dir Thomson Tour Operations Ltd 1993–94, md Airtours Holidays 1995–2001, chief exec Thomson Holidays (TUI Northern Europe) 2001–; MCIM 1989; *Recreations* skiing, squash, sailing; *Style—* Peter Rothwell, Esq

ROTTER, Prof (John) Michael; s of late Godfrey Cyril John Rotter, and late Gwendoline May Rotter; *b* 31 December 1948, Chesterfield, Derbys; *Educ* Clare Coll Cambridge (MA), Univ of Sydney (PhD); *Children* 1 s (Benedict Edward Godfrey b 1979), 1 da (Rebecca Victoria Elizabeth b 1981); *Career* lectr then sr lectr Univ of Sydney 1975–89, prof of civil engrg Univ of Edinburgh 1989– (head of dept 1989–92, head of div 1992–99); visiting prof (première classe) INSA Lyon 1996 and 2000; visiting prof: Tech Univ Graz 1997, 2001 and 2005, Tech Univ Vienna 2000; author of five books and over 300 pubns in jls and confs; CEng, FIE(Aust) 1987, FICE 1996, FREng 2004, FRSE 2005; *Recreations* hill walking, classical music, theatre; *Style—* Prof J Michael Rotter; ✉ 176 Mayfield Road, Edinburgh EH9 3AX (e-mail m.rotter@ed.ac.uk)

ROUCH, Peter Christopher; QC (1996); s of Rupert Trevelyan Rouch (d 1975), and Doris Linda, *née* Hayes (d 1982); *b* 15 June 1947; *Educ* Canton HS Cardiff, UC Wales Aberystwyth (LLB); *m* 1980, Carol Sandra, *née* Francis; 1 s (Robin Benjamin), 1 da (Hannah Jessica); *Career* called to the Bar Gray's Inn 1972, recorder 1992–; *Recreations* skiing, golf, fishing, cinema, reading; *Style—* Peter Rouch, Esq, QC; ✉ 9 Mayals Road, Mayals, Swansea SA3 5BT; Iscoed Chambers, 86 St Helen's Road, Swansea SA1 4BQ (tel 01792 652988); 9–12 Bell Yard, London WC2A 2LF (tel 020 7400 1800); 20 Archery Close, London W2 2BE

ROUECHÉ, Mossman (Jr); s of Col Mossman Roueché (d 2003), of Winter Park, Florida, and Elizabeth Molin, *née* Meier; *b* 14 December 1947; *Educ* Montgomery Blair HS Maryland, Kenyon Coll Ohio (BA), SUNY Buffalo (MA); *m* 29 July 1972, Charlotte Mary, da of Charles Percy Tunnard Wrinch (d 1999), of Guernsey, CI; 1 da (Alice b 1979), 1 s (Thomas b 1986); *Career* trainee Standard Chartered Bank plc 1973–75, dir Samuel Montagu & Co Ltd (now subsid of HSBC) 1986–96 (joined 1975), md and European head of transaction devpt HSBC Bank plc (formerly HSBC Markets Ltd) 1994–2006, chm Montagu Pension Trustees Ltd 1995–2000; dir HSBC Bank Pension Tst (UK) Ltd 2000–, chm Asset and Liability Ctee 2004–; memb: Advsy Cncl Inst of Classical Studies Univ of London 2003–, Advsy Cncl Warburg Inst Univ of London 2005–; tstee Lambeth Palace Library 2005–; *Recreations* swimming, Byzantine philosophy; *Style—* Mossman Roueché, Esq; ✉ 19 Bartholomew Villas, London NW5 2LJ; Talbot Cottage, Fisher's Lane,

R

Charlbury, Oxfordshire OX7 3RX; HSBC Bank plc, 8 Canada Square, London E14 5HQ (tel 020 7991 1500)

ROUND, Prof Nicholas Grenville; s of Isaac Eric Round, and Laura Christabel, *née* Poole; *b* 6 June 1938; *Educ* Launceston Coll, Pembroke Coll Oxford (MA, DPhil); *m* 2 April 1966, Ann, da of Louis Le Vin; 1 da (Grainne Ann b 1968); *Career* Queen's Univ Belfast: lectr in Spanish 1962–71, warden Alanbrooke Hall 1970–72, reader in Spanish 1971–72; Stevenson prof of hispanic studies Univ of Glasgow 1972–94, Hughes prof of Spanish Univ of Sheffield 1994–2003 (emeritus prof 2003–); former exec memb and vice-chm Clydebank/Milngavie Constituency Lab Pty; former exec memb: Strathclyde West Euro-Constituency Lab Pty, Strathclyde Regnl Lab Pty; pres Assoc Internac de Galdosistas 1999–2001; memb: ALL, MHRA, SSMLL, AHGBI, AIH; MITI 1990, FBA 1996; Oficial de la Orden de Isabel la Católica 1990; *Books* Unamuno: Abel Sánchez (1974), The Greatest Man Uncrowned: A Study of the Fall of Don Alvaro de Luna (1986), Tirso de Molina: Damned for Despair (1986), On Reasoning and Realism (1991), Libro llamado Fedrón (1993), Translation Studies in Hispanic Contexts (ed, 1998), New Galdo's Studies (ed, 2003); *Recreations* music, reading, drawing, hill walking, politics, all aspects of Cornwall; *Clubs* Queen's Univ Belfast Student's Union (hon life memb); *Style*— Prof Nicholas Round, FBA; ✉ 10 King's Road, Penzance, Cornwall TR18 4LG (tel 01736 362365, e-mail nickround@blue-earth.co.uk)

ROUNDELL, James; s of Charles Wilbraham Roundell, and Ann, *née* Moore; *b* 23 October 1951; *Educ* Winchester, Magdalene Coll Cambridge (BA, Cricket blue); *m* 3 May 1975, Alexandra Jane, da of Sir Cyril Stanley Pickard; 1 s (Thomas b 1979), 1 da (Rebecca b 1982); *Career* Christie's Fine Art Auctioneers: joined 1973, i/c 18th and 19th century English Drawings and Watercolours 1974–76, dir Old Master & Modern Prints 1976–86, dir Impressionist and Modern Pictures 1986–95 (during which time handled the sale of two of the three most expensive pictures ever sold); proprietor James Roundell Ltd 1995–; dir Simon C Dickinson Ltd 1998–; Liveryman Worshipful Co of Grocers 1981 (Freeman 1972); *Books* Thomas Shotter Boys (1975); *Recreations* cricket, sailing, opera; *Clubs* Hurlingham, MCC, I Zingari, various cricket clubs; *Style*— James Roundell, Esq; ✉ James Roundell Limited, 58 Jermyn Street, London SW1Y 6LX

ROUSE, Anne Barrett; da of William Dashiell Rouse, of Atlantic, Virginia, and Florence Irene, *née* Munson; *b* 26 September 1954; *Educ* W Springfield HS, Shimer Coll Ill, Bedford Coll London (BA); *Career* Islington MIND: employment worker 1988–91, dir 1991–94; state registered nurse 1982, registered mental nurse 1984; author of articles in The Independent and The Washington Post; poems published in: The Observer, TLS, New Statesman, London Review of Books, London Magazine, Atlantic Monthly; Hawthornden fell 1999, Royal Literary Fund writing fell Univ of Glasgow 2000–02; *Poetry* Sunset Grill (1993), Timing (1997); anthologies incl: New Women Poets (ed Carol Rumens, 1990), The Firebox (ed Sean O'Brien, 2000), The School of Night (2004); *Style*— Ms Anne Rouse; ✉ Bloodaxe Books, PO Box 1SN, Newcastle upon Tyne NE99 1SN (e-mail rouseanne@hotmail.com)

ROUSE, Christopher John; s of Cyril Rouse (d 1995), and Barbara, *née* Walkden; *b* 20 August 1941; *Educ* Alleyne's Sch Uttoxeter, The Hotel Sch of Coll of the Fylde; *Career* hotelier; postgrad mgmnt trg British Transport Hotels (Midland Hotel Manchester, Restaurant la Tour d'Argent Paris, Hotel Nassauer Hof Wiesbaden, Ritz and Palace Hotels Madrid) 1961–65, dep gen mangr Gleneagles Hotel 1969–73 (asst mangr and house mangr 1966–69); mangr: Old Course Hotel St Andrews 1973–76, Welcombe Hotel Stratford-upon-Avon 1976–78; gen mangr Turnberry Hotel 1978–98 (dir of holding co 1993–98), md CJ Rouse Consits Ltd 1998–; memb: Scottish Divnl Ctee BHA 1978–98, UK Ctee Leading Hotels of the World 1986–98, W of Scotland Ctee IOD 1993–98, Walpole Ctee 1993–98; hon memb Académie Culinaire de France; fndr memb Connoisseurs Scotland Ltd 1991– (chm 1998–); Master Innholder (memb Exec Ctee 1997–), tstee Master Innholders Charitable Tst 2003–; Hotelier of the Year (Caterer and Hotelkeeper) 1997; Freeman City of London, Liveryman Worshipful Co of Distillers; MIMgt 1976, FHCIMA 1978 (MHCIMA 1961), MInstD 1990; *Recreations* travel, golf, wine; *Clubs* Reform; *Style*— Christopher Rouse, Esq; ✉ Captain's House, 41 Fedden Village, Portishead, North Somerset BS20 8DN (tel 01275 845610)

ROUSE, Jon; s of James Clement Rouse, of Kettering, Northants, and Barbara Jean, *née* Fowler; *b* 23 May 1968; *Educ* Latimer Sch Kettering, Univ of Manchester (LLB), Univ of N London (MA), Univ of Nottingham (MBA); *m* 13 July 1991, Heulwen Mary, *née* Evans; *Career* private sec to min for Housing 1994–95, policy and communications mangr English Partnerships 1995–98, sec Govt Urban Task Force 1998–99, chief exec CABE 2000–04, chief exec Housing Corp 2004–, bd dir English Partnerships 2004–; FA qualified referee 2004–; Hon DUniv Oxford Brookes; Hon FRIBA 2001, Hon MRTPI 2002; *Recreations* tennis, hiking, French cinema; *Clubs* Queens Park Rangers FC, Nottingham Ambassadors; *Style*— Jon Rouse, Esq; ✉ The Housing Corporation, Maple House, 149 Tottenham Court Road, London W1T 7BN

ROUSE, Lucy Jane; da of Julian Spencer Rouse, of East Molesey, Surrey, and Pauline Ann Rouse, of Tunbridge Wells, Kent; *b* 3 June 1971; *Educ* Tunbridge Wells Girls' GS, Univ of York (BA, news ed Vision), Birkbeck Coll London (MA); *Career* journalist; with Government Group Publications 1992–95 (rising to ed Government Purchasing); Emap: dep ed M&M Europe 1995–97, assoc ed Mediaweek 1997–98, dep ed TV World 1998–99, features ed then ed Broadcast 1999–2002, sr ed Broadcast 2002–03; freelance journalist 2003– (incl for: Broadcast, Media Guardian and Sunday Times); memb: Broadcasting Press Guild, RTS; *Recreations* walking, reading, gardening, theatre and cinema; *Style*— Ms Lucy Rouse; ✉ mobile 07974 238386, e-mail rouse_lucy@hotmail.com

ROUSSEAU, Prof George Sebastian; s of Hyman Victoire Rousseau (d 1993), of NYC, and Esther, *née* Zacuto (d 2005); *b* 23 February 1941, NYC; *Educ* Amherst Coll USA (BA), Princeton Univ USA (MA, PhD); *Career* Osgood fell in Eng lit then Woodrow Wilson dissertation fell Princeton Univ 1965–66, instr and asst prof Harvard Univ 1966–68, asst prof then assoc prof UCLA 1968–69, German state lectr W Germany univs 1970, hon fell Wolfson Coll Cambridge 1974–75, prof of Eng and eighteenth century studies UCLA 1976–93, Regius Chalmers prof of Eng Univ of Aberdeen 1994–, research prof of humanities De Montfort Univ 1999–2002, prof Modern History Research Unit Univ of Oxford 2002–; overseas fell Univ of Cambridge 1979, visiting fell commoner Trinity Coll Cambridge 1982, sr Fulbright research scholar Sir Thomas Browne Inst The Netherlands 1983, visiting exchange prof King's Coll Cambridge 1984, Clark Library prof Univ of California 1985–86, sr fell Nat Endowment for the Humanities 1986–87, Nat Endowment for the Humanities and Westfield Center lectr National Mozart Symposium 1990–91, visiting fell Magdalen Coll Oxford 1993–94, sr US Fulbright prof Univ of Lausanne Switzerland 1994, visiting professorial fell New Coll and Merton Coll Oxford 1999; chm Inst Memberships and prog chm annual meeting American Soc for Eighteenth Century Studies 1971–72, pres Western Soc for Eighteenth Century Studies 1985–86, chm and tstee Soc for Lit and Sci 1985–92; delg Museums, Libraries and Archives Cncl (MLA) Assembly 1971–74; memb Exec Ctee: Div on Lit and Sci MLA 1985–89, Div on Comparative Studies in Eighteenth Century Lit 1989–92; book reviewer NY Sunday Times 1967–; Louis Gottshalk Prize American Soc for Eighteenth Century Studies 1987; memb History of Science Soc 1966; Dr (hc) Univ of Bucharest 2007; FRSM 1967, fell American Cncl of Learned Socs 1970, FRSA 1973; *Books* This Long Disease My Life: Alexander Pope and the Sciences (co-author, 1968), English Poetic Satire (co-author, 1969), The Augustan Milieu: Essays Presented to Louis A Landa (jt ed, 1970), Tobias Smollett: Bicentennial Essays Presented to Lewis M Knapp (jt ed, 1971), Organic Form: The Life of an Idea (ed, 1972), Goldsmith: The Critical Heritage (1974), The Ferment of Knowledge: Studies in the Historiography of Science (1980), The Letters and Private Papers of Sir John Hill (1981), Tobias Smollett: Essays of Two Decades (1982), Science and Imagination: The Berkeley Conference (ed, 1987), Sexual Underworlds of the Enlightenment (co-author, 1987), The Enduring Legacy: Alexander Pope Tercentenary Essays (co-author, 1988), Exoticism in the Enlightenment (co-author, 1990), The Languages of Psyche: Mind and Body in Enlightenment Thought (1990), Perilous Enlightenment: Pre- and Post-Modern Discourses: Sexual, Historical (1991), Enlightenment Crossings: Pre- and Post-Modern Discourses: Anthropological (1991), Enlightenment Borders: Pre- and Post-Modern Discourses: Medical, Scientific (1991), Hysteria Before Freud (co-author, 1993), Gout: The Patrician Malady (co-author, 1998), Framing and Imagining Disease (2003), Marguerite Yourcenar: Life and Times (2004), Nervous Acts: Essays on Literature and Culture (2005), Children and Sexuality: The Greeks to The Great War (ed, 2007); *Recreations* chamber music, hillside walking, gardening; *Clubs* Osler; *Style*— Prof George Rousseau; ✉ Modern History Faculty, Broad Street, Oxford University, Oxford OX1 3BD (tel 01865 224208, fax 01865 224173, e-mail george.rousseau@ntlworld.com)

ROUSSOUNIS, Dr Socrates Hercules; s of Hercules Roussounis, and Mary, *née* Evagoras; *b* 30 August 1937; *Educ* Howardian GS Cardiff, St George's Hosp Univ of London (MB BS, DCH, DObstRCOG); *m* 22 Nov 1968, Loucia, da of Stephan Stephanou (d 1987); 3 s (Alexander b 24 Feb 1972, Eracles b 2 Sept 1975, Stephan b 1 Oct 1979); *Career* res fell in clinical neurophysicology Hosp for Sick Children Gt Ormond St 1972–73, sr registrar in paediatrics and developmental medicine Charing Cross Hosp 1973–77, conslt in paediatric neurology St James's Univ Hosp 1977–2002, hon sr lectr in clinical paediatrics Univ of Leeds 1987–2002, medico-legal claims expert, dir i/c Regnl Child Devpt Centre St James's Univ Hosp Leeds; memb Br Neurology Assoc; FRCP 1989, FRCPCH 1996; *Publications* author of various papers on aspects of paediatric neurology incl: child devpt, epilepsy, cerebral palsy, and use of botulin toxin in the treatment of childhood spastic cerebral palsy; *Recreations* golf, photography; *Style*— Dr Socrates Roussounis; ✉ St James's University Hospital, Leeds LS9 7TF (tel 0113 243 3144)

ROUTLEDGE, (Katherine) Patricia; CBE (2004, OBE 1993); da of Isaac Edgar Routledge (d 1985), of Birkenhead, Cheshire, and Catherine, *née* Perry (d 1957); *b* 17 February 1929; *Educ* Birkenhead HS, Univ of Liverpool (BA); *Career* actress and singer; trained Bristol Old Vic and with Walther Gruner Guildhall Sch of Music; *Theatre* first professional appearance as Hippolyta in A Midsummer Night's Dream (Liverpool Playhouse) 1952, first West End appearance in Sheridan's The Duenna (Westminster Theatre) 1954, first Broadway appearance in How's the World Treating You? (Music Box NY, Whitbread Award) 1966, Darling of the Day (Broadway, Antoinette Perry Award) 1968, Love Match (Ahmanson Theatre Los Angeles) 1968–69, Cowardy Custard (Mermaid Theatre) 1972–73, Noises Off (Savoy Theatre) 1981, Queen Margaret in Richard III (RSC (Olivier Award Nomination)) 1984–85, The Old Lady in Candide (Old Vic (Olivier Award)) 1988–89, Come for the Ride (solo show) 1988, Carousel (RNT) 1993, The Rivals (Chichester) 1994, Beatrix (Chichester and tour) 1996, The Importance of Being Earnest (Chichester, Theatre Royal and Australian tour) 1999–2001, Wild Orchids (Chichester) 2002; *Television* incl: Sophia and Constance, A Woman of No Importance 1982 (Broadcasting Press Guild Critics Award), A Lady of Letters 1988 (BAFTA Nomination), First and Last, Missing Persons, Victoria Wood - As Seen on TV, Talking Heads (BBC, also staged Comedy Theatre) 1992, Hildegarde Of Bingen (BBC) 1994, Keeping up Appearances (BBC) 1995–2000, lead role in Hetty Wainthropp Investigates (BBC) 1998–2002, Anybody's Nightmare (Carlton) 2001, The Brontës (BBC) 2003; *Style*— Miss Patricia Routledge, CBE

ROUX, Albert Henri; OBE (2002); s of Henri Roux (d 1983), and Germaine Roux (d 2003); bro of Michel André Roux, *qv*; *b* 8 October 1935; *Educ* Ecole Primaire St Mandé France; *m* 1959, Monique; 1 s (Michel Albert b 1960), 1 da (Danielle b 1965); *Career* French Mil Serv Algeria; fndr (with bro) Le Gavroche Restaurant 1967 (moved to Mayfair 1981), fndr memb Académie Culinaire de Grande Bretagne; Maitre Cuisinièr de France 1968, Officier du Mérite Agricole 1987 (Chevalier 1975), Chevalier Legion d'Honneur 2005; Hon DSc Cncl for Nat Academic Awards 1987; *Books* with Michel Roux: New Classic Cuisine (1983), The Roux Brothers on Patisserie (1986), The Roux Brothers on French Country Cooking (1989), Cooking For Two (1991); *Recreations* fishing, racing; *Style*— Albert Roux, OBE; ✉ Le Gavroche, 43 Upper Brook Street, London W1Y 1PF (tel 020 7408 0881)

ROUX, Michel Albert; s of Albert Roux, *qv*, and Monique, *née* Merle; *b* 23 May 1960; *Educ* Emanuel Sch London; *m* 20 April 1990, Giselle Francoise, da of late Marcel Malbos; 1 da (Emily Amandine b 8 Feb 1991); *Career* chef; apprenticeship under Maître Patissier Paris 1976–79, trained under Alain Chapel at Mionay 1980–82; mil service Elysée Palace kitchens 1982–83; Boucherie Lamartine Paris 1983, Charcuterie Mothu Paris 1983, sous chef Gavers Restaurant London 1983–84, commis de cuisine Tante Claire London 1984, Mandarin Hotel Hong Kong 1984, Waterside Inn Bray 1985; chef of Roux Restaurants incl: Roux Patisserie, Roux Lamartine, Le Poulbot Brasserie, Le Gamin; chef de cuisine Le Gavroche London 1991– (three Michelin stars); memb Traditions et Qualité, memb Relais et Chateaux; fundraiser for VICTA (Visually Impaired Children Taking Action); Maitre Cuisinèr de France 2002; *Awards* The Carlton London Restaurant Awards 1999, The Carlton London Restaurant Awards Laurent Perrier Award of Excellence 2000, The Academy of Food and Wine Services 2000, Restrauteurs Restaurant of the Year Awards 2000; *Books* Le Gavroche Cookbook (2001), Marathon Chef Cookbook (2002), Matching Food and Wine Cookbook (2005), Vin de Constance Cookbook (2006); *Recreations* long-distance running, marathons, ultra endurance running, football; *Style*— Michel Roux, Jr; ✉ Le Gavroche, 43 Upper Brook Street, London W1K 7QR (tel 020 7408 0881, fax 020 7409 0939, e-mail bookings@le-gavroche.com, website www.le-gavroche.co.uk and www.michelroux.co.uk)

ROUX, Michel André; Hon OBE (2002); s of Henri Roux (d 1983), and Germaine, *née* Triger (d 2003); bro of Albert Henri Roux, *qv*; *b* 19 April 1941; *Educ* Ecole Primaire Saint Mandé France, Brevet de Maîtrise (Pâtisserie); *m* 1 (m dis 1979), Françoise Marcelle, *née* Becquet; 1 s (Alain b 1968), 2 da (Christine b 1963, Françine b 1965); m 2, 21 May 1984, Robyn Margaret, *née* Joyce; *Career* French Mil Serv 1960–62; Versailles 1960, Colomb Béchar Algeria 1961–62, awarded the Médaille Commémorative des Opérations de Securité et de Maintien de l'Ordre en AFC avec Agiape Sahara BOPP no 42; commis pâtissier and cuisinièr at Br Embassy Paris 1955–57, commis cook to Miss Cécile de Rothschild Paris 1957–59 (chef 1962–67); restaurants opened in England: Le Gavroche 1967, The Waterside Inn 1972 (3 Michelin stars 1985), Le Gavroche (moved to Mayfair) 1981, Roux Britannia 1986; memb: l'Académie Culinaire de France (UK branch), Assoc Relais et Desserts, Assoc Relais et Chateaux; Hon Dr of Culinary Arts Providence RI 2002; *Awards* Silver Medal des Cuisiniers Français (Paris) 1963, Silver Medal Ville de Paris 1966, Silver Medal Sucre Tiré et Soufflé (London) 1970, Prix International Taittinger (2nd, Paris) 1971, Gold Medal Cuisiniers Français (Paris) 1972, Meilleur Ouvrier de France en Pâtisserie (Paris) 1976, Vermeil Medal du Prestige des Cuisiniers Français (Paris) 1983, Lauréat Best Menu of the Year Prepared for a Private Function (Caterer and Hotel Keeper) 1984, Lauréat Restaurateur of the Year (Caterer and Hotel Keeper) 1985, Lauréat du Premier Hommage Veuve Cliquot aux Ambassadeurs de la Cuisine Française dans le Monde (Paris) 1985, Lauréat Personality of the Year Gastronomie dans le Monde (Paris) 1985, Lauréat Culinary Trophy Personality of the Year in Pâtisserie (Assoc of French

Pâtissiers de la Saint-Michel) 1986, Chevalier de l'Ordre National du Mérite 1987, Officier du Mérite Agricole 1987, The Man of the Year award (RADAR) 1989, Chevalier de l'Ordre des Arts et des Lettres (France) 1990, Chevalier dans l'Ordre de la Légion d'Honneur 2004, Lifetime Achievement Award London 2006; *Books* New Classic Cuisine (1983), Roux Brothers on Pâtisserie (1986), At Home with the Roux Brothers (1987), French Country Cooking (1989), Cooking for Two (1991), Desserts, a Lifelong Passion (1994), Sauces (1996), Life is a Menu (autobiography, 2000), Only the Best (2002), Eggs (2005); *Recreations* shooting, walking, skiing; *Clubs* The Benedicts; *Style*— Michel Roux, Esq, OBE; ✉ The Waterside Inn, Ferry Road, Bray, Berkshire SL6 2AT (tel 01628 771966/620691, fax 01628 789182, e-mail michelroux@btconnect.com)

ROWALLAN, 4 Baron (UK 1911); John Polson Cameron Corbett; s of 3 Baron Rowallan (d 1993), and his 1 w, Eleanor Mary, *née* Boyle; *b* 8 March 1947; *Educ* Eton, RAC Cirencester; *m* 1, 1971 (m dis 1983), (Susan) Jane Dianne; 1 s (Hon Jason William Polson Cameron b 1972), 1 da (Hon Joanna Gwyn Alice Cameron b 1974); m 2, 17 April 1984 (m dis 1994), Sandrew Filomena Bryson; 1 s (Hon (Jonathan Arthur) Cameron b 1985), 1 da (Hon Soay Mairi Cameron b 1988); m 3, 1995, Claire Dinning, da of Robert Laidler, of Gateshead, Tyne & Wear; *Heir* s, Hon Jason Corbett; *Career* estate agent; commentator; dir: Rowallan Activity Centre Ltd, Rowallan Holdings Ltd, Land Devpt Scotland Ltd, Rowallan Asset Management; chm Loch Goin Covenanters Tst; patron Depression Alliance; landowner (1000 acres); ARICS; *Recreations* skiing, equestrianism; *Style*— The Lord Rowallan; ✉ Meiklemosside, Fenwick, Ayrshire KA3 6AY (tel 01560 600667, fax 01560 600335, e-mail john.rowallan@btconnect.com)

ROWAN, Prof Alistair John; s of Francis Peter Rowan (d 1957), and Margaret Gemmell, *née* Scoular (d 1957); *b* 3 June 1938; *Educ* Campbell Coll Belfast, The Edinburgh Coll of Art/Univ of Edinburgh (DipArch, Swimming blue), Magdalene Coll Cambridge (PhD), Univ of Padua; *m* 1968, Ann Martha, da of Charles Percy Tunnard Wrinch; 1 da (Harriet Grace b 1975); *Career* corr Country Life 1967–77 (architectural ed 1966–67), lectr in fine art Univ of Edinburgh 1967–77, prof of history of art UC Dublin 1977–90, Slade prof of fine art Univ of Oxford 1988, princ Edinburgh Coll of Art and prof Heriot-Watt Univ 1990–2001, prof of art history UC Cork 2001–03; major works incl: Mr David Bryce (Edinburgh Univ Exhibition) 1976, The Buildings of Ireland - North West Ulster 1979, Designs for Castles and Country Villas by Robert and James Adam 1985, catalogue of Robert Adam Drawings (V&A) 1988, The Buildings of Ireland - North Leinster (with C Casey, 1993), Scottish Country Houses 1600–1914 (with Ian Gow) 1995; memb Historic Buildings Cncl for Scotland 1986–95; chm: The Irish Architectural Archive 1982–87, Heritage Advsy Ctee Dept of the Taoiseach Dublin 1987; pres: Soc of Architectural Historians of GB 1992–96, The Architectural Heritage Soc of Scotland 1992–2002; memb Patrick Allan Fraser Tst 1990–, chm The Paxton Tst 1993–, chm The Gunsgreen House Tst 1998–; Silver Medal RSA 1972; FRSE 1993; Cavaliere del Ordine al Merito 1983; *Recreations* gardening and broadcasting; *Style*— Prof Alistair Rowan

ROWAN, David; *b* 8 April 1965, London; *Educ* Haberdashers' Aske's, Gonville & Caius Coll Cambridge (MA); *Career* journalist; trainee journalist The Times 1988–89; launch ed Education and The Editor supplements and ed Comments and Letters, Analysis, Saturday Outlook and Guardian Unlimited The Guardian 1990–2000, writer, broadcaster and consIt ed (incl: launch ed Public Agenda and Career supplements and columnist The Times, media interviewer Evening Standard, contrib Sunday Times Magazine, The Times Magazine, Daily Telegraph Magazine and The Observer) 2001–05, ed Jewish Chronicle 2006–; ind filmmaker Channel 4 News; ✉ The Jewish Chronicle, 25 Furnival Street, London EC4A 1JT (tel 020 7415 1500, fax 020 7405 9040, e-mail editorial@thejc.com)

ROWAN, Patricia Adrienne; da of Henry Matthew Talintyre (d 1962), and Gladys, *née* Gould (d 1992); *Educ* Harrow County GS for Girls; *m* 1 April 1960, Ivan Settle Harris Rowan (d 2006); 1 s (Matthew Settle Nicholas b 1960); *Career* journalist; Time and Tide 1952–56, Sunday Express 1956–57, Daily Sketch 1957–58, News Chronicle 1958–60, Granada TV 1961–62, Sunday Times 1962–66, ed Times Educational Supplement 1989–97 (editorial staff 1972–89); memb Bd Nat Children's Bureau 1997–2003; chair Stroud Valley Project 2002– (memb Bd 2001–02); hon fell Inst of Education Univ of London 1997; Hon FRSA 1989; *Books* What Sort of Life? (1980), Education - The Wasted Years? (contrib, 1988); *Recreations* gardening, cooking, reading; *Clubs* Reform; *Style*— Mrs Patricia Rowan; ✉ Park View, Nupend, Horsley, Stroud, Gloucestershire GL6 0PY (tel 01453 833305)

ROWAN, (Thomas) Stanley; s of Thomas Rowan (d 1965); *b* 11 April 1935; *Educ* Wellington Sch, Univ of Natal (BA), Gonville & Caius Coll Cambridge (LLB); *m* 1964, Anne Strafford, *née* Sanderson; 1 s (Michael), 1 da (Vanessa); *Career* articled James Edwards & Co (now Arthur Andersen), internal auditor Br and Commonwealth Gp 1961–64, Jones Hutchinson & Co (now Hodgson Harris & Co) 1964–68; dir Singer & Friedlander Ltd 1975–87, dir Singer & Friedlander Holdings Ltd 1987–96, dir Singer & Friedlander Investment Management Ltd 1987–97; dir Singer & Friedlander (Jersey) 1976–99; Scottish Oriental Smaller Companies Tst plc 1995–; FCA 1971–2004 (ACA 1961); *Recreations* fine wine and food; reading, international travel; *Style*— Stanley Rowan Esq; ✉ Strafford House, Fulwith Road, Harrogate, North Yorkshire HG2 8HL (tel 01423 873137 and 01423 871350)

ROWBOTHAM, Brian William; s of Laurence William Edward Rowbotham (d 1967), of Surbiton, and Florence Madge Rowbotham (d 1975); *b* 27 May 1931; *Educ* Oakham Sch; *m* 19 Sept 1959, Carol Ann, da of Henry Nordheim Webster (d 1966), of Wallasey; 3 s (Anthony Charles William, Nigel Henry, Jonathan Brian Nicholas); *Career* Nat Serv Lt RA 1955–57; chm and chief exec Morgan-Grampian plc 1969–86, fndr chm Br Business Press 1984–86; chm: Periodical Publishers Assoc 1985–87, London Newspaper Group 1988–94, Charterhouse Communications Group plc 1988–2006, Allied Radio plc 1994–96; dep chm Adscene Group plc 1987–94; dir Advent Capital (Holdings) plc 1995–; FCA; *Clubs* RAC; *Style*— Brian Rowbotham, Esq; ✉ Robins Mount, Alma Road, Reigate, Surrey RH2 0DN

ROWBOTHAM, Dr Hugo Dalyson; s of George Frederick Rowbotham (d 1975), and Monica Dalyson, *née* Boyle, of Upton, nr Blewbury, Oxon; *b* 30 March 1942; *Educ* Dragon Sch Oxford, Shrewsbury, King's Coll Durham (MB BS, Hockey colours); *m* 8 Sept 1973, Gloria Geraldine; 1 s (Richard b 23 Jan 1976), 2 da (Louisa b 12 Aug 1980, Emily b 23 Feb 1982); *Career* house surgn and physician Newcastle Gen Hosp 1965–66, ENT sr house offr Royal Victoria Infirmary 1966–67, surgical res asst Royal Marsden Hosp 1968–71, private GP 1971–; visiting med offr: King Edward VII Hosp 1975–, The London Clinic 1975–; memb: BMA, Soc of Occupational Med, Sloane Soc, Chelsea Clinical Soc; *Recreations* hockey; *Clubs* Surbiton Hockey, Llamas Hockey, English Nat Ballet Co (Gold Card memb); *Style*— Dr Hugo Rowbotham; ✉ 11 Cromwell Crescent, London SW5 9QW (tel 020 7603 6967); 147 Harley Street, London W1G 6BL (tel 020 7935 4444, fax 020 7486 3782)

ROWBOTHAM, Dr Thomas Robert (Tom); *b* 9 June 1941; *Educ* Queen's Univ Belfast (BSc, Cross Country capt and blue), Univ of Surrey (MSc), Univ of Nottingham (PhD); *Career* British Telecommunications plc (formerly GPO): exec engr London 1964–68, sr exec engr Microwave Radio Castleton S Wales 1968–74, head Digital Transmission Res Section Martlesham 1974–78, chief of communications R&D Intelsat Washington 1978–80, head Site Servs Div Martlesham 1980–83, head Optical Transmission System Res Div Martlesham 1983–87, gen mangr Network Systems Res Dept Martlesham 1987–89, dir of networks technol Martlesham 1989–93, sr vice-pres Concert (a BT/MCI jt venture) 1993–95, dir of tech strategy BT 1995–2000; chm KCC Ltd 1988–99, chm Teltier Technologies 2001–02, vice-chm Flomerics plc 1999–; dir: Aravox Inc 2000–02, ERA Technologies 2001–, ERA Fndn 2002–; non-exec dir Piping Hot Networks 2000–01; vice-pres int affrs IEEE Communications Soc 1992–93, vice-chm IEE Electronics Divnl Bd 1999, memb IEE Cncl, non-exec dir IEEE Fndn 1998–01, non-exec dir IEEE Inc 2000–01; venture ptnr St Paul Venture Capital 2000–, advsr Carlyle European Venture Partners 2001–; prof (special chair) Univ of Nottingham 1986–89, visiting prof KCL 1993–; Sporting All Ireland Youths Cross Country Championships Winners Medal 1958 and 1959, vice-pres British Telecom Research Football Club; FREng 1992, FIEE; *Books* Communications Systems Analysis (with P B Johns, 1972); *Recreations* marathon running; *Clubs* In & Out; *Style*— Dr Tom R Rowbotham, FREng

ROWDEN, Ray; s of William Charles Rowden (d 1987), of Kent, and Joyce Vera, *née* Wood (d 1983); *b* 11 July 1952; *Educ* Sir William Nottidge Sch Kent; *m* 15 Dec 1973 (m dis 1990), Linda Margaret; 2 da (Helen Louise Victoria b 12 Sept 1974, Elizabeth Christabel b 25 Sept 1980); partner, Tom Sobel (civil partnership, 2007); *Career* trained as: registered mental nurse St Augustine's Hosp Kent 1970–73, SRN Kent and Canterbury Hosp 1976–78, oncology nurse Royal Marsden Hosp London and Surrey 1981; RCN: regnl N Wales 1978–79, sr offr Wales 1978–81, advsr in mgmnt London 1984–86; dir of nursing Royal Marsden Hosp Sutton 1981–84, unit gen mangr Mental Health Servs W Lambeth 1986–89, unit gen mangr Priority Servs W Lambeth DHA 1989–91, chief exec W Lambeth Community Care NHS Tst 1991–93, dir The Inst of Health Services Mgmnt 1993–96, dir Commissioning Bd for High Security Psychiatric Services NHS Exec 1996–98, visiting prof Dept of Health Studies Univ of York 1998–2002, dir Healthcare Progs Gatehouse Ltd 1999–, dir Mental Health Int Devpt 2005; reviewer Cmmn for Health Improvement 2002–; non-exec dir/vice-chm Lewisham & Guy's NHS Mental Health Tst 1994–96; memb: Open Govt Task Force Dept of Health 1994–, NHS Plan Task Force (Quality) Dept of Health 2001; memb Editorial Advsy Bd Health Services Jl 1993–96; memb: Lab Pty 1974–, RCN Nat Cncl 1979–81, Cncl for Music in Hosps 1985–, Corp Governance Task Force Dept of Health 1993–; chair NAHAT Primary Care Gp 1992–94; consIt in nursing and mgmnt to Govt of St Lucia 1990, visiting fell The Kings Fund Coll 1994–97, specialist advsr House of Commons Health Select Ctee 2000; advsr Invitation to the Ballet project (Royal Ballet) 1982–97, fndr/dir Reach 4 Dance 2004, advsr Ashiya Int Ballet Japan 2005; owner and md Palmlagoon Resorts Ltd Kerala 2001–; Hon Dr Kingston Univ 1999; MRCN 1970, MHSM 1987; *Books* Managing Nursing (1984); *Recreations* writing, ballet and other dance, music, politics, collecting bronze sculpture and paintings; *Style*— Ray Rowden; ✉ 8 Abinger Place, Lewes, Sussex BN7 2QA (e-mail ray@palmlagoon.com)

ROWE, Anthony; s of late Norman Oliver George Rowe, and Eunice Constance Mary Rowe; *b* 1945, Bristol; *Educ* W of Eng Acad of Art; *Career* artist and designer; scenic artist rising to theatre designer Bristol Old Vic Theatre Co 1971–75, head of design Bristol Old Vic Theatre Sch 1975–95, design co-ordinator RSC 1996–2003, jt dir Number 9 Gallery Winchcombe (with Judy Hill) 2004–; freelance design for opera, ballet and animation; design lectr: Shakespeare Inst, Univ of Birmingham; memb Panel SW Arts 1983–86; *Selected Exhibitions* The Guild Gallery Bristol, Ginger Gallery Bristol, The Gallery Oundle, The Other Place Gallery Stratford-upon-Avon, The Gallery Upstairs Henley-in-Arden, Royal Birmingham Soc of Artists, Venice in Peril (WH Patterson London), Llewellyn Alexander Gallery London, The New English Art Club, The Mall Galleries, D'Arcy Gallery Cheltenham; *Recreations* music, walking; *Style*— Anthony Rowe, Esq; ✉ 4 Corelli Close, Stratford-upon-Avon, Warwickshire CV37 9PU (e-mail anthonyjrowe@hotmail.com)

ROWE, Crispin; s of Peter Whitmill Rowe, of Cranbrook, Kent, and Bridget, *née* Moyle; *b* 28 May 1955, Burton on Trent; *Educ* Bryanston, Univ of Newcastle upon Tyne (BA, PGCE); *m* Aug 1977, Jillian, *née* Highton; 2 s (Thomas Patrick b 25 Oct 1981, Benjamin Peter b 16 May 1986), 1 da (Hannah Clare b 7 May 1983); *Career* history teacher: Watford Boys' GS 1978–80, Royal GS Newcastle upon Tyne 1980–92; King Edward's Sch Bath: dep head 1992–2004, headmaster 2004–; memb Assoc of Sch and Coll Ldrs; *Recreations* sport, music; *Style*— Crispin Rowe, Esq; ✉ King Edward's School, North Road, Bath BA2 6HU (tel 01225 464313, fax 01225 481363, e-mail headmaster@kesbath.biblio.net)

ROWE, Heather; da of Leonard Richard Rowe, of Welwyn, Herts, and Enid, *née* Livermore; *b* 16 October 1957; *Educ* Welwyn Garden City GS, Univ of Manchester (LLB); *Career* admitted slr 1981, articled clerk and slr Wilde Sapte 1979–83, SJ Berwin & Co 1983–85, Durrant Piesse 1985–88, ptnr Lovell's (formerly Lovell White Durrant) 1988–2004; former chm: ICC UK Ctee on Telecommunications and Information Technology, ICC Int Working Pty on Data Protection and Privacy; Freeman Worshipful Co of Slrs; memb Law Soc; *Recreations* fishing, birdwatching, gardening, painting, cars; *Clubs* Piscatorial Soc, Historic Rally Car Register; *Style*— Miss Heather Rowe; ✉ Teasel, Wilsford Cum Lake, Salisbury, Wiltshire SP4 7BL (tel 01980 623843, e-mail ht.olsen@virgin.net)

ROWE, John Richard; s of William Rowe (d 1990), of Wanstead, London, and Anne, *née* Radley (d 2000); *b* 1 August 1942; *Educ* St Barnabas Secdy Modern Sch; *m* 22 Oct 1966, Rosa Mary, da of Geoffrey Laurence Ball (d 1958), of Woodford Bridge, Essex; *Career* asst film librarian Twentieth Century Fox 1958–61, film researcher Rediffusion TV 1961–72 (progs incl: The Life and Times of Lord Mountbatten 1966–68, This Week), head of prodn res Thames TV 1972–82 (progs incl Emmy award winning World at War series 1972–74); Sky TV: head of programming 1982–84, head of prodn 1984–93; prodr Special Projects QVC The Shopping Channel 1994–95 (exec prodr 1993–94); fndr and exec prodr John Rowe Productions (ind prodr of film and TV prodns) 1995–; co-ordinating dir 1987 World Music Video Awards; prodr: The Pet Show series, Live from the Escape, Live from Rotterdam; prodr and dir: A Magical Disney Christmas, Ferry Aid Gala, Deadly Ernest Horror Show series 1989–91, Screeners 1997, Blues Clues 1997–2000 (6 series 2002–03), Havakazoo 2000; dir: The Gulf Aid Gala, Masters of History 1998, Reflections in the Eye: A documentary on the life of Anthony Quinn 2000, Monkey Makes 2002–04, Big Cook, Little Cook 2004 and 2005; writer, prodr and dir: Nickelodeon Live Tour 2002–04, The Big Story Book 2005; writer and dir Nickelodeon Jump Up Event 2006; *Recreations* cinema, walking, reading; *Style*— John Rowe, Esq; ✉ 24 Long Hill, Mere, Warminster, Wiltshire BA12 6LR (tel and fax 01747 861 966, e-mail john.rowe@clara.co.uk)

ROWE, Michael; *Educ* High Wycombe Coll of Art (DipAD), RCA (MA); *Career* in own silversmithing workshop 1972, sunglasses designer Polaroid (UK) Ltd 1971–72; spectacle designer: Optica Info Cncl fashion promotion 1973, Merx International Optical Co 1974–76; visiting lectr: Bucks Coll of Higher Educn 1973–82, Camberwell Sch of Art and Crafts 1976–82; visiting lectr and tutor RCA 1978–84; researcher (with Richard Hughes) into: colouring, bronzing and patination of metals Camberwell Sch of Art and Crafts 1979–82 (work published as manual by Crafts Cncl 1982), ancient patinated surfaces British Museum 1984–87; course leader Dept of Metalwork and Jewellery RCA 1984–; guest lectr: colls in Düsseldorf, Cologne, Schwabisch Gmund, Pforzheim and Munich 1983, Gerrit Rietreld Académie Amsterdam 1984, Oslo Statens Handverks-Og Kunstindustriskole 1985, Bezalel Coll of Art Jerusalem 1987; guest speaker: Soc of N American Goldsmiths Conf Toronto 1985, Jewellers and Metalsmiths Gp of Aust Fourth Biennial Conf Perth, First International Metal Arts Symposium Won-Kwang Univ 1995; memb jury: Mecca Dante Stakes Trophy Competition 1981 and 1982, Perrier Trophy Competition 1982, Das Tablett (int silversmithing competition) 1983, Chongju Int Craft Biennale Competition South Korea 1999; Hon Dr Buckinghamshire Chilterns UC 2004 Freeman City of London 1983, Freeman Worshipful Co of Goldsmiths 1983; FRCA 1987,

R

FRSA 1989; *Solo Exhibitions* Crafts Cncl Gallery London 1978, V&A Craft Show London 1985, Retrospective Exhibition (Princess of Museum Leeuwarden) 1988, Contemporary Applied Arts London 1988, The Eloquent Vessel (Museum für Angewandte Kunst Cologne, Museum für Angewandte Kunst Gera, and Deutsches Goldschmiedhaus Hanau) 1992, Studio Ton Berends The Hague 1993, Galerie Louise Smit Amsterdam 1995, Retrospective Exhibition (Birmingham Museum and Art Gallery, Manchester Art Gallery, City Art Gallery Leicester and tour) 2003–05; *Group Exhibitions* incl: Europalia '73 Brussels 1973, The Craftsman's Art (V&A) 1973, Collab '74 (Br Design and Craft and Philadelphia and World Crafts Exhibition Toronto) 1974, Sotheby Contemporary British Crafts at Auction Munich and London 1980, Galerie Ra Amsterdam 1983, Our Domestic Landscape (one of five selector/writer/exhibitors, London, Manchester and Aberystwyth) 1986, British Art and Design 1986 (Kunstlerhaus Vienna) 1986, Contemporary British Crafts (Br Cncl) 1988, Function Nonfunction (Rezac Gallery Chicago) 1989, New British Design Image and Object (Pompidou Centre Paris and Nat MOMA Kyoto) 1990, 20th Century Silver (Crafts Cncl London) 1993, The National Collection (Silver Tsts cmmns Goldsmiths Hall London) 1994, Design of the Times: 100 Years of the RCA (RCA) 1996, Objects of Our Time (Silver Jubilee exhibn Crafts Cncl London) 1996, First Choice (Museum Boymans van Beuningen Rotterdam) 1996, Design mit Zukunft (Focke Museum Bremen, Museum für Angewandte Kunst Cologne) 1997–98, European Prize for Contemporary Art and Design Led Crafts (Palais Harrach Vienna, Rohsska Museum Gothenburg, Musée des Arts Decoratifs Paris) 1998–99, Metalmorphosis: British Silver and Metalwork 1880–98 (Museum of Decorative Arts Prague, Brohan Museum Berlin) 1998–99, World Contemporary Craft Now (Cheongju Int Craft Biennale S Korea) 1999, Treasures of the 20th Century (Goldsmiths' Hall London) 2000, Cheongju Int Craft Biennale 2001, Torino 2002: Masterpieces 1902–2002 (Turin) 2002, Crafts Now: America, Europe and Asia (World Crafts Forum Kanazawa) 2003, Ars Ornata Europeana: Mais Perto/Closer (Nat Musuem of Art Lisbon) 2005, Transformations: The Language of Craft (Nat Gallery of Aust Canberra) 2005–06; *Work in Public Collections* incl: Birmingham City Museum and Art Galleries, Crafts Cncl London, Leeds City Art Gallery, V&A, Karlsruhe Museum, Art Gallery of Western Aust Perth, Shipley Art Gallery Gateshead, Stedelijk Museum Amsterdam, Nat MOMA Tokyo, Museum Boymans van Beuningen Rotterdam, Royal Museum of Scotland Edinburgh, Musée des Arts Decoratifs Paris, Vestlanske Kunstindustrimuseum Bergen, Worshipful Co of Goldsmiths, Nordenfjeldske Kunstindustrimuseum Trondheim, Museum of 21st Centruy Art Kanazawa, Manchester Art Gallery, Nat Gallery of Aust Canberra, Millennium Galleries Sheffield; *Commissions* incl: silver pomander for The Craftman's Art exhbn (V&A, cmmned by Crafts Cncl) 1972, silver pomander (V&A, cmmned by Liberty & Co) 1975, pair of silver candelabra for 10 Downing St (cmmned by The Silver Tst) 1994, silver vase (cmmned by Worshipful Co of Goldsmiths) 1997, silver cup for Millennium Cmmns (Sheffield Millennium Galleries, cmmned by Sheffield Assay Office) 2002, perm installation (cmmned by Middlesbrough Inst of Modern Art) 2005, silver jug (cmmned by Worshipful Co of Goldsmiths) 2005; *Awards* Frogmoor Fndn travelling scholarship 1967, dip World Crafts Cncl 1974, res award Camberwell Sch of Art and Crafts 1978, Sotheby Decorative Arts award 1988, awarded Japan Fndn Artists Fellowship 1993, Prize Winner European Prize for Contemporary Art and Design Led Crafts 1998, Golden Ring of Honour Gesellschaft Für Goldschmiedekunst Germany 2002; *Style*— Michael Rowe, Esq; ✉ Department of Metalwork and Jewellery, Royal College of Art, Kensington Gore, London SW7 2EU (tel 020 7590 4263, e-mail m.rowe@rca.ac.uk)

ROWE, Rita; da of Cecil Mason, of Belfast, and Marguarita Helen, *née* Dixon (d 1974); *Educ* St Helens Sch, St Helens Coll Merseyside; *m* 1, 1971, Gerald James Rowe; m 2, 1993, John Fagan Williams, s of Frank Thomas Williams; 1 step da (Kate Brannan); *Career* sales promotions exec Lancashire Evening Telegraph 1974–81, freelance journalist and broadcaster 1980–96, publicity offr Manchester Theatres 1981–84, conslt Staniforth Williams PR 1984–86, fndr and jt md Mason Williams PR 1986–, ceo Muse Gp; recipient 60 industry awards for PR work incl for Boots Opticians, News International, Waddingtons Games, Vauxhall, Dale Farm, Hasbro, Express Dairy and for business achievements; FInstD, FRSA, FCIPR; *Clubs* RAC, Soho House, Bluebird; *Style*— Ms Rita Rowe; ✉ Mason Williams, One Sekforde Street, Clerkenwell, London EC1R 0BE (tel 0845 094 1007, e-mail rita@mason-williams.com)

ROWE-BEDDOE, Baron (Life Peer 2006), of Kilgetty in the County of Dyfed; Sir David Sydney Rowe-Beddoe; kt (2000), DL (Gwent 2003); s of Sydney Rowe-Beddoe (d 1937), of Kilgetty, and Gwen Dolan, *née* Evans (d 1967); *b* 19 December 1937; *Educ* Llandaff Cathedral Sch, Stowe Sch, St John's Coll Cambridge (MA), Harvard Univ Grad Sch of Business Admin (PMD); *m* 1, 1962 (m dis 1982), Malinda, o da of Thomas Collison, of Calif; 3 da (Hon Lisa Dolan b 1964, Hon Samantha Olwen b 1967, Hon Amanda Sian b 1969); m 2, 1984, Madeleine Harrison, o da of late Walter Geminder; *Career* served RN, Sub-Lt Lt RNVR 1956–58, Lt RNR 1958–66; chief exec Thomas De La Rue & Co 1971–76 (joined 1961); Revlon Inc 1976–81 (pres: Latin America and Caribbean 1976–77, EMEA 1977–81); pres: GFTA Trendanalysen 1981–87, Morgan Stanley - GFTA Ltd 1983–91; chm: Cavendish Services Group 1987–93, European Hotels Corporation Ltd 2001–, Victoria Capital (UK) Ltd 2004–, gfta Analytics Ltd 2005–; dir: Development Securities plc 1994–2000, Toye Group plc 2002– (dep chm 2003–), Newport Networks Gp plc 2004–; chm: Welsh Devpt Agency 1993–2001, Devpt Bd for Rural Wales 1994–98, N Wales Economic Forum 1996–2001, Mid Wales Partnership 1996–2001, SE Wales Economic Forum 1999–2001, Wales Millennium Centre 2001–; memb: Welsh Economic Cncl 1994–96, Prince of Wales Ctee 1994–97; patron Prince's Trust Bro 1996–; dir: Int Film Festival of Wales 1998–2000; pres: Welsh Centre for Int Affrs (WCIA) 1999–2004, Celtic Film Festival 2000, Llangollen Int Musical Eisteddfod 2001–05, Royal Welsh Coll of Music and Drama 2004– (govr 1993–2004, chm Bd of Govrs 2000–04), Wales N America Business Cncl, Cardiff Business Club 2006– (chm 2002–06); chm Representative Body Church in Wales 2002–; Freeman: City of London, Worshipful Co of Broderers; Hon DUniv Glamorgan 1997, Hon DEconSc Univ of Wales 2004; hon fell: Univ of Wales Inst Cardiff 2002, Univ of Wales Coll Newport 1998, Univ of Cardiff 1999; FRSA, CCMI; *Recreations* music, theatre, country pursuits; *Clubs* Cardiff & County, Garrick, The Brook (NY); *Style*— The Lord Rowe-Beddoe, DL; ✉ Wales Millennium Centre, Bute Place, Cardiff CF10 5AL (tel 029 2063 6400)

ROWE-HAM, Sir David Kenneth; GBE (1986); s of Kenneth Henry Rowe-Ham (d 1990), and Muriel Phyllis, *née* Mundy (d 2002); *b* 19 December 1935; *Educ* Dragon Sch, Charterhouse; *m* 1 (m dis 1980), Elizabeth, *née* Aston; 1 s (Adrian); m 2, 1980, Sandra Celia, widow of Ian Glover; 1 s (Mark b 1981), and 1 adopted step s (Gerald); *Career* CA 1962; cmmnd 3 King's Own Hussars; sr ptnr Smith Keen Cutler 1972–82, conslt to Touche Ross & Co 1984–93; chm: Asset Trust plc 1982–89, Jersey General Investment Trust Ltd 1988–89, Olayan Europe Ltd 1989–, Brewin Dolphin Holdings plc 1992–2003, APTA Healthcare plc 1994–96, Coral Products plc 1995–2006, Peninsular South Asia Investment Co Ltd (formerly BNP Paribas South Asia Investment Co Ltd) 1995–, Gradus Group plc (jt chm) 1995–97, Arden Partners plc 2006–; dir: W Canning plc 1981–86, Savoy Theatre Ltd 1986–98, Williams plc 1992–2000, CLS Holdings plc 1994–99, Chubb plc 2000–03, Hikma Pharmaceuticals plc 2005–; regnl dir (London) Lloyds Bank 1985–91, memb Advsy Panel Guinness Flight Unit Trust Mangrs Ltd 1985–99 (chm 1987); Alderman City of London Ward of Bridge and Bridge Without 1976–2004, Sheriff City of London 1984–85, Lord Mayor of London 1986–87; JP City of London 1976–94, chief magistrate 1986–87; chm: Birmingham Municipal Bank 1970–72, Political Cncl Jr Carlton Club 1977; dep chm Political Ctee Carlton Club 1977–79; memb: Stock Exchange 1964–84, Birmingham City Cncl 1965–72, Ct City Univ 1981–86 (chllr 1986–87), Ct HAC 1976–2004; govr Royal Shakespeare Co 1988–2003, former tstee Friends of D'Oyly Carte; pres: Black Country Museum Devpt Tst, The Crown Agents Fndn 1996–2002; Liveryman: Worshipful Co of CAs in England and Wales (Master 1985–86), Worshipful Co of Wheelwrights; hon memb Worshipful Co of Launderers; Hon DLitt City Univ 1986; FCA; Commandeur de l'Ordre Mérite (France) 1984, Cdr Order of the Lion (Malawi) 1985, Order of the Aztec Eagle (Class II) Mexico 1985, Order of King Abdul Aziz (Class I) 1987, Grand Officier Order of Wissam Alouite (Morocco) 1987, Order of Diego Losada of Caracas (Venezuela) 1987; Pedro Ernesto medal (Rio de Janeiro) 1987; HM's Cmmn of Lieutenancy for City of London 1987–2004; KJStJ 1986; *Recreations* theatre, shooting; *Clubs* Carlton, Guildhall, Lord's Taverners; *Style*— Sir David Rowe-Ham, GBE; ✉ 140 Piccadilly, London W1J 7NS (tel 020 7245 4000)

ROWELL, Rt Rev (Douglas) Geoffrey; *see:* Gibraltar in Europe, Bishop of

ROWELL, Jack; OBE (1998); s of Edwin Cecil Rowell (d 1956), of Hartlepool, and Monica Mary, *née* Day (d 1991); *Educ* West Hartlepool GS, Univ of Oxford (MA); *m* 26 May 1969, Susan Rowell, JP, da of Alan Cooper; 2 s (Dominic John b 27 Aug 1972, Christian Michael b 24 Dec 1974); *Career* with Procter & Gamble until 1976, Lucas Ingredients Bristol 1976–88 (fin dir, chief exec), chief exec Golden Wonder 1988–92, exec dir Dalgety plc 1993–96; chm: Dolphin Computer Services Ltd 1994–99, OSI Holdings Ltd 1994–99, Marlar Bennett International Ltd 1994–99, Lyons Seafoods Ltd 1994–2003, UKR Product Group plc 2004–; non-exec chm: Pilgrim Foods Ltd 1996–2004, Coppice Ltd 2002–; dir: Celsis International plc 1994– (ceo 1998–, chm 2000), Oliver Ashworth Group plc 1997–99; memb Bd Sport England 2006–; Hon LLD Univ of Bath 1994; FCA; *Rugby career* joined Gosforth (later Newcastle Gosforth), appointed capt and later coach (winners John Player Cup Final); coach Bath RFC 1977–94 (winners John Player Specials Cup (later Pilkington Cup) 1984, 1985, 1986, 1987, 1989, 1990, 1992 and 1994, winners Courage League Div 1 1989, 1991, 1992, 1993 and 1994, winners Middx Sevens 1994), mangr England RFU team 1994–97 (5 Nations Grand Slam 1995, semi-finalists World Cup South Africa 1995, 5 Nations champions and Triple Crown 1996), dir Bristol Rugby Ltd until 2002, dir of rugby Bath RFC 2002–05, non-exec dir Bath Rugby 2005–; *Recreations* rugby, golf; *Style*— Jack Rowell, Esq, OBE; ✉ Middlehill House, Middlehill, Box, Wiltshire SN13 8QS (tel 01225 744576)

ROWEN, Paul; MP; *b* Rochdale; *Educ* Bishop Henshaw Memorial HS, Univ of Nottingham; *Career* teacher Kimberly Comp Nottingham 1977–80, head of chemistry St Albans RC HS 1980–86, head of sci Our Lady's RC HS 1986–90, dep head Yorkshire Martyrs Coll 1990–2005; cncllr (Lib Dem) Rochdale BC 1983–2007 (chair housing 1985–86, ldr Lib Dem Gp 1990–2005, ldr 1992–96), MP (Lib Dem) Rochdale 2005– (Parly candidate (Lib Dem) Rochdale 2001); *Style*— Paul Rowen, Esq, MP; ✉ House of Commons, London SW1A 0AA

ROWLAND, Gilbert Raymond David; s of Capt Norman Denis Rowland, and Effy May, *née* McEwen; *b* 8 October 1946; *Educ* Catford Secdy Sch, Royal Coll of Music; *Career* harpsichordist; major performances include: Wigmore Hall 1973–75, Greenwich Festival 1975–84, Purcell Room 1979, 1983 and 1985, Berlin 1985, Carlisle 1988, Lancaster 1989, 1991, 1993, 1996 and 2000, Peterborough Festival 1992, Leicester Early Music Festival 1998; broadcasts for BBC Radio 3 1977, 1978, 1983, 1984, and 1985; various solo recordings for Nimbus Records, Scarlatti sonatas for Kingdom Records, keyboard works of Fischer for Keyboard Records, complete harpsichord works of Rameau for Naxos Records, complete sonatas of Soler for Naxos Records; took part in: performance of Couperin's 27 Ordres 2005–06, Scarlatti's 250th anniversary celebrations 2007; piano and harpsichord teacher Epsom Coll 1969–; memb Br Harpsichord Soc; ARCO 1967, ARCM 1969; *Style*— Gilbert Rowland, Esq; ✉ 418 Brockley Road, London SE4 2DH (tel 020 8699 2549)

ROWLAND, John; QC (1996); s of Peter Rowland (d 1976), and Marion Agnes *née* Guppy; *b* 17 January 1952; *Educ* Aquinas Coll Perth, Univ of Western Aust (BSc), Univ of London (LLB); *m* 8 Dec 1979, Juliet Claire, da of Ernest John Hathaway; 3 s (Benjamin b 1985, Matthew b 1988, Luke b 1990), 2 da (Freya b 1992, Cassia b 1996); *Career* Pilot Offr RAAF 1971–72; tutor Kingswood Coll Univ of Western Aust 1973–74; called to the Bar: Middle Temple 1979, Victoria 2002; in practice 1979–; admitted to practice NSW and Victoria 2001; memb: London Common Law Bar Assoc 1984, COMBAR; *Recreations* cricket, walking, skiing; *Style*— Mr John Rowland, QC; ✉ 4 Pump Court, Temple, London EC4Y 7AN (tel 020 7842 5555, fax 020 7583 2036, e-mail jrowland@4pumpcourt.com)

ROWLAND, Jonathan (Jon); s of David Rowland, and Sara, *née* Porush; *b* 7 November 1946; *Educ* UCS, Univ Coll London, Architectural Assoc Sch of Architecture (AA Dipl), Univ of Sussex (MA); *m* 1 Feb 1972, Charlotte Ann, da of Gordon Scott Bessey; 1 da (Abigail Amber b 29 June 1976), 1 s (Adam Benjamin b 30 March 1979); *Career* conslt architect and urban designer; principal of Jon Rowland Urban Design; responsible for urban design strategies in Liverpool, York, South Bank London, Newcastle, Leeds, Bracknell, and Lewisham, city centre masterplans for Cardiff, Lincoln, Gloucester and Bristol; responsible for the Strategy for Architecture and the Built Environment in SW, urban design assistance to Crown Estates, urban design guidance for S Oxon, advsr spatial devpt strategy GLA, new urban villages at Runcorn and Warrington, new Millennium community at Telford; worked in Africa, S Asia, Far East, Caribbean on World Bank and ODA projects; other projects incl city centre masterplans in Lincoln, Cardiff and Bristol; memb: Ctee Urban Design Gp (chm 1992–97), English Partnerships National Design Advsy Panel, Design Panel NWDA; vice-chair Urban Design Alliance; enabler Cmmn for Architecture and the Built Environment (CABE) (rep SE Region); former visiting lectr: Architectural Assoc, Oxford Brookes Univ; memb Editorial Bd: Open House, Urban Design International; exhibitor at: Royal Acad London, Green Coll Oxford, Wolfson Coll Oxford; memb: RIBA, ARCUK, Royal Anthropological Inst, Urban Design Gp, Land Use Soc, Landscape Fndn; FRSA; *Publications* Community Decay (1973), Urban Design Futures (2006); author of numerous articles in various professional jls; *Recreations* music, art, walking; *Style*— Jon Rowland, Esq; ✉ Jon Rowland Urban Design, 65 Hurst Rise Road, Oxford OX2 9HE (tel 01865 863642, fax 01865 863502, e-mail jonrowland@jrud.co.uk, website www.jrud.co.uk)

ROWLAND, Prof Malcolm; s of Stanley Rowland (d 1973); *b* 5 August 1939; *Educ* Univ of London (BPharm, PhD, DSc); *m* 5 Sept 1965, Dawn; 2 da (Lisa Claire b 21 Dec 1968, Michelle b 1 July 1970); *Career* assoc prof of pharmacy and pharmaceutical chemistry Univ of Calif San Francisco 1970–75 (asst prof 1967–71); Univ of Manchester: prof of pharmacy 1975–2005, head Dept of Pharmacy 1988–91, dean Sch of Pharmacy 1998–2001, research prof 2002–05, prof emeritus 2002–; visiting prof Center for Drug Devpt Science Sch of Pharmacy Univ of Calif San Francisco at Washington DC 2005–; chief exec Medeval Ltd 1983–93 (pres 1993–98), fndr and princ NDA Partners 2003–; ed Jl of Pharmacokinetics and Pharmacodynamics (formerly Jl of Pharmacokinetics and Biopharmaceutics) 1973–2006; pres European Fedn of Pharmaceutical Scientists 1996–2000, vice-pres Int Pharmaceutical Fedn 2001–; Hon DSc Univ of Poitiers 1981, Hon DPh Univ of Uppsala 1989; fell: Royal Pharmaceutical Soc of GB 1987 (memb 1965), American Assoc of Pharmaceutical Scientists 1988; hon fell American Coll of Clinical Pharmacology; Hon MRCP, FIMA 1978, FMedSci 2001; *Books* incl: Clinical Pharmacokinetics: Concepts and Applications (with Dr T N Tozer, 3 edn 1995), Introduction to Pharmacokinetics and Pharmacodynamics (with Dr T N Tozer, 2006);

Style— Prof Malcolm Rowland; ✉ School of Pharmacy and Pharmaceutical Sciences, University of Manchester, Manchester M13 9PL (tel 0161 275 2348, fax 0161 273 8196)

ROWLAND PAYNE, Dr Christopher Melville Edwin; s of Maj Edwin Rowland Payne, and Rosemary Ann, *née* Bird; *b* 19 May 1955; *Educ* Clifton, Univ of London, Bart's Med Coll (MB BS, MRCP); *m* 28 May 1994, Wendy Margaret, da of Maxwell Mair, of Bermuda; 3 da (Anoushka Poppy Joy b 26 Sept 1997, Alexandra Katinka Heather b 25 March 1999, Araminta Lily Bird Mair b 19 Jan 2004); *Career* conslt dermatologist and landowner; house surgn St Bart's Hosp London 1978; house physician: Med Prof Unit Royal Infirmary Edinburgh 1978, Royal Marsden Hosp 1979; dermatological registrar St Thomas' Hosp London 1980–83, dermatological sr registrar Westminster Hosp 1983–89; professeur universitaire Faculté de Medecine de Paris 1985–86; conslt dermatologist: Kent and Canterbury Hosp 1990–94, William Harvey Hosp Kent 1990–97, Cromwell Hosp London 1990–2000, St Saviour's Hosp Kent 1990–2003, The London Clinic 1995–, Royal Marsden Hosp 1997–2001; clinical prof of dermatology Ross Univ NY 1990; visiting prof of dermatology Univ of Sci and Technol Kumasi Ghana 1995; HAC 1974–76; ed Jl of Cosmetic Dermatology 2000–04; Roxburgh prize 1977; Br Assoc of Dermatologists awards 1984, 1985, 1986, 1988, 1989 and 1993; Dowling Club prizes: 1985, 1986, 1987 and 1988, MRC project grant 1988–89; RCP award 1989; sec-gen Euro Soc for Cosmetic and Aesthetic Dermatology 1997– (pres 1998–99); hon memb Société Française de Dermatologie; memb: Br Assoc of Dermatologists, Int Soc for Dermatological Surgery; UK co-ordinator Euro Soc for Laser Dermatology; Freeman City of London, Liveryman Worshipful Soc of Apothecaries; *Publications* contrib: BMJ, Lancet, British Jl of Dermatology, Jl of Cosmetic Dermatology and others; *Recreations* shooting, cycling, military history; *Clubs* Cardiff and County; *Style—* Dr Christopher Rowland Payne; ✉ The London Clinic, 149 Harley Street, London W1G 6DE (tel 020 7224 1228, fax 020 7487 5479, e-mail crp@thelondonclinic.co.uk); 32 Warwick Square, London SW1V 2AD

ROWLANDS, Anthony Francis; s of Arthur Rowlands (d 1998), and Joan, *née* Shortt; *b* 11 August 1952; *Educ* Ryde Sch, The Queen's Coll Oxford (open scholarship), Churchill Coll Cambridge, Inst of Educn Univ of London; *m* 1981, Harriet Jane, da of late Alick Isaacs, FRS, and Dr Susanna Isaacs Elmhirst; 1 da (Alice Louisa b 13 June 1983), 1 s (Samuel Peter Harold b 4 March 1986); *Career* history teacher: Bristol GS 1976–79, Haberdashers' Aske's Sch 1979–89, Dr Challoner's GS Amersham 1990–98; dir Centre for Reform 2000–05, exec dir Centre Forum 2005–; cncllr St Albans City and Dist Cncl 1986–2003 and 2006–, cncllr Herts CC 1993–97; Parly candidate (Lib Dem) St Albans 1997, Parly candidate (Lib Dem) IOW 2005; *Recreations* running (completed 11 London marathons), cricket, football, supporting Burnley FC; *Clubs* MCC, National Liberal; *Style—* Anthony Rowlands, Esq; ✉ 106 Beaumont Avenue, St Albans, Hertfordshire AL1 4TP (tel 01727 839132, e-mail anthonyrowlands@hotmail.com)

ROWLANDS, Prof Brian James; *b* 18 March 1945; *Educ* Wirral GS Cheshire, Guy's Hosp Med Sch (MB BS), Univ of Sheffield; *m* 16 Oct 1971, Judith Thomas; 1 da (Rachel b 14 March 1975); *Career* lectr Dept of Surgery Univ of Sheffield 1974–77, fell surgical gastroenterology and nutrition Dept of Surgery Univ of Texas Med Sch Houston 1977–78; Univ of Texas Health Sci Centre Houston: instr surgery 1977–78, asst prof of surgery 1978–81, assoc prof of surgery 1981–86; prof and head Dept of Surgery Queen's Univ Belfast 1986–97, prof and head of Section of Surgery and Div of Gastrointestinal Surgery Queen's Medical Centre Univ of Nottingham 1997–; memb Surgical Res Soc, sec Assoc of Profs Surgery, chm Scientific Ctee Assoc of Surgns of GB and I 1997–; FRCS 1973, fell American Coll Surgns 1983; FRCSI 1988, FRCS (Ed) 1995, FRCPS (Glas) 1995; *Books* The Physiological Basis of Modern Surgical Care (jt ed, 1988); *Style—* Prof Brian J Rowlands; ✉ Queen's Medical Centre, University Hospital, Nottingham NG7 2UH (tel 0115 970 9245, fax 0115 970 9428, e-mail bjr.surgery@nottingham.ac.uk)

ROWLANDS, Chris; *Educ* Univ of London (LLB); *Career* early career with Barclays Bank, with 3i Gp plc 1984–96, ptnr and head of corp finance Arthur Andersen 1996–2002 (latterly memb UK Leadership Team); 3i Gp plc: memb Exec Ctee 2002–, head of gp markets and growth capital 2002–05, head of gp markets 2005–; non-exec dir Principality Building Soc 2005–; *Style—* Mr Chris Rowlands; ✉ 3i Group plc, 91 Waterloo Road, London SE1 8XP

ROWLANDS, Christopher John (Chris); s of Wilfred John Rowlands (d 1978), of Leeds, and Margaretta, *née* Roberts; *b* 29 August 1951; *Educ* Roundhay Sch Leeds, Gonville & Caius Coll Cambridge (MA Econ); *m* 1978, Alison Mary, da of Capt Edward Peter Craig Kelly RN; 2 da (Victoria Grace, Amy Louise (twins) b Aug 1981); *Career* Peat Marwick Mitchell: articled clerk 1973–75, CA 1975, mangr 1981, seconded as ptnr Lusaka Zambia 1981–83, sr mangr London Office 1983–85; Asda Group plc: controller business planning Asda Stores 1985–86, divnl dir gp finance 1986–88, dep md/fin dir all gp property devpt and investment cos 1988–92; HTV Group plc: gp fin dir 1992–93, chief exec 1993–97; chief exec The Television Corporation plc 1998–2001; chief operating offr and dep chm Apace Media plc 2005–; formerly non-exec dir: Access Plus Ltd, Bristol & London plc, iTouch plc 2002–05, currently non-exec dir Deutsche Equity Income Trust plc; memb ITVA Cncl 1993–97 (chm Engrg Policy Gp 1994–97); FCA 1975, CIMgt, FRSA; *Recreations* family, theatre, church, skiing, tennis, travel; *Style—* Chris Rowlands, Esq; ✉ Apace Media Group plc, Sheperds East, Richmond Way, London W14 0DQ

ROWLANDS, Sir David; KCB (2006, CB 1991); s of late George Joseph Rowlands, of Great Crosby, and Margaret, *née* Whittington; *b* 31 May 1947; *Educ* St Mary's Coll Great Crosby, St Edmund Hall Oxford (BA); *m* 8 Nov 1975, Louise Marjorie, da of late George Brown; 2 s (Iain George b 22 March 1980, Simon David b 2 Oct 1982); *Career* DTI: joined 1974, private sec to Min of State for Industry 1978–80, princ 1980–83; Dept of Tport: asst sec 1984–90, under sec 1990–93, dep sec 1993; dir railways, aviation, logistics, maritime and security Dept for Tport (previously DETR then DTLR) 1997–2003, perm sec Dept for Tport 2003–07; *Style—* Sir David Rowlands, KCB

ROWLANDS, Baron (Life Peer UK 2004), of Merthyr Tydfil and Rhymney in the County of Mid Glamorgan; Edward (Ted) Rowlands; s of William Samuel Rowlands (d 1966), of Rhondda; *b* 23 January 1940; *Educ* Rhondda GS, Wirral GS, King's Coll London; *m* 1968, Janice Williams (d 2004); 2 s, 1 da; *Career* res asst History of Parly Tst 1963–65, lectr in modern history and govr Welsh Coll of Advanced Technol 1965–66; MP (Lab): Cardiff N 1966–70, Merthyr Tydfil 1972–83, Merthyr Tydfil and Rhymney 1983–2001; Parly under-sec of state: for Wales 1969–70 and 1974–75, FCO 1975–76; min of state FCO 1976–79; oppn front bench spokesman on: Foreign and Cwlth Affairs 1979–81, Energy 1981–87; chm: All-Pty Gp on Publishing 1983–84, Select Ctee on Defence Trade and Industry and Foreign Affairs; memb Select Ctee on Foreign Affairs 1987–2001; memb: Governing Body and Exec of Cwlth Inst 1980–91, Academic Cncl Wilton Park 1983–90; judge: Booker McConnell Novel of the Year Competition 1984, Manchester Oddfellows Social Award Book; *Style—* The Rt Hon the Lord Rowlands; ✉ 42 Station Road, Kidwelly, Carmathenshire SA17 4UT

ROWLEY, Sir Charles Robert; 8 Bt (GB 1786) of Tendring Hall, Suffolk, and 7 Bt (UK 1836), of Hill House, Berkshire; s of Lt-Col Sir William Joshua Rowley, 6 Bt (d 1971); suc kinsman, Sir Joshua Francis Rowley, 7 Bt (d 1997) (proved claim 2002); *b* 15 March 1926; *Educ* Wellington; *m* 1952, Astrid, da of late Sir Arthur Massey, CBE; 1 da (Caroline Astrid (Mrs Edwin March Phillipps de Lisle) b 1955), 1 s (Richard Charles b 1959); *Heir* s, Richard Rowley; *Style—* Sir Charles Rowley, Bt; ✉ Naseby Hall, Northamptonshire NN6 6DP; 21 Tedworth Square, London SW3 4DR

ROWLEY, Prof David Ian; s of Sydney Garnett Rowley (d 1987), and Jessie, *née* Boot (d 1984); *b* 4 July 1951; *Educ* Wheelwright GS Dewsbury, Univ of Aberdeen (BMed Biol, MB ChB), Univ of Sheffield (MD); *m* 5 Aug 1975, Ingrid Ginette, da of K Mueller (d 1985); 1 da (Kristina Ann Ginette b 1976), 1 s (Andrew Graham David b 1979); *Career* lectr in orthopeadic surgery Univ of Sheffield 1981–85, sr lectr in orthopaedic surgery Univ of Manchester 1985–88, sr lectr in orthopaedic mechanics Univ of Salford 1986–88, prof of orthopaedic and trauma surgery Univ of Dundee 1988– (dep dean of medicine 2004–06); hon chair of surgical antomy and educn Univ of Edinburgh; RCS(Ed): dir of educn 2003–, memb Cncl 2003–; memb Cncl BOA 2004–06; Woolmer lectr Inst of Physics and Engrg and Medicine 1997, Livingstone lectr RCS Glasgow 1998; regnl advsr in surgery and examiner RCSEd, intercollegiate examiner on orthopaedic surgery/accident and emergency medicine; Symes prof and gold medallist RCS(Ed) 1995; non-exec memb Tayside Health Bd Appts 1999–2007; FRCSEd, FRCSGlas, FBOA, FRCS 2000; *Books* Skeletal Injuries in Old Age (1994), Surgery of Disorders of the Foot and Ankle (ed, 1996), Clinical Surgery (co-author and ed, 1996 and 2003), War Wounds with Fractures: A Guide to Surgical Management (1996 and 2002), The Musculoskeltal System (with J A Dent, 1997); *Style—* Prof David Rowley; ✉ Marclann Cottage, Kellie Castle, Arbirlot, Arbroath, Angus DD11 2PB (tel 01241 876466, fax 01241 431894); University Department of Orthopaedic Surgery, Ninewells Hospital and Medical School, Dundee DD1 9SY (tel 01382 425746, fax 01382 496200, e-mail d.i.rowley@dundee.ac.uk)

ROWLEY, Paul Keith; s of James Keith Rowley (d 1988), and Christine Mabel Stableford, *née* Damp; *b* 17 March 1966, Preston, Lancs; *m* 25 Aug 1995, Sara Elizabeth, *née* Douglas; 2 s (George Alexander b 3 Nov 1997, Lucus James b 10 July 2001); *Career* apprentice bricklayer 1982–87, mgmnt trainee Alfred McAlpine 1987–93, land and sales mangr Fairclough Homes 1991–93, md Rowland Homes 1993–; Property Entrepeneur of the Year NW 2003 and 2005; *Recreations* fell walking, skiing; *Style—* Paul Rowley, Esq; ✉ Rowland Homes, Farington House, Stanifield Lane, Leyland, Lancashire PR25 4UA (tel 01772 621166, fax 017772 623552, e-mail paul.rowley@rowland.co.uk)

ROWLEY-HILL, Sir John Alfred; 11 Bt (I 1779), of Brook Hall, Londonderry; s of Sir George Alfred Rowley Hill, 9 Bt (d 1985), and his 2 w, Jessie Anne, *née* Roberts (d 1995); suc half-bro, Sir Richard George Rowley Hill, 10 Bt (d 1992); *b* 29 February 1940; *m* 1966 (m dis 1981), Diana Anne, da of Donald Wilfred Walker, of Blaby, Leics; 1 adopted s (James Richard Rowley-Hill b 27 June 1974), 1 adopted da (Samantha Rowley-Hill b 9 July 1976); *Style—* Sir John Rowley-Hill, Bt; ✉ 5 Wherry Close, March, Cambridgeshire PE15 9BX

ROWLING, JK (Joanne Kathleen); OBE (2000); *Educ* Univ of Exeter; *m* 26 Dec 2001, Dr Neil Murray; *Career* children's writer; hon degree: Napier Univ 2000, Dartmouth Coll USA 2000, Univ of Exeter 2000, Univ of St Andrews 2000; FRSL; *Books* Harry Potter and the Philosopher's Stone (1997), Harry Potter and the Chamber of Secrets (1998), Harry Potter and the Prisoner of Azkaban (1999), Harry Potter and the Goblet of Fire (2000), Quidditch Through the Ages (2001), Fantastic Beasts & Where to Find Them (2001), Harry Potter and the Order of the Phoenix (2003), Harry Potter and the Half-Blood Prince (2005), Harry Potter and the Deathly Hallows (2007); *Awards* incl: Twice winner of Nestlé Smarties Book Prize Gold Medal 9–11 Years, FCBG Children's Book Award, Birmingham Cable Children's Book Award, The Young Telegraph Paperback of the Year, British Book Awards' Children's Book of the Year, The Sheffield Children's Book Award, Sorcières Prix 1999, Premio Cento per la Letteratura Infantile 1998, Whitbread Children's Book of the Year 2000, W H Smith Book of the Year 2006; *Style—* Ms Joanne Rowling, OBE; ✉ c/o The Christopher Little Literary Agency, Ten Eel Brook Studios, 125 Moore Park Road, London SW6 4PS (tel 020 7736 4455, fax 020 7736 4490)

ROWLINSON, Prof Sir John Shipley; kt (2000); s of Frank Rowlinson (d 1986), and Winifred, *née* Jones (d 1994); *b* 12 May 1926; *Educ* Rossall Sch Fleetwood, Trinity Coll Oxford (BSc, MA, DPhil); *m* 2 Aug 1952, Nancy, da of Horace Gaskell (d 1970); 1 s (Paul b 1954), 1 da (Stella (Dr Barczak) b 1956); *Career* res assoc Univ of Wisconsin 1950–51, sr lectr in chem Univ of Manchester 1957–60 (res fell 1951–54, lectr 1954–57), prof of chem technol Univ of London 1961–73, Dr Lee's prof of chem Univ of Oxford 1974–93, fell Exeter Coll Oxford 1974–, A D White prof-at-large Cornell Univ 1990–96; borough cncllr Sale 1956–59; physical sec and vice-pres Royal Soc 1994–99; hon foreign memb American Acad of Arts and Sci 1994; FRSC, FIChemE, FREng 1976, FRS 1970, Hon FCGI 1986; *Books* Liquids and Liquid Mixtures (1959), The Perfect Gas (1963), Thermodynamics for Chemical Engineers (1975), Molecular Theory of Capillarity (1982), JD van der Waals, On the Continuity of the Gaseous and Liquid States (ed, 1988), Van der Waals and Molecular Science (1996), Cohesion: A scientific history of intermolecular forces (2002); *Recreations* hill walking; *Clubs* Alpine; *Style—* Prof Sir John Rowlinson, FRS, FREng; ✉ 12 Pullen's Field, Oxford OX3 0BU (tel 01865 767507); Physical and Theoretical Chemistry Laboratory, South Parks Road, Oxford OX1 3QZ (tel 01865 275400, e-mail john.rowlinson@chem.ox.ac.uk)

ROWLINSON, Stephen Richard; s of Henry Robert Rowlinson (d 1988), of Godalming; *b* 25 December 1939; *Educ* Wanstead HS, Univ of Nottingham (BA); *m* 17 Aug 1967, Kathleen Ann (Kathy); 2 s (Benjamin Toby, Thomas Henry), 1 da (Emily Kate Louise); *Career* Sullivan Stauffer Colwell Bayles Inc 1961–62, Harris Lebus Ltd 1962–67, McKinsey and Co Inc 1967–74, TCK Gp Ltd 1974–77, Rowlinson Tomala and Assocs Ltd 1977–80, Bickerton Rowlinson Ltd 1980–85, Korn/Ferry Int Ltd 1985–89, Penna plc 1989–91, Merton Associates Ltd 1991–2001, chm Bartlett Merton Ltd 1998–2001, chief exec Daric plc 1998–2001, chm London Private Capital Ltd 2002–, chm Exton Estates Ltd 2002–05, chm Penna Consulting plc 2005–; *Recreations* sailing, skiing; *Clubs* Royal Thames Yacht; *Style—* Stephen Rowlinson, Esq; ✉ 16 Wallside, Barbican, London EC2Y 8BH (e-mail stephenrowlinson@hotmail.co.uk)

R

ROWNTREE, Graham Christopher; s of Christopher Rowntree, of Leicester, and Patricia Jane, *née* Lough; *b* 18 April 1971; *Educ* Hastings HS Hinckley, John Cleveland Coll Hinckley; *Career* rugby union prop; clubs: Nuneaton RFC 1979–86, Leicester Tigers 1986– (youth team, first team debut aged 19, winners Pilkington Cup 1993, Courage League Champions 1995, Zurich Premiership 2000 and 2001, Zurich Championship 2001, Heineken Cup 2001); represented: Leicestershire U14, Leicestershire and Midlands U16, U18 and U21, Midlands Div v All Blacks 1993, Barbarians v Newport 1993 and v East Midlands 1994; England: U16, U18, Colts, U21, A tour Canada 1993, memb sr squad tour South Africa 1994, memb squad tour North America 2001, first full cap when came on as sub v Scotland 1995 (sub since 1993), started v Italy and v Western Samoa World Cup South Africa 1995, 35 full caps; memb British Lions tour to South Africa 1997 and NZ 2005; non sporting career currently with P & G Blands Insurance Brokers Leicester; *Recreations* training, training and more training, golf; *Style—* Graham Rowntree, Esq; ✉ c/o Leicester RFC, The Clubhouse, Aylestone Road, Leicester LE2 7LF

ROWSON, Peter Aston; s of Dr Lionel Edward Aston Rowson, OBE, FRS (d 1989); *b* 8 October 1942; *Educ* St Edmunds Coll Ware; *m* 1967, Jennifer Mary, *née* Smyth; 1 s, 2 da; *Career* accountant; fin dir and co sec: Panther Securities plc, Panther Devpts Ltd, Panther Shop Investments Ltd, Panther Shop Investments (Midlands) Ltd, Westmead Building Company Ltd, Saxonbest Ltd, MRG Systems Ltd, Etonbrook Properties plc, Multitrust Property Investments Ltd, Yardworth Ltd, Excelchoice Ltd, Snowbest Ltd, Panther (Dover) Ltd, Surrey Motors Ltd, Panther (Bromley) Ltd; co sec: Perand Ltd, Dreamwish Ltd, Wenhedge Ltd; dir: Wenhedge Ltd, Northstar Property Investment Ltd (also sec), Northstar Properties Ltd, Northstar Land Ltd; dir and co sec: London Property Co plc, Eurocity Properties plc, Eurocity (Seaside) Ltd, Eurocity Properties (Central) Ltd, Eurocity Properties (Manchester) Ltd, Oak Properties Ltd, Oak II Properties Ltd, Trio Properties Ltd, Eurocity (Rugby) Ltd, CJV Properties Ltd, Eurocity (Crawley) Ltd; *Style—*

Peter Rowson, Esq; ✉ Panther House, 38 Mount Pleasant, London WC1X 0AN (tel 020 7278 8011)

ROXBURGH, Prof Ian Walter; s of Walter McRonald Roxburgh, and Kathleen Joyce, *née* Prescott; *b* 31 August 1939; *Educ* King Edward VII GS Sheffield, Univ of Nottingham (BSc), Univ of Cambridge (PhD); *m* 1960, Diana Patricia, *née* Dunn; 2 s, 1 da; *Career* research fell Churchill Coll Cambridge 1963, lectr in maths KCL 1964–66 (asst lectr 1963–64), reader in astronomy Univ of Sussex 1966–67; Queen Mary & Westfield Coll (formerly QMC) London: prof of applied maths 1967–87, head Sch of Mathematical Scis 1978–95, dir Astronomy Unit 1983–2001, prof of maths and astronomy 1987–, pro-princ 1987; chm Heads of Univ Depts of Mathematics & Statistics 1988–93; conslt European Space Agency; Parly candidate: (Liberal) Walthamstow W 1970, (SDP) Ilford North 1983; memb: European Physical Soc, European Astronomical Soc, Int Astronomical Union, London Mathematic Soc; hon chercheur associé Observatoire de Paris; CPhys, FInstP, FRAS; *Style—* Prof Ian W Roxburgh; ✉ 37 Leicester Road, Wanstead, London E11 2DW (tel 020 8989 7117)

ROXBURGH, Roy; s of William Addison Roxburgh (d 1970), of Dunfermline, and Elizabeth, *née* Melville; *b* 29 September 1950, London; *Educ* Owens GS Islington, Dunfermline HS, Univ of Edinburgh (LLB); *m* 15 March 1975, Joyce Ross, *née* Dickson; 1 da (Elisabeth b 6 Nov 1982), 1 s (Ross b 15 May 1985); *Career* admitted slr 1974; ptnr Iain Smith & Co 1977–; memb R3 Scottish Tech Ctee; memb Law Soc of Scotland 1974 (memb Insolvency Slrs Ctee); *Books* The Law and Practice of Receivership in Scotland (3rd edn 2005); *Recreations* skiing, golf, bridge, chess; *Clubs* Deeside Golf, Ballater Golf; *Style—* Roy Roxburgh, Esq; ✉ Iain Smith & Co, 18–20 Queen's Road, Aberdeen AB15 4ZT

ROXBURGH, Dr Stuart Thomas Dalrymple; s of Robert Roxburgh (d 2002), and Helen Roxburgh (d 2000); *b* 10 May 1950; *Educ* Camphill Sch, Univ of Glasgow (MB ChB); *m* 25 June 1975, Christine MacLeod Campbell, da of John Ramsay (d 1979); 1 s (Campbell b 27 March 1980), 1 da (Alison b 5 Oct 1982); *Career* conslt ophthalmologist Tayside Health Bd, hon sr lectr Dept of Ophthalmology Univ of Dundee (former head of Dept); vice-chm Acad of Royal Colleges and Facilities in Scotland 2003–05; FRCSEd 1979, FRCOphth 1988 (vice-pres, chm Examination Ctee 2000–04); *Recreations* golf, hill walking, painting; *Style—* Dr Stuart Roxburgh; ✉ 4 Craigie Knowes Avenue, Perth PH2 0DL (tel 01738 634347, e-mail stuart.roxburgh@blueyonder.co.uk); Ninewells Hospital and Medical School, Dundee DD1 9SY (tel 01382 660111, fax 01382 660130)

ROXBURGHE, 10 Duke of (S 1707); Sir Guy David Innes-Ker; 11 Bt (Premier Bt of Scotland or Nova Scotia, S 1625); also Lord Roxburghe (S before 31 March 1600), Earl of Roxburghe, Lord Ker of Cessford and Cavertoun (both S 1616), Marquis of Bowmont and Cessford, Earl of Kelso, Viscount of Broxmouth (S, with the Dukedom the last Peerages cr in the Peerage of Scotland, 1707), and Earl Innes (UK 1837); s of 9 Duke of Roxburghe (d 1974) and his 2 w (late Mrs Jocelyn Hambro); 1 Earl obtained a charter in 1648 of succession to the honour, to his gs 4 s of his da Countess of Perth, and after him the 3 s successively of his gda Countess of Wigton; Dukedom in remainder to whoever succeeds to Earldom; *b* 18 November 1954; *Educ* Eton, Magdalene Coll Cambridge; *m* 1, 1977 (m dis 1990), Lady Jane, *née* Grosvenor, da of 5 Duke of Westminster and Hon Viola Lyttelton, da of 9 Viscount Cobham;1 da (Lady Rosanagh Viola Alexandra b 1979), 2 s (Charles Robert George, Marquess of Bowmont and Cessford b 1981, Lord Edward Arthur Gerald b 1984); m 2, 3 Sept 1992, Virginia Mary, da of David Wynn-Williams; 1 da (Lady Isabella May b 1994), 1 s (Lord George Alastair b 1996); *Heir* s, Marquess of Bowmont and Cessford; *Career* formerly Lt RHG/1 Dragoons; landowner, co dir; Liveryman Worshipful Co of Fishmongers; *Recreations* fishing, shooting, golf, racing, skiing; *Clubs* White's, Turf; *Style—* His Grace the Duke of Roxburghe; ✉ Floors Castle, Kelso, Roxburghshire (tel 01573 224288); Roxburghe Estate Office, Kelso, Roxburghshire (tel 01573 223333, e-mail estate@floorscastle.com)

ROY, Prof Donald Hubert; s of William Hadland Roy (d 1987), and Winifred Elizabeth Margaret, *née* Davies (d 1993); *b* 5 April 1930; *Educ* Canton HS Cardiff, Univ of Wales (BA, MA, DipEd), Univ of Paris Sorbonne; *m* 1, 4 Aug 1955 (m dis 1959), Jane Elizabeth Ailwen Phillips (Sian Phillips); m 2, 25 Jan 1975, Arlette, da of James William Hopper, of Sutton, Surrey; 1 s (Gareth b 1978), 1 da (Francesca b 1980); *Career* Nat Serv cmmnd RAF 1954–56; asst lectr in French Univ of St Andrews 1958–59, lectr in French (former asst lectr) Univ of Glasgow 1959–63, dir and prof of drama (former lectr i/c and sr lectr) Univ of Hull 1963–95 (prof emeritus 1995–), visiting prof Univ of Delaware 1974, visiting dir Central Univ of Iowa 1987; FRSA 1984; *Books* Molière - Five Plays (1982), Plays by James Robinson Planché (1986), Jacques Copeau and the Cartel des Quatre (1993), Romantic and Revolutionary Theatre, 1789–1860 (2003); *Recreations* reading, gardening, hill walking; *Style—* Prof Donald Roy; ✉ Department of Drama, University of Hull, Hull, HU6 7RX (tel 01482 447566, fax 01482 466727)

ROY, Frank; MP; s of James Roy (d 1989), and Esther, *née* McMahon; *b* 29 August 1958; *Educ* St Josephs' HS Motherwell, Our Lady's HS Motherwell, Motherwell Coll (HNC), Glasgow Caledonian Univ (BA); *m* 17 Sept 1977, Ellen, da of Patrick Foy; 1 s (Brian), 1 da (Kelly-Anne); *Career* Ravenscraig Steelworks 1977–91, PA to Helen Liddell, MP 1994–97; MP (Lab) Motherwell and Wishaw 1997–, PPS to sec of state for Scotland Dr John Reid, MP 1999–2001, PPS to dep sec of state Helen Liddell, MP 1998–99, asst govt whip 2005–06, a Lord Cmmr of HM Treasy (Govt whip) 2006–; House of Commons: memb Social Security Select Ctee 1997–98, memb Defence Select Ctee 2001–05; *Recreations* gardening, reading, football; *Style—* Frank Roy, Esq, MP; ✉ House of Commons, London SW1A 0AA (tel 020 7219 3000)

ROY, Nicholas Guy; s of Dr Hiren Roy, of Sutton Coldfield, W Midlands, and Hilda Mary, *née* Dore (d 1995); *b* 14 November 1942, London; *Educ* St Paul's, UCL (LLB); *m* 1, 18 Jan 1964, Madeline Jean, *née* Plant (d 2000); 2 s (David Andrew Guy b 11 Dec 1963, Justin Nicholas b 17 April 1970); m 2, 14 Sept 2002, Stella Inglis, *née* Millar, wid of Donald Inglis; *Career* admitted slr 1969; Freeland & Passey: articled clerk 1967–69, asst slr 1969–72; ptnr: Watt & Morgan 1972–74, John Morgan 1974–89; sole princ 1989–2000, ptnr Jonas Roy Bloom 2000–; dep stipendiary magistrate (Stoke-on-Trent and Bradford) 1994–99; chm Sutton Coldfield Round Table 1980–81; *Recreations* gardening, entertaining, travelling, church; *Clubs* Coleshill & District 41; *Style—* Nicholas Roy, Esq; ✉ Jonas Roy Bloom, 190 Corporation Street, Birmingham B4 6QD (tel 0121 212 4111, fax 0121 212 1770, e-mail nicholas_roy@jonasroybloom.co.uk)

ROYALL, District Judge Martyn; s of late Frederick Bertram Royall, of Torquay, and Edna Doreen, *née* Ball; *b* 8 January 1948; *Educ* Bishop Wordsworth Sch Salisbury, Coll of Law Guildford; *m* 24 June 1972, Jacqueline Barbara, da of late Jack Thompson; 1 da (Anna Rebecca b 16 Jan 1974), 1 s (Jack Hain b 13 Oct 1975, Thomas Martyn b 2 July 1979); *Career* articled Thomas Eggar & Sons Chichester, qualified slr 1972, ptnr Hawkins 1973–92 (joined 1972), district judge 1992–, recorder 2000– (asst recorder 1997–2000); pres: Kings Lynn W Norfolk Law Soc 1988– (sec 1974–83), Assoc of District Judges 2004–05; chm Nat Young Slrs Gp 1982; memb The Law Soc; *Recreations* outdoor sports (incl shooting); *Clubs* Norfolk; *Style—* District Judge Martyn Royall; ✉ Norwich Combined Court, The Law Courts, Bishopsgate, Norfolk NR3 1UR (tel 01603 728200)

ROYALL OF BLAISDON, Baroness (Life Peer UK 2004), of Blaisdon in the County of Gloucestershire; Janet Anne (Jan) Royall; da of Basil Oscar Royall (d 1993), and Myra Jessie, *née* Albutt (d 1995); *b* 20 August 1955, Glos; *Educ* Royal Forest of Dean GS, Westfield Coll Univ of London (BA), South Bank Poly (Dip); *m* 6 Sept 1980, Stuart Henry James Hercock, s of late Henry Hercock; 1 da (Hon Charlotte Rebecca b 2 Sept 1984), 2 s (Hon Edwin Henry Frederick b 28 May 1986, Hon Henry Jonathan b 5 Feb 1989); *Career* Continental Farms Europe 1978, sec-gen Br Lab Gp European Parl 1979–85, Office of Ldr of the Oppn 1985–92, political advsr to Rt Hon Neil Kinnock MP 1992–94, cabinet memb to Rt Hon Neil Kinnock (as EU Cmmr) 1995–2001, Parly co-ordinator Press and Communications Dept European Cmmn 2001–03, head EC Office Cardiff 2003–04, Govt whip House of Lords 2005–; pres Autism Cymru, patron Kidney Wales Fndn; *Recreations* gardening, reading, swimming; *Style—* The Rt Hon the Lady Royall of Blaisdon; ✉ House of Lords, London SW1A 0PW (tel 020 7219 8652, e-mail royallj@parliament.uk)

ROYCE, Hon Mr Justice; Sir (Roger) John Royce; kt (2002); s of John Roger Royce (d 1990), and Margaret (Peggy), *née* Sibbald (d 2005); *b* 27 August 1944; *Educ* The Leys Sch Cambridge, Trinity Hall Cambridge (BA); *m* 12 May 1979, Gillian Wendy, da of Geoffrey Guy Adderley; 2 s (Andrew David Lyndon b 1986, David John Henry b 1989), 1 da (Joanna Katy Rachel b 1984); *Career* admitted slr 1969, called to the Bar Gray's Inn 1970, bencher 1997, recorder 1986–2002, QC 1987, dep High Ct judge (Queen's Bench Div) 1993, leader (Western Circuit) 1998–2001, judge of the High Court (Queen's Bench Div) 2002–, presiding judge Western Circuit 2006–; sport: Univ of Cambridge Hockey Blue 1965–66, East Hockey 1965–66, West Hockey 1972–73, capt Somerset Hockey 1976, qualified ski instr Austria 1969; *Recreations* skiing, cricket, golf, collecting corkscrews; *Clubs* Hawks' (Cambridge), St Enodoc GC; *Style—* The Hon Mr Justice Royce; ✉ Royal Courts of Justice, Strand, London WC2A 2LL

ROYDEN, Sir Christopher John; 5 Bt (UK 1905), of Frankby Hall, Co Palatine of Chester; s of Sir John Royden, 4 Bt (d 1976), of Battle, E Sussex, and (Dolores) Catherine (d 1994), da of Cecil Coward, of Lima, Peru; *b* 26 February 1937; *Educ* Winchester, ChCh Oxford (MA); *m* 1961, Diana Bridget, da of Lt-Col Joseph Henry Goodhart, MC (d 1975), of Kirkbymoorside, York, by Evelyn, yst da of Henry Beaumont, JP, DL; 2 s (John Michael Joseph b 1965, Richard Thomas Bland b 1967), 1 da (Emma Mary Bridget b 1971 d 2003); *Heir* s, John Royden; *Career* Nat Serv 2 Lt 16/5 The Queen's Royal Lancers 1955–57; Duncan Fox & Co Ltd 1960–71; stockbroker: Spencer Thornton & Co 1971–86, Gerrard Vivian Gray Ltd 1988–97, Greig Middleton & Co Ltd 1997–2000, Gerard Ltd 2000–04; FSI; *Recreations* shooting, fishing, gardening; *Clubs* Boodle's; *Style—* Sir Christopher Royden, Bt; ✉ Bridge House, Ablington, Bibury, Gloucestershire GL7 5NY

ROYDON, Terry Rene; s of Leon Roydon, and Lyanne, *née* Hamoniere; *b* 26 December 1946; *Educ* Clifton, Univ of London (BSc), Univ of Pittsburgh (MBA); *m* 29 Sept 1972, Carol Joycelyn, da of Stanley Norris; 1 da (Karen b 1977); *Career* md Comben Group plc 1970–84, chief exec Prowting plc 1985–98, chm Banner Homes Gp plc 1999–2002, chm Swallow Homes Ltd 2000–01; dir: Nat House Bldg Cncl 1981–2004, PPS Ltd 1996–, Dom Devpt SA (Poland) 1999–, County and Metropolitan plc 2003–05, McCann Homes Ltd 2003–, Gladedale plc 2005–07, Engel East Europe plc 2005–; pres: Housebuilder Fedn 1984, European Union of Housebuilders and Developers 1995–97; govr St Helen's Sch Northwood 1988–; *Style—* Terry Roydon, Esq; ✉ Kingsmill, The Marlins, Northwood, Middlesex HA6 3NP

ROYDS, Richard George; s of Nicholas Clyne Royds, and Sally Royds; *b* 15 November 1957; *Educ* Charterhouse; *m* Lucinda, da of Richard McClean; 1 s (George), 1 da (Isabella); *Career* sales exec: LWT 1976–79, Capital Radio 1979–82; dir The Media Shop 1982–86; md: Wardley Unit Trust Managers 1986–89, John Govett Unit Trust Managers 1989–92, Mercury Fund Managers Ltd 1992–2000; dir: Mercury Asset Management plc 1992–98, Mercury Life Assurance Co Ltd 1992–2000, Mercury Asset Management Ltd 1998–2000, Merrill Lynch Fund Managers 2000–; md mktg communications Merrill Lynch Investment Managers 2000–; *Recreations* golf, fishing, art, wine, eating, shopping; *Clubs* Sunningdale Golf, Royal St George's Golf, The Golf Match; *Style—* Richard Royds, Esq; ✉ Merrill Lynch Investment Managers, 33 King William Street, London EC4R 9AS (tel 020 7743 3000, fax 020 7743 1109)

ROYLE, Carol Buchanan (Mrs Julian Spear); da of Derek Stanley Royle (d 1990), and Jane Irene, *née* Shortt; *b* 10 February 1954; *Educ* Streatham HS for Girls, Pitmans Sch Wimbledon, Central Sch of Speech and Drama; *m* Julian David Barnaby Spear, s of Bernard Spear; 1 s (Taran Oliver Buchanan b 5 Nov 1983), 1 da (Talitha Mary-Jane Buchanan Royle Spear b 31 Aug 1995); *Career* actress; *Theatre* incl: Harrogate Repertory Co 1976–77; RSC 1980–82 and 1990–92 incl: Ophelia in Hamlet and Cressida in Troilus and Cressida 1980–82, Princess of France in Love's Labour's Lost and Mrs Arbuthnot in A Woman of No Importance; other roles incl: Titania in A Midsummer Night's Dream (Regent's Park) 1988, Kate in Harold Pinter's Old Times (Birmingham Rep) 1993, May in Fay Weldon's Four Alice Bakers (Birmingham Rep) 1999, Private Lives (Theatre Clwyd), Arcadia (Theatre Clwyd), Lady Bracknell in The Importance of Being Earnest (Northampton), See You Next Tuesday (West End), Festen (West End), Going Straight (nat tour), extensive work in Windsor; *Television* for BBC incl: Blakes 7 1979, Possibilities 1982, Bergerac 1983, Oxbridge Blues 1984, A Still Small Shout 1985, Life Without George (three series) 1987–89, Hedgehog Wedding 1987, Blackeyes 1989, Casualty 1990, The Bill; for ITV incl: The Professionals, Waxwork 1980, Heartland 1980; for Thames incl: Judgement Day 1983, Ladies in Charge 1985–86, The London Embassy 1987; other credits incl: The Cedar Tree (three series, ATV) 1977–79, Girl Talk (ATV) 1980, The Racing Game (YTV) 1980, Feet Foremost (Granada) 1982, The Outsider (YTV) 1983, Crime Traveller 1996, Thief Takers 1997, Heartbeat, Crossroads, Gil Mayo, Doctors; *Films* incl: Tuxedo Warrior 1982–83, When the Wall Comes Tumbling Down (EMI) 1984, Deadline (RSPCA) 1988; *Awards* London Drama Critics' Award for Most Promising Actress (for Ophelia) 1980; *Style—* Ms Carol Royle; ✉ c/o Emptage Hallett, 14 Rathbone Place, London W1T 1HT (tel 020 7436 0425)

ROYLE, Gavin Timothy; s of late Basil Victor Royle, and late Gwen Royle; *Educ* Epsom Coll, Charing Cross Med Sch London (entrance scholar, MB BS, MS, Cricket capt); *m* Katherine; 2 s (Matthew, Thomas), 1 da (Elisabeth); *Career* surgical trg Oxford and Harvard, former MRC research fell at MIT and lectr in surgery Massachusetts Gen Hosp, conslt gen surgn specialising in breast and endocrine disease Southampton Univ Hosps 1983–, currently hon sr lectr in surgery Univ of Southampton, clinical lead Nat Cancer Peer Review South Zone, lead cancer clinician Southampton Univ Hosps; memb: Br Breast Gp, Br Assoc of Surgical Oncology, Assoc of Surgery, BMA, Br Assoc of Endocrine Surgns; Oxford HA Surgery Prize 1977, Wessex Med Sch Tst TV South Award 1986; MRC fellowship 1980; LRCP 1970, FRCS 1974 (MRCS 1970); *Publications* author of papers on various aspects of gen surgery, especially breast disease; *Recreations* fishing, reading, clay pigeon shooting; *Clubs* MCC; *Style—* Gavin Royle, Esq; ✉ Royal South Hampshire Hospital, Brinton's Terrace, Southampton (tel 023 8082 5717); West Nuffield Hospital (tel 023 8025 8434)

ROZENBERG, Joshua Rufus; s of Zigmund Rozenberg (d 1982), and Beatrice Doris, *née* Davies (d 1995); *b* 30 May 1950; *Educ* Latymer Upper Sch, Wadham Coll Oxford (MA); *m* 31 March 1974, Melanie, da of Alfred Phillips; 1 s, 1 da; *Career* trainee journalist BBC 1975, admitted slr 1976; legal and constitutional affrs corr BBC News 1997–2000 (legal affrs corr 1985–1997), legal ed The Daily Telegraph 2000–; hon bencher Gray's Inn 2003; Hon LLD Univ of Hertfordshire 1999; *Books* Your Rights and The Law (with N Watkins, 1986), The Case For The Crown (1987), The Search For Justice (1994), Trial of Strength (1997), Privacy and the Press (2004); *Clubs* Garrick; *Style—* Joshua Rozenberg, Esq; ✉ The Daily Telegraph, 111 Buckingham Palace Road, London SW1W 0DT (tel 020 7931 2528, e-mail law@telegraph.co.uk)

RUANE, Christopher Shaun (Chris); MP; s of Michael Ruane (d 1974), and Esther, *née* Roberts; *b* 18 July 1958; *Educ* Blessed Edward Jones Comp Rhyl, Univ of Wales

Aberystwyth, Univ of Liverpool (PGCE); *m* 1994, Gill Roberts: 2 c; *Career* dep headmaster Ysgol Mair Primary Sch Rhyl 1991–1997; MP (Lab) Vale of Clwyd 1997–, PPS to Sec of State for Wales 2002–07; chair All-Pty Gp on Heart Disease 2002–, treas All-Pty Objective One Gp; memb Welsh Affairs Select Ctee 1999–2002; chair N Wales Gp of Lab MPs 2002–; former local cncllr; fndr and pres Rhyl Environmental Assoc; memb NUT (pres Vale of Clwyd branch 1989 and 1998); *Style—* Chris Ruane, MP; ✉ 25 Kinmel Street, Rhyl LL18 1AH (tel 01745 354626, fax 01745 334827, e-mail ruanec@parliament.uk); House of Commons, London SW1A 0AA (tel 020 7219 6378)

RUAUX, Her Hon Judge Gillian Doreen; da of Charles Edward Ruaux (d 1977), of Bolton, and Denise Maud, *née* Le Page; *b* 25 March 1945; *Educ* Bolton Sch - Girls' Div Bolton, Univ of Manchester (LLB, LLM); *m* 4 Sept 1968, William Derek Partington, s of Joseph Partington; 1 da (Victoria Louise b 24 Aug 1973); *Career* called to the Bar Gray's Inn 1968 (Gerald Moody scholar), pupillage with H K Goddard, QC, at 9 Albert Sq Manchester then tenancy at same (which transferred to Deans Ct Chambers Manchester), circuit judge (Northern Circuit) 1993–; memb Gray's Inn 1964; *Recreations* opera, theatre, horse-racing and cookery; *Clubs* Bolton Old Links Golf; *Style—* Her Hon Judge Ruaux

RUBENS, Prof Robert David; s of Joel Rubens, of London, and Dinah, *née* Hasseck; *b* 11 June 1943; *Educ* Quintin GS, King's Coll London (BSc), St George's Hosp Med Sch London (MB BS), Univ of London (MD); *m* 30 Oct 1970, Margaret, da of Alan Chamberlin, of Burncross, S Yorks; 2 da (Abigail b 15 Nov 1971, Carolyn b 10 June 1974); *Career* house and registrar appts St George's, Brompton, Hammersmith & Royal Marsden Hosps 1968–72, conslt physician Guy's Hosp 1975– (dir of oncology servs 1985–90), prof of clinical oncology Guy's and St Thomas' and King's Coll Hosps Sch of Med and Dentistry of King's Coll London 1985–2003 (chm Div of Oncology 1989–97); ICRF: memb scientific staff 1972–85, dir Clinical Oncology Unit 1985–97; chief med offr: Mercantile & General Reinsurance Co plc 1987–97 (conslt med offr 1977–97), Legal & General Assurance Society Ltd 1992– (conslt med offr 1978–), Swiss Re Life and Health Ltd 1997–; ed-in-chief Cancer Treatment Reviews 1992–2001; examiner RCP 1987–93; chm EORTC Breast Cancer Co-operative Gp 1991–93; pres Assurance Med Soc 2003–05 (memb Cncl 1982–90), memb Assoc of Cancer Physicians 1985; hon dir Inc Homes for Ladies with Limited Income 1983–2000; memb: BMA 1969, British Breast Gp 1976, American Assoc for Cancer Res 1977, American Soc of Clinical Oncology 1977; Freeman: City of London 1979, Worshipful Soc of Apothecaries 1978 (Liveryman 1983); FRCP 1984 (MRCP 1969); *Publications* A Short Textbook of Clinical Oncology (1980), Bone Metastases (1991), Cancer and the Skeleton (2000) pubns on experimental and clinical cancer therapy; *Recreations* golf, bridge; *Clubs* Royal Wimbledon Golf; *Style—* Prof Robert Rubens; ✉ 5 Currie Hill Close, Arthur Road, Wimbledon, London SW19 7DX (tel 020 8946 0422)

RUBERY, Dr Eileen Doris; CB (1998), QHP (1993); *b* 16 May 1943; *Educ* Univ of Sheffield (MB, ChB), Univ of London (Dip Med Radiotherapy), Univ of Cambridge (PGC Chemical Microbiology, PhD), Univ of London (MA); *m*; 1 da; *Career* Sheffield Royal Infirmary: house physician (endocrinology and therapeutics) 1966–67, house surgn 1967; MRC research fell 1968–71, Meres' sr research student St John's Coll Cambridge 1971–73; Addenbrooke's Hosp: sr registrar Dept of Radiotherapy and Oncology 1976–78 (registrar 1973–76), Wellcome sr clinical res fell Dept of Clinical Biochemistry and hon conslt Dept of Radiotherapy and Oncology 1978–82; Girton Coll Cambridge: sr res fell and dir of med studies 1980–82, registrar of the roll 1997–, visiting fell 1997–2000, sr res fell 2000–; DHSS (now Dept of Health): sr med offr Toxicology and Environmental Protection (TEP) Div 1983–88, princ med offr TEH and head of Food and Radiation Branch 1988, princ med offr and head Communicable Disease Branch 1988–89, sr princ med offr and head Communicable Disease and Immunisation Div 1989–91, seconded to E Anglian Regnl HA 1991, sr princ med offr and head of Health Promotion (Med) Div 1991–95, under sec and head of Health Aspects of Environment and Food Div 1995–97, under sec and head Protection of Health Div 1997–99; Univ of Cambridge: pt/t secondment as lectr in public health med Inst of Public Health 1993–95, pt/t sr res assoc Judge Inst of Mgmnt Studies 1997–2004, course dir MSt in community enterprise 2001–04, sr assoc Judge Inst 2004–; memb GMC disciplinary ctees 2000–06; conslt to public sector and other orgns on food safety and other public health issues; tutor in art history: Univ of Cambridge Inst of Continuing Educn 2004–, Rewley House Univ of Oxford 2005–; Helen P Tompkinson Award BMA, WHO Travelling Fellowship; memb Cncl Roedean Sch 2002–05; FFPHM, FRCR, FRSPH, FRCPath; *Publications* numerous articles in professional journals on biochemistry, radiation, public health, professional devpt, risk and uncertainty; *Recreations* reading, theatre, music (classical and opera), travel, Byzantine, Romanesque, Gothic art and art history; *Style—* Dr Eileen Rubery, CB, QHP; ✉ Girton College, Huntingdon Road, Cambridge (tel 01223 337025, e-mail roll@girton.cam.ac.uk and edr1001@cam.ac.uk)

RUBERY, His Hon Judge (Reginald) John; s of Reginald Arthur Rubery (d 1964), and Phyllis Margaret, *née* Payne (d 1992); *b* 13 July 1937; *Educ* Wadham House Hale, King's Sch Worcester; *m* 1, 10 June 1961 (m dis), Diana, da of Maurice Wilcock Holgate; 1 s (Mark John b 7 Feb 1968); m 2, 15 March 1974, Frances Camille, da of Thomas Murphy; 1 step da (Leonie); *Career* admitted slr 1963, ptnr Whitworths Manchester then Taylor Kirkman & Mainprice Manchester 1963–68, cncllr Manchester City Cncl 1968–74, hon sec Law Soc Manchester 1974–78, county court registrar then dist judge 1978–95, recorder of the Crown Court 1991–95 (asst recorder 1987–91), circuit judge (Midland & Oxford Circuit) 1995–, judge Court of Appeal St Helena 1997–, justice of appeal Falklands Islands, Br Indian Ocean Territory and Br Antarctic Territory; pt/t chm Immigration Appeal Tbnl 1998–2005, pt/t chm Mental Health Review Tbnl 2001–; memb: Law Soc, District Judges Assoc, Cncl of Circuit Judges; *Recreations* golf, swimming, gardening; *Clubs* Lansdowne, Hale Golf, Nefyn Golf, Market Drayton Golf; *Style—* His Hon Judge Rubery; ✉ Birkby, Charnes Road, Ashley, Market Drayton, Shropshire TF9 4LQ

RUBIN, Dr Anthony Paul; s of Henry Walter Rubin (d 1990), and Lily, *née* Hooberman (d 1999); *Educ* St Paul's, Gonville & Caius Coll Cambridge, London Hosp Med Sch (MA, MB BChir); *m* 14 June 1969, Gillian Mary, da of John Dolbear (d 1997); 2 da (Deborah Jane b 19 June 1971, Esther Louise b 12 June 1974); *Career* registrar then sr registrar in anaesthetics Charing Cross Hosp 1964–71, insr in anesthesiology Univ of Washington Seattle 1969–70; conslt anaesthetist: Charing Cross Hosp (later Chelsea and Westminster Hosp) 1971–97, Royal Nat Orthopaedic Hosp Stanmore 1975–2004; Royal Coll of Anaesthetists: former examiner, memb Cncl, gold medallist; memb Assoc of Anaesthetists 1964; FRCA 1966, FRSM 1969; *Books* Problems in Obstetric Anaesthesia (jtly, 1993); numerous chapters and scientific papers; *Recreations* association football, travel, music; *Clubs* Queen's; *Style—* Dr Anthony Rubin; ✉ 126 Harley Street, London W1G 7JS (tel 020 7935 9409, fax 020 7224 3490, e-mail rubin@easynet.co.uk)

RUBIN, Prof Peter Charles; s of Woolf Rubin (d 1980), of Redruth, Cornwall, and Enis Muriel, *née* Cowling (d 2003); *b* 21 November 1948; *Educ* Univ of Cambridge (MA), Univ of Oxford (DM); *m* 2 Oct 1976 (m dis 2006), Dr Fiona Anne, da of William Burns Logan (d 1967); 1 da (Victoria b 1979), 1 s (Jeffrey b 1984); *Career* American Heart Assoc fell Stanford Med Center 1977–79, sr registrar in med and clinical pharmacology Glasgow 1979–82, Wellcome Tst sr fell Glasgow 1982–87; Univ of Nottingham Med Sch: prof of therapeutics 1987–, chm Dept of Med 1991–97, dean Faculty of Med and Health Scis 1997–2003; chm: SAC in Clinical Pharmacology and Therapeutics RCP 1993–95, GMC Education Ctee 2002–, Postgrad medical Educn and Trg Bd 2005–; non-exec dir Nottingham HA 1998–2002; memb: MRC Grants Ctee 1992–96, Assoc of Physicians 1990, Bd HEFCE 2003–; FRCP 1989; *Books* Lecture Notes on Clinical Pharmacology (1981, 7 edn 2006), Prescribing in Pregnancy (1987, 4 edn 2007), Hypertension in Pregnancy (1988, 2 edn 2000); *Clubs* Oxford and Cambridge; *Style—* Prof Peter Rubin; ✉ Department of Medicine, University Hospital, Nottingham NG7 2UH (tel 0115 823 1063, fax 0115 823 1059, e-mail peter.rubin@nottingham.ac.uk)

RUBIN, (Robert) Stephen; OBE; s of Berko Rubin, and Minnie Gould; *b* 3 December 1937, Liverpool; *Educ* Canford, UCL (LLB); *m* 1958, Angela; 4 c; *Career* called to the Bar Inner Temple; chm Pentland Gp plc, dir La Chemise Lacoste; former dir: Reebok Int, Adidas AG; chm World Short Course Swimming Championships Manchester 2008, pres World Sports Forum, dir World Fedn of the Sporting Goods Industry, past pres World Sports Fedn, world pres Textile Inst; Lifetime Achievement Award Br Sports Industry; Hon LLD Lancaster Univ; FRSA, companion Textile Inst; *Recreations* anything to do with water, reading; *Clubs* Athenaeum, Travellers; *Style—* Stephen Rubin, Esq; ✉ Pentland Group plc, 8 Manchester Square, London W1U 3PH

RUBINSTEIN, Felicity Kate; da of Hilary Rubinstein, *qv*, and Helge, *née* Kitzinger; *b* 27 July 1958; *Educ* Godolphin & Latymer Sch, Camden Sch for Girls, Univ of Warwick; *m* 1991, Hon Roland Alexander Philipps, *qv*, s of 3 Baron Milford (d 1999); 1 s (Nathaniel Alexander b Dec 1996); *Career* literary agent; Rosenstone/Wender lit agency NY USA 1980–84, Viking Penguin Inc publishers NY USA 1985–86, dir William Heinemann Ltd publishers UK 1987–88, md Macmillan London publishers UK 1989–93, ptnr Lutyens and Rubinstein Literary Agency 1993–; *Recreations* more reading, food; *Style—* Ms Felicity Rubinstein; ✉ 231 Westbourne Park Road, London W11 1EB

RUBINSTEIN, Hilary Harold; s of Harold Frederick Rubinstein (d 1974), of London, and Lena, *née* Lowy (d 1939); *b* 24 April 1926; *Educ* Cheltenham Coll, Merton Coll Oxford (MA); *m* 6 Aug 1955, Helge, da of Gabriel Kitzinger (d 1963), of Herts; 3 s (Jonathan Paul b 1956, Mark Gabriel b 1961, Ben Hilary b 1963), 1 da (Felicity Kate Rubinstein, *qv*, b 1958); *Career* trainee pilot RAF 1944–47, later Educn Corps and Vocational Advice Serv; editorial dir Victor Gollancz Ltd 1952–63, special features ed The Observer Magazine 1964–65, md AP Watt Ltd Literary Agents 1965–92, md Hilary Rubinstein Books Literary Agents 1992–; memb Cncl Inst of Contemporary Arts 1976–92, tstee Open Coll of the Arts 1987–96; *Books* The Complete Insomniac (1974), The Good Hotel Guide (fndr ed, 1978–2000), Hotels and Inns - An Oxford Anthology (ed, 1984); *Recreations* hotel-watching, reading in bed; *Style—* Hilary Rubinstein, Esq; ✉ Hilary Rubinstein Books, 32 Ladbroke Grove, London W11 3BQ (home tel 020 7727 9550, office tel 020 7792 4282, e-mail hilaryrubinstein@pobox.com)

RUCK KEENE, Benjamin Charles (Ben); JP (Oxon 1992); o s of Capt John Henry Ruck Keene, OBE, DSC, RN (d 1967), and Patricia, *née* Gibbons (d 2005); *b* 2 September 1949; *Educ* Ampleforth, Univ of York (BA), Inns of Court Sch of Law; *m* 9 Sept 1972, Frances Anne Marylee, 2 da of Jocelyn Wiseman Fagan Morton; 2 s (Alexander Charles Edward b 21 Aug 1976, Dominic Nicholas John b 14 Feb 1982), 1 da (Hermione Katharine Mary b 28 June 1978); *Career* called to the Bar Gray's Inn 1971, in practice NE Circuit 1972–79; Univ of York 1979–83, assoc dir Credit Suisse Asset Management and memb Stock Exchange 1983–88, fell and bursar CCC Oxford 1989– (MA by decree 1989), a curator Oxford Univ Chest 1995–2000; memb: Investment Ctee Univ of Oxford 2000–, Property Investment Ctee Univ of Oxford 1995– (chm 1991–), Advsy Ctee Charities Property Fund 2000–, Abbot of Ampleforth's Advsy Ctee St Benet's Hall Oxford 2002–: govr: Pate's GS Cheltenham 1993–2007, Tudor Hall Sch 1999– (vice-chm 2005–); *Clubs* Brooks's (memb Ctee of Mangrs 2005–); *Style—* Ben Ruck Keene, Esq; ✉ Corpus Christi College, Oxford OX1 4JF (tel 01865 276736, fax 01865 248910, e-mail ben.ruckkeene@ccc.ox.ac.uk)

RUCK KEENE, David Kenneth Lancelot; s of Thomas Ruck Keene, of Ewelme, Oxford, and Anne Coventry, *née* Greig (d 1991); *b* 22 September 1948; *Educ* Eton; *m* 30 Oct 1976, Tania Caroline, da of William Anstey Preston Wild; 3 da (Katherine b 1981, Rosanna b 1983, Lucia b 1985); *Career* CA; Rowe & Pitman stockbrokers 1977–86 (ptnr 1982–86), dir SG Warburg Securities 1986–95, former dir UBS Ltd (formerly UBS Warburg, joined 1995), chm South Uist Estates Ltd; FCA 1974, MSI; *Recreations* country pursuits, tennis, golf; *Clubs* White's, Queen's, MCC; *Style—* David Ruck Keene, Esq

RUCKER, Jane; *see:* Campbell Garratt, Jane Louise

RUCKER, His Hon Judge Jeffrey Hamilton; s of Charles Edward Sigismund Rucker, MC (d 1965), of Ashmore, nr Salisbury, Wilts, and Nancy Winifred, *née* Hodgson (d 1993); *b* 19 December 1942; *Educ* Charterhouse, Univ of Heidelberg; *m* 15 May 1965, Caroline Mary, da of Col Philip Edward Salkeld (d 1975), of Blandford, Dorset; 3 s (Simon b 3 Nov 1970, Nicholas b 26 Sept 1972, James b 3 Feb 1978); *Career* called to the Bar Middle Temple 1967, recorder 1984–88, circuit judge (SE Circuit) 1988–; memb Cncl of Govrs of United Med and Dental Schs of St Thomas' and Guy's Hosps 1991–98; *Recreations* sailing, skiing, music; *Style—* His Hon Judge Jeffrey Rucker; ✉ Truro Combined Court Centre, Edward Street, Truro TR1 2PB

RUCKMAN, Eur Ing Robert Julian Stanley; s of William James Ruckman (d 1962), late of Chalfont, and Ida Marjorie, *née* Woodward (d 1989); *b* 11 May 1939; *Educ* Harrow Tech Coll, Cranfield Univ (MSc); *m* 16 Oct 1965, Josephine Margaret, da of Lieut RNVR George Colin Trentham, DSC (despatches) (d 1979); 1 s (Gordon b 1966 d 2005), 1 da (Helen b 1973); *Career* chartered engr, systems analyst; memb tech staff Systems Sci Corp VA 1966, sr engr Kent Instruments 1968, computer mangr Highways Agency DOT (design of Geographical Information Systems (GIS)) 1970–95, ret; author of various publications on digital systems; assessor Br Computer Soc Professional Review Panel, membership advsr IEE 1993–95; dep govr American Biographical Inst (ABI) Research Assoc; ABI Man of the Year 2005–07, ABI Sovereign Ambassador of the Order of American Ambassadors 2006, United Cultural Convention Int Peace Prize; fell ABI 2006; CEng, MIEE, MBCS, CITP, CMILT, FIAP; *Recreations* hill walking, classical music, watercolour painting; *Style—* Eur Ing Robert Ruckman; ✉ Flamingo, 13 Alexander Avenue, Droitwich, Worcester WR9 8NH (tel 01905 775286, e-mail robert_ruckman@tinyworld.co.uk)

RUDAIZKY, John Nicholas; s of Raymond Rudaizky, and Shirley Rudaizky; *Educ* King Alfred Sch Hampstead, City Univ London (BSc); *Career* Saatchi & Saatchi: joined 1987, youngest managing ptnr, running campaigns worldwide, awarded campaigns incl: leadership and launch NSPCC Full Stop campaign, Sony, Visa International Europe; chair (mktg and commercial) SnowsportGB (formerly Br Ski and Snowboard Fedn); launched Rudaizky Ryan Cmmns 2002, joined JWT 2005, global business dir Vodafone; memb Mktg Soc, MIPA, MInstD; *Recreations* snowboarding, golf, tennis; *Clubs* Soho House; *Style—* John Rudaizky, Esq

RUDD, Charlie Richard Cooper; s of Lewis Rudd, of Winchester, Hants, and Joan, *née* Bower; *b* 28 June 1967, London; *Educ* Bryanston, Royal Holloway Coll; *m* 17 June 1995, Katrina, *née* Woods; 2 s (Oliver b 27 July 1998, Toby b 11 Dec 2000); *Career* grad trainee rising to account mangr Ogilvy & Mather Ltd 1989–92, account mangr rising to bd dir Simons Palmer Denton Clemmow & Johnson Ltd 1992–98, bd dir J Walter Thompson Ltd 1998, head of account mgmnt and dep md Bartle Bogle Hegarty Ltd 1999–; *Recreations* family, sport, news junkie; *Style—* Charlie Rudd, Esq; ✉ Bartle Bogle Hegarty Limited, 60 Kingly Street, London W1B 5DS (tel 020 7734 1677, e-mail charlie.rudd@bbh.co.uk)

RUDD, Sir (Anthony) Nigel Russell; kt (1996), DL (Derbyshire); s of Samuel Rudd (d 1983), and Eileen, *née* Pinder (d 1999); *b* 31 December 1946; *Educ* Bemrose GS Derby; *m* 20 Sept 1969, Lesley Elizabeth, da of Bernard Thomas Hodgkinson (d 1990); 2 s (Timothy Nigel b 27 May 1971, Edward Thomas b 23 Sept 1973), 1 da (Jennifer Clare b 24 March 1978); *Career* chm: Williams plc 1982–2000, Pendragon plc 1989–, Pilkington plc 1995– (dir

1994–), Kidde plc 2000–03, Boots plc 2003–06 (non-exec dir 1999–, dep chm 2001–03), Alliance Boots plc 2006–; non-exec dir: Barclays plc 1996– (dep chm 2004–), BAE Systems plc 2006–; chm BAA 2007–; memb CBI Preident's Ctee; Liveryman Worshipful Co of Chartered Accountants, Freeman City of London; Hon DTech Loughborough 1998, Hon DUniv Derby 1998; *Recreations* golf, field sports, skiing, tennis; *Clubs* Brooks's, RAC, Chevin Golf, Notts Golf, London Capital, The China; *Style*— Sir Nigel Rudd, DL; ✉ Alliance Boots plc, Sedley Place, 361 Oxford Street, London W1C 2JL

RUDDOCK, Alan Stephen Dennis; s of John Alexander Ruddock, of Dublin, and Doreen, *née* Rocliffe; *b* 21 July 1960; *Educ* Coll of St Columba Dublin, Trinity Coll Dublin (BA); *m* 4 July 1986, Jacqueline, da of Howard Kilroy; 3 s (Matthew b 1989, Daniel b 1992, Cameron b 1995); *Career* journalist; with: Sunday Times 1992–96, Sunday Express 1996, Mirror Gp Newspapers 1996–98; ed: The Scotsman 1998–2000, Sunday Independent 2001–; *Recreations* watching sport, skiing, tennis, golf; *Style*— Alan Ruddock, Esq; ✉ Rathmore Park, Tullow, Co Carlow, Ireland (tel 353 5036 61179, e-mail ruddock@indigo.ie)

RUDDOCK, Joan; MP; da of Kenneth Charles Anthony (d 1981), and Eileen Messenger; *b* 28 December 1943; *Educ* Pontypool GS for Girls, Imperial Coll London (BSc); *m* 1963 (sep), Keith Ruddock (d 1996), s of Charles Ruddock (d 1966), of Yorks; *Career* mangr Citizens' Advice Bureau Reading, chairperson CND 1981–85; MP (Lab) Lewisham Deptford 1987–, shadow min for transport 1989–92, shadow min Home Office 1992–94, shadow min for environmental protection 1994–97, Parly under sec of state for women 1997–98; hon fell Goldsmiths Coll London, hon fell Laban Centre London; *Style*— Ms Joan Ruddock, MP; ✉ House of Commons, London SW1A 0AA

RUDDOCK, Michael (Mike); OBE (2006); s of Vernon James Ruddock (d 1997), of Blaina, and Margaret Mary, *née* Carroll; *b* 5 September 1959, Blaina, Gwent; *Educ* Nantyglo Secdy Sch; *m* 11 June 1987, Bernadette Mary (Bernie); 2 s (Ciaran Terence James, Rhys James), 1 da (Katie Mary); *Career* rugby union player and coach; played as back row forward for Blaina, Tredegar, Swansea (Swansea Player of the Year 1982) and Wales B, ret following industrial accident 1985; coach: Blaina 1986–88 (winners Monmouthshire Premier League 1987), Cross Keys 1988–90, Bective Rangers 1990–91, Swansea 1991–97 (beat Aust nat team 1992, Welsh League 1992 and 1994, Welsh Challenge Cup 1995), Leinster 1997–2000 (winners Irish Provincial Championship 1997, also coach Ireland A and asst coach Ireland 1998), Ebbw Vale 2000–03, Newport Gwent Dragons 2003–04, Wales nat team 2004–06 (winners Six Nations Championship and Grand Slam 2005, former coach Emerging Wales and Wales A and former asst nat team coach); Welsh Coach of the Year 1992 and 2005; hon fell: Cardiff Univ 2005, Newport Univ 2005; *Style*— Mr Mike Ruddock, OBE

RUDDOCK, Air Vice-Marshal Peter William David; CBE (2001); s of late William James Ruddock, and Evelyn Mary, *née* Besançon; *b* 5 February 1954; *Educ* Grosvenor HS Belfast, Advanced Staff Coll Bracknell, Ashridge Mgmnt Coll; *m* 1; 1 da (Alison Margaret b 17 July 1984), 1 s (David Alexander b 24 June 1988); m 2, 27 Oct 2001, Joanna Elizabeth, *née* Mitchell; *Career* cmmnd RAF 1974, completed tours 1978–88, qualified weapons instr (air defence) 1982, cmd Phantom Qualified Weapons Instr (QWI) course RAF Coningsby then RAF Leuchars 1986–88, gp weapons and Phantom desk offr HQ No 11 Gp RAF Bentley Priory 1988–90, advanced staff trg 1990, posted Defence Intelligence Serv (DIS) 1991–93, OC Ops Wing RAF Coningsby 1993–96, asst dir DIS 1996–99, cmd RAF Coningsby 1999–2000, Air Cdre Defensive Ops HQ No 1 Gp 2000–02, Dir of Air Staff 2002–04, Air Sec 2004–06, DG Saudi Armed Forces Project 2006–; display pilot Battle of Britain Meml Flight 1993–99; FRAeS; *Recreations* gliding, sailing, equestrian activities, most sports, military and family history; *Clubs* RAF; *Style*— Air Vice-Marshal Peter Ruddock, CBE, FRAeS; ✉ DGSAP, 8(S) Castlewood House, 77–91 New Oxford Street, London WC1A 1DT (tel 020 7829 8572)

RUDGE, Sir Alan Walter; kt (2000), CBE (1995, OBE 1987); *b* 17 October 1937; *Educ* Hugh Myddelton Sch, London Poly, Univ of Birmingham (PhD); 1969, Jennifer Joan Minott; 1 s, 1 da; *Career* researcher Illinois Inst of Technol Research Inst (IITRI) 1968–71, lectr Electronic and Engrg Dept Univ of Birmingham 1971–74, established Anglo-American Research Centre for Radio Frequency Technol Electrical Research Assoc (ERA) 1974, ERA acquired Research Centre 1979, md ERA Technology Ltd 1979–87; BT plc: dir Research and Technol 1987–89, gp technol and devpt dir 1989–90, main bd dir 1989–97, md devpt and procurement 1990–95, dep gp md 1995–96, dep chief exec 1996–97; chm: WS Atkins Ltd 1997–2001, ERA Technology Ltd 1997–2003, ERA Fndn 2001–; MSI Cellular: chief exec 2001–02, pres 2002–04; non-exec chm Metapath Software Int Inc 1999–2000; non-exec dir: Br Maritime technol Ltd 1984–89, Ricardo Consulting Engrs plc 1985–89, Telecom Securicor Cellular Radio 1989–90, MCI Communication Corp 1995–96, LucasVarity plc 1997–99, GEC (then Marconi plc) 1997–2002, GUS plc 1997–2006, MSI Cellular Investment Hldgs 1998–2002, Experian Gp plc 2006–; pres IEE 1993–94 (vice-chm 1989–91, dep pres 1991); chm: EPSRC 1994–99, Engrg Cncl 1996–99, Bd of Mgmnt Royal Cmmn for the Exhbn of 1851 2002– (memb 1997–); memb: Research and Technol Ctee CBI 1980–86, Systems and Electronics Bd Def Scientific Advsy Cncl MOD 1981–87, Cncl Royal Acad of Engrg 1987–90, Cncl Def Evalutation and Research Agency (DERA) MOD 1991–96, Cncl Royal Instn 1992–95, Cncl for Sci and Technol 1993–97; visiting prof Queen Mary and Westfield Coll London 1985–, pro-vice-chllr Univ of Surrey 2002–; chm of tstees Br Retinitis Pigmentosa Soc 1996–; Freeman City of London, Liveryman Worshipful Co of Engrs 1998; Faraday medal IEE 1991, Duncan Davies meml medal R&D Soc 1998, Fndr's medal IEEE 1998, Millennium medal IEEE 2000; Hon DEng: Univ of Birmingham 1991, Univ of Bradford 1994, Univ of Portsmouth 1994, Nottingham Trent Univ 1995; Hon DSc: Univ of Strathclyde 1992, Univ of Bath 1995, Loughborough Univ 1995, Westminster Univ 1996; Hon DUniv Surrey 1994; hon fell UCL 1998; FREng (FEng 1984), FRS 1992, Hon FIEE 2000, FIET; *Recreations* sailing, cycling; *Style*— Sir Alan Rudge, CBE, FREng, FRS

RUDGE, John Aulton; s of Kenneth James Rudge (d 1993), of Stivichall, Coventry, and Leigh, *née* Soames; *b* 29 August 1951; *Educ* Woodlands Sch Coventry, Sch of Architecture Univ of Nottingham (BA, BArch); *m* 19 Aug 1972, Christine, da of William Hollowood (d 1956); 2 da (Alexandra Jane b 25 Sept 1981, Sussanah Kate b 21 April 1987), 1 s (Robert Aulton b 7 May 1983); *Career* architect: Erewash DC Derbys 1975–79, de Brant Joyce and Partners London 1979–83; ptnr Percy Thomas Partnership 1986–94 (assoc 1983–86), chief exec Percy Thomas Partnership (Architects) Ltd 1996–2004 (dir 1994), dir of architecture Capita Percy Thomas 2004–; most notable works incl: Kenstead Hall, London residence for HRH King Fahd of Saudi Arabia, conversion of Grade 2 listed building (7 Albemarle St) into business and fine arts sch for Univ of Notre Dame, Royal Hosp Muscat, Armed Forces Hosp Muscat, Int Convention Centre and Symphony Hall Birmingham, Procurement Exec HQ for the Miny of Defence in N Bristol, Dorset County Hosp (Ph2), Wales Millennium Centre project Cardiff, Russels Hall Hosp Dudley, Def Trg Review PFI; dir: The Bristol Initiative 1991–92, Bristol 97 1991–94, PTP Seward 1995–97, PTP Hong Kong 2004; RIBA 1976, ARCUK 1975, FFB 1991, BCO 1996, MInstD 2003; *Style*— John Rudge, Esq; ✉ Capita Percy Thomas, 1 Proctor Street, London WC1V 6DW (tel 020 7492 0155, e-mail john.rudge@capita.co.uk); Capita Percy Thomas, Embassy House, Queens Avenue, Bristol BS8 1SB (tel 0117 311 2900)

RUDIN, Richard Duncan (professional name Richard Duncan); s of Arthur Derek Rudin (d 1981), and Margaret, *née* Swale; *b* 24 May 1957; *Educ* John Willmott GS Sutton Coldfield, Sutton Coldfield Coll of FE, Highbury Tech Coll, Open Univ (BA), Univ of Leicester (MA), holder City & Guilds Cert Techer in Further and Adult Educn; *m* 30 July 1983, Alison Marjorie, da of David Hay; 1 s (David Duncan Rudin b 2 June 1990); *Career* trainee newspaper reporter (NCTJ) Midland News Assoc 1976–79, newscaster/reporter Beacon Radio 1979–80, presenter/prodr BFBS Germany 1980–84, presenter Metro Radio Newcastle 1984–86, sr presenter Red Rose Radio Preston 1986–89, prog organiser BBC Radio Leeds (and on attachment as prodr BBC Radio Sheffield) 1989–92, prog controller Radio City Gold 1992–95, with media trg and PR Co CAT 1995–, lectr in journalism, public affairs, radio prodn etc Liverpool Community Coll 1995–98, sr lectr radio and journalism Liverpool John Moores Univ; also freelance writer and broadcaster (work broadcast on Radio 4); nominated Best Outside Broadcast Sony Radio Award 1988; memb: Radio Acad, NUJ, NATFHE; *Publications* An Introduction to Journalism (with Trevor Ibbotson, 2002), Encyclopedia of Radio (contrib, 2004); *Recreations* writing, reading, political biographies, histories and theory, walking, playing with son; *Style*— Richard Rudin, Esq; ✉ 1 Oakleigh, Skelmersdale, Lancashire WN8 9QU (tel and fax 01744 886505, e-mail richard@richardrudin.com, website www.richardrudin.com)

RUDING, Dr (Herman) Onno; s of Dr Roelof Ruding (d 1981), and Annie-Maria, *née* Fehmers; *b* 15 August 1939; *Educ* Gymnasium HS, Netherlands Sch of Economics Erasmus Univ Rotterdam (BA, MA, PhD); *m* 17 April 1971, Renée, *née* Hekking; 1 da (Barbara b 1 Sept 1973), 1 s (Martyn b 8 Feb 1974); *Career* Miny of Finance The Hague 1965–70, Amsterdam-Rotterdam Bank (AMRO Bank) Amsterdam 1971–76, exec dir IMF Washington DC 1977–80, memb Bd of Managing Directors Amsterdam-Rotterdam Bank and chm AMRO International Ltd London 1981–82, Min of Finance of The Netherlands 1982–89 (also chm Interim Ctee IMF 1985–89); chm Bd of Govrs: Asian Development Bank 1984, Inter American Development Bank 1989; chm Christian Federation of Employers (NCW) The Hague and memb Cncl of Presidents UNICE Brussels 1990–92, dir Citicorp 1990–, vice-chm Citicorp/Citibank 1992–; non-exec dir: Corning Inc, Corning, Pechiney Paris, Unilever NV, Unilever plc, RTL Group Luxembourg, Compass Ltd Bermuda; advsr Robeco Rotterdam; memb Bd of Tstees Mount Sinai Hosp New York; memb: Ctee for Monetary Union, Trilateral Cmmn, Bd of Tax Fndn; *Recreations* golf, history, chess; *Clubs* University, Blind Brook Golf, Noordwÿksche Golf and Country; *Style*— Dr Onno Ruding; ✉ Citicorp/Citibank, 399 Park Avenue, New York, NY 10043, USA (tel 00 1 212 559 2785, fax 00 1 212 559 4023)

RUDKIN, (James) David; s of David Jonathan Rudkin (d 1995), of Bosham, W Sussex, and Anne Alice *née* Martin (d 1969), of Armagh, NI; *b* 29 June 1936; *Educ* King Edward's Sch Birmingham, Univ of Oxford (MA); *m* 3 May 1967, (Alexandra) Sandra Margaret, da of Donald Thompson (d 1969); 2 s (Jamie b 1972, Tom (twin) b 1972 d 1997), 2 da (Sophie b 1977, Jess b 1978); *Career* Nat Serv RCS 1955–57, schoolmaster (classics and music) Co HS Bromsgrove 1961–64; playwright; Judith E Wilson fell Univ of Cambridge 1985, visiting prof Univ of Middlesex 2004–, hon prof Univ of Wales Aberystwyth 2006–; work incl: Afore Night Come 1960 (staged 1962), The Sons of Light 1964 (staged 1976), Ashes 1972 (staged 1974), Cries from Casement as his Bones are Brought to Dublin 1972 (radio 1973), Penda's Fen 1972 (TV film, shown 1974), The Triumph of Death 1976 (staged 1981), Hansel and Gretel 1979 (staged 1980), Artemis 81 1980 (TV film, shown 1981), The Saxon Shore 1983 (staged 1986), Testimony 1985 (film screenplay, released 1988), author/dir White Lady 1986 (TV film, shown 1987), December Bride 1988 (film screenplay, released 1990), John Piper in the House of Death 1985 (staged 1991), Broken Strings (libretto, staged 1992), The Lovesong of Alfred J Hitchcock 1989 (radio 1993), Symphonie Pathétique 1993 (revised 2000, unstaged), The Haunting of Mahler (radio 1994), The Woodlanders (film screenplay, released 1997), Trade 1997 (revised 2003, unstaged), Red Sun 2002 (staged 2003), The Master and the Margarita (Bulgakov, adaptation staged 2004), The Giant's Cause... 2004 (radio 2005); translations: The Persians 1965 (Aeschylus, radio 1965), Moses and Aaron 1965 (Schoenberg opera, staged 1965), Hecuba 1974 (Euripides, radio 1975), Hippolytus 1978 (Euripides, staged 1978), Peer Gynt 1982 (Ibsen, staged 1982), Deathwatch and the Maids 1987 (Genet, staged 1987), Rosmersholm 1989 (Ibsen, broadcast 1990), When We Dead Waken 1989 (Ibsen, staged 1990), Sir Gawain 1990 (TV adaptation, 1991), Dreyer's Vampyr 2004 (monograph, published 2005); *Recreations* bridge, languages, geology, music, the sea; *Style*— J D Rudkin, Esq; ✉ c/o Casarotto Ramsay & Associates Ltd, 60–66 Wardour Street, London W1V 4ND (tel 020 7287 4450, fax 020 7287 9128, website www.davidrudkin.com)

RUDLAND, Malcolm; s of Harold William Rudland (d 1966), of Leeds, and Marika, *née* Széll (d 1943); *b* 17 August 1941; *Educ* Ashville Coll Harrogate, St Paul's Cheltenham, Royal Acad of Music (BMus); *Career* music teacher Cirencester Sch; conductor; works incl: Fiddler on the Roof, West Side Story, Peter Pan; pianist and organist; music critic for: The Times, Opera, Musical Times; hon sec Peter Warlock Soc; FRCO, ARAM; Pro Cultura Hungarica; *Recreations* gliding, walking, reading; *Style*— Malcolm Rudland, Esq; ✉ 31 Hammerfield House, Cale Street, London SW3 3SG (tel and fax 020 7589 9595, e-mail mrudland@talk21.com, website malcolmrudland.org)

RUDLAND, Margaret Florence; da of Ernest George Rudland (d 1979), and Florence Hilda, *née* Davies; *b* 15 June 1945; *Educ* Sweyne Sch Rayleigh, Bedford Coll London; *Career* asst mathematics mistress Godolphin & Latymer Sch 1967–70, VSO Ilorin Nigeria 1970–71, asst mathematics mistress Clapham Co Sch 1971–72, asst mathematics mistress and head of mathematics St Paul's Girls' Sch 1972–83, dep headmistress Norwich HS 1983–85, headmistress Godolphin & Latymer Sch 1986–; govr: St Margaret's Sch Bushey 1996–, Merchant Taylor's Sch 1999–, St Mary's Sch Ascot 2002–; memb: Cncl UCL, Bd UCAS 2002–, General Teaching Cncl (GTC) 2002–; pres GSA 1996, memb Cncl Nightingale Fund 1996–; *Recreations* opera, travel, cinema; *Style*— Miss Margaret Rudland; ✉ The Godolphin & Latymer School, Iffley Road, Hammersmith, London W6 0PG (tel 020 8741 1936)

RUDLAND, His Hon Judge Martin William; s of Maurice Rudland, of Sheffield, S Yorks, and Patricia, *née* Crossley; *b* 13 March 1955; *Educ* Rowlinson Sch Sheffield, Univ of Sheffield (LLB); *m* 1, 1980, Norma Jane Lee; 2 s (Oliver William b 17 Dec 1983, Edward James Martin b 23 Jan 1987); m 3, 1997, Mrs Linda Sturgess Jackson, *née* Potter; 1 step s, 1 step da; *Career* called to the Bar Middle Temple 1977 (Harmsworth scholar 1977); in practice 1977–2002, jr NE Circuit 1985, recorder 1996–2002 (asst recorder 1992–96), circuit judge (Northern Circuit) 2002–; *Recreations* books, walking, cinema, travel; *Style*— His Hon Judge Rudland; ✉ Manchester Crown Court, Courts of Justice, Crown Square, Manchester M3 3FL (tel 0161 954 1800)

RUDMAN, Shelley-Marie; da of Jack Rudman, of Pewsey, Wilts, and Josephine-Ann, *née* Goddard; *b* 23 March 1981, Swindon, Wilts; *Educ* Pewsey Vale Sch, New Coll Swindon (BTEC), Univ of Bath (HND, Tugendhat Chllrs Award, Full Blue Award), St Mary's Coll Twickenham (BSc); *Career* skeleton bobsleigh: World Student Champion 2005, Silver medal European Championships 2006, Silver medal Winter Olympic Games 2006; athletics coach and gym instr Univ of Bath 1999–2001, cross country coach and gym instr American Community Int Sch Cobham Surrey 2001–02, classroom mangr Devizes Sch 2004–06; full time athlete 2006–; 100% Me Drugs Free in Sport ambass for UK; hon teaching fell Faculty of Health and Wellbeing Sheffield Hallam Univ; BBC West Sports Personality of the Year 2006; *Style*— Miss Shelley-Marie Rudman

RUDOFSKY, John Alec; s of Alexander Edward Rudofsky (d 1986), and Ethel, *née* Frost; *b* 13 December 1951; *Educ* St Clement Danes Sch, Selwyn Coll Cambridge (MA); *m* 1978, Susan Judith, da of late James Ernest Riley; 3 s (James Alexander b 1980, Nicholas John b 1984, Joshua Lewis b 1987); *Career* fin journalist: City Press 1973–76, BBC radio 1973–76, Investors Chronicle 1976–79, Daily Telegraph 1979–86; asst dir and fin communications conslt Streets Communications 1987–88, fndr dir and communications conslt Citigate Dewe Rogerson (formerly Citigate Communications Ltd) 1988–2000, dir Helsen Communications 2000–; *Style*— John Rudofsky, Esq; ✉ Helsen Communications, Bank Chambers, 2 The High Street, Thames Ditton, Surrey KT7 0RY (tel 020 8786 6699, website www.helsen.com)

RUDOLF, Anthony; s of Henry Cyril Rudolf, (d 1986), of London, and Esther, *née* Rosenberg; *b* 6 September 1942; *Educ* City of London Sch, Institut Britannique Paris, Trinity Coll Cambridge; *m* (m dis); 1 s (Nathaniel b 1974), 1 da (Naomi b 1976); *Career* fndr and publisher Menard Press 1969–; visiting lectr Faculty of Arts and Humanities London Metropolitan Univ 2001–03, Royal Literary Fund fell Univ of Hertfordshire 2003–04, Royal Literary Fund fell Univ of Westminster 2005–08; juror Neustadt Int Prize for Literature Oklahoma 1986, judge of translation prize Br Comparative Literature Assoc 1994–97; Adam lectr King's Coll London 1990, H H Wingate/Jewish Quarterly Prize for Non-Fiction 1991, Hawthornden fell 1993; patron Safer World Fndn 1990–2000; FRSL 2005; Chevalier de l'Ordre des Arts et des Lettres 2004; *Books* The Same River Twice: Poems (1976), After the Dream: Poems (1980), Selected Poems of Yves Bonnefoy (1985, 1995 and 2000), The Unknown Masterpiece: translation with essay of Balzac's story (1988), Wine from Two Glasses: Poetry and Politics (The Adam Lecture for 1990), At an Uncertain Hour: Primo Levi's War Against Oblivion (1990), I'm Not Even a Grown-Up: The Diary of Jerzy Feliks Urman (1991), The Poet's Voice (poems and translations, 1994), Engraved in Flesh (on Piotr Rawicz) (1996, revised edn 2007), The Arithmetic of Memory: autobiography (1999), Mandorla (poems, 1999, illustrated edn 2007), Kitaj (2001), Piotor Rawicz: Blood from the Sky (ed and introduced, 2004), Rescue Work: Memory and Text, Pierre Rouve Memorial Lecture 2001 (2004), Kafka's Doll (2007); *Recreations* listening to music, looking at paintings, watching cricket; *Style*— Anthony Rudolf, Esq; ✉ The Menard Press, 8 The Oaks, Woodside Avenue, London N12 8AR (e-mail menard.press@virgin.net)

RUEBAIN, David Ezra; *Educ* Lord Mayor Treloar Coll, Hampstead Sch, Oriel Coll Oxford (MA), Coll of Law (CPE); *Career* admitted slr 1989, with Levenes 1995– (head Dept of Educn and Disability Law); accredited mediator, non-exec dir Equality Works Consultancy; founding memb The Times Newspaper Law Panel, chair Mental Health and Disability Ctee Law Soc; memb: Educn Law Assoc, Educ Law Practitioners Gp, Disability Discrimination Act Advsrs Gp, Nat Autistic Soc panel of specialist educ law slrs, Disability Rights Cmmn panel of specialist disability discrimination slrs; memb Editorial Bd: Disability and Soc, Community Care Law Reports; peer reviewer Legal Servs Cmmn; conslt on disability discrimination law to FA Premier League; tstee Disability Discrimination Act Representation and Advice Project; hon legal advsr to ind panel for Special Educn Advice; RADAR Person of the Year 2002; fell Br American Project; *Books* Disability Discrimination Act Tool Kit (co-author), Taking Action, A Guide for Parents of Children with Special Educational Needs (co-author), Education Law and Practice (co-author), Atkin's Court Forms (co-author, vol on educ law), Disability Rights Law and Policy (contrib), Disability Discrimination: The Law and Practice (consltg ed), Disability Rights in Europe: From Theory to Practice (contrib), Disabled Children and the Law (co-author), The Good Schools Guide (contrib); *Recreations* swimming, exercise, watching Arsenal FC, socialising; *Style*— David Ruebain, Esq; ✉ Levenes Solicitors, Ashley House, 235–239 High Road, Wood Green, London N22 8HS (tel 020 8881 7777, e-mail druebain@levenes.co.uk)

RUFFELLE, Frances; da of Norman Albert Ruffell, and Sylvia, *née* Bakel; *b* 29 August 1966; *Educ* Gate House Learning Centre, Sylvia Young Theatre Sch; *m* 31 Aug 1990, John Newport Caird, s of George Bradford Caird; 1 da (Eliza Sophie b 15 April 1988), 2 s (Nathaniel George b 17 June 1990, Felix Manley b 24 May 1995); *Career* actress and singer; *Theatre* roles incl: Princess Louisa in The Sleeping Prince (Haymarket) 1983, Dinah in Starlight Express (Apollo) 1984, Eponine in Les Misérables (RSC and Palace 1985, Broadway 1987), Delilah in Apples (Royal Court) 1989, Yonah in Children of Eden (Prince Edward) 1991, Roxie in Chicago (Adelphi) 2003–04 and 2005; *Television* incl: Tuckers Luck (BBC) 1985, Eunice in P'Tang Yang Kipperbang (Channel 4) 1982, Sylvie in The Equalizer (CBS) 1987, Further Adventures of Robin Hood (Channel 5) 1999, Kitty in Headless (Channel 5) 2000, Dawn Daniel-Spears in Dream Team 2001–02; *Films* appeared as Angela Hall and Roxanne in the film Wildcats of St Trinian's 1980, Eleni in The Road to Ithaca 1999, Zeze in Last Chance 2000; *Recordings* contrib incl: cast of Les Misérables London 1985 and Broadway 1987, cast of Starlight Express 1984, duet with Christopher Cross on Back of My Mind 1988, featured on Ian Dury's Apples 1989, cast of Children of Eden 1991, duet with Michael Crawford on Michael Crawford Sings Andrew Lloyd Webber 1991; solo albums: Fragile 1996, Frances Ruffelle 1998, Showgirl 2004; Purify (as Patala) 2005; *Awards* for Les Misérables (Broadway): Tony Award for Best Featured Actress, Helen Hayes Award for Best Newcomer, Outer Circle Critics' Award for Best Newcomer, Theatre World Award; *Style*— Ms Frances Ruffelle

RUFFER, Jonathan Garnier; s of Maj J E M Ruffer; *b* 17 August 1951; *Educ* Marlborough, Sidney Sussex Coll Cambridge; *m* 1982, Jane Mary, da of Dr P Sequeira; 1 da (Harriet b 16 Oct 1990); *Career* Myers and Co Stock Exchange; called to the Bar Middle Temple (jr Harmsworth exhibitioner); J Henry Schroder Wagg 1977–79, Dunbar Group Ltd 1980–85 (dir Dunbar Fund Management Ltd 1981–85), dir CFS (Investment Management) Ltd 1985–88, md Rathbone Investment Management 1988–94, chief exec Ruffer LLP (formerly Ruffer Investment Management Ltd) 1994–; dir: Rathbone Bros plc 1989–94, Odey Asset Management 1992–2005, Fuel Tech NV 1994–98, Electric & General Investment Tst plc 2001–; chm Good Shepherd Mission Bethnal Green 1998–; *Books* The Big Shots (1977), Ruffer: Is Every Day Xmas Day? (2005); *Recreations* opera, sleeping; *Clubs* Athenaeum; *Style*— Jonathan Ruffer, Esq; ✉ Ugley Hall, Ugley, Bishop's Stortford, Hertfordshire CM22 6JB (tel 01799 543245); 4 Brunswick Mews, London W1H 7FB; Ruffer LLP, 80 Victoria Street, London SW1E 5JL (tel 020 7963 8138)

RUFFLES, Philip Charles; CBE (2001); s of Charles Richard Ruffles (d 1980), and Emily Edith, *née* Kemsley (d 1998); *b* 14 October 1939; *Educ* Sevenoaks Sch, Univ of Bristol (BSc); *m* 27 May 1967, Jane, *née* Connor; 2 da (Amy Jane b 12 June 1971, Laura Megan b 31 May 1974); *Career* Rolls-Royce: graduate apprentice 1961–63, engr preliminary design 1963–68, project devpt engr RB211 1968–75, mangr JT10D Team E Hartford 1976, chief engr RB211 1977–80, head of engrg Helicopters 1981–83, dir of design engrg 1984–89, tech dir 1989–90, dir of engrg 1991–96, dir of engrg and technol 1997–2001, tech advsr 2001–04; Royal Aeronautical Soc: Ackroyd Stuart prize 1987, Gold medal 1996; MacRobert Award Royal Acad of Engrg 1996, Royal Designer for Industry (RDI) 1997, James Clayton Prize IMechE 1998, Prince Philip Medal Royal Acad of Engrg 2001, Francois-Xavier Bagnout Aerospace Prize 2001, RTO Sawyer Award ASME 2002, Premio Internazionale Basanti & Matteucci Award 2002; hon prof Univ of Warwick, hon fell Imperial Coll London 2002; Hon DEng: Univ of Bristol 1995, Univ of Birmingham 1998, Univ of Sheffield 1999; Hon DSc City Univ 1998; Liveryman Worshipful Co of Engineers; FREng 1988, FRAeS, FIMechE, FRS 1998; *Recreations* rugby; *Style*— Philip Ruffles, Esq, CBE, FRS, FREng; ✉ 5 Ford Lane, Allestree, Derby DE22 2EX (tel 01332 553550, fax 01332 553211)

RUFFLEY, David Laurie; MP; *b* 18 April 1962; *Educ* Bolton Boys' Sch, Queens' Coll Cambridge (exhibitioner, fndn scholar, MA); *Career* slr with Clifford Chance (and predecessor company) 1985–91; special advsr to: Sec of State for Educn and Science 1991–92, Home Sec 1992–93, Chllr of the Exchequer 1993–96; econ consult Cons Pty 1996–97, MP (Cons) Bury St Edmunds 1997–; oppn whip 2004, oppn Treasy whip 2004–05; memb Select Ctee on Public Admin 1997–98, memb Treasy Select Ctee 1998–2004; sec: Finance Ctee 1999–2001, Home Affairs Ctee 1999–2001; vice-pres Small Business Bureau 1996–; advsr Grant Maintained Schs Fndn 1993–96; govr: Marylebone Sch 1992–94, Pimlico Sch 1994–96, Bolton Boys' Sch 1997–99; *Recreations* football, golf, film, thinking; *Clubs* Farmers' (Bury St Edmunds), Bury St Edmunds Golf; *Style*— David Ruffley, Esq, MP; ✉ House of Commons, London SW1A 0AA (tel 020 7219 2880, fax 020 7219 3998)

RUGBY, 3 Baron (UK 1947), of Rugby, Co Warwick; Robert Charles Maffey; 2 (but eldest surviving) s of 2 Baron Rugby (d 1990), and Margaret, *née* Bindley; *b* 4 May 1951, 1951; *m* 1974, Anne Penelope, yr da of David Hale, of Somerden, Chiddingstone, Kent; 2 s (Hon Timothy James Howard b 1975, Hon Philip Edward b 1976); *Heir* s, Hon Timothy Maffey; *Style*— The Rt Hon the Lord Rugby; ✉ Grove Farm, Frankton, Rugby CV23 9QG

RUMBELOW, His Hon Judge (Arthur) Anthony; QC (1990); *b* 9 September 1943; *Educ* Salford GS, Queens' Coll Cambridge (Squire scholar, BA); *Children* 3 da; *Career* called to the Bar Middle Temple 1967 (Harmsworth exhibitioner and Astbury scholar); recorder 1988, dep judge of the High Court (Family Div) 2000–, circuit judge (Northern Circuit) 2002–; chm: Med Appeal Tbnl 1988–2002, Mental Health Review Tbnl 2000–; *Style*— His Hon Judge Rumbelow, QC; ✉ Manchester County Court, Crown Square, Manchester M3 3FL (tel 0161 954 1800)

RUMBELOW, (Roger) Martin; s of Leonard Douglas Rumbelow (d 1980), and Phyllis Mary, *née* Perkins (d 1984); *b* 3 June 1937; *Educ* Cardiff HS, Univ of Bristol (BSc), Cranfield Inst of Technol (MSc); *m* 24 July 1965, (Marjorie) Elizabeth, da of Charles Richard Glover, of Macclesfield, Cheshire; *Career* Nat Serv RAF pilot and Flying Offr 1955–57; Concorde project mangr Br Aircraft Corp 1973–74 (tech sales 1960–67, dep prodn controller 1967–73); DTI: princ 1974–78, asst sec 1978–86, under sec Mgmnt Servs and Manpower Div 1987–92, under sec Electronics and Engrg Div 1992–96; freelance conslt and advsr 1996–; CEng, MRAeS; *Recreations* singing, tennis, theatre, electronics; *Clubs* RAF; *Style*— Martin Rumbelow, Esq; ✉ The Spinney, The Chase, Knott Park, Oxshott, Surrey KT22 0HR (tel 01372 842144, e-mail mrumbelow@aol.com)

RUMBLES, Michael John (Mike); MSP; s of Samuel Rumbles, of Jarrow, Tyne & Wear, and Joan, *née* Derrick; *b* 10 June 1956; *Educ* RMA Sandhurst, Univ of Durham (BEd), Univ of Wales (MSc); *m* 12 Oct 1985, Pauline Kinloch, *née* Sillars; 2 s (Andrew b 14 Nov 1987, Malcolm b 11 May 1990); *Career* Army Education and Trg Services Branch 1979–1994 (final rank Maj), team ldr in HR mgmnt and business mgmnt Aberdeen Coll 1995–99, MSP (Lib Dem) Aberdeenshire W and Kincardine 1999–; *Recreations* family, walking; *Style*— Mike Rumbles, Esq, MSP; ✉ Kinloch House, Birse Aboyne, Aberdeenshire AB34 5BY; The Scottish Parliament, Edinburgh EH99 1SP (tel 0131 348 5798); 6 Dee Street, Banchory, Kincardineshire AB31 5ST (tel 01330 820268)

RUMBOLD, Sir Henry John Sebastian; 11 Bt (GB 1779), of Wood Hall, Watton, Herts; s of Sir (Horace) Anthony Claude Rumbold, 10 Bt, KCMG, KCVO, CB (d 1983, formerly an ambass to Thailand and Austria), by his 1 w, Felicity (d 1984), da of late Lt-Col Frederick Bailey and Lady Janet, *née* Mackay (da of 1 Earl of Inchcape); *b* 24 December 1947; *Educ* Eton, William & Mary Coll Virginia USA; *m* 1978, Frances Ann, da of late Dr Albert Whitfield Hawkes, and formerly w of Julian Berry; *Heir* kinsman, Charles Rumbold; *Career* solicitor; currently ptnr Dawson Cornwell, formerly ptnr Stephenson Harwood; *Recreations* riding, shooting, reading; *Clubs* Boodle's, Brooks's, Groucho; *Style*— Sir Henry Rumbold, Bt; ✉ 19 Hollywood Road, London SW10 9HT; Hatch House, Tisbury, Salisbury, Wiltshire SP3 6PA; Dawson Cornwell, 15 Red Lion Square, London WC1R 4QT (tel 020 7242 2556)

RUMFITT, Nigel John; QC (1994); s of Alan Rumfitt, and Dorothy, *née* Ackroyd (d 2000); *b* 6 March 1950, Leeds; *Educ* Leeds Modern Sch, Pembroke Coll Oxford (MA, BCL); *m* 15 Sept 1984, Pamela, *née* Pouncey; *Career* teaching asst Northwestern Univ Sch of Law Chicago 1972–73; called to the Bar Middle Temple 1974 (Harmsworth law scholar); recorder of the Crown Court 1995– (asst recorder 1991–95); memb: Criminal Bar Assoc, Midland Circuit; *Recreations* skiing, sailing; *Style*— Nigel Rumfitt, Esq, QC; ✉ Chambers of David Farrer QC, 7 Bedford Row, London WC1R 4BU (tel 020 7242 3555, fax 020 7242 2511, e-mail clerks@7br.co.uk)

RUNCIMAN OF DOXFORD, Viscountess; Ruth; DBE (1998, OBE 1991); da of Joseph Michael Hellmann (d 1941), and Dr Ellen Hellmann (d 1982); *b* 9 January 1936; *Educ* Roedean Sch Johannesburg, Univ of the Witwatersrand (BA), Girton Coll Cambridge (BA); *m* 1, 1959 (m dis 1962), Denis Mack Smith; m 2, 1963, 3 Viscount Runciman of Doxford, CBE, *qv*; 2 da (Lisa b 18 Aug 1965, Catherine b 18 July 1969), 1 s (David b 1 March 1967); *Career* memb Advsy Cnl on the Misuse of Drugs 1974–95, memb Cncl Nat Assoc of CAB 1978–83, dir ENO 1978–83, dep chm Prison Reform Tst 1981–; chm: Mental Health Act Cmmn 1994–98, Nat AIDS Tst 2000– (tstee 1989–93), Central and NW London Mental Health NHS Tst 2001–; tstee: Prince's Tst Volunteers 1989–94, Mental Health Fndn 1990–96, The Pilgrim Tst 1999–, Sainsbury Centre for Mental Health 2001–03; memb PCC 1998–2001 (memb Charter Compliance Panel 2004–06); advice worker Kensington CAB 1986–2001; Hon LLD De Montfort Univ 1997, hon fell Univ of Central Lancs 2000, hon fell Girton Coll Cambridge 2001; *Recreations* gardening, tennis; *Style*— The Viscountess Runciman of Doxford, DBE; fax 020 7372 4668

RUNCIMAN OF DOXFORD, 3 Viscount (UK 1937); Sir Walter Garrison (Garry) Runciman; 4 Bt (UK 1906), CBE (1987); also Baron Runciman (UK 1933); s of 2 Viscount Runciman of Doxford, OBE, AFC, AE, DL (d 1989), and his 2 wife, Katharine Schuyler, *née* Garrison (d 1993); *b* 10 November 1934; *Educ* Eton, Trinity Coll Cambridge; *m* 17 April 1963, Ruth (Viscountess Runciman of Doxford, DBE, *qv*), da of Joseph Hellman, of Johannesburg, and former w of Denis Mack Smith; 2 da (Hon Lisa b 18 Aug 1965, Hon Catherine b 18 July 1969), 1 s (Hon David Walter b 1 March 1967); *Heir* s, Hon David Runciman; *Career* fell Trinity Coll Cambridge 1959–63 and 1971–; chm: Andrew Weir and Co Ltd 1991–2005, Runciman Investments Ltd; memb FSA (formerly SIB) 1986–98 (dep chm 1998); treas Child Poverty Action Gp 1972–97; pres Gen Cncl Br Shipping 1986–87 (vice-pres 1985–86); chm Royal Cmmn on Criminal Justice 1991–93; pres Br Acad 2001–05; Hon DLitt Univ of Oxford 2000; FBA 1975; *Books* Plato's Later Epistemology (1962), Social Science and Political Theory (1963), Relative Deprivation and Social Justice (1966), A Critique of Max Weber's Philosophy of Social Science (1972), A Treatise on Social Theory Vol I (1983), Vol II (1989), Vol III (1997), The Social Animal (1998); *Clubs* Brooks's; *Style*— The Rt Hon the Viscount Runciman of Doxford, CBE; ✉ Trinity College, Cambridge, CB2 1TQ

RUSBRIDGER, Alan Charles; s of G H Rusbridger, of Guildford, Surrey, and Barbara, *née* Wickham (d 1995); *b* 29 December 1953; *Educ* Cranleigh Sch, Magdalene Coll Cambridge (MA); *m* 1982, Lindsay, da of Baron Mackie of Benshie, CBE, DSO, DFC (Life Peer), *qv*; *Career* reporter Cambridge Evening News 1976–79, reporter, columnist and feature writer The Guardian 1979–86, TV critic The Observer 1986–87, Washington corr London Daily News 1987, features ed The Guardian 1989–93 (feature writer and ed Weekend Guardian 1987–93), ed The Guardian 1995– (dep ed 1993–95), exec ed The Observer 1997–; dir Bd: Guardian Newspapers Ltd (GNL) 1994, Guardian Media Group (GMG) 1999; memb: Code Ctee PCC 2004–, NUJ, Scott Tst; commended Br Press Awards 1977 and 1978, What the Papers Say Award Newspaper Ed of the Year 1996, 2001 and 2005, Nat Newspaper Ed of the Year Newspaper Focus Awards 1996, Freedom of the Press Award London Press Club Awards 1998; chm: Photographer's Gallery 2001–04, Nat Youth Orch 2004–; visiting fell Nuffield Coll Oxford 2004–, visiting prof Queen Mary's Coll London; *Publications* The Guardian Year (ed, 1994), Fields of Gold (with Ronan Bennett); also author of three children's books; *Recreations* golf, music; *Style*— Alan

R

Rusbridger, Esq; ✉ The Guardian, 119 Farringdon Road, London EC1R 3ER (tel 020 7278 2332, fax 020 7239 9997)

RUSEDSKI, Greg; *b* 6 September 1973, Canada; *m* Lucy Connor; 1 da (Scarlett b Jan 2006); *Career* tennis player; turned professional 1991; tournament victories: Miller Hall of Fame Championships Newport RI (first tour title) 1993, 2004 and 2005, Newport RI (doubles title) 1994, KAL Cup Seoul South Korea 1995, Beijing Open 1996, Swiss Indoors Basle 1997, Nottingham Open 1997, champion Paris Indoor Open 1998, champion European Community Championships Antwerp 1998, CA Trophy Vienna 1999, Grand Slam Cup Munich 1999, Sybase Open San Jose 2001, Heineken Open NZ 2002, RCA Championship Indianapolis 2002, Nottingham Open 2003; finalist in several tournaments incl: US Open 1997, ATP Champions' Cup Indian Wells CA 1998; highest ATP Tour ranking 6 1997; memb Br Davis Cup Team 1996–2007 (became Br subject in June 1995); ret 2007; BBC Sports Personality of the Year 1997, ITV British Sportsman of the Year 1997, Player of the Year LTA, Br Lawn Tennis Writers Assoc Award 1997, Sportsman of the Year Sports Writers Assoc of Britain 1997; *Recreations* Arsenal football, golf, cinema, James Bond; *Style*— Greg Rusedski, Esq; ✉ c/o Sharon Park, Ructions, PO Box 31369, London SW11 3GH (tel 020 7738 2080, e-mail sharon@park54.fsnet.co.uk)

RUSH, Michael Allen Frank; s of Colin Charles Rush (d 1968), of Richmond, Surrey, and Muriel Mary, *née* Hinds (d 1968); *b* 2 January 1933; *Educ* KCS Wimbledon, KCL (BSc); *m* 1, 26 July 1958 (m dis 1979), Janet Larema, da of Lt-Col David George Ogilvy Ayerst (d 1992); 1 s (David b 1959), 2 da (Susan b 1961, Lindy b 1970); m 2, 1 Sept 1980, Linda Evelyn, da of Maurice Stratton Townsend (d 1997); *Career* Flying Offr RAF 1954–56; mgmnt conslt A/C Inbucon 1961–65; W S Try Ltd: dir 1968, md 1972, chm of int subsid 1977–85, dep chm main UK subsid 1983–85; formed Michael Rush Associates mgmnt conslts 1985, project mangr Daily Mail and Evening Standard new devpt printing works 1985–93, chm Management Selection Consultants Ltd 1991–2002; pres Chiltern Soc 2003– (hon sec Rivers and Wetlands Conservation Gp 1994–95, vice-chm 1995–97, chm 1997–2002, vice-pres 2002–03), memb Chilterns Conservation Bd 2001–03; MICE 1958, MInstD 1975; *Recreations* horse riding, hunting, walking, conservation, sailing; *Clubs* RAF; *Style*— Michael A F Rush, Esq; ✉ 15 Northerwood House, Emery Down, Lyndhurst, Hampshire SO43 7DT (tel 02380 282395)

RUSH, Prof Michael David; s of Wilfred George Rush (d 1983), of Richmond, Surrey, and Elizabeth May Winifred, *née* Gurney (d 1985); *b* 29 October 1937; *Educ* Shene GS Richmond, Univ of Sheffield (BA, PhD); *m* 25 July 1964, Jean Margaret, da of George Telford (d 1987), of Golcar, W Yorks; 2 s (Jonathan b 1968, Anthony b 1971); *Career* Nat Serv RASC 1957–59; Univ of Exeter: asst lectr 1964–67, lectr 1967–81, sr lectr 1981–90, head Dept of Politics 1985–92, reader in Parliamentary govt 1990–94, prof of politics 1994–2003, emeritus prof of politics 2003–; visiting lectr Univ of Western Ontario 1967–68, visiting prof Univ of Acadia Nova Scotia 1981, res fell Carleton Univ Ottawa 1975, 1992 and 1999; chm Study of Parliament Gp 1990–93; memb Cncl Hansard Soc 1992–2001; FRSA 1992; *Books* The Selection of Parliamentary Candidates (1969), The MP and his Information (jtly, 1970), An Introduction to Political Sociology (jtly, 1971), The House of Commons: Services and Facilities (co-ed, 1974), Parliamentary Government in Britain (1981), The House of Commons: Services and Facilities 1972–82 (ed, 1983), The Cabinet and Policy Formation (1984), Parliament and the Public (1976 and 1986), Parliament and Pressure Politics (ed, 1990), Politics and Society: An Introduction to Political Sociology (1992), British Government and Politics Since 1945: Changes in Perspective (co-ed, 1995), The Role of the Member of Parliament Since 1868: From Gentlemen to Players (2001), Parliament Today (2005), The Palgrave Review of British Politics 2005 (co-ed, 2006), The Palgrave Review of British Politics 2006 (co-ed, 2007); *Recreations* listening to classical music, theatre, travel; *Style*— Prof Michael Rush; ✉ 2 St Loyes Road, Heavitree, Exeter EX2 5HA (tel 01392 254089, e-mail michaelrush@tinyonline.co.uk)

RUSHDIE, Sir (Ahmed) Salman; kt (2007); s of Anis Ahmed Rushdie (d 1987), and Negin, *née* Butt; *b* 19 June 1947, Bombay; *Educ* Rugby, King's Coll Cambridge; *m* 1, 1976 (m dis), Clarissa Luard; 1 s; m 2, 1988 (m dis), Marianne Wiggins; m 3, 1997 (m dis), Elizabeth West; 1 s; m 4, 2004, Padma Lakshmi; *Career* writer; former advertising copywriter; memb: Gen Cncl Camden Ctee for Community Relations 1975–82, Int PEN 1981–, Cncl ICA 1985–, Production Bd BFI 1986–; pres PEN American Center 2004–; Freedom of the City Mexico City 1999; hon prof of the humanities MIT 1993; FRSL 1983; Commandeur de l'Ordre des Arts et des Lettres (France) 1999; *Books* Grimus (1975), Midnight's Children (1981, Booker Prize, James Tait Black Meml Prize, E-SU Literary Award), Shame (1983, Prix du Meilleur Livre Etranger 1984), The Jaguar Smile: a Nicaraguan Journey (1987), The Satanic Verses (1988, Whitbread Award), Haroun and the Sea of Stories (1990), Imaginary Homelands (essays, 1991), The Wizard of Oz (1992), East, West (1994), The Moor's Last Sigh (1995, Whitbread Fiction Award 1996, Book of the Year Br Book Awards 1996, The EU's Aristeion Prize for Literature 1996), The Ground Beneath Her Feet (1999, Commonwealth Prize (Eurasic Section) 2000), Fury (2001), Step Across This Line: Collected Non-Fiction 1992–2002 (2002), Shalimar the Clown (2005, shortlisted Whitbread Novel of the Year 2005); *Television films* The Painter and the Pest 1985, The Riddle of Midnight 1988; *Style*— Sir Salman Rushdie; ✉ c/o The Wylie Agency, 17 Bedford Square, London WC1B 3JA (tel 020 7908 5900, fax 020 7908 5901)

RUSHMAN, Dr Geoffrey Boswall; s of William John Rushman (d 1967), of Northampton, and Violet Helen Elizabeth, *née* Richards (d 1999); *b* 20 August 1939; *Educ* Northampton GS, Univ of London, Bart's Med Coll London (MB BS); *m* 12 Oct 1963, Gillian Mary, da of George Leslie Rogers, of Alcester, Warks; 3 da (Alison b 1965, Ruth b 1967, Jacqueline b 1969); *Career* jr anaesthetist Bart's 1968–73, conslt anaesthetist Southend Hosp 1974–99; Assoc of Anaesthetists prize for contribs to anaesthesia; examiner final FRCA Royal Coll of Anaesthetists 1994–2000 (part I 1991–94) and Coll assessor 1993–99; memb Cncl Section of Anaesthesia RSM 1985–88 and 1991–2000 (sr sec 1992–93, pres 1999–2000), elected memb Cncl RSM 2001–05; lay reader Oxford Diocese; FFARCS 1970; *Books* Synopsis of Anaesthesia (ed 8–11, 1977, 1982, 1987, 1993), MCQ Self Test Companion (1994), A Short History of Anaesthesia (1996), Short Answer Questions in Anaesthesia (1997), Lee's Synopsis of Anaesthesia (12 edn, 1999); *Recreations* skiing, preaching The Gospel, mountain walking, fishing; *Clubs* RSM; *Style*— Dr Geoffrey Rushman; ✉ Aylesbury Road, Thame, Oxfordshire OX9 3AW

RUSHMAN, Nigel John; s of Maj Frederick William Edward Henry Rushman, and Irene Vera, *née* Beer; *b* 25 May 1956; *Educ* Gillingham Tech HS, Gravesend GS, Thanet Tech Coll; *m* 1, 21 Sept 1980 (m dis), Deborah Sally, da of Kenneth William White, of London; 1 da (Louise Amanda b 1986); m 2, 28 July 1989, Nicola Susan, da of David Polding, of Oare, Wilts; 1 da (Sophie b 1995); *Career* md Rushmans Ltd; dir: Cubavest Ltd, Modulec Ltd; *Recreations* fly fishing, shooting; *Style*— Nigel Rushman, Esq; ✉ Rushmans Ltd, PO Box 2391, Marlborough, Wiltshire SN8 3WJ (tel 01264 852010, fax 01264 852011)

RUSHTON, Prof David Nigel; s of Dr Roland Rushton, of Bromley, and Pamela Anne, *née* Galzini; *b* 21 December 1944; *Educ* King's Sch Canterbury, Trinity Coll Cambridge (BA), King's Coll Hosp Med Sch (MB BChir), Univ of Cambridge (MD); *m* 30 March 1968, Anne, da of Leo Gallagher (d 1967), of Liverpool; 2 da (Nicola b 1970, Susannah b 1976), 1 s (Samuel b 1982); *Career* clinical scientific staff MRC Neurological Prostheses Unit 1971–, reader Dept of Neurology Inst of Psychiatry 1990–92, prof of rehabilitation Univ of London (London Hosp Med Coll) 1993–97; hon conslt Maudsley Hosp 1979–92, hon conslt neurologist King's Coll Hosp 1984–92, conslt in rehabilitation King's Coll Hosp 1997–; contrib scientific articles on neurology and neurological prostheses; memb: Assoc of Br Neurologists, Physiological Soc, Br Soc for Rehabilitation Med; Freeman Worshipful Co of Spectacle Makers 1979; FRCP 1989; *Books* Treatment in Clinical Medicine - neurological disorders, Handbook of Neuro-Urology, Neurological Prostheses; *Recreations* medieval house reconstruction, steam road vehicles; *Style*— Prof David Rushton

RUSHTON, Kenneth John (Ken); s of Dr Martin Rushton (d 1996), and Halina, *née* Schoenfeld (d 2002); *b* 6 October 1944; *Educ* Uppingham, Trinity Coll Dublin (MA); *m* Sept 1970, Lesley Christine, da of Michael Jackson (d 2001); 2 s (Patrick b July 1973, Christopher b March 1982), 1 da (Jane b Feb 1976); *Career* ICI: joined 1968, various secretarial appts, asst co sec 1988–96, co sec 1996–99, ret; dir Inst of Business Ethics 2000–01, dir UK Listing Authority 2001–03; currently sr advsr to Nestor Advisors Ltd; FICS, FRSA; *Recreations* theatre, music, opera, skiing, golf; *Clubs* RSA, IOD; *Style*— Ken Rushton, Esq

RUSHTON, Prof Neil; s of John Allen Rushton (d 1996), and Iris, *née* Street (d 1987); *b* 16 December 1945; *Educ* Oglethorpe Sch Tadcaster, Middx Hosp London (MB BS), Univ of Cambridge (MD); *m* 12 June 1971, Sheila Margaret, da of Capt Geoffrey Greville Johnson (d 1997), of Southwold, Suffolk; 2 s (Mark b 25 Sept 1973, Timothy b 24 Jan 1980), 1 da (Nicola b 15 Aug 1975); *Career* Univ of Cambridge: dir Orthopaedic Res Unit 1983–, fell Magdalene Coll 1984–, prof of orthopaedics; hon orthopaedic conslt Addenbrooke's Hosp; Hunterian prof RCS; examiner Univs of Cambridge, Oxford and London; dep ed for Research Jl of Bone & Joint Surgery (B) 1996–2006; Hon MA Univ of Cambridge 1979; pres Euro Orthopaedic Research Soc, fndr memb Br Hip Soc, memb Br Orthopaedic Assoc, fell Br Orthopaedic Research Soc, FRSM, FRCS; *Books* Colour Atlas of Surgical Exposures of the Limbs (1985), Orthopaedics - The Principles and Practice of Musculoskeletal Surgery (contrib, 1987), Body Clock (contrib); *Recreations* dinghy sailing, snow skiing, scuba diving, wines; *Clubs* SCGB, Athenaeum; *Style*— Prof Neil Rushton; ✉ 37 Bentley Road, Cambridge CB2 2AW (tel 01223 353624, fax 01223 365889); Orthopaedic Research Unit, University of Cambridge, Box 180, Addenbrooke's Hospital, Cambridge CB2 2QQ (tel 01223 217551, fax 01223 214094, e-mail nr10000@cam.ac.uk)

RUSKIN, Paul; *b* 22 August 1958; *Educ* Hertford Coll Oxford (MA), Cranfield Sch of Mgmnt (MBA); *Career* Cambridge Consultants Ltd: joined 1980, business unit mangr Informatics 1995–2001, dir 1996–2001; dir and ind conslt Paul Ruskin Ltd 2001–05, dir of special projects Premier Performance Div UK Ford 2002–04, memb Mgmnt Gp PA Consulting 2005–; MIEE 1981, CEng; *Style*— Paul Ruskin, Esq

RUSSELL, Alec Charles Cumine; s of James Cecil Cumine Russell of Aden, CBE, and Diana Margaret, *née* White; *b* 21 October 1966; *Educ* Winchester, New Coll Oxford (BA); *Career* Daily Telegraph: Bucharest corr Jan-Dec 1990 (Turkey during Gulf War and Kurdish crisis), Yugoslav War corr 1991–92, SE Europe staff corr (based Bucharest) 1992–93, South Africa corr (based Johannesburg) 1993–98, asst foreign ed 1998–99, dep foreign ed 2000–01, foreign ed 2001–02, asst ed (foreign) 2002–; highly commended: Young Journalist of the Year Award 1990, David Blundie Freelance Corr Award 1991; *Publications* Prejudice and Plum Brandy (1993), Big Men Little People (1999); *Style*— Alec Russell, Esq; ✉ The Daily Telegraph, 1 Canada Square, Canary Wharf, London E14 5DT (tel 020 7538 5000)

RUSSELL, Alexander William (Sandy); CB; s of William Russell (d 1992), and Elizabeth Wallace Bennett, *née* Russell (d 1992); *b* 16 October 1938; *Educ* Royal HS Edinburgh, Univ of Edinburgh (MA), Manitoba Univ (MA); *m* 1, Nov 1962, Elspeth Rae, *née* Robertson (decd); m 2, Dec 1999, Patricia, *née* Moodie; *Career* Scottish Office: asst princ Scottish Devpt Dept 1961–64, private sec to Parly Under Sec of State 1964–65, princ Regnl Devpt Div and Scottish Devpt Dept 1965–72, princ private sec to Sec of State for Scotland 1972–73, Scottish Devpt Dept 1973–76, asst sec Civil Serv Dept 1976–79, under sec Mgmnt and Personnel Office 1979–82, head Treasury MPO Financial Mgmnt Unit 1982–85; HM Customs and Excise: dir of orgn 1985–90, dir of customs 1990–93, dep chm 1993–98; efficiency advsr to Cabinet Office 1999–2003; dir SITPRO 1999–2006 (advsr 2006–); strategic conslt 1999–; memb Cncl on Tbnls 2002–05; *Style*— Sandy Russell, Esq, CB; ✉ Flat 1, Hyndford House, 18 Fidra Road, North Berwick EH39 4NG (e-mail awrussell@compuserve.com)

RUSSELL, Andrew Neville; s of Herbert Mark Russell (d 1999), and Phyllis Mary, *née* Slade (d 1989); *b* 30 October 1940; *Educ* Highgate Sch; *m* 1964 (m dis 2004), Audrey Helen Roe; 1 da (Philippa Clare b 1968); *Career* articled clerk Neville Russell 1957–62, accountant Coopers & Lybrand 1963–66, ptnr Caldwell & Braham 1967–73, sr ptnr Mazars Neville Russell Brighton (formerly Neville Russell) 1974–2001, exec ptnr Mazars Neville Russell (UK Partnership) 1982–98; treas: Keep Sunday Special Campaign 1982–96, Brighton Int Festival 1988–92 and 1994–97, Ryder Cheshire 2000–; govr St Mary's Hall Brighton 2000– (chm 2003–); tstee The Charleston Tst 2002–, Target Tuberculosis 2003–; Liveryman Worshipful Co of Coachmakers and Coach Harness Makers 1972; FCA 1963; *Recreations* walking, music, visual arts; *Style*— Andrew N Russell, Esq; ✉ 18 Lewes Crescent, Brighton BN2 1GB (tel 01273 685459, e-mail andrewrussell18@ukonline.co.uk)

RUSSELL, Angus Charles; s of Kenneth John Russell (d 2002), and Nora, *née* Liversidge (d 1977); *b* 2 January 1956; *Educ* Bablake Sch Coventry, Coventry Univ; *Children* 2 da (Harriet Emily b 7 Dec 1988, Sophie Francesca b 21 July 1990); *Career* trainee CA PricewaterhouseCoopers 1975–80, in fin, mktg and business devpt ICI plc 1980–93, gp treas Zeneca Gp plc 1993–99, vice-pres (corp fin) Astrazeneca plc 1999, chief financial offr Shire Pharmaceuticals Gp plc 1999–; non-exec dir City of London Investment Tst plc 2003–; memb ICA 1979, FACT 1990; *Recreations* sailing and windsurfing, skiing, collecting art, antiques and contemporary ceramics; *Clubs* Royal Southern Yacht; *Style*— Angus Russell, Esq; ✉ Shire Pharmaceuticals Group plc, Hampshire International Business Park, Chineham, Basingstoke, Hampshire RG24 8EP (tel 01256 894222, fax 01256 894713, e-mail arussell@uk.shire.com)

RUSSELL, Rt Rev Dr Anthony John; *see:* Ely, Bishop of

RUSSELL, His Hon Judge Anthony Patrick; QC (1999); s of Dr Michael Hibberd Russell (d 1987), and Pamela, *née* Eyre; *b* 11 April 1951; *Educ* The King's Sch Chester, Pembroke Coll Oxford (MA); *Career* called to the Bar Middle Temple 1974; jr Northern Circuit 1977, recorder 1993–96 and 2001–04 (asst recorder 1989–93), standing counsel (Criminal) to the Inland Revenue 1994–96, circuit judge (Northern Circuit) 2004–06, sr circuit judge 2006–, hon recorder of Preston 2006–; memb Bar Cncl 1988–94; Guild of Church Musicians: memb Cncl 1985–93 and 1995–2004, hon fell 2001, vice-pres 2005; *Recreations* singing, listening to music, video photography, travel, the countryside; *Clubs* Oxford and Cambridge; *Style*— His Hon Judge Anthony Russell, QC; ✉ The Law Courts, Openshaw Place, Ring Way, Preston PR1 2LL (tel 01772 844700)

RUSSELL, Sir Charles Dominic; 4 Bt (UK 1916), of Littleworth Corner, Burnham, Co Buckingham; s of Sir Charles Russell, 3 Bt (d 1997); *b* 28 May 1956; *Educ* Worth Abbey Sch; *m* 1, 24 May 1986 (m dis 1995), Sarah Jane Murray, da of Anthony Chandor, of Haslemere, Surrey; 1 s (Charles William b 8 Sept 1988); m 2, 6 Sept 2005, Wandee Ruanrakrao; *Heir* s, Charles Russell; *Career* antiquarian book dealer; *Style*— Sir Charles Russell, Bt

RUSSELL, Christine Margaret; MP; da of John Alfred William Carr, of Holbeach, and Phyllis Carr; *b* 25 March 1945; *Educ* Spalding HS, London Sch of Librarianship, Poly of NW London; *m* 30 July 1971 (m dis 1991), Dr James Russell; 1 s, 1 da; *Career* librarian: London Borough of Camden 1967–70, Univ of Glasgow 1970–71, Dumbartonshire CC 1971–73; personal asst to: Lyndon Harrison, MEP 1989–91, Brian Simpson, MEP 1992–94; co-ordinator Advocacy Project MIND 1994–97; MP (Lab) City of Chester 1997–; ALA

1971; *Recreations* film, football and walking; *Style—* Ms Christine Russell, MP; ✉ House of Commons, London SW1A 0AA (tel 020 7219 6398, fax 020 7219 0943, e-mail russellcm@parliament.uk)

RUSSELL, Christopher Garnet; s of George Percival Jewett (d 1948), of Boscombe, Hants, and Marjorie Alice Boddam-Whetham, *née* Keeling-Bloxam; *b* 6 April 1943; *Educ* Westminster, New Coll Oxford (MA); *m* 23 June 1973, Agatha Mary, da of Stephen Joseph Culkin (d 1984); 2 da (Claire b 1974, Lucy b 1975), 1 s (Charles b 1976); *Career* called to the Bar Middle Temple 1971, ad eundum Lincoln's Inn 1985; *Style—* Christopher Russell, Esq; ✉ Penhayle, New Polzeath, Cornwall (tel 01208 862041); Framfield Place, Framfield, East Sussex (tel 01825 890021); 12 New Square, Lincoln's Inn, London WC2 (tel 020 7419 9411 or 020 7419 8000, fax 020 7419 1313, e-mail christopher.russell@newsquarechambers.co.uk, website www.12newsquare.co.uk); Third Floor East, 7 Stone Buildings, Lincoln's Inn, London WC2 (tel 020 7404 9739)

RUSSELL, Clare Nancy; JP (2003); da of Sir Ewan Macpherson-Grant, 6 Bt (d 1983), and Lady Macpherson-Grant; *b* 4 August 1944; *Educ* Scotland; *m* 1967, Oliver Henry Russell; 2 s, 1 da; *Career* head decorator Constance Spry 1962–65, sec to Fourth Clerk at the Table House of Commons 1965–67, dir Craigo Farms Ltd 1970–; estate owner and land mangr Ballindalloch 1979–, opened Ballindalloch Castle to the public 1993; chm Queen Mary's Clothing Guild 1990–93 (estab Queen Mary's Clothing Guild in Scotland 1986); memb: Cncl Nat Tst for Scotland 1985–88, Moray Health Cncl 1986–91, Exec Ctee Scotland's Garden Scheme 1987–93 (dist organiser Moray and Banff 1980–93), Bd Children's Hospice Assoc Scotland 1995–2002; Sunday sch teacher Inveraven Church 1982–; HM Lord-Lt Banffshire 2002– (DL 1991–98, Vice Lord-Lt 1998–2002); *Books* Favourite Recipes, Dried Flowers and Pot Pourri from Ballindalloch Castle (1993), Favourite Puddings from Ballindalloch Castle (1995), Favourite First Courses from Ballindalloch Castle (1996), Favourite Recipes from Ballindalloch Castle (1998), I Love Food (2004); *Recreations* dog-handling, gardening, flower arranging, piano, tapestry, knitting, cooking, historic houses, antiques; *Clubs* Sloane; *Style—* Mrs Clare Russell; ✉ Ballindalloch Castle, Banffshire AB37 9AX (tel 01807 500206, fax 01807 500210, e-mail enquiries@ballindallochcastle.co.uk)

RUSSELL, Hon David Whitney Erskine; s and h of 4 Baron Ampthill, CBE, PC, *qv* by his 1 w, Susan, da of Hon Charles Winn (s of 2 Baron St Oswald, JP, DL); *b* 27 May 1947; *Educ* Stowe; *m* 1, 15 Nov 1980 (m dis 1998), April, yst da of Paul Arbon, of New York; 2 da (Christabel b 1981, Daisy b 1983); m 2, 6 July 2002, Tia Ipsen, wid of Prince Rostislav Romanoff; *Career* memb: Rye Town Cncl 2003–, Rother DC 2007–; *Clubs* White's; *Style—* The Hon David Russell

RUSSELL, Prof Donald Andrew Frank Moore; s of Samuel Charles Russell (d 1979), and Laura, *née* Moore (d 1966); *b* 13 October 1920; *Educ* KCS Wimbledon, Balliol Coll Oxford (MA, DLitt); *m* 22 July 1967, Joycelyne Gledhill Dickinson (Joy) (d 1993), da of Percy Parkin Dickinson (d 1972); *Career* served WWII: Royal Signals 1941–43, Intelligence Corps 1943–45; St John's Coll Oxford: fell 1948–88 (emeritus fell 1988–), univ lectr in classical languages and lit 1952–78, reader in classical lit 1978–85, prof of classical lit 1985–88; J H Gray Lectures Univ of Cambridge 1981; visiting prof: Univ of N Carolina 1985, Stanford Univ 1989–91; FBA 1971; *Books* Longinus On the Sublime (1964), Plutarch (1972), Ancient Literary Criticism (with M Winterbottom, 1972), Criticism in Antiquity (1981), Menander Rhetor (with N G Wilson, 1981), Greek Declamation (1983), Anthology of Latin Prose (1990), Anthology of Greek Prose (1991), Dio Chrysostom, Orations 7, 12, 36 (1992), Plutarch: Selected Essays and Dialogues (1993), Libanius: Imaginary Speeches (1996), Quintilian (2001), Heraclitus: Homeric Allegories (with D Konstan, 2005); *Style—* Prof Donald Russell, FBA; ✉ 35 Belsyre Court, Oxford OX2 6HU (tel 01865 556135); St John's College, Oxford OX1 3JP

RUSSELL, Edwin John Cumming; s of Edwin Russell (d 1962), and Mary Elizabeth, *née* Cumming (d 1969); *b* 4 May 1939; *Educ* Brighton GS, Brighton Sch of Art, Royal Acad Schs (Cert RAS); *m* 7 Nov 1964, Lorne, da of Lt Cdr J A H McKean, RN (d 1981); 2 da (Rebecca b 21 Jan 1966, Tanya b 25 April 1968); *Career* sculptor; Gold Medal for Sculpture RA, Sir Otto Beit Medal 1991; FRBS 1970; *Works* sculptures incl: Crucifix St Paul's Cathedral 1964, St Catherine Westminster Abbey 1966, Bishop Bubwith W Front Wells Cathedral, forecourt sculpture Rank Xerox Int HQ 1989; shopping centre sculptures: Mad Hatters Tea Party Warrington 1984, Lion and Lamb Farnham 1987 (Best Shopping Centre Award); public works: Suffragette Meml London 1968, First Govr of Bahamas Sheraton Hotel Nassau 1968, Alice and the White Rabbit Guildford (Lewis Carroll commemorative sculpture) 1984, Panda World Wide Fund Int HQ 1988; sundials incl: Jubilee Dolphin dial Nat Maritime Museum Greenwich 1978, sundial Sultan Qaboos Univ Oman 1986, Botanical Armillary sundial Kew Gardens 1987, History of London sundial Tower Hill Underground 1992, 18 ft concrete dial Bracknell; *Private Collections* incl: Goodwood House, Arup Assocs, Trafalgar House plc, Cementation Int, John Mowlem & Co, City of London GS; *Recreations* sculpture and philosophy; *Style—* Edwin Russell, Esq; ✉ Lethendry, Polecat Valley, Hindhead, Surrey GU26 6BE (tel 01428 605655)

RUSSELL, Francis George Scott; s of Robert Scott Russell, CBE (d 2000), of East Hanney, Oxon, and Anne, *née* Ingle Finch; *b* 4 February 1949, Oxford; *Educ* Westminster, ChCh Oxford; *Career* Christie's: joined 1972, dir 1978, dep chm 2004; memb: Arts Panel, Nat Tst; FSA; *Publications* Portraits of Sir Walter Scott (1987), John, 3rd Earl of Bute: Patron and Collector (2004), Italian Places (2006); author of articles in magazines incl Burlington Magazine, Apollo, Master Drawings and Country Life and of contributions to exhbn catalogues; *Clubs* Beefsteak, Pratt's, Turf, White's; *Style—* Francis Russell, Esq; ✉ 30C Upper Montagu Street, London W1H 1RP (tel 020 7724 0054); The Grange, East Hanney, Wantage, Oxfordshire; Christie's, 8 King Street, St James's, London SW1Y 6QT (tel 020 7389 2073, fax 020 7724 0054)

RUSSELL, Lord Francis Hastings; s (by 2 m) of 13 Duke of Bedford (d 2002), and Lydia, Duchess of Bedford, *née* Yarde-Buller (d 2006); *b* 27 February 1950; *Educ* Eton; *m* 1, 1971 (m dis); 1 da (Czarina b 14 July 1976); m 2, 1996 (m dis), Sarah Clemence; 2 s (John Francis b 5 June 1997, Harry Evelyn Terence b 11 Nov 1999); *Career* chartered surveyor 1979, md and chm LFR & Co Ltd; MRICS; *Recreations* skiing, golf; *Style—* Lord Francis Russell; ✉ 10 Yeoman's Row, London SW3 2AH (tel 020 7581 4488, fax 020 7581 4944, e-mail francis@lfr.co.uk)

RUSSELL, Sir George; kt (1992), CBE (1985); s of William Henry Russell (d 1972), of Gateshead, Co Durham, and Frances Annie, *née* Atkinson (d 1973); *b* 25 October 1935; *Educ* Gateshead GS, Univ of Durham (BA); *m* 19 Dec 1959, Dorothy, da of Ernest Victor Brown (d 1969), of Gateshead, Co Durham; 3 da (Erica Frances b 1963, Livia Jane b 1966, Alison Victoria b 1969); *Career* successively graduate trainee, commercial res offr, sales rep then product manager ICI 1958–67; vice-pres and gen mangr: Welland Chemical Co of Canada 1968, St Clair Chemical Co Ltd 1968; dir Luxfer Holdings Ltd 1976; md: Alcan Aluminium (UK) 1977–81, Alcan UK Ltd 1981–82 (asst md 1977–81); md and chief exec British Alcan Aluminium 1982–86; dir: Alcan Aluminiumwerke GmbH Frankfurt 1982–86, Alcan Aluminium Ltd 1987–2000; chm: ITN Ltd 1988–89, Marley plc 1989–97 (chief exec 1986–89), 3i Group plc 1993–2001, Northern Development Company 1994–99, Camelot Group plc 1995–2002; dep chm Channel 4 Television Co Ltd 1987–88, non-exec dep chm Granada plc 2002–04, dep chm ITV plc 2003–; dir: Northern Rock plc (formerly Northern Rock Building Society) 1985–2006, Basys International Ltd 1987–88, Taylor Woodrow plc 1992–2004; visiting prof Univ of Newcastle upon Tyne 1978–81; chm: IBA 1989–90 (memb 1979–86), ITC 1991–96; memb: Bd Northern Sinfonia Orchestra 1977–80, Northern Industrial Bd 1977–80, Washington Corp 1978–80, Bd Civil Serv Pay Res Unit 1980–81, Megaw Inquiry into Civil Serv Pay 1981–82, CBI 1984–85, Widdicombe Ctee of Inquiry into Conduct of Local Authy Business 1985–86, Advsy Bd Skillcity 2004–05; memb Advsy Bd Mori 2005–; dir Wildfowl and Wetland Tst 2002–; tstee: Beamish Museum Tst 1985–89, Thomas Bewick Birthplace Tst 1986–89; memb Ct Univ of Newcastle upon Tyne 2004–; Hon DEng Univ of Newcastle upon Tyne 1985, Hon DBA Univ of Northumbria 1992; Hon LLD: Univ of Sunderland 1995, Univ of Durham 1997; Hon FRIBA, Hon FRTS, Hon FRAM, fell Inst of Industrial Mangrs, CIMgt, FRSA, FInstD; *Recreations* tennis, badminton, bird watching; *Style—* Sir George Russell, CBE; ✉ ITV plc, 200 Gray's Inn Road, London WC1X 8HF

RUSSELL, Prof Gerald Francis Morris; s of Maj Daniel George Russell, MC (d 1958), of Ventnor, IOW, and Berthe Marie Mathilde Ghislaine, *née* De Boe (d 1981); *b* 12 January 1928; *Educ* George Watson's Coll Edinburgh, Univ of Edinburgh (MB ChB, MD); *m* 8 Sept 1950, Margaret Euphemia, da of John Taylor (d 1956), of Edinburgh; 3 s (Malcolm b 1951, Nigel b 1956, Graham b 1957); *Career* Capt RAMC 1951–53, regtl med offr Queen's Bays; dean Inst of Psychiatry Univ of London 1966–70, prof of psychiatry Royal Free Hosp Sch of Med Univ of London 1971–79, hon conslt psychiatrist Royal Free Hosp and Friern Hosp 1971–79, prof of psychiatry Inst of Psychiatry Univ of London 1979–93, hon conslt psychiatrist Bethlem Royal and Maudsley Hosp 1979–93; conslt psychiatrist Priory Hosp Hayes Grove 1993–; chm: Section on Eating Disorders World Psychiatric Assoc 1989–99, Assoc of Univ Teachers of Psychiatry 1990–94, Sub-Ctee on Eating Disorders RCPsych 1992–95, Special Interest Gp on Eating Disorders RCPsych 1995–99; FRCP, FRCPEd, Hon FRCPsych; *Books* The Neuroses and Personality Disorders, vol 4 of The Handbook of Psychiatry (jtly, 1983), Scientific and Clinical Articles on Eating Disorders; author of numerous articles incl: original description of bulimia nervosa in Psychological Medicine (vol 9, 1979), confirmation of the benefits of family therapy in anorexia nervosa in Archives General Psychiatry (jtly, vol 4, 1987); *Recreations* art galleries, photography, music; *Style—* Prof Gerald Russell; ✉ Priory Hospital Hayes Grove, Prestons Road, Hayes, Kent BR2 7AS (tel 020 8462 7722, fax 020 8462 5028, e-mail geraldrussell@prioryhealthcare.com)

RUSSELL, Gerald William; s of Cyril Russell (d 2005), and Elizabeth, *née* Batten; *b* 21 May 1950, Twickenham, Middx; *Educ* St John's Beaumont Sch, Ampleforth; *m* 11 Dec 1976, Tessa Melanie, *née* Rumsey; 1 s (James Alexander b 13 June 1978), 4 da (Sophie Annabel b 17 March 1980, Lucy Victoria b 7 June 1983, Kate Elizabeth b 6 Oct 1985, Emma Rose b 1 Sept 1989); *Career* Whinney Murray (now Ernst & Young): joined 1969, Middle East 1977–79, ptnr 1983, managing ptnr Reading 1988–95, regnl managing ptnr South 1995–98, managing ptnr London 1998–2005, memb Cncl 2006–; memb Cncl and chair Audit and Assurance Faculty ICAEW 2005–; tstee and chair Finance Ctee NCH 2005–; govr Notre Dame Sch Cobham 2006–; FCA 1988 (ACA 1983); *Recreations* sailing, skiing, classic cars, carpentry; *Clubs* Aldeburgh Golf, Aldeburgh Yacht; *Style—* Gerald Russell, Esq; ✉ The White House, Castle Road, Weybridge, Surrey KT13 9QN (tel 01932 844498, e-mail gerald@russell.org.uk); Ernst & Young, 1 More London Place, London SE1 2AF (tel 020 7951 3434, e-mail grussell@uk.ey.com)

RUSSELL, Prof Ian John; s of Phillip William George Russell (d 1975), of Chestfield, Kent, and Joan Lilian, *née* Snook (d 1984); *b* 19 June 1943; *Educ* Chatham Tech Sch for Boys, QMC London (BSc), Univ of Br Columbia (NATO studentship, MSc), Univ of Cambridge (Trinity Hall research studentship, PhD); *m* 20 July 1968, Janice Marion, da of Gladstone Herbert Hall; 1 s (Simon Alexander b 14 Sept 1975), 1 da (Charlotte Louise b 3 Jan 1979); *Career* res fell Magdalene Coll Cambridge 1969–73, SRC res fell Univ of Cambridge 1969–71, Royal Soc res fell King Gustaf V Res Inst Stockholm 1970–71; Univ of Sussex: lectr in neurobiology 1971–79, MRC sr res fell 1979–81, reader 1979–87, prof of neurobiology 1987–, MRC sr res leave fell 1995–98; memb: Physiological Soc 1972, Soc of Experimental Biology 1966–1990, Assoc for Res in Otolaryngology 1993–, Acoustical Soc of America 1998–; FRS 1989; *Recreations* hockey, windsurfing, gardening, walking, music, reading and especially my family; *Style—* Prof Ian Russell, FRS; ✉ Little Ivy Cottage, Waldron, East Sussex TN21 0QX; School of Life Sciences, University of Sussex, Falmer, Brighton BN1 9QG (tel 01273 678632, fax 01273 678433, e-mail i.j.russell@sussex.ac.uk)

RUSSELL, Ian Simon MacGregor; CBE (2007); s of James MacGregor Russell, of Norwich, and Christine, *née* Clark; *b* 16 January 1953; *Educ* George Heriot's Sch Edinburgh, Univ of Edinburgh (BCom); *m* 25 Oct 1975, Fiona; 1 s (Ewan b 7 April 1982), 1 da (Lindsay b 9 July 1989); *Career* audit sr Thomson McLintock 1974–78, accountant Mars Ltd 1978–81, controller Pentos plc 1981–83, sub fin dir Hongkong and Shanghai Banking Corporation 1983–90, controller Tomkins plc 1990–94; Scottish Power plc: finance dir 1994–99, dep chief exec 1999–2001, chief exec 2001–06; non-exec dir: Johnston Press plc 2007–, JP Morgan Fleming Mercantile Tst plc; non-exec chm Remploy Ltd 2007–, dir Business in the Community Ltd; MICAS 1977; *Recreations* golf; *Clubs* RAC; *Style—* Ian Russell, Esq, CBE

RUSSELL, Jeremy Jonathan; QC (1994); s of Sidney Thomas Russell, of St Albans, Herts, and Maud Eugenie, *née* Davies; *b* 18 December 1950; *Educ* Watford Boys' GS, City of London Poly (BA), LSE (LLM); *m* 1987, Gillian Elizabeth, da of Hugh Giles; 1 s (Thomas Jonathan Giles b 8 Oct 1988), 1 da (Monica Eugenie Helen b 10 May 1990); *Career* called to the Bar Middle Temple 1975; in practice SE Circuit, salvage arbitrator Lloyd's 2000–05, CEDR accredited mediator; *Recreations* reading (particularly military history), gliding, classic cars; *Style—* Jeremy Russell, Esq, QC; ✉ Quadrant Chambers, Quadrant House, 10 Fleet Street, London EC4Y 1AU (tel 020 7583 4444, fax 020 7583 4455, e-mail jeremy.russell@quadrantchambers.com)

RUSSELL, John; s of Harold George Russell, and Joyce Caroline, *née* Morris; *b* 1 June 1953; *Educ* Westcliff HS for Boys, Univ of Southampton (LLB); *m* 23 July 1977, (Ingegerd) Maria, da of Rolf Erik Norén, KVO; 2 da (Samantha b 2 June 1982, Emma b 5 April 1985); *Career* admitted slr 1977, Linklaters & Paines London and Hong Kong 1975–85, investment banker Merrill Lynch International 1985–88, ptnr Simmons & Simmons 1988–; memb: Law Soc, Capital Markets Forum; MSI; *Recreations* skiing, walking, swimming, sailing; *Style—* John Russell, Esq; ✉ c/o Simmons & Simmons, CityPoint, One Ropemaker Street, London EC2Y 9SS (tel 020 7628 2020, fax 020 7628 2070)

RUSSELL, John Bayley; s of Frederick Charles Russell (d 1987), of Brisbane, Aust, and Clarice Emily Mander, *née* Jones (d 1959); *b* 22 January 1942; *Educ* C of E GS Brisbane, Univ of Queensland (BComm); *m* 27 Sept 1968, Virginia; 1 s (Simon b 1972); *Career* Deutsche Securities Aust Ltd (formerly Bain & Co Securities): ptnr 1972–92, ptnr i/c London Office 1980–84 and 1986–99, ptnr i/c NY office 1984–86; chm: Cedar Estates Ltd 2000–06, Thirty Five Ltd 2002–, Henderson Far East Income Tst plc 2007– (dir 2000–), Minster Pharmaceuticals plc 2007– (dir 2005–); dir Herencia Resources plc 2006–; memb: Aust Business in Europe 1990–2005, Victorian Advsy Ctee 1992–97; *Recreations* golf, reading; *Clubs* Univ and Schs (Sydney); *Style—* John Russell, Esq; ✉ 12 Rutland House, Marloes Road, London W8 5LE (e-mail jbr@jbrussell.com)

RUSSELL, (Henry) Kenneth Alfred (Ken); *b* 3 July 1927, Southampton; *Educ* Pangbourne Coll; *Family* 8 c (from 4 ms); *Career* film dir; early career as ballet dancer then briefly actor; began as dir on drama-documentaries for Monitor (BBC) incl Elgar and Delius; films incl: Tommy, Women in Love, Altered States, The Music Lovers, Savage Messiah, The Boy Friend, Listzomania, Valentino, The Devils; opera credits incl: Madam Butterfly, Faust, Rake's Progress, Princess Ida; other credits incl: Revenge of the Elephant Man, The Fall of the Louse of Usher, Elgar - Fantasy on a Composer on a Bicycle

R

(documentary); Chevalier de la Lagion d'Honneur (France); *Publications* incl Mike and Gaby's Space Gospel (novel), Directing: From Pitch to Premier, Brahms Gets Laid, Revenge of the White Worm, Elgar: The Erotic Variations, Delius: A Moment with Venus; *Style—* Prof Ken Russell

RUSSELL, Lucy; *Educ* Sherborne Sch for Girls, UCL (BA), The Poor Sch London, Sorbonne; *Career* actress; *Theatre* Semi-Monde (Lyric Theatre) 2001, The Cherry Orchard (Citizen's Theatre Glasgow) 2002, In the Name of Science (King's Head Theatre London) 2003; *Television* Rescue Me 2002, Cambridge Spies 2003, Murphy's Law 2003, Red Cap 2003; *Film* Following 1999, Left Turn 2001, Far From China 2002, Nude Descending 2002, L'Anglaise et le Duc (The Lady and the Duke) 2002, The Knowledge 2002, I Am David 2002, Animal 2003, Pour Le Plaisir 2003, Red Rose 2003, My Summer of Love 2004, Tristan and Isolde 2004; awarded Shooting Star Berlin Film Festival 2002; *Style—* Ms Lucy Russell

RUSSELL, Lynda Jane; da of Ivor Gordon Russell, of Stirchley, Birmingham, and Alison Jeanne, *née* Honeybourne; *b* 15 March 1952; *Educ* Swanshurst Bilateral Sch Kings Heath Birmingham, Royal Coll of Music London (Kathleen Ferrier Meml scholar); *m* 4 Jan 1991, Christopher William Royall, counter-tenor, s of late Gerald William Royall; 2 s (Timothy Gordon Russell Royall b 26 April 1988, Jonathan Charles William b 22 June 1994); *Career* soprano; studied with Meriel St Clair at RCM and with Eugénie Ludwig in Paris and Vienna, prizewinner Hertogenbosch and Paris Competitions; has appeared at numerous international opera houses incl London Coliseum, Covent Garden, Madrid, Nice, Venice, Vicenza, Bologna, Rome, Strasbourg and Met Opera NY, given concert and recital performances at numerous European festivals incl Athens, Barcelona, Granada, San Sebastian, Santander, Cuenca, Venice, Berne, Munich, Strasbourg, Dijon, Siena, Glyndebourne and BBC Proms; performed with orchs incl The Sixteen Choir and Orch, London Mozart Players, Bournemouth Symphony Orch, The Philharmonia, RPO and Royal Scottish Orch, worked with conductors incl Libor Pesek, Sir Yehudi Menuhin, Leonard Slatkin, David Hill, Richard Hickox, Simon Rattle, M Rostropovich, Walter Weller and Jesus Lopez-Cobos; *Performances* concert and recital performances incl: Rossini's Stabat Mater Strasbourg and Dijon festivals 1992, Handel's Messiah (with The Sixteen Choir and Orch under Harry Christophers for BBC TV on 250th anniversary of its composition Easter 1992, and with Sir Yehudi Menuhin in Spain and Moscow Autumn 1992), Brahms' Requiem (with Jesus Lopez-Cobos in San Sebastian and with Richard Hickox for BBC TV Wales in Tewkesbury Abbey 1992), Beethoven's Missa Solemnis (with Dresdner Staatskapelle), Mozart's Coronation Mass (with Peter Weller) Madrid, Beethoven's Ninth Symphony (with The Philharmonia under Leonard Slatkin) Royal Festival Hall, Mozart's Mass in C Minor (for RTE) Dublin, Haydn's Creation (with Sixteen Choir and Orch) Madrid, Dvorák's Stabat Mater (with RPO under Libor Pesek) Royal Festival Hall, Teixeira's Te Deum (with Sixteen Choir and Orch) BBC Proms 1992, Britten's Les Illuminations (with LSO under M Rostropovich) Barbican 1993, Britten's Quatre Chansons Française (with CBSO under Simon Rattle) Symphony Hall Birmingham 1993; operatic roles: title role in Handel's Partenope (nominated for Soc of West End Theatre Outstanding First Achievement award), various with companies incl Glyndebourne (festival and on tour), Opera North, Opera Northern Ireland, Garsington and ENO (US tour), made debut at Covent Garden as First Lady in Mozart's Magic Flute Nov 1993; *Recordings* incl: Vaughan Williams' Benedicite (with Bournemouth Symphony Orch under David Hill, Decca Argo) 1992, Teixeira's Te Deum (with The Sixteen Choir and Orch, Collins Classics) 1992, Bach's Christmas Oratorio 1993, Mahler's 4th Symphony with Antoni Wit and Polish Nat Radio Symphony Orch 1993; *Recreations* walking, entertaining, cooking; *Style—* Ms Lynda Russell

RUSSELL, Sir (Arthur) Mervyn; 8 Bt (UK 1812), of Swallowfield, Berkshire; s of Sir Arthur Edward Ian Montagu Russell, 6 Bt (d 1964); suc his, half-bro, Sir George Michael Russell, 7 Bt 1993; *b* 7 February 1923; *m* 1, 18 April 1945 (m dis), Ruth, da of Charles George Holloway; 1 s (Stephen Charles b 12 Jan 1949); m 2, 18 Feb 1956, Kathleen Joyce Searle (d 2005); 1 s (Ian Mervyn b 8 Dec 1957); *Heir* s, Stephen Russell; *Style—* Sir Mervyn Russell, Bt

RUSSELL, Prof Michael Anthony Hamilton; s of James Hamilton Russell (d 1981), and Hon Kathleen Mary, *née* Gibson; *b* 9 March 1932; *Educ* Diocesan Coll Cape Town, UC Oxford (MA, BM BCh, DPM); *m* 27 Jan 1962, Audrey Anne, da of Archibald Timms (d 1940); 2 s (James Hamilton b 16 March 1974, Nicholas Hamilton b 3 Sept 1977); *Career* house physician and surgn Guy's Hosp London 1957–58, registrar in pathology and sr registrar med Groote Schuur Hosp Univ of Cape Town 1959–64, med registrar Ruttonjee Sanatorium Hong Kong 1964–65, registrar and sr registrar in psychiatry Maudsley Hosp London 1965–69, lectr in psychiatry Inst of Psychiatry London 1969–73, sr lectr and hon conslt Maudsley Hosp London 1973–, on MRC External Scientific Staff 1978–98, prof of addiction Univ of London Inst of Psychiatry 1992–98 (reader in addiction 1985–92, prof emeritus 1998–), hon conslt ICRF Health Behaviour Unit UCL 1997– (hon dir 1988–97); numerous papers and articles on tobacco smoking in scientific jls; invited lectr RSS 1974, Robert Philip lectr RCP(Ed) 1978; WHO No-Tobacco medal 1989, Alton Ochsner Award American Coll of Physicians 1996, Ove Ferno Award Soc of Res on Nicotine and Tobacco 1998; memb: Cncl Action on Smoking and Health (ASH), Br Assoc of Psychopharmacology; hon fell Soc for the Study of Addiction 1999; FRCP 1982, FRCPsych 1980, FRSH 1988; *Books* Nicotine Psychopharmacology (with S Wonnacott and I P Stolerman, 1990); *Recreations* reading, travel, water sports, oil paintings; *Style—* Prof Michael Russell

RUSSELL, Michael William; MSP; s of Thomas Stevenson Russell (decd), and Jean Marjorie, *née* Haynes (decd), of Kirkcudbright; *b* 9 August 1953; *Educ* The Marr Coll Troon, Univ of Edinburgh (MA); *m* 30 March 1980, Cathleen Anne, *née* Macaskill; 1 s (b 13 Feb 1988); *Career* prodr and dir; creative prodr Church of Scotland 1974–77, dir Cinema Sgire 1977–81, exec dir Network Scotland Ltd 1983–91, dir Eala Bhan Ltd 1991–, sec gen Assoc of Film and TV in the Celtic Countries 1981–83; SNP: various branch offices 1974–87, candidate Clydsdale 1987, campaign manager Alex Salmond's leadership campaign 1990, vice-convenor publicity 1987–91, chief exec 1994–99, shadow min of parly, shadow min for culture, broadcasting and gaelic 1999–2000, shadow min for children and educn, incl culture 2000–03; MSP (SNP) Scotland South 1999–2003 and 2007–; contested SNP Leadership 2004, min for environment Scottish Parl 2007–; former dir Scottish Nat Photography Centre; former vice-chm Skeklers Theatre Co, former chair Save a Life in Scotland, former bd dir Glasgow Film Theatre, former tstee Celtic Film and TV Assoc; *Publications* Glasgow - The Book (ed, 1990), Edinburgh - A Celebration (ed, 1992), Poem of Remote Lives - The Enigma of Werner Kissling (1997), In Waiting: Travels in the Shadow of Edwin Muir (1998), A Different Country (2002), Stop the World - The Autobiography of Winnie Ewing (ed, 2004), Grasping the Thistle (with Dennis Macleod, 2006), The Next Big Thing (2007), The Price of Innocence (with Ian McKie, 2007); *Recreations* cookery, gardening; *Style—* Michael Russell, Esq, MSP

RUSSELL, Sir (Alastair) Muir; KCB (2001), DL (Glasgow, 2004); s of Thomas Russell (d 1988), and Anne, *née* Muir (d 1977); *b* 9 January 1949; *Educ* HS of Glasgow, Univ of Glasgow (BSc); *m* 19 Aug 1983, Eileen Alison Mackay, CB, FRSE, *qv*, da of Alexander William Mackay OBE (d 1967), of Dingwall, Ross-shire; *Career* Scottish Office 1970–99: seconded as sec to Scottish Devpt Agency 1975–76, asst sec 1981, princ private sec to Sec of State for Scotland 1981–83, under sec 1990, seconded to Cabinet Office 1990–92, under sec (housing) Environment Dept 1992–95 (dep sec 1995), sec and head Agric Environment and Fisheries Dept 1995–98, perm under sec of state Scottish Office 1998–99, perm sec Scottish Exec 1999–2003; princ and vice-chllr Univ of Glasgow 2003–; dir UCAS 2005, memb Cncl ACU 2006, convenor Univs Scotland 2006–08; non-exec dir Stagecoach Holdings plc 1992–95; memb Cncl Edinburgh Int Festival Soc 2004; Hon LLD Univ of Strathclyde 2000, Hon DUniv Glasgow 2001; Freeman City of London 2006; FRSE 2000, FInstP 2003, Hon FRCPSGlas 2005, CCMI (CIMgt 2001); *Clubs* Royal Cwlth Soc, Caledonian, New (Edinburgh); *Style—* Sir Muir Russell, KCB, DL, FRSE; ✉ The University of Glasgow, Glasgow G12 8QQ (tel 0141 330 5995)

RUSSELL, Sheriff (Albert) Muir Galloway; CBE (1989), QC (Scot 1965); s of Hon Lord Russell (d 1975, Senator of the Coll of Justice), and Florence Muir, *née* Galloway (d 1983); *b* 26 October 1925; *Educ* Edinburgh Acad, Wellington, BNC Oxford (BA), Univ of Edinburgh (LLB); *m* 9 April 1954, Margaret Winifred, da of Thomas McWalter Millar (d 1970), of Edinburgh; 2 s (Douglas b 27 April 1958, Graham b 14 June 1962), 2 da (Anne b 1 Nov 1960, Jennifer b 22 Jan 1964); *Career* Lt Scots Gds 1944–47, served BLA and BAOR; memb Faculty of Advocates (Edinburgh) 1951; standing jr counsel: BOT, Dept of Agric and Forestry Cmmn; Sheriff of Grampian Highlands and Islands at Aberdeen 1971–91, ret; memb Sheriff Court Rules Cncl 1977–86; vice-chm Bd of Mgmnt Southern Gp of Hosps Edinburgh 1964, govr Moray House Coll of Educn 1966–70; *Recreations* golf, music; *Style—* Sheriff Muir Russell, CBE, QC; ✉ Tulloch House, 1 Aultbea, Ross-shire IV22 2JB (tel 01445 731325); 9 St Fillans Terrace, Edinburgh EH10 5NH

RUSSELL, Prof Nicholas John; *Educ* Univ of Cambridge (MA, PhD); *Career* emeritus prof of microbiology Univ of Cardiff and Imperial Coll London; visiting prof Inst of Chemical Technol Prague; memb Sub-Ctee on Evolutionary Biology Scientific Ctee for Antarctic Research (SCAR), former memb Cncl UK Soc for Gen Microbiology; former ed Microbiology, memb Editorial Bd Extremophiles; Napoleon Balling Medal Inst of Chemical Technol Prague; *Style—* Prof Nicholas Russell; ✉ Imperial College London, Wye Campus, Ashford, Kent TN25 5AH

RUSSELL, Ven Norman Atkinson; s of Norman Gerald Russell, of Stormont, Belfast, and Olive Muriel, *née* Williamson; *b* 7 August 1943; *Educ* Royal Belfast Academical Instn, Churchill Coll Cambridge (MA), London Coll of Divinity (BD); *m* 1974, Victoria Christine, da of late Tadeusz Jan Jasinski; 2 s ((Dr) Edward John Norman b 1976, Timothy James Tadeusz b 1980); *Career* articled clerk Coopers & Lybrand 1966–67; curate: Christ Church with Emmanuel Clifton Bristol 1970–74, Christ Church Cockfosters (concurrently pt/t chaplain Middx Poly) 1974–77; rector Harwell with Chilton 1977–84; priest i/c: Gerrards Cross 1984–88, Fulmer 1985–88; rector of Gerrards Cross and Fulmer 1988–98, rural dean of Amersham 1996–98, archdeacon of Berkshire 1998–; prolocutor Lower House Convocation of Canterbury and memb Archbishops' Cncl 2005–; vice-chm Ecumenical Cncl for Corporate Responsibility 1999–2002; *Publications* Censorship (1972); *Recreations* downland walking, watching rugby football; *Style—* The Ven the Archdeacon of Berkshire; ✉ Foxglove House, Love Lane, Donnington, Newbury RG14 2JG (tel 01635 552820, fax 01635 522165, e-mail archdber@oxford.anglican.org)

RUSSELL, Peter John; s of Capt Raymond Colston Frederick Russell, of Bristol, and Marjorie Catherine, *née* Lock; *b* 14 December 1951; *Educ* Bedminster Down Sch Bristol, Univ of London (BA, LLM); *m* 7 April 1979, Dr Evelyn Mary, da of Sqdn Ldr Lorence Alan Scott, of Bridport, Dorset; 1 da (Sarah Anne b 1982), 1 s (Timothy Paul b 1985); *Career* called to the Bar Inner Temple 1975; in practice Northern Circuit 1979–93, lectr in law Univ of Manchester 1975–82; chm Employment Tbnls 1993– (pt/t 1992); memb: Manchester Wine Soc, La Commanderie de Bordeaux á Manchester, Hon Soc of the Inner Temple; *Recreations* wine tasting, gardening; *Style—* Peter Russell, Esq; ✉ Alexandra House, 14/22 The Parsonage, Manchester M3 2JA (tel 0161 833 0581, fax 0161 832 0249)

RUSSELL, Dr Philippa Margaret; CBE (2002, OBE 1999); da of Garth Rivers Stoneham (d 1987), of Barrow-in-Furness, Cumbria, and Nancy Wooler, *née* Leslie (d 1997); *b* 4 February 1938, Sheffield; *Educ* Barrow-in-Furness GS for Girls, St Hilda's Coll Oxford (BA); *m* 22 Aug 1959, Dr Alan Russell, OBE; 2 s (Simon Fitzgerald b 3 Nov 1963, James Christopher b 18 Oct 1964), 1 da (Emma Caroline b 18 Nov 1971); *Career* dir Cncl for Disabled Children 1976–2003, disability policy advsr Nat Children's Bureau 2003–; cmmr Disability Rights Cmmn 2002–; chair MOVE, memb Nat Learning Disability Task Force; tstee: Disability Partnership, Mental Health Fndn, ICAN, 4Children, Centre for Studies in Inclusive Educn; patron: United Response, Contact a Family; author of a wide range of articles, chapters and reports on policy issues relating to disabled children and young people and family carers; Rose Fitzgerald Kennedy Centenary Int Award 1990; Lifetime Achievement Award: 4Children 2004, Royal Assoc for Disability and Human Rights, RADAR (Royal Assoc of Disability and Rehabilitation) 2005; Hon Dr: King Alfred's Coll of HE Winchester, Univ of York; hon fell Univ of Central Lancs; Hon FRCPCH 1997, FRSA; *Recreations* art, music, walking, family life; *Style—* Dr Philippa Russell, CBE; ✉ 91 Hillway, Highgate, London N6 6AB (tel 020 8340 3376); National Children's Bureau, 8 Wakley Street, London EC1V 7QE (tel 020 7843 9708, fax 020 7843 6313, e-mail prussell@ncb.org.uk)

RUSSELL, Robert Edward (Bob); MP; s of Ewart James Russell (d 1989), and Muriel Alice, *née* Sawdy (d 1988); *b* 31 March 1946; *Educ* Myland Primary Colchester, St Helena Secdy Modern Colchester, North East Essex Tech Coll Colchester; *m* 1 April 1967, Audrey, da of Frank Blandon (d 1996); 2 s (Andrew, Mark (twins) b 5 March 1968), 2 da (Joanne b 16 May 1971 d 1978, Nicola b 9 April 1981); *Career* reporter Essex County Standard and also Colchester Gazette 1963–66, news ed Braintree and Witham Times 1966–68, ed Maldon and Burnham Standard 1968–69, sub-ed London Evening News 1969–72, sub-ed London Evening Standard 1972–73, press offr British Telecom (formerly Post Office Telecommunications) Eastern region 1973–85, publicity offr Univ of Essex 1986–97, MP (Lib Dem) Colchester 1997–, memb Home Affrs Select Ctee 1998–; memb Lib Dem Home and Legal Affairs Team 1997–99, sports spokesman 1999–2005; mayor of Colchester 1986–87, ldr Colchester BC 1987–91 (cncllr 1971–2002); *Recreations* football (Colchester United FC), promoting the town of Colchester; *Style—* Bob Russell, MP; ✉ House of Commons, London SW1A 0AA (tel 020 7219 5150, fax 020 7219 2365, e-mail brooksse@parliament.uk); constituency (tel 01206 506600, fax 01206 506610)

RUSSELL, Ronald; s of Samuel Russell (d 1988), of Glasgow, and Marion, *née* Hanley; *b* 14 January 1956, Glasgow; *Educ* St Mungo's Acad Glasgow, Caledonian Univ; *m* 1 Oct 1991, Sandra, *née* Cheyne; 2 da (Shonagh b 6 July 1992, Jill b 28 Feb 1997); *Career* finance dir: Southern Natural Gas (part of Sonat Inc) USA 1979–89, Healthcare Scotland Ltd 1989–2004; dir Affinity Hospitals Holdings Ltd; FCA 1976; *Recreations* supporting Celtic FC; *Style—* Ronald Russell, Esq; ✉ Healthcare Scotland, 35 Albert Street, Aberdeen AB25 1XU (tel 01224 648258)

RUSSELL, Prof Roy Robert Baird; *b* 7 May 1944, Dublin, Ireland; *Educ* Rossall Sch Fleetwood, Trinity Coll Dublin (BA), Univ of Melbourne (PhD); *m*; 2 c; *Career* research scientist Meat Research Lab CSIRO Brisbane 1970–73, postdoctoral fell Div of Biological Scis Nat Research Cncl of Canada Ottawa 1973–75, sr research fell then dir Dental Research Unit Dept of Dental Scis RCS 1975–91, prof of oral biology Univ of Newcastle upon Tyne 1991–; memb Editorial Bds: Caries Research, Odontology, Infection and Immunity, Oral Microbiology and Immunology, Jl of Dental Research; memb: American Soc for Microbiology, Soc for Gen Microbiology, Int Assoc for Dental Research, Br Soc for Dental Research; FDSRCS (by election) 1986; *Style—* Prof Roy Russell; ✉ Oral Biology, School of Dental Sciences, Framlington Place, Newcastle upon Tyne NE2 4BW (tel 0191 222 7859, fax 0191 222 6137, e-mail r.r.russell@newcastle.ac.uk)

RUSSELL, Rupert Edward Odo; s of David Hastings Gerald Russell (see Debrett's Peerage, Ampthill, B), of London, and Hester Clere, *née* Parsons; *b* 5 November 1944; *Educ* Selwyn

House Sch Montreal, Rannoch Sch Perthshire; *m* 9 Dec 1981, Catherine Jill, former Lady Brougham and Vaux, da of William Daniel Gulliver (d 1970); *Career* admitted slr 1973; ptnr: Blount Petre and Co 1979–86, Amhurst Brown Martin and Nicholson 1986–87, Payne Hicks Beach 1988–92, REO Russell & Co (own practice) 1992–; vice-pres Cities of London and Westminster Cons Assoc (former chm); memb Law Soc 1973; *Recreations* skiing, sailing, fishing, gardening; *Clubs* Buck's (former chm); *Style*— Rupert Russell, Esq; ✉ Highleaze, Oare, Marlborough, Wiltshire SN8 4JE (tel 01672 562487/564352, fax 01672 564163); Wassand Hall, Seaton, Hull HU11 5RJ (tel 01672 564352)

RUSSELL BEALE, Simon; CBE (2003); s of Lt-Gen Sir Peter Beale, RAMC, and Dr Julia Beale, *née* Winter; *b* 12 January 1961; *Educ* St Paul's Cathedral Choir Sch, Clifton, Gonville & Caius Coll Cambridge, GSM; *Career* actor; assoc artist: RSC, RNT, Almeida Theatre; *Theatre* Traverse Theatre credits incl: Die Hose, The Death of Elias Sawney, Sandra Manon; others incl: Look to the Rainbow (Apollo), Women Beware Women (Royal Court), A Winter's Tale, Everyman in His Humour, The Art of Success, The Fair Maid of the West, Speculators, The Storm, The Constant Couple, The Man of Mode, Restoration, Some Americans Abroad, Mary and Lizzie, Playing with Trains, Troilus and Cressida, Edward II, Love's Labour's Lost, The Seagull, Richard III, King Lear, The Tempest, Ghosts, The Duchess of Malfi (Greenwich and West End) 1995, Mosca in Volpone (RNT, Olivier Award for Best Supporting Performance 1996) 1995, Rosencrantz and Guildenstern are Dead (RNT) 1996, Othello (RNT) 1997–98, Candide, Money, Summerfolk, Battle Royal (RNT) 1999–2000, Hamlet 2001 (Evening Standard Best Actor Award 2001, Critics Circle Award 2001), Humble Boy (RNT) 2001, Twelfth Night, Uncle Vanya (Donmar Warehouse and NY, Evening Standard Best Actor Award 2003, Olivier Award 2003, Critics Circle Best Actor Award 2003), Jumpers 2003, Macbeth (Almeida) 2005, Julius Caesar (Barbican) 2005, The Philanthropist (Donmar Warehouse) 2005 (Evening Standard Best Actor Award 2005, Critics Circle Award 2005); *Television* A Very Peculiar Practice, The Mushroom Picker, Down Town Lagos, Persuasion, A Dance to the Music of Time (Best Actor: BAFTA 1998, RTS 1998), The Last Temptation of Franz Schubert, Alice inWonderland; *Film* incl: An Ideal Husband, Blackadder Back and Forth, The Gathering; *Style*— Simon Russell Beale, Esq, CBE; ✉ c/o The Richard Stone Partnership, 2 Henrietta Street, London WC2E 8PS (tel 020 7497 0849, fax 020 7497 0869)

RUSSELL-JOHNSTON, Baron (Life Peer UK 1997), of Minginish in Highland; Sir Russell Russell-Johnston; kt (1985); s of David Knox Johnston (d 1972); assumed by deed poll 1997 the surname Russell-Johnston in lieu of his patronymic; *b* 1932; *Educ* Portree HS Isle of Skye, Univ of Edinburgh (MA); *m* 1967, Joan Graham, da of Donald Menzies; 3 s; *Career* Nat Serv cmmnd Intelligence Corps 1958; history teacher Liberton Secdy Sch Edinburgh 1961–63; memb Exec Scottish Lib Pty 1961–; Scottish Lib Pty: res asst 1963–64, vice-chm 1965–70, chm 1970–74, leader 1974–87; MP (Lib until 1988, now Lib Dem): Inverness 1964–83, Inverness, Nairn and Lochaber 1983–97; Lib spokesman on: foreign and cwlth affrs 1970–75 and 1979–85, Scotland 1970–73, 1975–83 and 1985–87; Alliance spokesman on Scotland and Euro Community Affrs 1987; Lib Dem spokesman on: foreign and cwlth affrs 1988–89, Europe and East/West rels 1989–97; one of first UK Lib membs of Euro Parl 1973–75 and 1976–79 (vice-pres Political Ctee 1976–79), stood at first Euro direct election 1979 and 1984; pres Scottish Lib Dems 1988–94 (chm 1970–74, ldr 1974–88); dep ldr Lib Dems 1989–92; memb: Royal Cmmn on Scottish Local Govt 1966–69, Western Euro Union Assemb 1984–86 and 1987–, rep to Cncl of Europe Parly Assemb 1984–86 and 1987– (ldr Lib Gp 1994–99, pres Sub-Ctee on Youth and Sport 1992–95, pres Ctee on Culture & Educn 1996–99), pres Parly Assemb Cncl of Europe 1999–2002; vice-pres: Euro Lib Democratic and Reform Parties 1990–92, Liberal International; vice-chm Bd of Govrs Westminster Fndn for Democracy 1992–97; chm bd of govrs Int Inst for Democracy Strasbourg 2002–; winner of debating trophies: The Scotsman 1956 and 1957, The Observer Mace 1961; *Publications* Highland Development, 'To be a Liberal' and 'Scottish Liberal Party Conference Speeches' 1971–78 and 1979–86; books of collected speeches from presidency of Parly Assemb Cncl of Europe: 'Humankind has No Nationalitiy', 'Human Rights and Wrongs', 'Moralpolitik'; *Clubs* Scottish Liberal; *Style*— Lord Russell-Johnston; ✉ House of Lords, London SW1A 0PW (tel 020 7219 3218)

RUSSELL-JONES, Maj-Gen (Peter) John; OBE (1988); s of Lt-Col P R Russell-Jones (d 1986), and Margaret (Peggy), *née* Roberts (d 1998); *b* 31 May 1948; *Educ* Wellington, RMA Sandhurst, RMCS Shrivenham, Staff Coll, Royal Coll of Defence Studies; *m* 2 Oct 1976, Stella Margaret, da of D P R Barrett; 1 s (James b 1 April 1979), 1 da (Polly 2 Feb 1981); *Career* Lt-Col and CO Engr Tank Regt 1988–90, Col Defence Policy MoD London 1990, Brig and chief exec Royal Engr Trg Orgn 1991–94, RCDS 1995, dir Int Orgns MOD London 1996–97, Maj-Gen 1997, capability mangr Manoeuvre MoD London 1997–2001; Col Cmdt Royal Engr 1999; army advsr BAE Systems 2001–; *Recreations* golf, military history, rock and blues music, family, travel; *Style*— Maj-Gen P J Russell-Jones, OBE; ✉ RHQ RE, Brompton Barracks, Chatham, Kent ME4 4UG (tel 01634 822355)

RUSSELL-JONES, Dr Robin David; s of John Lewis Russell-Jones, JP (d 1970), of Saundersfoot, Pembrokeshire, and Mary Elizabeth, *née* Ebsworth (d 1997); *b* 5 March 1948; *Educ* Rugby, Peterhouse Cambridge (MA, MB BChir); *m* 1, 1 Nov 1975, Ann Hilary Fair (d 1991), da of Roger Brian Nixon (d 1988), of Cheltenham, Glos; 1 da (Joy b 1976), 1 s (Christopher b 1979); *m* 2, 18 Sept 1993, Nina, da of Kailash Salooja, of Goring-on-Thames, Oxon; 2 da (Eleanor b 1994, Lily b 1996); *Career* conslt dermatologist St Thomas' Hosp, Ealing Hosp and Hammersmith Hosp 1983–; sr lectr Dept of Med Royal Postgraduate Med Sch London; dir Skin Tumour Unit St John's Inst of Dermatology St Thomas' Hosp 1996–; chm: Friends of the Earth Pollution Advsy Ctee, Campaign for Lead Free Air 1984–89, UK Skin Lymphoma Gp 1999–; FRCP 1990 (MRCP 1973), FRCPath 2002; *Books* Lead Versus Health (1983), Radiation and Health (1987), Ozone Depletion (1989); *Recreations* skiing, sailing, golf; *Style*— Dr Robin Russell-Jones; ✉ Atholl House, Church Lane, Stoke Poges, Buckinghamshire SL2 4NZ

RUSSELL OF LIVERPOOL, 3 Baron (UK 1919); Simon Gordon Jared Russell; s of Capt Hon Langley Russell, MC, s of 2 Baron Russell of Liverpool, CBE, MC; suc gf 1981; *b* 30 August 1952; *Educ* Charterhouse, Trinity Coll Cambridge, INSEAD; *m* 1984, Gilda F, yst da of F Albano, of Salerno, Italy; 2 s (Hon Edward Charles Stanley b 1985, Hon William Francis Langley b 1988), 1 da (Hon Leonora Maria Kiloran b 1987); *Heir* s, Hon Edward Russell; *Career* mgmnt conslt; Liveryman Worshipful Co of Fishmongers; *Style*— The Rt Hon Lord Russell of Liverpool

RUSSELL-ROBERTS, Anthony de Villeneuve; CBE (2004); s of Francis Douglas Russell-Roberts (d 1973), and Edith Margaret Gertrudis, *née* Ashton (d 1990); *b* 25 March 1944; *Educ* Eton, New Coll Oxford; *m* 1 (m dis); *m* 2, 12 Dec 1975 (m dis), Anne, *née* Dunhill; 2 da (Tabitha b 10 March 1977, Juliet b 19 Dec 1979), 1 step s (Ingo Ferruzzi b 19 Feb 1972), 1 step da (Anita Ferruzzi b 19 Dec 1973); *m* 3, 10 March 2001, Jane, *née* Holkenfeldt; *Career* VSO Br Honduras (now Belize) 1961–62; gen mgmnt trainee Watney Mann 1965–68, ptnr Lane Fox and Ptnrs 1971–76 (joined 1968); stage mgmnt: Glyndebourne Festival Opera 1976, Kent Opera 1977; asst to gen dir Royal Opera House 1977–80, artistic admin Theatre Nationale de L'Opera de Paris 1981–83, admin dir Royal Ballet 1983–, dir Amarin Corp plc; *Recreations* gardening, golf; *Clubs* Garrick; *Style*— Anthony Russell-Roberts, CBE; ✉ Royal Ballet, Royal Opera House, Covent Garden, London WC2E 9DD (tel 020 7212 9158, fax 020 7212 9121, e-mail arr@roh.org.uk)

RUSSELL-SMITH, Penny; LVO (2000); da of Denham William Russell-Smith, of Cheltenham, Glos, and Barbara Cynthia, *née* Hemsley; *b* 22 October 1956; *Educ* Sherborne Sch for Girls, Girton Coll Cambridge; *Career* dep ed Whitaker's Almanack 1980–81, ed Navy

and Army pubns MOD 1982–84, press office MOD 1984–88 (incl Falkland Is), chief press offr Dept of Tport, EU desk News Dept FCO 1990–93, press sec to HM The Queen 2001– (asst press sec 1993–97, dep press sec 1997–2001); *Recreations* embroidery, walking, holidaying without mobile phone; *Style*— Miss Penny Russell-Smith, LVO; ✉ Press Secretary to HM The Queen, Royal Household, Buckingham Palace, London SW1A 1AA (tel 020 7024 4207)

RUSSILL, Patrick Joseph; *b* 9 September 1953; *Educ* Shaftesbury GS, New Coll Oxford (Margaret Bridges organ scholar, MA); *m* 28 April 1979, Jane Mary, *née* Rogers; 3 da (Francesca b 1981, Helen b 1985, Katherine b 1991), 2 s (Benjamin b 1983, Dominic b 1988); *Career* organist, choral dir and church music educator; dir of music London Oratory 1999– (asst organist 1976–77, organist 1977–99), organist for Papal Mass Wembley Stadium 1982; dir: Oxford Chamber Choir 1977–79, London Oratory Jr Choir 1984–2003, Europa Singers of London 1985–89; Royal Acad of Music: teacher of music techniques 1982–87, head of church music studies 1987–97, head of choral conducting 1997–, prof of organ 1999–; visiting lectr St George's Coll Jerusalem 1994–95, visiting prof of choral conducting Leipzig Hochschule für Musik 2001–; chief examiner Royal Coll of Organists 2005–; external examiner: UEA 1991–97, Univ of Leeds 2004–05; memb Exec Ctee Church Music Soc 1990–; given lectures to various bodies incl: Incorporated Assoc of Organists, Soc of St Gregory, Royal Sch of Church Music, Winchester Diocesan Synod, Yale Inst of Sacred Music, Hungarian Church Music Assoc, Br Inst of Organ Studies; tstee: Friends of St Marylebone Music 1993–, Nicholas Danby Tst 1999–; hon patron Herbert Howells Soc 1993–, memb Ctee Organists' Benevolent League 1994–, memb Cncl Royal Coll of Organists 1996–; Hon RAM 1993 (Hon ARAM 1989), Hon FGCM 1997, Hon FRCO 2002 (ARCO 1971); *Performances* organ recitals in UK, France, Germany, Near East and Asia incl Royal Festival Hall (debut 1986) and Queen Elizabeth Hall, UK premières of works by Hakim and Grier, CD solo recordings for ASV and Herald; work as choral director on EMI, Hyperion, Herald and Deutsche Grammophon Archiv; *Publications* editions of Howells and Sweelinck; music ed The Catholic Hymnbook 1998; author of numerous articles mainly on church music for jls and periodicals incl: The Organist, Organists' Review, British Institute of Organ Studies (BIOS) Journal, Royal College of Organists (RCO) Yearbook, Choir and Organ, Gramophone, The Cambridge Companion to the Organ 1998; *Style*— Patrick Russill, Esq; ✉ The Oratory, Brompton Road, London SW7 2RP (tel 020 7808 0911); Royal Academy of Music, Marylebone Road, London NW1 5HT (tel 020 7873 7331, e-mail p.russill@ram.ac.uk)

RUSSON, David; s of Thomas Charles Russon (d 1962), and Violet, *née* Jarvis (d 2001); *b* 12 June 1944; *Educ* Wellington GS, UCL (BSc), Univ of York; *m* 29 July 1967, Kathleen Mary, da of Frederick Gregory, of Morecambe, Lancs; 2 da (Katherine b 1971, Nicola b 1973), 1 s ((Charles) Benedict b 1975); *Career* various appts DES 1969–74; British Library: various appts 1974–85, dir Document Supply Centre 1985–88, DG for Sci Technol and Industry 1988–91, memb Bd 1988–2001, DG Boston Spa 1991–96, dep chief exec 1996–2001); pres Int Cncl for Scientific and Tech Information 1995–2001 (vice-pres 1992–95); contrib to various learned journals; CPhys, FInstP, FCLIP; *Recreations* tennis, badminton, golf; *Style*— David Russon, Esq; ✉ March House, Tollerton, York YO6 2ET (tel 01347 838253)

RUSTAGE, Christopher Charles; s of George Roland Rustage (d 1983), of Manchester, and Mary, *née* Killian (d 1993); *b* 7 June 1948; *Educ* De La Salle Coll Manchester, St Joseph's Coll Manchester; *m* 1, 1967 (m dis 1986), Ann, da of Herman Taylor; 2 da (Andre-Jayne b 1967, Joanne Marie b 1971), 1 s (Christopher George b 1974); *m* 2, Angela Parkin; *Career* franchiser; apprentice motor body fitter 1965–66, specialist importer of blending and roasting teas and coffees, labourer/driver 1968–69, grave digger, brewery asst, asst to lion tamer at Billy Smart's circus, watch assembler and shoe polish manufacturer 1969–73, fndr construction co 1973–79, livestock farmer 1979–83, inventor/manufacturer new health products 1983–87, property speculator and furniture manufacturer 1987–90, fndr Riverside International Ltd (largest privately owned franchising chain in Europe) 1990–; chm The Pet Club Great Britain Ltd; memb Manorial Soc of GB 1972, memb Confedn of Trades & Indust 1983, memb Prince's Tst 1983–84; Lord of the Manor of Edern; *Books* The Fax Book (1983); *Recreations* shooting, boating, travel, country pursuits; *Style*— Christopher Rustage, Esq

RUSTIN, Prof Gordon John Sampson; s of Maj Maurice Edward Rustin, MC (d 1972), of Hale, Cheshire, and (Barbara) Joan, *née* Goldstone; *Educ* Uppingham, Middx Hosp Med Sch (MB BS), Univ of London (MSc, MD); *m* 17 Feb 1977, Frances Phyllis, da of Lionel Rainsbury, of London; 1 s (Edward Samuel b 4 May 1981), 1 da (Jessica Leah b 3 Jan 1986); *Career* registrar Whittington Hosp and UCH 1974–76, res fell Hammersmith Hosp 1977–78, sr registrar Charing Cross Hosp 1978–84, sr lectr and hon conslt in med oncology Charing Cross Hosp and Mount Vernon Hosp 1984–95, dir of med oncology Mount Vernon Hosp 1995–, prof UCL and Univ of Herts; over 200 pubns on: tumour markers, vascular targeting therapy, germ cell, trophoblastic and ovarian tumours; memb Gynaecological Working Pty NCRI; memb: BMA 1971, RSM 1977, ACP 1985; FRCP 1992 (MRCP 1974), BACR 1979; *Recreations* tennis, golf, opera, skiing; *Style*— Prof Gordon Rustin; ✉ 15 Wellgarth Road, London NW11 7HP (tel 020 8455 5943); Director of Medical Oncology, Mount Vernon Hospital, Northwood, Middlesex HA6 2RN (tel 01923 844389, fax 01923 844840, e-mail grustin@nhs.net)

RUSTIN, Dr Malcolm Howard Albert; s of Maurice Edward Rustin, MC (d 1972), and Barbara Joan, *née* Goldstone; *b* 6 November 1951; *Educ* Uppingham, Middx Hosp Med Sch London (BSc, MB BS, MD); *m* Dr Joanna Rustin; 2 s (Jonathan b 1986, Benjamin b 1986), 1 da (Hannah b 1989); *Career* conslt dermatologist and hon sr lectr Royal Free and University Coll Med Sch 1989–; special clinical interest in connective tissue diseases and both a clinical and research commitment to atopic eczema; chm: Dermatitis and Allied Diseases Research Tst (Dermatrust), N Thames Specialist Training Ctee in Dermatology; memb Specialist Advsy Ctee in Dermatology; Gold medal American Acad of Dermatology; memb Br Assoc of Dermatologists, fell American Acad of Dermatology; previous appts: sr registrar (dermatology) UCHL and Middx Hosp London, Muir-Hambro res fell RCP; FRCP; *Publications* author of over 150 pubns on general dermatology and the pathogenesis and treatment of atopic eczema; *Recreations* walking, golf, skiing; *Style*— Dr Malcolm Rustin; ✉ 53 Wimpole Street, London W1G 8YH (tel 020 7935 9266, fax 020 7935 3060); Department of Dermatology, The Royal Free Hospital, Pond Street, London NW3 2QG (tel 020 7830 2376, fax 020 7830 2247)

RUTHERFORD, His Hon Judge Andrew; DL (Somerset); s of Robert Mark Rutherford, and Alison Wellington, *née* Clark; *b* 25 March 1948; *Educ* Clifton, Univ of Exeter (LLB); *m* 7 April 1994, Lucy Elizabeth, da of Prof Edmund Bosworth; 2 da (Isobel b 1 Dec 1996, Alexandra b 12 Oct 1999); *Career* called to the Bar Middle Temple 1970, recorder of the Crown Court 1993–95, circuit judge (Western Circuit) 1995–; *Clubs* Bath and County; *Style*— His Hon Judge Rutherford, DL; ✉ Western Circuit Office, 5th Floor, Greyfriars, Lewins Mead, Bristol BS1 2NR

RUTHERFORD, Lyn Malcolm; s of Wilfred Rutherford, and Margaret, *née* Robinson; *b* 20 January 1948, Consett, Co Durham; *Educ* Hookergate GS, Univ of Liverpool; *Partner* Vivien Medwell; *Career* admitted slr 1972; articles McKeags and Co 1970–72, slr Clayton Mott 1973, Dickinson Dees 1974– (currently ptnr and head Family Law Gp); tstee of cat and dog shelter; *Recreations* horse racing, football; *Style*— Lyn Rutherford, Esq; ✉ Dickinson Dees, One Trinity, Broad Chare, Newcastle NE1 2HF (tel 0191 279 9229, fax 0191 279 9130, e-mail lyn.rutherford@dickinson-dees.com)

R

RUTHERFORD, Michael John Cloette Crawford (Mike); s of Capt W H F Crawford Rutherford (d 1986), of Farnham, Surrey, and Annette, *née* Downing (d 1993); *b* 2 October 1950; *Educ* Charterhouse; *m* 13 Nov 1976, Angela Mary, da of Harry Downing; 2 s (Tom William b 4 Dec 1980, Harry John Crawford b 19 Nov 1987), 1 da (Kate Elizabeth b 19 Oct 1977); *Career* musician; fndr memb Genesis 1966 (with Peter Gabriel, *qv*, and Tony Banks), first single released 1969, seventeenth album released 1992; fndr Mike and the Mechanics gp 1985–; top ten single Over My Shoulder 1995 (from album Beggar on a Beach of Gold 1995); *Recreations* polo (Cowdray Park); *Style*— Mike Rutherford, Esq; ✉ c/o Hit & Run Music Ltd, 30 Ives Street, London SW3 2ND (tel 020 7581 0261, fax 020 7584 5774)

RUTHVEN, Prof Kenneth Borthwick Howard; *b* 1 February 1952, Edinburgh; *Educ* Univ of Edinburgh (DipEd), Moray House Coll Edinburgh (PGCE), Univ of Oxford (MA), Univ of Stirling (PhD), Univ of Cambridge (MA); *Career* teacher of mathematics and computing at schs in Edinburgh, Brighton and Cambridge 1974–83; Univ of Cambridge: lectr in educn 1983–98, reader in educn 1998–2005, prof of educn 2005–; Education Studies in Mathematics: ed 1994–95, ed-in-chief 1996–2000, advsy ed 2001–; author of 50 research papers in peer-reviewed jls; memb Br Soc for Res into Learning Mathematics 1983– (chair 2006–); tstee Sch Mathematics Project 1996– (dep chair 2004–05, chair 2006–); *Style*— Prof Kenneth Ruthven; ✉ University of Cambridge, Faculty of Education, 184 Hills Road, Cambridge CB2 2PQ (tel 01223 767600, fax 01223 767602, e-mail kr18@cam.ac.uk)

RUTLAND, 11 Duke of (E 1703); David Charles Robert Manners; also Earl of Rutland (E 1525), Baron Manners of Haddon (E 1679), Marquess of Granby (E 1703), and Baron Roos of Belvoir (E 1616); s of 10 Duke of Rutland (d 1999), by his 2 w, Frances, *née* Sweeny; *b* 8 May 1959; *Educ* Wellesley House Broadstairs, Stanbridge Earls; *m* 6 June 1992, Emma L, da of John Watkins, of Knighton, Powys; 3 da (Lady Violet Diana Louise b 18 Aug 1993, Lady Alice Louisa Lilly b 27 April 1995, Lady Eliza Charlotte b 27 July 1997), 2 s (Charles John Montague, Marquess of Granby b 3 July 1999, Lord Hugo William James b 24 July 2003); *Heir* s, Marquess of Granby; *Career* dir Belvoir Estate; chm Historic Houses Assoc in E Midlands until 1999; pres: Grantham branch Air Crew Assoc, Grantham Canal Restoration Soc; memb: Leics Ctee CLA, Civilian Ctee ATC Sqdn Grantham Lincs (47F Sqdn), Hereford Cattle Breeders Assoc; Freeman City of London, Liveryman Worshipful Co of Gunsmiths; *Recreations* shooting, fishing, flying; *Clubs* Turf, Annabel's; *Style*— His Grace the Duke of Rutland; ✉ Belvoir Castle, Grantham, Lincolnshire NG32 1PE (tel 01476 871005)

RUTTER, Claire; *Educ* Guildhall Sch of Music & Drama (AGSM), Nat Opera Studio (sponsored by Friends of Eng Nat Opera); *m* Stephen Gadd (baritone); *Career* soprano; Wigmore Hall recital debut 1994; *Roles* with Scottish Opera incl: Violetta in La Traviata, Countess Almaviva in The Marriage of Figaro, Elettra in Idomeneo, Gilda in Rigoletto, Fiordiligi in Cosi fan Tutte, Rosalinde in Die Fledermaus; other prodns incl: Violetta (WNO), Mimi in La Bohème (Hong Kong and Beijing International Festival), Beethoven No 9 Choral Symphony (BBC Scottish Symphony Orchestra), Songs of the Auvergne (with BBC Scottish Symphony Orch), Madama Butterfly (with Royal Liverpool Philharmonic Orch), Giovanna D'Arco in Ludwigshafen (Opera North), Violetta in La Traviata (ENO), Gilda in Rigoletto (ENO and WNO), Donna Anna in Don Giovanni (ENO and Montpellier), Verdi Requiem, Sea Symphony, Fiordiligi (Dallas, US debut) 2003, Amelia in Ballo in Maschera (ENO), Tosca (ENO), Elvira in Ernani (ENO), La Gioconda (Opera North); *Recordings* highlights of Madame Butterfly and La Bohème (with RPO) 1997, Illustrated Man (film score by Jerry Goldsmith, with Royal Scottish Nat Orch), Holst's Mystic Trumpeter (with Royal Scot Nat Orch), Christmas Classics with Carl Davis and Hallé 2003; *Style*— Ms Claire Rutter; ✉ c/o John McMurray, Intermusica, Artists' Management Ltd, 16 Duncan Terrace, London, N1 8BZ

RUTTER, Rev Canon (Allen Edward Henry) Claude; s of Rev Norman Rutter (d 1967), and Hilda, *née* Mason (d 1979); *b* 24 December 1928; *Educ* Monkton Combe, Dauntsey's Sch West Lavington, Queens' Coll Cambridge (MA, DipAgric), St John's Coll and Cranmer Hall Univ of Durham (DipTh); *m* 26 April 1960, Elizabeth Jane, da of Rt Rev Martin Patrick Grainge Leonard, DSO, MA (Bishop of Thetford, d 1963); 2 da (Patricia b 1961, Miranda b 1976), 2 s (Christopher b 1962, Timothy b 1965); *Career* scientific liaison offr East Malling Res Station 1953–56; curate: Bath Abbey 1959–60, East Dereham 1960–64; rector: Cawston Gp (and chaplain Cawston Coll) 1964–69, Gingindhlovu Zululand 1969–73 (also agric sec Helwel Diocese of Zululand), Queen Thorne 1973–96; rural dean Sherborne 1976–87, chm Salisbury Diocesan Lay Educnl and Trg Ctee 1984–92, canon and prebendary Salisbury Cathedral 1986–, diocesan co-ordinator Rural Miny Devpt 1987–92, diocesan rural link offr 1989–92, conslt Archbishops' Cmmn on Rural Areas 1989–91, vicar and RAF chaplain Ascension Island 1996–97, priest-in-charge Thorncombe with Forde Abbey, Winsham and Cricket St Thomas 1998–; played cricket for: Univ of Cambridge 1953, Wilts CCC 1948–55, Norfolk CCC 1961–65 (the only clergyman to have played in the Gillette Cup); played hockey for: Cambridge Univ Wanderers, Maidstone; Clergy Golf Champion 1977 and 1991; *Recreations* cricket, hockey, golf, farming, gardening, picture framing; *Clubs* Hawks' (Cambridge), MCC, Farmers', Oxford and Cambridge; *Style*— The Rev Canon Claude Rutter; ✉ Home Farm, Chilson, South Chard, Somerset TA20 2NX (tel 01460 221368)

RUTTER, Hadyn Michael; s of Herbert Rutter (d 1985), of Winsford, Cheshire, and Mabel Rutter; *b* 29 December 1946; *Educ* Verdin GS Winsford, Lincoln Coll Oxford (BA); *m* 1 April 1970, Susan, da of Charles Robert Johnson, of Winsford; 3 da (Tanya b 1974, Amanda b 1977, Lisa b 1981); *Career* admitted slr 1971; Richards Butler & Co London 1969–72, sr ptnr Bruce Campbell & Co Cayman Islands 1977–80 (joined 1972), own practice 1980–; pres Cayman Islands Law Soc 1979 (sec 1975–79); dir: Golf Links Publishing Ltd, Golf Links Int Ltd, Golf Links Int Inc; organiser World Pro-Am: Arizona, Acapulco, Hong Kong, Dubai, Las Vegas, Sun City, Thailand; Duke of Edinburgh Award (Gold) 1965; *Publications* Cayman Islands Handbook Tax Guide (1977), The Golf Rules Dictionary (1997, 4 edn 2004); *Recreations* cricket, golf, badminton, tennis; *Clubs* Oxford and Cambridge; *Style*— Hadyn Rutter, Esq; ✉ 18 Magestic Apartments, Onchan, Isle of Man IM3 2BN (tel 01624 661800, e-mail hadynrutter@manx.net, website www.golfrulesdictionary.com)

RUTTER, John Milford; CBE (2007); *b* 1945, London; *Educ* Highgate Sch, Clare Coll Cambridge; *Career* composer and conductor; dir of music Clare Coll Cambridge 1975–79, fndr Cambridge Singers 1979; guest-conductor and lectr worldwide incl Europe, Scandinavia, N America and Australasia; major compositions and incl: Requiem 1985, Magnificat 1990, Psalmfest 1993, Opera Choruses 1995, European Sacred Music 1996; hon fell Westminster Choir Coll Princeton 1980, fell Guild of Church Musicians 1988; Dr of Music Lambeth 1996; Hon Dr: Anglia Poly Univ 1999, Univ of Leicester 2005; *Publications* Mass of the Children (2003); *Style*— John Rutter, Esq, CBE

RUTTER, Dr (James) Michael; CBE (2002); s of James William Rutter (d 1996), of Kendal, Cumbria, and Lily, *née* Harriman (d 1986); *b* 20 August 1941; *Educ* Kendal GS, Royal (Dick) Sch of Vet Studies Univ of Edinburgh (BVM and S, BSc, PhD); *m* 1 July 1967, Jacqueline Patricia, da of late Thomas Anderson Watson; 1 da (Charlotte Sophie b 6 May 1977); *Career* Univ of Edinburgh: research scholar 1964–67, research asst 1967–69; Inst for Research on Animal Diseases Compton (later Inst for Animal Health): vet research offr 1969–73, princ vet research offr 1973–84, seconded to Dept of Educn and Science 1975–78, head Dept of Microbiology 1984–89, acting head Compton Lab 1986–89; dir of Vet Meds DEFRA (formerly MAFF) 1989–2002, chief exec Vet Meds Directorate 1990–2002, JMR Consultancy 2002–; expert conslt: ODA 1986, Food and Agric Orgn 1991–92, WHO 1997; assessor Animal Medicines Trg Regulatory Authy 2007–; memb EC Ctee for Vet Medicinal Products 1991–99, memb Mgmnt Bd European Meds Evaluation Agency 1996–2002; dir Vet Benevolent Fund 2004– (sec 2006–); MRCVS 1964, FRSM; *Books* Perinatal Ill Health in Calves (ed, 1973), Pasteurella and Pasteurellosis (co-ed, 1989); author of numerous scientific articles; *Recreations* gardening, ballet, theatre, outdoor sports; *Style*— Dr Michael Rutter, CBE; ✉ Charleswood, Mile Path, Hook Heath, Woking, Surrey GU22 0JX (tel 01483 760666)

RUTTER, Prof Sir Michael Llewellyn; kt (1992), CBE (1985); s of Llewellyn Charles Rutter, and Winifred Olive, *née* Barber; *b* 15 August 1933; *Educ* Wolverhampton GS, Bootham Sch York, Univ of Birmingham Med Sch (MB ChB, MD); *m* 28 December 1958, Marjorie, da of Richard Heys (d 1983); 2 da (Sheila b 22 April 1960, Christine b 18 Sept 1964), 1 s (Stephen b 5 April 1963); *Career* memb scientific staff MRC Social Psychiatry Research Unit 1962–65; Inst of Psychiatry Univ of London: sr lectr (later reader) 1966–73, prof of child psychiatry 1973–98, prof of developmental psychopathology 1998–; hon conslt physician Bethlehem Royal and Maudsley Hosps 1966–; hon dir: MRC Child Psychiatry Unit Inst of Psychiatry 1984–98, Social, Genetic & Developmental Psychiatry Research Centre 1994–98; pres Int Soc for Research in Child and Adolescent Psychopathology 1997–99, pres Soc for Research in Child Devpt 1999–2001; Hon Dr: Univ of Leiden 1985, Catholic Univ Louvain 1990, Univ of Jyvaskyla 1996; Hon DSc: Univ of Birmingham 1990, Univ of Chicago 1991, Univ of Minnesota 1993, Univ of Ghent 1994, Univ of Warwick 1999, UEA 2000; Hon MD Univ of Edinburgh 1990, Hon DUniv N London, hon prof Univ of Amsterdam 2001; Distinguished Scientific Contribution Award American Psychological Association 1995, Castilla del Pino Prize for Achievement in Psychiatry Cordoba Spain 1995, Helmut Horten Research Award Helmut Horten Stiftung Switzerland 1997, Etienne de Greef Prize Int Soc for Criminology 1998, Ruane Prize 2000, Sarnat Prize 2001, IMFAR Award 2002, G Stanley Award 2003, Brooke Garber Nerdich Award 2004; foreign assoc memb: Inst of Med US Nat Acad of Sciences 1988, US Nat Acad of Educn 1990; foreign hon memb American Acad of Arts and Sciences 1989; founding memb Academia Europaea 1988, hon memb Br Paediatric Assoc 1994; hon FRSM 1996, hon fell Inst of Child Health 1996, Hon FRCPsych 1997; fell KCL 1998, fndr fell and memb Cncl Acad of Med Scis 1998; FRS 1987; *Books* incl: A Neuropsychiatric Study in Childhood (with P Graham and W Yule, 1970), Maternal Deprivation Reassessed (1972, 2 edn 1981), The Child With Delayed Speech (ed with J A M Martin, 1972), Cycles of Disadvantage: A Review of Research (with N Madge, 1976), Changing Youth in a Changing Society: Patterns of Adolescent Development and Disorder (1979), Developmental Neuropsychiatry (ed 1983), Juvenile Delinquency: Trends and Perspectives (with H Giller, 1983), Language Development and Disorders (ed with W Yule, 1987), Straight and Devious Pathways from Childhood to Adulthood (ed with L Robins, 1990), Developing Minds: Challenge and Continuity Across the Lifespan (with Majorie Rutter, 1993), Child and Adolescent Psychiatry: Modern Approaches (ed with E Taylor and L Hersov, 3 edn 1994), Development Through Life (ed with D Hay, 1994), Stress, Risk and Resilience in Children and Adolescents: Processes, Mechanisms and Interventions (ed with R J Haggerty, L R Sherrod and N Garmezy, 1994), Psychosocial Disorders in Young People: Time trends and their causes (co-edited with David Smith, 1995), Behavioral Genetics (with R Plomlin, J DeFries and G E McClearn, 3 edn, 1997), Antisocial Behaviour by Young People (with H Giller and A Hagell, 1998), Sex Differences in Antisocial Behaviour: Conduct, Disorder, Delinquency and Violence in the Dunedin Longitudinal Study (with T Moffitt, A Caspi and P Silva, 2001), Child and Adolescent Psychiatry (ed with Eric Taylor, 4 edn 2002); *Recreations* grandchildren, fell walking, tennis, wine tasting, theatre; *Style*— Prof Sir Michael Rutter, CBE, FRS; ✉ 190 Court Lane, Dulwich, London SE21 7ED; Institute of Psychiatry PO80, De Crespigny Park, Denmark Hill, London SE5 8AF (tel 020 7848 0882, fax 020 7848 0881, e-mail j.wickham@iop.kcl.ac.uk)

RUTTLE, (Henry) Stephen Mayo; QC (1997); s of His Hon Henry Samuel Jacob Ruttle (d 1995), and Joyce Mayo, *née* Moriarty (d 1968); *b* 6 February 1953; *Educ* Westminster (Queen's scholar), Queens' Coll Cambridge (BA); *m* 24 Aug 1985, Fiona Jane, da of William Mitchell-Innes; 2 da (Emma Jane Mayo b 1988, Bethia Claire Mayo b 1993), 2 s (James Patrick Mayo b 1990, David Timothy Mayo b 1995); *Career* called to the Bar Gray's Inn 1976 (bencher 2004); currently practicing as specialist commercial and community mediator (also sits as reinsurance arbitrator); memb: Br Insurance Law Assoc, Lloyd's of London Arbitration Panel, Civil Justice Cncl ADR Sub-Ctee; CEDR accredited and registered mediator; contributor to numerous publications on mediation and conflict resolution; active church member, committed to dispute resolution at individual and community level; *Recreations* fly fishing, the countryside, mountains, oak furniture; *Clubs* Flyfishers'; *Style*— Stephen Ruttle, Esq, QC; ✉ Brick Court Chambers, 7–8 Essex Street, London WC2R 3LD (tel 020 7379 3550, fax 020 7379 3558, e-mail stephen.ruttle@brickcourt.co.uk)

RUZICKA, Jeffrey F; s of James Ruzicka (d 2003), of Chicago, and Blanca, née Friser (d 1993); *b* 8 January 1942; *Educ* Colgate Univ (BA), Columbia Univ, American Grad Sch of Int Mgmnt (MIM); *m* 20 April 1968, Pamela, da of John Lawrence Barnard (d 1977), of Stonington, CT; 2 da (Alexa b 1970, Christina b 1975); *Career* US Army 1965–68; with Northern Tst Co Chicago 1970–90 (gen mangr London Branch 1980–84, head Int 1984–90), md State Street Corp and State Street Bank Europe Ltd 1990–2003; dir: Westminster Forum Ltd 1997–, BritishAmerican Business Inc 2002–, State Street Bank Europe Ltd 2003–; memb Advsy Bd European Capital Markets Inst 1995–; dir Salt Marsh Opera; tstee Woolnoth Soc 1991–; *Recreations* sailing, shooting, tennis, golf; *Clubs* Buck's, City of London (memb Ctee); *Style*— Jeffrey Ruzicka, Esq; ✉ State Street Corporation, 1 Royal Exchange, London EC3V 3LL

RYALL, David John; s of John Bertram Ryall (d 1978), of Shoreham-by-Sea, W Sussex, and Gladys Lilian, *née* Bowles (d 1980); *b* 5 January 1936; *Educ* Shoreham GS, Wallington GS, RADA (scholar); *m* 1, 1964, Gillian, da of Rear Adm Eddison; 1 s (Jonathan Charles b 8 Feb 1966), 1 da (Imogen Victoria b 21 Sept 1967); m 2, 1985, Cathy, da of Benek Buchwald; 1 da (Charlotte Maria Grace b 15 Oct 1986); m 3, 2003, Penny Ann, da of Keith England; *Career* actor; *Theatre* repertory work at Salisbury, Leicester, Bristol and Birmingham (incl King Lear and The Masterbuilder); with NT at the Old Vic 1965–73: Armstrong's Last Goodnight, The Royal Hunt of the Sun, Rosencrantz and Guildenstern are Dead, A Flea In Her Ear, The Idiot, The Beaux Strategem, The National Health, Jumpers, The Front Page; RNT incl: A Month In The Country, Guys and Dolls, The Beggars' Opera, Coriolanus (Clarence Derwent Award 1985), Animal Farm, A Chorus of Disapproval, Rosmersholm, School for Wives, Wild Oats, Bacchai, The UN Inspector; devised, directed and performed for NT: A Leap in the Light (works by Edward Bond) 1984, Ego in the Cosmos (Diaries of James Agate) 1989; RSC 1996–97 incl: In the Company of Men, Hamlet, The Mysteries; other appearances incl: Twelfth Night (Peter Hall Co) 1991, Venice Preserved (Royal Exchange Co Manchester) 1994, Hamlet (NY and Washington, Helen Hayes Award nomination), The Invention of Love (Haymarket) 1998, Lenny (Queens) 1999, Tantalus (Denver Centre Theatre Co) 2000 (also UK tour and Barbican Theatre) 2001, Three Sisters (Chichester Festival Theatre) 2001, King Lear (Almeida) 2002, Democracy (RNT and Wyndhams) 2003–04, The UN Inspector (RNT) 2005, Everything is Illuminated (Hampstead) 2006, Don Juan in Soho (Donmar Warehouse) 2007; *Television* incl: The Knowledge, The Singing Detective, Inspector Morse, The Men's Room, Shelley, The Borrowers, Prime Suspect, To Play the King,

Lovejoy, A Touch of Frost, The Final Cut, Jake's Progress, Plotlands, Oliver Twist, Happy Birthday Shakespeare, Lucky Jim, Bertie and Elizabeth, State of Play, Byron, Foyle's War, Down to Earth, Le Grand Charles, The Worst Journey in the World, Clapham Junction, Outnumbered, Doc Martin; *Film* incl: The Elephant Man, Empire of the Sun, Wilt, Truly Madly Deeply, Revolver, Giorgino, Restoration, Carrington, Who Killed Victor Fox, Two Men Went to War, Blackball, Round the World in 80 Days, City of Ember; *Style*— David Ryall, Esq; ✉ c/o Scott Marshall Partners Ltd, 2nd Floor, 15 Little Portland Street, London W1W 8BW (tel 020 7637 4623, e-mail smpm@scottmarshall.co.uk)

RYAN, Prof Alan James; *b* 9 May 1940; *Educ* Christ's Hosp, Balliol Coll Oxford (Fawkes scholar, Powell English Essay Prize, MA), Univ of Oxford (DLitt); *m* 1971, Kathleen Alyson, *née* Lane; 1 da (Sadie Jane b 1976); *Career* asst lectr then lectr Keele Univ 1963–66, lectr Univ of Essex 1966–69, fell and tutor New Coll Oxford 1969, reader Univ of Oxford 1978–88 (lectr 1969–78), prof of politics Princeton Univ 1988–96, warden New Coll Oxford 1996–; visiting prof: Hunter Coll CUNY 1967–, Univ of Texas at Austin 1972, Univ of Calif Santa Cruz 1977, Univ of the Witwatersrand 1978 (visiting lectr 1973), Univ of Cape Town 1982, 1983, 1984; visiting fell Australian Nat Univ 1974–75 and 1979; de Carle lectr Univ of Otago 1983, Mellon visiting fell Inst of Advanced Study 1991–92, Whidden lectr McMaster Univ 1993, dir Rothermere American Inst 1999–; memb CNAA 1975–83, assoc ed Ethics 1991–; FBA 1986; *Books* The Philosophy of John Stuart Mill (1970, 2 edn 1987), The Philosophy of the Social Sciences (1970, 15 impression 1990), J S Mill (1975), Property and Political Theory (1984), Property (1987), Russell: A Political Life (1988), John Dewey and the High Tide of American Liberalism (1995), Liberal Anxieties and Liberal Education (1998); also ed of various books on political theory 1973–; *Style*— Prof Alan Ryan, FBA; ✉ New College, Oxford OX1 3BN (e-mail alan.ryan@new.ox.ac.uk)

RYAN, Chris John; s of Henry Patrick Ryan, of Melton, Suffolk, and Evelyn May, *née* Hill; *b* 16 June 1954; *Educ* Farlingaye Sch Woodbridge, Colchester Sch of Art; *m* 22 June 1982, Vanessa Faith, da of Colin Day; *Career* photographer; trained with Phil Jude, Tony Copeland and Van Pariser; own studio 1981–; major assignments incl: covers for Radio Times and Telegraph, Aston Martin cars, Vogue España magazine, annual reports for Duke of Westminster and Société Générale de Belgique; awards from D & AD and Assoc of Photographers; memb Assoc of Photographers 1976; *Recreations* anything hedonistic; *Style*— Chris Ryan, Esq; ✉ Chris Ryan Studio, 11 Wyfold Road, Studio 3, London SW6 6SE (tel 020 7386 8080, fax 020 7386 8041, mobile 078 3180 6963)

RYAN, David Stuart; s of David Ryan (d 2003), of Kingston upon Thames, and Eileen Inez, *née* Sullivan (d 1966); *b* 22 October 1943; *Educ* Wimbledon Coll, KCL (BA); *m* 16 June 1971, Jacqueline, da of Sydney Wills (d 1989), of Southfields, London; 1 da (Chloe Selena b 1972); *Career* author and advtg copywriter KDM Advertising; memb: DMA, IDM, IPG; winner of 24 nat and int advtg awards; *Publications* John Lennon's Secret (1982), India A Guide to the Experience (1983), America A Guide to the Experience (1986), The Lost Journal of Robyn Hood - Outlaw (1989), The Cream of the Troubadour Coffee House (1990), The Blue Angel - Marlene Dietrich's Life and Loves (1993); *Recreations* photography, travel, poetry, astrology; *Clubs* Poetry Soc; *Style*— David Ryan, Esq; ✉ KDM Advertising, 134 Elsenham Street, London SW18 5NP (tel 020 8874 8218, e-mail daver134@yahoo.com)

RYAN, Dr David William; s of Leslie Ryan (d 1989), and Fiona, *née* Gregson; *b* 2 May 1946; *Educ* Sheffield City GS, Univ of Sheffield (MB ChB); *m* 24 July 1969, Susan Margaret, da of James Edward Varley (d 1945); 2 s (James b 1973, Charles b 1976); *Career* conslt and hon lectr in anaesthesia Univ of Newcastle upon Tyne 1978–2006, conslt clinical physiologist 1981–2006; Freeman Hosp: conslt in charge Intensive Therapy Unit 1981–2002, const Adv Cardiothoracic ICU 2003–06; author of 9 book chapters and over 170 articles and res papers on intensive therapy, ed of 5 books, ed Care of The Critically Ill Jl (emeritus ed 2000–06); chm Metabolic Section Euro Soc of Intensive Care Medicine 1998–2001; memb Cncl: Intensive Care Soc 1983–89 (sec 1984–87), World Fedn of Intensive and Critical Care Med 1989–97 (treas 1993–97); memb: BMA 1970, Assoc of Anaesthetists 1972, Intensive Care Soc 1978; FFARCS 1974; *Books* Colour Atlas of Critical and Intensive Care (with G R Park, 1995), Current Practice in Critical Illness (ed, 8 chapters, Vol 1 1996, Vol 2 1997, Vol 3 1998); *Recreations* cricket, art, golf; *Style*— Dr David Ryan; ✉ Department of Anaesthetics, Freeman Hospital, Newcastle upon Tyne NE7 7DN (tel 0191 233 6161 ext 31059, e-mail dwryan@aol.com)

RYAN, Sir Derek Gerald; 4 Bt (UK 1919), of Hintlesham, Suffolk; o s of Sir Derek Gerald Ryan, 3 Bt (d 1990), and his 1 w, Penelope Anne, *née* Hawkings; *b* 25 March 1954; *Educ* Univ of Calif Berkeley (BAED); *m* 1986 (m dis 1990), Maria Teresa, da of Juan G Rodriguez, of Lexington, Kentucky; *Heir* kinsman, Desmond Ryan; *Career* with Fowler Ferguson Kingston Ruben architects Salt Lake City Utah 1977–79, Atelier d'Urbanisme en Montagne architects/urban planners Chambéry France June-Oct 1979; NBBJ architects/planners Seattle Washington 1980–99, Jeffrey Charles Williams Architects AIA Ketchum Idaho 1999–, ptnr Williams Partners Architects PC; memb Nat Cncl of Architects Registration Bd (NCARB) 1984, memb AIA 1999; *Recreations* skiing, guitar; *Style*— Sir Derek Ryan, Bt; ✉ PO Box 6966, Ketchum ID 83340, USA (tel 00 1 208 720 4153)

RYAN, Rt Hon Joan; PC (2007), MP; *m* Martin Hegarty; 1 s (Michael), 1 da (Julie); *Career* former teacher with Hammersmith and Fulham LEA; MP (Lab) Enfield N 1997–; PPS to Rt Hon Andrew Smith, MP, *qv*, until 2002, asst Govt whip 2002–03, Govt whip 2003–06, Parly under sec of state Home Office 2006–; Barnet Cncl: cncllr 1990–97, dep ldr 1994–97, chm Policy and Resources Ctee 1994–97; *Style*— The Rt Hon Joan Ryan, MP; ✉ House of Commons, London SW1A 0AA (tel 020 7219 3000, fax 020 7219 2335, e-mail ryanj@parliament.uk)

RYAN, John Gerald Christopher; s of Sir Andrew Ryan, KBE, CMG (d 1949), of East Bergholt, Suffolk, and Ruth Marguerite, *née* Van Millingen (d 1975); *b* 4 March 1921; *Educ* Ampleforth; *m* 3 Jan 1950, Priscilla Ann, da of Austin Blomfield (d 1968), of Chelsea, London; 2 da (Marianne b 1951, Isabel b 1957), 1 s (Christopher b 1954); *Career* served WWII Lincs Regt UK, India, Burma 1940–46, cmmnd 2 Lt 1941, demobilised Capt 1946; children's author, illustrator and cartoon film maker; cr Captain Pugwash, 45 pubns incl 19 Captain Pugwash titles 1955–, maker of BBC Captain Pugwash films and over 100 others incl Sir Prancelot and Mary Mungo & Midge 1956–80; cartoonist Catholic Herald 1964–2007; memb Soc of Authors; *Recreations* walking; *Style*— John Ryan, Esq; ✉ Gungarden Lodge, The Gungardens, Rye, East Sussex TN31 7HH (tel 01797 222034)

RYAN, John Patrick; s of James Patrick Ryan (d 1960), of Rhos-on-Sea, N Wales, and Marie Elsie, *née* Gaines (d 1988); *b* 19 August 1943; *Educ* St Mary's Coll Rhos-on-Sea N Wales, Queens' Coll Cambridge (MA); *m* 8 Feb 1969, Verna Marguerite, da of Capt Charles Edward Henry Mytton, of Hampstead Garden Suburb; 2 s (Nicholas b 26 Feb 1972, Alastair b 13 Sept 1976), 1 da (Annabel b 22 March 1974); *Career* actuarial supt Guardian Royal Exchange 1968, ptnr James Capel & Co 1972–76, vice-pres and princ Tillinghast (part of Towers Perrin Co) 1976–2001, md Heath Lambert Hybrid Solutions 2001–04, Hines Assocs 2004–; vice-pres Inst of Actuaries 1995–97 (memb Cncl 1997–2001), assoc Casualty Actuarial Soc USA 1979, memb American Acad of Actuaries USA 1979, fell Inst of Risk Mgmnt 1987; Freeman: City of London, Liveryman Worshipful Co of Needlemakers; FIA 1968, AMIIA 1973; *Recreations* travel, walking, theatre, old buildings, golf, racing; *Style*— John Ryan, Esq; ✉ 17 Highfields Grove, Highgate, London N6 6HN (tel 020 8348 0195, e-mail johnryanactuary@yahoo.co.uk)

RYAN, Michelle; da of Craig Ryan, and Tina Ryan; *Educ* Chace Community Sch Enfield (Govr's prize for outstanding achievement); *Career* actress; patron CLICSargent; memb BAFTA; *Theatre* credits incl: The Stars in our Eyes (HM's Theatre London), Smash (London Palladium), Hollywood and Broadway (Millfield Theatre), Next Stop...Broadway (Millfield Theatre), Who's the Daddy (Kings Head Islington); *Television* credits incl: The Worst Witch (ITV), Burnside (ITV), Zoe Slater in Eastenders (BBC) 2000–05, Miss Marple (ITV), Mansfield Park (ITV), Jekyll (BBC 1), Comic Relief 2007 (BBC 1), Bionic Woman (NBC); performed in Nat Dance Comp and Finals (HM's Theatre London); *Film* Cashback, Suzy, I Want Candy, Lila Owens, Flick; *Awards* BBC1 Best TV Moments of 2001, Best Single Episode British Soap Awards 2004; *Recreations* reading, theatre, cinema; *Style*— Miss Michelle Ryan; ✉ c/o Claire Maroussas, ICM, Oxford House, 76 Oxford Street, London W1D 1BS (tel 020 7636 6565); c/o Philip Grenz, William Morris Agency (tel 00 1 310 859 4000)

RYAN, Prof Paul; s of John Joseph Ryan (d 2006), and Mary Cecilia, *née* Walsh (d 1992); *b* 14 January 1947, Northampton; *Educ* LSE (MSc, BSc), Harvard Univ (PhD); *m* 1, 30 June 1970 (m dis); 1 s (Jude Sebastien b 20 March 1974); m 2, 2 May 1986, Gale, *née* Smith; 1 s (Stephen Jacob b 31 Oct 1986); *Career* lectr and sr lectr Faculty of Economics Univ of Cambridge 1977–2004, fell King's Coll Cambridge 1977–2004, prof of labour economics Dept of Mgmnt KCL 2004–; visiting prof Univ of California at Berkeley 1994–95; conslt: World Bank, ILO, OECD; memb: Royal Economic Soc, American Economic Assoc; *Publications* The Problem of Youth (1991), The Roles of Evaluation for Vocational Education and Training (1999); *Recreations* swimming, running, film, music, history; *Style*— Prof Paul Ryan; ✉ Department of Management, King's College London, 150 Stamford Street, London SE1 9NH (tel and fax 020 7848 3966, e-mail paul.ryan@kcl.ac.uk)

RYAN, Sean Matthew; s of Brendan Manus Ryan, of London, and Marion Celia, *née* Hinkley; *b* 14 September 1959; *Educ* King's Sch Worcester, Pembroke Coll Oxford (scholar, MA); *m* 12 May 1984, Carmel Mary, da of Kevin Campbell; 1 s (Alastair Matthew b 24 Aug 1988), 2 da (Charlotte Anne b 21 April 1990, Anna Marion b 19 April 2000); *Career* reporter Reading Evening Post 1982–85; Daily Mail 1985–90; Sunday Times: environment corr 1991–94, science corr 1994–95, dep news ed and science ed 1995–96, Focus ed 1996–97, foreign ed 1997–; Pfizer Award Young Journalist of the Year 1983, Team of the Year (Kosovo) British Press Awards 2000; memb Bd Watch Tst for Environmental Educn 1992–93, govr St Gabriel's Sch Newbury; *Recreations* walking, running; *Style*— Sean Ryan, Esq; ✉ The Sunday Times, 1 Pennington Street, London E1 9XW (tel 020 7782 5691, fax 020 7782 5050, e-mail sean.ryan@sunday-times.co.uk)

RYCROFT, HE Matthew; CBE; *b* 16 June 1968; *m* 1997, Alison Emma Victoria; 3 da; *Career* diplomat; entered HM Dip Serv 1989, third sec Geneva 1990, asst desk offr Security Policy Dept 1990–91, third sec then second sec (Chancery) Paris 1991–95, head of section Eastern Adriatic Unit FCO 1995–96, desk offr Policy Planners FCO 1996–98, first sec (political) Washington DC 1998–2002, private sec (foreign affrs) to PM 2002–04, ambass to Bosnia and Herzegovina 2005–; *Style*— HE Mr Matthew Rycroft, CBE; ✉ c/o Foreign & Commonwealth Office (Sarajevo), King Charles Street, London SW1A 2AH

RYCROFT, Sir Richard John; 8 Bt (GB 1784), of Calton, Yorks; s of late Cdr Henry Richard Rycroft, OBE, DSC, RN; suc cous Sir Richard Newton Rycroft (d 1999); *b* 15 June 1946; *Educ* Sherborne; *Heir* cous, Francis Rycroft; *Clubs* Royal Corinthian Yacht; *Style*— Sir Richard Rycroft, Bt

RYDER, Chris; s of late Dermod Ryder, and late Brigid, *née* Burns; *b* 9 May 1947; *Educ* St MacNissis Coll Garron Tower, St Mary's CBS Belfast; *m* 1, 1967 (m dis 1996), Anne, da of late John Henry; 3 s (Paul, Declan, Edward), 1 da (Michelle); m 2, 2000, Genevieve, da of Jack Belton; *Career* clerical offr Postmaster-Gen's Dept 1965–66, freelance journalist and publicist 1966–70, advtg and publicity mangr Bass Ireland Ltd 1970–71, freelance journalist 1971–72, news reporter The Sunday Times 1972–88, Irish corr The Daily Telegraph 1988–93, author, journalist and broadcaster 1993–; fndr memb NI Community Rels Cncl 1990–94, memb Police Authy for NI 1994–96; memb Ulster History Circle 2003– (sec 2007–); *Books* The RUC: A Force Under Fire (1989), The UDR: An Instrument of Peace? (1991), Inside the Maze (2000), Drumcree: The Orange Order's Last Stand (with Vincent Kearney, 2001), The Fateful Split: Catholics and the RUC (2004), A Special Kind of Courage: 321EOD Squadron Battling the Bombers (2005), Fighting Fitt (2006); *Recreations* music, reading; *Clubs* Ulster Reform; *Style*— Chris Ryder, Esq; ✉ 1 Clontonacally Road, Carryduff, Belfast BT8 8AG (tel 028 9081 7357, fax 028 9081 7351, e-mail chris@chrisryder.co.uk)

RYDER, Hon Mr Justice; Sir Ernest Nigel Ryder; kt (2004), TD (1996); s of Dr John Buckley Ryder, TD (d 1983), of Bolton, Lancs, and Constance, *née* Collier; *b* 9 December 1957; *Educ* Bolton Sch, Peterhouse Cambridge (MA, jr treas Cambridge Union Soc); *m* 1990, Janette Lynn Martin; 1 da; *Career* merchant banker Grindley Brandt & Co 1979–81; called to the Bar Gray's Inn 1981; QC 1997, recorder of the Crown Court 2000–04 (asst recorder 1997–2000), a dep judge of the High Court 2001–04, judge of the High Court of Justice (Family Div) 2004–; boundary cmmr for England 2000–04; counsel North Wales Tbnl of Inquiry 1996–98; TA: cmmnd Duke of Lancaster's Own Yeo 1981, Sqdn Ldr Duke of Lancaster's Yeo 1990, Sqdn Ldr Royal Mercian and Lancastrian Yeo 1992; *Publications* Clarke Hall and Morrison on Children (ed); *Recreations* listening, walking; *Clubs* Cwlth, RAC; *Style*— The Hon Mr Justice Ryder; ✉ Royal Courts of Justice, Strand, London WC2A 2LL

RYDER, Janet; AM; *b* 21 June 1955; *Educ* Northern Counties Coll of Educn (T Cert), Open Univ (BA); *m*; 3 c; *Career* teacher: Little Weighton Co Primary Sch, St Bede's Catholic Primary Sch Hull, Coleford Primary Sch Hull; Denbighshire County Cncl: memb for Rhuthun 1995–99, chair Children and Families Sub-Ctee 1995–98, chair Denbighshire Early Years Partnership 1996–98, chair Denbighshire Plan Partnership, memb working pty Denbighshire Community Care Charter; Mayor of Rhuthun 1998–2000 (Plaid Cymru town cncllr 1993–2003), memb Nat Assembly for Wales (Plaid Cymru) North Wales 1999–; shadow min for local govt and communities 1999–2003 (also with responsibility for finance 2002–03), shadow min for educn and lifelong learning 2003– (also with responsibility for skills 2006–); memb Plaid Cymru Nat Exec; chm Canolfan Awelon Mgmnt Ctee; former tstee Denbighshire Voluntary Services Cncl; memb: Rhuthun Community Action Gp, Rhuthun Action Gp (Youth Forum); former memb: North Wales Fire Authy, Denbighshire Access Gp, Denbighshire Strategic Planning Gp for People with Learning Disabilities, Cymdeithas Teulu Rhuthun Family Assoc; *Style*— Ms Janet Ryder, AM; ✉ National Assembly for Wales, Cardiff Bay, Cardiff CF99 1NA (tel 029 2089 8250, e-mail janet.ryder@wales.gov.uk); constituency address: The Machine, 65 Stryd y Ffynnon, Rhuthun LL15 1AG (tel 01824 704625, fax 01824 702739)

RYDER, Michael John; s of late John William Ryder, and late Eva, *née* Walden; *Educ* Southall GS; *m* March 1985, Geraldine; 3 c from first m (Lee b 1970, Mark b 1971, Suzanne b 1974); *Career* journalist; chief sub London Evening News, night desk ed The Sun, asst ed London Daily News, night ed Daily Mirror, asst ed The People, assoc ed Sunday Mirror 1996–; *Recreations* reading other people's newspapers; *Style*— Michael Ryder, Esq; ✉ Sunday Mirror, 1 Canada Square, Canary Wharf, London E14 5AP (tel 020 7293 3106, fax 020 7293 3939)

RYDER, Peter; CB (1994); s of Percival Henry Sussex Ryder (d 1976), and Bridget, *née* McCormack (d 1997); *b* 10 March 1942; *Educ* Yorebridge GS, Univ of Leeds (BSc, PhD); *m* 24 April 1965, Jacqueline Doris Sylvia, da of Douglas Rigby; 2 s (Andrew Stephen b 9 April 1966, Mark James b 19 Aug 1970), 1 da (Louise Pauline b 4 Feb 1972); *Career* res asst Physics Dept Univ of Leeds 1966–67; Meteorological Office: asst dir Cloud Physics Res 1976–82, asst dir Systems Development 1982–84, dep dir Observational Servs 1984–88, dep dir Forecasting Servs 1988–89, dir of Servs 1989–90; dep chief exec and dir ops Meteorological Office Executive Agency 1990–96; conslt on environmental info servs 1996–; chm: Thames Regnl Flood Defence Ctee 2003–, EuroGOOS 2003–; William Gaskell Meml Medal 1981, L G Groves Meml Prize for Meteorology 1982; FRMetS 2004 (memb Cncl 1980–83, memb Editorial Bd Quarterley Jl 1981–84, gen sec 2001–06); *Recreations* gardening, walking, fishing, photography; *Style*— Dr Peter Ryder, CB, FRMetS; ✉ 8 Sherring Close, Bracknell, Berkshire RG42 2LD (tel 01344 423380, fax 01344 421796)

RYDER, Sophie Marie-Louise; da of Wilfred Ryder (d 1981), of Twickenham, and Jacqueline, *née* Bazin; *b* 28 January 1963; *Educ* Chiswick Comp, Kingston Poly, Royal Acad Schs (Dip); *m* 5 Nov 1989, Harry Scott, s of James Scott (d 2000); 2 da (Maud Augusta Ryder b 24 Aug 1989, Nell Ryder Lucy b 8 Aug 1991); *Career* sculptor; residencies: Yorkshire Sculpture Park 1986, Grizedale Forest Cumbria 1986, Salisbury Cathedral 1987, Forest of Dean 1988, Kilkenny Eire 1992, Boulogne France 1996, Cheltenham Art Gallery and Museum 1997, Cheltenham Music Fetival 1997, Cheekwood Sculpture Park Nashville 1998; *Solo Exhibitions* incl: Edward Totah Gallery London 1987, Salisbury Cathedral 1987, St Paul's Gallery Leeds 1988, Berkeley Sq Gallery London 1989, 1995, 1996, 1997 and 1999, Courcoux & Courcoux Salisbury 1989, 1990, 1992 and 2002, Newport Museum & Art Gallery 1990, Yorkshire Sculpture Park 1991, Collage (Oxford Gallery) 1993, Winchester Cathedral 1994, Charlie Belloc Lowndes Gallery Chicago 1996, Willis Corroon Group HQ London 1997, O'Hara Gallery NY 1997, Cheltenham Art Gallery and Museum 1997, Victoria Art Gallery Bath 1999, Cartwright Hall Art Gallery Bradford 1999, Berkeley Sq Gallery London 1999, Br Cncl The Hague 1999, Veranneman Fndn Belgium 2000, Odapark Venray Holland 2000, Buschlen Mowatt Galleries Vancouver 2000, Gallerie de Bellefeuille Montreal 2001, Metropole Galleries Folkestone 2002, Buschlen Mowatt Galleries 2002, Pierrepoint Gallery 2002, Imago Gallery California 2004, Storey Gallery Lancaster 2004, Canary Wharf London 2005, Millfield Sch 2006, Imago Gallery California 2007, Blickachsen 6 2007, Meijer Sculpture Garden 2007; *Group Exhibitions* incl: Pick of the Graduates (Christies London) 1984, Dogwork (Interim Art London) 1984, Sophie Ryder & Harry Scott (Gallery 24 London) 1985, Bretton Menagerie (Yorkshire Sculpture Park) 1986, Freedom to Touch (Laing Art Gallery Newcastle) 1986, Animal in Photography (Photographers Gallery London) 1987, The Fabricated Landscape (Plymouth City Museum) 1989, Women Artists - Critics Choice (Bruton St Gallery London) 1992, Young British Art (Kunstforening AF 1847 Århus Festival Denmark) 1992, Art in the City (Finsbury Park) 1993, Exhibition for the Blind (Bury St Edmunds Art Gallery) 1993–94, Summer Exhibition (Bruton Gallery Bath) 1994, Young Contemporary's (Berkeley Sq Gallery London) 1994, Sculpture in Paradise (Chichester Cathedral) 1994, Sculpture at Goodwood 1994, Minotaurs Myths and Legends (Berkeley Sq Gallery London 1994, Chicago 1995), The Shape of the Century (Salisbury) 1999, Br Sculpture from the 20th Century (Carlow Arts Festival) 2001, Art Miami 2002, Palm Beach 2002, Art 2003 (Business Design Centre London) 2003, Newbury Arts Festival 2003, Aykley Heads Project Durham 2004, Victoria Gallery Bath 2004, Solomon Gallery Dublin 2005, Palm Beach 2006; *Public Collections* Newport City Museum, Yorkshire Sculpture Park, Barings Bank Collection, De Beers Collection, Conoco Ltd, Gerard and National Bank, National Trust (Buckland Abbey), EFG Private Bank Ltd, Le Trion Secdy Sch France, Cheekwood Sculpture Park Nashville, Cheltenham BC, Cheltenham Art Gallery and Museum, Victoria Art Gall Bath; *Style*— Ms Sophie Ryder; ✉ Lampits Farm, Winson, Cirencester, Gloucestershire GL7 5ER (e-mail harry@lampits.demon.co.uk)

RYDER, Susan Myfanwy Prudence; da of Capt Robert Edward Dudley Ryder, VC (d 1986), and Hilaré Myfanwy, *née* Green-Wilkinson (d 1982); *b* 14 March 1944; *Educ* Beaufront Sch Camberley, Byam Shaw Sch of Art (David Murray travel scholar, NDD); *m* Martin Graves Bates; 1 s (Oliver Robert Hunter b 29 March 1969), 1 da (Susannah Hilaré Myfanwy b 15 May 1970); *Career* artist; regular exhibitor: Royal Academy Summer Exhbn, Royal Soc of Portrait Painters, New English Art Club (memb 1980–); RP 1992 (currently vice-pres); *Solo Exhibitions* Haste Gallery 1979 and 1981, W H Patterson 1989, 1995 and 1999, Brian Sinfield Gallery 1993, Oakham Galleries 2004; *Portraits* HRH The Princess of Wales 1981, Miss Pears 1984, Christina Leder 1988, Miss Nicola Paget 1991, Sir Eric Ash 1993, Lord Porter 1994, HM The Queen 1996; *Awards* Barney Wilkins prize 1990, winner Alexon Portrait Competition 1991, first prize New English Art Club Critic's prize 1993 (second 1992); *Recreations* family and friends; *Style*— Miss Susan Ryder, RP, NEAC; ✉ 48 Stratford Road, London W8 6QA (website www.susanryder.co.uk)

RYDER OF WENSUM, Baron (Life Peer UK 1997), of Wensum in the County of Norfolk; Rt Hon Richard Andrew Ryder; PC (1990), OBE (1981); s of (Richard) Stephen Ryder, JP, DL (d 2003), and Margaret, *née* MacKenzie; *b* 4 February 1949; *Educ* Radley, Magdalene Coll Cambridge (BA); *m* 1981, Caroline Ryder, CVO, MBE, o da of late Sir David Stephens, KCB, CVO; 1 s (decd), 1 da; *Career* journalist; political sec to PM 1975–81; MP (Cons) Norfolk Mid 1983–97; PPS to: Fin Sec to the Treasy 1984, Sec of State for Foreign Affrs 1984–86; chm Cons Foreign and Cwlth Cncl 1984–89; Govt whip 1986–88, Parly sec MAFF 1988–89, econ sec to the Treasy 1989–90, paymaster-gen 1990, Parly sec to the Treasy (Govt chief whip) 1990–95; chm Eastern Counties Radio 1997–2001, vice-chm BBC 2002–04 (actg chm of govrs 2004), chm Inst of Cancer Research 2005–; dir of family businesses; *Style*— The Rt Hon Lord Ryder of Wensum, OBE, PC; ✉ House of Lords, London SW1A 0PW

RYDER RICHARDSON, Anna Carolyne; da of Colin Ryder Richardson, and Jill Macilwaine; *b* 29 January 1964; *Educ* Priors Field Godalming; *Partner* Colin MacDougall; 2 da (Bibi Belle b 11 May 2002, Dixie Dot b 7 April 2003); *Career* interior designer and TV personality; BBC credits incl: Good Morning with Anne and Nick, Pebble Mill The Terrace, Change That, Changing Rooms, Whose House, All The Right Moves, Girls on Top; winner Nat TV Award for Changing Rooms; involved with: Queen Mother's Hosp Glasgow, C of E Children's Soc; *Publications* Babies' Rooms; *Style*— Ms Anna Ryder Richardson; ✉ c/o Arlington Enterprises Ltd, 1–3 Charlotte Street, London W1T 1RD (tel 020 7580 0702, fax 020 7580 4994)

RYE, Renny Michael Douglas; s of Douglas Rye, of Maidstone, Kent, and Pamela, *née* Whitmore; *b* 2 December 1947; *Educ* Maidstone GS, St Catherine's Coll Oxford (BA); *m* 8 Aug 1970, Ann, da of (Andrew Frank) Peter Lynn, of Maidstone, Kent; 1 da (Helen b 1974), 1 s (Thomas b 1977); *Career* BBC: prodn ops asst BBC radio 1971–73, asst floor mangr TV plays dept 1973–79, prodr and asst ed Blue Peter 1979–81; freelance drama dir: The Box of Delights (BBC) 1983–84, The December Rose (BBC) 1985, Casualty (BBC) 1986, The Gemini Factor 1987, All our Children (BBC) 1987–89, Agatha Christie's Poirot 1988–91, The Other Side of Paradise 1991, Lipstick on Your Collar (Channel 4) 1992, Midnight Movie (film) 1993, Chandler & Co (BBC), Kavanagh QC 1994, Karaoke, Cold Lazarus (BBC/Channel 4) 1995, Family Money (Channel 4) 1996, Big Women (Channel 4) 1997, Oliver Twist (ITV) 1999, Close & True (ITV) 2000, Two Thousand Acres of Sky (BBC) 2001–02, Silent Witness (BBC) 2002–03, Midsomer Murders (ITV) 2003–06, Vital Signs (ITV) 2006; memb: BAFTA, DGGB; *Recreations* cricket, films, music; *Style*— Renny Rye, Esq; ✉ c/o Jessica Sykes, ICM Ltd, Oxford House, 76 New Oxford Street, London W1N 0XA (tel 020 7636 6565)

RYLANCE, His Hon Judge John Randolph Trevor; s of Dr Ralph Curzon Rylance (d 1983), and Margaret Joan Clare, *née* Chambers (d 2005); *b* 26 February 1944; *Educ* Shrewsbury; *m* 14 Dec 1974, Philippa Anne, da of Philip Sidney Bailey (d 1975); 2 da (Georgina b 1976, Charlotte b 1978); *Career* called to the Bar Lincoln's Inn 1968; res asst to Sir Edward Gardner, QC, MP 1971–73, recorder 1993–2003 (asst recorder 1989–93), circuit judge (SE Circuit) 2003–; memb Professional Conduct Ctee Bar Cncl 1992–94; govr Fulham Cross Sch 1977–88, branch chm Fulham Cons Assoc 1983–89 (memb Mgmnt Ctee 1980–90), memb Exec Ctee Fulham Soc 1988–, chm Fulham Palace Tst 1996– (tstee 1991–); *Clubs* Hurlingham; *Style*— His Hon Judge John Rylance; ✉ Guildford County Court, The Law Courts, Mary Road, Guildford, Surrey GU1 4PS (tel 01483 405300)

RYLAND, David Stuart; s of Sir William Ryland, CB (d 1988), of Croydon, Surrey, and Lady Sybil Ryland; *b* 27 October 1953; *Educ* Dulwich, Exeter Coll Oxford; *m* 18 July 1986, Anne Helen, da of Kenneth Wright, of Benfleet, Essex; *Career* admitted slr 1981; Clifford Chance 1981–88, ptnr SJ Berwin & Co 1988–; Freeman City of London; memb Law Soc; *Recreations* films, music, sport; *Style*— David Ryland, Esq; ✉ SJ Berwin & Co, 222 Gray's Inn Road, London WC1X 8HB (tel 020 7533 2222, fax 020 7533 2000)

RYLAND, His Hon Judge Timothy Richard Godfrey Fetherstonhaugh; s of Richard Desmond Fetherstonhaugh Ryland (d 1983), and Frances Katharine Vernon, *née* Plummer (d 1990); *b* 13 June 1938; *Educ* St Andrew's Coll, TCD (BA, LLB); *m* 22 June 1991, Jean Margaret Muirhead; *Career* called to the Bar Gray's Inn 1961; dep circuit judge 1978, recorder Crown Court 1983–88, circuit judge (SE Circuit) 1988–, Central London Civil Justice Centre 1994–; *Recreations* opera, wine; *Clubs* Lansdowne, Kildare St and Univ (Dublin); *Style*— His Hon Judge Ryland

RYLANDS, Patrick; s of Leo Rylands (d 1978), and Ada, *née* Hyde (d 1992); *b* 12 September 1942; *Educ* Hull Coll of Art (NDD), RCA (DesRCA); *m* Ljiljana, *née* Momčilović; *Career* toy designer; teacher: Sch of Ceramics Hornsey Sch of Art 1966–70, Sch of Architecture Poly of North London 1972–76; ceramic designer Grindley Hotel Ware Stoke-on-Trent 1966–70, visiting designer Creative Playthings USA 1970, freelance cmmns for Rosedale, Kurt Naef and Europlastic 1970–76, sole design conslt for Ambi Toys by Europlastic 1976–2002, conslt Tolo Toys Ltd (Hong Kong) 2003–04; memb juries: Design Cncl Design Index, Design Cncl Design Awards, RSA Burseries, Toymakers' Guild Prizes, Br Toy and Hobby Manufacturers' Assoc Prize Ctee; memb: Tstees Ctee V&A Bethnal Green Museum of Childhood, Artworkers Guild 1998; RDI 1999; *Recreations* drawing and photography; *Style*— Patrick Rylands, RDI; ✉ 76A Belsize Park Gardens, London NW3 4NG (tel 020 7586 0878, fax 020 7916 6836, e-mail patrickrylands@mac.com)

RYLE, Sallie Elizabeth; da of Barry Davidson Eaton Smith, MBE (d 1995), of Ilkley, W Yorks, and Mary Elizabeth, *née* Priest (d 1996); *b* 14 November 1950; *Educ* Ilkley GS; *m* 19 Sept 1981, Nicholas Peter Bodley Ryle, s of Michael Thomas Ryle, of Winsford, Somerset; 1 s (George David Bodley b 6 April 1987), 1 da (Vanessa Isabelle b 25 April 1990); *Career* Yorkshire TV: asst publicity offr 1982–84, head of publicity 1984–87, head of publicity and PR 1987–96; chief press offr Granada TV 1997–98, head of media relations (North) Granada and head of regnl affrs Yorkshire Television 1998–2004, dir Yorkshire Television 2004–; currently dir ITV prog publicity (controller 2004–07); memb: NUJ, RTS; *Recreations* equestrian sports, tennis, travel; *Style*— Ms Sallie Ryle; ✉ ITV Yorkshire, TV Centre, Leeds LS3 1JS (tel 0113 222 7118, fax 0113 244 0213, e-mail sallie.ryle@itv.com)

RYLE-HODGES, Carolyn; da of Harry Morton Neal, and Cecilia Elizabeth, *née* Crawford; *b* 10 June 1961; *Educ* Courtauld Inst of Art London (BA); *m* 2 June 1988, Rupert Ryle-Hodges, s of Edward Ryle-Hodges; 1 da (Eve b 1 May 1991), 1 s (William b 20 March 1993); *Career* ptnr Long & Ryle Art Gallery 1988–; corp clients incl: Lloyd Thompson, McKinsey's & Co, Cazenove & Co, Kreditbank, Morgan Grenfell, Société Générale, Mitsui Trust, HM Customs & Excise, Mitsubishi Corp plc, London Underground Ltd Canary Wharf, Barclays Bank, Paribas, Bank America Tst, Capsticks Slrs; memb: Worshipful Co of Carpenters, Friends of the Tate, Friends of the Royal Acad; *Recreations* visiting museums, walking; *Style*— Mrs Carolyn Ryle-Hodges; ✉ 4 Redesdale Street, London SW3; Long and Ryle Art Gallery, 4 John Islip Street, London SW1P 4PX (tel 020 7834 1434, fax 020 7821 9409, e-mail longandryle@btconnect.com, website www.longandryle.com)

RYOTT, Emma; *Educ* St James' Sch West Malvern, Francis Holland Sch, Trent Poly (BA); *Children* 1 s (Matthew); *Career* costume and set designer; asst to wardrobe supervisor and touring wardrobe asst Eng Nat Ballet 1981–85, costume supervisor and designer Royal Shakespeare Theatre 1985–97; *Productions* Kiss Me Kate (Old Vic and Savoy Theatre) 1986, Henceforward (Vaudeville Theatre) 1988, Macbeth (USA tour) 1988, Twelfth Night (Royal Shakespeare Theatre) 1989, Big Game (Nuffield Theatre Southampton) 1989, Sir Thomas More (Shaw Theatre) 1990, Archbishop Ceiling (Royal Shakespeare Theatre) 1990, Henry IV (Wyndhams Theatre)1990, Electra (Riverside Studios) 1992, Hamlet (Mediaeval Players) 1992, Francesca da Rimini (Bregenzerfestspiele Austria) 1994, Orlando (Flanders Opera) 1995, Rhapsody (Royal Ballet) 1995, Steptext (Royal Ballet) 1995, Shakespeare Revue (Vaudeville Theatre) 1995, Son of Man (Royal Shakespeare Theatre) 1995, The Entertainer (Hampstead Theatre) 1996, A Doll's House (Odeon Paris) 1997, Porgy and Bess (Bregenzerfestspiele) 1998, Hidden Variables (Royal Ballet) 1999, Un Ballo in Maschera (Bregenzerfestspiele) 1999 and 2000, The Merry Widow (Met Opera NY) 2000, Manon Lescaut (ENO) 2000, La Bohème (Bregenzerfestspiele) 2001, Manon Lescaut (Göteborg Operan Sweden) 2002, Nine (Malmo Musikteater Sweden) 2002, La Bohème (Bregenzerfestspiele) 2002, Ragtime (West End) 2003, Pearl Fishers (State Opera Kazan Russia) 2003, Lulu (Stuttgart Ballet) 2003, Marriage of Figaro (Savoy Opera) 2004, One Touch of Venus (Opera North) 2004, Le Peau Blanche (Stuttgart Ballet) 2005, Oedipus Rex (Epidaurus Festival Contemporary Theatre Athens) 2005, Berenice (Heidelberg Staattheater) 2005, Sandmann (Stuttgart Ballet) 2006, Rock & Roll (Royal Court and West End) 2006, Barber of Seville (Grange Park Opera) 2006, The Return of Ulysses (Royal Flanders Ballet) 2006, Damnation of Faust (Semper Opera Dresden) 2007; *Style*— Ms Emma Ryott; ✉ c/o Loesje Sanders, Pound Square, 1 North Hill, Woodbridge, Suffolk IP12 1HH (tel 01394 385260, fax 01394 388734, e-mail loesjev@aol.com)

S

SAATCHI, Charles; s of Nathan David Saatchi (d 2000), and Daisy Saatchi, of London; *b* 9 June 1943; *Educ* Christ's Coll Finchley; *m* 1, 1973, Doris Jean, da of Jack Lockhart of USA; m 2, 2003, Nigella Lawson, *qv*; *Career* assoc dir Collett Dickenson Pearce 1966–68, dir Cramer Saatchi 1968–70, dir Saatchi & Saatchi Co plc 1970–93 (hon pres 1993–95), fndr ptnr M&C Saatchi Ltd 1995–; Chm's Award for Outstanding Contribution to Commercials Indust (British TV Advtg Awards) 1994; *Recreations* karting; *Style—* Charles Saatchi, Esq; ✉ c/o Saatchi Gallery, 98A Boundary Road, London NW8 0RH (tel 020 7624 8299)

SAATCHI, Baron (Life Peer UK 1996), of Staplefield in the County of West Sussex; Maurice Saatchi; s of late Nathan Saatchi, and Daisy Saatchi; *b* 21 June 1946; *Educ* LSE (BSc); *m* 1984, Josephine Hart, novelist; 1 s ((Hon) Edward b 1985), 1 step s; *Career* chm Saatchi & Saatchi Co plc 1984–94; fndr ptnr M&C Saatchi Ltd 1995–, chm Finsbury Food Gp plc 1995–; House of Lords: oppn Treasy spokesman 1999–2003, oppn Cabinet Office spokesman 2001–03; co-chm Cons Pty 2003–05; dir Centre for Policy Studies 1999–; memb Cncl RCA 1997, dir Museum of Garden History 2001–; govr LSE; *Publications* The War of Independence (1999), Happiness Can't Buy Money (1999), The Bad Samaritan (2000), Poor People! Stop Paying Tax ! (2001), The Science of Politics (2001), If this is Conservatism, I am a Conservative (2005), In Praise of Ideology (2006); *Style—* The Lord Saatchi; ✉ M&C Saatchi plc, 36 Golden Square, London W1F 9EE (tel 020 7543 4510, fax 020 7543 4502)

SABIN, Paul Robert; DL (Kent 2001); s of Robert Reginald Sabin (d 1988), and Dorothy Maude, *née* Aston (d 1992); *b* 29 March 1943; *Educ* Oldbury GS, Aston Univ (DMS); *m* 19 June 1965, Vivien, da of Harry Furnival; 1 s (Martin Lawrence b 1969), 2 da (Ann Hazel b 1973, Caroline Jane b 1978); *Career* West Bromwich CBC 1959–69, chief fin offr Redditch Devpt Corp 1975–81 (joined 1969); City of Birmingham: joined 1981, city treas 1982–86, dep chief exec 1984–86; chief exec Kent CC 1986–97; chief exec Leeds Castle Foundation and Leeds Castle (Enterprises) Ltd 1998–2003; non-exec dir Folkestone and Dover Water Co; Hon Citizen of the City of Baltimore USA 1985; CPFA 1966, FTS, DMS, FCMI, FRSA; *Recreations* fine books, music; *Style—* Paul Sabin, Esq, DL; ✉ tel 01580 715603

SACH, Keith Howard; JP (Warks 1989); s of Cyril James Sach (d 1989), of Warks, and Jessie Annie, *née* Andlaw (d 1990); *b* 13 May 1948; *Educ* Strode's Sch Egham, King George V Sch, St Peter's Coll Birmingham, Open Univ; *m* 14 July 1990, Elizabeth Anne (Mrs Brierley), da of Geoffrey Ball (d 1990); 2 step da (Alexis b 1973, Kathryn b 1979), 1 step s (Jonathan b 1976); *Career* asst master Solihull Sch 1970–79, dir RLSS UK 1979–88 (chief Cwlth sec 1979–86, Cwlth vice-pres 1987), md S & P Safety 1988–90, dir: Safety Mgmnt Partnership Ltd 1992–95, Scalefast Systems Ltd 1996–, IQL UK Ltd 2001–06 (chm 2001–06); safety conslt to: Overseas Govts, HSE, Sport England, RLSS Aust, Leisure Connection, D C Leisure, Sports and Leisure Management, Fitness Express, Cannons Health and Fitness, 3D Leisure, Community Leisure Servs, SOLL Leisure, local authorities; broadcaster and writer; swimming pool health and safety advsr Royal Life Saving Soc UK 2007–; memb: Magistrates Assoc (chm Warks Branch 1998–2004 and 2005–, memb Nat Cncl 2001–05, tstee 2005), Safety in Leisure Research Unit (SAIL); Civil, Criminal and Coroners' Courts expert witness on swimming pool, leisure centre, sport and recreation accidents; chm: Nat Water Safety Ctee 1980–83, Nat Rescue Trg Cncl 1981–88 (tstee 1995–97); Hon Constable St Helier Jersey 1984, Hon Citizen Burlington Ontario 1985; *Books* Safety in Swimming Pools (contrib, 1988), Recreation Management Factfile (contrib, 1991/92), Quality in the Leisure Industry (contrib, 1992), Handbook of Sports and Recreational Building Design (contrib, 1993), Guide to Risk Assessment (jtly, 1993), Managing Health and Safety in Swimming Pools (contrib, 1999 and 2003), Magistrates' Courts Security Guide (contrib, 2004); *Recreations* theatre, music, travel, swimming; *Style—* Keith H Sach, Esq, JP; ✉ High Ash Farm, Great Packington, Warwickshire CV7 7JZ (tel 07831 608900, e-mail highashfarm@aol.com)

SACHAR, Jasbir Singh; s of late Balwant Singh, and late Inder Kaur, *née* Phul; *b* 12 December 1936; *Educ* Punjab Univ Amritsar (BA, BT, MA), Univ of Agra (LLB); *m* 8 Oct 1967, Kanwaljit (decd), da of late Avtar Singh Keer, of India; 1 da (Ruby b 26 Aug 1968), 1 s (Navi b 22 April 1970); *Career* headmaster Govt Middle Sch Chamyari Dist Amritsar 1957–59, princ SGN Int Coll Bareilly India 1964–67; winner numerous prizes for literary and academic achievement; sec Headmasters' Assoc India 1957–59, memb Allahabad Educn Bd 1964–67, pres Asian Welfare and Cultural Assoc E London 1975 (gen sec 1974), PR offr and hon sec Standing Conference of Asian Orgns in UK 1975–, dir of publicity and PR First Int Convention of Overseas Indians (Euro Section) London 1989, fndr and UK delegate First Int Convention NY 1989, hon gen sec Int Punjabi Soc (UK) 1993–; fndr memb and vice-pres GOPIO (Global Orgn People of Indian Origin) European Region 2002–06, fndr sec Sikh Forum (UK), fndr tstee WPO (World Punjabi Orgn) European Region 2002–; exec memb numerous other nat and int orgns; *Books* Asian Directory and Who's Who editions 1–18 (ed, 1975–2005), Asian Observer (ed monthly); *Recreations* gardening, socialising; *Clubs* Rotary Int (Redbridge); *Style—* Jasbir Sachar, Esq; ✉ 47 Beattyville Gardens, Barkingside, Ilford, Essex IG6 1JW (tel 020 8550 3745, fax 020 8551 0990, mobile 07985 141796, e-mail jsachar@asianwhoswho.com)

SACHRAJDA, Prof Christopher Tadeusz Czeslaw; s of Czeslaw Sachrajda (d 1959), and Hanna Teresa, *née* Grabowska; *b* 15 November 1949; *Educ* Finchley Catholic GS London, Univ of Sussex (BSc), Imperial Coll London (PhD); *m* 31 Aug 1974, Irena, da of Antoni Czyzewski, and Antonina Czyzewski; 2 s (Andrew Marian b 22 Sept 1978, Gregory Antoni Czeslaw b 23 Nov 1979), 1 da (Sophie Maria b 31 July 1992); *Career* Harkness fell (for study and travel in USA) Stanford Linear Accelerator Center Stanford Univ 1974–76, fell and staff memb CERN Geneva 1976–79; Dept of Physics and Astronomy Univ of Southampton: lectr 1979–86, sr lectr 1986–88, reader 1988–90, prof 1990–, head of dept 1997–2000; PPARC (formerly SERC): sr fell 1991–96, memb Cncl 1998–2004; CPhys 1989, FInstP 1989, FRS 1996; *Recreations* family activities, tennis, philately (early Polish), walking; *Clubs* Portswood Lawn Tennis; *Style—* Prof Christopher Sachrajda, FRS; ✉ 20 Radway Road, Southampton SO15 7PW (tel 023 8078 4208); School of Physics and Astronomy, University of Southampton, University Road, Highfield, Southampton SO17 1BJ (tel 023 8059 2105, fax 023 8059 5359, e-mail cts@phys.soton.ac.uk)

SACKLOFF, Gail Josephine; da of late Myer Sackloff, of London, and late Rachel, *née* Crivon (niece of late Robert Crivon, Dir of Cultural Affrs, Cncl of Europe, Strasbourg); *b* 15 December 1944; *Educ* Norfolk Coll for Girls Dublin; *Career* Euro import co-ordinator for May Dept Stores USA/Nigel French Fashion Consultancy 1970–78, merchandise mangr Batus Retail 1978–89, UK mktg dir Saks Fifth Ave Stores USA 1989–; dir Mgmnt Cncl Br Fashion Cncl (chm Int Ctee); honoured by UK Fashion Exports in recognition of outstanding export achievement 2004; *Recreations* theatre, boating; *Clubs* Network, Club 2000; *Style—* Ms Gail Sackloff; ✉ Saks Fifth Avenue UK Division, c/o AMC, 47 Great Portland Street, London W1N 5DG (tel 020 7468 0130, fax 020 7468 0132)

SACKMAN, Simon Laurence; s of Bernard Sackman (d 1986), and Mamie, *née* Epstein (d 2003); *b* 16 January 1951; *Educ* St Paul's, Pembroke Coll Oxford (MA); *m* 7 Feb 1982, Donna, da of Hon Solomon Seruya, OBE, of Gibraltar; 3 da (Sarah b 1984, Paloma b 1987, Claire b 1992); *Career* Norton Rose: articled clerk 1974–77, asst slr 1977–83, ptnr 1983–; memb: City of London Slrs Co 1982, Law Soc 1977, Int Bar Assoc 1989; *Recreations* theatre, music, gardening; *Clubs* City Univ, MCC; *Style—* Simon Sackman, Esq; ✉ Norton Rose, 3 More Riverside, London SE1 2AQ (tel 020 7283 6000, fax 020 7283 6500, e-mail simon.sackman@nortonrose.com)

SACKS, John Harvey; s of late Joseph Gerald Sacks, of London, and Yvonne, *née* Clayton; *b* 29 April 1946; *Educ* Perse Sch Cambridge, Univ of London (LLB); *m* 2 Dec 1969, Roberta Judith, da of late Archy Arenson, of Regent's Park, London; 2 da (Deborah b 7 Oct 1972, Rachel b 1 March 1976), 1 s (David b 19 Jan 1981); *Career* chief exec Arenson Group plc 1982–97, chm and md President Office Furniture Ltd, chm Bradley Gp Ltd 1999–, dir Luke Hughes and Co Ltd 1999–2000, md Samas Roneo Ltd 2000–01, md Roneo Systems Furniture Ltd 2001–; pres Fédération Européenne de Meubles de Bureau 1996–97; chm Office Furniture and Filing Mfrs' Assoc (OFFMA) 1990–96, past chm London & SE Furniture Manufacturing Assoc; Liveryman Worshipful Co of Furniture Makers; FCA, FRSA; *Recreations* cycling, chess, bridge, music; *Clubs* Savile; *Style—* John Sacks, Esq; ✉ Barlogan, Priory Drive, Stanmore, Middlesex HA7 3HL; JSA Consultancy Services, Atlas Chambers, Gray's Inn, London WC1R 5EP (tel 020 7269 7986, e-mail john.sacks@jsacs.co.uk, website www.jsacs.co.uk)

SACKS, Chief Rabbi Sir Jonathan Henry; kt (2005); s of late Louis David Sacks, of London, and Louisa, *née* Frumkin; *b* 8 March 1948; *Educ* Christ's Coll Finchley, Gonville & Caius Coll Cambridge (MA), New Coll Oxford, Univ of London (PhD), Jews' Coll London, Yeshivat Etz Hayyim London; *m* 14 July 1970, Elaine, da of Philip Taylor (d 1986); 1 s (Joshua b 1975), 2 da (Dina b 1977, Gila b 1982); *Career* lectr in moral philosophy Middx Poly 1971–73; Jews' Coll London: lectr Jewish philosophy 1973–76, lectr Talmud and Jewish philosophy 1976–82, Chief Rabbi Lord Jakobovits prof (first incumbent) in modern Jewish thought 1982–, dir rabbinic faculty 1983–90, princ 1984–90, Chief Rabbi of the United Hebrew Congregations of the Cwlth 1991–; Sherman Lecture Univ of Manchester 1989, Reith Lecture 1990, Cook Lecture 1997; visiting prof of philosophy Univ of Essex 1989–90; currently visiting prof: of philosophy Hebrew Univ, of theology and religious studies KCL; rabbi: Golders Green Synagogue London 1978–82, Marble Arch Synagogue London 1983–90; editor Le'ela, A Journal of Judaism Today 1985–90; memb CRAC; The Jerusalem Prize 1995; Hon Doctorates: Middlesex 1993, Cambridge 1993, Haifa (Israel) 1996, Liverpool 1997, Yeshiva (NY) 1997, St Andrews 1998, Lambeth 2001, Glasgow 2001; hon fell Gonville & Caius Coll Cambridge 1993, presentation fell KCL 1993; *Books* Torah Studies (1986), Tradition and Transition: Essays Presented to Chief Rabbi Sir Immanuel Jakobovits to Celebrate Twenty Years in Office (1986), Traditional Alternatives (1989), Tradition in an Untraditional Age (1990), The Reith Lectures 1990–, The Persistence of Faith (1991), Orthodoxy Confronts Modernity (ed, 1991), Crisis and Covenant (1992), One People? (1993), Will We Have Jewish Grandchildren? (1994), Community of Faith (1995), Faith in the Future (1995), The Politics of Hope (1997), Morals & Markets (1999), Celebrating Life (2000), A Letter in the Scroll (2000), Radical Then Radical Now (2001), The Dignity of Difference (2002), The Passover Haggadah (2003), From Optimism to Hope (2004), To Heal a Fractured World (2005), New Translation and Commentary of The Authorised Daily Prayer Book (4 edn, 2007); *Recreations* walking; *Style—* Chief Rabbi Sir Jonathan Sacks; ✉ Office of the Chief Rabbi, Adler House, 735 High Road, London N12 0US (tel 020 8343 6301, fax 020 8343 6310, e-mail info@chiefrabbi.org, website www.chiefrabbi.org)

SACKUR, Stephen John; s of Robert Neil Humphrys Sackur, of Spilsby, Lincs, and Sallie, *née* Caley; *b* 9 January 1964; *Educ* King Edward VI GS Spilsby, Emmanuel Coll Cambridge (BA), Harvard Univ (Henry fellowship); *m* May 1992, Zina, da of Saadallah Sabbagh; *Career* BBC: trainee 1986–87, prodr Current Affairs 1987–89, reporter World At One 1989–90, foreign affairs corr 1990–92, Middle East corr 1992–97, Washington corr 1997–2002, Europe corr 2002–05, presenter Hardtalk 2005–; *Books* On the Basra Road (1991); *Recreations* football, cinema, books, walking, day dreaming; *Style—* Stephen Sackur, Esq; ✉ BBC News and Current Affairs, BBC Television Centre, London W12 7RJ

SACKVILLE, Hon Thomas Geoffrey (Tom); yr s of 10 Earl De La Warr, DL (d 1988); *b* 26 October 1950; *Educ* Eton, Lincoln Coll Oxford (BA); *m* 1979, Catherine, da of late Brig James Windsor Lewis; 1 s, 1 da; *Career* formerly merchant banker; MP (Cons) Bolton W 1983–97; PPS to Min of State Treasy 1985–86, PPS to Min of State NI Office 1986–87, PPS to min of state for Social Security 1987–88, an asst Govt whip 1988–89, a Lord Cmmr of the Treasy (Govt whip) 1989–92, jt Parly under-sec of state Dept of Health 1992–95, Parly under-sec of state Home Office 1995–97; dir NewMedia Investors Ltd 1997–2000, chief exec Int Fedn of Health Plans 1998–; tstee Royal Hosp for Neurodisability 2004–; *Style—* Tom Sackville

SACRANIE, Sir Iqbal; kt (2005), OBE (1999); s of Abdul Karim Mussa Sacranie (d 1982), and Mariam Mussa, *née* Osman; *b* 6 September 1951, Malawi; *m* 30 Jan 1976, Yasmin, *née* Ismail; 2 da (Sameena (Mrs Ahmad), Raheena (Mrs Memi)), 3 s (Hamza, Mohammed, Abdul Karim); *Career* early career in accountancy, articled clerk 1972–77; sec gen Muslim Cncl of GB 2002–06 (founding sec gen 1997); dep pres World Memon Orgn 2004–, vice-pres Family Welfare Assoc; chair of tstees: Memon Assoc UK, Balham Mosque, Tooting Islamic Centre, Al Rissala Educn Tst; tstee Muslim Aid; Muslim News Award for Excellence, PM's Good Citizenship award; Hon LLD Leeds Met Univ 2005; FFA 1978; *Recreations* cricket, volleyball, golf; *Style—* Sir Iqbal Sacranie, OBE; ✉ Unit 1, Red Lion Business Park, Red Lion Road, Surbiton, Surrey KT6 7QD

SADEQUE, Shahwar; da of Ali Imam (d 1943), of Bangladesh, and Akhtar Banu; *b* 31 August 1942; *Educ* Dhaka Univ Bangladesh (BSc), Bedford Coll London (MPhil),

S

Kingston Poly (MSc); *m* 7 Oct 1962, Pharhad Sadeque, s of Abdus Sadeque (d 1961); 1 da (Schehrezade b 13 Nov 1963), 1 s (Fahim b 26 Jan 1971); *Career* computer programmer BARIC Services Ltd 1969–73, physics teacher Nonsuch HS for Girls Sutton 1973–84, pt/t res into application of artificial intelligence and vision systems to mfrg processes Kingston Univ (formerly Kingston Poly) 1985–92; educnl and ICT conslt 1997–, special rep of the Secretary of State FCO 1998–; dir TriEs Ltd 1991–; vice-chair Immigration Advsy Serv 2002–07 (memb 2000–02); assoc Hosp mangr SW London and St George's Mental Health NHS Tst 2004– memb: Cmmn for Racial Equality 1989–93, Bd of Govrs BBC 1990–95, Bd Waltham Forest Housing Action Tst 1991–2002, VAT Tbnls of England and Wales 1991–, Income and Corporation Taxes Tbnl 1992–, Sch Curriculum and Assessment Authy 1993–97, Nat Cncl for Educnl Technol 1994–97, Metropolitan Police Ctee 1995–2000, Bd of Govrs Kingston Univ 1995–2002, Cncl C&G 1995–, Marshall Aid Commemoration Cmmn FCO 1998–2004, Panel 2000 FCO 1998, MRC Working Gp for Operational and Ethical Guidelines 1998–2001, RCP Ctee on Ethical Issues in Medicine 1998–, Lord Chancellor's Advsy Cncl on Nat Records and Archives 1999–2004, Dept of Health Good Practice in Consent Advsy Gp 2000–01, Nuffield Cncl on Bioethics Working Party on Healthcare Related Res in Developing Countries 2000–02, Patient Information Advsy Gp Dept of Health 2001–04, Panel of Independent Persons UCL 2003–, patient and carer network RCP 2004–07; govr of Tstees Research into Ageing 1998–2001; tstee: Windsor Leadership Tst 1998–2005; involved with community work for the elderly and charity fundraising (Oxfam and UNICEF); formerly: memb various Cons Pty bodies incl Cons Women's Nat Ctee and Bow Gp Educn Standing Ctee, govr Riverview Co First Sch; voluntary worker St George's Hosp Tooting; MBCS 1991, FRSA 1994–2000; *Publications* papers: Education and Ethnic Minorities (1988), Manufacturing - Towards the 21st Century (1988), A Knowledge-Based System for Sensor Interaction and Real-Time Component Control (1988); *Recreations* collecting thimbles and perfume bottles, cooking Indian-style, keeping up-to-date with current affairs; *Style*— Mrs Shahwar Sadeque

SADGROVE, Very Rev Michael; s of Ralph Sadgrove, of London, and Doreen, *née* Leyser; *b* 13 April 1950; *Educ* UCS London, Balliol Coll Oxford (MA), Trinity Theol Coll Bristol; *m* 1974, Elizabeth Jennifer, *née* Suddes; 3 da (Joanna Elizabeth Marie b 1977, Philippa Thomasin Jane b 1979, Eleanor Jemima Clare b 1983), 1 s (Aidan Mark Daniel b 1982); *Career* ordained: deacon 1975, priest 1976; licensed to officiate Rural Deanery of Cowley 1975–77; Salisbury and Wells Theol Coll: lectr in Old Testament studies 1977–82, vice-princ 1980–82; hon vicar-choral Salisbury Cathedral 1978–82, vicar Alnwick Northumberland 1982–87, canon residentiary, precentor and vice-provost Coventry Cathedral 1987–95, provost of Sheffield 1995–2000, dean of Sheffield 2000–03, dean of Durham 2003–; memb Cathedrals Fabric Cmmn for England 1996–2006; Bishops' sr inspr of theol colls and courses 1982–; chm: Precentors' Conf of England and Wales 1991–94, Sheffield Common Purpose Advsy Gp 1996–99, Univ of Durham Ethics Advsy Ctee 2004–; memb Soc for Old Testament Studies 1978; memb Gen Synod of the Church of England 2003–; visitor St Chad's Coll Durham 2003–; memb Cncl: Univ of Durham 2003–, St John's Coll Durham 2003–, Coll of St Hild and St Bede Durham 2004–, Hatfield Coll Durham 2004–; pres St Cuthbert's Hospice Durham 2003–; FRSA 1997; *Books* A Picture of Faith (1995); contrib: Studia Biblica (1978), Lion Handbook of the World's Religions (1982, 2 edn 1994), Reflecting the Word (1989), Rethinking Marriage (1993), Coventry's First Cathedral (1994), The Care Guide (1995), Calling Time (2000), Dreaming Spires? (2006), The Eight Words of Jesus (2006); articles and reviews in theol jls; *Recreations* music, the arts, poetry and classical literature, walking the north-east of England, railways and trams, travels in Burgundy, European issues; *Clubs* Royal Over-Seas League; *Style*— The Very Rev Michael Sadgrove, Dean of Durham; ✉ The Deanery, Durham DH1 3EQ (tel 0191 384 7500, e-mail michael.sadgrove@durhamcathedral.co.uk)

SADLER, Ven Anthony Graham; s of Frank Sadler, of Sutton Coldfield, and Hannah, *née* Luckock; *b* 1 April 1936; *Educ* Bishop Veseys GS Sutton Coldfield, The Queen's Coll Oxford (MA), Lichfield Theol Coll; *Career* ordained: deacon 1962, priest 1963; curate St Chad Burton-upon-Trent 1962–65; vicar of: All Saints Rangemore and St Mary Dunstall 1965–72, St Nicholas Abbots Bromley 1972–79, St Michael Pelsall 1979–90; rural dean of Walsall 1982–90, priest i/c Bramshall, Gratwich, Checkley, Stramshall, Marchington, Marchington Woodlands and Kingstone 1990–97, priest i/c Leigh 1992–97, rector of Uttoxeter 1997 (priest i/c 1990–97), archdeacon of Walsall 1997–2004 (archdeacon emeritus 2004–), hon canon of Lichfield Cathedral 1997– (prebendary of Whittington 1987–97); *Recreations* music; *Style*— The Ven Anthony Sadler; ✉ Llldiant Newydd, Llanrhaeadr-ym-Mochnant, Oswestry SY10 0ED

SADLER, Brent Roderick; s of Philip Sadler (d 1996), and Ruth, *née* Dunkerley (d 1996); *b* 29 November 1950; *Educ* Royal Masonic Sch Bushey; *m* 15 Nov 2003, Dr Jelena Anicic; from previous marriages 2 s, 2 da; *Career* news reporter; formerly with: Harrow Observer, Reading Evening Post, Southern TV, Westward TV and HTV Bristol; ITN 1981–91 (ME corr 1986–91); assignments covered incl: hunger strikes Maze Prison Belfast 1981, Falklands war 1982, Israeli invasion of Lebanon 1982, Lebanese civil war 1981–89, Sabra and Chatila massacres 1983, US invasion of Grenada 1986, siege of Bourj al Barajneh Beirut 1987, Iran-Iraq war 1983–88, Gulf war 1991; sr int corr CNN (Lebanon) 1991–; assignments covered incl: release of Western hostages Beirut 1991, post-war Iraq (incl US missile strikes 1993), Somalia famine 1992–93, Bosnia Herzegovina 1993–96, PLO-Israeli peace agreement 1993, South African elections 1994, US intervention in Haiti 1994, Chechnya rebellion 1995–97, Israeli 'Grapes of Wrath' offensive against Lebanon 1996, death of Diana, Princess of Wales 1997, showdown in Iraq 1997, Kosovo 1998–99, NATO strikes on Yugoslavia 1999; bureau chief CNN Beirut 1997–; winner: Middx Co Press Journalist of the Year 1971, RTS Regional News Award 1980, RTS Int News Award 1987, BAFTA Awards (with ITN team) for Quality of Coverage from Lebanon 1983 and Best Actuality Coverage of Gulf War 1992, Emmy (US) for Somalia 1993, Overseas Press Club of America Award for Meritorious Reporting in Lebanon 1996, Cable Ace Award for Coverage of Russian Elections 1996; *Recreations* fly fishing, skiing, tennis, sailing; *Style*— Brent Sadler, Esq; ✉ Turner House, c/o CNNI, PO Box 2012, London W1A 2GX (tel +961 1 970300 or +961 3 437148)

SADLER, (Arthur) Edward; s of Arthur William Sadler (d 1969), and Hilda, *née* Suckling (d 1984); *b* 27 October 1947; *Educ* Adams' GS Newport, UC Oxford (MA), Coll of Law; *m* 1980, Patricia, da of Charles Cooper; 1 s (Matthew b 19 July 1981); *Career* articled clerk Farrer & Co 1971–73; ptnr: (specialising in corp tax) Clifford-Turner 1977 (joined Dept of Corp Tax 1973), Clifford Chance (following merger of Clifford-Turner and Coward Chance) 1987–97; memb: Corp Tax Sub Ctee of Revenue Ctee Law Soc, Revenue Ctee City of London Solicitors' Co 1978–97, Tax Ctee Int Bar Assoc 1980–97; dep special cmmr of Income Tax 2002–; Freeman Worshipful Co of Haberdashers 1974; memb: City of London Solicitors' Co, Law Soc, Int Bar Assoc; *Books* Equipment Leasing (with S C Reisbach and Marian Thomas, loose-leaf edn 1993); *Recreations* gardening, opera, hill walking, occasional sailing, Christian activities, 20th Century history; *Style*— Edward Sadler, Esq; ✉ Clifford Chance, 10 Upper Bank Street, London E14 5JJ (tel 020 7600 1000, fax 020 7006 1000)

SAFINIA, Dr Khosrow; s of Gholam-Reza Safinia (d 1951), and Mehrvash, *née* Mostofi (d 1999); *b* 18 April 1941; *Educ* Gosforth GS, Sutherland Dental Sch, King's Coll Durham (BDS, LDS RCS, DOrth RCS); *m* 9 April 1973, Dr Shirin Safinia, da of Mohammed-Ali Javad-Shahidi; 2 s (Farhad b 25 July 1975, Bahram b 3 March 1977); *Career* dental surgn, specialist in orthodontics; house offr Middx Hosp 1967–68, SHO Royal Dental Hosp and St George's Hosp 1968–69, orthodontic course Eastman Dental Hosp Inst of Postgraduate Dental Surgery 1969–70, registrar in orthodontics Eastman Dental Hosp 1970–72, Tweed fndn course Tucson AZ 1972; private practice: Tehran 1973–84, Harley St London 1984–; assoc prof of orthodontics Univ of Tehran 1973–79, sr dental offr Croydon HA 1984–90, clinical lectr Eastman Dental Hosp Inst of Postgrad Dental Surgery 1990–; memb: American Assoc of Orthodontics 1971, Br Orthodontic Soc, Specialist Register GDC; fndr memb Iranian Assoc of Orthodontics 1974; fell: Pierre Fauchard Acad 1996, World Fedn of Orthodontists; *Recreations* skiing, mountain hikes, classical music, photography; *Style*— Dr Khosrow Safinia; ✉ 128 Harley Street, London W1G 7JT (tel 020 7935 8811, fax 020 7935 8191)

SAGE, John George Patrick; s of Austin Sage, and Pauline, *née* Hussey; *Educ* Princethorpe Coll, Univ of Reading (BA); *m*; 1 s, 2 da; *Career* news ed Brighton Evening Argus 1993–95, asst news ed UK News 1995–96; Teletext Ltd: asst ed 1997–98, exec ed 1998–99, ed-in-chief 2000–; memb Soc of Editors 2000–; *Recreations* my family, squash, tennis, golf; *Style*— John Sage, Esq; ✉ Teletext Ltd, 101 Farm Lane, Fulham, London SW6 1QJ (tel 020 7386 3647, fax 020 7385 0348, e-mail johns@teletext.co.uk)

SAGE, Morley William; OBE (1984); s of William George Sage (d 1968), of Worle, Weston-super-Mare, and Grace Graves, *née* Smith (d 1977); *b* 15 January 1930; *Educ* Blundell's, Emmanuel Coll Cambridge (MA); *m* 30 April 1955, Enid Muriel, da of Herbert Sim Hirst (d 1987); 2 da (Caroline b 1957, Fiona b 1960), 1 s (Morley b 1962); *Career* chartered electrical engr and conslt; lab and energy mangr Corporate Lab ICI plc 1962–75, dir computing serv Univ of Southampton 1975–88, princ conslt Systems Technol Conslt 1980–2001; visiting fell Clare Hall Cambridge 1967–69 (life fell 1986); memb Univ Grants Technol Sub-Ctee 1974–79 (Computer Systems and Electronics Bd 1973–77); chm: Data Communications Protocol Steering Ctee CSERB 1977–81, Inter Univ Ctee on Computing 1983–85, Integrated Prodn Systems SERC 1975–76, Control Engrg Ctee SERC 1974–79 (memb Computing Sci Ctee 1976–79), N/SVQ Forum Engrg Cncl, Industrial Advsy Ctee Univ of Exeter 1995–2000; dep chm Resources and Methods Ctee ESRC 1982–85; vice-pres IEE 1984–88; memb: Br Computer Soc 1967, Inst of Measurement and Control 1977 (memb Cncl 1967–71); FIEE 1972, FREng 1987, FBCS, FInstMC; *Recreations* reading, gardening, caravanning, DIY, model railways; *Clubs* Royal Cwlth Soc; *Style*— Morley Sage, Esq, OBE, FREng; ✉ Wiltown Place, Wiltown, Curry Rivel, Langport, Somerset TA10 0HZ (tel 01458 251407, e-mail morley.sage@ukgateway.net)

SAGGAR, Prof Shamit; s of Krishan Dev Saggar, of Nairobi, Kenya, and Kamala, *née* Bhakoo (d 1974); *b* 14 August 1963; *Educ* Finchley Manorhill Sch, Univ of Essex (BA, PhD); *m* 23 July 1988, Rita Alfred; 3 c (Shelley b 1994, Shaan b 1998, Symran b 2001); *Career* early academic appts at Univ of Essex and Univ of Liverpool, reader in political behaviour Univ of London until 2001, seconded as sr policy advsr PM's Strategy Unit Cabinet Office 2001–03, prof of political sci Univ of Sussex 2004–; visiting appts: Yale Univ, UCLA, ANU, Univ of Western Aust, NYU; chm Legal Complaints Serv Law Soc 2005–, cmmr Better Regulation Cmmn 2006–; non-exec dir: FSA, NCC, Whittington Hosp NHS Tst, Ethics Standards Bd Accountancy Fndn; cmmr: RSA Migration Cmmn, Ind Asylum Cmmn 2006–; sometime conslt to Hansard Soc, Age Concern England, Cmmn for Racial Equality, Cwlth Cmmn on Respect and Understanding, BBC, Carlton Television and numerous UK and int govt depts; memb Advsy Cncl: Global Britons Prog Foreign Policy Centre, Inst for Citizenship, RNIB; memb Customer Impact Panel ABI 2006–; sr advsr Foreign Policy Centre and European Inclusion Index Br Cncl; govr Peabody Tst; Stein Rokkan postgrad fell 1988, Menzies fell 1992 and 1997, Harkness fell 1993, John Adams fell 2000, Yale world fell 2003–04; FRSA; *Books* incl: Race and Representation (2000), Pariah Politics (2008); *Recreations* travel, cooking, tennis, the company of my children; *Clubs* Cwlth; *Style*— Prof Shamit Saggar; ✉ c/o The Legal Complaints Service, Victoria Court, 8 Dormer Place, Leamington Spa, Warwickshire CV34 5AE (tel 01926 822186, e-mail s.saggar@sussex.ac.uk)

SAIDI, Samira Miriam (Sam); da of Hussein Ahmed Saidi, of Manchester, and Elizabeth Anne, *née* Bradshaw; *b* 8 July 1961; *Educ* Bush Davies Schs (ARAD), Royal Ballet Sch; *m* 28 Feb 1987, Alain Jacques Luis Dubreuil, s of Jacques E Dubreuil (d 1989), of Monaco; 2 s (Téo Jacques b April 1993, Louis Frederick b Jan 1996); *Career* dancer Birmingham Royal Ballet (formerly Sadler's Wells Royal Ballet) 1979– (currently first soloist); roles created incl: title role in David Bintley's The Snow Queen, Sybil Vane in The Picture of Dorian Gray, Giselle, Les Sylphides, Alice in Hobson's Choice, Kenneth Macmillan's Quartet, Odette/Odile in Swan Lake, and many other princ roles in co's repertoire; recreated second movement in Massine's Choreartium; ret dancing 1998; currently teacher: Dance Track prog Educ Dept Birmingham Royal Ballet, Royal Ballet Sch (teaching jr assocs); also choreographer Nat Youth Ballet; *Recreations* theatre, interior design, antiques; *Style*— Miss Samira Saidi; ✉ The Birmingham Royal Ballet, Birmingham Hippodrom, Thorp Street, Birmingham B5 4AU (tel 0121 622 2555, fax 0121 622 5038)

SAIL, Lawrence Richard; s of Gustav Hellmut Sail, and Barbara, *née* Wright; *b* 29 October 1942, London; *Educ* Sherborne, St John's Coll Oxford (open scholar, Trevelyan scholar, BA); *m* 1, 1965 (m dis 1981), Teresa Luke; 1 s (Matthew Charles b Feb 1972), 1 da (Erica Jocelyn b April 1974); m 2, 1994, Helen Bird; 2 da (Rose Arlette, Grace Romola (twins) b June 2003); *Career* admin offr ILEA then Planning Dept GLC 1965–66, head of modern languages Lenana Sch Nairobi 1966–70, freelance writer 1971–73 and 1991–; teacher of French and German: Millfield Sch 1973–74, Blundell's Sch 1976–80 (visiting writer 1980–81), Exeter Sch 1982–91; course tutor and guest reader Arvon Fndn 1978– (chm 1990–94), participant WH Smith Poets in Schs Scheme 1978–, prog dir Cheltenham Festival of Literature 1991, judge Whitbread Book of the Year Awards 1991, memb jury European Literature Prize 1994–96, co-dir 50th Anniversary Cheltenham Festival of Literature 1999; visited for Br Cncl: India 1993, Egypt 1996, Bosnia 1996, Ukraine 1999, Portugal 2006 and 2007; participant: Anglo-French Poetry Festival Paris 1993, Trois Rivières Poetry Festival Quebec 2003, Medellín Int Poetry Festival Colombia 2004; poems broadcast on BBC radio and TV; compiler and presenter: Time for Verse series (BBC Radio 4), edition of Poetry Now (BBC Radio 3); Hawthornden fell 1992, Writer's Bursary Arts Cncl 1993, Cholmondeley Award 2004; memb SCR St John's Coll Oxford; FRSL 1998; *Poetry* Opposite Views (1974), The Drowned River (1978), The Kingdom of Atlas (1980), Devotions (1987), Aquamarine (1988), Out of Land: New & Selected Poems (1992), Building into Air (1995), The World Returning (2002), Eye-Baby (2006); *Other Works* Children in Hospital (with Teresa Sail, 1974), Death of an Echo (radio play, 1980), Cross-currents (essays, 2005); as contrib: Mind Readings, Sightlines (short stories), work in numerous anthologies incl Palgrave's Golden Treasury and The Oxford Book of Christmas Poems; poems, reviews, articles and essays in various periodicals and newspapers; as ed: First and Always: Poems for Great Ormond Street Children's Hospital (1988), South West Review (1980–85), South West Review: A Celebration (1985), 100 Voices (1989); The New Exeter Book of Riddles (ed with Kevin Crossley-Holland, 1999), Light Unlocked: Christmas Card Poems (with Kevin Crossley-Holland, 2005); *Style*— Lawrence Sail, Esq; ✉ Richmond Villa, 7 Wonford Road, Exeter EX2 4LF

SAINSBURY, Jeffrey Paul; s of Walter Ronald Sainsbury, of Cardiff, and Joan Margaret, *née* Slamin (d 1974); *b* 27 June 1943; *Educ* Cardiff HS; *m* 1967, Janet Elizabeth; 1 s (Mark Christopher Paul b 1968), 1 da (Emma Louise b 1971); *Career* qualified CA 1966, md Exchange Registrars Ltd (part of Pannell Kerr Forster) 1994–2000, exec vice-pres Computershare Ltd 2000–; memb: Cardiff City Cncl 1969–96 (Dep Lord Mayor 1977–78,

Lord Mayor 1991–92), S Glamorgan CC 1973–76, S Glamorgan HA 1988–90; chm: Cardiff New Theatre 1984–89, S Glamorgan TEC 1994–99, SE Wales TEC 1999–2000; memb Bd Cardiff Bay Devpt Corp 1991–2000; govr Welsh Coll of Music and Drama 1992–2001; FRSA; OStJ; *Recreations* theatre, music, sport; *Clubs* Cardiff and County; *Style*— Jeffrey Sainsbury, Esq; ✉ 6 Druidstone House, Druidstone Road, St Mellons, Cardiff CF3 6XF (tel 01633 680397); Computershare Ltd, 68 Upper Thames Street, London EC4V 3BJ (tel 0870 703 6044, fax 0870 703 0351, mobile 07787 154477, e-mail jeff.sainsbury@computershare.com)

SAINSBURY, Prof (Richard) Mark; *b* 2 July 1943; *Educ* CCC Oxford (scholar, MA, DPhil); *Career* Radcliffe lectr in philosophy Magdalen Coll Oxford 1968–70, lectr in philosophy St Hilda's Coll Oxford 1970–73, Radcliffe lectr in philosophy BNC Oxford 1973–75, lectr in philosophy Univ of Essex 1975–78, lectr in philosophy Bedford Coll London 1978–84 (actg head of Philosophy Dept 1981–84); KCL: lectr in philosophy 1984–87, reader 1987–89, head Dept of Philosophy 1988–95, Susan Stebbing prof of philosophy 1989–; prof Philosophy Dept Univ of Texas at Austin 2002–; visiting research fell ANU 1992, Wittgenstein lectr and visiting prof Bayreuth Univ 1994, Leverhulme sr res fell 2000–02; ed MIND 1990–2000; currently tstee Philosophy in Britain; FBA 1998; *Books* Russell (1979), Paradoxes (1988, 2 edn 1995), Logical Forms (1991, 2 edn 2000), Departing from Frege (2002), Reference Without Referents (2005); also author of numerous articles and reviews in learned jls; *Style*— Prof Mark Sainsbury, FBA; ✉ Department of Philosophy, University of Texas at Austin, Austin, TX 78712, USA (tel 00 1 512 471 5433, e-mail marksainsbury@mail.utexas.edu)

SAINSBURY, Roger Norman; s of Cecil Charles Sainsbury (d 1989), of Hitchin, Herts, and Ivy Evelyn, *née* Pettengell (d 2000); *b* 11 June 1940; *Educ* Eton, Keble Coll Oxford (MA); *m* 16 May 1969, Susan Margaret, da of Henry William Higgs (d 1981); *Career* chartered civil engr; dir: John Mowlem & Co plc 1982–95, Greater Manchester Metro Ltd 1990–95, UK Detention Services Ltd 1991–95; non-exec chm Thomas Telford Ltd 1993–99; advsr to DG of Water Servs 1998–2000; memb Regulatory Policy Ctee Office of Water Services 2000–02; memb Advsy Bd Dept of Engrg Science Univ of Oxford 2000–04; pres Inst of Civil Engrs 1999 (vice-pres 1996–98); memb Cncl CIRIA 1997–2000 (vice-pres 1999–2000); awarded Inst of Civil Engrs: George Stephenson Medal, Reed and Mallik Medal, Parkman Medal; pres Keble Assoc 2000–04; FREng 1986, Hon IFASCE; *Recreations* European orchids, gardening, theatre; *Style*— Roger Sainsbury, Esq, FREng; ✉ 88 Dukes Avenue, Muswell Hill, London N10 2QA

SAINSBURY, Rt Hon Sir Timothy Alan Davan; kt (1995), PC (1992); yst s (by 1 m) of Baron Sainsbury; *b* 11 June 1932; *Educ* Eton, Worcester Coll Oxford (MA); *m* 26 April 1961, Susan Mary, da of late Brig James Alastair Harry Mitchell, CBE, DSO; 2 s (James b 1962, Alexander b 1968), 2 da (Camilla b 1962, Jessica b 1970); *Career* dir J Sainsbury plc 1962–83 and 1995–99 (non-exec), MP (Cons) Hove 1973–97; PPS to: Sec of State for the Environment 1979–83, Sec of State for Defence 1983; asst Govt whip 1983–85, a Lord Cmmr of the Treasy (Govt whip) 1985–87, Parly under sec of state for defence procurement at MOD 1987–89, Parly under sec of state FCO 1989–90, min of state for trade DTI 1990–92, min of state for industry DTI 1992–94; chm Somerset House Tst 1997–2002; non-exec chm: Pendennis Shipyard (Holdings) Ltd 1999–2007, Marlborough Tiles Ltd 1999–; memb: Cncl RSA 1981–83, Bd of Govrs Westminster Fndn for Democracy 1994–97; nat chm Cons Friends of Israel 1995–97 (pres 1997–2005); visitor Ashmolean Museum Oxford 2001–06, tstee V&A 2003–; Liveryman Worshipful Co of Vintners; hon fell Worcester Coll Oxford 1982; Hon FRICS, Hon FRIBA; *Style*— The Rt Hon Sir Timothy Sainsbury

SAINSBURY OF PRESTON CANDOVER, Baron (Life Peer UK 1989), of Preston Candover in the County of Hampshire; Sir John Davan Sainsbury; KG (1992), kt (1980); eldest s (by 1 m) of late Baron Sainsbury (Life Peer), of Drury Lane; *b* 2 November 1927; *Educ* Stowe, Worcester Coll Oxford; *m* 8 March 1963, Anya (Anya Linden, the Royal Ballet ballerina), da of George Charles Eltenton; 2 s, 1 da; *Career* J Sainsbury plc: dir 1958–92, vice-chm 1967–69, chm 1969–92, pres 1992–; dir The Economist 1972–80; chm Royal Opera House Covent Garden 1987–91 (dir 1969–85), dir Royal Opera House Tst 1974–84 and 1987–97, chm of tstees Royal Opera House Endowment Fund 2001–05; memb Cncl of Friends of Covent Garden 1969–91 (chm 1969–81); tstee: Nat Gallery 1976–83, Westminster Abbey Tst 1977–83, Tate Gallery 1982–83, Rhodes Tst 1984–98, Saïd Business Sch Fndn 2003–; jt hon treas Euro Movement 1972–75; pres: Br Retail Consortium 1993–97 (memb Cncl 1975–79), Sparsholt Coll 1993–2000; memb President's Ctee CBI 1982–84; vice-patron Contemporary Arts Soc 1984– (hon sec 1965–71, vice-chm 1971–74); a dir Friends of Nelson Mandela Children's Fund 1996–2000; chm Benesh Inst of Choreology 1986–87, chm of govrs Royal Ballet 1995–2003 (govr 1987–); govr Royal Ballet Sch 1965–76 and 1987–91, dir Rambert Sch of Ballet and Contemporary Dance 2003–05; visitor Ashmolean Museum 2003–, patron Dulwich Picture Gallery 2004– (chm of tstees 1994–2000), patron Sir Harold Hillier Gardens and Arboretum 2005–; memb Jt Parly Scrutiny Ctee on Draft Charities Bill 2004–05; Albert Medal RSA 1989; hon bencher Inner Temple 1985; hon fell Worcester Coll Oxford 1982, hon fell British Sch at Rome 2002; Hon DScEcon Univ of London 1985, Hon DLitt South Bank Univ 1992, Hon LLD Univ of Bristol 1993, hon DScEcon (hc) Univ of Cape Town 2000; FIGD 1973, Hon FRIBA 1993; *Clubs* Garrick, Beefsteak; *Style*— The Rt Hon Lord Sainsbury of Preston Candover, KG

SAINSBURY OF TURVILLE, Baron (Life Peer UK 1997), of Turville in the County of Buckinghamshire; David John Sainsbury; s of late Sir Robert Sainsbury; *b* 24 October 1940; *Educ* King's Coll Cambridge, Columbia Grad Sch of Business NY (MBA); *Career* J Sainsbury plc: joined 1963, dir 1966–98, fin controller 1971–73, fin dir 1973–90, dep chm 1988–92, chm 1992–98; chm Savacentre Ltd 1984–93, dir Shaw's Supermarkets Inc 1983–95; Parly under sec of state for science and innovation DTI 1998–2006; chm Governing Body London Business Sch 1991–98, chm Transition Bd Univ for Industry 1998–99; visiting fell Nuffield Coll Oxford 1987–95, memb Cmmn on Public Policy and Br Business IPPR 1995–97; tstee SDP 1982–90 (memb Steering Ctee 1981–82); Columbia Business Sch Award for Distinguished Leadership in Business 1990; hon fell LBS 1990, Hon LLD Univ of Cambridge 1997; Hon FREng 1994; *Publications* Government and Industry - A New Partnership (Fabian Soc), Wealth Creation and Jobs (with Christopher Smallwood, Public Policy Centre); *Style*— Lord Sainsbury of Turville; ✉ House of Lords, London SW1A 0BW (tel 020 7219 3000)

SAINT, (Prof) Andrew John; s of Rev Arthur James Maxwell Saint, and Elisabeth Yvetta, *née* Butterfield; *b* 30 November 1946; *Educ* Christ's Hosp, Balliol Coll Oxford (BA), Warburg Inst Univ of London (MPhil); *Career* teacher Univ of Essex 1971–74, architectural ed The Survey of London 1974–86, historian English Heritage 1986–95, prof of architecture Univ of Cambridge 1995–2006, gen ed Survey of London English Heritage 2006–; Alice Davis Hitchcock Medallion Soc of Architectural Historians (GB) 1978 and 1989; Hon FRIBA; *Books* Richard Norman Shaw (1976), The Image of the Architect (1983), Towards A Social Architecture (1986); *Style*— Andrew Saint, Esq; ✉ 14 Denny Crescent, London SE11 4UY (tel 020 7735 3863)

ST ALBANS, Bishop of 1995–; Rt Rev Christopher William Herbert; s of Walter Meredith Herbert, of Coleford, Glos, and Hilda Lucy, *née* Dibbin (d 1948); *b* 7 January 1944; *Educ* Monmouth, St David's UC Lampeter (BA, Badminton colours), Univ of Bristol (PGCE), Wells Theological Coll, Univ of Leicester (MPhil); *m* 27 July 1968, Janet Elizabeth, da of Eric Turner, of Headingley, Leeds; 2 s (Robin William b 1970, James Kimbell b 1973); *Career* curate St Paul's Tupsley and asst master Bishop's Sch Hereford 1967–71, dir of educn Diocese of Hereford 1976–81 (advsr in religious educn 1971–76), prebendary Hereford Cathedral 1977–81, vicar St Thomas on the Bourne Farham Surrey 1981–90, dir of post-ordination trg Diocese of Guildford 1983–90, hon canon Guildford Cathedral 1985–95, archdeacon of Dorking 1990–95; memb House of Lords 1999–; national chm: Hosp Chaplaincies Cncl, Cncl of Christians and Jews; Hon DLitt Univ of Hertfordshire 2003; *Books* The New Creation (1971), A Place to Dream (1976), St Paul's: a Place to Dream (1981), The Edge of Wonder (1981), Listening to Children (1983), On the Road (1984), Be Thou My Vision (1985), This Most Amazing Day (1986), Ways Into Prayer (1987), The Question of Jesus (1987), Alive to God (1987), Help in Your Bereavement (1988), Prayers for Children (1993), Pocket Prayers (1993), The Prayer Garden (1994), Words of Comfort (1994), Pocket Prayers for Children (1999), Pocket Words of Comfort (2004); *Recreations* walking, music, cycling, gardening; *Style*— The Rt Rev the Lord Bishop of St Albans; ✉ Abbey Gate House, Abbey Mill Lane, St Albans, Hertfordshire AL3 4HD

ST ALBANS, 14 Duke of (E 1684); Murray de Vere Beauclerk; also Baron Hedington and Earl of Burford (E 1676), Baron Vere of Hanworth (GB 1750); Hereditary Grand Falconer and Hereditary Registrar of Court of Chancery; s of 13 Duke of St Albans, OBE (d 1988), and his 1 w, Nathalie Chatham (d 1985), da of Percival Walker; gggggs of 1 Duke of St Albans, who was natural s of King Charles II and Eleanor (Nell) Gwynn; *b* 19 January 1939; *Educ* Tonbridge; *m* 1, 1963 (m dis 1974), Rosemary Frances, o da of Francis Harold Scoones, MRCS, LRCP, JP; 1 da (Lady Emma Caroline de Vere (Lady Emma Smellie) b 22 July 1963), 1 s (Charles Francis Topham de Vere, Earl of Burford b 22 Feb 1965); m 2, 1974 (m dis 2001), Cynthia Theresa Mary (d 2002), da of late Lt-Col William James Holdsworth Howard, DSO, and former w of late Sir Anthony Robin Maurice Hooper, 2 Bt; m 3, 2002, Gillian Anita, da of late Lt-Col Cyril George Reginald Northam, and wid of Philip Nesfield Roberts; *Heir* s, Earl of Burford (Charles Beauclerk, *qv*); *Career* chartered accountant; Govr-Gen Royal Stuart Soc, pres Beaufort Opera, patron Bestwood Male Voice Choir; Freeman City of London, Liveryman Worshipful Co of Drapers; FCA; *Style*— His Grace the Duke of St Albans; ✉ 16 Ovington Street, London SW3 2JB

ST ALDWYN, 3 Earl (UK 1915); Sir Michael Henry Hicks Beach; 11 Bt (E 1619); also Viscount St Aldwyn (UK 1906), Viscount Quenington (UK 1915); s of 2 Earl St Aldwyn, GBE, TD, PC (d Jan 1992), and Diana Mary Christian, *née* Mills (d July 1992); *b* 7 February 1950; *Educ* Eton, Univ of Oxford (MA); *m* 1, 1982, Gilda Maria, o da of Barão Saavedra (d 1984), and Baronesa Saavedra, of Ipanema, Brazil; 2 da (Lady Atalanta Maria b 1983, Lady Aurora Ursula b 1988); m 2, 2005, Mrs Louise Wigan; *Heir* bro, Hon David Hicks Beach; *Career* dir The Rank Fndn; Liveryman Worshipful Co of Mercers; *Clubs* Leander, White's, Pratt's; *Style*— The Rt Hon the Earl St Aldwyn; ✉ Williamstrip Park, Coln St Aldwyns, Cirencester GL7 5AT (tel 01285 750226, fax 01285 750463); International Fund Marketing (UK) Ltd, 5th Floor - Suite 7A, Berkeley Square House, Berkeley Square, London W1J 6BY (tel 020 7616 7400, fax 020 7616 7411, e-mail mstaldwyn@infunmar.com)

ST ANDREWS, Earl of; George Philip Nicholas Windsor; er s and h of HRH The Duke of Kent, KG, GCMG, GCVO (*see Royal Family Section*); *b* 26 June 1962; *Educ* Eton, Downing Coll Cambridge; *m* 9 Jan 1988, Sylvana Palma (b 28 May 1957), da of Max(imilian) Karl Tomaselli and Josiane Preschez; 1 s (Edward Edmund Maximilian George, Lord Downpatrick b 2 Dec 1988), 2 da (Lady Marina-Charlotte Alexandra Katharine Helen b 30 Sept 1992, Lady Amelia Sophia Theodora Mary Margaret b 24 Aug 1995); *Heir* s, Lord Downpatrick; *Career* attached FCO 1987–88, Christie's 1996–98; chm: GB-Sasakawa Fndn 2005– (tstee 1995–), Golden Web Fndn 2006–; tstee SOS Children's Villages (UK) 1998; patron: Assoc for Int Cancer Research 1995–, The Princess Margarita of Romania Tst 1997–, Prince George Galitzine Meml Library 2005–; *Style*— Earl of St Andrews

ST ANDREWS AND EDINBURGH, Archbishop of (RC) 1985–; His Eminence Cardinal Keith Michael Patrick O'Brien; s of Mark Joseph O'Brien, DSM (d 1988), of Edinburgh, and Alice Mary, *née* Moriarty (d 1955); *b* 17 March 1938; *Educ* St Patrick's HS Dumbarton, Holy Cross Acad Edinburgh, Univ of Edinburgh (BSc), St Andrew's Coll Drygrange, Moray House Coll of Educn (Dip Ed); *Career* ordained priest 1965, ordained bishop 1985, cr Cardinal Priest of the title SS Joachim and Anne ad Tusculanum 2003; asst priest: Holy Cross Parish Edinburgh 1965–66, St Bride's Cowdenbeath 1966–71 (sch chaplain and teacher St Columba's Secdy Sch Dunfermline), St Patrick's Parish Kilsyth 1972–75, St Mary's Bathgate 1975–78; spiritual dir St Andrew's Coll Drygrange 1978–80, rector St Mary's Coll Blairs 1980–85; Apostolic Administrator of the Diocese of Argyll and the Isles 1996–99; Hon LLD Univ of Antigonish Nova Scotia 2004, Hon DD St Andrews Univ 2004, Hon DD Univ of Edinburgh 2004; Grand Prior of the Scottish Lieutenancy of the Order 2001, Knight of the Grand Cross Order of the Holy Sepulchre of Jerusalem 2003 (Knight Cdr with Star Equestrian 1991), Bailiff Grand Cross of Honour and Devotion Sovereign Military Order of Malta 2005 (Grand Cross Conventual chaplain1985); *Recreations* music, hill walking; *Style*— His Eminence the Cardinal Archbishop of St Andrews and Edinburgh; ✉ Archbishop's House, 42 Greenhill Gardens, Edinburgh EH10 4BJ (tel 0131 447 3337, fax 0131 447 0816, e-mail cardinal@staned.org.uk)

ST ASAPH, Bishop of 1999–; Rt Rev John Stewart Davies; s of John Edward Davies (d 1991), and Dorothy Stewart, *née* Jones; *b* 28 February 1943; *Educ* St John's Sch Leatherhead, Univ of Wales Bangor (BA), Queens' Coll Cambridge (MLitt); *m* Joan; 2 s (John Reuben b 1970, Matthew William b 1973); *Career* curate Hawarden 1974–78, vicar Rhosymedre 1978–87, vicar Mold 1987–90, archdeacon of St Asaph 1991–99; *Publications* Bible Reading Fellowship Study Notes (contrib); *Style*— The Rt Rev the Bishop of St Asaph; ✉ Esgobty, St Asaph, Denbighshire LL17 0TW (tel 01745 583503)

ST AUBIN de TERAN, Lisa Gioconda; da of Cuthbert Jan Alwin Rynveld Carew, of Guyana, and Joan Mary St Aubin (d 1981); *b* 2 October 1953; *Educ* James Allen's Girls' Sch Dulwich; *m* 1, 1970, Jaime Cesar Terán Mejia Cifuentes Terán; 1 da (Iseult Joanna Teran St Aubin (Mrs Iseult Terán Ysenburg) b 5 May 1973); m 2, 1982, George Mann Macbeth; 1 s (Alexander Morton George Macbeth b 30 Sept 1982); m 3, 1989, Robbie Charles Duff-Scott, s of Frederick Duff-Scott (d 1989); 1 da (Florence Cameron Alexandra Rose Duff-Scott b 10 July 1990); *Career* plantation mangr and sugar farmer Venezuelan Andes 1972–78; writer; *Awards* Somerset Maugham Award 1983, John Llewelyn Rhys Prize 1983, Eric Gregory Award for Poetry 1983; trans into many languages, public readings worldwide; *Books* Keepers of the House (1983), The Slow Train to Milan (1984), The Tiger (1984), The Bay of Silence (1985), The High Place (poetry, 1986), The Marble Mountain (short stories, 1989), Joanna (1990), Venice the Four Seasons (essays, 1992), A Valley In Italy: Confessions of a House Addict (1994), The Hacienda (memoirs, 1997), The Palace (novel, 1997), South Paw (short stories, 1999), Memory Maps (memoirs, 2001); *Recreations* reading, falconry, herbal medicines; *Clubs* Groucho; *Style*— Mrs Lisa St Aubin de Terán

ST AUBYN, Hon Giles Rowan; LVO (1977); yst s of 3 Baron St Levan (d 1978), and Hon Clementina Gwendolen Catharine, *née* Nicolson (d 1995), da of 1 Baron Carnock; *b* 11 March 1925; *Educ* Wellington, Univ of Glasgow, Trinity Coll Oxford; *Career* master and house master Eton 1947–85; author; FRSL; *Books* Macaulay (1952), A Victorian Eminence (1957), The Art of Argument (1957), The Royal George (1963), A World to Win (1968), Infamous Victorians (1971), William of Gloucester: Pioneer Prince (1977), Edward VII, Prince and King (1979), The Year of Three Kings 1483 (1983), Queen Victoria, A Portrait (1991); *Clubs* Beefsteak, The Royal Over-Seas League; *Style*— The Hon Giles St Aubyn, LVO; ✉ Apartment 2, Saumarez Park Manor, Route de Saumarez, Câtel, Guernsey GY5 7TH (tel 01481 251789)

ST AUBYN, Nicholas Francis; s of Hon Piers St Aubyn, MC (d 2006), and Mary St Aubyn (d 1987); *b* 10 November 1955; *Educ* Eton, Trinity Coll Oxford (MA); *m* 1980, Jane Mary, da of William F Brooks; 2 s, 3 da; *Career* J P Morgan 1977–86, Kleinwort Benson 1986–87, American International Gp 1987–89, Gemini Clothescare 1989–93, Fitzroy Gp 1993–; MP (Cons) Guildford 1997–2001, memb Educn and Employment Select Ctee 1997–2001; dir: Arab Br Centre, Project Tst, Zebra Housing Assoc; fndr memb London International Futures Market 1982–84; *Recreations* riding, shooting, swimming, sailing; *Clubs* Brooks's, IOD, Surrey CC, Cornish, Mounts Sailing; *Style*— Nicholas St Aubyn, Esq

ST CLAIR, William Linn; *b* 7 December 1937; *Educ* Edinburgh Acad, St John's Coll Oxford; *Children* 2 da (Anna b 1967, Elisabeth b 1970); *Career* writer; formerly under sec HM Treasy, served Admiralty and FCO; conslt: OECD 1992–95, EU 1996; int pres Byron Soc; fell: All Souls Coll Oxford 1992–96 (visiting fell 1981–82), Trinity Coll Cambridge 1998– (visiting fell 1997–98); visiting fell Huntington Library Calif 1985; memb Ctee London Library 1996–2000; patron English PEN Writers-in-Prison Ctee; FRSL, FBA (memb Cncl 1997–2000); *Awards* Heinemann Prize for Lit 1973, Time Life Award for Br Non-Fiction 1990, Thalassa Forum Award for Culture 2000; *Books* Lord Elgin and the Marbles (1967, revised edn 1998), That Greece Might Still Be Free (1972), Trelawny (1978), Policy Evaluation - A Guide For Managers (1988), The Godwins and the Shelleys - The Biography of a Family (1989), Executive Agencies - A Guide to Setting Targets and Judging Performance (1992), Conduct Literature for Women 1500–1640 (jt ed with Irmgard Maassen, 2000), Mapping Lives: The Uses of Biography (jt ed with Peter France, 2002), Conduct Literature for Women 1640–1710 (jt ed with Imgard Maassen, 2002), The Reading Nation in the Romantic Period (2004), The Grand Slave Emporium, Cape Coast Castle and the British Slave Trade (2006, published in US as The Door of No Return (2007)); *Recreations* old books, Scottish mountains; *Style*— William St Clair; ✉ 52 Eaton Place, London SW1X 8AL (tel 020 7235 8329, e-mail ws214@cam.ac.uk); c/o Deborah Rogers, 20 Powis Mews, London W11 1JN

ST CLAIR-FORD, Sir James Anson; 7 Bt (GB 1793), of Ember Court, Surrey; o s of Capt Sir Aubrey St Clair-Ford, 6 Bt, DSO, RN (d 1991), and Anne, *née* Christopherson; *b* 16 March 1952; *Educ* Wellington, Univ of Bristol; *m* 1, 1977 (m dis 1985), Jennifer Margaret, da of Cdre J Robin Grindle, RN; m 2, 1987, Mary Anne, da of late Judge Nathaniel Robert Blaker, QC, DL, of Winchester, Hants; *Heir* cous, Colin St Clair-Ford; *Style*— Sir James St Clair-Ford, Bt

ST CLAIRE, Marian (Mrs Michael Beare); da of Matthew William Allsopp, of Leyland, Lancs and Margaret Taylor; *b* 11 May 1946; *Educ* Wellfield Secdy Sch Leyland, Loretto Sch of Dance Southport, Ballet Rambert Sch London; *m* 2 Aug 1985, Michael Walter Beare, s of Douglas Charles Beare; *Career* ballet dancer; soloist: Ballet Rambert 1966–67 (former memb Corps de Ballet), Cape Town Ballet Co SA 1967–69; princ dancer: Scottish Ballet 1969–75, New London Ballet 1975–76; ballerina Dame Margot Fonteyn's Farewell Tour of UK 1976–77, ballerina Harold King's Lunch Hour Ballet Arts Theatre London 1978, fndr, ballerina and asst artistic dir London City Ballet Co 1979–91; currently freelance guest ballerina, teacher and répétiteur; guest ballerina: Nat Ballet of Rhodesia 1977, London Festival Ballet 1977–78, Northern Ballet 1978, Wayne Sleep's Hot Shoe Show (London Palladium), Sleep with Friends, Bits and Pieces and World of Dance 1989; performed as guest artist in Canada, Tokyo, Zimbabwe, Stockholm and at Chicago, Cuba, Poland, Spain and Romania dance festivals; guest artist Weiner Ballet Theatre; *Performances* incl: Bluebird Pas de Deux in Sleeping Beauty (Cape Town Ballet and London Festival Ballet), Peasant Pas de Trois and Neopolitan Dance in Swan Lake (Cape Town Ballet), The Misfit (leading role created by Gary Burn, Cape Town Ballet), Beauty in Beauty and the Beast (Scottish Ballet), Sugar Plum Fairy in The Nutcracker (Scottish Ballet), Antonia in Tales of Hoffman (Scottish Ballet), Columbia in Le Carnival (Scottish Ballet), Desdemona in Othello (New London Ballet), Elgie Pas de Deux (New London Ballet), Faust Variations (New London Ballet), Soft Blue Shadows (New London Ballet), leading roles in Giselle (Scottish Ballet, London Festival Ballet, Northern Ballet, London City Ballet), La Sylphide (Scottish Ballet, Northern Ballet, London City Ballet), Cinderella (Northern Ballet, London City Ballet), Carmen (London City Ballet), Swan Lake (London City Ballet), Coppélia (London City Ballet), La Traviata (London City Ballet); *Recreations* teaching, keeping fit, designing and making wedding tiaras; *Style*— Ms Marian St Claire; ✉ 35 Milton Avenue, Barnet, Hertfordshire EN5 2EY (tel and fax 020 8447 0247)

ST CLEMENT, Pamela (Pam); *b* 11 May 1942; *Educ* The Warren Worthing, Rolle Coll, Rose Bruford Coll of Drama; *m* 1970 (m dis 1979), Andrew Louis Gordon; *Career* actress and presenter; involved in charity and other activities; pres W Herts RSPCA, vice-pres Scottish Terrier Emergency Care Scheme; patron: London Animal Day, Tusk Tst, Africat UK (SE), Leicester Animal Aid Assoc, Ridgeway Tst for Endangered Cats, Pro-Dogs, Pets as Therapy; involved with: Blue Cross, PDSA, Nat Animal Welfare Tst, Battersea Dogs Home, Kennel Club and Good Citizen Dog Scheme, Environmental Investigation Agency, Project Life Lion, Earth Kind, WSPA, Hearing Dogs for Deaf People, Int League for the Protection of Horses, Humane Educn Tst; memb Inst of Advanced Motorists; presented Duke of Edinburgh Awards St James's Palace 2000; *Theatre* incl: Joan Littlewood's Theatre Royal Stratford, Royal Shakespeare Theatre Co; other credits incl: Stringberg and Chekov (Prospect Theatre Co tour), Macbeth (Thorndike Theatre), I Am A Camera (Yvonne Arnaud Guildford and tour), Once a Catholic (Leeds Playhouse); *Television* incl: Within These Walls (2 series, LWT), Shall I See You Now? (BBC play), A Horseman Riding By (BBC series), Emmerdale Farm (YTV), Shoestring (BBC), Partners in Crime (LWT), Cats Eyes (TVS), The Tripods (BBC), Not For The Likes Of Us (BBC Play for Today), Pat Butcher in EastEnders (BBC) 1986–, Whipsnade 13 part Wildlife Series (2 Series, Anglia TV), Animal Planet, Adopt-a-Wild Animal, Wild at Heart, BBC Animal Awards; *Film* incl: Hedda, Dangerous Davies, The Bunker, Scrubbers; *Style*— Ms Pam St Clement; ✉ c/o Saraband Associates, 265 Liverpool Road, London N1 1LX (tel 020 7609 5313/4, fax 020 7609 2370); c/o BBC TV Studios, Clarendon Road, Borehamwood, Hertfordshire WD6 1JF (fax 020 8228 8868)

ST DAVIDS, Archdeacon of; *see:* Davies, Ven Graham

ST DAVIDS, Bishop of 2002–; Rt Rev Carl Norman Cooper; s of Joseph Cooper, of Wigan, Lancs, and Kathleen Mary, *née* Roby; *b* 4 August 1960; *Educ* Deanery HS Wigan, St Davids UC Lampeter (BA), Wycliffe Hall Oxford (CertTheol), Trinity Coll Carmarthen (MPhil); *m* 7 Aug 1982, Joy Erica, da of Eric Bowyer; 1 s (David b 13 March 1985), 2 da (Lora b 5 Aug 1987, Emma b 4 April 1990); *Career* curate Llanelli 1985–87, rector Llannerch Aeron, Ciliau Aeron, Dihewyd and Mydroilyn 1987–93, rector Dolgellau Rectorial Benefice 1993–2002, archdeacon of Meirionnydd 2000–02; pres Trinity Coll Carmarthen, visitor Univ of Wales Lampeter, visitor Llandovery Coll; *Recreations* reading, family holidays, fishing; *Style*— The Rt Rev the Bishop of St Davids; ✉ Llys Esgob, Abergwili, Caerfyrddin SA31 2JG (tel 01267 236597, fax 01267 237482, e-mail bishop.stdavids@churchinwales.org.uk)

ST DAVIDS, Dean of; *see:* Evans, Very Rev (John) Wyn

ST EDMUNDSBURY, Dean of; *see:* Collings, Very Rev Neil

ST EDMUNDSBURY, Provost of; *see:* Atwell, Very Rev James Edgar

ST GEORGE, Charles Reginald; s of William Acheson St George (d 1993), and Heather Atwood, *née* Brown (d 1978); *b* 20 April 1955; *Educ* Henley GS, Univ of Exeter (BA), Queen's Univ Kingston Ontario (MA); *m* 1, 19 July 1980 (m dis 1989); 1 da (Imogen Margaret b 15 Jan 1984), 1 s (Michael John b 31 Dec 1985); m 2, 17 Oct 1991; 2 s (Henry Peter b 19 May 1995, Edward Charles George b 23 April 1998); *Career* CBI: sec Smaller Firms Cncl 1979–82, head of secretariat 1982–83; account mangr Ian Greer Associates Ltd 1983–87, md Profile Political Relations Ltd 1989–90 (dir 1987–88), dir PPS Group Ltd 2001– (jt md 1990–2001); Parly candidate (Lib) Guildford 1980–82, Lib Alliance borough cncllr Guildford 1983–87; *Recreations* golf, tennis and skiing; *Style*— Charles St George, Esq; ✉ PPS Group Ltd, 9 North Court, The Courtyard, Woodlands Lane, Almondsbury, Bristol BS32 4NQ (tel 01454 275630, e-mail charles.stgeorge@ppsgroup.co.uk)

ST GERMANS, 10 Earl of (UK 1815); Peregrine Nicholas Eliot; also Baron Eliot (GB 1784); s of 9 Earl of St Germans (d 1988), by his 1 w Helen Mary (who d 1951, having m 2, 1947, Capt Ralph Benson, Coldstream Gds), da of Lt Charles Walters Villiers, CBE, DSO; *b* 2 January 1941; *Educ* Eton; *m* 1, 9 Oct 1964 (m dis 1990), Hon Jacquetta Jean Fredricka Lampson, da of 1 Baron Killearn; 3 s (Jago b 1966 d 2006, Hon Louis b 11 April 1968, Hon Francis b 16 Nov 1971); m 2, 20 April 1991 (m dis 1996), Elizabeth Mary, eldest da of Basil James Williams, of France; m 3, Catherine Elizabeth, da of Dr George Morrison Wilson; *Heir* gs, Lord Eliot; *Career* landowner; 30 years in a job without prospects; patron of three livings; *Recreations* sitting still; *Clubs* Pratt's, The Cornish; *Style*— The Rt Hon the Earl of St Germans; ✉ Port Eliot, St Germans, Cornwall PL12 5ND (tel 01503 230211)

ST GILES, Mark Valentine; s of late Austin Loudon Valentine St Giles, and Sybil Gladwin Sykes Thompson; *b* 4 June 1941; *Educ* Winchester, Clare Coll Cambridge (MA); *m* 1966, Susan Janet, da of late Edward Turner; 2 da (Emma b 1968, Lucy b 1970), 1 s (Edward b 1974); *Career* analyst Laurence Keen & Gardner stockbrokers 1964–69, dir Jessel Securities 1969–75, md Allied Hambro Ltd 1975–83, dir Hambros Bank 1975–83, dir (later md) GT Management plc 1983–88, chm Cadogan Management Ltd 1988–93, dir Framlington Group plc 1989–97, dir International Financial Strategy Ltd 1993–2000, ptnr Cadogan Financial 2000–; *Recreations* travel, sailing, gardening; *Clubs* Travellers; *Style*— Mark St Giles, Esq; ✉ Cadogan Financial, Higher House, West Lydford, Somerset TA11 7DG (tel 01963 240232, fax 01963 240655, e-mail stgiles@dial.pipex.com)

ST HELENS, 2 Baron (UK 1964); Richard Francis Hughes-Young; s of 1 Baron (d 1980), and Elizabeth (d 1956), da of late Capt Richard Blakiston-Houston (ggs of Sir Matthew Blakiston, 2 Bt); *b* 4 November 1945; *Educ* Nautical Coll Pangbourne; *m* 1983, Mrs Emma R Talbot-Smith; 1 s, 1 da; *Heir* s, Hon Henry Hughes-Young; *Style*— The Rt Hon the Lord St Helens

ST JOHN OF BLETSO, 21 Baron (E 1559); Sir Anthony Tudor St John; 18 Bt (E 1660); s of 20 Baron, TD (d 1978), and Katharine Emily, *née* von Berg; *b* 16 May 1957; *Educ* Diocesan Coll Cape Town, Univ of Cape Town (BA, BSc, BProc), Univ of London (LLM); *m* 16 Sept 1994, Dr Helen Jane Westlake, eldest da of Michael Westlake, of Bath, Avon; 2 s (Hon Oliver Beauchamp b 1995, Hon Alexander Andrew b 29 Aug 1996), 2 da (Athene b 24 Feb 1998, Chloe b 17 June 1999); *Heir* s, Hon Oliver St John; *Career* sits as Independent Peer in Lords (Parly interests foreign affairs, environment, financial and legal services), Extra Lord-in-Waiting to HM The Queen 1998–; dep chm All-Pty Parly SA Gp; memb: EC Select Ctee A (Trade, Finance and Foreign Affairs 1996–99, EU Sub-Ctee B Energy Internal Markets; solicitor and stockbroker; md Globix (UK) 1998–2002; chm: Eurotrust Ltd, Spiritel plc; conslt to Merrill Lynch plc London; non-exec dir Regal Petroleum 2003–; *Recreations* tennis, golf, skiing, running; *Clubs* Wisley Golf, Sunningdale Golf (conslt), Royal Cape, Hurlingham; *Style*— The Rt Hon The Lord St John of Bletso; ✉ House of Lords, London SW1A 0PW (e-mail asj@enterprise.net)

ST JOHN OF FAWSLEY, Baron (Life Peer UK 1987), of Preston Capes in the County of Northamptonshire; Norman Antony Francis St John-Stevas; PC (1979); s of late Stephen S Stevas, and Kitty St John O'Connor; *b* 18 May 1929; *Educ* Ratcliffe, Fitzwilliam Coll Cambridge, ChCh Oxford; *Career* called to the Bar 1952; former jurisprudence tutor; political corr The Economist 1959; author; contested (Cons) Dagenham 1951, MP (Cons) Chelmsford 1964–87; under sec of state for Educn 1972–73, min of state for Educn and Science with special responsibility for the Arts 1973–74, oppn spokesman the Arts 1974 and memb Shadow Cabinet 1974–79; Arts min 1979, leader House of Commons and chllr of Duchy of Lancaster 1979–81; vice-pres Theatres Advsy Cncl 1983–, chm Royal Fine Art Cmmn 1985–, Master Emmanuel Coll Cambridge 1991–; non-exec dir British Sky Broadcasting plc 1991–; former pres Cambridge Union; FRSL 1966; OStJ 1980, Order of Merit Italy 1965, KSLJ 1963; *Clubs* White's, Garrick, Pratt's; *Style*— The Rt Hon the Lord St John of Fawsley, PC; ✉ The Old Rectory, Preston Capes, Daventry, Northamptonshire; 7 Brunswick Place, Regent's Park, London NW1 4PS

ST LEVAN, 4 Baron (UK 1887); Sir John Francis Arthur St Aubyn; 5 Bt (UK 1866), OBE (2004), DSC (1942), DL (Cornwall 1977); s of 3 Baron (d 1978), and Hon Clementina Gwendolen Catharine, *née* Nicolson (d 1995), da of 1 Baron Carnock and sis of Sir Harold Nicolson (the author, d 1968); *b* 23 February 1919; *Educ* Eton, Trinity Coll Cambridge (BA); *m* 1970, Susan (d 2003), da of late Maj-Gen Sir John Noble Kennedy, GCMG, KCVO, KBE, CB, MC; *Heir* n, James Piers Southwell St Aubyn; *Career* slr 1948; Lt RNVR, ret; landowner and farmer, co dir; admin of St Michael's Mount of behalf of Nat Tst 1976–2003; High Sheriff Cornwall 1974, Vice Lord-Lt Cornwall 1992–95; pres: W Penwith Nat Tst Assoc, W Cornwall Branch Sail Training Assoc, Penwith and Isles of Scilly Dist Scout Cncl, Cornwall Maritime Trust, Cornwall Church Action with the Unemployed, Cornwall Branch Normandy Veterans' Assoc 1995–, St Ives Soc of Artists; past pres: London Cornish Assoc, Friends of Plymouth Museum, Royal Bath and West and Southern Counties Soc; vice-pres: Royal Cornwall Agric Assoc, Penlee Station Branch RNLI; patron: Nat Coastwatch Inst, West Country Writers Assoc; bard of Cornwall 1995–; FRSA; KStJ 1998; *Books* Illustrated History of St Michael's Mount; *Clubs* Brooks's, Royal Yacht Squadron; *Style*— The Rt Hon the Lord St Levan, OBE, DSC, DL; ✉ 8 St Mary's Terrace, Penzance, Cornwall TR18 4DZ

ST MARK, Carole; *b* 1943; *Educ* Douglas Coll Rutgers Univ (BA), Pace Univ New York (MBA), Wharton Sch Univ of Pennsylvania (AMP); *Career* early positions with General Electric, St Regis Paper Co and General Foods; Pitney Bowes: joined as dir Human Resources 1980–84, vice-pres Strategic Planning 1984–85, vice-pres Corp Planning and Devpt (also memb Corp Mgmnt Ctee) 1985–88, pres Pitney Bowes Business Supplies and Services Gp and pres Pitney Bowes Management Services 1988–90, pres Pitney Bowes Logistics Systems and Business Services 1990–94, pres Pitney Bowes Business Services and chm and chief exec Pitney Bowes Management Services Inc 1994– (also memb Mgmnt Ctee); non-exec dir: SuperValu Inc Minneapolis, Grand Metropolitan plc, Royal & Sun Alliance Gp plc 1998–; *Style*— Ms Carole St Mark; ✉ Pitney Bowes Management Services, World HQ, MSC 03–13, 1 Elmcroft Road, Stamford, CT 06926–0700, USA

ST MAUR SHEIL, Michael Patrick; s of John St Maur Sheil, and Doreen Victoria, *née* Bradley; *b* 31 October 1946; *Educ* Bloxham Sch, St Edmund Hall Oxford; *m* Janet Susan, o da of Cdr F Allford, RN (ret); 1 s (Ross Patrick), 1 da (Fiona Jean); *Career* photographer (specialising in corp, industrial, and editorial photography); assoc Black Star photographers' agency NY 1971–; clients incl: Anti-Slavery Int, Bechtel, EC, Time, Nat Geographic, NY Times; exhbns: Child Trafficking in West Africa 2002, Fields of Battle - Messines and Passchendale 2007; memb Guild of Battlefield Guides 2006; FRGS *Awards* NY Art Dirs' Assoc: Magazine Cover Award 1971, Best Travel Photography for Advertising (Colour) 1983; Br Assoc of Industrial Eds: Best Photography Award 1981 and 1993, Magazine Cover Award 1983; First Prize World Press Photo Awards 2002; *Publications* National Geographic Guide to Britain and Ireland (contrib photographer, 1983); numerous magazine and annual reports; *Recreations* fishing, cricket, walking, photographing fields of battle; *Style—* Michael St Maur Sheil, Esq; ✉ website www.westernfrontphotography.com

ST OSWALD, 6 Baron (UK 1885); Charles Rowland Andrew Winn; DL (W Yorks 2004); s of 5 Baron St Oswald (d 1999); *b* 22 July 1959; *m* 1985, Louise Alexandra, da of Stewart Mackenzie Scott; 1 s (Hon Rowland Charles Sebastian Henry b 1986), 1 da (Hon Henrietta Sophia Alexandra b 1993); *Heir* s, Hon Rowland Winn; *Career* landowner; *Style—* The Rt Hon the Lord St Oswald, DL

ST PIERRE, Roger; s of Alexander Richard St Pierre, MBE (d 1999), and Caroline Amelia Borrett (d 1985); *b* 8 November 1941; *Educ* Ilford County HS; *m* 10 Nov 1975, Lesley, da of Bernard Constantine, of Sheffield; 1 s (Richard b 1976), 2 da (Danielle b 1978, Nicole b 1979); *Career* author and journalist; editor: Disco International 1977–79, Voyager Magazine (British Midland in-flight Magazine) 1986–90, European Hotelier 1992–95, Pocket Guide Series 1993–97, Holiday and Leisure World 1995–, Entertain Magazine 1995–97, Cycling Today 1996–98, American Express Great Golf Hotel Guide 1997–2001; contrib to: Debrett's International Collection, London Evening Standard, The Dorchester Magazine, Travel GBI, Renaissance, The Times, Financial Weekly, Wish You Were Here, ABTA Magazine, Meridian, Conference and Incentive Travel, Incentive Travel and Corporate Meetings, DriveTime, De Vere Magazine, High Flyer, Independent Travel Trade News, Incentive Travel, Cycling Plus; motoring corr The Mercury; formerly PR mangr for: Diana Ross, Glen Campbell, Jerry Lee Lewis, Don Williams, James Brown, Jackson 5, Frankie Lane; author of more than 1,000 record/album sleeve notes; broadcaster BBC and www.solarradio.com; cycle racer in many countries, mangr of int cycle teams; specialist writer on: travel (118 countries visited), hotel industry, food and drink, music, motoring, cycling, leisure; memb Br Guild of Travel Writers; Hon Col Cwlth of Kentucky; *Books* incl: Book of The Bicycle (1973), The Rock Handbook (1986), Illustrated History of Black Music (1986), Marilyn Monroe (1987) Story of The Blues (1993), AA/Thomas Cook Guide to Orlando (1994), McDonalds - A History (1994), Tom Jones - In His Own Words (1996), Know the Game - Cycling (1996); *Recreations* cycling, music, travel; *Style—* Roger St Pierre, Esq; ✉ The Hoods, High Street, Wethersfield, Essex CM7 4BY (tel 01371 850238, fax 01371 851714, e-mail stpierre.roger@ukf.net)

ST QUINTON, Martin George; s of Eric St Quinton (d 2003), and Sybil, *née* Sanderson (d 1977); *b* 9 November 1957, Hull; *Educ* Univ of Durham (BA), Pacific Western Univ USA (MBA); *m* 6 August 1983, Judith, *née* Faughey; 2 da (Abigail b 17 Feb 1990, Caroline b 20 Sept 1991), 2 s (George b 8 Nov 1995, Charlie b 10 June 2000); *Career* ceo Saint Group 1980–93, ceo Danka International plc 1993–99, ceo and founder Azzurri Communications Ltd 2000–; fndr Saint Fndn Charitable Tst; Ernst & Young Technology Entrepreneur of the Year 2004; *Recreations* horseracing, travel; *Clubs* Loch Lomond Golf, Racehorse Owners'; *Style—* Martin St Quinton, Esq; ✉ Azzurri Communications Limited, St Anthony's House, Oxford Square, Oxford Street, Newbury, Berkshire RG14 1JQ (tel 01635 520360, fax 01635 520361, e-mail msq@azzu.co.uk)

ST VINCENT, 7 Viscount (UK 1801); Ronald George James Jervis; s of 6 Viscount (d 1940, himself ggs of 2 Viscount, who was in his turn n of 1 Viscount and Earl of St Vincent, whose title commemorated his victory over the Spaniards in 1797 despite being outnumbered 27 to 15 - the name title was chosen by George III himself; St Vincent, more modestly, had suggested Yarmouth and Orford, which did not call to mind his successful action) and Marion, *née* Broun; *b* 3 May 1905; *Educ* Sherborne; *m* 2 Oct 1945, Constance Phillida Anne, da of Lt-Col Robert Hector Logan, OBE, late Loyal Regt; 2 s, 1 da; *Heir* s, Hon Edward Jervis; *Career* served WW II, acting Lt Cdr RNVR; JP Somerset 1950–55; *Style—* The Rt Hon the Viscount St Vincent; ✉ Les Charrieres House, St Ouen, Jersey JE3 2LG (tel 0534 482118)

SAKO, Prof Mari (Lady Chakrabarti); da of Kanzo Sako, and Akemi, *née* Hiei; *b* 12 June 1960; *Educ* Univ of Oxford (BA), LSE (MSc(Econ)), Johns Hopkins Univ (Lessing-Rosenthal trg grant 1982–84, Univ fell 1982–84, MA), Univ of London (PhD); *m* Sir Sumantra Chakrabarti, *qv*; 1 da (Maya b 5 Sept 1995); *Career* research assoc The Technical Change Centre London 1984–86, research asst COMRES Imperial Coll London 1986–87; LSE: lectr in modern Japanese business 1987–92, lectr in industrial rels 1992–94, reader in industrial rels 1994–97; prof of mgmnt studies Univ of Oxford 1997–; fell Japanese Soc for the Promotion of Sci Econs Dept Kyoto Univ 1992, Japan Fndn fell Inst of Soc Sci Univ of Tokyo 1997; dir Zipangu Fund; memb Editorial Bd Industry and Innovation; memb: Br Univ Industrial Rels Assoc, Soc for the Advancement of Socio-Economics, Acad of Mgmnt; FRSA 2001; *Books* How the Japanese Learn to Work (with R Dore, 1989, 2 edn 1998), Prices, Quality and Trust: Inter-firm Relations in Britain and Japan (1992), Japanese Labour and Management in Transition: Diversity, Flexibility and Participation (co-ed with H Sato, 1997), Are Skills the Answer? (jtly with C Crouch and D Finegold, 1999), Shifting Boundaries of the Firm (2006); also author of numerous book chapters and articles in learned jls; *Recreations* music, travel; *Style—* Prof Mari Sako; ✉ Saïd Business School, University of Oxford, Park End Street, Oxford OX1 1HP (tel 01865 288925, fax 01865 288805)

SALEM, Maurice; *b* 19 January 1970, Lebanon; *Educ* Br Sch of Brussels, Carmel Coll, Univ of London (BA); *Career* trading and mgmnt of French govt bonds UBS 1991–94, md Wharton Asset Management UK Ltd 1994–; FSA 2000; *Style—* Maurice Salem, Esq

SALFORD, Bishop of (RC) 1997–; Rt Rev Terence John Brain; s of Reginald John Brain, of Coventry, Warks, and Mary, *née* Cooney; *b* 19 December 1938; *Educ* King Henry VIII GS Coventry, Cotton Coll, Oscott Coll Birmingham; *Career* ordained RC priest (Birmingham) 1964; asst priest St Gregory's Longton Stoke-on-Trent 1964–65, on staff Cotton Coll 1965–69, hosp chaplain Birmingham 1969–71, private sec to Archbishop of Birmingham 1971–82; parish priest: Bentilee Stoke-on-Trent 1982–88 (memb Staffordshire LEA Ctee 1982–91), St Austin's Stafford 1988–91; aux bishop of Birmingham and titular bishop of Amudarsa 1991–97; bishop for prisons 1994–; chm Bishop's Social Welfare Ctee 1992–2003; episcopal advsr: Union of Catholic Mothers 1993–, Nat Cncl of Lay Assocs 1993–; *Recreations* watercolour painting, crossword puzzles; *Style—* The Rt Rev Terence Brain; ✉ Wardley Hall, Worsley, Manchester M28 2ND (tel 0161 794 2825, fax 0161 727 8592, e-mail bishop@wardleyhall.org.uk)

SALIS, *see:* de Salis

SALISBURY, Bishop of 1993–; Rt Rev Dr David Staffurth Stancliffe; DD, FRSCM; s of Very Rev Michael S Stancliffe (d 1987 formerly Dean of Winchester), and Barbara Elizabeth, da of Rev Canon Tissington Tatlow; *b* 1 October 1942; *Educ* Westminster, Trinity Coll Oxford (MA), Cuddesdon Theol Coll; *m* 17 July 1965, Sarah Loveday, da of Philip Sascha Smith, of Mead House, Great Ayton; 2 da (Rachel b 1968, Hannah b 1969), 1 s (Benjamin b 1972); *Career* asst curate of St Bartholomew's Armley 1967–70, chaplain to Clifton Coll Bristol 1970–77, residentiary canon of Portsmouth Cathedral 1977–82, diocesan dir of ordinands and lay ministry advsr Portsmouth 1977–82, provost of Portsmouth 1982–93; chm: Southern Regional Inst 1979–81 and 1984–89, Diocesan Advsy Ctee 1982–93; memb: Gen Synod 1985–, Cathedrals Fabric Cmmn for England 1991–2001; vice-pres Assoc of European Cathedrals 1986–, chm C of E Liturgical Cmmn 1993–2005 (memb 1985–2005), pres Affirming Catholicism 1994–; memb House of Lords 1998–; DD Lambeth 2004, Hon DLitt Univ of Portsmouth 1993; hon fell: Trinity Coll Oxford 2003, St Chad's Coll Durham; FRSCM 2001; *Recreations* old music, Italy; *Style—* The Rt Rev Dr the Lord Bishop of Salisbury, DD, FRSCM; ✉ South Canonry, 71 The Close, Salisbury SP1 2ER (tel 01722 334031, fax 01722 413112, e-mail dsarum@salisbury.anglican.org)

SALISBURY, Dr Jonathan Richard; s of George Richard Salisbury (d 1971), and Patricia Doreen, *née* Jones; *b* 25 June 1956; *Educ* Hereford HS, UCL (BSc), UCH Med Sch (MB BS), King's Coll Sch of Med (MD); *m* 19 May 1984 (m dis 2004), Alyson Frances, da of Lister Wilfred Bumby (d 1996), of Herne Bay, Kent; 1 da (Elizabeth b 1989), 1 s (Joseph b 1992); *Career* GKT: sr lectr in histopathology 1987–97, reader in histopathology 1997–2004; conslt histopathologist KCH London 2004– (hon conslt 1987–2004); FRCPath 1997 (MRCPath 1986–97); *Style—* Dr Jonathan Salisbury; ✉ 84 Harbut Road, London SW11 2RE; Department of Histopathology, King's College Hospital, Bessemer Road, London SE5 9PJ (tel 020 3299 3093, fax 020 3299 3670, e-mail jon.salisbury@kch.nhs.uk)

SALISBURY, 7 Marquess of (GB 1789); Robert Michael James (Gascoyne-)Cecil; PC (1994), DL (Herts 2006); also Baron Cecil (E 1603), Viscount Cranborne (E 1604), Earl of Salisbury (E 1605); and Baron Gascoyne-Cecil (Life Peer UK 1999), of Essendon, Co Rutland; s of 6 Marquess of Salisbury (d 2003); received a Writ in Acceleration summoning him to the House of Lords in his father's Barony of Cecil 1992; *b* 30 September 1946; *Educ* Eton, ChCh Oxford; *m* 1970, Hannah Ann, da of Lt-Col William Joseph Stirling of Keir, gs of Sir William Stirling-Maxwell, 9 Bt (a Baronetcy dormant since 1956); 2 s (Robert Edward William, Viscount Cranborne b 1970, Lord James Richard b 1973), 3 da (Lady Elizabeth Ann b 1972, Lady Georgiana, Lady Katherine (twins) b 1977); *Heir* s, Viscount Cranborne; *Career* MP (Cons) Dorset S 1979–87; chm Afghanistan Support Ctee; PPS to Cranley Onslow as Min of State FCO April-May 1982 (when resigned to be free to criticise Govt Ulster devolution plans), Parly under sec of state MOD 1992–94, Lord Privy Seal and ldr of the House of Lords 1994–97, shadow spokesman on NI and shadow ldr of the House of Lords 1997–98, leave of absence House of Lords 2002–; chm RVC Cncl 1998–, chllr Univ of Hertfordshire 2005–; DL Dorset 1988–2006; *Style—* The Most Hon the Marquess of Salisbury, PC, DL; ✉ 2 Swan Walk, London SW3 4JJ

SALJE, Prof Ekhard Karl Hermann; s of Gerhard Salje, of Hanover, and Hildegard, *née* Drechsler; *b* 26 October 1946; *Educ* Herschel Sch Hanover, Univ of Hanover (Dip Physics, PhD); *m* 19 July 1952, Elisabeth, *née* Démaret; 1 s (Henrik b 26 June 1980), 4 da (Joelle b 16 Oct 1981, Jeanne b 2 April 1983, Léa-Cécile b 4 June 1985, Barbara b 25 April 1990); *Career* prof of crystallography Univ of Hanover 1978–87 (lectr in physics 1975–78); Univ of Cambridge: lectr in mineral physics 1987–88, reader 1988–92, prof 1992–94, prof of mineralogy and petrology 1994–, head Dept of Earth Sci 1999–, pres Clare Hall 2001–; co-dir IRC in superconductivity 1987–98; prog dir Cambridge-MIT Inst 2000–03; visiting prof: Univ of Paris 1981–82, Univ of Grenoble 1990–92, Japan 1996 (Monbusho prof), Univ of Le Mans 1998, Bayerisches Geoinstitut Bayreuth 1998–, Univ of Bilbao 1999, Univ of Hamburg 2003–; memb Bd: Max Planck Inst of Mathematics Leipzig 2003–, Univ of Hanover 2004– (senator 1980–82), Univ of Hamburg 2004–, Parly Office of Science and Technol 2007–; pres Alexander von Humboldt Assoc UK 2004–; Abraham Gottlieb Werner Medal 1994, Humboldt Prize 1999, Ernst Ising Prize for Physics 2002, Golden Medal Univ of Hamburg 2002, Agricola Medal for Applied Mineralogy 2006; hon fell Darwin Coll Cambridge 2002; fell: Mineralogical Soc 1990 (Schlumberger medal 1998), Acad of Science (Leopoldina) 1994; FInstP 1996, FGS 1996, FRS 1996, FRSA 1996; Chevalier dans l'Ordre des Palmes Académiques (France) 2003, First Class Cross of the Order of Merit Germany 2006; *Books* Phase Transitions in Ferroelastic and Co-elastic Crystals (1990, 2 edn 1993); author of over 300 scientific pubns; *Recreations* music, painting; *Style—* Prof Ekhard Salje, FRS; ✉ The President's House, Clare Hall, Cambridge CB3 9AL (tel 01223 332361); Department of Earth Sciences, University of Cambridge, Downing Street, Cambridge CB2 3EQ (tel 01223 333481, fax 01223 333478, e-mail es10002@esc.cam.ac.uk)

SALKELD, David John; s of William (Bill) Salkeld, and Freda Salkeld; *b* 23 February 1956, Middlesbrough; *Educ* Middlesbrough HS, Univ of London (BSc); *m* Catherine; 3 s (Andrew, Nicholas, Christopher); *Career* co industrial rels mangr Findus 1981–83, gp employee rels mangr Grand Metropolitan Retail 1983–86, personnel dir then ops dir Northern Foods plc 1986–90, md Northern Dairies (div of Northern Foods plc) 1990–95, ceo Arla Foods plc 1995–2003, gp ceo Grampian Country Foods Gp Ltd 2003–05 (non-exec dir 2002–03); sr ind dir Kelda Gp plc 2000–; non-exec dir: Vircol plc, T2 Communications, Yorkshire Financial Mgmnt; FIGD; *Recreations* running, keep fit, Leeds United FC, golf, family; *Style—* David Salkeld, Esq; ✉ e-mail david.salkeld@btinternet.com

SALLITT, Timothy William Baines; CBE (1991); s of Brig William Baines Sallitt, OBE (d 1979), and Mary Elaine, *née* Whincup (d 1997); *b* 21 March 1934; *Educ* Rugby, Bradford Poly, Borough Poly, Georgia Tech Atlanta; *m* 14 June 1958, Angela Mary, da of Dr Brian Laidlaw Goodlet, OBE (d 1961); 2 da (Amelia b 1960, Lucinda b 1965), 1 s (Henry b 1962); *Career* Nat Serv 2 Lt RE Cyprus 1955–57; BP 1957–59; divnl mangr: Brush Electrical Engineering 1959–66, Plessey Co 1966–70; sub-co md Hawker Siddeley Group 1970–77, gp dir Hawker Siddeley Group 1977–89, chm Sedgemoor plc 1991–99; former chm Electrical Technol Requirements Bd DTI; former memb Cncl Electrical Res Assoc, former pres BEAMA, dep chm Export Guarantees Advsy Cncl 1986–89; FIIM; *Recreations* shooting, gardening, crosswords; *Clubs* Boodle's; *Style—* Timothy Sallitt, Esq, CBE; ✉ Langham Cottage, Langham, Rutland LE15 7HY (tel 01572 724509)

SALMON, Kenneth Thomas; s of Thomas Salmon (d 1984), and Mary, *née* Jones (d 1984); *b* 16 April 1946, Stockport; *Educ* Salford Univ and Tech Coll, Coll of Law Liverpool; *m* 19 Oct 1968, Marjie, *née* Bate; 1 s (Nolan b 14 Sept 1972); *Career* admitted slr: Eng and Wales 1973, Ireland 2005; ptnr Kirk Jackson 1975–2001, ptnr and head of construction law Mace & Jones 2002–; regular contrib of articles Jl of CIArb, occasional contrib Building magazine; memb Law Soc, MCIArb (memb Ctee NW Branch); *Recreations* painting, cycling, five-a-side football; *Style—* Kenneth Salmon, Esq; ✉ Mace & Jones, Pall Mall Court, 61–67 King Street, Manchester M2 4PD (tel 0161 214 0500, e-mail kenneth.salmon@maceandjones.co.uk)

SALMON, Prof Michael John (Mike); s of Arthur Salmon (d 1972), and May, *née* Dadswell; *b* 22 June 1936; *Educ* Roundhay Sch Leeds, Univ of Leeds (BA, PGCE), Univ of Leicester (MEd); *m* 1, 5 April 1958 (m dis 1973), Angela, da of Leslie Winstone Cookson; 1 s (Andrew John b 17 April 1964); m 2, 17 Aug 1973, Daphne Beatrice (d 1996), da of Albert Ernest Bird; 1 s (Christopher Michael b 14 Dec 1984); m 3, 25 April 1998, Sheila Frances, da of Edward John Patterson; *Career* Flt Lt RAF 1957–62; lectr Letchworth Coll of Technol 1962–65, sr then princ lectr Leeds Coll of Technol 1965–68, princ lectr NE London Poly 1968–71, head Dept of Applied Economics and head Int Office NE London Poly 1971–77, dep dir Chelmer Inst of Higher Educn 1977–83, dir Essex Inst of Higher Educn 1983–89, dir Anglia Higher Educn Coll 1989–91, dir Anglia Poly 1991–92, vice-chllr Anglia Poly Univ 1992–95; dir: Proshare Ltd 1991–93, Essex TEC 1989–93; non-exec dir Mid Essex Hosp Servs NHS Tst 1993–95, chm Essex Rivers NHS Trust 1995–2005; chm Tendring Community Renewal Forum 1998–2001; memb various ctees and bds Cncl for Nat Academic Awards 1971–92; memb: Electricity Industry Trg Bd 1973–75, Educn Advsy Cncl IBA 1973–83, Poly and Coll Funding Cncl 1989–93, E Regn Cncl CBI 1989–93, Forum 2000 1993–, CVCP (chm Student Affairs Ctee 1992–95), Academic Ctee Royal Coll of Music 1995–2000, General Optical Cncl 1999– (vice-chm 2002–05, chm Educn 2002–05); govr: Norwich Sch of Art and Design 1996–2001 (chm of govrs 1999–2001), King Edward VI Sch Chelmsford (vice-chm 2000–01); Hon PhD Anglia Poly Univ 1995; memb Worshipful Co of Spectacle-Makers 2006–; hon fell: Fachhochschule für Wirtshaft Berlin 1994, Limburg Hogeschool Netherlands 1996; FRSA 1982, FIMgt 1982; *Recreations* hill walking, France, gardening; *Style—* Prof Mike Salmon; ✉ Barberries, Runsell Lane, Danbury, Essex CM3 4NZ (tel 01245 223734, e-mail profmike.salmon@gmail.com)

SALMON, Peter; s of late Patrick Joseph Salmon, and late Doreen Salmon; *b* 15 May 1956; *Educ* St Theodore's RC Comp Secdy Sch, Univ of Warwick, CAM (certificate in advtg and mktg), NCTJ qualification; *Family*; 4 s (Michael, David, Paul, Joseph), 2 step s (Thomas, Matthew); *Career* English teacher VSO Borneo 1977–78, with Miny of Overseas Devpt (now DFID) 1978–79, reporter Chatham News and Standard 1979–81, with BBC Radio & TV (series prodr Crimewatch, ed Nature, exec prodr 999) 1981–93, head of TV features BBC Bristol 1991–93, controller of factual progs Channel Four Television Corporation 1993–96, dir of progs Granada TV 1996–97, controller BBC1 1997–2000, dir of sport BBC 2000–05, chief exec The Television Corporation 2005–06, chief creative offr BBC Vision Studios 2006–; *Recreations* music, football, cycling, museums; *Clubs* Burnley FC; *Style*— Peter Salmon, Esq

SALMON, Timothy John (Tim); s of John Frederick Salmon, of Woldingham, and Esmé, *née* Lane; *b* 31 December 1960; *Educ* Caterham Sch, Univ of Exeter (BA); *m* 21 July 1990, Helen Sophia, da of late Anthony Jessup; 1 s (James Timothy (Jim) b 27 March 1997), 1 d (Georgina Helen (Gina) b 2 Feb 1999); *Career* Arthur Andersen: mangr 1987–93, ptnr 1993–2001, chief fin offr 1998–2001; interim finance dir Cons Central Office 2002, interim chief financial offr (business process mgmnt) Xansa plc 2003, finance dir Richards Butler 2004–07; FCA 1995 (ACA 1985); *Recreations* motoring, DIY, gardening, theatre, reading, watching sport; *Clubs* RAC; *Style*— Tim Salmon, Esq; ✉ Woodside, Slines Oak Road, Woldingham, Surrey CR3 7BH (e-mail salmons@ukgateway.net)

SALMOND, Rt Hon Alexander Elliot Anderson (Alex); PC (2007), MP; s of Robert Fyfe Findlay Salmond, of Linlithgow, Scotland, and Mary Stewart Milne; *b* 31 December 1954; *Educ* Linlithgow Acad, Univ of St Andrews (MA); *m* 6 May 1981, Moira French McGlashan; *Career* asst economist Govt Econ Serv 1978–80, economist Royal Bank of Scotland 1980–87; MP (SNP) Banff and Buchan 1987–, MSP (SNP) Banff and Buchan 1999–2001, MSP (SNP) Gordon 2007–; ldr Opposition Scottish Parliament 1999–2000; ldr SNP 1990–2000 and 2004– (dep ldr 1987–90); first min Scottish Exec 2007–; *Publications* numerous articles and conference papers on oil and gas economics; *Recreations* reading, golf; *Style*— The Rt Hon Alex Salmond, MP; ✉ Constituency Office, 17 Maiden Street, Peterhead, Aberdeenshire AB42 1EE (tel 01779 470444, fax 01779 474460)

SALMOND, Prof George Peacock Copland; s of John Brown Salmond (d 1998), and Joan Tennant Lambie, *née* Copland (d 1989); *b* 15 November 1952; *Educ* Bathgate Acad, Whitburn Acad West Lothian, Univ of Strathclyde (Malcolm Kerr Prize for Biology, BSc), Univ of Warwick (PhD), Univ of Cambridge (MA); *m* 1975 (m dis 1985), Christina Brown Adamson; partner, Carolyn Ann Alderson; 1 da (Kathryn Rebecca Salmond b 1996); *Career* post doctoral research fell Dept of Molecular Biology Univ of Edinburgh 1977–80, lectr in microbiology Biological Lab Univ of Kent 1980–83; Dept of Biological Sciences Univ of Warwick: lectr in microbiology 1983–89, sr lectr 1989–93, prof 1993–96; prof of molecular microbiology Dept of Biochemistry Univ of Cambridge 1996–, fell Wolfson Coll Cambridge 2000– (memb Governing Body 2000–); dir Cargenex Research Ltd 1997–2000; BBSRC: memb Plants and Microbial Sciences Ctees 1999–2001 (chm Natural Products Biology Steering Gp 2000–02), chm Plant and Microbial Sciences Panel for Scientific Quality Assessment of BBSRC Research Insts 2001, memb Integration Panel for BBSRC Inst Science Quality Assessment 2001, memb Cross Ctee Gp on Antimicrobial Research 2001, memb Sequencing Panel 2002–, memb Plant and Microbial Metabolomics Initiative Sift Panel 2002–, chm Research Equipment Initiative Ctee 2003–; Scot Exec Environment and Rural Affrs Dept (SEERAD): chm Quality of Science Assessment Panel (Plants) for Scot Research Insts 2002–, memb Integration Panel Quality of Science Assessment Panels 2002–; memb: Scientific Advsy Bd NSC Technologies Illinois 1996–2001, Panel for Jt Research Cncls Equipment Initiative (JREI) 2001, Pathogen Sequencing Advsy Gp Wellcome Tst Sanger Inst 2002–, Science Unions Ctee Royal Soc 2005–, Cncl Fedn of European Microbiological Socs 2004–; dir, tstee and memb Governing Cncl John Innes Centre Norwich 2003–, dir, tstee and memb Governing Body Scottish Crop Research Inst Dundee 2003–; sr ed Jl of Molecular Microbiology and Biotechnology 1998–; memb Ed Bd: Molecular Microbiology 1988–97, Molecular Plant Pathology-On-Line 1996–, Molecular Plant Pathology 1999–2002, Microbiology 1999–2000; assoc ed: European Jl of Plant Pathology 1992–98, Molecular Plant-Microbe Interactions 1993–98; Soc for Gen Microbiology: memb Cncl 1997–2001 and 2004–, convenor Physiology, Biochemistry and Molecular Genetics Gp Ctee 2002–, convenor and chm Physiology, Biochemistry and Molecular Genetics Gp Ctee 2002–, int sec 2004–; memb: Genetical Soc, Biochemical Soc, American Soc of Microbiology, Br Soc for Plant Pathology, Br Soc for Antimicrobial Chemotherapy, Soc for Industrial Microbiology; fell Cambridge Philosophical Soc FRSA 2001, FFCS 2001; *Publications* author of numerous articles in learned jls on molecular biology and bacterial genetics (incl studies on bacterial cell division, molecular phytopathology, antibiotics, quorum sensing, bacterial virulence and protein secretion); *Recreations* driving, poetry, accumulating Air Miles; *Style*— Prof George Salmond; ✉ Department of Biochemistry, University of Cambridge, Tennis Court Road, Cambridge CB2 1QW (tel 01223 333650, fax 01223 766108, e-mail gpcs@mole.bio.cam.ac.uk)

SALOMON, William Henry; s of Sir Walter Hans Salomon (d 1987), of Hamburg, and Kaete Gerda, *née* Jacoby; *b* 30 September 1957; *Educ* Lycée Français de Londres, Westminster, Magdalene Coll Cambridge (MA, LLB), Inns of Court Sch of Law; *m* 4 July 1992, Emma Georgina (Gigi), da of Maj H R Callander, MC (decd); 1 da (Bettina b 9 April 1994), 1 s (Alexander b 26 March 1996); *Career* trainee Welt am Sonntag Hamburg 1974, Brown Shipley & Co Ltd 1978–80, trainee Brown Brother Harriman NY 1980–81, Rea Brothers Ltd 1981–85, Finsbury Asset Management Ltd 1987–99; dir: Immuno International AG 1981–97, Manganese Bronze (Holdings) plc 1987–2002, Rea Brothers Group plc 1988–99 (dep chm until 1998, chm 1999), Adam & Harvey Group plc 1991–2002, Aquila International Fund Ltd 1994–, Ocean Wilson Holdings Ltd 1995– (dep chm 1999–), Hanseatic Asset Mgmnt LBG 1998–, Hansa Capital Ptnrs LLP 1998–, Aberdeen Emerging Markets Investment Tst 1999–2002, Close Asset Mgmnt Holdings Ltd 1999–2002 (vice-chm 1999–2000), Cathedral Capital plc 2002–06, New India Investment Tst plc 2004– (chm); memb Hon Soc of the Inner Temple 1986–; *Recreations* tennis, fishing; *Clubs* Norddeutscher Regatta Verein Hamburg, Rio de Janeiro Country, Hurlingham, Bath and Racquets, Brooks's; *Style*— William Salomon, Esq; ✉ Hansa Capital Partners LLP, 50 Curzon Street, London W1J 7UW (tel 020 7647 5750, fax 020 7647 5770); (tel 020 7647 5750, fax 020 7647 5770, e-mail info@hansacap.com)

SALOP, Archdeacon of; *see*: Hall, Ven John Barrie

SALSBURY, Peter Leslie; *Career* Marks and Spencer plc: jt md i/c clothing, home furnishings, direct mail, european retail, franchise operations, int franchise gp 1994–98 (previously dir i/c personnel and store operations), md i/c general merchandise 1998–99, chief exec 1998–2000; non-exec dir: TR Property Investment Tst plc 1997– (chm 2004–), Highway Insurance Holdings 2006–; currently with P&S Salsbury Ltd (Mgmnt Consultants); memb Cncl C&G; *Style*— Peter Salsbury; ✉ P&S Salsbury Ltd, 63 St Johns Avenue, London SW15 6AL

SALT, Dr (Robert) Barry; s of Francis Robert Salt (d 1975), and Margaret Jaffray, *née* Incoll (d 1965); *b* 15 December 1933; *Educ* Williamstown HS, Melbourne HS, Univ of Melbourne, NW Poly London, Birkbeck Coll London (BSc, PhD), London Sch of Film Technique; *Career* teacher Sunshine HS Melbourne 1955, dancer Ballet Guild Co Melbourne 1955–56, computist Cwlth Aeronautical Res Labs Melbourne 1956, dancer Western Theatre Ballet London 1957, computer programmer Int Computers & Tabulators London 1958–60, lectr in physics Sir John Cass Coll London 1965–66, dancer Ballet Minerva London 1966, freelance lighting cameraman 1968–71, supply teacher ILEA 1969–70, film teacher and res asst Slade Sch London 1970, lectr for post grad dip in film studies UCL 1973–78, pt/t lectr Slade Sch London 1978–82, tutor in film-making Sch of Film & TV RCA 1982–87, pt/t tutor in film-making for post grad dip Communications Dept Goldsmiths Coll London 1987–88, course dir London Int Film Sch 1988–; visiting lectr film schs and univs England and Europe 1977–; films directed incl: My Name is Errol Addison (documentary) 1965, Pop Up Into a New World (documentary) 1967, The Future Perfect (fictional short) 1968, Six Reels of Film to be Shown in any Order (fiction feature) 1971; organiser and presenter series of progs on film history Nat Film Theatre 1976–; invited speaker at many academic confs on film history in England and Europe 1976–; conslt and writer for Microsoft Encarta 1994–, author of numerous articles on dance, film and science subjects; *Books* Film Style and Technology - History and Analysis (1983, 2 edn 1992), Making Pictures: A Century of European Cinematography (jtly, 2003), Moving into Pictures (2006); *Recreations* reading; *Style*— Dr Barry Salt; ✉ tel 020 7240 0168

SALT, Christopher James; s of Lawrence Athelstan Salt (d 1994), of Woodbury, Devon, and Marion Agnes, *née* Manners (d 1999); *b* 11 January 1946; *Educ* Beaumont Coll, BRNC Dartmouth; *m* 29 Nov 1969, Jennifer, da of Douglas Thomas; 4 da (Rebecca Jane b 8 Aug 1971, Jessica Agnes b 3 Jan 1974, Harriet Clare b 23 Oct 1975, Elizabeth Ann b 1 June 1978); *Career* Gen List Offr RN 1964–86, customer servs mangr and sales & marketing servs mangr Calor Gas Ltd 1986–91, md Corps of Commissionaires Management Ltd 1992–98, dir Management Response Ltd (interim mgmnt conslts) 1998–2001, ops dir Fuelstretcher Ltd 2001–; *Recreations* fishing, walking, sailing, medieval history; *Clubs* Anchorites, Exeter Flotilla, RNSA, Exe Sailing; *Style*— Christopher Salt, Esq; ✉ c/o Fuelstretcher Ltd, Tamar Science Park, Derriford, Plymouth, Devon PL6 8BX (tel 01752 764423, fax 01752 764424, e-mail cjs@fuelstretcher.co.uk)

SALT, Julia Ann; da of Kenneth Gordon Richardson, and Nora, *née* McLachlan; *b* 4 May 1955; *Educ* St Mary's Senior HS Hull, St Hilda's Oxford (MA); *Family* 1 da (Freya b 12 Aug 1983), 1 s (Frederick b 17 July 1985); m 10 Aug 2000, Graham Bailey; *Career* Allen & Overy 1985–; memb: City of London Solicitors Co 1985, The Law Soc 1977; govr Rugby Sch 2000–; *Recreations* sailing, skiing, opera, languages; *Clubs* Royal Ocean Racing, Royal Thames Yacht, Royal Corinthian Yacht; *Style*— Mrs Julia A Salt; ✉ Allen & Overy LLP, 40 Bank Street, London E14 5DU

SALT, Sir (Thomas) Michael John; 4 Bt (UK 1899), of Standon, and of Weeping Cross, Co Stafford; s of Lt-Col Sir Thomas Henry Salt, 3 Bt (d 1965); *b* 7 November 1946; *Educ* Eton; *m* 1971, Caroline, eldest da of Henry Robert John Hildyard (d 1986); 2 da (Henrietta Sophia Meriel b 1978, Alexandra Georgia May b 1982); *Heir* bro, Anthony Salt; *Style*— Sir Michael Salt, Bt; ✉ Shillingstone House, Shillingstone, Dorset

SALT, Sir Patrick MacDonnell; 7 Bt (UK 1869), of Saltaire, Yorkshire; s of Cdr Sir John William Titus Salt, 4 Bt, RN (d 1952), and Stella Houlton, *née* Jackson (d 1974); suc bro, Sir Anthony Houlton Salt, 6 Bt, 1991; *b* 25 September 1932; *Educ* Stowe; *m* 1976, Ann Elizabeth Mary, da of late Dr Thomas Kay Maclachlan, and wid of Denys Kilham Roberts, OBE; *Heir* kinsman, Daniel Salt; *Style*— Sir Patrick Salt, Bt; ✉ Hillwatering Farmhouse, Langham, Bury St Edmunds, Suffolk IP31 3ED

SALTER, David Arthur; s of James Wardel Salter, and Kathleen Wright Salter; *b* 27 August 1948; *Educ* Ecclesfield GS, Pembroke Coll Cambridge (MA, LLM); *m* Anne Ruth; 2 s (Robin James Edward b 1 March 1977, William David Wardel b 17 April 1982), 1 da (Alice Rosemary b 9 May 1989); *Career* admitted slr 1972; asst slr: Mills & Reeve Norwich 1972–74 (formerly articled clerk), Barber Robinson Harrogate 1974–75; Addleshaw Goddard (formerly Addleshaw Booth & Co): asst slr 1975–78, ptnr 1978–, currently nat head Family Law Gp; recorder of the Crown Court 1995–; memb Family Procedure Rule Ctee, sometime memb Family Ctee Judicial Studies Bd, sometime chm Resolution; govr Harrogate Int Festival, organist and choirmaster Knaresborough Parish Church; pres European Chapter Int Acad of Matrimonial Lawyers; ARCO; *Books* Litigation Practice (gen ed), Matrimonial Consent Orders and Agreements (jtly), Humphreys' Family Proceedings (gen ed), Family Courts: Emergency Remedies in the Family Courts (jtly), Pensions and Insurance on Family Breakdown (gen ed), Debt and Insolvency on Family Breakdown (jtly), Butterworths Family Law Service (ed), Family Finance and Tax (jtly), The Family Court Practice (jtly); *Style*— David Salter, Esq; ✉ Addleshaw Goddard, Sovereign House, Sovereign Street, Leeds LS1 1HQ (tel 0113 209 2454, fax 0113 209 2611, e-mail david.salter@addleshawgoddard.com)

SALTER, Ian; s of Norman Salter, and Turid Salter; *b* 21 February 1968, Chatham, Kent; *Educ* King's Sch Rochester, Univ of Bristol (LLB), Coll of Law Guildford; *m* 27 Feb 1993, Caryn; 1 s (David), 1 da (Rhiannon); *Career* slr; Burges Salmon Solicitors 1990– (ptnr 1999–, currently head Environmental Law Unit); memb Law Soc 1990, Int Nuclear Lawyers' Assoc 1998; MRTPI 1996; *Recreations* golf; *Clubs* Reform; *Style*— Ian Salter, Esq; ✉ Burges Salmon LLP, Narrow Quay House, Prince Street, Bristol BS1 4AH (tel 0117 939 2000, fax 0117 902 4400, e-mail ian.salter@burges-salmon.com)

SALTER, Ian George; s of late Desmond Salter, and Diane Salter (d 1992); *b* 7 March 1943; *Educ* Hutchins Sch Hobart; *Career* md SG Investment Mgmnt Ltd (formerly Strauss Turnbull then Société Générale Strauss Turnbull) 2001–03, chm CCH International (formerly Emdex Trade) 2001–, dir Tilney Investment Mgmnt (London) 2003–; memb Hobart Stock Exchange 1965–69; London Stock Exchange: memb 1970–, memb Cncl 1980–91, non-exec dir 1986–2004, dep chm 1990–2004; inspr DTI 1984–87, memb Fin Reporting Cncl 1994–2002, memb Code Ctee Takeover Panel 2002–04; *Recreations* gardening, opera, travel; *Clubs* City of London; *Style*— Ian Salter, Esq; ✉ 36 Queen Street, London EC4 1BN (tel 020 7329 6363)

SALTER, Rev (Arthur Thomas Alexis) John; TD (1988); er s of Arthur Salter (d 1982), of The Tong-Norton Farm, Shropshire, and Dora May, *née* Wright (d 1985); the Salter family has been seated in Shropshire since the reign of King John, when John de le Sel is mentioned in the records of Shrewsbury Abbey 1211 (*see* Burke's Landed Gentry, 18 edn, vol III, 1972); *b* 22 November 1934; *Educ* Wellington GS, KCL (AKC 1960), St Boniface's Theol Coll Warminster; *Career* served Intelligence Corps 1954–55, RAMC 1955–56; ordained: deacon 1961, priest 1962; asst priest: St Peter's Mount Park Ealing 1961–65, St Stephen with St Thomas the Apostle Shepherd's Bush 1965–66, St Alban the Martyr Holborn with St Peter Saffron Hill 1966–70; priest-in-charge St Clement Barnsbury and St Michael the Archangel Islington 1970–79, vicar St Silas with All Saints Pentonville 1970–2000, guild vicar St Dunstan-in-the-West with St Thomas of Canterbury within the Liberty of the Rolls 1979–99; ordained Melkite Greek Catholic Patriarchal Priest 2002; cnsllr for Foreign Relations to his Sacred Beatitude the Melkite Greek Catholic Patriarch Gregory III of Antioch and all the East, of Alexandria and of Jerusalem 2002–; chm Wynford Estate's Old People's Club 1971–90, chaplain Law Courts Branch Edward Bear Fndn for Muscular Dystrophy 1979–99, chm Ctee Anglican and Eastern Churches Assoc 1990–2001 (gen sec 1975–90); Royal Army Chaplains' Dept 1975–94, CF IV (Capt) 1975–81, CF III (Maj); chaplain: 36 Signal Regt 1975–80, 257 (S) Gen Hosp RAMC (V) Duke of York's HQ 1980–94, Reg Army Reserve of Offrs 1994–96; hon chaplain HMTS Lancastria Assoc 1996–; memb: Ctee Nikaean Club Lambeth Palace 1999–2001, Societas Sanctae Crucis (SSC), Soc of Friends of St George's Windsor and Descendants of the Knights of the Garter, Coptic Cultural Centre Venice, Friends of the Holy Father; fell Sion Coll 1979; chaplain of jurisdiction and justice Order of St Lazarus of Jerusalem 1974, chaplain to HBM Consulate-Gen Istanbul 1975, Locum Tenens Apocrisarios to HAH The Ecumenical Patriarch and to His Sacred Beatitude the

Patriarch of Constantinople of the Armenians, hereditary Lord of Choulton and Eton 1982–; chm Pontifical Soc of St John Chrysostom 2002; Freeman City of London 1990; Hon Archimandrite's Cross of Byelo-Russian Autocephalic Orthodox Church-in-Exile 1979, Archpriest's Cross of Ethiopian Catholic Uniate Church (Eparchy of Asmara Eritrea) 1980, Archpriest's Cross Exarchate of Pope Shenouda III (Coptic Orthodox Patriarchate of Alexandria) 1981, Hon Knight Order of St Michael of the Wing (Royal House of Braganza Portugal) 1984, Companion of Honour Order of Orthodox Hospitallers (Ethnarchy of Cyprus and Greek Patriarchate of Antioch) 1985; *Recreations* travelling in Eastern Europe, genealogy, reading; *Clubs* Athenaeum, City Volunteers Officers'; *Style—* The Rev John Salter, TD, SSC, AKC; ✉ 1 St James Close, 1 Bishop Street, Islington, London N1 8PH (tel 020 7359 0250)

SALTER, Martin; MP; *Career* MP (Lab) Reading West 1997–; *Style—* Martin Salter, Esq, MP; ✉ House of Commons, London SW1A 0AA (tel 020 7219 3000)

SALTER, Rebecca; *b* 24 February 1955; *Educ* Bristol Poly; *Career* artist; research student Kyoto City Univ of Arts Japan (Leverhulme scholarship) 1979–81, living and working: in Japan 1981–85, in London 1985–; artist in residence Josef and Anni Albers Fndn CT 2003; research fell TrAIN (Transnational Art, Identity and Nation) Research Centre Univ of the Arts London; *Awards* incl: Greater London Arts Award 1985, Pollock-Krasner Fndn Award 1995 and 2003, Cheltenham Open Drawing Award 1997; *Solo Exhibitions* incl: Galerie Maronie Kyoto 1981, Amano Gall Osaka 1982, Gall Suzuki Kyoto 1983, Gall Te Tokyo 1984, Curwen Gall London 1984 and 1987, Art Forum Singapore 1985, Miller/Brown Gall San Francisco 1986, Ichikawa Gall Tokyo 1990, Greene Gall Connecticut 1991, Quay Arts Centre Isle of Wight 1992, Ishiyacho Gall Kyoto 1993, Jill George Gallery London 1994, 1996, 1998 and 2000, M-13/Howard Scott Gall NY 1997 and 1999, Galerie Pousse Tokyo 1998, Galerie Michael Sturm Stuttgart 1999, Feichtner & Mizrahi Vienna 1999, Gall Sowaka Kyoto 1999, Howard Scott Gall NY 2001 and 2004, Russell-Cotes Art Gall Bournemouth 2001, Hirschl Contemporary Art London 2002, Line Fosterart London 2004, Beardsmore Gall London 2006, Howard Scott Gall NY 2007; *Group Exhibitions* incl: Rijeka Drawing Biennale Yugoslavia 1982, Ryu Int Gall Tokyo 1982, Ljubljana Int Print Biennale Yugoslavia 1983 and 1985, Curwen Gall London 1984 and 1985, Osaka Contemporary Art Fair 1985, Norwegian Int Print Biennale 1986, Int Contemporary Art Fair London 1986, Chicago Int Art Exhibition 1986–92, Oxford Gall Oxford 1988, Art London '89 1989, RCA 1990, Basel Art Fair 1991, Cleveland Drawing Biennale 1991, Intaglio Gall London 1992, Mall Galleries London 1992, Eagle Gall London 1993, Jill George Gall 1994, Tate Gall London 1995, Turnpike Gall Leigh 1995, Cheltenham Open Drawing 1996, Galerie Michael Sturm Stuttgart 1996, Rubicon Gall Dublin 1997, 20th Century Art Fair London 1997 and 1998, Gainsborough's House Sudbury 1999, Art 2000 London 2000, Art 2001 London 2001, Working the Grid Lafayette Coll Easton PA 2002, Untitled: work on paper Hirschl Contemporary Art London 2003, Atlantic Fosterart London 2003, Yale Center for British Art 2005; *Work in Collections* incl: Tate Gall London, British Museum, Cleveland County Cncl, Unilever London, WH Smith plc, Govt Art Coll, The Mortgage Corp, Arthur Anderson & Co London, MSP Ltd, Leslie & Godwin Gp London, Pearl Assurance Peterborough, Gartmore Investment Mgmnt Ltd, San Francisco MOMA, Portland MOMA, JP Morgan NYC, World Print Cncl San Francisco, Heithoff Family Collection Calif, Lake Tower Collection Chicago, American Telephone and Telegraph Co, California Coll of Arts and Crafts, Library of Congress Washington DC, Frechen Kunstverein Germany, Yale Center for British Art, Victoria and Albert Museum London; *Commissions* incl: United Airlines, EPR Architects, many private cmmns; *Publications* Japanese Woodblock Printing (2001), Japanese Popular Prints: From Votive Slips to Playing Cards (2006); *Style—* Ms Rebecca Salter; ✉ Park Studios, 34 Scarborough Road, London N4 4LT (e-mail info@rebeccasalter.com)

SALTER, Richard Stanley; QC (1995); s of Stanley James Salter (d 1980), and Betty Maud, *née* Topsom (d 1974); *b* 2 October 1951; *Educ* Harrow Co Sch, Balliol Coll Oxford (MA); *m* 11 May 1991, Shona Virginia Playfair, o da of (Jack) Philip Cannon, *qv*; *Career* called to the Bar Inner Temple 1975 (bencher 1991), asst recorder 1997–2000, recorder 2000–, asst boundary cmmr 2000–; chm Inner Temple Scholarships Ctee 2002–; chm London Common Law and Commercial Bar Assoc 2004–05 (memb Ctee 1986–2001, vice-chm 2002–03); memb: Cncl of Legal Educn 1990–96 (chm Bd of Examiners 1992–93), Advocacy Studies Bd 1996–2000, Advsy Bd City Univ Inst of Law 2001–, Bar Cncl 2004–08 (ex-officio 2004–05, elected 2006–08); govr Inns of Court Sch of Law 1996–2001; ACIArb 1983; *Publications* contrib: Banks, Liability and Risk (1990, 3 edn 2001), Halsbury's Laws of England: Guarantee and Indemnity (4 edn, 1993), Banks and Remedies (2 edn, 1999); ed: All England Commercial Cases (1999–), Legal Decisions Affecting Bankers (vols 12–14, 2001); *Recreations* books, music, theatre, cricket; *Clubs* Savile, Shoscombe Village Cricket; *Style—* Richard Salter, Esq, QC; ✉ 3 Verulam Buildings, Gray's Inn, London WC1R 5NT (tel 020 7831 8441, fax 020 7831 8479)

SALTER, Prof Stephen Hugh; MBE (2004); s of Willoughby de Carle Salter (d 1993), of Mansfield, Notts, and Rachel, *née* Floyd (d 1984); *b* 7 December 1938; *Educ* Framlingham Coll, Sidney Sussex Coll Cambridge; *m* 24 April 1973, Prof Margaret Caldwell, da of James Donaldson (d 1947), of Aberfoyle, Perthshire; *Career* apprentice fitter tool maker Saunders Roe Ltd 1956–61, res asst Univ of Cambridge 1962–67, personal chair in engrg design Univ of Edinburgh 1986– (res fell 1967–71, lectr 1971–78, reader 1978–86); author of scientific papers on robotics, renewable energy, mine clearance, the suppression of explosions, hydraulic machines, climate change, flood prevention and water supply; FRSE 1991; *Recreations* photography, the invention of instruments and tools; *Style—* Prof Stephen Salter, MBE, FRSE; ✉ King's Buildings, Mayfield Road, University of Edinburgh EH9 3JL (tel 0131 650 5703, fax 0131 650 5702, e-mail shs@mech.ed.ac.uk)

SALTISSI, Dr Stephen; s of Victor Saltissi, of Leeds, and Betty, *née* Weinman; *b* 21 September 1950; *Educ* Roundhay Sch Leeds, King's Coll London (MB BS), Univ of London (MSc, MD); *m* 30 July 1972, Sandra Bernice, da of Maurice Aaron Bellman, of Leeds; 2 da (Nicola b 1978, Caroline b 1980); *Career* sr res fell St Thomas' Hosp 1979–80 (registrar 1977–78); sr registrar: N Tees 1981–82, Newcastle upon Tyne 1982–84; Royal Liverpool Univ Hosp: conslt physician and cardiologist 1984–, clinical sub dean 1991–2001, clinical dir of med 1992–96, head of cardiology 1998– (also Broadgreen Univ Hosp), assoc medical dir 2001–04 (also Broadgreen Univ Hosp), lead for clincial risk mgmnt 2001–04 (also Broadgreen Univ Hosp), lead cardiologist Cheshire and Merseyside Cardiac Clinical Network; hon lectr Univ of Liverpool 1984–; memb Appraisals Ctee Nat Inst for Clinical Excellence 2001–; past chm Library Ctee Royal Liverpool Univ Hosp, chm Liverpool Cardiac Rehabilitation Services; memb: Br Cardiac Soc 1985, Merseyside and N Wales Assoc Physicians 1984, Royal Liverpool Univ Hosp Clinical Risk Mgmnt Gp, Cncl Br Soc of Echocardiography 1998–2000; FRCP 1991 (MRCP 1975); *Recreations* tennis, supporter Liverpool FC, travel; *Style—* Dr Stephen Saltissi; ✉ Wansfell, 25 Hillside Drive, Woolton, Liverpool L25 5NR (tel 0151 428 2034, fax 0151 428 0137, e-mail stephensaltissi@blueyonder.co.uk); Royal Liverpool University Hospital, Prescot Street, Liverpool L7 8XP (tel 0151 706 3573 (sec), 0151 706 3574 (direct line), fax 0151 706 5833, e-mail stephen.saltissi@rlbuht.nhs.uk); 88 Rodney Street, Liverpool L1 9AR (tel 0151 709 7066, fax 0151 709 7279)

SALTONSTALL, James Edwin Rous; MBE (1997); s of Peter Rous Saltonstall, (d 1984), of Bridlington, E Yorks, and Antonia, *née* Ernste; *b* 22 July 1947; *Educ* St George's Secdy Sch; *m* 26 June 1971, Christine Ann, da of Norman Woodhouse, and Margaret Woodhouse; 1 s (Jeremy Richard Rous b 11 Dec 1981); *Career* served RN 1962–77; yacht racer and coach; yacht and dinghy racing commencing Royal Yorks Yacht Club 1952, RN dinghy team 1965–77 (capt 1974–76), sr nat racing coach RYA 1977–2000; attended over 100 int yacht and dinghy events (World, Euro, Olympic); achievements incl: runner-up J24 class World Championships Japan 1985, Euro champion J24 class Germany 1991, nat champion J24 class 1984–85; Yachtsman of the Year 1984 and Special Award 1995; Olympic Team coach: Atlanta 1996, Sydney 2000; *Books* RYA Race Training Manual (1983, 3 edn (RYA Book of Race Training) 1996, 4 edn (Race Training with Jim Saltonstall) 2006); *Recreations* sailing; *Style—* James Saltonstall, Esq, MBE; ✉ e-mail jimsaltonstall@btinternet.com

SALTOUN, Rt Hon Lady (twenty-first holder of title; S 1445); Flora Marjory; *née* Fraser; Chief of the Name of Fraser; family granted right to own Univ of Fraserburgh by King James VI; da of 20 Lord Saltoun, MC (d 1979), and Dorothy, da of Sir Charles Welby, 5 Bt, CB, by Maria, sis of 4 Marquess of Bristol; *b* 18 October 1930; *Educ* St Mary's Wantage; *m* 1956, Capt Alexander Ramsay of Mar, DL (d 2000); 3 da; *Heir* da, Hon Mrs Nicolson; *Career* sits as Independent in House of Lords; *Clubs* New; *Style—* The Rt Hon the Lady Saltoun; ✉ House of Lords, London SW1A 0PW

SALUSBURY-TRELAWNY, *see:* Trelawny

SALVESEN, Alastair Eric Hotson; s of Lt-Col Iver Ronald Stuart Salvesen (d 1957), and Marion Hamilton, *née* McClure (d 1997); Christian Salvesen (fndr of family business) emigrated from Norway to Edinburgh 1846; bro of Robin S Salvesen, DL, *qv*; *b* 28 July 1941; *Educ* Fettes, Cranfield (MBA); *m* 18 July 1979, Elizabeth Evelyn, da of Patrick Murray, WS, RNVR (d 2001), of Hawick, Roxburghshire; 1 da (Venetia Clare Johanna), 1 s (George Edward Thomas); *Career* chm: Dawnfresh Seafoods Ltd 1983– (md 1981–93), Dovecot Studios Ltd 2001–, Silvertrout Ltd 2004–; dir: Praha Investment Holdings Ltd 1985–, Richmond Foods plc 1994–2003, New Ingliston Ltd 1995–, Luing Cattle Soc 1996–99; pres Royal Highland & Agric Soc of Scot 2001–02; exec memb: UK Assoc of Frozen Food Prodrs 1990– (chm Shellfish Ctee 1984–96), British Frozen Foods Fedn 1992– (pres 1995–97); chm Shellfish Ctee Food & Drink Fedn 2007–; memb: Deregulation Taskforce for Food, Drink and Agriculture 1993–94, Cncl Shellfish Assoc of GB 2003 (also memb Ctee); estab Alastair Salvesen Art Scholarship 1989; memb Cncl Royal Soc of Arts 2005; govr: The Fettes Tst 1994–, Donaldson's Tst 1997–, Compass Sch 1994– (chm 1996–); memb The Queen's Body Guard for Scotland (The Royal Company of Archers); Liveryman Worshipful Co of Fishmongers; CA; Queen's Jubilee Medal; HRSA, FCIM, FCMI, FRSA, FSA Scot, ARAgS 2004; *Publications* Slekten Salvesen 1550–1995; *Recreations* shooting, archery, farming and forestry, contemporary Scottish art; *Clubs* New (Edinburgh); *Style—* Alastair E H Salvesen, Esq; ✉ Whitburgh, Pathhead, Midlothian EH37 5SR (tel 01875 320304, fax 01875 320766); Dawnfresh Seafoods Ltd, Bothwell Park Industrial Estate, Uddingston, Lanarkshire G71 6LS (tel 01698 810008, fax 01698 810088, e-mail alastair.salvesen@dawnfresh.co.uk)

SALVESEN, HE Dr (Charles) Hugh; s of John Salvesen, of Gullane, E Lothian, and Eelin, *née* Brown (d 2002); *b* 10 September 1955, Alyth, Perthshire; *Educ* Loretto Sch Musselburgh, Christ's Coll Cambridge (BA, PhD); *m* 17 Dec 1983, Emilie, *née* Ingenhousz; 2 s (Jonathan, Alexis (twins) b 28 Nov 1987), 1 da (Maria b 31 Oct 1990 d 1995); *Career* entered HM Diplomatic Service 1982; FCO 1982–84, first sec Br Mil Govt Berlin 1984–85, first sec Br Embassy Bonn 1985–88, FCO 1988–93, first sec Br Embassy Buenos Aires 1993–96, dep high cmmr Br High Cmmn Wellington 1996–2000, FCO 2000–05, ambass Montevideo 2005–; *Style—* HE Dr Hugh Salvesen; ✉ c/o FCO, King Charles Street, London SW1A 2AH (e-mail hugh.salvesen@fco.gov.uk)

SALVESEN, Robin Somervell; DL (E Lothian 1993); s of Iver Ronald Stuart Salvesen (d 1957), and Marion Hamilton, *née* McClure (d 1997); bro of Alastair Salvesen; *b* 4 May 1935; *Educ* Cargilfield Sch Edinburgh, Fettes, UC Oxford, Hendon Tech Coll; *m* 6 Aug 1960, Sari Frances Judith *née* Clarke; 4 da (Ferelith b 3 May 1961, Alice b 25 Dec 1962, Tabitha b 13 Feb 1964, Emily b 22 June 1970), 3 s (Francis b 26 Oct 1965, Thomas b 14 May 1967, Iver b 31 Jan 1969); *Career* 5 Bn QO Nigeria Regt 1955–56, Maj Royal Scots TA 52 Lowland Volunteers 1957–69; chm: Scot Cncl King George's Fund for Sailors 1982–2007, Lights Advsy Ctee 1987–2003; dir: The Murrayfield plc until 1992, Christian Salvesen plc until 2002; memb Gen Ctee and Scottish Ctee Lloyd's Register of Shipping 1974–91; dep chm Scot Veterans' Residences, chm Assoc for Protection of Rural Scotland 1994–2000; memb Merchant Co of the City of Edinburgh (former memb Ct of Assts); pres Edinburgh Area Scouts 1991– (Silver Acorn 2007); chm: Bells National Tst, Theodore Salvesen Tst; former chm Leith Nautical Coll; tstee Thistle Tst; elder of St Mary's Church Haddington (chm Congregational Bd 1988–2002); hon Danish consul for E Scotland 1972–89; moderator The High Constabulary of The Port of Leith 1994; Queen's Silver Jubilee Medal 1977, Queen's Golden Jubilee Medal 2002; memb Queen's Body Guard for Scotland (Royal Co of Archers) 1965–; FIMgt; Royal Order of the Chev of Dannebrog (Denmark) 1981 (first class 1989); *Publications* Biography/Memoirs (2003); *Recreations* shooting with long bow and shotgun; *Clubs* New (Edinburgh); *Style—* Robin S Salvesen, Esq, DL; ✉ Eaglescairnie House, Haddington, East Lothian EH41 4HN (tel 01620 810261, fax 01620 810775)

SALVIDANT, Sallie Christina Ellen; da of James Cooper (d 1990), and Nancy Cooper (d 2000); *b* 3 August 1950, Barnet, Herts; *Educ* Kenya HS, Univ of London (CertEd, BEd); *m* 1, 17 May 1968 (m dis 1970), Geoffrey Salvidant; 1 da (Rebecca Kirsty b 7 Aug 1969); m 2, 27 Dec 2001, Alan Lewis; *Career* teacher Taiz North Yemen 1970–72, class teacher Beckford Infants Sch West Hampstead 1977–81, class teacher Christchurch Primary Sch Regents Park 1981–85, head of lower sch Holmewood Boys Prep Sch 1985–87, headmistress Rupert House Prep Sch Henley 1987–93, headmistress Bute House Prep Sch for Girls (formerly St Paul's Girls' Prep Sch) Hammersmith 1993–; govr St Christopher's Sch Hampstead; former govr: Highfield Sch Maidenhead, Cranford House Sch; memb No10 Dist Ctee, Policy and Promotions Ctee and Inspections Ctee IAPS, ISC inspector; Tatler Best Headmistress of a Prep School 2004; IAPS 1987, AHIS 1987; *Recreations* breeding Siamese cats, gardening, walking dogs; *Style—* Mrs Sallie Salvidant; ✉ Bute House Preparatory School for Girls, Luxemburg Gardens, London W6 7EA (tel 020 7603 7381, e-mail ss@butehouse.co.uk)

SALWAY, Francis; s of Toby Salway, and Ann Salway; *b* 5 October 1957; *Educ* Rugby, Univ of Cambridge (MA); *m* 1 June 1985, Sarah; 1 s (Hugh), 1 da (Rachael); *Career* Richard Ellis 1979–82, Abacus Devpt 1982–85, Coll of Estate Mgmnt Reading 1985–86, Standard Life 1986–2000; Land Securities Gp plc: ceo Land Securities Portfolio Mgmnt 2000, memb Bd 2001, ceo Land Securities Devpt 2002, gp chief operating offr 2003, gp chief exec 2004–; vice-pres Br Property Fedn; memb Investment Property Forum; FRICS; *Books* Depreciation of Commercial Property (1986); *Recreations* tennis, walking; *Style—* Francis Salway, Esq; ✉ Land Securities Group plc, 5 Strand, London WC2N 5AF (tel 020 7413 9000, fax 020 7024 3777, e-mail francis.salway@landsecurities.com)

SALZ, Anthony Michael Vaughan; s of Michael Salz, of Yelverton, Devon, and Veronica, *née* Hall; *b* 30 June 1950; *Educ* Radley, Univ of Exeter (LLB); *m* 17 May 1975, Sally Ruth, da of Harold J Hagger, of Broughton, Hants; 1 s (Christopher b 1978), 2 da (Emily b 1980, Rachel b 1982); *Career* admitted slr 1974; Freshfields Bruckhaus Deringer: joined 1975, seconded to Davis Polk and Wardwell NY 1977–78, ptnr 1980–2006, head of corporate finance 1990–94, head of corporate 1994–96, sr ptnr 1996–2000, jt sr ptnr 2000–06; vice-chm BBC 2004– (acting chm 2006); memb Corp Advsy Gp Tate Gallery 1997– (chm 1997–2002); dir: Tate Fndn 2000–, Habitat for Humanity GB 2004–; tstee: Eden Project 2001–, Paul Hamlyn Fndn 2005–; memb Law Soc; *Publications* contrib to various learned jls; *Recreations* fly fishing, tennis, golf, Southampton FC and the family generally; *Clubs* MCC, Berkshire Golf, Walbrook; *Style—* Anthony Salz, Esq; ✉ Freshfields Bruckhaus Deringer, 65 Fleet Street, London EC4Y 1HS (tel 020 7936 4000, fax 020 7832 7392)

SAMANI, Vinay; s of Amritlal Samani, of London, and Jayaben, *née* Madlani; *b* 4 June 1970, Eldoret, Kenya; *Educ* Univ of Birmingham (LLB); *m* 2 Nov 1997, Komal, *née* Ondhia; 2 s (Pranav b 21 Aug 2001, Keshav b 19 Sep 2003); *Career* admitted slr 1994; ptnr Linklaters 2004–; *Style—* Vinay Samani, Esq; ✉ Linklaters, One Silk Street, London EC2Y 8HQ (tel 020 7456 2000)

SAMARAWICKRAMA, Prof Dayananda Yasasiri Dias; s of late Kornelis Dias Samarawickrama, of Galle, Sri Lanka, and late Alice, *née* Mirinchi Arachchi; *b* Sri Lanka; *Educ* Mahinda Coll Galle, Univ of Ceylon (BDS), The London Hosp Med Coll Univ of London (PhD); *m* August 1970, Padma Grace, *née* Kodithuwakku; 2 da (Amanda Kanchana Dias b Sept 1975, Samantha Thanuja Dias b Feb 1978); *Career* asst lectr in conservative dentistry Univ of Peradeniya Sri Lanka 1968, research fell Depts of Conservative Dentistry and Oral Pathology The London Hosp Med Coll 1970, sr lectr in restorative dentistry and dental materials sci Univ of Peradeniya 1981 (lectr in conservative dentistry 1975); The London Hosp Med Coll: lectr in conservative dentistry 1983, dir Dental Auxiliary Sch and sr lectr in conservative dentistry 1989–95; actg head Dept of Conservative Dentistry and sr lectr in conservative dentistry St Bartholomew's and the Royal London Sch of Med and Dentistry 1995, hon conslt in restorative dentistry Barts and The London NHS Tst 2000–, prof of conservative dentistry Queen Mary's Sch of Med & Dentistry Univ of London 2004– (sr tutor 2002–); GDC: specialist in restorative dentistry 2000–, specialist in endodontics 2001–; ed Cwlth Dental Assoc 2006–; memb: Cncl Br Assoc of Teachers of Conservative Dentistry 1995– (pres 1996–97), Cncl Sri Lankan Med and Dental Assoc in the UK (pres 1997–98), Dental Chapter Barts and The London Alumni Assoc (pres 2002–03); assessor int qualifying exam Gen Dental Cncl UK 2000–; external examiner: Univ of Liverpool 2005–, Univ of Manchester 2006–, Postgrad Inst of Medicine Sri Lanka 2006–; author of more than 100 pubns incl original papers, reviews, chapters in books and conf papers; WHO: fell in oral health 1976–77, fell in med educn 1980, memb and reporter WHO/FDI Jt Working Gp on Dental Educn and Trg 1982–86, conslt and advsr on oral health care Sri Lanka 1980–82; conslt: Miny of Health Trinidad & Tobago 1992–96, Miny of Health Barbados and Barbados Dental Cncl 2001–03; memb: BDA 1985–, Br Soc for Restorative Dentistry 1999–; FDSRCS 1992, FHEA 2007; *Recreations* hiking, gardening, reading; *Style—* Prof Dayananda Samarawickrama

SAMBAR, Dr David H; s of Habib David Sambar (d 1952), of Haifa, and Georgette, *née* El Khoury; *b* 19 August 1930; *Educ* Univ of London (BA), American Univ Beirut (MA), Faculty of Economics and Business Admin Lyons (Doctorate magna cum laude); *m* 15 Oct 1966, Salma Renee Sambar, da of Labib Y Zacca, of Beirut (d 1982); 1 s (Habib David b 1968), 1 da (Syma Karine b 1970); *Career* Chase Bank Beirut 1955–73 (auditor, asst mangr, mangr, vice-pres), vice-pres Chase NYC 1973–77, Strategic Investment Planning London 1982–85; chm: Sharjah Investment London 1977–81, Sambar International Investments Ltd 1984–, British American Properties NY 1990–, British American Capital NY 1990–; NE chm EMS Biomedical Vienna; memb Lloyd's of London 1984–; advsr to various companies, ed of articles and speeches for various US and Euro pubns and professional orgns; tstee Princeton in Asia 1965–; memb: Stanford Res Inst 1979–, Euro-Atlantic Gp, Guild of Int Bankers, RIIA; cnsllr in int affrs Peoples for UN NYC 1979–, govr Atlantic 2000; tstee: Woman's World Banking 1986–, Near East Fndn NY; memb Cons Pty; Hon Dr Mexican Acad of Int Law (fell); Freeman City of London; fell Atlantic Cncl, FInstD; *Recreations* tennis, skiing; *Clubs* Hurlingham,RAC; *Style—* Dr David Sambar; ✉ 31 Eaton Place, London SW1X 8BP (tel 020 7235 6815, e-mail dhsambar@aol.com)

SAMBROOK, Richard Jeremy; s of (Philip) Michael Sambrook (d 1980), of Ashford, Kent, and Joan Hartridge (d 1983); *b* 24 April 1956; *Educ* Maidstone Sch for Boys, Univ of Reading (BA), Birkbeck Coll London (MSc); *m* 3 Oct 1987, Susan Jane, da of John Fisher; 1 s (Huw b 17 July 1992), 1 da (Freya b 20 Jan 1994); *Career* journalist with Thomson Regional Newspapers (on Rhondda Leader and South Wales Echo) 1977–80; BBC: chief sub ed BBC Radio News 1980–84, prodr BBC TV News 1984–88, dep ed Nine O'Clock News 1988–92, news ed BBC TV and Radio News 1992–96, head of newsgathering BBC News 1996–99, dep dir BBC News 1999–2001, dir BBC News 2001–04, dir world service and global news 2004–; FRSA, FRTS; *Recreations* music, novels, tennis; *Style—* Richard Sambrook, Esq; ✉ BBC Global News, Room 312CB, Bush House, London WC2B 4PH (tel 020 7557 1400, fax 020 7557 1900)

SAMODUROV, Viacheslav; s of Vladimir Samodurov, of St Petersburg, and Irina Maimusova; *b* 19 May 1974, Tallin, Estonia; *Educ* Vaganova Acad of Ballet St Petersburg; *Career* ballet dancer; princ dancer Kirov Ballet Mariiensky Theatre St Petersburg 1998–2001 (joined 1992), Dutch Nat Ballet Amsterdam 2000–03, Royal Ballet Covent Garden 2003–; first prize Maya Plisetskaya Competition 1996; *Performances* with Kirov Ballet incl: Don Quixote, La Bayadère, La Sylphide, Le Corsaire, The Nutcracker, Giselle, Laurencia, Cinderella, Romeo and Juliet, Grand pas classique, Le Jeune Homme et la Mort, Petrushka, Schéhérazade, Tchaikovsky pas de deux, Symphony in C, Capriccio, The Fairy's Kiss, Middle Duet, Poem of Ecstasy; with Dutch Nat Ballet incl: La Sylphide, Sleeping Beauty, Apollo, Duo Concertante, Symphony in Three Movements, Violin Concerto, Brahms Schoenberg Quartet, The Four Temperaments, Les Noces, Choreartium, Symphonic Variations, Adagio Hammerklavier, Black Cake, Five Tangos, Andante Festivo, Four Last Songs, Approximate Sonata, The Vertiginous Thrill of Exactitude; with Royal Ballet: Romeo & Juliet, The Four Temperaments, Cinderella, Agon, Le Spectre de la Rose, L'Après-Midi d'Un Faune, Voices of Spring; *Recreations* watercolour painting, travel, reading; *Style—* Viacheslav Samodurov, Esq; ✉ c/o Suzanne Banki, 19 Tierney Road, London SW2 4QL (tel 020 8674 1670); Royal Opera House, Covent Garden, London WC2E 9DD (tel 020 7240 1200)

SAMPSON, Adam; *Educ* Maidstone GS, Brasenose Coll Oxford; *m*; 2 c; *Career* system probation offr Probation Service 1987–87, dep dir Prison Reform Tst 1989–94, dep prisons ombudsman Home Office 1994–97, chief exec Rehabilitation of Addicted Prisoners Tst (RAPt) 1998–2003, dir Shelter 2003–; *Recreations* cinema, football, music; *Style—* Adam Sampson, Esq; ✉ Shelter, 88 Old Street, London EC1V 9HU (tel 020 7505 2124, fax 020 7505 2176)

SAMPSON, Michael; s of late William Thomas Sampson, of Horsham, W Sussex, and Lilian Emma, *née* Edmonds; *b* 27 September 1942; *Educ* Collyers Sch Horsham, Univ of Southampton (BScEcon); *m* 7 June 1969, Elizabeth Victoria, da of late Cdr Alfred Bryant Hilliar, of Bishops Caundle, Dorset, and Dorothy Maud, *née* Brendon; 2 da (Anna b 1978, Caroline 1980); *Career* res analyst Simon & Coates stockbrokers 1964–77, Lloyd's investment mangr 1977–85; dir: John Govett & Co 1986–92, Broadgate Investment Trust 1992–2000; *Recreations* tennis, golf; *Style—* Michael Sampson, Esq; ✉ Oakhurst, Courtlands, London Road, Tonbridge, Kent TN10 3DA (tel 01732 354885)

SAMPSON, Nicholas Alexander; s of Charles Sampson, of Faversham, Kent, and Patricia, *née* Burgess; *b* 27 August 1958, Gillingham, Kent; *Educ* Gillingham GS, Howard Sch Rainham, Selwyn Coll Cambridge (MA), Westminster Coll Oxford (PGCE); *m* 18 Apr 1981, Nancy, *née* Threlfall; 2 da (Frances Isobel Rachel, Aurora Nancy Alys (twins) b 10 Apr 1994); *Career* HM inspr of taxes 1981–82, Wells Cathedral Sch 1984–94, headmaster Sutton Valence Sch 1994–2000, princ Geelong GS Australia 2000–04, master Marlborough Coll 2004–; *Recreations* literature, drama, music, sport; *Clubs* East India, Lansdowne, Athenaeum; *Style—* Nicholas Sampson, Esq; ✉ The Master's Lodge, Marlborough College, Marlborough, Wiltshire SN8 1PA (tel 01672 892400, fax 01672 892407, e-mail master@marlboroughcollege.org)

SAMS, Craig; *b* 1944, Nebraska; *Educ* Wharton Sch Univ of Pennsylvania (BSc), Kingston Univ (DBA); *m* 1991, Josephine Fairley; *Career* opened Seed (macrobiotic restaurant) 1967, co-fndr and prop Whole Earth Foods 1967–2003; Green & Black's Organic Chocolate: co fndr (with w, Josephine Fairley) 1991, first product to carry Fairtrade mark, pres 1991–, non-exec dir 2005–; chm: Soil Assoc 2001– (hon treas 1990–2001), Judges Bakery Ltd; *Publications* About Macrobiotics (1972), The Brown Rice Cookbook (1982, 2 edn 1992), The Little Food Book (1993); co-publisher Seed Magazine: The Journal of Organic Living 1972–77, contrib Natural Products News; *Style—* Craig Sams, Esq; ✉ c/o Soil Association, Bristol House, 40–56 Victoria Street, Bristol BS1 6BY (tel 0117 314 5000, fax 0117 314 5001)

SAMS, Jeremy Charles; s of late Eric Sams, of London, and late Enid, *née* Tidmarsh; *b* 12 January 1957; *Educ* Whitgift Sch Croydon, Magdalene Coll Cambridge, Guildhall Sch of Music; *Family* 1 s (Toby Oliver Sams-Friedman b 26 Nov 1994); *Career* composer, director, translator of opera and plays; freelance pianist 1977–82; *Theatre* dir: Schippel, The Plumber, Entertaining Mr Sloane (Greenwich), The Card (Newbury), Wind in the Willows (Tokyo), Neville's Island (Nottingham and West End), Enjoy (Nottingham), Wild Oats (RNT) 1995, The Wind in the Willows (Old Vic) 1995, Passion (Queen's) 1996, Marat/Sade (RNT) 1997, Enter the Guardsman (Donmar) 1997, Two Pianos Four Hands (Birmingham Rep and Comedy) 1999, Spend! Spend! Spend! (Piccadilly) 1999 (and tour 2001), Noises Off (RNT) 2000 (tour, West End and Broadway 2001), Benefactors (Albery) 2002; translations incl: The Rehearsal (Almeida and Garrick, Time Out Award 1991), Leonce and Lena (Sheffield Crucible), Becket (Theatre Royal Haymarket), The Miser (NT), Les Parents Terribles (RNT), Mary Stuart (RNT) 1996, Le Bourgeois Gentilhomme (Nottingham Playhouse) 1997, Colombe (Salisbury Playhouse) 1999, Waiting in the Wings (Broadway) 1999, Scapino (Chichester Festival Theatre) 2005; adaptations incl Chitty Chitty Bang Bang (London Palladium) 2002 and (Broadway) 2005, Amour (Broadway) 2002; *Opera* dir: The Reluctant King (Opera North); translations incl: The Magic Flute, Macbeth, Figaro's Wedding, Force of Destiny, La Bohème, The Ring (ENO), Cosi fan Tutte (Opera 80), Johnny Strikes Up, L'Étoile, Orpheus in the Underworld, The Reluctant King (Opera North), The Merry Widow (Royal Opera); *Scores* over 30 scores for theatre and TV: Kean (Old Vic), The Sneeze, A Walk in the Woods (West End), Persuasion (BAFTA Award for Original TV Music 1996), Have your Cake (BBC) 1997, The Mother (BBC) 2003, Enduring Love (Pathé) 2004 (Ivor Novello Award); at the RSC: Temptation, The Tempest, Measure for Measure, Merry Wives of Windsor, Midsummer Night's Dream; at RNT: Sunday in the Park With George (music dir), Ghetto (also lyrics), The Wind in the Willows (also lyrics), Arcadia; *Books* The Miser (trans, 1991), The Rehearsal (trans, 1991), Les Parents Terribles (trans, 1995), Wild Oats (1995), The Merry Widow (trans, 2000), Enigma Variations (trans, 2003), The Visitor (trans, 2003), Don Juan (trans, 2003), Antigone (trans, 2003); *Style—* Jeremy Sams, Esq; ✉ c/o The Agency, 24 Pottery Lane, Holland Park, London W11 4LZ (tel 020 7727 1346, fax 020 7727 9037)

SAMSON, Prof Thomas James (Jim); s of Edward Samson, of NI, and Matilda Jane, *née* Smyth; *b* 6 July 1946; *Educ* Queen's Univ Belfast (BMus), UC Cardiff (MMus, PhD, LRAM); *Career* res fell in humanities Univ of Leicester 1972–73; Univ of Exeter: lectr in music 1973–87, head of dept 1986–92, reader in musicology 1987–92, prof of musicology 1992–94; prof of music Univ of Bristol 1994–2002, prof of music Royal Holloway Univ of London 2002–: memb Cncl RMA; Order of Merit of the Polish Miny of Culture 1989; FBA 2000; *Books* Music in Transition: A Study in Tonal Expansion and Atonality (1977), The Music of Szymanowski (1980), The Music of Chopin (1985), Chopin Studies (1988), The Late Romantic Era, Man & Music 7 (1991), The Cambridge Companion to Chopin (1992), Chopin - the Four Ballades (1992), Chopin Studies 2 (with John Rink, 1994), Chopin (Master Musicians, 1996), The Cambridge History of Nineteenth-Century Music (2002), Virtuosity and the Musical Work: The Transcendental Studies of Liszt (2003); *Recreations* farming, astronomy; *Style—* Prof Jim Samson; ✉ Department of Music, Royal Holloway, University of London, Egham, Surrey TW20 0EX

SAMSWORTH, Jane Mary Catherine; da of James Gerard Brodie, and Elizabeth, *née* Griffiths; *b* 8 October 1951, London; *Educ* Univ of Sussex (BA), Coll of Law Lancaster Gate; *m* 30 May 1980, Robert Samsworth; 2 da (Chloe Eleanor b 18 Nov 1988, Esmé Verity Annabel b 25 Sept 1995); *Career* slr; Legal Dept GLC 1978–82, Legal Dept Br Telecom plc 1982–1987, Lovells 1987– (ptnr in Pensions Gp 1991–); pres Soc of Pension Conslts 1999–2001, chm Pension Advsrs Service 2004–06, memb Cncl Nat Assoc of Pension Funds (NAPF) 2007–; memb City of London Slrs Co; chm Harpenden Tangent Club 2004–05 (sec 2006–07); FPMI (APMI); *Publications* Guide to the Pensions Act 1995 (jtly, 1995); *Recreations* books, restaurants, family; *Style—* Mrs Jane Samsworth; ✉ Lovells, Atlantic House, 50 Holborn Viaduct, London EC1A 2FG (tel 020 7296 2000, fax 020 7296 2001, e-mail jane.samsworth@lovells.com)

SAMUEL, Andrew William Dougall; s of Capt Andrew Samuel, RN (d 1952), and Letitia Shearer Samuel (d 1999); *b* 12 July 1937; *Educ* Hutchesons' Boys' GS Glasgow, Glasgow Sch of Architecture; *m* 1, 20 Feb 1962 (m dis 1981), Sybille Marie Luise; 1 s (Craig Andrew Alexander Porter b 1966), 1 da (Katja Lilian Hamilton b 1969); *m* 2, 2 Oct 1981, Mary Carswell, da of John Bisset (d 1978), of Carmunock, Glasgow; *Career* chartered architect; princ and dir Andrew Samuel & Co Ltd 1968, chm Townhead Properties Ltd 1980, md Gavin Watson Ltd 1983, dir Johnstone Reid Investments Ltd; holder (with entry in Guinness Book of World Records): World Canoeing Record Loch Ness 1975–85, World Canoeing Record English Channel 1976–2005, World Canoeing K2 Doubles Record English Channel 1980–86; World Masters Games (with A Wilson) 1989: first K2 500m, first K2 5000m, third K2 Marathon; Scottish Nat Canoeing Racing Coach 1976–83, registered Int Canoe Fedn (ICF) official; chm former E Central Tourist Assoc (Scotland), former chm Central Scotland Tourist Assoc, festival dir Trossachs Water Festival 1973–76, sec Trossachs Tourist Assoc 1969–76 (past pres), initiated formation of Loch Lomond and Trossachs Nat Park 1970 (opened 2002); memb SME Consultative Gp to Scottish Exec Scottish Parl; memb: Cncl CBI Scotland, Cncl CBI/SME; FRIAS, RIBA, FIPD, FFB; *Recreations* boating, travel, canoeing, photography; *Clubs* Trossachs Canoe and Boat, West Kilbride Golf, Arran Yacht; *Style—* Andrew Samuel, Esq; ✉ Woodside Farm, By Beith, Ayrshire KA15 1JF (e-mail awdsamuel@gavinwatson.co.uk)

SAMUEL, Christopher John Loraine (Chris); *b* 1 July 1958; *Educ* Marlborough, St Edmund Hall Oxford (MA); *m* 1988, Alison Oralia; 2 da (Harriet Lucy b 12 Dec 1989, Alexandra Mary b 9 Dec 1991), 1 s (Oliver John Loraine b 19 Jan 1996); *Career* gp fin controller Prudential-Bache Int (UK) Group 1985–90, dir of fin Prudential-Bache Securities (Canada) Ltd 1990–91, chief fin offr Prudential Securities (Japan) Ltd 1991, sr vice-pres/int controller Prudential Securities Inc NY 1991–94, dir and chief operating offr Hill Samuel Asset Management Group Ltd 1995–97, dir and chief operating offr Gartmore Investment Management plc 1997–2005, gp chief financial offr Cambridge Place Investment Mgmnt 2006–; ACA 1983; *Clubs* MCC, Leander; *Style—* Chris Samuel, Esq; ✉ Cambridge Place Investment Management, Lexicon House, 17 Old Court Place, London W8 4PL (tel 020 7938 8873, fax 020 7938 5701, e-mail chris.samuel@cpim.co.uk)

SAMUEL, 3 Viscount (UK 1937), of Mount Carmel, and Toxteth in the City of Liverpool; David Herbert Samuel; OBE (1996); s of 2 Viscount Samuel, CMG (d 1978, gs of Edwin Samuel, whose yr bro Montagu cr Lord Swaythling), and Hadassah, *née* Goor (d 1986); *b* 8 July 1922; *Educ* High Sch Jerusalem, Balliol Coll Oxford (MA), Hebrew Univ (PhD);

m 1, 1950 (m dis 1957), Esther, *née* Berelowitz; 1 da (Hon Judith b 1951); m 2, 1960 (m dis 1978), Mrs Rinna Dafni, *née* Grossman; 1 da (Hon Naomi Rachel b 1962); m 3, 1980 (m dis 1993), Mrs Veronika Grimm, *née* Engelhardt; m 4, 1997, Eve Black; *Heir* bro, Hon Dan Samuel; *Career* Capt RA, served India, Burma and Sumatra 1942–45 (despatches); Weizmann Inst of Sci Israel: academic staff Neurobiology Dept 1949–, head Chemistry Gp Sci Teaching Dept 1967–84, head Centre for Neurosciences and Behavioural Research 1970–87, dean Faculty of Chemistry 1971–73, currently prof emeritus; post-doctoral fell Chemistry Dept UCL 1956; research fell: Chemistry Dept Harvard Univ 1957–58, Lab of Chemical Biodynamics (Lawrence Radiation Lab) Univ of Calif Berkeley 1965–66; visiting prof Sch of Molecular Sciences Univ of Warwick 1967, chm Bd of Studies on Chemistry Feinberg Grad Sch 1968–74, visiting Royal Soc prof MRC Neuroimmunology Unit Zoology Dept UCL 1974–75, visiting prof Pharmacology Dept Yale Sch of Med 1983–84, McLaughlin prof Sch of Med McMaster Univ (Canada) 1984; visiting prof Chemistry Dept Univ of York 1995–96 and 1997; memb: Bd US-Israel Educnl (Fulbright) Fndn 1969–74 (chm 1974–75), Bd Bat-Sheva de Rothschild Fndn for Advancement of Sci in Israel 1970–84, Bd Israel Center for Scientific and Technol Info 1970–74, Bd of Tstees Nat Inst of Psychobiology in Israel 1973–, Israel Exec Ctee American-Israel Cultural Fndn 1975–87 (chm 1985–87), Academic Advsy Bd Everyman's (Open) Univ 1977–83, Bd of Govrs Tel Aviv Museum of Art 1980–, Ctee for Chemical Educn Int Union of Pure and Applied Chemistry (IUPAC) 1982–90 (nat rep 1973–82), Israel Chem Soc (memb Cncl 1976–84), Royal Chemical Soc 1957– (fell 1996), Int Soc Neurochemistry (ISN) 1970–, Int Brain Res Orgn (IBRO) 1984–, Israel Britain and Cwlth Assoc (IBCA) 1984–94, Anglo-Israel Assoc 1985– (co-chm Anglo-Israel Colloquia 1997–), Br Israel Arts Fndn 1986–97, Bd of Govrs Bezalel Acad of Arts and Design 1977–, Bd Tstees Menninger Fndn (USA) 1989–; Shenkar Coll of Textile Technol and Fashion: memb Bd 1970–87, pres 1987–94, hon fell 2002; memb Fibre Soc 1990–; memb Editorial Bd: Brain Behaviour and Immunity, Alzheimer Disease and Associated Disorders, Journal of Labelled Compounds and Radiopharmaceuticals; author of over 300 pubns on chemistry, psychopharmacology, animal behaviour, neurochemistry and educn; Scopus Award Hebrew Univ 2000, Tercentenary Medal Yale Univ 2001; hon fell Shenkar Coll of Engrg and Design 2002; *Books* The Aging of the Brain (ed, 1983), Memory - How We Use It, Lose It and Can Improve It (1999); *Recreations* etching, archery; *Style*— The Rt Hon the Viscount Samuel, OBE; ✉ Department of Neurobiology, Weizmann Institute of Science, Rehovot 76100, Israel (tel 00 972 89344 229, or 00 972 89344 206, e-mail dhsamuel@gmail.com)

SAMUEL, Sir John Michael Glen; 5 Bt (UK 1898), of Nevern Square, St Mary Abbots, Kensington, Co London; s of Sir John Oliver Cecil Samuel, 4 Bt (d 1962), and Charlotte Mary Desmond; *b* 25 January 1944; *Educ* Radley, UCL; *m* 1, 24 Sept 1966, Antoinette Sandra, da of late Capt Anthony Hewitt, RE; 2 s (Anthony John Fulton b 1972, Rupert Casper James b 1974); m 2, March 1982, Mrs Elizabeth Ann Molinari, yst da of late Maj R G Curry, of Bournemouth; *Heir* s, Anthony Samuel; *Career* chm: Electric Auto Corporation (Detroit USA) 1978–82, Silver Volt Corporation (Freeport Bahamas) 1980–82, Whisper Electric Car A/S (Denmark) 1985–87, Synergy Research Ltd (UK) 1983–, Clean Air Transport (Hldgs) Ltd 1989–94, Zeus Energy Ltd 1995–98, RE-fuel technology Ltd 1999–; MIMechE, CEng; *Recreations* motor racing; *Style*— Sir John Samuel, Bt; ✉ e-mail synergy.gb@tiscali.co.uk

SAMUEL, William Edgar Foyle (Bill); s of Edgar Horace Samuel, and Winifred Olive, *née* Foyle; *Educ* Harrow; *Career* exec dir Investcorp Bank 1986–90; Turks and Caicos Islands: dir of tourism 1991, supt of banking and offshore fin 1992, dir Turks and Caicos Banking Ltd 1993–2000, UK rep Turks and Caicos Govt 1994–2004; dir W & G Foyle Ltd 1999–; FCA 1965; *Recreations* sailing, scuba, skiing, walking, reading, music; *Style*— Bill Samuel, Esq; ✉ c/o Foyles, 113–119 Charing Cross Road, London WC2H 0EB (tel 020 7440 3226, fax 020 7434 1575, mobile 07770 443789, e-mail bill@thecourtyard.co.uk)

SAMUELS, His Hon John Edward Anthony; QC (1981); s of Albert Edward Samuels (d 1982), and Sadie Beatrice Samuels (d 1991); *b* 15 August 1940; *Educ* Charterhouse, Queens' Coll Cambridge (MA); *m* 1967, Maxine, da of Lt-Col F D Robertson, MC (d 1998); 2 s (David b 1970, Adam b 1973); *Career* called to the Bar Lincoln's Inn 1964 (bencher 1990); dep judge of the High Court 1981–97, recorder of the Crown Court 1985–97, circuit judge (SE Circuit) 1997–2006 (dep circuit judge 2006–); chm Jt Regulations Ctee of the Inns' Cncl and the Bar Cncl 1987–90; memb: Senate of the Inns of Court and the Bar 1983–86, Bar Cncl 1992–97, Criminal Injuries Compensation Appeal Panel 1996–97, Ctee Cncl of HM Circuit Judges 2001– (chm Criminal Sub-Ctee 2002–), Cncl Centre for Crime and Justice Studies 2002–; asst Parly Boundary Cmmr 1992–95, lay chair NHS Complaints Panels 1996–97, judicial memb Parole Bd 2005–; chm Prisoners' Educn Tst 2006– (tstee 2000–), vice-pres Unlock (Nat Assoc of Ex-Offenders) 2007–; *Style*— His Hon John Samuels, QC; ✉ Treasury Office, Lincoln's Inn, London WC2A 3TL (tel 020 7405 1393)

SAMUELSON, David Wylie; s of George Berthold Samuelson (d 1947), and Marjorie Emma Elizabeth, *née* Vint (d 1991); bro of Michael Edward Wylie Samuelson, CBE (1998) and Sir Sydney Wylie Samuelson, CBE; *m* 1, 1949 (m dis 1973), Joan, da of Philip Woolf; 2 s (Paul, Adam), 2 da (Gail, Zoe); m 2, 1978, Elaine Witz; *Career* served RAF 1944–47; with Br Movietone News 1941–60, fndr dir Samuelson Group plc 1958–84, dir dSam Ltd 1984–; as cameraman filmed in over 40 countries and at 4 Olympic games; original inventions incl: through-the-lens video viewfinders for film cameras, remote control system for Louma camera crane, Samcine inclining prism; winner of many awards incl: SMPTE Special Commendation Award 1978, AMPAS Scientific and Engrg Award 1980, SMPTE Presidential Proclamation Award 1984, Acad Tech Achievement Award 1987, BSC 'Bert Easy' Tech Award 1994, Acad Award for remote control system for Louma camera crane 2005; govr London Int Film Sch 1981–94 (chm 1984–86), vice-pres Int Union of Film Tech Assocs 1974–80, chm Br Bd of Film Classification 1972–89 (memb 1969–94), memb Br Screen Advsy Cncl 1985–93; FRPS, FBKSTS (pres 1970–72, memb Cncl 1966–78 and 1984–90), FSMPTE, memb ACTT; *Books* Motion Picture Camera and Lighting Equipment, Motion Picture Camera Techniques, The Panaflex Users' Manual, The Cinematographers' Computer Calculator, Motion Picture Camera Data, The Samuelson Manual of Cinematography, American Cinematographer magazine (contrib ed, 1973–83), David Samuelson's Hands-on Manual for Cinematographers (1993); *Style*— D W Samuelson, Esq; ✉ 7 Montagu Mews West, London W1H 2EE (fax 020 7724 4025, e-mail dsam@compuserve.com)

SAMWORTH, David Chetwode; CBE (1985), DL (1984); s of Frank Samworth; *b* 25 June 1935; *Educ* Uppingham; *m* 1969, Rosemary Grace, *née* Cadell; 1 s (Mark b 1970), 3 da (Mary b 1972, Susannah b 1975, Victoria b 1977); *Career* Lt Sudan and Cyprus; chm Pork Farms Ltd 1968–81, dir Northern Foods Ltd 1978–81; chm: Meat and Livestock Cmmn 1980–84, Samworth Brothers (Holdings) Ltd 1984–2005 (pres 2005–); non-exec dir: Imperial Group 1983–85, Thorntons plc 1988–93; pres Br Meat Mfrs Assoc 1988–94, pres Leics Agric Soc 1996–99, pres RASE 2000–01, pres Young Enterprise Leics 2001–04; vice-chm Leics 33 Hosp Mgmnt Ctee 1970–74, memb Cncl of Univ of Nottingham 1975–76, chm Governing Body Uppingham Sch 1996–99 (vice chm 1980–89); High Sheriff of Leicestershire 1997; Liveryman Worshipful Co of Butchers; *Recreations* fishing; *Style*— David Samworth, Esq, CBE, DL

SANCROFT-BAKER, Raymond Samuel; s of Anthony Sancroft-Baker (d 1985), and Jean Norah, *née* Heron-Maxwell (d 1981); *b* 30 July 1950; *Educ* Bromsgrove Sch; *m* 29 Jan 1983 (m dis 1994), (Daphne) Caroline, da of Gp Capt Maurice Adams, OBE, AFC (d 1976); 2 s (Robert b 1985, Hugh b 1987); *Career* Christie's: head Coin and Metal Dept 1973, dir 1981–, dir Jewellery Dept 1988–; Freeman City of London 1972; Liveryman: Worshipful Co of Wax Chandlers 1973, Worshipful Co of Pattenmakers 1972 (memb Ct of Assts 1987, Master 1994); FRNS 1971, FGA 1992; *Recreations* tennis, squash, wood turning; *Style*— Raymond Sancroft-Baker, Esq; ✉ Christie's, 8 King Street, St James's, London SW1Y 6QT (tel 020 7839 9060, e-mail rsancroft-baker@christies.com)

SANDALL, Robert Paul; s of Arthur Sandall, of Rippingale, Lincs, and Irene Norah, *née* Chard; *b* 9 June 1952; *Educ* Haberdashers' Aske's Elstree, Lincoln Coll Oxford (exhibitioner, BA), Cornell Univ NY USA; *Career* freelance musican and composer 1976–84, writer, critic and broadcaster 1985–; currently: pop/rock critic Sunday Times, presenter Mixing It BBC Radio 3; presenter VH-1 MTV 1994–96; contributing ed GQ Magazine; occasional feature writer and fiction reviewer Sunday Times; memb Performing Rights Soc 1984; *Publications* Rolling Stones: Images of the World Tour 1989–90 (1991); *Recreations* skiing, tennis, scuba diving, fell walking; *Style*— Robert Sandall, Esq

SANDBACH, Richard Stainton Edward; s of Frank Stainton Sandbach (ka 1917), and Beatrice Emmeline, *née* Clifton (d 1963); *b* 13 June 1915; *Educ* Manchester Grammar, St John's Coll Cambridge (MA, LLM, Macmahon law student); *m* 10 Sept 1949, (Brenda Mary) Wendy, da of Charles Lionel Osborn Cleminson (d 1958), of Ickleford, Herts; 2 s (John Christopher Stainton b 1950, Richard Paul Stainton (Dickon) b 1956); *Career* Private VR Suffolk Regt 1939, OCTU 1940, 22 Cheshire Regt 1940–46, Jr Staff Coll 1941, Maj 1 Canadian Army 1943–44, Airborne Corps 1944–46, Lucknow Dist 1946; admitted slr 1946; sr ptnr Greenwoods Peterborough 1970–79 (ptnr 1951–79), clerk Huntingdon Freemen 1968–76; chm: DHSS Local Appeals Tbnl Peterborough 1980–88, Paten & Co Ltd 1988–96, QCCC Ltd 1989–97, QCCC Sales Ltd 1991–97; fndr chm Minster Gen Housing Assoc Ltd; dir: Arcade Properties (Peterborough) Ltd; past pres Peterborough and Dist Law Soc; past chm City and Cos Club Peterborough, memb and former chm Burgh Soc Peterborough; tstee Peterborough Cathedral Preservation Tst; chm Peterborough Diocesan Bd of Fin 1974–84, provincial grand master for Northamptonshire and Huntingdonshire Ancient Free and Accepted Masons of England 1984–90, memb Supreme Cncl Ancient and Accepted Rite 1989–2004 (sovereign grand cdr 2002–04), hon memb Supreme Cncl Ancient and Accepted Rite for Australia; Grand Master's Order of Serv for Masonry 2006; memb: Law Soc 1947, Royal Cwlth Soc; *Books* The Book of the Lodge (by G Oliver, contrib Introduction, 1986), Priest and Freemason (1988), Peterborough Booklets 1–5 (1990–92), Notes for a Candidate for Freemasonry (1991), Understanding the Royal Arch (1992), History of the Fitzwilliam Lodge 2533 (1994), Letter to a Master-Elect (1994), Talks for Lodge and Chapter (1996), History of The Clerestory Lodge 6551 (1998), Square Pomes (sic) (collection of verses, 1998), No Excuse (autobiography, 2007); *Recreations* hill walking, computers, photography, historic research; *Clubs* Oxford and Cambridge, Victory Services; *Style*— Richard Sandbach, Esq; ✉ 91 Lincoln Road, Peterborough PE1 2SH; (tel 01733 343012, fax 01733 314548); The Moorings, Fairbourne, Gwynedd LL38 2DJ; Drumnagarrachan, Kiltarlity, by Beauly, Inverness

SANDBERG, Alexander Logie John; s of John Forbes (d 1963), and Diana Margaret Ina, *née* Hurst (d 1999); *b* 15 July 1949; *Educ* Hawtreys, Milton Abbey; *m* 15 Sept 1979, Clare Angela Eli, da of Antony Colman; 2 s (James, Edward), 2 da (Serena, Louisa); *Career* chm and chief exec College Hill Associates; *Recreations* tennis, gardening, skiing, shooting; *Clubs* Queen's; *Style*— Alexander Sandberg, Esq; ✉ College Hill Associates, 78 Cannon Street, London EC4N 6HH (tel 020 7457 2020, fax 020 7248 3295)

SANDBERG, Baron (Life Peer UK 1997), of Passfield in the County of Hampshire; Sir Michael Graham Ruddock Sandberg; kt (1986), CBE (1982, OBE 1977); s of Gerald Arthur Clifford and Ethel Marion Sandberg; *b* 31 May 1927; *Educ* St Edward's Sch Oxford; *m* 1954, Carmel Mary Roseleen, *née* Donnelly; 2 s, 2 da; *Career* served 6 Lancers (Indian Army) and King's Dragoon Gds 1945; Hongkong and Shanghai Banking Corp: joined 1949, chm 1977–86; treas Univ of Hong Kong 1977–86, chm British Bank of the Middle East 1980–86; dir: New World Development Ltd, Winsor Ind Corp, Winsor Properties Holdings Ltd, Green Island Cement Ltd, A S Watson & Co Ltd; memb Exec Cncl of Hong Kong 1978–86, chm Bd of Stewards Royal Hong Kong Jockey Club 1981–86 (Hon Steward 1986), pres Surrey CCC 1987–88; JP Hong Kong 1972–86; Freeman City of London; FCIB 1977 (vice-pres 1984–87), FRSA 1983; *Publications* The Sandberg Watch Collection (1998); *Recreations* cricket, horology, racing; *Clubs* Garrick, White's, MCC, Surrey CCC, Hong Kong; *Style*— The Lord Sandberg, CBE; ✉ 33 St James's Square, London SW1Y 4JS (tel 020 7661 9697)

SANDBERG, Rosemary; da of Leslie Northcott (d 1969), and Constance, *née* Eley (d 1961); *b* 16 December 1939, London; *Educ* Claremont Sch for Girls Esher, KCL (BA); *m* Robin Sandberg; 2 da (Mary b 23 April 1969, Alice b 26 April 1971); *Career* marketing asst J Walter Thompson 1961–65, ed Fleetway Publications 1965–67, Puffin Club sec Puffin Books 1967–72, publisher paperbacks for children William Collins 1973–91, dir Rosemary Sandberg Ltd 1991–; *Recreations* travelling, ballet, family; *Clubs* Groucho, Hurlingham; *Style*— Mrs Rosemary Sandberg; ✉ 44 Bowerdean Street, London SW6 3TW (tel 020 7731 0794); Rosemary Sandberg Ltd, 6 Bayley Street, London WC1B 3HE (tel 020 7304 4110, e-mail rosemary@sandberg.demon.co.uk)

SANDELL, Michael Charles Caines; s of Christopher Sandell (d 1974), and Doris, *née* Waters (d 1997), of Amesbury, Wilts; *b* 30 September 1933; *Educ* Cheltenham Coll, RAC Cirencester; *m* 19 Sept 1959, (Janet) Heather, da of William Duncan Montgomery (d 1971); 2 da (Camilla (Mrs Thomas Newton) b 3 March 1962, Georgina (Mrs Clive Stoddart) b 1 April 1964); *Career* Nat Serv cmmnd RA, served Gibraltar 1952–53; asst agent Belvoir Castle Estate 1957–59; Fisher German (formerly Fisher & Co and Fisher Hoggarth): chartered surveyor and land agent 1959–2006, sr ptnr 1981–99, conslt 1999–2006; valuer Agricultural Mortgage Corporation plc 1976–2001; High Sheriff of Leicestershire 2001–2002; FRICS 1970; *Recreations* shooting, gardening, tennis, travel; *Style*— Michael Sandell, Esq; ✉ Village Farm, Sutton Bassett, Market Harborough, Leicestershire LE16 8HP (tel 01858 410435, fax 01858 410434)

SANDELSON, Bernice Helen; da of Maurice Wingate (d 1972), and Bella Davis (d 1991); *b* 29 March 1937; *Educ* Queens Coll London; *m* 10 June 1958, Victor Sandelson; 2 s, 2 da; *Career* owner and md Cartoon Originals 1974–77, prop and md Montpelier Sandelson (gallery specialising in 20th Century British Art) 1979–; *Recreations* gallery-crawling; *Clubs* Vanderbilt, Chelsea Arts; *Style*— Mrs Bernice Sandelson; ✉ Montpelier Sandelson Ltd, 24 Abbotsbury Road, London W14 8ER (tel 020 7727 8168)

SANDEMAN, David Robert; s of Robert John Sandeman, of Bridge of Allan, Stirlingshire, and Enid, *née* Webb; *b* 3 August 1954; *Educ* Trinity Coll Glenalmond, UCL (BSc), Westminster Med Sch London (MB BS, pres Westminster Students' Union); *m* Dr Alison Peters Sandeman, da of William Henry Cowin; 2 da (Isabel Laelia b 11 Oct 1988, Isla Alison b 13 Feb 2001), 1 s (Jonathan Donald b 17 Sept 1998); *Career* pre-registration houseman Westminster Hosp London 1979–80, A&E Luton and Dunstable Hosp 1980, gen surgery registrar (rotation) Birmingham 1980–83, SHO in neurosurgery Bristol 1984, registrar in neurosurgery Liverpool 1984–85 and 1986–87, research registrar UCH London and Inst of Neurology Queen's Square London 1985–86, sr registrar in neurosurgery Manchester Royal Infirmary and Hope Hosp Salford 1987–90, conslt neurosurgn Frenchay Hosp Bristol 1991–; research interests in neuro-oncology and laser application to neurosurgery, pioneer of interactive image directed surgical techniques, minimally invasive neurosurgery, neuro-endoscopy and surgical robotics; memb: Euro

Laser Assoc 1987, Soc of Br Neurosurgeons 1991, French Neurosurgical Soc 1992, Euro Stereotactic Assoc 1992; *Books* Lasers in Neurosurgery (1990); *Recreations* skiing, cycling, swimming, triathlon, hill walking; *Style*— David R Sandeman, Esq; ✉ Department of Neurosurgery, Frenchay Hospital, Bristol BS16 1LE (tel 0117 918 6614, fax 0117 970 1161, mobile 07831 451641, e-mail info@david-sandeman.com, website www.david-sandeman.com)

SANDERCOCK, Dr Peter Andrew Gale; s of Capt Michael John Gale Sandercock (d 1996), of Northwood, Middx, and Helen Betty, *née* Howland (d 1995); *b* 16 April 1951; *Educ* Shrewsbury, New Coll Oxford (MA, BMB Ch, DM); *m* 10 Sept 1977, Janet Mary, da of Peter Searell Andrews, of Little Addington, Northants; 3 s (David, Robert, Andrew), 1 da (Eleanor); *Career* actg clinical lectr Univ of Oxford 1981–85, lectr Univ of Liverpool 1985–87, sr lectr Univ of Edinburgh 1988–93, reader in Neurology Univ of Edinburgh 1993–99, prof 1999–; MRCP 1979, FRCP 1992; *Books* Stroke (1987); *Style*— Prof Peter Sandercock; ✉ Department of Clinical Neuroscience, Western General Hospital, Crewe Road, Edinburgh EH4 2XU (tel 0131 537 2928, fax 0131 332 5150)

SANDERS, Adrian; MP; *b* 25 April 1959; *Educ* Torquay Boys' GS; *Career* with Britannic Assurance 1978–85, joined Assoc of Lib (later Lib Dem) Cncllrs 1986–89, parly offr Lib Dem Whips' Office 1989–90, rejoined Assoc of Lib Dem Cncllrs 1990–92, with the office of Rt Hon Paddy Ashdown, MP 1992–93, with Nat Cncl for Voluntary Orgns (NCVO) 1993–94, joined Southern Assoc of Voluntary Action Gps for Europe (SAVAGE) 1994–97; MP (Lib Dem) Torbay 1997–, housing spokesman and regional whip (South and South West) 1997–99, local govt and housing spokesman 1999–2001, tourism spokesman 2001–; contested: Torbay 1992, Devon and East Plymouth Euro election 1994; *Recreations* soccer, music and films; *Style*— Adrian Sanders, Esq, MP; ✉ House of Commons, London SW1A 0AA (tel 020 7219 6304)

SANDERS, Prof Carol; da of Ronald Humphrey Sanders (d 1957), and Evelyn Maud, *née* Bradbury (now Mrs Payn); *b* 31 December 1944; *Educ* Univ of Cambridge (MA), Univ of London (PGCE), Univ of Paris (Doctorat de l'Université); *m* 29 July 1978, Peter Mary Eugene Figueroa, s of Rupert Aston (d 1969); 1 da (Emma Michelle b 1982), 1 s (James Michael b 1986); *Career* lectr in French: Univ of Reading 1969–72, Univ of W Indies 1972–76, Univ of Sussex 1977–84; reader then prof of French ANU Canberra 1984–88, prof of French Univ of Surrey 1988–2004 (now emeritus); fndn pres Assoc for French Language Studies, memb Ctee Soc for French Studies, ed Jl of French Language Studies; memb Assoc for French Language Studies, FIL; Chevalier dans l'Ordre des Palmes Académiques (France) 1983; *Books* F de Saussure - Cours De Linguistique Générale (1979), Cours De Français Contemporain (with M M Gervais, 1986), Lire Le Pacifique (with K Muller, 1989), Franc Exchange (with J Gladkow, 1991), French Today, Language in its Social Context (ed, 1993), Raymond Queneau (1994), Cambridge Companion to Saussure (ed, 2004), F de Saussure: Writings in General Linguistics (annotated translation and bibliography, jtly, 2002); *Recreations* travel, reading; *Style*— Prof Carol Sanders; ✉ Division of Culture and Communication, University of Surrey, Guildford GU2 5XH (tel 01483 683076, fax 01483 686237, e-mail c.sanders@surrey.ac.uk)

SANDERS, Prof Dale; s of Leslie G D Sanders, and Daphne M Sanders; *Educ* Univ of York (BA), Univ of Cambridge (PhD, ScD); *Career* Yale Univ Sch of Med: James Hudson Brown res fell 1978–79, res assoc 1979–83; Univ of York: lectr 1983–89, reader 1989–92, prof of biology 1992–, head Biology Dept 2004–; author of over 100 pubns in learned jls; President's Medal Soc for Experimental Biology 1987, Euro Sci Prize Körber Fndn 2001; FRS 2001; *Style*— Prof Dale Sanders; ✉ 120 The Mount, York YO24 1AS (tel 01904 637306); Biology Department Area 6, PO Box 373, University of York, York YO10 5YW (tel 01904 328555, fax 01904 328666, e-mail ds10@york.ac.uk)

SANDERS, (June) Deidre; da of Philip Ronald Heaton (d 1991), and Audrey Minton, *née* Harvey (d 1972); *b* 9 June 1945; *Educ* Harrow County GS for Girls, Univ of Sheffield (BA); *m* 12 Dec 1969, Richard James, 2 da (Susan b 1976, Phoebe b 1988); *Career* journalist, author, broadcaster; problem-page ed The Sun; memb: NSPCC Cncl, Br Assoc for Counselling; tstee Nat Family and Parenting Inst; patron: Youth Access, Nat Assoc for People Abused in Childhood; Jubilee Medal 1977; FRSA; *Books* Kitchen Sink or Swim? (1982), Women and Depression (1984), Woman Book of Love and Sex (1985), Woman Report on Men (1987); *Style*— Mrs Deidre Sanders; ✉ Freepost, 1 Virginia Street, London E98 1AX (tel 020 7782 4000, e-mail problems@deardeidre.org)

SANDERS, Dr Eric; s of Albert Sanders, and Caroline, *née* Johnson; *b* 22 October 1946; *Educ* Stanley GS Co Durham, Univ of Wales (BSc, MB); *m* 10 July 1971, Dianne Marilyn, da of David Denzil Harris Thomas, of Carmarthen; 2 s (Gareth Wyn b 20 June 1974, Gethyn Huw b 21 Sept 1976), 1 da (Angharad Jane b 4 June 1980); *Career* pre-registration house offr Royal Infirmary Cardiff 1971, SHO Univ Hosp Wales 1972–74, research registrar and lectr Kruf Inst Renal Disease Royal Infirmary Cardiff 1974–80, conslt physician and dir of dialysis servs W Wales Hosp Carmarthen 1980–93, cons diabetologist N Durham Acute NHS Tst 1993–; dir of med servs W Wales Hosp 1992–; tstee and hon treas Kidney Research Unit Wales Fndn, memb Cncl Wales Diabetes Research Tst, former pres and regnl offr Lions Int Dist 105W; memb: Renal Assoc GB, EDTA; FRCP 1990 (MRCP 1974); *Books* Nephrology Illustrated (1981), Clinical Atlas of the Kidney (1993); *Recreations* local community service, music; *Style*— Dr Eric Sanders; ✉ Dryburn Hospital, North Road, Durham DH1 5TW (tel 0191 333 2597)

SANDERS, Prof Jeremy Keith Morris; s of Sidney Sanders, and Sylvia, *née* Rutman (d 1983); *b* 3 May 1948; *Educ* Wandsworth Sch, Imperial Coll London (Edmund White Prize, BSc), Churchill Coll Cambridge (PhD), Selwyn Coll Cambridge (ScD); *m* 1972, Louise, da of Dr A Elliott, OBE; 1 s, 1 da; *Career* res assoc in pharmacology Stanford Univ 1972–73; Univ of Cambridge: demonstrator in chemistry 1973–78, lectr in chemistry 1978–92, reader and asst head Dept of Chemistry 1992–96, prof of chemistry 1996–, memb Cncl 1999–2002, head Dept of Chemistry 2000–06 (dep head 1998–2000), chm Allocations Ctee 1999–2000, dep vice-chllr 2006–, chair Cambridge Prog for Industry 2003–; fell: Christ's Coll Cambridge (Darwin Prize) 1972–76, Selwyn Coll Cambridge 1976–; visiting assoc prof and MRC fell Univ of Br Columbia 1979–80; assoc ed New Journal of Chemistry 1998–2000, chm Editorial Bd Chemical Society Reviews 2000–02, chair Chemistry Sub-Panel 2008 UK Research Assessment Exercise 2004–; Meldola Medal 1975, Hickinbottom Award 1981, Pfizer Academic Award (on nuclear Overhauser effect) 1984, Pfizer Academic Award 1988 (on NMR of whole cells), Josef Loschmidt Prize 1994, Pedler Medal and Prize 1996, Izatt-Christensen Award in Macrocyclic Chemistry (USA) 2003; fell Japan Soc for the Promotion of Science 2002; FRSC, CChem 1978, FRS 1995, FRSA 1997; *Books* Modern NMR Spectroscopy (with B K Hunter, 1987, 2 edn 1993); *Recreations* family, cooking, music, walking; *Clubs* Athenaeum; *Style*— Prof Jeremy Sanders, FRS; ✉ Department of Chemistry, University of Cambridge, Lensfield Road, Cambridge CB2 1EW (tel 01223 336411, fax 01223 336017, e-mail jkms@cam.ac.uk)

SANDERS, Michael David; s of Norris Manley Sanders, of Farringdon, Hants, and Gertrude Florence, *née* Hayley; *b* 19 September 1935; *Educ* Tonbridge, Guy's Hosp Med Sch (MB BS, DO); *m* 1 Nov 1969, Thalia Margaret, da of Thomas Garlick (d 1961), of Ashover, Derbys; 1 s (Rupert Miles b 16 March 1971), 1 da (Melissa Tryce b 25 May 1973); *Career* house surgn Guy's Hosp 1959, research offr Moorfields Eye Hosp 1963–67, Alexander Piggot Werner meml fell Univ of Calif San Francisco 1967–68; conslt ophthalmologist: Nat Hosp Nervous Diseases 1969–99, St Thomas' Hosp 1972–98; civil conslt ophthalmology RAF 1972; distinguished lectures: Middlemore 1985, Percival Hay 1986, Sir Stewart Duke-Elder 1987, Ida Mann 1987, Lettsomian 1988; Bowman Medal 1996; hon memb Pacific Coast Oto-Ophthalmological Soc, hon conslt Sydney Hosp Univ of Sydney; asst ed British Journal of Ophthalmology, chm Frost Fndn, memb Cncl Iris Fund for Prevention of Blindness 1994–2003; pres Int Neuro-Ophthalmology Soc; FRCP, FRCS, FCOpth; *Books* Topics in Neuro-Ophthalmology (1979), Computerised Tomography in Neuro-Ophthalmology (1982), Common Problems in Neuro-Ophthalmology (1997); *Recreations* golf; *Clubs* RAF, Hankley Cmmn; *Style*— Michael Sanders, Esq; ✉ Chawton Lodge, Chawton, Alton, Hampshire GU34 1SL (tel 01420 86681)

SANDERS, Prof Roy; s of Leslie John Sanders, and Marguerite Alice, *née* Knight; *b* 20 August 1937; *Educ* Hertford GS, Univ of London (BSc, MB BS); *m* 1, 25 July 1961 (m dis 1977), Ann Ruth, da of William Costar; 1 da (Lyvia Ann b 1963), 2 s (Andrew St John William b 1965, Charles St John David b 1966); m 2, 6 Jan 1984, Fleur Annette Chandler; *Career* HAC Gunner 1957–62, Regt MO 1963–75, HAC Co of Pikemen and Musketeers 1982–2005 (vice-pres 2004–06), OC HAC Light Cavalry 1996–2004; hon prof UCL; pres: Plastic Surgery Section RSM of London 1989–90, Br Assoc of Plastic Surgns 1993 (sec 1986–88); sec Br Assoc of Aesthetic Plastic Surgns 1985–87, chm Medical Equestrian Assoc 1985–86; Freeman City of London, Liveryman Worshipful Co of Barbers, Liveryman Worshipful Soc of Apothecaries; FRCS; *Recreations* equestrian activities, painting in watercolour; *Clubs* Garrick; *Style*— Prof Roy Sanders; ✉ 77 Harley Street, London WIG 8QN (tel 020 7935 7417, e-mail docact@btopenworld.com); Upper Rye Farmhouse, Moreton-in-Marsh, Gloucestershire (tel 01608 650542)

SANDERS, Dr Stuart; s of David Sadofsky (d 1955), and Florence, *née* Rakusen; *b* 20 November 1934; *Educ* Hymers Coll Hull, Univ of Leeds Medical Sch (MB, ChB, DCH, DObstRCOG, James and Mabel Gaunt Prize in Paediatrics); *m* 15 March 1979, Kathryn, da of Rudolf Bleichroeder; 2 s (Jonathan b 25 Dec 1979, Jeremy b 16 June 1983); *Career* paediatric house physician Leeds Gen Infirmary 1958–59, obstetric house surgn Manygates Maternity Hosp Wakefield 1959, medical SHO Pinderfields Gen Hosp Wakefield 1960–61, res pathologist Royal Free Hosp 1961–62, private physician and princ med advsr to public cos 1962–, GP NHS 1962–66, paediatric clinical asst Royal Free Hosp 1963–67, sr res fell Hosp for Sick Children Great Ormond St London 1966–74; author of publications in various medical journals and letters to The Times; memb: RSM, Chelsea Clinical Soc (hon treas), BMA (chm St Marylebone Div 1984–87); hon treas Cons Med Soc; pres Ind Doctors Forum (chm 1990–94); Gold Medal Hunterian Soc 1963, Silver Medal Ind Doctors' Forum 1994; JP 1976–80; Freeman City of London 1978, Liveryman Worshipful Soc of Apothecaries; FRCGP (by assessment), MRCS, LRCP; *Recreations* family, skiing, bridge, theatre, music; *Clubs* Savile, Annabel's, Mark's; *Style*— Dr Stuart Sanders; ✉ 22 Harmont House, 20 Harley Street, London W1G 9PH (tel 020 7436 5687, fax 020 7436 4387, car 07836 625905, e-mail drsanders@msn.com, website www.drsanders.net)

SANDERS, Prof Thomas Andrew Bruce; s of John Bruce Sanders (d 1992), of Eastbourne, E Sussex, and Annie, *née* Dewsberry (d 1990); *b* 29 December 1949; *Educ* Eastbourne Coll, Queen Elizabeth Coll London (BSc), Univ of London (PhD, DSc); *m* 20 Oct 1973, Linda Marie, *née* Fassbender; 1 da (Mila b 30 March 1978), 1 s (Toby b 11 July 1981); *Career* prog assoc UNICEF (Indonesia) 1971–73; res nutritionist SW Thames RHA 1974–77; Queen Elizabeth Coll London: Rank Prize Funds fell 1977–79, res fell 1979–82, lectr in nutrition 1982–84; KCL: lectr in nutrition 1984–91, reader 1991–94, prof of nutrition and dietetics 1994–, head of Dept 1995–2001, head Research Div of Nutritional Sciences, memb Cncl; sci govr Br Nutrition Fndn, hon nutritional dir Heart UK, chair Assoc of Profs of Human Nutrition; memb: Advsy Ctee on Novel Foods and Processes Food Standards Agency 1994–2001, Nutrition Soc, British Atherosclerosis Soc, RSM, UK Sci Advsy Ctee Jt Health Claims Initiative; tstee Br Nutrition Fndn; frequent contib to television and radio, author of numerous papers and contribs to scientific jls; *Books* The Vegetarian's Healthy Diet Book (1986), The Food Revolution (1991), You Don't Have to Diet (1994), Foods that Harm, Foods that Heal (1996), The Molecular Basis of Human Nutrition (2003); *Recreations* surfing, windsurfing, fishing, cinema, theatre, opera; *Style*— Prof Tom Sanders; ✉ Nutritional Sciences Division, King's College London, Franklin-Wilkins Building, 150 Stamford Street, London SE1 9NH (tel 020 7848 4273, fax 020 7848 4171, mobile 07768 414337, e-mail tom.sanders@kcl.ac.uk)

SANDERS, Timothy Simon (Tim); s of Robert Ernest Sanders, and Patricia Anne, *née* Tracy; *b* 13 March 1959; *Educ* Llandovery Coll (Thomas Phillips scholar), Thames Valley GS, Univ of London (LLB); *m* Kathrine, da of Brian Thomas Firth; 1 s (James Thomas b 22 Sept 1986), 1 da (Alice Caroline b 22 March 1992); *Career* qualified 1984; Theodore Goddard: assoc 1991–92, ptnr 1992, head Corp Tax Dept 1993–2000; ptnr Skadden, Arps, Slate, Meagher & Flom LLP 2001–; memb Law Soc 1984; CTA (fell); *Books* Butterworths Tax Indemnities & Warranties (1998), Tolley's Company Law (contrib), US Practising Law Handbook Series (contrib); *Recreations* gardening, golf, national heritage; *Clubs* Surrey CCC, Harlequins RFC, Kingswood GC; *Style*— Tim Sanders, Esq; ✉ Skadden, Arps, Slate, Meagher & Flom LLP, 40 Bank Street, Canary Wharf, London E14 5DS (tel 020 7519 7000, e-mail tsanders@skadden.com)

SANDERS-CROOK, William Stanley; MBE (1972); s of William Charles Herbert Crook (d 1966), of Twickenham, Middx, and Mary Amelia, *née* Green (d 1986); *b* 2 November 1933; *Educ* Latymer Upper Sch, RMA Sandhurst; *m* 1, 5 May 1962; 1 s (William b 1963), 1 da (Deborah b 1972); m 2, 20 Dec 1982, Jean Rosemary, da of Eric Ernest Walker (d 1973), of Barnstaple, N Devon; *Career* Regular Army 1953–77; Maj; served infantry and para: BAOR, Cyprus, Suez, Malaya, Borneo, Singapore, MOD, NI, Brunei; writer; dir: John Roberts Conslts 1977–79, Jean Kittermaster PR 1981–; ceo Globe Run 1991–; *Novels* Four Days (1979), Death Run (1980), Triple Seven (1981), Fighting Back (1992); *Recreations* riding, scuba diving, dogs, cabinet making, painting; *Clubs* Special Forces; *Style*— William Sanders-Crook, Esq, MBE; ✉ Jean Kittermaster Public Relations, 239 King's Road, Chelsea, London SW3 5EJ (tel 020 7352 6811, fax 020 7351 9215, e-mail wsc@ukonline.co.uk)

SANDERSON, Alison Kimberley; da of Brian Glanville Field, and Barbara Evelyn, *née* Waters; *b* 6 July 1958; *Educ* Twickenham Co Sch for Girls, Thames Valley Sixth Form Coll, Univ of Leeds (BA); *m* Antony Richard Sanderson; 1 da (Katherine Natalie b 2 Feb 1994); *Career* advtg exec; Price Waterhouse CAs 1980–84, Black & Decker Co 1984–90; PepsiCola North America: fin planning mangr Baltimore 1990–92, gp strategic planning mangr Somers NY 1992–93; N Europe planning mangr PepsiCola International Richmond Surrey 1993–94, commercial dir J Walter Thompson Co Ltd; ACA 1983; *Style*— Mrs Alison Sanderson

SANDERSON, Arthur Norman; MBE (1986); s of Very Rev Dr William Roy Sanderson, of E Lothian, and Annie Muriel, *née* Easton (d 2001); *b* 3 September 1943; *Educ* Glasgow Acad, Fettes, CCC Oxford (MA), Univ of Edinburgh (DipEd), Henley Mgmnt Coll (Dip Mgmnt); *m* 30 July 1966, Issy, *née* Halliday; 1 s (Angus William b 29 Sept 1968), 1 da (Emma b 27 Jan 1970); *Career* VSO tutor in mathematics and English Foso Trg Coll Ghana 1966–68, econs and careers master Daniel Stewart's Coll Edinburgh 1969–73; Br Cncl: asst dir Kano Nigeria 1974–76, regnl dir Recife Brazil 1976–80, Far East and Pacific Dept London 1980–83, asst then acting rep Ghana 1983–86, regnl dir Glasgow 1986–89, dir Enugu Nigeria 1989–91, dir S India 1991–95, dir Baltic States 1995–97; PR conslt Crown Agents Mozambique Customs Management Project (with special experience in drafting and translating new Customs legislation into English) 1997–2001; selector VSO 2001–; treas Claremont Tst 2002–; Scottish Parly candidate (Lib Dem) Glasgow Maryhill 2003, Parly candidate (Lib Dem) Glasgow S 2005, convener Gtr Glasgow Lib Dems 2003–; memb: Bd of Dirs Citizens Theatre Glasgow 2003–, Overseas Ctee Scottish Episcopal

Church, Soc of Authors; *Publications* Customs Reform Management, Mozambique - A Model for Partnership; *Recreations* hill walking, jogging, languages, Scottish country dancing, classical music; *Style*— Arthur N Sanderson, Esq, MBE; ✉ 1 Waterside Drive, Newton Mearns, Glasgow G77 6TL (tel 0141 639 8025, e-mail artandissy@tiscali.co.uk)

SANDERSON, Bryan Kaye; CBE (1999); s of Eric Sanderson (d 1973), and Anne, *née* Kaye; *b* 14 October 1940; *Educ* Dame Allan's Sch Newcastle upon Tyne, LSE (BSc(Econ)), IMEDE Business Sch Lausanne; *m* Oct 1966, Sirkka Aulikki, *née* Kärki; 1 da (Christina Elvira *b* Jan 1976), 1 s (Peter James Eric *b* Sept 1978); *Career* vol serv with UNA Peru 1962–64; BP Amoco plc (formerly British Petroleum): md and chief exec BP Nutrition 1987–90, chief exec BP Chemicals 1990–2000, an md (main bd dir) BP plc 1992–2000, chm BUPA 2001–06, chm Standard Chartered Bank 2003–06; chm Learning and Skills Cncl 2000–04; non-exec dir: Corus (formerly British Steel) 1994–2001, Six Continents 2001–03; pres CEFIC 1998–2000; memb: Advsy Gp to Lab Pty on Industrial Competition Policy 1997–98, DTI Steering Gp on Company Law Reform 1998–2001, DTI Ind Devpt Advsy Bd 2000; non-exec dir: Sunderland FC Ltd (chm 1998–2004), Durham CCC; chm Sunderland Area Regeneration Co 2001–, tstee Economist 2006–; memb Ct of Govrs LSE 1999– (vice-chm 1998–2003); Hon DUniv: Sunderland 1998, York 1999; *Recreations* reading, golf, walking, gardening; *Style*— Bryan Sanderson, Esq, CBE

SANDERSON, Eric Fenton; s of late Francis Kirton Sanderson, of Dundee, and Margarita Shand, *née* Fenton; *b* 14 October 1951; *Educ* Morgan Acad Dundee, Univ of Dundee (LLB, pres Students' Assoc), Harvard Business Sch (AMP); *m* 26 July 1975, Patricia Ann, da of late Lt-Cdr Donald Brian Shaw, and Mrs Pamela Shaw; 3 da (Anna *b* 1 June 1979, Caroline *b* 30 June 1982, Emma *b* 12 April 1985); *Career* articled clerk Touche Ross & Co Edinburgh, qualified CA 1976; The British Linen Bank Ltd: joined 1976, dir and head corp fin 1984, gp chief exec 1989–97; chief exec Bank of Scotland Treasury Services plc 1997–99 (also memb Bank of Scotland Mgmnt Bd); chm Kwik-Fit Insurance Services Ltd 2000–02; non-exec dir: MyTravel Group plc (formerly Airtours plc) 1987–2004 (dep chm 2001–02, chm 2003–04), English & Overseas Properties plc 1988–99, Oriel Leisure 1997–99, Docklands Light Railway Ltd 1999–, First Milk Lts 2006–; chm Marylebone Warwick Balfour Group plc 2005–, memb British Railways Bd 1991–94; gradiates assessor and memb Ct Univ of Dundee 2005–; FCIBS 1994 (MCIBS 1990); *Recreations* tennis, gardening, photography; *Clubs* New (Edinburgh); *Style*— Eric Sanderson, Esq; ✉ e-mail ericsanderson@blueyonder.co.uk

SANDERSON, Sir Frank Linton; 3 Bt (UK 1920), of Malling Deanery, South Malling, Co Sussex, OBE (2005); er s of Sir (Frank Philip) Bryan Sanderson, 2 Bt (d 1992), and Annette Irene Caroline (d 1967), da of late Col Korab Laskowski, of Warsaw, and gda of Gen Count Edouard de Castellaz; *b* 21 November 1933; *Educ* Stowe, Salamanca Univ; *m* 4 April 1961, Margaret Ann (Margot), da of John Cleveland Maxwell (d 1976), of New York; 2 s (David Frank *b* 1962, Michael John *b* 1965), 3 da (Caroline Ann *b* 1966, Nina Margaret, Katherine Claire (twins) *b* 1968); *Heir* s, David Sanderson; *Career* RNVR 1950–65; J H Minet & Co Ltd 1956–93 (dir 1985–93), dir Knott Hotels Co of London 1965–75, dir and chm Humber Fertilisers plc 1972–88; underwriting memb Lloyd's 1957–88; chm Thiepual Project 1998–2006; memb Chichester Dio Synod 1980–93; Master Worshipful Co of Curriers 1993–94; *Style*— Sir Frank Sanderson, Bt, OBE; ✉ Grandturzel Farm, Burwash, East Sussex TN19 7DE

SANDERSON, Prof John Elsby; s of Arthur John Sanderson, of Rhoose Glamorgan, and Ruth Megan, *née* Griffiths; *b* 1 May 1949; *Educ* Blundell's, Univ of Cambridge (MA, MD), Bart's Med Coll London (MB BChir); *m* 1, 1972 (m dis 1977), Susanna Marion, da of Richard Tewson, of Hempstead, Essex; *m* 2, 1980, Dr Julia Dorothy Billingham, da of David Billingham, of Crowhurst, E Sussex; 1 da (Vanessa Maureen *b* 1980), 1 s (Henry John Elsby *b* 1981); *Career* house physician and surgn Bart's London 1973–74, sr house physician Brompton and Hammersmith Hosps 1974–75, res fell (cardiology) RPMS Hammersmith Hosp 1975–78, lectr in cardiovascular med Univ of Oxford and John Radcliffe Hosp Oxford 1978–81, Wellcome Tst lectr St Mary's Hosp and hon lectr Univ of Nairobi Kenya (St Marys/Univ of Nairobi Hypertension project) 1981–83, conslt physician and cardiologist Taunton and Somerset Hosp and clinical tutor Univ of Bristol 1983–92, sr lectr in med (cardiology) and conslt cardiologist The Chinese Univ of Hong Kong Prince of Wales Hosp 1992–96, prof of med and head Div of Cardiology Chinese Univ of Hong Kong 1996–2005, prof of cardiology and conslt cardiologist Keele Univ Med Sch and Univ Hosp of N Staffs NHS Tst 2005–07, prof of clinical cardiology Univ of Birmingham Med Sch 2007–; memb: BMA, Br Cardiac Soc, Br Hypertension Soc, European Soc of Cardiology, N American Soc of Electrophysiology; fell American Coll of Cardiology; FRCP, FRSTM&H; *Publications* pubns and papers on heart failure, echocardiography, hypertension and Ischaemic heart disease; *Recreations* family, music, sailing, skiing and walking; *Clubs* Royal Hong Kong Yacht; *Style*— Prof John Sanderson; ✉ Dept of Cardiovascular Medicine, University of Birmingham Medical School, Edgbaston, Birmingham BI5 2TT (tel 0121 414 3917, fax 0121 414 3713, e-mail j.e.sanderson@bham.ac.uk)

SANDERSON, Timothy William; s of Dr Michael William Bristowe Sanderson, and Mrs Kay Glendinning, MBE, *née* Holman; *b* 3 March 1958; *Educ* Uppingham, UC Oxford (MA); *m* 9 Oct 1987, Damaris Stella Lavinia Margot Muir, da of Armitage Clifford Taylor (d 1967), of Hilden Hall, Penn, Bucks; 3 s (Hugh William Muir *b* 27 Nov 1990, Maximilian Henry Armitage *b* 14 July 1993, Alexander Edward Rohan *b* 6 Jan 1996); *Career* Hill Samuel Investment Management Group 1979–90, dir and chief investment offr Delaware International Advisers Ltd 1990–2000, chm and chief investment offr Sanderson Asset Management Ltd; tstee The Dunhill Medical Tst; assoc CFA (Chartered Financial Analyst) Inst; *Recreations* gardening, book collecting, literature, history, reading, wine, fly fishing; *Clubs* Buck's, Hurlingham; *Style*— Timothy Sanderson, Esq; ✉ Sanderson Asset Management Ltd, 20 Savile Row, London W1S 3PR (tel 020 7468 5970, fax 020 7468 5979, e-mail tsanderson@sandersonam.com)

SANDERSON OF BOWDEN, Baron (Life Peer UK 1985), of Melrose in the District of Ettrick and Lauderdale; Sir (Charles) Russell Sanderson; kt (1981), DL (Roxburgh, Ettrick and Lauderdale 1990); s of Charles Plummer Sanderson (d 1976), of Melrose, Roxburghshire, and (Martha) Evelyn (d 1954), da of Joseph Gardiner, of Glasgow; *b* 30 April 1933; *Educ* St Mary's Sch Melrose, Trinity Coll Glenalmond, Bradford Tech Coll, Scottish Coll of Textiles Galashiels; *m* 5 July 1958, (Frances) Elizabeth, da of Donald Alfred Ramsden Macaulay (d 1982), of Rylstone, N Yorks; 2 s (Hon (Charles) David Russell *b* 1960, Hon Andrew Bruce Plummer *b* 1968 *d* 1991), 2 da (Hon (Evelyn) Claire (Hon Dr Walker) *b* 1961, Hon (Frances) Georgina (Hon Mrs Riley) *b* 1963); *Career* cmmnd Royal Signals 1952, served 51 (Highland) Inf Div Signal Regt (TA) 1953–56, KOSB (TA) 1956–58; Scottish Cons & Unionist Assoc: vice-pres 1975–77, pres 1977–79, hon pres 1996–2000; Nat Union of Cons Assocs: memb Exec Ctee 1977–86, vice-chm 1979–81, chm 1981–86; Min of State Scottish Office 1987–90; chm: Scottish Cons Pty 1990–93, Scottish Peers' Assoc 1998– (vice-chm 1996–97, chm 1998–2000); ptnr Chas P Sanderson Wool and Yarn Merchants Melrose 1958–87; chm: Edinburgh Financial Trust 1983–87, Shires Investment Trust 1984–87, Hawick Cashmere Co 1991–, The Scottish Mortgage Trust plc 1993–2003 (dir 1991–2003); dir: Illingworth Morris plc 1981–87 and 1990–92, Clydesdale Bank 1985–87 and 1993–2000 (dep chm 1996–98, chm 1999–2004), Woolcombers plc 1992–95, Caros 1992–95, United Auctions Ltd 1992–99, Edinburgh Woollen Mills Ltd 1993–97, Watson & Philip plc 1993–99, Scottish Pride Holdings 1994–97, Morrison Construction plc 1995–2000, Develica Deutschland plc 2006–; memb Bd Yorkshire Bank plc 1999–2004; govr: St Mary's Sch Melrose 1978–87 (chm 1998–2004), Scottish Coll of Textiles 1980–87;

memb: Cncl Trinity Coll Glenalmond 1982–2000 (chm 1994–2000), British Cncl Independent Schs 1984–87, Ctee Governing Bodies 1984–87, Ct Napier Univ 1994–2001; pres Royal Highland and Agricultural Soc of Scotland 2002–03; cmmr Gen Assembly Church of Scotland 1972; Vice Lord-Lt Roxburgh, Ettrick and Lauderdale 2003–; memb Ct of Assts Worshipful Co of Framework Knitters 2000– (Under Warden 2003–04, Upper Warden 2004–, Master 2005–06); hon degree: Univ of Glasgow 2001, Napier Univ 2001; *Recreations* golf, fishing; *Clubs* Caledonian, Hon Co of Edinburgh Golfers; *Style*— The Rt Hon the Lord Sanderson of Bowden, DL; ✉ Becketts Field, Bowden, Melrose, Roxburghshire TD6 0ST (tel 01835 822736)

SANDFORD, Arthur; DL; s of Arthur Sandford (d 1990), and Lilian Sandford (d 1995); *b* 12 May 1941; *Educ* Queen Elizabeth's GS Blackburn, UCL (LLB); *m* 1963, Kathleen, da of James Entwistle (d 1976); 2 da (Allison *b* 1967, Janet *b* 1969); *Career* asst slr Preston CBC 1965–66 (sr asst slr 1966–68), asst slr Hampshire CC 1969–70; Nottinghamshire CC: second asst clerk 1970–72, first asst clerk 1972–74, dep dir of admin 1974–75, dir of admin 1975–77, dep clerk of CC and co sec 1977–78, clerk of the CC and chief exec 1978–90; chief exec: The Football League Ltd 1990–92, Manchester City Cncl 1992–98; chm Trent SHA 2002–04; *Recreations* sport, gardening; *Style*— Arthur Sandford, Esq, DL; ✉ 4 Wentworth Way, Edwalton, Nottingham NG12 4DJ (e-mail arthur.sandford@ntlworld.com)

SANDFORD, 2 Baron (UK 1945); Rev John Cyril Edmondson; DSC (1942); s of 1 Baron Sandford, DL, sometime MP Banbury, Lord Cmmr of the Treasy and Vice-Chamberlain HM's Household 1939–42 (d 1959), by his w Edith, *née* Freeman; *b* 22 December 1920; *Educ* Eton, RNC Dartmouth; *m* 4 Jan 1947, Catharine Mary, da of late Rev Oswald Andrew Hunt; 2 s, 2 da; *Heir* s, Hon James Edmondson; *Career* took Cons whip in House of Lords; RN: midshipman 1940, Eastern Med 1940–41, N African and Sicily Invasions 1942, Normandy Invasions 1944, Signal Offr 1945, House Offr RNC Dartmouth 1947, Flag Lt to Flag Offr cmdg 3 Aircraft Sqdn 1949, Flag Lt to flag offr air (Home) 1951, on Staff C-in-C Far East Station 1953, Cdr 1953, cmd HMS Tyne (Home Fleet Flagship) 1954–56, ret 1956; ordained 1958; curate Parish of St Nicholas Harpenden 1958–63, exec chaplain to Bishop of St Albans 1965–68; chm Herts CC Social Service 1966–69, chm Bd of Church Army 1969–70; oppn whip House of Lords 1966–70, Parly under-sec of state Dept of Environment 1970–73, Parly under-sec of state Dept of Educn and Sci 1973–74; memb Select Ctee on European Community Directive 1978–88; memb Bd Ecclesiastical Insurance Office 1978–89; pres: Anglo-Swiss Soc 1976–84, Assoc of Dist Cncls 1980–86; Church Cmmr, chm Redundant Churches 1982–89; chm SE Regnl Planning Cncl (SERPLAN) 1981–89; pres Offa's Dyke Assoc; fndr Sandford Award for Heritage Educn 1976; Hon FILA 1971; *Clubs* Stroke; *Style*— The Rev the Commander the Rt Hon the Lord Sandford, DSC, Hon FILA; ✉ 27 Ashley Gardens, Ambrosden Avenue, London SW1P 1QD (tel 020 7834 5722)

SANDHU, Prof Bhupinder Kaur; da of Malkiat Singh Sandhu, and Swaran Kaur, *née* Garcha; *b* 24 April 1951; *Educ* Moat Girls' Sch Leicester, Wyggeston Girls' Sch Leicester, UCL (MB BS), Univ of London (MD); *m* 1980, Richard Whitburn; s of George Whitburn (d 1994) and Anna, *née* Evans; 2 da (Tara *b* 1 Feb 1983, Jess *b* 27 Jan 1986); *Career* res fell and hon sr registrar Hosp for Sick Children Gt Ormond St London 1981–84, lectr in child health and hon sr registrar Charing Cross and Westminster Hosp Med Sch 1984–88, conslt paediatric gastroenterologist and head Gastroenterology Unit Royal Hosp for Sick Children Bristol 1988–, hon sr clinical lectr Univ of Bristol 1988–; temp advsr WHO; visiting prof of child health, gastroenterology and nutrition UWE 2000–; examiner: Univ of London 1989–94 and 2005–, Addis Ababa Univ 1993–95, RCPCH 1997–, Univ of Birmingham 1999–2001, Univ of Cardiff 2007–; chm Div of Paediatrics 1991–96, sec SW Paediatric Soc 1991–96, chair Res Working Gp Euro Soc of Paediatric Gastroenterology, Nutrition and Hepatology, convenor and sec Br Soc of Paediatric Gastroenterology and Nutrition 1993–96, memb Nutrition Ctee RCPCH 2001–; United Bristol Healthcare Tst: memb Equal Opportunities Advsy Gp 1991–99, sec Hosp Med Ctee 1996–2000; pres elect Cwlth Soc of Paediatric Gastroentrology and Nutrition 2006–, memb Cwlth Advsy Ctee on Health 2004–06, pres Medical Women's Fedn 2005–06 (hon treas 2002–04), memb Cncl and memb Conslts and Srs Ctee BMA 2006–; delivered numerous invited guest lectures in UK and overseas, chaired int meetings and symposia; chair: Regnl Advsy Ctee BBC West 1992–96, Clifton Branch Bristol W Lab Pty 1999–2003; memb Bd: Bristol Old Vic Theatre Sch 1990–, VSO 1998–2005, Food Standards Agency 2000–02; memb Maternity and Health Links 1989–91; chair of govrs Highgate Primary Sch London 1984–88, govr Clifton HS 1994–2005, dep chair Governing Bd UWE 2004– (memb 1996–); Professional of the Year Asian Women of Achievement Awards 2002; FRCP 1996 (MRCP 1978), FRCPCH 1997; *Publications* author of over 80 papers in int jls on subjects related to child health, gastroenterology and nutrition; *Recreations* coastal walking, theatre, travel; *Style*— Prof Bhu Sandhu; ✉ Royal Hospital for Children, Upper Maudlin Street, Bristol BS2 8BJ (tel 0117 342 8828, fax 0117 342 8845, e-mail bhupinder.sandhu@ubht.nhs.uk)

SANDHU, Sham; s of Kartar Singh Sandhu, of London, and Tarlochan Kaur, *née* Mangat; *b* 3 December 1971; *Educ* Ashmole Sch London, St Catherine's Coll Oxford (BA); *Career* BBC: prodn trainee Features Dept 1994–96, asst prodr Watchdog and Crimewatch 1996–97, dir and prodr Blue Peter and Live and Kicking 1997–99, devpt planner BBC One BBC Broadcast 1999–2000, head of new media and new channels BBC Prodn 2000–01; Five: controller Interactive Programming 2001–02, controller Youth and Music Programmes 2002–04, controller Special Events and Pop Features 2002–04; memb: Cncl RTS 2000–, Edinburgh TV Festival Exec Ctee 2004– (memb Advsy Ctee 2000–04), BAFTA; *Recreations* skiing, television, photography, 1950s Scandinavian design; *Clubs* Soho House; *Style*— Sham Sandhu, Esq; ✉ Five, 22 Long Acre, London WC2E 9LY (tel 020 7550 5555)

SANDHURST, 6 Baron (UK 1871); Guy Rhys John Mansfield; see: Guy Mansfield, QC

SANDIFER, Dr Quentin Dudley; s of Keith Dudley Sandifer (d 1982), and Joyce Eileen, *née* Lewis (d 1968); *b* 14 July 1960, Cardiff; *Educ* Univ of Wales Coll of Med (MB, BCh, MPH), London Business Sch, Columbia Univ NY (MBA); *m* 19 Jan 1985, Anne Griffiths, *née* Evans; 1 da (Charlotte *b* 11 Feb 1987), 2 s (Thomas *b* 22 June 1989, Christopher *b* 6 June 1991); *Career* house offr Singleton Hosp and North Tees Gen Hosp 1985–86; gen practice trainee: Royal Shewsbury Gp of Hosps 1986–89, St John's Hill Surgery Shrewsbury 1989–90; family physician and active staff physician Barrhead Clinic and Gen Hosp Alberta Canada 1990–92, specialist registrar in public health med South Glamorgan HA 1992–97; Iechyd Morgannwg (West/Mid Glamorgan) HA: conslt in public health med 1997–2000, exec dir of public health 2000–03; dir of public health Swansea Local Health Bd 2003–04, dir of public health and med dir Kent & Medway SHA 2004–05, exec dir of public health Kent & Medway SHA and Kent CC 2005–06, hon clinical sr lectr Univ of Kent 2005–, dep regnl dir of public health and med dir NHS SE Coast 2006–; author various papers in learned jls; memb Advsy Ctee on Microbiological Safety of Food Food Standards Agency 2001–06; RSM: Janet Nash travelling fell 1996, pres Section of Gen Practice 1998–99, hon sec 2004–, hon vice-pres Section of Gen Practice with Primary Health Care 2004–; DRCOG, FRCGP 2000 (MRCGP 1989), FRSH 2001, FFPH 2004 (MFPHM 1997), FRIPH 2005; *Recreations* opera; *Clubs* RSM; *Style*— Dr Quentin D Sandifer; ✉ 8 Linden Fields, Tunbridge Wells, Kent TN2 5QN

SANDILANDS, James Andrew Douglas; see: Torphichen, Lord

SANDISON, Francis Gunn; s of Capt Dr Andrew Tawse Sandison (d 1982), of Glasgow, and Dr Ann Brougham, *née* Austin; *b* 25 May 1949; *Educ* Glasgow Acad, Charterhouse,

S

Magdalen Coll Oxford (MA, BCL); *m* 5 Sept 1981 (m dis 2007), Milva Lou, da of Prof John Emory McCaw, of Des Moines, Iowa; 1 s (Gavin b 1985); *Career* admitted slr 1974; ptnr Freshfields Bruckhaus Deringer 1980–2004 (asst slr 1974–80); memb: Law Soc 1974– (memb Tax Law Ctee 1992–2004, chm Corporation Tax Sub-Ctee 1993–99), City of London Law Soc 1980– (chm Revenue Law Sub-Ctee 1991–97), Addington Soc 1987–, Advsy Bd Fulbright Cmmn 1995–97, VAT Practitioners Gp 1996–2004, Tax Law Review Ctee 1997–2004, Tax Law Rewrite Consultative Ctee 2005–; Distinguished Service Award City of London Law Soc 1997; *Books* Profit Sharing and Other Share Acquisition Schemes (1979), Whiteman on Income Tax (co-author 3 edn, 1988); *Recreations* fishing, wine, reading, cooking; *Clubs* Lansdowne; *Style*— Francis Sandison, Esq; ✉ The Shieling, Kirkmichael, Blairgowrie, Perthshire PH10 7NA (tel 01250 881352, e-mail frankspeycaster253@btinternet.com)

SANDLE, Prof Michael Leonard; s of Charles Edward Sandle, and Dorothy Gwendoline Gladys, *née* Vernon; *b* 18 May 1936; *Educ* Douglas HS, Douglas Sch of Art and Technol, Slade Sch of Fine Art (AFA); *m* 1, 1971 (m dis 1974), Cynthia Dora Koppel; m 2, 1988, Demelza Jane Spargo (m dis 2004); 1 s (George Benjamin Charles b 24 May 1992), 1 da (Genevieve Holly b 6 Nov 1996); *Career* various teaching posts in Britain 1961–64, lectr Coventry Coll of Art 1964–68, visiting prof Univ of Calgary 1970–71, assoc prof Univ of Victoria BC 1972–73, prof in sculpture Fachhochschule für Gestaltung Pforzheim 1977–80 (lectr 1973–77), sr research fell De Montfort Univ 1997–; has participated in exhibitions internationally 1957–: V Biennale Paris 1966, Documenta IV Kassel 1968, Documenta VI 1977; works exhibited in public collections including: Arts Cncl of GB, Tate Gallery, Australian Nat Gallery Canberra, Metropolitan Museum NY, Stzüki Museum Łódź, Nat Gallery of Warsaw, Wilhelm Lehmbruck Museum Duisburg, Hakone Open Air Museum; prof Akademie Für Bildenden Künste Germany 1980–99 ret; first Kenneth Armitage Fndn fell 2004–06; ARA 1980, RA 1990–97 (resigned) and 2004 (re-elected), FRBS 1994; *Style*— Prof Michael Sandle, RA, FRBS; ✉ c/o RBS, 108 Brompton Road, London SW7 3RA

SANDLER, Prof Merton; s of late Frank Sandler, of Salford, Lancs, and late Edith, *née* Stein; *b* 28 March 1926; *Educ* Manchester Grammar, Univ of Manchester (MB ChB, MD); *m* 1961, Lorna Rosemary, da of late Ian Michael Grenby, of Colindale, London; 2 s, 2 da; *Career* Capt RAMC; jr specialist in pathology 1951–53, res fell in clinical pathology Brompton Hosp 1953–54, lectr in chem pathology Royal Free Hosp Sch of Med 1955–58; prof of chem pathology Royal Postgrad Med Sch Inst of Obstetrics and Gynaecology Univ of London 1973–91 (now emeritus), conslt chem pathologist Queen Charlotte's Maternity Hosp 1958–91; visiting prof: Univ of New Mexico 1983, Chicago Med Sch 1984, Univ of S Florida 1988; recognised teacher in chem pathology 1960 (examiner various Br and foreign univs and Royal Colls); memb Standing Advsy Ctee Bd of Studies in Pathology Univ of London 1972–76 (Chem Pathology Sub-Ctee 1973–91); Inst of Obstetrics and Gynaecology: chm Academic Bd 1972–73, chm Bd of Mgmnt 1975–76; govr: Br Postgrad Med Fedn 1976–78, Queen Charlotte's Hosp for Women; memb Cncl and meetings sec Assoc of Clinical Pathologists 1959–70, memb Cncl Collegium Int Neuro-Psychopharmacologicum 1982–85, hon librarian RSM 1987–93; pres: section Med Experimental Med and Therapeutics 1979–80, Br Assoc for Psychopharmacology 1980 (hon memb 1993), Br Assoc for Postnatal Illness 1980–, W London Med Chirurgical Soc 1996–97; chm tstees Nat Soc for Res into Mental Health 1983–, memb Med Advsy Cncls of Migraine Tst 1975–80 (tstee 1987–92, chm Scientific Advsy Ctee 1985–92); memb: Schizophrenia Assoc of GB 1975–78, Parkinson's Disease Soc 1981; chm and sec Biology Cncl Symposium on Drug Action 1979, memb Bd of Mgmnt and chm Awards Sub-Ctee Biology Cncl 1983–91 (sec 1985–91); memb Exec Ctee: Marcé Soc 1983–86, Med Cncl on Alcoholism 1987–91, sec and memb Cncl Harveian Soc of London 1979–93 (pres 1992), memb Cncl of Mgmnt and patron Helping Hand Organisation 1981–87, foreign corresponding memb American Coll of Neuropsychopharmacology 1975; hon memb: Indian Acad of Neurosciences 1982, Hungarian Pharmacological Soc 1985; jt ed: British Journal of Pharmacology 1974–80, Clinical Science 1975–77, Journal of Neural Transmission 1979–82; jt ed-in-chief Journal of Psychiatric Research 1982–92, present or past memb editorial bds of 17 other sci jls; lectr to various learned socs incl: 1 Cummings Meml 1976, James E Beall II Meml 1980, Biol Cncl Lecture medal 1984, F B Smith Meml 1995, Jane Chomet Meml 1997, Marcia Wilkinson 2001; Anna Monika Int Prize for res on biological aspects of depression 1973, Gold Medal Br Migraine Assoc 1974, Senator Dr Franz Burda Int Prize for res on Parkinson's disease 1988, Arnold Friedman Distinguished Clinician/Researcher Award 1991, Br Assoc of Psychopharmacology/Zeneca Lifetime Achievement Award 1999, Concilium Int Neuro-Psycho Pharmacologicum (CINP)/Pfizer Pioneer Award for lifetime contribution to monoamine studies in human health and disease 2006; Hon DUniv Semmelweis Univ of Med Budapest 1992; FRCP, FRCPath, FRCPsych; *Books* Mental Illness in Pregnancy and the Puerperium (1978), The Psychopharmacology of Aggression (1979), Enzyme Inhibitors as Drugs (1980), Amniotic Fluid and its Clinical Significance (1980), The Psychopharmacology of Alcohol (1980), The Psychopathology of Anticonvulsants (1981), Nervous Laughter (1991); jtly: The Adrenal Cortex (1961), The Thyroid Gland (1967), Advances in Pharmacology (1968), Monoamine Oxidases (1972), Serotonin - New Vistas (1974), Sexual Behaviour: Pharmacology and Biochemistry (1975), Trace Amines and the Brain (1976), Phenolsulphotransferase in Mental Health Research (1981), Tetrahydroisoquinolines and B-Carbolines (1982), Progress towards a Male Contraceptive (1982), Neurobiology of the Trace Amines (1984), Psychopharmacology and Food (1985), Neurotransmitter Interactions (1986), Design of Enzyme Inhibitors as Drugs (Vol I 1987, Vol II 1993), Progress in Catecholamine Research (1988), Migraine: A Spectrum of Ideas (1990), 5-Hydroxytryptamine in Psychiatry (1991), Genetic Research in Psychiatry (1992), Monoamine Oxidase: Basic and Clinical Aspects (1993), Migraine: Pharmacology and Genetics (1996), Wine: a Scientific Exploration (2003); *Recreations* reading, listening to music, lying in the sun; *Clubs* Athenaeum; *Style*— Prof Merton Sandler; ✉ 33 Park Road, Twickenham, Middlesex TW1 2QD (tel 020 8892 9085, fax 020 8891 5370, e-mail m.sandler@imperial.ac.uk)

SANDLER, Michael Stephen; s of Carl Bernard Sandler (d 1998), and Taube Irene Barash (d 1980); *b* 17 October 1947; *Educ* Leeds GS, Boston Univ (BA); *m* 1973, Gail Michele, da of Dr David Granet, JP, of Scotland; 2 s (Andrew b 1975, Jonathan b 1978); *Career* qualified chartered surveyor; Conrad Ritblat & Co 1971–78, dir Streets Financial Ltd 1979–86, md Kingsway Financial Public Relations (Saatchi & Saatchi Co) 1986–88, chm Hudson Sandler Ltd 1988–; ARICS; *Recreations* theatre, cinema, golf, opera; *Style*— Michael Sandler, Esq; ✉ 2 Marston Close, London NW6 4EU (tel 020 7328 7510); Hudson Sandler Ltd, 29 Cloth Fair, London EC1A 7JQ (tel 020 7796 4133)

SANDS, (John) Derek; s of Reginald Sands (d 1971), of Manchester, and Elizabeth, *née* Whitlow (d 1988); *b* 26 January 1940; *Educ* Manchester Grammar, Univ of Manchester (LLB); *m* 1, 7 May 1966, Sylvia Rose (d 1981); 1 s (Christopher Andrew b 12 April 1967), 2 da (Amanda Melanie b 19 Dec 1968, Rachel Elizabeth b 15 Oct 1972); m 2, 7 Sept 1982, Kathleen; *Career* asst slr: Addleshaw Sons & Latham 1965–66 (articled clerk 1961–65), Cartwright & Backhouse 1966–67; ptnr Kirk Jackson (now Rowlands Slrs) 1968– (asst slr 1967–68); Law Soc: memb Cncl 1986–2000, chm Family Law Ctee 1990–91, chm Courts and Legal Servs Ctee 1996–99, chm of various Law Soc working parties and task forces; chm Manchester Young Slrs' Assoc 1973–74, memb Cncl Manchester Law Soc 1974–2000 (pres 1985–86); memb: Law Soc 1965, Manchester Law Soc 1965; *Recreations* tennis, reading, music, gardening, travel, food, wine; *Clubs* Swinton & Pendlebury Rotary; *Style*— Derek Sands, Esq; ✉ Rowlands Solicitors, 3 York Street, Manchester M2 2RW (tel 0161 835 2020, fax 0161 835 2525, e-mail jds@rowlands-solicitors.co.uk)

SANDS, Jonathan Peter; s of Peter Stuart Sands, of Buxton, Derbys, and Vivianne Anne, *née* Kidd; *b* 27 March 1961; *Educ* Normanton Sch, Stockport Coll of Technol; *m* 17 Sept 1983, Carolyn Jane, da of Norman Fletcher; 2 s (Thomas Charles b 9 March 1986, Henry George b 5 Oct 1993), 1 da (Polly Kate b 17 Sept 1992); *Career* IAS Advertising Macclesfield 1979–82, md Elmwood Design (pt of The Charles Wall Group before MBO 1989) 1985– (joined 1982); recipient numerous design awards incl Design Effectiveness, Clio, Mobius, Int Brand Packaging and NY Festivals; chm DBA 1995–97 (formerly dir), memb Cncl Design Cncl, former memb Cncl RSA; broadcaster and columnist; regular lectr at business confs, seminars and at univs on BA and MBA courses; memb DBA; memb Cncl RHS Yorkshire 2002–; Hon DSc Huddersfield Univ 2002; *Recreations* fast cars; *Clubs* Groucho, Harrogate Golf, Gullane Golf; *Style*— Jonathan Sands, Esq; ✉ Elmwood Design, Elmwood House, Ghyll Royd, Guiseley, Leeds LS20 9LT (tel 01943 870229, fax 01943 870191)

SANDS, Marc; s of Allan Sands and Ruth, *née* Buchholz; *b* 12 December 1963; *Educ* Univ Coll Sch London, Pembroke Coll Cambridge (MA), Univ of Bradford (MBA); *m* 11 Feb 1995, Lyndsay, *née* Griffiths; 2 s (Aldo, Emil); *Career* with: DMB & B London and NY offices 1987–91, SP Lintas 1992–93, Howell Henry Chaldecott Lury 1994–97; mktg dir Granada TV 1997–98, dir of brand mktg ONdigital (formerly BDB) 1998–2000, mktg dir Guardian Newspapers Ltd 2001–; *Recreations* Arsenal FC (season-ticket holder), running, skiing; *Style*— Marc Sands, Esq

SANDS, Peter; s of John Sands, of Whitley Bay, Tyne & Wear, and Jane Caroline, *née* Reay (d 1984); *b* 16 May 1955; *Educ* Whitley Bay GS, Huddersfield Poly (BA); *m* 29 March 1986, Pamela Jean, da of William Maurice Hutchinson; 3 s (Jack William b 1 March 1987, Daniel Peter b 12 July 1988, Thomas Joseph b 23 Sept 1996), 1 da (Anna Jane b 24 Feb 1993); *Career* reporter Shields Weekly News (N Shields) 1977–79, sub ed The Northern Echo 1979–81, chief sub ed The Evening Despatch (Darlington) 1981–84; The Northern Echo: night ed 1984–86, asst ed 1986–89, dep ed 1989–90, ed 1990–93; devpt ed Westminster Press 1993–95, dir The Editorial Centre Ltd 1995–; awards (for The Northern Echo): Newspaper Design Award for Provincial Morning Newspapers, Freedom of Information Newspaper Award, Newspaper Indust Awards for Design and Use of Photography 1991, NE Newspaper of the Year 1991; memb Soc of Editors; *Recreations* spending time with the family, Newcastle United FC, country pubs, newspapers, literature; *Clubs* Beckley Rangers FC (mangr and sponsor); *Style*— Peter Sands, Esq; ✉ The Editorial Centre, Hanover House, Marine Court, St Leonards, East Sussex (tel 01424 435991, fax 01424 445547, e-mail sands@editorial-centre.co.uk)

SANDS, Prof Philippe; QC; s of Alan Sands, of London, and Ruth, *née* Buchholz; *b* 17 October 1960, London; *Educ* Univ Coll Sch London, CCC Cambridge (BA, LLM); *m* 5 June 1993, Natalia Schiffrin; 1 s (Leo b 14 April 1995), 2 da (Lara b 16 May 1997, Katya b 11 April 2000); *Career* res fell St Catharine's Coll Cambridge 1984–88, lectr faculty of law KCL 1988–92, lectr, reader then prof SOAS Univ of London 1992–2001, prof of law UCL 2001–; *Publications* Principles of International Environmental Law (2 edn 2003), Lawless World (2005); *Recreations* skiing, Arsenal, Umbria; *Style*— Prof Philippe Sands, QC; ✉ 50 Willow Road, London NW3 1TP (tel 020 7404 3447, fax 020 7404 3448, e-mail p.sands@ucl.ac.uk)

SANDS, Sir Roger Blakemore; KCB (2006); s of Thomas Blakemore Sands (d 1980), and Edith Malyon, *née* Waldram (d 1986); *b* 6 May 1942; *Educ* UCS Hampstead, Oriel Coll Oxford (scholar, MA); *m* 24 Sept 1966, Jennifer Ann, da of Hugh T Cattell (d 1992); 1 da and 1 da decd; *Career* Clerks Dept House of Commons 1965–; princ clerk of: Overseas Office 1987–91, Select Ctees (and registrar of Members' Interests) 1991–94, Public Bills 1994–97, Legislation 1998–2001; clerk asst 2001–03, clerk and chief exec of House of Commons 2003–06; chm Study of Parliament Gp 1993–96, tstee History of Parliament Tst 2001–02 (sec 1974–80), tstee Industry and Parliament Tst 2001–02; *Style*— Sir Roger Sands, KCB; ✉ No 4 (The Ashurst Suite), Woodbury House, Lewes Road, East Grinstead, West Sussex RH19 3UD (tel 01342 302245)

SANDWICH, 11 Earl of (E 1660); John Edward Hollister Montagu; also Viscount Hinchingbrooke and Baron Montagu, of St Neots (both E 1660); s of (Alexander) Victor Edward Paulet Montagu (10 Earl of Sandwich, who disclaimed peerages for life 1964; d 1995), and his 1 w, Rosemary (Maud), *née* Peto (d 1998); *b* 11 April 1943; *Educ* Eton, Trinity Coll Cambridge (MA); *m* 1 July 1968, (Susan) Caroline, o da of Rev Canon Perceval Ecroyd Cobham Hayman, of Rogate, W Sussex; 2 s (Luke Timothy Charles Montagu, Viscount Hinchingbrooke b 1969, Hon Orlando William b 1971), 1 da (Jemima Mary b 1973); *Heir* s, Viscount Hinchingbrooke; *Career* editorial conslt; info offr Christian Aid 1974–86 (memb Bd 1999–2004), conslt ed Save the Children Fund 1987–92, conslt CARE Int 1989–94, memb Cncl Anti Slavery Int 1997–, govr Beaminster Sch 1997–2004; jt owner/admin Mapperton Estate Dorset; elected hereditary peer House of Lords 1999–; pres Samuel Pepys Club 1985–; *Books* Book of the World (1971), Prospects for Africa (jt ed, 1988), Prospects for Africa's Children (1990), Children at Crisis Point (1992), Hinch: A Celebration (jtly ed, 1997); *Style*— The Rt Hon the Earl of Sandwich; ✉ House of Lords, London SW1A 0PW

SANDYS, 7 Baron (UK 1802); Richard Michael Oliver Hill; DL (Worcs 1968); s of 6 Baron Sandys, DL (d 1961), and Cynthia Mary (d 1990), o da of Col Frederic Richard Thomas Trench-Gascoigne, DSO; *b* 21 July 1931; *Educ* RNC Dartmouth; *m* 1961, Patricia Simpson, da of late Capt Lionel Hall, MC; *Heir* kinsman, Marquess of Downshire; *Career* late Lt Royal Scots Greys; patron of one living; a lord-in-waiting to HM the Queen Jan to March 1974, oppn whip House of Lords 1974–79, Capt HM Body Guard of the Yeomen of the Guard (govt dep chief whip in House of Lords) 1979–82; Liveryman Worshipful Co of Goldsmiths; FRGS; *Clubs* Cavalry and Guards'; *Style*— The Lord Sandys, DL; ✉ Ombersley Court, Droitwich, Worcestershire WR9 0HH (tel 01905 620220)

SANFORD, Prof Anthony John; s of Edwin Sanford (d 1970), and Winnifred Olive, *née* Hurdman (d 1981); *b* 5 July 1944; *Educ* Waverley GS, Univ of Leeds (BSc), Pembroke Coll Cambridge (PhD); *m* 1, 3 Sept 1966, Valerie Ann, da of Frank Hines (d 1972); 1 da (Bridget Isobel b 27 March 1970); m 2, 24 Jan 1987, Linda Mae, da of John Moxey (d 2002); 1 s (Anthony Iain Moxey b 2 May 1992), 1 da (Heather Margaret Moxey b 4 May 1995); m 3, 28 June 2002, Alison Jane Sutherland, da of Peter Chesney; *Career* lectr in psychology Univ of Dundee 1971–74; Dept of Psychology Univ of Glasgow: sr lectr 1974–80, reader 1980–82, prof 1983–, head of dept 1983–86; Gifford lectr in natural theology 1983; FBPsS, FRSA, CPsychol; *Books* Understanding Written Language (with S Garrod, 1981), Models, Mind and Man (1983), Cognition and Cognitive Psychology (1985), The Mind of Man (1987), Communicating Quantities (with L Moxey, 1993), The Nature and Limits of Human Understanding (ed, 2003); *Recreations* hill walking (Munroist 1991, Corbetts 2004), industrial archeology, music, cooking; *Style*— Prof Anthony Sanford; ✉ Department of Psychology, University of Glasgow, Glasgow G12 8QQ (tel 0141 330 4058, fax 0141 339 8889, e-mail tony@psy.gla.ac.uk)

SANGER, Christopher; s of James Sanger, and Madeline Sanger; *b* 3 July 1970, London; *Educ* Shrewsbury, Lady Margaret Hall Oxford (MA), Warwick Business Sch (MBA); *m* 7 Sept 2002, Gillian; 1 da (Octavia b 28 Oct 2003), 1 s (Henry b 15 July 2005); *Career* chartered accountant Arthur Andersen 1992–98, head of business tax policy HM Treasy 1998–2001, dep chm Deloitte & Touche 2002–04, ptnr and head of tax policy Ernst & Young LLP 2005–; vice-chm Tax Faculty ICAEW, memb Tax Law Review Ctee Inst for

Fiscal Studies; CTA 1995, FCA 1996; *Recreations* tennis, squash, family, Scottish dancing; *Clubs* Hurlingham; *Style*— Christopher Sanger, Esq; ✉ Ernst & Young LLP, 1 More London Place, London SE1 2AF (tel 020 7951 0150, e-mail csanger@uk.ey.com or chris@csanger.com)

SANGER, Dr Frederick; OM (1986), CH (1981), CBE (1963); s of Frederick Sanger, and Cicely, *née* Crewdson; *b* 13 August 1918; *Educ* Bryanston, St John's Coll Cambridge; *m* 1940, M Joan, da of Alfred Howe; 2 s, 1 da; *Career* res scientist: Biochemistry Laboratory Univ of Cambridge 1943–61, MRC Laboratory of Molecular Biol Cambridge 1961–83, ret; winner Nobel Prize for Chemistry 1958 and jt winner 1980; Hon DSc Cambridge 1983; FRS; *Style*— Dr Frederick Sanger, OM, CH, CBE, FRS; ✉ Far Leys, Fen Lane, Swaffham Bulbeck, Cambridge CB5 0NJ (tel 01223 811610)

SANGER, James Gerald; s of Gerald Fountain Sanger, CBE, JP (d 1981), and (Margaret) Hope Sanger, MBE (d 1994); *b* 29 April 1939; *Educ* Shrewsbury, Worcester Coll Oxford (MA), Harvard Business Sch (MBA); *m* 21 Sept 1968, Madeline Mary, da of George William Jack Collis (d 1986); 1 s (Christopher James b 1970), 1 da (Katherine Hope b 1972); *Career* Farrow Bersey Gain Vincent & Co 1962–63 (articled 1957–59), asst to chm Associated Newspapers 1966–68 (joined 1963), md First Investors Ltd 1969–75, dir Henderson Administration 1974–75; fin dir: Blyth Greene Jourdain 1975–77, James Burrough plc 1977–84; exec dir: Tomkins plc 1985–88, Peek plc 1988–98, Associated Holdings Ltd 1998–2001, Liontrust Asset Mgmnt plc 1999–; dep chm: Stenoak Associated Services plc 1999–2001, Articon-Integralis AG 2000–05, DeRisk IT Ltd 2002–05; govr: Benenden Sch 1975–2002, Shrewsbury Sch 1985–99, Wellington Coll 2002–; dep chm Farnham Castle 1998–; FCA 1973; *Recreations* real and lawn tennis, golf, travel, poetry, listening, Richard III; *Clubs* Hurlingham (finance chm 2005–, dep chm 2006), RAC; *Style*— James Sanger, Esq; ✉ Moreton House, Brightwell-cum-Sotwell, Oxfordshire OX10 0PT (tel 01491 833655, fax 01491 836599, e-mail jim@jimsanger.com)

SANGHERA, District Judge Pal Singh; s of Harbans Singh, of London, and Mohinder, *née* Kaur; *b* 15 December 1953; *Educ* Southall GS, Middx Poly (BA), Coll of Law Chester; *m* 10 April 1977, Mohinder; 1 da (Sangeet b 1982), 1 s (Bhopinder b 1983); *Career* admitted slr 1979 (articles with Chapman Wells); asst slr Whiteley & Pickering 1979–82, slr Ian Burr 1982, ptnr Ian Burr & Co 1982, appointed dep district judge 1995, gained higher court rights of advocacy 1998, apppointed full time Coventry Combined Court Centre 1999, resident judge Nuneaton County Court, recorder of the Crown Ct 2003–; memb Assoc of District Judges 1999, assoc memb of Commonwealth Magistrates and Judges Assoc; fndr chm British Asian Business and Professionals Assoc 1991; senator Jr Chamber Int; tstee Sydenham Neighbourhood Initiatives; *Recreations* archery, voluntary organisations; *Style*— District Judge Sanghera

SANGSTER, Nigel; QC (1998); s of Dr H B Singh; *b* 16 February 1954; *Educ* Repton, Univ of Leeds (LLB); *Career* called to the Bar Middle Temple 1976; in practice specialising in fraud 1977–, recorder of the Crown Court 1997–; memb Bar Cncl 1994–2004, memb Criminal Bar Assoc; *Style*— Nigel Sangster, Esq, QC; ✉ 25 Bedford Row, London WC1R 4HD (tel 020 7067 1500, e-mail mail@nigelsangster.qc.com); St Paul's Chambers, 5th Floor, St Paul's House, 23 Park Square South, Leeds LS1 2ND (tel 0113 245 5866, fax 0113 245 5807)

SANKEY, Vernon Louis; s of Edward Sankey (d 1982), and Marguerite Elizabeth Louise, *née* Van Maurik (d 1962); *b* 9 May 1949; *Educ* Harrow, Oriel Coll Oxford (MA); *m* 5 June 1976, Elizabeth, da of Tom Knights (d 2000); 3 s (James Edward b 12 May 1979, Mark Henry b 14 July 1981, William Thomas b 1 Feb 1985), 1 da (Angela Louise (twin) b 14 July 1981); *Career* Reckitt & Colman plc: mgmnt trainee Food & Drink UK 1971–74, asst mangr Fin & Planning HQ London 1974–76, dir of planning Europe France 1976–78, gen mangr Denmark 1978–80, PA to chm and chief Exec HQ 1980–81, md France 1981–85, md Food & Drink Norwich 1985–89, chm and chief exec Reckitt & Colman Inc USA 1989–99, gp dir N America 1989–91, bd memb 1989–99, chief exec 1992–99; chm: Thomson Travel Group plc 2000, Gala Gp Holdings plc 2000–02, Beltpacker plc 2000–04, The Really Effective Devpt Co Ltd 2000–06, Photo-Me Int plc 2000–07; non-exec dir: Pearson plc 1993–2006, Allied Zurich plc 1998–2000, Zurich Allied AG 1998–2000, Zurich Fin Services 1998–, Taylor Woodrow 2004–, Vividas plc 2005– (chm designate), Atos Origin SA 2006–, Firmenich SA 2006–; memb Int Advsy Bd Korn/Ferry International 1994–2005; memb Bd: Grocery Mfrs of America (GMA) 1995–99, Food Standards Agency 2000–05, Cofra Holdings AG (Switzerland) 2001–; memb Advsy Bd: Proudfoot UK plc 2001–06, MCC Inc 2001–; MInstD 1995; FRSA 1999; *Recreations* jogging, tennis, fitness; *Clubs* Leander; *Style*— Vernon Sankey, Esq; ✉ c/o Sue Pullen, Zurich Financial Services, 9–15 Sackville Street, London W1A 2JP (tel 020 7437 7844, e-mail vernonsankey@hotmail.com)

SANT CASSIA, Louis Joseph; s of Maj Henri Emmanuel Sant Cassia, ED (d 1990), of St Paul's Bay, Malta, and Anna, *née* De Piro Gourgion (d 1995); *b* 19 September 1946; *Educ* Lyceum Malta, Royal Univ of Malta (MD), Univ of Nottingham (DM); *m* 11 July 1974, Antoinette, da of Gerald H Ferro, MVO, MBE (d 2005),of Sliema, Malta; 1 s (Henri b 1977), 1 da (Emma b 1980); *Career* cmmnd 1 Bn King's Own Malta Regt 1968–72; res fell Dept of Obstetrics and Gynaecology Nottingham 1981–83, conslt obstetrician and gynaecologist Coventry 1987–, lead clinician for gynaecological oncology in Warwickshire 1999–; Coventry Dist tutor RCOG 1988–94; visiting sr clinical lectr Univ of Warwick 1993; hon lectr Univ of Malta 1997; examiner MRCOG; chm: Coventry Med Res and Ethics Ctee 1993–2004, Med Advsy Ctee Warwickshire Nuffield Hosp 1995–2000, chm Sr Hosp Medical Staff Ctee Coventry 2004–; author various pubns on gynaecological oncology, subfertility, recurrent spontaneous abortions and research ethics; goalkeeper Malta water polo team Med Games 1967; FRCOG 1992 (MRCOG 1979); *Recreations* gardening, melitensia; *Style*— Louis Joseph Sant Cassia, Esq; ✉ Four Winds, Stoneleigh Road, Blackdown, Leamington Spa CV32 6QR (tel 01926 422147, e-mail ljsc@warwickshire-medical.com)

SANTA-OLALLA, Brig David Manuel; DSO (1995), MC (1976); s of Manolo Santa-Olalla, of Spain, and Ann Santa-Olalla; *b* 10 February 1953; *Educ* Mount St Mary's Coll, KCL (MA), RMA Sandhurst; *m* 17 July 1976, Joanna Mary, *née* Gilbert; 2 da (Lydia b 18 March 1980, Zoe b 25 Oct 1981), 2 s (Thomas b 15 Dec 1984, Harry b 10 Jan 1987); *Career* cmmnd Green Howards 1973, served in NW Europe, NI, Cyprus, Brunei and Hong Kong 1973–84, Army Staff Coll 1985, served in Germany, NI and USA 1986–92 (despatches 1991), CO 1 Bn Duke of Wellington's Regt NW Europe and Balkans 1992–94, CO 2 Inf Bde 2001–; *Recreations* golf, fishing, cricket; *Style*— Brig David Santa-Olalla, DSO, MC; ✉ HQ 2 Infantry Brigade, Sir John Moore Barracks, Folkestone, Kent CT20 3HF (tel 01303 225030, fax 01303 225145)

SANTO DOMINGO, Alejandro; s of Julio Mario Santo Domingo, of NYC, and Beatrice, *née* Davila; *b* 13 February 1977; *Educ* Harvard Coll (BA); *Career* md Quadrant Capital Advisors Inc NYC, vice-chm Latin America SABMiller plc, chm Bd Bavaria SA, chm Backus & Johnston, memb Bd Valorem; memb Bd: Aid for AIDS, DKMS; *Recreations* squash, hunting, reading; *Style*— Alejandro Santo Domingo, Esq; ✉ Quadrant Capital Advisors Inc, 499 Park Avenue, 24th Floor, New York, NY 10022 USA (tel 00 1 646 282 2600)

SANTS, Hector William Hepburn; s of (Hector) John Sants, of Oxford, and Elsie Ann Watt Hepburn; *b* 15 December 1955; *Educ* Clifton, CCC Oxford (MA); *m* 21 Dec 1987, Caroline Jane, da of Kenneth Ord Mackenzie; 3 s (Hector Alexander b 9 Jan 1989, Edward Kenneth Richard b 16 Oct 1990, Arthur Frederick Joseph b 15 May 1994); *Career* ptnr Phillips & Drew stockbrokers 1977–87, head of int securities Union Bank of Switzerland Securities Inc NY 1987–88, head of research Union Bank of Switzerland 1988, head of equities and vice-chm UBS Ltd 1988–98, chm DLJ Int Securities, head of int equities Donaldson Lufkin & Jenrette 1998–2000, head of int equities and vice-chm Credit Suisse First Boston 2000–01, ceo EMEA Credit Suisse First Boston 2001–04, md Wholesale and Institutional Markets FSA 2004–; advsr Public Tstee Office 1996–2000; memb: Stock Exchange Settlement Servs Bd 1990, Securities and Futures Authy Bd 1993–94, EASDAQ Bd 1996–99, London Stock Exchange Bd 1997–2001, Fin Law Panel 2001–02, Europe Bd NASDAQ 2001–03, FSA Practitioners Bd 2001–04, LCH Clearnet Bd 2003–04, Fin Reporting Cncl 2004–, Bd Nuffield Orthopaedic Centre NHS Tst 2002–, Advsy Bd Saïd Business Sch Univ of Oxford; *Recreations* painting, skiing, tennis, shooting; *Clubs* City of London; *Style*— Hector Sants, Esq

SAPHIR, Nicholas Peter George; s of Emanuel Saphir, MBE, and Anne Saphir; *b* 30 November 1944; *Educ* City of London, Univ of Manchester (LLB); *m* 1971, Ena, da of Raphael Bodin; 1 s; *Career* called to the Bar Lincoln's Inn 1967; dir Bodin and Nielsen Ltd 1975–; chm: Hunter Saphir plc 1987–97, Organic Milk Supplies Co-operative Ltd (OMSCO) 2003–, Rural Revival 2004–, Coressence 2006–; non-exec dir: Dairy Crest Ltd 1987–93, Albert Fisher Gp plc 1993–97, San Miguel SA 1993–98 and 2001–; pres Fresh Produce Consortium 1997–2000; chm: Central Cncl for Agricultural and Horticultural Corp (CCAHC) 1980–83, Food From Britain 1983–87, Agricultural Forum 2001–04; memb Food and Drinks EDC 1984–87; chm Br Israel C of C 1991–94; *Publications* Farmed Out (2001), London Wholesale Markets Review for DEFRA and Corpn of London (2002); *Recreations* modern art; *Clubs* Farmers'; *Style*— Nicholas Saphir, Esq

SAPOCHNIK, Carlos Luis; s of Leon Sapochnik (d 1985), of Argentina, and Clara Aronovich; *b* 18 July 1944; *Educ* Buenos Aires Nat Univ, Royal Coll of Art (MA), City Univ, Univ of East London (MA); *m* 1966, Victoria, da of Vicente Rosenberg; 1 da (Manuela Maria b 8 Sept 1972), 1 s (Miguel Vicente b 21 July 1974); *Career* freelance graphic designer and illustrator 1970–92; art dir Free Association Books 1984–88, creative dir Burnett Associates 1988–90, dir The Running Head Ltd; publishing clients incl: Methuen & Co, Tavistock Publications, Routledge, Hutchinson Educnl; local govt clients incl: London Borough of Hackney, GLC; theatre clients incl: Royal Court Theatre, Haymarket Leicester, Lyric Hammersmith; other clients incl: Midland Bank, CBS Records; pt/t lectr in graphic design: Chelsea Sch of Art 1981–84, Bath Acad of Art 1982–86; princ lectr in postgraduate design studies Middx Univ 1990–; Quality Assurance Agency specialist reviewer art and design 1998–2000; solo drawing exhibitions: Vortex Gallery 1989, Argile Gallery 1990, Diorama Gallery 1994, Espace Amigorena Paris 1994; two-man drawing exhibitions: Boundary Gallery 1988, Ben Uri Gallery 1996; group exhibitions incl: Dublin Arts Festival 1975, Warsaw Poster Biennale 1976, 1978 and 1980, Lahti Poster Biennale Finland 1978, 1979 and 1983, Brno Graphic Design Biennale Czechoslovakia 1984, 1986, 1988 and 1992, London Group Open 1992, Riviera Gallery 1994, Rexel Derwent Open 1994, Pastel Soc 1994, Ben Uri Gallery 1996, Cheltenham Open 1996; ind organizational conslt 2001–; memb: Tavistock Soc of Psychotherapists and Allied Professionals 2002, Int Soc for the Psychoanalytic Study of Organizations 2003; fell Int Soc of Typographic Designers 2000; FCSD 1991, FHEA 2002; *Style*— Carlos Sapochnik, Esq; ✉ 36A Southwood Avenue, London N6 5RZ (tel 020 8340 4873, e-mail c.sapochnik@blueyonder.co.uk)

SAPSFORD, Ralph Neville; s of Roland Geoffrey Sapsford (d 1973), of South Africa, and Doreen Inez Sapsford; *b* 30 October 1938; *Educ* St Andres's Sch Bloemfontein, Univ of Cape Town (MB ChB, ChM, class medal for jurisprudence), RCS (cert of completion of higher trg); *m* (m dis 1981) Simone André; 2 s, 1 da; *Career* MPILO Central Hosp Bulawayo Rhodesia: pre-registration house offr in gen surgery then gen med 1963, sr house offr in accident and orthopaedics then gen surgery 1964, registrar in gen surgery 1965; sr house offr in: radiotherapy Western Gen Hosp Edinburgh 1966, orthopaedics Princess Margaret Rose Hosp Edinburgh 1966–67; registrar in cardiothoracic surgery Papworth Hosp Cambridge 1967–68, asst lectr in cardiothoracic surgery Manchester Royal Infirmary 1968; sr registrar in: cardiothoracic surgery Killingbeck Hosp Leeds 1968–69, cardiac surgery Nat Heart Hosp London 1970, cardiothoracic surgery The Middx Hosp London 1970–71; res fell in cardiovascular surgery Dept of Surgery Univ of Alabama Birmingham USA 1972–73, sr registrar in thoracic surgery Harefield Hosp Uxbridge Middx 1974–75; Hammersmith Hosp London: sr registrar in cardiothoracic surgery 1971–72, 1973–74 and 1976–77, conslt/sr lectr in thoracic surgery 1977, ret 1989; hon conslt cardiothoracic surgn to St Mary's Hosp London 1981–90, in private practice Humana Hosp Wellington St John's Wood and Harley St 1990–; B merit award NHS 1987 (C merit award 1983); author of numerous learned articles and pubns; Freeman City of London; memb: Worshipful Soc of Apothecaries, Worshipful Co of Loriners; memb: Soc of Cardiothoracic Surgns GB and I 1969, Br Cardiac Soc 1977, Euro Soc of Cardio-Vascular Surgns 1977; FRCS 1967, FRCSEd 1967; *Recreations* collecting antique pistols and old Jaguars, cabinet making; *Clubs* United Wards, Aldersgate Ward, City Livery; *Style*— Ralph N Sapsford, Esq; ✉ 20 Birkdale Road, Ealing, London W5 1JZ

SARGEANT, Mark; s of Brian Anthony Sargeant, of Swanley, Kent, and Joan Rita Mollins; *b* 25 August 1973; *Educ* Oakwood Park GS Maidstone, West Kent Coll Tonbridge; *Career* commis chef Boodle's 1993–94; chef: Reads Restaurant 1994–96, Le Soufflé 1996, Coast 1996–97, Aubergine 1997–98, Gordon Ramsay Restaurant 1998–2001; chef de cuisine Gordon Ramsay at Claridges 2001– (1 Michelin Star, 3 AA Rosettes, Tatler Restaurant of the Year 2002); Young Chef of the Year 1996, Chef of the Year 2002; *Style*— Mark Sargeant, Esq; ✉ Gordon Ramsay at Claridges, 55 Brook Street, London W1A 2JQ (tel 020 7409 0812)

SARGENT, Wallace Leslie William; s of Leslie William Sargent (d 1979), and Eleanor, *née* Dennis (d 1964); *b* 15 February 1935; *m* 5 Aug 1964, Dr Anneila Sargent, da of Richard Cassells (d 1968), of Burntisland, Fife; 2 da (Lindsay Eleanor b 8 July 1970, Alison Clare b 25 Jan 1972); *Career* research fell Caltech 1959–62, sr research fell Royal Greenwich Observatory 1962–64, asst prof of physics Univ of Calif San Diego 1964–66; Caltech: asst prof 1966–68, assoc prof 1968–71, prof 1971–81, exec offr for astronomy 1975–81 and 1996–97, Ira S Bowen prof of astronomy 1981–, dir Palomar Observatory 1997–2000; visiting fell: Mount Stromlo Observatory Aust Nat Univ 1965 and 1967, Inst of Theoretical Astronomy Univ of Cambridge 1968–72, 1974–75, 1979, 1982 and 1987, Dept of Astrophysics Univ of Oxford 1973, Univ of Groningen 1978, Euro Southern Observatory 1980, 1982 and 1985, Univ of Florence 1981 and 2000, Institut d'Astrophysique Paris 1984, Royal Observatory Edinburgh 1990, MPIFA Heidelberg 1992, 1993 and 1994; memb: N Hemisphere Review Ctee SRC 1968–69, Visiting Ctee Univ of Arizona 1970–73, Ctee on Space Astronomy and Astrophysics Nat Acad of Sciences 1975–78, Study Gp for Space Telescope Science Inst Nat Acad of Sciences 1976, Harvard Coll Observatory Visiting Ctee 1979–86 (chm 1987–93), Editorial Bd Annual Reviews of Astronomy and Astrophysics 1977–81, Bd Harvard-Smithsonian Centre for Astrophysics 1983–, Science Steering Ctee Keck Observatory 1985– (co-chm 1985–89 and SUNY Stony Brook 1987, Astronomy Dept Univ of Calif Berkeley 1988, Space Telescope Science Inst 1989–91; memb: Astronomy and Astrophysics Survey Ctee Nat Acad of Sciences 1989–91 (co-chm Optical/IR Panel), Space Telescope Advsy Ctee 1990–91; Alfred P Sloane Fndn fell 1968–70, Helen B Warner prize American Astronomical Soc 1969, George Darwin lectr RAS 1987, Dirs distinguished lectr Lawrence Livermore Lab 1988, Dannie Heineman prize 1991, Bruce Gold medal 1994, Henry Norris Russell lectr American Astronomical Soc 2001; memb: American Astronomical Soc, RAS, Int Astronomical Union; FAAAS 1977, FRS 1981, ARAS 1998; *Recreations* watching sports, oriental rugs, music, reading;

S

Clubs Athenaeum (Pasadena); *Style—* Wallace Sargent, Esq, FRS; ✉ Astronomy Department, 105–24 California Institute of Technology, 1201 East California Boulevard, Pasadena, CA 91125, USA (tel 626 356 4055, fax 626 568 9352)

SARNE, Tanya; *see:* Gordon, Tanya Joan

SARPONG, June Kunadu; MBE (2007); da of Sam Sarpong, and Thelma, *née* Amihere; *b* 31 May 1977, London; *Educ* Connaught Sch for Girls London, Sir George Monoux Sixth Form Coll London; *Career* Kiss 100 FM 1992–95, BMG Music 1995–97, presenter: MTV 1997–2001, C4 (incl weekend show T4) 2001–, BBC 2006–; ambass Prince's Trust 2003, supporter Oxfam; *Recreations* reading, writing, sports, charity; *Style—* Ms June Sarpong, MBE; ✉ c/o A M Creative Limited, First Floor, 8–9 Stratton Street, London W1J 8LF (tel 020 7495 8378)

SARWAR, Mohammad; MP; *b* 18 August 1952, Faisalabad, Pakistan; *Educ* Univ of Faisalabad; *Career* former dir: United Wholesale Grocers Ltd, United Homestores Ltd; chair Islamic Centre 1985–88; cncllr Glasgow CC 1992–97; MP (Lab) Glasgow Govan 1997–; memb Scottish Affrs Select Ctee 1999–, chair Scottish Regnl Gp of Lab MP's 2002–; memb: UK Overseas Pakistan C of C, Ethnic Minority Enterprise Centre, GMB; *Style—* Mohammad Sarwar, Esq, MP; ✉ House of Commons, London SW1A 0AA

SASSOON, Adrian David; s of Hugh Meyer Sassoon, of London, and Marion Julia, *née* Schiff; *b* 1 February 1961; *Educ* Eton, Inchbald Sch of Design, Christie's Fine Arts Course; *Career* asst curator Dept of Decorative Arts J Paul Getty Museum Calif 1982–84 (curatorial asst 1980–82), dir Alexander & Berendt Ltd London 1990–92 (asst to md 1987–89); lectr on/dealer in French decorative arts, 18th century Sèvres porcelain and contemporary British ceramics and glass; treas and memb Ctee French Porcelain Soc 1989–95 (joined as memb 1985); memb: Cncl The Attingham Tst for the Study of the Country House 1990–95, Patrons of British Art Acquisitions Sub-Ctee Tate Gallery London 1997–99; tstee UK Friends of the Heritage Museum St Petersburg; articles on French 18th century decorative arts in the J Paul Getty Museum Jls 1981–85; *Books* Decorative Arts: A Handbook of the J Paul Getty Museum (1986), Catalogue of Vincennes and Sèvres Porcelain in the J Paul Getty Museum (1991), Vincennes and Sèvres Porcelain from a European Collection (2001); *Clubs* Lyford Cay (Nassau), Brooks's; *Style—* Adrian Sassoon, Esq; ✉ e-mail email@adriansassoon.com

SASSOON, James Meyer; s of Hugh Meyer Sassoon, of London, and Marion Julia, *née* Schiff; *b* 11 September 1955; *Educ* Eton, ChCh Oxford (exhibitioner, MA, Gibbs book prize); *m* 23 Oct 1981, Sarah Caroline Ray, da of Sir (Ernest) John Ward Barnes; 1 s (Frederick b 1 April 1987), 2 da (Alexandra b 6 Nov 1990, Victoria b 4 June 1994); *Career* Thomson McLintock & Co 1977–86, S G Warburg & Co Ltd 1987–95 (dir 1991–95); UBS Warburg (formerly Warburg Dillon Read): md 1995–2002, vice-chm Investment Banking 2000–02; HM Treasy: md Finance, Regulation and Industry 2002–06, Chllr's rep for promotion of the city 2006–; dir: HBV Enterprise 2000–02, Partnerships UK plc 2002–06, The Merchants Tst plc 2006–; contrib articles to art and fin jls; tstee: Nat Gallery Tst, Gerald Coke Handel Fndn; memb: Advsy Bd Resolution Fndn, Tate Gallery Patrons of New Art (memb Acquisition Ctee 1986), French Porcelain Soc; govr Ashdown House Sch 2001–06; FCA 1991 (ACA 1980); *Recreations* travel, the arts, watching sport; *Clubs* MCC; *Style—* James Sassoon, Esq; ✉ HM Treasury, 1 Horse Guards Road, London SW1A 2HQ (tel 020 7270 4399, e-mail james.sassoon@hm-treasury.x.gsi.gov.uk)

SATCHELL, John Timothy Moffatt (Tim); s of John Frederick Bridge, and Evelyn Adelaide, *née* Calvert; *b* 27 November 1946; *Educ* Haileybury and ISC; *m* 25 March 1975, Amanda Rowena, da of Edward Barrington Smyth; 2 da (Cordelia Victoria b 1 April 1985, Rowena Beatrice b 11 Jan 1988); *Career* media conslt; asst to Clive Graham Daily Express 1965, subsequently on staff Sunday Express and Daily Mail, int mangr Dart Records and dir Beautiful Music 1970–74; ed Insider, contrib Daily Telegraph (as Prof Ernst Andersen, KPMG) 1999–; former contrib: Books and Bookmen, London Evening News, Evening Standard, Hello!, Today; chm Insider Magazines plc 1995–98; chm thevirtual.org 1999–; Master Worshipful Co of Saddlers 2003–04; *Books* McQueen (1981), Royal Romance (1986), Astaire (1987), The Newest London Spy (ed Tim Heald, 1988), The Things We Do for Love (ed Frankie McGowan, 1994); *Recreations* bees, opera, fashion, farming, the pursuit of excellence; *Clubs* Groucho; *Style—* Tim Satchell, Esq; ✉ 15 Moreton Place, London SW1V 2NL (e-mail tim@thevirtual.org)

SATCHELL, Keith; s of Dennis Joseph Satchell, of Hemel Hempstead, and Joan Betty, *née* Elms; *b* 3 June 1951; *Educ* Hemel Hempstead GS, Aston Univ (BSc); *m* 1 July 1972, Hazel Dorothy, da of Douglas Burston, of Birmingham; 2 s (Paul b 1978, Richard b 1980), 1 da (Olivia b 1984); *Career* chief exec Friends Provident plc (Life Office) 1997–2006; FIA 1976; *Recreations* sport, theatre; *Style—* Keith Satchell, Esq; ✉ 54 The Panoramic, 152 Grosvenor Road, London SW1W 3JL

SATTERTHWAITE, Christopher James; s of Col Richard George Satterthwaite, LVO, OBE (d 1993), of Petersfield, W Sussex, and Rosemary, *née* Messervy; *b* 21 May 1956; *Educ* Ampleforth, Lincoln Coll Oxford (MA); *m* 30 Jan 1988, Teresa Mary, da of Cdr L Bailey; 2 s (James Richard b 29 Oct 1988, Henry Frank b 8 Nov 1989), 1 da (Eleanor Sara b 6 Feb 1992); *Career* graduate trainee H J Heinz Ltd 1979–81, IMP Ltd 1981–93 (md 1987–93), dir HHCL and Partners 1993–99, chief exec Bell Pottinger Communications 1999–2000, chief exec Chime Communications 2000–; non-exec dir Centaur Media plc 2007–; *Recreations* fly fishing, escapology, bombology, motorbikes, Scottish birds, Norwich culture; *Style—* Christopher Satterthwaite, Esq; ✉ Chime Communications, 14 Curzon Street, London W1J 5HN (tel 020 7861 8589, e-mail csatterthwaite@chime.plc.uk)

SAUL, Roger John; s of (Frederick) Michael Saul, of Chilcompton, Somerset, and Joan, *née* Legg; *b* 25 July 1950; *Educ* Kingswood Sch Bath, Westminster Coll London; *m* 23 July 1977, Marion Joan, da of Clifford Cameron; 3 s (William Michael, Cameron Robert, Frederick Jakes); *Career* fndr, creator, designer and pres Mulberry 1971–2002 (memb Bd until 2003), brand label in Br contemporary classic fashion worldwide; fndr Charlton House (Michelin Star restaurant and hotel) 1996, launched Monty's (beauty product and spa range) 2004, co-fndr bottletop charity (with son Cameron) to raise funds and awareness for disadvantaged youth worldwide 2004, launched Sharpham Park (rare breed meat) and Spelt Flour (bread pasta and cereal range) 2005, built first organic spelt flour mill in UK 2006; govr Kingswood Sch 2006; awarded Queen's Award for Export 1979, 1989 and 1996, BKCEC Exporter of the Year 1987–88, 1990 and 1996; *Recreations* tennis, historic car racing (winner Brooklands Trophy Porto Grand Prix and Irish Grand Prix in Motor Racing Legends Series with GP Alfa Romeo P3 2005–06), skiing, shooting, garden design; *Style—* Roger Saul, Esq; ✉ Charlton House, Shepton Mallet, Bath, Somerset BA4 4PR (tel 01749 342008, fax 01749 346362)

SAUMAREZ, *see:* de Saumarez

SAUMAREZ SMITH, Dr Charles Robert; s of William Hanbury Saumarez Smith, OBE (d 1994), and Alice Elizabeth Harness, *née* Raven; *b* 28 May 1954; *Educ* Marlborough, King's Coll Cambridge (scholar, MA), Harvard Univ (Henry fellow), Warburg Inst Univ of London (PhD); *m* Romilly Le Quesne, *née* Savage; 2 s (Otto Livingstone b 1987, Ferdinand Le Quesne b 1990); *Career* Christie's research fell and dir of studies (history of art) Christ's Coll Cambridge 1979–82; V&A: asst keeper (responsible for V&A/RCA MA course in history of design) 1982–90, head of research 1990–94; dir National Portrait Gallery 1994–2002, dir National Gallery 2002–07, sec and ceo Royal Acad 2007–; visiting fell Yale Center for British Art 1983, Benno M Forman fellowship H F du Pont Winterthur Museum 1988, South Square fell RCA 1990, Slade prof Univ of Oxford, visiting prof Grad Sch of Humanities Queen Mary 2007–; memb: Ctee Design History Soc 1985–89, Ctee Soc of Architectural Historians 1987–90, Editorial Bd Art History 1988–93, Exec Ctee Assoc of Art Historians 1990–94, Exec Ctee London Library 1992–96, Cncl Charleston Tst 1993–; tstee: Soane Monuments Tst 1988–, Prince's Drawing Sch 2003–, Public Catalogue Fndn 2003–; memb Advsy Cncl: Paul Mellon Centre for Studies in British Art 1995–99, Warburg Inst 1996–2003, Inst of Historical Research 1999–2003, Sch of Advanced Studies Univ of London 2003–07; pres Museums Assoc 2004–06 (memb Cncl 1998–2001, vice-pres 2002–04); govr Univ of the Arts 2001–; Alice Davis Hitchcock medallion 1990; Hon DLitt: UEA 2001, Univ of Westminster 2002, Univ of London 2003, Univ of Sussex 2003, Univ of Essex 2005; hon fell Christ's Coll Cambridge 2002; Hon FRCA 1991, FRSA 1995, FSA 1997, Hon FRIBA 2000; *Publications* The Building of Castle Howard (1990), Eighteenth-Century Decoration: Design and the Domestic Interior in England (1993), The National Portrait Gallery (1997); *Style—* Dr Charles Saumarez Smith, FSA; ✉ The Royal Academy of Arts, Burlington House, Piccadilly, London W1J 0BD (tel 020 7300 8006, fax 020 7300 8026, e-mail charles.saumarezsmith@royalacademy.org.uk)

SAUNDERS, Dr Ann Loreille; MBE; da of George Cox-Johnson (d 1941), and Joan Loreille, *née* Clowser (d 1980); *b* 23 May 1930; *Educ* Henrietta Barnett Sch, Queen's Coll Harley St, UCL (BA), Univ of Leicester (PhD); *m* 4 June 1960, Bruce Kemp Saunders, s of Kemp Alexander Saunders (d 1973); 1 s (Matthew Kemp b 1964), 1 da (Katherine Sophia Loreille b 1967 d 1984); *Career* dep librarian Lambeth Palace Library 1952–55, asst keeper Br Museum 1955–56, borough archivist St Marylebone Public Library 1956–63, asst to the Hon Ed Jl of the British Archaeological Assoc 1963–75, hon ed Costume Soc 1967–, hon ed London Topographical Soc 1975–; pt/t lectr: Richmond Coll Kensington 1979–92, City Univ 1981–2007; contrib to various jls incl Geographical Magazine, Burlington Magazine and The London Journal; fell UCL 1991 (hon research fell Dept of History 1995–); FSA; *Books* John Bacon RA, 1740–1799 (as Ann Cox-Johnson, 1961), Regent's Park: A Study of the Development of the Area from 1066 to the Present Day (1969), Arthur Mee's King's England Series: London North of the Thames (revised 1972), London: The City and Westminster (revised 1975), Regent's Park (revised, 1981), The Regent's Park Villas (1981), The Art and Architecture of London: An Illustrated Guide (won London Tourist Bd award for specialist guidebook of the year 1984, 2 edn 1988, reprinted 1992 and 1996), St Martin in the Fields: A Short History and Guide (1989), The Royal Exchange: a short history (1991, ed and co-wrote extended edn 1997), St Paul's: The Story of the Cathedral (2001), The History of the Merchant Taylors' Company (with Matthew Davies, 2004); *Recreations* reading, embroidery, cooking, walking, studying London, going to exhibitions and the theatre and to churches; *Style—* Dr Ann Saunders, MBE, FSA; ✉ 3 Meadway Gate, London NW11 7LA

SAUNDERS, Dr (William) Anthony; s of Robert Valentine Saunders (d 1997), of Sneyd Park, Bristol, and Mary Isabel, *née* Kerr; *b* 24 June 1940; *Educ* Clifton, Trinity Coll Cambridge (MA, MB BChir, DPM, DCH); *m* 11 Feb 1967, Angela Pauline, da of Charles Alan Rapson (d 1971), of Topsham, Exeter; 2 da (Emma b 13 March 1968, Annabel b 29 July 1972), 1 s (Jonathan b 7 May 1970); *Career* conslt in child and adolescent psychiatry 1973–, hon clinical lectr Univ of Southampton 1973–, conslt Marchwood Priory Hosp Southampton, conslt Winchester Coll; former chm Wessex Child Psychiatrists, past nat chm Ctee of Mgmnt Assoc for Professionals in Servs for Adolescents; Hospital Prize for Forensic Medicine; FRCPsych; *Style—* Dr Anthony Saunders; ✉ Meadow Cottage, Otterbourne, Winchester, Hampshire SO21 2EQ (tel 01962 713129)

SAUNDERS, David John; s of James Saunders (d 1986), and Margaret, *née* Christy; *b* 4 August 1953; *Educ* Kingston Poly (BSc), Aston Univ (PhD); *m* 6 Sept 1975, Elizabeth Jean, da of Mandel Coutier Hodgson; 2 da (Zoë Alice b 1 March 1977, Jessica Elizabeth b 23 March 1988), 2 s (Robin Edward James b 23 May 1979, Tobias David Oliver b 4 Jan 1982); *Career* mgmnt trainee Serck Ltd 1975–78; DTI: trg posts then successively asst private sec to sec of state and private sec to jr min 1978–84, on loan to OFT 1984–87 (dep head Mergers Branch 1986–87), with Privatisation of Br Steel Unit 1987–88, export dir SE Office 1988–90, regnl mgmnt support offr 1990, sec BOTB and dir Jt Export Promotion Directorate (JEPD) 1990–95, dir Nuclear Power Privatisation Team 1995–96, dir Oil and Gas Div 1996–98; regnl dir Govt Office for the SE (GOSE) 1998–2002, dir business support DTI 2002–04, dir consumer and competition policy 2004–; *Recreations* swimming, cycling, surfing, diving; *Style—* David Saunders, Esq; ✉ Department of Trade and Industry, 1 Victoria Street, London SW1H 0ET

SAUNDERS, David William; CB (1989); s of William Ernest Saunders (d 1993), of Hornchurch, Essex, and Lilian Grace, *née* Ward (d 1987); *b* 4 November 1936; *Educ* Hornchurch GS, Worcester Coll Oxford (MA); *m* 15 April 1963, Margaret Susan Rose, da of William Colin Bartholomew (d 1980), of London; *Career* Nat Serv RAF 1955–57 (Russian linguist), articled clerk later slr private practice 1960–69; Parly Counsel: asst counsel 1970–75, on loan to Law Cmmn 1972–74, sr asst counsel 1975–78, dep counsel 1978–80, counsel 1980–94, on loan to Law Cmmn as sr draftsman 1986–87, second counsel 1994–96, counsel 1996–99; counsel to chm of ctees House of Lords 1999–2005; memb Law Soc 1964; *Recreations* bridge, golf; *Style—* David Saunders, Esq, CB; ✉ Highfields, High Wych, Sawbridgeworth, Hertfordshire CM21 0HX (tel 01279 724736)

SAUNDERS, Prof George Albert; s of Barnett Stanley Saunders (d 1977), and Lilian Gladys Saunders (d 1976); *b* 4 January 1936; *Educ* Caterham Sch, Imperial Coll London (BSc, PhD, DIC); *m* 16 April 1960, Linda Mary, da of Edward and Ruth Butt; 2 s (Barnett Edward, Edward Alan); *Career* res fell Univ of Calif 1962–64, sr lectr (former lectr) Univ of Durham 1964–75, prof of physics Univ of Bath 1975–2001 (emeritus 2001–); FInstP 1970, CPhys 1980; *Recreations* mountaineering, ornithology; *Style—* Prof George Saunders; ✉ e-mail g.saunders@blueyonder.co.uk

SAUNDERS, Graham Eric; JP; s of Arthur Frank Saunders (d 1960), of York, and Ivy Ethel Saunders (d 2003); *b* 3 April 1945; *Educ* Archbishop Holgate's GS York, Univ of Durham (BSc, DipHSM); *m* 20 Dec 1969, Valerie, *née* Barton; 1 da (Elizabeth Helen b 23 Dec 1977), 1 s (Christopher Andrew b 25 Jan 1982); *Career* VSO 1966–67, nat admin trainee Sheffield Regnl Hosp Bd 1967–69, dep hosp sec Sunderland Gen Hosp 1969–70, sr admin asst Gp HQ Sunderland Hosp Mgmnt Ctee 1970–72, hosp sec Sunderland Royal Infirmary 1972–74, gen administrator (operational servs) Durham Health Dist 1974–77, dep chief administrator Leeds Eastern Health Dist 1977–81, dist gen mangr Harrogate HA 1985–92 (chief administrator 1982–85), chief exec Harrogate Health Care NHS Tst 1992–2001, chief exec W Yorks NHS Workforce Devpt Confedn 2001–05, policy advsr NHS Employers 2005–, ind healthcare conslt 2005–; dir N Yorks TEC 1989–92, memb Nat Cncl Inst of Health Servs Mgmnt 1987–93, Yorks chm 1996–97; govr Harrogate Coll 1985–97; FIHM 1999; *Recreations* walking, theatre, opera, good food; *Style—* Graham Saunders, Esq; ✉ 36 Ayresome Terrace, Leeds LS8 1BH (tel 0113 266 4729)

SAUNDERS, (William) Howard; *b* 29 June 1939; *Educ* Alleyn's Sch Dulwich; *m* 1, 29 Oct 1960, Rita Doris (d 1992), da of Thomas William Hardaway (d 1979); 2 s (Jeremy Howard b 31 March 1965, Jonathan James Howard b 29 July 1972); m 2, 22 May 1996, Moira Ann, sis of Rita Doris Hardaway; *Career* Nat Serv RAPC 1960–62; Keith, Bayley, Rogers & Co Ltd (formerly Keith Bayley & Rigg): joined 1955, ptnr 1970, sr ptnr 1982–2001; chm Ebbark Nominees Ltd, non-exec dir Walker, Crips, Weddle, Beck plc (incorporating Keith, Bayley, Rogers & Co Ltd) 2003– (exec dir 2001–03); chm St Mary's Westerham Heritage Tst 2001–; MSI 1992 (memb Stock Exchange 1970); *Recreations* theatre, music, reading news and encyclopedias; *Style—* Howard Saunders, Esq; ✉ Pilgrim House, Pilgrims Way, Westerham, Kent TN16 2DP (tel 01959 563495, fax 01959 565337, e-mail saundershoward@aol.com); Walker, Crips, Weddle, Beck plc, Sophia House, 76–80 City Road, London EC1Y 2EQ

SAUNDERS, Iain Ogilvy Swain; s of Leslie Swain Saunders (d 1988), and Elizabeth, *née* Culme Seymour (d 1963); *b* 7 November 1947; *Educ* Radley, Univ of Bristol (BSc); *m* 1976, Roberta Ann, da of David Allen Phoenix; 1 da (Christina Ann Swain b 1983); *Career* Arbuthnot Latham 1968–71; Robert Fleming: joined 1971, Jardine Fleming Hong Kong 1976–78, gen mangr Jardine Fleming Tokyo 1978–84, dir Robert Fleming Holdings 1984–, pres and ceo NY office 1985–89, chm Fleming Investment Mgmnt London 1990–94, dep chm Robert Fleming Asset Mgmnt 1994–2001; dir: JP Morgan Fleming American Investment Tst plc 1990–2005, JP Morgan Fleming Indian Investment Tst plc 1994–2006, Aberdeen Asia Smaller Companies Investment Tst plc 2004–06; chm: Czech and Slovak Investment Co 1995–, JP Morgan Fleming Funds 1996–, Baring Emerging Europe plc 2002–, MB Asia 2002–; memb Governing Cncl Euro Asset Mgmnt Assoc 1999–2001; *Recreations* sailing, gardening; *Style*— Iain Saunders, Esq; ✉ Duine, Ardfern, Argyll PA31 8QN (01852 500289)

SAUNDERS, Jennifer; *b* 6 July 1958, Lincolnshire; *m* 1985, Adrian Edmondson; *Career* actress, writer and comedienne; *Theatre* An Evening With French and Saunders (nat tour) 1989, Me and Mamie O'Rourke 1993, French and Saunders Live in 2000 2000; *Television* appearences incl: The Comic Strip Presents... 1982–98, The Young Ones 1982–84, The Dangerous Brothers 1986, Rita Rudner 1990, The Full Wax 1991–92, Queen of the East 1995, Roseanne 1998, Friends 1998, The Magicians House 1999, Mirrorball 2000; wrote and performed in: French And Saunders 1987–, Absolutely Fabulous 1992–2001; *Films* appearances incl: The Supergrass 1985, Eat the Rich 1987, Prince Cinders 1993, In the Bleak Midwinter 1995, Muppet Treasure Island 1996, Spice World 1997, Fanny and Elvis 1999; *Style*— Ms Jennifer Saunders; ✉ PFD, Drury House, 34–43 Russell Street, London WC2B 5HA

SAUNDERS, Prof John; s of John Saunders, and Queenie, *née* Thomas; *b* 27 August 1946; *Educ* Hatfield Secdy Modern Sch, Doncaster Tech Coll Loughborough Univ (BSc), Cranfield Inst of Technol (MBA), Univ of Bradford (DPhil); *m* 7 Aug 1981, Veronica Wai Yoke, da of Wong Peng Chow; 1 s (Paul), 1 da (Carolyne); *Career* successively: sales and marketing Hawker Siddeley Aviation, lectr Univ of Bradford Mgmnt Centre, lectr Univ of Warwick Business Sch, prof of marketing Loughborough Univ and dir Loughborough Univ Business Sch; currently dir Aston Business Sch and prof of mktg and pro-vice-chllr Aston Univ; fell European Mktg Acad, FBAM, FCIM, FRSA; *Books* Enterprise (1977), Practical Business Forecasting (1987), The Specification of Aggregate Marketing Phenomina (1987), The Best of Companies (1989), Competitive Positioning (1993), The Marketing Initiative (1994), Principles of Marketing: The European Edition (2001), Marketing Strategy and Competitive Positioning (2004); *Recreations* my family, travel, rock, literature, history, science and technology, exercise, DIY and gardening; *Style*— Prof John Saunders; ✉ Holme Leys Farm, Black Horse Hill, Appleby Magna, Leicestershire DE12 7AQ (tel 01530 272759)

SAUNDERS, John David; s of John Alan Saunders (d 1995), and Gladys-Anne Triptree (d 1972); *b* 15 March 1953; *Educ* Brentwood Sch Essex, Univ of Bristol (LLB); *Career* admitted slr 1977; Lord Chllr's Dept (now Dept for Constitutional Affrs): joined Legal Gp 1980, sec Cncl on Tbnls 1993–97, head of statute law revision Law Cmmn 1997–; memb Law Soc 1977; *Recreations* Victorian music hall, cinema; *Clubs* Players Theatre, Scotch Malt Whisky Soc; *Style*— John Saunders, Esq; ✉ Law Commission, Conquest House, 37–38 John Street, London WC1N 2BQ (tel 020 7453 1218)

SAUNDERS, Hon Mr Justice; Sir John Henry Boulton; kt (2007); s of Henry George Boulton Saunders (d 1984), and Kathleen Mary, *née* Brandle; *b* 15 March 1949; *Educ* St John's Coll Sch Cambridge, Uppingham (music scholar), Magdalen Coll Oxford; *m* 20 Dec 1975, Susan Mary, da of Charles William Paull Chick (d 1989); 2 da (Sarah Kate b 30 Nov 1977, Hannah May b 21 May 1979), 1 s (Daniel Paull b 26 Nov 1985); *Career* called to the Bar 1972; prosecuting counsel to the DHSS (now DSS) Midland & Oxford Circuit 1983–91, recorder 1990–2004 (asst recorder 1987–90), QC 1991, dep judge of the High Court 2000, sr circuit judge (Midland Circuit) 2004–07, judge of the High Court of Justice (Queen's Bench Div) 2007–; hon recorder of Birmingham 2004–; *Recreations* music, sailing; *Style*— The Hon Mr Justice John Saunders; ✉ c/o Royal Courts of Justice, Strand, London WC2A 2LL

SAUNDERS, Prof Max; s of Garry Saunders, and Diana Cohen, *née* Snow; *b* 24 June 1957, London; *Educ* Sevenoaks Sch, Queens' Coll Cambridge (entrance scholar, BA), Harvard Univ (AM), Selwyn Coll Cambridge (Le Bas Prize, PhD); *Children* 1 s (Alfred b 19 Aug 1991); *Career* research fell then coll lectr Selwyn Coll Cambridge 1983–89 (dir of studies for English Part II 1987, tutor 1988); KCL: univ lectr 1989–97, reader in English 1997–2000, prof of English 2000–, dir Centre of Life-Writing Research 2007; chair Ford Madox Ford Soc 1997; fell English Assoc 2005; *Publications* Ford Madox Ford: A Duel Life (Vols 1 and 2, 1996), Ford Madox Ford: Selected Poems (ed, 1997), Ford Madox Ford: War Prose (ed, 1999), Ford Madox Ford: Critical Essays (jt ed, 2002); *Style*— Prof Max Saunders; ✉ Department of English, King's College London, The Strand, London WC2R 2LS (e-mail max.saunders@kcl.ac.uk)

SAUNDERS, Prof Peter Robert; s of Albert Edward Saunders, of Orpington, Kent, and Joan Kathleen, *née* Swan; *b* 30 August 1950; *Educ* Selhurst GS Croydon, Univ of Kent (BA), Univ of London (PhD); *m* 15 April 1971 (m dis 1990), Susan Elisabeth, da of Dr Frank Ellis, of Redhill, Surrey; 1 s (Michael b 1971), 1 da (Claire Louise b 1973); *Career* res offr Univ of Essex 1973–76, prof of sociology Univ of Sussex 1988– (lectr 1976–84, reader 1984–88); research mangr Australian Institute of Family Studies 1999–2000; FRSA 1987; *Books* Urban Politics: A Sociological Interpretation (1979), Social Theory and the Urban Question (1981 and 1986), An Introduction to British Politics (1984, new edn 2000), Social Class and Stratification (1989), A Nation of Home Owners (1990), Privatisation and Popular Capitalism (1994), Capitalism: A Social Audit (1995), Unequal but Fair? A Study of Class Barriers in Britain (1996), Reforming the Australian Welfare State (2000); *Style*— Prof Peter Saunders; ✉ School of Social Sciences, University of Sussex, Falmer, Brighton BN1 9QN (tel 01273 678891, fax 01273 673563)

SAUNDERS, Richard; s of Edward Ernest Saunders (d 1971), of Henley-on-Thames, and Betty, *née* Belsey (d 1993); *b* 4 July 1937; *Educ* St Edmund's Sch Hindhead, Uppingham; *m* 1, 21 Sept 1961, Suzannah, da of Thomas Rhodes-Cooke (d 1985), of Chiswick; 1 s (Andrew b 1964); m 2, 12 June 1970, Alison, da of Maj J A Fiddes (d 1964), of Wimbledon; *Career* 2 Lt LG 1958–60, served in Germany; govr Royal Star and Garter Home 1984–; chartered surveyor; chm Baker Harris Saunders Gp plc 1986–92, conslt Herring Baker Harris Group plc 1992–93; dir: Br Property Fedn 1974–90, St Edmund's Sch Tst Ltd 1978–93, Star and Garter Trading and Promotions Ltd; chm: City Branch RICS 1979–80, Metropolitan Public Gdns Assoc 1984–91; dep for Ward of Candlewick 1983–2000; Sheriff City of London 1987–88; bd memb Gen Practice Finance Corp 1985–89; govr Bridewell Royal Hosp and King Edward's Sch Witley 1976–93, partnership conslt Christ's Hospital 1993–97 (govr and almoner 1980–93); memb: Cncl Br Property Fedn 1974–90 (hon treas 1974–85), Ct of Common Cncl Corp of London 1975–2000; pres Associated Owners of City Properties 1984–86, chm Ex-Servs Resettlement Gp 1991–93; Liveryman and memb Ct of Assts Worshipful Co of Clothworkers 1960 (Warden 1989–90, Master 2001–02), Liveryman Worshipful Co of Chartered Surveyors 1979–93; *Recreations* golf, tennis (lawn and real), music; *Clubs* MCC, City Livery; *Style*— Richard Saunders, Esq; ✉ The Old Rectory, Bagendon, Cirencester, Gloucestershire GL7 7DU (01285 831352)

SAUNDERS, Robin Elizabeth; *b* 8 June 1962, North Carolina, USA; *Educ* Florida State Univ; *m* 1992, Matthew Roeser; 2 da (Ella, Savannah (twins)); *Career* financier; successively with Northern Tst, Citibank, Chemical Bank and Deutsche Bank, head Principal Finance Unit WestLB 1998–2003, fndr Clearbrook Investments Ltd 2004–, managing ptnr Clearbrook Scotland GP Ltd 2004–; dir: Swan Gp until 2003, Formula One Holdings Ltd until 2003, Pubmaster Ltd until 2003, Whyte and Mackay Gp Ltd until 2003, BHS Gp Ltd 1999–2003, Odeon Ltd 2003, Office of the Rail Regulator until 2004, Lanterndrive Ltd 2004–, Eclipse Scientific Gp Ltd 2005–; *Recreations* the Arts; *Style*— Ms Robin Saunders; ✉ Clearbrook Capital Partners LLP, 25 Grosvenor Street, London W1K 4QN

SAUNDERS, Steven Philip; s of David Saunders, of Ipswich, Suffolk, and Joy Saunders; *b* 8 June 1961; *Educ* St Joseph's Coll of HE nr Ipswich, Suffolk Coll of Higher and Further Educn; *Family* 2 da (Serena b 17 Sept 1988, Stefanie b 16 April 1991); *Career* mgmnt trainee The Savoy 1979–81, gen mangr White Hart Great Yeldham 1981–86; chef and proprietor: The Pink Geranium Restaurant Melbourn 1986–, The Sheene Mill Melbourn (hotel, brasserie and deli) 1997–, Steven Saunders at The Lowry 2000– (opened by HM The Queen 2000, awarded Best Building of the Year); proprietor: Hawthorn Ventures Ltd, Steven Saunders Enterprises, Steven Saunders Organic Cookery Sch UK; fndr: Organica 2001 (UK's first organic catering co), Steven Saunders at Home; chef presenter: Good Morning (BBC1), Ready Steady Cook (BBC2), Here's One I Made Earlier (Channel 4), Afternoon Live's Remote Control Cookery (Carlton), Sky Int, NBC; food writer Organic Life magazine; regular features in: Caterer and Hotelkeeper, Hello!, OK; resident chef/writer Organic & Natural Living magazine; presenter: own radio show BBC Radio Cambridgeshire 1987–, Talk Radio UK; launched Tibard (Steven Saunders Chefs clothing range) 2001, Organica (first organic catering co in UK); conslt Bonterra Organic Wines; introduced Work Based Degree for Chefs Master Chefs of GB; patron Born Free Fndn, vice-patron Addenbrooke's Hosp; memb Soil Assoc; fell Master Chef of GB; *Awards* Catey Award for Young Restaurateur of the Year 1991; for the Pink Geranium: Assoc of Catering Excellence Restaurant of the Year 1995, FT Top Ten Restaurants in the UK 1996, Michelin Red M, Ackerman Four Leaf Clover, Egon Ronay Arrow, Good Food Guide 7/10, 3 AA Rosettes, Business Person of the Year; *Books* Only the Best (1993), Chef's Secrets (1996), Here's One I Made Earlier (1997), Short Cuts (1998), Feng Shui Food '99 (1999), Manchester on a Plate (2001), Quick Cuisine (2001), Bonterra Organic Recipes (2002), Choose Your Food to Change Your Mood (2003); *Recreations* tennis, squash, theatre, diving, travel, entertaining; *Style*— Steven Saunders, Esq; ✉ c/o PR @ Sheene Mill Hotel & Brasserie, Station Road, Melbourn, Cambridgeshire SG8 6DX (tel 01763 261393, fax 01763 261376, websites www.stevensaunders.com or www.sheenemill.co.uk)

SAVAGE, Prof Caroline Olive Sylvia; *b* 24 November 1953; *Educ* Tonbridge Sch for Girls, Royal London Hosp Med Sch (Edith Forbes scholar, BSc, MB BS, Sutton Prize), Univ of London (PhD, MD); *m*; 2 da; *Career* house physician Med Unit then Renal Unit and genito-urinary med Royal London Hosp 1979, house surgn Whipps Cross Hosp London 1979–80, SHO in renal and immunological med Southmead Hosp Bristol 1980–81, SHO in cardiology and gen med Hammersmith Hosp 1981, registrar in gen med, cardiology and rheumatology Ealing Hosp 1981–82, registrar in med Renal and Immunology Unit Hammersmith Hosp 1982–83, MRC trg fell and hon sr registrar in renal and immunological med Royal Postgrad Med Sch London 1983–87, sr registrar in nephrology and gen med Hammersmith Hosp 1987–89, MRC travelling fell Dept of Pathology Brigham & Women's Hosp and Harvard Med Sch 1989–90, MRC clinical scientist and conslt nephrologist Clinical Res Centre Harrow 1990–93, hon conslt nephrologist Renal Unit Hammersmith Hosp 1990–93, sr lectr in nephrology Med Sch Univ of Birmingham 1993–98, prof of nephrology Univ of Birmingham and hon conslt physician Queen Elizabeth Hosp Birmingham 1998–, prog dir Wellcome Tst Clinical Res Facility Birmingham 2000–; Mary Evelyn Lucking Prize in Nephrology 1991, Wegener prize 1993; academic vice-pres and tstee Renal Assoc 2007–, tstee Kidney Research UK 2007–; memb: Med Res Soc, Euro Renal Assoc, Br Soc for Immunology, Br Transplantation Soc, RSM, Assoc of Physicians, American Soc of Nephrology, Int Soc of Nephrology; FRCP 1996 (MRCP 1981), FMedSci; *Publications* Immunological Aspects of the Vascular Endothelium (jt ed, 1995); author of numerous book chapters and articles in learned jls; *Style*— Prof Caroline O S Savage; ✉ Renal Immunobiology, Division of Immunity and Infection, The Medical School, University of Birmingham, Edgbaston, Birmingham B15 2TT (tel 0121 415 8620, fax 0121 414 6819, e-mail c.o.s.savage@bham.ac.uk)

SAVAGE, David Jack; s of Arthur Jack Savage (d 1953), of Farnborough, Hants, and Sylvia Maude, *née* Bacon (d 1993; descendant of Sir Nicholas Bacon, Lord Keeper of the Great Seal to Queen Elizabeth I); *b* 7 August 1939; *Educ* Hurstpierpoint Coll, Weissenhaus Holstein Germany, Alliance Francaise, Univ of London (LLB), Coll of Law; *m* 16 May 1981, Elizabeth Mary, da of late Dr and Mrs Ives; 2 s (Nicholas David St John b 1982, Louis Arthur Ives b 1983); *Career* admitted slr 1963; sr ptnr Foster, Savage & Gordon of Farnborough 1984–2001, conslt 2001–05, estab David Savage & Co (Notaries Public) 2005; NP 1988; cmmr of income tax 1969–90, vice-chm N Hants Local Valuation Tbnl 1984–90 (memb 1976–90); pres Hants Inc Law Soc 1983–84 (memb Ctee 1972–2002), dir Slrs' Benevolent Assoc 1984–96, chm Reading Legal Aid Funding Review Ctee 2000–02; memb: No 3 Southern Area Legal Aid Ctee 1989–2000 (vice-chm 1999–2000), Cncl Law Soc 1990–2002 (memb Criminal Law Ctee 1988–2002); life memb Berks Bucks and Oxon Law Soc (memb Ctee 1990–2002); Law Soc rep to UINL (Int Union of Latin Notaries) 1997–98; cncllr: Farnborough UDC 1964–73 (vice-chm 1972–73), Rushmoor BC 1973–80; Parly candidate (Cons): Birmingham Sparkbrook 1974, Birmingham Smallheath 1979; govr Swinton Cons Coll 1971–74, vice-pres Aldershot Divnl Cons Assoc 1973– (chm 1969–73); dir Aldershot FC 1971; chm of govrs Farnborough GS 1970–72; memb Ct Univ of Southampton 2000–; Freeman City of London 1989; Liveryman: Worshipful Co of Arbitrators 1989, Worshipful Co of Scriveners 1990, Worshipful Co of Woolmen 1991; ACIArb 1988; *Recreations* travel (preferably by train), browsing, bricklaying, ornithology; *Style*— David Savage, Esq; ✉ Ridgeway, 16 Clockhouse Road, Farnborough, Hampshire GU14 7QY; David Savage & Co, Ridgeway Chambers, Clockhouse Road, Farnborough, Hampshire GU14 7QY (tel and fax 01252 372858)

SAVAGE, Graeme Peter; s of Peter Samuel Savage, of Hove, E Sussex, and Patricia, *née* Kerr; *b* 12 August 1952; *Educ* Univ of Reading (BA); *m* 1, 12 Dec 1972 (m dis 1992); 1 da (Tamara Jane b 26 Nov 1972), 2 s (Jonathan Peter b 10 Nov 1975, Joseph Graeme b 16 Nov 1979); m 2, Sharon Elizabeth; 3 s (Alexander Gannon b 20 Dec 1990, Connor George b 2 May 1996, Calum Charles b 6 Sept 1997); *Career* magazine sales rep Thomson Magazines Ltd (grad trainee 1974–75); RIBA Services Ltd: sales rep 1976–77, field sales mangr 1977–78, sales mangr 1978–81, publisher 1981–82, publishing dir 1982–87, dep md 1987–91, md 1991–94; md Wedgwood Markham Associates Ltd 1994–; FInstD 1991–; *Recreations* music, rugby, travel; *Style*— Graeme Savage, Esq; ✉ Wedgwood Markham Associates Ltd, The Coach House, Ealing Green, London W5 5ER (tel 020 8579 8184, fax 020 8579 3991)

SAVAGE, Valerie (Mrs Paul Ridout); *b* 1944; *Educ* N London Collegiate Sch, Central Sch of Speech & Drama; *m* Paul Ridout; 1 da (Lucy); *Career* speech and language conslt, specialist in communication disorders and teaching broadcasting skills to news reporters; formerly chief speech and language therapist Nuffield Hearing and Speech Centre (helped launch Nuffield Dyspraxia Prog), currently in private practice working internationally and particularly in the Arabian Gulf, own clinic in Doha Qatar; *Publications* incl professional articles on speech disorders in the pre-school child and teaching progs to treat them; *Recreations* theatre, Indian cookery, opera; *Style*— Miss Valerie Savage; ✉ Pinero House, 115A Harley Street, London W1G 6AR (tel 020 7486 0503, fax 020 7034 4490)

S

SAVAGE, Wendy Diane; da of William George Edwards (d 1984), and Anne, *née* Smith (d 1943); *b* 12 April 1935; *Educ* Croydon HS, Girton Coll Cambridge (BA), London Hosp Med Coll (MB BCh), LSHTM (MSc); *m* 27 July 1960 (m dis 1973), Miguel Babatunde Richard (Mike) Savage, s of Richard Gabriel Akiwande Savage (d 1993), of Edinburgh; 2 da (Yewande Patricia b 9 April 1961, Wendy Claire b 28 May 1962), 2 s (Nicholas Richard b 10 June 1964, Jonathan Chukuma b 18 April 1969); *Career* res fell Harvard Univ 1962–64, MO Awo-omama and Enugu Nigeria 1964–67; registrar: Kenyatta Hosp Nairobi Kenya 1967–69, Royal Free Hosp London 1969–71; various posts Tower Hamlets, Islington Borough and Pregnancy Advsy Serv 1971–73, specialist in obstetrics Cook Hosp NZ 1973–76, lectr London Hosp 1976–77, sr lectr in obstetrics and gynaecology London Hosp Med Coll and hon conslt Royal London Hosp 1977–2000, ret; hon visiting prof Faculty of Social Sciences Middx Univ 1991–; PR offr Doctors For Women's Choice on Abortion; former tstee Simon Population Tst; former patron and tstee Pregnancy Advsy Serv; advsr Maternity Alliance; fndr memb: Women in Med (now disbanded), Women in Gynaecology and Obstetrics; chair Forum on Maternity and the Newborn RSM 1987–89; memb GMC 1989–, memb Cncl BMA 2000–02; pres: Med Women's Fedn 1992–93, Exec Ctee Safe Motherhood (UK) 1993–94 (resigned); tstee Attlee Fndn 2002–03; FRCOG 1985 (MRCOG 1971); RSA 1992–99; *Books* Hysterectomy (1982), Coping with Caesarian Section and Other Difficult Births (with Fran Reader, 1983), A Savage Enquiry (1986), Caesarean Birth in Britain (with Colin Francome, Helen Churchill and Helen Lewison, 1993); *Recreations* reading novels, playing piano duets, travel; *Style—* Mrs Wendy Savage; ✉ 19 Vincent Terrace, London N1 8HN (tel and fax 020 7837 7635, e-mail w.d.savage@qmul.ac.uk)

SAVIDGE, Prof Geoffrey Francis; *b* 16 December 1940; *Educ* Univ of Cambridge (MB BChir, MA), Karolinska Inst Stockholm Sweden (MD); *m* Paula Margaretha; 2 s (Tor b 1964, Kevin b 1975), 1 da (Kim b 1966); *Career* lectr: Dept of Neurology Karolinska Hosp Stockholm 1969–71, Dept of Pathology and Clinical Chemistry St Goran's Hosp Stockholm 1974–77 (Dept of Med 1971–74); res assoc Inst of Coagulation Res Karolinska Inst Stockholm 1976–79, physician Dept of Coagulation Disorders Karolinska Hosp Stockholm 1977–79; St Thomas' Hosp London: dir Haemophilia Reference Centre 1979–, sr lectr and hon conslt 1979, dir of coagulation res Rayne Inst 1988–, prof of coagulation med 1997–; memb: Br Soc of Thrombosis and Haemostasis 1983, NY Acad of Sci 1986, American Soc of Haematology 1988, American Assoc for Advancement of Sci; fell American Heart Assoc (memb 1989); fell Int Acad of Clinical and Applied Thrombosis/Hemostasis 2004; *Books* Factor VIII - von Willebrand Factor (2 vols, 1989); *Recreations* music, reading, sport; *Clubs* Oxford and Cambridge; *Style—* Prof Geoffrey Savidge; ✉ Centre for Haemostasis and Thrombosis - Haemophilia Reference Centre, St Thomas' Hospital, Lambeth Palace Road, London SE1 7EH (tel 020 7620 0378, fax 020 7401 3125)

SAVIDGE, Malcolm Kemp; s of late David Savidge, and late Jean, *née* Kemp; *b* 9 May 1946; *Educ* Wallington County GS for Boys, Univ of Aberdeen (MA), Aberdeen Coll of Educn; *Career* prodn/stock control and computer asst Bryans' Electronic Ltd 1970 and 1971; mathematics teacher: Greenwood Dale Secdy Sch Nottingham 1971, Peterhead Acad 1972–73, Kincorth Acad Aberdeen 1973–97; MP (Lab) Aberdeen N 1997–2005; cncllr Aberdeen CC 1980–96 (convener Fin and General Purposes Ctee, vice-convener Policy and dep leader 1994–96); govr: Robert Gordon's Inst of Technol 1980–88 (convener Staff Affrs Ctee 1985–88), Aberdeen Coll of Educn 1980–87; Nuclear Free Authorities: memb Scot and UK Steering Ctee 1985–96, vice-convener 1992–94, convener 1994–96; dir Scot Nat Orch 1985–86; memb: Local Advsy Ctee IBA 1986–88, Convention of Scot Local Authorities 1994–96; dep Scot Constitutional Convention 1989–94 (memb 1994–96); JP 1984–86 and 1988–96, memb Justice's Ctee 1984–86, 1988–94 and 1995–96; memb: Lab Pty 1971–, Educnl Inst of Scotland, TGWU, Scientists for Global Responsibility, United Nations Assoc, Socialist Environment and Resources Assoc, Co-operative Pty, Amnesty Int, World Disarmament Campaign; hon fell Robert Gordon Univ (Hon FRGU)1997; *Recreations* exploring life, spectator sports, crosswords and puzzles, reading, real ale, the arts, heraldry; *Style—* Malcolm Savidge, Esq

SAVILE, 3 Baron (UK 1888); George Halifax Lumley-Savile; JP (Borough of Dewsbury 1955), DL (W Yorks 1954); patron of two livings; s of 2 Baron (d 1931), of Rufford Abbey, Notts, and Esmé Grace Virginia (d 1958), da of John Wolton; *b* 24 January 1919; *Educ* Eton; *Heir* n, John Lumley-Savile; *Career* formerly Capt Duke of Wellington's Regt, attached 1 Bn Lincs Regt, Burma 1943–44; chm St John Cncl S and W Yorks 1980, pres W Yorks SSAFA - Forces Help 1986; landowner (18,000 acres); CStJ 1983; *Recreations* walking, listening to classical music; *Clubs* Brooks's, Huddersfield, Sloane; *Style—* The Lord Savile, CstJ, JP, DL; ✉ Gryce Hall, Shelley, Huddersfield, West Yorkshire (tel 01484 602774); Carter Jonas, Savile Estate Office, Thornhill, Dewsbury, West Yorkshire (tel 01924 462341)

SAVILL, Prof John; *Career* former dir MRC/Univ of Edinburgh Centre for Inflammation Research, currently prof of med and head Coll of Med and Vet Med Univ of Edinburgh; MRC: memb Cncl, chair Physiological Systems and Clinical Sciences Bd; chair and govr Health Fndn, memb Clinical Interest Gp Wellcome Tst; memb Lothian Health Bd; *Style—* Prof John Savill; ✉ The Queen's Medical Research Institute, 47 Little France Crescent, Edinburgh EH16 4TJ

SAVILL, Rosalind Joy; CBE (2000); da of Dr Guy Savill, and Lorna, *née* Williams; *b* 12 May 1951; *Educ* Wycombe Abbey, Châtelard Sch Montreux, Univ of Leeds (BA), The Study Centre for the Fine and Decorative Arts (Dip); *Children* 1 da (Isabella Dove Savill b 23 Dec 1989); *Career* museum asst V&A 1973–74; The Wallace Collection: museum asst 1974–78, asst to the dir 1978–92, dir 1992–; fndr ctee memb French Porcelain Soc (chm 1988–94, pres 1999–); memb: Cncl Attingham Summer Sch 1980–92 (fndr chm Scholarship Ctee), Vetting Ctee Annual Int Ceramics Seminar and Fair London 1981–, Advsy Ctee Treasure Houses of Britain exhbn Nat Gall of Art Washington DC 1985, Comité Scientifique Versailles, Tables Royales exhbn Château de Versailles 1993–94, Nat Tst Arts Panel 1995–, Advsy Ctee Nat Museums and Galleries of Wales 1998–2003, Museums and Collections Advisy Ctee (MUSAC) English Heritage 1998–2003, Registration Ctee MLA 1999–, Advsy Ctee Royal Mint 1999–; tstee: Somerset House 1997–2004, Campaign for Museums 1999–, Holburne Museum Bath 2004–; author of numerous articles in art jls; govr Camden Sch for Girls 1996–; Arts & Media Award European Woman of Achievement 2005; Hon Doctorate Univ of Bucks and Chilterns 2005; FRSA 1990, FSA 1990; *Books* The Wallace Collection - Sèvres Porcelain (1980), Treasure Houses of Britain - Five Hundred Years of Private Patronage and Art Collecting (contrib, 1985), The Wallace Collection Catalogue of Sèvres Porcelain (3 vols, 1988), The Wallace Collection - French Gold Boxes (1991), Boughton House - The English Versailles (contrib, 1992); *Recreations* music, birds, wildlife, gardens; *Style—* Miss Rosalind Savill, CBE, FSA; ✉ The Wallace Collection, Hertford House, Manchester Square, London W1U 3BN (tel 020 7563 9512, fax 020 7224 2155, e-mail rosalind.savill@wallacecollection.org)

SAVILLE OF NEWDIGATE, Baron (Life Peer UK 1997), of Newdigate in the County of Surrey; Sir Mark Oliver Saville; kt (1985), PC (1994); s of Kenneth Vivian Saville, and Olivia Sarah Frances, *née* Gray; *b* 20 March 1936; *Educ* Rye GS, BNC Oxford (Vinerian scholar, BA, BCL); *m* 30 June 1961, Jill Whitworth; 2 s (William Christian b 8 March 1962, Henry Oliver b 8 Aug 1964); *Career* Nat Serv 2 Lt Royal Sussex Regt 1954–56; called to the Bar Middle Temple 1962 (bencher 1983); QC 1975, judge of the High Court of Justice (Queen's Bench Div) 1985–94, a Lord Justice of Appeal 1994–97, a Lord of Appeal in Ordinary 1997–; hon fell BNC Oxford 1998; Hon LLD London Guildhall Univ 1997; *Recreations* sailing, flying, computers; *Clubs* Garrick; *Style—* The Rt Hon Lord Saville of Newdigate, PC; ✉ House of Lords, London SW1A 0PW

SAVOURS, *see:* Campbell-Savours

SAVULESCU, Prof Julian; s of Radu Ion Savulescu (d 1998), and Valda Jean, *née* Thewlis; *b* 22 December 1963; *Educ* Haileybury Coll Melbourne (scholar), Monash Univ Melbourne (MB BS, PhD), Univ of Oxford (Sir Robert Menzies med scholar); *Career* clinical ethicist Oxford Radcliffe Hosps 1995–97, Logan research fell Monash Univ Melbourne 1997–98, dir Bioethics Prog Centre for Study of Health and Society Univ of Melbourne 1998–2002, Ethics of Genetics Prog Murdoch Children's Research Inst Royal Children's Hosp Melbourne 1998–2002, Uehiro chair in practical ethics Univ of Oxford 2002–, dir Oxford Uehiro Centre for Practical Ethics 2002–; chm Dept of Human Services Victoria Ethics Ctee 1998–2002; ed Jl of Med Ethics 2001–04; *Publications* Medical Ethics and Law: The Core Curriculum (jtly, 2003); over 100 articles in BMJ, Lancet, Australian Jl of Philosophy, Bioethics, Jl of Med Ethics, American Jl of Bioethics, Med Jl of Australia, Philosophy, Psychiatry and Psychology and New Scientist; *Recreations* skiing, surfing, cycling, swimming, rollerblading, film, wine; *Style—* Prof Julian Savulescu; ✉ Oxford Uehiro Centre for Practical Ethics, Littlegate House, Oxford OX1 1PT (tel 01865 286888, fax 01865 286886, e-mail ethics@philosophy.ox.ac.uk)

SAVVAS, Michael; s of M Savvas, and Rebecca, *née* Hermogenou; *b* 16 March 1957; *Educ* Holloway Sch, London Hosp Med Coll (MB BS); *Career* house surgn N Middx Hosp 1980–81, house physician Whipps Cross Hosp 1981, SHO A/E London Hosp 1982 (Dept of Obstetrics and Gynaecology 1981–82), SHO Dept of Obstetrics and Gynaecology Whipps Cross Hosp 1982–83, SHO/acting registrar Dept of Endocrinology Jessop Hosp for Women Sheffield 1983–84, registrar in obstetrics and gynaecology Westminster Hosp, St Stephen's Hosp and Hillingdon Hosp 1984–86, res registrar KCH and Dulwich Hosp 1986–88, sr registrar KCH, Lewisham Hosp and Greenwich District Hosp 1988–92, conslt Dept of Obstetrics and Gynaecology Lewisham Hosp and hon sr lectr UMDS (now GKT) 1992–2001, conslt obstetrician and gynaecologist KCH London 2002–; author of numerous scientific pubns; Galen Prize for advances in infertility Hellenic Med Soc; memb: Int Menopause Soc, Br Menopause Soc, Blair Bell Research Soc, Hellenic Med Soc, Int Soc of Gynaecological Endocrinology; MRCOG, FRSM (memb Cncl); *Recreations* classical and medical history, theatre, classical music; *Style—* Michael Savvas, Esq; ✉ Department of Gynaecology, The Blackheath Hospital, 40–42 Lee Terrace, London SE3 9UD (tel 020 8318 7722)

SAWARD, Rev Canon Michael John; s of Donald Saward (d 1992), and Lily, *née* Kendall (d 1991); *b* 14 May 1932; *Educ* Eltham Coll London, Univ of Bristol (BA), Tyndale Hall Bristol; *m* 3 April 1956, Jackie, da of Col John Atkinson, DSO, OBE, TD (d 1945), and Eileen Atkinson, MBE (d 1976); 3 da (Rachel b 1960, Jill, Susan (twins) b 1965), 1 s (Joe b 1961); *Career* 2 Lt RA (Royal W African Frontier Force 1951–52); asst curate: Christ Church Croydon 1956–59, Edgware Parish Church 1959–64; warden Holy Trinity Inter-Church Centre Liverpool 1964–67, sec Liverpool Cncl of Churches 1964–67, C of E radio and TV offr 1967–72, memb Lambeth Conf Preparatory Ctee 1967–68, hon curate St John Beckenham 1969–72; vicar: St Matthew Fulham 1972–78, Ealing 1978–91; priest i/c St Paul Northfields Ealing 1986–89, canon theologian St Michael Sanibel FL 2001–02; canon treas St Paul's Cathedral 1991–2000 (prebendary Caddington Major 1985–91, memb Sch Cncl 1991–2000, Millennium Hymn Competition 1998–99, canon emeritus 2001–); Church Cmmr for England 1978–93 (memb: Redundant Churches Ctee 1978–81, Houses Ctee 1981–88, Bd of Govrs 1986–93, Pastoral Ctee 1988–93); Gen Synod C of E: Broadcasting Cmmn 1970–73, memb 1975–95, Dio in Europe Working Pty 1977–79, Rite A Revis Ctee 1978–79, Partners in Mission Working Pty 1979–81, Dioceses Cmmn 1981–89; London Diocesan Synod: memb 1973–95, memb Vacancy-in-See Ctee 1975–95, memb Bishop's Cncl 1989–91, memb Pastoral Ctee 1989–92, memb Fin Ctee 1989–94; memb: Willesden Area Synod 1980–91 (vice-pres 1985–88), Ealing E Deanery Synod 1978–91 (area dean 1979–84), Sion Coll 2001–; memb Cncl: BCMS 1964–76, Tyndale Hall 1968–72, Trinity Coll Bristol 1974–78, Church Pastoral Aid Soc 1992–98; memb: RTS 1970–72, Archbishops' Cncl on Evangelism 1975–78, C of E Evangelical Cncl 1976–93, Anglican Evangelical Assembly 1983–95; tstee: Bowman Ecclesiastical Tst 1978–91, Jubilate Hymns Charitable Tst 1980–2007, Hartlebury Castle Tst 1983–88, Bowman Charitable Tst 1987–91, Christian Evidence Soc 1992–98; dir Jubilate Hymns Ltd 1980–2006 (chm 2000–01); hon chaplain Ealing Royal Br Legion 1979–90; Burma Star 1979–90; religious advsr to film Cromwell 1971; editor, journalist, columnist, reviewer, hymnwriter (105 hymns) and broadcaster (650 progs); judge Times Preacher of the Year Competition 2000; winner: Southern TV Hymn for Britain Competition 1966, BBC Songs of Praise New Hymn Competition 1985; Polly Bond Journalism Award USA 1990; Winston Churchill Travelling Fellowship 1984; Freeman City of London 1993, Liveryman Worshipful Co of Gardeners 1997–2000; *Books* Leisure (1963), Christian Youth Groups (1965), Task Unfinished (1973), Don't Miss the Party (1974), Cracking the God Code (1975), And So to Bed? (1975), God's Friends (1978), All Change (1983), Evangelicals on the Move (1987), These are the Facts (1997), A Faint Streak of Humility (1999), Jubilate Everybody (2003), Signed, Sealed, Delivered (2004), Christ Triumphant (2006); words ed: Hymns for Today's Church (1982), Sing Glory (1999), Sing to the Lord (2000); contrib: Broadcasting, Society and the Church (1973), Christian Initiation (1991), Prayers for Today's World (1993), Has Keele Failed? (1995), The Post-Evangelical Debate (1997), 366 Graces (1999); also contrib to 222 hymnbooks worldwide; *Recreations* being faithful to Sophia Loren, hymn-writing, reading (especially military history), music, cricket, travel, food and drink; *Clubs* Athenaeum (memb Gen Ctee 1997–2000), Sion Coll; *Style—* The Rev Canon Michael Saward; ✉ 6 Discovery Walk, London E1W 2JG (tel and fax 020 7702 1130)

SAWBRIDGE, Edward Henry Ewen; s of Henry Raywood Sawbridge, CBE (d 1990), of Kingsgate, Kent, and Lilian, *née* Wood (d 1991); *b* 14 August 1953; *Educ* Radley, Balliol Coll Oxford (MA); *m* 23 July 1983, Angela Rose Louisa, da of Maj Anthony James MacDonald Watt (d 1991), of Longwood, Sunninghill, Berks; 3 s (Jack William Hugo b 1986, Hugh Anthony Edward b 1988, Arthur Henry James b 1991); *Career* Peat Marwick Mitchell & Co 1976–83, ACLI Metals (London) Ltd 1983–85, fin dir Lehman Brothers Commodities Ltd 1985–98, exec dir Lehman Brothers International Ltd 1991–98, fin dir Natixis Commodity Markets Ltd (formerly Natexis Metals Ltd) 1998–, chief operating offr Natixis London 2006–; FCA, FRSA; *Recreations* bridge, fishing, cooking, lawns; *Clubs* Oxford and Cambridge; *Style—* Edward Sawbridge, Esq; ✉ Natixis Commodity Markets Limited, 4th Floor, Capital House, 85 King William Street, London EC4N 7BL (e-mail edward@sawbridge.net)

SAWCZUK, Basil; s of Petro Sawczuk (d 2000), of Brockworth, Glos, and Maria, *née* Perik; *b* 22 May 1954; *Educ* Chosen Hill GS Churchdown, Leicester Poly (DipArch), Open Univ (Dip Mgmnt, MBA), CEM Univ of Reading; *m* 19 May 1979, Sonia Elizabeth, da Stefan Szewczuk (d 1987), of Leicester; 1 s (Luke Sebastian b 24 Oct 1988); *Career* project architect Harper Fairley ptnrs Birmingham 1979–80, assoc Malcolm Payne and Assocs Birmingham 1980–83; DGI: joined 1983, exec dir DGI International plc 1986–91 and Overseas Business Devpt 1992–95, exec DGI Group plc 1991–92; divnl dir (following takeoverby W S Atkins) W S Atkins (Midlands)/Atkins DGI 1996–99, dir WS Atkins Architects Ltd 1999–2000; mktg dir: W S Atkins Property Design Gp 1999–2001, W S Atkins Property Services 2001–02, Lee Crowder Solicitors 2002–04; business devpt dir: Accord Housing Servs 2005–06, Accord Housing and Environmental Servs 2006–; responsible for: computer centre GDS Swindon and SWEB HQ Bristol, various projects in Western Siberia, food distribution study in Tyumen region Russia for EC, Paediatric Polyclinic Nefteugansk Russia, several projects for the BBC; memb: Main Ctee Birmingham AA 1980–83 (ed BAA Gazette 1982–83), Ctee Housing Centre Tst 1980, Birmingham and Sutton Coldfield Crime Prevention Panel 1981–82, Ctee of Midland Study Centre 1984, RIBA Parly Action Lobby 1982–83; chm Midland Jr Liaison Organisation 1984; visiting prof Tyumen Univ Russia 1992–93; external examiner: Leicester Sch of Architecture 1990–94, Univ of Nottingham Sch of Architecture 1996–2000; visiting external lectr: De Montfort Univ Leicester, Univ of Nottingham, Univ of Central England; memb W Midlands Arbitration Discussion Gp 1990–2001, registered mediator 1991, memb Acad of Experts 1990–99 (memb ADR Ctee 1993), memb Ctee Professional Marketing Forum 1997–99, memb Construction Ctee London C of C 2000–02, memb Fundraising Ctee Nat Inst of Conductive Education 2000–02; Freeman City of London 1983, Freeman Worshipful Co of Arbitrators 1983–94; MInstD 1999–2001, memb Br Soc of Clinical Hypnosis 2003; RIBA 1979, FCIArb 1989–2006 (ACIArb 1980, memb Panel of Arbitrators 1991, memb Ctee Midlands branch 1995–98), FCIM 2001; *Books* Risk Avoidance for the Building Team (1996); various articles in professional jls; *Recreations* painting, reading, fishing; *Style—* Basil Sawczuk, Esq; ✉ e-mail basil@potentialise.com

SAWER, David Peter; *b* 14 September 1961; *Educ* Univ of York (BA, DPhil), Staatliche Hochschule für Musik Rheinland; *Career* composer in assoc Bournemouth Orchs 1995–96; *Awards* DAAD scholarship (to study with Mauricio Kagel in Köln) 1984, Sony Radio Award (for Swansong) 1990, Fulbright Fellowship 1992, Paul Hamlyn Fndn Award 1993, Arts Fndn Composer Fellowship 1995; *Compositions* for theatre: Etudes 1984, Food of Love 1988, The Panic 1991; for orch: Byrnan Wood 1992, The Memory of Water 1993/1995, Trumpet Concerto 1994, Tiroirs 1996, the greatest happiness principle 1997, Musica ficta 1998, Piano Concerto 2002; chamber music: Cat's-Eye 1986, Take Off 1987, Good Night 1989, Rhetoric 1989, Hollywood Extra 1996, Rebus 2004; choral music: Songs of Love and War 1990, Sounds Three Kandinsky Poems 1996 and 1999, Stramm Gedichte 2002, Mutability 2004; opera: From Morning to Midnight 1998–2001; instrumental: Solo Piano 1983, The Melancholy of Departure 1990, Between 1998; *Style—* David Sawer, Esq; ✉ c/o Allied Artist Agency, 42 Montpelier Square, London SW7 1JZ (tel 020 7589 6243, fax 020 7581 5269, e-mail info@alliedartists.co.uk)

SAWERS, Sir (Robert) John; KCMG (2007, CMG 1996); s of Colin Simon Sawers, and Daphne Anne, *née* Davis; *Educ* Beechen Cliff Sch Bath, Univ of Nottingham (BSc), St Andrews Univ; *Career* FCO appointments: Damascus 1982, London 1984, Pretoria/Cape Town 1988; head EU Presidency Unit 1992, princ private sec to foreign sec 1993, int fell Harvard Univ 1995–96, cnsllr Washington 1996, foreign affrs private sec to PM 1999, ambass Cairo 2001–03, UK special envoy to Iraq May-July 2003, political dir FCO 2003–07, UK Perm Rep to the UN NY 2007–; *Recreations* theatre, tennis; *Style—* Sir John Sawers, KCMG; ✉ c/o Foreign & Commonwealth Office, King Charles Street, London SW1A 2AH

SAWFORD, Philip; *b* 26 June 1950; *Educ* Kettering GS, Ruskin Coll Oxford, Univ of Leicester (BA); *m* Rosemary; 2 s (Lee, Andrew); *Career* former apprentice carpenter/joiner construction industry until 1977, with British Steel Corp1977–80, in full-time educn 1980–85, joined Wellingborough Community Relations Cncl 1985 and subsequently with a training partnership in Wellingborough until 1997; MP (Lab) Kettering 1997–2005; cncllr Desborough Town Cncl 1977–97, ldr Kettering BC 1991–97 (cncllr 1979–83 and 1986–97); *Style—* Philip Sawford, Esq

SAWLE, Dr Guy Victor; s of Victor Sawle, and Joan, *née* Roots; *Educ* Univ of Nottingham Med Sch (DM); *m* 18 July 1981, Fiona, *née* Alldis; 1 da (Chloe b 13 Sept 1983), 2 s (Oliver b 13 Oct 1985, Tristan b 5 Sept 1992); *Career* neurology trg Addenbrooke's Hosp Cambridge and St Thomas', Hammersmith and Nat Hosps London, currently conslt neurologist Queens Med Centre Nottingham; past pres Notts Medico Legal Soc; memb Assoc of Br Neurologists 1990, memb Movement Disorder Soc 1990; FRCP 1998; *Publications* Movement Disorders in Clinical Practice (ed, 1999); over 100 works incl pubns on functional brain imaging, movement disorders and neurological complications of pregnancy; *Recreations* music, koi, microscopy, astronomy; *Style—* Dr Guy Sawle; ✉ Department of Neurology, Queens Medical Centre, Nottingham NG7 2UH (tel 0115 970 9792, fax 0115 960 4253)

SAWYER, Anthony Charles (Tony); CB (1999); s of Charles Bertram Sawyer (d 1999), and Elisabeth, *née* Spinks (d 1992); *b* 3 August 1939; *Educ* Redhill Tech Coll; *m* 1962, Kathleen Josephine, *née* McGill; 2 s (Stephen b 1965, Andrew b 1967), 1 da (Sarah Ann b 1969); *Career* Customs and Excise: joined 1963, princ 1978–82, dep collector S Wales 1983–84, collector Edinburgh 1984–88, cmmr of Customs and Excise 1991–99, dir Outfield 1991–94 (dep dir 1988–91), dir Enforcement 1994–99; fiscal expert IMF 1999– (expert missions to Bulgaria, Kenya, Kyrgyzstan, Nigeria, Romania, Tanzania, Tajikistan, Pakistan and the Philippines); fiscal advsr to: Kyrgyz Repub 2000, Egypt 2003–04, Ethiopia 2004; non-exec dir Retail Banking Bd Royal Bank of Scotland plc 1994–97; dir Customs Annuity and Benevolent Fund 1998–2004; FCMI, FInstD, FRMetS, FRSA; *Recreations* travelling, cricket, sailing; *Clubs* National Liberal, Royal Scots (Edinburgh); *Style—* Anthony C Sawyer, Esq, CB; fax 01892 661962, e-mail acskjs@hotmail.com

SAX, Richard Noel; s of late Lt-Col George Hans Sax, of Whatlington, E Sussex, and Yvonne Anna Marcelle Sax; *b* 26 December 1938; *Educ* Tonbridge, St John's Coll Oxford (MA); *m* 8 April 1967, Margaret, da of Ronald Frank Penny (d 1988); 3 da (Catherine b 1968, Josephine b 1971, Charlotte b 1974); *Career* Nat Serv cmmnd 2 Lt RASC 1957, attached 1 Gds Bde Irish Gds Cyprus (GSM Cyprus Clasp), Lt 1959; admitted slr 1967; managing ptnr Rubinstein Callingham 1984–93 (equity ptnr 1968–94), ptnr then conslt Manches 1994–; dep dist judge Princ Registry Family Div 1990–; chm Slrs Family Law Assoc 1987–99; memb: Law Cmmn Working Pty on Family Property 1974, Family Law Ctee Law Soc 1990–2000, Bd Children and Family Court Advsy Serv (CAFCASS); memb Law Soc 1967, past pres European Chapter and fell IAML, govr Skinners Sch for Girls Hackney; Liveryman Worshipful Co of Skinners; *Recreations* current affairs, gardening, history and archaeology, travel, art; *Clubs* MCC; *Style—* Richard Sax, Esq; ✉ 29 Kelsey Way, Beckenham, Kent BR3 3LP (tel 020 8650 8272); Manches, Aldwych House, 81 Aldwych, London WC2B 4RP (tel 020 7404 4483, fax 020 7430 1133, e-mail richard.sax@manches.com)

SAXBEE, Rt Rev Dr John Charles; *see:* Lincoln, Bishop of

SAXBY, Graham; s of Flinton Saxby (d 1972), and Eleanor Cora, *née* Pratt (d 1985); *b* 4 November 1925; *Educ* West Buckland Sch, UC of SW (now Univ of Exeter), Univ of London (BSc), Univ of Manchester (PGCE), Open Univ (BA (twice)); *m* Christine Mary, da of Ernest Smalley (d 1980); 1 step da; *Career* RAF: joined as photographer 1947, served Singapore, Hong Kong, Bahrain and Germany, latterly chief technician, cmmnd educn offr (tech) 1966, OC Photographic Science Flight Jt Sch of Photography until ret as Sqdn Ldr 1974; Wolverhampton Tech Teachers' Coll (later part of Univ of Wolverhampton): lectr in educnl technol 1974–90, estab Holography Unit 1986, hon res fell in holography 1990–93; tech advsr Holography Dept RCA 1985–96; memb Int Soc for Optical Engrg (SPIE) 1997–2007; FBIPP 1981 (MBIPP 1956), Hon FRPS 1988 (memb 1946, FRPS 1981), FInstP 2005 (MInstP 2002); *Awards* Technical Writers' award (Specialist Div) 1981, second prize Diplome de la Musée de la Photographie (Prix Louis-Philippe Clerc) 1983, nominee King Feisal Award for Science Writing 1988, Kraszna-Krausz Award for Photographic Writing 1993 and 2002, City and Guilds Insignia Award (photographic technol) 1970; *Publications* The Focal Guide to Slides (1979), Holograms: How to Make and Display Them (1980), Newnes Book of Photography (contrib, 1983), Practical Holography (1988, 1994 and 2003), Manual of Practical Holography (1991), The Science of Imaging (2001), The Oxford Companion to the Photograph (contributing ed, 2005), author of numerous technical articles in professional jls; *Recreations* photography, music, vegetable gardening; *Style—* Graham Saxby, Esq; ✉ 3 Honor Avenue, Goldthorn Park, Wolverhampton, West Midlands WV4 5HF (tel 01902 341291, e-mail grahamsaxby@sagainternet.co.uk)

SAXBY, John; s of George Saxby, and Veronica, *née* Flynn; *b* 29 September 1949; *Educ* St Mary's Coll Crosby Liverpool, King's Coll London (BA), Univ of Cologne, MA (1992), MBA (1993); *m* 15 Nov 1986, Janet Adelyne, da of Harold Livesey; 1 da (Emily-Jane Christine b 7 Nov 1989); *Career* chief exec Co Durham and Darlington NHS Tst 2002–; *Recreations* distance running, fell running, cycling; *Style—* John Saxby, Esq; ✉ University of North Durham, Durham DH1 5TW (tel 0191 333 2151, e-mail john.saxby@cddah.nhs.uk)

SAXON, Prof David Harold; OBE (2005); s of Rev Canon Eric Saxon, of Bramhall, Manchester, and Ruth, *née* Higginbottom; *b* 27 October 1945; *Educ* Manchester Grammar, Balliol Coll Oxford (Brackenbury scholar, BA, Scott prize, DSc), Jesus Coll Oxford (MA, DPhil); *m* 13 July 1968, Margaret, da of Rev John Flitcroft; 1 s (Philip Jeffrey b 28 Feb 1972), 1 da (Patricia Alice b 6 Dec 1974); *Career* Univ of Oxford: jr res fell Jesus Coll 1968–70, res offr Dept of Nuclear Physics 1969–70; res assoc Columbia Univ 1970–73; Rutherford Appleton Laboratory: res assoc 1974–75, sr scientific offr 1975–76, princ scientific offr 1976–89, grade 6 1989–90; Univ of Glasgow: Kelvin prof of physics 1990–, head Dept of Physics and Astronomy 1996–2001, vice-dean of physical sciences 2000–02, dean of physical sciences 2002–; chm Governing Ctee Scottish Univs Summer Sch in Physics 1997–2003 (dir 1993); memb: Selection Panel SERC Particle Physics Experiment 1989–92, High Energy Particle Physics Ctee Inst of Physics 1989–93, Nuclear Physics Div Ctee Inst of Physics 1990–93, Detector R&D Ctee CERN 1990–93, Particle Physics Ctee SERC 1991–94 (chm 1992), Nuclear Physics Bd SERC 1992–93, UK Ctee on CERN 1992–95 and 1998–, Scientific Policy Ctee CERN 1993–98, Physics Res Ctee DESY 1993–99, Research Assessment Physics Panel 1996, Cncl PPARC 1997–2001 (chm Particle Physics Ctee 1994–95, chm Public Understanding of Sci Panel 1997–2001), MRC Scientific Advsy Gp on Technol 1999 (Discipline Hopping Panel 2000 and 2006), Cncl Central Laboratories for Research Cncls 2000–01 and 2005–07 (chm Particle Physics Users Advsy Ctee 1998–2004, memb Resources Allocation Ctee 2006–07), External Review Ctee CERN 2001–02, Cncl RSE 2001–04 (res convener 2002–05), Univ of Trento Sci Advsy Panel 2002–04, Br cncl Tavel Awards Panel 2006, Cmmn C11 Int Union of Pure and Applied Physics (IUPAP) 2006–; chm: UK Inst of Physics Conf 1993, 27th Int Conf on High Energy Physics 1994, chm Inst of Physics in Scotland 2003–05 (vice-chm 2001–03); CPhys, FInstP 1985, FRSE 1993, FRSA 1997, FRAS 2004; *Style—* Prof David H Saxon, OBE, FRSE; ✉ Faculty of Physical Sciences, University of Glasgow, Glasgow G12 8QQ (tel 0141 330 4673, fax 0141 330 4371, e-mail d.saxon@physics.gla.ac.uk)

SAXON, Richard Gilbert; CBE (2001); s of Rev Canon Eric Saxon, QHC, of Stockport, and Ruth, *née* Higginbottom; *b* 14 April 1942; *Educ* Manchester Grammar, Univ of Liverpool (BArch, MCD); *m* 14 Sept 1968, (Elizabeth) Anne, da of Samuel Shaw Tatton, of Barwick in Elmet, Leeds; *Career* architect; Building Design Partnership (BDP): assoc 1970–77, ptnr 1977–97, head of architectural profession London Office 1991–96, chm London Office 1993–99, gp chm 1996–2002, dir 1997–2005, dir mktg 2000–05; princ Consultancy for the Built Environment (client and practice advsr) 2005–; design ptnr: J P Morgan HQ London 1986–91, Paddington Basin Redevelopment 1989–92, All England Lawn Tennis Club Redevelopment 1992–95, Adam Opel AG Headquarters Rüsselsheim Germany 1993–97; relationship dir Marks and Spencer 1995–, conslt Shell 2001; awards incl: RIBA Halifax Bldg Soc HQ 1975, Europa Nostra medal and Civic Tst Durham Milburngate Centre 1978, Civic Tst commendation Merseyside Maritime Museum Masterplan 1981, New City Architecture award JP Morgan HQ 1993, Civic Tst commendation All England Lawn Tennis Club No 1 Court 1998, BCO Award Halifax HQ 2000; bldg advsr EDC 1984–86; memb: Bldg Sub-Ctee Sci and Engrg Res Cncl 1987–90, Electronic Applications Sub-Ctee NEDO 1991–92, DTI Task Force on Construction Deregulation 1993, Bd Br Cncl for Offices 1990–99 (pres 1995–96), Bd Reading Construction Forum 1995–2002 (chair 1999–2002), Design Build Fndn 1997–2002, Building Ctee Univ of Cambridge 2004–; chm: Good Practice Panel Construction Industry Bd 1996–99, Collaborating for the Built Environment 2002–05; memb Strategic Forum for Construction 2001–02; Freeman City of London 1988, Master Worshipful Co of Chartered Architects 2005–06 (memb Ct of Assts 1992–); memb The Bond; RIBA 1968 (vice-pres 2002–08), MCIM, FRSA 1987, MInstD; *Books* Atrium Buildings, Development and Design: Architectural Press (1983 and 1986), Moscow (1987), Kajima Press Japan (1988 and 1993), Bardon Chinese Agency ROC (1994), chapter Atrium Buildings Wiley/AIA Encyclopaedia of Architecture (1988), The Atrium Comes of Age (1993), Kenchiku Gijutsu Japan (1995), Be Valuable: A guide to creating value in the built environment (2005); *Recreations* travel, photography, music, theatre, film, writing; *Style—* Richard Saxon, Esq, CBE; ✉ Consultancy for the Built Environment, 9 Whistlers Avenue, London SW11 3TS (tel 020 7585 1976, e-mail richard@saxoncbe.com, website www.saxoncbe.com)

SAXTON, Dr Robert Louis Alfred; s of Capt Ian Sanders Saxton, barr-at-law, of London, and Dr Jean Augusta Saxton, *née* Infield; *b* 8 October 1953; *Educ* Bryanston, St Catharine's Coll Cambridge (MA), Worcester Coll Oxford (BMus, DMus); *Partner* 1979–, Teresa Cahill, *qv*; *Career* visiting tutor Univ of Oxford 1980–82, lectr Univ of Bristol 1984–85, visiting fell Princeton Univ 1986, composer in residence City Univ 1987–89, head of Composition Dept GSM 1990–98 (composition tutor 1979–84 and 1986–90), artisitic dir Opera Lab 1993–99, visiting fell in Composition Univ of Bristol 1995–2000, head Composition Dept RAM 1998–99, univ lectr and tutorial fell Worcester Coll Oxford 1999–; composer of over 40 published works, over 20 commercial recordings; contrib to various music jls; several radio and TV appearances; memb: Cncl SPNM 1978–90 (memb Exec Ctee 1979–82), Artistic Bd Blackheath Concert Halls 1987–89, BBC Score Reading Panel 1988–, Arts Cncl of GB Music Advsy Panel 1989–93, Site Devpt Bd South Bank Centre 1996–97, Governing Bd South Bank Centre 1997–; hon pres Assoc of English Singers and Speakers 1997–; PRS 1976, FGSM 1986, MCPS 1990; *Recreations* theatre, cinema, reading biography, history and philosophy; *Style—* Dr Robert Saxton; ✉ c/o Music Sales, 8/9 Frith Street, London W1V 5TZ (tel 020 7434 0066, fax 020 7278 6329); c/o University of York Music Press, Department of Music, University of York, Heslington, York Y10 5DD (tel 01904 432434, fax 01904 432450, e-mail uymp@york.ac.uk)

SAXTON, Robert Michael; s of Arthur Colin, and Joyce, *née* Dulson; *b* 12 August 1952; *Educ* Magdalen Coll Oxford (MA); *Career* publisher; Studio Vista 1975–80, exec ed Mitchell Beazley 1980–91 (responsible for lists on gardening, design, architecture and photography), editorial dir Duncan Baird Publishers UK 1991– (int co-edn titles and illustrated reference); *Poetry* The Promise Clinic (1994), Manganese (2003), Local Honey (2007); *Recreations* ornithology, modern jazz, learning jazz piano, world music, poetry, Indian classical music; *Style—* Robert Saxton, Esq; ✉ Duncan Baird Publishers, Castle House, 75–76 Wells Street, London W1T 3QH

SAYE AND SELE, 21 Baron (E 1447 and 1603); Nathaniel Thomas Allen Fiennes; DL (Oxon 1979); s of 20 Baron, OBE, MC (Ivo Murray Twisleton-Wykeham-Fiennes, d 1968), and Hersey, da of late Capt Sir Thomas Dacres Butler, KCVO; relinquished by deed poll 1965 the additional surnames of Twisleton and Wykeham; *b* 22 September 1920; *Educ* Eton, New Coll Oxford; *m* 1958, Mariette Helena, da of Maj-Gen Sir (Arthur) Guy

S

Salisbury-Jones, GCVO, CMG, CBE, MC (d 1985), and Hilda (d 1995), da of Rt Hon Sir Maurice de Bunsen, 1 and last Bt, GCMG, GCVO, CB; 4 s (2 decd), 1 da; *Heir* s, Hon Martin Fiennes; *Career* Rifle Bde (despatches twice) 1939–45; chartered surveyor; ptnr Laws & Fiennes; regnl dir Lloyds Bank 1983–90; tstee Ernest Cook Tst 1959–95 (chm 1964–90); fell Winchester Coll 1967–83; *Style—* The Lord Saye and Sele, DL; ✉ Broughton Castle, Banbury, Oxfordshire OX15 5EB (tel 01295 262624)

SAYEED, Dr (Abulfatah) Akram; OBE (1976); s of Mokhles Ahmed (d 1967), of Pirwalistan, Jessore, Bangladesh, and Noor Jehan Begum, *née* Munshi (d 1987); *b* 23 November 1935; *Educ* St Joseph's Sch Khulna, Univ of Dhaka (MB BS); *m* 11 Oct 1959, Hosne-ara, da of Al-Haj M Sabet Ali; 1 da (Dina Jesmin b 17 June 1963), 2 s (Rana Ahmed b 10 March 1967, Reza Abu b 15 April 1972); *Career* trained in Bangladesh, USA and UK, started Gen Practice 1963, ret 2003; author of numerous articles on medico-politics; writer, lectr and broadcaster on med educn and trg in Bangladesh; fndr memb Leicester Cncl for Community Rels 1965–; memb: CRC 1968–77, BBC Asian Programme Advsy Ctee 1972–77, Leics Family Practitioners' Ctee 1977–86, Unit Mgmnt Team 1977–86, Leics Med Ctee 1977–2002, Home Sec's Advsy Cncl on Community Rels 1983–88, DHSS Working Gps (Asian health, treatment of overseas visitors); unit advsr NCCI 1965–68; nat chm: Standing Conf of Asian Orgns in UK 1973–77 (vice-chm 1970–73, pres 1973–84), Stop Rickets Campaign Leics 1979–82; chm Asian Mother and Baby Campaign (Leicester) 1983–85, UK delg First World Conf on Muslim Educn King Abdul Aziz Univ Mecca 1977, vice-pres Fedn of Bangladeshi Orgns in UK and Europe 1984–90, sec Inst of Transcultural Health Care 1985–93, co-ordinator and facilitator in UK for Bangladesh Coll of Physicians and Surgeons 1990–2004, hon advsr Miny of Health Govt of Bangladesh 1991–; pres Leicester Med Soc 2001–02; memb Editorial Bd: ODA News Review 1979–96, Asian Who's Who (18 edn 2005–06), Ethnicity and Health 1990–2002; Overseas Doctors' Assoc: fndr chm 1975, gen sec 1975–77, vice-pres 1979–84, chm S Trent Div 1981–90, vice-chm 1984, chm Annual Representative Meeting 1990–93, chm 1993–96; BMA: memb 1961, memb Agenda Ctee 1992–96 and 1998, pres Leics Div 1993–94, memb Gen Med Servs Ctee 1993–99, elected memb GMC 1999–2004; feasibility study to establish undergrad gen practice in certain Bangladeshi med schs (short-term consultancy) WHO 2000; memb: Bangladesh Med Assoc UK 1972–, Ophthalmic Soc of Bangladesh (life memb); associate Med Journalists' Assoc; journalist and writer 2003–; weekly columns The Letter From Leicester in The Bangladesh Today; FODA 1985, Hon FCGP (Bangladesh) 1991, Hon FCPS Bangladesh 1992, FRCPE 1994, fell BMA 1995, FRCGP 1998 (MRCGP 1992); *Books* Caring for Asians in General Practice (contrib, 1989), Letters From Leicester Vol I (2004), Letters From Leicester Vol II (2005), Shesher Adhaya (Bangla novel, 2005), Rahu Grash (2006), In the Shadow of My Taqdir (memoirs, 2006), Letters From Leicester Vol III (2007); *Recreations* oriental music, listening to talking books, information materials and current affairs programmes (suffers from severe visual impairment and registered semi-blind); *Style—* Dr A Akram Sayeed, OBE; ✉ Ramna, 2 Mickelton Drive, Leicester LE5 6GD (tel 0116 241 6703, fax 0116 241 5753, e-mail akram.sayeed@runbox.com)

SAYER, Michael John; s of Maj Douglas James William Sayer, MBE, TD, JP (d 2005), of Sparham Hall, Norfolk, and Mary Elizabeth, *née* Weddall; *b* 11 October 1947; *Educ* Repton, Pembroke Coll Oxford (MA, BLitt); *Career* landowner, author; CLA: memb Norfolk Branch Ctee 1972, memb Water Sub-Ctee 1980–84, memb Tax Sub-Ctee 1989–93, memb Cncl 1993– (memb exec 1999–), chm Norfolk Branch 1995–98; tax cmmr 1979– (chm St Faith's and Aylsham Div 1988–2005, chm Central Norfolk Div 2006–); memb: Norwich Diocesan Synod 1973–82 (Pastoral Ctee 1974–82), Tax Ctee Historic Houses Assoc 1990–; chm Norfolk Churches Tst 1984–86; jt rep Duke of Norfolk on Cmmn d'Information et de Liaison des Associations de Noblesse d'Europe (CILANE) 1994–, vice-pres Friends of the Countryside 1998–, delg European Landowners' Orgn UN Framework Convention on Climate Change 1999–2001; FSA 1982; *Books* English Nobility: The Gentry, The Heralds and The Continental Context (1979), Norfolk section of Burke's and Savill's Guide to Country Houses, vol III, East Anglia (1981), The Disintegration of a Heritage: Country Houses and their Collections 1979–1992 (1993), Sea-Level Rise and Coastal Defence in the Southern North Sea (jt ed, 2004), Climate Change and the European Countryside (jtly, 2006); *Recreations* history, architecture, shooting; *Clubs* Norfolk; *Style—* Michael J Sayer, Esq, FSA; ✉ Sparham House, Norwich NR9 5PJ

SAYER, Paul Anthony; s of John Sayer (d 1992), of South Milford, nr Leeds, and Adelaide, *née* Lambert (d 1985); *b* 4 October 1955; *Educ* Tadcaster GS; *m* 31 Jan 1981, Anne, da of James Bell (d 1997); 1 s (Simon b 19 Dec 1984); *Career* author; shop asst 1973–76, RMN 1979, psychiatric nurse 1976–81 and 1986–89, shop keeper 1981–84, storeman 1984–85, author 1989–; memb Soc of Authors 1988; *Books* The Comforts of Madness (1988, Constable Trophy for Fiction, Whitbread First Novel Award, Whitbread Book of the Year Award), Howling at the Moon (1990), The Absolution Game (1992), The Storm-Bringer (1994), The God Child (1996), Men in Rage (1998); *Recreations* lifelong supporter of York City FC, and other hopeless causes; *Style—* Paul Sayer, Esq; ✉ Jane Conway-Gordon, 1 Old Compton Street, London W1V 5PH (e-mail paulsayer@fsmail.net)

SAYER, Philip William; s of Edward George Poulton Sayer, of Basingstoke, Hants, and Jean, *née* Kennedy; *b* 7 January 1947; *Educ* Queen Mary's GS Basingstoke; *m* Dec 1984, Joan Katherine, da of Ronald Frederick Taylor; 1 da (Rosie b Sept 1985), 1 s (Joseph b 21 July 1991); *Career* photographer; asst to Maurice Broomfield, photographer Butlins Holiday Camp Bognor 1965–67, photographic printer Derek Robinson Partnership 1967–70, freelance editorial photographer 1970–; currently contrib to various magazines incl: Domus (RA magazine), Crafts, Blueprint, World of Interiors, GQ (USA), Travel & Leisure (USA), ES, The Times - Saturday Review; currently photographer numerous design gps Europe and USA; solo exhibitions: Portraits for Print (Norwich Sch of Art) 1983, The Face of Craft (Br Crafts Centre) 1984, Portraits (Impressions Gallery York) 1985, permanent exhibition of portraits (The Blueprint Café Design Museum London) 1989, The 100 Mile City (exhibition Architectural Fndn London) 1992, The Making of the Modern World (Science Museum) 1993, The Hermitage, St Petersburg (Pentagram Gallery) 1995, Eye to Eye (Barrett Marsden Gallery London) 2002, Icons of Icons (RCA) 2003; FCSD 1983; *Books* Building of Faith - Westminster Cathedral (1995), Critical Mass (Royal Acad, 1998), Alexander 'Greek' Thompson (with Gavin Stamp, 1999), West Wing (2005); *Recreations* painting, cycling, music (jazz, country and western), reading; *Style—* Philip Sayer, Esq; ✉ Philip Sayer Partnership, Lynwood House, Church Road, Cookham Dean, Berkshire SL6 9PD (tel and fax 01628 890960)

SAYER, Robert; s of Kenneth Sayer (d 1979) and Ellen; *b* 16 January 1952; *Educ* Salvatorian Coll Harrow Weald, Univ of Swansea (BA); *m* 1997, Catherine Hunt; *Career* founder and sr ptnr Sayer Moore & Co 1983; Law Soc: memb 1979–, vice-pres 1995–96 and 1998–99 (dep vice-pres 1997–98), dep treas 1996–97, treas 1997–99, pres 1999–2000; memb: Law Soc of Ireland 1996, Cwlth Law Assoc; assoc memb America's Bar Assoc 1995–, hon memb Inst of Advanced Legal Studies; *Publications* numerous articles in Law Soc Gazette, The Lawyer, New Law Journal, Solicitors Journal, American Studies; *Recreations* sailing, writing; *Clubs* Naval and Military; *Style—* Robert Sayer, Esq; ✉ Sayer Moore & Company, 190 Horn Lane, Acton, London W3 6PL (tel 020 8993 7571, fax 020 8993 7763)

SAYER, Stephen Thomas; s of late Charles Martin Sayer, of Epping, Essex, and late Justina, *née* Marsden Jones; *b* 8 July 1945; *Educ* Framlingham Coll, Coll of Law; *m* 1, 20 July 1968 (m dis 1987), Gillian Susan, da of John Talbot Warwick, of Rustington, W Sussex; 2 s (Edward b 1971, Timothy b and d 1973), 1 da (Harriet b 1976); m 2, 30 Jan 1988, Aileen, da of Roy Victor Wegener, of Toowoomba, Aust; *Career* admitted slr 1968; articles Tuffe Sweet & Co, ptnr Richards Butler 1974–2005 (asst slr 1968), sr lawyer Said Al-Shahry Law Office Muscat; memb Advsy Bd Inst of Law City Univ; Freeman City of London 1978, Liveryman Worshipful Co of Slrs 1975; memb: Law Soc 1968, Lawyers Club 1980, Soc of English and American Lawyers, UK Assoc of Euro Law; *Books* Joint Ventures with International Partners, International Joint Venture and Agency and Distribution sections of Longman's Commercial Precedents, Negotiating International Joint Ventures; *Recreations* real tennis, rackets, theatre, history; *Clubs* Reform, Queen's; *Style—* Stephen Sayer, Esq; ✉ Reed Smith, Richards Butler LLP, Beaufort House, 15 St Botolph Street, London EC3A 7EE (e-mail sts@saslo.com)

SAYERS, Allan Langley; s of Wilfrid William Sayers (d 1977), and Ivy Florence Amelia, *née* Braun (d 1987); *b* 30 June 1939; *Educ* St Paul's; *m* 30 May 1962, Susan Mary, *née* Fisher; 2 s (Andrew John b 18 April 1965, Christopher Allan b 19 Dec 1978); *Career* dir: A Sayers Ltd 1962–86 (chm 1977–86), Menswear Association of Britain 1986–91 (pres 1979–80, dir Menswear Fair Ltd 1978–93); chief exec British Shops and Stores Association 1991–99; chm Distributive Industries Trg Advsy Cncl 1999–2002; memb: EDC for the Distributive Trades 1980–85 (Technology Working Pty for the Distributive Trades 1980–83), Retail Ctee Br Chambers of Commerce 1993–96, Mgmnt Bd British Retail Consortium 1993–99 (Cncl 1980–85); chm Euro Assoc of Textile Retailers Int Platform (AEDT) 1999–; UK representative: Euro Assoc of Nat Organisations of Textile Retailers 1992–99, Euro Federation of Furniture Retailers 1993–98; employers' rep Non-Food Wages Cncl 1986–93; chm Wembley Round Table 1970–71, pres Northwick Park Rotary Club 1980–81; Freeman City of London 1994, Liveryman Worshipful Co of Glovers 1994; FCMI 1979, FRSA 1993; *Recreations* travel, playing at golf, photography, bowls, bridge; *Style—* Allan Sayers, Esq; ✉ 20 Ross Way, Northwood, Middlesex HA6 3HU (tel 01923 828685); A Sayers Ltd, 5 New Broadway, Ealing, London W5 5AW (tel 020 8567 4485, car 07710 874350)

SAYERS, Michael Patrick; QC (1988); s of Maj (Herbert James) Michael Sayers, RA (ka 1943), and Sheilah de Courcy Holroyd, *née* Stephenson (d 1969); *b* 28 March 1940; *Educ* Harrow, Fitzwilliam Coll Cambridge (Evelyn Rothschild scholar, MA); *m* 12 March 1976, Moussie Brougham, *née* Hallstrom; 1 da (Nicola b 27 Dec 1980), 1 s (Frederick b 3 Dec 1981), 1 step s (Henry Brougham b 12 Nov 1971); *Career* called to the Bar Inner Temple 1970 (bencher 1994); jr Central Criminal Court Bar Mess 1975–78, supplementary prosecuting counsel to the Crown Central Criminal Court 1977–88, dep circuit judge 1981, recorder of the Crown Court 1986–2005 (asst recorder 1982); memb Ctee Barrs' Benevolent Assoc 1991–2007; chm Harrow Assoc 1991–97 (vice-pres 1999); *Recreations* shooting, stalking, theatre, Sweden; *Clubs* Garrick, Pratt's, Swinley Forest Golf; *Style—* Michael Sayers, Esq, QC; ✉ 2 King's Bench Walk, Temple, London EC4Y 7DE (tel 020 7353 1746, fax 020 7583 2051/4571)

SAYERS, Michael Warwick; s of Warwick Sayers (d 1977), and Sheila, *née* Carr; *b* 25 August 1943; *Educ* Charterhouse, Univ of Oxford; *m* 23 Aug 1969, Elizabeth Ruth, *née* Wood; 1 da (Rachel b 26 Dec 1970), 1 s (Jeremy b 24 Feb 1973); *Career* called to the Bar 1967; legal advsr Central Criminal Court 1966–72, advocate Criminal Injuries Compensation Bd 1972–76, legal advsr Law Cmmn 1976–78, sec Cncl on Tbnls 1981–87 (legal advsr 1978–81); Lord Chllr's Dept: head Criminal Policy and Professional Practice Div 1987–88, head Judicial Appts Div 1988–91, head Family Law Div 1991–94; chief exec and sec Law Cmmn 1994–2003; UK Sports Dispute Resolution Panel: chm Panel of Arbitrators 2000–, memb Panel Appts and Review Bd 2005–; gen sec Cwlth Assoc of Law Reform Agencies 2004–; law reform conslt 2004–; legal chm NHS Tbnl 1996–2000, chm Parole Local Ctees 1987–95, memb Clergy Discipline Cmmn of the C of E 2004–; first chm Editorial Bd Tribunals 1994; govr Aldro Sch 1983– (chm 2006–); FRSA; *Publications* Tribunals Practice and Procedure (jtly, 1985), The Council on Tribunals: New Developments in Research (1985), The Council on Tribunals (1986), Tribunals, Inquiries and Ombudsmen (jtly, 1987), Franks Revisited: A Model of the Ideal Tribunal (jtly, 1990), The Importance and Variety of Tribunals (1994), Co-operation between Commonwealth Law Reform Agencies (2000), International Co-operation in Law Reform (2003), Best Practices in Law Reform (2005), Law Reform: International Dimensions (2005); *Recreations* involvement in local church, sport; *Clubs* Varsity Squash (Guildford); *Style—* Michael Sayers, Esq; ✉ e-mail thesayers@hotmail.com

SAYLE, Alexei David; s of Joseph Henry Sayle (d 1984), of Liverpool and Malka, *née* Mendelson; *b* 7 August 1952; *Educ* Alsop HS Liverpool, Southport Art Sch, Chelsea Sch of Art (DipAD), Garnet Coll Roehampton (CertEd); *m* Linda Eleanor, da of Noel Rawsthorn; *Career* comedian, actor and writer; master of ceremonies: Comedy Store Club 1979–80, Comic Strip Club 1980–81; various solo tours as stand-up comedian; *Television* incl: The Young Ones 1982–85, The Strike 1987, Alexei Sayle's Stuff 1988–91, Night Voice 1990, Itch 1991, Selling Hitler 1991, The All-New Alexei Sayle Show 1994 and 1995, Paris 1995, Sorry About Last Night (writer and actor, BBC) 1995, Great Railway Journeys of the World 1996, Hospital! (Channel 5) 1997, Alexei Sayle's Merry Go Round (BBC) 1998; *Films* Gorky Park 1983, Supergrass 1985, Siesta 1986, Indiana Jones and the Last Crusade 1989, Swing 1999; *Recordings* single released Ullo John! Gotta New Motor? 1984; *Radio* presenter Fourth Column (Radio 4) 1994; *Columnist* Time Out, Sunday Mirror, The Observer Magazine, The Independent, Esquire, Car; *Awards* Best Comedy Awards incl: Pye Radio 1981, RTS 1988, Broadcast Press Guild 1988, International Emmy 1988, Bronze Rose of Montreux; *Books* Train to Hell (1982), Geoffrey the Tube Train and the Fat Comedian (1987), Great Bus Journeys of the World (1988), Barcelona Plates (2000), The Dog Catcher (2001), Overtaker (2003), The Weeping Women Hotel (2006); *Recreations* cycling; *Clubs* Chelsea Arts; *Style—* Alexei Sayle; ✉ c/o Cassie Mayer Ltd, 5 Old Garden House, The Lanterns, Bridge Lane, London SW11 3AD

SAYWELL, (John Anthony) Telfer; JP (Richmond 1985); s of John Rupert Saywell (d 1948), of London, and Winifred, *née* Green (d 1980); *b* 19 August 1939; *Educ* Abingdon Sch, Open Univ (BA); *m* 8 June 1968, June Mary, da of Maurice Thomas Hunnable (d 1972), of Rivenhall, Essex; 1 da (Polly b 1969), 2 s (Thomas b 1971, Henry b 1977); *Career* CA; Fincham Vallance & Co 1958–63, Tansley Witt & Co 1963–69; Layton Fern & Co Ltd (coffee and tea specialists): joined 1969, md 1970, chm 1975–; pres UK Coffee Trade Benevolent Soc; chm Mediation in Divorce 1997–2001, chm Richmond upon Thames Magistrates Court 2004–, chm London Bench Forum 2006–; govr RSC 1982–; treas: Harlequin FC 1971–78, Union Soc City of Westminster 1985–98, St Luke's Educnl Centre 1989–99; hon auditor Richmond upon Thames Disabled Assoc 1973–98, Master Billingsgate Ward Club 1987–88; Freeman City of London 1981, Master Worshipful Co of Carmen 1998, memb Worshipful Co of Parish Clerks 2000; FCA 1964; *Recreations* sailing, studying, skiing; *Clubs* Harlequin FC, Leander, Frinton Working Men's; *Style—* Telfer Saywell, Esq; ✉ 2 Cumberland Road, Kew Gardens, Richmond, Surrey TW9 3HQ (tel 020 8940 0298, fax 020 8287 3486); Layton Fern & Co Ltd, Fern House, Onslow Court, Kingsland, Basingstoke, Hampshire RG24 8QL (tel 01256 355661, fax 01256 355044)

SCADDING, Dr Glenis Kathleen; *b* 3 October 1947; *Educ* Newnham Coll Cambridge (sr scholar, MA), Middx Hosp Med Sch (Florence Johnstone and Stoney clinical studentship, Freeman scholar in obstetrics, MB BChir), Univ of Cambridge (MD, Ralph Noble prize); *m*; 4 c; *Career* house physician Middx Hosp 1972–73, house surgn Kettering Gen Hosp 1972–73, SHO in neurology Walton Hosp Liverpool 1973–74, MO Shining Hosp Pokhara Nepal 1974–75, SHO Med Unit Brompton Hosp 1974–75, Abbott research fell and hon registrar in endocrinology Royal Free Hosp 1976–80, hon lectr in med Royal Free Med Unit 1978, Wellcome research fell Dept of Neurological Scis 1980–83, sr registrar Dept of Immunology Middx Hosp 1983–87, conslt physician in rhinology and allergy Royal Nat Throat, Nose and Ear Hosp and hon sr lectr Dept of Immunology UCL Sch of Med 1987–, Joseph Sr White fell RCP 1988–92; memb: RSM (pres Section of Immunology), BMA, Br Soc for Immunology, Antibody Club, Br Soc for Allergy and Clinical Immunology (chm ENT/Allergy Immunology Sub-Ctee), Euro Rhinological Soc, Br Assoc of Paediatric Otolaryngologists; assoc memb: RCPath, Zoological Soc; FRCP 1995 (MRCP); *Books* Clinical Immunology (co-ed), Immunology of ENT Disorders (ed, 1995), Investigative Rhinology (with Prof V J Lund, 2004); *Style*— Dr Glenis K Scadding; ✉ Royal National Throat, Nose & Ear Hospital, Gray's Inn Road, London WC1X 8DA (tel 020 7915 1542, fax 020 7915 1430, e-mail g.scadding@ucl.ac.uk)

SCALES, Prunella Margaret Rumney; CBE (1992); da of John Richardson Illingworth (d 1977), and Catherine, *née* Scales (d 1982); *Educ* Moira House Eastbourne, Old Vic Theatre Sch London; *m* 1963, Timothy West, *qv*, s of H Lockwood West, of Brighton, E Sussex; 2 s (Samuel, *qv*, b 1966, Joseph b 1969); *Career* actress, dir and teacher; frequent broadcasts, readings, poetry recitals and fringe productions, has directed plays at Bristol Old Vic, Arts Theatre Cambridge, Billingham Forum, Almost Free Theatre London, Nottingham Playhouse, West Yorkshire Playhouse and Nat Theatre of WA Perth; teacher at several drama schools; Hon DLitt: Univ of Bradford 1995, UEA 1996; *Theatre* seasons at Stratford-on-Avon and Chichester Festival Theatre 1967–68; credits incl: The Promise 1967, Hay Fever 1968, It's a Two-Foot-Six-Inches-Above-The-Ground-World 1970, The Wolf 1975, Breezeblock Park 1978, Make and Break (Haymarket) 1980, An Evening with Queen Victoria 1980, The Merchant of Venice 1981, Quartermaine's Terms (Queen's) 1981, When We Are Married (Whitehall) 1986, Single Spies (RNT) 1989, School for Scandal (RNT) 1990, Long Day's Journey into Night (RNT) 1991, Some Singing Blood (Royal Court) 1992, The Editing Process (Royal Court) 1995, Staying On 1997, Just the Three of Us 1997, The Birthday Party 1999, The Cherry Orchard 2000, The External 2001, A Day in the Death of Joe Egg 2001, Too Far to Walk (King's Head) 2002, A Woman of No Importance (Theatre Royal London) 2004, Gertrude's Secret (New End Theatre London) 2007; *Television* incl: Sybil Fawlty in Fawlty Towers (BBC) 1975–79, Doris and Doreen, A Wife like the Moon, Grand Duo, The Merry Wives of Windsor 1982, Outside Edge, Mapp and Lucia 1985, After Henry 1990, The Rector's Wife (Channel 4) 1994, Signs and Wonders (BBC) 1994, The World of Lee Evans (Channel 4) 1995, Searching (ITV) 1995, Emma (Meridian/ITV) 1996, Lord of Misrule (BBC) 1996, Breaking the Code (BBC) 1996, Midsomer Murders, The Ghost of Greville Lodge 2000, Looking for Victoria, Mr Loveday's Little Outing 2006; *Films* incl: The Lonely Passion of Judith Hearne 1989, A Chorus of Disapproval 1989, Howards End 1990, Wolf 1994, An Awfully Big Adventure 1994, Stiff Upper Lips 1996, An Ideal Husband 1999; *Recreations* gardening, canal boat; *Style*— Prunella Scales, CBE; ✉ c/o Conway van Gelder Ltd, 18–21 Jermyn Street, London SW1Y 6HP (tel 020 7287 0077, fax 020 7287 1940)

SCALLY, Dr Gabriel John; s of Bernard Gabriel Scally, and Maureen, *née* Hopkins; *b* 24 September 1954; *Educ* St Mary's GS Belfast, Queen's Univ Belfast (MB BCh, BAO), London Sch of Hygiene and Tropical Med London (MSc), FFPHM, MFPHMI, MRCGP; *m* 1990, Rona Margaret, *née* Campbell; 2 da; *Career* trainee in gen practice 1980–81, sr tutor Dept of Community Med Queen's Univ Belfast 1984–86, chief admin MO and dir of public health Eastern Health and Social Servs Bd Belfast 1989–93 (conslt in public health med 1986–88); regnl dir of public health: SE Thames RHA 1993–94, S and W RHA 1994–96, SW Region 1996–; memb: NI Bd for Nursing, Health Visiting and Midwifery 1988–93, Cncl BMA 1985–86 and 1988–89 (chm Jr Membs Forum 1988–89), GMC 1989–99, Nat Treatment Agency for Substance Misuse 2004–; author of papers on med research and health policy in med jls; *Recreations* sailing, traditional and contemporary Irish music, theatre, London Irish RFC; *Style*— Dr Gabriel Scally; ✉ 11 Dowry Square, Bristol BS8 4SH (tel 0117 926 8510); Regional Public Health Group, Government Office for the South West, 2 Rivergate Temple Quay, Bristol BS1 6ED (tel 0117 900 3530, fax 0117 900 1911, e-mail gscally.gosw@go-regions.gsi.gov.uk)

SCAMELL, Ernest Harold; s of Capt Ernest Harold Scamell (d 1981), and Lilian Kate, *née* Hall; *b* 9 March 1928; *Educ* Frays Coll Uxbridge, King's Coll London (LLB, LLM, AKC); *m* 1, 22 Aug 1952 (m dis), Patricia Annie, da of Percy Bullock (d 1979); 2 s (Grant b 11 Nov 1956, Adrian b 9 July 1958), 2 da (Joanna b 9 May 1960, Amanda b 19 Oct 1963); *m* 2, 11 Sept 1977, Ragnhild Bennedsen, da of Viggo Holdt, of Nyborg, Denmark; 1 step s (Cleere b 16 Nov 1967); *Career* called to the Bar Lincoln's Inn 1949; memb Hogarth Chambers 5 New Sq Lincoln's Inn until 2005 (head of chambers at 5 New Sq 1971–91); vice-provost UCL 1978–84, prof emeritus of English law Univ of London 1990– (reader 1960–66, prof 1966–90); memb Bar Cncl; *Books* Land Covenants (1996), Butterworths Property Law Handbook (6 edn 2005); *Recreations* dog walking, moving house; *Clubs* Holy Trinity Meccano, The George Formby Soc; *Style*— Ernest Scamell; ✉ The White House, 273 Sandown Road, Deal, Kent CT14 6QU (tel 01304 371280, e-mail ernest@scamell.com)

SCANLAN, Charles Denis; s of late Francis Joseph Winsloe Scanlan, and late Eileen, *née* Terry; *b* 23 December 1944; *Educ* St Benedict's Sch Ealing, Balliol Coll Oxford (BA); *m* 11 Sept 1971, Dorothy, da of late Frederick Albert Quick, of Laleston, Mid Glam; 2 s (Christopher b 1977, Stephen b 1980); *Career* admitted slr 1970; Simmons & Simmons: articled clerk 1967–70, asst slr 1970–73, ptnr 1973–; Freeman City Slrs Co; memb Law Soc; *Books* Know Your Rights (jtly, 1975), Pensions: The New Regime (jtly, 1997); *Style*— Charles Scanlan, Esq; ✉ Simmons & Simmons, CityPoint, One Ropemaker Street, London EC2Y 9SS (tel 020 7628 2020, fax 020 7628 2070)

SCANLON, Mary; MSP; da of John Charles Campbell (d 1981), and Anne, *née* O'Donnell (d 2001); *b* 25 May 1947; *Educ* Craigo Secdy Sch Montrose, Univ of Dundee (MA); *m* 26 Sept 1970, James Scanlon; 1 da (Claire b 26 Jan 1973), 1 s (Grant James b 11 Oct 1974); *Career* various admin and secretarial posts 1963–70; lectr: Dundee Inst of Technol 1982–85, Perth Coll 1985–88, Univ of Abertay 1988–94, Inverness Coll 1994–99; MSP (Cons) Highlands and Islands 1999–; MIPD; *Recreations* hill walking, swimming, gardening; *Style*— Mary Scanlon, MSP; ✉ 25 Miller Street, Inverness IV2 3DN (tel 01463 718951, fax 01463 241164); The Scottish Parliament, Edinburgh EH99 1SP (tel 0131 348 5650, fax 0131 348 5656, mobile 07775 830480, e-mail mary.scanlon.msp@scottish.parliament.uk)

SCANNELL, Rick; *Educ* Univ of East London (BA), Univ of Cambridge (LLM); *Career* called to the Bar 1986; practising barr specialising in immigration and asylum cases, currently memb of chambers 2 Garden Court; notable cases in House of Lords incl: Oladehinde and Alexander v Sec of State for the Home Dept (SSHD) 1991, M v Home Office 1994, T v SSHD 1996, Sepet and Bulbul v SSHD 2001, Saadi and others v SSHD 2001; chair Immigration Law Practitioners' Assoc (ILPA) 2000– (memb 1983–); special advocate Special Immigration Appeals Cmmn 1998–; memb: Administrative Law Bar Assoc, Justice, Haldane Soc, Legal Action; *Publications* Immigration: Recent Developments (co-writer, 1985–2003), Current Law (edns 1996, 1997, 1999 and 2002), Butterworths Immigration Law Service (co-ed, 1997–), Immigration, Nationality and Asylum under the Human Rights Act 1998 (contrib, 1999), Macdonald's Immigration Law and Practice (contrib, 5 edn 2001, 6 edn 2004) Freedom of Movement of Persons in the Enlarged European Union (co-writer, 2004), Halsbury's Laws of England, Vol 4 (2): British Nationality, Immigration and Asylum (contrib); *Recreations* circus skills (flying trapeze,

acro-balance, unicycling and juggling), car and motorbike racing; *Style*— Rick Scannell, Esq

SCANNELL, Vernon; *b* 23 January 1922; *Educ* Univ of Leeds; *m* 1 Oct 1954, Josephine, da of Lt-Col Claude Higson, of Edenbridge, Kent; 2 da (Jane b 1955, Nancy b 1957), 3 s (Toby b 1959, John b 1961, Jacob b 1967); *Career* 70 Bn Argyll & Sutherland Highlanders 1940–42, 5/7 Bn Gordon Highlanders 1942–45; poet in residence: Berinsfield Oxfordshire 1975–76, King's Sch Canterbury 1979, Wakefield Dist Coll 1987, Mount Sch York 1987; awards: Heinemann Award for Lit 1961, Cholmondeley Poetry Prize 1974, Travelling Scholarship Soc of Authors 1987; FRSL 1961; *Books* A Sense of Danger (1962), Walking Wounded (1965), Epithets of War (1968), The Tiger and the Rose, An Autobiography (1971), New and Collected Poems (1980), Argument of Kings (1987), A Time For Fires (1991), Drums of Morning - Growing Up in the Thirties (1992), Collected Poems 1950–1993 (1993), The Black and White Days, Poems (1996), Views and Distances: Poems (2000), Feminine Endings (2000), Of Love and War - New and Selected Poems (2002); *Style*— Vernon Scannell, Esq, FRSL; ✉ 51 North Street, Otley, West Yorkshire LS21 1AH (tel 01943 467176)

SCARBOROUGH, Vernon Marcus; s of George Arthur Scarborough (d 1962), of London, and Sarah Florence, *née* Patey (d 1986); *b* 11 February 1940; *Educ* Brockley Co GS, Westminster Coll; *m* 1966, Jennifer Bernadette, *née* Keane, da of Capt Barney St John Keane; 3 da (Rowena b 1970, Karen b 1972, Ursula b 1980); *Career* HM Dip Serv: CRO 1961, Bombay, Dacca 1962, CRO 1964 Karachi 1965, vice-consul Brussels 1969, third sec Banjul 1971, second sec FCO 1977, second sec Muscat, HM consul Lagos 1980, first sec Kuala Lumpur 1984, first sec FCO 1987, chargé d'affaires San Salvador 1988, dep consul-gen Auckland 1990, dep head of mission Suva and HM ambass to Palau, Federated States of Micronesia, Marshall Islands 1995–2000, dep high cmmr Tarawa 2002–05, ret; memb Cncl Pacific Soc of UK and Ireland (PSUKI); *Recreations* photography, golf; *Clubs* Royal Commonwealth Soc, Defence (Fiji), Rotary (Fiji), Returned Servicemen's and Ex-Servicemen's Assoc (Fiji); *Style*— Vernon Scarborough, Esq

SCARD, Dennis Leslie; s of late Charles Leslie Scard (d 1998), of Harrow, and Doris Annie Scard (d 1976); *b* 8 May 1943; *Educ* Lascelles County Secdy Sch, Trinity Coll of Music; *m* Linda Christine, *née* Perry; 2 s from prev m (Timothy Martin b 27 Feb 1969, Christopher Robin b 18 July 1974); *Career* professional musician (horn player) 1962–85 (worked with various symphony and chamber orchs and other musical combinations, opera, ballet, recording and theatre work); Musicians' Union: memb Exec Ctee 1979–85, dist official E and NE area 1985–90, gen sec 1990–2000; chair Shoreham Port Authy; memb Bd Symphony Hall/Town Hall Birmingham; memb Central Arbitration Ctee DTI, lay memb Employment Tbnl Serv; chair Music Students Hostel Tst; Hon FTCL; memb Royal Soc of Musicians 1983, FRSA; *Recreations* music, theatre, cooking, walking; *Style*— Dennis Scard, Esq; ✉ 6 Cranborne Avenue, Meads, Eastbourne, East Sussex BN20 7TS (tel and fax 01323 648364, e-mail calverton100@hotmail.com)

SCARDINO, Dame Marjorie Morris; DBE (2001); da of Robert Weldon Morris (d 1990), of Texas, and Beth, *née* Lamb; *b* 25 January 1947; *Educ* Baylor Univ TX (BA), George Washington Univ Law Sch, Univ of San Francisco Law Sch (JD); *m* 1974, Albert J Scardino; 1 da (Adelaide b 1978), 2 s (William b 1979, Albert b 1984); *Career* ptnr Brannen Wessels Searcy law firm Savannah Ga 1975–85, publisher The Georgia Gazette 1978–85 (winner Pulitzer Prize 1983), pres The Economist Newspaper Gp Inc New York 1985–92, chief exec The Economist Gp plc London 1992–96, gp chief exec Pearson plc 1997–; non-exec dir Nokia Corp; memb various charitable and advsy bds incl: The Carter Center, John D and Catherine T MacArthur Fndn, V&A; *Style*— Dame Marjorie Scardino, DBE; ✉ Pearson plc, 80 Strand, London WC2R 0RL

SCARFE, Gerald Anthony; s of Reginald Thomas Scarfe, and Dorothy Edna, *née* Gardner; *b* 1 June 1936; *m* Jane Asher, *qv*, da of Dr Richard Asher (d 1968), of London; 1 da (Katie Geraldine b 11 April 1974), 2 s (Alexander David b 16 Dec 1981, Rory Christopher b 10 Dec 1983); *Career* designer and director; political cartoonist of the Sunday Times 1967–; designer and dir of animation Pink Floyd's The Wall (MGM); exhbns: UK tour 2001 and 2003, Sheffield Galleries 2005, Fine Art Soc 2005; 6 sculptures of the Br Character (Millennium Dome) 2000; Hon Dr Arts Univ of Liverpool, Hon DLitt Univ of Kent, Hon DLitt Univ of Dundee 2007; *Theatre* numerous scenery and costume credits incl: Orpheus in the Underworld (London Coliseum), What a Lucky Boy (Manchester Royal Exchange), Ubu Unchained (Traverse Theatre), Magic Flute (LA Opera), An Absolute Turkey (Globe), Mind Millie for Me (Haymarket), Scarfe at the NPG (one man show at Nat Portrait Gallery) 1998, Fantastic Mr Fox (LA Opera) 1998, The Magic Flute (Seattle Opera) 1999 and (San Francisco Opera) 2007, Peter and the Wolf (Holiday on Ice Paris and world tour) 2000, The Nutcracker (ENB London Coliseum and nat tour) 2002–03, animation sequence for Miss Saigon (UK tour) 2004–05; *Television* dir of films for the BBC: Hogarth 1970, Scarfe by Scarfe 1986, Scarfe's Follies 1987, I Like The Girls Who Do 1988, Scarfe on... 1989, Scarfe on Sex 1991, Scarfe on Art 1991, Scarfe in Paradise 1992, Scarfe on Class 1993; *Film* prodn designer and character design for Walt Disney's Hercules 1997; *Books* Scarfe by Scarfe (1986), Scarfe's Seven Deadly Sins (1987), Scarfe's Line of Attack (1988), Scarfeland (1989), Scarfe on Stage (1992), Scarfe Face (1993), Hades - The Truth at Last (1997), Heroes and Villains (2003), Gerald Scarfe: Drawing Blood (2005); *Recreations* skiing; *Clubs* Brooks's; *Style*— Gerald Scarfe, Esq

SCARFFE, Prof (John) Howard; s of late Andrew Ernest Scarffe, of Douglas, IOM, and Nancy May, *née* Fargher; *b* 11 March 1947; *Educ* King William's Coll IOM, St Bartholomew's Hosp Med Coll Univ of London (MB BS, MD); *m* 8 Jan 1972, Sheila Elizabeth, da of Alfred Coyte, of Broadstairs, Kent; 1 s (Christopher), 1 da (Elizabeth); *Career* house surgn Addenbrooke's Hosp Cambridge 1971–72, sr house offr gen med Bart's 1972–74 (house physician 1971); Univ of Manchester: lectr and hon registrar 1974–76, lectr and hon sr registrar 1976–80, sr lectr and hon conslt 1980–91, reader and hon conslt 1991–96, prof of med oncology and hon conslt 1996–99; dir Regnl Acute Leukaemia and Bone Marrow Transplant Unit Christie Hosp, med dir and head of careers The Wellcome Tst 2000–01, conslt med oncologist E and N Herts Cancer Unit 2002–06; contrib chapters to a number of oncological textbooks; memb: Teaching Faculty Int Union Against Cancer 1980, S Manchester Health Authy 1983–89, NW Regnl Advsy Ctee for Oncology Services 1985–91, Assoc of Cancer Physicians Ctee 1991–94, Ctee on Safety of Meds Med Control Agency 2000–01, Academic Ctee RCP 2000–01; MRCS 1970, FRCP 1986 (MRCP 1973, LRCP 1970); *Recreations* rugby, walking, reading; *Clubs* Lymm Rugby Football; *Style*— Prof J Howard Scarffe; ✉ Westcroft, 46 The Crofts, Castletown, Isle of Man IM9 1LZ (tel 01624 823443, e-mail hscarffe@manx.net)

SCARISBRICK, Diana; da of Charles Wood (d 1994), and Genevieve, *née* Sutherland (d 1995); *b* 8 October 1928; *Educ* Christ's Hosp, St Hugh's Coll Oxford (exhibitioner, MA); *m* 5 July 1955, Peter Ewald Scarisbrick, s of Charles Ewald Scarisbrick (d 1966); 1 da (Sophie Hastings-Bass b 15 May 1956); *Career* freelance lectr and writer on jewellery and engraved gems; jewellery ed Harpers & Queen Magazine 1990–93; contrib to: Burlington Magazine, Apollo Magazine, Country Life, Il Giornale Dell'Arte, exhibition and museum catalogues in Britain, Sweden, Germany, France, USA and Japan; memb: Soc of Antiquaries, Soc of Jewellery Historians; *Books* The Ralph Harari Collection of Finger Rings (with Prof John Boardman, 1977), Jewellery (1984), Il Valore Dei Gioielli e Degli Orologi da Collezione (1984 and 1987), 2500 Years of Rings (1988), Ancestral Jewels (1989), Rings (1993), Jewels in Britain 1066–1837 (1994), Classical Gems, Ancient and Modern Intaglios and Cameos in the Fitzwilliam Museum, Cambridge (with Dr Martin Henig and Mary Whiting, 1994), Tudor and Jacobean Jewellery (1995), Chaumet, Master

S

Jewellers from 1780 (1995), Chaumet: Two Centuries of Fine Jewellery (catalogue of exhbn at Musée Carnavalet Paris, 1998), Crowning Glories: Two Centuries of Tiaras (catalogue of exhbn at Museum of Fine Arts Boston, 2000), Three Thousand Years of Rings (catalogue of exhbn of Hashimoto ring collection at Teien Met Art Museum Tokyo, 2000), From the Renaissance to Art Deco: Jewellery 1540–1940 (catalogue of exhbn at Teien Met Art Museum Tokyo 2003), Historic Rings: Four Thousand Years of Craftsmanship (2004), Napoléon Amoureux (exhbn at 12 Place Vendôme, Paris 2004), Dignity and Beauty: The Story of the Tiara (exhbn at Bunkamura Museum Tokyo 2007); *Recreations* walking, sight-seeing; *Style—* Mrs Diana Scarisbrick; ✉ 11 Chester Terrace, London NW1 4ND (tel 020 7935 9928, e-mail dianascarisbrick@aol.com)

SCARISBRICK, Prof John Joseph; s of Thomas Stuart (d 1934), and Margaret Mary Baines (d 1972); *b* 6 October 1938, London; *Educ* John Fisher Sch Purley, Christ's Coll Cambridge (MA, PhD); *m* 2 Jan 1965, Nuala Ann, *née* Izod; 2 da (Emma Mary b 14 May 1966, Sarah Ann b 29 April 1968); *Career* lectr in history QMC London 1954–69, prof of history Univ of Warwick 1969–94; visiting lectr: Univ of Ghana 1959–60, Wellesley Coll MA 1967–68; co-fndr and chm LIFE 1970–, chair Zoe's Place Tst; FRHistS 1958, FRSL 1968; *Publications* Henry VIII (1968), The Reformation and the English People (1984); *Recreations* listening to music, DIY, fighting weeds; *Style—* Prof John Scarisbrick; ✉ 35 Kenilworth Road, Leamington Spa, Warwickshire CV32 6JG (tel 01926 428255, fax 01926 336497)

SCARLETT, Sir John McLeod; KCMG (2007, CMG 2001), OBE (1987); s of Dr James Henri Stuart Scarlett (d 1961), of Bromley, Kent, and Clara Dunlop, *née* Morton (d 2006); *Educ* Epsom Coll, Magdalen Coll Oxford (MA); *m* 1970, Gwenda Mary Rachel, da of Norman Howard Stilliard; 3 da (Alexia b 1971, Victoria b 1976, Rhiannon b 1979), 1 s (John b 1986); *Career* joined HM Dip Serv 1971, third sec Nairobi 1973–74, second sec Moscow 1976–77; first sec: FCO 1977–84, Paris 1984–88, FCO 1988–91; political cnsllr Moscow 1991–94, cnsllr FCO 1994–2001, chm Jt Intelligence Ctee 2001–04, chief Secret Intelligence Service (MI6) 2004–; *Clubs* Oxford and Cambridge; *Style—* Sir John Scarlett, KCMG, OBE

SCARONI, Paolo; *b* 1946, Vicenza, Italy; *Educ* Bocconi Univ Milan, Columbia Univ NY (MBA); *Career* exec positions Saint Gobain Gp 1973–84 (head Flat Glass Div 1984), vice-chm and ceo Techint SpA 1985–96, gp chief exec Pilkington plc 1996–2002, chief exec Enel SpA 2002–05, ceo ENI SpA 2005–; non-exec chm Alliance UniChem plc 2005– (non-exec dir 2002–); non-exec dir: BAE Systems plc 2000–04, Marzotto SpA; memb Supervisory Bd ABN AMRO Bank NV; memb Exec Ctee Confindustria, pres Unindustria Venezia, memb Bd Columbia Univ Business Sch NY; *Style—* Paolo Scaroni, Esq; ✉ Alliance UniChem plc, Alliance House, 2 Heath Road, Weybridge, Surrey KT13 8AP

SCARPELLO, Dr John Hugh; s of late William John Scarpello, of Nottingham, and Pauline Frances, *née* Berney; *b* 23 July 1947; *Educ* Haberdashers' Aske's, Univ of Wales Coll of Med (MB BCh, MD); *m* 20 April 1974, Barbara Jean, da of William John Erasmus; 2 da (Kay Elizabeth b 11 July 1975, Tracey Jane b 30 July 1977), 1 s (Robert John b 27 April 1981); *Career* house offr Univ Hosp of Wales 1971–72, SHO Nottingham Gen Hosp 1972–74, med registrar Royal Hosp Sheffield 1974–76, sr registrar Royal Hallamshire Hosp 1976–81, hon clinical tutor Univ of Sheffield 1976–81, conslt physician Univ Hosp of N Staffs 1981–, sr lectr Keele Univ 1992– (formerly sr research fell); memb: Scientific Section Diabetes UK, Euro Assoc for Study of Diabetes; FRCP 1989 (MRCP 1974); *Recreations* swimming, walking; *Style—* Dr John Scarpello; ✉ Newlyn, Seabridge Lane, Newcastle, Staffordshire ST5 3LS (tel 01782 613682); Department of Diabetes and Endocrinology, University Hospital of North Staffordshire, Stoke-on-Trent, Staffordshire ST4 6QG (tel 01782 553425, fax 01782 553427)

SCASE, Prof Richard; *Educ* Thetford GS, Univ of Leicester (MA), Univ of Kent (PhD); *m* 1967 (m dis 1987), Anita Scase; 2 da (Camilla b 23 June 1969, Katrina b 10 March 1976); *Career* research fell Univ of East Anglia 1965–67; Univ of Kent: asst lectr 1967–69, lectr 1969–76, sr lectr 1976–84, prof of organisational behaviour 1984–; currently prof of mgmnt Univ of Kent; visiting prof: Univ of London, Univ of Auckland, Monash Univ Aust, Tilburg Univ the Netherlands, Univ of Essex; fndr media co part of Capital Gp UK; fndr (with two others) business to business co providing on-line learning materials for corp mgmnt devpt progs; memb: DTI Retail and Consumer Services Panel, DTI Design for Living in an Ageing Soc Working Gp, EC Working Pty 1998–2000; keynote speaker at corp and indust events; voted by Personnel Today as ninth most influential person in Br on personnel and human resource mgmnt; *Publications* 21 authored and co-authored books incl Reluctant Managers (1989) and Corporate Realities (1995), Britain 2010: The Changing Business Landscape (2000), Living in the Corporate 200 (2002); contrib to national newspapers, professional magazines, radio and tv progs; *Clubs* Athenaeum; *Style—* Prof Richard Scase; ✉ University of Kent at Canterbury, 10 St Stephen's Hill, Canterbury, Kent CT2 7AX (tel 01227 764000, e-mail r.scase@ukc.ac.uk, website www.sfb.co.uk/portfolio/richardscase)

SCHAEFER, Prof Stephen Martin; s of Gerhardt Martin Schaefer, OBE (d 1986), of Bramhall, Cheshire, and Helga Maria Schaefer (d 1992); *b* 18 November 1946; *Educ* Manchester Grammar, Univ of Cambridge (MA), Univ of London (PhD); *m* 26 July 1969, Teresa Evelyn; 2 s (Maximilian b 1974, Joshua b 1977); *Career* London Business Sch: research offr, sr research offr and lectr 1970–79; asst prof Stanford Univ 1979–81; London Business Sch: sr research fell and prof of finance 1981–, dir Inst of Fin and Accounting 1985–92, research dean 1992–95; visiting asst prof: Univ of Chicago, Univ of Calif Berkeley 1977; visiting prof: Univ of Venice 1991, Univ of Cape Town 1996; dir: Lawtex plc 1974–91, Securities Assoc 1990–91, Securities and Futures Authy 1991–96, Tokai Derivative Products Ltd 1998–99; non-exec dir: Tokai Bank Europe 2000–02, Leo Fund Managers 2004–; tstee Smith Breeden Mutual Funds 1992–2000; memb American Fin Assoc; *Style—* Prof Stephen Schaefer; ✉ London Business School, Sussex Place, Regents Park, London NW1 4SA (tel 020 7262 5050, fax 020 7724 3317, e-mail sschaefer@london.edu)

SCHAFF, Alistair Graham; QC (1999); s of John Schaff, and Barbara Dorothy, *née* Williams; *b* 25 September 1959; *Educ* Bishop's Stortford Coll, Magdalene Coll Cambridge (MA); *m* 13 April 1991, (Marie) Leona, *née* Burley; 1 s (Dominic Michael b 21 Jan 1994), 1 da (Eleanor Marcella b 4 Sept 1996); *Career* called to the Bar 1983; *Recreations* family life, foreign travel, history, spectator sports; *Style—* Alistair Schaff, Esq, QC; ✉ 7 King's Bench Walk, Temple, London EC4Y 7DS (tel 020 7583 0404, fax 020 7583 0950, e-mail clerks@7kbw.law.co.uk)

SCHAPIRA, Prof Anthony Henry Vernon; s of Marcus Schapira (d 1994), of Yorkshire, and Hannah Constance (d 1982); *Educ* Bradford GS, Westminster Med Sch (entrance scholar, Berridge research scholar, BSc, MB BS, MD, DSc, AKC); *m* 1; 1 da (Sarah Victoria Constance b 1983); m 2, 2003, Laura, da of Robert Swan Johnson; *Career* house physician to Sir Richard Bayliss, Chief Physician to HM The Queen 1979, med trg Hammersmith and Whittington Hosps, Nat Hosp for Neurology and Neurosurgery and St Thomas' Hosp 1980–84, trg in neurology Royal Free Hosp and Nat Hosp for Neurology and Neurosurgery 1983–88, Wellcome research fell 1985–87; Royal Free and UC Med Sch and Inst of Neurology London: sr lectr and conslt in neurology 1988–90, univ chair of clinical neurosciences 1990–; conslt neurologist Royal Free Hosp, Nat Hosp for Neurology and Neurosurgery; hon prof of neurology Mount Sinai Med Sch NY 1995; Queen Square Prize 1986, Graham Bull Prize for Clinical Sci RCP 1995, European Prize for Clinical Science 1998, Buckston Browne Medal Harveian Soc 1995, Opprecht Prize 1999, Duchenne Prize 2005; memb: Movement Disorders Soc, Harveian Soc 1994; FRCP 1992, FMedSci 1999; *Books* Mitochondrial Disorders in Neurology (1994), Mitochondria: DNA, Protein and Disease (1994), Muscle Diseases (1999), Clinical Cases in Neurology (2001), Mitrochondrial Disorders in Neurology 2 (2002), Mitochondrial Function and Dysfunction (2002), Current Treatment of Parkinson's Disease (2005), Textbook of Neurology and Clinical Neuroscience (2005); *Recreations* chess (Yorkshire champion 1966), motor racing, European history, international affairs; *Style—* Prof Anthony Schapira; ✉ University Department of Clinical Neurosciences, Royal Free and University College Medical School, Rowland Hill Street, London NW3 2PF (tel 020 7830 2012, fax 020 7431 1577)

SCHEER, Cherrill Sheila; da of Maurice Hille (d 1968), and Ray Hille (d 1986); *b* 29 March 1939; *Educ* Copthall Co GS, Architectural Assoc London, Architectural Dept Kingston Sch of Art; *m* 3 Dec 1961, Ian Scheer, s of Oscar Scheer (d 1988); 1 s (Ivan), 1 da (Danielle Ann (Mrs Benson)); *Career* mktg dir Hille International Ltd 1970–83 (mktg mangr 1961–70); dir: Print Forum Ltd 1965–, S Hille & Co (Holdings) Ltd 1970–; dir gp mktg: Hille Ergonom plc 1983–89, Scott Howard Furniture Ltd 1989–91, Cherrill Scheer & Associates 1991–; congress dir Design Renaissance 1993 Int Design Congress; vice-pres Design & Industry Assoc (chm 1976–78); govr London Met Univ; memb Office Furniture, Furniture and Filing Mfrs' Assoc (past chm); hon fell in design Arts Inst at Bournemouth; Liveryman Worshipful Co of Furniture Makers; FCSD (past memb Cncl), FInstSMM, FRSA; *Style—* Mrs Cherrill Scheer; ✉ 16 Kerry Avenue, Stanmore, Middlesex HA7 4NN (tel 020 8954 3839); Cherrill Scheer & Associates, Hille House, 132 St Albans Road, Watford, Hertfordshire WD24 4AE (tel 01923 242769, fax 01923 228110, e-mail csa@hillehouse.co.uk)

SCHERER, Paul Joseph; s of François Joseph Scherer (d 1961), of Folkestone, Kent, and Florence, *née* Haywood (d 1977); *b* 28 December 1933; *Educ* Stonyhurst; *m* 4 April 1959, Mary, da of Claude Fieldus; 1 s (Jonathan b 9 Nov 1961), 3 da (Clare b 14 March 1963, Joanna b 26 June 1965, Lucy b 3 Jan 1968); *Career* Nat Serv 1952–54, cmmnd Buffs (Royal E Kent Regt); Bailey Bros & Swinfen Ltd 1954–56, jr ed G Bell & Sons Ltd 1956–58, sales mangr Penguin Books 1958–63, gp sales dir Paul Hamlyn Ltd 1963–68, md Int Div William Collins Sons & Co Ltd 1968–77, pres Collins & World USA 1974–75, md Mills & Boon Ltd 1977–82; Transworld Publishers Ltd: md and chief exec 1982–95, chm 1995–96; sr vice-pres Bantam Doubleday Dell Publishing Group Inc 1990–98, dir Book Tokens Ltd 1995–2002, chm Curtis Brown Ltd 1996–2004, vice-chm Bloomsbury Publishing plc 2004–06 (dir 1993–2006); memb Bd: Book Devpt Cncl 1971–74, Book Mktg Cncl 1977–84 (chm 1982–84), British Library 1996–2000; pres The Book Trade Benevolent Soc 1995–98; Publishers Assoc: memb Cncl 1982–84 and 1989–94, vice-pres 1990 and 1993, pres 1991–93; fndr chm Unicorn Sch Kew 1970–73, govr Worth Sch 1993–96; chm Whizzkidz 1998–2000 (tstee 1996–2002); *Clubs* Hurlingham, Garrick; *Style—* Paul Scherer, Esq; ✉ 18 Carlyle Mansions, Cheyne Walk, London SW3 5LS

SCHIEMANN, Rt Hon Sir Konrad Hermann Theodor; kt (1986), PC (1995); s of Helmuth Schiemann (d 1945), and Beate, *née* von Simson (d 1946); *b* 15 September 1937; *Educ* King Edward's Sch Birmingham, Freiburg Univ, Pembroke Coll Cambridge (MA, LLB); *m* 1965, Elisabeth Hanna Eleonore, da of late John Holroyd-Reece; 1 da (Juliet b 1966); *Career* called to the Bar Inner Temple 1962 (bencher 1985, reader 2002, treas 2003), jr counsel to the Crown (Common Law) 1978–80; QC 1980, recorder of the Crown Court 1985, judge of the High Court of Justice (Queen's Bench Div) 1986–95, a Lord Justice of Appeal 1995–2003, judge Court of Justice of the European Communities 2004–; chm Cncl St John's Smith Square 1995–2003 (memb 1984–95, tstee 1990–95), vice-chm Parole Bd 1991–92 (memb 1990): memb advsy bd: Centre for Euro Legal Studies Univ of Cambridge 1996–, Centre of Euro Private Law Münster Univ 1999–, Acad of European Law 2004–, European Competition Jl 2005–, European Law Review 2006–; memb Cncl of Mgmnt Br Inst of Int and Competition Law 2000–06; contrib to English and German legal books and journals; govr English Nat Ballet 1995–2001, dir Acad of Ancient Music 2001–03, vice-chm Temple Music Fndn 2002–03; patron Busoga Tst 1999– (chm 1989–99); hon fell Pembroke Coll Cambridge 1998; *Recreations* music, reading, walking, water sources in Uganda; *Style—* The Rt Hon Sir Konrad Schiemann

SCHIFF, Andras; s of Odon Schiff, and Klara, *née* Csengeri; *b* 21 December 1953; *Educ* Franz Liszt Acad of Music Budapest (with Pal Kadosa, Ferenc Rados and Gyorgy Kurtag), private study with George Malcolm; *m* Oct 1987, Yuuko, *née* Shiokawa; *Career* concert pianist; regular orchestral engagements: NY Philharmonic, Chicago Symphony, Vienna Philharmonic, Concertgebouw Orchestra, Orchestre de Paris, London Philharmonic, London Symphony, Royal Philharmonic, Philharmonia, Israel Philharmonic, Washington Nat Symphony; orchestral conductor: Baltimore Symphony, Chamber Orchestra of Europe, City of Birmingham Symphony, LA Philharmonic, Philadelphia, Philharmonia; cr Cappella Andrea Barca (own orch) 1999; festivals incl: Vienna, Feldkirch, Salzburg, Lucerne, Edinburgh; fndr and artistic dir Musiktage Mondsee Festival 1989–98, co-fndr (with Heinz Holliger) Ittinger Pfingst Konzerte Kartause Ittingen 1995, started Hommage to Palladio series Teatro Olimpico Vicenza 1998; *Awards* Premio della Academia Chigiana Siena 1987, Wiener Flotenuhr (Mozart Prize of the City of Vienna) 1989, Bartók Prize 1991, Instrumentalist of the Year Int Classical Music Awards 1992, Claudio Arrau Meml Medal Robert Schumann Soc 1994, Instrumentalist of the Year Royal Philharmonic Soc 1994, Kossuth Prize 1996, Leonie Sonnings Music Prize Copenhagen 1997, Penna d'Oro della Cittá di Vicenza 2003, Musikfest-Preis Bremen 2003; *Recordings* incl: all the Mozart Piano Concertos (with The Camerata Academica Salzburg and Sandor Vegh), Bach Concertos (with The Chamber Orchestra of Europe), all the Schubert Piano Sonatas, Mozart Sonatas and Chamber Music (on Mozart's own instruments), Beethoven Piano Concertos (with The Staatskapelle Dresden and Bernard Haitink), Bartok Piano Concertos (with The Budapest Festival Orchestra and Ivan Fischer), Lieder (with Peter Schreier, Robert Holl, Cecilia Bartoli and Juliane Banse); *Recreations* theatre, art, cinema, literature, languages, soccer; *Style—* Andras Schiff, Esq; ✉ c/o Terry Harrison Artists Management, The Orchard, Market Street, Charlbury, Oxfordshire OX7 3PJ (tel 01608 810330, fax 01608 811331, e-mail artists@harrisonturner.co.uk, website www.harrisonturner.co.uk)

SCHILD, Geoffrey Christopher; CBE (1993); s of Christopher Schild (d 1963), of Sheffield, and Georgina Schild (d 1970); *b* 28 November 1935; *Educ* High Storrs GS Sheffield, Univ of Reading (BSc), Univ of Sheffield (PhD), Univ of Reading (DSc); *m* 1 Aug 1961, Tora, da of Canon Peter Madland (d 1977), of Bergen, Norway; 2 s (Øystein Christopher b 1962, Peter Geoffrey b 1969), 1 da (Ingrid b 1965); *Career* lectr in virology Univ of Sheffield 1963–67; dir World Influenza Centre at MRC Nat Inst for Med Res 1969–75 (memb scientific staff MRC 1967–75), dir and chief exec Nat Inst for Biological Standards and Control 1985–2002 (head Div of Virology 1975–85), dir MRC Directed Prog of AIDS Res 1987–94; visiting prof in vaccinology Univ of Bergen 1998–; chm: MRC Working Gp on Hepatitis Vaccines, Euro Community Working Pty on Biotechnology 1986–93; memb: Dept of Health Jt Ctee on Vaccination and Immunisation 1975–, MRC Ctee on Vaccines and Immunological Procedures 1975–93, Ctee on Safety of Medicines, Sub-Ctee on Biologicals 1977–, Nat Biological Standards Bd 1985–, MRC Aids Research Co-ordinating Ctee; WHO: memb Special Advsy Gp on Vaccine Devpt 1989–, memb Advsy Task Force WHO Global Prog on Vaccines and Immunization, memb Strategic Task Force Children's Vaccine Initiative, memb Steering Ctee on AIDS Res 1989–; memb and vice-chm Bd of Tstees Int Vaccines Inst Seoul, memb Bd UK Health Protection Agency 2003–; professional affrs offr UK Soc for Gen Microbiology 2002–; visiting prof Univ of Bergen Norway 1996–, academic attachment Imperial Coll London; Freeman City of London 1988; Hon DSc Univ of Sheffield 2002; Hon FRCP 1999; FIBiol 1977, FRCPath

1993, FRCPEd 1998, FMedSci 2001; *Recreations* ornithology, music; *Style*— Dr Geoffrey C Schild, CBE; ✉ 17 Sunnyfield, Mill Hill, London NW7 4RD (tel 020 8959 5767, fax 020 8906 3978, e-mail the.schilds@btinternet.com)

SCHLAGMAN, Richard Edward; s of Jack Schlagman, of London, and Shirley, *née* Goldston (d 1992); *b* 11 November 1953; *Educ* UCS Hampstead, Brunel Univ; *Career* publisher; co-fndr, jt chm and md Interstate Electronics Ltd 1973–86, purchased Bush name from Rank Organisation and renamed IEL Bush Radio Ltd 1981, floated Bush Radio on London Stock Exchange 1984, Bush Radio plc sold 1986; acquired Phaidon Press Ltd 1990, chm and publisher Phaidon Press Ltd 1990–, pres Phaidon Press Inc 1998–; memb Bd Judd Fndn Texas 1999– (pres 1999–2001); memb: Exec Ctee Patrons of New Art Tate Gallery 1994–97, Alan Fletcher Circle of Patrons Design Museum; patron: Bayreuth, Salzburger Festspiele, Whitechapel Art Gallery, Schbertiade Festival, Acad de Verbier; memb: Royal Opera House Trust, Glyndebourne Festival Soc, Br Design and Art Direction; FRSA; *Recreations* music, art, architecture; *Clubs* Chelsea Arts; *Style*— Richard Schlagman, Esq; ✉ Phaidon Press Ltd, Regent's Wharf, All Saints Street, London N1 9PA (tel 020 7843 1000, fax 020 7843 1010)

SCHLEE, Ann Acheson; da of Duncan Cumming (d 1979), and Nancy Houghton Cumming (d 1967); *b* 26 May 1934; *Educ* Downe House, Somerville Coll Oxford (MA); *m* 27 July 1956, Nicholas Schlee; 3 da (Emily b 1958, Catherine b 1960, Hannah b 1965), 1 s (Duncan b 1963); *Career* writer; FRSL 1997; *Books* Rhine Journey (1981), The Proprietor (1983), Laing (1987), The Time in Aderra (1997); *Style*— Mrs Ann Schlee, FRSL; ✉ c/o Bruce Hunter, David Higham Associates, 5–8 Lower John Street, Golden Square, London W1R 4HA (tel 020 7437 7888, fax 020 7437 1072)

SCHMIDT, Michael Norton; OBE (2006); s of Carl Bernhardt Schmidt (d 1971), and Elizabeth Norton, *née* Hill (d 1990); *b* 2 March 1947; *Educ* The Hill Sch Pottstown PA, Christ's Hosp (ESU scholar), Harvard Univ, Wadham Coll Oxford (exhibitioner, MA, pres OU Poetry Soc); *m* (m dis), Claire Patricia Harman; 2 s (Charles Bernhardt b 1980, Benedict William b 1985), 1 da (Isabel Claire b 1982); *Career* fndr md and editorial dir Carcanet Press Ltd 1969–; Univ of Manchester: Gulbenkian fell of poetry 1971–74, special lectr and sr lectr in poetry Dept of English 1974–98, dir The Writing Sch (formerly The Poetry Centre) 1993–98, dir Writing Sch and prof of English Manchester Metropolitan Univ 1998–2005, prof of poetry Univ of Glasgow 2006–; fndr and gen ed PN Review (formerly Poetry Nation) 1972–; NW theatre critic The Independent 1986–88, Northern theatre critic The Daily Telegraph 1988–93; Br delegate at literary congresses in Liège Murcia Valencia and Paris; memb Arts Cncl Touring Panel 1991–94; adjudicator Translation Awards Br Comparative Literature Assoc 1992; advsr Finnish Literature Bd 1990–; selector Globe Theatre Awards 1993–95; dir Modern Poetry Archive Project Rylands; memb Finnish Literature Soc; FRSL 1994; *Books* British Poetry since 1960 (with G Lindop, 1972), Ten English Poets (1976), Flower and Song: Aztec Poetry (trans with E Kissam, 1977), Fifty Modern British Poets (1979), Fifty English Poets 1300–1900 (1979), Five American Poets (with J Mathias, 1979), Eleven British Poets (1980), British Poetry since 1970 (1980), The Colonist (published as Green Island in USA, 1983, LA Times Book Award, 1984), On Poets & Others (trans, 1986), The Dresden Gate (1988), Reading Modern Poetry (1989), New Poetries (1994), Lives of the Poets (1998), The First Poets: Lives of the Ancient Greek Poets (2004); *Poetry* Black Buildings (1969), It Was My Tree (1970), Bedlam and the Oakwood (1970), Desert of the Lions (1972), My Brother Gloucester (1976), A Change of Affairs (1978), Choosing a Guest (1983), The Love of Strangers (1988), Selected Poems (1996), The Harvill Book of Twentieth-Century Poetry in English (1999), The Story of Poetry (2001), Lives of the First Poets (2004); *Clubs* PEN, Savile; *Style*— Michael Schmidt, Esq, OBE, FRSL; ✉ c/o Carcanet Press Ltd, 4th Floor, Alliance House, 30 Cross Street, Manchester M2 7AQ (tel 0161 834 8730, fax 0161 832 0084)

SCHMIEGELOW, Ian Lunn; *b* 16 March 1943; *Educ* Oundle, Magdalene Coll Cambridge (MA); *m* 1, 1966, Penelope (d 1992); 3 da (Alexandra, Catrina, Antonia); m 2, 1997, Samantha; *Career* called to the Bar Inner Temple 1967, in practice 1967–69; Hambros Bank Ltd: joined 1969, dir 1978–85, exec dir 1982–85; sr vice-pres and chm Mgmnt Cncl for EMEA First National Bank of Chicago 1985–87, chm Hamilton Lunn Gp of Cos 1988–; *Clubs* Turf; *Style*— Ian Schmiegelow, Esq; ✉ Audley House, 13 Palace Street, London SW1E 5HX (tel 020 7630 3350. fax 020 7630 3360)

SCHOFIELD, Prof Andrew Noel; s of Rev John Nöel Schofield (d 1986), of Farnborough, Hants, and Winifred Jane Mary, *née* Eyles (d 1999); *b* 1 November 1930; *Educ* Mill Hill Sch, Christ's Coll Cambridge (MA, PhD); *m* 17 June 1961, Margaret Eileen, da of Oswald Green (d 1963), of Cambridge; 2 s (Ben b 1963, Matthew b 1965), 2 da (Polly b 1962, Tiffany b 1967); *Career* asst engr Scott Wilson Kirkpatrick & Ptnrs (Malawi) 1951–54, lectr Univ of Cambridge 1959–68 (res student and demonstrator 1954–59), res fell Caltech 1963–64, fell Churchill Coll Cambridge 1964–66 and 1974–, prof of civil engrg UMIST 1968–74, prof of engrg Univ of Cambridge 1974–98; chm: Andrew N Schofield & Assocs Ltd (ANS&A) 1984–2000, Centrifuge Instrumentation and Equipment Ltd (ciel) 1987–97; FICE 1972, FREng 1986, FRS 1992; *Books* Critical State Soil Mechanics (with C P Wroth, 1968), Land Disposal of Hazardous Waste (with J R Gronow and R K Jain, 1988), Centrifuges in Soil Mechanics (with W H Craig and R G James, 1988); *Style*— Prof Andrew N Schofield, FRS, FREng; ✉ Cambridge University Engineering Department, Trumpington Street, Cambridge CB2 1PZ (tel 01223 332717/460555, fax 01223 460777, e-mail ans@eng.cam.ac.uk)

SCHOFIELD, Angela Rosemary; da of Donald George Tym (d 1958), of Sheffield, and Clara Annie, *née* Bird; *b* 5 July 1951; *Educ* Grange GS Sheffield, Univ of York (BA); *m* 1989, Michael Schofield; *Career* higher clerical offr Royal Hosp Sheffield 1975–76, unit administrator Lightwood House Hosp Sheffield 1976–78, dep sector administrator Royal Infirmary Sheffield 1978–79, sr admin asst Sheffield Area Health Authy 1979–80; hosp administrator: Weston Park Hosp, Charles Clifford Dental Hosp Sheffield 1980–85; unit gen mangr: N Derbyshire Health Authy 1985–88, St Mary's Hosp Manchester 1988–89; sr fell Health Servs Mgmnt Unit Univ of Manchester 1989–92, chief exec Calderdale Healthcare NHS Trust 1992–95, formerly sr fell Health Servs Mgmnt Unit Univ of Manchester; chm: Regnl Cncl Trent Region IHSM 1986–87, Quality Assurance Ctee for Managing Health Servs IHSM; *Recreations* horse riding, golf; *Style*— Mrs Angela Schofield

SCHOFIELD, Dr Jennifer Anne; da of Stanley Stephen Goy (d 1979), and Mary Catherine, *née* Jones (d 2005); *b* 12 July 1946; *Educ* Rosebery GS Epsom, Middlesex Hospital Med Sch (MB BS); *m* 1 Oct 1977, Neil McCallum Schofield, s of Fred Schofield (d 2000); 3 s (Guy b 11 May 1980, Stuart b 25 Oct 1981, Max b 17 April 1992), 1 da (Olivia b 13 March 1983); *Career* ships surgn MN P&O Shipping Co 1973–74; anaesthetist Duchess of Kent Children's Hosp Hong Kong 1975–76, sr registrar in anaesthetics Hosp for Sick Children Gt Ormond St London 1977, med offr Grendon Underwood Prison Aylesbury 1979–81, conslt anaesthetist Stoke Mandeville Hosp Aylesbury 1981–2007 (clinical dir Critical Care Directorate 1996–99); chm Oxford Regnl Anaesthetic Advsy Ctee 1991–94; FRCA 1975; *Recreations* needlework, family life; *Style*— Dr Jennifer Goy; ✉ Perrotts Farm, Bicester Road, Long Crendon, Aylesbury, Buckinghamshire HP18 9BP (tel 01844 201585)

SCHOFIELD, Kenneth Douglas; CBE (1996); s of Douglas Joseph Schofield (d 1978), and Jessie, *née* Gray (d 1994); *b* 3 February 1946; *Educ* Auchterarder HS; *m* 12 June 1968, Evelyn May, da of Arthur Gordon Sharp (d 1973); 2 da (Susan b 28 Jan 1971, Evonne b 13 Nov 1973); *Career* mangr Dunblane branch Perth Trustee Savings Bank 1969–71 (joined 1962), dep to press and PR dir George Simms Organisation 1971–74, first exec dir PGA Tournament Players Div (now PGA European Tour) 1975–; memb Cncl Golf Fndn; assoc Savings Bank Inst 1966–71; *Books* Pro Golf (1972–75), John Player Golf Yearbook (1973–75); *Recreations* golf, all main sports, walking; *Clubs* Wentworth (hon memb), Crieff Golf (hon memb), Auchterarder Golf (hon memb), Foxhills Golf & County, Royal & Ancient, Caledonian; *Style*— Kenneth D Schofield, Esq, CBE; ✉ PGA European Tour, Wentworth Drive, Virginia Water, Surrey GU25 4LX (tel 01344 840400, fax 01344 840451, e-mail kschofield@europeantour.com)

SCHOFIELD, Paul Robert; s of Robert Schofield, of Blackburn, Lancs, and Margaret, *née* Platt; *b* 23 May 1955, Rossendale, Lancs; *Educ* St Mary's Coll GS Blackburn, Univ of Manchester (LLB), Coll of Law Chester; *m* Patricia, *née* Birkett; 2 da (Katy b 18 Feb 1982, Lucy b 15 July 1984), 1 s (James Paul b 14 Aug 1990); *Career* admitted slr 1980; Farleys Slrs: joined as trainee 1977, equity ptnr 1982–; supervisor Serious Fraud Panel 2000; duty slr 1984; memb: Law Soc 1980, Criminal Law Solicitors' Assoc 2000; *Recreations* travel, football, sailing, foreign property investment; *Clubs* Blackburn Rovers; *Style*— Paul Schofield, Esq; ✉ Farleys Solicitors, 22–27 Richmond Terrace, Blackburn BB1 7AQ (tel 01254 606000, fax 01254 272319, e-mail paul.schofield@farleys.com)

SCHOFIELD, Phillip Bryan; s of Brian Homer Schofield, and Patricia, *née* Parry; *b* 1 April 1962; *Educ* Newquay GS; *m* March 1993, Stephanie, da of John Lowe; 2 da (Molly b July 1993, Ruby b Jan 1996); *Career* BBC TV: anchorman Children's TV 1985–87, co-presenter (with Sarah Greene) Going Live until 1993, presenter Schofield's Europe 1990–93, presenter Television's Greatest Hits 1992–93, also The Movie Game (3 series), Schofield's Europe, Take Two (4 series); presenter: Schofield's TV Gold 1993–96, Schofield's Quest 1994–96, Talking Telephone Numbers 1994–, One in a Million 1996, National Lottery Winning Lines 2001–04 (BBC 1); co-host: Test the Nation 2002–04, This Morning 2002–, Best Ever... (ITV) 2004–, Dancing on Ice (ITV) 2006–; performed title role in Joseph and the Amazing Technicolor Dreamcoat (London Palladium 1992–93, nationwide tour 1993–96), title role in Doctor Dolittle 1998–2001; Top Man on TV 1987–88, Number 1 TV personality in all maj teenage magazines 1987–88, Best Dressed Man of the Year 1992, Variety Club Show Business Personality of the Year 1992; involved in: Children's Royal Variety Performance 1987–88, Royal Variety Performance 1992, Stars Orgn for Spastics, NSPCC, Br Heart Fndn; *Style*— Phillip Schofield, Esq; ✉ c/o James Grant Management, 94 Strand on the Green, London W4 3NN (tel 020 8742 1950, fax 020 8742 4951)

SCHOFIELD, Dr Roger Snowden; s of Ronald Snowden Schofield (d 1970), of Leeds, and Muriel Grace, *née* Braime (d 1972); *b* 26 August 1937; *Educ* Leighton Park Sch Reading, Clare Coll Cambridge (BA, PhD, LittD); *m* 3 Sept 1961; 1 da (Melanie b 1972); *Career* fell Clare Coll Cambridge 1969– (res fell 1962–65), sr res offr Cambridge Group 1966–73, dir SSRC Cambridge Group for the History of Population and Social Structure 1974–94, sr res assoc Cambridge Group for the History of Population and Social Structure 1994–97; hon readership in historical demography Univ of Cambridge 1991–97; ed: Local Population Studies 1968–97, Population Studies 1979–97; Br Soc for Population Studies: memb Cncl 1979–87, treas 1981–85, pres 1985–87; memb: Population Investigation Ctee 1976–97 (treas 1987–97), Historical Demography Ctee Int Union for the Scientific Study of Population 1983–91 (chm 1987–91); FRHistS 1970, FRSS 1987, FBA 1988; *Publications* The Population History of England 1541–1871: A reconstruction (with E A Wrigley, 1981, 2 edn 1989), English Marriage Patterns Revisited (Journal of Family History, 1985), The State of Population Theory: forward from Malthus (contrib, 1986), Famine, Disease and Crisis Mortality in Early Modern Society (contrib with J Walter, 1989), The Decline of Mortality in Europe (with David Reher and Alain Bideau, 1991), Old and New Methods in Historical Demography (with David Reher, 1993), English Population History from Family Reconstitution (with E A Wrigley et al, 1997), Through a Glass Darkly (Social Science History, 1998), Taxation under the Early Tudors, 1485–1547 (2004); various articles on historical demography and research methods; *Style*— Dr Roger Schofield, FBA; ✉ Clare College, Cambridge CB2 1TL (tel 01223 333267, e-mail rss1@cam.ac.uk)

SCHOLAR, Sir Michael Charles; KCB (1999, CB 1991); s of Richard Herbert Scholar (d 1993), of Grampound, Cornwall, and Mary Blodwen, *née* Jones (d 1985); *b* 3 January 1942; *Educ* St Olave's and St Saviour's GS Orpington, St John's Coll Cambridge (MA, PhD), Univ of Calif Berkeley, Harvard Univ; *m* 26 Aug 1964, Angela Mary, da of William Whinfield Sweet (d 1984), of Wylam, Northumberland; 3 s (Thomas b 1968, Richard b 1973, John b 1980), 1 da (Jane b 1976 d 1977); *Career* asst lectr in philosophy Univ of Leicester 1968, fell St John's Coll Cambridge 1969 (hon fell 1999), asst princ HM Treasy 1969, private sec to Chief Sec HM Treasy 1974–76, sr int mangr Barclays Bank plc 1979–81, private sec to PM 1981–83, dep sec HM Treasy 1987–93 (under sec 1983); perm sec: Welsh Office 1993–96, DTI 1996–2001; chm Civil Service Sports Cncl 1998–2001; pres St John's Coll Oxford 2001–, pro-vice-chllr and chm Conf of Colls Univ of Oxford 2005–; memb Cncl of Mgmnt NIESR 2001–05; non-exec dir Legal and General Investment Management (Holdings) plc 2002–; chm Benton Fletcher Tst 2004–; fell: Univ of Wales Aberystwyth 1996, Univ of Cardiff 2003; Hon Dr Univ of Glamorgan 1999; ARCO 1965; *Recreations* playing the piano and organ, walking, gardening; *Style*— Sir Michael Scholar, KCB; ✉ e-mail president@sjc.ox.ac.uk

SCHOLEFIELD, Prof John Howard; s of Frank Scholefield, and Beryl Scholefield; *b* 28 September 1959; *Educ* Bradford GS, Univ of Liverpool (Bromley scholarship, MB ChB, ChM); *Career* house offr Broadgreen Hosp Liverpool 1983–84, SHO (A&E and orthopaedic surgery) Walton Hosp Liverpool 1984–85, SHO (oncology, gastroenterology, urology and gen surgery) Northern Gen Hosp Sheffield 1985–86, Peri-Fellowship registrar rotation Royal Hallamshire Hosp Sheffield 1986–87, clinical res fell Imperial Cancer Res Fund Colorectal Unit St Mark's Hosp London 1987–89 (hon clinical asst and postgrad tutor 1988–89), lectr in surgery (registrar rising to sr registrar) Univ Dept of Surgery Clinical Sciences Centre Northern Gen Hosp Sheffield 1989–93, res surgical offr St Mark's Hosp London 1993–94; Section of Surgery Univ of Nottingham: sr lectr 1994–97 reader 1997–99, prof of surgery 2000–; hon conslt surgn Univ Hosp NHS Tst 1994–; chm Nat Cancer Res Inst Colorectal Gp 2001–; memb: Cncl Assoc of Coloproctology of GB and Ireland 1997–2000, Ctee Soc of Academic Surgns 1997–2000, Cancer Ctee RCS 2000–; memb Editorial Bd: Aird's Companion to Surgical Studies, Surgery (speciality ed for gen surgery); presented papers and many nat and int meetings of learned socs; memb: Surgical Res Soc, Br Assoc of Coloproctology, Assoc of Surgns of GB and Ireland (regnl rep 2002–), American Soc of Colon and Rectal Surgns, Br Soc for Gastroenterology, RSM (Coloproctology, Surgery and Oncology Sections), St Mark's Assoc, E Midlands Surgical Soc; FRCSEd 1987, FRCS 1988 *Awards* Nordic Travel Scholarship RSM 1990, NY Travelling Scholarship RCS 1991, Ethicon Fndn Travel Award RCS 1991, Surgical Res Soc Travelling Fellowship 1992, Br Digestive Fndn Travel Award 1992, RSM Travelling Fellowship 1993 (to American Soc of Colon and Rectal Surgns 1994), Japan Surgical Soc Travelling Scholarship 1996, John Arderne Medal RSM Section of Coloproctology 1989, Raven Prize Br Assoc of Surgical Oncology 1989, N of England Gastroenterology Soc Res Prize 1990, Hunterian prof RCS 1991; *Publications* Challenges in Colorectal Cancer (ed, 2000 and 2005); numerous book chapters, refereed papers, reviews, letters and published abstracts; *Recreations* squash, golf; *Style*— Prof John Scholefield; ✉ Division of GI Surgery, Queen's Medical Centre, Nottingham NG7 2UH (tel 0115 849 3323 or 0115 993 2009)

SCHOLES, Paul; *b* 16 November 1974, Salford; *m* Claire; 1 s, 1 da; *Career* professional footballer (midfielder); Manchester United 1993–: over 400 appearances, over 100 goals;

S

winners FA Premiership 1994, 1996, 1997, 1999, 2000, 2001, 2003 and 2007, FA Cup 1994, 1996, 1999 and 2004, Charity Shield 1994, 1995, 1996 and 1997, European Champions League 1999; England: debut 1997, 66 full caps and 14 goals, memb squad World Cup 1998, memb squad European Championships 2000 and 2004, ret 2004; *Style*— Paul Scholes, Esq; ✉ c/o Manchester United FC, Old Trafford, Manchester M16 0RA

SCHOLES, Richard Thomas; TD; *b* 12 May 1945; *Educ* Stowe; *Career* articled clerk Porter Matthews & Marsden Blackburn 1965–69, Arthur Andersen & Co 1969–70, ptnr Joseph Sebag & Co 1976–78 (joined 1970), Carr Sebag & Co 1978–82, Grieveson Grant 1982–86, dir Dresdner Kleinwort Benson 1986–2001; non-exec dir: British Vita plc 1993–2003, Bodycote International 1998–, Keller Group plc 2002–, Chaucer Holdings plc 2003–, Crest Nicholson plc 2003–07, Marshalls plc 2003–; dep chm RCO Holdings plc 1993–2000; FCA; *Recreations* family, rural; *Clubs* Boodle's; *Style*— R T Scholes, Esq; ✉ 37 Doneraile Street, London SW6 6EW (e-mail mail@richardscholes.com); Office tel and fax 020 7736 2756

SCHOLEY, Sir David Gerald; kt (1987), CBE (1976); *b* 28 June 1935; *Educ* Wellington, ChCh Oxford; *m* 1960, Alexandra Beatrix, da of Hon George Drew, and Fiorenza Drew, of Canada; 1 s (Christopher), 1 da (Fiorenza); *Career* Nat Serv 9 Queen's Royal Lancers 1953–55; with: Thompson Graham & Co (Lloyd's Brokers) 1956–58, Dale & Co (Insurance Brokers) Canada 1958–59, Guinness Mahon & Co Ltd 1959–64; UBS AG: joined S G Warburg & Co Ltd 1964 (dir 1967, dep chm 1977, jt chm 1980–84), chm S G Warburg Group plc 1980–95, chm SBC Warburg (following acquisition by Swiss Bank Corporation) July-Nov 1995, currently sr advsr UBS; chm Int Advsy Cncl Swiss Bank Corporation July 1995–97; non-exec chm Close Brothers 1999–2006; non-exec dir Anglo American plc 1999–2005; dir: Orion Insurance Co Ltd 1963–87, Stewart Wrightson Holdings Ltd 1972–81, Union Discount Co of London Ltd 1976–81, Bank of England 1981–98, British Telecommunications plc 1986–94, The Chubb Corporation (USA) 1991–, The General Electric Company plc 1992–95, J Sainsbury plc 1996–2000, Vodafone Gp plc 1998–2005; sr advsr International Finance Corp World Bank Gp 1996–2005; memb: Euro Advsy Cncl General Motors 1988–97, Mitsubishi Int Advsy Ctee 2001–, Sultanate of Oman Fin Servs Advsy Gp 2002–; dir: INSEAD 1991–2004 (chm UK Cncl 1992–97, chm Int Cncl 1995–2003), London First 1993–96, LSE 1993–96; govr BBC 1994–2000; dep chm Export Guarantees Advsy Cncl 1974–75, chm Construction Exports Advsy Bd 1975–78, memb Cncl IISS 1984–93 (hon treas 1984–90); govr: NIESR 1984–, LSE 1993–96, Wellington Coll 1978–88 and 1996–2004 (vice-pres 1998–2004); memb: Pres's Ctee Business in the Community 1988–91, Industry and Commerce Gp Save the Children Fund 1989–95 (chm Save the Children Fund 75th Birthday Private Appeal), London Symphony Orch Advsy Cncl 1998–2004, Lord Mayor's Appeal Ctee Save the Children Fund 2002–03, Fitch Int Advsy Ctee 2001–, Ctee Action Japan 1985–90; chm of tstees Nat Portrait Gallery 2001–05 (tstee 1992–2005), tstee Glyndebourne Arts Tst 1989–2002; Hon DLitt London Metropolitan Univ 1993, Hon BSc UMIST 1999, hon alumnus INSEAD 2000, hon student ChCh Oxford 2003; *Style*— Sir David Scholey, CBE; ✉ UBS Investment Bank, 1 Finsbury Avenue, London EC2M 2PP (tel 020 7568 2400, fax 020 7568 4225, e-mail david.scholey@ubs.com)

SCHOLEY, Sir Robert; kt (1987), CBE (1982); *b* 8 October 1921; *Educ* King Edward VII Sch Sheffield, Univ of Sheffield; *m* 2 da; *Career* served REME 1943–47; engr Steel Peech & Tozer Rotherham 1947, formerly of United Steel Companies Ltd (head office 1972, md Strip Mills Div 1972); Br Steel Corp: memb Bd of Dirs 1973, dep chm and chief exec 1976, chm 1986–92, ret; pres Pipeline Industries Guild 1987–89, dir Eurotunnel Bd 1987–92, pres Inst of Metals 1989–90, non-exec dir Nat Health Serv Policy Bd 1989–, vice-pres Eurofer 1990– (pres 1985–90), vice-chm Int Iron and Steel Inst 1990– (chm 1989–90), ex-chm Ironbridge Gorge Museum Devpt Tst, ex-memb ECSC Consultative Ctee; winner: Bessemer Gold medal Inst of Metals 1988, Gold medal BIM 1988; Hon BSc Univ of Teeside 1996; Hon PhD Engrg Univ of Sheffield 1987; Hon FCGI, FREng 1990, FIM 1990; *Style*— Sir Robert Scholey, CBE, FREng

SCHOLTES, Prof Stefan; *b* 22 November 1960, Trier, Germany; *Educ* Univ of Karlsruhe (Dip, PhD), Cornell Univ; *Career* researcher and lectr Univ of Karlsruhe 1990–96; Judge Business Sch Univ of Cambridge: lectr and reader 1996–2002, prof of mgmnt science 2002–, currently dir of research; visiting positions: Stanford Univ, MIT, London Business Sch; author of 24 articles in professional jls; *Books* On Convex Bodies and Some Applications to Optimization (1990), System Modelling and Optimization: Methods, Theory and Applications (jt ed, 2000); *Style*— Prof Stefan Scholtes

SCHOONMAKER, Tim; s of Tom Schoonmaker, of Philadelphia USA, and Ann Schoonmaker; *b* 4 July 1957, New York, USA; *Educ* Dartmouth Coll USA (BA), London Business Sch (MBA); *m* Lucille; 2 s (Robert b 7 April 1990, James b 11 Aug 1993); *Career* general mgmnt positions with EMAP 1983–2004, launched EMAP Radio 1990, chief exec EMAP Performance 1999–2004, chm EMAP Advtg until 2004; chief exec Odeon Cinemas Ltd 2004, non-exec chm Diamond FM 2006–; sometime bd memb Commercial Radio Companies Assoc (CRCA), founding dir Radio Advertising Bureau; corp fell Industry & Parliament Tst; *Recreations* tennis, music; *Style*— Tim Schoonmaker, Esq

SCHOTT, Ben; s of Dr Geoffrey D Schott, of London, and Judith C, *née* Ross; *b* 26 May 1974, London; *Educ* Gonville & Caius Coll Cambridge (MA); *Career* writer; *Publications* Schott's Original Miscellany (2002), Schott's Food & Drink Miscellany (2003), Schott's Sporting, Gaming & Idling Miscellany (2004), Schott's Almanac (annually, 2005–); *Recreations* adsignification; *Clubs* Reform; *Style*— Ben Schott, Esq; ✉ c/o Rogers Coleridge & White, 20 Powis Mews, London W11 1JN (tel 020 7221 3717, website www.benschott.com)

SCHOUVALOFF, Alexander; s of Count Paul Schouvaloff (d 1960), and Anna, *née* Raevsky, MBE (d 1991); *b* 4 May 1934; *Educ* Harrow, Jesus Coll Oxford (MA); *m* 1, 18 Feb 1959 (m dis), Gillian Baker; 1 s (Alexander b 1959); m 2, 18 Nov 1971, Daria Antonia Marie, da of late Marquis de Mérindol, and formerly wife of Hon (Geoffrey) Patrick Hopkinson Chorley; *Career* Nat Serv 2 Lt RMP SHAPE Paris 1957–59, Award of Merit Eaton Hall OCS; asst dir Edinburgh Festival 1965–67; dir: NW Arts Assoc 1967–74, Rochdale Festival 1971, Chester Festival 1973; fndr curator Theatre Museum V&A 1974–89; tstee London Archives of the Dance, memb Ctee for Dance Division NY Public Library for the Performing Arts, memb Scientific Ctee Institut national d'histoire de l'art Paris; radio plays Radio Four: Summer of the Bullshine Boys 1981, No Saleable Value 1982; Order of Polonia Restituta (Poland) 1971; *Books* Summer of the Bullshine Boys (1979), Stravinsky on Stage (with Victor Borovsky, 1982), Catalogue of Set and Costume Designs in Thyssen-Bornemisza Collection (1987), The Theatre Museum (1987), Theatre on Paper (1990), Léon Bakst - the Theatre Art (1991), The Art of Ballets Russes: the Serge Lifar Collection of Theater Designs, Costumes and Paintings at the Wadsworth Athenaeum, Hartford, Connecticut (1997); *Clubs* Garrick; *Style*— Alexander Schouvaloff, Esq; ✉ 10 Avondale Park Gardens, London W11 4PR (tel and fax 020 7727 7543)

SCHRODER, (Baron) Bruno Lionel; s of Baron Helmut William Bruno Schroder (d 1969), s of Baron Bruno Schroder or von Schröder, sr ptnr the London branch of the Banking House of J Henry Schroder & Co, cr Freiherr by Kaiser Wilhelm II aboard the yacht 'Hohenzollern' on 27 July 1904; the Baron's er bro Rudolph was cr Freiherr eight months later, and Margaret Eleanor Phyllis (d 1994), eld da of Sir Lionel Darell, 6 Bt, DSO, JP, DL; *b* 17 January 1933; *Educ* Eton, Université de Tours, Sch of Languages Hamburg, UC Oxford (MA), Harvard Business Sch (MBA); *m* 30 May 1969, Patricia Leonie Mary (Piffa), da of Maj Adrian Holt (d 1984); 1 da (Leonie b 1974); *Career* 2 Lt The Life Gds 1951–53; dir: Schroders plc 1963– (joined 1960), Schröder Gebrüder Bank Hamburg 1954–55, J Henry Schroder & Co Ltd 1966–, Schroders Inc 1984–; tstee Schroder Charity Tst 1960–, tstee Schroder Fndn 2004–; dir Fine Art Fund 2002–; tstee Univ Coll Membs' Tst 1992–98; memb Bd of Tstees Br Urological Fndn (chm 1998–2002, tstee 2002–), former memb Cncl of Mgmnt Educn Univ of Oxford, memb Exec Ctee The Air Sqdn 1996–2002, memb Cncl Household Cavalry of the Life Guards 2003–, memb Cncl Air League 2007–; vice-chm Br Friends of the Harvard Business Sch; govr English Nat Ballet 1994–2000; tstee Argyllshire Piping Tst 1995–; steward and sr steward Argyllshire Gathering 1985–2000; Prime Warden of Worshipful Co of Goldsmiths 2001–02 (Freeman 1973, Liveryman 1976, memb Ct of Assts 1987–), Liveryman Guild of Air Pilots and Air Navigators; Queen Beatrix of the Netherlands Wedding Medal, Cross of the Order of Merit of the Federal Rep of Germany; *Recreations* flying, stalking, shooting; *Clubs* Brooks's, White's, Leander; *Style*— Bruno Schroder; ✉ Schroders plc, 31 Gresham Street, London EC2V 7QA (tel 020 7658 6000, fax 020 7658 2006, telex 885029)

SCHRÖDER, Prof Martin; s of Hermann Schröder (d 1971), and Edith, *née* Kruusna (d 1999); *b* 14 April 1954; *Educ* Slough GS, Univ of Sheffield (BSc), Imperial Coll London (PhD, DIC); *m* Leena-Kreet, da of Härm Kore; *Career* Royal Society/Swiss Nat Fndn postdoctoral fell Laboratorium für Organische Chemie Eidgenössische Technische Hochschule Zurich 1978–80, postdoctoral research asst Univ Chemical Laboratories Cambridge 1980–82; Univ of Edinburgh: sr demonstrator in inorganic chemistry Dept of Chemistry 1982–83, lectr 1983–91, reader 1991–94, personal chair in inorganic chemistry Dept of Chemistry 1994–95; Univ of Nottingham: prof and head of inorganic chemistry Dept of Chemistry 1995–, head Sch of Chemistry 1999–2005; visiting prof Lash Miller Laboratories Univ of Toronto 1990, Mellor visiting prof Univ of Dunedin 1995, visiting prof Sch of Chemistry Univ Louis Pasteur Strasbourg 2004; memb various SERC panels and ctees incl Inorganic Chemistry Sub-Ctee 1990–93; memb various EPSRC panels and ctees and also chm and memb Inorganic Synthesis Panel, memb Dalton Cncl and Conference Ctee RSC 1998–2007; author of over 380 publications in learned jls; support research fell RSE 1991–92, Leverhulme Tst sr research fell 2005–06, Wolfson Merit Award Royal Soc 2005–10; Corday-Morgan Medal and Prize RSC 1989, Tilden lectr RSC 2000–01, Transition Metal Chemistry Award RSC 2003; Hon Dr Tech Univ of Tallinn 2005; CChem, FRSC 1994, FRSE 1994; *Style*— Prof Martin Schröder; ✉ School of Chemistry, University of Nottingham, University Park, Nottingham NG7 2RD (tel 0115 951 3490, fax 0115 951 3563, e-mail m.schroder@nottingham.ac.uk)

SCHULTEN, Christopher Francis (Chris); *b* 5 January 1953; *Educ* Victoria Univ of Manchester (BA); *m* Oct 1978, Elizabeth; 2 s (Stephen Richard b 25 Sept 1984, Andrew Mark b 22 April 1987); *Career* audit supervisor Arthur Young & Co (London, Manchester, Brussels, Bermuda) 1974–80, comptroller Walton Insurance Ltd (Bermuda) 1980–81, chief accountant Petroleum Products Gp Phillips Petroleum London 1981–84, corp fin mangr DRI Holdings Ltd Staines 1984–86, dep gp fin dir and co sec WPP Group plc London 1986–93, chief exec Richards Butler (slrs) London 1995– (fin dir 1993–95); FCA 1977, MCT 1986; *Recreations* golf, skiing; *Style*— Chris Schulten, Esq; ✉ Richards Butler, Beaufort House, 15 St Botolph Street, London EC3A 7EE (tel 020 7247 6555, fax 020 7247 5091)

SCHUTZ, Prof Bernard Frederick; s of Bernard Frederick Schutz, of Plainview, NY, and Virginia M, *née* Lefebure (d 1986); *b* 11 August 1946; *Educ* Bethpage HS NY, Clarkson Coll of Technol NY (BSc), Caltech (PhD); *m* 1, 13 Aug 1968 (m dis 1973), Joan Catherine, *née* Rankie; m 2, 16 Sept 1977 (m dis 1981), Susan, *née* Whitelegg; m 3, 22 Dec 1985, Sian Lynette, da of John Alexander Easton Pouncy, of Neath, W Glamorgan; 3 da (Rachel b 1984, Catherine b 1986, Annalie b 1989); *Career* postdoctoral res fell Univ of Cambridge 1971–72, instructor in physics Yale Univ 1973–74 (postdoctoral res fell 1972–73), prof Univ of Wales Cardiff 1984– (lectr 1974–76, reader 1976–84), dir Max Planck Inst for Gravitational Physics (The Albert Einstein Inst) Golm Germany 1995–; Amaldi Medal Italian Soc for Gravitation 2006; memb: German Physical Soc, Soc of Sigma XI, Royal Acad of Arts and Sciences Uppsala Sweden, Deutsche Acad Leopoldina; hon prof: Univ of Potsdam 1998–, Univ of Hanover; fell American Physical Soc, FRAS, FInstP; *Books* Geometrical Methods of Mathematical Physics (1980), A First Course in General Relativity (1985), Gravitational Wave Data Analysis (1989), Gravity from the Ground Up (2003); *Recreations* singing, skiing, sailing; *Style*— Prof Bernard Schutz; ✉ MPI Gravitational Physics, Am Muehlenberg 1, D-14476 Golm, Germany (tel 00 49 331 5677220, fax 00 49 331 5677298, e-mail bernard.schutz@aei.mpg.de)

SCHWAB, Ann Dorothy (Annie); MBE (1999); da of William Henry Clovis, and Dorothy, *née* Taylor; *b* 28 November 1946; *Educ* Burnholme Sch York; *m* 1; 3 s (Barry Devlin b 4 July 1965, Neil Devlin b 12 July 1966, Ian Devlin b 23 July 1968); m 2, 31 Oct 1977, Germain Eric Schwab, *qv*; *Career* hotelier; The Olde Worlde Club York 1972–74, Hans and Gerda's Restaurant Findlenhof Zermatt Switzerland 1976–83, Hotel Poste Zermatt Switzerland 1983–84, Beck Farm Restaurant York 1984–88, Winteringham Fields Winteringham 1988– (2 Michelin stars 1999); memb: Restaurant Assoc 1993, Hospitality Assoc 1993, Food Writers' Guild, Acad of Food and Wine Serv, Writers' Guild of Great Britain 1994, Euro Toque '96, Exec Ctee Restaurant Assoc of Great Britain; cmmr Euro Toques UK; chair Young Chef and Young Waiter Competition; FRSA 2002; *Recreations* journalism; *Clubs* Sloane; *Style*— Mrs Annie Schwab, MBE; ✉ Lerignac, 16480 Ste Souline, France (tel 00 33 5 45 98 57 05, e-mail euroannie@aol.com)

SCHWAB, Germain Eric; s of Eric Herbert Schwab (d 1967), of Switzerland, and Therese Marie Anne, *née* Unternahrer; *b* 5 December 1950; *Educ* Ecole Chantemerle Moutier Suisse, Ecole D'Aptitude Professionnelle Delémont Suisse, Ecole De Formation Professionnelle de Cuisinier Bienne Suisse, Diplome De Fin D'Apprentis Palais Des Congres Bienne; *m* 31 Oct 1977, Ann Dorothy Schwab, MBE, *qv*, da of William Henry Clovis; *Career* chef; Hotel Central Tavanne Switzerland 1970, La Grenette Fribourg Switzerland 1970, Gstaad Palace Gstaad Switzerland 1970, Portledge Hotel Bideford England 1971, Frederick Restaurant Camden London 1971, Chesterfield Hotel Mayfair London 1971, Dorchester Hotel London 1972, St Moritz Club Wardour St London 1973, Seiler Haus Mount Cervin Zermatt Switzerland 1974, Le Mirabeau Hotel Zermatt 1975, Le Bristol Hotel Zermatt 1977, Beck Farm Restaurant Wilberfoss England 1980, Winteringham Fields Winteringham 1988– (Michelin star 1994, Which? Good Hotel Guide Humberside Hotel of the Year 1996, 9 out of 10 Good Food Guide 1999, 2 Michelin stars 1999); County Restaurant of the Year: Good Food Guide 1990, La Ina 1990; Restaurant of the Year The Independent 1990, English Estates Humberside Rural Employment award 1990, English Estates Humberside county winner (Tourism) 1990, Booker Prize Best Chef and Best Restaurant 1995, AA Chef of the Year 2006; memb: Société Master Chefs (UK) Feb 1983, Euro Toque 1990, Académie Culinaire de France; *Recreations* sketching; *Clubs* Sloane; *Style*— Germain Schwab, Esq; ✉ Lerignac, 16480 Ste Souline, France (tel 00 33 5 45 98 57 05)

SCHWARTZ, Prof Steven; *b* 5 November 1946, NYC; *Educ* Brooklyn Coll City Univ NYC (BA), Syracuse Univ (MSc, PhD); *Family* 2 s (Seth b 25 May 1969, Greg b 23 Jan 1976), 1 da (Tricia b 18 April 1972); m, 9 Nov 2001, Claire Mary; *Career* cmmnd offr and grad fell US Public Health Serv NIH Washington DC 1967–68, clinical psychologist Veteran Admin Hosp Syracuse 1969–70, asst prof Dept of Psychology Northern Illinois Univ DeKalb 1971–75, research scientist Depts of Psychiatry, Community Med and Public Health Univ of Texas Med Branch Galveston 1975–78, sr lectr Dept of Psychology Univ of WA 1978–79, prof and head Dept of Psychology Univ of Qld 1980–90, pres Academic Bd Univ of Qld 1991–93, exec dean Faculty of Med and Dentistry Univ of WA 1994–96, vice-chllr and pres Murdoch Univ 1996–2002, vice-chllr and princ Brunel Univ 2002–06;

visiting research fell: NATO Brussels 1978, Int Brain Research Orgn Lausanne 1982; visiting prof: Stanford Univ 1983, Dept of Health Policy and Mgmnt Harvard Sch of Public Health 1987; Royal Soc and Australian Acad of Science exchange fell ICRF Labs London 1988, visiting fell Wolfson Coll Oxford 1994, Morris Leibovitz fell Univ of Southern Calif 1995; chair UK Govt Review into HE 2003–, memb Productive Industries Cmmn GLA 2003–; pres Sigma Xi The Scientific Research Soc 1986–90; memb Bd: Cncl for Int Educn Exchange (CIEE) 1997–, Cncl for Industry and HE 2002–, Fndn for Int Educn 2003–; memb Editorial Bd: Texas Reports in Biology and Med 1976–78, Jl of Research in Personality 1978–90, Applied Psycholinguistics 1980–84, Brain and Cognition 1991–95, Med Decision Making, Australian Autism Review, Jl of Child Clinical Psychology (special ed), The Behavioural and Brain Sciences, Current Psychological Reviews and Reports, Psychological Bulletin; memb: NY Acad of Sciences, Public Health Assoc of Australia, Soc for Med Decision Making, AAAS, Judgement and Decision Making Soc, Int Assoc of Univ Presidents, American Psychological Assoc; Travel Fellowship American Psychological Assoc 1973, Career Scientist Devpt Award NIH 1977, Brain Research Award Br Red Cross Soc 1988, ALIS Award Br Cncl 1988; govr: Henley Mgmnt Coll 2002–, Richmond the American Univ in London 2003–; ambass City of Perth 1999–; fell: Acad of Social Sciences Australia 1991, Australian Inst of Mgmnt 2000, Australian Inst of Co Dirs 2001; *Publications* Human Judgement and Decision Processes (ed with M F Kaplan, 1975), Human Judgement and Decision Processes in Applied Settings (ed with M F Kaplan, 1977), Language and Cognition in Schizophrenia (ed, 1978), Psychopathology of Childhood: An Experimental Approach (with J H Johnson, 1981, revised edn 1985), Measuring Reading Competence (1984), Medical Thinking: The Psychology of Medical Judgement and Decision-Making (with T Griffin, 1986), Classic Studies in Psychology (1986), Pavlov's Heirs (1987), Case Studies in Abnormal Psychology (ed, 1992), Classic Studies in Abnormal Psychology (1993), Abnormal Pscyhology (2000); also author of book chapters, reviews, conf papers, and articles in newspapers, magazines and learned jls; *Style*— Prof Steven Schwartz

SCICLUNA, Martin Anthony; s of late William Scicluna, and Miriam Scicluna; *b* 20 November 1950; *Educ* Berkhamsted Sch, Univ of Leeds (BCom); *m* 1979 (m dis 2000); 2 s (Mark William b 26 April 1984, Edward James b 2 Feb 1989), 1 da (Claire Alexandra b 11 Aug 1987); *Career* chartered accountant; Touche Ross (now Deloitte): joined 1973, ptnr 1982–, head London Audit Div 1990–95, chm 1995–2007; memb Bd of Directors and Governance Ctee Deloitte Touche Tohmatsu 1999–2007; chm: London Soc of Chartered Accountants ICAEW 1988–89, Cncl ICAEW 1990–95; memb Company Law Review Steering Gp and chm Accounting and Reporting Working Gp Company Law Review 1999–2001, govr NIESR; memb Finance Ctee V&A; Freeman City of London, memb Worshipful Co of Chartered Accountants in England and Wales; FCA 1980 (ACA 1976), CIMgt 1996 (MIMgt 1976), FRSA; *Recreations* tennis, gardening, wine; *Style*— Martin A Scicluna, Esq; ✉ Deloitte, Stonecutter Court, 1 Stonecutter Street, London EC4A 4TR (tel 020 7303 5002)

SCLATER, Prof John George; s of John George Sclater, and Margaret Bennet Glen; *b* 17 June 1940; *Educ* Stonyhurst, Univ of Edinburgh (BSc), Univ of Cambridge (PhD); *m* 1, 1968, Fredrica Rose Feleyn; 2 s, (Iain, Stuart); m 2, 1985, Paula Anne Edwards; m 3, Naila Gloria Burchett; *Career* asst res geophysicist Scripps Instn of Oceanography 1967–72 (postgrad res asst 1965–67), prof MIT 1977–83 (asst prof 1972–77), dir Joint Prog in Oceanography and Ocean Engrg (with Woods Hole Oceanographic Instn) MIT 1981–83, The Instn for Geophysics Univ of Texas of Austin 1983–91 (assoc dir, sr res scientist, Shell distinguished prof in geophysics), prof UCSD/Scripps Instn of Oceanography 1991–; assoc ed Jl of Geophysical Res 1971–74; memb: Ocean Sciences Ctee US Nat Acad of Sciences 1972–76, Nat Sci Review Ctee on Oceanography 1974–77, Review Ctee IDOE Nat Science Fndn 1974, Heat Flow Panel JOIDES 1968–74, Science Fndn 1974, Ocean Crisis Panel IPOD 1974–76, Indian Ocean Panel JOIDES 1968–74, Indian Ocean Panel Ocean Drilling Prog 1985–88 (Lithesphere panel 1984–86), Ocean Studies Bd/Naval Panel 1985–; chm Ocean Studies Bd US Nat Acad of Sciences 1988–91 (memb 1985–92); Rosenstiel Award 1979, Bucher Medal AGU 1985; Guggenheim fell 1998–99; fell: Geological Soc of America, American Geophysical Union; fell: AAPG, Nat Acad of Sciences; FRS; *Publications* numerous contribs to Jl of Geophysical Res, Bulletin Earthquake Res, Earth and Planetary Science Letters, Geophysical Jl RAS, Tectonophysics, and other learned jls; *Style*— Prof John Sclater, FRS; ✉ Geosciences Research Division - 0220, Scripps Institution of Oceanography, University of California, San Diego, La Jolla, CA 92093–0220, USA

SCLATER, Patrick Henry; s of Henry Nicolai Sclater (d 2003), of Stockbridge, Hants, and Suzanna Mary, *née* Agnew (d 1993); *b* 9 January 1944; *Educ* Charterhouse, RAC Cirencester; *m* 6 July 1968, Rosalyn Heather, da of Urban George Eric Stephenson, of Frith House, Stalbridge, Dorset; 3 s (William b 1969, Alastair b 1971, Peter b 1976), 1 da (Heather b 1978); *Career* estate agent: sole princ Sclater Real Estate Dorchester 1974–83, Symonds Sampson & Sclater 1983–87, local dir Fulljames & Still Dorchester 1987; relocation agent: princ Sclater Property Search 1988–, chm Compass Relocation Ltd 1995–; partner in family farm; FRICS; *Recreations* shooting, sailing, walking, gardening, reading, travel; *Clubs* Farmers'; *Style*— Patrick H Sclater, Esq; ✉ Sclater Property Search, Frith Old Farmhouse, Stalbridge, Sturminster Newton, Dorset DT10 2SD (tel 01963 251363, fax 01963 251373, e-mail info@sclaterpropertysearch.co.uk, website www.sclaterpropertysearch.co.uk)

SCLATER WALL, Madeleine Elizabeth Ramsden; *Educ* Manchester HS for Girls, Victoria Univ of Manchester (LLB); *Career* admitted slr England & Wales 1972, admitted Attorney California Bar USA 1982, admitted Attorney US Supreme Ct Bar 2003; asst gen counsel ITEL Corp Inc USA 1978–82, vice-pres and gen counsel Clarendon Gp USA 1982–85, vice-pres and chief counsel McDonnell Douglas Corp International USA 1985–90, gp dir of legal regulatory affairs Cable & Wireless plc 1990–99, sr vice-pres gen counsel Equant NV Holland 1999–2001, gen counsel The European Lawyer 2001–05, pres Elizabeth Wall Int LLC (NY) (estab 2005); non-exec dir Legal & General Assurance plc 1998–2001; memb: Bd of Govrs Coll of Law 1995–2006, Bd of Tstees Civilia Fndn 1996–1999; chair US Bd of Dirs American Corp Counsel Assoc 2002–03 (memb 1997–, vice-chm 2001–02), pres European Capter of American Corporate Counsel Assoc 2003–04; int seminar and conf speaker; The Lawyer Magazine In-House Co Commercial Lawyer of the Year Award 1994, American Soc of Int Law Prominent Woman in Int Law Award 1994, ACCA USA Excellence in Corp Practice Award 1999; memb: Law Soc 1972– (chm Commerce & Indust Gp 1996–97), Int Bar Assoc, Assoc of Corporate Counsel; MInstD; *Recreations* travel, the arts, interior design, watching professional golf and rugby; *Style*— Elizabeth Wall; ✉ Elizabeth Wall International LLC, 245 Park Avenue, New York, NY 10167, USA (tel 001 212 792 4215, e-mail elizabeth@elizabethwallintl.com)

SCOBIE, Kenneth Charles; s of Charles Smith Scobie (d 1965), and Shena Bertram, *née* Melrose (d 1990); *b* 29 July 1938; *Educ* Daniel Stewart's Coll, Univ of Edinburgh (CA); *m* 29 Sept 1973, (Adela) Jane, da of Keith Somers Hollebone (d 1991), of Bampton Castle, Oxon; 1 da (Deborah b 19 May 1975), 1 s (Charles b 11 Oct 1976); *Career* CA; profit planning BMC (Scotland) Ltd 1961–63, dep fin dir Motor Car Div Rolls Royce 1963–66, sr mgmnt conslt and ptnr Robson Morrow & Co 1966–70, memb Main Bd and Exec Ctee Black and Decker Euro Gp 1971–72, md Vavasseur SA Ltd 1972–76, chief exec and dir Vernon Orgn 1977, md H C Sleigh UK Ltd 1979–82, gp md Blackwood Hodge plc 1984–90, non-exec dir Albrighton plc 1990–93, dir Postern Executive Group Ltd 1991–97, actg chm, dep chm and chief exec Brent Walker Group plc 1991–93; chm: Lovells Confectionery Ltd 1991–98, William Hill Group 1992–93, Cardinal Data Ltd 1993–94, Allied Leisure plc 1994–2000, Chemring plc 1997–; dep chm/chief exec Addis Ltd 1993–94; non-exec dir: Gartmore Indosuez UK Recovery (Group) Ltd 1993–98, Gartmore 1990 Ltd; pres London Scottish Football Club Ltd 1997–2001, chm Exec Bd Scottish Rugby Union 2000–03; CA 1961, CIMgt 1987; *Recreations* rugby, golf, tennis, cricket; *Clubs* Stewart's Melville, London Scottish RFC, Huntercombe Golf, The Durban; *Style*— Kenneth Scobie, Esq

SCOBLE, Peter Ernest Walter; er s of Walter George Scoble (d 1984), and Muriel Phyllis Mary, *née* Buckley (d 1999); *b* 8 March 1938; *Educ* Malvern Coll; *m* 1, 29 June 1963, (Marjorie) Lesley (d 1988), yr da of James Durban Wilkinson; 2 da (Karen Lesley b 20 Oct 1967, Anna Jill b 2 July 1969), 1 s (Mark Walter James b 7 Sept 1972); m 2, 3 Nov 1990, Carolyn Antonia Pilmore-Bedford, *née* Newnham; *Career* slr; articled clerk Joynson-Hicks & Co, admitted slr 1962; Boodle Hatfield: joined 1962, ptnr 1964–2001, sr ptnr 1994–99, conslt 2001–02; conslt Pemberton Greenish 2002–07; past pres City of Westminster Law Soc, memb Cncl Law Soc 1986–92; past chm Papplewick Educnl Tst Ltd; memb: Nat Tst, RHS; *Recreations* music, garden, philately; *Clubs* MCC, Kent CCC, Lowtonian Soc (treas 1995–2002), Country Landowners; *Style*— Peter Scoble, Esq; ✉ Still Waters, Burnt Lodge Lane, Ticehurst, East Sussex TN5 7LE (e-mail carpet@p-bplus.fsnet.co.uk)

SCOFIELD, (David) Paul; CH (2001), CBE (1956); s of Edward Henry Scofield (d 1976), of Hurstpierpoint, W Sussex, and Mary, *née* Wild; *b* 21 January 1922; *Educ* Hurstpierpoint C of E Sch, Varndean Sch for Boys Brighton; *m* 15 May 1943, Joy Mary, da of Edward Henry Parker (d 1967); 1 s (Martin Paul b 6 March 1945), 1 da (Sarah b 22 Aug 1951); *Career* actor; Birmingham Repertory Theatre 1942–45; Stratford-upon-Avon 1946, 1947 and 1948; Hon LLD Univ of Glasgow 1968; Hon DLitt: Univ of Kent 1973, Univ of Sussex 1985, Univ of St Andrews 1998, Univ of Oxford 2001; *Theatre incl* Adventure Story and The Seagull (St James's) 1949, Ring Round the Moon (Globe) 1950–52, Much Ado About Nothing (Phoenix) 1952, The River Line (Edinburgh Festival, Lyric Hammersmith, Strand) 1952, Richard II, The Way of the World and Venice Preserved (Lyric Hammersmith) 1952–53, A Question of Fact (Piccadilly) 1953–54, Time Remembered (New Theatre) 1954–55, Hamlet (Moscow) 1955, Paul Scofield-Peter Brook Season 1956, The Power and the Glory, Hamlet and Family Reunion (Phoenix), A Dead Secret (Piccadilly) 1957, Expresso Bongo (Savile) 1958, The Complaisant Lover (Globe) 1959, A Man for All Seasons (Globe 1960, Anta Theatre NY 1961–62), Coriolanus and Love's Labour's Lost (Shakespeare Festival Theatre Stratford, Ontario), King Lear (Stratford and Aldwych 1962–63, Moscow, W Berlin, Prague, Warsaw, Budapest, Bucharest, Belgrade and New York 1964), Timon of Athens (Stratford) 1965, The Government Inspector and Staircase (Aldwych) 1966, Macbeth (Stratford, Russia, Finland) 1967, A Hotel in Amsterdam (Royal Court and New) 1968, Uncle Vanya (Royal Court) 1970, Savages (Royal Court and Comedy) 1973, The Tempest (Wyndham's) 1975, I'm Not Rappaport (Apollo) 1986–87; NT (1971–83): Captain of Köpenick, The Rules of the Game, Volpone, Amadeus, Othello, Don Quixote; Heartbreak House (Theatre Royal Haymarket) 1992, John Gabriel Borkman (RNT) 1996; *Television* numerous TV plays, Martin Chuzzlewit (BBC serial, 1994); *Films* That Lady, Carve Her Name with Pride, The Train, A Man for All Seasons, Bartleby, King Lear, Scorpio, A Delicate Balance, Anna Karenina, Nineteen Nineteen, The Attic, When the Whales Came, Henry V, Hamlet, Utz, Quiz Show, The Crucible; *Awards* Evening Standard 1956 and 1963, New York Tony 1962, Oscar and Br Film Academy 1966, Danish Film Academy 1971, Hamburg Shakespeare Prize 1972, Variety Club 1956, 1963 and 1987, Evening Standard Award For Best Actor (for John Gabriel Borkman) 1996, BAFTA Award for Best Supporting Actor (for The Crucible) 1997, Shakespeare Birthday Award 1999; *Recreations* walking, reading; *Clubs* Athenaeum; *Style*— Paul Scofield, CH, CBE

SCOON, HE Sir Paul; GCMG (1979), GCVO (1985), OBE (1970); *b* 1935; *Career* taught in Grenada 1953–67, former Cabinet sec, govr-gen Grenada 1978–92; *Publications* Survival for Service: My Experiences as Governor General of Grenada (2003); *Style*— Sir Paul Scoon, GCMG, GCVO, OBE; ✉ PO Box 180, St George's, Grenada (tel 473 440 2180)

SCOPES, Richard Henry; s of Eric Henry Scopes, of Funtington, W Sussex, and Ida Lucy Mary (Sally), *née* Hare (d 1991); *b* 6 June 1944; *Educ* Univ Coll Sch, Magdalene Coll Cambridge (LLB); *m* 29 March 1969, Jacqueline Elizabeth Mary, da of Maj Ronald Walter Monk (d 1973), of Blackheath; 1 da (Katie b 1972); *Career* admitted slr 1969; Ashurst Morris Crisp & Co 1963–69, dir Scopes & Sons 1970–75, ptnr Wilde Sapte 1980–2000 (joined 1976), ptnr Denton Wilde Sapte 2000–01; memb City of London Slrs Co 1981; memb: Law Soc, Insolvency Lawyers Assoc, Assoc of Business Recovery Professionals; MIPA; *Recreations* gardening, painting; *Clubs* Oxford and Cambridge; *Style*— Richard Scopes, Esq; ✉ Westfield House, River Hill, Flamstead, Hertfordshire AL3 8DA

SCORER, Timothy Rowland (Tim); s of Derek Rowland Scorer, TD, of Naples, Florida, and Margaret Shirley, *née* Staveacre (d 1998); *b* 25 June 1941; *Educ* Repton; *m* 1, 10 Oct 1965 (m dis 1981), Wendy Ann, da of Edward Thomas Glazier (d 1978); 2 s (Craig b 29 Jan 1967, Jamie b 3 July 1969); m 2, 25 Sept 1982 (m dis 1989), Julia Jane, da of Jeremy John Booth; 1 da (Lucinda b 29 Oct 1987); m 3, 7 May 1993, Julie Emma, da of Alan Baker; 2 s (Alexander b 3 Sept 1992, Cameron b 2 July 1996); *Career* admitted slr 1965; ptnr Josselyn & Sons Ipswich 1967, asst sec Law Soc 1976; ptnr: Barlow Lyde & Gilbert London 1980, Jarvis & Bannister 1992, DLA 1997, Thomas Cooper & Stibbard 2001–; chm and fndr Lawyers' Flying Assoc, int vice-pres Lawyer Pilots' Bar Assoc USA; hon slr: Helicopter Club of GB, Euro Gen Aviation Safety Fndn, Guild of Air Pilots and Air Navigators; Freeman City of London 1987, Liveryman Guild of Air Pilots and Air Navigators 1988 (Freeman 1985); memb Law Soc 1966; MRAeS; *Recreations* flying, photography, travel; *Style*— Tim Scorer, Esq; ✉ Toad Hall, White Colne, Colchester, Essex CO6 2PW (tel 01787 224294); Thomas Cooper & Stibbard, 42–47 Minories, London EC3N 1HA (tel 020 7390 2224, fax 020 7480 6097, mobile 07860 557766, e-mail tim.scorer@tcssol.com)

SCOTLAND, Tony; s of Peter Whitmore Scotland (d 1997), and Elizabeth Ann, *née* Dunn (d 1954); *b* 29 May 1945; *Career* TV reporter Look East BBC Norwich 1968–69, sub ed BBC Radio News London 1969–72, prodr The Arts Worldwide BBC Radio 3 1972–80, announcer Radio 3 1972–92; conslt and presenter Classic FM 1992–98, freelance writer 1992–; articles published in The Spectator, Harpers & Queen, Sunday Telegraph, The Independent, House & Garden, Catholic Herald, Erotic Review; fndr and administrator Bulgarian Orphans Fund 2000–; *Books* The Empty Throne - The Quest for an Imperial Heir in the People's Republic of China (1993), Six Story Ballets in Words and Music (writer and narrator, 1997); *Recreations* travel, research; *Style*— J A Scotland, Esq; ✉ e-mail scotlandsyard@aol.com

SCOTLAND OF ASTHAL, The Rt Hon the Baroness (Life Peer UK 1997), of Asthal in the County of Oxfordshire; Patricia Janet Scotland; PC (2001), QC (1991); da of Arthur Leonard Scotland, of Ilford, Essex; *b* 19 August 1955; *Educ* Univ of London (LLB); *m* 1985, Richard Martin Mawhinney, s of Raymond Johnston Mawhinney; 2 s (Hon Matthew Jackson b 1992, Hon Benjamin James b 1994); *Career* called to the Bar Middle Temple 1977 (bencher 1997), memb Bar of Antigua and Cwlth of Dominica; recorder 2000 (asst recorder 1994), dep judge of the High Ct (Family Div) 2000, fndr memb and former head of chambers 1 Gray's Inn Sq, former door tenant Bridewell Chambers; Parly under-sec of state FCO 1999–2001, Parly sec Lord Chllr's Dept (now Dept for Constitutional Affrs) 2001–03, min of state for the criminal justice system and law reform Home Office 2003–05, min of state for the criminal justice system and offender mgmnt

S

Home Office 2005–07, Attorney-Gen for England and Wales 2007–, alternate UK Govt rep European Convention 2002–03, spokesperson for DTI on women & equality issues House of Lords; memb: Govt Caribbean Advsy Gp, PLP Women's Gp, Advsy Panel of Br American Project; former chm: ILEA Disciplinary Tbnl, HMG Caribbean Advsy Gp; former memb: Millennium Cmmn 1994–99, House of Commons Working Party on Child Abduction, Ctee Cmmn for Racial Equality, Legal Advsy Panel Nat Consumer Cncl, Advsy Ctee on Mentally Disordered Offenders; former memb Bar Ctees incl: Public Rels, Race Rels, Judicial Studies Bd Ethnic Minority Advsy Ctee; memb: Thomas More Soc, Lawyer's Christian Fellowship; former hon pres Trinity Hall Law Soc; Black Woman of the the Year (Law) 1992, Peer of the Year House Magazine Awards and Channel 4 Political Awards 2004, Parliamentarian of the Year Political Studies Assoc Awards 2004, Spectator Parliamentarian of the Year 2005; hon fell: Soc of Advanced Legal Studies, Wolfson Coll Cambridge, Cardiff Univ; Hon Dr: Univ of Westminster, Univ of Buckingham, Univ of Leicester, Univ of E London; Dame Sacred Mil Constantinian Order of St George 2003; *Style*— The Rt Hon the Baroness Scotland of Asthal, PC, QC; ✉ c/o Trudy Hughes, House of Lords, London SW1A 0PW (e-mail hughest@parliament.uk)

SCOTT, Rev Adam; TD (1979); s of Brig Fraser Scott, of Broxbourne, Herts, and Bridget Penelope, *née* Williams; *b* 6 May 1947; *Educ* Marlborough, ChCh Oxford (MA), City Univ Business Sch (MSc); *m* 30 Sept 1978, Prof Oona MacDonald, PhD, FCSP, da of Prof R J D Graham (d 1950), of St Andrews, Fife; *Career* OUOTC 1965–68, CVHQ RA, 94 Locating Regt 1968–81, cmd Reserve Meteorologists, Capt 1975, ret 1981; reader St Aldate's Oxford 1970–75; ordained (Southwark): deacon 1975, priest 1976; asst curate St Michael and All Angels Blackheath Park 1975–; dean: Ministers in Secular Employment, Woolwich Episcopal Area 1990–2000; trained as intellectual property lawyer 1970–74; called to the Bar Inner Temple 1972; with: ITT 1974–77, PO 1977–81; BT: corp planner 1981–86, dir Office of Iain Vallance (chm of BT) 1986–88, dir of int affairs 1988–92, chm apparatus supply business 1992–94, ret 1997; sr advsr Europe Economics 1998–2000; memb: Competition Cmmn Appeal Tbnls 2000–2003, Guernsey Utility Appeal Panel 2002–, Competition Appeal Tbnl 2003–; Univ of St Andrews: fell St Andrews Mgmnt Inst 1994–96, professorial fell 1996–97, sr research fell 1998–; holding tstee House of St Barnabas Soho; Freeman City of London 1993; CEng, FIET (FIEE 1994, MIEE 1981), FRSA 1995, FHEA 2007; *Recreations* gardening, walking; *Clubs* Cannons; *Style*— The Rev Adam Scott, TD; ✉ 19 Blackheath Park, Blackheath, London SE3 9RW (tel 020 8852 3286, fax 020 8852 6247)

SCOTT, Adrian Eason Bailey; s of Deric Sidney Scott (d 1997), and Margaret Emeline, *née* Bailey (d 1993); *b* 12 February 1938, Bournemouth, Dorset; *Educ* Canford Sch, Nat Assoc of Funeral Dirs (Dip Funeral Directing); *Career* Nat Serv Royal Signals 1956–58 (Gen Serv Medal); dir, jt md then chm Deric S Scott Ltd Funeral Directors 1960–97; chm European Gp Selected Ind Funeral Homes 1976–77, pres Bournemouth and Dist Assoc of Funeral Dirs; fndr chm Bournemouth Jr Chamber 1967 (also chm 1974); co-chm Bournemouth Deanery Synod 1979–84 (memb 1970–98), memb Gen Synod C of E 1980–90 (memb Liturgical Cmmn and Diocesan Synod), churchwarden St Stephen's Church Bournemouth 1975–85 and 2002–07, churchwarden Major Parish of Bournemouth Town Centre 1986–87 and 1995–2000; memb The Samaritans, govr Talbot Heath Sch 1982–95 (chm governing body 1994–95); tstee: Vitalis Tst, Pier Project Bournemouth Crime and Disorder Reduction Partnership; former dir Rotary Housing Assoc; Paul Harris fell Rotary Int; High Sheriff Dorset 2007–08; memb Br Inst of Embalmers; *Recreations* travel, dining out, music; *Clubs* East India, Rotary, No Name Dining, Nikaean, Sixty-Six (sec 1987–94), William Temple Assoc; *Style*— Adrian Scott, Esq; ✉ 7 Byron House, 28 Boscombe Cliff Road, Bournemouth, Dorset BH5 1JP (tel and fax 01202 397983, e-mail adrian@ebscott.fsnet.co.uk)

SCOTT, Andrew John; CBE (2006); s of late Cyril John Scott, and Gertrude Ethel, *née* Miller; *b* 3 June 1949; *Educ* Bablake Sch Coventry, Univ of Newcastle upon Tyne (BSc, MSc), Univ of Huddersfield (DMS); *m* 1972, Margaret Anne, *née* Benyon; *Career* civil engr Local Water Authy Tyneside, London and W Yorks 1971–84, actg dir W Yorks Tport Museum 1984–86, keeper of technol Bradford City Museums 1986–87, dir London Tport Museum 1988–94, head Nat Railway Museum 1994– (winner Euro Museum of The Year Award 2001); author various essays for museological jls; tstee: Locomotion Tst, Friends of the LT Museum; chm York Tourism Bureau; chm of advsrs Int Assoc of Tport Museums, vice-pres Assoc of Br Tport and Engrg Museums; MICE 1976, FMA 1993 (AMA 1987); *Books* North Eastern Renaissance (1991), Making Histories in Transport Museums (with C Divall, 2001); *Recreations* travel, railways, ecclesiastical architecture; *Style*— Andrew Scott, Esq, CBE; ✉ National Railway Museum, Leeman Road, York YO26 4XJ (tel 01904 686200, fax 01904 686203, e-mail andrew.scott@nrm.org.uk)

SCOTT, Dr (Christine) Angela; da of William Hurst Roy Grundy (d 1994), of Salisbury, Wilts, and Margaret, *née* Drury (d 2006); *b* 19 June 1946; *Educ* Harrogate Coll, King's Coll Med Sch London (MB, BS); *m* 7 June 1969, (John) Nigel (David) Scott, s of Lt-Col George William Inglis Scott, RA, DSO (d 1976); 3 s (Andrew b 1974, Robin b 1976, Alan b 1980); *Career* Salisbury NHS Fndn Tst (formerly Salisbury Health Care NHS Tst): conslt histopathologist and cytologist 1981–2007, med dir of pathology 1989–92, clinical dir Clinical Support 2001–07, ret; FRCPath 1988; *Recreations* squash, gardening; *Style*— Dr Angela Scott; ✉ Pathology Department, Salisbury District Hospital, Odstock, Salisbury, Wiltshire SP2 8BJ (tel 01722 336262 ext 4110)

SCOTT, Sir Anthony Percy; 3 Bt (UK 1913), of Witley, Surrey; s of Col Sir Douglas Scott, 2 Bt (d 1984), and Elizabeth Joyce, née Glanley (d 1983); *b* 1 May 1937; *Educ* Harrow, ChCh Oxford; *m* 1962, Caroline Teresa Anne, er da of (William Charles) Edward Bacon, of Mobberley, Cheshire; 2 s (Henry Douglas Edward b 1964, Simon James b 1965), 1 da (Miranda Claire b 1968); *Heir* s, Henry Scott; *Career* called to the Bar Inner Temple 1960; ptnr in stockbroking firm Laurie Milbank & Co 1974–; chm and md L M (Moneybrokers) Ltd 1986–1995; Liveryman Worshipful Co of Haberdashers; *Style*— Sir Anthony Scott, Bt; ✉ Chateau la Coste, 81140 Larroque, France

SCOTT, Prof Bill; s of George Barclay Scott (d 1975), of Moniave, Dumfriesshire, and Jeanie Stuart, *née* Waugh (d 1962); *b* 16 August 1935; *Educ* Morton Acad, Dumfries Acad, Edinburgh Coll of Art (Dip, Postgrad Dip), Ecole des Beaux Arts Paris (travel scholar, Clason Harvie Bequest prize); *m* 25 March 1961, Phyllis Owen, da of William Lauderdale Fisher; 1 s (Ian Alexander b 1 Jan 1962), 2 da (Phyllis Elizabeth b 7 July 1962, Jeanie May b 27 July 1971); *Career* sculptor; temp teacher Fife 1960–61, pt/t teacher Edinburgh Coll of Art 1961–63; Sculpture Sch Edinburgh Coll of Art: lectr 1963–76, sr lectr 1976–90, head of sch 1991–97, prof 1994; chm Bd of Dirs Edinburgh Sculpture Workshop 1998–; memb: Cncl Soc of Scottish Artists 1970–73, Ctee Br Sch at Rome 1980–85, Bd Fruit Market Gallery 1983–91; chm Awards Panel Arts Ctee Scottish Arts Cncl 1990–93 (memb Art Ctee 1989–93); RSA 1984 (sec 1998–); *Solo Exhibitions* Compass Gallery Glasgow 1972, Stirling Gallery 1974, New 57 Gallery Edinburgh 1979, Artspace Art Gallery Aberdeen 1980, Kirkcaldy Museum and Gallery 1985, Talbot Rice Art Centre 1994, Working Drawings (Fettes Coll Gallery) 2002, Drawing and Sculpture (Scottish Arts Club) 2002, Demarco 2003, Kunstverein Heinsberg 2004, RBS Gallery London 2005; *Group Exhibitions* 11 Scottish Sculptors (Fruit Market Gallery Edinburgh) 1975, Small Sculptures (Scottish Arts Cncl Edinburgh) 1978, British Art Show (Mappin Gallery Edinburgh, Hatton Gallery and Arnolfini) 1979–80, V Int Exhibition of Small Sculpture Budapest 1981, Built in Scotland (Third Eye Centre Glasgow, City Arts Centre Edinburgh, Camden Arts Centre London) 1982–83, One Cubic Foot Exhibition (Aberdeen and Glasgow) 1986, Scandex Exhibition Norway 1994, Selected Exhibition of Medals by the British Art Medals Soc (York, NY and Colorado) 1997, Transistors (Hashimoto Art Museum Japan), Ten Invited Artists (City of Viersen Gallery) 1999, Sudbahnhof Gallery Krefeld 2000, Int Medaillen Kunst Weimar 2000, Kunstransfer Heinsberg 2002, Insider - Box Art (Oriel Davies Gallery Newtown) 2003, Derby Museum 2004, Aberystwyth Museum 2004, Canterbury Museum 2005; *Commissions* New Byre Theatre St Andrews 1969, Cumbernauld Shopping Centre 1980, Kentigern House Glasgow 1985, meml sculpture for Sir Alec Douglas-Home at The Hirsel Coldstream 1998, Elizabeth Chrichton sculpture Dumfries 2000, Sorley Maclean portrait 2003; *Style*— Prof Bill Scott, RSA

SCOTT, (John) Brough; s of Mason Hogarth Scott (d 1971), of Broadway, Worcs, and Irene Florence, *née* Seely (d 1976); *b* 12 December 1942; *Educ* Radley, CCC Oxford; *m* 3 Nov 1973, Susan Eleanor, da of late Ronald Grant MacInnes, of Abinger Common, Surrey; 2 da (Sophie Diana b 20 July 1974, Tessa Irene b 3 Nov 1984), 2 s (Charles Ronald Brough b 21 Jan 1976, James Seely b 14 Feb 1979); *Career* amateur and professional jump jockey (100 winners incl Imperial Cup and Mandarin Chase) 1962–70; TV journalist: ITV 1971–84 (chief racing presenter 1979–), Channel 4 1985–2001; sports journalist: Evening Standard 1972–74, Sunday Times 1974–90, Independent on Sunday 1990–92, Sunday Times 1993–95, Sunday Telegraph 1995–; dir Racing Post 1985– (editorial dir 1988–); Lord Derby Award (racing journalist of the year) 1980, Clive Graham Trophy (services to racing) 1982, Sports Feature Writer of the Year 1985, 1990 and 1992; vice-pres Jockeys' Assoc 1969–71; chm Injured Jockeys' Fund, tstee Moorcroft Racehorse Welfare Centre; *Books* World of Flat Racing (1983), On And Off The Rails (1984), Front Runners (1991), Willie Carson - Up Front (1993), Racing Certainties (1995), Galloper Jack (2003); *Recreations* riding, books, making bonfires; *Style*— Brough Scott, Esq; ✉ Coneyhurst Ltd, Willow House, 35 High Street, Wimbledon Common, London SW19 5BY (tel 020 8946 9671)

SCOTT, Charles Clive; s of Lt-Col Sir James Walter Scott, 2 Bt (d 1993), of Rotherfield Park, Alton, Hants, and Anne Constantia, *née* Austin; *b* 31 July 1954; *Educ* Eton, Trinity Coll Cambridge, INSEAD; *m* 1979, Caroline Frances, da of Hugh Grahame Jago; 3 da (Eleanor, Rose, Alice); *Career* formerly with Macfarlanes slrs, dir de Zoete & Bevan Ltd 1988–1995, dir UK Barclays Private Bank Ltd 1996–2004; Freeman City of London 1977, Master Worshipful Co of Mercers 2004; memb Law Soc, MSI; *Clubs* Leander; *Style*— Charles Scott, Esq; ✉ 2 Bunhouse Place, London SW1W 8HU

SCOTT, Charles Thomas; *b* 22 February 1949; *m*; 2 c; *Career* articles Binder Hamlyn 1967–72, chief accountant Itel Corporation 1972–77, chief fin offr IMS International Inc 1985–89 (controller 1978–84); Saatchi & Saatchi Company plc: chief fin offr 1990–91, chief operating offr 1991–92, ceo 1993–95; chm: Cordiant plc 1995–97, Cordiant Communications Gp plc 1997–2003, William Hill plc 2004–; currently non-exec dir: InTechnology, Profile Media Gp plc, Emcore Corporation, Flybe Gp Ltd; formerly non-exec dir: adidas AG, Joe's Developments Ltd, TBI plc; FCA 1979 (ACA 1972); *Recreations* golf, tennis; *Style*— Charles Scott, Esq

SCOTT, Prof Clive; s of Jesse Scott, of Outwell, Cambs, and Nesta Vera, *née* Morton; *b* 13 November 1943; *Educ* Bishop's Stortford Coll, St John's Coll Oxford (state scholar, Casberd exhibitioner, MA, MPhil, DPhil); *m* 1, 13 Aug 1965 (m dis 1983), Elizabeth Anne, da of Rowland Drabble; 1 da (Katherine Sophie b 27 Nov 1969), 1 s (Benjamin Nicholas b 24 Aug 1972); m 2, 21 July 1984, Marie-Noëlle, da of Jean Guillot; 2 s (Samuel William b 28 July 1985, Thomas Alexander b 3 Feb 1991); *Career* UEA: asst lectr 1967–70, lectr 1970–88, reader 1988–91, prof of European literature 1991–, head Sch of Literature and Creative Writing 2004–05; dir of studies Br Cncl summer sch for Soviet teachers of English 1983–88; FBA 1994; *Books* French Verse-Art: A Study (1980), Anthologie Éluard (1983), A Question of Syllables: Essays in Nineteenth-Century French Verse (1986), The Riches of Rhyme: Studies in French Verse (1988), Vers Libre: The Emergence of Free Verse in France 1886–1914 (1990), Reading the Rhythm: The Poetics of French Free Verse 1910–1930 (1993), The Poetics of French Verse: Studies in Reading (1998), The Spoken Image: Photography and Language (1999), Translating Baudelaire (2000), Channel Crossings: French and English Poetry in Dialogue 1550–2000 (2002, R H Gapper Book Prize 2004), Translating Rimbaud's Illuminations (2006), Street Photography: From Alger to Cartier-Bresson (2007); *Style*— Prof Clive Scott, FBA; ✉ School of Literature and Creative Writing, University of East Anglia, University Plain, Norwich NR4 7TJ (tel 01603 592135, fax 01603 250599)

SCOTT, David Griffiths; s of Wilfred Emberton Scott (d 1967), and Gwenith, *née* Griffiths (d 2000); *b* 15 February 1942; *Educ* Adams GS Newport, Christ's Coll Cambridge (MA), London Business Sch (MSc); *m* 1969, Alison Jane Fraser; 2 da (Helen b 1971, Katherine b 1976), 1 s (James b 1974); *Career* md: ISC Alloy Ltd 1975–84, Impalloy Ltd 1978–84, Kleen-e-ze Holdings plc 1984–88, Yale Security Products Ltd 1989–91; dir: Ops Bd Newman Tonks plc 1991–94, David Scott Associates Ltd 1994–; ops dir Intelek plc 1994–99; CEng, FIMechE; *Recreations* golf, sailing, cricket, watercolours; *Style*— David Scott, Esq; ✉ The Barn, Main Street, Wick, Pershore, Worcestershire WR10 3NZ (tel 01386 554185, fax 01386 553713, e-mail dgscott@btinternet.com)

SCOTT, David Morris Fitzgerald; s of Rev Canon William Morris Fitzgerald Scott (d 1959), of Birkenhead, Cheshire, and Nora Compigné, *née* Shaw (d 1995); *b* 7 June 1946; *Educ* St Lawrence Coll Ramsgate, The Hotchkiss Sch Lakeville CT, CCC Oxford (scholar, MA); *m* 10 June 1972, Jacqueline Mary, da of Kenneth Percy Pool; 2 da (Elizabeth b 1976, Sarah b 1978), 1 s (Michael b 1981); *Career* ptnr Kitcat & Aitken 1974–80 (investment analyst 1967–74), vice-pres Bank of NY 1980–83; dir: Warburg Investment Mgmnt Int 1983–85, Mercury Warburg Investment Mgmnt 1985–87, Mercury Rowan Mullens 1987–89, Mercury Asset Mgmnt Private Investors Gp 1990–2000, Singer & Friedlander Investment Mgmnt 2000–; lay fell Sion Coll; tstee Officers Assoc, memb Ct New England Co; Freeman City of London, Past Master Worshipful Co of Scriveners; AIIMR, FSI (Dip); *Recreations* reading; *Clubs* Brooks's, City of London; *Style*— David Scott, Esq; ✉ Windmill House, Windmill Lane, Wadhurst, East Sussex TN5 6DJ (tel and fax 01892 782683); Singer & Friedlander Investment Management, One Hanover Street, London W1S 1AX (tel 020 3205 5900, fax 020 3205 5905)

SCOTT, David Richard Alexander; CBE (2006); s of Lt Cdr Robert Irwin Maddin Scott, OBE (d 1968), of Lyddington, Rutland, and (Margaret Sylvia) Daphne, *née* Alexander; *b* 25 August 1954; *Educ* Wellington; *m* 1 Aug 1981, Moy, da of Air Chief Marshal Sir John Barraclough, KCB, CBE, DFC, AFC; 1 s (Alexander b 8 Aug 1982), 1 da (Arabella b 11 Jan 1985); *Career* CA Peat Marwick Mitchell & Co Blackfriars 1972–81, Channel Four Television Corporation (Channel Four Television Co Ltd until 1993): controller of fin and co sec 1981–88, dir of fin 1988–97, md 1997–2002, md and dep chief exec 2002–05; FCA 1976, FRTS 2004; *Recreations* opera, theatre, ballet, bridge, sailing, country pursuits; *Clubs* Guards Polo; *Style*— David Scott, Esq, CBE

SCOTT, Douglas Keith (Doug); CBE (1994); s of George Douglas Scott, of Nottingham, and Edith Joyce Scott; *b* 29 May 1941; *Educ* Cottesmore Secdy Modern Sch, Mundella GS Nottingham, Loughborough Teachers' Trg Coll (Cert); *m* 1, 1962 (m dis 1988), Janice Elaine, da of Thomas Arthur Brook, of Notts; 1 s (Michael b 1963), 2 da (Martha b 1973, Rosie b 1978); m 2, 17 Sept 1993 (m dis 2002), Sharavati (Sharu), da of Ramchandra Sandu Prabhu and Kalyani Ramchandra Prabhu; 2 s (Arran b 1994, Euan b 1996); *Career* mountaineer; began climbing aged 12, visited Alps aged 17 and most years thereafter; pres Alpine Climbing Gp 1976–82, pres Alpine Club 1999–2001, vice-pres Br Mountaineering Cncl 1994–97; Hon MA: Univ of Nottingham 1991, Loughborough Univ 1994; Hon MEd Nottingham Trent Univ 1995; *Expeditions* first ascents incl: Tarso Teiroko Tibesti Mountains Sahara 1965, Cilo Dag Mountains SE Turkey 1966, S face

Koh-i-Bandaka (6837m) Hindu Kush Afghanistan 1967, E pillar of Mt Asgard Baffin Island Expedition 1972, Changbang (6864m) 1974, SE spur Pic Lenin (7189m) 1974, Mt McKinley (6226m, first alpine ascent of S face via new route, with Dougal Haston) 1976, E face direct Mt Kenya 1976, Ogre (7330m) Karakoram Mountains 1977, N Ridge route Kangchenjunga 1977 (and without oxygen 1979), N summit Kussum Kangguru 1979, N face Nuptse 1979, Kangchungtse (7640m, alpine style) 1980, Shivling E pillar (13–day alpine style push) 1981, N face to central summit Changlang (with Rheinhold Messner) 1981, Pungpa Ri (7445m) 1982, Shishapangma S face (8046m) 1982, Lobsang Spire (Karakoram) 1983, Broad Peak (8047m) 1983, Mt Baruntse (7143m) 1984, E summit Mt Changlang (7287m, and traverse over unclimbed central summit alpine style to within 100m of summit) 1984, rock climbs Southern India 1986, rock climbs Wadi Rum Jordan 1986, S face Mt Jitchu Drake (6793m, alpine style) Bhutan 1988, Indian Arete Latok III 1990, Hanging Glacier Peak S (6294m, via S ridge) 1991, Chombu E (5745m) 1996, Drohmo Central Summit (6855m, via S pillar alpine style with Roger Mear) 1998, Targo Ri (6572m) 2000; first Br ascent Salathé Wall El Capitain Yosemite 1971, first alpine style ascent Diran (7260m) 1985, first Br ascent Chimtarga (5482m) Fansikye Mountains Tadzhikistan 1992, climed Mt Vinson (4897m, highest point in Antarctica) 1992, attempt on Nanga Parbat (8135m) via Mazeno Ridge 1992, climbed three Mazeno Peaks 1993 (also Mazeno Spire and West Peak), climbs and explorations in Tierra del Fuego 1994, original route and new route up N face V Carstenez Pyramid (4884m) 1995, second ascent NE ridge Teng Kongma (6215m) 1998, first ever foreigner (with Greg Child) to explore mountains of central Arunachal Pardesh 1999; memb other expdns incl: Euro Mt Everest Expedition to SW face 1972; Br Mt Everest Expedition to SW face 1972 (autumn), Br Mt Everest Expedition (reached summit with Dougal Haston, via SW face, first Britons on summit) 1975; *Publications* Big Wall Climbing (1974), Shishapangma, Tibet (with Alex MacIntyre, 1984), Himalayan Climber (1992); contributor to Alpine Journal, American Alpine Journal and Mountain Magazine, Himal Magazine; *Recreations* rock climbing, organic gardening; *Clubs* Alpine, Alpine Climbing Gp, Nottingham Climbers; *Style*— Doug Scott, Esq, CBE; ✉ Warwick Mill, Warwick Bridge, Carlisle, Cumbria CA4 8RR (tel 01228 564488, e-mail dougscott25@hotmail.com or info@catreks.com)

SCOTT, Dougray; *Educ* Kirkcaldy Coll of Technol (later Fife Coll), Welsh Coll of Music and Drama; *Career* actor; *Theatre* Wallace (Scottish Theatre), Welcome Home (Old Red Lion), To Kill A Mockingbird (SNAP Theatre Co), This Island's Mine (Gay Sweatshop), Indigo (Almedia), The Power and the Glory (Chichester Festival Theatre), Unidentified Human Remains (Traverse), And the True Nature of Love (Hampstead), The Rover (Jacob Street), To The Green Fields Beyond (Donmar Warehouse); *Television* incl: Crow Road 1996, Arabian Nights 2000, Heist 2006, Desperate Housewives 2006–07; *Film* incl: Mission: Impossible II 2000, Enigma 2001, Ripley's Game 2002, To Kill A King 2003 (also assoc prodr), The Poet 2003, One Last Chance 2004 (also exec prodr), Things to Do Before You're 30 2004, Dark Water 2005, Perfect Creature 2007; *Style*— Dougray Scott, Esq; ✉ c/o Public Eye Communications, Suite 318, 535 King's Road, London SW10 0SZ (tel 020 7351 1555, fax 020 7351 1010)

SCOTT, Dr Eleanor Roberta; da of late William Ettles, and Roberta, *née* Reid; *b* 23 July 1951; *Educ* Bearsden Acad, Univ of Glasgow (MB ChB); *m* 1977 (m dis 1994) David Scott; 1 da (Tania Emily 10 July 1982), 1 s (Robert David b 7 July 1985); partner, Rob Gibson, MSP, *qv*; *Career* various jr hosp dr posts 1974–78, trainee in gen practice Nairn 1979, community paediatrician Inverness 1980–87, community paediatrician Ross and Cromarty 1987–2003, MSP (Green) Highlands and Islands 2003–07; memb Scottish Green Pty 1989–; *Recreations* traditional music, gardening; *Style*— Dr Eleanor Scott; ✉ 8 Culcairn Road, Evanton IV16 9YT (tel 01349 830388, fax 01349 830599)

SCOTT, Finlay McMillan; TD (1984); s of Finlay McMillan Scott (d 1985), and Anne Cameron Robertson, *née* Coutts (d 1972); *b* 25 May 1947; *Educ* Greenock HS, Open Univ (BA), Univ of Durham (MSc); *m* 1, 17 May 1969 (m dis 2001), Eileen Frances, da of Ronald Francis Marshall; 1 da (Karen Anne Coutts b 21 Dec 1972), 1 s (Finlay Alan McMillan b 18 July 1975); m 2, Prof Elizabeth Susan Perkins; *Career* Dept for Educn 1975–94 (under sec (grade 3) 1990), seconded as sec Univs Funding Cncl 1990–92, seconded as sec and dep chief exec HEFCE 1992–94, chief exec and registrar GMC 1994–; memb: NI Higher Educn Cncl 1994–, Med Workforce Standing Advsy Ctee 1996–2001, Postgrad Medical Educn and Trg Bd 2003–; TA: Intelligence Corps 1973–76, RAOC 1976–94, Lt Col 1989, Royal Logistic Corps 1994–95, RARO 1995–; govr: London Guildhall Univ 1996–2002, London Metropolitan Univ 2003–; *Recreations* Dartmoor letter boxing, squash, tennis, hill walking; *Style*— Finlay Scott, Esq, TD; ✉ General Medical Council, Regents Place, 350 Euston Road, London NW1 3JN

SCOTT, (Celia) Gay; da of Ivor Norman Bailey (d 1986), and Enid Alice, *née* Sherwood (d 1997); *b* 25 March 1944; *Educ* St Angela's Providence Convent London, NW London Poly, Brighton Coll of Librarianship; *m* 18 May 1967, Michael James Frederick Scott, s of Capt John Bristol Irwin Scott (d 1991), of Bedford; 1 s (Charles b 1982); *Career* Membs' Info Serv House of Commons 1973–74, head of Euro Unit Greater London Cncl 1976–80, fndr and dir European Information Ltd (acquired by Eurofi 1982) 1980–, dir Eurofi 1982–; assoc Library Assoc 1967, MIInfSc 1977; *Publications* The European Economic Community (1979), A Guide to European Community Grants and Loans (annually 1980–), Money for Research and Development (jtly, 1986), Eurobrief (monthly 1981–83); *Recreations* riding, walking, cookery, tennis, theatre-going, gardening; *Style*— Mrs Michael Scott; ✉ Butler's, Brisley, Dereham, Norfolk NR20 5AA (tel and fax 01362 667079); Eurofi House, 37 London Road, Newbury, Berkshire RG13 1JL (tel 01635 31900, fax 01635 37370, e-mail gayscott@btinternet.com)

SCOTT, Graham Robert; s of Robert Alexander Scott, of Alness, Ross-shire, and Helen, *née* Tawse (d 1987); *b* 8 December 1944; *Educ* Bryanston, Univ of Nottingham (BSc); *m* 19 Aug 1967, Wendy Jean, da of Harry Mumford (d 1983); 1 s (Andrew), 1 da (Harriet); *Career* gen mangr Unitrition Int Ltd 1984–86, md BP Nutrition (UK) Ltd 1987–89, area chief exec BP Nutrition Specialities 1989–90, chief exec BP Nutrition Petfoods 1991–93, gp chief exec JLI Group plc 1994–95, chief exec NWF Group plc 1995–2007; non-exec dir: Buxton Arts Festival Ltd 1997–, Butcher's Pet Care Ltd 2001–; non-exec chm Dee Valley Group plc 1998–2002 and 2003–; CEng 1971, MIChemE 1971; *Style*— Graham Scott, Esq

SCOTT, Dr Hazel R; da of Very Rev Dr Hugh R Wyllie, of Hamilton, Strathclyde, and Eileen, *née* Cameron; *b* 31 January 1965; *Educ* Hutchesons' GS, Univ of Glasgow (MB ChB, MD); *m* 16 Sept 1994, Alastair E Scott; 2 s (Iain b 1 April 1999, Alexander b 9 June 2004); *Career* sr registrar W Glasgow Hosps Univ NHS Tst until 1996, conslt physician (with an interest in respiratory med) Wishaw Gen Hosp NHS Tst 1996–; dir Med Educn Lanarkshire Acute Hosps Tst 2001–; dir of medical educn and continuing professional devpt (CPD) RCPSGlas 2006–; treas Royal Medicochirurgical Soc of Glasgow 1996–2000 and 2003–; FRCP; *Recreations* music, gardening; *Style*— Dr Hazel R Scott; ✉ Department of Medicine, Wishaw General Hospital NHS Trust, Wishaw, Lanarkshire ML2 0DP (tel 01698 361100)

SCOTT, Hugh Johnstone; s of Hugh Johnstone Scott (d 1961), and Agnes Alison Leckie, *née* Storie (d 1994); *Educ* Paisley GS, Glasgow Sch of Art (DA), Jordanhill Coll (CertEd); *m* 23 Dec 1960, Mary Smith Craig, da of James Hamilton; 1 s (David b 7 Oct 1961), 1 da (Caroline b 18 Sept 1963); *Career* Nat Serv 1958–60; art teacher various schs 1971–84 (latterly head of art Lomond Sch Helensburgh); full time author 1984–; writer in residence City of Aberdeen 1991 (Scottish Arts Cncl bursary), pt/t lectr in creative writing Adult and Continuing Educn Dept Univ of Glasgow 1988–, tutor with the Arvon Fndn 1994, pt/t lectr in drawing and painting Adult and Continuing Educn Dept Univ of Glasgow 1998–2003, ind tutor of drawing and painting and of creative writing 2003–, columnist and cartoonist for The Park Free Press (formerly The Press & Post) 2003–; winner Woman's Realm Children's Story Competition 1982, Scottish Arts Cncl bursary 1988–89, Whitbread Children's Category Book of the Year 1989, Scottish Arts Cncl bursary 1993–94 and 1997; memb Soc of Authors 1988; *Books* incl: The Shaman's Stone (1988), The Plant That Ate The World (1989), Why Weeps The Brogan? (1989, short-listed for the McVitie prize 1990), Freddie and the Enormouse, The Haunted Sand, The Camera Obscura, The Summertime Santa, Something Watching, The Gargoyle (1991), Change the King! (1991), A Box of Tricks (1991), A Ghost Waiting (1993), The Place Between (1994), The Ghosts of Ravens Crag (1996), The Grave-Digger (1997), The Secret of the Pit (1998), Giants (1999); *Recreations* weight training, reading, exploring England, painting; *Style*— Hugh Scott, Esq; ✉ c/o Walker Books Ltd, 87 Vauxhall Walk, London SE11 5HJ (tel 020 7793 0909, fax 020 7587 1123)

SCOTT, Prof Ian Richard; s of Ernest Richard Scott (d 1971), of Geelong, Aust, and Edith Miriam Scott (d 1976); *b* 8 January 1940; *Educ* Geelong Coll, Queen's Coll, Univ of Melbourne (LLB), King's Coll London (PhD); *m* 1 Oct 1971, Ecce Scott, da of Prof Boris Norman Cole, of Leeds; 2 da (Anneke b 1 Jan 1978, Kaatye b 3 Jan 1981); *Career* barr and slr Supreme Court of Victoria 1964–, called to the Bar Gray's Inn 1995 (hon bencher 1988); Univ of Birmingham: reader judicial admin 1976–78, dir Inst of Judicial Admin 1976–82, Barber prof of law 1978–2000, dean Faculty of Law 1985–94, prof of law 2000–05, emeritus prof 2005–; visiting research prof Whittier Coll California 1978–79, exec dir Victoria Law Fndn 1982–84, non-exec dir Royal Orthopaedic Hosp NHS Tst 1996–2000; gen ed The White Book 2007– (contributing ed 1989–2006); memb: Lord Chllr's Review Body on Civil Justice 1985–88, Policy Advsy Gp Nat Health Serv Litigation Authy 1997–2000, Alternative Dispute Resolution sub-ctee of Civil Justice Cncl 1998–2002; chm Home Sec's N Yorks Magistrates' Courts Inquiry 1989; *Style*— Prof I R Scott; ✉ Faculty of Law, University of Birmingham, Birmingham B15 2TT (tel 0121 414 3637)

SCOTT, Ian Russell; s of William Russell Scott (d 1974), and Winifred Mabel, *née* Morgan; *b* 12 September 1942; *Educ* Sherborne, Univ of London (LLB); *m* 3 May 1969, Mary Peverell, da of Robert Riggs Wright, TD (d 1998); 2 da (Katharine b 1971, Louise b 1973), 1 s (William b 1975); *Career* asst slr Sharpe Pritchard & Co 1967–68, ptnr Ashurst Morris Crisp (now Ashurst) 1972–2002 (asst slr 1968–72, sr advsr 2002–); memb Law Soc 1965; *Recreations* theatre, tennis, hockey, golf, sailing; *Clubs* City of London; *Style*— Ian Scott, Esq; ✉ The Court House, Ryme Intrinseca, Sherborne, Dorset DT9 6JX; Flat 2, 32 Pembridge Villas, London W8 3EL; Ashurst, Broadwalk House, 5 Appold Street, London EC2A 2HA (tel 020 7638 1111, fax 020 7638 1112)

SCOTT, Prof James; s of Robert Bentham Scott (d 1976), and Iris Olive, *née* Hill, of Melton Mowbray, Leics; *b* 13 September 1946; *Educ* Univ of London (scholar, BSc), London Hosp Med Coll (MB BS, MSc, MRCP); *m* 1976, Diane Marylin, da of Herbert Lowe; 2 s (William b 30 July 1981, Edward b 10 Sept 1984), 1 da (Lucy b 20 Jan 1990); *Career* house offr: London Hosp 1971–72, Hereford Co Hosp 1972; SHO Midland Centre for Neurosurgery and Neurology and Queen Elizabeth Hosp Birmingham 1972–73; registrar in med: Gen Hosp Birmingham 1973–74, Academic Dept of Med Royal Free Hosp London 1975–76; MRC research fell and hon sr registrar Royal Postgraduate Med Sch and Hammersmith Hosp London 1977–80, Euro Molecular Biology Orgn fell Dept of Biochemistry Univ of Calif San Francisco 1980–83, MRC clinical scientist and hon conslt physician MRC Clinical Research Inst and Northwick Park Hosp 1983–91, hon dir MRC Molecular Med Gp 1992–, prof of med and chm Dept of Med Imperial Coll Sch of Med at Hammersmith Hosp (Royal Postgraduate Med Sch until merger 1997) 1992, dir of med and chief of serv med cardiology Hammersmith Hosps NHS Tst 1994, dir Genetics and Genomics Research Inst Imperial Coll (dep princ Research); Humphrey Davy Rolleston lectr RCP 1989, guest lectr MRS 1990, Pfizer lectr Clinical Research Inst Montreal 1990, guest lectr Japan Atherosclerosis Soc 1992, medallist and visiting prof RSM/American Heart Assoc 1992, Montreal Merck Frosst-McGill lectr in lipid metabolism 1992, Simms lectr 1995; Graham Bull Prize RCP 1989, Squibb Bristol-Myers Award 1993 (for cardiovascular research); memb: Grants Ctee B MRC Systems Bd until 1990, Research Fund Ctee Br Heart Fndn until 1992, Research Ctee RCP 1988–; external examiner (BSc Clinical Scis) 1991 and internal examiner (MB BS) 1993 Univ of London; author of numerous book chapters, reviews and refereed papers; Euro ed Arteriosclerosis, Thrombosis and Vascular Biology (American Heart Assoc jl); fell Queen Mary & Westfield Coll London 1998; memb: Biochemical Soc, RSM, Euro Molecular Biology Orgn 1993; FRCP 1986, FRS 1997, FIBiol 1998, FMedSci 1998, hon fell Assoc of Physicians of GB and I 1998; *Recreations* family and friends, the twentieth century novel, British impressionist and modern painting, long distance running and swimming; *Style*— Prof James Scott, FRS; ✉ Genetics and Genomics Research Institute, Imperial College School of Medicine, South Kensington Campus, Exhibition Road, London SW7 2AZ (tel 020 7594 3614, fax 020 7594 3653)

SCOTT, James Empson; s of James Christopher Scott (d 1979), and Phyllis Margaret, *née* Empson (d 1985); *b* 8 November 1942; *Educ* King's Sch Canterbury, Oriel Coll Oxford, Middx Hosp Med Sch (MA); *m* 1, 1967 (m dis), Mary, da of Sir Brian Fairfax-Lucy (d 1974); 2 da (Sophie b 1970, Charlotte b 1974); m 2, 1980, Katherine Henrietta, da of Sir Michael Cary (d 1978); 2 s (Matthew b 1984, Ned b 1985), 1 da (Molly b 1990); *Career* successively: sr registrar (orthopaedic surgery) Middx Hosp and Royal Nat Orthopaedic Hosp, Fulbright scholar and fell in orthopaedic surgery Massachusetts Gen Hosp, conslt orthopaedic surgn St Stephen's Hosp, St Mary Abbott's Hosp and Westminster Hosps, conslt orthopaedic surgn Chelsea and Westminster Hosp London; sr examiner (MB BS) Univ of London, memb Cncl Orthopaedic Section RSM; ed Jl of Bone and Joint Surgery; FRCS, FBOA; *Recreations* paintings; *Clubs* Athenaeum; *Style*— James Scott, Esq; ✉ 8 Rectory Grove, London SW4 0EA (tel 020 7622 0571); The Lister Hospital, Chelsea Bridge Road, London SW1W 8RH (tel 020 7259 9216, fax 020 7259 9221)

SCOTT, Sir James Jervoise; 3 Bt (UK 1962), of Rotherfield Park, Hants; s of Sir James Walter Scott, 2 Bt, DL (d 1993), and Anne Constantia, *née* Austin; *b* 12 October 1952; *Educ* Eton, Trinity Coll Cambridge; *m* 13 Oct 1982, Judy Evelyn, da of Brian Trafford, of Tismans, W Sussex; 1 s (Arthur Jervoise Trafford b 2 Feb 1984), 1 da (Alexandra Lilian b 1986); *Heir* s, Arthur Scott; *Career* ed Big Farm Weekly 1984–88; memb Hants CC 2001–05; High Sheriff Hants 2004–05; pres Hants Branch CLA 2005– (chm 1996–98); Liveryman Worshipful Co of Mercers; *Style*— Sir James Scott, Bt; ✉ Rotherfield Park, East Tisted, Alton, Hampshire GU34 3QE

SCOTT, Sir (Walter) John; 5 Bt (UK 1907), of Beauclerc, Bywell St Andrews, Co Northumberland; s of Maj Sir Walter Scott, 4 Bt, JP, DL (d 1992), and Diana Mary, *née* Owen (d 1985); *b* 24 February 1948; *Educ* privately; *m* 1, 1969 (m dis 1971), Lowell Patria, da of late Gp Capt Pat Vaughan Goddard, of Auckland, NZ; 1 da (Rebecca b 1970); m 2, 1977, Mary Gavin, o da of Alexander Fairley Anderson, of Gartocharn, Dunbartonshire; 1 da (Diana Helen Rose b 1977), 1 s (Walter Samuel b 1984); *Heir* s, Walter Scott; *Career* farmer, columnist, author and TV broadcaster; *Recreations* field sports; *Style*— Sir John Scott, Bt

SCOTT, John; JP, MSP; s of William Scott, of Ballantrae, Ayrshire, and Elizabeth Haddow, *née* Graham; *b* 7 June 1951; *Educ* George Watson's Coll Edinburgh, Univ of Edinburgh (BSc); *m* 7 June 1975, Charity Nadine Mary (d 2000), da of Lt-Col G M T Bousfield; 1 s (Gordon John b 12 June 1977), 1 da (Caroline Mary Elizabeth b 1 May 1979); *Career*

S

farmer W Scott & Son partnership Balkissock 1973–, ptnr Doorstep Dishes and Events in Tents 1986–2000, estab fertiliser selling agency 1987, fndr dir Ayrshire Country Lamb Ltd 1988–93, estab Ayrshire Farmers Markets 1999, MSP (Cons) Ayr 2000–; memb Tport and Environment Ctee Scot Parl 2001–03, Scot Cons spokesman on the environment 2001–03, memb Corporate Body Scot Parl 2003–, dep convenor Petitions Ctee Scot Parl 2003–; policy cmmr (rural affrs) Rifkind Policy Cmmn Scot Cons Pty 1998, dep chm Carrick Cumnock and Doon Valley Cons Pty 1999–2000; NFU of Scot: convenor Hill Farming Ctee 1993–99, pres Ayrshire Exec 1994–96; chm: Ayrshire and Arran Farming and Wildlife Advsy Gp 1993–99, S of Scot Regnl Wool Ctee 1996–99, Advsy Gp Hill Sheep and Native Woodland Project 1999–, Scot Area Ctee UK Cons Countryside Forum 1999–2000; fndr chm: Scot Assoc of Farmers' Markets 2001, Ayrshire Farmers' Markets 2001; *Recreations* geology, curling, bridge, rugby; *Style—* John Scott, Esq, MSP; ✉ Constituency Office, 1 Wellington Square, Ayr KA7 1EN (tel 01292 286251, fax 01292 280480); Scottish Parliament, Edinburgh EH99 1SP (tel 0131 348 5664, fax 0131 348 5617, e-mail john.scott.msp@scottish.parliament.uk)

SCOTT, John Gavin; LVO (2004); s of Douglas Gavin Scott, and Hetty, *née* Murphy; *b* 18 June 1956; *Educ* Queen Elizabeth GS Wakefield, St John's Coll Cambridge (organ scholar, MA, MusB); *m* 28 July 1979, Carolyn Jane, da of David James Lumsden; 1 da (Emma Jane b 27 Dec 1984), 1 s (Alexander Gavin b 29 Oct 1987); *Career* asst organist: Wakefield Cathedral 1970–74, St Paul's and Southwark Cathedrals 1978–84; organist and dir of music St Paul's Cathedral 1990–2004 (sub-organist 1984–90), organist and dir of music St Thomas Church Fifth Avenue NY 2004–; debut Henry Wood Proms 1977, Royal Festival Hall debut March 1979; frequent solo tours, dir of St Paul's Cathedral Choir in numerous concerts, tours and recordings; awarded first prize: Manchester International Organ Competition 1978, Leipzig J S Bach Competition 1984; International Performer of the Year Award American Guild of Organists 1998; Liveryman Worshipful Co of Musicians; Hon RAM 1990, Hon FGCM 1996, Hon FRSCM 2006; *Recordings* as soloist: Liszt's Ad Nos, Ad Salutarem Undam 1984, Organ Music by Marcel Dupré 1986, Organ Music by Maurice Duruflé 1989, Organ Music by Mendelssohn, Janácek's Glagolitic Mass 1990, Organ Music by Elgar, Harris and Bairstow 1992, Organ Music by William Mathias 1993, Great European Organs No 40 1996, 20th Century Masterpieces 1998, Marcel Dupré Vol II 1998, Organ Music by Percy Whitlock 2004; as conductor with St Paul's Choir: Christmas Music 1986, My Soul Doth Magnify the Lord 1987, Herbert Howell's Church Music 1987, My Spirit Hath Rejoiced 1988, Praise to the Lord 1989, The English Anthem Vol 1–8 1989–2004, Stainer's Crucifixion 1990, Hear my Prayer 1991, Cathedral Music by Kenneth Leighton 1992, Music by William Croft 1993, RPO Christmas Concert 1993, Christmas Carols 1994, Psalms Vol 1–12 1994–2000, Passiontide 1996, Music for St Paul's 1998, Advent at St Paul's 1998, Epiphany at St Paul's 2001, Remembrance 2003; as conductor with St Thomas Choir: Christmas on 5th Avenue 2005, Easter on 5th Avenue 2006; *Publications* The New St Paul's Cathedral Psalter (1997), Ash Wednesday to Easter for Choirs (1998), St Paul's Cathedral Descant Book (2001), Epiphany to All Saints for Choirs (2004); *Recreations* reading, travel; *Style—* John Scott, Esq, LVO; ✉ 202 West 58th Street, New York, NY 10019, USA (tel 00 212 757 7013, e-mail jscott@saintthomaschurch.org)

SCOTT, John Philip Henry Schomberg; s of late Christopher Bartle Hugh Scott, and late Anne Margaret D'Arcy, *née* Kerr, of Galashiels, Scotland; *b* 20 June 1952; *Educ* Eton, Magdalene Coll Cambridge (MA), INSEAD Fontainebleau (MBA); *m* 6 Dec 1977, Jacqueline Dawn, da of Colin Rae, MC, of Bunbury, Cheshire; 2 s (Alexander Hugh Frere b 8 Dec 1982, James Julian Frere b 1 April 1985); *Career* Jardine Matheson & Co Ltd Hong Kong 1974–80; dir: Lazard Brothers & Co Ltd London 1988–2001 (joined 1981), Xaar plc 2001–, Dunedin Income Growth Investment Tst plc 2001– (chm 2006–), Miller Insurance Services Ltd 2001–, Scottish Mortgage Investment Tst plc 2001–, Martin Currie Pacific Tst plc 2002–, JP Morgan Claverhouse Investment Tst plc 2004–, Schroder Japan Growth Fund plc 2004–; non-exec dep chm Endace Ltd (formerly chm); memb Queen's Body Guard for Scotland (Royal Co of Archers); Freeman City of London 1981, Liveryman Worshipful Co of Grocers 1992 (memb Ct of Assts 2002); FCII 1980, FSI 2005 (MSI 1993); *Recreations* outdoor sports; *Clubs* New (Edinburgh), Boodle's, Forest (Selkirk), '71 (Cambridge); *Style—* John Scott, Esq; ✉ Hollybush, by Galashiels, Selkirkshire TD1 3PU (tel 01896 753549)

SCOTT, (Ian) Jonathan; CBE (1995); s of Col Alexander Brassey Jonathan Scott, DSO, MC (d 1978), of Lasborough, Tetbury, and Rhona Margaret, *née* Stewart; *b* 7 February 1940; *Educ* Harrow, Balliol Coll Oxford (BA); *m* 12 June 1965, Annabella Constance, JP, da of Francis William Hope Loudon (d 1985), of Olantigh, Kent, and his w Lady Prudence, *née* Jellicoe, da of 1 Earl Jellicoe (d 2000); 2 s (Alexander b 1966, Justin b 1970), 1 da (Julia b 1969); *Career* dir: Charterhouse Japhet Ltd 1973–80, Barclays Merchant Bank Ltd 1980–85, Barclays de Zoete Wedd Ltd 1985–92; chm Reviewing Ctee on the Export of Works of Art 1985–95; tstee: Imperial War Museum 1984–98, V&A Museum 1995–2003 (dep chm 1997–2003); chm Acceptance in Lieu Panel 2000–; FSA 1980; *Books* Piranesi (1975), Salvator Rosa (1995), The Pleasures of Antiquity (2003); *Clubs* Brooks's; *Style—* Jonathan Scott, Esq, CBE, FSA; ✉ Lasborough Manor, Tetbury, Gloucestershire GL8 8UF; Flat 8, 25 Queen's Gate, London SW7 5JE

SCOTT, Judith Margaret; da of Robert Wright, of Halstead, Essex, and Marjorie, *née* Wood (d 1983); *b* 4 October 1942, Altrincham, Cheshire; *Educ* St Monica's Sch Clacton, Univ of St Andrews (BSc), Univ of Cambridge (Dip); *m* 23 March 1972, Gordon Robert Scott (d 1996); 2 da (Alison Catherine b 2 Oct 1974, Maureen Lesley b 24 Dec 1976); *Career* Defence Electronics Canada 1966–68, Computer Servs Canada 1968–79, product mktg dir Gandalf Data Ltd Canada 1979–82, dir of corp strategy Gandalf Technologies Inc Canada 1982–87, md Gandalf Digital Communications Ltd UK 1987–95, chief exec BCS 1995–2002; memb PPARC 2001–06; chm Wokingham and Dist CAB; tstee: Menerva Educnl Tst, Wokingham and Dist Cancer Care Tst; chm Sonning Dearery Synod; memb Cncl Univ of Reading; hon degree Univ of Staffordshire 2002; memb Worshipful Co of Information Technologists; FBCS 1995, CEng 1995; *Recreations* walking, gardening; *Style—* Mrs Judith Scott

SCOTT, (Norman) Keith; CBE (1989); s of Norman Scott (d 1986), and Dora Scott (d 1979); *b* 10 February 1927; *Educ* Preston GS, Univ of Liverpool Sch of Architecture (BArch, MA), Univ of Liverpool Sch of Planning (DipCD), MIT (MArch); *m* 19 Jan 1952, Dorothy Anne, da of Frederick Walker (d 1958); 2 da (Louise Amanda b 22 Nov 1953, Hilary Jane b 7 June 1956), 2 s (Quentin Nicholas b 3 Sept 1959, (Timothy) Tarquin b 7 March 1964); *Career* architect to Dean and Chapter Liverpool Cathedral 1979–98; chm: Awards Panel RIBA 1982–84, BDP 1984–89 (ptnr 1963, conslt 1989–93); private architect and planning conslt 1993–; memb Bd: Lake Dist Summer Music Festival 1984–95 (chm 1990–95), Rural Buildings Tst 1994–; govr Lancashire Poly (now Univ of Central Lancashire) 1988–92; chm: N Lancs Soc of Architects 1966–67, BDP Music Soc 1968–, Friends of London Int Piano Competition 1991–; memb Preston City Vision Bd 2004–; life memb Victorian Soc; memb Lambda Alpha International 1994–; FRIBA, MRTPI; *Books* Shopping Centre Design (1989), Would You Care To Say Something (1998); *Recreations* music, fell walking, sketching; *Clubs* Oriental; *Style—* N Keith Scott, CBE; ✉ Overleigh House, East Cliff, Preston PR1 3JE (tel 01772 253545,e-mail normanscott25@aol.com)

SCOTT, Lee; MP; s of Sidney Scott (d 1997), and Rennee, *née* Cain (d 1983); *b* 6 April 1956, Stratford, London; *Educ* Clarkes Coll Ilford; *m* 18 May 1987, Estelle King; 3 da (Sara b 8 Dec 1977, Hana b 28 Oct 1981, Rachel b 24 July 1988), 2 s (Daniel b 28 June 1979, Ben b 16 May 1984); *Career* campaign dir United Jewish Israel Appeal 1988–98; former cncllr (Cons) Redbridge BC, Parly candidate (Cons) Waveney 2001, MP (Cons) Ilford N 2005–; *Style—* Lee Scott, Esq, MP; ✉ House of Commons, London SW1A 0AA (tel 020 7219 8326, fax 020 7219 0970, e-mail scottle@parliament.uk); Constituency Office tel 020 8551 4333, fax 020 8551 4801, website www.leescott.co.uk

SCOTT, Malcolm James; s of David Scott, of Edinburgh, and Florence, *née* Purdie; *b* 13 November 1963, Edinburgh; *Educ* Fettes, Harper Adams Agric Coll; *m* 2 March 1991, Rona, *née* Melville; 2 s (Oliver b 21 Aug 1991, Charles b 6 July 1999), 1 da (Joanna b 26 Nov 1995); *Career* md and fndr Dunalastair Estates Ltd 1993–, md Dunalastair Philip Wilson Ltd 1996–; memb Devpt Ctee Prince's Tst 2005–; treas Scottish Cons 2006–; founding tstee Pakistan Human Devpt Fund; hon consul of Pakistan (Scotland) 2004–; Devpt of the Year (Ireland) 2004; *Recreations* running, gardening, antiques; *Clubs* New (Edinburgh); *Style—* Malcolm Scott, Esq; ✉ 9 Blair Street, Edinburgh EH1 1QR (tel 0131 225 3040, fax 0131 225 3009)

SCOTT, Maj Gen Michael Ian Eldon (Mike); CB (1997), CBE (1987), DSO (1982); s of Col Eric Scott (d 2005), and Rose-Anne Scott (d 1994); *b* 3 March 1941; *Educ* Bradfield Coll, RMA Sandhurst; *m* Veronica Daniell; 1 s, 1 da; *Career* cmmnd Scots Gds 1960, served UK, E Africa, NI and BAOR, psc 1974, MA 2 to Chief of Gen Staff, returned NI, COS Task Force Delta (now 12 Armd Bde) BAOR, Armed Forces Staff Coll USA, cmd 2 Bn Scots Gds London, Falklands Conflict 1982 and Cyprus, on Directing Staff Staff Coll Camberley 1984, cmd 8 Infantry Bde NI 1984–86, RCDS 1987, Dep Mil Sec (B) MOD 1987–93, GOC Scotland and Govr of Edinburgh Castle 1993–95, Mil Sec 1995–97; Complaints Cmmr Bar Cncl 1997–2006; *Recreations* art, travel, outdoor pursuits; *Style—* Maj Gen M I E Scott, CB, CBE, DSO

SCOTT, Michael James; s of Arthur James Scott, and Phyllis, *née* Ravenhill (d 1970); *b* 7 December 1942; *Educ* Sutton Valence, Univ of Edinburgh (MA); *m* 10 May 1969, Suzette; 1 da (Polly Elizabeth b 2 Sept 1971), 1 s (Edward James b 6 Sept 1980); *Career* CA 1968; Arthur Andersen 1970–72, ptnr Grant Thornton 1975–2001 (joined 1972), conslt 2001–02; memb Advsy Cncl Philharmonia Orch 2003–; govr Southill Lower Sch 2007–; *Recreations* music, skiing, tennis, France; *Clubs* SCGB, DHO, Grasshoppers, Racket & Anchor; *Style—* Michael Scott, Esq; ✉ The Old Vicarage, Old Warden, Bedfordshire SG18 9HQ (tel 01767 627505, e-mail mjs@scott712.fsnet.co.uk)

SCOTT, Sir Oliver Christopher Anderson; 3 Bt (UK 1909), of Yews, Undermilbeck, Westmorland; s of Sir Samuel Haslam Scott, 2 Bt (d 1960), and his 2 wife, Nancy Lilian, *née* Anderson (d 1935); *b* 6 November 1922; *Educ* Charterhouse, King's Coll Cambridge (MA); *m* 1951, Phoebe Anne, er da of Desmond O'Neill Tolhurst, of Chelsea; 2 da (Hermione Mary (Mrs Miles R Stanford) b 1952, Camilla Nancy (Mrs David B Withington) b 1956), 1 s (Christopher James b 1955); *Heir* s, Christopher Scott; *Career* High Sheriff of Westmorland 1966; dir Res Unit of Radiobiology British Empire Cancer Campaign 1966–69, conslt Inst of Cancer Res 1974–82, radiobiologist St Thomas' Hosp London 1982–88; Liveryman Worshipful Co of Skinners; Hon FRCR 1998; *Clubs* Brooks's; *Style—* Sir Oliver Scott, Bt, MD; ✉ 31 Kensington Square, London W8 5HH

SCOTT, Patricia Mary; da of Gordon James Rouse (d 1978), and Hilda May, *née* Marchant; *b* 28 November 1954; *Educ* Hreod Burna Sr HS, Portsmouth Poly; *m* 1 Aug 1975, Anthony Vincent Scott, s of Thomas Arthur David Scott; 1 s (Adam James b 27 May 1991), 1 adopted da (Anna Louise b 7 July 1995); *Career* various appts Thorn Television Rentals Ltd and Thorn EMI plc 1974–85, accountant Burmah Oil Exploration Ltd 1985; Thorn EMI plc: gp tax mangr 1986–89, dir Taxation and Treasury 1989–94; chief exec The Chieveley Consulting Group Ltd 1995–97 and 1998–, gp treas Redland plc 1997–98; dir: Woodbridge Ptnrs Ltd 2002–, Scott Young Ltd 2002–07; dir and fndr: Leadership in Finance 2005–06, The Rivendell Centre Ltd incorporating Leading Edge Change 2006–; non-exec dir: Warden Housing Assoc 1995–2006, Housing Ops Bd Home Housing Gp 2006–; hon treas St Augustine's Church 1985–2002, tstee One Small Step charity for the disabled 1993–96; govr Downe House Sch 1995–97; fell Chartered Assoc of Certified Accountants 1989 (memb 1984); memb Tax Law Review Ctee 1994–2004; fell Assoc of Corporate Treasurers 1998 (memb 1990); *Publications* Having their Cake - How the City and Big Bosses are Consuming UK Business (co-author, 2004); *Recreations* gardening, walking, reading; *Style—* Patricia Scott; ✉ Rivendell, 5 The Clays, Market Lavington, Devizes, Wiltshire SN10 4AY (tel 01380 816077, fax 01380 816077, e-mail pat.scott@rivendellcentre.com and pat.scott@leadingedgechange.com)

SCOTT, Prof Sir (George) Peter; kt (2007); *Educ* Merton Coll Oxford (BA), Univ of Calif Berkeley Graduate Sch of Public Policy (visiting scholar, Harkness fell); *Career* reporter then news ed TES 1967–69, reporter The Times 1969–71, dep ed The Times Higher Educational Supplement 1971–73, leader writer The Times 1974–76, ed The Times Higher Educational Supplement 1976–92; Univ of Leeds: prof of educn 1992–97, dir Centre for Policy Studies in Educn 1992–97, pro-vice-chllr (external affrs) 1996–97; vice-chllr Kingston Univ 1997–; chm: governing body S Thames Coll 1985–92, Exec Ctee UKCOSA 1992–98; memb: Continuing Educn Working Pty 1985–86, Nat Advsy Body for Public Sector Higher Educn 1985–86, Further Educn Unit 1993, Further Educn Staff College Review Gp, Further Educn Funding Cncl 1993, Lord Chllr's Advsy Ctee on Legal Educn and Conduct 1994–99 (vice-chm 1996), Bd of Mgmnt FE Devpt Assoc 1994–, HEFCE Working Pty on Higher Educn in Further Educn 1995 Advsy Ctee on Academic Standards Bolton Inst of Higher Educn 1996–, Nat Advsy Gp on Continuing Educn and Lifelong Learning (Fryer Ctee) 1997–, Bd of Directors Educn Counselling Service Br Cncl 1999–, Bd of Directors HESA 2000–, HEFCE Review Panel Inst of Educn Univ of London 2000, Bd HEFCE 2000–06, Cncl Euro Univ Assoc (EUA) 2002–; Hon LLD Univ of Bath, Hon DLitt CNAA, Hon DLitt Grand Valley State Univ, Hon DPhil Anglia Poly Univ; hon fell UMIST, hon fell Bath Coll of HE; memb Academia Europaea; AcSS 2000, fell Soc for Research into HE, FRSA; *Books* Strategies for Postsecondary Education (1976), The Crisis of the University (1984), Knowledge and Nation (1990), The New Production of Knowledge: the dynamics of science and research in contemporary societies (jtly, 1994), The Meanings of Mass Higher Education (1995), Governing Universities: Changing the Culture? (jtly, 1996); also author of numerous book chapters and articles in learned jls; *Style—* Prof Sir Peter Scott; ✉ Kingston University, River House, 53–57 High Street, Kingston upon Thames, Surrey KT1 1LQ (tel 020 8547 7010, fax 020 8547 7009, e-mail p.scott@kingston.ac.uk)

SCOTT, Peter Anthony; s of J Barclay Scott, and Doris Scott; *b* 24 April 1947; *Educ* Manchester Poly; *m* May 1969, Lynne Scott, *née* Smithies; 1 da (Deborah Ann b 26 July 1972) 1 s (Steven Anthony b 10 Oct 1975); *Career* fin accountant: Fothergill & Harvey plc 1962–75, Crane Fruehauf Ltd 1975–77; Peel Holdings plc: co sec 1977–84, fin dir 1984–85, md 1985–; FCCA 1979; *Style—* Peter A Scott, Esq; ✉ Peel Holdings plc, Peel Dome, The Trafford Centre, Manchester M17 8PL (tel 0161 629 8200, fax 0161 629 8333, e-mail pscott@peel.co.uk)

SCOTT, Peter Denys John; QC (1978); s of John Ernest Dudley Scott, and Joan Steinberg, *née* Clayton-Cooper; *b* 19 April 1935; *Educ* Monroe HS Rochester NY, Balliol Coll Oxford (MA); *Career* Nat Serv Lt RHA; called to the Bar Middle Temple 1960; chm Gen Cncl of the Bar 1987 (vice-chm 1985–86), judicial chm City Disputes Panel; chm The Takeover Panel 2000–; chm Bd of Tstees: Kensington Housing Tst 1998–2002, Nat Gallery 2000–; memb Investigatory Serv Tbnl 2000–; *Style—* Peter Scott, Esq, QC; ✉ 4 Eldon Road, London W8 5PU (tel 020 7937 3301, fax 020 7376 1169); Fountain Court, Temple, London EC4Y 9DH (tel 020 7583 3335, fax 020 7353 0329)

SCOTT, Dr Peter Richard; s of Peter Robert Scott (d 2002), of Nottingham, and Doreen Elizabeth, *née* Jebb; *b* 23 March 1950; *Educ* Nottingham HS, St John's Coll Oxford (MA),

Pembroke Coll Oxford (DPhil); *m* 14 Aug 1976, Susan Margaret, da of Harry Dean; 2 da (Joanna Carol b 17 Nov 1982, Catherine Lucy b 19 July 1986); *Career* asst master Charterhouse 1974–91 (dir of studies and housemaster), dep head Royal GS Guildford 1991–96, headmaster Bancroft's Sch Woodford Green 1996–; govr: Ripley Ct Sch 1990–96, Northants GS 1997–2005, Gatehouse Sch 2001– (chm); Freeman of The Worshipful Company of Drapers 2007; *Books* incl: Energy Levels in Atoms (1994); *Style*— Dr Peter Scott; ✉ Bancroft's School, Woodford Green, Essex IG8 0RF (tel 020 8505 4821, fax 020 8559 0032, e-mail headmaster@bancrofts.essex.sch.uk)

SCOTT, Philip Edward Hannay; s of Edward Beattie Scott, MBE, and Mary, *née* Potter; *b* 6 April 1957; *Educ* Millfield, Cricklade Coll Andover; *m* 23 Sept 1989, Victoria, *née* Byles; 1 s (Frederick Charles Edward b 27 Nov 2001); *Career* formerly worked in film indust Tor Films Ltd (Tarka the Otter); paralysed in motor racing accident 1977; illustrator 1978–, freelance journalist and broadcaster BBC 1979–1986 (Radio 4, World Service, Local Radio); currently an equity trader in Fin Ind; fndr Kudos Capital Partners 2003–; work with the disabled 1979–; achievements incl: fndr memb Project 81, fndr memb Hampshire Centre for Ind Living 1982, became one of first people to be completely supported in the community by a health authy; promotor of interests of the disabled through aviation achievements incl: fndr Operation Ability Ltd 1984, first tetraplegic to pass a Civil Aviation Authy med to gain private pilots' licence, private pilots' licence 1999 involved first G tests for tetraplegic person 1985; Man of the Year award for serv to disabled community 1988, awarded The Gerald Frewer Meml Trophy 1992, Br Microlight Aircraft Assoc Chairman's Award 1999; Freeman: City of London, Worshipful Co of Haberdashers 1978; AMRAeS 1985, MIED 1992; *Recreations* art, engineering, travel, flying, calligraphy, aviation; *Style*— Philip Scott, Esq

SCOTT, Philip Gordon; s of John Theophilus Scott (d 1973), of Great Yarmouth, and Grace Virginia, *née* Cole (d 1999); *b* 6 January 1954; *Educ* Great Yarmouth GS, KCL; *m* 9 Feb 1974, Helen Rebecca Evelyn, da of James Richard Blair Fearnley (d 1985); 1 da (Rebecca Jane b 11 Dec 1978); *Career* Aviva plc: joined 1973, qualified as actuary 1979, asst actuary for NZ 1981–84, asst investment mangr 1984–87, investment mangr 1987–88, sr investment mangr 1988–92, gen mangr (Fin) 1992–93, gen mangr (Life and Pensions) 1993–98, dir 1993–, chief exec (Life) 1998–2002, gp exec dir Avivia Int and chm Morley Fund Mgmnt 2003–06, gp finance dir Aviva plc 2007–; FIA 1979, FRSA; *Recreations* sailing, gardening, apples; *Clubs* Annabel's; *Style*— Philip G Scott, Esq; ✉ Whitegate Farm, Burgh St Margaret, Great Yarmouth, Norfolk NR29 3DB (tel 01493 369599); Aviva plc, St Helen's, 1 Undershaft, London EC39 3DQ (tel 020 7662 2264, fax 020 7662 2678, e-mail philip.scott@aviva.com)

SCOTT, Primrose Smith; da of Robert Scott (d 1978), of Uphall, W Lothian, and Jeannie McLaughlan, *née* Pollock (d 1962); *b* 21 September 1940; *Educ* Ayr Acad; *Career* trainee Stewart Gilmour & Co, qualified CA 1963, various managerial positions leading to ptnr Deloitte Haskins & Sells Edinburgh 1981–87, in own practice The McCabe Partnership (formerly Primrose McCabe & Co) 1987–99; dir: Dunfermline Building Society 1990–2005, Lothian and Edinburgh Enterprise Ltd 1995–99, Ecosse Unique Ltd 2004–; non-exec dir Northern Venture Trust plc 1995–; ICAS: memb Cncl 1987–95, chm Gen Practice Ctee 1990–93, pres 1994–95, head of Quality Review 1999–2002; tstee: New Lanark Tst 2002–06, Bield Housing Assoc 2005–; hon treas Hospitality Industry Tst Scotland 1994–2002, hon treas Age Concern Scotland 2004; hon fell SCOTVEC 1994; *Recreations* keep fit and dog walking; *Style*— Miss Primrose Scott; ✉ The Cleugh, Redpath, Earlston, Berwickshire TD4 6AD (tel 01896 849042)

SCOTT, Sir Ridley; kt (2003); *b* 30 November 1937, South Shields; *Career* film dir; *films*; incl: The Duellists 1977, Alien 1979, Blade Runner 1982, Legend 1986, Someone To Watch Over Me 1987, Black Rain 1989, Thelma & Louise 1991 (BAFTA nomination for Best Dir 1991, Academy Award nomination for Best Dir 1991), 1492 - Conquest Of Paradise 1992, White Squall 1996, GI Jane 1997, Gladiator 2000 (Academy Award nomination for Best Dir 2001, BAFTA nomination for Best Dir 2001, Golden Globe nomination for Best Dir 2001; voted Best Film at BAFTA's 2001 and Academy Awards 2001), Hannibal 2001, Black Hawk Down 2001 (Oscar nomination for Best Director 2002), Matchstick Men 2003, Kingdom of Heaven 2005, A Good Year 2006; *Style*— Sir Ridley Scott; ✉ c/o Julie Payne, 42–44 Beak Street, London W1R 3DA

SCOTT, Robert Avisson (Bob); CBE (2002); *b* 6 January 1942; *Career* gp chief exec General Accident plc 1996–98, gp chief exec CGU plc 1998–2000 (following merger between Commercial Union and General Accident), gp chief exec CGNU plc 2000–01 (following merger with Norwich Union); chm Yell Group plc 2003–; non-exec dir: Royal Bank of Scotland 2001–, Jardine Lloyd Thompson Group Ltd 2002–, Swiss Reinsurance Co Zurich 2002–; memb Ct of Assts Worshipful Co of Insurers; sr assoc Australian and NZ Inst of Insurance and Finance; FCIBS, Hon FCII; *Style*— Bob Scott, Esq, CBE; ✉ Axford Lodge, Axford, Hampshire RG25 2DZ (tel 01256 389259)

SCOTT, His Hon Judge Roger Martin; s of Hermann Albert Scott (d 1965), of Morley, Leeds, and Sarah Margaret, *née* Craven (d 1989); *b* 8 September 1944; *Educ* Mill Hill Sch, Univ of St Andrews (LLB, univ hockey team); *m* 10 Sept 1966, Diana Elizabeth, da of John Hayes Clark; 2 s (Martin John b 23 Nov 1967, Andrew Charles b 21 March 1970), 1 da (Katherine Anne b 29 July 1972); *Career* called to the Bar 1968; memb NE Circuit 1968–93, pupillage at 38 Park Square Leeds with H A Richardson, a fndr of new chambers at St Paul's House Park Sq 1981 (head of chambers 1985–91), recorder 1989–93 (asst recorder 1985–89), circuit judge (NE Circuit) 1993–; *Recreations* reading, theatre, walking, golf and watching all sports; *Style*— His Hon Judge Scott; ✉ Bradford Crown Court, Exchange Square, Drake Street, Bradford BD1 1JA (tel 01274 840274)

SCOTT, Sebastian Simon Frere; s of Christopher Hugh Bartle Frere Scott, and Anne Margret D'Arcy Kerr; *b* 1 August 1961; *Educ* Univ of Bristol (BA); *Career* studio mangr and reporter BBC Radio 1983–86, researcher That's Life and Kilroy BBC TV 1986–87, researcher and reporter Network Seven Sunday Prodns 1989, reporter Six O'Clock Show and Eyewitness LWT 1989–90, ed and series prodr Reportage and Rough Guide BBC TV 1990; Planet 24: ed The Word Channel 4 1991, exec prodr (features) 1992, ed The Big Breakfast Channel 4 1992–96; md and exec prodr Princess Productions 1996– (prodns incl: Model Behaviour, The Restaurant, Wright Stuff, Light Lunch, The Friday Night Project, Date My Mom); memb BAFTA 2003–; *Style*— Sebastian Scott, Esq

SCOTT, Tavish Hamilton; MSP; s of John H Scott, of Bressay, Shetland, and Wendy Scott; *Educ* Anderson HS Lerwick, Napier Univ (BA); *m* (sep) Margaret; 1 da (Lorna Katherine b 3 July 1992), 2 s (Alasdair Duncan b 10 Aug 1993, Cameron James John b 11 Feb 2000); *Career* research asst to Jim Wallace MP 1989–90, press offr SLD 1990–92, cncllr Shetland Islands Cncl 1994–99 (vice-chm Roads and Tport Cmmn); MSP (Lib Dem) Shetland 1999–; dep min for parl 2000–01, dep min for finance, public services and parly business 2003–05, min for tport 2005–07; chm Lerwick Harbour Tst 1997–99; *Recreations* golf, current affairs, Up-Helly-Ha; *Style*— Tavish Scott, Esq, MSP; ✉ The Scottish Parliament, Edinburgh EH99 1SP (tel 0131 348 5815, fax 0131 348 5807, e-mail tavish.scott.msp@scottish.parliament.uk)

SCOTT, Dr (James) Thomas; s of James Basil Spence Scott (d 1937), of London, and Alice Fawsitt, *née* Taylor (d 1987); *b* 10 November 1926; *Educ* Univ Coll Sch, St Mary's Hosp Univ of London (MB BS, MD); *m* 29 Oct 1956, Faith Margaret, da of William Ernest Smith (d 1944), of Fishguard, Pembs; 3 s (Humphrey, Matthew, Richard); *Career* RAMC 1952–54; conslt physician: Postgrad Med Sch 1962–65, Hammersmith Hosp 1962–65, Charing Cross Hosp 1966–91; hon physician Kennedy Inst of Rheumatology 1966–91, conslt physician in rheumatology Royal Navy 1970–91; past pres Med Soc of London, vice-pres Arthritis Research Campaign; FRSM 1960, memb Assoc of Physicians 1964, FRCP 1968 (MRCP 1952); hon memb: Australasian Assoc of Rheumatology 1983, American Coll of Rheumatology 1984; *Books* Copeman's Textbook of the Rheumatic Diseases (ed, 5 edn 1978, 6 edn 1986), Arthritis and Rheumatism - The Facts (1980); *Recreations* fly fishing, numismatics; *Style*— Dr Thomas Scott; ✉ Winter's Lodge, Huish Champflower, Taunton, Somerset TA4 2BZ (tel 01984 624632); Charing Cross Hospital, Fulham Palace Road, London W6 8RF (tel 020 8846 1234)

SCOTT, Dr Walter Grant; s of Thomas Scott (d 1979), and Marion Urie Roberts; *b* 13 May 1947; *Educ* Eastwood HS, Univ of Edinburgh (BSc), Trinity Hall Cambridge (PhD); *m* 1973, Rosemary Ann Clark, da of Alfred W C Lobban (d 1987), of Beds; 1 s (Matthew), 2 da (Rachel, Diana); *Career* dir Ivory & Sime Ltd 1972–82, chm Walter Scott & Partners Ltd 1982–, chm Walter Scott International 1983–; tstee The Walter Scott Research Fndn 1984–; *Recreations* rowing, running, flying, gardening; *Clubs* Leander, New (Edinburgh), New York Athletic; *Style*— Dr Walter Scott; ✉ One Charlotte Square, Edinburgh EH2 4DZ (tel 0131 225 1357)

SCOTT-BARRETT, Jonathan; s of John Scott-Barrett (d 1968), and Doreen, *née* Robottom (d 1976); *b* 13 April 1944; *Educ* Prince of Wales Sch Nairobi, Ellesmere Coll; *m* 1, 1968 (m dis 1980), Jane, *née* Colchester; 2 s (Marcus b 25 Sept 1970, Dominic b 13 July 1972), 1 da (Miranda b 31 July 1977); m 2, 22 Sept 1983, Malise, *née* Menzies; *Career* Capt 15/19 King's Royal Hussars 1963–68; chartered surveyor Savills 1969–72, ptnr Knight Frank & Rutley (Paris) 1972–76, partner Kapnist International Cap d'Antibes 1976–81, dir Hong Kong Hi Speed Ferries Ltd 1982–86, dir Centaur Publishing Ltd (magazine titles incl Marketing Week, Money Marketing, Design Week, Creative Review) 1986–2002, chm Perfect Information Ltd 1996–2002, ceo Eureka Mining plc 2006–; non-exec dir: Hanson plc 1991–2000, Xtempus Ltd 2002–, Keith Chapman Prodns 2004–, Aerial Camera Systems 2004–, MG Capital plc 2004–; exec dir Celtic Resources plc 2007–; FRICS 1971; *Recreations* tennis, shooting, gym; *Clubs* Cavalry and Guards', Annabel's; *Style*— Jonathan Scott-Barrett, Esq; ✉ Walnut Cottage, Midgham Park, Midgham, Berkshire RG7 5UG; tel 020 7225 2088, e-mail jsb@eurekamining.co.uk

SCOTT-BOWDEN, Brig Robert Logan; MBE (1992); s of Maj-Gen L Scott-Bowden, CBE, DSO, MC*, and J H Scott-Bowden, *née* Price; *b* 6 June 1955; *Educ* Wellington, RMA Sandhurst, RMCS Shrivenham; *m* 16 Aug 1980, Nicola Frances Kimberley, *née* Phillips; 1 da (Camilla Frances b 20 Sept 1984), 1 s (Christopher William b 15 March 1987); *Career* cmmnd The Royal Scots (The Royal Regt) 1974 (mentioned in despatches 1976); Adj 1 Bn 1981–83, instr RMA Sandhurst 1983–85, SO3 G3 HQ Falkland Islands 1985, Staff Coll Camberley 1986–87, Co Cdr 1 Royal Scots 1988–89, SO2 G3 (Operational Requirements) 1990–91, Co Cdr and chief instr RMA Sandhurst 1992–93, instr Staff Coll Camberley 1994, CO 1 Royal Scots 1994–97, SO1 J3 (Land) Perm Jt HQ 1997–98, integrated project team ldr Defence Procurement Agency 1998–2001, cmd 52 Lowland Bde 2001–02, cmd 52 Inf Bde 2002–04, Dir of Inf 2005–; Queen's Commendation for Valuable Serv 1996; *Recreations* hill walking, skiing, sailing, rugby, Italian cooking; *Style*— Brig Robert Scott-Bowden, MBE; ✉ Regimental Headquarters, The Royal Scots (The Royal Regiment), The Castle, Edinburgh EH1 2YT (tel 0131 310 5014)

SCOTT-GALL, His Hon Judge Anthony Robert Gall; s of Sidney Robert Gall (d 1994), and Daphne Margaret, *née* Williamson (d 1990); *b* 30 March 1946; *Educ* Stowe, New Coll Oxford (BA); *m* 8 Sept 1973, Caroline Anne, da of David Charles Roger Scott; 1 s (Alexander David Robert b 6 Aug 1975), 1 da (Henrietta Charlotte Anne b 16 Dec 1976); *Career* called to the Bar Middle Temple 1971; recorder 1993–96, circuit judge (SE Circuit) 1996–; *Recreations* gardening, travel, music, rugby union, cricket, country pursuits; *Clubs* Richmond FC, Armadillos Cricket; *Style*— His Hon Judge Scott-Gall; ✉ Lewes Combined Court, High Street, Lewes, East Sussex BN7 1YB

SCOTT-JOYNT, Rt Rev Michael Charles; *see:* Winchester, Bishop of

SCOTT-MANDERSON, Marcus Charles William; QC (2006); s of Dr William Scott-Manderson (d 2001), and Pamela Scott-Manderson; *b* 10 February 1956; *Educ* Harrow, ChCh Oxford (BCL, MA), Dept of Forensic Med Univ of Glasgow, The Hague Acad of Int Law 1980; *m* 5 July 2003, Melinda Penelope Tillard; *Career* called to the Bar Lincoln's Inn 1980, Queen's Counsel 2006; sec Family Law Bar Assoc Conciliation Bd 1992–96, memb Legal Working Gp Reunite Int Child Abduction Centre 2004– (memb 1999–); memb: Br Acad of Forensic Sci, Forensisch Medisch Genootschap The Netherlands 1983–98; *Publications* Butterworths Essential Family Practice (contrib, 2001 and 2002 edns); *Recreations* ancient history, archaeology, fencing, travel; *Clubs* Lansdowne; *Style*— Marcus Scott-Manderson, QC; ✉ 17 Burlington Road, London SW6 4NP (tel 020 7731 1476); Park House, The Strand, Ashton-in-Makerfield, Wigan, Lancashire; 4 Paper Buildings, Temple, London EC4Y 7EX (tel 020 7583 0816, fax 020 7353 4979, e-mail msm@4pb.com, website www.4pb.com)

SCOTT-MONCRIEFF, Lucy Ann; da of Lt Col William Scott-Moncrieff (d 1997), and Rosemary, *née* Knollys; *b* 26 March 1954; *Educ* St Mary's Sch Calne, Guildford Tech Coll, Univ of Kent at Canterbury (BA); *Partner*, 1985–95, John Dowie; 2 s (Stephen Harry b 1 March 1987, Robert Arthur b 7 Nov 1989); *Career* admitted slr 1978; specialises in mental health law; ptnr Offenbach and Co until 1987, sole practitioner 1987 (subsequent partnerships with Tony Harbour and then Lydia Sinclair), managing ptnr Scott-Moncrieff, Harbour & Sinclair 2000–; sometime Mental Health Act cmmr; memb Editorial Advsy Bd Community Care Law Reports; Law Soc: fndr memb Mental Health and Disability Ctee 1983– (co-chair 2003–04), memb Cncl 2002–), chair Access to Justice Ctee 2004– (memb 2002–); memb Advsy Panel Coll of Law London; hon lectr Univ of Kent at Canterbury; *Recreations* walking my dogs, woodcarving; *Style*— Ms Lucy Scott-Moncrieff; ✉ Scott-Moncrieff, Harbour & Sinclair, 19 Greenwood Place, London NW5 1LB (tel 020 7485 5588, fax 020 7485 5577, e-mail scomo@scomo.com)

SCOTT OF FOSCOTE, Baron (Life Peer UK 2000), of Foscote in the County of Buckinghamshire; Sir Richard Rashleigh Folliott Scott; kt (1983), PC (1991); s of Lt-Col Curtis Wilson Folliott Scott, OBE, 2/9 Gurkha Rifles, and Katharine, *née* Rashleigh; *b* 2 October 1934; *m* 8 Aug 1959, Rima Elisa, da of Salvador Ripoll and Blanca Korsi de Ripoll, of Panama City; 2 s (Richard Salvador Folliott b 9 June 1960, Jonathan Ripoll Folliott b 21 Dec 1963), 2 da (Katharine Blanca b 27 April 1962, Mariella Louisa (Mrs Karim Lahham) b 4 July 1967); *Career* called to the Bar Inner Temple 1959 (bencher 1981); QC 1975, attorney-gen Duchy of Lancaster 1980–83, chm of the Bar 1982–83, judge of the High Court of Justice (Chancery Div) 1983–91, vice-chllr Co Palatine and Duchy of Lancaster 1987–91, a Lord Justice of Appeal 1991–94, head Inquiry into defence related exports to Iraq 1992–96, Vice-Chllr of the Supreme Court 1994–2000, head of Civil Justice 1995–2000, a Lord of Appeal in Ordinary 2000–, non-perm judge of the Hong-Kong Court of Final Appeal 2003–; Hon LLD: Univ of Birmingham 1996, Univ of Buckingham 1999; *Style*— The Rt Hon Lord Scott of Foscote; ✉ House of Lords, London SW1A 0PW

SCOTT OF NEEDHAM MARKET, Baroness (Life Peer UK 2000), of Needham Market in the County of Suffolk; Rosalind Carol (Ros) Scott; da of Kenneth Leadbeater (d 1996), of Felixstowe, and Carol, *née* Young (d 2007); *b* 19 August 1957; *Educ* Whitby GS, UEA (BA); *Children* 1 da (Sally Rebecca b 1984), 1 s (Jamie Alan b 1987); *Career* memb and ldr Suffolk CC 1993–, chair Local Govt Assoc Tport Exec 1997–2004, memb UK Delgn Ctee of Regions EU 1998–2002, memb Cmmn for Integrated Tport 2001–07; non-exec dir: Anglia TV 2002–05, Lloyds Register 2004–; memb Bd: Entrust plc 2000–, Audit Cmmn; patron: E Coast Sailing Tst, Wings of Hope; *Recreations* choral singing, walking; *Clubs* Royal Commonwealth; *Style*— The Rt Hon the Baroness Scott of Needham Market;

✉ House of Lords, London SW1A 0PW (tel 020 7219 8660, fax 020 7219 8602, e-mail scottrc@parliament.uk)

SCOTT PLUMMER, (Patrick) Joseph; s of Charles Humphrey Scott Plummer (d 1991), of Mainhouse, Kelso, Roxburghshire, and Hon Pamela Lilias, *née* Balfour; *b* 24 August 1943; *Educ* Radley, Magdalene Coll Cambridge (MA); *m* 1, 12 March 1970 (m dis 1977), Elizabeth-Anne, da of Col Anthony Way, MC, of Kincairney, Perthshire; 1 s (Charles b 18 Aug 1972), 1 da (Annabel b 26 June 1974); m 2, 15 Sept 1977, Mrs Christine Margaret Hermione Roberts, da of Hon Anthony Gerard Bampfylde (d 1968), of Boyton House, Suffolk; 1 s (Guy b 13 Aug 1978); *Career* ptnr Cazenove and Co 1974–80; Martin Currie Ltd: dir 1981–2005, md 1991–96, chief exec 1996–99, chm 1999–2005; dir: Candover Investments plc 1985–2003, Merchants Trust plc 1997–, Martin Currie Portfolio Investment Tst plc 1999–2005; FCA 1967; *Recreations* foxhunting, shooting, tennis; *Clubs* New (Edinburgh), Pratt's, Royal Caledonian Hunt, Boodle's; *Style*— Joseph Scott Plummer, Esq; ✉ Mainhouse, Kelso, Roxburghshire (tel 01573 223327); 29 Castle Terrace, Edinburgh (tel 0131 229 0228); Martin Currie Ltd, Saltire Court, 20 Castle Terrace, Edinburgh (tel 0131 229 5252)

SCOVELL, Brian Souter; s of Percy Henry John Scovell (d 1991), of IOW, and Maude Janet Scovell (d 1978); *b* 21 November 1935; *Educ* Ventnor Coll, Elgin Acad, NCTJ (Cert, Dip); *m* 1 Oct 1965, Audrey Esther (d 2000), da of Eric William O'Sullivan; 1 da (Louise Jayne b 8 Oct 1967), 1 s (Gavin Richard Souter b 25 Oct 1969); *Career* journalist; trainee reporter Isle of Wight Guardian 1952–57, gen reporter Wolverhampton Express and Star 1957–58; sports reporter: Norwich Evening News and Eastern Daily Press 1958, Press Assoc 1959–60; cricket corr and dep football corr Daily Sketch 1960–71, cricket and football corr Daily Mail 1971–; maj events covered incl: football World Cups 1966, 1982, 1986 and 1990, cricket World Cups 1975, 1979 and 1983, over 280 test matches and 300 int football matches; chm Football Writers Assoc 1982, sec Cricket Writers Club 2004– (chm 1985–89); Cricket Writer of the Year Wombwell Cricket Lovers Soc 1963, highly recommended in sports news section Sports Cncl Writing Awards 1991; FA soccer coach 1966, MCC cricket coach 1977; *Books* Everything That's Cricket (1963), Whose Side Are You On Ref? (1973), The Big Match (1976), The Diary of a Season (1979), Not Out (1979), Trevor Brooking (1981), Ken Barrington - A Tribute (1982), Glory, Glory (1984), Revelations of a Soccer Manager (1985), The Big Match Soccer Anthology (1987), And the Next Voice You Will Hear (1987), Gary Sobers - Twenty Years at the Top (1988), Handbook of Soccer (1988), Beating the Field - Brian Lara's Story (1995), Dickie: A Tribute to Umpire Dickie Bird (1996), Chelsea Azzurri (1997), Sixty Years on the Back Foot: Sir Clyde Walcott's Life in Cricket (1999), Football Gentry (2005), The England Managers: The Impossible Job (2006), Jim Laker 19–90 (2006), Brian Lara: Cricket's Troubled Genius (2007); *Recreations* watching and playing cricket, watching and writing on football, going on cricket tours abroad, reading, theatre, walking, cinema; *Clubs* Woodpeckers CC; *Style*— Brian Scovell, Esq; ✉ Daily Mail, Northcliffe House, 2 Derry Street, London W8 5TT (tel 020 8464 4133, mobile 07879 612690)

SCREECH, Rev Prof Michael Andrew; s of Richard John Screech, MM (d 1986), of Plymstock, Devon, and Nellie Ernestine, *née* Maunder (d 1977); *b* 2 May 1926; *Educ* Sutton HS Plymouth, UCL (BA); *m* 4 April 1956, (Ursula) Anne Grace, da of John William Reeve (d 1960), of Byfleet, Surrey; 3 s (Matthew Erasmus John b 30 Jan 1960, Timothy Benjamin Mark b 28 Sept 1961, Toby Daniel Luke b 3 Oct 1963); *Career* other rank Intelligence Corps (mainly Far East) 1944–47; successively asst lectr, lectr then sr lectr Univ of Birmingham 1951–61, reader then prof of French UCL 1961–71, Fielden prof of French language and literature UCL 1971–84, Johnson prof Inst for Res in the Humanities Madison Wisconsin 1978, Campion lectr Regina Saskatchewan 1983, Dorothy Ford Wiley prof of Renaissance culture N Carolina 1986, Zaharoff lectr Oxford 1988; visiting prof: Collège de France 1989, La Sorbonne 1990; fell and chaplain All Souls Coll Oxford 2001–03 (sr res fell 1984–93, emeritus fell 1993–2001 and 2003–), hon fell Wolfson Coll Oxford 2001– (extraordinary fell 1993–2001), occasional lectr Oxford Ministry Course 1994–96; ordained: deacon 1993, priest 1994; memb comité: d' Humanisme et Renaissance 1958–, des Textes Littéraires Français 1958–, du patronage des Textes Classiques de la Renaissance 1986–; corresponding memb: Inst Archéologique et Historique Geneva 1990, L'Académie des Inscriptions et Belles-Lettres 2000; tstee Lambeth Palace Library 1994–2006; formerly memb Whitchurch St Mary's PCC, Whitchurch Parish Cncl, formerly chm of Mangrs Whitchurch Primary Sch; Médaille de la Ville de Tours 1984; fell UCL 1982; DLitt: Birmingham 1960, London 1982, Oxford 1990; Hon DLitt Exeter 1993, Hon D(Th) Geneva 1998; FBA 1981, FRSL 1989; Chevalier dans l'Ordre National du Mérite France 1983, Chevalier dans la Légion d'Honneur 1992; *Books* The Rabelaisian Marriage (1958), L'Evangélisme de Rabelais (1959), Marot Evangélique (1967); Rabelais edns: Tiers Livre (1964), Gargantua (1970), Prognostication (1975); Regrets and Antiquitez de Rome (by Du Bellay, ed 1964), Rabelais (1979), Erasmus - Ecstasy and the Praise of Folly (1980), Montaigne and Melancholy (1983), Apology for Raymond Sebond (by Montaigne, trans 1987), A New Rabelais Bibliography (1988), Montaigne - The Complete Essays (1991), Some Renaissance Studies (1992), Clément Marot, a Renaissance poet discovers the Gospel (1993), Warden Mocket of All Souls College: Doctrina et politia Ecclesiae anglicanae (ed, 1995), Monumental Inscriptions in All Souls Coll Oxford (1997), Laughter at the Foot of the Cross (1998), Montaigne's Copy of Lucretius (1998), Rabelais: Gargantua and Panagruel (translator, 2006); *Recreations* walking, gardening; *Clubs* Athenaeum, Pangbourne Working Men's; *Style*— The Rev Prof M A Screech, FBA, FRSL; ✉ 5 Swanston Field, Whitchurch-on-Thames, Reading RG8 7HP (e-mail michael.screech@btinternet.com); All Souls College, Oxford OX1 4AL; Wolfson College, Oxford OX2 6UD (tel and fax 0118 984 2513)

SCRIMGEOUR, Alastair James; s of late Robin Neville Carron Scrimgeour, of Wilts, and Deirdre Elizabeth Blundell, *née* Brown; *b* 17 April 1956; *Educ* Eton, Univ of Bristol (BSc); *Career* chartered accountant; ptnr: Binder Hamlyn London 1986–94 (joined 1978), Arthur Andersen 1994–2002, Deloitte & Touche 2002–; FCA; *Recreations* hunting, shooting, racing, gardening, squash, tennis; *Clubs* RAC, Turf; *Style*— Alastair Scrimgeour, Esq; ✉ Deloitte & Touche, Athene Place, 66 Shoe Lane, London EC4A 3BQ (tel 020 7007 2993, fax 020 7007 1051)

SCRIMGEOUR, Angus Muir Edington; s of Dr David Muir Scrimgeour (d 1977), and May Burton Clair, *née* Edington (d 1988); *b* 19 February 1945; *Educ* Westminster, New Coll Oxford (MA), UCL (MSc); *m* 21 Dec 1968, Clare Christian Gauvain, da of Dr Ronald Ormiston Murray, MBE; 1 s (Alexander b 1971); *Career* vice-pres Citibank NA 1974–84, chief exec Edington plc merchant bank 1984–90, dep chm Henry Cooke Group 1990–91 (jt chief exec 1988–90), chief exec Bankside Underwriting Agencies Ltd 1992–95; Corporation of Lloyds: dir CSU 1993–96, head of market mgmnt 1995–96; vice-pres and chief fin offr World Bank (MIGA) Washington DC 1997–02, chm Scrimgeour & Co 1983–, chm Solar Products Ltd 2003–, pres Int Assoc for Digital Pubns 2004–; *Recreations* design, chess, music; *Clubs* Oxford and Cambridge, IOD, Berkshire Golf; *Style*— Angus Scrimgeour, Esq; ✉ 3134 P Street NW, Washington DC 20007, USA (tel 00 1 202 337 2781)

SCRIVEN, Jane Katherine; da of Sir Peter Gibbings, of London, and Elspeth, *née* Macintosh; *b* 5 October 1959, England; *Educ* Millfield, KCL (LLB); *m* 13 June 1987, Simon Scriven; 1 da (Harriet Clare b 22 Aug 1990), 1 s (Frederick Charles b 10 June 1994); *Career* slr Norton Rose 1986–87, commercial mangr Elders IXL Hong Kong 1987–89, strategy and investment mangr Elders Finance 1989–91; Geest plc: devpt dir 1991–2000, memb Bd 1996–2005, md Continental Europe 2000–05; non-exec dir Greene King plc 2005–, chm Origin8 Deli-Cafés Ltd 2006–; memb Law Soc 1986; *Recreations* skiing, equestrianism; *Style*— Mrs Jane Scriven

SCRIVEN, Pamela; QC (1992); da of Maurice Scriven (d 1979), and Evelyn Lavinia, *née* Stickney; *b* 5 April 1948; *Educ* UCL (LLB); *m*; 2 c; *Career* called to the Inner Temple Bar 1970, bencher 1995; recorder of the Crown Ct 1996– (asst recorder 1993–96), dep judge of the High Ct (Family Div); Chm Family Law Bar Assoc 1999–2001 (memb 1991–); *Recreations* theatre and travel; *Style*— Pamela Scriven, QC; ✉ 1 King's Bench Walk, 2nd Floor, Temple, London EC4Y 7DB

SCRIVEN, Peter John Keith; s of Sydney Verdun Scriven, of Dudley, W Midlands, and Mona Patricia, *née* Gaston (d 1974); *b* 25 July 1956; *Educ* Alexandra GS Midlands, UCW Aberystwyth (BScEcon), Leicester Poly (DMS); *m*; 3 s (Thomas Edward b Feb 1990, Matthew Alexander b Nov 1994, Oliver William b Dec 1996); *Career* UK mktg mangr Barclays Bank 1977–83, investment mktg mangr Charterhouse Merchant Bank 1983–84, strategic planning mangr Citicorp UK 1984–86, Euro business planning mangr Chase Manhattan Bank 1986–87, gp head of business devpt National and Provincial Building Society 1987–90, sr vice-pres and gen mangr Middle East Visa International Service Association 1990–; MInstM; *Recreations* flying, skiing, foreign travel, ocean sailing; *Clubs* MCIM, BMAA; *Style*— Peter Scriven, Esq

SCRIVENER, Anthony Frank; QC (1975); s of Frank Bertram Scrivener (d 1995), of Kent, and Tonia, *née* Mather (d 2002); *b* 31 July 1935; *Educ* Kent Coll Canterbury, UCL; *m* m 1, Iren Becze; 1 da (Zsuzsa b 4 Oct 1966), 1 s (Zoltan b 10 Oct 1968); m 2, Ying Hui Tan; *Career* called to the Bar Gray's Inn 1959 (Holt scholar); lectr Ghana 1959–61, in practice 1961–, recorder of the Crown Court 1975, head of chambers 1992–2001; bencher Lincoln's Inn, chm Bar Cncl 1991; UK judge FIA Int Court of Appeal, RAC steward; *Recreations* walking with family dog Blackie, chess, cards, croquet; *Style*— Anthony Scrivener, Esq, QC; ✉ 2–3 Gray's Inn Square, Gray's Inn, London WC1R 5JH (tel 020 7242 4986, fax 020 7504 1166)

SCRIVENER, Richard; *Educ* Univ of Hull (BA); *m* Ann-Janine Murtagh; 1 s (Conrad b 20 Dec 2001); *Career* ed Disney magazine 1983–87, licensing agent 1987–89 (projects incl: Lucasfilm, Asterix the Gaul, NSPCC), sr ed rising to publishing dir Puffin Books 1989–2000; Scholastic Ltd: publishing dir 2000–02, publisher Scholastic Children's Books 2002–; *Recreations* reading anything, watching and discussing football; *Style*— Richard Scrivener, Esq; ✉ Scholastic Children's Books, Commonwealth House, 1–19 New Oxford Street, London WC1A 4NU (tel 020 7421 9000, fax 020 7421 9032)

SCROGGS, Cedric Annesley; s of Richard Brian Harry Scroggs (d 2003), and Vera Wesley, *née* Coombs (d 1960); *b* 2 January 1941; *Educ* Reading Sch, St John's Coll Oxford (Sir Thomas White scholar, BA); *m* 1964, Patricia Mary Sutherland Ogg, da of late George Sutherland Ogg; 2 s (Duncan John b 1965, James Richard Sutherland b 1971), 1 da (Joanna Mary b 1967); *Career* mktg exec: AEI-Hotpoint Ltd 1962–67, General Foods Ltd 1967–73; mktg dir: Cadbury Ltd 1974–76 (joined 1973), Leyland Cars 1976–78; Fisons plc: md Scientific Equipment Div 1979–81, chm Scientific Equipment Div and main bd dir 1981–92, gp chief exec 1992–93; non-exec dir: Caradon plc 1988–89, YJL plc (now Renew Gp plc) 1990–2004 (chm 1999), Huntsworth plc (formerly Holmes & Marchant Group plc) 1997–2000; chm SE Oxfordshire PCT 2001–02; dep chm: GENUS plc 1995–2000, Sarginsons plc 1999–; non-exec memb: Milk Mktg Bd 1991–94, Hillingdon Hosp NHS Tst 1991–92, CBI Nat Mfrg Cncl 1992–94, Oxfordshire Mental Healthcare NHS Tst 1995–2001 and 2007–; visiting fell Nuffield Coll Oxford 1993–2001; pres BEAMA 1991–92; *Recreations* boating, golf, diving; *Clubs* Leander, Huntercombe Golf; *Style*— Cedric Scroggs, Esq; ✉ The Priory, Brightwell-cum-Sotwell, Wallingford, Oxfordshire OX10 0RH (tel 01491 836188, fax 01491 824437)

SCROPE, Simon Egerton; s of Richard Ladislas Scrope (d 1990), of Danby, and Lady Jane Egerton (d 1978), da of 4 Earl of Ellesmere; *b* 23 December 1934; *Educ* Ampleforth, Trinity Coll Cambridge; *m* 23 July 1970, (Jennifer) Jane, da of Sir Kenneth Wade Parkinson, DL (d 1981), of N Yorks; 1 da (Emily Katherine b 24 May 1972), 1 s (Simon Henry Richard b 3 Sept 1974); *Career* Nat Serv 2 Lt Coldstream Guards 1953–55; insurance broker, memb Lloyd's 1956; chm Richards Longstaff Group (then RL Insurance Ltd) 1974–2005; dir: Gibbs Hartley Cooper Ltd (now HSBC Insurance Brokers) 1993–98, R F Kershaw Ltd 1993–96; farmer and landowner; memb York Race Ctee 1981–2005, chm Pontefract Park Race Co Ltd 1997, dir Hosp of St John and St Elizabeth, chm Brampton Tst 2003; *Recreations* shooting, fishing, gardening, racing; *Clubs* Brooks's; *Style*— Simon Scrope, Esq; ✉ Danby on Yore, Leyburn, North Yorkshire DL8 4PX (tel 01969 623297, fax 01969 624260); 5 Kendal Steps, St Georges Fields, London W2 2YE (tel 020 7402 3265)

SCRUTON, Prof Roger Vernon; s of John Scruton, of High Wycombe, Bucks, and Beryl Clarys, *née* Haines (d 1967); *b* 27 February 1944; *Educ* Royal GS High Wycombe, Jesus Coll Cambridge (MA, PhD); *m* 1, 1975 (m dis 1979), (Marie Genevieve) Danielle, da of Robert Laffitte, of Orthez, France; m 2, 1996, Sophie Jeffreys, da of late 2 Baron Jeffreys; *Career* called to the Bar Inner Temple 1974, fell Peterhouse Cambridge 1969–71, prof of aesthetics Dept of Philosophy Birkbeck Coll London (formerly lectr and reader), Univ Profs Prog Boston Univ 1992–94; ed Salisbury Review 1982–2000; FRSL 2003; *Books* Art and Imagination (1974), The Aesthetics of Architecture (1979), The Meaning of Conservatism (1980), Fortnight's Anger (1981), A Dictionary of Political Thought (1983), Sexual Desire (1986), Thinkers of the New Left (1986), A Land Held Hostage (1987), The Philosopher on Dover Beach (1990), Francesca (1991), Xanthippic Dialogues (1993), Modern Philosophy: An Introduction and Survey (1994), Animal Rights and Wrongs (1996), An Intelligent Person's Guide to Philosophy (1996), The Aesthetics of Music (1997), On Hunting (1998), An Intelligent Person's Guide to Modern Culture (1998), Perictione in Colophon (2000), England: an Elegy (2000), The West and the Rest (2002), News From Somewhere (2004), Death-Devoted Heart (2004), Gentle Regrets (2005); *Recreations* music, hunting; *Style*— Prof Roger Scruton; ✉ Sunday Hill Farm, Brinkworth, Wiltshire SN15 5AS

SCUDAMORE, Jeremy Paul; s of Clifford John Scudamore (d 1977), and Iris Scudamore; *b* 27 April 1947, Bristol; *Educ* Birkenhead Sch, Univ of Nottingham (BA), INSEAD (AMP); *m* 29 April 1972, Ruth, *née* Skelton; 1 s (James Robert b 19 May 1976), 1 da (Sarah Jane b 5 March 1978); *Career* various roles rising to gen mangr ICI Gp 1971–93; Zeneca Gp (demerged from ICI): gen mangr 1993–94, successively business dir Zeneca Agrochemicals, md Zeneca Seeds and regnl exec Eastern Europe 1994–97, ceo Zeneca Specialities and chm Zeneca Manufacturing Partnership 1997–99; Avecia Gp: ceo 1999–2006, chm 2005–06; non-exec chm: Cyprotex plc 2001–03, Oxford Advanced Surfaces Ltd; non-exec dir: ARM Holdings plc 2004–, Stem Cell Sciences plc, Oxford Catalysts Gp plc, Board Link Gp Ltd; chm NW Science Cncl; memb: Advsy Bd Chemical & Engrg News (USA) 2001–03, Editorial Advsy Bd European Chemical News 2002–06, Bd Chemical Leadership Cncl 2004–06 (chm Innovation Team), Bd Manchester Knowledge Capital; *Recreations* sport, gardening, walking; *Clubs* MCC; *Style*— Jeremy Scudamore, Esq; ✉ c/o North West Regional Development Agency, PO Box 37, Renaissance House, Warrington, Cheshire WA1 1XB

SCULLY, Prof Crispian; CBE (2000); s of Patrick Scully and Rosaleen, *née* Richardson; *b* 24 May 1945; *Educ* Univ of London (BDS, BSc, MB BS, PhD), Univ of Bristol (MD, MDS); *m* 5 Oct 1977, Zoë Boucoumani; 1 da (Frances b 31 Jan 1982); *Career* lectr: Univ of London (oral immunology) 1977–79, Univ of Glasgow (oral med and pathology) 1979–81; sr lectr Univ of Glasgow (oral med and pathology) 1981–82, prof of oral med, surgery and pathology Univ of Bristol 1982–94, head Univ of Bristol Dental Sch 1986–90, dean

Eastman Dental Inst Univ of London 1994–, prof of special needs dentistry Univ of London 1997– (prof of oral med, pathology and microbiology 1994–), adjunct prof Univ of Helsinki 2005–, visiting prof Univ of Edinburgh 2006–; conslt: UCLH Tst, Gt Ormond St Hosp, Nuffield Orthopaedic Centre, John Radcliffe Hosp Oxford; sec-gen Int Acad of Oral Oncology, past pres European Assoc of Oral Med; past chm Central Examining Bd for Dental Hygienists; past pres Br Soc for Oral Med; past memb Central Research and Devpt Ctee Dept of Health; DSc; FDSRCS, FDSRCSE, FDSRCPS, FFDRCSI, FRCPath, FMedSci, FHEA; *Books* incl: Multiple Choice Questions in Clinical Dentistry (jtly, 1985), Hospital Dental Surgeon's Guide (1985), Slide Interpretation in Oral Diseases and the Oral Manifestations of Systemic Disease (jtly, 1986), Dental Surgery Assistant's Handbook (jtly, 2 edn 1993), Colour Aids in Oral Medicine (jtly, 3 edn 1999), Dental Patient Care (1989), Atlas of Stomatology (jtly, 1989), Occupational Hazards to Dental Staff (jtly, 1990), Radiographic Interpretation in Oral Disease (jtly, 1991), Clinical Virology in Oral Medicine and Dentistry (jtly, 1992), Colour Aids in Medicine and Surgery (jtly, 2 edn 1999), Colour Atlas of Orofacial Diseases in Childhood and Adolescence (jtly, 1993, 2 edn 2001), Colour Atlas of Oral Pathology (jtly, 1995), Oral Health Care for those with HIV Infection and Other Special Needs (jtly, 1995), Innovations and Development in Non-invasive Orofacial Health Care (jtly, 1996), Oxford Handbook of Dental Care (jtly, 1999), Diagnostic Handbook of Oral Disease (1999), Dermatology of the Lips (jtly, 2000), Applied Basic Science in Dentistry (2002), Periodontal Manifestations of Local and Systemic Disease (jtly, 2003), Textbook of General and Oral Medicine (jtly, 1999 and 2003), Oral Medicine for the Dental Team (jtly, 2003), Oral and Maxillofacial Medicine (2004), Oral Diseases (jtly, 3 edn 2004), Medical Problems in Dentistry (jtly, 5 edn 2004), Human Disease for Dental Students (jtly, 2005), Culturally Sensitive Oral Health Care (jtly, 2006), Special Care in Dentistry (jtly, 2007); *Recreations* swimming, hill walking, skiing, travelling, music, windsurfing, sailing; *Style*— Prof Crispian Scully, CBE; ✉ Eastman Dental Institute, 256 Gray's Inn Road, London WC1X 8LD (tel 020 7915 1038, fax 020 7915 1039, e-mail cscully@eastman.ucl.ac.uk)

SCULLY, Sean; *b* 1945, Dublin; *Educ* Croydon Coll of Art, Univ of Newcastle upon Tyne, Harvard Univ; *Career* artist; lectr: Chelsea Sch of Art and Goldsmiths' Sch of Art 1973–75, Princeton Univ 1977–83; recipient: Guggenheim fellowship 1983, Artist's fellowship (Nat Endowment for the Arts) 1984; subject of numerous articles and reviews; *Solo Exhibitions* incl: Rowan Gallery London 1973, 1975, 1977, 1979 and 1981, Tortue Gallery Santa Monica Calif 1975 and 1976, Duffy-Gibbs Gallery NY 1977, Nadin Gallery NY 1979, Susan Caldwell Gallery NY 1980, Museum fur (Sub-) Kultur Berlin 1981, Sean Scully: Paintings 1971–81 (Ikon Gallery Birmingham and touring) 1981, David McKee Gallery NY 1983, 1985 and 1986, Gallery S65 Aaslt Belgium 1984, Drawings (Barbara Kraków Gallery Boston Mass) 1985, Monotypes (Pamela Auchincloss Gallery Santa Barbara Calif, David McKee Gallery NY, Douglas Flanders Contemporary Art Minneapolis) 1987, Galerie Schmele Düsseldorf 1987, Art Inst of Chicago 1987, Fuji TV Gallery Tokyo 1988 and 1994, David McKee Gallery NY 1989 and 1990, Whitechapel Art Gallery London and tour 1989, Pastel Drawings (Grob Gallery London) 1989–90, Karsten Greve Gallery Cologne 1990, Galerie de France Paris 1990, Monotypes (Pamela Auchincloss Gallery NY) 1990, Sean Scully - Paintings and Works on Paper 1982–88 (Whitechapel Gallery London, Lenbachhaus Munich and Palacio de Velázquez Madrid 1989, Jamileh Weber Galerie Zurich and McKee Gallery NY 1991), Waddington Galleries London 1992 and 1995, The Catherine Paintings (Modern Museum of Fort Worth 1993, Palais des Beaux-Arts Charleroi Belgium and Kunsthalle Bielefeld 1995, Galerie Nationale de Jeu de Paume Paris 1996), Paintings, Works on Paper (Galerie Bernd Kluser Munich) 1993, Galleria Gian Ferrari Arte Contemporánea Milano Italy 1994, Galeria El Diario Vasco San Sebastian Spain 1995, Galerie de l'Ancien Coll Chatellerault France 1995, Bernd Kluser Galerie Munchen Germany 1995, Sean Scully: Twenty Years (Hirshhorn Museum and Sculpture Garden Washington DC, High Museum of Art Atlanta Georgia, La Caixa des Pensiones Barcelona, MOMA Dublin and Schirn Kunsthalle Frankfurt) 1995–96, Drawing Exhibition (Graphische Sammlung Munchen and Museum Folkwang Essen) 1996; *Group Exhibitions* incl: John Moores Liverpool Exhibition 8 (prizewinner) 1972, La Peinture Anglaise Aujourd'hui (MOMA Paris) 1973, British Painting (Hayward Gallery London) 1974, Certain Traditions (travelling exhibition Canada) 1978, Aspects of All-Over (Harm Boukaert Gallery NY) 1982, Part 1: Twelve Abstract Painters (Siegel Contemporary Art NY) 1984, Art on Paper (Weatherspoon Art Gallery Greensboro N Carolina) 1985, Structure/Abstraction (Hill Gallery Birmingham Mississippi) 1986, Harvey Quaytman & Sean Scully (Helsinki Festival Island) 1987, Logical Foundations (Pfizer Inc NY) 1987–88, Drawings and Related Prints (Castelli Graphics NY) 1989, Drawing: Paul Beus, Paul Rotterdam, Sean Scully (Arnold Herstand & Co NY) 1990, Sean Scully/Donald Sultan: Abstraction/Representation (Stanford Art Gallery Stanford Univ) 1990, Artist in the Abstract (Univ of N Carolina at Greensboro) 1990, La Metafisica della luce (NY) 1991, Four Series of Paintings (John Berggruen Gallery San Francisco) 1992, workshop (Harvard Univ) 1992, Geteilte Bilder (Museum Folkwang Essen) 1992, Behind Bars, Thread Waxing Space (NY) 1992, Color Block Prints of the 20th Century (Associated American Artists NY) 1992, Turner Prize Exhibition (Tate) 1993, Partners (Annely Juda Fine Art London) 1993, British Abstract Art (Flowers East Gallery London) 1994, Seven from the Seventies (Knoedler Gallery NY) 1995; *Collections* work in numerous public collections worlwide incl: Carnegie Museum of Art Pittsburgh, MOMA NY, Arts Cncl of GB, British Cncl, Tate Gallery, V&A, Aust Nat Gallery Canberra; *Style*— Sean Scully; ✉ c/o Timothy Taylor Gallery, 24 Dering Street, London W1S 1TT (tel 020 7409 3344, fax 020 7409 1316)

SCULTHORPE, Paul; s of Douglas Rae Sculthorpe, and Linda Margaret, *née* Griffiths; *b* 22 September 1977, Burnley; *Educ* Counthill Sch Oldham; *m* Lindsay, *née* McCulloch; 1 s (Jake b 18 March 2000), 1 da (Lucy Jo b 11 Nov 2003); *Career* rugby league player; amateur clubs: Mayfield RLFC, Waterhead RLFC, Rosebridge RLFC; professional clubs: Warrington RLFC 1994–98, St Helens RLFC 1998– (transferred for £375,000, world record for a forward, capt 2004–); winner: Grand Final 1999, 2000, 2002 and 2006, World Club Championship 2001 and 2007, Challenge Cup 2001, 2004 and 2006); England 1995– (4 caps, also former capt under 16s), GB 1996– (25 caps, capt 2005–), Lancashire (3 appearances); awarded full testimonial 2008; Rugby League drug free sport ambass to UK Sport; regular panelist and mystery guest on A Question of Sport (BBC); Freeman Knowsley Borough; *Awards* Players' Player of the Year 2001, Liverpool Echo Rugby League Player of the Year 2001, Sky Viewers Player of the Year 2001, Rugby League Writers Player of the Year 2001, Man of Steel 2001 and 2002, BBC NW Rugby League Player of the Year 2001 and 2002, Rugby League Express readers Player of the Year 2001 and 2002, memb Rugby League Dream Team 2001, 2002 and 2004, runner-up Golden Boot Award 2001 and 2002, BBC NW Sportsman of the Year 2002, memb Rugby League World Dream Team 2002, winner Opta Statistics 2002, Scouseology Award for Sport 2005; Gillette Face of Rugby League 2004–07; *Recreations* golf, snooker, music, bulldog ("Boss"); *Style*— Mr Paul Sculthorpe; ✉ c/o Steve Williams, SJW Management, 7 Compton Road, Pedmore, Stourbridge, West Midlands DY6 0TE (tel 01562 887232, fax 01562 887232, mobile 07740 085112, e-mail steve@sjwmanagement.com, website www.sjwmanagement.com); St Helens RLFC, Knowsley Road, St Helens, Merseyside WA10 4AD

SCUPHAM, John Peter; s of John Scupham, OBE (d 1990), of Thorpe St Andrew, Norwich, Norfolk, and Dorothy Lacey, *née* Clark (d 1987); *b* 24 February 1933; *Educ* Perse Sch Cambridge, St George's Harpenden, Emmanuel Coll Cambridge (BA); *m* 10 Aug 1957, Carola Nance, da of Hermann Justus Braunholtz, CBE (d 1963); 3 s (Christopher, Giles, Roger), 1 da (Kate); *Career* Nat Serv 1952–54; head of English St Christopher Sch Letchworth 1961–80, fndr The Mandeville Press 1974–; Cholmondeley Award Society of Authors Awards 1996; FRSL; *Books* The Snowing Globe (1972), Prehistories (1975), The Hinterland (1977), Summer Palaces (1980), Winter Quarters (1983), Out Late (1986), The Air Show (1988), Watching the Perseids (1990), Selected Poems (1990), The Ark (1994), Night Watch (1999), Collected Poems (2002); *Recreations* book collecting; *Style*— Peter Scupham, Esq, FRSL; ✉ Old Hall, Norwich Road, South Burlingham, Norwich NR13 4EY

SCURR, John Henry; s of Henry Scurr (d 1981), of Slough, Berks, and Joyce, *née* Standerwick; *b* 25 March 1947; *Educ* Langley GS, Middx Hosp Med Sch London (BSc, MB BS); *m* 1, 16 July 1969 (m dis 1986), Gillian Margaret Mason; m 2, 5 April 1986, Nicola Mary Alexandra, da of Ivor S Vincent (d 1994), of London; *Children* 3 da (Ruth b 1971, Ingrid b 1972, Victoria b 1986), 3 s (James b 1976, Edward b 1984, Thomas b 1990); *Career* conslt surgn Middx Hosp and UCH, sr lectr in surgery Univ of London, hon conslt surgn St Luke's Hosp for the Clergy; memb Aeromedical Practitioners Assoc; Freeman Worshipful Soc of Apothecaries 1989, Freeman Guild of Air Pilots and Air Navigators 1994 (Liveryman 1999); FRSM 1972, FRCS 1976; *Books* Microcomputer Applications in Medicine (1987); *Recreations* flying, walking; *Clubs* RAF; *Style*— John Scurr, Esq; ✉ The Grange, Cloatley Road, Hankerton SN16 9LQ (tel 01666 577630); Lister Hospital, London SW1W 8RH (tel 020 7730 9563, fax 020 7834 6315, e-mail jscurr@uk-consultants.co.uk, website www.jscurr.com)

SEABECK, Alison Jane; MP; da of Michael Ward, of Rochester, Kent, and Lilian, *née* Lomas; *b* 20 January 1954, Dagenham; *Educ* Harold Hill GS Essex, NE London Poly; *m* 12 July 1975 (sep 2007), Denis Seabeck; 2 da (Elese b 31 Dec 1981, Emma b 24 Oct 1985); *Career* Parly asst Rt Hon Roy Hattersley, MP 1987–92, advsr Rt Hon Nick Raynsford, MP 1992–2005; MP (Lab) Plymouth Devonport 2005–, asst Govt whip 2007–; memb ODPM Select Ctee, memb Regulatory Reform Select Ctee 2005–07, chm All Pty Parly Gp on Local Govt 2006–07, parly convenor Lab Housing Gp 2005–07, vice-chair PLP ODPM Ctee 2006–07, vice-chair SW Gp of Lab MPs 2006–07; memb: Amicus (branch sec), S London Co-op Pty, Fawcett Soc, Lab Women's Network; patron Devon Lupus Gp, hon pres 47th Plymouth Scout Gp; *Recreations* reading, swimming, walking; *Style*— Ms Alison Seabeck, MP; ✉ House of Commons, London SW1A 0AA (tel 020 7219 6431, e-mail seabecka@parliament.uk); Constituency Office tel 01759 362649

SEABROOK, Michael Richard; s of Robert Henry Seabrook (d 1983), of Solihull, and Clara, *née* Berry (d 2000); *b* 24 March 1952; *Educ* King Edward's Sch Birmingham, Univ of Exeter (LLB); *m* 1 Sept 1979, Hilary Margaret Seabrook, JP, da of Anthony John Pettitt, of Bromley, Kent; 2 s (Nicholas b 1983, William b 1986); *Career* admitted slr 1976; articled clerk Lovell White & King 1974–76, asst slr Clifford-Turner 1976–79; ptnr: Needham & James 1981–86 (asst slr 1980), Eversheds 1986– (dep sr ptnr 1994–2003); memb Cncl Birmingham C of C and Industry 1995–2003, non-exec dir W Midlands Enterprise; memb Law Soc 1976; MSI 1992; *Recreations* sporting; *Clubs* Copt Heath Golf, East India and Public Schools, Warwickshire Imps Cricket, Knowle & Dorridge Cricket, Warwickshire Pilgrims Cricket, Bacchanalians Golf Soc; *Style*— Michael R Seabrook, Esq; ✉ 2 Granville Road, Dorridge, Solihull, West Midlands B93 8BY (tel 01564 773732); Eversheds, 115 Colmore Row, Birmingham B3 3AL (tel 0121 232 1000, fax 0121 232 1900, e-mail michaelseabrook@eversheds.com)

SEABROOK, Peter John; MBE (2005); s of Robert Henry Seabrook (d 1987), of Galleywood, Essex, and Emma Mary, *née* Cottey (d 1989); *b* 2 November 1935; *Educ* King Edward VI GS Chelmsford, Essex Inst of Agric Writtle (MHort, Dip Hort); *m* 14 May 1960, Margaret Ruth, da of Arthur Wilfred Risbey (d 1990), of Churchdown, Glos; 1 s (Roger b 9 Feb 1962), 1 da (Alison b 13 May 1964); *Career* Nat Serv RASC 1956–58; author of books and presenter of TV progs on gardening; horticultural advsr and dir Cramphorn plc 1958–66, tech rep Bord na Mona 1966–70, horticultural conslt 1971–; dir: William Strike Ltd 1972–95, Roger Harvey Ltd 1981–99; gardening corr: Nurseryman and Garden Centre 1964–2003, The Sun 1977–, The Yorkshire Post 1981–92, Amateur Gardening 1986–; hon fell Writtle Coll 1997, assoc of honour RHS 1996, Victoria Medal of Honour RHS 2003; FIHort; *Radio* presenter: In Your Garden 1965–70, Gardeners' Question Time 1981–82; *Television* presenter gardening features Pebble Mill at One BBC 1 1975–86; presenter: WGBH TV Boston USA 1975–97, Gardener's World BBC 2 1976–79, Chelsea Flower Show 1976–89, Gardeners' Direct Line BBC TV 1982–90, Peter Seabrook's Gardening Week BBC 1 1996, Great Gardeners HGTV 1997–98; *Books* Shrubs For Your Garden (1973), Complete Vegetable Gardener (1976), Book of the Garden (1979), Good Plant Guide (1981), Good Food Gardening (1983), Shrubs for Everyone (1997); *Recreations* gardening; *Clubs* Farmers'; *Style*— Peter Seabrook, Esq, MBE; ✉ 212A Baddow Road, Chelmsford, Essex CM2 9QR

SEABROOK, Robert John; QC (1983); s of Alan Thomas Pertwee Seabrook, MBE (d 2001), and Mary, *née* Parker (d 1977); *b* 6 October 1941; *Educ* St George's Coll Harare, UCL (LLB); *m* 19 Oct 1965, Liv Karin, da of Rev Bjarne Djupvik (d 1983), of Bergen, Norway; 2 s (Justin b 20 Dec 1969, Magnus b 23 April 1975), 1 da (Marianne b 23 Oct 1971); *Career* called to the Bar Middle Temple 1964 (bencher 1991, treas 2007); recorder 1984–2007, dep judge of the High Court 1991–, ldr SE Circuit 1989–92; chm Bar Cncl 1994; memb: Interception of Communications Tbnl 1995–2000, Criminal Justice Consultative Cncl 1995–2002, Investigating Powers Tbnl 2000–, Regulation of Investigatory Powers Guernsey Tbnl 2006–; memb Court Univ of Sussex 1988–93, vice-pres Brighton Coll (govr 1993–2004, chm 1998–2004); Master Worshipful Co of Curriers 1995 (Liveryman 1972); memb Les Six; *Recreations* wine, listening to music, travel; *Clubs* Athenaeum; *Style*— Robert Seabrook, QC; ✉ 1 Crown Office Row, Temple, London EC4Y 7HH (tel 020 7797 7500, fax 020 7797 7550, DX 1020, e-mail robert.seabrook@1cor.com)

SEAFIELD, 13 Earl of (S 1701); Ian Derek Francis Ogilvie-Grant; Lord Ogilvy of Cullen and Viscount Seafield (S 1698), Lord Ogilvy of Deskford and Cullen and Viscount Reidhaven (S 1701); s of Countess of Seafield (12 in line, d 1969) and Derek Studley-Herbert (who assumed by deed poll 1939 the additional surnames of Ogilvie-Grant, the present Peer being recognised in those surnames by warrant of Lord Lyon 1971); *b* 20 March 1939; *Educ* Eton; *m* 1, 1960 (m dis 1971), Mary Dawn Mackenzie, da of Henry Illingworth; 2 s (James Andrew, Viscount Reidhaven b 1963, Hon Alexander b 1966); m 2, 1971, Leila, da of Mahmoud Refaat, of Cairo; *Heir* s, Viscount Reidhaven; *Clubs* White's; *Style*— The Rt Hon The Earl of Seafield; ✉ Old Cullen, Cullen, Banffshire AB56 4XW

SEAFORD, 6 Baron (UK 1826); Colin Humphrey Felton Ellis; s of Maj William Felton Ellis (d 1977), and Edwina, *née* Bond (d 1976); *b* 19 April 1946, Sussex; *Educ* Sherborne, RAC Cirencester; *m* 1, 1971 (m dis 1992), Susan, *née* Magill; 2 da (Hon Harriett Fay b 4 April 1973, Hon Charlotte Susan b 17 Oct 1975), 2 s (Hon Benjamin Felton Thomas b 17 Dec 1976, Hon Humphrey Henry Guysulf b 10 March 1983); m 2, 1993, Penelope Mary Bastin, *née* Goulson; *Heir* s, Hon Benjamin Ellis; *Career* resident agent Ely Lodge Enniskillen 1968–70, farmer Dorset 1970–93 (dir Blackmore Farms 1982–92), farmer Wilts 1993–; sec Br Bison Assoc, memb various ctees; MRICS; *Recreations* shooting, fishing, writing limericks; *Style*— The Rt Hon the Lord Seaford; ✉ Bush Farm, West Knoyle, Warminster, Wiltshire BA12 6AE (tel 01747 830263, e-mail info@bisonfarm.co.uk)

SEAGER, Chris; s of David Seager (d 2002), and Mamie, *née* Harrison (d 1973); *b* 10 November 1949; *Educ* Monks Park Comp Sch Bristol, Guildford Sch of Art (Dip Film and TV); *m* 3 March 1995, Erica Banks; 2 s (Daniel b 23 Feb 1983, Calum b 16 Sept 1995), 1 da (Rosana b 15 July 1989); *Career* cinematographer; Education TV Unit Wessex TV, trainee studio camera operator BBC Technical Ops, camera asst rising to lighting cameraman BBC Film Dept Ealing Studios; freelance dir of photography 1994–; memb BSC 1996 (memb Bd of Govrs 2002–); *Television* incl: Arena: Scarfe on Scarfe (BAFTA Award), Just Good Friends, Only Fools and Horses, Bergerac, South of the Border, Ashenden 1991, Nice Town 1992, The Vampyr (opera) 1993 (winner Prix Italia Music and Arts), The Peacock Spring 1995, A Dance to the Music of Time 1997, See Saw 1997, The Passion 1998, Bad Blood 1998, In the Name of Love 1999, Madame Bovary 1999, The Sins 2000, Lorna Doone 2000 (nominated BAFTA Photography and Lighting Award 2001), The Way We Live Now 2001 (nominated BAFTA Photography and Lighting Award 2002), Lenny Blue 2001, Ella & The Mothers 2001, State of Play 2003 (RTS Best Photography - Drama Award 2003), Suspicion 2003, Sex Traffic 2004; TV films: Here is the News 1991, They Never Slept 1991, My Sister Wife 1992, Bad Girl 1992, The Bullion Boys 1993, Bambino Mio 1993, Skallagrigg 1994, Cold Comfort Farm 1994, Big Cat 1998, Frenchman's Creek 1998 (nominated RTS Best Photography - Drama Award 1999), Murder Rooms 2000, The Young Visiters 2003; *Film* Stonewall 1994, Beautiful Thing 1995, Fever Pitch 1996, Alive and Kicking 1996, Vent de Colere 1997, The Biographer 2000, Ashes and Sand 2002, White Noise 2003; *Recreations* gym, tennis; *Clubs* Soho House, Blacks; *Style*— Chris Seager, Esq, BSC; ✉ c/o Flic McKinney, McKinney Macartney Management Ltd, The Barley Mow Centre, 10 Barley Mow Passage, London W4 4PH (tel 020 8995 4747, fax 020 8995 2414, e-mail mail@mckinneymacartney.com)

SEAGROVE, Jennifer Ann (Jenny); da of Derek Claud Seagrove, of Penang, Malaysia, and Pauline Marjorie, *née* Pilditch (d 1993); *Educ* St Hilary's Godalming, Queen Anne's Caversham, Kirby Lodge Cambridge, Bristol Old Vic Theatre Sch; *m* 19 May 1984 (m dis 1988), Madhav Sharma; *Career* actress; *Theatre* incl: title role in Jane Eyre (Chichester Festival Theatre), King Lear in New York (Chichester), Present Laughter (Globe), The Miracle Worker (Comedy and Wyndhams), Dead Guilty (Apollo), Hurly Burly (Queen's), Hamlet (Ludlow Festival), Brief Encounter (Lyric), Female Odd Couple (Apollo), The Constant Wife (Apollo), The Secret Rapture (Apollo), The Night of the Iguana (Lyric), The Letter (Wyndhams); *Television* incl: A Woman of Substance, Hold the Dream, Diana, Lucy Walker, The Woman in White, Judge John Deed; for American television: The Hitchhiker, In Like Flynn, Deadly Games, Incident at Victoria Falls, The Betrothed; *Films* incl: To Hell and Back in Time for Breakfast, A Shocking Accident, Local Hero, Savage Islands, Tattoo, Moonlighting, The Sign of Four, Appointment with Death, A Chorus of Disapproval, The Guardian, Miss Beatty's Children, Don't Go Breaking My Heart, Zoe; *Recreations* country walks with dog, running, writing poetry, gardening, theatre, cinema, campaigning for animal welfare and the environment; *Style*— Miss Jenny Seagrove; ✉ c/o Duncan Heath, ICM Ltd, Oxford House, 76 Oxford Street, London W1N 0AX (tel 020 73636 6565)

SEAL, Dr Barry Herbert; s of Herbert Seal, and Rose Ann Seal; *b* 28 October 1937; *Educ* Univ of Bradford, Harvard Business Sch; *m* 1963, Frances Catherine Wilkinson; 1 s (Robert), 1 da (Catherine); *Career* chem engr, control engr, univ lectr; former ldr Bradford Cncl Labour Gp; MEP (Lab) Yorkshire W 1979–99; former ldr Br Lab Gp in European Parl; memb European Parly: Tport Ctee, Social Affairs Ctee; chair of Delgn to USA; chm: Brookfields Int 1999–2003, N Kirklees Primary Care Tst 2002–06, Bradford Dist NHS Care Tst; Hon Freeman Borough of Calderdale 2000; *Books* Dissertations on Computer Control; *Recreations* walking, bridge, reading, riding; *Style*— Dr Barry Seal; ✉ Brookfields Farm, Brookfields Road, Wyke, Bradford BD12 9LU (tel 01274 671888, e-mail barryseal@aol.com)

SEAL, Michael Jefferson; s of Maj Jefferson Seal, TD (d 1977), and Florence Eileen, *née* Herbert (d 1980); *b* 17 October 1936; *Educ* Marlborough; *m* 22 Sept 1962, Julia Mary Seton, da of late Malcolm Sinclair Gaskill, of Hale, Cheshire; 1 s (Jonathan Michael Jefferson), 2 da (Heather Caroline Seton (Mrs Manners), Rosanne Julia (Mrs Nieboer)); *Career* Nat Serv 1955–57, TA 1957–68; Carborundum Co Ltd 1957–59; ptnr: Jefferson Seal & Co 1961–68 (joined 1959), Seal Arnold & Co 1968–72, D Q Henriques Seal & Co 1972–75, Charlton Seal Dimmock & Co 1975–87; chm: Charlton Seal Ltd 1987–88, Charlton Seal Schaverien Ltd 1988–90; non-exec chm CST Emerging Asia Trust plc 1989–92; dir Wise Speke Ltd 1990–96 (conslt 1997–), dir Wise Speke Holdings Ltd 1990–96, sr div dir Wise Speke (div of Brewin Dolphin Securities Ltd) 1998–2000; dir Jefferson Seal Ltd (Jersey) 1986–93; ret 2003; tstee: MGS Tst, Humane Soc for the Hundred of Salford, Wood St Mission, Wythenshawe Hosp Transplant Fund, Gtr Manchester Educnl Tst, Clonter Farm Music Tst, Cheadle Royal Hosp Tst; *Recreations* opera, country sports; *Clubs* St James's (Manchester); *Style*— Michael Seal, Esq; ✉ Burrows Farm, Heaton, Rushton Spencer, Macclesfield, Cheshire SK11 0RD (tel 01260 226555)

SEAL, né Sealhenry Samuel; *m* 2005, Heidi Klum, the model; *Career* singer and songwriter; debut single Killer (with Adamski) reached UK number 1 for 4 weeks 1990, first solo single Crazy reached number 1 in 3 countries 1990; *Albums* Seal (UK no 1, US Top 20, 1991), Seal (UK no 1, 1994), Human Being (1998), Seal IV (2003); Best Male Artist, Best Album, Best Video (for Killer) BRIT Awards 1992, Best Song, Best Record, Best Male Pop Vocal (for Kiss From a Rose) Grammy Awards 1996, International Hit of the Year Ivor Novello Awards 1996; *Style*— Seal

SEALE, Sir John Henry; 5 Bt (UK 1838), of Mount Boone, Devonshire; patron of one living; s of Sir John Carteret Hyde Seale, 4 Bt (d 1964); *b* 3 March 1921; *Educ* Eton, ChCh Oxford; *m* 1953, Ray Josephine, da of late R G Charters, MC, of Christchurch, New Zealand; 1 s, 1 da; *Heir* s, Robert Seale; *Career* Capt RA; architect; RIBA; *Style*— Sir John Seale, Bt; ✉ Slade, Kingsbridge, Devon TQ7 4BL

SEALEY, Barry Edward; CBE (1990); s of Edward Sealey (d 1995), and Queenie Katherine, *née* Hill (d 1981); *b* 3 February 1936; *Educ* Dursley GS, St John's Coll Cambridge (MA); *m* 21 May 1960, Helen, da of Dr Frank Martyn (d 1979), of Grimsby; 1 da (Margaret (Mrs Cave) b 1962), 1 s (Andrew b 1964); *Career* Nat Serv RAF 1953–55; Christian Salvesen plc: trainee 1958, dir 1969, md 1981, md and dep chm 1987, dep chm 1989, ret 1990; dir of cos incl: Scottish American Investment Co 1983–2001, Scottish Equitable plc 1984–99, The Caledonian Brewing Co Ltd 1990–2004, Stagecoach Holdings plc 1992–2001, Wilson Byard Ltd (chm) 1992–2003, Optos plc (chm) 1992–2006, Edinburgh Healthcare NHS Tst (chm) 1993–99, Scottish Equitable Policyholders Tst Ltd 1993–2006, Lothian Health Bd 1999–2002, Lothian Univ Hosps Tst (chm) 1999–2002, ESI Investors Ltd 1999–, Archangel Informal Investment Ltd (chm) 2000–, CXR Biosciences plc 2001–, Northern 3 VCT plc 2001–, Scottish Health Innovations Ltd (chm) 2002–07, LAB 901 Ltd (chm) 2002–, The Dundas Commercial Property (Gen Ptnr) Ltd 2002–, Indigo Lighthouse Group Ltd (chm) 2004, EZD Ltd 2005–, The Landmark Trustee Co Ltd 2006–; CIMgt; *Recreations* walking, music; *Clubs* New (Edinburgh); *Style*— Barry E Sealey, Esq, CBE; ✉ 4 Castlelaw Road, Edinburgh EH13 0DN (tel 0131 441 9136, fax 0131 441 6085, e-mail bes@morago.co.uk)

SEALY, Prof Leonard Sedgwick; s of Alfred Desmond Sealy (d 1964), and Mary Louise, *née* Mark (d 1967); *b* 22 July 1930; *Educ* Stratford HS NZ, Univ of Auckland (MA, LLM), Univ of Cambridge (PhD, Yorke prize); *m* 11 Aug 1960, Beryl Mary, da of Richard Edwards; 2 da (Elizabeth Helena b 23 Jan 1963, Louise Caroline b 3 Dec 1969), 1 s (Mark Edward Byers b 4 Sept 1964); *Career* called to the Bar NZ and admitted barr and slr 1953; Univ of Cambridge: asst lectr 1959–61, lectr 1961–91, SJ Berwin prof of corp law 1991–97; Gonville & Caius Coll Cambridge: fell 1959–, tutor 1960–70, sr tutor 1970–75; ed Cambridge Law Jl 1982–88; gen ed: British Company Law and Practice 1989–, International Corporate Procedures 1991–2005; Cwlth ed Gore-Browne on Companies 1996–2005; *Books* Cases and Materials in Company Law (1971, 8 edn with S Worthington 2007), Benjamin's Sale of Goods (with A G Guest and others, 1974, 7 edn 2006), Company Law and Commercial Reality (1984), Disqualification and Personal Liability of Directors (1986, 6 edn 2000), Guide to the Insolvency Legislation (with D Milman, 1987, 9 edn 2006), Commercial Law, Text and Materials (with R J A Hooley, 1994, 3 edn 2003); *Style*— Prof Leonard Sealy; ✉ Gonville & Caius College, Cambridge CB2 1TA (tel 01223 332400, fax 01223 332456)

SEAMAN, Christopher Bertram; s of Albert Edward Seaman (d 1960), of Canterbury, Kent, and Ethel Margery, *née* Chambers (d 1985); *b* 7 March 1942; *Educ* Canterbury Cathedral Choir Sch, King's Sch Canterbury, King's Coll Cambridge (Scholar, MA); *Career* princ timpanist and memb Bd London Philharmonic Orch 1964–68; princ conductor: BBC Scot Symphony Orch 1971–77 (asst conductor 1968–70), Northern Sinfonia Orch 1974–79; chief guest conductor Utrecht Symphony Orch 1979–82, conductor in res Baltimore Symphony Orch 1987–98, music dir Rochester Philharmonic 1998–; music dir Naples (Florida) Philharmonic Orch 1993–2004; appears as guest conductor worldwide; FGSM 1972; *Recreations* people, reading, shopping, theology; *Style*— Christopher Seaman; ✉ c/o Harrison/Parrott Ltd, 12 Penzance Place, London W11 4PA (tel 020 7229 9166, fax 020 7221 5042)

SEAMAN, (Marvin) Roy; s of late Charles Seaman, of Harleston, Norfolk, and late Mary Elizabeth, *née* Goldsmith; *b* 11 September 1945; *Educ* Stradbroke Secdy Modern Sch, RAF Tech Trg Coll; *m* 19 Oct 1977, Judy, da of late Joseph Ragobar, of Marabella, Trinidad; 2 s (Christian b 1978, Jonathan b 1982), 1 da (Michelle-Anne b 1981); *Career* RAF 1961–67; int mgmnt conslt to Br firms 1968–81, fndr and chm Franchise Development Services Ltd 1981– (offices in 14 countries worldwide); publisher: The UK Franchise Directory 1984–, The Franchise Magazine 1985–, Franchise International 1998–, The Irish Franchise Magazine 1999–, European Franchising 2000–, The Scottish Franchise Magazine 2004–; visiting lectr seminars and confs on franchising and licensing (servs to estab franchisors, prospective franchisors, franchise publications, public relations, seminars, exhibitions and marketing); acknowledged by IOD as Europe's franchise boss and Britain's greatest franchise mastermind; hon prof Beijing Normal Univ 2005; memb: Int Christian C of C, Full Gospel Businessmen's Fellowship Int, CBI; FInstD, MCIM, MInstEx, CFE; *Recreations* deep sea fishing, walking, relaxing with family; *Style*— Roy Seaman, Esq; ✉ Cedar Lodge, Ipswich Road, Tasburgh, Norfolk NR15 1NS (tel 01508 470686); Franchise Development Services Ltd, Franchise House, 56 Surrey Street, Norwich NR1 3FD (tel 01603 620301, fax 01603 630174, e-mail roy@fdsltd.com, website www.fdsfranchise.com)

SEARLE, Geoffrey John; TD (1976); s of late William Ernest Searle, of Cornwall, and Eileen Edith, *née* Girling; *b* 21 June 1945; *Educ* Bancroft's Sch; *m* 25 Sept 1971, Nicole Nicette Suzanne, da of Gilbert Andre Paul Cochonneau, of Tours, France; 2 s (Dominic b 1973, Yann b 1976), 1 da (Olivia b 1984); *Career* TA RCS 1963–77, ret actg Maj; admitted slr 1968; asst clerk of Cncl Brentwood UDC 1969–73, managing ptnr Denton Hall slrs 1988–92 (asst slr 1973–76, ptnr 1977–94), in own practice 1994–; pres Environment and Legislation Ctee FIABCI Worldwide 1994–98, memb Ctee of Mgmnt Br Chapter FIABCI (Int Real Estate Fedn) (pres 1996–97); fndr memb UK Environmental Law Assoc; Freeman City of London, Liveryman Worshipful Co of Slrs; memb Law Soc; FRSA; *Books* Development Land Tax (1985); *Recreations* reading, walking, family history (including the life and times and tracing the descendants of Thomas Taylor (1758–1835), Platonist, four-times great grandfather); *Clubs* Athenaeum; *Style*— Geoffrey Searle; ✉ Geoffrey Searle Planning Solicitors, One Star Lane Mews, Stamford, Lincolnshire PE9 1PE (tel 01780 480133, fax 01780 754182, e-mail gjs@geoffreysearle.com, website www.geoffreysearle.com)

SEARLE, Graham William; s of Frederick William Searle (d 1969), and Margaret, *née* Hewitt (d 1961); *b* 26 September 1946; *Educ* Sir George Monoux GS Walthamstow, SW Essex Tech Coll, King's Coll London (BSc, pres Students' Union 1967–68), Sir John Cass Coll London; *m* 4 Aug 1984 (m dis 1996), Francesca Vivica, *née* Parsons; 1 s (Frederick b 1 June 1991), 1 da (Rebecca b 7 March 1989); *Career* fndr and dir: Friends of the Earth Ltd London 1971, Earth Resources Research Ltd London 1973 (exec dir 1975); advsr Dept of Urban Affrs Fed Govt of Canada 1976, liaison offr Environment Liaison Centre Nairobi Kenya 1977, prog offr UN Environment Prog Nairobi 1978, ind environmental mgmnt conslt 1979–92, exec dir Euro Organic Reclamation and Composting Assoc Brussels and ed Recycling and Resource Management 1991–92, non-exec dir Shanks and McEwan Environmental Services Ltd 1992–94; currently: pres Composting Assoc, hon vice-pres Suffolk Wildlife Tst (chm 1994–95); memb: Ind Cmmn on Tport Planning 1973, UK Standing Ctee on Nat Parks 1975, Standing Ctee of UK Waste Mgmnt Advsy Cncl 1975, Environmental Advsy Bd SME, Rivers Advsy Ctee Nat Rivers Authy (Anglia Region) 1988–94, Conservation Working Gp and Broads Plan Steering Ctee Broads Authy 1992–93; FGS; *Books* Project Earth (1973), Changing Directions (contrib, 1974), Rush to Destruction (1975), The Politics of Physical Resources (contrib, 1975), Energy (1977), Automatic Unemployment (co-author, 1979), The Habitat Handbook (1980), Major World Bank Projects (1987); *Recreations* watching cricket and rugby, supporter of Ipswich Town FC; *Clubs* Suffolk Agricultural Assoc; *Style*— Graham Searle, Esq; ✉ Blacksmiths Cottage, Huntingfield, Halesworth, Suffolk IP19 0PZ (tel 01986 798123)

SEARLE, Ronald William Fordham; CBE (2004); s of William James Searle (d 1967), and Nellie, *née* Hunt (d 1991); *b* 3 March 1920; *Educ* Cambridge Sch of Art; *m* 1 (m dis 1967), Kaye Webb, MBE (d 1996), da of Arthur Webb; 2 c (John, Kate (twins) b 17 July 1947); m 2, Monica Ilse Koenig; *Career* artist and illustrator; Sapper 287 Field Co RE 1939–46 (Japanese POW, Siam and Malaya 1942–45), dept psychological warfare Allied Force HQ Port Said Ops 1956; contrib Punch 1947–61, special features artist Life Magazine 1955–62, contrib New Yorker Magazine 1966–, Le Monde (Paris) 1995–, designer commemorative medals to the French Mint 1975– and BAMS 1984–; RDI, AGI; Chevalier de la Légion d'honneur (France) 2006; *Films* designer: John Gilpin, On the Twelfth Day, Energetically Yours, Germany 1960, Toulouse-Lautrec, Dick Deadeye; designer of animation sequences: Those Magnificent Men in their Flying Machines 1965, Monte Carlo or Bust! 1969, Scrooge 1970; *Exhibitions* one-man exhibitions 1950–2001 incl: Leicester Galleries London, Imperial War Museum, Br Museum, Kraushaar Gallery NY, Bianchini Gallery NY, Kunsthalle Bremen, Bibliothèque Nationale Paris, Stadtmuseum Munich, Neue Galerie Vienna, Wilhelm Busch Museum Hannover 1965, 1976, 1996 and 2001 (jt exhbn with Monica Searle); *Collections* work in permanent collections incl: V&A London, Br Museum London, Imperial War Museum London, Cooper-Hewitt Museum NY, Univ of Austin Texas, Bibliothèque Nationale Paris, Wilhelm Busch Museum Hannover, Prussian Nat Museums Berlin; *Awards* LA Art Dirs Club Medal 1959, Philadelphia Art Dirs Club Medal 1959, Nat Cartoonists Soc Award 1959 and 1960, Gold Medal III Biennale Tolentino Italy 1965, Prix de la Critique Belge 1968, Grand Prix de l'Humour Noir (France) 1971, Prix d'Humour Festival d'Avignon 1971, Medal of French Circus 1971, Prix Internationale 'Charles Huard' 1972, La Monnaie de Paris Medal 1974, Bundesrechtsanwaltskammer Award from the German Legal Profession 1998; *Books incl* Forty Drawings (1946), John Gilpin (1952), Souls in Torment (1953), Rake's Progress (1955), Merry England (1956), Paris Sketchbook (1957), The St Trinian's Story (with Kaye Webb 1959); with Alex Atkinson: The Big City (1958), USA for Beginners (1959), Russia for Beginners (1960); Refugees (1960), Which Way did He Go? (1961), Escape from the Amazon (1963), From Frozen North to Filthy Lucre (1964), Those Magnificent Men in their Flying Machines (1965), Haven't We Met Before Somewhere? (with Heinz Huber 1966), Searle's Cats (1967), The Square Egg (1968), Hello - Where did all the People Go? (1969), Secret Sketchbook (1970), The Second Coming of Toulouse-Lautrec (1970), The Addict (1971), More Cats (1975), Designs for Gilbert and Sullivan (1975), Paris! Paris! (with Irwin Shaw 1977), Searle's Zoodiac (1977), Ronald Searle (monograph 1978), The King of Beasts (1980), The Big Fat Cat Book (1982), Illustrated Winespeak (1983), Ronald Searle in Perspective (monograph 1984), Ronald Searle's Golden Oldies 1941–1961 (1985), Something in the Cellar (1986), To the Kwai - and Back (1986), Ah Yes, I Remember It Well...: Paris 1961–75 (1987), Non-Sexist Dictionary (1988), Slightly Foxed - but still desirable (1989), Carnet de Croquis (1992), The Curse of St Trinian's (1993), Marquis de Sade meets Goody Two-Shoes (1994), Ronald Searle dans Le Monde (1998), The Face of War (with Simon Rae, 1999), The Scrapbook Drawings (2005); subject of biography Ronald Searle (by Russell Davies, 1990); *Clubs* Garrick; *Style*— Ronald Searle, Esq, CBE; ✉ The Sayle Literary Agency, 1 Petersfield, Cambridge CB1 1BB (tel 01223 303035, fax 01223 301638, e-mail rachel@sayleliteraryagency.com, website www.ronaldsearle.com)

SEARS, Dr Charles Alistair Newton; s of Dr (Harold) Trevor Newton Sears (d 1995), and Dr Janet Sorley, *née* Conn (d 1994); *b* 30 December 1952; *Educ* Sandbach Sch, Middx Hosp Med Sch London (MB BS); *m* 6 May 1978, Judith Lesley, da of Dr Leslie Victor Martin, of Oxbridge, Dorset; 3 s (James b 1979, Robert b 1982, Nicholas b 1986); *Career* house offr Middx Hosp 1978; SHO: neurosurgery Royal Free Hosp 1978–79, med Queen Elizabeth Hosp Birmingham 1979–82; ptnr in gen practice Salisbury 1983–, clinical asst Learning Disability 1986–2006 (clinical asst Rheumatology 1985–92); trainer in gen practice Salisbury Dist Vocational Trg Scheme; memb: Cncl RCGP 1991–95, Health Cncl of Disability Partnership 1992–2007, Med and Social Servs Ctee Muscular Dystrophy Campaign 1993–2003, NHS Exec Commissioning Gp for R&D in Complex and Physical Disability 1994–98, Jt Specialty Ctee for Rehabilitation Med RCP 1994–, Devpt Gp National Back Pain Guidelines RCGP 1996 and 1999, Devpt Gp Faculty of Occupational Med Back Pain Guidelines 1999–2000, Editorial Bd Guidelines in Practice 1999–2003, Ctee of Safety Devices 2001–; vice-pres Backcare 2003– (tstee 1994–2002); RCGP nominee to Back Pain Sub-Gp Clinical Standards Advsy Gp 1992–95; memb: Br Inst of Musculoskeletal Med, Br Soc of Rehabilitation Medicine, Centre for the Advancement of Interprofessional Educn; FRCGP 2003 (MRCGP 1988), FRIPH 2005; *Style*— Dr Charles Sears; ✉ Grove House Surgery, 18 Wilton Road, Salisbury, Wiltshire SP2 7EE (tel 01722 333034, fax 01722 410308)

SEARS, (Robert) David Murray; QC (2003); s of (Robert) Murray Sears, and Janet Leslie, *née* Heape; *b* 13 December 1957, Haslemere, Surrey; *Educ* Eton, Trinity Coll Oxford (MA); *m* 14 July 1984 (m dis 2007), Victoria Jane, *née* Morlock; 1 s (Benedict b 7 May 1994), 1 da (Cordelia b 31 Jan 1996); *Career* MOD 1979–83, barr 4 Pump Court Temple 1985–; *Recreations* sailing, motorcycling, supporting Ipswich Town FC; *Clubs* Leander, Vincent's (Oxford); *Style*— David Sears, Esq, QC; ✉ 4 Pump Court, Temple, London EC4Y 7AN (tel 020 7842 1140, fax 020 7583 2036, e-mail dsears@4pumpcourt.com)

SEATON, Prof Anthony; CBE (1997); s of Dr Douglas Ronald Seaton (d 1986), of Ipswich, Suffolk, and Julia, *née* Harrison; bro of Dr Douglas Seaton and James Ronald Seaton, *qqv*; *b* 20 August 1938; *Educ* Rossall Sch, King's Coll Cambridge (BA, MB, MD); *m* 4 April 1964, Jillian Margaret Duke; 2 s (Andrew b 1966, Jonathan b 1969); *Career* qualified in med 1962, asst prof of med Univ of W Virginia 1969–71, conslt chest physician Univ of Wales 1971–77, dir Inst of Occupational Med Edinburgh 1978–90, prof Univ of Aberdeen 1988–2003 (head Dept of Environmental and Occupational Med), emeritus prof Univ of Aberdeen 2003–, sr conslt Inst of Occupational Med Edinburgh 2004–; Tudor Edwards lectr RCP and RCS, Hunter lectr Faculty of Occupational Med, Gehrmann lectr American Coll of Occupational and Environmental Med, Warner lectr Br Occupational Hygiene Soc, Meiklejohn lectr Soc of Occupational Med; author of numerous pubns in jls; memb: Br Occupational Med and Thoracic Socs (pres Br Thoracic Soc 1999), Ctee on Med Effects of Air Pollution Dept of Health; chm expert panel on air quality standards DOE 1991–2001, memb Royal Soc and Royal Acad of Engrg Working Gp on Nanoscience 2003–04; Br Thoracic Soc Medal 2006; DSc (hc) Univ of Aberdeen 2007; FRCP 1977 (MRCP 1964), FRCPE 1986, FFOM 1985, FMedSci 1998; *Publications* Occupational Lung Diseases (with W K C Morgan 1975, 3 edn 1995), Thorax (ed, 1977–81), Respiratory Diseases (with D Seaton and A G Leitch, 1989, 2 edn 2000), Practical Occupational Medicine (1994, 2 edn 2005); *Recreations* keeping fit, opera, painting; *Clubs* St Andrew Boat; *Style*— Prof Anthony Seaton, CBE; ✉ 8 Avon Grove, Barnton, Edinburgh EH4 6RF (tel 0131 336 5113, fax 0131 336 2710, e-mail a.seaton@abdn.ac.uk)

SEATON, Dr Douglas; s of Dr Douglas Ronald Seaton (d 1986), of Ipswich, Suffolk, and Julia, *née* Harrison; bro of Prof Anthony Seaton, CBE and James Ronald Seaton, *qqv*; *b* 5 February 1946; *Educ* Rossall Sch Fleetwood, Univ of Liverpool (MB ChB, MD); *m* 1 Aug 1970, Anja Elisabeth, da of Frits Coenraad Neervoort, of Bussum, Netherlands; 3 s (Edward b 31 Aug 1972, Bart b 8 Feb 1974, Michael b 20 May 1978); *Career* sr med registrar United Liverpool Hosps 1976, instr in med W Virginia Univ USA 1977, conslt physician in gen and respiratory med The Ipswich Hosp 1979–, asst ed Thorax 1980–82; author of med papers on respiratory diseases, contrib chapters in med textbooks; MRCS, FRCP (MRCP), FRCPEd; *Books* Crofton and Douglas's Respiratory Diseases (with A Seaton and A G Leitch, 1989 and 2000); *Recreations* country walking, church architecture; *Style*— Dr Douglas Seaton; ✉ King's Field, 23 Park Road, Ipswich, Suffolk IP1 3SX (tel 01473 216671, fax 01473 212011)

SEATON, James Ronald; s of Douglas Ronald Seaton (d 1986), of Ipswich, Suffolk, and Julia, *née* Harrison; bro of Dr Douglas Seaton and Prof Anthony Seaton, CBE, *qqv*; *b* 3 March 1955; *Educ* Rossall Sch Fleetwood, Wirral GS Bebington, Univ of Birmingham (BA); *m* 7 Oct 1978, Jessica Ruth, da of Arthur Barwell Hampton; 1 da (Rachel Amelia b 2 Aug 1980), 1 s (Nicholas James b 12 March 1985); *Career* knitwear and clothing designer/mfr: J & J Seaton 1978– (2 collections annually), Seaton 1995– (2 collections annually), Toast (mail order) 1997– (2 collections annually); *Books* The Seaton Collection (1989); *Recreations* paleo-ethno botany; *Style*— James Seaton, Esq; ✉ J & J Seaton, Llanfynydd, Carmarthen, Dyfed SA32 7TT (tel 01558 668825, fax 01558 668875)

SEAWARD, Prof Mark Richard David; *b* 10 August 1938; *Educ* City GS Lincoln, Univ of Birmingham (BSc, Dip Ed), Univ of Nottingham (MSc), Univ of Bradford (PhD, DSc); *Career* head of biology Brigg GS 1960–65, lectr Loughborough Trg Coll 1965–67, sr lectr Trinity and All Saints Colls 1967–73; Univ of Bradford: chm Post Grad Sch of Environmental Sci 1980–88, chm Bd of Studies and Higher Degrees Ctee 1981–84, memb Cncl 1984–90, memb Senate 1984–97, prof of environmental biology 1990–, head Dept of Environmental Sci 1991–95; hon visiting prof Univ of Lincoln, hon research fell Manchester Museum; chm Ctee Heads of Environmental Sciences 1996–99; vice-pres Linnean Soc 1997–2001 and 2006–; hon memb: Br Lichen Soc (memb Cncl), Japan Lichenology Soc, Polish Lichenology Soc, Italian Lichenology Soc; ed The Naturalist; author of over 400 scientific papers and assoc ed of 2 jls; Ursula Duncan Award Br Lichen Soc, Acharius Medal Int Lichenology Assoc; pres Leeds Philosophical Literary Soc 2003–; exec memb: Yorkshire Naturalists Union, Tennyson Soc; Nummo Aureo Univ of Wroclaw, Dr (hc) Univ of Wroclaw; FIBiol, FLS; *Books* Lichen Ecology (1977), Lichenology in the British Isles 1568–1975 (1977), A Handbook for Naturalists (1980), Urban Ecology (1982), Atlas of the Lichens of the British Isles (1982), Lichen Atlas of the British Isles (1995–), Richard Spruce, Botanist and Explorer (1996), Lichenology in Latin America (1998), Ecology of the Chagos Archipelago (1999), Biodeterioration of Stone Surfaces (2004); *Recreations* book collecting, music, philately, postal history; *Clubs* Linnean; *Style*— Prof Mark Seaward; ✉ University of Bradford, Bradford BD7 1DP (tel 01274 234212, fax 01274 234231, e-mail m.r.d.seaward@bradford.ac.uk)

SEAWRIGHT, Paul; s of William James Seawright, and Isobel, *née* McComb; *Educ* Belfast Royal Acad, Univ of Ulster, W Surrey Coll of Art (BA); *Career* photographer; Univ of Ulster: pt/t lectr in art and design 1990–92, assoc lectr in photography 1991–94; Univ of Wales Coll Newport: sr lectr in documentary photography 1994–95, course ldr documentary photography 1995–97, head of res Dept of Media Arts 1997–2000, currently head Centre for Photographic Res; visiting prof Ecole Nationale Superior des Beaux Arts Paris 1996; founding ed Source; chm Photo Works North 1992–94; memb Visual Arts Panel Arts Cncl of NI 1992–94, advsr to bd Gall of Photography Dublin 1994–97; *Solo Exhibitions* Mikkelin Valokuvakesus Finland 1989, Gallery Vapauden Aukion Helsinki 1989, The Photographer's Gall London 1991 and 1995, The Gall of Photography Dublin 1992 and 1995, Impressions Gall York 1992, The Int Center of Photography NY 1992, The Old Museum Belfast 1993, Arts Cncl Gall Belfast 1993, UN Gen Assembly Building NY 1993, Blue Sky Gall Portland Oregon 1993 and 1997, Cornerhouse Manchester 1994, Ffotogallery Cardiff 1996, Houston Fotofest 1996, Françoise Knabe Gall Frankfurt 1997, Le Lieu l'Orient France 1997, Galerie du Jour / Agnes b Paris 1998 and 2001, Rena Bransten Gall San Francisco 1998 and 2000, Rhona Hoffman Gall Chicago 1998 and 2000, Angles Gall Santa Monica 1998 and 2001, Kerlin Gall Dublin 1999, Centro de Fotografia Univ of Salamanca 2000, Maureen Paley/Interim Art London 2000, Photo.doc Forum Box Helsinki 2000, Bonakdar Jancou Gall NY 2000, Grieder Von Puttkamer Berlin 2000, Museum of Contemporary Art Zagreb 2000, Hasselblad Centre Kunst Museum Gothenberg 2001, Douglas Hyde Gall Dublin 2001, Fndn Marangoni Florence 2002; *Group Exhibitions* Show of Hands (Photographers' Gall London) 1988, Death (Cambridge Darkroom Gall/Kettles Yard) 1988, Shocks to the System (Arts Cncl of GB RFH and Ikon Gall Birmingham) 1991, NI Cultural Counterpoint Conf (SUNY Binghamton) 1991, Current Account (RPS Bath and Mai de la Photo Riems) 1992–93, Through the Lens (Arts Cncl of NI touring exhbn) 1992, Recent Acquisitions (Ulster Museum Belfast) 1992, History of the Photographic Image (Rencontres Intls de la Photographie Arles) 1992, Godowsky Awards (PRC Gall Boston) 1993, Documentary Dilemmas (Brit Cncl touring Euro, S America and Ireland) 1993–94, Nervous Landscapes (Southeast Museum of Photography Florida) 1994, Different Stories (Photo Int and Nederlands Foto Instituut Rotterdam) 1994, Ceasefire (Wolverhampton Museum and Art Gall) 1994–95, L'Imaginaire Irlandais (Ecole des Beaux Arts Paris) 1996, Inside Out (Galerie du Jour/Agnes b Paris) 1996, Kerlin Gall Dublin 1996, Lie of the Land (touring exhbn, Gall of Photography Dublin, Centre Nationale de la Photographie Paris, Copenhagen, Salamanca, Athens and Prague) 1996–97, Irish MOMA/Glen Dimplex Artists Award (Irish MOMA) 1997, Recent Acquisitions (Irish MOMA) 1997, NGBK Contemporary British Photography (Berlin) 1997, Residue (Douglas Hyde Gall Dublin) 1997, Political Spaces - Three Person (Rena Bransten San Francisco) 1997, The Missing - Three Person Exhibition (Nederlands Foto Instituut Rotterdam) 1997, Photos Leurres (French Inst Prague) 1998, Le Primtemps (Cahor France) 1998, Sightings - New Photographic Art (ICA London) 1998, Europe in Decay (Light Hall Kuopio and Helsinki Cathedral) 1998, Troubled, Photography and Video from Northern Ireland (The Light Factory and Contemporary Art Museum Raleigh N Carolina) 1998, Declinations of the Boundaries (Galerie Lichtblick Cologne) 1999, Revealing Views; Images from Ireland (RFH) 1999, Under Exposed (Public Art Project Stockholm) 1999, Contemporary Art (Arts Cncl of Ireland Collection, Limerick City Art Gall) 1999, Silent Presence (Staatliche Kunsthalle Baden-Baden Germany) 1999, Concern for the Document (Vox Populi Le Mois de la Photo Montreal Canada) 1999, Contemporary Art (Ormeau Baths Gall Belfast) 1999, Fragments of Document & Memory (Tokyo Photo Bienalle, Tokyo Met Museum of Photography) 1999, Surveying the Landscape (Lombard/Fried Fine Arts NY) 1999, Engaging Tradition (Hotbath Gall Bath), 0044 (PS1 NY, Albright-Knox Art Gall Buffalo) 1999 and Ormeau Baths Gall Belfast and Crawford, Municipal Art Gall Cork) 2000, Lautlose Gegenwart (Bielefelder Kunstverein) 2000, Foto Biennale Rotterdam 2000, Irish Art Now: From the Poetic to the Political (McMullen Museum of Art Boston Coll, Art Gall of Newfoundland and Labrador Canada, Chicago Cultural Centre Chicago) 2000 and Irish MOMA 2001, British Art Show 5 (tour venues incl Scottish Nat Gall of Modern Art, Southampton City Art Gall, Ffotogallery Cardiff and Ikon Birmingham) 2000, Auto Werke (Deichtorhallen Hamburg, with Gillian Wearing, *qv*, et al) 2000, 50 Years of Irish Art (Irish MOMA) 2001, On the Margins (Barbara Krakow Gall Boston) 2001, Depicting Abscence/Implying Prescence (San Jose Inst of Contemporary Art Calif) 2001, Werner Mertz Prize (Centrum Beeldende Kunst Maastricht Netherlands) 2001, A470 (Oriel Gall Llandudno Wales and Chapter Cardiff) 2001, New Directions (Winston Wachter Fine Art Seattle) 2001, The Gap Show - Critical Art from Great Britain (Museum am Ostwall Dortmund Germany) 2002, Gewaltbilder - Gewalt in der Gegenwartskunst (Museum Bellerive Zurich) 2002; collections incl: Arts Cncl of GB, Cncl of Ireland, Int Center of Photography NY, Art Gall of Ontario Canada, Vereins-und Westbank Hamburg, Worcester City Art Gall and Museum, Deutsche Bank Frankfurt, AIB Collection Dublin, ACC Bank Dublin, Simmons and Simmons London, Waterford RTC, Museum of Contemporary Art Strasbourg, San Francisco MOMA, Art Inst Chicago, BMW Munich; *Awards* Photoworks in Progress Cmmn Netherlands Foto Inst 1997, Irish MOMA/Glen Dimplex Artists Award 1997, BMW Auto Werke Cmmn Munich 1998, Ville de Paris Artist Award 1999, In Context Cmmn S Dublin CC 2000, War Artist Cmmn Afghanistan Imp War Museum 2002; *Publications* numerous exhibition catalogues and features in magazines and jls; *Style*— Paul Seawright, Esq; ✉ University of Wales College Newport, PO Box 179, Newport NP18 3YG (tel 01633 432642, fax 01633 432168, e-mail paul.seawright@newport.ac.uk)

SEBAG-MONTEFIORE, Charles Adam Laurie; s of Denzil Charles Sebag-Montefiore (d 1996), and Ruth Emily, *née* Magnus; *b* 25 October 1949; *Educ* Eton, Univ of St Andrews (MA); *m* 5 Oct 1979, Pamela Mary Diana, da of Archibald Tennant (d 1955); 2 da (Elizabeth Anne b 1982, Laura Rose b 1984), 1 s (Archibald Edward Charles b 1987); *Career* initial career with Touche Ross & Co CAs, ptnr Grieveson Grant & Co 1981–86, dir Kleinwort Benson Securities Ltd 1986–94, dep chm Harvill Press Ltd 1994–2002; dir: Euclidian plc 1994–99, Elderstreet Corporate Finance Ltd 1997–99, IDJ Ltd 1999–2004, Govett European Enhanced Investment Trust plc 1999–2004 (chm 2003–04), Kiln plc 2001–06; chm Community Careline Services Ltd 2001–02, non-exec dep chm West 175 Media Gp 2001–06 (dir 2000–06), non-exec dir Hightex Gp plc 2006–; tstee HSBC Common Funds for Growth and Income 1994–2002; dir Ludgate Investments Ltd 2004–; chm: Projects Ctee Nat Art-Collections Fund 1977–86, London Historic House Museums Tst 1992– (tstee 1987–); hon treas: Friends of the Nat Libraries 1990–, Friends of the British Library 1990–95, Friends of Lambeth Palace Library 1990–, The London Library 1991–2003, The Walpole Soc 1992–; govr of Patrons of the Nat Gallery of Scotland 1992–, treas Roxburghe Club 2002–; tstee: Samuel Courtauld Tst 1992–, Nat Art Collections Fund 2000–, Nat Manuscripts Conservation Tst 2000–, Montefiore Endowment 2004–, Oxford Centre for Hebrew and Jewish Studies 2004–, Strawberry Hill Tst 2004–; jt sec Soc of Dilettanti 2002–; Liveryman Worshipful Co of Spectacle Makers 1973; FCA 1974, FRSA 1980, FSA 1995; *Recreations* visiting picture galleries, collecting books, opera; *Clubs* Brooks's, Beefsteak; *Style*— Charles Sebag-Montefiore, Esq, FSA; ✉ 21 Hazlewell Road, London SW15 6LT (tel 020 8789 5999, fax 020 8785 4071); Ludgate Investments Ltd, 46 Cannon Street, London EC4N 6JJ (tel 020 7236 0973, fax 020 7329 2100, e-mail csmontefiore@ludgate.com)

SEBASTIAN, Timothy (Tim); s of Peter Sebastian, CBE, of Hove, E Sussex, and Pegitha, *née* Saunders; *b* 13 March 1952; *Educ* Westminster, New Coll Oxford (BA), UC Cardiff (Dip Journalism); *m* 4 June 1977 (m dis 1995), Diane, da of John Buscombe, of Frensham, Surrey; 1 s (Peter b 1981), 2 da (Clare b 1983, Caroline b 1986); *Career* BBC TV: eastern Europe corr 1979–82, Moscow corr 1984–85, Washington corr 1986–89, presenter Hardtalk 1997–2004; fndr and chm The Doha Debates 2004–; *Books* Nice Promises (1984), I Spy in Russia (1985), The Spy in Question (1987), Spy Shadow (1989), Saviour's Gate (1990), Exit Berlin (1992), Last Rights (1993), Special Relations (1994), War Dance (1995), Ultra (1997); *Style*— Tim Sebastian, Esq

SECCOMBE, Baroness (Life Peer UK 1991), of Kineton in the County of Warwickshire; Dame Joan Anna Dalziel Seccombe; DBE (1984); da of Robert John Owen (d 1941), of Solihull, W Midlands, and Olive Barlow Owen; *b* 3 May 1930; *Educ* St Martin's Sch Solihull; *m* 1950, Henry Lawrence Seccombe, s of Herbert Stanley Seccombe (d 1951), of Lapworth, Warks; 2 s (Hon Philip Stanley b 1951, Hon Robert Murray b 1954); *Career* memb: W Midlands CC 1977–81 (chm Trading Standards 1979–81), Midlands Elec Consultative Cncl 1981–90; chm: Cons Womens Nat Ctee 1981–84, Nat Union of Cons & Unionists Assoc 1987–88 (vice-chm 1984–87), Lord Chllr's Advsy Ctee, Solihull Magistrates 1975–93, Solihull Bench 1981–84; vice-pres Inst of Trading Standards Admin 1992–; vice-chm Cons Party 1987–97; memb: W Midlands Police Ctee 1977–81 and 1985–91, Admin and Works Sub-Ctee 1991–94, Offices Ctee House of Lords 1991–94 and 1997–2000, Broadcasting Ctee 1994–97, Finance and Staff Sub-Ctee 1994–97, Personal Bills Ctee 1994–97; oppn whip House of Lords 1997–2001 (dep chief oppn whip 2001–); Nuffield Hosps: govr 1988–2001, dep chm 1993–2001, chm tstees Pension Fund 1992–2001; extra Baroness in Waiting to HM the Queen 2004–; pres St Enedoc Golf Club 1991–; JP Solihull 1968–2000; *Recreations* skiing, golf, needlework; *Style*— The Rt Hon Lady Seccombe, DBE; ✉ House of Lords, London SW1A 0PW (tel 020 7219 4558)

SECKER, Prof Philip Edward; s of Cyril Edward Secker (d 1980); *b* 28 April 1936; *Educ* Haberdashers' Aske's, Univ of London; *m* 1968, Judith Andrea, da of Douglas Eric Lee (d 1981); 2 s; *Career* chartered engr; lectr Univ of London 1961–64, visiting asst prof MIT 1964–65; UCNW: lectr 1965–69, sr lectr 1969–73, reader 1973–75, prof 1975–80; md IDB (UCNW) Ltd 1971–80, engrg dir Royal Doulton Ltd 1980–87, visiting prof Dept of Physics Keele Univ 1985–; md IEE 1999–2001 (acting chief exec 1998–99, dep chief exec 1990–97); exec sec ERA Fndn 2002–05; dir: UWB Enterprises Ltd, IDB (UBW) Ltd 2001–06 (chm 2006–), Young Engrs Ltd 2001–; *Recreations* refurbishing classic cars, gardening; *Style*— Prof Philip Secker; ✉ Gwel-y-Don, Cae Mair, Beaumaris, Anglesey LL58 8YN (tel 01248 810771, e-mail psecker@cherry-garden.demon.co.uk)

SECKER-WALKER, Dr Jonathan; s of Geoffrey Secker-Walker (d 1968), of Farnborough, Hants, and Joan Alice, *née* Diplock (d 1995); *b* 19 October 1942; *Educ* Sherborne, UCL (BSc), UCH Med Sch (MB BS); *m* 20 July 1968, Jan Lilian, da of Charles James Goodwin (d 1998), of Ryde, IOW; 1 da (Katherine Louise b 16 Aug 1971), 1 s (Thomas Adam b 30 April 1973); *Career* registrar (anaesthetics): UCH 1970–72, Gt Ormond St 1972; sr registrar (anaesthetics) St Thomas' Hosp 1973, clinical asst Toronto Sick Children's Hospital 1974, conslt anaesthetist and sr lectr UCH 1975, sr lectr in clinical audit UCL 1988–94, gen mangr UCL Hosps 1992–94, med dir Merrett Health Risk Management Ltd 1994–98, sr lect Univ of Wales Coll of Med 1999–2003, emeritus conslt UCL Hosps 1994–; FRCA 1972, FRSM; *Recreations* skiing, sailing, walking, theatre; *Style*— Dr Jonathan Secker-Walker; ✉ Brook House, Stogumber, Somerset TA4 3SZ (tel 01984 656701)

SECKL, Prof Jonathan Robert; s of Josef Seckl, and Zehava, *née* Segal; *b* 15 August 1956; *Educ* William Ellis Sch London, UCL (BSc, MB BS, Filliter Prize, Magrath scholarship, Fellowes Gold Medal, Achison exhbn), Westminster Hosp Med Sch London (PhD); *m* 9 Nov 1986, Molly, *née* Sifnugel; 1 s (Benjamin b 15 July 1988), 1 da (Joanna b 4 Nov 1989); *Career* Univ of Edinburgh: Sir Jules Thorn research fell 1984, Wellcome Tst/RSE sr clinical research fell 1989, hon conslt physician 1989, sr lectr in med 1993, prof of endocrinology 1996, Moncrieff-Arnott prof of molecular med 1997, head Dept of Med Sciences 2001, head Sch of Molecular and Clinical Med 2002, dir of research Coll of Medicine and Veterinary Med 2005–; memb: Lloyds TSB Ctee RSE, Scottish Science Advsy Ctee (SSAC); Soc for Endocrinology Medal 1998; PhD (hc) Umea Univ 2001; memb Assoc of Physicians 1991; MRCP 1983, FRCPEd 1993, FMedSci 1999, FRSE 2002; *Publications* approximately 250 papers, reviews and chapters on endocrinology, notably on glucocorticoid biology in relation to brain ageing and obesity/type 2 diabetes; author of several patents; *Recreations* tennis, skiing; *Style*— Prof Jonathan Seckl; ✉ Edinburgh University, The Queen's Medical Research Institute, 47 Little France Crescent, Edinburgh EH16 4TJ (tel 0131 242 6777, fax 0131 242 6779, e-mail j.seckl@ed.ac.uk)

SECONDÉ, Sir Reginald Louis; KCMG (1981, CMG 1972), CVO (1968, MVO 1957); s of Lt-Col Emile Charles Secondé (d 1952); *b* 28 July 1922; *Educ* Beaumont Coll, King's Coll Cambridge; *m* 1951, Catherine Penelope (d 2004), da of Thomas Ralph Sneyd-Kynnersley, OBE, MC; 1 s, 2 da; *Career* Maj WWII Coldstream Gds in N Africa and Italy (despatches); Dip Serv 1949–82: UK Delgn to United Nations and British Embassies in Portugal, Cambodia, Poland and Brazil 1949–69, head S European Dept FCO 1969–72, RCDS 1972–73; ambass: Chile 1973–76, Romania 1977–79, Venezuela 1979–82 (ret 1982); *Clubs* Cavalry and Guards'; *Style*— Sir Reginald Secondé, KCMG, CVO; ✉ Stowlangtoft Hall, Stowlangtoft, Bury St Edmunds, Suffolk IP31 3JY (tel 01359 230927)

SECUNDE, Nadine Rekeszus; da of John Philip Secunde, of the USA, and Patricia Margaret, *née* Bousi; *b* 21 December 1951; *Educ* Oberlin Conservatory of Music Oberlin Ohio, Univ of Indiana; *m* Heiner Rekeusus; 1 da (Anja Maria b 1989), 1 s (Jan-Philipp b 1992); *Career* soprano; studied with Margaret Harshaw at Univ of Indiana, Fulbright scholarship to Germany 1979, memb Hessisches Staatstheater Ensemble Wiesbaden 1980–84, with Cologne Opera 1984–89, Bayreuth Festspiele 1987–92; numerous guest appearances at major opera houses incl Munich, Vienna, Berlin, San Francisco, Chicago, Paris, Barcelona; *Recordings* incl: Prokofiev's The Fiery Angel (DDG), Strauss' Elektra (Phillips), Bayreuther Ring (Sieglinde), laser disc of Britten's Turn of the Screw; *Recreations* rare books; *Style*— Ms Nadine Secunde; ✉ c/o Ingpen & Williams Ltd, 7 St George's Court, 131 Putney Bridge Road, London SW15 2PA (tel 020 8874 3222, fax 020 8877 3113)

SEDDON, Nicholas Paul (Nick); s of Clive Seddon, of Congleton, Cheshire, and Alison Helen, *née* Dale; *b* 11 July 1960; *Educ* Sandbach GS, Univ of Birmingham (LLB); *Career* admitted slr 1984; ptnr: Needham & James Birmingham 1988–93 (joined 1982), currently md Asia DLA Piper (formerly Dibb Lupton Alsop); memb Law Soc; Freeman City of London, Liveryman Worshipful Co of Basketmakers; *Recreations* motor sport, gardening, photography, wine; *Style*— Nick Seddon, Esq; ✉ DLA Piper, 40th Floor Bank of China Tower, 1 Garden Road, Central, Hong Kong (e-mail nick.seddon@dlapiper.com)

SEDDON, Patsy Frances Jane; da of Richard Hayes, of Pembrokeshire, and Cynthia, *née* Shelley; *Educ* Tudor Hall, Winkfield Coll; *m* 1971 (m dis 2002), Julian Seddon; 1 s (Alexander James Dyson b 2 May 1973), 1 da (Zoe Louisa b 8 May 1974); *Career* Browns South Molton St London 1970–73; Phase Eight Ltd (fashion and design): fndr 1979, chm 1979–2001, pres 2001–05; fndr Hazelbury Ltd (trades as Thyme & Spice) 2004; runner-up Entrepreneur of the Year 2001; *Recreations* plants, flowers, cooking, decoupage, skiing; *Style*— Mrs Patsy Seddon; ✉ 109 Hazlebury Road, London SW6 3HR

SEDGWICK, (Ian) Peter; *b* 13 October 1935; *m* 6 Aug 1956, (Verna) Mary; 1 s (Paul b 17 March 1961), 1 da (Carey Anne b 30 Nov 1962); *Career* National Provincial Bank 1952–59, Ottoman Bank Africa and the ME 1959–69, J Henry Schroder Wagg & Co Ltd 1969–90, chief exec Schroder Investment Management Limited 1985–94; Schroders plc: gp md investment mgmnt 1987–95, dep chm 1995–2000, chm 2000–02; chm Schroder UK Growth Fund 1994–2002, chm Schroder & Co Inc 1996–2000 (non-exec dir 1991), pres and ceo US Holdings Inc NY (formerly Schroders Inc NY) 1996–2000; non-exec vice-pres Equitable Life Assurance Society 1991–2001; INVESCO City & Commercial Investment Trust plc (formerly New City & Commercial Investment Trust plc) 1992–2001; chm Queen Elizabeth's Fndn 2007– (tstee 2002–); *Recreations* golf; *Style*— Peter Sedgwick, Esq

SEDGWICK, Peter Norman; s of late Norman Victor Sedgwick, of Dorset, and Lorna Clara, *née* Burton; *b* 4 December 1943; *Educ* Westminster Cathedral Choir Sch, Downside, Lincoln Coll Oxford (MA, BPhil); *m* 17 Feb 1984, Catherine Jane, da of Barry Donald Thomas and Janet Saunders; 2 s (Richard b 30 Dec 1986, Christopher b 14 April 1988), 2 da (Victoria b 6 July 1989, Rebecca Elizabeth b 3 Dec 1990); *Career* HM Treasy: econ asst 1969, econ advsr 1971, sr econ advsr 1977, under-sec 1984, dep dir 1995–99; vice-pres and memb Mgmnt Ctee European Investment Bank Luxembourg 2000–06, dir European Investment Fund 2002–06, chm 3i Infrastructure Ltd 2007–; memb London Symphony Chorus 1972– (chm 1979–84); *Recreations* singing, gardening, walking; *Style*— Peter Sedgwick, Esq; ✉ 20 Skeena Hill, Southfields, London SW18 5PL

SEDLEY, Rt Hon Lord Justice; Rt Hon Sir Stephen John; kt (1992), PC (1999); s of William Sedley (d 1984), and Rachel Sedley (d 1987); *b* 9 October 1939; *Educ* Mill Hill Sch, Queens' Coll Cambridge (open scholar and exhibitioner, BA); *m* 1, 1968 (m dis), Ann Tate; 3 c (Jane May b 5 May 1970, Benjamin Anthony b 9 May 1972, Sarah Ann b 27 Sept 1975); m 2, 1996, Teresa (Tia) Cockrell; *Career* called to the Bar: Inner Temple 1964 (bencher 1989), Trinidad and Tobago 1986; QC 1983, asst recorder 1985–92, judge of the High Court of Justice (Queen's Bench Div) 1992–, Lord Justice of Appeal 1999– memb Int Cmmn on Mercenaries (Angola) 1976, pres Nat Reference Tbnls for coalmining industry 1983–87, chair Inquiry into the death of Tyra Henry (Lambeth) 1986–87, fndr memb and dir Public Law Project 1988–93, chm Sex Discrimination Ctee Bar Cncl 1992–95; pres Br Inst of Human Rights 2000–, hon vice-pres Administrative Law Bar Assoc 1993– (memb Ctee 1987–92), chair Br Cncl Advsy Ctee on Governance 2002–05; ad hoc judge European Court of Human Rights 2000–01; hon prof of law: Univ of Wales at Cardiff 1992–, Univ of Warwick 1993–; visiting professorial fell Univ of Warwick 1981, distinguished visitor Hong Kong Univ 1992, Bernard Simons Meml Lecture 1994, Paul Sieghart Meml Lecture on Human Rights 1995, Radcliffe lectr Univ of Warwick 1996, Hamlyn Lectures 1998, Laskin prof and lectr Osgoode Hall Toronto 1997 (visiting fell 1987), Atkin lectr 2002, Blackstone lectr 2006; pres Holdsworth Soc Univ of Birmingham 2005; Hon Dr Univ of N London 1996; Hon LLD: Nottingham Trent Univ 1997, Univ of Bristol 1999, Univ of Warwick 1999, Univ of Durham 2001, Univ of Hull 2002, Univ of Southampton 2003, Univ of Exeter 2004; *Publications* From Burgos Gaol (translation, 1964), The Seeds of Love (anthology, 1967), Inside the Myth (contrib, 1984), Civil Liberties (contrib, 1984), Police, the Constitution and the Community (contrib, 1985), Challenging Decisions (1986), Public Interest Law (contrib, 1987), Whose Child? (report of the Tyra Henry Inquiry, 1987), Civil Liberties in Conflict (contrib, 1988), Law in East and West (contrib, 1988), Citizenship (contrib, 1991), A Spark in the Ashes: the pamphlets of John Warr (ed with introduction, 1992), Administrative Law and Government Action (contrib, 1995), The Making and Remaking of the British Constitution (with Lord Nolan, 1997), The Golden Metwand and the Crooked Cord (contrib, 1998), Freedom, Law and Justice (1998 Hamlyn Lectures, 1999), Freedom of Expression and Freedom of Information (contrib, 2000), Judicial Review in International Perspective (contrib, 2000), Discriminating Lawyers (contrib, 2000); contrib Oxford DNB; also various articles in: Public Law, Modern Law Review, Journal of Law and Society, Civil Justice Quarterly, London Review of Books, Industrial Law Journal, Law Quarterly Review, Osgoode Hall Law Journal; *Style*— The Rt Hon Lord Justice Sedley; ✉ c/o Royal Courts of Justice, Strand, London WC2A 2LL

SEED, Paul; *b* 18 September 1947; *Educ* Manchester Grammar, Univ of Manchester (BA); *Career* director; actor 1970–1981; credits as dir incl: Too Late to Talk to Billy (trilogy, BBC) 1982–83, Wynne & Penovsky (BBC, US title The Man from Moscow) 1984, Inappropriate Behaviour (BBC) 1986, Capital City (Euston Films) 1988–89, House of Cards (BBC) 1990, To Play the King (BBC) 1993, Disaster at Valdez (HBO/BBC, US title Dead Ahead) 1992, The Affair (HBO/BBC) 1994–95, Have your Cake and Eat It (BBC/Initial) 1996, Playing the Field (Tiger Aspect/BBC) 1997, A Rather English Marriage (Wall to Wall/BBC) 1998, Every Woman Knows a Secret (Carnival/ITV) 1998–99, Murder Rooms (BBC, US title The Dark Beginnings of Sherlock Holmes) 1999, Dirty Tricks (Little Bird/Carlton) 2000, My Beautiful Son (Showtime/Granada, US title Strange Relations) 2001, Auf Wiedersehen, Pet (BBC) 2001–02, Ready When You Are, Mr McGill (WTTV/ITV) 2002–03, The Booze Cruise (YTV) 2003, New Tricks (BBC) 2003–04, Christmas Lights (Granada) 2004; *Style*— Paul Seed, Esq; ✉ c/o Tim Corrie, PFD, Drury House, 34–43 Russell Street, London WC2B 5HA (tel 020 7344 1000, fax 020 7836 9543)

SEED, Ven Richard Murray Crosland; s of Denis Briggs Seed, of Harrogate, N Yorks, and Mary Crosland Seed (d 1986); *b* 9 May 1949; *Educ* St Philips Sch Burley-in-Wharfedale, Univ of Leeds (MA), Edinburgh Theological Coll; *m* 1974, Jane Margaret, da of John Berry; 3 da (Emily b 1975, Lucy b 1977, Miriam b 1980), 1 s (Tim b 1983); *Career* curate Christ Church Skipton 1972–75, curate Baildon 1975–77, team vicar Kidlington 1977–80, chaplain Campsfield House Detention Centre 1977–80, vicar of Boston Spa 1980–99, archdeacon of York 1999–; fndr chm Martin House Hospice for Children 1982–; *Recreations* walking, dogs, travel, gardening; *Style*— The Ven the Archdeacon of York; ✉ Holy Trinity Rectory, 81 Micklegate, York YO1 6LE (tel 01904 623798, fax 01904 628155, e-mail archdeacon.of.york@yorkdiocese.org)

SEEDS, Prof Alwyn John; s of Harry Seeds (d 1987), and Margaret Mary, *née* Ferguson; *b* 24 July 1955; *Educ* Dover GS, Chelsea Coll London (BSc), UCL (PhD), Univ of London (DSc); *m* 1986, Angela Carolyn, da of Ronald Williams; 1 da (Caroline Emily Margaret b 1993); *Career* staff memb Lincoln Laboratory MIT 1980–83, lectr Dept of Electrical and Electronic Engrg QMC London 1983–86; Dept of Electronic and Electrical Engrg UCL: lectr 1986–91, sr lectr 1991–93, reader 1993–95, prof of optoelectronics 1995–, head of dept 2006–; chm Lightwave Ctee IEEE Microwave Theory and Techniques Soc 1998–2001, chm Cmmn D Int Union for Radio Sci 1998–2001, chm IEE Photonics Professional Network 2001–, memb and panel chm Peer Review Coll UK EPSRC 1995–, memb Technical Evaluation Ctee Agence Nationale de Recherche France, prog chair IEEE Indium Phosphide and Related Materials Conf 2005–06, memb Bd of Govrs IEEE Lasers and Electro-optics Soc 2007–, dir Syn Optika Ltd; conslt: Alcatel, BBC, Euro Space Agency, Thales Ltd, Nortel, Euro Cmmn, Lincoln Laboratory MIT, QinetiQ plc; chm Elm Park and Chelsea Park Residents Assoc 1991–; FIEE, FIEEE, FREng; *Publications* author of over 250 publications on microwave devices and circuits, lasers, optoelectronics and optical communications; *Recreations* audio engineering, music, opera; *Style*— Prof Alwyn Seeds; ✉ Department of Electronic and Electrical Engineering, University College London, Gower Street, London WC1E 6BT (tel 020 7679 7928, fax 020 7388 9325, e-mail a.seeds@ee.ucl.ac.uk, website www.ee.ucl.ac.uk)

SEEISO, HRH Prince Seeiso Bereng; s of King Moshoeshoe II of Lesotho (d 1996), and Queen 'Mamohato, *née* Mojela (d 2003); *b* 16 April 1966; *Educ* Ampleforth, Nat Univ of Lesotho (BA), Univ of Birmingham (MA), Beijing Language Inst; *m* 15 Dec 2001, HRH Princess 'Mabereng, *née* Makara; 1 s (Prince Bereng Selala Seeiso), 1 da (Princess 'Masentle Thabitha Seeiso); *Career* appointed princ chief Matsieng 1991; Lesotho diplomat; memb: Nat Constituent Assembly 1991, Senate 1993; dep chairperson Coll of Chief 1994, high cmmr to UK 2005–; memb Parly Reform Ctee 2004; memb: CPA, Cncl of Traditional Ldrs Southern African Devpt Community (SADC); co-patron Sentebale Prince's Trust; *Recreations* horse riding, hiking, tennis; *Style*— HRH Prince Seeiso Bereng Seeiso; ✉ 4 Holne Chase, Hampstead Garden Suburb N2 0QN; Lesotho High Commission, 7 Chesham Place, London SW1X 8HN (tel 020 7235 5686, fax 020 7235 5023, e-mail hicom@lesotholondon.org.uk)

SEEKINGS, John Charles; s of late Leonard Charles Seekings, of Shrewsbury, and Joan Margaret, *née* Lemming; *b* 25 October 1955; *Educ* Worthing Technical HS, Univ of Southampton (BSc); *m* 1 June 1985, Andrea Katrina, da of late James Peter Hamilton MBE; 2 da (Charlotte Elise b 30 April 1986, Emily Alexandra b 1 March 1989), 2 s (Matthew Charles b 10 Sept 1991, Alexander James b 4 June 1999); *Career* freelance stage and prodn mangr 1977–78; ROH: tech mangr 1979–87, asst tech dir 1988–92, dep tech dir 1993–95, devpt dir 1995–98, dir of ops and devpt 1998–; co sec ROH Covent Garden Ltd 2002–; dir: ROH Developments Ltd 1996–, ROH Management Ltd 1997–, ROH Holdings Ltd 1997–, ROH Trading Ltd 2000–; ROH Pensions tstee 2006–; TTTS Ltd: conslt to Bd 1992–95, dir and chm 1995–; chm Bd Arts Devpt Tst 2004–, memb Cncl Nat Cncl for Drama Trg 2005–, memb Soc of London Theatres 2006–; FRGS 1977; *Recreations* family, travel, reading; *Style*— John Seekings, Esq; ✉ Royal Opera House, Covent Garden, London WC2E 9DD (tel 020 7212 9350, fax 020 7212 9512, e-mail john.seekings@roh.org.uk)

SEELY, Sir Nigel Edward; 5 Bt (UK 1896), of Sherwood Lodge, Arnold, Notts and Brooke House, Brooke, Isle of Wight; s of Sir Victor Seely, 4 Bt (d 1980), by 1 w, Sybil Helen (later Baroness Paget of Northampton, *née* Gibbons (d 1994), widow of Sir John Bridger Shiffner, 6 Bt; *b* 28 July 1923; *Educ* Stowe; *m* 1, 1949, Loraine, da of late Wilfred W Lindley-Travis; 3 da; m 2, 1984, Trudi, da of Sydney Pacter; *Heir* half-bro, Maj Victor Seely; *Career* with Dorland International; *Clubs* Buck's, Royal Solent Yacht; *Style*— Sir Nigel Seely, Bt; ✉ 3 Craven Hill Mews, London W2 3DY

SEFTON, Catherine; *see:* Waddell, Martin

SEGAL, Prof Anthony Walter; s of Cyril Segal, and Doreen, *née* Hayden; *b* 24 February 1944; *Educ* Univ of Cape Town (MB ChB, MD), Univ of London (MSc, DSc, PhD); *m* 18 Dec 1966 (m dis), Barbara Ann, da of Justice Solomon Miller (d 1987), of Durban, South Africa; 3 da (Terry b 1969, Jessica b 1972, Penelope b 1975); *Career* Charles Dent prof of med UCL 1986–, fell UCL 2002; FRCP, FRS 1998, FMedSci 1998; *Recreations* golf, sailing, art, theatre; *Style*— Prof Anthony Segal, FRS; ✉ Department of Medicine, University College London, University Street, London WC1E 6JJ (tel 020 7679 6175, fax 020 7679 6211)

SEGAL, Michael John; s of Abraham Charles Segal (d 1981), of London, and Iris Muriel, *née* Parsons (d 1971); *b* 20 September 1937; *Educ* Strode's Sch Surrey; *m* 1 March 1963, Barbara Gina, da of Dr Joseph Leon Fluxman (d 1954), of Johannesburg, South Africa; 1 da (Leila b 10 Sept 1966); *Career* 7th Royal Tank Regt 1956–57; called to the Bar Middle Temple 1962; practised on Midland & Oxford circuit 1963–84, dist judge Princ Registry Family Div 1985–; memb: Queen's Bench Procedure Ctee 1975–80, Civil and Family Ctee Judicial Studies Bd 1990–94; dep stipendiary magistrate 1980–84; memb Medico-Legal Soc, fndr memb Trollope Soc, memb Soc of Indexers 2004; FLS 2004; *Publications* Butterworths Costs Service (jt ed), Supreme Court Practice (jt ed 1993–95), Costs Advocacy; regular contrib Protecting Children Update; *Recreations* reading, music, logic; *Clubs* East India; *Style*— Michael Segal, Esq; ✉ 28 Grange Road, London N6 4AP (tel 020 8348 0680); Principal Registry, Family Division, First Avenue House, 42–48 High Holborn, London WC1V 2NP

SEGALL, Anne (Mrs David Evans); *b* 20 April 1948; *Educ* St Paul's Girls' Sch London, St Hilda's Coll Oxford (exhibitioner, MA); *m* David Howard Evans, QC; 2 s (Oliver, Edward); *Career* economics and banking corr Investors' Chronicle 1971–76, banking corr The Economist 1976–80, banking then economics corr Daily Telegraph 1980–2001, freelance journalist/writer 2001–; Harold Wincott award 1975; *Recreations* swimming, theatre, reading; *Style*— Ms Anne Segall; ✉ e-mail annesegall@hotmail.com

SEHDEV, District Judge Vijay Kumar; s of Tarlok S Sehdev, and Surjit, *née* Kaur; *Career* admitted slr 1981, dep district judge 1981, district judge (Midland Circuit) 2000– (nominated for public law); memb Law Soc, memb Assoc of District Judges; *Recreations* aikido (3 dan), golf, fountain pens; *Style*— District Judge Sehdev; ✉ Birmingham County Court, Civil Justice Centre, The Priory Courts, 33 Bull Street, Birmingham B4 6DS (tel 0121 681 6441, fax 0121 681 3001)

SEIFERT, John Michael; s of Lt-Col Richard Seifert, and Josephine Jeanette, *née* Harding; *b* 17 February 1949; *Educ* Mill Hill Sch, Bartlett Sch of Architecture, UCL (BSc, Dip Arch); *m* 1 Feb 1985, Johanna Marion, da of Elias Hofmann; 2 s (James, Edward), 1 da (Elizabeth), 1 step s (Marlon); *Career* architect; co-fndr Seifert International 1984, fndr and chm John Seifert Architects Ltd 1991, fndr RCP Seifert Interior Design 2005; major projects incl: Cutlers Gardens 1983, Mermaid Theatre 1983, Bank of Chicago House 1984, Sheraton Hotel Lagos 1985, Bishopsbridge 1985, MISR Bank Tower 1986, South Quay Plaza 1987, Swiss Banking Corporation 1988, Hambros Bank 1988, Sceptre Court 1988, Greenwich View 1989, Glengall Bridge 1989, Hilton Hotel Paris 1991, HMP Parc 1994; major competitions won: Surrey Docks Shopping Centre 1983, Limehouse Basin 1985, Heathrow Hotel 1988, Sandwell Mall 1988, Frankfurt Hilton 1995, RAC HQ 1997; Liveryman Worshipful Co of Glaziers and Painters of Glass 1967; RIBA 1976, CROAIF (France) 1981, NCARB (USA) 1983; *Recreations* painting, sculpture, numismatics; *Clubs* Carlton, Arts; *Style*— John Seifert, Esq; ✉ John Seifert Architects, 2–20 Capper Street, London WC1E 6JA (tel 020 7908 7979, fax 020 7908 7999)

SEIFERT, Dr Martin Howard; s of Dr Victor Max Seifert (d 1974), of Winchmore Hill, London, and Sophie Seifert (d 1980); *b* 16 November 1939; *Educ* Highgate Sch, London Hosp Med Coll Univ of London (MB BS); *m* Nov 1974, Dr Jackie Morris, *qv*, da of Prof Norman Morris, *qv*, of Hampstead, London; 1 da (Victoria Charlotte b 1975), 1 s (Benjamin William D'Avigdor b 1978); *Career* house surgn The London Hosp 1965, registrar in rheumatology The Middx Hosp 1969 (SHO 1967–69), sr registrar and chief asst in rheumatology St Thomas' Hosp 1971–74, res fell in rheumatology Univ of Colorado Med Center Denver USA 1973, conslt rheumatologist St Mary's Hosp London 1974–2007, conslt physician The Charterhouse Rheumatism Clinic London 1975–84; RCP: regnl advsr in med for NW Thames Region 1991–95, regnl advsr for continuing med educn 1995–96, hon sec Ctee on Rheumatology 1995–98, chm Specialist Advsy Ctee on Rheumatology 1999–2003, rep on Central Conslts and Specialists Ctee BMA 1996–2001; chm Educn Ctee Arthritis and Rheumatism Cncl 1987–90; Br Soc for Rheumatology: treas 1984–87 (Heberden Rounds-man 1996), memb Cncl and tstee 1995–98, rep on UEMS/European Bd of Rheumatology Brussels 1999–2003; RSM: pres Rheumatology and Rehabilitation Section 1989 (vice-pres 1990), memb Cncl 1990–95; Med Soc of London: memb Cncl 1990–96, hon sec 1993–95, vice-pres 1995–96, pres 2003–04, librarian 2005–; numerous papers and contribs to textbooks on rheumatic diseases; FRCP 1980; *Recreations* family, book collecting, the arts, being sous chef to Dr Jackie Morris; *Clubs* Athenaeum; *Style*— Dr Martin Seifert; ✉ 23 Balcombe Street, Dorset Square London, NW1 6HE (tel 020 7258 3548); The Hospital of St John and St Elizabeth, 60 Grove End Road, London NW8 9NH (tel 020 7806 4062)

SEIFERT, Dr Ruth; da of Sigmund Seifert (d 1979), and Connie, *née* Shine; *b* 20 December 1943; *Educ* Camden Sch for Girls, Guy's Hosp Med Sch London; *m* 1971, Dr Charles Richard Astley Clarke, *qv*, s of Prof Sir Cyril Astley Clarke, KBE, FRS; 2 da (Rebecca b 3 Feb 1973, Naomi b 7 Sept 1976); *Career* jr hosp appts 1968–73, post grad trg in psychiatry Maudsley Hosp 1973–80, conslt in psychological med Bart's 1980–98, ret (dep chm Med Cncl 1988–90), regnl advsr in psychiatry NE Thames RHA 1993–97; MO Himal Kisthwar Expdn (to climb Bramah in the Himalayas) 1971; FRCPsych 1988 (MRCPsych 1975); *Recreations* opera, cinema, cooking; *Style*— Dr Ruth Seifert; ✉ tel 020 7226 1990

SEITLER, Jonathan; QC (2003); *Educ* Univ of Oxford (BA, Dip Law); *Career* called to the Bar Inner Temple 1985 (Duke of Edinburgh scholar); practising barr specialising in property law and professional negligence litigation, memb Wilberforce Chambers 1995–, qualified mediator 2003; memb: Commercial Bar Assoc, Professional Negligence Bar Assoc; *Publications* Property Finance Negligence: Claims Against Solicitors and Valuers (co-author, 1996), Commercial Property Disputes: Law and Practice (1999); *Recreations* football (referee under-9's games); *Style*— Jonathan Seitler, Esq, QC; ✉ Wilberforce Chambers, 8 New Square, Lincoln's Inn, London WC2A 3QP (tel 020 7306 0102, fax 020 7306 0095, e-mail jseitler@wilberforce.co.uk)

SEITZ, Hon Raymond George Hardenbergh; s of John Francis Regis Seitz, and Helen Stewart Johnson Hardenbergh; *b* 8 December 1940, Hawaii; *Educ* Yale Univ (BA); *m* 10 May 1985, Caroline, *née* Richardson; 2 s (Royce Manning Barr b 24 Sept 1966, Thomas McKeen Cutler b 10 April 1974), 1 da (Hillary Helen Brewster b 1 Jan 1969); *Career* American Dip Serv until 1994: consular offr Montreal 1968–69, political offr Nairobi and concurrently vice-consul Seychelles 1969–70, princ offr Bukavu Zaïre 1970–72, staff offr later dir Secretariat Staff Washington 1972, special asst to DG Foreign Serv 1972–75, political offr London 1975–79 (DG's Award for Reporting), dep exec sec Dept of State Washington 1979–81, dep asst sec for public affrs 1981–82, exec asst to Sec of State 1982–84, min London 1984–89, asst sec of state for Euro and Canadian affrs Washington 1989–91, ambass to Ct of St James's 1991–94; chm Authoriszor 1999–; vice-chm Lehman Brothers International (Europe) 1996–2003 (sr md 1995–96); non-exec dir: Telegraph Group plc 1994–, Chubb Corporation 1994–, Cable & Wireless plc 1995–2002, British Airways plc 1995–2002, Marconi plc (formerly GEC plc) 1995–2002, Rio Tinto plc 1996–2002; memb Special Ctee of the Bd Hollinger Int Inc 2003–; tstee: National Gallery 1996–2001, Royal Acad 1996–; chm Whitbread Book of the Year and Literary Awards 1999; Presidential Award for Meritorious Service 1986 and 1988; Knight Cdr's Cross (Germany) 1991; Benjamin Franklin Medal RSA 1996; hon doctorates: Univ of Reading 1992, Richmond Coll 1992, Univ of Bath 1993, Univ of Leeds 1994, Univ of Durham 1994, Heriot-Watt Univ 1994, Univ of Buckingham 1998; *Publications* Over Here (1998); *Recreations* literature, architecture; *Clubs* Garrick, Beefsteak; *Style*— The Hon Raymond Seitz

SELBORNE, 4 Earl of (UK 1882); John Roundell Palmer; KBE (1987), DL (Hants 1982); also Baron Selborne (UK 1872), Viscount Wolmer (UK 1882); s of Viscount Wolmer (k on active service 1942; s of 3 Earl) and Priscilla (*see* Baron Newton); suc gf 1971. Lord Selborne's gggf, the 1 Earl, was Lord Chllr 1872–74 and 1880–85 and his ggf was First Lord of the Admiralty 1900–05 and helped establish the RNVR, the RFR, Osborne and Dartmouth Naval Colleges and the Designs Committee which resulted in the Royal Navy being equipped with Dreadnoughts; *b* 24 March 1940; *Educ* Eton, ChCh Oxford; *m* 1969, Joanna Van Antwerp, da of Evan James, of Upwood Park, Abingdon (and sis of late Countess Baldwin of Bewdley); 3 s (William Lewis, Viscount Wolmer b 1971, Hon George, Hon Luke (twins) b 1974), 1 da (Lady Emily b 1978); *Heir* s, Viscount Wolmer; *Career* sits as Cons in House of Lords, chm Sub-Ctee D (Agric and Food) House of Lords' Select Ctee on Euro Communities 1991–93 and 1999–2003, chm Select Ctee on Science and Technology 1993–97; chm: Hops Marketing Bd 1978–82, Agric and Food Res Cncl 1983–89 (memb 1975–89, dep chm 1982), Joint Nature Conservation Ctee 1991–97, Agricultural Mortgage Corporation 1994–2002; pres RIPHH 1991–98, pres RGS, with IBG 1997–2000, vice-pres Fndn for Science and Technology 1993–, memb Royal Cmmn on Environmental Pollution 1993–98; non-exec dir: Lloyds Bank plc 1994–95, Lloyds TSB Group plc 1995–2004; chllr Univ of Southampton 1996–; chm Bd of Tstees Royal Botanic Gardens Kew 2003–; former vice-chm Apple and Pear Devpt Cncl, treas Bridewell Royal Hosp (King Edward's Sch Witley) 1972–83; memb UNESCO World Cmmn on the Ethics of Scientific Knowledge and Technology 1999–2003; memb Ct of Assts Worshipful Co of Mercers; FRS 1991; *Clubs* Travellers; *Style*— The Rt Hon the Earl of Selborne, KBE, FRS, DL; ✉ Temple Manor, Selborne, Alton, Hampshire GU34 3LR (tel 01420 473646)

SELBY, Bishop of 2003–; Rt Rev Martin William Wallace; s of Derek Philip William Wallace, and Audrey Sybil, *née* Thomason; *Educ* Varndean GS Brighton, Taunton's Sch Southampton, KCL (Winchester scholarship, BD, AKC), St Augustine's Theol Coll Canterbury; *m* Diana; 1 da (Caroline b 1973), 1 s (Matthew b 1975); *Career* ordained: deacon 1971, priest 1972; asst curate: Attercliffe Sheffield 1971–74, New Malden 1974–77; vicar St Mark's Forest Gate London 1977–93, chaplain Forest Gate Hosp 1977–80, rural dean Newham E London 1982–91; priest-in-charge: Emmanuel Forest Gate 1985–89, All Saints Forest Gate 1991–93; urban offr Chelmsford Dio 1991–93, rector Bradwell-on-Sea and St Lawrence Essex 1993–97, industrial chaplain Maldon & Dengie 1993–97, hon canon Chelmsford Cathedral 1989–97, archdeacon of Colchester 1997–2003; *Publications* Healing Encounters in the City (1987), City Prayers (1994), Pocket Celtic Prayers (1996), Celtic Reflections (1996), The Celtic Resource Book (1998), Worship, Window of the Urban Church (contrib, 2007); *Recreations* local history, garden design; *Style*— The Rt Rev the Bishop of Selby; ✉ Bishop's House, Barton-le-Street, Malton, York YO17 6PL (e-mail bishselby@clara.net)

SELBY, Prof Peter John; CBE (2001); s of Joseph Selby, and Dorothy, *née* Cross; *b* 10 July 1950; *Educ* Lydney GS, Univ of Cambridge (MA, MB, MB BChir, MD); *m* 8 July 1972, Catherine Elisabeth, da of Peter Thomas; 1 da (Alexandra b 1980), 1 s (David b 1985); *Career* conslt physician Royal Marsden Hosp London 1985–88, prof of cancer medicine and conslt physician Univ of Leeds and St James's Univ Hosp Leeds 1988– (dir Cancer Research UK Clincal Research Centre 1993–), dir of clinical research ICRF 1997–2001, lead clinician Leeds Cancer Centre 1997–2005; ed Br Jl Cancer 1987–92; dir Nat Cancer Research Network 2001–05, dir UK Clinical Research Network 2005–; memb Ctee: Assoc of Cancer Physicians, Br Assoc for Cancer Research, Br Oncological Assoc (pres 1992–94), MRC, Euro Orgn for Research and Treatment of Cancer; FRCP, FRCR, FMedSci; *Books* Hodgkin's Disease (1987), Confronting Cancer: Cause and Prevention (1993), Cancer in Adolescents (1995), Malignant Lymphomas (2002), Cell and Molecular Biology of Cancer (2005); *Recreations* reading, music, running; *Style*— Prof Peter Selby; ✉ 17 Park Lane, Roundhay, Leeds LS8 2EX; Cancer Research UK Clinical Research Centre, St James's University Hospital, Beckett Street, Leeds LS9 7TF (tel 0113 206 5668, fax 0113 242 9886)

SELBY, Rona; *Educ* Beckenham GS for Girls, Univ of Exeter (BA); *m* 2 Sept 1978, David Selby; 1 s (Ben b 11 May 1983), 1 da (Tamsin Alexandra b 4 May 1985); *Career* The Bodley Head Publishers 1975–88 (memb Bd 1987–88), publisher Methuen Children's Books 1988–92, conslt S4C Wales 1992, children's book devpt conslt to BBC 1992–96, head of BBC Children's Publishing (Video, Books and Audio) 1996–97, fndr The Children's Media Consultancy 1997–2004, editorial dir Andersen Press Ltd 2004–; *Books* Angela Anaconda: The Secret Life of Teachers (2002), Families and How to Survive Them (2002), Gordy Loves Gina (2003),Wallace and Gromit: Welcome to West Wallaby Street (2003); *Publications* articles on children's media published in The Author and The Bookseller; *Recreations* sailing; *Style*— Rona Selby; ✉ Andersen Press Ltd, 20 Vauxhall Bridge Road, London SW1V 2SA (tel 020 7840 8706, fax 020 7233 6263)

SELDON, Dr Anthony; *b* 2 August 1953; *Educ* Tonbridge, Worcester Coll Oxford (BA), LSE (PhD), KCL (PGCE, Blackwell Teaching Prize), PCL (MBA); *m*; 1 s, 2 da; *Career* research fell and tutor LSE 1980–82, head of politics Whitgift Sch Croydon 1983–89, head of

S

history and sixth form gen educn Tonbridge Sch 1989–92, dep headmaster then actg headmaster St Dunstan's Coll Catford 1993–97, headmaster Brighton Coll 1997–2005, master Wellington Coll 2006–; visiting fell Dept of Int History Univ of Kent 1992–94; founding dir Inst of Contemporary British History; historical advsr to orgns incl Rio Tinto-Zinc Corp; ed: Whitgiftian 1984–87, Tonbridge Today 1991–92, Modern History Review, Politics Review, Contemporary Record, Making Contemporary Britain (book series); regular broadcaster and newspaper contrib; FRSA, FRHistS; *Publications* books incl: Churchill's Indian Summer (1981), The Thatcher Effect (1989), The Conservative Century (1994), John Major: A Political Life (1997), Number 10: An Illustrated History (1999), The Blair Effect (2001), Governing Before New Labour (2003), Tony Blair: A Biography (2004); pamphlets: Public and Private Education: the divide must end (2001), A New Conservative Century (2001), Partnership not Paternalism (2002); regular book reviewer for TLS, academic jls and newspapers; *Recreations* drama, music, sport; *Style*— Dr Anthony Seldon; ✉ Wellington College, Crowthorne, Berkshire RG45 7PU

SELF, William Woodard (Will); s of Peter John Otter Self, of Canberra, Aust, and Elaine, *née* Rosenbloom; *b* 26 September 1961; *Educ* Christ's Coll, Exeter Coll Oxford (MA); *m* June 1989 (m dis 1996), Katharine Sylvia Anthony, da of John Chancellor; 1 s (Alexis b June 1990), 1 da (Madeleine b Sept 1992); m 2, 1997, Deborah Jane Orr, *qv*; 2 s (Ivan William Scott b Sept 1997, Luther James David b Aug 2001); *Career* writer; columnist The Observer 1995–97, The Times 1997–99, The Independent on Sunday 1999–2001, Evening Standard 2002–; Geoffrey Faber Meml Award 1992; *Books* The Quantity Theory of Insanity (1991), Cock and Bull (1992), My Idea of Fun (1993), Grey Area (1994), Junk Mail (1995), The Sweet Smell of Psychosis (1996), Great Apes (1997), Tough Tough Toys for Tough Tough Boys (1998), How the Dead Live (2000), Perfidious Man (2000), Sore Sites (2000), Feeling Frenzy (2001), Dorian (2002), Dr Mukti (2004), The Book of Dave (2006); *Style*— Will Self, Esq

SELIGMAN, Mark Donald; s of Spencer Walter Oscar Seligman (d 2001), of London, and Joanne Winifred Rhoda, *née* Bye; *b* 24 January 1956; *Educ* Eton, Lincoln Coll Oxford (MA); *m* 17 April 1982, Louise Angela Mary, da of Sir Philip De Zulueta (d 1989); 1 s (Jocelyn David b 9 April 1983), 2 da (Lucinda Marie Joanne b 27 April 1985, Iona Louise b 22 Sept 1990); *Career* Price Waterhouse 1977–80, fin analyst Chloride Gp plc 1981–83, dir SG Warburg & Co Ltd 1989–95 (joined 1983); head UK investment banking BZW 1997 (joined 1995); Credit Suisse First Boston: head UK investment banking 1997–99, dep chm 1999–2005, chm UK investment banking 2003–05, sr advsr 2005–; non exec dir Gp 4 Securicor plc 2006–, chm Corp Fin Ctee London Investment Bankers Assoc 1999–2001; memb Panel of Takeovers and Mergers 1999–2001 (alternate memb 2006–); memb Lord Mayor's Appeal Ctee 2003; memb Heart of the City Advsy Bd 2006–, dir Industrial Development Advisory Bd 2005–; memb Rector's Cncl Lincoln Coll Oxford 2004–; co-pres Winchester House Sch Look to the Future Appeal 2005; tstee Aston Martin Heritage Tst 2004–; Freeman City of London 2003; ACA 1980; *Recreations* stalking, music; *Clubs* Northern Meeting, Beefsteak, Pilgrims, Guild of International Bankers; *Style*— Mark Seligman, Esq; ✉ Credit Suisse, 1 Cabot Square, London E14 4QJ (tel 020 7888 8888)

SELKIRK OF DOUGLAS, Baron (Life Peer UK 1997), of Cramond in the City of Edinburgh; James Alexander Douglas-Hamilton; PC (1996), QC (Scot 1996), MSP; disclaimed Earldom of Selkirk for life 1994; 2 s of 14 Duke of Hamilton and Brandon, KT, GCVO, AFC, PC (d 1973); *b* 31 July 1942; *Educ* Eton, Balliol Coll Oxford (MA, Boxing blue, pres Oxford Union, pres OUCA), Univ of Edinburgh (LLB); *m* 1974, Hon Priscilla Susan (Susie), *née* Buchan, da of 2 Baron Tweedsmuir (d 1996), and Baroness Tweedsmuir of Belhelvie (d 1978); 4 s (Hon John Andrew, Master of Selkirk b 8 Feb 1978, Hon Charles Douglas b 1979, Hon James Robert, Hon Harry Alexander (twins) b 1981); *Heir* s, Hon John Andrew, Master of Selkirk; *Career* offr TA 6/7 Bn Cameronians Scottish Rifles 1961–66, TAVR 1971–73, Capt 2 Bn Lowland Volunteers; advocate 1968–76; MP (Cons) Edinburgh W Oct 1974–97 (Parly candidate (Cons) Hamilton Feb 1974); Scottish Cons whip 1977, a Lord Cmmr of the Treasy 1979–81, PPS to Malcolm Rifkind MP 1983–87 (as Min FO 1983–86, as sec of state for Scotland 1986–87), Parly under sec of state for home affrs and environment 1987–92 (incl local govt at Scottish Office 1987–89, additional responsibility for local govt fin 1989–90 and for the Arts in Scotland Sept 1990–92), Parly under sec of state for educn and housing Scottish Office 1992–95, min of state for home affrs and health (with responsibility for roads & tport and construction) Scottish Office 1995–97, appointed Scottish Cons spokesman for the Arts, culture and sport 1998; MSP (Cons) Lothians 1999–, chief whip and business mangr Scottish Cons Gp of MSPs 1999–2001, princ home affrs spokesman Scottish Cons Gp of MSPs 2001–03, Educn spokesman 2003–; memb Scottish Select Ctee on Scottish Affrs 1981–83; hon sec: Cons Parly Constitutional Ctee, Cons Parly Aviation Ctee 1983–97; chm Scottish Parly All-Pty Penal Affrs Ctee 1983; hon pres Scottish Amateur Boxing Assoc 1975–98; pres: Royal Cwlth Soc (Scotland) 1979–87, Scottish Nat Cncl UN Assoc 1981–87, Int Rescue Corps 1995–; memb Queen's Body Guard for Scotland (Royal Co of Archers); official patron Hope and Homes for Children 2002– (chm Edinburgh Support Gp 2002–07 (vice-chm 2007–)); pres Scottish Veterans Garden City Assoc Inc 2003–; Hon Air Cdre No 2 Maritime HQ Unit (RAAF) 1995–, Hon Air Cdre 603 (City of Edinburgh) Squadron RAAF; cncllr Murrayfield and Cramond 1972–74; life memb Nat Tst for Scotland (memb Cncl 1977–82); *Books* Motive for a Mission: The Story Behind Hess's Flight to Britain (1971), The Air Battle for Malta: the Diaries of a Fighter Pilot (1981), Roof of the World: Man's First Flight over Everest (1983), The Truth About Rudolf Hess (1993); *Recreations* golf, forestry, debating, history, boxing; *Style*— The Rt Hon Lord Selkirk of Douglas, PC, QC, MSP; ✉ House of Lords, London SW1A 0PW

SELLARS, John Ernest; CBE (1994); s of late Ernest Buttle Sellars, and late Edna Grace Mordaunt; *b* 5 February 1936; *Educ* Wintringham GS Grimsby, Univ of Manchester (BSc, MSc); *m* 20 Dec 1958, Dorothy Beatrice, da of late Maj Douglas Norman Morrison; 3 da (Karen b 1961, Fiona b 1962, Ann b 1964); *Career* res engr English Electric (GW) Ltd 1958–61, lectr Royal Coll of Advanced Technol (now Univ of Salford) 1961–67, head of mathematics Lanchester Coll of Technol 1967–71, head of computer science Lanchester Poly (now Coventry Univ) 1971–74, chief offr Business Educn Cncl 1974–83, dir and chief exec Business and Technology Educn Cncl 1983–94, dir City Technol Colls Tst 1989–94; London Guildhall Univ: govr 1994–2000, vice-chm of govrs 1995–2000, chm Fin and Employment Ctee 1995–2000; dir and tstee Gatsby Technical Educn Projects 1999–2005; memb Engrg Cncl 1994–95; memb RoSPA: Exec Ctee 1994–2002, Policy Ctee 1997–99, Fin Ctee 1997–2002; memb Br Accreditation Cncl for Independent Further and Higher Educn 1999–2002; hon fell Nene Coll of HE; Hon DUniv Sheffield Hallam Univ, Hon DTech London Guildhall Univ; *Recreations* walking, travel; *Clubs* Reform, Middlesex CCC, MCC; *Style*— John Sellars, Esq, CBE; ✉ 306 Cassiobury Drive, Watford, Hertfordshire WD17 3AW (tel 01923 233055)

SELLARS, Dr Leslie; s of Robert Norman Sellars (d 1980), of Flimby, Cumbria, and Hannah Elizabeth, *née* Pickering (d 2004); *b* 14 January 1951; *Educ* Workington GS, Univ of Newcastle upon Tyne (MB BS, MD); *m* 29 June 1974, Joan, da of William Steele (d 1993), of Maryport; 2 da (Kathryn Jane b 1978, Julia Anne b 1979); *Career* registrar in med Royal Victoria Infirmary Newcastle 1977–78, first asst in med (nephrology) Univ of Newcastle upon Tyne 1981–85, conslt physician and nephrologist Hull and East Yorkshire Hosps NHS Tst 1985–; memb: Renal Assoc 1979, Br Hypertension Soc 1981, Euro Dialysis and Transplant Assoc; FRCPEd 1988, FRCP (London) 1993; *Recreations* fishing, fell-walking; *Style*— Dr Leslie Sellars; ✉ 20 The Triangle, North Ferriby, North Humberside HU14 3AT (tel 01482 631760); The Renal Unit, Hull Royal Infirmary, Anlaby Road, Hull (tel 01482 674881)

SELLERS, Geoffrey Bernard; CB (1991); s of Bernard Whittaker Sellers (d 1991), of Stockport, and Elsie, *née* Coop (d 1963); *b* 5 June 1947; *Educ* Manchester Grammar, Magdalen Coll Oxford (Mackinnon scholar, BCL, MA); *m* Susan Margaret (d 1995), da of Arthur Donald Faulconbridge (d 1989); 2 s (Daniel b 1981, John b 1987), 2 da (Anna b 1984, Katherine b 1989); *Career* called to the Bar Gray's Inn 1971; legal asst Law Cmmn 1971, Cmmn on Industrial Relations 1971–74, Office of Parly Counsel 1974, Law Cmmn 1982–85 and 1991–93, Inland Revenue 1996–99; Parly counsel 1987–; *Clubs* RAC; *Style*— Geoffrey Sellers, Esq, CB; ✉ 53 Canonbury Road, London N1 2DG (tel 020 7359 7606)

SELLERS, Dr Susan Mary; da of Geoffrey Noel Sellers, of Esher, Surrey, and Mary McNeil, *née* Boswell; *b* 13 January 1949; *Educ* Birkenhead HS, Univ of Manchester (MB ChB, MD); *m* 16 July 1983, Andres Lopez, s of Andres Lopez Gil, of Murcia, Spain; 2 s (James b 3 Dec 1984, Teo b 10 Nov 1986), 1 da (Susannah b 24 May 1989); *Career* obstetrician and gynaecologist; registrar Southmead and Frenchay Hosps Bristol 1976–78; John Radcliffe Hosp Oxford: clinical lectr 1982–87, conslt 1988–2001; conslt obstetrician St Michael's Hosp Bristol 2001–; memb: Claims Ctee Med Protection Soc, Expert Advsy Gp on AIDS; FRCOG 1993 (MRCOG 1977); *Recreations* music, family, cookery, travelling; *Style*— Dr Susan Sellers; ✉ Level E, St Michael's Hospital, Southwell Street, Bristol BS2 8EG

SELLEY, Prof Richard Curtis; JP (1981); s of Harry Westcott Selley (d 1967), and Dorothy Joan, *née* Curtis (d 1999); *b* 21 September 1939; *Educ* Eastbourne Coll, Univ of London (BSc, PhD), Imperial Coll London (DIC); *m* 15 May 1965, Pauline, da of John Fletcher; 2 da (Helen b 24 Aug 1967, Andrea b 2 April 1969); *Career* Imperial Coll London: post doctoral res fell 1963–66, lectr in sedimentology 1966–69, reader in petroleum geology 1974–89, head Dept of Geology 1988–93, prof of applied sedimentology 1989–2000, emeritus prof in sedimentology and petroleum geology 2000–, sr res fell 2000–; visiting res fell Natural History Museum 1990–92; sr sedimentologist Oasis Oil Co of Libya 1969–71, sr geologist Conoco Europe Ltd 1971–74; dir: R C Selley & Co Ltd 1982–2000, Tooting Constitutional Club Ltd 1972–; chm SE Surrey Bench 2003–05 (dep chm 1999–2001); memb: Cncl Geological Soc of London 1992–97 (vice-pres 1992–94, hon sec Foreign and External Affairs 1994–97), Cncl Euro Fedn of Geologists 1994–97, Cncl Science and Technol Institutes 1994–97, Cncl Geologists' Assoc 2000–03; Hon DSc Kingston Univ 2006; hon memb Wine Guild of the UK 2005; Silver Medal Geological Soc of London 2003; hon memb Petroleum Exploration Soc of GB 2006; CGeol, FGS 1962, AAPG 1971, PESGB 1971, SPE 1981, EurGeol 2002, CSci 2004; *Books* Ancient Sedimentary Environments (1970, 4 edn 1996), Introduction to Sedimentology (1976, 2 edn 1982), Elements of Petroleum Geology (1985, 2 edn 1998), Applied Sedimentology (1988, 2 edn 2000), African Basins (1997), The Winelands of Britain (2004), The Box Hill and Mole Valley Book of Geology (2006); *Recreations* researching the geology of British vineyards; *Clubs* Surrey Magistrates', Chaps; *Style*— Prof Richard Selley; ✉ Department of Earth Sciences and Engineering, Royal School of Mines, Imperial College, Prince Consort Road, London SW7 2BP (e-mail r.selley@imperial.ac.uk)

SELLORS, Sir Patrick John Holmes; KCVO (1999, LVO 1990); *b* 11 February 1934; *Educ* Rugby, Oriel Coll Oxford (MA, BM BCh), Middx Hosp Med Sch (entrance scholar, state scholar, Douglas Cree prize in med); *m*; 3 c; *Career* conslt ophthalmic surgn: Royal Marsden Hosp until 1998, St Luke's Hosp for The Clergy until 1998; hon conslt ophthalmic surgn: St George's Hosp, Croydon Eye Unit; surgn-oculist to HM The Queen until 1999; author of various papers for presentation and jls and of chapters in med books; memb Gen Optical Cncl until 1997, vice-pres Cncl until 1996 and Exec Ctee until 1996 Royal Coll of Ophthalmologists, pres Section of Ophthalmology RSM 1992–94, memb Cncl Med Def Union; tstee Anne Allerton Tst for Ophthalmic Research; Liveryman Worshipful Soc of Apothecaries; FRCS 1965, FCOphth 1990; *Books* An Outline of Ophthalmology (jtly, 1985, 2 edn 1996); *Style*— Sir Patrick J Holmes Sellors, KCVO; ✉ Summer House, Sandy Lane, West Runton, Cromer, Norfolk NR27 9NB

SELLS, Andrew; s of Sir David Perronet Sells (d 1993), and Lady Sells (d 1997); *b* 30 November 1948; *Educ* Wellington, Univ of London (MSc); *m* (m dis); 1 s, 1 da; *Career* CA 1972; Schroders plc 1972–82, Thompson Clive & Partners 1982–87, md Sovereign Capital 1990–2000; chm: Linden plc 1991–, Westerleigh Group plc 1992–2002, RHS Enterprises Ltd 1995–2004, Team 1000 1996–2000, Medical Gas Servs Ltd 2004–; dir: Stourbridge Properties 1997–, Everest Gp 2004–, Indigo Retail Holdings Ltd 2005–; memb Cncl RHS 2003–; *Recreations* travel, reading, cricket, trees; *Clubs* Boodle's, MCC; *Style*— Andrew Sells, Esq; ✉ Sandy Farm, Sopworth, Chippenham, Wiltshire SN14 6PP (tel 01666 840200); 42 Artillery Mansions, London SW1H 0HZ (tel 020 7233 2133, e-mail andrewsells@easynet.co.uk)

SELLS, David James Guthrie; s of Henry James Sells (d 1967), of Birmingham, and Anne Guthrie, *née* Milne (d 1990); *b* 21 December 1928; *Educ* King Edward's Sch Birmingham, Merchant Taylors' Northwood, Lincoln Coll Oxford; *m* 17 Sept 1952 (m dis 1984), Pauline Alice, *née* Hill; 2 s (Adrian David Guthrie b 1957, Christopher James Guthrie b 1961); *Career* news correspondent; Reuters: London 1952–54, Rome 1954–57, Warsaw 1957–60, chief corr Bonn 1960–64, Brussels mangr 1964–65; BBC Radio/TV: London 1966–71, Beirut 1971–76, Newsday 1976–78, Assignment 1978–79, Newsnight 1980–2006; BBC Radio presenter: World in Focus 1976, World Tonight 1986–91; *Recreations* reading, swimming, travel; *Style*— David Sells Esq; ✉ tel 020 7603 1026, e-mail david.sells@zen.co.uk

SELLS, Oliver Matthew; QC (1995); s of Sir David Perronet Sells (d 1993), of Royston, Herts, and Beryl Cecilia, *née* Charrington (d 1997); *b* 29 September 1950; *Educ* Wellington, Coll of Law London; *m* 30 Aug 1986, Lucinda Jane, da of Gerard William Mackworth-Young (d 1984), of Fisherton de la Mere, Wilts; 1 s (Hugo William b 17 June 1988), 1 da (Rosanna Mary b 30 June 1991); *Career* called to the Bar Inner Temple 1972 (bencher 1996); in practice SE Circuit, supplementary counsel to The Crown 1981–86, recorder of the Crown Court 1991– (asst recorder 1987–91); chm SE Circuit Liaison Ctee 2002–memb: Gen Cncl of the Bar 1977–80 and 1985–89, Cwlth Law Assoc; hon memb American Bar Assoc; dir Music for Charity; chm of tstees St Mary's Church Houghton-on-the-Hill 2000–, tstee Breckland Soc 2004–; *Recreations* shooting, cricket, fishing; *Clubs* Boodle's, MCC, Norfolk (Norwich), Royal W Norfolk Golf; *Style*— Oliver Sells, Esq, QC; ✉ 5 Paper Buildings, Temple, London EC4Y 7HB (tel 020 7583 6117, fax 020 7353 0075)

SELLS, Prof Robert Anthony; s of Rev William Blyth Sells (d 1977), of Portsmouth, and Eleanor Mary Sells; *b* 13 April 1938; *Educ* Christ's Hosp, Univ of London Guy's Hosp (MB BS); *m* 1, 1964 (m dis 1976), Elizabeth Lucy, *née* Schryver; 2 s (Rupert William Blyth b 1967, Henry Perronet b 1968), 1 da (Katherine b 1970); m 2, 10 May 1977, Dr Paula Gilchrist, da of Stephen Muir (d 1988), of Denbigh, Clwyd; 2 s (Edward Anthony b 1981, Patrick David b 1982); *Career* lectr: Dept of Surgery Univ of London Guy's Hosp 1967–68, Dept of Surgery Cambridge Univ 1968–70; MRC travelling scholar Peter Bent-Brigham Hosp Harvard Univ 1970–71, dir Regnl Transplant Unit; conslt surgn: Royal Liverpool Hosp 1971, Liverpool HA 1978, ret; pres Liverpool Med Inst 1997–98; pres The British Transplantation Soc 1983–86, vice-pres The Transplantation Soc 1990–94 (cncllr 1982–88), chm Int Forum for Transplant Ethics 1995–, pres Moyinhan Chirurgical Club 2000–01; hon prof Univ of Liverpool (chair Immunology and Surgery Dept Faculty of Med); MA Cambridge Univ; memb BMA 1962, FRCS, FRCSEd; *Books* Transplantation Today (1982), Organ Transplantation: Current Clinical and Immunological Concepts (1989); *Recreations* conductor, Crosby symphony orchestra;

Clubs Moynihan Chirurgical (pres 2000–01), The XX; *Style*— Prof Robert Sells; ✉ Cil Llwyn, Llandyrnog, Denbighshire LL16 4HY (tel 01745 710296)

SELOUS, Andrew; MP; s of Cdr G M B Selous, OBE, VRD (d 2007), of Langley, Norfolk, and Miranda, *née* Casey (d 1995); *b* 27 April 1962; *m* 28 Aug 1993, Harriet Victoria, da of late Jeremy Marston; 3 da (Camilla b 20 July 1995, Laetitia b 7 March 1997, Maria b 30 Oct 2000); *Career* MP (Cons) Bedfordshire SW 2001–; *Style*— Andrew Selous, Esq, MP; ✉ House of Commons, London SW1A 0AA

SELSDON, 3 Baron (UK 1932); Sir Malcolm McEacharn Mitchell-Thomson; 4 Bt (UK 1900); s of 2 Baron Selsdon, DSC (d 1963), and his 1 w, Phoebette (d 1991), da of Crossley Swithinbank; *b* 27 October 1937; *Educ* Winchester; *m* 1, 1965, Patricia Anne, da of Donald Smith; 1 s; m 2, 1995, Gabrielle, *née* Williams; *Heir* s, Hon Callum Mitchell-Thomson; *Career* Sub Lt RNVR; banker with Midland Bank Gp, British delg to Cncl of Europe and WEU 1972–78, chm Ctee of Middle East Trade (Comet) 1979–86, memb British Overseas Trade Bd 1983–86, memb E European Trade Cncl 1983–87, pres Br Exporters' Assoc (BEXA) 1992–98; elected herditary peer House of Lords 1999–; chm Greater London and SE Cncl for Sport and Recreation 1978–83; *Recreations* tennis, lawn tennis, skiing, sailing; *Clubs* MCC; *Style*— The Rt Hon the Lord Selsdon

SELWAY-SWIFT, Paul; *b* 20 May 1944; *Educ* Allhallows Sch, Sloan Sch of Mgmnt MIT; *Family* 3 da; *Career* HSBC Gp: joined 1962, gp gen mangr Hong Kong and China HongKong and Shanghai Bank 1988–96 (appointed exec dir 1992), chm HSBC Investment Bank Asia until 1996, dir Hang Seng Bank until 1996, dep chm HSBC Investment Bank London 1996–98, chm Samuel Montagu 1996–98, chm HSBC Capital Markets India 1996–98, dep chm Guyerzeller Bank Zurich 1996–98; chm: Novae Group plc (formerly SVB Hldgs plc) 1998–, Singer and Friedlander Gp plc 2003–05 (non-exec dir 2000–05); non-exec chm Chivers Communications plc 2000–01 (non-exec dir 2000) currently dir: Alba plc, Asia Investment Corporation, Atlantis China Fund plc, Forman Hardy Hldgs Ltd (dep chm), Li & Fung Ltd, Temenos Gp AG; formerly dir: Cathay Pacific Airways Ltd, Hutchison Wampoa Ltd, Hong Kong Electric Co Ltd, Visa Int (Asia Pacific), Hong Kong Building and Loan Agency Ltd, Regent Int Hotels; formerly: chm Hong Kong Assoc of Banks, steward Royal Hong Kong Jockey Club, dir Hong Kong Trade Devpt Cncl, advsr Hong Kong SAR Land Fund; memb Sports Broadcasting Monitoring Ctee; *Recreations* golf, horse racing, rugby, fly fishing, wine, music; *Style*— Paul Selway-Swift, Esq; ✉ Old Rectory, Upper Pendock, Malvern, Worcestershire WR13 6JP (tel 01684 833669, fax 01684 833435, e-mail paul@selway-swift.com)

SELWYN GUMMER, *see:* Gummer

SEMPILL, 21 Lord (S 1489); James William Stuart Whitemore Sempill; s of Ann Moira, Lady Sempill (20 in line; d 1995), and her 2 husband Lt-Col Stuart Whitemore Chant-Sempill, OBE, MC, late Gordon Highlanders (d 1991); *b* 25 February 1949; *Educ* Oratory Sch, St Clare's Hall and Hertford Coll Oxford; *m* 1977, Josephine Ann Edith, da of Joseph Norman Rees, of Kelso; 1 s (Hon Francis, Master of Sempill b 4 Jan 1979), 1 da (Hon Cosima b 20 April 1983); *Heir* s, Master of Sempill; *Career* tobacco exec Gallaher Ltd 1972–80, brand mangr South African Breweries Johannesburg 1982–86; account dir: Bates Wells Pty Ltd (Advertising Agency) 1986–87, Partnership in Advertising Johannesburg 1988–90; client serv dir Ogilvy and Mather Cape Town 1990–92, trade mktg dir Scottish & Newcastle Breweries Edinburgh 1993–95, Angus Dundee Distillers plc 2001–03, dir of mktg Caledonian Brewing Co Edinburgh 2003–06, dir The Gathering 2009 Ltd; memb Standing Cncl of Scottish Chiefs 1996–; sat as cross-bench peer House of Lords 1996–99, prospective Parly candidate (Cons) Scottish Parl 1998–; chm Edinburgh N and Leith Cons Assoc 1999–2001; *Recreations* walking, rugby, scuba diving; *Clubs* New (Edinburgh); *Style*— The Lord Sempill; ✉ 3 Vanburgh Place, Leith, Edinburgh EH6 8AE (e-mail jsempill@lumison.co.uk)

SEMPLE, Dr Colin Gordon; s of Dr Thomas Semple, and Elspeth Roubaix, *née* Dewar; *Educ* Loretto, BNC Oxford (MA), Univ of Glasgow (MB ChB, MD); *m* 31 March 1979, Elaine Elizabeth, *née* Rankin; 1 s (Alan b 1981), 1 da (Gillian b 1983); *Career* Southern Gen Hosp: conslt physician 1988–, assoc postgrad dean 2002–; chm Specialist Advsy Ctee in Gen Med of the Jt Ctee of Higher Med Trg 1999–2003; author of various papers on diabetes and endocrinology; vice-pres RCPSGlas 2005–07 (hon sec 1998–2001); FRCP (Glasgow, Edinburgh, London); *Recreations* golf, fishing, gardening; *Style*— Dr Colin Semple; ✉ Diabetes Centre, Southern General Hosptial, Glasgow G51 4TF (tel 0141 201 1100, fax 0141 201 2399)

SEMPLE, Margaret Olivia (Maggie); OBE (2001); da of Robert Henry Semple, and Olivia Victorine, *née* Shuffler (d 1992); *b* 30 July 1954; *Educ* Shelburne Girls' HS London, UC Worcester, Univ of London (Advanced Dip), Univ of Sussex (MA); *Career* teacher Parliament Hill Girls' Sch London 1975–79, ILEA advsy dance teacher White Lion Centre London 1979–80, head of performing arts N Westminster Sch London 1980–88; Arts Cncl London: dir AEMS project 1988–91, dir of educn and trg 1991–97; nat prog dir of Learning Experience New Millennium Experience Co 1997–2001, chief exec and dir The Experience Corps 2001, sr assoc The King's Fund 2001–04, chm Nat R&D Centre Inst of Educn Univ of London 2004–, chm Wellcome Wolfson Dana Centre Science Museum London 2004–; res dir Extemporary Dance Theatre 1985–88; reader Open Univ; pres Laban Guild UK 1994–2000; external examiner Liverpool Inst for Performing Arts 1997–2000; memb Govt's Nat Advsy Gp for Continuing and Lifelong Learning, Civil Service cmmr 2001–07; chm Nat Youth Music Theatre; memb Jury Bonnie Bird Choreographic Award 1991–97; memb Bd: Rambert Dance Co 1998–2006, Teacher Trg Agency 2000–03, The Roundhouse Tst 2000–06, The Women's Library 2000–04, The Arts Educnl Schs Tst 2000–, De Montfort Univ 2000–, Br Sch 2003–, Arts Cncl London 2003–06; memb: Nat Curriculum Working Gp for Physical Educn 1989–90, Cwlth Inst Educn Ctee 1992–94, All Souls Gp Oxford 1994–, Further Educn Funding Cncl's Widening Participation Ctee 1995–97, e-Learning Task Force DfES 2002–03, Nat Policy Gp for the YMCA, Cncl of Europe's Expert Gp on Creativity and Youth Initiative, Cncl of Euro Cultural Centre of Delphi, Windsor Leadership Tst, HM Ct Service 2007; tstee: Barnado's 1997–2000, Nat Museums of Science and Industry (NMSI) 2003, Balance Fndn for Unclaimed Assets 2004–07, Br Library 2007; memb Cncl: RSA 1998–2003 (tstee 1992–98), Inst of Educn Univ of London 2003, City and Guilds 2006; dir Sadlers Wells Theatre; fell Br American Project (BAP) 1992–; UK expert on EC Kaleidoscope Ctee 1994–97; contrib to books and jls; Hon DEd De Montfort Univ; FCGI 2005; *Recreations* reading; *Clubs* Gorilla; *Style*— Dr Maggie Semple, OBE; ✉ mobile 07711 118386, e-mail maggie.semple@experience-corps.co.uk

SEMPLE, Dr Peter d'Almaine; DL (Renfrewshire 2000); s of Thomas Semple, of Renfrewshire, and Elspeth Roubaix, *née* Dewar; *b* 30 October 1945; *Educ* Loretto, Univ of Glasgow (MB ChB, MD); *m* 1979, Judith (Judy) Mairi, da of late Frank Abercromby, of Oban; 2 da (Catriona Mairi b 3 May 1981, Emma Dewar b 15 Dec 1982); *Career* conslt physician and chest specialist Inverclyde Dist 1979–, hon sr clinical lectr Univ of Glasgow 1981–; RCPSGlas: dir of med audit and memb Cncl 1993–99, property convenor 1999–2004; past chm Med Audit Ctee Home and Health Dept Scottish Office; various contribs to med periodicals 1975–2000; chm: St Petersburg Charity Forum 1997–2005, Cncl Ardgowan Hospice 2004–; past chm W of Scot Branch Br Deer Soc; FRCPGlas 1984, FRCPEd 1988, FRCP London 1996; *Recreations* field sports, gardening; *Style*— Dr Peter Semple, DL; ✉ High Lunderston, Inverkip PA16 0DU (tel 01475 522342); Inverclyde Royal Hospital, Greenock PA16 0XN (tel 01475 633777, fax 01475 637340)

SEN, Prof Amartya Kumar; Hon CH (2000); s of late Dr Ashutosh Sen, and Amita Sen; *b* 3 November 1933, Santiniketan, India; *Educ* Presidency Coll Calcutta (BA), Trinity Coll Cambridge (Adam Smith prize, Wrenbury scholar, sr scholar, Stevenson prize, research scholar, MA, PhD); *m* 1, 1960 (m dis 1975), Nabaneeta Dev; 2 da; m 2, 1978, Eva Colorni (d 1985); 1 da, 1 s; *Career* prof of econs Jadavpur Univ Calcutta 1956–58, fell Trinity Coll Cambridge 1957–63, prof of econs Delhi Sch of Econs Univ of Dehli 1963–71, prof of econs LSE 1971–77, prof of econs Univ of Oxford and fell Nuffield Coll 1977–80, Drummond prof of political economy Univ of Oxford and fell All Souls Coll 1980–88; Harvard Univ: prof of econs and philosophy 1987–98, Thomas W Lamont univ prof 1988–98, prof emeritus 1998–, sr fell Harvard Soc of Fells 1989–98; master Trinity Coll Cambridge 1998–2003; visiting asst prof MIT 1960–61, visiting assoc prof Stanford Univ 1961, visiting prof Univ of Calif Berkeley 1964–65, visiting prof Harvard Univ 1968–69, Andrew D White prof at large Cornell Univ 1978–84; pres: Devpt Studies Assoc 1980–82, Econometric Soc 1984, Int Econ Assoc 1986–89 (hon pres 1989–), Indian Econ Assoc 1989, American Econ Assoc 1994; hon vice-pres Royal Econ Soc 1988–; hon fell: Inst of Soc Studies The Hague 1982, LSE 1984, Inst of Devpt Studies Univ of Sussex 1984, Trinity Coll Cambridge 1991, SOAS Univ of London 1998, Darwin Coll Cambridge, Nuffield Coll Oxford, LSHTM, St Edmund's Coll Cambridge; hon prof Delhi Univ; Hon DLitt: Saskatchewan Univ 1980, Visva-Bharati Univ 1983, Georgetown Univ 1989, Jadavpur Univ 1990, Kalyani Univ 1990, London Guildhall Univ 1991, Williams Coll 1991, New Sch for Soc Research USA 1992, Calcutta Univ 1993, Oberlin Coll USA 1993, Univ of Oxford 1996, Rabindra Bharati Univ India 1998, Univ of Leicester 1998, Kingston Univ 1998, Columbia Univ 1998, McGill Univ 1998, Chhatrapati Shahu Ji Maharaj Univ India 1998, UEA 1999, Univ of Nottingham 1999, Heriot Watt Univ 1999, Univ of Allahabad 2000, Assam Univ 2000, Univ of Strathclyde 2000, Univ of Kerala 2000, Univ of Mumbai 2002, Univ of North Bengal 2002; Hon DSc: Univ of Bath 1984, Univ of Edinburgh 1995, Univ of Dhaka 1999, Assam Agricultural Univ 2000, Univ of Birmingham 2000, Univ of London 2000, Univ of Sussex 2003, Univ of Michigan 2006; Hon DUniv: Essex 1984, Rabindra Bharati Univ 1998; Dr (hc): Caen 1987, Univ of Louvain 1989, Univ of Athens 1991, Univ of Valencia 1994, Univ of Zurich 1994, Antwerp Univ 1995, Bard Coll 1997, Kiel Univ 1997, Univ of Delhi 1999, Kingston Univ 1999, Univ of Athens 1999, Univ de la Méditerranée Marseille 1999, Tech Univ of Lisbon 2001, Univ Jaume I Castellón 2001, Univ of Tokyo 2002, Clark Univ Worcester USA 2002, Open Univ 2002, Univ of Southampton 2002, Univ Pierre Mendès Grenoble 2002, Santa Clara Univ 2002, Bidhan Chandra Krishi Viswavidyalaya India 2003, Ritsumeikan Univ Japan 2003, Univ of York 2004, Rhodes Univ South Africa 2004, Koc Univ Turkey 2004, York Univ Toronto 2004, Univ Rovira I Virgili Tarragona 2004, Simmons Coll Boston 2005, Gottingen Univ 2005, Univ of the Witwatersrand 2007, Sorbonne 2007, UCD 2007, Univ Osnabruck 2007; Dr (ad honorem) Univ of Bologna 1988; Hon LLD: Tulane Univ 1990, Queen's Univ Canada 1993, Harvard Univ 2000, Mount Holyoke Coll USA 2003, Univ of Toronto 2004, Univ of Connecticut 2006; Hon DHumLit: Syracuse Univ 1994, Wesleyan Univ 1995, Univ of Massachusetts Lowell 2006; Hon PhD: Univ of Stockholm 1996, Jawaharlal Nehru Univ India 1998; Laurea (hc): Padova Univ 1998, Univ of Florence 2000, Univ of Pavia 2005; Hon DSocSci Chinese Univ of Hong Kong 1999; Hon DCL Univ of Durham 2002; DEc Univ of Natal 2004; DEcSci Cape Town 2006; Frank E Seidman Distinguished Award for Political Economy 1986, Senator Giovanni Agnelli Int Prize in Ethics 1990, Alan Shawn Feinstein World Hunger Award 1990, Jean Mayer Global Citizenship Award 1993, Indira Gandhi Gold Medal Award Royal Asiatic Soc 1994, Edinburgh Medal 1997, 9th Catalonia Int Prize 1997, Nobel Prize for Economics 1998, Bharat Ratna 1999, Leontief Prize 2000, Ordem do Merito Cientifico Brazil 2000, Eisenhower Medal 2000, Presidency of the Italian Republic Medal 2000, Bruno-Kreisky Award for Political Book of the Year 2001, Electricité de France European Economics Book Prize 2002, Ayrton Senna Grand Prix of Journalism 2002, Barnard Coll Medal of Distinction 2005, Silver Banner Florence 2005, George C Marshall Award 2005, Sidharth Maitra Meml Lecture Award 2006; Frances Perkins fell American Acad of Political and Social Science, distinguished fell All Souls Coll Oxford; memb Accademia Nazionale dei Lincei, foreign hon memb American Acad of Arts and Sciences, memb American Philosophical Assoc, memb Universal Acad of Cultures; fell Econometric Soc, FBA 1977, Hon FRSE, Hon FMedSci; *Books* Choice of Techniques (1960, 3 edn 1968), Collective Choice and Social Welfare (1970), Growth Economics (ed, 1970), Guidelines for Project Evaluation (jtly, 1972), On Economic Inequality (1973), Employment, Technology, and Development (1975), Poverty and Families: An Essay on Entitlement and Deprivation (1981), Utilitarianism and Beyond (jtly, 1982), Choice, Welfare and Measurement (1982), Resources, Values and Development (1982), Commodities and Capabilities (1985), The Standard of Living (jtly, 1987), On Ethics and Economics (1987), Hunger and Public Action (1989), The Political Economy of Hunger (3 vols, jtly, 1990–91), Inequality Re-examined (1992), The Quality of Life (jtly, 1993), India: Economic Development and Social Opportunity (jtly, 1995), Indian Development: Selected Regional Perspectives (jtly, 1997), Development as Freedom (1999), Rationality and Freedom (2002), India: Development and Participation (2002), The Argumentative Indian (2005), Identity and Violence: The Illusion of Destiny (2006); also author of numerous articles in learned jls; *Style*— Prof Amartya Sen

SENINGTON, David James; s of Victor Samuel Colston Senington, of Bristol, and Ella Matilda, *née* Ridout; *b* 28 March 1947; *Educ* Queen Elizabeth's Hosp Bristol, Coll of Commerce Bristol; *m* 31 Aug 1974, Julie Elizabeth, da of Thomas Park Hill; 1 s (Richard James b 31 December 1980), 1 da (Helen Louisa b 21 June 1984); *Career* reporter New Observer Bristol 1966–67, news sub-ed then features sub-ed Western Daily Press Bristol 1969–70 (reporter 1967–69); travelling 1970–71: Europe, Middle East, India, Australia; Parly reporter The West Australian Perth W Australia 1971; travelling 1971–72: Australia, New Zealand, Pacific, N America; news sub-ed: Western Daily Press 1972–73, Daily Telegraph London 1973, Daily Mail London 1973–74; travelling 1974–75: N & S America, W & N Africa; freelance sub-ed London 1975–76, contrib Sunday Express 1979–91 (Sunday Times 1977–78); Evening Standard: news sub-ed 1976–79, overnight dep chief sub-ed 1979–84, dep chief sub-ed 1984–85, chief sub-ed 1985–93, copy ed 1993–2006; memb: NUJ 1966, Soc of Genealogists 1982, Nat Tst 1988; *Recreations* writing, genealogy, numismatics, travel, gardening and garden design, reading; *Style*— David Senington, Esq; ✉ e-mail dsenington@rocketmail.com

SENIOR, Grahame; s of Raymond Senior, of Huddersfield, W Yorks, and Evelyn, *née* Wood; *b* 21 October 1944; *Educ* King James Sch; *m* 10 July 1965, Prudence Elizabeth, da of William Holland; 2 da (Claire Elizabeth b 30 Oct 1967, Charlotte Elizabeth b 26 Sept 1980), 1 s (Adam Michael b 3 June 1970); *Career* mgmnt trainee then asst publicity exec Royal Insurance Group 1963–65, writer Radio Caroline 1965, copywriter Vernons 1965–66, writer Royds 1966–67; Brunnings: copy chief 1967–69, creative dir 1969–73, md 1978–79; fndr Senior King Ltd 1980 (currently chm and chief exec), fndr MKA Films 1981, fndr Media Options Ltd (media independent) 1984 (currently chm); fndr and pres IN Int Network of Agencies; chm Bugscang & Associates Ltd; author of various articles and booklets on mktg, market targeting and tourism mktg 1973–87; chm Northern Publicity Assoc, organiser Northern NABS fundraising initiatives, fndr Liverpool Gold Medal Awards for Man of the Year; dir: Spaghetti House Restaurants Ltd, Associated Hotel Services Ltd; parish church warden, chm Friends of Tring Church; ACII 1965, MIPA 1967, MInstM 1969; *Recreations* dry fly fishing, gardening, ballet, tennis, painting, reading, wine, cooking; *Clubs* Reform, RAC, IOD; *Style*— Grahame Senior, Esq; ✉ Greenways, Grove Road, Tring, Hertfordshire HP23 5PD (tel 01442

822770); Senior King Ltd, 14–15 Carlisle Street, London W1V 5RE (tel 020 7734 5855, fax 020 7437 1908, mobile 07774 234008, e-mail gsenior@seniorking.co.uk)

SENIOR, Dr Michael; DL (Gwynedd 1989); s of Geoffrey Senior (d 1957), of Glan Conwy, N Wales, and Julia Elaine, *née* Cotterell (d 1984); *b* 14 April 1940; *Educ* Uppingham, Open Univ (BA, PhD); *Career* writer and farmer; radio play The Coffee Table (1964); memb Bd of Tstees Civic Tst for Wales 1998–2004; Hon RCA 2000; *Books* Portrait of North Wales (1973), Portrait of South Wales (1974), Greece and its Myths (1978), Myths of Britain (1979), The Age of Myth and Legend in Heroes and Heroines (1980), Sir Thomas Malory's Tales of King Arthur (ed, 1980), The Life and Times of Richard II (1981), Who's Who in Mythology (1985), Conwy: The Town's Story (1977), The Crossing of the Conwy (1991), Son et Lumière Script: A Place in History (1991), Gods and Heroes in North Wales, a Mythological Guide (1992), North Wales in the Making (1995), Figures in a Landscape (part 1 1997, part 2 1999), Did Lewis Carroll Visit Llandudno? (2000), Llys Helig, and the myth of lost lands (2002), Back from Catraeth (poems, 2002), The Standing Stones of North-Western Wales (2003), Did Prince Madog Discover America? (2004), Hillforts of Northern Wales (2005), Cromlechs and Cairns (2006); author of additional local history booklets 1982–99; *Recreations* hill walking, painting, croquet; *Style*— Dr Michael Senior, DL; ✉ Bryn Eisteddfod, Glan Conwy, Colwyn Bay, North Wales LL28 5LF; c/o David Higham Associates Ltd, 5–8 Lower John Street, London W1R 4HA

SENIOR, Robert; *b* 5 December 1964, Middlesbrough, Cleveland; *Educ* Univ of Durham; *m* Inge; 3 c (Lotte, Bas, Sanne); *Career* began career in advtg at Burkitt Weinreich Bryant; DMB&B: joined 1989, memb bd 1992–94; client services dir TBWA Simons Palmer 1994–98; co-fndr and managing ptnr Fallon 1998–; *Style*— Robert Senior, Esq; ✉ Fallon London, 67–69 Beak Street, London W1F 9SW (tel 020 7494 9120)

SENNETT, Prof Richard; s of Maurice Reid Sennett (d 1993), and Dorothy, *née* Vorontsev-Zhnezetsky; *b* 1943, Chicago; *Educ* Juliard Sch of Music, Univ of Chicago (BA), Harvard Univ (PhD); *m* 1982, Saskia, *née* Sassen; 1 c (Hilary b 1976); *Career* prof NY Univ 1972–97, dir NY Inst for the Humanities 1976–85 and 1997, chair and prof LSE 1998– (academic govr 2006–); chm UN Cmmn on Urban Studies 1988–93, pres American Cncl on Work 1993–97; Amalfi Award for Sociology 1999, Friedrich Ebert Award for Service to Social Democracy 1999; Chevalier de l'Ordre des Arts et des Lettres (France) 1996; FRSL 1996, FRSA 2005; *Publications* incl: Flesh and Stone: The Body and the City in Western Civilization (1994), The Corrosion of Character: the Personal Consequences of Work in the New Capitalism (1998), Respect: The Formation of Character in a World of Inequality (2003), The Culture of the New Capitalism (2006); *Recreations* cooking, chamber music; *Clubs* Century Assoc (NY), Signet (Harvard); *Style*— Prof Richard Sennett; ✉ London School of Economics and Political Science, Houghton Street, London WC2A 2AE (tel 020 7955 6076, fax 020 7955 7697, e-mail r.sennett@lse.ac.uk)

SENNITT, His Hon John Stuart; s of Stuart Osland Sennitt (d 1985), and Nora Kathleen, *née* Stockings (d 1982); *b* 5 March 1935; *Educ* Culford Sch Bury St Edmunds, St Catharine's Coll Cambridge (MA, LLB); *m* 30 April 1966, Janet Ann; 2 da, 1 s; *Career* admitted slr 1961, ptnr Wild Hewitson & Shaw Slrs Cambridge 1963–83, registrar Cambridge County Court then dist judge 1983–94, recorder of the Crown Court 1992–94 (asst recorder 1988–92), circuit judge (SE Circuit) 1994–2007; *Style*— His Hon John Sennitt

SENTAMU, Most Rev Dr John Tucker Mugabi; *see:* York, Archbishop of

SENTANCE, Andrew William; s of William Thomas Wulfram Sentance, and Lillian, *née* Bointon; *b* 17 September 1958; *Educ* Eltham Coll London, Clare Coll Cambridge (MA), LSE (MSc, PhD); *m* 3 Aug 1985, Anne Margaret, da of Raymond Austin Penfold; 1 s (Timothy Michael b 4 March 1989), 1 da (Rebecca Louise b 21 March 1991); *Career* petrol station mangr Petrocell Ltd 1980–81, mgmnt trainee NCB 1982–83; CBI: economist with Economic Affrs Directorate 1986–89, dir economic affrs CBI 1989–93; sr res fell London Business Sch 1994–95, dir Centre for Economic Forecasting London Business Sch 1995–97, chief economic advsr Br Retail Consortium 1995–97; British Airways plc: chief economist 1998–2006, head of environmental affrs 2003–06; memb Cmmn for Integrated Transport 2006–, memb Monetary Policy Ctee Bank of England 2006–; visiting prof of economics Royal Holloway Univ of London 1998–, visiting prof Cranfield Univ 2001–; memb: RPI Advsy Ctee 1989 and 1992–94, CSO Advsy Ctee 1992–95, HM Treasy Ind Panel of Economic Forecasting Advsrs 1992–93, Cmmn on Wealth Creation and Social Cohesion 1994–95, NAPF Retirement Income Inquiry 1994–95, ONS Advsy Ctee 1996–99, Advsy Bd Air Transport Action Gp 2000–; Soc of Business Economists: memb 1988–, memb Cncl 1991–2003, chm 1995–2000, dep chm 2000–03, fell 2001–; tstee: Harvest Help 1996–2006, Anglo-German Fndn 2001–, BA Pension Funds 2002–06; professional fell Univ of Warwick 2006–; FRAeS 2004; *Recreations* playing piano, guitar, writing and performing music; *Style*— Dr Andrew Sentance; ✉ Bank of England, Threadneedle Street, London EC2R 8AH (tel 020 7601 5189, e-mail andrew.sentance@bankofengland.co.uk)

SERGEANT, John; s of Ernest Sergeant (d 1985), and Olive Stevens, *née* Cook, of Devon (d 2004); *b* 14 April 1944; *Educ* Millfield, Magdalen Coll Oxford (BA); *m* 1969, Mary, *née* Smithies; 2 s (William b 1973, Michael b 1975); *Career* freelance writer and broadcaster; appeared with Alan Bennett in his comedy series On The Margin (BBC) 1966, trainee Liverpool Daily Post & Echo 1967–70; BBC TV and Radio: news reporter 1970–80, political corr 1980–88, chief political corr 1988–2000; political ed ITN 2000–02; assignments as reporter in 25 countries incl: Vietnam, Rhodesia, NI, Turkish invasion of Cyprus, Israeli invasion of Lebanon; also acting corr in Dublin, Paris and Washington, sometime presenter of Radio 4 current affrs programmes incl World at One, Today and PM, frequent guest on television and radio light entertainment programmes incl Have I Got News For You, UK Theatre tour 'An Audience with John Sergeant' 2003–06; winner Broadcasting Press Guild award for most memorable outside broadcast of 1990 (Mrs Thatcher interrupting live broadcast outside Paris Embassy to announce participation in second round of Cons Pty leadership ballot), winner Best Contribution to TV Award 2000 (Listener and Viewer Assoc); pres Johnson Soc 2003–04, memb Hansard Soc Cmmn on the Communication of Parliamentary Democracy; *Books* Give Me Ten Seconds (memoirs, 2001), Maggie: Her Fatal Legacy (2005); *Recreations* sailing; *Style*— John Sergeant; ✉ c/o Anita Land, Capel and Land Ltd, 29 Wardour Street, London W1D 6PS (tel 020 7734 2414)

SERGEANT, Sir Patrick John Rushton; kt (1984); s of George Sergeant, and Rene Sergeant; *b* 17 March 1924; *Educ* Beaumont Coll; *m* 1952, Gillian, *née* Wilks; 2 da (Harriet, Emma); *Career* Lt RNVR 1945; asst city ed News Chronicle 1948, city ed Daily Mail 1960–84 (dep city ed 1953), fndr and md Euromoney Publications 1969–85 (chm 1985–92, pres 1992–); dir: Associated Newspapers Group 1971–83, Daily Mail and Gen Tst 1983–2003; Wincott Award Financial Journalist of the Year 1979; Freeman City of London; Domus fell St Catherine's Coll Oxford 1988; FRSA; *Books* Another Road to Samarkand (1955), Money Matters (1967), Inflation Fighters Handbook (1976); *Recreations* tennis, swimming, talking; *Clubs* RAC, Mark's, All England Lawn Tennis and Croquet, Queen's; *Style*— Sir Patrick Sergeant; ✉ No 1 The Grove, Highgate Village, London N6 6JU; Euromoney Institutional Investor plc, Nestor House, Playhouse Yard, London EC4V 5EX (tel 020 7779 8879, fax 020 7779 8880, e-mail psergeant@euromoneyplc.com)

SERLE, Christopher Richard (Chris); s of Frank Raymond Serle (d 1988), of Bristol, and Winifred Mary, *née* Pugsley (d 1989); *b* 13 July 1943; *Educ* Clifton, Trinity Coll Dublin; *m* 1, 22 Jan 1983 (m dis), Anna Southall, *qv*, da of Stephen Readhead Southall, of Clifford, Hereford and Worcester; 2 s (Harry b 1983, Jack b 1987); m 2, 8 April 2006, Alison Fraser, da of Malcolm Fraser, of Weymouth, Dorset; *Career* actor 1964–68, prodr BBC radio and TV 1968–78, TV and radio journalist and presenter; programmes incl: That's Life, In At The Deep End, People, Pick of the Week; *Recreations* gliding, jazz drumming; *Style*— Chris Serle, Esq; ✉ tel 0117 946 6673

SERMON, (Thomas) Richard; s of Eric Thomas Sermon (d 1978), of Nottingham, and Marjorie Hilda, *née* Parsons (d 1969); *b* 25 February 1947; *Educ* Nottingham HS; *m* 10 Oct 1970, Rosemary Diane, da of Thomas Smith (d 1971), of Sheffield; 1 s (Thomas Christopher b 1971), 1 da (Catherine Marjorie b 1975); *Career* co sec Crest Hotels Ltd 1969–74, dep chm Good Relations Gp Ltd 1974–79; md: Shandwick Consultants Ltd 1979–87; chief exec: Shandwick Europe plc 1988–90, Shandwick International plc 1990–96; chm: Gryphon Corporate Counsel Ltd 1996–, Shandwick Consultants Ltd 1996–2000; PR advsr Goldman Sachs International 1992–96; dir: Gryphon Ptnrs Ltd 1994–, Jardine Lloyd Thompson Group plc 1996–2006, Newmond plc 1997–2000, Defence Storage and Distribution Agency 1999–2006, Wrightson Wood Ltd 2002–, The PBN Co Ltd 2003–, Eloqui Public Relations Ltd 2003–; appointed memb PPP Healthcare 1994–98; vice-pres: RADAR 1987–, Providence Row 1997–; memb Nat Advsy Cncl on Employment of People with Disabilities (NACEPD) 1994–98; dir The City of London Sinfonia Ltd 1995–2001; chm: Fedn of London Youth Clubs 1996– (hon treas 1995–96), Home Improvement Tst 1997–; memb Cncl: The Foundation for Manufacturing and Industry 1994–98, The City and Guilds of London Inst 1994– (memb Exec Ctee 1999–, jt hon sec 2005–); Freeman City of London 1968; memb Ct of Assts: Worshipful Co of Wheelwrights 1990 (Master 2000–01), Worshipful Co of Chartered Secs and Administrators 1991; FCIS 1972, Hon FCGI 2004; *Clubs* City of London, City Livery, Mark's, Walbrook; *Style*— Richard Sermon, Esq; ✉ Friars Well, Aynho, Banbury, Oxfordshire OX17 3BG (tel 01869 810284, fax 01869 810634); Gryphon Corporate Counsel Ltd, 1 Duchess Street, London W1W 6AN (tel 020 7323 9857, fax 020 7323 9859, e-mail richardsermon@gryphoncorporate.com)

SEROTA, His Hon Judge Daniel; QC (1989); *b* 27 September 1945; *Educ* Univ of Oxford (MA); *m*; 2 da; *Career* called to the Bar Lincoln's Inn 1969; recorder of the Crown Court 1989–99, circuit judge (SE Circuit) 1999–; *Style*— His Hon Judge Serota, QC; ✉ Milton Keynes County Court, 351 Silbury Boulevard, Witan Gate East, Central Milton Keynes MK9 2DT (tel 01908 302800)

SEROTA, (Hon) Sir Nicholas Andrew; kt (1999); o s of Baroness Serota (d 2002); does not use courtesy prefix of Hon; *b* 27 April 1946; *Educ* Haberdashers' Aske's, Christ's Coll Cambridge (BA), Courtauld Inst of Art London (MA); *m*; 2 da; *Career* regnl art offr and exhibition organiser Arts Council of GB 1970–73; dir: MOMA Oxford 1973–76, Whitechapel Art Gallery 1976–88, The Tate Gallery 1988–; chm VAAC British Cncl 1992–98 (memb 1976–98), cmmr Cmmn for Architecture and the Built Environment (CABE) 1999–2006; memb Olympic Delivery Authy 2006–; tstee: Public Art Devpt Tst (PADT) 1983–87, Architecture Fndn 1991–99, Little Sparta Tst 1995–; Hon DArts: London Guildhall Univ 1990, Univ of Plymouth 1993; Hon DLitt: Keele Univ 1994, South Bank Univ 1996, Univ of Exeter 2000, London Inst 2001, Univ of Essex 2002; Hon DUniv Wimbledon Sch of Art (Univ of Surrey) 1997; hon fell: Queen Mary & Westfield College London 1988, Goldsmiths Coll London 1994, Christ's Coll Cambridge 2002; sr fell RCA 1996; Hon FRIBA 1992; *Books* Experience or Interpretation: The Dilemma of Museums of Modern Art (1997); *Style*— Sir Nicholas Serota; ✉ Tate, Millbank, London SW1P 4RG (tel 020 7887 8004, fax 020 7887 8010)

SERVICE, Alastair Stanley Douglas; MVO (2007), CBE (1995); s of Lt Cdr Douglas Service (d 1976), and Evelyn Caroline, *née* Sharp (d 1986); *b* 8 May 1933; *Educ* Westminster, The Queen's Coll Oxford; *m* 1, 1959 (m dis 1984), Louisa Anne Service, OBE, JP, *qv*, da of Lt-Col Harold Hemming, OBE, MC (d 1976); 1 s (Nicholas), 1 da (Sophia); m 2, 1992, Zandria Madeleine, da of John E Pauncefort (d 1981); *Career* Midshipman RNR 1952; writer and campaigner, former merchant banker and publisher; worked in Brazil and USA 1958–59; hon parly campaigns organiser for reforms of family planning, abortion, adoption and divorce laws 1964–75; chm Birth Control Campaign 1970–74, nat chm Family Planning Assoc 1975–79, chm Population Concern Int 1975–79, vice-chm Health Educn Cncl 1979–87, gen sec Family Planning Assoc 1980–89, dep chm Health Educn Authy 1987–89; chm: Wessex RHA NHS 1993–94 (memb 1989–94), Wilts HA 1992–2000, Publications Ctee Victorian Soc 1982–89; co-fndr and memb Ctee ARK (Action for the River Kennet) 1991– (hon sec 1991–2002), co-fndr and chm Wilts Health and Social Servs Strategic Forum 1996–2000; The Prince of Wales Fndn: tstee 1999–, chm Regeneration Through Heritage Gp 2000–; tstee Population Concern International 1998; chm The Avebury Soc (Civic Tst) 2002–; life memb: Soc for Protection of Ancient Buildings, Victorian Soc, Soc of Architectural Historians of GB, Family Planning Assoc of UK; *Books* incl: A Birth Control Plan for Britain (jtly, 1972), Edwardian Architecture (1977), The Architects of London, 1066–Today (1979), Lost Worlds (1981), A Guide to the Megaliths of Europe (jtly, 1981), Anglo-Saxon and Norman Buildings of Britain (1982), Edwardian Interiors (1982), Victorian and Edwardian Hampstead (1989), The Standing Stones of Europe (1993); *Libretto* The Sky Speaker (opera, composer James Harpham, 1999), The Angel Cantata (composer Robin Nelson, 2003); *Recreations* cycling, opera (especially Verdi and Bellini), dalmatians, the pursuit of stone circles, mounds and historic buildings; *Clubs* Garrick; *Style*— Alastair Service, Esq, MVO, CBE; ✉ Swan House, Avebury, Wiltshire SN8 1RA (tel 01672 539312, fax 01672 539634)

SERVICE, Louisa Anne; OBE (1997); da of Lt-Col Henry Harold Hemming, OBE, MC (d 1976), of London, and Alice Louisa Hemming, OBE, *née* Weaver (d 1994); *b* 13 December 1931; *Educ* schs in Canada, France, USA and UK, St Hilda's Coll Oxford (MA); *m* 28 Feb 1959 (m dis 1984), Alastair Stanley Douglas Service, CBE, *qv*, s of Lt Cdr Douglas Service (d 1976), of London; 1 s (Nicholas Alastair McFee Douglas b 9 May 1961), 1 da (Sophia Alice Louisa Douglas b 20 April 1963); *Career* export dir Ladybird Electric 1955–59; dir Glass's Information Services Ltd 1971– (dep chm 1976–81, chm 1981–95); jt chm: Municipal Group of Cos 1976– (fin dir 1966–76), Hemming Publishing 1985–; dir Opera Circus Ltd; chm: Mayer-Lismann Opera Workshop 1976–91, Youth and Music 1990–2000 (memb Cncl 1987–), Jacqueline du Pré Music Bldg 2000–06; memb Cncl: Friends of Covent Garden 1982–2005 (memb Mgmnt Ctee 1982–95 and 1997–2002), Haydn/Mozart Soc 1990–92; memb Advsy Bd Rudolfe Kempe Soc; hon sec Women's India Assoc 1967–74, dep chm Paddington Probation Hostel 1976–86; chm: Hackney Juvenile Ct 1975–82, Westminster Juvenile Ct 1982–88, Hammersmith and Fulham Juvenile Ct 1988–92, Hammersmith and Fulham Family Proceedings Ct and Youth Ct 1992–94, Family Proceedings Ct and Youth Ct 1994–2001; memb: London Magistrates Cts Ctee 1995–2001 (chm Audit Ctee), Dept of Trade's Consumer Credit Appeals Panel 1981–2006, FIMBRA Appeals Tribunal 1989–92, Adjudication and Appeals Ctee Slrs' Complaints Bureau 1992–93; JP 1969–2001; tstee: Women's India Tst 1989–, Performing Arts Lab 1996–99; memb St Hilda's Coll Oxford Devpt Ctee, treas St Hilda's Coll Law Network 1998–2002; FRGS; *Recreations* music, travel, reading; *Clubs* Athenaeum (memb: Gen Ctee 2003–, Exec Ctee 2004–); *Style*— Ms Louisa A Service, OBE; ✉ c/o Hemming Publishing Ltd, 32 Vauxhall Bridge Road, London SW1V 2SS (tel 020 7973 6404, fax 020 7233 5049)

SERWOTKA, Mark Henryk; s of Henryk Josef Serwotka, of Aberdare, S Wales, and Audrey Phylis Serwotka; *b* 26 April 1963, Cardiff; *Educ* Bishop Healey RC Comp Sch Merthyr Tydfil; *m* 6 April 2001, Ruth Louise, da of Robert Cockcroft; 1 da (Imogen b 6 Nov 1994), 1 s (Rhys b 26 June 1997); *Career* Public and Commercial Servs Union: lay rep 1980–2002, personal case offr 1995–98, gen sec 2001–; DHSS: clerical offr 1980–2000, exec offr

2000–02; *Recreations* sport, walking, reading; *Style*— Mark Serwotka, Esq; ✉ Public and Commercial Services Union, 160 Falcon Road, London SW11 2LN (tel 020 7924 2727, fax 020 7924 6377, e-mail mark@pcs.org.uk)

SESSIONS, John Gibb; *né* Marshall; s of John Craig Marshall, of St Albans, Herts, and Esmé Richardson; *b* 11 January 1953; *Educ* Verulum Sch St Albans, Univ of Bangor (MA), RADA; *Career* actor; *Theatre* Liverpool Everyman: Chameleon Blue, A Midsummer Night's Dream; Phoenix: The American Napoleon, The Common Pursuit; Riverside Studios: Christmas Show, Salute to Doctor Johnson, Lives of the Great Composers, The Life of Napoleon; other credits incl: Limbo Tales (Gate), Waiting for Godot (Young Vic), One Flew Over the Cuckoo's Nest (Manchester Royal Exchange), Hamlet (Sheffield Crucible), Man is Man (Almeida), The Alchemist (Lyric Hammersmith), The Orton Diaries (NT), Die Fledermaus (Royal Opera House), Tartuffe (Playhouse), Chestnuts Old and New (King's Head), The Life of Napoleon (Albery), Travelling Tales (Haymarket and nat tour), The Soldier's Tale (Barbican), Daniel in My Night with Reg (Theatre Upstairs Royal Court and Criterion), Paint Said Fred (Royal Acad), The Soldier's Tale (Barbican, with LSO); *Solo Shows* at: Liverpool Everyman, Young Vic, Cottesloe, Royal Exchange, Gate; The Eleventh Hour (Donmar Warehouse) *Television* Channel 4 incl: Girls on Top, The Madness Museum, Porterhouse Blue, Gramsci, Whose Line Is It Anyway?, A History of Psychiatry, The Christmas Show; BBC: The Cellar Show, Saturday Review, Laugh I Nearly Paid My Licence Fee, Tender is the Night, The Lenny Henry Show, Jute City, Have I Got News for You, Life with Eliza, The Full Wax, Some Enchanted Evening, On the Spot, Tall Tales, Tom Jones, Likely Stories, In the Red, Stella Street (series I, II, III and IV), Splendour in the Grass: In the Footsteps of Wordsworth and Coleridge, The Man, Gormenghast, Randall and Hopkirk (Deceased), Murder Rooms, Well-Schooled in Murder; LWT: After Midnight, The Ackroyd Dickens; Yorkshire: The New Statesman, A Day in Summer; other credits incl: Boon (Central), Menace Unseen (Thames), The Treasure Seekers (Carlton), The Inspector Linley Mysteries, The Lost Prince, Judge John Deed, Midsomer Murders, Dalziel and Pascoe, George Eliot - A Life, Hawking, Absolute Power, QI 2005–06, The English Harem 2005, Jackanory Annivrsary Special 2006, The Moving Finger 2006, Low Winter Sun 2006, The Ronni Ancona Show 2006, New Tricks 2007, Hotel Babylon 2007, Reichenbach Falls (BBC 4) 2007; *Radio* incl: New Premises, Whose Line Is It Anyway?, Beachcomber By the Way, Figaro gets Divorced, Poonsh, Aunt Julia and the Scriptwriter, Mightier than the Sword, The Reith Affair, Saturday Night Fry, Good Opera Bad Opera, The Destiny of Nathalie X, Season's Greetings, Reconstructing Louis, The Man Who Came To Dinner, The Haunting, The Titanic Enquiry, St Graham and St Evelyn, Pray for Us, In the Company of Men, The Possessed (BBC Radio 3), Atlee Confidential (BBC Radio 4), Zazie on the Metro (BBC Radio 4); *Film* incl: Faith, The Sender, The Bounty, Gunbus, Whoops Apocalypse, Castaway, Henry V, Sweet Revenge, The Pope Must Die, Princess Caraboo, In the Bleak Midwinter, Pinocchio, My Night with Reg, Cousin Bette, A Midsummer Night's Dream, 1 of the Hollywood 10, The Gangs of New York, High Heels and Low Life, Flight of Fancy, Five Children and It, The Merchant of Venice, Stella Street: The Movie, Rag Tale, Funny Farm 2006, The Good Shepherd 2006; *Recreations* socialising, reading, travelling; *Clubs* Groucho; *Style*— John Sessions, Esq; ✉ c/o Markham & Froggatt Ltd, 4 Windmill Street, London W1P 1HF (tel 020 7636 4412, fax 020 7637 5233)

SETCHELL, David Lloyd; s of Raymond Setchell (d 1967), and Phyllis Jane, *née* Lloyd (d 1952); *b* 16 April 1937; *Educ* Woodhouse GS, Jesus Coll Cambridge (MA); *m* 11 Aug 1962, Muriel Mary, *née* Davies; 1 da (Justine (Mrs Nicholas Panay) b 1967), 1 s (Andrew b 1970); *Career* Peat Marwick London 1960–64, Shawinigan Ltd 1964–71; mktg mangr Gulf Oil Chemicals (Europe) 1971–77 (vice-pres 1978–82), md Gulf Oil 1982–98; dir: RAF Personnel and Trg Cmd Bd 2000–06, Univ of Glos (chair 2002–); FEI (pres 1996–98), FCA; *Recreations* golf, music, theatre; *Clubs* Oriental, MCC, St George's Hill Golf, Cotswold Hills Golf; *Style*— David Setchell, Esq; ✉ South Hayes, Sandy Lane Road, Cheltenham, Gloucestershire GL53 9DE (tel 01242 571390)

SETCHELL, Marcus Edward; CVO (2004); s of Eric Headley Setchell (d 1980), of Cambridge, and Barbara Mary, *née* Whitworth (d 1992); *b* 4 October 1943; *Educ* Felsted, Univ of Cambridge, St Bartholomew's Hosp Med Coll (MA, MB BChir); *m* 1973, Sarah Loveday, da of Vernon Alfred Robert French (d 1967), of Northwood, Middx, and Dr Margaret French, *née* Davies (d 1981); 2 da (Anna b 1974, Catherine b 1980), 2 s (Thomas b 1976, David b 1984); *Career* conslt gynaecologist and obstetrician: St Bartholomew's Hosp and Homerton Hosp 1975–2000, Whittington Hosp 2000–, King Edward VII Hosp for Offrs, St Luke's Hosp for the Clergy; dir Fertility Unit Portland Hosp 1987–94, med dir Homerton Hosp 1994–97; surgn/gynaecologist to HM The Queen 1990–; regnl assessor Maternal Mortality Enquiry 1992–; speciality advsr (gynaecology) to Nat Patient Safety Agency 2003–06; chm Med Ctee King Edward VII Hosp 1998–2005; RSM: memb Cncl, pres Section of Obstetrics and Gynaecology 1994–95; memb Cncl RCOG 1994–2000; tstee and memb Cncl WellBeing 2003–; Liveryman Worshipful Soc of Apothecaries; FRCS, FRCSEd, FRCOG; *Publications* Progress in Obstetrics and Gynaecology (1987), Scientific Foundations of Obstetrics and Gynaecology (ed, 1991), Reconstructive Urology (1993), Ten Teachers Gynaecology (1995), Ten Teachers Obstetrics (1995), MCQ's in Obstetrics and Gynaecology (1996), Shaw's Textbook of Operative Gynaecology (2001), Self-Assessment in Gynaecology and Obstetrics (2001), General Surgical Operations (2006); *Recreations* tennis, skiing, sailing, travel, gardening; *Clubs* All England Lawn Tennis & Croquet, RSM, Fountain, St Albans Medical; *Style*— Marcus Setchell, Esq, CVO; ✉ 64 Wood Vale, London N10 3DN (tel 020 8444 5266); 5 Devonshire Place, London W1G 6HL (tel 020 7935 4444, fax 020 7486 3446)

SETCHELL, Michael Robert; s of George Robert Setchell (d 1989), of Bedford, and Violet, *née* Cooper (d 1996); *b* 22 March 1944; *Educ* Bedford Modern Sch, Guy's Hosp Dental Sch London (BDS, LDS); *m* 5 Aug 1967, Mary, da of late Cecil Richardson; 1 da (Joanna Mary b 26 May 1973), 1 s (Alexander Michael b 19 April 1976); *Career* dental practitioner; Guy's Hosp London: resident house surgn 1966–67, registrar in dental conservation 1967–69, lectr (dental sch) in conservative dentistry 1969–72; gen practice Dulwich 1968–70, full time practitioner Devonshire Place London 1972–; memb: RSM, BDA, Dental Soc of London (pres 1996–97), Royal Inst; MFGDP RCS; *Recreations* gardening, photography, hill walking; *Clubs* Rotary Int, Langley Park Rotary (past pres); *Style*— Michael Setchell, Esq; ✉ 35 Devonshire Place, London W1G 6JP (tel 020 7935 3342, e-mail msetchell@dial.pipex.com)

SETH, Vikram; Hon CBE (2001); s of Premnath Seth, and Leila, also *née* Seth; *b* 20 June 1952; *Educ* Doon Sch Dehradun India, Tonbridge, Corpus Christi Coll Oxford (open scholarship, MA), Stanford Univ (MA, full fellowship), Nanjing Univ China; *Career* writer; sr ed Stanford Univ Press 1985–86; Guggenheim Fellowship 1986, Commonwealth Poetry Prize 1986, Sahitya Akademi Award 1988, W H Smith Literary Award and Cwlth Writers Prize (for A Suitable Boy) 1994; hon fell Corpus Christi Coll Oxford 1994; FRSL; Chevalier de l'Ordre des Arts et des Lettres (France) 2001; *Books* Mappings (poems, Calcutta, 1982), From Heaven Lake - Travels Through Sinkiang and Tibet (1983, Thomas Cook Travel Book Award), The Humble Administrator's Garden (poems, 1985), The Golden Gate - A Novel in Verse (1986), All You Who Sleep Tonight (poems, 1990), Beastly Tales From Here and There - Fables in Verse (Penguin India, 1992), Three Chinese Poets (translations, 1992), A Suitable Boy (novel, 1993), Arion and the Dolphin (libretto, 1994), An Equal Music (1999), Two Lives (2005); *Recreations* Chinese calligraphy, swimming, music; *Style*— Vikram Seth; ✉ c/o Little, John, Time Warner Books, Brettenham House, Lancaster Place, London WC2E 7EN (tel 020 7911 8000)

SETON, Sir Charles Wallace; 13 Bt (NS 1683), of Pitmedden, Aberdeenshire; suc uncle, Sir James Christall Seton, Bt (d 1998); *b* 25 August 1948; *m* 1974, Rebecca, da of Robert Lowery; *Heir* bro, Bruce Seton; *Style*— Sir Charles Seton, Bt

SETON, Sir Iain Bruce; 13 Bt (NS 1663), of Abercorn, Linlithgowshire; s of Sir (Christopher) Bruce Seton, 12 Bt (d 1988); *b* 27 August 1942; *Educ* Colchester, Chadacre Agric Inst; *m* 1963, Margaret Ann, o da of Walter Charles Faulkner (d 1998), of Barlee Road, W Australia: 1 s (Laurence Bruce b 1968), 1 da (Amanda Jane b 1971); *Heir* s, Laurence Seton; *Style*— Sir Iain Seton, Bt; ✉ 16 Radiata Drive, Albany, Western Australia 6330, Australia

SEVER, Prof Peter Sedgwick; s of Harry Sedgwick Sever, of London, and Lillian Maria, *née* Moran (d 1990); *b* 23 July 1944; *Educ* Manchester Grammar, Trinity Hall Cambridge (MA, MB BChir), St Mary's Hosp Med Sch (Lord Moran schor), Univ of London (PhD); *Career* SHO: in gen med and cardiology St Mary's Hosp London 1969–70, in chest diseases The Brompton Hosp 1970; MRC jr research fell Dept of Biochemistry St Mary's Hosp Med Sch and hon med registrar to the Professorial Med Unit 1971–74, lectr in med and pharmacology St Mary's Hosp Med Sch and hon sr registrar St Mary's Hosp 1974–76, sr lectr in med St Mary's Hosp Med Sch and hon conslt physician 1976–89, prof of clinical pharmacology and therapeutics St Mary's Hosp Med Sch 1980–; prog conslt Wellcome Tst/Kenya/St Mary's Research Unit 1980–85, chm Specialist Advsy Ctee on Clinical Pharmacology Jt Ctee on Higher Med Trg 1984–90, memb Br Heart Fndn Grant Awards Ctee 1988–92, govr Imperial Coll of Sci Technol and Med 1989–93, memb Exec Scientific Ctee Euro Soc of Cardiology 1991–93; ed: Clinical Science 1980–87, Jl of Hypertension 1983–89, Jl of Human Hypertension 1987, Jl of Drug Development 1988; memb: Br Pharmacological Soc 1976, Int Soc of Hypertension 1978; sec: London Hypertension Soc 1977–85, Euro Blood Pressure Gp 1979–82; pres: Br Hypertension Soc 1989–91, European Cncl for Blood Pressure and Cardiovascular Research 1998–99; memb Cncl Br Heart Fndn 2002– (chm Fellowships Ctee); fell Euro Soc of Cardiology, FRCP; *Books* Clinical Atlas of Hypertension (with Peart and Swales, 1992), Cardiovascular Disease - Practical Issues for Prevention (with Poulter and Thom, 1993), also editor of several books on cardiovascular disease and hypertention and author of over 300 papers on cardiovascular disease and clinical pharmacology; *Recreations* sport (tennis and rugby), theatre, travel; *Clubs* Wig & Pen; *Style*— Prof Peter Sever; ✉ Hedgerley House, Hedgerley, Buckinghamshire SL2 3UL; Department of Clinical Pharmacology, Imperial College School of Medicine at St Mary's, Queen Elizabeth the Queen Mother Wing, London W2 1NY (tel 020 7886 1117, fax 020 7886 6145, e-mail p.sever@ic.ac.uk)

SEVERIN, Prof Dorothy Sherman; Hon OBE (2003); da of late Wilbur B Sherman, and Virginia, *née* Tucker; *b* 24 March 1942; *Educ* Harvard Univ (AB, AM, PhD); *m* 24 March 1966 (m dis 1979), Giles Timothy Severin; 1 da (Ida); *Career* tutor Harvard Univ 1964–66, visiting lectr Univ of W Indies 1967–68, asst prof Vassar Coll NY 1968–69, lectr Westfield Coll London 1969–82, Gilmour prof of Spanish Univ of Liverpool 1982– (ed Bulletin of Hispanic Studies 1982–); visiting prof: Harvard Univ 1982, Columbia Univ NY 1985, Yale Univ 1985, Univ of Calif Berkeley 1996; pro-vice-chllr Univ of Liverpool 1989–92; memb: NI HE Cncl 1993–2001, Int Courtly Lit Soc (former pres Br Branch), Peer Review AHRC 2005–, Research Assessment Exercise Sub-Panel (Iberian) HEFCE 2005–; tstee: Modern Humanities Res Assoc, Res Panel Humanities Res Bd Br Acad 1994–96, Junta Assoc Hispánica de Literatura Medieval 1997–99, Junta Convivio 2004–, Junta Asociación Internacional de Hispanistas 2004–; memb Assoc of Hispanists of GB and I; FSA; *Books* Celestina (edns 1969, 1987), Memory in La Celestina (1970), Diego de San Pedro, La pasión trobada (1973), La Lengua de Erasmo romançada por muy elegante estilo (ed, 1975), Diego de San Pedro, Poesía (ed with Keith Whinnom, 1979), Cosas sacadas de la crónica del rey Juan II (ed with Angus Mackay, 1982), Celestina with the Translation of James Mabbe 1631 (ed, 1987), Tragicomedy and Novelistic Discourse in Celestina (1989), Cancionero de Oñate-Castañeda (1990), The Paris Cancioneros (with F Maguire and M Garcia, 1993 and 1997), Witchcraft in Celestina (1995), Animals in Celestina (with Vicenta Blay, 1999), Two Spanish Songbooks (2000), Del manuscrito a la imprenta en la época de Isabel la Católica (2004), Religious Parody in the Spanish Sentimental Romance (2005); *Style*— Prof Dorothy Severin, OBE, FSA; ✉ Hispanic Studies, Modern Languages Building, University of Liverpool, Chatham Street, Liverpool L69 7ZR (tel 0151 794 2773/4, fax 0151 794 2785, e-mail d.s.severin@liv.ac.uk)

SEVERIN, Giles Timothy (Tim); s of Maurice Watkins, and Inge Severin; *b* 25 September 1940; *Educ* Tonbridge, Keble Coll Oxford (MA, BLitt); *m* 1966 (m dis 1979), Dorothy Virginia Sherman; 1 da; *Career* author, film maker, historian, traveller; expeditions: led motorcycle team along Marco Polo route 1961, river Mississippi by canoe and launch 1965, Brendan Voyage from W Ireland to N America 1977, Sindbad Voyage from Oman to China 1980–81, Jason Voyage from Iolkos to Colchis 1984, Ulysses Voyage from Troy to Ithaca 1985, First Crusade route by horse to Jerusalem 1987–88, travels on horseback in Mongolia 1990, trans-Pacific bamboo raft from Hong Kong 1993, Prahu voyage Eastern Indonesia 1996, Pacific Ocean travels in search of the white whale, Caribbean travels for castaway histories 1998; films: The Brendan Voyage, The Sindbad Voyage, The Jason Voyage, Crusader, In Search of Genghis Khan, The China Voyage, The Spice Islands Voyage, In Search of Moby Dick; Founder's medal RGS, Livingstone medal RGS (Scotland), Sir Percy Sykes medal RSAA; Hon DLitt: Univ of Dublin, UC Cork; *Books* Tracking Marco Polo (1964), Explorers of the Mississippi (1967), The Golden Antilles (1970), Vanishing Primitive Man (1973), The African Adventure (1973), The Oriental Adventure (1978), The Brendan Voyage (1978), The Sindbad Voyage (1982), The Jason Voyage (1985), The Ulysses Voyage (1987), Crusader (1989), In Search of Genghis Khan (1991), The China Voyage (1994), The Spice Islands Voyage (1997), In Search of Moby Dick (1999), Seeking Robinson Crusoe (2002), Viking (novel, 2005), Corsair (novel, 2007); *Style*— Tim Severin, Esq

SEVERN, David Benjamin; s of Benjamin Henry Severn (d 1976), and Winifred, *née* Jackson (d 1985); *b* 17 June 1948; *Educ* Open Univ (BA); *m* 1 (m dis 1979), Clare Olivia Ann, *née* Grafe; m 2, Christine Mary, *née* O'Connor; *Career* formerly with: Barclays Bank, DHSS, Building Societies Cmmn, SIB, PIA; currently head of retail investments policy FSA; FRSA; *Recreations* horse racing; *Style*— David Severn, Esq; ✉ The Financial Services Authority, 25 The North Colonnade, Canary Wharf, London E14 5HS (tel 020 7066 5438, fax 020 7066 9717)

SEVERN, Prof Roy Thomas; CBE (1992); s of Ernest Severn (d 1985), of Great Yarmouth, Norfolk, and Muriel Breeta, *née* Woollatt (d 1978); *b* 6 September 1929; *Educ* Deacon's Sch Peterborough, Great Yarmouth GS, Imperial Coll London (BSc, PhD, DSc); *m* 12 Sept 1957, Hilary Irene, da of Harold Batty Saxton, of Douglas, IOM; 2 da (Fiona Rae b 1960, Elizabeth Louise b 1962); *Career* 2 Lt RE (Survey) 1954–56; lectr Imperial Coll London 1952–54; Univ of Bristol: lectr 1956–65, reader 1965–68, prof 1968–95, pro-vice-chllr 1981–84, currently sr research fell and prof emeritus; dir Earthquake Engrg Research Centre; memb: UGC Tech Sub-Ctee 1982–89, Engrg Bd SERC 1986–90; pres ICE 1990–91; FICE, FREng 1982; *Books* Advances in Structural Engineering (1982); *Recreations* sailing, gardening, bee-keeping; *Style*— Prof Roy Severn, CBE, FREng; ✉ Department of Civil Engineering, University of Bristol, Bristol BS8 1TR (tel 0117 928 9769, fax 0117 928 7783)

SEVILLE, Prof Jonathan Peter Kyle; *b* 5 February 1956; *Educ* Gonville & Caius Coll Cambridge (entrance scholar, MA, MEng), Univ of Surrey (PhD); *m* 1994, Elizabeth Jane, *née* Pope; 2 da (Rosie Elizabeth b 1989, Alice Minnie Judith b 1993); *Career* chemical engr Res Div Courtaulds Ltd 1979–81; sr lectr Univ of Surrey 1991–94 (lectr 1984–91); Univ of Birmingham: prof of chemical engrg 1994–, head Dept of Chemical Engrg 1998–;

visiting prof Univ of Br Columbia 1989–90, visiting prof Tech Univ of Denmark Copenhagen 1997–99, hon prof S China Univ of Technol Guangzhou 1999–; external examiner Universiti Putra Malaysia (UPM) 1999–2001; co-fndr dir Particle Consits Ltd; numerous consultancies incl conslt on particle technol Unilever Res 1985–; ed-in-chief Powder Technology 1995–; IChemE: memb Ctee Particle Technol Subject Gp 1985– (sec 1991–95, chm 1995–97), memb Pubns Ctee 1986–88, memb Product-Process Working Pty 1998–2000, memb Cncl 2003–; memb: Ctee Particle Characterisation Gp RSC 1984–88, Working Pty on Single Particle Light Interaction BSI 1985–86, Particulate and Coal Technol Sub-Ctee SERC 1988–91, Cncl Filtration Soc 1992–94 (memb Editorial Advsy Ctee Filtration and Separation 1992–94), Coll EPSRC 1994–, Steering Gp Particle Technol UK Forum 1998– (fndr memb), Exec Ctee Standing Conf of Profs and Heads of Dept of Chemical Engrg 1999–; UK rep Agglomeration Working Pty Euro Fedn of Chemical Engrg 1994–2006; CEng, FIChemE 1997, FREng 2004; *Books* Gas Cleaning at High Temperatures (jt ed, 1993), Processing of Particulate Solids (jtly, 1997), Gas Cleaning in Demanding Applications (ed, 1997), Granulation (jt ed, 2007); author of numerous articles in learned jls; *Recreations* theatre; *Style*— Prof Jonathan Seville; ✉ Department of Chemical Engineering, University of Birmingham, Edgbaston, Birmingham B15 2TT (tel 0121 414 5322, e-mail j.p.k.seville@bham.ac.uk)

SEVITT, Dr Michael Andrew; s of Simon Sevitt (d 1988), of Birmingham, and Betty, *née* Woolf (d 2006); *b* 13 October 1944; *Educ* King Edward's Sch Birmingham, King's Coll Cambridge, UCH Med Sch London; *m* 12 Sept 1970, Dr Jennifer Margaret Duckham, da of William John Duckham, of London, and Peggy Duckham (d 2002); 1 s (Timothy b 1974), 1 da (Deborah b 1976); *Career* lectr in psychiatry Univ of Southampton 1974–76, conslt in child and adolescent psychiatry 1978–; memb UK Cncl for Psychotherapy; MRCP 1971, MRCPsych 1974, MInstGPAnal 1979; *Recreations* theatre, singing, dancing, gardening, travelling; *Style*— Dr Michael Sevitt; ✉ 7 Upper Park Road, Kingston upon Thames, Surrey KT2 5LB (tel 020 8546 4173, fax 020 8546 8825, e-mail mike@sevduck.fsnet.co.uk)

SEWARD, Desmond; s of W E L Seward, MC (d 1975), and Eileen Bennett (d 2002); *b* 22 May 1935, Paris; *Educ* Ampleforth, St Catharine's Coll Cambridge (BA); *Career* author; Knight SMOM 1978, Knight Constantinian St George (Parma) 2001; *Books* The First Bourbon (1971), The Monks of War (1972, new edn 2000, Spanish trans 2004), Prince of the Renaissance (1973), The Bourbon Kings of France (1976), Eleanor of Aquitaine (1978), The Hundred Years War (1978, new edn 1996), Monks and Wine (1979, French trans 1982), Marie Antoinette (1981), Richard III (1983, new edn 1998), Naples (1984), Italy's Knights of St George (1986), Napoleon's Family (1986), Henry V (1987), Napoleon and Hitler (1988, Russian translation 1996), Byzantium (with Susan Mountgarret, 1988), Metternich (1991, German translation 1993), Brooks's: a social history (jt ed with Philip Ziegler, 1991), The Dancing Sun (1993); Sussex (1995), The Wars of the Roses (1995), Caravaggio (1998, Japanese translation 2000), Eugènie (2004), Savonarola (2006); *Recreations* walking, France, Italy; *Clubs* Brooks's, Pratt's, Puffins (Edinburgh); *Style*— Desmond Seward, Esq; ✉ c/o Marsh Agency, 11–12 Dover Street, London W1S 4LJ

SEWARD, Dame Margaret Helen Elizabeth; DBE (1999, CBE 1994); da of Frederick Oldershaw, and Gwen, *née* Rappaporte; *b* 5 August 1935; *Educ* Latymer Sch London, London Hosp Dental Sch (BDS, FDS RCS, MCCD, MDS); *m* 5 May 1962, Prof Gordon Robert Seward, CBE; 1 da (Pamela Elizabeth b 31 May 1964), 1 s (Colin Robert b 9 Sept 1966); *Career* registrar Oral Surgery Dept and dental offr to the Nursing Staff London Hosp Whitechapel 1960–62 (resident dental house surgn 1959–60), sr hosp dental offr Highlands Gen Hosp London 1962–64, hon clinical asst Dental Health Study Unit London Hosp Med Coll 1967–75; locum conslt: Highlands Gen Hosp London 1969–70, N Middx Hosp London 1970; chief dental offr Dept of Health 2000–02; pt/t sch/community dental offr Cheshunt 1970–75, pt/t sr research fell Br Postgrad Med Fndn 1975–77, Cncl of Europe travelling fell The Netherlands 1978, ed Br Dental Jl 1979–92 (ed designate 1978–79); pres BDA 1993–94 (pres designate 1992), pres GDC 1994–99 (memb 1976–); ind dir Quality Assurance Agency in HE 1997–2000; vice-chm Standing Dental Advsy Ctee 1990–94 (memb 1984–94), vice-dean Bd of Faculty RCS 1990–91 (memb 1980–88), pres Section of Odontology RSM 1991–92; hon pres Women in Dentistry 1988–92; ed Int Dental Jl (Fédération Dentaire Internationale) 1990–2000; memb Advsy Bd DENPLAN 1999–2000 and 2002–; tstee EFFORT 1999–2000; memb: Br Paedodontic Soc 1969 (nat sec 1975–78), Br Assoc of Oral and Maxillofacial Surgns 1965, Br Assoc for the Study of Community Dentistry 1974 (fndr memb), Br Dental Eds Forum 1980 (chm 1983–85), Med Protection Soc - Dental Protection 2003–; hon memb Br Orthodontic Soc 1998; chm of govrs The Latymer Sch London 1983–94; author of various book chapters and of numerous papers in learned jls; hon memb American Dental Assoc 1992, fell American Coll of Dentists New Orleans 1994, hon fell Acad of Dentistry Int Vancouver 1994, hon fell Queen Mary & Westfield Coll London 1997–98; Hon DDSc Univ of Newcastle upon Tyne 1995, Hon DDS Univ of Birmingham 1995, Hon DSc Univ of Sheffield 2002, Hon DSc Univ of Portsmouth 2005; Hon FDSRCSE 1995, Hon FDSRCPS 1998, Hon FRCA 2001, Hon FGDP 2001; *Video* Nothing but the Tooth (teething disturbances and treatment); *Recreations* walking, entertaining at home, United Reform Church (sec Richmond Hill St Andrews Bournemouth); *Clubs* Lansdowne, RSM; *Style*— Dame Margaret Seward, DBE; ✉ 1 Wimpole Street, London W1M 8AL (e-mail gordon.seward@btinternet.com)

SEWEL, Baron (Life Peer UK 1996), of Gilcomstoun in the District of the City of Aberdeen; John Buttifant Sewel; CBE (1984); *b* 1946; *Educ* Hanson Boys' GS Bradford, Univ of Durham, Univ Coll Swansea, Univ of Aberdeen; *Children* 1 s, 1 da; *Career* Univ of Aberdeen 1969–97: successively research fell, lectr, sr lectr, prof, dean Faculty of Economic and Social Scis 1989–94, vice-princ and dean Faculty of Social Scis and Law 1995–97, prof 1999–, vice-princ 1999–2001, sr vice-princ 2001–; oppn spokesman on Scotland House of Lords 1996–97, Parly under sec of state Scottish Office (with responsibility for agric, environment, fisheries and for Forestry Cmmn) 1997–99; ldr Aberdeen City Cncl 1977–80 (cncllr 1974–84); pres Convention for Scottish Local Authorities 1982–84; memb: Accounts Cmmn for Scotland 1987–96, Scottish Constitutional Cmmn 1994–95; *Style*— The Lord Sewel, CBE; ✉ House of Lords, London SW1A 0PW

SEWELL, Brian; *Career* art critic Evening Standard; British Press Awards: Critic of the Year 1988, Arts Journalist of the Year 1994; Hawthornden Prize for Art Criticism 1995, Foreign Press Award (Arts) 2000; *Books* South from Ephesus (1988), The Reviews that caused the Rumpus (1994), An Alphabet of Villains (1995); *Style*— Brian Sewell, Esq; ✉ The Evening Standard, Northcliffe House, 2 Derry Street, Kensington, London W8 5EE (tel 020 7938 6000, fax 020 7937 2648)

SEWELL, Prof Herb; *Educ* Univ of Birmingham (BDS, MSc, PhD), Univ of Leicester (MB ChB); *Career* academic appts Univ of Glasgow and Univ of Aberdeen, prof of immunology Univ of Nottingham 1990– (head Div of Immunology until 2002), currently pro-vice-chllr (research) Univ of Nottingham; chair: Jt Ctee on Immunology and Allergy RCP and RCPath 1994–98, Special Advsy Ctee on Immunology RCPath; memb: UK Advsy Gp on Quarantine 1998, Advsy Cncl on Novel Foods 1998–2001, Cncl MRC 2004–, Nuffield Cncl on Bioethics; UK rep WHO Consultation on Xenotransplantation, cmmr UK Meds Cmmn; Hon DDS Univ of Birmingham 2001, Hon DSc Univ of the WI 2003; FRCP, FRCPath, FMedSci; *Books* The Immunological Basis of Surgical Science and Practice (ed with Oleg Eremin, 1992); *Style*— Prof Herb Sewell; ✉ Medical School, Queen's Medical Centre, Nottingham NG7 2UH

SEWELL, Prof John Isaac; s of Harry Sewell (d 1975), of Kirkby Stephen, Cumbria, and Dorothy, *née* Brunskill (d 1977); *b* 13 May 1942; *Educ* Kirkby Stephen GS, Univ of Durham (BSc, DSc), Univ of Newcastle upon Tyne (PhD); *m* 6 May 1989, Ruth Alexandra, da of Walter Baxter (d 1986), of Edinburgh; *Career* Univ of Hull: lectr 1968–76, sr lectr 1976–84, reader in integrated electronic systems 1984–85; Univ of Glasgow: prof of electronic systems 1985–2005 (emeritus prof 2005–), dean of engrg 1990–93, memb Univ Ct 2000–04; visiting research prof Univ of Toronto 1995; winner IEE J J Thomson Paper Premium 1992 (jtly); FIEE 1986, FIEEE 1992; *Recreations* climbing, swimming; *Style*— Prof John Sewell; ✉ 16 Paterson Place Bearsden, Glasgow G61 4RU (tel 0141 586 5336); Department of Electronics and Electrical Engineering, University of Glasgow, Glasgow G12 8LT (tel 0141 330 4253, fax 0141 330 4907, e-mail sewell@elec.gla.ac.uk, website www.elec.gla.ac.uk)

SEWELL, Rufus Frederick; *b* 29 October 1967; *m* 1999, Yasmin Abdullah; *Career* actor; *Theatre* credits incl: Royal Hunt of the Sun, Comedians (both Compass Theatre Co), The Lost Domain (Watermill Theatre Newbury), Peter and the Captain (BAC), Pride and Prejudice (Royal Exchange Manchester), The Government Inspector, The Seagull, As you Like It (all Crucible Sheffield), Making it Better (Hampstead and Criterion), Arcadia (RNT), Translations (Plymouth Theatre NY), Rat in the Skull (Duke of Yorks), Macbeth (Queen's Theatre), Luther (NT), Rock'N'Roll (Royal Court and Duke of York) 2006 (Best Actor Critics Circle Awards 2006); *Television* credits incl: The Last Romantics (BBC), Gone to Seed (Central), Middlemarch (BBC), Dirty Something (Skreba), Citizen Locke, Cold Comfort Farm (Thames), Henry IV (BBC), Arabian Nights, Helen of Troy, Charles II: The Power and the Passion; *Films* credits incl: Twenty-One, Dirty Weekend, A Man of No Importance, Carrington, Victory, Hamlet, The Woodlanders, The Honest Courtesan, Martha - Meet Frank, Daniel & Laurence, In a Savage Land, Bless the Child, A Knight's Tale, Extreme Ops, Tristan & Isolde; *Style*— Rufus Sewell, Esq; ✉ c/o Julian Belfrage Associates, 46 Albemarle Street, London W1S 4DF (tel 020 7491 4400, fax 020 7493 5460)

SEYDOU, HE Adamou; *Career* diplomat; ambass to the Ct of St James's 2003–; *Style*— HE Mr Adamou Seydou; ✉ Embassy of the Republic of Niger, 154 rue de Longchamp, 75116 Paris, France

SEYFRIED, David John; *see:* Herbert, 19 Baron

SEYMOUR, Anya; *see:* Hindmarch, Anya

SEYMOUR, David; CB (2005); s of Graham Seymour, of Sanderstead, Surrey, and Beatrice (Betty), *née* Watson (d 1992); *b* 24 January 1951; *Educ* Trinity Sch Croydon, The Queen's Coll Oxford (open exhibitioner, BA), Fitzwilliam Coll Cambridge (LLB); *m* 1972, Elisabeth, da of Ronald and Muriel Huitson; 1 s (Nicholas b 16 Feb 1977), 2 da (Rachel b 10 June 1979, Charlotte b 21 Dec 1981); *Career* civil servant; law clerk Rosenfeld Meyer & Susman (attorneys) Beverly Hills Calif 1972–73; called to the Bar: Gray's Inn 1975 (Holt scholar, bencher 2001), NI 1997; Home Office: joined as legal asst 1976, princ asst legal advsr 1994–96, dep legal advsr 1996–97, legal advsr 2000–; legal sec to the Law Offrs 1997–2000; memb NI Criminal Justice Review 1998–2000; visiting lectr Sch of Law Univ of Connecticut 1986; *Recreations* hockey, squash, walking; *Clubs* MCC; *Style*— David Seymour, Esq, CB; ✉ Home Office, 2 Marsham Street, London SW1P 4DF

SEYMOUR, Jane; da of late John Frankenberg, of Hillingdon, Middx, and Mieke, *née* van Tricht; *b* 15 February 1951; *Educ* Wimbledon HS, Arts Educnl Tst; *m* 1, 1971 (m dis), Michael John Attenborough, *qv*; m 2, 1977 (m dis), Geoffrey Planer; m 3, 1981, David Flynn, s of Lloyd Flynn, of Santa Barbara, California; 1 da (Katherine Jane b 1982), 1 s (Sean Michael b 1985); m 4, 1993, James Keach; 2 s (John Stacy, Kristopher Steven (twins) b 1995); *Career* actress; int ambassador Childhelp USA, ambassador UNICEF nat chm Cityhearts, active involvement in CLIC UK, hon chm RP Fndn USA (fighting blindness), hon citizen Illinois USA 1977; *Theatre* incl: Amadeus (Broadway) 1981, Not Now Darling (Canterbury Repertory), Ophelia in Hamlet (Harrogate Repertory), Lady Macbeth in Macbeth, Nora in A Dolls House; *Television* incl: The Onedin Line 1973, Strauss Family 1973, Captains and Kings 1976 (Emmy nomination), Seventh Avenue 1977, Awakening Land 1978, Battlestar Galactica 1978, Dallas Cowboy Cheerleaders 1979, East of Eden 1981 (Golden Globe Best Actress), The Scarlet Pimpernel 1982, The Haunting Passion 1983, The Phantom of the Opera 1983, The Sun Also Rises 1984, Dark Mirror 1984, The Leather Funnel 1984, Jamaica Inn 1985, The Hanged Man 1985, Obsessed with a Married Man 1985, The Woman He Loved (Golden Globe nomination) 1988, Onassis (Emmy Award) 1988, War and Remembrance (Emmy nomination) 1989, Jack the Ripper 1989, Angel of Death, Matters of the Heart, Are You Lonesome Tonight?; most recently Dr Quinn - Medicine Woman (160 episodes, Golden Globe winner), Sunstroke, Praying Mantis, A Passion for Justice - The Hazel Brannon -Smith Story, The Absolute Truth, A Marriage of Convenience, A Memory of the Heart, Murder in the Mirror, Enslavement - The True Story of Fanny Kemble, Blackout, Yesterday's Children; *Films* incl: Oh, What a Lovely War 1969, Sinbad and the Eye of the Tiger 1972, Young Winston 1973, Live and Let Die 1973, Four Feathers, Somewhere in Time 1980, Oh Heavenly Dog 1980, Lassiter 1984, Head Office 1986, The Tunnel 1987, Keys to Freedom 1989, Le Revolution Français, Swiss Family Robinson 1997, Dr Quinn the Movie 1999; *Books* Jane Seymour's Guide to Romantic Living (1987); This One and That One series: Yum (jtly, 1998), Splat (jtly, 1998), Boing (jtly, 1999), Eat (jtly, 1999), Me & Me (jtly, 1999), Play (jtly, 1999), Talk (jtly, 1999); *Style*— Miss Jane Seymour

SEYMOUR, Miranda; da of George Fitzroy Seymour, JP, DL (d 1994), of Thrumpton Hall, Notts, and Hon Rosemary Nest Scott Ellis, da of 8 Baron Howard de Walden; *b* 8 August 1948; *Educ* private sch, Bedford Coll London (BA); *m* 1, 1972 (m dis 1981), Andrew Sinclair; 1 s (Merlin b 1973); m 2, 1989 (m dis 2005), Anthony Gottlieb; *Career* writer; visiting prof Nottingham Trent Univ 1996; FRSL 1996, FRSA; *Books* for children: Mumtaz the Magical Cat (1984), The Vampire of Verdonia (1986), Caspar and the Secret Kingdom (1986), Pierre and the Pamplemousse (1990); The Madonna of the Island - Tales of Corfu (short stories, 1980); historical novels: The Stones of Maggiare (1974), Count Manfred (1976), Daughter of Darkness - Lucrezia Borgia (1977), The Goddess (1978), Medea (1981); modern novels: Carrying On (1984), The Reluctant Devil (1990), The Telling (1997, US edn The Summer of 39, 1999); other writing: A Ring of Conspirators - Henry James and his Literary Circle (biography, 1989, reissued 2004) Ottoline Morrell: A Life on the Grand Scale (1992); Robert Graves: Life on the Edge (1995, reissued 2003), Mary Shelley: a Biography (2000), A Brief History of Thyme and Other Herbs (2002), The Bugatti Queen (2004), In My Father's House: Elegy for an Obsessive Love (memoir, 2007); *Style*— Ms Miranda Seymour, FRSL, FRSA; ✉ c/o David Higham Literary Agency, 5–8 Lower John Street, London W1 (tel 020 7437 7888, fax 020 7437 1072)

SEYMOUR, Prof Philip Herschel Kean; s of William Kean Seymour (d 1975), of Alresford, Hants, and Rosalind Herschel, *née* Wade, OBE (d 1989); *b* 9 March 1938; *Educ* Kelly Coll Tavistock, Univ of Oxford (BA), Univ of St Andrews (MEd), Univ of Dundee (PhD); *m* 26 Jan 1962, Margaret Jean Dyson (Jane), da of Prof William Ian Clinch Morris, of Springfield, Fife; 2 s (Patrick b 1962, Dominic b 1975), 2 da (Emma b 1964, Mary Marcella b 1978); *Career* Nat Serv RAEC 1957–59; Univ of Dundee: lectr and sr lectr 1966–82, reader 1982–88, prof 1988–2003, emeritus prof 2003–; chm Scot Dyslexia Assoc 1987; memb Br Psychological Soc; *Books* Human Visual Cognition (1979), Cognitive Analysis of Dyslexia (1986); *Recreations* gardening, fishing; *Style*— Prof Philip Seymour; ✉ Edenfield House, Springfield, by Cupar, Fife (tel 01334 653177); Department of Psychology, The University, Dundee DD1 4HN (tel 01382 344614, fax 01382 229993, e-mail p.h.k.seymour@dundee.ac.uk)

SEYMOUR, Prof Richard; s of Bertram Seymour, of Scarborough, N Yorks, and Annie Irenie, *née* Sherwood; *b* 1 May 1953; *Educ* Scarborough HS for Boys, Royal Coll of Art (MA(RCA)); *m* April 1980, Anne Margaret, da of Steven Hart; 1 da (Peggy Teresa b 12 June 1982), 1 s (Arthur William b 25 Sept 1985); *Career* product designer; freelance art dir within various London advtg agencies incl JWT, Holmes Knight Ritchie and Michael Bungey DFS 1977–79, creative dir Blazelynn Advertising London 1979–82 (various D&AD awards), freelance designer working specifically on advtg and new product devpt projects 1982–83, fndr designer Seymour-Furst specialising in film prodn design 1983–84, fndr (with Dick Powell, *qv*) Seymour-Powell 1984– (clients incl Yamaha, Tefal, Casio, Nokia, Ford and Aqualisa); external assessor BA Product Design course Central St Martin's Coll of Art and Design 1990– (memb Jt Course Advy Ctee Product Design Dept 1989–90), external examiner RCA Transportation Design course 1993–, visiting prof of product and transportation design RCA 1995–; inaugural product design judge BBC Design Awards 1987, memb Panel of Judges D&AD Product Design Section 1987, main speaker Blueprint Moving Up seminars 1988; memb: Exec Ctee Design Business Gp 1988–, Int Advsy Ctee Design Museum 1989–, Steering Ctee Lead Body for Design 1991–, Bd of Tstees Design Museum London 1994–, Exec Ctee D&AD 1997– (pres 1999); Hon Dr Coll for Creative Studies Michigan; FRSA 1993, FCSD 1993; regular contrib British design press, *Television* contrib BBC Design Classics, Designs on Britain and several children's progs featuring design and future thinking 1986, subject of Channel 4 Designs on Your... series 1998, Better By Design (six part series, Channel 4) 2000, Innovation Nation (BBC); *Awards* Best Overall Design and Product Design (for Norton F1 motorcycle) Design Week Awards 1990, D&AD Silver Award (for Technophone Cellular Telephone) 1991, ID Award and D&AD Silver Award (for MuZ Skorpion motorcycle) 1993, winner Product Design category BBC Design Awards 1994, CSD Minerva Award (for MuZ Skorpian) 1994, ID Award (for Sun Voyager) 1994, D&AD President's Award (for outstanding contribution to design) 1995, DBA Design Effectiveness Award 1995, 2002 and 2003, Special Commendation Prince Philip Designers Prize 1997, winner Janus (France) 1998, shortlisted Prince Philip Designers Prize 2003, Gerald Frewer Meml Trophy Inst of Engrg Designers 2003, Corp Film Samsung European Premium Design 2003, Star Pacic Award 2003; *Books* The Mirrorstone (conceived and designed 1985, words by Michael Palin, Smarties Award for Innovation in Book Design 1985, Hatchard's Top Ten Authors Award 1985); *Recreations* playing the cello, piano and organ, Early English music, motorcycles; *Style*— Prof Richard Seymour; ✉ Seymour Powell, 327 Lillie Road, London SW6 7NR (tel 020 7381 6433, fax 020 7381 9081, e-mail design@seymourpowell.com, website www.seymourpowell.com)

SEYMOUR, His Hon Judge Richard William; s of late Albert Percy Seymour, of Bude, Cornwall, and Vera Maud, *née* Greenfield; *b* 4 May 1950; *Educ* Brentwood Sch, Royal Belfast Academical Instn, Christ's Coll Cambridge (scholar, De Hart prize, coll prize, MA); *m* 14 Aug 1971, Clare Veronica, da of Stanley Victor Peskett; 1 da (Victoria Jane Rebecca b 29 Aug 1979), 1 s (Edward Patrick James b 4 Nov 1981); *Career* called to the Bar Gray's Inn 1972 (Holker jr exhbn and sr scholarship); pupil barrister 5 Essex Court Temple 1972–73, chambers of R I Threlfall QC 1973, in practice 1973–2000, QC 1991, recorder of the Crown Court 1995–2000 (asst recorder 1991–95), judge of the Technol and Construction Court 2000–05, sr circuit judge (SE Circuit) 2000–, assigned to High Court of Justice (Queen's Bench Div) 2005–; pres Mental Health Review Tbnl 2000; *Books* The Quantum of Damages (jt ed, 1975, 4 edn), Practice and Procedure for the Quantity Surveyor (contrib 8 edn, 1980), The Architect in Practice (contrib 6 edn, 1981), Courtroom Skills for Social Workers (with Clare Seymour, 2007); *Recreations* archaeology, walking, foreign travel; *Style*— His Hon Judge Seymour; ✉ Royal Courts of Justice, Strand, London WC2A 2LL

SEYMOUR, Timothy Massingham (Tim); s of William George Massingham Seymour, and Georgina Edmée, *née* Rouillard; *b* 29 June 1948; *Educ* Michaelhouse, Univ of Natal (BSc), Oriel Coll Oxford (Rhodes scholar, MA, Rugby blue); *Career* articled clerk Price Waterhouse 1974–77, corp fin exec S G Warburg & Co Ltd 1977–80, dir County Bank Ltd 1983–87 (corp fin exec 1980–82), fndr dir Gilbert Eliott Corporate Finance Ltd 1987–91, corp fin dir and dept head Rea Brothers Limited 1991–2001, fndr dir Stafford Corporate Consulting Ltd 2001–; FCA (ACA 1977); *Style*— Tim Seymour, Esq; ✉ Stafford Corporate Consulting, 19 Old Queen Street, London SW1H 9JA (tel 020 7222 2828)

SHACKLE, Prof Christopher; s of Francis Mark Shackle (d 1943), and Diana Margaret, *née* Harrington (d 1990); *b* 4 March 1942; *Educ* Haileybury, Merton Coll Oxford (BA), St Antony's Coll Oxford (Dip Social Anthropology, BLitt), Univ of London (PhD); *m* 1 (m dis), Emma Margaret, *née* Richmond; 2 da (Mary b 15 Feb 1967, Zoe b 13 Sept 1974), 1 s (Guy b 16 April 1969); m 2, Shahrukh, *née* Husain; 1 s (Adam b 24 May 1982), 1 da (Samira b 16 July 1987); *Career* SOAS Univ of London: fell in Indian Studies 1966, lectr in Urdu and Panjabi 1969–79 reader 1979–85, prof of modern languages of S Asia 1985–, pro-dir for Academic Affrs 1997–2002, actg dir 2001, pro-dir 2002–03; Royal Asiatic Soc Medal 2006; FBA 1990 (memb Cncl 1995–96 and 2000–04); Sitara-i-Imtiaz 2005 (awarded by Pres of Pakistan); *Books* Teach Yourself Punjabi (1972), An Anthology of Classical Urdu Love Lyrics (1972), The Siraiki Language of Central Pakistan (1976), A Guru Nanak Glossary (1981), An Introduction to the Sacred Language of the Sikhs (1983), The Sikhs (1984), Urdu Literature (1985), Ismaili Hymns from South Asia (1992), The Indian Narrative (1992), Qasida Poetry in Islamic Asia and Africa (1996), Hali's Musaddas (1997), Treasury of Indian Love Poetry (1999), Sikh Religion, Culture and Ethnicity (2001), SOAS Since the Sixties (2003), Teachings of the Sikh Gurus (2005), The Art of Spiritual Flight (2006), Stories of Mazhar ul Islam (2006); *Style*— Prof Christopher Shackle, FBA; ✉ Department of South Asia, School of Oriental and African Studies, Thornhaugh Street, Russell Square, London WC1H 0XG (tel 020 7637 2388)

SHACKLETON, Fiona Sara; LVO (2006); da of Jonathan Philip Charkham, CBE (d 2006), of London, and Moira Elizabeth Frances, *née* Salmon; *b* 26 May 1956; *Educ* Benenden, Univ of Exeter (LLB); *m* 26 Sept 1985, Ian Ridgeway, s of Lt-Col Richard John Shackleton, MBE (d 1977); 2 da (Cordelia Molly Louise b 25 May 1988, Lydia Elizabeth Moira b 6 July 1989); *Career* slr; articled clerk Herbert Smith & Co 1978–80, admitted slr 1980; ptnr: Brecher & Co 1981–84 (joined 1980), Farrer & Co 1986–2000 (joined 1984), Payne Hicks Beach 2001–; slr to HRH The Prince of Wales 1996–2005, slr to TRH Princes William and Harry of Wales 1996–; memb: Law Soc, International Acad Matrimonial Lawyers, Slrs' Family Law Assoc; govr Benenden Sch 1985–; *Books* The Divorce Handbook (with Olivia Timbs, 1992); *Recreations* bridge, food, opera and calligraphy; *Style*— Mrs Fiona Shackleton, LVO; ✉ Payne Hicks Beach, 10 New Square, Lincoln's Inn, London WC2A 3QG (tel 020 7465 4300, fax 020 7465 4380)

SHACKLOCK, Timothy Anthony (Tim); s of Anthony Shacklock (d 1976), and Netta Joan, *née* Payne; *b* 12 July 1956, Nottingham; *Educ* Nottingham Boys' HS; *m* (m dis); 3 da (Antonia, Georgina (twins) b 26 Aug 1990, Daniella b 27 Oct 1995); *Career* CA 1980; Spicer & Pegler until 1980, Pannell Kerr Forster 1980–88 (ptnr 1985), dir Kleinwort Benson 1989 (joined 1988), head of corporate finance Dresdner Kleinwort Benson 1996–2001, dep chm Dresdner Kleinwort Wasserstein 2001–02, fndr and ceo Gleacher Shacklock 2003–; FCA; *Recreations* skiing; *Style*— Tim Shacklock, Esq; ✉ Gleacher Shacklock LLP, Cleveland House, 33 King Street, London SW1Y 6RJ (tel 020 7484 1120, fax 020 7484 1160)

SHAFER, Prof Byron Edwin; *b* 8 January 1947; *Educ* Yale Univ (BA), Univ of Calif Berkeley (PhD, Peter B Odegard Prize); *m*; 1 s; *Career* resident scholar Russell Sage Fndn 1977–84, assoc prof of political science Florida State Univ 1984–85, Andrew W Mellon prof of American govt Univ of Oxford 1985–2001, acting warden Nuffield Coll Oxford 2000–01, Glenn B and Cleone Orr Hawkins prof of political science Univ of Wisconsin 2001–; memb Editorial Bd: Jl of Policy History 1993–, Annual Review of Political Science 2003–; author of numerous pubns in learned professional jls; memb: American Political Science Assoc, American Historical Assoc, Political Studies Assoc UK, Br Assoc for American Studies; American Political Science Assoc: E E Schattschneider Award 1980, Franklin L Burdette Pi Sigma Alpha Award 1990, Jack L Walker Award 2000; Hon MA Univ of Oxford 1985; *Style*— Prof Byron Shafer; ✉ Department of Political Science, University of Wisconsin, Madison, WI 53706, USA (tel 00 1 608 263 1909, fax 00 1 608 265 2663, e-mail bshafer@polisci.wisc.edu)

SHAFFER, Sir Peter Levin; kt (2001), CBE (1987); s of Jack Shaffer (d 1987), of London, and Reka, *née* Fredman; *b* 15 May 1926; *Educ* St Paul's, Trinity Coll Cambridge; *Career* playwright; Cameron Mackintosh prof of contemporary drama Univ of Oxford 1994; fndr memb Euro Acad of Yuste 1999; Hamburg Shakespeare Prize 1987, William Inge Award USA 1992; FRSL; *Plays* The Salt Land (1955), Five Finger Exercise (1958, Evening Standard Award 1959), The Private Ear, The Public Eye (1961), The Royal Hunt of the Sun (1964), Black Comedy (1965), White Liars (1966), The Battle of Shrivings (1970), Equus (1973, Antoinette Perry Award NY and NY Critics Award 1975), Amadeus (1979, Best Drama Evening Standard Awards 1980, Antoinette Perry Award NY 1981), Yonadab (1985), Lettice and Lovage (1987, Best Comedy Evening Standard Awards 1988), The Gift of the Gorgon (1992); screenplays: Equus (1977), Amadeus (1984, Academy Award); radio play: Whom Do I Have The Honour of Addressing? (1989, adapted for stage 1996); *Recreations* walking, music, architecture; *Clubs* Garrick, Arts; *Style*— Sir Peter Shaffer, CBE, FRSL; ✉ c/o MacNaughton Lord 2000 Ltd, 19 Margravine Gardens, London W6 8RL (tel 020 8741 0606)

SHAH, Bharat Kumar Hansraj; s of Hansraj D Shah, and Lalitaben H Shah; *b* 20 December 1949, Nairobi, Kenya; *Educ* Univ of Bath (BPharm); *m* 29 July 1974, Jayoti; 2 s (Hatul b 26 Oct 1978, Rajiv b 15 Jan 1985); *Career* Sigma Pharmaceuticals plc: retail pharmacy 1975–1985, wholesale and distribution of pharmaceuticals 1982–, md 1982–; memb: Pharmaceutical Soc of GB, Inst of Pharmaceutical Mgmnt; Ferris Gold Medal in Pharmacy, Glory of India Award, Ernst & Young Entrepreneur of Year (UK central region), GG2 Entrepreneur of the Year; memb: Bal Bhavan gurukul, Shree Digamber Jain Assoc; tstee: Shri Vallabh Nidhi, Sigma Charitable Trust; FRSA, fell Inst of Br Engrs; *Recreations* sports, travelling; *Style*— Bharat Shah, Esq; ✉ Unit 1–7, Colonial Way, PO Box 233, Watford, Hertfordshire WD24 4YR (tel 01923 444999, fax 01923 444998, e-mail bharat@sigpharm.co.uk)

SHAH, Navnit Shankerlal; *b* 9 December 1933; *Educ* Bombay Univ (MB BS), RCP (DLO), RCS (FRCS); *m* Frances, *née* Murphy; *Career* currently: hon conslt surgn Royal Nat Throat Nose and Ear Hosp London, hon conslt otologist Nuffield Hearing and Speech Centre London, former hon sr lectr Inst of Laryngology and Otology, hon prof Portmann Fond Bordeaux France, sr vice-pres Hearing Int; memb Sections of Laryngology and Otology RSM (pres Section of Otology 1990–91), former vice-chm and hon med advsr Cwlth Soc for the Deaf (latterly Sound Seekers); visiting prof in otolaryngology Madidol Univ Bangkok Thailand; formerly: vice-dean and chm Acad Bd Inst of Laryngology and Otology, sr lectr/dep dir Professorial Unit and chm Med Cncl Royal Nat ENT Hosp, pres Indian Med Assoc of GB; memb: Br Assoc of Otolaryngologists, Br Assoc of Audiological Physicians, BMA, Med Soc of London; FRSM; *Recreations* reading, current affairs; *Style*— Navnit Shah, Esq; ✉ 6 Holmdene Avenue, London NW7 2LX (tel 020 8959 3711)

SHAH, Samir; OBE (2000); s of Amrit Shah, of Bombay, India, and Uma, *née* Chaudhary (d 1973); *b* 29 January 1952; *Educ* Latymer Upper Sch, Univ of Hull (BSc), St Catherine's Coll Oxford (DPhil); *m* 18 Dec 1983, Belkis Bhegani, da of Jan-Mohammed Hassam, of Kampala, Uganda; 1 s (Cimran Temur b 19 Oct 1986); *Career* memb Home Office 1978–79; LWT 1979–87: reporter Skin, researcher Weekend World then series prodr Eastern Eye and Credo, The London Programme; BBC: dep ed news and current affrs progs BBC TV 1987–89, ed weekly and special progs BBC News and Current Affrs 1990–93, head of political progs BBC 1994–98; ceo Juniper Communications 1998–; non-exec dir BBC 2007–; chair Runnymede Tst 1999–; tstee V&A 2004–; FRTS; *Style*— Samir Shah, Esq, OBE; ✉ Juniper Communications, 52 Lant Street, London SE1 1RB (tel 020 7407 9292)

SHAKERLEY, Lady Elizabeth Georgiana; *née* Anson; granted style, rank and precedence of an Earl's da 1961; da of Lt-Col Thomas William Arnold, Viscount Anson (d 1958), and HH Princess Anne of Denmark, *née* Anne Bowes-Lyon (d 1980); sis of 5 Earl of Lichfield (d 2005); *b* 7 June 1941, (HM King George VI stood sponsor); *m* 1972, as his 2 wife, Sir Geoffrey Adam Shakerley, 6 Bt, *qv*; 1 da (Fiona Elizabeth Fenella b 1973); *Career* proprietor Party Planners; dir Mosimann's (a members only dining club); chm: Cadogan Co, Rupert Lund Property Development; past pres Action for ME; *Books* Lady Elizabeth Anson's Party Planners Book (1986); *Style*— The Lady Elizabeth Shakerley; ✉ 56 Ladbroke Grove, London W11 2PB (tel 020 7727 7686, fax 020 7727 6001, e-mail lea@party-planners.co.uk and lizashakerley@yahoo.co.uk)

SHAKERLEY, Sir Geoffrey Adam; 6 Bt (UK 1838), of Somerford Park, Cheshire; s of Maj Sir Cyril Holland Shakerley, 5 Bt (d 1970), and Elizabeth Averil, MBE (d 1990), da of late Edward Gwynne Eardley-Wilmot, gggda of Sir John Eardley Eardley-Wilmot, 1 Bt; *b* 9 December 1932; *Educ* Harrow, Trinity Coll Oxford; *m* 1, 1962, Virginia Elizabeth (d 1968), da of W E Maskell; 2 s; m 2, 1972, Lady Elizabeth Shakerley, *qv*; 1 da; *Heir* s, Nicholas Shakerley; *Career* 2 Lt KRRC; md Photographic Records Ltd 1970–; Liveryman Worshipful Co of Skinners; *Books* Henry Moore - Sculptures in Landscape (1978), The English Dog at Home (1986); *Style*— Sir Geoffrey Shakerley, Bt; ✉ Brent House, North Warnborough, Hampshire RG29 1BE

SHAKESPEARE, Nicholas William Richmond; s of John William Richmond Shakespeare, and Lalage Ann, *née* Mais; *b* 3 March 1957; *Educ* The Dragon Sch Oxford, Winchester, Magdalene Coll Cambridge (MA); *Career* asst prodr BBC TV 1980–84, dep arts/literary ed The Times 1985–87; literary ed: London Daily News 1987, Daily Telegraph 1988–91, Sunday Telegraph 1989–91; FRS 1999, FRSL 1999; *Publications* The Men Who Would Be King (1984), Londoners (1986), The Vision of Elena Silves (1989, Somerset Maugham prize, Betty Tst Prize), The High Flyer (1993), The Dancer Upstairs (1995, American Library Assoc Award for Best Novel 1997), Bruce Chatwin (1999); for television: The Waugh Trilogy (BBC), Return to the Sacred Ice (BBC), Iquitos (Channel 4), For the Sake of the Children (Granada, US Christopher Award), In the Footsteps of Bruce Chatwin (BBC); *Recreations* travelling, drawing; *Clubs* Beefsteak, Literary Soc; *Style*— Nicholas Shakespeare, Esq

SHAKESPEARE, Dr (Sir) Thomas William; 3 Bt (UK 1942), of Lakenham, City of Norwich, but does not use the title; er s of Sir William Geoffrey Shakespeare, 2 Bt (d 1996), and Susan Mary, *née* Raffel; *b* 11 May 1966; *Educ* Radley, Pembroke Coll Cambridge (MA), King's Coll Cambridge (MPhil, PhD); *Family* by Lucy Ann Broadhead: 1 da (Ivy Connor Broadhead b 7 June 1988); by Judy Brown: 1 s (Robert Samuel Brown b 19 Nov 1988); m, 12 Oct 2002, Caroline Emily, da of Lloyd Bowditch, of Victoria, Aust; *Heir* bro, James Shakespeare; *Career* lectr in sociology Univ of Sunderland 1993–99, research fell in sociology Univ of Leeds1996–99, dir of outreach Policy Ethics and Life Sciences Research Inst Newcastle 1999–2005 (research fell 2005–07); chair NE Regnl Arts Cncl and memb Arts Cncl England 2004–; *Publications* The Sexual Politics of Disability (1996), The Disability Reader (1998), Exploring Disability (1999), Help (2000), Disability and

Postmodernism (2002), Genetic Politics (2002), Disability Rights and Wrongs (2007); *Style—* Dr Thomas Shakespeare; ✉ 22 Derby Crescent, Hebburn, Tyne & Wear NE31 2TP (e-mail tomshakespeare@blueyonder.co.uk); Department of Social Policy, University of Newcastle upon Tyne NE1 7RU

SHALE, Prof Dennis John; s of Samuel Edward Shale, of Leicester, and Winifred Beatrice, *née* Newstead (d 1986); *b* 19 February 1948; *Educ* Charles Keene Coll, Univ of Newcastle upon Tyne (BSc, MB BS, MD); *m* 1, 23 March 1970 (m dis 1993), Kathleen Patricia, da of Harry Clark, of Great Glen, Leics; 1 da (Victoria b 1975), 1 s (Matthew b 1978); m 2, 1 May 1993, Pamela Joan, da of Charles Lawrence, of Penarth, S Glamorgan; 1 s (George b 1994), 1 da (Rosie b 1996), 1 adopted da (Kate b 1987); *Career* lectr in physiology Univ of Newcastle upon Tyne 1976–78, jr trg posts in med Newcastle upon Tyne and Oxford 1978–81, sr registrar in respiratory med Oxford 1981–84, sr lectr in respiratory med Univ of Nottingham 1985–90, David Davies prof of respiratory and communicable diseases Univ of Wales Coll of Med 1991–; author of chapters in books on respiratory med and original articles in aspects of respiratory med incl shock lung and cystic fibrosis in int jls, contrib editorials and reviews to med jls; assoc ed Thorax 1986; hon regnl advsr to Cystic Fibrosis Tst; memb WHO Advsy Ctee on future mgmnt of cystic fibrosis; memb: Br Thoracic Soc 1983, Med Res Soc 1984, Societas Euro Pneumonology 1985, American Throacic Soc 1989; FRCP 1991 (MRCP 1980); *Recreations* gardening, archaeology, English and American literature, baroque music; *Style—* Prof Dennis Shale; ✉ University of Wales College of Medicine, Section of Respiratory Medicine, Llandough Hospital, Penarth, South Glamorgan CF64 2XX

SHALIT, Jonathan Sigmund; s of David Manuel Shalit, and Sophie Shalit, JP, *née* Gestetner; *b* 17 April 1962; *Educ* City of London Sch; *Career* chm Shalit Global Entertainment + Management 1987–; tstee: Variety Club of GB (also vice-pres), Chicken Shed Theatre Co, Regain; Freeman City of London, Liveryman Worshipful Co of Coachmakers and Harness Makers; MInstD; *Recreations* sailing, squash and triathlon; *Clubs* Annabel's, RAC, Tramp, Queen's; *Style—* Jonathan Shalit, Esq; ✉ 53 Campden Hill Gate, Duchess of Bedford Walk, London W8 7QJ; Shalit Global Entertainment and Management, 7 Moor Street, London W1D 5NB

SHAMTALLY, Bhye Mahmood (Danny); s of Hadjee Abdool Raffick Shamtally, of Mauritius, and Bibi Afroze, *née* Hisaindee; *b* 7 June 1951; *Educ* Mauritius Coll, Bhujoharry Coll, Univ of Durham Business Sch (MBA); *m* 19 Sept 1973, Carmelita Panaligan, da of late Francisco Panaligan; 1 s (Reza b 2 Dec 1976), 1 da (Natasha b 17 Jan 1979); *Career* staff nurse Belmont Hosp 1974–76, offr-in-charge London Borough of Sutton Social Serv 1977–85 (asst offr-in-charge 1976–77), princ ptnr Care Unlimited (formerly Private Nursing Homes) 1983–; dir Solution Avant Ltd 1999–; memb: NSPCC, Nat Tst; gold friend Benjamin Waugh Fndn NSPCC; memb Rotary Club Reigate; fell Durham Univ Soc 1994; RN 1974, FIWO 1985, FRSH 1985, MCMI 1994, FRIPH 1995, MIHE 1998, MInstD; *Recreations* country walks, antiques, collectors' cars, poetry; *Clubs* Royal Over-Seas League; *Style—* Danny Shamtally, Esq; ✉ Care Unlimited, Chaldon Rise Mews, Rockshaw Road, Merstham, Surrey RH1 3DB (tel 01737 645171, fax 01737 642634, e-mail info@careunlimited.co.uk)

SHAND, Charles Stuart; s of Maj C W Shand, OBE, BEM (d 2006), and Sybil, *née* James (d 2005); *b* 10 July 1945; *Educ* Portsmouth, London, Seattle, LA and Boston (courses in engrg, business studies and mktg); *m* 1977, Penelope Sue, da of Sydney John Valentine (d 1969), of Wimbledon, London; 1 s (Charles William Valentine b 1986); *Career* dir Childs Greene Public Relations Ltd 1971–73, md United Kingdom Sales Promotion Ltd 1971–73, jt md CGA Marketing Group Ltd 1971–73, dir/Euro mangr Young & Rubicam Group Ltd 1973–80, dir J Walter Thompson Ltd 1980–81, dir int mktg mangr Cadbury Schweppes plc 1981–84, dir of client servs Minale Tattersfield & Partners 1984–88, dir The Page Factory Ltd 1988–91, dep chm Field Wiley & Company Ltd 1988–91; chm: The Shand Group SC 1992–2003, Studio 36 International 1992–2003, Universal Shand Group Inc 2003–; vice-chm Shand International Management Ltd 1986–; dir: Christian Shand BV 1995–2003, Mission Dynamics Group 1995–2003; involved with major design projects (corp and brand identities, new product devpt, architectural projects, etc); awards incl: 3 Silver Awards D&AD (for Irish Distillers Packaging, Gold Mastercard (NatWest Bank) and BP Int Packaging), 2 Certs of Distinction NY Art Dirs' Club (for Hundhaar Schnapps Packaging and Forte Hotels), Best Literature Award DBA/Mktg Design Effectiveness Awards (for MOMI), Best Brochure Award (for MOMI) and Best Poster Award (for Charlie Chaplin Exhbn, MOMI) NY Festivals; chm SwimStars Fndn 2003–; memb Assoc of Masters in Business Admin, MIAA 1982, MIPR 1984, memb D&AD 1987, FInstD 1989, FRSA 1994; *Recreations* cycling, gymnastics, motoring; *Clubs* Headliners' (Dallas), Socio Merito, Societa del Passatore (Faenza), Millionaires in Motion (San Diego), Velo Club St Raphaël; *Style—* Charles Shand, Esq; ✉ Universal Shand Group Inc, Scottsdale House, 16 Eversley Road, Surbiton, Surrey KT5 8BG (tel 020 8399 8535, fax 020 8287 8096, e-mail swimstars@blueyonder.co.uk)

SHAND, His Hon John Alexander Ogilvie; DL (Staffs 1998); s of Alexander Shand, MBE, QPM (d 1968), of West Bridgford, Notts, and Marguerite Marie, *née* Farcy (d 1994); *b* 6 November 1942; *Educ* Nottingham HS, Queens' Coll Cambridge (MA, LLB, Chancellor's Medal for Law 1965); *m* 1, 18 Dec 1965 (m dis 1988), Patricia Margaret, da of Frederick Toynbee, of Nottingham (d 1958); 2 s (James b 1967, Simon b 1972), 1 da (Juliet b 1969); m 2, 10 Aug 1990, Valerie Jean, da of William Bond, of Lichfield; *Career* called to the Bar Middle Temple 1965; Midland & Oxford circuit 1965–70 and 1973–81, asst lectr fell and tutor Queens' Coll Cambridge 1970–73, recorder 1981–88, circuit judge (Midland & Oxford Circuit) 1988–2006, ret; chm Industrial Tbnls 1981–88; chllr: Dio of Southwell 1981–2005, Dio of Lichfield 1989–2006; *Books* Legal Values in Western Society (co-author, 1974); *Style—* His Hon John Shand, DL; ✉ Stafford Courts Group Manager, Stafford Combined Court Centre, Victoria Square, Stafford ST16 2SE (tel 01785 610801)

SHAND, Terence Richard; s of Terence James Shand, and Dorothy Joyce, *née* Shackell; *b* 27 October 1954; *Educ* Borehamwood GS; *m* 1 (m dis 1985) Maureen; 1 s (Elliot James b 1977); m 2 (m dis 1995), Arja, da of Paavo Saren; 1 s (Terence Elias b 1984), 2 da (Natalia Sirka b 1988, Eleanor Veronica Grace b 2000); *Career* dir Stage One Records Ltd 1978–83; chm: Castle Communications plc 1983–97, Eagle Rock Entertainment Ltd 1997–; *Recreations* tennis, shooting, music, reading; *Clubs* Carlton; *Style—* Terence Shand, Esq; ✉ Eagle Rock Entertainment Ltd, Eagle House, 22 Armoury Way, London SW18 1EZ (tel 020 8870 5670)

SHAND, William Stewart; s of William Paterson Shand (d 1990), of Derby, and Annabella Kirkland Stewart, *née* Waddell (d 1952); *b* 12 October 1936; *Educ* Repton, St John's Coll Cambridge (MA, MB BChir, MD); *m* 26 Aug 1972, (Anne) Caroline Dashwood (d 2005), da of late Patrice Edouard Charvet, of Cheltenham, Glos; 2 s (Robert b 1974, James b 1976), 2 step da (Claire b 1964, Sophie b 1966), 1 step s (Tom b 1967); *Career* hon consulting surgn Bart's and the Royal London Hosps 1997– (conslt surgn Bart's 1973–96); hon conslt surgn St Mark's Hosp for Diseases of the Colon and Rectum 1985–95; govr Sutton's Hosp in Charterhouse 1989–; Penrose-May teacher RCS (Penrose-May tutor 1980–85, memb Ct of Examiners RCS 1985–91); licensed reader C of E; memb Ct of Assts: Worshipful Soc of Apothecaries 1974 (Master 2004–05), Worshipful Co of Barbers 1981 (Master 2001–02); fell: Assoc of Surgns of GB and I, Hunterian Soc, Harveian Soc of London, Travelling Surgical Soc (pres 1994–97); FRCS 1969, FRCSEd 1970; *Books* The Art of Dying (jtly, 1989); *Recreations* stained glass window making, painting, fishing, walking; *Style—* William Shand, Esq; ✉ Dan-y-Castell, Castle Road, Crickhowell, Powys NP8 1AP (tel 01873 810452)

SHANES, Eric; s of Mark Shanes (d 1993), of London, and Dinah, *née* Cohen (d 1977); *b* 21 October 1944; *Educ* Whittingehame Coll Brighton, Regent Street Poly Sch of Art, Chelsea Sch of Art (DipAD); *m* Jacky, da of Kenneth Darville (d 1969), of Windsor; 1 da (Anna b 1976), 1 s (Mark b 1979); *Career* author, journalist and artist; classical music critic Daily Mail 1988–89, numerous contribs to Burlington Magazine, Apollo, and Modern Painters jls; fndr ed: Turner Studies, Art Book Review; lectr: Chelsea Sch of Art (pt/t) 1966–88, Dept of Art History Univ of Cambridge, Royal Coll of Music; lecture tours: N America 1982, 1983, 1984, 1986 and 2002, Switzerland 1987, Malaysia 1988; Br Cncl Cultural Exchange award as official visitor: Romania 1982, Czechoslovakia 1984; Yorkshire Post Art Book award 1979; vice-pres Turner Soc 1994– (chm 1988–94 and 2000–); awarded Nuclear Electric scholarship 1995 (to research and exhibit Turner's Colour-Beginnings at Tate Gallery 1997); fndr chm Save Acton Swimming Baths campaign; *Exhibitions* numerous studio shows of paintings and prints; Splinter Gallery London 1992, Wall-to-Wall Gallery London 2004; guest exhibition curator: J M W Turner - the Foundations of Genius (Taft Museum Cincinnati) 1986, Masterpieces of English Watercolour from the Hickman Bacon Collection and the Fitzwilliam Museum Cambridge (touring Japan) 1990–91, Turner's Watercolour Explorations (Tate Gallery) 1997, Turner in 1066 Country (Hastings Art Gallery) 1998, J M W Turner: The Great Watercolours (Royal Acad of Arts London) 2000–01, The Golden Age of Watercolours: The Hickman Bacon Collection (Dulwich Picture Gallery) 2001–02, Yale Center for British Art 2002, Winslow Homer, Poet of the Sea (Dulwich Picture Gallery) 2006; *Books* Turner's Picturesque Views in England and Wales (1979), Turner's Rivers, Harbours and Coasts (1981), The Genius of the Royal Academy (1981), Hockney Posters (1987), Constantin Brancusi (1989), Turner's England (1990), Turner: The Masterworks (1990), Turner's Human Landscape (1990), Dali: The Masterworks (1990), Warhol: The Masterworks (1991), Jack Beal: American Realist (1992), Turner: The Master Painter (1992), Warhol: The Master Painter (1993), Dali: The Master Painter (1994), Impressionist London (1994), Jake's Legacy: A History of Whittingehame College (2000), Turner: The Life and Masterworks (2004), Warhol: The Life and Masterworks (2004), The Pop Art Tradition (2007); photographic essay in Gustav Mahler: Songs and Symphonies of Death (Donald Mitchell, 1985); *Recreations* music appreciation, swimming; *Style—* Eric Shanes, Esq; ✉ 7 Cumberland Road, Acton, London W3 6EX (tel 020 8992 7985, fax 020 8993 3146, e-mail ericshanes@aol.com, website www.ericshanes.com)

SHANIN, Prof Teodor; OBE (2002); s of Meir Zajdsznur (d 1954), and Rebeka, *née* Jaszunski (d 1988); *b* 29 October 1930; *Educ* Univ of Jerusalem (BA), Univ of Birmingham (PhD), Univ of Manchester (MSc); *m* 1 (m dis 1962), Neomi; m 2, 1970, Prof Shulamith Ramon; 2 da (Anna b 1970, Aelita b 1976); *Career* 6 Regt of Commando (Palmakh) Israeli Army 1948–49; probation offr Miny of Welfare (former social worker Youth Care Servs) Tel Aviv 1952–56, dir Rehabilitation Centre (former rehabilitation offr for handicapped) Miny of Labour 1956–63, lectr in sociology Univ of Sheffield 1965–70 (seconded to Centre for Russian and E Euro Studies Univ of Birmingham 1968–70), assoc prof Haifa Univ Israel 1971–73 (sr lectr 1970–71), visiting sr fell St Antony's Coll Oxford 1973–74, prof of sociology Univ of Manchester 1974– (head of dept 1976–81); commoner Trinity Coll Cambridge 1990–91, co-pres InterCentre Moscow 1993–, rector Moscow Sch of Social and Economic Scis; fell: Wilson Center Washington DC 1987, Russian Acad of Agric Scis; memb Br Sociological Assoc; *Books* Peasants and Peasant Societies (1971), The Awkward Class (1972), Russia as a 'Developing Society' (1985), Revolution as a Moment of Truth (1986), Defining Peasants (1990); *Recreations* fell walking, theatre; *Style—* Prof Teodor Shanin, OBE; ✉ Department of Sociology, University of Manchester, Manchester M13 9PL (tel 0161 275 2503)

SHANKS, Duncan Faichney; s of Duncan Faichney Shanks (d 1956), of Uddingston, Strathclyde, and Elizabeth Provan, *née* Clark (d 1943); *b* 30 August 1937; *Educ* Uddingston GS, Glasgow Sch of Art (post dip, travelling scholarship to Italy); *m* 1 Aug 1966, Una Brown, da of Laurence George Gordon (d 1965), of Hartwood, Strathclyde; *Career* pt/t lectr Glasgow Sch of Art 1962–79, full time artist 1979–; memb RGI 1982, RSW 1987, RSA 1990 (ARSA 1972); *Recreations* music; *Style—* Duncan Shanks, Esq, RSA

SHANKS, Prof Ian Alexander; s of Alexander Shanks, of Dumbarton, and Isabella Affleck, *née* Beaton; *b* 22 June 1948; *Educ* Dumbarton Acad, Univ of Glasgow (BSc), CNAA (PhD); *m* 14 May 1971, Janice Smillie, da of J Coulter, of Dumbarton, Dunbartonshire; 1 da (Emma b 1977); *Career* projects mangr Scottish Colorfoto Labs Alexandria 1970–72, princ sci offr RSRE Malvern 1973–82, princ scientist Unilever Research 1982–86, visiting prof of electrical and electronic engrg Univ of Glasgow 1985–, chief scientist Thorn EMI plc 1986–94; vice-pres physical and engrg sciences Unilever 2001–03; memb: Optoelectronics Ctee The Rank Prize Funds 1985–, Steering Gp for Science and Engrg Policy Studies Unit 1988–90, Sci Consultative Gp BBC 1989–91, Advsy Bd for the Res Cncls (ABRC) 1990–93, Advsy Bd for Inst of Nanotechnology 2001–; memb Cncl and vice-pres The Royal Soc 1989–91; chm Inter-Agency Ctee on Marine Science and Technol 1991–93; Clifford Paterson medal Inst of Physics 1984; Hon DEng Univ of Glasgow 2002; FIEE, FRS 1984, FREng 1992, FRSA 1993, FRSE 2000, Hon FIoN (hon fell Inst of Nanotechnology) 2005; *Recreations* music, antique clocks and pocket watches, Art Deco sculpture; *Style—* Prof Ian Shanks, FRS, FREng, FRSE; ✉ 23 Reres Road, Broughty Ferry DD5 2QA (e-mail ianshanks@mail.com)

SHANKS, Prof Robert Gray (Robin); CBE (1997); s of Robert Shanks, and Mary, *née* Gray; *b* 4 April 1934; *Educ* Methodist Coll Belfast, Queen's Univ Belfast (MB, MD, BSc, DSc); *m* 1, 10 Dec 1960, Denise Isabelle Sheila (d 1998), da of Victor Cecil Woods (d 1971), of Bangor, NI; 4 da (Amanda b 1961, Melanie b 1962, Deborah b 1962, Rachel b 1968); m 2, 24 June 2000, Mary Carson, da of Samuel McPeak (d 1980); 1 step s (Richard b 1964), 1 step da (Gillian b 1967); *Career* head of cardiovascular pharmacology Pharmaceutical Div ICI Ltd 1962–66; Queen's Univ Belfast: lectr and conslt in clinical pharmacology 1967–72, prof of clinical pharmacology 1972–77, Whitla prof and head Dept of Therapeutics and Pharmacology 1977–98, dean Faculty of Med 1986–91, pro-vice-chllr 1991–95, sr pro-vice-chllr 1995–97, acting vice-chllr 1997; pres Ulster Med Soc 1993–94; memb GMC 1987–91; Hon LLD Queen's Univ Belfast; MRIA 1987, FRCP, FACP; *Recreations* golf, gardening; *Clubs* Royal County Down Golf; *Style—* Prof Robin Shanks, CBE; ✉ Whitla Lodge, 15 Lenamore Park, Lisburn, Co Antrim BT28 3NJ

SHANLEY, Patrick; *b* 18 April 1954; *Educ* Joseph Whitaker Sch, Sherwood Hall GS, West Notts Tech Coll, Nottingham Trent Univ/Univ of Derby; *m* Julia; 1 da (Nicola), 1 s (Paul); *Career* British Coal: fin trainee 1971–73, mgmnt accountant 1973–77, investment accountant 1977–78; Courtaulds plc: mgmnt accountant 1978–82, fin accountant/controller 1982–85, fin offr Pulp ops 1986–87, vice-pres Fin for North American Coatings 1987–89, area fin dir (responsible for fibres, films, chemicals and North American Coatings) 1989–94, gp fin controller 1994–97, fin dir 1997–99; dep ceo/chief fin offr Acordis 2002–03 (chief fin offr 1999–2002), ceo Corsadi 2003–; assoc memb CIMA 1978; *Recreations* sport (particularly golf, skiing and swimming); *Style—* Patrick Shanley, Esq; ✉ Corsadi, 1 Holme Lane, Derby DE21 7BP

SHANNON, Jim; MLA; s of Richard James Shannon, and Mona Rhoda Rebecca, *née* Hamilton; *b* 25 March 1955; *Educ* Coleraine Academical Inst; *m* 6 June 1987, Sandra, da of Robert George; 3 s (Jamie b 3 March 1988, Ian b 29 Aug 1991, Luke b 10 June 1993); *Career* Ulster Def Regt 1973–74 and 1975–77 (GSM), 102 Royal Artillery Air-Def 1977–88; joined DUP 1977; memb Ards Cncl 1985– (mayor 1991–92), memb NI Forum for Political Dialogue 1996–98; MLA (DUP) Strangford 1998–; Apprentice Boys of Derry (Comber), sec Loyal Orange Inst Kircubbin LOL 1900, past dist master Royal Black Preceptory No 11 Dist, sec Royal Black Preceptory Ballywalter No 675; memb: Greyabbey branch Royal Br Legion, NSPCC, Mid Ards branch Ulster Farmers Union, Ulster-Scots Language Soc, Comber Wildfowlers, Countryside Alliance 1973–; *Recreations* field sports, football, conservation, Ulster-Scots language; *Clubs* Carrowdore Shooting; *Style*— Jim Shannon, Esq, MLA; ✉ Northern Ireland Assembly, Parliament Buildings, Stormont Estate, Belfast BT4 3XX; Strangford Lodge, 40 Portaferry Road, Kircubbin BT22 2RY (tel 028 4278 8581, fax 028 4278 8581); 34A Francis Street, Newtownards BT23 7DN (tel 028 9182 7990, fax 028 9182 7991)

SHANNON, 9 Earl of (I 1756); Richard Bentinck Boyle; Baron Carleton (GB 1786); also Viscount Boyle and Baron Castle-Martyr (both I 1756); s of 8 Earl of Shannon (d 1963), and Marjorie, *née* Walker (d 1981); *b* 23 October 1924; *Educ* Eton; *m* 1, 1947 (m dis 1955), Donna Catherine Irene Helen, da of Marchese Demetrio Imperiali di Francavilla (cr by King Victor Amadeus III of Sardinia 1779); m 2, 1957 (m dis 1979), Susan Margaret, da of late John Russell Hogg; 1 s, 2 da; m 3, 1994, Mrs Almine Barton, da of late Rocco Catorsia de Villiers, of Cape Town, South Africa; *Heir* s, Viscount Boyle; *Career* Capt Irish Gds and RWAFF 1942–54; sec Fedn of Euro Indust Co-op Res Orgns 1975–86, chm Fndn Sci and Technol 1977–83; dir Ctee Dirs Res Assoc 1969–85, vice-pres Inland Waterways Assoc; dep speaker and dep chm of ctees House of Lords 1968–78, chm British-Armenian Parly Gp 1992–99; Provincial Grand Master Masonic Province of Surrey 1967–99, patron The Freemen of England and Wales 2000–; FRSA, FCMI, FBHI; *Recreations* horology, inland waterways; *Clubs* White's; *Style*— The Rt Hon the Earl of Shannon; ✉ Pimm's Cottage, Man's Hill, Burghfield Common, Berkshire RG7 3BD

SHANNON, Prof Robert William Ernest; CBE (2001); *b* 10 October 1937; *Educ* Belfast Tech HS, Belfast Coll of Technol (HNC, Inst of Marine Engrs Prize for Heat Engines, Belfast Assoc of Engrs Prize for Best Student, Capt J S Davidson Meml Prize for Best Student of the Year, RAeS (Belfast Branch) Prize for Best Student in Aeronautics), Queen's Univ Belfast (fndn scholar, BSc, PhD); *m* Annabelle; 2 c; *Career* laboratory technician James Mackie & Sons Ltd (Belfast) 1954–55; Short Brothers & Harland Ltd (Belfast): aircraft engrg apprentice 1955–58, aerodynamicist Light Aircraft Div Design Office 1958–62 (pt/t 1959–62), pt/t stressman 1962–63; Queen's Univ Belfast: asst lectr Dept of Aeronautical Engrg 1963–66, res fell Dept of Mechanical Engrg 1966–70, lectr Dept of Mechanical Engrg 1970; pt/t engrg conslt 1966–70; R&D Div British Gas plc (formerly British Gas Corporation): specialist in fracture 1970–74 (seconded to Civil Engrg Dept Queen's Univ Belfast 1970–72), successively asst div mangr, mangr, chief project engr, asst dir then dir of on-line inspection 1974–89, HQ dir of engrg res 1989–91, dir of devpt 1991–93; gp dir of special projects British Gas Global 1993–96 (ret); exec dir ERA Technology Ltd 1997–99; professorial fell Queen's Univ Belfast 1996–; pres Inst of Gas Engrs 1994–95 (memb Cncl 1990–98, chm Fin and Gen Purposes Ctee 1995–96, chm R&T Ctee 1998–); pres Inst of Mechanical Engrs 1996–97 (memb Cncl and its Exec Ctee 1989–, memb Engrg Quality Bd 1993–96, memb Engrg Quality Advsy Bd 1993–96, chm Fin Bd 1994–96, chm Res Ctee 1998–, chm Cncl Awards Ctee 1998–), vice-pres and hon int sec Royal Acad of Engrg 1998–2003, vice chm UK Nat Cmmn for Unesco Natural Sciences Ctee 2005–; memb: Technol and Innovation Ctee CBI 1994–96, Industrial Res and Technol Unit Bd NI Office (chm NIGC/IRTU Foresight Steering Ctee 1996–), Mgmnt Bd SEPSU 1991–94, Bd European Prize Charitable Tst 1998–; chm Euro Ctee for Standardisation CEN TC/54 1997–; memb: Res Ctee Poly and Colls Funding Cncl 1989–92, governing body Warwick Sch 2001–, Royal Soc Wolfson Fndn Ctee 2002–; memb Advsy Ctee Dept of Mechanical Engrg: Univ of Sheffield 1989–, Univ of Newcastle upon Tyne 1995–, Sheffield Hallam Univ 1998–2000; chm Engrg Policy Ctee Sheffield Hallam Univ 2000–; memb Senate Engrg Cncl 1996–99; memb Exec Bd: Euro-CASE 1998–2005 (treas and chm Fin Ctee 2001–05), FEANI 1999–; chm: Membership Ctee (Panel 1) 1995–98, Int Ctee Royal Acad of Engrg 1998– (also vice-pres), Ethics Ctee IMechE 2002–; chm NI Science Park Fndn 1999–2004, chm NI Science Park Holdings Ltd 2000–04; author of numerous pubns concerned with gas pipelines; Gold Medal Inst of Gas Engrs 1982, MacRobert Award 1989, President's Honour Lecture Br Inst of Non-Destructive Testing 1990, Mullard Award Royal Soc 1992; chm governing body Warwick Sch Redhill 2001–, memb Reigate Coll Corp 2002–, vice chm Surrey Govrs Assoc 2005–; Hon DSc Queen's Univ Belfast, Hon DTech Staffordshire Univ; Freeman City of London 1997, Liveryman Worshipful Co of Engrs 1997; MRAeS, fell Br Inst of Non-Destructive Testing, FIMechE, FIGE, FIEI, FREng 1987, FIAcadE 2001; *Style*— Prof Robert Shannon, CBE, FREng; ✉ Lindisfarne, 16 Friths Drive, Reigate, Surrey RH2 0DS (tel 01737 223559, fax 01737 223559, e-mail ermest.shannon@btinternet.com)

SHAO, En; *b* 1954; *Educ* Beijing Centre Music Conservatory, RNCM (Lord Rhodes fellow); *Career* conductor; made to stop music studies due to Cultural Revolution 1966–70; awarded first Eduard Van Beinum Fndn Scholarship 1988, winner Hungarian Television Int Conductor's Competition 1989; second princ conductor Chinese Broadcasting Symphony Orch for 5 years, princ guest conductor Central Philharmonic Orch of China, princ guest conductor Nat Youth Orch China, conductor Hungarian Radio Orch and State Symphony Orch 1989, assoc conductor BBC Philharmonic Orch 1990–92, princ conductor and artistic advsr Ulster Orch 1992–95, princ guest conductor Euskadi Symphony Orch Spain 1994–97, currently music dir Guildford Philharmonic Orch; guest conductor: Bournemouth Symphony Orch, all BBC Orchs, Northern Sinfonia, Royal Liverpool Philharmonic Orch, Hallé Orch, Royal Scottish Nat Orch, Oslo Philharmonic Orch, Helsinki Philharmonic Orch, Berlin Symphonic Orch, Czech Philharmonic Orch, ABC Orchs Australia 1991, 1993 and 1994, Toronto Symphony Orch, Vancouver Symphony, Colorado Symphony Orch, Nat Symphony Orch Johannesburg (debut 1996); debut BBC Proms 1995; *Recreations* Chinese cooking, contemporary interior design and architecture, ballet, jazz, environmental issues; *Style*— En Shao, Esq; ✉ c/o Kathryn Naish, IMG Artists Europe, Lovell House, 616 Chiswick High Road, London W4 5RX (tel 020 8233 5814, fax 020 8233 5801)

SHAPIRO, David I; *Career* slr advocate and mediator; sr founding ptnr and head of litigation Dickstein Shapiro Morin & Oshinsky (USA) until 1996, currently conslt SJ Berwin; visiting fell Dept of Law LSE; former dir and chief mediator JAMS Endispute Europe; vol counsel City of St Petersburg 1991–92 (estab Russia's first food bank); chm Panel of Ind Mediators; memb: Commercial Mediation Panel Law Soc, Commercial Court's Working Pty on ADR, Panel of Distinguished Mediators CPR Inst for Dispute Resolution NY; MCIArb, fell Int Acad of Mediators; *Style*— David I Shapiro, Esq; ✉ SJ Berwin, 222 Gray's Inn Road, London WC1X 8XF (tel 020 7533 2421, fax 020 7533 2000)

SHAPIRO, Dr Leonard Melvyn; s of Joseph Shapiro, of London, and Stella, *née* Solomon; *b* 9 March 1951; *Educ* Leyton County HS London, Univ of Manchester (BSc, MB ChB, MD); *Children*1 da (Laura Diana b 10 Sept 1980), 1 s (Paul Richard b 3 May 1984); *Career* sr registrar Nat Heart Hosp 1983–88, conslt cardiologist Papworth and Addenbrooke's Hosps Cambridge 1988–; special interests: athlete's heart, coronary artery disease, interventional cardiology; med advsr FA, dir Cardiac Servs 1998–2002; co-fndr and founding pres Br Soc of Echocardiography; fell American Coll of Cardiology; FRCP 1993 (MRCP 1978); *Books* A Colour Atlas of Hypertension (with K M Fox, 1985, 2 edn with M Bucalter, 1991), A Colour Atlas of Angina Pectoris (with K M Fox and C Warnes, 1986), A Colour Atlas of Heart Failure (with K M Fox, 1987, 2 edn 1995), A Colour Atlas of Physical Signs in Cardiovascular Disease (with K M Fox, 1988), A Colour Atlas of Palpitations and Syncope (with K M Fox, 1989), A Colour Atlas of Congenital Heart Disease in the Adult (with K M Fox, 1989), A Colour Atlas of Coronary Artery Atherosclerosis (1990, 2 edn 1992), Mitral Valve Disease (with F C Wells, 1996), An atlas of echocardiography (with A Kenny, 1997); *Style*— Dr Leonard Shapiro; ✉ Cardiac Unit, Papworth Hospital, Papworth Everard, Cambridge CB3 8RE (tel 01480 831284, fax 01480 831035, e-mail lms@lmshapiro.com)

SHAPPS, Grant; MP; *b* 14 September 1968, Watford, Herts; *Educ* Watford GS, Manchester Poly (HND); *m* Belinda; 2 s (Hadley b 2001, Noa b 2004), 1 da (Tabytha (twin) b 2004); *Career* PrintHouse Ltd: fndr 1990, dir 1990–2000, chm 2000–; Parly candidate (Cons): N Southwark and Bermondsey 1997, Welwyn Hatfield 2001; MP (Cons) Welwyn Hatfield 2005–, vice-chm (campaigning) Cons Pty, shadow housing min 2007–; *Style*— Grant Shapps, Esq, MP; ✉ House of Commons, London SW1A 0AA (e-mail grant@shapps.com, website www.shapps.com)

SHARIF, Omar; *né* Michel Shalhoub; s of Joseph M Shalhoub (d 1978), and Claire Saada; *b* 10 April 1932; *Educ* Victoria Coll Cairo; *m* 1, 5 Feb 1955 (m dis 1967), Faten, da of Ahmed Hamama; 1 s (Tarek b 1957); m 2, 7 Jan 1973; *Career* actor; Best Actor awards in film festivals of: Alexandria, Valencia, Bastia; *Theatre* The Grand Duke in The Sleeping Prince (Chichester and Haymarket Theatre) 1983–84; *Television* incl: The Far Pavilions (mini series) 1982, Edge of the Wind (BBC Play of the Month) 1984, Huis Clos (BBC Play of the Month) 1985, Peter the Great (mini series) 1984–85, Gulliver's Travels 1996, Shaka Zulu: The Citadel 2000, Urban Myths 2004; *Film* incl: Lawrence of Arabia 1962 (Oscar nomination, Golden Globe Award), The Fall of the Roman Empire 1964, Behold a Pale Horse 1964, The Yellow Rolls Royce 1964, Genghis Khan 1965, Dr Zhivago 1965 (Golden Globe Award), The Night of the Generals 1966, Marco the Magnificent 1966, More Than a Miracle 1967, McKenna's Gold 1968, Funny Girl 1968, Mayerling 1968, The Appointment 1969, Che! 1969, The Last Valley 1970, The Horsemen 1971, The Burglars 1971, The Tamarind Seed 1974, Juggernaut 1974, The Mysterious Island of Captain Nemo 1974, Funny Lady 1975, Crime and Passion 1975, Ace up the Sleeve 1976, The Pink Panther Strikes Again 1976, The Right to Love, Ashanti 1979, Bloodline 1979, Oh Heavenly Dog 1980, The Baltimore Bullet 1980, Green Ice 1981, Chanel Solitaire 1981, Top Secret 1984, The Rainbow Thief 1985, Mountains of the Moon 1990, Journey of Love 1990, Mysteries of Egypt 1998, The 13th Warrior 1999, Mr Ibraïm and les Fleurs du Coran 2003 (French César for Best Actor), Hidalgo 2004; *Books* The Eternal Male (autobiography, 1977), My Life in Bridge; *Recreations* bridge, owning, breeding and racing horses; *Style*— Omar Sharif, Esq; ✉ c/o Steve Kenis & Co, Royalty House, 72–74 Dean Street, London W1D 3SG (tel 020 7534 6001, fax 020 7287 6328)

SHARIFF, Yasmin; da of Chottu Amirali Alibhai Shariff (d 1992), and Shirin Popat Jiwa; *b* 7 April 1956; *Educ* Kenya HS, AA Sch of Architecture, SOAS Univ of London (MA), Bartlett Sch of Architecture UCL (DipArch); *m* 8 Dec 1983, Dennis Charles Sharp, *qv*; 1 s (Deen b 1984); *Career* architect; former appts: Lobb Partnership, ACP, Pringle Brandon, Jestico and Whiles; ptnr Dennis Sharp Architects 1992–; chair Eastern Regn RIBA 1999–2001, rep RIBA Cncl 1998–2004, sr lectr in architecture Univ of Westminster, EU Framework 5 evaluator 1999–2001, Civic Tst adjudicator 1999–; memb: UK Round Table on Sustainable Devpt 1999–2001, Bd E of England Devpt Agency 2001–06, Cncl E England Arts 2003–06, Bd Architects Registration Bd 2003–06; memb: ARCUK, RIBA; FRSA; *Publications* contrib: The Illustrated Dictionary of Architecture (ed D Sharp, 1991), The Guinness Book of Records 1492 (ed D Manley, 1992), The Encyclopedia of Vernaculr Architecture (ed P Oliver, 1998); contrib articles to architectural jls, author of conf papers; *Style*— Ms Yasmin Shariff; ✉ Dennis Sharp Architects, 1 Woodcock Lodge, Epping Green, Hertfordshire SG13 8ND (tel 01707 875253, fax 01707 875286, e-mail mail@sharparchitects.co.uk)

SHARKEY, John; *b* 24 September 1947; *Educ* Univ of Manchester (BSc Maths); *m* 3 da; *Career* formerly with: Benton & Bowles, KMP; Saatchi & Saatchi: joined 1984, dep chm 1986, md 1987; chm: Broad Street Group, BDDP; fndr jt chm and ceo BST-BDDP (formerly Bainsfair Sharkey Trott) 1990–97, jt chm BDDP GGT (following merger with GGT Advertising) 1997–98; md Europe Manpower plc 1998; *Style*— John Sharkey, Esq

SHARMA, HE Kamalesh; s of Kashyap Krishan Sharma, and Sheela, *née* Misra; *b* 30 September 1941, Varanasi, India; *Educ* St Stephen's Coll Univ of Delhi (BA, MA), King's Coll Cambridge (MA); *m* 22 April 1967, Babli, *née* Dubey; 1 s (Aditya b 4 Feb 1968), 1 da (Devyani b 22 Oct 1971); *Career* Indian diplomat; Indian Foreign Service 1965–2002, under-sec-gen of the UN to East Timor 2002–04, high cmmr to UK 2004–; fell Harvard Univ (Weatherhead Centre for Int Affairs), fell Foreign Policy Assoc of the United States, govr Ditchley Fndn, vice-pres Royal Over-Seas League; Hon LLD De Montfort Univ; US Foreign Policy Assoc medal; *Books* Imagining Tomorrow: Rethinking the Global Challenge (ed, 1999), Mille Fleurs: Poetry from Around the World (ed, 2000); *Recreations* literature, religious and mystical traditions, cosmology, development, global affairs and multilateralism, human society, cricket, Indian classical music, jazz; *Clubs* Athenaeum, Travellers, Delhi Gymkhana, India International Centre; *Style*— HE Mr Kamalesh Sharma; ✉ High Commission of India, Aldwych, London WC2B 4NA (tel 020 7836 2556, fax 020 7240 4688, e-mail hc.london@mea.gov.in)

SHARMA, Rita; OBE (2007); da of Varindar Kumar (d 1998), and Raj Rani, *née* Prakash Sangar (d 1995); *b* 29 July 1960, India; *m* 12 Jan 1987, Rahul Sharma; 1 da (Ria b 20 Oct 1988), 1 s (Rohan b 8 Feb 1991); *Career* founder and md Worldwide Journeys 1986–; memb Bd TiE UK; Hon PhD Univ of E London 2005; *Style*— Mrs Rita Sharma, OBE; ✉ Worldwide Journeys, Worldwide House, 10–12 Berners Mews, London W1T 3AP

SHARMAN, Alison Jane; da of Frank Sharman (d 1995), of Manchester, and Bel, *née* Thompson; *b* 18 March 1965; *Educ* Ellesmere Park Comp, Eccles Sixth Form Coll, Newcastle upon Tyne Poly (BA); *m* 16 Sept 1989, Andrew Thompson; 2 da (Abigail b 22 May 1995, Olivia b 11 Oct 1996); *Career* TV prodr; prodn sec Watchdog (BBC) 1986–88, sec and researcher TV-am 1988–89, prodr and presenter BSkyB 1989–90, researcher Travelog (Channel 4) 1990–92; BBC: successively researcher, dir, prodr and series prodr Holiday 1992–98, ed devpt Daytime 1998–2000, creative dir Gen Factual 2000–01, controller Daytime 2002–05, controller CBBC 2005–06; dir Factual & Daytime ITV 2006–; Media Guardian Edinburgh TV Festival Advsy Chair; *Recreations* sport, children, food, cinema; *Style*— Ms Alison Sharman; ✉ ITV, 200 Grays Inn Road, London WC1X 8HF (tel 020 7843 8132, fax 020 7843 8166, e-mail alison.sharman@itv.com)

SHARMAN, Baron (Life Peer UK 1999), of Redlynch in the County of Wiltshire Colin Morven; OBE (1980); *b* 19 February 1943; *m* Angela; 1 s (Richard b 1972), 1 da (Sarah b 1969); *Career* qualified chartered accountant Woolgar Hennel & Co 1965; KPMG (and predecessor firms): joined 1966, expanded practice Benelux Scandinavia and the Netherlands 1977–81, large scale investment London 1981–87, sr ptnr Nat Mktg and Industry Gps and chm KPMG Mktg Ctee 1987–90, sr mgmnt consultancy ptnr 1989–90, sr regnl ptnr for London and South East 1990–94, chm KPMG Management Consultancy International 1991–94, UK sr ptnr 1994–98, chm KPMG International 1997–99; chm: Aegis Gp plc 1999–, Aviva 2006– (non-exec dir 2005–), Le Gavroche Ltd; non-exec dir: AEA Technology plc 1996–2002, Young & Co's Brewery 1999–2002, BG Gp 2000–, Reed Elsevier 2002–, Group 4 Securicor 2003–05; memb Supervisory Bd ABN Amro NV; chair Foresight Crime Prevention Panel DTI; memb Advsy Bd The George Washington Inst for Mgmnt; hon memb Securities Inst; ambass for Merseyside 1998–; Hon Dr Cranfield Univ 1998; Hon MSI, FCA (ACA 1965), CIMgt; *Recreations* outdoor and field sports, shooting, sailing; *Clubs* Reform, Bembridge Sailing; *Style*— The Rt Hon the Lord Sharman, OBE

S

SHARMAN, Helen Patricia; OBE (1992); da of John David Sharman, of Sheffield, and Lyndis Mary, *née* Barrand; *b* 30 May 1963; *Educ* Jordanthorpe Comp Sch Sheffield, Univ of Sheffield (BSc); *Career* dep head Coatings Section MOV Hammersmith (formerly Marconi-Osram Valve, GEC subsid) 1985–87 (joined 1984), res technologist Mars Confectionery Slough 1987–89; selected as UK astronaut for Project Juno (jt venture between USSR and Antequera Ltd) 1989, trained at Yuri Gagarin Cosmonaut Trg Centre USSR 1989–91, became first Br person in space during mission 1991; currently scientific lectr and presenter; Geoffrey Pardoe award RAeS, Bronze medal Br Interplanetary Soc, Friendship of the People of the Soviet Union medal, The Worshipful Guild of Air Pilots and Air Navigators award, Gold Medal of the Royal Aero Club, Pres's Medal of the Soc Chemical Industry, Univ of Sheffield Chancellor's medal for achievement; Freeman City of Sheffield; CChem, Hon FRSC 1993, Hon MSc Univ of Birmingham 1991, Hon Master of Univ Univ of Surrey 1992; Hon DSc: Univ of Kent 1995, Southampton Inst 1997, Univ of Staffordshire 1998; Hon DTech: Univ of Plymouth 1995, The Robert Gordon Univ 1996; memb Br Interplanetary Soc (fell 1996); hon memb Soc of Chemical Industry (SCI) 1992; sr fell Univ of Sheffield, fell Sheffield Hallam Univ; FRGS 1995, FRAeS 1995 (MRAeS 1991); *Recreations* cycling, swimming, running, playing piano and saxophone, listening to music, theatre, art, travelling; *Style*— Dr Helen Sharman, OBE

SHARMAN, Mark; s of Stanley Brian Sharman, of Leamington Spa, Warwicks, and Beryl Mary, *née* Brown; *b* 2 January 1950; *Educ* John Port GS Etwall; *m* 1981, Patricia, da of Ivor Goodier (d 1987); 2 s (Matthew b 7 Oct 1981, Luke b 4 Nov 1984); *Career* reporter Derby Evening Telegraph 1967–71, reporter Raymond's News Agency 1971, sports reporter Derby Evening Telegraph 1972, sports sub-ed then chief sub-ed Birmingham Evening Mail 1972–76, sports journalist ATV Ltd Birmingham 1976, sports prodr London Weekend Television 1977–81 (incl prog ed ITV coverage of 1978 World Cup and 1980 Olympics), head of sport, head of news and sport then contoller of news and sport TVS 1981–88 (responsible for ITV network progs incl Emergency 999 and Police International), ed ITV Olympics 1988, md Chrysalis Television plc 1988–91, head of progs London News Network 1992–94, dep head Sky Sports 1997–98 (dir of programming 1994–97), controller of sport Channel 4 TV 1998–2000, dir broadcasting prodn Sky Networks 2000–03, dep md Sky Networks 2003, conslt 2003–05, dir ITV Sport 2005–; *Style*— Mark Sharman, Esq

SHARMAN, Patrick George; s of Charles A Sharman (d 1988), of Peterborough, and Betty, *née* Roll; *b* 8 July 1939; *Educ* Marlborough, Pembroke Coll Cambridge (MA); *m* 1; 1 s (Robert b 2 April 1969), 1 da (Caroline b 21 Oct 1964); m 2, 26 July 1978, Wendy, *née* Read; 2 s (Timothy b 12 Oct 1978, Algernon b 19 Aug 1980); *Career* admitted slr 1965; articled clerk Theodore Goddard & Co, ptnr Bircham & Co 1968–73, dir and slr Sharman Newspapers Ltd 1973–89, chm Sharman & Co Ltd 1989–98; fndr chm Hereward Radio plc, dir Anglia TV Ltd 1979–99; Freeman City of London, Liveryman City of London Slrs' Co; memb Law Soc 1965; *Recreations* tennis; *Style*— Patrick Sharman, Esq; ✉ 5 Chaucer Road, Cambridge CB2 2EB (tel 01223 356927)

SHARP, Sir Adrian; 4 Bt (UK 1922), of Warden Court, Maidstone, Kent; s of Sir Edward Herbert Sharp, 3 Bt (d 1985), and Beryl Kathleen, *née* Simmons-Green (d 1994); *b* 17 September 1951; *Educ* Boxhill Sch, Nat Business Coll Cape Town; *m* 1, 1976 (m dis 1986), Hazel Patricia, only da of James Trevor Wallace, of Pietersburg, South Africa, and former w of William Ian Barrett Bothwell; m 2, 1994, Denise, o da of Percy Edward Roberts, of Ironbridge, Shropshire; 1 s (Hayden Sean b 27 Aug 1994); *Heir* s, Hayden Sharp; *Career* exec mangr Toyota Motor Co; *Style*— Sir Adrian Sharp, Bt; ✉ 27 Donkin Avenue, Tableview 7441, Cape, South Africa; 31 Hamble Court, Broom Park, Teddington, Middlesex TW11 9RW

SHARP, Christopher Francis; QC (1999); s of Peter Sharp (d 1995), of Milford-on-Sea, Hants, and Corona, *née* Bradshaw; *b* 17 September 1952; *Educ* Canford Sch, Worcester Coll Oxford (MA); *m* 1978, Sarah Margot, JP, da of Norman Cripps; 1 da (Melanie Sarah b 16 Oct 1980), 1 s (Charles Michael Francis b 9 June 1982); *Career* called to the Bar Inner Temple 1975; fndr memb St John's Chambers Bristol 1978, head of chambers 2000– (dep head of chambers 1988–2000), recorder 2005–; visiting fell Faculty of Law UWE 2003–; fndr chm Family Law Bar Assoc (Bristol) 1990–96; author of various articles in legal jls; memb Advsy Cncl Worcester Coll Soc 2006–; *Recreations* holidays, real tennis, sailing, skiing, mountain walking; *Clubs* Bristol and Bath Tennis; *Style*— Christopher Sharp, Esq, QC; ✉ St John's Chambers, 101 Victoria Street, Bristol BS1 6PU (e-mail christopher.sharpqc@stjohnschambers.co.uk)

SHARP, David John; s of Norman Sharp, of Viggory Lodge, Horsell Common, Woking, Surrey, and Freda Madeleine, *née* Wakeford; *b* 15 April 1949; *Educ* Lancing, St Mary's Hosp Med Sch London (MB BS, FRCS, MD); *m* 7 Sept 1982, Marisa Nicole, *née* Parnes; 2 s (Oliver b 1985, William b 1986), 1 da (Augusta b 1990); *Career* registrar on orthopaedic higher surgical trg scheme Royal Orthopaedic Hosp Birmingham 1981–83, sr registrar on orthopaedic higher surgical trg scheme Northampton and Royal Postgrad Med Sch London 1983–88, research fell Materials Dept QMC London 1986, conslt orthopaedic and spinal surgn The Ipswich Hosp 1988–; memb Br Orthopaedic Research Soc, memb Exec Ctee Br Assoc of Spinal Surgns; tstee DISCS charity for spinal research; FBOA; *Recreations* vintage car, drawing, squash, opera, sailing; *Style*— David Sharp, Esq; ✉ Peartree, Farm, Charsfield, Woodbridge, Suffolk IP13 7QE (tel 01473 737266, e-mail dj.m.sharp@btinternet.com)

SHARP, Prof Deborah; *b* 11 November 1951; *Educ* Lady Margaret Hall Oxford (BA, BM BCh), DRCOG, Univ of London (PhD); *Career* currently prof of primary health care (chair funded by NHS Exec S&W) Univ of Bristol; FRCGP; *Books* Prevention of Anxiety and Depression in Primary Care (contrib, 1992); *Style*— Prof Deborah Sharp; ✉ Division of Primary Health Care, Cotham House, Cotham Hill, Bristol BS6 6LJ (tel 0117 954 6641, fax 0117 954 6647, mobile 077 7083 3257, e-mail debbie.sharp@bristol.ac.uk)

SHARP, Dennis Charles; s of Walter Charles Henry Sharp (d 1976), and Elsie, *née* Evans (d 1998); *Educ* Bedford Modern Sch, AA Sch of Architecture London (AADipl), Univ of Liverpool (MA); *m* 1, 1963 (m dis 1973), Joanna Leighton, da of William Scales (d 1986); 1 da (Melanie Clare); m 2, 8 Dec 1983, Yasmin Shariff, *qv*; 1 s (Deen b 1984); *Career* architect, writer, editor and designer; Dennis Sharp Architects London and Hertford 1964–; Leverhulme fell in architecture Univ of Liverpool 1960–63, lectr in architecture Univ of Manchester 1964–68; AA: sr lectr i/c history course AA Sch 1968–72, sr tutor and lectr 1973–81, gen ed AA Quarterly/AA Papers 1968–82, hon sec AA 1997–99, vice-pres 2007–; prof Int Acad of Architecture, special prof Sch of Architecture Univ of Nottingham 1996–99; visiting lectr: Imperial Coll London 1969–70, Royal Univ of Malta 1971, 1972 and 1974, PNL 1977–78, Univ of Sheffield 1988–89, UCL 1990–92; distinguished visiting critic Finnish Assoc of Architects 1980–81, visiting prof Columbia Univ of NY 1981, distinguished visiting scholar Univ of Adelaide SA 1984; exec ed World Architecture 1989–92, ed International Architecture 1993–; chair DOCOMOMO-UK 2002–; Graham Fndn lectures Chicago 1974 and 1986, John Player lectr NFT 1977; Silver medal Académie d'Architecture Paris 1991, special mention UIA 1993; chair CICA 1979–; external examiner: Bartlett Sch UCL 1971–78, Univs of Oxford, Sheffield, Bristol, Manchester, Liverpool and Kingston; ARIBA 1959 (vice-pres RIBA 1992–93); *Books* Modern Architecture & Expressionism (1966), Sources of Modern Architecture (1967, 1981), The Picture Palace (1969), A Visual History of 20th Century Architecture (1972), Glass Architecture (ed, 1972), The Rationalists (1978 and 2000), Muthesius H: The English House (ed, 1979 and 2007), Illustrated Dictionary of Architects and Architecture (ed, 1991 and 2001), Twentieth Century Architecture: A Visual History (1991, 3 edn 2002), The Bauhaus (1993), Santiago Calatrava (ed, 1992 and 1994), Connell, Ward and Lucas (1994), Bilbao 2000 (1995), Kisho Kurokawa (1998, 2 edn 2002), Manfredi Nicoletti (1999), The Modern Movement in Architecture (2000); *Recreations* photography, investigating towns and buildings; *Clubs* Royal Over-Seas League, Architecture; *Style*— Dennis Sharp; ✉ Dennis Sharp Architects, 1 Woodcock Lodge, Epping Green, Hertford SG13 8ND (tel 01707 875253, fax 01707 875286, e-mail dsharp@sharparchitects.co.uk, website www.sharparchitects.co.uk)

SHARP, Lesley; *Educ* Guildhall Sch of Music and Drama (Gold Medal); *Career* actress; AGSM; *Theatre* RSC: Cyrano de Bergerac, King Lear, Maydays, The Body, Macbeth, Mary and Lizzie, Playing with Trains; Royal Court: Gone, Who Knew McKenzie, Road, Shirley, Greenland, Our Country's Good/The Recruiting Officer, Top Girls (also tour); RNT: Command or Promise, True Dare Kiss, Tin Tang Mine, Six Characters in Search of an Author, Fathers and Sons, On, Murmuring Judges, Uncle Vanya, Mother Courage; other credits incl: Green (Contact Theatre Manchester) Face Value (Contact Theatre Manchester), Cavern of Dreams (Liverpool Playhouse) Hindle Wakes (Liverpool Playhouse), A Family Affair (Cheek by Jowl), Summerfolk (Chichester Festival Theatre); *Television* Debt, Road, Voice, Tartuffe, Josie, Wedded, Top Girls, Rides, Frank Stubbs, Dandelion Dead, Prime Suspect III: The Lost Child, Common as Muck, Moonstone, Playing the Field (three series), Great Expectations, Daylight Robbery, Nature Boy, Clocking Off, Bob and Rose, The Second Coming, Carrie's War, Carla, Afterlife, Our Hidden Lives, True Voice of Murder, True Voice of Prostitution; *Film* The Love Child, Rita, Sue and Bob Too, The Rachel Papers, Close my Eyes, Priest, Naked, The Full Monty, From Hell, Cheeky, Inkheart; *Awards* for Bob and Rose: Outstanding Dramatic Actress of the Year Monte Carlo Television Festival, RTS Best Actress Award, Northwest Centre Award, nominated Best Actress BAFTA, nominated Best Actress Br Comedy Awards; Broadcasting Press Guild TV Actress Award 2001 (for Bob and Rose and Clocking Off); for Afterlife: Best Female Actor RTS Awards, Outstanding Dramatic Actress of the Year Monte Carlo TV Festival 2006 (nominee 2007), Hamilton Deane Award for Outstanding Acting 2006; nominated: Olivier Award for Best Comedy Performance 1986, Olivier Award for Best Supporting Actress 1992, RTS Awards for Clocking Off, Best Actress in a Supporting Role BAFTA (for The Full Monty); *Style*— Ms Lesley Sharp; ✉ c/o ICM, Oxford House, 76 Oxford Street, London W1D 1BS

SHARP, Dr Lindsay Gerard; s of Clifford Douglas Sharp, FIA, of Wyke, Dorset, and Olive, *née* Joyce (d 2001); *b* 22 August 1947; *Educ* Univ of Oxford (DPhil); *m* 1, 1968, Margaret M, *née* Sommi; 1 s (Lindsay Thomas b 1975); m 2, 1981, Robyn C Stringer, *née* Peterson; 1 da (Meaghan Catherine b 1988); *Career* with Nat Museum of Science and Industry (Science Museum) London 1976–78, ldr sponsorship and mgmnt team Powerhouse Museum Sydney 1978–88, dir entertainment and leisure Merlin Int Properties 1988–90, ceo/exec conslt Earth Exchange Sydney 1990–94, dep dir and sr museum conslt Miken Family Fndn Santa Monica 1994–97, pres and ceo Royal Ontario Museum 1997–2000, dir Science Museum/Nat Museum of Science and Industry 2000–05; tstee Beacon Fellowship Tst; *Style*— Dr Lindsay Sharp

SHARP, Peter John; s of John Frederick Sharp, of Plumstead, N Norfolk, and Joan Brimelow, *née* Hotchkiss; *b* 16 April 1956; *Educ* Berkhamsted, Univ of Oxford (BA); *m* 22 Dec 1984, Philippa Joanna, da of Sqdn Ldr William Ronald Stanley Body, of Drinkstone Green, Suffolk; 3 s (Samuel Frederick b 1985, William Rodric Peter b 1991, Christopher Patrick Brimelow b 1996), 2 da (Holly Rose b and d 1987, Florence Emily b 1989); *Career* admitted slr 1982; ptnr Wilde Sapte 1984–95 (memb Managing Bd 1990–92), ptnr Le Boeuf Lamb Greene & MacRae (founding English ptnr London office) 1995–; dep chm Prince's Youth Business Tst S London 1993–94 (chm 1991–93); memb: Law Soc, Little Ship Club; *Recreations* yachting, motor racing, cycling; *Style*— Peter Sharp, Esq; ✉ Le Boeuf Lamb Green & MacRae, 6th Floor, 1 Minster Court, Mincing Lane, London EC43R 7A (tel 020 7459 5000, fax 020 7459 5099)

SHARP, Hon Richard Simon; s of Baron Sharp of Grimsdyke (d 1994), and Marion, *née* Freeman; *b* 8 February 1956; *Educ* Merchant Taylors', ChCh Oxford (MA); *m* 29 Aug 1987, Victoria Susan, da of Lloyd Nelson Hull; 1 da (Caroline Nicola b 17 Oct 1989), 2 s (James Eric Halle b 6 June 1992, Alexander Simon Lloyd b 30 April 1994); *Career* Morgan Guaranty Trust Co 1978–84, ptnr Goldman Sachs 1994–; *Style*— The Hon Richard Sharp; ✉ Goldman Sachs, Peterborough Court, 133 Fleet Street, London EC4A 2BB (tel 020 7774 1000)

SHARP, Steven Michael; s of Clarence Sharp, of Willerby, E Yorks, and Anne, *née* Price; *b* 5 July 1950; *Educ* Ainthorpe HS Kingston upon Hull, Hull Poly (Hotel and Catering Inst, City and Guilds of London Inst); *Family* 1 da (Emma Louise b 3 Feb 1978), 1 s (Daniel James b 21 Aug 1979); m, 18 Oct 1996, Lesley Sharp, *née* Mair; 2 da (Amelia Grace b 9 Jan 1997, Freya Rose b 16 Dec 2003); *Career* hotel mgmnt positions 1969–73, sales and mktg mgmnt positions in food distribution 1973–78, dir Bejam Agencies Jersey CI, mktg mangr Bejam Group plc 1978–83, head of retail mktg Argyll Group plc 1983–87, mktg dir Asda Group plc 1987–89, mktg dir Debenhams plc 1989–92, mktg dir The Burton Group plc 1992–2004, chm Steven Sharp plc 1997–, gp mktg dir Arcadia plc 2001–2004, exec dir mktg Marks & Spencer plc 2004–; visiting prof Glasgow Caledonian Univ; FCIM; *Recreations* shooting, skiing, music, art; *Clubs* RAC, IOD, Soho House; *Style*— Dr Steven Sharp

SHARP OF GUILDFORD, Baroness (Life Peer UK 1998), of Guildford in the County of Surrey; Margaret Lucy Sharp; da of Osmund Hailstone, and Sydney Mary Ellen, *née* White; *b* 21 November 1938; *Educ* Tonbridge Girls' GS, Newnham Coll Cambridge (MA); *m* 1962, Thomas Sharp; 2 da; *Career* asst princ Bd of Trade and HM Treasy 1960–63, lectr in economics LSE 1963–72, pt/t guest fell Brookings Instn Washington DC 1973–76, econ advsr NEDO 1977–81, res fell Sussex Euro Res Centre Univ of Sussex 1981–84, sr fell Science Policy Res Unit Univ of Sussex 1984–; Parly candidate (SDP/Alliance) Guildford 1983 and 1987, Parly candidate (Lib Dem) Guildford 1992 and 1997, memb Lib Dem Fed Policy Ctee 1992–2003; memb Advsy Cncl Save Br Sci; tstee: Age Concern Surrey, Nancy Seear Tst; *Books* The State, the Enterprise and the Individual (1974), The New Biotechnology: European Governments in search of a strategy (1985), Europe and the New Technologies (ed, 1985), Managing Change in British Industry (with Geoffrey Shepherd, 1986), Strategies for New Technologies (ed with Peter Holmes, 1987), European Technological Collaboration (with Claire Shearman, 1987), Technology and the Future of Europe (jt ed, 1992), Technology Policy in the European Union (with John Peterson, 1998); author of articles in learned jls dealing with science and technology policy; *Recreations* walking, reading, theatre, listening to music; *Style*— The Rt Hon the Baroness Sharp of Guildford; ✉ House of Lords, London SW1A 0PW (tel 020 7219 3121, fax 020 7219 5979, e-mail sharpm@parliament.uk)

SHARPE, Prof David Thomas; OBE (1986); s of Albert Edward Sharpe, of Swanscombe, Kent, and late Grace Emily, *née* Large; *b* 14 January 1946; *Educ* GS for Boys Gravesend, Downing Coll Cambridge, Univ of Oxford Med Sch (MB BChir); *m* 1, 23 Jan 1971 (m dis 2000), Patricia Lilian, da of Brinley Meredith (d 1965); 1 s (Timothy Richard Brinley b 4 Aug 1972), 2 da (Katherine Anna b 24 June 1974, Caroline Louise b 2 Nov 1978); m 2, 11 June 2004, Tracey Louise, da of Peter Bowman and Sandra Wade; *Career* plastic surgeon; house surgn Radcliffe Infirmary Oxford 1970–71, SHO in plastic surgery Churchill Hosp Oxford 1971–72, Pathology Dept Radcliffe Infirmary 1972–73 (Accident Service 1972), gen surgery Royal United Hosp Bath 1973–75; registrar: Plastic Surgery Unit Chepstow 1976–78 (plastic surgeon 1976), Canniesburn Hosp Glasgow 1978–80; sr registrar in plastic surgery Leeds and Bradford 1980–84, chm and md Plastech Research and Design Ltd 1984–, dir Plastic Surgery and Burns Research Unit Univ of Bradford 1986–, prof of plastic and reconstructive surgery Univ of Bradford, chm Breast Special Interest Gp Br Assoc of Plastic Surgns 1997–; conslt plastic surgn St Luke's Hosp Bradford, Bradford Royal Infirmary and Huddersfield Royal Infirmary 1985–, visiting conslt plastic surgn Yorkshire Clinic Bradford, BUPA Hosp Elland W Yorkshire and Cromwell Hosp London 1985–; author of various chapters, leading articles and papers on plastic surgery topics, major burn disaster management, tissue expansion and breast reconstruction; memb Cncl British Assoc of Aesthetic Plastic Surgeons 1989– (pres 1997–99); former chm Yorks Air Ambulance; FRCS 1975; *Recreations* painting, shooting, flying (PPL H); *Style*— Prof David T Sharpe, OBE; ✉ Hazelbrae, Calverley, Leeds LS28 5QQ (e-mail profsharpe@hotmail.com); The Yorkshire Clinic, Bradford Road, Bingley, West Yorkshire BD16 1TW (tel 01274 560311, fax 01274 510760)

SHARPE, John Harald; s of John William Sharpe (d 1961), and Eva Mary, *née* Harrison (d 1994); *b* 31 December 1941; *Educ* King Edward VI GS Retford, King Edward VI GS Sheffield, Univ of Liverpool (BSc); *m* 1969, Maureen, da of Roland W Norris, of Umkomaas, South Africa; 2 s (James Alexander b 29 June 1970, Oliver John b 30 June 1973), 1 da (Sarah Jane b 24 April 1976); *Career* Unilever plc and subsids: mgmnt trainee 1963–65, various mktg positions in UK, South Africa, USA and Philippines 1965–78, chm Sunlight AG Switzerland 1981–83 (mktg dir 1978–80), sr international mktg and advtg exec detergents 1983–86, chm Elida Gibbs UK 1986–92, chm Birds Eye Wall's 1993–95, chief exec Lever Europe 1995–96, pres Unilever - Home & Personal Care - Europe 1996–2001; ind conslt 2001–; pres Union Savonneries Suisse (Swiss Detergents Assoc) 1981–83, pres Euro Cosmetics, Toiletries and Perfumery Assoc (COLIPA) 1991–92, chm Cosmetics Toiletries and Perfumery Assoc UK 1988–90, chm UK Assoc of Frozen Food Prodrs 1994–95, dir Br Quality Fndn 1994–98, memb Governing Ctee European Fndn for Quality Mgmnt (EFQM) 1999–2001; FRSA 1993; *Recreations* travel, golf; *Clubs* RAC; *Style*— John Sharpe, Esq

SHARPE, Thomas Anthony Edward; QC (1994); s of late James Sharpe (d 1981), and Lydia, *née* de Gegg; *b* 21 December 1949; *m* 1, 14 June 1974 (m dis), Sheena Carmichael, da of late Baron Carmichael of Kelvingrove (Life Peer); 2 c; m 2, 16 Feb 1988, Phillis, da of late W P Rogers; 2 c; *Career* called to the Bar Lincoln's Inn 1976 (bencher 2004); fell Wolfson Coll and Nuffield Coll Oxford 1987; chm New London Orch 1998–2000; *Recreations* music, art, furniture, travelling; *Clubs* Reform; *Style*— Thomas Sharpe, Esq, QC; ✉ 1 Essex Court, Ground Floor, Temple, London EC4Y 9AR (tel 020 7583 2000, fax 020 7583 0118)

SHARPE, Thomas Ridley (Tom); s of Rev George Coverdale Sharpe (d 1944), and Grace Egerton, *née* Brown (d 1975); *b* 30 March 1928; *Educ* Lancing, Pembroke Coll Cambridge (MA); *m* 1969, Nancy Anne Looper; 3 da (Melanie, Grace, Jemima); *Career* RM 1946–48; social worker Johannesburg 1951–52, teacher Natal 1952–56, photographer South Africa 1956–61, deported from South Africa on political grounds 1961, teacher trg Cambridge 1962–63, lectr in history Cambridge Coll of Arts and Technology 1963–71, novelist 1971–; XXXIIIème Grand Prix de l'Humoir Noir Xavier Fouchat 1986; *Books* Riotous Assembly (1971), Indecent Exposure (1973), Porterhouse Blue (1974), Blott on the Landscape (1975), Wilt (1976), The Great Pursuit (1977), The Throwback (1978), The Wilt Alternative (1979), Ancestral Vices (1980), Vintage Stuff (1982), Wilt on High (1984), Granchester Grind (1995), The Midden (1996), Wilt in Nowhere (2004); *Recreations* photography, old typewriters, gardening, reading, cats, talking; *Style*— Tom Sharpe, Esq; ✉ 38 Tunwells Lane, Great Shelford, Cambridge CB2 5LJ

SHARPE-NEWTON, Geraldine; da of late Jesse J Sharpe, of New York City, and Adrienne Rosaire; *Educ* Univ of Illinois (BA), Univ of Pittsburgh (MLS); *m* 1, 1962 (m dis 1974), Thomas Alan Newton; 1 da (Jennifer Jesse b 1965), 1 s (Matthew Ross b 1968); m 2, 1992, John Peter Bluff; *Career* assoc dir special projects Burson Marsteller PR 1974–77, vice-pres Niki Singer Inc 1977–79, vice-pres of PR Simon and Schuster 1979–80, dir Info Servs CBS News 1980–83, head of Press and Public Affrs ITN 1983–91, strategic dir of communications WWF UK 1991–94, sr vice-pres Int PR Turner Broadcasting System Inc 1994–98, md GSN Communications 1998–2001, ptnr Sharpe/McKenna Ltd 2002–06, md Sharpe Connections 2006–; assoc dir Critical Eye 2005–; chm Forum UK 1997–99; pres Media Soc 2006–; memb: BAFTA, RTS, Forum UK, Benjamin West Gp Royal Acad; *Recreations* gardening, travelling, art, books, writing; *Clubs* Soho House, Reform (counsel memb Media Gp), Groucho, Hurlingham; *Style*— Mrs Geraldine Sharpe-Newton; ✉ c/o Critical Eye, 20–21 The Bakehouse, Bakery Place, 119 Altenburg, London SW11 1JQ (tel 020 7350 5107, e-mail gsn@sharpeconnections.net)

SHARPLES, Christopher John; s of Baroness Sharples, *qv*, and Sir Richard Sharples, KCMG, OBE, MC (assass 1973); *b* 24 May 1947; *Educ* Eton, Business Sch of Neuchâtel; *m* 1975, Sharon, da of late Robert Sweeny, DFC; 3 c; *Career* VSO India 1965–66; C Czarnikow Ltd (sugar brokers) 1968–72, co fndr and dir Inter Commodities Ltd (brokers in futures and options, renamed GNI Ltd in 1984 following partial acquisition by Gerrard & National plc) 1972–78, dir GNI Holdings Ltd 1981–2000, fndr dir and chm ICV Ltd (vendors of real-time financial data incl London Stock Exchange trading system) 1981–98, dir Royal Blue plc (systems integration house) 1982–90, vice-chm International Petroleum Exchange 1986–87 (dir 1981–87); dir: Hiscox Dedicated Insurance Fund plc 1995–96, Futures and Options Assoc 1998–2000, Digital River Ltd 1998–2000, Unigestion (UK) Ltd 2000–, Grandeye Ltd 2004–; chm: Assoc of Futures Brokers and Dealers (self-regulatory body designated under Fin Servs Act 1986) 1987–91, SFA 1991–95, Lombard Street Research Ltd 1997–2000, Datastream International Ltd 1996–98, Membertrack Ltd 1999–2000; memb Takeover Panel 1991–95; served Ctees: London Commodity Exchange (PR), London International Financial Futures Exchange (Clearing), Br Fedn of Commodity Assocs (Taxation), London Commodity Exchange Regulatory Advsy Gp, Advsy Panel SIB 1986; MSI; *Recreations* sailing, flying; *Clubs* Royal Yacht Squadron, Air Squadron, White's, Pratt's; *Style*— Christopher Sharples; ✉ Unigestion Ltd, 105 Piccadilly, London W1J 7NJ

SHARPLES, Prof Mike; *b* 14 December 1952; *Educ* St Andrews Univ (BSc), Univ of Edinburgh (PhD); *Career* res fell Open Univ 1981–82, res fell Univ of Edinburgh 1982–84, lectr in artificial intelligence Univ of Sussex 1984–93, sr lectr Sch of Cognitive and Computing Sci Univ of Sussex 1993–97, Kodak/Royal Acad of Engrg res prof of educnl technol Univ of Birmingham 1997–2003, prof of educnl technol 2003–05, prof of learning sciences and dir Learning Sciences Research Inst Univ of Nottingham 2005–; founder mLearn int conference series on mobile learning; dep scientific mangr Kaleidoscope European Network of Excellence on Technol Enhanced Learning; memb Editorial Bd: Computers and Composition 1994–, Jl of Computer Assisted Learning 2001–; fndr and memb Ctee Writing and Computers Assoc 1991–; memb: Soc for the Study of Artificial Intelligence and Simulation of Behaviour 1989–, Soc of Authors 1990–; MIEEE 1999, FRSA 2002; *Books* Cognition, Computers and Creative Writing (1985), Computers and Thought: a Practical Introduction to Artificial Intelligence (1989), Benefits and Risks of Knowledge-based Systems (1989), Computers and Writing: Issues and Implementations (ed, 1992), Computer Supported Collaborative Writing (ed, 1993), The New Writing Environment: Writers at Work in a World of Technology (ed with T van der Geest, 1996), How We Write: An Account of Writing as Creative Design (1999); also author of 35 articles in learned jls, 75 refereed conf papers, and 60 book chapters; *Style*— Prof Mike Sharples; ✉ University of Nottingham, Exchange Building, Jubilee Campus, Wollaton Road, Nottingham NG8 1BB (tel 0115 951 3716, fax 0115 846 7931, e-mail mike.sharples@nottingham.ac.uk, website www.nottingham.ac.uk/lsri)

SHARPLES, Baroness (Life Peer UK 1973), of Chawton in the County of Hampshire; Pamela Swan; da of Lt Cdr Keith William Newall, RN (d 1937), and Violet Ruby, *née* Ashton (who m 2, Lord Claud Nigel Hamilton, GCVO, CMG, DSO, s of 2 Duke of Abercorn, and d 1986); *b* 11 February 1923; *Educ* Southover Manor Lewes, Florence Italy; *m* 1, 1946, Sir Richard Christopher Sharples, KCMG, OBE, MC, govr of Bermuda (assass in Bermuda 1973), s of Richard William Sharples, OBE; 2 s ((Hon) Christopher John Sharples, *qv* b 1947, Hon David Richard b 1955), 2 da (Hon Fiona (Hon Mrs Paterson) b 1949, Hon Miranda (Hon Mrs Larkins) b 1951); m 2, 1977, Patrick David de Laszlo (d 1980); m 3, 1983, (Robert) Douglas Swan (d 1995); *Career* served WAAF 1941–46, Armed Forces Pay Review Bd 1979–81; sits as Cons peer in House of Lords; chm TVS Tst 1981–92; *Recreations* golf, tennis, gardening; *Clubs* Royal Cape Golf SA, Mid Ocean Bermuda, Parliamentary Golf Assoc, Rushmoor Golf; *Style*— The Rt Hon the Lady Sharples; ✉ 60 Westminster Gardens, Marsham Street, London SW1P 4JG (tel 020 7821 1875); Well Cottage, Higher Coombe, Shaftesbury, Dorset SP7 9LR (tel 01747 852971)

SHARPLES, Prof Ray Martin; s of Wilfred Sharples, of Widnes, Cheshire, and Irene, *née* Lamb (d 1983); *b* 13 January 1955, Widnes, Cheshire; *Educ* Wade Deacon GS Widnes, Univ of St Andrews (BSc, class medal), Univ of Edinburgh (PhD); *m* 31 Oct 1988, Heather Webster Scott; 2 s (Alasdair Gordon Scott b 15 April 1992, Stuart David Scott b 17 Dec 1994); *Career* staff astronomer Anglo-Australian Observatory 1984–90; Univ of Durham: lectr 1990–95, reader 1995–2002, prof 2002–, head Astronomical Instrumentation Gp; author of 120 scientific pubns; memb Optical Soc of America; MInstP, FRAS; *Recreations* rock climbing, mountaineering; *Style*— Prof Ray Sharples; ✉ Department of Physics, Rochester Building, Science Laboratories, South Road, Durham DH1 3LE (tel 0191 334 3719, fax 0191 334 3609, e-mail r.m.sharples@durham.ac.uk)

SHARPLES, Prof Robert William; s of William Arthur Sharples (d 1988), of Meopham, Kent, and Joan Catherine, *née* Affleck; *b* 28 May 1949; *Educ* Dulwich Coll, Trinity Coll Cambridge (MA, PhD); *m* 24 July 1976, Grace Elizabeth (d 2004), da of William Nevard (d 1979), of Mill Hill, London; 1 da (Elizabeth b 1984); *Career* res fell Fitzwilliam Coll Cambridge 1972–73; UCL: lectr in Greek and Latin 1973–91, reader in Greek and Latin 1991–94, prof of classics 1994–; sec Cncl of Univ Classical Depts 1983–87 (chair 1999–2001); ed Phronesis 1993–97; *Books* Alexander of Aphrodisias on Fate (1983), Plato - Meno (1985), Alexander of Aphrodisias - Ethical Problems (1990), Cicero On Fate and Boethius Consolation of Philosophy (1991), Alexander of Aphrodisias - Quaestiones (1992 and 1994), Theophrastus of Eresus (co-author, 1992, 1995, 1998 and 2003), Stoics, Epicureans and Sceptics (1996), Alexander of Aphrodisias - Supplement to On the Soul (2004), Pseudo-Aristoteles, Supplementa Problematorum (co-author, 2006); *Recreations* computing; *Style*— Prof Robert Sharples; ✉ Department of Greek and Latin, University College London, Gower Street, London WC1E 6BT (tel 020 7679 7522, fax 020 7679 7475, e-mail r.sharples@ucl.ac.uk)

SHARPSTON, Eleanor Veronica Elizabeth; QC (1999); da of Charles Sharpston, and Pauline, *née* Bryant; *b* 13 July 1955; *Educ* St Paul's Girls' Sch (scholarship), Bedales (scholarship), Konservatorium der Stadt Wien Vienna, King's Coll Cambridge (MA), CCC Oxford (Rowing blue, pres Oxford Univ Women's Boat Club 1978–80; Squash blue), Inns of Court Sch of Law; *m* 1991, David John Lyon, naval historian (d 2000); *Career* called to the Bar Middle Temple 1980 (Jules Thorn scholar 1980, Sir Peter Bristow scholar 1981, bencher 2005), Bar of Ireland 1986, Bar of Gibraltar 1999; practising barr specialising in EC law, jt head Hailsham Chambers; référendaire to Advocate Gen Sir Gordon Slynn at EC Court of Justice Luxembourg 1987–90, lectr and dir European Legal Studies UCL 1990–92; Univ of Cambridge: fell in law King's Coll 1992–, lectr 1992–98, affiliated lectr 1998–, sr fell Centre for European Legal Studies 1998–; advocate gen European Court of Justice 2006–; chm Bar European Gp 2003–04; memb COMBAR; FSA; *Publications* Interim and Substantive Relief in Claims Under Community Law (Butterworths, Current EC Legal Devpt Series, 1993), numerous academic articles; *Recreations* theatre, classical music, european literature, sailing square riggers, rowing, squash, scuba diving, skiing; *Clubs* Leander, Athenaeum; *Style*— Miss Eleanor Sharpston, QC; ✉ Court of Justice of the European Communities, L-2925 Luxembourg (tel 00 352 4303 2215)

SHARROCK, Ivan; s of William Arthur Sharrock, and Gladys Muriel, *née* Roberts; *b* 17 July 1941; *Educ* Newquay GS, Cornwall Tech Coll; *m* 5 Oct 1974, Suzanne Jacqueline Clare, da of Jack Cecil Edward Haig, of Sutton Coldfield; 1 s (Sky Kelly Ivan b 1975); *Career* film prodn sound mixer; memb: Acad of Motion Picture Arts and Sciences, Cinema Audio Soc (USA), BAFTA, BECTU, BKSTS, IATSE Local 659; joined BBC 1961, trained in film sound techniques at Ealing Film Studios 1961–64, outside broadcasts BBC TV 1964–65, freelance sound mixer with Alan King Assocs 1965–81; *Film* has recorded over 60 feature films incl: The Shining 1980, The French Lieutenant's Woman 1981 (Br Acad Award), Greystoke 1984 (Br Acad nomination), The Last Emperor 1987 (Oscar), The Sheltering Sky 1990, Patriot Games 1992, Little Buddha 1993, Mary Shelly's Frankenstein 1994, The Saint 1996, The English Patient 1996 (Br Acad nomination), The Talented Mr Ripley 1999 (Br Acad nomination), U571 2000 (Oscar nomination), Gangs of New York 2002 (Oscar and Br Acad nominatons), Cold Mountain 2003 (Br Acad nomination), Brothers Grimm 2004, Closer 2004, The Da Vinci Code 2005, Blood Diamond 2006 (Oscar nomination), Speed Racer 2007; *Recreations* sailing, skiing, windsurfing, music, reading, vintage car renovation and trialling; *Style*— Ivan Sharrock, Esq; ✉ 9 Burghley Road, London NW5 1UG (tel 020 7267 3170 and 020 7284 4306, fax 020 7284 4250, e-mail ivan@raspberry-ss.com)

SHARROCK, Thea Zoe; da of Peter Sharrock, of London, and Victoria Brittain; *b* 11 December 1975; *Educ* King Alfred Sch London, St Paul's Girls' Sch, Univ of Oxford; *m* 11 Sept 2004, Paul Handley; *Career* theatre director; trained Anna Scher Theatre 1987–97, asst to head NT Studio 1996; artistic dir: Southwark Playhouse 2001–03, Gate Theatre 2004–07; tstee James Menzies-Kitchin Meml Tst, patron Anna Scher Theatre; sometime player Arsenal Ladies FC; *Plays* Top Girls (Battersea Arts Centre) 2000 (James Menzies-Kitchin Meml Tst Young Dir of the Year 2000), Art (assoc dir, Wyndham's Theatre, Whitehall Theatre and nat tour) 2001–02, The Sleepers Den (Southwark Playhouse) 2001, Top Girls (Oxford Stage Co nat tour) 2001, Top Girls (Aldwych Theatre and nat tour) 2002, Free (NT Loft) 2002, Trip's Cinch (Southwark Playhouse) 2002, Mongoose (Southwark Playhouse) 2003, The Fight for Barbara (Peter Hall Season Theatre Royal Bath) 2002, The Deep Blue Sea (Theatre Royal Bath) 2003, A Doll's House (Southwark Playhouse) 2003, Don Juan and Blithe Spirit (both Peter Hall Season Theatre Royal Bath) 2004, Tejas Verdes (Gate Theatre), Private Lives (Peter Hall Season Theatre Royal Bath), The Chairs (Gate Theatre) 2006, Equus (Gielgud Theatre) 2007; *Recreations* Arsenal FC; *Style*— Miss Thea Sharrock; ✉ c/o Michael Foster, ARG, 4 Great Portland Street, London W1W 8PA (tel 020 7436 6400, fax 020 7436 6700)

SHATTOCK, Sir Gordon; kt (1985); s of Frederick Thomas Shattock (d 1974), of Exeter, Devon, and Rose May Irene, *née* James (d 1988); *b* 12 May 1928; *Educ* Hele's Sch Exeter, RVC London (MRCVS); *m* 1 17 July 1952, Jeanne Mary (d 1984), da of Austin Edwin Watkins (d 1970), of Exeter, Devon; 1 s (Simon John b 1954), 1 da (Clare Lucinda b 1956); m 2, 17 Sept 1988, Mrs David Sale (wid); *Career* sr ptnr St David Veterinary Hosp Exeter 1951–84, dir and vice-chm Veterinary Drug Co plc 1982–97, divnl bursar Western Area Woodard Schs 1988–2002; fndr chm (pres 1989–93) Devon Euro Constituency Cons Cncl; chm: local Cancer Res Campaign 1972–88, Grenville Coll 1973–88 (also memb Sch Cncl), Western Area Cons Pty (Avon, Somerset, Devon and Cornwall) 1982–85 (pres 1989–92), Exeter Cathedral Music Fndn 1985–2004; fell Woodward Corp of Schs 1973–88; pres Br Veterinary Hosps Assoc 1974, Old Heleans' Soc 1999–; memb: Exec Cncl Animal Health

S

Tst 1974–98, Political Advsy Bd TSW 1985–90, Exeter HA 1985–93, Exec Cncl Guide Dogs for the Blind 1985–97; hon memb Br Veterinary Assoc 1989; Freeman City of London 1978, Liveryman Worshipful Co of Farriers (Master 1992–93, memb Ct of Assts), Jr Grand Warden United Grand Lodge of England 1997–98; FRSA 1990, Hon FRVC 1994; *Recreations* gardening, restoration of old houses; *Clubs* RSM; *Style—* Sir Gordon Shattock; ✉ Bowhill, Riverside Road, Topsham, Exeter EX3 0LR (tel 01392 876655, fax 01392 875588, e-mail sirgordonshattock@blueyonder.co.uk)

SHAVE, Prof Terry; *b* 8 June 1952, Suffolk; *Educ* Ipswich Sch of Art, Loughborough Coll of Art (BA), Slade Sch London (Higher Dip Fine Art); *Career* artist; prof of fine art and head Fine Art Dept Staffordshire Univ; work subject of numerous exhibition catalogues, magazine and newspaper articles; *Solo Exhibitions* Staffordshire Poly Gallery 1983, Some Kind of Eden (Morley Gallery London) 1983, The Minories Colchester (and tour) 1985, Notes from an Ordinary Hell (Ikon Gallery Birmingham) 1986, The Fall to Pandemonium series (Gallery N Kirby Lonsdale) 1989, Anderson O'Day Gallery London 1990, Wolf-at-the-Door Gallery Penzance 1990, Accumulations (City Museum and Art Gallery Stoke-on-Trent) 1993, Tour to Mead Gallery (Univ of Warwick) 1993, Works on Paper (Midlands Contemporary Art Birmingham) 1993, Behind the View (Ainscough Gallery Liverpool) 1995, Loaded (Ikon Gallery Birmingham) 1996, Reloading (Real Gallery NY) 1997, Comes the Flood (Flaxman Studios Stoke-on-Trent); *Group Exhibitions* incl: British Printmaking Now (Thumb Gallery London) 1978, Six Attitudes to Print (Aspex Gallery Portsmouth) 1982, 4th Tolly Cobbold/Eastern Arts Nat Exhibition (prizewinner) 1983, Place (Gimpel Fils London) 1983, John Moores Liverpool Exhibition 15 (prizewinner) 1987, The Presence of Painting (S Bank Centre/Arts Cncl touring) 1989, The Language of Landscape (Anderson O'Day London) 1990, 4 UK Artists (Norlino Gallery NY) 1990, Landscape Visions (selected by Peter Fuller, Pears Gallery Aldeburgh) 1990, A Tribute to Peter Fuller (Beaux-Arts Bath) 1990, 11th Bradford Int Print Biennale (RCA London) 1991, Beyond the Wow Factor (New York State Univ) 1993, first Harlech Int Contemporary Art Exhibition (invited artist) 1994, Foreign Bodies (Shinjuki Cultural Centre Tokyo) 1996, Warming Up (Arcus Nurnberg) 1996, Aid (Hellenic American Union Gallery Athens) 2003; *Work in Public and Corporate Collections* Arts Cncl of GB, Ipswich Corp, Birmingham Museum and Art Gallery, Stoke-on-Trent Museum and Art Gallery, Bedfordshire CC, St Thomas' Hosp London, Colgate/Palmolive Ltd, Unilever Ltd, Coopers & Lybrand Ltd, Univ of Warwick; *Style—* Prof Terry Shave; ✉ 19 Park Avenue, Wolstanton, Newcastle-under-Lyme, Staffordshire ST5 8AX

SHAW, Antony Michael Ninian; QC (1994); s of Harold Anthony Shaw, of Newhaven, E Sussex, and Edith Beatrice Sanbach, *née* Holmes, of Iden Green, Kent; *b* 4 October 1948; *Educ* King's Sch Canterbury, Trinity Coll Oxford (major history scholar, BA); *m* Louise Göta (d 2006), da of Louis Carl Faugust (d 1971); 1 s (James William Hugo b 19 Jan 1984), 2 da (Antonia Elizabeth Göta b 21 June 1985, Olivia Louise Beatrice b 22 Aug 1990); *Career* res in constitutional law and human rights in Anglophonic Africa financed by Ford Fndn 1970–71, res offr Legal Res Unit Bedford Coll London 1972–75, called to the Bar Middle Temple 1975 (Astbury scholar, bencher 2003), visiting lectr London Coll of Printing 1975–76, pupillage 1976, tenancy at 4 Brick Court chambers of Barbara Calvert, QC, 1977, head of chambers 4 Brick Court 1988–99; asst recorder 1997–2000, recorder 2000–; criminal defence work including drugs and serious fraud; vice-chm Legal Aid and Fees Ctee Bar Cncl 1995–97, govr Int Students House 1999–2003, memb Criminal Bar Assoc; contrib to numerous publications and jls; *Books* Archbold's Criminal Pleadings and Practice (co-ed, 1990–); *Recreations* history, reading; *Style—* Antony Shaw, QC; ✉ 18 Red Lion Court, London EC4A 3EB (tel 020 7520 6000, e-mail tony.shaw@18rlc.co.uk)

SHAW, Prof Bernard Leslie; s of Tom Shaw (d 1971), and Vera, *née* Dale (d 1989); *b* 28 March 1930; *Educ* Hulme GS Oldham, Univ of Manchester (BSc, PhD); *m* 2 June 1951, Mary Elizabeth, da of William Birdsall Neild; 3 s (John Ewart Hardern b 1953, Andrew b and d 1956, Jonathan Bernard b 1960); *Career* sci offr Civil Serv 1953–56, res sci ICI 1956–61, prof Univ of Leeds 1971– (lectr 1962–66, reader 1966–71); FRS 1978; *Recreations* pottery; *Style—* Prof Bernard Shaw, FRS; ✉ 14 Monkbridge Road, Leeds LS6 4DX (tel 0113 275 5895); School of Chemistry, University of Leeds, Leeds LS2 9JT (tel 0113 343 6454, fax 0113 343 6565, e-mail b.l.shaw@leeds.ac.uk)

SHAW, Carolyn; *b* 24 April 1947; *Educ* West Kirby GS for Girls, Goldsmiths Coll London (BA), Univ of Liverpool (PGCE); *m* 1974, Dr Charles Shaw; 1 s (Timothy b 20 Dec 1978), 1 da (Anna b 23 May 1981); *Career* English teacher La Sainte Union Convent Bath 1972–74, head of English Mount St Agnes Acad Bermuda 1974–78, full time mother 1978–86, pt/t marketing position with export co 1986–89, English teacher and univ advsr Cheltenham Ladies' Coll 1989–96, headmistress St Mary's Sch Calne 1996–2003, headmistress Roedean Sch 2003–; memb: Girls' Schs Assoc 1996–, Independent Schools Examination Bd 1998– (vice-chm 2003–); *Publications* English for the Community Bound (in The English Jl, Nov 1977); *Recreations* music, theatre, walking, travel; *Style—* Mrs Carolyn Shaw; ✉ Roedean School, Brighton BN2 5RQ (tel 01273 667500, fax 01273 680791, e-mail headmistress@roedean.co.uk)

SHAW, Sir Charles de Vere; 8 Bt (UK 1821), of Bushy Park, Dublin; s of late Capt John Frederick de Vere Shaw, yr s of 6 Bt; suc unc, Sir Robert Shaw, 7 Bt (d 2002); *b* 1 March 1957; *Educ* Michaelhouse, RMA Sandhurst; *m* 1985, Sonia, elder da of Geoff Eden and Meera Eden, of Farnham, Surrey; 1 da (Alexandra Frances b 1986), 1 s (Robert Jonathan de Vere b 1988); *Heir* s, Robert Shaw; *Career* served Europe, Central America and Middle East with 5th Royal Inniskilling Dragoon Guards (subsequently the Royal Dragoon Guards) 1975–87, Major; dir of consultancy Safetynet plc 1989–94; md Morgan Lovell plc 1994–2000, ceo Intellispace 2001–05, md Arlington Property Services 2005–; non-exec dir The Shaw Travel Co; *Recreations* leading expeditions including to the Geographic North Pole in 1997, most sports, photography, wine; *Clubs* Army and Navy, RGS; *Style—* Sir Charles Shaw, Bt; ✉ Pigeon Farmhouse, Greenham, Newbury, Berkshire RG19 8SP (e-mail charles@leadershipdynamics.co.uk)

SHAW, Prof Charles Timothy (Tim); s of Charles John Shaw (d 1985), and Constance Olive, *née* Scotton (d 1961); *b* 10 October 1934; *Educ* Diocesan Coll Rondebosch, Univ of the Witwatersrand (BSc), McGill Univ Montreal (MSc); *m* 1 Sept 1962, Tuulike Raili, da of Dr Artur Aleksander Linari-Linholm (d 1984); 2 da (Karen b 1 Sept 1963, Nicolette b 29 Jan 1966), 1 s (Jeffrey Charles b 15 Sept 1973); *Career* Johannesburg Consolidated Investment Co Group: employed variously 1960–65, head of computing 1966–69, mangr 1969–71, consulting engr (Randfontein Estates, GM Co Ltd, Consolidated Murchison Ltd) 1971–73; consulting engr and dir Rustenburg Platinum Mines Ltd 1973–75, chief consulting engr and alternative dir Johannesburg Consolidated Investment 1975–77, md Western Areas Gold Mining Co Ltd 1975–77; assoc prof Virginia Poly Inst and State Univ Blacksburg Virginia USA 1977–80, emeritus prof of mining Royal Sch of Mines Imperial Coll London 2000– (prof 1980–2000, dean 1991–95); hon prof Inst of Archaeology UCL; chm Special Sub Ctee on Engrg Qualifications Mining Qualifications Bd 1986–87, ed Mineral Resources Engineering 1988–2002; memb: Professional Engrs 1977, Scientific Ctee Inst for Archaeo-Metallurgical Studies 1982–92, Safety in Mines Res Advsy Bd UK 1985–88, Ctee of Mgmnt Inst of Archaeology 1985–87, Cncl Royal Sch of Mines Assoc 1982 (pres 1988–89); sec gen Societät der Bergbaukunde (Soc of Mining Professors) 1990–2005; govr Camborne Sch of Mines 1982–90; fell: South African Inst of Mining and Metallurgy 1961, Inst of Mining and Metallurgy 1980 (memb Cncl 1981–88 and 1989–93), Inst of Mining Engrs 1981 (memb Cncl 1988–96, pres Southern Counties Branch 1988–89 and 1990–91), Inst of Quarrying 1981; Hon PhD Miskolc University Hungary 1995, Dr (hc) Moscow State Mining Univ 1999; CEng 1980; *Style—* Prof Tim Shaw; ✉ Imperial College of Science, Technology and Medicine, South Kensington, London SW7 (tel 020 8878 5005, fax 020 8876 0243)

SHAW, Chris Thomas; s of John Dennis Bolton Shaw (d 1989), of Sussex, and Isabel, *née* Loewe (d 1985); *b* 19 June 1957; *Educ* Westminster, Balliol Coll Oxford; *Career* trainee LBC 1980–81, bulletin ed Independent Radio News 1981–85, chief sub-ed ITN 1987–89 (writer 1985–87), sr prodr Sky News 1990–91; ITN: rejoined 1992, foreign and home news ed Channel 4 News 1992–93, prog ed News at Ten 1993–96, ed ITN news service for Channel Five 1996–98; Channel Five Broadcasting: controller of news, current affrs and documentaries 1998–2001, sr prog controller 2001–; *Style—* Chris Shaw, Esq; ✉ Channel Five Broadcasting Ltd, 22 Long Acre, London WC2E 9LY (tel 020 7421 7123)

SHAW, Christopher Nigel (Chris); s of Jack Shaw, of Clowne, Derbys, and Vera, *née* Gould; *b* 31 March 1962; *Educ* Cardiff High Sch, LSE (BSc); *m* 4 Sept 1993, Caroline Margaret, da of Francis Flynn; 2 da (Phoebe Helena b 15 March 1997, Isobel Louise b 7 Oct 1998); *Career* media trainee rising to media supr McCann-Erickson 1984–89; Publicis: sr media planner 1989–90, media mangr 1990–91, media account dir 1991–92; media account dir and bd dir Optimedia (following merger with Geers Gross and FCB) 1992–93, European media account dir Initiative Media 1993–95, jt md then pres EMEA Universal McCann 1997–2006 (fndr dir 1995), 19 Entertainment 2006– (working on Honda Racing F1 Team account); *Style—* Chris Shaw, Esq; ✉ 19 Entertainment Limited, 33 Ransomes Dock, 35–37 Parkgate Road, London SW11 4NP

SHAW, David Lawrence; *b* 14 November 1950; *Educ* KCS Wimbledon, City of London Poly; *m* 1986, Dr Lesley Christine Shaw, *née* Brown; 1 s (b 1989), 1 da (b 1994); *Career* with Coopers & Lybrand 1971–79, County Bank 1979–83, fndr and chm Sabrelance Ltd 1983–, dep chm The Adscene Group plc 1986–99, chm RRI plc 1994–2000, chm and tstee The David Shaw Charitable Tst 1994–, chm 2020 Strategy Ltd 1997–; fin dir Nettec plc 2003–05; MP (Cons) Dover 1987–97 (Parly Candidate (Cons) Leigh 1979 and Kingston & Surbiton 2001); memb Social Security Select Ctee House of Commons 1991–97, vice-chm Cons Pty Finance Ctee 1990–97, chm Cons Pty Smaller Businesses Ctee 1991–97, former co-chm All-Pty Dolphin Protection Gp, fndr Bow Gp/Ripon Soc Transatlantic Confs (chm Bow Gp 1983–84); joined Cons Pty 1970, cncllr Royal Borough of Kingston upon Thames 1974–78, vice-chm Kingston and Malden Cons Assoc 1979–86, chm Bow Gp 1983–84; memb Cncl PITCOM 1995–97; hon vice-pres IPI 1996–; MInstD, FCA (ACA 1974); *Clubs* Carlton; *Style—* David Shaw, Esq, FCA; ✉ 66 Richborne Terrace, London SW8 1AX (tel 020 7735 6965, fax 020 7582 9380, e-mail david@davidshaw.net, website www.davidshaw.net)

SHAW, Donald Gordon Brian; *b* 14 January 1956; *Educ* Edinburgh Acad, Univ of Aberdeen (LLB); *m* May 2000, Susan Edith Shaw; 2 da (Alexandra, Georgia); *Career* admitted slr 1979 (articled Shepherd & Wedderburn); Dundas & Wilson LLP: ptnr 1985–, Real Estate industry ldr 2000–, managing ptnr 2006–; ptnr Garretts 1997–2002; ldr Real Estate Law Andersen Legal 1998–2002; memb Law Soc of Scotland; fell Soc Advanced Legal Studies 1998, WS, NP; *Recreations* psychology, music, history, art, wine, travel; *Style—* Donald Shaw, Esq; ✉ Dundas & Wilson LLP, North West Wing, Bush House, Aldwych, London WC2B 4EZ (tel 020 7759 3559, fax 020 7240 2448, e-mail donald.shaw@dundas-wilson.com)

SHAW, Fiona Mary; Hon CBE (2002); da of Dr Denis Joseph Wilson, of Cork, Ireland, and Mary Teresa, *née* Flynn; *b* 10 July 1958; *Educ* Scoil Mhuire Cork, UC Cork, RADA; *Career* actress; hon prof of drama Trinity Coll Dublin, Hon LLD Nat Univ of Ireland 1996; Hon PhD: Open Univ 1997, Trinity Coll Dublin 2001, Univ of Ulster 2004; Officier de l'Ordre des Arts et des Lettres (France) 2000; *Theatre* Julia in The Rivals (NT) 1983, Mary Shelley in Bloody Poetry (Leicester and Hampstead) 1984; RSC 1985–88: Tatyana Vasilyevna in Philistines, Celia in As You Like It, Madame de Volange in Les Liaisons Dangereuses, Erika Brückner in Mephisto, Beatrice in Much Ado About Nothing, Portia in The Merchant of Venice, Mistress Carol in Hyde Park, Katherine in The Taming of the Shrew, Lady Frampul in New Inn, title role in Electra (Best Actress Olivier Awards 1989, Theatre Critics's Award 1989); title role in Mary Stuart (Greenwich) 1988, Rosalind in As You Like It (Old Vic, Best Actress Olivier Awards 1989), Shen Te/Shui Ta in The Good Person of Sichuan (NT, London Theatre Critics' Award 1989, Best Actress Olivier Awards 1989), title role in Hedda Gabler 1991 (Abbey Theatre Dublin and Playhouse London, nominated Best Actress Olivier Awards 1992, winner London Theatre Critics' Award 1992), Machinal (RNT, Best Actress Evening Standard Award 1993, Best Actress Olivier Awards 1994), Footfalls (Garrick, 1 week) 1994, title role in Richard II (RNT) 1995, Millamant in The Way of the World (RNT) 1995, The Waste Land (Paris and Canada, winner Drama Desk Award NY 1997) 1996, speaker in Honegger's Joan of Arc at the Stake (BBC Proms) 1997, The Prime of Miss Jean Brodie (RNT) 1998; dir Widower's Houses (RNT) 1999, Medea (Abbey Theatre Dublin) 2000 (Irish Times Best Actress Award 2000), Medea (Queen's Theatre) 2001 (Best Actress Evening Standard Award 2002), The Powerbook (RNT) 2002, Medea (US tour) 2003 (Elliot Norton Award, Obie Award, NY Tony nomination), The Seagull (Edinburgh Festival) 2003, The Powerbook (Paris, Rome) 2003, Julius Caesar (Barbican) 2005, My Life is a Fairytale (NY) 2005, Readings (Theatre Nationale de Chaillot Paris) 2005, Dido and Anaeas (Vienna Festival) 2006, Woman and Scarecrow (Royal Court) 2006, Happy Days (RNT) 2007; *Television* incl: Elspeth in Fireworks for Elspeth 1983, Hedda Gabler 1993, Persuasion 1994, Jane Eyre 1994, The Waste Land 1995, Gormenghast 1999, The British Face 2005; *Film* My Left Foot 1988, The Mountains of the Moon 1988, Three Men and a Little Lady 1990, London Kills Me 1991, Super Mario Brothers 1993, Undercover Blues 1993, Anna Karenina 1996, The Butcher Boy 1996, The Avengers 1997, The Last September 1998, RKO 281 1999, The Triumph of Love 2000, Harry Potter and the Philosopher's Stone 2000, Harry Potter and the Chamber of Secrets 2002, Harry Potter and the Prisoner of Azkaban 2003, The Black Dahlia 2005, Catch and Release 2005, Fracture 2006; *Books* Players of Shakespeare (1987), Clamorous Voices (contrib, 1988), Conversation with Actresses (1990); *Recreations* travel, reading, running, painting; *Style—* Miss Fiona Shaw; ✉ c/o ICM Ltd, Oxford House, 76 Oxford Street, London W1N 0AX (tel 020 7636 6565, fax 020 7323 0101, e-mail shawassist@aol.com)

SHAW, (John) Howard; s of Arthur Shaw, and late Edith, *née* Richardson, of Oldham, Lancs; *b* 6 September 1948; *Educ* The Hulme GS Oldham, Bristol Univ (LLB); *m* 30 Dec 1972, Mary Charlotte, da of Rev Charles Strong, MBE (d 1959); 2 s (Alister Cameron, Duncan Howard); *Career* grad entry scheme Tstee and Income Tax Dept National Westminster Bank 1970–72; called to the Bar Inner Temple 1973; 3 Dr Johnson's Bldg: pupillage with Her Hon Judge Adrianne Uziell-Hamilton then His Hon Judge K Machin, QC, 1973–74, in practice 1973–87, admin of chambers 1987–90, head of chambers 1990–96; moved chambers to 29 Bedford Row; admitted to the Bar Rep of Ireland (King's Inn); memb: Family Law Bar Assoc, Professional Negligence Bar Assoc, Personal Injury Bar Assoc; *Style—* Howard Shaw, Esq

SHAW, Prof Sir John Calman; kt (1995), CBE (1989); s of Arthur John Shaw (d 1978), of Edinburgh, and Dorothy, *née* Turpie (d 1959); *b* 10 July 1932; *Educ* Strathallan Sch, Univ of Edinburgh (BL); *m* 2 Jan 1960, Shirley, da of James Botterill (d 1936), of Yedingham, N Yorks; 3 da (Jane b 14 Jan 1961, Gillian b 31 Jan 1963, Catherine b 9 Oct 1966); *Career* local sr ptnr Deloitte Haskins & Sells Edinburgh (formerly Graham Smart & Annan)1960–86, first exec dir Scottish Financial Enterprise 1986–90 (chm 1995–99), govr Bank of Scotland 1999–2002 (non-exec dir 1990, dep govr 1991–99); non-exec dir of various investment trusts and investment cos 1982–2003; Johnstone Smith prof of accountancy Univ of Glasgow 1977–82; public appts with: Scottish Industrial Devpt Advsy Bd, Financial Reporting Cncl, Scottish Enterprise, Univs Funding Cncl (chm Scot Ctee), Scottish HE Funding Cncl (chm), HE Funding Cncl for Eng, Scottish Economic Council, tstee David Hume Inst 1995–2001, first chm Advanced Mgmnt Prog in Scotland 1995–2005; dep chm Edinburgh Int Festival Soc 1990–2000; receiver-gen Priory of Scotland Order of St John of Jerusalem 1992–2002; hon degrees from: Univ of Edinburgh, Univ of Glasgow, Univ of St Andrews, Univ of Abertay Dundee, Napier Univ; CA 1954 (pres 1983–84), FCMA 1958, MBCS 1975, FRSE 1992, KStJ 1994; *Books* The Audit Report (1980), Bogie on Group Accounts (3 edn, 1973); *Recreations* walking, opera, foreign travel; *Clubs* New (Edinburgh), Caledonian; *Style*— Prof Sir John Shaw, CBE, FRSE; ✉ Tayhill, Dunkeld PH8 0BA (fax 01350 728981)

SHAW, John Dennis; s of Frederick Shaw (d 2003), of Chapeltown, Sheffield, and Dorothy, *née* Wilson (d 1958); *b* 11 July 1938; *Educ* Ecclesfield GS, Univ of Sheffield Med Sch (MB ChB); *m* 5 Sept 1964, Margaret, da of William John Jones, of Dymock, Glos; 1 da (Susan b 1965), 1 s (Simon b 1966); *Career* rotating registrar United Sheffield Hosp 1965–67, sr registrar in otolaryngology Cardiff Royal Infirmary and Singleton Hosp Swansea 1967–70, res fell Wayne State Univ Detroit 1970, conslt ENT surgn Royal Hallamshire Hosp Sheffield 1971–94, currently hon conslt ENT surgn; memb Cncl Sections of Otology and Laryngology RSM, regnl advsr in otolaryngology RCS Trent, memb Ct of Examiners RCS; FRCSEd 1967, FRCS 1969; *Books* Fibreoptic Endoscopy of the Upper Respiratory Tract; *Style*— John Shaw, Esq; ✉ The Gables, Sandygate Road, Sheffield S10 5UE (tel 0114 230 7784)

SHAW, Jonathan; MP; *Career* MP (Lab) Chatham and Aylesford 1997–; asst Govt whip 2006–; *Style*— Jonathan Shaw, Esq, MP; ✉ House of Commons, London SW1A 0AA (tel 020 7219 6919); Constituency Office, 411 High Street, Chatham, Kent ME4 4NU

SHAW, Dr Mark Robert; s of William Shaw (d 1993), of Drayton St Leonard, Oxon, and Mabel Courtenay, *née* Bower; *b* 11 May 1945; *Educ* Dartington Hall Sch, Oriel Coll Oxford (MA, DPhil); *m* 11 July 1970, Francesca Dennis, da of Rev Dennis Wilkinson (d 1971); 2 da (Zerynthia b 23 Dec 1972, Melitaea b 19 April 1978); *Career* research asst Dept of Zoology Univ of Manchester 1973–76, research fell Univ of Reading 1977–80; Nat Museums of Scotland (formerly Royal Scottish Museum): asst keeper Dept of Natural History 1980–83, keeper of natural history 1983–96, keeper of geology and zoology 1996–2005, hon research assoc 2005–; frequent contrib to various pubns on entomology; FRES 1974, FRSE 2004; *Recreations* field entomology, family life; *Style*— Dr Mark R Shaw; ✉ Royal Museum of Scotland, Chambers Street, Edinburgh EH1 1JF (tel 0131 247 4246, fax 0131 220 4819, e-mail m.shaw@nms.ac.uk)

SHAW, Martin; s of Albert Cyril Shaw (d 1967), of Leeds, and Letitia Whitehead (d 1978); *b* 31 October 1944; *Educ* Leeds GS, UCL (LLB); *m* 1, 19 Aug 1967 (m dis 1995), Christine Helen, da of Maurice Grenville Whitwam (d 1986), of Leeds; 1 da (Sarah b 25 Nov 1970), 2 s (Simon b 17 March 1973, Jonathan b 4 Aug 1978); *m* 2, 2 Aug 1996, Christine Elizabeth St Lawrence, da of Ivor St Lawrence Morris (d 1991), of Collingham, W Yorks; *Career* Simpson Curtis (merged with Pinsent & Co to form Pinsent Curtis 1995, now Pinsent Masons): articled clerk 1966–69, slr 1969–71, ptnr 1971–, head Corporate Dept 1980–88, managing ptnr 1992–94, head Corporate Dept Leeds 1999–2007, head Corporate Europe 2007–; chm: Minstergate plc 1985–89, ABI Caravans Ltd 1986–88, Minster Corporation plc 1988–90, Legal Resources Group 1988–91; dir Leeds Business Venture 1982–95; govr: Richmond House Sch 1977–92, Gateways Sch 1985– (currently chm); memb: Headingley Rotary Club, Variety Club of GB (chm Yorks region 1995); memb: Law Soc 1969, Leeds Law Soc 1969, Slrs Euro Gp 1975, ABA 1985, IBA 1985; *Recreations* running, golf, squash, tennis; *Clubs* Alwoodley Golf, Chapel Allerton Lawn Tennis and Squash; *Style*— Martin Shaw, Esq; ✉ Holly House, Smithy Lane, Bardsey, Leeds LS17 9DT (tel 01937 572888); Pinsent Masons, 1 Park Row, Leeds LS1 5AB (tel 0113 244 5000, fax 0113 244 8000)

SHAW, Rev (Ralph) Michael; s of late Stanley Shaw, and late Mary Ann Shaw; *b* 20 September 1945; *Educ* King Sch Pontefract, Lichfield Theological Coll, Univ of London (DipAE); *m* 26 July 1970, Eileen, *née* Scott; 2 s (Jeremy Paul b 21 March 1974, Matthew David b 13 Dec 1978); *Career* asst curate All Saints Dewsbury 1970, team vicar Redcar in Kirkleatham 1974, youth advsr St Albans Dio 1976, ceo John Grooms (charity) 1992–, chm VODG 1997–2000; dir: Dio of St Albans Community Project 1978–91, Mitrecrest Travel 1984–91, Acevo 1999–; chm Prince's Tst-Action Herts 1986–98; vice-chm Field Lane Fndn 2004– (chm 2001–04); memb Prince of Wales Gp on Disability, memb Dio of St Albans BSR, vice-chm Townsend C of E Sch 1986–91, govr St John's C of E Sch Digswell 1992–2001, tstee Church Action on Disability 1998–2002; *Books* Training Games & Exercises (1978); *Recreations* sailing, reading, arts, walking; *Style*— Rev Michael Shaw; ✉ John Grooms, 50 Scrutton Street, London EC2A 4QX (tel 020 7452 2000, fax 020 7452 2001)

SHAW, Murray William Anderson; s of Leslie Conway Shaw (d 1992), and Adeline Georgina, *née* Young; *b* 25 September 1957, Dundee; *Educ* Devonport GS, Bristol GS, Tudor Grange GS Solihull, Solihull Sixth Form Coll, Univ of Dundee (LLB); *m* 4 Oct 1986, Grace Yeun Hym, *née* Wong; 2 s (Adam David b 22 March 1990, Frazer Conway b 13 Oct 1992); *Career* slr specialising in construction and planning law; asst slr Biggart Baillie (formerly Biggart Baillie & Gifford) 1982–85 (apprentice 1980–82), asst Speechly Bircham 1985–86, ptnr Biggart Baillie & Gifford 1987– (asst slr 1986–87); memb: Licensing and Disciplinary Ctees ACCA, Planning Law Ctee Law Soc; memb Law Soc of Scot 1982; ACIArb 2003; *Recreations* golf, watching sport, cinema, theatre; *Clubs* Whitecraigs Golf; *Style*— Murray Shaw, Esq; ✉ Biggart Baillie, 310 St Vincent Street, Glasgow G2 5QR (tel 0141 228 8000, fax 0141 228 8310, e-mail mshaw@biggartbaillie.co.uk)

SHAW, Prof Richard Wright; CBE (1997); s of George Beeley Shaw (d 1965), and Bella, *née* Wright (d 1982); *b* 22 September 1941; *Educ* Lancaster Royal GS, Sidney Sussex Coll Cambridge (MA); *m* 2 April 1965, Susan Angela, da of Lewis Birchley; 2 s (David Lewis b 24 Sept 1970, James Lachlan b 29 July 1977); *Career* Univ of Leeds: asst lectr in mgmnt 1964–66, lectr in economics 1966–69; Univ of Stirling: lectr in economics 1969–75, sr lectr in economics 1975–84, head Dept of Economics 1982–84; Paisley Coll: prof and head Dept of Economics and Mgmnt 1984–86, vice-princ 1986, princ 1987–92; princ and vice-chllr Univ of Paisley 1992–2001; visiting lectr in economics Univ of Newcastle NSW 1982; dir: Renfrewshire Enterprise 1991–2000, Univs and Colls Employers Assoc 2000–01; chm Lead Scotland 2001–; convenor Ctee of Scottish Higher Educn Principals 1996–98; memb: Scottish Economic Cncl 1995–97, Scottish Business Forum 1998–99; fell Scottish Vocational Educn Cncl 1995; Hon DUniv Glasgow 2001; FRSA; *Books* Industry and Competition (with C J Sutton, 1976); *Recreations* walking, listening to music, sketching, painting; *Style*— Prof Richard Shaw, CBE

SHAW, Prof Robert Alfred; s of Walter Schlesinger (d 1964), and Lily Karoline, *née* Plahner (d 1954); *b* 2 November 1924; *Educ* Univ of London (BSc, PhD, DSc); *m* 23 Aug 1980, Dr Leylâ Süheylâ Shaw, da of Yusuf Gözen, of Tarsus, Turkey; 1 s (Robert b 28 March 1984), 1 da (Lily b 30 May 1989); *Career* WWII Royal Fusiliers and Queen's Royal Regt UK, India, SE Asia command 1944–47; Birkbeck Coll Univ of London: asst lectr 1953–56, lectr 1956–65, prof of chemistry 1965–90, prof emeritus 1990–; co-dir of an EC sponsored int research project in chemistry with Poland 1994–, co-dir of int research projects in chemistry: with Indian Inst of Science Bangalore 1971–81, with Turkey 1998– and 2002–; pioneer in interdisciplinary and international res collaboration interested in teamwork and leadership issues; author of numerous articles dealing with chemistry, educn, and third world countries; plenary lectr to Turkish Chemical Congress Konya 2002 and Kars 2004; memb Academic Policy Ctee of the Inter-Univ Cncl for Higher Educn Overseas 1976–81, UNESCO conslt to Turkish Govt 1977, main speaker and memb Organising Ctee of Conf sponsored by Institut Mondial du Phosphate Rabat Morocco 1977, main speaker on Life-long Educn in Koblenz W Germany 1978, fndr memb and was on steering ctee of Univ of the Third Age London; Dr (hc): Univ Paul Sabatier Toulouse 1978, Gebze Inst of Technol Turkey 2005; memb Soc of Chemical Indust; CChem, FRSC; *Recreations* reading, music, travelling, skiing, fencing; *Style*— Prof Robert A Shaw; ✉ Brettargh Holt, Camden Way, Chislehurst, Kent BR7 5HT (tel 020 8467 5656, e-mail brettargh.holt@dsl.pipex.com); School of Biological and Chemical Sciences, Birkbeck College (University of London), Malet Street, London WC1E 7HX

SHAW, Prof Robert Wayne; CBE (2002); s of Arthur Stanley Shaw (decd), of Colwyn Bay, Clwyd, and Margery Maud, *née* Griffiths (decd); *b* 25 June 1946; *Educ* Priory GS Shrewsbury, Univ of Birmingham (MB ChB, MD); *m* 6 March 1980, Mary Philomena; 1 s (Robert Andrew b 31 Dec 1982), 1 da (Hilary Mary b 21 June 1985); *Career* prof Dept of Obstetrics and Gynaecology: Royal Free Hosp Sch of Med 1983–92, Univ of Wales Coll of Med 1992–2001; currently at Sch of Human Devpt Univ of Nottingham; pres RCOG 1998–2001 (vice-pres 1995–98); memb: American Soc of Reproductive Med 1982, Br Fertility Soc 1985; dir World Endometriosis Soc; FRCSEd, FRCOG; *Books* Atlas of Endometriosis (1993, 2 edn 2002), Gynaecology (ed jtly, 1993, 3 edn 2002), Endometriosis - Current Understanding and Management (1995); *Recreations* sailing, hill walking; *Clubs* Athenaeum; *Style*— Prof Robert Shaw, CBE; ✉ Derby City General Hospital, Clinical Sciences Building, Uttoxeter Road, Derby DE22 3DT (tel 01332 724668, fax 01332 724697, e-mail robert.shaw@nottingham.ac.uk)

SHAW, Sarah Margaret Foulkes; *b* 2 June 1958; *Educ* Penarth GS, Univ of Birmingham (LLB, Sir Henry Barber Law Scholar, Gregg Memorial Prize), Coll of Law; *m* Prof Rory J Shaw; 2 da; *Career* slr Freshfields 1982–86 (articled clerk 1980–82), slr Cadbury Schweppes plc 1986–89, legal advsr Reed International plc 1989–91, gp co sec and legal advsr Signet Group plc 1992–95, gp co sec and head of legal BBA Group plc 1997–; memb Law Soc; *Style*— Mrs Sarah Foulkes Shaw; ✉ BBA Group plc, 20 Balderton Street, London W1K 6TL (tel 020 7514 3999, e-mail sshaw@bbagroup.com)

SHAW, Simon Dalton; MBE (2004); *b* 1 September 1973, Nairobi, Kenya; *Educ* King's Coll, Runneymede Coll, Godalming Sixth Form Coll, UWE; *Career* rugby union player (lock); clubs: Otago NZ, Bristol RUFC 1993–97, London Wasps RUFC 1997– (winners Tetley's Bitter Cup 1999 and 2000, Parker Pen Challenge Cup 2003, Zurich Championship 2003, 2004 and 2005, Heineken Cup 2004 and 2007); England: 38 caps, debut v Italy 1996, winners Six Nations Championship 2000 and 2003 (Grand Slam 2003), ranked no 1 team in world 2003, winners World Cup Aust 2003, memb squad World Cup France 2007; memb squad British and Irish Lions tour to South Africa 1997 and NZ 2005; *Style*— Simon Shaw, Esq, MBE; ✉ c/o Rugby Football Union, Rugby House, Rugby Road, Twickenham, Middlesex TW1 1DS

SHAW, Stephen; s of Ivan Shaw, and Phyllis, *née* Niechcicki; *b* 20 December 1952; *Educ* Harrow Co GS, Univ of Birmingham (LLB); *m* 26 Sept 1978, Fabia Melanie, da of John Alexander; 2 s (Gideon David b 20 Sept 1982, Aaron Alexander b 7 Jan 1987), 2 da (Gabrielle Leah b 25 March 1984, Rachel Rose Sybil b 24 July 1991); *Career* called to the Bar Gray's Inn 1975; pt/t lawyer chm London Rent Assessment Panel and Leasehold Valuation Tbnl; accredited CEDR mediator; MCIArb; *Books* contrib New Law Journal and Estates Gazette on landlord and tenant matters; *Recreations* amateur magic, jazz, cycling; *Style*— Stephen Shaw, Esq; ✉ Lamb Chambers, Lamb Building, Temple, London EC4Y 7AS (tel 020 7797 8300, fax 020 7797 8308, e-mail stephenshaw@lambchambers.co.uk)

SHAW, Dr Stephen; CBE (2004); s of Walter Arthur Shaw (d 1976), and Gwendolyn Primrose, *née* Cottrell; *b* 26 March 1953; *Educ* Rutlish Sch Merton, Univ of Warwick (BA), Univ of Leeds (MA), Univ of Kent (PhD); *m* 23 April 1977, Christine Elizabeth, da of Michael Robinson; 2 s (with Jane Angela Skinner); *Career* lectr: Coventry Tech Coll 1975–76, Mid-Kent Coll of Technol 1977–79; res offr: Nat Assoc for the Care and Resettlement of Offenders 1979–80, Home Office 1980–81; dir Prison Reform Trust 1981–99; prisons ombudsman 1999–2001, prisons and probation ombudsman 2001–; DUniv Univ of Central England 2000; *Publications* numerous publications on criminal justice and economic isssues; *Recreations* family life, watching Fulham FC; *Style*— Stephen Shaw; ✉ Prisons and Probation Ombudsman, Ashley House, 2 Monck Street, London SW1P 2BQ (tel 020 7035 2876, fax 020 7035 2860, e-mail stephen.shaw@ppo.gsi.gov.uk)

SHAW OF NORTHSTEAD, Baron (Life Peer UK 1994), of Liversedge in the County of West Yorkshire; Sir Michael Norman Shaw; kt (1982), JP (Dewsbury 1953), DL (W Yorks 1977); eld s of late Norman Shaw; *b* 9 October 1920; *Educ* Sedbergh; *m* 1951, Joan Mary Louise, da of Sir Alfred Law Mowat, 2 and last Bt, DSO, OBE, MC (d 1968); 3 s (Hon Charles Michael Mowat b 1952, Hon James William b 1955, Maj Gen the Hon Jonathan David b 1957); *Career* MP: (Lib and Cons) Brighouse and Spenborough 1960–64, (Cons) Scarborough and Whitby 1966–74, Scarborough 1974–92; PPS: to Min of Lab and Nat Serv 1962–63, to Sec of State for Trade and Industry 1970–72, to Chllr of the Duchy of Lancaster 1973–74; memb UK Delgn European Parl 1974–79; Liveryman Worshipful Co of Chartered Accountants; FCA; *Style*— The Rt Hon Lord Shaw of Northstead, DL; ✉ Duxbury Hall, Liversedge, West Yorkshire WF15 7NR (tel 01924 402270)

SHAW OF TORDARROCH, John; 22 Chief of the Highland Clan of Shaw; s of late Maj Charles John Shaw of Tordarroch, MBE, TD, DL, JP; *b* 1937; *Educ* Eton, Magdalene Coll Cambridge (MA); *m* 1960, Silvia Margaret, da of late Rev David John Silian Jones; 1 s; *Heir* s, Iain Shaw; *Career* late 2 Lt Seaforth Highlanders 1955–57; memb Queen's Body Guard for Scotland (Royal Co of Archers); hon vice-pres Clan Chattan Assoc (UK); memb standing Cncl of Scottish Chiefs; *Books* A History of Clan Shaw (ed); *Clubs* New, Turf, Puffins; *Style*— John Shaw of Tordarroch; ✉ Apartado de Correos No 5, 07510 Sineu, Majorca, Balearic Islands, Spain

SHAWCROSS, His Hon Judge Roger Michael; s of Michael Campbell Shawcross (d 1945), of London, and Friedel Marie Partington, *née* Freund (d 1983); *b* 27 March 1941; *Educ* Radley, ChCh Oxford (MA); *m* 15 Feb 1969, Sarah, da of Maurice Henry Peter Broom (d 1987), of Farnham, Surrey; 1 da (Miranda b 1972), 1 s (Philip b 1974); *Career* called to the Bar Gray's Inn 1967, recorder Western circuit 1985–93, circuit judge (Western circuit) 1993–, dep designated family judge Hants and IOW 2005–; *Recreations* tennis, music, literature, history, travel; *Style*— His Hon Judge Shawcross

SHAWCROSS, Valerie; CBE (2002), AM; *b* 9 April 1958; *Educ* Queen Elizabeth HS Manchester, Univ of Liverpool (BA), Univ of London (MA); *Career* ILEA Further and Higher Educn Div 1984–86, campaign offr World Univ Service (UK) 1986–87, project mangr Cwlth Secretariat 1987–91, head of Public Affairs Nat Fedn of Women's Insts 1991–92, Nat Women's Offr Lab Pty 1993, cncllr London Borough of Croydon 1994–2000 (chair Educn Ctee 1995–97, dep ldr 1996–97, ldr 1997–2000); GLA: memb London Assembly (Lab) Lambeth & Southwark 2000–, chair London Fire and Emergency Planning Authy 2000–; memb GLA: Audit Panel 2000–, Planning Ctee; memb Lab Pty 1979–; *Recreations* swimming, poetry, theatre; *Style*— Ms Valerie Shawcross, CBE, AM; ✉ London Assembly, City Hall, Queens Walk, Southwark, London SE1 2AA (tel 020 7983 4371, fax 020 7983 4418, e-mail valerie.shawcross@london.gov.uk, website www.valshawcross.com)

S

SHAWCROSS, (Hon) William Hartley Hume; s (by 2 m) Baron Shawcross (Life Peer, d 2003); *b* 28 May 1946; *Educ* Eton, UC Oxford; *m* 1, 1972 (m dis 1980), Marina Warner, *qv*, da of Col Esmond Pelham Warner, TD (d 1982), of Cambridge; 1 s (Conrad Hartley Pelham b 1977); m 2, 1981 (m dis), Michal, da of late A J Levin by his w Leah; 1 da (Eleanor Joan Georgina b 1983); m 3, 1993, Olga Polizzi, CBE, *qv*, eldest da of Baron Forte (Life Peer), and wid of Marchese Alessandro Polizzi di Sorentino; *Career* writer and broadcaster; chm Article 19: The Int Centre on Censorship 1986–96; memb Bd Int Crisis Gp 1995–2006; memb Informal Advsy Gp UNHCR 1996–2001; memb Govr's World Service Consultative Gp BBC 1997–2004; memb Cncl Disasters Emergency Ctee 1998–2002; assoc prodr and presenter Queen and Country (BBC TV series) 2002; *Books* Dubcek (1970), Crime and Compromise (1974), Sideshow (1979), The Quality of Mercy (1984), The Shah's Last Ride (1989), Rupert Murdoch (1992), Deliver Us from Evil: Warlords, Peacekeepers and a World of Endless Conflict (2001), Queen and Country (2002), Allies: The United States, Britain and the War in Iraq (2003); *Style*— William Shawcross; ✉ c/o Green and Heaton Ltd, 37 Goldhawk Road, London W12 8QQ (tel 020 7289 8089, website www.williamshawcross.com)

SHAWYER, Peter Michael; s of Edward William Francis Shawyer (d 1986), of Brookmans Park Herts, and Marjorie Josephine Shawyer; *b* 11 September 1950; *Educ* Enfield GS, Univ of Sheffield (BA); *m* 23 June 1979, Margot Anne, da of Wing Cdr Norman Edwin Bishop (d 1975), of Sidmouth, Devon; 1 da (Emily b 3 Dec 1980), 1 s (Richard b 14 March 1984); *Career* CA; Deloitte & Touche (formerly Touche Ross): joined 1972, memb Bd, managing ptnr, memb Euro Mgmnt Bd, memb Central Europe Bd; specialist in taxation and author of numerous tax articles in specialist journals; FCA 1975; *Recreations* golf; *Clubs* Hadley Wood Golf, Brocket Hall Golf; *Style*— Peter Shawyer, Esq; ✉ Deloitte & Touche, Stonecutter Court, 1 Stonecutter Street, London EC4A 4TR (tel 020 7303 5764, fax 020 7353 8648, telex 884739 TRLNDN G)

SHEA, Dr Jamie Patrick; *b* 11 September 1953; *Educ* Univ of Sussex (BA), Lincoln Coll Oxford (DPhil); *Family* m with 2 c; *Career* NATO: admin Cncl Ops Section of Exec Secretariat 1980–82, head of youth programmes 1982–85, head of external relations conferences and seminars 1985–98, asst to sec-gen 1988–91, dep head and sr planning offr Policy Planning Unit and Multilateral Affairs Section of Political Directorate 1991–93, spokesman and dep dir of info and press 1993–2000 (the public voice of NATO during the Kosovo conflict March-June 1999), dir of info and press 2000–, dep asst sec-gen 2003–; PR Week Euro Communicator of 1999; hon fell Atlantic Cncl of UK, external assoc Centre for Defence and Security Studies Univ of Manitoba Winnipeg Canada, fndn year fell, 21st Century Fndn, assoc memb Institut Royal des Relations Internationales Brussels; vice-pres and memb of bd of govrs Centre d'Etudes de Relations Internationales et Stratégiques Univ Libre de Bruxelles 1988– (Jean Monnet visiting prof), prof of int relations American Univ Washington DC 1985–99, lectr in defence studies Univ of Lille 1987–90, adjunct prof of int relations James Madison Coll Michigan State Univ 1987–, dir MSU Summer Sch Brussels 1987–, course instr Int Relations MA Boston Univ 1991–94, lectr in US/Euro Relations Univ of Antwerp 1993–; memb: Advsy Bd Centre d'Etudes et de Prospectives Stratégiques Paris, Trans-Atlantic Policy Network, Centre for Euro Policy Studies Brussels, Euro-Atlantic Movement, Int Studies Assoc USA; *Publications* The NATO Executive Secretariat (1983), NATO and Public Opinion (1986), The Myths of Anti-Americanism (1986), The Atlantic Gap: National Differences and the Future of the Alliance - Options for Action by the Private Sector (1987), NATO Public Opinion Survey (1987, 1988 and 1989), NATO's Future (1989), NATO 2000: The View from Brussels (1990), Moving on from the London Declaration: The Political Role of NATO in the new Europe (1992), The Impact of the Moscow Coup on NATO (1992), Coping with Disorder in Europe (1993), NATO in the 1990s (with Prof Michael Schechter, 2001); also articles in jls and book chapters; *Style*— Dr Jamie Shea; ✉ NATO, Division of Public Diplomacy, NATO Headquarters, Blvd Leopold III, 1110 Brussels, Belgium (tel 02 707 44 13, fax 02 707 45 79, e-mail j.shea@hq.nato.int)

SHEA, Michael Sinclair MacAuslan; CVO (1987, LVO 1985), DL; s of James Michael Shea, of Lenzie, Strathclyde; *b* 10 May 1938; *Educ* Gordonstoun, Univ of Edinburgh (MA, PhD); *m* 1968, Mona Grec Stensen, da of Egil Stensen, of Oslo, Norway; 2 da; *Career* FO 1963, former first sec Bonn, head of Chancery Bucharest 1973, DG Br Info Servs NY 1976, press sec to HM The Queen 1978–87; dir of public affairs Hanson plc 1987–93; nat memb for Scot ITC 1996–2003; chm: N2N Enviro UK Ltd 1999–2003, Royal Lyceum Theatre Co 1998–2004; chm Exec Ctee Edinburgh Military Tattoo, chm Scottish Nat Photographic Centre 2001–, former tstee Nat Galleries of Scotland, govr Gordonstoun Sch; author; *Books* Britain's Offshore Islands (1981), Tomorrow's Men (1982), Influence (1988), Leadership Rules (1990), Personal Impact (1992), Spin Doctor (1995), The British Ambassador (1996), To Lie Abroad (1996), Berlin Embassy (1998), The Primacy Effect (1998), Spinoff (1999), From The Sidelines (2003), The Freedom Years (2006) and six novels under the name Michael Sinclair; The Rich Tide (with Sir David Frost, *qv*, 1986), The Mid-Atlantic Companion (with Sir David Frost, 1986); *Recreations* writing; *Clubs* Garrick; *Style*— Michael Shea, Esq, CVO, DL; ✉ 1A Ramsay Garden, Edinburgh EH1 2NA (tel 0131 220 1456, e-mail shea@dial.pipex.com)

SHEAR, Warren Ivor; s of Alec Shear, of New Wanstead, and Edith Bessie, *née* Onnie (d 1989); *b* 8 August 1937; *Educ* East Ham GS, Univ of Sheffield, Royal Coll of Surgeons (LDS); *m* 1961, Marion, da of Aron Hollander; 1 s (Daniel Marc b 3 Dec 1968), 1 da (Sarah Jane b 20 Jan 1970); *Career* dentist; joined Prof H Singer's practice Holland Park 1964, own practice Wimpole St 1967–, pt/t clinical lectr in restorative dentistry Royal Dental Hosp London 1975, pt/t sr clinical lectr in restorative dentistry UCL 1982–91, pt/t UMDS (now GKT) 1992–; memb: RSM 1985, BDA 1962, London Dental Fellowship 1984 (pres 1992–93), Soc for Advancement of Anaesthesia in Dentistry; *publications:* author of various articles published in dental jls; *Recreations* reading, walking, swimming, working for human rights; *Style*— Warren Shear, Esq; ✉ 19 Wimpole Street, London W1M 7AD (tel 020 7580 3863)

SHEARD, Rodney Kilner (Rod); s of Saville Kilner Sheard (d 1990), and Margaret Helen, *née* Gibson; *b* 11 September 1951, Brisbane, Aust; *Educ* Indooroopilly HS Queensland, Queensland Inst of Technol (DipArch); *m* 30 July 1988, Catherine Marie Elisabeth, *née* Nouqueret; 2 s (Pierre Saville b 25 Nov 1989, Louis Alexandre b 21 July 1999); *Career* architect; specialist in stadia and creator of Stadia Generations concept; ptnr Howard Lobb and Ptnrs 1981 (joined 1975), chm LOBB 1993, currently sr princ and memb Bd HOK Sport+Venue+Event (formerly HOK+LOBB); work exhibited at Royal Acad and by Design Cncl; memb Venue Mgmnt Assoc; Hon DSc Univ of Luton 2002; RIBA 1977, FRSA, MRAIA; *Projects* incl: Croke Park Masterplan Dublin 1989–90, Royal Selangor Turf Club Kuala Lumpur 1989–93, Alfred McAlpine Stadium Huddersfield 1991–93 (RIBA Building of the Year Award 1995), Arsenal FC North Stand 1991–93, Chelsea FC North Stand 1993–94, Reebok Stadium Bolton Wanderers FC 1994–97, Millennium Stadium Cardiff 1995–99, Kempton Park Racecourse Main Stand 1995–97, Westpac Trust Stadium Wellington 1996–2000, Telstra Stadium (formerly Stadium Australia) Sydney 1996–99, Telstra Dome (formerly Colonial Stadium) Melbourne 1996–2000, Wembley National Stadium 1998–, Ipswich Town FC North Stand 1999–2002, Members' Facilities All England Lawn Tennis & Croquet Club Wimbledon 1999–2002, Arsenal Stadium Arsenal FC 1999–, Suncorp Stadium Brisbane 2000–03, Ascot Racecourse 2001–, Centre Court All England Lawn Tennis & Croquet Club Wimbledon 2002–; *Publications* Sports Architecture (2001), Stadia: A Design & Development Guide (with Prof Geraint John, *qv*, 1994); *Recreations* fly fishing, sailing, skiing, reading; *Clubs* RAC; *Style*— Rod Sheard, Esq; ✉ HOK Sport + Venue + Event, Unit 14, Blades Court, 121 Deodar Road, Putney, London SW15 2NU (tel 020 8874 7666, fax 020 8874 7470)

SHEARER, Alan; OBE (2001); s of Alan Shearer, and Anne, *née* Collins; *b* 13 August 1970; *Educ* Gosforth HS Newcastle upon Tyne; *m* Lainya; 1 s (Will), 2 da (Chloe, Hollie); *Career* professional footballer; clubs: Southampton FC 1988–92 (over 100 appearances), Blackburn Rovers 1992–96 (transferred for then Br record of £3.2 million, winners FA Premier League 1994/95), Newcastle United 1996– (transferred for then world record fee of £15m, player-coach 2005–); England: 63 full caps (30 as captain) and 30 goals (scored on debut v France 1992), capt England 1996–2000, memb squad European Championships 1992, 1996 and 2000, memb squad World Cup 1998, ret 2000; Sport Writers Player of the Year 1994, PFA Player of the Year 1995 and 1997, third FIFA World Player of 1996 Awards, Premier League Overall Player of the Decade 2003, Domestic Player of the Decade 2003; *Style*— Alan Shearer, Esq, OBE; ✉ c/o SFX Sports Group (Europe) Ltd, 9 Hockley Court, 2401 Stratford Road, Hockley Heath, West Midlands B94 6NW

SHEARER, Anthony Patrick (Tony); s of James Francis Shearer, CBE (d 1997), of London, and Judith Margaret, *née* Bowman; *b* 24 October 1948; *Educ* Rugby; *m* 1, 1 Dec 1972 (m dis 2007), Jennifer, da of Alfred Dixon (d 1981); 2 da (Juliet b 19 Aug 1980, Lauretta b 30 March 1982); m 2, 31 March 2007, Pam; *Career* ptnr Deloitte Haskins & Sells 1980–88 (joined 1967), chief operating offr M & G Group plc 1988–96, chief exec Electronic Share Information Ltd 1996–97, chief execMellon Fund Administration Ltd 1997–98, dep chief exec Old Mutual International 1998–2001; chm: Planet Recruit Ltd 2000–03, Updata plc 2001–03, Uruguay Mineral Exploration Inc 2002–, Caxton FX 2006–, Jerrold Hldgs 2006–; chief exec Singer & Friedlander Gp 2003–05; non-exec dir: Gremlin Group plc 1997–98, Wogen plc 2005–; govr Rugby Sch 1994–2004, chm of govrs Packwood Haugh Sch 2000–06; FCA; *Recreations* skiing, tennis, rock 'n' roll; *Clubs* Brooks's, City; *Style*— Tony Shearer, Esq; ✉ 10 Napier Road, London W14 8LQ (tel 020 7602 1570, fax 020 7371 2682, e-mail tony@tonyshearer.com)

SHEARER, Patrick John; QPM (2007); *Educ* Univ of Aberdeen (MA, LLB); *Career* Grampian Police: joined 1983, asst chief constable 2001–05, dep chief constable 2005–07; chief constable Dumfries and Galloway Constabulary 2007–; *Style*— Patrick Shearer, Esq, QPM; ✉ Dumfries and Galloway Constabulary, Cornwall Mount, Dumfries DG1 1PZ (tel 01387 242201, e-mail executive@dg.pnn.police.uk)

SHEARER, Dr Raymund Michael; s of Patrick Shearer (d 1959), of Belfast, and Elizabeth, *née* Toolan (d 1957); *b* 6 November 1930; *Educ* Irish Christian Brothers Belfast, Queen's Univ Belfast (MB BCh, BAO, MD); *m* 1, 3 Sept 1956, Frances Mary, da of Peter Lenfestey; 3 s (Raymond Patrick b 27 Feb 1958, Cormac Peter b 10 Feb 1960, Lawrence John Paul b 14 Oct 1964), 2 da (Paula Elizabeth b 25 March 1961, Elizabeth Anne b 4 Sept 1962); m 2, 3 March 1987, Deborra Jane, da of Henry Desmond Milling; 2 s (Desmond John b 9 March 1988, Kevin Raymund b 30 April 1989), 1 da (Emer Jane Diana b 27 June 1990); *Career* rotating house offr Mater Infirmorum Hosp Belfast 1954–55, locum tenens 1955, pt/t GP asst 1955–56, locum tenens 1956, GP's asst 1956–57, GP 1957–, pt/t med dir N & W Community Unit of Mgmnt (unit clinician 1983–94); memb: Eastern (formerly Belfast) Local Med Ctee 1958–, NI Gen Med Servs Ctee 1960– (hon vice-chm 1997–), Eastern Health and Social Servs Bd 1978–81, Pemberton Ctee NI (concerning prescribing and social security costs); vice-chm NI GP Obstetric Ctee 1965–97; BMA: memb 1974, NI rep 1990–, chm Cncl NI 1994–98; memb GMC 1994–99; *Recreations* ice skating, weight lifting (Bronze medal British Amateur Weight-Lifters' Association 1950); *Style*— Dr Raymund Shearer; ✉ 13 Deramore Drive, Malone Road, Belfast BT9 5JQ (tel 028 9066 4421, fax 028 9020 9134); practice: 26 Springfield Road, Belfast (tel 028 9059 3334)

SHEARS, Philip Peter; QC (1996); s of Arthur Geoffrey Shears (d 1969), of Hong Kong, and Olave, *née* Grain (d 1967); *b* 10 May 1947; *Educ* The Leys Sch Cambridge, Univ of Nottingham (LLB), Univ of Cambridge (LLB); *m* 2, 1990, Sarah; 3 c by prev m (James b 1977, Eleanor b 1980, Michael b 1981); *Career* called to the Bar Middle Temple 1972; memb Midland Circuit, recorder of the Crown Court 1990– (asst recorder 1985), specialist in commercial fraud and serious crime; memb Criminal Bar Assoc; *Recreations* sailing, country sports; *Clubs* Bar Yacht, Royal London Yacht (Vice Cdre); *Style*— Philip Shears, Esq, QC; ✉ 7 Bedford Row, London WC1R 4BU (tel 020 7242 3555, fax 020 7242 2511, mobile 07970 545615)

SHEARSMITH, Reeson Wayne (Reece); s of Reece Shearsmith, of Hull, and Christine, *née* Don; *b* 27 August 1969; *Educ* Bretton Hall Coll (BA); *m* 17 Feb 2001, Jane, *née* Welch; 1 da (Holly Madeline b 16 Sept 2002), 1 s (Daniel Finbar b 23 June 2004); *Career* comedian, actor and writer; Hon Dr Univ of Huddersfield 2003; *Theatre* A Local Show for Local People (Theatre Royal London and UK tour) 2000–01, Art (Whitehall Theatre London) 2002–03, As You Like It (Wyndham's Theatre London) 2005; *Television* BBC: Alexei Sayle's Merry-Go-Round 1998, Lenny Goes to Town 1998, In the Red 1998, The League of Gentlemen 1999, 2000 and 2002, Randall & Hopkirk (Deceased) 2000, TLC 2002, Catterick 2003; other credits incl: Spaced (Channel 4) 1999, The All Star Comedy Show (ITV) 2004, Max and Paddy's Road to Nowhere (Channel 4) 2004; *Radio* On the Town with the League of Gentlemen (Radio 4) 1997; *Film* This Year's Love 1999, Birthday Girl 2001, Shaun of the Dead 2003, The League of Gentlemen's Apocalypse 2005; *Awards* Perrier Award 1997, Sony Silver Award for Radio Comedy 1998, Golden Rose of Montreux 1999, Best Entertainment Award RTS 2000, Best Comedy Series BAFTA 2000, NME Readers' Poll 2001, Best Comedy South Bank Show 2003; *Publications* A Local Book for Local People (2000), The League of Gentlemen (script book, 2003); *Recreations* drawing (caricatures, cartoons), magic, conjuring; *Style*— Reece Shearsmith, Esq; ✉ c/o PBJ Management Ltd, 7 Soho Street, London W1D 3DQ (tel 020 7287 1112, fax 020 7287 1191, website www.pbjmgt.co.uk)

SHEASBY, (John) Michael; s of (Herbert) Basil Sheasby, OBE, JP (d 1993), of Maidenhead, Berks, and (Edith) Barbara, *née* Parker (d 1989); *b* 31 May 1936; *Educ* Haileybury; *m* 3 June 1961, Juliet Sylvia Gillett; 1 s (Christopher Mark Andrew b 30 Nov 1966); *Career* qualified CA 1958; Arthur Young & Co UK and Italy 1953–63, fin dir then md Gp Admin RCA Ltd 1964–81, vice-pres fin and planning Squibb Europe Inc 1982–88, fin ptnr Ernst & Young 1989–90, gp controller then dir of gp internal audit Glaxo Wellcome plc (formerly Glaxo Holdings plc) 1990–98; advsy dir American C of C 1990–98; chm Internal Audit Ctee ICAEW Audit Faculty 2002–06; hon treas BAAS 1994–2002; memb Audit Ctee: Crestco Ltd 1997–99, Natural History Museum 1999–, HEFCE 2003–; memb S Bucks DC 1999–2003; memb Cncl Brunel Univ 1998–2006, memb Ct Henley Mgmnt Coll 2002–06; FCA 1958, FIIA 1998; *Recreations* drawing and painting, watching rugby, sailing, bee keeping, rowing; *Clubs* Harlequin FC, London Irish RFC, Maidenhead RC (vice-pres 2005); *Style*— J Michael Sheasby, Esq; ✉ The Red House, Old Beaconsfield Road, Farnham Common, Buckinghamshire SL2 3LR (tel 01753 642656)

SHEBBEARE, Sir Thomas Andrew (Tom); KCVO (2003, CVO 1996); s of late Robert Austin Shebbeare, and Frances Dare Graham; *b* 25 January 1952; *Educ* Malvern, Univ of Exeter (BA); *m* 1976, Cynthia Jane Cottrell; 1 s, 1 da; *Career* World University Service (UK) 1973–75, gen sec British Youth Cncl 1975–80, admin Cncl of Europe 1980–85, exec dir Euro Youth Fndn 1985–88, chief exec The Prince's Tst 1998–2003 (dir 1988–98), dir of charities to HRH The Prince of Wales 2004–; dir: Gifts in Kind 1996–, UK Skills 1998–, Skills Festivals Co 1999–; tstee The Nations Tst 1995–; Hon LLD Univ of Exeter 2005; *Recreations* family, cooking, gardening, food and drink; *Style*— Sir Tom Shebbeare; ✉ HRH The Prince of Wales' Household, Clarence House, London SW1A 1BA (tel 020 7024 5756)

SHEDDEN, Dr (William) Ian Hamilton; s of George Shedden (d 1966), of Bathgate, Scotland, and Agnes Hamilton, *née* Heigh (d 1979); *b* 21 March 1934; *Educ* The Acad Bathgate, Univ of Edinburgh (BSc, MB ChB), Univ of Birmingham (MD), City Univ London (Dip Law); *m* 21 March 1960, Elma Joyce, da of Lewis M Jobson (d 1985), of Edinburgh; 3 s (Malcolm b 1960, Andrew b 1962, Colin b 1971), 1 da (Clare b 1968); *Career* cmmnd Capt RAMC 1961–67, regtl MO Hallamshire Bn York and Lancaster Regt 1961–67; lectr Univ of Sheffield 1960–64, sr res fell MRC 1964–67, dir R&D Lilly Industries Ltd 1968–77, vice-pres Eli Lilly & Co USA 1977–83, prof of med Univ of Indiana USA 1979–, md Glaxo Group Research Ltd 1983–86; dir: Speywood Group, The Speywood Laboratory 1991–97, Speywood Pharmaceuticals 1994–97; non-exec dir Evolutec Ltd 2000–01; asst dep coroner City of London 1987–99, conslt physician Institut Henri Beaufour Paris 1998–2001; Freeman City of London 1975, Liveryman Worshipful Soc of Apothecaries 1974; CBiol, FIBiol 1969, FRCPEd 1983, FACP 1981, FFPM 1990, FRCP 1991; *Books* Vinca Alkaloids in the Chemotherapy of Malignant Disease (ed vol 1–3, 1968–70); *Recreations* golf, travel (especially in the Antarctic); *Clubs* Naval and Military, The Dalmahoy; *Style—* Dr Ian Shedden; ✉ Beachamwell House, Beachamwell Road, Swaffham, Norfolk PE37 8BF (tel 01760 724126, fax 01760 724135, e-mail ian.shedden@ukgateway.net)

SHEEHAN, Sheriff Albert Vincent; s of Richard Greig Sheehan, of Bo'ness, and Mary, *née* Moffat; *b* 23 August 1936; *Educ* Bo'ness Acad, Univ of Edinburgh (MA, LLB); *m* 1965, Edna Georgina Scott (d 2000), da of Andrew Hastings, of Coatbridge; 2 da (Wendy b 1968, Susan b 1971); *Career* Capt Royal Scots (The Royal Regt) 1959–61; slr; depute procurator fiscal 1961–74, Leverhulme fell 1971–72, dep crown agent for Scot 1974–79, Scot Law Cmmn 1979–81; sheriff: Edinburgh 1981, Falkirk 1983–2005; *Recreations* naval history, travel, gardening; *Style—* Sheriff Albert Sheehan

SHEEHAN, Prof Antony; s of Thomas Sheehan (d 1977), of Cork, Ireland, and Mary Kerr, *née* Hood; *b* 10 September 1964, Cannock, Staffs; *Educ* Cardinal Griffin RC Sch Cannock, Staffs Coll (CertEd), St George's Psychiatric Sch Stafford, Manchester Met Univ (BEd), Univ of Nottingham (MPhil), Univ of Keele (DipHSM); *m* 26 March 2001, Andrea, *née* Coleman; 1 s (Ashley Thomas b 2 March 1984), 2 da (Bonnie Michelle b 2 Jan 1988, Ellie b 10 Aug 2006); *Career* mental health nurse; formerly: dir and mgmnt conslt European Nursing Devpt Agency, dir of serv devpt Fndn NHS Tst Staffs, asst regnl dir of public health NHS Exec W Midlands; Department of Health: jt head of mental health then ceo Nat Inst for Mental Health in Eng (NIMHE) and dir of mental health until 2003, DG Care Servs 2003–06, DG Health and Care Partnerships 2006–07, memb Corporate Mgmnt Bd; chief exec Leicestershire Partnership NHS Tst 2007–; chair and memb numerous Govt, departmental and NHS ctees and gps; prof of health and social care strategy Univ of Central Lancashire; visiting prof Univ of Central England; memb Panel of Inquiry Gray Report 1995; conslt: Int Cncl of Nurses and WHO Geneva 1990, WHO Copenhagen 1994, Ivan Sechenov Acad Moscow 1994; memb Editorial Bd Public Serv Leadership Jl, author of more than 50 pubns; patron AS-IT, former pres No Panic; registered nurse; Hon DSc Univ of Wolverhampton 2003, Hon Dr Univ of Staffordshire 2005; MHSM, Hon MFPH; *Recreations* walking with dogs, film, photography, fast cars; *Style—* Prof Antony Sheehan; ✉ Leicestershire Partnership NHS Trust, George Hine House, Gipsy Lane, Leicester LE5 0TD (tel 0116 2256547, fax 0116 2256679, e-mail mala.dhakk@leicsport.nhs.uk)

SHEEHY, Sir Patrick; kt (1991); s of Sir John Francis Sheehy, CSI (d 1949), and Jean Newton Simpson (d 1993); *b* 2 September 1930; *Educ* Australia, Ampleforth; *m* 1964, Jill Patricia Tindall; 1 s, 1 da; *Career* Nat Serv 2 Lt Irish Gds 1948–50; British-American Tobacco Co: joined 1950, various appts Nigeria, Ghana, Ethiopia and West Indies, mktg advsr London 1962–67, gen mangr Holland 1967, memb Gp Bd 1970, memb Chm's Policy Ctee and chm Tobacco Div 1975; BAT Industries plc: dep chm 1976–81 (chm BATCo Bd), vice-chm 1981–82, chm 1982–95; chm: Marlborough Underwriting 1996, Perpetual Income Investment Trust Ltd 1996–2007; non-exec dir: British Petroleum Company plc 1984–98, Asda Property Holdings 1994–, Abdela Holdings UK Ltd 1996, Sherritt International Corp 1996–, Celtic plc 1996, EFG Private Bank Ltd 1996, Cluff Mining 1997–; memb Cncl of Int Advsrs Swiss Bank Corporation 1985–97, memb Bd The Spectator 1988–2004; formerly memb: President's Ctee CBI, European Roundtable of Industrialists, Action Ctee for Europe, Cncl RIIA; estab Franco British Colloque 1990–, chm Home Office Inquiry into Police Responsibility and Rewards; Chevalier de la Légion d'Honneur (France) 1995; *Recreations* golf, reading, skiing; *Style—* Sir Patrick Sheehy

SHEEPSHANKS, Robin John; CBE (1990), DL (Suffolk 1979); s of Maj Richard Sheepshanks, DSO, MVO (d 1951), by his w Hon Bridget, *née* Thesiger (d 1983), da of 1 Viscount Chelmsford; *b* 4 August 1925; *Educ* Eton; *m* 1951, Lilias Mulgrave, da of Maj Sir Humphrey Noble, 4 Bt, MBE, MC (d 1968), of Walwick Hall; 4 s (David b 1952, Richard b 1955, Andrew b 1960, Christopher b 1964); *Career* Capt 1 King's Dragoon Gds 1943–52; farmer 1952–; memb E Suffolk CC 1963–74, chm Suffolk CC 1982–84 (memb 1974–93); High Sheriff Suffolk 1981; chm: Suffolk Police Authority, Standing Conference of E Anglian Local Authorities 1987–93, Felix Cobbold Trust 1985–93, Crimestoppers Anglia Region 1994–97, Radgrade Ltd 1981–; dir East Coast Cable Ltd 1989–93; memb Worshipful Co of Gunmakers; OStJ; *Recreations* shooting, golf, fishing, gardening; *Clubs* Cavalry and Guards', Pratt's; *Style—* Robin Sheepshanks, Esq, CBE, DL; ✉ The Rookery, Eyke, Woodbridge, Suffolk IP12 2RR (tel 01394 460226)

SHEERMAN, Barry John; MP; s of William Sheerman; *b* 17 August 1940; *Educ* Hampton GS, LSE (BSc), Univ of London (MSc); *m* 1965, Pamela Elizabeth, *née* Brenchley; 1 s, 3 da; *Career* former univ lectr; MP (Lab): Huddersfield E 1979–83, Huddersfield 1983–; memb: Public Accounts Ctee 1980–83, Parly Univ Gp; chm: Parly Advsy Cncl for Tport Safety, Educn and Skills Ctee 1999–; chair: Parly Manufacturing Industry Gp, Parly Gp for Design and Innovation, Cross Pty Advsy Gp on Preparation for EMU, Urban Mines, Networking for Industry (formerly Made In The UK), Cross-Pty Gp on European Economic Reform 2005–; oppn front bench spokesman on employment and educn with special responsibility for devpt of educn policy and trg for over-16s 1983–87, spokesman on employment 1987–97, home affairs front bench spokesman on police, prisons, crime prevention, drugs, civil defence and fire serv, dep to Rt Hon Roy Hattersley MP 1988–92, shadow min for disability rights 1992–94, memb Sec of State for Trade and Industry's Manufacturing Task Force; chair World Bank Global Road Safety Partnership 2002–04, chair John Clare Educn and Environment Tst 2005–; Hon DEd: Kingston Univ 2006, Univ of Bradford 2006; *Books* Harold Laski (with Isaac Kramnick, 1993); *Recreations* social entrepreneuring, walking, music; *Style—* Barry Sheerman, Esq, MP; ✉ House of Commons, London SW1A 0AA (tel 020 7219 5037, constituency office 01484 451382, e-mail sheermanb@parliament.uk)

SHEFF, Sylvia Claire; MBE (1995), JP (1976); da of Isaac Glickman (d 1981), of Prestwich, Manchester, and Rita, *née* Bor (d 1976); *b* 9 November 1935; *Educ* Stand GS for Girls, Univ of Manchester (BA); *m* 28 Dec 1958, Alan Frederick Sheff (d 1986); 1 da (Janine Rachel b 1960), 1 s (Marcus Jeremy b 1963); *Career* teacher 1958–77; fndr and dir Friendship with Israel All-Pty Gp (in European Parl) 1979–90, asst nat dir Cons Friends of Israel 1985–89 (nat projects dir 1974–85), assoc dir Manchester Jewish Cultural Centre 1990–94; chm and pres Manchester 35 Gp Women's Campaign for Soviet Jewry 1980– (fndr chm 1972–80), fndr memb Bury Family Conciliation Serv Mgmnt Ctee 1985–87, hon sec Nat Cncl for Soviet Jewry UK 1987–89 (memb Cncl 1975–90), del Bd of Deps of Br Jews 1987–, int co-ordinator Yeled Yafeh Fellowship Children of Chernobyl Project 1990–94, memb UK Assoc of Jewish Lawyers and Jurists 2001–; delg and lectr Jewish Rep Cncl of Gtr Manchester; concert promoter/dir Manchester Jewish Community's Musical Tribute to HM The Queen on Her Golden Jubilee 2002–; *Recreations* bridge, theatre, opera, travel; *Style—* Mrs Sylvia Sheff, MBE; ✉ 6 The Meadows, Old Hall Lane, Whitefield, Manchester M45 7RZ (tel 0161 766 4391, fax 0161 766 4391)

SHEFFIELD, Graham; *Educ* Univ of Edinburgh (BA); *m*; 2 c; *Career* music prodr BBC Radio 1976–90 (series incl: Ragas and the Republic, Music Weekly and Tasting Notes (Sony Radio Award 1990)), music dir South Bank Centre 1990–95 (fndr Meltdown Festival), artistic dir Barbican 1995–; chair Int Soc of Performing Arts 2004–06, chm Royal Philharmonic Soc 2005–, cncl memb Arts Cncl Eng, int artistic assoc Luminato Festival Toronto 2007–; Hon Dr of Arts City Univ; Chevalier de l'Ordre des Arts et des Lettres (France) 2005, Chevalier de Tastevin de Bourgogne (France) 2005; *Recreations* wine, cricket, skiing, piano; *Style—* Graham Sheffield, Esq; ✉ Barbican Centre, Silk Street, London EC2Y 8DS

SHEFFIELD, Bishop of 1997–; Rt Rev John (Jack) Nicholls; s of James William Nicholls (d 1997), of Rossendale, Lancs, and Nellie, *née* Bann (d 1986); *b* 16 July 1943; *Educ* Bacup & Rawtenstall GS, King's Coll London (AKC, Jelf Prize for Theol); *m* 1969, Judith, da of William Ernest Dagnall; 2 s (Antony Paul b 15 May 1971, Michael Patrick David b 11 Nov 1973), 2 da (Rachel Elizabeth b 4 Dec 1977, Clare Frances b 18 April 1979); *Career* curate St Clement with St Cyprian Ordsall Salford 1967–69, vicar All Saints and Martyrs Langley 1972–78 (curate 1969–72), dir of pastoral studies Coll of the Resurrection Mirfield 1978–83, residentiary canon of Manchester Cathedral 1983–90, bishop of Lancaster 1990–97; memb House of Lords 2002–; warden of the community of St Mary the Virgin Wantage 1987–98; fell Univ of Central Lancashire 1997; *Books* A Faith Worth Sharing? A Church Worth Joining? (jtly, 1995); *Recreations* music, reading, listening to and telling stories; *Clubs* Royal Over-Seas League; *Style—* The Rt Rev the Lord Bishop of Sheffield; ✉ Bishopscroft, Snaithing Lane, Sheffield S10 3LG (tel 0114 230 2170, fax 0114 263 0110, e-mail bishop.jack@bishopscroft.idps.co.uk)

SHEFFIELD, (John) Julian Lionel George; DL (Hants 2001); s of John Vincent Sheffield, CBE (himself 4 s of Sir Berkeley Sheffield, 6 Bt, JP, DL); *b* 28 August 1938; *Educ* Eton, Christ's Coll Cambridge; *m* 1961, Carolyn Alexandra, er da of late Brig Sir Alexander Abel Smith, TD, by his 1 w, Elizabeth (da of David B Morgan, of N Carolina); 3 s (John b 1963, Simon b 1964, Lionel b 1969), 1 da (Nicola b 1973); *Career* industrialist; chm: Portals Group plc (papermaking co) 1979–95 (Queen's Award for Export 1966, 1977 and 1982), Norcros plc 1989–96 (joined 1974); dep chm Guardian Royal Exchange 1981–99; dir: Newbury Racecourse plc 1988–2005, Inspec Group plc 1995–98, De La Rue plc until 1998; chm North Foreland Lodge Ltd 1987–97, chm N Hants Med Tst 2002; chm Hosp of St Cross; tstee: Henry Smith Charity 1971– (chm 1997–), Winchester Cathedral Tst, Portsmouth Cathedral Devpt Tst until 2006; High Sheriff Hants 1998–99; Liveryman Worshipful Co of Gunmakers; *Recreations* outdoor sports, collecting; *Clubs* White's, MCC; *Style—* Julian Sheffield, Esq, DL; ✉ Spring Pond, Laverstoke, Whitchurch, Hampshire RG28 7PD (tel 01256 895130)

SHEFFIELD, Sir Reginald Adrian Berkeley; 8 Bt (GB 1755), of Normanby, N Lincs; DL (Lincs 1985); s of Maj Edmund Sheffield, JP, DL (d 1977), of Sutton Park, Sutton-on-the-Forest, York; (s of 6 Bt), and Nancie Miriel Denise, wid of Lt Cdr Glen Kidston, RN, and yst da of Edward Roland Soames (d 1997); suc unc, Sir Robert Sheffield, 7 Bt 1977; *b* 9 May 1946; *Educ* Eton; *m* 1, 1969 (m dis 1975), Annabel Lucy Veronica, da of late Timothy Angus Jones, and late Hon Mrs Pandora Astor; 2 da (Samantha Gwendoline (Mrs David Cameron), *qv*, b 1971, Emily Julia (Mrs Tom Mullion) b 1973); m 2, 1977, Victoria Penelope, da of late Ronald Clive Walker, DFC; 1 s (Robert Charles Berkeley b 1984), 2 da (Alice Daisy Victoria b 1980, Lucy Mary b 1981); *Heir* s, Robert Sheffield; *Career* chm Normanby Estate Holdings and subsidiaries; cncllr (Cons) Ermine Ward Humberside CC 1981–89, vice-chm S Humberside Business Advice Centre Ltd; landowner (7,500 acres); memb: CLA, IOD; *Recreations* shooting, stalking; *Clubs* White's, Pratt's, Lincolnshire; *Style—* Sir Reginald Sheffield, Bt, DL; ✉ Thealby Hall, Thealby, Scunthorpe, North Lincolnshire DN15 9AB; Estate Office, Normanby, Scunthorpe, North Lincolnshire DN15 9HS (tel 01724 720618, fax 01724 721565); 4 Needham Road, London W11 2LR (tel 020 7727 4160); Sutton Park, Sutton-on-the-Forest, York YO61 1DP (tel 01347 810249, e-mail norestate@fsbdial.co.uk)

SHEFFIELD AND ROTHERHAM, Archdeacon of; *see:* Blackburn, Ven Richard Finn

SHEIKHOLESLAMI, Prof (Ali) Reza; s of Sultan Ali Sultani Sheikholeslami (d 1972), and Shah Zadeh, *née* Mansuri; *b* 21 July 1941; *Educ* Hadaf HS Tehran, Columbia Univ (BA), Northwestern Univ (MA), UCLA (PhD); *m* 2, 1996, Scheherezade, da of Ibrahim Vigeh; *Career* asst prof of political science Univ of Washington 1975–85, sr research fell Harvard Univ 1985–88; Univ of Oxford: visiting sr fell St Antony's Coll 1988–90, Soudavar prof of Persian studies and professorial fell Wadham Coll 1990–; *Books* The Political Economy of Saudi-Arabia, The Structure of Central Authority in Qagar Iran 1871–1896; *Recreations* reading, cycling, travelling; *Style—* Prof Reza Sheikholeslami; ✉ Oriental Institute, University of Oxford, Pusey Lane, Oxford OX1 2LE (tel 01865 278200, fax 01865 278190, e-mail ali.sheikholeslami@orinst.oxford.ac.uk)

SHEIL, Anthony Leonard; s of William Anthony Sheil (d 1945), and Flora Aileen, *née* MacDonnell (d 1982); *b* 18 May 1932, London; *Educ* Ampleforth, ChCh Oxford; *m* 23 Nov 1997, Annette, *née* Worsley-Taylor; *Career* fndr and chm Anthony Sheil Associates (literary agency) 1962–; co-fndr and dir: Sources of History Ltd 1970–75, Wallace Aitken & Sheil 1972–89; chm Sheil Land Associates 1990–99; chm Authors Agents Assoc 1981–84; *Recreations* walking, reading, philhellenism; *Clubs* Beefsteak; *Style—* Anthony Sheil, Esq; ✉ 3/57 Drayton Gardens, London SW10 9RU (tel 020 7835 0221, fax 020 7835 0846, e-mail anthony.sheil@gmail.com); c/o Gillon Aitken Associates Ltd, 18 Cavaye Place, London SW10 9PT (tel 020 7373 8672, fax 020 7373 6002, e-mail anthony@gillonaitken.co.uk)

SHEIL, Rt Hon Lord Justice; Rt Hon Sir John Joseph; kt (1989), PC (2005); s of Hon Mr Justice (Charles Leo) Sheil (d 1968), and Elizabeth Josephine, *née* Cassidy (d 1984); *b* 19 June 1938; *Educ* Clongowes Wood Coll, Queen's Univ Belfast (LLB), TCD (MA); *m* 18 April 1979, Brenda Margaret Hale, da of Rev Forde Patterson (d 1982), and Elizabeth, *née* Irwin (d 1977); 1 s (Michael Forde b 23 Oct 1980); *Career* called to the Bar: NI 1964, Gray's Inn 1974, Ireland 1976; QC 1975, judge of the High Court of Justice NI 1989–2004, Lord Justice of Appeal NI 2004–; memb Governance Advsy Ctee Br Cncl 2002–; *Recreations* golf, travel; *Style—* The Rt Hon Lord Justice Sheil; ✉ Royal Courts of Justice, Chichester Street, Belfast BT1 3JF (tel 028 9023 5111)

SHEINKMAN, Elizabeth; da of Shepard A Sheinkman, and Katherine, *née* Ruben; *b* 1 June 1971, NY; *Educ* Sidwell Friends HS Washington DC, Columbia Univ NY (BA); *m* 2 July 2005, Hon James Byng; *Career* asst ed: Oxford Univ Press NY 1993–94, Alfred A Knopf 1994–96; literary agent Elaine Markson Literary Agency NY 1996–2004, dir Elaine Markson Agency Ltd UK 2004–06, sr agent and dir Book Bd Curtis Brown Gp Ltd 2006–; co-chair Young Lions Ctee NY Public Library 2003–05, visiting fell Bread Loaf Writers' Conf 2000, 2001 and 2006, visiting lectr Chenango Valley Writers' Conf 1998 and 1999; memb: PEN 1999–, Women in Publishing (NYC Chapter) 2001–04; *Recreations* music, yoga; *Clubs* Soho House; *Style—* Ms Elizabeth Sheinkman; ✉ 151 Chesterton Road, London W10 6ET (tel 020 8964 8883, fax 020 8969 8524); Curtis Brown Group Ltd, Haymarket House, 28–29 Haymarket, London SW1Y 4SP (tel 020 7393 4426, e-mail elizabeth@curtisbrown.co.uk)

SHEINMAN, Dr Bryan David; s of Neville Sheinman, of London, and Anita Sheinman (d 1988); *b* 23 June 1950; *Educ* Woodhouse GS Finchley, Univ of London (BPharm), Bart's

(MB BS), RCP (MRCP), Univ of London (MD); *m* 27 May 1991, Marilyn Phillips, da of Alec Kesselman; *Career* house offr in med and oncology Bart's 1977, house surgn in gen surgery Royal Berks Hosp 1977–78; sr house offr in: med, diabetes, chests and geriatrics Whittington Hosp 1978–79, neurology Bart's 1979–80; registrar in med and cardiology Royal Free Hosp 1980–83, res fell in thoracic med Bart's 1983–86, lectr Cardiothoracic Inst 1986–87; currently: in private practice Harley St, assoc specialist in Chest and Allergy St Mary's Hosp London; memb Worshipful Soc of Apothecaries; memb: Br Thoracic Soc, Br Soc of Allergy and Clinical Immunology, RSM; *Recreations* sailing, jazz; *Style—* Dr Bryan Sheinman; ✉ 5th Floor Consulting Rooms, Wellington Hospital South, Wellington Place, London NW8 9LE; 7 Kidderpore Gardens, London NW3 (tel 020 7794 0664)

SHEINWALD, HE Sir Nigel; KCMG (2001); s of Leonard Sheinwald (d 2006), and Joyce, *née* Posener; *b* 26 June 1953, London; *Educ* Harrow Co Sch for Boys, Balliol Coll Oxford (MA); *m* 20 Aug 1980, Julia, *née* Dunne; 3 s; *Career* HM Diplomatic Service: joined 1976, postings in Moscow, Washington DC, Brussels, London, press sec and head News Dept FCO 1995–98, dir Europe FCO and UK ambass and permanent rep to the EU Brussels 2000–03; foreign policy advsr to the PM and head of Cabinet Office Def and Overseas Secretariat 2003–07, ambass to US 2007–; *Style—* HE Sir Nigel Sheinwald, KCMG; ✉ c/o Foreign and Commonwealth Office (Washington DC), King Charles Street, London SW1A 2AH

SHEKHDAR, James (Jim); s of Nariman Shekhdar (d 1988), and Amy Doris Shekhdar (d 1965); *b* 13 November 1946, Leamington Spa, Warks; *Educ* Leamington Coll for Boys, QMC; *m* 13 Aug 1977, Jane, *née* Riley; 2 da (Anna b 28 May 1979, Sarah b 22 April 1981); *Career* ocean rower; civil engr UK, Africa, Aust, Middle East, NZ and New Guinea 1970–81, prop of own IT business then sales and mktg role Epson 1982–85, mgmnt conslt CEE Bratislava 1985– (pt/t 1997–), ocean rower, project planner and speaker 1997–; world record unassisted and solo row of the Pacific Ocean in 274 days; supporter: Williams Fund, Saving Faces, BASICS, Population Concern; *Books* Bold Man of the Sea (2001); *Recreations* sport, adventure and exploration; *Clubs* Northwood Cricket; *Style—* Jim Shekhdar, Esq; ✉ 35 Roy Road, Northwood Middlesex HA6 1EQ (tel and fax 01923 822411, e-mail jim.shekhdar@btinternet.com)

SHELDON, Brig Geoffrey Paul; s of William Sheldon, of Matlock, Derbys, and Margaret, *née* Aitken; *b* 9 October 1953; *Educ* Dunfermline HS, Magdalen Coll Oxford (MA); *m* 28 March 1978, Elizabeth Ruscoe, *née* Hill; *Career* CO 1 Bn Queen's Lancashire Regt 1991–94, directing staff Army Staff Coll 1994–95, dir Kuwait Jt Command & Staff Coll 1995–98, RCDS 1999, Cdr Br Forces Falkland Is 2000, dir Land Digitalization MOD 2001–04, account dir Defence Consulting EDS 2007; Col Queen's Lancashire Regt 2001–06, memb Queen's Lanc Regtl Cncl; *Recreations* cricket, sailing, running, military history; *Style—* Brigadier Geoffrey Sheldon; ✉ EDS, 1–3 Bartley Wood Business Park, Barley Way, Hook, Hampshire RG27 9XA (tel 01256 742000, fax 01256 742666, e-mail geoffrey.sheldon@eds.com)

SHELDON, (Timothy) James Ralph (Jamie); s of Anthony John Sheldon, and Elizabeth Mary, *née* Ferguson; *b* 9 July 1956; *Educ* Eton, Univ of Exeter (BA); *m* 25 Feb 1984, Susan Jean (Susie), da of John Ridell Best; 1 s (Charles b 14 Oct 1985, Richard b 30 June 1990), 1 da (Sophie b 23 Nov 1987); *Career* CA; Armitage & Norton 1978–82, Robert Fleming & Co Ltd 1982–87; chief exec GNI Ltd 1987–99; dir: GNI Holdings Ltd 1992–99, Gerrard Group plc 1994–99; chm Immersive Educn Ltd 2000–; non-exec dir: Harry Ferguson Ltd 1983–, Mathengine plc; ACA; *Recreations* sailing, skiing, farming, flying, tennis, piano; *Clubs* Royal Yacht Squadron, Royal Thames Yacht, Air Squadron; *Style—* Jamie Sheldon, Esq

SHELDON, Mark Hebberton; CBE (1997); s of George Hebberton Sheldon (d 1971), and Marie, *née* Hazlitt (d 1974); *b* 6 February 1931; *Educ* Stand GS, Wycliffe Coll, CCC Oxford (MA); *m* 16 June 1971, Catherine Eve, da of Edwin Charles James Ashworth (d 1968); 1 da (Alice b 1972), 1 s (Edward b 1976); *Career* Nat Serv Lt Royal Signals 1949–50, TA 1950–53; admitted slr 1957; Linklaters & Paines: articled 1953–56, asst slr 1957–59, ptnr 1959–94, resident ptnr New York 1972–74, sr ptnr 1988–91, jt sr ptnr 1991–93, conslt 1994–96; govr PPP Fndn (now The Health Fndn) 1998–2002 (chm 1999–2001), non-exec dir Coutts & Co 1996–98; Law Soc: memb Cncl 1978–96, treas 1981–86, pres 1992–93; pres City of London Law Soc 1987–88; chm Bar Cncl Working Pty on Barristers' Rights to Conduct Litigation 1999–2000; memb: Cncl of JUSTICE 1993–2005, Advsy Cncl of Centre for Socio-Legal Studies Univ of Oxford 1995–2003, Panel of Conciliators of Int Centre for Investment Disputes 1995–2003, Cncl Corp of Lloyd's 1989–90 (chm Working Pty on Voting Rights 1993), Cadbury Ctee on Fin Aspects of Corp Governance 1991–95, Financial Reporting Cncl 1990–98, Financial Law Panel 1993–98, Sr Salaries Review Body 1994–99; tstee Oxford Inst of Legal Practice 1993–, tstee and dir Court Based Personal Support (personal support unit at Royal Courts of Justice) 2002–; govr: Yehudi Menuhin Sch 1996–; memb Ct City of London Slrs' Co 1975– (Master 1987–88); hon bencher Inner Temple 1993; hon memb: Canadian Bar Assoc 1993–, Soc of Public Teachers of Law 1993–; hon fell CCC Oxford 1995; *Recreations* music, English watercolours, wine and food, swimming; *Clubs* Travellers, City of London, Hurlingham; *Style—* Mark Sheldon, Esq, CBE; ✉ 5 St Albans Grove, London W8 5PN (tel 020 7460 7172, fax 020 7938 4771)

SHELDON, Richard Michael; QC (1996); s of Ralph Maurice Sheldon, of Maidenhead, Berks, and Ady, *née* Jaudel; *b* 29 September 1955; *Educ* Bolton Sch, Maidenhead GS, Jesus Coll Cambridge (MA, pres CUMC); *m* 1983, Helen Mary, da of John Lake; 1 da (Laura Jane b 1986), 2 s (Nicholas James b 1988, William Mark b 1991); *Career* called to the Bar Gray's Inn 1979; *Publications* Halsbury's Laws of England (Vol 7 (3), Companies 4 edn, 1996); *Recreations* music, bassoon; *Style—* Richard Sheldon, Esq, QC; ✉ 3/4 South Square, Gray's Inn, London WC1R 5HP (tel 020 7696 9900, fax 020 7696 9911)

SHELDON, Baron (Life Peer UK 2001), of Ashton-under-Lyne in the County of Greater Manchester; Robert Edward Sheldon; PC (1977); *b* 13 September 1923; *Educ* Whitworth scholar, BSc; *m* 1, 1945, Eileen Shamash (d 1969); 1 s, 1 da; m 2, 1971, Mary Shield; *Career* trained as engr; Parly candidate (Lab) Manchester Withington 1959, MP (Lab) Ashton-under-Lyne 1964–2001; oppn spokesman on Treasy matters, civil service and machinery of Govt 1970–74; min of state: CSD 1974, Treasy 1974–75; fin sec to Treasy 1975–79, oppn front bench spokesman on Treasy and econ affrs 1981–83; memb: Select Ctee on Treasy and Civil Service until 1981 (and chm Sub-Ctee), Public Expenditure Ctee 1972–74 (chm gen sub-ctee); chm: Public Accounts Ctee 1983–97 (memb 1965–70 and 1975–79), Standards and Privileges Ctee 1997–2001, Liaison Ctee 1997–2001, Public Accounts Cmmn 1997–2001; vice-chm All Pty Arts and Heritage Gp 1997–2001 (pres 2001–); chm: Lab Parly Econ Affrs and Fin Gp 1967–68, NW Gp of Lab MPs 1970–74; dir Manchester C of C 1964–74; *Style—* The Rt Hon the Lord Sheldon, PC; ✉ 2 Ryder Street, London SW1 (tel 020 7839 4533, fax 020 7930 1528); 27 Darley Avenue, Manchester M20 8ZD (tel 0161 445 3489)

SHELDRICK, Dr (Evelyn) Carol; da of Clement Gordon Sheldrick (d 1979), and Doris Evelyn, *née* Sackett (d 1982); *b* 29 March 1942; *Educ* Woodford HS, Univ of Oxford (MA, BM BChir), Univ of London (MPhil); *m* 17 Dec 1983; *Career* conslt: Maudsley Hosp 1978–97 (formerly house offr, research asst, registrar then sr registrar), Blackheath Hosp 1997–2005; author of articles and chapters on changing diagnosis in psychiatry, delinquency, sexual abuse and risk; FRCPsych 1989; *Recreations* music, theatre, gardening, walking; *Style—* Dr Carol Sheldrick

SHELFORD, Peter Bengt McNeill; s of Leonard Vere McNeill Shelford (d 1993), and Kerstin Olivia, *née* Lindberg (d 1979); *b* 20 February 1951; *Educ* St John's Sch Leatherhead, Guildford Tech Coll, Univ of Southampton, Guildford Coll of Law; *m* 2 July 1977, Patricia Evelyn, da of Comet Norman Pullen; 1 s (Andrew b 21 Sept 1979), 2 da (Sarah b 30 May 1983, Emma b 25 Oct 1985); *Career* admitted slr: England and Wales 1975, Hong Kong 1996; Clyde & Co: articled clerk 1973–75, asst slr 1975–79, ptnr 1979–2001 (Hong Kong office 1996–2001); ptnr DLA Piper Rudnick Gray Cary 2001– (cuurently managing ptnr Bangkok office); memb: Regnl Panel Singapore International Arbitration Centre, Panel Singapore Chamber of Maritime Arbitration; fell Singapore Inst of Arbitrators; *Recreations* tennis, golf, bridge, swimming; *Clubs* Hurst Green Tennis (hon sec 1989–95), Hong Kong CC; *Style—* Peter Shelford, Esq; ✉ DLA Piper Rudnick Gray Cary, 47th Floor, Unit 4707, Empire Tower, 195 South Sathorn Road, Yannawa, Sathorn, Bangkok, 10120, Thailand

SHELLEY, Howard Gordon; s of Frederick Gordon Shelley (d 1979), and Katharine Anne, *née* Taylor; *b* 9 March 1950; *Educ* scholar: Highgate Sch, RCM; *m* 7 June 1975, Hilary Mary Pauline, *née* Macnamara; 1 s (Alexander Gordon b 1979), 1 step s (Peter Cullivan b 1962); *Career* concert pianist and conductor; London debut Wigmore Hall 1971, Henry Wood Prom debut (TV) 1972, conducting debut London Symphony Orch Barbican 1985, concert performances worldwide; has had piano concertos written for him by Cowie, Chapple and Dickinson; performed first cycle of the complete solo piano works of Rachmaninov at Wigmore Hall 1983; Two-Piano duo with Hilary Macnamara (debut 1976); princ guest conductor London Mozart Players 1992–98 (assoc conductor 1990–92), musical dir and princ conductor Uppsala Chamber Orch 2000–03; memb Worshipful Co of Musicians; FRCM, ARCO; *Recordings* incl: complete solo piano works and concertos of Rachmaninov, piano concerto cycles of Mozart, Mendelssohn, Hummel, Herz, Moscheles and Cramer, Chopin recitals, Schumann recital, Gershwin piano concerto and rhapsodies, piano concertos by Vaughan Williams, Carwithen, Alwyn, Rubbra, Tippett, Howard Ferguson and Peter Dickinson, Mozart and Schubert symphonies with RPO, Reinecke symphonies; *Awards* Chappell Gold medal 1971, Silver medal of Worshipful Co of Musicians, Dannreuther Concerto prize; *Style—* Howard Shelley, Esq; ✉ 38 Cholmeley Park, Highgate, London N6 5ER; Caroline Baird Artists, Pinkhill House, Oxford Road, Eynsham, Oxfordshire OX29 4DA (tel and fax 01865 882771, e-mail caroline@cbartists.com)

SHELLEY, John Philip Bernhard (né Seales); s of Philip Edward Seales (d 1964), and Jessica, *née* Thompson (d 1960); *b* 24 May 1932; *Educ* Clyde House Swindon, Swindon Tech Coll, RMCS Shrivenham; *m* 17 Dec 1952, Mary Elisabeth, *née* Lewis; *Career* professional photographer 1948–, Royal photographer 1978–; photographer Swindon Town Speedway 1950–52, mangr Leeds Cameras London 1974–1980; md and prop: JS Library Int 1978–, John Shelley Photographic Ltd, John Shelley Photography, John Shelley Int, and Library and Gallery Int 1980–81; photographer Saudi Royal Family 1975–81, private photographer to Sir Lynden Pindling PM of Bahamas 1982–83; travel and photography lectr 1980–, interviewed, photographed and prepared features on many celebrities 1983–; nat and int exhbns 1952– (incl The Royal Jubilee Display FCO 2002 and up to 180 countries worldwide for Golden Jubilee 2002); travelled to 101 countries worldwide since 1970s; fndr memb, chm and sec Assoc Buckingham Palace Accredited Photographers 1982–; chm and treas Swindon Town Young Conservatives 1949–50, sec NUPE Swindon 1953–54; *Publications* incl: The Man From Rome (photography, 1982), Anne: The Working Princess (photography, 1987), Down to Earth: speeches and writings of His Royal Highness Prince Philip Duke of Edinburgh on the relationship of man with his environment (photography, 1988), Charles & Diana, A 10th Anniversary Celebration (photography, 1991), Elizabeth, A Biography of Her Majesty the Queen (photography, 1996); provided illustrations for numerous books and magazines; *Recreations* cooking, fine wines and food, gardening, travelling the world, collecting books and films, photography; *Clubs* Guards Polo; *Style—* John Shelley, Esq; ✉ J S Library International, 101A Brondesbury Park, London NW2 5JL (tel 020 8451 2668, fax 020 8459 0223, e-mail js@online24.co.uk, website www.jslibrary.com and jslibraryprints.com)

SHELLEY, Dr (Sir) John Richard; 11 Bt (E 1611) of Michelgrove, Sussex (but does not use the title); s of John Shelley (d 1974); suc gf, Maj Sir John Frederick Shelley, 10 Bt (d 1976); *b* 18 January 1943; *Educ* King's Sch Bruton, Trinity Coll Cambridge (MA), St Mary's Hosp Univ of London (MB BChir); *m* 1965, Clare, da of Claud Bicknell, OBE; 2 da (Diana Elizabeth b 1970, Helen Ruth b 1972); *Heir* bro, Thomas Shelley; *Career* general practitioner; ptnr Drs Shelley, Doddington & Gibb (med practitioners), ret; farmer; DObstRCOG, MRCGP; *Style—* Dr John Shelley; ✉ Shobrooke Park, Crediton, Devon EX17 1DG (e-mail jack@shobrookepark.com)

SHELTON, Graham John; s of Alfred Thomas Shelton (d 1987), of Derby, and Louisa Emily, *née* Clarke (d 1984); *b* 26 October 1950; *Educ* Bemrose GS for Boys Derby, Univ of Wolverhampton (BA), Univ of Birmingham (scholar, MSocSci), DipHSM; *m* 15 Dec 1979, Noelle Margaret, da of James Minihan, of Limerick, Ireland; 3 s (Matthew William Henry b 31 Dec 1982, James Eoin b 11 Oct 1984, Piers Thomas b 25 Jan 1992), 2 da (Lydia Louise b 9 April 1987, Naomi Marie b 18 July 1989); *Career* trainee in health servs mgmnt Trent RHA, subsequently various appts in W Midlands and E Anglian regions, dep unit admin The Royal Hallamshire Hosp Sheffield 1983–85, unit admin Raigmore Hosp Inverness 1985–86, dir and unit gen mangr Mental Health Servs Norwich HA 1986–93 (acting dist gen mangr 1988–89), chief exec Norfolk Mental Health Care NHS Tst 1993–2000, head of Mental Health NHS Exec Eastern 2000–03, md Graham Shelton Partnership Ltd 2003–; memb Mental Health Review Tbnl 2002–; formerly: hon research fell UEA, pt/t lectr in health servs mgmnt Sheffield Hallam Univ; author of various jl pubns on mgmnt and mental health servs; MHSM 1976; FRSA 1999; *Recreations* family, church, music, theatre, memb Taverham Band; *Clubs* Norfolk; *Style—* Graham Shelton, Esq; ✉ e-mail admin@grahamsheltonpartnership.co.uk

SHEMILT, Prof Elaine Katherine Mary; da of Harold J Shemilt, and Margarita Isabel Diaz Medina; *b* 7 May 1954; *Educ* Bloomfield Collegiate Sch Belfast, Brighton Sch of Art, Winchester Sch of Art (BA), Royal Coll of Art (MA); *m* 1, 1977 (m dis 1984) David A Duly; 2 s (Benjamin b 1979, Emile Josef b 1980); m 2, 1985 (sep 1997), Dr T J C Murphy; 1 da (Genevieve Clare b 1988); *Career* artist; art teacher 1979–80, artist and printmaker in residence South Hill Park Arts Centre Berks 1980–82, fell in fine art and printmaking Winchester Sch of Art 1982–84, sr lectr and course dir Dept of Printmaking Sch of Fine Art Duncan of Jordanstone Coll of Art Dundee 1989– (lectr 1985–88, reader in fine art 2003–), vice-chm and dir Dundee Printmakers Workshop/Seagate Gallery Dundee 1989–96, external assessor for printmaking UWE 1991–95, external assessor for printmaking Humberside Univ 1996–99, external assessor for printmaking Norwich Sch of Art and Design 1999–2001, artist in residence Univ of Wollongong NSW Aust 2000; visiting lectr: Univ of Sydney Aust, Univ of Canberra Aust; professional memb Scottish Soc of Artists 1992 (memb Cncl 1995–98), pres elect Soc of Scottish Artists; Shackleton scholar; FRSA; *Exhibitions* incl: Serpentine Gallery 1976, ICA 1978, Minories Gallery Colchester 1979, Hayward Gallery 1979, Ikon Gallery Birmingham 1980, South Hill Park Main Gallery Berks 1981, The Winchester Gallery 1984, Aspects Gallery Exeter 1984, Tom Allen Centre London 1984, The London Group Barbican 1987, Gallery Twerenbold Lucerne Switzerland 1988, Bellfrie Gallery Copenhagen 1988, Courtauld Gallery 1993, Roger Billcliffe Gallery Glasgow 1993, Scotland National Gallery of Modern Art 1993, Gallerie Centre d'Arl en Lille Geneva 1993, The Demarco European Art Fndn Edinburgh Festival 1993, Gallerie Beeldspraak Amsterdam 1995, Lamont Gallery London 1996, Kansas State Univ Gallery 1997, Moorhead State Univ Minnesota 1997, Seagate Gallery Dundee 1997, Brazen Head Gallery Norfolk 1998, Cooper Gallery DJCAD 1999,

CentreSpace Dundee Contemporary Arts 1999, Dick Institute Kilmarnock 1999, Peacock Aberdeen 2000, European Media Art Festival Osnabruck Germany, Traces of Conflict Imp War Museum London 2002; *Work in Collections* BBC, Landesbank Stuttgart, Arts Cncl, Dundee City Museums and Art Galleries, Lincoln and Humberside Arts, Scottish Arts Cncl, Southern Arts; *Important Works* incl: Hayward Annual Installation 1979, Behind Appearance (toured across midwest of USA) 1997, Chimera (with, Stephen Partridge, winner of Adobe Software Award) 1998; *Style*— Prof Elaine Shemilt; ✉ School of Fine Art, DJCAD, University of Dundee, Perth Road, Dundee DD1 4HT (tel 01382 345145, fax 01382 200983, e-mail e.shemilt@dundee.ac.uk)

SHENKIN, Prof Alan; *b* 3 September 1943; *Educ* Hutchesons' GS Glasgow, Univ of Glasgow (BSc, MB ChB, PhD); *m* 27 June 1967, Leonna Estelle, da of Godfrey Jacob Delmonte (d 1978), of Glasgow; 2 da (Susie b 1970, Trudi b 1971), 1 s (Stephen b 1975); *Career* lectr in biochemistry Univ of Glasgow 1970–74, Royal Soc European exchange fell Karolinska Inst Stockholm 1976–77; conslt in clinical biochemistry Glasgow Royal Infirmary 1978–90 (sr registrar 1974–78), prof of clinical chemistry Univ of Liverpool 1990–; European ed Nutrition jl 1986–, author of various research papers and book chapters on nutritional support and micronutrients; pres Assoc of Clinical Biochemists 2000–03 (chm Scientific Ctee 1994–96); vice-pres: European Soc of Parenteral and Enteral Nutrition 2002 (treas 1988–92), Br Nutrition Fndn 2005–; memb Cncl and Exec RCPath 1995–98 (also chm Specialty Advsy Ctee on Chemical Pathology), memb Cncl Nutrition Soc 1995–98 and 2005– (ctee memb Clinical Metabolism and Nutritional Support Gp 1988–94), chm Intercollegiate Gp on Nutrition 1996–2006, chm Intercollegiate Ctee on Metabolic Med 2001–03; hon memb Czechoslovakian Med Soc and Czechoslovakian Soc for Parenteral and Enteral Nutrition 1990; FRCPath 1990, FRCPGlas 1990, FRCP 1993; *Recreations* golf, word games, travel; *Style*— Prof Alan Shenkin; ✉ 10 Rockbourne Green, Woolton, Liverpool L25 4TH (tel 0151 428 9756); Department of Clinical Chemistry, University of Liverpool, Liverpool L69 3GA (tel 0151 706 4232, fax 0151 706 5813, e-mail shenkin@liverpool.ac.uk)

SHENNAN, Francis Gerard; s of Thomas Gerard Shennan, of Tadley, Hants, and Cecelia Shennan; *b* 14 September 1949; *Educ* Preston Catholic Coll, St Joseph's Coll Dumfries, Univ of Edinburgh (LLB); *m* 1998, Marion Young; 1 da (Lorna Young b 4 Sept 1980), 1 s (Neil Young b 7 July 1984); *Career* writer and journalist; news sub ed: Daily Mirror Manchester 1975–76, Scottish Daily Record 1976–88; recruitment columnist the Scotsman 1988–89, fndr prop The Shennan Agency 1988–2007, Scot business ed The Sunday Times 1989–90, currently dir Casino Training UK Ltd, formerly dir Footie Index Ltd; law examiner for Scot Nat Cncl for the Trg of Journalists 1981–84, external examiner of media law Napier Poly Edinburgh 1984–92; law lectr: Napier Univ, Strathclyde Univ, Glasgow Caledonian Univ, Telford Coll Edinburgh, Glasgow Metropolitan Coll, Cardonald Coll, NUJ, Associated Newspapers, Johnstone Press; speaker: Law Soc of Scotland, Nat Employment Conf, Nat Investment Forum, NW Writers' Assoc, SE Writers' Assoc; contrib to: The Herald, The Times, The Guardian, Scotland on Sunday, The Scotsman, CA Magazine, Investors' Chronicle, Mail on Sunday, and various business, media and women's magazines in UK and abroad; also corp work for Govt and Scottish enterprise agencies; UK Regnl Finance Writer of the Year 2001 and 2005 (shortlisted 1999, runner-up 2000), runner-up Scottish Financial/Business Writer of the Year 1999, shortlisted BIBA Regnl Finance Writer 2007; *Books* The Life, Passions, and Legacies of John Napier (1990), Rebels in Paradise: The Inside Story of the Battle for Celtic Football Club (with D Low); *Recreations* travelling; *Style*— Francis Shennan, Esq; ✉ 64 Ashton Lane, Glasgow G12 8SJ (tel 0141 579 5040, e-mail info@francisshennan.com)

SHENTON, David William; s of Sir William Edward Leonard Shenton (d 1967), and Erica Lucy, *née* Denison (d 1978); *b* 1 December 1924; *Educ* Westminster, Magdalen Coll Oxford (BA); *m* 1, 1972 (m dis 1987), Della, da of F G Marshall (d 1977), of Sutton, Surrey; m 2, 12 May 1988, Charmian Nancy Lacey, LVO, da of Christopher William Lacey (d 1966), of Walmer, Kent; *Career* WWII Lt Coldstream Gds 1943–46, served Italy (despatches); admitted slr 1951; ptnr Lovell White and King 1955, conslt Lovell White Durrant 1988–89; int arbitrator; conslt Studio Legale Ardito 1990–91; chm Slrs' Euro Gp of Law Soc 1980–81, memb Ctee D of Section on Business Law and Ctee 20 of Section on General Practice Int Bar Assoc 1983– (life chm emeritus Ctee D 1987–); memb: Editorial Ctee Int Business Lawyer 1986–88, Chm's Advsy Ctee Int Bar Assoc 1988–90; pres Coldstream Guards Assoc Isle of Wight branch 1999–; Freeman City of London 1950; Liveryman: Worshipful Co of Grocers 1954, Worshipful Co of Slrs 1970; *Recreations* sailing, visiting ancient sites and buildings, stone carving, collection of stone carvings, photography, enjoying fine wine; *Clubs* RYS, Household Division Yacht, Carlton; *Style*— David Shenton, Esq; ✉ Compton Undermount, Bonchurch Village Road, Ventnor, Isle of Wight PO38 1RG (tel 01983 855654, fax 01983 854266, mobile 07968 214375)

SHENTON, Marilyn Jennifer; da of Ivan Harold Leak (d 1998), and June, *née* Dennett (d 1978); *b* 15 December 1950; *Educ* Fallowfield C of E HS Manchester, Northern Counties Teacher Trg Coll, Univ of Birmingham, Rotherham Coll of Art and Technol; *m* 15 Sept 1971, David Lister Shenton, s of William Shenton; 2 s (Andrew Lister b 26 Jan 1979, Simon Peter b 20 April 1980); *Career* photographer; work exhibited at Bircham Gallery Norfolk, provided images for Photonica, Alamy and Getty int picture libraries, work featured in int photography and art magazines; exhibited BIPP Int Photographic Awards Exhbn 2000–01, 2001–02 and 2002–03, On the Edge (fine art and photographic exhbn, Sheringham Norfolk, in conjunction with N Norfolk Exhbn Project) 2002, Social Documentary of Gypsy Horse Fairs exhbn Gressenhall Rural Life Museum Norfolk 2002–03, N Norfolk Coastline exhbn Fine Art Landscapes N Norfolk Cncl 2003; speaker on: photographic trg overseas Cyprus 2005, art in the landscape and passion for the horse 2005–; Master Photographers' Assoc awards: Press and PR Photographer of the Year 1999, 2000, 2001 and 2002, Pictorial Photographer of the Year 2000, Fashion and Illustrative Photographer of the Year 2001, Master Photographer of the Year 2001 (nominated 2002 and 2003), Black and White Photography Award 2002; BIPP Int Photographic Awards: winner Press and PR Category 2001 (nominated 2002, bronze 2003), Art of Illustration Award 2003 (gold), New Art of Science Award 2003 (gold); assoc Master Photographers' Assoc 1997, ARPS 1997, LBIPP 2000; *Recreations* photography and art (including digital art); *Style*— Mrs Marilyn Shenton

SHEPHARD OF NORTHWOLD, Baroness (Life Peer UK 2005), of Northwold in the County of Norfolk; Gillian Patricia Shephard; PC (1992), DL (Norfolk 2003); *b* 22 January 1940; *Educ* North Walsham Girls' HS, St Hilda's Coll Oxford; *Career* MP (Cons) Norfolk South West 1987–2005; PPS to Economic Sec to Treasy 1988–89, Parly under-sec of state DSS 1989–90, min of state HM Treasy 1990–92, sec of state for employment 1992–93, min of agriculture, fisheries and food 1993–94, sec of state for educn 1994–95, sec of state for educn and employment 1995–97; shadow ldr of the House of Commons 1997–98, shadow sec of state for environment, tport and the regions 1998–99; Cons Pty: dep chm 1991–92 and 2002–04, head of candidate devpt 2001–03; chm Assoc of Cons Peers 2006–; memb Ctee on Standards in Public Life 2003–; chm: E of Eng Bio-Fuels Forum 2003–, Video Standards Cncl 2005–; tstee Workers Educnl Assoc 2006–; hon fell St Hilda's Coll Oxford 1991, memb Cncl Univ of Oxford 2000–; *Style*— The Rt Hon the Lady Shephard of Northwold, PC, DL

SHEPHERD, David Robert; MBE (1997); s of Herbert Howell Shepherd (d 1962), of Bideford, Devon, and Doris Sarah, *née* Smallridge (d 1990); *b* 27 December 1940; *Educ* Barnstaple GS, St Luke's Coll Exeter; *Partner* Jennifer Margaret Hoare; *Career* cricket umpire; player: English Schs 1959, Devon 1959–64, Gloucestershire CCC 1965–79 (awarded county cap 1969), total 282 first class matches; scored 108 on debut Glos v Univ of Oxford; appointed first class umpire 1981–: first match at Oxford, first one day int Pakistan v Sri Lanka 1983, first test match England v Aust 1985, umpired 81 test matches; other matches umpired incl: World Cup England 1983, World Cup India and Pakistan 1987, MCC Bicentenary Lord's 1987, Asia Cup Sri Lanka, World Cup Aust and NZ 1992, World Cup India, Pakistan and Sri Lanka (incl final in Lahore) 1996, World Cup UK (incl final at Lord's) 1999, World Cup South Africa (incl final in Johannesburg) 2003, 147 one day internationals, numerous domestic cup finals Lord's; *Recreations* all sports, stamp collecting; *Style*— David Shepherd, Esq, MBE; ✉ England and Wales Cricket Board, Lord's Cricket Ground, London NW8 8QN (tel 020 7286 4405)

SHEPHERD, 3 Baron (UK 1946) Graeme George; s of 2 Baron Shepherd, PC (d 2001); *b* 6 January 1949; *m* 1971, Eleanor; 1 s (Hon Patrick Malcolm); *Heir* s, Hon Patrick Shepherd; *Clubs* Hong Kong, Oriental (London); *Style*— The Rt Hon the Lord Shepherd; ✉ The Hong Kong Club, 1 Jackson Road, Central, Hong Kong

SHEPHERD, Prof James; s of James Bell Shepherd, of Ardbeg, Bute, and Margaret McCrum, *née* Camick; *b* 8 April 1944; *Educ* Hamilton Acad, Univ of Glasgow (BSc, MB ChB, PhD); *m* 5 July 1969, Jan Bulloch, da of William Bulloch Kelly, of Motherwell; 1 s (Ewen James b 7 Feb 1974), 1 da (Fiona Elizabeth b 7 July 1976); *Career* lectr in biochemistry Univ of Glasgow 1969–72; Dept of Pathological Biochemistry Univ of Glasgow and Glasgow Royal Infirmary: lectr 1973–77, sr lectr and hon conslt 1977–84, prof and head of dept 1988–2006, prof emeritus 2006–; clinical dir Laboratories Glasgow Royal Infirmary 1993–; asst prof of med Methodist Hosp Houston TX 1976–77, visiting prof of med Cantonal Hosp Geneva 1984; dir W of Scotland Coronary Prevention Study 1989–96, dir Prospective Study of Pravastatin in the Elderly at Risk (PROSPER) 1998–2002; chm Euro Atherosclerosis Soc 1993–96; memb: Coronary Prevention Gp, Int Atherosclerosis Soc; FRSE 1996, FMedSci 1998, FRCP, FRCPath; *Books* incl: Lipoproteins in Coronary Heart Disease (jtly, 1986), Atherosclerosis: Developments, Complications and Treatment (jtly, 1987), Lipoprotein Metabolism (1987), Coronary Risks Revisited (ed jtly, 1989), Human Plasma Lipoproteins (ed jtly, 1989), Preventive Cardiology (ed jtly, 1991), Lipoproteins and the Pathogenesis of Atherosclerosis (ed jtly, 1991), Cardiovascular Disease: Current perspectives on the Asian-Pacific Region (ed jtly, 1994), Clinical Biochemistry: An illustrated colour text (co-author, 1995, 3 edn 2005), Lipoproteins in Health and Disease (ed jtly, 1999), Statins: The HMGCoA reductase inhibitors in perspective (ed jtly, 2000, 2 edn 2004), Lipids and Atherosclerosis Annual 2001 (ed jtly, 2001), Lipids and Atherosclerosis Annual 2003 (ed jtly, 2003); *Style*— Prof James Shepherd, FRSE; ✉ 17 Barriedale Avenue, Hamilton ML3 9DB (tel 01698 428259, fax 01698 286281); Department of Pathological Biochemistry, Royal Infirmary, Glasgow G4 0SF (tel 0141 211 4628, fax 0141 553 1703, telex 779234 HLAGLA G, e-mail jshepherd@gri-biochem.org.uk)

SHEPHERD, John H; s of Dr Henry Robert Shepherd, DSC, of Enfield, Middx, and Mimika, *née* Martaki; *b* 11 July 1948; *Educ* Blundell's, Bart's Med Coll (MB BS); *m* 27 May 1972, Alison Sheila, da of Capt Henry Stephen Brandram-Adams, MBE, of Wootton, IOW; 1 s (David b 1976), 2 da (Katy b 1978, Emily b 1985); *Career* conslt gynaecological surgn: Bart's 1981–, Chelsea Hosp for Women 1983–84, Royal Marsden Hosp 1983–; prof of surgical gynaecology Bart's and the London Sch of Medicine and Dentistry Queen Mary Westfield Coll London; hon conslt King Edward VII Hosp for Offrs 1993–; Hunterian prof RCS 2006–07; author of numerous chapters and scientific articles on med topics relating to cancer, gynaecology and obstetrics; pres Section of Obstetrics and Gynaecology RSM 2006–07 (hon sec 1997–98); memb: Cncl RCOG 1984–87, 1989–95 and 2004–, Cncl Soc of Pelvic Surgns 2004– (vice-pres 1999, pres-elect 2007), Working Pty in Gynaecological Oncology MRC; chm Gynaecological Cancer Sub Ctee of UK Co-ordinating Ctee for Cancer Res 1994–97; memb: Soc of Gynaecologic Oncologists, Chelsea Clinical Soc, Academia Europaea, NY Acad of Science; Liveryman Worshipful Soc of Apothecaries; memb BMA 1971; fell: Belgian Royal Acad of Med 1986, Singaporian Acad of Med 1987; hon fell Flemish Soc of Obstetrics and Gynaecology (VVOG) 2002; FRSM 1972, FRCS 1975, MRCOG (Gold Medal) 1978, FACOG 1981, FRCOG 1996; *Books* Clinical Gynaecological Oncology (1985, 2 edn 1990); *Recreations* skiing, sailing, cricket, squash, classical music; *Clubs* MCC, Royal Ocean Racing; *Style*— John Shepherd, Esq; ✉ Pickwick Cottage, 31 College Road, Dulwich, London SE21 7BG (tel 020 8693 6342); 5 Devonshire Place, London W1G 6HE (tel 020 7935 4444, fax 020 7935 6224)

SHEPHERD, Michael Charles; s of Henry Robert Shepherd, and Mimika; *b* 1 October 1953; *Educ* Blundell's, Univ of Surrey (BSc); *m*; 3 c; *Career* London Hilton 1976–79, Lesotho Hilton 1979–81, asst to sr vice-pres for Europe Hilton International EMEA 1981–84, exec asst mangr Istanbul Hilton 1984–86, mangr Athens Hilton 1986–88, mangr Corfu Hilton 1987; gen mangr: Cyprus Hilton 1988–92, Nile Hilton 1992–93, The Langham Hilton 1993–97; md The Savoy Hotel London 1997–2003, gen mangr London Hilton on Park Lane 2003–; chm London Regnl Br Hospitality Assoc (BHA), memb Nat Exec BHA; trainer HCITB 1978–; memb Advsy Bd Dept of Mgmnt Univ of Surrey; Freeman Llantrisant Wales, Freeman City of London, Master Innholder; FHCIMA; *Awards* Hilton Int Gp Hotel Gen Mangr of the Year 1990, nominated Hilton UK Gen Mangr of the Year 1996, Worldwide Exec Travel Awards Hotel of the Year (Savoy Hotel) 1997, National Catey Award Corp Hotel of the Year (Savoy Hotel) 1998, Condé Nast Travel Readers Award Top Business Hotel 1998, Best Br Hotel Telegraph Travel Awards 1999 and 2000, 5 Star RAC Gold Ribbon 2002 and 2003, 5 Star AA Red Star Award 2002 and 2003, Business Traveller Magazine Best Business Hotel in Western Europe 2005, Business Traveller Magazine Best Business Hotel in Europe 2006, Visit London Large Hotel of the Year 2006, Visit Britain/Enjoy England Excellence Silver Award Large Hotel of the Year 2007; *Recreations* gardening, tennis, walking, reading, travel, int economical and political current affairs; *Style*— Michael Shepherd, Esq; ✉ The London Hilton on Park Lane, 22 Park Lane, London W1K 1BE

SHEPHERD, Philip Alexander; QC (2003); s of Col John Ernest Shepherd, of Cobham, Surrey, and Eve, *née* Zachariou; *b* 1 May 1950; *Educ* St Georges Coll Weybridge, LSE (BSc); *m* 17 March 1983, Amanda Robin, da of Gavin Clezy, OBE, of Beausale, Warks; 2 s (Freddy b 12 Dec 1985, William b 28 Oct 1987); *Career* called to the Bar Gray's Inn 1975; recorder 2000–, memb of chambers and ldr Aviation and Travel Gp 24 Old Buildings; memb: Br Italian Law Assoc, Commercial Bar Assoc, Chancery Bar Assoc, European Air Law Assoc, Geneva Panel of Arbitrators, Hong Kong Int Arbitration Center Panel, Int Bar Assoc, Lawyers Flying Assoc; LCIA arbitrator; MCIArb, MCIAeS; *Recreations* flying, opera, walking, skiing; *Clubs* RAC; *Style*— Philip Shepherd, Esq, QC; ✉ 24 Old Buildings, Lincoln's Inn, London WC2A 3UP (tel 020 7691 2424, fax 0870 460 2178, e-mail philip.shepherd@xxiv.co.uk)

SHEPHERD, Richard Charles Scrimgeour; MP; s of Alfred Shepherd, and Davida Sophia, *née* Wallace; *b* 6 December 1942; *Educ* LSE, Johns Hopkins Sch of Advanced Int Studies (MSc Econ); *Career* dir: Partridges of Sloane Street Ltd, Shepherd Foods Ltd; memb SE Econ Planning Cncl 1970–74; MP (Cons) Aldridge Brownhills 1979– (Parly candidate (Cons) Nottingham E Feb 1974); memb Select Ctee on: Treasy and CS 1979–83, Modernisation of the House of Commons 1997–, Public Admin 1997–2000; sec Cons Ctees on Euro Affairs and Indust 1980–81, vice-chm Cons Pty Ctee for Constitutional Affairs Scotland and Wales 1999– (jt vice-chm 1999–), memb All-Pty Br Cncl Gp 1999–, memb Jt Ctee on Human Rights; co-chm Campaign for Freedom of Information; memb: Cons Euro Reform Gp, Fresh Start Gp; sponsor: Crown Immunity Bill 1986, Protection of

Official Information Bill 1988, Referendum Bill 1992, Public Interest Disclosure Bill; Cons Whip withdrawn 1994–95; Backbencher of the Year 1987, Campaign for Freedom of Information Award 1988, voted one of 10 most effective MPs 1988, Spectator-Highland Park Parliamentarian of the Year 1995; underwriting memb Lloyd's 1974–94; *Clubs* Carlton, Beefsteak, Chelsea Arts; *Style*— Richard Shepherd, Esq, MP; ✉ House of Commons, London SW1A 0AA (tel 020 7219 3000, constituency tel and fax 01922 451449)

SHEPHERD, Dr Robert John; s of Reginald John Stuart Shepherd (d 1973), of Gloucester, and Ellen, *née* Pritchard; *b* 16 January 1946; *Educ* King's Sch Gloucester, Univ of Liverpool (MB ChB); *Career* med registrar Nat Heart Hosp London, sr med registrar Radcliffe Infirmary Oxford; conslt physician Dept of Med for the Elderly Leics DHA 1977–93, conslt physician Leicester General Hosp NHS Tst 1993–2000, conslt physician Leicester Univ Hospitals Tst 2000–03; locum conslt physician: Dept of Med for the Elderly Countess of Chester Hosp 2004–05, Univ Hosp of Coventry and Warwick 2005–06, James Cook Univ Hosp 2006, James Paget Univ Hosp 2006–; regional serv advsr (Trent region) for geriatric med 1997–99; memb Exec and Cncl Br Geriatric Soc 1996–2002 (hon dep treas 1996–99, dir and treas 1999–2002), chm Trent Br Geriatric Soc 1996–99 (hon treas 1991–93, hon sec 1993–96); memb BMA; MRCP (UK), FRCPEd 1992, FRCP 1995, FRCPGlas 1997; *Publications* Syncope in Myxoedema due to Transient Ventricular Fibrillation (PostGrad Med Jl), Normal Pressure Hydrocephalus Presenting as Parkinsonian Syndrome (Thorax), Unusual Presentation of Systemic Lupus Erythematosus (Hospital Update, 1996), Age Related Variations in Presentation and Outcome in Wegener's Granulomatosis (Jl of RCP, 1997), also author of various other papers; *Recreations* travel, photography, collecting antiques; *Style*— Dr R J Shepherd; ✉ Ty Gwyn, 37 Ashfield Road, Stoneygate, Leicester LE2 1LB (tel 01162 707029, fax 01162 708438)

SHEPPARD, Andy; s of Philip Charles Sheppard, of Salisbury, and Irene, *née* Rhymes; *b* 20 January 1957; *Educ* Bishop Wordsworth GS; *m* 2, Rebecca Sian, da of Rod Allerton; 1 da (Phoebe Rose b 30 Sept 1992), 1 s (Charles Benjamin b 12 Sept 1995); *Career* jazz saxophonist; composer for TV, film, theatre and dance; self-taught at age of 18, busker Paris Metro; worked with numerous bands incl Urban Sax; musicians worked with incl: Gil Evans, George Russell, Carla Bley; formed several bands incl: In Co Motion, Big Co Motion, Inclassificables, Moving Image (toured of UK Europe and world); patron: Music Space, Bristol Harbourside; Br Jazz Awards: best instrumentalist 1989 and 1990, best album 1990, best big band 1991; Hon MMus Univ of West of England 1993; *Recordings* Introductions in the Dark, Soft on the Inside, In Co Motion, Rhythm Method, Inclassificables, Songs with Legs, Moving Image, Delivery Suite, Learning to Wave, Dancing Man and Woman, Nocturnal Tourist, Music for a New Crossing, PS; *Recreations* deck chair, gin and tonic; *Clubs* Ronnie Scott's; *Style*— Andy Sheppard, Esq

SHEPPARD, Howard William; *b* 2 November 1944; *Educ* Kingston Sch of Architecture (DArch), Heriot-Watt Univ (MSc); *m*; 3 c; *Career* asst architect Marani Routhwaith & Dick Architects Toronto 1966–67, architect with various private practices 1969–72; GLC: architect planner Transportation and Planning (Central London) 1972–76, project architect Dept of Architecture (Housing) 1976–79, devpt planner Transportation and Planning (NW London) 1979–81; London Docklands Devpt Corp: sr architect planner 1981–86, area dir (Devpt) Wapping and Limehouse 1986–89 (Isle of Dogs and Wapping 1989–91), dir City Design and Planning 1991–97, planning advsr Canary Wharf Gp London 1998–, memb Bd Docklands Business Club 1999–; visiting prof of architecture and urban studies Virginia Poly Inst and State Univ 1976–77, memb Awards Panel American Inst of Planning (Virginia) Williamsburg 1977, speaker Int Forum Waterfront 2001 Osaka 1991; memb Planning Tech Ctee Br Property Fedn 2002–, cmmr Town and Country Planning Assoc 2004–06; memb: Nat Tst, Consumer Assoc; corp memb: RIBA, RTPI; FRSA; *Style*— Howard Sheppard, Esq; ✉ Number One St Agatha's Drive, Kingston upon Thames, Surrey KT2 5SH (tel 020 8541 4081, e-mail howard.sheppard@canarywharf.com)

SHEPPARD, Maurice Raymond; s of Wilfred Ernest Sheppard (d 1976), and Florence Hilda Sheppard (d 2002); *b* 25 February 1947; *Educ* Haverfordwest GS, Eisteddfod Maldwyn, Loughborough Coll of Art, Kingston Coll of Art (DipAD), RCA (MA); *Career* artist, draughtsman and watercolourist; cmmnd to paint The Golden Valley (for Lord Attenborough's film Shadowlands) 1993; Br Instn Award 1971, David Murray Landscape Award 1972, Geoffrey Crawshay Meml travelling scholar Univ of Wales 1973; memb Nat Art Collection Fund; ARWS 1974, RWS 1977, VPRWS 1979, PRWS 1984–87 (tstee 1983–95, hon retired memb 2002), NEAC 2000; *Major Exhibitions* Fairfax-Lucy, Hayes, Sheppard (New Grafton Gallery) 1976, Maurice Sheppard (New Grafton Gallery) 1979, Maurice Sheppard (Christopher Wood Gallery) 1989, Beard, Jane Carpanini, Sheppard (Attic Gallery Swansea) 2007; *Group Exhibitions* incl: Royal Acad Summer Exhibition 1971–, Royal Watercolour Soc 1974–2002, Mall Gallery, Agnews, John Nevil Gallery Canterbury, Leonie Jonleigh Gallery Guildford, Tom Caldwell Belfast and Dublin, Prouds Pty Sydney, Mitsokoshi Japan; formed gp with Pamela Kay, Paul Newland and Jacqueline Rizvi showing at Alresford Gallery 2003 and Abbott and Holder 2004 and 2005, Alpha House Gallery Sherbourne 2007; *Collections* public collections: Br Museum, V&A, Nat Museum of Wales, City of Birmingham Museum and Art Gallery, Beecroft Museum and Art Gallery Westcliffe-on-Sea, Tullie House Museum Carlisle, UCW Aberystwyth, Nat Library of Wales, Topsham Museum Devon; private collections: HM The Queen, Lord Pym, Lord Inglewood, Lady Jane Wellesley, Lady Serena Rothchild, Lady Alice Fairfax-Lucy, Sir Francis Beaumont, Andrew Wilton, Lord Young; corporate collections: Boots plc, WH Smith, Blue Circle plc, HOR Oil (UK) plc, MBNA International Bank of America Ltd (11 works, 1972–95), Canary Wharf Devpt Corp; *Recreations* cycling, music, a small garden, quiet; *Style*— Maurice Sheppard, Esq; ✉ 33 St Martin's Park, Crow Hill, Haverfordwest, Pembrokeshire SA61 2HP

SHEPPARD, Maj Gen Peter John; CB (1995), CBE (1992, OBE 1982); s of Kenneth Wescombe Sheppard (d 2002), of Tynemouth, Tyne & Wear, and Margaret, *née* Coleman (d 1993); *b* 15 August 1942; *Educ* Welbeck Coll, RMA Sandhurst (RE Instn Prize, rugby 1st XV), Univ of London (BSc(Eng), rugby 1st XV); *m* 15 Aug 1964, Sheila Elizabeth, *née* Bell; 1 da (Sara Jane b 3 August 1968), 1 s (Timothy Peter b 22 Jan 1971); *Career* cmmnd 2 Lt Royal Engrs 1962, Univ of London 1962–65, Lt 1 Div RE Germany then Libya 1966–67; promoted Capt 1968, Intelligence Offr 1 Div RE Germany 1968, 2 i/c 3 Field Sqdn RE England then N Ireland 1968–70, Staff Capt MOD 1970–72, RMCS 1973, psc 1974; promoted Maj 1975, GSO2(W) weapons and fighting vehicles Br Army Staff Washington DC 1975–77, OC 29 Field Sqdn RE Germany then N Ireland 1977–79 (despatches N Ireland 1978), GSO2 HQ 1st Br Corps Germany 1979–80; promoted Lt Col 1980, GSO1 mil ops MOD 1980–82, CO 35 Engr Regt Germany 1982–84; Col 1984, Col Gen Staff HQ 1st Br Corps Germany 1984–86; Brig 1986, Cdr Corps RE HQ 1st Br Corps Germany 1986–89, Dir of Army Plans and Progs MOD 1989–91; Maj Gen 1991, COS BAOR 1991–93, DG Logistic Policy (Army) MOD 1993–94, COS HQ Quartermaster General 1994–96, ret 1996; chief exec SSAFA - Forces Help 1996–2004 (ret); Col Cmdt RE 1996–2007; special advsr House of Commons Defence Select Ctee 1997–2001; chm of govrs The Royal Sch Hampstead 1997–2004, chm RE Officers' Widows' Soc 2000–2007, dir Army Charitable Advsy Co 2004–, tstee Army Benevolent Fund 2006–; *Recreations* golf, philately, walking, travel; *Clubs* Army and Navy; *Style*— Maj Gen Peter Sheppard, CB, CBE; ✉ Wescombe House, Barton Stacey, Winchester, Hampshire SO21 3RH

SHEPPARD OF DIDGEMERE, Baron (Life Peer UK 1994), of Roydon in the County of Essex; Sir Allen John George Sheppard; kt (1990), KCVO (1998); s of John Baggott Sheppard (d 1985), and Lily Marjorie, *née* Palmer (d 2000); *b* 25 December 1932; *Educ* Ilford Co HS, LSE (BSc); *m* 1, 1958 (m dis 1980), Damaris, da of David Jones (d 1964); m 2, 1980, Mary, da of Harry Stewart, of London; *Career* with Ford UK and Ford of Europe 1958–68, dir Rootes Gp 1968–71, dir British Leyland 1971–75; Grand Metropolitan plc: joined as chief exec subsid Watney Mann & Truman Brewers, gp md 1982, chief exec 1986–93, chm 1987–96; non-exec chm: UBM plc 1983–85 (non-exec dir 1981–83), Mallinson-Denny Gp Ltd 1985–87, Gp Tst plc 1994–2001, McBride plc 1995–2007, BrightReasons Gp plc 1995–96 (non-exec dir 1994–95), Unipart Gp of Cos 1996–, GB Railways plc 1996–2004; non-exec dep chm Meyer Int plc 1992–94 (non-exec dir 1989–92); non-exec dir: Rexam plc (formerly Bowater plc) 1994–95, High Point Rendel 1997–2003, Gladstone plc 1999–2001, Nyne Ltd 1999–, OneClick HR plc 1999–, Transware plc 2001–03; chm Namibian Resources plc 2004–; pt/t memb British Railways Bd 1985–90; memb Nat Trg Task Force 1989–92 (concurrently chm Sub-Gp on Investors in People); vice-pres: Business in the Community (chm 1994–97), Int Business Ldrs Forum 1990–95; chm: Prince's Youth Business Tst 1990–94, Advsy Bd Br-American C of C 1991–94, London First 1992–, Admin Cncl Prince's Tst 1995–98; co-chm London Pride Partnership 1994–98, tstee English Nat Stadium Tst 1996–98, dir London Waste Action Ltd 1997–98, dir London Devpt Partnership; vice-pres: Brewers Soc 1987–, United Response, Blue Cross; memb: Cons Pty Bd of Mgmnt 1992–98, Exec Ctee Animal Health Tst; govr LSE; chllr Middlesex Univ 2000; hon fell: London Business Sch 1993, LSE 2001; Gold Medal Inst of Mgmnt 1993, Int Hall of Fame Award Mktg Soc 1994; Hon Dr: Int Mgmnt Centre 1989, Brunel Univ 1994, South Bank Univ 1994, Univ of East London 1997, Univ of Westminster 1998, Middlesex Univ 1999; FCMA, FCIS, CIMgt, FRSA, FCIM, Hon FCGI 1993; *Books* Your Business Matters (jtly, 1958), Maximum Leadership (jtly, 1995); *Recreations* gardens, reading, red setter dogs; *Style*— The Rt Hon Lord Sheppard of Didgemere, KCVO; ✉ House of Lords, London SW1A 0PW

SHEPPERD, John William; s of John Walter Shepperd, of Lancing, E Sussex, and Joan Mary, *née* Owen; *b* 26 February 1951; *Educ* Tottenham GS, UCW Aberystwyth (BSc(Econ)), Univ of Manchester (MA(Econ)); *m* 7 Aug 1975, Margot, *née* Hickey; 2 da (Clare b 19 Sept 1986, Emer b 7 Dec 1990); *Career* lectr Calgary Univ 1973–78, mangr macroeconomic forecasting Economic Models Ltd 1978–80, economist Laing & Cruickshank 1980–82, economist Mullens & Co 1982–86, dir sterling bond research Warburg Securities 1986–93, chief economist Yamaichi International (Europe) Ltd 1993–98, dir Dresdner Kleinwort Wasserstein plc 1998–; *Recreations* tennis, listening to Bob Dylan; *Clubs* Reform; *Style*— John Shepperd, Esq; ✉ 44 Priory Gardens, Highgate, London N6 5QS (tel 020 8341 9456); Dresdner Kleinwort Wasserstein plc, 20 Fenchurch Street, London EC3P 3DB (tel 020 7623 8000, fax 020 7623 4069, e-mail john.shepperd@drkw.com)

SHEPSTONE, Dr Basil John; s of James John Shepstone (d 1957), of Bloemfontein, South Africa, and Letitia Isabel, *née* Robinson (d 1984); *b* 4 August 1935; *Educ* Brebner HS Bloemfontein, Univ of the Orange Free State (BSc, MSc, DSc), Univ of South Africa (BA), Univ of Oxford (BM BCh, MA, DPhil), Univ of Cape Town (MD); *m* 23 Sept 1961, (Brenda) Victoria, da of James Dudley Alen, of Cambridge; 1 s (Jonathan James b 21 Nov 1962), 1 da (Charlotte Isabel b 8 Dec 1965); *Career* jr lectr in radiation physics Univ of The Orange Free State and hosp physicist Nat Prov Hosp Bloemfontein SA 1958–60, house offr in paediatrics and thoracic surgery United Oxford Hosps 1969, head of Dept of Nuclear Med Univ of Cape Town and Groote Shuur Hosp Cape Town 1972–78 (sr specialist Dept of Radiotherapy 1970–72), dean of degrees Wolfson Coll Oxford 1980–, univ lectr and hon conslt in radiology Oxford Univ and Oxfordshire Health Authy 1981–, head of Dept of Radiology Oxford Univ 1984– (clinical lectr 1978–81), dir of clinical studies Oxford Univ Med Sch 1988–91 (dep dir 1985–88); contrib to jls and books on solid state physics, radiobiology, radiotherapy, radiodiagnosis, nuclear med and med educn; memb: Br Inst of Radiology, Br Nuclear Med Soc; fell Wolfson Coll Oxford; FInstP, LRCP, MRCS, FRCR; *Recreations* art history, reading, travelling; *Style*— Dr Basil Shepstone; ✉ Department of Radiology, University of Oxford, The Radcliffe Infirmary, Woodstock Road, Oxford OX2 6HE (tel 01865 224679)

SHER, Sir Antony; KBE (2000); s of Emanuel Sher, and Margery, *née* Abramowitz; *b* 14 June 1949; *Educ* Sea Point Boys HS Cape Town, Webber-Douglas Acad of Dramatic Art London, Post Grad drama course Manchester Univ Drama Dept and Manchester Poly Sch of Theatre; *partner* (civil partnership 2005) Gregory Doran, *qv*; *Career* actor, author and artist; DLitt (hc) Univ of Liverpool 1998, Hon DUniv Exeter 2004, Hon DLitt Univ of Warwick 2007; *Theatre* assoc artist RSC, roles incl: Richard III, Shylock in Merchant of Venice, The Fool in King Lear, Vindice in The Revenger's Tragedy, Tartuffe, Johnnie in Hello and Goodbye, title role in Singer, title role in Tamburlaine 1993, title role in Cyrano de Bergerac 1997, Leontes in The Winter's Tale 1999, title role in Macbeth 1999, Domitian Caesar in The Roman Actor 2002, Malevole in The Malcontent 2002, Iago in Othello 2004; other roles incl: Arnold in Torch Song Trilogy (Albery) 1985, title role in Arturo Ui (RNT) 1991, Astrov in Uncle Vanya (RNT) 1992, Henry Carr in Travesties (Savoy) 1994, Titus Andronicus (Market Theatre Johannesburg, transfered to RNT, TMA Best Actor Award) 1995, Stanley (RNT and Broadway) 1996, Tsafendas in ID (Almeida) 2003, Primo (Cape Town RNT and Broadway) 2004–05, title role in Kean (Apollo) 2007; dir Breakfast with Mugabe (RSC); *Television* incl: Howard Kirk in The History Man (BBC) 1980, Genghis Cohn (BBC) 1993, Macbeth (Channel 4) 2001, The Jury (Granda) 2002, Home (BBC4) 2003, Churchill the Hollywood Years 2004; *Films* incl: Alive and Kicking 1996, Mrs Brown 1997, *Exhibitions* A Cast of Characters (London Jewish Cultural Centre) 2007; *Awards* Best Actor Awards for Richard III incl: Drama Magazine Award 1984, Evening Standard Award 1985 and Olivier Award 1985; other Olivier Awards for Best Actor incl: Torch Song Trilogy 1985, Stanley 1997; Evening Standard Peter Sellers Film Award for Disraeli in Mrs Brown 1997, NY Drama Desk and Outer Critics Circle Awards and South African Fleur du Cap Award all for Best Solo Performance for Primo 2006; *Books* Year of the King (actor's diary and sketchbook, 1985), Middlepost (1988), Characters (painting and drawings, 1989), The Indoor Boy (1991), Cheap Lives (1995), Woza Shakespeare! (with Gregory Doran, 1996), The Feast (1998), Beside Myself (autobiography, 2001), ID (2003), Primo Time (2005), Primo (stage play, 2005); *Style*— Sir Antony Sher, KBE; ✉ c/o Paul Lyon-Maris, ICM, Oxford House, 76 Oxford Street, London W1D 1BS (tel 020 7636 6565)

SHER, Samuel Julius (Jules); QC (1981); s of Philip Sher (d 1985), and Isa Phyllis, *née* Hesselson; *b* 22 October 1941; *Educ* Athlone HS, Univ of the Witwatersrand (BCom, LLB), Univ of Oxford (BCL); *m* 29 Aug 1965, Sandra, da of Michael Maris, of Johannesburg, South Africa; 1 s (Brian b 10 July 1967), 2 da (Joanne b 8 Aug 1969, Debby b 6 May 1974); *Career* called to the Bar Inner Temple 1968 (bencher 1988), recorder 1987–2005, dep judge of the High Ct, head of chambers Wilberforce Chambers 2006–; *Recreations* tennis; *Style*— Jules Sher, Esq, QC; ✉ 12 Constable Close, London NW11 6TY (tel 020 8455 2753); Wilberforce Chambers, 8 New Square, Lincoln's Inn, London WC2A 3QP (tel 020 7306 0102, fax 020 7306 0095)

SHERFIELD, 2 Baron (UK 1964), of Sherfield-on-Loddon, Co Southampton; Christopher James Makins; s of 1 Baron Sherfield, GCB, GCMG, FRS (d 1996), and Alice, *née* Davis (d 1985); *b* 23 July 1942; *Educ* Winchester, New Coll Oxford; *m* 1975, Mrs Wendy Catherine Cortesi, er da of late John Whitney, of Evergreen, Colorado, USA; 1 da (Hon Marian Whitney b 7 Oct 1980); *Heir* bro, Hon Dwight Makins; *Career* HM Dip Serv 1964–75; fell All Souls Coll Oxford 1963–77; vice-pres The Aspen Inst 1989–97, pres The Atlantic Cncl of the United States 1999–; *Clubs* Pratt's, Metropolitan (Washington), Alibi

(Washington); *Style*— The Rt Hon the Lord Sherfield; ✉ 3034 P Street, NW, Washington, DC 20007, USA (tel 202 333 7314)

SHERIDAN, Christopher Julian; s of Mark Sheridan, and Olive Maud, *née* Hobbs; *b* 18 February 1943; *Educ* Berkhamsted Sch; *m* 1972, Diane Virginia, *née* Wadey; 1 da (Kate *b* 20 April 1974); *Career* Samuel Montagu & Co Ltd: joined International Div 1962, exec dir responsible for Dealing Div activities 1974–81, md Dealing Div 1981–84, chief exec 1984–94, dep chm 1988–94; chm Yorkshire Building Society 1995–2006; non-exec dir: Hanover Acceptances Ltd 1995–, Minerva plc 1996–, Coutts Consulting Gp 1997–99, Willmott Dixon Ltd 1999–2003, Standard Bank London Ltd 1999–, Alpha Bank London Ltd 2004–; dep chm Inspace plc 2005–; FCIB, CIMgt; *Recreations* theatre, tennis; *Clubs* Buck's; *Style*— Christopher Sheridan, Esq; ✉ c/o Buck's Club, 18 Clifford Street, London W1X 1RG (tel 020 7734 2337)

SHERIDAN, David Martin; s of Vernon Arthur Sheridan (d 1990), and Ruth Eleanor, *née* Caminer (d 2003); *b* 31 August 1950; *Educ* Haberdashers' Aske's, King's Coll London (BSc); *m* 1 July 1978, Christine Lesley, *née* White; 2 da (Hillary Ann *b* 17 June 1984, Deborah Lynn *b* 15 April 1987); *Career* chartered accountant; i/c Statistics Dept Marians Bloodstock Agency 1972–74, buyer Racal-BPL 1974–75, articles Mercer & Hole 1975–78, qualified ACA 1978, exec dir Brand Packaging Jefferson Smurfit Group 1980–82 (joined as PA to divnl fin dir 1978), chm Veruth Holdings Ltd 1991–, md Europa Components & Equipment plc 1991– (fin & mktg dir 1982–90), dir SIBA (UK) Ltd 1995–; pres Beds, Bucks & Herts Soc of Chartered Accountants 1988–89, memb Cncl ICAEW 1993–96 (past memb of numerous ctees), ICAEW rep jt ICAEW/ICAS Working Pty Breaking the Code 1999; Bd of Chartered Accountants in Business (BCAB): chm Working Pty 1992, co-vice-chm 1993–96, co-opted memb 1996–2000; treas Owens Sch Assoc 1997–2002; memb St Albans Round Table 1983–91, sports offr Area 28 (Round Table) 1989–91, chm Elstree and Borehamwood Twin Town 20th Anniversary 2001–02; *Recreations* work, more work, my family, squash, riding, crosswords; *Clubs* 41 (St Albans); *Style*— David Sheridan, Esq; ✉ Europa Components & Equipment plc, Europa House, 108 Ripon Way, Borehamwood, Hertfordshire WD6 2JA (tel 020 8207 0440, fax 020 8207 6646, mobile 07711 699096, e-mail david@lynton-ave.demon.co.uk)

SHERIDAN, James; MP; s of Frank Sheridan (d 1995), of Glasgow, and Annie Burke (d 1990); *b* 24 November 1952; *m* 15 Oct 1977, Jean McDowell, da of William McDowell; 1 s (Alan *b* 19 Nov 1980), 1 da (Joanne *b* 3 Sept 1984); *Career* MP (Lab) Renfrewshire W 2001–; *Style*— James Sheridan, Esq, MP; ✉ House of Commons, London SW1A 0AA

SHERIDAN, Paul Francis; s of Stanislaus Sheridan (d 1994), and Mary Patricia, *née* Keown; *b* 4 July 1960, Kesh, Co Fermanagh; *Educ* St Patrick's Coll Belfast, Richard Huish GS Taunton, Univ of Southampton (LLB); *m* 30 Jan 1999, Alice Naomi Jane; 1 s (Theo Huxley *b* 20 Oct 2001), 1 da (Amy Natasha *b* 16 Jan 2005); *Career* slr specialising in environment law; ptnr CMS Cameron McKenna LLP; *Style*— Paul Sheridan, Esq; ✉ CMS Cameron McKenna LLP, Mitre House, 160 Aldersgate Street, London EC1A 4DD (tel 020 7367 2186, e-mail paul.sheridan@cms-cmck.com)

SHERIDAN, Paul Richard; TD (1982, Bar 1991); s of Patrick William Sheridan (d 1991), of Grimsby, and Claire Sheridan, JP, *née* Marklew (d 1990); *b* 19 July 1951; *Educ* Havelock Sch Grimsby, Grimsby Coll of Technol, Univ of Kent (BA); *m* 30 June 1985, Beverley, *née* Seagger; 1 da (Cordelia Scarlet *b* 17 Dec 1996); *Career* RCT TA, Maj 1985–93 (Cadet 1969, 2 Lt 1970, Lt 1972, Capt 1977), Staff Coll (TA) 1991, RARO II 1993–2006; admitted slr 1979; ptnr Wilkin Chapman 1982–, NP 1985; Cmmr for Oaths 1990; pres Grimsby & Cleethorpes Law Soc 2005–06; chm League of Friends of Grimsby Hosps 1985–88 (hon membership offr 1988–95), chm Community Fund Raising Panel MRI £1m Scanner Appeal 1992–94; patron Nat Domesday Ctee 1986; Lord of the Manor of Aspenden Herts 1985–; memb: Law Soc 1979, Notaries Soc 1985; ind memb Standards Ctee West Lindsey DC 2007–; Freeman City of London 1985, Liveryman Worshipful Co of Carmen 1986; *Recreations* heraldry; *Clubs* Victory Services, London; *Style*— Paul R Sheridan, Esq, TD; ✉ Folly Cottage, 9 Church Street, Caistor, Market Rasen, Lincolnshire LN7 6UG (tel 01472 852070); Wilkin Chapman, PO Box 16, Town Hall Square, Grimsby, North East Lincolnshire DN35 1HE (tel 01472 262626, fax 01472 360198)

SHERIDAN, Richard Jonathan; s of Dr Morris (Roger) Sheridan, of London, and late Yvonne, *née* Brook; *b* 20 December 1956; *Educ* City of London Sch, Guy's Hosp Med Sch Univ of London; *Career* conslt obstetrician and gynaecologist Watford Gen Hosp; memb Cncl and former vice-pres Obstetrics and Gynaecology Section Royal Soc of Med; Freeman City of London, Liveryman Worshipful Soc of Apothecaries; FRCS 1985, FRCOG 1998 (MRCOG 1985); *Papers* Fertility in a Male with Trisomy 21 (1989); *Recreations* squash, skiing, riding; *Style*— Richard Sheridan, Esq; ✉ Bupa Hospital, Heathbourne Road, Bushey, Hertfordshire WD2 1RD (tel and fax 020 8421 8537); Watford General Hospital, Vicarage Road, Watford (tel 01923 217935)

SHERIDAN, Sylvia; OBE (2001); adopted da of Joseph Ford, and Margaret Ford; *b* 26 March 1948; *Educ* Pendower HS for Girls Newcastle upon Tyne, Shepherd's Commercial Coll Newcastle upon Tyne, Open Univ (BA); *m* 1969, Chris Sheridan; 1 da (Victoria *b* 2 Oct 1973); *Career* newsdesk copy taker BBC Newcastle 1970–71, sales exec Tyne Tees TV 1971, prodn sec Granada TV 1972–81, prodn sec, community educn offr and prog researcher Thames TV 1981–86, community educn offr Anglia TV 1986–87, head of community affrs TV-am 1987–89, fndr, chm and chief exec Independent Media Support Ltd 1989–; memb Cncl of Mgmnt BBFC 1999–; memb Bd of Tstees RNID 1999–2002, tstee Herts Hearing Advsy Serv 2001–02; memb RTS; *Recreations* flying light aircraft, travel, cooking, golf; *Clubs* Naval and Military, Home House; *Style*— Mrs Sylvia Sheridan, OBE; ✉ Pheasant Field, Frithsden Rise, Ashridge Park, Berkhamsted, Hertfordshire HP4 1NP; Independent Media Support Ltd, 21 Soho Square, London W1D 3QP (tel 020 7440 5400, fax 020 7440 5410, mobile 07796 690980, e-mail sylvia.sheridan@ims-media.com)

SHERLING, Clive Richard; s of late Philip Sherling, and Maureen Vivienne, *née* Gulperin, of Northwood, Middx; *b* 20 October 1949; *Educ* Woodhouse GS, LSE (BSc Econ); *m* 3 March 1993, Sally Ann; 2 s (Adrian Mark, William David (twins) *b* 31 Oct 1977); *Career* articled clerk then ptnr Arthur Andersen 1970–87, with Apax Partners Worldwide 1987–2004, vice-chm Wembley National Stadium Ltd; non-exec dir: Blacks Leisure Gp plc, Standard Life European Private Equity Tst; former chm: Sports Aid Fndn Charitable Tst, Football Licensing Authy, BVCA; MSI, FCA (ACA 1973); *Recreations* soccer, theatre, walking; *Style*— Clive Sherling, Esq; ✉ Lincoln House, Woodside Hill, Chalfont St Peter, Buckinghamshire SL9 9TF (tel 01753 887454)

SHERLOCK, David Christopher; CBE (2006); s of Frank Ernest Sherlock (d 1987), and (Emily) Edna, *née* Johnson (d 1993); *b* 6 November 1943; *Educ* Blakesley Sch, Rutlish Sch Merton, Coll of Art & Industrial Design Newcastle upon Tyne, Univ of Nottingham (BA, MPhil); *m* 1, 1969 (m dis 1975) Jean, *née* Earl; *m* 2, 1976, Cynthia Mary, da of Norman Lovell Hood; 1 da (Zoë Virginia Mary *b* 10 Feb 1977), 1 s (Nicholas David *b* 12 Oct 1978); *Career* Nottingham Coll of Art & Design 1967–70, Trent Poly 1970–74, dep dir Nat Coll of Art & Design Dublin 1975–80; princ: Winchester Sch of Art 1980–87, Central St Martin's Coll of Art & Design 1988–91; asst rector London Inst 1988–91, dir of devpt RCA 1991–93, regnl sr inspr and nat sr inspr for art and design Further Educn Funding Cncl 1993–97, chief exec and chief inspr Training Standards Cncl 1997–2001, chief inspr Adult Learning and chief exec Adult Learning Inspectorate 2000–07, dir Beyond Standards Ltd 2007–; regular columnist Times Educational Supplement 2003–; conslt industrial designer and sometime advsr to EC, UN and govts of Bangladesh, Somalia, Ghana, Portugal and Turkey; FRSA 1975, FCGLI 2007, MInstD 2007;

Recreations sailing, mountain biking; *Clubs* Royal Southern Yacht; *Style*— David Sherlock, Esq, CBE; ✉ Poplar Farm, West Tytherley, Salisbury SP5 1NR (e-mail info@beyondstandards.net)

SHERLOCK, Nigel; OBE (2003); s of Horace Sherlock (d 1967), and Dorothea, *née* Robinson (d 1980); *b* 12 January 1940; *Educ* Barnard Castle Sch, Univ of Nottingham (BA); *m* 3 Sept 1966, Helen Diana Frances, da of M Sigmund (d 2004); 2 s (Andrew *b* 27 July 1968, Mark *b* 7 July 1976), 1 da (Emma *b* 5 Sept 1970); *Career* stockbroker; chief exec Wise Speke (Div) 1993–2000, dir Ockham Holdings 1993–98, dir Brewin Dolphin Securities 1998–2005, dir Brewin Dolphin Holdings plc 1998–2002; non-exec memb: Cncl Nat Assoc of Pension Funds 1988–90, London Stock Exchange 1995–2001 (memb Bd), Skipton Building Soc 1998–2007, Church of England Pensions Bd 1998–; non-exec dep chm Assoc of Private Client Investment Managers and Stockbrokers 1995–2003; memb Cncl NE Regional C of C 1997–2004 (pres 2000–01); memb Bd of Govrs Royal GS Newcastle upon Tyne 1998–2005 (chm 2000–05); Univ of Newcastle upon Tyne: pro-chllr and chm 1993–2002, memb Ct 2002–; pres Northumberland Co Scouts 2000– (memb Cncl 1980–98), vice-pres Community Fndn of Tyne & Wear 2001– (fndr memb 1988), patron Northumbria Coalition Against Crime 2001– (vice-patron 1995–2001); tstee: William Leech Charity 1990–, Bede Museum Tst (now Fndn) 1980–90 (chm 1985–90); memb Bd Northern Sinfonia Orchestral Soc 1974–95 (chm 1990–95), memb Northern Sinfonia Devpt Tst 1980–2001 (chm 1981–2001, tstee 1980–2001), memb Bd Northern Sinfonia Orchestra 1984–96, memb Bd and chm Fundraising Ctee North Music Tst (The Sage Gateshead) 2000–05, jt pres St John Ambulance Northumbria 2001–; memb Newcastle Diocesan Bd of Fin 1973–87 (chm 1978–87), memb Bishop's Cncl Dio of Newcastle 1975–94, chm Newcastle Cathedral Cncl 2002–05, hon lay canon Durham Cathedral 2007– (hon fin advsr dean and chapter 1997–), chm Crown Nominations Cmmn for the Appt of the Archbishop of York 2005; High Sheriff Tyne & Wear 1990–91, HM Lord-Lt Tyne & Wear 2000– (DL 1995–2000); Freeman: City of Newcastle, City of London, Hostmen's Co; Liveryman Worshipful Co of Scriveners (London and Newcastle); hon fell St John's Coll Durham 1997 (memb Cncl 1984–95), hon bro of Trinty House Newcastle upon Tyne 1995; Hon DCL: Univ of Newcastle upon Tyne 2002, Univof Northumbria; FSI 1999, CCMI 2000; K St J 2002; *Recreations* music, theatre, the countryside, family skiing; *Clubs* Brooks's, City of London, New (Edinburgh), Northern Counties (Newcastle); *Style*— Nigel Sherlock, Esq, OBE; ✉ 14 North Avenue, Gosforth, Newcastle upon Tyne NE3 4DS

SHERRARD, Michael David; CBE (2003), QC (1968); s of Morris Sherrard (d 1965), and Ethel Sherrard (d 1983); *b* 23 June 1928; *Educ* King's Coll London (LLB); *m* 6 April 1952, Shirley, da of Maurice and Lucy Bagrit (both d 1973); 2 s (Nicholas *b* 9 June 1953, Jonathan *b* 5 Aug 1957); *Career* called to the Bar Middle Temple 1949 (bencher 1977, treas 1996); memb Winn Ctee on Personal Injury Litigation 1966–68, recorder of the Crown Court 1974–93, bench rep on Senate 1978–80, inspr Dept of Trade under Companies Acts (London Capital Gp) 1975–77; chm Normansfield Hosp Public Inquiry 1977–78, memb Bar Assoc of City of NY 1986–95, memb Cncl of Justice 1985–2000, dir Middle Temple Advocacy 1994–2003; FRSA 1991; *Publications* contrib British Accounting Standards - The First 10 years (1981); *Recreations* travel, listening to opera, oriental art; *Style*— Michael Sherrard, Esq, CBE, QC; ✉ 26 Eton Avenue, London NW3 3HL (tel 020 7431 0713, fax 020 7433 1605)

SHERRARD, Scott Rathman; s of John Alfred Sherrard (d 1999), of Buckhaven, Fife, and Mary Stephen, *née* Stiven; *b* 19 May 1954; *Educ* Dundee HS, Galashiels Acad, Gonville & Caius Coll Cambridge (BA, vice-pres JCR); *m* 1, 7 July 1978, Lorna Jane (d 1985), da of Allan William Clark; 1 s (Nicholas Clark Stiven *b* 25 Dec 1982); *m* 2, 28 Aug 1987, Susan Elizabeth, da of William Graham Clark; 1 da (Katherine Jane *b* 15 Sept 1988); *Career* Scottish & Newcastle Breweries Ltd: joined as mgmnt trainee 1975, brand mangr 1976–78, mktg mangr 1978–81; fndr ptnr: Cockman Thompson Wilding Ltd 1981–83, Grierson Cockman Craig & Druiff Ltd 1983–85; Grey London Ltd advtg agency: planning dir 1985–88, creative devpt dir 1988–90, md 1990–95; chief exec The Cambridge Centre 1995–, chm Collett Dickenson Pearce 1995–2000, dir Theatre of Ideas Ltd 1999–; writer/prodr of musical for Edinburgh Festival; chm Borders Young Libs; memb: Devpt Ctee Bridget's Tst, Mktg Soc; *Recreations* children, piano, golf, fishing; *Clubs* Tyneside Anglers Syndicate, Durham CCC; *Style*— Scott Sherrard, Esq; ✉ Greenside House, Greenside, Ryton, Tyne & Wear NE40 4AA (tel 0191 413 1458, fax 0191 413 1000, e-mail scott.sherrard@thecambridgecentre.co.uk)

SHERRARD, Simon Patrick; s of Patrick Sherrard (d 1997), and Angela Beatrice, *née* Stacey (d 1988); *b* 22 September 1947; *Educ* Eton; *m* 23 Aug 1975, Sara Anne, da of Maj Peter Pain Stancliffe, MBE; 3 da (Emma *b* 11 Jan 1977, Kate *b* 4 Aug 1978, Polly *b* 6 April 1983), 1 s (James *b* 19 Oct 1984); *Career* Samuel Montagu & Co Ltd 1968–74, Jardine Matheson & Co Ltd Hong Kong 1974–84; Bibby Line Group Ltd Liverpool: md 1985–97, chm 1997–; chm Port of London Authy 2001–; chm A&P Gp 2002–; non-exec dir: Cooke Bros (Tattenhall) Ltd 1991–2005 (chm 2005), Lloyd's Register 1992– (dep chm 2002–), Johnson Service Gp plc 2000– (chm 2004–); pres Chamber of Shipping 2000–01; memb Bd of Tstees Liverpool Sch of Tropical Medicine 1998–2007 (dep chm 2002–07), memb Cncl Mission to Seafarers, memb Cncl White Ensign Assoc, tstee Royal Liverpool Philharmonic Hall Diamond Jubilee Fndn 1996–2005; elder bro Trinity House; High Sheriff Cheshire 2004–05; Freeman Worshipful Co of Watermen and Lightermen of the River Thames, Liveryman Worshipful Co of Shipwrights; *Recreations* tennis, golf, breeding rare sheep; *Clubs* Boodle's, MCC; *Style*— Simon Sherrard, Esq; ✉ Port of London Authority, Bakers Hall, 7 Harp Lane, London EC3R 6LB (tel 020 7743 7924, fax 020 7743 7995, e-mail simon.sherrard@pola.co.uk)

SHERRATT, Dr Brian Walter; OBE (1995), JP; s of late Walter Eric Sherratt, and Violet Florence, *née* Cox-Smith; *b* 28 May 1942; *Educ* Univ of Leeds (BA, PGCE), Univ of London (AcDipEd, MA), Univ of Birmingham (PhD); *m* 1966, (Pauline) Brenda Hargreaves; 2 s, 2 da; *Career* asst master Normanton GS 1965–67, head Religious Studies Dept Selby GS 1967–70, sr lectr in religious studies and warden Avery Hill Coll of Educn 1970–73, asst master Kidbrooke Sch 1970–71, warden Mile End Teachers' Centre Avery Hill Coll 1971–73, dep head Sandown Court Sch Tunbridge Wells 1976–79 (sr master 1973–76), headmaster and warden Kirk Hallam Sch and Community Centre 1979–84, headmaster Great Barr Sch Birmingham 1984–2005; hon lectr Sch of Educn Univ of Birmingham 1988–; chm: Eco-Schs Advsy Panel 1997–2001, Green Code Prog for Schs Advsy Panel 1998–2005; memb: Ct Univ of Birmingham 1986–90, Organising Ctee Going for Green 1994–96, Sutton Coldfield Coll Corporation 1994–98, Centre for Policy Studies 1994–, Politeia 1995–, Civitas 2000–; non-exec dir: Going for Green Limited 1996–2000, ENCAMS (Environmental Campaigns) 1998–2005 (vice-chm 2003–05, memb Resources Ctee 2002–03 and Audit Ctee 2003–05, chm Devolution Ctee 2004–05); memb: Educn Cmmn 2002–05, Academic Advsy Cncl Univ of Buckingham 2005–; tstee ENCAMS Pension Funds 1999–2005, dir Nottingham Park Estate Ltd 2005–; Queen Mother's Birthday Award for the Environment 1999, George Cadbury Prize in Educn 2005, British Educnl Leadership Mgmnt and Admin Soc (BELMAS) Best PhD Thesis of the Year Award 2005; Freeman Guild of Educators 2003; FIMgt 1984, FRSA 1984; *Publications* Gods and Men: a survey of world religions (1971), Local Education Authorities Project: Locally Managed Schools (1998), Opting for Freedom: a stronger policy on grant-maintained schools (Centre for Policy Studies, Policy Study No 138, 1994), Grant-Maintained Status: considering the options (1994), A Structured Approach to School and Staff Development: from theory to practice (co-author, 1996), Radical Educational Policies and Conservative Secretaries of State (co-author, 1997), Headteacher

S

Appraisal (co-author, 1997), Leadership and Professional Knowledge in Education (contrib, 1999); contrib TES; *Recreations* classical music, literature, antiques, buildings; *Clubs* Athenaeum; *Style—* Dr Brian Sherratt, OBE, JP; ✉ Oakhurst, 17 Lenton Road, The Park, Nottingham NG7 1DQ (e-mail brian.sherratt@ntlworld.com)

SHERREN, Graham Veere; s of Veere George Sherren (d 1986), and Janet Cecelia Maude, *née* McLachlan; *b* 6 December 1937, Kent; *Educ* Dover Coll; *m* 1, 1961 (m dis 1970), Deirdre Jane, *née* Wright; 4 da (Sally, Caroline, Fiona, Kate); m 2, 1975, Judy Mary Hayes, *née* Newington; *Career* gen mangr Medical News Ltd 1962–64, chm and ceo Morgan-Grampian Ltd 1964–82, chm and ceo Centaur Media plc 1982–; *Recreations* golf; *Clubs* White's, Buck's, Racquet (NY), Sunningdale Golf; *Style—* Graham Sherren, Esq; ✉ Centaur Media plc, St Giles House, 50 Poland Street, London W1F 7AX (tel 020 7970 4504, fax 020 7970 4519, e-mail graham.sherren@centaur.co.uk)

SHERRIN, Edward George (Ned); CBE (1997); s of Thomas Adam Sherrin (d 1965), and Dorothy Finch, *née* Drewett (d 1980); *b* 18 February 1931; *Educ* Sexey's Sch Bruton, Exeter Coll Oxford (MA); *Career* producer, director, presenter and writer for film, theatre, radio and television; 2 Lt Royal Corps of Signals 1949–51; called to the Bar Gray's Inn; ATV 1956–58, BBC 1958–65 (TW3, Tonight); *Theatre* incl: Side by Side by Sondheim, Jeffrey Bernard is Unwell, The Mitford Girls, Sing a Rude Song, Mr and Mrs Nobody, Ratepayer's Iolanthe, Metropolitan Mikado, Bookends, Victor Spinetti's Private Diary, Our Song (London and Athens), A Passionate Woman 1994, Salad Days (Vaudeville) 1996, Good Grief (1998), Bing Bong (1999), A Saint She Ain't (1999); *Radio* Loose Ends; *Films* incl: The Virgin Soldiers 1967, The National Health 1972; *Books* Cindy Ella or I Gotta Shoe, Rappell 1910, Benbow Was His Name, A Small Thing Like an Earthquake (autobiography), Cutting Edge, Loose Neds, Ned Sherrin's Theatrical Anecdotes; Ned Sherrin in his Anecdotage (1993), Oxford Dictionary of Humorous Quotations (ed, 1995), Scratch an Actor (novel, 1996), Diary: Sherrin's Year (1996), I Wish I'd Said That (ed, 2004), Ned Sherrin: The Autobiography (2005); *Recreations* eating, theatre; *Clubs* Groucho, Garrick; *Style—* Ned Sherrin, Esq, CBE; ✉ c/o D & J Arlon, 12 Newburgh Street, London W1F 7RP (tel 020 7494 9088)

SHERRINGTON, Prof David; s of James Arthur Sherrington, KSG (d 1986), of Middlesbrough, Cleveland, and Elfreda, *née* Cameron (d 1996); *b* 29 October 1941; *Educ* St Mary's Coll Middlesbrough, Univ of Manchester (BSc, PhD); *m* 20 July 1966, Margaret, da of Richard Gee-Clough (d 1980), of Blackpool, Lancashire; 1 s (Andrew Damian b 20 Feb 1967), 1 da (Lesley Jane b 14 Jan 1971); *Career* lectr in theoretical physics Univ of Manchester 1967–69 (asst lectr 1964–67), prof of physics Imperial Coll London 1983–89 (lectr in theoretical solid state physics 1969–74, reader 1974–83), Wykeham prof of physics Univ of Oxford 1989–, Ulam scholar Los Alamos Nat Laboratory 1995–96, external prof Santa Fe Inst 2004–; jls ed: Communications on Physics 1975–78, Advances in Physics 1984–, Journal of Physics A: Mathematical and General 1989–93; contrib many articles in scientific jls; fell New Coll Oxford 1989–; hon MA Univ of Oxford 1989; FInstP 1974, fell American Physical Soc 1984; FRS 1994; *Books* Phase Transitions in Soft Condensed Matter (co-ed, 1989), Spontaneous Formation of Space - Time Structures and Criticality (co-ed, 1991), Phase Transitions and Relaxation in Systems with Competing Energy Scales (co-ed, 1993), Physics of Biomaterials: Fluctuations, Selfassembly and Evolution (co-ed, 1995), Dynamical Properties of Unconventional Magnets (co-ed, 1997), Landscape Paradigms in Physics and Biology: Concepts, Structures and Dynamics (co-ed, 1997), Stealing the Gold: A Celebration of the Pioneering Physics of Sam Edwards (co-ed, 2005); *Style—* Prof David Sherrington, FRS; ✉ Theoretical Physics, University of Oxford, 1 Keble Road, Oxford OX1 3NP (tel 01865 273947, fax 01865 273418, e-mail d.sherrington1@physics.ox.ac.uk)

SHERRY, Prof Norman; s of Michael Sherry, and Sarah, *née* Taylor; *b* 6 July 1935; *Educ* Univ of Durham (BA), Univ of Singapore (PhD); *m* 1, June 1960, Dulcie Sylvia, da of Samuel William Brunt; m 2, Sept 1990, Carmen Sherry, *née* Flores; 1 s (John Michael Graham b 6 June 1990), 1 da (Ileana Taylor b 29 Dec 1993); *Career* lectr in English literature Univ of Singapore 1961–66, lectr and sr lectr of literature Trinity Univ San Antonio TX 1983–; fell Humanities Res Center N Carolina 1982, fell Guggenheim Fndn 1989–90, first holder of Roydon B Davis Chair Georgetown Univ Washington DC 1998; FRSL 1986; *Books* Conrad's Eastern World (1966, reprinted 1971, reissued 2005), Jane Austen (1966), Charlotte and Emily Bronte (1969), Conrad's Western World (1971, reissued 2005), Conrad and His World (1972), Conrad - The Critical Heritage (1973), Conrad in Conference (1976), The Life of Graham Greene Vol One 1904–39 (1989, Edgar Allan Poe Award 1990), The Life of Graham Greene Vol Two 1939–55 (1994, nominated Edgar Allan Poe Award 1994, included in NY Times as one of Best Eleven Books of 1995, featured in NY Times Books of the Century 1998), The Life of Graham Greene Vol Three 1955–91 (2004, nominated Edgar Allan Poe Award 2005); ed Conrad Edns: Lord Jim (1967, 1974), An Outpost of Progress, Heart of Darkness (1973), Nostromo (1974), The Secret Agent (1974), The Nigger of The Narcissus, Typhoon, Falk and Other Stories (1975); contrib: The Academic American Encyclopedia, Guardian, Daily Telegraph, Oxford Magazine, Modern Language Review, Review of English Studies, Notes and Queries; BBC book contrib: Kenneth Muir Festschrift (1987), Creativity (1989); TV and radios; Conrad and His Critics BBC Radio 3 1981, film on Graham Greene Arena BBC TV 1989, in-depth TV interview on Greene's Life and Letters Global Catholic Network 2005, TV interview with LA Theater Works on play The Living Room 2005; *Recreations* talking, writing, reading, public speaking, jogging, table tennis; *Clubs* Savile; *Style—* Prof Norman Sherry

SHERRY, Patrick; *b* 29 September 1947; *Educ* Univ of Birmingham (BCom), London Stock Exchange Exam; *m*; 4 c; *Career* chartered accountant and mgmnt conslt; joined Coopers & Lybrand 1969, subsequently with Hoare Govett; currently with PricewaterhouseCoopers (formerly Coopers & Lybrand before merger): ptnr 1986–, former ptnr in mgmnt consulting, former chm Int Financial Servs, former managing ptnr Int Affrs in UK Firm and memb UK Bd, memb Int Exec Ctee and int exec ptnr Coopers & Lybrand International 1995–98, memb PricewaterhouseCoopers Global Mgmnt Team 1998–2001, sr ptnr Govt Practice 2001–, sr ptrnr Healthcare Practice 2005–, chm PwC Economics; FCA; *Style—* Patrick Sherry, Esq; ✉ PricewaterhouseCoopers, 1 Embankment Place, London WC2N 6RH (tel 020 7212 4910, fax 020 7212 5100)

SHERSTON-BAKER, Sir Robert George Humphrey; 7 Bt (GB 1796), of Dunstable House, Richmond, Surrey; o s of Sir Humphrey Dodington Benedict Sherston-Baker, 6 Bt (d 1990), and Margaret Alice, *née* Binns; *b* 3 April 1951; *m* 2 Nov 1991, Vanessa R A, yst da of C E A Baird, of Grouville, Jersey; 1 s (David Arbuthnot George b 1992), 1 da (Amy Margaret b 8 Feb 1994); *Heir* s, David Sherston-Baker; *Style—* Sir Robert Sherston-Baker, Bt; ✉ Wealden House, North Elham, Kent CT4 6UY

SHERWOOD, Bishop of 1989–; Rt Rev Alan Wyndham Morgan; s of Albert Wyndham Morgan (d 1987), and Daisy Eleanor, *née* Campbell (d 1991); *b* 22 June 1940; *Educ* Boys' GS Gowerton, St David's UC Lampeter (BA, colours in tennis, hockey and badminton), St Michael's Coll Llandaff; *m* 25 Jan 1965, (Margaret) Patricia, da of William Oswald Williams (d 1985); 1 s (Jonathan Charles b 7 Jan 1966), 1 da (Eleanor Jane b 22 Aug 1968); *Career* asst curate: Llangyfelach with Morriston 1964–69, Cockett 1969–71, St Mark's Coventry 1972; team vicar St Barnabas Coventry E 1972–78, bishop's offr for social responsibility Dio of Coventry 1978–83, archdeacon of Coventry 1983–89; memb Gen Synod 1981–89, chm House of Clergy Coventry Diocesan Synod 1982–88, chm E Midlands Churches Forum 1998, chm Gen Synod Bd of Social Responsibility's Working Pty which produced pubn Something to Celebrate; pres: Nottingham Help the Homeless Assoc 1989–2001, Framework Housing 2001, Nottingham Assoc of Voluntary Orgns, Mansfield DIAL (Disabled Info Advice Line), Mansfield Educn Forum (chm 1992–2000); vice-pres NCVO (chm 1986–89); chm: Gtr Nottingham TEC Additional Needs 1990–96, Mansfield Social Strategy Gp 1994–2003, N Notts TEC Additional Needs 1996–2001, Coalfields Regeneration Tst 1998, E Midlands Awards Ctee Nat Lottery Charities Bd 1994–2000, Notts Community Fndn 2001–; bd dir: Gtr Nottingham 1990–96, N Notts TEC 1996–2001, Notts Enterprise 2001–03; tstee Charities Aid Fndn (CAF) 1997–2002; memb: Dep PM's Coalfield Task Force, Mansfield Area Partnership Exec Bd, Governing Cncl Family Policy Studies Centre 1994–99; *Publications* Working Together: Partnerships in Local Social Service (1981), A Time to be Born and a Time to Die (1985), Partnership for Health (1987); *Recreations* walking, reading, gardening; *Style—* The Rt Rev the Bishop of Sherwood; ✉ Dunham House, Westgate, Southwell, Nottinghamshire NG25 0JL (tel 01636 819133, fax 01636 819085, e-mail bishopsherwood@southwell.anglican.org)

SHERWOOD, Charles N C; *b* 30 September 1959; *Educ* Univ of Cambridge (Whittaker scholar, MA), Harvard Univ Grad Sch of Business Admin (Baker scholar, MBA); *m*; 3 c; *Career* assoc conslt Boston Consulting Gp 1981–1983, gen ptnr Business Sch Travel 1984–85, ptnr Permira (formerly Schroder Ventures) 1985–; non-exec dir: Homebase 2001–02, The AA 2004–, Sea Containers Inc 1996–; *Recreations* snow, rock and ice climbing, skiing and ski mountaineering, scuba diving, paragliding, guitar, reading; *Style—* Charles Sherwood, Esq; ✉ Permira Advisers LLP, 20 Southampton Street, London WC2E 7QH (tel 020 7632 1032, fax 020 7947 2174, e-mail charles.sherwood@permira.com)

SHERWOOD, James Blair; s of William Earl (d 1996), and Florence Balph Sherwood (d 2005); *b* 8 August 1933; *Educ* Yale Univ (BA); *m* 31 Dec 1977, Shirley Angela, da of Geoffrey Masser Briggs (d 1993), of Hinton Waldrist, Oxon; 2 step s (Charles Nigel Cross Sherwood b 1959, Simon Michael Cross Sherwood b 1960); *Career* Lt (jr grade) US Naval Reserve 1955–58; mangr French Ports and asst gen freight traffic mangr United States Lines Co (Le Havre and NY) 1959–62, gen mangr Container Transport International Inc 1963–64, fndr and pres Sea Containers Ltd (Bermuda) 1965–2006, chm Orient-Express Hotels Ltd 1987–; estab Harry's Bar (with Mark Birley) London 1979; restored and brought into regular service Venice Simplon-Orient-Express 1982; dir Hotel Cipriani SpA; memb Cncl Save Venice Inc; tstee Solomon R Guggenheim Fndn NY; hon citizen Venice; Order of the Southern Cross (Brazil); *Recreations* tennis, skiing, golf, sailing; *Clubs* Pilgrims, Mory's, Hurlingham, Mark's, Idle Hour Country; *Style—* James Sherwood, Esq; ✉ tel 020 7921 4002

SHERWOOD, (Peter) Louis Michael; s of Peter Louis Sherwood, and Mervyn De Toll; *b* 27 October 1941; *Educ* Westminster, New Coll Oxford (MA), Stanford Univ Sch of Business (MBA); *m* 22 Aug 1970, Nicole, da of Albert Dina, of Voiron, France; 1 s (Christopher b 1974), 2 da (Anne b 1975, Isabelle b 1978); *Career* corp fin exec Grenfell & Co Ltd 1965–68, asst to Chm Fine Fare Ltd 1968–69, md Melias Ltd 1969–72, retailing exec Cavenham Ltd 1972, dir Anglo-Continental Investment & Finance Co Ltd 1972–79, sr vice-pres for devpt Grand Union Co (New Jersey) 1979–85, pres Gt Atlantic & Pacific Tea Co 1985–88, dir Gateway Corporation 1988–89, chm and chief exec Gateway Foodmarkets Ltd 1988–89; non-exec dir: ROK plc 1990–2006, Birmingham Midshires Building Society 1991–96, United Bristol Healthcare NHS Trust 1991–98, ASW Holdings plc 1993–2002, Wessex Water Services Ltd 1998–2006, Halifax Gp plc 1999–2004, HBOS plc 2001–2004; non-exec chm: Magnet Gp plc 1990–92, HTV Gp plc 1991–97 (non-exec dir 1990–97), HTV West 1995–99, New Look plc 1994–96, Govett Euro Technol and Income Tst plc (formerly The First Ireland Investment Co) 1999–2003 (non-exec dir 1998–99), Clerical Medical Investment Gp 2000–01 (non-exec dir 1990–2004), Insight Investment Management Ltd 2001–; chm: Bristol C of C and Initiative (now Business West) 1993–95 (non-exec dir 1989–), The Harbourside Centre Ltd (formerly Centre for the Performing Arts (Bristol) Ltd) 1995–2001; dep chm At Bristol (formerly Bristol 2000 Ltd) 1995–; *Recreations* mountain walking, fine wine collecting, English watercolours collecting; *Clubs* Soc of Merchant Venturers (Bristol), Lansdowne, Garrick; *Style—* Louis Sherwood, Esq; ✉ 10 College Road, Clifton, Bristol BS8 3HZ

SHERWOOD, Martin William; s of Peter Louis Sherwood (d 1992), and Mervyn, *née* De Toll (d 2005); *Educ* Westminster, New Coll Oxford (BA); *Career* grad trainee, account exec and supervisor Ogilvy Benson & Mather advtg agency 1967–74, mktg mangr, sales mangr, controller shop-in-shops, then md (subsid) Debenhams plc 1974–85, md Retail Detail Ltd 1985–87, md MMI plc financial mktg gp 1987–94, chief exec Investment Finance Div Mills & Reeve 1994–97, dir Teather & Greenwood Ltd Stockbrokers 1997–2004, dir Smith & Williamson 2004–, dir EIS companies; non-exec dir Notting Hill Housing Tst 1981–1997 (memb Fundraising Ctee), non-exec dir and chm Audit Ctee Chelsea & Westminster Hospital NHS Tst 2000–03; memb NEDO Ctee 'Better Made in Britain' 1984, memb: Cncl and dir Enterprise Investment Scheme Assoc, Securities Inst; fndr and tstee CRUSAID 1986–97; *Recreations* charity, bridge, opera, horse racing, travel; *Style—* Martin Sherwood, Esq; ✉ Smith & Williamson, 25 Moorgate, London EC2R 6AY (tel 020 7131 4326, e-mail martin.sherwood@smith.williamson.co.uk)

SHERWOOD, Oliver Martin Carwardine; s of Nathaniel Edward Carwardine Sherwood (d 1998), of Easthorpe, nr Colchester, Essex, and Heather Patricia Motion, *née* Carolin; *b* 23 March 1955; *Educ* Radley; *Children* 2 da (Davina Ruth b 7 July 1984, Sabrina Coral b 14 Oct 1994), 2 s (Peter Frederick Carwardine b 27 Oct 1986, Archie William Nathaniel b 17 April 1997); *Career* racehorse trainer; asst trainer to: G Pritchard-Gordon Newmarket 1975–76, Arthur Moore Ireland 1976–79, Fred Winter Lambourn 1979–84; racehorse trainer Rhonehurst Upper Lambourn 1984–; trainer of 500 winners incl winners of: EBF Novice Hurdle Final Cheltenham 1986, Glenlivet Hurdle Liverpool 1987, Sun Alliance Novices Hurdle Cheltenham 1987 and 1988, Sun Alliance Novices Steeplechase Cheltenham 1988, Bic Razor Gold Cup Handicap Hurdle Lingfield 1989, Rapid Raceline Scottish Champion Hurdle Ayr 1989, Gerry Fielden Hurdle Newbury 1989, Charles Heidsieck Champagne Bula Hurdle Newbury 1989, New Year's Day Hurdle Windsor 1990, ASW Hurdle Ascot 1990, Ekbalco Handicap Hurdle Newcastle 1990, Hennessy Cognac Gold Cup Steeplechase Newbury 1990, Tingle Creek Handicap Chase Sandown 1990, Baring Securities Tolworth Hurdle Sandown 1990, First Nat Steeplechase Ascot 1990, Cheltenham Grand Annual Challenge Cup Handicap Chase Cheltenham 1991, BMW Champion Novices' Hurdle Punchestown 1991, Challow Hurdle 1994, Tote Gold Trophy 1994; champion amateur rider (ridden 95 winners incl 3 Nat Hunt Cheltenham Festival winners); *Recreations* shooting, cricket; *Style—* Oliver Sherwood, Esq; ✉ Rhonehurst, Upper Lambourn, Newbury, Berkshire RG16 7RG (tel 01488 71411, fax 01488 72786, e-mail oliver.sherwood@virgin.net)

SHEW, Edmund Jeffrey; s of Edmund Robert Shew (d 1952), of Bosbury, Herefords, and Dorothy May, *née* Teague (d 1988); *b* 23 December 1936; *Educ* Rossall Sch Fleetwood; *m* 1, 24 June 1960 (m dis); 1 s (Michael b 14 June 1962), 1 da (Dorothy b 19 May 1966); m 2, 21 Nov 1987, Vivien Dawn, da of Meirion Jones; *Career* Nat Serv RAF 1960–62; articled clerk 1954–59, ptnr Stanley Marsh & Co CAs St Helens 1962–66, princ Edmund Shew & Co CA St Helens 1966–2002, dir North West Accounting Services Ltd 2002–; pres Liverpool Soc of CAs 1983–84, memb Cncl ICAEW 1989–95; FCA (ACA 1960), CTA (ATII 1965), FCCA 1982, FCMI (FIMgt 1986); *Recreations* meteorology, gardening, agriculture, golf; *Style—* Edmund Shew, Esq; ✉ 46 Crank Road, Billinge, Wigan, Lancashire WN5 7EZ (tel 01744 895361, e-mail vivien.shew@btinternet.com); 8 Le Golf, Gros Bissinges, 74500 Evian-les-Bains, France (tel 00 33 04 50 75 27 91); North West

Accounting Services Ltd, 35 Westfield Street, St Helens, Merseyside WA10 1QD (tel 01744 730888, fax 01744 451785)

SHIACH, Allan George; s of Maj Gordon Leslie Shiach, WS (d 1948), and Lucie Sybil, *née* de Freitas; *b* 16 September 1941; *Educ* Gordonstoun, McGill Univ Montreal (BA); *m* 12 Nov 1966, Kathleen Beaumont, da of Richard B Swarbreck (d 1977), of Rhodesia; 2 s (Dominic Leslie b 1967, Luke Allan b 1974), 1 da (Philippa Lucie b 1969); *Career* chm Macallan-Glenlivet plc 1980–96, dir Rafford Films Ltd 1984–; screenwriter/producer 1970–; writer/co-writer: Don't Look Now 1975, Joseph Andrews 1979, The Girl from Petrovka 1978, Tenebrae 1982, DARYL 1984, Castaway 1985, The Witches 1988, Cold Heaven 1990, Two Deaths 1995, The Preacher's Wife 1996, In Love and War 1996, Regeneration 1996, The Fourth Angel 2000, and others; memb Cncl of Scotch Whisky Assoc; dir: SMG plc, Caledonian Publishers Ltd; chm: Scottish Film Cncl, Scottish Screen; govr British Film Inst; Freeman City of London 1988, Liveryman Worshipful Co of Distillers; memb: BAFTA, WGA, American Acad of Motion Picture Arts and Scis; *Clubs* Savile; *Style—* Allan Shiach, Esq

SHIELDS, Elizabeth Lois; da of Thomas Henry Teare (d 1977), and Dorothy Emma Elizabeth, *née* Roberts-Lawrence (d 1977); *b* 27 February 1928; *Educ* Whyteleafe Girls' GS Surrey, UCL (BA), Univ of York (MA); *m* 12 Aug 1961, David Cathro Shields, s of Arthur William Strachan Shields; *Career* teacher: classics at St Philomena's Carshalton, Jersey Coll for Girls, St Swithun's Winchester, Trowbridge HS, Queen Ethelburga's, Harrogate, Malton Sch; lectr: Univ of Hull 1989–90, WEA Leeds and York Univ 1991–; memb Lib Dem Pty, Lib Dem spokesman on the environment for Yorks and Humberside 1990–95, chm Yorks and Humberside Lib Dems Candidates' Ctee 1993–97, pres Yorks and Humberside Regn for Lib Dems 1997–; Ryedale DC: cncllr 1980–, chm 1989, chm Community Servs 1991–, chm Environment, Health and Housing Ctee 1992–2001, chm Community Servs and Licensing Ctee 2001–07, chm Overview and Scrutiny Ctee Ryedale DC 2007–; MP (Lib Dem) Ryedale May 1986–June 1987, re-selected prospective Parly candidate Ryedale; memb Ryedale Housing Assoc (chm 1990–91, currently chm Devpt Ctee), chm Yorks and Humber Housing Forum 2001–; govr Norton Sch 1980–92, chm of govrs Langton CP Sch 1992–94, memb Ct Univ of York 1996–, chm Malton Sch PTA, patron Malton and Norton Boys' Club; pres: Ryedale Motor Neurone Disease Assoc 1990–95, Ryedale Cats Protection League 1991–; *Books* A Year to Remember (1995); *Clubs* National Liberal; *Style—* Mrs Elizabeth Shields; ✉ Firby Hall, Kirkham Abbey, Westow, York YO60 7LH (tel 01653 681474, e-mail elizabethshields@btclick.com)

SHIELDS, Frank Cox; s of Joseph F Shields (d 1973), of Dublin, and Alice, *née* Cox (d 1972); *b* 10 September 1944; *Educ* Harvard Univ (AB), Wharton Sch of Fin and Commerce (MBA); *m* 9 Oct 1971, Elizabeth Jean, da of John Blythe Kinross, CBE, of London; 1 da (Henrietta b 1973), 2 s (Oliver b 1975, Alexander b 1980); *Career* res staff LSE 1969–71; stockbroker: Cazenove & Co 1971–73, Grieveson Grant & Co 1973–78; exec dir: European Banking Co Ltd 1978–85, EBC AMRO Bank Ltd 1985–86; sr rep Maruman Securities Co Ltd London 1987, dir and gen mangr Maruman Securities (Europe) Ltd 1987–92, sr private banker and vice-pres Merrill Lynch International Bank Ltd 1992–94, head of real estate and tstee services National Bank of Kuwait (International) plc 1995–99; dir of investor rels and mktg: Emerging Markets Partnership (Europe) Ltd 2000–05, Mid Europa Partners LLP 2005–06, EMP Global 2006–; *Recreations* architecture, reading, travel; *Clubs* Brooks's, The Nassau (Princeton NJ), The Fly (Cambridge Mass); *Style—* Frank Shields, Esq; ✉ 24 Church Row, Hampstead, London NW3 6UP (tel 020 7435 1175, e-mail fcshields@msn.com); EMP Global, Saski Crescent, Królewska 16, 00–103 Warsaw, Poland (tel 00 48 (22) 330 6301, fax 00 48 (22) 330 6300, e-mail shieldsf@empglobal.com, website www.empglobal.com)

SHIELDS, (Robert) Michael Coverdale; CBE (2002); s of Thomas Shields, and Dorothy Shields; *b* 23 January 1943; *Educ* Durham Johnston Grammar Tech Sch, Univ of Durham (BSc), Univ of Newcastle upon Tyne (DipTP); *m* 1965, Dorothy Jean Dennison; 2 s, 1 da; *Career* with Planning Depts: Newcastle upon Tyne 1964–65, Durham CC 1965–69, Nottingham 1969–73; dep dir of planning Leeds City Cncl 1973–78, city tech servs offr and dep chief exec Salford City Cncl 1978–83; chief exec: Trafford BC 1983–87, Trafford Park Devpt Corp 1987–98, NW RDA 1998–2003; dir Innvotec NW Tst Ltd 1998–2001, inaugural chief exec Manchester Knowledge Capital 2003–04, princ URC Associates 2003–, assoc Amion Consltg 2004–, chm United Utilities Trust Fund 2005, chm Liverpool Land Devpt Co 2005–; govr Altrincham GS 1988–98 (chm 1988–93); Univ of Salford: pro-chllr 1993–99, chm Cncl 1997–99, dep 1999–2003; tstee Mfrg Inst 2006–; Hon DSc Univ of Salford, Hon DLitt UMIST, Hon LLD Univ of Manchester; MRTPI, FRSA; *Recreations* family, books; *Style—* Michael Shields, Esq; ✉ tel 0161 928 2320, e-mail mike.shields@urca.co.uk

SHIER, Jonathan Fraser; s of Frank Eric Shier (d 1993), and Margery Mary, *née* Dutton (d 1995); *b* 18 October 1947, Melbourne, Aust; *Educ* Geelong C of E GS, Monash Univ Melbourne (LLB, BEC); *m* 1993 (m dis 2005), Susan, *née* Pugsley; 1 s (Charles Cameron Crossland Shier); *Career* private sec to Dep Senate Ldr and AG of Aust 1973–76, mktg controller and dir of sales and mktg Scottish TV 1977–85, dir of sales and mktg Thames TV plc 1985–93, dep chief exec Thames TV plc 1990–93; chm ITV Marketing Ctee 1989–91; ceo (Central and Eastern Europe) Nethold 1994–97, commercial dir TV3 Broadcasting Group 1998–99, md Aust Broadcasting Corp 2000–01; chm Continental Ventures 2002–; *Recreations* travel, theatre; *Clubs* Hurlingham, East India, Melbourne CC; *Style—* Jonathan Shier, Esq; ✉ 1701/81 Macleay Street, Potts Point, Sydney, NSW 2011, Australia (tel 00 612 9331 6603, fax 00 612 9331 6605, e-mail jfsprivate@imap-mail.com)

SHIFFNER, Sir Henry David; 8 Bt (UK 1818), of Coombe, Sussex; s of Maj Sir Henry Burrows Shiffner, 7 Bt, OBE (d 1941); *b* 2 February 1930; *Educ* Rugby, Trinity Hall Cambridge; *m* 1, 1951 (m dis 1956), Dorothy, da of W G Jackson, of Coventry, Warks; 1 da (Elizabeth Marilyn b 1953); m 2, 1957 (m dis 1970), Beryl, da of George Milburn, of Saltdean, E Sussex; 1 da (Linda Mary b 1957); m 3, 1971, Joaquina Ramos Lopez, of Madrid; *Heir* kinsman, George Shiffner; *Career* company dir; *Style—* Sir Henry Shiffner, Bt

SHILLING, David; s of late Ronald Shilling, and Gertrude Shilling (d 1999); *b* 27 June 1953; *Educ* St Paul's; *Career* designer, artist; designs incl: menswear, womenswear, lingerie, furs, jewellery, fine china limited edition pieces, ceramic tiles, wallpapers, upholstery fabrics and designs for film, theatre, ballet and opera; important solo shows incl: The Hats (Ulster Museum exhibition, exhibited Worthing, Plymouth, Salisbury, Durham, Leeds and Exeter Museums) 1981–, David Shilling - A Decade of Design (Chester Museum) 1991; other solo exhibitions incl: Angela Flowers London, Tino Ghelfi Vicenza Italy, Rendezvous Gallery Aberdeen, Phillip Francis Sheffield, Richard Demarco Gallery Edinburgh, Sotheby's Stockholm, Salamo-Caro Gallery Cork St London 1993, British Cncl Köln 1995, Dubai 1999, Hatworks Museum Stockport 2001, National Horseracing Museum Newmarket 2001, Int Museum of the Horse Lexington KY 2002, Newmarket Racecourse 2002, Henley Festival 2003, Galerie Ferrero Nice 2004, Musee Chapeau Lyon 2004–05, Ferrero Gallery Nice 2005, Regent's Park London 2005, Holdenby Northampton 2006; work in museum collections: V&A, Met NY, Los Angeles County, Mappin Gallery Sheffield, Musée de l'Art Décoratif Paris, Philadelphia Museum of Art; UN sr conslt for design and product adaptation for developing countries (projects in S America, Asia and Africa) 1990–; pres Valdivia Ecuador; *Books* Thinking Rich (1986); *Recreations* sleeping on aeroplanes, exploring, jet-skiing, jam making; *Style—* David Shilling, Esq; ✉ website www.davidshilling.com

SHILSTON, Andrew Barkley; s of Alan Shilston, and Patricia Shilston; *b* 20 October 1955; *Educ* Epsom Coll, Keble Coll Oxford (MA); *m* 30 Aug 1980, Catherine; 2 da (Sophie b 1985, Emma b 1988), 1 s (James b 1987); *Career* Arthur Andersen 1977–81, BP 1981–83, Abbott Laboratories 1983–84, fin dir Enterprise Oil plc 1985–2002, fin dir Rolls-Royce plc 2003–; non-exec dir: AEA Technology plc 1996–2004, Cairn Energy 2004–; ACA 1980, MCT 1989; *Recreations* tennis, skiing, rugby, opera; *Clubs* RAC; *Style—* Andrew Shilston, Esq; ✉ Rolls-Royce plc, 65 Buckingham Gate, London SW1E 6AT (tel 020 7227 9487, e-mail andrew.shilston@rolls-royce.com)

SHIMELL, William Douglas John; s of William George Shimell, of Cawsand, Cornwall, and F Elizabeth Bowen; *b* 23 September 1952; *Educ* Westminster Abbey Choir Sch, St Edward's Sch Oxford, Guildhall Sch of Music, National Opera Studio; *m* 1996, Olga Slavka; *Career* baritone; *Roles* incl: Count Almaviva in The Marriage of Figaro (Glyndebourne Festival 1984, La Scala Milan 1987 and 1989, Geneva Opera 1989, Vienna Staatsoper 1990, 1993, 1994 and 1995, Zurich Opera 1990, Chicago Lyric Opera 1991, Champs Elysees Theatre Paris 1997), Marcello in La Bohème (Royal Opera House Covent Garden 1990, Vienna Staatsoper 1991, San Francisco 1993, Metropolitan NY 1996), title role in Don Giovanni (WNO 1984, ENO 1985, Amsterdam 1989 and 1992, Zurich 1991, Aix-en-Provence Festival 1993, Munich 1994, Berlin 1994, San Francisco 1995, Vienna Straatsoper 1997), Dandini in La Cenerentola (Glyndebourne Touring Opera 1983, Le Châtalet Paris 1986), Malatesta in Don Pasquale (Netherlands Opera) 1987, Nick Shadow in The Rake's Progress (San Francisco Opera 1988, Opèra de Lyon 1995, Munich 2002, Metropolitan NY 2003), Guglielmo in Cosi fan Tutte (Covent Garden, Geneva Opera, Zurich Opera, Tokyo, Bolshoi Theatre Moscow with La Scala Co 1989), Dourlinski in Lodoiska (La Scala Milan under Riccardo Muti, also recorded live for Sony) 1991, Don Alfonso in Cosi fan Tutte (Rome 1995, Paris 1996, Metropolitan NY 1997), Sharpless in Madame Butterfly (Rome 1996, Metropolitan NY 1999 and 2002), title role in Hercules (Aix-en-Provence Festival) 2004; *Recordings* Joseph in Berlioz L'Enfance du Christ (with English Chamber Orch under Léger, Thames Television), Bach B minor Mass (with Chicago Symphony Orch under Sir Georg Solti, Decca), Vaughan Williams Sea Symphony (with Royal Liverpool Philharmonic under Vernon Handley, EMI), Lambert Summer's Last Will and Testament (with English Northern Philharmonic under David Lloyd-Jones), Stravinsky Pulcinella (with Amsterdam Concertgebouw under Chailly, Decca), title role in Don Giovanni (with Vienna Philharmonic under Riccardo Muti, EMI); *Style—* William Shimell, Esq; ✉ c/o IMG Artists, Lovell House, 616 Chiswick High Road, London W4 5RX (tel 020 8747 9977, fax 020 8742 8758)

SHINDLER, Dr Colin; s of Israel Shindler, of Prestwich, Manchester, and Florence, *née* Weidberg; *b* 28 June 1949; *Educ* Bury GS, Gonville & Caius Coll Cambridge (MA, PhD); *m* 23 Sept 1972, (Nancy) Lynn, da of Prof Robert Stephen White (d 2005), of Santa Barbara, CA; 1 da (Amy b 1975), 1 s (David b 1977); *Career* film, television writer and producer: res fell American Film Inst Beverly Hills 1972; as prodr incl: Love Story series (BBC) 1981, East Lynne (BBC) 1982, The Worst Witch (Central, American Cable Emmy) 1985, A Little Princess (LWT, BAFTA) 1986, Lovejoy (BBC, series V 1993, series VI 1994), Wish Me Luck (LWT) 1987, 1914 All Out (YTV, first prize Reims Int Film Festival) 1989; as writer and prodr: Young Charlie Chaplin (Thames/PBS, US Prime Time Emmy nomination), The Scarlet Thread (NBC) 1992, Madson (BBC) 1995, Manchester United Ruined My Life (BBC) 1998, Footballers' Lives 2003; author of screenplay Buster (feature film) 1988; Radio: Warner Bros Goes to War (BBC Radio 3) 1995, Second City Blues (BBC Radio 4) 1999, Mothers, Daughters and Chicken Soup (BBC Radio 4) 2002; memb BAFTA; lectr Faculty of History Univ of Cambridge 1998–; *Books* Hollywood Goes to War (1979), Buster (1988), Hollywood in Crisis (1996), Manchester United Ruined My Life (1998), High on a Cliff (1999), Fathers, Sons and Football (2001), First Love, Second Chance (2002), George Best and 21 Others (2004); *Recreations* cricket, soccer, golf, tennis, badminton, theatre, music, fell walking in the Lake District; *Style—* Dr Colin Shindler; ✉ c/o ICM Ltd, Oxford House, 76 Oxford Street, London W1N 0AX (tel 020 7636 6565, fax 020 7323 0101)

SHINDLER, Geoffrey Arnold; s of Israel Shindler (d 2004), of Manchester, and Florence, *née* Weidberg (d 1962); *b* 21 October 1942; *Educ* Bury GS, Gonville & Caius Coll Cambridge (WM Tapp scholar, MA, LLM); *m* 20 Feb 1966, Gay, da of late Harry Kenton; 3 da (Freya b 29 Dec 1966, Nicola b 8 Oct 1968, Caroline b 29 Jan 1971); *Career* ptnr March Pearson & Skelton 1971–86 (articled clerk 1966–68, asst slr 1968–71), ptnr Halliwell Landau Manchester 1986–2005, sr memb Halliwells LLP 2005–06, ptnr Lane-Smith & Shindler LLP 2006–; memb: Bd of Visitors HM Prison Manchester 1973–84, Salford FPC 1984–89, Exec Ctee NW Arts 1984–91; chm: Local Review Ctee (Parole) HM Prison Manchester 1979–84, Soc of Tst and Estate Practitioners 1994–98, Inst for Fiscal Studies NW region 1996–98; pres Soc of Tst and Estate Practitioners 2006– (vice-pres 1998–2006); memb Tst Law Ctee, memb Bd of Advsrs Int Compliance Assoc; hon assoc Centre For Law and Business Univ of Manchester 1990–; dir: Opera North 1995–97, Royal Exchange Theatre Co 2003–, Manchester Camerata; recipient Muriel Goodwin trophy 1993; memb: Manchester Literary and Philosophical Soc, Soc of Legal Scholars, Int Academy of Estate and Tst Law; chm Devpt Ctee Royal Exchange Theatre Manchester; tstee Portico Library Manchester; MSI; *Books* Law of Trusts (with K Hodkinson, 1984); *Publications* Trusts and Estates Law and Tax Jl (conslt ed), Wills and Trusts Law Reports (memb bd); *Recreations* theatre, music, opera, books; *Clubs* Lancashire CCC (memb Ctee 2006–), MCC, Portico Library; *Style—* Geoffrey A Shindler, Esq; ✉ 10 Bury Old Road, Prestwich, Manchester M25 0EX (tel 0161 740 2291); Lane-Smith & Shindler LLP, Colwyn Chambers, 19 York Street, Manchester M2 3BA (tel 0845 658 4848, fax 0845 658 4849)

SHINDLER, Nicola; da of Geoffrey Shindler, of Manchester, and Gay, *née* Kenton; *b* 8 October 1968; *Educ* Bury GS, Gonville & Caius Coll Cambridge (BA); *Children* 1 da (Abby Shindler Greenhalgh b 8 March 2003); *Career* early work incl: script ed Cracker 1993, asst prodr Our Friends in the North 1994–95, prodr Hillsborough 1995–96, prodr Heart 1997; fndr Red Prodn Co 1998–, co-fndr Red Wall Prodn Co; prodr/exec: Queer As Folk (2 series), Love in the 21st Century, Clocking Off (4 series), Linda Green (2 series), Bob & Rose, The Second Coming, Sparkhouse, Flesh and Blood, Burn It (2 series), Mine all Mine, Jane Hall's Big Bad Bus Ride, Conviction, Casanova, Dead Man Weds, Big Dippers; *Awards* BAFTA: Best Single Drama 1996, Best Series 2000; RTS: Drama Series 2001, Best Drama 2002, Best Drama Series 2002; RTS NW: Best Drama Series 2001, Best Prog 2001, Best Drama 2001, Best Network Drama 2001, Best Drama 2002, Best Prog Produced by NW Independent 2003, Best Network Drama Prog 2003, Best Cable Prog 2003; Indies: Drama Award 2001, Best Drama 2002, Best TV Prog of Year 2002; Indie-vidual Award 2002, TV Prog of the Year Prix Europe TV Fiction 2003, Best Single Drama Broadcast Awards 2003; *Clubs* Manchester United FC (season ticket holder); *Style—* Ms Nicola Shindler; ✉ Red Production Company, c/o Granada TV, 1 Quay Street, Manchester M60 9EA (tel 0161 827 2530, fax 0161 827 2518, e-mail nicola@redlimited.co.uk)

SHINGLER, Timothy Hugh; s of Hugh Shingler (d 1993), and Enid Mary, *née* Stuffins; *b* 10 August 1955; *Educ* Bromley Tech HS for Boys; *m* 1, 1979 (m dis 1985), Laura Muriel, *née* Mill; 1 da (Sarah Laura b 23 Dec 1983); m 2, 11 June 1988, Susan, da of Dennis Arthur Edgar Elmes; 2 da (Helen Elizabeth b 21 April 1992, Nicola Joanne b 27 Jan 1998); *Career* geological data supervisor and co scout Shell UK Exploration and Production 1973–81, sr project co-ordinator Petroleum Information Ltd 1981–86, assoc Petroleum Servs Div James Capel & Co 1990–91 (oil exec 1986–89), business devpt/mktg dir Petroleum Servs Gp Arthur Andersen (now Andersen) 2000– (sr mangr 1991–99); dir

Borough 19 Motor Club Ltd; memb: Petroleum Exploration Soc of Great Britain 1986–, London Oil Analyst Gp, SE Asia Petroleum Exploration Soc; MInstPet 1986; *Recreations* motor sport, skiing, gardening, cooking; *Style*— Timothy Shingler, Esq; ✉ Andersen, 180 Strand, London WC2R 1BL (tel 020 7438 3880, fax 020 7438 3881, e-mail timothy.h.shingler@uk.andersen.com)

SHINGLES, Godfrey Stephen (Geoff); CBE (1987); s of Sidney Shingles, and Winifred, *née* Moss; *b* 9 April 1939; *Educ* Paston Sch North Walsham, Univ of Leeds (BSc); *m* 1, (m dis); 2 s (Jonathan b 19 Feb 1968, James b 29 April 1970); m 2, 2 Jan 1997, Frances Margaret; 1 da (Emma b 9 March 1998); *Career* Digital Equipment Co 1965–94 (latterly chm and chief exec), chm Imagination Technologies Group plc 1996– (dep chm 1994–96); dir: Speed-trap, Retento, Sarantel, Corsair, Interregnum Venture Marketing Ltd until 2006; FInstD, FBCS, FIEE; *Recreations* painting, skiing, sailing, rugby, golf; *Clubs* Royal Ocean Racing, MCC; *Style*— Geoff Shingles, Esq, CBE

SHINGLETON, Andrew Philip; s of Wilfrid James Shingleton (d 1984), and Grace Bernadina Shingleton, *née* Pole; *b* 28 June 1943; *Educ* Douai Sch; *m* 1, 1967, Vanessa Jane (d 1977), da of Capt John Liley, of Marbella, Spain; 3 s (Toby John-James b 1972, Alexander William, Barnaby Andrew (twins) b 1975); m 2, 1982, Wendy Elizabeth, da of Alec Barnes, of South Lancing, W Sussex; *Career* McCann Erickson Advertising: dir 1987–, vice-pres McCann Erickson Worldwide 1994–; memb Bd of Tstees Care Int UK 2001–; MIPA 1972, memb CAM 1973; *Recreations* walking the Cornish cliffs, golf, 18th century French history; *Style*— Andrew P Shingleton, Esq; ✉ Bossiney, 75 Orchehill Avenue, Gerrards Cross, Buckinghamshire SL9 8QH (tel 01753 887985, e-mail shingleton.aw@tesco.net); McCann Erickson Advertising, 36 Howland Street, London W1A 1AT (tel 020 7312 6410)

SHIPLEY, Her Hon Judge Jane; da of John Roberts Shipley, and late Maureen Anne Shipley; *b* 5 January 1952; *Educ* Maltby GS (head girl), St Hugh's Coll Oxford (MA, pres Oxford Law Soc); *m* 22 May 1977, David Arthur Farnsworth; 2 da (Emma, Sarah); *Career* called to the Bar Gray's Inn 1974, joined NE Circuit 1974, recorder of the Crown Court 1995–2000 (asst recorder 1991–95), circuit judge (NE Circuit) 2000–; *Recreations* gardening; *Style*— Her Hon Judge Jane Shipley; ✉ Sheffield Law Courts, 50 West Bar, Sheffield S3 8PH (tel 0114 281 2400)

SHIPPEY, Prof Thomas Alan; s of Ernest Shippey (d 1962), and Christina Emily, *née* Kjelgaard; *b* 9 September 1943; *Educ* King Edward's Sch Birmingham, Queens' Coll Cambridge (MA, PhD); *m* 1, 27 Dec 1966 (m dis 1983), Susan Margaret, da of John Veale, of Bingley, W Yorks; 2 da (Louise b 1970, Gillian b 1972), 1 s (John b 1973); m 2, 19 June 1993, Catherine Elizabeth, da of John Barton, of Bromley, Kent; *Career* lectr Univ of Birmingham 1965–72, fell St John's Coll Oxford 1972–79, prof of English language and medieval English literature Univ of Leeds 1979–93, Walter Ong chair Dept of English St Louis Univ 1993–; *Books* Old English Verse (1972), Poems of Wisdom and Learning in Old English (1976), Beowulf (1978), The Road to Middle-Earth (1982), Fictional Space (1991), Fiction 2000 (1992), Oxford Book of Science Fiction Stories (1992), Oxford Book of Fantasy Stories (1994), Beowulf: The Critical Heritage (1998), Tolkien: Author of the Century (2000), The Shadow-walkers (2005), Roots and Branches (2007); *Recreations* walking, running, science fiction; *Style*— Prof Thomas Shippey; ✉ English Department, St Louis University, St Louis, MO 63103, USA (tel 00 1 314 977 7196, fax 00 1 314 977 1514, e-mail shippey@slu.edu)

SHIPWRIGHT, Adrian John; s of Jack Shipwright, and Jennie, *née* Eastman; *b* 2 July 1950; *Educ* King Edward VI Sch Southampton, ChCh Oxford (MA, BCL); *m* 17 Aug 1974, Diana Evelyn, da of Percival Denys Treseder (d 1971); 1 s (Henry b 1983), 1 da (Fiona b 1985); *Career* asst slr Linklaters & Paines 1977, official student and tutor in law ChCh Oxford 1977–82, ptnr Denton Hall Burgin & Warrens 1984–87 (asst slr 1982–84), ptnr SJ Berwin & Co 1987–92 (conslt 1992); called to the Bar Lincoln's Inn 1993, in practice Pump Court Tax Chambers 1993–2004, with Moore & Blatch 2004–07, conslt Clarke Willmott 2007–; dep special cmmr and pt/t chm VAT Tbnl; memb Tst Law Ctee; KCL: hon lectr in laws 1986–90, prof of business law 1992–96, visiting prof 1996–; govr King Edward VI Sch Southampton 1982–96; FTII, FRSA, AIIT, TEP; *Books* CCH British Tax Reporter Vol 5 (1986) Tax Planning and UK Land Development (1988, 3 edn 2001), Capital Gains Tax Strategies in the New Regime (1989), UK Tax and Intellectual Property (1990, 2 edn 1996), VAT, Property and the New Rules (1990), UK Tax and Trusts (1991, 2 edn 2000), Strategic Tax Planning (ed and contrib), Textbook on Revenue Law (1997, 3 edn 2000); *Recreations* music; *Style*— Adrian Shipwright, Esq; ✉ Clarke Willmott, Burlington House, Botleigh Grange Business Park, Hedge End, Southampton SO30 2DF (tel 01489 77000)

SHIRAISHI, Yuko; da of Masahiro Shinoda, of Tokyo, Japan, and Kazuko Shiraishi; *b* 6 March 1956; *Educ* Shinmei Jr Sch Tokyo, Myojyo HS Tokyo, Chelsea Sch of Art (Br Cncl scholar, BA, MA); *m* 1983, David Juda, *qv*; *Career* artist; projects: Field Inst Hombroich, Stiftung Insel Hombroich Museum Neuss 2001, BBC White City Project 2001–03, Moorfields Eye Hosp London 2006; *Solo Exhibitions* Edward Totah Gallery 1988, 1990 and 1992, Shigeru Yokota Gallery Tokyo 1989, 1992, 1997 and 2001, Galerie Konstruktiv Tendens Stockholm 1990, 1994, 1997 and 2006, Gallery Kasahara 1993, 1996 and 2001, Galerie Hans Mayer Düsseldorf 1996, EAF Adelaide 1996, Annely Juda Fine Art 1997, 2001 and 2005, Ernst Museum Budapest 1998, Tate Gallery St Ives 1999, Museum Wiesbaden 2002, Mead Gallery Warwick Arts Centre Coventry 2002, Leeds City Art Gallery 2003, Crawford Municipal Art Gallery Cork 2003, Waygood Gallery Newcastle 2003, Leonard Hutton Galerie NY (with Joseph Albers) 2006; *Group Exhibitions* incl: New Contemporaries (ICA) 1980, The Presence of Painting: Aspects of British Abstraction 1957–88 (Arts Cncl Mappin Gallery Sheffield and touring) 1988, Kunstlerinnen des 20 Jahrhunderts (Museum Wiesbaden Germany) 1990, Geteilte Bilder (Folkwang Museum, Germany) 1992, A Sense of Purpose (Mappin Art Gallery Sheffield) 1992, Recent British Painting (Arts Cncl touring exhbn) 1993, Zwei Energie Haus fur Konstructive und Konkrete Kunst (Zurich) 1993; Jerwood Painting Prize Royal Scottish Acad Edinburgh/The Royal Acad of Arts London 1994, Clear and Saturated (arti et Amicitiae Amsterdam) 1998, Geometrie als Gestalt (Neue Nationalgalerie Berlin) 1999, Blue (New Art Gallery Walsall) 2000, Monochrome (Mucsarnok Budapest) 2002, Art Unlimited Basel 2003, Kyoto Art Walk Nijo Castle 2005, MOT London 2006, Busan Biennale Sea Art Festival 2006; *Work in Public Collections* Unilever, Br Museum, IBM, Arthur Andersen collection, Seibu Japan, McCrory Corporations NY, Arts Cncl of GB, Contemporary Art Soc, Graves City Art Gallery Sheffield, Ohara Museum Japan, Weishaupt Forum Germany, Daimler Benz Stuttgart Germany, British Cncl London, Govt Collection London, Sammlung Albertina Vienna, Ludwig Museum Budapest, Nat Museum of Art Osaka; *Style*— Ms Yuko Shiraishi; ✉ Acme Studio, Studio F, 15 Orsman Road, London N1 5RA

SHIRLEY, Malcolm Christopher; s of Lt Cdr Leonard Noel Shirley, RN (d 1988), of Burford, Oxon, and Edith Florence, *née* Bullen (d 1999); *b* 10 April 1945; *Educ* Churcher's Coll Petersfield, BRNC Dartmouth, RN Engrg Coll (BSc); *m* 18 April 1970, Lucilla Rose Geary, da of Cdr Thomas Geary Dyer, RN, of Bradford-on-Avon, Wilts; 3 s (Guy b 1 March 1975, Ben b 1 March 1977, Hugo b 2 Jan 1979); *Career* RN: Midshipman 1964, Sub Lt 1965–69, Lt 1969, dep marine engr offr HMS Zulu 1970–73, trg offr HMS Eastbourne 1973–75, sr engr offr HM Yacht Britannia 1975–77, Lt Cdr 1976, RN Staff Coll 1977–78, Ship Design Authy MOD Bath 1978–79, marine engr off HMS Coventry 1980–81, asst naval attaché Paris (1982–84), manning and trg policy desk offr MOD Whitehall 1984–86, OC Machinery Trials Unit 1987–89, Capt 1989, asst dir MOD Bath 1989–91, UK military rep NATO (SHAPE) Belgium 1992–94, Cdre 1995, i/c Rating Study Gp, cmdg offr HMS Sultan 1995–98; DG Engrg Cncl 1998–2001, sec Royal Cmmn for the Exhbn of 1851 2002–; Freeman City of London, Liveryman Worshipful Co of Engineers 1999; CEng 1973, FIMarEST (FIMarE 1980), FRSA 2002; *Recreations* sailing, music, fine wine; *Clubs* RNSA, Royal Yacht Sqdn; *Style*— Mr Malcolm Shirley; ✉ 1851 Royal Commission, Sherfield Building, Imperial College, London SW7 2AZ (tel 020 7594 8790, e-mail royalcom1851@imperial.ac.uk)

SHIRLEY, Dame Stephanie (Steve); DBE, (2000, OBE 1980); da of late Arnold Buchthal, and Margaret, *née* Schick; arrived in UK on Kindertransport as child refugee in 1939; f moved from being friendly enemy alien (one of the Dunera boys) prior to UK Army, to US Army (serving at Nuremberg trials) later German equivalent of High Ct Judge, changed name on naturalisation to Brook to honour Rupert Brooke; *b* 16 September 1933; *Educ* Sir John Cass Coll London (BSc); *m* 14 Nov 1959, Derek George Millington Shirley, s of George Millington Shirley (d 1970); 1 s (Giles Millington d 1998); *Career* PO Res Station Dollis Hill 1951–59, CDL 1959–62; Xansa (previously FI GROUP plc) fndr dir 1962–93, ceded control to workforce 1991, life pres 1993–; non-exec dir: AEA Technology plc (formerly UKAEA) 1992–2000, Tandem Computers Inc 1992–97, John Lewis Partnership plc 1999–2001; European Advsy Bd Korn/Ferry Int 2001–4; chair Women of Influence 1993; vice-pres City & Guilds Inst 2000–05; memb: Computer, Systems and Electronics Requirements Bd 1979–81, Electronics and Avionics Requirements Bd 1981–83, Cncl Work Fndn 1984–90, NCVQ 1986–89, Br-N American Ctee 1991–2001, Cncl 1992 Cwlth Studies Conf; RITA Award (recognition of IT achievement) 1985, Inst of Mgmnt Gold Medal 1991, Mountbatten Medal 1999; US Nat Women's Hall of Fame 1995, Beacon Fellowship 2003, Br Computer Soc Lifetime Achievement Award 2004; tstee Help The Aged 1987–90; pres: Br Computer Soc 1989–90; fndr tstee: The Kingwood Tst 1994–99, The Shirley Fndn 1996–, Prior's Ct Fndn 1998–2003, Autism Cymru 2001–02, Autism Speaks (formerly Nat Alliance for Autism Research) 2004–; patron: Disablement Income Gp 1989–2001, Centre for Tomorrow's Company 1997–; memb Cncl Buckingham Univ 1993–96; Freeman City of London 1987, Master Worshipful Co of Info Technologists 1992–93; fndn fell Balliol Coll Oxford 2001; hon fell: Manchester Metropolitan Univ 1989, Staffs Univ 1991, Sheffield Hallam Univ 1992, Birkbeck Coll London 2002, New Hall Cambridge 2002; Hon DSc: Buckingham Univ 1991, Aston Univ 1993, Nottingham Trent/Southampton 1994, Univ of Derby 1997, Solent Univ of Southampton 2003, Brunel Univ 2005; Hon DTech: Loughborough Univ 1991, Kingston Univ 1995; Hon DLitt: De Montfort Univ 1993, London Guildhall Univ 1998, Univ of Stirling 2000; Hon DBA: UWE 1995, Int Mgmnt Centres 1999, City Univ 1999; Hon DUniv: Leeds Met 1993, Edinburgh 2003; Hon DLaws: Univ of Leicester 2005, Univ of Bath 2006; Hon FCGI 1989, FBCS 1971, CCMI (CIMgt 1984), CEng 1990, FREng 2001; *Publications* The Art of Prior's Court School (2002); articles in professional jls; *Recreations* wishful thinking; *Style*— Dame Stephanie Shirley, DBE; ✉ 47 Thames House, Phyllis Court Drive, Henley-on-Thames, Oxfordshire RG9 2NA (tel 01491 579004, fax 01491 574995, e-mail steve@steveshirley.com, website www.steveshirley.com)

SHIRRIFFS, Dr George Geddes; OBE (2002); s of William Skinner Shirriffs, and Mary Allan Shirriffs; *b* 10 February 1940; *Educ* Aberdeen GS, Univ of Aberdeen (MB ChB, MEd); *m* 1965, June Valerie; 2 c (Lesley, Brian); *Career* princ in gen practice Aberdeen 1969–; gen practice trainer 1975–95, assoc regnl advsr (CME) Grampian 1978–89, JCPT visitor 1988–92; memb: Regnl Postgrad Med Educn Ctee NE Scotland 1989–2001, Scottish Cncl on Postgrad Med and Dental Educn 1993–2001, Jt Med Advsy Ctee for the HE Funding Cncl of England, Scotland and Wales 1996–2001; chm Educn Network RCGP 1996–99; pt/t sr clinical lectr Dept of Gen Practice Univ of Aberdeen 1995–; gen practice appraiser 2004–; Murray Scott Educn Lecture NE Faculty RCGP 1993; President's Medal RCGP 2001; FRCGP 1982 (MRCGP 1974); *Recreations* hill walking, golfing, allotment keeping; *Clubs* Deeside Golf; *Style*— Dr George Shirriffs, OBE; ✉ 19 Richmondhill Place, Aberdeen AB15 5EN (tel 01224 311044, e-mail g.shirriffs@btopenworld.com)

SHIVAS, Mark; s of James Dallas Shivas (d 1986), of Banstead, Surrey, and Winifred Alice, *née* Lighton (d 1978); *b* 24 April 1938; *Educ* Whitgift Sch, Merton Coll Oxford (MA); *Career* TV and film producer; co-fndr and asst ed Movie Magazine 1961–64, dir, prodr and presenter Granada TV 1964–68, drama prodr BBC TV 1969–79, dir Southern Pictures 1979–81 (exec prodr Winston Churchill the Wilderness Years and Bad Blood); BBC TV: head of drama gp 1988–93, head of films 1993–97; chm Headline Pictures Ltd 2005–; BBC prodns incl: The Six Wives of Henry VIII, Casanova, To Encourage the Others, The Evacuees, 84 Charing Cross Road, Abide with Me, The Glittering Prizes, Rogue Male, She Fell Among Thieves, Professional Foul, On Giants Shoulders, Telford's Change; prodr: The Price (Channel 4) 1985, What if it's Raining? (Channel 4) 1986, The Storyteller (Channel 4) 1987, Talking Heads 2 (BBC) 1998, Telling Tales (BBC) 2000, Cambridge Spies (BBC) 2003; exec prodr: Truly, Madly, Deeply 1991, Enchanted April, The Grass Arena, The Snapper, Priest, Small Faces, Jude, The Van, Hideous Kinky, I Capture the Castle; film prodr: Moonlighting 1982, A Private Function 1985, The Witches 1989; FRTS; *Recreations* swimming, gardening, Italy; *Clubs* Groucho; *Style*— Mark Shivas, Esq; ✉ 38 Gloucester Mews, London W2 3HE (tel 020 7723 4678, fax 020 7262 1415, e-mail markshivas@hotmail.com)

SHLAIM, Prof Avi; s of Joseph Shlaim, and Aida, *née* Obadiah; *b* 31 October 1945; *Educ* Jesus Coll Cambridge (BA), LSE (MSc), Univ of Reading (PhD); *Career* Nat Serv 1964–66; lectr and reader in politics Univ of Reading 1970–87; Alistair Buchan reader in international relations Univ of Oxford 1987–96, prof of international relations Univ of Oxford 1996–, fell St Antony's Coll Oxford; memb: RIIA, IISS, Br Soc for Middle Eastern Studies; *Books* British Foreign Secretaries since 1945 (jtly, 1977), The United States and the Berlin Blockade, 1948–49: A Study in Crisis Decision Making (1983), Collusion Across the Jordan: King Abdullah, the Zionist Movement, and the Partition of Palestine (1988), The Politics of Partition (1990), War and Peace in the Middle East: A Concise History (1995), The Iron Wall: Israel and the Arab World (2000); *Recreations* tennis, travel; *Style*— Prof Avi Shlaim; ✉ 8 Chalfont Road, Oxford OX2 6TH (tel 01865 556244); St Antony's College, Oxford OX2 6JF (tel 01865 274460, e-mail avi.shlaim@sant.ox.ac.uk)

SHNEERSON, Dr John Michael; s of Gregory Shneerson (d 2004), of Orpington, Kent, and Alfreda, *née* Ledger (d 1980); *b* 27 September 1946; *Educ* St Paul's, St Edmund Hall Oxford (MA, DM), St Mary's Hosp London; *m* 15 March 1975, Dr Anne Shneerson, da of Dr Kenneth Maclean, of Oxted, Surrey; 2 da (Joanna b 1979, Catherine b 1981), 1 s (Robert b 1983); *Career* sr registrar Westminster & Brompton Hosps London 1978–80; conslt physician: Newmarket Gen Hosp 1980–, Papworth Hosp 1980–, Addenbrooke's Hosp 1980–96, W Suffolk Hosp 1983–2002; dir: Assisted Ventilation Unit Newmarket Gen Hosp 1981–92, Respiratory Support and Sleep Centre Papworth Hosp 1992–; FRCP 1986, FCCP 1993; *Books* Manual of Chest Medicine (1986), Disorders of Ventilation (1988), Two Centuries of Real Tennis (1998), Handbook of Sleep Medicine (2000), Sleep Medicine: A Guide to Sleep and its Disorders (2005); *Recreations* squash, golf, tennis, gardening; *Style*— Dr John Shneerson; ✉ Papworth Hospital, Papworth Everard, Cambridge CB3 8RE (tel 01480 830541, fax 01480 364568)

SHONE, Richard Noel; *b* 8 May 1949; *Educ* Wrekin Coll, Clare Coll Cambridge (BA); *Career* writer and exhbn curator; ed The Burlington Magazine 2003– (assoc ed 1979–2003); selected and catalogued: Portraits by Duncan Grant 1969, Portraits by Walter Sickert 1990, co-selector Sickert exhbn Royal Acad 1992–93, purchaser Arts Cncl Collection 1994–96, selector New Contemporaries exhbn Liverpool and London 1996; curator: Head First (Arts Cncl tour) 1998–99, The Art of Bloomsbury (Tate and US tour) 1999–2000;

contrib numerous articles on modern Br art and Bloomsbury to: The Spectator, The Observer, Artforum, The Burlington Magazine; closely involved in restoration and opening of Charleston Farmhouse Sussex (home of Vanessa Bell and Duncan Grant) 1980–; memb: Jury Turner Prize 1988, Advsy Ctee Govt Art Collection 1990–94; *Publications* Bloomsbury Portraits: Vanessa Bell, Duncan Grant and their Circle (1976, new edn 1993), The Century of Change: British Art Since 1900 (1977), Sisley (1979), Augustus John (1979), The Post Impressionists (1980), Walter Sickert (1988), Rodrigo Moynihan (1988), Alfred Sisley (1992), Damien Hirst (2001); *Style*— Richard Shone, Esq; ✉ The Burlington Magazine, 14–16 Duke's Road, London WC1H 9SZ (e-mail shone@burlington.org.uk)

SHORE, Andrew; s of Frank Shore (d 1969), of Oldham, Lancs, and Edith, *née* Ashton (d 1963); *b* 30 September 1952; *Educ* Counthill GS Oldham, Univ of Bristol (BA), Royal Northern Coll of Music, London Opera Centre; *m* 1976, Fiona Mary, da of John Macdonald; 3 da (Sarah Jane b 12 Sept 1983, Emily Ann b 22 Sept 1985, Harriet Mary Edith b 16 March 1990); *Career* stage mangr and singer Opera for All tours (Frosch in Die Fledermaus, Fiorello in The Barber of Seville, Giacomo in Fra Diavolo, Marquis in La Traviata) 1977–79; Kent Opera: joined chorus 1979, subsequent roles incl Antonio in Marriage of Figaro, Pasha Selim in Il Seraglio, Dr Bartolo in The Barber of Seville and Papageno in The Magic Flute, deviser and presenter of educnl material; Opera North roles incl: King Dodon in The Golden Cockerel (debut 1985), Sacristan in Tosca, Leander in The Love for Three Oranges, Varlaam in Boris Godunov, Don Inigo in L'Heure Espagnole, Dr Bartolo, The Mayor in The Thieving Magpie, Don Jerome in Gerhard's Duenna, Geronimo in Cimarosa's Secret Marriage, title roles in Don Pasquale, Gianni Schicchi, King Priam, Wozzeck and Falstaff; Scottish Opera roles incl: Mr Flint in Billy Budd (debut 1987), Baron in La Vie Parisienne, Don Alfonso in Cosi Fan Tutte; ENO roles incl: Cappadocian in Salome (debut 1987), Doeg in Philip Glass's Planet 8, Don Alfonso, Falstaff, Papageno, Frank in Die Fledermaus, Dr Bartolo, Don Pasquale, Gianni Schicchi, Shishkov in House of the Dead, Dulcamara in Elixir of Love, Faninal in Der Rosenkavalier, Alberich in The Ring; Glyndebourne Festival roles incl: Baron Douphol in La Traviata (debut 1988), Vicar in Albert Herring, Falstaff, Kolenaty in Makropulos Case, Dikoj in Katya Kabanova, Dr Bartolo and Don Alfonso with Glyndebourne Touring Opera; WNO roles incl: Dr Bartolo (debut 1990, also Vancouver and Ottawa 1991), Sacristan in Tosca, Kolenaty, Papageno; debuts: Royal Opera House Covent Garden as Baron Trombonok in Rossini's Il Viaggio a Reims 1992, Paris Opera Bastille as Sacristan in Tosca 1995, Dulcamara in L'Elisir d'amore San Diego 1996 and Copenhagen 1999, Barcelona and Hamburg as Kolenaty 1999, La Monnaie Brussels as Kothner in Die Meistersinger, Chicago Lyric Opera in The Great Gatsby 2000, Santa Fe Festival as Falstaff 2001, Met Opera NY as Dulcamara 2006, Bayreuth Festival as Alberich in The Ring 2006; prodr for various amateur and professional gps: Nabucco, Manon Lescaut, Carmen, Orpheus in the Underworld, Bastien and Bastienne, Der Freischütz, Hugh the Drover, La Traviata, Romeo & Juliet, Handel's Faramondo, Wolf-Ferrari's School for Fathers; Tim Brandt Award in Opera Prodn 1977, nominated Olivier Award for Outstanding Achievement in Opera 1999; *Recordings* Nightingale by Charles Strouse 1983, Barber of Seville (role of Dr Bartolo) 1995, Don Pasquale (title role) 1998, L'Elisir d'amore (role of Dulcamara) 1999, Don Giovanni (role of Leporello) 2001, Falstaff (role of Falstaff) 2002, Andrew Shore Great Operatic Arias 2002, Wozzeck (title role) 2003; *Style*— Andrew Shore, Esq; ✉ c/o Ingpen & Williams Ltd, 7 St George's Court, 131 Putney Bridge Road, London SW15 2PA (tel 020 8874 3222, fax 020 8877 3113)

SHORE, Darryl Francis; *b* 30 August 1946; *Educ* De La Salle Coll Sheffield, Sheffield Univ Med Sch (MB ChB); *Career* house surgn Royal Infirmary Sheffield 1972 (house physician 1971–72), demonstrator in pathology Univ of Sheffield 1972–73, sr house offr orthopaedic surgery Royal Hosp Sheffield 1973, sr house offr in gen surgery Bristol Royal Infirmary 1974 (sr house offr in urology 1973–74), sr house offr in orthopaedic surgery Dept of Orthopaedics Bristol 1974–75, registrar in paediatric surgery Children's Hosp Sheffield 1975–76, registrar in gen and vascular surgery Royal Infirmary Sheffield 1976 (registrar in gen surgery 1975); registrar in cardiothoracic surgery: Royal Infirmary and Children's Hosp and Cardiothoracic Unit Northern Gen Hosp Sheffield 1976–78, Brompton Hosp London 1978; res fell in cardiothoracic surgery Albert Einstein Coll of Med NY USA 1979; sr registrar in cardiothoracic surgery: Brompton Hosp London 1980, Hosp for Sick Children Gt Ormond St London 1981; sr registrar in cardiac surgery Nat Heart Hosp London 1982, conslt in cardiac surgery to the Southampton and SW Hampshire Health Authy and clinical teacher Univ of Southampton 1982–87; Royal Brompton Hosp: conslt cardiac surgn in adult and paediatric cardiac surgery 1987–, clinical dir of surgery 1990–95; *Publications* incl: Urinary Lithiasis in Childhood in the Bristol Clinical Area (jtly in Br Jl of Urology, 1975), Results of Mitral Valvuloplasty with Suture Plication Technique (jtly in Jl of Thoracic and Cardiovascular Surgery, 1980), Atresia in Left Atrio-Ventricular Connection (jtly in Br Heart Jl, 1982), Oral Veraparmil Fails to Prevent Supraventricular Tachycardia Following Coronary Artery Surgery (jtly in Int Jl of Cardiology, 1985), Thirteen Years Evaluation of the Bjork-Shiley Isolated Mitral Valve Prosthesis (jtly in Jl of Cardiovascular Surgery, 1989), Surgical Treatment for Infarct-Related Ventricular Septal Defects (jtly in Jl of Thoracic Surgery, 1990); *Style*— Darryl Shore, Esq; ✉ Royal Brompton Hospital, Sydney Street, London SW3 6NP (tel 020 7351 8211)

SHORROCK, (John) Michael; QC (1988); s of James Godby Shorrock (d 1987), and Mary Patricia, *née* Lings (d 2001); *b* 25 May 1943; *Educ* Clifton, Pembroke Coll Cambridge (MA); *m* 25 Nov 1971, Marianne, da of Jack Mills (d 1983); 2 da (Amabel b 13 Dec 1971, Rose b 1 Sept 1974); *Career* called to the Bar Inner Temple 1965 (bencher 1995); recorder of the Crown Court 1982–, head of chambers 1992–2005; memb: Criminal Injuries Compensation Bd 1995–2000, Criminal Injuries Compensation Appeals Panel 1997–; govr William Hulme's GS 1999–2006; *Style*— Michael Shorrock, Esq, QC; ✉ Atkinson Bevan Chambers, 2 Harcourt Buildings, Temple, London EC4Y 9DB (tel 020 7353 2112, fax 020 7353 8339)

SHORT, Prof (Charles) Alan; s of Charles Ronald Short, and Dorothea Henrietta Winterfeldt; *b* 23 March 1955; *Educ* Lower Sch of John Lyon Harrow, Trinity Coll Cambridge (MA), Harvard Univ Graduate Sch of Design; *Career* architect; ptnr Edward Cullinan Architects 1981–86; fndr: Peake, Short & Ptnrs 1986, Short and Associates 1997–; dean Faculty of Art and Design De Montfort Univ 1998–2001, elected prof of architecture and head of dept Univ of Cambridge 2001; winner Green Building of the Year Award (for Queens Building Leicester) 1995, High Architecture Low Energy Award (for Simonds Farsons CISK Malta) 1995, Building Magazine Building of the Year (for Lanchester Library Coventry) 2000; RIBA Awards: Contact Theatre 2000, Poole Arts Centre 2003, Sch of Slavonic and E European Studies 2006; CIBSE Environmental Initiation of the Year, BDA Public Building of the Year (for Sch of Slavonic and E European Studies) 2006; DipArch, RIBA, FRSA; *Recreations* collecting drawings; *Clubs* Oxford and Cambridge, Chelsea Arts; *Style*— Prof Alan Short; ✉ Short and Associates, 24A Marshalsea Road, Borough, London SE1 1HF (tel 020 7407 8885, e-mail post@short-assoc.demon.co.uk, website shortandassociates.co.uk)

SHORT, Rt Hon Clare; PC (1997), MP; da of Frank Short, and Joan Short; *b* 15 February 1946; *Educ* Keele Univ, Univ of Leeds (BA); *m* 1981, Alexander Ward Lyon (d 1993), former MP (Lab) York; *Career* civil servant Home Office 1970–75; dir: All Faiths for One Race Birmingham 1976–78, Youth Aid and the Unemployment Unit 1979–83; MP (Lab) Birmingham Ladywood 1983–; front bench spokesperson on: employment 1985–88, social

security 1988–91, environmental protection 1992–93, women 1993–95; elected to Shadow Cabinet 1995; chief oppn spokesperson on: tport 1995–96, overseas devpt 1996–97; sec of state for International Devpt 1997–2003; chm All-Pty Parly Gp on Race Rels 1985–86, memb Home Affrs Select Ctee 1983–85; memb Lab Pty NEC 1988–98; *Publications* Talking Blues - A Study of Young West Indians' Views of Policing (1978), Handbook of Immigration Law (1978), Dear Clare (1991), An Honourable Deception? (2004); *Recreations* family and friends, swimming; *Style*— The Rt Hon Clare Short, MP; ✉ House of Commons, London SW1A 0AA

SHORT, David; WS; s of Maurice Short (d 1990), and Nancy, *née* Straker; *b* 25 January 1958, North Shields, Tyne & Wear; *Educ* Blyth Ridley HS, Univ of Dundee (MA), Univ of Strathclyde Univ (DipLP); *m* 12 June 1992, Caroline, *née* Watt; 1 s (Tom b 31 Dec 1994); *Career* managing ptnr Lawford Kidd slrs (joined 1982); Scottish sec Assoc of Personal Injury Lawyers; NP, memb Law Soc of Scotland 1986; *Recreations* golf, travel; *Clubs* Hallion; *Style*— David Short, Esq, WS; ✉ 10 Ravelrig Drive, Balerno, Midlothian EH14 7NQ (tel 0131 449 9521, e-mail ds.mail@btinternet.com); Lawford Kidd, 12 Hill Street, Edinburgh EH2 3LB (tel 0131 225 5214, fax 0131 226 2069, e-mail david.short@lawfordkidd.co.uk)

SHORT, Nigel David; MBE (1999); s of David Malcolm Short, of Lancs, and Jean, *née* Gaskell; *b* 1 June 1965; *Educ* Bolton Sch; *m* 24 Aug 1987, Rhea Argyro, da of Nikolaos Karageorgiou; 1 da (Kyveli Aliki b 7 July 1991), 1 s (Nicholas Darwin b 18 Dec 1998); *Career* professional chess player; int master 1980, grandmaster 1984; achievements incl: Br lightning chess champion 1978 and 1980, equal first Br Championship 1979, runner-up World Jr Championship 1980, Br champion 1984 and 1987, memb England Olympiad team 1984–2004 (Silver medals 1984, 1986 and 1988, Bronze medal 1990), World Championship candidate 1985–94 (defeated Anatoly Karpov in semi-finals Spain 1992, finalist 1993, challenger to World Champion Garry Kasparov 1993), English champion 1991, Cwlth champion 2004; other titles won: BBC Master Game 1981, OHRA Tournament Amsterdam 1982, Baku Azerbaijan 1983, Wijk Aan Zee 1986 and 1987, Reykjavik 1987, first equal Subotica Interzonal 1987, Hastings 1988 and 1989, VSB Amsterdam 1988 (first equal 1991 and 1992), Parnu 1996, Parnu 1998, Dhaka 1999, Gibraltar 2003 and 2004, Taiyuan 2004; highest ever rating achieved by Br player (2685) 1992; fndr memb and dir Professional Chess Assoc 1993, sec gen Cwlth Chess Assoc 2005; chess columnist: Sunday Telegraph 1996–2005, The Guardian 2005–; hon fell Bolton Inst of HE; *Recreations* cricket, music, olive farming, swimming, economics; *Style*— Nigel Short, Esq, MBE

SHORT, Philip; s of Wilfred Short (d 1976), and Marion, *née* Edgar; *b* 17 April 1945; *Educ* Sherborne, Queens' Coll Cambridge (MA); *m* 1, 9 Aug 1968 (m dis), Christine Victoria, da of (Francis) Donald Baring-Gould; 1 s (Sengan b 1 March 1971); *m* 2, 1 Sept 1992, Renquan, da of Zhen Gu; 1 s (Benedict b 10 May 1993); *Career* journalist and author; corr BBC (postings incl Moscow, Peking, Paris, Tokyo and Washington) 1972–97; sometime journalism teacher Univ of Iowa; *Books* Banda (1974), The Dragon and The Bear (1982), Mao: A Life (1999), Pol Pot: Anatomy of a Nightmare (2005); *Recreations* Chinese porcelain; *Style*— Philip Short, Esq

SHORT, Rodney Neil Terry; s of late Flt Lt Cyril Herbert Terry Short, AFC, of Burnham-on-Sea, Somerset, and Deborah Allen, *née* Hobbs; *b* 4 August 1946; *Educ* Sherborne, Coll of Law, INSEAD (MBA); *m* 16 April 1977, Penelope Anne, da of late Capt Emile William Goodman, OBE; 1 s (Jonathan b 1980), 1 da (Anna b 1983); *Career* admitted slr 1970, asst slr Freshfields 1970–73 and 1975–77, Corp Fin Dept Kleinwort Benson 1974–75; Clifford Chance (formerly Coward Chance) 1977–: Dubai office 1978–81, Bahrain office 1981–83, ptnr 1982–, Paris office 1989–91, Washington DC office 1999–2001, Frankfurt office 2001–03; Freeman City of London Solicitors' Co 1983; memb: Law Soc 1970, IBA 1982; *Recreations* tennis, golf, shooting, skiing; *Clubs* Roehampton; *Style*— Rodney Short, Esq; ✉ 1 Vineyard Hill Road, London SW19 7JL (tel 020 8879 1677); Clifford Chance, 10 Upper Bank Street, London E14 5JJ (tel 020 7006 1000, fax 020 7006 5555, e-mail rodney.short@cliffordchance.com)

SHORTHOUSE, Prof Andrew John; s of George Sydney Shorthouse, and Dorothy Enid, *née* Baxter; *b* 25 April 1947, Market Bosworth, Leics; *Educ* Univ of London (BSc, MS), St Mary's Hosp London (MB BS); *m* 21 Jan 1977, Christine Elizabeth, *née* Tyrrell-Gray; 1 s (Dr James Richard Shorthouse b 3 Jan 1979), 1 da (Alice Mary b 26 March 1982); *Career* sr surgical registrar St George's Hosp London 1981–86, hon sr lectr Univ of Sheffield 1986–, conslt gen and colorectal surgn Royal Hallamshire Hosp Sheffield 1986–2004, conslt colorectal surgn Northern Gen Hosp Sheffield 2004–, currently lead colorectal clinician Sheffield Teaching Hosps NHS Tst, hon prof Sheffield Hallam Univ 2005–; author of book chapters and over 60 articles in med jls; hon sec Br Assoc of Surgical Oncology 1995–96, pres Assoc of Coloproctology of GB and I 2005–06 (hon sec 1997–2000), pres elect European Soc of Coloproctology 2006– (fndr memb 2001, hon sec 2001–04); memb: Worshipful Co of Apothecaries; memb: Assoc of Surgns of GB and I, RSM (Section of Coloproctology), Grey Turner Surgical Club (pres 2002–03), St Mark's Assoc, American Soc of Colon and Rectal Surgns; fndr memb European Soc of Coloproctology 2006; FRCS 1975; *Recreations* flyfishing, painting (HS Hilliard Soc); *Clubs* Derwent Flyfishing; *Style*— Prof Andrew Shorthouse; ✉ Department of Colorectal Surgery, Northern General Hospital, Herries Road, Sheffield S5 7AU (tel 0114 226 9333, e-mail shorthouse@doctors.org.uk)

SHORTRIDGE, Sir Jon Deacon; KCB (2002); s of Eric Creber Deacon Shortridge (d 1979), and Audrey Joan, *née* Hunt (d 1990); *b* 10 April 1947; *Educ* Chichester HS, St Edmund Hall Oxford (MA), Univ of Edinburgh (MSc); *m* 1972, Diana Jean, da of Dr E G Gordon; 1 da (Clare b 2 Dec 1975), 1 s (James b 9 Oct 1978); *Career* various jobs Miny of Housing, Countryside Cmmn and DOE 1969–75; various planning jobs Shropshire CC 1975–84; Welsh Office: joined 1984, private sec to Sec of State for Wales 1987–88, head Fin Div (grade 5) 1988–92, Head Local Govt Re-Organisation Gp (grade 3) 1992–95, head Local Govt Gp 1995–97, dir Econ Affairs (grade 2) 1997–99 (perm sec 1999); perm sec Nat Assembly for Wales 1999–; MRTPI 1974–96, CIMgt; *Books* Information Systems for Policy Planning in Local Government (jt ed, 1984); *Recreations* family, tennis, rowing, modern history; *Clubs* Oxford and Cambridge; *Style*— Sir Jon Shortridge, KCB; ✉ National Assembly for Wales, Cathays Park, Cardiff CF10 3NQ (tel 029 2082 3289, fax 029 2082 5649)

SHORTT, Denys Christopher; s of Peter Shortt, of Winchcombe, Glos, and Rosemary, *née* Meredith (d 2001); *b* 30 May 1964, Cheltenham; *Educ* Warwick Sch; *m* 21 April 1990, Deborah, *née* Moty; 1 s (Charles b 10 Oct 1991), 1 da (Lydia b 20 Oct 1993); *Career* with Shakespeare (family business) 1982–94; fndr: DCS Europe 1994, Enable Software 2000, Enable Infomatrix Ltd 2004; vice-pres County Air Ambulance, memb Business Devpt Bd Scope, govr Cheltenham Coll; *Awards* Entrepreneur of the Year 2000 (nominated 2003), ranked tenth in Management Today 's Top 100 Entrepreneurs 2004 (ranked eighteenth 2002); CBI Growing Business Awards: winner Int Initiative of the Year 2001, nominee Entrepreneur of the Year 2003, nominee Technology in Business 2003; DCS listed in Fast Track 100, Enable listed in Tech Track 100; *Recreations* helicopter pilot, hockey (England under 21 int), farming, shooting, 4x4; *Clubs* Helicopter Club of GB, Ladykillers Hockey; *Style*— Denys Shortt, Esq; ✉ DCS Europe plc, Timothy's Bridge Road, Stratford-upon-Avon, Warwickshire CV37 9YL (tel 01789 208000, fax 01789 208031, e-mail denys@dcseurope.com, website www.dcseurope.com); website www.denysshortt.com

SHOTTER, Very Rev Edward Frank; s of Frank Edward Shotter (d 1970), and Minnetta, *née* Gaskill (d 1976); *b* 29 June 1933; *Educ* Humberstone Fndn Sch Clee, Sch of Architecture King's Coll Newcastle, St David's Coll Lampeter, Univ of Wales (BA), St Stephen's House Oxford; *m* 9 Dec 1978, Dr Jane Edgcumbe, da of Dr John Oliver Pearce Edgcumbe; 2 s (James b 1982, Piers b 1984), 1 da (Emma b 1987); *Career* ordained: deacon 1960, priest 1961; asst curate St Peter's Plymouth 1960–62, intercollegiate sec Student Christian Movement London 1962–66; dir: London Medical Gp 1963–89, Inst of Medical Ethics 1974–89; chaplain Univ of London 1969–89, prebendary St Paul's Cathedral London 1977–89, dean of Rochester 1989–2003 (now emeritus), memb Gen Synod 1994–2003, sec Assoc of English Cathedrals 1994–2002, chm Diocese of Rochester Thames Gateway Co-ordinating Gp 1997–2000; jt chm Kent Ecumenical Police Chaplaincy Ctee 1993–2001 (Force chaplain 1995–2001); chm Governing Body King's Sch Rochester 1989–2003, pres St Bartholomew's Hosp Rochester 1989–2003, dir Firmstart Medway 1991–2001; chm: Medway Enterprise Agency 1993–98, Medway Business Support Partnership 1994–98, Medway Business Point Ltd 1996–98, HMS Cavalier Meml Steering Gp 2000–; vice-pres Inst of Med Ethics 1999– (Amulree fell 1991–99 and 2003–); chm: East Europe Subcommittee Liberal Party Foreign Affrs Panel 1974–81, Working Party on Ethics of Prolonging Life and Assisting Death 1993–97, Univ of Greenwich Research Ethics Ctee 1995–2003, Ctee on Welfare of Czech and Slovak Med Students in Britain 1968–69; memb: Editorial Bd Journal of Medical Ethics (fndr 1975), Archbishop of Canterbury's Cnsllrs on Foreign Rels 1971–82, BCC East West Rels Advsy Ctee 1971–81, Educn Ctee St Christopher's Hospice 1982–89, Church Heritage Forum 1999–2003; FRSM 1976, Hon FRCP 2007; Patriarchal Cross Romanian Orthodox Church (Oeconomos Stavrophor) 1975; *Books* Matters of Life and Death (ed, 1970), Life Before Birth (jt author, 1986); *Recreations* East European affairs, domestic architecture, gardening; *Clubs* Reform; *Style*— The Very Rev Edward Shotter; ✉ Hill House, Westhall, Halesworth, Suffolk IP19 8QZ (tel 01502 575364)

SHOVELTON, Dame Helena; DBE (1999); da of the late Denis George Richards, OBE, of Highgate, London, and the late Barbara, *née* Smethurst; *b* 28 May 1945; *Educ* N London Collegiate Sch, Regent St Poly (HND Business Studies), Strathclyde Grad Business Sch Univ of Strathclyde (MBA); *m* 1968, Walter Patrick Shovelton, CB, CMG, s of Sydney Taverner Shovelton, CBE (d 1968); *Career* mgmnt trainee then industrial market research asst Urwick Orr & Partners 1965–67, in-house magazine and business digest writer/PR handler Alfred Pemberton Ltd (advtg agency) 1967–69, PA to Accountant then to MD Computer Sciences International 1969–71, bursar Wellgarth Nursary Trg Coll 1972–74, vol work 1978–85 (chair City of London Appeal for King George's Fund for Sailors 1984); md Good Companions Ltd 1985–87, mangr Tunbridge Wells CAB 1987–94; chair Nat Assoc of Citizens Advice Bureaux 1994–99 (vice-chair 1990–94); cmmr then dep chair Local Govt Cmmn for England 1995–98, chair Continuing Care Review Panel for E Sussex Brighton and Hove HA 1996–98, ind memb: Dept of Health's Panel for Recruitment of Non-Exec Dirs 1996–98, Cabinet Office's Better Regulation Task Force 1997–99, Banking Code Standards Bd (formerly Ind Review Body for the banking and mortgage lending codes) 1997–2000; cmmr then chair: Audit Cmmn 1995–2001, Nat Lottery Cmmn 1999–2000; memb Competition Cmmn (formerly Monopolies and Mergers Cmmn) 1997–2004; chief exec Br Lung Fndn 2002–; dir Energy Saving Tst 1998–, tstee RAF Benevolent Fund 1998–2006; CIMgt 2000; FRSA 1995, hon FRCP 2006; *Recreations* reading, friends and family; *Style*— Dame Helena Shovelton, DBE; ✉ 73/75 Goswell Road, London EC1V 7ER (tel 020 7688 5555, e-mail helena.shovelton@blf-uk.org)

SHRAGER, Robert Neil; s of Benjamin Shrager, of London, and Rose Ruth, *née* Kempner; *b* 21 May 1948; *Educ* Charterhouse, St John's Coll Oxford (MA), City Univ Business Sch (MBA); *m* 1982, Elizabeth Fiona, da of Mortimer Stuart Bogod (d 1964); 2 s (James b 1985, Edward b 1987); *Career* chm: House of Fraser plc 1999–2000, Tempo Holdings Ltd 1999–2001, The Food Doctor Ltd 2001–, Courts plc 2002–04; dir: Morgan Grenfell & Co Ltd 1985–88, Dixons Group plc 1988–98; non-exec dir: UK Coal plc 1994–2004, Matalan plc 1998–2006, easyInternetCafe Ltd 2001–03, Autodex Ltd 2003–, Autodex Fleet Leasing Ltd 2003–, RAB Capital plc 2004–, Four Seasons Country Club Ltd 2004–; *Recreations* family, golf, arts; *Style*— Robert Shrager, Esq; ✉ Woodstock, 5 Hollycroft Avenue, London NW3 7QG (tel 020 7435 4367, fax 020 7431 7445, e-mail robert@rshrager.freeserve.co.uk)

SHRAPNEL, John Morley; s of Norman Shrapnel, of Far Oakridge, Glos, and Mary Lillian Myfanwy, *née* Edwards; *b* 27 April 1942; *Educ* Stockport Sch Cheshire, City of London Sch, St Catharine's Coll Cambridge (MA); *m* 1975, Francesca Anne, da of Sqdn Ldr Anthony Charles Bartley, and Deborah Kerr, the actress; 3 s (Joe Sebastian b 1976, Alexander Carey b 1979, Thomas Heydon b 1981); *Career* actor; fndr memb Nat Youth Theatre; Merit Award for narration (Int Wildlife Film Festival) 1997; *Theatre* in rep Nottingham Playhouse and Birmingham; NT: Banquo in Macbeth, Pentheus in The Bacchae, Endicott in Front Page, Orsino in Twelfth Night 1973–75, Capt Brackett in South Pacific 2001–02; Timon in Timon of Athens (Bristol Old Vic) 1979; RSC: Agamemnon in The Greeks 1980, Jeremy in May Days 1985, Sigmund in The Archbishop's Ceiling 1986, Foustka in Havel's Temptation 1988, Oedipus in Oedipus Rex 1989, Angelo in Measure for Measure 1990, Creon in Thebans 1991–92, Azriel in The Dybbuk 1991–92, Claudius in Hamlet 1992–93; other roles incl: Leonard Brazil in City Sugar (premiere, Bush), Brutus in Julius Caesar (Riverside); West End credits incl: Andrey in Three Sisters, Tesman in Hedda Gabler, Gibbs in Pinter's The Hot House, Caesar in Julius Caesar (Barbican, Paris and Madrid); *Television* The Earl of Suffolk in Elizabeth R, McKendrick in Professional Foul, Erzberger in Gossip from the Forest, Hardinge in Edward and Mrs Simpson, Sakharov in People from the Forest, Glyde in Woman in White, Myshlaevsky in White Guard, Cyril Burt in The Intelligence Man, Creon in Sophocles' Theban Plays, BBC Shakespeare Series (Hector in Troilus and Cressida, Alcibiades in Timon of Athens, Kent in King Lear), Rev Eland in the Burston Rebellion, Steyne in Vanity Fair, Blake in Potter's Black-Eyes, Schulte-Hiller in Selling Hitler, Dr Jacobs in GBH, Dunning in Between The Lines, Archibald Hall in The Ladies' Man, Kavanagh QC, Black Easter, McIntyre in Bodyguards, Rev Glasson in True Tilda, Morse, Marshall Bentley in Invasion Earth, Midsummer Murders, Hornblower, Jonathan Creek, Mary and Jesus, Tenth Kingdom, Monty Sinclair in Gentleman Thief, Nick in The Fairy Godfather, Raymond Brooks in Foyle's War; extensive commentaries and narrations for Wildlife progs; *Radio* extensive radio work incl: Morse in Inspector Morse, Death and the Maiden, Gielgud's celebratory King Lear, Pinter's 70th birthday celebratory Moonlight; *Film* Petya in Nicholas and Alexandra, Fr James in Pope Joan, Semper in Wagner, Lionel in Personal Services, Zdhanov in Testimony, Mendalbaum in How to Get Ahead in Advertising, Cinca in Two Deaths, Skinner in 101 Dalmatians, Cain in Solo Shuttle, Jeremy in Notting Hill, Gaius in Gladiator, Cohen in The Body, Vandenberg in Claim, Hannah in Alone, Bratayev in K-19 the Widowmaker, The General in Mathilde, Nestor in Troy, Archbishop in The Hangman's Tale, Michael Kuhn in Alien Autopsy, Bernie in Sparkle, Lord Howard in The Golden Age; *Recreations* mountaineering, walking, skiing, music, reading, family; *Style*— John Shrapnel, Esq; ✉ c/o Jonathan Altaras Associates, 11 Garrick Street, London WC2E 9AR (tel 020 7836 8722, fax 020 7836 6066)

SHREWSBURY, Bishop of 2001–; Rt Rev Dr Alan Gregory Clayton Smith; s of Frank Eric Smith (d 1985), and Rosemary Clayton, *née* Barker; *b* 14 February 1957; *Educ* Trowbridge GS for Boys, Univ of Birmingham (BA, MA), Wycliffe Hall Oxford (CertTheol), Univ of Wales Bangor (PhD); *Career* curate St Lawrence Pudsey 1981–84, chaplain Lee Abbey Fellowship 1984–90, diocesan missioner and team vicar St Matthew's Walsall 1990–97, archdeacon of Stoke-upon-Trent 1997–2001, hon canon of Lichfield Cathedral; chair Shropshire Strategic Partnership; *Recreations* travel, music, skiing, squash; *Style*— The Rt Rev the Bishop of Shrewsbury; ✉ Athlone House, 68 London Road, Shrewsbury, Shropshire SY2 6PG (tel 01743 235867, fax 01743 243296, e-mail bishop.shrewsbury@lichfield.anglican.org)

SHREWSBURY, Bishop of (RC, cr 1851) 1995–; Rt Rev Brian Michael Noble; s of late Thomas Joseph Noble, and Cecilia, *née* Tasch; *b* 11 April 1936; *Educ* Catholic Coll Preston, Ushaw Coll Durham; *Career* ordained priest 1960, curate St Ignatius Preston 1960–68, curate Our Lady and St Patrick Maryport 1968–72, chaplain Lancaster Univ 1972–80, lectr in pastoral studies Pontifical Beda Coll Rome 1980–87, parish priest and dean of West Cumbria St Benedict's Whitehaven 1987–95, canon Lancaster Cathedral 1994–95; *Recreations* music, reading poetry and novels, walking; *Style*— The Rt Rev the Bishop of Shrewsbury; ✉ Curial Offices, 2 Park Road South, Prenton, Wirral CH43 4UX (tel 0151 652 9855, fax 08701 671935, e-mail curia@dioceseofshrewsbury.org)

SHREWSBURY AND WATERFORD, 22 Earl of (E 1442, I 1446 respectively); Charles Henry John Benedict Crofton Chetwynd Chetwynd-Talbot; DL (Staffs); Premier Earl (on the Roll) in peerages both of England and Ireland; Baron Talbot (GB 1723), Earl Talbot and Viscount Ingestre (GB 1784); Hereditary Lord High Steward of Ireland and Great Seneschal; patron of 11 lvings; s of 21 Earl (d 1980) by 1 w, Nadine, Countess of Shrewsbury (d 2003); *b* 18 December 1952; *Educ* Harrow; *m* 1974, Deborah Jane, da of Noel Staughton Hutchinson, of Ellerton House, Sambrook, Salop; 1 da (Lady Victoria Jane b 7 Sept 1975), 2 s (James Richard Charles John, Viscount Ingestre b 11 Jan 1978, Hon Edward William Henry Alexander b 18 Sept 1981); *Heir* s, Viscount Ingestre; *Career* dep chm Britannia Building Soc 1988–91 (dir 1983–92); patron St Giles Hospice, hon pres SSAFA - Forces Help (Wolverhampton); vice-pres: Shropshire Bldg Preservation Tst, Staffordshire Small-bore Rifle Assoc; pres: Bldg Socs Assoc 1992–97, British Institute of Innkeepers 1996–97, Gun Trade Assoc; chm Firearms Consultative Ctee 1994–99; dir: Minibus Plus Ltd 1997–2001, Earthport plc 2000–01; chm Br Shooting Sports Cncl; patron Albrighton Moat Project; chllr Univ of Wolverhampton 1993–99; Hon LLD Univ of Wolverhampton 1994; *Recreations* all field sports; *Style*— The Rt Hon the Earl of Shrewsbury and Waterford, DL; ✉ Wanfield Hall, Kingstone, Uttoxeter, Staffordshire ST14 8QR (tel and fax 01889 500275, e-mail shrewsbury@dungarvanestates.co.uk)

SHRIGLEY, David; *b* 17 September 1968, Macclesfield, Cheshire; *Educ* Glasgow Sch of Art; *Career* artist; *Solo Exhibitions* Transmission Gallery Glasgow 1995, Catalyst Arts Belfast 1996, Photographers' Gallery London 1997, Galleri Nicolai Wallner Copenhagen 1997, 1998 and 2000, Stephen Friedman Gallery London 1997, 1999 and 2001, Francesca Pia Bern 1997 and 1999, CCA Glasgow 1997, Hermetic Gallery Milwaukee 1997, Galerie Yvon Lambert Paris 1998, 1999 and 2001, Bloom Gallery Amsterdam 1998, CCS Museum Bard Coll NY 2001, Camden Arts Centre 2002; *Group Exhibitions* In Here (Transmission Gallery Glasgow) 1992, New Art in Scotland (CCA Glasgow) 1994, Some of My Friends (Galerie Campbells Occaisionally Copenhagen) 1994, Scottish Autumn (Bartok 32 Galeria Budapest) 1995, Toons (Galerie Campbells Occaisionally Copenhagen) 1996, White Hysteria (Contemporary Art Centre of S Aust Melbourne) 1996, Big Girl/Little Girl (Collective Gallery Edinburgh) 1996, Fucking Biscuits and other drawings (Bloom Gallery Amsterdam) 1996, The Unbelievable Truth (Stedelijk Museum Bureau Amsterdam and Tramway Glasgow) 1996, Absolute Blue & White (Inverleith House Edinburgh) 1996, Sarah Staton Superstore (Up & Co NY) 1996, Slight (Norwich Gallery) 1997, Appetizer (Free Parking Toronto) 1997, Young British Photography (Stadthaus Ulm) 1997, About Life in the Periphery (Wacker Kunst Darmstadt) 1997, Caldas Biennale (Caldas de Rainha Portugal) 1997, Blueprint (De Appel Amsterdam) 1997, Tales of the City (Stills Gallery Edinburgh) 1997, Real Life (Galleria SALES Rome) 1998, Works on Paper (Alexander & Bonin NY) 1998, Habitat (Centre for Contemporary Photography Melbourne) 1998, Surfacing (ICA London) 1998, Common People: British Art Between Phenomenon & Reality (Fondazione Sandretto Rebaudengo Per L'Arte Guarene D'Alba) 1999, Bildung (Kunstverien Graz) 1999, Green (Exedra Hilversum) 1999, Zac 99 (Musee D'Art Moderne de la Ville de Paris) 1999, Diary (Cornerhouse Manchester) 1999, Love Bites (Ikon Gallery Birmingham and tour) 1999, Becks Futures (ICA London and tour) 2000, The British Art Show 5 (City Art Centre Edinburgh and tour) 2000, Open Country (Musee Cantonal des Beaux Arts Lausanne) 2000, The Fantastic Repetition of Certain Situations (Isabell II Madrid and tour) 2001, Under Bridges and Along the River (Casino Luxembourg) 2001, Rendezvous III (Collection Lambert Avignon) 2001; *Magazine Projects* insert in Parkett (number 53) 1998, weekly cartoon Independent on Sunday Review 1999–2000, Cabinet magazine (issue 1) 2001; *Publications* Slug Trails (1991), Merry Eczema (1992), Blanket of Filth (1994), Enquire Within (1995), Let Not These Shadows Fall Upon Thee (1996), Err (1996), Drawings Done Whilst On Phone To Idiot (1996), Blank Page and Other Pages (1998), Centre Parting (1998), This (1998), To Make Meringue You Must Beat The Egg Whites Until They Look Like This (1998), Why We Got The Sack From The Museum (1998), The Beast Is Near (1999), Hard Work (2000), Grip (2000), Do Not Bend (2001), Human Achievement (2002), Evil Thoughts (2003), Who I Am and What I Want (2003), Yellow Bird with Worm (2003), Kill Your Pets (2004), Let's Wrestle (2004), Joy (2005); *Style*— David Shrigley, Esq; ✉ Stephen Friedman Gallery, 25–28 Old Burlington Street, London W1S 3AN (tel 020 7494 1434)

SHRIMPLIN, Roger Clifford; s of Clifford Walter Shrimplin (d 1987), and Grace Florence, *née* Davis; *b* 9 September 1948; *Educ* St Albans Sch, Jesus Coll Cambridge (MA, DipArch); *m* 21 Sept 1974, Catalina Maria Eugenia, da of L Alomar-Josa (d 1982); 3 s (Robert b 1977, Richard b 1980, Edward b 1985); *Career* architect; ptnr and princ C W & R C Shrimplin (Chartered Architects and Chartered Town Planners) 1975–; occasional lectr: Univ of Cambridge Sch of Architecture, AA; external examiner: Bartlett Sch of Architecture Univ of London, Oxford Brookes Univ; memb Cncl: ARCUK 1985–88 and 1994–97, RIBA 1995–2001 and 2004–; memb various ctees of RIBA, ARCUK, ACE and ARB (hon sec RIBA 1999–2001); dir RIBA Insurance Agency 2002–; tstee Temple Island Henley (chm 1987–99), chm Beds Architectural Heritage Tst 2001–; hon sec and vice-pres (Europe) Cwlth Assoc of Architects (CAA) 2000–03; tstee The London Stained Glass Repository (chm Mgmnt Ctee 1994–99), dir Glaziers Hall Ltd 2002–; Lord of the Manor of Shimpling Norfolk 1987; Freeman and Liveryman: City of London, Worshipful Co of Glaziers & Painters of Glass 1974 (Master 2001–02); RIBA 1974, FRTPI 1985, FCIArb 1986, MIL 1994; Arquitecto Colegiado (Baleares) 1990; *Style*— Roger Shrimplin, Esq; ✉ 11 Cardiff Road, Luton, Bedfordshire LU1 1PP

SHRIMPTON, David Everard; s of late Col G H T Shrimpton, CBE, TD, of Dulwich, and Joyce Margaret, *née* Little; *b* 19 May 1943; *Educ* Dulwich Coll; *m* 25 Oct 1969, Rosemary Sarah, da of Frank Victor Fone; 3 s (Matthew John b 3 Nov 1972, Benjamin James b 24 May 1975, Daniel Thomas b 11 April 1978); *Career* student trainee mangr Deloitte Haskins & Sells 1961–75, princ Industrial Devpt Unit DTI 1975–77, corp fin exec Midland Bank plc 1977–79; BDO Stoy Hayward: ptnr in charge corp fin 1979–89, gen practice ptnr 1989–2001; memb Exec Ctee Quoted Companies Alliance 2000–; dir: Mark Warner Ltd 2002–, Ruxley Holdings Ltd 2002–, Cashtec Services Ltd 2002–; chm Broomleigh Housing Assoc; Freeman City of London, Liveryman Worshipful Co of Chartered Accountants; FCA 1967; *Recreations* tennis, rugby and Fulham FC; *Style*— David Shrimpton, Esq; ✉ BDO Stoy Hayward, 8 Baker Street, London W1M 1DA (tel 020 7486 5888, fax 020 7487 3686, e-mail david.shrimpton@bdo.co.uk)

SHROPSHIRE, John Bourne; OBE (1996); s of Guy Stuart Shropshire, and Joan, *née* Olivant (d 1962); *b* 6 April 1955, Newmarket; *Educ* Oundle, Univ of Newcastle upon Tyne (BSc); *m* 14 July 1979, Patricia Sheila, *née* Wallis; 1 da (Davina Helen b 19 Feb 1981), 3 s (Guy William b 25 May 1983, Charles John b 27 March 1986, Henry James b 13 Aug 1991); *Career* joined GS Shropshire & Sons (family business) 1976; FRAgS, FIHort; memb Worshipful Co of Fruiterers; National Agricultural Award 2001; *Recreations* reading, walking, travel, countryside, shooting, skiing, tennis; *Clubs* Farmers'; *Style*— John Shropshire, Esq, OBE; ✉ Hainey Farm, Barway, Ely, Cambridgeshire CB7 5TZ (tel 01353 727200)

SHUBROOK, Brian Ralph; s of Ronald Kenneth Shubrook, and Audrey Gwendoline, *née* Jones; *b* 22 June 1950; *m* 20 May 1972, Pauline, da of George Frederick Edgill, MBE, of Leigh-on-Sea, Essex; 2 da (Nicola Jane b 9 Aug 1974, Jessica Anne b 8 Jan 1979); *Career* sr foreign exchange dealer Lloyds Bank Int London 1968–74, foreign exchange mangr Banco de Santander London 1974–81, treas Bayerische Hypotheken und Wechsel Bank London 1981–86, first vice-pres and treas Swiss Volksbank London 1986–93, treas mangr Bayersiche Hypotheken-und Wechsel Bank AG (Hypobank) 1993–94, asst gen mangr Treasury Banco Santander London 1994–95, asst gen mangr and treas Bank Brussels Lambert London 1995–2001; co dir: Bowerpark Ltd 2001–04, Shubrook Developments Ltd 2002–, Quest End Devpts Ltd 2005–; memb Foreign Exchange Ctee Foreign Banks Assoc London; *Recreations* golf, squash, tennis; *Style*— Brian Shubrook, Esq; ✉ 10 High Elms, Chigwell, Essex IG7 6NF (tel 020 8502 6715, fax 020 8502 6745, e-mail brian@shubrook.com)

SHUCKBURGH, Julian John Evelyn; s of Sir Evelyn Shuckburgh, GCMG, CB (d 1994), and Hon Nancy, *née* Brett (d 1999), da of 3 Viscount Esher (d 1963); *b* 30 July 1940; *Educ* Winchester, Peterhouse Cambridge; *m* 1, 1963 (m dis 1969), Faith, da of Sir Paul Wright, KCMG, OBE; 1 da (Matilda b 1964), 1 s (Benjamin b 1967); m 2, 1976 (m dis 1992), Sarah, eld da of Sir David Willcocks, CBE, MC, *qv*; 2 da (Amy b 1977, Hannah b 1979), 1 s (Alexander b 1982); *Career* publisher; Methuen & Co: publicity asst 1961, asst ed Academic Dept 1963, commissioning ed Academic Dept 1964–65; Weidenfeld & Nicolson Ltd: sr ed Reference Books 1965, sr ed Academic Dept 1966–68, dir Academic Dept 1968–72; read for the Bar Middle Temple 1972–73; editorial dir W H Allen Ltd 1973–75, publishing dir and md of Pitkin Pictorials Ltd Garrod & Lofthouse (Printers) 1975–78, md and fndr Shuckburgh Reynolds Ltd 1978–87, md Barrie & Jenkins Ltd 1987–2000, assoc publisher Ebury Press 1992–2000; *Books* The Bedside Book (1979), The Second Bedside Book (1981), London Revealed (2003), Spectacular London (2005); *Recreations* music (memb Bach Choir), walking, food and wine; *Clubs* Garrick; *Style*— Julian Shuckburgh, Esq; ✉ 22 Ellingham Road, London W12 9PR (tel 020 8749 7197)

SHUCKBURGH, Sir Rupert Charles Gerald; 13 Bt (E 1660), of Shuckburgh, Warwickshire; s of Sir Charles Gerald Stewkley Shuckburgh, 12 Bt, TD, JP, DL (d 1988), and his 2 w Nancy Diana Mary, OBE (d 1984), da of late Capt R Egerton Lubbock, RN, bro of 1 Baron Avebury; *b* 12 February 1949; *Educ* Worksop Coll; *m* 1, 1976 (m dis 1987), Judith, da of late William Gordon Mackaness, of Paddock Lodge, Everdon, Daventry; 2 s (James Rupert Charles b 1978, Peter Gerald William b 1982); m 2, 1987, Margaret Ida, da of late William Evans, of Middleton, Derbys; *Heir* s, James Shuckburgh; *Style*— Sir Rupert Shuckburgh, Bt

SHUCKSMITH, Prof Mark; s of Thomas David Shucksmith (d 2005), and Inga Shucksmith; *b* 25 August 1953, Hillingdon; *Educ* Sidney Sussex Coll Cambridge (MA), Univ of Newcastle upon Tyne (MSc, PhD); *m* 1979, Janet Susan Shucksmith; 2 da (Clare Louise b 29 Aug 1984, Anna Katherine b 10 May 1989); *Career* asst lectr in agricultural economics Univ of Newcastle upon Tyne 1977–81; Univ of Aberdeen: lectr, sr lectr then reader Dept of Land Economy 1981–93, prof of land economy 1993–2004, dir Arkleton Centre for Rural Devpt Research 1995–2004; dir Scottish Centre for Research on Social Justice 2001–04, prof of planning Univ of Newcastle upon Tyne 2005–; visiting prof Centre for Rural Research Univ of Trondheim Norway 2004–06; memb Bd Countryside Agency 2005–06, memb Affordable Rural Housing Cmmn 2005–06, cmmr Cmmn for Rural Communities 2006–; chair Ctee of Inquiry on Crofting 2007–08; memb: European Soc of Rural Sociology, Int Rural Sociological Assoc (first vice-pres 2004–08); *Publications* No Homes for Locals? (1981), Rural Housing in Scotland (1987), Housebuilding in Britain's Countryside (1990), Rural Scotland Today (1996), Exclusive Countryside? Social Inclusion and Regeneration in Rural Britain (2000), Housing in the European Countryside (2002), Young People in Rural Europe (2003), The CAP and the Regions: The Territorial Impact of the Common Agricultural Policy (2005); author of more than 60 articles in learned jls and chapters in books; *Recreations* maintaining a sense of wonder, listening to music, reading novels, hill-walking, drinking coffee; *Style*— Prof Mark Shucksmith; ✉ School of Architecture, Planning and Landscape, University of Newcastle upon Tyne, Newcastle upon Tyne NE1 7RU (tel 0191 222 6808, e-mail m.shucksmith@ncl.ac.uk)

SHUKMAN, David Roderick; s of Dr Harold Shukman, of St Antony's Coll Oxford, and Rev Dr Ann Shukman, *née* King-Farlow; *b* 30 May 1958; *Educ* Eton, Univ of Durham (BA); *m* Jessica Therese, da of David Pryce-Jones; 2 s (Jack b 5 Dec 1989, Harry b 20 April 1992), 1 da (Kitty b 3 Nov 1994); *Career* reporter Coventry Evening Telegraph 1980–83; BBC TV: news trainee 1983–85, reporter BBC TV Northern Ireland 1985–87, defence and foreign affrs corr News and Current Affrs 1987–95, Europe corr 1995–99, world affrs corr 1999–2003, environment and sci corr 2003–; memb: Int Inst for Strategic Studies 1988, Royal Inst for Int Affrs 1988; *Books* All Necessary Means: Inside the Gulf War (with Ben Brown, 1991), The Sorcerer's Challenge: Fears and Hopes for the Weapons of the Next Millenium (1995); *Recreations* diving, cooking; *Clubs* Frontline; *Style*— David Shukman, Esq; ✉ BBC News and Current Affairs, BBC Television Centre, Wood Lane, London W12 7RJ (tel 020 8743 8000)

SHULMAN, Alexandra; OBE (2005); da of Milton Shulman (d 2004), and Drusilla Beyfus, *qv*; *m* 26 May 1994 (m dis 2005), Paul Spike, s of late Rev Dr Robert W Spike, of NYC, and Alice Spike of El Paso TX; 1 s (Samuel Robert b 6 April 1995); *Career* successively: features ed Tatler Magazine, women's ed Sunday Telegraph, features ed Vogue Magazine; ed: GQ Magazine 1990–92, Vogue Magazine 1992–; PPA Magazine Ed of the Year 1997; tstee National Portrait Gallery 1999–; *Style*— Ms Alexandra Shulman, OBE; ✉ Vogue Magazine, Vogue House, Hanover Square, London W1R 1JU (tel 020 7499 9080, fax 020 7493 1345)

SHULMAN, Jeremy Ian; s of David Shulman (d 1974), of Leeds, and Lilo Shulman; *b* 3 March 1952; *Educ* Leeds GS, Univ of Birmingham (LLB); *m* 6 Nov 1977, Angela Elaine Lewin; 1 s (David Charles b 1 Oct 1979); *Career* admitted slr 1975; currently chm Shulmans (fndr 1981); nat chm Young Slrs' Gp 1986–87, memb Cncl Law Soc 1991–97; past memb Law Soc Employment Law Ctee; pt/t chm Employment Tbnls, pres Interlegal Network 1999–2001, pres Leeds Law Soc 2001–02, vice-chm Park Lane Coll Leeds 2000–04, chm Yorkshire Lawyer Awards, sec Interlegal Network, memb Cncl of Leeds C of C and Industry, memb Leeds Fin Services Steering Gp; former memb Gen Advsy Cncl IBA, chm Local Radio Advsy Ctee; memb Massada Fellowship; memb Law Soc 1975; *Recreations* playing tennis and golf, walking (particularly in Yorkshire Dales), bird watching, watching cricket and rugby, music, reading; *Clubs* MCC, Moor Allerton Golf, Chapel Allerton Lawn Tennis and Squash, Yorkshire CCC; *Style*— Jeremy Shulman, Esq; ✉ Shulmans, 120 Wellington Street, Leeds LS1 4LT (tel 0113 245 2833, fax 0113 246 7326, e-mail jshulman@shulmans.co.uk)

SHULMAN, Neville; CBE (2005, OBE 1990); *m* 8 Jan 1970, Emma, *née* Broide; 2 s (Alon Hamilton b 9 Sept 1970, Lee Hamilton b 23 June 1973), 1 da (Lauren Hamilton b 8 Aug 1984); *Career* CA in private practice 1961–; ed magazine Industry 1967 and 1968; mangr actors and film dirs 1973–, prodr theatrical prodns, documentaries and short films; chm and dir Int Theatre Inst 1985–, chm Land and City Families Tst 1987–95, tstee Camden Arts Centre 1988–2000; sec Fedn of Industrial Devpt Assocs 1965–68, offr and memb Theatres Advsy Cncl 1985–2002, chm Theatres Forum 2002; vice-pres NCH Action for Children 1989–; prison visitor Pentonville 1966; pres Rotary Club of London 1992–93 (vice-pres 1991–92), chm George Thomas Educnl Tst 2002; Liveryman of the Worshipful Co of Blacksmiths 1992; Freeman of the City of London 1992; Hon Col Tennessee Army 1977–; memb: NUJ 1967–, Bhutan Soc 1995; fell Explorers Club 2002 (memb 1993); FCA 1971 (ACA 1961), FRGS 1990, FRSA 1992; *Books* Exit of a Dragonfly (1985), Zen In the Art of Climbing Mountains (1992), On Top of Africa (1995), Zen Explorations in Remotest New Guinea (1997), Some Like It Cold (2001), Climbing the Equator (2005); *Recreations* contemporary art, travel, archaeology, film, theatre, mountaineering; *Style*— Neville Shulman, Esq, CBE; ✉ 35A Huntsworth Mews, Gloucester Place, London NW1 6DB (tel 020 7616 0777, fax 020 7724 8266)

SHUTTLE, Penelope Diane; da of Jack Frederick Shuttle, of Middlesex, and Joan Shepherdess Lipscombe; *b* 12 May 1947; *m* Peter William Redgrove (d 2003), s of G J Redgrove, of Hampstead; 1 da (Zoe b 1976); *Career* writer and poet; poetry recorded for Poetry Room Harvard and The Poetry Archive; Arts Cncl Award 1969, 1972 and 1985, Greenwood Poetry Prize 1972, EC Gregory Award for Poetry 1974, Authors' Fndn Grant 1993, Hawthornden fell 2005; chair Falmouth Poetry Gp; Cholmondeley Award 2007; *Radio* plays: The Girl who Lost her Glove 1975 (jt third prize winner Radio Times Drama Bursaries Competition 1974), The Dauntless Girl 1978; *Novels* An Excusable Vengeance (1967), All the Usual Hours of Sleeping (1969), Wailing Monkey Embracing a Tree (1974), The Terrors of Dr Treviles (with Peter Redgrove, 1974), Rainsplitter in the Zodiac Garden (1976), Mirror of the Giant (1979); *Poetry* Nostalgia Neurosis (1968), Midwinter Mandala (1973), Photographs of Persephone (1973), Autumn Piano (1973), Songbook of the Snow (1973), The Hermaphrodite Album (with Peter Redgrove, 1973), Webs on Fire (1977), The Orchard Upstairs (1981), The Child-Stealer (1983), The Lion from Rio (1986), Adventures with my Horse (PBS Recommendation 1988), Taxing The Rain (1992), Building a City for Jamie (1996), Selected Poems (PBS Recommendation 1998), A Leaf out of His Book (PBS Recommendation 1999), Redgrove's Wife (2006 reprinted 2007; shortlisted: The Forward Prize, the T S Eliot Award), Adventures with my Horse (2007); *Psychology* The Wise Wound (with Peter Redgrove, 1978 re-issued 1986, 1994,1999 and 2005), Alchemy for Women (with Peter Redgrove, 1995); *Recreations* gardening, walking, yoga, travel, reading; *Style*— Ms Penelope Shuttle; ✉ c/o David Higham Associates, 5–8 Lower John Street, Golden Square, London W1R 4HA (tel 020 7437 7888, fax 020 7437 1072)

SHUTTLEWORTH, 5 Baron (UK 1902); Sir Charles Geoffrey Nicholas Kay-Shuttleworth; 6 Bt (UK 1850), JP 1997; s of 4 Baron Shuttleworth, MC (d 1975), and Anne Elizabeth (d 1991), da of late Col Geoffrey Francis Phillips, CBE, DSO; *b* 2 August 1948; *Educ* Eton; *m* 1975, Ann Mary, da of James Whatman and former w of late Daniel Henry Barclay; 3 s; *Heir* s, Hon Thomas Kay-Shuttleworth; *Career* memb House of Lords 1975–99; dir Burnley Building Society 1978–82, chm National and Provincial Building Society 1994–96 (dir and dep chm 1983–93), dep chm Abbey National plc 1996–99 (dir until 2004); chartered surveyor; ptnr Burton Barnes and Vigers 1977–96; dir Rank Foundation 1993–; memb Bd Skelmersdale Development Corporation 1982–85; govr Giggleswick Sch 1982– (chm of Govrs 1984–97); chm: Rural Devpt Cmmn 1990–97, Yorks Dales Millennium Tst 2000–05; memb Cncl: Lancaster Univ 1990–93, Duchy of Lancaster 1998– (chm 2006–); Hon Col 4 Bn The Queen's Lancashire Regt 1996–99, Hon Col Lancastrian and Cumbrian Volunteers 1999–2005; HM Lord-Lt and Custos Rotulorum of Lancashire 1997–; hon fell Univ of Central Lancashire 1996, hon fell and patron Myerscough Coll 2003; KStJ 1997; *Clubs* Brooks's; *Style*— The Rt Hon the Lord Shuttleworth; ✉ Leck Hall, Carnforth, Lancashire LA6 2JF

SHUTTLEWORTH, Dr Kenneth Owen; s of Owen William Shuttleworth, of Birmingham, and Ilene Doris, *née* Peakman; *Educ* Handsworth GS Birmingham, City of Leicester Poly (Dip Arch); *m* 30 May 1987, Seana Ann, da of Patrick James Brennan; 1 s (Jo b 28 April 1990), 1 da (Jaime b June 1993); *Career* architect; Harry Bloomer & Sons 1972–73, Essex Goodman & Suggitt Birmingham 1973–74; ptnr/dir Foster & Partners (formerly Sir Norman Foster & Partners, joined 1974) until 2003, fndr Make 2003–; projects incl: Willis Faber & Dumas Ipswich, Hong Kong Bank Hong Kong, Televisa Mexico, Century Tower Tokyo, ITN HQ London, BP HQ London, King Faisal Fndn Riyadh, Cranfield Library, Nîmes Mediatech France, Hong Kong Airport, British Gas Thames Valley Park, Wembley Stadium, GLA Mayor's Office London, Crescent House Wiltshire, Swiss Re HQ London; cmmr CABE 2002–; Hon Dr of Design De Montfort Univ 1994; memb: ARCUK 1977, RIBA 1977; *Awards* RIBA: Willis Faber & Dumas 1977, Regnl Award 2002; Civic Tst: Renault Centre Swindon 1984, Crescent Wing Sainsbury Centre for Visual Arts 1992; Royal Gold Medal for Architecture 1983, Crescent House Wilts Concrete Award 2000, Benny Award 2003; numerous other awards; *Recreations* drawing, design, photography, painting, landscape design; *Style*— Dr Kenneth Shuttleworth; ✉ Make, 55–65 Whitfield Street, London W1T 4HE

SHUTTLEWORTH, Maj Noel Charles; s of Rev Richard Charles Shuttleworth (d 1955), and Doris Marian, *née* Sims (d 1978); *b* 4 January 1933; *Educ* Haileybury and ISC, RMA Sandhurst; *Career* Scots Guards 1953–63, served Germany, Canada, Kenya, UK, ret Maj 1963; fndr and chm The English Courtyard Assoc 1979– (winners of 6 Civic Tst Commendations, 10 Housing Design awards from DOE, RIBA and NHBC for excellence in housing design), dir Les Blancs Bois Ltd Guernsey 1987–, jt fndr Retirement Plus Ltd 2004; life pres and vice-chm The Elderly Accommodation Cncl 2004– (govr 1987–, chm 1992–2004); vice-pres Devizes Constituency Cons Assoc 1980– (chm 1977–80); *Recreations* cricket (played for Kenya and E Africa 1962–63), tennis; *Clubs* Cavalry and Guards'; *Style*— Maj Noel Shuttleworth; ✉ Crabtree, Savernake Forest, Marlborough, Wiltshire; The English Courtyard Association, Prospect House, The Broadway, Farnham Common, Buckinghamshire SL2 3PP (tel 01753 669866, fax 01753 669866)

SHUTZ, Roy Martin; s of Joseph Shutz (d 1969), of Birmingham, and Alice, *née* Susz (d 1989); *b* 23 January 1943; *Educ* King Edward's Five Ways Sch Birmingham, Univ of Birmingham (LLB), Coll of Law; *Career* teacher Longsands Sch Cambridge 1966–68, admin asst Univ of Warwick 1968–69, asst to Academic and Fin Secs LSE 1969–74, chm Romar Investments Ltd 1969–; barr 1974–90; Barnet BC: memb 1982–98, chm Educn Ctee 1985–90, mayor 1990–91, leader 1991–94; chm Mill Hill RFC 1996–99, memb Corporation of Hendon Coll 1998–2000, memb Middx Area Probation Ctee 1986–94, non-exec dir Barnet Community Healthcare Tst 1991–94; dir Maze Restaurants Ltd 2001–06; memb Gen Advsy Cncl Br Property Fedn (BPF) 2002–06; FInstD, chm Cambs Branch Ctee IoD 2003–05 (memb 2001–06); *Recreations* golf, rugby union, singing, theatre; *Clubs* Huntingdon RFC, Reform; *Style*— Roy Shutz, Esq; ✉ Dean Courtyard, High Street, Lower Dean, Huntingdon PE28 0LL (tel 01480 860874)

SIBBALD, Graham; s of Walter Inglis Sibbald, and Eileen Hilda, *née* Waddell; *b* 20 February 1961, Inverness; *Educ* George Heriot's Sch Edinburgh, Univ of Edinburgh (LLB, DipLP); *m* 21 June 1996, Diane Elizabeth, *née* Nicol; 1 da (Catherine Elsie), 1 s (James William Inglis); *Career* slr; NP; head of corp gp Bird Semple (now DLA Piper) until 1997, ptnr Dundas & Wilson CS LLP 1997– (head of media gp and practice area ldr for corp gp Glasgow); memb Law Soc of Scot; *Recreations* family, golf, skiing, cinema, reading;

S

Style— Graham Sibbald, Esq; ✉ Dundas & Wilson CS LLP, 191 West George Street, Glasgow G2 2LD (tel 0141 304 6025)

SIBBETT, Prof Wilson; CBE (2001); s of John Sibbett (d 1985), and Margaret, *née* McLeister (d 1983); *b* 15 March 1948; *Educ* Ballymena Tech Coll, Queen's Univ Belfast (BSc, PhD); *m* 20 Sept 1979, Barbara Anne, *née* Brown; 3 da (Hannah Margaret b 8 Dec 1980, Ruth Anne b 16 May 1983, Rachael Annette b 30 April 1985); *Career* Imperial Coll London: lectr in physics 1977–84, reader in physics 1984–85; Univ of St Andrews: head Dept of Physics 1985–87, head Sch of Physics and Astronomy 1987–94, dir of research Sch of Physics and Astronomy 1994–2003, Wardlaw prof of physics 1997–; chair Scot Sci Advsy Ctee 2002–06; Rank Prize in Optoelectronics 1997, Rumford Medal Royal Soc 2000; Hon LLD Univ of Dundee, Hon DSc TCD; FInstP 1986, FRSE 1988, FRS 1997, fell Optical Soc of America 1998; *Publications* author of around 300 pubns in laser physics and optoelectronics; *Recreations* golf; *Clubs* Rotary (St Andrews), New Golf (St Andrews), Royal and Ancient Golf; *Style—* Prof Wilson Sibbett, CBE, FRS; ✉ School of Physics and Astronomy, University of St Andrews, North Haugh, St Andrews, Fife KY16 9SS (tel 01334 463100, fax 01334 463104, e-mail ws@st-and.ac.uk)

SIBLEY, Dame Antoinette; DBE (1996, CBE 1973); da of Edward George Sibley, of Kent, and Winifred Maude, *née* Smith; *b* 27 February 1939; *Educ* Arts Educnl Sch Tring, Royal Ballet Sch; *m* 1, 1964 (m dis 1973), Michael George Somes, CBE (d 1994); m 2, 1974, Richard Panton Corbett, *qv*, s of William Corbett, of Shropshire; 1 da (Eloise b 1975), 1 s (Isambard b 1980); *Career* graduated into the Royal Ballet 1956, took over the role of Odette/Odile in Swan Lake at short notice Covent Garden 1959, promoted to soloist 1959 and to princ dancer 1960; noted for interpretation of Aurora in Sleeping Beauty, title role in Giselle, title role in Ashton's Cinderella, Juliet in Macmillan's Romeo and Juliet, Titania in The Dream (created for her by Ashton), title role in Manon (created for her by Macmillan), Dorabella (created for her by Ashton), Chloë in Ashton's Daphnis and Chloë, Ashton's A Month in the Country, numerous other roles; has toured N and S America, USSR, Aust and Europe; prima ballerina role in film The Turning Point; pres Royal Acad of Dance 1991– (vice-pres 1989–91); *Publications* Sibley and Dowell (1976), Antoinette Sibley (1981), Antoinette Sibley - Reflections of a Ballerina (1986); *Recreations* opera-going, reading, music, gardening; *Style—* Dame Antoinette Sibley, DBE; ✉ c/o The Royal Opera House, Covent Garden, London WC2

SIBLEY, Edward; s of William Sibley (d 1941), of Rhymney, Gwent, and Myfanwy, *née* Williams (d 1987); *b* 21 July 1935; *Educ* Rhymney GS Gwent, UCW Aberystwyth (LLB, Samuel Evans Prize), Coll of Law; *m* 3 Aug 1957, Sonia, da of Harold Beynon; 2 s (Stephen b 6 Dec 1965, Neil Edward b 24 May 1970), 1 da (Deborah Jane b 1 Dec 1962); *Career* articled clerk Clifford-Turner 1962–65, admitted slr 1965, ptnr Berwin & Co 1967 (joined as asst slr 1965), sr ptnr Berwin Leighton Paisner (fndr ptnr 1970), sr ptnr Sibley & Co (fndr ptnr 2000); qualified NY Bar USA 1985; memb Worshipful Co of Slrs 1985; memb: Law Soc, ABA, IBA, UIA; FCIArb 2000; *Recreations* skiing, running, opera, theatre, literature; *Clubs* Reform, MCC; *Style—* Edward Sibley, Esq; ✉ Berwin Leighton Paisner, Adelaide House, London Bridge, London EC4R 9HA (tel 020 7760 1000, fax 020 7760 1111)

SIBLEY, Richard Edmonde Miles Phillippe; s of William Alfred Sibley, JP (d 1992), of Crowfield, Suffolk, and Florence May, *née* Marsh (d 2004); *b* 23 May 1949; *Educ* Clark's Coll London, Anglican Regnl Coll; *m* 5 June 1976, Hannelore, da of Hans Njammasch, of Germany; 1 s (Alexander b 21 March 1979); *Career* chief exec Ogilby Housing Society Ltd 1987–, chm Calderwood Housing Assoc 1992–2004; dir Sibley Property Co Ltd; chm NE London Valuation Court (rating) 1981–90; chm London (NE) Valuation and Community Charge Tbnl 1990–; Rotarian 1982– (pres 1993–94); Freeman City of London 1980, Liveryman and memb Court of Assts Worshipful Co of Coopers (Upper Warden 1994–95); *Recreations* painting, volcanology, fungi; *Clubs* Bishopsgate Ward; *Style—* R E M P Sibley, Esq; ✉ Ogilby Housing Society Ltd, Estate Office, Greenways Court, Butts Green Road, Hornchurch, Essex RM11 2JL (tel 01708 475115/6)

SIDDALL, Peter John; s of John Siddall (d 1999), of Burston, Stafford, and Helen, *née* Wood (d 1998); *b* 15 October 1942; *Educ* Rydal Sch; *m* 9 Sept 1972, Ena; 2 da (Kirsten b 16 Feb 1977, Tara b 28 July 1980); *Career* mgmnt conslt; md Siddall & Co Ltd 1978–; chm: Churchill China plc 1987–96, Martello Textiles Ltd 1989–92, Horticulture Research International 1998–2004; author of numerous articles in business jls and books; FCA 1977 (ACA 1966), FIMC 1993, FRSA 2000; *Recreations* yachting, skiing, croquet, amateur dramatics; *Style—* Peter Siddall, Esq; ✉ Siddall & Company Ltd, 16 Tideway Yard, Mortlake High Street, London SW14 8SN (tel 020 8392 5900, fax 020 8878 4438, e-mail peter.siddall@siddall.co.uk)

SIDDALL, Robert Guy; s of Sir Norman Siddall (d 2002), of Mansfield, Notts, and Pauline, *née* Arthur; *b* 28 January 1945; *Educ* Nottingham HS, Univ of Nottingham (BSc); *m* 1970, Gillian Elaine, da of Philip Morley, and Violet, *née* Fenton; 4 da (Anna-Louise b 1973, Naomi Sarah b 1975, Charlotte Elaine b 1978, Laura Mary b 1980); *Career* National Coal Board 1968–95; trainee 1966–68, various jr mgmnt positions 1968–71, undermangr Sherwood Colliery 1971–73, dep mangr Rufford Colliery 1973–75, colliery mangr Blidworth Colliery 1975–80, sr mining engr Planning & Surveying North Notts 1980–83, chief mining engr Doncaster area 1983–85; dep dir: Mining North Derbys 1985–87, Selby North Yorks 1987–88, Mining North Yorks area 1988–90; gp dir: North Yorks Gp 1990–91, South Yorks Gp 1991–93; dir Opencast 1991–93; conslt 1996–; dir Shelton Trenching Systems Ltd 1996–97; conslt mining engr; pres: Midland Inst of Mining Engrs 1992–93, Instn of Mining Engrs 1995–96; winner Futers Medal Instn of Mining Engrs 1992; author of several pubns in tech jls; FIMMM, FREng 1995; *Recreations* industrial archaeology; *Style—* Eur Ing Robert Siddall, FREng; ✉ Stud Farm House, Ossington Lane, Sutton-on-Trent, Nottinghamshire NG23 6QR (tel 01636 821991, 01636 822677, e-mail rgsiddall@aol.com)

SIDDIQUI, Prof Mona; da of Abdul Ali (d 1999), and Hasina Khatoon (d 1997); *b* 3 May 1963; *Educ* Univ of Leeds (BA), Univ of Manchester (MA, PhD); *m* 29 June 1991, Farhaj Siddiqui; 3 s (Suhaib b 2 Jan 1995, Zuhayr b 27 June 1996, Fayz b 23 Nov 2000); *Career* Univ of Glasgow: lectr in Islamic studies 1995–2002, sr lectr in Islamic studies 2002–05, prof of Islamic studies and public understanding 2006–; external examiner Univ of Aberdeen; chair Scottish Religious Advsy Cncl and memb Central Religious Advsy Cncl BBC; Hon DLitt Univ of Wolverhampton 2002; FRSE 2005, FRSA 2005; *Publications* author of articles in learned jls and books incl Encyclopaedia of the Qur'an and Jl of the American Academy of Religion; *Recreations* cooking, interior design; *Style—* Prof Mona Siddiqui; ✉ Department of Theology and Religious Studies, Glasgow University, Glasgow G12 8QQ (tel 0141 330 6525, fax 0141 330 4943, e-mail msi@arts.gla.ac.uk)

SIDDLE, Prof Kenneth; s of Fred Siddle, of Morecambe, Lancs, and Vera, *née* Sunderland; *b* 30 March 1947; *Educ* Morecambe GS, Downing Coll Cambridge (scholar, Bye fell, MA, PhD); *m* 1, 1971 (m dis 1994), Yvonne Marie, *née* Kennedy; 1 s (Paul b 1977); m 2, 1996, Anne Elizabeth Willis; 1 s (Edward John Willis b 2000); *Career* lectr Dept of Med Biochemistry Welsh Nat Sch of Med 1971–78; Univ of Cambridge: Meres sr student for med res St John's Coll 1978–81, fell Churchill Coll 1982–, Wellcome lectr Dept of Clinical Biochemistry 1981–90, prof of molecular endocrinology 1990–; visiting scientist Joslin Diabetes Center and Harvard Med Sch 1989–90; chm Biochemical Jl 1995–99; memb: Biochemical Soc 1970–, Diabetes UK (formerly Br Diabetic Assoc) 1972–, Br Soc for Cell Biology 1980–, Assoc of Clinical Biochemists 1985–; sr treas Cricket Club Univ of Cambridge; author of over 100 articles in scientific jls; *Recreations* mountaineering, cricket, gardening; *Clubs* Lancashire CCC, MCC, Hawks' (Cambridge); *Style—* Prof Kenneth Siddle; ✉ Department of Clinical Biochemistry, University of Cambridge, Addenbrooke's Hospital, Cambridge CB2 2QR (tel 01223 336789, fax 01223 330598, e-mail ks14@mole.bio.cam.ac.uk)

SIDDLE, Roger; s of William Siddle, of Bath, and Mary Siddle; *Educ* Hampton Sch, Sidney Sussex Coll Cambridge (MA), Harvard Business Sch (MBA); *m* 11 July 1992, Helen; 2 s (Huw b April 1995, Gareth b March 2002), 1 da (Carys b May 1998); *Career* Andersen Consulting 1983–88; Bain & Co Inc UK: joined 1990, ptnr 1995–2007, managing ptnr UK 2001–07, chm European Operating Ctee 2006–07; chief exec BPP Hldgs plc 2007–; cncllr London Region CBI; *Recreations* family, wine, skiing, Newcastle United; *Style—* Roger Siddle, Esq; ✉ BPP Holdings plc, Aldine Place, London W12 8AA (tel 020 8740 2222)

SIDNEY, Elizabeth Anne; OBE (1998); *Educ* Sherborne Sch for Girls, Univ of Oxford (MA), Univ of London (MA); *m* (m dis), Deryck Malcolm Sidney; 1 s, 3 da; *Career* psychologist Civil Service Cmmn 1957–72, trg dir Family Planning Assoc 1970–74, fndr and managing ptnr Mantra Consultancy Group (conslts and trainers in public and private sectors UK, Europe, USA, India, Far East); memb Kensington Chelsea and Westminster Area Health Authy 1972–80, pres Women's Liberal Fedn 1982–84, chm Lib Pty Policy Panel on Employment 1980–83, dep chm Candidates Ctee Lib Pty 1986–87, pres Women Lib Dems 1988–91, chm Lib Dems Working Pty on Industrial Democracy 1990–; chm: Int Network of Lib Women 1997–2000, WAFE (Int Fedn of Women Against Fundamentalism and For Equality) 2004–; Lib Dem rep on Exec Women's Nat Cmmn 1993–98; tstee: New Economics Fndn 1980–88, Environmental Law Fndn 1996–; chm The Green Alliance 1984–89; former JP; CPsychol, FBPsS, FPTD, FRSA; *Books* The Skills of Interviewing (1961), Case Studies of Management Initiative (1967), The Industrial Society (1970), Skills with People: A Guide for Managers (1973), Future Woman: How to Survive Life (1982), ed Managing Recruitment (1989), One to One Management (1991), The Status of Women (1995), Working to End Domestic Violence (1997); *Recreations* political work, environment, travel; *Clubs* RSA; *Style—* Ms Elizabeth Sidney, OBE; ✉ 25 Ellington Street, London N7 8PN (tel 020 7607 6592, e-mail mantra@psinet.co.uk)

SIDOLI, Robert Andrew; s of Primo Sidoli, of Merthyr Tydfil, Glamorgan, and Barbara, *née* Bryant; *b* 21 June 1979; *Educ* Bishop Hedley HS, Univ of Cardiff (BSc); *Partner* Nicola; *Career* rugby union player; domestic: Crawshays RFC, Pontypridd RFC 1998– (player of the year 2000–01 and 2002–03); international: Wales Youth 1998 (played in FIRA Jr World Cup), Wales U21 2000, Wales A 2002, Wales 2002– (24 caps, debut v South Africa 2002, memb squad World Cup Aust 2003, winners Six Nations Championship 2005); pres Cefn Coed RFC; *Recreations* snooker, cards, socialising; *Clubs* Merthyr RFC, Pontypridd RFC, Celtic Warriors; *Style—* Robert Sidoli, Esq; ✉ c/o Adam Palfrey, 3 Bogo Street, Cardiff CF11 9JJ

SIDOR, Neven Joseph; Krešo Sidor, of Wimbledon, London, and Blanka, *née* Novak; *b* 8 May 1953; *Educ* Univ of Nottingham (BA, BArch), RIBA (part III exam); *m* Hanya Chlala; 1 da (Alexa); *Career* architect Rock Townsend London 1978–81; Grimshaw Architects LLP (formerly Nicholas Grimshaw & Partners Ltd): joined 1981, assoc 1984–92, dir 1992–; projects incl: LSE, Lincoln's Inn Fields, Frankfurt Trade Hall, Engineering Building UCL, KPMG HQ Berlin, The Minerva Building London, Ijburg bridge Amsterdam, Bijlmer Station Amsterdam, Ludwig Erhard Haus Berlin, Waterloo International Terminal London, Lloyds TSB HQ London, Sainsbury Devpt Camden Town, Oxford Ice Rink, Herman Miller distribution facility; winning competition entries incl: Frankfurt Trade Hall, bridges Ijburg Devpt, Pusan High Speed Rail Complex, Berlin Stock Exchange & Communications Centre, UK Pavilion at EXPO 92; FRIBA; *Recreations* music, jazz guitarist; *Style—* Neven Sidor, Esq; ✉ Grimshaw Architects LLP, 57 Clerkenwell Road, London EC1M 5NG

SIEFF, Hon Sir David Daniel; kt (1999); s (by 1 m) of Baron Sieff of Brimpton (Life Peer, d 2001); *b* 1939; *Educ* Repton; *m* 1962, Jennifer, da of H Walton, of Salford Priors, Worcs; 2 s (Simon Marcus b 1965, Jonathan David b 1966); *Career* Marks & Spencer plc: dir 1972–97, non-exec dir 1997–2001; chm: Nat Lottery Charities Bd until 1999, Br Retail Consortium until 2002, UK Betting plc until 2004; currently chm Newbury Racecourse plc; *Style—* The Hon Sir David Sieff

SIEFKEN, Prof Hinrich Gerhard; s of Werner Johann Hinrich Siefken (d 1968), and Lisel, *née* Menne (d 1963); *b* 21 April 1939; *Educ* Carl Duisberg Gymnasium Leverkusen, Univ of Tübingen (DPhil), Univ of Nottingham (DLitt); *m* 1 Aug 1968, Marcia Corinne, da of Harry Birch (d 1989), of Sheffield; 1 da (Brigitte Christiane 14 March 1970), 1 s (Kristian Hinrich b 8 August 1973); *Career* tutor Univ of Tübingen 1962–65, lectr Univ Coll of N Wales Bangor 1965–66, wissenschaftlicher asst Univ of Tübingen 1966–67, sr lectr St David's Univ Coll Lampeter 1973–79 (asst lectr 1967–68, lectr 1968–73); Univ of Nottingham: prof of German 1979–97 (prof emeritus 1997–), head Sch of Modern Languages 1986–88, dean Faculty of Arts 1988–92, dir Inst of German, Austrian and Swiss Affrs 1992–94; hon prof of modern languages Univ of Wales Bangor 1999–; ed Trivium 1978–79 (subject ed 1974–79), gen ed Renaissance and Modern Studies 1986–88, memb Editorial Bd New Manchester German Texts 1986–91; *Books* Kudrunepos (1967), Ungeduld und Lässigkeit - Kafka (1977), Thomas Mann - Goethe Ideal der Deutschheit (1981), Theodor Haecker (1989), Theodor Haecker, Tag - und Nachtbücher (ed, 1989), Die Weisse Rose, Student Resistance to National Socialism (ed, 1991), Resistance to National Socialism: Arbeiter, Christen, Jugendliche, Eliten (ed, 1993), Die Weisse Rose und ihre Flugblätter (1994), Theodor Haecker: Leben und Werk (ed, 1995), Kunst und Widerstand (ed, 1995), Experiencing Tradition - Essays of Discovery (ed, 2003); *Recreations* music, walking, gardening; *Style—* Prof Hinrich Siefken; ✉ 6 Mountsorrel Drive, Westbridgford, Nottingham NG2 6LJ (tel 0115 981 1617, e-mail hinrichsiefken@hotmail.com)

SIEGHART, Mary Ann Corinna Howard; da of Paul Sieghart (d 1988), and Felicity Ann, *née* Baer; *b* 6 August 1961; *Educ* Cobham Hall, Bedales, Wadham Coll Oxford (major scholarship); *m* 17 June 1989, David Stephens Prichard, s of Maj Michael Prichard; 2 da; *Career* journalist Eye to Eye Publishing 1978–79, reporter Sunday Express 1979, arts ed rising to news ed Cherwell 1979–80, ldr and feature writer Daily Telegraph 1980–82, Eurobond corr rising to Lex Columnist Financial Times 1982–86, city ed Today 1986, political corr The Economist 1986–88, presenter The World This Week 1988, presenter The Week in Westminster (Radio 4); The Times: ed op-ed page 1988–91, arts ed 1989–90, acting ed Monday edn 1997–99, currently asst ed, columnist and political leader writer; chairwoman The Brains Trust (BBC 2), contrib Start the Week (Radio 4); vice-pres Nat Assoc for Gifted Children, tstee Radcliffe Tst; treas Nat Cncl for One-Parent Families 1986–89; memb: Steering Ctee and Advsy Cncl New Europe 1999–2006, Social Studies Advsy Bd Univ of Oxfordn 1999–2003, Steering Ctee No Campaign 1999–2004; tstee Heritage Lottery Fund 1997–2002; vice-chair N Fulham New Deal for Communities 2000–06; founding ctee memb Women in Journalism 1995–98; runner up young journalist of the year Br Press Awards 1983, Harold Wincott prize for Young Financial Journalist of the Year 1983, winner Laurence Stern fellowship 1984 (worked for the Washington Post); *Recreations* rollerblading, trekking in remote places, doodling, choral singing, classic cars, reading novels on holiday, listening to music, art, architecture; *Style—* Ms Sieghart; ✉ The Times, 1 Pennington Street, London E98 1TA (direct tel 020 7782 5160, fax 020 7782 5229, e-mail maryann.sieghart@thetimes.co.uk)

SIGWART, Prof Ulrich; s of Dr August Robert Sigwart, and Elizabeth Augusta Sigwart; *b* 9 March 1941; *Educ* Univ of Basel, Univ of Munster Medical Sch, Univ of Freiburg; *m* 2 Sept 1967, Christine Rosemary, da of Peter Sartorius; 2 da (Ann Elizabeth b 27 Feb 1969, Catherine Isabel b 16 Oct 1976), 2 s (Philip Martin Christopher b 10 Aug 1970, Jan

Michael Pierre b 27 April 1973); *Career* intern Community Hosp Lörrach, res Framington Union Hosp 1968–71, chief of cath lab Gollwitzer Meier Inst Bad Oeynhausen 1973–79, chief of invasive cardiology Univ Hosp Lausanne 1979–89, conslt cardiologist and dir of invasive cardiology Royal Brompton London; academic career: prof of med Univ of Düsseldorf, assoc prof of cardiology Univ of Lausanne, prof and chief of cardiology Univ Hosp Geneva; memb Editorial Bd: Clinical Cardiology, JACC (Jl of the American Coll of Cardiologists), Interventional Cardiology (asst ed), Frontiers in Cardiology, Handbook of Cardiovascular Interventions, Stent, Egyptian Heart Jl, Int Jl of Cardiovascular Interventions, Indian Jl of Cardiology, Asean Heart Jl, Jl of American Coll of Cardiology, Heart Views, Circulation (guest ed); memb: Br Cardiac Soc, American Heart Assoc, Swiss Soc of Cardiology, German Soc of Cardiology; chm: Working Gp on Myocardial Function, Working Gp on PTCA & Lysis SSC; ESC Grüntzig Award 1996 and 2006, King Faisal Prize for Medicine 2004, Suen Effeul Prize 2004, Gozer Prize 2007, ACC Interiat Award 2007; hon memb Polish Soc of Cardiology, hon fell Russian Soc of Interventional Cardiology; Dr (hc) Univ of Lausanne 1999; FRCP, FACC, FESC; *Books* Automation in Cardiac Diagnosis (1978), Ventricular Wall Motion (1984), Coronary Stents (1992), Endoluminal Stents (1995); *Recreations* flying, sailing, music, skiing, photography; *Style*— Prof Ulrich Sigwart; ✉ 1 Avenue de Miremont, CH-1206, Geneve, Switzerland

SIKORA, Prof Karol; s of Witold Karol Sikora (d 1966), and Thomasina Sikora; *b* 17 June 1948; *Educ* Dulwich Coll, Univ of Cambridge (MA, PhD, MB BChir), Middx Hosp; *m* 6 Dec 1975, Alison Mary; 1 s (Simon b 1977), 2 da (Emma b 1980, Lucy b 1982); *Career* formerly: prof and head Dept of Clinical Oncology Imperial Coll Sch of Med at Hammersmith Hosp (Royal Postgrad Med Sch until merger 1997), jt dir of cancer servs Hammersmith and Charing Cross Hosps; former chief WHO Cancer Prog; currently: dean Brunel Univ and Univ of Buckingham Med Sch, visiting prof of cancer med Imperial Coll Sch of Med at Hammersmith Hosp, scientific dir Medical Solutions plc, medical dir Cancer Ptnrs UK; FRCR 1980, FRCP 1987, FFPM 2001; *Books* Monoclonal Antibodies (1984), Fight Cancer (1989), Cancer: a positive approach (1995), Treatment of Cancer (5 edn 2005); *Recreations* boating, climbing; *Clubs* Athenaeum, Polish Hearth; *Style*— Prof Karol Sikora; ✉ 79 Harley Street, London W1G 8PZ (tel 020 7518 0780, fax 020 7518 0781, e-mail karolsikora@hotmail.com)

SILBER, Hon Mr Justice; Sir Stephen Robert Silber; kt (1999); s of Julius Joseph Silber (d 1975), of London, and Marguerite Silber (d 2004); *b* 26 March 1944; *Educ* William Ellis Sch, Trinity Coll Cambridge, UCL; *m* 1982, Frances Nina Lucinda, da of Lt Col D St J Edwards; 1 s, 1 da; *Career* called to the Bar Gray's Inn 1968 (bencher 1999); QC 1987, memb Judicial Studies Bd (Criminal Law Ctee) 1994–99, law cmmr for England and Wales 1994–99, recorder of the Crown Court 1987–99, dep judge of the High Court 1995–99, judge of the High Court of Justice (Queen's Bench Div) 1999–, judge of the Employment Appeal Tribunal 2004–; *Recreations* music, walking, theatre, watching sport; *Style*— The Hon Mr Justice Silber; ✉ Royal Courts of Justice, Strand, London WC2A 2LL

SILBERSTON, Prof (Zangwill) Aubrey; CBE (1987); s of Louis Silberston (d 1975), of London, and Polly, *née* Kern (d 1976); *b* 26 January 1922; *Educ* Hackney Downs Sch, Jesus Coll Cambridge (BA, MA), Univ of Oxford (MA); *m* 1, 1945 (m dis), Dorothy Marion, da of A S Nicholls (d 1965), of London; 1 da (Katharine b 1948 d 1982), 1 s (Jeremy b 1950 d 2006); m 2, 1985, Michèle, da of Vitomir Ledić (d 2004), of Zagreb; *Career* Royal Fusiliers 1942–45, served in Iraq, Egypt, N Africa and Italy; economist Courtaulds Ltd 1946–50; Univ of Cambridge: res fell St Catharine's Coll 1950–53, lectr in economics 1951–71, fell St John's Coll 1958–71; official fell Nuffield Coll Oxford 1971–78 (dean 1972–78); Univ of London: prof of economics Imperial Coll 1978–87, prof emeritus Univ of London 1987–, sr research fell Tanaka Business Sch Imperial Coll 1987–2005; sr advsr London Economics 1992–2004; memb: Monopolies Cmmn 1965–68, Bd Br Steel Corp 1967–76, Royal Cmmn on the Press 1974–77, Royal Cmmn on Environmental Pollution 1986–96, Restrictive Practices Ct 1986–92, Cncl of Experts Intellectual Property Inst 1992–; specialist advsr Sub-Ctee B European Communities Ctee House of Lords 1993; pres Confedn of Euro Econ Assocs 1988–90, vice-pres Royal Econ Soc 1992– (memb 1946, sec gen 1979–92); *Books* The Motor Industry (jtly, 1959), Economic Impact of the Patent System (jtly, 1973), The Steel Industry (jtly, 1974), The Multi-Fibre Arrangement and the UK Economy (1984), The Future of the Multi-Fibre Arrangement (jtly, 1989), Beyond the Multi-Fibre Arrangement (jtly, 1995), Environmental Economics (jt ed, 1995), The Changing Industrial Map of Europe (jtly, 1996), Anti-Dumping and Countervailing Action: Limits imposed by Economic and Legal Theory (jtly, 2007); *Recreations* opera, ballet; *Style*— Prof Aubrey Silberston, CBE; ✉ Rue Jules Lejeune 2, B-1050 Brussels, Belgium (e-mail asilberston@yahoo.co.uk)

SILK, *see also:* Kilroy-Silk

SILK, Prof David Baxter A; *b* 14 April 1944; *Educ* Univ of London (MB BS, LRCP); *Career* lectr in med Dept of Med and Gastroenterology Bart's 1971–75, MRC Travelling fell and visiting assoc prof Univ of Calif San Francisco 1975–76, sr lectr and conslt Liver Unit KCL 1976–78, conslt physician and dir Dept of Gastroenterology and Nutrition Central Middx Hosp London 1978–; appointed to Editorial Bd: Gut 1978, Jl of Clinical Nutrition and Gastroenterology 1985, Gastroenterology in Practice 1987; chm Br Assoc of Parenteral and Enteral Nutrition 1994–99; memb: Euro Soc of Parenteral and Enteral Nutrition, American Soc of Parenteral and Enteral Nutrition; British Soc of Gastroenterology Res Medal, Nutricia Int Clinical Nutrician Award; memb Assoc of Physicians, MRCS 1968, MD 1974, FRCP 1983 (MRCP); *Books* Nutritional Support in Hospital Practice (1983), Artificial Nutrition Support in Clinical Practice (1994), Coping with IBS (1997), Understanding Your IBS (1998); author of over 300 articles in learned jls; *Style*— Prof David Silk; ✉ Department of Gastroenterology and Nutrition, Central Middlesex Hospital, Acton Lane, Park Royal, London NW10 7NS (tel 020 8453 2205, fax 020 8453 2538)

SILK, Dennis Raoul Whitehall; CBE (1995), JP (Oxon 1973); s of Rev Dr Claude Whitehall Silk (d 1974), and Louise Enicita, *née* Dumoret (d 1936); *b* 8 October 1931; *Educ* Christ's Hosp, Sidney Sussex Coll Cambridge (MA, Cricket blues, Rugby Football blues); *m* 6 April 1963, Diana Merilyn, da of William Frank Milton (d 1970), of Taunton, Somerset; 2 da (Katharine b 1964, Alexandra b 1966), 2 s (Thomas b 1967, William b 1970); *Career* housemaster Marlborough Coll 1957–68 (asst master 1955–68), warden Radley Coll 1968–91; dir Imperial War Museum; memb: Ctee MCC 1965–2002 (pres 1992–94), ECB (formerly TCCB) 1984–96 (chm 1994–96); *Books* Cricket for Schools (1964), Attacking Cricket (1965); *Recreations* gardening, fishing, reading; *Clubs* Hawks' (Cambridge), East India Sports, Devonshire; *Style*— Dennis Silk, Esq, CBE; ✉ Sturts Barn, Huntham Lane, Stoke St Gregory, Taunton, Somerset TA3 6EG (tel 01823 490348, fax 01823 490641)

SILLARS, James; s of Matthew Sillars (d 1987), and Agnes, *née* Sproat (d 1942); *b* 4 October 1937; *Educ* Ayr Acad; *Career* mgmnt conslt; MP (Lab 1970–76, SLP 1976–79) S Ayrshire 1970–79, MP (SNP) Glasgow Govan 1988–92; jt fndr Scot Lab Pty 1976, joined SNP 1980 (former dep ldr); asst to Sec-Gen Arab-Br C of C 1993–; memb Scot Enterprise Bd 1996–2002; formerly: railway fireman, radio operator RN, firefighter, Labour Pty official and trade union official, chief exec Scottish Consultants International; *Style*— James Sillars, Esq; ✉ 97 Grange Loan, Edinburgh EH9 2ED (tel 0131 667 6658)

SILLARS, Michael Gordon; s of Derek Gordon Sillars, of Greendales, Nether Silton, Thirsk, North Yorkshire, and Patricia Dora, *née* Lovell; *b* 2 August 1943; *Educ* Forres Sch Rondebosch, Diocesan Coll Rondebosch; *m* 16 June 1973 (dis 1993), Lavinia Charlotte, da of Eric James Fletcher; 2 da (Amanda Louise b 16 July 1976, Emma Charlotte b 23 Nov 1979); m 2, 24 June 2000, Sheila Townsend; *Career* Peat Marwick Mitchell & Co: articled clerk Middlesbrough 1963–69, qualified chartered accountant 1969, London 1970–71, Johannesburg SA 1971–73; Haggie Rand Ltd Johannesburg SA: chief accountant Haggie Rand Industrial Products Ltd 1973–74, fin accountant Haggie Steel Ropes Ltd 1974–75, project accountant Haggie Rand Wire Ltd 1975–77; ptnr: H H Kilvington Chartered Accountants Hartlepool Cleveland 1978–80 (joined 1977), WT Walton & Son Hartlepool (following merger) 1980–87, BDO Binder Hamlyn (following merger) 1987–91, Waltons & Clark Whitehill Waltons (now known as Horwath Clark Whitehill) 1991–; chm Teeside Soc of Chartered Accountants 1989–90; treas Hartlepool div SSAFA 2000; FCA 1979 (ACA 1969); *Recreations* golf, tennis, music, art and drawing, photography; *Style*— Michael Sillars, Esq; ✉ Horwath Clark Whitehill, 40 Victoria Road, Hartlepool, Cleveland (tel 01429 234414)

SILLEY, Jonathan Henry; s of Henry Arthur John Silley, CBE (d 1972), and Betty Stewart, *née* Cotton (d 1981); *b* 2 May 1937; *Educ* Winchester; *m* 17 June 1961, Alison Mary, da of Richard Kenneth May (d 1965), of Purley, Surrey; 3 da (Jennifer Mary b 1964, Jane Elizabeth b 1965, Nichola Anne b 1969); *Career* Nat Serv 1955–57, 2 Lt Queen's Royal Regt; joined Samuel Hodge Gp 1959; dir: Surface Protection 1959–84 (chm 1971–84), E Wood Ltd 1963–84 (chm 1971–84), Hodge Clemco Ltd 1965–2001 (chm 1971–2001), Victor Pyrate Ltd 1965–2001 (chm 1971–2001), S Hodge Ltd 1965–2003 (chm 1971–2003), Hodge Separators Ltd 1976–2001 (chm), Stetfield Ltd 1987–97 (chm), Western Selection plc 1988–91, Teknequip Ltd 1993–2001 (chm), Breconcherry Ltd 1999–2001 (chm); memb HAC 1988; *Recreations* golf, tennis, racquets; *Clubs* City of London; *Style*— Jonathan Silley, Esq; ✉ Oudle House, Much Hadham, Hertfordshire SG10 6BT (tel 01279 842359)

SILLITOE, Alan; s of Christopher Archibald (d 1959), and Sabina Burton (d 1986); *b* 4 March 1928; *Educ* Radford Boulevard Sch Nottingham; *m* 19 Nov 1959, Ruth, da of Leslie Alexander Jonas Fainlight, of Sussex; 1 da (Susan Dawn b 1961), 1 s (David Nimrod b 1962); *Career* air traffic control 1945–46, RAF wireless operator 1946–49; writer 1948–; visiting prof of English de Montfort Univ Leicester 1993–97; Hon Degree: Manchester Poly 1976, Nottingham Poly 1990, Univ of Nottingham 1994, De Montfort Univ; *Books* Saturday Night and Sunday Morning (1958, Authors' Club award 1958, film 1960, play 1964), The Loneliness of the Long Distance Runner (1959, Hawthornden prize, film 1962), Key to the Door (1961), Raw Material (1972), The Widower's Son (1976), The Storyteller (1979), Her Victory (1982), The Lost Flying Boat (1983), The Open Door (1989), Last Loves (1990), Leonard's War (1991), Snowstop (1993), Life Without Armour (autobiography, 1995), Leading the Blind (1995), Collected Stories (1995), Alligator Playground (1997), The Broken Chariot (1998), The German Numbers Woman (1999), Birthday (2001), A Man of His Time (2004), A Flight of Arrows (essays, 2004); poetry collections incl: The Rats and Other Poems (1960), A Falling Out of Love (1964), Snow on the North Side of Lucifer (1979), Tides and Stone Walls (1986), Collected Poems (1993); for children: Marmalade Jim City Adventures (1967), Marmalade Jim at the Farm (1980), Marmalade Jim and the Fox (1985); *Recreations* short wave morse listening, travel, cartography; *Style*— Alan Sillitoe, Esq; ✉ 14 Ladbroke Terrace, London SW11 3PG

SILVER, Clinton Vita; CBE (1993); s of Sidney (Mick) Silver (d 1973), of London, and Mina, *née* Gabriel (d 1980); *b* 26 September 1929; *Educ* Upton House Sch, City of London Coll, Univ of Southampton (BSc(Econ)); *m* 1973, Patricia Ann (Jill), da of John Vernon (d 1958); 1 s (Michael John b 1974), 1 da (Suzy Jane b 1978); *Career* Nat Serv 1950–52; Marks and Spencer plc: joined 1952, alternate dir 1974–78, dir 1978–94, md 1990–94, dep chm 1991–94; chm Br Fashion Cncl 1994–97; non-exec dir: Hillsdown Holdings plc 1994–98, Tommy Hilfiger Corp 1994–2006, Pentland Group plc 1994–99; patron Devpt Bd Univ of Southampton; Hon DLitt Univ of Southampton 1997; CCMI, Companion Textile Inst, FRSA 1994; *Recreations* family, garden, music; *Clubs* Athenaeum, Phyllis Court; *Style*— Clinton Silver, Esq, CBE

SILVER, Prof Ian Adair; s of Capt George James Silver (d 1937), and Nora Adair, *née* Seckham (d 1979); *b* 28 December 1927; *Educ* Rugby, CCC Cambridge (MA), Royal Vet Coll London (FRCVS); *m* 1, 30 June 1950, Marian (d 1994), da of Dr Frederick John Scrase (d 1981); 2 da (Alison b 1956 (who m Andrew Lorimer Hunter, *qv*), Fiona (Mrs Rainer Grün) b 1959), 2 s (Alastair b 1960, Angus b 1963); m 2, 6 May 1996, Maria, da of Prof Kazimierz Erecinski (d 1980); *Career* RN 'Y' Scheme 1945, Cambridge Univ, trans to Tech and Scientific Regt 1948; Univ of Cambridge: demonstrator in zoology 1952–57, lectr in anatomy 1957–70, fell and sr grad tutor Churchill Coll 1965–70; Univ of Bristol: prof of comparative pathology 1970–81, prof and chm Dept of Pathology and Microbiology 1981–93 (emeritus prof of pathology 1993–), dean Faculty of Med 1987–90, sr research fell 1995–; prof of neurology Univ of Pennsylvania 1977–2006; visiting prof: Louisiana Tech Univ 1973, Cayetana Heredia Univ Lima 1976, Royal Soc prof Federal Univ Rio de Janeiro 1977; chm: Inst of Clinical Neurosciences 2000–, Burden Neurological Inst 2006–; chm Southmead Health Servs NHS Tst 1992–99 (non-exec dir 1991–92); memb Research Cncl Ctees: MRC, SERC, AFRC, ARC; chm Laminitis Tst 2002–; pres: RCVS 1985–86 and 1987, Int Soc for Study of O Transport to Tissue 1977 and 1986; *Books* edited 7 scientific books, published over 200 learned papers; *Recreations* exploration, DIY, fishing; *Style*— Prof Ian Silver; ✉ c/o Department of Anatomy, School of Veterinary Science, Southwell Street, University of Bristol, Bristol BS2 8EJ (tel 0117 928 8362, fax 0117 925 4794, e-mail ian.a.silver@bris.ac.uk)

SILVERMAN, Prof Bernard Walter; s of Elias Silverman, of London, and Helen, *née* Korn (d 1989); *b* 22 February 1952; *Educ* City of London Sch, Univ of Cambridge (MA, PhD, ScD); *m* 9 March 1985, Dr Rowena Fowler; 1 s (Matthew b 1989); *Career* res fell Jesus Coll Cambridge 1975–77, devpt mangr Sinclair Radionics Ltd 1976–77, lectr Univ of Oxford 1977–78; Univ of Bath: lectr 1978–80, reader 1981–84, prof of statistics 1984–93, head Sch of Mathematical Sciences 1988–91; Univ of Bristol: prof of statistics 1993–2003, Henry Overton Wills prof of mathematics 1999–2003, provost Inst for Advanced Studies 2000–03, prof emeritus 2003; master St Peter's Coll Oxford 2003–; ed International Statistical Review 1991–94, ed Annals of Statistics 2007–, author of over one hundred papers in jls; Chartered Statistician; hon sec Royal Statistical Soc 1984–90, pres Inst of Mathematical Statistics USA 2000–01; chair: Jt Mathematical Cncl of the UK 2003–06, UK Mathematics Tst 2004–, Peer Review Panel Dept for Tport Project for the Sustainable Devpt of Heathrow 2005–06, Statistics Panel HEFCE Research Assessment Exercise 2005–; non-exec dir Defence Analytical Services Agency 2003–, memb Govt GM Science Review Panel 2002–03; Guy Medal in Bronze Royal Statistical Soc 1984, President's Award Ctee of Presidents of Statistical Socs USA 1991, Guy Medal in Silver Royal Statistical Soc 1995; ordained C of E: deacon 1999, priest 2000; assoc parish priest St Paul's Clifton and St Mary's Cotham 2003–05 (curate 1999–2003), proctor in convocation (Gen Synod) 2000–03, licence to officiate Dio of Oxford 2005–; hon fell Jesus Coll Cambridge 2003; FRS 1997, Academia Europea 2001; *Books* Density Estimation for Statistics and Data Analysis (1986), Nonparametric Regression and Generalized Linear Models (with P J Green, 1994), Functional Data Analysis (with J O Ramsay, 1997, 2 edn 2006), Applied Functional Data Analysis (jtly, 2002); *Clubs* Cwlth, Oxford and Cambridge; *Style*— Prof Bernard Silverman, FRS; ✉ St Peter's College, New Inn Hall Street, Oxford OX1 2DL

SILVERMAN, Prof (Hugh) Richard; OBE (2000); s of S G Silverman (d 1985), and N E Silverman, of New South Wales; *b* 23 September 1940; *Educ* Brighton Coll of Art and Craft (DipArch), Univ of Edinburgh (MSc); *m* 24 Feb 1963, Aase Kay, da of Knud Sonderskov Madsen; 2 da (Jennifer Solvej b 24 April 1971, Sophia Annelise b 23 Nov 1974); *Career* dir Alec French Partnership (Architects) Bristol 1984–86, head The Welsh

Sch of Architecture Cardiff 1986–97; memb: Bd Cardiff Bay Devpt Corp 1990–2000 (chm Devpt Advsy Panel); dir Edward Ware Homes Ltd 2002–04; dir Under The Sky Urban Renewal; emeritus prof Univ of Cardiff 2001–; ARIBA 1965, FRSA 1989; *Style*— Prof Richard Silverman

SILVESTER, Simon Charles Arthur; *b* 25 January 1962; *Educ* The King's Sch Chester, Trinity Hall Cambridge (MA, ed Cantab magazine); *Career* account planner Boase Massimi Pollitt 1983–87, copywriter Delaney Fletcher Delaney 1987–89, sr planner Gold Greenlees Trott 1989–90; planning dir: Burkitt Weinreich Bryant 1990–95; md Silvester Research 1996–98, global planning dir Ammirati Puris Lintas 1998–2000, head of planning McCann Erickson Germany 2000–02, exec planning dir Young and Rubicam EMEA 2002–; awards: Merit NY One Show 1988, Silver ILR Radio Awards 1988, Pyramid Epica Awards 1988, Merit Euro Awards 1988, WPP Atticus prizes 2003, 2004 and 2005; memb: MRS 1983, Mktg Soc 1992; *Publications* Spoilt Brats (1990), Invasion of Essex Men (1991), Eurokids - The Single Youth of the Single Market (1992), Is Research Killing Advertising? (1992), World Waves (1997), So You Think You Have a Global Brand? (2002), You're Getting Old (2002), How to Become an Icon (2003), Service With a Snarl (2004), Spam (2005), All You Need is Envy (2005), My Brain Hurts (2006); *Recreations* travel, art; *Style*— Simon Silvester, Esq; ✉ e-mail simonsilvester@hotmail.com, website www.silvester.com

SIM, Prof Edith; da of Joseph Dunbar Strachan, and Edith Mary Hay, *née* Pont; *Educ* Morgan Acad Dundee, Univ of Edinburgh (BSc), Univ of Oxford (DPhil); *Career* Centre d'Etudes Nucleaires 1976–78, fell Royal Soc European Exchange Grenoble; Univ of Oxford: demonstrator Dept of Biochemistry 1978–83, Florey res fell LMH 1981–84, fell in biochemistry St Peter's Coll 1990, Wellcome sr lectr Dept of Pharmacology 1983–99, head Dept of Pharmacology 1999–2005, dir of grad trg Div of Medical Sciences 2006–; SAC Arthritis and Rheumatism Cncl 1985–9; memb: Biochemical Soc 1976, Br Biophysical Soc 1978, BSI 1979, Br Toxicology Soc 1983, Int Soc for the Study of Xenobiotics (ISSX) 2000, Br Pharmacological Soc 2000, RSM 2007; MCMB memb MRC 2004; *Publications* Biological Membranes (1982), Humoral Factors in Natural Immunity (ed, 1993); over 100 res articles in learned jls; *Recreations* gardening, dancing; *Style*— Prof Edith Sim; ✉ Department of Pharmacology, Mansfield Road, Oxford OX1 3QT (tel 01865 271884, e-mail edith.sim@pharm.ox.ac.uk)

SIMEON, Prof (Sir) Richard Edmund Barrington; 8 Bt (UK 1815), of Grazeley, Berks (but does not use title); s and h of Sir John Simeon, 7 Bt, by his w, Anne Mary Dean; *b* 2 March 1943; *Educ* St George's Sch Vancouver, Univ of Br Columbia (BA), Yale Univ (MA, PhD); *m* 1, 6 Aug 1966 (m dis 1989), Agnes Joan, o da of George Frederick Weld; 1 s (Stephen George Barrington b 1970), 1 da (Rachel Elizabeth b 1973); m 2, 17 April 1993, Maryetta, da of Edward John Cheney; *Heir* s, Stephen Simeon; *Career* Queen's Univ Kingston Canada: prof Dept of Political Studies 1968–91, dir Inst of Intergovernmental Relations 1976–83, dir Sch of Public Admin 1986–91; prof of political sci and law Univ of Toronto 1991–, William Lyon Mackenzie King visiting prof of Canadian studies Harvard Univ 1998 and 2006–08; res co-ordinator Royal Cmmn on the Economic Union and Canada's Devpt Prospects 1983–85, vice-chm Ontario Law Reform Cmmn 1989–95; FRSC 2004; *Books* Federal-Provincial Diplomacy (1972, reissued 2006), Federalism and the Economic Union (with K Norrie and M Krasnick, 1985), Politics of Constitutional Change (ed with Keith Banting, 1984), State, Society and the Development of Canadian Federalism (with Ian Robinson, 1990), In Search of a Social Contract (1994), Rethinking the Federal Idea: Citizens, Politics and Markets (ed with K Knop, S Ostry and K Swinton, 1995), Degrees of Difference: Canada and the United States in a Changing World (with K Banting and G Hoberg, 1996); *Style*— Prof Richard Simeon; ✉ Department of Political Science, University of Toronto, Toronto, Ontario, Canada M5S 1A1 (tel 00 1 416 978 3346, fax 00 1 416 978 5566, e-mail rsimeon@chass.utoronto.ca and rsimeon@wcfia.harvard.edu)

SIMKIN, (Richard) Graham; s of Frederick Simkin (d 1986), and Edna, *née* Turner; *b* 14 July 1952; *Educ* Univ of Leeds (LLB); *Children* 3 da (Elizabeth b 1980, Sarah b 1981, Rachel b 1986), 1 s (Matthew b 1989); *Career* slr; ptnr Boodle Hatfield 1978–90, chief exec Terre Armée Group 1994–98 (dep chief exec 1990–93), ptnr Richards Butler 1999–2004, ptnr Fulbright & Jaworski International LLP 2004–; memb Law Soc 1976; *Recreations* theatre, photography; *Style*— Graham Simkin, Esq; ✉ Fulbright & Jaworski International LLP, 90 Long Acre, London WC2 (tel 020 7010 8307, mobile 07768 278089, e-mail gsimkin@fulbright.com)

SIMM, John; eld s of Ronald James Simm, and Brenda Lily, *née* Chamberlain; *b* 10 July 1970; *Educ* Edge End HS, Blackpool and Fylde Coll of Further and Higher Educn, Drama Centre London (Dip); *Children* 1 s (Ryan John Magowan b 13 Aug 2001); *Career* actor; *Theatre* Goldhawk Road (Bush Theatre), Danny Rule (Royal Court); *Television* Rumpole of the Bailey, Men of the World, Chillers - The Mirror Man, Meat, Cracker, The Lakes (two series), Forgive and Forget, Never Never, Crime and Punishment, State of Play, Canterbury Tales: The Knight's Tale, Sex Traffic, Life on Mars (two series); *Films* Understanding Jane, Diana & Me, Boston Kickout (Best Actor Valencia Film Festival 1995), Human Traffic, Wonderland, 24 Hour Party People, Miranda, Blue/Orange, Devilwood; *Recreations* music, football (Manchester United); *Clubs* Century; *Style*— John Simm, Esq; ✉ c/o Harriet Robinson, ICM, Oxford House, 76 Oxford Street, London W1D 1BS (tel 020 7636 6565, fax 020 7323 0101)

SIMM, Dr Robert James (Bob); s of Alfred Simm (d 1992), of Manchester, and Vera, *née* Lowe (d 2003); *b* 2 March 1948; *Educ* St John's Coll, Lancaster Univ, Univ of Oxford, Cranfield Univ, INSEAD; *m* 7 May 1977 (m dis 1995), Sally Elizabeth, da of Edward McNamara; 2 s (Richard James Alfred b 5 Jan 1982, James Edward Alexander b 26 April 1984), 1 da (Katherine Elizabeth Jane b 4 April 1989); *Career* Marks and Spencer plc: grad trainee 1971–74, Head Office 1974–75, head Store Mgmnt Trg 1975–77; sr mangr Price Waterhouse 1977–84; KPMG Peat Marwick: head Human Resources 1984–85, ptnr 1985–94, chm Int Human Resources Steering Ctee 1986–91, sr ptnr Mgmnt Consltg 1990, memb Bd 1991, chm UK Mgmnt Consltg 1993–94; chm Harley St Medical Ltd; art conslt; Inst of Mgmnt Conslts: chm UK Professional Devpt Ctee 1988–90 (London Regnl Ctee 1985–88), memb Cncl; memb Cncl Mgmnt Conslts Assoc, memb Devpt Ctee Nat Portrait Gallery; MITD 1974, master of Transactional Analysis 1975, FIMC 1985, ACA 1991, FRSA 1992; nominated: Man of the Year American Biographical Institute (listed in pubn Great Minds of the 21st Century), International Peace Prize Consulate of the United Cultural Convention General-in-Residence; *Recreations* collecting and sponsoring art; *Style*— Dr Bob Simm; ✉ 77 Greenhill, Prince Arthur Road, London NW3 5TZ (tel 020 7431 8335, mobile 07968 797243)

SIMMERS, Graeme Maxwell; CBE (1998, OBE 1982); s of William Maxwell Simmers (the Scottish rugby int, d 1972), and Gwenyth Reinagle, *née* Sterry (Wightman Cup tennis champion); gm Mrs C R Sterry, *née* Cooper (5 times Wimbledon tennis champion); *b* 2 May 1935; *Educ* Glasgow Acad, Loretto; *m* 10 Sept 1965, Jennifer Margaret Hunter, da of William Roxburgh, OBE, of Fife; 2 s (Mark William b 1967, Peter Hunter Maxwell b 1973), 2 da (Corinne Charlotte b 1969, Kirstin Margaret b 1970); *Career* Nat Serv Lt RM 1959–61; CA 1959, ptnr Kidson Simmers 1959–88, chm Scottish Highland Hotels Group Ltd 1972–92, non-exec Forth Valley Health Bd 2002–; chm Hotel and Catering Benevolent Assoc Scotland 1984–87; memb: Scottish Tourist Bd 1979–86, Nat Exec Br Hospitality Assoc 1991–97; chm Championship Ctee Royal and Ancient Golf Club 1988–91, govr The Queen's Coll Glasgow 1989–93, chm Scottish Sports Cncl 1992–99; chm of govrs Loretto Sch, elder and treas of Killearn Kirk; memb Ct Univ of Stirling 2001–; Hon Col RMR Scotland 2000–06; *Recreations* golf, tennis, skiing; *Clubs* Royal & Ancient (capt 2001–02), All England Lawn Tennis; *Style*— Graeme M Simmers, Esq, CBE; ✉ Kincaple, Boquhan, Balfron, Glasgow G63 0RW (tel 01360 440375, fax 01360 440985)

SIMMONDS, Adam Christopher; s of George Simmonds, of Leighton Buzzard, Beds, and Christine, *née* White; *b* 12 February 1971, Welwyn Garden City, Herts; *Educ* Vandyke Upper Sch Leighton Buzzard, Barnfield Catering Coll Beds; *Career* chef; FortySeven Park Street London 1989, Halkin Hotel London 1990–91, Ritz Hotel London and Ritz Carlton Colorado USA 1991–92, demi chef then chef de partie The Lanesbrough London 1992–94 and Les Saveurs London 1994–95, jr sous chef L'Escargot London 1995–96, sous chef Jean-Christophe Novelli de Les Saveurs London 1996–97 and Heathcote's Longridge 1997–98, successively chef de partie, sr chef de partie and jr sous chef Le Manoir aux Quat Saisons 1998–2001, head chef The Greenway 2001–02 (3 AA Rosettes), head chef Ynyshir Hall Powys 2003–07 (1 Michelin Star 2006, 4 AA Rosettes, 2 Egon Ronay Stars, 8 out of 10 Good Food Guide), head chef Oak Room Restuarant Danesfield House Hotel 2007–; nat winner Chaine des Rotisseurs competition 1995, Br Meat Chef of the Year 1998, Gold medal class winner Hospitality Week cook and serve 1999, runner up Cotswold Chef of the Year 2003; *Recreations* snowboarding, scuba diving, football; *Style*— Adam Simmonds, Esq; ✉ Danesfield House Hotel and Spa, Henley Road, Marlow-on-Thames, Buckinghamshire SL7 2EY (tel 01628 891010, website www.danesfieldhouse.co.uk)

SIMMONDS, Andrew John; QC (1999); s of Ernest Simmonds (d 1992), and Sybil Vera Erica Allen, *née* Hedley; *b* 9 May 1957; *Educ* Sevenoaks Sch, St John's Coll Cambridge (MA), Coll of Law (Astbury scholar of the Middle Temple); *m* 15 Aug 1981, Kathleen Claire, da of David Moyse; 1 da (Imogen Ria Hedley b 23 July 1994); *Career* called to the Bar 1980; practising barr specialising in contentious pensions and professional negligence litigation, dep High Court judge 2006–; memb Pension Litigation Court Users Ctee; *Recreations* skiing, running; *Style*— Andrew Simmonds, Esq, QC; ✉ 5 Stone Buildings, Lincoln's Inn, London WC2A 3XT (tel 020 7242 6201, fax 020 7831 8102)

SIMMONDS, Andrew Keith John (Andy); s of Reginald Arthur Simmonds (d 1989), and Hilda Violet, *née* Hunnisett; *b* 10 August 1952; *Educ* Rye GS, Univ of Manchester (BSc); *m* 1978, Janet, da of A Stanley Hore; 2 da (Beth b 1981, Laura b 1984); *Career* articled clerk Deloitte & Co CAs 1973–77, sr lectr Accountancy Tuition Centre 1977–85 (lectr in financial accounting 1977–80), princ Tech Dept Touche Ross (now Deloitte & Touche) 1985–, ptnr Deloitte & Touche 1999–; memb Accounting Standards Bd 2007–; ICAEW: chm Fin Reporting Ctee, memb Urgent Issues Task Force until 2007; FCA (ACA 1977); *Books* Mastering Financial Accounting (Macmillan, 1986), Accounting for Europe (Touche Ross, 1989), Accountants Digest: Accounting for Subsidiary Undertakings (Accountancy Books, 1992), FRS 9 - A Practical Guide (1999); *Recreations* music, golf; *Style*— Andy Simmonds, Esq; ✉ Deloitte & Touche, Hill House, 1 Little New Street, London EC4A 3TR (tel 020 7303 4605, fax 020 7353 9820, e-mail asimmonds@deloitte.co.uk)

SIMMONDS, Prof Kenneth; s of Herbert Marshall Simmonds, and Margaret, *née* Trevurza; *b* 17 February 1935; *Educ* Univ of NZ (BCom, MCom), Harvard Univ (DBA), LSE (PhD), Univ of de Deusto Spain (MGCE), JDipMA; *m* 19 June 1960, Nancy Miriam, *née* Bunai; 2 s (John, Peter), 1 da (Jane); *Career* clerk Guardian Trust Co Wellington 1950–53, asst co sec Gordon & Gotch Ltd Wellington 1953–55, chief accountant William Cable Ltd Wellington 1955–59; conslt: Arthur D Little Inc Cambridge Mass 1959–60, Harbridge House Inc Boston 1962–64; sr lectr Cranfield Inst of Tech 1963–64, asst prof of int business Indiana Univ Bloomington 1964–66, prof of mktg Univ of Manchester 1966–69, Ford Fndn prof of int business Univ of Chicago 1974–75, prof of mktg and int business London Business Sch 1969–2000 (emeritus prof 2000–), fell Saïd Business Sch Univ of Oxford 2002–; mktg advsr International Publishing Corp 1967–78; dir: British Steel Corp 1970–72, Redpath Dorman Long Ltd 1972–74, EMAP plc 1981–96, MIL Research Gp plc 1986–89, Aerostructures Hamble Ltd 1990–92, Enviros Ltd 1996–98, Diagnology Ltd 1997–2000, Manor House Gp Ltd 1997–; chm Planners Collaborative 1985–88; govr London Business Sch 1980–86, chm London Business Gp 1988–91, chief ed Int Jl of Advertising 1982–96; Chartered Inst of Mktg: memb senate 1994–, vice-dean 1996–; memb: Textile Cncl UK 1968–70, Ctee Social Science Res Cncl UK 1971–72, Ctee CBI 1971–74, Electrical Engrg Econ Devpt Ctee UK 1982–86; fell: Inst of CAs NZ, NZ Inst of Cost and Mgmnt Accountants, Acad of Int Business, Acad of Mktg; FCIS, FCMA, FCIM; *Books* International Business and Multinational Enterprises (1973, 4 edn 1989), Case Problems in Marketing (1973), Strategy and Marketing (1982, 2 edn 1986), Short Cases in Marketing (1987); *Style*— Prof Kenneth Simmonds; ✉ London Business School, Regents Park, London NW1 4SA (tel 020 7262 5050, e-mail ksimmonds@london.edu)

SIMMONDS, Mark Jonathan Mortlock; MP; s of Neil Mortlock Simmonds, and Mary Griffith, *née* Morgan; *b* 12 April 1964; *Educ* Worksop Coll, Trent Poly (BSc); *m* 1994, Lizbeth Josefina, *née* Hanomancin-Garcia; 3 c; *Career* surveyor Savills 1986–88, ptnr Strutt and Parker 1988–96, dir Hillier Parker 1997–99, chm Mortlock Simmonds Brown 1999–; memb Wandsworth BC 1990–94 (chm Property Ctee 1991–92, chm Housing Ctee 1992–94); Parly candidate (Cons) Ashfield 1997, MP (Cons) Boston and Skegness 2001–; PPS to Michael Ancram QC MP, *qv*; sec All-Pty Latin America Gp 2001–; memb Select Ctee on Educn and Skills 2001–03, shadow min for educn 2003–04, shadow min for foreign affrs 2004–05, shadow min for int devpt 2005–07, shadow min for health 2007–; Bow Gp: memb, chair Foreign Affrs Ctee 1993–94, memb Housing Gp reporting to PM on Housing Policy; memb Putney Cons Assoc 1990– (vice-chm (Political) 1995–); MRICS 1987; *Recreations* family, rugby, tennis, hockey, history, reading; *Clubs* Naval and Military; *Style*— Mark Simmonds, Esq, MP; ✉ House of Commons, London SW1A 0AA (tel 020 7219 6254, fax 020 7219 1746, e-mail simmondsm@parliament.uk)

SIMMONDS, Richard James; CBE (1996); s of Reginald A C Simmonds, and Betty, *née* Cahusac; sis Posy Simmonds the illustrator and cartoonist; *b* 1944; *m* 1967, Mary, *née* Stewart; 1 s, 2 da; *Career* nat vice-chm Young Cons 1973–75, fndr vice-chm Young Euro Democrats 1974; PA to Rt Hon Edward Heath, MBE, MP 1973–75, PPS to Sir James Scott-Hopkins as Ldr EDG 1979–82; MEP (EPP): Midlands West 1979–84, Wight and Hampshire East 1984–94; memb: Agric and Budget Control Ctees, Environment, Public Health & Consumer Protection Ctee; spokesman: Youth and Educn 1982–84, Budget Control 1984–87; Br whip 1987–89, chief whip 1992–94; chm The Countryside Cmmn 1995–99, advsr to European Cmmn 1996–, chm Ind Tport Cmmn 1999–2001; chm London and Economic Properties 2002–, pres A > B Global Inc 2004; memb Berkshire CC (chm 4 ctees) 1972–79; chm Bd of Govrs Berks Coll of Agric 1979–91, fndr pres Mounted Games Assoc 1984–, travelling fell Waitangi Fndn 1995–96, memb Cncl PDSA 1995–2001, pres Jersey Cattle Soc 1997; fell Parl and Indust Tst (attached to Marks and Spencer and DuPont International); *Publications* The Common Agricultural Policy, A Sad Misnomer (1979), A to Z of Myths and Misunderstandings of EEC (1981, 1988 and 1992), World Hunger - The European Community's Response (1981), European Parliament Report on Farm Animal Welfare (1985, 1987 and 1990), The Production, Processing, Politics and Potential of New Zealand Meat (1996), The Cork Declaration on CAP Reform (co-author, 1996); *Recreations* resisting bureaucracy, getting things done; *Clubs* Ancient Britons, OPB Sailing (hon cdre 1998–); *Style*— Richard Simmonds, Esq, CBE; ✉ Dyars, Cookham Dean, Berkshire SL6 9PJ

SIMMONS, His Hon Judge Alan Gerald; s of Maurice Simmons (d 1949), of Bedford, and Sophie, *née* Lasserson (d 1952); *b* 7 September 1936; *Educ* Bedford Modern and Quintin Sch; *m* 26 Nov 1961, Mia, da of Emanuel Rosenstein (d 1957), and Lisa, *née* Rinsler (d

1981); 1 s (Richard b 1964), 1 da (Joanne b 1966); *Career* Nat Serv RAF 1956–58; dir: Aslon Laboratories Ltd, Record Productions (Surrey) Ltd, Ashcourt Ltd; called to the Bar Gray's Inn 1968 (Holker sr exhbn, Lee essay prize); recorder 1989 (asst recorder 1985), circuit judge (SE Circuit) 1990–; memb Mental Health Review Tbnl; memb Bd of Deps of Br Jews 1982–88, former memb Cncl of United Synagogue; *Recreations* music, reading, formerly fencing; *Style*— His Hon Judge Simmons; ✉ South Eastern Circuit Office, New Cavendish House, 18 Maltravers Street, London WC2R 3EU (tel 020 7936 7235)

SIMMONS, Allan Frank; s of Michael Philip Simmons (d 1971), and Elda Dineen, *née* Malpas; *b* 7 June 1943; *Educ* Bournemouth Sch for Boys; *m* 9 Sept 1967, Elizabeth Ann, da of Edwin Waring Mathison; 2 s (Jonathan Michael Harman b 9 May 1973, Alexander Waring b 3 June 1975), 1 da (Katie Ann b 14 April 1980); *Career* Malpas Simmons (merged with Smith and Williamson CAs 1987): trainee 1959, ptnr 1969–2003; High Sheriff Dorset 2004–05; *Recreations* sailing, walking, reading; *Clubs* Poole Yacht, Farmers; *Style*— Allan Simmons, Esq; ✉ 4 Branksome Grange, Lakeside Road, Poole, Dorset BH13 6LR (e-mail allan_simmons@fastmail.fm)

SIMMONS, Marion Adèle; QC (1994); da of Sidney Simmons (d 1983), of London, and Bella, *née* Byer (d 2003); *b* 11 April 1949; *Educ* Hendon County GS, QMC London (LLB, LLM); *Career* called to the Bar Gray's Inn 1970 (bencher 1993); recorder 1998– (asst recorder 1990–98); memb Mental Health Review Tbnl (restricted panel) 2000–, pt/t chm Competition Appeal Tbnl 2003–; asst boundary cmmr 2000–; vice-chm Appeal Ctee ICAEW 2000–05, memb Panel of Chairmen Accountancy Investigation and Disciplinary Bd 2005–, chm Disciplinary Ctee Taxation Disciplinary Bd 2005–; memb RSM; *Clubs* Athenaeum; *Style*— Miss Marion Simmons, QC; ✉ 3–4 South Square, Gray's Inn, London WC1R 5HP (tel 020 7696 9900, fax 020 7696 9911)

SIMMONS, Richard John; CBE (1995); s of John Eric Simmons, and Joy Mary, *née* Foat; *b* 2 June 1947; *Educ* Moseley GS Birmingham, LSE (BSc Econ), Univ of Calif Berkeley Business Sch; *m* 23 April 1983, Veronica, da of Richard Sinkins; 1 s, 1 da; *Career* chartered accountant; asst sec to IASC 1973–75, sr ptnr Arthur Andersen 1996–2001; dir The Constable Educational Trust Ltd 2003–; chm: BDP Media Gp Ltd 2002–, Chameleon Nursery Ltd 2002–; non-exec dir: Cranfield Info Technol Inst 1987–89, Westminster Forum Ltd 1999–; advsr Oxford Resources 2002–04; tstee Fndn for Social and Economic Thinking 2003–; memb: Devpt Bd Royal Acad of Arts 1990–2002, Shadow National Accounts Cmmn 2000–01, Bd of Treasurers Cons Pty 2001–03; hon treas Political Ctee Carlton Club 1992–2001; chm Bow Gp 1980–81 (tstee); chm and govr Moat Sch; FCA 1971, FRSA; *Recreations* horse racing, tennis, gardening; *Style*— Richard Simmons, Esq, CBE; ✉ BDP Media, The Leathermarket, Weston Street, London SE1 3ER (tel 020 7848 4781, e-mail richardsimmons@bdpmedia.com)

SIMMONS, Prof Robert Malcolm (Bob); s of Stanley Laurence (d 1982), and Marjorie, *née* Amys (d 1988); *b* 23 January 1938; *Educ* Brighton Coll, KCL (BSc), Royal Inst London (PhD), UCL (MSc); *m* 1967, Mary Ann (Anna), da of Archibald Denison Ross (decd); 1 da (Rebecca b 1968), 1 s (Nicholas b 1970); *Career* UCL: Sharpey scholar Dept of Physiology 1967–70, lectr 1970–79, MRC research fell 1979–81; KCL: MRC staff scientist 1981–83, prof of biophysics 1983–2002, hon dir MRC Muscle & Cell Motility Unit 1990–2002, dir Randall Centre for Molecular Mechanisms of Cell Function 1999–2002, emeritus prof 2002–; memb: Physiological Soc, Br Biophysical Soc; FRS 1995, FKC 1997, FIBiol 1999; *Recreations* music, fishing; *Style*— Prof Robert Simmons, FRS; ✉ Edmunds Ground, Woodborough Road, Pewsey, Wiltshire SN9 5NH

SIMMS, Alan John Gordon; s of Edward Gordon Clark, formerly Januszkiewiscz (d 1981), of Aigburth, Liverpool, and Hilda Mary, *née* Gordon; *b* 3 April 1954; *Educ* Liverpool Collegiate GS, Univ of London (LLB, MA, BL); *m* 2 Aug 1980, Julia Jane, da of Paul Ferguson, of Leintwardine, Salop; 2 c (Jack Edward Paul Januszkiewiscz, Charlotte Jane Januszkiewiscz (twins) b 28 Feb 1996); *Career* called to the Bar: Lincoln's Inn 1976, King's Inn 2002; ad eundum Northern Circuit 1980–; memb Criminal Bar Assoc; sec Inst of Advanced Motorists 1986–88, chm RoSPA Chester (RoSPA Advanced Drivers Assoc Class One and Diploma holder), memb's rep Nat Exec Ctee RoSPA, legal memb Mental Health Review Tbnl 1994–; univ external examiner in forensic sci 1998–; advocacy tutor Northern Circuit; memb: Br Motor Racing Marshals Club, Br Automobile Racing Club (Oulton Park), Hon Soc of Lincoln's Inn 1976, Br Acad of Forensic Sci 1978, Bar Assoc of Commerce Fin and Industry 1980, Br Psychological Soc 1994, Forensic Sci Soc 1995, Philological Soc 1996, Hon Soc of King's Inn 2002, RUSI; qualified memb London Chauffeurs Guild; assoc fell Soc of Advanced Legal Studies 2001; *Recreations* reading, motor racing, motor racing marshalling, road safety, blues and jazz music, guitar playing, chess, crime (theory only); *Style*— Alan Simms, Esq; ✉ Chavasse Court Chambers, 2nd Floor, Chavasse Court, 24 Lord Street, Liverpool (tel 0151 707 1191, e-mail clerks@chavassecounsel.plus.com)

SIMMS, (Dr) Brendan Peter; s of David John Simms, of Dublin, and Anngret, *née* Erichson; *b* 3 September 1967; *Educ* St Kilian's German Sch Dublin, Heinrich-Hertz Gymnasium Bonn, Trinity Coll Dublin (scholar, Gold medal), Univ of Tübingen, Peterhouse Cambridge; *m* 3 Sept 1993, Anita Mary, da of Richard John Bunyan; 1 da (Constance Maria b 21 April 1998), 1 s (Hugh Edward b 10 June 2002); *Career* res fell ChCh Oxford 1992–93; fell and dir of studies in history Peterhouse Cambridge 1993– (admissions tutor (humanities) 1997–2002); Newton Sheehy teaching fell in int rels Univ of Cambridge Centre of Int Studies 1998–; tstee Bosnian Inst London 1998–, memb Exec Ctee Br Irish Assoc 1998–2002, memb Editorial Bd German History; *Books* The Impact of Napoleon (1997), The Struggle for Mastery in Germany, 1780–1850 (1998), Unfinest Hour: Britain and the Destruction of Bosnia (2001); *Recreations* hill walking, football; *Style*— Brendan Simms; ✉ Peterhouse, Cambridge CB2 1RD (tel 01223 338200, fax 01223 337578)

SIMMS, Sir Neville Ian; kt (1998); *Educ* Univ of Newcastle upon Tyne (BSc), Univ of Glasgow (MEng); *Career* structural engr Ove Arup and Partners 1966–69, with AM Carmichael Ltd Edinburgh 1969–70; Tarmac Gp: joined 1970, chief exec Tarmac Construction Ltd 1988–92, dir Bd Tarmac plc 1988–99, gp chief exec Tarmac plc 1992–99, dep chm Tarmac plc 1994–99; chm: Carillion plc 1999–2005, International Power plc 2000–; non-exec dir: Bank of England 1995–2002, National Power plc 1998–2000; currently: co-chm Transmanche Link, operating ptnr Duke St Capital; memb Pres's Ctee CBI 1996–, Business Advsy Panel Trade Partners UK 2001–03; chm: Balsall Heath Birmingham Employers Forum 1994–97, Regnl Leadership Team Business in the Community West Midlands 1998–2001, Regnl Leadership Team Business in the Community Solent 2005–; former chm National Contractors Gp; former memb: Overseas Project Bd DTI, Chancellor of Exchequer's Private Finance Panel 1993–97; chm Bretrust 2005–; govr: Stafford GS 1998–2004, Ashridge Mgmnt Coll 2000–; former govr Brooklands Sch Stafford; Hon DTech Univ of Wolverhampton 1997, Dr (hc) Univ of Edinburgh 2000, Hon DEng Univ of Glasgow 2001; MIHT, CIMgt, FICE, FCIBS, FREng; *Style*— Sir Neville Simms, FREng

SIMON, Anthony J B; s of John Murray Simon, of Ide Hill, Kent, and Sheila Beatrice Simon; *b* 26 April 1945, Fulmer, Berks; *Educ* Westminster, The Queen's Coll Oxford (MA), INSEAD (MBA); *m* 9 Feb 1974, Maja Brita Mechelsen; 1 da (Antonia b 10 Nov 1974), 1 s (Carl-Michael b 1 May 1976); *Career* Bowater Paper Corp 1966–67, various roles latterly corp offr responsible for global strategy and global core businesses CPC International Inc (latterly Bestfoods) 1968–2000, pres mktg and memb Foods Div Bd Unilever Bestfoods 2000–04; memb Bd Huhtamaki; sr advsr to World Business Cncl for Sustainable Devpt, memb Bd INSEAD Sustainability Activities; occasional lectr on

business in Europe, integrated mktg, brands, future of the food industry and the role of business in tomorrow's soc; friend UN Fndn, participant Clinton Global Initiative; *Recreations* summer house in Sweden, golf, dabbling in the "Brussels scene" as an engaged global European; *Style*— Anthony Simon, Esq; ✉ Avenue du Golf 61, B-1640 Rhode-St-Genese, Belgium (tel 00 32 478 21 70 63, fax 00 32 23 58 50 99, e-mail simon.anthony@skynet.be); Sweden (fax 00 46 431 36 32 99)

SIMON, 3 Viscount (UK 1940); Jan David Simon; s of 2 Viscount Simon, CMG (d 1993); *b* 20 July 1940; *Educ* Westminster, Dept of Navigation Univ of Southampton, Sydney Tech Coll; *m* 26 April 1969, Mary Elizabeth, da of late John J Burns (d 1966), of Sydney, NSW; 1 da (Fiona Elizabeth b 1971); *Heir* none; *Career* dep chm ctees House of Lords 1998–, dep speaker House of Lords 1999–; memb Select Ctee on: Procedure of the House of Lords 1999–2002, Personal Bills 2004–, Standing Orders (Private Bills) 2004–; *Style*— The Viscount Simon; ✉ House of Lords, London SW1A 0PW (tel 020 7219 5353)

SIMON, Josette; OBE (2000); da of Charles Simon, of Leicester, and Eileen, *née* Petty; *Educ* Alderman Newton's GS for Girls, Central Sch of Speech Training and Dramatic Art; *m* 27 Oct 1996, Mark Padmore; 1 da (Maisie b Sept 2000); *Career* actress; Hon MA Univ of Leicester (for services to the Arts) 1995, Pioneers and Achievers Award for services to the Arts 1998; *Theatre* RSC: Macbeth, Antony and Cleopatra, Much Ado About Nothing, The Tempest, Peer Gynt, The Custom of the Country, The Merchant of Venice, Love's Labour's Lost, Golden Girls, The Party, The War Plays, The Mystery of the Charity of Joan of Arc, Measure for Measure, A Midsummer Night's Dream, Don Carlos; RNT: The White Devil, After the Fall (Best Actress Evening Standard Drama Awards 1990, Plays and Players Awards 1990, Critics' Circle Awards 1991, London Theatre Awards 1991, Laurence Olivier Awards 1991); others incl Ibsen's The Lady from the Sea (Lyric Hammersmith) 1994, The Taming of the Shrew (Leicester Haymarket) 1995, The Maids (Donmar) 1997; concert performances: The Fairy Queen (with The Sixteen, conducted by Harry Christophers, Tel Aviv) 1994, King Arthur (with Les Arts Florrissante, conducted by William Christie, France) 1995; *Television* incl: The Squad, The Cuckoo Waltz, Pob's Programme, 123 Go, Umbrella, The Sharpeville Six, Somewhere to Run, Trumpet of a Prophesy, Here is the News, King, Tecx, Two Dogs and Freedom, Thompson, The Pyrates, When Love Dies, Capital City, Runaways, Nice Town, Seekers, Henry IV, Bodyguards, Kavanagh QC, Silent Witness, Dalziel and Pascoe, The Last Detective, Harry Enfield's 'Celeb'; *Radio* incl: Goldoni's Mirandolina, Cromwell Mansions, Dictator Gal (nominated Prix Futura Award Berlin 1993), Gertrude Stein's Listen to Me, The Roads of Freedom, Sealed with a Kiss, Medea, Selections from the Old Testament, Something Understood, Poetry Please, Twelfth Night; *Film* incl: Dardanelle, Cry Freedom, Milk and Honey (Best Actress: Atlantic Film Festival Canada 1988, Paris Film Festival 1990; nominated Best Actress Canadian Acad Award 1989), A Child from the South, Bitter Harvest, Bridge of Time; *Recreations* learning French and Italian, reading, cinema, music, travel, gardening, cooking; *Style*— Josette Simon, OBE; ✉ c/o Conway van Gelder Ltd, 18–21 Jermyn Street, London SW1Y 6HP (tel 020 7287 1070, fax 020 7287 1940)

SIMON, Lloyd; s of Astrid Weiner, *née* Niditch; *b* 14 July 1966; *Educ* Hasmonean GS London; *m* 9 July 1995, Lauren, *née* Fox; 2 s (Alexander Harry b 18 Feb 1998, Daniel Scott Ross b 30 June 2000); *Career* estate agent; ptnr Baker Lorenz (now Dunlop Heywood Lorenz) 1983–, chm Western Ridge Properties; memb 20th Century Soc; *Recreations* boxing, running, art; *Clubs* Tramp; *Style*— Lloyd Simon, Esq; ✉ Western Ridge Properties, 36 Queen Anne Street, London W1G 8HF (tel 020 44092121, e-mail lsimon@westernridge.co.uk)

SIMON, Hon Mr Justice; Sir Peregrine Charles Hugo Simon; kt (2002); s (by 2 m) of Baron Simon of Glaisdale, PC, DL (Life Peer); *b* 1950; *Educ* Westminster, Trinity Hall Cambridge (MA); *m* 1980, Francesca, da of Maj T W E Fortescue Hitchins, of Brewham, Somerset; 2 da (Polly Harriet Artemis b 1982, Lucy Persephone Frances b 1984), 2 s ((Alexander Edward) Orlando b 1986, Ferdinand William Hugo b 1989); *Career* called to the Bar Middle Temple 1973 (bencher 1999); memb Midland & Oxford Circuit, QC 1991, recorder NE Circuit 1998, dep judge of the High Court 1999, judge of the High Court of Justice (Queen's Bench Division) 2002–; FLS; *Style*— The Hon Mr Justice Simon

SIMON, Peter; *b* 4 August 1949, Columbo; *Career* founded Monsoon 1972, created Accessorize 1984, exec chm Monsoon Accessorize plc; fndr and tstee Monsoon Tst; *Style*— Peter Simon, Esq; ✉ Monsoon Accessorize Ltd, Monsoon Building, 179 Harrow Road, London W2 6NB

SIMON, Robin John Hughes; s of Most Rev William Glyn Hughes Simon, Archbishop of Wales (d 1972), and Sarah Ellen (Sheila), *née* Roberts (d 1963); *b* 23 July 1947; *Educ* Cardiff HS, Univ of Exeter (BA), Courtauld Inst of Art (MA); *m* 1, 1971, Margaret, *née* Brooke; m 2, 1979, Joanna, *née* Ross; 1 s (Benet Glyn Hughes b 1974), 2 da (Alice Emily Hughes b 1976, Poppy Candida Hughes b 1991); *Career* art historian; lectr in history of art and English Univ of Nottingham 1972–78, hist bldgs rep The Nat Tst 1979–80, dir Inst of European Studies London 1980–90, art critic The Daily Mail 1990– (arts corr 1987–90), ed Apollo magazine 1990–97, head of publications NACF, ed Art Quarterly and Review 1997–98, founding ed The Br Art Jl 1999–; selector: The Discerning Eye 1992, The Critics' Choice: New British Art 1993, Royal Watercolour Soc Summer Exhbn 1996; visiting prof of history of art and architecture Westminster Coll 1989; memb: Ctee Courtauld Inst Assoc of Former Students 1991– (chm 1998–), Advsy Cncl Paul Mellon Centre for Studies in British Art 1993–98, Exec Ctee Assoc of Art Historians 1993–96, Ctee of Honour Lord Leighton Centenary Tst 1994–96, The Johnson Club 1995–, Exec Ctee Walpole Soc 2005– (memb Cncl 1991–96); Delmas fndn fell Venice 1978; FSA 1998; *Books* The Art of Cricket (jtly, 1983), The Portrait in Britain and America (1987), Buckingham Palace: A complete guide (ed, 1993), The King's Apartments, Hampton Court Palace (ed, 1994), The National Trust 1895–1995: 100 great treasures (jt ed, 1995), Lord Leighton 1830–1896 and Leighton House (ed, 1996), A Rake's Progress: From Hogarth to Hockney (jt ed, 1997), Enlightened Self-interest: The Foundling Hospital and Hogarth (jt ed, 1997), Oxford: Art and architecture (ed, 1997), Somerset House: The building and collections (ed, 2001), Public Artist, Private Passions: The world of Edward Linley Sambourne (ed, 2001) The Tyranny of Treatment: Samuel Johnson, his friends, and Georgian medicine (jt ed, 2003), Hogarth, France and British Art (2007); articles in various jls, papers and magazines; *Recreations* cricket (capt Poor Fred's XI), music; *Clubs* Garrick, MCC; *Style*— Robin Simon, Esq, FSA; ✉ The British Art Journal, 46 Grove Lane, London SE5 8ST

SIMON, Siôn Llewelyn; MP; *b* 23 December 1968, Doncaster; *Educ* Handsworth GS, Magdalen Coll Oxford; *m* (m dis); 3 c; *Career* research asst George Robertson MP 1990–93, sr mangr Guinness plc 1993–95, freelance speechwriter 1995–97, columnist: Daily Telegraph, News of the World, Spectator; MP (Lab) Birmingham Erdington 2001–; memb: AMICUS, NUJ, Fabian Soc; *Style*— Siôn Simon, Esq, MP; ✉ House of Commons, London SW1A 0AA

SIMON OF HIGHBURY, Baron (Life Peer UK 1997), of Canonbury in the London Borough of Islington; Sir David Alec Gwyn Simon; kt (1995), CBE (1991); s of Roger A Simon (d 1993), of Shoreham, W Sussex, and Barbara, *née* Hudd (d 2000); *Educ* Christ's Hosp, Gonville & Caius Coll Cambridge (MA), INSEAD (MBA); *m* 1, 1964 (m dis 1987), Hanne, da of Ehrling Mohn, of Oslo, Norway; 2 s (Hon Nicholas b 1964, Hon Alexander b 1967); m 2, 1992, Sarah, da of Frederick Roderick Smith (d 1994), of Much Wenlock, Salop; *Career* British Petroleum plc: mktg dir BP Oil UK 1980–82, md BP Oil International 1982–85, a gp md 1986–95, chief operating offr 1990–92, gp dep chm 1990–95, gp chief

S

exec 1992–95, chm 1995–97; memb Court of Bank of England 1995–97; non-exec dir: Grand Metropolitan plc 1989–96, The RTZ Corporation plc 1995–97 (non-exec dir CRA Ltd Dec 1995–97); advsy dir Unilever plc 2000–; sr advsr Morgan Stanley 2000–; memb: Supervisory Bd Allianz AG 1996–97, Int Cncl and UK Advsy Bd INSEAD, Advsy Cncl Deutsche Bank 1991–97, Advsy Bd Fortis 2001–04, Bd Suez Gp, Advsy Bd LEK Consulting 2000–05, Fitch Int Advsy Ctee 2001–, Supervisory Bd Volkswagen AG 2002–; min for Trade and Competitiveness in Europe DTI and HM Treasy 1997–99, advsr to the PM on Modernisation of Govt 1999–2003, memb Advsy Gp on Reform of the EU 1999 and 2003; chm Cambridge Univ Fndn 2000–05, memb Univ of Cambridge Cncl 2005–; tstee Hert Fndn 2000; Liveryman: Worshipful Co of Tallow Chandlers, Worshipful Co of Carmen; *Recreations* music, golf, reading; *Style*— Lord Simon of Highbury; ✉ House of Lords, London SW1A 1PW

SIMONDS-GOODING, Anthony James Joseph; s of Maj Hamilton Simonds-Gooding (d 2003), of Dooks, Co Kerry, and Dorothy, *née* Reilly; *b* 10 September 1937; *Educ* Ampleforth, BRNC Dartmouth; *m* 1, 1961, Fiona; 4 s (Rupert, Benedict, George, Harry d 1996), 2 da (Lucinda, Dominique); m 2, 1982, Marjorie Anne, da of William John Pennock (d 1987), and Wendy, *née* Trollope; 1 step s (Daniel Porter); *Career* RN 1953–59; Unilever 1960–73, Whitbread & Co plc 1973–85 (mktg dir, md, gp md), chm and chief exec all communication and advertising companies worldwide for Saatchi & Saatchi plc 1985–87, chief exec British Satellite Broadcasting 1987–90, chm Ammirati Puris Lintas Ltd (formerly S P Lintas) 1994–96; currently chm Design and Art Directors Assoc; non-exec dir: Robinson & Sons Ltd 1993–99, Community Hospitals plc 1995–2000, Interbrand Newell & Sorrell (formerly Newell & Sorrell) 1996–99, Clark & Taylor 1996– (chm 1998–2000), Blick plc 1997–, Kunick plc 1997–, Corporate Edge plc 1999–; chm: OMG plc 2002–, Design Business Assoc 2003–; dir: Macmillan Cancer Relief, Inst of Contemporary Art until 1995, Brixton Prison Board until 1996; tstee Rainbow Tst Children's Charity 2002–04; *Recreations* family, opera, tennis, fishing, reading, painting, travelling, skiing; *Clubs* Hurlingham, Sloane, Garrick; *Style*— Anthony Simonds-Gooding, Esq; ✉ c/o Design and Art Directors Association, 9 Graphite Square, Vauxhall Walk, London SE11 5EE (tel 020 7840 1111)

SIMONS, Prof John Philip; s of Mark Isaac Simons (d 1974), of London, and Rose, *née* Pepper (d 1962); *b* 20 April 1934; *Educ* Haberdashers' Aske's, Sidney Sussex Coll Cambridge (BA, PhD, ScD); *m* 1, 1 Dec 1956, Althea Mary (d 1989), da of Robert Douglas Screaton (d 1988), of Nottingham; 3 s (Thomas John b 1960, Joseph Robert b 1962, Benjamin David b 1965); m 2, 25 Jan 1992, Mrs Elizabeth Ann Corps; *Career* Univ of Birmingham: ICI fell 1960, reader 1975, prof of photochemistry 1979–81; prof of physical chemistry Univ of Nottingham 1981–93, Dr Lee's prof of chemistry Univ of Oxford and fell Exeter Coll 1993–99, Miller prof Univ of Calif Berkeley 2000, emeritus prof; memb: SERC Chemistry Laser Facility Ctees, NATO Sci Ctees; pres Faraday Div Royal Soc of Chemistry 1993–95, memb Cncl Royal Soc 1999–2000; Hon DSc Univ of Birmingham 2002; CChem, FRSC 1979, FRS 1989; *Awards* RSC: Tilden 1983, Chemical Dynamics 1993, Polanyi medal 1996, Spiers Medal 1999, Citoyen s'Honneur de la Ville de Toulouse 1997, Humphry Davy lectr Royal Soc 2001, Liversidge Lectureship 2007; *Books* Photochemistry and Spectroscopy (1970); *Recreations* verse; *Style*— Prof John Simons, FRS; ✉ Physical and Theoretical Chemistry Laboratory, University of Oxford, South Parks Road, Oxford OX1 3QZ (tel 01865 275400, fax 01865 275410, e-mail john.simons@chem.ox.ac.uk)

SIMONS, Jonquil Edwina; da of Jack Albert Simons (d 1996), of Brighton, and Rose Simons; *b* 3 March 1953; *Educ* Brighton & Hove HS for Girls GPDST; *m* 1990, Robert David Tracy, s of Arthur Herbert Tracy (d 1962); *Career* asst to Publicity Mangr Robert Hale & Co publishers 1971–72, publicity asst Evans Bros educnl publishers 1972–73, PR asst Sussex Police 1973–76, PRO Gardner Centre Theatre Sussex 1976–77, assoc dir Public Relations Counsel Ltd PR consultancy 1980–82 (account exec 1977–80), head of PR Alan Pascoe Associates Ltd 1982–84, freelance PR conslt 1984–88, ptnr The Matthews Simons Partnership 1988–93, sr ptnr The Simons Partnership 1993–; CIPR: chm London & SE Gp Ctee 1986 and 1987 (memb 1983–93, hon sec 1983–85), memb Cncl 1989, 1990 and 1991, memb Educn and Trg Ctee 1989–95, chm Student Devpt Working Pty 1993, judge Sword of Excellence 1992 and 1993, memb Fells Forum Working Pty 1996–98; tstee St Margaret's Hospice Somerset 2002–06; memb British Mensa; FCIPR 1991 (MCIPR 1981); *Recreations* theatre, canal and river cruising; *Style*— Ms Jonquil Simons; ✉ The Simons Partnership, The Penthouse, Merton Place, Western Lane, Minehead, Somerset TA24 8BZ (tel 01643 708843, fax 01643 706671, mobile 078 6046 6959, e-mail jonquilsimons@aol.com)

SIMONS, Paul; s of Francis Simons (d 1966), and Kathleen, *née* Ruddy (d 1983); *b* 11 March 1948; *Educ* Bridley Moor HS, Kingston Poly, Lancaster Univ (MA); *m* 1 (m dis), Lesley Bailey; 2 s (Neil b 27 Dec 1968, Nicholas b 6 Sept 1971); m 2, Ann, da of William Perry, of Long Ashton, Bristol; 1 da (Kate b 7 Dec 1984), 1 s (Harry Jonathan b 27 Oct 1991 d 7 Jan 1993); *Career* Cadbury Schweppes 1972–75 (asst product mangr, product mangr), gp product mangr Imperial Tobacco Foods 1975–76, mktg mangr United Biscuits 1976–78, Cogent Elliott 1978–84 (account dir, client serv dir); Gold Greenlees Trott 1984–88 (client serv dir, dep md, vice-chm), chm and chief exec Simons Palmer Clemmow Johnson Ltd 1988–97, chief exec TBWA Simons Palmer (following merger) 1997–98, chm TBWA UK Group (following merger of TBWA International and BDDP Worldwide) 1998–99, chm and chief exec Ogilvy & Mather 1999–2002 (also chm Ogilvy & Mather Holdings Ltd), chm Investment Consortium 2002–, estab Paul Simons and Partners strategic consultancy 2002 (currently managing ptnr), chief exec Cagney Gp plc; non-exec chm Unique Digital Marketing Ltd, non-exec dir In Cup Plus plc; rock musician (guitar) 1963–67, played with several bands (started first band with late John Bonham of Led Zeppelin), released various unsuccessful records; author of numerous articles; estab Harry Simons Tst to provide funds for res into Reyes Syndrome 1993; FIPA, FInstD, fell Marketing Soc; *Recreations* golf, gym, sailing, concerts, travel; *Clubs* Home House; *Style*— Paul Simons, Esq; ✉ 65 Clarendon Court, Maida Vale, London W9 1AJ (tel 020 7289 1998, e-mail paul.simons@paulsimonsandpartners.com); Cagney plc, Holden House, 57 Rathbone Place, London W1T 1JU (tel 020 7637 4198, fax 020 7580 2649)

SIMONS, Prof Peter Murray; s of Jack Simons (d 1990), and Marjorie Nita, *née* Brown (d 1972); *b* 23 March 1950, London; *Educ* Univ of Manchester (BSc, MA, PhD), Univ of Salzburg; *m* 21 July 1973, Susan Jane, *née* Walker; 1 s (Rupert Daniel b 17 Sept 1981), 1 da (Rebecca May b 7 Jan 1984); *Career* asst librarian Univ of Manchester 1975–77, lectr in philosophy Bolton Inst of Technol 1977–80, lectr in philosophy Univ of Salzburg 1980–95, prof of philosophy Univ of Leeds 1995–; hon prof of philosophy Univ of Salzburg 1996–; pres: European Soc for Analytic Philosophy 1993–96, Int Bernard Bolzano Soc 1993–98; ed History and Philosophy of Logic 1993–2001, author of 200 essays, articles and reviews; dir Franz Brentano Fndn, industrial conslt Ontek Corp Calif 1989–2001; Cultural Prize City of Salzburg 1986; FBA 2004; memb Academia Europaea 2006; *Books* Das Naturrecht heute and morgen: Gedächtnisschrift für Rene Marcic (ed with Dorothea Mayer-Maly, 1983), Parts: A Study in Ontology (1987), Philosophy and Logic in Central Europe from Bolzano to Tarski: Selected Essays (1992), Metaphysik - neue Zugänge zu alten Fragen (ed with J Brandl and A Hieke, 1996), Formal Ontology (ed with R Poli, 1996), Applied Ethics in a Troubled World (ed with E Morscher and O Neumaier, 1998); *Recreations* walking, choral singing, skiing; *Style*— Prof Peter Simons; ✉ School of Philosophy, University of Leeds, Leeds LS2 9JT

SIMONS, Richard Brian; s of Harry Simons (d 1984), of High Wycombe, Bucks, and Ann Lily, *née* Gold; *b* 5 November 1952; *Educ* Royal GS High Wycombe, Exeter Coll Oxford (BA); *Children* 1 s (Harry b 26 Oct 1985), 1 da (Kate b 19 April 1988); *Career* ITN 1974–91: joined as grad trainee TV journalist 1974, news ed News at One 1977, news ed News at Ten 1979, news ed General Election 1983 and 1987, sports ed 1985–86, special productions exec 1989; head of features Carlton TV 1991–96; cmmns with Carlton incl: Hollywood Women, Hollywood Kids (BAFTA nominee for Best Documentary), Hollywood Men, Hollywood Pets, The Visit I, II and III (NY Film Festival Gold Award), Special Babies, Blues & Twos, Sport in Question, Animal Detectives, The Day I Nearly Died, Paranormal World of Paul McKenna I and II, SAS - Soldier's Story, Police Camera Action, Oddballs, Beyond Belief I and II, Champion Children, ITV Panasonic Sports Award, Police Stop!; Meridian Broadcasting Ltd (now part of ITV plc): controller of Programmes and Production 1996–2000, memb Bd 1997–2001; md Squirrel Networks Ltd 2001–, consltg head of devpt GMTV, devpt dir New Media Prodn United Broadcasting and Entertainment; memb RTS; *Recreations* tennis, TV, piano, cinema; *Clubs* Groucho; *Style*— Richard Simons, Esq

SIMONS, Susannah Catherine; da of Peter Simons, of Windsor, and Betty, *née* Edwards; *b* 19 April 1948; *Educ* Langley GS, GSM; *m* 17 July 1976, Richard Percival Taylor, s of Percival Taylor; 1 da (Sarah Kate b 7 May 1980), 1 s (Sebastian Richard b 29 Oct 1982); *Career* TV and radio presenter; radio drama studio mangr BBC 1970–73 (BBC trainee 1969), prodr and presenter Capital Radio 1973; presenter: IRN 1975, Tonight (BBC) 1977, PM (BBC Radio) 1977, various BBC Radio 4 news and current affairs progs 1977–87 (The World at One, The World This Weekend, Radio 4 Budget Special, 1981 Royal Wedding, 1987 General Election, also The Jimmy Young Show on Radio 2 and The News Quiz), The Business Programme (Channel 4) 1986, Business Daily (Channel 4) 1987–92, Today (Radio 4), Answering Back (Channel 4) 1992, Classic FM 1992–2002, Around Westminster (BBC 2) 1993, TUC Conf coverage (BBC 2) 1995; GWR Gp: head of Corporate Liaison Dept 1998–2001, dir of communications 2001–; head of public affrs and outreach BBC Radio and Music 2002–; dir Business Television 1990–92; chair: Nat Youth Dance Tst, London Advsy Bd Arts & Business, Bd Orch of the Age of Enlightenment; memb Royal Ballet Advsy Bd 1998–99, tstee More House Sch; Variety Club Female Radio Personality of the Year 1984, Broadcasting Press Best Radio Prog 1992; AGSM, FRSA; *Recreations* reading, theatre, opera, walking, skiing, cooking; *Style*— Ms Susannah Simons; ✉ Room 4128, BBC Broadcasting House, Portland Place, London W1A 1AA (tel 020 7765 0806, e-mail susannah.simons@bbc.co.uk)

SIMPKIN, Andrew Gordon; s of Ronald William Simpkin, of Menorca, and Garry, *née* Braidwood; *b* 31 March 1947; *Educ* Chethams Hosp Sch Manchester, Coll of Law; *m* 9 Sept 1972, Gail Yvonne, da of John Hartley Turner, of Knutsford, Cheshire; 2 s (Robert Gordon b 1974, James William b 1976); *Career* slr; ptnr: Ogden & Simpkin 1973–78, Pannone LLP 1978–2007 (conslt lawyer 2007–); non-exec dir Trafford Park Estates plc 1986–99; memb Bd: City Coll Manchester 1998–, Arawak Housing Assoc 1999–; govr City Coll Manchester 1999–; memb: Young Slrs' Gp Law Soc 1972–82, Equal Opportunities Cmmn 1986–91; *Recreations* mountaineering; *Clubs* Law Soc; *Style*— Andrew G Simpkin, Esq; ✉ Pannone LLP, 123 Deansgate, Manchester M3 2BU (tel 0161 909 3000, fax 0161 909 4444)

SIMPKIN, Dr Paul; *b* 17 August 1945; *Educ* Queen Elizabeth GS Wakefield, St Thomas' Hosp Med Sch London (scholar, MB BS); *m* 1980, Marie-Louise, da of Dr Albert Edward Meechan Sieger; 2 da (Arabella Louise b 1981, Victoria Lucy b 1983); *Career* hon clinical asst Chest Dept St Thomas' Hosp 1975–80 (jr med appts 1970–75); conslt staff physician: GLC 1975–86, ILEA 1975–90; consulting occupational health physician 1980–, med advsr London Residuary Body 1986–93, md Medicine At Work Ltd 1989–; med advsr to numerous cos, professional instns and local govt authorities; MRCP (UK) 1974, AFOM 1982; *Style*— Dr Paul Simpkin; ✉ 2 Upper Wimpole Street, London W1G 6LD (tel 020 7935 5614)

SIMPSON, Alan; MP; s of Reg and Marjorie Simpson; *b* 20 September 1948; *Educ* Bootle GS, Nottingham Poly (BScEcon); *Children* 2 da, 2 s; *Career* pres Nottingham Poly Students' Union 1969–70, asst gen sec Nottingham Cncl of Voluntary Serv 1970–74 (estab Home Office pilot project for non-custodial treatment of young offenders 1971), community worker on anti-vandalism project 1974–78, res and info offr Nottingham Racial Equality Cncl 1979–92, MP (Lab) Nottingham South 1992–; cncllr Notts CC 1985–93; offr Socialist Campaign Gp of Lab MPs 1994–; chair Parl Warm Homes Gp 1997–, vice-chair All-Pty Gp on Complementary Health 1998–, chair Social Science and Policy Gp 2000–; memb UNISON; author of various books and articles on community development, housing, employment, policing policies, Europe, environmental sustainability and racism; *Recreations* sport, vegetarian cooking, music, reading; *Style*— Alan Simpson, MP; ✉ House of Commons, London SW1A 0AA (simpsona@parliament.uk)

SIMPSON, Alan Francis; OBE (2000); s of Francis Simpson (d 1947), and Lilian, *née* Ellwood (d 1988); *b* 27 November 1929; *Educ* Mitcham GS; *m* 1958, Kathleen (d 1978), da of George Phillips (d 1975); *Career* author and scriptwriter 1951– (in collaboration with Ray Galton, OBE, *qv*); *Theatre* incl: Way out in Piccadilly 1966, The Wind in the Sassafras Trees 1968, Albert och Herbert (Sweden) 1981; *Television* incl: Hancock's Half Hour 1956–61, Comedy Playhouse 1962–63, Steptoe and Son 1962–74, Galton and Simpson Comedy 1969, Clochemerle 1971, Casanova 1974, Dawson's Weekly 1975, The Galton and Simpson Playhouse 1976, Camilo e Filho (Portugal Steptoe) 1995, Paul Merton In Galton & Simpson's... (series) 1996 and 1997, Pfeifer (Germany) 2000, Fleksnes Fataliteter (Scandanavia) 2002; *Radio* with Ray Galton: Hancock's Half Hour 1954–59, Steptoe and Son 1966–73, The Frankie Howerd Show, Back with Braden, The Galton and Simpson Radio Playhouse 1998–99, Fleksnes Tataliter (Norway) 2002; *Film* incl: The Rebel 1960, The Bargee 1963, The Wrong Arm of the Law 1963, The Spy with a Cold Nose 1966, Loot 1969, Steptoe and Son 1971, Den Siste Fleksnes (Norway) 1974; *Awards* incl: Scriptwriters of the Year (Guild of TV Prodrs and Dirs) 1959, Best TV Comedy Series (Steptoe and Son, Screenwriters' Guild) 1962/3/4/5, John Logie Baird Award 1964, Best Comedy Series (Steptoe and Son, Dutch TV) 1966, Best Comedy Screenplay (Screenwriters' Guild) 1972, Writers' Guild of GB Lifetime Achievement Award 1997, BPI Gold Disc for 100,000 sales of Hancock's Half Hour (BBC Radio Collection audio cassette) 1998; *Books* with Ray Galton: Hancock (1961), Steptoe and Son (1963), The Reunion and Other Plays (1966), Hancock Scripts (1974), The Best of Hancock (1986), Hancock - The Classic Years (1987), The Best of Steptoe and Son (1988), Steptoe and Son (2002), Fifty Years of Hancock's Half Hour (2004); *Recreations* gastronomy, football, travelling, after dinner speaking; *Clubs* Hampton Football (pres), Hampton Cricket (pres); *Style*— Alan Simpson, Esq, OBE; ✉ c/o Tessa Le Bars Management, 54 Birchwood Road, Petts Wood, Kent BR5 1NZ (tel and fax 01689 837084)

SIMPSON, Alasdair John; s of James White Simpson (d 1987), and Joan Margaret, *née* Ebsworth (d 1997); *b* 10 March 1943; *Educ* Queen Elizabeth GS Carmarthen, Univ of London (LLB); *m* 1, 11 March 1966 (m dis 1998), (Judith) Jane, da of Sidney Zebulun Manches (d 1999), of St John's Wood, London; 1 s (Thomas), 2 da (Emily, Sarah); m 2, 16 July 1999, Tanya *née* Rose; 1 s (Jake); *Career* admitted slr 1967; sr ptnr Manches 1982–2003 (asst slr 1967, ptnr 1968), ptnr Addleshaw Goddard 2003–; memb Law Soc 1967; *Recreations* tennis, thoroughbreds, claret, Provençe and Arsenal FC; *Clubs* RAC, Turf; *Style*— Alasdair Simpson, Esq

SIMPSON, Bernard Keith; s of John Stanley Simpson (d 1979), and Rose Hilda Simpson (d 1993); *b* 29 January 1948; *Career* dir: International Stores 1979–85, Gateway Food Markets 1985–89, Nationwide Building Society 1989–; memb Inst of Mgmnt Information

Systems; FRSA; *Recreations* sailing, shooting, photography; *Style*— Bernard Simpson, Esq; ✉ Nationwide Building Society, Nationwide House, Pipers Way, Swindon SN38 1BS (tel 01793 655783)

SIMPSON, David; MP, MLA; *Educ* Killicomaine HS, Coll of Business Studies Belfast; *Career* cncllr (DUP) Craigavon BC 2001–, memb NI Assembly (DUP) Upper Bann, MP (DUP) Upper Bann 2005– (Parly candidate (DUP) Upper Bann 2001); vice-pres DUP, vice-chair DUP Victims Ctee, vice-chair DUP Cncl Assoc; *Style*— David Simpson, Esq, MP, MLA; ✉ House of Commons, London SW1A 0AA; Northern Ireland Assembly, Parliament Buildings, Belfast BT4 3XX

SIMPSON, David Macdonald; s of James Simpson (d 1990), and Helen Macdonald, *née* Butters; *b* 25 May 1941; *Educ* Fettes, ChCh Oxford (MA); *m* Elizabeth Cochran, da of James Cochran Hamilton (d 1987); 1 s (Andrew b 1971), 1 da (Shona b 1974); *Career* gen mangr and sec Standard Life Assurance Co 1994–96 (investment mangr 1973–88, gen mangr (investment) 1988–94); non-exec dir: Wickes plc 1996–2000, Royal Mail Pensions Tstees 1997–2003, Fidelity European Values plc 1998–, Edinburgh Income and Value 1999–2005, F&C Private Equity Tst plc 1999–; FFA 1966; *Recreations* golf, curling, hill walking, skiing; *Clubs* Elie Golf House, Bruntsfield Links GS, Hon Co of Edinburgh Golfers, R&A; *Style*— David Simpson, Esq; ✉ 27 Succoth Park, Edinburgh EH12 6BX (tel and fax 0131 476 0922)

SIMPSON, David Richard Salisbury; OBE (1989); s of late Richard Salisbury Simpson, and Joan Margaret, *née* Braund; *b* 1 October 1945; *Educ* Merchiston Castle Sch Edinburgh; *Career* VSO teacher W Pakistan 1963–64; CA; joined Peat Marwick Mitchell & Co 1964–72, Scottish dir Shelter (Campaign for the Homeless) 1972–74; dir: Amnesty Int (Br Section) 1974–79, Action on Smoking and Health (ASH) 1979–90; fndr and dir International Agency on Tobacco and Health 1991–, visiting prof Dept of Epidemiology and Population Health London Sch of Hygiene and Tropical Med; Hon MFPHM 1991; *Books* Doctors and Tobacco, Medicine's Big Challenge (2000), Tobacco: A Global Threat (with J Crofton, 2002); *Recreations* reading, music, hill walking, Orkney; *Style*— David Simpson, OBE; ✉ International Agency on Tobacco and Health, Tavistock House, Tavistock Square, London WC1H 9LG (tel 020 7387 9898, fax 020 7387 9841, e-mail admin@iath.org)

SIMPSON, Dr Graeme Kenneth; s of late Kenneth Caird Simpson, of Grangemouth, Stirlingshire, and Edna Muriel, *née* Graham; *b* 25 September 1956; *Educ* Grangemouth HS, Univ of Edinburgh Med Sch (BSc, MB ChB); *m* 6 May 1978, Jacqueline Sara, da of late Andrew Auchterlonie, of Edinburgh; 1 s (David Malcolm b 1978), 2 da (Elspeth Margaret b 1981, Patricia Hannah b 1984); *Career* SHO: Med Renal Unit Royal Infirmary Edinburgh 1981–82, Med Unit Roodlands Hosp Haddington 1982–83 (house surgn 1981); registrar in med Eastern Gen Hosp Edinburgh 1983–86 (house physician 1980–81), sr registrar in gen and geriatric med Newcastle upon Tyne 1986–89, conslt physician and clinical dir geriatric med Royal Alexandra Hosp Paisley 1989–; memb: Collegiate Membs Ctee RCP 1985–89 (chm and memb Coll Cncl 1988–89), Br Geriatric Soc; life memb Royal Med Soc; MRCP 1983, FRCPE 1995, FRCPGlas 2001; *Books* contrib Body Weight Control (1988); *Recreations* golf, swimming, gardening; *Style*— Dr Graeme Simpson; ✉ Weybridge, 18 Stanely Drive, Paisley, Strathclyde; Royal Alexandra Hospital, Paisley, Strathclyde

SIMPSON, Graham; *b* 5 September 1951; *Educ* Torells Boys' Sch, Univ of Southern Calif, AA Sch of Architecture (AADipl), Univ of Westminster (RIBA); *m* 1, 16 Aug 1980 (m dis 1990); 1 s (Bertram Rupert Oscar), 1 da (Chloë March Louise); m 2, 25 Nov 1995, Pauline Lucy, da of Leslie Allan Watson (d 1964); *Career* architect; CZWG 1987–90 (projects incl The Circle London SE1 apartments, houses, business units, shops and courtyards), Prince Turki Abdullah Abdulrahman 1991–95 (projects incl private residences in Riyadh), Sir Norman Foster and Partners 1995–2000 (projects incl Al Faisaliah Centre, Riyadh hotel, apartments, office, banquet hall and retail centre), Houses Apartments Hotels 2001– (projects incl private residences in Sydney and New Zealand); RAIA, RIBA; *Recreations* cricket, cycling, history, travel; *Clubs* Middx CCC, Travellers; *Style*— Graham Simpson, Esq; ✉ 59 Worple Road, Isleworth, Middlesex TW7 7BA (tel 020 8560 0621, fax 020 8560 0271, e-mail gplsimpson@aol.com)

SIMPSON, Harry Arthur (aka Camp-Simpson); AE; s of Cyril Simpson (d 1950), of Ferndown, Dorset, and Nellie, *née* Buckley (d 1967); *b* 16 December 1914; *Educ* Moseley GS; *m* 1, 10 July 1943 (m dis 1983), Lilian Jackson, *née* Macdonald; 2 da (Dianne Gail b 13 March 1945, Julie Jackson b 11 Dec 1956), 1 s (Roger Graham b 13 Feb 1948 d 1974); m 2, 9 May 1984 (m dis 2001), Deborah Jane, da of Philip J Camp, of Bookham, Surrey; *Career* Nat Serv WWII RAF, specialist 'N' Symbol Award 1942, Pilot Gen Duties, Sqdn Ldr; contract Bakelite Ltd 1930–39; fndr chm and chief exec Flexible Abrasives Ltd 1947–65, dir John Oakey & Sons Ltd 1963–65, fndr chm and chief exec Arrow Abrasives Ltd 1966–93, fndr and exec chm Electro-Motive Ltd 1995–2004; European Ctee Exec Concerning Safety of Power Tools 1989–2004; author 2004–; FRMetS, FInstD; *Recreations* yachting, fishing; *Clubs* Royal Thames Yacht, RAC, RAF; *Style*— Harry Simpson, Esq, AE; ✉ 6 King William's Gate, The Square, Petersfield, Hampshire GU32 3HP (mobile 07768 903804)

SIMPSON, Prof Hugh Walter; s of Rev Ian Simpson (d 1976), and Dr Elenora Simpson, *née* Howie (d 1989); *b* 4 April 1931; *Educ* Bryanston, Univ of Edinburgh (MB ChB, MD), Univ of Glasgow (PhD); *m* 21 March 1959, Myrtle Lilias, da of Maj H Emslie; 3 s (Robin Gordon b 5 Jan 1960, Bruce Brian b 7 Feb 1961, Rory Drummond b 13 Jan 1968), 1 da (Rona O'Clanis b 17 June 1962); *Career* MO Br Antarctic Survey Hope Bay 1955–58, leader of many scientific expeditions to polar regns, pathologist then prof and head of div Glasgow Royal Infirmary and Univ of Glasgow 1959–93, sr res fell Univ of Glasgow and Dept of Surgery Royal Infirmary 1993–; inventor of Chronobra for detection of breast pre-cancer risk; author of over 160 scientific pubns; examiner RCPath 1984–93, chm Ethical Ctee Glasgow Royal Infirmary 1987–92; Polar Medal 1964, Mungo Park Medal 1970, J Y Simpson Medal Lecture RCS(Ed) 1995, Pery Medal 1996; FRCPath, FRCP; *Recreations* polar exploration, skiing; *Style*— Prof Hugh Simpson; ✉ Farleiter, Kincraig, Inverness-shire PH21 1NU (tel 01540 651 288, fax 01540 651813, e-mail simpsonhwsimpson@aol.com)

SIMPSON, Sheriff Ian Christopher; QC (2005); s of Maj David Francis Simpson, WS (d 1994), of St Andrews, and Joss, *née* Dickie (d 1975); *b* 5 July 1949; *Educ* Trinity Coll Glenalmond, Univ of Edinburgh (LLB); *m* 7 Aug 1973, (Christine Margaret) Anne, da of Duncan D Strang, of Crieff; 2 s (Richard David b 1977, Graham Mark b 1979); *Career* appointed Sheriff of S Strathclyde Dumfries and Galloway (floating) 1988, Sheriff at Airdrie 1991–2003, Sheriff of Tayside Central and Fife at Dunfermline 2003–06, Sheriff of Lothians and Borders at Edinburgh 2006, ret; temporary judge 2004–07; memb Faculty of Advocates 1974; *Recreations* golf, travel, reading; *Clubs* R&A, Luffness Golf, Bruntsfield Golf; *Style*— Sheriff Ian Simpson, QC; ✉ 30 Cluny Drive, Edinburgh EH10 6DP (tel 0131 447 3363)

SIMPSON, Prof (William) James; s of Ronald, and Margaret Simpson; *b* 16 March 1954; *Educ* Scotch Coll Melbourne, Univ of Melbourne (BA), Univ of Oxford (Paget Toynbee Dante prize, MPhil), Univ of Cambridge (MPhil, PhD); *Career* tutor Univ of Melbourne 1977–78, lectr Westfield Coll London 1981–89; Univ of Cambridge: lectr 1989–99, prof of medieval and Renaissance English 1999–2003; Girton Coll Cambridge: official fell and coll lectr 1989–99, professorial fell 1999–2003, life fell 2004–; Donald P and Katherine B Loker prof of English and American literature Harvard Univ 2004–; visiting distinguished prof Univ of Connecticut 1997, visiting prof Chaucer-Langland Nat Endowment for the Humanities Inst Boulder Colorado 1995, visiting distinguished prof Stanford Univ 1999; *Publications* Medieval English Religious and Ethical Literature: Essays in Honour of G H Russell (jt ed, 1986), Parisian Libraries (1989), Piers Plowman: An Introduction to the B-Text (1990), Sciences and the Self in Medieval Poetry: Alan of Lille's 'Anticlaudianus' and John Gower's 'Confessio amantis' (1995), Images, Idolatory and Iconoclasm in Late Medieval England (jt ed), Reform and Cultural Revolution 1350–1547 (2002); author of numerous articles in books and learned jls; *Recreations* conversation; *Style*— Prof James Simpson; ✉ Harvard University Department of English and American Literature and Language, Barker Center, 12 Quincy Street, Cambridge, MA 02138, USA

SIMPSON, James; s of late William Watson Simpson, and Beatrice Hilda, *née* Dixon; *b* 16 April 1944; *Educ* Barton Peveril GS Eastleigh, Univ of London (LLB); *m* 28 Dec 1968 (m dis 1982), Patricia Vivian (Tricia), da of late Michael Joseph Sheridan, of Southampton; 1 s (Toby b 1973), 1 da (Charlotte b 1975); *Career* RNR 1965, cmmnd Sub Lt 1966, Lt 1969, resigned cmmn 1974; admitted slr 1969, asst litigation slr Coffin Mew & Clover Southampton 1969–70, prosecuting slr Hants CC Portsmouth 1970–72; Brutton & Co Fareham: asst slr 1972–73, ptnr 1973–87, sr ptnr 1987–89; dep High and Co Ct registrar 1978–89; called to the Bar Middle Temple 1990; hon sec Hants Inc Law Soc 1987–89, pt/t chm Employment Tbnls 1996–, pt/t immigration judge 1998–; fndr chm Hamble Valley Round Table 1975–76 (chm Area I 1981–82); ward cncllr Fareham Borough Cncl 1978–82; *Recreations* flying, foreign travel, photography, golf; *Clubs* Hamble Valley Stick, Cams Hall Estate Golf; *Style*— James Simpson, Esq; ✉ 12 East Street, Titchfield, Hampshire PO14 4AD (tel 01329 846639, e-mail englishflyer@aol.com)

SIMPSON, (Judith) Jane; s of Sidney Manches (d 1999), and Judith, *née* Hydleman; *b* 15 July 1942, Westminster, London; *m* 11 March 1966 (m dis), Alasdair John Simpson, s of James Simpson; 2 da (Emily (Mrs Banks) b 27 March 1968, Sarah b 2 Dec 1969), 1 s (Thomas b 7 Nov 1974); *Career* slr; chm Manches LLP (also fndr and head Family Law Dept); co-fndr Slrs Family Law Assoc (now Resolution, chm 1993–95), former memb Lord Chllr's Family Law Advsy Bd; former vice-chm Tavistock Portman NHS Tst; *Recreations* music, food, travel, garden; *Style*— Mrs Jane Simpson; ✉ Manches LLP, Aldwych House, 81 Aldwych, London WC2B 4RP (tel 020 7753 7519, fax 020 7404 1838, e-mail jane.simpson@manches.com)

SIMPSON, Joe; s of Lt-Col I L Simpson, and Geraldine Elizabeth, *née* McGuire; *b* 13 August 1960; *Educ* Ampleforth, Univ of Edinburgh (MA); *Career* author, mountaineer, guide and motivational speaker; memb Alpine Climbing Gp; ASC Speaker of the Year 2003; Hon Dr: Univ of Sheffield 2005, Sheffield Hallam Univ 2005, Leeds Metropolitan Univ 2005, Univ of Edinburgh 2006; *Books* Touching the Void (non-fiction, 1988, trans into 14 foreign languages, Boardman Tasker Prize 1988, NCR Book Award for Non-Fiction 1990, Literaturpreis des Deutschen Alpenvereins 1990, Cardo d'argento Premio ITAS del libro di Montagna 1993), The Water People (novel, 1992), This Game of Ghosts (autobiography, 1993), Storms of Silence (non-fiction, 1996), Dark Shadows Falling (non-fiction, 1997), The Beckoning Silence (non-fiction, 2002, winner Nat Outdoor Book Award USA 2003); *Film* Touching the Void (drama documentary, 2004, Outstanding Br Film of the Year BAFTA Awards 2004, Evening Standard Best Film of the Year 2004, Best Feature Film Banff Mountain Film Festival, Prix Special du Jury Festival International du Film d'Autrans Montagne & Aventure, Grand Prize Kendal Mountain Film Festival, People's Choice Kendal Mountain Film Festival, People's Choice Llanberis Mountain Film Festival); *Recreations* photography, paragliding, gardening, rock climbing, diving, fly fishing, travel; *Style*— Joe Simpson; ✉ c/o Vivienne Schuster, Curtis Brown, 4th Floor, Haymarket House, 28–29 Haymarket, London SW1Y 4SP (tel 020 7396 6600); Corporate Motivational Speaking, Parliament Communications Ltd, Marek Kriwald, Suite 16, Roddis House, 12 Old Christchurch Road, Bournemouth BH1 1LG (tel 01202 242424, e-mail parlcom@aol.com); website www.noordinaryjoe.co.uk

SIMPSON, John Andrew; s of Robert Morris Simpson, and Joan Margaret, *née* Sersale; *b* 13 October 1953; *Educ* Dean Close Sch Cheltenham, Univ of York (BA, Hockey colours), Univ of Reading (MA); *m* 25 Sept 1976, Dr Hilary Simpson, da of Edmund Wilfred Croxford; 2 da (Katharine Jane b 1982, Eleanor Grace b 1990); *Career* ed Concise Oxford Dictionary of Proverbs 1978– (3 edn 1998), sr ed Supplement to the Oxford English Dictionary 1980–84 (asst ed 1976–78), chief ed Oxford English Dictionary 1993– (ed new words 1984–85, co-ed 1986–93, 3 edn online 2000–), ed Oxford Dictionary of Modern Slang (with John Ayto) 1992; Oxford English Dictionary Additions series: ed Vols 1 and 2 (with Edmund Weiner) 1993, gen ed Vol 3 1997; fell Kellogg Coll Oxford 1991–; memb: English Faculty Univ of Oxford 1993–, Philological Soc 1994–, European Fedn of Nat Institutions for Language 2002– (memb Exec Ctee 2003–), Advsy Bd Opera del Vocabolario Italiano 2003–; Hon DLitt ANU 1999; *Recreations* cricket (Holton CC); *Style*— John Simpson, Esq; ✉ Chestnut Lodge, 7 St Mary's Close, Wheatley, Oxford OX33 1YP (tel 01865 875140); Oxford English Dictionary, Oxford University Press, Great Clarendon Street, Oxford OX2 6DP (tel 01865 353728, fax 01865 353811, e-mail john.simpson@kellogg.ox.ac.uk)

SIMPSON, John Cody (FIDLER-); CBE (1991); s of Roy Simpson Fidler-Simpson (d 1980), of Dunwich, Suffolk, and Joyce Leila Vivienne, *née* Cody (d 1983); *b* 9 August 1944; *Educ* St Paul's, Magdalene Coll Cambridge (MA); *m* 1, 14 Aug 1965 (m dis 1996), Diane Jean, da of Dr Manville Petteys, of La Jolla, Calif, USA; 2 da (Julia Anne b 1969, Eleanor Mary b 1971); m 2, 8 May 1996, Adèle Krüger, da of Johan Krüger, of Johannesburg, South Africa; 1 s (Rafe b 2006); *Career* with the BBC; sub ed Radio News 1966, corr Dublin 1972; foreign corr: Brussels 1975, Johannesburg 1977; diplomatic corr TV News 1978, political ed 1980, presenter Nine O'Clock News 1981, diplomatic ed 1982, foreign affairs ed 1988–; assoc ed The Spectator 1991–95, columnist The Sunday Telegraph 1995–; awards: RTS TV Journalist of the Year 1990, BAFTA Richard Dimbleby Award 1992, Columnist of the Year Nat Magazine Awards 1993, RTS Award for Best Foreign Documentary 1997, Peabody Award USA 1997 and 2000, BAFTA and RTS Awards for reporting from Belgrade 2000, 2 RTS Awards for reporting from Afghanistan 2002, Int Emmy 2002, War Corr Award Bayeux 2002, GQ Writer of the Year Award 2003, RTS Current Affairs Award for Panorama: In the Line of Fire 2004; Hon DLitt: De Montfort Univ, Univ of Nottingham, Univ of Dundee; Hon DUniv Southampton 2003; hon fell Magdalene Coll Cambridge 1999; FRGS 1990; *Books* The Best of Granta (jt ed, 1966), Moscow Requiem (novel, 1980), A Fine and Private Place (novel, 1982), The Disappeared (1985), Behind Iranian Lines (1988), Despatches from the Barricades (1990), From the House of War (1991), The Darkness Crumbles (1992), In the Forests of the Night (1993), Lifting the Veil (jtly, 1995), Oxford Book of Exile (1995), Strange Places, Questionable People (autobiography, 1998), A Mad World My Masters (2000), News from No Man's Land (2002), The Wars Against Sadam (2003); *Recreations* books, travelling, diving; *Clubs* Garrick, Travellers, Chelsea Arts, Nat Yacht, Dun Laoghaire; *Style*— John Simpson, Esq, CBE; ✉ 370–372 Old York Road, London SW18 1SP (tel 020 8877 0200)

SIMPSON, Prof John Harold; s of Frederick Harold Simpson (d 1990), and Margaret Morrison, *née* Lees-Wallace; *b* 21 May 1940; *Educ* Bootham Sch York, Exeter Coll Oxford (BA), Univ of Liverpool (PhD, DSc); *m* 31 Aug 1964, Frances Mary, da of Thomas Estell Peacock (d 1989); 3 da (Amanda b 1967, Rachel b 1968, Joanna b 1970); *Career* Univ of Wales Bangor: lectr in physical oceanography 1965, res fell Nat Inst of Oceanography 1969–70, personal chair in physical oceanography 1982, established chair in physical oceanography 1986–2005, head Sch of Ocean Scis 1996–2000, research prof of oceanography 2005–; visiting prof of physical oceanography Virginia Inst of Marine

Sciences USA 1989; NERC: memb Ctee AAPS 1975–79, memb Cncl 1982–88, chm North Sea Project Scientific Steering Gp 1987–92, chm LOIS Shelf Edge Study Steering Gp 1992–98; memb: Cncl Scottish Marine Biological Assoc 1985–91, Cncl Netherlands Inst for Sea Research 2000–; pres Challenger Soc for Marine Sci 1994–96; *Recreations* hill walking, sailing, gardening; *Style*— Prof John Simpson; ✉ School of Ocean Sciences, University of Wales, Bangor, Menai Bridge, Anglesey LL59 5AB (tel 01248 382844, fax 01248 382812, e-mail j.h.simpson@bangor.ac.uk)

SIMPSON, Keith Robert; MP; s of Harry Simpson, and Jean Betty, *née* Day; *b* 29 March 1949; *Educ* Thorpe GS Norfolk, Univ of Hull (BA), King's Coll London (postgrad research); *m* 1984, Pepita Maria, da of Norman Hollingsworth; 1 s (George Harry b 1991); *Career* sr lectr in war studies RMA Sandhurst 1973–86, head of foreign affrs and defence Cons Research Dept 1986–88, special advsr to sec of state for defence 1988–90, dir Cranfield Security Studies Inst Cranfield Univ 1991–97; MP (Cons) Norfolk Mid 1997–; oppn frontbench spokesman for defence 1998–99, oppn whip Treasy and Health 1999–2001, oppn frontbench spokesman for environment, food and rural affrs 2001–02, shadow min for Def 2002–05, shadow min for FO (Middle East) 2005–; sec Cons Parly Backbench Defence Ctee 1997–98; memb: RUSI 1971–, IISS 1976–, Br Cmmn for Military History 1973–, House of Commons Catering Ctee 1997–98; Hon Col RMP; *Books* The Old Contemptibles (1981), A Nation in Arms (ed, 1982), History of the German Army (1985), The War the Infantry Knew 1914–1919 (1986), Waffen SS (1991); *Recreations* walking dogs, cinema, collecting books, walking battlefields, observing ambitious people; *Clubs* Norfolk; *Style*— Keith Simpson, Esq, MP; ✉ House of Commons, London SW1A 0AA (tel 020 7219 4053, fax 020 7219 0975)

SIMPSON, Norman; s of James Robert Simpson (d 1942), of Warsop, Notts, and Alice May Lody, *née* Eaton (d 1982); *b* 22 September 1933; *Educ* Warsop Infants' and Secdy Sch, Mansfield Tech Sch, Mansfield Sch of Art, Nottingham Sch of Architecture, Nottingham Poly (Dip Landscape Design); *m* 2 Sept 1958, Margaret Audrey, da of Frederick Israel Woodhouse (d 1969), of Sutton in Ashfield, Notts; *Career* retired architect in private practice; over 40 leisure projects throughout UK; award-winning projects incl: W Burton 'A' Power Station (Civic Tst Award 1968 and Countryside Award 1970), Nat Watersport Centre Holme Pierrepont; former chm East Midland Landscape Group; currently company architect Trinity Holdings (East Midlands) Ltd; hon architect: Nottinghamshire Rural Community Cncl, Nottinghamshire Assoc of Village and Community Halls; assoc Inst of Sport and Recreation Mgmnt; lay chair Gedling Deanery Synod Southwell and Nottingham Dio; ARCUK 1964, FRIBA 1968 (ARIBA 1964), ALI 1976, FIMgt 1982; *Recreations* photography and sketching; *Style*— Norman Simpson; ✉ Studio, 16 Allens Walk, Arnold, Nottingham NG5 8HF (tel 0115 920 2731, fax 0115 920 3785)

SIMPSON, Paul Graham; s of Graham James Simpson, of Nuneaton, Warks, and Valerie Ann, *née* Chilton; *b* 27 August 1961; *Educ* Manor Park GS Nuneaton, King Edward VI Coll Nuneaton, Univ of Kent at Canterbury (BA); *m* Lesley Ann Simpson, *née* Turner; 1 s (Jack Aron Bickerton); *Career* editorial asst MW Publishers Edgware 1982–84; Litho Week (Haymarket Publishing): reporter 1984–85, features ed 1985, news ed 1985, dep ed 1986–87, ed 1987–90 (youngest ever ed); ed: Newspaper Focus magazine (Haymarket Publishing) 1990–94, Four Four Two magazine (Haymarket Publishing) 1994–96, The Box 1996–, Demon magazine 1999–2000, Army magazine 2000–01, Freedom magazine 2001–, Champions magazine 2004–, FA Cup Final Prog 2005; ed-in-chief: Four Four Two magazine 1997–98, Haymarket R&D 1997–98, Focus magazine (Gruner and Jahr) 1998–99; *Awards* for Newspaper Focus: nominated Business Magazine of the Year Media Week Awards 1991, Business Magazine of the Year PPA Awards 1992; nominated Ed of the Year PPA Awards 1992, Consumer Magazine of the Year PPA Awards (for Four Four Two), Customer Magazine of the Year PPA Awards 2002 (for Army); *Books* Construction Yearbook (1983), British Printing Industry (1987), European Printing Industry (1992), European Newapaper Industry (1993), Football Intelligence (1997), Rough Guide to Online Shopping (2000), Paul Gascoigne (2001), Rough Guide to Cult Movies (2001), Rough Guide to Elvis (2002), Rough Guide to Cult TV (2002), Rough Guide to James Bond (2002), Rough Guide to Cult Pop (2003), Rough Guide to Cult Football (2003), Rough Guide to Lord of the Rings (2003), Rough Guide to Superheroes (2004), Rough Guide to Cult Fiction (2004); *Recreations* reading American thrillers, writing, listening to Elvis Presley records; *Style*— Paul Simpson, Esq; ✉ 64 Crescent Road, Shepperton, Middlesex TW17 8BP

SIMPSON, Prof Peter; *Educ* Bournemouth and Poole Coll of Art; *m* Dec 1970, Jennifer Carol, *née* Johnson; 2 da (Rebecca Caroline b 21 Sept 1972, Naomi Rosalind Mary b 18 July 1975); *Career* ceramic designer; currently emeritus prof of art Sch of Art and Design Univ of Derby (asst dean until 1999); visiting tutor and lectr in ceramics; memb Craftsmen Bursary Panel Southern Arts Assoc 1976–79 (memb Visual Arts Panel 1976–78), exhibition memb The Contemporary Applied Arts London; *Exhibitions* incl: one-man exhibition (Pace Gallery and Design Centre London) 1970, Ceramics '71 (Bradford City Art Gallery and Design Centre London) 1971, More British Potters (Keetles Yard Cambridge) 1972, International Ceramics '72 (V&A) 1972, Craftsman's Art (V&A) 1973, Modern British Crafts (Royal Scottish Museum Edinburgh) 1973, Gordon Baldwin, Peter Simpson (British Crafts Centre London) 1974, Chunichi 3 Int Exhibition of Ceramic Art Tokyo 1975, 6 Studio Potters (V&A) 1976, 2–man show (British Crafts Centre London) 1979, 4–man show (CPA London) 1980, Pottery Now (Sotheby's Gallery Belgravia London) 1985; numerous works in public collections incl Royal Scottish Museum (Edinburgh) and V&A (London); *Style*— Prof Peter Simpson

SIMPSON, His Hon Judge Peter Robert; o s of Surgn Capt (D) Donald Lee Simpson, RN (d 1985), of Barnet, Herts, and Margaret Olive, *née* Lathan; *b* 9 February 1936; *Educ* St John's Coll Southsea; *m* 1, 1968 (m dis 1994), Mary Elizabeth, yr da of late Thomas Kirton, and Frances Florence Cecilia Kirton; 2 s; m 2, 1995, Megan Elizabeth, da of late Kenneth John Dodd, and Melva Dodd; *Career* admitted slr 1960; called to the Bar Inner Temple 1970, ad eundem Lincoln's Inn 1972, practised on the South Eastern Circuit then at Chancery Bar (mainly in property and conveyancing matters), rec 1987–89, appointed circuit judge (SE Circuit)1989, London County Courts 1989–94, second judge Mayors & City of London Court 1994–; former memb Herts and Essex Sessions bar mess; *Recreations* reading legal and political biographies, dipping into books of history, listening to music, playing chess, dining out; *Clubs* Guildhall; *Style*— His Hon Judge P R Simpson; ✉ 12 New Square, Lincoln's Inn, London WC2A 3SW (tel 020 7405 3808); Mayors and City of London Court, Guildhall Buildings, Basinghall Street, London EC2V 5AR (tel 020 7796 5400)

SIMPSON, Prof Richard John; s of John Taylor Simpson, and Margaret Norah *née* Coates; *b* 1942; *Educ* Univ of Edinburgh; *Career* princ in gen practice 1970–99 (sr ptnr 1987–99), psychiatrist Forth Valley Health Bd Area 1970–99, dir Forth Valley Primary Care Res Gp, med advsr on adoption and fostering Clackmannanshire Stirling and Falkirk Authorities 1982–2000, conslt in addictions; pt/t lectr on social work Univ of Stirling 1972–1990, hon prof of psychology Univ of Stirling; MSP (Lab) Ochil 1999–2003; dep min for Justice 2001–02; chair Strathcarron Hospice 1988–92, memb Med Section (Scot) Br Agencies for Adoption and Fostering 1982– (chair 1985–89), pres Scot Union of Students 1967–69, memb Ct Heriot-Watt Univ 1969–78; hon pres Heriot-Watt Students Assoc 1969–75; FRCPsych 1994, MRCGP; *Recreations* golf, music; *Style*— Prof Richard Simpson

SIMPSON, Dr Roderick Howard Wallace; s of Dr Robert Wallace Simpson (d 1991), of Salisbury, and Betty Noreen, *née* Mollett (d 1994); *b* 10 January 1951; *Educ* King's Sch Bruton, Univ of St Andrews (BSc), Univ of Dundee (MB ChB), Univ of Stellenbosch (MMed); *m* 10 Nov 1979, (Alethea) Avrille, da of Cecil Alfred Milborrow, of Johannesburg, South Africa (d 1993); 3 s (Andrew b 1980, Richard b 1983, Nicholas b 1993), 1 da (Eleanor b 1987); *Career* registrar in pathology Guy's Hosp 1976–79, lectr in pathology Univ of Stellenbosch 1980–82, sr lectr in pathology and neuropathology Univ of the Witwatersrand 1982–85, conslt pathologist and sr lectr Univ of Exeter and Royal Devon and Exeter Hosps 1985–; invited lectr at nat and int conferences incl: Int Acad of Pathology Nice 1998, Dubai 2000, Amsterdam 2002 Brisbane 2004 and Montreal 2006, Pakistan Soc of Pathology Peshawar 1996, UAE Pathology Congress Dubai 1999, Euro Soc congresses 1995, 1997, 1999, 2001, 2003 and 2005, Intercontinental Congress of Pathology Madeira 2000 and Iguaçu 2004; sec Euro Soc of Pathology 2003– (memb Exec Ctee 1997–2001), memb Expert Panel for Revised WHO Histopathological Classification of Head and Neck Tumors; FRCPath 1996 (MRCPath 1983); *Publications* Choroby slinných z̆áz (Diseases of the salivary glands, with I Stárek and L Černý); author of 5 chapters in med textbooks and over 90 pubns in med jls on aspects of histopathology (in particular tumours of the head and neck); *Recreations* cricket, travel, the past; *Clubs* East India; *Style*— Dr Roderick Simpson; ✉ Iron Pool, Dry Lane, Christow, Exeter, Devon EX6 7PF (tel 01647 252034); Area Department of Pathology, Church Lane, Heavitree, Exeter, Devon EX2 5DY (tel 01392 402941)

SIMPSON, Prof Stephen James; s of Arthur Leonard Simpson, and Patricia Simpson; *b* 26 June 1957; *Educ* C of E GS Brisbane, Univ of Qld (BSc), Univ of London (PhD), Univ of Oxford (MA); *m* 1984, Lesley Kathryn; 2 s (Nicholas, Alastair); *Career* Univ of Oxford: MRC post-doctoral res asst Dept of Experimental Psychology 1982–83, demonstrator Dept of Zoology 1983–86, curator Hope Entomological Collections 1986–2005, lectr in entomology 1986–98, princ curator Univ Museum of Nat History 1989–92, reader in zoology 1996–98, prof 1998–2004, assoc head Dept of Zoology 2000–04, visiting prof 2005–; fell: Linacre Coll Oxford 1986–88, Jesus Coll Oxford 1988–2004; fedn fell Sch of Biological Sciences Univ of Sydney 2005–; guest prof in animal behaviour Univ of Basel 1990, distinguished visiting prof Univ of Arizona 1999; fell Wissenschaftskolleg (Inst for Advanced Study) Berlin 2002–03, fell Aust Acad of Sci 2007; *Publications* The Right Fly (1996), Anglers' Flies (1997); ed of books and 150 scientific papers; *Recreations* fishing, cooking; *Style*— Prof Stephen Simpson

SIMPSON, William George; s of William Anion Simpson (d 1961), of Liverpool, and Sarah Jane Simpson (d 1972); *b* 27 June 1945; *Educ* Liverpool Inst, Univ of Liverpool (BA), Univ of Aberdeen (Gilroy scholar), Dublin (MA); *m* 2 Nov 1968, Margaret Lilian, da of Bertram Pollard, of Liverpool; 2 da (Nicola Margaret b 1969, Fiona Sarah b 1974); *Career* asst librarian Univ of Durham 1969–73, John Rylands Library Univ of Manchester 1973–85 (asst librarian, sub-librarian, sr sub-librarian); univ librarian: Univ of Surrey 1985–90, Univ of London 1990–94; librarian and coll archivist Trinity Coll Dublin 1994–2002, dir John Rylands Library and univ librarian Univ of Manchester 2002–07; curator Oxford Univ Libraries 2002–07; memb: SCONUL 1985–, Br Library London Servs Advsy Ctee 1990–94, Nat Cncl for Orientalist Library Resources 1991–96, An Chomhairle Leabharlanna 1995–2002, COLICO 1995–2002 (chair 1998–2000), Mgmnt Ctee Nat Preservation Office 1996–2002 (chair 1999–2002), Consultative Cncl on National Policy for Libraries and Information Services (Ireland) 1997–99; chm: American Studies Library Gp 1987–94, Guildford Inst 1987–90, CONUL 1997–99, Standing Ctee on Legal Deposit 1998–2001; dir: CURL 1992–97 and 2003–05, IRIS 1994–2004; sec LIBER Div of Library Mgmnt and Admin 2002–, memb Int Editorial Bd Jl of Library Administration 2004–; tstee: The Worth Library 1997–, The People's History Museum 2003–05, Working Class Movement Library 2007–; Memorial Medal Charles Univ Prague 1998; MCLIP, FRSA, FRAS; *Publications* Libraries, Languages and the Interpretation of the Past (1988), The Book of Kells on CD-ROM (ed, 2000); author of articles and reviews in learned and professional jls; *Recreations* astronomy, genealogy, languages, travel; *Style*— William Simpson, Esq; ✉ White Cottage, 30 New Road, Milford, Godalming, Surrey GU8 5BE (tel 01483 860234); John Rylands Library, University of Manchester, Oxford Road, Manchester M13 9PP (tel 0161 275 3700, fax 0161 275 3759, e-mail bill.simpson@manchester.ac.uk)

SIMPSON OF DUNKELD, Baron (Life Peer UK 1997), of Dunkeld in Perth and Kinross; George Simpson; s of William Simpson (d 1979), of Dundee, Scotland, and Eliza Jane, *née* Wilkie (d 1982); *b* 2 July 1942; *Educ* Morgan Acad Dundee, Dundee Inst of Technol (Dip Business Admin); *m* 5 Sept 1963, Eva, da of William Chalmers, of Dundee; 1 s (Hon George Anthony b 22 Feb 1965), 1 da (Hon Gillian b 23 Oct 1966); *Career* sr accountant Scottish Gas 1964–68, sr fin position British Leyland 1969–77, fin dir Leyland Truck & Bus Ltd 1978–79; md: Coventry Climax 1980–82, Freight Rover 1983–85, Rover Group Commercial Vehicles 1986–87; chief exec Leyland DAF 1987–88, chm and chief exec Rover Group plc 1989–92, memb Supervisory Bd DAF NV 1989–94, chm Rover Group and dep chief exec British Aerospace plc (parent co) 1992–94; chief exec Lucas Industries plc 1994–96; Marconi plc (formerly GEC plc): md 1996–99, chief exec 1999–2001; non-exec dir: Pilkington plc 1992–99, ICI plc 1995–2001, Alstom SA 1998–, Nestlé SA 1999–, NW Venture Capital Fund Ltd, Bank of Scotland 2001–; pres: SMMT 1995–96 (formerly vice-pres), West Midlands Development Agency 1993–95; industrial prof Univ of Warwick 1991–, memb Govt Advsy Ctee on Business and Environment 1991–93; memb Cmmn on Public Policy and Br Business Inst of Public Policy Research 1995–97; memb Senate Engrg Cncl, memb Euro Round Table, govr London Business Sch; FCCA, ACIS, FIMI, FCIT, FRSA; *Recreations* golf; *Clubs* Royal Birkdale Golf, New Zealand Golf, Pine Valley Golf, Blairgowrie Golf; *Style*— The Rt Hon Lord Simpson of Dunkeld

SIMS, Prof Andrew Charles Petter; s of Dr Charles Henry Sims (d 1994), of Exeter, and Dr Norah Winnifred Kennan, *née* Petter (d 1998); *b* 5 November 1938; *Educ* Monkton Combe Sch, Emmanuel Coll Cambridge (MA, MB BChir, MD), Westminster Hosp Med Sch London; *m* 25 April 1964, Ruth Marie, da of Dr John Cuthbert Harvey (d 1988), of Birmingham; 2 s (David b 1965, John b 1968), 2 da (Mary b 1966, Ann b 1970); *Career* house surgn Westminster Hosp 1963–64, registrar Manchester Royal Infirmary 1965–68, conslt psychiatrist All Saints' Hosp Birmingham 1971–76, sr lectr and hon conslt psychiatrist Univ of Birmingham 1976–79, prof of psychiatry Univ of Leeds 1979–2000; ed Advances in Psychiatric Treatment 1993–2003, asst ed Br Jl of Psychiatry 1994–2005, ed Developing Mental Health 2002–05; pres RCPsych 1990–93 (dean 1987–90); chm: Confidential Inquiry into Homicides and Suicides of Mentally Ill People 1992–95, Schizophrenia Report of Clinical Standards Advsy Gp 1993–95, Spirituality and Psychiatry Special Interest Gp RCPsych 2003–05; memb GMC 1994–99; MD (Lambeth) 1995; FRCPsych 1979 (Hon FRCPsych 1994), FRCPEd 1993, FRCP 1997; fell Coll of Physicians and Surgns Pakistan 1994, fell Coll of Psychiatrists South Africa 1997, fell Assoc of European Psychiatrists 2002; *Books* Neurosis in Society (1983), Psychiatry CMT (5 edn, 1983), Lecture Notes in Behavioural Science (1984), Symptoms in the Mind (1988), Anxiety in Clinical Practice (1988), Angsttherapie in der Klinischen Praxis (1993), Psychiatry (6 edn, 1993), Speech and Language Disorders in Psychiatry (1995), Symptoms in the Mind (1988, 3 edn 2003), Disorders of Volition (1998); *Recreations* music, theatre, hill walking, gardening; *Clubs* Christian Medical Fellowship, RSM, Athenaeum; *Style*— Prof Andrew Sims; ✉ Church Farm House, Alveley, Bridgnorth, Shropshire WV15 6ND

SIMS, Frank; s of Frank Sims (d 1986), and Doris Elizabeth, *née* Hayes; *b* 21 July 1943; *Educ* Hitchin GS, Univ of Sheffield (BA); *m* 29 Oct 1966, Jean Caroline, da of Edward Francis Whitworth; 1 da (Claire b 1972), 1 s (Richard b 1974); *Career* CA; Price

Waterhouse 1967–72, Wallace Sassoon Bank 1972–74; ptnr: Binder Hamlyn 1974–97, Arthur Andersen 1997–2002; conslt Mercer & Hole 2002–05; Freeman City of London 1977, Liveryman Worshipful Co of Glovers; FCA 1970; *Recreations* golf, music, travel; *Style—* Frank Sims, Esq; ✉ Birchdale, 24 Oakland Place, Buckhurst Hill, Essex IG9 5JZ (tel 020 8505 0019)

SIMS, John Haesaert Mancel; s of Harold Mancel Sims (d 1958), and Jeanie Emilie Anne, *née* Haesaert (d 1965); *b* 16 December 1929; *Educ* Highfield Sch Wandsworth, Brixton Sch of Bldg; *Career* Nat Serv RE 1948–50; various appts with quantity surveyors' firms in private practice 1950–73, in sole practice as bldg contracts conslt; lectr, writer, arbitrator, adjudicator and mediator 1973–, author of numerous articles on bldg contracts for Building 1975–89; pres Soc of Construction Arbitrators 1992–95, chm CIArb 1994–95 (vice-pres 1991–95), memb DTI Departmental Advsy Ctee on Arbitration Law 1990–96; Freeman City of London 1981, Liveryman Worshipful Co of Arbitrators 1982; FRICS 1967 (ARICS 1954), FCIArb 1970, MAE 1988, FRSA 1995; *Books* with Vincent Powell-Smith: Building Contract Claims (1983, 4 edn by David Chappell 2004), Contract Documentation for Contractors (1985, 3 edn with Christopher Dancaster 2000), Determination and Suspension of Construction Contracts (1985), The JCT Management Contract: A Practical Guide (1988), Construction Arbitrations: A Practical Guide (1989, 2 edn with Christopher Dancaster 1998); The Arbitration Act 1996: A Practical Guide (with Margaret Rutherford, QC, 1996); *Recreations* classical music, choral singing, reading; *Clubs* Commonwealth; *Style—* John H M Sims, Esq; ✉ Common Farm, The Common, Leiston, Suffolk IP16 4UN (tel 01728 833852, fax 01728 832107, e-mail jhmsims@toucansurf.com)

SIMS, Monica Louie; OBE (1971); da of Albert Charles Sims (d 1959), and Eva Elizabeth, *née* Preen; *Educ* Denmark Rd HS for Girls Gloucester, St Hugh's Coll Oxford (MA, LRAM, LGSM); *Career* tutor in English and drama Dept of Adult Educn Univ Coll of Hull 1947, educn tutor Nat Fedn of Women's Insts 1950; BBC: radio talks prodr 1953, TV prodr 1956, ed Woman's Hour 1964, head of children's progs (TV) 1967, Controller Radio 4 1979, dir of progs (radio) 1983; dir of prodn Children's Film and Television Foundation 1985–97; vice-pres Br Bd of Film Classification 1985–98; memb Cncl Univ of Bristol 1990–99; Hon DLitt Univ of Bristol 2000; FRSA 1984; *Recreations* theatre, cinema, gardening; *Style—* Miss Monica Sims, OBE; ✉ 97 Gloucester Terrace, London W2 3HB (tel 020 7262 6191)

SIMS, Neville William; MBE (1974); s of William Ellis Sims (d 1954), of Whitchurch, Cardiff, and Ethel Stacey Colley, *née* Inman (d 1980); *b* 15 June 1933; *Educ* Penarth Co Sch; *m* 2 April 1964, Jennifer Ann, da of Horace George Warwick (d 1999), of Rhiwbina, Cardiff; 2 s (Jeremy b 1971, Matthew b 1981), 2 da (Heather b 1973, Caroline b 1980); *Career* articles with T H Trump, qualified CA 1957; Ernst & Young: ptnr 1960–85, managing ptnr Cardiff Office 1974–84, ret 1985; conslt Watts Gregory 1986–; dir: Compact Cases Ltd 1986–89, Peter Evans Flooring Ltd 1992–; pres S Wales Soc of Chartered Accountants 1977–78, chm CAs for Business in Wales (CABW) 1992–2002; chm: Wales Area Young Cons 1960–63, Barry Cons Assoc 1962–72; vice-chm Postwatch Wales 2001–; hon treas: YWCA Centre Cardiff 1963–70, Cardiff Central Cons Assoc 1987–93; memb: Welsh Regnl Bd Homeowners' Friendly Soc 1984–88, Standing Fin Ctee Welsh Nat Bd for Nursing, Midwifery and Health Visiting 1989–93, Post Office Users' Cncl for Wales 1992–2000, Exec UK 200 Group 1992–2000, Audit Ctee Welsh Funding Cncl for HE Colls 1996–99; chm of govrs Howell's Sch Llandaff 1981–2006; memb Cncl: ICAEW 1981–99, AAT 1989–92; Liveryman Welsh Livery Guild 1997; FCA; *Recreations* theatre, music, gardening; *Clubs* Cardiff and County; *Style—* Neville Sims, Esq, MBE; ✉ The Chimes, 15 Westminster Crescent, Cyncoed, Cardiff CF23 6SE (tel 029 2075 3424, fax 029 2075 6752, e-mail nevillesims@hotmail.com)

SIMS-WILLIAMS, Prof Nicholas John; s of Rev Michael Vernon Sims Sims-Williams (d 1992), and Kathleen Marjorie, *née* Wenborn (d 1996); twin bro of Prof Patrick Sims-Williams, FBA, *qv*; *b* 11 April 1949; *Educ* Borden GS Sittingbourne, Trinity Hall Cambridge (MA, PhD); *m* 1 July 1972, Ursula Mary Judith, da of (George) Hugh Nicholas Seton-Watson, CBE, FBA (d 1984); 2 da ((Jennifer) Helen Seton b 1986, Frances Mary Seton b 1989); *Career* research fell Gonville & Caius Coll Cambridge 1975–76; Univ of London: lectr in Iranian languages SOAS 1976–89, reader in Iranian studies 1989–94, prof of Iranian and Central Asian studies 1994–2004, research prof of Iranian and Central Asian studies 2004–; research reader British Acad 1992–94, Leverhulme maj research fellowship 2002–04; visiting prof: Collège de France 1998–99, Macquarie Univ Sydney 1998–2000, Univ La Sapienza Rome 2001; adjunct prof Macquarie Univ Sydney 2004–06; assoc ed Encyclopaedia Iranica NY 2002–; chair Corpus Inscriptionum Iranicarum 2002– (sec 1985–2002), pres Philological Soc 2003–07 (sec 1998–2001), chair Section H4 (Linguistics and Philology) Br Acad 2004–07, elected memb Bd Int Union of Academics Brussels 2006–; Prix Ghirshman Institut de France 1988; Hirayama prize Inst of Silk Road Studies 1996; corresponding fell Aust Acad of Scis 1989, associé étranger Académie des Inscriptions et Belles-Lettres Institut de France 2002 (correspondant étranger 2000); FBA 1988; *Books* The Christian Sogdian Manuscript C2 (1985), Sogdian and Other Iranian Inscriptions of the Upper Indus, I (1989) and II (1992), Documents Turco-Sogdiens du IXe-Xe Siècle de Touen-Houang (with James Hamilton, 1990), Partita (1993), Serenade for ten wind instruments (1997), New Light on Ancient Afghanistan: the decipherment of Bactrian (1997), Bactrian documents from Northern Afghanistan, I (2001), In Memoriam for string trio (2002); *Recreations* composing music, playing French horn; *Style—* Prof Nicholas Sims-Williams, FBA; ✉ 11 Park Parade, Cambridge CB5 8AL; School of Oriental and African Studies, University of London, Thornhaugh Street, Russell Square, London WC1H 0XG (e-mail ns5@soas.ac.uk)

SIMS-WILLIAMS, Prof Patrick; s of Rev Michael Vernon Sims-Williams (d 1992), and Kathleen Marjorie, *née* Wenborn (d 1996); twin bro of Prof Nicholas Sims-Williams, FBA, *qv*; *b* 11 April 1949; *Educ* Borden GS Sittingbourne, Trinity Hall Cambridge (MA), Univ of Birmingham (PhD); *m* 1986, Prof Marged Haycock, da of Emrys J Haycock; 1 da (Gwen Kathleen b 11 Nov 1990), 1 s (Gwilym Emrys b 10 Sept 1993); *Career* Univ of Cambridge: fell St John's Coll 1977–93, lectr Dept of Anglo-Saxon, Norse and Celtic 1977–93, reader in Celtic and Anglo-Saxon 1993; prof of Celtic studies Univ of Wales Aberystwyth 1994–; British Acad research reader 1988–90; ed Cambrian Medieval Celtic Studies; O'Donnell lectr: Univ of Oxford 1981–82, Univ of Edinburgh 1986, Univ of Wales 2000–2001; Leverhulme Tst Major Research Fellowship 2003–06; Sir Israel Gollancz prize British Acad, Antiquity prize; FBA 1996; *Books* Religion and Literature in Western England, 600–800 (1990), Britain and Early Christian Europe (1995), Ptolemy: Towards a Linguistic Atlas of the Earliest Celtic Place-Names of Europe (2000), The Celtic Inscriptions of Britain (2003), New Approaches to Celtic Place-Names in Ptolemy's Geography (2005), Ancient Celtic Place-Names in Europe and Asia Minor (2006), The Iron House in Ireland (2006), Additions to Alfred Holder's Celtic Thesaurus (2006); *Recreations* music, sailing, carpentry; *Style—* Prof Patrick Sims-Williams, FBA; ✉ Department of Welsh, University of Wales, Aberystwyth, Ceredigion SY23 2AX (tel 01970 622137)

SIMSON, Peregrine Anthony Litton; s of Brig Ernest Clive Litton Simson, of Aston Rowant, Oxon, and Daphne Camilla Marian, *née* Todhunter (d 1982); *b* 10 April 1944; *Educ* Charterhouse, Worcester Coll Oxford (BA); *m* 6 May 1967 (m dis 1979), Caroline Basina, da of Frank Hosier (d 1962), of Wexcombe Manor, Marlborough, Wilts; 1 s (Christian Edward Litton b 9 April 1970), 1 da (Camilla Basina Litton b 12 July 1972); *Career* slr; ptnr: Clifford-Turner 1972–87, Clifford Chance (merged firm of Clifford Turner and Coward Chance) 1987–; Liveryman Worshipful Co of Slrs 1974; memb Law Soc 1970; *Recreations* shooting, tennis, travel; *Clubs* City, Hurlingham, Annabel's; *Style—* Peregrine Simson, Esq; ✉ Corn Hall, Bures St Mary, Suffolk; Clifford Chance, 10 Upper Bank Street, London E14 5JJ (tel 020 7600 1000)

SINCLAIR, Dr Andrew Annandale; s of Stanley Charles Sinclair, CBE (d 1973), and Kathleen, *née* Nash-Webber; *b* 21 January 1935; *Educ* Eton, Trinity Coll Cambridge, Harvard Univ, Columbia Univ NY; *m* 1 (m dis 1971), Marianne Alexandre; 1 s (Timon Alexandre); m 2 (m dis 1984), Miranda Seymour; 1 s (Merlin George); m 3, Sonia, Lady Melchett; *Career* Ensign Coldstream Gds 1953–55; ed and publisher Lorrimer Publishing 1968–87, md Timon Films 1968–; FRSL 1970, fell Soc of American Historians 1970, FRSA 2007; *Novels* The Breaking of Bumbo (1957), My Friend Judas (1958), The Project (1960), The Hallelujah Bum (1963), The Raker (1964), Gog (1967), Magog (1972), A Patriot for Hire (1978), The Facts in the Case of E A Poe (1980), Beau Bumbo (1985), King Ludd (1988), In Love and Anger (1994); *Non-Fiction* Prohibition The Era of Excess (1962), The Available Man The Life Behind the Mask of Warren Gamaliel Harding (1965), The Better Half The Emancipation of the American Woman (1965), A Concise History of the United States (1967), The Last of the Best - The Aristocracy of Europe in the Twentieth Century (1969), Che Guevara (1970), Jack - A Biography of Jack London (1977), John Ford (1979), Corsair - The Life of J Pierpoint Morgan (1981), The Other Victoria - The Princess Royal and the Great Game of Europe (1981), The Red and the Blue (1986), Speigel (1987), War Like a Wasp (1989), The War Decade (1989), The Need to Give the Patrons and the Arts (1990), The Naked Savage (1991), The Sword and the Grail (1992), Francis Bacon, His Life and Violent Times (1993), In Love and Anger: A View of the 'Sixties (1994), Arts & Cultures: A History of the Fifty Years of the Arts Council of Great Britain (1995), Jerusalem: The Endless Crusade (1996), Death by Fame: A Life of Elisabeth, Empress of Austria (1998), The Discovery of the Grail (1998), Dylan the Bard: a Life of Dylan Thomas (1999), The Secret Scroll (2001), Blood & Kin (2002), The Anatomy of Terror (2003), Rosslyn (2005), Viva Che! (2006), The Grail (2007), The Reivers' Trail (2007); *Films* Under Milk Wood, Dylan on Dylan; *Recreations* visiting ruins; *Clubs* Chelsea Arts, Garrick; *Style—* Dr Andrew Sinclair; ✉ Flat 20, Millennium House, 132 Grosvenor Road, London SW1V 3JY (tel 020 7976 5454, fax 020 7976 6141)

SINCLAIR, Dr Bruce David; s of William Sinclair, of Comins Coch, Aberystwyth, and Muriel Elma, *née* Bruce; *b* 18 April 1961; *Educ* Ardwyn GS and Penglais Comp Aberystwyth, Univ of St Andrews (Thomson entrance bursary, BSc, PhD, J F Allen prize, Neil Arnot prize, class medal); *m* 17 Aug 1991, Marina Elizabeth, da of John Kenneth Blair, and Carita Maria, *née* Schwela; 2 s (Callum Dennis b 28 June 1993, Paul Bruce b 30 Oct 1995); *Career* Sch of Physics and Astronomy Univ of St Andrews: res asst in nonlinear optics in fibres 1986–87 then in diode pumped lasers 1987–89, Wolfson lectr (temp) in laser physics 1989, lectr 1989–96, sr lectr 1996–2001, reader 2001–; Inst of Physics: local organiser Scot branch 1991–, hon sec Quantum Electronics Group 1994–98 (ctee memb 1992–95), chair Advsrs Ctee to Physical Scis Centre of UK Learning and Teaching Support Network 2002–; dir 1998 EU-sponsored int summer sch on advances in lasers and applications; hon pres Students Voluntary Serv Univ of St Andrews; *Books* contrib chapter to Optoelectronic Devices (ed Des Smith, 1995), Advances in Lasers and Applications (ed, 1999); also author of over 40 publications in refereed jls and over 80 papers at confs and tech meetings; *Recreations* family, tandem, gardening, walking, swimming, DIY; *Style—* Dr Bruce Sinclair; ✉ School of Physics and Astronomy, University of St Andrews, North Haugh, St Andrews, Fife KY16 9SS (tel 01334 463118, fax 01334 463104, e-mail b.d.sinclair@st-andrews.ac.uk)

SINCLAIR, Charles James Francis; s of late Sir George Evelyn Sinclair, CMG, OBE, and Katharine Jane, *née* Burdekin (d 1971); *b* 4 April 1948; *Educ* Winchester, Magdalen Coll Oxford (BA); *m* 1974, Nicola, da of Maj W R Bayliss, RM; 2 s (Jeremy b 1977, Robert b 1979); *Career* ACA 1974; Dearden Farrow CAs London 1970–75; Associated Newspapers Holdings Ltd: joined 1975 asst md 1986, dep md 1987, md 1988, md and gp chief exec Daily Mail and General Trust plc 1989–; non-exec dir: Schroders plc 1990–2004, Reuters Gp plc 1994–2005, SVG Capital plc 2005–; chm of tstees Minack Theatre Tst (Porthcurno Cornwall); memb UK Ctee VSO 2006–; FCA 1980; *Recreations* opera, fishing, skiing; *Clubs* Athenaeum, Vincent's, Flyfishers'; *Style—* Charles Sinclair, Esq; ✉ Daily Mail and General Trust plc, Northcliffe House, 2 Derry Street, London W8 5TT (tel 020 7938 6614, fax 020 7938 3909, e-mail charles.sinclair@dmgt.co.uk)

SINCLAIR, Dr Clive John; s of David Sinclair, of Hendon, and Betty, *née* Jacobovitch; *b* 19 February 1948; *Educ* UEA (BA), Univ of Calif Santa Cruz, Univ of Exeter, UEA (PhD); *m* 1979, Frances, da of Sydney Redhouse (d 1994); 1 s (Seth Benjamin b 1981); *Career* writer; copywriter Young & Rubicam 1973–76, literary ed The Jewish Chronicle 1983–87, British Cncl writer in residence Univ of Uppsala Sweden 1988, Royal Literary Fund fell UEA 2005; Bicentennial Arts fell 1980–81, Somerset Maugham prize 1981, Br Library Penguin Writer's fell 1996, Jewish Quarterly Prize for fiction 1997, PEN Silver pen for fiction 1997, one of 20 Best Young British Novelists 1983; memb: Soc of Authors, PEN 1979–; FRSL 1983; *Fiction* Bibliosexuality (1973), Hearts of Gold (short stories, 1979), Bedbugs (short stories, 1982), Blood Libels (1985), Cosmetic Effects (1989), For Good or Evil (short stories, 1991), Augustus Rex (1992), The Lady with the Laptop (short stories, 1996), Meet the Wife (2002); *Non-Fiction* The Brothers Singer (biography, 1983), Diaspora Blues (travel, 1987), A Soap Opera from Hell (essays, 1998); *Recreations* travel and football and letter writing; *Style—* Dr Clive Sinclair, FRSL; ✉ c/o Picador, Pan Macmillan, 20 New Wharf Road, London N1 9RR (tel 020 7014 6000)

SINCLAIR, Sir Clive Marles; kt (1983); s of George William Carter Sinclair, and Thora Edith Ella, *née* Marles; *b* 30 July 1940; *Educ* Highgate Sch, Reading Sch, St George's Coll Weybridge; *m* 1962 (m dis 1985), Ann, *née* Trevor Briscoe; 2 s, 1 da; *Career* ed Bernards (publishers) 1958–61; chm: Sinclair Radionics 1962–79 (produced pocket TV), Sinclair Research Ltd 1979–, Cambridge Computer Ltd 1986–90; fndr Sinclair Browne (publishers) 1981–85 (annual Sinclair Prize for Fiction); dir: Shaye Communications Ltd 1986–91, Anamartic Ltd; visiting fell Robinson Coll Cambridge 1982–85; visiting prof: Imperial Coll of Science and Technol London 1984–92 (hon fell 1984), UMIST 1984 (hon fell); chm Br Mensa 1980–98; Mullard Award Royal Soc 1984; Hon DSc: Univ of Bath 1983, Univ of Warwick 1983, Heriot-Watt Univ 1983; *Publications* Practical Transistor Receivers (1959), British Semiconductor Survey (1963); *Recreations* music, poetry, mathematics, science, poker; *Clubs* RAC, Nat Liberal; *Style—* Sir Clive Sinclair; ✉ 1A Spring Gardens, Trafalgar Square, London SW1A 2BB (tel 020 7839 7744)

SINCLAIR, David Grant; s of Leslie Sinclair (d 1978), of London, and Beatrice Zena (d 1979); *b* 12 February 1948; *Educ* Latymer Upper Sch; *m* 7 June 1970, Susan Carol, da of Alexander Merkin (d 1963), of London; 2 s (Alexander James b 1972, Julian Lloyd b 1974); 1 da (Olivia Lesley b 1982); *Career* fndr and sr ptnr Sinclair Assocs Chartered Accountants 1972–; jt fndr and dir International Corporate Compliance Ltd and assoc cos 1991–, chm Investment Ventures plc 2000–, chm and fndr Axiom Capital Ltd 2001–, dir Economic Lifestyle Ltd 1995–; recognised expert in forensic accounting; FCA 1978 (ACA 1972); *Recreations* bridge, charity work; *Style—* David G Sinclair, Esq; ✉ Sinclair Associates, Roman House, 296 Golders Green Road, London NW11 9PT (tel 020 8455 0011, fax 020 8455 1199, mobile 07977 466121, e-mail dgs@sinclairsilverman.com)

SINCLAIR, David William Jonathan; s of James Daniel Sinclair, of Glasgow, and Barbara Kathleen, *née* Barclay-Bishop; *b* 24 October 1952; *Educ* Eltham Coll London, Univ of Warwick (BA); *m* 1 May 1986, Prudence Evelyn, da of late Sir Evelyn Hone; 1 s (Jack b 23 Dec 1990), 1 da ((Josephine) Faith b 23 Aug 1989); *Career* music writer and broadcaster; former drummer/vocalist in groups incl: Empire Made 1976–77, Tidal

Waveband 1977–78, Blunt Instrument 1978–79, London Zoo 1979–81, TV Smith's Explorers 1981–82, Laughing Sam's Dice 1983–85; contrib to magazines and newspapers incl: One Two Testing 1983–85, Guitar Heroes 1983–84, The History of Rock 1983–84, Kerrang! 1983–85, The Times 1985–, Q Magazine 1986–, Billboard (ed Global Music Pulse column) 1991–, Rolling Stone 1992–97, Mojo 1999–; researcher BBC TV (progs incl Eight Days A Week, Wogan, The Rock'n'Roll Years and Rock School) 1984–86; regular appearances on: Sunday Edition (BBC Radio 5) 1991–92, Sunrise Morning News (Sky TV) 1991–92, The Breakfast Show (BBC GLR) 1992–96; judge Mercury Music Prize 1994–; *Books* Tres Hombres - The Story of ZZ Top (1986), Rock on CD - The Essential Guide (1992, revised and updated 1993); *Recreations* tennis, badminton, bridge; *Clubs* Polytechnic of Central London; *Style*— David Sinclair, Esq; ✉ c/o The Arts Desk, The Times, 1 Pennington Street, Wapping, London E1 9XN (tel 020 7782 5000, fax 020 7782 5046)

SINCLAIR, Franklin; s of Eddie Sinclair (d 1988), and Sheila, *née* Cohen (d 1995); *b* 28 June 1958, Manchester; *Educ* Manchester Grammar, Univ of Manchester (LLB), Coll of Law Chester; *m* 26 Oct 1989 (m dis 2000); 1 s (Miles b 8 April 1990), 2 da (Mica b 5 July 1992, Nikita b 23 Sept 1993); *Career* admitted slr 1982; sr ptnr Tuckers Slrs 1984– (joined 1983); higher courts advocate 2002; chm Criminal Law Slrs Assoc 1999–2002, pres Manchester Law Soc 2005; *Recreations* golf, music (disc jockey 1975–89); *Clubs* Durham Forest Golf (Cheshire); *Style*— Franklin Sinclair, Esq; ✉ Tuckers Solicitors, 63–65 Mosley Street, Manchester M2 3HZ (tel 0161 233 4321, fax 0161 233 4344, e-mail sinclairf@tuckerssolicitors.com)

SINCLAIR, Iain Macgregor; s of Dr Henry Macgregor Sinclair (d 1989), and Doris, *née* Jones (d 1991); *b* 11 June 1943; *Educ* Cheltenham Coll, London Sch of Film Technique, Trinity Coll Dublin, Courtauld Inst of Art London; *m* (Mary) Annabel Rose, *née* Hadman; 2 da (Farne b 8 July 1972, Madeleine b 14 Jan 1980), 1 s (William Llewelyn b 21 Oct 1975); *Career* writer; *Books* incl: The Kodak Mantra Diaries (historical documentary, 1971), Lud Heat (poetry/essays, 1975), Suicide Bridge (poetry/essays, 1979), White Chappell, Scarlet Tracings (fiction, 1987), Flesh Eggs and Scalp Metal (poetry, 1989), Downriver (fiction, 1991), Radon Daughters (fiction, 1994), Lights Out for the Territory: Nine Excursions in the Secret History of London (1997), Slow Chocolate Autopsy (stories, 1997), Crash (film essay, 1999), Rodinsky's Room (documentary investigation, 1999), Landor's Tower (novel, 2001), London Orbital (2002), Dining on Stones (novel, 2004), Edge of the Orison (2005), London: City of Disappearances (ed, 2006); *Style*— Iain Sinclair, Esq; ✉ c/o John Parker, MBA Literary Agents, 62 Grafton Way, London W1P 5ZD (tel 020 7387 2076, fax 020 7387 2042)

SINCLAIR, Sir Ian McTaggart; KCMG (1977, CMG 1972), QC (1979); s of John Sinclair (d 1950), of Whitecraigs, Renfrewshire, and Margaret Wilson Gardner, *née* Love (d 1965); *b* 14 January 1926; *Educ* Merchiston Castle Sch Edinburgh, King's Coll Cambridge (BA, LLB); *m* 24 April 1954, Barbara Elizabeth, da of Stanley Lenton (d 1982), of Grimsby, Lincs; 1 da (Jane b 1956), 2 s (Andrew b 1958, Philip b 1962); *Career* Intelligence Corps 1944–47; called to the Bar Middle Temple 1952 (bencher 1980); entered Dip Serv 1950; legal cnsllr: NY and Washington 1964–67, FCO 1967–71; dep legal advsr FCO 1971–72, second legal advsr 1973–75, legal advsr 1976–84; barr 1984–2005, ret; memb Int Law Cmmn 1981–86; memb Institut de Droit Int 1987– (assoc memb 1983–87); hon memb: American Soc of Int Law 1987, Permanent Court of Arbitration 1992–2003; FRGS 1987; *Books* Vienna Convention on the Law of Treaties (1973, 2 edn 1984), International Law Commission (1987); *Recreations* bird watching, reading; *Style*— Sir Ian Sinclair, KCMG, QC; ✉ Lassington, Chithurst, Petersfield, Hampshire GU31 5EU (tel 01730 815370)

SINCLAIR, Jeremy; s of Donald Alan Forrester Sinclair (d 1987), of London; *b* 4 November 1946; *m* Jan 1976, Jacqueline Margaret, da of Jack Metcalfe (d 1994); 1 da (Naomi b 26 Jan 1979), 2 s (Leon b 21 Oct 1981, David b 13 March 1985); *Career* worldwide creative dir and dep chm Saatchi & Saatchi plc until 1995 (resigned); M&C Saatchi: ptnr 1995–, chm 2004–; *Style*— Jeremy Sinclair, Esq; ✉ M&C Saatchi Ltd, 36 Golden Square, London W1R 4EE (tel 020 7543 4500)

SINCLAIR, Karen; AM; *b* 20 November 1952; *Educ* Grove Park Girls Sch Wrexham; *m* Mike; 1 da (Helen), 1 s (Thomas); *Career* memb Nat Assembly for Wales (Lab) Clwyd S 1999–; business min 2003–05; memb N Wales Regnl Ctee; cncllr: Glyndwr DC 1988–95, Denbighshire CC 1997–99; formerly: contracted care mangr Wrexham Soc Servs, advsr CAB, govr Dinas Bran Sch Llangollen; *Recreations* reading, walking; *Style*— Ms Karen Sinclair, AM; ✉ 6 Oak Mews, Oak Street, Llangollen, Denbighshire LL20 8RP (tel 01978 869105, fax 01978 869464); Room B302, National Assembly for Wales, Cardiff Bay, Cardiff CF99 1NA (tel 029 2089 8724, fax 029 2089 8305, e-mail karen.sinclair@wales.gov.uk)

SINCLAIR, Dr Leonard; s of Sidney Sinclair (d 1973), of London, and Blanche, *née* Appele (d 1988); *b* 23 September 1928; *Educ* Rochelle Sch, Raine's Fndn Sch, Middx Hosp Med Sch Univ of London (Meyerstein Scholar, James McIntosh scholar, BSc, MB BS, Lyell Gold medal, Football colours); *m* 22 March 1959, Ann, da of Frederick Franks; 1 da (Judith b 19 Dec 1959), 3 s (Jonathan b 31 Oct 1962, David b 5 Feb 1964, Anthony b 27 Aug 1969); *Career* Queen Elizabeth Hosp for Children 1956–57 (med registrar 1960–62), jr lectr and hon registrar Guy's Hosp Med Sch 1957–60, sr paediatric registrar Chelsea and Westminster Children's Hosp 1962–66, hon conslt paediatrician Hosp of St John and St Elizabeth 1965–75, formerly conslt paediatrician St Stephen's Hosp, Westminster Hosp, Westminster Children's Hosp and Charing Cross Hosp, currently emeritus consIt paediatrician Chelsea and Westminster Hosp; visiting prof: Mount Sinai Hosp 1969, St Sophia's Children's Hosp Univ of Rotterdam 1983; hon sr lectr Faculty of Med UCL 1984; dep pres Paediatric Section RSM 1974–75 (sec Paediatric Section 1971–73); DCH 1957, FRCP 1974 (MRCP 1960), FRSM 1966, memb BMA 1969, FRCPCH 1997; *Books* Metabolic Disease in Childhood (1979), Enfermedades Metabolicas en la Infancia (1981), BMA Complete Family Health Encyclopedia (paediatric section, 1990); author of other scientific and med papers; *Recreations* tennis, old books, other people's problems; *Clubs* Athenaeum, RSM; *Style*— Dr Leonard Sinclair; ✉ 152 Harley Street, London W1G 7LH (tel 020 7935 3834); 34 Armitage Road, London NW11 8RD (tel 020 8458 6464, fax 020 8905 5433)

SINCLAIR, (Donald) Malcolm; s of Donald Sinclair, and Joyce Patricia, *née* Ellis; *Educ* Trinity Sch of John Whitgift Croydon, Univ of Hull (BA), Bristol Old Vic Theatre Sch; *Career* actor; speaker: Mendelssohn's Midsummer Night's Dream (Boston Symphony Orch, Boston and Carnegie Hall), Schoenberg's A Survivor in Warsaw (Boston Symphony Orch, Boston and London), Stravinsky's A Soldier's Tale (Nash Ensemble, BBC Radio 3), Prokofiev's Peter and the Wolf (East of England Orch), Bliss's Morning Heroes (Royal Liverpool Philharmonic Orch), Ivor Gurney recital (Purcell Room); recording Life of Tchaikovsky (Naxos); *Theatre* rep seasons: Bristol, Birmingham, Sheffield, York, Leicester, Nottingham; RSC: Hamlet (regnl tour), Comedy of Errors (regnl tour), Serebryakov in Uncle Vanya (Young Vic), Buckingham in Richard III (Stratford-upon-Avon); RNT: The Misanthrope, Kingston in Racing Demon, Clarence in Richard III, Gavin Ryng-Mayne in House/Garden (Clarence Derwent Award 2000), Cajetan in Luther; other prodns incl: Malvolio in Twelfth Night (Crucible Theatre Sheffield), Little Lies (Wyndhams Theatre London), London Cuckolds (Lyric Theatre Hammersmith), Anatole (Gate Theatre London), Façades (Lyric Theatre Hammersmith), The Millionairess (Greenwich Theatre), Dark River (Orange Tree Theatre Richmond), The Case of Rebellious Susan (Orange Tree Theatre Richmond), Splendids (Lyric Theatre Hammersmith), Jeeves in By Jeeves (Duke of York's Theatre London), Mazzini Dunn in Heartbreak House (Almeida Theatre London), Richard Greatham in Hay Fever (Savoy Theatre London and tour), William Blagrave in Cressida (Almeida at the Albery Theatre London), Maj Giles Flack in Privates on Parade (Donmar Warehouse London, Olivier Award nomination 2001), Col Pickering in My Fair Lady (Theatre Royal Drury Lane London), Duke of Buckingham in Richard III (RSC Stratford); *Television* credits incl: Esther Waters (BBC), Byron in Byron - A Personal Tour (BBC), Rassendyll and The King in Prisoner of Zenda (BBC), Ronnie in Me and the Girls (BBC), Everyone a Winner (Channel 4), Rumpole of the Bailey (Thames TV), Poirot (LWT), The Bill (Thames TV), John Le Mesurier in Hancock (BBC), Big Battalions (Carnival for Channel 4), A Question of Guilt (BBC), The Scarlet and the Black (BBC), Scarlett (US mini series), Pie in the Sky (SelecTV for BBC), Writing on the Wall (Little Bird Prodns), McLibel, Casualty (BBC), Kavanagh QC (Carlton Prodns), Midsomer Murders (Bentley Prodns), Fish (Principal Pictures for BBC), Prince Shcherbatsky in Anna Karenina (Co for Channel 4), Lord Conyngham in Victoria & Albert (Allahoo Ltd), Blythe in Murder Rooms (BBC), Julian in Relic Hunter (Firecorp VII Prodns), Clive Thornton in A&E (Granada TV), Nicholas Purnell, QC in Anybody's Nightmare (Carlton), Commander Denville in Making Waves (Carlton), Coroner in The Brief (BBC), Quentin Glazer in Rosemary and Thyme (Carnival for ITV); *Radio* Noel Coward in: Design for Murder (BBC Radio 4), Blithe Spy (BBC Radio 4), A Bullet at Balmains (BBC Radio 4); *Film* Success is the Best Revenge, Now That It's Morning, God on the Rocks, Young Poisoner's Handbook, Keep the Aspidistra Flying, Secret Passage, The Statement; *Publications* Look Back in Pleasure, Noel Coward Reconsidered (contrib); *Recreations* classical music; *Style*— Malcolm Sinclair, Esq; ✉ c/o Caroline Dawson Associates, 125 Gloucester Road, London SW7 4TE (tel 020 7373 3323, fax 020 7373 1110, website www.malcolmsinclair.com)

SINCLAIR, 18 Lord (S c 1449, confirmed 1488–9); Matthew Murray Kennedy St Clair; s of 17 Lord Sinclair, CVO (d 2004); 1 Lord resigned the Earldoms of Orkney and Caithness to the crown 1470, 10 Lord obtained Charter under Great Seal 1677 confirming his honours with remainders to male heirs whatsoever; *b* 9 December 1968; *Educ* Glenalmond, RAC Cirencester; *Career* md Saint Property; MRICS; *Clubs* New (Edinburgh); *Style*— The Rt Hon the Lord Sinclair; ✉ Knocknalling, Dalry, Castle Douglas DG7 3ST; Saint Property tel 0131 478 4533, e-mail mstc@saintproperty.com

SINCLAIR, Michael; *see:* Shea, Michael Sinclair MacAuslan

SINCLAIR, Nicholas Hilary; s of Hugh Sinclair (d 1962), actor, of Sussex, and Rosalie, *née* Williams; *b* 28 January 1954; *Educ* Christ's Hosp, Univ of Newcastle upon Tyne; *Career* photographer; chm North Star Studios 1983–93; *Solo Exhibitions* Gardner Arts Centre Univ of Sussex 1983, Photogallery St Leonards-on-Sea 1985, Photography Centre of Athens 1986, Brighton Museum and Art Gallery 1995, Tom Blau Gallery London 1996, Brighton Museum and Art Gallery 1995, 1997, 2004 and 2007, Luciano Inga Pin Gallery Milan 1999, Focus Gallery London 2000 and 2002; *Selected Group Exhibitions* Nat Theatre 1985, Northern Centre for Contemporary Art Sunderland 1989, Br Cncl touring exhibition W Germany 1990–91, Angela Flowers Gallery London 1993, Nat Portrait Gallery London 1994, 1998–99, 2000 and 2001, Joseloff Gallery Univ of Hartford USA 1995, Tom Blau Gallery 1995, Kunsthalle Vienna 1997, Galerie Rudolfinum Prague 1997, Padglione d'Art Contemporanea Milan 1999, Culturgest Lisbon 1999, Caterina Gualco Gallery Genova 2000, Muée de l'Elysée Lausanne 2000, Giacomo Zaza Gallery Bisceglie 2001, Kunsthalle Wurth Kunzelsau 2003, Musee d'Art et Histoire Fribourg 2004, UBS Zurich 2005, Nat Museum of Wales Cardiff 2006, Kettle's Yard Cambridge 2006; *Public Collections* incl: Nat Portrait Gallery, V&A, Nat Museum and Galleries of Wales Cardiff, Nat Library of Wales Aberystwyth, Brighton Museum and Art Gallery, Staatsgalerie Stuttgart, Folkwang Museum Essen, Kunsthalle Wurth Kunzelsau, Musée de l'Elysée Lausanne; *Books* Sussex Churches and Chapels (1989), The Chameleon Body (1996), Franko B (1998), Portraits of Artists (2000), Crossing the Water (2002), Kyffin Williams (2004); *Monographs* The Chameleon Body (1996), Franko B (1998), Portraits of Artists (2000), Crossing the Water (2002, Berlin: Imagining the Tri Chord (2007); *Recreations* swimming, music, theatre, cinema; *Style*— Nicholas Sinclair, Esq; ✉ North Star Studios, 65 Ditchling Road, Brighton BN1 4SD (tel 01273 730289, e-mail nicholas.sinclair@virgin.net, website www.nicholassinclair.com)

SINCLAIR, Sir Patrick Robert Richard; 10 Bt (NS 1704), of Dunbeath, Caithness; s of Alexander Robert Sinclair (d 1972, bro of 8 Bt), and Mabel Vera, *née* Baxendale (d 1981); suc his cousin, Sir John Rollo Norman Blair Sinclair, 9 Bt (d 1990); *b* 21 May 1936; *Educ* Winchester, Oriel Coll Oxford (MA); *m* 1974, Susan Catherine Beresford, eldest da of Geoffrey Clive Davies, OBE, of Holbrook, Ipswich, Suffolk; 1 s (William Robert Francis b 1979), 1 da (Helen Margaret Gwendolen b 1984); *Heir* s, William Sinclair; *Career* RNVR; called to the Bar Lincoln's Inn 1961, bencher 1994, in practice at Chancery Bar; *Clubs* Pin Mill Sailing (Suffolk); *Style*— Sir Patrick Sinclair of Dunbeath, Bt; ✉ Hogarth Chambers, 5 New Square, Lincoln's Inn, London WC2A 3SA (tel 020 7404 0404)

SINCLAIR, Ross; *b* 12 April 1966, Glasgow; *Educ* Glasgow Sch of Art (BA, MFA), Calif Inst of the Arts LA; *Career* artist; Paul Hamlyn Award 1998–2000, Arendt Oetker Atelier Stipendium Galerie für Zeitgenossische Kunst Leipzig 1999, Baloise Prize 2001; *Solo Exhibitions* incl: Fanclub (Stills Gallery Edinburgh) 1991, National Virus (Transmission Gallery Glasgow) 1991, Black Flags for USA '92 (Lime Gallery LA) 1992, We Don't Love You Anymore (Transmission Gallery Glasgow) 1993, Galerie Knoll Vienna 1993–94 and 2000, Art Zombies (Catalyst Arts Belfast) 1994, As Good As New (Smart Gallery Amsterdam) 1995, Studio Real Life (Galerie Campbells Occasionally Copenhagen) 1995, I Never Felt More Like Singin the Blues (De Paraplujfabrik Nijmegen) 1995, Real Life Rocky Mountain (CCA Glasgow) 1996, Containerize (Kunstwerke Berlin) 1997, Mercer Union (Toronto) 1997, Irving Gallery Aberdeen 1997, The Agency Contemporary Art London 1997, 1998, 2001, 2002 and 2004, Galerie Walcheturm Zurich 1998, Pier Arts Centre Stromness 1998, Fruitmarket Gallery Edinburgh 1999, Journey to the Edge of the World (Aspex Gallery Portsmouth) 2000, South London Gallery 2001, Badischer Kunstverein Karlsruhe 2001, Kunsthalle Hamburg (room installation) 2002, Galerie Yvon Lambert Paris 2002, Galleria Raffaella Cortese Milan 2002, Wewerka Pavillion Muenster 2002, Dundee Centre for Contemporary Arts 2003, Van Ram Gallery Gent 2004, The Agency 2005; *Group Exhibitions* incl: International Departures (Gesellschaft für Aktuelle Kunst Bremen) 1993, Return of the Exquisite Corpse (Drawing Center NY) 1993, Left Luggage (Hou Hanru Paris and HU Obrist Vienna) 1993, 3+3+3 (Fruitmarket Gallery Edinburgh) 1994, GOL (Mark Boote Gallery NY) 1994, Easter Show, Summer Show LA 1994, Some Of My Friends (Galerie Campbells Occasionally Copenhagen) 1994, Wish You Were Here (Leeds) 1994, Modern Art (Transmission Gallery Glasgow) 1994, Museum of Despair (The Royal Mile (Aerial) Edinburgh) 1994, It is not Like it Used to be (Bartok 32 Galeria Budapest) 1994, Institute of Cultural Anxiety (ICA London) 1994, Eigen + Art at IAS (Independent Artspace London) 1995, Club Berlin (Kunstwerke at the Venice Biennale) 1995, Shift (De Appel Fndn Amsterdam) 1995, How to Dress (Kunsthalle Vienna) 1995, Shopping (CAPC Museum Bordeaux) 1995, Scottish Autumn (Uljak Exhbn Hall Budapest) 1995, 30 seconds plus Title (Art Gallery of Ontario Toronto) 1995, Fairytale in the Supermarket (Fotofeis Glasgow) 1995, 6eme Semaine Internationale de Video (Geneva) 1995, Make me Clean Again (Alpenmilchzentrale Vienna) 1996, Art for People (Transmission Gallery Glasgow) 1996, A4 Favours (Three Month Gallery Liverpool) 1996, Notell Hotel (Moat House Glasgow) 1996, Host (OB Projects Amsterdam) 1996, City Limits (Staffs Univ Stafford) 1996, Shopping (SoHo Art Week NY) 1996, Sarah Staton's Supastore De-Luxe (Up & Co NY) 1996, Speel (Artis Den Bosch) 1997, One Night Stands (The Norwich Gallery) 1997, Glasgow (Kunsthalle Bern) 1997, New Art from Glasgow (Museet For Samtidskunst Oslo) 1998, Do All Oceans Have Walls? (GAK & Kunstlerhaus Bremen) 1998, This Island Earth (An Turrain Art Centre Isle of Skye) 1998, From Here (High St project Christchurch NZ) 1998, Word Enough To Save a Life (Dilston Gove Church London) 1999, If I Ruled the World (Living Art Museum Iceland) 1999, LKW (OK Centre for Contemporary Arts Linz) 1999, For Those About to Rock (Galerie der Stadt Schwaz) 2000, The Blue Chamber (Duff House Banff) 2000, If I Ruled the World (CCA Glasgow) 2000, New Life (Expo Leipzig) 2000, Living in the Real World (Museum Dhont Dhanens Ghent) 2000, Video Vibe (Br Sch of Rome) 2000, LKW (Kunstverein Bregenz and Centre Pasquart Biel) 2000, A Shot in the Head (Lisson Gallery London) 2000, PICAF 2000 (Pusan Art Festival Korea) 2000, Landscape (Br Cncl touring exhbn) 2000–01, Black Box Recorder (Br Cncl London) 2000–01, PS1 NY 2001, City Racing, 10 Years (ICA London) 2001, Aesthetic Terrorism (The Agency London) 2001, Circles (ZKM Karlsruhe) 2001, G3 NY (Casey Kaplan NY) 2001, Gravita Zero (Fondazione Olivetti Rome) 2001, Dundee Centre for the Arts 2001, Air Guitar (MKG Milton Keynes) 2002, No One Ever Dies Here (Hartware projects Dortmund) 2002, Tent (Rotterdam) 2002, Arte Contemporanea & Montagu Aosta 2003, Glasgow MOMA 2003, Home at Last (Harewood House) 2003, Independence (South London Gallery) 2003, Words (Arts Cncl Collection, touring exhbn) 2003, Air Guitar (Milton Keynes Gallery) 2003, Skin Deep (MART Museum Rovereto) 2003, Galleria Sonia Rossi Pardone 2004, Art Metropol Toronto 2004, Villa Arson Nice 2004, Aichi Expo Nagoya Japan 2005; *Style*— Ross Sinclair, Esq

SINCLAIR, Rt Rev (Gordon) Keith; *see:* Bishop of Birkenhead

SINCLAIR-JONES, Ruth E; da of Philip Knopp (d 1975), and Ellen, *née* Sinclair; *b* 9 October 1957, Kent; *Educ* Bromley HS GPDST, Hertford Coll Oxford (scholar, MA); *m* 1982, David E Sinclair-Jones; 2 da (Catherine b 1989, Christina b 2002), 1 s (Philip b 1992); *Career* London Borough of the City of Westminster 1982–85, London Borough of Hammersmith and Fulham 1985–87; British Cncl: joined 1987, subsequent postings incl Bangkok, Warsaw and Vienna, currently change prog mangr Brussels; memb CIPFA 1986, MSP registered practitioner 2005; *Recreations* reading, music, skiing, Scottish country dancing; *Clubs* British (Bangkok); *Style*— Mrs Ruth Sinclair-Jones; ✉ British Council, Rue du Trône 108, 1050 Brussels, Belgium (tel 00 32 2 554 0460, fax 00 32 2 227 0849)

SINCLAIR-LOCKHART, Sir Simon John Edward Francis; 15 Bt (NS 1636), of Murkle, Co Caithness, and Stevenson, Co Haddington; s of Sir Muir Edward Sinclair-Lockhart, 14 Bt (d 1985), and Olga Ann, *née* White-Parsons; *b* 22 July 1941; *m* 1973, Felicity Edith, da of late Ivan Lachlan Campbell Stewart, of Havelock North, NZ; 2 s (Robert Muir b 1973 d 2001, James Lachlan (twin) b 1973), 1 da (Fiona Mary b 1979); *Heir* s, James Sinclair-Lockhart; *Style*— Sir Simon Sinclair-Lockhart, Bt

SINCLAIR TAYLOR, (Robin) James; s of late Bob Sinclair Taylor, and Wendy, *née* Cox; *b* 9 March 1948, Hastings, Sussex; *Educ* Grenville Coll, Univ of Leicester (BSc); *Children* 1 da (Jessica); *Career* admitted slr 1976; trained with Vivash Hunt, slr North Kensington Law Centre 1976–80, researcher American Legal Servs Cmmn 1980, sr slr Hounslow Law Centre 1981, fndr Sinclair Taylor & Martin 1981, ptnr Russell-Cooke (following merger) 1983–; tstee: Camden Charities, Ajahma Tst, Prairie Tst; govr Kensington and Chelsea Coll; memb Lord Chancellor's Legal Aid Advsy Ctee; treas Law Centre Fedn; chair Pregnancy Advsy Service; memb: Law Soc, Charity Law Assoc; *Books* Voluntary Sector Legal Handbook (1996 and 2001), Company Handbook and Register for Voluntary Sector Companies Limited by Guarantee (2002); *Recreations* sailing cruisers and dinghies, gardening, walking, fringe theatre; *Clubs* London Corinthian Sailing, Swanage Sailing; *Style*— James Sinclair Taylor, Esq; ✉ Russell-Cooke, 2 Putney Hill, Putney, London SW15 6AB (tel 020 8394 6480, fax 020 8394 6535, e-mail taylorj@russell-cooke.co.uk)

SINDALL, Barry John; s of Reginald Sindall (d 1978), and Kathleen, *née* Kellison (d 2002); *b* 20 October 1945, Birkenhead, Cheshire; *Educ* Rock Ferry HS Birkenhead, Univ of Exeter (MEd); *m* 1975, Margaret, da of Fredrick Barker; 1 da (Roberta Karen b 6 March 1977), 1 s (Jon Grendon b 1 Sept 1978); *Career* teacher Duncan Bowen Sch Ashford 1967–68, head of humanities R M Bailey Sch Nassau 1968–76, dir of studies Colyton GS 1976–88, dep headteacher Torquay Boys' GS 1988–90, headteacher Colyton GS 1990–; memb Nat GS Ctee; FRSA 1992; *Recreations* amateur dramatics, skiing, fell walking, cricket; *Style*— Barry Sindall, Esq; ✉ Colyton Grammar School, Colyford, Devon EX24 6HN (tel 01297 552327, fax 01297 553853, e-mail bsindall@colytongrammar.devon.sch.uk)

SINDEN, Sir Donald Alfred; kt (1997), CBE (1979); s of Alfred Edward Sinden (d 1972), and Mabel Agnes, *née* Fuller (d 1959); *b* 9 October 1923; *m* 3 May 1948, Diana (d 2004), da of Daniel Mahony (d 1981); 2 s (Jeremy b 14 June 1950 d 29 May 1996, Marcus (Marc), *qv* b 9 May 1954); *Career* actor; first stage performance 1942; assoc artist RSC 1967–; pres: Fedn of Playgoers' Socs 1968–93, Royal Theatrical Fund 1983–, Theatre Museum Assoc 1985–1995; patron: Green Room Club Benevolent Fund 1998–2005, Ellen Terry Theatre 2001–, Irving Soc 2001–; tstee Br Actors' Equity Assoc 1988–2004; Hon DLitt Univ of Leicester 2005; Freeman City of London; FRSA *Television* incl: Two's Company, Never the Twain, Discovering English Churches, Judge John Deed; *Film* Rank Orgn 1952–60 appearing in 23 films incl: Doctor in the House, The Cruel Sea; *Awards* incl: Drama Desk Award (for London Assurance) 1974, Variety Club of GB Stage Actor of 1976, Evening Standard Drama Award Best Actor 1977 (both for King Lear), Pragnell Shakespeare Award 2006; *Books* A Touch of the Memoirs (autobiography, 1982), Laughter in the Second Act (autobiography, 1985), The Everyman Book of Theatrical Anecdotes (ed, 1987), The English Country Church (1988), The Last Word (ed, 1994); *Recreations* serendipity; *Clubs* Garrick (tstee 1980–2000, life memb), Beefsteak, MCC; *Style*— Sir Donald Sinden, CBE; ✉ Number One NW11 6AY

SINDEN, Marcus Andrew (Marc); s of Sir Donald Alfred Sinden, CBE, *qv*, of London, and Diana, *née* Mahony (d 2004); *b* 9 May 1954; *Educ* Hall Sch Hampstead, Edgeborough Sch, Stanbridge Earls Sch, Bristol Old Vic Theatre Sch; *m* 20 Aug 1977 (m dis 1997), Joanne Lesley, da of Geoffrey Gilbert (decd), of Dorset; 1 s (Henry (Hal) b 6 Feb 1980), 1 da (Bridie b 1 Sept 1990); *Career* actor and prodr; jeweller and goldsmith H Knowles-Brown Ltd Hampstead 1973–78; actor 1978–, artistic dir Mermaid Theatre 1993–94, md Smallhythe Productions Ltd 1996–97, assoc prodr Bill Kenwright Ltd 1997–98, md Marc Sinden Productions 2000–, md The One Night Booking Co Ltd 2003–, md UK Theatre Availabity Ltd 2003–; patron Design Museum; Freedom City of London, Liveryman Worshipful Co of Innholders; FZS; *Theatre* as prodr: Seven Deadly Sins Four Deadly Sinners, An Evening With... (series with Julian Clary, Gyles Brandreth and Sir Donald Sinden), Merely Players, Sex Wars, Straker Sings Brel, The Glee Club, East (Stage Award Best Ensemble Work), Shakespeare's Villains (also dir, nominated SOLT/Oliver award for Best Entertainment), Lady Windermere's Fan, Pygmalion (also co-dir), An Ideal Husband, Just The Three of Us, Catch Me If You Can, My Fat Friend, Huckleberry Finn, Dangerous to Know, Aladdin, Noel & Gertie, Passion, Fallen Angels, Woman in Black, Move Over Mrs Markham, Times Up, An Ideal Husband (Australian tour), That Good Night; as actor West End incl: The Beaux Stratagem, Over my Dead Body, Ross, Two into One, School for Scandal, Underground, Her Royal Highness, Enjoy; other roles incl: over 40 plays on tour and in rep incl: Death and the Maiden, Sting in the Tale, Mansfield Park, Private Lives, Dangerous Obsession, There's a Girl in my Soup, John Bull's Other Island (Gaiety Dublin), Major Barbara (Chichester Festival), Death on the Nile, Chorus Girls (Stratford East), Importance of Being Earnest, Under Milk Wood, While the Sun Shines, Pygmalion, Privates on Parade, Julius Caesar, Norman Conquests; *Television* incl: Judge John Deed, The Island, The Politicians Wife, Against All Odds, Century Falls, The Country Boy, Emmerdale, Magnum PI, Never the Twain, Bergerac, Rumpole of the Bailey, If You Go Down to the Woods Today, All at No 20, Wolf to the Slaughter, Crossroads, Home Front, Dick Turpin; as exec prodr Business Profiles; *Film* as actor incl: Puckoon, The Brylcreem Boys, The Mystery of Edwin Drood, Carry on Columbus, Decadence, Princess, Mangeuses d'Homme, White Nights, The Wicked Lady, Clash of Loyalties; assoc prodr That Good Night; *Other Work* many voice-overs on radio and TV incl: Fosters Lager, Apple Computers (nominated for Sony award), Bassetts Allsorts; actor on numerous radio plays and audio-visual commentaries; prodr of audio-CDs incl: The Ballad of Reading Gaol, Oscar Wilde Fairy Tales; *Recreations* theatrical history, zoology, ethology, Sicilian mafiology, motor racing, history of stunt-work, landscape photography; *Style*— Marc Sinden, Esq; ✉ Marc Sinden Productions, 3 Grand Union Walk, Camden Town, London NW1 9LP (tel 020 8455 3278, e-mail mail@sindenproductions.com, website www.sindenproductions.com)

SINFIELD, Prof (Robert) Adrian; s of Robert Ernest Sinfield (d 1983), of Diss, Norfolk, and Agnes Joy, *née* Fouracre (d 1995); *b* 3 November 1938; *Educ* Mercers' Sch, Balliol Coll Oxford (BA), LSE (Dip); *m* 17 Sept 1964, Dorothy Anne, da of George Stanley Palmer (d 1992), of Watford, Herts; 2 da (Beth b 1965, Laura b 1969); *Career* jr admin Lutheran World Service Hong Kong 1961–62, res asst LSE 1963–64, res assoc NY State Mental Health Res Unit Syracuse 1964–65, Univ of Essex 1965–79 (asst lectr, lectr, sr lectr, reader sociology); prof of social policy Univ of Edinburgh 1979–95 (emeritus 1995–); visiting posts: Graduate Sch of Social Work and Soc Res Bryn Mawr Coll Pa 1969, NY Sch of Social Work Univ of Columbia 1969, Euro Chair of Social Policy Eötvös Loránd Univ Budapest 1996, 1999, 2001 and 2005, Dept of Applied Social Studies City Univ of Hong Kong 1999, Inst of Public Policy Auckland Univ of Technol 2004; conslt: on long term unemployed OECD Paris 1965–68, on industrial social welfare UN NY 1970–72, on income maintenance servs N Tyneside CDP 1975–78, on tax benefits ILO Geneva 1999; exec Child Poverty Action Gp 1974–78 and 2001– (vice-chair 2003–), co-fndr and chair Mgmnt Ctee Unemployment Unit 1981–91; pres: Sociology and Social Policy BAAS 1993, Social Policy Assoc 1996–2001 (chair 1986–89); Hon PhD Eötvös Loránd Univ Budapest 2004; *Books* The Long-Term Unemployed (1968), Industrial Social Welfare (1971), What Unemployment Means (1981), The Workless State (co-ed with Brian Showler, 1981), Excluding Youth (co-author, 1991), The Sociology of Social Security (co-ed, 1991), Poverty, Inequality and Justice (ed, 1993), Tax Routes to Welfare in Denmark and the United Kingdom (co-author, 1996); *Recreations* reading, walking, travel; *Style*— Prof Adrian Sinfield; ✉ 12 Eden Lane, Edinburgh EH10 4SD (tel 0131 447 2182); University of Edinburgh, School of Social and Political Studies, Adam Ferguson Building, George Square, Edinburgh EH8 9LL (tel 0131 650 3924, fax 0131 650 3919, e-mail adrian.sinfield@ed.ac.uk)

SINGER, Prof Albert; s of Jacob Singer (Capt in Polish Army, d 1989), of Sydney, Aust, and Gertie, *née* Sadik (d 1986); *b* 4 January 1938; *Educ* Sydney GS, Univ of Sydney (MB BS, PhD), Univ of Oxford (DPhil); *m* 27 June 1976, Talya, da of Maurice Goodman (d 1991); 3 da (Leora b 1978, Rebecca b 1980, Alexandra b 1983); *Career* Nat Serv Royal Aust Air Force 1956–57, Univ Sqdn Flt Lt 1960, active serv with RAAF Reserve in Vietnam 1968–69; Commonwealth fell Oxford 1970, visiting fell to Europe and USA 1968–69, pt/t conslt WHO 1969–70, in res 1970–73, sr lectr then reader Univ of Sheffield 1973–80, conslt gynaecologist Whittington Hosp London 1980–, prof UCL; has published extensively on subject of gynaecological surgery and res into causes of female cancer; served on numerous govt panels and ctees primarily concerned with female cancer; memb RSM, FRCOG; *Books* The Cervix (with J Jordan), The Colour Atlas of Gynaecological Surgery (6 vols with David Lees), Lower Genital Tract Pre-Cancer (with J Monaghan); *Recreations* sport, especially tennis, swimming and sailing; *Clubs* Oxford and Cambridge; *Style*— Prof Albert Singer; ✉ First Floor Consulting Rooms, 212–214 Great Portland Street, London W1N 5HG (tel 020 7390 8442, fax 020 8458 0168)

SINGER, His Hon Harold Samuel Singer; s of Ellis Singer (d 1982), and Minnie, *née* Coffman (d 1964); *b* 17 July 1935; *Educ* Salford GS, Fitzwilliam House Cambridge (MA); *m* 1966, Adele Berenice, da of Julius Emanuel; 1 s (Andrew b 1967), 2 da (Rachel b 1970, Victoria b 1974); *Career* called to the Bar Gray's Inn 1957; recorder of the Crown Court 1981–84, circuit judge (Northern Circuit) 1984–2003; govr Delamere Forest Sch 1998; *Recreations* music, reading, painting, photography; *Style*— His Hon Harold Singer

SINGER, Nicky Margaret; da of Geoffrey William Singer (d 1970), and Sheila Anne, *née* King (d 1987); *b* 22 July 1956; *Educ* Queen Anne's Caversham, Univ of Bristol (BA); *m* 17 Sept 1983, (Timothy) James Stephen King-Smith; 2 s (Roland James Singer-Kingsmith 28 Dec 1987, Edmund John Singer-Kingsmith b 26 Sept 1991), 1 da (Molly Rose Singer-Kingsmith b 23 July 1996); *Career* assoc dir of lectures and seminars ICA 1980–83, researcher Voices (Channel 4) 1983–84, programme conslt for David Puttnam at Enigma Film and TV 1984–85, literature offr SE Arts 1985–86, co-fndr and co-dir Performing Arts Labs charity 1987–96; presenter six films Labours of Eve (BBC) 1995; chair Literature Ctee Brighton Festival 1988–93, memb Bd SE Arts Bd 2000–02; short drama cmmnd The Sins of the World (Channel 4) 1990, story ed Asylum Wall (multi-media narrative) 1996–99; *Books* novels: To Still the Child (1992), To Have and to Hold (1993), What She Wanted (1996), My Mother's Daughter (1998); children's fiction: Feather Boy (2002, Blue Peter Book of the Year 2002, BBC dramatisation 2004 (winner BAFTA Best Drama), Feather Boy the Musical (written jtly) 2006), Doll (2003, shortlisted Booktrust Teenage Prize), The Innocents' Story (2005), GemX (2006); non-fiction: The Tiny Book of Time (with Kim Pickin, 1999), The Little Book of the Millenium (with Jackie Singer, 1999); *Style*— Ms Nicky Singer; ✉ c/o Conville and Walsh, 118–120 Wardour Street, London W1V 3LA

SINGER, Hon Mr Justice; Sir (Jan) Peter Singer; kt (1993); s of late Dr Hanus Kurt Singer, and late Anita, *née* Muller; *b* 10 September 1944; *Educ* King Edward's Sch Birmingham, Selwyn Coll Cambridge; *m* 2 Jan 1970 (m dis 2006), Julia Mary, da of Norman Stewart Caney (d 1988); 1 da (Laura b 1983), 1 s (Luke b 1985); *Career* called to the Bar Inner Temple 1967 (bencher 1993); recorder of the Crown Court 1987–93 (asst recorder 1983–87), QC 1987, judge of the High Court of Justice (Family Div) 1993–; Family Law Bar Assoc: sec 1980–83, treas 1983–90, chm 1990–92; Bar nominee: Matrimonial Causes Rule Ctee 1981–85, Nat Legal Aid Ctee Law Soc 1984–89; memb: Senate of the Inns of Court and the Bar 1983–86, Legal Aid and Fees Ctee Bar Cncl 1986–92; ex officio memb: Gen Cncl of the Bar 1990–92, Bar Ctee Gen Cncl of the Bar 1990–92; vice-pres Int Acad of Matrimonial Lawyers (Euro Chapter) 1992–93; *Publications* Rayden on Divorce (jt ed, 14 edn 1983), At A Glance: Essential Court Tables for Ancillary Relief (jt ed, annually 1992–), Essential Family Practice (jt consulting ed, annually 2000–02), @eGlance (software, 2001–), Care (software, 2003–); *Recreations* travel, walking; *Style*— The Hon Mr Justice Singer; ✉ Royal Courts of Justice, Strand, London WC2A 2LL

SINGER, Susan Honor (Sue); da of Brig John James McCully, DSO, (d 1985), and Honor Goad, *née* Ward (now Mrs Edward Basil Elliott), of Deal, Kent; *b* 23 February 1942; *Educ* St Mary's Sch Calne, Open Univ (BA), Garnett Coll London (PGCE); *m* 18 April 1964, Christopher Ronald Morgan Singer; 1 s (Humphrey Stewart Morgan b 14 Dec 1965), 2 da (Charlotte Honor b 20 Sept 1967, Hermione Juliet b 24 Jan 1971); *Career* set up and ran pre-sch playgroup 1968–74; St Paul's Girls' Sch: mathematics teacher 1980–91, head of Middle Sch 1988–91, head of mathematics 1990–91; headteacher Guildford HS 1991–2002; educational conslt 2002–; GSA: memb 1991–2002, chm Educ Ctee 1998–2000, jt chm GSA/HMC Educn/Acad Policy Ctee 1998–2000, pres 2001; memb: Reference Gp for Tomlinson Enquiry into A Level Standards 2002, Steering Gp Post 14 Inquiry into Mathematics 2003; pres Mathematical Assoc 2005–06; RSA 1994; *Recreations* off shore sailing; *Style—* Mrs Sue Singer; ✉ 39 East Sheen Avenue, London SW14 8AR (tel 020 8876 4031, fax 020 8876 4615, e-mail sue.singer@btconnect.com)

SINGH, Dr Ajeet; s of Wir Singh (d 1961), and Jagchanan Kaur; *b* 6 June 1935; *Educ* King George Med Coll Lucknow India (MB BS), Univ of Bombay (DA); *m* 5 Aug 1962, Sharda, da of Mangesh Nadkarny, of Bankikiodla, India; 1 s (Bobby b 15 June 1963), 2 da (Aarti, Vineeta); *Career* asst prof of anaesthetics Bombay 1964–67, sr registrar anaesthesia Liverpool 1969–72, conslt anaesthetist West Midland RHA 1972–; former dir Midland Community Radio Coventry, former chm Radio Harmony Coventry, fndr memb and former pres Rotary Club of Coventry Jubilee, former memb Exec Ctee Relate Rugby; memb: Med Research Inst Appeal Ctee Univ of Warwick, Assoc of Anaesthetists GB and Ireland, Intractable Pain Soc, Midland Soc of Anaesthetists, Rugby Med Soc; former minute sec Obstetric Anaesthetist Soc; life memb Guru Nanak Gurdwara Rugby; FFARCS; *Publications* author of six papers in professional jls; *Recreations* music, photography, painting, broadcasting; *Clubs* Rotary (Coventry), Jubilee, Whitefield Golf (fndr memb), Rugby 16; *Style—* Dr Ajeet Singh; ✉ Hospital of St Cross, Barby Road, Rugby CV22 5PX (tel 01788 813207, e-mail ajeet@larbreck.fsbusiness.co.uk)

SINGH, Prof Ajit; *b* 11 September 1940; *Educ* Punjab Univ (BA), Howard Univ Washington DC (MA), Univ of Cambridge (MA), Univ of Calif Berkeley (PhD); *Career* Univ of Cambridge: research offr 1964–65, asst univ lectr 1965–68, univ lectr 1968–91, ad hominem reader 1991–95, prof of economics 1995–; Queens' Coll Cambridge: lectr and fell 1965, dir of studies in economics 1972–95, sr fell 1992; Dr William M Scholl visiting prof of int economics Univ of Notre Dame 1987–94; currently ed Cambridge Jl of Economics; conslt: ILO Geneva 1988–, World Bank Washington DC 1989–, UNCTAD 1990–, South Cmmn and subsequently South Centre 1990–; sr economic advsr: Govt of Mexico 1978–82, Govt of Tanzania 1982–85; Academician UK Acad of Social Sciences 2004; *Publications* author of several books and numerous articles in leading academic jls; *Style—* Prof Ajit Singh; ✉ Queens' College, Cambridge CB3 9ET (fax 01223 740479, e-mail ajit.singh@econ.cam.ac.uk)

SINGH, Amolak; MBE (2003); *b* 16 June 1934; *Educ* King Edward VII Sch Taiping, Elphinstone Coll Univ of Bombay, Nair Hosp Dental Coll Univ of Bombay (BDS), Royal Dental Sch Queen's Univ Belfast (LDS RCS), Univ of London (LLB), KCL (Dip Med Ethics and Law); *m*; *Career* princ in gen dental practice 1961–; chief exec Gen Dental Practitioners' Assoc 1991–2004, past pres Anglo-Asian Odontological Gp; fndr memb BUPA Dental Cover (also Advsy Ctee); memb: Cncl Br Dental Health Fndn 1990–92, Employment Tbnls (sec of state appt) 1992–2004, Criminal Injuries Compensation Appeals Panel (Home Office appt) 1997–, Gen Dental Services Ctee BDA 1990–2003; chm Cncl of Managerial and Professional Staffs; author of numerous pubns on legal and medico-legal topics for dentists; memb: GDC, BDA; FGDP RCS, fell Pierre Fauchad Acad (FPFA); *Recreations* skiing, reading, walking, swimming, gardening; *Style—* Amolak Singh, Esq, MBE; ✉ Knightons, Keston, Kent BR2 6AG (tel 01689 856354)

SINGH, Indarjit; OBE (1996), JP (Wimbledon 1984); *Educ* MBA; *Career* journalist and broadcaster; hon dir Network of Sikh Orgns UK, hon ed Sikh Messenger; fndr memb and former co-chair Interfaith Network UK, chair Sikh Cncl for Interfaith Rels, tstee World Congress of Faiths; memb: Religious Advsy Cncl UN Assoc, Inner Cities Religious Advsy Cncl DETR, Gene Therapy Advsy Ctee, Central Religious Advsy Ctee BBC and Independent Broadcasting Authy; Home Office conslt on the pastoral care of Sikhs in penal estabs 1976–; former memb: Home Sec's Advsy Cncl on Race Rels, Bd of Visitors Brixton Prison 1981–84, Med Ethics Ctee BMA 1993–98; frequent lectr on race rels at maj univs and other instns in UK and abroad; World Congress of Faiths Sir Francis Younghusband Meml Lecture 1990; frequent contrib: The Times, The Independent, and other newspapers and magazines in UK and abroad, Pause for Thought (BBC World Serv), Thought for the Day (BBC Radio 4); recipient: UK Templeton Prize (for furtherance of spiritual and ethical understanding) 1989, Interfaith Medallion (for servs to religious broadcasting) 1991, included in The Independent's Good List 2006; Hon LLD Univ of Leicester, Hon DLit Univ of Coventry; MComm, CEng, MIMinE; *Style—* Dr Indarjit Singh, OBE; ✉ Network of Sikh Organisations UK, 43 Dorset Road, Merton Park, London SW19 3EZ (tel 020 8540 4148)

SINGH, Karamjit Sukhminder; CBE (2000); s of Tara Singh (d 1986), of Punjab, India, and Chanan, *née* Kaur (d 2001); *b* 11 March 1950; *Educ* Univ of Warwick (MA); *m* 1972, Jaswir Kaur, da of Malkit Singh; 2 s; *Career* res assoc Industrial Rels Res Unit Univ of Warwick 1971–75, caseworker Leicester Community Rels Cncl 1975–78, sr exec offr Cmmn for Racial Equality 1978–82, princ offr W Midlands CC 1982–84, asst co clerk Leics CC 1984–87, memb Police Complaints Authy (England and Wales) 1987–90 and 1991–94, memb Parole Bd for England and Wales 1994–97, memb Criminal Cases Review Cmmn 1997–2006, memb Data Protection Tbnl 1997–2003, cmmr Electoral Cmmn 2001–, memb QC Selection Panel for England and Wales 2005–, NI Judicial Appts Ombudsman 2006–; pt/t Civil Serv cmmr 1996–2000; memb: Area Manpower Bd for Coventry and Warks 1984–87, Industrial Tbnls Panel for England and Wales 1986–96, W Midlands Police Authy 1994–96, Complaints Audit Ctee Immigration and Nationality Dept 1994–97, Judicial Studies Bd 1994–99, Regulatory Decisions Ctee FSA 2002–06; non-exec dir Coventry HA 1996–2001; hon memb Working Gp Justice 1993–94; hon tstee Citizenship Fndn 1993–2000, tstee Lloyds TSB Fndn for England and Wales 2001–06, tstee Br Lung Fndn 2006–; govr Coventry Univ 1994–99; Harkness Fellowship 1990–91; *Recreations* family, reading, charity work in India; *Clubs* Reform; *Style—* Karamjit Singh, Esq, CBE; ✉ Electoral Commission, Trevelyan House, 30 Great Peter Street, London SW1P 2HW (tel 020 7271 0603, e-mail ksingh@electoralcommission.org.uk)

SINGH, HE Laleshwar Kumar Narayan; s of late Mr and Mrs Narayan, of Windsor Forest, Guyana; *b* 2 April 1941; *Educ* Windsor Forest Govt Sch, Indian Educn Tst Coll, Clerk to the Justices; *m* 10 Sept 1971, Latchmin, *née* Ramrattan; 2 c (Ashwindra b 22 Nov 1976, Vashti b 17 Oct 1987); *Career* Guyanan diplomat; migrated to Britain 1961; offr Inner London Ctee of Magistrates until 1993, high cmmr to UK 1993– (concurrently non-resident ambass to the Netherlands, France, Russian Fedn, Czech Republic and the Holy See); *Style—* HE Mr Laleshwar Singh; ✉ Guyana High Commission, 3 Palace Court, Bayswater Road, London W2 4LP (tel 020 7229 7684/8, fax 020 7727 9809, e-mail ghc.1@ic24.net)

SINGH, Marsha; MP; s of Harbans Singh, and late Kartar Kaur; *b* 11 October 1954; *Educ* Belle Vue Boys Upper Sch, Loughborough Univ (BA); *m* 1, Sital Kaur (d 2001); 1 s (Ravinder Singh Sohal), 1 da (Hardev Kaur Sohal); m 2, 21 Sept 2006, Kuldip Mann; 1 step s (Sukhinder), 1 Step da (Serena); *Career* grad trainee Lloyd's Bank 1976–79, with Bradford Community Relations Cncl 1980–81, Bradford Law Centre 1981–83, princ educn offr 1983–90, serv quality advsr and sr devpt mangr Bradford Community Health 1990–97; MP (Lab) Bradford W 1997–; memb: Home Affrs Select Ctee, Intl Devpt Select Ctee 2005–; *Recreations* chess, bridge, reading; *Style—* Marsha Singh, Esq, MP; ✉ House of Commons, London SW1A 0AA (tel 020 7219 4516)

SINGH, Dr Simon Lehna; MBE; s of Mengha Singh, and Sawarn, *née* Kaur; *b* 19 September 1964, Wellington, Somerset; *Educ* Imperial Coll London (BSc), Univ of Cambridge (PhD); *Career* TV producer and dir 1991–96, writer and broadcaster 1997–; *Books* Fermat's Last Theorem (1997), The Code Book (1999), Big Bang (2004); *Style—* Dr Simon Singh, MBE; ✉ c/o Patrick Walsh, Conville and Walsh Ltd, 2 Ganton Street, London W1F 7QL (tel 020 7287 3030, e-mail patrick@convilleandwalsh.com)

SINGLETON, (Richard John) Basil; s of Richard Carl Thomas Singleton (d 2002), of Crumlin, Co Antrim, and Marion Frances, *née* Campbell (d 1981); *b* 25 April 1935; *Educ* Foyle Coll Londonderry, Campbell Coll Belfast, Hong Kong Univ; *m* 14 Sept 1957, Florence Elizabeth, da of Albert McRoberts, of Dunmurry, Co Antrim (d 1981); 1 s (Richard David b 1961 d 1975), 1 da (Wendy Marion Jane b 1964); *Career* RA 1953–55; Ulster TV Ltd: mktg exec 1959–64, mktg mangr 1965–73; md AV Browne Advertising Ltd 1973–82, chm and chief exec Basil Singleton Ltd 1982–; dir: Brookville Trading Co Ltd 1982–, Mandalay Enterprises Ltd 1993–, European Magazine Services Ltd 1998–, PPA Ireland Ltd 2002–; memb Belfast Jr C of C 1961–75; chm: Publicity Assoc of NI 1969–70, Ulster Branch Irish Hockey Union 1976–88; pres: NI Civil Service Hockey Club 1973–78, Old Campbellian Soc 1999; MCIM, MIPR; *Recreations* hockey, tennis; *Clubs* Ulster Reform; *Style—* Basil Singleton, Esq; ✉ Basil Singleton Ltd, 72 Circular Road, Belfast, County Antrim BT4 2GD (tel 028 9076 8330)

SINGLETON, Sir Roger; kt (2006), CBE (1997); s of Malcolm Singleton (ka 1944), and Ethel, *née* Drew; *b* 6 November 1942; *Educ* City GS Sheffield, Univ of Durham (MA), Univ of Bath (MSc), Univ of London (Dip Soc Studies), Univ of Leeds (CertEd); *m* 30 July 1966, Ann, da of late Lawrence Edmond Hasler; 2 da (Jane b 1968, Katharine b 1969); *Career* various appts in care and educn of deprived and delinquent young people 1961–71, professional advsr to Children's Regnl Planning Ctee 1971–74, chief exec Barnardo's 1984–2006 (dep dir 1974–84), conslt and govt advsr 2006–, chm Ind Barring Bd; accredited mediator; dir Capacity Builders; contribs to various jls; chm: Princess of Wales Memorial Fund, Perennial (Gardeners' Royal Benevolent Soc); tstee: Inst for Global Ethics, Children's High Level Gp; former: treas Nat Cncl of Voluntary Child Care Organisations (chm 1990–92); memb: Nat Youth Bureau, Central Cncl for Educn and Trg of Social Workers; memb various Govt ctees and inquiries; CCMI 1994, FRSA 1991; *Recreations* timber framed buildings; *Clubs* Reform; *Style—* Sir Roger Singleton, CBE; ✉ e-mail randasingleton@aol.com

SINGLETON, Valerie; OBE (1994); da of Wing Cdr Denis Gordon Singleton, OBE, and Catherine Eileen Singleton, LRAM; *b* 9 April 1937; *Educ* Arts Educnl Sch London, RADA; *Career* broadcast personality and writer; Bromley Rep 1956–57; subsequently: No 1 tour Cambridge Arts Theatre, theatre work, TV appearances in Compact and Emergency Ward 10, top voice over commentator for TV commercials and advtg magazines; BBC1: continuity announcer 1962–64, presenter Blue Peter 1962–72, Nationwide 1972–78, Val Meets the VIPs (3 series), Blue Peter Special Assignment (4 series), Blue Peter Royal Safari with HRH The Princess Anne, Tonight and Tonight in Town 1978–79, Blue Peter Special Assignments Rivers Yukon and Niagara 1980; BBC2: Echoes of Holocaust 1979, The Migrant Workers of Europe 1980, The Money Programme 1980–88; Radio 4: PM 1981–93, several appearances Midweek; freelance broadcaster and travel writer 1993–; presenter: Back-Date (daily quiz prog, Channel Four) 1996, Playback (series, History Channel) 1998; numerous appearances in TV advertising and coporate work; memb Equity; *Recreations* travelling, photography, exploring London, sailing, walking, visiting salesrooms, museums; *Style—* Miss Valerie Singleton, OBE; ✉ c/o Lili Panagi, PanMedia UK, 18 Montrose Crescent, London N12 0ED (tel 020 8446 9662, e-mail v.panagi@btinternet.com)

SINGLETON-GREEN, Brian; s of John Singleton-Green (d 1974), and Edna, *née* Hargreaves (d 1999); *b* 26 April 1951; *Educ* Eltham Coll, Clare Coll Cambridge; *m* 26 April 1986, Barbara Ann, *née* Dyer; *Career* Deloitte & Co 1973–76, HM Treasy 1977–78, Binder Hamlyn 1979–80, Tech Directorate ICAEW 1980–89, ed Accountancy 1990–; FCA 1976; *Style—* Brian Singleton-Green, Esq

SINHA, 6 Baron (UK 1919); Arup Kumar Sinha; s of 5 Baron Sinha (d 1999); *b* 23 April 1966; *m* 1, 1993 (m dis 1995), Deborah Jane, da of Tony Tidswell; m 2, July 2001, Penny Marie, da of Ellen Kramer, and Clair Kramer; *Heir* bro, Hon Dilip Sinha; *Style—* The Rt Hon the Lord Sinha

SINHA, Prof Brajraman Prasad; s of Shree B N Sinha (d 1966), of Hazipur, India, and S *née* Devi (d 1982); *b* 20 December 1936; *Educ* Patna Univ (BSc Civil), Univ of Liverpool (Dip Building Sci), Univ of Edinburgh (PhD, DSc); *m* 10 June 1962, N, da of S Sahaya; 3 c (Sangeeta b 24 April 1964, Saurabh b 18 Jan 1970, Shameek b 12 Jan 1973); *Career* asst engr Patna Univ Works Dept India 1957–59, asst engr Bihar State Electricity Bd India 1959–60; PWD Bihar India: asst engr 1960–63, design engr 1968–69; Univ of Edinburgh Dept of Civil Engrg: research fell then lectr 1969–85, sr lectr 1985, reader 1995, prof 1999–2002, emeritus prof 2002–; visiting prof: Biher Coll of Engrg 1986, Univ of Arcona 1999, Santa Catrina Brazil 1999, Indian Inst of Sci Bangalore 2000 and 2003, Univ of Dresden 2003; chm Hindu Temple & Cultural Centre 1985–86; pres Indian Arts Cncl 1994; memb: Boroughmuir Sch Cncl 1981, Senate Univ of Edinburgh 1984–2000; chair Lothian Racial Equality Cnc 2004–; Henry Adam Bronze Medal IStructE 1971–72, prize from Inst of Engineers India 1991–92, univ scholarship in intermediate sci Bihar Univ India; FIStructE 1983, FICE 1992, MASCE 1998, CEng; *Books* Reinforced and Prestressed Masonry (contrib, 1989), Design of Masonry Structures (co-author, 1998), Structured Masonry for Developing Countries (co-ed, 1992); contrib over 110 articles to professional jls; *Recreations* reading, overseas travel, photography, table tennis, writing; *Style—* Prof Brajraman Sinha; ✉ School of Engineering and Electronics, William Rankine Building, King's Buildings, West Mains Road, Edinburgh EH9 3JN (tel 0131 650 5726, fax 0131 6506781, e-mail bsinha@ed.ac.uk)

SINHA, Indra; s of Capt Bhagvati Prasad Sinha, of Bombay and Goa, India, and Irene Elizabeth, *née* Phare (d 1986); *b* 10 February 1950; *Educ* Mayo Coll Ajmer Rajasthan India, Oakham Sch, Pembroke Coll Cambridge (BA); *m* 9 Sept 1978, Viktoria Jane Yvette, da of Maj Arthur Henry Lionel Pilkington; 1 da (Tara Pauline Elizabeth b 6 Oct 1981), 2 s (Dan Alexander Iqbal b 28 Aug 1984, Samuel Barnaby Prem b 14 May 1988); *Career* writer; advtg copywriter: The Creative Business 1976–79, Ogilvy & Mather 1980–83; with Collett Dickenson Pearce & Partners 1984–95, chm and creative ptnr Chaos Communication Ltd 1995; memb D&AD; *Books* Kama Sutra (new trans, 1980), Tantra (1994), The CyberGypsies (1998); *Recreations* travel, reading, cybertravel, folk music, butterflies; *Clubs* Sussex CCC, Cassoulet; *Style—* Indra Sinha, Esq

SINNETT, Prof Dudley Hugh; s of Hugh Sinnett, and Ruth, *née* Matthews; *Educ* Dynevor GS Swansea, Charing Cross Med Sch London, Univ of London (MS); *m* 27 Sept 1975, Jill Christine, *née* Morris-Jackson; 1 s (Tim), 1 da (Katie); *Career* sr surgical registrar Bart's London 1980–84, conslt surgn and hon sr lectr Royal Marsden Hosp London 1984–89, conslt breast surgn Charing Cross Hosp London 1989–, prof of breast surgery Imperial Coll London 2005; examiner Univ of London, memb Ct of Examiners RCS (also memb Intercollegiate Bd of Examiners for FRCS); jt author of papers in learned jls; supporter: Royal Med Benevolent Fund, Haven Tst for Women with Breast Cancer, Women's Nat Cancer Control Campaign, Breast Cancer Care Med Advsy Panel; Freeman City of London, Liveryman Worshipful Soc of Apothecaries; FRCS 1976; *Recreations* watching sport, playing golf, reading, travel; *Clubs* RAC, Walton Heath Golf; *Style—* Prof Dudley Sinnett; ✉ Charing Cross Hospital, Fulham Palace Road, London W6 8RF (tel 020 8846 7303, fax 020 8846 1624, e-mail dsinnett@hhnt.org)

SINNOTT, Kevin Fergus; s of Myles Vincent Sinnott (d 1974), of Wales, and Honora, *née* Burke (d 1993); *b* 4 December 1947; *Educ* St Roberts Aberkenfig, Cardiff Coll of Art (fndn course), Glos Coll of Art and Design (DipAD), RCA (MA); *m* 30 Aug 1969, Susan Margaret, da of Lawrence Hadyn Forward, and Rita, *née* Terry; 3 s (Matthew b 22 Aug 1971, Gavin b 6 June 1975, Thomas b 4 March 1983), 1 da (Lucy Anne b 24 Aug 1984); *Career* artist; visiting lectr: Ruskin Sch of Drawing Oxford 1975–76, Canterbury Coll of Art 1981–88; pt/t teacher St Martin's Sch of Art London 1981–93; *Solo Exhibitions* House Gallery London 1980 and 1983, Ikon Gallery Birmingham 1980, Riverside Studios London

1981, St Paul's Gallery Leeds 1981, Blond Fine Art London 1982 and 1984, Chapter Arts Centre Cardiff 1984, Bernard Jacobson Gallery (London 1986, London and NY 1987, NY 1988, London 1990), Jan Turner Gallery LA 1987, Roger Ramsay Gallery Chicago 1988, Anne Berthoud Gallery London 1990, Flowers East London 1992, 1994 and 1996, Gallery Henrik Kampmann Copenhagen 1996, Flowers East London 1998, Martin Tinney Gallery 1999, 2001, 2003, 2005 and 2007, Caldwell/Snyder NY 2000, Caldwell/Snyder San Francisco 2001 and 2002, Depot Haus Grafenwald Germany 2004 and 2006; *Group Exhibitions* incl: Whitechapel Open London 1978 and 1980, John Moores Liverpool 1978, 1980 and 1991, Ruskin Sch of Art Oxford 1981, Blond Fine Art London 1982–85, LA Louver Gallery 1986, Bernard Jacobson Gallery London 1986, Lefevre Gallery London 1988, The Contemporary Arts Centre Cincinnati 1988, Oriel Mostyn 2002; *Work in Public Collections* Br Cncl, Arts Cncl of GB, IOM Arts Cncl, RCA, The Whitworth Manchester, Br Museum, Wolverhampton City Art Gallery, Metropolitan Museum of Art NY, Deutsche Bank AG London, Unilever, Contemporary Art Soc of Wales, The Nat Museum of Wales, Univ Catholic Chaplaincy Oxford, Ashmolean Museum Oxford; *Publications* Behind the Canvas (autobiography, 2007); *Clubs* Chelsea Arts, Ogmore; *Style*— Kevin Sinnott, Esq; ✉ Ty'r Santes Fair, Pont-y-Rhyl, Bridgend, Mid Glamorgan CF32 8LJ (tel 01656 871 854, e-mail mail@kevinsinnott.co.uk)

SINYOR, Joe; s of Samuel Joseph Sinyor, and Claire, *née* Mizrahi; *b* 16 August 1957; *Educ* Manchester Grammar, Jesus Coll Cambridge (BA), London Business Sch (MBA); *m* 22 Dec 1987, Pamela Caroline Neild, da of Michael Collis; 2 s (Joshua Samuel Michael b 17 Nov 1988, Benjamin Johnathan b 30 June 1990), 1 da (Jessica Claire Rachel b 1 Jan 1994); *Career* slr Nabarro Nathanson London 1979–81, corp fin exec J Henry Schroder Wagg 1984–85, sr engagement mangr McKinsey & Co Inc 1985–90, gp chief exec Pepe Group plc 1990–93, md Dillons The Bookstore 1994–98, md Sony United Kingdom Ltd 1998–2000, chief exec (newspapers) Trinity Mirror plc 2000–03, md Terra Firma Capital Partners 2003–06, md Strategic Valve Partners LLP 2007–; memb: Cncl Booksellers' Assoc 1995–98, Bd Channel Four TV Corp 1998–2004; *Recreations* family, opera, walking, skiing; *Style*— Joe Sinyor, Esq; ✉ Strategic Valve Partners LLP, 5 Savile Row, London W1S 3PD (tel 020 7758 7800)

SISSONS, Dr Clifford Ernest; s of George Robert Percival Sissons (d 1964), and Elsie Emma, *née* Evans (d 1993); *b* 26 January 1934; *Educ* Liverpool Inst HS for Boys, Univ of Liverpool Med Sch (MB ChB); *m* 1, 28 Dec 1956 (m dis 1997), Mary Beryl, da of James Davies (d 1941); 2 s (Mark Christopher John, Guy Richard James), 1 da (Amanda Jane Elizabeth); m 2, 29 Nov 1997, Gweneth Dianne, da of Roy Williams; *Career* Nat Serv Capt RAMC 1959–61; house physician and house surgn Liverpool Stanley Hosp 1958–59; med registrar: Birkenhead Gen Hosp 1962–67, Professorial Med Unit Liverpool Royal Infirmary 1967–69; sr med registrar David Lewis Northern and Sefton Gen Hosp Liverpool 1969–72, conslt physician Wrexham War Memorial and Maelor Hosps 1972–98, conslt physician Classic Yale Hosp, Wrexham and Grosvenor Nuffield Hosp 1974–; memb Cncl RCP 1985–87 (regnl advsr 1982–87), examiner in med RCP (London) 1991–; memb: BMA, Br Soc of Echocardiography, Br Hyperlipidaemia Assoc; FRCP 1977 (MRCP 1966); *Recreations* languages, travel, reading, painting; *Style*— Dr Clifford Sissons; ✉ Classic Yale Hospital, Croesnewyd Road, Wrexham LL13 7YP (tel 01978 291306, fax 01978 291397)

SISSONS, (Thomas) Michael Beswick; s of Capt T E B Sissons (ka 1940), and Marjorie, *née* Shepherd; *b* 13 October 1934; *Educ* Winchester, Exeter Coll Oxford (MA); *m* 1, 1960 (m dis), Nicola Ann, *née* Fowler; 1 s, 1 da; m 2, 1974 (m dis), Ilze, *née* Kadegis; 2 da; m 3, 1992, Serena, *née* Palmer; *Career* Nat Serv 2 Lt 13/18 Royal Hussars 1953–55; lectr in history Tulane Univ New Orleans 1958–59, AD Peters & Co Ltd Literary Agency 1959–88 (dir 1965, chm and md 1973–88), jt chm The Peters Fraser & Dunlop Group (PFD) Ltd 1994–99 (jt chm and md 1988–94, sr conslt 1999–), dir London Broadcasting Co 1973–75; pres Assoc of Authors' Agents 1978–81, memb Ctee MCC 1984–87 and 1993–2000 (chm Arts and Library Sub-Ctee 1985–93, chm Mktg and Public Affrs Sub-ctee 1995–2000); memb Bd: Groucho Club plc 1985–2001, BFSS 1994–95, Countryside Movement 1995–97; *Books* Age of Austerity (ed with Philip French, 1963, 2 edn 1986), A Countryside For All (ed, 2001); *Recreations* gardening, cricket, music; *Clubs* Groucho, MCC, Boodle's; *Style*— Michael Sissons, Esq; ✉ The White House, Broadleaze Farm, Westcot Lane, Sparsholt, Wantage, Oxfordshire OX12 9PZ (tel 01235 751215, fax 01235 751561); PFD, Drury House, 34–43 Russell Street, London WC2B 5HA (tel 020 7344 1000, fax 020 7836 9539, e-mail msissons@pfd.co.uk)

SISSONS, (John Gerald) Patrick; s of Gerald William Sissons (d 1966), and Georgina Margaret, *née* Cockin (d 1960); *b* 28 June 1945; *Educ* Felsted, St Mary's Hosp Med Sch London (MB BS, MD); *m* April 1971 (m dis 1985), Jennifer Anne Scovell; 2 da (Sarah b 1973, Rebecca b 1974); *Career* registrar and hon lectr Royal Postgrad Med Sch London 1973–76, NIH Fogarty fell and asst memb Scripps Clinic San Diego 1977–80, reader in infectious diseases Royal Postgrad Med Sch 1987 (Wellcome sr lectr 1980–86); Univ of Cambridge: prof of med 1988–2005, regius prof of physic 2005–; author of pubns on pathogenesis of virus infections; fell Darwin Coll Cambridge; FRCP, FRCPath, FMedSci 1998; *Recreations* travel; *Style*— Patrick Sissons, Esq; ✉ Department of Medicine, University of Cambridge Clinical School, Hills Road, Cambridge CB2 2QQ (tel 01223 336849)

SISSONS, Peter George; s of George Robert Percival Sissons (d 1964), and Elsie Emma, *née* Evans (d 1993); *b* 17 July 1942; *Educ* Liverpool Inst HS for Boys, Univ Coll Oxford (MA); *m* Sylvia; 2 s (Michael Peter, Jonathan Richard), 1 da (Kate Victoria); *Career* TV journalist and presenter; ITN 1964–89: gen trainee then script writer, gen reporter, foreign correspondent, news ed, industry correspondent, industry ed, presenter News at One 1978–82, presenter Channel Four News 1982–89; chm Question Time BBC TV 1989–93, presenter 6 O'Clock News BBC 1989–93, presenter 9 O'Clock News BBC 1994–2000, presenter 10 O'Clock News BBC 2000–03, presenter BBC News 24 2003–, presenter Breakfast with Frost 2003–05; Broadcasting Press Guild's Best Front of Camera Performer 1984, RTS's Judges Award 1989, TRIC Newscaster of the Year 2001; hon fell Liverpool John Moores Univ 1997; Hon LLD Univ of Liverpool 2002; *Recreations* relaxing; *Style*— Peter Sissons, Esq

SITKOVETSKY, Dmitry; s of Julian Sitkovetsky, violinist, and Bella Davidovich, pianist; *b* 1954, Baku, USSR; *Educ* Moscow Conservatoire, Juilliard Sch NY; *Career* violinist and conductor; winner Kreisler competition Vienna 1979; fndr and music dir New European Strings 1990–, princ conductor Ulster Orchestra 1996–2001 (now conductor laureate), music dir Greenboro Symphony Orch 2003–, princ guest conductor Russian State Orch 2003–; artist-in-residence: Orchestre de Castilla and Leon 2006, Bodensee Festival 2007; artistic dir: Korsholm Festival Finland 1983–93, Umea Festival Sweden 1991–93, Seattle International Music Festival 1993–; a founding artist Tuscan Sun Festival 2003–; guest conductor: Stuttgart Chamber Orch, MDR Leipzig Orch, chamber ensemble of St Martin in the Fields (tour of Germany) 1994, Vienna Virtuosi, Academia di Santa Cecilia, New York Chamber Symphony, Detroitt Symphony, BBC Philharmonic; worked with numerous major conductors incl Claudio Abbado, Vladimir Ashkenazy, Andrew Davis, Sir Colin Davis, Christoph Dohnányi, Sir Neville Marriner, Gennadi Rozhdestvensky, Wolfgang Sawallisch, Michael Tilson Thomas, Mariss Jansons, Yuri Temirkanov and Kurt Masur; given recital performances at various international venues and festivals incl Salzburg, Lucerne, Edinburgh, Ravinia and Mostly Mozart, BBC Proms (première of Casken's Violin Concerto) 1995; was the first postwar Russian emigré musician to return to Moscow at the official invitation in 1988; subject of South Bank Show 1993; *Recordings* incl: Bach (sonatas and partitas for solo violin), Haydn, Mozart, Beethoven, Mendelssohn, Brahms, Elgar, Bartók, Prokofiev and Shostakovich violin concerti; *Publications* author of over 20 transcriptions incl: Bach Goldberg Variations for String Trio and Goldberg Variations for String Orch, Dohnányi Serenade, Shostakovich String Symphony Opus 73 for String Orch, Tchaikovsky String Symphony Opus 30; *Style*— Dmitry Sitkovetsky, Esq; ✉ Greensboro Symphony Orchestra, 200 North Davie Street, Greensboro, NC 27401, USA

SITWELL, Sir (Sacheverell) Reresby; 7 Bt (UK 1808), of Renishaw, Derbyshire; DL (Derbyshire 1984); s of Sir Sacheverell Sitwell, 6 Bt (d 1988), by his w, Georgia Louise, *née* Doble (d 1980); *b* 15 April 1927; *Educ* Eton, King's Coll Cambridge; *m* 1952, Penelope, yr da of Col Hon Donald Alexander Forbes, DSO, MVO (d 1938), s of 7 Earl of Granard; 1 da (Alexandra Isobel Susanna Edith (Mrs Richard Hayward) b 1958); *Career* former Lt 2 Bn Grenadier Gds, BAOR Germany 1946–48; advtg and PR exec 1948–60, vending machines operator 1960–70, wine merchant 1960–75; landowner 1965–; Lord of the Manors of Eckington and Barlborough in Derbys and of Whiston and Brampton-en-le-Morthen in S Yorks; High Sheriff of Derbys 1983; Freeman City of London 1984; hon fell Grey Coll Durham 2001, LittD Univ of Sheffield 2004; *Publications* Mount Athos (with John Julius Norwich and A Costa, 1964), Hortus Sitwellianus (epilogue, 1984); *Recreations* travel, music, architecture, racing; *Clubs* White's, Brooks's, Pratt's, Pitt (Cambridge), County (Derby), Soc of Dilettanti; *Style*— Sir Reresby Sitwell, Bt, DL, LittD; ✉ Renishaw Hall, Renishaw, Sheffield S21 3WB (tel 01246 432042, fax 01246 430760); 4 Southwick Place, London W2 2TN (tel and fax 020 7262 3939)

SIXSMITH, (George) Martin; s of George Francis Sixsmith, of Walton, Cheshire, and Joyce Lythgoe, *née* Sutton; *b* 24 September 1954; *Educ* Manchester Grammar, Sorbonne, New Coll Oxford (open scholar, MA), Leningrad Polytechnical Inst, Harvard Univ, St Antony's Coll Oxford; *m* 4 Sept 1976, Mary Winifred, da of Francis Cooney; 2 da (Joanna Mary b 19 Dec 1979, Rebecca Helen b 11 Oct 1988), 2 s (Patrick Martin b 7 Jan 1983, Daniel Thomas b 30 Oct 1985); *Career* Harkness fell and tutor in slavics Harvard Univ 1977–79; BBC: trainee journalist London 1980–82, Western Europe reporter Brussels 1982–85 then Geneva 1985–86, Eastern Europe corr Warsaw 1986–88, Moscow corr TV News 1988–91, Washington corr TV News 1991–95, Moscow corr TV News 1995–97; dir of information DSS until 1999, dir of communications Marconi plc 1999–2001, dir of communications DTLR 2001–02, freelance journalist and author 2002–; memb Young Königswinter Confs 1986; *Books* Vladislav Xodasevic: k 40–letiju so dnja smerti (critical biog of Vladislav Khodasevich the Russian poet, 1979), The Harvard Guide to France (1980), Jobit's Journal: A history of the French campaigns in Ireland (trans, 1982), Moscow Coup: the death of the Soviet system (1991), Spin, a novel (2004), I Heard Lenin Laugh (2006), The Litvinenko File: the true story of a death foretold (2007); *Recreations* serious music, Russian literature, Liverpool FC; *Style*— Martin Sixsmith, Esq

SIZER, Prof John; CBE (1989); s of John Robert Sizer, and Mary Sizer; *b* 14 September 1938; *Educ* Univ of Nottingham (BA), Loughborough Univ (DLitt); *m* 1965, Valerie Claire Davies; 3 s; *Career* accountancy asst Ross Group Ltd Grimsby 1954–57, sr cost clerk Eskimo Foods Ltd Cleethorpes 1957–58, asst accountant Clover Dairies Ltd Grimsby 1958–61, fin advsr Guest Keen & Nettlefolds Ltd 1964–65, Univ of Edinburgh 1965–68 (teaching fell, lectr), London Graduate Sch of Business Studies 1968–70 (sr lectr in accounting, asst academic dean); Loughborough Univ: prof of fin mgmnt 1970–96, dean Sch of Human & Environmental Studies 1973–76, sr pro-vice-chllr 1980–82, fndr and head Dept of Mgmnt Studies 1971–80, 1982–84 and 1990, dir Business Sch 1991–92, visiting prof 1996–2005, emeritus prof 2005–; visiting prof Lancaster Univ 1993–94, memb Science and Engrg Base Coordinating Ctee 1993–2001, memb Steering Gp Foresight Prog 1996–2001; chief exec and memb Scottish Higher Educn Funding Cncl 1992–2001, chief exec and memb Scottish Further Educn Funding Cncl 1999–2001; Nat Forum for Mgmnt Educn & Devpt 1987–96 (memb Exec Ctee, chm Fin and Resourcing Ctee), advsr Business & Mgmnt Studies UFC 1989–92; memb: Univ Grants Ctee 1984–89, Jt CVCP UFC Steering Ctee on Performance Indicators 1989–92, UFC NI Ctee 1989–92; chm OECD IMHE (Institutional Management for Higher Education) 1980–84, vice-pres Soc for Res into Higher Educn 1995– (chm 1992–93); memb Editorial Bd: Financial Accountability and Mgmnt 1985–96, Higher Educn 1990–2007, Educn Economics 1993–2001, Tertiary Educn and Mgmnt 1994–2001; memb: Cncl Chartered Inst of Mgmnt Accountants 1981–88 (chm Int Ctee 1982–86, chm Fin Ctee 1986–88), Public Sector and Not-for-Profit Ctee Accounting Standards Bd 1994–98, Scot Parl Fin Issues Advsy Gp 1998–99, Knowledge Economy Task Force Scot Office 1998–99, Scottish Executive 1999–2000; tstee Nat Centre for Social Research 2007– (chm Audit Ctee); advsr Bertelsmann Fndn Germany 1989–90; Hon LLD: Univ of Abertay Dundee, Univ of St Andrews; Hon DSc (Econ) Univ of Hull; fell Chartered Inst of Mgmnt Accountants, fell Chartered Mgmnt Inst, FRSA; *Books* An Insight into Management Accounting (1969, 3 edn 1989), Case Studies in Management Accounting (1974), Perspectives in Management Accounting (1981), Resources and Higher Education (jt ed, 1983), A Casebook of British Management Accounting (jtly 1984, 1985), Institutional Responses to Financial Reductions in the University Sector (1987); *Recreations* walking; *Style*— Prof John Sizer, CBE; ✉ Charnwood, 15 Selwyn Road, Burntwood, Staffordshire W57 9HU (tel 01543 674361, fax 01543 675712, e-mail profsizer@aol.com)

SKAN, Martin; s of Reginald Norman Skan (d 1985), of Worcester, and Millicent May, *née* Vaughan (d 1977); *b* 28 December 1934; *Educ* Haileybury, Harvard Sch Calif (exchange scholar); *m* 1, 1970 (m dis 1988), Sally Elizabeth Margaret, da of John Eric Wade; 2 da (Lara Julie b 1971, Tilly Matina b 1975); m 2, 1989, Brigitte Berta, da of late Erwin Heinrich Joos, of Winterthur, Switzerland; *Career* cmmnd Dorset Regt 1955–57; British Market Research Bureau Ltd (subsid of JWT Advertising) 1957–58, Kinloch (PM) Ltd 1958–89; dir: Skan Taylor & Co Ltd 1959–65, J A & P Holland Ltd 1962–65, Parkinsons (Doncaster) Ltd 1962–65, Holland Distributors Ltd 1962–65, Harper Paper Group (and subsid cos) 1962–65, LMS (Consultants) Ltd 1986–91; chm Chewton Glen (Hotels) Ltd 1966–2006 (pres 2006–); for Chewton Glen Hotel: Egon Ronay Hotel of The Year 1976, Michelin Star 1981–, The Hoteliers' Hotelier The Observer 1988, Times Hotel Restaurant of the Year 1990, Tourism Catey award 1990, American Express Country Hotel of the Year 1991 and 1992, 5 Red Stars (AA and RAC) 1993, Condé Nast Traveller Magazine Best Resort Hotel in Britain 1998, Booker Award of Excellence for Best British Hotel 1998, Gourmet Magazine Best Country House Hotel in the World 2000, Best Small Hotel (under 60 rooms) World Gallivanters Guide 2003, Best Hotel Spa in Europe Gala Magazine Germany 2003, Best Hotel (under 100 rooms) Worldwide Gallivanters Guide 2004, Best Hotel in Britain Conde Nast USA 2006; Personality of the Year 1990, Master Innholder 1991, Hotelier of the Year 1991, Director of the Year 1999 (PricewaterhouseCoopers), AA/AXA Lifetime Hospitality Award 2006–07; memb: Relais Château 1972–2006, Leading Hotels of the World 1972–99; fndr memb The Walpole Ctee; hon memb Académie Culinaire de France; Freeman City of London 1991; RSA; *Recreations* tennis, golf, cycling, skiing; *Clubs* IoD, Hamptworth Golf, Ascona Golf (Switzerland), Royal Lymington Yacht; *Style*— Martin Skan, Esq; ✉ Honeysuckle Cottage, Bramshaw, Hampshire SO43 7JH (tel 023 8081 2149, e-mail mskan@skanenterprises.com)

SKELDING, Barry Howard; s of late Denis Howard Skelding, and Stella, *née* Scott Elliott; *b* 2 January 1945; *Educ* The Stationers' Co's Sch; *m* 27 Aug 1977, Margaret Marion, da of Gordon David Carnegie (d 1969); 2 da (Katie b 1981, Sarah b 1983); *Career* admitted slr 1970; assoc ptnr Gamlens 1970, gp property slr EMI Ltd 1970–80, ptnr Rowe and

S

Maw 1980–92, assoc Jaques & Lewis and Eversheds 1993–95, ptnr Park Nelson 1995–2004, conslt Lester Aldridge (incorporating Park Nelson) 2004–05 and 2007; memb Law Soc 1970; Freeman City of London 1996; *Recreations* lawn tennis, squash rackets, music; *Clubs* Cumberland, Radlett LT and SRC, Broxbourne SC, Escorts SRC, Veterans' Squash Club of GB, Veterans' Lawn Tennis Club of GB; *Style*— Barry H Skelding, Esq; ✉ 2 Folly Pathway, Radlett, Hertfordshire WD7 8DS

SKELLERN, Peter; s of John Skellern, of Lancs, and Margaret, *née* Spencer (d 1987); *b* 14 March 1947; *Educ* The Derby Sch Bury, Guildhall Sch of Music and Drama (AGSM); *m* 1970, Diana Elizabeth, da of Edward Dampier Seare (d 1997); 1 s (Timothy Seare b 29 Nov 1971), 1 da (Katherine Daisy b 22 June 1974); *Career* pianist, singer, composer; trombonist Nat Youth Brass Band 1963, memb March Hare pop gp 1968–70; wrote song You're a Lady (reached No 1 in 6 countries) 1972, writer for Stop the Week (BBC Radio 4) 1970s, made autobiographical TV series 1981, scriptwriter, composer and actor Happy Endings TV series of mini-musicals 1982, co-wrote (with Richard Stilgoe) and appeared in Who Plays Wins (Vaudeville) 1985 and has toured with their two-man show every year until 2001; *Recordings* 15 albums incl: Astaire (1980), Oasis (with Julian Lloyd Webber and Mary Hopkin, 1982); *Publications* Trolls (musical for children, 1990, published by J B Cramer), Six Simple Carols for SATB Choirs (published by Novello & Co, 1998); other anthems and sacred music published by Royal Sch of Church Music for whom he holds choral workshops throughout the country; *Recreations* painting, golf; *Clubs* MCC, Lord's Taverners, Soc of Amateur Artists; *Style*— Peter Skellern, Esq

SKELLETT, Colin Frank; *b* 13 June 1945; *Educ* City Univ, North Staffordshire Poly (MSc); *Career* various operational mgmnt positions in water and sewerage industry until 1986; Wessex Water (previously Wessex Water Authy): div mangr 1986–88, gp md 1988–94, gp chief exec 1995–99, chm 1996–; chm Jarvis plc 2000–02, vice-chm Azurix 1999–2001, dir YTL Utilities UK 2003–; tstee Wateraid 1995–2003; fell Assoc of Churchill Fells 1983; CChem, FRSC, FCIWEM; *Style*— Colin Skellett, Esq; ✉ Wessex Water, Claverton Down, Bath BA2 7WW (tel 01225 526000, fax 01225 528000)

SKELMERSDALE, 7 Baron (UK 1828); Roger Bootle-Wilbraham; s of Brig 6 Baron Skelmersdale, DSO, MC (d 1973), and Ann (d 1974), da of Percy Quilter and gda of Sir Cuthbert Quilter, 1 Bt; *b* 2 April 1945; *Educ* Eton, Lord Wandsworth Coll; *m* 1972, Christine, da of Roy Morgan, of Hamel Evercreech, Somerset; 1 da (Hon Carolyn Ann (Mrs Staton) b 1974), 1 s (Hon Andrew b 1977); *Heir* s, Hon Andrew Bootle-Wilbraham; *Career* horticulturist; dir Broadleigh Nurseries 1991– (md 1973–81); pres Somerset Tst for Nature Conservation 1980–, pres Br Naturalists Assoc 1980–95; Lord-in-Waiting to HM The Queen 1981–86; Parly under sec of state: DOE 1986–87, DHSS 1987–88, DSS 1988–89, NI Office (DHSS and Agric) 1989–90; dep chm of Ctees House of Lords 1991–95, dep speaker House of Lords 1995–2003, elected to sit in House of Lords 1999, oppn whip 2003–05, spokesman on work and pensions 2005–; parly conslt 1991–96; memb Jt Ctee on Statutory Instruments 1991–2003, memb Sub-Ctee B (Euro energy, industry and tport) 1996–2003, memb House of Lords Procedure Ctee 1997–2000; chm The Stroke Assoc 1993–2004; govr Castle Sch Taunton 1992–96; memb RHS, tstee Hestercombe Gardens Tst 2001–; FLS; *Recreations* gardening, reading, bridge, walking; *Style*— The Rt Hon Lord Skelmersdale; ✉ House of Lords, London SW1A 0PW (tel 020 7219 3224, fax 020 7630 0088, e-mail skelmersdaler@parliament.uk)

SKELTON, Nick David; s of David Frank Skelton, of Odnull Farm, Wase Lane, Berkswell, and Norma, *née* Brindley; *Children* 2 s (Daniel b 9 April 1985, Harry b 20 Sept 1989); *Career* show jumper; ridden 100 World Cup classes and 116 Nations Cup teams; jr Euro champion 1975, Br champion 1981, winner 10 classes Wembley 1981, 3 team Gold medals Euro Championships (individual Bronze), 4 team Silver medals and 4 team Bronze medals World Championships (individual Bronze), memb Olympic team 1988, 1992 and 1996, winner Hickstead Derby 3 times (runner up twice); Grand Prix wins: Dublin 4 times, NY twice, Aachen 3 times; GB high jump record Olympia 1975; *Recreations* skiing, farming; *Style*— Nick Skelton, Esq; ✉ c/o British Show Jumping Association, British Equestrian Centre, Stoneleigh, Kenilworth, Warwickshire CV8 2LR

SKELTON, Robert William; OBE (1989); s of John William Skelton (d 1989), of South Holmwood, Surrey, and Rosa Ellen Victoria Ena, *née* Wright (d 1969); *b* 11 June 1929; *Educ* Tiffins Sch Kingston; *m* 31 July 1954, Frances, da of Lionel Aird (d 1990), of Clapham; 3 s (Oliver b 1957, Gregory b 1959, Nicholas b 1962); *Career* V&A: dep keeper Indian Section 1972–77 (asst keeper 1960–72), keeper Indian Dept 1978–88; tstee: Asia House Tst 1977–, The Indian Nat Tst for Art and Cultural Heritage (INTACH) UK 1991–; memb Cncl: Soc for S Asian Studies 1984–94, Royal Asiatic Soc 1970–73, 1975–78 and 1988–92; Col James Tod Award Maharana Mewar Fndn 1997; *Books* Indian Miniatures from the XVth to XIXth Centuries (1961), Rajasthani Temple Hangings of The Krishna Cult (1973), Indian Painting (jtly, 1978), Arts of Bengal (jtly, 1979), The Indian Heritage (jtly, 1982); *Recreations* chamber music, walking; *Style*— Robert Skelton, Esq, OBE; ✉ 10 Spencer Road, South Croydon, Surrey CR2 7EH (>e-mail< robertskelton@blueyonder.co.uk)

SKEMPTON, Maj-Gen Keith; CBE, DL; s of Dr Ivor Skempton (decd), and Leslie Skempton (decd), of Little Sutton, Cheshire; *Educ* Birkenhead Sch, Liverpool Coll of Building, Army Staff Coll Camberley; *m* 1971, Sue, *née* Lawrence; 1 da (Kyra b 1979); *Career* cmmnd Cheshire Regt 1969; served UK, Europe, Middle East and Far East; COS HQ 33 Armoured Bde Germany 1982–83, mil asst to GOC NI 1986–88, CO 1 Bn Cheshire Regt 1988–91, Deputy COS 1 Armoured Div 1991–93, DACOS G4 Ops and Plans HQ Land Command 1993–96, COS Br Forces Cyprus 1996–98, Deputy COS Support HQ ARRC, Asst COS HQ AFSOUTH 2001–03; Col Cheshire Regt 1999–2006; business devpt dir Denis Ferranti Gp 2006–07; dir of ops Chester Cathedral 2007–; Queen's Commendation for Valuable Service (Kosovo), CBE for logistic aspects of ops in Rwanda, Angola, Kuwait, Yugoslavia, twice mentioned in despatches; Dep-Lt Cheshire 2006; MInstD, FCMI; *Recreations* interest in most sports, motor vehicles, travel, architecture, walking, shooting, sailing, skiing; *Clubs* Cheshire Regt Assoc, Army and Navy, Chester City; *Style*— Major General Keith Skempton, CBE; ✉ RHQ Cheshire Regiment, The Castle, Chester (tel 01244 327617)

SKENE, Charles Pirie; OBE (1992); *b* 30 April 1935; *Educ* Loretto, Robert Gordon Univ (DBA); *m* 9 May 1964, Alison Jean Katherine Lamont; 2 da (Jennifer b 1966, Pamela b 1972), 1 s (Richard b 1967); *Career* gp chm and chief exec of The Skene Group of Companies; pres: Jr Chamber Aberdeen 1967, Aberdeen C of C 1983–85, Assoc of Scot Chambers of Commerce 1985–86; fndr Aberdeen Civic Soc 1968, nat sec Jr Chamber Scot 1970 (dir 1969); chm: NE Branch of Lorettonian Soc 1976–86, Royal Northern and Univ Club 1981–82, Industry Year Grampian Area 1986, Industry Matters Grampian Area 1987–89; dir Aberdeen and NE Soc for the Deaf 1973–97, assessor to Dean of Guild 1983–95, industry conslt Scot Educn Indust Ctee 1986–87, former memb Exec Ctee Scot Cncl Devpt and Industry; Robert Gordon Univ: govr 1985–96, visiting prof of entrepreneurship, endowed chair of entrepreneurship 2001, Centre of Enterprise renamed Charles P Skene Centre of Entrepreneurship 2002; memb: Economic Affrs Ctee SCUA 1986–97, Exec Ctee CBI (Scot) 1988–94 and 1995–, Open Univ Enterprise in Higher Educn Advsy Ctee for Scot 1990–92; chm: RGIT Enterprise Mgmnt Ctee 1988–93, Scot Industrialists' Cncl Grampian Branch, Scotland Educn Ctee CBI 1993–94, Enterprise Gp CBI (Scot) 1994–96; donor of the annual Skene Aberdeen Int Youth Festival Award 1976–2000; initiator Skene Young Entrepreneurs Award 1987–2004; author of paper Educating Scotsmen and Women 1987; MSC Fit for Work Award, European Year of the Environment (conservation award, design award commendation), Queen's Award for Enterprise Promotion 2005; FRSA, FBIPP; *Style*— Charles P Skene, Esq, OBE; ✉ The Skene Group, 96 Rosemount Viaduct, Aberdeen AB25 1AX (tel 01224 627171, fax 01224 626866)

SKENE, Prudence; CBE (2000); da of Robert Worboys Skene (d 1988), and Phyllis Monica, *née* Langley (d 1982); *b* 9 January 1944; *Educ* Francis Holland Sch; *m* 12 Sept 1986, Brian Henry Wray (d 2002); 2 step c (Nicholas Wray, Jacqueline Plant); *Career* admin Granada Films 1967–69, tour mgmnt UK and Australia 1969–71, mangr Castle Opera 1972, dep admin Round House Chalk Farm 1973–75, admin rising to exec dir Ballet Rambert 1975–86, exec prodr English Shakespeare Co 1987–90, freelance conslt 1991–, dir The Arts Fndn 1993–98, advsy dir Performing Arts Labs 1998–99; non-exec dir Theatre Royal Bath Ltd 1998–2003, chm Rambert Dance Co 2000–; Arts Cncl of England: chm Dance Advsy Panel 1992–96, ACE/Royal Opera House Monitoring Ctee 1994–96, chm Lottery Advsy Panel 1996–2000, memb Audit Ctee; chm Arvon Fndn 2001–05; chm Dancers' Resettlement Tst and vice-chm and tstee Dancers' Resettlement Fund 1988–92; non-exec dir RUH NHS Tst Bath 1999–2003; tstee: Cardiff Old Library Tst 1996–2000, Stephen Spender Meml Fund 2000–, NESTA 2006–07; memb Cncl of Mgmnt Theatrical Management Assoc 1984–96 (pres 1991–92, vice-pres and chm Fin Ctee 1985–89); FRSA 1992; *Recreations* travel, reading, food; *Style*— Ms Prudence Skene, CBE; ✉ 19A Eccleston Street, London SW1W 9LX (tel 020 7259 9174, e-mail prudence.wray@virgin.net)

SKIDELSKY, Baron (Life Peer UK 1991), of Tilton in the County of East Sussex; Robert Jacob Alexander Skidelsky; s of Boris J Skidelsky (d 1982), and Galia V, *née* Sapelkin (d 1987); *b* 25 April 1939; *Educ* Brighton Coll, Jesus Coll Oxford (MA, DPhil); *m* 2 Sept 1970, Augusta Mary Clarissa, da of John Humphrey Hope (d 1974); 2 s (Hon Edward b 1973, Hon William b 1976), 1 da (Hon Juliet b 1981); *Career* res fell Nuffield Coll Oxford 1965–68, assoc prof Johns Hopkins Univ 1970–76; Univ of Warwick: prof of int studies 1978–90, prof of political economy 1990–2006; memb: Lord Chllr's Advsy Cncl on Public Records 1987–92, Schools Examination and Assessment Cncl 1992–93 (resigned); chm: Charleston Tst 1987–92, Social Market Fndn 1991–2001, Hands Off Reading Campaign 1994–97; tstee Manhatten Inst 1994–; dir: Stillwell Fin Servs 2000–02, Janus Capital Gp 2003–, Greater Europe Fund 2005–; advsr Deutsche Bank 2006–, tstee Humanitas 1991–2000, tstee Moscow Sch of Political Studies 1999–; govr Brighton Coll 1998– (chm Bd of Govrs 2004–); memb Wilton Park Acad Cncl 2002–; sits in House of Lords (as Cons until 2001, then as cross-bencher), oppn spokesman on culture, media and sport House of Lords 1997–98, princ oppn spokesman on treasy affairs House of Lords 1998–99; memb Cncl Royal Econ Soc 2007; FRHistS 1973, FRSL 1978, FBA 1994; *Books* Politicians and the Slump (1967), English Progressive Schools (1970), Oswald Mosley (1975), John Maynard Keynes (I 1983, II 1992, III 2000, single vol edn 2003), World After Communism (1994), Beyond the Welfare State (1997); *Recreations* tennis, bridge, opera; *Style*— The Rt Hon Lord Skidelsky, FBA; ✉ Saxon Lodge, Saxon Lane, Seaford BN25 1QL (e-mail skidelskyr@parliament.uk); Centre for Global Studies tel 020 7219 8721

SKIDMORE, (Frederic) David; OBE (1984); s of Frederick Ernest Skidmore (d 1990), of Bexhill on Sea, E Sussex, and Mary Elizabeth Skidmore (d 1980); *b* 10 December 1939; *Educ* Gonville & Caius Coll Cambridge (MA, MB BChir, MD), Birmingham Med Sch; *m* 2 July 1966 (m dis 1983), Yvonne, da of John Steel (d 1979); 1 da (Rebecca Mary b 1969), 1 s (David James Benedict b 1970); m 2, 1983, Diana Sarah; *Career* former: demonstrator in anatomy Cambridge, Br Heart Fndn res fell, lectr in surgery Univ of Manchester; currently: conslt surgn London & Kent, hon sr clinical lectr Dept of Surgery Royal Free UC Med Sch, examiner in surgery Univ of London; Freeman: City of London, Worshipful Co of Tylers and Bricklayers, Worshipful Soc of Apothecaries; memb: RIIA, RSM, Br Assoc for Surgical Oncology; FRCSEd 1968, FRCS 1970; *Books* Studies on Development of the Heart and Great Vessels (1973); *Publications* Cardiac Embryology, Trauma and Intensive Care; 37 papers on various surgical and cancer topics in peer-reviewed jls; *Recreations* swimming, windsurfing, ornithology; *Clubs* Hawks' (Cambridge), Otter, Lansdowne; *Style*— David Skidmore, Esq, OBE; ✉ 2 The Close, London SE3 0UR; London Bridge Hospital, London SE1 2PR (tel 020 8318 6923, car 07836 714137, fax 020 8852 6919, e-mail dskidmore@doctors.org.uk, website www.cancersurgeonconsultant.co.uk)

SKILLING, Raymond Inwood; s of late Dane Skilling, and Elizabeth Skilling, *née* Burleigh; *b* 14 July 1939; *Educ* Campbell Coll Belfast, Queen's Univ of Belfast (LLB, Marquess of Dufferin and Ava Medal for debate, McKane Medal in Jurisprudence), Law Sch Univ of Chicago (JD); *m* 1982, Alice Mae, da of late Robert J and Catherine Welsh, of Indiana, USA; 1 s (from previous marriage); *Career* Cwlth fell Univ of Chicago 1961–62, Fulbright fell 1961–63, Bigelow teaching fell Law Sch Univ of Chicago 1962–63; joined Clifford-Turner (now Clifford Chance) 1963, admitted slr 1966, ptnr Clifford-Turner 1969–76, admitted bar Illinois, USA 1974; dir and exec vice-pres Aon Corp (and predecessor companies) 1976–2003, sr advsr Aon Corp 2004–; dir London General Insurance Co Ltd 1985–, dir Combined Insurance Companies of Europe Ltd 1985–; memb Bd of Overseers RAND Inst for Civil Justice 2001– (chm Bd 2004–); dir Queen's Univ Belfast Fndn 2001–, nat dir Lyric Opera Chicago 2003–; tstee Chicago Symphony Orchestra 2002–, memb Int Advsy Bd Br American Business Cncl 2004–; *Recreations* music, travel, avoiding physical exercise; *Clubs* Buck's, Carlton, City of London, Cercle de L'Union Interalliée (Paris), Chicago, Racquet (Chicago); *Style*— Raymond I Skilling, Esq; ✉ 200 East Randolph Street, Chicago 60601 USA (tel 00 312 381 3025)

SKILTON, Prof David John; s of Henry Charles Stanley Skilton (d 1999), of London, and Iris Flora Marion, *née* Redfern (d 1975); *b* 10 July 1942; *Educ* Tollington GS London, King's Coll Cambridge (MA, MLitt), Univ of Copenhagen; *m* 1, 29 Oct 1976 (m dis 1981), Marvid Elaine Graham, da of David King Wilson (d 1976); m 2, 12 April 1984, Joanne Vivien, da of Norman Louis Papworth, of Hunts; 1 s (Adam Jonathan b 1989), 1 da (Hannah Catherine b 1985); *Career* sr lectr Univ of Glasgow 1978–80 (lectr 1970–80), dean Faculty of Arts St David's Univ Coll Lampeter 1983–86 (prof of English 1980–86), prof of English and head Dept of English UWIST 1986–88; Cardiff Univ: prof of English 1988–, head Sch of English, Communication and Philosophy 1988–2002, dep princ 1992–95, pro-vice-chllr 1995–96, dean of Humanities and Social Studies 1997–2000, dir Centre for Editorial and Intertextual Research 2004–; founding ed Jl of Illustration Studies 2007–; memb Nat Curriculum English Working Gp 1988–89, literary advsr to Trollope Soc 1988–, tstee and chair of Advsy Bd Roald Dahl Arts Project Tst; FRSA 2001, fell English Assoc 2002; *Books* Anthony Trollope and his Contemporaries (1972), Defoe to the Victorians: Two Centuries of the English Novel (1978), The Complete Novels of Anthony Trollope (gen ed), Critical Approaches: The Early and Mid-Victorian Novel (1992), Anthony Trollope, An Autobiography (ed 1996); *Recreations* music; *Style*— Prof David Skilton; ✉ Cardiff University, Humanities Building, Colum Drive, Cardiff CF10 3EU (tel 029 2087 4040, fax 029 2087 4502, e-mail skilton@cf.ac.uk)

SKINGLE, HE Diana; *b* 3 May 1947; *Partner* Christopher John Marshall Carrington; *Career* diplomat; entered HM Dip Serv 1966; posted: Kampala 1970, Abidjan 1974, Vila 1975, Prague 1977, Casablanca 1979; second sec FCO 1982–85, second sec (aid and commercial) Georgetown 1985–86, second sec (devpt) Bridgetown 1986–88, first sec (info) UKDEL NATO Brussels 1988–93, first sec FCO 1993–2001, dep head of mission Addis Ababa 2001–04, high cmmr to Seychelles 2004–; *Style*— HE Ms Diana Skingle; ✉ c/o Foreign & Commonwealth Office (Victoria), King Charles Street, London SW1A 2AH

SKINNER, Alan Kenneth; s of Kenneth Alfred Skinner of Grayshott, Surrey, and Millicent Louise, *née* Chapman; *b* 27 August 1948; *Educ* Sutton Valence; *m* 24 March 1973, Heather, da of Peter Campbell; 1 da (Hannah b 13 June 1978); *Career* Edward Moore & Sons (now

Menzies): articled clerk 1966–70, qualified 1970, ptnr 1975, sr ptnr Kingston upon Thames office 1975–; chm Accreditation of Trg Offices Surrey Bd ICAEW 1984–93, chm SW London Dist Soc of CAs 1981–82, external examiner Accountancy Fndn Course Kingston Univ 1986–94; non-exec dir Kingston Hosp 1990–97; former non-exec dir: Hadleigh Products Ltd, Kingston University Campus Enterprises Ltd; memb: Kingston Round Table 1976–89, Kingston Rotary 1998–; FCA 1979 (ACA 1970); *Recreations* travel, golf, rugby and nature; *Style—* Alan Skinner, Esq; ✉ Green Hayes, Forest Road, Pyrford, Woking, Surrey GU22 8LU; Menzies, Neville House, 55 Eden Street, Kingston upon Thames, Surrey KT1 1BW (tel 020 8974 7500, fax 020 8541 5820, e-mail askinner@menzies.co.uk)

SKINNER, Prof Andrew Stewart; s of Andrew Paterson Skinner (d 1975), of Cardross, Dunbartonshire, and Isabella Bateman, *née* Stewart (d 1986); *b* 11 January 1935; *Educ* Kiel Sch Dumbarton, Cornell Univ, Univ of Glasgow (MA, BLitt); *m* 29 Aug 1966, Margaret Mary Dorothy, da of William Robertson (d 1986), of Alloway, Ayrshire; *Career* Queen's Univ Belfast 1960–62, Queen's Coll Dundee 1962–64; Univ of Glasgow: clerk of senate 1983–90, Daniel Jack chair of political economy 1985–94, Adam Smith chair 1994–97, vice-princ (Arts) 1991–96; Hon DUniv Glasgow 2001; FRSE 1988, FBA 1993; *Books* Sir James Steuart Principles of Political Economy (ed, 1966, and 1998 with N Kobayashi and H Mizuta), Adam Smith - The Wealth of Nations (ed with R H Campbell and W B Todd, 1976), A System of Social Science - papers relating to Adam Smith (1979, 2 edn, 1996), Adam Smith Reviewed (ed with P Jones, 1992), Index to Smith's Works (with K Haakommssem); *Recreations* gardening; *Clubs* Naval; *Style—* Prof Andrew Skinner, FRSE, FBA; ✉ Glen House, Cardross, Dunbartonshire G82 5ES (tel 01389 841603); Department of Political Economy, University of Glasgow, Glasgow G12 8RT (tel 0141 330 4657, fax 0141 330 4940, telex 777070 UNIGLA)

SKINNER, Angus; s of Dr Theodore Skinner (d 1988), and Morag, *née* MacKinnon (d 1989); *b* 4 January 1950; *Educ* Univ of Edinburgh (BSc), Univ of London, Univ of Strathclyde (MBA); *m* (sep 1995); 1 s (Aidan b 11 July 1980), 2 da (Jenny b 20 Sept 1982, Caitlin b 9 May 1985); *Career* social worker Cheshire and Kent Cncls 1971–75, social work mangr Lothian and Borders Cncls 1975–91, chief inspr Scottish Office 1992– (chief social work advsr 1991–92); *Books* Another Kind of Home (1992); *Recreations* family, friends, learning, theatre; *Style—* Angus Skinner, Esq; ✉ Scottish Executive, Victoria Quay, Edinburgh EH16 6QQ (tel 0131 244 5414, fax 0131 244 5496)

SKINNER, Caroline Mary Louise; da of Robin Mark Hill Griffiths, of Glan-y-Wern, Llandyrnog, and Rosemary Alison, *née* Collins; *b* 30 January 1969; *Educ* Wycombe Abbey, Homerton Coll Cambridge (BEd), London Sch of Publishing and PR (DipPR); *m* 28 July 2001, Justin Skinner, s of Peter Skinner; *Career* teacher Burdett Coutts Primary Sch Westminster 1991–94, Phipps PR 1994–95, Consumer Mktg Team Charles Barker BSMG 1995–99, dir Counsel PR 1999–; *Recreations* tennis, skiing, golf; *Clubs* Campden Hill Lawn Tennis, David Lloyd Health and Fitness; *Style—* Mrs Caroline Skinner; ✉ Counsel, 15–17 Huntsworth Mews, London NW1 6DD (tel 020 7298 6502, e-mail caroline.griffiths@counsel-huntsworth.com)

SKINNER, Prof Christopher John (Chris); s of Richard N Skinner, of Bexhill-on-Sea, East Sussex, and Daphne R, *née* Edginton; *b* 12 March 1953, London; *Educ* St Dunstan's Coll London, Trinity Coll Cambridge (BA), LSE (MSc), Univ of Southampton (PhD); *m* 1, 1979, 2 s (Thomas b 18 May 1976, Samuel b 5 March 1980); *m* 2, 1998, Sheila; *Career* asst statistician Central Statistical Office 1976–77, research asst LSE 1977–78, temp lectr rising to sr lectr Univ of Southampton 1978–94, prof Div of Social Statistics Univ of Southampton 1994–, fell Centre for Microdata Methods Inst for Fiscal Studies 2001–06, visiting fell Nat Centre for Social Research 2002–05, dir ESRC Centre for Applied Social Surveys 2001–05 (dep dir 1995–2001), dir ESRC Nat Centre for Research Methods 2004–; visiting asst prof: Univ of Wisconsin Madison 1985, Iowa State Univ 1990; series ed Wiley Survey Methodology Series 1997–; assoc ed: Biometrika 1989–93, Jl of the Royal Statistical Soc Series B 1990–91 and 2000–04, Jl of the Royal Statistical Soc Series C (Applied Statistics) 1993–97, Jl of Official Statistics 1994–2000, Int Statistical Review 1995–99, Survey Methodology 1995–; memb Cncl Royal Statistical Soc 2005– (chair Social Statistics Section 1996–98 (memb 1987–91), memb Honours Ctee 1997–2002); Int Assoc of Survey Statisticians: scientific sec 1993–95, vice-pres 1995–97, chair Jury of Cochran-Hansen Prize 2001–03 (memb 2000–01); ordinary memb Int Statistical Inst 2001; FRSS 1977, fell American Statistical Assoc 1994, AcSS 2001, FBA 2004; *Style—* Prof Chris Skinner; ✉ Division of Social Statistics, School of Social Sciences, University of Southampton, Southampton SO17 1BJ (fax 023 8059 5763)

SKINNER, Dennis Edward; MP; s of Edward Skinner; *b* 11 February 1932; *Educ* Tupton Hall GS, Ruskin Coll Oxford; *m* 12 March 1960, Mary, da of James Parker; 1 s, 2 da; *Career* former miner; joined Lab Pty 1950, MP (Lab) Bolsover 1970–; NEC: memb Lab Pty Home Policy Ctee 1978–, memb Lab Pty Orgn Policy Ctee 1978, Lab Pty chm 1988–89; memb: Campaign Gp Labour MPs 1982–, Lab Pty Youth Ctee until 1982, Tribune Gp until 1982; memb Clay Cross Cncl 1960–72, pres Derbyshire Miners 1966–70; *Style—* Dennis Skinner, Esq, MP; ✉ House of Commons, London SW1A 0AA

SKINNER, Frank (né Chris Collins); *b* 28 January 1957; *Career* comedian, presenter and writer; sometime English tutor Halesowen Coll Birmingham, first stand-up gig at the Birmingham Anglers' Association 1987; stand-up incl: Frank Skinner Live at the Apollo 1994, Frank Skinner Live at the London Palladium 1996, Frank Skinner Live in Birmingham 1998; Perrier Award 1991, Sony Radio Award nomination for Baddiel and Skinner World Cup Podcast 2006; Hon DUniv Central England in Birmingham; *Theatre* incl: Art 1999, Cooking with Elvis 2000; *Television* incl: Packet of Three 1991, Fantasy Football League 1994, The Frank Skinner Show 1995–, Fantasy World Cup 1998, Baddiel and Skinner Unplanned 2000–, Shane 2004–; *Books* Frank Skinner on Frank Skinner (2001); *Singles* writer and singer (with David Baddiel, qv, and The Lightning Seeds): Three Lions (official song for Euro '96, UK no 1 twice), Germany no 17, NME Brat Award 1996), Three Lions '98 (UK no 1); *Recreations* supporting West Bromwich Albion FC; *Style—* mid-life crisis chic; ✉ c/o Avalon Public Relations, 4A Exmoor Street, London W10 6BD (tel 020 7598 8000, fax 020 7598 7300)

SKINNER, Jeremy John Banks; s of R Banks Skinner (d 1978), of Moor Park, Herts, and Betty, *née* Short; *b* 15 November 1936; *Educ* Rugby, Clare Coll Cambridge (BA); *m* 31 Aug 1963, Judith Anne, da of Jack William Austin (d 1986), of Letchworth, Herts; 2 da (Sophie (Mrs Payne) b 24 Nov 1964, Sasha (Mrs Wellings) b 9 July 1968), 1 s (Spencer b 13 July 1966); *Career* Nat Serv 2 Lt 16/5 The Queen's Royal Lancers 1956–57; ptnr Linklaters & Paines 1967–96; memb Cncl Inst of Fiscal Studies, memb Ct of Assts Worshipful Co of Cordwainers (former Master); *Recreations* hunting; *Style—* Jeremy Skinner, Esq; ✉ Stocking Farm, Stocking Pelham, Buntingford, Hertfordshire SG9 0HU (tel 01279 777287, fax 01279 777988)

SKINNER, Sir (Thomas) Keith Hewitt; 4 Bt (UK 1912), of Pont Street, Borough of Chelsea; s of Sir (Thomas) Gordon Skinner, 3 Bt (d 1972), and his 1 w, Mollie Barbara, *née* Girling (d 1965); *b* 6 December 1927; *Educ* Charterhouse; *m* 29 April 1959, Jill, da of late Cedric Ivor Tuckett, of Tonbridge, Kent; 2 s; *Heir* s, James Skinner; *Career* dir Reed International 1980–90, chm and chief exec Reed Publishing 1982–90; *Style—* Sir Keith Skinner, Bt; ✉ Wood Farm, Reydon, Southwold, Suffolk IP18 6SL

SKINNER, Michael Gordon (Mick); s of Geordie Skinner, of Newcastle upon Tyne, and Chrissie, *née* Jackson; *b* 26 November 1958; *Educ* Wallbottle GS; *m* Anna, *née* Palmer; 1 da (Emily Elizabeth b 4 July 1995), 3 s (Maximilian George b 7 Sept 1997, Zachary Jack, Barnaby John (twins) b 16 Oct 1998); *Career* former rugby union flanker; clubs: Blaydon

RFC 1974–79, Blackheath RFC 1979–84 and 1992–94, Harlequins FC 1984–92 (winner John Player Cup 1988 and Pilkington Cup 1991); capt Barbarians' Easter tour of Wales 1990; rep: Blaydon Colts (winner Durham Co Colts Cup), Northumberland U21, Kent, London Div, England B (debut v France 1987); England: debut v France 1988, memb World Cup runners-up team 1991 (was the only England forward to score a try in the World Cup), memb Grand Slam winning team 1992, 21 caps; currently TV and newspaper rugby pundit; freelance computer conslt; *Style—* Mick Skinner, Esq

SKINNER, Paul David; s of William Skinner, and Elizabeth Skinner; *Educ* Palmer's Sch Grays, Pembroke Coll Cambridge (BA, Association Football blue), Manchester Business Sch (MBA); *m* 1971, Rita Jacqueline Oldak; 2 s; *Career* Royal Dutch/Shell Gp of Cos: joined 1966, assigned UK, Greece 1974–76 and Nigeria 1976–78, chm Shell NZ 1984–87, md Norske Shell 1987–91, pres Shell Int Trading and Shipping Co Ltd 1991–96, pres Shell Europe Oil Products 1998–99, chief exec Oil Products 1999–2003, gp md Royal Dutch/Shell 2000–03; chm Rio Tinto plc 2003– (non-exec dir 2001–); non-exec dir: Standard Chartered plc 2003–, Tetra Laval Gp 2005–, Air Liquide SA 2006–; pres UK Chamber of Shipping 1997–98; memb Bd INSEAD Business Sch Fontainebleu 1999–, chm ICC UK 2005–, memb Mgmnt Bd MOD 2006–; Liveryman Worshipful Co of Shipwrights; *Recreations* golf, skiing, fly fishing, opera; *Clubs* Hawks' (Cambridge), Roehampton, RAC; *Style—* Paul Skinner, Esq

SKINNER, Peter; MEP (Lab) South East England; s of James and Jean Skinner; *Educ* Univ of Bradford (BSc), Univ of Warwick (postgrad cert industrial rels), Univ of Greenwich (PGCE); *m* 1, 14 July 1990 (m dis 2006), Julie Doreen; *m* 2, Nov 2006, Kim Strycharz-Skinner; *Career* industrial rels offr 1982–84, union organiser 1984–86, lectr NW Kent Coll and Univ of Greenwich 1989–94; MEP (Lab): Kent W 1994–99, SE England 1999–; *Recreations* most sports, especially football; *Style—* Peter Skinner, Esq, MEP; ✉ 99 Kent Road, Dartford, Kent DA1 2AJ (tel and fax 01622 892222, e-mail southeast@peterskinnermep.eu)

SKINNER, Prof Quentin Robert Duthie; s of Alexander Skinner, CBE (d 1979), and Winifred Rose Margaret, *née* Duthie (d 1982); *b* 26 November 1940; *Educ* Bedford Sch, Gonville & Caius Coll Cambridge (MA); *m* 31 Aug 1979, Prof Susan Deborah Thorpe James, da of Prof Derrick James, of London; 1 da (Olivia b 7 Dec 1979), 1 s (Marcus b 13 July 1982); *Career* Univ of Cambridge: fell Christ's Coll 1962–, prof of political sci 1978–96, regius prof of modern history 1996–, pro-vice-chllr 1999; Hon LittD: Univ of Chicago 1992, UEA 1992, Univ of Helsinki 1997, Univ of Oxford 2000, Univ of Leuven 2004, Harvard Univ 2005, Univ of St Andrews 2005, Univ of Athens 2007, Univ of Aberdeen 2007; hon fell: Gonville & Caius Coll Cambridge 1997, QMC London 2000; FRHS 1970, FBA 1980; *Books* The Foundations of Modern Political Thought (2 vols, 1978), Machiavelli (1981), Meaning and Context (1988), Reason and Rhetoric in the Philosophy of Hobbes (1996), Liberty Before Liberalism (1998), Visions of Politics (3 vols, 2002), Hobbes and Republican Liberty (2008); *Style—* Prof Quentin Skinner, FBA; ✉ Faculty of History, University of Cambridge, West Road, Cambridge CB3 9EF (e-mail qrds2@cam.ac.uk)

SKINNER, Richard; *Career* radio and TV personality; BBC Radio 1 1973–92: fndr presenter/reporter Newsbeat 1973–79, hosted Rock On, Saturday Live, Rockshow and The Saturday Sequence, specialist interviewer of most major int rock stars; BBC Radio 1 documentary series incl: Beeb's Lost Beatles Tapes (Sony Award), profiles of Mark Knopfler, Elton John and Ronnie Spector; BBC TV: former regular presenter Top of the Pops and Whistle Test, one hour special documentaries (for BBC 2) interviewing Genesis, Joni Mitchell, Bryan Ferry, Paul McCartney and Peter Gabriel; presenter The Morning Show GLR 1990–92, jt programming dir and morning show presenter Virgin Radio (national independent radio station) 1993– Oct 1996, with Magic 105.4 (formerly Melody FM) 1997–; other work: opening voice and anchorman (for BBC TV) Live Aid 1985, The Nelson Mandela Tribute (for BBC) 1987, also regular contrib to BBC World Service, The British Forces Broadcasting Service and Westwood One radio networks (USA); *Style—* Richard Skinner, Esq; ✉ c/o Magic 105.4, Mappin House, 4 Winsley Street, London W1N 8HF (tel 020 7436 1515, e-mail richard.skinner@magicradio.com)

SKIPWITH, Sir Patrick Alexander d'Estoteville; 12 Bt (E 1622), of Prestwould, Leicestershire; s of Grey d'Estoteville Townsend Skipwith (ka 1942), and Sofka (d 1994), da of Prince Peter Alexandrovitch Dolgorouky; suc gf, Sir Grey Humberston d'Estoteville Skipwith 1950; *b* 1 September 1938; *Educ* Harrow, TCD (MA), Imperial Coll London (PhD); *m* 1, 1964 (m dis 1970), Gillian Patricia, adopted da of late Charles Frederick Harwood; 1 da (Zara Alexandra Jane d'Estoteville b 1967), 1 s (Alexander Sebastian Grey d'Estoteville b 1969); *m* 2, 1972 (m dis 1997), Ashkhain (d 2006), da of late Bedros Atikian; *m* 3, 1997, Martine Sophie Yvonne, da of Joseph de Wilde; 2 s (Grey Camille d'Estoteville, Louis Peyton d'Estoteville (twins) b 1997); *Heir* s, Alexander Skipwith; *Career* marine geologist Ocean Mining Inc 1966–70, Directorate-Gen of Mineral Resources Jeddah Saudi Arabia 1970–73, geological ed Bureau de Recherches Géologiques et Minières Jeddah Saudi Arabia 1973–86; md Immel Publishing Ltd 1988–89; freelance editing (GeoEdit), translating and public relations 1986–96; head of translation BRGM Orléans France 1996–2003; Aprotrad; *Recreations* riding, sailing, hill walking, tennis; *Clubs* Chelsea Arts; *Style—* Sir Patrick Skipwith, Bt; ✉ 76 rue de Pont-aux-Moines, 45450 Donnery, France (tel 00 33 2 38 59 24 13, e-mail patrick@donnery.com)

SKIPWORTH, Mark; s of George Skipworth, of Kingston upon Hull, E Yorks, and Jean Marjorie Skipworth; *b* 27 January 1959; *Educ* Sydney Smith Sch Hull, St John's Coll Oxford (BA); *m* 29 Aug 1981, Julie Alison Patricia, da of Frank Deegan; 2 s (Hunter b 31 Oct 1987, Patrick b 2 May 1992), 1 da (Zoe b 16 April 1994); *Career* reporter Sheffield Star 1980–84, writer Which? Magazine 1984–89, reporter Daily Telegraph 1989; Sunday Times: consumer affairs corr 1990–93, dep insight ed 1994–95, news ed 1995–97, managing ed (news) 1998–; *Awards* Yorkshire Young Journalist of the Year 1982, Nat Newspapers' Consumer Journalist of the Year 1991, commended Reporter of the Year Br Press Awards 1991, Scoop of the Year 1994, What the Papers Say Investigations of the Year 1994, Br Press Awards Exclusive of the Year 1994, Br Press Awards Team Journalism Award 1994, What the Papers Say Scoop of the Year 2006, Br Press Awards Team of the Year 2007; *Books* Oxford Type: The Best of ISIS (with Andrew Billen, 1984), The Scotch Whisky Book (1987), Class (with Greg Hadfield, 1994); *Recreations* piano and piano accordion; *Style—* Mark Skipworth, Esq; ✉ The Sunday Times, 1 Pennington Street, London E1 9XW (tel 020 7782 5653, fax 020 7782 5731)

SKLAR, Dr Jonathan; s of Vivian Sklar, of London, and Joyce, *née* Longworth (d 1991); *b* 9 June 1949; *Educ* Latymer Upper Sch, Royal Free Hosp Univ of London (MB BS), Inst of Psychoanalysis London; *Family* 2 da (Clea b 1 Aug 1978, Livia b 31 Oct 1981); *Career* psychoanalyst; sr registrar in psychiatry Friern and Royal Free Hosps 1978–79, sr registrar in psychotherapy Tavistock Clinic 1979–83, conslt psychotherapist Cambridge HA 1983–95; head of Dept of Psychotherapy Addenbrooke's Hosp 1989–95, visiting prof Århus Univ and Psychiatric Hosp 1991–92, in private psychoanalytic practice; sec Psychotherapy Exec of Joint Ctee of Higher Psychiatric Trg 1990–92; Freedom City of Cusco Peru 1989; trg analyst Br Psychoanalytical Soc 1998 (assoc memb 1984, memb 1991); LRCP, MRCS, MRCPsych 1977; *Recreations* reading, opera; *Style—* Dr Jonathan Sklar; ✉ 58 Grafton Terrace, London NW5 4HY (tel 020 7485 6974, e-mail jonathan@sklar.co.uk)

SKLAR, Prof Kathryn Kish; da of William Edward Kish, and Elizabeth Sue, *née* Rhodes; *b* 26 December 1939, Columbus, OH; *Educ* Harvard Univ (BA), Univ of Michigan (PhD); *m* 1, 1958; 1 s (Leonard b 1959), 1 da (Susan b 1964); *m* 2, 1988, Thomas Dublin; *Career* asst prof Univ of Michigan 1969–74 (chair ctee to design a women's prog 1972–73), assoc

S

prof then prof UCLA 1974–88 (chair ctee to design and administrate Women's Studies Prog 1974–75, prog administrator 1976–77, 1977–78, 1979–80 and 1980–81, memb Ctee 1983–84 and 1986–87, memb American Antiquarian Soc 1977, chair Advsy Ctee Center for the Study of Women 1984–85), distinguished prof of history State Univ of NY 1988–2005, co-fndr and co-dir Center for the Historical Study of Women and Gender State Univ of NY 1998–, Harmsworth prof of US history Univ of Oxford 2005–; memb: Coordinating Ctee on Women in the Historical Profession 1973–, Cncl American Studies Assoc 1978–80, California Cncl for the Humanities 1981–85, Advsy Bd Southern California Inst for Historical Research and Servs 1981–88, Basic Research in Behavorial and Social Scis Ctee Gender Studies Working Gp Nat Research Cncl 1985, Soc of American Historians 1987, NY Cncl for the Humanities 1992–99 (memb Exec Ctee and chair Awards Ctee 1995–96), Scholars Working Gp Nat Ctee on Civic Renewal Inst for Philosophy and Public Policy Univ of Maryland 1996–98, Advsy Bd Working Gp on Catholic Women Cushwa Center for the Study of American Catholicism Univ of Notre Dame 1998–2000; evaluator Stanford Inst on Women's History 1977–79, various positions within the Orgn of American Historians 1977–, fndr and coordinator Workshop on Teaching US Women's History 1978–88; memb Editorial Bd: American Quarterly 1976–79, Jl of American History 1978–81, America: History and Life 1984–, Jl of Women's History 1987–2004, History of Women Religious Newsletter 1988–92, American National Biography 1990–2000, Feminist Press 1990–2001, Women's History Review 1990–, Hayes Historical Jl: A Jl of the Gilded Age 1991–94, Historical Encyclopaedia of Chicago Women 1992–2001; memb Scholarly Advsy Bd Ms 1980–84; pres: Pacific Coast Branch American Historical Assoc (AHA) 1987–88 (chair Ctee on Women Historians 1980–83, vice-pres 1986–87), Soc for Historians of the Gilded Age and Progressive Era 1994–95 (memb Cncl 1989–93, vice-pres 1993–94); Daniels fell American Antiquarian Soc 1976, Rockefeller Fndn humanities fell 1981–82, Woodrow Wilson Int Center fell 1982, NEH fell 1982–83 and 1998–99, Guggenheim fell 1985–86, Univ Award for Excellence in Research State Univ of NY 1998, American Assoc of Univ Women Fndrs fell 1990–91, Univ Scholar-in-Residence Award American Assoc of Univ Women Educn Fndn (jtly) 2000–02, Chllr's Award for Excellence in Teaching and in Scholarship and Creative Activities State Univ of NY 2002; fell: Radcliffe Inst Cambridge Massachusetts 1973–74, Nat Humanities Inst Yale Univ 1975–76, Center for Advanced Study in the Behavorial and Social Scis Stanford Univ 1987–88, Woodrow Wilson Int Center for Scholars 1992–93, Nat Humanities Center Research Triangle Park 1995–96; *Books* Catharine Beecher: A Study in American Domesticity (1973, winner Berkshire Prize 1973, shortlisted Nat Book Award 1974), Catherine Beecher, A Treatise on Domestic Economy (ed, 1977), Harriet Beecher Stowe: Uncle Tom's Cabin, or Life among the Lowly; The Minister's Wooing; Oldtown Folks (ed, 1981), The Autobiography of Florence Kelley: Notes of Sixty Years (ed, 1986), Women and Power in American History: A Reader (co-ed, 1991, 2 edn 2001), The Social Survey Movement in Historical Perspective (co-ed, 1992), US History as Women's History: New Feminist Essays (co-ed, 1995), Florence Kelley and the Nation's Work: The Rise of Women's Political Culture, 1830–1900 (1995, Berkshire Prize 1996, Assoc for Research on Nonprofit Orgns and Voluntary Action Prize 1998), Cambridge Dictionary of American Biography (memb Editorial Bd, 1995), Social Justice Feminists in the United States and Germany: A Dialogue in Documents, 1885–1933 (co-ed, 1998), Social Work Dictionary (memb Editorial Bd, 1999), Women's Rights Emerges within the Anti-slavery Movement: A Short History with Documents, 1830–1870 (2000), Harriet Martineau's Writing on the British Empire (advsy ed, 2003), Harriet Martineau: Writings on British History and Military Reform (advsy ed, 2005), Selected Letters of Florence Kelley, 1869–1932 (co-ed, 2007), Women's Rights and Transatlantic Slavery in the Era of Emancipation (co-ed, 2007); *Style*— Prof Kathryn Sklar; ✉ Department of History, State University of New York, Binghamton, NY 13902, USA

SKOOG, Matz; s of Nils Skoog, and Jane, *née* Antoniazzi; *b* Stockholm; *Educ* Royal Swedish Ballet Sch, Vagnova Sch Leningrad, Kirov Theatre Leningrad; *Career* ballet dancer and artistic dir; dancer: Royal Swedish Ballet, Nederlands Dance Theatre, English Nat Ballet 1979–91; staged La Sylphide and Napoli Act III (Rome Opera Ballet) 1991, ballet master London City Ballet 1992–93, asst dir Ater Balletto Italy 1993–94, dancer and teacher Rambert Dance Co 1994, artistic dir Royal NZ Ballet 1996–2001, artistic dir English Nat Ballet 2001–05; guest teacher: San Francisco Ballet, Cullberg Ballet, Royal Danish Ballet, Grand Theatre De Genéve, Royal Ballet; *Style*— Matz Skoog, Esq

SKORUPSKI, Prof John Maria; s of Wactaw Skorupski (d 1991), of Warsaw, Poland, and late Wanda, *née* Pankiewicz; *b* 19 September 1946; *Educ* St Benedict's Sch Ealing, Christ's Coll Cambridge (MA), Univ of Cambridge (PhD); *m* 18 Sept 1971, Barbara, da of Ernest Robert Taylor; 2 da (Katharine Wanda Taylor b 3 Nov 1978, Julia Zofia Taylor b 9 Feb 1982); *Career* visiting lectr Univ of Ife Nigeria 1971–72, visiting prof Univ of Louvain Belgium 1974; res fell UC Swansea Univ of Wales 1974–76, lectr Dept of Philosophy Univ of Glasgow 1976–84, prof of philosophy Univ of Sheffield 1984–90, prof of moral philosophy Univ of St Andrews 1990–; gen ed: OUP OPUS paperbacks, The International Research Library of Philosophy; memb Editorial Bd: Ratio, The Philosophical Quarterly, Utilitas; pres Aristotelian Soc 1990–91; hon fell Centre for the Study of Political Thought Jagiellonian Univ Kraków Poland 1991–; memb Exec Ctee Mind Assoc 1992–; FRSE 1992; *Books* Symbol and Theory, A Philosophical Study of Theories of Religion in Social Anthropology (1975), John Stuart Mill (1989), English Language Philosophy 1750–1945 (1993), Ethical Explorations (1999), Why Read Mill Today? (2006); *Recreations* walking, skiing, music; *Style*— Prof John Skorupski, FRSE; ✉ Department of Moral Philosophy, University of St Andrews, St Andrews, Fife KY16 9AL (tel 01334 462483)

SKOULDING, Peter Michael; MBE (2007); s of Frederick Clarence Skoulding (d 1989), and Lilian Dorothy, *née* Sampson (d 1995); *b* 31 May 1931; *Educ* March GS, Wisbech GS; *m* 18 July 1953, Marjorie Joan, *née* Collins; 2 s (John Michael b 30 May 1954, Robert Frederick b 29 Sept 1957), 1 da (Cindy Ann b 25 Jan 1963); *Career* dir: Snowmountain Enterprises Ltd (founded 1964), Gemdome Ltd, Longhill Energy Ltd; underwriter Lloyds 1972; urban dist cncllr 1960, cncllr (Cons) Fenland DC 1974–, cncllr March Town Cncl (mayor 2001–02); *Style*— Peter Skoulding, Esq, MBE; ✉ Mill Hill Lodge, Mill Hill Lane, Knights End, March, Cambridgeshire PE15 9QB (tel 01354 652024); Marwich House, Station Road, March, Cambridgeshire PE15 8XA (tel 01354 653649, fax 01354 657081, e-mail peter@snowmarch.co.uk)

SKREIN, (Stephen Peter) Michael; *b* 1947; *Educ* UCS, Univ of Oxford (MA), Univ of Southern Calif (AM), Coll of Law; *Career* Richards, Butler & Co: admitted slr 1973, ptnr Richards Butler 1976–2006, head Commercial Litigation Gp 1990–96; ptnr Reed Smith Richards Butler LLP 2007–; elected Honor Soc of Phi Kappa Phi; Freeman City of London, Liveryman City of London Slrs' Co; memb: Law Soc, Int Bar Assoc, Int Trademark Assoc, RTS, Br Literary and Artistic Copyright Assoc, The Media Soc; fell Soc for Advanced Legal Studies; *Style*— Michael Skrein, Esq; ✉ Reed Smith Richards Butler LLP, Beaufort House, 15 St Botolph Street, London EC3A 7EE (tel 020 7247 6555, fax 020 7247 5091, e-mail spms@reedsmith.com)

SLACK, Martin Richard; *b* 29 June 1949, Hull; *Educ* Churchill Coll Cambridge (MA); *m* 1971, Kate; *Career* Lane Clark & Peacock LLP: joined 1970, ptnr 1975–, sr ptnr 1996–; chm Assoc of Consulting Actuaries 1998–2000 (hon treas 1995–98), memb OPB 1992–97; FIA 1972; *Recreations* flying, gardening, horse riding; *Style*— Martin Slack, Esq; ✉ Lane Clark & Peacock, 30 Old Burlington Street, London W1S 3NN (tel 020 7439 2266, fax 020 7439 0183)

SLACK, Prof Paul; *Career* Univ of Oxford: princ Linacre Coll 1996–, prof of early modern social history; FBA; *Books* incl: Crisis and Order in English Towns, 1500–1700: Essays in Urban History (ed with Peter Clark, 1972), Poverty in Early-Stuart Salisbury (1975), English Towns in Transition 1500–1700 (with Peter Clark, 1976), Rebellion, Popular Protest, and the Social Order in Early Modern England (ed, 1984), The Impact of Plague in Tudor and Stuart England (1985), Poverty and Policy in Tudor and Stuart England (1988), The English Poor Law, 1531–1782 (1990), Epidemics and Ideas: Essays on the Historical Perception of Pestilence (ed with Terence Ranger, 1992), From Reformation to Improvement: Public Welfare in Early Modern England (1999), Environments and Historical Change (1999), The Peopling of Britain: The Shaping of a Human Landscape (ed with Ryk Ward, 2002), Managing Water Resources Past and Present (ed with Julie Trottier, 2004); *Style*— Prof Paul Slack; ✉ Linacre College, St Cross Road, Oxford OX1 3JA

SLACK, Dr Richard Charles Bewick; s of Dr Horace George Bewick Slack (d 1966), of Bramhall, Cheshire, and Dorothy Edith, *née* Smith (d 1997); *b* 4 March 1944; *Educ* Manchester Grammar, Jesus Coll Cambridge (MA, MB BChir); *m* 10 May 1969, Dr Patricia Mary Slack, da of Dr Arthur Hamilton Cheshire (d 1982), of Brewood, Staffs; 2 s (Benjamin b 1972, William b 1974), 2 da (Clare b 1976, Eleanor b 1981); *Career* house surgn St Mary's Hosp London 1969–70; lectr: Middx Hosp Med Sch 1971–73, Univ of Nairobi 1973–77; sr lectr Univ of Nottingham 1978–, hon conslt PHLS and Nottingham HA 1978–, conslt in communicable disease control 1990–, temp conslt WHO Special Programme AIDS 1987–88; pres Assoc of Med Microbiologists, chm Fed Infection Soc, memb Exec RIPH; memb Ski Club of GB and Br Mountaineering Gp; MRCPath 1977; *Books* Antimicrobial Chemotherapy (2000), Medical Microbiology (2002), Public Health (ed); *Recreations* fell walking, skiing, forestry; *Style*— Dr Richard Slack; ✉ 5 Magdala Road, Mapperley Park, Nottingham, NG3 5DE (tel 0115 960 5940); Department of Microbiology, University of Nottingham Medical School, Queen's Medical Centre, Nottingham NG7 2UH (tel 0115 924 9924, fax 0115 942 2190); Health Protection Unit (tel 0115 912 3350, fax 0115 912 3351)

SLACK, Robert William Talbot; s of Sir William Slack, of Somerset, and Lady (Joan) Slack; *b* 29 August 1953; *Educ* Winchester, Bart's Med Sch, Univ of Bristol; *m* 18 June 1982, Dr Nicola Slack, *née* Caporn; 1 da (Amy b 15 June 1984), 1 s (Edward b 9 Feb 1986); *Career* sr registrar ENT Surgery Bristol and Bath 1985–90, conslt ENT surgn Royal United Hosp Bath 1990–; memb GMC 1999–; Liveryman Worshipful Co of Barbers; FRCS 1984; *Recreations* real tennis, rackets, sailing; *Style*— Robert Slack, Esq; ✉ Royal United Hospital, Combe Park, Bath BA1 2NG (tel 01225 824556)

SLACK, Timothy Willatt; LVO (1995); s of Cecil Moorhouse Slack, MC (d 1986), and Dora, *née* Willatt (d 1978); *b* 18 April 1928; *Educ* Winchester, New Coll Oxford (MA); *m* 1, 31 Aug 1957, Katharine (d 1993), da of Norman Hughes (d 1982); 3 da (Caroline b 1960, Louisa b 1966, Rebecca b 1969), 1 s (Henry b 1962); m 2, 19 July 1996 (m dis 2003), Shuna (d 2006), *née* Black; *Career* Nat Serv RN; asst master: Lycée de Garçons Rennes France 1951–52, Schule Schloss Salem W Germany 1952–53, Repton 1953–59; headmaster: Kambawsa Coll Burma 1959–62, Bedales Sch Hants 1962–74, Hellenic Coll London 1983–84; princ St Catharine's Fndn Cumberland Lodge Windsor 1985–95; dir: FCO Wiston House Conf Centre 1977–83 (asst dir 1975–77), Nat Tenants Resource Centre 1990–; Parly candidate: (Lib) Petersfield Feb and Oct 1974, (Alliance) Enfield Southgate 1984, (Alliance) Fareham 1987; chm: Soc of Headmasters of Ind Schs 1965–67, Cwlth Round Table 1994–2001, Sir Heinz Koeppler Tst 2001–05; chm of govrs Royal Sch Windsor Great Park 1988–95; *Style*— Timothy Slack, Esq, LVO; ✉ Greenlands, Stoner Hill, Steep, Petersfield, Hampshire GU32 1AG

SLADE, Adrian Carnegie; CBE (1988); s of George Penkivil Slade, KC (d 1942), and Mary Albinia Alice, *née* Carnegie (d 1988); *b* 25 May 1936; *Educ* Eton, Trinity Coll Cambridge (BA); *m* 22 June 1960, Susan Elizabeth, da of Edward Forsyth (d 1978); 1 da (Nicola b 28 March 1962), 1 s (Rupert b 15 Jan 1965); *Career* writer J Walter Thompson 1959–64, dir S H Benson (advertising) 1969–71 (writer 1964–71), co fndr Slade Monico Bluff (later Slade Bluff & Bigg then Slade Hamilton Fenech) 1971–91, dir Longslade Media Trg 1991–97, mktg conslt 1991–2004; mgmnt Wandsworth Cncl for Community Rels 1967–81; chm: ONE plus ONE Marriage and Partnership Research 1990–97, Orange Tree Theatre Ltd Richmond 1991–98, ADZIDO Pan African Dance Ensemble 2001–04; Parly candidate (Lib) Putney 1966 and 1974, Parly candidate (Alliance) Wimbledon 1987; memb GLC Richmond 1981–86 (ldr Alliance Gp 1982–86); pres Lib Pty 1987–88, jt pres Lib Dems 1988 (vice-pres 1988–89); *Recreations* theatre, music, photography, piano playing; *Style*— Adrian Slade

SLADE, Sir Benjamin Julian Alfred; 7 Bt (UK 1831), of Maunsel House, Somerset; s of Capt Sir Michael Niall Slade, 6 Bt (d 1962), and Angela (d 1959), da of Capt Orlando Chichester; *b* 22 May 1946; *Educ* Millfield; *m* 1977 (m dis 1991), Pauline Carol, da of Maj Claude Myburgh; *Career* chm and md Shirlstar Holdings Ltd, dir Pyman Bell Ltd; Freeman City of London 1979, memb Worshipful Co of Ironmongers; *Recreations* racing, polo, bridge, shooting; *Clubs* Turf, Old Somerset Dining, Sloane, White's, 1980 Dining; *Style*— Sir Benjamin Slade, Bt; ✉ Maunsel, North Newton, Bridgwater, Somerset (tel 01278 663413, fax 01278 661074, estate office 01278 661076, e-mail bensladebt@aol.com, website www.maunselhouse.co.uk); South West Conference Centre Ltd, The Loop Centre, Bittern Road, Sowton Industrial Estate, Exeter, Devon EX2 7LW (tel 0870 240 8684, fax 0870 240 8681, e-mail info@swconferencing.co.uk)

SLADE, Elizabeth Ann; QC (1992); da of late Dr Charles Slade, and Henriette Slade; *b* 12 May 1949; *Educ* Wycombe Abbey, LMH Oxford (exhibitioner, MA); *m* 1975; 2 da; *Career* called to the Bar Inner Temple 1972 (bencher 1990); recorder 1998– (asst recorder 1995–98), dep judge of the High Court 1998–, pt/t judge Employment Appeal Tbnl 2000–03; chm Employment Law Bar Assoc 1995–97 (hon vice-pres 1997–); chm Bar Cncl Sex Discrimination Ctee 2000–02; tstee Free Representation Unit 1998–2002; memb Admin Tbnl of the Bank for Int Settlements 1999–; *Books* Tolleys Employment Handbook (ed then co-ed, 1–7 edn, 1978–90); *Recreations* theatre, art, music, walking; *Style*— Miss Elizabeth Slade, QC; ✉ 11 King's Bench Walk, Temple, London EC4Y 7EQ

SLADE, Laurie George; s of Humphrey Slade (d 1983), of Nairobi, Kenya, and Constance Laing, *née* Gordon (d 1997); *b* 12 February 1944; *Educ* Duke of York Sch Nairobi, Magdalen Coll Oxford (MA); *Career* called to the Bar Lincoln's Inn 1966, advocate High Court Kenya 1976, 18 years in consumer dispute resolution, legal advsr and registrar Chartered Inst of Arbitrators and dep registrar London Court of Int Arbitration 1982–88, ombudsman Insurance Ombudsman Bureau London 1994–96 and 1999–2000 (dep ombudsman 1988–94), ind investigator FSA (formerly SIB) 1996–99; chm FSA Ombudsman Steering Gp 1998; memb IBRC (sec of state appointee) 1997–98; memb Br and Irish Ombudsman Assoc 1993; registered psychoanalytic psychotherapist UKCP 1999, memb Guild of Psychotherapists 1999, fndr memb Int Neuro-Psychoanalysis Soc 2000, memb Confedn of Analytical Psychologists 2002; FCIArb 1993–2002; *Style*— Laurie Slade, Esq; ✉ 71 Netheravon Road, London W4 2NB (tel 020 8995 0528)

SLADEK, Nancy; da of Dr Milan Sladek, of Geneva, Switzerland, and Hana, *née* Kozeluhova; *Educ* Heathfield Sch Ascot, Univ of Geneva (LèsL); *Children* 1 s (Lorenzo Michael b 21 Oct 2004); *Career* ed Literary Review 1999– (dep ed 1996–99); *Clubs* Academy; *Style*— Ms Nancy Sladek; ✉ Literary Review, 44 Lexington Street, London W1F 0LW (tel 020 7437 9392, fax 020 7734 1844, e-mail nancy@literaryreview.co.uk)

SLAPAK, Maurice; CBE (1999); s of Abraham Szlapak (d 1965), of Nairobi, Kenya, and Rachel Szlapak; *b* 15 February 1930; *Educ* Prince of Wales Sch Nairobi, Millfield, Downing Coll Cambridge (MA, MB MChir); *m* 16 June 1960, Catherine Elisabeth, da of Arthur Ellis (d 1966), of Ottawa, Canada; 2 da (Gabrielle Isobel b 16 Jan 1964, Alexander Rachel b 10 Feb 1968); *Career* Capt RAMC: RMO i/c Household Cavalry Regt 1959, MO i/c SHAPE Paris; assoc prof of surgery Harvard Med Sch 1972, co chm first Int Symposium Organ Preservation 1973, sr asst surgn Univ of Cambridge 1972–75, conslt and co dir Transplant Unit St Mary's Hosp Portsmouth, Hunterian prof of surgery RCS, memb Editorial Advsy Bd Transplantation Proceedings; pres: World Transplant Games, Transplant Section RSM; fndr and pres Transplant Olympic Games 1978, vice-pres Euro Soc for Organ Transplantation; FRCS 1964, FRCS (Canada) 1967, FACS 1971; *Publications* Experimental and Clinical Methods in Fulminant Liver Failure Support (1973), The Acute Abdomen (in Tice Sloane Practice of Medicine, 1972); *Recreations* tennis, squash, windsurfing, reading; *Clubs* All England Lawn Tennis, Queen's, Hurlingham; *Style*— Maurice Slapak, Esq, CBE; ✉ Abbey House, Itchen Abbas, Hampshire SO21 1BN (tel 01962 779233, fax 01962 779673, e-mail slapakhamlet@aol.com); 30 Rutland Gate, London SW5; Cromwell Hospital (tel 020 7370 4233)

SLARK, Gavin; s of Vincent Slark, of Leicestershire, and Moira Rose, *née* Smith; *b* 6 April 1965, Sunderland; *Educ* North Leamington Sch Royal Leamington Spa, London Business Sch; *m* 12 July 1986, Lori Mary, *née* Hall; 2 s (Daniel James b 30 March 1993, Jacob William b 18 Oct 1995); *Career* BSS Gp plc: md PTS Plumbing Trade Supplies and exec dir 2002–05, chief operating offr 2005–06, chief exec 2006–; *Recreations* travel, golf, Sunderland FC; *Style*— Gavin Slark, Esq

SLATER, Arnold; s of Arnold Slater, of Holmfirth, W Yorks, and Pauline Margaret, *née* Shaw-Parker; *b* 26 March 1948; *Educ* Hadham Hall Sch, Regent St Poly; *m* 21 Oct 1972, Judith Helen, da of Philip Ellison, of Bishop's Stortford, Herts; 1 s (Ross Adrian b 24 Sept 1973), 1 da (Anthea Helen b 15 Feb 1978); *Career* chief photographer Herts and Essex Observer 1973–78; photographer: Press Assoc 1978–87, London Daily News 1987, Sunday People 1987–88, The Mirror 1988–; winner: Simeon Edmunds award for best young press photographer, Ilford Press Photographer of the Year 1987; *Recreations* squash, skiing, fly tying, fly fishing; *Style*— Arnold Slater, Esq; ✉ c/o The Picture Desk, The Mirror, One Canada Square, Canary Wharf, London E14 5AP (tel 020 7293 3851)

SLATER, David; *b* 21 October 1960; *Educ* Vyne Sch Basingstoke, Basingstoke Tech Coll, Bournemouth and Poole Coll of Art; *Career* designer; Raymond Loewy 1983, Allied International Designers 1983–86, Lansdown Euro 1986–87, assoc dir Fitch & Co 1987–89, creative dir Wolff Olins Hall 1989–90, freelance designer 1990–92; creative dir: Tango Design Consultancy 1992–95, Vista Design 1995–96, e-fact 1996–98, Saatchi & Saatchi Design 1998–2000, Addison Design 2000–01; md and creative dir IDVista 2002–; *Style*— David Slater, Esq; ✉ IDVista tel 01424 812256

SLATER, Dr David Homfray; CB (1996); s of William Dennis Slater, and Edna Florence, *née* Homfray; *b* 16 October 1940; *Educ* Ardwyn GS, UCW (BSc), Univ of Wales (PhD); *m* 18 April 1964, Edith Mildred, da of Geoffrey Edward Price; 4 da (Ellen Louise b 7 March 1965, Sian Juliet b 1 July 1966, Melanie Lynne b 18 March 1968, Emma Wynne b 22 Feb 1970); *Career* res asst Ohio State Univ 1966–69, sr res fell Univ of Southampton 1969–70, lectr Dept of Chemical Engrg and Technol Imperial Coll London 1970–75, ptnr Cremer & Warner 1979–81 (conslt 1975–79), fndr dir Technica Ltd (London) 1981, chm and chief exec Technica Inc (USA) 1987–91, dir and chief inspr HM Inspectorate of Pollution 1991–95, dir Pollution Prevention and Control and chm Policy Gp Environment Agency 1995–97; chm Task Force on Risk Assessment DETR 1997–98; conseiller DGXI E Euro Cmmn 1997–98; specialist advsr House of Commons Environment Tport and Regional Affrs Select Ctee 1999–2000; environmental advsr to Cabinet Office's Better Regulation Taskforce 2000–; md OXERA Environmental 1998–2001, princ ptnr ACONA Gp 2001–, dir Cambrensis 2002–, chm RLtec 2003–, chm Nirex CLG 2005–; prof Warren Centre for Advanced Engineering Univ of Sydney 1985–86, hon prof of life sciences UCW 1991–, assoc fell Environmental Change Unit Univ of Oxford 1998–, chm Environmental Gp Regulatory Policy Inst Oxford 2001–2002, Royal Acad of Engrg prof UMIST 2002–06, adjunct prof Centre for Risk Mgmnt KCL 2003–06; CChem, CEng, FRSC; *Recreations* music, horses, walking the dogs; *Clubs* Athenaeum; *Style*— Dr David Slater, CB; ✉ Ruxton Farm, King's Caple, Herefordshire HR1 4TX (tel 01432 840568, fax 01432 840731)

SLATER, Prof Gillian Lesley; DL (Dorset 2006); da of Leonard William Henry Filtness (d 1978), of Sutton, Surrey, and Adeline Mary, *née* Rowland (d 2005); *b* 13 January 1949; *Educ* Sutton HS for Girls, St Hugh's Coll Oxford (IBM scholar, MSc, DPhil, MA); *m* 1, 1970 (m dis 1983), John Bruce Slater; 2 da (Rosemary Jane Slater b 16 May 1977, Eleanor Ann Slater b 21 Jan 1981); m 2, 1988, Ian David Huntley, s of Desmond Ernest Huntley; *Career* lectr in mathematics Poly of S Bank 1973–79, sr lectr then princ Sheffield City Poly 1979–86; Manchester Metropolitan Univ (formerly Manchester Poly): head Dept of Mathematics and Physics 1986–89, asst dir and dean of sci and engrg 1989–92, pro-vice-chllr 1992–94; vice-chllr Bournemouth Univ 1994–2005; FIMA (1982), CMath 1991, FRSA 1992; *Books* Essential Mathematics for Software Engineers (1987), Mathematics for Software Construction (with A Norcliffe, 1991); also author of numerous articles in learned jls; *Recreations* birdwatching, music; *Style*— Prof Gillian Slater; ✉ 31 Leven Avenue, Bournemouth, Dorset BH4 9LH

SLATER, John Christopher Nash; QC (1987); s of late Lt-Col Leonard Slater, CBE; *b* 14 June 1946; *Educ* Sedbergh, UC Oxford (MA); *m* 1971, Jane Schapiro; 2 s, 1 da; *Career* called to the Bar Middle Temple 1969 (Harmsworth scholar, bencher 1996); recorder 1990– (asst recorder 1987–90), dep High Court judge 1994–, head of chambers 1996–99; *Recreations* golf, acting, travel; *Clubs* Hampstead Golf, Hampstead Cricket; *Style*— John Slater, Esq, QC; ✉ 41 Wood Vale, London N10 3DJ (tel 020 8442 0689); Crown Office Chambers, 2 Crown Office Row, Temple, London EC4Y 7HJ (tel 020 7797 8100, fax 020 7797 8101, e-mail jslaterqc@crownofficechambers.com)

SLATER, Adm Sir John Cunningham Kirkwood (Jock); GCB (1992, KCB 1988), LVO (1971), DL (Hants 2000); s of Dr James K Slater, OBE, MD, FRCPE (d 1965), of Edinburgh, and Margaret Claire Byrom, *née* Bramwell; *b* 27 March 1938; *Educ* Edinburgh Acad, Sedbergh, Dartmouth; *m* 1972, Ann Frances, da of late William Patrick Scott, OBE, DL, of Orkney Islands; 2 s (Charles b 1974, Rory b 1977); *Career* RN; Equerry to HM The Queen 1968–71; CO: HMS Soberton (minesweeper) 1965, HMS Jupiter (frigate) 1972–73, HMS Kent (guided missile destroyer) 1976–77; Royal Coll of Def Studies 1978; CO: HMS Illustrious (aircraft carrier) 1981–83, HMS Dryad & Capt Sch of Maritime Ops 1983–85; ACDS (Policy and Nuclear) 1985–87; Flag Offr Scotland and N Ireland, Naval Base Cdr Rosyth, NATO Cdr N sub area E Atlantic, Cdr Nore sub area Channel 1987–89, Chief of Fleet Support 1989–91, C-in-C Fleet, Allied C-in-C Channel and C-in-C Eastern Atlantic 1991–92, Vice Chief of the Def Staff 1993–95, First Sea Lord and Chief of Naval Staff 1995–98, First and Princ Naval ADC to HM The Queen 1995–98; vice-chm RUSI 1993–95 (vice-pres 1995–98); non-exec dir: VT Gp plc 1999–2004, Lockheed Martin (UK) 2000–; conslt Bristow Helicopters Ltd 2001–04; chm: Imperial War Museum 2001–06 (tstee 1999–2006), RN Club (1765–85) 2001–04, White Ensign Assoc 2002–05 (memb Cncl 1999–), RNLI 2004– (memb Cncl 1999–, chm Ops, Ctee 2001–02, dep chm 2002–04); memb Nat Youth Orchestra 1955; govr Sedbergh Sch 1997–2002, Elder Bro Trinity House 1995 (Yr Bro 1978), Freeman City of London 1989, Liveryman Worshipful Co of Shipwrights 1991 (memb Ct of Assts 2005–, Fifth Warden 2007–); Cdr Legion of Merit (US) 1997; Hon DSc Univ of Cranfield 1998; *Recreations* the outdoors; *Clubs* Army and Navy, Liphook Golf; *Style*— Adm Sir Jock Slater, GCB, LVO, DL

SLATER, Dr John Morton; s of Rev Percy William Slater (d 1988), of Winston, and Evelyn Maude Morton Slater (d 1978); *b* 21 August 1938; *Educ* Durham Sch, Univ of Nottingham (BSc), Univ of Toronto (MS), Univ of Illinois (PhD, L J Norton Memorial fell); *m* 30 Sept 1972, Susan Mary Black, da of Rev Dr John Park, of Stormont, Belfast; 2 s (William John Park b 26 April 1974, Philip James Morton b 10 May 1976), 1 da (Helen Mary Elizabeth b 15 Sept 1979); *Career* lectr Univ of Manchester 1965–70, conslt FAO 1966–67; MAFF: econ advsr 1970–84, head Econ and Stats (Food) Div 1984–92, head Econ (Int) Div 1992–96, head Econ and Stats Gp 1996–98, special advsr House of Lords Select Ctee on Sci and Technol 1999–2000; independent agric economic conslt 1998–; chm Millennium Masters Assoc 2003–06; govr Corporation of Sons of the Clergy 2001–; Freeman City of London 1972, Master Worshipful Co of Turners 1999–2000 (memb Ct of Assts 1990); MRI; *Books* Fifty Years of the National Food Survey 1940–1990 (ed); *Recreations* squash (Durham Co squash 1971–73), cricket, golf, bridge; *Clubs* City Livery (hon sec 2002–03), MCC, United Wards; *Style*— Dr John Slater; ✉ 28 Swains Lane, London N6 6QR (tel and fax 020 7485 1238, e-mail j.slater@slaterconsult.demon.co.uk)

SLATER, Mark; s of R M K Slater (d 2001), and Barbara, *née* Murdoch (d 1999); *b* 4 March 1954, Lima, Peru; *Educ* Wellington, St Edmund Hall Oxford (MA), KCL (PGCE); *m* 17 Aug 1985 (m dis), Joanna, *née* Coulson; 2 da (Catherine b 15 March 1987, Jennifer b 7 Jan 1991); *Career* teacher of Spanish Lord Wandsworth Coll 1979–82, head of Spanish and housemaster Wellington Coll 1982–96, headmaster St Lawrence Coll 1996–2004, headmaster The Leys Sch 2004–; memb HMC 1996–; *Recreations* walking, skiing, tennis; *Clubs* East India, St James's; *Style*— Mark Slater, Esq; ✉ Headmaster's House, The Leys School, Cambridge CB2 2AD (tel 01223 508903, fax 01223 505303, e-mail mos@theleys.net)

SLATER, Mark William; s of James Derrick Slater, of Cranleigh, Surrey, and Helen Slater; *b* 13 May 1969, London; *Educ* Oundle, Peterhouse Cambridge (MA); *m* July 2005, Maritzina, *née* Caltagirone; 2 s; *Career* chm and fndr Slater Investments Ltd 1994–, fndr Internet Indirect plc 1998–2000 (subsequently non-exec dir New Media Spark 2000–01), chm Galahad Capital plc (now Galahad Gold) 2001–03 (non-exec dir 2003–06), dir Union Investment Mgmnt 2006–; *Recreations* salmon fishing, cinema; *Clubs* Brooks's, Mark's, George, Annabel's, Aspinalls; *Style*— Mark Slater, Esq; ✉ Slater Investments Limited, 39 Cornhill, London EC3V 3RR (tel 020 7256 3950, fax 020 7929 2918)

SLATER, Nigel; *Career* cookery writer; food ed Marie Claire 1988–93, food columnist The Observer 1993–; *Awards* Glenfiddich Award 1989, 1995, 1999 and 2004, Cookery Writer of the Year Award 1995 and 1999, Glenfiddich Trophy 1995, BBC Media Personality of the Year 1997, Guild of Food Writers Broadcaster of the Year 1999, André Simon 2001 and 2004, People's Choice Book of the Year 2004, British Biography of the Year 2004; *Books* Real Fast Food (1992), Real Fast Puddings (1993), The 30-Minute Cook (1994), Real Good Food (1995), Real Cooking (1997), Nigel Slater's Real Food (to accompany eight-part television series 1998), Appetite (2000), Thirst (2002), Toast: The Story of a Boy's Hunger (2003), The Kitchen Diaries (2005), Eating for England (2007); *Style*— Nigel Slater, Esq

SLATER, Prof Nigel Kenneth Henry; *Educ* Univ of Cambridge (MA, PhD); *Career* lectr in chemical engrg Univ of Cambridge 1979–85, bioprocessing section mangr Unilever, head of bioprocess devpt Wellcome plc, currently prof of chemical engrg Univ of Cambridge and fell Fitzwilliam Coll Cambridge; former chair BBSRC Chemicals and Pharmaceuticals Directorate; memb: BBSRC Biochemical Engrg Review Panel, BBSRC Technol Interaction Bd, EPSRC Process Engrg Coll, SERC Process Engrg Ctee, SERC Separations Sub-Ctee; non-exec memb Bd Cobra Bio-manufacturing plc; FIChemE 1996, FREng 2004; *Style*— Prof Nigel Slater; ✉ Department of Chemical Engineering, University of Cambridge, New Museums Site, Pembroke Street, Cambridge CB2 3RA

SLATER, Prof Peter James Bramwell; *b* 26 December 1942; *Educ* Univ of Edinburgh (BSc, PhD, DSc); *m*; 2 s; *Career* demonstrator Zoology Dept Univ of Edinburgh 1966–68 (Shaw Macfie Lang fell 1964–66), lectr in biology Univ of Sussex 1968–84; Univ of St Andrews: Kennedy prof of natural history 1984–, chm Dept of Zoology and Marine Biology 1984–87, head Sch of Biological and Medical Scis 1992–97, dean Faculty of Science 1998–2002; pres Assoc for the Study of Animal Behaviour 1986–89 (hon sec 1973–78, medallist 1999), chm Heads of Univ Biological Scis UK 1994–96; FRSE 1991; *Books* Sex Hormones and Behaviour. Studies in Biology (1978), Animal Behaviour (ed jtly, vol 1 Causes and Effects 1983, vol 2 Communication 1983, vol 3 Genes, Development and Learning 1983), An Introduction to Ethology (1985), The Collins Encyclopedia of Animal Behaviour (ed, 1986), Behaviour and Evolution (ed jtly, 1994), Bird Song: Biological Themes and Variations (jtly, 1995), Essentials of Animal Behaviour (1999); *Style*— Prof Peter Slater, FRSE; ✉ School of Biology, Bute Medical Building, University of St Andrews, St Andrews, Fife KY16 9TS (tel 01334 463500, fax 01334 463600, e-mail pjbs@st-andrews.ac.uk)

SLATER, Richard; s of Dennis Slater (d 1979), and Freida, *née* Hodgson; *b* 18 August 1948; *Educ* UCS, Pembroke Coll Cambridge (MA); *m* Julie Norma, da of Gordon Jolley Ward; 2 s (Samuel Rupert b 1980, Frederick James b 1985), 1 da (Amy Louise b 1982); *Career* Slaughter and May: articled clerk 1970–72, asst slr 1972–79, ptnr 1979–2005; commercial travel photographer 2005–; *Recreations* tennis, theatre, cinema, opera, ballet, horse racing, watching football, rugby and cricket; *Clubs* MCC; *Style*— Richard Slater, Esq; ✉ Triptik Images, 105 Clifton Hill, London NW8 0JR (tel 020 7328 8513, fax 020 7372 2364, e-mail richard.slater@triptikimages.com)

SLATFORD, Rodney Gerald Yorke; OBE (2007); s of Frederick Charles Slatford (d 1951), and (Irene) Vida Yorke, *née* Robinson (d 1991); *b* 18 July 1944; *Educ* Bishop's Stortford Coll, Royal Coll of Music; *Career* double bassist, broadcaster; memb Nat Youth Orch of GB 1961–62, RCM 1963–65; princ bass: London Soloist's Ensemble 1965, Midland Sinfonia (later English Sinfonia) 1965–74, Nash Ensemble of London 1965–94, Purcell Room recital debut 1969, freelance Acad of St Martin-in-the-Fields 1972–74, co-princ double bass English Chamber Orch 1974–81, soloist Henry Wood Promenade Concert 1974, Wigmore Hall Double Bass Forum 1974, world recital tour (India, Sri Lanka, Singapore, Aust, NZ, Nepal) 1975, soloist Aix Festival English Chamber Orch 1977, artist in residence (one month) Cairo Conservatoire 1981, artist in residence Kusatsu Int Summer Acad Japan 1984; md and fndr Yorke Edn 1969–, prof RCM 1974–84, fndr and dir Isle of Man Int Double Bass Competition and Workshop 1978, examiner for Assoc Bd Royal Schs of Music 1979–96 and 2002–, admin Young Musicians Scheme Greater London Arts Assoc 1980–82, chm ESTA Music Competition Report 1982, head of School of Strings RNCM 1984–2001 (sr tutor in double bass 1980–84), fndr and chm The Yorke Tst 1984–, guest tutor Beijing Conservatoire 1984, organiser Manchester Bass Week 1985, reg presenter BBC Radio 3 1986–96, guest tutor Toho Sch of Music Tokyo 1988, chm ESTA Int Conf Manchester 1989, Portsmouth 1999; memb: Advsy Ctee Br Cncl Music 1989, Gowrie Ctee review of the London Music Conservatoires 1990, Exec Ctee European String Teachers' Assoc; chm Br Branch ESTA 1992–96; tstee Loan Fund for Musical Instruments 2005–; has made numerous broadcasts and recordings, juror and examiner at numerous nat and int venues, has lectured extensively since 1964, author of various reports and contrib to Grove's Dictionary of Music; Hon RCM 1976, FRNCM 1987; *Recreations* music publishing, gardening, cooking, walking; *Style*— Rodney

Slatford, Esq, OBE; ✉ Grove Cottage, Southgate Road, South Creake, Norfolk NR21 9PA

SLATKIN, Leonard; s of Felix Slatkin, and Eleanor Aller; *b* 9 January 1944, LA; *Educ* Aspen Music Sch, Juilliard Sch; *m* Linda Hohenfeld; 1 s (Daniel); *Career* conductor; music dir Nat Symphony Orch Washington DC 1996–, chief conductor BBC Symphony Orch 2000–04; conductor laureate St Louis Symphony Orch 1996– (music dir 1979–96); princ guest conductor: Philharmonia Orch 1997–2000, Royal Philharmonic Orch 2005–; performed with numerous orchs incl: NY Philharmonic, NHK Symphony, Royal Concertgebouw, Berlin Philharmonic, Orchestre de Paris, Vienna Symphony, Czech Philharmonic, Orchestra del Teatro Comunale di Firenze; dir Cleveland Orch Blossom Festival 1992–99, fndr and dir Nat Conducting Inst USA; over 100 recordings and winner four Grammy Awards (fifty nominations); *Style*— Leonard Slatkin, Esq; ✉ c/o Askonas Holt Ltd, Lonsdale Chambers, 27 Chancery Lane, London WC2A 1PF

SLATTERY, Tony Deklan; s of Michael Slattery, and Margaret Slattery; *b* 9 November 1959; *Educ* London Jesuit GS, Trinity Hall Cambridge (exhibitioner, MA, pres Footlights); *Career* improviser and actor; repertoire incl: drama, revue, film, comedy, musicals, presenting, soap opera, current affrs; rector Univ of Dundee 1998–; memb Br Humanist Soc; *Theatre* work incl: Edinburgh Fringe Festival, Me and My Girl (Adelphi Theatre London), Comedy Store Leicester Square, Radio Times (Queen's Theatre London), Neville's Island (Apollo Theatre London, Olivier nomination); *Television* incl: Whose Line Is It Anyway? (Channel 4), This is David Harper (Channel 4), Drowning in the Shallow End (BBC), writer and presenter Saturday Night at the Movies (ITV), S & M (Channel 4, Special Jury Prize Montreux TV Festival), An English Hareem 2005, Ahead of The Class 2005, Coronation Street 2005–06; *Films* incl: Peter's Friends, The Crying Game, Up n Under; Perrier Award Edinburgh Festival; *Recreations* psychopharmacology, the wines of Alsace, designing ouija boards; *Style*— Tony Slattery

SLAUGHTER, Andrew Francis; MP; *b* 29 September 1960; *Educ* Univ of Exeter; *Career* barrister; Hammersmith and Fulham BC: cncllr 1986–2006, dep cncl ldr 1991–96, cncl ldr 1996–2005; MP (Lab) Ealing Acton and Shepherd's Bush 2005– (Parly candidate (Lab) Uxbridge 1997 (by-election)); memb: Co-op Pty, Amicus; *Style*— Andrew Slaughter, Esq, MP; ✉ House of Commons, London SW1A 0AA

SLAYMAKER, Paul Ellis; s of Ellis Hamilton Slaymaker (d 2001), of Surrey, and Barbara Joan, *née* Langfield; *b* 10 March 1945; *Educ* Sunbury GS (BA), Ealing Tech Coll; *m* 1968, Ann Elizabeth, da of Edward Michael Frederick Piercey (d 1982), of IOW; 1 s (Nicholas b 1978), 1 da (Emma b 1975); m 2, 1991, Frances Margaret Illingworth; *Career* advertising; mgmnt conslt McKinsey & Co Inc 1975–76, head of mktg CPC (UK) Ltd 1977–80, dep md Leo Burnett Ltd 1980–86; Delaney Fletcher Bozell: md 1986–95, exec vice-pres Bozell Worldwide 1995–; *Recreations* photography, flying, shooting; *Style*— Paul Slaymaker, Esq; ✉ Bozell Worldwide, 25 Wellington Street, London WC2E 7DA (tel 020 7836 3474)

SLEE, Very Rev Colin B; OBE (2001); *b* 1945; *Educ* Ealing GS, King's Coll London (BD, AKC, Univ of London Rowing colours), St Augustine's Coll Canterbury; *m* 1971, Edith, *née* Tryon; *Career* ordained: deacon 1970, priest 1971 (St Francis Norwich); curate St Mary the Great with St Michael Cambridge and chaplain Girton Coll Cambridge 1973–76, chaplain and tutor King's Coll London 1976–82, sub-dean Cathedral and Abbey Church of St Alban 1982–94, provost The Cathedral and Collegiate Church of St Saviour and St Mary Overie Southwark 1994, dean of Southwark 2000–; newcomen warden St Saviour's Charities 2000–03; chm: Tutu Fndn UK 2004–, Homicide Review Advsy Gp 2005–; memb Cncl Corp of the Sons of the Clergy 1999, memb Ctee of Visitors Harvard Univ 2001; tstee: Crisis 1995–2005, Parents for Children, The Millennium Footbridge 1999–2002, Borough Market 2000–; govr Inform; Winston Churchill fell 2003; FKC 2001; *Recreations* rowing, bee keeping, gardening; *Style*— The Very Rev the Dean of Southwark, OBE; ✉ Provost's Lodging, 51 Bankside, London SE1 9JE; Southwark Cathedral, London Bridge, London SE1 9DA (tel 020 7367 6731, fax 020 7367 6725, e-mail colin.slee@southwark.anglican.org)

SLEEMAN, Prof Brian David; s of Richard Kinsman Sleeman (d 2002), and Gertrude Cecilia, *née* Gamble (d 1998); *b* 4 August 1939; *Educ* Canterbury Rd Sch Morden, Tiffin Boy's Sch Kingston upon Thames, Battersea Coll of Technol (BSc), Univ of London (PhD), Univ of Dundee (DSc); *m* 7 Sept 1963, Juliet Mary, da of Frederick James John (d 1972); 1 da (Elizabeth b 15 Sept 1966), 2 s (Matthew b 19 Feb 1969, David b 12 June 1972); *Career* Univ of Dundee: asst lectr 1965–67, lectr 1967–71, reader 1971–78, prof of applied analysis 1978–93, head Dept of Mathematics and Computer Sci 1986–89, Ivory prof of mathematics 1993–95, hon prof of mathematics 1995–; Univ of Leeds: prof of applied mathematics 1995–2004, prof emeritus 2004–; various hon visiting professorships at univs in USA, Canada, Sweden, France, Chile and China; visiting prof mathematical biology Univ of Abertay Dundee 2004–; chm Scot Branch IMA 1982–84, pres of Edinburgh Mathematical Soc 1988–89; life memb Clare Hall Cambridge 2002–; Erskine Fell Univ of Canterbury Christchurch NZ 2003, Endowment Fund for the Future Fell Univ of Alberta Canada 2003; FIMA 1972, FRSE 1976, CMath 1991; *Books* Multiparameter Spectral Theory in Hilbert Space (1978), Differential Equations and Mathematical Biology (1983, revised edn 2003); *Recreations* choral music, hill walking; *Style*— Prof Brian Sleeman, FRSE; ✉ School of Mathematics, University of Leeds, Leeds LS2 9JT (tel 0113 343 5188, fax 0113 343 5090, e-mail bds@maths.leeds.ac.uk)

SLEEP, Wayne Philip Colin; OBE (1998); s of stepfather Stanley Sleep, of Plymouth, Devon, and Joan Gwendoline Maude Sleep (d 1994); *b* 17 July 1948; *Educ* West Hartlepool Tech Sch, Royal Ballet Sch Richmond Park (Leverhulme scholarship); *Career* dancer, choreographer; joined Royal Ballet 1966 and in 1973 became princ dancer in over 50 leading roles incl: Puck in The Dream, Jester in Cinderella, Blue Boy in Les Patineurs, Petrushka, Alain and Widow Simone in La Fille Mal Gardée, Dr Coppélius in Coppélia (ENB tour) 1994; roles created for him by Sir Frederick Ashton incl: Koila in A Month in the Country, G R Sinclair in Elgar's Enigma Variations, Squirrel Nutkin and one of the Bad Mice in the film The Tales of Beatrix Potter; worked with other choreographers incl: Dame Ninette De Valois, Sir Kenneth Macmillan, Rudolph Nureyev, Joe Layton, Norman Main, Nigel Lythgoe; choreographer of: David and Goliath (London Contemporary Dance), dance sequence in Death on the Nile, The Hot Shoe Show (BBC TV), Harry Nilsson's The Point (and played leading role, Mermaid), Savoy Suite (Savoy Theatre reopening benefit for ENB) 1993, Promenade (for ENB Sch Festival) 1994, Alice in Wonderland (Nat Youth Ballet) 1997; acting roles incl: Ariel in The Tempest (New Shakespeare Co), Truffelino in The Servant of Two Masters, title role in Pinocchio (Birmingham rep), Tony Lumpkin in She Stoops to Conquer (BBC Radio), the Soldier in The Soldiers Tale (Festival Hall), The First Great Train Robbery, The Virgin Soldiers, original co of Cats 1981, Song and Dance 1982, Emcee in Gillian Lynn's Cabaret (West End), Puck in A Midsummer Night's Dream (Shakespeare Festival Brighton, Leeds and Nottingham) 2002, played in numerous pantomime seasons; formed own dance gp with nat and int tours under the names of Dash, The Hot Shoe Show and Bits and Pieces 1982–85, made several guest appearances, directed Carnival for the Birds (Royal Opera House), toured UK with cabaret show, revival of Song and Dance (West End and UK tour) 1992, Hollywood and Broadway - The Musicals (with Lorna Luft) 1992, directed royal ballet gala for Benesh Dance Notation charity 1993, Wayne's World of Dance tour 1993, Hollywood and Broadway Part II (UK tour) 1994, starred in and choreographed royal charity gala 90 Years of Dance 1995, own dance company tour Dance 1995, directed and starred in royal charity gala A Night of Stars (HM's Theatre) 1997, Hollywood and Broadway Part III (UK tour) 1997, starred in Le Fil Mal Gardé (Scottish Ballet) 1997, directed and starred in Lord Mayor of London charity gala A Celebration of Dance (Britten Theatre) 1997, directed and starred in Wayne Sleep Gala 50 Winks at Wayne Sleep 1998, directed and starred in Dash to the Coliseum 1998, Wayne's World of Classic Ballet tour 1998, starred in Aladdin Blackpool Grand 1998, directed and starred in Aspects of Dance (UK tour) 1999, choreographed Carousel (nat tour) 2000, star and choreographer Ready Steady Dance (UK tour) 2001, directed Dame Beryls Gray's 75th Birthday Gala (Sadlers Wells) 2002; fndr Wayne Sleep Dance Scholarship 1998, jazz ballet and tap teacher and coach; compere own radio show LBC 1987–97, subject of Special South Bank Show 1998; Show Business Personality of the Year 1983, two entries in Guinness Book of Records; Hon DUniv Exeter, Hon BA Teesside Univ 1999; FRSA; *Books* Variations on Wayne Sleep (1982), Precious Little Sleep (autobiography); *Clubs* Groucho; *Style*— Dr Wayne Sleep, OBE; ✉ c/o Alex Jay Personal Management, 8 Higher Newmarket Road, Newmarket, Nailsworth, Gloucestershire GL6 0RP (e-mail alexjay@alex-jay-pm.freeserve.co.uk)

SLEIGH, Prof Michael Alfred; s of Cyril Button Sleigh (d 1978), of Bath, and Ida Louisa, *née* Horstmann (d 1987); *b* 11 June 1932; *Educ* Taunton Sch, Bristol GS, Univ of Bristol (BSc, PhD, DSc); *m* 28 Dec 1957, Peggy, da of Maurice Arthur Mason (d 1982), of Calne, Wilts; 2 s (Roger b 1960, Peter b 1965), 1 da (Anne b 1962 d 2000); *Career* Nat Serv Flying Offr RAF Educn Branch 1957–58; lectr in zoology Univ of Exeter 1958–63, lectr and reader in zoology Univ of Bristol 1963–74, prof of biology Univ of Southampton 1975–97 (emeritus prof 1998–); managing ed European Jl of Protistology 2000–; chm Romsey Univ of the Third Age 2007–; sec Soc for Experimental Biology (nat) 1965–69, vice-pres Int Soc of Protozoologists 1987–88 (pres Br section 1982–85); memb: Marine Biological Assoc of the UK, Freshwater Biological Assoc; Eduard Reichenow medal Deutsche Gesellschaft für Protozoologie 2001; FIBiol 1977; *Books* The Biology of Cilia and Flagella (1962), The Biology of Protozoa (1973), Cilia and Flagella (1974), Microbes in the Sea (1987), Protozoa and other Protists (1989), Evolutionary Relationships Among Protozoa (1998), A Century of Protozoology in Britain (2000); *Recreations* travel, gardening, microscopy, walking, photography, local, family and natural history; *Style*— Prof Michael Sleigh; ✉ School of Biological Sciences, University of Southampton, Biomedical Sciences Building, Bassett Crescent East, Southampton SO16 7PX

SLEIGHT, Sir Richard; 4 Bt (UK 1920), of Weelsby Hall, Clee, Co Lincoln; s of Sir John Frederick Sleight, 3 Bt (d 1990), and Jacqueline Margaret, *née* Carter; *b* 27 May 1946; *m* 1978, Marie-Thérèse, da of O M Stepan, of London; 2 s (James Alexander b 1981, Nicholas Edward b 1985); *Heir* s, James Sleight; *Style*— Sir Richard Sleight, Bt; ✉ c/o National Westminster Bank, 6 High Street, Teddington, Middlesex TW11 8EP

SLEVIN, Dr Maurice Louis; s of David Slevin, of Cape Town, South Africa, and Nita, *née* Rosenbaum; *b* 2 July 1949; *Educ* De La Salle Coll East London, Univ of Cape Town (MB ChB); *m* 1, 5 Jan 1975 (m dis 1988), Cherry Lynn; 2 da (Lindi b 1978, Amy b 1981); m 2, 1993, Nicola Jane Harris; 1 da (Susannah b 1996), 1 s (Jamie b 1997); *Career* med registrar Groote Schuur Hosp Cape Town 1977, registrar and sr registrar Dept of Med Oncology Bart's London 1978–82, conslt physician and med oncologist Depts of Med Oncology Bart's and Homerton Hosps London 1982–2007, hon conslt physician and med oncologist Depts of Med Oncology Bart's and London NHS Tst 2007–; chm Cancerbacup (formerly Br Assoc Cancer United Patients), founder memb Doctors of Reform; MD 1984, FRCP 1989 (MRCP 1978); *Books* Randomised Trials in Cancer: A Critical Review by Sites (jt ed, with Maurice Staquet), Challenging Cancer: From Chaos to Control, Cancer: The Facts (with Michael Whitehouse, 1996), Cancer: How Worthwhile is Non Curative Treatment (1998), Challenging Cancer: Fighting Back, Taking Control, Finding Options (2002); *Style*— Dr Maurice Slevin; ✉ London Oncology Clinic, 95 Harley Street, London W1G 6AF (tel 020 7317 2525, fax 020 7009 4225)

SLIGO, 11 Marquess of (I 1800); Jeremy Ulick Browne; sits as Baron Monteagle (UK 1806); also Baron Mount Eagle (I 1760), Viscount Westport (I 1768), Earl of Altamont (I 1771), Earl of Clanricarde (I 1543 and 1800, with special remainder); s of 10 Marquess of Sligo (d 1991), and José, *née* Gauche; *b* 4 June 1939; *Educ* St Columba's Coll, RAC Cirencester; *m* 1961, Jennifer June, da of Maj Derek Cooper, MC, of Dunlewey, Co Donegal, and Mrs C Heber Percy; 5 da (Lady Sheelyn Felicity b 1963, Lady Karen Lavinia b 1964, Lady Lucinda Jane b 1969, Lady Clare Romane b 1974, Lady Alannah Grace b 1980); *Heir* cous, Sebastian Browne; *Clubs* Kildare Street; *Style*— The Most Hon the Marquess of Sligo; ✉ Westport House, Westport, Co Mayo, Republic of Ireland

SLIM, 2 Viscount (UK 1960); John Douglas Slim; OBE (1973), DL (Greater London 1988); s of Field Marshal 1 Viscount (Sir William Joseph) Slim, KG, GCB, GCMG, GCVO, GBE, DSO, MC, sometime GOC Allied Land Forces SE Asia, govr-gen Aust and govr and constable Windsor Castle (d 1970), and Aileen, *née* Robertson (d 1993); *b* 20 July 1927; *Educ* Prince of Wales Royal Indian Mil Coll Dehra Dun; *m* 1958, Elisabeth, da of Arthur Rawdon Spinney, CBE (decd); 2 s, 1 da; *Heir* s, Hon Mark Slim, *qv*; *Career* cmmnd Indian Army 6 Gurkha Rifles 1945–48, Lt Argyll and Sutherland Highlanders 1948, Staff Coll 1961, Jt Serv Staff Coll 1964, Cdr 22 SAS Regt 1967–70, GSO1 (Special Forces) HQ UK Land Forces 1970–72, ret 1972; Morgan Crucible Co 1973–76, chm Peek plc 1977–91 (dep chm 1991–97); dir Trailfinders Ltd and various other cos; pres Burma Star Assoc, vice-pres Br-Aust Soc, vice-chm Arab-Br C of C and Industry 1977–96, pres Special Air Serv Assoc, tstee Royal Cwlth Ex-Services League; elected memb House of Lords 1999; Master Worshipful Co of Clothworkers 1995–96; FRGS 1983; *Clubs* White's, Special Forces; *Style*— The Rt Hon the Viscount Slim, OBE, DL; ✉ House of Lords, London SW1A 0PW

SLIM, Hon Mark William Rawdon; s and h of 2 Viscount Slim, OBE, DL, *qv*; *b* 13 February 1960; *m* 15 Feb 1992, Harriet Laura, yr da of Jonathan Harrison, of Beds; 3 s (Rufus William Rawdon b 15 April 1995, William James Harrison b 6 July 1999, Kit Cosmo John b 20 Aug 2004); *Career* Mark Slim and Partners (real estate conslts); tstee Burma Star Assoc; Liveryman Worshipful Co of Clothworkers; *Recreations* shooting, fishing, history; *Clubs* White's, Aldeburgh Yacht; *Style*— The Hon Mark Slim; ✉ Mark Slim and Partners, 1 Poultry, London EC2R 8JR (tel 020 7643 2229, e-mail mark@markslim.co.uk)

SLINGER, His Hon Judge Edward; s of Thomas Slinger (d 1957), of Lancs, and Rhoda, *née* Bradshaw (d 1987); *b* 2 February 1938; *Educ* Accrington GS, Balliol Coll Oxford (BA); *m* 31 July 1965, Rosalind Margaret, da of Stanley Albert Jewitt, of Chiddingfold, Surrey; 2 da (Nicola b 1967, Emma b 1971), 2 s (Giles b 1969, Fergus b 1975); *Career* admitted slr 1961; dep dist registrar High Court 1981–88, recorder of the Crown Court 1992–95 (asst recorder 1988–92, Higher Courts Advocacy Qualification 1994), circuit judge (Northern Circuit) 1995–, memb Immigration Appeal Tribunal 1998–2005; vice-chm: Lancs CCC 1987–98 (vice-pres 2000–), ECB (formerly TCCB) Disciplinary Ctee 1989– (memb 1987–); memb ECB Working Pty on Structure of First Class Cricket; govr: Westholme Sch Blackburn, St Leonard-the-Less C of E Sch Samlesbury Preston; *Clubs* Lancashire CCC, MCC, Lansdowne; *Style*— His Hon Judge Slinger; ✉ c/o Courts Administrator's Office, Sessions House, Lancaster Road, Preston, Lancashire PR1 2PD (tel 01772 821451, fax 01772 884767)

SLINN, David Arthur; OBE (2000); s of Ronald Geoffrey Slinn, of Northampton, and Christine Mary, *née* Kingston; *b* 16 April 1959, Northampton; *Educ* Northampton GS, Univ of Salford (BA); *Career* diplomat; joined FCO 1981, third sec UK Perm Rep to Conf on Disarmament (UKDis) Geneva 1983, second sec Ulaanbaatar 1987, second sec Pretoria and Cape Town 1990, FCO 1993, chargé d'affaires Tirana 1995, first sec Belgrade 1996, head Br Govt Office Pristina 1999, on loan to NATO/EU Macedonia 2001, ambass to North Korea 2002–05; FRSA 2005; *Recreations* rugby, golf, malt whisky; *Style*— David Slinn, Esq, OBE; ✉ c/o Foreign & Commonwealth Office, King Charles Street, London SW1A 2AH (e-mail davidslinn@hotmail.com)

SLIPMAN, Sue; OBE (1994); da of Max Slipman (d 1971), of London, and Doris *née* Barham (d 1972); *b* 3 August 1949; *Educ* Stockwell Manor Sch, Univ of Wales (BA), Univ of London (PGCE); *Children* 1 s (Gideon Max b 1988); *Career* pres NUS 1977–78, vice-chm Br Youth Cncl 1977–78, memb Cncl Open Univ 1978–81; memb: Nat Union of Public Employees 1970–85, EC Econ and Social Ctee 1990–92; dir: Nat Cncl for One Parent Families 1985–95, London East TEC 1989–, London TEC Cncl 1995–96, Gas Consumers' Cncl 1996–98; dir for social responsibility Camelot Gp plc 1998–2003, chm Bd Financial Ombudsman Service 2003–04, dir Foundation Trust Network NHS Confedn 2004–; chair: Better Regulation Task Force 1997–2001, Corporate Responsibility Gp 2002; memb Working Gp on Women's Issues to Sec of State for Employment; *Books* Helping Ourselves to Power: A Training Manual for Women in Public Life Skills (1986), Helping One Parent Families to Work (1988), Maintainance: A System to Benefit Children (1989), Making Maintainance Pay (1990); *Style*— Ms Sue Slipman, OBE

SLIWERSKI, Trevor Zygmunt; s of Zdzislaw Andrzej Sliwerski (d 2002), and Irene Sliwerski (d 1990); *b* 30 December 1950; *Educ* John Fisher Sch Purley; *m* Lynn, da of Leonard Arthur Francis (d 1991); 1 da (Claire Louise b 1983), 1 s (Jeremy Andrew Zbigniew b 1987); *Career* dealer: Savory Milln 1968–71, R Layton 1971–74, Nomura 1978–80; dir RBT Fleming 1980–85, dir i/c Japanese equity warrants Baring Securities 1985–95, AJG Investments Ltd 1995–96, head of convertible and warrant sales Investec Bank (UK) Ltd (formerly Guinness Mahon & Co Ltd) 1996–2001, dir MSG and Partners Ltd 2001–; proprietor Noah's Ark Nursery 1990–2004; *Recreations* walking, flying; *Clubs* Surrey Walking, Stock Exchange Athletic; *Style*— Trevor Z Sliwerski, Esq; ✉ Stratton Street Capital LLP, 10 Babmaes Street, London SW1Y 6HD (tel 020 7766 0810, e-mail trevorsliwerski@strattonstreet.com)

SLOAM, Nigel Spencer; s of Maurice Sloam (d 1991), of London, and Ruth, *née* Davis (d 1998); *b* 17 December 1950; *Educ* Haberdashers' Aske's, Corpus Christi Coll Oxford (MA); *m* 3 Sept 1978, Elizabeth Augusta, da of Arnold Hertzberg; 1 da (Natalia Sylvia Caroline b 1979), 1 s (Oliver Julian Richard b 1983); *Career* trainee actuary Messrs Bacon & Woodrow 1972–76, actuary Sahar Insurance Co of Israel 1976–77, mangr Actuarial Dept Charterhouse Magna Assurance Co 1977–78, dir Messrs Bevington Lowndes Ltd 1978–79, sr ptnr Nigel Sloam & Co 1979–; Freeman City of London, Liveryman Worshipful Co of Basketmakers, Liveryman Worshipful Co of Actuaries; FIA 1977, ASA 1987, CMath 1991, MIMA; *Clubs* Oxford and Cambridge, City Livery, PHIATUS, Goose and Beast (pres), The Maccabeans; *Style*— Nigel Sloam, Esq; ✉ Nigel Sloam & Co, Roman House, 296 Golders Green Road, London NW11 9PY (tel 020 8209 1222, fax 020 8455 3973, e-mail nigel@nigelsloam.co.uk)

SLOAN, Eur Ing Gordon McMillan; s of Samuel Sloan, of Muirkirk, Ayrshire, and Christine McMillan, *née* Turner; *b* 30 December 1934; *Educ* Muirkirk Sch, Kilmarnock Acad, Glasgow Royal Tech Coll; *m* 5 Aug 1961, Patricia Mary, da of William Stewart McKim (d 1979); 1 s (John), 4 da (Christine, Elizabeth, Mary, Rachel); *Career* dir: Parsons Brown & Newton Consulting Engineers 1973–81, McMillan Sloan & Partners Consulting Engineers 1981–; notable works incl: studies, master plans, reports and detailed plans for major new ports at Dammam (Saudi Arabia), and Muara (Brunei), study and re-devpt plan with designs for Cardiff Port, design of floating port Aqaba (Jordan), detailed study of abandonment and removal of major N Sea prodn platform; advsr to developers of energy and transportation projects in Far East; professional examiner IMechE 1996–2001; Freeman City of London 1967, Liveryman Worshipful Co of Turners 1968 (memb Ct of Assts 1987, Upper Warden 1994–95, Master 1995–96, Dep Master 1996–97); CEng 1967, FInstPet 1974, FIMechE 1978, MSocIS (France) 1978, FPWI 1988, Eur Ing 1989, MIET 2006; *Recreations* music appreciation, property restoration; *Style*— Eur Ing Gordon Sloan; ✉ Glebe Cottage, Church Street, Henstridge, Somerset BA8 0QE (tel and fax 01963 362665)

SLOAN, Ronald Kenneth (Ronnie); *b* 21 July 1943; *Educ* Edinburgh Acad; *m* 29 May 1965, Sandra; 2 s (Elliot b 1969, Moray b 1971), 1 da (Hazel b 1978); *Career* Standard Life 1960–67, Friends Provident 1967–70; dir: Antony Gibbs Pensions Ltd 1970–71, Martin Paterson Assocs Ltd 1972–87; divnl dir and actuary Buck Paterson Conslts Ltd 1987–93, ind conslt actuary 1993–94, ptnr Punter Southall & Co 1994–2000, ind consulting actuary 2000–; chm Scottish Gp NAPF 1997–99 (Nat Assoc of Pension Funds); pres Edinburgh Academical RFC 1992–94 (capt 1973–74), govr Scottish Sports Aid Fndn, chm Raeburn Place Appeal; fundraiser for Children 1st (formerly RSSPCC) running 33 marathons around the world dressed as tartan Superman raising over £220,000; FFA 1967, FPMI 1977, FInstD 1980; *Recreations* tennis, rugby, running, Scottish country dancing; *Clubs* New (Edinburgh); *Style*— Ronnie Sloan, Esq; ✉ 20 Lomond Road, Edinburgh EH5 3JR (tel 0131 551 5471)

SLOANE, Prof Peter James; s of John Joseph Sloane (d 1992), and Elizabeth, *née* Clarke (d 2004); *b* 6 August 1942; *Educ* Cheadle Hulme Sch, Univ of Sheffield (BA), Univ of Strathclyde (PhD); *m* 30 July 1969, Avril Mary, da of Kenneth Urquhart (d 1984); 1 s (Christopher Peter b 1971); *Career* asst lectr and lectr in political economy Univ of Aberdeen 1966–69, lectr in industrial economics Univ of Nottingham 1969–75, econ advsr Unit for Manpower Studies Dept of Employment 1973–74, prof of economics and mgmnt Paisley Coll 1975–84; Univ of Aberdeen: prof of political economy 1984–2002 (now emeritus), Jaffrey prof of political economy 1985–2002, vice-princ and dean of social scis and law 1996–2002; dir Welsh Economy Labour Market Evaluation and Research Centre (WELMERC) Dept of Economics Univ of Wales Swansea; visiting prof: McMaster Univ Hamilton Ontario 1978 (Cwlth fell), Indiana Univ 1996, Univ of Melbourne 2007; hon res fell Inst for Labor Studies Bonn 2001–; vice-pres Int Assoc of Sports Economists 2000–; memb: ESRC 1979–85, Sec of State for Scotland's Panel of Econ Conslts 1981–91, Cncl Scottish Econ Soc 1983–2001, Ct Univ of Aberdeen 1987–91 and 1993–2002, Royal Economic Soc, Br Univs Industrial Rels Assoc, Euro Assoc of Labour Economists; FRSA 1997, FRSE 1997; *Books* Changing Patterns of Working Hours (1975), Sex Discrimination in the Labour Market (with B Chiplin, 1975), Sport in the Market? (1980), Women and Low Pay (ed 1980), The Earnings Gap Between Men and Women in Great Britain (1981), Equal Employment Issues (with H C Jain, 1981), Tackling Discrimination in the Workplace (with B Chiplin, 1982), Labour Economics (with D Carline, et al 1985), Sex at Work: Equal Pay and the Comparable Worth Controversy (1985), Low Pay and Earnings Mobility in Europe (ed with R Asplund and I Theodossiou, 1998), Employment Equity and Affirmative Action (with H Jain and F Horwitz, 2003), The Economics of Sport (with M Rosentraub and R Sandy, 2004); plus contributions to various academic jls; *Recreations* sport; *Clubs* Pennard Golf; *Style*— Prof Peter Sloane, FRSE; ✉ 5 Willowbrook Gardens, Mayals, Swansea SA3 5EB (tel 01792 517511); WELMERC, School of Business and Economics, University of Wales Swansea, Richard Price Building, Singleton Park, Swansea SA2 8PP (tel 01792 513319, fax 01792 295 872, e-mail p.j.sloane@swansea.ac.uk)

SLOBODA, Prof John Anthony; s of Mieczyslaw Sloboda (d 1981), and Mary, *née* Bregazzi; *b* 13 June 1950, London; *Educ* St Benedict's Sch Ealing, The Queen's Coll Oxford (MA), UCL (PhD); *m* 1980 (m dis 1991), Judith, *née* Nussbaum; 1 da (Miriam Anne b 14 Feb 1982); *Career* Keele Univ: memb Sch of Psychology 1974–, dir Unit for the Study of Musical Skill and Devpt 1991–, hon research fell Sch of Politics, Int Rels and the Environment (SPIRE); sometime pres: Psychology Section and Gen Section BAAS, European Soc for the Cognitive Sciences of Music; memb Editorial Bd: Musicae Scientiae (jl of European Soc for the Cognitive Sciences of Music), Psychology of Music, Music Perception, Psychology Teaching Review; Pres's Award for Distinguished Contributions to Psychological Knowledge Br Psychological Soc 1998; exec dir Oxford Research Gp, co-fndr Iraq Body Count Project; FBPsS, FBA; *Publications* The Musical Mind: The Cognitive Psychology of Music (1985), Generative Processes in Music: The Psychology of Performance, Improvisation and Composition (1988), Musical Beginnings: Origins and Development of Musical Competence (jtly, 1996), Perception and Cognition of Music (jtly, 1997), Music and Emotion: Theory and Research (ed jtly, 2001), Exploring the Musical Mind (2004), Psychology for Musicians (jtly, 2007), Beyond Terror: The truth about the real threats to our world (jtly, 2007); also author of research papers and jl articles; *Recreations* choral singing, conducting; *Style*— Prof John Sloboda; ✉ 7 Commonside Close, Stafford ST16 3FP (tel 01785 251246); Department of Psychology, Keele University, Newcastle, Staffordshire ST5 5BG (e-mail j.a.sloboda@keele.ac.uk)

SLOCOCK, Caroline Ann; da of Horace Slocock, and (Florence) Joyce, *née* Wheelton; *Educ* Talbot Heath Sch Bournemouth, UCL (BA); *m* John Nightingale; *Career* joined Dept of Employment 1982, private sec to sec of state for Employment 1985–87, memb Next Steps Project Team Cabinet Office 1988–89, private sec (home affrs) to PM 1989–91, head of Treasy personnel 1993–96, sr policy advsr on expenditure HM Treasy 1997–2000, jt head Early Years and Childcare Unit DfES 2000–02, chief exec Equal Opportunities Cmmn 2002–; *Recreations* gardening, photography, painting, reading; *Style*— Ms Caroline Slocock; ✉ Equal Opportunities Commission, 36 Broadway, London SW1H 0BH (tel 020 7960 7427, fax 020 7222 2810, e-mail caroline.slocock@eoc.org.uk)

SLOCOCK, (David) Michael; s of Maj Arthur Anthony Slocock (d 1995), and Elizabeth Anthea, *née* Sturdy (d 1990); *b* 1 February 1945; *Educ* Radley, Lincoln Coll Oxford (BA); *m* 12 April 1969, Theresa Mary, da of Maj Anthony Clyde-Smith (d 1989), of Jersey, CI; 1 da (Lucinda Sheila Mary b 1971), 2 s (Julian Mark Anthony b 1973, Mark David Philip b 1976); *Career* The Sunday Telegraph 1967–69, Hill Samuel & Co Ltd merchant bankers 1969–71, dir various cos including Normans Group plc, Empire Plantations & Investments, L K Industrial Investments 1971–79; chief exec: Normans Group plc 1973–90, Selections Mail Order 1991–; *Recreations* sailing, skiing, golf, gardening; *Clubs* Royal Motor Yacht; *Style*— Michael Slocock, Esq; ✉ Southover House, Tolpuddle, Dorchester, Dorset DT2 7HF (tel 01305 848220, fax 01305 848516)

SLOCOMBE, Sue; OBE (1994); da of Capt Leonard William Ellis, MBE (d 1977), and Phyllis Muriel, *née* Chick (d 1984); *b* 8 June 1949; *Educ* Nailsea GS, Bedford Coll of Physical Educ, Univ of Bristol; *m* 1, 5 Aug 1972, Martin Charles Slocombe, s of Charles Slocombe (d 1976); *m* 2, 30 June 2000, David Whitaker, OBE; *Career* teacher Clifton HS for Girls 1970–74; lectr: Coll of St Matthias 1974–76, Faculty of Educn Bristol Poly 1976–98; princ lectr and dir of studies UWE (formerly Bristol Poly); currently dir Performance Conslts Ltd; course dir MSc in coaching and devpt in business 2002–; sportswoman; int hockey player: Outdoor World Cup 1979, Euro Bronze medallist 1985, indoor capt 1985–88; coach England Ladies Sr Hockey Team 1986–94 (Euro Silver medal 1987, 4th in World Cup 1990, Euro Gold medal 1991), coach GB Ladies Olympic Hockey Squad 1993– (asst coach 1989–90, 4th in Atlanta Olympic Games 1996); memb: Coaches Advsy Panel Br Olympic Assoc, Exec Bd Nat Coaches Assoc 1993–, Exec Bd Nat Coaching Fndn 1993–, Sports Cncl Women in Coaching Advsy Gp 1993–; involved in hockey coaching to club and int standard (also children's hockey coach); winner Coach of the Year award 1991; expert advsr Sport England 2000–; prog dir Business, Women & Success in the 21st Century 2000; tstee Children our Ultimate Investment; memb: NASC, PE Assoc of GB and NI, BAALPE; *Books* Indoor Hockey (1985), Make Hockey Fun - Hockey for 8–12 year olds (1985); *Style*— Mrs Sue Slocombe, OBE; ✉ Brackenwood, 2 Folleigh Close, Long Ashton, Bristol BS41 9HX (tel 01275 394116, e-mail sue_slocombe@performanceconsultants.co.uk)

SLOGROVE, Richard Paul; s of Wing Cdr A P H Slogrove (d 1974), and Margaret Anne (Margot), *née* Hannam-Clark (d 1997); *b* 1 November 1945; *Educ* The King's Sch Ely, RAF Coll Cranwell (Sword of Honour, Queen's Medal), Univ of London (BA); *m* 6 June 1970, Judyth Anne (Jo), da of James Peacock (d 1999); 1 da (Emma b 1 June 1972); *Career* RAF 1963–76 (Sqdn Ldr); md Telex UK Ltd 1985–88; Memorex Telex: vice-pres Personal Computer Div 1988–90, pres Canada 1990–92, vice-pres N America Sales and Serv 1992–94; British Telecommunications plc: dir Global Mktg 1994–97, pres Asia Pacific 1997–2000, pres Operations BT Ignite 2000–01; former memb Bd: Albacom Italy, Bharti Televentures India, ESAT Ireland, Maxis Malaysia, Mediaset Italy, Rogers Cantel Canada, SmarTone Hong Kong, StarHub Singapore, sunrise Switzerland, Telenordia Sweden; chm Bd of Govrs King's Sch Ely 2005–; *Recreations* gardening, music; *Clubs* RAF; *Style*— Richard Slogrove, Esq; ✉ 9 Houghton Gardens, Ely, Cambridgeshire CB7 4JN (e-mail richardslogrove@btinternet.com)

SLOWE, Victoria Jane (Vikki); da of David Ross, of London, and Sybil, *née* Harris; *b* 24 May 1947; *Educ* Camden Sch for Girls, London Coll of Fashion (City & Guilds Dip); *m* 1966, Martin A M Slowe; 2 da (Emily b 1970, Hannah b 1973); *Career* abstract artist of constructions and prints; fell Royal Soc of Painter-Printmakers; *Group Exhibitions* incl: Realities Nouvelles Paris, VOK Moscow, NY, Ottawa, Singapore, Royal Academy, Royal W of England Academy and Royal Soc of Painter-Printmakers London; *Work in Collections* incl: Smithsonian Instn Washington DC, Tel Aviv Museum, Ashmolean Museum Oxford; *Recreations* exhibitions, travel, theatre; *Style*— Mrs Vikki Slowe

SLYNN OF HADLEY, Baron (Life Peer UK 1992), of Eggington in the County of Bedfordshire; Sir Gordon Slynn; kt (1976), PC (1992); er s of John and Edith Slynn; *b* 17 February 1930; *Educ* Sandbach Sch, Goldsmiths Coll London, Trinity Coll Cambridge; *m* 1962, Odile Marie Henriette, da of Pierre Boutin; *Career* called to the Bar Gray's Inn 1956 (bencher 1970, treas 1988); lectr in air law LSE 1958–61, jr counsel Miny of Labour 1967–68, jr counsel Treasy 1968–74, recorder 1971 (hon recorder Hereford 1972–76), QC 1974, leading counsel Treasy 1974–76, judge of the High Court of Justice (Queen's Bench Div) 1976–81, pres Employment Appeal Tbnl 1978–81, judge Court of Justice of Euro Communities 1988–91 (advocate gen 1981–88), a Lord of Appeal in Ordinary 1992–2002, pres Court of Appeal Solomon Islands 2001–; visiting prof of law: Univ of Durham 1981–88, KCL 1986–90 and 1995–, Univ of Technol Sydney 1990–, Nat Univ of India Bangalore 1994–; visitor: Mansfield Coll Oxford 1996–, Univ of Essex 1996–2000; hon vice-pres Union Internationale des Avocats 1976–, chm Exec Cncl Int Law Assoc 1988–, pres Acad of Experts 1992–96; chief steward Hereford 1978– (dep chief steward 1977–78), Freedom City of Hereford 1997; pres: Bentham Club 1992, Holdsworth Club 1993; fell Int Students' Tst 1985– (govr 1979–85 and 1992–), govr Sadler's Wells Theatre 1988–95, memb Cncl Pilgrims 1992–2005; hon memb: Canadian Bar Assoc, Colegio de Abagados de Buenos Aires; hon fell American Coll of Trial Lawyers; memb American Law Inst; Master Worshipful Co of Broderers 1994–95; Hon Decanus Legis Mercer USA; hon fell: UC Buckingham 1982, St Andrews Coll Sydney 1991, Trinity Coll Cambridge 1991, Liverpool John Moores Univ 1992, Goldsmiths Coll London 1993, KCL 1995, Northampton Coll; Hon LLD Univs of: Birmingham 1983, Buckingham 1983, Exeter 1985, Technol Sydney 1991, Bristol Poly (CNAA) 1992, Sussex 1992, Stetson USA 1993, Saarlandes 1994, Staffordshire 1994, Pace (NY) 1995, Kingston 1996, Pondicherry (India) 1997, London 1999, Strathclyde 1999, Hertfordshire 2003; Hon DCL: Univ of Durham 1989, City Univ 1994; Hon DUniv Museo Social Buenos Aires 1994; Cordell Hull Medal Stamford Univ Al 1993; FCIArb, ADR Chambers accredited mediator; Commandeur d'Honneur de Bontemps de Medoc et des Graves, Commandeur Confrèrie de St Cunibert

(Luxembourg), Chevalier de Tastevin, Grande Croix de l'Ordre de Merite (Luxembourg), Knight Order of Merit (Poland), KStJ (Prior of England and the Islands OStJ), Officer Order of Merit (Hungary); *Clubs* Beefsteak, Garrick, White's; *Style—* The Rt Hon Lord Slynn of Hadley, PC; ✉ House of Lords, London SW1A 0PW

SMALL, Harry; s of Eric James Small, of London, and Brenda, *née* Bedford; *b* 20 April 1957; *Educ* St Alban's Boys' GS, Oriel Coll Oxford (MA); *Career* asst slr Linklaters & Paines 1981–86 (articled clerk 1979–81); Baker & McKenzie: assoc Hong Kong 1986–87, assoc London 1987–89, ptnr Intellectual Property IT Dept 1989–, head IT and Communications Gp 2002–; visiting lectr in trade mark law Queen Mary Coll London 1984–85, lectr in designs law Intellectual Property Dip Univ of Bristol 1993–, expert EU Economic and Social Ctee on various EU copyright and IT law proposals 1990–; author of numerous articles on IT matters; chm Soc for Computers and Law 1997–; memb: Law Soc England 1981–, Law Soc Hong Kong 1986–87, Computer Law Gp 1990–; *Recreations* travel, food, drink, sleeping; *Clubs* Lansdowne; *Style—* Harry Small, Esq; ✉ Baker & McKenzie, 100 New Bridge Street, London EC4V 7JA (tel 020 7919 1000, e-mail harry.small@bakernet.com)

SMALL, Peter John; CB (2000); s of John Small, of Belfast, and Kathleen, *née* Keys; *b* 21 July 1946; *Educ* Grosvenor GS Belfast, Univ of London (LLB); *m* 11 Aug 1971, Pamela; 2 s (Alan b 7 March 1974, Colin b 18 Sept 1976); *Career* dir of finance NI Civil Service 1983–88, dir of personnel NI Civil Service 1988–94, head Social Security Policy and Health Service 1994–96, perm sec Dept of Agriculture and Rural Devpt (NI) 1996–2003; ret; *Recreations* gardening, reading, music, soccer (Liverpool FC), cricket, golf (handicap 17); *Style—* Peter Small, Esq, CB

SMALLMAN, Prof (Edward) Raymond; CBE (1992); s of David Smallman, and Edith, *née* French; *b* 4 August 1929; *Educ* Rugeley GS, Univ of Birmingham (BSc, PhD, DSc); *m* 6 Sept 1952, Joan Doreen, da of George Faulkner, of Wolverhampton; 1 da (Lesley Ann (Mrs Grimer) b 1955), 1 s (Robert Ian b 1959); *Career* sr scientific offr AERE Harwell 1953–58; Univ of Birmingham: lectr Dept of Physical Metallurgy 1958–63, sr lectr 1963–64, prof of physical metallurgy 1964–69, Feeney prof of metallurgy and materials sci 1969–93, head Physical Metallurgy and Sci of Materials 1969–81, head Dept Metallurgy and Materials 1981–88, dean Faculty of Sci and Engrg 1984–85, dean Faculty of Engrg 1985–87, vice-princ 1987–92, prof of metallurgy and materials sci 1993–2001, emeritus prof of metallurgy and materials sci 2001–; visiting prof: Univ of Pennsylvania 1961, Stanford Univ 1962, UC Berkley 1978, Univ of NSW Australia 1974, Cape Town 1982; hon prof Univ of Hong Kong 1990–; academic advsr: Univ of Queensland 1995, Univ of Hong Kong 1996–99, Ghulam Ishaq Khan Inst of Engrg Sciences and Technol Pakistan 1996–2002; Sir George Beilby Gold medal 1969, Rosenhain medal 1972, Elegant Work prize 1979, Platinum medal 1989, Acta Materialia Gold medal 2004; pres Birmingham Metallurgical Assoc 1972, vice-pres Metals Soc 1980–85, vice-pres Inst of Materials 1995–98 (memb Cncl 1992–98), pres Federated Euro Materials Socs 1994–96 (vice-pres 1992–94); SERC: memb Materials Cmmn 1988–92, memb Cncl 1992–94; Warden Assay Office Birmingham 1994–97 (guardian 1997–2000); non-exec dir Univ Hosp Birmingham NHS Tst 1995–99; Hon DSc: Univ of Wales, Univ of Novi Sad Yugoslavia 1990, Univ of Cranfield 2001; hon foreign memb: China Ordnance Soc 1993, Czech Soc for Metal Sci 1995; foreign assoc US Nat Acad of Engrg (NAE) 2005; FIM 1965, FRS 1986, FREng 1991; *Books* Modern Physical Metallurgy (1962, 4 edn 1985), Modern Metallography (1966), Structure of Metals and Alloys (1969), Defect Analysis in Electron Microscopy (1975), Vacancies '76 (1976), Metals and Materials (1994), Modern Physical Metallurgy and Materials Engineering (1999); articles on microstructure and properties of materials in learned jls; *Recreations* golf, bridge, travel; *Clubs* South Staffs Golf; *Style—* Prof Raymond Smallman, CBE, DSc, FRS, FREng; ✉ 59 Woodthorne Road South, Tettenhall, Wolverhampton WV6 8SN (tel and fax (home) 01902 752545, e-mail ray.smallman@btopenworld.com); work (tel 0121 414 7368, fax 0121 414 7368, e-mail r.e.smallman@bham.ac.uk)

SMALLMAN, Timothy Gilpin; s of Stanley Cottrell Smallman (d 1965), of Kenilworth, Warks, and Grace Mary Louise, *née* Wilson (d 1990); *b* 6 November 1938; *Educ* Stowe; *m* 18 April 1964, Jane, da of Edward Holloway (d 1988), of Acocks Green, Birmingham; 2 s (Guy b 1965, Simon b 1967); *Career* chm: Smallman Lubricants (Hereford) Ltd 1972–2000, WF Smallman and Son Ltd 1978–2000 (md 1965–2000), Smallman Lubricants Ltd 1978–2000 (md 1978–96), Coronet Oil Refineries Ltd 1979–2000, Needwood Oils and Solvents Ltd 1984–2000, ret; nat pres Br Lubricants Fedn Ltd 1983–85 (dir 1977–89); FInstD 1965, FInstPet 1968; *Recreations* bridge, ornithology, nature and wildlife conservation; *Style—* Timothy Smallman, Esq; ✉ Luddington Manor, Stratford-upon-Avon, Warwickshire CV37 9SJ

SMALLWOOD, Christopher Rafton; s of James Rafton Smallwood, of Sandbach, Cheshire, and Josephine, *née* Mortimer; *b* 13 August 1947, Morecambe, Lancs; *Educ* Royal GS Lancaster, Exeter Coll Oxford (open exhibitioner, BA), Nuffield Coll Oxford (MPhil); *m* 28 July 1979, Ingeborg Hedwig Eva, *née* Wiesler; 1 s (Nicholas Joseph Christopher b 20 Sept 1982), 1 da (Stephanie Ingeborg b 22 Nov 1985); *Career* Harkness fell Harvard Univ 1968–69, lectr in economics Exeter Coll Oxford 1971–72, lectr in economics Univ of Edinburgh 1972–76, special advsr Cabinet Office Constitution Unit 1974–75, economic advsr HM Treasy 1976–81, dir of policy SDP 1981–83, chief economist British Petroleum Co plc 1983–86, economics ed Sunday Times 1986–89, gp economist and strategic devpt dir TSB Gp 1989–94 (also dir TSB Bank), ptnr Makinson Cowell Ltd 1994–98, ptnr Brunswick Gp Ltd 1998–2001, chief economic advsr Barclays plc 2001–05, dir Lombard Street Assocs 2005–; memb Competition Cmmn 2001–; policy advsr Prince of Wales Charitable Fndns 2005–; memb Advsy Cncl ECGD 1991–94; visiting fell Centre for Business Strategy London Business Sch 1987–88; dir UnLTD 2001– (chm Investment Ctee); *Recreations* opera, theatre, golf; *Clubs* Reform; *Style—* Christopher Smallwood, Esq

SMALLWOOD, Prof Rodney Harris (Rod); s of William Frederick Smallwood (d 1997), and Muriel, *née* Smith (d 2006); *b* 14 July 1945; *Educ* Withernsea HS, UCL (BSc), Lancaster Univ (MSc), Univ of Sheffield (PhD); *m* 3 Aug 1968, Anna Mary, *née* Treharne; 1 s (Ben b 15 Nov 1984); *Career* basic grade, sr grade, princ grade then top grade med physicist NHS 1970–96; Univ of Sheffield: prof of med engrg 1995–2003, prof of computational systems biology 2003–, dir of research (engrg) 2003–; author of and contrib to books and sci pubns; pres Inst of Physics and Engrg in Med 1999–2001; FREng 2001, Hon FRCP 2002, FIEE, FInstP, fell Inst of Physics and Engrg in Med (FIPEM); *Recreations* fell running, mountaineering, cycling; *Style—* Prof Rod Smallwood; ✉ Department of Computer Science, University of Sheffield, Regent Court, 211 Portobello Road, Sheffield S1 4DP (tel 0114 222 1840, e-mail r.smallwood@dcs.shef.ac.uk, website www.dcs.shef.ac.uk/rod)

SMALLWOOD, Dr Stuart David; s of James Smallwood, of Canterbury, Kent, and Pamela Smallwood; *b* 21 February 1962; *Educ* Harvey GS Folkestone, Univ of Leeds (BSc), Univ of Cambridge (PhD), Univ of Bristol (PGCE, NPQH); *m* 9 April 1988, Charlotte, *née* Burlend; 1 da (Eleanor b 1991), 2 s (Oliver b 1995, Benedict b 2000); *Career* teacher of geography, head of geography and head of humanities Sir Thomas Rich's Sch Gloucester 1989–98, headmaster Bishop Wordsworth's Sch Salisbury 2002– (dep headmaster 1998–2002); memb ASCL; *Recreations* ornithology, running, classical music, clarinet; *Style—* Dr Stuart Smallwood; ✉ Bishop Wordsworth's School, 11 The Close, Salisbury, Wiltshire SP1 2EB (tel 01722 333851, fax 01722 325899, e-mail sds@bws.wilts.sch.uk)

SMART, Adrian Michael Harwood; s of Harold Leslie Harwood Smart (d 1976), of Cuckfield, W Sussex, and Moira, *née* Scanlon (d 1986); *b* 20 November 1935; *Educ* Eastbourne Coll; *m* 14 Sept 1963, Anne Sara, da of Richard Buxton Morrish; 1 da (Amanda Hilary Harwood b 6 Oct 1964), 1 s (Richard Anthony Harwood b 29 March 1967); *Career* Slaughter and May: articled clerk 1957–61, asst slr 1961–68, ptnr 1969–93; dir: Baring Stratton Investment Trust plc 1994–98, Pillar Property plc (formerly Pillar Property Investments plc) 1994–2000; chm: Gatton Park Educn Trust 1998–, The Gatton Trust 2001–, Gatton Park Lettings Ltd 2001–; memb Bd of Mgmnt Royal Alexandra and Albert Sch Fndn 1996– (chm 2000–06); *Recreations* gardening, fishing; *Clubs* Boodle's, Hong Kong; *Style—* Adrian M H Smart, Esq; ✉ Little Santon Farm, Trumpet Hill, Reigate Heath, Surrey RH2 8QY (tel 01737 242285, fax 01737 226577)

SMART, Edward Christopher (Ted); *b* 9 April 1943; *Educ* St Edward's Sch Oxford; *m* Nicola; 3 s (Alex b 1976, Tim b 1978, Mat b 1982); *Career* with Royal Hong Kong Police 1963–71, fndr The Book People Ltd 1988–; patron Deaf and Blind Children's Home Sreepur Bangladesh; *Recreations* reading, travel, keeping parrots; *Style—* Ted Smart, Esq; ✉ The Book People Ltd, Catteshall Manor, Godalming, Surrey GU7 1UU (tel 01483 860215)

SMART, John Dalziel Beveridge; JP; s of George Beveridge Smart (d 1987), and Kirsty, *née* MacDonald (d 1976); *b* 12 August 1932, Edinburgh; *Educ* Harrow, Admin Staff Coll; *m* 1 Oct 1960, Valerie Bigelow, da of Col H K Blaber, CBE (d 1976); 2 s (James Bigelow Beveridge b 14 Nov 1962, Robert John Beveridge b 11 May 1967); *Career* Nat Serv The Black Watch (RHR) Korea 1951–53 (PA to COS, wounded), with J & J Smart (Brechin) Ltd 1953–64 (dir 1954), dir Don Brothers Buist & Co Ltd 1964–87 (md 1985–87), chm British Polyolefin Textiles Assoc 1986–97; memb St Andrews Mgmnt Inst 1989; HM Lord-Lt Kincardineshire 1999– (DL 1993); chm Scottish American Community Relations Ctee 1990–93; dean Guildry of Brechin 1991–93; memb Queen's Body Guard for Scotland (Royal Co of Archers); *Recreations* shooting, skiing; *Style—* John Smart, Esq; ✉ Kincardine, 9A The Glebe, Edzell, Brechin DD9 7SZ (tel 01356 648416, e-mail smart@woodmyre.freeserve.co.uk)

SMART, John Robert; s of Arthur Smart, and Amy, *née* Williams; *b* 18 June 1944; *Educ* Glan Taf HS Cardiff; *m* Janet (decd); 2 s (Alexander b 17 Jan 1973, Gareth b 17 March 1979); partner, Kathy Bowles; *Career* articled to HMR Burgess & Ptnrs architects, then with various leading architects in Cardiff; fndr (with w, Janet) J R Smart (Builders) Ltd; dir Cardiff RFC; *Style—* John Smart, Esq; ✉ J R Smart (Builders) Ltd, 7–8 Park Place, Cardiff CF10 3DP (tel 02920 398844, fax 02920 398855)

SMEDLEY, Brig John Edward Bruce; s of Edward Smedley (d 1986), and Veronica, *née* McCabe (d 1976); *b* 14 December 1946; *Educ* Felsted (scholar, head of sch), Univ of Reading (BA); *m* 3 April 1976, Lavinia, *née* Lane; 2 s (Rupert b 26 Jan 1979, Charles b 30 March 1981); *Career* cmmnd Royal Tank Regt 1966; Cdr UN Peacekeeping Force in Cyprus (UNFICYP) Support Regt 1988–91, ACOS HQ Br Army of Rhine 1992–94, Cdr Armd Reconnaissance Ace Rapid Reaction Corps 1995, COS Staff Coll Camberley 1996, Dep Cdr 1 (UK) Armd Div 1997–2001; private sec to TRH The Earl and Countess of Wessex 2002–; FInstM; *Recreations* offshore sailing (RYA Yachtmaster), skiing, cricket; *Clubs* Cavalry and Guards'; *Style—* Brigadier John Smedley; ✉ Holmrooke House, Chitterne, Wiltshire BA12 0LG

SMEE, Clive Harrod; CB (1997); s of Victor Woolley Smee (d 1991), of Kingsbridge, Devon, and Leila Olive, *née* Harrod (d 1956); *b* 29 April 1942; *Educ* Royal GS Guildford, LSE (BEcon), Business Sch Indiana Univ (MBA), Inst of Cwlth Studies Oxford; *m* 5 April 1975, Denise Eileen, da of Edward Ernest Sell (d 1968), of Shafton, S Yorks; 2 da (Anna b 1978, Elizabeth b 1985), 1 s (David b 1981); *Career* Br Cncl Nigeria 1966–68, econ advsr ODM 1969–75, sr econ advsr DHSS 1975–82, Nuffield and Leverhulme travelling fell USA and Canada 1978–79, advsr Central Policy Review Staff 1982–83, sr econ advsr HM Treasy 1983–84; chief econ advsr: DHSS 1984–89, Dept of Health 1989–2002; princ social policy advsr NZ Treasy 2002–; conslt NZ Govt 1988, 1991 and 1996–; visiting prof of econ Univ of Surrey 1995–; chm: Social Policy Working Pty OECD 1987–89, Co-Ordinating Ctee Cwlth Fund 1997–; Queen Elizabeth the Queen Mother fell 2003; *Recreations* running, gardening, family; *Style—* Prof Clive Smee, CB; ✉ c/o The Treasury, 1 The Terrace, Wellington, New Zealand (tel 006444715013, fax 006444724942, e-mail clive.smee@treasury.govt.nz)

SMERDON, Richard William; s of late John Conran Smerdon, of Cheltenham, and late Monica Rosewarne, *née* Woollen; *b* 20 May 1942; *Educ* King Edward GS Aston Birmingham, ChCh Oxford (open Smith choral scholar, MA); *m* 1, 13 Aug 1966 (m dis 1991), Alison Lorna, *née* Webb; 1 s (Edward b 14 May 1968), 2 da (Helen b 2 Jan 1970, Jane b 26 August 1972); m 2, 19 Oct 1991, Dr Caroline Mary Kynaston Bowden, da of John Kynaston Williams; *Career* asst slr Slaughter and May 1965–69 (articled 1963–65), ptnr Osborne Clarke 1970–2004; memb: Stock Exchange (Midland and Western) Working Pty on Smaller Co Markets 1994, Sub-Ctee on Corp Governance Int Devpts and Ctee on Negotiated Acquisitions American Bar Assoc; ed Practical Governance 2001–; memb Editorial Bd Walters Kluwer Corp Practice Serv; founding chm Coach House Small Business Centre 1982–85, chm Bath Festival Fndn 1988–91; tstee and faculty memb The Fndn for Ind Dir; ed Practical Governance; tstee Nat Fndn for Educn and Research 2003–; memb Bd Henri Ogijike Dance Co 2003–; *Books* Butterworth's Company Law Service (co-ed, 1987), Palmer's Company Law Manual (ed, 2001), A Practical Guide to Corporate Governance (3 edn 2007); *Recreations* singing early music, trekking with wife, grandchildren, sculling, gardening; *Clubs* Athenaeum; *Style—* Richard Smerdon, Esq; ✉ 5 Merthyr Terrace, London SW13 9DL (tel 020 8741 0630)

SMETHURST, Richard Good; s of Thomas Good Smethurst (d 1981), of Abingdon, Oxon, and Madeleine Nora, *née* Foulkes (d 1987); *b* 17 January 1941; *Educ* Liverpool Coll, Worcester Coll Oxford (Henriques scholar), Nuffield Coll Oxford (G Webb Medley jr scholar, BA, MA); *m* 1, 1964 (m dis), (Dorothy) Joan, da of William James Mitchenall (d 1951), of Shrewsbury; 2 da (Katharine b 1969, Frances b 1976), 2 s (James b 1971, Jonathan b 1979); m 2, 2000, Dr Susan Gillingham, da of Lance Mull (d 1965), of Bradford; 2 step da (Abigail b 1980, Esther b 1984); *Career* fell and tutor in econs St Edmund Hall Oxford 1965–66 (res fell 1964–65), conslt UN/FAO World Food Prog Inst for Cwlth Studies Oxford 1965–66; Univ of Oxford: fell and tutor in econs Worcester Coll and univ lectr in econs 1967–76, dir Dept for External Studies and professorial fell Worcester Coll 1976–86; dep chm Monopolies and Mergers Cmmn 1986–89 (pt/t memb 1978–86); Univ of Oxford: chm Gen Bd of the Faculties 1989–91, provost Worcester Coll 1991–, pro-vice-chllr 1997–, chm Conf of Colls 2001–03; pt/t econ advsr HM Treasy 1969–71, pt/t policy advsr PM's Policy Unit 1975–76; non-exec dir: Investment Mgmnt Regulatory Orgn 1987–2000, Nuffield Orthopaedic Centre NHS Tst 1992–2000; memb: Advsy Cncl for Adult and Continuing Educn DES 1977–83, Continuing Educn Standing Ctee UGC/NAB 1984–88, Cncl Templeton Coll Oxford Centre for Mgmnt Studies 1982–2001, Consumer Panel FSA 1998–2005; chm: Unit for Devpt of Adult Continuing Educn 1991–92, Academic Consultative Ctee Open Univ 1986–92, Advsy Bd Music at Oxford 1988–94; tstee: Euro Community Baroque Orchestra 1986–93, Oxford Philomusica 2003–; pres: WEA Thames and Solent 1992–2002, Nat Inst for Adult Continuing Educn (NIACE) 1994–2001; life govr Liverpool Coll; fndn hon fell Kellogg Coll Oxford 1990, hon fell St Edmund Hall Oxford 1991, hon fell St Catharine's Coll Cambridge 2002; *Publications* Impact of Food Aid on Donor Countries (with G R Allen, 1967); contrib: New Thinking About Welfare (1969), The Economic System in the UK (1977, 2 edn 1979), New Directions in Adult and Continuing Education (1979), Continuing Education in Universities and Polytechnics (1982); various articles in Jl of Development Studies and Oxford Review of Education; *Recreations* good food, eating out and occasionally cooking;

Style— Richard Smethurst, Esq; ✉ The Provost's Lodgings, Worcester College, Oxford OX1 2HB (tel 01865 278362, fax 01865 793106, e-mail provost@worc.ox.ac.uk)

SMIDDY, (Francis) Paul; s of Francis Geoffrey Smiddy, of Leeds, and Thelma Vivenne Smiddy; *b* 13 November 1953; *Educ* Winchester, Univ of Manchester; *Career* mangr Price Waterhouse 1978–82, fin analyst J Sainsbury 1982–84, res analyst Capel-Cure Myers 1984–85, assoc dir Wood Mackenzie 1985–88; dir: Retail Res Kleinwort Benson Securities 1988–93, Retail Res Nomura Research Institute - Europe Ltd 1993–95, Credit Lyonnais Securities Europe 1995–2002, RW Baird Ltd 2002–05, dir European retail research HSBC 2006–; Freeman Guild of Air Pilots and Air Navigators; FCA 1988; *Recreations* flying, motor sport, France, skiing; *Clubs* Naval and Military; *Style*— Paul Smiddy, Esq; ✉ HSBC Bank plc, 8 Canada Square, London E14 5HQ

SMIETANA, Krzysztof; Wlodzimierz Smietana, of Kraków, Poland, and Irena, *née* Ludwig (d 1985); *b* 11 October 1956; *Educ* Secdy Music Sch Kraków, Kraków Acad of Music, Guildhall Sch of Music and Drama; *Career* violinist; formerly soloist with the Polish Chamber Orch, came to London 1980 to study under Yfrah Neaman at (and now teacher at) the Guildhall Sch of Music; performed throughout Europe, made several tours of Germany, appeared at most major London venues, appeared at Proms Festival 1997, appeared at BBC Proms Festival, regularly broadcast on BBC Radio 3, guest leader LSO; memb London Mozart Trio 1999–; prizewinner numerous int competitions, winner numerous Polish honours; FGSM 1996; *Recordings incl* Panufnik's Violin Concerto (CD Review magazine CD of the Month) 1989, Fauré Sonantas (CD for Meridian, Retailers Assoc Award for Best Chamber Music Recording 1995) 1993, Brahms Violin Sonatas (CD for ASV), Stravinsky Violin Concerto conducted by Robert Craft (CD for Music Masters), Polish XX Century Music for Piano Trio (CD for Polygram); *Style*— Krzysztof Smietana, Esq; ✉ 14 Kersley Road, London N16 0NP (tel 020 7254 8876, fax 020 7254 8860, e-mail ksmietana@aol.com)

SMILEY, Lt-Col Sir John Philip; 4 Bt (UK 1903), of Drumalis, Larne, Co Antrim, and Gallowhill, Paisley, Co Renfrew; o s of Sir Hugh Houston Smiley, 3 Bt, JP, DL (d 1990), and Nancy Elizabeth Louise Hardy, *née* Beaton (d 1999); *b* 24 February 1934; *Educ* Eton, RMA Sandhurst; *m* 1963, Davina Elizabeth, eldest da of Denis Charles Griffiths (d 1949); 1 da (Melinda Elizabeth Eirène (Mrs Jonathon Baker) b 1965), 2 s (Christopher Hugh Charles b 1968, William Timothy John b 1972); *Heir* s, Christopher Smiley; *Career* cmmnd Grenadier Guards 1954, served in BAOR, Cyprus and Hong Kong, ADC to Govr of Bermuda 1961–62, ret 1986; dir of admin Russell Reynolds Assocs 1986–89; govr Oundle Schs 1987–99; memb Ct of Assts Worshipful Co of Grocers 1987– (Master 1992–93); *Clubs* Army and Navy; *Style*— Lt-Col Sir John Smiley, Bt; ✉ Cornerway House, Chobham, Woking, Surrey GU24 8SW (tel 01276 858992)

SMILEY, Philip David; s of Col David de Crespigny Smiley, LVO, OBE, MC, of London, and Moyra Eileen, *née* Montagu-Douglas-Scott; bro of Xan de Crespigny Smiley, *qv*; *b* 26 August 1951, W Germany; *Educ* Eton, Univ of St Andrews (MA); *m* 3 March 1995, Sohyung, da of Gen and Mrs Young-Woo Kim; 2 s (Francis Hugh Kim b 13 Jan 1996, Dominic David b 14 Dec 1998), 1 da (Flora Ruby b 3 Nov 2000); *Career* HM Overseas Colonial Serv 1974–85: Miny of Home Affrs Solomon Islands 1974–76, Judicial Dept Solomon Islands 1976–80, Civil Serv Branch Hong Kong 1981–83, Economic Servs Branch Hong Kong 1983–85; WI Carr Group 1985–90: research co-ordinator and dir Hong Kong 1985–87, md WI Carr (Far East) Ltd Hong Kong 1988–89, gp dir of fin and admin London 1989–90; Jardine Fleming Group 1990–2001: dir Jardine Fleming International Holdings Ltd, dir JF Asia Select Ltd, dir JF Asian Realty Inc, md Jardine Fleming International Securities Ltd Singapore, branch mangr Seoul Office 1990–96; chm: Jardine Matheson (Thailand) Ltd 2001–06, PXP Vietnam Fund 2004–, Vietnam Emerging Equity Fund 2006–, Vietnam Lotus Fund 2007–, Advsy Bd Emerging Beachfront Land Investment Fund 2007–; dir: Hyundai International Merchant Bank 1990–95, Arisaig India Fund 1999–, Asia Commercial Bank 2002–06, Tantallon BRIC Fund 2006–, Tantallon Asian Smaller Cos Fund 2006–; chm: Br C of C Korea, Bd Euro C of C Korea 1995–96; Solomon Islands Independence Medal 1976; *Recreations* books, travel, dogs; *Clubs* White's, Special Forces, Foreign Correspondents (Hong Kong), Hong Kong; *Style*— Philip Smiley, Esq; ✉ Chateau St Jean d'Anglès, St Arailles 32350, France (tel and fax 00 33 5 62 64 19 69, e-mail pds@smileys.cc)

SMILEY, Xan de Crespigny; s of Col David de Crespigny Smiley, LVO, OBE, MC, and Moyra, widow of Maj Hugo Tweedie, and da of Lt-Col Lord Francis Montagu Douglas Scott, KCMG, DSO (6 s of 6 Duke of Buccleuch and Queensberry); bro of Philip David Smiley, *qv*; *b* 1 May 1949; *Educ* Eton, New Coll Oxford (MA); *m* 1983, Hon Jane Lyon-Dalberg-Acton, 6 and yst da of 3 Baron Acton, CMG, MBE, TD (d 1989), and sis of 4 Baron Acton, *qv*; 2 s (Ben Richard Philip de Crespigny b 1985, Adam David Emerich b 1988), 2 step da (Charlotte Pugh b 1978, Rebecca Pugh b 1979); *Career* journalist and broadcaster; commentator BBC Radio External Serv current affrs 1974–75, corr Spectator and Observer in Africa 1975–77, ed Africa Confidential newsletter 1977–81 (dir 1981–2004), ldr writer The Times 1982–83, foreign affrs staff writer then Middle East ed The Economist 1983–86, Moscow corr Daily Telegraph 1986–89, Washington corr The Sunday Telegraph 1990–92; The Economist: political ed and Bagehot columnist 1992–94, Europe corr 1994–95, Europe ed 1996–2004, Middle East and Africa ed 2004–; publisher The Soviet Analyst 1990–91; Noel Buxton lectr in African politics 1980; *Recreations* food, sport (memb Br ski team 1969, winner of Downhill Oxford v Cambridge 1969), shooting, travel, genealogy; *Clubs* Pratt's, Beefsteak, Polish Hearth, Grillion's; *Style*— Xan Smiley, Esq; ✉ Lower Farm, Taston, Charlbury, Oxfordshire OX7 3JL; c/o The Economist, 25 St James's Street, London SW1A 1HG (tel 020 7830 7000, fax 020 7930 5549, e-mail xansmiley@economist.com)

SMILLIE, Carol Patricia; da of George Smillie, of Glasgow, and Isobel, *née* Blackstock; *b* 23 December 1961; *m* 30 Aug 1991, Alex Knight; 2 c; *Career* television presenter; BBC credits incl: Hearts of Gold, The Travel Show, Holiday Memories, National Lottery Live, Smillie's People (talk show), Changing Rooms, Star Secrets, Holiday Swaps, Holiday, Summer Holiday; other credits incl: The Big Breakfast (Channel Four), The Jamesons (Radio 2), Radio Clyde (own talk show), Get It On (STV), Wheel of Fortune (ITV), Dream Holiday Home (Channel 5); subject of This is Your Life, winner 2 Gotcha Oscars Noel's House Party; *Style*— Ms Carol Smillie; ✉ c/o David Anthony Promotions, PO Box 286, Warrington, Cheshire WA2 8GA (tel 01925 632496, fax 01925 416589)

SMITH, His Hon Judge Adrian Charles; s of Fred Smith (d 1993), and Jenny Smith (d 1994); *b* 25 November 1950; *Educ* Blackpool GS, Queen Mary Coll London (LLB); *m* 14 July 1973, Sally Ann, da of Peter Derek Monteverde Palmer; 2 da (Sophie Louise Elizabeth b 1977, Olivia Rose b 3 Aug 1979); *Career* called to the Bar Lincoln's Inn 1973; barr Northern Circuit 1974–96, recorder of the Crown Court 1994–96, circuit judge (Northern Circuit) 1996–; Crown Court liaison judge to Oldham Justices; memb Mgmnt Ctee Liverpool Witness Support 1990–93, legal memb NW Mental Health Review Tbnl 1994– (memb Restricted Panel 2000–); *Recreations* world travel, theatre, fell walking; *Clubs* Waterloo RUFC; *Style*— His Hon Judge Adrian Smith; ✉ c/o Manchester Crown Court, Minshull Street, Manchester M1 3FS (tel 0161 954 7500)

SMITH, Alan Frederick; *b* 21 July 1944; *Children* 1 da (Julia Ann 1971), 1 s (Michael b 1973); *Career* Colchester Borough Cncl 1961–66, Ipswich Borough Cncl 1966–73, asst county treas Suffolk CC 1973–74, fin mangr Anglian Water 1974–75, asst fin dir Southern Water Authy 1975–80, fin dir Anglian Water Authy 1980–90, gp md Anglian Water plc 1990–97 (gp fin dir 1989–90); chm: Acambis plc (formerly Peptide Therapeutics Group plc) 1995–, Avlar Bioventures Ltd (formerly Quantum Healthcare Fund Manager Ltd) 1999–; memb CIPFA; *Style*— Alan Smith, Esq

SMITH, Prof Alan Gordon Rae; s of Alan Fife Smith (d 1976), and Jean Reid, *née* Lightbody (d 1971); *b* 22 December 1936; *Educ* Glasgow HS, Univ of Glasgow (Macfarlane scholar, MA), Univ of London (PhD); *m* 1972, Isabel, da of Neil McKechnie Robertson and Helen Brown; 1 da (Stella Jean b 1975), 1 s (Donald Alan Neil b 1979); *Career* research fell Inst of Historical Research Univ of London 1961–62; Univ of Glasgow: asst lectr in modern history 1962–64, lectr 1964–75, sr lectr 1975–85, reader 1985–92, head Dept of Modern History 1991–94, prof in modern history 1992–95, chm of history examiners 1993–94, head Sch of History and Archaeology 1993–95, prof of early modern history 1995–2002, emeritus prof 2002–; memb Governing Bd Inst of Historical Research Univ of London 1994–99 and 2003–; FRHistS (memb Cncl 1990–94), FRSE 1996, FRAS 1997; *Publications* author of ten books incl: Servant of the Cecils (1977), The Emergence of a Nation State (1984); *Recreations* watching sport; *Style*— Prof Alan Smith, FRSE; ✉ 5 Cargil Avenue, Kilmacolm, Inverclyde PA13 4LS; Department of Modern History, University of Glasgow, Glasgow G12 8QQ (tel 0141 330 4509)

SMITH, Rt Rev Alan Gregory Clayton; *see:* Shrewsbury, Bishop of

SMITH, Alan Keith Patrick; *Educ* Univ of Edinburgh; *Career* exec dir Marks & Spencer plc 1978–93 (joined 1964), chief exec Kingfisher plc 1993–95, non-exec chm Mothercare plc 1996–2002, non-exec chm Space NK Ltd 1997–; non-exec dir: Colefax & Fowler Group plc 1994–, Whitehead Mann plc 1997–2006; memb Bd South Bank Centre 1995–; tstee Arts & Business 1999–; *Style*— Alan Smith, Esq

SMITH, Prof (Murdo) Alasdair Macdonald; DL (East Sussex 2001); s of John Smith (d 1970), and Isabella, *née* Mackenzie (d 2004); *b* 9 February 1949, Stornoway; *Educ* Nicolson Inst Stornoway, Univ of Glasgow (MA), LSE (MSc, Ely Devons Prize), Univ of Oxford (DPhil); *m* Sherry, *née* Ferdman; 2 da (Katie b 1979, Laura b 1981); *Career* lectr in econs: Univ Coll Oxford 1970–72, LSE 1972–81; Univ of Sussex: prof of econs 1981–, dean Sch of European Studies 1991–94, sr pro-vice-chllr 1997–98, vice-chllr 1998–2007; research fell Centre for Economic Policy Research 1983–2002; visiting positions: Columbia Univ, Univ of Rochester, Univ of California San Diego, Univ of Michigan, Coll of Europe Bruges and Natolin, European Univ Inst; convenor 1994 Gp of Univs 2001–05; memb Bd: Univ of Brighton 1998–2006, Univs and Colls Employers Assoc 2000–07, Univs UK 2003–07; chair of tstees Inst Devpt Studies 1998–2007; memb Prison Serv Pay Review Body 2001–04; govr: Holloway Sch London 1973–81 (vice-chm 1973–78, chm 1978–79); memb: SE Eng Regnl Assembly 1993–2003, Brighton and Hove Econ Partnership 2001–07; Hon DSc Univ of Warsaw 2004; *Publications* incl: A Mathematical Introduction to Economics (1982), Empirical Studies of Strategic Trade Policy (jt ed and contrib, 1994), Competitiveness and Cohesion in EU Policies (jt ed and contrib, 2001); author of 70 jl articles and book chapters; *Recreations* gardening; *Clubs* Athenaeum; *Style*— Prof Alasdair Smith, DL; ✉ University of Sussex, Sussex House, Falmer, Brighton BN1 9RH (tel 01273 678028, fax 01273 678254, e-mail alasdair@sussex.ac.uk)

SMITH, Allan Keppie; CBE; s of Allan Smith (d 1977), of Kincardineshire, and Margaret Isobel, *née* Keppie (d 1992); *b* 18 May 1932; *Educ* Univ of Aberdeen (BSc); *m* 2 Sept 1965, Mary Bridget, *née* Love, of Paisley; 1 s (Stephen Allan b 4 March 1971), 3 da (Valerie May b 18 May 1976, Fiona Margaret Keppie b 5 Dec 1981, Leanne Isabel b 20 May 1983); *Career* Nat Serv 1953–55, cmmnd REME 1954; Babcock and Wilcox: graduate trainee 1955–57, welding engr Metallurgical and Welding Dept 1957–62, facilities engr Indust Engrg Dept 1962–65, indust engrg mangr 1965–74, production dir Renfrew Works 1974–76; md: Renfrew and Dumbarton Works 1976–86, Babcock Thorn Ltd 1986–93, Rosyth Royal Dockyard plc 1986–93; dir Babcock International Group plc 1989–93; md Facilities Mgmnt Div Babcock International Group 1991–97; chm: Babcock Rosyth Defence Ltd 1993–97, Rosyth Royal Dockyard plc 1993–97, Babcock New Zealand Ltd 1994–97, Railcare Ltd 1995–2001, Fife Enterprise Ltd 1999–2000; former pres Scot Engrg Employers Assoc, past chm Cncl Welding Inst, past memb Scot Indust Devpt Advsy Bd, fell Univ of Paisley; Hon DUniv Paisley 1997; FREng 1990, FIMechE, FWeldI; *Recreations* DIY, shooting, gardening, restoration of farm carts; *Style*— Allan Smith, Esq, CBE, FREng; ✉ tel 0131 319 1668, e-mail allanksmith@btinternet.com

SMITH, Dr Andrew Benjamin; s of Benjamin Butler Smith, of Stonehaven, Grampian, and Elsie Marjory, *née* Flemming; *b* 6 February 1954; *Educ* Mackie Acad Stonehaven, Univ of Edinburgh (BSc), Univ of Exeter (PhD); *m* 18 Aug 1976, Mary Patricia Cumming, da of David Cumming Simpson; 2 da (Katherine Heather b 22 Jan 1985, Fiona Margaret b 18 April 1987); *Career* postdoctoral research asst Univ of Liverpool 1979–81 and 1982–83 (temp lectr in geology 1981–82), research scientist Dept of Palaeontology The Natural History Museum 1983–; Bicentenary Medal Linnean Soc 1993, Bigsby Medal Geological Soc 1995, Lyell Medal Geological Soc 2002, Linnean Medal Linnean Soc 2005; Hon DSc Univ of Edinburgh 1989; FRSE 1996, FRS 2002; *Books* Echinoid Palaeobiology (1984), Systematics and the fossil record: discovering evolutionary patterns (1994); *Style*— Dr Andrew Smith, FRS, FRSE; ✉ Department of Palaeontology, The Natural History Museum, Cromwell Road, London SW7 5BD (tel 020 7938 8925, fax 020 7938 9277, e-mail a.smith@nhm.ac.uk)

SMITH, Hon Mr Justice; Sir Andrew Charles Smith; kt (2000); *Educ* Univ of Oxford (BA); *Career* called to the Bar Middle Temple 1974 (bencher 1999), QC 1990, judge of the High Court of Justice (Queen's Bench Div) 2000–, presiding judge North Eastern Circuit 2003–06; *Style*— The Hon Mr Justice Andrew Smith; ✉ Royal Courts of Justice, Strand, London WC2A 2LL

SMITH, Rt Hon Andrew David; PC (1997), MP; s of late David E C Smith, and Georgina H J Smith; *b* 1 February 1951; *Educ* Reading Sch, St John's Coll Oxford (BA, BPhil); *m* 26 March 1976, Valerie, da of William Labert; 1 s; *Career* Oxford City Cncl: cncllr 1976–87, chm Recreation and Amenities Ctee 1980–83, chm Planning Ctee 1985–87, chm Race and Community Relations Ctee 1985–87; relations offr Oxford and Swindon Co-op Soc 1979–87; MP (Lab) Oxford E 1987–; oppn front bench spokesman: on higher educn 1988–92, on Treasy & econ affrs 1992–94; shadow chief sec to Treasy 1994–96, shadow sec of state for tport 1996–97; min of state Dept for Educn and Employment (employment, welfare to work and equal opportunities) 1997–99, chief sec to Treasy 1999–2002, sec of state for Work and Pensions 2002–04; memb Social Servs Select Ctee 1988–89, jt sec All-Pty Gp for Overseas Devpt 1987–94; memb USDAW; chm Govrs of Oxford Brookes Univ (formerly Oxford Poly) 1987–93; *Clubs* Blackbird Leys Community Assoc; *Style*— The Rt Hon Andrew Smith, MP; ✉ 4 Flaxfield Road, Blackbird Leys, Oxford OX4 5QD; Constituency (tel 01865 772893); House of Commons, London SW1A 0AA (tel 020 7219 5102); DWP (tel 020 7238 0654)

SMITH, Andrew Keith; *b* 1964; *Educ* Benton Park GS, Univ of Wales Cardiff (BSc Econ), Inst of Mktg (Dip); *Career* with Touche Ross & Co 1985–92, dir Henry Cooke Corporate Finance 1993–97, dir Brown Shipley & Co 1997–2004, md Westhouse Securities 2004–; chm Quoted Companies Alliance; ACA 1988; *Style*— Andrew Smith, Esq; ✉ Westhouse Securities LLP, Clements House, 14–18 Gresham Street, London EC2V 7NN (tel 020 7601 6100, fax 020 7796 2713, e-mail andrew.smith@westhousesecurities.com)

SMITH, Prof Andrew Paul (Andy); *b* 3 August 1952, Liss, Hampshire; *Educ* Cambridgeshire HS, UCL (BSc, PhD); *m*; 1 s, 2 da; *Career* post-doctoral res fell Dept of Experimental Psychology Univ of Oxford 1976–82, scientist MRC Perceptual and Cognitive Performance Unit Univ of Sussex 1982–88, Charles Hunnisett res fell Laboratory of Experimental Psychology Univ of Sussex 1989–90, dir Health Psychology Res Unit and reader Sch of Psychology UWCC 1990–93, prof Dept of Psychology Univ of Bristol

S

1993–99, prof Sch of Psychology and dir Centre for Occupational and Health Psychology Univ of Cardiff 1999–; memb Mgmnt Ctee Agro-Food Quality Link Prog; CPsychol, FBPsS, FRSM; *Publications* author of numerous articles in learned periodicals; *Style*— Prof Andy Smith; ✉ tel 029 2087 4757, fax 029 2087 4758, e-mail smithap@cardiff.ac.uk

SMITH, Angela; MP; da of Patrick and Emily Evans; *b* 7 January 1959; *Educ* Chalvedon Sch Basildon, Leicester Poly (BA); *m* Dec 1978, Nigel Smith; *Career* trainee accountant London Borough of Newham 1981–83, sometime head of political and public relations League Against Cruel Sports 1983–95, Parly researcher to Alun Michael MP, *qv*, as Shadow Min for Home Affrs 1995–97; MP (Lab) Basildon 1997–; PPS to Paul Boateng, *qv* (Home Office Min) 1999–2001, asst Govt whip 2001–02, Parly under-sec of state NI Office 2002–06, Parly under sec of state Dept for Communities and Local Govt 2006–, Parly prive sec to the PM 2007–; cncllr Essex CC 1989–97; memb: Amnesty Int, T&GWU; *Style*— Angela Smith, MP; ✉ House of Commons, London SW1A 0AA (tel 020 7219 6273, fax 020 7219 0926)

SMITH, Angela; MP; *b* 16 August 1961; *Educ* Univ of Nottingham, Newnham Coll Cambridge; *Career* MP (Lab) Sheffield Hillsborough 2005–; Sheffield City Cncl: cncllr, cabinet memb for Educn; memb Amicus; *Style*— Ms Angela Smith, MP; ✉ House of Commons, London SW1A 0AA

SMITH, Hon Lady; Anne; da of John Mather (d 1963), of London, and Jessica, *née* Douglas; *b* 16 March 1955; *Educ* Jordanhill Coll Glasgow, Cheadle County GS for Girls, Univ of Edinburgh (LLB, medallist in Criminal Law); *m* 22 Sept 1979, David Alexander Smith, WS, s of William Duncan Smith (d 1998); 1 s (William Iain b 6 Aug 1983), 1 da (Charlotte Alexandra b 14 Aug 1985); *Career* apprenticed Shepherd & Wedderburn, WS 1977–79, pupil of Lord McGhie 1979–80, admitted Faculty of Advocates 1980, in practice 1980–2001, QC (Scot) 1993, senator Coll of Justice 2001–; chm Cncl St George's Sch for Girls 2003–, tstee RSNO Fndn; *Recreations* music (piano), keeping fit, hill walking, gardening, skiing; *Style*— The Hon Lady Smith; ✉ Court of Session, Parliament House, Edinburgh EH1 1RF (tel 0131 225 2595)

SMITH, Anthony David; CBE (1987); s of Henry Smith (d 1951), and Esther Smith; *b* 14 March 1938; *Educ* Harrow Co Sch, BNC Oxford (BA); *Career* current affrs prodr BBC TV 1960–71, fell St Antony's Coll Oxford 1971–76, dir BFI 1979–88, memb Bd Channel Four TV Co 1980–84, pres Magdalen Coll Oxford 1988–2005; memb: Writers and Scholars Educn Tst 1982–99, Arts Cncl of GB 1990–94; chm Hill Fndn 2000–; Hon Dr of Arts Oxford Brookes Univ 1997; *Books* The Shadow in the Cave: The Broadcaster, the Audience and the State (1973), British Broadcasting (1974), The British Press since the War (1976), Subsidies and the Press in Europe (1977), The Politics of Information (1978), Television and Political Life (1979), The Newspaper: An International History (1979), Newspapers and Democracy (1980), Goodbye Gutenberg - The Newspaper Revolution of the 1980's (1980), The Geopolitics of Information (1980), The Age of Behemoths - the Globalisation of Mass Media Firms (1991), From Books to Bytes (1993), Software for the Self (1995), Television - An International History (1998); *Style*— Anthony Smith, Esq, CBE; ✉ Albany, Piccadilly, London W1J 0AX (e-mail anthony.smith@magd.ox.ac.uk)

SMITH, Anthony John Francis; s of Hubert J F Smith (d 1984), of Dorset, and Diana, *née* Watkin (d 1990); *b* 30 March 1926; *Educ* Blundell's, Balliol Coll Oxford (MA); *m* 1, 1956 (m dis 1983), Barbara Dorothy, da of Maj-Gen Charles Richard Newman CB, CMG, DSO (d 1954), of Ottery St Mary, Devon; 1 s (Adam b 1963), 2 da (Polly b 1968, Laura b 1969); *m* 2, 1984, Margaret Ann (formerly Mrs Holloway), da of George Hounsom (d 1987); 1 s (Quintin b 1986); *Career* RAF 1944–48; reporter Manchester Guardian 1953–57, sci corr Daily Telegraph 1957–63, freelance broadcaster, author and journalist 1964–; FRGS 1966, FZS 1969; *Books* Blind White Fish in Persia (1953), High Street Africa (1961), Throw Out Two Hands (1963), The Body (1968), The Dangerous Sort (1970), Mato Grosso (1971), The Human Pedigree (1975), Wilderness (1978), A Persian Quarter Century (1979), The Mind (1984), Smith & Son (1984), The Great Rift (1988), Explorers of the Amazon (1990), The Free Life (1995), Sex, Genes and All That (1997), The Human Body (1998), Survived (1998), Ballooning (1998), The Weather (2000), Machine Gun (2002), The Lost Lady of the Amazon (2003); for children: Which Animal Are You? (1988), Best Friends (1990), Swaps (1992); *Recreations* ballooning; *Clubs* Explorers (NY); *Style*— Anthony Smith, Esq; ✉ 10 Aldbourne Road, London W12 0LN (tel 020 8248 9589); St Aidan's, Bamburgh, Northumberland

SMITH, Antony Gervase; s of Gervase Gorst Smith, JP (d 1963), and Gladys Alford (d 1968); *b* 31 July 1927; *Educ* Haileybury; *m* 4 Nov 1955, Penelope, da of Pearson Faux, of Durban, Natal (d 1964); 1 s (Julian Gervase b 21 Feb 1958), 2 da (Miranda b 9 March 1962, Philippa b 30 April 1963); *Career* Belt of Honour 60th Rifles OCTU, served KRRC 1945–48, Capt Queen Victoria's Rifles 1948–52; dir Long Till & Colvin 1960–68, md Astley & Pearce (Sterling) 1980, chm MH Cockell Ltd 1987–94; princ Baltic Exchange and underwriting memb Lloyd's 1956–91; church warden St Mary-le-Bow; Freeman City of London, Liveryman Worshipful Co of Turners 1969; *Recreations* shooting, walking a labrador; *Clubs* Army and Navy, Royal Green Jackets; *Style*— Antony Gervase Smith, Esq; ✉ Cozen's House, Orcheston, Salisbury, Wiltshire SP3 4RW (tel 01980 620257, e-mail pcozens@waitrose.com)

SMITH, (Brian) Arthur John; s of Sydney Frederick Smith, of Bath, and Hazel Nora, *née* Kirk; *b* 27 November 1954; *Educ* Roan Sch, UEA (BA); *Career* writer and comedian; former teacher and road sweeper, fndr memb National Revue Co, hosted First Exposure (BBC) and Paramount City (BBC), reg contrib Loose Ends (Radio 4), fndr comedy double act Fiasco Job Job with Phil Nice (C4 series Arthur and Phil Go Off 1985); author of plays: Live Bed Show (nominated for Perrier and Independent Theatre Awards 1989, Garrick Theatre 1995), Trench Kiss, An Evening With Gary Lineker (with Chris England, Edinburgh Festival then Duchess Theatre and Vaudeville Theatre (nominated Best Comedy Olivier Awards 1992)) 1991–92, Arthur Smith sings Andy Williams (Edinburgh, London, NY) 1992–93, Sod (with Nigel Cole) 1993; presenter: Sentimental Journeys (BBC Radio 4) 1994–2000, Excess Baggage (BBC Radio 4); wrote and performed: Hamlet 1995, The Smith Lectures (BBC Radio 2) 1996–; screenplay My Summer with Des (BBC 1) 1998, Arthur Smith sings Leonard Cohen (Edinburgh) 2000, Dante's Inferno 2003, Arthur Smith's Swan Lake 2005; self-proclaimed Greatest Artist in the World, Artwart (exhibition Edinbugh, 2007); *Books* Trench Kiss (1990), An Evening With Gary Lineker (with Chris England, 1992), Pointless Hoax (1997); *Recreations* giving up smoking, sleeping; *Clubs* Kilcoynes; *Style*— Arthur Smith, Esq

SMITH, Barrie Edwin; OBE (1994); *m* June; 2 da (Dawn, Helen); *Career* chartered accountant and conslt; Nat Serv 1959–61; articled clerk JE Forsdike & Co 1953–58; Franklin Greening: audit mangr 1961, ptnr 1964, co merged with PKF 1971, taxation ptnr 1971, managing ptnr 1988–92, chm S Yorks practice 1993–96, conslt 1996–98; chm Congregational & General Charitable Tst; past pres: Sheffield C of C, Sheffield and District Soc of Chartered Accountants; elder Central United Reformed Church, tstee Yorks Historic Churches Tst, tstee Music at Swinglee; JP Sheffield 1979–2005; Freeman City of London, memb Worshipful Co of Chartered Accountants; FRSA, FCMI; *Recreations* gardening, maintaining a Victorian house and garden, keeping fit, fell walking, keen interest in soccer; *Style*— Barrie E Smith, Esq, OBE; ✉ Cliffe House, 4 Cavendish Road, Sheffield S11 9BH (tel and fax 0114 255 0900, e-mail barrieesmith@the-cliffe.demon.co.uk)

SMITH, (Donald) Barry; *b* 22 May 1948; *m* 1 Nov 1975, Sophie Janina, *née* Pasko (Rachel b 1978, Claire b 1980, Alice b 1986); *Career* divnl fin accountant Showerings Vine Products & Whiteways Ltd 1971–73, accountant CH Beazer Holdings plc 1973–78, sr ptnr Rossiter

Smith & Co Chartered Accountants 1978–; Dolphin Packaging plc: fin dir 1987–89, chm 1989–90, dep chm 1990–2000; FCA 1971, ATII 1972; *Style*— Barry Smith, Esq; ✉ Rossiter Smith & Co, Bank House, 1 Burlington Road, Bristol BS6 6TJ (tel 0117 973 0863, fax 0117 923 7929, e-mail barrysmith@rossitersmith.co.uk)

SMITH, Prof Barry Edward; s of Ernest Edward Smith (d 1977), and Agnes Mary, *née* DeFraine (d 1957); *b* 15 November 1939; *Educ* Dr Challoner's GS Amersham, Royal Melbourne Tech Coll, Hatfield Tech Coll, Univ of Exeter (BSc), Univ of E Anglia (PhD); *m* 7 Sept 1963, Pamela Heather, *née* Pullen; 1 da (Tamzin Sarah b 23 Nov 1964), 1 s (Joel Dominic Barnaby b 4 Feb 1968); *Career* trainee chemist ICIANZ Central Research Labs 1956–59, lab asst Polymers Div ICI 1959–60, Univ of Exeter 1960–64, UEA 1964–66, research fell Univ of Washington Seattle 1966–68, SRC research fell Physical Chemistry Lab Univ of Oxford 1968–69, sr princ scientific offr ARC Unit of Nitrogen Fixation 1985 (sr scientific offr 1969–74, princ scientific offr 1974–85), asst dir Unit of Nitrogen Fixation 1986, head and dep chief scientific offr Nitrogen Fixation Laboratory AFRC Inst of Plant Science Research 1987–94, assoc research dir John Innes Centre Norwich 1994–2000 (emeritus fell John Innes Fndn 2000–04); Univ of Sussex: hon reader Sch of Chemistry and Molecular Sciences Univ of Sussex 1985, hon reader in biochemistry Sch of Biological Sciences 1986, hon professorial fell 1989–95; hon prof Sch of Chemical Scis UEA 1995–; visiting prof Univ of Essex 1988–2000; memb Int Steering Ctee for Int Symposia on Nitrogen Fixation 1988–2004, convenor Enzyme Cmmn Panel on Nomenclature of Molybdenum Enzymes; memb: Biochemical Soc, Br Biophysical Soc; ed Biochemical Jl 1988–95, author of numerous pubns in scientific jls; Leverhulme emeritus fell 2001–03; MRSC; *Recreations* gardening and bridge; *Style*— Prof Barry Smith; ✉ 61 Church Lane, Eaton, Norwich NR4 6NY (tel 01603 453779, e-mail prof.barrysmith@btinternet.com)

SMITH, Barry Howard; *b* 8 September 1949; *Educ* QMC London (LLB); *Career* admitted slr 1974; media and entertainment ptnr Richards Butler 1980–2007, ptnr Reed Smith Richards Butler 2007–; *Recreations* art, cinema, theatre; *Style*— Barry Smith, Esq; ✉ Reed Smith Richards Butler, Beaufort House, 15 St Botolph Street, London EC3A 7EE (tel 020 7247 6555, fax 020 7247 5091, e-mail bhs@richardsbutler.com)

SMITH, Bob; s of Frederick Brill, and Deirdre, *née* Borlaise; *Educ* Wandsworth Comp, Univ of Reading (BA), Goldsmiths Coll London (MA); *Career* artist, one half of Bob and Roberta Smith; memb Bd Chisenhale Gallery, dir and fndr (with Jessica Voorsanger, *qv*) Leytonstone Center for Contemporary Art; Rome scholarship 1985–87, Harkness fell 1987–90; trumpeter in Ken Ardley Playboys; *Exhibitions* Don't Hate Sculpt (Chisenhale Gallery) 1997, Intelligence (Tate Britain) 2000, Improve the Cat (Galleria Carbone Turin) 2001, It's not Easy being a famous Artist (Galleria Praz Delavacade Paris) 2002, Useless Women/Stupid Men (Anthony Wilkinson Gallery London) 2002, Art Amnesty (Pieroggi 2000 NY) 2003, Independance (South London Gallery) 2003, No Man is an Island (GAK Breman) 2003, Help Build the Ruins of Democracy (The Baltic Gatehead) 2004; *Publications* A is for book (2001), Inconsistant (2001), Make Your Own Damn Art (2004); *Recreations* going to work; *Style*— Bob Smith, Esq; ✉ c/o Hales Gallery, Tea Building G3, 5–11 Bethnal Green Road, London E1 6JJ

SMITH, Brenda; *Educ* Merchant Taylors', Univ of Manchester, Manchester Business Sch (MBA); *m*; 2 da; *Career* sr accountant Business Consultancy Div Arthur Andersen 1978–91; Granada Television: various financial roles 1981–83, prog mangr then operational line mangr Granada Film 1983–89, gen mangr Facilities Div 1989–93, dir of resources 1993–97, md Granada Television Ltd 1997–2004, md Granada Studios 1997–2004; EMEA gp md Ascent Media Gp 2004–; dir: Castlefield Properties Ltd (subsid of Granada Television), NW Regnl Devpt Agency, Liverpool European Capital of Culture 2008, Jt Industry Grading Scheme Ltd; non-exec dir: Liverpool Vision, MIDAS, Manchester Airport Aviation Services Ltd, AFM Lighting Ltd; chm London Forum Skillset; memb: NW Business Leadership Team, NW Vision, Business in the Community, CAMPUS, Cultural Consortium, Community Loan Fund NW, Ravensbourne Advsy Bd, Int Media Centre (IMC) Advsy Bd Univ of Salford, Bd Women in Film; non-exec memb NW Regnl Economic Panel; formerly: dir NW Film Television Cmmn, memb Manchester:Liverpool Vision Study, Skillset Steering Gp; other non-exec roles: Manchester HA 1992–96, Mental Health Services of Salford 1996–2000; Hon DLitt Univ of Salford; ACA, FRSA; *Recreations* all sports, theatre; *Style*— Ms Brenda Smith

SMITH, Rt Rev Brian Arthur; *see:* Edinburgh, Bishop of

SMITH, Brian Roy; s of Arthur Roy Smith (d 1971), and Phyllis Edith Smith (d 1990); *b* 18 August 1937; *Educ* Sir George Monoux GS; *m* 4 July 1959, Barbara Gladys, da of James Richard Beasley (d 1980); 1 s (Stewart Spencer b 26 Jan 1963), 1 da (Justine Caroline b 10 April 1967); *Career* RAF 1956–58; English & American INSCE Co 1959–68, B R Smith and Others (Lloyd's Syndicate) 1969–97; chm Garwyn Ltd 1972–2006; non-exec dir: Reed Stenhouse Syndicates Ltd 1976–85, Cotesworth and Co Ltd 1985–98, Bankside Syndicates Ltd 1985–99, Bankside Members Agency Ltd 1985–99, Bankside Underwriting Agencies Ltd 1985–99, QBE Lloyd's Agency 1996–2006; memb Lloyd's 1972–98 (memb Non Marine Assoc Ctee 1985–97); *Recreations* golf, tennis, theatre, opera, boating; *Clubs* Weald Park Golf; *Style*— Brian Smith, Esq; ✉ The Old Place, Ugley Green, Bishop's Stortford CM22 6HL (tel 01279 816351)

SMITH, Brian Ward; s of Frederick George Smith (d 1979), and Violet Barbara, *née* Whitbread (d 1983); *b* 15 July 1937; *Educ* Trinity Sch of John Whitgift Croydon, Christ's Coll Cambridge (coll scholar, BA), Univ of Calif Berkeley (Fulbright scholar, MS); *m* 9 Feb 1963, Ann Buckingham; 2 s (Jonathan Ward, Matthew Simon (twins) b 26 May 1966), 1 da (Sarah Jane b 18 June 1969); *Career* civil and structural engr; design engr Ove Arup and Partners 1961, Univ of Calif 1962–64; Flint & Neill (consulting engrs): joined 1964, assoc 1974, ptnr 1977, sr ptnr 1993–97, conslt 1997–; memb Exec Cncl Int Assoc for Shell and Spatial Structures, Building Research Estab visitor 1992–97; author of various specialist articles for the technical press; FICE, FIStructE, FASCE, MConsE, FREng 1994; *Recreations* painting/drawing, walking, skiing; *Clubs* St Stephen's; *Style*— Brian Smith, Esq, FREng; ✉ Flint & Neill Partnership, Bridge House, 4 Borough High Street, London SE1 9QQ (tel 020 7940 7600, fax 020 7940 7600, e-mail bws@flintneill.co.uk)

SMITH, (William Wilson) Campbell; s of Stanley Smith (d 1993), of Glasgow, and Winifred Agnes Erskine, *née* Wilson (d 2002); *b* 17 May 1946; *Educ* Glasgow Acad, St Catharine's Coll Cambridge (exhibitioner, MA), Univ of Glasgow (LLB); *m* 13 April 1974, Elizabeth Margaret, da of Maj Tom Richards (d 1994); 2 da (Emma Jane Campbell b 24 May 1977, Catherine Elizabeth Campbell b 30 Oct 1979); *Career* trainee slr Biggart Lumsden & Co Glasgow (qualified 1972), asst slr Herbert Smith & Co London 1972–73, ptnr Biggart Baillie Slrs Glasgow and Edinburgh 1974– (managing ptnr 1997–2003); chm Glassford Sheltered Housing Tst 2002–04, tstee The Lennoxlove Tst 2000–04; Freeman City of Glasgow; memb: Incorporation of Barbers Glasgow 1970– (deacon 1989–90), Incorporation of Cordiners Glasgow 1975–; memb Law Soc of Scot 1972; *Recreations* barbershop singing, golf, croquet; *Clubs* Glasgow Golf; *Style*— Campbell Smith; ✉ Parklea, 16 Dargarvel Avenue, Dumbreck, Glasgow G41 5LU (tel 0141 427 0267, e-mail campbell@dargarvel.freeserve.co.uk); Biggart Baillie, Dalmore House, 310 St Vincent Street, Glasgow G2 5QR (tel 0141 228 8000, fax 0141 228 8310); Biggart Baillie, 7 Castle Street, Edinburgh EH2 3AP (tel 0131 226 5541, fax 0131 226 2278, e-mail csmith@biggartbaillie.co.uk)

SMITH, Sir Charles Bracewell; *see:* Bracewell-Smith, Sir Charles

SMITH, Charles William Peter; s of Peter Christopher Smith, of Windermere, FL, and Simone Hilary, *née* Collett; *b* 5 August 1969, Lowestoft, Suffolk; *Educ* St Joseph's Coll

Ipswich, Cannock House Chelsfield; *m* 25 Aug 1998, Jane Elizabeth, *née* Thomas; 1 da (Rosie Isobel b 25 Dec 2001), 2 s (William Clifford Peter b 3 June 2003, Oliver James b 2 Aug 2005); *Career* Hiscox 1988–93, Foxtons 1993–98, Sotheby's International Realty 1998–; *Recreations* family, travel, art, classic literature; *Style*— Charles Smith, Esq; ✉ Linden, Ray Park Avenue, Maidenhead, Berkshire SL6 8DS; Sotheby's International Realty, 26A Conduit Street, Mayfair, London W1S 2XY (tel 020 7495 9580, fax 020 7495 9589, e-mail charles.smith@sothebysrealty.com, website www.sothebyshomes.com)

SMITH, Colin Deverell; *b* 21 May 1947, Lincolnshire; *Educ* Univ of Liverpool; *m* 1971, Kathy Morgan; 2 s; *Career* early career with Arthur Andersen; Safeway plc (formerly Argyll Group plc): joined 1979, financial controller and co sec Argyll Foods 1980–83, co sec and gp financial controller 1983–89, main bd dir 1984–99, finance dir 1989–93, gp chief exec 1993–99; chm: Poundland Holdings 2002–, Assured Food Standards 2003–; non-exec dir McBride plc 2002–; FCA; *Style*— Colin Smith, Esq; ✉ Assured Food Standards, Kings Building, 16 Smith Square, London SW1P 3JJ

SMITH, Colin Hilton; s of Reginald Walter Smith (d 1982), and Barbara, *née* Milligan; *b* 21 February 1953; *Educ* Falmouth Sch of Arts, RCA, Yale Univ; *m* 1, 1976 (m dis 1980), Barbara Ann, da of William Henry Spicer; m 2, 1983 (m dis 1992), Rosemary Victoria, da of Gerald Henry Dean; 1 s (William Lawrence Hilton b 1986); *Career* artist; Great London Arts Assoc Award 1982, London Arts Bd Award 1995, Abbey Award in Painting Br Sch at Rome 1996; Harkness fell and res assoc Faculty of Fine Art Yale Univ 1983–86; *Solo Exhibitions* Nicola Jacobs Gallery London 1982, 1984, 1987 and 1989, Ruth Siegal NY 1986, Anderson O'Day Gallery London 1991, Kunstlandschaft Europa Kunstverein Freiburg 1991, Gallery Three Zero NYC 1993, Big Paintings for the Barbican London 1993, Galleri M Stockholm 1995, Univ of Northumbria Gallery 1995, Wilmer Cutler and Pickering Berlin 1995, The Chelsea Arts Club 1995 and 2004, Galleria Arte X Arte Buenos Aires 1996, Galleri M Stockholm 1997, Six Chapel Row Contemporary Art Bath 1998, Br Cncl Art Centre Buenos Aires 1998, Adair Margo Gallery Elpaso TX 1999, Rockwell Gallery London 2004, Reigate Sch of Art Gallery 2004; *Group Exhibitions* The First Exhbn (Nicola Jacobs Gallery) 1979, Sculpture and works on paper (Nicola Jacobs Gallery) 1980, Fourteenth Int Festival of Painting Cagnes-sur-Mer-France 1982, Tolly Cobbold Eastern Arts Fourth Nat Exhbn and tour 1983, The Figurative Exhibition II (Nicola Jacobs Gallery) 1983, New Talent (Hal Bromm NYC) 1984, The Image as Catalyst (Ashmolean Museum Oxford) 1984, Royal Over-Seas League Annual Exhbn (jt first prize winner) 1987, Academicians Choice (Mall Galleries London and The Eye Gallery Bristol) 1990, The London Gp Exhbn (RCA) 1990, Foregrounds and Distances (touring) 1992–93, Retour à la Peinture Montreal 1992, The Figure The City NYC 1993, Ian Jones and Colin Smith (Barbican) 1993, John Moores Exhbn 18 (Walker Art Gallery Liverpool) 1993, Painting The City (Corr Contemporary Art London) 1995, Mostra (Br Sch at Rome) 1996, The Motor Show - Cars in Art (touring exhbn) 1996; *Work in Collections* Tate Gallery London, Royal Palm Hotel Phoenix Arizona, NatWest Gp London, Br Cncl Buenos Aires, RCA, Unilever London, Arts Cncl of GB, Prudential Holborn, Pepsi Cola London, Contemporary Art Soc, Arthur Andersen Ltd, British Airways, EMI Ltd, Kettering Art Gallery, Carlton Communications, Coopers Lybrand, Virgin Airways London, The Duke and Duchess of Westminster, Amerivox Scandanavia Stockholm, Arthur Andersen Newcastle, Wilmer Cutler and Pickering Berlin, BML Corp Mgmnt Frankfurt, Scottish Equitable Edinburgh; *Publications* An Interview with Richard Diebenkorn (Artscribe 1992), Karl Weschice (The Whistler Magazine, 1996); *Recreations* reading, films; *Clubs* Chelsea Arts; *Style*— Colin Smith, Esq; ✉ 27 Orsman Road, Hoxton, London N1 5RA (tel 020 7739 3067)

SMITH, His Hon Judge Colin Milner; QC (1985); s of Alan Milner Smith, OBE (d 1999), of Otford, Kent, and Vera Ivy, *née* Cannon (d 1973); *b* 2 November 1936; *Educ* Tonbridge, BNC Oxford (MA), Univ of Chicago (JD); *m* 14 Dec 1979, Moira Soraya, da of Charles Reginald Braybrooke, (d 1989) of Lower Layham, Suffolk; 1 s (Alexander b 1982), 1 da (Camilla b 1987); *Career* Nat Serv Lt RM (3 Commando Bde) 1955–57; called to the Bar Gray's Inn 1962; recorder 1987–91, circuit judge (SE Circuit) 1991–; *Recreations* cricket, skiing, reading; *Clubs* MCC; *Style*— His Honour Judge Colin Smith, QC; ✉ 3 Verulam Buildings, Gray's Inn, London WC1R 5NT (tel 020 7831 8441)

SMITH, Colin Roland Francis; s of Roland Smith (d 1993), of Sutton Coldfield, and Anne, *née* Colley (d 1954); *b* 6 September 1944; *Educ* John Willmott GS; *m* Sylvia, da of Sydney Skillett, of Guernsey; 1 da (Helena b 1964), 1 s (Gavin b 1966); *Career* Royal Signals Jr Leaders' Regt; harbour corr Guernsey Evening Press 1962–63; reporter on several local newspapers and Daily Sketch until 1968; The Observer: joined 1968, chief roving corr 1972–77, ME corr (based in Cyprus, Cairo and Jerusalem) 1977–85, chief roving corr 1985–88, Asia ed based in Bangkok 1988–90, asst ed and roving corr 1990, Washington corr 1993; roving corr The Sunday Times 1993–94; contrib: The Sunday Times 1995–, Prospect magazine 1997–, New Statesman 1999–, The Oldie 2005, The Literary Review 2006–; Int Reporter of the Year 1975 and 1985; *Books* The Palestinians (1975), Carlos - Portrait of a Terrorist (1976, revised edn 1995), Fire in the Night: Wingate of Burma, Ethiopia and Zion (with John Bierman, 1999), Alamein - War Without Hate (with John Bierman, 2002), Singapore Burning: Heroism and Surrender in World War Two (2005); *Novels* Cut-Out (1980), The Last Crusade (1991); *Recreations* tennis, military history; *Style*— Colin Smith, Esq; ✉ PO Box 20827, Nicosia 1664, Cyprus (website www.colin-smith.info)

SMITH, (William) Dallas; s of William Smith, and Estelle Smith; *Educ* Aldenham, Univ of Ulster (BA); *Career* talent agent; worked in theatre admin: Mayfair Theatre London, Arts Theatre Cambridge, Royal Exchange Manchester, Palace Theatre Watford, Roundhouse Theatre London; gen mangr Hampstead Theatre London 1980–90, talent agent 1990–, dir PFD 1999–; dir LAMDA; FRSA; *Recreations* travel, food, theatre, cinema; *Clubs* Century; *Style*— Dallas Smith, Esq; ✉ PFD, Drury House, 34–43 Russell Street, London WC2B 5HA (tel 020 7344 1010, fax 020 7836 9544, e-mail dsmith@pfd.co.uk)

SMITH, Prof (Anthony) David; s of Rev William Beddard Smith (d 1985), and Evelyn, *née* Eagle (d 1987); *b* 16 September 1938; *Educ* Kingswood Sch Bath, ChCh Oxford (Bostock exhibitioner, MA, DPhil); *m* 1, 1962 (m dis 1974), Wendy Diana, *née* Lee; 1 da (Catherine Anne b 1965), 1 s (Richard David b 1968); m 2, 1975, Dr Ingegerd Östman; 1 s (Niklas Carl William b 1987); *Career* Univ of Oxford: Royal Soc Stothert res fell 1966–70, res lectr ChCh 1966–71, Wellcome res fell 1970–71, univ lectr in pharmacology and student of ChCh 1971–84, prof and head Dept of Pharmacology 1984–2005, hon dir MRC Anatomical Neuropharmacology Unit 1985–98, fell LMH Oxford 1984–, dir Oxford Project to Investigate Memory and Ageing (OPTIMA) 1988–, dep head Div of Med Sciences 2000–05; ed and contrib articles in various jls; memb: Gen Bd of the Faculties Oxford 1980–84, Neurosciences Bd MRC 1983–85; chair Sicentific Advsy Bd Alzheimer's Res Tst 1997–2002; Hon Dr Szeged Univ 1993, Hon Dr Med Lund Univ 1998; seventh Gaddum Meml Prize Br Pharmacological Soc 1979, Decade of the Brain lectr 1993, memb Norwegian Acad of Sci and Letters 1996, hon memb Hungarian Acad of Scis 1998, Dana Alliance for the Brain 2000; hon res fell Alzheimer's Res Tst 2006; memb: Physiological Soc, Pharmacological Soc; FMedSci 2000; *Recreations* music, travel; *Style*— Prof David Smith; ✉ University Laboratory of Physiology, Parks Road, Oxford OX1 3PT (tel 01865 285837, e-mail david.smith@pharm.ox.ac.uk)

SMITH, David Andrew; s of John William Smith (d 1968), of London, and Patricia Mary Smith; *b* 5 March 1952; *Educ* Finchley GS, Lincoln Coll Oxford (MA, ed Cherwell (univ newspaper)); *m* 1, 18 Oct 1980 (m dis 1994), Pamela, da of Douglas Keith Reading; 2 s (Mark Patrick Reading b 30 Dec 1982, Matthew Louis Reading b 29 May 1986); m 2, 16 Nov 1996, Sonia, da of Francisco Ruseler; 1 da (Alegria Ruseler-Smith b 14 Jan 1998), 1 s (Nelson Ruseler-Smith b 15 July 2000); *Career* corr Italy Reuters 1977–78 (Spain 1975–76); ITN corr: Africa 1979–81, Israel 1982–86, Soviet Union 1988–90, USA 1991–; visiting prof Univ of Michigan 1986–87; International Reporter of the Year (for despatches from Lebanon) RTS Awards 1983; *Books* Mugabe (1981), Prisoners of God - The Conflict of Arab and Jew (1987); *Style*— David Smith, Esq

SMITH, Cdre David Andrew Harry McGregor; CBE (2002); *Educ* Lancing, RCDS; *Career* served HMY Britannia 1986–88, staff of Naval Sec 1988–91, dir (Future Devpts) Navy Logistics Staff 1992–95, EA/DEPSACLANT USA 1995–98, RCDS 1998, Cdre HMS Nelson 1999–2000, dir Navy Personnel Corporate Programming 2000–01; memb Advsy Bd Origo Inc 2002; dir of markets City of London 2003–; tstee King William IV Naval Fndn 2003; Liveryman Worshipful Co of Cooks of London; Freeman City of London; FHCIMA 1994, FCIPD 2001; *Publications* Confucianism - Signpost to China's Future Relations with her East Asian Neighbours (1998); *Clubs* Royal Thames Yacht, Royal Naval and Royal Albert Yacht, Anchorites; *Style*— Cdre David Smith, CBE; ✉ PO Box 270, Guildhall, London EC2P 2EJ (mobile 07760 352233)

SMITH, David Bruce Boyter; OBE (1994); s of Bruce Aitken Smith (d 1993), of Dunfermline, and Helen Brown, *née* Boyter (d 1996); *b* 11 March 1942; *Educ* Dunfermline HS, Univ of Edinburgh (MA, LLB); *m* 7 Aug 1965, Christine Anne, da of Robert McKenzie (d 1972); 1 s (Andrew b 1 Aug 1969), 1 da (Caroline b 1 July 1974); *Career* admitted slr 1968, NP 1969, slr Standard Life Assurance Co 1969–73; Dunfermline Building Society: sec 1974, gen mangr 1981, dep chief exec 1986, chief exec 1987–2001, ret; dep chm Glenrothes New Town Devpt Corp 1990–96; dir: Fife Enterprise Ltd 1991–2000, Building Socs Investor Protection Bd 1991–2002; BSA: chm BSA London 1999–2000, chm Scottish Ctee 1996–98 (vice-chm 1994–96); chm: Northern Assoc of Building Socs 1997–98, Building Societies Trust Ltd 1998–2001; memb Bd NHBC 2004–, chm Scotland NHBC 2004–; memb: Scottish Advsy Bd BT 1996–98, Scottish Conveyancing Bd 1996–2003, Exec Ctee Cncl of Mortgage Lenders 1998–2001; vice-chm Scottish Fisheries Museum Tst Ltd 2002–06; vice-chm Ct and finance convener Univ of Edinburgh 1991–2003, chm Univ of Edinburgh Endowment Tst, vice-chm Lauder Coll 1993–98, vice-chm Scottish Opera 2000–04; life tstee: Carnegie Tst for the Universities of Scotland, Carnegie UK, Dunfermline and Hero Fund Tsts; tstee Scottish Lime Centre 2006–; memb Law Soc of Scotland 1968; vice-pres Euro Mortgage Fedn 2000–02; memb Registers of Scotland Ministerial Advisory Bd 2002–; Dr (hc) Univ of Edinburgh 2000; FRSA 1992, FInstD 1994 (chm Scottish Div 1994–97); *Recreations* golf, sailing, the arts; *Clubs* New (Edinburgh), Dalgety Bay Sailing, Dunfermline Golf; *Style*— Dr David Smith, OBE; ✉ 26 Donibristle Gardens, Dalgety Bay, Dunfermline KY11 9NQ (tel 01383 829994)

SMITH, Sheriff David Buchanan; s of William Adam Smith (d 1955), of Elderslie, Renfrewshire, and Irene Mary Calderwood, *née* Hogarth (d 1976); *b* 31 October 1936; *Educ* Paisley GS, Univ of Glasgow (MA), Univ of Edinburgh (LLB); *m* 1 April 1961, Hazel Mary, da of James Alexander Walker Sinclair, MBE (d 1960), of Edinburgh; 2 s (David Ewan b 1962, d 1986, Patrick Sinclair b 1965), 1 da (Alison Mary b 1963); *Career* advocate 1961–75, standing jr counsel to Scottish Educn Dept 1968–75; tutor Faculty of Law Univ of Edinburgh 1964–72; sheriff of N Strathclyde at Kilmarnock 1975–2001; pres Kilmarnock and Dist History Gp 1985–2007, treas The Sheriffs' Assoc 1979–89 (archivist 1989–, cncl memb 1998–2001); cncl memb: Scot Nat Dictionary Assoc 1995–2002, Stair Soc 1995–98 (vice-chm 1998–), Scottish Language Dictionaries 2002–; memb Scot Records Advsy Cncl 2000–; res assoc Nat Museums of Scotland 2002–; tstee Scot Curling Museum Tst 1980–, pres Ayr Curling Club 1995–96, pres Eglinton County Curling Game 2000–03; Lifetime Achievement Award Royal Caledonian Curling Club 2005; FSA Scot; *Books* Curling: an Illustrated History (1981), The Roaring Game: Memories of Scottish Curling (1985), The Sheriff Court (in The Stair Memorial Encyclopedia of the Laws of Scotland vol 6, 1988), George Washington Wilson in Ayrshire (1991), Macphail: Sheriff Court Practice (contrib 2 edn, 1998), Sport, Scotland and the Scots (contrib chapter on curling, 2000), The Oxford Companion to Scottish History (contrib, 2001), Encyclopedia of Traditional British Rural Sports (contrib, 2005); *Recreations* history of the laws and institutions of Scotland, curling, collecting curliana, music, architecture, grandchildren; *Clubs* Glasgow Art; *Style*— Sheriff David B Smith; ✉ 72 South Beach, Troon, Ayrshire KA10 6EG (tel 01292 312130, e-mail dbsmith@omne.uk.net)

SMITH, Sir David Cecil; kt (1986); s of William John Smith, and Elva Emily, *née* Deeble; *b* 21 May 1930; *Educ* St Paul's, The Queen's Coll Oxford (MA, DPhil); *m* 1965, Lesley Margaret, da of Henry John Mollison Mutch (d 1946); 2 s (Adam, Cameron), 1 da (Bryony); *Career* 2 Lt RA 1955–56; Swedish Inst scholar Uppsala Univ 1951–52, Brown res fell The Queen's Coll Oxford 1956–59, Harkness fell Univ of Calif Berkeley 1959–60, lectr Dept of Agric Univ of Oxford 1960–74, tutorial fell and tutor for admissions Wadham Coll Oxford 1971–74 (Royal Soc res fell 1964–71), Melville Wills prof of botany Univ of Bristol 1974–80 (dir of biological studies 1977–80), Sibthorpian prof of rural economy Univ of Oxford 1980–87, princ and vice-chllr Univ of Edinburgh 1987–94, pres Wolfson Coll Oxford 1994–2000; Hon DSc: Univ of Liverpool 1986, Univ of Exeter 1986, Univ of Hull 1987, Univ of Aberdeen 1990, Napier Univ 1993, Oxford Brookes Univ 1996, Univ of Bradford 2001; Hon DL: Univ of Pennsylvania 1990, Queen's Univ (Ontario) 1991; Hon DUniv Heriot-Watt 1993, Hon Dr (hc) Univ of Edinburgh 1994; FRS 1975, FRSE 1988; *Books* The Biology of Symbiosis (with A Douglas, 1987); *Clubs* Farmers'; *Style*— Sir David Smith, FRS, FRSE; ✉ 13 Abbotsford Park, Edinburgh EH10 5DZ (tel 0131 446 0230)

SMITH, David Henry; s of Charles Henry Smith (d 1990), and Elizabeth Mary, *née* Williams (d 1963); *b* 3 April 1954; *Educ* West Bromwich GS, UC Cardiff (BSc(Econ), Tassie medallion), Birkbeck Coll London (MSc(Econ)); *m* 1980, Jane Howells; 2 s (Richard Howell b 1981, Thomas David b 1983), 2 da (Emily Victoria b 1987, Elizabeth Jane b 1992); *Career* econ report writer Lloyds Bank 1976–77, economist Henley Centre 1977–79, econ writer Now! magazine 1979–81, asst ed Financial Weekly 1981–84, econ corr The Times 1984–89, econ ed The Sunday Times 1989– (currently also policy advsr and asst ed); commended Journalist of the Year Br Press Awards 1992 and 1999, Business Columnist of the Year PPA Awards 1995 and 1996, Wincott Fndn Sr Financial Journalist of the Year 2004; FRSA 1999; *Books* The Rise and Fall of Monetarism (1987), North and South (1989, 2 edn, 1994), Mrs Thatcher's Economics (1989), Mrs Thatcher's Economics: Her Legacy (1991), From Boom to Bust (1992), UK Current Economic Policy (1995, 2 edn 1999), Eurofutures (1997), Will Europe Work? (1999), Welfare, Work and Poverty (ed, 2000), Free Lunch (2003), The Dragon and the Elephant: China, India and the New World Order (2007); *Recreations* golf, squash; *Clubs* Bexley Tennis & Squash; *Style*— David Smith, Esq, FRSA; ✉ The Sunday Times, 1 Pennington Street, London E98 1ST (tel 020 7782 5750, fax 020 7782 5237, e-mail david.smith@sunday-times.co.uk, website www.economicsuk.com)

SMITH, Rt Rev David James; s of Stanley James Smith (d 1965), and Gwendolen Emie, *née* Nunn (d 1960); *b* 14 July 1935; *Educ* Hertford GS, KCL (AKC), St Boniface Coll Warminster; *m* 2 Dec 1961, Mary Hunter, da of Eric John Moult (d 1970); 1 da (Rebecca Clare b 9 Feb 1965), 1 s (Christopher Michael b 16 Sept 1966); *Career* asst curate: All Saints Gosforth 1959–62, St Francis High Heaton 1962–64, Longbenton 1964–68; vicar: Longhirst with Hebron 1968–75, St Mary Monkseaton 1975–81, Felton 1982–83; archdeacon of Lindisfarne 1981–87, bishop of Maidstone 1987–92, bishop to HM Forces 1990–92, bishop of Bradford 1992–2002; memb House of Lords 1997–2002; Hon DUniv

S

Bradford 2001; FKC; *Recreations* walking, reading novels; *Style*— The Rt Rev David Smith

SMITH, Derek Graham; s of Albert Edward Smith (d 1993), and Rosetta Alexandra, *née* Lyme (d 2001); *b* 16 May 1947; *Educ* Royal Liberty Sch Romford, Univ of Kent (BA); *m* 25 April 1981, Margaret Elizabeth, *née* Harris; 1 da (Michelle Helen b 7 Sept 1982), 1 s (Fraser James b 8 June 1987); *Career* Coopers and Lybrand 1969–77: joined as articled clerk 1969, subsequently supervisor then mangr; Mazars Neville Russell (formerly Neville Russell) 1977–: mangr then sr mangr, ptnr 1980–, chm Mgmnt Bd London Office 1991–, nat managing ptnr 1993; memb Exec Gp Mazars & Guérard Gp; memb Cncl St Martin's Church Ongar; Freeman City of London 1992; FCA 1972, FIMC 1987; *Books* Management and Control of Time in an Accountancy Practice (1982); *Recreations* DIY, local church; *Clubs* National; *Style*— Derek Smith, Esq; ✉ Springfield Orchard, Epping Road, Ongar, Essex CM5 0BD; Mazars Neville Russell, 24 Bevis Marks, London EC3A 7NR (tel 020 7377 1000, fax 020 7377 8931)

SMITH, Derek Vincent; s of Arthur Edmund Smith, of Cheshire, and Hazel, *née* Proudlove (d 1989); *b* 26 September 1948; *Educ* Sale Co Boys' GS, UC Swansea (BSc(Econ)), Univ of Strathclyde (Postgrad Dip Russian); *Family* 1 da (Claire-Louise b 17 Nov 1976), 2 s (Matthew James b 24 Oct 1978, Benjamin Harrison b 14 Sept 2001); m, 17 May 2003, Ruth Harrison; *Career* NHS nat admin trainee Scotland 1972–74, asst sector administrator Falkirk and Dist Royal Infirmary 1974–76, administrator (serv planning) Ayrshire and Arran Health Bd 1976–79, dist planning offr Southmead Dist Avon Area HA 1979–82; Frenchay Hosp Bristol: administrator 1982–85, gen mangr 1985–87; district gen mangr S Bedfordshire HA 1987–90, chief exec Camberwell HA 1990–93, chief exec King's Healthcare NHS Tst 1993–99, md London Underground Ltd 1999–2001 (also dir London Transport), chief exec Hammersmith Hosps 2001–; Dip HSM 1975, MHSM 1979; *Recreations* squash rackets, tennis, classical music, sailing, golf; *Clubs* RAC; *Style*— Derek Smith, Esq

SMITH, Prof (Stanley) Desmond; OBE; s of Henry George Stanley Smith (d 1969), and Sarah Emily Ruth Weare; *b* 3 March 1931; *Educ* Cotham Bristol, Univ of Bristol (BSc, DSc), Univ of Reading (PhD); *m* 1 July 1956, Gillian Anne, da of Howard Stanley Parish; 1 s (David), 1 da (Nicola); *Career* SSO RAE Farnborough 1956–59; research asst Meteorology Dept Imperial Coll London 1959–60, reader Univ of Reading 1966–70 (lectr 1960–66), prof of physics and dept head Heriot-Watt Univ 1970–96; chm and dir: Edinburgh Instruments Ltd 1971–, Edinburgh Sensors Ltd 1988–; dir Edinburgh C of C 1981–84; memb: cabinet ACOST 1987–88 (formerly ACARD 1985–87), Def Science Advsy Cncl MOD 1985–91; Hon DSc Heriot-Watt Univ 2003; FRMetS 1962, FRSE 1973, FInstP 1976, FRS 1976; *Recreations* mountaineering, skiing, tennis, golf, raising the temperature; *Clubs* Royal Soc; *Style*— Prof Desmond Smith, OBE, FRS, FRSE; ✉ Tree Tops, 29D Gillespie Road, Colinton, Edinburgh EH13 0NW (tel 0131 441 7225); 106 Corniche du Pinateau, 05260 Chaillol 1600, Hautes Alpes, France (tel 00 33 492 50 08 81, e-mail desmond.smith@wanadoo.fr); Edinburgh Instruments Ltd, 2 Bain Square, Livingston EH54 7DQ (tel 01506 425301, fax 01506 425320, e-mail des.smith@edinst.com)

SMITH, (Brian) Douglas; s of Henry Charles Smith (d 1958), of Crouch End, London, and Ruby Constance, *née* Hall (d 1976); *b* 17 August 1935; *Educ* Stationers' Co Sch Hornsey, King's Coll London, LSE (BA, Cricket purple); *m* 1, 1961, Verity Anne, da of late William Wright; 2 da (Tracy McClure, Francesca McClure); m 2, 1985, Mary Barbara, *née* Gillman; 1 da (Rebecca Barbara); *Career* London publicity offr Cons Party Central Office 1960–62, head of publicity Fire Protection Assoc 1962–64, sec Int Co-operation Year Ctee 1964–66, dir Intercapita Public Relations 1966–68, assoc dir Planned Public Relations 1968–71, dir MDA Public Relations 1971–85, md PRCI Ltd (later Countrywide Political Communications) 1985–90; chm: Westminster Advisers Ltd 1990–, Political Intelligence Ltd 1996–, Parliamentary Perceptions Ltd 2004–; cncllr Hornsey BC 1961–65 (chm Housing Ctee 1963–65); Haringey Cncl: cncllr 1964–86, dep ldr Cons Gp 1966–70, dep mayor 1968–69, chm Planning and Devpt Ctee 1968–70, chm Personnel Ctee 1969–71, ldr Cons Oppn 1980–84; pres Hornsey and Wood Green Cons Assoc 2000–03; chm PR Conslts Assoc 1984–85 (treas, vice-chm), pres IPR 1990 (fndr chm Govt Affrs Gp 1986–87), pres CERP Consultants 1992–94; PR Week Award for outstanding career achievement in PR 1990, IPR Sword of Excellence Award 1997, Public Affairs News Award for lifetime achievement 2005; chm St Stephen's Club 2003–; MCAM, Hon FCIPR, Hon FBEng; *Publications* Legitimate Lobbying (with Peter Morris, 1997), Votes for Cricket (with David Lemmon, 2000); *Recreations* watching and talking cricket, visiting old pubs; *Clubs* Kent CCC, St Stephen's, Middlesex CCC; *Style*— Douglas Smith, Esq; ✉ 1 Astral House, Regency Place, London SW1P 2EA (tel 020 7828 0828, fax 020 7931 0893, e-mail douglassmith@btinternet.com)

SMITH, (John) Edward Kitson (Ed); s of Jack Kitson Smith (d 1992), and Edith, *née* Taylor; *b* 24 October 1954, Calcutta, India; *Educ* St Dunstan's Coll Catford, London Met Univ (BA); *m* 11 July 1981, Jennifer Maude, *née* Linton; 1 s (Nicholas b 27 Feb 1987), 2 da (Jessica b 28 Nov 1988, Anna b 13 Sept 1997); *Career* PricewaterhouseCoopers: joined 1977, head of educn practice 1989–93, exec ptnr UK audit 1994–97, global ldr learning and devpt 1998–99, memb UK Bd 2000–03, currently sr ptnr and global assurance chief operating offr and ldr strategy; fin advsr DES 1987–89, memb Accounting for People Taskforce DTI 2003; govr Univ of N London 1991–95; memb: Audit Ctee Poly and Colls Funding Cncl 1990–92, Bd HEFCE 2004–, Advsy Bd Opportunity Now; FCA 2000 (ACA 1980), FRSA; *Publications* Breakpoint/Breakthrough Strategies for Worklife Balance in the 21st Century (co-author, 1999), Accounting for People (2003), Diversity Dimensions (2004), Papering Over the Cracks? (co-author, 2006); *Recreations* golf, cooking, wine collecting, opera; *Clubs* Carlton, Westerham Golf; *Style*— Ed Smith, Esq; ✉ Old Mill Leat, Vicarage Hill, Westerham, Kent TN16 1TJ (tel 01959 564008); PricewaterhouseCoopers LLP, 1 Embankment Place, London WC2N 6RH (tel 020 7212 4697, fax 020 7213 3852, e-mail ed.k.smith@uk.pwc.com)

SMITH, Elaine; MSP; da of late William Dornan, and Mary McGill; *b* 7 May 1963, Coatbridge; *Educ* St Patrick's HS Coatbridge, Glasgow Coll, St Andrews Teacher Trg Coll; *m* 31 Dec 1986, James Vann Smith; 1 s (Vann b 5 May 1996); *Career* MSP (Lab) Coatbridge and Chryston 1999–; convenor Lab's Campaign for Socialism; memb: Gen Teaching Cncl, TGWU; Free Spirit Award Scottish Politician of the Year 2002; *Recreations* swimming, bowling, reading, family; *Style*— Mrs Elaine Smith, MSP; ✉ The Scottish Parliament, Edinburgh EH99 1SP

SMITH, Elizabeth Jean; OBE (2004); da of Lt-Gen Sir Robert Hay, KCIE (d 1980); *b* 15 August 1936; *Educ* St George's Sch Edinburgh, Univ of Edinburgh (MA); *m* 23 Feb 1960, Geoffrey Peter Smith, s of William Stanley Smith (d 1958), of Wallasey, Cheshire; 1 da (Catherine b 1965), 1 s (Graham b 1968); *Career* BBC: studio mangr 1958–61, prodr radio news 1961–70, dep ed consumer affrs Radio 4 1970–78, prodr TV current affrs 1978–79, sr asst Secretariat 1979–81, Cwlth fellowship to study the impact of satellite TV on India 1984, asst head central talks and features World Service 1981–84, head current affrs World Service 1984–88, controller English Services World Service 1988–94; sec gen Cwlth Broadcasting Assoc 1994–; monthly columnist The Listener 1975–78; chair Voice of the Listener and Viewer Tst; memb: Cncl RIIA 1992–95, Bd of Govrs Westminster Fndn for Democracy 1998–2001; fell Radio Acad; *Books* Healing Herbs (jtly, 1978), Sambo Sahib (as Elizabeth Hay, 1981); *Style*— Mrs Elizabeth Smith, OBE; ✉ CBA, 17 Fleet Street, London EC4Y 1AA (tel 020 7583 5550, fax 020 7583 5549)

SMITH, Emily Frances; da of late Oliver Ronald Smith, and late Moyra Elizabeth, *née* Blandy; *Educ* Cranborne Chase Sch, New Hall Cambridge (BA); *m* 1982, Sir Michael Wheeler-Booth, KCB , *qv*; 2 da (Kate b 1985, Charlotte b 1987), 1 s (Alfred James b 1990); *Career* author; called to the Bar Inner Temple 1975; legal advsr Dairy Trade Fedn 1976–80; reporter East Anglian Daily Times 1980–82, reporter and sub-ed Windsor Express Series 1982–85; *Books* Astrid the Au Pair from Outer Space (1999, Smarties Silver Award, 6–8 category), The Shrimp (2001, Smarties Gold Award, 6–8 category), Annie and the Aliens (2001), What Howls at the Moon in Frilly Knickers? (2001), Robomum (2003), When Mum Threw Out The Telly (2003), Patrick the Party Hater (2004), Joe v The Fairies (2005), A Stain on the Stone: A Jack Young Mystery (2006); *Style*— Ms Emily Smith; ✉ c/o David Higham Associates, 5–8 Lower John Street, Golden Square, London W1R 4HA (tel 020 7437 7888, fax 020 7437 1072, e-mail dha@davidhigham.co.uk)

SMITH, Prof Francis William; s of Capt William Smith, RAMC (d 1978) of Harare, Zimbabwe, and Frances Marrianne May, *née* Emslie (d 1992); *b* 8 January 1943; *Educ* Prince Edward Sch Harare, Univ of Aberdeen (MB ChB, DMRD, MD); *m* 5 Dec 1970, Pamela Anne, da of James Cox (d 1958), of Gateshead, Co Durham; 1 da (Jane b 1971), 1 s (James b 1976); *Career* dir of clinical magnetic resonance res Aberdeen Royal Infirmary 1980 (conslt in nuclear med 1979–97); conslt radiologist Grampain Univ Hospitals NHS Tst 1997–; prof of health sciences Robert Gordon Univ 1999–, prof of radiology Univ of Aberdeen 2005–; chief ed Magnetic Resonance Imaging 1985–91, assoc ed Jl of Magnetic Resonance Imaging 1991–2001; club dr: Montrose FC 1990–95, Dundee United FC 1995–; pres Soc for Magnetic Resonance Imaging 1983; FFR RCSI 1978, FRCPEd 1992, Dip in Sports Med 1992, FRCR 1997, FRCSEd 2005, FFSEM 2007; *Books* Magnetic Resonance in Medicine and Biology (1984), Practical Nuclear Medicine (1989); *Recreations* swimming, walking, entomology, fly fishing, golf; *Style*— Prof Francis Smith; ✉ 7 Primrosehill Road, Cults, Aberdeen AB15 9ND (tel 01224 868745, e-mail franciswsmith@hotmail.com); Department of Radiology, Woodend Hospital, Eday Road, Aberdeen AB15 6XS (tel 01224 681818 ext 56040, fax 01224 556232)

SMITH, Frank Arthur; s of George Frederick Stanley Smith (d 1984), of Nottingham, and Doris Hannah, *née* Simcock (d 1984); *b* 18 December 1941; *Educ* King Edward VII Sch Sheffield, Trinity Coll Oxford (MA); *m* 1, 14 Oct 1967, Eva June (d 1990), da of George Henry Larner, of Haverfordwest; 1 da (Anna Margaret b 23 March 1969), 1 s (Thomas Louis b 19 March 1972); m 2, 23 Oct 1993, Karin Ulrika, da of Axel Ludwig Bäck, of Eksjö, Sweden; 3 step da (Anna Rachel b 7 June 1963, Miriam Elna b 28 Dec 1966, Rebecca Karin b 4 Dec 1968); *Career* RSM Robson Rhodes 1963–2000 (nat tax ptnr 1983–93), seconded as head Int Dept RSM Salustro Reydel Paris 1993–2000; memb Tax Ctee ICAEW 1984–93, memb Tax Ctee London C of C and Industry 1978–86; tstee and vice-chm Geffrye Museum 1989–; memb Ctee Otter Housing Soc 1991–93; chm Blackheath Soc 2003–, dir Blackheath Preservation Tst 2004–, hon treas Greengates 2000–; FCA 1966, CTA (fell 1979); *Recreations* walking, reading, gardening, jazz, travel; *Style*— Frank Smith, Esq; ✉ Eastnor Garden House, 73 Tranquil Vale, Blackheath, London SE3 0BP (tel 020 8852 6390, fax 020 8318 4471, e-mail frankarthursmith@aol.com)

SMITH, Prof Frank Thomas; s of Leslie Maxwell Smith, of Havant, Hants, and Catherine Matilda, *née* Wilken; *b* 24 February 1948; *Educ* Kinson CP Sch, Bournemouth GS, Jesus Coll Oxford (BA, DPhil); *m* 16 Sept 1972, Valerie Sheila, da of Albert Alfred Hearn; 3 da (Helen b 1976, Natalie b 1978, Amy b 1987); *Career* res fell Theoretical Aerodynamics Unit Southampton 1972–73, lectr Imperial Coll London 1973–78, visiting prof Univ of W Ontario 1978–79, reader and prof Imperial Coll London 1979–84, Goldsmid prof in applied maths UCL 1984–, dir Lighthill Inst 2006–, dir London Taught Course Centre 2007–; FRS 1984; *Books* Boundary - Layer Separation (with Prof Susan Brown 1987); *Recreations* sports, reading, family; *Style*— Prof Frank T Smith, FRS; ✉ Mathematics Department, University College, Gower Street, London WC1E 6BT (tel 020 7679 2839, fax 020 7383 5519, e-mail frank@math.ucl.ac.uk)

SMITH, Prof George David William; s of George Alfred William Smith (d 1989), and Grace Violet Hannah Dayton, *née* Bloom; *b* 28 March 1943; *Educ* St Benedict's Sch Aldershot, Salesian Coll Farnborough, CCC Oxford (open scholar, graduate scholar, MA, DPhil); *m* 1968, Josephine Ann, da of Edwin Walter Halford; 2 s (Timothy George Edwin b 1969, Richard Charles Edwin b 1972); *Career* Univ of Oxford: SRC research fell 1968–70, postdoctoral research fell 1970–75, sr research fell 1975–77, lectr in metallurgy 1977–92, George Kelley reader in metallurgy 1992–96, prof of materials science 1996–2000, head Dept of Materials 2000–05; research fell Wolfson Coll Oxford 1972–77 (jr research fell 1968–72), fell St Cross Coll Oxford 1977–91 (emeritus fell 1992–), professorial fell Trinity Coll Oxford 1996– (tutorial fell 1991–95); Oxford Nanoscience Ltd (formerly Kindbrisk Ltd): md 1987–2002, chm 2002–04, R&D 100 award 1993, Prince of Wales' Award for Innovation 1997, Millennium Product Designation 1998, Nat Award for Innovative Measurement 2004; non-exec chm Polaron plc 2004–06; co-chm UK Materials Congress 1998; memb: Materials Research Soc (USA) 1987–, Minerals, Metals and Materials Soc (USA) 1992–, Office of Science and Technol Foresight Panel for Materials 1999–2003, HE Funding Cncl Research Assessment Panel for Materials 1999–2001; Sir George Beilby Medal and Prize 1985, Acta Materialia Gold Medal 2005; Inst of Materials: memb 1963–, Vanadium Award (jtly) 1985, Rosenhain Medal and Prize 1991, memb Cncl 1997–, vice-pres 2002–, Platinum Medal 2006; memb Exec Cncl Royal Soc 2002–04; Liveryman Worshipful Co of Armourers and Braziers 2003 (Freeman 1998), Freeman City of London 1999; CEng 1978, CPhys 1996; FInstP 1996 (MInstP 1978), FIM 1996, FRS 1996, FRSA 1997, FRSC 2003, memb European Acad of Science and Arts 2006; *Books* Atom Probe Microanalysis: Principles and Application to Materials Problems (with M K Miller, 1989), Atom Probe Field Ion Microscopy (jtly, 1996); *Recreations* walking, fishing, bird watching, travel; *Style*— Prof George Smith, FRS; ✉ Department of Materials, University of Oxford, Parks Road, Oxford OX1 3PH (tel 01865 273762, fax 01865 273738, e-mail george.smith@materials.oxford.ac.uk)

SMITH, Geraldine; MP; da of Sidney John Smith, and Ann, *née* Hughes; *b* 29 August 1961; *Educ* Morecambe HS, Morecambe & Lancaster Coll; *Career* postal offr 1980–97, MP (Lab) Morecambe and Lunesdale 1997–; area rep Communication Workers Union; memb: Deregulation Select Ctee 1997–, Sci and Technol Select Ctee, Parly delegation to the Cncl; former cncllr Lancaster City Cncl; *Recreations* playing chess, walking; *Style*— Miss Geraldine Smith, MP; ✉ House of Commons, London SW1A 0AA (tel 020 7219 5816, fax 020 7219 0977)

SMITH, Gillian Sara; da of Nathan Abraham Oppenheim, of Edinburgh, and Eve Renee, *née* Halson; *b* 26 January 1953; *Educ* St George's Sch for Girls Edinburgh, Newnham Coll Cambridge (MA, Roman Law Prize); *m* 5 Oct 1987, Lindsay Meredith Smith; 1 s (Simon Alexander b 25 May 1989); *Career* asst slr Linklaters & Paines 1977–81 (articled clerk 1975–77), in-house counsel Nordic Bank 1981–83; SJ Berwin: joined 1983, ptnr 1985–, seconded Watchell Lipton Rosen & Katz New York 1987–89, banking ptnr 1989–, head of banking 1992–; *Recreations* reading, entertaining, gardening; *Style*— Mrs Gillian Smith; ✉ SJ Berwin LLP, 10 Queen Street Place, London EC4R 1BE (tel 020 7111 2647, fax 020 7111 2000, e-mail gillian.smith@sjberwin.com)

SMITH, Godfrey; s of Flying Offr Reginald Montague Smith, RAF (d 1975), of Bexhill, and Ada May, *née* Damen; *b* 12 May 1926; *Educ* Surbiton Co Sch, Eggar's GS, Worcester Coll Oxford (MA, pres Oxford Union); *m* 23 June 1951, Mary (d 1997), da of Jakub Schoenfeld (d 1966), of Vienna; 3 da (Deborah b 1956, Amanda b 1959, Candida b 1964); *Career* RAF 1944–47; Sunday Times: PA to Lord Kemsley 1951, news ed 1956, asst ed 1959, magazine ed 1965–72, dir 1968–81, assoc ed 1972–91, ed Weekly Review 1972–79, columnist 1979–2004; Regent's lectr Univ of Calif 1970; author; FRSL 1995; *Novels* The Flaw in the Crystal (1954), The Friends (1957), The Business of Loving (1961, Book Soc choice), The Network (1965), Caviare (1976); *Non-fiction* The English Companion (1984), The English Season (1987, revised edn 1994), The English Reader (1988); *Anthologies* The Best of Nat Gubbins (1978), A World of Love (1982), Beyond the Tingle Quotient (1982), How it Was in the War (1989), Take the Ball and Run (1991); *Recreations* chums; *Clubs* Garrick, Savile, Leander, MCC, RAF; *Style*— Godfrey Smith, Esq, FRSL; ✉ 10 Kensington Park Mews, London W11 2EY (tel 020 7727 4155, fax 020 7221 7543); Village Farmhouse, Charlton, Malmesbury, Wiltshire SN16 9DL (tel 01666 822479, fax 01666 824094)

SMITH, Prof Gordon Campbell Sinclair; s of Robert S Smith, of Glasgow, and Peggy M, *née* Fergusson; *b* 11 May 1965, Glasgow; *Educ* Stonelaw HS Glasgow, Univ of Glasgow (BSc, MB ChB, MD, PhD); *m* 2 Aug 1986, Nicola Wilkinson; 2 da (Jessica b Sept 1991, Alice b June 1994); *Career* jr hosp positions obstetrics and gynaecology Glasgow 1991–96, Wellcome Tst clinical research fell Univ of Glasgow 1992–93, Wellcome Tst advanced clinical research fell Cornell Univ 1996–99, trainee maternal-foetal med Glasgow 1999–2001, prof of obstetrics and gynaecology Univ of Cambridge 2001–; memb: Perinatal Research Soc USA 2000, Soc of Gynaecological Investigation USA 2002, Gynaecological Visiting Soc 2004, Soc for Maternal Fetal Medicine USA; MRCOG 1995; *Publications* author of articles in learned jls incl: New England Jl of Med, Nature, Lancet, Jl of the American Med Assoc, BMJ; *Style*— Prof Gordon Smith; ✉ Department of Obstetrics and Gynaecology, University of Cambridge, The Rosie Hospital, Robinson Way, Cambridge CB2 2SW (tel 01223 336871, fax 01223 215327, e-mail obgyn-headofdept@lists.cam.ac.uk)

SMITH, Graham Alan; s of Sydney Horace Smith (d 1970), and Joan Olive, *née* Tame; *b* 29 October 1947; *Educ* Beckenham GS for Boys; *m* Aug 1978, Joan Louise; 1 s (Patrick Henry James Smith b Nov 1984); *Career* sales asst then exec ABC TV/Thames TV 1966–70, media gp head Boase Massimi Pollitt Advertising 1970–73, successively business devpt mangr, business devpt dir then vice-chm Saatchi & Saatchi Advertising 1973–92, exec vice-pres Ogilvy & Mather Europe 1992–94, dir and ptnr Warman & Bannister 1994– (formerly Leopard Advertising Ltd until 1997); memb Mktg Soc 1986; *Recreations* motor racing, photography, cricket; *Style*— Graham Smith, Esq; ✉ Warman & Bannister Ltd, 40 Marsh Wall, London E14 9TP (tel 020 7512 1000, fax 020 7512 1999)

SMITH, Graham Paul; s of James Alfred Smith (d 1985), and Elsie Winifred, *née* Cleathero; *b* 25 December 1949; *Educ* Royal GS High Wycombe, Univ of Durham (BA), Osgoode Hall Law Sch Toronto (LLM); *m* 14 Sept 1991, Mary, da of Edward T Ray (d 1986), of Southwold, Suffolk; 1 da (Charlotte b 1994); *Career* slr Supreme Court 1975; ptnr: Clifford-Turner 1981–87, Clifford Chance 1987–2000; conslt Clifford Chance 2000–; Liveryman City of London Slrs' Co; memb Law Soc 1975; *Books* contrib chapters to: The Encyclopaedia of Information Technology Law (1990), Computer Law (3 edn, 1996); *Recreations* opera, cricket; *Clubs* MCC, RAC; *Style*— Graham Smith, Esq; ✉ Clifford Chance, 10 Upper Bank Street, London E14 5JJ (tel 020 7006 1000, fax 020 7006 5555, e-mail graham.smith@cliffordchance.com)

SMITH, Graham Richard Elliott; s of Donald Smith (d 1978), and Betty Lillian, *née* Elliott; *b* 24 February 1958; *Educ* Royal GS Guildford, Univ of Nottingham (BA); *m* 19 Sept 1987, Sharon Elizabeth Peterson, da of Aubrey Owen Mulroney, of Nortonbury, Morgans Rd, Hertford, Herts; 2 s (Sebastian Guy Elliott b 5 November 1991, Willem Peter Elliott b 5 April 1994), 1 da (Leone Jane Peterson b 4 June 1990); *Career* admitted slr 1982; Wilde Sapte: articled clerk 1980–82, slr 1982–87, ptnr 1987–98; ptnr Allen & Overy 1998– (currently global head Structured & Asset Finance Gp); Freeman Worshipful Co of Slrs 1986–; memb: Law Soc, Int Bar Assoc; *Recreations* skiing, fine wine, travel; *Style*— Graham Smith, Esq; ✉ Allen & Overy LLP, 40 Bank Street, London E14 5NR

SMITH, Iain; MSP; s of William Smith, and Jane Allison, *née* Farmer; *b* 1 May 1960; *Educ* Bell Baxter HS Cupar, Univ of Newcastle upon Tyne (BA); *Career* ldr of opposition and Lib Dem Gp Fife Regnl Cncl 1986–99 (cncllr 1982–99); MSP (Lib Dem) NE Fife 1999–; Scot Parl: dep min for Parl 1999–2000, memb Local Govt Ctee 2000–03, memb Local Govt and Tport Ctee 2003–05, convenor Procedures Ctee 2003–05, convenor Educn Ctee 2005–; Scot Lib Dem spokesperson: local govt 2000–03, local govt and tport 2003–05, Europe and external rels 2005–; *Recreations* sport (mainly football and cricket), cinema, travel, reading; *Style*— Iain Smith, MSP; ✉ The Scottish Parliament, Edinburgh EH99 1SP (tel 0131 348 5817, fax 0131 348 8962, e-mail iain.smith@msp.scottish.parliament.uk); Constituency Office, 16 Millgate, Cupar, Fife KY15 5EG (tel 01334 656361, fax 01334 654045, website www.iainsmith.org)

SMITH, Iain Alastair Robertson; s of Nathaniel Lawrence Albert Smith, and Anne Cameron, *née* Urquhart; *Educ* Jordanhill Coll Sch, London Film Sch; *Career* film prodr; prodr My Childhood (BFI), fndr prodn co (with Jon Schorstein) working on TV commercials, documentaries, children's feature films and low budget dramas; prodn mangr Deathwatch 1978, unit location mangr Chariots of Fire 1979; line prodr: Local Hero, The Killing Fields, The Mission; prodr: The Frog Prince, Seven Years in Tibet, Entrapment; fndr Applecross Productions 1987; co-prodr: Hearts of Fire, Killing Dad, City of Joy, Mary Reilly, The Fifth Element; exec prodr: 1492 - Conquest of Paradise, Spy Game, Cold Mountain; prodr: Alexander, The Fountain, Children of Men; dir Children's Film and TV Fndn, vice-pres Prodn Guild of GB; dep chm: Br Film Advsy Gp, Br Film Cmmn; founding memb Scottish Film Trg Tst, memb: Br Screen Advsy Cncl and Skillset, Bd UK Film Cncl, Bd Scottish Screen, BAFTA, BFI; former memb: Scottish Film Cncl, Scottish Film Prodn Fund, Trade Ctee BFTPA, Trade Ctee AIP, Trade Ctee PACT; former govr Nat Film and TV Sch; *Recreations* reading, theatre, cinema, Scottish painting, walking, philosophy, travel; *Clubs* Groucho, Glasgow Art; *Style*— Iain Smith, Esq; ✉ c/o Sandra Marsh, Marsh Management, 9150 Wilshire Boulevard, Beverly Hills, CA 90212, USA (tel 00 1 310 285 0303, fax 00 1 310 285 0218)

SMITH, Ian Anderson; s of Sidney Victor Smith, and Mary, *née* Anderson; *b* 13 June 1948, Edinburgh; *Educ* London Business Sch (Sr Exec Prog), Inst of Electrical Engineers (HNC); *m* 18 July 1970, Jennifer Margaret, *née* Chrisp; 2 s (Robert Duncan b 29 July 1977, Andrew Douglas b 11 Dec 1981); *Career* customer service dir Digital UK, Ireland and Middle East 1987–90, dir European office Digital USA 1990–91, dir business ptnrs Digital Equipment Corp 1991–94, md customer service BT UK 1994–99, regnl sr vice-pres and md Oracle Corporation Ltd UK, Ireland, Israel and South Africa; pres Inst Customer Service, chair Leadership & Mgmnt Advsy Panel; memb Bd: Specialist Schs and Acads Tst (SSAT), London Skills and Educn Bd, Business in the Community; CITP, FIET, FBCS; *Recreations* football, rugby; *Style*— Ian Smith, Esq; ✉ Oracle Corporation UK Ltd, 510 Oracle Parkway, Thames Valley Park, Reading, Berkshire RG6 1RA (tel 0118 924 3566, fax 0118 924 3710, e-mail ian.smith@oracle.com)

SMITH, Prof Ian Edward; s of David N Smith, of Dundee, and Netty T, *née* Millar; *b* 16 May 1946; *Educ* Dundee HS, Univ of Edinburgh (Bsc, MB ChB, MD, Ettles scholar, Leslie Gold medal), Univ of Illinois (Carnegie scholar), Harvard Univ; *m* 1978, Suzanne D, *née* Mackey; 3 da (Emily b 31 Oct 1979, Rebecca b 24 March 1982, Katy b 12 Dec 1984); *Career* Edinburgh Royal Infirmary: house physician 1971–72, house surgn 1972, SHO Dept of Med 1972–73, med registrar Med Professorial Unit Royal Marsden Hosp 1974–75, Royal Marsden res fell Dept of Med and Biophysics Inst of Cancer Research 1975–76, UICC travelling fell Sidney Farber Cancer Inst Harvard Med Sch 1976–77, lectr in med Inst of Cancer Research and hon sr med registrar Royal Marsden Hosp 1977–78, conslt med oncologist Royal Marsden Hosp 1978–2000, med dir Royal Marsden Hosp 2000–, prof of cancer med Inst of Cancer Research 2000–; invited lectrs worldwide on various aspects of lung and breast cancer treatment and biology; chm MRC Lung Cancer Working Party 1997, head Section of Med Inst of Cancer Research 1991– (hon sr lectr 1979–); chm: Assoc of Cancer Physicians 1996–, Sub-Ctee UK Coordinating Ctee on Cancer Research, Specialist Advsy Ctee on Med Oncology RCP; pres Euro Winter Oncology Conf 1997–98; former pres Edinburgh Royal Med Soc; memb: American Soc of Clinical Oncology 1980, Br Assoc for Cancer Research 1981, Br Assoc for Cancer Physicians 1982, Br Breast Gp 1982, Euro Soc of Med Oncology 1986, Br Oncological Assoc 1986; FRCP Edin 1986, FRCP 1988; *Books* Autologous Bone Marrow Transplantation in Solid Tumours (jt ed, 1984), Medical Management of Breast Cancer (jt ed, 1991); author of over 300 pubns on breast cancer, lung cancer and cancer biology; *Recreations* skiing, outdoors, reading; *Style*— Prof Ian Smith; ✉ Royal Marsden Hospital, Fulham Road, London SW3 6JJ (tel 020 7808 2751, fax 020 7352 5441, e-mail ian.smith@rmh.nhs.uk)

SMITH, Prof Ian Moffat; s of John Smith (d 1981), and Elizabeth, *née* Martin (d 1995); *b* 29 April 1940; *Educ* Glasgow HS, Univ of Glasgow (BSc, PhD), Univ of Calif (MS), Victoria Univ of Manchester (DSc); *m* 1979, Janet, *née* Bairstow; 1 da (Catherine b 1981); *Career* Victoria Univ of Manchester (now Univ of Manchester): lectr 1967–73, sr lectr 1973–78, reader 1978–84, prof 1984–; FREng 1998, FICE 1984 (MICE 1972); *Publications* author of numerous articles in learned jls; *Recreations* gardening, golf; *Style*— Prof Ian Smith, FREng

SMITH, Ian Richard; *b* 22 January 1954; *Educ* Univ of Oxford (MA), Univ of Hull (PhD), Harvard Business Sch (MBA); *Career* early career Royal Dutch/Shell Group of Cos, md Monitor Co Europe until 1998; Exel plc: gp commercial dir Ocean Gp plc (subsequently merged with Exel) 1998, memb Exec Bd 2001, ceo consumer, retail and health (Europe) until 2003, ceo EMEA 2003–04; chief exec: General Healthcare Gp 2004–07, Taylor Woodrow plc 2007–; non-exec dir Galiform plc (formerly MFI Furniture Gp plc); memb Competitiveness Cncl, advsr to govt on industrial policy; *Style*— Ian Smith, Esq

SMITH, Dr Ian Robertson; s of Robert Smith (d 1988), and Mary Elizabeth Boyd, *née* Loudon (d 1951); *b* 1 August 1943; *Educ* Paisley GS, Univ of Glasgow (MB ChB); *m* 1968, Margaret Foster, da of Provost Harry Clunie (d 1993); 1 da (Angela Elizabeth b 9 Nov 1969), 1 s (Michael Stuart b 31 July 1971); *Career* house physician Paisley Infirmary 1968–69, house surgn Inverness Royal Infirmary 1969, SHO in obstetrics Inverness Raigmore 1969–70, GP Inverness 1970–2006; chm Ness DOC (GP Cooperative) 1996–98 (dir 1998–2001); dir Highland Hospice 1998–2005; gen practice trainer 1986–95, assoc advsr in gen practice 1987–92; memb Highland Health Bd Gp Educn Ctee 1978–2001; memb: BMA 1970, Highland Med Soc 1970 (pres 1994–95); FRCGP 1991 (N of Scotland Faculty: hon sec 1975–87, chm 1991–93, provost 2003–); *Recreations* medical advisor Inverness Caledonian Thistle FC and Scottish Football Assoc; *Clubs* Nairn Golf, Torness Curling; *Style*— Dr Ian Smith; ✉ Dromard, 43 Midmills Road, Inverness IV2 3NZ (tel 01463 236741)

SMITH, Prof Ian William Murison; s of Dr William Murison Smith (d 1981), and Margaret Moir, *née* Forrest; *b* 15 June 1937; *Educ* Giggleswick Sch, Christ's Coll Cambridge (MA, PhD); *m* 25 March 1961, Susan, da of Dr John E Morrish; 2 s (Fraser b 5 March 1967, Andrew b 28 Aug 1968), 2 da (Katie b 11 Jan 1972, Tracey b 5 Aug 1973); *Career* Christ's Coll Cambridge: research fell 1963–66, staff fell and lectr 1966–85, asst to sr tutor 1968–69, full tutor 1969–76, dir of studies in nat sci 1972–85, dir of studies in chemistry 1982–85, fell commoner 2002–; postdoctoral fell Dept of Chemistry Univ of Toronto 1964–65; Univ of Cambridge: ICI research fell Dept of Physical Chemistry 1965–66, univ demonstrator in Physical Chemistry 1966–71, univ lectr in Physical Chemistry 1971–85, sr res fell 2002–; Univ of Calif: visiting scientist Dept of Chemistry 1972, visiting fell NATO sr scientist 1980; Univ of Birmingham: prof of chemistry 1985–91, head of Sch of Chemistry 1989–93, Mason chair of chemistry 1991–2002, emeritus prof 2002–; visiting prof Univ of Rennes 1999, visiting fell Univ of Colorado 2000; pres Faraday Div RSC 2001–03; *Awards* RSC: special award in reaction kinetics 1982, Tilden Medal and lectureship 1983–84, Polanyi Medal 1990, Liversidge lectureship 2001–02, EU Descartes Prize 2000, Jost Memorial Lectures Germany 2003; FRSC 1985, FRS 1995; *Publications* Kinetics and Dynamics of Gas Reactions (1980), over 260 papers in scientific lit; two edited books; *Recreations* family, (occasional) golf and tennis, theatre, gardening 'under instruction'; *Style*— Prof Ian Smith, FRS; ✉ University Chemical Laboratories, Lensfield Road, Cambridge CB2 1EW (tel 01223 357456, fax 01223 336362, e-mail iwms2@cam.ac.uk or e-mail i.w.m.smith@bham.ac.uk)

SMITH, Ivo; s of Guy Sydney Smith (d 1972), of Market Rasen, Lincs, and Florence Maud, *née* Titmarsh (d 1981); *b* 31 May 1931; *Educ* De Aston GS Market Rasen, Jesus Coll Cambridge (MA, MChir), St Mary's Hosp Med Sch Univ of London; *m* 17 Feb 1962, Janet, da of George James Twyman (d 1936), of Deal, Kent; 1 da (Mary b 1965), 2 s (Robin b 1966, Simon b 1969); *Career* Nat Serv RAF (Educn Branch) 1950–51; conslt surgn, lectr and author on surgery of the breast and the breast in art; med chm Pension Appeals Tbnls; Freeman City of London 1965, Liveryman Worshipful Soc of Apothecaries 1964; FRCS; *Recreations* my family, fishing; *Style*— Ivo Smith, Esq; ✉ 229 Princes Gardens, London W3 0LU (tel 020 8992 0939)

SMITH, Prof Ivor Ramsay; s of Howard Smith (d 1966), of Birmingham, and Elsie Emily, *née* Underhill (d 1980); *b* 8 October 1929; *Educ* Univ of Bristol (BSc, PhD, DSc); *m* 3 Jan 1962, Pamela Mary, da of Alfred Voake (d 1976), of Birmingham; 3 s (Laurence David b 12 May 1963, Andrew Paul b 25 June 1965, Michael Jonathan b 8 Nov 1968); *Career* design and devpt engr GEC Birmingham 1956–59, reader (also lectr and sr lectr) Univ of Birmingham 1959–74; Loughborough Univ: prof of electrical power engrg 1974–, head Dept of Electronic and Electrical Engrg 1980–90, dean of engrg 1983–86, pro-vice-chllr 1987–91; CEng 1974, FIEE 1974, FREng 1988; *Publications* author/co-author of over 350 pubns (incl 2 books) in the areas of electrical machine control and the production, conditioning and use of high voltage and high current pulses of electrical energy; *Recreations* gardening, walking, reading; *Style*— Prof Ivor Smith, FREng; ✉ 83 Nanpantan Road, Loughborough, Leicestershire LE11 3ST; Department of Electronic and Electrical Engineering, Loughborough University, Leicestershire LE11 3TU (tel 01509 227005, fax 01509 227053, e-mail i.r.smith@lboro.ac.uk)

SMITH, Jack; s of John Edward Smith (d 1984), and Laura Amanda, *née* Booth (d 1949); *b* 18 June 1928; *Educ* Netheredge GS Sheffield, Sheffield Coll of Art, St Martins Sch of Art, RCA (ARCA); *m* 23 June 1956, Susan, da of Brig Gen Hugh Marjoribanks Craigie Halkett (d 1951); *Career* Nat Serv RAF 1946–48; artist; exhibitions: Beaux Arts Gallery London 1952–58, Catherine Viviano Gallery NY 1958, 1962 and 1963, Whitechapel Gallery 1959 and 1971, Matthiesen Gallery 1960 and 1963, Grosvenor Gallery 1965, Marlborough Fine Art 1968, Fischer Fine Art 1981 and 1983, 1983, Angela Flowers Gallery 1990, 1991, 1992, 1996, 2000, 2003 and 2007; work shown: Venice Biennale 1956, Br Painting Madrid 1983 et al; work in permanent collections incl: Tate Gallery, Arts Cncl, Contemporary Art Soc, Br Cncl; subject of monograph Jacksmith by Norbert Lynton; *Style*— Jack Smith, Esq; ✉ 29 Seafield Road, Hove, East Sussex BN3 2TP (tel 01273 738 312)

SMITH, Jacqueline Jill (Jacqui); PC (2003), MP; da of Michael Smith, and Jill, *née* Burley; *b* 3 November 1962; *Educ* Dyson Perrins HS Malvern, Hertford Coll Oxford (BA), Worcester Coll of HE (PGCE); *m* Richard Timney; 2 s (James b 28 Aug 1993, Michael b 3 June 1998); *Career* teacher 1986–97, MP (Lab) Redditch 1997–; Parly under sec of state for school standards 1999–2001, min of state for mental health and social care 2001–03, min of state for industry and the regions and dep min for women and equality 2003–05, min of state for school standards 2005–06, Govt chief whip and Parly sec to the Treasy 2006–07, sec of state Home Office 2007–; *Recreations* family, football; *Style*— The Rt Hon Jacqui Smith, MP; ✉ House of Commons, London SW1A 0AA (tel 020 7219 3000)

SMITH, Prof James Cuthbert (Jim); s of Leslie Cuthbert Smith (d 2000), of Pinner, Middx, and Freda Sarah, *née* Wragg; *b* 31 December 1954; *Educ* Latymer Upper Sch, Christ's Coll Cambridge (MA, Frank Smart prize in zoology), Univ of London (PhD); *m* 22 Sept 1979, Fiona Mary, da of David Mackie Watt (d 2000); 2 s (Angus James MacDougall b 15 May 1994, Gavin Robert Benedict b 3 May 2002), 1 da (Kirsty Flora Elizabeth (twin) b 3 May 2002); *Career* NATO postdoctoral fell Sidney Farber Cancer Inst and Harvard Med Sch 1979–81; ICRF postdoctoral fell 1981–84; Nat Inst for Med Research: memb scientific staff 1984, sr scientist 1990, head Div of Developmental Biology 1991–2000, head Genes and Cellular Controls Gp 1997–2000; chm and John Humphrey Plummer prof of developmental biology Wellcome Tst/Cancer Research UK Gurdon Inst Cambridge 2001– (chm designate 2000–01), scientific fell Zoological Soc, Wellcome visiting prof 1991–92, int res scholar Howard Hughes Med Inst 1993–98; ed-in-chief Development; author of numerous pubns and articles in scientific jls; chm British Soc for Developmental Biology 1994–99; memb: EMBO 1992 (medal 1993), Academia Europaea 2000; Scientific Medal Zoological Soc 1989, Otto Mangold Prize German Soc for Developmental Biology 1991, Feldberg Fndn Award 2000, William Bate Harvey Prize 2001; FRS 1993, FIBiol 1997, FMedSci 1998; *Recreations* reading, family, cycling, running; *Style*— Prof Jim Smith, FRS; ✉ Wellcome Trust/Cancer Research UK Gurdon Institute, Tennis Court Road, Cambridge CB2 1QN (tel 01223 334132, fax 01223 334134, e-mail jim@gurdon.cam.ac.uk)

SMITH, James Edward; s of James Joseph Smith, of Liverpool, and Dorothy, *née* Roberts; *b* 31 March 1950; *Educ* Univ of Liverpool (BA, Duke of Edinburgh Gold award), Liverpool Univ Business Sch (Post Grad Degree in Mktg), Inst of Mktg (Dip MInstM); *m* 1979, Celia Margaret, da of John Nairm; 2 da (Emma Lindsey b 25 Sept 1980, Rebecca Caroline b 20 July 1982); *Career* articled clerk Harwood Banner & Co 1968–71, mktg mangr Mobil Oil 1971–73, student 1973–74, mktg mangr Lonrho 1974–76, mktg dir rising to md Graham Poulter Group 1976–85, client servs dir J Walter Thompson 1988–90 (bd dir 1985–88); chm: JWT Group Manchester until 1996, chm Conquest Creative Services; md Clear Marketing Communications Ltd (formerly Nairn Smith Partnership Ltd); MInstM; *Recreations* music, wine, skiing, basketball (10 caps England Youth Int), travel; *Clubs* Young Presidents' Organisation; *Style*— James Smith, Esq

SMITH, Jan Eileen; da of Harold Douglas Smith (decd), of Morecambe, and Lena, *née* Barrett; *b* 5 April 1947; *Educ* Casterton Sch Kirkby Lonsdale, Univ Coll of Rhodesia Salisbury (BA London); *Career* Int Div Midland Bank plc London 1970–79, TSB Bank 1980–86, Lloyds Bank plc 1986–88, mktg dir First Direct 1989–90, dir of network mktg TSB Bank plc 1990–92; mktg dir Mazda Cars (UK) Ltd 1992–95, gp strategic dir RAC 1995–98, md The Virtual Co Ltd 1998–; currently non-exec dir: Royal Mint, Govt Actuary's Dept, Saffron Building Soc, Disposal Servs Agency MOD; winner Product Excellence Award Mktg Soc 1990; memb Mktg Soc; MInstD, FIDM; *Recreations* motor racing, classic car rallying, reading, yoga; *Style*— Miss Jan E Smith

SMITH, Rt Hon Lady Justice; Rt Hon Dame Janet Hilary (Dame Janet Mathieson); DBE (1992), PC (2002); da of Alexander Roe Holt (d 1970), and Margaret Holt, *née* Birchall (d 1991); *b* 29 November 1940; *Educ* Bolton Sch; *m* 1, 6 June 1959 (m dis 1982), Edward Stuart Smith, s of Edward Austin Carruthers Smith (d 1990); 2 s (Richard b 1959, Alasdair b 1963), 1 da (Rachel b 1962); m 2, 12 Oct 1984, Robin Edward Alexander Mathieson, s of Alexander John Mathieson, MC (d 1974), of Yoxall, Staffs; *Career* called to the Bar Lincoln's Inn 1972; QC 1986, recorder of the Crown Court 1988, memb Criminal Injuries Compensation Bd 1988–92, judge of the High Court of Justice (Queen's Bench Div) 1992–2002, judge Employment Appeal Tbnl 1994–2002, presiding judge (NE Circuit) 1995–98, Lord Justice of Appeal 2002–; pres Cncl of the Inns of Court 2006–; chm: Civil Ctee Judicial Studies Bd 2000–04, Security Vetting Appeals Panel 2000–, Shipman Inquiry 2001–05; chllr Manchester Metropolitan Univ 2003–; *Style*— The Rt Hon Lady Justice Smith, DBE; ✉ Royal Courts of Justice, Strand, London WC2A 2LL

SMITH, Janice Ann; da of Frank Charles Henry Smith, MBE, of Tunbridge Wells, Kent, and Mary Elizabeth, *née* Bridges (d 1989); *b* 24 March 1960, Chiswick, London; *Educ* Tunbridge Wells Girls' GS, Univ of Leeds (LLB), Guildford Coll of Law; *m* 9 March 1996, Rev Robert John Dando; *Career* admitted slr; specialises in clinical negligence cases and risk mgmnt; Herbert Smith 1983–86, Beckman & Beckman 1987–89, Capsticks 1990– (ptnr 1991–); assoc non-exec dir Milton Keynes Gen NHS Tst, memb Clinical Negligence and Serious Injury Ctee Civil Justice Cncl; vice-pres London Dist Boys' Brigade, chair Baptist World Congress Ctee; memb Law Soc 1985; *Recreations* theatre, good food, shopping; *Style*— Miss Janice Smith; ✉ Capsticks, 77–83 Upper Richmond Road, London SW15 2TT (tel 020 8780 4712, e-mail jsmith@capsticks.co.uk)

SMITH, Joan Alison; da of Alan Smith (d 1985), and Ann Anita, *née* Coltman; *b* 27 August 1953; *Educ* Girls GS Stevenage, HS for Girls Basingstoke, Univ of Reading (BA); *Career* journalist: Evening Gazette Blackpool 1976–78, Piccadilly Radio Manchester 1978–79, Sunday Times 1979–84; freelance writer 1984–; chair Writers in Prison Ctee English Pen 2000–04; associate prof Sch of Communications and Multi-Media Edith Cowan Univ WA 2002–05; memb FCO Freedom of Expression Panel 2002–04; hon assoc Nat Secular Soc; FRSA; *Books* Clouds of Deceit (1985), A Masculine Ending (1987), Why Aren't They Screaming? (1988), Misogynies (1989), Don't Leave Me This Way (1990), Femmes de Siècle (ed, 1992), What Men Say (1993), Full Stop (1995), Hungry For You: From Cannibalism to Seduction - A Book of Food (1996), Different For Girls: How Culture Creates Women (1997), Moralities: Sex, Money and Power in the 21st Century (2001), What Will Survive (2007); *Style*— Ms Joan Smith; ✉ c/o William Morris Agency (UK) Limited, 52–53 Poland Street, London W1F 7LX

SMITH, (Edward Ernest) John; s of Ernest Frederick Smith, DCM, of Chiswick, London, and Elizabeth, *née* Reilly; *b* 13 August 1950; *Educ* Latymer Upper Sch London, Emmanuel Coll Cambridge (MA, MD, BChir), St Thomas' Hosp Med Sch London; *m* 23 April 1984, Muriel Susan, da of Daniel Shannon, of Ayr; 2 da (Susan b 1985, Katherine b 1987), 1 s (David b 1989); *Career* conslt cardiothoracic surgn St George's Hosp London and Royal Surrey Co Hosp Guildford; memb BMA 1974; FRCS 1978; *Recreations* opera, golf, skiing; *Clubs* London Rowing, Royal Wimbledon Golf; *Style*— John Smith, Esq; ✉ Homewood, 4A Drax Avenue, Wimbledon SW20 0EH (tel 020 8946 1893, fax 020 8946 3130, e-mail eejmss@supanet.com); St Anthony's Hospital, North Cheam SM3 9DW (tel 01243 869940)

SMITH, John; MP; s of John Henry Smith, and Mary Margaret, *née* Collins; *b* 17 March 1951; *m* Kathleen, *née* Mulvaney; 1 da (Melanie Jayne b 17 Sept 1971), 2 s (Nathan John b 4 Jan 1974, Theo Anthony b 14 Sept 1979); *Career* with RAF 1968–72, chm Wales Lab Pty 1988–89; MP (Lab) Vale of Glamorgan 1989–92 (by-election) and 1997–; PPS to: Dep Ldr Lab Pty 1989–92, Min of State for Armed Forces 1997–98, Min of Tport 1998–; chm: All-Pty Gp on DVT Awareness, Lab Parly Def Ctee; memb North Atlantic Assembly 1997–; chm Wales Anti-Apartheid Movement 1987–95; *Style*— John Smith, Esq, MP; ✉ House of Commons, London SW1A 0AA (tel 020 7219 3000); tel 01446 743769

SMITH, John Allan Raymond; s of Alexander MacIntyre Smith (d 1979), of Edinburgh, and Evelyn Joyce, *née* Duthie (d 1988); *b* 24 November 1942; *Educ* Boroughmuir Sch Edinburgh, Univ of Edinburgh (MB, ChB), Univ of Aberdeen (PhD); *Family* 3 da (Jane b 1966, Sheri b 1970, Sara b 1975), 2 s (Richard b 1967, Michael b 1968); m 18 April 1979, Valerie, da of James Fullalove (d 1988), of Eaglescliffe; *Career* house offr Royal Infirmary Edinburgh 1966–67, Dept of Surgery Univ of Aberdeen 1974–76, sr surgical registrar Aberdeen Teaching Hosp 1976–78, sr lectr in surgery Univ of Sheffield and hon conslt surgn Royal Hallamshire Hosp 1978–85, conslt surgn Northern Gen Hosp Sheffield 1985–; contrib of numerous chapters in textbooks; FRCS (Eng), FRSCEd 1972 (pres 2003–); *Books* Pyes Surgical Handicraft: Complications in Surgery; *Style*— John A R Smith, Esq; ✉ Northern General Hospital, Herries Road, Sheffield S5 7AU (tel 0114 271 4969)

SMITH, John Barry; s of Kenneth William Smith, and Elsie, *née* Jackson; *Educ* Derby Shelton Sch, S London Coll, Harvard Business Sch; *Career* audit clerk Bocock Bew Chartered Accountants 1973–75; BR Gp Commercial Subsidiaries: mgmnt trainee 1975–81, fin manager and head customer serv Seaspeed Hovercraft 1981–83; head of insurance rising to corp fin manager BR Board 1983–89; BBC: gp chief accountant 1989–92, fin controller Network TV 1992–96, dep fin dir 1996–97, dir of fin 1997–2000, dir of fin, property and business affrs then chief operating offr 2000–04, currently chief exec BBC Worldwide; non-exec dir Severn Trent 2003–; former memb: Accounting Standards Bd, Public Services Productivity Panel HM Treasy, 100 Gp of Fin Dirs; dir UK Enterprise Advsy Bd Zurich Fin Services until 2001; *Recreations* country pursuits, opera, cinema, sports cars, skiing, sailing; *Style*— John Smith, Esq; ✉ BBC Worldwide, 80 Wood Lane, London W12 0TT (tel 020 8433 3533, mobile 07850 717762, fax 020 8433 2953, e-mail john.smith.01@bbc.co.uk)

SMITH, John William; s of William Stanley Smith, of Bromley, Kent (d 1981), and Stella, *née* Etherington (d 1998); *b* 14 January 1945, Bromley, Kent; *Educ* Univ of Newcastle upon Tyne (BA), LSE (MScEcon); *m* 15 Dec 1978, Yvonne, *née* Lukey; 2 da (Alice Lukey-Smith b 14 Nov 1979, Sara Lukey-Smith b 9 March 1983); *Career* Dept of Environment London 1977–90 (posts incl sr economic advsr Local Govt Finance, head Water Quality Div and head Waste Mgmnt Div), dir of regnl servs then dir of regulation Anglian Water Services Ltd 1990–97, dir of regulation & govt Railtrack plc 1997–2002, ind conslt 2003 and 2006–, princ conslt Indepen Consulting Ltd 2004–06 (assoc 2006–); non-exec memb Steering Bd Marine & Fisheries Agency 2006–, memb Reporting Panel and Utilities Panel Competition Cmmn 2005–; tstee and hon treas Groundwork N London; MInstD 2002; *Publications* Structure of the Water Industry in England: Does It Remain Fit for Purpose? (co-author DEFRA and OFWAT report, 2003); various articles on UK utility regulation; *Recreations* choral singing, country walking, travel, films, theatre; *Style*— John Smith, Esq

SMITH, Jon; s of Michael Smith, of Toronto, Canada, and Rosemary, *née* Leavey (d 1968); *Educ* Orange Hill GS, Kingsway Coll of FE; *m* 1, Lee (decd); m 2, 20 July 1986, Janine, da of Martin Jaffe (d 1992), and Bernice Jaffe; 2 s (Ross Alexander b 10 Nov 1988, Scott b 12 April 1991); *Career* ptnr Anglo House Estates 1980–86, owner Green Light prodn co (sold 1981), fndr First Artist Corp plc 1986 (currently ceo); chief exec London Monarchs 1990s; patron Br Stammering Assoc, tstee Lee Smith Research Fndn, former memb Bd Inst of Child Health; FInstD 1987; *Recreations* motor racing, football, paying school fees; *Style*— Jon Smith, Esq; ✉ First Artist Corporation plc, First Artist House, 87 Wembley Hill Road, Middlesex HA9 8BU (tel 020 8900 1818, fax 020 8903 2964, e-mail jons@firstartist.com)

SMITH, Sir Joseph William Grenville; kt (1991); s of Douglas Ralph Smith (d 1987), of Cardiff, and Hannah Leticia Margaret, *née* Leonard (d 1968); *b* 14 November 1930; *Educ* Cathays HS for Boys Cardiff, Welsh Nat Sch of Med (MB BCh), Univ of London, Univ of Wales (MD); *m* 3 Aug 1954, Nira Jean, da of Oliver Davies (d 1964), of Burry Port; 1 s (Jonathan b 1955); *Career* Nat Serv RAF 1954–56, Flying Offr Med Branch (later Flt Lt), MO RAF SYLT, 2 TAF BAOR; lectr (later sr lectr) bacteriology and immunology LSHTM 1960–65, conslt clinical bacteriologist Radcliffe Infirmary Oxford 1965–69, head of bacteriology Wellcome Res Laboratories 1969, princ in gen practice Islington 1970–71, dep dir epidemiological res lab Public Health Laboratory Serv 1971–76; dir: Nat Inst for Biological Standards and Control 1976–85, Public Health Laboratory Serv of England and Wales 1985–92; special prof Univ of Nottingham 1989–94; chm: Tropical Med Research Bd MRC 1989–91, Bd of Mgmnt LSHTM 1995–97, WHO Euro Region Cmmn 1996–2006; Global Cmmn for the Certification of Poliomyelitis Eradication 2001–03; memb: Br Pharmacopoea Cmmn 1976–85, Jt Ctee on Vaccination and Immunisation 1976–87, Ctee on Safety of Meds 1978–87 (chm Biologicals Sub-Ctee 1981–87), Cncl Royal Coll of Pathologists 1988–90, MRC 1988–92, MAFF Advsy Gp on Rabies Quarantine 1997–98; FRCPath 1975, FFPHM 1976, FRCP 1987; *Books* Tetanus (jtly, 1969); *Style*— Sir Joseph Smith; ✉ 95 Lofting Road, London N1 1JF

SMITH, Julian Arthur Vaughan; s of Neil Lindsey Vaughan Smith, of Appledore, Kent, and Frances Marguerite Katharine, *née* Coleridge; *b* 7 February 1969, London; *Educ* Charterhouse (fndn and sr fndn scholar), Peterhouse Cambridge (Lord North scholar, BA), Coll of Law London; *m* 10 Sept 1994, Suzanne Elaine, *née* Hearne; 2 da (Emma Frances Vaughan b 18 Aug 1998, Katherine Grace Vaughan b 18 Aug 1998); *Career* admitted slr 1994; Farrer & Co slrs: trainee 1992–94, asst slr Charities Team 1994–2000, ptnr 2000–, ldr Charity and Community Team 2004–; visiting lectr Centre for Charity Effectiveness Cass Business Sch; memb Advsy Bd European Assoc for Planned Giving; memb Advsy Ctee: Charinco, Charishare, Charishare Tobacco Restricted Common Investment Funds; tstee Carthusian Tst; memb: Law Soc 1994, Charity Law Assoc 1994 (currently memb Ctee); *Publications* The Charities Act 2000 (jntly); *Recreations* family and friends; *Style*— Julian Smith, Esq; ✉ Farrer & Co, 66 Lincoln's Inn Fields, London WC2A 3LH (tel 020 7242 2022, fax 020 7917 7408, e-mail jas@farrer.co.uk)

SMITH, Kate; da of Reginald Ernest Bayston, of Co Durham, and Mabel, *née* Jackson; *b* 8 May 1951; *Educ* Orpington Co Secdy Sch, Wilby Carr HS Doncaster, Doncaster Coll of Technol, Univ of Leeds (BA), Wine & Spirit Educn Tst (higher cert in wines & spirits, instructors cert in wines & spirits Dip pt A&B); *m* 14 Oct 1973, Richard Francis Smith, s of late William Henry Bernard Smith; 2 s (Giles Edward b 25 April 1983, Rupert James b 29 Aug 1995); *Career* asst mangr Restaurant and Banqueting Div Trust House Forte London 1974–75, lectr in food and beverages North Devon Coll 1976–77; Royal Garden Hotel London: project mangr Garden Cafe 1978, acting banqueting mangr 1978–80, promotions mangr 1980; sales and mktg dir Hyatt Carlton Tower London 1982, conslt Rank Hotels Ltd 1982–84, dir Smith Giddings Ltd (parent co of The Beetle & Wedge Hotel Moulsford-on-Thames Oxon); winner: Pub of the Year Award The Royal Oak 1985, Badoit Restaurant of the Year Award Beetle & Wedge 1991, Gonzalez Byass Customer Care Award Beetle & Wedge 1992, Good Hotel Guide César Award 1993, Hosts of the Year Egon Ronay Guide Beetle & Wedge 1995; Master Innholder until 1995, memb Académie Culinaire de France; *Recreations* skiing, theatre, interior design, wine and food; *Style*— Mrs Kate Smith; ✉ The Beetle & Wedge Hotel, Moulsford-on-Thames, Oxfordshire OX10 9JF (tel 01491 651381, fax 01491 651376)

SMITH, Prof Keith; s of Joseph Smith (d 1972), and Catherine Maria, *née* Carr (d 1985); *b* 9 January 1938; *Educ* Hyde Co GS, Univ of Hull (BA, PhD); *m* 29 July 1961, Muriel Doris, da of George Hyde (d 1988); 1 da (Fiona b 1966), 1 s (Matthew b 1968); *Career* tutor in geography Univ of Liverpool 1963–65, lectr in geography Univ of Durham 1965–70, prof of geography Univ of Strathclyde 1982–86 (sr lectr 1971–75, reader 1975–82); Univ of Stirling: prof of environmental science 1986–98, head Sch of Natural Sciences 1994–96, dean Faculty of Natural Sciences 1996–97, emeritus prof of environmental science 1998–;

FRSE 1988; *Books* Water in Britain (1972), Principles of Applied Climatology (1975), Human Adjustment to The Flood Hazard (1979), Environmental Hazards (1992, 4 edn 2004), Floods (with R C Ward, 1998); *Recreations* gardening, hill walking; *Style*— Prof Keith Smith, FRSE; ✉ 11 Grinnan Road, Braco, By Dunblane, Perthshire FK15 9RF (tel 01786 880359, e-mail kmds@btinternet.com); Department of Biological and Environmental Sciences, University of Stirling, Stirling FK9 4LA (tel 01786 467750, fax 01786 446896)

SMITH, Kenneth David; s of Percival Smith (d 1985), and Doris Lillian, *née* Townsend (d 2004); *b* 27 February 1944; *Educ* Beckenham Tech Sch, Beckenham Art Sch, SE London Tech Coll; *m* 1 (m dis 1993); 1 s, 2 da; m 2, 19 Nov 1993, Marilyn Susan, *née* Brittain; *Career* designer; Elsom Pack Roberts (chartered architects, and town planners) 1978–86, ptnr EPR Design Partnership 1985–89, md EPR Design Ltd 1988–92; KDS & Associates: md 1992–2003, chm 2004–; memb City Architecture Forum; Freeman City of London 1981; FCSD; *Recreations* art, theatre, music; *Style*— Kenneth Smith, Esq; ✉ 10 Edward Henry House, Cornwall Road, Waterloo, London SE1 8YF; KDS & Associates Ltd, 101 The Blackfriars Foundry, 156 Blackfriars Road, London SE1 8EN (tel 020 7721 7091, fax 020 7721 7093)

SMITH, Lawrence George Albert; s of Lawrence Cyril Smith (d 1966), of Worcs, and Ida Mildred Smith, *née* Moule (d 1970); *b* 17 December 1930; *Educ* King Charles I Sch Kidderminster, Univ of Birmingham (LLB); *m* 12 Nov 1955, Tess, da of Bertram Bishop (d 1957), of Worcs; 3 da (Sally b 1960, Rachel b 1963, Rebecca b 1968); *Career* Nat Serv Lt S Staffs Regt; BAOR 1955; admitted slr 1954; ptnr Thursfields 1964–92, NP 1977–, clerk Clare Witnell & Blount Charity 1973–91; pres Kidderminster and Dist C of C 1984–86, dep chm Kidderminster Cons Assoc 1971–73; assoc Inst of European Law Univ of Birmingham 1991–, dir West Mercia C of C and Industry Ltd 1992–95, memb Nat Cncl Assoc of British Cs of C 1993–95, govr Kidderminster Coll 1994–96; *Recreations* rugby football, gardening, rambling, politics, golf; *Style*— Lawrence Smith, Esq; ✉ Bracton House, 5 Westville Avenue, Kidderminster, Worcestershire DY11 6BZ (tel 01562 824806); Thursfields, 14 Church Street, Kidderminster, Worcestershire DY10 2AS (tel 01562 820575, fax 01562 66783)

SMITH, Dr Lindsay Frederick Paul; s of Frederick Jean Orlando Smith and Audrey Joyce Smith, of Yeovil, Somerset; *Educ* Univ of Bristol (BSc, MB ChB, MD), Univ of Western Ontario Canada (MClinSci); *m* 1990, Caroline Patricia, da of David Taylor; 4 s (William b 14 March 1992, James b 1 Oct 1993, Charles b 22 Feb 1996, Henry b 5 Jan 1998); *Career* princ in gen med practice Somerset 1988–; research fell Univ of Bristol 1988–94, RCGP research trg fell 1990–91, lectr Inst of Gen Practice Univ of Exeter 1995–96, hon conslt sr lectr Queen Mary & Westfield Coll London 1996–99; chair clinical network RCGP 1996–99; chm Assoc for Community Based Maternity Care 1995–2000; author of original research/academic papers in scientific jls; memb Editorial Bd Br Jl of Gen Practice 1997–; memb Health Technology Appraisal Ctee NICE 2003–; FRCP, FRCGP, FHEA; *Recreations* duplicate bridge; *Style*— Dr Lindsay Smith; ✉ ESReC, Westlake Surgery, West Coker, Somerset BA22 9AH (tel 01935 862624, fax 01935 862042, e-mail research@esrec.nhs.uk)

SMITH, Prof Lorraine Nancy; da of Geoffrey Leonard Millington, and Ida May, *née* Attfield; *b* 29 June 1949; *Educ* Univ of Ottawa (BScN), Univ of Manchester (MEd, PhD); *m* Christopher Murray, s of Herbert Murray Smith (d 1990); 1 s (Nicholas Geoffrey Murray b 13 Nov 1979), 1 da (Jennifer Eugenie b 17 Dec 1983); *Career* staff nurse 1971–75, sister 1975–76; lectr Dept of Nursing Studies Univ of Manchester 1976–90; Univ of Glasgow: prof 1990–, head of sch 1990–2001; chair RCN Research Soc (Scot) 1999–2005, chair Workgroup of Euro Nurse Researchers 2005–; memb: Members Advsy Bd MRC, Acute Healthcare Res Ctee 1991–94, UK Clinical Standards Advsy Gp 1994–99, Turning Point (Scotland) 1996, RCN (UK); memb Editorial Bd: Clinical Rehabilitation, Jl of Psychiatric and Mental Health Nursing; *Recreations* bridge, sailing, golf, skiing; *Clubs* S Caernarvonshire Yacht, Golff Abersoch; *Style*— Prof Lorraine N Smith; ✉ Nursing & Health Care, University of Glasgow, 59 Oakfield Avenue, Glasgow G12 8LW (tel 0141 330 5498, fax 0141 330 3539, e-mail l.n.smith@clinmed.gla.ac.uk)

SMITH, Dr Malcolm; s of Ralph Smith (d 1988), and Hilda, *née* Joseph (d 1998); *b* 11 March 1949, Mid Wales; *Educ* Univ of London (BSc), Univ of Kent and Tropical Products Inst London (PhD); *m* 25 Oct 2002, Vivien Conway; *Children* 2 da (Clare b 24 July 1975, Annabel b 7 Dec 1981), 1 s (Thomas b 24 May 1979); *Career* research mangr Unilever plc 1973–75; Nature Conservancy Cncl: asst regnl offr N Wales 1975–86, dep head Sci and Policy Unit Wales HQ 1986–89, head Sci and Policy Branch Wales HQ 1989–91; Countryside Cncl for Wales: chief ecologist 1991–95, dir of policy and sci 1995–98, sr dir and chief scientist 1998–2004; memb: Terrestrial and Freshwater Sciences Bd NERC 1999–2000, Welsh Consumers Cncl 2004–, Bd Environment Agency 2004– (memb with special responsibility for Wales); freelance writer on environment, wildlife, travel and sci 1982–; *Publications* numerous feature articles on environment, wildlife, heritage and travel in a range of UK and int pubns; *Recreations* gardening, bird watching, travel; *Style*— Dr Malcolm Smith

SMITH, Malcolm Bryan; s of Brian Frederick Smith, and Barbara Ruth Smith; *b* 7 December 1964; *Educ* Brisbane GS, Univ of Queensland, Yale Univ; *m* 4 April 1992, Dr Penelope Smith; *Career* architect; sr architect John Simpson Assocs Brisbane 1989–91, founding dir Integrated Urbanism Unit Arup; reviewer Cmmn for Architecture and the Built Environment; assoc: Royal Aust Inst of Architects 1987, Queensland Bd of Architects 1989; fell Royal Soc of Architects; *Recreations* golf, drawing, walking, sailing, skiing; *Style*— Malcolm Smith, Esq; ✉ Arup, 38 Fitzroy Square, London W1T 6EY (tel 020 7555 5555)

SMITH, Margaret; MSP; da of John Murray (d 1983), and May, *née* Rintoul; *Educ* Broughton HS, Univ of Edinburgh (MA); *m* 12 Nov 1983 (m dis 2003), Douglas Robert Smith; 1 s (Andrew b 12 June 1988), 1 da (Jennifer b 19 Dec 1991); civil partnership 31 March 2006, Suzanne Main; 3 step s (Joseph 10 Aug 1988, David b 13 May 1991, Michael b 7 Feb 1999); *Career* civil servant 1983–88; tour guide and freelance journalist 1988–90; voluntary sector organiser UNA; Lib Dem Constituency Organiser 1995–96, Local Authy Cncllr City of Edinburgh Cncl (Cramond Ward) 1995–99, MSP (Lib Dem) Edinburgh W 1999–; *Style*— Ms Margaret Smith, MSP; ✉ West Edinburgh Liberal Democrats, 3 Drumbrae Avenue, Edinburgh EH12 3TE (tel 0131 317 7292)

SMITH, Dame Margaret Natalie Cross (Maggie); DBE (1990, CBE 1970); da of Nathaniel Smith, and Margaret Little, *née* Hutton; *b* 28 December 1934; *Educ* Oxford HS for Girls, Oxford Playhouse Sch; *m* 1, 1967 (m dis 1975), Robert Stephens, actor (later Sir Robert Stephens; d 1995); 2 s (Christopher (actor under name of Chris Larkin), Toby); m 2, 1975, Beverley Cross (d 1998); *Career* actress; debut as Viola in Twelfth Night (OUDS) 1952, NY debut as comedienne in New Faces (Ethel Barrymore Theatre) 1956; dir United Br Artists 1982–; Hon DLitt: Univ of St Andrews 1971, Univ of London 1991, Univ of Cambridge 1994; Shakespeare Prize 1991, BAFTA Special Achievement Award 1993, Channel 4 Lifetime Achievement Award 1995; *Theatre* for Old Vic Co 1959–60 credits incl: The Double Dealer, As You Like it, Richard II, The Merry Wives of Windsor, What Every Woman Knows; NT credits incl: The Recruiting Officer 1963, Othello, The Master Builder, Hay Fever 1964, Much Ado About Nothing, Miss Julie 1965, A Bond Honoured 1966, The Beaux' Stratagem 1970 (also USA), Hedda Gabler 1970 (Evening Standard Best Actress Award), War Plays 1985, Coming in to Land 1986; at Festival Theatre Stratford Ontario: Antony and Cleopatra, The Way of the World, Measure for Measure, The Three Sisters 1976, A Midsummer Night's Dream, Richard II, The Guardsman, As You Like it, Hay Fever 1977, As You Like It, Macbeth, Private Lives 1978, Virginia, Much Ado About Nothing 1980; other credits incl: Share My Lettuce (Lyric Hammersmith) 1957, The Stepmother (St Martin's) 1958, Rhinoceros (Strand) 1960, Strip the Willow (Cambridge) 1960, The Rehearsal (Globe) 1961, The Private Ear and the Public Eye (Globe) 1962 (Evening Standard Drama Award Best Actress), Mary Mary (Queen's) 1963 (Variety Club of GB Best Actress of the Year), The Country Wife (Chichester) 1969, Design for Living (LA) 1971, Private Lives (Queen's) 1972 (also Globe 1973, NY 1975, Variety Club of GB Stage Actress Award 1972), Peter Pan (Coliseum) 1973, Snap (Vaudeville) 1974, Night and Day (Phoenix) 1979, Virginia (Haymarket) 1981 (Evening Standard Best Actress Award 1982), The Way of the World (Chichester and Haymarket) 1984 (Evening Standard Best Actress Award 1985), Interpreters (Queen's) 1985, Lettice and Lovage (Globe) 1987 (also NY 1990, Tony Award Best Leading Actress 1990), The Importance of Being Earnest (Aldwych) 1993, Three Tall Women (Wyndhams) 1994 and 1995 (Evening Standard Best Actress Award 1994), Talking Heads (Chichester) 1996 (also London 1997), A Delicate Balance (Haymarket) 1997, The Lady in the Van (Queen's) 1999, Breath of Life (Haymarket) 2002–03, Talking Heads (Aust and NZ tour) 2004, The Lady from Dubuque (Haymarket Theatre) 2007; *Television* incl: Bed Among the Lentils (as part of Alan Bennett's Talking Heads, BBC (RTS Award)) 1989, Memento Mori (BBC) 1992, Suddenly Last Summer (BBC) 1993, David Copperfield (BBC) 1999, All The King's Men (BBC) 1999, Capturing Mary 2007; *Film* The VIP's 1963, The Pumpkin Eater 1964, Young Cassidy 1965, Othello 1966, The Honey Pot 1967, Hot Millions 1968 (Variety Club of GB Award), The Prime of Miss Jean Brodie 1968 (Oscar, SFTA Award), Oh! What a Lovely War 1968, Love and Pain (and the Whole Damned Thing) 1973, Travels with my Aunt 1973, Murder by Death 1976, California Suite 1977 (Oscar), Death on the Nile 1978, Quartet 1981, Clash of the Titans 1981, Evil Under the Sun 1982, The Missionary 1982, A Private Function 1984 (BAFTA Award Best Actress 1985), The Loves of Lily 1985, A Room with a View 1986 (Variety Club of GB Award, BAFTA Award Best Actress 1986), The Lonely Passion of Judith Hearne 1989 (Evening Standard British Films Award 1988, BAFTA Award Best Film Actress 1988), Hook 1992, Sister Act 1992, The Secret Garden 1993, Richard III 1996, First Wives Club 1996, Washington Square 1998, Tea With Mussolini 1999, The Last September 2000, Harry Potter and the Philosopher's Stone 2001, Gosford Park 2001 (Oscar nomination for Best Supporting Actress 2002), Divine Secrets of the Ya-Ya Sisterhood 2002, Harry Potter and the Chamber of Secrets 2002, Harry Potter and the Prisoner of Azkaban 2004, My House in Umbria 2004, Ladies in Lavender 2004, Harry Potter and the Goblet of Fire 2005, Keeping Mum 2005, Becoming Jane 2007, Harry Potter and the Order of the Phoenix 2007; *Style*— Dame Maggie Smith, DBE; ✉ c/o 41 Warbeck Road, London W12 8NS

SMITH, Mark Aynsley; s of Frank Sidney Smith (d 1987), and Sheila Gertrude, *née* Cowin (d 1987); *b* 24 May 1939; *Educ* KCS Wimbledon; *m* 3 Oct 1964, Carol Ann, da of Harold Jones (d 1983); 1 s (Jeremy b 1973), 1 da (Melissa b 1975); *Career* chartered accountant Peat Marwick Mitchell & Co London 1958–66; SBC Warburg: joined 1966, dir 1971, vice-chm 1990–93, non-exec dir 1993–95; dir: The Laird Group plc 1993–2004, Bradford & Bingley Building Society 1994–2000, Renold plc 1994–2006, Bradford & Bingley plc 2000–04; Br Merchant Banking and Securities Houses Assoc: memb Corp Fin Ctee 1988–92, dep chm 1989–90, chm 1991–92; memb Take-Over Panel 1991–92; FCA 1973 (ACA 1963); *Recreations* golf, walking, collecting; *Style*— Mark Smith, Esq; ✉ 38 Meadway, Esher, Surrey KT10 9HF (tel 01372 462689, fax 01372 468595)

SMITH, Martin Gregory; s of Archibald Gregory Smith, OBE (d 1981), of St Albans, Herts, and Mary Eleanor Smith (d 1975); *Educ* St Albans Sch, St Edmund Hall Oxford (MA), Stanford Univ (MBA, AM Econ); *m* 2 Oct 1971, Elise Becket, da of late George Campbell Becket, of Lakeville, CT; 1 s (Jeremy b 28 Jan 1974), 1 da (Katie b 5 Aug 1975); *Career* asst brewer Arthur Guinness Son and Co Dublin Ltd 1964–69, engagement mangr McKinsey and Co Inc 1971–73, vice-pres and dir head of corp fin Citicorp Int Bank Ltd 1974–80, sr vice-pres and chm Bankers Trust International Ltd 1980–83; dir: Phoenix Securities Ltd 1983–97, Phoenix Partnership 1991–2000, Odgers, Ray & Berndtson plc; chm: Phoenix Fund Managers Ltd 1991–2000, DLJ European Investment Banking Gp 1997–2000, Amerindo Internet Fund plc 2000–06, GP Bullhound; dir New Star Asset Management Ltd; sr advsr: Bain Capital; memb Advsy Bd IDDAS Ltd; dir and chm Cncl of Advsrs Orchestra of the Age of Enlightenment; chm: ENO 2001–05, Bath Mozartfest; dep chm: South Bank Centre 1992–97, Science Museum; tstee: Wigmore Hall, IMS Prussia Cove, Becket Collection, Tetbury Music Festival, Ashmolean Museum (visitor), Royal Acad of Music, Glyndebourne Arts Tst; Hon FRAM; *Recreations* music, riding, sailing, skiing, golf; *Clubs* Brooks's, Garrick, Cape Cod Nat Golf, Minchinhampton Golf; *Style*— Martin Smith, Esq; ✉ New Star Asset Management Ltd, 1 Knightsbridge Green, London SW1X 7NE (tel 020 7225 9221, fax 020 7225 9321, e-mail mgsmith@newstaram.com)

SMITH, Martin Stephen; s of Cyril George Smith, of Ferring, W Sussex, and Irene Mildred, *née* Harrison; *b* 1 July 1952; *Educ* Purley GS, Fitzwilliam Coll Cambridge (MA); *m* 24 Feb 1979, Krystyna Maria, da of Josef Parkitny; 2 da (Louisa Aniela b 10 Nov 1982, Natalia Maria b 24 Sept 1985); *Career* freelance writer and actor 1974, account mangr Ogilvy Benson & Mather advtg 1976–78 (copywriter 1975–76), account supervisor Saatchi & Saatchi 1978–80, account dir TBWA 1980–82; Bartle Bogle Hegarty: fndr ptnr 1982–2000, chm Lexington Street (below-the-line gp) 1989, md 1996–98, dep-chm 1998–2000; chief exec Grey Worldwide London 2000–02, fndr ptnr Rapley Smith & Jones Ltd 2002, ind communication strategist 2003, fndr ptnr Grounds Morris Smith 2004, currently worldwide ceo The Law Firm; *Style*— Martin Smith, Esq; ✉ 19 Grand Avenue, London N10 3AY (e-mail martin@thelawfirmgroup.com)

SMITH, Maureen; *b* 30 July 1947; *m* 8 Nov 1978, Alan Lewis Sutherland; 1 da (Natasha b 1980); *Career* md: BBDO PR Ltd 1972 (dir 1971), Good Relations Ltd 1973; chief exec: Good Relations Group Ltd 1975, Good Relations Group plc; chm The Communication Group plc (PR consultancy); *Style*— Ms Maureen Smith; ✉ The Communication Group plc, 19 Buckingham Gate, London SW1E 6LB (tel 020 7630 1411, fax 020 7931 8010)

SMITH, Maxwell; TD (1967); *b* 19 December 1929; *Educ* Royal Liberty Sch Romford, Univ of London (BSc, DipEd); *m* 29 Sept 1956, Anne; 2 da (Helen (Mrs Notter) b 1962, Isobel (Mrs Smales) b 1965), 1 s (Duncan b 1970); *Career* RE TA 1951–67 (Maj 1964–67); South Bank Poly: head Dept of Estate Mgmnt 1970–77, dean of Faculty 1972–77, asst and dep dir 1977–86; co dir and mgmnt conslt 1986–, memb and vice-chm Corp Southwark Coll 1992–, chief exec Co of Chartered Surveyors Youth Trg Tst 1991–92; chm: CNAA Surveying Bd 1975–81, SERC Bldg Sub-Ctee 1980–86; memb Gen Cncl RICS 1975–86 (divnl pres 1977–78); memb Worshipful Co of Chartered Surveyors 1977; hon fell London South Bank Univ 1988; FRICS 1965 (ARICS 1951); *Books* Manual of British Standards in Building Construction and Specification (2 edn, 1987), South Bank Century (1992); *Recreations* walking, music, painting; *Style*— Maxwell Smith, Esq, TD; ✉ 50 Pickwick Road, Dulwich Village, London SE21 7JW (tel 020 7274 9041)

SMITH, Melvyn Kenneth (Mel); s of Kenneth Smith (d 1984), of Chiswick, London, and Vera Ellen Elizabeth, *née* Flemming; *b* 3 December 1952; *Educ* Latymer Upper Sch, New Coll Oxford; *m* 30 April 1988, Pamela, *née* Gay-Rees; *Career* actor, writer and director; dir: TalkBack, Midfield Films, Lucky Elliot; *Theatre* Charlie's Aunt 1983 (actor), The Gambler (author, actor and dir), Not In Front Of The Audience (actor and dir), Big in Brazil (dir), Summer With Monica (dir); asst dir Royal Court prodns: When Did You Last See My Mother, Nobody Knew They Were There, Dr Jekyll and Mr Hyde; assoc dir Crucible and Young Vic prodns: Carnation Gang, Old Times, My Fair Lady, Hitting

S

Town, Loot; *Television* comedy series incl: Not the Nine O'Clock News 1979–82, Alas Smith & Jones (with Griff Rhys Jones) 1984–, The World According to Smith & Jones 1986–87, Small Doses 1989, Colin's Sandwich, Smith & Jones 1991–; drama incl: Muck & Brass, Milner 1994; dir numerous TV commercials; *Film* Bloody Kids 1979, Babylon 1980, Bullshot 1983, Slayground 1983, National Lampoon's European Vacation II 1985, Restless Natives 1985, Number One 1985, Morons From Outer Space (author of screenplay) 1985, The Princess Bride 1987, The Wolves of Willoughby Chase 1988, Wilt 1989, The Tall Guy (dir) 1989, Lame Ducks 1991, Radioland Murders (dir) 1994, Bean (dir) 1997, High Heels and Low Lifes (dir) 2000, Blackball 2003; *Records* Bitter & Twisted, Scratch 'n' Sniff, Alas Smith & Jones, Not the Nine O'Clock News, Rockin' around the Christmas Tree (with Kim Wilde); *Awards* Emmy Award for Alas Smith & Jones, Br Comedy Top Entertainment Series Award for Smith & Jones 1991, Br Comedy Top Entertainment Performer (with Griff Rhys Jones) for Smith & Jones 1991; *Books* The Lavishly Tooled Smith & Jones (1986), Janet Lives With Mel and Griff (1988), Head to Head (1992); *Clubs* Groucho; *Style*— Mel Smith, Esq; ✉ c/o Talkback Management, 20–21 Newman Street, London W1P 3HB (tel 020 7861 8060, fax 020 7861 8061)

SMITH, (James David) Michael (Mike); s of William Smith (d 1988), and Elizabeth Mary, née Lewis (d 1996); b 24 September 1939; *Educ* Midsomer Norton GS, UCL (BSc); m 1974, Susan Sheridanne, da of David William Burges; 2 s (Guy Edward b 1977, Owen James b 1979); *Career* various positions in Chemicals and Carbon Dioxide Divs The Distillers' Co 1960–69; BTR plc: md BTR Silvertown Ltd 1973–76 (chemical plant business mangr 1969–72, dir and commercial mangr 1972–73), chief exec Industrial Products Gp 1976–79, dir BTR Industries Ltd (and chief exec various divs) 1979–87, exec dir Europe BTR plc 1988–95 (non-exec dir 1995–96); dir: Octopus Publishing Gp plc 1985–88, Bullough plc 1996–2003, Cobham plc 1996–2005, Terranova Food plc 1998–99, PZ Cussons plc 2000–; chm APV plc 1996–97 (dir 1995–97); *Recreations* rugby, golf, skiing, squash, reading, theatre, wine, music; *Style*— Mike Smith, Esq; ✉ Meadowcroft, Sterlings Field, Cookham Dean, Berkshire SL6 9PG (tel 01628 488108, fax 01628 488109, mobile 07831 621193, e-mail jdmsmith@aol.com)

SMITH, Most Rev Michael; see: Meath, Bishop of (RC)

SMITH, Michael Forbes; s of Forbes Weir Smith (d 2000), and Elizabeth, née Mackie (d 1972); b 4 June 1948, Aberdeen; *Educ* Aberdeen GS, Univ of Southampton (BSc); m 1986, Claire Helen, née Stubbs; 1 da (Amelia b 1989), 1 s (Alastair b 1992), 1 other da (Sabina b 1965); *Career* Bd of Trade 1966–68, cmmnd Gordon Highlanders 1971 (ret as Capt 1978); entered HM Dip Serv 1978, second sec FCO 1978–79, second later first sec and head of Chancery Addis Ababa 1979–83, political advsr to govr Port Stanley 1983–85, SE Asia Dept then FO spokesman FCO 1985–89, consul (commercial) Zürich 1990–94, head of press and public affrs Bonn 1994–99, dep high cmmr Islamabad 1999–2003, first resident ambass to Tajikistan 2002–04, ret; fndr Tempered and True Consultancy (dip skills devpt) 2004, advsr Gulf International Minerals Ltd 2004–06, DG Chartered Inst of Arbitrators 2006–; vice-pres St Thomas More PC Bonn 1996–99, memb Appeal Ctee and Church Cncl Farm St Church Mayfair 1986–90; chm Bonn Caledonian Soc 1995–99; contrib Piping Times; FRGS 1971, FRSA 1991, FSA Scot 1995; *Recreations* music, Scotland, sailing, field and winter sports, entertaining and conviviality; *Clubs* Army and Navy, Royal Northern and Univ (Aberdeen), Royal Findhorn Yacht; *Style*— Michael Forbes Smith, Esq; ✉ The Chartered Institute of Arbitrators, 12 Bloomsbury Square, London WC1A 2LP

SMITH, Michael (Paul) Marshall; s of Prof David M Smith, of Loughton, Essex, and Margaret, née Harrup; b 3 May 1965; *Educ* Chigwell Sch, King's Coll Cambridge (MA); m Paula Grainger; *Career* writer; ptnr Smith & Jones Film Production; Cambridge Footlights: memb 1984–87, memb Ctee 1987, performer/writer nat tour 1987 and tour of USA 1988; memb: Equity, Musicians Union; *Awards* Icarus Award 1990, BFS Award for Best Short Story 1990, 1991 and 1996, August Delerth Award for Best Novel 1995, Philip K Dick Award 2001; *Books* Only Forward (1994), Spares (1996), One of Us (1998), What You Make It (1999), The Straw Men (2002); short stories incl: Dark Terrors, Dark Voices, Dark Lands, The Mammoth Books, Omni; film and television adaptations: Clive Barker's Weaveworld, Robert Faulcon's Nighthunter, Jay Russell's Celestial Dogs; writer/performer (as Michael Rutger) And Now In Colour (BBC Radio 4, 2 series and 2 Christmas specials); *Recreations* music, art and design, foreign travel, cats (owner Spangle and Lintilla); *Clubs* Soho House, Groucho; *Style*— Michael Marshall Smith, Esq; ✉ c/o Jonny Geller, Curtis Brown, Haymarket House, 28–29 Haymarket, London SW1Y 4SP (tel 020 7396 6600)

SMITH, (George) Neil; CMG (1987); s of George William Smith (d 1982), of Sheffield, and Ena Hill (d 1993); b 12 July 1936; *Educ* King Edward VII Sch Sheffield; m 5 May 1956, Elvi Vappu, da of Johannes Hämäläinen (d 1962), of Finland; 1 da (Helen b 1957), 1 s (Kim b 1959); *Career* joined Dip Serv 1953, Nat Serv RAF 1954–56; commercial attaché Rangoon 1958–61, second sec (commercial) Berne 1961–65, Dip Serv Admin 1965–66, first sec Cwlth Office 1966–68, Br Mil Govt Berlin 1969–73, FCO (European Integration and N America Depts) 1973–77, cnsllr (commercial) Helsinki 1977–80, consul-gen Zurich and Principality of Liechtenstein 1980–85, head of Trade Rels and Exports Dept FCO 1985–88, RCDS 1988, ambass to Repub of Finland 1989–95, ret; sec-gen Soc of London Art Dealers 1996–2001, sec Br Art Market Fedn 1996–2001; *Recreations* music and golf; *Style*— Neil Smith, Esq, CMG

SMITH, Prof Neilson Voyne (Neil); s of Voyne Smith (d 1991), and Lilian Freda, née Rose (d 1973); b 21 June 1939; *Educ* Trinity Coll Cambridge (MA), UCL (PhD); m 2 July 1966, Dr Saraswati Keskar, da of Dr Govind Raghunath (d 1963); 2 s (Amahl b 4 June 1967, Ivan b 13 July 1973); *Career* lectr in linguistics and W African languages SOAS Univ of London 1970–72 (lectr in W African languages 1964–70); UCL: reader in linguistics 1972–81, prof of linguistics 1981–, head Dept of Phonetics and Linguistics 1982–90; memb: Linguistics Assoc of GB (pres 1980–86), Philological Soc 1964– (sometime memb Cncl), SSRC 1973–89; pres Assoc of Heads and Profs of Linguistics 1993–94; hon memb Linguistic Soc of America 2000; FBA 1999; *Books* An Outline Grammar of Nupe (1967), The Acquisition of Phonology (1973), Modern Linguistics (with Deirdre Wilson, 1979), Mutual Knowledge (ed, 1982), The Twitter Machine (1989), The Mind of a Savant (with I Tsimpli, 1995), Chomsky: Ideas and Ideals (1999, 2 edn 2004), Language, Bananas and Bonobos (2002), Language, Frogs and Savants (2005); *Recreations* travel, music, walking; *Style*— Prof Neil Smith; ✉ 32 Long Buftlers, Harpenden, Hertfordshire AL5 1JE (tel 01582 761313); Department of Phonetics and Linguistics, University College London, Gower Street, London WC1E 6BT (tel 020 7679 7173, fax 020 7679 3262, e-mail neil@linguistics.ucl.ac.uk)

SMITH, Norman Jack; s of Maurice Leslie Smith (d 1967), of Newton Abbot, Devon, and Ellen Dorothy, née Solly (d 1994); b 14 April 1936; *Educ* Henley GS, Oriel Coll Oxford (MA), City Univ (MPhil); m 4 March 1967, Valerie Ann, da of Capt Arthur Ernest Frost (d 1978), of Ramsgate, Kent; 1 s (Malcolm b 1970), 1 da (Gail b 1974); *Career* market analyst Dexion Ltd 1957–60, commercial evaluation mangr Vickers Ltd 1960–69, business devpt mangr Baring Bros and Co Ltd 1969–80; md Smith Rea Energy Associates Ltd 1983–98; dir: Burntisland Engineers and Fabricators Ltd 1974–76, Zenith Reed Ltd 1975–76, International Economic Services Ltd 1975–76, SAI Tubular Services Ltd 1983–88, Atkins Oil and Gas Engineering Ltd 1984–86, Smith Rea Energy Analysts Ltd 1985–98, Gas Transmission Ltd 1989–95, Smith Rea Energy Aberdeen Ltd 1990–98, Capcis Ltd 1998–2000, Smith Rea Energy Ltd 1999–2000; DG Offshore Supplies Office 1978–80; chm: British Underwater Engineering Ltd 1981–83, Mentor Engineering

Consultants Ltd 1988–92, Petroleum Venture Mgmnt Ltd 2001–05; chm Friends of the Canterbury Archaeological Tst 2003–07, memb Tst Cncl Canterbury Archaeological Tst 2003–07; patron Oriel Coll Devpt Tst 2003–; FIE, FInstD, fell Soc of Business Economists; *Recreations* archaeology, history, walking, swimming, gardening; *Clubs* Oxford and Cambridge; *Style*— Norman Jack Smith, Esq; ✉ c/o Oxford and Cambridge Club, 71 Pall Mall, London SW1Y 5HD (tel 020 7930 5151, fax 020 7930 9490)

SMITH, Paul Adrian; s of Clifford Bryce Smith, and Marjorie Doreen, née Walker; b 16 January 1947, Belfast; *Educ* Royal Belfast Academical Instn; m Sarah; 1 da (Lucy), 1 s (Sam); *Career* trainee projectionist rising to dir BBC 1966–73, freelance TV prodr and dir 1973–81, fndr chm and md Complete Video 1981–95, also estab The Edit Works and The Shooting Crew, former head of A&R LWT's record label, sold Celador Int and Celador Prodns 2006; currently: chm Complete Communications Corp Ltd (estab 1988), chm Celador Films (estab 2000); *Television* creator It'll Be Alright on the Night (winner Silver Rose of Montreux and nomination Br Acad Award for It'll Be Alright on the Night 2 1980); prodr and dir of shows in UK and US incl: An Audience with Jasper Carrott (LWT), The Pink Medicine Show (LWT), London Night Out (Thames), Bruce's Big Night (LWT), Oh Boy (ATV), Peter Cook and Company (LWT, Gold Medal NY TV Festival), TV's Censored Bloopers (NBC); Celador prodns incl: Who Wants to be a Millionaire? (ITV1, Best Light Entertainment Prog BAFTA Awards 1999, Outstanding Game or Audience Participation Prog Emmy Awards 2000 and 2001), Winning Lines (BBC 1), Jasper Carrott - Back to the Front (BBC 1), The Detectives (BBC 1), Ruby Wax's Commercial Breakdown (BBC 1), Talking Telephone Numbers (ITV), Auntie's Bloomers (BBC 1), The Hypnotic World of Paul McKenna (ITV), All About Me (BBC 1), You Are What You Eat (Channel 4); *Film* Dirty Pretty Things 2002 (Best Film Evening Standard Film Awards 2002, nominated Best British Film BAFTA Awards 2002, Best Film Br Ind Film Awards 2003, special for excellence in film making Nat Bd of Review), The Descent 2005, Separate Lies 2005; *Recreations* photography, cinema, collecting original sixties records, family and home; *Style*— Paul Smith, Esq; ✉ Complete Communications Corporation, 39 Long Acre, London WC2E 9LG (tel 020 7845 6802, fax 020 7836 1117, e-mail psmith@completecomms.com)

SMITH, Paul Alick; s of Walter Alick Smith, and Valerie, née Cupit; b 31 October 1960, Carshalton, Surrey; *Educ* Greenshaw Comp Sutton, Colchester Inst (HND); m 22 June 1985, Jackie, née Shelley; 2 da (Felicity b 15 March 1987, Verity b 30 Jan 2001), 1 s (James b 12 April 1989); *Career* photojournalist Anglia Press Agency 1978–82, opened Brewsters 1982–84, Strutt Daughters 1984–86 (acquired 4 branches and opened further 16); Spicerhaart: currently chief exec, opened Spicer McColl 1989, launched Mortgages Direct 1990, acquired 72 Cornerstone Branches (renamed Spicer McColl) 1995, acquired Wolton Chartered Surveyors 1996, opened Felicity J Lord 1998, acquired 173 Woolwich Property Services branches (renamed Haart) 1999, acquired 47 Darlows branches 2000; Colchester Businessman of the Year 2005–06, Essex Countywide Businessman of the Year 2006–07; fell Inst of Sales & Mktg Mgmnt; *Recreations* Chelsea FC supporter; *Clubs* Colchester Colne Round Table (chm 1993–94 and 2005–06); *Style*— Paul Smith, Esq; ✉ Spicerhaart, Wellington House, Butt Road, Colchester, Essex CO3 3DA (tel 01206 732429, fax 01206 366984, e-mail paul.smith@spicerhaart.com)

SMITH, Sir Paul Brierley; kt (2000), CBE (1994); s of late Harold Smith, and late Marjorie Smith; b 5 July 1946; *Educ* Beeston Fields Sch; m 24 Nov 2000, Pauline Denyer; *Career* clothes designer; fndr and chm Paul Smith Ltd Nottingham 1970; currently wholesales in 42 countries around the world with Paul Smith shops in London, Nottingham, LA, NY, Paris, Milan, Moscow, Hong Kong, Singapore, Taiwan, Korea and over 250 in Japan; memb Design Cncl; finalist Design Cncl's Prince Philip Prize for the Designer of the Year 1992 and 1993; Hon MDes Nottingham Poly (now Nottingham Trent Univ) 1991; Hon Freedom City of Nottingham 1997; RDI 1991, Hon FRIBA 2007; *Style*— Sir Paul Smith, CBE; ✉ Paul Smith Ltd, 20 Kean Street, London WC2B 4AS (tel 020 7836 7828)

SMITH, Paul David John; s of Ernest Smith, of Walton on the Naze, Essex, and Margaret Lillian, née Taylor; b 12 June 1949; m Helen Mary, née Verlander; 2 s (Joel Julian Verlander, Giles James Verlander); *Career* art dir Collet Dickenson and Pearce 1973–87 (bd dir 1975–87), creative dir Allen Brady & Marsh 1987–91, int creative dir Lowe Howard-Spink 1991–94, exec int creative dir Grey Advertising 1994–99; Ogilvy: regnl creative dir EMEA 1999–, vice-chm Ogilvy Europe 1999–; vice-chm S D Lime Sustainable Business Development Co; all nat and int awards incl: 4 D&AD, Cannes Lions (Gold, Silver and Bronze), New York One Show; *Recreations* tennis, horse riding; *Clubs* Soho House, The Fox; *Style*— Paul Smith, Esq; ✉ Ogilvy, 10 Cabot Square, Canary Wharf, London E14 4QB (tel 020 7345 3205, e-mail paul.smith@ogilvy.com)

SMITH, Paul John; s of John Joseph Smith, of Sunderland, Tyne & Wear, and Mary Patricia, née Maher; b 25 July 1945; *Educ* Ampleforth, Univ of Newcastle upon Tyne (MB BS); m 14 July 1972, Anne Westmoreland Snowdon; 1 s (Mark b 1977), 3 da (Jaime b 1980, Victoria b 1982, Francesca b 1982); *Career* asst lectr in anatomy 1969–71; surgical registrar: Glasgow Western Infirmary 1971–76, Wexham Park Hosp 1976–78; res asst Microsurgical Laboratory Univ of Louisville 1978; Christine Kleinert fell in hand surgery Louisville 1978, resident and instructor in plastic surgery Duke Univ N Carolina 1979; conslt plastic surgn: Mount Vernon Hosp 1982–, Gt Ormond St Hosp for Sick Children 1988–; memb: Cncl Br Hand Soc 1988–90, Editorial Bd Journal of Hand Surgery 1989–91; sec Plastic Surgery Royal Soc of Med 1990; FRCSGlas 1974; Hayward foundation scholar 1978, 1st prize American Assoc Hand Surgery Toronto 1979, Pulvertaft Prize British Hand Soc 1983; memb: BMA, RSM, BSSH, BAPS, BAAPS; *Books* Principles of Hand Surgery (1990), Lister's The Hand - Diagnosis and Indications (2002); *Recreations* skiing; *Style*— Paul Smith, Esq; ✉ Kimble Farm, Fawley, Henley, Oxfordshire RG9 6JP (tel 01491 638870, office 01923 828100)

SMITH, Paul Jonathan; OBE (1999); s of late Arthur Godfrey Smith (d 1987), and Constance Mildred, née Phelps (d 2001); b 30 May 1956; *Educ* King Edward's Sch Birmingham, Queens' Coll Cambridge (MA, PhD); m 30 Aug 1997, Viveka Kumari; 3 c (Mrinal Sinh Smith b 4 Dec 1985, Nikhil Arthur Sinh Smith b 5 Nov 1994, Radheka Farah Kumari b 19 Oct 1996); *Career* lectr in English literature St Stephen's Coll Delhi Univ 1978–80, tripos supervisor Faculty of English Univ of Cambridge 1980–83; Br Cncl: asst dir Kano Nigeria 1983, asst rep Lagos Nigeria 1985, dep dir Drama and Dance 1987, AG rep Chile 1990, AG dir Berlin 1990, arts conslt 1991, AG dir Burma 1991, dep dir Bangladesh 1992, dir NZ 1995, dir Arts 1999, dir W India 2000–05, dir Egypt 2005–; theatre dir: Twelfth Night, Rosencrantz and Guildenstern are Dead, Love's Labour's Lost, Murder in the Cathedral, Everyman, Krapp's Last Tape, A Midsummer Night's Dream, Hamlet; *Publications* The St James Press Reference Guide to English Literature (contrib, 1990); *Recreations* literature, theatre, cinema, theology; *Style*— Paul Smith, Esq, OBE; ✉ British Council, 192 El Nil Street, Agouza, Cairo, Egypt (tel 00 202 300 1666, e-mail paul.smith@britishcouncil.org.eg)

SMITH, Peter Alan; s of Dudley Vaughan Smith (d 1983), and Beatrice Ellen, née Sketcher; b 5 August 1946; *Educ* Mill Hill Sch, Univ of Southampton (BSc), Wharton Sch Univ of Pennsylvania (AMP); m 2 Oct 1971, Cherry, da of Thomas A Blandford (d 1986); 2 s (Nicholas David b 1975, Richard James b 1977); *Career* RAFVR 1964–67, cmmnd actg PO 1967; PricewaterhouseCoopers (formerly Coopers & Lybrand before merger): joined 1967, ptnr 1975–2000, managing ptnr London City Office 1989–94, memb Partnership Bd 1990–2000, chm Coopers & Lybrand 1994–98, sr ptnr 1998–2000; chm: RAC plc 2003–05, Savills 2004–; non-exec dir: N M Rothschild & Sons 2001–, Equitable Life Assurance Soc 2001– (dep chm), Safeway plc 2002–04, Templeton Emerging Markets

Investment Tst plc 2004–, Associated British Foods plc 2007–; memb: Fin Ctee The Nat Tst 1991–98 and 2001–05, Prince of Wales Business Leaders' Forum 1994–2000, President's Ctee CBI 1994–98, Fin and Gen Purpose Ctee 1999–, Ctee on Corp Governance 1996–98; memb Cncl ICAEW 1997–2003 (treas 2001–03); former hon treas UK Housing Tst; Liveryman Worshipful Co of Chartered Accountants 1993; CCMI, FCA, FRSA; *Books* Housing Association Accounts and their Audit (1980); *Recreations* golf, gardens; *Clubs* Carlton, Beaconsfield Golf; *Style—* Peter Smith, Esq; ✉ New Court, St Swithins Lane, London EC4P 4DU (tel 020 7280 5419, fax 020 7280 5562)

SMITH, Most Rev Peter David; *see:* Cardiff, Archbishop of (RC)

SMITH, Prof Peter Frederick; s of Harold Frederick Smith (d 1987), and Irene May, *née* Shepherd (d 1990); *b* 24 December 1930; *Educ* Liverpool Inst HS, Queens' Coll Cambridge (MA), Univ of Manchester (PhD); *m* 1958, Jeannette Alexandra, da of Alexander Ferguson; 2 da (Karen Ann b May 1960, Pamela Jane b August 1962), 1 s (Michael James b March 1965); *Career* princ in architectural practice Ferguson Smith and Associates (later Partners) Sheffield 1968–89 (projects incl low energy housing devpts and churches as well as the restoration of listed bldgs such as the President's Lodge Queens' Coll Cambridge); chm and md Equity Homes Ltd (designers and builders of low cost extendible homes) 1983–87; sr lectr Univ of Sheffield 1974–86 (lectr 1965–74); Leeds Metropolitan Univ (formerly Leeds Poly): prof and head Dept of Architecture and Landscape 1986–90, actg head Dept of Construction 1988–90, prof and head Dept of Architecture and asst dean 1990, emeritus prof of architecture 1990; prof of architecture Sheffield Hallam Univ 1997–2002, special prof of sustainable energy Univ of Nottingham 2004–; research activity incl: EC contract to conduct intensive univ staff workshops in the UK, Ireland and Sweden on sustainability issues 1998–2000, EPSRC contract to investigate the feasibility of measures to upgrade the housing stock of England and Wales 1998–2001; memb Construction Indust Cncl Energy and Environment Ctee 1989–; RIBA: memb Yorks Regnl Cncl 1986– (chm 1990–91), chm Nat Environment and Energy Ctee 1988–96, memb Nat Cncl 1988–91 and 1997–, chm Euro Educn Ctee 1990–92, chm Jt RIBA/Dept of Energy Steering Ctee for the commissioning and prodn of Best Practice pubns and CPD environment and energy progs for the UK 1991–93, chm Sustainable Futures Ctee 1997–2002, vice-pres for Sustainable Development 2000–03; dir Pilkington Energy Efficiency Tst 1998–; lectr and keynote speaker at numerous architectural confs in Europe and the US; various interviews on environmental issues for BBC 1, Radio 4 and BBC World TV; script writer and presenter: Frank Lloyd Wright (ITV) 1972, Future Trends in Urbanism (ITV) 1972, The Soul of the City (BBC 1) 1973; FRIBA 1970, FRSA 1980; *Books* Third Millennium Churches (1973), The Dynamics of Urbanism (1975), The Syntax of Cities (1977), Architecture and the Human Dimension (1979), Architecktur und Asthetik (1981), Architecture and the Principal of Harmony (1987), Options for a Flexible Planet (1996), Concepts in Practice: Energy - Building for the Third Millennium (with A C Pitts, 1997), Architecture in a Climate of Change (2001, expanded 2 edn 2005), Sustainability at the Cutting Edge - Emerging Technologies for Low Energy Buildings (2002), Eco-Refurbishment - a Practical Guide to Creating an Energy Efficient Home (2003), The Dynamics of Delight - Architecture and Aesthetics (2003); written evidence to House of Commons Environment, Food and Rural Affrs Cmmn report 2005; contribs to other books and author of articles, papers and submissions to govt on energy related topics; *Recreations* painting, writing, travel; *Clubs* Oxford and Cambridge; *Style—* Prof Peter Smith; ✉ 50 Endcliffe Hall Avenue, Sheffield S10 3EL (tel and fax 0114 266 1722, e-mail pfsmith@ukonline.co.uk)

SMITH, Peter Michael; s of Peter William Smith (d 1944), of Reading, and Margaret, *née* Gilchrist (d 1971); *b* 10 January 1938; *Educ* St George's Coll Weybridge; *m* 1, 6 Dec 1975 (m dis 1998), Sarah Diana, da of John Seyfried; 2 s (Benjamin b 18 June 1977, Matthew b 17 Oct 1981); m 2, 19 July 2003, Carolyn Marie Noel-Johnson, da of Anthony Petit; *Career* served BSA Police Rhodesia 1956–59; Barclays Bank plc 1955–56, Barclays Bank Int 1959–62; PR and mktg mgmnt: Total Oil Products Central Africa 1962–66, Gallaher plc 1966–70; PR advsr Booker McConnell plc (responsible for early devpt of Booker Prize for Fiction) 1970–78, public affrs mangr Powell Duffryn plc 1978–85, dir of corp rels Reed Int plc 1985–87, jt managing ptnr City and Corporate Counsel (co-fndr 1987) 1987–93, dir UK Radio Devpts 1990–92, tstee One World Broadcasting Tst 1991–96, fndr chief exec The Strategic Partnership (London) Ltd 1994–2004; dir: Threadneedle Gp plc (co-fndr 1987–2000), Elixir Mktg Communications Ltd 1992–, A T Hudson Ltd 1993–; chm Worldaware (Centre for World Devpt Educn) 1992–95, chm RSA Tomorrow's Company Inquiry Network 1993–95; BESO: dep pres and chm Fin and Gen Purposes Ctee 1997–2003, dep chm and chm Audit Ctee 2003–05; cncllr London Borough of Camden 1968–71; Parly candidate (Cons): Rowley Regis and Tipton 1970, West Bromwich W Feb 1974; joined SDP 1982, currently memb Lib Dem Party; memb Nat Cncl and Exec Ctee Euro Movement in UK 1981–82; chm PR Educn and Res Tst 1984–89; Royal Cwlth Soc: vice-pres, fndr and chm Focus Gp 1975–78, pres Focus Gp 1978–83, dep chm 1980–83; pres IPR 1984 (chm City and Fin Gp 1981–82, chm Govt Affrs Gp 1991–95); Investor Rels Soc: co-fndr 1980, memb Ctee 1980–92, chm 1986–89, memb Professional Affrs Ctee 1989–2004; memb Worshipful Co of Mgmnt Conslts 2000– (memb Ct of Assts 2002–04), awarded Stephen Tallents Medal 1995; Freeman City of London 2000; FCIPR (Hon FIPR 1998), FRSA 1985–2005, FInstD 1987–2005, MIRS (Hon MIRS 1989), MIMC 1990–2005, CMC; *Recreations* golf, reading, music; *Style—* Peter Smith, Esq; ✉ La Grange, Liffernet, 46100 Lunan, Figeac, France (tel 00 33 5 65 34 99 36, e-mail psmith@lagrangeliffernet.com); 2 Vestry Mews, Vestry Road, London SE5 8NS (tel 020 7277 2798)

SMITH, His Hon Judge Peter William; s of William Smith (d 1995), and Bessie, *née* Hall (d 1986); *b* 31 December 1945; *Educ* Arnold Sch Blackpool, Downing Coll Cambridge (MA); *m* Vanessa, da of John Wildash; 1 s (Matthew b 29 May 1974); *Career* called to the Bar Middle Temple 1969, in practice Northern Circuit, circuit judge (Northern Circuit) 1994–; *Style—* His Hon Judge Peter Smith; ✉ c/o Preston Law Courts, Ring Way, Preston PR1 2LL

SMITH, Hon Mr Justice; Sir Peter Winston; kt (2002); s of George Arthur Smith (d 1993), and Iris Muriel, *née* Winstanley (d 1986); *b* 1 May 1952; *Educ* Bridlington Sch, Selwyn Coll Cambridge (MA), Coll of Law Chancery Lane London (Hardwicke scholar, Tancred scholar, Megarry pupillage award); *m* 13 Sept 1980, Diane, da of Charles Webster Dalgliesh; 2 da (Laura b 13 July 1980, Katy b 15 Feb 1982), 1 s (James b 3 May 1983); *Career* called to the Bar Lincoln's Inn 1975 (bencher 2000); QC 1992; examiner of title HM Land Registry 1976–82, lectr Univ of Manchester 1977–83; practising N Circuit: 460 Royal Exchange Manchester 1979–87, 40 King St Manchester 1987–2002; dep High Court judge 1996–2002, recorder 1997–2002 (asst recorder 1994–97), judge of the High Court of Justice (Chancery Div) 2002–; acting deemster IOM 2000; *Books* Conveyancing Law-Practice (2 edn 1982); *Recreations* reading military history, avid student of Jackie Fisher, football, memb Titanic Historical Soc and Br Titanic Soc; *Style—* The Hon Mr Justice Peter Smith; ✉ Royal Courts of Justice, Strand, London WC2A 1LL

SMITH, Phil; s of Emmanuel Smith, and Rosemary Smith; *Career* promotion asst Pinnacle Records 1976–79, head of regnl promotion Pye Records 1979–81, head of promotion Magnet Records 1981–82, head of promotion MCA/Universal Records 1982–92, prop Double Impact Ltd 1992–95, with First Artist Corp plc 1993– (currently chief operating offr); patron Lee Smith Leukaemia Orgn; football coach: Wealdstone FC, Maccabi GB; *Recreations* football (player and coach); *Style—* Phil Smith, Esq; ✉ First Artist Corporation plc, First Artist House, 87 Wembley Hill Road, Wembley, Middlesex HA9 8BU (tel 020 8900 1818, fax 020 8903 2984, mobile 07831 527804, e-mail phils@firstartist.com)

SMITH, Philip Henry; s of Alfred Henry Smith (d 1977), of Leicester, and Georgina May, *née* Ives (d 1969); *b* 24 November 1946; *Educ* Loughborough Coll GS, Leicester Regnl Coll of Technol, Nottingham Poly; *m* 27 Dec 1968, Sonia Idena, da of Ivan Garnet Moody (d 1964), of Leicester; 1 da (Melissa b 21 June 1969), 2 s (Christian Philip b 13 June 1972, Philip Raoul b 28 Feb 1975); *Career* sr audit asst Leics CC 1964–69, gp accountant Lusaka City Cncl Zambia 1969–72, branch accountant Dairy Produce Bd Zambia 1972–74, divnl dir and sec Dorada Holdings plc 1974–81, divnl fin dir Brook Tool Engineering Holdings plc 1981–83, gp treas Asda Group plc 1983–91, dir of treasy National Power plc 1991–99; non-exec chm: Intercontinental Utilities (Group) plc 1999–, Pan African Sports Investments Ltd 2000–, Global Utilities (Holdings) Ltd 2002–, Prosports Events Ltd 2003–, Pulse Generation (Tidal) Ltd 2005–; non-exec dir: Leading Edge Technologies BVI 2002–, The Environmental Tst Scheme Regulatory Body Ltd 2002–, Damhead Energy Ltd 2003–, Miles Invest Inc BVI 2003–, United Water Developers Ltd 2003–, Optimised Hybrid Desalination Ltd 2004–, Ela Hldgs Ltd 2007–; govr De Montfort Univ 2001–, assoc govr Kingsbrook Business and Enterprise Coll; chm Milton Keynes branch IOD; vice-pres: Broomleys CC, Eversholt CC; life memb Clifton Rangers Youth Football; memb IPFA 1971, FCMA 1974, FIMgt 1974, FCT 1988 (memb Cncl 1996–2001); *Recreations* sports, wine, gardening, political and economic affairs; *Clubs* Royal Navy, Royal Yacht Portsmouth; *Style—* Philip H Smith, Esq; ✉ The Old White Horse, Main Street, Padbury, Buckingham MK18 2AY (tel 01280 814848, e-mail phs@oldwhitehorse.fsbusiness.co.uk)

SMITH, Philip Henry; s of Reginald Smith, and Grace, *née* Howgate; *b* 14 July 1934; *Educ* Leeds GS, Univ of Leeds (MB ChB); *m* 13 Aug 1960, Margaret, da of Wilfred Glover (d 1967); 4 da (Alison (Mrs Belfield) b 1962, Catherine b 1964 d 1964, Anne (Mrs Johnson) b 1967, Rosemary b 1967), 1 s (Richard b 1965 d 1988); *Career* Nat Serv and OC 50 FST Br Cameroons, OC Surgical Div Tidworth Mil Hosp; head Dept of Urology St James Hosp Leeds 1967–98, urologist to Regnl Spinal Injuries Unit Pinderfields Hosp Wakefield 1967–91; sec Urology Gp of European Orgn for Research on Treatment of Cancer 1979–82 (chm 1976–79); chm: Prostatic Cancer Sub Gp MRC 1985, Urology Working Party MRC 1988–91, Data Monitoring Ctee European Randomised Study for Screening for Prostate Cancer 1994–; memb: BAUS, European Assoc of Urology, Bd European Orgn for Research on Treatment of Cancer 1997–2000; FRCS 1960; *Books* Bladder Cancer (ed, 1984), Combination Therapy in Urological Malignancy (ed, 1988); *Recreations* grandchildren, gardening; *Style—* Philip Smith, Esq; ✉ tel 0113 267 3616

SMITH, Phillip; s of Jeffrey Smith, and Rene Smith; *Educ* Quarry Bank HS Liverpool, Univ of Southampton (BA), Loughborough Coll (CertEd); *Career* teacher 1972–95; Br Horseracing Bd: handicapper 1995–98, sr jumps handicapper 1998–2006, head of handicapping 2007–; footballer: Br Univs 1970–72, Altrincham FC 1973–75, Northwich Victoria 1976–78; *Publications* 21 Years of the Pattern (1992); *Recreations* golf; *Clubs* Gay Hill Golf; *Style—* Phillip Smith, Esq; ✉ c/o British Horseracing Board, 151 Shaftesbury Avenue, London WC2H 8AL (e-mail psmith@bhb.co.uk)

SMITH, Richard Lloyd; QC (2001); *b* 28 January 1963; *Educ* Wellsway Sch Keynsham, KCL (LLB); *m* 1990, Anna Sara; 1 da (Giorgia), 1 s (Joe Luca); *Career* called to the Bar Middle Temple 1986; recorder of the Crown Court 2000–; lawyer: England rugby team Rugby World Cup Aust 2003, Br and Irish Lions rugby team tour NZ 2005; memb: Chm's Panel, Sports Dispute Resolution Panel; *Style—* Richard Smith, Esq, QC; ✉ Guildhall Chambers, 23 Broad Street, Bristol BS1 2HG

SMITH, Prof Richard Michael; s of Louis Gordon Smith (d 1971), of Essex, and Elsie Fanny, *née* Ward; *Educ* Earls Colne GS Essex, UCL (BA, Rosa Morison prize), St Catharine's Coll Cambridge (MA, PhD); *m* 1971, Margaret Anne, da of William D McFadden; *Career* post doctoral res fell Univ of Chicago 1971–73, lectr in population studies Plymouth Poly 1973–74; Univ of Cambridge: asst lectr in population and historical geography 1974–76, fell Fitzwilliam Coll 1977–83; Univ of Oxford: lectr in historical demography 1983–89, professorial fell All Souls Coll 1983–94, reader in history of med and dir Wellcome Unit for the History of Med 1990–94; Univ of Cambridge: fell Downing Coll, reader in historical demography and dir Cambridge Gp for the History of Population and Social Structure 1994–2003 (sr res offr 1976–81, asst dir 1981), prof of historical geography and demography 2003–; fndn lectr Fitzwilliam Coll Cambridge 1989, Sir John Neal's lectr UCL 1995; fell UCL 2004; pres Economic History Soc 2007–; FRHistS 1985, FBA 1991; *Books* Sources on English Society 1250–1800: The Sir Nicholas Bacon Collection (1973), Bastardy and its Comparative History (1980), Land, Kinship and Life-Cycle (1984), The World We Have Gained: Histories of Population and Social Structures (1986), Life, Death and the Elderly: Historical Perspectives (1991), Medieval Society and the Manor Court (1996), The Locus of Care: Families, communities, institutions and the provision of welfare since antiquity (1997); *Recreations* walking in Norfolk, listening to music; *Style—* Prof Richard Smith, FBA; ✉ Cambridge Group for the History of Population and Social Structure, Sir William Hardy Building, Department of Geography, Downing Place, Cambridge CB2 3EN (tel 01223 333181, fax 01223 333183, e-mail rms20@cam.ac.uk)

SMITH, Prof Richard Sydney William; CBE (2000); s of Sydney Frederick Smith, and Hazel Nora, *née* Kirk; *b* 11 March 1952; *Educ* Roan GS for Boys, Univ of Edinburgh Med Sch (BSc, MB ChB), Graduate Sch of Business Stanford Univ (MSc); *m* Oct 1977, Linda Jean, da of Alexander Rae Arnott; 2 s (Freddie Paris b April 1982, James Arthur b Feb 1984), 1 da (Florence Harriet Rose b March 1991); *Career* house offr: Eastern Gen Hosp Edinburgh 1976–77, Dunfermline and West Fife Hosp 1977; jr doctor Auckland and Green Lane Hosps Auckland NZ 1977–78, chief exec BMJ Publishing Group and ed British Medical Journal 1991–2004 (asst ed 1979–91), chief exec UnitedHealth Europe 2004–; prof of medical journalism Dept of Med Univ of Nottingham 1993–2001, visiting prof LSHTM 1996–; television doctor: BBC Breakfast Time 1982–86, TV-AM 1988–89; chm Foresight Ctee on Info and Health 2020 2000; memb: BMA 1979, Med Journalists' Assoc 1980, RCP working pty on alcohol 1985–87, RCP working pty on prison med 1987–90, bd ed Nat Med Jl of India 1991–2001, Int Ctee Med Jl Eds 1991–2004, Bd World Assoc of Med Eds 1994–2000, RCOG ind ctee Inquiry 1995, Bd Project HOPE UK 1996–2002, Editorial Bd Canadian Med Assoc Jl 1997–2001, Scientific Advsy Ctee of Univ of Lausanne 1997–2002, RCP working pty into Structure and Functions of RCP 1998, Bd Public Library of Science 2004–, Governing Cncl St George's Univ of London 2004–, Advsy Bd Global Trial Bank 2005–, Medicines Partnership Task Force Nat Prescribing Centre 2006–, UK Panel for Health and Biomedical Research Integrity 2006–; advsr to Dept Health Ind Inquiry into Inequalities in Health 1998; contrib Comment is Free The Guradian website 2006–; fell Acad of Gen Educn Manipal Karnataka India 1993; MFPHM 1991, FRCPE 1992, FRCP 1995 (MRCP 1993), FRCGP 1997, FFPHM 1997, FAMS 1998, FRCSEd 1999; *Awards* Med Journalists' Assoc Young Journalist of the Year 1980, Periodical Publishers' Assoc Specialist Writer of the Year 1981, runner up Med Journalists' Assoc Journalist of the Year 1983 and 1985; *Books* Alcohol Problems (1982), Prison Health Care (1984), Unemployment and Health (1987), The Good Health Kit (1987), Health of the Nation (ed, 1991), Rationing in Action (1993), Management for Doctors (ed jtly, 1995), Scientific Basis of Health Services (1996), The Trouble with Medical Journals (2006); *Television* That's Family Life (BBC1, 1983), Compulsions (Thames, 1987), Fashion Victims (BBC2, 1991), Breakthrough or Ballyhoo (BBC2, 1992); *Recreations* music (particularly jazz and chamber), theatre, wine, running, hill walking; *Style—* Prof Richard

Smith, CBE; ✉ UnitedHealth Europe, 15 Greycoat Place, London SW1P 1SB (tel 020 7202 0800)

SMITH, Sir Robert Courtney; kt (1987), CBE (1980); s of John Smith, JP, DL (d 1954), of Glasgow and Symington, and Agnes, *née* Brown (d 1969); *b* 10 September 1927; *Educ* Kelvinside Acad Glasgow, Sedbergh, Trinity Coll Cambridge (MA); *m* 6 March 1954, Moira Rose, da of Wilfred Hugh Macdougall (d 1948); 2 s (Nigel b 1956 d 1971, Christopher b 1961), 2 da (Lorna Bromley-Martin b 1958, Rosalind (Mrs Lindsay Buchan) b 1964); *Career* RM 1945–47, RMFVR 1951–57; CA 1953; ptnr Arthur Young McClelland Moores 1957–78; chm: Standard Life 1982–88, Alliance Trust 1984–96; dir: Sidlaw Group plc 1977–97 (chm 1980–88), Volvo Truck and Bus Ltd 1979–98, British Alcan Aluminium plc 1979–99, Edinburgh Investment Tst plc 1983–98, Bank of Scotland 1985–97; tstee Carnegie Tst for Univs of Scotland 1982–2002, memb Scottish Industries Devpt Bd 1972–88 (chm 1981–88), chllr's assessor Univ of Glasgow 1984–96; Hon Col Royal Marines Reserve Scot 1992–96; Hon LLD: Univ of Glasgow 1978, Univ of Aberdeen 1991; FRSE 1988; CStJ 2004; *Clubs* East India, Western (Glasgow), Hawks' (Cambridge); *Style*— Sir Robert Smith, CBE, FRSE; ✉ The Old Rectory, Cathedral Street, Dunkeld, Perthshire PH8 0AW (tel 01350 727574)

SMITH, Robert Daglish; CMG (1998); s of Robert Ramsay Smith (d 1992), of Sidcup, Kent, and Jessie, *née* Daglish; *b* 2 July 1934; *Educ* Dulwich Coll (State scholar), Queens' Coll Cambridge (MA); *m* 1984, Ursula, da of Peter Josef Stollenwerk; *Career* Nat Serv 2 Lt Royal Signals 1953–55; The King's Sch Canterbury 1960–65 (dir King's Week Arts Festival 1962–65), lectr Newland Park Coll of Educn Bucks 1965–67, Wells Management Consultants Ltd 1968–70, freelance mgmnt conslt in fundraising (arts admin) 1970–74, dir E Midlands Arts Assoc 1974–80 (sec then chair Standing Ctee of Regnl Arts Assocs 1976–80), exec dir UK Ctee for UNICEF (UN Children's Fund) 1980–99; cmmr Howard League Inquiry into Violence in Penal Institutions for Young People 1994–95; memb Cncl (treas) Children's Rights Alliance for Eng (formerly Children's Rights Office) 1992–2004, tstee NSPCC 1999–; memb Bd UN Assoc 2002–; memb Cncl Shakespeare's Globe 2005– (memb Int Ctee 2000–05); FRSA 1990; *Recreations* music, opera, theatre, travel; *Style*— Robert D Smith, Esq, CMG; ✉ 37E Westbourne Gardens, London W2 5NR (tel 020 7221 0890)

SMITH, Sir Robert Hill; 3 Bt (UK 1945), of Crowmallie, Co Aberdeen, MP; s (by 2 m) of Sir Gordon Smith, 2 Bt, VRD (d 1983); *b* 15 April 1958; *Educ* Merchant Taylors', Aberdeen Univ; *m* 13 Aug 1993, Fiona, da of Col J D Cormack; 3 da (Helen, Kirsty, Elizabeth); *Heir* bro, Charles Smith; *Career* MP (Lib Dem) W Aberdeenshire and Kincardine 2001–; memb Lib Dem Tport and Environment Team 1997–98, memb Lib Dem Scot Affrs Team (police, prisons, tport and environment) 1998–99, vice-chm Parly All-Pty UK Offshore Oil and Gas Industry Gp 1998–99, memb Scottish Affrs Select Ctee 1999–, Scottish Affrs spokesman 1999–2001, memb Trade and Industry Select Ctee 1999–2001, memb Procedure Ctee 2001–, dep chief whip 2001–06, memb Int Devpt Select Ctee 2007–; *Recreations* sailing; *Clubs* Royal Thames Yacht; *Style*— Sir Robert Smith, Bt, MP; ✉ Constituency Office, 6 Dee Street, Banchory, Kincardinshire, AB31 5ST (tel 01330 8203300, fax 01330 820338, e-mail bobsmith@cix.co.uk)

SMITH, Robert James; s of Mervyn Daniel Smith (d 1982), of Wickwar, Glos, and Marjorie Irene, *née* Griffin; *b* 22 July 1945; *Educ* King's Coll Taunton, Royal Holloway Coll London (BA); *m* 20 Aug 1970, Anne Rosemary, da of Brendan Fitzpatrick (d 1993), of London; 1 da (Kate b 1979), 1 s (Daniel b 1983); *Career* managing ed Gower Press Ltd, Xerox Corp Inc 1971–75, editorial mangr Octopus Books Ltd 1975–78, editorial dir Ebury Press Nat Magazine Co Ltd 1979–85, publishing dir Sidgwick and Jackson Macmillan Publishers Ltd 1985–90, chm and md Smith Gryphon Ltd 1990–97, md Robert Smith Literary Agency Ltd 1997–; memb Assoc of Authors' Agents; *Recreations* conservation, theatre, local history, collecting antiques and antiquarian books; *Clubs* Groucho; *Style*— Robert Smith, Esq; ✉ Robert Smith Literary Agency Ltd, 12 Bridge Wharf, 156 Caledonian Road, London N1 9UU (tel 020 7278 2444, fax 020 7833 5680)

SMITH, Robert James; s of James Alexander Smith, of Crawley, W Sussex, and Rita Mary, *née* Emmott; *b* 21 April 1959; *Educ* Notre Dame RC Middle Sch Crawley, St Wilfrid's RC Comp Crawley; *m* 13 Aug 1988, Mary Theresa, da of John Richard Poole; *Career* pop singer, musician and song-writer; stage debut with Malice (school group) 1976, name changed to Easy Cure (debut concert 1977), band now called The Cure (debut concert 1978); first tours: Britain 1979, Europe 1979, USA 1980, Antipodes 1980, Japan 1984; has performed in over 1000 concerts worldwide; other work incl: guitarist Siouxsie and the Banshees Sept-Oct 1979 and Oct 1982–May 1984, co-fndr The Glove (studio project, one album Blue Sunshine) 1983; *Albums* Three Imaginary Boys (US version Boys Don't Cry) 1979, Seventeen Seconds 1980, Faith 1981, Pornography 1982, Japanese Whispers (compilation) 1983, The Top 1984, Concert - The Cure Live 1984, Concert and Curiosity - Cure Anomalies 1977–84 1984, The Head on the Door 1985, Standing On The Beach (compilation) 1986, Kiss Me Kiss Me Kiss Me 1987, Disintegration 1989, Mixed Up (compilation) 1990, Entreat (live) 1991, Wish 1992, Show (live) 1993, Paris (live) 1993, Wild Mood Swings 1996, Galore (singles compilation) 1997, Bloodflowers 1999, Greatest Hits 2001, Join the Dots (compilation) 2004, The Cure 2004; *Videos* incl: Staring at the Sea (singles compilation) 1986, The Cure in Orange (concert) 1986, Picture Show (singles compilation) 1991, Playout (live) 1991, Show (concert) 1993, Galore (singles compilation) 1997; *Awards* Best Video (for Lullaby) BPI 1989, Best US Radio Song (for Lovesong) ASCAP 1989, Best British Group BPI 1990, Best Video (for Friday I'm in Love) MTV 1992, Best US Radio Song (for Friday I'm in Love) ASCAP 1993; *Publications* Ten Imaginary Years (offical Cure biography, jtly 1987), Songwords (co-author and ed, 1989); *Recreations* deep sea diving, hot air ballooning, reading, writing, staring into space...; *Style*— Robert Smith, Esq

SMITH, Robert Lee (Rob); CB (2004); s of John Joseph Smith, and Joan Margaret, *née* Parry; *b* 9 February 1952; *Educ* St Dunstan's Coll, Magdalene Coll Cambridge (open scholar, MA); *m* 24 May 1986, Susan Elizabeth, da of Raymond and Elizabeth Armfield; 1 da (Anna Elizabeth b 15 Sept 1989), 1 s (Andrew John b 18 July 1991); *Career* Civil Serv admin trainee 1974–76; Dept for Educn and Employment: princ private sec to Sec of State 1985–87, under sec 1994–95, dir for Pupils, Parents and Youth 1995–98, dir for Pupil Support and Inclusion 1998–2000; DG Regnl Co-Ordination Unit 2000–04, DG Regnl Devpt Gp ODPM 2004–05; co-chm: Inst of Mgmnt Civil Serv Network 1995–2000, Social Policy Forum 2003–; tstee: Nat Literacy Tst 2005– (dep chair 2006–), Place2be 2006–; *Recreations* folk dancing and music, package holidays; *Style*— Rob Smith, Esq, CB

SMITH, Robin Anthony; TD (1978, Bar 1984), DL (W Yorks 1991); s of Tom Sumerfield Smith (d 1990), of Wetherby, W Yorks, and Mary, *née* Taylor (d 1998); *b* 15 February 1943; *Educ* St Michael's Coll Leeds, Univ of Manchester (LLB); *m* 5 Oct 1967, Jennifer Elizabeth, da of Eric Anthony Roslington (d 1978), of Leeds; 1 s (Jonathan b 1969), 1 da (Sarah b 1972); *Career* cmmnd KOYLI 1966, 5 Bn The Light Inf 1967–86, ret as Lt-Col 1986; admitted slr 1966; DLA Piper (formerly Dibb Lupton Alsop): ptnr 1968–87, managing ptnr 1987–93, sr ptnr 1993–98, conslt 1998–2007; non-exec dir: Leeds Building Soc 1998– (chm 2007–), Town Centre Securities plc 1998–; local dir Coutts & Co 1999–2006; memb Law Soc 1966– (memb Cncl 1982–91); govr Stonyhurst Coll 1990–98; KSG 2002; *Recreations* cricket, golf, tennis; *Clubs* Army and Navy, Leeds, Alwoodley Golf, MCC, Yorkshire CCC (pres 2000–04, chm 2003–06); *Style*— Robin Smith, Esq, TD, DL; ✉ c/o DLA, Princes Exchange, Princes Square, Leeds LS1 4BY (tel 0113 369 2222, fax 0113 369 2799, e-mail robin.smith@dla.com)

SMITH, Prof Roderick Arthur; *b* 26 December 1947, Oldham, Lancs; *Educ* The Hulme GS Oldham, St John's Coll Oxford (BA), Queens' Coll Cambridge (PhD, Gas Cncl res scholar); *m* 1975, Yayoi Yamanoi, of Tokyo; *Career* student engr apprentice and serv engr David Brown Corp 1966–71, Godfrey Mitchell res fell Queens' Coll Cambridge 1975–78, lectr Engrg Dept Univ of Cambridge 1980–88 (asst lectr 1977–80), official fell and dir of studies in engrg Queens' Coll Cambridge 1978–88; Univ of Sheffield: prof of mechanical and process engrg 1988–2000, head of dept 1992–95, warden Stephenson Hall 1992–2000 (sr warden 1997–2000), chm Advanced Railway Res Centre (ARRC) 1993–2000, Royal Acad of Engrg/Br Rail res prof of advanced railway engrg 1995–2000; Imperial Coll London: head Dept of Mechanical Engrg 2000–05, Royal Acad of Engrg research prof and chm Future Rail Research Centre 2006–; visiting prof Univ of York and Univ of Kyushu 1997–99, visiting chair of tport systems engrg Univ of Tokyo 1998–99, hon prof Central Queensland Univ 1999–, hon prof Chinese Acad of Railway Sci Beijing 2002–, sr visiting research fell St John's Coll Oxford 2005–06; chm and non-exec dir Coll of Railway Technol Derby 1996–97; conslt: Br Steel plc 1987–90, HSE, BR (memb Res and Tech Ctee 1992–96); chm BR Crashworthiness Devpt Steering Gp 1993–96, chm Japanese Railway Soc 1996–, dir AEA Technol Engrg Dept Univ of Cambridge, Advanced Technol Centre 1998–, memb AEA Technol Sci and Engrg Ctee 1997–; memb Editorial Bd: Int Jl of Fatigue, Fatigue of Engrg Materials, Condition Monitoring and Diagnostic Technol; memb American Soc of Engrs, memb Cncl IMechE 1999–; tstee Nat Museum of Sci and Industry 2002–; ScD Univ of Cambridge 1998; FREng, CEng, FIMechE, FIM, FCGI 2000; *Publications* ed books on: fatigue and fracture mechanics, innovative teaching, engrg for crowd safety, railway engrg, condition monitoring; approx 290 published papers in areas of fatigue and fracture mechanics, finite element stress analysis railway and environmental engrg; *Recreations* mountaineering: ldr of expeditions to Arctic Norway, Everest region and Karakoram; *Clubs* Alpine, Reform; *Style*— Prof Roderick Smith, FREng; ✉ Department of Mechanical Engineering, Imperial College of Science, Technology and Medicine, South Kensington, London SW7 2AZ (tel 020 7594 7007, e-mail roderick.smith@imperial.ac.uk)

SMITH, Dr Roger; s of Sylvanus Joseph Smith (d 1973), of Newcastle-under-Lyme, Staffs, and Winifred Beatrice, *née* Adams (d 1979); *b* 3 February 1930; *Educ* Newcastle-under-Lyme HS, Trinity Coll Cambridge (MA, MD), UCH London (PhD); *m* 25 June 1955, Barbara Ann, da of Harold Willatt (d 1987), of Newcastle-under-Lyme, Staffs; 3 da (Philippa b 7 Dec 1956, Clare b 6 April 1962, Katharine b 3 April 1966), 1 s (Julian b 22 May 1960); *Career* served: Rifle Bde 1948, Intelligence Corps 1949; sr Wellcome res fell UCH London 1965–68, clinical reader Nuffield Depts of Med and Orthopaedic Surgery Oxford 1969–77, fell Nuffield Coll Oxford 1971–77, conslt physician in metabolic med John Radcliffe Hosp and Nuffield Orthopaedic Centre Oxford 1977–95, hon conslt physician Nuffield Orthopaedic Centre Oxford 1995–; fell Green Coll Oxford 1984–95 (emeritus fell 1995); memb Cncl RCP 1985–89 (regnl advsr 1981–85), chm Med Staff Cncl and Med Exec Ctee Oxford Hosps 1987–89; memb: Cncl Nat Osteoporosis Soc, Assoc of Physicians; FRCP; *Books* Electrolyte Metabolism in Severe Infantile Malnutrition (1968), Biochemical Disorders of the Skeleton (1979), Osteoporosis (1990), Clinical and Biochemical Disorders of the Skeleton (2005); *Recreations* painting, tennis; *Style*— Dr Roger Smith; ✉ 6 Southcroft, Elsfield Road, Old Marston, Oxford OX3 0PF; Nuffield Orthopaedic Centre, Headington, Oxford OX3 7LD (tel 01865 741155)

SMITH, Roland Hedley; CMG (1994); s of Alan Hedley Smith (d 1997), of Sheffield, and Elizabeth Louise, *née* Froggatt; *b* 11 April 1943; *Educ* King Edward VII Sch Sheffield, Keble Coll Oxford (MA); *m* 27 Feb 1971, Katherine Jane, da of Philip Graham Lawrence (d 1975), of Brighton; 2 da (Rebecca b 1972, Ursula b 1975); *Career* HM Dip Serv: third sec FO 1967, second sec Moscow 1969, second later first sec UK Delgn to NATO Brussels 1971, first sec FCO 1974, first sec and cultural attaché Moscow 1978, FCO 1980, attached to Int Inst for Strategic Studies 1983, political advsr and head of Chancery Berlin 1984, Sci Energy and Nuclear Dept FCO 1988, head of Non Proliferation and Def Dept FCO 1990–92, min and dep permanent rep UK Delgn to NATO Brussels 1992–95, dir (Int Security) FCO 1995–98, ambass to Ukraine 1999–2002, ret; dir St Ethelburga's Centre for Reconciliation and Peace 2002–04, clerk to the tstees Wakefield Tst 2004–; *Books* Soviet Policy Towards West Germany (1985); *Recreations* music, choral singing; *Style*— Roland Smith, Esq, CMG; ✉ Wakefield Trust, Attlee House, 28 Commercial Street, London E1 6LR (tel 020 7377 6614, fax 020 7377 9822, e-mail roland.smith@wakefieldtrust.org.uk)

SMITH, Ronald; s of William Smith, of Lerwick, Shetland Islands, and Daisy, *née* Manson (d 2005); *b* 9 June 1951, Lerwick, Shetland Islands; *Educ* Anderson Educnl Inst, Univ of Aberdeen (MA), Aberdeen Coll of Educn (PGCE); *m* 10 April 1976, Mae, *née* Lambie; 1 da (Kirstin b 17 April 1982), 1 s (Craig b 9 Oct 1984); *Career* teacher then princ teacher of Latin and modern studies Broxburn Acad 1973–88; Educnl Inst of Scotland: asst sec 1988–95, gen sec 1995–; pres: Educn Int (Europe) 2006– (memb European Ctee 1995–), European Trade Union Ctee for Educn 2006– (memb Exec Bd 1995–); FEIS 2003; *Recreations* Livingston FC, Island of Foula; *Style*— Ronald Smith, Esq; ✉ Educational Institute of Scotland, 46 Moray Place, Edinburgh EH3 6BH (tel 0131 225 6244, fax 0131 220 3151, e-mail rsmith@eis.org.uk)

SMITH, Sean; *b* 1959, London; *family* 3 c; *Career* photographer; The Guardian 1988–; memb British Press Photographers Assoc; memb Burt Bacharach and Hal David Fan Club; *Publications* Five Thousand Days (contrib, 2004, also exhbn RNT); *Recreations* drinking and other associated pleasures; *Style*— Sean Smith, Esq; ✉ The Guardian, 119 Farringdon Road, London EC1R 3ER (tel 020 7239 9585)

SMITH, Col Stanley Jackman; s of George Stanley Smith (d 1960), of Purley, Surrey, and Dorothy Ellen, *née* Jackman (d 1980); *b* 16 September 1921; *Educ* St Paul's, The Law Soc's Sch of Law; *m* 15 Feb 1958, Gisela, da of Kurt Flessa, of Minden, Germany; 3 da (Karoline Susanne b 4 Feb 1959, Jennifer Christine b 9 June 1960, Helen Deborah b 20 April 1962); *Career* articled clerk Evill & Coleman Solicitors London 1938–42, admitted slr 1944; served Army 1942–75: RA 1942–43, Intelligence Corps 1943–46 (active serv Burma Campaign 1944–45), Staff Capt (Legal) and Dep Asst Judge Advocate Gen (Indian Army) 1946–47, Prosecuting Offr Japanese and German War Crimes Trials (Singapore, Malaya, Burma, Borneo, Hong Kong, Germany) 1946–50, Mil Dept Office of the Judge Advocate Gen of the Forces 1947–48, joined Directorate of Army Legal Services 1948, promoted Maj 1951, Dep Asst Dir Army Legal Services 1951–60 (served BAOR, Korea (active serv), Japan, Middle East Land Forces, Egypt, Kenya), promoted Lt Col 1960, Asst Dir Army Legal Services 1960–67 (War Office, BAOR), promoted Col 1967, Dep Dir Army Legal Services (Far East Land Forces 1969–71, MOD 1971–73), CO Army Legal Aid Section Germany 1973–75, Col RARO 1975–; decorations: 1939–45 Star, Burma Star, Defence Medal 1939–45, War Medal 1945, Queen's Medal for Korea, UN Medal for Korea 1953, Gen Serv Medal (Clasp Canal Zone); prosecuting slr Hampshire Constabulary 1975–85; lay memb Investigation Ctee ICAEW 1988–97, summary writer Criminal Appeal Office of Court of Appeal (Criminal Div) 1989–; memb: Law Soc 1959, Int Soc for Military Law and the Law of War (UK Gp) 1993; *Recreations* reading history, gardening, walking, The USA; *Clubs* Army and Navy; *Style*— Col Stanley Smith; ✉ 5 St Lawrence Close, Stratford sub Castle, Salisbury, Wiltshire SP1 3LW (tel 01722 500133)

SMITH, Prof Stanley William (Stan); s of Stanley Smith (d 1980), and Edith, *née* Barlow (d 1997); *b* 12 January 1943; *Educ* Boteler GS, Jesus Coll Cambridge (MA, PhD); *m* (m dis); 1 da (Caroline Elizabeth b 2 July 1965), 2 s (Philip Malcolm b 2 Oct 1967, Stephen Mark b 31 March 1971); *Career* asst lectr in English Univ of Aberdeen 1967–68; Univ of

Dundee: lectr in English 1968–85, sr lectr 1985–88, reader 1988–89, prof 1989–98, head of dept 1989–92 and 1992–94; research prof in literary studies Nottingham Trent Univ 1999–; visiting prof: Univ of Florence 1987, Univ of Zaragoza 1996; memb: Steering Ctee Standing Conf of Arts and Social Sciences 1990–2001, Bd European Soc for the Study of English 1991–93, SOED Postgraduate Awards Ctee 1993–98; chm Cncl for Univ English 1991–93 (memb Steering Ctee 1989–94), vice-chm Scottish Ctee of Profs of English 1993–95 (memb 1990–99), memb Steering Ctee Cncl of Univ Deans of Arts and Humanities 1997–2002; poetry reviews ed The Literary Review 1979–81; gen ed: Longman Critical Reader series 1988–, Longman Studies in Twentieth Century Literature 1991–, Visions and Revisions: Irish Writers series 2005–; co-ed Keywords 2001–; founding fell English Assoc 2000– (chm Fellowship Ctee 2000–04); memb: Modernist Research Project Univ of La Rioja 2002–07, Exec of English Assoc 2003–06; tstee English Asoc 2006–; *Books* A Sadly Contracted Hero: The Comic Self in Post-War American Fiction (1981), Inviolable Voice: History and Twentieth-Century Poetry (1982), Twentieth-Century Poetry (ed, 1983), W H Auden (1985), Edward Thomas (1986), W B Yeats: A Critical Introduction (1990), The Origins of Modernism: Eliot, Pound, Yeats and the Rhetorics of Renewal (1994), Auden issue: Critical Survey (ed, 1994), W H Auden (1997), Modernism Issue: Miscelánea (ed Zaragoza, 1999), The Country (by Edward Thomas, ed and intro, 1999), Critical Survey (Postmodern Poetries issue, 2002), Cambridge Companion to W H Auden (ed, 2004), Storm Jameson's In the Second Year (ed and intro, 2004), Studies in Travel Writing: Modernist Travels (guest ed, 2004), Irish Poetry and the Construction of Modern Identity (2005), Globalisation and its Discontents: Writing the Global Culture (ed, 2006), EREA Special Issue Right/Left/Right: Revolving Commitment in Britain and France 1929–1950 (guest ed, 2006), Poetry and Displacement (2007), Family Fortunes: A Sonnet Sequence (2008); *Recreations* classical music, foreign travel, family history, archaeology; *Style*— Prof Stan Smith; ✉ School of Arts and Humanities, Nottingham Trent University, Clifton Campus, Clifton Lane, Nottingham NG11 8NS (tel 0115 941 8418, personal extension 0115 848 3084, fax 0115 848 6632, e-mail stan.smith@ntu.ac.uk or stan.smith1@ntlworld.com)

SMITH, Stephen; s of Joseph Leslie Smith (d 1980), and Audrey May, *née* Wright (d 1998); *b* 8 August 1948; *Educ* Loughborough GS, Regent's Park Coll Oxford (MA, PGCE); *m* 25 July 1970, Janice Susan, da of Wilfred Allen; 1 da (Rachael Jane b 19 Jan 1972), 1 s (Adam Mark b 28 Dec 1974); *Career* Loughborough GS: asst history teacher 1970–87, head of first year 1974–78, housemaster junior boarders 1976–79, head of third year 1978–83, head of general studies 1983–87, head of history 1987–93; dep head Birkenhead Sch 1993–96, head Bedford Modern Sch 1996–; chm HMC/GSA Sports Sub Ctee; *Recreations* music and drama, sport; *Clubs* East India; *Style*— Stephen Smith, Esq; ✉ Bedford Modern School, Manton Lane, Bedford MK41 7NT (tel 01234 332500, fax 01234 332550, e-mail stephens@bedmod.co.uk)

SMITH, Prof Stephen Kevin; s of Albert Smith, DFC, of Birkenhead, and Drusilla, *née* Hills; *b* 8 March 1951; *Educ* Birkenhead Sch, Univ of London (MB BS, MD, DSc), Univ of Cambridge (MA); *m* 8 July 1978, Catriona Maclean, da of Alan Maclean Hobkirk, of Edinburgh; 1 s (Richard Alan), 2 da (Lucinda Jane, Alice Charlotte); *Career* lectr Univ of Sheffield 1982–85, conslt in obstetrics and gynaecology MRC Reproductive Biology Unit and Lothian Health Bd 1985–88, prof of obstetrics and gynaecology Univ of Cambridge 1988–2003 (fell Fitzwilliam Coll), princ Faculty of Med Imperial Coll London 2003–; author of various scientific and med pubns; FRCOG, FIBiol, FMedSci; *Recreations* walking, flying, politics, history, music; *Style*— Prof Stephen Smith; ✉ Faculty of Medicine, Imperial College London, Level 2 Faculty Building, South Kensington Campus, London SW7 2AZ (tel 020 7594 8800, fax 020 7594 9833)

SMITH, Prof Steven Murray (Steve); s of William Smith, and Doris Smith; *b* 4 February 1952; *Educ* Univ of Southampton (BSc, MSc, PhD, DSc); *Partner* Jeannie Forbes; *Career* lectr in politics Huddersfield Poly 1976–78, lectr, sr lectr then prof of int relations UEA 1979–92, prof of int politics UCW Aberystwyth (later Univ of Wales Aberystwyth) 1992–2002 (pro-vice-chllr 1999–2002), vice-chllr Univ of Exeter 2002–; pres Int Studies Assoc 2003–04; AcSS 2000; *Books* Foreign Policy Adaptation (1981), Politics and Human Nature (ed with I Forbes, 1983), Foreign Policy Implementation (ed with M Clarke, 1985), International Relations (ed, 1985), The Cold War Past and Present (ed with R Crockatt, 1987), British Foreign Policy: Tradition, Change, and Transformation (ed with M Smith and B White, 1988), Belief Systems and International Relations (ed with R Little, 1988), Explaining and Understanding International Relations (with M Hollis, 1990), Deciding Factors in British Politics: A Case-Studies Approach (with J Greenaway and J Street, 1992), European Foreign Policy (ed with W Carlsnaes, 1994), International Relations Theory Today (ed with K Booth, 1995), International Theory: Positivism and Beyond (ed with K Booth and M Zalewski, 1996), The Globalization of World Politics (ed with J Baylis, 1997, 3 edn 2004); *Recreations* Norwich City FC, theatre, music, firework displays, arctophile; *Style*— Prof Steve Smith; ✉ Vice-Chancellor's Office, University of Exeter, Northcote House, Queen's Drive, Exeter EX4 4QJ (tel 01392 263000, e-mail vice-chancellor@ex.ac.uk)

SMITH, Stuart Crawford; s of David Norman Smith, of Spain, and Sheila Marie, *née* Hallowes; *b* 17 September 1953; *Educ* City of Bath Boys' Sch, Wadham Coll Oxford (major scholar, BA), Univ of Sussex (MA); *m* 23 Dec 1987, Hilary Joy Phillips; *Career* ed Marketing Week Magazine 1988– (joined as sub ed 1982); *Recreations* skiing, reading, riding; *Style*— Stuart Smith, Esq; ✉ Centaur Publishing, St Giles House, 49–50 Poland Street, London W1F 7AX (tel 020 7970 4000, fax 020 7970 6721)

SMITH, Susan Lorraine (Susy); da of Clifford Bryce Smith (d 1999), and Marjorie Doreen Walker (d 1991); *b* 15 August 1957; *Educ* Grosvenor HS Belfast, Central Sch of Art London (BA); *Partner* Alex Evans; 2 da (Constance Marjorie (Connie), Harriet Anne (Hattie) (twins) b 6 March 1998); *Career* layout artist My Guy 1980, jr designer Ideal Home 1982, homes asst Homes & Gardens 1983, style ed In Store 1985, freelance stylist and design conslt 1987; House Beautiful magazine: style and design ed 1988–93, assoc ed 1993–95; ed Country Living 1995–; Innovation of the Year BSME 1999 (for Country Living's Farmer Wants a Wife), Best Coverage of Environmental Issues by a Consumer Magazine British Environment and Media Awards (BEMAS) 20003, Consumer Lifestyle Magazine of the Year PPA 2004; *Recreations* gardening, walking, birdwatching; *Clubs* Blacks; *Style*— Ms Susy Smith; ✉ National Magazine Company, 72 Broadwick Street, London W1F 9EP (tel 020 7439 5294, e-mail susy.smith@natmags.co.uk)

SMITH, Terence Barriston (Terry); s of Herbert William Smith, of Arundel, W Sussex, and Elsie Eva, *née* Hasker; *b* 12 July 1941; *Educ* N Hammersmith Sch of Art, Ealing Tech Coll, Open Univ (BA); *m* (m dis), Marion; 1 da (Justine Emma b 2 Aug 1966), 1 s (Richard Adam b 19 Jan 1968); partner, Jean Douglas-Withers; *Career* mgmnt trainee Metal Box Co 1960–62; systems analyst: Ford Motor Co 1962–65, J Stone Ltd 1965–67; BBC: systems analyst 1967–68, sr systems analyst 1968–70, chief systems analyst 1970–73, asst head of TV computer projects 1973–76, head of TV computer servs 1976–91, head of IT BBC TV 1991–95; md Business Solutions 1995–; Freeman City of London 1988, Liveryman Worshipful Company of Information Technologists 1988; FBCS 1976, CEng; *Recreations* golf, opera, cricket, wine; *Clubs* Gerrards Cross Golf, Harleyford Golf, Middlesex CC, Phyllis Court, La Sella Golf; *Style*— Terry Smith, Esq; ✉ Business Solutions and Castle Mews Group, 11 Misbourne House, Amersham Road, Chalfont St Giles, Buckinghamshire HP8 4RY (tel and fax 01494 870026, e-mail tsbarriston@aol.com)

SMITH, Terence Charles (Terry); s of Ernest George Smith (d 1985), of London, and Eva Ada, *née* Bruce (d 2001); *b* 15 May 1953; *Educ* Stratford GS, UC Cardiff (BA), Mgmnt Coll Henley (MBA); *m* 31 Aug 1974, Barbara Mary, da of Ivor Thomas George, of Ebbw Vale; 2 da (Katy b 1981, Emily b 1984); *Career* mgmnt trainee, branch mangr, fin mangr Barclays Bank 1974–83, bank analyst W Greenwell and Co 1984–86, dir, bank analyst, head of fin desk Barclays de Zoete Wedd 1986–88, bank analyst James Capel and Co 1989–90, dep md and head of UK company research UBS Phillips & Drew 1990–92 (dismissed following publication of book on suspect UK financial accounting techniques), dir Collins Stewart stockbrokers 1992–, ceo Collins Stewart Inc 1999–, ceo Collins Stewart Tullett plc 2000–06, chm Collins Stewart plc 2006–, ceo Tullett Prebon plc 2006–; rated leading banking sector analyst 1984–90; ACIB, MSI; *Books* Accounting for Growth (1992, 2 edn 1996); *Recreations* boxing, shooting, flying; *Style*— Terry Smith, Esq; ✉ The Old Rectory, Danbury, Essex CM3 4NG (tel 01245 226414); Collins Stewart plc, 9th Floor, 88 Wood Street, London EC2V 7QR (tel 020 7200 7337)

SMITH, Thomas James (Tom); s of Geoffrey Smith (d 1977), and Alison, *née* Bell; *b* 31 October 1971; *Educ* Rannoch Sch, Univ of Abertay Dundee (BA); *m* 5 June 1999, Zoe, *née* Schlesinger; 1 s (Angus James b 8 Jan 2001), 1 da (Amélie Rose Alice b 1 June 2002); *Career* professional rugby union player; clubs: Caledonian Reds 1996–99, CA Brive Corrèze 1999–2001, Northampton Saints 2001–; int: Scotland Schools U18, Scotland U21, Scotland A, Scotland (46 caps, winners Five Nations Championship 1999, memb squad World Cup Aust 2003); memb Br Lions tour: South Africa 1997 (3 full caps), Australia 2001 (3 full caps); Scotland Player of the Year 2000–01; patron Enlighten Action for Epilepsy Edinburgh and Hong Kong; *Recreations* family, golf; *Style*— Tom Smith, Esq; ✉ c/o Bart Campbell, Global Sports Management Ltd, Hyde Park House, 5 Manfred Road, London SW15 2RS (tel 020 8871 3712, fax 020 8871 2051, e-mail info@gsmworld.co.uk)

SMITH, Thomas William David; s of George Ernest Smith, of Sheffield, and Dora Staniforth; *b* 4 August 1939; *Educ* Selwyn Coll Cambridge (MA, MB BChir), St Mary's Hosp Med Sch; *m* 24 Nov 1967, Christina Mary, da of William O'Connor, of Dublin; 3 s (Nicholas William Patrick b 1968, Thomas Fitzgerald George b 1972, Hugh Francis Niall b 1974), 2 da (Gillian Mary b 1970, Alexandra Gwen b 1972); *Career* orthopaedic registrar Oxford 1968–70, sr orthopaedic registrar Sheffield 1970–73, lectr Univ of Sheffield 1973–76, conslt orthopaedic surgn Sheffield 1976–; Liveryman Worshipful Co of Pattenmakers; FRCS, FRCSEd; *Recreations* fly fishing, skiing; *Style*— Thomas Smith, Esq; ✉ Cleveland House, 3 Whitworth Road, Sheffield S10 3HD (tel 0114 230 8398); Orthopaedic Department, Northern General Hospital, Herries Road, Sheffield S5 7AU (tel 0114 243 4343)

SMITH, Timothy John; s of late Capt Norman Wesley Smith, CBE (sometime Cdre Orient Steam Navigation Co), and late Nancy Phyllis, da of Engr Capt F J Pedrick, RN; *b* 5 October 1947; *Educ* Harrow, St Peter's Coll Oxford (MA); *m* 1980, Jennifer Jane, da of late Maj Sir James Sidney Rawdon Scott-Hopkins, MP, MEP; 2 s (Henry b 1982, Charles b 1984); *Career* articled Gibson Harris & Turnbull 1969–71, sr auditor Peat Marwick Mitchell 1971–73, co sec Coubro & Scrutton Holdings 1973–79, sec Parly and Law Ctee ICAEW 1979–82, ptnr HM Williams CAs 2001–, dir Nevill Hovey & Co Ltd CAs 2002–; dir Harbour Centre Plymouth 2005–; chm Abbeyfield Launceston Soc 2003–; MP (Cons): Ashfield 1977–79, Beaconsfield 1982–97; PPS to Rt Hon Leon Brittan 1983–85, Parly under-sec NI Office 1994; memb: NI Select Ctee 1994–97, HM Treasury Financial Reporting Advsy Bd 1996–97, Inland Revenue Tax Law Rewrite Steering Ctee 1996–97; vice-chm Cons Backbench Fin Ctee 1987–92, sec Cons Backbench Trade and Industry Ctee 1987–92, memb Public Accounts Ctee 1987–92 and 1995–97, vice-chm and jt treas Cons Pty 1992–94; treas St Petrocs Soc 2005–; FCA, CTA; *Style*— Timothy Smith, Esq

SMITH, William James; s of William Smith, and Alice, *née* Divers; *b* 2 December 1954; *Educ* St Aloysius Coll Glasgow, Heriot-Watt Univ (BSc); *m* 3 July 1978, Marion Anne, da of Hugh Charles Slevin (d 1989); 3 da (Sarah b 1981, Hannah b 1985, Moya b 1994), 1 s (Alastair b 1983); *Career* asst investment mangr Standard Life Assurance Co 1977–84, jt md Prudential-Bache 1986–90, dir BZW Securities 1990–97, global head of equity research UBS 1997–98; Barclays Bank plc: chief exec Savings & Investment 1998–99, md Products Retail Financial Services 1999, chief admin offr Products Retail Financial Services 1999–2000, head of equities Europe and emerging markets ABN AMRO Bank NV 2000–; FFA 1982, FIMA 1993; *Recreations* running; *Style*— William Smith, Esq; ✉ ABN AMRO Bank NV, 250 Bishopsgate, London EC2M 4AA (mobile 07776 223850)

SMITH-DODSWORTH, Sir John Christopher; 8 Bt (GB 1784), of Newland Park and Thornton Watlass, Yorks; s of Sir Claude Matthew Smith-Dodsworth, 7 Bt (d 1940); *b* 4 March 1935; *Educ* Ampleforth; *m* 1, 1961 (m dis 1971), Margaret Anne, da of Alfred Jones, of Pludds, Glos; 1 da (Cyrilla Denise b 1962), 1 s (David John b 1963); m 2, 1972, Margaret Theresa (d 1990), da of Henry Grey, of Auckland, NZ; 1 s (Daniel Leui'i b 1974); m 3, 10 March 1991 (m dis 2005), Lolita, da of Romeo Pulante, of Laur, Philippines; 1 da (Joanna Marie b 23 April 1992), 1 s (John Joseph b 12 April 1995); m 4, 29 April 2006, Nerrisa, da of Mateo Feratero, of Manila, Philippines; *Heir* s, David Smith-Dodsworth; *Publications* incl: New Zealand Ferns and Allied Plants (with P J Brownsey, 1989, 2 edn 2001), New Zealand Native Shrubs and Climbers (1991); *Style*— Sir John Smith-Dodsworth, Bt; ✉ Driving Creek, PO Box 26, Coromandel, New Zealand (tel and fax 07 8667698)

SMITH-GORDON, Sir (Lionel) Eldred Peter; 5 Bt (UK 1838); s of Sir Lionel Eldred Pottinger Smith-Gordon, 4 Bt (d 1976); *b* 7 May 1935; *Educ* Eton, Trinity Coll Oxford; *m* 1962, Sandra Rosamund Ann, da of late Wing Cdr Walter Farley, DFC; 1 s (Lionel George Eldred b 1964), 1 da (Isobel Charlotte Laura b 1966); *Heir* s, Lionel Smith-Gordon; *Career* chm Smith-Gordon and Co Ltd scientific, technical and med publishers 1988–; *Style*— Sir Eldred Smith-Gordon, Bt; ✉ 13 Shalcomb Street, London SW10 0HZ (tel 020 7352 8506)

SMITH-MARRIOTT, Sir Hugh Cavendish; 11 Bt (GB 1774), of Sydling St Nicholas, Dorset; s (by 1 m) of Sir Ralph George Smith-Marriott, 10 Bt (d 1987); *b* 22 March 1925; *Educ* Bristol Cathedral Sch; *m* 1953, Pauline Anne (d 1985), da of Frank Fawcett Holt, of Bristol; 1 da (Julie Anne (Mrs David A Graveney) b 1958); *Heir* bro, Peter Smith-Marriott; *Career* md Drawing Office Co 1956, gp mktg exec Bryan Bros Gp 1976, PR and mktg exec dir 1987–, dir H S M Mktg Ltd 1988–; dir Royal Br Legion Festival of Remembrance Bristol 1966–2006; pres Bristol Musical Comedy Club; *Recreations* theatre, golf, water colour painting; *Clubs* Gloucestershire CCC, MCC, Bristol Savages, Bristol RFC, Old Cathedralians Soc (chm), Royal Mariners Assoc; *Style*— Sir Hugh Smith-Marriott, Bt

SMITH OF CLIFTON, Baron (Life Peer UK 1997), of Mountsandel in the County of Londonderry; Prof Sir Trevor Arthur Smith; kt (1996); s of late Arthur James Smith, of Newnham-on-Severn, Glos, and Vera Gladys, *née* Cross; *b* 14 June 1937; *Educ* LSE (BSc); *m* 1, 14 Feb 1960 (m dis 1973), Brenda Susan, *née* Eustace; 2 s (Hon Adam James William b 6 June 1964, Hon Gideon Matthew Kingsley b 14 May 1966); m 2, 9 Aug 1979, Julia Donnithorne, *née* Bullock; 1 da (Hon Naomi Thérèse b 8 June 1981); *Career* school teacher LCC 1958–59, temp asst lectr Univ of Exeter 1959–60, res offr Acton Soc Tst 1960–62, lectr in politics Univ of Hull 1962–67 visiting assoc prof California State Univ Los Angeles 1969; QMC (later Queen Mary & Westfield Coll) London: lectr (later sr lectr) in political studies 1967–83, head of dept 1972–85, dean of social studies 1979–82, prof 1983–91, pro-princ 1985–87, sr pro-princ 1987–89, sr vice-princ 1989–91; vice-chllr Univ of Ulster 1991–99; dir: Job Ownership Ltd 1978–85, New Society Ltd 1986–88, Statesman and Nation Publishing Co Ltd 1988–90, Gerald Duckworth & Co Ltd 1990–95; chm Conf of Rectors in Ireland 1987, chm Political Studies Assoc of UK 1988–89 (vice-pres 1989–91 and 1993–, pres 1991–93); govr: Sir John Cass and Redcoats Sch 1979–84, Univ of Haifa

1985–92, Bell Educn Tst 1988–93; memb Tower Hamlets DHA 1987–91 (vice-chm 1989–91), vice-pres Patients Assoc of UK 1988–97, dep pres Inst of Citizenship Studies 1991–, non-exec dir N Yorks HA 2000–02; pres Belfast Civic Tst 1995–99; memb: Administrative Bd Int Assoc of Univs 1995–96, Editorial Bd Government and Opposition 1995–, Bd A Taste of Ulster 1996–99, Bd of Opera Northern Ireland, UK Socrates Cncl 1993–99 (chm 1996–99); Parliamentary candidate (Lib) Lewisham West 1959; House of Lords: Lib Dem Spokesman on NI, memb Select Ctee on Science and Technology Sub-Ctee on Complementary and Alternative Med 1999–2000, memb British-Irish Inter-Parliamentary Body 2000–, memb EU Select Ctee E (Law and Institutions) 2001, chm Select Ctee on Animals in Scientific Proceedures 2001–2002, memb Select Ctee on Communications 2004–06, memb Select Ctee on Constitution 2005–, memb Sub-Ctee on Lords' Interests 2006–; dir Joseph Rowntree Reform Trust Ltd 1975–2006 (chm 1987–99), dir Democratic Audit Ltd 2007–; Hon LLD: Dublin 1992, Hull 1993, Belfast 1995, NUI 1996; Hon DHL Alabama 1998, Hon DLitt Univ of Ulster 2002; hon memb Senate Fachhochschule Augsburg 1994, hon fell Queen Mary Univ of London 2003; AcSS 2001; FRHistS 1986, CIMgt 1992, FRSA 1994, FICPD 1998; *Clubs* Reform; *Style*— Prof Lord Smith of Clifton; ✉ House of Lords, London SW1A 0PW

SMITH OF FINSBURY, Baron (Life Peer UK 2005), of Finsbury in the London Borough of Islington; Christopher Robert (Chris) Smith; PC (1997); s of Colin Smith, and Gladys, *née* Luscombe; *b* 24 July 1951; *Educ* George Watson's Coll Edinburgh, Pembroke Coll Cambridge (PhD), Harvard Univ (Kennedy scholar); *Career* housing devpt worker 1976–83, MP (Lab) Islington S and Finsbury 1983–2005 (Parly candidate (Lab) Epsom and Ewell 1979); oppn front bench spokesman on Treasy and econ affrs 1987–92, memb Shadow Cabinet 1992–97, chief oppn spokesman on environmental protection 1992–94, shadow sec of state for Nat Heritage 1994–95; chief oppn spokesman on: social security 1995–96, health 1996–97; sec of state DCMS 1997–2001; dir Clore Leadership Programme 2003–; memb Environment Select Ctee 1983–87; chm: Tribune Group of MPs 1988–89 (sec 1984–88), Lab Campaign for criminal justice 1985–88; memb Ctee on Standards in Public Life 2001–04; pres Lab Environment Campaign (SERA) 1992–2007; visiting prof Univ of the Arts London 2002–; sr advsr Walt Disney Co 2001–07; cnclir London Borough of Islington 1978–83 (chief whip 1978–79, chm Housing Ctee 1981–83); ASTMS branch: sec 1978–80, chm 1980–83; chm Bd Tribune Newspaper 1990–93, chm Bd New Century Magazine 1993–96; chm: Classic FM Consumer Panel 2002–07, Wordsworth Tst 2002– (tstee 2001–02), Donmar Warehouse Theatre 2004– (memb Bd 2002–04), London Cultural Consortium 2004–, Advertising Standards Authy 2007–; non-exec memb Bd Phonographic Performance Ltd 2006–, tstee John Muir Tst 1991–97; memb: Cncl for Nat Parks 1978–88, Bd of Shelter 1987–92, Exec Ctee NCCL 1986–88, Bd Sadler's Wells Theatre 1986–93, Exec Ctee Fabian Soc 1992–97 (vice-chm 1995–96, chm 1996–97), Exec Ctee Nat Tst 1995–97, Bd RNT 2001–; hon fell Pembroke Coll Cambridge 2004–; *Publications* Creative Britain (1998), Suicide of the West (jtly, 2006); *Recreations* literature, music, theatre, mountaineering; *Style*— The Rt Hon the Lord Smith of Finsbury, PC; ✉ House of Lords, London SW1A 0PW

SMITH OF GILMOREHILL, Baroness (Life Peer UK 1995), of Gilmorehill in the District of the City of Glasgow; Elizabeth Margaret Smith; DL (City of Edinburgh); da of late Frederick William Moncrieff Bennett; *b* 4 June 1940; *Educ* Univ of Glasgow; *m* 5 July 1967, Rt Hon John Smith, QC, MP (d 1994), son of late Archibald Leitch Smith, of Dunoon, Argyll; 3 da (Hon Sarah b 22 Nov 1968, Hon Jane b 28 July 1971, Hon Catherine b 4 May 1973); *Career* memb PCC 1995–2001; non-exec dir: Deutsche (Scotland) Ltd 1996–2003, Hakluyt Fndn 1998–2001, City Inn 2001; memb BP Advsy Bd for Scotland 1996–2003, chm Edinburgh Festival Fringe Soc; cncl memb Russo-British Chamber of Commerce; pres: Scottish Opera, Birkbeck Coll London 1996–2002; govr ESU; tstee: Centre for Euro Reform, John Smith Meml Tst, 21st Century Tst 2002–; memb Advsy Bd Beacon Fellowship 2002–; *Style*— The Rt Hon Lady Smith of Gilmorehill, DL; ✉ House of Lords, London SW1A 0PW

SMITH OF LEIGH, Baron (Life Peer UK 1999), of Wigan in the County of Greater Manchester; Peter Richard Charles Smith; s of Ronald Ernest Smith, and Kathleen, *née* Hocken; *b* 24 July 1945; *Educ* Bolton Sch, LSE (BSc), Garnet Coll London (CertEd), Univ of Salford (MSc); *m* 1968, Joy Lesley Booth; 1 da; *Career* lectr: Walbrook Coll London 1969–74, Manchester Coll of Art and Technol 1974–2001; Wigan MBC: cncllr 1978–, chair of fin 1982–91, ldr 1991–; vice-pres Br Epilepsy Assoc; *Recreations* gardening, jazz, sport (particularly rugby league); *Clubs* Hindley Green Labour; *Style*— The Lord Smith of Leigh; ✉ Mysevin, Old Hall Mill Lane, Atherton, Manchester M46 0RG (tel 01942 676127); Wigan Council, Town Hall, Library Street, Wigan WN1 1YN (tel 01942 827001, e-mail leader@wiganmbc.gov.uk)

SMITHAM, Peter; s of Brinley James Smitham, and Violet May, *née* Linden; *b* 11 May 1942; *Educ* Univ Coll Swansea (BSc), Univ of Salford (DMS), Stanford Univ (Sr Exec Prog); *m* Lynne Helen, *née* Wolfendale; 2 da (Andrea, Samantha); *Career* mgmnt Co-operative Wholesale Society 1964–67, ops dir then gen mangr ITT 1967–71, gen mangr Barclay Securities 1971–73, md Jermyn Holdings 1973–83, md European electronics Lex Service plc 1983–85, ptnr Permira Advisers (formerly Schroder Ventures) 1985– (managing ptnr London office 1994–98, ldr European business 1998–2000); non-exec chm Memec Inc 2001–, dir various other companies; *Style*— Peter Smitham, Esq

SMITHERMAN, Mark William; QFSM; s of William Richard Smitherman, and Audrey, *née* Holmes; *b* 21 April 1961, London; *Educ* Univ of Kingston (DMS), Univ of Greenwich (MBA); *m* 4 Aug 1995, Christian, *née* Kerr; 2 s (Robbie, Jamie), 1 da (Isla); *Career* divnl offr London Fire Brigade 1992, sr divnl offr Strathclyde Fire Brigade 1995, dep chief fire offr Nottinghamshire Fire and Rescue Serv 2000, chief fire offr South Yorkshire Fire and Rescue Serv 2004–; memb: Int Assoc of Fire Chiefs 1998, Soc of Local Authy Chief Execs 2005; MCIM 1988, MIFireE 1986; *Recreations* sky diving, judo, hill walking, keeping fit; *Style*— Mark Smitherman, Esq, QFSM; ✉ South Yorkshire Fire and Rescue Service, Command Headquarters, Wellington Street, Sheffield S1 3FG (tel 0114 272 7202, fax 0114 253 2266, e-mail msmitherman@syfire.org.uk)

SMITHERS, Prof Alan George; s of Alfred Edward (d 1976), of London, and Queenie Lilian, *née* Carmichael (d 1994); *b* 20 May 1938; *Educ* Barking Abbey, KCL (BSc, PhD), Univ of Bradford (MSc, PhD), Univ of Manchester (MEd); *m* 27 Aug 1962 (m dis 2003), Angela Grace, da of David Wykes, of Exeter; 2 da (Vaila Helen b 1967, Rachel Hilary b 1969); *Career* lectr in botany Birkbeck Coll London 1964–67, sr lectr in educn Univ of Bradford 1969–75 (research fell 1967–69), prof of educn Univ of Manchester 1976–96, prof of educn (policy research) Brunel Univ 1996–98, Sydney Jones prof of educn Univ of Liverpool 1998–2004, prof of educn and dir Centre for Educn and Employment Research Univ of Buckingham 2004–; special advsr House of Commons Educn and Skills Ctee; former memb Nat Curriculum Cncl, memb Beaumont Ctee on Nat Vocational Qualifications; CPsychol, fell Soc for Research in HE; *Books* Sandwich Courses: An Integrated Education? (1976), The Progress of Mature Students (jtly, 1986), The Growth of Mixed A Levels (jtly, 1988), The Shortage of Mathematics and Physics Teachers (jtly, 1988), Increasing Participation in Higher Education (jtly, 1989), Graduates in the Police Service (jtly, 1990), Teacher Provision in the Sciences (jtly, 1990), Gender, Primary Schools and the National Curriculum (jtly, 1991), The Vocational Route into Higher Education (1991), Teacher Provision: Trends and Perceptions (jtly, 1991), Staffing Secondary Schools in the Nineties (jtly, 1991), Every Child in Britain (Report of Channel 4 Education Commission, 1991), Beyond Compulsory Schooling (jtly, 1991), Technology in the National Curriculum (jtly, 1992), Technology at A Level (jtly, 1992), Assessing the Value (jtly, 1992), General Studies: Breadth at Level? (jtly, 1993), Changing Colleges: Further Education in the Market Place (jtly, 1993), All Our Futures: Britain's Education Revolution (1993), Technology Teachers (jtly, 1994), The Impact of Double Science (jtly, 1994), Post-18 Education: Growth, Change, Prospect (jtly, 1995), Affording Teachers (jtly, 1995), Co-educational and Single Sex Schooling (jtly, 1995), Trends in Higher Education (jtly, 1996), Technology in Secondary Schools (jtly, 1997), Staffing Our Schools (jtly, 1997), The New Zealand Qualifications Framework (1997), Co-educational and Single Sex Schooling Revisited (jtly, 1998), Degrees of Choice (jtly, 1998), Assessment in Primary Schools (1998), Teacher Supply: Old Story or New Chapter? (jtly, 1999), Further Education Re-Formed (jtly, 2000), Coping with Teacher Shortages (jtly, 2000), Talking Heads (jtly, 2000), Attracting Teachers (jtly, 2000), Teachers Leaving (jtly, 2001), Teacher Qualifications (jtly, 2003), Factors Affecting Teachers' Decisions to Leave the Profession (jtly, 2003), The Reality of School Staffing (jtly, 2003), England's Education (2004), Teacher Turnover: Wastage and Movements Between Schools (jtly, 2005), Physics in Schools and Colleges (jtly, 2005, Five Years On (jtly, 2006), Patterns and Policies in Physics Education (jtly, 2006), The Paradox of Single Sex and Coeducation (jtly, 2006), Bucking the Trend (jtly, 2007), School Headship: Present and Future (jtly, 2007); *Recreations* theatre, walking; *Style*— Prof Alan Smithers; ✉ Centre for Education and Employment Research, University of Buckingham, Buckingham MK18 1EG (tel 01280 820270, fax 01280 820343, e-mail alan.smithers@buckingham.ac.uk)

SMITHERS, Andrew Reeve Waldron; s of Prof Sir David Waldron Smithers, MD, FRCP, FRCS, FRCR (d 1995), of Knockholt, Kent, and Gwladys Margaret, *née* Angel; gs of Sir Waldron Smithers, MP for 30 yrs Chislehurst and Orpington; *b* 21 September 1937; *Educ* Winchester, Clare Coll Cambridge (MA); *m* 8 June 1963, (Amanda) Jill, da of Edward Gilbert Kennedy; 2 s ((Matthew) Pelham b 10 Oct 1964, (Jonathan) Kit b 6 Dec 1967); *Career* chm: Whatman plc (formerly Whatman Reeve Angel plc) 1969–2002 (dir 1960–2002), Smithers & Co Ltd (Economic Conslts) 1989–; dir: S G Warburg Securities 1967–89 (joined co 1962), Mercury Selected Trust 1977–96; *Books* Japan's Key Challenges for the 21st Century (jtly, 1998), Valuing Wall Street (jtly, 2000); *Recreations* conversation, reading, performing arts; *Clubs* Brooks's; *Style*— Andrew Smithers, Esq; ✉ Smithers & Co Ltd, 20 St Dunstan's Hill, London EC3R 8HL (tel 020 7283 3344, fax 020 7283 3345, e-mail info@smithers.co.uk)

SMITHSON, Dr (William) Henry; s of Ronald Geoffrey Smithson (d 1965), of Wetherby, W Yorks, and Harriet, *née* Gregson (d 2005); *Educ* Leeds GS, Univ of Dundee (MB ChB), Univ of York (MSc); *m* 24 June 1982, Jeanne Rachael, da of John Edmund Smales, of Roos, E Yorks; 1 s (William John b 6 May 1984), 1 da (Elizabeth Anne b 13 June 1988); *Career* GP trainee York Vocational Trg Scheme 1977–80, assoc family physician The Pas Manitoba Canada 1980–82, princ in gen practice Escrick York 1982–; GP trainer 1986–91, vol trg course organiser York 1991–2000, prescribing lead and memb Bd Selby Primary Care Gp 1999–2001; hon clinical sr lectr Hull York Med Sch 2003–; RCGP: memb Yorks Faculty 1989–, chm Yorks Faculty 1996–99, Prince of Wales educnl fell in epilepsy 1996–98; memb: BMA 1982, York Med Soc 1983; professional memb Br Epilepsy Assoc 1994; chair Epilepsy Guidelines Gp Nat Inst for Clinical Excellence (NICE) 2002–04, Leading Practice Through Research grant holder Health Fndn 2003–05; DRCOG, FRCGP (MRCGP); *Publications* Epilepsy: A General Practice Problem (1997), Integrating the Algorithm into Community Practice (1999), Net Based Education (2000), Neuropathic Pain (2001), National Clinical Sentinel Audit on Epilepsy Related Death (2001), Epilepsy: Death in the Shadows (2002); *Recreations* cricket, writing, foreign travel; *Clubs* York Wanderers Cricket; *Style*— Dr Henry Smithson; ✉ Drs Smithson, Butlin, Lenthall and Hanly, The Surgery, Escrick, York YO19 6LE (tel 01904 728243, fax 01904 728826, e-mail henry.smithson@gp-b82018.nhs.uk)

SMITHSON, Simon; s of Peter D Smithson (d 2003), and Alison M, *née* Gill (d 1997); *b* 28 June 1954; *Educ* Univ of Cambridge (BA, DipArch), Harvard Univ Graduate Sch of Design (MA); *Career* architect; George Candelis Paris 1976–77, Foster Associates 1979–80, Cambridge Seven Associates USA 1982–85, Civitas Inc USA 1985–88, Nicholas Hare Architects 1989–91, Richard Rogers Partnership 1991– (assoc dir 1996–), dir Richard Rogers SL (Spain) 2005; lectr: Harvard Univ, Univ of Colorado Denver, Univ of Madrid; *Projects* incl: General Cinema Corp refurbishment strategy, Williams Coll Athletic Facilities USA, street furniture for 16th Street Mall Denver USA, BAT HQ Staines, Shanghai Masterplan, Heathrow Airport Terminal 5, Daiwa Europe House, Lloyd's Register of Shipping, ParcBIT Masterplan Palma, Welsh Assembly Building, Antwerp Law Courts, T4 Madrid Barajas Airport, Pabilion de Estado Madrid Barajas, Abengoa HQ Seville, multi use building Campus de Justicia Madrid; masterplans: Coto de Macairena Granada, Vallodolid Este, Castilla Leon Spain; *Clubs* London Rowing; *Style*— Simon Smithson, Esq; ✉ Richard Rogers Partnership, Thames Wharf, Rainville Road, London W6 9HA

SMOUHA, Brian Andrew; s of Wing Cdr Edward Ralph Smouha, OBE (d 1992), and Yvonne Annie, *née* Ades; *b* 3 September 1938; *Educ* Harrow, Magdalene Coll Cambridge; *m* 28 Dec 1961, Hana Smouha, da of Simon Btesh (d 1974); 2 s (Joe, *qv*, b 20 Jan 1963, Stephen b 12 April 1965); *Career* chartered accountant; ptnr Deloitte & Touche 1970–2001, seconded under-sec Industrial Devpt Unit Dept of Industry 1979–80, seconded Deloitte & Touche LLP USA 1997–2000, dep chm Dawnay, Day International Ltd; liquidator of: Banco Ambrosiano 1983, BCCI 1991; pres Cambridge Athletics Union 1961, rep UK at athletics; FCA 1973; *Recreations* skiing, tennis, walking, opera; *Style*— Brian Smouha, Esq; ✉ Dawnay, Day International Ltd, 17 Grosvenor Gardens, London SW1W 0BD

SMOUHA, Joe; QC (2003); s of Brian Smouha, *qv*, and Hana, *née* Btesh; *b* 20 January 1963; *Educ* Magdalene Coll Cambridge (MA), NYU Sch of Law (Fulbright Scholar, LLM); *Career* called to the Bar Middle Temple 1986; practising barr specialising in int commercial law and art litigation, memb Essex Court Chambers 1987–; memb: Commercial Bar Assoc, London Common Law and Commercial Bar Assoc; govr Royal Sch, dir English Concert, tstee young@now; *Style*— Joe Smouha, Esq, QC; ✉ Essex Court Chambers, 24 Lincoln's Inn Fields, London WC2A 3EG

SMOUT, Prof (Thomas) Christopher; CBE (1994); s of Arthur Smout (d 1961), of Sheriffs Lench, Worcs, and Hilda, *née* Follows (d 1979); *b* 19 December 1933; *Educ* Leys Sch Cambridge, Clare Coll Cambridge (MA, PhD); *m* 15 Aug 1959, Anne-Marie, da of Alfred Schøning, of Charlottenlund, Denmark; 1 da (Pernille Anne b 1961), 1 s (Andrew b 1963); *Career* prof of econ history Univ of Edinburgh 1971 (asst lectr 1959); Univ of St Andrews: prof of Scottish history 1980–91, dir St John's House Centre for Advanced Historical Studies 1992–97, dir Inst for Environmental History 1992–2000; historiographer Royal Scotland 1993–; memb Royal Cmmn on Ancient and Historical Monuments (Scotland) 1986–2000, dep chm Bd Scottish Nat Heritage until 1996, memb Royal Cmmn on Historic Manuscripts until 2003, memb Advsy Ctee on Public and Historical Records 2003; tstee Nat Museum of Scotland until 1995; hon fell Trinity Coll Dublin 1995, Hon DSocSc Queen's Univ Belfast 1995, Hon DSSS Univ of Edinburgh 1996, Hon DLitt Univ of St Andrews 1999, Hon DLitt Univ of Glasgow 2001, Hon DUniv Stirling 2002; FRSE 1978, FBA 1988, FSA Scot 1991; *Books* A History of the Scottish People (1969), A Century of the Scottish People (1986), Scottish Voices (with Sydney Wood, 1990), Prices, Food and Wages in Scotland 1550–1780 (with A J S Gibson, 1995), Nature Contested (2000), A History of the Native Woodlands of Scotland 1500–1920 (with A R MacDonald and F Watson, 2004); *Recreations* birds, butterflies, moths, dragonflies and bees; *Style*— Prof

Christopher Smout, CBE, FBA, FRSE; ✉ Chesterhill, Shore Road, Anstruther, Fife KY10 3DZ (tel 01333 310330, e-mail tcs1@st-andrews.ac.uk)

SMOUT, (Peter Alun) Clifford; s of Peter Smout (d 2006), and Mary Patricia, *née* Chadbourne; *b* 26 July 1956; *Educ* Kimbolton Sch, Clare Coll Cambridge (BA); *m* 26 Oct 1985, Eileen Frances, *née* Roots (d 2005); 1 da (Jennifer Frances b 17 May 1988), 1 s (Alistair David b 17 Aug 1991); *Career* Bank of England: Int Div 1978–83, Money Markets Div 1983–86, fndr memb Wholesale Markets Supervision Div 1986–87, dep govr's private sec 1987–89, portfolio mangr Foreign Exchange Div 1989–91, sr mangr Supervision of US Banks 1991–93, head of Supervisory Policy Div 1993–98, head of Foreign Exchange 1998–2002, fin dir 2002–06; fin services advsy Deloitte 4 Touche 2006–; memb: RSPB, Herts & Middx Wildlife Tst, Herts Bird Club; *Recreations* birdwatching, football (Northampton Town supporter); *Style—* Clifford Smout, Esq; ✉ Deloitte 4 Touche LLP, Stonecutter Court, 1 Stonecutter Street, London EC4A 4TR (tel 020 7303 6390)

SMYTH, Christopher Jackson; s of Col Edward Hugh Jackson Smyth, FRCS, of Churt, Surrey, and Ursula Helen Lucy, *née* Ross (d 1984); *b* 9 August 1946; *Educ* St Lawrence Coll, Trinity Hall Cambridge (MA); *m* 9 Dec 1972, Jane Elizabeth, da of Dr Robert Alexander Porter (d 1981); 3 da (Deborah-Jayne b 1976, Sophie b 1979, Amanda b 1982); *Career* Lt RN 1966–76, Lt Cdr Sussex Div RNR 1978–82; called to the Bar Inner Temple 1972; recorder of the Crown Court 1994; dist chm Appeal Service Tbnl 2004, chm and exec dir Resolve: the Christian Mediation and Arbitration Service; pres (UK) Int Christian C of C; *Recreations* sailing, fly fishing, gardening; *Clubs* National, RNSA; *Style—* Christopher Smyth, Esq; ✉ c/o National Club, 69 St James Street, London SW1A 1PJ

SMYTH, His Hon Judge David William; QC (1989); s of William McKeag Smyth (d 1954), and Eva Maud, *née* Moran (d 1992); *b* 12 November 1948; *Educ* Methodist Coll Belfast, Queen's Univ Belfast (Porter scholar, LLB); *m* 23 July 1977, Anthea Linda Hall-Thompson, DL, da of Lloyd Hall-Thompson (former MP, d 1992); 3 da (Rachel Anthea b 13 Feb 1979, Hannah Sophia b 31 Dec 1983 d 1984, Rebecca Charlotte b 21 May 1987), 1 s (Alasdair Lloyd William b 26 Aug 1980); *Career* called to the NI Bar 1972 (bencher 1997), political res London 1972–74, called to the Bar Gray's Inn 1978, called to the Bar of Ireland 1989; County Court judge: Fermanagh and Tyrone 1990–97, Antrim 1997–; chm: Legal Aid Advsy Bd NI 1994–2005, NI Cncl on Alcohol 1996–98, Bd of Advsrs Inst of Criminology Queen's Univ Belfast 2002, Cncl of County Court Judges 2005–; memb: Criminal Justice Working Gp on Drugs 2002, Ctee Anglo-French Judicial Gp 2002, Youth Conferencing Advsy Gp 2003; Winston Churchill Fellowship 2001; pres NI Community Addiction Service 1998, tstee N Belfast Working Mens' Club 1974–; *Recreations* cycling, history, opera, theatre; *Style—* His Hon Judge Smyth, QC; ✉ Royal Courts of Justice, Chichester Street, Belfast BT1 3JE (tel 028 9751 1621, e-mail dsmyth.rcj@courtsni.gov.uk)

SMYTH, (Joseph) Desmond; CBE (2000); s of Andrew Smyth (d 1991), and Annie Elizabeth, *née* Scott; *b* 20 April 1950; *Educ* Limavady GS, Queen's Univ Belfast (BSc); *m* 23 April 1975, (Irene) Janette, da of John Dale (d 1991); 1 s (Stuart b 1976), 1 da (Kerry b 1978); *Career* Ulster Television: accountant 1975–76, co sec and fin controller 1976–83, md 1983–99; dir Viridian plc 1996–2005; pres NI C of C and Industry 1991–92; FCA, FRTS, MInstD; *Recreations* cycling, cinema, fishing; *Style—* Desmond Smyth, Esq, CBE

SMYTH, Rev (William) Martin; s of James Smyth, JP (d 1982), of Belfast, and Minnie Kane; *b* 15 June 1931; *Educ* Methodist Coll Belfast, Magee UC Londonderry, Trinity Coll Dublin (BA, BD), Presbyterian Coll Belfast; *m* 1957, Kathleen Jean, da of David Johnston (d 1978), of Ballymatoskerty, Toomebridge; 2 da (and 1 da decd); *Career* ordained Raffrey Presbyterian Church 1957, installed Alexandra (Belfast) 1963–82, minister without charge April 1982; grand master: Grand Orange Lodge of Ireland 1972–96, World Orange Cncl 1973–82; hon dep grand master Orange Order: USA, NZ, NSW; hon past grand master Canada; elected NI Assembly Oct 1982–86, chm of Assembly Health and Social Services Ctee; MP (UUP) Belfast S 1982–2005, UU Pty spokesman on health, social security, chief whip 1995–97, pres UU Cncl 2000–04; vice-chm Parly Social Servs Panel; memb: Br Exec IPU 1985–92 and 1994–2005, Social Servs Select Ctee 1983–90, UK Exec CPA 1989–2005, Health Select Ctee 1991–97; hon sec Parly and Scientific Ctee 2003–05 (treas 2000–03); vice-chm: Br-Brazilian Gp, Br-Taiwan Gp; sec Br-Israel Gp, treas Br-Indo Gp; fell: Industry and Parl Tst, Parly Police Scheme; *Recreations* reading, photography, travel; *Style—* The Rev Martin Smyth; ✉ 6 Mornington, Annadale Avenue, Belfast BT7 3JS (tel 028 9064 3816, fax 028 9064 3816)

SMYTH, Michael Thomas; 2 s of Rev Kenneth Smyth, and Freda Smyth; *Educ* Royal Belfast Academical Inst, Clare Coll Cambridge (MA); *m* Joyce Smyth, *née* Young; 1 s (William), 1 da (Rachel); *Career* slr; ptnr and head of public policy Clifford Chance; chm Public Concern at Work; visiting fell Univ of Essex 2003–06; FRSA; *Books* Business and the Human Rights Act (2000); *Clubs* Reform; *Style—* Michael Smyth, Esq; ✉ Clifford Chance, 10 Upper Bank Street, London E14 5JJ (tel 020 7006 1000, fax 020 7006 5555, e-mail michael.smyth@cliffordchance.com)

SMYTH, Peterjohn Jeremy Vignaux; s of late Eric Thomas William Smyth, and Olive Cecily Smyth; *b* 14 April 1940; *Educ* Ampleforth (Cambridge exhibitioner), Clare Coll Cambridge (BA, Dip Arch); *m* Jan 1966, Julia, da of Hubert Alwyn Child; 1 s (Timothy Christian b 15 Sept 1966), 2 da (Rhoda b 9 Jan 1970, Dorothy Vignaux b 21 April 1973); *Career* architect; Morton Lupton & Smith Wallingford Berks 1963–66; Percy Thomas Partnership (Architects) Ltd (formerly Sir Percy Thomas & Son then Percy Thomas Partnership): joined 1966, assoc 1972–80, ptnr 1980–94, dir 1994–, chm 2003; ldr and co-ordinating architect Prince of Wales' new urban village Poundbury (Dorchester) 1993; memb: Urban Villages Forum 1994–, Princes Fndn; work experience incl healthcare, university, housing, urban design and gen architecture projects; contrib articles to various pubns and sometime speaker and lectr; RIBA 1966; *Awards* winner int competition for 600 bed hosp Cairo 1975, int competition for 1000 bed hosp Avellino (Italy) 1992; *Recreations* golf; *Style—* Peterjohn Smyth, Esq

SMYTH, Richard Ian; s of Ronald Smyth (d 1987), and Elsa, *née* Martin (d 1976); *b* 19 November 1951, Sunderland; *Educ* Sedbergh, Emmanuel Coll Cambridge (Turner exhibitioner, MA, PGCE, Cricket blue, Rugby half blue); *m* 1983, Nicole Adrienne, *née* Ryser; 2 da (Helen b 23 Dec 1985, Esther b 17 Feb 1990), 1 s (Stuart b 23 June 1987); *Career* teacher Christ's Hosp Horsham 1975–77, family business Sunderland and Darlington 1977–81, licensed asst to Anglican vicar of Berne Switzerland 1981–82, teacher Gresham's Sch Holt 1982–85, teacher Wellington Coll 1985–92, headmaster King's Sch Bruton 1993–2004, headmaster St Peter's Sch York 2004–; memb: HMC 1993, ASCL; *Recreations* cricket, rugby, alpine flowers; *Clubs* East India, MCC, Free Foresters; *Style—* Richard Smyth, Esq; ✉ St Peter's School, York YO30 6AB (tel 01904 527408, fax 01904 527302, e-mail r.smyth@st-peters.york.sch.uk)

SMYTH, (John) Rodney; s of John Clifford Smyth, of Heswall, Merseyside; *b* 23 August 1953; *Educ* Shrewsbury, Magdalene Coll Cambridge (MA); *m* 20 July 1990, Sarah, *née* Johnson; 1 s (Edward John Richard b 13 Oct 1995); *Career* barr 1975–79; admitted slr 1980; asst slr Holman, Fenwick & Willan 1980–82, ptnr Lovell White Durrant (formerly Durrant Piesse) 1985–95 (asst slr 1982–85), head of legal servs L G T Asset Management plc 1997–98 (asst compliance offr 1995–96), head of legal INVESCO UK Ltd 2002–04 (slr 1998–2002); memb Law Soc; *Recreations* birdwatching, weather, dogs; *Style—* Rodney Smyth, Esq; ✉ Brickhouse Farm, Cuckold's Green Road, St Mary Hoo, Rochester, Kent ME3 8RP (tel 01634 270 326, e-mail rodneysatbhf@aol.com)

SMYTH, Stephen Mark James Athelstan; s of Marcus Smyth (d 1965), of Ditchling, E Sussex, and Ann, *née* Symons; *b* 28 December 1946; *Educ* Hurstpierpoint Coll, Alliance Française; *m* 22 May 1981, Bridget Rosemary Diana, da of Maj (Arthur) Creagh Gibson (d 1970), of Glenburn Hall, Jedburgh; 2 da (Lalage Vivien b 5 Jan 1986, India b 24 May 1989); *Career* worked way around world 1966–67, PA to Greville Janner, MP 1973; called to the Bar Inner Temple 1974, recorder 2001– (asst recorder 1994–2001); chm Churchill Clinic IVF Ethical Ctee 1995; *Recreations* books, sailing; *Clubs* Bosham Sailing; *Style—* Stephen Smyth, Esq; ✉ 2 Harcourt Buildings, Temple, London EC4 (tel 020 7353 2112, fax 020 7353 8339)

SMYTH, Dr Sir Timothy John; 2 Bt (UK 1956), of Teignmouth, Co Devon; s of Julian Smyth (d 1974, himself 2 s of Brig Rt Hon Sir John Smyth, 1 Bt, VC, MC (d 1983)), and his w Philomena Mary, *née* Cannon; *b* 16 April 1953; *Educ* Univ of NSW (MB BS, LLB, MBA); *m* 1981, Bernadette Mary, da of Leo Askew; 2 s, 2 da; *Heir* s, Brendan Smyth; *Career* health lawyer; *Style—* Dr Sir Timothy Smyth, Bt; ✉ PO Box A2188, Sydney South, NSW, Australia 1235

SNAPE, Baron (Life Peer UK 2004), of Wednesbury in the County of West Midlands; Peter Charles Snape; s of Thomas Snape, and Kathleen Snape; *b* 12 February 1942; *Educ* St Joseph's Stockport, St Winifred's Stockport; *m* 1963 (m dis 1980); 2 da; *Career* former railway signalman then guard, soldier (RE & RCT), British Rail clerk; MP (Lab) West Bromwich E Feb 1974–2001, memb Cncl of Europe and WEU 1975, asst Govt whip 1975–77, Lord Cmmr of the Treasury (Govt whip) 1977–79; oppn front bench spokesman: on defence and disarmament 1981–82, home affrs 1982–83, transport 1983–92; *Style—* The Rt Hon the Lord Snape

SNASHALL, Dr David Charles; s of Cyril Francis Snashall (d 1998), of London, and Phyllis Mary, *née* Hibbitt (d 1970); *b* 3 February 1943; *Educ* Haberdashers' Aske's, Univ of Edinburgh (MB ChB), LSHTM (MSc, DIH, DTM&H), Univ of Wales Cardiff (LLM); *Children* (Lesley b 1963, Rebecca b 1978, Corinna b 1996); *Career* resident posts in hosp med and gen practice UK, Canada and France 1968–75, chief MO Majes Consortium Peru 1975–76, chief med advsr Tarmac 1977–81, project MO Mufindi Project 1981–82, chief MO Costain Group of Companies 1982–89, med advsr to House of Commons 1982–91, hon conslt and clinical dir of staff occupational health servs W Lambeth HA 1982–93, sr lectr in occupational health GKT 1982–, chief med advsr FCO 1989–98, chief med advsr Health and Safety Exec 1998–2003; clinical dir occupational health servs Guy's and St Thomas' Hosp Tst 1993–; pres Faculty of Occupational Medicine RCP 2005–, chair Research Ethics Ctee Health and Safety Exec 2003–; memb: Health Servs Advsy Ctee HSE (BMA nominated) 1987–92, GMC 1989–96 and 1999–2003, Editorial Ctee Occupational and Environmental Med 1994–, Fitness to Practise Panel 2003–; SE Thames regnl speciality advsr 1989–2005; FFOM 1987 (AFOM 1981, MFOM 1983), FRCP 1993 (MRCP 1972), FFOM 2004, FFTMGlas 2006; *Publications* incl: Searching for Causes of Work-related Diseases: An Introduction to Epidemiology at the Work Site (jtly, 1991), ABC of Work-related Disorders (ed, 1997), ABC of Occupational and Environmental Medicine (ed, 2003); *Recreations* travel, European languages, jazz music, mountaineering, cooking, gardening; *Clubs* Ronnie Scott's; *Style—* Dr David Snashall; ✉ 2 Charity Cottages, Petsoe End, Olney, Buckinghamshire MK46 5JN (tel 01234 711072); King's College London, School of Medicine, Occupational Health Department, St Thomas' Hospital, London SE1 7EH (tel 020 7188 4147)

SNEATH, Christopher George; s of Arthur George Sneath (d 1972), and Dorothy, *née* Knight (d 1989); *b* 27 June 1933; *Educ* Canford Sch; *m* 12 May 1962, Patricia Lesley, da of Anthony Spinks (d 1982); 1 da (Deborah Jane b 16 July 1963), 1 s (James Rupert b 19 Jan 1966); *Career* CA 1957; sr ptnr specialising in int business matters KPMG Peat Marwick 1978–94 (ptnr 1971–94), dep sec gen Peat Marwick Int 1978–80; receiver gen Order of St John 1991–98; dir: Spirax-Sarco Engineering plc 1994–2002, Millennium & Copthorne Hotels plc 1999–; vice-pres Saracens RFC (hon treas 1980–2005), dir Saracens Ltd 1996–2003; chm of govrs Queenswood Sch Herts 1999–2005 (govr 1989–2005), tstee The Sir Thomas Lipton Meml Home; FCA; KStJ 1991; *Books* Guide to Acquisitions in the US (1989); *Recreations* watching cricket and rugby football, maintaining Lotus motor cars; *Clubs* Carlton, MCC, Pilgrims; *Style—* Christopher Sneath, Esq; ✉ Ascot House, Paradise Drive, Eastbourne, East Sussex BN20 7SX (tel 01323 725709, e-mail csneath@aol.com)

SNEATH, Christopher Gilbert; s of Colin Frank Sneath, of Brookmans Park; *b* 25 June 1938; *Educ* Framlingham Coll; *m* 25 May 1963, Elizabeth Mary, da of Bernard Stephen Copson, of Potters Bar, Herts; 2 da (Lucy Jane b 1965, Julia Elizabeth b 1967); *Career* Nat Serv RCS 1957–59; md Barrett & Wright Group Ltd 1971–92, dir Phab UK Ltd 1991, sales and mktg dir A G Manly Group Ltd 1992–1999, dir C J Bartley & Co Ltd 1995–2000, conslt BSC Consulting; pres Heating & Ventilating Contractors Assoc 1990–91 and 1996; assessor Latham Review of Construction Industry 1994, conslt Building Services Research and Information Assoc 1998–2001, chm Construction Industry Sector Advsy Gp 1999–2001, dep chm Construction Industry Bd 1999–2001, chm Plumbing and Heating Industry Alliance 2001–, chm Dep PM's Construction Health and Safety Task Ctee 1999–2001; chm Potters Bar and Dist Abbeyfield Soc 2002–03; capt Brookmans Park Golf Club 1980–81 (pres 1994–99), chm London Area Clubs Physically Handicapped Able Bodied 1987; govr Mount Grace Sch; memb Worshipful Co of Plumbers 1991 (membe Ct of Assts 2006); CEng, FCIBSE; *Recreations* golf, marathon running; *Clubs* Brookmans Park Golf, Thorpeness Golf, RAC; *Style—* Christopher Sneath, Esq; ✉ 31 Brookmans Avenue, Brookmans Park, Hatfield, Hertfordshire AL9 7QH (tel 01707 658709, fax 01707 661570, e-mail cgsneath@dial.pipex.com)

SNEDDEN, David King; s of David Snedden; *b* 23 February 1933; *Educ* Daniel Stewart's Coll Edinburgh; *m* 1958; 2 s (Keith b 1961, Stuart b 1963), 1 da (Ann); *Career* formerly: investment advsr Guinness Mahon Ltd, dir Radio Forth Ltd, memb Press Cncl; md: Belfast Telegraph Newspapers 1966–70 (dir 1979–82), Scotsman Publications 1970–79; Thomson Regional Newspapers Ltd: dir 1974–, gp asst md 1979–80, jt md 1980–82; Trinity Int Holdings plc: md and chief exec 1982–93, non-exec dir 1993–98, chm 1994–98; exec chm Headway Home and Law Publishing Gp Ltd 1993, chm Norcor Holdings plc 1994–99; non-exec dir BSkyB Ltd 1994–97; dir: Reuters Holdings plc 1987–94, The Press Assoc 1984–92 (chm 1989–91); *Recreations* golf, fishing; *Clubs* Bruntsfield Links Golfing Soc, Isle of Harris Golf, Grantown on Spey; *Style—* David K Snedden, Esq; ✉ Flat 29, Ravelston Heights, Edinburgh EH4 3LX (tel 0131 343 3290, fax 0131 332 0578)

SNELGROVE, Anne; MP; *b* 7 August 1957, Wokingham; *Educ* Bracknell Ranelagh Sch, King Alfred's Coll Winchester, City Univ; *Career* former teacher, former LEA advsr; MP (Lab) Swindon S 2005–; memb: Co-op Pty, Amicus, Amnesty Int; *Style—* Ms Anne Snelgrove, MP; ✉ House of Commons, London SW1A 0AA

SNELL, Richard Owen; s of Richard Henry Snell, and Mildred, *née* Ratcliffe; *b* 5 September 1947; *Educ* Univ of Leeds (BSc); *m* Sheila; 1 s (Richard James b 1976); *Career* section engr Sir William Halcrow & Partners Ltd; BP Exploration: engr Marine Branch 1980–83, head Civil Engineering (UK) 1983–86, sr conslt Structures Div 1986–2000, ldr Structures and Naval Architecture 1992–2000, sr advsr 2000–; memb Segment Engrg Tech Authy; chm Offshore Structures Standards Ctee Int Standards Orgn; FREng, FICE 1996, FIStructE 2007; *Publications* author of several learned jls; *Recreations* yachting, travel, history; *Clubs* RYA, WMYC, RNVRYC; *Style—* Richard Snell, Esq, FREng; ✉ BP Exploration, Chertsey Road, Sunbury-on-Thames, Surrey TW16 7LN (tel 01932 774803, fax 01932 774833, e-mail snellro@bp.com)

SNOAD, Harold Edward; s of Sidney Edward Snoad, of Eastbourne, E Sussex, and Irene Dora, *née* Janes; *b* 28 August 1935; *Educ* Eastbourne Coll; *m* 1, 21 Sept 1957 (m dis 1963) Anne Christine, *née* Cadwallader; m 2, 6 July 1963, Jean, da of James Green (d 1968), of London; 2 da (Helen Julie b 1969, Jeanette Clare b 1975); *Career* Nat Serv RAF 1954–56; with BBC 1957–96: prodr and dir 1970–83, exec prodr and dir 1983–96; currently working freelance 1996–; produced and directed many successful comedy series for the BBC incl: The Dick Emery Show, Rings on their Fingers, The Further Adventures of Lucky Jim, Tears Before Bedtime, Hilary, Don't Wait Up, Ever Decreasing Circles, Brush Strokes, Keeping up Appearances, The Memoirs of Hyacinth Bucket (BBC Worldwide America); dir feature film Not Now Comrade, re-wrote Dad's Army for radio, dir Say Who You Are (theatre); scripted original comedy series: Share and Share Alike and It Sticks Out Half a Mile (radio), High and Dry (TV); *Books* Directing Situation Comedy (1988); *Recreations* swimming, gardening, theatre-going, DIY, motoring; *Style*— Harold Snoad, Esq; ✉ Fir Tree Cottage, 43 Hawkewood Road, Sunbury-on-Thames, Middlesex TW16 6HL (tel and fax 01932 785887)

SNOOK, John Thomas; s of Bert Snook, and Elice, *née* Brew (d 1967); *b* 22 March 1954, Manchester; *Educ* Trinity Coll Cambridge (MA); *m* Amanda, *née* Chumas; *Career* chartered accountant; Deloitte, Haskins & Sells 1975–79, 3i 1979–83, Cinven 1983–85, co-fndr and md Close Brothers Private Equity 1985–; ACA 1979, MSI 1996; *Recreations* golf, vintage sports cars, reading; *Clubs* Royal Automobile; *Style*— John Snook, Esq; ✉ Close Brothers Private Equity LLP, 10 Throgmorton Avenue, London EC2N 2DL (tel 020 7065 1100, fax 020 7588 6815, e-mail john.snook@cbpel.com)

SNOW, Antony Edmund; s of Thomas Maitland Snow, CMG (d 1997), and Phyllis Annette Hopkins, *née* Malcolmson; *b* 5 December 1932; *Educ* Sherborne, New Coll Oxford; *m* 31 March 1961, Caroline, da of Comar Wilson (d 1961); 2 da (Arabella b 1 Feb 1964, Henrietta b 2 April 1970), 1 s (Lucian b 21 Aug 1965); *Career* 10 Royal Hussars, cmmnd 1952–53; dep chm Charles Barker & Sons 1971–76, vice-pres Market Planning Stueben Glass NY 1976–78, dep dir Corning Museum of Glass USA 1978–79, dir Rockwell Museum USA 1979–83; dir: Charles Barker plc 1983–90 (chm and chief exec 1983–87), Hogg Group plc 1988–94; chm Hill and Knowlton (UK) Ltd 1992–98 (chm Mgmnt Ctee Europe 1994–99, non-exec dir 1999–), ret; tstee: Arnott Museum USA 1980–84, Corning Museum of Glass USA 1983–, V&A 1995–2002; chm Fraser Tst 1996–2001, non-exec dir Fraser CRE 2001–; memb: Ctee of Mgmnt Courtauld Inst of Art 1985–89, Exec Ctee The Art Fund 1985–, Cncl RCA 1994–2002; cncllr Design Cncl 1989–94, tstee Monteverdi Choir 1988–2001, memb AMAC Ctee English Heritage 1989–92; FIPA, FIPR; *Recreations* English watercolours, fishing; *Clubs* Cavalry and Guards'; *Style*— Antony Snow, Esq; ✉ 1 Tedwoth House, 1 Tedworth Square, London SW3 4DU (tel 020 7351 9139); Fyfield Hill Barn, Marlborough, Wiltshire (tel 01672 861498)

SNOW, Jonathan George (Jon); s of Rt Rev George D'Oyly Snow, Bishop of Whitby (d 1977), and Joan Monica, *née* Way; *b* 28 September 1947; *Educ* St Edward's Sch Oxford, Univ of Liverpool; *Children* 2 da (Leila Snow Colvin b 1982, Freya Snow Colvin b 1986); *Career* dir New Horizon Youth Centre Covent Garden 1970–73; journalist: LBC and IRN 1973–76, ITN 1976– (Washington corr 1983–86, diplomatic ed 1986–89); presenter Channel Four News 1989–; memb NUJ; visiting prof: Nottingham Trent Univ 1992–2001, Univ of Stirling 2001–; chllr Oxford Brookes Univ 2001–; tstee: Nat Gallery 1999–, Tate Gallery 1999–04 (chair Tate Modern Cncl); dep chair Media Tst 1997–; chair New Horizon Youth Centre 1986–; *Books* Atlas of Today (1987), Sons and Mothers (1996), Shooting History: A Personal Journey (2004); *Style*— Jon Snow; ✉ ITN Ltd, 200 Gray's Inn Road, London WC1X 8XZ (tel 020 7430 4237, fax 020 7430 4609)

SNOW, Peter John; CBE (2006); s of Brig John Fitzgerald Snow, CBE (Somerset LI, d 1973), and Peggy Mary, *née* Pringle (d 1970); *b* 20 April 1938; *Educ* Wellington, Balliol Coll Oxford (BA); *m* 1, 30 Sept 1964 (m dis 1975), Alison Mary, da of late George Fairlie Carter, of Piltdown, E Sussex; 1 s (Shane Fitzgerald b 1966), 1 da (Shuna Justine b 1968); m 2, 15 May 1976, Ann Elizabeth, da of Dr Robert Laidlaw MacMillan, of Toronto, Canada; 1 s (Daniel Robert b 1978), 2 da (Rebecca Olwen b 1980, Katherine Peggy b 1983); *Career* Nat Serv 2 Lt Somerset LI 1956–58; dip and def corr ITN 1966–79 (reporter and newscaster 1962–66); presenter BBC TV: Newsnight and election progs 1979–97, Tomorrow's World 1997–2001, election progs 1997–2005; presenter (with s, Dan Snow) BBC TV: Battlefield Britain 2004, 20th Century Battles 2007, What Makes Britain Rich? 2007; BBC Radio 4: question master Mastermind, question master Masterteam 1998–2005, presenter Random Edition; Judges' Award for Outstanding Contribution to TV Journalism RTS Sports and Journalism Awards 1998; vice-patron Jubilee Sailing Tst; *Books* Leila's Hijack War (1970), Hussein: A Biography (1972), Battlefield Britain (with Dan Snow, 2004), The World's Greatest 20th Century Battlefields (with Dan Snow, 2007); *Recreations* tennis, sailing, skiing, model railways; *Style*— Peter Snow, Esq, CBE; ✉ c/o BBC TV, BBC White City, Wood Lane, London W12 7TS (tel 020 8752 5252)

SNOW, Terence Clive; s of Ernest William George Snow (d 1968), and Elsie May, *née* Baynes (d 1992); *b* 18 September 1931; *Educ* Poly of N London Sch of Architecture; *m* 28 March 1953, Phyllis (d 2006), da of Frank Mann (d 1971); 4 s (Graeme b 1956, David b 1958, Phillip b 1960, John b 1969), 1 da (Patricia b 1971); *Career* Nat Serv RAF 1956–58; conslt Architects Co-Partnership 1995 (dir 1973, md 1991–95); vice-pres RIBA 1979–81 (memb Cncl 1979–86); chm: RIBA Services Ltd 1982–94, Library Planning Consultants Ltd 1982–94, National Building Specification Ltd 1982–94; dir RIBA Cos Ltd 1986–, chm NBS Services Ltd 1990–94; FRIBA 1970 (ARIBA 1960); *Recreations* magic; *Clubs* The Magic Circle; *Style*— Terence Snow, Esq; ✉ 130 Park Road, New Barnet, Hertfordshire EN4 9QN (tel 020 8449 1277)

SNOWBALL, Joseph; s of Joseph Snowball (d 1960), and Gwendoline Alice, *née* Miles (d 1990); *b* 30 April 1946; *Educ* Cardiff HS; *m* 24 Oct 1970, Priscilla, da of Joseph Bennett; 1 s (Joseph Philip b 7 Sept 1973), 1 da (Carys Anne b 17 March 1976); *Career* Coopers & Lybrand CAs: articled clerk with predecessor firm 1962–68, ptnr in associate firm Lagos Nigeria 1978–81, ptnr in UK firm S Wales 1981–88, ptnr Gloucester office 1988–94; ptnr Gloucester office Guilfoyle Sage & Co 1994–; FCA 1978 (ACA 1968); *Recreations* golf, rugby; *Clubs* Ross on Wye Golf; *Style*— Joseph Snowball, Esq; ✉ Guilfoyle Sage & Co, 58 Eastgate Street, Gloucester GL1 1QN (tel 01452 309363, fax 01452 311088, e-mail joes@guilfoylesageglos.co.uk)

SNOWBALL, Patrick Joseph Robert; s of Brig Edward Snowball, OBE (d 1987), and June Burlton (d 2001); *b* 12 June 1950; *Educ* Harrow, RMA Sandhurst, Lincoln Coll Oxford (MA); *m* 1975, Jennifer, da of James Longmore, CBE, and Hon Mrs Jean Longmore; 3 s (Robert b 1981, Thomas b 1984, Edward b 1990); *Career* Offr 4/7 Royal Dragoon Gds 1970–87 (Army Staff Coll 1983); recruitment conslt GKR 1987–88, commercial dir and md Ajax Insurance 1988–94; Norwich Union plc (merged into CGNU plc 2000 then renamed Aviva plc 2002): md General Insurance (Intermediaries) 1994–2000, md and chief exec Norwich Union Insurance 2000–03, dir Main Bd 2001–07, exec dir General Insurance Aviva plc 2003–07; *Recreations* sailing, skiing, field sports; *Clubs* Royal Yacht Sqdn, Army and Navy; *Style*— Patrick Snowball, Esq; ✉ The Old Rectory, Longham, Dereham, Norfolk NR19 2RG

SNOWDEN, Prof Christopher Maxwell; s of William Arthur Snowden, of Cottingham, and Barbara Jeanne, *née* Locking; *b* 5 March 1956; *Educ* Univ of Leeds (BSc, MSc, PhD); *m* 8 Jan 1993, Irena, *née* Lewandowska; 2 s (James b 12 March 1994, William b 6 Aug 1996); *Career* applications engr Mullard Applications Lab Surrey 1977–78, lectr Dept of Electronics Univ of York 1982–83; Univ of Leeds: lectr rising to sr lectr Dept of Electronic and Electrical Engrg 1983–92, prof of microwave engrg (personal chair) 1992–2005, head Sch of Electronic and Electrical Engrg 1995–98, dir Inst of Microwaves and Photonics 1997–98; Filtronic plc: exec dir of technol 1998–99, jt chief exec 1999–2001, ceo compound semiconductors 2001–03, ceo Filtronic ICS 2003–05; univ prof, vice-chllr and chief exec Univ of Surrey 2005–; visiting prof physics Univ of Durham 2004–05; staff scientist M/A-COM Inc Corp R&D MA 1990–91; vice-chm European Microwave Assoc 2003–; tstee Inst of Engrg and Technol (vice-pres 2006–07, dep pres 2007–09); dir: Engrg Technol Bd 2006–, Defence Scientific Advsy Cncl 2007–; chair: Employability, Business and Industry Policy Ctee UK 2007–, S E England Science Engrg and Technol Advsy Cncl 2005–; memb Engrg and Physical Sciences Research Cncl 2006–; non-exec dir: Cenamps Ltd 2003–06, Intense Ltd 2004–; chm The Daphne Jackson Charitable Tst 2005–, chm Hero Ltd 2006–; advsr First Ventures 2005–; patron Surrey Community Devpt Tst 2005–; memb Cncl for Industry and HE 2006–; IEEE distinguished lectr (electron devices) 1996–2006, IEEE Microwave Prize 1999, Silver Medal Royal Acad of Engrg 2004; memb MIT Electromagnetics Acad; FIEE 1993, FIEEE 1996, FRSA 2000, FREng 2000, FRS 2005, FCGI 2005; *Publications* author of eight books and over 300 refereed journal and conference papers incl: Introduction to Semiconductor Device Modelling (1986, Japanese trans 1988), INCA Interactive Circuit Analysis (1988), Semiconductor Device Modelling (1988), Compound Semiconductor Device Modelling (1993); *Recreations* photography, oil painting; *Style*— Prof Christopher Snowden; ✉ Vice-Chancellor's Office, University of Surrey, Guildford, Surrey GU2 7XH (tel 01483 689249, fax 01483 689518, e-mail c.snowden@surrey.ac.uk)

SNOWDON, 1 Earl of (UK 1961); Sir Antony Charles Robert Armstrong-Jones; GCVO (1969); also Viscount Linley (UK 1961), and Baron Armstrong-Jones (Life Peer UK 1999), of Nymans in the County of West Sussex; sits as Baron Armstrong-Jones; s of Ronald Owen Lloyd Armstrong-Jones, MBE, QC, DL (d 1966), of Plas Dinas, Caernarfon, and Anne, *née* Messel, later Countess of Rosse (d 1992); *b* 7 March 1930; *Educ* Eton, Jesus Coll Cambridge; *m* 1, 6 May 1960 (m dis 1978), HRH The Princess Margaret Rose (d 2002), yr da of HM the late King George VI; 1 s, 1 da; m 2, 15 Dec 1978, Lucy Mary, da of Donald Brook Davies, of Hemingstone Hall, Ipswich, and formerly w of Michael Lindsay-Hogg (film dir, s of Edward Lindsay-Hogg, gs of Sir Lindsay Lindsay-Hogg, 1 Bt, JP); 1 da (Lady Frances b 17 July 1979); *Heir* s, Viscount Linley (*see* Royal Family section); *Career* photographer and designer; artistic advsr Sunday Times and Sunday Times Publications 1962–90, The Telegraph Magazine 1990–95, consultative advsr to Design Cncl London 1962–87, editorial advsr Design Magazine 1962–87; designer: Snowdon Aviary for London Zoo (in collaboration with Cedric Price and Frank Newby, Grade 2 listed 1998) 1965, for investiture of HRH the Prince of Wales at Caernarfon Castle (in collaboration with Carl Toms, CBE and John Pound, CBE) 1969, electrically-powered wheelchair for disabled people (Chairmobile) 1972; pres: Contemporary Art Soc for Wales until 1995, Civic Tst for Wales, Welsh Theatre Co, Gtr London Arts Assoc, Int Year of Disabled People England (1981), ADAPT (Access for Disabled People to Arts Premises Today) 1995–; vice-pres Bristol Univ Photographic Soc; memb: Cncl of Nat Fund for Research into Crippling Diseases, Faculty of Designers for Industry, The Prince of Wales Advsy Gp on Disability; patron: Metropolitan Union of YMCAs, British Water Ski Fedn, Welsh Nat Rowing Club, Physically Handicapped and Able-Bodied, Circle of Guide Dog Owners, Demand, Disabled Water Skiing Assoc; fndr Snowdon Award Scheme for Disabled Students 1980; provost RCA 1995– (sr fell 1986); Constable of Caernarfon Castle 1963–; Liveryman Worshipful Co of Clothworkers; fell Manchester Coll of Art and Design, hon fell Inst of Br Photographers; Hon DUniv Bradford 1989; Hon LLD: Univ of Bath 1989, Univ of Southampton 1993; RDI, FRSA, FSIAD, FRPS; *Exhibitions* Photocall London 1958, Assignments (Photokina) 1972, London 1973, Brussels 1974, Los Angeles, St Louis, Kansas, New York and Tokyo 1975, Sydney and Melbourne 1976, Copenhagen 1976, Paris 1977, Amsterdam 1977; Serendipity Brighton 1989 (also at Bradford 1989, Bath 1990), Photographs by Snowdon - a retrospective (Nat Portrait Gallery) 2000 (also at City Arts Centre Edinburgh 2000, Kunst Haus Wien Vienna 2001, Yale Center for British Art New Haven 2001); *Television* TV films: Don't Count the Candles (CBS 1968, winner two Hollywood Emmys, St George Prix, Venice Dip, Prague and Barcelona Film Festival award), Love of a Kind (BBC 1969), Born to be Small (ATV 1971, Chicago Hugo award), Happy being Happy (ATV 1973), Mary Kingsley (BBC 1975), Burke and Wills (1975), Peter, Tina and Steve (ATV 1977), Snowdon on Camera (BBC 1981, BAFTA nomination); *Awards* Art Dirs Club of NY Certificate of Merit 1969; Soc of Publication Designers: Cert of Merit 1970, Designers Award of Excellence 1973; Wilson Hicks Cert of Merit for Photocommunication 1971, Design and Art Directors Award 1978, Royal Photographic Soc Hood Award 1979; *Books* Malta (in collaboration with Sacheverell Sitwell, 1958), London (1958), Private View (in collaboration with John Russell and Bryan Robertson, 1965), Assignments (1972), A View of Venice (1972), The Sack of Bath (1972), Inchcape Review (1977), Pride of the Shire (in collaboration with John Oakley, 1979), Personal View (1979), Tasmania Essay (1981), Sittings (1983), My Wales (in collaboration with Viscount Tonypandy, 1986), Israel - a First View (1986), Stills 1984–1987 (1987), Public Appearances 1987–1991 (1991), Wild Flowers (1995), Snowdon on Stage (1996), Wild Fruit (1997), London Sight Unseen (1999), Snowdon - a Retrospective (2000), Snowdon on Russia (2005); *Style*— The Rt Hon the Earl of Snowdon, GCVO; ✉ 22 Launceston Place, London W8 5LR (tel 020 7937 1524, fax 020 7938 1727)

SNOWDON, Graham Richard; s of Thomas Richard Snowdon (d 1970), of Doncaster, S Yorks, and Edna Mary, *née* Storm (d 1997); *b* 8 February 1944; *Educ* Doncaster GS; *m* 5 Aug 1967, Peta Dawn, da of Frederick Alfred Rawlings (d 1992), of Lowestoft, Suffolk; 1 da (Jessica Louise (Mrs Andrew Friend) b 21 March 1972), 1 s (Frazer Richard b 6 March 1974); *Career* jr reporter: Barnsley Chronicle 1960–61, Yorkshire Evening News 1961–63; family sports agency Doncaster 1963–64, competitions press offr RAC Motor Sport Div London 1964–66, northern press offr RAC Manchester 1966–70, freelance sports journalist 1969–, regular contrib Daily Telegraph 1969–2007; cycling corr: The Guardian 1985–97, Press Assoc 1990–2007; ptnr (with Peta Snowdon) Snowdon Sports Editorial (sports press agency) 1970–, md Snowdon Sports Media Ptnrs Ltd (official collators of nat sporting leagues and competitions) 2002–07; conslt Guinness Book of Records 1971–95; *Recreations* food and drink, walking, travel, motoring, autonumerology; *Clubs* Sports Journalists' Assoc of GB, Assoc Internationale des Journalistes du Cyclisme, Assoc Internationale de la Presse Sportive, NUJ (life memb 2006); *Style*— Graham Snowdon, Esq; ✉ 6 Hallam Grange Croft, Fulwood, Sheffield S10 4BP (tel 0114 230 2233, e-mail 6hgc@snowdons.co.uk); 43 Eastgate, Pickering, North Yorkshire YO18 7DU (tel 01751 477581); Snowdon Sports Media Group, PO Box 100, Sheffield S6 6YB (tel 0114 232 5555, fax 0114 232 5577)

SNOWIE, Malcolm McDonald; s of James Tait Snowie, of East Gogar, Stirling (d 1977), and Sheila Fenwick, *née* McDonald; *b* 31 March 1959, Bridge of Allan, Stirlingshire; *Educ* Morrisons Acad Crieff; *m* 1, 25 June 1982 (m dis 2003), Heather, *née* Raeburn; 1 da (Lesley b 30 June 1987), 1 s (Calum b 3 March 1990); m 2, 6 May 2006, Amanda, *née* Buitelaar; 1 step s (James b 3 Aug 1985), 1 step da (Sarah b 3 Aug 1994); *Career* farmer; md and shareholder: Snowie Holdings Ltd, Snowie Ltd, Northern Hydroseeding Ltd; dir and shareholder M&A Ind Trading Co Ltd; shareholder Moonen Yachts BV Ltd; former dir Royal Highland Agricultural Soc, memb Bd Oatridge Agric Coll; memb Inst of Waste Mgmt; *Recreations* hunting, shooting, sailing; *Style*— Malcolm Snowie, Esq; ✉ West Gogar, Blairlogie, Stirling FK9 5QB (tel 01259 727600, fax 01259 722146, e-mail malcolm@snowie.co.uk)

SNOWMAN, Daniel; s of Arthur Mortimer Snowman (d 1982), and Bertha, *née* Lazarus (d 1997); *b* 4 November 1938; *Educ* Jesus Coll Cambridge, Cornell Univ NY (MA); *m* 17 Dec 1975, Janet Linda, *née* Levison; 1 s (Benjamin b 1977), 1 da (Anna b 1978); *Career* broadcaster, writer and lectr; lectr Univ of Sussex 1963–67; prodr features arts and education BBC Radio 1968–95; prodns incl: A World in Common, The Vatican, Reith Lectures, Northern Lights (BBC Arctic Festival), variety of historical and cultural programmes; visiting prof of history Calif State Univ 1972–73; contrib to British and US newspapers and jls; *Books* America Since 1920 (1968), Eleanor Roosevelt (1970), Kissing Cousins: An Interpretation of British and American Culture, 1945–75 (1977), If I Had Been ... Ten Historical Fantasies (1979), The Amadeus Quartet: The Men and the Music (1981), The World of Plácido Domingo (1985), Beyond the Tunnel of History (1990), Pole Positions: The Polar Regions and the Future of the Planet (1993), Plácido Domingo's Tales from the Opera (1994), Fins de Siècle (with Lord Briggs, *qv*, 1996), PastMasters: The Best of History Today (2001), The Hitler Emigrés: The Cultural Impact on Britain of Refugees from Nazism (2002), Historians (2007), Hallelujah! An Informed History of the London Philharmonic Choir (2007); *Recreations* singing with London Philharmonic Choir (former chm); *Style—* Daniel Snowman, Esq; ✉ 46 Molyneux Street, London W1H 5JD (website www.danielsnowman.org.uk)

SNOWMAN, (Michael) Nicholas; s of Kenneth Snowman (d 2002), and Sallie, *née* Moghi-Levkine (d 1995); *b* 18 March 1944; *Educ* Hall Sch, Highgate Sch, Magdalene Coll Cambridge (BA); *m* 1983, Margo Michelle Rouard; 1 s; *Career* asst to Head of Music Staff Glyndebourne Festival Opera 1967–69, co-fndr and gen mangr London Sinfonietta 1968–72, admin Music Theatre Ensemble 1968–71, artistic dir Institut de Recherche et de Co-ordination Acoustique/Musique (IRCAM) Centre d'Art et de Culture Georges Pompidou 1972–86; Ensemble InterContemporain Paris: co-fndr 1975, artistic advsr 1975–92, memb Bd 1992–, vice-chm 1998–; The South Bank Centre: gen dir (Arts) 1986–92, chief exec 1992–98; gen dir Glyndebourne Festival Opera 1998–2000, chm Wartski 2002– (co-chm 1997–2002), gen dir Opéra National du Rhin (Strasbourg, Mulhouse, Colmar) 2002–; govr Royal Acad of Music 1998– (Hon RAM); memb Music Ctee Venice Biennale 1979–86; Festival d'Automne de Paris: artistic dir Stravinsky 1980, Webern 1981, Boulez 1983; prog conslt Cité de la Musique La Villette Paris 1991; memb Br Section Franco-Br Cncl 1995–2000; tstee New Berlioz Edn 1996–, memb Comité Hector Berlioz 2000–; Officier de l'Ordre des Arts et des Lettres (France) 1990 (Chevalier 1985), Order of Cultural Merit (Poland) 1990, Chevalier dans l'Ordre National du Mérite (France) 1995; *Books* The Best of Granta (co-ed, 1967), The Contemporary Composers (series ed); author of papers and articles on music, architecture and cultural policy; *Recreations* films, eating, spy novels, France; *Clubs* Garrick; *Style—* Nicholas Snowman

SNYDER, Michael John; s of Percy Elsworth Snyder (d 1953), and Pauline Edith, *née* Davenport; *b* 30 July 1950; *Educ* Brentwood Sch, City of London Coll; *m* 14 Dec 1974, Mary Barbara, da of Rev Wilfrid Edgar Dickinson; 2 da (Julia Caroline b 10 Nov 1976, Susanna Jane b 9 Sept 1978); *Career* chartered accountant; Kingston Smith: joined 1968, ptnr 1974, managing ptnr 1979–, sr ptnr 1990–; chm: Kingston Smith Consultants Ltd, Devonshire Corp Fin Ltd, HR Insight Ltd, Blacktower Financial Advisers Ltd; chm Govts Accountants Working Gp Assoc of Practising Accountants; memb Ct of Common Cncl City of London; Corp of London: chm Policy and Resources Ctee, memb Fin Ctee, memb Investment Ctee, memb Audit Ctee, memb Establishment Ctee, memb City Lands and Bridge House Estates Ctee; London Metropolitan Univ: govr, chm Audit Ctee; dir Gateway to London, memb Thames Gateway London Partnership, memb Lee Valley Regnl Park Authy, memb Bd Film London; tstee Acad Sponsor Tst, vice-chair London Cncls and Ldrs Ctee; hon treas Bow Bells Assoc; hon treas and vice-chm of govrs Brentwood Sch, memb Bd of Govrs City of London Sch for Girls; Freeman City of London 1980; Past Master and Liveryman Worshipful Co of Needlemakers, Liveryman and memb Ct of Assts Worshipful Co of Tallow Chandlers; DSc City Univ 2001; FCA 1978 (ACA 1973), FInstD, MSI; Grand Cross Order of Merit (Germany) 1998; *Recreations* inland waterways, music, bridge; *Clubs* City Livery, Cordwainer Ward (vice-pres); *Style—* Michael Snyder, Esq; ✉ Kingston Smith LLP, Devonshire House, 60 Goswell Road, London EC1M 7AD (tel 020 7566 4000, fax 020 7566 4010, mobile 07768 233233)

SOAMES, Hon Emma Mary; da of Baron Soames, GCMG, GCVO, CH, CBE, PC (Life Peer; d 1987), and Lady Soames, DBE, *qv*, *née* Spencer-Churchill; sis of Hon Rupert Soames, *qv* and Hon Nicholas Soames, MP, *qv*; *b* 6 September 1949; *m* 4 July 1981 (m dis 1989), James MacManus, assist ed The Times, s of Dr Niall MacManus, of London; 1 da (Emily Fiona b 1983); *Career* formerly: journalist Evening Standard, ed Literary Review, features ed Vogue, ed Tatler, freelance journalist, dep ed The Oldie 1991–92, ed ES Magazine (Evening Standard) 1992–94; ed Telegraph Magazine 1994–2002, ed Saga Magazine 2002–; tstee Rehabilitation of Addicted Prisoners Tst (RAPT); *Clubs* Groucho; *Style—* The Hon Emma Soames; ✉ 26 Eland Road, London SW11 5JY

SOAMES, Eveline Virginia (Evie) (Lady Duff Gordon); da of Samuel Soames, of London, and Margaret Temple Dolan (d 1983); *b* 30 April 1947; *Educ* Downe House, Trinity Coll Dublin (BA); *m* 1975, Sir Andrew Duff Gordon, 8 Bt, *qv*; 3 s (William b 1977, Thomas b 1979, Frederick b 1981); *Career* dir Charles Barker BSMG 1975–, md Charles Barker Watney Powell 1976–91, chief exec Charles Barker Public Affairs 1991–97, conslt Weber Shandwick 2003–; dir: Liberty plc until 1998, Franco-Br Parly Rels Ctee 1975–; *Clubs* Kington Golf; *Style—* Ms Evie Soames; ✉ Weber Shandwick, Fox Court, 114 Gray's Inn Road, London WC1X 8WS (tel 020 7067 0328)

SOAMES, Baroness; Hon Mary; LG (2005), DBE (1980, MBE Mil 1945); da of late Rt Hon Sir Winston Leonard Spencer Churchill, KG, OM, CH, TD, PC, FRS (d 1965, gs of 7 Duke of Marlborough), and Baroness Spencer Churchill (Dame Clementine Ogilvy, GBE, cr Life Peer 1965, da of late Col Sir Henry Montague Hozier, KCB, bro of 1 Baron Newlands, and Lady (Henrietta) Blanche Ogilvy, da of 5 (10 but for attainder) Earl of Airlie, KT); *b* 1922; *m* 1947, Capt Christopher Soames (later Baron Soames, GCMG, GCVO, CH, CBE, PC, d 1987); 3 s, 2 da; *Career* formerly Jr Cdr ATS; memb Cncl Winston Churchill Meml Tst 1978–97 (chm of tstees 1991–2002), chm Royal Nat Theatre Bd 1989–95; patron Nat Benevolent Fund for the Aged 1978–; govr Harrow Sch 1981–95; hon fell Churchill Coll Cambridge; Hon DLitt: Univ of Sussex 1989, Univ of Kent 1997, Univ of the South Tennessee USA 2004; Hon LLD Univ of Alberta 2004; FRSL 2000 Chevalier de la Légion d'Honneur (France) 1995; *Books* Clementine Churchill by Her Daughter Mary Soames (1979, revised and updated edn 2002), A Churchill Family Album (1982), The Profligate Duke: George Spencer Churchill, 5th Duke of Marlborough and his Duchess (1987), Winston Churchill: His Life as a Painter - A Memoir by his daughter Mary Soames (1990), Speaking for Themselves: the Personal Letters of Winston and Clementine Churchill - edited by their daughter Mary Soames (1998); *Style—* The Lady Soames, LG, DBE

SOAMES, Hon (Arthur) Nicholas Winston; MP; s of Baron Soames, GCMG, GCVO, CH, CBE, PC (Life Peer; d 1987), and Lady Soames, DBE, *qv*, *née* Spencer-Churchill, da of late Sir Winston Churchill and Baroness Spencer-Churchill; bro of Hon Rupert Soames, *qv* and Hon Emma Soames, *qv*; *b* 12 February 1948; *Educ* Eton; *m* 1, 1981 (m dis 1988), Catherine, da of Capt Tony Weatherall, of Dumfries; 1 s (Arthur Harry David b 1985); m 2, 21 Dec 1993, Serena Mary, da of Sir John Lindsay Eric Smith, CBE, JP, DL, of Shottesbrooke Park, Maidenhead, Berks; 1 da (Isabella b 1996), 1 s (Christopher b 2001); *Career* served 11 Hussars 1967–70, extra equerry to HRH The Prince of Wales 1970–72, Lloyd's insurance broker 1972–74, PA to Sir James Goldsmith 1974–76, PA to US Senator Mark Hatfield 1976–78, asst dir Sedgwick Group 1979–81; Parly candidate (Cons) Central Dumbartonshire 1979; MP (Cons): Crawley 1983–97, Sussex Mid 1997–; PPS to Rt Hon John Selwyn Gummer as Min of State for Employment and Chm of the Cons Party 1984–86, sec Cons Foreign Affrs Ctee 1986–87, PPS to the Rt Hon Nicholas Ridley 1987–89, PPS to Sec of State DTI 1989–92, Parly sec Min of Agric Fisheries and Food 1992–94, min of state (armed forces) MOD 1994–97, shadow sec of state for defence 2003–05; *Clubs* White's, Turf, Pratt's; *Style—* The Hon Nicholas Soames, MP; ✉ House of Commons, London SW1A 0AA

SOAMES, Hon Rupert Christopher; s of Baron Soames, GCMG, GCVO, CH, CBE, PC (Life Peer; d 1987), and Lady Soames, DBE, *qv*, *née* Spencer-Churchill; bro of Hon Emma Soames, *qv* and Hon Nicholas Soames, MP, *qv*; *b* 18 May 1959; *Educ* Eton, Worcester Coll Oxford (BA, pres Oxford Union 1980); *m* 1988, Camilla Rose, eldest da of Sir Thomas Raymond Dunne, of Gatley Park, Leominster, Herefordshire; 2 s (Arthur Christopher b 3 Feb 1990, Jack Winston b 20 Sept 1994), 1 da (Daisy b 2 April 1992); *Career* GEC plc: joined 1981, former md subsid Avery Berkel UK; Misys plc: joined 1997, chief exec Misys Banking and Securities Div, chief exec Aggreko plc 2003–; non-exec dir Electrocomponents plc 2007–; *Clubs* Turf, White's, Pratt's; *Style—* The Hon Rupert Soames

SOANE, James; s of Alastair Soane, and Elizabeth Soane; *b* 31 August 1966; *Educ* Univ of Cambridge (MA), Bartlett Sch of Architecture UCL (DipArch, RIBA pt III); *Partner* Christopher Ash; *Career* architect and designer; dir Project Orange 2001–; projects incl: MyHotel Chelsea London 2002, Monsoon Store London 2003, 40 Under 40 (Victoria and Albert Museum exhibition) 2005, Farnham Estate Hotel Ireland 2006, Park Hotel Mumba India 2007, Orange Cottage Lavenham 2007, 1st Floor Smiths London 2007; dir Conran & Partners 1999–2001 (joined 1992), studio master Bartlett 2001–04; projects incl: Das Triest Hotel Vienna 1996, Blueprint Cafe, Rex Bar Reykjavik 1998, Fitzwilliam Hotel Dublin 1998, Ark Hills Club Tokyo 1998, Myhotel London 1999, Forest Court Housing Tokyo 1999, Bridgemarket New York 2000 (Landmark Restoration Award 2000), Great Eastern Hotel London 2000; cartographer Cadogan Guide to New York 1990; studio teacher Kingston Univ 1992–97, visiting lectr Univ of Cape Town 1997; visiting critic: Univ of Cambridge, RCA, South Bank Univ; speaker: 100% Design London 2006; *Publications* New Homes (2003), Catalogue (2003); *Recreations* walking, travelling, eating out, dancing, saunas, shopping; *Style—* James Soane, Esq; ✉ Project Orange, 2nd Floor, Morelands, 5–23 Old Street, London EC1V 9HL (tel 020 7566 0410, fax 020 7566 0411, e-mail mail@projectorange.com)

SOBOLEWSKI, Dr Stanislaw; s of Kazimierz Sobolewski (d 1979), of Scunthorpe, and Bronislawa Sobolewska (d 1989); *b* 9 February 1943; *Educ* Bialystok GS Poland, Med Acad of Bialystok Poland (MB BS), Univ of Bradford (PhD); *m* 1, 1968 (m dis 1976), Elizabeth, *née* Olszewska; 2 da (Marta b 1970, Anastasia b 1972), 1 s (Edward b 1974); m 2, Patricia, da of George Pearson (decd), of Rawmarsh, Rotherham, S Yorks; *Career* Grajewo Hosp Poland 1967, Olecko Hosp Poland 1968–70, sr house offr in rheumatology Harrogate 1971–72, registrar in pathology Sheffield 1974–77 (registrar in clinical haematology 1972–74), sr registrar in haematology Leeds and Bradford, conslt haematologist Trent RHA S Lincs Dist Boston; regnl rep RCPath, fndr chm Trent Region Haematology Sub Ctee, chm Boston Leukaemia and Cancer Fund, memb Med Exec Ctee Pilgrim Hosp; ACP 1974, memb Br Soc of Haematology 1976, MRCS 1976, LRCP 1976, MRCPath 1979; *Books* A New Function of Megakaryoctes in Malignancy (1986); *Recreations* classic cars restoration, swimming, football; *Clubs* Polish Social (Scunthorpe); *Style—* Dr Stanislaw Sobolewski; ✉ Pinewood, 32 Linden Way, Boston, Lincolnshire PE21 9DS (tel 01205 351655); Consultant Haematologist, Pilgrim Hospital, Sibsey Road, Boston Lincolnshire PE21 9QS (tel 012053 64801)

SODANO, Sandro; s of Massimo Sodano, and Alfonsina, *née* De Vita; *b* Newport, Wales; *Educ* St Joseph's RC Comp Sch Newport, Newport Coll of Art and Design, St Martin's Sch of Art (BA); *m* 4 Sept 1998 (m dis 2003), Piera Beradi; 1 da (Constanza Velvet b 19 June 2001); *Career* photographer; estab ABOUD SODANO with Alan K Aboud, *qv* 1990 (currently creative dir); photographer Royal Mail Stamp collection 2001; subject of documentary: Shillouette (Japan) 2001, Jigsaw (ITV) 2003; *Awards* D&AD Silver 1997; *Publications* Growing (co-author, 1995), subject of The End (2002); *Recreations* film, cooking; *Style—* Sandro Sodano, Esq; ✉ ABOUD SODANO, Studio 26, Pall Mall Deposit, 124–128 Barlby Road, London W10 6BL (tel 020 8968 6142, fax 020 8968 6143, e-mail mail@aboud-sodano.com, www.aboud-sodano.com)

SODOR AND MAN, Bishop of 2003–; Rt Rev Graeme Paul Knowles; s of Stanley Knowles, and Grace Edith Ellen, *née* Pratt; *b* 25 September 1951; *Educ* KCL (AKC), St Augustine's Coll Canterbury (Bishop Hanson prize); *m* 1973, Susan Gail, *née* Marsden; *Career* ordained: deacon 1974, priest 1975; curate St Peter in Thanet 1974–79, sr curate and precentor Leeds Parish Church 1979–81, chaplain precentor Portsmouth Cathedral 1981–87, vicar of Leigh Park 1987–93, rural dean of Havant 1990–93, archdeacon of Portsmouth 1993–98, dean of Carlisle 1998–2003; chm Cncl for the Care of Churches 2003–; memb Legislative Cncl Tynwald Ct; *Recreations* music (Victorian and Edwardian ballads), novels of E F Benson; *Style—* The Rt Rev the Lord Bishop of Sodor and Man; ✉ The Bishop's House, Quarterbridge Road, Douglas, Isle of Man IM2 3RF

SOFER, Anne Hallowell; da of Baron Crowther (Life Peer, d 1972); does not use courtesy style of Hon; *b* 1937; *Educ* St Paul's Sch, Swarthmore Coll USA, Somerville Coll Oxford (MA); *m* 1958, Jonathan Sofer (d 2003); 2 s, 1 da; *Career* sec Nat Assoc of Govrs and Mangrs 1972–75, additional memb ILEA Educn Ctee 1974–77, cncllr (Lab until 1981 whereafter SDP) GLC for St Pancras N 1977–86, chm ILEA Schs Sub Ctee 1978–81, chief educn offr London Borough of Tower Hamlets 1989–97; columnist The Times 1983–87; dir Channel Four Television Co Ltd 1981–83, tstee Nuffield Fndn 1991–2005, chm National Children's Bureau 2000– (vice-chm 1996–2000); *Books* The School Governors' Handbook (with Tyrrell Burgess, 1978 and 1986), The London Left Takeover (1987); *Style—* Mrs Anne Sofer; ✉ 46 Regent's Park Road, London NW1 7SX (tel 020 7722 8970)

SOHAL, Naresh; s of Des Raj Sohal (d 1996), and Tarawati (d 1993); *b* 18 September 1939, Harsipind, Panjab, India; *Educ* Univ of Panjab, City Literary Inst, London Coll of Music, Univ of Leeds (Arts Cncl Bursary); *Partner* Janet Swinney, writer; *Career* composer; copyist Boosey & Hawkes 1962–70; *Works* orchestral: Asht Prahar 1965, Concerto for Harmonica and Strings 1966, Aalaykhyam I 1970, Aalaykhyam II 1972, Indra-Dhanush 1973, Dhyan I 1974, Tandava Nritya 1984, Violin Concerto 1986, Lila 1995, Satyagraha 1996, Hymn of Creation 2001; stage: Gautama Buddha (ballet) 1987, Madness Lit by Lightning (libretto by Trevor Preston) 1989, Maya (libretto by Trevor Preston) 1998; chamber and instrumental: Hexad 1971, Chiaroscuro I 1971, Oblation 1971, Octal 1972, A Mirage 1974, Shades I 1974, Shades II 1975, Hexahedron 1975, Chiaroscuro II 1976, Monody 1976, Undulation 1976, Shades III 1978, Chakra 1979, Shades IV 1983, Brass Quintet 1983, Shades V 1988, Trio 1988, Concertino for Violoncello & Strings 2000, Shades VI 2000; vocal and choral: Kavita I 1965, Poems of Tagore I 1970, Surya 1970, Night's Post 1971, Kavita II 1972, Kavita III 1972, Poets to Come 1975, Poems of Tagore II 1977, Inscape 1979, The Wanderer 1981, From Gitanjali 1985, The Unsung Song 1993, Poems of Tagore III 1994, Songs of Desire 1, 2, 3 2002, Songs of the Five Rivers 2002; for television: The World at Your Feet, Sir William in Search of Xanadu, Monarchy, Apartheid, End of Empire, Simla - A Summer Place (dir), Moral Combat - Nato at War 2000; for films: Manika; *Awards* BBC Young Composer's Forum (for Hexad) 1974, Padma Shri (Order of the Lotus) 1987; *Recreations* photography, chess, cricket, badminton, yoga;

S

Style— Naresh Sohal, Esq; ✉ 55 Drakefell Road, London SE14 5SH (tel 020 7635 5132, e-mail nareshsohal@hotmail.com, website www.nareshsohal.org.uk)

SOKOLOV, Dr Avril; da of Frederick Cresswell Pyman (d 1966), and Frances Gwenneth, *née* Holman (d 1964); *b* 4 May 1930; *Educ* privately, Newnham Coll Cambridge (exhibitioner, Arthur Hugh Clough scholar, BA), Univ of Cambridge (PhD); *m* 1963, Kirill Konstantinovich Sokolov, s of Konstantin Mikhailovich Sokolov (d 1972); 1 da (Irina b 1965); *Career* Br Cncl scholar Leningrad 1959–61, freelance translator, researcher and writer Moscow 1963–74; Univ of Durham: pt/t lectr 1976–78, lectr 1978–86, sr lectr 1986–89, reader 1989–96, reader emeritus 1996–; memb Assoc of Writers (Translating Sector); FIL 1949, FBA 1996; *Books* as Avril Pyman: Life of Aleksander Blok vol 1: The Distant Thunder (1979), Life of Aleksander Blok vol 2: The Release of Harmony (1980, Russian trans 2005), History of Russian Symbolism (1994, Russian trans 1998), Anna Akhmatova, Requiem (trans with engravings by K Sokolov, 2003), Fedor Tiutchev, A Selection of Poems (trans with engravings by K Sokolov, 2003); also written and translated numerous books, articles and poetry; *Recreations* art, theatre, travelling; *Style*— Dr Avril Sokolov, FBA; ✉ Department of Russian, University of Durham, Elvet Riverside, New Elvet, Durham DH1 3JT (tel 0191 374 287, fax 0191 374 7795)

SOLARI, Vivien Juliet Emma; da of Victor Solari (d 2004), of Hants, and Annette Anderson, of Cheshire; *b* 11 November 1978, Aruba; *Educ* Ridge Danyers Coll Stockport, Univ of Leicester; *m* 20 July 2001, Nick Mills; *Career* fashion model 1998–; face of Radical Fashion exhbn V&A 2001–02; campaigns incl: Giorgio Armani cosmetics, Versace Versus perfume, Giorgio Armani Mania perfume, Calvin Klein, Christian Dior cosmetics, Jil Sander perfume, Vera Wang perfume, DKNY, Ralph Lauren, GAP, Sportmax, Bottega Veneta, Missoni, Burberry, Hermes, Patek Phillipe, Evian, Joop, Oil of Olay, Issey Miyake, Clarins skincare, Very Valentino perfume; catwalk shows (NY, Paris, Milan and London) incl: Calvin Klein, DKNY, Bottega Veneta, Christian Dior, Kenzo, Paul Smith, Burberry, Helmut Lang, Christian Lacroix, Fendi, Chanel, Nicole Farhi, Julien MacDonald, Diane von Furstenberg, VH1 Fashion Awards, Prince's Tst Fashion Rocks; appeared on cover of int magazines incl: Vogue (France, UK, Aust and Spain), Numero (France), Marie Claire (Italy and France), Elle (Italy and France), Surface (USA), Oyster (Aust), Amica (Italy), Donna (Italy), L'Officiel (France); featured in numerous editorials for magazines incl: W, Vogue (USA, UK, Italy, France, Aust, Russia and Germany), Elle (UK, USA and France), ID, Dazed and Confused, The Face, Visionnaire, Marie Claire (UK, Italy and France), 10; *Recreations* running, music, gardening; *Clubs* New Forest Runners; *Style*— Ms Vivien Solari; ✉ c/o ICM Models, 2nd Floor, 2 Henrietta Street, London WC2E 8PS (tel 020 775 5110)

SOLESBURY, William Booth; s of William and Hannah Solesbury; *b* 10 April 1940; *Educ* Hertford GS, Univ of Cambridge (BA), Univ of Liverpool (MCD); *m* 1966, Felicity; 1 s, 2 da; *Career* London CC 1961–65; planning asst: London Borough of Camden 1965–66, City of Munich 1966–67, Miny of Housing 1967–72; NATO res fell Univ of Calif Berkeley 1973, Dept of the Environment 1974–89, Gwilym Gibbon res fell Nuffield Coll Oxford 1989–90, sec Econ and Social Res Cncl UK 1990–95; conslt 1995–2000; sr visiting research fell Centre for Evidence-Based Policy and Practice KCL; *Publications* Policy in Urban Planning (1974); various articles in Public Administration, Policy and Politics; *Recreations* home life, films, reading, travel; *Style*— William Solesbury, Esq

SOLEY, Baron (Life Peer UK 2005), of Hammersmith in the London Borough of Hammersmith and Fulham; Clive Stafford Soley; *b* 7 May 1939; *Educ* Downshall Secdy Modern, Newbattle Abbey Adult Educn Coll, Univ of Strathclyde (BA), Univ of Southampton (Dip Applied Soc Servs); *Career* probation offr 1970–75, sr probation offr 1975–79; MP (Lab): Hammersmith N 1979–83, Hammersmith 1983–97, Ealing, Acton and Shepherd's Bush 1997–2005; chm PLP 1997–2001; oppn front bench spokesman: on NI 1981–82 and 1983–84, on home affrs 1984–87, on housing and local govt 1987–89, on housing and planning 1989–92; chm NI Affairs Select Ctee 1995–97 (memb 1994–97), memb Modernisation House of Commons Select Ctee 1997–2001; memb Standing Ctee: Prevention of Terrorism Bill 1983–84, Criminal Justice Bill 1987–88, Housing Bill 1987–88, Local Govt and Housing Bill 1988–89, Planning and Compensation Bill 1990–91, Freedom and Responsibility of the Press Bill 1992–93; memb NEC Lab Pty; fell Industry and Parliament Tst; memb GMB; campaign dir Future Heathrow 2005–; chair: Mary Seacoll Meml Statue Appeal 2003–, Arab-Jewish Forum 2003–; *Publications* Regulating the Press (with Tom O'Malley); *Recreations* walking, photography, scuba diving; *Style*— The Rt Hon the Lord Soley

SOLOMON, David; s of Leslie Ezekiel Solomon, of London, and Peggy, *née* Shatzman; *b* 6 August 1948; *Educ* Clarks Coll, City of London Coll; *m* 1, 15 July 1973 (m dis 1986), Sarah-Lou Reekie; 1 s (Tony Daniel b 1980); m 2, 25 Nov 1997, Carol Stern; *Career* began in advertising with Garland-Compton, fndr Pink-Soda Fashion Co 1983– (opened Euro Office in Paris 1988); winner Queen's Award for Export Achievement 1987, BKCEC Award for Export Achievement (awarded by HRH The Princess Royal); MInstMSM; *Recreations* running; *Style*— David Solomon, Esq; ✉ 22 Eastcastle Street, London W1W 8DE (tel 020 7636 9001, fax 020 7637 1641, e-mail david@pinksoda.co.uk)

SOLOMON, Prof David Henry; AM (1990); s of H J Solomon, and Mary Solomon; *b* 19 November 1929, Adelaide, Aust; *Educ* Sydney Tech Coll (Dip), NSW Univ of Technol (BSc, MSc), Univ of NSW (PhD, DSc); *m* 28 Jan 1954, Harriet Valerie Dawn, da of Albert Henry Charles Newport; 3 da; *Career* with BALM Paints Ltd 1946–63 (ldr Resin and Polymer Resin 1955–63), demonstrator and teaching fell NSW Inst of Technol 1953–55; CSIRO: chief research scientist Div of Applied Mineralogy 1963–70, chief research scientist Div of Applied Chemistry 1970–74, chief Div of Chemicals and Polymers 1974–89, dep dir Inst of Industrial Technol 1989–90; ICI Aust-Masson prof of chemistry and head Sch of Chemistry Univ of Melbourne 1990–94, professorial fell Dept of Chemical and Biomolecular Engrg Univ of Melbourne 1996–; dir Gradipore Ltd 1989–91; memb: Steering Ctee Strategic Review of Chemistry Research in Aust RACI 1991–92, Selection Ctee Aust Acad of Sci 1991–, Pubns Ctee and Activities Ctee Aust Acad of Technological Sci and Engrg 1991–; pres RACI 1979–80; Archibald D Olle Prize RACI 1967, H G Smith Meml Medal RACI 1971, David Syme Research Prize Univ of Melbourne 1976, Polymer Medal RACI 1977, Applied Research Medal RACI 1980, Leighton Meml Medal and Lecture RACI 1985, CSIRO Medal 1987 and 1990, Australian Bicentennial Science Achievement Award 1988, Ian William Wark Medal and Lecture Australian Acad of Science 1989, Clunies Ross Science and Technol Award 1994, Centenary Medal 2003, Victoria Prize 2006; numerous named lectrs; FRACI 1966, fndn fell Aust Acad of Technological Sci and Engrg (FTSE) 1975, FAA 1975, FRS 2004; *Books* Chemistry of Organic Film Formers (1967, 2 edn 1977), Step-Growth Polymerizations: Kinetics and Mechanisms (ed, 1972), The Catalytic Properties of Pigments: Technical Association of the Pulp and Paper Industry Inc (1977), Chemistry of Pigments and Fillers (1983), The Chemistry of Free Radical Polymerization (1995), The Chemistry of Radical Polymerization (2006); *Recreations* fishing; *Style*— Prof David Solomon, AM; ✉ Department of Chemical and Biomolecular Engineering, University of Melbourne, Victoria 3010, Australia (tel 00 61 3 8344 8200, fax 00 61 3 8344 4153, e-mail davids@unimelb.edu.au)

SOLOMON, David Joseph; s of Sydney Solomon (d 1963), of Bournemouth, and Rosie, *née* Joseph (d 1978); *b* 31 December 1930; *Educ* Torquay GS, Univ of Manchester (LLB); *m* 5 April 1959, Hazel, da of Joseph Boam, of London; 1 s (Jonathan b 1961), 2 da (Ruth b 1963, Joanne b 1966); *Career* slr; ptnr Nabarro Nathanson 1961–68; D J Freeman: head Property Dept 1976–90, chief exec 1990–93, sr ptnr 1992–96; chm The Oriental Art Fund plc 1996–; tstee Highgate Literary and Scientific Instn 1999–2006 (pres 1993–98); memb Cncl Oriental Ceramics Soc 1989–92, 1994–97, 1998–2001 and 2002–06; tstee Public Art Devpt Tst 2000–02 (chm 1997–2000); *Recreations* Chinese ceramics, music, architecture, art, wine; *Clubs* Athenaeum; *Style*— David Solomon, Esq; ✉ Russell House, 9 South Grove, London N6 6BS (tel and fax 020 8341 6454); Longecourt Les Culetre, 21230 Arnay le Duc, France (tel and fax 00 33 3 80 90 05 55)

SOLOMON, Nathaniel; s of Leopold Solomon (d 1984), and Fanny, *née* Hartz (d 1991); *b* 20 November 1925; *Educ* Owen's Sch London, Emmanuel Coll Cambridge (MA); *m* 24 Feb 1951, Patricia, da of Arthur Creak (d 1954); 2 s (Max b 1957 d 2006, Justin b 1962), 1 da (Claire b 1959); *Career* Midshipman Fleet Air Arm 1944–47; joined Unilever 1949; dir: United Africa Co Ltd 1964–72, William Baird plc 1972–74; md Associated Leisure plc 1974–84, chm Pleasurama plc 1984–88; dir: Bally Manufacturing Corp 1989–91, Jefferies International 1985–99, Harrap Publishing Gp 1989–92, Fastrack Gp 1992–2000 (chm 1997–99), Wolsey Gp Ltd 2000–; chm: Crown Leisure 1993–99, Gala Gp Ltd 1997–2000, RAL Holdings Ltd 2000–03; dep chm: Grass Roots Gp plc 1985–, Berry Recruitment Ltd 2001–03; leisure industry advsr Livingstone Guarantee 2003–; conslt: Aberdeen Murray Johnstone Private Equity 2004–, Talarius plc; Tottenham Hotspur plc: chm 1991, dep chm 1991–92, life vice-pres 1992–; CIMgt 1986; *Recreations* bridge, tennis, wine, opera, theatre, watching soccer (especially Tottenham Hotspur); *Clubs* Reform, MCC, Harvard Business Sch, The Wimbledon; *Style*— Nathaniel Solomon, Esq; ✉ Livingstone Guarantee, 15 Adam Street, London WC2N 6RJ (tel and fax 020 7938 4506)

SOLOMON, Stephen Edward; s of Maj William Edward Solomon (d 1977), and Winifred Constance, *née* Day; *b* 29 November 1947; *Educ* Royal GS Guildford, Univ of Manchester; *m* (m dis 1995) Maureen Diane, da of William Robert Wilkins, of Tenby, Dyfed; 2 s (Robert William Petrie b 1980, John Christopher Petrie b 1981); *Career* admitted slr 1973; ptnr: Crossman Block and Keith slrs 1978–87 (joined 1976), Withers Crossman Block 1988–89, Crossman Block 1989–93; tstee The Law Debenture Corp plc 1994–95, ptnr W Davies & Son 1996–; memb: Guildford Round Table 1979–89, Guildford XRT; memb Law Soc; *Recreations* golf, skiing, gliding, astronomy, plumbing; *Clubs* Bramley Golf; *Style*— Stephen Solomon, Esq

SOLOMONS, Edward Brian; s of Emanuel Montague Solomons, of Ruislip, and Jeanette Flora, *née* Karamelli; *b* 9 October 1953; *Educ* Orange Hill County GS, Middlesex Poly (BA); *m* 20 Feb 1977, Jacqueline Eve, *née* Lampert; 3 da (Lydia Jane b 1979, Gillian Tamara b 1982, Tanya Zoë b 1985); *Career* slr; Brian Thompson & Partners: asst slr 1979–81, salaried ptnr 1981–84, equity ptnr 1984–94; Treasy Slrs Dept: Grade 6 lawyer 1995–96, sr civil servant, asst treasy slr 1996–2001, Dep Official Slr to the Supreme Ct and Dep Public Tstee 2001–06; dir of legal servs Met Police 2006–; memb: Cncl Law Soc of England and Wales 2001–05 (memb Standards Bd 2002–05), Bd Slrs Regulation Authy 2006– (chair Rules and Ethics Ctee 2003–); pres City of Westminster and Holborn Law Soc 2003–04; *Style*— Edward Solomons, Esq; ✉ Directorate of Legal Services, Metropolitan Police, Wellington House, 67–73 Buckingham Gate, London SW1E 6BE (tel 020 7230 7353, fax 020 7230 7521)

SOLTMANN, Diana-Margaret (Diana); da of HE Dr Otto Soltmann (d 2001), of Koblenz, W Germany, and Ethel Margaret, *née* Oakleigh-Walker; *b* 29 October 1952; *Educ* Rosemead Sch Littlehampton, Keele Univ (BA), LSE (Dip Personnel Mgmnt); *m* 16 June 1980, Timothy Congreve Stephenson, *qv*; 3 s (Christopher (Kit) b 2 Feb 1983, William b 8 July 1985, James b 1 Dec 1989); *Career* dir: Good Relations Technol 1978–85, The Communication Group 1985–89; head corp communications Blue Arrow plc 1988–89, md Millbank Public Relations 1990–99, currently gp chief exec Flagship Group; chm S London Ctee for the Employment of People with Disabilities 1994–97; memb Strategic Advsy Gp Mencap 1998–; AIPM, MIPR; *Recreations* reading, theatre; *Style*— Miss Diana Soltmann; ✉ Flagship Consulting, The Media Centre, 19 Bolsover Street, London W1W 5NA

SOLYMAR, Prof Laszlo; *b* 24 January 1930; *Educ* Tech Univ of Budapest (Dip Electrical Engrg, PhD); *m*; 2 da (Gillian Kathy Lacey-Solymar b 1963, Lucy Suzanne Solymar b 1970); *Career* lectr Tech Univ Budapest 1952–53; research engr: Research Inst for Telecommunications Budapest 1953–56, Standard Telecommunications Laboratories Ltd Harlow 1956–66; Univ of Oxford: fell and tutor BNC 1966–86, lectr Dept of Engrg Sci 1971–86, Donald Pollock reader in engrg sci Dept of Engrg Sci 1986–, professorial fell Hertford Coll 1986–, prof of applied electromagnetism 1992–97 (prof emeritus 1997–, Leverhulme emeritus fell 1997–99); visiting positions and consultancies: visiting prof Laboratoire de Physique École Normale Superieure Univ of Paris 1965–66, visiting prof Tech Univ of Denmark 1972–73, conslt Tech Univ of Denmark 1973–76, visiting scientist Thomson-CSF Research Laboratories Orsay France 1984, conslt BT Research Laboratories 1986–88, conslt Hirst Research Laboratories GEC 1986–88, visiting prof Dept of Physics Univ of Osnabruck Germany 1987, visiting prof Optical Inst Tech Univ Berlin 1990, conslt Pilkington plc 1990, visiting prof Dept of Physics of Materials Univ Autónoma Madrid 1993 and 1995, visiting prof Dept of Electrical and Electronic Engrg Imperial Coll London 2003–; Faraday Medal IEE 1992; author of 3 radio plays for BBC Radio 4 (with late John Wain) 1991: Anaxagoras, Archimedes, Hypatia; FIEE 1978, FRS 1995; *Books* Lectures on the Electrical Properties of Materials (with D Walsh, 1 edn 1970), Superconductive Tunnelling and Applications (1972), A Review of the Principles of Electrical and Electronic Engineering (4 volumes, ed, 1974), Lectures on Electromagnetic Theory (1 edn 1976), Volume Holography and Volume Gratings (with D J Cooke, 1981), Solutions Manual to Accompany Lectures on the Electrical Properties of Materials (1988) Lectures on Fourier Series (1989), The Physics and Applications of Photorefractive Materials (1996), Getting the Message; a History of Communications (1999); *Recreations* languages, twentieth century history particularly that of the Soviet Union, theatre, chess, swimming, bridge; *Style*— Prof Laszlo Solymar; ✉ Department of Engineering Science, University of Oxford, Oxford OX1 3PJ (e-mail laszlo.solymar@eng.ox.ac.uk)

SOMERLEYTON, 3 Baron (UK 1916); Sir Savile William Francis Crossley; 4 Bt (UK 1863), GCVO (1999, KCVO 1994), DL (Suffolk 1964); s of 2 Baron, MC, DL (d 1959), and Bridget, Baroness Somerleyton (d 1983); *b* 17 September 1928; *Educ* Eton; *m* 1963, Belinda Maris, da of late Vivian Loyd, of Kingsmoor, Ascot; 4 da (Hon Isabel (Hon Mrs (Mark) Cator) b 1964, Hon Camilla (Hon Mrs Sandy Soames) b 1967, Hon Alicia (Hon Mrs Bobby Pawson) b 1969, Hon Louisa (Hon Mrs Nick Marcq) b 1974), 1 s (Hon Hugh b 1971); *Heir* s, Hon Hugh Crossley; *Career* cmmnd Coldstream Gds 1948, Capt 1956; former co cncllr E Suffolk, non-political lord-in-waiting to HM The Queen (permanent) 1978–91; Master of the Horse 1991–98; farmer; patron of one living; dir Essex and Suffolk Water plc; ret 1997; landowner (5000 acres); *Recreations* hunting, shooting; *Clubs* Pratt's, White's; *Style*— The Rt Hon the Lord Somerleyton, GCVO, DL; ✉ Blocka Hall Farm, Herringfleet, Lowestoft, Suffolk NR32 5NW (tel 01493 484921, fax 01493 484923)

SOMERS COCKS, Hon Anna Gwenllian (Hon Mrs Allemandi); da of John Sebastian Somers Cocks, CVO, CBE (d 1964), and Marjorie Olive, *née* Weller (d 2002), and sister of 9 Baron Somers; raised to the rank of a baron's da 1996; *b* 18 April 1950; *Educ* Convent of the Sacred Heart Woldingham, St Anne's Coll Oxford (MA), Courtauld Inst Univ of London (MA); *m* 1, 1971 (m dis 1977), Martin Alan Walker; m 2, 1978 (m dis 1990), John Julian Savile Lee Hardy; 1 s (Maximilian John Lee b 10 Feb 1980), 1 da (Katharine Isabella Eugenia b 15 Feb 1982); m 3, 30 Nov 1991, Umberto Allemandi; *Career* asst keeper: Dept of Metalwork V&A 1973–85, Dept of Ceramics V&A 1985–87; ed Apollo 1987–90, ed-in-chief The Art Newspaper 1994–95, chm Umberto Allemandi & Co Publishing (publishers of The Art Newspaper) 1995–96, ed-in-chief The Art Newspaper 1996–2003, gp editorial dir Umberto Allemandi Publishing 2003–; chm Venice in Peril Fund 1999–; tstee The Gilbert Collection 1998–; memb Cncl The Attingham Tst 1998–, memb Advsy Bd Sotheby's Inst 2002–; expert advsr to Heritage Lottery Fund; tstee Cass Sculpture Fndn 2004–; European Women of Achievement Award (Art and Media) 2006; memb Worshipful Co of Goldsmiths 1989; FSA; Commendatore Ordine della Stella della Solidarietá Italiana 2004; *Publications* The Victoria and Albert Museum - The Making of the Collection (1980), Princely Magnificence - Court Jewels of the Renaissance (ed and jt author, 1980), Renaissance Jewels, Gold Boxes and Objets de Vertu in the Thyssen Bornemisza Collection (1985); *Recreations* skiing, entertaining, travelling, walking; *Style*— The Hon Anna Somers Cocks, FSA; ✉ San Defendente 52, Canale d'Alba, Piedmont, Italy

SOMERSET, 19 Duke of (E 1547); Sir John Michael Edward Seymour; 17 Bt (E 1611), DL (Wilts 1993); also Baron Seymour (E 1547); s of 18 Duke of Somerset, DL (d 1984), and Gwendoline Collette (Jane), née Thomas (d 2005); *b* 30 December 1952; *Educ* Eton; *m* 20 May 1978, Judith-Rose, da of John Hull; 2 s (Sebastian Edward, Lord Seymour b 1982, Lord Charles Thomas George b 1992), 2 da (Lady Sophia b 1987, Lady Henrietta Charlotte b 1989); *Heir* s, Lord Seymour; *Career* pres RFS 1993–95; FRICS; *Style*— His Grace the Duke of Somerset, DL; ✉ Estate Office, Berry Pomeroy, Devon TQ9 6LR

SOMERVILLE, Prof Jane; da of Capt Bertram Platnauer, MC, of London, and Pearl Annie, *née* Backler (d 1969); *b* 24 January 1933; *Educ* Queen's Coll London, Guy's Hosp Med Sch London (MB BS, MD); *m* 2 Feb 1957, Walter Somerville (d 2005), s of Patrick Somerville (d 1954), of Dublin; 1 da (Kate b 1961), 3 s (Lorne b 1963, Rowan b 1966, Crispin b 1972); *Career* sr lectr Inst of Cardiology London 1964–74, hon conslt physician Hosp For Sick Children 1968–88; hon sr lectr: Nat Heart and Lung Inst Univ of London 1974–98, Inst of Child Health until 1988; conslt physician and cardiologist Royal Brompton and Nat Heart Hosp (formerly Nat Heart Hosp) 1974–99, conslt cardiologist St Bartholomew's 1988–91, conslt physician for congenital heart diseases and dir Grown Up Congenital Heart Unit Royal Brompton and Nat Heart and Lung Hosp 1991–99; currently: hon conslt cardiologist Grown Up Congenital Heart Unit Middx Hosp/UCL, hon conslt advsr Congenital Heart Centre, emeritus prof of cardiology Imperial Coll London; memb Ctee on Cardiology RCP 1985–90, advsr on congenital heart disease for Sec of State's Hon Med Advsy Panel On Driving And Disorders Of The Cardiovascular System 1986 (published Heart Supplement 2002), advsr Congenital Heart Servs NATO Project Baltic States 2002–, chm Working Party Grown Up Congenital Heart Defects for British Cardiac Soc, chm Working Gp Grown Up Congenital Heart Disease European Soc of Cardiologists, pres Grown Up Congenital Heart Patients Assoc 2004–; Queen's Coll London: chm Bd of Govrs 1990–96, chm Cncl 2000–06; hon pres World Congress Pediatric Cardiology and Cardio Surgery 2001–2005; FACC 1972, FRCP 1973, FESC; *Recreations* collecting objets d'art, opera, roof gardening; *Style*— Prof Jane Somerville; ✉ 81 Harley Street, London W1G 8PP (tel 020 7262 2144, fax 020 7724 2238)

SOMERVILLE, Julia; *b* 1947; *Career* journalist and broadcaster; BBC: joined 1973, news reporter then industrial/labour corr BBC Radio News 1979–1984, newscaster BBC TV 1984–87; newscaster with ITN 1987–2001, presenter LBC Radio 1999–2001; chm Govt Art Collection Advsy Ctee 2003–; *Style*— Ms Julia Somerville

SOMERVILLE, Dr Kevin William; *b* 21 November 1950; *Educ* Lynfield Coll Auckland, Univ of Auckland (sr scholar in human biology, BSc, MB ChB, Beecham prize in physiology, sr prize in med, T W J Johnson prize in postgrad med), Univ of Nottingham (DM); *Career* physician with special interests in insurance med and risk assessment; house offr posts in Auckland and Nelson 1974–76, med registrar Auckland and Greenlane Hosps 1976–79, clinical research fell Gastrointestinal Unit Western General Hosp Edinburgh 1979–80, lectr and hon sr registrar Dept of Therapeutics Univ of Nottingham 1981–85, conslt gen physician Middlemore Hosp Auckland 1986, sr registrar Div of Geriatric Med Radcliffe Infirmary Oxford 1986–89, sr lectr Dept of Med Barts Med Coll and hon conslt physician Barts 1989–97, clinical dir Dept of Med for the Elderly Barts NHS Gp 1989–95, med conslt to Swiss Re 1997–; research and pubns on disease aetiology and pharmaco-epidemiology in older people; Elizabeth Brown prize Br Geriatrics Soc 1987; memb: Br Geriatrics Soc, Christian Med Fellowship, Br Soc of Gastroenterology, Assurance Med Soc, American Acad of Insurance Med; FRACP 1981, FRCP 1995; *Style*— Dr Kevin Somerville; ✉ 33 Oxhey Road, Watford, Hertfordshire WD19 4QG (tel 01923 240827, fax 020 7933 5749, e-mail kevin_somerville@swissre.com)

SOMMERS, Paul; s of Arthur Sommers (d 1998), and Nesta Sommers (d 2000); *m* 18 Dec 1993, Jenny, *née* Zamit; 2 da (Holly b 17 Feb 1998, Scarlet b 18 March 2000); *Career* television prodr; former dir Aspect Film and Television, currently head Factual & Documentary Tiger Aspect Productions; prodr: The Real Don Giovanni (Channel 4, Best Music Documentary Award Midem Cannes) 1999, Cop Shop (ITV) 1999, Howard Goodall's Big Bangs (BAFTA Award 2000, Peabody Award 2000, nominee Int Emmy, nominee RTS) 2000, Harry Enfield's Real Kevins (BBC1) 2000, Kevin and Perry's Girlfriends (BBC1) 2000, Country House (four series, BBC2) 2002–04, A Place in France (two series, Channel 4) 2002 and 2004, When She Died the Death of a Princess (Channel 4 and Trio Channel USA) 2002; exec prodr: Omnibus: The Billy Elliott Boy (nominee RTS) 2001, Future Fighting Machines (2 series, Bravo and Tech TV USA) 2001, Doubletake and Doubletake Xmas Special (BBC2, BAFTA Award 2002, nominee Golden Rose) 2001 and 2003, The Crucified Soldier (Channel 4) 2002, Howard Goodall's Great Dates (Channel 4, 2002), The Men from the Agency (BBC4) 2003, Heist (Court TV USA) 2003, The Highest Bidder (BBC2) 2003, Country Parish (2 series, BBC2) 2003 and 2004, More than Love (Channel 4) 2003, A Place in Italy, A Place in Spain, A Place in Greece (Channel 4) 2004, Howard Goodall's 20C Greats (Channel 4) 2004, The Body of... JFK, Hitler, Marilyn Monroe (Discovery US and BBC3) 2004; *Recreations* sky diving, polo; *Clubs* Groucho, Electric; *Style*— Paul Sommers, Esq; ✉ Tiger Aspect Productions, 5 Soho Square, London W1D 3QA (tel 020 7544 1616, fax 020 7287 1448, e-mail paulsommers@tigeraspect.co.uk)

SONDHI, Ranjit; CBE (1999); s of Prem Lal Sondhi (d 2004), and Kanta Sondhi; *b* 20 October 1950, India; *Educ* St John's HS Chandigarh, Bedford Sch, Univ of Birmingham (BSc); *m* 1979, Anita Bhalla; 1 da (Maya Zareen b 1983), 1 s (Kabir Prem b 1985); *Career* worked on inner city community projects incl Handsworth Action Centre 1972–76, fndr Asian Resource Centre Handsworth 1976–85, sr lectr Dept of Community and Youth Studies Westhill Coll Univ of Birmingham 1985– (co-ordinator undergrad degree in race and ethnic studies 1997–2001); cmmr then dep chair Cmmn for Racial Equality 1989–95, chm Refugee Employment, Trg and Educn Forum 1990–95; memb: Ethnic Minority Ctee Judicial Studies Bd 1991–95, Lord Chllr's Advsy Ctee on Legal Educn and Conduct 1996–2000, Home Sec's Race Rels Forum 1998–2002, Race Equality Advsy Panel 2003–; former memb: Birmingham TEC, Disability Task Force on Disability Rights DfEE, Strategic Gp on Tackling Racial Harassment in the NHS Dept of Health; memb: Ind Broadcasting Authy 1987–90, Radio Authy 1990–95, Bd of Govrs BBC 1998–2006 (chm English Nat Forum); memb Civil Serv Cmmn 2006–; non-exec dir Birmingham HA 1998–2002, chm Heart of Birmingham Teaching Primary Care Tst 2002–; tstee: Nat Gall 2000–, Baring Fndn 2002–, Bryant Tst 2003–, Teaching Awards Tst until 2006; former tstee: Prince's Tst, Feeney Tst; involved with projects incl Second City Second Chance, Brimingham Focus on Blindness and sampad; memb Lunar Soc Birmingham; Hon DUniv Univ of Central England 2003; FRSA; *Publications* Ethnicity and the Media (jtly, 1977), Asian Resource Centre: Problems, Perspectives, Progress (ed, 1979), Divided Families (ed, 1985), Educational Interventions (jtly, 1997), An Experiment in Moral Education (jtly, 1997), Twenty Years after the Act (jt ed, 1999); contrib to books and author of articles in jls; *Recreations* music, books, travel; *Style*— Ranjit Sondhi, Esq, CBE; ✉ Bartholomew House, 142 Hagley Road, Birmingham B16 9PA (tel 0121 224 4740, e-mail ranjit.sondhi@hobtpct.nhs.uk)

SONG, Prof Yong-Hua; *Educ* Sichuan Univ (BEng), China Electric Power Research Inst (MSc, PhD), Brunel Univ (DSc); *Career* postdoctoral research fell Tsinghua Univ 1989–91, research offr Univ of Bath 1992–93, lectr Liverpool John Moores Univ 1993–94, lectr Univ of Bath 1995–97; Brunel Univ: Royal Acad of Engrg/British Energy/BNFL/Siemens research prof of power systems 1997–2001, prof of network systems 2002–, pro-vice-chllr (grad studies), dir Brunel Advanced Inst of Network Systems (BRAINS); Royal Soc visiting fell Univ of Bristol 1991–92, external assessor and visiting prof Chinese Acad of Sciences 2002–; visiting prof: Tsinghua Univ, Xian Jiaotong Univ, N China Electric Power Univ; sr advsr China Electricity Reform Project UN Devpt Prog (UNDP) 2001–, science advsr to Macao Govt 2002–; chief ed Jl of Modern Electric Power; FRSA 2001, FIEE 2001, FREng 2004; *Books* Modern Optimisation Techniques in Power Systems (ed, 1999), Flexible AC Transmission Systems (jt ed, 1999), Optimal Operation and Planning of Power Systems (jtly, 2003), Operation of Market-oriented Power Systems (jt ed, 2003); *Style*— Prof Yong-Hua Song; ✉ School of Engineering and Design, Brunel University, Uxbridge, Middlesex UB8 3PH

SONNABEND, Yolanda; da of late Dr H Sonnabend, and late Dr F Sandler; *b* 26 March 1935, Rhodesia; *Educ* Eveline HS Rhodesia, Académie des Beaux-Arts Geneva, McGill Univ Montreal, Slade Sch of Fine Art London (Boise postgrad travelling scholarship); *Career* artist; visiting tutor: Camberwell Sch of Art 1964–70, Central Sch of Art (stage design) 1969–; lectr Slade Sch of Fine Art 1988–; numerous gp exhibitions 1956–, designed plays (most recently Camino Real (RSC) 1997), operas and ballet; ballet designs incl: Requiem, My Brother My Sisters, Swan Lake (Royal Ballet) 1987, costumes for Bayadère (Royal Ballet) 1988, Camino Reale Tennessee Williams (RSC) 1997, Antony and Cleopatra (RSC) 1999, The Rite of Spring (ENB) 2000, Swan Lake (K Ballet Tokyo) 2003, The Nutcracker (K Ballet Tokyo) 2006; travel award to Venice 1977, Br Cncl grant to Prague (Baroque Theatre) 1979, Arts Cncl bursary to Geneva (mask making) 1979, Garrick-Milne Prize for Theatrical Portraiture 2000; fell UCL 2002; *Solo Exhibitions* Whitechapel Art Gallery 1975, Serpentine Gallery 1985–86, Fischer Fine Art 1989; *Public Collections* Arts Cncl of GB, British Cncl, Theatre Museum, V&A, Nat Portrait Gallery (portraits incl Stephen Hawking and Sir Kenneth Macmillan), Science Museum, Unilever, Library of Performing Arts, Lincoln Center NYC, Unilever, Fitzwilliam Museum, British Museum, Wellcome Library (portrait of Prof Patrick Way) 2006; *Style*— Ms Yolanda Sonnabend

SONNET, Keith Robert; s of Leonard Henry Sonnet, and Dorothy Sonnet; *Educ* LSE (BSc, DMA), IPM; *Career* trade union official 1973–; asst gen sec NALGO 1990– (chief negotiator for local govt employees, ldr first nat strike in local govt 1989); UNISON: asst gen sec 1993–2001, dep gen sec 2001–, chief negotiator for local govt employees; memb: Gen Cncl TUC, Bd Improvement and Devpt Agency, Cwlth Local Govt Forum, Central Arbitration Ctee; author of numerous press articles and features; *Recreations* restaurants, theatre, travel, watching West Ham FC; *Style*— Keith Sonnet, Esq; ✉ UNISON, 1 Mabledon Place, London WC1H 9AJ (tel 020 7388 2366, fax 020 7387 0679, e-mail k.sonnet@unison.co.uk)

SOOKE, Thomas Peter (Tom); s of Dr Paul Sooke (d 1992), of London, and Gertrude, *née* Klinger (d 1969); *b* 8 January 1945; *Educ* Westminster, Pembroke Coll Cambridge (MA), Columbia Univ NY (MBA); *m* 6 June 1975, Ceridwen Leeuwke Bathurst, da of Derek Matthews; 1 s (Alastair b 1981), 1 da (Leonie b 1985); *Career* Price Waterhouse 1967–70, Wallace Bros Bank 1972–76, dir Granville Holdings plc and Venture Funds 1976–87 (co fndr Br Venture Capital Assoc 1983), corp fin ptnr Deloitte & Touche 1988–91, chm CitiCourt Assocs Ltd 1991; non-exec dir: Quester VCT plc, Matrix Income and Growth VCT and VCT3and private cos; FCA 1979; *Recreations* tennis, golf, old watercolours; *Clubs* Oxford and Cambridge, MCC, Isle of Purbeck Golf; *Style*— Tom Sooke, Esq; ✉ 4 Monmouth Road, London W2 5SB (tel 020 7229 5253, e-mail tom.citicourt@btinternet.com)

SOOLE, Michael Alexander; QC (2002); s of Brian Alfred Seymour Soole (d 1974), and Rosemary Una, *née* Salt; *b* 18 July 1954; *Educ* Berkhamsted Sch (scholar), UC Oxford (scholar, MA, pres Oxford Union); *m* 2002, Catherine Gavine Marshall, *née* Gardiner; 3 step s, 2 step da; *Career* called to the Bar Inner Temple 1977; practising barr 1978–, recorder of the Crown Court 2000–; Parly candidate Aylesbury (SDP/Liberal Alliance) general elections 1983 and 1987; memb Bd Christian Aid 1991–2002, tstee Oxford Literary and Debating Union Tst 2005–; *Recreations* conversation; *Style*— Michael Soole, Esq, QC; ✉ 4 New Square, Lincolns Inn, London WC2A 3RJ (tel 020 7822 2000, fax 020 7822 2001)

SOOTHILL, Prof Peter William; *b* 30 October 1957; *Educ* Guy's Hosp Med Sch London (MB BS), Univ of London (BSc, MD, MRCOG); *Career* KCH London: lectr then hon sr registrar in obstetrics and gynaecology and dir Day Assessment Unit 1989–91, subspeciality fell/sr registrar in fetal med 1991–92; sr lectr in obstetrics and gynaecology UCL Med Sch and Inst of Child Health Univ of London 1992–95, hon conslt UCH (dir Fetal Med Unit) and Gt Ormond St Hosp London 1992–95, prof of maternal and fetal med Univ of Bristol 1995–; author of numerous articles in learned jls; *Style*— Prof P W Soothill; ✉ University Department of Obstetrics and Gynaecology, Fetal Medicine Research Unit, St Michael's Hospital, Southwell Street, Bristol BS2 8EG (tel 0117 928 5513, fax 0117 928 5683, e-mail peter.soothill@bristol.ac.uk)

SOPER, Rt Rev (Andrew) Laurence; OSB; s of Alan Soper, of Angmering-on-Sea, W Sussex, and Anne, *née* Morris; *Educ* St Benedict's Sch Ealing, St Benet's Hall Oxford, Collegio Sant Anselmo Rome (STL, STD), St Mary's Coll Twickenham (PGCE); *Career* Barclays Bank 1960–64; entered monastery Ealing 1964; ordained: deacon (Assisi) 1969, priest 1970; St Benedict's Sch Ealing: teacher 1973–83, bursar 1975–91, prior 1984–91, ruling abbot 1991–2000; titular abbot St Albans 2000–; episcopal vicar for Religious in Archdiocese of Westminster Western Area 1995–2000; delg to Gen Chapter (sec) 1985 and 1989; pt/t chaplain Harrow Sch 1981–91, visiting chaplain Feltham YOI 1988–2000; chm Union of Monastic Superiors 1995–99, gen treas Int Benedictine Confedn 2002–; Freeman City of Norcia Italy; FRSA 1975; *Books* The Thoughts of Jesus Christ (1970), T H Green as Theologian (1972); *Recreations* walking; *Style*— The Rt Rev Laurence Soper, OSB; ✉ Badia Primaziale S Anselmo, Piazza Cavalieri di Malta 5, I-00153, Rome, Italy

SOPHER, Ivan; s of James Joseph Sopher, of London, and Sophie Sopher; *b* 27 August 1949; *m* 1973, Helen; 1 s, 2 da; *Career* sole proprietor Ivan Sopher & Co CAs; dir: Professional Publications Ltd, Delta Financial Management plc, DJS Securities Ltd, Media Advisory Group Ltd, Shish Restaurants Ltd; FCA, FCCA, ATII, MIMgt; *Recreations* travel, sport; *Style*— Ivan Sopher, Esq; ✉ 5 Elstree Gate, Elstree Way, Borehamwood, Hertfordshire WD6 1JD (e-mail ivans@ivansopher.co.uk)

SORABJI, Prof Richard Rustom Kharsedji; CBE (1999); s of Prof Richard Kaikushru Sorabji (d 1950), of Oxford, and Mary Katharine Monkhouse (d 1990); *b* 8 November 1934; *Educ* Charterhouse, Pembroke Coll Oxford (BA, BPhil); *m* 1958, Margaret Anne Catherine, da of Kenneth Taster (d 1958); 1 s (Richard Jon Francis b 29 March 1959), 2 da (Cornelia Katharine b 23 Dec 1961, Tahmina Lucy b 28 Dec 1964); *Career* positions rising to assoc prof with tenure Sage Sch of Philosophy Cornell Univ NY 1962–69; Univ of London: positions rising to current position of prof of ancient philosophy Dept of Philosophy KCL 1970–, chm Bd of Philosophical Studies 1979–82, head Philosophy Dept KCL 1984–85 (acting head 1975, 1983 and 1987), designer and first dir King's Coll Centre for Philosophical Studies 1989–91, fell KCL 1990–, dir Inst of Classical Studies 1991–96; British Academy research prof 1996–99; pres Aristotelian Soc 1985–86, fndr and organiser Int Project on the Aristotle Commentators 1985–; memb Common Room: Wolfson Coll Oxford 1991–96, Pembroke Coll Oxford 1992–; sr fell Cncl of Humanities Princeton Univ 1985, sr res fell Soc of the Humanities Cornell Univ 1979, fell Wolfson Coll Oxford 1996–; Townsend lectr Cornell Univ 1991; Gifford lectr St Andrews Univ 1997, Gifford lectr Edinburgh Univ 1997; hon foreign memb American Acad of Arts and Scis 1997–; Choice Award for Outstanding Academic Books 1989–90; FBA 1989; *Books* Aristotle on Memory (1972), Articles on Aristotle (co-ed, 4 vols, 1975–79), Necessity, Cause and Blame (1980), Time, Creation and the Continuum (1983), Philoponus and the Rejection of Aristotelian Science (ed, 1987), Aristotle Transformed: The Ancient Commentators and Their Influence (ed, 1989) Translations of the Ancient Commentators on Aristotle (ed of 40 vols 2000–), Matter, Space and Motion (1988), Animal Minds and Human Morals (1993), Aristotle and After (ed 1997), Emotion and Peace of Mind: From Stoic Agitation to Christian Temptation (2000); *Recreations* archaeology, architecture; *Style*— Prof Richard Sorabji, CBE, FBA; ✉ Department of Philosophy, King's College, Strand, London WC2R 2LS (tel 020 7873 2231, fax 020 7873 2270)

SORBIE, Trevor; MBE (2004); s of Robert Sorbie (d 1992), of Harlow New Town, and Edna, *née* Saxby (d 1979); *b* 13 March 1949; *Educ* Richard Henry Sch of Hairdressing; *m* 1, Susan Harré; m 2 (m dis), Kris Szewczyk; 1 c (Jade b 12 Oct 1978); *Career* hair stylist; apprentice barber Ilford 1964, opened own shop Edmonton 1969; stylist: Henri Loughton 1971, Selfridges Ilford 1971, Vidal Sassoon 1972–73; artistic dir Vidal Sassoon 1973–78, stylist and session hairdresser Toni & Guy then John Frieda 1978, opened own salons Covent Garden 1979 and 1999, created Trevor Sorbie Professional product line 1986 (relaunched 1999); launched: Mg product range 2000, Style Solutions product line 2001, The Professional Range 2001, Long Hair Range 2002, Professional Rejuvenate Range 2003, Electrical Range 2005; subject of: Visions in Hair by Kris Sorbie and Jacki Wadeson, Legends, Trevor Sorbie by Jacki Wadeson (2003); patron: Terrence Higgins Tst, Headlines; patron of honour Fellowship of Australian Hairdressers 2003; FCGI 2003; *Awards* British Hairdresser of the Year 1985, 1986, 1991, and 1992 (finalist 1995 and 1996), Nat Hairdresser of the Year 1985, London Stylist of the Year 1986 and 1989, Avant Garde Stylist of the Year 1989, Peluquerias magazine Foreign Stylist of the Year 1990 and 1991, British Hairdressing Hall of Fame 1991, Patron D'Honneur Lifetime Hairdressing Award 1993, Best Educn Award (USA) 1993, Living Legend Award NY 1995, World Congress Hall of Fame 1995, Most Newsworthy Male Worldwide (Int Beauty Show Award) 1996 and 1997, Best Haircutter Worldwide 1997, Grand Trophy of the Professional Press AIPP 2001, Aveda Master of the Arts 2002, Pantene Pro-V Celebrity Hairdresser of the Year 2002, British Master Award 2003; *Recreations* cooking, walking, motor racing; *Clubs* The Wellington; *Style*— Trevor Sorbie, Esq, MBE; ✉ 27 Floral Street, Covent Garden, London WC2E 9DT (tel 0870 920 1103, fax 020 7395 2909); c/o Jacki Wadeson @ JWPR, 1421–1423 London Road, Norbury, London SW16 4AH (tel 020 8679 5010, fax 020 8679 8086, e-mail jacki@jackiwadeson.demon.co.uk)

SORENSEN, Eric; *b* 1944; *Educ* Bedford Sch, Keele Univ (BA); *m*; 2 s, 1 da; *Career* voluntary work in India then various posts DOE, private sec to Rt Hon Peter Shore as Sec of State for the Environment 1977, regnl dir Manchester Office Depts of Environment and Tport 1980–81, head Merseyside Task Force 1981–84, head Inner Cities Directorate (responsible for DOE urban policy) 1984–87, head of Cabinet Office Urban Policy Unit 1987–88, dir of personnel DOE 1988–90, dep sec Housing and Construction Command 1990–91; chief exec: London Docklands Devpt Corp 1991–97, Millennium Commission 1997–98, London Devpt Partnership 1998–, currently chm Royal Docks Tst; *Style*— Eric Sorensen, Esq

SØRENSEN, (Nils Jorgen) Philip; *see:* Philip-Sørensen, Nils Jorgen

SORIANO, Kathleen; da of Salvador Soriano, of London and Valencia, and Kathleen, *née* O'Neill; *b* 18 July 1963, London; *Educ* Putney HS, Spalding Univ Louisville KY (ESU scholar), Univ of Leicester (BA); *m* 22 July 2005, Peter Greenhough; 1 da (Martha Amelia Scarlett b 3 June 1998); *Career* Royal Academy of Arts 1985–89, head of exhbns and collections Nat Portrait Gallery 1989–2006, dir Compton Verney 2006–; Clore Leadership Prog fell 2004–05; Kentucky Col, hon capt Louisville Belle paddle steamer 1982; memb Museums Assoc; FRSA 2004; *Recreations* red wine, good food, reading, gardening, walking, theatre; *Clubs* Arts; *Style*— Kathleen Soriano; ✉ Compton Verney, Warwickshire CV35 9HZ (tel 01926 645500, e-mail kathleen.soriano@comptonverney.org.uk)

SORKIN, (Alexander) Michael; s of Joseph Sorkin (d 1984), and Hilda Ruth, *née* Fiebusch; *b* 2 March 1943; *Educ* St Paul's Manchester Univ (BA); *m* 27 Nov 1977, Angela Lucille, da of Leon Berman (MC), of London; 2 da (Zoe b 1979, Kim b 1980), 1 s (Jacob b 1983); *Career* Hambros Bank Ltd: joined 1968, dir 1973, exec dir 1983, vice-chm 1987–95, dep chm 1995–98; dir Hambros plc 1986–98, md SG Hambros 1998–2001, vice-chm N M Rothschild 2001–; *Recreations* opera, golf, tennis; *Style*— Michael Sorkin, Esq; ✉ N M Rothschild & Sons, New Court, St Swithin's Lane, London EC4P 4DU (tel 020 7280 5000, fax 020 7283 4656)

SORRELL, Frances M; *née* Newell; *m* John Sorrell, CBE, *qv*; 3 c; *Career* fndr and co chm Newell and Sorrell Ltd (identity and brand consits) 1976–97, chair Interbrand Fndn (following merger) 1997–2000, fndr and tstee The Sorrell Fndn 1999–; dir: Bd Royal Acad Enterprises 1996–99, Bd Inst for Employment Studies 2000–02; memb: City & Guilds Nat Advsy Ctee for Craft Design and Art 1994–96, Advsy Bd Nat Museum of Photography, Film & TV 1997–, City & Guilds Affairs & Awards Ctee 1999–2001, Arts Advsy Gp QCA 2000–, Colour Gp, NHS Design Advsy Gp, Br Cncl Design Advsy Gp; tstee Mencap 1999–; godparent to the NMEC Millennium Dome Garden Zone 1999; judge: BBC Design Awards, D&AD Awards, RIBA Awards; hon memb City & Guilds; FRSA, FCD, FRIBA; *Awards* 11 Design Effectiveness Awards, five Silver D&AD Awards, five Clios, five Gold Awards NY Festival, Grand Award for BA Corporate Identity, two Art Director's Club of Euro Awards; *Style*— Frances Sorrell; ✉ The Sorrell Foundation (tel 020 7014 5300, fax 020 7014 5301)

SORRELL, John W; CBE (1996); *m* Frances Sorrell, *qv*, *née* Newell; 3 c; *Career* fndr and co chm Newell & Sorrell Ltd (identity and design consits) 1976–97, sole chm Interbrand Newell & Sorrell Ltd (following merger) 1997–2000; chm The Sorrell Fndn 1999–; chm: DBA 1990–92, Design Cncl 1994–2000, NHS London Design Advsy Gp 2001–03, CABE 2004–; co-chm Br Abroad Task Force 2000–03; memb: BR Architecture and Design Panel 1991–93, RSA Design Advsy Gp 1991–93, Panel 2000 1998–2000, London Design Festival 2003–; govr Design Dimension 1991–93; memb: Encouraging Innovation Competitiveness working party DTI 1998, Qualifications and Curriculum Authority Advsy Gp for Media and Culture 1998–, Culture and Creativity Advsy Gp DCMS 2002–03, London Challenge Ministerial Advsy Gp DfES 2002–, Public Diplomacy Strategy Bd 2002–, Advsy Gp on Design of Sch Bldgs DfES 2002–04; tstee RIBA Tst 2004–05; 'godparent' to the NMEC National Identity Zone; vice-pres CSD 1989–92; RSA Bicentenary Medal 1998; Hon Dr of Design De Montfort Univ 1997, Hon PhD London Inst 1999; hon memb Romanian Design Centre; memb: D&AD, Strategic Planning Soc, IOD; FCSD, FRSA; *Publications* Creative Island (2002), joinedupdesignforschools (2005); *Recreations* architecture, Arsenal, art, film; *Clubs* Groucho, Bluebird, Arts; *Style*— John Sorrell, Esq, CBE

SORRELL, Sir Martin Stuart; kt (2000); s of Jack Sorrell, of Mill Hill, London; *b* 14 February 1945; *Educ* Haberdashers' Aske's, Christ's Coll Cambridge, Harvard Business Sch; *m* 1971 (m dis 2005), Sandra Carol Ann, *née* Finestone; 3 s; *Career* gp fin dir Saatchi & Saatchi Co plc (mktg serv) 1977–86, gp chief exec WPP Group plc (communications servs) 1986–; non-exec dir: Storehouse plc 1994–97, Colefax & Fowler 1997–2003, Nasdaq 2001–04; chm Int Advsy Bd Br-American Business Inc; memb: Governing Body London Business Sch (dep chm), Advsy Bd Instituto de Estudios Superiores de la Empresa (IESE), Panel 2000, Advsy Bd Harvard Univ Grad Sch of Business and Administration, Advsy Bd Boston Univ Sch of Mgmnt, Bd Indian Sch of Business, Bd Engrg and Technol Bd, Cncl for Excellence in Mgmnt in Leadership DfEE, Ctee Special Olympics (memb Bd until 2005), Int Advsy Bd CBI; tstee: Univ of Cambridge Fndn, The Conference Bd, RCA Fndn; Br ambass for business; *Recreations* skiing, cricket; *Clubs* Reform, Harvard, MCC; *Style*— Sir Martin Sorrell; ✉ WPP Group plc, 27 Farm Street, London W1J 5RJ (tel 020 7408 2204)

SORRELL, Richard; s of Alan Sorrell (d 1974), of Thundersley, Essex, and Elizabeth, *née* Tanner (d 1991); *b* 24 September 1948; *Educ* Eton House Sch Thorpe Bay, Walthamstow Art Sch, Kingston Coll of Art (DipAD), Royal Acad Schs (Post Grad Cert, bronze and silver medals); *m* 1974 (m dis), Dodie, da of Michael Burke; 2 s (William b 1978, Edmund b 1981); *Career* artist (painter, draughtsman and printmaker) 1972–; memb Art Workers' Guild, memb Ctee Nat Artists' Assoc 1995–96; chief hanger RWS 1999–2001; govr Mall Galleries 2000–; RBA De Lazlo medal 2002; RBA 1989 (ARBA 1988), NEAC 1995 (memb Ctee), VPRWS 2002 (ARWS 1975, RWS 1978, elected pres PRWS 2006); *Works* aerial views incl: Blickling Hall, Ickworth and Uppark (all for National Tst), Stonor Park for Lord Camoys, Antony House for Sir Richard Carew-Pole, Settrington House for Sir Richard Storey, Buscot Park for Lord Faringdon, Summer Fields Sch Oxford, Channel Tunnel workings Shakespeare Cliff for V&A, model of Charlecote Park and Gatehouse 1998; painting of HM Queen Elizabeth the Queen Mother's 100th birthday parade 2001 (presented to HM Queen Elizabeth the Queen Mother) *Exhibitions* incl: Royal Acad 1971–, Royal Watercolour Soc 1975–, Royal Soc of Br Artists 1988–, Nat Portrait Gallery 1980, 1983 and 1984, Lutyens Exhbn Hayward Gallery 1980, Artists in National Parks (V&A) 1988, Agnews 1990, Cadogan Gallery 1992, Leamington Spa Art Gallery and Museum 1997, Bourne Gallery Reigate 2000, The Sheen Gallery 2001, Thompsons Gallery Stow-on-the-Wold 2002, Galleries Sternberg Chicago 2004; *Collections* work in public collections incl: V&A, Museum of London, National Tst, Worshipful Co of Fishmongers; *Style*— Richard Sorrell, Esq; ✉ The White House, Chapel Lane, Mickleton, Chipping Campden, Gloucestershire GL55 6SD (tel and fax 01386 438860, e-mail sorrellr@aol.com, website www.richardsorrell.co.uk)

SORRELL, Stephen Terence; s of Terence Sorrell, of Stockport, Cheshire, and Christine Mary, *née* Smith; *b* 5 October 1959, Stockport, Cheshire; *Educ* Marple Hall GS Stockport, Univ of Manchester (LLB), Chester Law Sch; *m* 23 June 1984, Jane Louise, *née* Goodman; 2 da (Ruth Hannah b 15 Aug 1986, Imogen Anne b 16 April 1989); *Career* slr; ptnr: Abson Hall & Co 1987–89, Eversheds (formerly Alexander Tatham) 1989– (currently head Developer Sector Gp); projects incl: Cwlth Games Manchester, Manchester FC stadium, Govt Millennium community projects, Olympic Games London; tstee Manchester Art Gallery, chm of tstees Manchester Library Theatre, chm Business in the Arts NW, memb Regeneration and Devpt Ctee Br Property Fedn; memb Law Soc 1984; *Publications* author of numerous articles on regeneration in property periodicals; *Recreations* contemporary art, theatre, cinema, Manchester City FC; *Style*— Stephen Sorrell, Esq; ✉ Eversheds LLP, Senator House, 85 Queen Victoria Street, London EC4V 4JL (tel 0845 497 9797, fax 0845 497 4919, e-mail stephensorrell@eversheds.com)

SOUEIF, (Dr) Ahdaf; da of M I Soueif, of Cairo, and Fatma Moussa; *b* Cairo; *Educ* Cairo Univ (BA), American Univ Cairo (MA), Lancaster Univ (PhD); *m* 1981, Ian Hamilton (d 2001); 2 s (Omar Robert b 1984, Ismail Richard b 1989); *Career* author; numerous appearances on Arab, American and Br TV and radio; memb: Bd Caine Prize for African Lit, Egyptian Writers' Union, Egyptian-Br Soc, PEN Egypt, PEN UK, Ctee for the Advancment of Arab-Br Understanding, Amnesty Int; patron: Palestine Solidarity Campaign; Hon PhD Lancaster Univ 2004, Hon DLitt London Metropolitan Univ; fell Lannan Fndn 2002, fell Bogliasco Fndn 2002, FRSL; *Publications* incl: Aisha (short stories, 1983, shortlisted Guardian Fiction Prize 1983), In the Eye of the Sun (novel, 1992), Sandpiper (short stories, 1996, Best Collection of Short Stories Cairo Int Book Fair 1996), The Map of Love (novel, 1999, shortlisted Booker Prize for Fiction 1999), Mezzaterra: Fragments from the Common Ground (essays, 2004), I Think of You (short stories, 2007); translations incl: In Deepest Night (1998), I Saw Ramallah (by Mourid al-Barghouti, 2000); author of numerous essays, short stories and reviews in English and Arabic published in various newspapers and jls; *Clubs* Gezira (Cairo); *Style*— Ahdaf Soueif; ✉ c/o Wylie Agency, 17 Bedford Square, London WC1B 3JA (tel 020 7908 5900, fax 020 7843 2151, e-mail kmarino@wylieagency.co.uk)

SOUHAMI, Mark J; s of John F Souhami (d 1996), and Freda Souhami (d 2006); *b* 25 September 1935; *Educ* St Marylebone GS; *m* 1964, Margaret, da of Joseph Austin; 2 da (Emma b 1966, Charlotte b 1968); *Career* Dixons Group plc: joined as gp mktg dir 1970, md 1973, gp md 1986–92, dep chm 1992–2003; chm Codic SA & NV 1998–; chm Br Retail Consortium 1994–98; memb Metropolitan Police Ctee 1995–99; *Clubs* Savile, RAC; *Style*— Mark Souhami, Esq

SOULSBY, Sir Peter Alfred; kt (1999), MP; s of Robert Soulsby, and Mary Josephine, *née* Reed; *b* 27 December 1948; *Educ* Minchenden GS Southgate, City of Leicester Coll of Educn (BEd); *m* 26 July 1969, Alison, *née* Prime; 3 da (Cassandra b 23 Nov 1975, Eleanor b 22 May 1978, Lauren b 14 Oct 1983); *Career* memb Leicester City Cncl 1973–2003 (ldr 1981–94 and 1995–99, memb Audit Cmmn 1994–2000), election agent to Jim Marshall MP 1997 and 2001 gen elections, MP (Lab) Leicester S 2005–; memb Select Ctee on: Environment, Food and Rural Affrs 2005–, Modernisation of the House of Commons 2007–, Crossrail Bill; memb British Waterways Bd 1998–2004 (vice-chm 2000–04), vice-chm Waterways Tst 1999–2004; chair Leicester City Challenge 1994–98, memb E Midlands EU's Ctee of the Regions 1994–2002; currently convenor Exec Ctee General Assembly Cncl of Unitarian and Free Christian Churches; *Recreations* canal cruising, cycling and swimming; *Style*— Sir Peter Soulsby, MP; ✉ House of Commons, London SW1A 0AA

SOULSBY OF SWAFFHAM PRIOR, Baron (Life Peer UK 1990), of Swaffham Prior in the County of Cambridgeshire; Prof Ernest Jackson Lawson Soulsby; s of William George Lawson Soulsby; *b* 23 June 1926; *Educ* Queen Elizabeth GS Penrith, Univ of Edinburgh (MRCVS, DVSM, PhD), Univ of Cambridge (MA); *m* 1962, Georgina Elizabeth Annette, da of John Whitmore Williams, of Cambridge; 1 da (Hon Katrina Yvonne b 1950), 1 s (Hon John Angus Lawson b 1954); *Career* vet offr City of Edinburgh 1949–52, lectr in clinical parasitology Univ of Bristol 1952–54, lectr in animal pathology Univ of Cambridge 1954–64, prof of parasitology Univ of Pennsylvania 1964–78 (chm Dept of Pathobiology 1965–78), prof of animal pathology and dean Sch of Vet Med Univ of Cambridge 1978–93, professorial fell Wolfson Coll Cambridge 1978–93 (emeritus fell 1993–); advsr and conslt to numerous univs, orgns and govts; author or co-author of 14 books and approximately 200 articles in scientific jls; chm: Study Gp on Parasitic Diseases Walter Reed Army Inst of Research Washington DC 1973–77, Animal Research Grants Bd AFRC 1985–88, Vet Advsy Ctee Horserace Betting Levy Bd 1985–97; memb: Tropical Med and Parasitology Study Section NIH Washington DC 1968–72, Scientific Advsy Panel Pan American Health Orgn Zoonosis Centre Buenos Aires 1974–85; pres:

RCVS 1984–85, RSM 1998–2000, RIPH 2003; corresponding memb: Argentine Assoc of Vet Parasitologists 1984–, Academie Royale de Med de Belgique 1992–; hon memb: German Soc of Parasitologists 1980–, Br Soc of Parasitologists 1989–, Helminthological Soc of Washington 1990–, BVA 1991–; hon life memb Br Small Animal Vet Assoc 1999; RN Chaudhury Gold Medal Calcutta Sch of Tropical Med 1976, Behring-Bilharz Prize Cairo 1977, Ludwig-Schunk Prize Justus Liebig Univ Giessen 1979, Frederich Messenmeier Medal Humboldt Univ Berlin 1990, Chiron Award BVA 1998, Distinguished Service Award St George's Univ Grenada 2006; House of Lords: pres Pet Advsy Ctee, pres Parly and Scientific Ctee, vice-pres All-Pty Gp on Animal Welfare, chm Sub-Ctee of Enquiry into Antimicrobial Resistance, chm Sub-Ctee of Enquiry into Fighting Infection, memb Select Ctee on Science and Technol; patron: Fund for the Replacement of Animals in Med Experiments, Wildlife Information Network; Hon DSc Univ of Pennsylvania 1985 (Hon AM 1972), Hon DVMS Univ of Edinburgh 1990, Hon DVM Univ of Leon 1993, Hon DSc Univ of Peradeniya 1994, Hon DVM&S Univ of Glasgow 2001, Hon DVM Univ of Liverpool 2004; CBiol, Hon FRSM 1996, Hon FRCVS 1997 (MRCVS 1948), FMedSci 1998, FIBiol 1998; *Style*— The Rt Hon the Lord Soulsby of Swaffham Prior

SOUNDY, Andrew John; s of Maj Harold Cecil Soundy, MBE, MC, TD (d 1969), and Adele Monica Templeton, *née* Westley (d 2005); *b* 29 March 1940; *Educ* Boxgrove Sch Guildford, Shrewsbury, Trinity Coll Cambridge (MA); *m* 12 Oct 1963, Jill Marion, da of Frank Nathaniel Steiner, of Gerrards Cross, Bucks; 1 s (Mark b 1964), 2 da (Emma b 1967, Victoria b 1969); *Career* admitted slr 1966; former sr ptnr Ashurst Morris Crisp slrs; former chm EW Fact plc; vice-pres The Lord Slynn of Hadley Euro Law Fndn 1998–; dir: St Michael's Hospice Basingstoke 1996– (chm 2007–), Anglo-Russian Opera and Ballet Tst 2001–; memb Bd of Govrs De Montfort Univ 2001–05; churchwarden parish of Mattingley 2002–; FRSA; *Recreations* farming, countryside, opera, tennis, fellowship; *Clubs* Cavalry and Guards', City Law, Bishopsgate Ward; *Style*— Andrew J Soundy, Esq; ✉ Bartletts Farm, Mattingley, Hook, Hampshire RG27 8JU (tel 0118 932 6279, fax 0118 932 6335, e-mail andrewsoundy@compuserve.com)

SOUTAR, Michael James (Mike); s of David Soutar, of Dundee, and Patricia Shanks, *née* Buik; *b* 8 November 1966; *Educ* Glenrothes HS, Univ of Michigan Exec Business Sch; *m* 8 April 1994, Beverly; 1 s (Alfie b 18 June 1991), 1 step s (Jai Francois b 25 Aug 1987); *Career* ed: Smash Hits 1990–94, FHM 1994–97; md Kiss FM Radio Ltd 1997–99, ed-in-chief Maxim (USA) 1999–2000, md Men's Div IPC Media 2000–03, chm Wallpaper Magazine Gp 2001–03, gp editorial dir IPC Media 2003–06, founding dir Crash Test Media 2006–; Magazine of the Year UK (for FHM) 1997, Sony Gold Award (for Kiss FM) 1999, Magazine of the Year USA (for Maxim) 2000; tstee bd memb Comic Relief 2003–; *Style*— Mike Soutar, Esq; ✉ Crash Test Media, 4th Floor, 53 Parker Street, London WC2B 5PT (tel 020 7400 7799, e-mail mike@crashtestmedia.com)

SOUTHALL, Anna; da of Stephen Southall, of Herefordshire, and Philippa, *née* Cadbury; *b* 9 June 1948; *Educ* The Mount Sch York, UEA (BA), Gateshead Tech Coll (Postgrad Dip Picture Conservation); *m* 1983 (m dis), Chris Serle, *qv*; 2 s (Harry b 1983, Jack b 1987); *Career* Ecclesiastical Insurance Office 1970, Advsy Bd for Redundant Churches Church Cmmrs 1970–71, secdy school teacher in Shoreditch 1972–74, sr conservation offr Area Museum Service for SE England 1975–81, sr conservator Tate Gallery 1981–96, dir Nat Museums & Galleries of Wales 1998–2002 (asst dir 1996–98), chief exec Museums Libraries and Archives Cncl 2002–03; chair Icon (Inst of Conservation) 2005–06; vice-chair Big Lottery Fund 2006–; memb: Spoliation Advsy Panel 2000–, Exec Bd Assoc of Charitable Fndns 2004–, Advsy Panel Futurebuilders 2005–07; memb: Fawcett Cmmn on Women 2004, Barrow Cadbury's Cmmn on Young People 2005; tstee Barrow Cadbury Tst (chair 1996–2006); *Publications* author of several articles on painting conservation and artists' materials and techniques; *Recreations* family, museums, conservation, countryside; *Style*— Anna Southall

SOUTHAMPTON, Bishop of 2004–; Rt Rev Paul Roger Butler; s of Denys Michael Butler, and Jean Florence, *née* Giddy; *b* 18 September 1955, Kingston upon Thames; *Educ* Kingston GS, Univ of Nottingham (BA), Wycliffe Hall Oxford (BA, CertTheol); *m* 11 Sept 1982, Rosemary Jean, *née* Johnson; 2 da (Caroline Mary b 17 Aug 1985, Sarah Bethany b 22 Feb 1994), 2 s (David Peter b 27 March 1987, Andrew Paul b 28 May 1989); *Career* travelling sec UCCF 1978–80, curate All Saints with Holy Trinity Wandsworth 1983–87, dep head of missions Scripture Union 1992–94 (inner London evangelist 1987–92), team rector Walthamstow 1994–2004, area dean Waltham Forest 2001–04, canon Byumba Cathedral Rwanda 2001–; chair Friends of Byumba Tst; tstee: Church Mission Soc, Five Talents UK; pres Southampton YMCA; *Publications* Reaching Children (1992), Following Jesus (1993), Friends of God (1993), Want to be in God's Family? (1994), Growing Up in God's Family (1994), Reaching Families (1995), Temptation and Testing (2007); *Recreations* gardening, walking, reading; *Style*— The Rt Rev the Bishop of Southampton; ✉ Ham House, The Crescent, Romsey, Hampshire SO51 7NG (tel and fax 01794 516005, e-mail paul.butler@bpsotonoffice.clara.co.uk)

SOUTHAMPTON, 6 Baron (GB 1780); Charles James FitzRoy; o s of Charles FitzRoy (d 1989), who suc as 5 Baron Southampton 1958, but disclaimed his peerage for life, and his 1 w, Margaret, *née* Drake (d 1931); *b* 12 August 1928; *Educ* Stowe; *m* 1, 29 May 1951, Pamela Anne (d 1997), da of late Edward Percy Henniker; 1 da (Hon Geraldine Anne (Hon Mrs Fuller) 1951), 1 s (Hon Edward Charles b 8 July 1955), and 1 s decd; m 2, 25 Oct 1997, Alma, da of Elidia Perez Pascual; 1 s (Hon Charles James b 8 June 1998), 1 da (Hon Isabelle Elidia Margaret b 7 Dec 1999); *Heir* s, Hon Edward FitzRoy; *Career* Master: the Easton Harriers 1968–71, the Blankney Foxhounds 1971–72; *Style*— The Rt Hon the Lord Southampton; ✉ Stone Cross, Stone Lane, Chagford, Devon

SOUTHBY, Sir John Richard Bilbe; 3 Bt (UK 1937), of Burford, Co Oxford; s of Sir (Archibald) Richard Charles Southby, 2 Bt, OBE (d 1988) and his 2 w, Olive Marion (d 1991), da of late Sir Thomas Bilbe-Robinson, GBE, KCMG; *b* 2 April 1948; *Educ* Peterhouse Rhodesia, Loughborough Univ (BSc); *m* 1971, Victoria Jane, da of John Wilfred Sturrock, of Tettenhall, Wolverhampton; 2 s (Peter John b 20 Aug 1973, James William b 1984), 1 da (Sarah Jane b 1975); *Heir* s, Peter Southby; *Career* gen mangr East Midlands Electricity plc, ret; pres: Milton Keynes Branch Inst of Mgmnt 1995–98, Milton Keynes Rotary Club 1997–98; non-exec dir Milton Keynes Gen Hosp NHS Tst 2001–; chm Milton Keynes Police Area Advisory Team 1995–99; memb Milton Keynes Business Ldrs (formerly Milton Keynes Large Employers Assoc) 1998– (chm 1994–98); memb Bd: Milton Keynes Economic Partnership 1995–1998, Milton Keynes Theatre & Gallery Co 1995–2000; asst govr Rotary Int (Beds, Herts and Bucks) 2006– (district sec 1999–2004); FIMgt, MIEE; *Recreations* gardening, DIY, photography, skiing, travel; *Clubs* Milton Keynes Rotary, Milton Keynes Concrete Cattlemen's; *Style*— Sir John Southby, Bt; ✉ Lomagundi, High Street, Nash, Buckinghamshire MK17 0EP (e-mail john@southby.org.uk, website www.southby.org.uk)

SOUTHEND, Archdeacon of; *see:* Lowman, Ven David

SOUTHERN, Graham; *b* 1960, Cornwall; *m* Antje; 2 da (Anneke, Caitlin); *Career* Modern and Impressionist Dept and Modern Br Dept Christie's London 1985–90, dir Christie, Manson & Woods 1990–2001, dir Christie's Contemporary London 1997–2001, dir Anthony D'Offay Gallery 2001–, fndr (with Harry Blain, *qv*) Haunch of Venison 2002–; *Clubs* Chelsea Arts; *Style*— Graham Southern, Esq; ✉ Haunch of Venison, 6 Haunch of Venison Yard, London W1K 5ES (tel 020 7495 5050, fax 020 7495 4050, e-mail graham@haunchofvenison.com)

SOUTHGATE, Crispin John; s of Brig John Terence Southgate, OBE, and Stancia Lillian, *née* Collins; *b* 16 February 1955; *Educ* Christ's Hosp, Merton Coll Oxford (MA); *m* 15 Sept 1979, Joanna Mary, da of Gerald Norman Donaldson, TD; 1 da (Eleanor b 1985), 2 s (William b 1987, Richard b 1990); *Career* Price Waterhouse & Co 1977–82; Charterhouse Bank Ltd: joined 1982, dir 1987, md 1992–94; dir S G Warburg 1994–95, md Merrill Lynch 2001–05 (dir 1996–2001); treas Rainer Fndn 1984–97; ACA 1980; *Style*— Crispin Southgate, Esq

SOUTHGATE, Gareth; s of Clive Stanley Southgate, and Barbara Ann, *née* Toll; *b* 3 September 1970; *Educ* Hazelwick Sch W Sussex; *Career* professional footballer; player: Crystal Palace FC 1987–95 (capt 1993–95, champions Div One 1993–94), Aston Villa FC 1995–2001 (capt 1997–2001, winners Coca Cola Cup 1996, finalists FA Cup 2000), Middlesbrough FC 2001–06 (winners Carling Cup 2004, finalists UEFA Cup 2006); England: 50 full caps (1 goal), debut v Portugal 1995, memb squad European Championship 1996 and 2000, World Cup 1998 and 2002; mangr Middlesbrough FC 2006–; *Style*— Gareth Southgate

SOUTHGATE, Robert; s of Robert Bevis Southgate (d 1958), and Anne, *née* Boyes (d 1985); *b* 20 January 1934; *Educ* Morecambe GS; *m* 1, 7 Sept 1957 (m dis 2002), Elizabeth, da of Robert Benson; 4 s (Paul Robert b 30 Nov 1958, Mark Nicholas b 6 Oct 1960, Jonathan Michael b 8 March 1962, Andrew James b 28 Sept 1965); m 2, 25 Oct 2002, Ann, da of Edward James Yeandle; *Career* reporter Morecambe Guardian 1949–52, sub ed News Chronicle 1955–56, night chief sub ed Daily Mirror Manchester 1956–60, sub ed Daily Herald 1960–62, freelance newscaster/reporter BBC and ABC 1962–64, dep Northern ed The Sun 1964–68, newscaster/reporter ITN 1968–79, reporter Thames News and TV Eye Thames Television 1979–82, controller of news and current affrs TVS 1982–85; Central Television: controller of news and regnl progs 1985–92, md Central Broadcasting 1993–94 (dep md 1992–93), ret as md 1994, non-exec dir 1994–97; non-exec dir: Meridian Television 1993–97, 021 Television 1993–94; ed The Cook Report (Central) 1995; memb Arts Cncl of England 1994–97 (memb Arts Cncl of GB 1992–94), chm W Midlands Regnl Arts Bd 1992–97, chm Birmingham Royal Ballet 2000– (dep chm 1994–99), dir Birmingham Repertory Theatre 1996–2002; *Recreations* Lyric theatre, food, wine; *Style*— Robert Southgate, Esq

SOUTHGATE, Dr Vaughan Robert; s of Stanley Robert Double Southgate, of Kempston, Beds, and Peggy, *née* Dean; *b* 13 May 1944, Kempston, Beds; *Educ* Bedford Modern Sch, Univ of Wales Aberystwyth (BSc), Christ's Coll Cambridge (PhD); *m* 13 Aug 1966, Marilyn, *née* Kuhn; 1 da (Antonia Claire b 10 July 1969), 1 s (Crispin Robert William b 22 Dec 1971); *Career* Nat History Museum: jr res fell 1968, band 4 1971, band 3 1974, head Experimental Taxonomy Div 1983, head Biomedical Parasitology Div and band 2 1992–2004, currently res assoc Dept of Zoology; CBiol 1980; memb Cncl and chm Autumn Symposium Ctee Br Soc for Parasitology; Zoological Soc of London: memb Publications Ctee 1975–80 and 1981–85, memb and chm Zoological Record Advsy Ctee 1982–86, memb Zoological Record Editorial Bd 1983–87; RSTMH: memb Cncl 1979–82 (ex-officio memb 1982–86), memb Meetings Ctee 1980 (chm 1981–85), hon sec 1986–91, vice-pres 1993–95, chm Electronic Publishing Working Pty 1996–98; WHO: dir Collaborating Centre for the Identification and Characterisation of Schistosome Strains and their Snail Intermediate Hosts 1983–2004, memb Working Gp on Schistosomiasis 1986–91, memb Expert Panel on Parasitic Diseases 2003–; Linnean Soc of London: memb Cncl 1989–92 and 1997–, vice-pres 1997–, zoology sec 1997–; ed Jl of Natural History 1972–83; memb Editorial Bd: Parasitology 1985–95, Transactions of the Royal Society of Tropical Medicine & Hygiene 1983–90 (chm 1990–91); author and co-author of 160 scientific papers and book chapters; external examiner for higher degrees in univs in UK, France, Belgium, Spain and the Netherlands; High Sheriff Beds 2007–08; chm of tstees Friends of Cople Church; tstee John Spedan Lewis Tst 2002–; hon fell Dept of Biology UCL; C A Wright Meml Medal Br Soc of Parasitology 1990; FIBiol 1988 (MIBiol 1980), FRSM 2003; *Recreations* family, game fishing (trout and salmon), game shooting, photography, skiing, walking, travel; *Clubs* Biggleswade Ivel Rotary (fndr memb), Roxton Flyfishers; *Style*— Dr Vaughan Southgate; ✉ The Coach House, Woodlands Close, Cople, Bedford MK41 3UE (tel 01234 838714, e-mail v.southgate714@btinternet.com)

SOUTHWARD, Sir Nigel Ralph; KCVO (2003, CVO 1995, LVO 1985); s of Sir Ralph Southward, KCVO (d 1997), and Evelyn, *née* Tassell; *b* 8 February 1941; *Educ* Rugby, Trinity Hall Cambridge (MA, MB BChir); *m* 24 July 1965, Annette, da of Johan Heinrich Hoffmann, of Strandvejen, Denmark; 1 s (Nicholas b 1966), 2 da (Karen b 1968, Emma b 1970); *Career* house surgn Middlesex Hosp 1965, house physician Royal Berkshire Hosp Reading 1966, house physician Central Middlesex Hosp 1966, casualty MO Middlesex Hosp 1967, visiting MO King Edward VII Hosp for Offrs 1972–2003; apothecary to HM The Queen; apothecary to the household and to the households of: Princess Alice Duchess of Gloucester, the Duke and Duchess of Gloucester, Duke and Duchess of Kent and Prince and Princess Michael of Kent 1975–2003; apothecary to the households of HM the late Queen Elizabeth the Queen Mother and the late Princess Margaret Countess of Snowdon 1975–2002; hon Freeman and Liveryman Worshipful Soc of Apothecaries; *Recreations* sailing, hunting, skiing; *Clubs* RYS, RCC; *Style*— Sir Nigel Southward, KCVO; ✉ Drokesfield, Bucklers Hard, Beaulieu, Hampshire SO42 7XE (tel 01590 616252, mobile 07836 757557, e-mail nsouthward@doctors.org.uk)

SOUTHWARK, Dean of; *see:* Slee, Very Rev Colin B

SOUTHWARK, Archbishop of (RC) 2003–; Most Rev Kevin John Patrick McDonald; s of Michael McDonald (d 1980), and Eileen McDonald (d 1999); *b* 18 August 1947; *Educ* Univ of Birmingham (BA), Gregorian Univ Rome (STL), Angelicum Univ Rome (STD); *Career* lectr Oscott Coll Birmingham 1976–85, staff memb Pontifical Cncl for Christian Unity Rome 1985–93, chaplain to His Holiness the Pope (appointed monsignor) 1988, parish priest Sparkhill Birmingham 1993–98, rector Oscott Coll 1998–2001, canon Birmingham RC Cathedral Chapter 1998–2001, bishop of Northampton 2001–03; Bishops Conference: chm Ctee for Other Faiths 2001–, chm Ctee for Catholic-Jewish Rels 2001–, chm Dept of Dialogue and Unity 2004–; co-sec Anglican-RC Int Cmmn (ARCIC) 1985–93, memb Pontifical Cncl for Interreligious Dialogue 2002–; *Publications* various articles on moral theology, ecumenism and inter-faith in Clergy Review, L'Osservatore Romano, Briefing; *Recreations* music, reading, walking; *Style*— The Most Rev the Archbishop of Southwark; ✉ Archbishop's House, 150 St George's House, Southwark, London SE1 6HX (tel 020 7928 2495, fax 020 7928 7833)

SOUTHWARK, Bishop of 1998–; Rt Rev Dr Thomas Frederick Butler; s of Thomas John Butler (decd), and Elsie, *née* Bainbridge (decd); *b* 5 March 1940; *Educ* Univ of Leeds (BSc, MSc, PhD), Coll of the Resurrection Mirfield; *m* Barbara Joan, *née* Clark; 1 s (Nicholas Roland b 1967), 1 da (Anna Clare b 1969); *Career* ordained: deacon 1964, priest 1965; curate: St Augustine's Wisbech 1964–66, St Saviour's Folkestone 1966–68; lectr and chaplain Univ of Zambia 1968–73, actg dean Holy Cross Cathedral Lusaka Zambia 1973, chaplain to Univ of Kent at Canterbury 1973–80, archdeacon of Northolt 1980–85, area bishop of Willesden 1985–91, bishop of Leicester 1991–1998; memb House of Lords 1996–; Hon LLD Univ of Leicester 1996, Hon DSc Loughborough Univ 1997, Hon LLD De Montfort Univ 1998, Hon DLitt South Bank Univ 2005, Hon DD Univ of Kent 2005; CEng, MIEE; memb Royal Commonwealth Soc; *Publications* Just Mission (with Barbara Butler, 1992), Just Spirituality in a World of Faiths (with Barbara Butler, 1996); *Recreations* walking, reading; *Style*— The Rt Rev the Lord Bishop of Southwark; ✉ Bishop's House, 38 Tooting Bec Gardens, London SW16 1QZ (tel 020 8769 3256, fax 020 8769 4126, e-mail bishops.house@dswark.org.uk)

S

SOUTHWELL, 7 Viscount (I 1776); Sir Pyers Anthony Joseph Southwell; 10 Bt (I 1662); also Baron Southwell (I 1717); s of late Hon Francis Joseph Southwell, 2 s of 5 Viscount; suc unc 1960; *b* 14 September 1930; *Educ* Beaumont Coll, RMA Sandhurst; *m* 1955, Barbara Jacqueline, da of A Raynes; 2 s; *Heir* s, Hon Richard Southwell; *Career* Capt 8 Hussars 1951–55; company dir; int mgmnt and mktg conslt; *Clubs* MCC; *Style*— The Rt Hon the Viscount Southwell

SOUTHWELL, Richard Charles; QC (1977); s of late Sir Philip Southwell, CBE, MC, and Mary, *née* Scarratt; *m* 1962, Belinda Mary, da of late Col F H Pownall, MC; 2 s, 1 da; *Career* called to the Bar Inner Temple 1959 (reader 2001, treas 2002); past judge of the Courts of Appeal of Jersey and Guernsey; pres Lloyd's Appeal Tbnl; chm of govrs: St Mary's Sch Calne, Warminster Sch; tstee Tropical Health and Educn Tst, lay canon Salisbury Cathedral; *Style*— Richard Southwell, Esq, QC; ✉ Serle Court Chambers, 6 New Square, Lincoln's Inn, London WC2A 3QS (tel 020 7242 6105, fax 020 7405 4004, e-mail clerks@serlecourt.co.uk)

SOUTHWELL AND NOTTINGHAM, Bishop of 1999–; Rt Rev George Henry Cassidy; s of Joseph Abram Cassidy (d 1979), and Ethel, *née* McDonald (d 1973); *b* 17 October 1942; *Educ* Belfast HS, Queen's Univ Belfast (BSc), UCL (MPhil), Oak Hill Theol Coll; *m* 17 Dec 1966, Jane Barling, da of Rev Frank Hayman Stevens; 2 da (Sarah, Gael); *Career* civil servant: NI 1967–68, Govt of Kenya 1968–70; curate Christ Church Clifton Bristol 1972–75; vicar: St Edyth's Sea Mills Bristol 1975–82, St Paul's Portman Sq 1982–87; archdeacon of London and canon residentiary of St Paul's Cathedral 1987–99, sub dean Most Excellent Order of the Br Empire 1996–99; memb Cathedrals Fabric Cmmn 2001; memb House of Lords 2004–; Hon DLitt Heriot Watt Univ 2005; Freeman City of London 1988, Hon Freeman Worshipful Co of Founders 1994, Liveryman Worshipful Co of Tylers and Bricklayers 1988; *Recreations* rugby, art, chamber music, walking in Quantocks; *Clubs* National, Nottingham; *Style*— The Rt Rev the Bishop of Southwell and Nottingham; ✉ Bishop's Manor, Southwell, Nottinghamshire NG25 0JR (tel 01636 812112, fax 01636 815401, e-mail bishop@southwell.anglican.org)

SOUTHWORTH, Helen; MP; *Career* MP (Lab) Warrington S 1997–; currently PPS to Rt Hon Paul Boateng, *qv*; *Style*— Ms Helen Southworth, MP; ✉ House of Commons, London SW1A 0AA (tel 020 7219 3000)

SOUTTER, William Patrick (Pat); s of William Paterson Soutter, of Glasgow, and Eleanore Louise, *née* Siekawitch; *b* 12 January 1944; *Educ* Glasgow HS, Univ of Glasgow (MB ChB, MD), Univ of Strathclyde (MSc); *m* 30 June 1973, Winifred Christine, da of William Hanworth, of Paisley; 2 da (Elizabeth b 1980, Eleanor b 1986); *Career* lectr in obstetrics and gynaecology Univ of Glasgow 1978–81, sr lectr in obstetrics and gynaecology Univ of Sheffield 1981–85, reader in gynaecological oncology Inst of Obstetrics and Gynaecology 1985–2006; FRCOG 1988; *Recreations* fishing, golf; *Style*— Pat Soutter, Esq; ✉ Institute of Obstetrics & Gynaecology, Imperial College School of Medicine at Hammersmith Hospital, Du Cane Road, London W12 0HS (tel 020 8383 326, fax 020 8383 8065)

SOUVIRON-CRESPO, HE Maria Beatriz; da of Alberto Souviron, and Victoria, *née* Crespo; *b* 12 November 1966, La Paz, Bolivia; *Educ* Universidad Simón Bolivar Caracas, Universidao del Salvador Buenos Aires; *Partner* Ricardo Roca; *Career* Bolivian diplomat; worked in social area of public sector and devpt projects 1993–2003, fundraiser for social and devpt progs Int Cooperation 2003–06, ambass to the Ct of St James's 2006–; *Style*— HE Ms Maria Souviron-Crespo; ✉ Embassy of Bolivia, 106 Eaton Square, London SW1W 9AD (tel 020 7235 4248, fax 020 7235 5286, e-mail bolivianembassy@yahoo.co.uk)

SOWARD, Prof Andrew Michael; *b* 20 October 1943; *Educ* St Edward's Sch Oxford, Queens Coll Cambridge (open exhibition, BA, PhD), Univ of Cambridge (ScD); *m* 1968; 1 da, 1 s; *Career* visiting memb Univ of NY Courant Inst of Mathematical Sciences 1969–70; visiting fell Co-op Inst for Res in Environmental Sciences Boulder Colorado 1970–71; Univ of Newcastle upon Tyne: SRC res fell 1971, lectr 1971–81, reader in fluid mechanics 1981–86, head Dept of Applied Mathematics 1985–88, prof of fluid dynamics 1986–95, head Div of Applied Mathematics 1989–95; prof of applied mathematics Univ of Exeter 1996–; res and teacher Inst of Geophysics and Planetary Physics UCLA 1977–78; on staff Geophysical Fluid Dynamics Summer Sch Woods Hole Oceanographic Instn MA 1978 and 1987; ed Jl of Geophysical and Astrophysical Fluid Dynamics 1991– (memb Editorial Bd 1986–89, assoc ed 1989–90); FRS 1991, FIMA 2003; *Publications* Book series ed The Fluid Mechanics of Astrophysics and Geophysics (with M Ghil); author of over 100 scientific papers; *Style*— Prof Andrew Soward, FRS; ✉ Department of Mathematical Sciences, University of Exeter, Exeter EX4 4QE (tel 01392 269279, fax 01392 217965, e-mail a.m.soward@exeter.ac.uk)

SOWDEN, Prof David Stewart; s of John Stewart Sowden (d 1980), and Elisabeth Ann, *née* Barford (d 1991); *b* 27 April 1956; *Educ* Cranbourne Bilateral Sch, Queen Marys Sixth Form Coll, Leeds Med Sch (MB ChB, DCH, DFFP); *m* 1981, Dr Maureen Patricia Burnett; *Career* house offr: (surgery) Leeds Gen Infirmary 1979–80, (med) Chapel Allerton Hosp Leeds 1980; GP vocational trg scheme Lincoln 1980–83, ptnr and full time princ in gen practice Measham 1983–2000; Univ of Leicester: clinical tutor to Dept of Gen Practice 1983–97, dir Gen Practice Postgraduate Educn Dept 1995–2000 (assoc regnl advsr 1991–95, chm Summative Assessment Bd 1997–2000); Leicester Vocational Trg Scheme: vocational trainer 1986–97, vocational course organiser 1988–91; postgrad dean of med Univ of Nottingham 2000–, dean dir Trent Multi-Professional Deanery 2005–07, dean dir E Midlands Healthcare Workforce Deanery 2007–; lead visitor Jt Ctee on Postgrad Trg for Gen Practice (JCPTGP) 2000–05 (nat lead dean obstetrics and gynaecology and cardiothoracic surgery 2001–, nat lead dean sports and exercise medicine 2005–), lead visitor Postgraduate Medical Education and Training Bd (PMETB) 2006– (memb Quality Assurance Sub-Ctee 2004–05); chair English Deans Ctee 2006–; non-exec dir Jt Mgmnt Bd WRT and NWP 2005–; visiting prof Univ of Lincoln 2006–; FRCGP, FFSEM, FRCOG ad eundem; *Recreations* golf, Alpine skiing, photography, travel; *Style*— Prof David Sowden; ✉ 18 Tower Gardens, Ashby de la Zouch, Leicestershire LE65 2GZ (tel 01530 411119); 15th Floor, Tower Building, University of Nottingham, Nottingham NG7 2RD (tel 0115 846 7102, fax 0115 846 7107, e-mail david.sowden@nottingham.ac.uk)

SOWDEN, Susan; da of Albert Henry Letley, and Ethel May Letley; *b* 10 June 1951; *Educ* Clarendon House GS for Girls, KCL (BSc, AKC, PGCE), Open Univ (Advanced Dip Educational Mgmnt); *m* 1, 18 Aug 1973; 3 c; m 2, 19 Aug 2000; *Career* teacher of geography, geology and environmental sci Peers Sch Oxford 1973–77 and 1984–85; various posts incl geography teacher, head of geography, housemistress (day girls), head of year and second dep head Headington Sch Oxford 1985–94; headmistress St Mary's Sch Wantage 1994–2006, registrar Headington Sch Oxford 2007–; examination work 1973–94; chief examiner CSE (E Midlands Regnl Examinations Bd (EMREB)) 1983–87 and GCSE (Southern Examinations Gp (SEG)) 1987–89, sr asst chief examiner A Level (Jt Matriculation Bd (JMB)/Northern Examinations and Assessment Bd (NEAB)) 1988–94, team ldr for Teacher In Serv Trg (INSET) for SEG and NEAB; memb: Central ISIS Fin and Gen Purposes Ctee 1995–98, GSA Membership Ctee 1996–2001, The Bloxham Project Steering Ctee 1998–2005 (chm 1999–2005); voluntary teacher Leafield Primary Sch 1984–85; community serv work 1997–: Rotary Club, Dist Cncl Safety Ctee and Drugs Sub-Ctee; parish duties St Giles' Church Horspath 1988–94, asst ldr of Young Church Wychwood Parishes 1984–88; memb Leafield PC 1983–85; Anglican lay min 1993–; *Recreations* touring, canoeing, camping, walking with my family, visiting Nat Tst and Heritage sites, music, concerts, theatre, reading, cooking, handicrafts, watching sport (especially motor racing); *Clubs* Univ Women's, Lansdowne; *Style*— Mrs Sue Sowden; ✉ Headington School, Oxford 0X3 7TD (tel 01235 759115, e-mail ssowden@headington.org)

SPACKMAN, Kim; da of Arthur Albert Spackman (d 1983), and Hilary Denise, *née* Maidment; *b* 29 October 1957; *Educ* Walthamstow Hall Kent; *Career* Thames TV plc 1980–92: sometime prog mangr, prodn mangr, assoc prodr, line prodr; line prodr Dark Horse Productions 1992; Reg Grundy Productions: prodn mangr 1992–94, head of prog mgmnt 1994–97; head of prog mgmnt Pearson TV UK Productions 1997–2001, head of prog mgmnt Thames TV Ltd 2001–; *Recreations* swimming, opera, reading, cinema; *Style*— Ms Kim Spackman; ✉ Thames Television Ltd, 1 Stephen Street, London W1T 1AL (tel 020 7691 6504, fax 020 7691 6086)

SPACKMAN, Michael John; s of Geoffrey Bertram Spackman (d 1976), and Audrey Ivy Elizabeth, *née* Morecombe (d 1998); *b* 8 October 1936; *Educ* Malvern Coll, Clare Coll Cambridge (MA), Queen Mary Coll London (MScEcon); *m* 27 Feb 1965, Judith Ann, da of Walter Henry Leathem (d 1966); 2 s (Sean Michael b 1968, Keir David b 1972), 2 da (Juliet Sarah Helen Christina b 1977, Helena Claire Nicola b 1982); *Career* Mil Serv 2 Lt RA 1955–57; physicist UKAEA Capenhurst 1960–69, sr physicist/engr The Nuclear Power Group Ltd 1969–71, princ scientific offr then economic advsr Dept of Energy 1971–77, dir of economics and accountancy Civil Serv Coll 1979–80; HM Treasy: economic advsr 1977–79, head Public Servs Economics Div 1980–85, under sec and head Public Expenditure Economics Gp 1985–91 and 1993–95; chief economic advsr Dept of Tport 1991–93; Gwilym Gibbon fell Nuffield Coll Oxford 1995–96, special conslt NERA Economic Consulting 1996–, visiting fell Centre for Analysis of Risk and Regulation LSE 2001–; *Recreations* climbing; *Style*— Michael Spackman, Esq; ✉ 44 Gibson Square, Islington, London N1 0RA (tel 020 7359 1053)

SPALDING, Frances; CBE (2005); da of Hedley Stinston Crabtree (d 1985), and Margaret, *née* Holiday (d 1989); *b* 16 July 1950; *Educ* Farringtons Sch Chislehurst, Univ of Nottingham (BA, PhD); *m* 20 April 1974 (m dis 1991), Julian Spalding; 1 s (Daniel b 11 Aug 1983); *Career* art historian and biographer; lectr Sheffield City Poly 1978–88, indep scholar 1989–2000, research co-ordinator for the Writers-in-Prison Ctee English PEN 1991–93, ed The Charleston Magazine 1992–2000, reader Univ of Newcastle upon Tyne 2002 (lectr 2000); Paul Mellon sr research fell and visiting research fell Newnham Coll Cambridge 2005–06; memb: Soc of Authors, PEN, Charleston Tst 1991–, Exec Ctee English PEN 1997–2000; Hon FRCA, FRSL 1984; *Publications* Magnificent Dreams: Burne-Jones and the late Victorians (1978), Whistler (1979, revised edn 1994), Roger Fry: Art and Life (1980), Vanessa Bell (1983), British Art since 1900 (1986), Stevie Smith: A Critical Biography (1988, revised edn 2002), Twentieth Century Painters and Sculptors (Dictionary of British Art series, 1990), Dance till the Stars Come Down: A Biography of John Minton (1991, revised edn 2005), Virginia Woolf: Paper Darts (selected and introduced, 1991), Duncan Grant (1997), The Bloomsbury Group (1997, revised edn 2005), The Tate: A Centenary History (1998), Gwen Raverat: Friends, Family and Affections (2001), John Piper in the 1930s: Abstraction on the Beach (with David Fraser Jenkins, 2003), Ravilious in Public (2003); *Recreations* music; *Style*— Frances Spalding, CBE, FRSL; ✉ c/o Rogers, Coleridge & White Ltd, 20 Powis Mews, London W11 1JN (tel 020 7226 5876)

SPALDING, John Anthony (Tony); s of John Eber Spalding (d 1964), of Wrexham, Denbighshire, and Katherine, *née* Davies; *b* 17 February 1938; *Educ* Wellington, BNC Oxford; *m* 1 (m dis); 2 da; m 2; 1 step da, 1 step s; *Career* journalist 1959–61, Public Affairs Dept Ford Motor Co 1961–64 and 1966–73, PR offr Vauxhall Motors Ltd Ellesmere Port 1964–66; dir of PR: British Leyland 1974–79 (car PR mangr 1973), Wilkinson Match 1979–80, Spillers 1980, Dalgety 1980–81; dir of communications Sea Containers/Seaco 1981–84, dir of public affairs Battersea Leisure/Alton Towers 1984–85, dir of external affairs Whitbread 1985–86; dir of public affairs: Dalgety 1986–89, Vauxhall Motors Ltd 1989–99; exec dir EU Affairs Gen Motors Europe 1999–2003; FIPR 1988, FRSA 1988; *Style*— Tony Spalding, Esq

SPALDING, Julian; s of Eric Spalding, and Margaret Grace, *née* Savager; *b* 15 June 1947; *Educ* Chislehurst and Sidcup GS for Boys, Univ of Nottingham (BA, Dip Museums Assoc); *m* 1, 1974 (m dis 1991), Frances; 1 s; m 2, 1991, Gillian, *née* Tait; *Career* art asst: Leicester Museum and Art Gallery 1970–71, Durham Light Infantry Museum and Arts Centre 1971–72; keeper Mappin Art Gallery 1972–76; dir: Sheffield City Cncl 1982–85 (dep dir 1976–82), Manchester City Art Galleries 1985–89, Glasgow Museums 1989–98; acting dir Nat Museum of Labour History 1987–88; dir: Scottish Football Museum Tst 1995–99, Niki de Saint Phalle Fndn 1995–; BBC broadcaster (talks and reviews incl Third Ear (BBC Radio 3) 1988); res fell Museum of Denmark 1999–2000; chm: Exhibitions Sub-Ctee Arts Cncl 1981–82 and 1986, Drawing Power 2000–; memb: Art Panel 1978–82, Art Galleries Assoc 1987– (fndr and memb Ctee 1976–), Visual Arts Advsy Ctee Br Cncl 1990–; master Guild of St George John Ruskin's Guild 1996–2005 (companion 1978, dir 1983); Crafts Cncl: memb Projects and Orgn Ctee 1985–87, memb 1986–90, memb Purchasing Ctee 1986, memb Exhibitions Ctee 1986–90; Lord Provost's Prize for Services to the Visual Arts in Glasgow 1999; FMA 1983; *Books* L S Lowry (1979), Three Little Books on Painting (1984), Is There Life in Museums? (1990), The Poetic Museum - Reviving Historic Collections (2002), The Eclipse of Art - Tackling the Crisis in Art Today (2003), The Art of Wonder: A History of Seeing (2005, Bannister Fletcher Prize 2006); exhibition catalogues incl: Modern British Painting (1975), Glasgow's Great British Art Exhibition (1990), Gallery of Modern Art Glasgow (1996); contrib Burlington Magazine; *Style*— Julian Spalding, Esq; ✉ 90 Grassmarket, Edinburgh EH1 2JR (tel and fax 0131 226 3798)

SPALDING, Richard Lionel; s of Frederick Lionel Spalding, MD, FRCS (d 1966), of Worcester, and Ines Sylvia, *née* Salkeld (d 1994); *b* 21 May 1938; *Educ* Malvern Coll; *m* 1, 1963, Jane (d 2000), da of late Dr P C King-Lewis; 2 da (Henrietta b 1966, Frederica b 1968), 1 s (William b 1973); m 2, 2003, Elaine Vellacott, da of V D Watford, and wid of James Lindsay-German; *Career* Hubert Leicester & Co accountants Worcester 1957–63, KPMG London 1963–97 (managing ptnr Guildford office 1986–91); dir: Hampstead Theatre Fndn 1998–2003, Worcester Community Housing 2003–; admin Compton Verney Opera Project 1997–2002, tstee Awards for Young Musicians 1998–2004; memb: Capital Devpt Gp, Three Counties Appeal for Acorns Children's Hospice 2000–05, memb The Research Network Parkinsons Disease Soc 2002–; ACA 1963; *Recreations* opera, gardens, churches; *Clubs* Brooks's; *Style*— Richard Spalding, Esq; ✉ 3 Britannia Square, Worcester WR1 3DG (e-mail rlspalding@tiscali.co.uk)

SPALL, Timothy; OBE (2000); *Career* actor; hon vice-pres The Archie and Gwen Smith Meml Tst Fund; FRSA 2000; *Theatre* NT incl: Bottom in A Midsummer's Night Dream, Ligurio in Mandragola, Dauphin in Saint Joan, Le Bourgeois Gentilhomme; RSC incl: Andre in The Three Sisters, Rafe in Knight of the Burning Pestle, Waxford Squeers/Mr Folair in Nicholas Nickleby, Simple in The Merry Wives of Windsor, Ivan in Suicide, Mech in Baal; Birmingham Rep incl: Boucicault in Heavenly Bodies, Gratiano in The Merchant of Venice, Harry Trevor/Baptista in Kiss Me Kate, Lawrence in Mary Barns (also Royal Court); other credits incl: Martin in Aunt Mary (Warehouse), Khelstakov in The Government Inspector (Greenwich), Vic Maggot in Smelling A Rat (Hampstead), Derek in Screamers (Playhouse Studio Edinburgh); *Television* BBC incl: Phil in A Nice Day at the Office, Jimmy Beales in Roots, Chico in La Nona, Francis Meakes in Broke, Paul in Body Contact, Clevor Trevor in Arena - Night Moves, Hawkins in Guest of the Nation, Gordon in Home Sweet Home, Sgt Baxter in A Cotswold Death, Yepikhodov in The Cherry Orchard, Shorty in The Brylcreem Boys, Wainwright in Vanishing Army,

Pathologist in Murder Most Horrid, Dread Poets Society, Our Mutual Friend; other credits incl: Barry in Auf Wiedersehen Pet, Webster in Boon (Central), Frank Stubbs in Frank Stubbs Promotes (2 series), Kevin in Outside Edge (3 series, Best TV Comedy Drama Br Comedy Awards 1994 for series 1 and 2), Donald Caudell in Stolen, Porfiry in Great Writers - Dostoyevsky, Lyndon in Dutch Girls, Pilot in A Class Act, Andrei in The Three Sisters, Pig Robinson in The Tale of Little Pig Robinson, Gordon Neville's Island, Oswold Bates, Shooting the Past, Vince in The Thing About Vince, Cunningham in Young Indiana Jones, Tommy Rag in Vacuuming Completely Nude in Paradise, Irving in Perfect Strangers, Barry in Auf Wiedersehen Pet 2002 and 2004, Mitchel Greenfield in Bodily Harm 2002, Malcolm Harvey in Mr Harvey Lights a Candle 2005, Terry Cannings in Cherished 2005, Eddie McEvoy in The Street 2006, Bill Ainscow in Mysterious Creatures 2006; *Film* incl: Harry in Quadrophenia 1979, Jim in SOS Titanic 1979, Douglas in Remembrance 1982, Paulus in The Bride 1985, Polidari in Gothic 1986, Igor in To Kill A Priest 1988, Peck in Dream Demon 1988, Reverant Miln in Crusoe 1988, Aubrey in Life is Sweet 1990, Eric Lyle in The Sheltering Sky 1990, Ramborde in 1871 1990, Hodkins in White Hunter Black Heart 1990, Nick Watt in The Nihilist's Double Vision, African Footsteps, Maurice in Secrets and Lies 1996, Rosencrantz in Hamlet 1996, Det Inspr Healey in Wisdom of Crocodiles 1997, Beano Bagot in Still Crazy 1998, Mr Stirling in Clandestine Marriage 1998, Richard Temple in Topsy Turvy 1999, Don Armado in Love's Labour's Lost 1999, Gourville in Vatel 1999, The Mayor in The Old Man who read Love Stories 2001, Andy in Intimacy 2001, Mats in Rock Star 2001, Cliff Gumble in Lucky Break 2001, Thomas in Vanilla Sky 2001, Charles Cheeryble in Nicholas Nickleby 2002, Phil Basset in All or Nothing 2002, Quinty in My House in Umbria 2003, Darren Barrington in Getting Square 2003, Simon Graham in The Last Samurai 2003, Peter Pettigrew in Harry Potter and the Prisoner of Azkaban 2004, Mr Poe in Lemony Snicket's A Series of Unfortunate Events 2004, Peter Pettigrew in Harry Potter and the Goblet of Fire 2005, Albert Pierrepoint in Pierrepoint 2006, Sugarman in Death Defying Acts 2007, Nathaniel in Enchanted 2007, Beadle Bamford in Sweeney Todd 2008, Voice and Churchill in Jackboots in Whitehall 2008; *Clubs* Colony, Dean Street Soho; *Style*— Timothy Spall, OBE; ✉ c/o Markham & Froggatt Ltd, Julian House, 4 Windmill Street, London W1P 1HF (tel 020 7636 4412, fax 020 7637 5233)

SPALTON, David John; *b* 2 March 1947; *Educ* Buxton Coll, Westminster Med Sch (MB BS); *m* 26 May 1979, Catherine, da of Donald George Bompas, CMG, of Petts Wood, Kent; 3 s (George b 1980, James b 1983, Benjamin b 1992); *Career* sr registrar Moorfields Eye Hosp 1976–77; conslt ophthalmic surgn: Charing Cross Hosp 1981–83, St Thomas' Hosp 1983, King Edward VII Hosp for Offrs London; hon conslt ophthalmic surgn Royal Hosp Chelsea, ophthalmic advsr to the Met Police, hon sr lectr in ophthalmology UMDS; Liveryman Worshipful Soc of Apothecaries; FRCS 1975, FRCOphth 1988, FRCP 1990; *Books* Atlas of Clinical Ophthalmology (1985, 3 edn 2004, BMA Award for Best Medical Textbook of the Year); *Recreations* fly fishing; *Style*— David Spalton, Esq; ✉ Consulting Rooms, King Edward VII's Hospital, 37A Devonshire Road, London W1G 6QA (tel 020 7935 6174, fax 020 7467 4376)

SPARKES, HE Andrew; CMG (2007); *b* 4 July 1959; *Educ* Manchester Grammar, Trinity Hall Cambridge; *m* 1985, Jean Mary, *née* Meakin; 1 s (Edward b 1988), 1 da (Laura b 1992); *Career* diplomat; entered HM Dip Serv 1982, second sec (Chancery) Ankara 1985–88, first sec FCO 1988–92, first sec (political) Bangkok 1992–95, first sec rising to cnsllr FCO 1995–97, on loan to DTI 1997–99, dep head of mission Jakarta 1999–2001, dep high cmmr Pretoria 2001–04, ambass to Democratic Repub of Congo 2004–07 (concurrently non-resident ambass to Congo); *Style*— HE Mr Andrew Sparkes, CMG; ✉ c/o Foreign & Commonwealth Office (Kinshasa), King Charles Street, London SW1A 2AH

SPARKS, Ian Leslie; OBE (1999); s of Ronald Leslie Sparks (d 2004), and Hilda, *née* Bullen (d 1996); *b* 26 May 1943; *Educ* Holt HS Liverpool, Brunel Univ (MA), Kingston Univ (DMS); *m* 1 July 1967, Eunice Jean, da of Reginald Robinson (d 1983); 1 da (Clare b 1973); *Career* social worker Merseyside 1971, asst divnl dir Barnardos 1974, chief exec The Children's Soc 1986–2002 (social work dir 1981); chair: End Child Poverty 2002–04, Frontier Youth Tst 2004–; chm Br Agencies for Adoption and Fostering 1996–2000; tstee: NCVCCO 1986–2002, Haven House Fndn, Tyn-y-Nant Christian Centre, ChildAid, Int Anglican Family Network 2002–; *Recreations* piano playing, gardening in miniature; *Style*— Ian Sparks, Esq; ✉ 16 Frating Crescent, Woodford Green, Essex IG8 0DW (tel 020 8505 4962, e-mail iansparks@btinternet.com)

SPARKS, Leslie Thomas (Les); OBE (1997); s of Eric Sparks (d 1977), of Yeovil, and Dorothy Leonie, *née* McQuillen (d 1987); *b* 3 March 1943; *Educ* Kingston Coll of Art (DipArch), Central London Poly (Dip Town and Country Planning); *m* 26 Aug 1967, Yvonne Ann, da of Alfred George Sawyer; 1 da (Heidi Jane b 15 March 1969), 1 s (Richard James b 12 Oct 1972); *Career* princ planning offr London Borough of Lambeth 1968–73, architect/planner for Hugh Wilson and Lewis Womersley 1973–74, chief planner New Ideal Homes 1974–75, Severn Gorge projects mangr Telford Devpt Corp 1975–80, dir of environmental services Bath City Cncl 1980–91, dir of planning and architecture Birmingham City Cncl 1991–99, pt/t planning inspr 1999–2002, cmmr Cmmn for Architecture and the Built Environment (CABE) 1999–2006 (chm CABE Design Review Panel 2004–06), cmmr English Heritage 2001– (memb Advsy Ctee, regnl cmmr for E Midlands, chm English Heritage/CABE Urban Panel); conslt Terence O'Rourke plc 1999–, planning advsr Joseph Rowntree Fndn 1999–2007, advsr Nottingham City Cncl 2001–, architectural advsr Crown Estate 2002–; visiting prof: Faculty of Built Environment UCE 1995–99, UWE 1999– (external examiner Faculty of Built Environment 1991–94); chm: Historic Buildings and Land Panel Heritage Lottery Fund 1999–2001, Bath and NE Somerset Urban Regeneration Panel 2004–, W Midlands Region Design Review Panel 2007–; memb: Urban Villages Forum Steering Ctee 1992–96, Historic Buildings Advsy Gp MOD 1994–, Mgmnt Ctee Nat Cncl for Habitat II (The City Summit) Conf 1995–96, Urban Capacity Sub-Gp Sec of State's UK Round Table on Sustainability 1996–97, Process Sub-Gp Dep PM's Urban Task Force 1998–99, Town Planning Panel Research Assessment Exercise 2001 HEFCE 1999–2001, Review of Heritage Protection Steering Gp DCMS 2003–06; memb DOE/DETR/DTLR Steering Gps 1996–2002 (Planning for Sustainability, The Role and Effectiveness of Planning Briefs, Design in the Planning System, Urban Green Spaces Task Force); patron Urban Design Gp 1997–, tstee Birmingham Conservation Tst 1999–; non-exec dir Birmingham Groundwork 1999–2001; hon life memb English Historic Towns Forum 1992; Hon DDes UWE 2000; corp memb RIBA 1971; MRTPI 1974, FRSA 1982; *Style*— Les Sparks, Esq, OBE; ✉ tel 0121 415 4547

SPARKS, Prof (Robert) Stephen John; s of Kenneth Grenfell Sparks, and late Ruth Joan, *née* Rugman; *b* 15 May 1949; *Educ* Wellington, Bingley GS, Imperial Coll London (BSc, PhD); *m* 19 June 1971, Ann Elizabeth, da of Frederick Currie Talbot (d 1986); 2 s (Andrew Robert James b 24 Aug 1978, Daniel Joseph b 1 May 1982); *Career* Royal Exhibition of 1951 fell Lancaster Univ 1974–76, NATO fell Univ of Rhode Island 1976–78, lectr in geology Univ of Cambridge 1978–89, prof of geology Univ of Bristol 1989–; pres Geological Soc of London 1994–; chief scientist Montserrat Volcano Observatory; prof NERC Research 1998–2003; pres Int Assoc of Volcanology and Chemistry of the Earth's Interior 1999–2003; memb: Grants Ctee NERC 1985–88 and 2001–05, various ctees Royal Soc; Bakerian Lecture Royal Soc 2000; Wager Medal Int Assoc of Volcanology and Chemistry of the Earth's Interior, Bigsby Medal Geological Soc London, Murchison Medal Geological Soc London, Arthur Day Medal Geological Soc America, Arthur Holmes Medal European Geosciences Union; Hon Dr: Lancaster Univ, Blaise Pascal Université, Institut de Physique du Globe de Paris; FRS 1988, FGS, fell American Geophysical Union; *Books* Tephra Studies (co-ed with S Self, 1980), Volcanic Plumes (with John Wiley, 1997), Physics of Explosive Volcanic Eruptions (co-ed with J Gilbert, 1998), Santorini Volcano (1999), State of the Planet (monograph); author of 280 published scientific papers; *Recreations* cricket, music, theatre; *Style*— Prof Stephen Sparks, FRS; ✉ Walnut Cottage, 19 Brinsea Road, Congresbury BS49 5JF (tel 01934 834306); Department of Earth Sciences, University of Bristol, Bristol BS8 1RJ (tel 0117 928 7789, e-mail steve.sparks@bristol.ac.uk)

SPASOV, HE Gjorgji; s of Nikola Spasov (d 1985), of Negotino, Macedonia, and Cveta, *née* Cekova (d 2005); *b* 11 August 1949, Negotino, Macedonia; *Educ* Faculty of Political Science Belgrade, Univ of Skopje (PhD); *m* 1, 16 Sept 1973, Zorica; 1 s (Nikola b 6 April 1981); m 2, 2 Sept 2004, Slavica, *née* Nikolovska; *Career* Macedonian diplomat; TV journalist 1972–93, researcher Inst for Sociological, Legal and Political Research Univ of Skopje 1973–93, ambass to Bulgaria and Moldavia 1994–97, min of justice 1997–98, MP 1998–2003, sec gen Social Democratic Union of Macedonia 1998–2002, prof of political science Faculty of Law Univ of Skopje 1999, chief of delgn to Assembly of WEU 2003, ambass to the Ct of St James's 2003–; memb RIIA; Madarski Kumamik of the First Range (Bulgaria) 1997; *Style*— HE Mr Gjorgji Spasov; ✉ BU1 'Vasil Gorgov', 20/57 Skopje, Republic of Macedonia; Embassy of the Republic of Macedonia, Suites 2.1 and 2.2, Buckingham Court, 75–83 Buckingham Gate, London SW1E 6PE (tel 020 7976 0535, e-mail spasov@macedonianembassy.org.uk)

SPATHIS, Dr Gerassimos Spyros (Memo); s of Spyros Andrew Spathis (d 1975), of Cephalonia, Greece, and Olga, *née* Georgopoulos (d 1999); *b* 20 April 1935; *Educ* The King's Sch Canterbury, Exeter Coll Oxford (MA, DM), Guy's Hosp London; *m* 3 June 1967, Maria, da of Demetrius Messinezy, of Tinos and Geneva; 2 da (Anna b 1969, Sonia b 1971); *Career* various positions held at: Guy's Hosp, Osler Hosp Oxford, Addenbrooke's Hosp Cambridge, St Thomas' Hosp, Central Middlesex and Middlesex Hosps London; physician St Helier Hosp Carshalton 1972–98, hon physician Royal Marsden Hosp Sutton, hon sr lectr St George's Hosp Med Sch, first sub dean St Helier Hosp 1986–93; prof and chm Faculty of Med Kigezi Int Sch of Med 2000–04; vice-chm SW Thames RHA 1989–93 (memb 1984–93), memb Cncl NAHAT 1989–93; memb Criminal Injuries Compensation Appeals Panel (CICAP) 2000–06; former JP (Youth Bench); Liveryman Worshipful Soc of Apothecaries; FRCP 1977, DPMSA; *Recreations* hill walking, photography; *Style*— Dr G S Spathis; ✉ e-mail spathis@doctors.org.uk

SPAVEN, Dr Patrick John; OBE (1997); s of John Basil Spaven (d 1960), and Marie, *née* Burford; *b* 2 November 1949; *Educ* Felsted, Univ of Sussex (MA), Univ of Warwick (PhD); *m* 1976, Kirsti, da of Hans-Jacob Hallvang; 1 s (Thomas b 8 June 1983), 1 da (Rebecca b 10 Oct 1990); *Career* tutor in industrial studies Univ of Sheffield 1974–76, Nuffield research assoc Univ of Warwick 1976–77, industrial relations offr Advisory Conciliation and Arbitration Service 1977–80; British Council: industrial relations advsr 1980–84, asst rep Kenya 1984–88, head of employment relations 1988–91, dir Barcelona 1991–96, dir Sweden 1997–2000, head of research and evaluation 2000–05; lead conslt Spaven Research and Evalutation 2005–; hon memb Anglo-Catalan Soc 1993–; MCIPD; *Style*— Dr Patrick Spaven, OBE; ✉ British Council, 10 Spring Gardens, London SW1A 2BN

SPEAIGHT, Anthony Hugh; QC (1995); s of George Victor Speaight (d 2005), of Kew Gardens, Surrey, and Mary Olive, *née* Mudd (d 2005); *b* 31 July 1948; *Educ* St Benedict's Sch Ealing, Lincoln Coll Oxford (MA); *m* 3 Aug 1991, Gabrielle Anne Kooy-Lister; 2 s (Edmund William Laurier b 18 July 1992, Lawrence Frederick Joseph b 28 May 1996), 1 da (Isabella Louise Annunziata b 14 Sept 1994); *Career* called to the Bar Middle Temple 1973 (bencher); elected memb Gen Cncl of the Bar 1987–91 and 1998–2000, memb Bar Cncl Working Pty on Televising Cts 1988; chm Editorial Bd Counsel (Jl of the Bar of Eng and Wales) 1991–95, chm Bar Cncl Access to the Bar Ctee 2004–06; nat chm Fedn of Cons Students 1972–73, chm Youth Bd of the Euro Movement (UK) 1974–75, dep chm Cons Gp for Europe 1977; Freeman City of London; Schuman Silver medal (awarded by FVS Fndn of Germany) 1976; *Books* The Law of Defective Premises (with G Stone, 1982), The Architects Journal Legal Handbook (jtly, 1985–2004), Butterworths Professional Negligence Service (jt ed, 2000); *Recreations* theatre, cricket; *Clubs* Carlton, Hurlingham; *Style*— Anthony Speaight, Esq, QC; ✉ 4 Pump Court, Temple, London EC4 (tel 020 7842 5555, fax 020 7583 2036)

SPEAKMAN, Prof John Roger; s of Ernest Wilcock Speakman, and (Miriam) Freda Speakman; *b* 29 November 1958, Leigh, Lancs; *Educ* Univ of Stirling (BSc, PhD), Univ of Aberdeen (DSc); *m* 9 Aug 1980, Mary Magdelene; 1 da (Emily Ann b 14 April 1993), 1 s ((Alasdair) Jack b 17 July 1995); *Career* Univ of Aberdeen: successively lectr, sr lectr and reader 1989–97, prof 1997–, head of integrative physiology 2003–; seconded pt/t to Rowett Research Inst 2000–05; memb Advsy Bd Mars Masterfoods 2001–; dir Co of Biologists 2004–; Scientific Medal Zoological Soc of London 1997, Scottish Science Medal Saltire Soc 2004; FRSE 2004; *Publications* Doubly Labelled Water: Theory and Practice (1997), Body Composition in Animals: A Handbook of Non-Invasive Methods (ed, 2001); author of more than 225 articles and papers in scientific pubns; *Recreations* photography; *Style*— Prof John Speakman

SPEARING, Prof Anthony Colin; s of Frederick Spearing, and Gertrude, *née* Calnin; *b* 31 January 1936; *Educ* Alleyn's Sch Dulwich, Jesus Coll Cambridge (MA); *m* 1961; 1 s, 1 da; *Career* research on Piers Plowman under supervision of C S Lewis and Elizabeth Salter 1957–60; Univ of Cambridge: W M Tapp fell Gonville & Caius Coll 1959–60, asst lectr in English 1960–64, supernumerary fell Gonville & Caius Coll 1960; Queens' Coll Cambridge: asst dir of studies in English 1960–67, lectr in English 1964–85, dir of studies in English 1967–85, sec Faculty of English 1970–71, chm Degree Ctee Faculty of English 1977–79, reader in Medieval English literature 1985–87, chm Faculty of English 1986–87, official fell 1960–87, life fell 1987–; Univ of Virginia: visiting prof of English 1979–80 and 1984, Center for Advanced Studies 1987–89, prof of English 1987–89, William R Kenan prof of English 1989–; external examiner: Univ of Bristol 1974, MA in Medieval Studies Univ of York 1974–76; Studentship Selection Ctee UK Dept of Educn and Science 1976–79; William Matthews lectr Birkbeck Coll London 1983–84; Lansdowne visiting fell Univ of Victoria BC 1993, Benjamin Meaker visiting prof Univ of Bristol 2003, Conway lectr Univ of Notre Dame 2007, visiting lectr at numerous univs in Britain, Europe, Canada and USA; *Publications* Criticism and Medieval Poetry (1964, 2 edn 1972), An Introduction to Chaucer (with Maurice Hussey and James Winny, 1965), The Gawain Poet: A Critical Study (1970), Chaucer: Troilus and Criseyde (1976), Medieval Dream-Poetry (1976), Medieval to Renaissance in English Poetry (1985), Readings in Medieval Poetry (1987), The Medieval Poet as Voyeur (1993), The Cloud of Unknowing (trans, 2001), Textual Subjectivity: The Encoding of Subjectivity in Medieval Romances and Lyrics (2005); contrib to numerous learned jls; *Style*— Prof A C Spearing; ✉ Department of English, 219 Bryan Hall, PO Box 400121, University of Virginia, Charlottesville, VA 22904–4121, USA (e-mail acs4j@virginia.edu)

SPEARING, (David) Nicholas; s of George David Spearing, of Caterham, Surrey, and Josephine Mary, *née* Newbould; *b* 4 May 1954; *Educ* Caterham Sch, Hertford Coll Oxford (MA); *Family* 2 da (Laura b 1982, Elizabeth b 1987), 2 s (James b 1989, George b 1992); m, 2004, Caroline, *née* Butler; *Career* slr; articled Gordon Dadds & Co 1976–78; Freshfields: asst slr 1978–84, ptnr 1984–; past chm Law Soc Slrs' Euro Gp; past pres Fielding Soc; chm St Jude's Community Centre; memb City of London Slrs' Co; *Publications* contrib: Encyclopaedia of Forms and Precedents, Butterworths Competition Law; author of articles in professional jls; *Recreations* modern art, reading, antiques;

Style— Nicholas Spearing, Esq; ✉ 8 Gullivers Wharf, Wapping Lane, London E1W 2RR (tel 020 7480 5644, fax 020 7680 0015); 65 Fleet Street, London EC4Y 1HS (tel 020 7832 7127, fax 020 7832 7233, e-mail nicholas.spearing@freshfields.com)

SPEARMAN, Sir Alexander Young Richard Mainwaring Spearman; 5 Bt (UK 1840), of Hanwell, Middlesex; s of Sir Alexander Bowyer Spearman, 4 Bt (d 1977); *b* 3 February 1969; *m* 1, 1994 (m dis 1997), Anne Stine, da of Kaj Munch, of Hyllinge, Denmark; m 2, 1997, Theresa Jean, da of Dr Thomas Sutcliffe, of Cape Town; 1 s (Alexander Axel b 1999); *Heir* s, Alexander Axel; *Style—* Sir Alexander Spearman, Bt

SPEARMAN, John Litting; s of Thomas Spearman, and Elizabeth Alexandra, *née* Leadbeater; *b* 25 November 1941; *Educ* Trinity Coll Dublin (MA); *m* 1, 1966, Susan Elizabeth, *née* Elmes; 1 s (Thomas Crawford John), 1 da (Laragh Elizabeth Jane); m 2, 1988, Angela Josephine, *née* van Praag; 1 da (Ottoline); *Career* graduate trainee Unilever 1964, account dir Lintas Advtg 1969, account dir and assoc bd dir Leo Burnett 1969–73, account dir, md then chm and chief exec Collett Dickenson Pearce 1973–90, chm Lazer Sales (sales and mktg subsid of LWT) 1990–92, dep chm Classic FM Radio 1997–98 (chief exec 1992–97); chm Playback (mgmnt trg video co) 1990–, operating ptnr Electra 1998–; bd dir Royal Philharmonic Orch 1993–96, memb Industry Lead Body for Design, patron dir RIBA, tstee World Monuments Fund, pres Music Therapy Appeal Ctee; memb Arts Cncl 1996–98; *Recreations* music, theatre, reading, gardening, walking, skiing, sailing; *Clubs* Athenaeum, Royal Irish Yacht, Hurlingham; *Style—* John Spearman, Esq

SPEARMAN, Richard; QC (1996); s of late Clement Spearman, CBE, and Olwen Regina, *née* Morgan; *b* 19 January 1953; *Educ* Bedales, King's Coll Cambridge (MA); *m* 30 April 1983, Alexandra Elizabeth, da of late Bryan A Harris; 3 da (Olivia b 6 July 1985, Annabel b 11 Oct 1987, Lucinda b 16 Jan 1992); *Career* called to the Bar Middle Temple 1977 (bencher 2006); recorder 2000– (asst recorder 1998–2000); *Books* Sale of Goods Litigation (with F A Philpott, 1983, 2 edn 1994), Information Rights (contrib, 2004, 2 edn 2007); *Recreations* lawn tennis, real tennis, skiing, family; *Clubs* Brooks's, Hurlingham, MCC; *Style—* Richard Spearman, Esq, QC; ✉ 4–5 Gray's Inn Square, Gray's Inn, London WC1R 5AY (tel 020 7404 5252, fax 020 7242 7803, e-mail chambers@4-5.co.uk)

SPECULAND, Bernard; s of Cyril Speculand (d 1953), and Hannah, *née* Shelower (d 1999); *b* 26 August 1949; *Educ* City of Norwich GS, Univ of Bristol (BDS, MDS); *m* 19 Dec 1975, Christine, da of Alec Turner; 2 da (Caroline b 1977, Mary b 1980), 1 s (Alex b 1982); *Career* sr registrar: Royal Adelaide Hosp 1977, Bristol Royal Infirmary, Bristol Dental Hosp and Frenchay Hosp 1978–85; City Hosp Birmingham, Queen Elizabeth Hosp Birmingham and Birmingham Dental Hosp: conslt oral and maxillo-facial surgn 1985–, chm Local Research Ethics Ctee 1997–2005; pres Birmingham Medico Legal Soc 1993–95 (vice-pres 1991–93), hon sec Assoc Res Ethics Ctees 2002–06, vice-chm Central Ctee for Hosp Dental Servs Br Dental Assoc 2006–; fell BAOMS, FRACDS 1977, FDSRCS 1975, FFDRCSI 1975; *Books* The Mouth and Peri-Oral Tissues in Health and Disease (contrib, 1989); *Recreations* squash, running, windsurfing, skiing; *Style—* Bernard Speculand, Esq; ✉ Department of Oral & Maxillofacial Surgery, City Hospital, Birmingham B18 7QH (tel 0121 554 3801, fax 0121 507 4315, e-mail bernard.speculand@swbh.nhs.uk)

SPEDDING, Prof Sir Colin Raymond William; kt (1994), CBE (1988); s of late Rev Robert K Spedding, and Ilynn, *née* Bannister; *b* 22 March 1925; *Educ* Univ of London (BSc, MSc, PhD, DSc); *m* 6 Sept 1952, Betty Noreen (d 1988), da of late A H George; 2 s (Peter George b 1954 d 1958, Geoffrey Robert b 1957), 1 da (Lucilla Mary (Mrs Weston) b 1960); *Career* Sub Lt RNVR 1943–46; Grassland Res Inst 1949–75 (dep dir 1972–75); Univ of Reading: visiting prof then pt/t prof Dept of Agric and Horticulture 1970–75, prof of agric systems Dept of Agric 1970–90, head Dept of Agric and Horticulture 1975–83, dir Centre for Agric Strategy 1981–90, dean Faculty of Agric and Food 1983–86, pro-vice-chllr 1986–90, emeritus prof 1990–; Lands Improvement Holdings plc: dir 1986–99, dep chm 1990–99; dir Centre for Economic and Environmental Devpt; pres: Euro Assoc of Animal Prodn Study Cmmn on Sheep and Goat Prodn 1970–76, Br Soc of Animal Prodn 1979–80; ed Agricultural Systems 1976–88, vice-chm Prog Ctee Int Livestock Centre for Africa Addis Ababa 1980–83 (memb 1976–80); chm: Bd of UK Register of Organic Food Standards 1987–99, Farm Animal Welfare Cncl 1988–99, Nat Resources Policy Gp Inst of Biology 1988–92, Apple and Pear Res Cncl 1989–97, Scientific Advsy Panel of World Soc for Protection of Animals 1989–98, Kintail Land Res Fndn 1990–2004, Nat Equine Forum 1992–, The Sci Cncl (formerly CSTI) 1994–2000, Assured Chicken Prodn Ltd 2000–04, Poultry Sector Bd 2004–; dir Assured Food Standards 2001–; Inst of Biology: vice-pres 1987–91 and 1997–2000, pres 1992–94, chm of PR Bd 1997–2000; sr conslt to Agric & Food Res Cncl 1992–94; dep chm PDSA 1988–2003; memb: Media Resource Services Steering Ctee 1985–2000, Governing Body Inst of Grassland and Environmental Res 1987–91, Food Safety Policy Gp Inst of Biology 1990–92; conslt dir Centre for Agric Strategy 1990–99; chm of tstees Farm Animal Welfare Trust 2003–; advsr Companion Animal Welfare Cncl 1999–, patron Family Farmers' Assoc; special advsr to DG World Soc for Protection of Animals 2003– (advsy dir 1998–2003); specalist advsr House of Lords Select Ctee on EC sub-ctee D (agric, fisheries and food) 1999, head UK delgn to Int Whaling Cmmn Workshop on Whale Killing Methods Grenada 1999; hon memb RSM 1998–; vice-pres RSPCA 2002–; awards: Canadian Inst of Agric Recognition Award 1971, George Hedley Meml Award 1971, Wooldridge Meml lectr and medallist (BVA) 1982, Massey Ferguson National Agricultural Award 1991, Hawkesbury Centenary Medal of Honour Univ of Western Sydney Aust 1991, Bawden Meml lectr 1992, Hammond Meml lectr 1995, Hume Meml lectr 1996, Paul Lynch address 1996, Robert Antoine Meml lectr 1997, Burntwood Meml lecture 2000, Victory Medal Central Veterinary Soc 2000; Hon DSc Univ of Reading 1995; hon life memb Br Soc of Animal Sci, hon assoc RCVS 1994, Hon FIBiol 1994; FZS 1962, FIBiol 1967, CBiol 1984, FRASE 1984, FIHort 1986, FRAgS 1986, FRSA 1988, MInstD 1992–99, FLS 1994; *Books* Sheep Production and Grazing Management (2 edn, 1970), Grassland Ecology (1971), Grasses and Legumes in British Agriculture (ed with E C Diekmahns, 1972), The Biology of Agricultural Systems (1975), Vegetable Productivity (ed, 1981), Biological Efficiency in Agriculture (with J M Walsingham and A M Hoxey, 1981), Fream's Agriculture (ed, 1983), An Introduction to Agricultural Systems (2 edn, 1988), Fream's Principles of Food & Agriculture (ed, 1992), Agriculture and the Citizen (1996), Animal Welfare (2000), The Natural History of a Garden (2003), The Second Mouse Gets the Cheese: Proverbs and their uses; *Clubs* Athenaeum, Farmers'; *Style—* Prof Sir Colin Spedding, CBE; ✉ Vine Cottage, Orchard Road, Hurst, Berkshire RG10 0SD (tel 0118 934 1771, fax 0118 934 2997)

SPEED, James Nicholas; s of J R G Speed, of The Cedar House Gallery, Ripley, Surrey, and J Speed, *née* Williamson; *b* 24 December 1958; *Educ* Wellington; *Career* hotelier; three year's experience at The Lancaster Hotel Paris; dir Durrant's Hotel London (Which London Hotel of the Year 1992 and 1993), former co-owner and fndr Thethaicollection.com (website and shops in Koh Samui and Bangkok selling shoes, clothes and jewellery); *Recreations* collecting fine wines, interior design, travel; *Style—* James Speed, Esq

SPEIRS, Robert (Bob); s of John Speirs (d 1969), and Isabella, *née* Clark (d 1993); *b* 23 October 1936; *Educ* Alleynes GS Uttoxeter; *m* 15 March 1958, Patricia; 2 s (John b 29 Aug 1969, Julian b 28 May 1971); *Career* Inland Revenue 1954–58, Dept of Taxes Fed of Rhodesia and Nyasaland 1958–64, sr tax mangr Coopers & Lybrand 1964–68, UK tax administrator Texaco Ltd 1968–77, fin dir BNOC/Britoil plc 1977–88, fin dir Olympia York Canary Wharf Ltd 1988–93, fin dir Royal Bank of Scotland Gp plc 1993–98; chm: Bell Gp plc 1999–2004, Miller Gp Ltd 1999–, Stagecoach Gp plc 2002– (non-exec dir 1995–); non-exec dir Canary Wharf Gp plc 1999–2004; *Recreations* gardening, travel, history, family (5 grandchildren); *Style—* Robert Speirs, Esq; ✉ Arden, Pitts Haven, Pitts Lane, Binstead, Isle of Wight PO33 3AX (tel 01983 568708, mobile 07710 068147)

SPEKE, (Ian) Benjamin; s of Col Neil Hanning Reed Speke, MC, TD (d 1996), of Aydon White House, Northumberland, and Averil Allgood, *née* Straker; *b* 12 March 1950; *Educ* Eton; *m* 30 July 1983, Ailsa Elizabeth, da of Matthew Hall Fenwick, of Capheaton, Newcastle upon Tyne; 2 da (Zara b 1988, Thea b 1990), 1 s (Toby b 1989); *Career* 9/12 Royal Lancers (Prince of Wales) 1968–72, Northumberland Hussars (Queen's Own Yeo) 1974–87; Pinchin Denny 1974–77, Hoare Govett Equity sales 1977–80, ptnr Wise Speke & Co 1980–87, dir Wise Speke Ltd 1987–98, dir Brewin Dolphin Holdings plc 2002–; memb Int Stock Exchange 1980; High Sheriff Northumberland 2005–06; *Recreations* field sports; *Clubs* Pratt's, Turf, Northern Cos; *Style—* Benjamin Speke, Esq; ✉ Thornbrough High House, Corbridge, Northumberland NE45 5PR (tel 01434 633080); Wise Speke, Commercial Union House, 39 Pilgrim Street, Newcastle upon Tyne NE1 6RQ (tel 0191 279 7300, fax 0191 279 7301)

SPELLAR, Rt Hon John Francis; PC (2001), MP; s of William David Spellar; *b* 5 August 1947; *Educ* Dulwich Coll, St Edmund Hall Oxford; *m* 1981, Anne (d 2003); 1 da; *Career* nat offr EETPU 1969–82 and 1983–92; MP (Lab): Birmingham Northfield 1982–83, Warley W 1992–97, Warley 1997– (Parly candidate (Lab): Bromley 1970, Birmingham Northfield 1983 and 1987); memb Commons Select Ctee on Energy 1982–83, sec All-Pty Construction Ctee 1992–, oppn whip (Employment and Trade and Industry) 1992–94; oppn spokesman on: NI 1994–95, Defence 1995–97; Parly under sec of state MOD 1997–99, min of state for Armed Forces 1999–2001, min for Tport 2001–03, min of state for NI 2003–05; *Recreations* reading, gardening; *Clubs* Rowley Regis and Blackheath Labour; *Style—* The Rt Hon John Spellar, MP; ✉ House of Commons, London SW1A 0AA (tel 020 7219 0674, e-mail spellarj@parliament.uk)

SPELLER, Dr Vivienne Marilyn (Viv); da of Edward Speller (d 1998), and Rosina Clara, *née* Bell; *b* 28 July 1953; *Educ* Univ of Manchester (BSc, PhD); *Children* 1 da (Laura Jane Pottinger b 8 May 1983), 1 s (Matthew Bowman Pottinger b 6 July 1987); *Career* health educn offr Manchester AHA 1978–80, health educn offr King's/Camberwell Health Dist London 1980–84, dist health promotion mangr Wandsworth HA 1984–86, dist health promotion mangr Winchester HA 1986–92, regnl health promotion mangr and regnl Health of the Nation co-ordinator Wessex RHA and Wessex Inst for Public Health Med 1992–96, sr lectr in health promotion Univ of Southampton 1996–2000, exec dir of public health devpt and memb Bd Health Devpt Agency 2000–04; temp advsr WHO 2002–04, regnl leader Int Union for Health Promotion and Educn (IUHPE) European Effectiveness Project 2005–, ind public health conslt 2004–, visiting sr research fell Univ of Southampton 2007–; generalist specialist UK Voluntary Register for Public Health Specialists 2006; FFPH 2006; *Publications* author of numerous books, reports, peer-reviewed articles and book chapters; *Recreations* yoga, horse riding, gardening, reading; *Style—* Dr Viv Speller; ✉ Denmead, Hampshire (tel 023 9225 1765, e-mail viv.speller@healthdevelopment.co.uk)

SPELLMAN, (Irene) Ruth; *née* Hewlett; OBE (2007); *b* Pyle, Glamorgan; *Educ* Croesyceiliug GS, Girton Coll Cambridge (MA); *m* 14 April 1979, Dr William Spellman; 3 c (Fiona, William, Rhiannon); *Career* NCB 1972–76, NEDO 1976–86, HR dir Eastern Region Coopers & Lybrand 1986–91, HR dir NSPCC 1991–98, chief exec Investors in People UK 1998–2006, chief exec IMechE 2006–; FCIPD (FIPD 1996), FRSA 2000; *Recreations* music, politics, English literature; *Style—* Mrs Ruth Spellman, OBE; ✉ Institution of Mechanical Engineers, 1 Birdcage Walk, Westminster, London SW1H 9JJ

SPELMAN, Caroline Alice; MP; da of Marshall Cormack (d 2000), and Helen Margaret, *née* Greenfield (d 1994); *b* 4 May 1958; *Educ* Herts and Essex GS (Joan Ashdown Scholar), Queen Mary Coll London (DAAD Scholarship to Freiburg, Drapers' Co Prize, BA); *m* 25 April 1987, Mark Gerald Spelman, s of Denis Gerald Spelman (d 2001); 1 da (Eleanor b 27 April 1991), 2 s (David b 12 Sept 1992, Jonathan b 7 Nov 1994); *Career* sugar beet advsr to NFU of England and Wales 1981–84, dep dir Int Confdn of Euro Beetgrowers 1984–89, dir Spelman, Cormack & Assocs (agric conslts) 1989–; MP (Cons) Meriden 1997–; oppn whip 1998–1999, oppn spokesman on health 1999–2001, shadow min for women 1999–, shadow sec of state for int devpt 2001–03, shadow secretary of state for the environment 2003–04, shadow sec of state for local and devolved govt affrs 2004–06, shadow sec of state for communities and local govt 2006–07, chm Cons Pty 2007–; tstee Snowdon Awards Scheme; *Publications* A Green and Pleasant Land (Bow Gp paper, 1991), Non Food Uses of Agricultural Raw Materials (1994); *Recreations* tennis, skiing, cooking, choral singing; *Style—* Mrs Caroline Spelman, MP; ✉ House of Commons, London SW1A 0AA (tel 020 7219 4189, fax 020 7219 0378, e-mail spelmanc@parliament.uk)

SPENCE, Christopher Alexander; CBE (2006, MBE 1992); s of Robert Donald Spence (d 1993), and Margaret, *née* Summerford (d 1994); *b* 24 April 1944; *Educ* Bromsgrove Sch; *m* 1990, Nancy Corbin, da of late Max Meadors; *Career* freelance cnsllr 1976–86; London Lighthouse: fndr dir 1986–96, pres 1997–2000; fndr chair Pan London HIV/AIDS Providers Consortium 1992–96, chair The HIV Project 1997–2000; chief exec: Nat Centre for Volunteering 1998–, Volunteering England 2004–; tstee and chair Grants Ctee Diana, Princess of Wales Meml Fund 1998–2006 (chm of bd 1999–2006), tstee and vice-chm Timebank 1999–2002, pres Euro Volunteer Centre Brussels 2001–; private sec to Speaker of the House of Commons; dir of courses Urban Ministry Project, dir Task Force; non-exec dir Oxfordshire Learning Disability NHS Tst 1996–2002 (vice-chair 1998–2002); lectr Counselling Dip Course London; hon fell Univ of Wales; FRSA 1998–; *Publications* A Homecoming and the Harvest: A Counsellor's View of Death, Dying and Bereavement, At Least 100 Principles of Love (with Nancy Kline), AIDS: An Issue for Everyone, AIDS: Time to Reclaim Our Power, On Watch: Views from the Lighthouse; *Style—* Christopher Spence, Esq, CBE; ✉ Lower Farm Orchard, Preston Crowmarsh, Wallingford, Oxfordshire OX10 6SL (tel 01491 835266, fax 01491 824595, e-mail christopher.spence@volunteeringengland.org)

SPENCE, Christopher John; s of Brig Ian Fleming Morris Spence, OBE, MC, TD, ADC (d 1966), of London, and Ruth, *née* Peacock (d 1961); *b* 4 June 1937; *Educ* Marlborough; *m* 1, 1960 (m dis 1968), Merle Aurelia, er da of Sir Leonard Ropner, 1 Bt, MC, TD (d 1977); 1 da (Miranda (Mrs Patrick Barran) b 1963), 1 s (Jeremy b 1964 d 1982); m 2, 1970, Susan, da of Brig Michael Morley, MBE (d 1990), of Wiltshire; 1 da (Lara b 1972), 1 s (Jonathan b 1975); *Career* 2 Lt 10 Royal Hussars (PWO) 1955–57, Royal Wilts Yeo 1957–66; memb London Stock Exchange 1959–78; chm English Trust Co Ltd 1991–2001 (md 1978–91); sr steward Jockey Club 1998–2003; High Sheriff Berks 1996–97; *Recreations* racing, shooting, golf; *Clubs* Jockey, Pratt's, Swinley Forest Golf; *Style—* Christopher Spence, Esq; ✉ Chieveley Manor, Newbury, Berkshire RG20 8UT (tel 01635 248208)

SPENCE, David Lane; s of Dr A S Spence, and Edith F, *née* Lane; *b* 5 October 1943; *Educ* Fettes; *m* 1966, Beverley Esther, da of Gp Capt Jasper Cardale (d 1981); 2 da (Sally b 1976, Sarah b 1980), 1 s (William b 1978); *Career* CA; C F Middleton & Co 1962–67; Grant Thornton (formerly Thornton Baker): joined 1967, ptnr 1970–2006, ptnr Euro practice 1974–80, chm Investigations Panel 1975–84 and 1990–98, exec ptnr 1984–89, London sr ptnr 1998; DTI inspr 1989 and 1992; pres ICAS 1998–99 (previously vice-pres), chm CAs Joint Ethics Ctee 1995–97; Liveryman Worshipful Co of Glaziers; *Recreations* golf, occasional cycling, tinkering with old MGs; *Clubs* Caledonian, R&A, Sunningdale Golf; *Style—* David Spence, Esq; ✉ tel 01276 451309

SPENCE, James William (Bill); DL (Orkney 1988); s of James William Spence (d 2002), of Stromness, Orkney, and Margaret Duncan, *née* Peace (d 2004); *b* 19 January 1945; *Educ* Firth Jr Secdy Sch Orkney, Leith Nautical Coll Edinburgh, Robert Gordon's Inst of Technol Aberdeen (Master Mariner), Univ of Wales Cardiff (BSc); *m* 1, 31 July 1971, Margaret Paplay (d 2000), da of Henry Stevenson (d 1983), of Stromness, Orkney; 3 s (James b 1976, Steven b 1978, Thomas b 1980); m 2, 1 Nov 2003, Susan Mary, da of Air Vice-Marshal Robert George Price, CB, of W Heslerton, N Yorks; *Career* Merchant Navy 1961–74; apprentice deck offr Watts Watts & Co Ltd 1961–65, certificated deck offr P&O Steam Navigation Co Ltd 1965–74; Micoperi SpA 1974–75, temp asst site co-ordinator Scapa Flow Project; John Jolly: mangr 1975, jr ptnr 1976–77, sr ptnr 1977–78, md and proprietor 1978–, chm 2003–; consul Norway 1978 (vice-consul 1976–78), vice-consul The Netherlands 1978–94, chm Assoc of Hon Norwegian Consuls in the UK and Ireland 1993–95 (vice-chm 1991–93); chm RNLI Kirkwall Lifeboat Station Branch Ctee 1997–2004 (dep Launching Authy 1976–87, Station hon sec 1987–96); memb: Kirkwall Community Cncl 1978–82, Orkney Pilotage Ctee 1979–88; chm: Kirkwall Port Employers' Assoc 1979–87 (memb 1975), BHS Orkney Riding Club 1985–92 (memb 1984), Bd of Tstees Pier Arts Centre Tst Orkney 1989–91 (tstee 1980–91); Hon Sheriff Grampian, Highland and Islands (Kirkwall) 2000; MNI 1972, MICS 1979; Cdr Royal Norwegian Order of Merit 1987, Chevalier in the Order of Orange-Nassau (Netherlands) 1994; *Recreations* oenophilist, equestrian matters, Orcadian history, vintage motoring; *Clubs* Caledonian; *Style*— J William Spence, Esq, DL; ✉ Alton House, Kirkwall, Orkney KW15 1NA; John Jolly, PO Box 2, Kiln Corner, Kirkwall, Orkney KW15 1HS (tel 01856 872268, fax 01856 875002, car 07885 200860, telex 75253, e-mail cons.kirkwall@johnjolly.co.uk)

SPENCE, John Alexander; OBE (2005), DL (Kent 2001); s of James Alexander Spence (d 1960), of Maidstone, Kent, and Edith Charlotte, *née* Barden; *b* 11 April 1936; *Educ* Maidstone Tech Sch, Royal Dockyard Sch Chatham; *m* 2 July 1973, Patricia, o da of Oliver G A Pocock; *Career* engr (ret 1984); non-exec dir Radio Invicta Ltd 1995–2000, non-exec chm/dir various small private cos; chm: Kent Ambulance Serv 1986–93, Medway HA 1986–93, Medway NHS Tst 1993–97; memb Shadow Bd W Kent Health Commissioning Agency 1991–93, formerly memb Cncl NAHA; pres Gillingham Cons Assoc 2002–06 (chm 1963–66, hon treas 1966–73, vice-pres 1973–); memb Gillingham BC 1961–72, memb Kent CC 1973–93 (chief whip Cons Gp 1985–92), memb ACC 1982–93 (memb Police Ctee 1982–93, chm Local Govt Fin Ctee 1991–93), chm UK Standing Ctee on Local Govt Superannuation 1992–93; Kent Police Authy: memb 1973–93, vice-chm 1973–77, chm 1981–86; memb Police Negotiating Bd and Central Ctee for Common Police Servs 1982–89, memb Police Trg Cncl and Bd of Govrs Bramshill Police Staff Coll 1989–93; memb: Exec Bd Kent Inst of Med and Health Scis 1995–2001, Cncl Univ of Kent 1995–2003 (chm Audit Ctee), Ct Univ of Kent 1995–, Chatham Historic Dockyard Tst 1984–, Ct Rochester Bridge Tst 1987– (Jr Warden 1991–92 and 2001–03, Sr Warden 1992–94 and 2003–05), Rochester Cathedral Cncl 2001–; tstee New Coll of Cobham 1991–2007 (pres 1991–94 and 2001–05), Rochester Cathedral Tst 2003–; chm: Bridge Wardens Coll Univ of Kent 1996–2005, Medway Educn Business Partnership 1998–2006, Medway Learning Partnership 2000–; varied charitable work; hon fell South Bank Univ 1993; Hon DCL Univ of Kent 2003; FRSA; *Recreations* The National Trust; *Style*— John A Spence, Esq, OBE, DL; ✉ 175 Fairview Avenue, Gillingham, Kent ME8 0PX (tel 01634 232538)

SPENCE, John Andrew; MBE (1999); *b* 30 January 1951; *Educ* George Watson's Coll Edinburgh, Trinity Coll Dublin (BA), Harvard Business Sch (PMD); *m* 26 Oct 1974, Yvonne; 1 s (Euan b 6 Oct 1977), 2 da (Lindsay b 8 March 1979, Catherine b 2 Nov 1981); *Career* Lloyds TSB Gp plc (formerly Lloyds Bank plc): joined 1973, head of business banking 1994–96, md 1996–98, chief exec Lloyds TSB Bank Scotland plc 1998–2000, dir of branch network 2000, dir of distribution 2001, dir of policy co-ordination and risk 2003; non-exec dir Edrington Gp 2001–; pres Enable, dep fin chm Business in the Community, tstee Blind in Business; chm Fin Ctee Chelmsford Cathedral; church cmmr 2005–; FRSA 1996, fell Chartered Inst of Bankers in Scotland (FCIOBS) 2001, FCIB 2003 (ACIB 1976); *Recreations* committees, cooking, swimming, motorcycling, theatre; *Style*— John Spence, MBE; ✉ Lloyds TSB Bank plc, 25 Gresham Street, London EC2V 7HN (tel 020 7356 2182, fax 020 7356 1237)

SPENCE, Prof John Edward (Jack); OBE (2002); s of John Herbert Spence (d 1946), of Krugersdorp, South Africa, and Violet, *née* Brown (d 1976); *b* 11 June 1931; *Educ* Boys' HS Pretoria, Univ of the Witwatersrand (BA), LSE (BSc); *m* 27 June 1959, Susanne Hilary Spence; 1 da (Rachel b 1967); *Career* lectr Dept of History and Politics Univ of Natal Pietermaritzburg 1958–60, Rockefeller jr res fell LSE 1960–62, reader Dept of Governmental Political Theory UC Swansea 1972–73 (asst lectr 1962–63, lectr 1963–68, sr lectr 1968–72), prof Dept of Politics Univ of Leicester 1973–91 (head of Dept of Politics 1974–81 and 1986–91, pro-vice-chllr 1981–85), dir of studies RIIA 1991–97 (assoc fell 1997–); academic advsr RCDS 1997–; visiting prof KCL 1997–; pres African Studies Assoc UK 1977–78, chm Br Int Studies Assoc 1986–88, memb Hong Kong Cncl for Academic Awards 1986–90; memb RIIA 1961; hon fell: Univ of Staffs 1992, UC Swansea 1993, Nene Coll 1995; Hon LLD Univ of Witwatersrand 1997, Hon DLitt Nottingham Trent Univ 1998, Hon DLitt Univ of Leicester 2001; *Books* Republic Under Pressure (1965), Lesotho - Politics of Dependence (1968), Political and Military Framework of Investment in South Africa (1976), British Politics in Perspective (ed with R Borthwick, 1985), Change in South Africa (1994), Violence in Southern Africa (1997), After Mandela: The 1999 South African Election (1999), Seaford House Papers (2000–06); *Recreations* collecting Faber poetry volumes, walking dogs; *Clubs* RAC, Caledonian; *Style*— Prof J E Spence, OBE; ✉ Cross of the Tree Farm, Lingen, Bucknell, Shropshire SY7 0EE; c/o Department of War Studies, King's College, The Strand, London WC2R 2LS (e-mail war.admissions@kcl.ac.uk)

SPENCE, Dr Joseph Arthur Francis; s of Joseph Arthur Cuthbert Spence (d 1987), and Lenice, *née* Woolley (d 1992); *b* 18 December 1959, Coventry; *Educ* St Philip's GS Edgbaston, The Salesian Coll Battersea, Univ of Reading (BA), Birkbeck Coll Univ of London (PhD); *m* 29 June 1985, Angela Margaret Alexander, *née* Fiddes; 1 da (Katharine (Kitty) b 27 June 1987), 2 s (William b 28 June 1989, James b 19 Dec 1992); *Career* asst master Eton Coll 1988–2002 (master in coll 1992–2002), headmaster Oakham Sch 2002–; govr of schs incl St George's Windsor Castle, St John's Coll Sch Cambridge and St Anselm's Bakewell; tstee Demarco Archive Tst; ed vols on Yeats, Shaw and Swift (Duckworth's The Sayings of... series) 1991–93; *Recreations* theatre, music, art, football, reading, writing; *Clubs* East India; *Style*— Dr Joseph Spence; ✉ Deanscroft, Station Road, Oakham, Rutland LE15 6QU (tel 01572 758775, e-mail jafs@oakham.rutland.sch.uk); Oakham School, Chapel Close, Oakham, Rutland LE15 6DT (tel 01572 758800, e-mail headmaster@oakham.rutland.sch.uk)

SPENCE, Julie Anne; OBE (2006); da of Alan Edwin Thomas Miller (d 2004), and Rita Margaret, *née* Moore; *b* 7 August 1955, Framlingham, Suffolk; *Educ* Colchester Co HS for Girls, I M Marsh Coll of PE, Univ of Liverpool (BEd), UWE (LLB), Univ of Exeter (MA), Henley Mgmnt Coll, Brunel Univ (MBA), Univ of Cambridge (Dip); *m* 18 April 1987, (Alfred) John Spence; *Career* head of girls' PE Sidcot Sch Winscombe 1977–78; Constable rising to Supt Avon and Somerset Constabulary 1978–99, Asst Chief Constable Thames Valley Police 1999–2004; Cambridgeshire Constabulary: Dep Chief Constable 2004–05, Chief Constable 2005–; pres British Assoc of Women in Policing; Network Woman of Achievement Award 1997, Leadership Award Int Assoc of Women Police 2002, Champions Award Opportunity Now 2006; *Recreations* walking, travelling, keeping fit, listening to smooth jazz; *Style*— Mrs Julie Spence, OBE; ✉ Cambridgeshire Constabulary HQ, Hinchingbrooke Park, Huntingdon, Cambridgeshire PE29 6NP (tel 01480 422319, fax 01480 432323, e-mail julie.spence@cambs.pnn.police.uk)

SPENCE, Malcolm Hugh; QC (1979); s of Dr Allan William Spence (d 1990), and Martha Lena, *née* Hutchison (d 1981); *b* 23 March 1934; *Educ* Stowe, Gonville & Caius Coll Cambridge (MA, LLM); *m* 18 March 1967, (Jennifer) Jane, da of Lt-Gen Sir George Sinclair Cole, KCB, CBE (d 1973); 1 da (Annabelle Irene b 1969), 1 s (Robert William b 1971); *Career* Nat Serv 1 Lt Worcestershire Regt 1952–54; called to the Bar Gray's Inn 1958 (James Mould scholar, sr Holker exhibitioner, Lee prizeman, bencher 1988); entered Chambers of John Widgery, QC, pupil to Nigel Bridge (now Lord Bridge of Harwich) 1958; asst recorder 1982–85, recorder 1985–99, dep judge of the High Court 1988–99; chm Planning and Environment Bar Assoc 1994–98; chartered arbitrator 2003–, accredited mediator 2006–; landowner (1100 acres); chm Wagner Soc 2002–; Freeman City of London 2001, Liveryman Worshipful Co of Arbitrators 2001; FCIArb; *Books* Rating Law and Valuation (jtly, 1961), The Chambers of Marshall Hall: 125 years (2005); *Recreations* salmon and trout fishing, golf; *Clubs* Hawks' (Cambridge), Caledonian; *Style*— Malcolm Spence, Esq, QC, FCIArb; ✉ 2–3 Gray's Inn Square, London WC1R 5JH (tel 020 7242 4986, fax 020 7405 1166); Scamadale, Arisaig, Inverness-shire PH39 4NS (tel 01687 450698, fax 01687 450303)

SPENCE, Prof Robert; s of Robert Whitehair Spence (d 1988), and Minnie Grace, *née* Wood (d 1984); *b* 11 July 1933; *Educ* Hymers Coll Hull, Hull Coll of Technol (BSc), Imperial Coll London (DIC, PhD, DSc); *m* 18 April 1960, Kathleen (d 2003), da of George Potts; 1 s (Robert b 1963), 1 da (Merin b 1966); *Career* Imperial Coll London: lectr 1962, reader 1968, prof of info engrg 1984–, head of Dept of Electrical and Electronic Engrg 1997–99, sr res investigator 2000–, emeritus prof 2000; Erskine fell Univ of Canterbury NZ 2002, visiting prof Univ of Manchester 2003–; founding dir and chm Interactive Solutions Ltd 1985–90; author of numerous papers; Dr RCA 1998; hon prof Univ of Waikato 2007; FIEE, FIEEE, FCGI; FREng 1990; Officier De L'ordre Du Palme Académique (France) 1996; *Books* Linear Active Networks (1970), Tellegen's Theorem and Electrical Networks (1970), Resistive Circuit Theory (1974), Modern Network Theory - An Introduction (1978), Sensitivity and Optimisation (1980), Circuit Analysis by Computer (1986), Tolerance Design of Electronic Circuits (1988), Information Visualization (2001, 2007); *Recreations* concrete aspects of gardening, bass player in steel band; *Style*— Prof Robert Spence, FREng; ✉ Department of Electrical and Electronic Engineering, Imperial College of Science Technology and Medicine, Exhibition Road, London SW7 2BT (tel 020 7594 6259, fax 020 7581 4419, e-mail r.spence@ic.ac.uk)

SPENCE, Prof Robin John Summerford; s of Donald Spence (d 1993), and Margaret, *née* Summerford (d 1994); *b* 7 August 1941; *Educ* Univ of Cambridge (MA, PhD), Cornell Univ (MSc); *m* 1, 12 Feb 1966 (m dis 1983), Fenella, da of Jock Butler; 2 s (Peter b 9 April 1969, Andrew b 30 Sept 1971); m 2, 30 May 1986, Bridget, da of Peter McKeigue; 1 da (Emily b 16 Dec 1986); *Career* structural engr Ove Arup & Partners 1963–69, lectr in civil engrg Univ of Zambia 1969–71, research asst Engrg Dept Univ of Cambridge 1971–73, research offr Intermediate Technol Devpt Gp 1973–75; Univ of Cambridge: lectr in architecture 1975–96, dir (later jt dir) Martin Centre for Architectural and Urban Studies 1987–, dir Cambridge Univ Centre for Risk in the Built Environment (CURBE) 1997–, prof of architectural engrg 2002–; fell and dir of studies in architecture Magdalene Coll Cambridge 1975– (tutor 1993–96); visiting posts: Islamic Architecture Prog MIT 1987, Bartlett Sch of Architecture UCL 1987, 1988, 1991 and 1992, Architecture Dept Univ of Naples 1987, 1988, 1989 and 2001, Architecture Dept UCLA 1991, Faculty of Architecure Georgia Inst of Technol Atlanta 1994, Earth Sciences Dept Macquarie Univ Sydney 1997; Li Ka Shing Fndn visiting lectr TsingHua Univ Beijing, Xi'an Univ of Architecture and Technol, Tong Ji Univ Shanghai and Hong Kong Univ 2001; dir Cambridge Architectural Research Ltd 1987– (chm 1990–2001), dir CARtograph Ltd 1990–97; resident European Assoc for Earthquake Engrg 2002–; memb: Built Environment Coll EPSRC 1995–97, Royal Soc Steering Gp for the Int Decade for Nat Disaster Reduction 1997–99; Murray Buxton Award IStructE 1987; hon prof Xi'an Univ of Architecture and Technol 2001; *Books* incl: Building Materials in Developing Countries (with D J Cook, 1983), Earthquake Protection (with A Coburn, 1992, 2 edn 2002), Interdisciplinary Design in Practice (ed with S Macmillan and P Kirby, 2001); *Style*— Prof Robin Spence; ✉ Department for Architecture, 6 Chaucer Road, Cambridge CB2 2EB (tel 01223 331710, fax 01223 331700, e-mail rspence@carltd.com)

SPENCE, Prof Roy Archibald Joseph; OBE (2001), JP (1998); s of Robert Spence (d 1988), of Belfast, and Margaret, *née* Gilmore; *b* 15 July 1952; *Educ* Queen's Univ Belfast (MB BCh, MA, MD); *m* 26 Sept 1979, Diana Mary, da of Dr C Burns, OBE (d 1989), of Ballymoney; 2 s (Robert b 20 July 1982, Andrew b 14 Sept 1984), 1 da (Katharine b 11 Feb 1987); *Career* conslt surgn Belfast City Hosp 1986–; exec dir Belfast City Hosp Tst Bd 1993–97; hon lectr in surgery, anatomy and oncology and hon prof Queen's Univ of Belfast; Univ of Ulster: hon prof 1998–, pro-chllr 2002–; Penman Visiting Prof Univ of Cape Town 2005; examiner: MRCS RCS(Ed) 2000–, Intercolliegate FRCS in Surgery 2000–; memb: BMA, Assoc of Surgns, Br Soc of Gastroenterology, World Assoc of Hepato-Biliary Surgns; memb: Police Authy NI 1994–2001 (chm Community Rels Ctee 1996–98), Bd Crimestoppers NI, Bd of Govrs and Bd of Tstees Wallace HS Lisburn 1993–99; FRCSEd 1981, FRCSI 1981, FRCS (ad eundum) 2006; *Books* Pathology for Surgeons (1986, 2 edn 1993), Colorectal Disease for Physicians and Surgeons (1997), Synopsis of Systematic Pathology for Surgeons (2001), Oncology - a Core Text (2001), Oncologic Emergencies (2002), Handbook of Oncology (2002), Genetics for Surgeons (2005), Illustrated Clinical Anatomy (2005), Emergencies in Oncology (2006), Infection in Oncological Patients (2006); also author of 165 jl papers and 14 chapters in books; *Recreations* history; *Style*— Prof Roy Spence, OBE; ✉ 7 Downshire Crescent, Hillsborough, Co Down BT26 6DD (tel 028 9268 2362, fax 028 9268 2418); Level 2, Belfast City Hospital, Lisburn Road, Belfast BT9 7AB (tel 028 9032 9241, e-mail roy.spence@bch.n-i.nhs.uk)

SPENCE, His Hon Stanley Brian; s of George Henry Spence (d 1941), and Sarah, *née* Hoad (d 1961); *b* 3 May 1937; *Educ* Portsmouth GS, BRNC Dartmouth; *m* 3 April 1961, Victoria Rosaleen, da of Lionel Charles Tapper; 1 s (Adrian Charles b 8 Nov 1961), 1 da (Henrietta Louise b 12 Aug 1965); *Career* entered BRNC Dartmouth 1953, voluntary ret from RN 1975; called to the Bar 1968, Office of Judge Advocate Gen (Army & RAF) 1975–91, recorder 1987–91, circuit judge (SE Circuit) 1991–2006, resident judge Reading Crown Court 1999–2006; *Recreations* maintaining cottage in France, wine; *Style*— His Hon Stanley Spence; ✉ The Crown Court, Old Shire Hall, The Forbury, Reading RG1 3EH (tel 0118 967 4400)

SPENCE, Stephen Frederick; s of Frederick Spence, of Tyne & Wear, and Veronica, *née* Scullion; *b* 23 December 1961; *Educ* Univ of Manchester (BA), AA Sch of Archtecture London (Dip); *m* 9 Dec 1995, Yasmin, da of Awni Al-Ani; 2 s (Cooper b 13 Oct 1999, Mac b 13 July 2001), 1 da (Sadie b 15 Aug 2004); *Career* architect; Richard Rogers Architects Ltd 1987–98; architectural asst projects incl: Royal Docks 1987, Terminal 5 competition Heathrow 1988, Tokyo Forum 1988, Canary Wharf 1988; project architect: Farnborough Air Terminal 1989, Grosvenor Road 1989–90, Chiswick Park 1990, Stockley Park 1990, Daiwa HQ 1990–91, Inland Revenue competition (runner-up) 1991–92, Berlin Underground competition (winner) 1992, VR Techno Japan 1993–94, TVU Resource Centre 1994–96, Stephen Strasse Frankfurt 1995–98; assoc dir: Broadwick St London 1996–98, Visual Control Tower Heathrow 1996, Pusan Station competition Korea (runner-up) 1996, Pilkington plc HQ 1997; dir Spence Associates Ltd 1998–; projects incl: TVU Masterplan Feasability 1998, TVU Media Centre 1998, NEC Pavillion competition 1998, River Café Reception 1999, private residence Kensington London 2000, LSE 2001, Turner Gallery Margate 2001, Northbank pedestrian bridge 2003, New Wear crossing 2005; tutor AA 1989–90, advsr RIBA 2003; AA Dip Year Prize 1986–87; RIBA 2002; *Exhibitions* The New Breed-Sydney Aust 1988, Zurich Architecural Museum 1990, AA 1991, Sci Museum London 1999, RA 2000, Cube Gallery Manchester 2001, V&A 2003; *Style*— Stephen Spence, Esq; ✉ Spence Associates, 53 Dymock Street, London SW6 3ET (tel 020 7224 9294, e-mail post@spenceassociates.co.uk)

SPENCE, Toby; s of Dr Magnus Peter Spence, of Datchworth, Herts, and Gillian Sara, *née* Squire (d 1991); *b* 22 May 1969; *Educ* Uppingham, New Coll Oxford (choral scholar), Guildhall Sch of Music and Drama; *m* Suzanne Elizabeth, da of Brandon Vaughan Edwards; *Career* opera singer; tenor; princ operatic roles incl: Idamante in Mozart's Idaomeneo under Sir Charles Mackerass 1995–96, Pane in Cavalli's La Calisto under René Jacobs, Verdi's Alzira under Elder 1995–96, in Mitridate under Norrington 1996–97, Tamino in Mozart's Die Zauberflöte under Robertson 1996–97, Telemachus in Monteverdi's Il Ritorno D'Ulisse in Patria (Netherlands Opera), Almaviva in Il Barbiere Di Seviglia (ENO), David in Die Meistersinger under Pappano; sung with various orchestras incl: Cleveland Orchestra under von Dohnanyi, Bournemouth Symphony Orchestra under Hickox, Monteverdi Choir and Orchestra under Eliot Gardiner, Los Angeles Philharmonic under Tilson Thomas, Deutsches Symphonie-Orchester Berlin; performed at various festivals incl: Brighton, Cheltenham, Salzburg, Edinburgh, Montreux, BBC Proms; memb and co princ ENO; *Recordings* incl: Philips Classics (St Matthew Passion with Orchestra of the Eighteenth Century under Frans Brüggen), Deutsche Gramaphon, Decca, BMG, Collins, Hyperion, EMI; *Style*— Toby Spence, Esq

SPENCER, 9 Earl (GB 1765); Charles Edward Maurice Spencer; also Viscount Spencer, Baron Spencer (both GB 1761), and Viscount Althorp (GB 1765 and UK 1905); s of 8 Earl Spencer, LVO, DL (d 1992), and his 1 w, Hon Frances Ruth Burke Roche (d 2004), da of 4 Baron Fermoy; bro of late Diana, Princess of Wales (d 1997); *b* 20 May 1964; *Educ* Maidwell Hall, Eton, Magdalen Coll Oxford; *m* 1, 16 Sept 1989 (m dis 1997), (Catherine) Victoria, o da of John Lockwood, of Barnes, London; 3 da (Lady Kitty Eleanor b 28 Dec 1990, Lady Eliza Victoria, Lady Katya Amelia (twins) b 10 July 1992), 1 s (Louis Frederick John, Viscount Althorp b 14 March 1994); m 2, 15 Dec 2001, Caroline Freud, *née* Hutton; 1 s (Hon Edmund Charles b 6 Oct 2003), 1 da (Lady Lara Caroline b 16 March 2006); *Heir* s, Viscount Althorp; *Career* page of honour to HM The Queen 1977–79; TV correspondent NBC News 1987–91 and 1993–96, reporter Granada Television 1991–93; *Publications* Althorp: The Story of an English House (1998), The Spencer Family (1999), Blenheim: Battle for Europe (2004), Prince Rupert: Last of the Cavalries (2007); *Style*— The Rt Hon the Earl Spencer, DL; ✉ Althorp, Northampton NN7 4HQ

SPENCER, Christopher Paul; er s of Anthony John Spencer (d 2005), of Weybridge, Surrey, and Elizabeth, *née* Carruthers (d 1991); *b* 7 July 1950; *Educ* St George's Coll Weybridge; *m* 28 June 1975, Margaret Elizabeth, da of Lt-Col Cyril Meredith Battye Howard, OBE, of Walton-on-Thames, Surrey; 2 da (Katherine b 13 Aug 1978, Anna Lisa b 24 July 1981); *Career* chartered accountant; ptnr: Midgley Snelling Spencer & Co 1978–83, Pannell Kerr Forster (CI) 1984–2000; chm Guernsey Post Ltd 2001–03; chm Guernsey Branch IOD 1994–96; pres Guernsey Soc of Chartered and Certified Accountants 1996–97; FCA; *Recreations* sailing, skiing, tennis; *Clubs* United, Guernsey Yacht, Ski Club of GB; *Style*— Christopher Spencer, Esq; ✉ Whitewings, Les Camps Du Moulin, St Martins, Guernsey (tel 01481 237637, fax 01481 237857, e-mail chris@cpspencer.com)

SPENCER, Dr David Anthony; s of late Henry William George Spencer, and Veronica Clare, *née* Bonanno; *b* 7 November 1963; *Educ* Raine's Fndn GS London, Univ of Exeter (BSc), Imperial Coll London (MSc, DIC), Swiss Fed Inst of Technol Zurich (DrScNat); *m* m (m dis), Prof PD Dr Cinzia Cervato; 1 da (Francesca Louise Spencer b 13 April 1998); partner, Christina Beales; 1 s (Conrad Francis Spencer b 25 May 2003); *Career* visiting scientist Univ of Beijing and ldr Exeter Univ Geological Expdn to China 1986; Swiss Fed Inst of Technol Zurich (ETH-Zurich): pre-doctoral research fell 1988–89, research and teaching asst and doctoral research fell 1989–92, visiting ETH doctoral research fell 1992–93, visiting postdoctoral research fell 1993–94 and 1997, postdoctoral research fell 1994–97; visiting scientist Tokyo Inst of Technol 1996, Swiss Nat Science Fndn sr research fell 1997–99, research asst prof and lectr in structural geology Univ of Maine 1997–98, visiting prof Univ of the Punjab Lahore 1997–2000 (visiting lectr 1995), hon assoc prof Albert Schweitzer Int Univ Geneva 2001; sr reservoir geologist Roxar Sofware Solutions Roxar Ltd 2003–; gifted and talented mentor, learning mentor and learning support asst Behaviour Unit Raine's Fndn Sch London 2002–03 (also publicity offr and devpt offr); delivered scientific lectures at numerous univs, also made over 150 scientific presentations at int scientific confs worldwide; platinum exploration geologist Impala Platinum Ltd SA 1986–87, hydrogeological conslt Philippines 1992–94, staff geologist/reservoir devpt structural geologist Section for Reservoir Geology and Geophysics Dept of Reservoir Devpt Saga Petroleum ASA Norway 1998–99 (worked in Section for Wells Dept of Petroleum Technol and Drilling 1999–2000), estab Spencer Structural Conslts 2000; currently assoc ed The Professional Geologist, European regnl ed Himalayan Notes 1994–97; Imperial Coll/Swiss Fed Inst of Technol Scholarship 1988–89, Geochron Research Award 1991, Swiss Acad of Natural Sciences Travel Scholarship 1992, Huber-Kudlich Fndn Visiting Lectureship 1996, Outstanding Young Scientist Award Swiss Fed Inst of Technol 1996; memb Research Bd of Advsrs (Int Div) American Biographical Inst, nat and int advsr American Biographical Inst Research Assoc, hon memb Advsy Cncl Int Biographical Centre; tstee Raine's Fndn 2002–, fndn govr Raine's Fndn Sch London 2002–; climbed to south summit of Mt Everest 2000; Freeman City of London 2001, Liveryman Worshipful Co of Scientific Instrument Makers 2001 (Freeman 2001); fell: Geological Assoc of Canada, Geological Soc of India, Geological Soc of SA, Mineralogical Soc of GB and I, American Inst of Chemists, American Geographic Soc; memb: Soc of Petroleum Engrs, American Inst of Mining, Metallurgical and Petroleum Engrs, SA Instn of Mining and Metallurgy, Energy Inst (MEI), SocAcad; CGeol, EurGeol (European Geologist), AIPG-CPG (Certified Professional Geologist), AAPG-CPG (Certified Petroleum Geologist), PrSciNat (Professional Natural Scientist), PGeo (Professional Geologist), CHGeol (Certified Swiss Geologist), CIPES (Certified Ind Professional Earth Scientist), CPhys, EurPhys (European Physicist), CSci, CChem, EurChem (European Chemist), ARSGS (Professional Assoc of RSGS), RegSciTech (Registered Sci Technician), LCGI, MRI, MISTC, MIEnvSc MInstP, MInstPet, MIMMM, MRSC, MACS, FGS, FRAS, FRGS, FRSA, FLS, FICPD, FMinSoc; *Recreations* mountaineering, playing guitar, long distance walking, campanology, flying, reading travel books, skiing, family history research, travelling, listening to the BBC World Service, reading the Times; *Style*— Dr David A Spencer; ✉ e-mail david@davidaspencer.com, website www.davidaspencer.com

SPENCER, Sir Derek Harold; kt (1992), QC (1980); s of Thomas Harold Spencer (d 1991), of Waddington, Lancs, and Gladys, *née* Heslop (d 1989); *b* 31 March 1936; *Educ* Clitheroe Royal GS, Keble Coll Oxford (MA, BCL); *m* 1, 30 July 1960 (m dis), Joan, da of late James Nutter, of Clitheroe, Lancs; 2 s (David John b 1966, Andrew Duncan b 1970), 1 da (Caroline Jane b 1964); m 2, 26 Nov 1988, Caroline Alexandra (d 2003), da of Dr Franziskus Pärn, of Hamburg; 1 s (Frederick Thomas Francis b 27 Oct 1990); *Career* 2 Lt KORR 1954–56, served Nigeria; called to the Bar Gray's Inn 1961 (bencher 1991); recorder of the Crown Court 1979–92 and 1997–2001, slr-gen 1992–97; MP (Cons): Leicester S 1983–87, Brighton Pavilion 1992–97; jt sec Cons Back Bench Legal Ctee 1985–86; PPS: to David Mellor as Min of State at the Home Office 1986, to Sir Michael Havers as Attorney Gen 1986–87; vice-chm St Pancras N Cons Assoc 1977–78, cncllr London Borough of Camden 1978–83 (dep ldr Cons Gp 1980–81); *Recreations* reading, gardening, travelling; *Style*— Sir Derek Spencer, QC; ✉ 18 Red Lion Court, London EC4A 3EB (tel 020 7520 6000, fax 020 7520 6248)

SPENCER, Ivor; MBE (2002), DL (London 1985); *b* 20 November 1924; *m* 1948, Estella; 1 s (Nigel), 1 da (Philippa); *Career* professional toastmaster 1956–; fndr and life pres Guild of Int Professional Toastmasters 1990 (first toastmaster to receive Outstanding Lifetime Achievement Award 1998); voted Toastmaster of Year 2000 by Guild of Int Professional Toastmasters; estab Guild of Int Professional Toastmasters Best After-Dinner Speakers Award of the Year (now The Ivor Spencer Best After Dinner Speaker of the Year) 1967 (past recipients incl Baroness Thatcher, Lord Redcliffe-Maud, Bob Monkhouse (only three times recipient), Denis Norden, Jimmy Tarbuck, Lord Tonypandy and Sir Peter Ustinov); has officiated at well over 1000 Royal events UK and overseas (first toastmaster to achieve this 1992); princ Ivor Spencer Sch for Professional Toastmasters 1977–; princ: Ivor Spencer International School for Butler Administrators/Personal Assistants UK and USA 1981–, Ivor Spencer Professional Toastmasters' Authy 1998–, Ivor Spencer Int Coll for Hotel Mgmnt; princ and md Ivor Spencer Enterprises Ltd; pres: of Toastmasters for Royal Occasions 1970, Guild of Professional After Dinner Speakers 1978, Guild of Int Butler Administrators/Personal Assistants 1982; chief exec Br Professional Toastmasters Authy 1995–; AMInstD 1997; *Recreations* after-dinner speaking and organising special events; *Clubs* IOD; *Style*— Ivor Spencer, Esq, DL, MBE; ✉ 12 Little Bornes, Alleyn Park, Dulwich, London SE21 8SE (tel 020 8670 5585, fax 020 8670 0055, website www.ivorspencer.com)

SPENCER, James; QC (1991); s of James Henry Spencer, and Irene Dulcie, *née* Wilson; *b* 27 May 1947; *Educ* The King's Sch Pontefract, Univ of Newcastle upon Tyne (LLB); *m* 1 (m dis); 1 da ((Jane) Emma b 1971), 2 s ((James) Adam b 1976, (John) Joseph b 1979); m 2, Christine Anne Egerton; 1 s (Oswald Wilson b 1998), 1 da (Dulcie Bee b 2000); *Career* admitted slr 1971, called to the Bar Gray's Inn 1975, recorder of the Crown Court 1990–2001, circuit judge (NE Circuit) 2001–, memb Parole Bd 2002–; pres MHRT 1999; *Style*— His Hon Judge Spencer, QC; ✉ The Court Service, Group Manager's Office, Symons House, Belgrave Street, Leeds LS2 8DD (tel 01132 459611)

SPENCER, Prof John Rason; Hon QC (2003); s of Donald Spencer, and Mary Spencer; *Educ* Univ of Cambridge (LLB, MA); *m* Rosemary, *née* Stewartson; 1 s, 2 da; *Career* Univ of Cambridge: asst lectr Law Faculty 1973–76, lectr 1976–91, reader 1991–95, prof 1995–, chm Faculty 1995–97; fell Selwyn Coll Cambridge 1970–; academic bencher Inner Temple 2003, hon memb of chambers: Hardwicke Building 2003, 15 New Bridge St 2004; Docteur en droit (hc) Univ of Poitiers 2004; Chevalier de l'Ordre des Palmes Académiques 1999; *Style*— Prof J R Spencer; ✉ Selwyn College, Cambridge CB3 9DQ

SPENCER, John William James; s of Capt John Lawrence Spencer, DSO, MC (d 1967), and Jane Lilian, *née* Duff (d 2004); *b* 26 December 1957; *Educ* Sedbergh, Magdalene Coll Cambridge (MA), Open Univ Business Sch (MBA); *m* 2 Oct 1987, Jane Elizabeth, da of Andrew Young (d 1974); 1 s (Charles b 1990), 2 da (Rosanagh b 1991, Caitlin b 1996); *Career* dir: Dewey Warren & Co Ltd 1986–88, PWS North America 1988–89, BMS Special Risk Services Ltd 1989–95, Lloyd's America Ltd 1995–97; BMS Associates Ltd: dir 1997–, chief operating offr 2000–02, gp chief exec 2002–; *Style*— J W J Spencer, Esq; ✉ Ghyllas, Sedbergh, Cumbria LA10 5LT; 8 Bushwood Road, Kew, Surrey TW9 3BQ

SPENCER, Johnny; s of Charles Thomas Spencer, and Ellen Patricia Spencer; *Educ* Goldsmiths Coll London, Camberwell Sch of Arts and Crafts (BA); *Career* artist; assoc researcher Copenhagen Free Univ 2001–; *Exhibitions* The Golden Age (ICA London) 1999, British Art Show 5 2000, Century Cities (Tate Modern) 2001; *Publications* New Neurotic Realism (1998), Young British Art: the Saatchi Decade (2000), Here, There and Elsewhere (2002); *Recreations* music; *Clubs* RFH; *Style*— Johnny Spencer, Esq; ✉ 57 Nithdale Road, Plumstead, London SE18 3PE (tel 020 8244 0962, e-mail johnny@artio.demon.co.uk); c/o Anthony Wilkinson Gallery, 242 Cambridge Heath Road, London E2 9DA (tel 020 8980 2662, fax 020 8980 0028, e-mail info@anthonywilkinsongallery)

SPENCER, Dr Jonathan Page; CB (2002); s of John Austin Spencer (d 2004), of Bath, and Doreen, *née* Page (d 1991); *b* 24 April 1949; *Educ* Bournemouth Sch, Downing Coll Cambridge (MA), Univ of Oxford (ICI res fell, jr res fell ChCh, DPhil); *m* 1976, Caroline Sarah; 2 da, 1 s; *Career* DTI: admin trainee 1974–77, princ 1977–83, private sec to Secs of State 1982–83, asst sec 1983–91, under sec and head Insurance Div 1991–97, DG Resources and Services 1997–2000, DG Business Competitiveness 2000–01; DG Clients and Policy Lord Chancellor's Dept (latterly Dept for Constitutional Affrs) 2002–05; currently public policy conslt and co dir; memb: Cncl on Tbnls 2005–, Slrs Regulation Authy 2006–; author of various articles in scientific jls; sch govr; *Recreations* making and listening to music, keeping the house up and the garden down; *Style*— Dr Jonathan Spencer, CB

SPENCER, Michael Alan; s of Oscar Alan Spencer (d 1983), and Diana, *née* Walker; *b* 30 May 1955; *Educ* Worth Abbey, CCC Oxford (MA); *m* 9 July 1983, Lorraine Geraldine, da of Ronald Murphy; 2 s (Patrick b 8 May 1988, Thomas b 20 Feb 1990), 1 da (Alexandra b 17 June 1992); *Career* analyst Simon & Coats 1976–80, vice-pres Drexel Burnham Lambert 1981–83, dir Charles Fulton 1983–86, chm Intercapital 1986–99, ceo ICAP 1999–, chm Numis 2003–; treas Cons Pty 2007–; *Recreations* running, riding, shooting, wine, art, politics; *Clubs* London Capital; *Style*— Michael Spencer, Esq; ✉ ICAP plc, 1–2 Broadgate, London EC2M 7UR (tel 020 7050 7400, fax 020 7050 7116, e-mail mas@icap.com)

SPENCER, Paul; s of Dr Seymour Spencer, of Oxford, and Margaret Spencer (d 1999); *b* 3 January 1950, Oxford; *Educ* Ampleforth, Thames Poly (BA); *m* Sept 1975, Lorna, *née* Nykerk; 1 da (Deborah b 1977), 2 s (Richard b 1980, Charles b 1986); *Career* analyst ICI Pension Fund 1970–75, overseas fin mangr British Leyland plc 1975–80, gp treas Rolls Royce plc 1980–86, gp treas and assoc dir Hanson plc 1986–96; Royal and Sun Alliance plc: gp fin dir 1996–99, chief exec UK 1999–2003; currently chm: NS&I (Nat Savings and Investments), State Street Managed Pension Fund Ltd, Sovereign Reversions plc; non-exec dir: Resolution plc, WPP Gp plc; FCMA 1978, FCT 1982; *Clubs* Hurlingham; *Style*— Paul Spencer, Esq; ✉ tel 07768 462077, e-mail paulspencer120@hotmail.com

SPENCER, Paul Arnold; s of John Spencer, of Yorkshire, and Maria Helena, *née* Rozenbroek; *b* 1 February 1960; *Educ* Beverley GS, Univ of Nottingham; *m* Karen Lesley; 1 s (Angus); *Career* prodr Radio Comedy BBC 1983–89, freelance TV prodr 1989–91; head of comedy: Central TV 1991–94, Carlton TV 1994–95; controller of network comedy ITV Network Centre 1995–98, controller of comedy & entertainment Yorkshire Television Ltd 1998–2000; *Recreations* horse riding; *Clubs* Lansdowne, Soho House; *Style*— Paul Spencer, Esq

SPENCER, Prof Paul Samuel John; OBE (1994); s of Albert Owen Spencer (d 1986), of Leicester, and Constance Christina, *née* Brass; *b* 24 October 1934; *Educ* Wyggeston Sch Leicester, Leicester Colls of Art and Technol, Univ of London; *m* 17 Aug 1957, Avril Dorothy, da of Thomas Spriggs (d 1972), of Leicester; 1 s (Jonathan b 1963), 2 da (Isobel b 1961, Rosemary b 1965); *Career* pre-registration pharmacist Middx Hosp London 1957–58, asst lectr Sch of Pharmacy Univ of London 1959–62, princ pharmacologist Allen & Hanburys (now Glaxo Research) Ware 1962–65, sr lectr then reader in pharmacology Sch of Pharmacy Aston Univ 1965–70, head of sch Welsh Sch of

Pharmacy UWIST Cardiff 1978–97 (prof of pharmacology 1971–), first dean Faculty of Health and Life Sciences Univ of Wales Coll Cardiff 1988–91, dep princ and pro-vice chllr Cardiff University 1994–98, prof of pharmacy and pharmacology Cardiff University; former memb: Educn Ctee and various working parties on professional educn and pharmacology RPharmS, Medicines Cmmn 1992–95, various CNAA Ctees, CRM Psychotropics Sub Ctee, Standing Pharmaceutical Ctee for England and Wales, Welsh Standing Pharmaceutical Ctee in Welsh Office (former chm); memb Bd of Tstees Motor-Neurone Disease Assoc (MNDA) 1998–; author of over 120 res and professional articles and reviews specialising in pharmacology of psychotropic drugs and pharmaceutical educn; Hon DSc De Montfort Univ 1994; FIBiol 1972, FRPharmS 1978, MCPP 1981, CBiol 1984, DSc (Wales) 1986; *Recreations* music, photography, sport; *Style*— Prof Paul Spencer, OBE; ✉ c/o Welsh School of Pharmacy, Cardiff University, King Edward VII Avenue, Cathays Park, Cardiff CF1 3XF (tel 029 2087 4781, fax 029 2087 4149, e-mail spencerps@cf.ac.uk)

SPENCER, Raine, Countess; Raine; da of Alexander McCorquodale (1 cous of 1 Baron McCorquodale of Newton, PC) by his 1 w Dame Barbara Cartland, DBE (d 2000); *b* 9 September 1929; *m* 1, 1948 (m dis 1976), as his 1 w, 9 Earl of Dartmouth (d 1997); 3 s (William, 10 Earl of Dartmouth, Hon Rupert, Hon Henry), 1 da (Lady Charlotte (Duchesa di Carcaci)); m 2, 1976, as his 2 w, 8 Earl Spencer, LVO, DL (d 1992); m 3, 1993 (m dis 1996), as his 2 w, Comte Jean-François Pineton de Chambrun, 3 s of Marquis de Chambrun; *Career* formerly a LCC Voluntary Care Ctee worker in Wandsworth and Vauxhall, and actively involved in the welfare of the elderly in other areas; memb Lewisham W LCC 1958–65; memb: GLC (Richmond) 1967–73, GLC Gen Purposes Ctee 1971–73; former memb BBC Nat Agric Advsy Ctee, chm Govt Working Pty on the Human Habitat for UN Conference on the Environment (which produced The Dartmouth Report, How Do You Want To Live?), and a UK delegate at the Conf in Stockholm 1972; chm: GLC Historic Bldgs Bd 1968–71, Covent Gdn Devpt Ctee 1971–75, UK Exec Ctee of European Architectural Heritage Year 1975; memb: English Tourist Bd 1971–75, BTA Infrastructure Ctee 1972–, Advsy Cncl V&A 1980–, BTA 1982–93, Ctee Prestige Tourism for City of Nice, Special Jury for the Improvement of the Promenade des Anglais Nice; chm: BTA Spas Ctee 1981–83, BTA Commendation Schemes Panel 1982–89, BTA Hotels and Restaurants Ctee 1983–87, BTA Accommodation Ctee 1987–93, BTA Devpt Ctee 1987–93, BTA Britain Welcomes Japan Ctee of Honour and Exec Ctee 1989, BTA Come to Britain Awards 1990–93, Ctee for Business Sponsorship of the Arts; dir Harrods International 1996– (with special interest in the 70 shops abroad, airport duty free shops and the devpt and licensing of new products), dir Harrods Management Ltd 2001–, dir Harrods Estates 2006–; awarded a gold medal for public speaking, and a former guest speaker at Oxford Univ and Cambridge Univ debates; lectr at Holloway, Maidstone and Wandsworth Prisons; *Books* The Spencers on Spas (with photographs by Earl Spencer); *Style*— Raine, Countess Spencer

SPENCER, Ritchie Lloyd; s of Capt P Lloyd Spencer; *b* 27 September 1942; *Educ* St Bees Sch, Univ of Manchester (BA), LSE; *m* 1965, Catherine Dilys, da of Dr John Naish; 3 s (Hal b 1968, Patrick b 1969, James b 1972); *Career* dir Sunderland Shipbuilders Ltd 1972–76, md Reliant Motors plc 1976–86, dir Nash Industries plc 1980–86, chief exec GKN Powder Metallurgy Div 1986–90; chm: Bound Brook Lichfield Ltd 1986–90, Firth Cleveland Sintered Products Ltd 1986–90, Sheepbridge Sintered Products Ltd 1986–90; pres: Bound Brook Italia SpA Brunico 1986–90, Saini SpA Milan 1986–90; dir: Mahindra Sintered Products Pune Ltd India 1986–90, Sintermex SA de CV Mexico 1986–90; md: European Industrial Services Ltd 1990–94, Nettlefolds Ltd 1990–94, Unifix Ltd 1990–94, Unifix (Belgium) NV/SA 1990–94, Unifix (Netherlands) BV 1990–94, EIS Depots Ltd 1990–94; chief exec ThyssenKrupp Woodhead Ltd 1994–, gen dir ThyssenKrupp Indusa Mure SLU Spain 2003–; memb Cncl Soc Motor Manufacturers & Traders 1978–87, dir Motor Industry Res Assoc 1997– (chm 1984–97); MIPM; *Recreations* theatre, music, gardening, skiing; *Style*— Ritchie Spencer, Esq; ✉ Skelbrooke Hall, Skelbrooke, Doncaster, South Yorkshire (tel and fax 01302 728408); Dorlinn View, Argyll Terrace, Tobermory, Isle of Mull (tel 01688 302324); ThyssenKrupp Woodhead Ltd, 177 Kirkstall Road, Leeds LS4 2AQ (tel 0113 244 1202, e-mail spencer@tka-wo.thyssenkrupp.com)

SPENCER, Robin Godfrey; QC (1999); s of Eric Spencer (d 1992), of Chester, and Audrey Elaine, *née* Brown; *b* 8 July 1955; *Educ* King's Sch Chester, Emmanuel Coll Cambridge (MA); *m* 5 Aug 1978, Julia Margaret Eileen, da of Eric John Bennet Burley, of Chester; 3 da (Jennifer b 1983, Susanna b 1984, Laura b 1987); *Career* called to the Bar Gray's Inn 1978 (bencher 2004); in practice Wales & Chester Circuit, recorder of the Crown Court 1998– (asst recorder 1993–98), dep judge of the High Court 2001–, ldr Wales & Cheshire Circuit 2004–; *Recreations* cricket, music, Methodist history; *Style*— Robin Spencer, Esq, QC; ✉ Sedan House, Stanley Place, Chester CH1 2LU (tel 01244 348282, fax 01244 342336); 9–12 Bell Yard, London WC2A 2JR (tel 020 7400 1800, fax 020 7404 1405)

SPENCER, Sarah Ann; CBE (2007); da of Dr Ian Osborne Bradford Spencer (d 1978), of Tynemouth, and Elspeth, *née* Strang; *b* 11 December 1952; *Educ* Univ of Nottingham (BA), UCL (MPhil); *m* 1978, Brian Hackland; 2 s (James b 30 Aug 1986, Nick b 24 July 1989); *Career* pt/t lectr Univ of London and researcher Law Faculty UCL 1977–79; Cobden Tst: research offr 1979–84, dir 1984–85; dir Nat Cncl for Civil Liberties 1985–89; IPPR: research fell 1990–95, dir Citizenship and Governance Prog 1999–2002, sr assoc 2002–03, seconded as pt/t advsr PM's Strategy Unit Cabinet Office 2000 and 2003; dir of policy research Centre on Migration, Policy and Society (COMPAS) Univ of Oxford 2003–05 (assoc dir 2005–), assoc memb Nuffield Coll Oxford 2004–, visiting prof Human Rights Centre Univ of Essex 2005–; chair Equality and Diversity Forum 2002–, cmmr Cmmn for Racial Equality 2002–06 (dep chair 2003–05); memb: Cmmn on the Future of Multi-Ethnic Britain (Parekh Cmmn) Runnymede Tst 1998–2000, Human Rights Act Taskforce Home Office 1998–2001, Advsy Bd Transnational Communities Prog ESRC 1998–2002, Advsy Ctee Effective Govt Structures for Children Gulbenkian Fndn 1999–2000, Governance Advsy Ctee Br Cncl 1999–2006, Citizenship Educn Ctee Br Cncl 2000–02, Advsy Ctee on Ethnic Minorities in the Labour Market Cabinet Office 2001–02, Human Rights Forum DCA 2002–, Taskforce Cmmn on Equality and Human Rights DTI 2003–05; advsr Cambridge Ind Review of UK Anti-Discrimination Legislation 2000–01; govr Br Inst of Human Rights 2002–; FRSA 1999; *Books* incl: Police Authorities during the Miners' Strike (1985), The Constitution of the United Kingdom (co-author, 1991), Immigration as an Economic Asset, the German Experience (ed, 1994), Migrants, Refugees and the Boundaries of Citizenship (1995), Mainstreaming Human Rights in Whitehall and Westminster (co-author, 1999), Time for a Ministry of Justice? The future of the Home Office and LCD (2001), Reluctant Witness (co-author, 2001), Age Equality Comes of Age (co-author 2003), Age as an Equality Issue: Legal and Policy Perspectives (jt ed, 2003), The Politics of Migration: Managing Opportunity, Conflict and Change (ed, 2003); *Style*— Sarah Spencer, CBE; ✉ COMPAS, University of Oxford, 58 Banbury Road, Oxford, OX2 6QS (e-mail sarah.spencer@compas.ox.ac.uk)

SPENCER, His Hon Judge Shaun Michael; QC (1988); s of Edward Michael Spencer, of Leeds, and Barbara Joan Patricia Spencer; *b* 4 February 1944; *Educ* Cockburn HS, Univ of Durham (LLB); *m* 9 June 1971, Nicola, da of Frederick George Greenwood, of Tockwith, N Yorks; 3 s (Robert Phillip b 1972, Samuel James Edward b 1982, Edward Frederick Claudio b 1993), 2 da (Eleanor Jane b 1979, Elizabeth Anne b 1980); *Career* lectr in law Univ of Sheffield 1966–68 (asst lectr in law 1965–66), called to the Bar Lincoln's Inn 1968 (Hardwicke & Mansfield scholar, bencher 1997), barr NE Circuit 1969, recorder of the Crown Ct 1985–2002, circuit judge (NE Circuit) 2002–; Master of Hounds Claro Beagles 1982–88; *Recreations* cookery, books, singing; *Style*— His Hon Judge Shaun Spencer, QC; ✉ 34A Rutland Drive, Harrogate, North Yorkshire HG1 2NX (tel 01423 523162); Snook House, Holy Island, Northumberland TD15 2SS (tel 01289 389229)

SPENCER, Thomas Newnham Bayley (Tom); s of Thomas Henry Newnham Spencer (d 1979); *b* 10 April 1948; *Educ* Nautical Coll Pangbourne, Univ of Southampton; *m* 1979, Elizabeth Nan, *née* Bath; 2 da and 1 step da; *Career* Peat Marwick Mitchell CAs 1972–75, asst dir Britain in Europe referedum campaign 1975, J Walter Thompson advtg 1975–79; MEP (EPP): Derbyshire 1979–84, Surrey West 1989–94, Surrey 1994–99; Cons spokesman on: Social Affairs and Employment 1979–82, External Trade 1982–84; Cons dep chief whip Euro Parl 1989–91, permanent rapporteur on climate change EPP 1991–99, chm British Section EPP Gp Euro Parl 1994–97; former chm Euro Parl's Ctee on Foreign Affrs, Security and Defence Policy, pres GLOBE Int (Global Legislators for a Balanced Environment) 1995–99, chm Euro Union of Cons and Christian Democratic Students 1971–74; currently: exec dir Euro Centre for Public Affrs (founding exec dir 1987–89), visiting prof of global governance Surrey Euro Mgmnt Sch Univ of Surrey Guildford 2000–03, visiting prof of public affrs Brunel Univ 2003–; memb Religious and Scientific Ctee Religion, Science and Environment Symposia; memb Advsy Cncl Centre for Corp and Public Affrs Manchester Met Univ; writer, lectr and broadcaster; memb Editorial Bd: Jl of Public Affrs; assoc dean Templeton Coll Oxford 1984–89, memb Ct Univ of Surrey; Forum for the Future Green Ribbon Award 1999; Great Golden Medal for Merit (Austria) 1996; *Books* Public Affairs and Power: Essays in a Time of Fear (2003), Everything Flows: Essays on Public Affairs and Change (2005); *Recreations* gardening, opera; *Clubs* Carlton; *Style*— Tom Spencer, Esq; ✉ Barford Court, Lampard Lane, Churt, Surrey GU10 2HJ (tel 01428 712375, website www.tomspencer.info)

SPENCER-CHURCHILL, *see:* Churchill

SPENCER-NAIRN, Angus; s of late Michael Alastair Spencer-Nairn, of Baltilly House, Ceres, Fife, and Ursula Helen, *née* Devitt; *b* 23 January 1947; *Educ* Eton, RAC Cirencester (MRAC); *m* 6 July 1968, Christina Janet, da of late Col Hugh Gillies, of Kindar House, New Abbey, Dumfriesshire; 1 da (Fiona b 1974), 1 s (Michael b 1975); *Career* chartered accountant; sr ptnr Rawlinson & Hunter, in practice St Helier Jersey; *Recreations* motor racing, flying, tennis, deer stalking, golf; *Clubs* Royal and Ancient Golf (St Andrews), New (Edinburgh); *Style*— Angus Spencer-Nairn, Esq; ✉ La Fontaine, Rue Du Pont, St John, Jersey JE3 4FF (tel 01534 861716); Ordnance House, Box 83, 31 Pier Road, St Helier, Jersey JE4 8PW (tel 01534 825200, fax 01534 825250)

SPENCER-NAIRN, Sir Robert Arnold; 3 Bt (UK 1933), of Monimail, Co Fife, DL (Dist of Fife 1995); s of Lt-Col Sir Douglas Leslie Spencer Spencer-Nairn, TD, 2 Bt (d 1970), and his 1 w, Elizabeth Livingston Henderson; *b* 11 October 1933; *Educ* Eton, Trinity Hall Cambridge; *m* 1963, Joanna Elizabeth, da of late Lt Cdr George Stevenson Salt, RN, s of 2 Bt (cr 1899); 1 da (Katharine Elizabeth b 1964), 2 s (James Robert b 1966, Andrew George b 1969); *Heir* s, James Spencer-Nairn; *Career* late Lt Scots Gds; Vice Lord-Lt Dist of Fife 1996; *Style*— Sir Robert Spencer-Nairn, Bt, DL; ✉ Barham, Cupar, Fife KY15 5RG

SPENCER-SMITH, Sir John Hamilton; 7 Bt (UK 1804), of Tring Park, Herts; s of Capt Sir Thomas Cospatric Spencer-Smith, 6 Bt (d 1959), and Lucy Ashton, da of late Thomas Ashton Ingram; *b* 18 March 1947; *Educ* Milton Abbey, Lackham Coll of Agric; *m* 1980 (m dis 1992), Mrs Christine Sandra Parris, da of late John Theodore Charles Osborne, of Durrington, W Sussex; 1 da (Jessica Kirsten b 1985); *Heir* kinsman, Michael Spencer-Smith; *Clubs* Cowdray Park Polo; *Style*— Sir John H Spencer-Smith, Bt

SPENS, David Patrick; QC (1995); s of Lt-Col Hugh Stuart Spens, MC, MBE, TD (d 1988), and Mary Jean Drake, *née* Reinhold; *b* 2 May 1950; *Educ* Rugby, Univ of Kent (BA); *m* 7 April 1979 (m dis 2003), Daniele, da of Robert William Irving, MBE (d 1994); 2 da (Dominique b 1982, Sophie-Claire b 1986); *Career* called to the Bar Inner Temple 1973; jr counsel to the Crown at the Central Criminal Court 1988–95, recorder of the Crown Court 1994–, ldr South Eastern Circuit 2007–; chm Central Bar Mess 1997–2000, chm Criminal Bar Assoc 2004–05; *Style*— David Spens, Esq, QC; ✉ Garden Court Chambers, 57–60 Lincoln's Inn Fields, London WC2A 3LS (tel 020 7993 7600, fax 020 7993 7700, e-mail david.spens@gclaw.co.uk)

SPENS, John Alexander; MVO, RD (1970), WS; s of late T P Spens and Nancy Farie Spens (d 1996); *b* 1933; *Educ* BA, LLB; *m* Finella Jane Gilroy; 2 s, 1 da; *Career* Carrick Pursuivant of Arms 1974–85, Albany Herald of Arms 1985–; ptnr Maclay Murray & Spens (Slrs) 1960–90 (conslt 1990–98); dir: Scottish Amicable Life Assurance Soc 1963–98 (chm 1978–81), Standard Property Investment plc 1977–87; *Style*— John A Spens, Esq, MVO, RD, WS, Albany Herald of Arms; ✉ The Old Manse, Gartocharn, Dunbartonshire G83 8RX (tel 01389 83329)

SPENS, Michael Colin Barkley; s of Richard Vernon Spens (d 1996), and Margaret, *née* Barkley; *b* 22 September 1950; *Educ* Marlborough, Selwyn Coll Cambridge (MA); *m* Deborah Susan, da of A George Lane; 1 s (William b 21 Jan 1993), 2 da (Tatiana b 8 Oct 1994, Georgina b 18 Feb 1997); *Career* with United Biscuits 1972–74; housemaster and head of careers Radley Coll 1974–93, headmaster Caldicott Sch 1993–98, headmaster Fettes Coll 1998–; Freeman City of London, Liveryman Worshipful Co of Grocers; *Recreations* running, golf, crosswords, electronics, bridge, gardening, wood turning; *Clubs* Hawks' (Cambridge), New (Edinburgh), Denham Golf; *Style*— Michael Spens, Esq; ✉ Headmaster's Lodge, Fettes College, Edinburgh EH4 1QX (tel 0131 311 6701, fax 0131 311 6714, e-mail mcb.spens@fettes.com)

SPERRYN, Simon George; s of George Roland Neville Sperryn, of Hampton Lucy, Warks, and Wendy, *née* King; *b* 7 April 1946; *Educ* Rydal Sch Clwyd, Pembroke Coll Cambridge (MA), Cranfield Sch of Mgmnt (MBA); *m* 11 Sept 1993, Jessica Alice Hayes; 2 s, 1 da; *Career* Chamber of Commerce and Industry: Birmingham 1967–77, chief exec Northants 1979–85, chief exec Manchester 1986–92, chief exec London 1992–2000; chm Manchester Camerata Ltd 1989–92; dir: Manchester TEC 1990–92, Business Link London 1995–2000; chief exec Lloyd's Market Assoc 2001–07; Br Chambers of Commerce: memb Bd of Dirs 1998–2000; pres Br Chambers of Commerce Executives 1994–95; dep chm World Chambers Fedn 2000; chm City of London Early Years Devpt and Childcare Partnership 1998–2000; memb: Met Police Serv Jt Steering Gp for Community Safety in London 1998–2000, Greater London Ctee FEFC 1996–2000, Cncl CII 2004–07; tstee UNIAID Fndn 2003–; CCMI (CIMgt), FRSA; *Style*— Simon Sperryn, Esq; ✉ Apt. 12, The Beldevere, Homerton Street, Cambridge CB2 0NT (tel 01223 213821, mobile 07950 269296, e-mail simon@sperryn.org)

SPICER, Sir (William) Michael Hardy; kt (1996), MP; s of Brig Leslie Hardy Spicer (d 1981), and Muriel Winifred Alice Spicer; *b* 22 January 1943; *Educ* Wellington, Emmanuel Coll Cambridge (MA); *m* 1967, Patricia Ann, da of Patrick Sinclair Hunter (d 1981); 1 s, 2 da; *Career* asst to ed The Statist, dir Cons Systems Res Centre 1968–70, md Economic Models Ltd 1970–80; MP (Cons): Worcs S 1974–97, Worcs W 1997–; PPS to Trade Mins 1979–81, vice-chm Cons Pty 1981–83, dep chm Cons Pty 1983–84, Parly under sec of state Dept of Transport 1985–86, min for aviation 1986–87, Parly under sec of state Dept of Energy 1987–90, min of state for housing and planning 1990, chm Parly Office of Sci and Technol 1992, chm Parly and Scientific Ctee 1996–99, memb Treasy Select Ctee 1997–2001, chm Treasy Sub-Ctee 1998–2001, chm 1922 Ctee 2001– (memb Exec Ctee 1997–98), memb Bd Cons Pty 2001– (chm Finance Ctee 2007–); pres Assoc of Electricity Prodrs 1991–; govr Wellington Coll 1992–2005; *Books* Final Act (1983), Prime Minister, Spy (1986), Cotswold Manners (1989), Cotswold Murders (1991), Cotswold Mistress (1992),

S

A Treaty Too Far - A New Policy for Europe (1992), Cotswolds Moles (1993), The Challenge of the East (1996); *Recreations* painting, writing, tennis, bridge; *Clubs* Garrick, Pratt's, Lords and Commons Tennis (capt/chm 1997–2006); *Style—* Sir Michael Spicer, MP; ✉ House of Commons, London SW1A 0AA (tel 020 7219 3000)

SPICER, Sir Nicholas Adrian Albert; 5 Bt (UK), of Lancaster Gate, Borough of Paddington; s of (Sir) Peter James Spicer, 4 Bt, who did not use the title (d 1993), and Margaret, *née* Wilson; *b* 28 October 1953; *Educ* Eton, Univ of Birmingham (MB ChB); *m* 1992, Patricia Carol, 2 da of Warwick Dye, of Auckland, NZ; 2 s (James Peter Warwick b 12 June 1993, Andrew Nicholas Kingsley b 1 Aug 1995); *Heir* s, James Spicer; *Career* medical practitioner; Liveryman Worshipful Co of Fishmongers; *Style—* Sir Nicholas Spicer, Bt; ✉ The Old Rectory, Malvern Road, Stanford Bishop, Worcester WR6 5TT

SPICER, Paul Cridland; s of John Harold Vincent Spicer, Kings Bromley, Staffs, and late Joan Sallie, *née* Hickling; *b* 6 June 1952; *Educ* New Coll Sch Oxford, Oakham Sch, Univ of London (BMus), Univ of Durham (PGCE), Royal Coll of Music (ARCO, ARCM, Walford Davies prize, top organ award); *Career* asst dir of music Uppingham Sch 1974–78, dir of music Ellesmere Coll 1978–84, prodr BBC Radio Three 1984–86, sr prodr Radio Three Midlands 1986–90, artistic dir Lichfield Int Arts Festival 1990–2001; dir: Chester Bach Singers 1982–84, Leicester Bach Choir 1984–92, Birmingham Bach Choir 1992–, Royal Coll of Music Chorus 1996–97; fndr dir Finzi Singers 1987–; princ conductor: Royal Coll of Music Chamber Choir 1995–, Birmingham Conservatoire Chamber Choir 2002–; guest conductor: Netherlands Radio Choir 1995–, Nat Chamber Choir of Ireland 2006–; prof of choral conducting: Royal Coll of Music 1998–, Birmingham Conservatoire 2003–; memb Cncl: Assoc of Br Choral Dirs 1989–92 and 2004–05, Birmingham Contemporary Music Gp 1991–94; memb: RCO, Assoc of Br Choral Conductors, Victorian Soc; vice-chm British Arts Festivals Assoc 1994–97; tstee Finzi Tst and chm Finzi Tst Friends, tstee Eleesmere Coll Schulze Organ Tst, dir Abbotsholme Arts Soc 1990–2001, memb Cncl Lichfield Cathedral 2000–; freelance record prodr; freelance conductor, conductor of choral workshops and masterclasses; frequent broadcaster and organ recitalist Radio 3; composer of choral, organ, instrumental and chamber music; hon res fell Univ of Birmingham, hon fell Birmingham Conservatoire; FRSA; *Compositions* princ works incl: Easter Oratorio (chorus, soloists and orchestra), The Deciduous Cross (choir and winds), On The Power of Sound (chorus, soloists and orchestra), The Darling of The World (chorus, soloist and orchestra), Piano Sonata, Song for Birds (cycle), Dies Natalis (a Capella), Kiwi Fireworks (organ), Man, Wretched Man (chorus and organ), Pilgrimages (piano), Suite for Organ; church music incl: Come Out Lazar, Magnificat and Nunc Dimittis (New Coll service); *Publications* English Pastoral Partsongs, A Biography of Herbert Howells; author of articles in many musical periodicals; *Recreations* architecture, preserving mystery, promoting British music, middle distance running; *Clubs* Athenaeum; *Style—* Paul Spicer, Esq; ✉ 4 The Close, Lichfield, Staffordshire WS13 7LD (tel 01543 306277, e-mail paul@paulspicer.com, website www.paulspicer.com)

SPICER, Paul George Bullen; s of Col Roy Godfrey Bullen Spicer, CMG, MC (d 1946), and Margaret Ina Frances, *née* Money; *b* 6 February 1928; *Educ* Eton; *m* 10 Sept 1954, June Elizabeth Cadogan, da of Antony Fenwick (d 1954), of Kiambu, Kenya, and Brinkburn Priory, Northumberland; 1 s (Rupert b 1955), 1 da (Venetia b 1959); *Career* Lt Coldstream Gds 1945–49, served UK, Palestine and Libya; Shell International Petroleum: joined 1949, London, Kenya, Tanzania, USA, Canada, South Africa and Cyprus, rising to md Overseas until 1970; Lonrho plc: joined 1970, main bd dir 1978–94, dep chm 1991–94; *Recreations* books, music, horses; *Clubs* Brooks's, White's; *Style—* Paul Spicer, Esq; ✉ 22 Ovington Gardens, London SW3 1LE

SPIEGELBERG, Richard George; s of Francis Edward Frederick Spiegelberg (d 1979), and Margaret Neville, *née* Clegg (d 1999); *b* 21 January 1944; *Educ* Marlborough, Hotchkiss Sch USA, New Coll Oxford (MA); *m* 1, 1970 (m dis 1979), Coralie Eve, *née* Dreyfus; 2 s (Rupert b 1971, Maximilian b 1974); m 2, 1980, Suzanne Louise *née* Dodd; 1 s (Assheton b 1981), 1 da (Henrietta b 1984); *Career* Economist Intelligence Unit 1965–67, business journalist and mgmnt ed The Times 1967–74, princ Dept of Indust 1974–75, NEDO 1975–76; assoc dir: J Walter Thompson & Co 1976–80, Coopers & Lybrand 1980–84; dir and jt md Streets Financial 1984–87; exec dir corp communications Merrill Lynch Europe/Middle East and Merrill Lynch International Bank Ltd 1987–98, dir Chancery Communications Ltd 1999–2003, dir Cardew Group Ltd 2003–; *Books* The City (1973); *Recreations* walking, golf, opera; *Clubs* Brooks's, Berkshire Golf; *Style—* Richard Spiegelberg, Esq; ✉ 27 Rowan Road, London W6 7DT

SPIERS, (John) Anthony (Tony); MBE (2005); *b* 19 September 1944; *Educ* Bishop Vesey's GS; *m* 1; 1 s (Jonathan); m 2, 1971 Anne; 2 s (Benjamin, Gerald), 2 da (Catherine, Hannah-May); *Career* slr; ptnr: Peter Peter & Wright 1970–96, Withy King Bath 2000–05, Michelmoves 2005–; clerk to Blanchminster Charity 1976–84; memb Cornwall CC 1981–88, dir Slrs' Benevolent Assoc 1991–93, fndr chm W of England Soc of Tst and Estate Practitioners 1992–94, sec Devon and Exeter Law Soc 1994–, chm of Tbnls in Appeals Service 1997–; sec Bath Law Soc 2001–02, memb Assoc of Contentious Tst and Probate Specialists; memb Law Soc Wills and Equity Ctee 2004–; FRSA (memb Cncl 1995–97, chm SW Regnl Ctee 1996–97); *Recreations* walking, driving, fishing, vegetable growing in my allotment, reading, family; *Style—* Tony Spiers, Esq, MBE; ✉ 2 Claremont Grove, Exeter EX2 4LY (tel 01392 420229, e-mail tony@aspiers.com)

SPIERS, Sir Donald Maurice; kt (1993), CB (1987), TD (1966); s of Harold Herbert Spiers (d 1968), and Emma, *née* Foster (d 1978); *b* 27 January 1934; *Educ* Trinity Coll Cambridge (MA); *m* 13 Dec 1958, Sylvia Mary, da of Samuel Lowman (d 1963); 2 s (Simon b 1965, Philip b 1969); *Career* 2 Lt RE 1952–54, devpt engr de Havilland 1957–60, operational res Air Miny 1961–66, scientific advsr Far East AF 1967–70, asst chief scientist RAF 1971–78, MOD PE 1978–84, dep controller Aircraft 1984–86, Controller Estab Res & Nuclear Programmes 1987–89, Controller Aircraft 1989–94; aerospace conslt 1994–; chm: Computing Devices Co Ltd 1997–2001 (non-exec dir 1994–2001), European Helicopter Industries Ltd 1997–2003, Meggitt plc 1998–2001 (non-exec dir 1995–2003), Agusta Westland Int Ltd 2003–, Farnborough Aerospace Consortium 2003–; non-exec dir: Smiths Industries Aerospace and Defence Ltd 1995–97, Messier-Dowty Int Ltd 1998–2004, TAG Aviation (UK) Ltd 1999–2005, General Dynamics UK Ltd 2001–; pres: RAeS 1995–96, Popular Flying Assoc 1997–2000; *Style—* Sir Donald Spiers, CB, TD; ✉ 20 Paddock Close, Camberley, Surrey GU15 2BN (tel 01276 28164, e-mail donald.spiers@ntlworld.com)

SPIERS, Prof John Raymond; s of H H Spiers (d 1956), and Kate, *née* Root (d 1976); *b* 30 September 1941; *Educ* Red Hill Sch E Sutton, Hornsey Coll of Art and Design, Catford Coll of Commerce, Univ of Sussex (BA); *m* 1, 24 June 1967 (m dis 1981), Prof Margaret Ann Boden, OBE, *qv*, da of Leonard Forbes Boden, OBE (d 1987); 1 s (Ruskin b 19 June 1968), 1 da (Jehane b 21 Jan 1972); m 2, 14 Jan 2003, Leigh Richardson, *née* Radford; 1 da (Lorna b 6 Aug 1978), 1 s (Philip b 6 April 1982); *Career* publisher and author 1960–; fndr, chm and md: The Harvester Press Ltd 1970–88, Harvester Microform Publications Ltd 1973–87, Wheatsheaf Books Ltd 1980–88; fndr and chm John Spiers Publishing Ltd 1988–, fndr chm Civitas Inst for the Study of Civil Society 1999–2000; chm Soc of Young Publishers 1972–73 (treas 1971–72), exec Independent Publishers Guild 1972–77; Parly candidate (Lab) Dorking 1974, resigned Lab Pty 1977, memb Cons Pty 1979–99; a special advsr to Rt Hon Sir Peter Morrison, MP (dep chm) Cons Central Office 1989–90, conslt dir Cons Central Office 1990–95; pres Brighton Kemp Town Cons Assoc 1991–95, dep treas Cons Pty SE Area England 1990–92; chm: Brighton Theatre Ltd 1984, Brighton Business Group 1989–95, Brighton Health Authy 1991–92, Brighton Healthcare NHS Tst 1992–94, David Salomon's Mgmnt Devpt Centre (SETRHA) 1993–94, Brighton Healthcare Arts Tst 1993–94, Advsy Bd Centre for Health Care Mgmnt Univ of Nottingham 1994–96, The Patients' Assoc 1995–97 (actg chief exec 1995–96), Health Policy Gp Centre for Policy Studies 1997–99; memb: Advsy Cncl IEA Health Unit 1989–92 and 1997–99, Communications Advsy Gp and Patients' Charter Advsy Gp NHS Mgmnt Exec 1991–94, Strategic Ctee on Women's Issues SE Thames RHA 1992–94, King's Fund NAHAT Public Participation Advsy Gp 1992, Governance in the NHS (Induction and Trg) Working Pty NHS Mgmnt Exec 1993, Ministerial Advsy Gp on Design in Healthcare 1993–98, PM's Advsy Panel on The Citizen's Charter 1994, Policy Advsy Gp Inst of Health Services Mgmnt 1994–98, NHSME Working Pty on Open Govt 1994, Bd Int Health Care Mgmnt Inst 1994–98, NHS Exec Patient Responsiveness Gp 1996–97, memb Bd Nat Cmmn on Care Standards 2001–03, Advsy Cncl Reform 2001–; Nat Assoc of Health Authorities and Tsts: memb Cncl 1992–94, memb Exec 1993–94, vice-chm Provider Ctee 1993–94, chm Conf Ctee 1993–94 (memb 1992); health policy advsr The Social Market Fndn 1994–99; visiting fell: NHS Staff Coll Wales 1995–, King's Fund Mgmnt Coll 1996–; research fell Inst of Economic Affrs 1997–99 (sr research fell 1999–2000 and 2003–), head of health care studies 1999–2000, adjunct scholar Cascade Policy Centre Portland OR 1999; external prof: Business Sch Univ of Glamorgan 1998–2001, Humanities and Social Studies Sch Univ of Glamorgan 2001–; sr research fell Inst of English Studies Univ of London 2003–, visiting fell Ruskin Prog Lancaster Univ 2005–; founding dir Southern Sound Radio plc 1980–87; dir: Radical Soc 1988–91 (co chm 1990–2000), Center for Intelligence Studies Washington DC 1990–93; pres The Gissing Fndn 2005–; tstee: Brighton Int Arts Festival 1989–96, Choice in Educn (grant maintained schs) 1989–92, Grant Maintained Schs Fndn 1992–99 (vice-chm 1992–99), The Trident Tst 1992–99 (vice-chm 1993, chm 1994–97), English Schs Orchestra and Choir 1998–2005, The League of Mercy 1999–2005 (companion 2002), Shakespeare Authorship Tst 2002–2005, The Ruskin Fndn 2002–; distinguished sr fell Center for Cons Studies Washington DC 1992; librarian and memb Nat Cncl Francis Bacon Soc 1998–2005; organiser: The Rediscovery of George Gissing Exhbn 1971, Centenary Conference, Gissing and the City 2003; memb: Exec Ctee William Morris Soc 1973–76, Advsy Bd Centre for Study of Social History Univ of Warwick 1979–82, RSA; Univ of Sussex: memb Ct 1987–, vice-pres Univ of Sussex Alumni Soc 2002– (chm 1983–2004), memb Chllr's Advsy Gp 1986–98, hon fell Univ of Sussex Soc 1999–; JP (E Sussex) 1989–91; Queen's Award for Export Achievement 1986; Freeman City of London 2000; Hon DUniv Sussex 1994; Companion of the Guild of St George 1979 (fndr and ed The Companion 2001–05, dir 2002–05); FRSA 1994; hon fell Inst of Econ Affrs 2003–; Knight Cdr with Star Order of St Stanislaus 1997 (Knight Grand Cross 1998); *Books* The Rediscovery of George Gissing (with Pierre Coustillas, 1971), The Invisible Hospital and The Secret Garden: An Insider's Account of the NHS Reforms (1995), Sense and Sensibility in Health Care (co-author, 1996), Who Owns Our Bodies: Making Moral Choices in Health Care (1997), Dilemmas in Health Policy (ed, 1998), The Realities of Rationing (1999), Coming, Ready or Not: The Politics, Present and Future of the NHS (2002), Patients, Power and Responsibility. The First Principles of Consumer-Driven Reform (2003), Land of Promise (ed, 2005), Gissing and the City (ed, 2006); *Recreations* collecting books, reading them, supporting The Arsenal, canal boats, walking, travelling in railway carriages, natural history; *Clubs* Hoxton Hawks Vintage Cycling (pres 2006–); *Style—* Prof John Spiers; ✉ e-mail jr.spiers@virgin.net

SPIERS, Shaun Mark; s of (Charles) Gordon Spiers (d 1990), and Ann Kathleen, *née* Hutton; *b* 23 April 1962; *Educ* Brentwood Sch, St John's Coll Oxford (BA), King's Coll London (MA); *Career* political offr SE Co-op 1987–94, MEP (Lab Co-op) London SE 1994–99; chief exec Assoc of Br Credit Unions 1999–2004; chief exec Campaign to Protect Rural England (CPRE) 2004–; *Style—* Shaun Spiers; ✉ 83 Humber Road, London SE3 7LR

SPILLER, David; *Educ* Slade Sch of Art; *Career* artist; *Exhibitions* Zeitkunst Gall Innsbruck and Cologne 1987 and 1988, Eugene Lendel Gall Gras 1987, Kunstverein Mannheim 1987, Woord and Reeld (Museum Hedendaagse Kunst Utrecht) 1987, Twinings Gall NY 1988 and 1989, Kana Contemporary Arts Gall Berlin 1988, Alexander Roussos Gall 1990, Ariadne Gall Vienna 1990 and 1991, Willy Schoots Gall Eindhoven 1991, Reflex Gall Amsterdam 1992, Pop Artvertising (Museum Van Bommel Venlo) 1992, Gall Naviglio Milan and Venice 1992 and 1993, Gall Moderne Silkeborg 1994, Gall Cotthem Knokke 1995, 1998, 2000 and 2003, Gall Cotthem Barcelona 1997, Rokoko Gallery Stuttgart 1998, Beaux Arts London 1998, 1999, 2000, 2001, 2002, 2004 and 2005, Cartoons and Comics (Virgin Atlantic) 1999, Gall Moderne Silkeborg 1999, Gall Moderne Denmark 2000, Guy Pieters Belgium 2000 and 2003, Gallery Camino Real Boca Raton 2000, Galerie Klaus Peter Goebel Stuttgart 2000, Galerie Wild Frankfurt 2001, Museum Espace Belleville Paris 2002, Royal West of England Acad 2003, Ernst Hilger Vienna 2004, Raab Galerie Berlin 2004; art fairs incl: Chicago, Cologne, Frankfurt, Miami, Los Angeles, FIAC Paris, Art98, Art99; *Style—* David Spiller, Esq

SPILLER, Prof Eric; s of Leonard Spiller, of Wombourne, Staffs, and Helen, *née* Holder; *b* 19 August 1946; *Educ* Central Sch of Art & Design London, Royal Coll of Art London (MA); *m* Carolyn; 2 s (Charles b 12 Sept 1974, Rufus b 8 Nov 1977), 1 da (Nancy b 11 July 1980); *Career* jewellery designer and lectr: pt/t lectr Fashion Dept Harrow Sch of Art 1971–73, lectr in silversmithing and jewellery 1973–75, Dept of Three-Dimensional Studies NI Poly, lectr i/c of jewellery 1975–81 (Dept of Design Grays Sch of Art, Robert Gordon's Inst of Technol Aberdeen), prog ldr BA (Combined Studies) Crafts Crewe and Alsager Coll of HE 1981–83, princ lectr/dep head of dept 1983–85 (Dept of Silversmithing Jewellery and Allied Crafts, Sir John Cass Faculty of Art City of London Poly); head of sch: Sch of Design Portsmouth Coll of Art Design and Further Educn 1985–87, Grays Sch of Art Robert Gordon's Inst of Technol Aberdeen 1987–92, asst princ Robert Gordon Univ 1992–2000, vice-princ Falmouth Coll of Arts (now UC Falmouth) 2000; visiting lectr: Univ of Ulster, West Surrey Coll of Art, Loughborough Coll of Art, S Glamorgan Inst of HE, Brighton Poly, San Diego State Univ; public collections incl: Goldsmiths Hall, Crafts Cncl, W Midlands Arts, NW Arts, Aberdeen Art Gallery, Nat Museum of Scotland; private collections worldwide; numerous exhibitions incl: Craftmans Art (V&A) 1973, Aberdeen Art Gallery 1977, New Jewellery (Royal Exchange Theatre Manchester) 1984, New York 1983, Kyoto 1984, Tokyo 1984–85, Munich 1989, 1991 and 1996; memb Cncl: Crafts Cncl 1993–99, Scottish Arts Cncl 1994–99 (chm Craft Ctee 1994–99); FRSA; *Style—* Prof Eric Spiller; ✉ University College Falmouth, Wood Lane, Falmouth, Cornwall TR11 4RA

SPILLER, John Anthony; MBE (1979); s of C Finn and step s of C H Spiller (d 1993), and Sarah, *née* Walsh (d 1988); *b* 29 December 1942; *Educ* Bideford Sch, N Devon Tech Coll, Bideford Art Coll; *m* 1 Sept 1972, Angela, da of Surtees Gleghorn (d 1971); 1 da (Sarah b 16 July 1974), 1 s (Ben b 23 Feb 1976); *Career* chm Devon Young Libs 1960–62, asst agent to Mark (Lord) Bonham-Carter Torrington Parly constituency 1962–64, constituency agent Cornwall N Parly constituency to John W Pardoe MP 1965–71; N regnl organiser and election agent: to Cyril Smith, MP Rochdale by-election, to Alan Beith, MP Berwick-upon-Tweed by-election 1972; nat agent Lib Central Assoc 1973–78, advsr to Joshua Nkomo African Peoples Union Zimbabwe (then Rhodesia) Independence Elections 1979–80, marginal seats advsr (UK) Lib Pty 1981–82, sec gen Lib Pty 1983–86, liaison offr for Devonshire PHAB 1991–92; co sec Estuary Seascapes Ltd 1994–96, sr exec Western Approaches Ltd 1992–96; nat pres Assoc of Lib Agents and Organisers 1983–84; memb: Bd Mgmnt Gladstone Benevolent Fund 1980–95 (sec and tstee 1995–98), Shelter, RNLI (S West); delegate Democracy conf Vilnius Lithuania 1992 and 1994,

Electoral Reform Soc delegate Democracy Conf Tallin Estonia 1995; delegate: Citizens and Democracy Conf Moscow Russia 1995, Democracy Conf Yerevan Repub of Armenia 1995; Office for Democratic Instns and Human Rights (ODIHR) observer for state elections Repub of Georgia Nov 1995, Office of Int Monitoring (OSCE) observer for elections Bosnia and Herzegovina Sept 1996, trg conslt political orgn Zagreb Croatia Oct 1996 and Jan 1997, lectr for FCO Eastern Slavonia, Vukorav and Erdut Feb 1997, tech advsr OSCE/ODIHR Mission Office Yugoslavia 1998, observer for state elections Estonia (OSCE) 1999; *Recreations* travel, watching amateur boxing, music (folk); *Style*— John Spiller, Esq, MBE; ✉ 4 Branksome Dene Road, Westbourne, Bournemouth, Dorset BH4 8JW; Keogh, Moycullen, County Galway, Eire

SPILLER, Richard John; s of Capt Michael Macnaughton Spiller, of Belfast, and Agnes Gall, *née* Algie; *b* 31 December 1953; *Educ* Royal Belfast Academical Inst, Univ of Exeter (LLB), London Guildhall Univ (MA); *m* 17 Sept 1982, Hilary, da of William Wright, of Kingston upon Thames; 1 s (James b 1984), 1 da (Emily b 1987); *Career* admitted slr 1980; ptnr: D J Freeman 1985–2003, Kendall Freeman 2003–; Freeman: City of London 1986, Worshipful Co of Slrs 1986 (memb Insurance Law Ctee); memb Law Soc; *Style*— Richard Spiller, Esq; ✉ Kendall Freeman, One Fetter Lane, London EC4A 1JB (tel 020 7583 4055, fax 020 7353 7377)

SPILMAN, John Ellerker; JP (1984), DL (Humberside, 1990); s of Maj Harry Spilman, MC, JP, DL (d 1980), and Phyllis Emily, *née* Hind (d 1998); *b* 9 March 1940; *Educ* Sedbergh, RAC Cirencester; *m* 25 Oct 1975, Patricia Mary, da of Gilbert Sutcliffe (d 1988), of Cleethorpes; 1 s (David b 1984), 1 da (Joanna b 1980); *Career* md farming co, dir Aylesby Manor Farms Ltd; High Sheriff Humberside 1989–90; church warden; tstee McAulay Meml Tst; *Recreations* fishing, shooting, tennis, music, Rotary (club pres 1991–92); *Clubs* Farmers; *Style*— John E Spilman, Esq, DL; ✉ Aylesby Manor, Grimsby, North East Lincolnshire DN37 7AW (tel 01472 871800); Manor Farm, Aylesby, Grimsby (tel 01472 872550, fax 01472 873032)

SPINETTI, Victor George Andrew; s of Guiseppe Spinetti (d 1985), and Lily, *née* Watson; *b* 2 September 1933; *Educ* Monmouth Sch, Royal Welsh of Music and Drama; *Career* actor and director; fell Coll of Music and Drama Cardiff; *Theatre* with Joan Littlewood's Theatre Workshop Stratford East 1959–65; numerous West End and Broadway appearances 1964–; one man show Victor Spinetti's Very Private Diary (Edinburgh Festival 1981, Donmar and Apollo Theatres London 1989, Sydney Opera House 1990, NY 1992), Windy City, Pirates of Penzance, Super Ted, Peter Pan, Comic Cuts, Oliver, One for the Pot; RSC at Stratford 1995–96; debut as dir NT 1968; plays directed incl: Hair (Amsterdam and Rome), Jesus Christ Superstar (Paris), Déjà Revue (London); devised and wrote revue Off The Peg (Arts Theatre), co-author (with John Lennon) play In His Own Write; *Television* recent credits incl: The Paradise Club, Vincent van Gogh, Singles, Maxwell's House, An Actor's Life for Me, Secrets (by Judith Krantz), In the Beginning; *Films* recent credits incl: Voyage of the Damned, Mistral's Daughter, Sins, Under the Cherry Moon, The Attic, The Krays, Julie and the Cadillacs; *Awards* Broadway Tony Award and Paris Int Festival first prize (for Oh! What A Lovely War 1965); *Recreations* reading, writing, walking; *Style*— Victor Spinetti, Esq; ✉ c/o Barry Burnett Organisation Ltd, 3 Clifford Street, London W1S 2LF (tel 020 7839 0202, fax 020 7839 0438)

SPINK, Air Marshal Clifford Rodney; CB (2002), CBE (1992, OBE 1989); s of Ronald Charles Spink (d 1990), and Beryl, *née* Phillips (d 2002); *b* 17 May 1946; *Educ* RAF Coll Cranwell; *m* 1, 3 April 1971, Christine Janet Grove (d 1973); m 2, 9 April 1977, Caroline Anne, da of Anthony Francis Smith; 1 da (Laura Claire b 2 Dec 1978), 1 s (Robert Alun b 13 Jan 1982); *Career* cmmnd RAF 1968, subsequently 111 (Fighter) Sqdn RAF Wattisham 1970–73, 56 (Fighter) Sqdn Akrotiri Cyprus 1974 (involved in conflict), 56 (Fighter) Sqdn Wattisham until 1976, instr RMAS 1976–79 (following courses at RMAS and Sch of Infantry Warminster), Flight Cdr 111 (Fighter) Sqdn RAF Leuchars 1979–82, NDC Latimer and subsequently HQ RAF Germany, Cdr 74 (Fighter) Sqdn RAF Wattisham 1986–89, Cdr RAF Mount Pleasant and Dep Cdr British Forces Falklands 1989–90, Cdr RAF Coningsby 1990–92, Detachment Cdr Dhahran (Gulf conflict) 1991, Air Cdre 1993, RCDS 1993 subsequently SASO HQ 11 Gp 1993–95, COS HQ 18 Gp, Air Vice-Marshal and First Air OC 11/18 Gp 1996–98, DG MOD Saudi Armed Forces Project 1998–2002; non-exec chm London Ashford Airport, dir Contingency Planning Associates Ltd, md Clifford Spink Associates Ltd; chm: Spitfire Ltd, Classic British Aircraft Shares; pres Royal Observer Corps Assoc; Liveryman Guild of Air Pilots and Air Navigators; FRAeS 1997; *Recreations* vintage aircraft, golf, garden; *Clubs* RAF; *Style*— Air Marshal Clifford Spink, CB, CBE, FCMI, FRAeS, RAF; ✉ Clifford Spink Associates Ltd, April Lodge, Loop Road, Keyston, Huntingdon, Cambridgeshire PE28 0RE

SPINK, Ian Alexander; s of John Arthur Spink, of Melbourne, Australia, and Lorna Kathleen, *née* Hart; *b* 8 October 1947; *Educ* Highett HS, Aust Ballet Sch; *m* 1, 1972 (m dis 1975), Gail Mae Ferguson; m 2, 1986 (m dis 1992), Michele Ashmore Smith; m 3, Lucinda Adele Bevan 1998; *Career* dancer Australian Ballet Co 1968–74, dancer and choreographer Dance Co of NSW 1975–77, dancer Richard Alston & Dancers Co 1978–79, fndr, dancer, dir and choreographer Ian Spink Dance Group 1978–82, co-fndr Second Stride (dance theatre) 1982–97 (became sole dir 1988), currently artistic dir CityMoves Dance Agency Aberdeen; theatre choreography for RSC, Ro Theatre (Holland) and The Crucible (Sheffield), opera choreography for Opera North, WNO, Royal Opera House, Scot Opera, Opera de Nice, ENO and Glyndebourne Festival Opera; dir: Fugue by Caryl Churchill (Channel Four) 1988, Judith Weir's The Vanishing Bridegroom (Scot Opera) 1990, The Pelican (Glasgow Citizens Theatre) 1992, Orlando (Batignano Opera Festival) 1992, Daughter of the Regiment (ETO) 1998–99, The Striker (Caryl Churchill, Aberystwyth) 2000, Orfeo (Purcell Sinfonia Japan) 2001, L'Enfant et les Sortilege and L'Heure Espagnole (Opera Zuid Maastricht) 2002, Private Lives (Glasgow Citizens Theatre) 2003, A Tragedy of Fashion (Rambert Dance Co) 2004; *Recreations* music, cooking, choreographing, growing avocado trees, thinking; *Style*— Spink

SPINK, Dr Robert (Bob); MP; *b* 1 August 1948; *Educ* Univ of Manchester (BSc(Eng)), Cranfield (MSc(IndustEng), CDipAF, PhD); *Family* 4 c; *Career* served RAF 1964–66, invalided; apprentice then engr EMI Electronics Ltd 1966–77, industrial mgmnt conslt 1977–80 and 1984–92, dir and co-owner Seafarer Navigation International Ltd 1981–84, dir Bournemouth International Airport plc 1989–93; MP (Cons) Castle Point 1992–97 and 2001–; memb: Educn Select Ctee 1992–94, Bd Parly Office of Science and Technol 1993–97; PPS to Ann Widdecombe MP, *qv*, 1994–2005; dir Harold Whitehead & Partners Mgmnt Conslts 1997–; Dorset CC: cncllr 1985–93, dep ldr Cons Gp 1989–90, memb Dorset Police Authy 1985–93; MInstD; *Style*— Dr Bob Spink, MP; ✉ House of Commons, London SW1A 0AA (e-mail spinkr@parliament.uk)

SPITTLE, His Hon Judge Leslie; s of Samuel Spittle (d 1942), and Irene, *née* Smith; *b* 14 November 1940; *Educ* Acklam Hall GTS, Constantine Coll of Technol, Univ of Hull (LLB); *m* 7 Sept 1963, Brenda, da of Charles Alexander Clayton (d 1961); 3 s (Nicholas b 21 June 1968, Jonathan b 23 Sept 1971, Matthew b 14 Dec 1981); *Career* Univ of Hull Air Sqdn RAFVR; mgmnt trainee 1956–62, lectr and sr lectr Teeside Poly 1965–70; called to Gray's Inn 1970, recorder 1990–96, circuit judge (NE Circuit) 1996–; pres Magistrates' Assoc N Yorks; former chm Round Table; govr Univ of Teesside; ACIS 1960; *Recreations* travel, golf, various charitable bodies; *Clubs* Eaglescliffe Golf, Rotary (Teesside West, fndr pres); *Style*— His Hon Judge Spittle

SPITTLE, Dr Margaret Flora; OBE (2004); da of Edwin William Spittle (d 1977), and Ada Florence, *née* Axam; *b* 11 November 1939; *Educ* KCL (MSc, AKC), Westminster Hosp Med Sch; *m* 1, 2 Jan 1965 (m dis 1977), Clive Lucas Harmer, s of Cecil Norman Harmer (d 1986); 2 da (Kasha Jane Lucas b 1968, Victoria Margaret Lucas b 1971); m 2, 31 May 1986, David John Hare, s of John Robinson Hare (d 1982), of Southrepps, Norfolk; *Career* conslt clinical oncologist Meyerstein Inst of Clinical Oncology The Middx Hosp, St John's Dermatology Centre St Thomas' Hosp and Cromwell Hosp, Harley Street Cancer Centre 1971–; vice-pres and dean RCR 1994–97, vice-pres RSM 1994– (pres Oncology Section 1987, pres Radiology Section 1989, pres Open Section 2000), pres Head and Neck Oncologists of GB 1991; memb: Govt Ctee on Breast Screening, Nat Radiological Protection Bd, Govt Ctee on Med Aspects of Radiation in the Environment; tstee of many cancer charities; Freeman City of London, Liveryman Worshipful Soc of Apothecaries (memb Ctee); memb RSM; FRCP, FRCR; *Publications* many articles and chapters on breast cancer, head and neck and skin cancer and AIDS-related malignancies; *Recreations* family, golf, music, flying; *Clubs* RAC; *Style*— Dr Margaret Spittle, OBE; ✉ The Manor House, Beaconsfield, Claygate, Surrey KT10 0PW (tel 01372 465540, fax 01372 470470); Meyerstein Institute of Clinical Oncology, The Middlesex Hospital, Mortimer Street, London W1N 3AA (tel 020 7380 9090, fax 020 7436 0160)

SPIVEY, Dr Nigel Jonathan; s of Rev A J Spivey, and Jennifer, *née* Norman; *Educ* Caterham Sch, Emmanuel Coll Cambridge (Athletics blue), Br Sch Rome, Univ of Pisa; *Career* Emmanuel Coll Cambridge: res fell 1986–89, lectr in classics 1991–, fell 1991–; lectr in classics St David's Univ Coll 1989–91; Runciman Prize 1997; *Books* Understanding Greek Sculpture (1996), Greek Art (1997), Etruscan Art (1997), Enduring Creation (2001), The Ancient Olympics (2004), How Art Made the World (2005), Songs on Bronze (2005); *Recreations* discus throwing, vegetable growing, family; *Clubs* Achilles; *Style*— Dr Nigel Spivey; ✉ Emmanuel College, Cambridge CB2 3AP (tel 01223 334224, e-mail njs11@cam.ac.uk; c/o PFD, Drury House, 34–43 Russell Street, London WC2B 5HA

SPOFFORTH, (David) Mark; s of Michael Gordon Spofforth (d 1987), and Joan Mary, *née* Marsh; *b* 26 July 1956; *Educ* Bradfield Coll, Univ of Durham (BSc); *m* 31 July 1983, Dorothy Lesley, *née* Payne; 1 da (Gemma Mary b 17 Nov 1987), 1 s (Peter Michael b 25 Jan 1990); *Career* articled clerk Coopers & Lybrand 1980–82, managing ptnr Spofforths Chartered Accountants 1997–2000 (joined 1983, ptnr 1984–); ICAEW: memb Tech Ctee 1985–94, memb Cncl 1993– (chm 2003–05), memb Gen Practitioner Bd 1993–99 (chm 1995–98), memb Exec Ctee 1998–2007, memb Members' Directorate 1998–2000, chm Educn and Trg 2000–03 and 2005–07, memb Regulation Review Working Pty, 2005 Working Pty; SE Soc of Chartered Accountants: memb Main Ctee 1990–, dep pres 1998–99, pres 1999–2000; broadcaster BBC Southern Counties Radio; Freeman City of London, Renter Warden Worshipful Co of Horners 2007, memb Worshipful Co of Chartered Accountants; FCA 1982, CTA 2005; FRSA 1994; *Publications* Profitable and Sustainable Practice (report, 2003); *Recreations* rugby, skiing, scuba diving; *Clubs* City Livery, Carlton; *Style*— Mark Spofforth, Esq; ✉ Spofforths, Donnington Park, Birdham Road, Chichester, West Sussex PO20 7AJ (tel 01243 787627, fax 01243 532757, e-mail markspofforth@spofforths.co.uk)

SPOKES, Christopher Daniel; s of John Dacre Spokes (d 1976), and Joyce Margaret, *née* Sheppard (d 1998); *b* 29 July 1947; *Educ* Wellingborough Sch, Northampton Coll of Technol, Northampton Coll of Agric (NCA), Shuttleworth Coll (NDA), UCW Aberystwyth (BSc Econ); *m* May 1983, Gillian Stewart, da of Alec Neil Donaldson; 1 da (Charlotte Kate b April 1985), 1 s (Alexander James b Oct 1987); *Career* articled clerk Cooper Bros (later PricewaterhouseCoopers) 1973–76; Bidwells chartered surveyors: joined 1977, ptnr 1986–, currently chm Professional Services Div; pres: Cambridge Soc of Chartered Accountants 1990–91, E Anglian Soc of Chartered Accountants 1997–98; chm: Business Membs Gp E Anglian Soc of Chartered Accountants 1991–98, Regnl Strategy Bd ICAEW; govr Cambridge Regnl Coll; FCA 1981 (ACA 1976), FICPD; *Recreations* tennis, billiards, cinema, walking; *Clubs* Farmers; *Style*— Christopher Spokes, Esq; ✉ Brooklands House, 167 Caxton End, Bourn, Cambridge CB3 7ST (tel 01954 719288); Bidwells, Trumpington Road, Cambridge CB2 2LD (tel 01223 841841, fax 01223 559562, e-mail cspokes@bidwells.co.uk)

SPON-SMITH, Robin Witterick; s of Alan Witterick Spon-Smith (d 1997), and Joyce Margaret, *née* Bache (d 1988); *b* 11 October 1942; *Educ* Eltham Coll,Univ of Greenwich (LLM); *m* 11 June 1966, Jennifer Dorothy, da of William Frederic Delabere Walker; 2 s (Jolyon b 1973, Phillip b 1975); *Career* 1 Bn London Scottish (TA) 1960–65; admitted slr 1965, called to the Bar Inner Temple 1976; recorder 1987–; conslt ed Family Court Reporter 1996–99; memb President's Adoption Ctee 1996–; cncllr London Borough of Bromley 1968–71; govr Eltham Coll 1974–96; Freeman City of London 1980; *Books* Guide to Oaths and Affirmations, Rayden & Jackson on Divorce and Family Matters (specialist contrib 18 edn); *Style*— Robin Spon-Smith, Esq; ✉ 1 Hare Court, Temple, London EC4Y 7BE (tel 020 7797 7070, fax 020 7797 7435, e-mail rss@spon-smith.com)

SPOONER, Dr David; s of Rev Reginald H Spooner (d 1982), and Lucy Ellen, *née* Read; *b* 12 January 1949; *Educ* Magdalen Coll Sch Brackley, Univ of Birmingham (MB, BSc); *m* Diana Lilian, da of Frederick John Mason, of Banbury; 2 s (John, Andrew), 1 da (Rebecca); *Career* res fell Cancer Res Inst Sutton Surrey 1979–81, sr registrar in radiotherapy Royal Marsden Hosp London 1981–82 (registrar 1976–79); conslt in radiotherapy and oncology: Queen Elizabeth Hosp, Birmingham Children's Hosp, Royal Orthopaedic Hosp Birmingham; memb Cncl Royal Coll of Radiologists; FRCP, FRCR; *Style*— Dr David Spooner

SPOONER, Graham Michael; s of Ronald Sidney Spooner (d 1968), of Westcliff-on-Sea, Essex, and Kitty Margaret, *née* Cole (d 1985); *b* 23 August 1953; *Educ* Westcliff HS, St John's Coll Cambridge (MA); *m* Virginia Mary, *née* Barker; *Career* ICFC (now part of 3i Group plc): joined 1974, area mangr Nottingham 1983, local dir in London 1986, dir 3i plc 1987–93; head of corp fin Olliff & Partners plc 1993–95, dir Rea Brothers Limited 1995–96, nat dir of corp fin HLB Kidsons 1996–2000; dir: Downing Classic VCT plc 1999–2003, Downing Classic VCT 2 plc 2000–03, Downing Classic VCT 3 plc 2000–03, Classic Fund Mgmnt Ltd 2000–04, Mentor UK Ltd 2000–05, Dunn-Line plc 2004–06, Dowgate Capital plc 2007–; venture capital advsr to Cwlth Devpt Corporation 1993, special advsr UN Devpt Prog 1993; memb Treasy and Strategy Ctees Metropolitan Housing Tst 1998–99; tstee BDA Pension & Life Assurance Scheme 2005–; sr vice-patron Diabetes UK (memb Advsy Cncl 2003–, treas 2005–), dir Br Diabetic Assoc 2005–, chm Diabetes UK Servs Ltd 2006–, memb Ctee Johnian Soc 2007–; memb Devpt Bd RSA 2006–; FRSA 1998; *Publications* Raising Venture Capital, A Guide to Venture Capital for Accountants, The Corporate Finance Manual (ed, 2000–03), Venture Capital and Private Equity: A Practitioner's Manual (ed), A Practitioner's Guide to Venture Capital Law (contrib), The Director's Manual (contrib); memb ed bd Accountants Digest 1999–2002, memb Editorial Bd Corporate Money 1997–2000; *Recreations* rugby union, classic cars, heritage; *Clubs* Oxford and Cambridge; *Style*— Graham Spooner, Esq; ✉ 4 Barrow Court, Barrow Gurney, North Somerset BS48 3RP (tel 01275 463690); 22 Remington Street, London N1 8DH (tel 020 7490 8728, e-mail gmspooner@beeb.net)

SPOONER, Sir James Douglas; kt (1981); o s of Vice Adm Ernest John Spooner, DSO (d 1942), and Megan, *née* Foster (d 1987); *b* 11 July 1932; *Educ* Eton, ChCh Oxford; *m* 1958, Jane Alyson, da of Sir Gerald Glover (d 1986); 2 s, 1 da; *Career* former ptnr Dixon Wilson & Co; chm: Coats Viyella 1969–89, Morgan Crucible 1983–97; dir: John Swire & Sons 1970–2003, J Sainsbury 1981–94, Barclays Bank 1983–94; chm Tstees British Telecom Pension Scheme 1992–97, chm Navy Army and Air Force Inst 1973–86, dir ROH 1987–97; fell and chm Cncl KCL 1986–97, fell Eton Coll 1990–2002, govr Royal Acad of

Music 1996–2006; *Recreations* history, music; *Clubs* Beefsteak, Brooks's; *Style*— Sir James Spooner; ✉ The Chapel, Pytchley, Kettering, Northamptonshire NN14 1EN

SPOONER, Richard Hamilton; s of Derek Richard Spooner (d 1978), and Patricia Sackville, *née* Hamilton; *b* 17 February 1952; *Educ* King's Sch Ely, Lanchester Sch of Business Studies (BA); *m* 8 April 1978, Susan Elizabeth Ann, da of Anthony John Rowntree (d 1998); 3 da (Victoria, Catherine, Elizabeth); *Career* audit mangr Howard Tilly 1976–79, chief accountant Yeoman Aggregates Ltd 1979–83; dir: Yeoman Heavy Haulage Ltd 1980–83, Buckingham Computers Ltd 1981–84, HTA 1983–88; md: Howard Tilly Associates Ltd 1984–88, H T A Property Systems Ltd 1987–97; chm Baker Tilly Consulting 1988–; ptnr: Howard Tilly 1986–88, Baker Tilly 1988–; memb Acad of Experts; ACA, MInstD, MIMgt; *Recreations* golf, cricket, bridge, good food; *Style*— Richard Spooner, Esq; ✉ Orchard House, off Elkins Road, Hedgerley, Buckinghamshire (tel and fax 01753 645357); Baker Tilly, 2 Bloomsbury Street, London WC1B 3ST (tel 020 7413 5100, fax 020 7413 5101, e-mail richard.spooner@bakertilly.co.uk)

SPORBORG, Christopher Henry; CBE (2001); s of Henry Nathan Sporborg, CMG (d 1985), of Albury, Herts, and Mary, *née* Rowlands; *b* 17 April 1939; *Educ* Rugby, Emmanuel Coll Cambridge; *m* 1961, Lucinda Jane, da of Brig Richard Nigel Hanbury (d 1971), of Braughing, Herts; 2 da (Sarah (Mrs James Hopkins) b 1964, Eliza (Mrs James S de Uphaugh) b 1967), 2 s (William b 1965, Simon b 1972); *Career* Nat Serv Lt Coldstream Gds; Hambros Bank Ltd 1962–95; dep chm Hambros plc 1990–98 (dir 1983); chm: BFSS Investments Ltd 1980–2005, Atlas Copco Group in GB 1984–2005, Countrywide Assured Group plc 1986–, Hambro Insurance Services Group plc 1992–99, Racecourse Holdings Tst Ltd 1998–2003, Chesnara plc 2004–; dep chm C E Heath plc 1994–97; jt master Puckeridge Foxhounds; fin steward The Jockey Club 1995–97; landowner; *Recreations* racing, hunting (MFH); *Clubs* Boodle's, Jockey; *Style*— Christopher Sporborg, Esq, CBE; ✉ Brooms Farm, Upwick Green, Ware, Hertfordshire SG11 2JX (tel 01279 771444)

SPOTTISWOODE, Clare Mary Joan; CBE (1999); da of Tony Spottiswoode, and Charlotte Spottiswoode; *b* 20 March 1953; *Educ* Cheltenham Ladies' Coll, Clare Coll Cambridge (MA), Yale Univ (Mellon fellowship, MPhil); *m* 1977, Oliver Richards, s of Robin Richards; 3 da (Imogen b 15 Sept 1980, Camilla b 13 April 1982, Olivia b 8 May 1990), 1 s (Dominic b 9 Dec 1991); *Career* economist HM Treasy 1977–80, sole proprietor Spottiswoode Trading (import business) 1980–84, chm and md Spottiswoode & Spottiswoode (microcomputer software house) 1984–90, tutor London Business Sch and software conslt 1990–93, DG Ofgas 1994–98, sr vice-pres European Water Azurix 1998–99; chm: Buyenergyonline.com 2000–01, Economatters 2000–, Bergesen AG 2003–; non-exec dir: Booker plc 1995–2000, Caminus 2000–03, Advanced Technology UK 2000–, British Energy plc 2001–07 (ind dep chm 2002–), Tullow Oil plc 2002–, Busy Bees 2002–05, Biofuels Corporation 2004–07; memb Mgmnt Gp PA Consulting Gp 1999–2000, memb Bd of Dirs Bergesen AG 2003–; policy holder advocate Aviva 2006–; Hon DSSc Brunel Univ 1997; CIGE 1994; *Books* Quill (1984), Abacus (1984); *Recreations* children, gardening, theatre; *Style*— Ms Clare Spottiswoode, CBE

SPRAGUE, Christopher William; s of Coulam Alfred Joseph Sprague (d 1997), and Joan Gertrude, *née* Jackson (d 1986); *b* 19 August 1943; *Educ* St Edward's Sch Oxford, ChCh Oxford (MA); *m* 24 April 1971, Clare, da of Dr John Russell Bradshaw (d 1968), and Jennie Winifred, *née* Bruce-Rayner (d 2005); 4 da (Katharine b 1972, Alison b 1974, Hannah b 1979, Alexandra b 1981); *Career* articled Simmons & Simmons, admitted slr 1970, conslt Ince & Co (asst slr 1970–75, ptnr 1975–2004); specialist in insurance and maritime law, lectr on maritime law and assoc subjects; subscribing memb Assoc of Average Adjusters, supporting memb London Maritime Arbitrators Assoc, memb Law Soc; pres Thames Regnl Rowing Cncl 2005–06, chm Thames Regnl Umpires Cmmn 2003– (memb 1981–, sec 1981–88), holder FISA int rowing umpire's license; govr Royal Sch Haslemere 2001–; Freeman City of London, memb Ct of Assts Worshipful Co of Barbers (Master 2004–05), Liveryman City of London Solicitors' Co, Craft Owning Freeman Co of Watermen and Lightermen; *Recreations* reading, history, rowing; *Clubs* Oxford and Cambridge, London Rowing (chm 2006–), Leander; *Style*— C W Sprague, Esq; ✉ Pasturewood, Woodhill Lane, Shamley Green, Guildford, Surrey GU5 0SP (e-mail chris.sprague1@btinternet.com)

SPRATT, Prof Brian Geoffrey; s of Clarence Albert Spratt (d 1966), of Rye, E Sussex, and Marjory Alice, *née* Jeffreys (d 1999); *b* 21 March 1947; *Educ* Tonbridge, UCL (BSc, PhD); *m* 1, (m dis 1995), Jennifer Broome-Smith; 1 s (Timothy Peter b 22 April 1988); m 2, Jiaji Zhou; 1 s (Henry Jestyn b 16 Feb 1995); *Career* res fell Dept of Biochemical Scis Princeton Univ 1973–75, res fell Dept of Genetics Univ of Leicester 1975–80; Univ of Sussex: lectr in biochemistry 1980–87, reader 1987–89, prof of molecular genetics 1989–97; princ res fell Wellcome Tst 1989–, prof of biology Univ of Oxford 1997–2001, prof of molecular microbiology Imperial Coll London 2001–; hon prof LSHTM 2002–; chair: Wellcome Tst Infection and Immunity Panel 1995–98, Acad of Med Sciences Report on Academic Bacteriology in the 21st Century 2001, chair Royal Soc Report on Health Hazards of Depleted Uranium Munitions 2001–02; author of numerous publications on microbiology in learned jls; Squibb lectures Rutgers Univ 1985, RS Leeuwenhoek lecture 2003; Fleming Award Soc for Gen Microbiology 1982, Pfizer Academic Award 1983, Hoechst-Roussel Award American Soc for Microbiology 1993, Kitasato Medal for Microbial Chemistry 1995; FRS 1993, FMedSci 1998, fell American Acad of Microbiology 2003; *Style*— Prof Brian Spratt, FRS; ✉ Department of Infectious Disease Epidemiology, Imperial College London, St Mary's Hospital, London W2 1PG (tel 020 7594 3398, fax 020 7402 3927, e-mail b.spratt@imperial.ac.uk)

SPRATT, Sir Greville Douglas; GBE (1987), TD (1962, and bar 1968), JP (City Bench 1978), DL (Gtr London 1986); er s of Hugh Douglas Spratt, of Henley-on-Thames, Oxon, and Sheelah Ivy, *née* Stace; *b* 1 May 1927; *Educ* Leighton Park Sch Reading, Charterhouse, RMA Sandhurst; *m* 1954, Sheila Farrow (d 2002), yst da of late Joseph Wade, Langstone, Hants; 3 da; *Career* Coldstream Gds 1945–46, cmmnd 1946, seconded to Arab Legion, served Palestine, Jordan and Egypt 1946–48, GSO III (Ops and Intelligence); joined HAC as Private 1950, re-cmmnd 1950, Capt 1952, Maj 1954, CO (Lt-Col) 1962–65, Regtl Col 1966–70, memb Ct of Assts HAC 1960–70 and 1978–95; Lloyd's 1948–61 (underwriting memb 1950–98); J & N Wade Gp of Cos: joined 1961, dir 1969–76, md 1972–76 (when gp sold); regnl dir and chm (City and West End) National Westminster Bank 1989–92; dir: Williams Lea Gp 1989–96, Forest Mere Ltd 1991–95 (chm 1993–95), Charterhouse Enterprises Ltd 1989–95; chm Kingsmead Underwriting Agency Ltd (formerly Claremount Underwriting Agency Ltd until 1996) 1994–99; memb City TAVRA 1960– (vice-chm 1973–77, chm 1977–82), vice-pres TAVRA for Gtr London 1994– (memb Exec and Fin Ctee 1977–94, chm 1992–94); Hon Col: City and NE sector London ACF 1983–99, 8 Bn The Queen's Fusiliers 1988–92, The London Regt 1992–95; memb Cncl Reserve Forces Assoc 1981–84; pres: London Fedn of Old Comrades Assocs 1983–2003, Alzheimer's Disease Soc Haslemere; dep pres London Br Red Cross 1983–91 (vice-pres 1993–); patron Emily Appeal; memb: Blackdown Ctee Nat Tst 1977–87, Ctee GSM 1978–80 and 1989– (hon memb GSM 1988), Court City Univ 1981–95 (chllr 1987–88), Governing Bodies of Girls' Schs Assoc 1982–90, City of London Police Ctee 1989–91, Planning and Communications Ctee 1990–91, Surrey Scout Cncl 1990–; govr: St Ives Sch 1976– (vice-chm 1977–86, chm 1986–90), King Edward's Sch Witley 1978– (vice-pres 1989–95), Christ's Hosp 1978–95, Bridewell Royal Hosp 1978–95, City of London Sch for Girls 1981–82, Malvern Girls' Coll 1982–90, St Paul's Cathedral Sch 1985–99, Charterhouse 1985–99 (chm Governing Body 1989–95), City of London Freemen's Sch 1992–95; life govr Corp of the Sons of the Clergy 1985–, patron Int Centre for Child Studies 1985–, vice-pres Not Forgotten Assoc 1990–; Royal Br Legion: pres Haslemere 1989–, vice-pres St James' 1991–99; chm: Action Research 1989–99 (memb Haslemere Ctee 1971–82, memb Cncl 1982–), Ct of Advsrs St Paul's Cathedral 1993–99, Anglo Jordanian Soc 1994–97, Wildlife Conservation Fndn 1996–, Carthusian Soc; memb Anglo-Arab Assoc; ADC to HM The Queen 1973–78, Alderman City of London (Castle Baynard Ward) 1978–95, Sheriff City of London 1984–85, Lord Mayor of London 1987–88; church cmmr 1993–95; tstee: Chichester Theatre, Chichester Cathedral, Endowment of St Paul's Cathedral, Children's Res Int, Trekforce; special tstee St Bartholomew's Hosp 1990–95, patron Surrey Charity Gp 1989–93; Freeman City of London 1977, Liveryman Worshipful Co of Ironmongers 1977 (Master 1995–96); Hon DLitt City Univ 1988; FRSA, KStJ 1987 (OStJ 1985), FRGS; Chevalier de la Légion d'Honneur 1961, Commandeur de l'Ordre Nationale du Mérite (France) 1984, Cdr Order of the Lion (Malawi) 1985, memb Nat Order of Aztec Eagle (Mexico) 1985, Order of Merit (Norway) 1988, Order of Merit (Senegal) 1988; *Recreations* tennis, music, military history, stamp, coin and bank note collecting; *Clubs* United Wards, City Livery, Guildhall; *Style*— Sir Greville Spratt, GBE, TD, DL; ✉ Rowans, Pathfields Close, Haslemere, Surrey GU27 2BL (tel 01428 664367)

SPRENT, Prof Janet Irene; OBE (1996); da of James William Findlater, and Dorothy May Findlater; *b* 10 January 1934; *Educ* Slough HS for Girls, Imperial Coll of Science and Technol London (BSc, ARCS), Univ of Tasmania (PhD), Univ of London (DSc); *m* 1955, Peter Sprent; *Career* scientific offr Rothamsted Experimental Station 1954–55, ICIANZ research fell Univ of Tasmania 1955–58, botany mistress Rochester Girl's GS 1959–61, lectr then sr lectr Goldsmiths Coll London 1960–67; Univ of Dundee: successively research fell, lectr, sr lectr and reader 1967–89, dean Faculty of Sci and Engineering 1987–89, prof of plant biology 1989–, head Dept of Biological Scis 1992–95, dep princ 1995–98; hon research prof Scottish Crop Research Inst 1991–; chm of govrs Macaulay Land Use Research Inst 1995–2001 (govr 1990–); various overseas visits and int meetings in respect of nitrogen fixing crops and tree research; memb: NERC 1991–95, Scottish HEFC 1992–96, Jt Nature Conservation Ctee 1993–2000 and 2005–07, Panel for Individual Merit Promotions UK Research Cncl 1992–98, Bd Scottish Natural Heritage 2001–, Royal Cmmn on Environmental Pollution 2002–, Scottish Cncl for Marine Science 2005–, Strategic Science Advsy Panel SEERAD 2006–; tstee Royal Botanic Gardens Edinburgh 2007–; hon memb Br Ecological Soc; memb: Soc for Experimental Biology, Soc for Gen Microbiology, Botanical Soc of Scotland, Aust Soc of Plant Physiologists; emeritus prof, Leverhulme fell 1998–2000; FLS, FRSA, FRSE 1990; *Books* The Ecology of the Nitrogen Cycle (1987), Nitrogen Fixing Organisms: Pure and Applied Aspects (with P Sprent, 1990), Advances in Legume Systematics, 5. The Nitrogen Factor (co-ed with D McKey, 1994), Nodulation in Legumes (2001); numerous book chapters and papers in scientific jls; *Recreations* hill walking, gardening, music; *Style*— Prof Janet Sprent, OBE, FRSE; ✉ 32 Birkhill Avenue, Wormit, Newport on Tay, Fife DD6 8PW (tel 01382 541706, fax 01382 542989, e-mail jisprent@aol.com); School of Life Sciences, University of Dundee, Dundee DD1 4HN

SPRING, Richard John Grenville; MP; s of late H J A Spring, and late Marjorie, *née* Watson-Morris; *b* 24 September 1946; *Educ* Rondebosch, Univ of Cape Town, Magdalene Coll Cambridge; *m* 13 Dec 1979 (m dis 1993), Hon Jane Henniker-Major, da of 8 Baron Henniker, KCMG, CVO, MC, DL (d 2004); 1 s, 1 da; *Career* vice-pres Merrill Lynch Ltd 1976–86 (joined 1971), dep md Hutton International Associates 1986–88, exec dir Shearson Lehman Hutton 1988–90, md Xerox Furman Selz 1990–92; Parly candidate (Cons) Ashton-under-Lyne 1983; MP (Cons): Bury St Edmunds 1992–97, Suffolk W 1997–; PPS to: Sir Patrick Mayhew (as Sec of State for NI) 1994–95, Rt Hon Tim Eggar (as Min of State DTI) 1996, Hon Nicholas Soames and James Arbuthnot (as Mins of State MOD) 1996–97; oppn frontbench spokesman on culture, media and sport 1997–2000, oppn frontbench spokesman on foreign and Cwlth affrs 2000–04, oppn frontbench treasury spokesman 2004–05, vice-chm Cons Pty 2006–; memb House of Commons Select Ctee for Employment 1992–94, memb House of Commons Select Ctee for NI 1994–97, memb Home Affrs Select Ctee 2006–07, vice-chm Cons Backbench Arts and Heritage Ctee 1992–94, jt sec N Ireland Cons Backbench Ctee 1993–95, vice-chm All Pty Racing and Bloodstock Gp 1996–97, co-chm Cons City Circle 2006–, jt sec All Pty Drugs Misuse Gp; Small Business Bureau: vice-chm 1992–97, dep chm 1997–, chm of its Parly Advsy Gp 1992–; govr Westminster Fndn for Democracy 2000–; held various offices Westminster Cons Assoc 1976–87; dir Br-Syrian Soc 2003–, chm Br-Ukranian Soc 2007–; *Recreations* country pursuits, tennis, swimming; *Clubs* Boodle's; *Style*— Richard Spring, Esq, MP; ✉ House of Commons, London SW1A 0AA (tel 020 7219 5192, website www.richardspringmp.com)

SPRING, Stephanie (Stevie); da of William Harold Spring (d 2001), and Marlene Green, *née* Coleman; *b* 10 June 1957, London; *Educ* Eggars GS Alton, Univ of Kent (LLB); *Career* mktg mangr Alpine Holdings 1978–82, devpt mangr TVam 1982–84, business dir Grey Advertising 1984–88, dep md GGT 1988–92; md: WMGO 1992–94, Young & Rubicam 1994–2000; ceo: Clear Channel UK 2000–06, Future plc 2006–; chm Fedn of Groundwork Tsts 2000–; tstee: Nat Advtg Benevolent Soc (NABS) 1990–, Arts and Business 2006–; fell: Inst of Practitioners in Advtg 1996, Mktg Soc 2004; *Recreations* socialising, swimming, spinning; *Clubs* Soho House, Women's Advtg, Blake 7; *Style*— Ms Stevie Spring; ✉ Future plc, 2 Balcombe Street, London NW1 6NW (tel 020 7042 4000, e-mail sspring@futurenet.co.uk)

SPRING RICE, Hon Charles James; s and h of 6 Baron Monteagle of Brandon; *b* 24 February 1953; *Educ* Harrow; *m* 1987, Mary Teresa Glover; 4 da (Helena Maire b 1987, Charlotte Etain b 1988, Agnes Imogen b 1991, Thea Teresa b 1995); *Career* secdy sch teacher; currently head English Dept Holy Family Coll Walthamstow London 1992–; *Style*— Charles Spring Rice, Esq; ✉ 26 Malvern Road, London E8 3LP

SPRINGMAN, Prof Sarah Marcella; OBE (1997); *b* 26 December 1956; *Educ* Wycombe Abbey, Univ of Cambridge (Roscoe meml prize, coll prize, MA, MPhil, PhD, Squash blue, played in 11 Varsity matches in 6 different sports); *Career* Univ of Cambridge OTC TA: commissioned 1978, trg offr 1978, cmd Royal Engineer Wing 1980 and 1983–85, Lt 1980, Capt 1983–85; Sir Alexander Gibb & Partners: various positions Geotechnical Dept, seconded to Public Works Dept and Monasavu Hydro-Electric Scheme Fiji, Adelaide and Canberra Offices 1975–83; Univ of Cambridge: SERC studentship Dept of Engrg 1983–84, research asst Soil Mechanics Gp Dept of Engrg 1985–89, res fell Magdalene Coll 1988–90, lectr Soil Mechanics Gp 1993–96 (asst lectr 1990–93), fell and college lectr in soil mechanics Magdalene Coll 1991–96, chair and initiator Language Prog for Engrs 1992–96; prof of geotechnical engrg Inst for Geotechnical Engrg Eidgenössische Technische Hochschule (ETH) Zürich 1997–, head Inst of Geotechnical Engrg 2001–05; memb EPSRC Peer Review Coll 2006–; memb: Women's Engrg Soc 1983, British Geotechnical Assoc 1988, Swiss Geotechnical Soc 1998, Swiss Natural Hazards Competence Centre 1998–, Swiss Engineers and Architects 1999, Swiss Sci and Technol Cncl 2000–07; govr: Marlborough Coll 1991–95, Wycombe Abbey Sch 1993–96; CEng, MIRE 1990, life fell RSA 2005, FICE 2006 (MICE 1983); *Sporting Career* 11 times British Triathlon champion, European Triathlon champion 1985, 1986 and 1988, 5 European Team Gold medals, S Pacific Squash champion 1982, champion Swiss Open Quadruple Sculls 1998, 2000 and 2003, champion Swiss Open Eights 1999, 2000, 2001, 2002 and 2003, vice-pres Int Triathlon Union 1992–96 (co-chair Women's Cmmn 1990–92), govr World Masters Games 1992–2002, memb GB Sports Cncl 1993–96 (UK Sports Cncl 1997–2001), memb Exec Bd Br Triathlon Assoc 2005–06, pres and chair Bd Br Triathlon

Fedn 2007–, chair ETHZ Natural Hatands Gp, memb Mgmnt Bd ETH Competence Centre for Environmental Sustainability 2007–; Cosmopolitan-Clairol Women of Achievement Award 1991; *Publications* Constitutive and Centrifuge Modelling: Two Extremes (ed, 2002), Permafrost (jt ed, 2003); *Clubs* Rob Roy Boat, Cambridge Triathlon, Belvoir Ruder; *Style*— Prof Sarah Springman, OBE; ✉ Institut für Geotechnik, Eidgenössische Technische Hochschule, Zürich CH 8093, Switzerland (tel 00 41 44 633 3805, fax 00 41 44 633 1079, e-mail sarah.springman@igt.baug.ethz.ch)

SPROAT, Iain MacDonald; s of William and Lydia Sproat; *b* 8 November 1938; *Educ* Melrose, Winchester, Magdalen Coll Oxford; *m* 1979, Judith Kernot, *née* King; 1 step s (Charles); *Career* MP (Cons) Aberdeen S 1970–83, Parly candidate Roxburgh and Berwickshire 1983, MP (Cons) Harwich 1992–97; PPS to sec of state for Scotland 1973–74; memb: Br Parly Delgn to oversee S Vietnamese Elections 1973, Br Parly Delgn to Soviet Union 1974; chm Soviet & East Euro Gp of Cons Foreign Affairs Ctee 1975–81; leader Cons Gp on Scottish Select Ctee 1979–81, chm Scottish Cons Ctee 1979–81; leader Br Parly Delgn to Austria 1980; Parly under-sec of state Dept of Trade 1981–83; special advsr to PM Gen Election 1987, Parly under-sec of state Dept of National Heritage 1993–95, min of state Dept of National Heritage 1995–97; conslt N M Rothschild & Sons Merchant Bankers Ltd 1983–; chm: Milner and Co Ltd, Cricketers' Who's Who Ltd; former dir D'Arcy Masius Benton and Bowles Ltd, dir Coll of Petroleum Studies Oxford; tstee: African Medical and Research Fndn 1987–, Scottish Self-Governing Schs Tst; Cricket Writer of the Year Wombwell Cricket Lovers' Soc 1983; *Books* Cricketers' Who's Who (ed annually, 1980–), Wodehouse at War (1981), Edward Heath - A Pictorial Biography, The British Prime Ministers (contrib); with Adam Sykes: The Wit of Sir Winston, The Wit of Westminster, The Wit of the Wig, The Harold Wilson Bunkside Book, The Cabinet Bedside Book; *Clubs* Oxford and Cambridge; *Style*— Iain Sproat, Esq

SPROTT, Duncan; s of Hugh Sprott, and Brenda, *née* Grieves; *b* 2 December 1952; *Educ* Newport GS Essex, Univ of St Andrews, Heatherley Sch of Art; *Career* writer; *Books* 1784 (1984), The Clopton Hercules (1991, US title The Rise of Mr Warde), Our Lady of the Potatoes (1995), Sprottichronicon (2000), The Ptolemies Quartet: The House of the Eagle (2004), Daughter of the Crocodile (2006); *Style*— Duncan Sprott, Esq; ✉ c/o Rogers, Coleridge & White Ltd, 20 Powis Mews, London W11 1JN (tel 020 7221 3717, fax 020 7229 9084)

SPRY, Christopher John; CBE (2002); s of Reginald Charles Spry (d 1962), and Kathleen Edith, *née* Hobart (d 2005); *b* 29 August 1946; *Educ* Sir Roger Manwood's Sch Sandwich, Univ of Exeter (BA); *m* 1, 1968 (m dis 1989), Jean Banks; 2 s (Matthew Alan b 16 Aug 1974, Michael John b 24 Nov 1978); *m* 2, 1989, Judith Christina, *née* Ryder; *Career* nat trainee 1967–69, admin asst Doncaster Royal Infirmary 1969–70, dep hosp sec Lewisham Hosp 1970–73, hosp sec Nottingham Gen Hosp 1973–75, dist admin S Nottingham 1978–81 (asst dist admin 1975–78), dist gen mangr Newcastle HA 1984–89 (dist admin 1981–84), regnl gen mangr SW Thames RHA 1989–94, regnl dir S Thames Region of NHS Executive 1994–96, chief exec Gtr Glasgow Health Bd 1996–2001, dir OD Partnerships Network 2001–, visiting prof Univ of Glasgow 2001–, non-exec dir W Dorset Hosps NHS Tst 2005–; MIHSM 1972; *Recreations* books, enjoying townscapes, travel, keeping fit; *Style*— Christopher J Spry, Esq, CBE; ✉ OD Partnerships Network, 2 Braemar Gardens, West Wickham BR4 0JW (tel 020 8916 9855, e-mail chrisspry@odpn.co.uk)

SPUFFORD, Francis; s of Peter Spufford, LittD, FBA, and Margaret Spufford, LittD, FBA; *b* 1964; *Career* freelance author and broadcaster; regular appearances on BBC Radio 4; regular contrib Condé Nast Traveller magazine; Young Writer of the Year Sunday Times 1977; FRSL 2007; *Publications* as ed: The Chatto Book of Cabbages and Kings: Lists in Literature (1989), The Chatto Book of the Devil (1992), Cultural Babbage: Technology, Time and Invention (with Jenny Uglow, 1996), The Vintage Book of the Devil (1997); as author: I May Be Some Time: Ice and the English Imagination (1996, Best Non-Fiction Book Writers' Guild Award 1996, Somerset Maugham Award 1997), The Child That Books Built (2002), The Backroom Boys: The Secret Return of the British Boffin (2003); *Style*— Francis Spufford, Esq; ✉ c/o Faber and Faber Ltd, 3 Queen Square, London WC1N 3AU

SPUFFORD, Prof Peter; s of Douglas Henry Spufford (d 1967), and Nancy Gwendoline, *née* Battagel; *b* 18 August 1934; *Educ* Kingswood Sch Bath, Jesus Coll Cambridge (MA, PhD, LittD); *m* 7 July 1962, Prof Margaret Spufford, *née* Clark; 1 s (Francis Peter b 22 April 1964), 1 da (Bridget Margaret b 17 April 1967 d 1989); *Career* research fell Jesus Coll Cambridge 1958–60, asst lectr rising to reader Dept of History Keele Univ 1960–79 (sometime actg head of dept), lectr, reader in economic history then prof of European history Faculty of History Univ of Cambridge 1979–2001 (emeritus prof 2001–), fell Queens' Coll Cambridge 1979–; chm Br Records Soc 1985– (sec 1960–79, sometime gen ed), vice-pres Soc of Genealogists 1997–; Medal Royal Numismatic Soc 2005; FRHistS 1968, FSA 1990, FBA 1994; *Books* incl: Origins of the English Parliament (1967), Monetary Problems in the Burgundian Netherlands (1970), Handbook of Medieval Exchange (1986), Money and its use in Medieval Europe (1988), Profit and Power: The Merchant in Medieval Europe (2002); *Style*— Prof Peter Spufford; ✉ Queens' College, Cambridge CB3 9ET (tel 01223 335511, fax 01223 335522, e-mail ps44@cam.ac.uk)

SPURLING, (Susan) Hilary; CBE (2007); da of Judge Gilbert Alexander Forrest (d 1977), and Emily Maureen, *née* Armstrong; *b* 25 December 1940; *Educ* Clifton HS Bristol, Somerville Coll Oxford; *m* 4 April 1961, John Spurling; 1 da (Amy Maria b 1972), 2 s (Nathaniel Stobart b 1974, Gilbert Alexander Fettiplace b 1977); *Career* Spectator: arts ed 1964–69, lit ed 1966–69; book reviewer: The Observer 1970–87 and 2006–, Daily Telegraph 1987–2006; *Books* Ivy When Young - The Early Life of I Compton-Burnett 1884–1919 (1974), Handbook to Anthony Powell's Music of Time (1977), Secrets of a Women's Heart - The Later Life of I Compton-Burnett 1919–69 (1984), Elinor Fettiplace's Receipt Book (1986), Paul Scott: a life (1990), Paper Spirits (1992), The Unknown Matisse - A Life of Henri Matisse, Vol 1 1869–1908 (1998), La Grande Thérèse (1999), The Girl from the Fiction Dept (2002), Matisse The Master: A Life of Henri Matisse vol 2 1909–1954 (2005, Whitbread Book of the Year and Whitbread Biography Prize); *Style*— Ms Hilary Spurling, CBE; ✉ David Higham Associates, 5–8 Lower John Street, Golden Square, London W1R 4HA

SPURLING, John Antony; s of Antony Cuthbert Spurling (d 1984), and Elizabeth Frances, *née* Stobart (d 1990); *b* 17 July 1936; *Educ* Dragon Sch, Marlborough, St John's Coll Oxford (BA); *m* 4 April 1961, Susan Hilary, da of Gilbert Alexander Forrest; 1 da (Amy Maria b 6 May 1972), 2 s (Nathaniel Stobart b 31 May 1974, Gilbert Alexander Fettiplace b 2 Dec 1977); *Career* Nat Serv 2 Lt RA 1955–57; plebiscite offr Southern Cameroons 1960–61, BBC Radio announcer 1963–66, freelance writer and broadcaster 1966–, Henfield writing fell Univ of E Anglia 1973, art critic The New Statesman 1976–88; playwright and novelist; *Plays* for stage: Macrune's Guevara (NT) 1969, In the Heart of the British Museum (Traverse Edinburgh) 1971, The British Empire Part One (Birmingham Repertory) 1980, Coming Ashore in Guadeloupe (Cherub Co Harrogate, Edinburgh and London) 1982–83, Racine at the Girls' Sch (Cheltenham Literary Festival) 1992, King Arthur in Avalon (Cheltenham Literary Festival) 1999, Robinson Crusoe Meets His Maker (HM Prison Albany) 2003; for BBC Radio 3: Dominion Over Palm and Pine 1982, The Christian Hero 1982, The Day of Reckoning 1985, Discobolus 1989, The Butcher of Baghdad 1993 (also staged by Cherub Co London 1993), Macrune's Guevara 1993, Heresy 2001; for BBC Radio 4: Fancy Pictures 1988, A Household in Hove 2002; *Novels* The Ragged End (1989), After Zenda (1995); *Style*— John Spurling, Esq;

✉ MacNaughton Lord 2000 Ltd, 19 Margravine Gardens, London W6 8RL (tel 020 8741 0606, fax 020 8741 7443, e-mail info@ml2000.org.uk)

SPURRELL, Dr Roworth Adrian John; s of Ivor Pritchard Spurrell (d 1968), and Marjorie, *née* Cheney; *b* 27 May 1942; *Educ* Oundle, Univ of London (MD, BSc, MB BS); *m* 28 April 1973, Susan Jane, da of George Kemp (d 1984); 2 da (Emma Louise, Clare Alexandra); *Career* registrar in cardiology: St George's Hosp London 1969–70, Nat Heart Hosp 1970–71; sr registrar in Cardiology Guy's Hosp 1971–74, conslt in charge of cardiology Bart's Hosp 1976–2001 (conslt 1974–2001) ret; FRCP, FACC; *Recreations* sailing, flying; *Clubs* Royal Yacht Sqdn, RAF; *Style*— Dr Roworth Spurrell; ✉ Suite 501, 50 Wimpole Street, London W1M 7DG (tel 020 7935 3922)

SPURRIER, Steven; s of John Spurrier (d 1988), of Derbys, and Pamela, *née* Neame (d 2002); *b* 5 October 1941, Cambridge; *Educ* Rugby, LSE (BSc); *m* 31 Jan 1968, Arabella, *née* Lawson; 1 s (Christian b 21 Feb 1971), 1 da (Kate b 10 July 1973); *Career* entered London wine trade 1964; prop: Caves de la Madeleine Paris (wine shop) 1970–88, L'Academie du Vin Paris 1973–88 (hosted California wine tasting 'The Judgement of Paris' 1976); ind wine conslt 1988–, clients incl Harrods, Delta Air Lines, Hediard and Singapore Airlines; fndr Christie's Wine Course London 1982; conslt ed Decanter magazine; chm Decanter Wine Awards and Japan Wine Challenge, judge int wine competitions; pres Circle of Wine Writers (formerly chm and vice-pres); *Books* incl: L'Academie du Vin Wine Course, L'Academie du Vin Guide to French Wines, How to Buy Fine Wine, The Clarke-Spurrier Fine Wine Guide (with Oz Clarke, qv, 1999, new edn 2001); *Recreations* looking at and collecting art, drinking wine; *Clubs* Boodle's, Chelsea Arts; *Style*— Steven Spurrier, Esq; ✉ 10 Playfair Mansions, Queen's Club Gardens, London W14 9TR (tel 020 7385 3855, fax 020 7385 4059, e-mail steven@stevenspurrier.com); Decanter, The Blue Fin Building, 110 Southwark Street, London SE1 0SU (tel 020 3148 5000, fax 020 3148 8524, website www.decanter.com)

SPURRIER-KIMBELL, David Henry; s of Norman Kenneth Bernard Kimbell, FRCOG (d 1982), of Warmington, Northants, and Mary Pamela, da of Sir Henry Spurrier; *b* 24 September 1944; *Educ* Oundle, Heidelberg Univ; *m* 25 July 1970, Maureen Patricia, da of Dr Eric Charles Elliot Golden; 2 da (Antonia b 1977, Deborah b 1979), 1 s (Henry b 1986); *Career* Br Leyland Motor Corp Ltd 1966–78, overseas dir Leyland Vehicles Ltd 1978; Spencer Stuart & Associates Ltd: joined 1979, int ptnr 1983, md UK 1985, int chm 1987–2003, UK chm 1992–; *Recreations* golf, tennis; *Clubs* Oriental; *Style*— David Spurrier-Kimbell, Esq; ✉ Chalkpit House, Ecchinswell, Hampshire RG20 4UQ (tel 01635 298269); Spencer Stuart & Associates Ltd, 16 Connaught Place, London W2 2ED (tel 020 7298 3333)

SPURWAY, (Marcus) John; s of Marcus Humphrey Spurway (d 1994), of Goudhurst, Kent, and Eva, *née* Mann (d 1980); *b* 28 October 1938; *Educ* Archbishop Tenison's Sch Croydon; *m* 23 Oct 1963, Christine Kate, da of Robert Charles Townshend (d 1981), of Canterbury, Kent; 2 s (Marcus John Charles b 1967, Edward Lewis David b 1969); *Career* Nat Serv 4 Regt RHA; insurance broker; dir Morgan Reid & Sharman Ltd (Lloyd's brokers, formerly B & C Aviation Insurance Brokers), ret 1999; specialist in aviation insurance; *Books* Aviation Insurance Abbreviations, Organisations and Institutions (1983), Aviation Insurance, The Market and Underwriting Practice (1991), Aviation Law and Claims (1992); *Style*— John Spurway, Esq; ✉ Lomeer, Common Road, Sissinghurst, Kent TN17 2JR

SPYER, Prof (Kenneth) Michael (Mike); s of Harris Spyer (d 1982), and Rebecca, *née* Jacobs (d 1982); *b* 15 September 1943; *Educ* Coopers Company's Sch, Univ of Sheffield (BSc), Univ of Birmingham (PhD, DSc); *m* 25 Aug 1971, Christine, da of John Roland Spalton; 2 s (Simon Jeremy b 20 Nov 1976, Nicholas Henry b 26 Oct 1979); *Career* res fell Dept of Physiology Univ of Birmingham Med Sch 1969–72, Royal Soc Euro prog fell Instituto di Fisiologia Umana Pisa 1972–73, sr res fell Department of Physiology Univ of Birmingham Med Sch 1978–80 (res fell 1973–78); Royal Free Hosp Sch of Med (RFHSM): Sophia Jex-Blake prof of physiology Dept of Physiology 1980–, dir British Heart Fndn Neural Control Gp 1985–, chm Basic Med Sciences 1991–94; head Depts of Physiology RFHSM and UCL 1994–99, dir Autonomic Neuroscience Inst RFHSM 1997–; (dean Royal Free & UC Med Sch 2001–06 (dean Royal Free Campus 1998–2001), vice-provost (enterprise) UCL 2006– (vice-provost (biomedicine) 2002–07); Crisp lectr Univ of Leeds 1988, Glaxo lectr Dept of Pharmacology Univ of Edinburgh 1993; visiting prof: Univ of Shanghai 1989, Georg-August Univ Göttingen 1990, Northwestern Univ Chicago 1990, Univ Vittoria Brazil 1991; Annual Review Lecture Physiological Soc 1994, Carl Ludwig Lecture American Physiological Society 1998; chm: Physiological/Pharmacological Panel Wellcome Tst 1993–96, Euro Biomedical Research Assoc 1996–; memb Ctee: Animal Procedures Home Office 1990–98, Benevolent Fund Physiological Soc 1993–99; memb Scientific Panel Brain Research Tst 1993–99, hon life memb Centre for Neuroscience UCL 1984, field ed News in Physiological Science 1992–96; Wolfson Univ Award 1989–92; Hon MD Univ of Lisbon 1991; memb: Physiological Soc 1972–, Brain Research Assoc 1973–, Euro Neuroscience Assoc 1976–, Research Defence Soc 1976– (hon sec 1986–89), Int Brain Research Orgn 1980–, Harveian Soc 1983– (hon sec 1987–89), Zoological 1983–96, Clinical Autonomic Soc 1983–, German Physiological Soc 1984–93, Soc for Neuroscience 1986–, American Physiological Soc 1997–; author of numerous pubns in learned jls; Hon FRCP 2002, FMedSci; *Recreations* armchair sports, fly fishing, travelling (particularly in Italy), gardening, books, fine arts; *Style*— Prof Mike Spyer; ✉ University College London, Gower Street, London WC1E 6BT (tel 020 7679 9851, fax 020 7679 9852, e-mail k.spyer@ucl.ac.uk)

SQUIRE, David Michael; s of Denis Arthur Squire (d 1999), of Esher, Surrey, and (Patricia) Mary Joyce, *née* Davis; *b* 26 February 1949; *Educ* St Edward's Sch Oxford, UC Oxford (MA); *m* 1 June 1974, Karen StClair, da of Peter Edward Hook (d 1982); 3 da (Isabelle b 1976, Eleanor b 1980, Madeline b 1982); *Career* CA 1973; ptnr PricewaterhouseCoopers (formerly Price Waterhouse before merger) 1981– 2000 (joined London Office 1970), ldr Assurance and Business Advsy Servs Bahrain 1998–2000, chm Soc Genealogist Enterprises Ltd 2001–03, dir Zernike (UK) Ltd 2001–, non-exec dir NW London Hospitals NHS Tst 2005–; tstee Ealing Jr Music Sch 1996–2001, govr Notting Hill and Ealing HS 2003–; FCA 1979, FSG 1998; *Recreations* sailing, tennis, family history, hill walking; *Clubs* Bahrain Yacht (treas 1998–2000), Redclyffe Yacht; *Style*— David Squire, Esq; ✉ 2 St Stephen's Avenue, London W13 8ES (tel 020 8997 5906, fax 020 8998 2708, e-mail david@squireuk.com); Zernike (UK) Ltd, The Grove, High Street, Sawston, Cambridge CB2 4HT (tel 01223 528980, e-mail dsquire@zernikeuk.com)

SQUIRE, Giles; professional name of Peter Giles Eyre-Tanner; s of Peter Ralph Eyre-Tanner, of Oak Tree House, Bucks, and Jean Rae, *née* Beaver; *b* 7 February 1954; *Educ* Wellington; *m* 2, 21 May 1988, Julie Anne, da of Brian Jay Stokoe; 1 s (Giles Lawrence b 14 Aug 1980), 1 da (Lucy Victoria b 28 July 1989); *Career* head of special programming UBN 1973–74 (disc jockey 1970–73), songwriter 1980–84; Metro Radio: joined 1974, sr presenter 1983–84, presentation prodr 1984–87, sr prodr 1987, asst prog controller 1987–88, prog controller Metro FM 1988–89, assoc dir of progs 1989–91, prog controller Metro FM and GNR 1991–97, prog dir Metro FM 1992–97, gp controller Tyne Tees 1993, formerly md TFM Radio (part of EMAP plc), gp prog dir Radio Partnership Ltd 1997–99, gp prog dir Forever Broadcasting plc 2000–; Sony Best Pop Prog award 1987; memb: Performing Rights Soc, BASCA, Equity; *Style*— Giles Squire, Esq

SQUIRE, Prof John Michael; s of George Victor Vincent Squire (d 1998), and Mary Hilton, *née* Clarke (d 1999); *b* 27 June 1945; *Educ* Fettes, KCL (BSc, AKC, PhD); *m* 12 Aug 1969, Melanie Rae, *née* Chandy; 4 da (Deborah Rae b 1 Nov 1970, Emily Jane b 17 July 1973, Katherine Emma b 29 Sept 1975, Beth Mary b 30 Dec 1979); *Career* amanuensis and lektor Biophysics Inst Aarhus Univ 1969–71 (chm Governing Body Biophysics Inst 1971), visitor Biophysics Dept KCL 1971, higher scientific offr AFRC Muscle Unit Dept of Zoology Univ of Oxford 1972; Imperial Coll London: lectr and head Biopolymer Gp 1972–82, MRC fell 1982–84, reader in biophysics and head Muscle Gp Dept of Materials Science 1982–83 and Dept of Physics 1983–95, prof of structural biophysics Biophysics Gp Dept of Physics 1995–99, prof of structural biophysics Biomedical Sciences Division 1999–, dep head of div (teaching) 2000–03, head Biological Structure and Function Section; Univ of London: memb Bd of Studies in Biophysics, memb Special Advsy Ctee in Crystallography; visiting scientist NIH Washington DC 1986, Japan Soc for the Promotion of Science fell Tohoku Univ 1987; fndr and chm Imperial Muscle Initiative 2002–, fndr and occasional organiser London Muscle Conf; invited lectr at numerous courses and confs; chm: SRFC Beam Allocation Panel F 1989–92, Biological Structures Gp Br Crystallographic Assoc (BCA) 1990–94, MRC/EPSRC/BBSRC Biology Section Panel 1994–97; memb: SERC Biological Sciences Ctee Advsy Gp IV 1979–82, MRC Assessment Panel for Research and Advanced Course Studentships 1985–88, Cncl BCA 1987–95, SERC Synchrotron Radiation Facilities Ctee 1989–92, MRC/SERC Jt Review Ctee for Biology at Daresbury 1992–94, SERC Biological Sciences Ctee 1993–94, MRC/EPSRC/BBSRC/CCLRC Biology Jt Review Ctee 1994–97, EPSRC/BBSRC Collaborative Computing Projects Panel 1995–99 and 2002–, Synchrotron Radiation Users Forum (SRSUF) 1996–97; ed The Fibre Diffraction Review, former ed Crystallography News; memb Editorial Bd: Jl of Muscle Research and Motility, Jl of Structural Biology, Reports on Progress in Physics; memb: AUT 1972, Br Biophysical Soc 1974, Biophysical Soc of America 1977, BCA 1982, Anatomical Soc 1999; CPhys, CBiol, FRMS 1977, FInstP 1999, FIBiol 2001; *Publications* The Structural Basis of Muscular Contraction (1981), Muscle: Design, Diversity and Disease (1986), Fibrous Protein Structure (ed with P J Vibert, 1987), Molecular Mechanisms in Muscular Contraction (ed, 1990); also author of over 100 scientific pubns incl articles in The Encyclopedia of Life Sciences and The Encyclopedia of Neuroscience; *Recreations* music (piano, cello, composition), DIY, gardening, films; *Style*— Prof John Squire; ✉ Biological Structure and Function Section, Biomedical Sciences Division, Imperial College London, Exhibition Road, London SW7 2AZ (tel 020 7594 3185, fax 020 7594 3169, e-mail j.squire@imperial.ac.uk)

SQUIRE, Air Chief Marshal Sir Peter Ted; GCB (2001, KCB 1997), DFC (1982), AFC (1979); s of Wing Cdr Frank Squire, DSO, DFC (d 1992), and Margaret Pascoe, *née* Trump (d 1980); *b* 7 October 1945; *Educ* King's Sch Bruton, RAF Coll Cranwell; *m* 10 Oct 1970, Carolyn; 3 s (Christopher b 8 May 1972, Richard b 11 Sept 1974, Edward b 11 Sept 1980); *Career* cmmnd RAF 1966, advanced flying and operational trg 1966–68, pilot No 20 Sqdn Singapore (Hunters and Pioneers) 1968–70, flying instr RAF Valley (Hunters) 1970–73, Sqdn Ldr 1973, Flt Cdr No 3(F) Sqdn Germany (Harriers) 1975–78, memb UK Air Forces TACEVAL Team HQ Strike Cmd 1978–80, attended Royal Naval Staff Coll Greenwich 1980, CO No 1(F) Sqdn RAF Wittering (Harriers) 1981–83, ldr Cmd Briefing and Presentation Team then PSO to AOC-in-C HQ Strike Cmd 1984–86, promoted Gp Capt 1985, CO Tri-National Tornado Trg Estab RAF Cottesmore 1986–88, Air Plans Dept MOD London 1988–89, promoted Air Cdre 1989, Dir Air Offensive MOD 1989–91, promoted Air Vice-Marshal 1991, Sr Air Staff Offr HQ Strike Cmd and Dep Chief of Staff Ops UK Air Forces 1991–93, AOC No 38 Gp 1993, AOC No 1 Gp 1993–94, Asst Chief of Air Staff 1994–95, promoted Air Marshal 1996, dep CDS Programmes and Personnel 1996–99, Air ADC to HM The Queen 1999–, promoted Air Chief Marshal 1999, AOC-in-C Strike Cmd and Cmdr Allied Air Forces NW Europe 1999–2000, CAS 2000–03; vice-chm Cwlth War Graves Cmmn 2005–; chm of tstees Imperial War Museum 2006–; sr warden King's Sch Bruton 2004–; FRAeS; *Recreations* cricket, golf; *Style*— Air Chief Marshal Sir Peter Squire, GCB, DFC, AFC, DSc, FRAeS; ✉ c/o NatWest Bank, 5 South Street, Wincanton, Somerset BA9 9DJ

SQUIRES, Richard John; s of Richard George Squires (d 1982), of Dulwich, London, and Lilian Florence, *née* Fuller (d 1987); *b* 9 December 1937; *Educ* Alleyn's Sch Dulwich; *m* 19 Aug 1961, Valerie Jean, da of Richard Wotton Wood, of Southfields, London; 1 da (Fiona Jane b 1967), 1 s (Paul Julian b 1970); *Career* asst actuary: Imperial Life Assurance of Canada 1963–65, Canada Life Co 1965–68; dir Save & Prosper Group Ltd 1981–94 (gp actuary 1969–89), ptnr Watson Wyatt Partners 1990–97, dir Merill Lynch Pensions Ltd 1997–2003; Freeman City of London, Liveryman Worshipful Co of Actuaries; FIA 1962; *Recreations* golf, gardening, painting; *Clubs* Bletchingley Golf, National Liberal; *Style*— Richard Squires, Esq; ✉ 6 The Highway, Sutton, Surrey SM2 5QT (tel 020 8642 7532)

STABLEFORD, Brian Michael; s of William Ernest Stableford, of Denton, Lancs, and Joyce Wilkinson; *b* 25 July 1948; *Educ* Manchester Grammar, Univ of York (BA, DPhil); *m* 1, 1973 (m dis 1985), Vivien Wynne, da of Caradog Owen; 1 s (Leo Michael b 5 April 1975), 1 da (Katharine Margaret b 21 Oct 1978); m 2, 1987, Roberta Jane, da of Charles Cragg; *Career* lectr Sociology Dept Univ of Reading 1976–88; freelance writer (latterly full time); pt/t lectr in cultural and media studies UWE 1995–97, pt/t lectr in creative writing UC Winchester 2000–05; *Awards* incl: European SF Award 1984, Distinguished Scholarship Award Int Assoc for the Fantastic in the Arts 1987, J Lloyd Eaton Award 1987, Pioneer Award Science Fiction Research Assoc 1996, Science Fiction Research Assoc Pilgrim Award 1999; *Fiction and Science Fiction* incl: Hooded Swan (series, 1972–78), Man In a Cage (1976), The Mind Riders (1976), Daedalus (series, 1976–79), Realms of Tartarus (1977), The Last Days of the Edge of the World (1978), The Walking Shadow (1979), Asgard (trilogy, 1982–90), The Empire of Fear (1988), The Werewolves of London (trilogy, 1990–94), Sexual Chemistry - Sardonic Tales of the Genetic Revolution (1991), Young Blood (1992), Genesys (trilogy, 1995–97), The Hunger and Ecstasy of Vampires (1996), Inherit the Earth (1998), Architects of Emortality (1999), The Fountains of Youth (2000), Year Zero (2000), The Cassandra Complex (2001), Dark Ararat (2002), The Omega Expedition (2002), The Stones of Camelot (2006); *Non-Fiction* incl: The Science in Science Fiction (1982), The Third Millennium (1985), Scientific Romance in Britain (1985), Yesterday's Bestsellers (1998), Glorious Perversity: The Decline and Fall of Literary Decadence (1999), Science Fact and Fiction: An Encyclopedia (2006); *Reference* contribs incl: The Encyclopedia of Science Fiction, The Survey of Science Fiction Literature, Anatomy of Wonder, Science Fiction Writers, The Survey of Modern Fantasy Literature, Supernatural Fiction Writers, The Cambridge Guide to Literature In English, Fantasy Literature, Horror Literature; *Style*— Brian Stableford, Esq; ✉ 113 St Peter's Road, Reading, Berkshire RG6 1PG (tel 0118 961 6238)

STABLEFORTH, Dr David Edward; s of Edward Victor Stableforth (d 1975), of Weymouth, Dorset, and Una Alice Stableforth; *b* 23 February 1942; *Educ* Truro Sch, St Catharine's Coll Cambridge, St Mary's Hosp Paddington; *m* 11 May 1967, Penelope Jane, da of David Ivor Phillips, MC (d 1976), of Finchley, London; 2 da (Abigail b 1972, Emily b 1979), 1 s (William b 1973); *Career* sr med registrar Brompton Hosp and St James' Hosp Balham 1973–77, hon sr lectr Univ of Birmingham 1977–2005, currently emeritus conslt physician Birmingham Heartlands and Solihull Hosps Tst; pres Midland Thoracic Soc 1995–98; memb: Br Thoracic Soc, BMA; FRCP 1985; *Recreations* walking, cycling, sailing and canoeing, cooking, theatre and concert-going; *Style*— Dr David Stableforth; ✉ Solihull Hospital, Lode Lane, Solihull, West Midlands B91 2JL (tel 0121 424 5670, e-mail docs@stableforth.fslife.co.uk)

STACE, Victoria Penelope (Vikki); da of Leonard H Stace (d 1981), of Cheltenham, and Gina, *née* Pluckrose; *b* 21 August 1950; *Educ* Malvern Girls' Coll, Univ of Bristol; *m* (m dis 1990), Gavin J Graham; 1 da (Chloe Alexandra b 23 July 1982), 1 s (Toby James Christopher b 8 June 1984); m 2, Tom F Tremlett; *Career* PR conslt; formerly: English teacher Nepal, journalist; publisher; mktg dir Sidgwick & Jackson, fndr Vikki Stace Associates subsequently Powerhouse 1985–98 (consumer and corp PR consultancy), md MacLaurin (following merger with Powerhouse) 1998–, dir hatch-group 2001–, ceo Trimedia Communications UK (following acquisition by Huntsworth plc) 2004–06, chm Trimedia Harrison Cowley (following merger) 2007–, dir of business devpt Huntsworth plc 2007–; chm: Internet Learning Tst, London Bd Princess Royal Tst for Carers; former chm Publishers Publicity Assoc; MIPR, FRSA; *Recreations* golf, skiing, opera, theatre, gardening; *Clubs* Beaufort Polo, Groucho; *Style*— Ms Vikki Stace; ✉ Yew Tree House, Sopworth, Wiltshire SN14 6PR (tel 01454 238344); Trimedia Harrison Cowley, Trimedia House, Lexington Street, London W1F 9AH (tel 020 7025 7500, e-mail vikki.stace@trimediahc.com)

STACEY, Prof Derek Norton; s of Albert Edward Stacey, and Rose, *née* Norton; *Educ* Tettenhall Coll, Balliol Coll Oxford (MA, DPhil); *Career* Univ of Oxford: dept demonstrator Clarendon Lab 1963–65, res fell Ford Fndn St Catherine's Coll 1965–68, univ lectr Clarendon Lab 1969–, tutorial fell University Coll 1969–87, student ChCh 1989–, prof of physics 1996–; visiting fell Jt Inst for Lab Astrophysics Boulder Colorado 1968–69, sr fell SERC 1982–87; sec Atomic and Molecular Sub-Ctee Inst of Physics 1972–5, memb Euro Gp for Atomic Spectroscopy (memb Bd 1972–75, chm 1975–79); Euro Physical Soc: memb Bd Atomic and Molecular Div 1975–89, memb Cncl 1987–91; *Publications* author of papers on experimental and theoretical physics incl measurements of quantum electrodynamic effects in hydrogen and parity-violating optical rotation; *Recreations* squash, tennis, music, literature; *Style*— Prof Derek Stacey; ✉ 14 Barlow Close, Wheatley, Oxford OX33 1NL; Clarendon Laboratory, Parks Road, Oxford OX1 3PU (tel 01865 272293, fax 01865 272400, e-mail d.stacey1@physics.oxford.ac.uk)

STACEY, Gloria Rose; da of Solomon Israel Cooklin (d 1950), and Amelia Simmie, *née* Nieman (d 1989); *Educ* Thornbank Sch Malvern, Kenton Coll, City & Guilds Sch of Art; *m* 1954 (m dis 1987), Nicholas Anthony Howard Stacey (d 1997), s of Marius Szecsi; *Career* artist specializing in collage pictures; dir Swedish Fashions 1953–60; exhibitions: Lasson Gallery London 1971, Marcel Bernheim Paris 1973, Fabian Carlsson Sweden 1978, Galleri Fleming Sweden 1978; pictures in numerous public and private collections; *Recreations* swimming, gardening, Dachshunds, looking at paintings, cooking; *Style*— Mrs Gloria Stacey; ✉ 12a Shelley Court, Tite Street, London SW3 4JB (tel and fax 020 7352 2019)

STACEY, Marianne Luise; da of Wilhelm Alois Ehrhardt, of Friedrichshafen, Federal Republic of Germany, and Viktoria, *née* Hollenzer; *b* 2 May 1950; *Educ* Graf Zeppelin Gymnasium Friedrichshafen, Staatliche Hochschule fur Musik Freiburg; *m* 10 March 1987, Nicholas Anthony Howard Stacey (d 1997); *Career* flautist; fndr and musical dir Ondine Ensemble (19th and 20th century classical chamber music ensemble) 1979–, fndr Platform (charitable tst promoting young composers' unpublished works internationally) 1990–; cmmnd and premiered numerous major compositions, major tours and broadcasts in Germany and the USA; Cross of the Order of Merit (Germany); *Recreations* reading, browsing in bookshops and libraries, astrology, research in subtle energies; *Style*— Mrs Marianne Stacey; ✉ 2 The Red Houses, Green Street, Avebury, Wiltshire SN8 1RE

STACEY, Thomas Charles Gerard (Tom); s of David Henry Stacey (d 1986), and Isobel Gwen, *née* Part; *b* 11 January 1930; *Educ* Eton (fndr Wotton's Soc 1947), Worcester Coll Oxford; *m* 5 Jan 1952, Caroline Susan, da of Charles Nightingale Clay (d 1961); 4 da (Emma b 1952, Mathilda b 1954, Isabella b 1957, Tomasina b 1967), 1 s (Sam b 1966); *Career* formerly: staff writer Picture Post, chief roving corr Sunday Times and others; author, screenwriter, publisher and penal reformer; chm Stacey International (publishers) 1974–; fndr and dir Offender's Tag Assoc 1982–; fndr Pilgrimage 2000; John Llewelyn Rhys Meml Prize 1954, Granada Award (as foreign corr) 1961; FRSL 1977 (memb Cncl 1987–92); *Books* The Hostile Sun (1953), The Brothers M (1960), Summons to Ruwenzori (1963), To-day's World (1970), Immigration and Enoch Powell (1972), Peoples of the Earth (deviser and supervisor, 20 vols, 1973–74), The Living and The Dying (1976), The Pandemonium (1980), The Twelfth Night of Ramadan (under nom de plume Kendal J Peel, 1983), The Worm in the Rose (1985), Deadline (novel and screenplay, 1988), Bodies and Souls (short stories, 1989), Decline (1991), Tribe: the Hidden History of the Mountains of the Moon (2003), Thomas Brassey, 1805–70: Greatest Railway Builder in the World (2005), The First Dog to be Somebody's Best Friend (children's book, 2007); *Shorter Fiction* The Same Old Story (1999), The Tether of the Flesh (2001), Golden Rain (2002), Grief (2004), The Swap (2006), Boredom, Or, the Yellow Trousers (2007); *Recreations* trees, music; *Clubs* White's, Beefsteak, Pratt's; *Style*— Tom Stacey, Esq, FRSL; ✉ 128 Kensington Church Street, London W8 4BH (tel 020 7221 7166, fax 020 7792 9288, e-mail tom@stacey-international.co.uk, website www.tomstacey.com)

STACK, Rt Rev George; s of Gerald Stack, and Elizabeth, *née* McKenzie; *b* 9 May 1946; *Educ* St Aloysius Coll Highgate, St Edmund's Coll Ware, St Mary's Coll Strawberry Hill (BEd); *Career* ordained priest 1972, curate St Joseph's Hanwell 1972–75, Diocesan Catechetical Office 1975–77, curate St Paul's Wood Green 1977–83, parish priest Our Lady Help of Christians Kentish Town 1983–90, vicar-gen Archdiocese of Westminster 1990–93, prelate of honour to His Holiness 1993, admin Westminster Cathedral 1993–2001; hon canon emeritus St Paul's Cathedral 2001, auxiliary bishop of Westminster 2001, titular bishop of Gemellae in Numidia 2001; Knight Equestrian Order of the Holy Sepulchre 2000; *Style*— The Rt Rev George Stack; ✉ Archbishop's House, Westminster, London SW1P 1QJ (tel 020 7798 9381)

STACY, Neil Edwin; s of Edwin Frank Dixon Stacy (d 1997), of Hinton, Glos, and Gladys Emily, *née* Wallis (d 1980); *b* 15 May 1941; *Educ* Hampton GS, Magdalen Coll Oxford (MA, DPhil); *Career* actor; historian; FRHistS; *Theatre* incl: The Soldier's Fortune, A Room with a View, The Importance of Being Earnest, Richard II (Prospect Prodns) 1964–68, Enemy (Saville) 1969, The Recruiting Offr (Bristol and Edinburgh Festival) 1979, A Patriot for Me (Chichester Festival) 1983, Canaries Sometimes Sing (Albery) 1987, Captain Carvallo (Greenwich) 1988, Blithe Spirit (Lyric Hammersmith) 1989, Single Spies (RNT tour) 1990, The Letter (Lyric Hammersmith) 1995, Mrs Warren's Profession (Lyric Hammersmith) 1996, Cause Célebre (Lyric Hammersmith) 1998, Real Inspector Hound (Comedy Theatre) 1998, Gasping (nat tour) 2000, A Perfect Gentleman (King's Head) 2001, Luther (RNT) 2001, The Deep Blue Sea (nat tour) 2003, Three Men in a Boat (nat tour) 2006; *Television* incl: War and Peace, Barlow at Large, Colditz, The Pallisers, To Serve Them All My Days, Shackleton, The Fourth Arm, Duty Free, Three Up Two Down, The House of Windsor, Get Well Soon; *Publications* Henry of Blois and the Lordship of Glastonbury (1999), Surveys of the Estates of Glastonbury Abbey (2001), Charters and Custumals of Shaftesbury Abbey (2006); *Style*— Neil Stacy, Esq; ✉ c/o Shepherd Management, 4th Floor, 45 Maddox Street, London W1S 2PE (tel 020 7495 7813, fax 020 7499 7535)

STADLEN, Nicholas Felix; QC (1991); s of Peter Stadlen (d 1996), concert pianist and former Daily Telegraph chief music critic, and Hedi, *née* Simon (d 2004); *b* 3 May 1950; *Educ* St Paul's (scholarship), Hackley Sch NY (English Speaking Union scholar), Trinity Coll Cambridge (open scholar, BA, pres Cambridge Union); *m* 9 Dec 1972, Frances Edith, da of Maj T E B Howarth, MC (d 1988); 3 s (Matthew Benedict b 1979, William Gabriel b 1981, Thomas Barnaby b 1986); *Career* called to the Bar Inner Temple 1976 (first in Order of Merit Part 1 Bar exams); recorder (SE Circuit) 2000–; sec Br Irish Assoc 1973–74, memb Public Affrs Ctee Bar Cncl 1987; *Publications* Gulbenkian Foundation Reports on Drama and Music Education (jtly, 1974 and 1975), Convention - an Account of the 1976

Democratic Party Presidential Convention (contrib, 1976); *Recreations* listening to classical music; *Style—* Nicholas Stadlen, Esq, QC; ⊠ Fountain Court, Temple, London EC4Y 9DH (tel 020 7583 3335, fax 020 7353 0329)

STAFFORD, Andrew Bruce; QC (2000); s of Cyril Stafford, of Newcastle upon Tyne, and Audrey, *née* Burman; *b* 30 March 1957; *Educ* Royal GS Newcastle upon Tyne, Trinity Hall Cambridge; *m* 2 Oct 1982, Catherine Anne, da of Derek Johnson; 4 da (Rebecca b 30 Sept 1983, Charlotte b 21 July 1985, Flora b 11 Dec 1986, Holly b 10 Dec 1988), 1 s (Benjamin b 29 May 1994); *Style—* Andrew Stafford, Esq, QC; ⊠ Littleton Chambers, 3 King's Bench Walk North, Temple, London EC4Y 7HR (tel 020 7797 8600, fax 020 7797 8699)

STAFFORD, 15 Baron (E 1640); Francis Melfort William Fitzherbert; DL (Staffs 1994); s of 14 Baron (d 1986), and Morag Nada, da of late Lt-Col Alastair Campbell, of Altries, Milltimber, Aberdeenshire; *b* 13 March 1954; *Educ* Ampleforth, Univ of Reading, RAC Cirencester; *m* 1980, Katharine Mary, 3 da of John Codrington, of Barnes, London; 2 s (Hon Benjamin John Basil b 1983, Hon Toby Francis b 1985), 2 da (Hon Teresa Emily b 1987, Hon Camilla Rose Jane b 1989); *Heir* s, Hon Benjamin Fitzherbert; *Career* pro-chllr Keele Univ 1993–2004; non-exec dir: Tarmac Ind Products Div 1987–93, The Fndn NHS Tst 1991–99, Hanley Economic Building Soc 1993– (vice-chm 2000–); pres: Staffs Environmental Fund 2002– (dir 1997–2002), Staffs Prince's Tst 1995–, Lord's Taverners (NW 1996–), Staffs CCC 1999–; chm Harper Adams Agric Coll 2004– (vice-chm 1990–); High Sheriff Staffs 2005; Hon DUniv: Keele, Staffs; *Recreations* cricket, shooting, golf; *Style—* The Rt Hon the Lord Stafford, DL, ARAgS; ⊠ Swynnerton Park, Stone, Staffordshire ST15 0QE

STAFFORD, Bishop of 2005–; Rt Rev (Alfred) Gordon Mursell; s of Philip Riley Mursell (d 1965), and Sheena Nicolson, *née* Black (d 2001); *b* 4 May 1949; *Educ* Ardingly, Pontifical Inst of Sacred Music Rome, BNC Oxford (MA), Cuddesdon Theol Coll (BD, ARCM); *m* 2 Sept 1989, Dr Anne Muir, da of William Muir; *Career* curate Walton Parish Church Liverpool 1973–77, vicar St John's East Dulwich London 1977–86, tutor Salisbury and Wells Theological Coll 1986–91, team rector Stafford 1991–99, provost of Birmingham 1999–2001, dean of Birmingham 2001–05; *Books* The Theology of the Carthusian Life (1988), Out of the Deep (1989), The Wisdom of the Anglo-Saxons (1996), English Spirituality (2001); *Recreations* music, hill walking; *Clubs* Athenaeum; *Style—* The Rt Rev the Bishop of Stafford; ⊠ Ash Garth, 6 Broughton Crescent, Barlaston, Stoke-on-Trent ST12 9DD (tel 01782 373308, fax 01782 373705, e-mail bishop.stafford@lichfield.anglican.org)

STAFFORD, Peter Moore; s of Harry Shaw Stafford (d 1981), and May Alexandra, *née* Moore (d 1994); *b* 24 April 1942; *Educ* Charterhouse; *m* 29 Sept 1973, Elspeth Anne, da of James Steel Harvey; 2 c (Gayle b 3 Sept 1975, Christopher b 9 March 1977); *Career* Garnett Crewdson 1966–68; ptnr: Garnett Crewdson & Co 1968–71, Spicer & Oppenheim 1971–90 (national managing ptnr 1990); Touche Ross (later Deloitte & Touche): ptnr 1990–2000, memb Bd of Ptnrs 1990–2000, chm 1992–95; dir Rathbone Training 2002–; memb: Cncl for Industry and Higher Educn 1993–97, Professional Standards Directorate ICAEW 1998–2002; govr Terra Nova Sch Tst Ltd 1976–2004; FCA (ACA 1965); *Recreations* travel, gardening, restoring antique launches; *Clubs* Royal Over-Seas League, St James's (Manchester; hon treas 2002–04); *Style—* Peter Stafford, Esq; ⊠ Twemlow Edge, Twemlow, Holmes Chapel, Cheshire CW4 8BG (tel 01477 533339, e-mail pmsviola@hotmail.com)

STAFFORD-CLARK, Maxwell Robert Guthrie Stewart (Max); s of David Stafford-Clark, and Dorothy Crossley, *née* Oldfield; *b* 17 March 1941; *Educ* Felsted, Riverdale Country Day Sch NYC, Trinity Coll Dublin; *m* 1, 1971, Carole, *née* Hayman; m 2, 1981, Ann, *née* Pennington; 1 da (Kitty b 28 Aug 1988); *Career* artistic director; Traverse Theatre Edinburgh 1968–70, Traverse Theatre Workshop 1971–72, Joint Stock Theatre Group 1974–79, Royal Court Theatre 1979–93, Out of Joint Theatre Co 1993–; visiting prof Royal Holloway and Bedford New Coll London 1993–94, Maisie Glass prof Univ of Sheffield 1995–96, visiting prof Univ of Herts 1999–, hon prof Univ of York 2002–; Hon DLitt: Oxford Brookes Univ 2000, Univ of Herts 2000, Univ of Warwick 2006; *Books* Letters to George (1988), Taking Stock (2006); *Clubs* Classic Car; *Style—* Max Stafford-Clark, Esq; ⊠ c/o Out of Joint, 7 Thane Works, Thane Villas, London N7 7PH (tel 020 7609 0207, fax 020 7609 0203)

STAGG, HE (Charles) Richard Vernon; CMG (2001); s of Walter Stagg, and Elise Patricia, *née* Maxwell; *Educ* Winchester, Oriel Coll Oxford; *Career* joined FCO 1977; served: Sofia 1979, The Hague 1982; first sec FCO 1985, UK rep to EU Brussels 1987, FCO 1988, UK rep to EU (press spokesman) Brussels 1991, private sec to foreign sec 1993, head EU (External) Dept 1996, ambass to Bulgaria 1998–2001, dir public servs and info FCO 2001–03, DG of corp affrs FCO 2003–07, high cmmr to India 2007–; *Recreations* racing, gardening; *Clubs* Turf, Millennium; *Style—* HE Mr Richard Stagg, CMG; ⊠ c/o Foreign & Commonwealth Office (New Delhi), King Charles Street, London SW1A 2AH

STAHEL, Rolf; s of Hermann Stahel (d 1997), of Jona, Switzerland, and Bluette Stahel; *b* 21 April 1944; *Educ* Handels Matura Lucerne; *m* Ewa; 2 s (Martin, Philip); *Career* sales admin Rhone Poulenc Switzerland 1963–67; Wellcome: rep UK 1967, asst mangr Switzerland 1968, gen mangr Italy 1969–74, md Thailand 1974–79, md Singapore 1979–90, dir of mktg Wellcome plc 1990–94; chief exec Shire Pharmaceuticals Gp plc 1994–2003, fndr chm Chesyl Pharma Ltd 2003–; non-exec chm: Newron Pharmaceuticals 2004–, Cosmo Pharmeceuticals 2006, Eusa Pharma Inc 2007; CEO of the Year (pharmaceutical industry global award) 2001, techMARK Mediscience Award (for most significant contribution to UK lifesciences) 2003; *Recreations* golf, classical music; *Clubs* RAC, S Winchester Golf, IOD London; *Style—* Rolf Stahel, Esq; ⊠ Neatham, Sleepers Hill, Winchester, Hampshire SO22 4NB (tel 01962 868224, fax 01962 861441, e-mail rstahel@chesyl.com)

STAHL, Andrew; s of Adam Jack Stahl, of London, and Sheena Penelope, *née* Simms; *b* 4 July 1954; *Educ* Slade Sch of Fine Art; *m* 1, 1988 (dis 1999), Jean Oh Mei Yen, da of Henry Oh Sui Hong; 1 s (Matthew b 1992), 2 da (Rosie, Juno (twins) b 1995); m 2, 2001, Kumiko, da of Wataru Tsuna; 1 da (Miyu b 2002); *Career* artist; head of undergraduate painting Slade Sch of Fine Art; Abbey Major Rome scholar 1979–81, fell in printmaking RCA 1989, Rome Award in painting Br Sch at Rome 1989, Wingate scholar 1991; artist in residence: Chiangmai Univ Thailand 2000, Silpakorn Univ Bangkok 2003, Univ of NSW 2004, Mahasarakarm Univ Thailand 2005, Br Cncl Bangkok 2006; *Solo Exhibitions* Air Gallery London 1981 and 1983, Paton Gallery London 1984 and 1988, Flowers East 1992, 1995 and 1998, Worthing Museum and Art Gallery 1993, Prints and Drawings (Flowers East) 1993, Maidstone Library Gallery 1994, Wolverhampton Art Gallery and Museum 1995, Fenderesky Gallery Belfast 1999, Chiangmai Univ Museum Thailand 2000, ac.t art Zirndorf Germany 2000–01, Silapakorn Univ Bangkok 2002, Tonson Gallery Thailand 2003–04, 2 weeks in Sydney (COFA Univ of NSW) 2004, Panya Vijinthanasarn & Andrew Stahl: Conversations, Collaborations and New Paintings (100 Tonson Gallery Bangkok) 2006, New Paintings (Robert Steel Gallery NY) 2007; *Group Exhibitions* incl: British Drawing (Hayward Gallery) 1982, Pagan Echoes (Riverside Studios) 1983, selections from 10 years at Air (Air Gallery) 1985, 17 International Festival of Painting Cagnes France 1985, Walking & Falling (Interim Art & Kettles Yard Cambridge) 1986, British Painting (touring Malaysia, Singapore, Hong Kong, Thailand) 1987, Artists Choice (V&A) 1987, London Group (RCA) 1988, Figuring out the 80's (Laing Art Gallery Newcastle), Whitechapel Open 1989, Rome Scholars 1980–90 (RCA) 1990, Selected Line (William Jackson Gallery) 1992, Biella Print Biennale 1993, 5 Artists (Angela Flowers Gallery) 1994, East Open Exhbn (Norwich Art Gallery) 1994, John Moores Liverpool Exhibition 1995, 3 Painters (Plymouth Arts Centre) 1996, Sad (Gasworks Studio) 1996, Life Live (MOMA Paris, invitation by David Medalla) 1996, Angela Flowers Gallery 1997 (Flowers East Gallery) 1997, Artists Camp (Nat Gallery Sri Lanka, selected by Br Cncl) 1997, British Figuration (Angela Flowers Gallery) 1997, Flowers West LA 1998, Millennium (Flowers East Gallery), London Bienniale 3 Artists Domingo St London 2000, Artists Choice (Flowers East Gallery) 2000, Small is Beautiful (Flowers East Gallery) 2002–04, Artskool (ENSBA Paris, Dover, Calais, Nimes and Central St Martins Coll of Art and Design) 2004, Figure, Place and Time (Art Space Gallery London) 2005, Royal Acad Summer Exhbn 2005, Painting from the 90s (Flowers Central) 2005, Monologue/Dialogue UK-Thai art today (Bangkok Univ Gallery) 2006, Heads (Flowers East Gallery) 2006, Portraits Small is Beautiful (Flowers Central) 2006; *Work in Public Collections* Metropolitan Museum of Art New York, Arts Cncl of GB, Br Cncl, Contemporary Arts Soc, Br Museum, City Museum Peterborough, Leicestershire Educn Authy; *Style—* Andrew Stahl; ⊠ 1 Old Oak Road, London W3 7HN (e-mail andrewstahl@hotmail.com)

STAINES, Christopher John (Chris); s of Trevor John Staines, of Bury St Edmunds, Suffolk, and Susan Anne, *née* Bugg; *b* 20 February 1975; *Educ* Thurston Upper Sch Bury St Edmunds, West Suffolk Coll (NVQ); *Career* commis chef Angel Hotel Bury St Edmunds 1993–94, chef de partie Llangoed Hall Powys 1994–95, work placement Keswick Hall Keswick VA and Inn at Perry Cabin St Michaels MD 1995, jr sous chef Lucknam Park Country House Hotel 1995–99, Chez Nico at 90 Park Lane 1998–2000, chef de cuisine The Oakroom Marco Pierre White 2000–02, chef de cuisine Foliage Restaurant Mandarin Oriental Hotel (1 Michelin Star) 2002–; *Recreations* reading, music; *Style—* Chris Staines, Esq; ⊠ Foliage, Mandarin Oriental Hyde Park, 66 Knightsbridge, London SW1X 7LA (tel 020 7235 2000 ext 3034, fax 020 7201 3811)

STAIR, 14 Earl of (S 1703); Sir John David James Dalrymple; 15 Bt of Stair (S 1664) and 11 of Killock (S 1698); also Viscount Stair and Lord Glenluce and Stranraer (S 1690), Viscount Dalrymple and Lord Newliston (S 1703), Baron Oxenfoord (UK 1841); s of 13 Earl of Stair, KCVO, MBE (d 1996), and Davina Katharine, *née* Bowes Lyon; *b* 4 September 1961; *Educ* Harrow; *Heir* bro, Hon David Dalrymple; *Career* cmmnd Scots Gds 1982; *Style—* The Rt Hon the Earl of Stair; ⊠ Lochinch Castle, Stranraer, Wigtownshire

STALLARD, Baron (Life Peer UK 1983), of St Pancras in the London Borough of Camden; Albert William Stallard; s of Frederick Stallard, of Tottenham; *b* 5 November 1921; *Educ* Low Waters Public Sch, Hamilton Acad Scotland; *m* 1944, Julie, da of William Cornelius Murphy, of Co Kerry; 1 s (Hon Richard b 1945), 1 da (Hon Brenda b 1949); *Career* engr 1937–65, tech trg offr 1965–70; memb St Pancras BC 1953–59 (alderman 1962–65); chm: Public Health Ctee 1956–59 and 1962–65, Housing and Planning Dept 1956–59; memb Camden BC 1965–70 (alderman 1971–78); MP (Lab): St Pancras N 1970–74, Camden Div of St Pancras N 1974–83; PPS: min of Agric 1973–74, min of Housing and Construction 1974–76; govt whip 1978–79 (asst 1976–78), Lords Cmmr Treasy, chm Lords All-Pty Gp on Ageing 1989–; memb and chm Camden Town Disablement Advsy Ctee 1951–83, vice-pres Camden Assoc of Mental Health; memb AEU Order of Merit 1968, former memb Inst of Trg & Devpt; *Style—* The Rt Hon the Lord Stallard; ⊠ House of Lords, London SW1A 0PW

STALLWORTHY, Jon Howie; s of Sir John Arthur Stallworthy (d 1993), and Margaret Wright, *née* Howie (d 1980); *b* 18 January 1935; *Educ* Rugby, Univ of Oxford (MA, BLitt); *m* 25 June 1960, Gillian (Jill), da of Sir Claude Humphrey Meredith Waldock, CMG, OBE, QC (d 1981); 2 s (Jonathan b 1965, Nicolas, *qv*, b 1970), 1 da (Pippa b 1967); *Career* Nat Serv 1953–55, 2 Lt Oxon and Bucks LI, seconded Royal W African Frontier Force; visiting fell All Souls Coll Oxford 1971–72, dep academic publisher OUP 1972–77, Anderson prof of Eng lit Cornell Univ 1977–86, professorial fell Wolfson Coll and reader in Eng lit Univ of Oxford 1986–92, ad hominem prof of English lit Univ of Oxford 1992–2000, sr fell Wolfson Coll Oxford 2000–; Hon DUniv Surrey, Hon DLitt Westminster Coll USA; FRSL, FBA 1990; *Books* incl: Between the Lines, WB Yeats's Poetry in the Making (1963), Vision and Revision in Yeats's Last Poems (1969), Alexander Blok, The Twelve and Other Poems (trans with Peter France, 1970), Wilfred Owen (winner Duff Cooper Meml Prize, W H Smith & Son Literary Award, E M Forster Award, 1974), The Penguin Book of Love Poetry (ed, 1973, 2 edn 2003), Wilfred Owen - The Complete Poems and Fragments (ed, 1983), Boris Pasternak, Selected Poems (trans with Peter France, 1984), The Oxford Book of War Poetry (ed, 1984), The Anzac Sonata - New and Selected Poems (1986), First Lines - Poems Written in Youth from Herbert to Heaney (ed, 1987), Henry Reed - Collected Poems (ed, 1991), Louis MacNeice (1995, winner Southern Arts Lit Prize), The Guest from the Future (1995), The Norton Anthology of Poetry (4 edn, ed with Margaret Ferguson and Mary Jo Salter, 1996), Singing School: the Making of a Poet (1998), Rounding the Horn: Collected Poems (1998), The Norton Anthology of English Literature (7 edn, with M H Abrams and others, 2000), Anthem for Doomed Youth (ed, 2002), Body Language (2004); *Style—* Prof Jon Stallworthy; ⊠ Long Farm, Elsfield Road, Old Marston, Oxford OX3 0PR; Wolfson College, Oxford OX2 6UD (tel 01865 274100)

STALLWORTHY, Nicolas; s of Prof Jon Stallworthy, FBA, FRSL , *qv*, of Oxford, and Jill, *née* Waldock; *b* 10 June 1970; *Educ* Radley, ChCh Oxford; *m* 10 April 1999, Blaise Dawn, da of Nicholas Dudley, FRCS; 1 s (Macnair Jon b 11 Nov 2001), 1 da (Constance Alba b 26 April 2003); *Career* called to the Bar 1993; specialist in law relating to occupational pension schemes; *Style—* Nicolas Stallworthy, Esq; ⊠ Outer Temple Chambers, 222 Strand, London WC2R 1BA

STAMER, Sir (Lovelace) Anthony; 5 Bt (UK 1809), of Beauchamp, Dublin; s of Sir Lovelace Stamer, 4 Bt (d 1941), and Mary, *née* Otter (d 1974; her mother Marianne was seventh in descent from 4 Baron North); *b* 28 February 1917; *Educ* Harrow, Trinity Coll Cambridge (MA), RAC Cirencester; *m* 1, 1948 (m dis 1953), Stella Huguette, da of late Paul Burnell Binnie; 1 s, 1 da; m 2, 1955 (m dis 1959), Margaret Lucy, da of late Maj T A Belben, IA; m 3, 1960 (m dis 1968), Marjorie June, da of late T C Noakes; m 4, 1983, Elizabeth Graham Smith (d 1992), da of late C J R Magrath; m 5, 16 April 1997, Pamela Grace Cheston, da of late E A Hawkins; *Heir* s, Peter Stamer; *Career* PO RAF 1939–41, 1 Offr Air Tport Aux 1941–45; exec dir: Bentley Drivers Club Ltd 1969–73, Bugatti and Ferrari Owners Clubs 1973–74; hon treas Ferrari Owners Club 1976–81; *Style—* Sir Anthony Stamer, Bt; ⊠ Old Timbers, Church Street, Moreton-in-Marsh, Gloucestershire GL56 0LN (tel 01608 652394)

STAMP, Gavin Mark; s of Barry Hartnell Stamp, and Norah Clare, *née* Rich; *b* 15 March 1948; *Educ* Dulwich Coll, Gonville & Caius Coll Cambridge (MA, PhD); *m* 12 Feb 1982 (sep), Alexandra Frances, da of Frank Artley, of Redcar; 2 da (Agnes Mary b 1984, Cecilia Jane b 1986); *Career* architectural historian and author; sr lectr Mackintosh Sch of Architecture Glasgow until 2003; hon prof Univ of Glasgow, Mellon sr fell and bye-fell Gonville & Caius Coll Cambridge 2003–04; contrib: The Spectator, Daily Telegraph, Independent, Herald, Architects Jl, Private Eye etc; chm Thirties Soc (now the Twentieth Century Soc), fndr and chm Alexander Thomson Soc 1991; Hon FRIAS 1994, Hon FRIBA, FSA 1998; *Books* The Architects Calendar (1974), The Victorian Buildings of London (with C Amery, 1980), Temples of Power (with G Boyd Harte, 1979), Robert Weir Schultz and His Work for The Marquesses of Bute (1981), The Great Perspectivists (1982), The Changing Metropolis (1984), The English House 1860–1914 (1986), Telephone Boxes (1989), Greek Thomson (ed with S McKinstry, 1994), Alexander 'Greek' Thomson (1999),

S

Edwin Lutyens: Country Houses (2001), Lutyens Abroad (ed with A Hopkins, 2002), An Architect of Promise (2002), The Memorial to the Missing of the Somme (2006); *Style*— Gavin Stamp; ✉ 15 Belle Vue Court, Devonshire Road, London SE23 3SY

STAMP, Dr Gillian Penelope; da of late Guy St John Tatham, of Johannesburg, South Africa; *Educ* Univ of the Witwatersrand (BA), Brunel Univ (MA) BIOSS Brunel Univ (PhD); *m* 27 Dec 1958, Hon (Jos) Colin Stamp (d 2001), s of 1 Baron Stamp, GCB, GBE (d 1941); 2 s (Robbie, Jonathan); *Career* dir Brunel Inst of Orgn and Social Studies (BIOSS); res consultancy work for numerous nat and int cos; visiting prof Indian Inst of Technol New Delhi; memb Ed Bd Indian Journal of Training and Development; memb: Cncl St George's House Windsor 1995–2001, Bd Nat Sch of Govt 2006; fell: Windsor Leadership Tst 2000, Sunningdale Inst 2006; Hon DPhil 1991; FRSA 1992; *Publications* Well-Being at Work (with Colin Stamp, 1993); *Style*— Dr Gillian Stamp; ✉ 12 Ullswater Road, London SW13 (tel 020 8748 2782, fax 020 8255 7579); Brunel Institute of Organisation and Social Studies, Brunel University, Uxbridge, Middlesex (tel 01895 270072, fax 01895 254760)

STAMP, Malcolm Frederick; CBE (2002); *b* 29 December 1952; *Educ* Stand GS; *Career* unit gen mangr (Acute) N Manchester HA 1985–88; dist gen mangr: Crewe HA 1988–90, Liverpool HA 1990–92; chief exec: Royal Liverpool Univ Hosp Tst 1992–94, Norfolk & Norwich Health Care NHS Tst 1994–2002, Cambridge Univ Hosps 2002–06; memb Bd Fndn Tst Network; former chm of govrs Peel Brow Primary Sch; Hon DCL UEA 2000; memb: Inst of Mgmnt Servs, Inst of Health Service Mgmnt; MHSM; *Recreations* football, reading, family; *Style*— Malcolm F Stamp, Esq, CBE

STAMP, Terence Henry; s of Thomas Stamp (d 1983), and Ethel Esther *née* Perrot (d 1985); *b* 22 July 1938; *Educ* Plaistow Co GS; *Career* actor; Doctor of Arts (hc) 1993; *Films* incl: Billy Budd 1960, The Collector 1964, Far from the Madding Crowd 1966, Tales of Mystery 1967, Theorom 1968, Meeting with Remarkable Men 1977, Superman I and II 1977, The Hit 1984, Legal Eagles 1985, Wall Street 1987, Young Guns 1988, The Sicilain 1988, Prince of Shadows 1991, Priscilla, Queen of the Desert 1994, Limited Edition 1998, Bowfinger 1999, The Limey 1999, My Boss's Daughter 2002, The Haunted Mansion 2003; *Books* Stamp Album (1987), Coming Attractions (1988), Double Feature (1989), The Night (novel, 1992), Wheat and Dairy Free Cook Book (with Elizabeth Buxton, 1998); *Recreations* film; *Clubs* New York Athletic; *Style*— Terence Stamp, Esq; ✉ c/o Markham & Froggatt Ltd, 4 Windmill Street, London W1T 2HZ

STAMP, 4 Baron (UK 1938) Trevor Charles Bosworth Stamp; s of 3 Baron Stamp (d 1987); *Educ* Leys Sch, Gonville & Caius Cambridge (BA), St Mary's Hosp Med Sch (MB BCh); *m* 1, 1963 (m dis 1971), Anne Carolynn, da of John Kenneth Churchill, of Tunbridge Wells; 2 da; m 2, 1975 (m dis 1997), Carol Anne, da of Robert Keith Russell, of Farnham, Surrey; 1 s, 1 da; *Heir* s, Hon Nicholas Stamp; *Career* med registrar Professorial Med Unit St Mary's Hosp 1964–66; Dept of Human Metabolism UCH and Med Sch: hon sr registrar 1968–73, hon sr lectr 1972–73; conslt physician and dir Dept of Bone and Mineral Metabolism Inst of Orthopaedics Royal Nat Orthopaedic Hosp 1974–99; hon conslt physician and sr lectr Middx Hosp and UCL Sch of Med 1974–99; emeritus conslt UCL Hosps 1999–; hon conslt physician RNOH 1999–; Prix André Lichtwitz France 1973; FRCP 1978; *Style*— The Lord Stamp; ✉ 15 Ceylon Road, London W14 0PY; Royal National Orthopaedic Hospital, Stanmore, Middlesex

STANBROOK, Clive St George Clement; OBE (1988), QC (1989); s of Ivor Robert Stanbrook, former MP for Orpington, and Joan, *née* Clement; *b* 10 April 1948; *Educ* Dragon Sch Oxford, Westminster, UCL (LLB); *m* 3 April 1971, Julia Suzanne, da of Victor Hillary; 1 s (Ivor Victor Hillary), 3 da (Fleur Elizabeth, Sophie Noelette, Isabella Grace); *Career* called to: the Bar Inner Temple 1972, the Turks and Caicos Bar 1986, the NY Bar 1988; memb Bd World Trade Center Assoc (London) 1977–83, fndr and sr ptnr Stanbrook & Hooper (int lawyers) Brussels 1977–; pres Br C of C for Belgium and Luxembourg 1985–87; *Books* Extradition the Law and Practice (jtly, 1980, 2 edn 2000), Dumping Manual on the EEC Anti Dumping Law (1980), International Trade Law and Practice (co ed, 1984), Dumping and Subsidies (jtly, 1996); *Recreations* tennis, sailing; *Style*— Clive Stanbrook, Esq, OBE, QC; ✉ Stanbrook & Hooper, 245 Rue Père Eudore Devroye, Brussels 1150, Belgium (tel 32 2 230 5059, fax 32 2 230 5713, e-mail clive.stanbrook@stanbrook.com)

STANCER, Rosie; da of Samuel Witterong Clayton, of The Great Park, Windsor, and Lady Mary, *née* Leveson Gower; *b* 25 January 1960; *Educ* Heathfield Sch Ascot, King James Coll Henley-on-Thames, Oxford and County Sch; *m* 9 July 1993, William Wordie Stancer, s of John Stancer; 1 s ('Jock' Wordie Stancer b 4 June 2001); *Career* jobs incl: developing The Princess Royal Tst for Carers 1991, dir of PR The Park Lane Hotel London 1992–97, lectr, travel writer and freelance journalist based in Prague 1997–2001; trained and worked in Polar expdns incl first all-women expdn to the N Pole (McVities Penguin North Pole Relay) 1997, first Br all-women expdn to the S Pole (M&G ISA Challenge) 1999–2000 and Snickers S Pole solo and unsupported expdn 2004; actively involved with Special Olympics; FRGS; *Recreations* writing accounts of own expeditions, cross country running, skiing, fencing, collecting Polar memorabilia, travelling anywhere off the track, shooting and missing overhead birds; *Style*— Ms Rosie Stancer; ✉ 44 Clavering Avenue, Barnes, London SW13 8DY (tel 020 8748 1481)

STANCLIFFE, David Staffurth; *see:* Salisbury, Bishop of

STANDAGE, Simon; *Career* fndr memb: English Concert 1973, Salomon String Quartet 1981, Collegium Musicum 90 1990; prof of baroque violin Royal Academy of Music; assoc dir Academy of Ancient Music 1991–95; recordings incl: Vivaldi Four Seasons (nominated for Grammy Award), Mozart Concertos, numerous works by Vivaldi, Telemann and Haydn; *Style*— Simon Standage, Esq; ✉ Collegium Musicum 90, 106 Hervey Road, Blackheath, London SE3 8BX (tel 020 8319 3372, fax 020 8856 1023, e-mail standages@pobox.com)

STANDEN, John Francis; s of Dr Edward Peter Standen (d 1976), and Margaret, *née* O'Shea (d 1995); *b* 14 October 1948; *Educ* St James' Sch Burnt Oak, Univ of Durham (BA); *m* 9 Aug 1975, Kathleen Mary, da of Joseph Quilty, of Co Galway, Ireland; 1 da (Aine b 1979), 2 s (Luke b 1981, Owen b 1984); *Career* Barclays de Zoete Wedd Ltd: md Corp Fin 1990–92, ceo Corp Finance UK 1992–93, chief exec Corp Finance Worldwide 1993–95, ceo Emerging Markets 1995–96; dir special projects Barclays plc 1997–98; non-exec chm: Chapelthorpe plc 2002–07, Z Group plc 2005–, Stanelco plc 2007–, Xploite plc 2007–; non-exec dir Lavendon plc 2005–; chm Cncl Univ of Hull 2006–; ACIB 1974; *Recreations* running, sailing, golf, family fun, theatre, opera; *Clubs* Brooks's, St James's, Hanbury Manor Golf (Ware), Glandore Harbour Yacht (Cork); *Style*— John Standen, Esq; ✉ 17 Ropemakers Fields, Narrow Street, London E14 8BX (tel 020 7517 7883)

STANDING, John Ronald; Sir John Ronald Leon, 4 Bt, but prefers to be known by professional name of John Standing; s of Sir Ronald George Leon, 3 Bt (d 1964), and his 1 w, Dorothy Katharine (the actress Kay Hammond; d 1980), da of Cdr Sir Guy Standing, KBE (d 1937), and who m 2, Sir John Clements, CBE; *b* 16 August 1934; *Educ* Eton, Millfield, Byam Shaw Sch of Art; *m* 1, 1961 (m dis 1972), Jill, da of Jack Melford, actor; 1 s (Alexander John b 1965); m 2, 7 April 1984, Sarah Kate, da of Bryan Forbes, film dir; 2 da (India b 25 June 1985, Octavia b 3 Nov 1989), 1 s (Archie b 28 July 1986); *Heir* s, Alexander Leon; *Career* actor; 2 Lt KRRC 1953–55; artist (watercolours); *Theatre* incl: The Importance of Being Earnest 1968, Ring Round the Moon 1969, Arms and the Man 1970, Sense of Detachment 1972, Private Lives 1973, St Joan 1973, Jingo 1976, The Philanderer 1978, Plunder 1978, Close of Play 1979, Tonight at 8.30 1981, Biko Inquest 1984, Rough Crossing 1985, Hayfever (Albery) 1992, A Month in the Country (Albery) 1994, Son of Man (RSC) 1996, A Delicate Balance 1998; *Television* UK incl: The First Churchills, Charley's Aunt, Tinker Tailor Soldier Spy, King Solomon's Mines; USA incl: Lime Street 1985, Murder She Wrote 1989, LA Law 1990, St Joan 1999, Longitude 1999, Gulliver's Travels 1997, Love in a Cold Climate 2001, The Falklands War 2002, The Real Jane Ansien 2002, A Line of Beauty; *Film* incl: King Rat 1965, Walk Don't Run 1965, The Eagle Has Landed 1976, Rogue Male 1976, The Legacy 1977, Mrs Dalloway, Rogue Trader 1998, Mad Cows 1998, Eight and a Half Women 1998, Queens Messenger 2000, The Good Woman, V for Vendetta, Kerala, The Shooter, Oui Law; *Recreations* painting, fishing; *Clubs* MCC; *Style*— John Standing, Esq

STANES, Ven Ian Thomas; s of Sydney Stanes (d 1966), of Bath, and Iris, *née* Hulme (d 1996); *b* 29 January 1939; *Educ* City of Bath Boys' Sch, Univ of Sheffield (BSc), Linacre Coll Oxford (MA), Wycliffe Hall Oxford; *m* 8 Sept 1962, Sylvia Alice, da of George John Drew; 1 da (Sally Rachael b 12 Aug 1968), 1 s (Alan Thomas (decd) b 18 Jan 1971); *Career* ordained: deacon 1965, priest 1966; curate Holy Apostles Leicester 1965–69, vicar St David's Broom Leys Coalville (Dio of Leicester) 1969–76, priest/warden Marrick Priory (Dio of Ripon) 1976–82, offr for mission miny and evangelism Willesden (Dio of London) 1982–92, continuing ministerial educn offr Willesden 1984–92, preb St Paul's Cathedral 1989–92, archdeacon of Loughborough (Dio of Leicester) 1992–2005 (archdeacon emeritus 2005–); *Recreations* hockey, rock climbing, walking, photography, singing, music and art appreciation, drama; *Style*— The Ven Ian Stanes; ✉ 192 Bath Road, Bradford-uopn-Avon, Wiltshire BA15 1SP (tel 01225 309036, mobile 07883 059643, e-mail ianstanes@surefish.co.uk)

STANES, Sara Jayne; OBE (2007); *b* London; *Educ* Convent of St Marie Auxiliatrice London; *m* 1994, Richard James Stanes; *Career* early career as documentary and television advtg film prodr; currently chocolatier, freelance food writer, lectr and broadcaster specialising in chocolate; dir Acad of Culinary Arts 1996– (dir of marketing and PR 1986–95); Guild of Food Writers: memb 1987–, memb Ctee 1994–98, vice-chm 1996–98, memb Food Policy Ctee; chm Acad of Chocolate; judge: Guild of Food Writers Awards for Radio and Television 1998–2001, Organic Food Awards 2000–, Nat Training Awards 2002–; external verifier for BSc in Culinary Arts Thames Valley Univ 2001–; tstee: Adopt a Sch Tst, The ARK Fndn; memb Ctee: Sustain Grab 5!, UK Skills; hon fell Thames Valley Univ 2004; Hon Freeman Worshipful Co of Cooks 2006, Freeman City of London 2007; *Publications* Chocolate: The Definitive Guide (2000), Chocolate (2005, best book in its category World Cookbook Fair 2006); *Awards* incl: Jeremy Round Award Guild of Food Writers 2000, Best Book in the English Language World Cookbook Fair Awards 2000, nomination André Simon Awards 2000, Ladle nomination Australian Jacob's Creek Media Awards 2001; *Recreations* chocolate, music, books, tennis, provenance of food, drink, the environment; *Style*— Mrs Sara Jayne Stanes; ✉ Academy of Culinary Arts, 53 Cavendish Road, London SW12 0BL (tel 020 8673 6300, fax 020 8673 6543, mobile 07789 874808, e-mail sarajaynestanes@academyofculinaryarts.org.uk)

STANFIELD, Prof Peter Robert; s of late Robert Ainslie Stanfield, of Woodstock, Oxford, and Irene Louisa, *née* Walker; *b* 13 July 1944; *Educ* Portsmouth GS, Univ of Cambridge (MA, PhD, ScD); *m* 21 Sept 1987, Philippa (d 2004), da of Eric Moss (d 2005), of Leicester; 2 step s (Edward McMillan Barrie b 1968, William McMillan Barrie b 1970); *Career* SRC res fell MBA laboratory Plymouth 1968–69, fell Clare Coll Cambridge, univ demonstrator in physiology Univ of Cambridge 1969–74; Univ of Leicester: lectr in physiology 1974–81, reader 1981–87, prof 1987–2001, head Dept of Physiology 1989–93; prof of molecular physiology Univ of Warwick 2001–; visiting prof: Purdue Univ Indiana 1984–85, Univ of Illinois at Chicago 1993–98; ed Journal of Physiology 1980–88, assoc ed Pflügers Archiv (European Jl of Physiology) 1993–; memb Physiological Soc 1973– (memb Ctee 1985–90 and 1995–99, hon sec 1996–99), hon memb Hungarian Physiological Soc 2001–; FMedSci 2003; *Books* Ion Channels: Molecules in Action (with D J Aidley, 1996); author of scientific papers on physiology of cell membranes; *Style*— Prof Peter Stanfield; ✉ Department of Biological Sciences, University of Warwick, Coventry CV4 7AL (tel 024 7657 2503, fax 024 7652 3701, e-mail p.r.stanfield@warwick.ac.uk)

STANFORD, Adrian Timothy James; s of Ven Leonard John Stanford (d 1967), former Archdeacon of Coventry, and Dora Kathleen, *née* Timms (d 1939); *b* 19 July 1935; *Educ* Rugby, Merton Coll Oxford (MA); *Career* Nat Serv 2 Lt The Sherwood Foresters 1954–55; merchant banker; dir Samuel Montagu & Co Ltd 1972–95 (joined 1958); memb Exec Ctee Georgian Gp (treas 1996–2001), chm Louis Franck INSEAD Scholarship Fund, tstee Old Broad St Charity Tst; advsr: Royal Fine Art Cmmn Tst, Building of the Year Award; *Recreations* gardening, architecture; *Clubs* Boodle's, Brooks's; *Style*— Adrian Stanford, Esq; ✉ 15 North Court, Great Peter Street, Westminster, London SW1P 3LL

STANFORD, Rear Adm Christopher David (Chris); CB (2002); s of Joseph Gerald Stanford, and Dr Elspeth Stanford, *née* Harrison; *b* 15 February 1950; *Educ* St Paul's, BRNC Dartmouth, Merton Coll Oxford (MA), RN Staff Coll Greenwich, RCDS; *m* 1972, Angela Mary, da of Cdr Derek G M Gardner, VRD, RSMA; 1 s, 3 da; *Career* joined RN 1967; various sea appts in navigational and warfare posts 1967–94; served HM Ships: Puma, Jupiter, Hubberston, Exmouth, Newcastle, Antrim, Brilliant (second in command), Fife (second in command); CO HMS Boxer 1988–89, CO HMS Coventry and 1 Frigate Sqdn 1993–94; MOD: dir of Naval Staff 1995–97, dir of Operational Capability 1997–99, COS to Surgeon General 1999–2002; ptnr Odgers Ray and Berndtson 2002–, chm Healthcare and Life Sciences Practice; chm Somerset and Dorset Sea Cadet Assoc 2003–; vice-pres N Dorset Rugby Club; yr bro Trinity House; Freeman City of London, Freeman Hon Co of Master Mariners; Hon DUniv Central England 2002; FNI 1999 (MNI 1988, sr vice-pres and memb Cncl until 2007), FRSA 2003; OStJ 2001; *Publications* contrib numerous articles on maritime, environmental, leadership and medical issues to learned and professional journals; *Recreations* rugby, art, maritime affairs, travel; *Clubs* Anchorites (past pres), Army and Navy, Woodroffe's; *Style*— Rear Adm Chris Stanford, CB; ✉ Church Farm Cottage, Cucklington, Wincanton, Somerset BA9 9PT (e-mail christopher_stanford@hotmail.com)

STANFORD, Peter James; s of Reginald James Hughes Stanford (d 2004), and Mary Catherine, *née* Fleming (d 1998); *b* 23 November 1961; *Educ* St Anselm's Coll Birkenhead, Merton Coll Oxford (BA); *m* 1995, Siobhan Cross; 1 s, 1 da; *Career* reporter The Tablet 1983–84, ed The Catholic Herald 1988–92 (news ed 1984–88), freelance journalist and broadcaster 1984– (incl BBC, The Guardian, The Observer, The Independent, The Independent on Sunday, The Tablet, presenter C4 series Catholics and Sex and on BBC Radio2, BBC Radio 4, Channel 5 and Viva! Radio); chm: ASPIRE (Assoc for Spinal Res, Rehabilitation and Reintegration) 1991–2001 and 2005–, Media Advsy Gp CAFOD; patron: CandoCo Dance Co, Ways With Words; dir Frank Longford Charitable Tst; *Books* Hidden Hands: Child Workers Around the World (1988), Believing Bishops (with Simon Lee, 1990), The Seven Deadly Sins (ed, 1990), Catholics and Sex (with Kate Saunders, 1992), Basil Hume (1993), Lord Longford (1994, revised and reissued as The Outcasts' Outcast 2003), The Catholics and Their Houses (with Leanda de Lisle, 1995), The Devil: A Biography (1996, televised 1998), The She-Pope (1998, televised 1998), Bronwen Astor: Her Life and Times (2000), Heaven: A Traveller's Guide (2002), Being a Dad (2004), Why I'm Still a Catholic (ed, 2005), C Day-Lewis: A Biography (2007); *Recreations* vases, photography, old cars; *Clubs* PEN; *Style*— Peter Stanford, Esq; ✉ c/o AP Watt, 20 John Street, London WC1N 2DR (e-mail peterstanford@easynet.co.uk, website www.peterstanford.co.uk)

STANFORD-TUCK, Michael David; s of Wing Cdr Roland Robert Stanford-Tuck, DSO, DFC and two bars (d 1987), and Joyce, *née* Carter (d 1985); *b* 3 November 1946; *Educ* Radley,

Univ of Southampton (LLB); *m* 30 June 1973, Susan Penelope, da of Raymond John Lilwall, of St Peters, Kent; 1 s (Alexander b 1976), 2 da (Olivia b 1978, Camilla b 1984); *Career* admitted slr 1972; barr and attorney Supreme Court of Bermuda 1978; ptnr: Appleby Spurling & Kempe Bermuda 1978–83, Taylor Wessing London 1985–; memb Ctee The Bermuda Soc; Freeman City of London 1989, Liveryman City of London Slrs' Co 1989 (Freeman 1973); memb Law Soc; *Recreations* golf, country sports, skiing; *Clubs* Royal St George's Golf, White's; *Style*— Michael Stanford-Tuck, Esq; ✉ Taylor Wessing, Carmelite, 50 Victoria Embankment, London EC4 (tel 020 7300 7000, fax 020 7300 7100, telex 268014)

STANGER, David Harry; OBE (1987); s of Charles Harry Stanger, CBE (d 1987), of Knole, Somerset, and Florence Bessie Hepworth, *née* Bowden (d 2001); *b* 14 February 1939; *Educ* Oundle, Millfield; *m* 20 July 1963, Jill Patricia, da of Reginald Arthur Barnes, of Brussels, Belgium; 2 da (Vanessa b 1966, Miranda b 1967), 1 s (Edward b 1972); *Career* served RE 1960–66, seconded Malaysian Engrs 1963–66, operational serv Kenya, Northern Malaysia and Sarawak, Capt RE; joined R H Harry Stanger 1966, ptnr Al Hoty Stanger Ltd Saudia Arabia 1975–; chm: Harry Stanger Ltd 1972–90, Stanger Consultants Ltd 1990–93; first sec-gen European Orgn for Testing and Certification 1993–97 (UK rep on Cncl 1990–93), dir David H Stanger sprl 1997–2001, conslt materials engr 2001–; conslt Int Trade Centre (UNCTAD/WTO); chm: Assoc of Consulting Scientists 1981–83, NAMAS Advsy Ctee 1985–87, Standards Quality Measurement Advsy Ctee 1987–91, Advsy Bd Brunel Centre for Mfrg Metrology 1991–93, Lab Ctee Int Lab Accreditation Co-Operation (ILAC, memb Exec Ctee 1998–2002); memb: Steering Ctee NATLAS 1981–85, Advsy Cncl for Calibration and Measurement 1982–87, Br C of C in Belguim 1997–; Conseil National des Inqenieurs et des Scientifiques de France (CNISF): memb Br Section 1975–, memb Belgian Section 2002–; Union Int des Laboratoires Independent (UILI): memb Governing Bd 1997–, sec-gen 1984–93 and 2001–03, rep to ISO/CASCO 2001–; vice-pres IQA 1986–2007 (chm Cncl 1990–93); chm Br Measurement and Testing Assoc 1990–93; Freeman Worshipful Co of Water Conservators 1989; FRSA 1987 (memb Belgium section); *Publications* Responsibility for Quality within British Industry (1989), Supporting European Quality Policies (1995), Customer Connection to a Global Laboratory Service (2000), Laboratory Services in a Global Marketplace (2002); *Recreations* collecting vintage wines; *Style*— D H Stanger, Esq, OBE; ✉ Rue du Tabellion 41, B-1050 Brussels, Belgium (tel and fax 00 32 2 345 1242, e-mail dhs@dhs.be)

STANIER, Capt Sir Beville Douglas; 3 Bt (UK 1917), of Peplow Hall, Market Drayton, Shropshire; s of Brig Sir Alexander Beville Gibbons Stanier, 2 Bt, DSO, MC, JP, DL (d 1995), and Dorothy Gladys, *née* Miller (d 1973); *b* 20 April 1934; *Educ* Eton; *m* 23 Feb 1963, (Violet) Shelagh, da of Maj James Stockley Sinnott (ka 1941), of Tetbury, Glos; 2 da (Henrietta (Mrs Magnus Morgan) b 1965, Lucinda (Mrs James Martin) b 1967), 1 s (Alexander James Sinnott b 1970); *Heir* s, Alexander Stanier; *Career* serv Welsh Gds 1952–60 (2 Lt 1953, Lt 1955, Capt 1958), UK, Egypt, Aust; ADC to Govr-Gen of Aust (Field Marshal Viscount Slim) 1959–60; stockbroker, ptnr Kitcat & Aitken 1960–76; farmer 1974–; conslt Hales Snails Ltd 1976–88; chm Buckingham Constituency Cons Assoc 1999–2003, chm Oxfordshire and Buckinghamshire Area Conservatives 2003–04; memb Aylesbury Vale DC 1999– (cabinet 2001–); memb Whaddon Parish Cncl 1976– (chm 1983–); *Recreations* shooting, cricket; *Clubs* MCC; *Style*— Capt Sir Beville Stanier, Bt; ✉ Kings Close House, Whaddon, Buckinghamshire MK17 0NG (tel 01908 501738, fax 01908 522027, e-mail bdstanier@aol.com); Home Farm, Shotover Park, Wheatley, Oxfordshire OX33 1QP (tel 077 7830 5419)

STANLEY, Ailsa; OBE (1976); da of Albert Smith (d 1979), of Hull, and Ellen, *née* Dunn (d 1962); *b* 3 June 1918; *Educ* Eversleigh HS Hull, Woods Coll Hull; *m* 19 June 1948, Harry Ronald Stanley, s of Harry Stanley; *Career* sec London N Eastern Railway Co 1934–38, sec to gen mangr Hull Daily Mail 1938–39, organiser Hull Daily Mail Comfort Fund 1939–45, business mangr and ed monthly jl 1946–48, sometime freelance journalist Nottingham Evening Post, ed The Soroptimist (jl of the Fedn of Soroptimist Clubs of GB & I) 1962–90, ed The International Soroptimist 1976–91; currently life pres Radio Trent (fndr bd memb 1975–) and RAM FM Ltd; life vice-pres Mapperley Hosp League of Friends (fndr memb 1955, sometime chm), formerly memb Metrication Bd, memb Consumer Policy Ctee BSI 1965– (chm 1967–70), memb Mgmnt Ctee Nottingham CAB (co fndr, sometime chm), memb Bd Nottingham Playhouse; JP Nottingham 1957–88; *Recreations* walking, theatre, entertaining; *Clubs* Soroptimist International of Nottingham, European Union of Women, Fawcett Soc; *Style*— Mrs Ailsa Stanley, OBE; ✉ Radio Trent Ltd, 29–31 Castle Gate, Nottingham NG1 7AP (tel 0115 952 7000, fax 0115 952 7003)

STANLEY, Barbara Elizabeth; da of Master John Morrison Hunter, CBE (d 1999), of Bangor, NI, and Elizabeth, *née* McKeag; *b* 2 July 1950, Belfast; *Educ* Glenlola Collegiate Sch Bangor NI, Queen's Univ Belfast (foundation scholar, BA), Univ of Leicester (PGCE); *m* 1978, Graham Stanley; 2 da (Louise b 25 Oct 1979, Jillian b 25 May 1982); *Career* teacher 1973–78 and 1986–; head of house Forest Sch Snaresbrook 1986–90, head of geography St Bernard's Convent Slough 1990–92, dep head Channing Sch Highgate 1992–95, headmistress Bedford HS 1995–2000, princ Alexandra Coll Dublin 2000–02, headmistress The Abbey Sch Reading 2002–; involved with Corrymeela Community NI, church and parish cncls; FRGS 2001; *Recreations* outdoor activities, travel, community involvement, book group; *Clubs* Univ Women's; *Style*— Mrs Barbara Stanley; ✉ The Abbey School, Kendrick Road, Reading RG1 5DZ (tel 0118 987 2256, fax 0118 987 1478, e-mail head@theabbey.co.uk)

STANLEY, Rt Hon Sir John Paul; kt (1988), PC (1984), MP; s of Harry Stanley (d 1956), and Maud Stanley (d 1993); *b* 19 January 1942; *Educ* Repton, Lincoln Coll Oxford; *m* 1968, Susan Elizabeth Giles; 2 s, 1 da; *Career* Cons Res Dept (Housing) 1967–68, res assoc IISS 1968–69, fin exec RTZ Corporation 1969–74; MP (Cons) Tonbridge and Malling Feb 1974–, memb Parly Select Ctee on Nationalised Industries 1974–76, PPS to Rt Hon Margaret Thatcher 1976–79, min for housing and construction with rank of min of state (DOE) 1979–83, min of state for armed forces MOD 1983–87, min of state for NI 1987–88; memb Parly Select Ctee on Foreign Affrs 1992–; *Recreations* music, arts, sailing; *Style*— The Rt Hon Sir John Stanley, MP; ✉ House of Commons, London SW1A 0AA

STANLEY, Martin Edward; s of Edward Alan Stanley, of Northumberland, and Dorothy, *née* Lewis; *b* 1 November 1948; *Educ* Royal GS Newcastle upon Tyne, Magdalen Coll Oxford (exhibitioner, BA); *m* 1971 (m dis 1991), Marilyn Joan, *née* Lewis; 1 s (Edward b 8 April 1983); partner Janice Munday; 2 s (Nicholas decd, Joshua b 4 July 1998); *Career* various positions Inland Revenue 1971–80; DTI: various positions 1980–90, princ private sec 1990–92, head Engrg, Automotive and Metals Div 1992–96, dir of infrastructure and energy projects 1996–98; dir Regulatory Impact Unit Cabinet Office 1998–99, chief exec Postal Services Cmmn 2000–04, chief exec Competition Cmmn 2004–; ed: www.civilservant.org.uk, www.vauxhallandkennington.org.uk; formerly non-exec dir: American Express, IBM, Atmaana Ltd; *Publications* How to be a Civil Servant; *Recreations* travel, walking, sailing; *Style*— Mr Martin Stanley; ✉ Competition Commission, Victoria House, Southampton Row, London WC1B 4AD

STANLEY, Oliver Duncan; s of late Bernard Stanley, and late Mabel *née* Best; *b* 5 June 1925; *Educ* Rhyl GS, ChCh Oxford (MA), Harvard Univ; *m* 7 Sept 1954, Ruth Leah Stanley (d 2002); 3 da (Nicola b 1955, Katherine b 1960, Sarah b 1963), 1 s (Julian b 1958); *Career* served 8 Hussars 1943–47; called to the Bar Middle Temple 1963; HM inspr of taxes 1952–65; dir: Gray Dawes Bank 1966–72, Rathbone Brothers plc 1971– (chm 1984–97, dir 1984–2000), Axa Equity & Law plc 1992–97; chm Profile Books 1996–2005; memb: Cncl of Legal Educn 1992–96, Nat Museums and Galleries Merseyside Devpt Tst 1994–96; govr IOC Law Sch 1996–99; *Books* Guide to Taxation (1967), Taxology (1971), Creation and Protection of Capital (1974), Taxation of Farmers and Landowners (1981, 20 edn 2007), Hotel Victoire (2007); *Recreations* music, tennis, French; *Clubs* Travellers; *Style*— Oliver Stanley, Esq; ✉ Rathbone Brothers plc, 159 New Bond Street, London W1Y 9PA (e-mail oliver@oduncan.wanadoo.co.uk)

STANLEY, Peter Henry Arthur; s of Col F A Stanley, OBE (d 1979), of Liphook, Hants, and Ann Jane, *née* Collins (d 1997); *b* 17 March 1933; *Educ* Eton; *m* 1, 7 May 1965 (m dis), Gunilla Margaretha Antonia Sophie, da of Count Wilhelm Douglas (d 1987), of Schloss Langenstein, Baden Wurttemberg; 1 da (Louisa b 1966), 1 s (Robin b 1968); m 2, 21 May 1990 (m dis), Mrs Lucy Campbell, da of James A Barnett, of Bel Air, CA; m 3, 29 May 1999, Hon Mrs Caroline Parr, da of Baron Renton, KBE, TD, PC, QC, DL (Life Peer); *Career* Grenadier Gds 1951–53; CA; trainee Dixon Wilson 1953–58, Peat Marwick (NY and Toronto) 1959–60, ptnr Hill Chaplin & Co (stockbrokers) 1961–68, chm and ceo Williams de Broë plc 1984–93 (dir 1968–93), chm BWD Securities plc 1995–2000 (dir 1994–2000), chm Manchester & London Investment Tst 2001– (dir 1997–); memb Cncl Stock Exchange 1979–86, dir Securities Assoc 1986–91 (chm Capital Ctee); FCA 1958; *Recreations* tennis, golf, shooting; *Clubs* White's, Swinley Forest Golf; *Style*— Peter Stanley, Esq; ✉ Cundall Hall, Helperby, North Yorkshire YO61 2RP (tel 01423 360252, fax 01423 360663, e-mail pstanyork@hotmail.com)

STANLEY OF ALDERLEY, 8 Baron (UK 1839); Sir Thomas Henry Oliver Stanley; 14 Bt (E 1660), DL (Gwynedd 1985); also Baron Sheffield (I 1783) and Baron Eddisbury of Winnington (UK 1848); s of Lt-Col the Hon Oliver Hugh Stanley, DSO, JP, DL (d 1952, s of 4 Baron; descended from Sir John Stanley of Alderley, yr bro of 1 Earl of Derby), and Lady Kathleen, *née* Thynne (d 1977), da of 5 Marquess of Bath; suc cous, 7 Baron (who preferred to be known as Lord Sheffield) 1971; *b* 28 September 1927; *Educ* Wellington; *m* 30 April 1955, Jane Barrett, da of late Ernest George Hartley; 3 s (Richard, Charles, Harry), 1 da (Lucinda); *Heir* s, Hon Richard Stanley; *Career* sat as Cons in House of Lords until 1999; Capt (ret) Coldstream Gds and Gds Ind Parachute Co; farmer in Anglesey and Oxfordshire; chm Thames Valley Cereals Ltd 1979–81; vice-pres RNLI 2003– (memb Ctee of Mgmnt 1981–2003, chm Fund Raising Ctee 1986–94); govr St Edwards Sch Oxford 1979–98; patron Ucheldre Centre Maritime Museum; memb: Friends of St Cybi Holyhead, Anglesey Antiquarian Soc; FRAgS; *Publications* Stanley's of Alderley 1927–2001; *Recreations* sailing, fishing, skiing; *Clubs* Farmers', Pratts; *Style*— The Rt Hon the Lord Stanley of Alderley, DL; ✉ Trysglwyn Fawr, Rhosybol, Amlwch, Anglesey (tel 01407 830364, fax 01407 830364); Rectory Farm, Stanton St John, Oxford (tel 0186 351214)

STANSALL, Paul James; s of James Douglas Stansall (d 1984), of Newark, Notts, and Vera Jean, *née* Hall (d 2002); *b* 21 September 1946; *Educ* Winifred Portland Secdy Tech Sch Worksop, RCA (MA), Leicester Poly (DipArch); *m* 1, 1 Jan 1970 (m dis 1993), Angela Mary, da of Alexander Burgon (d 1954), of Beeston, Notts; 1 da (Alexandra b 1984); m 2, 15 July 2000, Moira Alison, da of Basil Fionn Young, of Thurso, Scotland; *Career* res asst UCL (memb Space Syntax Res Team) 1975–80, assoc DEGW Architects Planners and Designers (memb ORBIT 2 Team) 1980–89, visiting prof Cornell Univ 1987–88, founding ptnr Allinson Stansall Partnership conslt architects 1989–90, dir Tectus Architecture Ltd 1991–2003, dir Tectus Space Mgmnt 2003–; visiting lectr in property mgmnt Civil Service Coll 1991–2003, visiting lectr various UK univs; corp memb Br Cncl for Offices; former memb Editorial Bd Jl of Property Mgmnt 1993; conslt to int cos, govt depts and local authorities (incl: Nat Audit Office, BA, The Wellcome Tst, Nomura Bank, DTI, City Univ, Winchester City Cncl) on space mgmnt; published numerous res papers and articles 1974–; memb: ARCUK 1981, Amnesty Int 2003–; RIBA 1987; *Recreations* history of science, walking, cooking, Tai Chi, choral music; *Style*— Paul Stansall, Esq; ✉ Tectus Space Management Ltd, 2 Frankley Buildings, Bath BA1 6EG (tel and fax 01225 444217, e-mail paul.stansall@virgin.net, website www.tectus-spacemanagement.co.uk)

STANSBIE, (John) Michael; s of John Albert Stansbie, MBE, of Willersey, Worcs, and Norah Lydia, *née* Hopkins; *b* 2 October 1941; *Educ* Bolton Sch, ChCh Oxford (MA), Middlesex Hosp Med Sch (BM BCh); *m* 12 April 1969, Patricia, da of Joseph Arthur Dunn of St Arvans, Gwent; 2 s (Nicholas b 1973, Nigel b 1975); *Career* house surgn Middx Hosp London 1967, house physican Hillingdon Hosp Middx 1967–68, casualty offr Kettering Gen Hosp 1969, ENT registrar and sr ENT house offr Queen Elizabeth Hosp Birmingham 1970–71, sr ENT registrar W Midlands Trg Scheme 1972–76, conslt ENT surgn Walsgrave Hosps NHS Tst Coventry 1977–2001; lectr in anatomy Leicester/Warwick Med Sch 2001–; W Midlands regnl advsr in otolaryngology RCS 1988–94, chm W Midlands Region Trg Sub-Ctee in Otolaryngology 1991–94, sec Midland Inst of Otology 1981–90; memb Panel of Examiners Intercollegiate Specialty Bd in Otolaryngology RCS 1996–2001; sec Shows Ctee Br Cactus and Succulent Soc 2004– (chm Coventry and Dist Branch 1987–90); FRCS 1972, FRSM 1977; *Recreations* natural history, cactus collecting and judging; *Style*— Michael Stansbie, Esq; ✉ 76 Bransford Avenue, Cannon Park, Coventry CV4 7EB (tel 024 7641 6755, e-mail mstansbie@doctors.org.uk)

STANSBY, John; s of Dumon Stansby (d 1980), and Vera Margaret, *née* Main (d 1972); *b* 2 July 1930; *Educ* Oundle, Jesus Coll Cambridge (scholar, MA); *m* 22 July 1966, Anna-Maria, da of Dr Harald Kruschewsky; 1 da (Daniela b 1967), 1 step s (Oliver b 1957), 1 step da (Veronica b 1960); *Career* Nat Serv cmmnd Queen's Royal Regt with Somaliland Scouts Br Somaliland 1949–50, Essex Regt TA 1950–55; domestic fuels mktg mangr Shell Mex & BP Ltd 1955–62, sr mktg conslt AIC Ltd 1962–65, dir Rank Leisure Services Ltd 1966–70, dir Energy Div P&O Steam Navigation Co 1970–74; chm: Dumon Stansby & Co Ltd 1974–, UIE (UK) Ltd (Bouygues Offshore) 1974–99, SAUR (UK) Ltd 1986–89, Bouygues (UK) Ltd 1986–91, Cementation-SAUR Water Services plc 1986–88, SAUR Water Services plc 1988–89, London Minsk Development Co plc 1993–96; dep chm: London Transport Exec 1978–80, Energy Resources Ltd 1990–92; dir Bouygues UK Ltd 1997–2005; FInstPet, FCIT, FRSA; Chevalier de l'Ordre National du Mérite; *Recreations* music, theatre, history; *Clubs* Travellers; *Style*— John Stansby, Esq; ✉ Apartment 5, Cranley Gardens, London SW7 3BD (tel 020 7835 1913, fax 020 7370 5259)

STANSFIELD, Lisa; da of Keith Stansfield, and Marion, *née* Kelly; *b* 11 April 1966; *Educ* Redbrook Middle Sch Rochdale, Oulder Hill Community Sch Rochdale; *Partner* Ian Owen Devaney; *Career* pop singer; formed band Blue Zone (with Andy Morris and Ian Devaney) 1986; solo albums: Affection (UK no 2) 1989, Real Love 1991 (jt album sales of over 8m), So Natural (1993), Lisa Stansfield (1997); recorded version of Cole Porter's Down In The Depths for Red Hot and Blue LP (raising funds for Aids Research) 1990; numerous maj tours 1990–92 incl Rock in Rio concert (audience 100,000) 1990 and world tour (UK, Europe, N America, Japan and SE Asia) 1992; other charity work: Trading Places (breast cancer), Prince's Tst, Simple Truth concert (for the Kurds), Red Hot and Blue and Red Hot and Dance, Freddie Mercury Tribute concert for Aids Awareness (Wembley Stadium, audience 75,000) 1992; *Awards* Best Female Artist BRIT Awards 1990–91 and 1991–92 (Best Newcomer 1989–90), Best Contemporary Song (All Around The World) Ivor Novello Awards 1990, Best Int Song Ivor Novello Awards 1991, Best New Artist Silver Clef Awards 1990, Best Newcomer US Billboard Awards 1990, Best New Female Singer Rolling Stone magazine 1991, Best Br Artist World Music Awards Monte Carlo 1991, two Grammy Award nominations 1991; *Recreations* painting, cooking, crosswords, drinking; *Style*— Ms Lisa Stansfield

S

STANSFIELD SMITH, Sir Colin; kt (1993), CBE (1988); s of Mr Stansfield Smith, and Mary, *née* Simpson; *b* 1 October 1932; *Educ* William Hulmes GS, Univ of Cambridge (MA, DipArch); *m* 17 Feb 1961, Angela Jean Earnshaw, da of Eric Maw (d 1970), of Rustington, W Sussex; 1 da (Sophie b 1967), 1 s (Oliver b 1970); *Career* Nat Serv Intelligence Corps 1951–53; ptnr Emberton Tardrew & Partners 1965–71, dep co architect Cheshire CC 1971–73, co architect Hants 1973–92 (conslt co architect 1992–), prof of architectural design Sch of Architecture Portsmouth Univ 1990–; vice-pres RIBA 1983–86; chm Estates Sub Ctee MCC 1978–84; Royal Gold Medal for Architecture RIBA 1991; ARIBA; *Recreations* painting, golf; *Clubs* MCC, Hockley Golf; *Style—* Prof Sir Colin Stansfield Smith, CBE; ✉ e-mail c.stansfieldsmith@talk21.com

STANSGATE, Viscountcy of; *see:* Benn, Rt Hon Anthony Neil Wedgwood, MP

STANTON, David; CB (2000); *b* 5 November 1942; *Educ* Worcester Coll Oxford (BA), LSE (MSc); *Career* Nuffield fell Central Planning Bureau Uganda 1965–67, lectr Brunel Univ 1967–70, on staff Highway Economics Unit Miny of Tport 1970–71, economic advsr DOE 1971–74, economic advsr HM Treasy 1974–75, seconded as sr economic advsr Hong Kong Govt 1975–77; Dept of Employment: sr economic advsr Unit for Manpower Studies 1977–80, economic analyst Economics Branch 1980–83, dir EMRU 1983–87, chief economist 1988–92; dir Analytical Servs Div DSS 1992–; *Style—* David Stanton, Esq, CB

STANTON, David Leslie; s of Leslie Stanton (d 1981), of Birmingham, and C Mary, *née* Staynes (d 2001); *b* 29 April 1943; *Educ* Bootham Sch York, Balliol Coll Oxford (BA); *m* 6 May 1989, Rosemary Jane, da of Kenneth Brown; 1 da (Acadia Elena b 27 April 1995); *Career* asst princ ODM 1965–69, SSRC sr scholarship Univ of Oxford 1969–71, princ ODA 1971–75, first sec Office of UK Perm Rep to EC 1975–77, memb Bd of Dirs Asian Devpt Bank 1979–82, head of dept ODA 1982–92, fin and admin advsr (on secondment) EBRD 1990–91, dir World Bank Gp 1992–97, memb Exec Bd and UK perm delg (with personal rank of ambass) UNESCO 1997–2003 (chair Fin and Admin Cmmn 2000–01), chair of tstees UNICEF UK 2004–; chair Exec Ctee Int Campaign for the Establishment of the Nubia Museum in Aswan and the Nat Museum of Egyptian Civilization in Cairo 2002–03; govr Canonbury Sch 2003–06 (vice-chair 2005–06); *Recreations* mountains, gardens, painting; *Style—* David Stanton, Esq; ✉ UNICEF UK, Africa House, 64–78 Kingsway, London WC2B 6NB (tel 020 7405 5592, fax 020 7405 2332)

STANTON, Prof Graham Norman; s of Norman Schofield Stanton, and Gladys Jean Stanton; *Educ* King's HS Dunedin, Univ of Otago (BA, MA, BD), Univ of Cambridge (Lewis and Gibson scholar, PhD); *m* 1965, Valerie Esther Douglas; 2 s, 1 da; *Career* temp lectr Princeton Theological Seminary 1969, Naden post-doctoral student St John's Coll Cambridge 1969–70; KCL: lectr 1970–77, prof of New Testament studies 1977–98, dean Faculty of Theology and Religious Studies 1982–84, head Dept of Biblical Studies 1982–88, Gresham Prof of Divinity 1984–97, head Dept of Theology and Religious Studies 1996–98; Univ of Cambridge: Lady Margaret's prof of divinity 1998–, chm Faculty Bd of Divinity 2001–03; fell Fitzwilliam Coll Cambridge; delivered numerous invited lectures in UK and overseas; ed: Oxford Bible Series (with P R Ackroyd) 1979–94, New Testament Studies 1982–90, Society for New Testament Studies Monograph Series 1982–91; gen ed International Critical Commentaries 1984–; pres Studiorum Novi Testamenti Societas 1996–97 (memb 1975–, sec 1976–82), chm Br Soc of New Testament Studies 1989–92; Burkitt Medal for Biblical Studies Br Acad 2006; Hon DD Univ of Otago; FKC; *Books* Jesus of Nazareth in New Testament Preaching (1974, 2 edn 1977, new edn 2004), The Interpretation of Matthew (ed, 1983, revised edn 1994), The Gospels and Jesus (1989, revised edn 2002), A Gospel for a New People: Studies in Matthew (1992), Resurrection: Essays in Honour of J L Houlden (ed with Stephen Barton, 1994), Gospel Truth? New Light on Jesus and the Gospels (1995, revised edn 1997), Tolerance and Intolerance in Early Judaism and Christianity (ed with G G Stroumsa, 1998), Reading Texts, Seeking Wisdom (ed with D F Ford, 2003), Lady Margaret Beaufort and her Professors of Divinity at Cambridge (with P Collinson and R Rex, 2003), Jesus and Gospel (2004), The Holy Spirit and Christian Origins (ed with S C Barton and B W Longenecker, 2004); *Recreations* gardening, walking, music, cricket; *Style—* Prof Graham Stanton; ✉ 11 Dane Drive, Cambridge CB3 9LP (tel 01223 740560); Faculty of Divinity, University of Cambridge, West Road, Cambridge CB3 9BS (tel 01223 763042, fax 01223 763003, e-mail gns23@cam.ac.uk)

STANTON, Dr Lyndon; s of Joseph Reginald Stanton (d 1986), and Violet Hazel, *née* Sears; *b* 1942, Newport, Monmouthshire; *Educ* Newport HS for Boys, Univ of Wales (BSc, PhD); *m* 1964, Carol Ann, *née* Smith; 2 da (Victoria Jane (Dr McLean) b 1969, Leonie Alexandra b 1971); *Career* Salters' research fell Emmanuel Coll Cambridge, various commercial and technical appts ICI Ltd 1969–79; Arco Chemical Europe: gen mangr sales and mktg 1979–81, mangr M&A 1981–83, business mangr Urethanes 1983–88, dir Business Devpt 1988–91, vice-pres Business Mgmnt 1991–94, pres and ceo 1994–98; pres and ceo Lyondell Chemical Europe (following merger) 1998–2000; non-exec dir: Environment Agency 2002– (chm Industry Sub-Ctee, chm Southern Region Advsy Panel), Nuclear Decommissioning Authy 2004–; author of scientific papers on nonlinear light scattering and atomic and molecular physics in learned jls; tstee: Prince of Wales's Phoenix Tst 1996–2004 (chm 2003–04), Earthwatch Europe 1997–2002, Churches Conservation Tst 1999–2005 (dep chm 2001–05), Norden Farm Centre for the Arts 2002– (chm Finance and Mgmnt Ctee); *Recreations* watersports (especially scuba diving), collecting antique furniture and antiquarian scientific textbooks, photography and music; *Clubs* Athenaeum; *Style—* Dr Lyndon Stanton; ✉ Broadley, 11 Woodlands Ride, Ascot, Berkshire SL5 9HP (tel 01344 626904, fax 01344 627045, e-mail lyndon.stanton@btinternet.com)

STANTON, Prof Stuart Lawrence; s of Michael Arthur Stanton (d 1968), and Sarah, *née* Joseph (d 1992); *b* 24 October 1938; *Educ* City of London Sch, London Hosp Med Sch (MB BS); *m* 1, 25 Feb 1965; 3 da (Claire b 1967, Talia b 1970, Joanna b 1972); m 2, 17 Feb 1991; 1 da (Tamara b 1991), 1 s (Noah b 1994); *Career* conslt urogynaecologist St George's Hosp 1984–2003, prof St George's Hosp Med Sch 1997– (hon sr lectr 1984–97); assoc: Br Assoc of Urological Surgns, European Assoc of Urologists; memb: Blair Bell Res Soc, Int Continence Soc; MRCS LRCP 1961, FRCS 1966, FRCOG 1987; *Books* Clinical Gynaecologic Urology (1984), Surgery of Female Incontinence (co ed with Emil Tanagho, 1986), Principles of Gynaecological Surgery (1987), Gynaecology in the Elderly (1988), Gynaecology (co-ed, 1992, 2 edn 1997), Clinical Urogynaecology (co-ed, 1999), Urinary Tract Infection in the Female (co-ed, 2000); *Recreations* photography, travel, opera, theatre, modern ceramics; *Style—* Prof Stuart Stanton; ✉ Flat 10, 43 Wimpole Street, London W1G 8AE (tel 020 7486 0677, fax 020 7486 6792, website www.urogyn.co.uk)

STAPLE, George Warren; CB (1996), Hon QC (1997); s of Kenneth Harry Staple, OBE (d 1978), and Betty Mary, *née* Lemon (d 2000); bro of William Philip Staple, *qv*; *b* 13 September 1940; *Educ* Haileybury; *m* Jan 1968, Olivia Deirdre, da of William James Lowry (d 1952), of Mtoko, Southern Rhodesia; 2 da (Alice b 1969, Polly b 1970), 2 s (Harry b 1976, Edward b 1978); *Career* admitted slr 1964; conslt Clifford Chance 2001– (ptnr 1967–92 and 1997–2001); DTI inspr: Consolidated Gold Fields plc 1986, Aldermanbury Trust plc 1988 (reported Dec 1990); dir the Serious Fraud Office 1992–97; chm of tbnls Securities and Futures Authy 1988–92, chm Fraud Advsy Panel 1998–2003; chm Review Bd for Govt Contracts 2002–; memb: Commercial Court Ctee 1978–92, Court of Govrs London Guildhall Univ 1982–94, Cncl Law Soc 1986–2000 (treas 1989–92), Law Advsy Ctee Br Cncl 1998–2001, Sr Salaries Review Body 2000–04, Accountants Disciplinary Tribunal 2005–; tstee Royal Humane Soc; chm of govrs Haileybury 2000–; hon bencher Inner Temple 2000; *Recreations* cricket, hill walking; *Clubs* Brooks's, City of London, MCC; *Style—* George Staple, Esq, CB, QC; ✉ Clifford Chance, 10 Upper Bank Street, London E14 5JJ (tel 020 7006 1000, fax 020 7006 5555)

STAPLE, William Philip; s of Kenneth Harry Staple, OBE (d 1978), and Betty Mary, *née* Lemon (d 2000); bro of George Warren Staple, CB, QC, *qv*; *b* 28 September 1947; *Educ* Haileybury, Coll of Law; *m* 14 May 1977 (m dis 1986), Jennifer Frances, da of Brig James Douglas Walker, OBE, of Farnham; 1 s (Oliver b 1980), 1 da (Sophia b 1982); *Career* called to the Bar 1970; exec Cazenove & Co 1972–81, dir N M Rothschild and Sons Ltd 1986–94 (asst dir 1982–86) and 1996–99, DG Panel on Takeovers and Mergers 1994–96, md Benfield Advisory 1999–2001, dir Brown, Shipley Corp Fin 2001–04, md Westhouse Securities 2004–; non-exec dir Grampian Holdings plc 1984–91; *Recreations* a variety of sports, theatre; *Clubs* White's, City of London; *Style—* William Staple, Esq; ✉ Westhouse Securities Ltd, Clements House, 14–18 Gresham Street, London EC2V 7NN (tel 020 7601 6100)

STAPLETON, Anthony Elliott Hopewell; s of Lt-Col B A Stapleton, CBE, MC, TD (d 1996), and Ann Elliott, *née* Batt (d 1973); *b* 11 August 1940; *Educ* Wrekin Coll; *m* 29 Aug 1964, Deana Mary (decd), da of James McCauley; 1 s (Andrew Elliot b 7 April 1969); *Career* trainee Selfridges London 1958–61, asst mangr Lewis's Leicester 1961–62, asst buyer Lewis's London 1962, asst to gen mangr (on acquisition of Ilford Store) 1962–63, sales mangr Lewis's Bristol 1963–67, special accounts controller S Reece & Son Liverpool 1967–68; floor controller: Lewis's Liverpool 1969–70 (asst to Promotions Dir 1968–69), Lewis's Birmingham 1970–73; asst gen mangr: Lewis's Leicester 1973–74, Lewis's Birmingham 1974–76; gen mangr Selfridges Oxford 1976–79, merchandise dir Selfridges London 1979–85, gen mangr John Radcliffe Hosp Oxford 1985–93, Associated Nursing Services plc 1994–96, Speciality Care plc 1996–98, ret; currently advsr to small companies; parish cncllr; dir Lindeth Coll Cumbria 1996–98; chm Oxford Crime Prevention Ctee 1977–79, memb Oxford St Traders' Assoc 1979–85, memb Steering Ctee Better Made in Britain 1983, exec Textile Benevolent Assoc 1980–85, memb Clothing Panel NEDO 1980–85; *Recreations* family, home brewing, gardening, photography, golf, travel; *Clubs* Oxford Management, Probus (former chair), Springs Golf Wallingford (former capt); *Style—* Anthony Stapleton, Esq; ✉ Cedars, Slade End, Brightwell cum Sotwell, Wallingford, Oxfordshire OX10 0RD (tel 01491 838886)

STAPLETON, Nigel John; s of Capt Frederick Ernest John Stapleton, of Winchmore Hill, London, and Katie Margaret, *née* Tyson; *b* 1 November 1946; *Educ* City of London Sch, Fitzwilliam Coll Cambridge (MA); *m* 20 Dec 1982, Johanna Augusta, da of Johan Molhoek, of Vienna, Austria; 1 s (Henry James b 1988), 1 da (Elizabeth Jane Cornelia b 1990); *Career* Unilever plc: various commercial appts 1968–83, vice-pres fin Unilever (United States) Inc 1983–86; Reed International plc: fin dir 1986–96, dep chm 1994–97, chm 1997–99; co-chief exec Reed Elsevier plc 1996–99 (chief fin offr 1993–96, chm 1996–98); chm: Veronis Suhler Int Ltd 1999–2002, Uniq plc 2001–, Cordiant Communications Gp plc 2003; non-exec dir: Allied Domecq plc (Allied-Lyons plc until 1994) 1993–99, Marconi plc 1997–2002, Sun Life and Provincial Holdings plc 1999–2000, AXA UK plc 2000–02, Royal Opera House Tst 2000–01, London Stock Exchange plc 2001–, Reliance Security Gp plc 2002–; chm Postal Services Cmmn 2004–; hon fell Fitzwilliam Coll Cambridge 1998–; FCMA 1987 (ACMA 1972); *Recreations* classical music, travel, tennis, opera; *Clubs* Oxford and Cambridge; *Style—* Nigel Stapleton, Esq; ✉ Postal Services Commission, Hercules House, 6 Hercules Road, London SE1 7DB (tel 020 7593 2102, fax 020 7593 2142, e-mail nigel.stapleton@psc.gov.uk)

STARK, Peter Harry Geoffrey; s of Geoffrey Stark (d 1981), of Bournemouth, Dorset, and Barbara, *née* Willis; *b* Guildford, Surrey; *Educ* Bournemouth Sch, Royal Coll of Music, Vienna Meisterkurse; *Family* 1 s (Harry b 1983), 1 da (Joanna b 1986); *Career* violinist: WNO 1978–88 (princ 2nd violin 1985–88), RPO 1981–83; freelance conductor 1990–; Leverhulme prof of conducting Nat Youth Orch of GB 1985–, prof of conducting Jr Acad Royal Acad of Music 1989–, sr fell of conducting and orchestral studies Trinity Coll of Music 1997–2004, prof of conducting Royal Coll of Music 2007–; artistic dir: Parnassus 1999–, W of Eng Philharmonic Orch 2000– (also conductor); princ conductor: Ernest Read Symphony Orch 1989–, Herts Co Youth Orch 1995–, Cambridge Univ Chamber Orch 2002–; conducted orchs incl: BBC Concert Orch, BBC Nat Orch of Wales, Berlin Symphony Orch, English Chamber Orch, Guildford Philharmonic Orch, LSO, Malaysian Philharmonic Orch, Orch of the Age of Enlightenment, Orch of the Maggio Musicale Fiorentino, WNO, Nat Youth Chamber Orch, Nat Children's Orch; worked with soloists incl: Prof Nicholas Daniel, Stephen Isserlis, CBE, John Lill, CBE, *qqv*; performed in major concert halls in London (incl Royal Festival Hall and Barbican) and UK; toured: Belguim, Bermuda, Denmark, France, Germany, Holland, Italy, Malta, Poland, Sweden, Switzerland, USA; asst to conductors incl: Sir Colin Davis, CH, CBE, Sir Andrew Davis, CBE, Sir Simon Rattle, CBE, *qqv*, Baron Menuhin, OM, KBE, Klaus Tennstedt; numerous recordings for BBC Radio; prizewinner Third Leeds Comp for Conductors 1987, finalist Vittorio Gui Int Comp 1980; Royal Coll of Music: Adrian Boult Conducting Scholarship 1977, Theodore Steir Conducting Prize 1977, Arthur Bliss Prize 1977, Tagore Gold Medal 1977; Allcard Grant Worshipful Co of Musicians 1979; Hon DMus UWE 2000; GRSM 1976, ARCM 1977, Hon ARAM 1996, Hon FTCL 1996; *Style—* Dr Peter Stark; ✉ Flat 1, 101 Walm Lane, Willesden Green, London NW2 4QG (tel and fax 020 8208 1709, e-mail pstark@mac.com)

STARKEY, Dr David; CBE (2007); *b* 1945; *Educ* Kendal GS, Fitzwilliam Coll Cambridge (open scholar, major state studentship, MA, PhD); *Career* research fell Fitzwilliam Coll Cambridge 1970–72, lectr in history Dept of Int History LSE 1972–98, visiting fell Fitzwilliam Coll Cambridge 1998–2001 (bye-fell 2001–); visiting Vernon prof of biography Dartmouth Coll NH 1987 and 1989, Br Cncl specialist visitor Australia 1989; contrib various newspapers, diary columnist The Sunday Times and Spectator, reg panellist Moral Maze (BBC Radio 4) 1992–2001, presenter weekend show Talk Radio 1995–98; presenter/writer: This Land of England (3 part series, Channel Four) 1985, Henry VIII (3 part series, Channel Four) 1998, Elizabeth I (4 part series, Channel Four) 2000, The Six Wives of Henry VIII (Channel Four) 2001, David Starkey's Henry VIII (Channel 4) 2002 (Indie Documentary Award 2002), The Unknown Tudors (Channel 4) 2002, Monarchy (Channel 4) 2004–07; memb Editorial Bd History Today 1980–, memb Commemorative Plaques Working Gp English Heritage 1993–2007, pres Soc for Court Studies 1996–2004; vice-pres Tory Campaign for Homosexual Equality (TORCHE) 1994–, hon assoc Rationalist Press Assoc 1995–, hon assoc Nat Secular Soc 1999–; historical advsr to quincentennial exhbn Henry VIII at Greenwich Nat Maritime Museum 1991; guest curator: Elizabeth exhbn Greenwich Nat Maritime Museum 2003, Lost Facts exhbn Philip Mould Gallery 2007; Norton Medlicott Medal for Services to History Historical Assoc 2001; Freeman Worshipful Co of Barbers 1992 (Liveryman 1999); Hon DLitt Lancaster Univ 2004, Hon DLitt Univ of Kent 2006; FRHistS 1984, FSA 1994; *Books* This Land of England (with David Souden, 1985), The Reign of Henry VIII: Personalities and Politics (1985, 2 edn 1991), Revolution Reassessed: Revisions in the History of Tudor Government and Administration (ed with Christopher Coleman, 1986), The English Court from the Wars of the Roses to the Civil War (ed, 1987), Rivals in Power: the Lives and Letters of the Great Tudor Dynasties (ed, 1990), Henry VIII: a European Court in England (1991), The Inventory of Henry VIII: Vol 1 (ed with Philip Ward, 1998), Elizabeth: Apprenticeship (2000, W H Smith Book Award), Six Wives: The Queens of Henry VIII (2003), Monarchy: the Beginnings (2004), Monarchy: from the Middle Ages to Modernity (2006); also author of numerous articles in learned jls; *Style—* Dr David Starkey, CBE, FSA; ✉ c/o Speakers for Business, 1–2 Pudding Lane, London EC3R 8AB (tel 020 7929

5559, fax 020 7929 5558, e-mail david.starkey@sfb.co.uk); Fitzwilliam College, Cambridge CB3 0DG

STARKEY, Hannah; da of George Howard Stalberger (d 1994), and Elizabeth Bernadette, *née* Starkey; *b* 12 July 1971; *Educ* Napier Univ (BA), RCA (MA); *m* Sept 1998, Nathaniel Paul Sharman; 2 da (Molly Elizabeth b 19 Nov 2000, Ella Kate b 14 April 2002); *Career* artist; *Solo Exhibitions* Hannah Starkey, Scottish Homes (Stills Gallery Edinburgh) 1995, Maureen Paley Interim Art London 1998, 2000, 2002 and 2004, Galleria Raucci/Santamaria Naples 1999, Cornerhouse Manchester 1999, Nederlands Foto Institut Rotterdam 1999, Progetto (Castello di Rivoli Turin) 2000, Irish MOMA Dublin 2000, Monica de Cardenas Milan 2002, Lisboa Photo 2005, Tankya Bonakdar Gallery NY 2006, Maureen Paley London 2007; *Group Exhibitions* John Kobal Foundation (Nat Portrait Gallery London) 1997, Modern Narratives: The domestic and the social (Artsway London) 1998, Shine, Photo '98 (Nat Museum of Film and Photography Bradford) 1998, Sightings, New Photographic Art (ICA London) 1998, Real Life (Galleria SALES Rome) 1998, Look at me (Kunsthal Rotterdam (Br Cncl touring exhbn) 1998, Remix: Images Photographiques (Musée des Beaux-Arts Nantes) 1998, Silver & Syrup: A Selection from the History of Photography (V&A) 1998, 3rd International Tokyo Photo Bienalle (Tokyo Met Museum of Photography) 1999, Clues (Monte Video Netherlands Media Art Inst Amsterdam) 1999, Galerie Rodolphe Janssen Brussels 1999, Give and Take: The Contemporary Art Society at the Jerwood (JerwoodSpace London) 2000, Imago (Universidad de Salamanca) 2000, Suspendidos (Centro de Fotograffa Universidad de Salamanca) 2000, Citibank Private Bank Photography Prize (The Photographers' Gallery London) 2001, Instant City (MuseoPecci Prato) 2001, Extended Painting (Monica de Cardenas Milan) 2001, No World Without You, Reflections of Indentity in New British Art (Herzliya Museum of Art Tel Aviv) 2001, Telling Tales: Narrative Impulses in Recent Art (Tate Liverpool) 2001, Melancholy (Northern Gallery for Contemporary Art Sunderland) 2001, Painted, Printed and Produced in Great Britain (Grant Selwyn Fine Art NY) 2002, Landscape (Saatchi Gallery London) 2002, Comin of Age (New Art Gallery Walsall) 2002, The St James Group Ltd Photography Prize 2002 (Flowers East London) 2002, Sodium Dreams (Center for Curatorial Studies Museum Bard Coll NY) 2003, Take Five! (Huis Marsellie Amsterdam) 2004, Berlin Photography Festival 2005, The Portrait (Harris Museum and Art Gallery Preston) 2006, Jugend von heute (Schim Kunsthalle Frankfurt) 2006, Between Today and Yesterday (Turnpike Gallery Wigan) 2007, Visual Dialogues (Manchester Art Gallery) 2007, Something That I'll Never Really See (Sainsbury Centre for Visual Art Norwich) 2007; *Commissions* Scottish Homes Nat Housing Agency for Scotland 1995, Nat Museum of Photography, Film and Television 1998, 1st Commission Level 1 Bookstore Tate Modern London 2000; *Awards* Nat Housing Body for Scotland 1995, John Kobal Portrait Award 1997, Deloitte and Touche Fine Art Award 1997, The Sunday Times Award 1997, Vogue Condé Nast Award 1997, The Photographers' Gallery Award 1997, Award for Excellence 3rd Int Tokyo Photo Bienalle 1999, City Bank shortlist 2001, Arts Fndn 10th Anniversary Award 2000, Vic Odden Award Royal Photographic Soc 2003; *Publications* Hannah Starkey Photographs 1997–2007 (monograph, 2007); *Style*— Ms Hannah Starkey; ✉ c/o Maureen Paley, 21 Herald Street, London E2 6JT (tel 020 7729 4112)

STARKEY, Sir John Philip; 3 Bt (UK 1935) of Norwood Park, Parish of Southwell and Co of Nottingham, DL (Notts 1981); s of Lt-Col Sir William Randle Starkey, 2 Bt (d 1977); *b* 8 May 1938; *Educ* Eton, ChCh Oxford (MA), London Business Sch (Sloan fell); *m* 1966, Victoria Henrietta Fleetwood, da of late Lt-Col Christopher Herbert Fleetwood Fuller, TD; 1 s, 3 da; *Heir* s, Henry Starkey; *Career* cmmnd Rifle Bde 1956–58; merchant banker and fruit grower; with Antony Gibbs & Sons Ltd 1961–71; chm: Starkey's Fruit Ltd, Norwood Park Golf Course Ltd; JP Notts 1982–88; church cmmr 1985–91; High Sheriff of Notts 1987–88; memb Exec Ctee and chm E Midlands Region Nat Tst 1986–97; chm Notts Branch Country Landowners Assoc 1977–80; vice-pres (UK) Confederation of European Agric 1988–2000; pres Newark Chamber of Commerce 1980–82; memb Ct Cncl Univ of Nottingham 1980–98; memb Archbishop of Canterbury's Cmmn on Rural Areas (ACORA); *Recreations* cricket, painting; *Style*— Sir John Starkey, Bt, DL; ✉ Norwood Park, Southwell, Nottinghamshire NG25 0PF

STARKEY, Dr Phyllis Margaret; MP; da of John Williams (d 2000), and Catherine Hooson, *née* Owen (d 1976); *b* 4 January 1947; *Educ* Perse Sch for Girls Cambridge, Lady Margaret Hall Oxford (BA), Clare Hall Cambridge (PhD); *m* 1969, Hugh Walton Starkey; 2 da (Laura b 14 Dec 1974, Claire b 1 Sept 1977); *Career* research scientist: Strangeways Laboratory Cambridge 1974–81, Sir William Dunn Sch of Pathology Oxford 1981–84; lectr in obstetrics and gynaecology Univ of Oxford 1984–93 (fell Somerville Coll 1987–93), head of assessment Biotechnology and Biological Sciences Research Cncl 1993–97; MP (Lab) Milton Keynes SW 1997–; PPS to Min for Europe 2001–05; memb Select Ctee on Modernisation of House of Commons 1997–99, memb Foreign Affairs Select Ctee 1999–2001, chair Parly Office of Sci and Technol 2001–05, chair Select Ctee on Dept for Communities and Local Govt 2005–; ldr Oxford City Cncl 1990–93 (cncllr 1983–97), chm Local Govt Information Unit 1992–97; tstee Theatres Tst 1998–; memb Biochemical Soc 1970; *Publications* author of over 70 scientific publications (1973–96); *Recreations* cinema, walking, gardening; *Style*— Dr Phyllis Starkey, MP; ✉ Labour Hall, Newport Road, New Bradwell, Milton Keynes, Buckinghamshire MK13 0AA (tel 01908 225522, fax 01908 320731, e-mail phyllis.starkey@gmail.com); House of Commons, London SW1A 0AA (tel 020 7219 0456)

STARKIE, Martin Sidney; s of Henry Starkie (d 1947), of Burnley, Lancs, and Pauline Anne, *née* Martin (d 1971); *b* 25 November 1922; *Educ* Burnley GS, Exeter Coll Oxford (MA, pres John Ford Dramatic Soc, fndr and first pres William Morris Soc, capt athletics, fndr and first pres OU Poetry Soc and OU Broadcasting Soc), LAMDA (ALAM), London Sch of Film Technique; *Career* actor/dramatist and prodr/dir; fndr and dir: Chaucer Festival Canterbury 1985–, Chaucer Centre Canterbury 1985–2002, Chaucer Festival London 1987–, Chaucer-Caxton Exhbition Chapter House Westminster Abbey 1992, Chaucer Heritage Tst 1992–, Chaucer's World Canterbury 1998–2002, Chaucer 600th Commemoration Exhbn Canterbury 2000, Chaucer Books exhbn Caxton to Coghill Canterbury 2001; actor Shanklin Theatre Co 1947–48, actor and poetry reader BBC Radio 1948–66 (recommended by Dylan Thomas), numerous leading roles ITV and BBC TV 1949–64 (incl L'Aiglon Napoleon's son in Rostand's L'Aiglon, Baranowski in Arrow to the Heart, dir Rudolf Cartier), starred in Robert Bolt's first play for the BBC, actor Canterbury Festivals 1949–51, actor and dir Watergate Theatre London 1949–53 (incl premiere of Shaw's final play Far-fetched Fables, dir Maire O'Neill in Synges' Riders to the Sea and The Tinker's Wedding), asst dir to Esmé Percy 1949–53 (incl James Joyce's Exiles' Q Theatre London 1950), poetry organiser for Sir Herbert Read ICA 1948–51 (incl Forty Thousand Years of Modern Art exhbn), played Dauphin opposite Rachel Kempson and Robert Shaw in St Joan (Q Theatre) 1953, broadcasting overseas NHK Japan, All India and Far East Networks 1951–71, one man recitals incl From Chaucer to Dylan Thomas for British Council et al in UK, Europe, USA, USSR, Near East, India, Ceylon, Japan and Far East 1951–2003, writer and presenter Schools TV (Rediffusion/ITV) 1962–65, reader (with Nerys Hughes) for 50th commemoration of the death of Dylan Thomas Westminster Abbey 2003; chm and md: Classic Presentations Ltd 1960–, Chanticleer Presentations Ltd 1967–; tstee Peter Nathan Cultural and Charitable Tsts 1967–, memb Cncl Kensington Soc 1992–, conslt Thorney Island Soc Westminster 1995–; FRSA 1997; *Productions* trans (with D Rancic) Turgenev's Torrents of Spring (dramatised/prodr Oxford Playhouse 1959 then Comedy Theatre London 1962, adapted for BBC with Brian Deakin 1963), dramatised (with Brian Deakin) The Bostonians by Henry James (BBC) 1963, dramatised/dir A Beach of Strangers by John Reeves (Criterion Theatre London) 1967, prodr Holy Bedroc (by Kevin Sheldon & Sir Adrian Beecham, LAMDA Theatre London) 1967; conception/writer/prodr/dir of numerous prodns of The Canterbury Tales incl: Oxford Playhouse (first ever stage version) 1964, Phoenix Theatre London (the musical, incl book with Nevill Coghill) 1968–73 ('Variety' Critics' Circle Award for Best Br Musical 1968), Eugene O'Neill Theatre NY (Tony Award and 4 Tony nominations) 1969, TV series from The Canterbury Tales (BBC) 1969, theatres in Sydney, Melbourne, Brisbane and Perth 1971–72, Her Majesty's Theatre Melbourne 1976, Shaftesbury Theatre London (Nevill Coghill 80th Birthday prodn) 1979, Marlowe Theatre Canterbury 1985 and 1986; prodn conslt for 20 international prodns 1969–2000; dir/prodr credits incl: Canterbury Tales in Cabaret (with Fenella Fielding, Arts Theatre London) 1990 and 1991, When Knights Were Bold (Mermaid Theatre London) 1993, Love, Lust and Marriage (Gulbenkian Theatre Canterbury 1995, Arts Theatre London 1996), Oracle by Jackie Skarvellis (King's Head Theatre London) 1996, Canterbury Pilgrims' Revue (with Doreen Wells, Lady Londonderry) Canterbury Festival 2000; several plays by Sir Richard Parsons incl: Man with Sparrow (co-author, White Bear Theatre London and Brighton Festival) 1993, Killing Time (Jermyn Street Theatre London), Aspects of Eve (Pentameters Theatre Hampstead) 1995, Is There a Diva in the House? (King's Head Theatre London, Jermyn Street Theatre London) 1996, Lady from the Snows (King's Head Theatre London) 2003; *Recordings* incl: Shakespeare's Sonnets and Scenes from the Plays (solo; HMV Victor Records) 1964, The Canterbury Pilgrims (solo; Polydor/DGG (Grammy nomination for Best Spoken Word Recording)) 1968, The Death of Patroclus with Vanessa Redgrave (77 Records and Spoken Arts NY) 1968, The Canterbury Tales with Prunella Scales 1982 (EMI, re-issued 1995), The Canterbury Tales with Fenella Fielding (Durkin/Hayes Canada) 1995; conslt Chaucer's Work, Life and Times (CD-ROM for Primary Source Media) 1995; *Publications* Oxford Poetry (ed with Roy MacNab, preface by Lord David Cecil, 1947), Canterbury Tales (the musical with Nevill Coghill, 1968), More Canterbury Tales (the musical with Nevill Coghill, 1976), Officina Bodoni edn of Chaucer's Prologue, dedicated to HIH Prince Naruhito of Japan (Chanticleer Presentations Ltd, 1989); *Recreations* reading, listening to chamber music, playing the piano, people, pigeons, cats, travel; *Style*— Martin Starkie, Esq; ✉ Horbury Villa, 85 Ladbroke Road, London W11 3PJ (tel 020 7727 9445, fax 020 7229 0635)

STARLING, David Henry; s of Brig John Sieveking Starling, CBE (d 1986), of Jersey, and Vivian Barbara, *née* Wagg (d 1983); gs of Prof Ernest Henry Starling, FRS, physiologist (Starling's Law of the Heart), pioneer of hormones and endocrinology (d 1927); *b* 11 August 1935; *Educ* Eton; *m* 1 Aug 1967, Judith Penelope, er da of Sir Laurence Lindo, GCVO, CMG, OJ; 1 s (Christopher Henry Boris b 9 Aug 1969), 1 da (Belinda Jane b 7 April 1972 d 2006); *Career* cmmnd RN 1953–58; sr ptnr Galloway & Pearson stockbrokers 1983–84 (joined 1959), dir W I Carr Group following takeover of Galloway & Pearson 1984–94, conslt Hambros Equities UK Ltd 1994–96; memb Cncl Stock Exchange 1975–79; chm of govrs Maidwell Hall Sch 1993–99; *Recreations* gardening, ceramics; *Clubs* Boodle's, Essex, Royal Naval Sailing Assoc; *Style*— David Starling; ✉ Porters Farm, Kelvedon, Essex CO5 9DD (tel 01376 584810)

STARLING, Melvin James; s of James Albert Starling, and Jean, *née* Craddock; *b* 15 July 1954; *Educ* Vyners GS Andover, UCL (BSc, DipArch); *m* 26 July 1978, Miriam Claire; 1 da (Jemma Alice b 23 May 1984), 1 s (Thomas William b 15 May 1986); *Career* ptnr Pringle Brandon Architects 1986–; RIBA 1985; *Recreations* golf, sailing, sport, family; *Clubs* Farleigh Court Golf; *Style*— Melvin Starling, Esq; ✉ Pringle Brandon Architects, 10 Bonhill Street, London EC2A 4QJ (tel 020 7466 1000)

STARMER, Keir; QC (2002); *b* 1962; *Educ* Univ of Leeds (LLB), Univ of Oxford (BCL); *m* Victoria Alexander; *Career* called to the Bar 1987; legal offr Liberty until 1990; practising barr specialising in human rights law, memb Doughty Street Chambers 1990–; fell Human Rights Centre Univ of Essex; conslt on human rights issues ACPO, human rights advsr NI Policing Bd 2003–; memb: Foreign Sec's Death Penalty Panel 2002–, Cncl Justice, Governance Advsy Ctee Br Cncl; Justice/Liberty Human Rights Lawyer of the Year Award 2000; *Publications* incl: Justice in Error (ed, 1995), Three Pillars of Liberty, Political Rights and Freedoms in the United Kingdom (1996), Miscarriages of Justice (ed, 1999), European Human Rights Law (1999), Blackstone's Human Rights Digest (2001), Criminal Justice, Police Powers and Human Rights (2001), Human Rights Principles (contrib, 2001), Mithani's Directors' Disqualification (contrib, 2001), Human Rights and Civil Practice (contrib, 2001); author of numerous articles in newspapers and jls; *Style*— Keir Starmer, Esq, QC; ✉ Doughty Street Chambers, 10–11 Doughty Street, London WC1N 2PL

STARMER-SMITH, Nigel Christopher; s of Harry Starmer-Smith (d 2002), and Joan Mary, *née* Keep (d 1985); *b* 25 December 1944; *Educ* Magdalen Coll Sch Oxford, UC Oxford (MA, Rugby blues); *m* 25 Aug 1973, Rosamund Mary, da of Wallace Bartlett; 1 da (Charlotte Alice Mary b 2 May 1975 d 1991); 2 s (Charles Jeremy Nigel b 5 June 1978, Julian Edward Giles b 9 April 1982 d 2001); *Career* schoolmaster Epsom Coll 1967–70, BBC Radio Outside Broadcasts 1970–73, sports commentator and presenter BBC TV (mainly rugby union and hockey) 1973–, ed-in-chief Rugby World magazine 1984–93, conslt/offical commentator Int Rugby Bd 2002–; minister's rep on Southern Sports Cncl 1989–93; tstee Reading and District Hospitals Charity 1992–, govr Shiplake Coll 2002–; *Former Sportsman* rugby: Oxford Univ, Oxfordshire, Harlequins, Surrey, Barbarians, England; hockey: Oxford Univ, Oxfordshire; cricket: Territorial Army; *Books* The Official History of the Barbarians (1977), Rugby - A Way of Life (1986); numerous rugby annuals and books; *Recreations* tennis, golf, piano-playing, family; *Clubs* Leander, Harlequin FC, Wig & Pen; *Style*— Nigel Starmer-Smith, Esq; ✉ Cobblers Cottage, Skirmett, Henley-on-Thames, Oxfordshire RG9 6TD (e-mail nstarmersmith@aol.com)

START, Glenn William; s of William Alfred John Start, of Leytonstone, and Marjorie Masie, *née* Short; *b* 23 January 1950; *Educ* Aveley Tech HS; *Children* 1 da (Felicity Louise b 30 Aug 1980), 1 s (Gregory William b 5 May 1982); *Career* articled clerk Elliotts CAs (became Kidsons Impey 1990) 1967–74, CA 1974, ptnr 1976, memb Kidsons Nat Exec 1989, managing ptnr East region 1990 (London 1989), currenty office managing ptnr (now Baker Tilly); Freeman City of London 1989, Liveryman Worshipful Co of Gold and Silver Wyre Drawers 1990; FCA; *Clubs* City Livery; *Style*— Glenn Start

STARY, Erica Frances Margaret; da of Eric Halstead Smith (d 1987), and Barbara Maud, *née* Creeke (d 1947); *b* 20 January 1943; *Educ* Hunmanby Hall, LSE (LLM); *m* 1, 1966; m 2, 1971, Michael McKirdy Anthony Stary, s of John Henry Stary (presumed dead 1939); 1 da (Philippa b 1977); *Career* admitted slr 1965; lectr then sr lectr Coll of Law 1966–73, Inland Revenue 1974–75, successively asst ed, ed and consulting ed British Tax Review 1976–, tech offr Inst of Taxation 1981–86, city lawyer 1986–98, district judge 1998–, asst recorder then recorder 1996–; memb Nat Ctee of Young Slrs 1969–77, chm London Young Slrs Gp 1972, dir Slrs Benevolent Assoc 1973–77, dir and tstee London Suzuki Group and Tst 1984–89, asst clerk then clerk Second East Brixton Gen Cmmrs of Income Tax 1987–98; memb Cncl: Chartered Inst of Taxation 1989–98 (chm Technical Ctee 1993–94), Assoc of Taxation Technicians 1991–98 (pres 1994–95); tstee: Nat Children's Orch 1989–98, Tax Advsrs Benevolent Assoc 1996–98; Liveryman City of London Solicitors' Co, Master Worshipful Co of Tax Advrs 2005–06 (memb Ct of Assts 1995–); CTA (fell) 1984; *Recreations* sailing, cycling, music, theatre; *Style*— Mrs Michael Stary; ✉ c/o Barclays Bank, 3 Church Street, Weybridge KT13 8DD

S

STASSINOPOULOS, Mary; da of John Stassinopoulos (d 1975), of Athens, and Pauline, *née* Kalliodis; *b* 9 January 1943; *Educ* Greece, Geneva Univ; *m* 1, 1963 (m dis 1977), Michael E Xilas; 1 s (Elias b 1965), 1 da (Irene b 1967); m 2, 1985, John G Carras; *Career* dir Vacani Sch of Dancing, examiner and memb Ctee Cecchetti (classical ballet) Soc; fell Imperial Soc of Teachers of Dancing; *Recreations* theatre, classical music, reading; *Clubs* Harry's Bar; *Style—* Miss Mary Stassinopoulos; ✉ 20 Norfolk Road, London NW8 6HG (tel 020 7586 3691)

STATMAN, His Hon Judge Philip Richard; s of Martin Statman, of Thorpe Bay, Essex, and Evelyn Statman, *née* Silver; *b* 28 March 1953; *Educ* Westcliff HS for Boys, Mid-Essex Tech Coll (LLB), Inns of Court Sch of Law; *m* 18 Oct 1998, Dr Mary Louise Cameron (d 2006); 2 s (Samuel Alexander b 1 June 1999, Angus Joseph David b 19 Nov 2001); *Career* called to the Bar 1975; tenant Chambers of Barbara Calvert, QC 1976–89, tenant Chambers of Rock Tansey, QC, *qv*, 1989–2002, asst recorder 1997, recorder 2000, circuit judge (SE Circuit) 2002–; *Recreations* travel, cinema, antiques, reading, association football; *Style—* His Hon Judge Statman; ✉ Maidstone Combined Court Centre, Barker Road, Maidstone ME16 8EQ (tel 01622 202000)

STATON, Roger Anthony; s of Harry James Staton (d 1977), of Coventry, and Janet, *née* Palmer; *b* 25 November 1945; *Educ* Bablake Sch Coventry, Univ of Manchester (BSc); *m* 23 May 1970, Angela, da of Joseph Armstrong; 2 s (David b 14 Sept 1971, Adam b 5 Aug 1973); *Career* trg offr GEC Telecommunications Ltd Coventry 1968–69 (apprentice 1963–68), prodn ed The Rugby Review 1969–71, dep ed Radio Communication magazine 1971–73; account exec: Scott Mactaggart Associates 1973–74, Golley Slater Public Relations 1974–76; fndr md Roger Staton Associates (renamed Six Degrees Ltd 2004) 1976–; dir: The Pegasus Press Ltd 1984–, ArtHaus Visual Communications Ltd 1987–, The RSA Group Ltd 1995–; FCIPR 2004 (MIPR); *Recreations* art history, reading, classic cars, cooking, walking; *Clubs* Wig & Pen; *Style—* Roger Staton, Esq; ✉ Six Degrees Ltd, Old Trinity Church, Trinity Road, Marlow, Buckinghamshire SL7 3AN (tel 01628 480280, fax 01628 487223, e-mail roger.staton@sixdegreespr.com)

STAUGHTON, Rt Hon Sir Christopher Stephen Thomas Jonathan Thayer; kt (1981), PC (1988); yr s of Simon Thomas Samuel Staughton, and Edith Madeline, *née* Jones; *b* 24 May 1933; *Educ* Eton, Magdalene Coll Cambridge; *m* 1960, Joanna Susan Elizabeth, er da of George Frederick Arthur Burgess; 2 da; *Career* served 2 Lt 11 Hussars; called to the Bar Inner Temple 1957 (reader 1996, treas 1997); QC 1970, recorder of the Crown Court 1972–81, judge of the High Court of Justice (Queen's Bench Div) 1981–87, a Lord Justice of Appeal 1987–97; int arbitrator 1997–, cmmr under the Police Act 1998–2000, judge Court of Appeal Gibraltar 2000–06 (pres 2005), appeal adjudicator (Enemy Property) 2000–; memb Br Library Advsy Bd 1999–2001; FCIArb 1998; *Style—* The Rt Hon Sir Christopher Staughton; ✉ 20 Essex Street, London WC2R 3AL (tel 020 7842 1200, fax 020 7842 1270, e-mail clerks@20essexst.com)

STAUGHTON, (Simon) David Howard Ladd; s of Simon Staughton (d 1967), and Madeline Somers-Cox, *née* Jones (d 1974); *b* 24 January 1931; *Educ* Eton; *m* 12 Oct 1957, Olivia Katharine, da of Egbert Cecil Barnes (d 1987); 1 s (James b 1959), 2 da (Julia b 1960, Fiona b 1963); *Career* Nat Serv, 2 Lt 10 Royal Hussars (PWO); sr ptnr Lee & Pembertons solicitors 1986–96, chm St Austell Brewery Co Ltd 1979–2000; *Clubs* Cavalry and Guards'; *Style—* David Staughton, Esq; ✉ Westward, Trenance, Mawgan Porth, Cornwall TR8 4BZ (tel 01637 860217)

STAUGHTON, Dr Richard Charles David; s of Thomas Richard Staughton (d 1989), and Bardi Dorothy, *née* Cole (1989); *b* 15 August 1944; *Educ* Wellingborough Sch, Emmanuel Coll Cambridge (MA), Bart's Med Coll (MB BChir); *m* 1, 1979 (m dis 1988), Jenny, da of Sir Anthony Quayle (d 1989); 1 s (Jack Anthony b 29 Dec 1982); m 2, 1991, Clare, o da of Sir Mark Evelyn Heath, KCVO, CMG; *Career* successively: house surgn then SHO Bart's, registrar King Edward VII Hosp Windsor, registrar (dermatology) St Thomas' Hosp, sr registrar (dermatology) Westminster Hosp, conslt dermatologist Addenbrooke's Hosp Cambridge; currently conslt dermatologist Chelsea and Westminster Hosp and hon conslt to King Edward VII Hosp Beaumont St, Royal Hosp Chelsea and The Royal Brompton Hosp; hon corresponding memb Soc Français de Dermatologie; memb: Br Assoc of Dermatologists, St John's Soc (pres 1987); FRCP; *Books* Cutaneous Manifestations of HIV Disease (1988, 2 edn 1994), Atopic Skin Disease (1996), Vulval Disease (1994, 2 edn 1997); *Recreations* gardening, matters Orcadian; *Clubs* Garrick, Chelsea Arts; *Style—* Dr Richard Staughton; ✉ Chelsea and Westminster Hospital, 369 Fulham Road, London SW10 9NH (tel 020 8746 8170, fax 020 8746 8578); Lister Hospital, Chelsea Bridge Road, London SW1W 8RH (tel 020 7584 5384, fax 020 7581 6242, e-mail rstaughton@lineone.net)

STAUNTON, Henry Eric; s of Henry Staunton (d 1976), and Joy Evelyn, *née* Brownlow; *b* 20 May 1948; *Educ* Univ of Exeter; *m* Karen; 1 s (James b 1977), 1 da (Clare b 1980); *Career* audit ptnr Price Waterhouse 1970–93, gp finance dir Granada Compass plc (following merger between Granada Gp plc and Compass Gp plc in 2000) 1993–2004, finance dir and dep chm Media Ventures Granada plc 2000–04, finance dir ITV plc 2004–06; non-exec dir: EMAP plc 1995–2002, Ashtead Gp plc 1997–2004 (chm 2001–04), Legal & General Gp plc 2004–, Ladbrokes plc 2006–; former non-exec dir: BSkyB plc, ITN Ltd; FCA; *Recreations* tennis, golf, theatre, travel; *Clubs* RAC; *Style—* Henry Staunton, Esq

STAUNTON, Marie; da of Austin Staunton, of Grange-over-Sands, Cumbria, and Ann, *née* McAuley; *b* 28 May 1952; *Educ* Larkhill House Sch Preston, Lancaster Univ (BA), Coll of Law; *m* 15 March 1986, James Albert Provan, s of William Provan, of Wallaceton, Perthshire; 2 da (Lucy Maryanne b 1987, Amy Clare b 1994); *Career* slr; successively: legal offr Nat Cncl for Civil Liberties, dir Br Section Amnesty Int (memb Int Exec Ctee), ed Solicitors Jl, publishing dir FT Law and Tax, dep exec dir UK Ctee UNICEF; chief exec Plan International UK 2000–; UK ind memb Mgmnt Bd EU Fundamental Rights Agency 2007–; FRSA; *Recreations* children, theatre, gardening; *Style—* Ms Marie Staunton; ✉ 18 Grove Lane, London SE5 8ST (tel 020 7701 9191); Plan International UK, 5–6 Underhill Street, London NW1 7HS (tel 020 7485 6612, fax 020 7485 2107)

STAVLING, Åke; *Educ* Stockholm Sch of Economics (BBA); *Career* Atlas Copco 1974–86, sr vice-pres of corp fin control Ericsson 1986–93, exec vice-pres and chief fin offr Astra AB 1993–99, exec dir business devpt AstraZeneca plc 1999–; *Style—* Åke Stavling, Esq

STEAD, Prof Christian Karlson; ONZ (2007), CBE (1985); s of James Walter Ambrose Stead (d 1971), and Olive Ethel, *née* Karlson (d 1975); *b* 17 October 1932, Auckland NZ; *Educ* Mt Albert GS, Univ of Auckland (MA, DLitt), Univ of Bristol (Michael Hiatt Baker scholar, PhD); *m* 8 Jan 1955, Kathleen Elizabeth, *née* Roberts; 1 s (Oliver William b 7 Aug 1963), 2 da (Charlotte Mary b 14 Dec 1966, Margaret Hermione b 9 Feb 1970); *Career* author; lectr in English Univ of New England NSW 1956–57; Univ of Auckland: lectr, sr lectr then assoc prof of English 1960–64, prof of English 1967–86 (now emeritus); Nuffield fell London 1965, Katherine Mansfield fell Menton France 1972, visiting fell UCL 1977, visiting sr fell St John's Coll Oxford 1996–97; winner: NZ Book Award for Poetry 1975 and 1988, NZ Book Award for Fiction 1984 and 1994; chm: NZ Literary Fund Advsy Ctee 1973–75, NZ Authors Fund Advsy Ctee 1986–89; vice-pres NZ PEN 1980–85; Hon DLitt Univ of Bristol; FRSL 1994, FEA 2004; *Publications* author of eleven novels (recent novels incl Talking About O'Dwyer, Mansfield and My Name was Judas (2006)), two collections of short stories, fourteen collections of poems, six books of literary criticism (incl The New Poetic, Yeats to Eliot) and several ed vols; *Recreations* music, walking, swimming, talking; *Style—* Prof C K Stead, ONZ, CBE, FRSL

STEAD, Prof Philip John; OBE (1966); s of William Thomas James Stead (d 1961), and Matilda, *née* Simpson (d 1978); *b* 5 February 1916, Swinton, N Yorks; *Educ* Holgate GS Barnsley, Pembroke Coll Oxford; *m* 19 Nov 1947, Judith Irene, *née* Freeder; *Career* Br Army 1940–46, Home Office 1946–53, dean of academic studies Police Staff Coll Bramshill 1953–74, prof and dean of grad studies John Jay Coll of Criminal Justice City Univ of NY 1974–82; memb Critics Circle London 1940; FRSL 1950; *Publications* incl: The Charlatan (1948), Fausta (1950), Mr Punch (1950), Vidocq (1953), Second Bureau (1959), Pioneers in Policing (1977), The Police of France (1983), Police in Britain (1983), Sounding Recall (2004); *Style—* Prof Philip John Stead, OBE

STEADMAN, Alison; OBE (2000); da of George Percival Steadman (d 1991), and Margorie, *née* Evans (d 1996); *b* 26 August 1946; *Educ* Childwall Valley HS for Girls, East 15 Acting Sch; *Children* 2 s (Toby Leigh b 3 Feb 1979, Leo Leigh b 15 Aug 1981); *Career* actress; patron: Haringey Phoenix Gp (people with visual impairment), Friends of Carers (Nat Carers Assoc); Hon MA Univ of E London, Hon DUniv Essex 2003, Hon DLitt Univ of Liverpool 2006; *Theatre* credits incl: The Prime of Miss Jean Brodie (Theatre Royal, Lincoln), Soft for a Girl, The Fish in the Sea, The Foursome (all Everyman, Liverpool), Othello, Travesties (both Nottingham Playhouse), The Sea Achor (Upstairs, Royal Court), The King (Shaw Theatre), Wholesome Glory (Upstairs, Royal Court), The Pope's Wedding (Exeter/Bush Theatre), Abigail's Party (Hampstead), Joking Apart (Globe), Uncle Vanya (Hampstead), Cinderella and Her Naughty Sisters, A Handful of Dust (both Lyric, Hammersmith), Tartuffe (RSC/Pit), Maydays (RSC/Barbican), Kafka's Dick (Royal Court), Cat on A Hot Tin Roof (RNT), The Rise and Fall of Little Voice (RNT and Aldwych), Marvin's Room (Hampstead and Comedy Theatre), When We Are Married (Chichester and Savoy Theatre), The Provok'd Wife (Old Vic), The Memory of Water (Vaudeville Theatre), Entertaining Mr Sloane (Arts Theatre and tour), Horse and Carriage (W Yorks Playhouse), The Woman Who Cooked Her Husband (New Ambassadors Theatre), Losing Louis (Whitehall Theatre, Hampstead Theatre and Trafalgar Studios); *Television* BBC credits incl: Girl, Hard Labour, He's Gone, Nuts in May, Flesh and Blood, Esther Waters, Through the Night, Pasmore, Abigail's Party, Nature in Focus, The Singing Detective, Virtuoso, Newshound, Pride and Prejudice, No Bananas, A Small Morning, The Cappuccino Years, Dalziel and Pascoe, Let Them Eat Cake, The Worst Week of My Life, Gavin and Stacey; other credits incl: The Caucasian Chalk Circle (Thames), Coming Through (Central), The Finding (Thames), Monster Maker (Henson Organisation), Selling Hitler (Euston), Gone to Seed (Central), Without Walls: Degas and Pissaro Fall Out (Channel Four), Wimbledon Poisoner (BBC/ABTV), Six Sides of Coogan - The Curator (Pozzitive Television), Rory Bremnar Who Else (Vera Prodns), The Missing Postman (BBC Scotland), Fat Friends (Yorkshire TV), Fat Friends (Series 2, 3 and 4, Yorkshire TV), Celeb (Tiger Aspect), Gone to the Dogs (Central), Who Gets the Dog (ITV), Miss Marple; *Film* Champions, P'Tang Yang Kipperbang, Number One, A Private Function, Clockwise, The Short & Curlies, Stormy Monday, The Adventures of Baron Munchausen, Shirley Valentine, Wilt, Life is Sweet, Blame it on the Bellboy, Topsy Turvy, Happy Now, Chunky Monkey, The Life and Death of Peter Sellers; *Short* DIY Hard; *Awards* Evening Standard Best Actress Award 1979, Olivier Award for Best Actress 1993; *Style—* Ms Alison Steadman, OBE; ✉ c/o PFD, Drury House, 34–43 Russell Street, London WC2B 5HA (tel 020 7344 1000, fax 020 7379 6790)

STEADMAN, Dr Philip; s of late Melvyn Steadman, and Mary Elisabeth, *née* Jenkins (now Mrs Davies); *b* 3 April 1953, South Wales; *Educ* Ystalyfera GS, Cwmtawe Comp Sch, UCL (BSc), Imperial Coll London (MSc, Dip), Guy's Medical Sch (MB BS); *m* 26 Dec 1978, Kay, *née* Manning; 2 s (Jared b 27 Sept 1982, Jack b 14 June 1989), 3 da (Lucy b 3 Aug 1984, Emily b 19 Oct 1987, Katie b 12 Dec 1992); *Career* psychiatrist; hosp house positions then various jobs in psychiatric health 1989–99, conslt psychiatrist Oxleas Mental Health NHS Fndn Tst 1999–; former memb Cncl and dir BMA, currently memb BMA Regnl Conslts Ctee and Regnl Local Negotiating Ctee; RCPsych: dep chm Equivalence Ctee, memb Overseas Doctors Ctee; MRCPsych 1996; *Publications* Child and Adolescent Mental Health: A guide for healthcare professionals; contrib to various jls and pubns in particular for BMA Bd of Sci and Educn; *Recreations* current affairs, films, reading, listening to music (mainly 1960s and 70s); *Style—* Dr Philip Steadman

STEADMAN, Timothy; s of Ronald Herbert Steadman, and Beatrice Dorothy, *née* Hunt; *b* 13 January 1955, Birmingham; *Educ* Ludlow GS, Hertford Coll Oxford (MA); *m* 6 Sept 1986, Alison Claire, *née* Spankie; 1 da (Anna), 2 s (Jack, Robert); *Career* slr; Lovells 1976–82, Baker & McKenzie 1982–97, Clifford Chance 1997–; author of articles in professional and firm pubns; memb: Law Soc, Int Bar Assoc; *Recreations* family, cooking, travel; *Style—* Timothy Steadman, Esq; ✉ Clifford Chance, 10 Upper Bank Street, Canary Wharf, London E14 5JJ (tel 020 7006 1000, fax 020 7006 5555, e-mail tim.steadman@cliffordchance.com)

STEARNS, Michael Patrick; s of Cdr Eric Gascoyne Stearns, OBE, and Evelyn, *née* Sherry; *b* 19 January 1947; *Educ* Guy's Hosp London (BDS, MB BS); *m* Elizabeth Jane Elford Smith; *Career* registrar (later sr registrar) Guy's Hosp 1977–84; conslt head and neck surgn and otolaryngologist: Royal Free Hosp 1984–, Barnet Gen Hosp 1984–; sec Euro Acad of Facial Surgery 1989–98, treas Int Fedn of Facial Plastic Surgical Socs 2000–01; fell: Univ of Washington 1982, Univ of Oregon 1983; FRCS 1978, FRSM 1982; *Style—* Michael Stearns, Esq; ✉ Suite 14, 30 Harley Street, London W1G 9PW (tel 020 7631 4448)

STEDMAN, John Edward Rooney; s of John Edward Stedman, MC (d 1983), of Blackheath, London, and Emily Rosina Yeo, *née* Rooney (d 1975); *b* 18 May 1936; *Educ* Rugby, UCL (BA); *Career* schoolmaster Stubbington House, King's Sch Worcester and Summerfields 1957–66, dir English Language Tutors Sussex 1967, sr ptnr English Language Tutors Madrid 1968–, dir European Holiday Courses SA Madrid 1968–; tstee Tello Fernandez Trust Madrid 1989–; landowner in Cumberland until 1989, 28 lord of the manor of Irthington Cumberland; reader C of E 1962–; memb: The Sidney Smith Assoc, Heraldry Soc, White Lion Soc, Prayer Book Soc; govr Corp of the Sons of the Clergy 1993; FRSA 1963; *Recreations* art, heraldry, opera, country pursuits; *Clubs* The Arts; *Style—* John Stedman, Esq; ✉ 14 Rue Jacquemont, 62140 Hesdin, France (tel 00 33 321 05 71 42)

STEDMAN JONES, Prof Gareth; s of Lewis and Joan Olive Stedman Jones; *b* 17 December 1942; *Educ* St Paul's, Lincoln Coll Oxford (BA), Nuffield Coll Oxford (DPhil); *Children* 1 s by Prof Sally Alexander, 1 s by Prof Miri Rubin; *Career* research fell Nuffield Coll Oxford 1967–70, sr assoc memb St Antony's Coll Oxford 1971–72, Humboldt Stiftung Dept of Philosophy Goethe Univ Frankfurt 1973–74; Univ of Cambridge: lectr in history 1979–86, reader in history of social thought 1986–97, co-dir Centre for History and Economics 1991–, prof of political sci 1997–; memb Editorial Bd New Left Review 1964–81, jt fndr and jt ed History Workshop Jl 1976–; *Publications* Outcast London (1971), Languages of Class (1983), Klassen, Politik, Sprache (1988), Charles Fourier, The Theory of the Four Movements - trans 1: Patterson (ed, 1994), Karl Marx and Friedrich Engels, The Communist Manifesto (2002), An End to Poverty? A Historical Debate (2004); *Recreations* country walks, collecting old books, cricket; *Style—* Prof Gareth Stedman Jones; ✉ King's College, Cambridge CB2 1ST (tel 01223 331197)

STEED, Mark Stephen; s of David Paul Steed, and Pamela, *née* Lloyd; *b* 22 September 1965; *Educ* King Edward VI GS Chelmsford, Fitzwilliam Coll Cambridge (MA, Athletics blue), Univ of Nottingham (MA); *m* 24 Dec 1988, Patricia Louise, *née* Newman; 1 da (Anastasia Patricia Catharine b 29 Aug 1992), 2 s (William Mark Sebastian b 28 Aug 1994, Jeremy Charles Sandle b 11 Feb 1998); *Career* teacher: The Leys Sch Cambridge 1987–88, Radley Coll 1988–91, Oundle Sch 1991–2001 (head of religious studies 1993–98, housemaster

1997–2001); headmaster Kelly Coll Tavistock 2001–; govr St Michael's Sch Tawstock; *Recreations* running, fives, walking, stained glass, art and architecture; *Clubs* East India, Hawks' (Cambridge), Achilles; *Style—* Mark S Steed, Esq; ✉ Headmaster's House, Kelly College, Tavistock, Devon PL19 0HZ (tel 01822 813126); Kelly College, Parkwood Road, Tavistock, Devon PL19 0HZ (tel 01822 813127, fax 01822 813110, e-mail headmaster@kellycollege.com)

STEED, Mark Wickham; s of Richard David Steed, and Jennifer Mary, *née* Hugh-Jones; gs of Henry Wickham Steed, editor of The Times; *b* 31 October 1952; *Educ* Downside; *m* 3 June 1989, Carola Dawn (m dis 1994), da of Dorian Joseph Williams, of Foscote Manor, Buckingham; *Career* CA; dir: Oxford Investments Ltd 1981–86, Beckdest Ltd 1981–88, Colt Securities Ltd 1983–95, Global Portfolio Management Ltd 1996–98, Amstel Securities 2002–, Rocktron Ltd 2007–; ACA, MSI, MCIM; *Recreations* shooting, realising dreams; *Clubs* Naval and Military; *Style—* Mark Steed, Esq; ✉ Keepers Cottage, The Shaw, Leckhampstead, Buckingham MK18 5PA

STEEDMAN, Prof Carolyn Kay; da of Ellis Kay Pilling (d 1977), of Streatham Hill and Gypsy Hill, London, and Edna Dawson (d 1983); *b* 20 March 1947; *Educ* Rosa Bassett GS for Girls London, Univ of Sussex (BA), Newnham Coll Cambridge (MLitt, PhD); *m* 1971 (m dis 1986), Mark Jerome Steedman, s of George Steedman (d 1998); *Career* class teacher in primary schs E Sussex and Warks 1974–81, project asst Schs Cncl Language in the Multicultural Primary Classroom Project Dept of Eng Inst of Educn Univ of London 1982–83, fell Sociological Research Unit Inst of Educn Univ of London 1983–84, reader Dept of Arts Educn Univ of Warwick 1991–93 (lectr 1984–88, sr lectr 1988–91), prof of social history Centre for the Study of Social History Univ of Warwick 1995– (reader 1993–95), prof History Dept Univ of Warwick 1998–; Helen Gamble research student Newnham Coll Cambridge 1970–71, visiting prof of history Univ of Michigan Ann Arbor 1992, Sir Simon research fell Dept of Sociology Univ of Manchester 1990–91, ESRC research prof 2004–07; ed History Workshop Jl 1983–1990; memb Panel for Validation and Review Cncl for Nat Academic Awards; external examiner: Univ of Portsmouth (formerly Portsmouth Poly) 1990–93, Keele Univ 1992–95, Univ of Leicester 1997–2000, Univ of Manchester 2002–; Nuffield Fndn small grant in social scis for work on Margaret McMillan (1860–1931) and the idea of childhood 1983, History Twenty Seven Fndn grant Inst of History Research 1983; *Publications* incl: The Tidy House: Little Girls Writing (1982, awarded Fawcett Soc Book prize 1983), Policing the Victorian Community: the Formation of English Provincial Police Forces 1856–1880 (1984), Language Gender and Childhood (jt ed, 1985), Landscape for a Good Woman (1986), The Radical Soldier's Tale (1988), Childhood Culture and Class In Britain: Margaret McMillan 1860–1931 (1990), Past Tenses: Essays on Writing, Autobiography and History 1980–90 (1992), Strange Dislocations: Childhood and the Idea of Human Interiority 1780–1930 (1995), Dust (2001), Master and Servant: Love and Labour in the English Industrial Age (2007); *Style—* Prof Carolyn Steedman; ✉ University of Warwick, Coventry CV4 7AL (tel 024 7652 3523 ext 3624, e-mail c.k.steedman@warwick.ac.uk)

STEEDMAN, Prof Mark; s of George Steedman (d 1998), and Nan, *née* Saunders; *b* 18 September 1946; *Educ* Univ of Sussex (BSc), Univ of Edinburgh (PhD); *m* 1987, Prof Bonnie Lynn Webber, *née* Gerzog; *Career* research fell Univ of Sussex 1974–77, lectr Univ of Warwick 1977–83, lectr then reader Univ of Edinburgh 1983–88, assoc prof then prof Univ of Pennsylvania 1988–98, prof of cognitive science Univ of Edinburgh 1998–; fell American Assoc for Artificial Intelligence 1993, FRSE 2002, FBA 2002; *Books* Surface Structure and Interpretation (1996), The Syntactic Process (2000); *Recreations* hill walking, reading, jazz; *Clubs* Ortlieb's Jazzhaus, Philadelphia; *Style—* Prof Mark Steedman; ✉ School of Informatics, University of Edinburgh, 2 Buccleuch Place, Edinburgh EH8 9LW (tel 0131 650 4631, fax 0131 650 6626)

STEEDMAN, Robert Russell; OBE (1997); s of Robert Smith Steedman (d 1950), and Helen Hope, *née* Brazier; *b* 3 January 1929; *Educ* Loretto, Sch of Architecture Edinburgh Coll of Art (DA), Univ of Pennsylvania (MLA); *m* 1, July 1956 (m dis 1974), Susan Elizabeth, da of Sir Robert Scott, GCMG, CBE (d 1982), of Peebles, Scotland; 1 s (Robert Scott b 1958), 2 da (Helena Elizabeth b 1960, Sarah Aeliz b 1962); m 2, July 1977, Martha, da of Rev John Edmund Hamilton; *Career* Nat Serv Lt RWAFF 1947–48; ptnr Morris and Steedman Edinburgh 1959–2002; memb: Countryside Cmmn for Scotland 1980–88, Royal Fine Art Cmmn for Scotland 1984–95; dir Friends of the Royal Scottish Acad 1985–93; govr Edinburgh Coll of Art 1974–88, memb Edinburgh Festival Soc 1978–98, memb Cncl Royal Scottish Acad 1981– (sec 1983–90, dep pres 1982–83 and 1999–2000); former memb Cncl: Royal Incorporation of Architects in Scotland, Soc of Scottish Artists, Scottish Museums 1984–90; memb Cncl Nat Tst for Scotland 1999–2005; chm Central Scotland Woodlands Tst 1984–87; memb: Sir Patrick Geddes Award Panel 1994–2002, Assoc for the Protection of Rural Scotland Award Panel 1995–99; awards: Civic Tst (ten times) 1963–88, Br Steel 1971, Saltire 1971, RIBA award for Scotland 1974 and 1989, Euro Architectural Heritage Medal 1975, Assoc for the Protection of Rural Scotland 1977, 1983 and 1989; Hon DLitt Univ of St Andrews 2006; RSA 1979, RIBA, FRIAS, MLI; *Clubs* New (Edinburgh), Royal & Ancient; *Style—* Robert Steedman, Esq, OBE, RSA; ✉ Muir of Blebo, Blebocraigs, by Cupar, Fife KY15 5UG (tel and fax 01334 850781)

STEEDMAN, Dr (Robert) Scott; s of Robert Russell Steedman, of Blebocraigs, Fife, and Susan Elizabeth Sym, *née* Scott; *b* 10 September 1958; *Educ* Edinburgh Acad, UMIST (BSc), Queens' Coll Cambridge (MPhil), St Catharine's Coll Cambridge (PhD); *m* 1, 5 Sept 1981 (m dis 2002), Zoreh, da of Dr Ebrahim Kazemzadeh (d 1993), of Mashad, Iran; 1 s (Nicholas Robert Cyrus b 1985), 1 da (Hannah Hope Eliza b 1990); m 2, 18 Nov 2005, Hon Deborah Jane, da of Lord Keith of Kinkel, GBE (Life Peer, d 2001), of Perthshire; *Career* fell St Catharine's Coll Cambridge 1983–93, lectr Dept of Engrg Univ of Cambridge 1983–90, with EQE (safety and risk mgmnt conslts) 1990–92; dir: Gibb Ltd (engrg conslts) 1993–2000, Whitby Bird & Partners Ltd (engrg design conslts) 2000–03, High-Point Rendel (construction and mgmnt conslts); visiting prof MIT 1987; vice-pres: Royal Acad of Engrg 2003–, ICE 2005–; chm Thomas Telford Ltd (publishers) 2003–07; CEng 1988, FICE 1994 (MICE 1988), FRSA 1996, FREng 2001; *Books* Geotechnical Centrifuge Modelling (contrib, 1995), Environment, Construction and Sustainable Development (contrib, 2001); *Recreations* the children, Bhutan, skiing, sailing, messing about in boats; *Clubs* New (Edinburgh); *Style—* Dr Scott Steedman; ✉ Flat 1, 25 Eldon Square, Reading, Berkshire RG1 4DP (tel 0118 950 4837)

STEEDS, Prof John Wickham; s of John Henry William Steeds (d 1987), of London, and Ethel Amelia, *née* Tyler; *b* 9 February 1940; *Educ* Haberdashers' Aske's, UCL (BSc), Univ of Cambridge (PhD); *m* 7 Dec 1969, Diana Mary, da of Harry Kettlewell (d 1984), of Harlaxton; 2 da (Charlotte b 7 Dec 1971, Lucy b 12 Dec 1973); *Career* res fell Selwyn Coll Cambridge 1964–67; Dept of Physics Univ of Bristol: lectr 1967–77, reader 1977–85, prof 1985–, dir Interface Analysis Centre 1990–2001, head of dept 2001–05, Henry Overton prof of physics 2002–; memb Sci and Engrg Cncl ctees 1982–88, chm Sci Res Fndn Emerson Green 1988–99, chm Cmmn on Electron Diffraction Int Union of Crystallography, chm Emersons Innovations Ltd 1999–2006; pres West of England Metals and Materials Assoc 2003–; Holweck Medal and Prize Inst of Physics and Société Française de Physique 1996; FRS 1988, FInstP 1991; *Books* Introduction to Anisotropic Elasticity Theory of Dislocations (1973), Electron Diffraction of Phases in Alloys (1984); *Recreations* tennis, cycling, travel; *Style—* Prof John Steeds, FRS; ✉ 21 Canynge Square, Clifton, Bristol BS8 3LA (tel 0117 973 2183); Physics Department, University of Bristol, Bristol BS8 1TL (tel 0117 928 8730, fax 0117 925 5624, e-mail j.w.steeds@bristol.ac.uk)

STEEL, Hon Mr Justice; Sir David William Steel; kt (1998); s of Sir Lincoln Steel (d 1985), and Barbara Isobel Thorburn, *née* Goldschmidt (d 1994); *b* 7 May 1943; *Educ* Eton, Keble Coll Oxford (MA); *m* 1970, Charlotte Elizabeth, da of Lt Cdr David A R M Ramsay, DSM (d 1981); 2 s (Jonathan b 1971, Timothy b 1974); *Career* called to the Bar Inner Temple 1966 (bencher 1991); jr counsel to Treasury (Admiralty and Common Law) 1978–81, QC 1981, recorder 1988, dep judge of the High Court of Justice 1993–98, judge of the High Court of Justice (Queen's Bench Div) 1998–, Admiralty judge 1998–, nominated judge of the Commercial Court 1998–, presiding judge Western Circuit 2002–06; former head of chambers; wreck cmmr for Eng and Wales 1982–98; memb: Panel Lloyd's Salvage Arbitrators 1981–98, Lord Chllr's Advsy Ctee on Legal Educn and Conduct 1991–97; ed: Temperley, Merchant Shipping Acts (1975), Kennedy on Salvage (1985); *Recreations* theatre, shooting, fishing, golf; *Style—* Hon Mr Justice Steel; ✉ c/o Royal Courts of Justice, Strand, London WC2A 2LL

STEEL, Her Hon Elizabeth Mary; DL (Merseyside 1991); da of His Hon Judge Edward Steel (d 1976), of Warrington, Cheshire, and Mary Evelyn Griffith, *née* Roberts (d 1987); sis of Dame Heather Steel, DBE, *qv*; *b* 28 November 1936; *Educ* Howells Sch Denbigh, Univ of Liverpool (LLB); *m* 8 April 1972, Stuart Christie, *qv*, s of Samuel Albert Christie; 1 da (Elspeth Victoria b 19 Nov 1976), 1 s (Iain Duncan b 17 Feb 1978); *Career* asst slr Percy Hughes & Roberts 1960–67 (articled clerk 1955–60); ptnr: John A Behn Twyford & Co 1968–80 (asst slr 1967–68), Cuff Roberts North Kirk 1980–91; recorder 1989–91, circuit judge (Northern Circuit) 1991–2007; nat vice-chm Young Cons 1965–67; memb: Cripps Ctee 1967–69, Race Relations Bd 1970–78, Gen Advsy Cncl BBC 1979–82; chm: NW Advsy Cncl BBC 1979–82, Steering Ctee Hillsborough Slrs Gp 1989–91; dep and vice-chm Bd of Dirs Liverpool Playhouse 1980–88 (memb Bd 1968–94, vice-pres 1994–99); Liverpool Law Soc: vice-pres 1988–89, pres 1989–90, memb Ctee, former chm Legal Educn Sub-Ctee; non-exec dir Bd Royal Liverpool Univ Hosp Tst 1990–91, govr Liverpool John Moores Univ 2001–, pres Merseyside branch ESU 2006–; memb: Law Soc 1960, Liverpool Law Soc 1960; Hon LLD Liverpool Univ 2007; *Recreations* theatre (watching professional and performing/directing amateur), music, needlework, cooking, reading, entertaining, being entertained; *Clubs* Univ Women's, Athenaeum (Liverpool; vice-pres 2001–02, pres 2002–03); *Style—* Her Hon Elizabeth Steel, DL

STEEL, Dame (Anne) Heather; DBE (1993); da of His Hon Edward Steel (d 1976), of Warrington, Cheshire, and Mary Evelyn Griffith, *née* Roberts (d 1987); sis of Her Hon Judge Elizabeth Steel, DL, *qv*; *b* 3 July 1940; *Educ* Howells Sch Denbigh North Wales, Univ of Liverpool (LLB); *m* 1967, David Kerr-Muir Beattie, s of Harold Beattie (d 1957), of Manchester; 1 da (Elinor b 1970), 1 s (Andrew b 1972); *Career* called to the Bar Gray's Inn 1963, practised Northern Circuit, prosecuting counsel for DHSS 1984–86, recorder of the Crown Court 1984–86, circuit judge 1986–93, judge of the High Court of Justice (Queen's Bench) 1993–2001; memb Judicial Studies Bd Criminal Ctee 1992–95; pres Faculty of Law Soc Univ of Liverpool 1994–, pres Merseyside Medico-Legal Soc 1992–94 (patron); bencher Gray's Inn 1993; Master Worshipful Co of Pattenmakers 2003–04, Freeman City of London; *Recreations* theatre, art, antiques, gardening; *Style—* Dame Heather Steel, DBE; ✉ The Royal Courts of Justice, Strand, London WC2A 2LL

STEEL, John Brychan; QC (1993); s of late Lt-Col John Exton Steel, of Swindon Hall, nr Cheltenham, Glos, and late Marianne Valentine, *née* Brychan Rees; *b* 4 June 1954; *Educ* Harrow, UC Durham (BSc, capt ski club, pres athletic union); *m* 6 June 1981, Susan Rebecca, da of Dr Robert Fraser (d 1979), of Yarm, Co Durham; 2 s (Charles John Robert b 1984, Henry James Edward b 1989), 1 da (Sophie Rosanagh b 1986); *Career* Lt Inns of Court and City Yeomanry TA 1977–81; called to the Bar Gray's Inn 1978, appointed to Attorney General's List of Counsel (Common Law) 1989, recorder 2000–; hon legal advsr to local authorities World Heritage Forum, hon legal advsr and memb Cncl The Air League; Gray's Inn prizewinner 1978; dir Busoga Tst 1982–2000; chm: Gray's Inn Field Club 1978–79, Kandahar Ski Club 1992–97, K Racing 1998–2000; dep chm: Ski Club of GB 1989–91, Durham Inst Univ of Durham 2000–; memb The Air Sqdn; Freeman GAPAN; FRGS, FRAeS; *Recreations* skiing, walking, flying; *Clubs* Boodle's, Travellers, Kandahar; *Style—* John Steel, Esq, QC; ✉ Great Rollright Manor, Chipping Norton, Oxfordshire OX7 5RH; 4–5 Gray's Inn Square, Gray's Inn, London WC1R 5AY (tel 020 7404 5252, fax 020 7242 7803)

STEEL, Prof (Christopher) Michael; s of Very Rev Dr David Steel (d 2002), of Edinburgh, and Sheila Eunice Nanette, *née* Martin (d 1993); *b* 25 January 1940; *Educ* Prince of Wales Sch Nairobi, George Watson's Coll Edinburgh, Univ of Edinburgh (Ettles scholar, BSc, MB ChB, PhD, DSc, Leslie Gold Medal in Med); *m* 1 Aug 1962, Judith Margaret, da of Frederick David Spratt; 2 s (Andrew David b 15 Feb 1968, Robert Michael b 22 Nov 1969), 1 da (Heather Judith b 3 May 1974); *Career* jr hosp appts Edinburgh Teaching Hosps 1965–68, univ research fell Edinburgh Med Sch 1968–71, MRC travelling research fell Univ of Nairobi Med Sch 1972–73, memb Clinical Scientific Staff MRC Human Genetics Unit Edinburgh 1973–94 (asst dir 1979–94), prof of med sci Univ of St Andrews 1994–2004 (emeritus prof 2005–); T P Gunton Award BMA (for research and educn in the cancer field) 1993–94; memb: UK Gene Therapy Advsy Ctee 1994–2000, MRC Advsy Bd 1999–2005; FRCPE, FRCSEd, FRCPath, FRSE 1994, FMedSci 1998; *Books* Biochemistry: A Concise Text for Medical Students (1992); *Recreations* golf, skiing, theatre; *Clubs* RSM; *Style—* Prof Michael Steel, FRSE; ✉ University of St Andrews, Bute Medical School, St Andrews, Fife KY16 9TS (tel 01334 463558, fax 01334 463482, mobile 07732 970751, e-mail cms4@st-and.ac.uk)

STEEL, Robert John Beveridge; *b* 6 August 1954; *Educ* Whitehill Sch Glasgow, Mackintosh Sch of Architecture Univ of Glasgow (BArch, DipArch, Joe Park student prize in architecture); *m*; 1 c; *Career* architectural asst: Dorward Matheson Gleave and Partners 1974–76, Fewster Valentine and Partners 1976–78, Rayack Construction Ltd 1978–80, McLean Gibson and Associates 1980–83; architect Building Design Partnership 1983–87; Reiach and Hall Architects: architect 1987–89, assoc 1989–91, dir 1991–; RIBA 1987, ARIAS 1987, memb ARCUK 1987; *Awards* for Lanark Architectural Heritage Trail: CDC Environmental Award Scheme 1986, Civic Tst Award 1988; for Life Association of Scotland HQ Edinburgh: EAA Silver Medal Commendation 1990, Patent Glazing Contractors Assoc Award 1991, Civic Tst Award 1991; for Strathclyde Graduate Business Sch Glasgow: Scottish Civic Tst Dip of Excellence 1992, Civic Tst Commendation 1993, RIBA Regional Award 1993; for Wemyss Bay Station Restoration: Int Brunel Award 1994, Ian Allan Railway Heritage Award 1994, Civic Tst Commendation 1994; *Recreations* architecture (issues, trends, debate), golf, skiing, swimming, badminton, travel, music, cinema; *Style—* Robert Steel, Esq

STEEL, Roger Cameron; s of David Ian Steel, of Scarborough, N Yorks, and Sylvia Margaret, *née* Youngman (d 1966); *b* 18 February 1952; *Educ* Scarborough HS for Boys, UCL (LLB); *m* 14 June 1975, Harriet Dorothy (Prue), da of George Michael Gee (d 2004); 2 da (Louise b 1982, Eleanor b 1985); *Career* admitted slr 1976 specialising in employment law; Frere Cholmeley Bischoff (formerly Frere Cholmeley): qualified 1976, ptnr 1982–98; ptnr Eversheds (following merger) 1998–; memb: Employment Lawyers Assoc, Int Bar Assoc, Law Soc, City of London Law Soc; *Recreations* gardening, photography, travel; *Style—* Roger Steel, Esq; ✉ Stane End House, 22 Grays House, Surrey KT21 1BU (tel 01372 272083); Eversheds, Senator House, 85 Queen Victoria Street, London EC4V 4JL (tel 0845 497 9797, fax 0845 497 4919, e-mail steelr@eversheds.com)

STEEL OF AIKWOOD, Baron (Life Peer UK 1997), of Ettrick Forest in The Scottish Borders; Sir David Martin Scott Steel; KT (2004), KBE (1990), PC (1977), DL (Ettrick and Lauderdale and Roxburghshire 1990); s of Very Rev Dr David Steel, Moderator of the

Gen Assembly of the Church of Scotland 1974–75; *b* 31 March 1938; *Educ* Prince of Wales Sch Nairobi, George Watson's Coll Edinburgh, Univ of Edinburgh (MA, LLB); *m* 1962, Judith Mary, da of W D MacGregor, CBE; 2 s, 1 da; *Career* sometime journalist, asst sec Scottish Lib Pty 1962–64, BBC TV interviewer in Scotland 1964–65 and later presenter of religious programmes for STV, Granada and BBC; MP (Lib until 1988, then Lib Dem): Roxburgh, Selkirk and Peebles 1965–83, Tweeddale, Ettrick and Lauderdale 1983–97 (stood down); MSP (Lib Dem) Lothians 1999–2003; pres Anti-Apartheid Movement of GB 1966–69, memb Parly Delgn to UN 1967, sponsored Abortion Act 1967, Lib chief whip 1970–75, spokesman on foreign affrs 1975–76, ldr of Lib Pty 1976–88, memb Select Ctee on Privileges 1979–86, pres Lib International 1994–96; presiding offr Scot Parl 1999–2003; fndr bd memb Int Inst for Democracy and Electoral Assistance (Stockholm) 1995; non-exec dir: Hall Advertising Ltd Edinburgh 1971–76, Border Television plc 1993–99, Heritage Oil & Gas Co Ltd 1995–97, One Planet Partnership Ltd (private policy consultancy) 1995–98, General Mediterranean Holding SA 1996–, Blue Planet European Financials Investment Tst 1999–; vice-pres The Countryside Alliance 1998–99; hon pres The Stationery Office Scotland 1997–98; chm Shelter Scotland 1969–73, memb Br Cncl of Churches 1971–74, rector Univ of Edinburgh 1982–85; regular contribs to newspapers incl The Scotsman and The Guardian; Freedom of Tweeddale 1988, Freedom of Ettrick and Lauderdale 1990; Chubb fell Yale Univ 1987, Hon Dr Univ of Stirling 1991, Hon DLitt Univ of Buckingham 1993, Hon DUniv Heriot-Watt 1996, Hon LLD Univ of Edinburgh 1997, Hon Dr Univ of Strathclyde 2000, Hon DUniv Open Univ 2001, Hon LLD Univ of Aberdeen 2001, Hon LLD Univ of St Andrews 2003, Hon LLD Glasgow Caledonian Univ 2004; Cdr's Cross of the Order of Merit (Germany) 1992; Chevalier de la Legion d'Honneur 2004; *Books* Boost for the Borders (1964), Out of Control (1968), No Entry (1969), The Liberal Way Forward (1975), A New Political Agenda (1976), Militant for the Reasonable Man (1977), A House Divided (1980), Partners in One Nation (1985), Border Country (with Judy Steel, 1985), The Time Has Come (1987), Mary Stuart's Scotland (with Judy Steel, 1987), Against Goliath (autobiography, 1989); *Recreations* classic cars, fishing; *Style*— The Rt Hon the Lord Steel of Aikwood, KT, KBE, DL; ✉ House of Lords, London SW1A 0PW

STEELE, Prof Robert James Campbell; s of Robert Steele, and Elizabeth Sheridan, *née* Campbell; *b* 5 March 1952; *Educ* Daniel Stewart's Coll Edinburgh, Univ of Edinburgh (BSc, MB ChB, MD); *Career* research fell, registrar and lectr in surgery Univ of Edinburgh 1980–85, lectr in surgery Chinese Univ of Hong Kong 1985–86, lectr in surgery Univ of Aberdeen 1986–90, sr lectr and reader in surgery Univ of Nottingham 1990–96, prof of surgical oncology Univ of Dundee 1996–2003, prof of surgery and head Dept of Surgery and Molecular Oncology Univ of Dundee 2003–; dir Scottish Colorectal Cancer Screening Cancer Pilot; chair: Colorectal Cancer Screening Project Bd, chair UK Colorectal Cancer Screening Exec Gp, Colorectal Sub-Gp Clinical Standards Bd for Scotland, Colorectal Cancer Focus Gp Scottish Intercollegiate Guidelines Network; memb MRC Advsy Bd, memb Colorectal Clinical Studies Gp Nat Cancer Research Inst; FRCSEd 1984 (Gold Medal), FRCS (ad eundem), 1995, fell Coll of Surgns Hong Kong 1995; *Publications* five books, three guidelines, 37 book chapters and 161 peer reviewed articles; *Style*— Prof R J C Steele; ✉ Department of Surgery and Molecular Oncology, Ninewells Hospital and Medical School, Level 6, Dundee DD1 9SY (tel 01382 632174, fax 01382 496361, e-mail r.j.c.steele@dundee.ac.uk)

STEELE, Tommy; né Thomas Hicks; OBE (1979); s of Thomas Walter Hicks (d 1980), and Elizabeth Ellen Bennett (d 1982); *b* 17 December 1936; *Educ* Bacon's Sch for Boys Bermondsey; *m* 1960, Ann, *née* Donoghue; 1 da (Emma b 1969); *Career* actor; stage debut (Sunderland) 1956, London stage debut (Dominion Theatre) 1957; Hon DLitt South Bank Univ 1998; *Theatre* incl: Cinderella (Colliseum) 1958, She Stoops to Conquer (Old Vic) 1960, Half a Sixpence (Cambridge Theatre London) 1963–64 and (Broadhurst Theatre NY) 1965, The Servant of Two Masters (Queen's) 1969, Dick Whittington (London Palladium) 1969, Meet Me in London (Adelphi) 1971, The Yeomen of the Guard (City of London Festival) 1978, The Tommy Steele Show (Palladium) 1973, Hans Andersen (Palladium 1974 (dir/prodr 1977 presentation and tour)), one-man show (Prince of Wales) 1979 and 1995, Scrooge (UK tour) 2003–04; dir of all prodns of Singin' in the Rain and Some Like it Hot; *Films* Kill Me Tomorrow 1956, The Tommy Steele Story, The Duke Wore Jeans, Tommy the Toreador, Light Up the Sky, It's All Happening, The Happiest Millionaire, Half a Sixpence, Finian's Rainbow, Where's Jack?; *Other Work* incl: Quincy's Quest (wrote and acted for TV) 1979, My Life, My Song (composed and recorded) 1974, A Portrait of Pablo (composed) 1985, Rock Suite - an Elderly Person's Guide to Rock (composed) 1987; *Books* Quincy (1981), The Final Run (1983), Bermondsey Boy (autobiography, 2006); *Recreations* squash, painting; *Style*— Tommy Steele, Esq, OBE; ✉ c/o Laurie Mansfield, International Artistes Ltd, 4th Floor, Holborn Hall, 193–197 High Holborn, London WC1V 7BD

STEELE-PERKINS, Christopher Horace (Chris); s of Alfred Horace Steele-Perkins (d 1963), and Mary, *née* Lloyd (d 2001); *b* 28 July 1947; *Educ* Christ's Hosp, Univ of Newcastle upon Tyne (BSc); *m* 17 July 1999, Miyako Yamada, da of Shinsei Lee; 2 s (Cedric Angelo b 16 Nov 1990, Cameron Benjamin b 18 June 1992); *Career* photographer; Magnum Photos: memb 1982, pres 1995–98; vice-pres Magnum Photos Japan 1998–2003; visiting prof Musashino Art Univ Tokyo 2000; *Exhibitions* The Pleasure Principle (FNAC Paris) 1990, Africa (Perpignon France) 1992, Cross Section (Hong Kong Festival) 1993, No Mans Land (PGI Tokyo) 1999, Afghanistan (UK tour) 2000, Fuji (MAC Birmingham and Grandship Japan) 2001, Teds (Howard Greenburg Gall NY) 2003, Echoes (FNAC Paris) 2004; *Awards* Oskar Barnak Award 1988, Robert Capa Gold Medal 1989, Tom Hopkinson Award 1989, La nacion Premier Photojournalism Award 1994, Co-operative Soc and One World Award (for film Dying for Publicity) 1994, Sasakawa Fndn Grant 1999 and 2004, World Press Award 2000; *Books* The Teds (1979), About 70 Photographs (1980), Survival Programmes (jtly, 1982), Beirut: Frontline Story (1983), The Pleasure Principle (1989), Afghanistan (2000), Fuji (2001), Echoes (2004); *Recreations* squash, chess, walking, music, literature, film; *Style*— Chris Steele-Perkins, Esq; ✉ Magnum Photos, 63 Gee Street, London EC1V 3RS (tel 020 7490 1771)

STEELE-PERKINS, Crispian; s of Dr Guy Steele-Perkins, and Sylvia de Courcey Steele-Perkins; *b* 18 December 1944; *Educ* Marlborough, Guildhall Sch of Music; *m* 1, 29 April 1967, Angela (d 1991), da of William Scambler Hall (d 1967); 2 da (Emma Victoria b 20 March 1968, Kathleen b 28 Oct 1970), ((Michael) Guy (twin) b 28 Oct 1970); m 2, 6 April 1995, Jane Steele-Perkins (second cous); *Career* trumpeter, specialising in Baroque period; with Sadler's Wells Opera/ENO 1966–73, dir London Gabrieli Brass Ensemble 1973–84, with English Chamber Orch 1973–76, asst princ trumpeter Royal Philharmonic Orch 1976–80, prof of trumpet Guildhall Sch of Music 1980–90, solo trumpeter with The English Baroque and The King's Consort 1980–, gives about 50 solo recitals and masterclasses a year; made over 800 recordings (incl 80 film soundtracks and 17 solo albums) incl: The English Trumpet, Trumpets Ancient and Modern, Classical Trumpet Concertos; *Style*— Crispian Steele-Perkins, Esq; ✉ 5 Westfield Gardens, Dorking, Surrey RH4 3DX (e-mail crispiansp@trumpet1.co.uk, website www.crispiansteel-perkins.co.uk)

STEEN, Anthony David; MP; s of late Stephen N Steen, of London; *b* 22 July 1939; *Educ* Westminster, Gray's Inn; *m* Carolyn Steen, JP, *née* Padfield; 1 s (Jason), 1 da (Xanthe); *Career* youth club ldr in E London Settlement 1959–64, called to the Bar Gray's Inn 1962, practised 1962–76; fndr dir: Task Force 1964–68, Community Project Fndn (formerly Young Volunteer Force) 1968–74; former Lloyd's underwriter (resigned); MP (Cons): Liverpool Wavertree 1974–83, South Hams 1983–97, Totnes 1997–; memb: Select Ctee on Immigration and Race Relations 1975–79, Select Ctee on Environment 1989–92, Euro Legislation Select Ctee 1997–, Deregulation Select Ctee 1997–; jt nat chm Impact 80s Campaign 1980–82, Cons Central Office co-ordinator for Critical Seats 1982–87, PPS to Sec of State for Nat Heritage 1992–94, PM's appointee to generate new activity amongst MPs in constituency work 1994; jt sec 1922 Ctee 2001– chm: Cons Party Backbench Ctee on Cities, Urban and New Town Affrs 1979–83, Urban and Inner City Ctee 1983–87, Cons Backbench Sane Planning Gp 1987–92, Cons Deregulation Ctee 1993–97; sec Cons Backbench Trade and Industry Ctee 1997–2000; chm All-Pty Gp on the Trafficking of Women and Children 2006–; vice-chm: Health and Social Servs Ctee 1979–81, Environment Ctee 1979–81, All-Pty Fisheries Gp, All-Pty Gp on St Helena, All-Pty South Africa Gp, All-Pty Maldives Gp, All-Pty Caribbean Gp 1979–, sec Public Admin Ctee 2001–02; exec memb Population and Devpt Gp 1989–97, treas All-Pty Parly Hepatology Gp 2003–; memb All-Pty: Child Abuse Ctee, Animal Welfare Gp, Human Rights Gp, Gp on Underground Space, Gp on Corporate Social Responsibility, Parly Small Business Gp, Mexico Gp, China Gp, Tibet Gp; memb: House of Commons Catering Ctee 1991–95, Parly Sustainable and Renewable Energy Gp, BDA Parly Panel; chm West County Members 1992–94, chm Minority Party Campaigns Unit Cons Central Office 1999–2001; advsr: English Vineyards Assoc, BMI British Midland Airways; conslt The Communications Group plc, advsr to various British airlines; vice-pres: Int Centre for Child Studies, Assoc of District Cncls; memb Cncl for Christians and Jews; tstee: Educn Extra, Dartington Summer Sch; advsy tutor to Sch of Environment PCL 1982–83; *Publications* Tested Ideas for Political Success (1976, revised edns 1983 and 1991), New Life for Old Cities (1981), Public Land Utilisation Management Schemes (PLUMS) (1988); *Recreations* piano playing, tennis; *Clubs* Brixham, Totnes & Ashburton Conservative, Royal North Cape, RAC; *Style*— Anthony Steen, Esq, MP; ✉ House of Commons, London SW1A 0AA (tel 020 7219 5045, e-mail steena@parliament.uk, website www.anthonysteen.org.uk)

STEEN, David; s of Edward Steen (d 1959), and Mary, *née* Heal (d 2003); *b* 16 February 1936, London; *m* 18 March 1961, Shirley, *née* Flack; 2 da (Charlotte b 1961, Georgina b 1969), 2 s (David Paul b 1963, James b 1965); *Career* photographer; joined as asst to photographers Picture Post 1951, Army photographer ME Nat Serv 1954–56, Daily Mail 1959–60, Queen magazine 1962, freelance for advtg, magazines and pubns incl Sunday Times, Daily Telegraph and Nova 1963–; Br Press Pictures of the Year Encyclopaedia Britannica 1958; *Publications* Heroes and Villains (2005); *Style*— David Steen, Esq

STEEN, (David) Michael Cochrane Elsworth; OBE (2007); s of Prof Robert Elsworth Steen, MD (d 1981), and Elizabeth Margaret, *née* Cochrane (d 2002); *b* 5 March 1945; *Educ* Eton, RCM, Oriel Coll Oxford (MA); *m* 18 Dec 1971, Rosemary Florence, da of Maj William Bellingham Denis Dobbs; 3 da (Jane b 1973, Lucy b 1975, Rosalie b 1977), 1 s (Peter b 1977); *Career* KPMG (formerly Peat Marwick Mitchell & Co): joined 1968, ptnr 1982–98, head of audit servs 1987–90, head of UK insurance practice 1991–92, bd memb 1992–98, head of risk mgmnt 1996–98; dir: Old Mutual South Africa Trust plc 1998–, Molins plc 2000–; memb Gaming Bd for GB 1999–2005, cmmr Gambling Cmmn 2005–; tstee: The King's Consort 1998–99, Friends of the V&A 2003– (chm 2005–), Gerald Coke Handel Fndn 2006–; chm RCM Soc 1998–2005; Hon RCM 2006 (ARCM); *Books* Guide to Directors Transactions (1983), Audits & Auditors: What the Public Thinks (1989), The Lives and Times of the Great Composers (2003); *Recreations* music (organ playing), bicycling, reading; *Clubs* Carlton, Leander; *Style*— Michael Steen, Esq, OBE; ✉ Nevilles, Mattingley, Hampshire RG27 8JU (tel 01256 762144, e-mail dmc@steen1.freeserve.co.uk)

STEEN, Prof William Maxwell; s of late Stourton William Peile Steen, and Marjorie Gordon, *née* Maxwell; *b* 30 September 1933; *Educ* Kingswood Sch Bath, Univ of Cambridge (MA), Imperial Coll London (PhD, DIC); *m* April 1960, Margaret, da of John Thomas Porkess Frankish, of Scunthorpe, Lincs; 1 s (Preston b 6 Oct 1963), 1 da (Melanie b 6 May 1965); *Career* Nat Serv Pilot RAF 1952–54; process engr APV Co Ltd 1958–62, Methodist Missionary Soc Bankura Christian Coll India 1962–65, sr lectr Imperial Coll London 1985–87 (lectr 1965–85), James Bibby prof of engrg manufacture Univ of Liverpool 1987–98 (emeritus prof 1998–), distinguished research fell Metallurgy Dept Univ of Cambridge 1998–; pres: Liverpool Metallurgical Soc 1991–92, Assoc of Industrial Laser Users 1995–2003; ed Christ's Coll Magazine Cambridge 2000–06; Freeman City of London 1983, Liveryman Worshipful Co of Goldsmiths; fell Laser Inst of America; FIMMM, CEng; *Publications* over 250 incl Laser Material Processing (1993, 3 edn 2003); *Recreations* gardening, swimming, walking, woodwork incl model ship building; *Style*— Prof William Steen; ✉ PO Box 147, Liverpool L69 3BX (tel 0151 794 4839/40, fax 0151 794 4892, telex 627095, e-mail w.steen@btinternet.com)

STEER, Dr Christopher Richard; s of Eric Arthur Steer (d 1975), of Chistlehurst, Kent, and Joan, *née* Bowden; *b* 30 May 1947; *Educ* St Olave's GS London, Univ of Edinburgh (BSc, MB ChB, DCH Glas); *m* 1, 20 Dec 1970 (m dis 1986), Patricia Ann, da of James Gallacher (d 1985); 1 s (Paul Christopher), 1 da (Jane Elizabeth); m 2, 1986, Patricia Mary Lennox; 1 s (Jamie Alisdair), 1 da (Rosemary Gillian); *Career* conslt paediatrician Fife 1983–, clinical dir Acute Unit Fife Health Bd 1990–, lead clinician paediatrics Kirkcaldy Acute Hosp 1999; memb: BMA 1978, Scottish Paediatric Soc 1978, Paediatric Res Soc 1978; assoc GMC 2000; FRCPE, FRCPCH, FRSM 2000; *Recreations* gardening; *Style*— Dr Christopher Steer; ✉ 14 Bellhouse Road, Aberdour, Fife KY3 0TL (tel 01383 860738); Paediatric Department, Victoria Hospital, Hayfield Road, Kirkcaldy, Fife KY2 5AH (tel 01592 643355, e-mail christophersteer@aol.com)

STEER, Clive Allen; s of Allan Edwin Steer (d 1986), of Guildford, Surrey, and Majorie, *née* Allen (d 1976); *b* 11 May 1938; *Educ* Northmead Sch Guildford, Royal Aircraft Estab Coll Farnborough, Central Sch of Art and Design London; *m* 24 Feb 1962, Janet, da of Arthur F E Evans, OBE; 3 da (Rebecca b 8 Feb 1966, Georgina b 27 Oct 1970, Jacqueline b 23 Sept 1972), 1 s (Jonathan b 21 Sept 1967); *Career* industrial designer; Rediffusion Vision Limited London 1964–69, head of industrial design Philips Electrical (UK) Ltd 1969–79, Philips Singapore 1979–82, assoc Business Design Group 1985–89, dir On the Line Design (conslts) 1989–90, princ Steer Associates 1990–94, accompanying offr FCO 1994–95, business advsr Business Link 1995–2005, freelance conslt 2005–; speaker on design and mktg at Design Cncl courses; awards: Design Cncl award for Philips Design Team Product (consumer and contract goods) 1975, 1984 Oscar for Invention and Gold medal Int Exposition of Invention Geneva; former: memb Judging Panel Design Cncl Consumer and Contract Goods Awards, memb Jury Bursary Awards RSA, chm Product Gp (A1) CSD, chm Membership Bd CSD, memb Fellowship Bd CSD, govr St Martin's Sch of Art, vice-pres and memb Cncl CSD; FRSA 1978, FCSD 1979; *Recreations* gardening, walking; *Clubs* Beaujolais Old Friends Soc (BOFS); *Style*— Clive Steer, Esq; ✉ Westview, Shere Road, West Horsley, Leatherhead, Surrey KT24 6EW (tel 01483 284686)

STEER, David; QC (1993); s of Alcombe Steer, of St Helens, Merseyside, and Nancy, *née* Smart; *b* 15 June 1951; *Educ* Rainford HS, Manchester Poly (BA); *m* 28 Sept 1974, Elizabeth May, da of James Basil Hide; 1 s (Oliver James Alcombe b 9 Aug 1982); *Career* called to the Bar Middle Temple 1974 (bencher 2001); recorder 1991–, head of chambers 1992–, ldr Northern Circuit 2002–04; memb Bar Cncl 1995–97 and 2002–04; *Recreations* rugby league, gardening; *Style*— David Steer, Esq, QC; ✉ Pyke's Farm, Clay Lane, Eccleston, St Helens, Merseyside WA10 5PX (tel 01744 36952); 7 Harrington Street, Liverpool L2 9YH (tel 0151 242 0707, fax 0151 236 2800)

STEER, Brig Francis Richard (Frank); MBE (1985); s of Terence Anthony Steer, and Doris Elizabeth, *née* Smith; *b* 25 August 1946; *Educ* St Ignatius' Coll London, RMA Sandhurst,

Army Staff Coll, NATO Defence Coll; *m* 30 Dec 1967, Virginia Rosemary Elizabeth, da of Aubrey Hill; 3 da (Victoria Angela b 22 Oct 1970, Virginia Melanie b 10 March 1972, Rosalynne Mary b 23 Dec 1975), 2 s (Richard Francis b 23 Dec 1973, Christopher Anthony b 29 Nov 1977); *Career* Cdr (supply) Berlin 1987–90, Cdr (supply) Gulf War Saudi Arabia 1991, dir Logistic Ops MOD 1994–96, dir Equipment Support (Army) 1997–99, DG Inst of Quality Assurance 1999–; tstee: Royal Army Ordnance Corps Tst, Royal Logistics Corps Museum; memb C&G 1979, FILT, FCIPS; *Books* Arnhem: The Fight to Sustain (2000), Arnhem: Oosterbeek and the Landing Grounds (2002), Arnhem: The Bridge (2003), Very Exceptional Soldiers (2005), To the Warrior His Arms: The Story of the Royal Army Ordnance Corps (2005); *Recreations* ornithology, authorship, skiing, squash; *Clubs* Army and Navy; *Style—* Brig Frank Steer, MBE; ✉ Institute of Quality Assurance, 12 Grosvenor Crescent, London SW1X 7EE (tel 020 7245 6722, fax 020 7245 0299, e-mail foxtrot.sierra@virgin.net)

STEFANOU, Stelio H; OBE (2004); s of George Stefanou (d 1979), of Surbiton, Surrey, and Katina, *née* Heracleiou; *b* 6 November 1952; *Educ* Hollyfield Sch Surbiton, Tiffin GS Kingston upon Thames, Imperial Coll London (BSc), RCS (ARCS); *m* 3 Sept 1977 (m dis), Rosemarie Ann, da of Sydney Gordon, of London; *Career* product devpt Johnson Matthey 1974–77, mktg exec Esso UK plc 1977–80, dir John Doyle Construction Ltd 1980–87, gp md and chief exec John Doyle Group plc 1987–99; Accord plc: chief exec 1999–2005, chm 2005–; CBI: chm Hertfordshire County Gp 1992–94, memb Nat Cncl 1994–97, chm Eastern Regnl Cncl 1995–97, memb Pres's Ctee 1996–97, memb Public Servs Strategy Bd 1997–, chm Local Govt Panel 1997–, chm Hertfordshire Learning and Skills Cncl 2001–03; memb: East of England Devpt Agency 1999–2001, DETR Best Value Steering Panel, Bank of England Eastern Regn Economic Advsy Panel; non-exec dir: East of England Investment Agency 1997–2001, Business Link Hertfordshire; memb Lighthouse Club; Freeman City of London 1994, Liveryman Worshipful Co of Founders; FInstD; *Recreations* tennis, photography, cooking; *Style—* Stelio H Stefanou, Esq, OBE; ✉ Accord plc, Accord House, Albany Place, Welwyn Garden City, Hertfordshire AL7 1HX

STEFFEN, Wilfried; *b* 5 June 1955; *Educ* Albertus-Magnus Univ Cologne (MBA); *m* Anne; 3 c; *Career* corporate auditor rising to mangr (controlling products and projects) Daimler-Benz 1981–93, gen mangr (corp controlling) then vice-pres (finance and controlling) Mercedes-Benz of North America 1993–99, vice-pres DaimlerChrysler AG 1999, ceo and md DaimlerChrysler Switzerland AG 2000–03, pres and ceo DaimlerChrysler UK Ltd 2003–; memb Br-German C of C; *Recreations* travel, music (jazz), sports (golf, football, tennis), arts, history, family; *Clubs* RAC; *Style—* Wilfried Steffen, Esq; ✉ DaimlerChrysler UK Limited, Tongwell, Milton Keynes, Buckinghamshire MK15 8BA (tel 01908 668899, fax 01908 245802)

STEIN, Brian; s of Abraham Stein (d 1994), and Lillian Stein (d 1991); *b* 28 August 1943, Johannesburg, SA; *Educ* King Edward VII Johannesburg, Johannesburg Sch of Art; *Career* vol Israeli Def Force 1964–66, Frugal Sound Folk Music 1967–70, fashion photographer 1969–72, fndr Maxwells Restaurant Gp (incl Café de Paris nightclub) 1972–; vol pilot St John's Ambulance Air Wing 1985–1992; Freeman Guild of Air Pilots and Navigators 1985; *Recreations* polo, aviation, painting, shooting; *Clubs* Guards Polo (memb Bd of Dirs 2000), Royal Co of Berks (RCB) Polo, Stoke Park; *Style—* Brian Stein, Esq; ✉ 22 Henrietta Street, London WC2E 8ND (tel 020 7379 6132, fax 020 7379 5025, e-mail post@maxwells.co.uk)

STEIN, Christopher Richard (Rick); OBE (2003); s of Eric Stein (d 1965), of Cornwall, and Dorothy Gertrude, *née* Jackson (d 1999); *b* 4 January 1947; *Educ* Uppingham, New Coll Oxford (BA); *m* 21 Sept 1975, Jill, da of Jack Newstead; 3 s (Edward b 16 Jan 1979, Jack b 31 Oct 1980, Charles b 14 Sept 1985); *Career* chef and restaurateur; estab (with Jill Stein) The Seafood Restaurant Cornwall 1975–; other business interests: St Petroc's Hotel and Bistro, Rick Stein's Café, Stein's Delicatessen, The Padstow Seafood School, Stein's Gift Shop, Stein's Patisserie, Stein's Fish & Chips; presenter: Rick Stein's Taste of the Sea (BBC 2) 1995 (Television Programme of the Year Glenfiddich Awards 1996), Rick Stein's Fruits of the Sea (BBC 2) 1997, Rick Stein's Seafood Odyssey (BBC 2) 1999, Fresh Food (BBC 2) 1999, The Seafood Lover's Guide 2000, Rick Stein's Food Heroes (BBC 2) 2002, Rick Stein's Food Heroes, Another Helping (BBC 2) 2003 and 2004, Rick Stein's French Odyssey (BBC 2) 2005, Rick Stein's Mediterranean Escapes (BBC 2) 2007; BBC Good Food TV Personality of the Year 1996, winner Glenfiddich Trophy 2001; *Books* English Seafood Cookery (1988, Glenfiddich Food Book of the Year 1989), Rick Stein's Taste of the Sea (1995, André Simon Cookery Book of the Year 1996, BBC Good Food of the Year 1996), Fish (1996), Fruits of the Sea (1997), Rick Stein Cooks Fish (1997), Rick Stein Cooks Seafood (1998), Rick Stein's Seafood Odyssey (1999), Rick Stein's Seafood Lover's Guide (2000), Rick Stein's Seafood (2001, James Beard Award for US edn 2005), Rick Stein's Food Heroes (2002), Rick Stein's Guide to the Food Heroes of Britain (2003), Rick Stein's Food Heroes, Another Helping (2004), Rick Stein's French Odyssey (2005), Rick Stein's Mediterranean Escapes (2007); *Recreations* swimming; *Style—* Rick Stein, Esq, OBE; ✉ Seafood Restaurant, Riverside, Padstow PL28 8BY (tel 01841 532700, fax 01841 533344, e-mail reservations@rickstein.com, website www.rickstein.com)

STEIN, Prof John Frederick; s of Eric Stein (d 1965), of Churchill, Oxon, and Dorothy, *née* Jackson (d 1999); *b* 20 February 1941; *Educ* Winchester, New Coll Oxford, St Thomas' Hosp Med Sch London (univ scholar); *m* 1, July 1964, Frances, *née* Hill; 1 s (William b 16 Nov 1965), 1 da (Polly b 8 July 1970); m 2, 14 Jan 1978, Clare, *née* Watson; 2 da (Lucy b 29 April 1979, Kate b 7 June 1981); *Career* med house appts St Thomas' Hosp London and Oxford and Leicester Hosps 1966–68, MRC research fell Radcliffe Infirmary Oxford 1968–70, fell and tutor in med Magdalen Coll Oxford 1970–; memb: BMA 1966, AUT 1970, Physiological Soc 1975, Assoc of Br Neurologists 1980, Br Dyslexia Assoc 1980, Movement Disorders Soc 1990, US Soc for Neuroscience; FRCP 1995; *Books* Introduction to Neurophysiology (1980), Cerebellum and Control of Movement (1985), Sensory Basis of Dyslexia (1995); *Recreations* gardening, squash; *Style—* Prof John Stein; ✉ Magdalen College, Oxford OX1 3AU; University Laboratory of Physiology, Parks Road, Oxford OX1 3PT (tel 01865 272552, fax 01865 272469, e-mail jfs@physiol.ox.ac.uk)

STEINBERG, Prof Hannah; da of late Dr Michael Steinberg, and Marie, *née* Wein; *Educ* Putney HS, Queen Anne's Sch Caversham, Univ of Reading (Cert Commerce), Denton Secretarial Coll, UCL (BA, PhD, Troughton scholar), Univ of London (postgrad studentship in psychology, pres Students Union, DSc); *Career* sec to md Omes Ltd until 1944; UCL: joined 1950 as hon research asst, asst lectr then lectr in pharmacology, reader in psychopharmacology, prof of psychopharmacology (first in Western Europe and USA) 1970–92, head of Psychopharmacology Gp 1979–92, hon research fell in psychology 1992–; prof emeritus in psychopharmacology Univ of London 1989–; visiting research prof Sch of Social Science Middx Univ 1992–2001; hon consltg clinical psychologist Dept of Psychological Med Royal Free Hosp 1970, visiting prof in psychiatry McMaster Univ Ontario (briefly) 1971; vice-pres: Collegium Internationale Neuro-Psychopharmacologicum 1968–74 (emeritus fell 1995–), Br Assoc for Psychopharmacology 1974–76 (hon memb 1989–); convener Academic Women's Achievement Gp 1979–92, special tstee Middx Hosp 1988–92; memb Editorial Bd: Br Jl of Pharmacology 1965–72, Psychopharmacologia 1965–80, Pharmacopsychoecologia 1987; memb: MRC Working Parties, Experimental Psychological Soc, Br Pharmacological Soc, Euro Behavioural Pharmacology Soc (fndr memb 1986), Euro Coll of Neuro-Psychopharmacology (fndr memb 1986), Br Assoc of Sport and Exercise Sciences (accredited sport and exercise scientist 1992–), European Health Psychology Soc; distinguished affiliate American Psychological Assoc Div of Psychopharmacology 1978; Br Assoc for Psychopharmacology/AstraZeneca Lifetime Achievement Award 2001; CPsychol 1990, FBPsS 1959 (ed Bulletin 1955–62); *Publications* Animals and Men (trans and jt ed, 1951), Animal Behaviour and Drug Action (jt ed, 1963), Scientific Basis of Drug Dependence (1968), Psychopharmacology: Sexual Disorders and Drug Abuse (1972), Exercise Addiction (1995), Quality and Quantity in Sport and Exercise Psychology (1996), How Teams Work (1996), Cognitive Enhancement (1997), What Sport Psychologists Do (1998), Sport Psychology in Practice: the Early Stages (2000); author of numerous scientific and semi-popular articles and chapters on psychopharmacology, drug addiction, drug combinations, psychological benefits and risks of physical exercise, exercise addiction, creativity and writer's block, academic women's issues, and also planning law in conservation areas: initiator with E A Sykes of The Steinberg Principle on new devpts in conservation areas (Town and Country Planning Act, Listed Buildings Act, 1990); *Style—* Prof Hannah Steinberg; ✉ c/o Pharmacology Department, University College London, London WC1E 6BT (tel 020 7267 4783, fax 020 7267 4780)

STEINBERG, Baron (Life Peer UK 2004), of Belfast in the County of Antrim; Leonard Steinberg; s of Jack Steinberg (d 1955), of Manchester, and Esther, *née* Lazarus (d 1968); *b* 1 August 1936, Belfast; *Educ* Royal Belfast Academical Instn; *m* 15 July 1962, Beryl, da of late Maurice Cobden, of Hull, E Yorks; 1 da (Hon Lynne Rochelle Ferster b 4 Dec 1964), 1 s (Hon Jonathan b 15 March 1967); *Career* fndr and chm Stanley Leisure 1957–2006 (life pres 2006–), estab Centre for Gambling and Commercial Gaming Univ of Salford 1997; memb Br Casino Assoc 1974–2005; dep treas Cons Pty 1994–2002; Hon DLitt Univ of Salford; *Recreations* cricket, stamp collecting, art, reading; *Clubs* RAC, Carlton; *Style—* The Rt Hon the Lord Steinberg; ✉ 151 Dale Street, Liverpool L2 2JW; House of Lords, London SW1A 0PW

STEINBY, Prof Eva Margareta; da of Kaarlo Erkki Wilén and Doris Margareta Steinby; *b* 21 November 1938; *Educ* Univ of Helsinki (Hum Kand, Fil Kand, Fil Lic, Fil Dr), Univ of Oxford (MA); *Career* Institutum Romanum Finlandiae Rome: asst 1973–77, dir 1979–82 and 1992–94; docent in history Univ of Helsinki 1977–, sr research fell Finnish Acad Helsinki 1985–92, prof of archaeology of the Roman Empire and fell All Souls Coll Oxford 1994–; visiting fell All Souls Coll Oxford 1990–91; fell: Suomen Historiallinen Seura 1978, Societas Scientiarum Fennica 1983, Pontificia Accademia Romana di Archeologia 1993–95 (corresponding fell 1982); corresponding fell Deutsches Archäologisches Institut 1984, foreign hon fell Archaeological Inst of America, fell Academia Scientiarum Fennica 2000 Medaglia d'Oro per Benemeriti Culturali (Italy) 1983, Medaglia Daria Borghese 2002, prize of Finnish Cultural Fndn 2003; FSA 1997; Offr 1st class Order of White Rose (Finland) 1991; *Books* La cronologia delle figlinae doliari urbane (1976), Lateres signati Ostienses (vols I-II, 1977–78), Indici complementari ai bolli doliari urbani (CIL, XV, 1, 1987), Lacus Iuturnae I (ed, 1989), Lexicon Topographicum Urbis Romae (6 vols, 1993–2000), Ianiculum - Gianicolo (ed, 1997), La necropoli della Via Triumphalis Roma (2003); also author of numerous articles in Italian, German and Finnish learned jls; *Style—* Prof Eva Margareta Steinby, FSA; ✉ All Souls College, Oxford OX1 4AL (tel 01865 279379)

STEINER, Prof George; s of F G Steiner (d 1968), and E Steiner (d 1981); *b* 23 April 1929; *Educ* Paris (BésL), Univ of Chicago (BA), Harvard Univ (MA), Univ of Oxford (DPhil), Univ of Cambridge (PhD); *m* 7 July 1955, Zara; 1 s (David b 1958), 1 da (Deborah b 1960); *Career* memb staff The Economist 1952–56, Inst for Advanced Study Princeton 1956–58, Gauss lectr Princeton 1959–60, fell Churchill Coll Cambridge 1961; prof of English and comparative literature Univ of Geneva 1974–94, visiting prof Collège de France 1992, visiting prof of Euro and comparative literature Univ of Oxford 1994, Lord Weidenfeld visiting prof of comparative literature Univ of Oxford 1994–95, Carles Elliot Norton prof of poetry Harvard Univ 2001–02; lectures: Massey 1974, Leslie Stephen Cambridge 1986, W P Ker Univ of Glasgow 1986, Page Barbour Univ of Virginia 1987; Fulbright professorship 1958–69, O Henry short story award 1958, Guggenheim fellowship 1971–72, Zabel award of Nat Inst of Arts and Letters of the US 1970, Faulkner stipend for fiction PEN 1983, Gifford lectr 1990, Truman Capote lifetime award for lit USA 1998, Ludwig Börne prize 2003; doctorate (hc): Univ of Louvain 1980, Univ of Salamanca 2002; Hon DLitt Univs of: East Anglia 1976, Bristol 1989, Glasgow 1990, Liège 1990, Ulster 1993, Durham 1995, Kenyon Coll 1996, Trinity Coll Dublin 1996, Rome 1998, Sorbonne 1998, Univ of Athens 2004; hon fell: Balliol Coll Oxford 1995, St Anne's Coll Oxford 1995; corresponding memb Germany Academy, hon memb American Acad of Arts and Sciences; FRSL 1964, FBA 1998, Hon RA 2000; Commandeur de l'Ordre des Arts et des Lettres (France) 2000, Legion d'Honneur; *Books* Tolstoy or Dostoevsky (1958), The Death of Tragedy (1960), Anno Domini (1964), Language and Silence (1967), Extraterritorial (1971), In Bluebeard's Castle (1971), The Sporting Scene: White Knights in Reykjavik (1973), After Babel (1975), Heidegger (1978), On Difficulty and other Essays (1978), The Portage to San Cristabal of AH (1981), Antigones (1984), George Steiner, a reader (1984), Real Presences (1989), Proofs and Three Parables (1992, Macmillan Silver Pen Award for Fiction PEN), No Passion Spent (1996), The Deeps of the Sea and Other Fiction (1996), Homer in English (ed, 1996), Errata (1997), Grammars of Creation (2001), Lessons of the Masters (2003); *Recreations* chess, music, hill walking, old English sheepdog; *Clubs* Athenaeum, Harvard Club of NYC; *Style—* Prof George Steiner, FBA; ✉ Churchill College, Cambridge CB3 0DS

STEINER, Jeffrey Josef; s of Beno Steiner, and Paula Borstein; *b* 3 April 1937; *Educ* Bradford Inst of Technol, City and Guilds Inst London; *m* 1, 1957 (m dis 1970), Claude; 1 s (Eric b 25 Oct 1961), 2 da (Natalia b 14 Sept 1965, Thierry Tama Tama (foster) b 31 Dec 1970); m 2, 6 March 1976 (m dis 1983), Linda, *née* Schaller; 1 s (Benjamin b 3 April 1978), 1 da (Alexandra b 1980); m 3, 19 March 1987 (m dis), Irja, *née* Eckerbrant Bonnier; *Career* mangr Metals and Controls Div Texas Instruments 1959–60 (mgmnt trainee 1958–59), pres Texas Instruments 1960–66 (Argentina, Brazil, Mexico, Switzerland, France), pres Burlington Tapis 1967–72, chm and pres Cedec SA Engrg Co 1973–84, chm, pres and ceo The Fairchild Corporation (NYSE) 1985–, chm and ceo Banner Aerospace Inc (NYSE); memb: Anti-Defamation League, Boys Town of Italy, Montefiore Med Centre, Bd Israel Museum; Hon Dr Yeshiva Univ 1994; Chevalier de l'Ordre des Arts et des Lettres (France) 1990, Chevalier de l'Ordre National du Mérite 1992; *Recreations* tennis, sailing, art collecting; *Clubs* Annabel's, Polo of Paris, Racing de France, Harry's Bar, St James's, Mark's; *Style—* Jeffrey Steiner, Esq; ✉ The Fairchild Corporation, 110 East 59th Street, New York, NY 10022, USA (tel 00 1 212 308 6700 and 703 478 5800, fax 00 1 212 888 5674)

STEINFELD, Alan Geoffrey; QC (1987); s of Henry C Steinfeld (d 1967), of London, and Deborah, *née* Brickman; *b* 13 July 1946; *Educ* City of London Sch, Downing Coll Cambridge (BA, LLB); *m* 19 Feb 1976, Josephine Nicole, da of Eugene Gros, of London; 2 s (Martin b 28 Jan 1980, Sebastian b 1 Nov 1981); *Career* called to the Bar Lincoln's Inn 1968 (bencher 1996), barr specialising in commercial Chancery law, dep judge of the High Court (Chancery and Queen's Bench Divs) 1994–; memb: Bar Cncl 1997, Assoc of Contentious Tst and Probate Specialists, Chancery Bar Assoc, Commercial Bar Assoc, Hong Kong Bar Assoc, Insolvency Lawyers Assoc; *Publications* Palmers Company Law Manual (conslt ed), Professional Negligence and Liability (contrib); *Recreations* lawn tennis, skiing, sailing, opera, cinema, lying in Turkish baths; *Clubs* RAC; *Style—* Alan Steinfeld, Esq, QC; ✉ 21 Wadham Gardens, London NW3 3DN (tel 020 7483 3450); Villa

S

Raphael, Cap d'Antibes, France; 24 Old Buildings, Lincoln's Inn, London WC2A 3UJ (tel 020 7404 0946, fax 020 7405 1360, e-mail alan.steinfeld@xxiv.co.uk)

STEINFELD, Michael Robert; *b* 3 December 1943; *Educ* William Ellis Sch London, Pembroke Coll Oxford (BA); *m* 28 May 1980, Elizabeth Ann, *née* Watson; 2 da (Rebecca Hannah b 25 Feb 1981, Jemimah Francine b 15 Oct 1983), 1 s (Jonathon Henry b 29 Oct 1992); *Career* Titmuss Sainer & Webb (now Dechert): articled clerk 1968–70, asst slr 1970–72, ptnr 1972–; memb Law Soc; *Recreations* sport, food, cinema, newspapers, music, France; *Style*— Michael Steinfeld, Esq; ✉ Dechert, 2 Serjeants' Inn, London EC4Y 1LT (tel 020 7583 5353, fax 020 7353 3683, e-mail michael.steinfeld@eu.dechert.com)

STELLA-SAWICKI, Dr Marek Andrzej; s of Jan Stella-Sawicki (d 1984), of Poland, and Stanislawa, *née* Lissowska (d 2002); *b* 21 February 1948; *Educ* Henry Jordan Sch, Tech Univ Cracow (MSc), KCL (PhD); *m* 27 July 1974, Teresa, da of Capt Antoni Witczak (d 1973), of London, and Helena, *née* Skrzyszowska (d 2005); 2 da (Dominika Helena b 1976, Joanna Jadwiga b 1978); *Career* sr systems engr United Biscuits (McVities) Ltd 1975–78, sr projects engr Metal Box plc 1978–82, projects engrg mangr Computer Field Maintenance Ltd 1982–85, gen mangr DPCE Computer Servs plc 1985–86, dir engrg ops MBS plc 1986–88, dir Computacenter Ltd 1988–95, strategic mktg and tech dir Computeraid Services Ltd 1995–2001, UK tech dir and chief tech offr Pink Roccade 2001–04, chief technol offr Services Architecture Global Services Delivery LogicaCMG plc 2004–; developer of corp and global strategy WASP and KNOWLEDGEfirst; launched e-Services Portal Platform V&A 2000; conslt Cover Pubns 1976–79, ed Video World 1979–81, publishing dir and editorial dir Video Press 1981–85; visiting prof Dept of Computer Science UCL 2007–; memb Polish Landowners Assoc; sponsorship: W Middx Lawn Tennis Club, Video Press Falklands Appeal; memb Cncl: Engrg Inst, AFSM (USA); life memb Ognisko Polskie, hon treas Assoc Polonoise des Chevaliers de Molte; memb Stewards Enclosure Henley Royal Regatta; MCIM, FIEE; *Books* Investigation into Computer Modelling Simulation and Control of the Stirling Engine (1978), Video A-Z (10 vols, 1981–83), A-Z of Personal Computers (10 vols, 1983–86), Which Appliance (2 edns, 1984–86), Business Process Re-Engineering (6 vols, 1996–97); *Recreations* skiing, shooting, bridge, target shooting (Bisley); *Clubs* Hurlingham, Leander, Nat Rifle Assoc, Classic Rally Assoc; *Style*— Dr Marek Stella-Sawicki; ✉ e-mail drmarksawicki@hotmail.com

STEMBRIDGE, Andrew William; s of David William Stembridge, of Melrose, Roxburghshire, and Edith Jean, *née* Banks; *b* 27 April 1971, Ratho, Midlothian; *Educ* Edinburgh Acad, Selkirk HS, Earlston HS, Univ of Strathclyde (BA), Cornell Univ; *m* 17 July 1999, Alison Charlotte; 1 s (Harry Logan b 7 March 2004), 1 da (Charlotte Emma b 1 May 2006); *Career* front of house mangr One Devonshire Gardens Glasgow 1994, food and beverage mangr Malmaison Glasgow and Edinburgh 1995, asst gen mangr Blantyre Lenox MA 1995, ops mangr Chewton Glen 1997, gen mangr Scotsman Hotel Edinburgh 2001, md Chewton Glen 2003–; FHCIMA 2005; Master Innholder 2005; *Style*— Andrew Stembridge, Esq; ✉ Chewton Glen, Christchurch Road, New Milton, Hampshire BH25 6QS (tel 01425 275341, fax 01425 272310, e-mail astembridge@chewtonglen.com)

STEMBRIDGE, David Harry; QC (1990); s of Percy Gladstone Stembridge (d 1959), of Droitwich, Worcs, and Emily Winifred, *née* Wright; *b* 23 December 1932; *Educ* Bromsgrove, Univ of Birmingham (LLB); *m* 2 April 1956, Theresa Cecilia, da of Max Furer, of Mulhouse, France; 3 s (Michael b 1957, Peter b 1960, Philip b 1968), 1 da (Helen b 1963); *Career* called to the Bar Gray's Inn 1955; practised Midland & Oxford Circuit, recorder of the Crown Court 1977–97, ret; *Recreations* organ, sailing; *Clubs* Bar Yacht; *Style*— David Stembridge, Esq, QC; ✉ 5 Fountain Court, Steelhouse Lane, Birmingham B4 6DR (tel 0121 606 0500, fax 0121 606 1501)

STEMMER, Philip; s of Emanuel Stemmer, of London, and Regina Stemmer; *b* 12 December 1949; *Educ* Manchester Jewish GS, Turner Dental Sch Manchester (BDS, represented Univ of Manchester soccer team); *m* 22 Dec 1976, Elissa, da of Myer Freedman; 4 da (Shiri Debra b 12 Aug 1979, Daniella Civia b 15 Dec 1981, Natalie Ruth b 30 Nov 1985, Anna Sophie Rose b 14 Dec 1994), 1 s (Raphael Steven b 2 Dec 1993); *Career* dental surgn; gen practice (with Phillip Wander) Manchester 1974–76, opened new practice Manchester 1976–84, opened branch practice Droylsden 1982–84, practised in Israel 1984–86 (affiliated to Periodontal Dept Tel Aviv Dental Sch), in private practice Harley St then Devonshire Place 1986–, owner of practice North Finchley 1987–89, opened UK's first fresh breath centre to combat oral malodour 1995; memb: BDA, Alpha Omega, Dental Post Grad Soc of Manchester, Insight Gp, Int Soc of Breath Odor Res (ISBOR); rep Lancs Chess Team 1964; *Recreations* swimming, music (opera, cantorial, good modern), chess; *Style*— Philip Stemmer, Esq; ✉ 2 Devonshire Place, London W1G 6HJ (tel 020 7935 7511/0407, mobile 07977 990490)

STENNING, Christopher John William (Kit); s of Col Philip Dives Stenning, of Sunnyside, Elie, Fife, and Cynthia Margaret, *née* Rycroft; *b* 16 October 1950; *Educ* Marlborough; *m* 1, 19 Sept 1981, Ruth Marian, da of late George Thomas Chenery Draper; 1 da (Rachel b 1983), 1 s (Jonathan b 1985); m 2, 21 April 2001, Christine Louise, da of John Walter Baxter; *Career* slr 1970–82, slr to Prudential Corp 1982–88, dir of corp fin David Garrick 1988–90, proprietor Kit Stenning Assocs 1990–91, ptnr Messrs Kennedys Slrs 1991–96; conslt McFadden 1996–; Freeman: City of London 1971, Worshipful Co of Haberdashers 1971; *Books* The Takeover Guide (1988); *Recreations* sport; *Clubs* Hurlingham; *Style*— Kit Stenning, Esq

STENNING, Prof Keith; s of Luis Charles Stenning (d 1992), of Beaconsfield, Bucks, and Marjorie, *née* Warren; *b* 15 June 1948; *Educ* Royal GS High Wycombe, Trinity Coll Oxford (exhibitioner, MA), Rockefeller Univ (PhD); *m* 1980, Dr Lynn Michell, da of Maj Leonard Dodd; 1 s (Nye b 2 June 1981); *Career* res assoc Rockefeller Univ 1975–76, lectr in psychology Univ of Liverpool 1976–83; Univ of Edinburgh: lectr in cognitive science 1983–88, dir Human Communication and Res Centre 1988–98, prof of human communication 1998–; author of numerous papers on human communication and reasoning; *Recreations* sailing; *Style*— Prof Keith Stenning; ✉ Human Communication Research Centre, University of Edinburgh, 2 Buccleuch Place, Edinburgh EH8 9LW (tel 0131 650 4444, fax 0131 650 4587, e-mail k.stenning@ed.ac.uk)

STENT, John Julian; s of Marion Hutchinson; *b* 2 March 1955; *Educ* Woking GS, Univ of Bristol (BA); *m* 1984, Morag Patrice; 1 s (Daniel b 1986), 3 da (Chloë b 1987, Charlotte b 1991, Jessica b 1995); *Career* BAA plc: joined 1988, md Stansted Airport 1997–2002, md Terminal 5 programme 2002–; memb Nat Audit Ctee LSC; FCA 1989 (ACA 1979); *Recreations* soccer, music; *Clubs* Old Wokingians FC; *Style*— John Stent, Esq; ✉ BAA plc, Longford House, 420 Bath Road, Longford, West Drayton UB7 0NX (tel 020 8745 1601, fax 020 8745 7615, e-mail ejohnstent@t5.co.uk)

STEPAN, Prof Alfred; s of Alfred C Stepan, Jr, and Mary Louise Quinn; *b* 22 July 1936; *Educ* Univ of Notre Dame (BA), Balliol Coll Oxford (MA), Columbia Univ (PhD); *m* 1964, Nancy Leys; 1 s, 1 da; *Career* special corr Economist 1964, staff memb Soc Sci Dept Rand Corp 1966–69; Yale Univ: successively asst prof, assoc prof then prof of political sci 1970–83; Columbia Univ: dean sch of Int and Public Affrs 1983–91, prof of political sci 1983–87, Burgess prof of political sci 1987–93; first rector and pres Central European Univ Budapest, Prague and Warsaw 1993–96; Gladstone prof of govt and fell All Souls Coll Oxford 1996–; visiting prof and lectr to numerous academic bodies and confs (USA, Europe, S America and Asia); dir Concilium on Int and Area Studies 1982–83; memb Ed Bd: Jl of Democracy 1989–, Government and Opposition 1996–; FAAAS, FBA 1997; *Books* The Military in Politics: changing patterns in Brazil (1971), The State and Society: Peru in comparative perspective (1978), Rethinking Military Politics. Brazil and the Southern cone (1988), Problems of Democratic Transition and Consolidation: Southern Europe, South America and post-Communist Europe (with J Linz, 1996); also author of numerous articles in learned jls; *Recreations* opera, gardening, walking; *Style*— Prof Alfred Stepan, FBA

STEPHEN, (John) David; s of John Stephen (d 1968), and Anne Eileen Stephen (d 1991); *b* 3 April 1942; *Educ* Luton GS, King's Coll Cambridge (MA), Univ of Essex (MA); *m* 28 Dec 1968, Susan Dorothy, *née* Harris; 3 s (John b 1972, Edward b 1977, Alexander b 1982), 1 da (Sophy b 1974); *Career* Runnymede Tst 1970–75 (dir 1973–75), Latin American regnl rep Int Univ Exchange Fund 1975–77, special advsr to Sec of State for Foreign and Cwlth Affrs 1977–79, freelance writer and conslt 1979–84, memb Gen Mgmnt Bd and dir of corporate rels Cwlth Devpt Corp 1984–92, princ offr Exec Office of the Sec-Gen United Nations NYC 1992–96, dir UN Verification Mission Guatemala 1996–97, dir UN Political Office for Somalia Nairobi Kenya 1997–2002, rep of UN sec-gen for Guinea-Bissau 2002–04, dir European Movement 2004–06; Parly candidate (Alliance) N Luton 1983 and 1987; *Style*— David Stephen, Esq; ✉ Raggot Hill Cottage, North Tamerton, Holsworthy, Devon EX22 6RJ

STEPHEN, Prof Kenneth William; s of William Stephen (d 1970), and Agnes Eleanor, *née* Rankin (d 1999); *b* 1 October 1937; *Educ* Hillhead HS, Univ of Glasgow (BDS, DDSc); *m* Anne Seymour, da of John Gardiner; 1 da (Linda Jane b 22 Nov 1966), 1 s (Grant MacLean b 8 Sept 1970); *Career* general dental practitioner 1960–64, house offr Dept of Oral Surgery Glasgow Dental Hosp 1964–65; Univ of Glasgow: lectr in conservative dentistry 1965–68, sr lectr in oral med 1971–80 (lectr 1968–71), reader 1980–84, head Dept of Oral Med and Pathology 1980–92, prof of community dental health 1984–95, prof of dental public health 1995–2001 (emeritus prof 2001–), head Dept of Adult Dental Care 1992–95; conslt in charge Glasgow Sch of Dental Hygiene 1979–96; hon lectr in oral physiology Univ of Newcastle upon Tyne 1969–70; memb: Int Assoc for Dental Res, Fédération Dentaire Internationale, Euro Orgn for Caries Res, BDA, Br Soc for Dental Res; hon memb: Finnish Dental Soc 1979, Hungarian Dental Assoc 1993; pres Glasgow Odontological Soc 1995 (vice-pres 1994–95); ORCA Rolex Prize 1990, E W Borrow Meml Award IADR 1992; Higher Dental Dip 1965, FDS 1967, FDSRCPS 2001; *Publications* author of 150 papers in scientific jls and contrib to 11 books; *Recreations* skiing, hill walking, gardening, swimming, cycling; *Style*— Prof Kenneth Stephen; ✉ University of Glasgow Dental School, 378 Sauchiehall Street, Glasgow G2 3JZ (tel 0141 211 9853, fax 0141 332 7053, e-mail k.stephen@dental.gla.ac.uk)

STEPHEN, Dr (George) Martin; s of Sir Andrew Stephen, KB (d 1980), of Sheffield, and Frances, *née* Barker (d 1999); *b* 18 July 1949; *Educ* Uppingham, Univ of Leeds (BA), Univ of Sheffield (DipEd, DPhil, PhD); *m* 21 Aug 1971, Jennifer Elaine, da of George Fisher, of Polloch, Invernesshire; 3 s (Neill b 22 July 1976, Simon b 31 Aug 1978, Henry b 20 March 1981); *Career* various posts in remand homes 1966–71, teacher of English Uppingham Sch 1971–72, housemaster and teacher of English Haileybury Coll and ISC 1972–83, second master Sedbergh Sch 1983–87, headmaster The Perse Sch 1987–94, high master The Manchester Grammar Sch 1994–2004, high master St Paul's Sch 2004–; assoc memb of the room Gonville & Caius Coll Cambridge 1988–94; HMC: memb 1987–, chm Community Serv Ctee 1992–95, memb HMC/GSA Univ Working Pty 1994–, chm 2004–; memb: The Naval Review 1991–, CSU Educn Advsr Ctee, Cncl The Project Tst, Bd Royal Exchange Theatre 1999–; govr: Withington Sch Manchester 1994–2002, Pownall Hall Sch Wilmslow 1994–, Ducie HS, The Hall Sch Hampstead, Orley Farm Harrow, Durston House Ealing; memb Ct Univ of Salford 2001–; visiting lectr Dept of English and American Studies Univ of Manchester 2001–; Hon Dr in Educn De Montfort Univ 1997; FRSA 1996; *Books* An Introductory Guide to English Literature (1982), Studying Shakespeare (1982), British Warship Designs Since 1906 (1984), English Literature (1986, 3 edn 1999), Sea Battles in Close Up (1987, 2 edn 1996), Never Such Innocence (1988, 3 edn 1993), The Fighting Admirals (1990), The Best of Saki (1993, 2 edn 1996), The Price of Pity (1996), The Desperate Remedy (2002), The Conscience of the King (2003), The Galleon's Grave (2004), The Rebel Heart (2006); *Recreations* sailing, scuba diving, rough shooting, writing, theatre; *Clubs* Athenaeum, East India Devonshire Sports & Public Sch (hon memb); *Style*— Dr Martin Stephen; ✉ St Paul's School, Lonsdale Road, Barnes, London SW13 9JT

STEPHEN, Michael; s of late Harry L Stephen; *b* 25 September 1942; *Educ* King Henry VIII Sch Coventry, Stanford Univ, Harvard Univ; *m* 27 May 1989, Virginia Mary, da of late Charles de Trensé; *Career* admitted slr 1964, called to the Bar Inner Temple 1966; Lt The Life Gds 1966–70; Harkness Fellowship USA (LLM Stanford) 1970–72, research fell Harvard 1972, asst legal advsr to UK Ambassador to UN 1972, practising barr 1972–92, int lawyer 1997–; MP (Cons) Shoreham 1992–97 (Parly candidate (Cons) Doncaster N 1983), PPS at MAFF 1996–97; author: Section 36 Criminal Justice Act 1988, Bail (Amendment) Act 1993; memb Trade and Industry and Environment Select Ctees and European Standing Ctee of House of Commons 1994–97, vice-chm Cons Parly Home Affairs and Legal Ctees; chm Constitutional Ctee Soc of Cons Lawyers 1997–2000; Industry and Parliament Tst Fellowship (British Rail) 1993–94; co cncllr Dunmow Div Essex 1985–91, memb Nat Exec Assoc of CCs 1989–91; chm Severnside Airport Consortium 2000–; memb RIIA 1984–; author of pamphlets and articles on Home Office and legal affrs, foreign affrs and housing; Evelyn Wrench meml lectr (annually, six years) USA; *Books* The Cyprus Question (4 edn 2001); *Style*— Michael Stephen, Esq; ✉ e-mail kkrkyz@gmail.com

STEPHEN, Nicol; MSP; s of R A Nicol Stephen, and Sheila G Stephen; *b* 23 March 1960, Aberdeen; *Educ* Robert Gordon's Coll Aberdeen, Univ of Aberdeen (LLB), Univ of Edinburgh (DipLP); *Partner* Caris Doig; 2 s, 2 da; *Career* slr, sr corp mangr, project mangr, co dir; cncllr Grampian Regnl Cncl 1982–91, MP (Lib Dem) Kincardine and Deeside 1991–92, MSP (Lib Dem) Aberdeen South 1999–, ldr Scot Lib Dems 2005–, dep first min Scot Parl 2005–07; *Recreations* golf; *Style*— Nicol Stephen, Esq, MSP; ✉ 173 Crown Street, Aberdeen AB11 6JA (tel 01224 252728, fax 01224 590926, e-mail nicol.stephen.msp@scottish.parliament.uk)

STEPHENS, Barbara Marion; OBE (2002); da of late Sydney Davis Webb, and Edna Marion, *née* Finch; *b* 25 August 1951; *Educ* Colchester Co HS, Mid-Essex Tech Coll (HNC Engineering), NE London Poly (Dip Mgmnt Studies), City Univ (MBA); *m* 28 March 1970, Trevor James Stephens; *Career* mech technician apprentice Marconi Co 1969–73, various tech and managerial posts Marconi Communication Systems Ltd 1973–88, asst industry advsr then industry advsr NEDO 1988–92; W Cumbria Devpt Agency: dir of ops 1993–95, chief exec 1995–98; chief exec Local Govt Cmmn for England 1998–2002, head of public sector practice KMC International 2002–07; memb Cncl (now Senate) Engrg Cncl 1990–96; dir and tstee: Assoc of MBAs 2001–06 (memb Advsy Cncl 1998–2001), Editorial Broadcasting Services Tst 2002–; chair NHSU 2003–05; memb: HEFCE 1995–2001, Advsy Forum for the Devpt of RN Personnel 1995–2002 (chm 2001–02), Bd New Opportunities Fund 2001–04, Bd Univ of Cumbria 2007–, Investigation Ctee Taxation Disciplinary Bd 2007–; non-exec dir Cumbria Ambulance Service NHS Tst 1996–98; lay memb Professional Conduct and Complaints Ctee Gen Cncl of the Bar 2000– (lay vice-chair 2006–); Hon DUniv Bradford 2005; IEng 1976, AMIPE 1976, MIEIE 1992, FIMgt 1994 (MBIM 1978), FRSA 1992; *Style*— Ms Barbara Stephens, OBE; ✉ Crook Hall, 28 High Seaton, Workington, Cumbria CA14 1PD (tel 01900 871095, e-mail contact@crook-hall.com)

STEPHENS, Dr John David; s of Sydney Brooke Stephens (d 1982), and Thora Gladys Stephens (d 1993); *b* 9 April 1944; *Educ* Highfields GS Wolverhampton, Guy's Hosp Med

Sch (MB BS, MD); *m* 19 July 1967 (m dis 1976), Amanda; 1 s (Damian b 1 Nov 1969); *Career* house physician and surgn Royal Surrey Co Hosp Guildford 1967–68, house surgn Guy's Hosp 1968–69, house physician Churchill Hosp Oxford 1969–70, registrar in med UCH 1970–72, registrar in cardiology Brompton Hosp 1972–73 (house physician 1970), res fell in cardiology Harvard Univ Med Sch Boston 1973–74, sr registrar in cardiology St Bartholomew's Hosp 1974–81, conslt cardiologist and head Cardiovascular Res Unit Queens Hosp Romford and St Bartholomew's Hosp (Barts and the London Tst) 1981–; author of pubns in various int med jls on original res in coronary blood flow, congestive heart failure and cardiovascular pharmacology; memb Br Cardiac Soc; FRCP 1993 (MRCP 1970); *Books* Cardiovascular Responses to Vasodilators in Man (1979); *Recreations* skiing, opera; *Clubs* RAC; *Style*— Dr John Stephens; ✉ 29 Crossways, Shenfield, Essex CM15 8QY (tel 01277 221254)

STEPHENS, John Lindsay; s of Rev Grosvenor Stephens (d 1992), and Olive, *née* Voysey-Martin (d 1987); *b* 23 July 1951; *Educ* Christ's Hosp, Coventry Univ (BA); *m* 30 Aug 1975, Nicola Elizabeth (Nikki), da of Neville Brouard, of St Saviour, Guernsey, CI; 1 s (David b 1982), 1 da (Joanna b 1980); *Career* admitted slr 1977; ptnr Clarke Willmott & Clarke; *Recreations* family, music, food and wine, photography, working out; *Clubs* City of London, King George's Sports and Social; *Style*— John Stephens, Esq; ✉ Clarke Willmott and Clarke, Burlington House, Botleigh Grange Business Park, Hedge End, Southampton, Hampshire SO30 2DF (tel 01489 70000, fax 01489 770190)

STEPHENS, Malcolm George; CB (1991); s of late Frank Ernest Stephens, and Annie Mary Janet, *née* Macqueen; *b* 14 July 1937; *Educ* St Michael and All Angels and Shooters Hill GS, St John's Coll Oxford (Casberd scholar, MA); *m* 5 Dec 1975, Lynette Marie, da of late John Patrick Caffery; *Career* Dip Serv: joined 1953, Ghana 1959–62, Kenya 1963–65, Exports Credits Guarantee Dept 1965–82, princ 1970, seconded to Civil Service Staff Coll as dir of economics and social admin course 1971–72, asst sec 1974, estab offr 1977, under sec 1978, head project gp 1978–79, princ fin offr 1979–82; int fin dir Barclays Bank International 1982, export fin dir and dir Barclays Export Servs with Barclays Bank 1982–87, chief exec Export Credits Guarantee Dept (ECGD) 1987–92, chief exec London C of C and Industry 1992–93, sec gen Int Union of Credit and Investment Insurers (Berne Union) 1992–98 (pres 1989–92), md and dep chm Commonwealth Investment Guarantee Agency (CIGA) Ltd 1998–99, chm International Financial Consulting 1998–, first exec dir Int Inst for Practitioners in Credit Insurance and Surety 2000–01, chm Del Credere Insurance Services Ltd until 2001, chm IFC Training 2001–; dir: European Capital 1992–2000, Maj Projects Assoc 1996–99, Berry Palmer & Lyle, Euler Int 1998–2000; advsr CDR International; exec vice-pres SGA International Florida 1998–2000; visiting scholar IMF 1998–99; conslt: World Bank 1997–98 and 1999, EU PHARE Prog 1997, 1998 and 1999, EU Cmmn 1998, 1999 and 2000, OECD (Russia) 2000 and 2001; conslt to govts of: Chile 1999, Bangladesh 1999, Sri Lanka 2000, Iran 2000 and 2001, South Africa 2000 and 2001, Australia 2000, 2001, 2002 and 2003, New Zealand 2001, Turkey 2001, Canada 2001 and 2003, Fiji 2003; special advsr People's Insurance Co of China (PICC) 2000–; memb: Overseas Projects Bd 1985–87, British Overseas Trade Bd 1987–92, Inst of Credit Mgmnt; FIEx, FIB; *Recreations* gardening, fitness centre, reading, swimming, tapestry, watching cricket and football (Charlton Athletic); *Clubs* Travellers; *Style*— Malcolm Stephens, Esq, CB

STEPHENS, His Hon Judge (Stephen) Martin; QC (1982); s of Abraham Stephens (d 1977), of Swansea, and Freda, *née* Ruck (d 1995); *b* 26 June 1939; *Educ* Swansea GS, Wadham Coll Oxford (MA); *m* 1965, Patricia Alison, da of Joseph Morris (d 1981), of Nottingham; 1 s (Richard b 1966) and 1 s decd, 1 da (Marianne b 1971); *Career* called to the Bar Middle Temple 1963 (bencher 2004); recorder of the Crown Court 1979–86, circuit judge (Wales & Chester Circuit) 1986–99, Central Criminal Court 1999–; memb: Criminal Ctee Judicial Studies Bd (JSB) 1995–2000, Parole Bd 1995–2001, Main Bd JSB 1997–2000; Liveryman Worshipful Co of Curriers; *Recreations* theatre, cricket; *Style*— His Hon Judge Stephens, QC; ✉ c/o Central Criminal Court, Old Bailey, London EC4M 7EH

STEPHENS, Prof Meic; s of Herbert Arthur Lloyd Stephens (d 1984), and Alma, *née* Symes (d 1994); *b* 23 July 1938; *Educ* Pontypridd Boys' GS, UCW Aberystwyth (BA), Univ of Rennes (DipFrench), UCNW Bangor (DipEd), Univ of Wales (DLitt); *m* 14 Aug 1965, Ruth Wynn, da of Rev John Ellis Meredith (d 1981); 3 da (Lowri b 1966, Heledd b 1968, Brengain b 1969), 1 s (Huw b 1981); *Career* teacher of French Ebbw Vale GS 1962–66, ed Poetry Wales 1965–73, journalist Western Mail Cardiff 1966–67, lit dir Welsh Arts Cncl 1967–90; ed, journalist, literary conslt 1990–, columnist Western Mail 1991–; dir Combrógos Literary Agency; visiting prof of English Brigham Young Univ UT 1991; lectr: Univ of Glamorgan 1994–2001, Centre for Journalism Studies Univ of Cardiff 1998–99; Univ of Glamorgan: lectr in writing 1999–, prof of Welsh writing in English 2001–06 (emeritus 2006–); hon fell St David's UC Lampeter 1986–, life memb the Welsh Acad 1990 (fell 1999); sec Rhys Davies Tst 1990–; hon memb (White Robe) Gorsedd of Bards 1976; Hon MA Univ of Wales 2000; *Books* Triad (1963), The Lilting House (co-ed, 1969), Writers of Wales (co-ed, 100 vols, 1970–), Artists in Wales (ed, 3 vols, 1971/73/77), The Welsh Language Today (ed, 1973), Exiles All (1973), A Reader's Guide to Wales (ed, 1973), Linguistic Minorities in Western Europe (1976), Green Horse (co-ed, 1978), The Arts in Wales 1950–75 (ed, 1979), The Curate of Clyro (ed, 1983), The Oxford Companion to the Literature of Wales (ed, 1986), A Cardiff Anthology (ed, 1987), The White Stone (trans, 1987), A Book of Wales (ed, 1988), A Dictionary of Literary Quotations (1989), The Gregynog Poets (ed, 12 vols 1989–90), The Bright Field (ed, 1991), The Oxford Illustrated Literary Guide to Great Britain and Ireland (ed, 1992), A Most Peculiar People (ed, 1992), Changing Wales (ed, 12 vols 1992–97), A Rhondda Anthology (ed, 1993), Take Wales: Cinema in Wales (1993), Literature in 20th Century Wales: a Select Bibliography (1995), The Collected Poems of Harri Webb (ed, 1995), For the Sake of Wales (trans, 1996), The Basques (trans, 1996), The Collected Poems of Glyn Jones (ed, 1996), The Collected Stories of Rhys Davies (ed, 3 vols, 1996–98), Ponies, Twynyrodyn (1997), No Half-Way House: Selected Political Journalism of Harri Webb (ed, 1997), Cydymaith i Lenyddiaeth Cymru (ed, 1997), How Green Was My Valley (ed, 1997), Monica (trans, 1997), A Little Book of Welsh Quotations (1997), The New Companion to the Literature of Wales (ed, 1998), A Militant Muse: Selected Literary Journalism of Harri Webb (ed, 1998), A Little Book of Welsh Sayings (1998), Illuminations: An Anthology of Welsh Short Prose (trans, 1998), A White Afternoon (trans, 1998), Shadow of the Sickle (trans, 1998), Return to Lleifior (trans, 1999), Welsh Names for Your Children (1999), Wales in Quotation (1999), The Literary Pilgrim in Wales (2000), Looking Up England's Arsehole: the Patriotic Poems and Boozy Ballads of Harri Webb (ed, 2000), Rhys Davies: Decoding the Hare (ed, 2001), A History of the Parish of Llanegryn (trans, 2002), The Corgi Series (ed, 24 vols, 2003–05), A Community and its University: Glamorgan 1913:2003 (co-ed, 2003), A Semester in Zion (2003), The Plum Tree (trans, 2004), Poetry 1900–2000 (ed, 2007); *Recreations* the world of Wales; *Style*— Prof Meic Stephens; ✉ 10 Heol Don, Whitchurch, Cardiff CF14 2AU (tel 029 20 623359)

STEPHENS, Nicholas Edward Egerton; DL (Shropshire 2000); s of Brian Alexis Fenwick Stephens, and Cynthia Mary Denise, *née* Prideaux-Brune; *b* 12 May 1946; *Educ* Charterhouse; *m* 10 Sept 1970, Avril Rose, da of Morgan Henry Birch Reynardson; 2 da (Samantha Jane (Mrs Adrian Boyes) b 12 June 1975, Clare Diana (Mrs Henry Cecil) b 17 June 1978); *Career* articled clerk R M March Son & Co (chartered accountants) 1965–69, Ionian Bank 1969–72, ptnr James Capel & Co 1978–80 (joined 1972), ptnr then dir (on incorporation) Albert E Sharp & Co (now Arbuthnot) 1980–2006; Parly candidate (Cons) Walsall North Gen Election 1983; High Sheriff of Shropshire 1995–96; tstee Hospital Mgmnt Tst 2004–; Co Cmmr of Scouts 1983–88, fell Woodard Corp 1987–2006 (vice-provost Midlands Dive 1998–2000), custos Ellesmere Coll 1992–99; patron of two livings; FCA; *Recreations* shooting, fishing, golf, opera, sailing; *Clubs* Boodle's, Pratt's, Turf; *Style*— Nicholas Stephens, Esq, DL; ✉ Grafton Lodge, Montford Bridge, Shrewsbury SY4 1HE (tel 01743 850262)

STEPHENS, Rev Prof (William) Peter; s of Alfred Cyril William Joseph Stephens (d 1942), of Penzance, Cornwall, and Jennie Eudora, *née* Trewavas (d 1982); *b* 16 May 1934; *Educ* Truro Sch, Univ of Cambridge (MA, BD), Univ of Strasbourg (Docteur es Sciences Religieuses), Univ of Lund, Univ of Munster; *Career* asst tutor in Greek and New Testament Hartley Victoria Coll Manchester 1958–61, methodist minister Nottingham and univ chaplain 1961–65, minister Shirley Church Croydon 1967–71, Ranmoor chair in church history Hartley Victoria Coll Manchester 1971–73 (Fernley Hartley lectr 1972), Randles chair in historical and systematic theol Wesley Coll Bristol 1973–80, James A Gray lectr Duke Univ N Carolina 1976; Queen's Coll Birmingham: res fell 1980–81, lectr in church history 1981–86, Hartley lectr 1982; prof of church history Univ of Aberdeen 1986–99 (dean Faculty of Divinity 1987–89); supt minister Plymouth Methodist Mission 1999–2000, minister Mint Methodist Church Exeter 2000–02, chaplain Univ of Exeter 2000–02 (visiting prof 2001–04), supt minister Liskeard and Looe Methodist Circuit 2002–03, chm and gen supt Methodist Church in The Gambia 2003–04, min Uckfield and Lewes 2004–06, min Camborne Circuit 2006–, supt min 2007–; sec Soc for the Study of Theol 1963–77, emb Central Ctee Conf of European Churches 1974–92, pres Soc for Reformation Studies 1995–98, pres Conf of the Methodist Church in Britain 1998–99; memb Bristol City Cncl 1976–83; Max Geilinger Prize 1997; *Books* The Holy Spirit in the Theology of Martin Bucer (1970), Faith and Love (1971), Methodism in Europe (1981), The Theology of Huldrych Zwingli (1986), Zwingli - An Introduction to His Thought (1992), The Bible The Reformation and the Church (ed, 1995), Zwingli: Einführung in sein Denken (1997), Zwingli le Théologien (1999); *Recreations* squash, swimming, surfing, cliff and hill walking, theatre, opera; *Style*— The Rev Prof W P Stephens; ✉ Trewavas House, Polwithen Road, Penzance, Cornwall TR18 4JS

STEPHENS, Philip Francis Christopher; s of Haydn Stephens, of London, and Teresa, *née* Martin; *b* 2 June 1953; *Educ* Wimbledon Coll, Worcester Coll Oxford (BA); *Partner* Patricia Jean Hemingway; 1 da (Jessica Rose b 24 Nov 1989), 1 s (Benedict Haydn b 24 March 1993); *Career* asst ed Europa Publications 1974–76, ed Commerce International 1976–79, corr Reuters London and Brussels 1979–83; Financial Times: econs corr 1983–88, political ed 1988–94, assoc ed and political commentator 1995–99, ed UK Edition 1999–2003, chief political commentator 2003–; Fulbright fell; commended Br Press Awards 1991, David Watt Award for Outstanding Political Journalism 2002; *Books* Politics and the Pound: The Conservatives' Struggle with Sterling (1996), Tony Blair, The Price of Leadership (2004); *Style*— Philip Stephens, Esq

STEPHENS, Simon William; s of Graham Stephens (d 2001), of Stockport, and Carole Stephens; *b* 6 February 1971; *Educ* Stockport Sch, Univ of York (BA), Inst of Educn Univ of London (PGCE); *m* Polly Heath; 2 s (Oscar Dylan b 6 Oct 1998, Stanley Samuel b 6 Feb 2002); *Career* writer; schoolteacher Eastbrook Sch Dagenham 1998–2000; Royal Court Theatre: resident dramatist 2000, writers' tutor Young Writers' Prog 2001–; Pearson attached playwright Royal Exchange Theatre Manchester 2000; *Plays* Bring Me Sunshine (Assembly Rooms Edinburgh, Riverside Studios London) 1997, Bring Me Sunshine (Royal Exchange) 2000, Bluebird (Royal Court Young Writers Festival) 1998, Herons (Royal Court) 2001 and (Stuttgart Staatstheater) 2003 (nomination Most Promising Playwright Olivier Awards 2001), Five Letters Home to Elizabeth (radio play, BBC Radio 4) 2001, Port (Royal Exchange) 2002 and (Graz Staatstheater) 2004 (Pearson Award for Best New Play), One Minute (Sheffield Crucible/Actors Touring Co) 2003 and (Stuttgart Staatstheater) 2004, Christmas (Ape Theatre Co/Bush Theatre) 2003–04, Country Music (Actors Touring Co/Royal Court Theatre) 2004 and (Essen Staatstheater) 2005, On the Shore of the Wide World (Royal Exchange/RNT) 2005; musician and fndr memb The Country Teasers 1993– (tours of America and Europe, several single and album releases); *Publications* Herons (2001), Port (2002), One Minute (2003), Christmas (2003), Country Music (2004), Collected Plays 1 (2005), On the Shore of the Wide World (2005); *Recreations* playing music, playing pool, my cat Mckenzie, the poetry and short stories of Raymond Carver; *Style*— Simon Stephens, Esq; ✉ c/o Mel Kenyon, Casarotto Ramsay & Associates, National House, 60–66 Wardour Street, London W1V 3HP (tel 020 7287 4450)

STEPHENSON, (Robert) Ashley Shute; LVO (1989, MVO 1979); s of James Stephenson (d 1960), and Agnes Maud, *née* Shute (d 1983); *b* 1 September 1927; *Educ* Heddon-on-the-Wall Sch, Walbottle Secdy Sch; *m* 21 May 1955, Isabel, da of Edward Dunn (d 1960); 1 da (Carol b 1959), 1 s (Ian Ashley b 1964); *Career* apprentice Newcastle upon Tyne Parks Dept 1942; served RASC Palestine and Cyprus 1946; landscape gardener Donald Ireland Ltd 1949, student RHS's gardens Wisley 1952; The Royal Parks: joined 1954, supt Regent's Park 1969, supt Central Royal Parks 1972, bailiff 1980–90; landscape conslt Trusthouse Forte (now Forte) 1990–93; freelance gardening corr (gardening corr The Times 1982–87), contrib to TV and radio progs; chm Britain in Bloom 1991–2000, dir Gardens for Pleasure 1987–94; memb: Ctee Royal Gardeners' Benevolent Fund, Ctee Rotten Row 300, Prince of Wales Royal Parks Tree Ctee 1979, Floral Ctee RHS 1981–; former memb Ctee London Children's Flower Soc; pres Br Pelargonium and Geranium Soc 1983–94, pres SE in Bloom Ctee English Tourist Bd 2000– (chm 1990–2000, judge Britain in Bloom competition), hort advsr Cincinnati Flower and Garden Show Soc USA 1990–2000; vice-pres PHAB 1992; FIHort 1998; *Books* The Garden Planner (1981); *Recreations* golf, walking, reading, gardening; *Clubs* Rotary (Seaford); *Style*— Ashley Stephenson, Esq, LVO; ✉ 17 Sandore Road, Seaford, East Sussex BN25 3PZ (tel 01323 891050)

STEPHENSON, (Marjorie) Gail; da of James Midgley (d 1978), and Ina, *née* Simpson (d 1992); *b* 28 July 1953; *Educ* Pendleon HS for Girls Salford, Manchester Sch of Orthoptics Manchester Royal Eye Hosp (DBO), Manchester Poly; *Career* sr orthoptist Royal Albert Edward Infirmary Wigan 1974–76, student teacher Manchester Royal Eye Hosp 1976–78; orthoptic teacher Manchester Royal Eye Hosp: full time 1978–81, pt/t 1982–91; pt/t locum head of Trg Sch Leeds Gen Infirmary 1987–89, pt/t research orthoptist St Paul's Eye Hosp Liverpool 1989–91, full time head Dept of Orthoptics Univ of Liverpool 1991– (responsible for writing and introducing one of UK's two 3 year honours degree courses in orthoptics); vision science advsr: Manchester United FC 1997–, Subaru World Rally Team 1998, Lawn Tennis Assoc 1998, Benetton Formula One 1998–; invited memb Woman of the Year Lunch 1993, 1994, 1995 and 1997; Br Orthoptic Soc: chm Nat Scientific Ctee 1989–92, chm Nat Educn Ctee 1990–92, memb Nat Exec Cncl 1989–, memb Working Pty into Post-Basic Orthoptic Qualifications 1989–, Br rep on selection panel for Int Orthoptic Assoc Fellowship 1990–, chm Professional Devpt Ctee 1992–; UK rep World Cncl of Orthoptists 2005–; Orthoptists Bd Cncl for Professions Supplementary to Med: memb 1990–, memb Registration Ctee 1990–, memb Disciplinary Ctee 1990–, chm Educn Ctee 1994–95; examiner (final examination) DBO 1991, external examiner (BSc Orthoptics) Glasgow Caledonian Univ 1994; memb Editorial Bd Br Orthoptic Jl 1991–, reviewer of neuro-ophthalmology papers submitted to Br Jl of Ophthalmology 1993–, author of various pubns, book reviews and presentations; *Recreations* all sport, watching tennis and football, playing tennis and squash, swimming; *Style*— Ms Gail Stephenson; ✉ Department of Orthoptics, PO Box 147, University of Liverpool, Liverpool L69 3BX

(tel 0151 794 5731, fax 0151 794 5781, mobile 07973 247828, e-mail rocket@liverpool.ac.uk)

STEPHENSON, Geoffrey Charles; s of Edmund Charles Stephenson, and Hilda Rose, *née* Bates; *b* 19 August 1943; *Educ* Bromley GS; *m* 3 Sept 1966, Margaret, da of Frank Wirth (d 1989); 2 da (Louise Elizabeth b 26 March 1970, Rebecca Dorothy b 8 Feb 1972), 1 s (Alistair James b 2 May 1974); *Career* Legal and General Assurance Society Ltd 1964–72; called to the Bar Gray's Inn 1971, ad eundem Lincoln's Inn 1991, admitted to State Bar Texas 1991; FCII; *Recreations* sport; *Clubs* St James's, Sundridge Park Lawn Tennis and Squash Rackets (chm); *Style—* Geoffrey Stephenson, Esq; ✉ 2/3 Grays Inn Square, London WC1R 5JH (tel 020 7242 4986, fax 020 7405 1166, e-mail gstephenson@barristernet.co.uk)

STEPHENSON, Prof Geoffrey Michael; s of Maurice Stephenson (d 1958), of Kenton, Middx, and Laura, *née* Sharp (d 1975); *b* 16 April 1939; *Educ* Harrow Co Sch for Boys, Univ of Nottingham (BA, PhD); *m* 14 April 1962 (m dis 1981), Marguerite Ida, da of James Lindsay (d 1986), of Kettering; 1 s (Lawrence James b 1963), 1 da (Katherine b 1965); m, 10 Jan 1989, Jennifer Ann, da of Frederick Williams, of St Mellon, Cardiff, and Elsie Williams; 1 s (David Field William b 1989); *Career* prof of social psychology and head of dept Univ of Kent Canterbury 1978–98 (emeritus prof 1998–); visiting prof of psychology Heriot-Watt Univ 1997–2001; res prof of psychology Univ of Greenwich 2000–, hon prof of psychology London South Bank Univ 2005–; ed Community and Applied Social Psychology 1991–; chm Social Psychology Section Br Psychological Soc 1977–80; memb Euro Assoc of Experimental Social Psychology 1972– (pres 1984–87); chm: IBA Advtg Advsy Ctee 1988–90, ITC Advtg Advsy Ctee 1991–92; CPsychol, FBPsS 1980; *Books* incl: The Development of Conscience (1966), The Social Psychology of Bargaining (with Ian Morley, 1976), The Psychology of Criminal Justice (1992); *Recreations* sailing, violin playing; *Style—* Prof Geoffrey Stephenson; ✉ e-mail g.m.stephenson@kent.ac.uk

STEPHENSON, Sir Henry Upton; 3 Bt (UK 1936), of Hassop Hall, Co Derby, TD; s of Lt-Col Sir (Henry) Francis Blake Stephenson, 2 Bt, OBE, TD, JP, DL (d 1982), and Joan, *née* Upton (d 2000); *b* 26 November 1926; *Educ* Eton; *m* 1962, Susan, da of late Maj John Ernest Clowes, of Clifton, Ashbourne, Derbys; 4 da (Fiona Kathleen b 1964, Annabel Mary b 1965, Emma Frances b 1968, Lucy Clare b 1970); *Heir* 1 cous, Timothy Stephenson, TD, JP; *Career* High Sheriff Derbys 1975; late Capt Yorkshire Yeo; former dir Stephenson Blake (Holdings) Ltd; *Style—* Sir Henry Stephenson, Bt, TD; ✉ Tissington Cottage, Rowland, Bakewell, Derbyshire DE45 1NR

STEPHENSON, Prof John; OBE (2000); s of George Stephenson, of Eastbourne, E Sussex, and Joyce, *née* Sirett (d 1992); *b* 28 May 1952; *Educ* Ewell Castle Sch, Kingston Art Sch (BA), RCA (MA); *Partner* Lesja Liber; 3 c (Natalka Liber Ivanovna b 5 Dec 1985, Samuel Liber Ivanovich, Hana Liber Ivanovna (twins) b 13 July 1989); *Career* special effects/puppet designer/film maker and commercials director; creative supr Jim Henson's Creature Shop 1986–; other work incl shop interiors for Ryder branches London 1981; currently dir Jim Henson Organisation and Jim Henson Productions; advsr/interim shadow design dir Design Cncl 1994; prof of moving image Camberwell Sch of Art 2003–; *Films* earlier work incl: The Dark Crystal 1980, Return to Oz 1983, Greystoke - The Legend of Tarzan Lord of the Apes 1984, various other films and videos 1984–86; other work incl: Teenage Mutant Ninja Turtles 1990, The Flintstones 1993 (Scientific and Engrg Award Acad of Motion Picture Arts & Scis), Pinocchio (2nd unit dir) 1996, Lost In Space (2nd unit dir) 1998, Animal Farm 1999, 5 Children and It 2004; *Style—* Prof John Stephenson, OBE; ✉ Jim Henson Organisation, 30 Oval Road, London NW1 7DE (tel 020 7428 4000)

STEPHENSON, John William; JP (1980); s of Kenneth George Stephenson (d 1979), and Madeline Alice, *née* Ounsworth (d 1974); *b* 23 June 1938; *Educ* Harrow Co Sch; *m* 7 Sept 1963, Lesley Helen, da of Flt Lt Harold Douglas Hopper (d 1980); 2 da (Joanna Margaret b 1968, Sarah Elizabeth b 1970); *Career* surveyor; Fuller Peiser: joined 1959, ptnr 1970–99, sr ptnr 1998–99; memb Wood Ctee: to review rating of plant and machinery 1991, to review rating of plant and machinery in prescribed industries 1996; chm Music in the Round Ltd 1993–2006 (dir and vice-chm 1988–93); chm: Cncl St John Ambulance Derbys 2004–07 (memb Co Mgmnt Bd 2001–03), Sheffield GS Exhbn Fund 2005– (tstee 1999–); tstee Sheffield Town 1986–; FRICS 1970; SBStJ; *Recreations* music, literature, walking; *Clubs* Royal Over-Seas League; *Style—* John Stephenson, Esq; ✉ Borgen, Grindleford, Hope Valley S32 2HT (tel 01433 630288)

STEPHENSON, Kate Frances; da of Air Vice Marshal Tom Birkett Stephenson, and Rosemary Patricia, *née* Thornton Kaye; *Educ* Wadhurst Coll, Univ of Nottingham (Wells Award for Industrial Relations); *Career* regnl media dir (Greater China) Leo Burnett 1991–96, client serv dir and founding memb Carat Asia Pacific 1996–98, md OMD SE Asia 1998–2001, md OMD International 2001–; memb Young Presidents Orgn Singapore 2000–; *Recreations* water skiing, riding, skiing, cycling; *Style—* Ms Kate Stephenson; ✉ OMD Europe, Seymour Mews House, 26–37 Seymour Mews, London W1H 6BN

STEPHENSON, Martin Richard; s of Richard Stephenson (d 1986), and Gladys, *née* Wheatley (d 1975); *b* 20 February 1959, London; *Educ* Therfield Secdy Modern Leatherhead; *Partner* Belinda Morgan; 1 s (Henry b 1992), 2 da (Beatrice b 1994, Jemima b 1999); *Career* estab first co SSC Ltd 1984–, took over the running of Stephenson Shuttering Ltd 1987–; estab: Stephenson Holdings Ltd 1995–, Stephenson Devpts Ltd 2001–, M R Stephenson Ltd 2003–, Stephenson Gp 2007–; co-fndr Morespace Ltd 2006–, Webbliworld Ltd 2006–, Sparkzmedia Ltd 2006–; chm Construct 2007–, memb Bd Cares; *Recreations* classic car motor racing, tennis, golf, wine, travel, design; *Clubs* Goodwood Road Racing, IOD; *Style—* Martin Stephenson, Esq; ✉ Stephenson Group, Oakwood House, Guildford Road, Bucks Green, West Sussex RH12 3JJ (tel 01403 824960, fax 01403 824961, e-mail m.s@stephenson-ssc.co.uk, website www.stephenson-ssc.co.uk)

STEPHENSON, Paul R; QPM (2000); s of Jack Stephenson (d 1999), and Rose Catherine, *née* Sullivan; *b* 26 September 1953; *Educ* Fearns Co Secdy Sch, Bacup and Rawtenstall GS; *m* 8 June 1974, Lynda, da of James Alexander Parker (d 1995); 3 da (Shelley Marie b 18 April 1975, Lisa Kathryn b 31 Aug 1977, Rebecca Faye b 9 Nov 1983); *Career* Lancs Constabulary: Constable 1975, Sgt 1982, Inspr 1983, Chief Inspr 1986, Supt 1988, Sub-Divnl Cdr Accrington, on secondment Banbridge RUC, Divnl Cdr Preston (previously Sub-Divnl Cdr); Asst Chief Constable Merseyside 1994–99, Dep Chief Constable Lancs 1999–2002, Chief Constable Lancs 2002–05, Dep Cmmr Met Police 2005–; *Recreations* music, reading, family pursuits; *Style—* Paul R Stephenson, Esq, QPM; ✉ Metropolitan Police Service, New Scotland Yard, Broadway, London SW1H 0BG

STEPHENSON, Timothy Congreve; s of Augustus William Stephenson (d 2000), of Cowden, Kent, and Mary Gloria (d 1992), only and posthumous child of Maj William La T Congreve, VC, DSO, MC; *b* 7 March 1940; *Educ* Harrow, London Business Sch; *m* 1, 14 April 1966 (m dis 1980), Nerena Anne, da of Maj the Hon William Nicholas Somers Laurence Hyde Villiers; 2 da (Lucinda (Mrs Guy Denison-Smith) b 1967, Henrietta (Mrs Ben Dyer) b 1975), 2 s (Guy b 1969, Frederick b 1978); m 2, 16 June 1980, Diana-Margaret Soltmann, *qv*, da of HE Dr Otto Soltmann (d 2001), of Koblenz, Germany; 3 s (Christopher b 1983, William b 1985, James b 1989); *Career* Welsh Gds 1959–65; Gallaher Ltd 1965–79, md Grafton Ltd and chm Grafton Office Products Inc 1980–86, md Stephenson Cobbold Ltd 1987–95, chm Stephenson and Co 1996–; former memb Industrial Tbnls, fndr memb Bd of Lab Rels (ACAS) NI; *Recreations* shooting, gardening; *Clubs* Brooks's, Beefsteak, Pratt's, City of London, MCC; *Style—* T C Stephenson, Esq; ✉ Stephenson and Co, Linden House, Sarson Lane, Amport, Hampshire SP11 8HX (tel 01264 772700, fax 01264 771355, e-mail tcs@stephensonandco.com)

STEPNEY, Bishop of 2003–; Rt Rev Stephen John Oliver; s of John Oliver, of Bovey Tracey, and Nora, *née* Greenalgh; *b* 7 January 1948; *Educ* Manchester Central GS, KCL, St Augustine's Coll Canterbury; *m* 1969, Hilary Joan, da of Rev Basil Barkham; 2 s (Simon Andrew b 1971, Adam David b 1973); *Career* curate Clifton Team Miny 1970–74, vicar Christ Church Newark 1974–79, rector St Mary's Plumtree 1979–85, chief prodr Religious Progs BBC 1985–91, rector of Leeds 1991–97, canon residentiary St Paul's Cathedral 1997–2003, bishop of Stepney 2003–; hon canon Ripon Cathedral 1996; memb BBC Task Force 1991, memb Liturgical Cmmn C of E 1991–2001; chm: Govrs Leeds Girls High Sch 1993–96, Govrs Agnes Stewart High Sch 1994–96; *Style—* The Rt Rev the Bishop of Stepney; ✉ 63 Coborn Road, London E3 2DB

STEPTOE, Prof Andrew Patrick Arthur; s of Patrick Christopher Steptoe, CBE (d 1988), and Sheena McLeod, *née* Kennedy (d 1990); *b* 24 April 1951; *Educ* Uppingham, Gonville & Caius Coll Cambridge (choral exhibitioner, hon sr scholar and Swann prize for biology, MA), Magdalen Coll Oxford (DPhil, MA (incorporated)), Univ of London (DSc); *m* 1, 1980 (m dis 1984), Jane Furneaux, da of Hugh Horncastle; 1 s (William Arthur Hugh b 1981); m 2, 1991, Frances Jane, da of Peter Wardle; 1 s (Matthew Peter Steptoe Wardle b 1984); *Career* Dept of Psychiatry Univ of Oxford: MRC research student 1972–75, MRC trg fell 1975–77; St George's Hosp Med Sch London: lectr in psychology 1977–81, sr lectr 1981–87, reader 1987–88, prof of psychology 1988–2000; Br Heart Fndn prof of psychology UCL 2000– (dep head Dept of Epidemiology and Public Health 2005–); visiting prof Dept of Public Health Univ of Tokyo 1992; memb: Research Progs Bd ESRC 1994–96, Educn and Psychosocial Research Ctee Cancer Research Campaign 1994–2000; assoc ed: Health Psychology, Psychophysiology 1982–86, Jl of Psychophysiology 1987–89, Annals of Behavioral Med 1991–97, Br Jl of Clinical Psychology 1992–95, Jl of Psychosomatic Research 1994–97 (asst ed 1989–93), Int Jl of Rehabilitation and Health 1995–2002; ed Br Jl of Health Psychology 1995–2001; memb Editorial Bd: Int Jl of Behavioral Med, Psychoneuroendocrinology, Jl of Hypertension, Brain Behavior and Immunity; essay prize in clinical psychology (Mental Health Fndn) 1972, Kenneth Reeves essay prize (Soc for Psychosomatic Research) 1977; hon fell Swedish Soc of Behavioural Med 1988, fell Academiae Europaeae 2003; memb: Int Soc of Behavioural Med (pres 1994–96), Soc for Psychosomatic Research (pres 1983–85), Soc for Psychophysiological Research USA (memb Bd of Dirs 1984–87); FBPsS (memb Scientific Affrs Bd 1991–93); AcSS; *Books* Psychological Factors in Cardiovascular Disorders (1981), Problems of Pain and Stress (1984), Health Care and Human Behaviour (with A Mathews, 1984), Essential Psychology for Medical Practice (with A Mathews, 1988), Stress, Personal Control and Health (with A Appels, 1989), Psychosocial Processes and Health (with J Wardle, 1994); non-medical: The Mozart-Da Ponte Operas: The Cultural and Musical Background to Le nozze di Figaro, Don Giovanni and Cosi fan tutte (1988), Mozart: Everyman - EMI Music Companion (1997), Genius and the Mind (1998); *Recreations* music, theatre, reading, family; *Style—* Prof Andrew Steptoe; ✉ Department of Epidemiology and Public Health, University College London, 1–19 Torrington Place, London WC1E 6UT (tel 020 7679 1804, fax 020 7916 8542, e-mail a.steptoe@ucl.ac.uk)

STEPTOE, Roger Guy; s of Charles Steptoe, of Winchester, and Norah Constance, *née* Shaw; *b* 25 January 1953; *Educ* Univ of Reading (BA), Royal Acad of Music (LRAM); *Career* composer and pianist; composer-in-residence Charterhouse 1976–79; RAM: admin Int Composer Festivals 1987–93, prof of composition 1980–91; prof Harmony and Composition Analysis Ecole Nationale de Musique de Danse et d'Art Dramatique Brive-la-Gaillarde France 2001–; journalist and Limusin corr French Times 1999–; freelance composer, works regularly as a soloist, chamber pianist and accompanist, compositions performed internationally; has performed in: UK, IOM, Russia, Sweden, Portugal, France, Spain, Scotland, Germany, USA; 50th birthday celebrations in UK, USA and France; memb: Inc Soc of Musicians, RAM Club; ARAM 1986; *Compositions* incl: King of Macedon (opera), Concertos for cello, oboe, tuba, clarinet and flute, Sinfonia Concertante for violin and string orchestra, Aubade for clarinet and string orchestra, 4 String Quartets, Piano Trio, Piano Quartet (Quatre romances sans paroles d'après Paul Verlaine), Four Sonnets for brass quintet, various song cycles for all voices and piano, instrumental works for different combinations, Oboe Quartet, 3 Piano Sonatas, Prélude for piano La Dame de Labenche (en hommage à Claude Debussy), Prélude for viola and piano (en hommage à Toru Takemitsu), 2 Violin Sonatas, In Winter's Cold Embraces Dye (for soprano, tenor, chorus and chamber orch), Life's Unquiet Dream (for baritone, chorus and chamber orch), Cheers! (for chamber orch), The Passionate Shepherd to his Love (for childrens' voices), Impressions Corrèziennes, nineteen variations for orchestra, This Side of Winter (symphonic poem), Clarinet Sonata, Dance Music for symphonic brass, Three-Tango Rhapsody for Symphony Orch, Sinfonietta for orga and 15 strings, Sonata for tuba, Dourando as trevas for two tubas and vibraphone, L'angèlus du matin à l'angèlus du soir for four Cristal Baschet; *Recordings* incl: the Songs of Ralph Vaughan Williams with Peter Savidge, the Piano Quartets of Walton and Frank Bridge, Elegy on the Death and Burial of Cock Robin (James Bowman), Sinfonietta for organ and strings, oboe and clarinet concertos, Tuba Concerto, Dourando as trevas for two tubas and vibraphone, L'angèlus du matin à l'angèlus du soir; *Recreations* travel, music, gardening, food and drink and seeing friends; *Style—* Roger Steptoe, Esq; ✉ c/o 7 rue Jean Gentet, 19140 Uzerche, France (tel 00 33 555 73 75 99, fax 00 33 555 98 80 93, e-mail roger.steptoe@nordnet.fr, website www.impulse-music.co.uk/rogersteptoe)

STERLING, Prof John Adrian Lawrence; s of Francis Thomas Sterling (d 1942), of Melbourne, Aust, and Millicent Lloyd, *née* Pitt (d 1989); *b* 17 April 1927; *Educ* Scotch Coll Melbourne, CEPS Mosman NSW, Barker Coll NSW, Univ of Sydney (LLB); *m* 6 Nov 1976, Caroline Snow, da of Octavius Samuel Wallace (d 1984), of Strabane, Co Tyrone; *Career* admitted to the Bar NSW 1949, called to the Bar Middle Temple 1953; dep DG Int Fedn of Phonographic Industry 1961–73, professorial fell Queen Mary & Westfield Coll London 1996, visiting prof King's Coll London 1999; vice-pres Br Copyright Cncl 2003, memb Advsy Bd Br Literary and Artistic Copyright Assoc; *Books* various publications incl: The Data Protection Act (1984), Copyright Law in the UK and the Rights of Performers, Authors and Composers in Europe (1986), Encyclopedia of Data Protection (co-ed, 1991), Intellectual Property Rights in Sound Recordings, Film and Video (1992, supplement 1994), World Copyright Law (1998, 2 edn 2003); *Recreations* reading, music, medieval iconography; *Style—* Prof J A L Sterling; ✉ Lamb Chambers, Lamb Building, Temple, London EC4Y 7AS (tel 020 7797 8300, fax 020 7797 8308)

STERLING, Prof Michael John Howard; s of Richard Howard Sterling, of Hampton, Middx, and Joan Valeria, *née* Skinner; *b* 9 February 1946; *Educ* Hampton GS, Univ of Sheffield (BEng, PhD, DEng, Hon DEng 1995); *m* 19 July 1969, Wendy Karla, da of Charles Murray Anstead (d 1978), of Milton Libourne, Wilts; 2 s (Christopher b 1972, Robert b 1975); *Career* AEI student apprentice 1964–68, res engr GEC Elliot Process Automation 1968–71, sr lectr in control engrg Univ of Sheffield 1978–80 (lectr 1971–78), prof of engrg Univ of Durham 1980–90, vice-chllr and princ Brunel Univ 1990–2001, vice-chllr Univ of Birmingham 2001–; dir: COBUILD, 2001–, UCAS 2001–, Universitas 21 2001–, TPIC 2001–; chm: SERC Electrical and Power Industries Sub-Ctee 1987–89, SERC/Central Electricity Generating Bd Co-funded Res Ctee 1987–92, Electro Mechanical Engrg Ctee SERC 1989–91 (memb 1987–89), HE Statistics Agency (HESA) 1992–2003 (chm Mgmnt Ctee 1992–93, chair HESA Services 1997–2003), Jt Performance Indicators Working Gp HEFCE-SHEFC-HEFCW 1992–95, Univs Statistical Record Review Gp 1992–95, Sub-Ctee on Res Performance Indicators CVCP-UFC 1992–93, Midman 2001–02, Royal Acad of Engrg Membership Panel 3 2003–; memb Royal Acad of Engrg Membership Panel 2001–02; pres IEE 2002–03 (memb Cncl 1991–93 and 1997, vice-pres 1997–2000, dep pres 2001–02, chm Qualifications Bd); memb: Electricity Supply Res Cncl 1987–89, Engrg Bd SERC 1989–92, Main Ctee UUK 1990–, Performance Indicators Ctee CVCP-UFC 1991–93, CICHE 2 Br Cncl 1991–94, CVCP Euro Ctee 1991–95, Mechanical, Aeronautical and Prodn Engrg Assessment Panel HEFCE 1992 and 1996, Quality Assessment Ctee HEFCE 1992–95, Standing Ctee for Educn, Trg and Competence to Practise Royal Acad of Engrg 1993–97, Cncl CVCP 1994–95, CVCP Student Numbers Steering Group 1995–96, UUP Info Systems Sector Gp 1995–, Bd for Engrs' Regulation Review Gp 1995, New Bd for Engrs' Regulation Working Gp 1995, Review Gp of Mechanisms for Providing Acad Advice to External Bodies Royal Acad of Engrg 1997–, UUK Working Gp on the Funding Method for Teaching 1997–, CVCP Res and Knowledge Transfer Steering Gp 1996–97, Bd West London TEC 1999–2001, Bd West London TEC Charitable Tst 1999–2001, Bd W Midlands HE Authy (WMHEA) 2001–, Bd AWM 2003– (memb AWM Broadband Steering Gp 2001–02), Research Base Funders Forum 2003–, CSTI 2004–; memb Engrg Cncl 1994–96 (Standing Ctee for the Engrg Profession 1994–96, Standing Ctee for the Regions and Assembly 1994–95); chm: OCEPS Ltd 1990–, WASMACS Ltd 1994–2002; chm of govrs Hampton Sch Middx 1997–2001 (govr 1991–2001), govr Burnham GS Bucks 1990–2001, pres Elmhurst Sch for Dance 2002–; tstee: Hillingdon Partnership Tst 1993–98, Barber Inst of Fine Art 2002–; Freeman City of London 1996, Liveryman Worshipful Co of Engrs 1997; CEng 1975, FInstMC 1983 (vice-pres 1985–88, pres 1988, memb Cncl 1983–91), FRSA 1984, FIEE 1985, FREng 1991; *Books* Power System Control (1978); author of 120 papers in learned jls; *Recreations* gardening, DIY, computers, model engineering; *Style*— Prof Michael Sterling, FREng; ✉ University of Birmingham, Birmingham B15 2TT (tel 0121 414 4536, fax 0121 414 4534)

STERLING, Dr (Isobel Jane) Nuala; CBE (1993); da of Prof Fred Bradbury (d 1948), and Florence Jane, *née* Ratcliff (d 1982); *b* 12 February 1937; *Educ* Friends' Sch Saffron Walden, KCL, St George's Hosp London (MB BS); *m* 26 August 1961, Dr Graham Murray, s of George Sterling (d 1987); 5 s (Charles b 1963, Guy b 1967, Andrew b 1974, Mark b 1977, Thomas b 1981), 1 da (b and d 1972); *Career* St George's Hosp London: house physician/surgn 1960–61, SHO 1961–62, med registrar 1965–67; in gen practice Oxford 1968–69, lectr Dept of Med Univ of Calif San Francisco 1969–70; Southampton Univ Hosps: sr registrar then lectr Dept of Med 1972–79, conslt physician in geriatric med 1979–2002 (emeritus 2002–); pres Med Women's Fedn 1989–90, chm Standing Med Advsy Ctee 1990–94 (memb 1984–96), vice-chm Regnl Advsy Ctee Distinction Awards (Wessex) 1999–2000 (Southern) 2000–03, memb Clinical Standards Advsy Gp 1992–94, memb Independent Review Panel on Advtg of Med 2000–, tstee Wessex Med Tst 1999–2004, tstee King Edward VII Hosp Midhurst 2002–06; FRCP 1982 (MRCP 1971); *Recreations* golf, music, orchids, gardening; *Style*— Dr Nuala Sterling, CBE, FRCP; ✉ Vermont House, East Boldre, Hampshire SO42 7WX

STERLING OF PLAISTOW, Baron (Life Peer UK 1991), of Pall Mall in the City of Westminster; Sir Jeffrey Maurice Sterling; GCVO (2002), CBE (1977); s of late Harry Sterling, and Alice Sterling; *b* 27 December 1934; *Educ* Reigate GS, Preston Manor Co Sch, Guildhall Sch of Music; *m* 1985, Dorothy Ann, *née* Smith; 1 da; *Career* Paul Schweder & Co (Stock Exchange) 1955–57, G Eberstadt & Co 1957–62, fin dir General Guarantee Corp 1962–64, md Gula Investments Ltd 1964–69, chm Sterling Guarantee Trust plc 1969 (merged with P&O 1985), memb Bd of Dirs British Airways 1979–82, exec chm The Peninsular and Oriental Steam Navigation Company 1983–2005 (dir 1980–2005), chm P&O Princess Cruises 2000–03; special advsr to Sec of State for Industry (later Trade and Industry) 1982–90; World ORT Union: memb Exec 1966–, chm Orgn Ctee 1969–73, chm ORT Technical Servs 1974–, vice-pres British ORT 1978–; pres: Gen Cncl of Br Shipping 1990–91, EC Shipowners' Assocs 1992–94; chm The Queen's Golden Jubilee Weekend Tst 2002, dep chm and hon treas London Celebrations Ctee for Queen's Silver Jubilee; Motability: co-fndr 1977, chm Exec Ctee 1977–, vice-chm 1977–94, chm 1994–; chm: Young Vic Co 1975–83, Bd of Govrs Royal Ballet Sch 1983–99; govr Royal Ballet 1986–99; tstee Nat Maritime Museum 2005–; Hon Capt RNR 1991, elder brother Trinity House 1991; Freeman City of London; Hon DBA Nottingham Trent Univ 1995, Hon DCL Univ of Durham 1996; Hon FIMarE 1991, Hon FICS 1992, Hon MRICS 1993, FISVA 1995, Hon FRINA 1997; KStJ 1998, Grand Offr Order of the May (Argentina) 2002, Officer's Cross of the Order of Merit (Germany) 2004; *Recreations* music, swimming, tennis; *Clubs* Garrick, Hurlingham; *Style*— The Rt Hon the Lord Sterling of Plaistow, GCVO, CBE

STERN, Anthony Edward; s of David Stern, and Joy Stern; *b* 28 May 1948, London; *Educ* Marlborough, Univ Coll Oxford, Manchester Business Sch; *m* 1975, Elizabeth; 2 da (b 1979 and 1984); *Career* formerly: treas Dixons Gp, vice-pres Chase Manhattan Bank; InterContinental Hotels (formerly Bass plc): dir of treasy 1988–2003, dir UK Pension Tst 2004–; panel memb Competition Cmmn 2005–; pres Assoc of Corporate Treasurers 2001–02; FRSA; *Publications* Economist Intelligence Unit pubn on European pensions (contrib, 2004); *Recreations* theatre, opera, skiing, walking the South Downs Way; *Style*— Anthony Stern, Esq

STERN, (John) Chester; s of Julius Charles Stern (d 1983), of Littlehampton, W Sussex, and Bertha Margaret, *née* Baker (d 2001); *b* 6 September 1944; *Educ* Parktown Boys' HS Johannesburg, Broad Green Coll Croydon; *m* 25 March 1967, Rosemary Ann, da of Wilfred Harold Symons; 2 da (Carolyn Joy b 28 Sept 1969, Paula Jane b 26 Feb 1972); *Career* asst librarian Wills Library Guy's Hospital Medical Sch 1964–65, ed asst Food Processing & Marketing 1965–66, freelance broadcaster BBC Radio London 1970–74, freelance sportswriter The Sunday Telegraph 1973–76; Metropolitan Police New Scotland Yard: publicity asst 1966–68, head of News Gp 1968–71, PRO Traffic Warden Service 1971–74, press and publicity offr London Airport Heathrow 1974–75, press and publicity offr S London 1975–77, head Press Bureau 1977–82; crime corr The Mail on Sunday 1982–2001, controller of public affrs Harrods 2001–04, dir of corp affrs Fulham FC 2001–04; freelance sportswriter and media conslt 2004–; pres Crime Reporters' Assoc 1995 (chm 1993), capt Press Golfing Soc 1999; memb: Sports Journalists' Assoc, Football Writers' Assoc; Winston Churchill fell 1975; FRGS 1964, MIPR 1971; *Books* Dr Iain West's Casebook (1996), The Black Widow (2002); *Recreations* golf; *Clubs* Mensa, Groucho; *Style*— Chester Stern, Esq; ✉ 101 Norfolk Avenue, Sanderstead, Surrey CR2 8BY (tel 020 8657 3649, fax 020 8409 0652, mobile 07841 697834, e-mail chesrose.stern@btinternet.com)

STERN, Dr Jeremy Samuel; s of late Harold Ian Stern, of Sheffield, and late Daphne, *née* Moses; *b* 12 January 1967; *Educ* Ecclesfield Sch Sheffield, King Edward VII Sch Sheffield, Christ's Coll Cambridge (MA), UCL, Middx Sch of Med London (MB BChir); *Career* house surgn Basildon and Orsett Hosps 1991–92, house physician Southampton Gen Hosp 1992, SHO in med Guy's Hosp 1992–94, registrar in geriatrics St George's Hosp London 1994–95; registrar in neurology: Atkinson Morley's Hosp 1995–96, Chelsea & Westminster Hosp 1996–97; research fell (neurology) Hammersmith Hosp 1997–2000, specialist registar in neurology Nat Hosp for Neurology and Neurosurgery and Addenbrooke's Hosp 2000–03, conslt neurologist Frimley Park Hosp and St George's Hosp 2004–; Tourette Syndrome Assoc: tstee 1990–2000, chair 2002–07, medical dir 2007–; asst sec Assoc of Br Neurology Trainees 1998–2001; memb (youngest ever) GMC 1994–99; memb Br Neuropsychiatry Assoc 1992, memb Assoc of Br Neurologists 1995; memb Chopin Soc; memb Worshipful Soc of Apothecaries 2000 (Dip in History of Med 1995); MRCP 1994; *Recreations* eating, playing the didgeridoo, drama, mandarin; *Style*— Dr Jeremy Stern; ✉ Ground Floor, Atkinson Morley's Wing, St Geroge's Hospital, Blackshaw Road, London SW17 0QT (tel 020 8725 4631, fax 020 8725 4700, e-mail jeremy.stern@stgeorges.nhs.uk)

STERN, John Andrew; s of Peter Stern (d 2002), and Gillian, *née* Bannister; *b* 12 March 1970, London; *Educ* King's Sch Canterbury, Univ of Manchester (BA); *m* 17 April 2004, Clare Alison, *née* Henderson; 2 step da (Eloise b 19 Oct 1994, Georgie b 16 Oct 1997); *Career* reporter Hayters Sports Agency 1992–97, freelance sports writer 1997–2001, contrib Wisden Cricketers' Almanack 1999–, dep ed Wisden Cricket Monthly 2001–03, ed The Wisden Cricketer 2003–; cricket columnist Sunday Times 2003–; *Recreations* football, cricket (Wendover CC) travel, food and wine; *Clubs* MCC, Lord's Taverners, Cricket Writers'; *Style*— John Stern, Esq; ✉ The Wisden Cricketer, 46 Loman Street, London SE1 0EH (>e-mail< john.stern@wisdencricketer.com)

STERN, Prof Sir Nicholas Herbert (Nick); kt (2004); s of Adalbert Stern, and Marion Fatima, *née* Swann; *b* 22 April 1946; *Educ* Latymer Upper Sch, Peterhouse Cambridge (BA), Nuffield Oxford (DPhilEcon); *m* 7 Sept 1968, Susan Ruth, da of Albert Edward Chesterton (d 1978), of Pinner, Middx; 1 da (Helen b 1976), 2 s (Daniel b 1979, Michael b 1980); *Career* jr res fell Queen's Coll Oxford, fell and tutor in econs St Catherine's Coll Oxford 1970–77 (hon fell 2000), lectr in industrial mathematics Univ of Oxford 1970–77, prof of economics Univ of Warwick 1978–85, Sir John Hicks prof of econs LSE 1986–94, chief economist and special advsr EBRD 1994–99, sch prof of economics LSE 1999 (on leave 2000–07), chief economist and sr vice-pres World Bank 2000–03, second perm sec HM Treasy and head Govt Economic Serv 2003–07 (dir of policy and research PM's Cmmn for Africa 2004, ldr and author Stern Review on the Economics of Climate Change HM Treasy 2005–06), IG Patel prof prof LSE 2007–; ed Jl of Public Economics 1981–97; res assoc/visiting prof: MIT 1972, Ecole Poly 1977, People's Univ China Beijing 1988 (hon prof 2001); Indian Statistical Inst: overseas visiting fell Br Acad 1974–75, Ford Fndn visiting prof 1981–82; foreign hon memb American Acad of Arts and Scis 1998–; fell Econometric Soc 1978; FBA 1993; *Books* An Appraisal of Tea Production on Smallholdings in Kenya (1972), Theories of Economic Growth (ed jtly, 1973), Crime, the Police and Criminal Statistics (jtly, 1979), Palanpur: The Economy of an Indian Village (jtly, 1982), The Theory of Taxation for Developing Countries (jtly, 1987), Economic Development in Palanpur over Five Decades (jtly, 1998); numerous articles in learned jls; *Recreations* walking, reading, watching football; *Style*— Prof Sir Nicholas Stern, FBA

STERNBERG, Michael Vivian; s of Sir Sigmund Sternberg, *qv*, and Beatrice Ruth, *née* Schiff (d 1994); *b* 12 September 1951; *Educ* Carmel Coll, Queens' Coll Cambridge (MA, LLM); *m* 20 July 1975, Janine Lois, da of Harold Levinson; 2 da (Rachel Serena b 2 Feb 1980, Sarah Jessica b 4 Jan 1988), 1 s (Daniel Isaiah b 24 Sept 1982); *Career* called to the Bar Gray's Inn 1975; asst sec Family Law Bar Assoc 1986–88; tstee: London Jewish East End Museum 1984–94, Sternberg Charitable Settlement; memb Cncl of Christians and Jews 1988; govr: N London Collegiate Sch 1992–; Lloyd's underwriter 1978–96; Freeman City of London 1983, Liveryman Worshipful Co of Horners 1987; FRSA 2007; Medaglia D'Argento di Benemerenza of the Sacred Military Constantinian Order of St George 1990; *Recreations* walking, reading, theatre; *Clubs* Reform; *Style*— Michael Sternberg, Esq; ✉ 4 Paper Buildings, Temple, London EC4Y 7EX (tel 020 7583 0816, fax 020 7353 4979, e-mail clerks@4paperbuildings.co.uk)

STERNBERG, Sir Sigmund; kt (1976), JP; s of late Abraham Sternberg, and Elizabeth Sternberg; *b* 2 June 1921, Budapest; *m* 1970, Hazel, *née* Everett-Jones; 1 s, 1 da, 1 step s, 1 step da; *Career* chm: Martin Slowe Estates Ltd 1971–; dep chm Lab Fin and Industry Gp 1972–93; chm St Charles Gp HMC 1974; pres Friends of Cruse 1993–; sr vice-pres Royal Coll of Speech and Language Therapists 1995–; chm Inst for Archaeo-Metallurgical Studies; patron Int Cncl of Christians and Jews; memb Bd of Deputies of Br Jews, govr Hebrew Univ of Jerusalem; life pres Sternberg Centre for Judaism 1996–, pres Reform Synagogues of GB 1998–; fndr: Three Faiths Forum (Christians, Muslims and Jews Dialogue Gp) 1997; memb Advsy Cncl Inst of Business Ethics 1986– (vice-pres 2002–), co-ordinator Religious Component World Economic Forum 2002–; life memb: Magistrates Assoc 1965, RSM; hon life pres Labour Fin and Indy Gp 2002–; memb Ct Univ of Essex, visiting prof Moderna Univ Lisbon 1998; memb John Templeton Fndn 1998– (Templeton Prize for Progress in Religion 1998); Paul Harris fell 1989; Liveryman Worshipful Co of Horners, Freeman City of London 1965; Medal of Merit Warsaw Univ 1995; Hon DUniv: Essex 1996, Open Univ 1998, Hebrew Union Coll Cincinnati 2000; hon fell UCL 2001; FRSA 1979, Hon FRSM 1981, Hon FCST 1989; Order of the Orthodox Hospitallers 1st Class with Star and Badge of Religion 1986, OStJ 1988, KCSG 1985, Silver Pontifical Medal 1986, Benemerenti Medal (Vatican) 1988 (in Silver 1990), Order of Merit (Poland) 1989, Order of the Gold Star (Hungary) 1990, Medaglia d'Argento di Benemerenza Sacred Mil Constantinian Order of St George 1991, Cdr's Cross 1st Class (Austria) 1992, Cdr's Cross Order of Merit (Poland) 1992, Cdr of the Order of Civil Merit (Spain) 1993, Cdr's Cross Order of Merit (Germany) 1993, Cdr Order of Honour (Greece) 1996, Cdr of the Royal Order of the Polar Star (Sweden) 1997, Wilhelm Leuschner Medal (Wiesbaden) 1998, Order of Commandatore of the Italian Republic (Italy) 1999, Cdr's Cross with a Star of the Order of Merit (Poland) 1999, Order de Mayo al Merito en el Gardo de Gran Oficial (Argentina) 1999, Order of Bernardo O'Higgins Grado de Gran Cruz (Chile) 2000, Order of Ukraine for Public Services (Ukraine) 2001, Order of Merit (Portugal) 2002, Order of the Madara Horsemen (Bulgaria) 2003, Order of the White Two-Armed Cross (Slovakia) 2003, Légion d'Honneur (France) 2003, Order of Francisco de Miranda (Venezuela) 2004, Knight Cdr's Cross Order of Merit (Germany) 2006; *Recreations* golf, swimming; *Clubs* Reform, City Livery; *Style*— Sir Sigmund Sternberg; ✉ 80 East End Road, London N3 2SY (fax 020 7485 4512)

STEUART FOTHRINGHAM, Robert; DL (Angus 1985); eld s of Maj Thomas Scrymsoure Steuart Fothringham, MC, DL, JP, TD (d 1979, 2 s of Lt-Col Walter Thomas James Scrymsoure Steuart Fothringham, of Pourie-Fothringham and Tealing, Angus, and of Grantully and Murthly, Perthshire, who took the name Steuart on succeeding Sir Archibald Douglas Stewart, 8 and last Bt, in the lands of Grantully and Murthly in 1890), and Carola Mary (d 1989), da of Maj the Hon Charles Hubert Francis Noel, OBE (d 1947); bro of Henry Steuart Fothringham of Grantully, OBE, *qv*; *b* 5 August 1937; *Educ* Fort Augustus Abbey, Trinity Coll Cambridge, RAC Cirencester; *m* 16 Feb 1962, Elizabeth Mary Charlotte (d 1990), da of Thomas Hope Brendan Lawther (d 1994), of Earl's Court, London SW5; 2 da (Mariana (Mrs Christopher Pease) b 1966, Ilona (Mrs Christopher Boyle) b 1969), 2 s (Thomas b 1971, Lionel b 1973); *Career* CA; memb Royal Co Archers; *Recreations* shooting, fishing, archery, music; *Clubs* Puffin's, Turf, New (Edinburgh); *Style*— Robert Steuart Fothringham of Pourie, DL; ✉ Fothringham, Forfar, Angus DD8 2JP (tel 01307 820231, fax 01307 820200)

STEUART FOTHRINGHAM OF GRANTULLY, Henry; OBE (1995); yst s of Maj Thomas Scrymsoure Steuart Fothringham, 21 of Pourie-Fothringham, MC, DL, JP (d 1979), of Fothringham, Forfar, Angus, and Carola Mary (d 1989), da of Maj the Hon Charles Hubert Francis Noel, OBE (d 1947); bro of Robert Steuart Fothringham, DL, *qv*; inherited the barony of Grantully from uncle, Maj Patrick Scrymsoure Steuart Fothringham, 22 of Grantully, DSO (d 1953); *b* 15 February 1944, Edinburgh; *Educ* Fort Augustus Abbey, RAC Cirencester; *m* 20 May 1972, Cherry Linnhe Stewart, 14 of Achnacone (d 2001), da of Brig Ian Macalister Stewart, 13 of Achnacone, DSO, OBE, MC, DL (d 1987), of Achnacone, Appin, Argyll; 3 s (Patrick yr of Grantully b 23 April 1973, Charles 15 of Achnacone b 6 April 1974, Ian b 13 Jan 1976); *Career* specialist in Scottish silver, writer and researcher; prop Grantully Castle Antiques 1966–68; ptnr (with late bro, Walter) specialising in Scottish silver 1968–72, promoting Norman Orr (crystal engraver, artist and designer) 1968–89; dir Logierait Bridge Co 1995– (vice-chm 1997–); memb: Tay Salmon Fisheries Bd 1977–80, Reviewing Ctee on the Export of Works of Art 1982–94, Advsy Cncl on the Export of Works of Art 1982–94, Hist Ctee Scottish Goldsmiths Tst 2001–; govr Heartland Radio Fndn Ltd 1995–2000; Freeman: Worshipful Co of Goldsmiths 1993, City of London 1994; memb: The Silver Soc 1977 (chm 1993–94), The Stewart Soc 1963 (hon vice-pres 1971–, pres 1995–98), Incorporation of Goldsmiths of the City of Edinburgh 1990 (Freeman 2000); MInstD, FRSA, FSA Scot, FRPSL; *Books and Publications* The Family of Fothringham of Pourie (1990, 3 edn 1995); contrib: Jackson's Silver and Gold Marks of England, Scotland and Ireland (1989), Scottish Gold and Silver Work (ed and co-author, 1991 edn), Bradbury's Book of Hallmarks (1991 edn); author of numerous articles in learned jls, book and exhbn reviews; regular contrib The Stewarts magazine; articles in Jl of The Silver Soc incl: The Darnley Jewel (2001), The Strathmore Silver Inventory of 1695 (2001), Scottish Goldsmiths' Apprenticeships (2002), St Eloi (2003), Scottish Goldsmiths' Weights (2003); *Recreations* Scottish silver studies, books, history, writing, the Arts and Sciences, Scotland, the countryside, trees and gardens; *Clubs* Royal Over-Seas League, Antiquaries Dining (Edinburgh), Puffins (Edinburgh); *Style*— Henry Steuart Fothringham, Esq, OBE; ✉ The Lagg, Aberfeldy, Perthshire PH15 2EE (tel 01887 820020, fax 01887 829582, e-mail hsfothringham@hotmail.com)

STEVELY, Prof William Stewart; CBE (2004); s of Robert Reid Stevely (d 1992), of Saltcoats, Ayrshire, and Catherine Callow, *née* Stewart; *b* 6 April 1943; *Educ* Ardrossan Acad, Univ of Glasgow (BSc, DipEd), Univ of Oxford (DPhil); *m* 1968, Sheila Anne, *née* Stalker; 3 s, 2 da; *Career* successively asst lectr, lectr then sr lectr in biochemistry Univ of Glasgow 1968–88; Univ of Paisley (formerly Paisley Coll of Technol): prof and head Dept of Biology 1988–92, vice-princ 1992–97; princ and vice-chllr Robert Gordon Univ 1997–2005; UCAS: memb Bd 2000–05, chm 2001–05; convenor Universities Scotland 2002–04; dir: John Ritchie Ltd Kilmarnock, Scot Cncl for Devpt and Industry, Scottish Agric Coll, Scottish Univ for Industry; chm NHS Ayrshire and Arran 2006–; memb: Nat Bd for Scotland of Nursing Midwifery and Health Visiting 1993–2002, Scottish HE Funding Cncl 1994–97, Bd Quality Assurance Agency for HE 1998–2002, Cncl Inst for Learning and Teaching in HE 1999–2000; memb: Biochemical Soc 1968, Soc of Gen Microbiology 1973; FIBiol 1988; *Style*— Prof William Stevely, CBE

STEVENS, Alan Michael; s of Raymond Alfred George Stevens, of Bournemouth, Dorset, and Joan Patricia, *née* Drury; *b* 8 April 1955; *Educ* Malvern Coll, Selwyn Coll Cambridge (MA); *m* 2 May 1987, Lynn Sarah, da of Henry B Hopfinger, of Coventry, Warks; 2 da (Eloise b 1988, Natalia b 1993), 2 s (Thomas b 1990, Benjamin b 1992); *Career* admitted slr 1980; ptnr Linklaters 1987–2003 (joined 1978), ptnr Carey Olsen Group 2003–; memb Law Soc; Freeman Worshipful Co of Slrs; *Recreations* tennis, skiing, sailing, golf; *Clubs* Royal Hong Kong Yacht, St Helier Yacht, Hurlingham, Banyan Tree; *Style*— Alan Stevens, Esq; ✉ Carey Olsen, 47 Esplanade, St Helier, Jersey JE1 0BD

STEVENS, Brian Turnbull Julius; s of Maj John Osmond Julius Stevens, MBE, and Kathleen, *née* Forman; *b* 3 November 1938; *Educ* Eton; *m* 5 Dec 1970, Hon Henrietta Maria, da of Lt-Col 1 Baron St Helens, MC (d 1980); 3 da (Flora Matilda Julius b 25 Feb 1973, Harriet Maria Julius b 11 Jan 1975, Louisa Elizabeth Julius b 15 Oct 1976); *Career* admitted slr 1962; currently conslt Withers; memb Law Soc; *Recreations* field sports, gardening; *Clubs* Boodle's, Pratt's; *Style*— Brian Stevens, Esq; ✉ Withers, 16 Old Bailey, London EC4M 7EG (tel 020 7597 6000, fax 020 7597 6543)

STEVENS, David Franklin; s of John Stanley Stevens (d 1969), of Guildford, Surrey, and Margaret Madelene, *née* Gale (d 1949); *b* 8 January 1928; *Educ* Sherborne; *m* 1947, Patricia Mary, da of Charles Campbell; 1 s (Alastair David b 1948), 1 da (Bryony Jane Carolyn b 1951); *Career* Nat Serv Capt Queen's Royal Regt, served Far East 1946–48, TA 1S9/23 SAS 1953–60; MW 1961; Rigby & Evens Ltd wine shippers Bristol 1949–56, md Rigby & Evens (Liverpool) Ltd 1957–69, chm Rigby & Evens (Wine Shippers) Ltd Liverpool and London 1969–76; dir Matthew Clark & Sons (Holdings) Ltd London 1967–81; estab own wine consultancy 1981–87, first exec dir Inst of Masters of Wine 1987–94 (chm 1973–74, pres 1994–97); wine columnist Literary Review 1987–92; memb Wine Ctee Int Wine and Food Soc; Freeman City of London, Liveryman Worshipful Co of Distillers 1993; memb: Confrérie des Chevaliers du Tastevin, Académie du Vin de Bordeaux, Commanderie du Bon Temps de Medoc et des Graves; *Books* contrib: Wines of the World (ed Serena Sutcliffe, 1979), The Oxford Companion to Wine (Jancis Robinson, 1994); *Recreations* writing, travelling, good wine, the cinema, all sports (active tennis player); *Style*— David Stevens, Esq; ✉ The Three Cottages, Meadle, Buckinghamshire HP17 9UD (tel and fax 01844 343825)

STEVENS, David Frederick; CBE (2006), QPM (1998); s of Frederick John Stevens (d 2001), and Kathleen Ann, *née* Leftley; *b* 27 March 1951; *Educ* LSE (LLB); *m* 1974, Patricia Ann, *née* True; 2 da (Sarah b 1978, Rebecca b 1984), 1 s (Paul b 1980); *Career* Constable rising to Chief Supt Surrey Police 1973–94; Beds Police: Asst Chief Constable 1994–96, Dep Chief Constable 1996–98; Chief Constable Essex Police 1998–2005; chair Performance Mgmnt Business Area ACPO 2001–04; chair Police Sport UK 2003–, hon sec Police Athletic Assoc 2002–03 (memb Cncl 1994–); CCMI 2001; *Style*— David Stevens, Esq, CBE, QPM; ✉ The Old Bakery, 49 Post Street, Godmanchester, Huntingdon PE29 2AQ

STEVENS, Dr David Laurence; s of Laurence Sydney Stevens (d 1987), of Ampney Crucis, Glos, and Ida May, *née* Roberts (d 1989); *b* 15 September 1938; *Educ* High Pavement Sch Nottingham, Guy's Hosp Med Sch Univ of London (MB BS, MD); *m* 20 Feb 1965, (Karin) Ute, da of Friedrich Heinrich Rudolf Holtzheimer (d 1966), of Berlin, Germany; 2 s (Michael b 1967, Andrew b 1970); *Career* registrar in neurology Derbyshire Royal Infirmary 1966–67, sr registrar in neurology Leeds Gen Infirmary 1967–73, res fell dept of genetics Univ of Leeds 1969–70; conslt neurologist 1973–2000 (Glos Royal Hosp, Cheltenham Gen Hosp, Frenchay Hosp Bristol); memb Editorial Bd Br Jl of Hosp Med 1985–96, assoc ed Jl of Neurological Sciences 1990–96; author of articles on neurology in med jls, contribs to various books; sec gen Res Gp on Huntington's Chorea World Fedn of Neurology 1983–91 (memb Res Ctee 1973–); pres SW England Neurosciences Assoc 1984–85, chm Fin Ctee and memb Orgn Ctee World Congress of Neurology 1997–2001, tstee variant Creutzfeldt-Jakob Disease (vCJD) Tst 2002–; Sydney Watson-Smith lectr RCPE 1996; Faculté de Médicine Medal Univ of Lille 1998, Annual Medal Assoc of Br Neurologists 2004; Membre d'honneur á Titre Étranger Societé Française de Neurologie 1999, memb Assoc of Br Neurologists (hon treas 1998–2003); FRCP 1980 (MRCP 1966), FRCPE 1997; *Publications* Handbook of Clinical Neurology (contrib); author of many papers on neurological subjects and on the delivery of neurological services; *Recreations* travel, photography, skiing, talking (a lot); *Style*— Dr David Stevens; ✉ Springfield Lawn, The Park, Cheltenham, Gloucestershire GL50 2SD (tel 01242 237921, fax 01242 522424, e-mail dls@david-stevens.demon.co.uk)

STEVENS, Dr Handley Michael Gambrell; s of Dr Ernest Norman Stevens (d 1991), and Dr Kathleen Emily Gambrell (d 1986); *b* 29 June 1941; *Educ* The Leys Sch, Phillips Acad Andover Mass, King's Coll Cambridge (MA, PhD); *m* 5 March 1966, Anne Frances, da of Robert Ross (d 2005); 3 da (Hilary b 1970, Lucy b 1971, Mary b 1980); *Career* Dip Serv 1964–70 (Kuala Lumpur 1966–69); asst private sec Lord Privy Seal 1970–71, Civil Serv Dept 1970–73, DTI 1973–83, under sec Dept of Tport 1983–94 (Int Aviation 1983–87, Finance 1988–91, Public Tport in London 1991–94); research assoc Euro Inst LSE 1994–; *Publications* Tport Policy in Britain (1998), Brussels Bureaucrats? (2000), Transport Policy in Europe (2003); *Recreations* Anglican lay reader, music, walking; *Style*— Dr Handley M G Stevens; ✉ 18A Belsize Lane, London NW3 5AB (tel 020 7794 0874)

STEVENS, Sir Jocelyn Edward Greville; kt (1996), CVO (1992); s of Maj (Charles) Greville Bartlett Stewart-Stevens, formerly Stevens, JP (d 1972, having m subsequently (1936) Muriel Athelstan Hood, *née* Stewart, 10 Lady of Balnakeilly, Perthshire, and adopted (1937) the name Stewart-Stevens), and late Mrs Greville Stevens (d 1932), da of Sir Edward Hulton (who owned the Evening Standard until 1923, when he sold it to 1 Baron Beaverbrook); *b* 14 February 1932; *Educ* Eton, Trinity Coll Cambridge; *m* 1956 (m dis 1979), Jane Armyne, LVO (1993), da of John Vincent Sheffield; 2 s (1 decd), 2 da; *Career* Nat Serv The Rifle Bde 1950–52; journalist Hulton Press Ltd 1955–56, chm and md Stevens Press Ltd and ed Queen Magazine 1957–68, dir Beaverbrook Newspapers 1971–77 (md 1974–77), md Evening Standard Co Ltd 1969–72, md Daily Express 1972–74, dep chm and md Express Newspapers 1975–81, dir Centaur Communications Ltd 1982–85, publisher and ed The Magazine 1982–84, rector and vice-provost RCA 1984–92, chm English Heritage 1992–2000, chm Royal Cmmn on the Historical Monuments of England (RCHME) 1999–2000; dep chm ITC 1991–96; non-exec dir: Lowe Group plc 1988–90, The Television Corporation 1996–2002; special advsr on Stonehenge to sec of state for culture, media and sport 2000–; pres The Cheyne Walk Tst 1989–93, vice-chm The Prince's Fndn 2000–02; chm: The Silver Trust 1989–93, The Prince of Wales's Phoenix Tst 2000–03, The Prince's Regeneration through Heritage Tst 2002–03; tstee: Mental Health Fndn 1972–94, Eureka! The Museum for Children 1986–2000, The Butrint Fndn 2000–05; govr: ICSTM 1985–92, Winchester Sch of Art 1986–89; Hon DLitt: Loughborough Univ, Buckingham Univ; sr fell RCA, hon fell CSD; FRSA; *Recreations* skiing; *Clubs* White's, Buck's; *Style*— Sir Jocelyn Stevens, CVO; ✉ 136 Oswald, Chelsea Bridge Wharf, 374 Queenstown Road, London SW8 4PJ (e-mail jocelyn.stevens32@btinternet.com)

STEVENS, John Christopher Courtney; *b* 23 May 1955; *Educ* Winchester, Magdalen Coll Oxford (BA); *Career* foreign exchange dealer Bayerische Hypotheken Wechselbank Munich 1976–77; fin corr Il Messaggiero Rome 1978; foreign exchange dealer: Banque Indosuez Paris 1979–80, Morgan Grenfell & Co Ltd London 1980–84; dir Morgan Grenfell International (and head of Euro Govt Bond Trading) 1985–89, advsr on foreign exchange and interest rates to J Rothschild Investment Management 1989–2005; MEP (Cons) Thames Valley 1989–99; advsr THS Ptnrs 1999–; dir: Airtrack Railways Ltd 2002–, ESV A/S Ltd 2005–; *Books* A Conservative European Monetary Union (1990), On Line in Time - The Case for a Smart Citizen's Card for Britain; *Style*—John Stevens, Esq; ✉ 40 Smith Square, London SWP 3HL (tel 020 7222 0770, fax 020 7976 7172)

STEVENS, Dr (Katharine) Lindsey Haughton; da of Richard Haughton Stevens (d 1977), and Rachel Vera Joyce, *née* Huxstep; *b* 17 July 1954; *Educ* Harrogate Ladies' Coll, Runton Hill Sch, Gresham's Sch, Churchill Coll Cambridge (MA), Middx Hosp Med Sch (MB BChir); *m* 1989, David Barrett McCausland, s of John McCausland, of Pett, E Sussex; 2 s (Duncan James Stevens b 1989, Theodore Richard Stevens b 1994), 1 da (Beth Mary Stevens b 1991); *Career* conslt/mangr A&E St George's Hosp 1985–96, clinical dir A&E Services St Helier Hosp 1996–99: Epsom and St Helier NHS Tst: dir A&E Services 1999–, dir Fndn Prog 2006–; hon sr lectr Univ of London 1985–, course dir and instr in advanced trauma life support RCS 1989 fndr St George's Start-a-Heart campaign and fund 1986, instructor in advanced life support 2006–; research into: psychological effects of trauma and bereavement, domestic violence, water safety, resuscitation, cardiac illness, physiotherapy; dep dist surgn St John Ambulance Bde; sec S Thames A&E Conslts Ctee 2000–, memb Br Assoc of Emergency Med 1985; A&E Section Royal Soc of Med: treas 1992–95, editorial rep 1995–97, library rep 1997–99; regnl sub-speciality advsr RCS 1990–93; memb RSM 1989; FCEM 1993, FRCP 1994 (MRCP 1983), FRSA 2002; *Books* Emergencies in Obstetrics and Gynaecology, Violence against Women (contrib), Rape (contrib); *Style*— Dr Lindsey Stevens; ✉ Accident and Emergency Services, Epsom and St Helier NHS Trust, Wrythe Lane, Carshalton SM5 1AA (tel 020 8296 2276)

STEVENS, Matthew John Hamilton (Matt); s of Russell John Stevens, and Georgina Hamilton Kelly; *b* 1 October 1982, Durban, South Africa; *Educ* Kearsney Coll Durban, Univ of Cape Town, Univ of Bath; *Career* rugby union player (front row forward); clubs: South Africa Univs (capt), Western Province, Bath Rugby 2002–; England: 15 caps, debut v NZ 2004, memb squad World Cup France 2007; memb British and Irish Lions touring squad NZ 2005; also played for and captained South Africa under 18 and under 19 teams; *Recreations* scuba diving, horse riding, guitar playing; *Style*— Mr Matt Stevens

STEVENS, Patrick Tom; s of Tom Stevens, of Norfolk, and Gwendoline, *née* Nurse; *b* 21 August 1949; *Educ* Paston GS; *Career* tax specialist Coopers & Lybrand 1975–79, tax ptnr BDO Stoy Hayward (and predecessor firms) 1979–96, tax ptnr and managing ptnr (entrepreneurial services) Ernst & Young 1996–; memb Cncl Chartered Inst of Taxation; Liveryman Worshipful Co of Glass Sellers; FCA 1972, CTA (fell) 2003 (ATII 1975); *Recreations* theatre, golf; *Style*— Patrick Stevens, Esq; ✉ Longacre, Sandhurst Road, Bodiam, East Sussex; Ernst & Young, 1 More London Place, London SE1 2AF(tel 020 7951 2334, fax 020 7951 9337)

STEVENS, Peter Rupert; s of late Surgn Capt R W Stevens, RN; *b* 14 May 1938; *Educ* Winchester, Taft Sch (USA); *m* 1963, Sarah Venetia Mary, da of late Air Vice Marshal H A V Hogan, CB, DSO, DFC; 3 c; *Career* 2 Lt KRRC; stockbroker; sr ptnr Laurie Milbank 1981–86 (ptnr 1969–86), head Sterling Fixed Interest International Chase Manhattan Investment Bank; chief exec GT Management plc 1989–94; dir Corporate Governance LGT Gp 1994–98; chm Tradepoint Fin Networks/Virt-x 1997–2006; memb: Stock Exchange Cncl 1974–87 and 1988–91 (dep chm 1988–90), Bd of The Securities & Futures Authy 1986–2001; *Recreations* opera, country pursuits; *Style*— Peter Stevens, Esq; ✉ Highmead House, Alton, Hampshire GU34 4BN (tel 01420 83945)

STEVENS, Rachel; da of Michael, and Linda Stevens; *b* 9 April 1978; *Educ* Ashmore Southgate, London Coll of Fashion; *Career* singer and actress; memb S Club (formerly S Club 7) 1999–2003 (with Brad McIntosh, Jon Lee, Tina Barrett, Jo O'Meara and Hannah Spearritt); promotional ptnrs incl: BT, Procter & Gamble, Pepsi, WWF; supporter: WWF, Children in Need, Woolworth's Kids First; *Singles* Bring It All Back (UK no 1, 1999), S Club Party (UK no 2, 1999), Two in a Million/You're My Number One (UK no 2, 1999), Reach (UK no 2, 2000), Natural (UK no 3, 2000), Never Had a Dream Come True (UK no 1, 2000), Don't Stop Movin' (UK no 1, 2001), Have You Ever (UK no 1, 2001), You (UK no 2, 2002); *Albums* S Club (UK no 2, 1999), 7 (UK no 1, 2000), Sunshine (UK no 3, 2001); *Television* series: Miami 7, LA 7, Hollywood 7; specials: Back to the 50s, Boyfriends & Birthdays, Artistic Differences, The Christmas Special; documentaries: S Club Go Wild, Don't Stop Movin'; *Video and DVDs* S Club Party 2001, S Club Carnival 2002; *Awards* 1999: Best Newcomers Smash Hits, Best TV Programme TV Hits, Best Selling Debut Album by a British Artist Music Week, Highest Rating Kids TV Prog of the Year; 2000: Best Br Newcomers BRIT Awards, Favourite Gp Disney Awards, Favourite TV Prog Disney Awards, Best Album TV Hits; 2001: Best Recording Artists Variety Club Awards, Record of the Year (Don't Stop Movin') Br TV Viewers; 2002: Best Song (Don't Stop Movin') Brit Awards, Best Concert (S Club Carnival) Capital Radio Music Awards; *Recreations* seeing friends, going for dinner, shopping, watching movies, going to the gym; *Style*— Ms Rachel Stevens; ✉ c/o 19 Entertainment Ltd, 33 Ransomes Dock, 35–37 Parkgate Road, London SW11 4NP (tel 020 7801 1919, fax 020 7801 1920)

STEVENS, Rear Adm Robert Patrick; CB (2000); s of late Major Phillip Joseph Stevens, RMP, and late Peggy, *née* Marshall; *b* 14 March 1948; *Educ* Prince Rupert Sch Wilhelmshaven, BRNC Dartmouth; *m* 1973, Vivien Roberts; 1 s, 1 da; *Career* CO HMS

Odin 1979–81, CO qualifying course HMS Dolphin 1983–85, CO HMS Torbay 1985–88, USN War Coll 1988–89, asst dir Strategic Systems MOD 1989–91, Capt 7 Frigate Sqdn and CO HMS Argonaut 1992–93, memb Navy Presentation Team 1993–94, dir Jt Warfare MOD 1994–98, Flag Offr Submarines 1998–2001, Cdr Submarines (NATO) E Atlantic 1998–2001, COS (Ops) to C-in-C Fleet 1998–2001, COS COMNAVSOUTH 2002–05; ceo Br Marine Fedn 2006–; pres RN Football Assoc 1998–2004; MRUSI 1992; *Recreations* hockey, skiing, cricket, sailing, tennis; *Clubs* Royal Navy of 1765 and 1785, RNSA, SW Shingles Yacht; *Style*— Rear Adm Robert Stevens, CB

STEVENS, Prof Stanley James; s of Harold Stevens (d 1987), of 84 Sandalwood Rd, Loughborough, and Gladys Mary, *née* Swain (d 1981); *b* 11 April 1933; *Educ* Bablake Sch Coventry, Univ of Nottingham (MSc), Cranfield Inst of Technol (MSc), Loughborough Univ (PhD); *m* 1 Sept 1956, Rita Lillian Stevens, da of Charles Lloyd (d 1986), of 5 Meredith Rd, Coventry; 2 da (Carol Anne b 3 June 1961, Kathryn Diane b 3 Nov 1965); *Career* engrg apprenticeship Armstrong-Siddely Motors Ltd 1950–55, project engr Siddeley Engines Ltd Bristol 1955–61; Loughborough Univ of Technol: lectr in aeronautics 1961–70, sr lectr 1970–76, reader 1976–81, prof of aircraft propulsion 1987–; ctee memb Loughborough Royal Aeronautical Soc, pres Leicestershire Lawn Tennis Assoc; Freeman City of Coventry 1956; MIMechE, MRAeS, CEng; *Recreations* tennis, walking, water colour painting; *Style*— Prof Stanley Stevens; ✉ 101 Valley Road, Loughborough, Leicestershire LE11 3PY (tel 01509 215139); Department of Aeronautical & Automotive Engineering and Transport Studies, Loughborough University of Technology, Loughborough, Leicestershire LE11 3TU (tel 01509 223404, fax 01509 267613, telex 34319)

STEVENS, Stuart Standish; s of Maj Edward Aloysious Stevens (d 1948), and Virginia Mary, *née* D'Vaz; *b* 30 April 1947; *Educ* St Joseph's Euro HS Bangalore, Acton County GS, Royal Holloway Coll London; *Children* 4 s (Uther Edward b 1984, Stuart William b 1989, Alexander George b 1993, Maximilian Richard b 1994), 1 da (Isabella Eda b 1986); *Career* called to the Bar Gray's Inn 1970; head of chambers; specialist in white collar and corp fraud; Freeman City of London 1991; *Style*— Stuart Stevens, Esq; ✉ Holborn Chambers, The Chambers of Stuart Stevens, 6 Gate Street, Lincoln's Inn Fields, London WC2 (tel 020 7242 6060, fax 020 7242 2777, e-mail stevens@holbornchambers.co.uk)

STEVENS, Rt Rev Timothy John; *see:* Leicester, Bishop of

STEVENS OF KIRKWHELPINGTON, Baron (Life Peer UK 2005), of Kirkwhelpington in the County of Northumberland; Sir John Arthur Stevens; kt (2000), QPM, DL (Gtr London 2001); *Educ* St Lawrence Coll Ramsgate, Univ of Leicester (LLB), Univ of Southampton (MPhil); *Career* joined Met Police Force 1964, Asst Chief Constable Hampshire 1986–88, Dep Chief Constable Cambridgeshire 1988–91, Chief Constable Northumbria 1991–98, Metropolitan Police Cmmr 2000–05 (Dep Cmmr 1998–2000); HM Insp of Constabulary 1996–98; head of inquiries into: alleged malpractice at NCIS 1989–92, alleged collusion between paramilitaries and security forces in NI 1989–2003, the deaths of Diana, Princess of Wales and Dodi Fayed 2004–06, alleged corruption in football Premier League player transfers 2006; former: chm ACPO Crime Prevention Ctee, chm Behavioural Science Ctee, advsr to Forensic Science Service, visiting prof City Univ NY, memb directing staff Police Staff Coll; advsr on policing to SA, Jamaican, Bugarian, Romanian, Quatar and Greek govts; non-exec chm Quest 2005–, non-exec dir Travelex 2005–; fell Wolfson Coll Cambridge, hon fell Soc of Advanced Legal Studies; Freeman City of London 2002; LLD Univ of Leicester 2000, Hon DCL Univ of Northumbria 2001; Rotary Paul Harris Fell 2000; Star of Romania 2000; *Recreations* sport as both spectator and participant; *Style*— The Rt Hon the Lord Stevens of Kirkwhelpington, QPM, DL

STEVENSON, George William; s of Harold Stevenson, of Maltby, S Yorks, and Elsie, *née* Bryan; *b* 30 August 1938; *Educ* Queensbury Road secdy modern sch; *m* 1958, Doreen June (d 1989); 2 s, 1 da; m 2, 1 June 1991, Pauline Margaret, *née* Brookes; *Career* MEP (Lab) Staffs E 1984–94, MP (Lab) Stoke-on-Trent S 1992–2005; memb: Tport Select Ctee, Euro Select and Standing Ctees, Chairman's Panel Ways and Means Ctee; chair All Pty Tibet Gp; Stoke-on-Trent City Cncl: dep ldr 1972–83, chm Highways Ctee; Staffordshire CC: dep ldr 1981–85, chm Social Services and Establishment Ctees; chm: Br Labour Gp Euro Parl 1987–88, Euro Parly Delgn for Relations with South Asia 1989; *Recreations* reading, travel; *Style*— George Stevenson; ✉ Stoke South Constituency Office, 2A Stanton Road, Meir, Stoke-on-Trent ST3 6DD (tel 01782 593393, fax 01782 593430, e-mail psteven745@aol.com)

STEVENSON, Hugh Alexander; *b* 7 September 1942; *Educ* Harrow, UC Oxford (BA); *m* 23 Oct 1965, Catherine, *née* Peacock; 2 s, 2 da; *Career* Linklaters & Paines slrs 1964–70, joined S G Warburg & Co 1970, dir S G Warburg Group plc 1987–95; chm: Mercury Asset Management Group plc 1992–98 (dir 1986–98), Equitas Ltd 1998–, The Merchants Tst plc 2000–; non-exec dir: Standard Life Assurance Co 1999–, FSA 2004–; tstee: Inst of Child Health Gen Charitable Tst, Stevenson Family's Charitable Trust, Welton Fndn, Sir Siegmund Warburg's Voluntary Settlement; *Style*— Hugh Stevenson, Esq; ✉ Equitas Limited, 33 St Mary Axe, London EC3A 8LL (tel 020 7342 2000)

STEVENSON, (Tallulah) Jessica Elina; *Educ* Kingston Coll; *Career* actress and writer; supporter of various charities incl Breast Cancer Res and Romanian Orphanage Fund; *Theatre* Night Heron (Royal Court) 2003; *Television* credits incl: Alice in Staying Alive 1995, Cheryl in The Royle Family 1996, Daisy in Spaced 1997–2000 (co-writer), Holly in Bob and Rose 2001; *Film* credits incl: Helga in Swing Kids 1992, midwife in Baby of Macon 1992, Victoria in Tomorrow La Scala; *Awards* Best Comedy Female Newcomer 1999, Best Comedy Actress 2001; nominated: Olivier Award 2003, BAFTA Award 2003; *Recreations* walking, church; *Style*— Miss Jessica Stevenson; ✉ c/o Jonathan Altaras Associates Ltd, 11 Garrick Street, London WC2E 9AR (tel 020 7836 8722)

STEVENSON, Juliet Anne Virginia; CBE (1999); da of Brig Michael Guy Stevens, MBE, and Virginia Ruth, *née* Marshall; *b* 30 October 1956; *Educ* Hurst Lodge Sch, St Catherine's Sch Bramley, RADA (Gold Bancroft Medal); *Partner* Hugh Brody; 1 da (Rosalind b 1994), 1 s (Gabriel b 2000); *Career* actress; currently assoc artist RSC; *Theatre* RSC 1978–86 incl: Madame de Tourvel in Les Liaisons Dangereuses, Rosalind in As You Like It, Cressida in Troilus and Cressida (nominated for Olivier Best Actress Award), Isabella in Measure for Measure (nominated for Best Actress Award, winner Drama Magazine Best Actress Award), Titania/Hippolyta in A Midsummer Night's Dream, Susan in The Witch of Edmonton, Clara Douglas in Money, Lady Percy in Henry IV Parts I and II, Miss Chasen in Once in a Lifetime, Yeliena in The White Guard, Aphrodite/Artemis in Hippolytus, Octavia/Iras in Antony and Cleopatra, Caroline Thompson in The Churchill Play; other credits incl: Emma/Betsy in Other Worlds (Royal Court) 1982, Paulina in Death and the Maiden (Royal Court and Duke of York's, Best Actress Time Out Awards and Olivier Awards 1992), Anna in Burn This (Hampstead/Lyric), Fanny in On the Verge (Sadler's Wells), title role in Yerma (NT) 1987 (nominated for Olivier Best Actress Award), Hedda in Hedda Gabler (NT) 1989, Galactia in Scenes from an Execution (Mark Taper Forum Los Angeles), The Duchess of Malfi (Wyndham's) 1995, The Caucasian Chalk Circle (RNT) 1997, Not I 1997, Footfalls 1997, Amanda in Private Lives (RNT) 1999, Corinne in The Country (Royal Court) 2000, A Little Night Music (NYC Opera) 2003, We Happy Few (Gielguld Theatre) 2004, The Alice Trilogy (Royal Court) 2005, The Seagull (RNT) 2006; *Television* for BBC incl: Nora in a Dolls House, Claire in The March, Rape Victim in Omnibus - Rape, Lucy Sadler in Aimée, Ruth in Out of Love, Hilda Spencer in Stanley, Rosalind in Life Story (winner Ace Cable TV Network Award Best Supporting Actress), Antigone in Oedipus at Colonus, title role in Antigone, Elizabeth Von Reitburg in Freud, Fliss in Bazaar and Rummage, Joanna Langton in Maybury, Stone Scissors Paper; other credits incl: Margaret in In The Border Country (Channel Four), Vicky in Living With Dinosaurs (Jim Henson Organisation, winner Emmy Award for Best Children's Film), Barbara Mallen in The Mallens (Granada), The Politician's Wife (Channel Four, The Broadcasting Press Guild Award for Best Actress 1996) 1995, Mother in Cider with Rosie (Carlton) 1998, Trial By Fire (ITV) 1999, The Road from Coorain 2001, The Pact (Lifetime TV) 2002, Hear the Silence 2003, Ordeal by Innocence 2007; *Films* incl: Nina in Truly Madly Deeply, Alice in Ladder of Swords, Cissie II in Drowning By Numbers, Fraulein Burstner in The Trial, Isobel in The Secret Rapture 1994, Mrs Elton in Emma 1996, Play (part of the Beckett on Film series) 2000, Bend It Like Beckham 2002, Food of Love 2002, Nicholas Nickleby 2002, Mona Lisa Smile 2003, Infamous 2005, Red Mercury Rising 2005, Pierrepoint 2005, When Did You Last See Your Father? 2007; *Books* Clamorous Voices (co-author, 1988), Shall I See You Again (co-ed, 1994); *Recreations* talking, walking, reading, piano, travelling, cinema, theatre, music; *Style*— Juliet Stevenson, CBE

STEVENSON, Rt Rev Dr Kenneth William; *see:* Portsmouth, Bishop of

STEVENSON, Michael Charles; s of Michael Anthony Stevenson, and Ena Elizabeth Stevenson, of Doncaster; *b* 14 August 1960; *Educ* Doncaster GS, ChCh Oxford (open scholarship, MA); *m* 1987, Deborah Frances, da of Baron Taylor of Gosforth (Life Peer, d 1997); 1 s (Thomas b 1991), 2 da (Celia b 1994, Beatrice b 1998); *Career* BBC: trainee BBC Radio Sport 1983–84, prodr Talks & Documentaries BBC Radio 1984–88, prodr On the Record BBC1 1988–90, chief asst Policy & Planning 1990–91, dep ed On the Record 1991–92, sec 1992–96, dep dir Regional Broadcasting 1996–99, dir Educn 1999–2003, jt dir Factual and Learning 2000–2003; DfES: dir Strategy and Communications 2003, dir technol and chief info offr 2005–06; vice-pres global educn and devpt Cisco Systems 2007–; memb Bd Resource (Cncl for museums, archives and libraries) 2000–06, non-exec dir Granada Learning 2007–; *Recreations* tennis, music; *Style*— Michael Stevenson, Esq; ✉ Cisco Systems, 9 New Square Park, Bedfont Lakes, Feltham, Middlesex TW14 8HA

STEVENSON, Patricia Mary; da of Dr Frank Bernard Anstey (d 1985), and Muriel Elizabeth, *née* Goodwin; *b* 17 December 1957, Bradfield, Berks; *Educ* Queen Anne's Sch Caversham, Univ of Surrey (BSc); *m* 29 June 1991, Gordon Cunningham Stevenson; 2 s (Luke Alexander Blackwood b 18 Oct 1994, Theodore James Anstey b 17 Aug 2000); *Career* sales exec Thomson Regnl Newspapers 1980–81, sr sales exec Mind Your Own Business Magazine 1981–84, advertisement mangr A La Carte magazine IPC Magazines 1984–87, head of business devpt Thames TV 1987–92; Condé Nast Pubns: promotions dir Tatler and Vanity Fair 1993–2000, publisher Tatler 2001–; *Recreations* skiing, horse riding, art, travelling, books; *Style*— Mrs Patricia Stevenson; ✉ Tatler, Condé Nast Publications Limited, Vogue House, Hanover Square, London W1S 1JU (tel 020 7152 3006)

STEVENSON, Robert Wilfrid (Wilf); s of James Alexander Stevenson (d 1993), and Elizabeth Anne, *née* Macrae (d 2006); *b* 19 April 1947; *Educ* Edinburgh Acad, UC Oxford (MA), Napier Poly pt/t (FCCA); *m* 1, 15 April 1972 (m dis 1979), Jennifer Grace, da of David Grace Antonio (d 1986), of Edinburgh; m 2, 19 April 1991, Elizabeth Ann, da of John Cavin Minogue, of Harrogate; 2 da (Iona Jane Minogue b 13 March 1992, Flora Kathleen Minogue b 19 Dec 1994), 1 s (Tobin James Minogue b 28 July 1993); *Career* res offr Univ of Edinburgh Students' Assoc 1970–74, sec Napier Univ Edinburgh 1974–87, dir: Br Film Inst 1988–97 (dep dir 1987–88), The Smith Inst 1997–; hon prof Univ of Stirling 1991–96; *Books* Gordon Brown Speeches 1997–2006 (ed, 2006), Moving Britain Forward (ed, 2006); *Recreations* cinema, bee keeping, gardening; *Style*— Wilf Stevenson, Esq; ✉ Missenden House, Little Missenden, Amersham, Buckinghamshire HP7 0RD (tel 01494 890689, fax 01494 868127, e-mail wilfstevenson@msn.com)

STEVENSON, (James Alexander) Stewart; MSP; s of James Thomas Middleton Stevenson (d 1990), and Helen Mary Berry, *née* MacGregor (d 1984); *Educ* Bell-Baxter Sch, Univ of Aberdeen (MA); *m* 1969, Sandra Isabel, *née* Pirie; *Career* with Bank of Scotland 1969–99 (positions incl: head of devpt servs, head of technol planning, dir of technol innovation); MSP (SNP) Banff & Buchan (by-election) 2001– (Scot Parl candidate Linlithgow 1999); min of transport, infrastructure and climate change Scottish Parliament 2007–; memb SNP 1961–; *Recreations* private flying, photography, public speaking; *Clubs* Town and County Banff, Edinburgh Flying; *Style*— Stewart Stevenson, Esq, MSP; ✉ Reidside, Ord, Banffshire AB45 3BL; 17 Maiden Street, Peterhead AB42 1EE (tel 01779 470444, fax 01779 474460, e-mail msp@stewartstevenson.net)

STEVENSON, Struan John Stirton; MEP (Cons) Scotland; s of Robert Harvey Ure Stevenson (d 1992), and Elizabeth, *née* Robertson Stirton (d 1986); *b* 4 April 1948; *Educ* Strathallan Sch Perthshire, West of Scotland Agric Coll Auchincruive Ayr (DipAg); *m* 9 Sept 1974, Patricia Anne, da of late Dr Alastair Taylor; 2 s (Ryan b 30 April 1977, Gregor b 2 July 1980); *Career* MEP (Cons) Scotland 1999– (Parly candidate (Cons): Carrick Cumnock & Doon Valley 1987, Edinburgh S 1992, Dumfries 1997; Euro Parly candidate (Cons) NE Scotland (by-election) 1998); pres Fisheries Ctee Euro Parl 2002–04; cncllr and gp ldr Convention of Scottish Local Authorities (COSLA) 1986–88; cncllr: Kyle & Carrick DC 1974–92 (ldr 1986–88), Girvan DC 1970–74; chm Scottish Cons Parly Candidates Assoc 1992–97; dir: J&R Stevenson Ltd 1968–, PS Communication Conslts Ltd 1994–99, Saferworld 1992–94; vice-pres European People's Party-European Democrats (EPP-ED) European Parly 2005–; memb NFU of Scotland, memb Advsy Ctee BBC Broadcasting Cncl 1984–88; Hon DSc State Medical Acad Semipalatinsk Kazakhstan 2000; Freedom City of Semipalatinsk Kazakhstan 2003, State Shapagat (Charity) Medal Repub of Kazakhstan 2007; *Recreations* contemporary art, music, opera, theatre, cinema, poetry, cycling, dogs; *Clubs* New (Edinburgh); *Style*— Struan Stevenson, Esq, MEP; ✉ European Parliament, Rue Wiertz, B-1047, Brussels (tel 00 322 284 7710, fax 00 322 284 9710, e-mail sstevenson@europarl.eu.int)

STEVENSON, Timothy Edwin Paul (Tim); OBE (2004), DL (Oxon 2007); s of Derek Stevenson, and Pamela, *née* Jervelund; *b* 14 May 1948; *Educ* Canford Sch, Worcester Coll Oxford (MA), London Business Sch (Sloan fell); *m* 1973, Marion Emma Lander, da of Robin Johnston; 3 da (Molly b 29 April 1979, Beatrice b 15 May 1982, Isobel b 12 July 1984); *Career* called to the Bar Inner Temple (Duke of Edinburgh scholar); Burmah Castrol plc: asst gp legal advsr 1975–77, gp planning mangr 1977–81, chief exec Castrol Spain 1981–85, mktg mangr 1985–86, corp devpt mangr 1986–88, chief exec Expandite Gp 1988–90, chief exec Fuels Gp 1990–93, dir Lubricants 1993–98, chief exec 1998–2000; chm: Travis Perkins plc 2001–, Morgan Crucible 2006–; non-exec dir: DfES 1997–2004, National Express Gp plc 2001–05, Partnerships UK plc 2001–04, Tribal Gp plc 2004–; chm of govrs Oxford Brookes Univ 2004–; memb Cncl of Mgmnt Oxford MOMA (latterly Modern Art Oxford) 1996–2004; *Recreations* hill walking, reading, music; *Clubs* Oxford and Cambridge; *Style*— Tim Stevenson, Esq, OBE, DL; ✉ Travis Perkins plc, Ryehill House, Ryehill Close, Lodge Farm Industrial Estate, Northampton NN5 7UA (tel 01604 752424)

STEVENSON, (Arthur) William; TD (1980), QC (1996); s of Arthur John Stevenson (d 1996), and Olivia Diana, *née* Serocold (d 1996); *b* 17 October 1943; *Educ* Marlborough, Trinity Coll Oxford (Evan Williams exhibitioner, MA); *m* 31 May 1969, Bridget Laura, da of late Laurence Frederick York; 1 da (Rebecca Clare b 25 April 1971), 2 s (Henry Laurence b 10 Jan 1973, Robert Frederick John b 13 April 1978); *Career* called to the Bar Lincoln's Inn 1968 (Hardwicke and Droop scholar, bencher 2001); in practice London, recorder of the Crown Court 1992–; *Recreations* country sports, skiing; *Style*— William Stevenson, Esq, TD, QC; ✉ Crown Office Chambers, Temple, London EC4Y 7HJ (tel 020 7797 8100, fax 020 7797 8101, e-mail wstevenson@crownofficechambers.com)

S

STEVENSON OF CODDENHAM, Baron (Life Peer UK 1999), of Coddenham in the County of Suffolk; Sir (Henry) Dennistoun Stevenson (Dennis); kt (1998), CBE (1981); s of Alexander James Stevenson, of Scotland, and Sylvia Florence, *née* Ingleby; *b* 19 July 1945; *Educ* Glenalmond Coll, King's Coll Cambridge (MA); *m* 15 Feb 1972, Charlotte Susan, da of Air Cdre Hon Sir Peter Beckford Rutgers Vanneck, GBE, CB, AFC; 4 s (Alexander, Heneage, Charles, William); *Career* chm: SRU Group 1972–96, Intermediate Technology Development Group 1984–90, AerFi Gp plc (formerly GPA Gp plc) 1993–2000, Pearson plc 1997–2005 (dir 1986–2005), HBOS plc (formerly Halifax plc) 1999– (non-exec dir 1999), Aldeburgh Music Ltd 2000–, House of Lords Appts Cmmn 2000–; dir: National Building Agency 1977–81, British Technology Group 1979–89, London Docklands Development Corporation 1981–88, Tyne Tees TV 1982–87, Manpower Inc (formerly Blue Arrow) 1988–2006, Thames Television plc 1991–93, J Rothschild Assurance plc 1991–99, English Partnerships 1993–99, British Sky Broadcasting Group plc 1994–2000, Cloaca Maxima Ltd 1996–2004, St James' Place Capital plc 1997–2002 (hon pres 2002–), Lazard Brothers 1997–2000, The Economist 1998–, Glyndebourne Productions Ltd 1998–, Schroder Ventures Ltd 2001–, London Qualifications Ltd 2003–04, Western Union Co 2006–; chm: Govt Working Pty on role of vol movements and youth in the environment 1971 (50 Million Volunteers (HMSO)), Independent Advsy Ctee on Pop Festivals 1972–76 (Pop Festivals, Report and Code of Practice (HMSO)), Aycliffe & Peterlee Corporation 1972–81, NAYC 1973–81, Intermediate Technology Devpt Gp 1983–90, Tstees of Tate Gallery 1988–98, Sinfonia 21 (formerly Docklands Sinfonietta) 1989–99, independent memb Panel on Takeovers and Mergers 1992–2000, British Cncl 1997–2003, Halifax plc 1999–; special advsr to PM and Sec of State for Educn on the use of Information Technology in Educn 1997–2000; memb Admin Cncl Royal Jubilee Tst 1978–80; govr LSE 1996–2002, govr London Business Sch 1999–2002; chllr London Inst (now Univ of the Arts London) 2000–; *Recreations* home; *Clubs* MCC, Brooks's; *Style—* The Rt Hon the Lord Stevenson of Coddenham, CBE; ✉ e-mail dennis@hdstevenson.co.uk

STEWART, Sir Alan D'Arcy; 13 Bt (I 1623), of Ramelton, Co Donegal; s (by 1 m) of Sir Jocelyn Harry Stewart, 12 Bt (d 1982); *b* 29 November 1932; *Educ* All Saints, Bathurst NSW; *m* 1952, Patricia, da of Lawrence Turner, of Ramelton; 2 s, 2 da; *Heir* s, Nicholas Stewart; *Career* yacht builder, marine engr; *Style—* Sir Alan Stewart, Bt; ✉ One Acre House, Church Street, Ramelton, Co Donegal

STEWART, Alastair James; OBE (2006); s of Gp Capt James Frederick Stewart, of Winslow, Bucks, and late Joan Mary, *née* Lord; *b* 22 June 1952; *Educ* St Augustine's Abbey Sch, Univ of Bristol; *m* 8 April 1978, Sally Ann, da of Frederick Harold Rudolph Jung (d 1968); 3 s (Alexander b 1982, Frederick b 1993, Oscar b 1997), 1 da (Clementine b 1985); *Career* dep pres NUS 1974–76; Southern Independent TV: editorial trainee 1976, industrial reporter and presenter of progs (incl Energy - What Crisis?) 1976–80; ITN: industrial corr 1980–82, newscaster (incl News at Ten and Channel 4 News) 1982–89 and 1990–92, Washington corr 1990; news anchor London News Network 1993–2004, currently newsreader London Tonight (ITV London); presenter: Missing (LWT/ITV Network) 1993–96, Alastair Stewart's Sunday (BBC Radio 5) 1994, The Sunday Programme with Alastair Stewart (GMTV) 1994, Police Stop! (Carlton TV/ITV Network) 1994, The Carlton Debates (Carlton TV) 1995, Police, Camera, Action! (Carlton TV/ITV Network) 1995–2003, Fire Live! (LWT/ITV Network) 1996, Devolution: The Future of the Union (LWT/ITV Network) 1997, Who Wants to be a London Mayor? (Carlton TV/LWT) 2000, King of the Castle (Carlton TV) 2001, ITV News Channel 2003, Live with Alastair Stewart (ITV News Channel), Cities at War (with Walter Cronkite, ITV) 2006, Legacy of War (with Walter Cronkite, ITV) 2007, ITV Lunchtime News and ITV News at 1030 2007–, The Moral of the Story (ITV) 2007–; presenter various news progs incl: The Budget 1982–92 and 2004–06, General Election 1987, 1992, 1997 and 2005, State Opening of Parliament 1988–89 and 2004–05 weddings of Prince of Wales and Duke of York, funeral of Pope John Paul II; subject of This is Your Life (BBC TV) 1999; Face of London Award RTS 2002, Presenter of the Year RTS 2004; vice-pres: Homestart UK, NCH Action for Children; patron: The Zito Tst, Lord Mayor Treloar Coll, HOPE, Samantha Dixon Tst, Loomba Tst 2005; vice-patron: Mental Health Fndn, SANE; tstee Just a Drop; memb Scrutiny Panel N and Mid Hants HA; govr Ravensbourne Coll; *Recreations* reading, music, antique maps; *Clubs* Reform, Century; *Style—* Alastair Stewart, OBE; ✉ ITN, 200 Gray's Inn Road, London WC1X 8XZ (tel 020 7833 3000)

STEWART, Sheriff Alastair Lindsay; QC (Scot 1995); s of Alexander Lindsay Stewart (d 1977); *b* 28 November 1938; *Educ* Edinburgh Acad, St Edmund Hall Oxford, Univ of Edinburgh; *m* 1, 1968 (m dis), Annabel Claire, da of Prof William McCausland Stewart (d 1989); 2 s; m 2, 1991, Sheila Anne, da of David Hynd Flockhart (d 1999), wid of William Neil Mackinnon; *Career* tutor Faculty of Law Univ of Edinburgh 1963–73, standing jr counsel Registrar of Restrictive Trading Agreements 1968–70, advocate depute 1970–73; Sheriff: South Strathclyde, Dumfries and Galloway at Airdrie 1973–79, Grampian, Highland and Islands at Aberdeen 1979–90, Tayside, Central and Fife at Dundee 1990–2004; temp judge Supreme Courts of Scotland 1996–, interim Sheriff Princ Lothian and Borders, Glasgow and Strathkelvin 2005; govr Robert Gordon's Inst of Technol 1982–90; hon prof Sch of Law Univ of Dundee 2001–; chm: Grampian Family Conciliation Serv 1984–87, Scottish Assoc of Family Conciliation Servs 1986–89; memb Judicial Studies Ctee 2000–04; ed Scottish Civil Law Reports 1992–95; *Books* The Scottish Criminal Courts in Action (1 edn 1990, 2 edn 1997), Macphail's Sheriff Court Practice (jt ed, 2 edn, vol 1 1998, vol 2 2002), Stair Memorial Encyclopaedia of the Laws of Scotland (Evidence reissue, 2006); *Recreations* reading, music, walking; *Clubs* New (Edinburgh); *Style—* Sheriff Alastair L Stewart, QC; ✉ 86 Albany Road, Broughty Ferry, Dundee DD5 1SQ (tel 01382 477580, e-mail als281138@aol.com)

STEWART, Sir Alastair Robin; 3 Bt (UK 1960), of Strathgarry, Co Perth; s of Sir Kenneth Dugald Stewart, 1 Bt, GBE (d 1972), and Noel, *née* Brodribb (d 1946); suc bro, Sir David Brodribb Stewart, 2 Bt (d 1992); *b* 26 September 1925; *Educ* Marlborough; *m* 1953, Patricia Helen, MBE, RIBA, da of late John Alfred Merrett, of Forest Green, Surrey; 3 da (Judith Patricia b 1954, Lucy Janetta b 1956, Catherine Helen b 1958), 1 s (John Kenneth Alexander b 1961); *Heir* s, John Stewart; *Career* Lt Royal Glos Hussars; md Stewart & Harvey Ltd (ret); *Clubs* Travellers; *Style—* Sir Alastair Stewart, Bt; ✉ Walter's Cottage, Little Baddow, Chelmsford, Essex CM3 4TQ

STEWART, Andrew Marshall (Andy); s of Dr John Stewart (d 1982), of Essex and Dr Mabel Stewart, *née* Linscott (d 1980); *b* 15 August 1951, London; *Educ* Felsted Sch, Mid-Essex Tech; *m* 4 Oct 1975, Judith, *née* Stewart; 2 s (Mark b 3 Aug 1978, Paul b 22 Jan 1981); *Career* stockbroker and ptnr Simon and Coates 1968–86, chief exec Chase Manhattan Securities (following merger) 1986–90, fndr and chief exec Collins Stewart 1991–2003 (led MBO and IPO 2000), fndr Cenkos Securities 2005–; memb London Stock Exchange; *Recreations* National Hunt horse racing (owner of 25 race horses); *Clubs* Royal Ascot; *Style—* Andy Stewart, Esq; ✉ Cenkos Securities, 6.7.8 Tokenhouse Yard, London EC2R 7AS (tel 020 7397 8989, fax 020 7397 8901, e-mail astewart@cenkos.com)

STEWART, Andrew William; s of William Stewart (d 2002), and Rose Stewart; *b* 27 December 1960; *Educ* Northolt HS, Hertford Coll Oxford, Inns of Court Sch of Law; *m* Mar 1992, Michelle; *Career* called to the Bar Middle Temple 1983; with Treasy Slrs Dept 1986–96 and 2000–, DTI 1997–2000; attends St Martin-in-the-Fields Church; *Style—* Andrew Stewart, Esq

STEWART, Angus; QC (Scot 1988); s of Archibald Ian Balfour Stewart, CBE (d 1998), and Ailsa Rosamund Mary Massey; *b* 14 December 1946; *Educ* Edinburgh Acad, Balliol Coll Oxford (BA), Univ of Edinburgh (LLB); *m* 14 June 1975, Jennifer Margaret, da of John Faulds Stewart (d 1980), of Edinburgh; 1 da (Flora b 13 Sept 1981); *Career* barr 1975–; keeper of the Advocate's Library 1994–2002; chm: Abbotsford Library Project 1995–2002, Scottish Cncl of Law Reporting 1997–2001; convenor Human Rights Ctee of Faculty of Advocates 2000–; tstee: Int E Boat Class Assoc 1993–, Nat Library of Scotland 1994–, Stewart Heritage Tst 1994–2001, Stewart Soc 1998–, Robert Louis Stevenson Club 2001–; *Publications* articles on law, history and literature; *Style—* Angus Stewart, Esq, QC; ✉ 8 Ann Street, Edinburgh EH4 1PJ (tel 0131 332 4083)

STEWART, Sir Brian John; kt (2002), CBE (1996); s of Ian Mann Stewart, and Christina Stewart; *b* 9 April 1945; *Educ* Perth Acad, Univ of Edinburgh (MSc); *m* 16 July 1971, Seonaid; 2 s (Alistair b 1974, Duncan b 1980), 1 da (Emily b 1976); *Career* articled clerk J & R Morison CAs Perth 1962–67, chief mgmnt accountant Ethicon Ltd Edinburgh 1969–76; Scottish and Newcastle plc: joined 1976, various commercial and financial positions in Scottish Brewers and William Younger subsids and Retail and Beer Prodn divisions, corp devpt dir 1985–88, gp fin dir 1988–91, gp chief exec 1991–2003, dep chm 1997–2000, exec chm 2000–03, non-exec chm 2003–; non-exec dir: Booker plc 1993–99, Standard Life Assurance Company 1993–2007 (non-exec chm 2003–07); chm Brewers' and Licensed Retailers' Assoc (formerly Brewers' Soc) 1996–98 (vice-chm 1994–96), vice-pres Br Beer & Pub Assoc; memb Ct Univ of Edinburgh 1991–98; MICAS 1967; *Recreations* golf, skiing; *Style—* Sir Brian Stewart, CBE; ✉ Scottish & Newcastle plc, 28 St Andrew Square, Edinburgh EH2 1AF (tel 0131 203 2000, fax 0131 203 2300)

STEWART, Callum John Tyndale; s of Air Vice-Marshal William Kilpatrick Stewart CB, CBE, AFC, QHP (d 1967), and Audrey Wentworth, *née* Tyndale (who m 2 1970, Sir Bryan Harold Cabot Matthews, CBE (d 1986); *b* 2 February 1945; *Educ* Wellington; *m* 1, 18 July 1975 (m dis 1982), Elaine Alison, da of Francis Bairstow (d 1979); m 2, 20 April 1991 (m dis 1998), Anna Rosemary, da of Peter Balmer (d 1995); 2 s (Rory William Kilpatrick b 13 Feb 1992, Finlay James Heriot b 19 May 1993); m 3, 21 April 2004, Licia Outtes Wanderley; *Career* exec dir Bland Welch & Co Ltd 1963–72; dir: CE Heath (International) Ltd 1972–75, Fielding & Ptnrs 1975–86 (dep chm 1984–86); md: Heath Gp plc (formerly CE Heath plc) 1997– (dir 1986–1998), Heath Lambert Reinsurance 1999–; *Recreations* music, travel, antiques; *Style—* Callum Stewart, Esq; ✉ Heath-Lambert Group, Friary Court, Cruched Friars, London EC3N 2NP (tel 020 7560 3338, fax 020 7560 3795)

STEWART, Danielle Caroline; da of Edward Elieza Harris, of London, and Deanna Sylvia, *née* Levy (now Mrs Morgan-Russell); *b* 6 November 1961; *Educ* Sutton HS for Girls GPDST, Nonsuch HS for Girls, Kingston Poly; *Children* 2 da (Francesca Anne Forristal b 19 Dec 1995, Isabelle Roberta Forristal b 8 Oct 1998); *Career* Myers Davis Chartered Accountants 1980–82, Halpern & Woolf Chartered Accountants 1982–84, Bright Grahame Murray 1985–87, self-employed 1987–88, ptnr Warrener Stewart 1988–2004 (conslt 2004–); dir: A Plus Ltd, A Plus Software Ltd, God in the Boardroom Ltd, Stratethica Ltd, Pentagon Protection plc; co sec Campus Media plc; devised and released Auditplus audit system 1991; memb: Accounting Standards Bd Ctee on Accounting for Smaller Entities (CASE) 1997–, Auditing Practices Bd Tech Advsy Gp; industrial fell Kingston Univ; winner Young Accountant of the Year Award 1994; FCA, FCCA; *Books* Auditplus (1991), A Practitioner's Guide to the Company Law Review (2002); *Recreations* spiritual matters generally; *Style—* Ms Danielle C Stewart; ✉ tel 07876 032222, e-mail daniellestewart@hotmail.com

STEWART, David John; s of John and Alice Stewart; *b* 5 May 1956; *Educ* Inverness HS, Paisley Coll (BA), Univ of Stirling (Dip Social Work, CQSW), Open Univ Business Sch (Dip Mgmnt); *m* 6 Aug 1982, Linda Ann, *née* MacDonald; 1 s (Andrew b 14 Jan 1987), 1 da (Kirsty b 1 Jan 1993), 1 s decd (Liam d 1991); *Career* social work asst Edinburgh 1980; social worker: Dumfries 1981–86, Dingwall 1986–87; team mangr Inverness 1987–97; MP (Lab) Inverness E, Nairn and Lochaber 1997–2005; cncllr Inverness DC 1988–96, govr Eden Court Theatre 1992–96; *Recreations* keep fit, sport, football, travel; *Style—* David Stewart, Esq; ✉ Queensgate Business Centre, Fraser Street, Inverness IV1 1DY (tel 01463 237441, fax 01463 237661)

STEWART, Capt Sir David John Christopher; 7 Bt (UK 1803), of Athenree, Tyrone; s of Sir Hugh Charlie Godfray Stewart, 6 Bt (d 1994), and his 1 w, Rosemary Elinor Dorothy, *née* Peacocke (d 1986); *b* 19 June 1935; *Educ* Bradfield, RMA Sandhurst; *m* 7 Nov 1959, Bridget Anne, er da of late Patrick Wood Sim; 3 da (Siobhan Amanda b 1961, Selina Godfray (Mrs Jeremy West) b 1964, Sophie Caroline (Mrs Jonathan A'Court-Wills) b 1966); *Heir* half-bro, Hugh Stewart; *Career* Capt (ret) Royal Inniskilling Fus (seconded Trucial Oman Scouts); sometime dir Maurice James (Hldgs) Ltd; hon treas Friends of Somerset SSAFA Forces Help (FOSS) 1998–2005; Medal of the Order of the Tower of Al Qasimi 2003; *Recreations* cricket, golf, music; *Clubs* MCC, XL, Royal N Devon Golf; *Style—* Capt Sir David Stewart, Bt; ✉ Tower View, 8 Silver Street, Wiveliscombe, Taunton, Somerset TA4 2PA

STEWART, David Purcell; s of Maurice Edward Stewart (d 1967), and Joyce Ethel Stewart (d 2000); *b* 8 September 1941; *Educ* Rutlish Sch Merton Park; *m* 14 Sept 1968, Judith Esther, da of Charles Owen (d 1983), of Bexleyheath, Kent; 1 da (Susannah Celia b 23 April 1977); *Career* chartered accountant; PricewaterhouseCoopers (formerly Deloitte Haskins & Sells and then Coopers & Lybrand): joined 1958, ptnr 1967–96, nat tax ptnr 1982–90, exec ptnr i/c Central London office 1990–94; chm Euro Human Resource Advsy Gp Coopers & Lybrand Europe 1994–98; dep chm Asda Property Holdings plc 1998–2001; dir ECB 2002–, chm Surrey CCC 2003– (treas 1997–2003); chm: Haig Homes 2000–, Tomorrow's People 2004–; tstee Royal Sch for the Deaf Margate 2005–; Freeman City of London 1982; FCA 1963, FInstD 1982; *Recreations* numismatics, theatre, opera, cricket; *Clubs* RAC, MCC; *Style—* David Stewart, Esq; ✉ 21 St Michaels, Wolfs Row, Limpsfield, Oxted, Surrey RH8 0QL

STEWART, Ed; *né* Mainwaring; s of R M Mainwaring (d 1989), of Church Knowle, Dorset, and Peggy Stewart, *née* Fraser; *b* 23 April 1941; *Educ* Glengyle Putney, Eagle House Sandhurst, St Edward's Sch Oxford; *m* Chiara Francesca Marinella, da of James McGrath Henney; 1 da (Francesca b 27 May 1975), 1 s (Marco Ray James b 23 March 1977); *Career* TV and radio presenter; capt Variety Club of GB Golfing Soc 1982 and 1983; Bait Rat Grand Order of Water Rats; nat pres PHAB; *Radio* Keith Prowse Records 1960–61; Hong Kong 1961–65: Radio Hong Kong, Commercial Radio, Rediffusion; Radio London (offshore) 1965–67; BBC Radio 1 1967–79: Junior Choice, Sunday Sport, Newsbeat, Roadshow; BBC Radio 2 1980–84 (Ed Stewart Show, Family Favourites), ILR Radio Mercury 1984–90, BBC Radio 2 1990–; *Television* Exit The Way Out Show (Rediffusion) 1967, Anything You Can Do (Granada) 1969, Stewpot (LWT) 1970–71, Ed and Zed (BBC) 1970, Crackerjack (BBC) 1975–79, Wish You Were Here (Thames) 1982–84; *Awards* Variety Club Broadcaster of the Year 1975, The Sun Top Children's Personality 1975; *Recreations* golf, cricket, tennis, football, cycling, travelling; *Clubs* Wig & Pen; *Style—* Ed Stewart, Esq; ✉ tel 07970 970890, e-mail ed.stewpot@virgin.net

STEWART, Prof Frances Julia; da of Nicholas Kaldor (d 1986), and Clarissa, *née* Goldschmidt (d 1995); *b* 4 August 1940; *Educ* Univ of Oxford (MA, DPhil, Webb Medley jr and sr prizes); *m* 23 June 1962, Michael Stewart, s of J I M Stewart; 3 da (Lucy b 1964, Anna b 1966 (decd), Kitty b 1970), 1 s (David b 1974); *Career* econ asst HM Treasy 1961–62, econ asst then advsr NEDO and Dept of Econ Affrs 1962–67, lectr Univ of Nairobi 1967–69; Queen Elizabeth House Univ of Oxford: sr research offr 1972–93, dir 1993–2003, dir Centre for Research on Inequality, Human Security and Ethnicity 2003–; fell Somerville Coll Oxford 1975–; overseer Thomas Watson Inst Brown Univ RI; pres Devpt

Studies Assoc 1990–92, memb UN Ctee for Devpt Policy; *Books* Technology and Underdevelopment (1976), Adjustment with a Human Face (jtly, 1987), War and Underdevelopment (jtly, 2001), Defining Poverty in the Developing World (jtly); *Recreations* gym, walking, children and grandchildren; *Style*— Prof Frances Stewart; ✉ Queen Elizabeth House, 3 Mansfield Road, Oxford OX1 3TB (tel 01865 281811, fax 01865 281801, e-mail frances.stewart@qeh.ox.ac.uk)

STEWART, Gordon; s of Archibald Leitch Stewart (d 1997), of Luton, Beds, and Christina Macpherson, *née* Taylor (d 1976); *b* 18 April 1953; *Educ* Luton GS, Univ of Durham (BA); *m* 2 Oct 1982, Teresa Violet, da of Sir James Holmes Henry, 2 Bt, CMG, MC, TD, QC (d 1997), of Hampton, Middx; 2 s (Edmund James b 24 May 1985, Roland Valentine b 16 Jan 1988); *Career* asst slr Slaughter & May 1978–83 (articled clerk 1976–78); ptnr: Simmons & Simmons 1985–99 (asst slr 1983–85), Richards Butler 1999–2004, Haarmann Hemmelrath 2004–06, conslt Squire, Sanders & Dempsey 2006–; memb Law Soc; *Recreations* motoring, food and wine; *Style*— Gordon Stewart, Esq; ✉ Squire, Sanders & Dempsey, Tower 42, 25 Old Broad Street, London EC2N 1HQ (tel 020 7382 4860, fax 020 7382 4833)

STEWART, Gordon Colin; s of Alan Alexander Fergus Stewart, of Glasgow, and Helen Somerville, *née* Curr; *b* 16 May 1956; *Educ* Buckhurst Hill Co HS, Hutchesons' Boys GS Glasgow, UC Oxford (MA); *m* 1987, Fiona Annabel, da of Jack Gatchfield (d 2003), of Welwyn Garden City, Herts; 2 da (Jessica b 1989, Amelia b 1995), 1 s (Alexander b 1992); *Career* ptnr: Cameron Markby 1983–88 (articled and asst slr 1978–83), Allen & Overy 1989–; pres Soc of Practitioners of Insolvency 1996–97; memb: City of London Slrs' Co, Int Bar Assoc 1995, INSOL International; hon memb Assoc of Business Recovery Professionals; *Books* Administrative Receivers and Administrators (1987), Leasing Law in the European Union (contrib, 1994), Directors in the Twilight Zone (ed and contrib, 2001, 2 edn 2005); *Recreations* running, golf, literature, humour; *Clubs* Roehampton, Holmes Place Health (Barbican); *Style*— Gordon Stewart, Esq; ✉ Allen & Overy LLP, One Bishops Square, London E1 6AO (tel 020 3088 0000, fax 020 3088 0088, e-mail gordon.stewart@allenovery.com)

STEWART, Ian; MP; s of John Stewart, and Helen, *née* Miller; *b* 28 August 1950; *Educ* Calder Street Secdy Sch Blantyre, Alfred Turner Secdy Modern Irlam, Stretford Technical Coll, Bolton Coll of Art and Design, Manchester Metropolitan Univ, Univ of Manchester (PhD in progress); *m* 9 Aug 1968, Merilyn, da of Arthur Holding, and Joyce Holding; 2 s (Robert b 14 Aug 1970, Alexander b 2 June 1977), 1 da (Lorna b 23 June 1979); *Career* apprentice electrician 1967–71; chemical plant operator: Lankro 1965–66, Shell Chemicals 1972–78; regnl offr T&GWU 1978–97; MP (Lab) Eccles 1997–; PPS to: Brian Wilson, MP 2001–03, Stephen Timms, MP 2003–05, Alan Johnson, MP (as Sec of State for Trade and Industry) 2005–06; Govt rep for defence sports; memb House of Commons: Deregulation Select Ctee 1997–, Information Select Ctee 1998–, Parly IT Ctee, Nominet Advsy Bd; chair: Gp for Vaccine Damaged Children, UK China Forum Industry Ctee; vice-chair All-Pty Br-China Gp 1997–, vice-chair All-Pty Gp on Kazakhstan, chair and fndr All-Pty Gp on Community Media, chair All Pty Parly Gp for the Prevention of Bullying and Work Related Violence, exec GB China Centre; visiting fell Univ of Salford; fndr Euro Fndn for Social Partnership and Continuing Trg Initiatives; memb: Int Soc of Industrial Rels, Manchester Industrial Rels Soc, UK Soc of Industrial Tutors, Cncl Euro Informatics Market (EURIM); fell Industry and Parliament Tst (placement with IBM); *Recreations* walking, running, reading, painting, tai chi, physical training traditions, music and performance events, research into religious, philosophical and political systems; *Style*— Ian Stewart, Esq, MP; ✉ House of Commons, London SW1A 0AA (tel 020 7219 6175, fax 020 7219 0903, e-mail ianstewartmp@parliament.uk)

STEWART, Prof Ian Nicholas; s of Arthur Reginald Stewart (d 2004), of Folkestone, Kent, and Marjorie Kathleen, *née* Diwell (d 2001); *b* 24 September 1945; *Educ* Univ of Cambridge (MA), Univ of Warwick (PhD); *m* 4 July 1970, Avril Bernice, *née* Montgomery; 2 s (James Andrew b 15 Nov 1973, Christopher Michael b 13 Jan 1976); *Career* Univ of Warwick: lectr 1969–84, reader 1984–90, prof 1990–; Humboldt fell Tübingen Univ 1974, visting fell Univ of Auckland 1976, assoc prof Univ of Connecticut Storrs 1977–78, prof Univ of Southern Illinois Carbondale 1978, prof Univ of Houston 1983–84; Gresham prof of geometry Gresham Coll 1994–98; delivered televised Royal Instn Christmas Lectures 1997; Michael Faraday Medal Royal Soc 1995, Jt Policy Bd for Mathematics Communications Award 1999, Gold Medal IMA 2000, Ferran Sunyer i Balaguer Prize Institut d'Estudis Catalans 2001, Chaos Award Liege 2001, Award for the Public Understanding of Science and Technol AAAS 2001; Hon DSc: Univ of Westminster 1998, Université Catholique de Louvain 2000, Kingston Univ 2003; fell AAAS 2001, FRS 2001; *Books* Nut-Crackers (with J Jaworski, 1971), Concepts of Modern Mathematics (1975), Get Knotted! (with J Jaworski, 1976), Catastrophe Theory and its Applications (with T Poston, 1978), The Problems of Mathematics (1987), Singularities and Groups in Bifurcation Theory (with M Golubitsky and D Schaeffer, 1988), Game, Set and Math (1989), Fearful Symmetry (with M Golubitsky, 1992), Another Fine Math You've Got Me Into (1992), The Collapse of Chaos (with J Cohen, 1994), Nature's Numbers (1995), From Here to Infinity (1996), Figments of Reality (with J Cohen, 1997), The Magical Maze (1997), Life's Other Secret (1998), The Science of Discworld (with Terry Pratchett, *qv*, and J Cohen, 1999), Wheelers (with J Cohen, 2000), Flatterland (2000), What Shape is a Snowflake? (2001), The Annotated Flatland (2001), The Symmetry Perspective (with M Golubitsky, 2002), The Science of Discworld 2: The Globe (with Terry Pratchett and J Cohen, 2002), Evolving the Alien (with J Cohen, 2002), Math Hysteria (2004), Heaven (with J Cohen, 2004), The Science of Discworld 3: Darwin's Watch (with Terry Pratchett and J Cohen, 2005), The Mayor of Uglyville's Dilemma (2005), Letters to a Young Mathematician (2006), How to Cut a Cake (2006), Why Beauty is Truth (2007); *Recreations* science fiction, guitar, geology, Egyptology; *Style*— Prof Ian Stewart; ✉ Mathematics Institute, University of Warwick, Coventry CV4 7AL (tel 024 7652 3740, fax 024 7652 4182, e-mail ins@maths.warwick.ac.uk)

STEWART, His Hon Judge James Simeon Hamilton; QC (1982); s of Henry Hamilton Stewart, MA, MD, FRCS (d 1970), and Edna Mary, *née* Pulman (d 2000); *b* 2 May 1943; *Educ* Cheltenham Coll, Univ of Leeds (LLB); *m* 1, 19 April 1972, Helen Margaret (d 1998), da of (Thomas) Kenneth Whiteley (d 1993); 2 da (Alexandra b 18 Jan 1974 d 2003, Georgina b 27 Nov 1975); *m* 2, 3 Jan 2006, Deborah Marion Rakusen, da of Harry Rose; *Career* called to the Bar Inner Temple 1966 (master 1992–); recorder of the Crown Ct 1982–2002, dep judge of the High Court 1993–, jt head of chambers 1996–2002, circuit judge (NE Circuit) 2002–, judge Court of Appeal (Criminal Div) 2005–; *Recreations* cricket, golf, gardening, tennis; *Clubs* Sloane, Bradford, Leeds Taverners, Royal Suva Yacht (Fiji); *Style*— His Hon Judge James Stewart, QC; ✉ Leeds Combined Court Centre, 1 Oxford Row, Leeds LS1 3BG

STEWART, Prof John David; s of David Stewart (d 1970), and Phyllis, *née* Crossley (d 1986); *b* 19 March 1929; *Educ* Stockport GS, Balliol Coll Oxford, Nuffield Coll Oxford; *m* 27 July 1953, Theresa, da of John Raisman (d 1980); 2 s (David b 7 Oct 1955, Henry b 27 June 1959), 2 da (Lindsey b 16 Feb 1957, Selina (Lady Hunt of Kings Heath) b 12 March 1962); *Career* Industrial Rels Dept NCB; Inst of Local Govt Studies Univ of Birmingham: sr lectr 1966–71, assoc dir 1970–76, prof 1971–96, dir 1976–83, hon prof 1996–99, emeritus prof 1999–; head of Sch of Public Policy Univ of Birmingham 1990–92; memb Academic Advsy Panel on Local Government DETR 1997–98, memb Layfield Ctee on Local Govt Fin, vice-pres RIPA 1988–92; *Books* British Pressure Groups (1958), Management in Local Government (1971), Corporate Planning in Local Government (with

R Greenwood, 1974), The Responsive Local Authority (1974), Approaches in Public Policy (jt ed with S Leach, 1982), The Case for Local Government (with G Jones, 1983), Local Government: Conditions of Local Choice (1983), The New Management of Local Government (1986), Understanding the Management of Local Government (1988, 2 edn 1995), The General Management of Local Government (with Michael Clarke, 1990), Choices for Local Government (with Michael Clarke, 1991), The Politics of Hung Authorities (with S Leach, 1992), Management in the Public Domain (with Stewart Ranson, 1994), The Changing Organisation and Management of Local Government (with Steve Leach and Keiron Walsh, 1994), Citizenship: Community, Rights and Participation (with David Prior and Keiron Walsh, 1995), Local Government in the 1990s (jt ed with G Stoker, 1995), The Nature of British Local Government (2000), Modernising British Local Government (2003); *Style*— Prof John Stewart; ✉ 15 Selly Wick Road, Birmingham B29 7JJ (tel 0121 472 1512)

STEWART, Sheriff John Hall; s of Cecil Francis Wilson Stewart (d 1964), and Mary Fyffe, *née* Hall; *b* 15 March 1944; *Educ* Airdrie Acad, Univ of St Andrews (LLB); *m* 29 Nov 1968, Marion, da of Donald MacCalman (d 1978); 1 s (Alan Breck b 1973) 2 da (Rohan Mhairi b 1975, Katryn MacCalman b 1978); *Career* enrolled slr 1971–77, advocate 1978–85; sheriff S Strathclyde Dumfries and Galloway: at Airdrie 1985–96, at Hamilton 1996–; memb Faculty of Advocates 1978; *Recreations* scuba diving, golf, spectator rugby football and soccer; *Clubs* Uddinton Rugby Football (past pres), Uddington Cricket and Sports (past pres); *Style*— Sheriff John H Stewart; ✉ 43 Grieve Croft, Bothwell, Glasgow G71 8LU (tel 01698 853854); Sheriff's Chambers, Sheriff Court House, Hamilton (tel 01698 282957)

STEWART, Sir John Young (Jackie); kt (2001), OBE (1972); s of Robert Paul Stewart (d 1972), and Jean Clark Young; *b* 11 June 1939; *Educ* Dumbarton Acad; *m* 1962, Helen McGregor; 2 s (Paul b 1965, Mark b 1968); *Career* former racing driver; memb Scottish and Br Team for clay pigeon shooting; former Scottish, English, Irish, Welsh and Br Champion, won Coupe des Nations 1959 and 1960; first raced 1961, competed in 4 meetings driving for Barry Filer Glasgow 1961–62, drove for Ecurie Ecosse and Barry Filer winning 14 out of 23 starts 1963, 28 wins out of 53 starts 1964, drove Formula One for Br Racing Motors (BRM) 1965–67 then for Ken Tyrrell 1968–73, has won Australian, NZ, Swedish, Mediterranean, Japanese and many other non-championship maj int motor races, set new world record by winning 26 World Championship Grand Prix (Zandvoort) 1973, 27 (Nürburgring) 1973, third in World Championship 1965, second in 1968 and 1972, World Champion 1969, 1971 and 1973; fndr Stewart Grand Prix; Br Automobile Racing Club Gold Medal 1971 and 1973, Daily Express Sportsman of the Year 1971 and 1973, BBC Sports Personality of the Year 1973, Segrave Trophy 1973 and 2000, Scottish Sportsman of the Year 1968 and 1973, USA Sportsman of the Year 1973; film: Weekend of a Champion 1972, Racing Stewart 1997; pres Scottish Dyslexia Tst, pres Dyslexia Scotland, vice-pres Br Dyslexia Assoc; fndr, tstee and chm Grand Prix Mechanics Charitable Tst, vice-pres Scottish Int Educn Tst; global ambass Royal Bank of Scotland 2004, ambass Rolex; dir Moët Hennessy UK Ltd; memb Int Advsy Bd Scottish Parl; chm Steering Ctee Cranfield Univ; pres Springfield Club; Hon PhD Lawrence Inst of Technol USA 1986, Hon PhD Glasgow Caledonian Univ 1993, hon degree Cranfield Univ 1998, hon dr Univ of Edinburgh 2006; Hon DEng: Heriot-Watt Univ 1996, Univ of Stirling 2001 (also hon prof); *Books* World Champion (with Eric Dymock, 1970), Faster! (with Peter Manso, 1972), On the Road (1983), Jackie Stewart's Principles of Performance Driving (with Alan Henry, 1986), The Jackie Stewart Book of Shooting (1991), Racing Stewart - The Birth of a Grand Prix Team (with Jon Nicholson & Maurice Hamilton, 1997); *Recreations* shooting, golf; *Clubs* RAC, RSAC, Br Racing Drivers' (pres 2000–06, vice-pres 2006–), Scottish Motor Racing (pres), R&A, Prestwick Golf, Gleneagles Golf, Loch Lomond Golf, Sunningdale Golf, Wentworth Golf, Ellesborough Golf, Geneva Golf, Domain & Imperial Golf; *Style*— Sir Jackie Stewart, OBE; ✉ c/o The British Racing Drivers' Club, Silverstone Circuit, Northamptonshire NN12 8TN

STEWART, Joseph Martin (Joe); OBE (1994); s of Joseph A Stewart (d 1990), and Annie M, *née* Friel; *b* 5 November 1955; *Educ* St Patrick's Coll Belfast, Queen's Univ Belfast (LLB), Univ of Ulster (DMS); *m* Sept 1978, Deirdre Ann, *née* Ritchie; *Career* dir Engrg Employers Fed NI Assoc Belfast 1985–90 (joined 1978), dir Harland & Wolff Shipbuilding and Heavy Industries Ltd Belfast 1990–95, sec and chief exec Police Authy for NI 1995–2001 (authy memb 1988–94, vice-chm 1990–94), sr dir of human resources Police Service of NI 2001–; dir Police Rehabilitation and Retraining Tst; memb Bd: Labour Relations Agency 1986–90, Justice Sector Skills Cncl; chm chm NI Country Gp; fndr memb NI Growth Challenge; former JP; FCIPD; *Recreations* game shooting, motorcycling, country pursuits; *Clubs* Reform; *Style*— Joe Stewart, Esq, OBE; ✉ Police Service of Northern Ireland, Department of Human Resources, 42 Montgomery Road, Belfast BT6 9LD (tel 028 9070 0928, fax 028 9070 0943)

STEWART, Marshall; s of Frederick Stewart (d 1988), and Gwendoline Miriam, *née* Bryant (d 2006); *m* 1977, Emma Christine, da of late J L Wood, of Harthill, S Yorks; *Career* ed Today prog BBC London 1970–74, chief ed IRN and LBC 1974–77, advsr IBA 1978, head of information BBC London 1978–82; Central Independent Television plc: dir of public affrs 1982–87, dir of corp strategy and main bd dir 1987–92, corp advsr 1992–94; dir: Central Television Enterprises 1988–94, Informed Sources International Ltd 1993–96, Earlybird Media Analysis Ltd 1996–; chm Harthill Communications Ltd 1992–, sr ptnr Harthill Partnership Ltd 2004–; memb: RTS, BAFTA, Assoc of European Journalists; *Recreations* theatre; *Clubs* Garrick; *Style*— Marshall Stewart; ✉ 3 Motcomb Street, London SW1X 8JU (mobile 07785 232831, e-mail msharthill@aol.com)

STEWART, Col (Robert) Michael; OBE (1973), TD (1964), DL (N Yorks 1996); s of Col Evan George Stewart, DSO, OBE (d 1958), of St Pauls Coll Hong Kong, and Dorothy Sarah, *née* Lander (d 1990); *b* 17 May 1931; *Educ* Monkton Combe Sch, UCL (BSc), Univ of London (Postgrad Dip); *m* 20 Oct 1962, (Vera) Patricia, da of Andrew Catley Hills (d 1983), of Sevenoaks, Kent; 2 da (Frances b 1963, Isobel b 1965); *Career* Army: cmmnd Royal Signals 1950, served in Austria and Germany 1950–51, in 56, 50 and 34 Signal Regts TA 1951–73, CO 34 Regt 1970–73, Col 1973; Dep Cmd: NE Dist TA 1973–76, 12 Signal Bde 1976–79; Cleveland County Cadet Cmdt 1979–84, Hon Col 34 Signal Regt 1981–88, Col Cmdt Royal Signals 1987–93, Hon Col Cleveland ACF 1992–2001; ICI: plant mangr 1956–59, design engr 1959–66, sec mangr 1966–74, mangr Supply Dept 1974–77, works engr 1977–78, works mangr 1978–81; gen mangr Phillips-Imperial Petroleum Ltd 1981–92, private sector liaison mangr City Challenge 1992–97; dir Tees and Hartlepool Port Authy 1985–94; chm: Royal Jubilee Tst Ctee for Cleveland 1981–85, 'Industry Year 1986' Steering Ctee for Cleveland; TAVRA: chm N England 1984–90, chm Cncl Jt Civilian Staff Ctee 1987–90, memb TAVR Advsy Ctee 1987–90, vice-chm Cncl 1988–90, tstee Cncl's Pension Fund 1992–98; civil rep Cncl of RFEA 1986–97; pres: Guisborough Branch Royal Br Legion 1989–, Cleveland SATRO 1990–99, E Cleveland Dist Scouts 1992–; vice-pres N Yorks Scouts 1998–, pres Cleveland Co Scouts 2002–; dir N Tees Health NHS Tst 1991–96; chm of govrs Prior Purseglove Coll 2001–03 (vice-chm 1992–2001), tstee 34 Signal Regt Tst 1980–, tstee Cleveland Community Fndn 1992–2006 (dep chm 1995–2006), govr HMS Trincomalee Tst 1993– (vice-chm 1994 chm 2000); chm: E Middlesbrough Community Venture Bd 1994–2002, Teesside Youth Devpt Prog 1994–2003; dir Archon 2000 Ltd 1997–2006; memb RFCA County Employers Liaison Team 1998–, chm Advsy Bd Local Network Fund for Children 2002–06, memb Bd Community Ventures Ltd 2002–, memb Bd HMS Trincomalee (1817) Enterprise Co Ltd

2007–; ADC to HM The Queen 1975–80; DL Cleveland 1975–96, High Sheriff of Cleveland 1990–91; MIEE 1960, MInstMC 1962, FRSA 1986; *Recreations* skiing, sailing, climbing; *Clubs* Army and Navy; *Style*— Col Michael Stewart, OBE, TD, DL; ✉ Hutton House, Hutton Gate, Guisborough, Cleveland TS14 8EQ (tel 01287 632420, fax 01287 207426, e-mail r.m.stewart@ntlworld.com)

STEWART, Mike (né Michael Stewart Mrowiec); s of Francis Joseph Mrowiec (d 1990), and Frances, *née* Lyall (d 2001); *b* 30 January 1946; *Educ* Henry Cavendish Sch Derby, Central Sch Derby, Sch for Business and Language Studies Oostkamp Bruges; *m* Barbara Kosilla; *Career* reporter and sports ed Staffordshire Advertiser and Chronicle 1965–71, chief reporter and news ed Staffordshire Newsletter 1971–73, sr newsman BRMB Radio Birmingham 1974–76, head of news and sport Beacon Radio Wolverhampton 1976–81, head of news and sport and prog controller Radio West Bristol 1981–84, prog controller Radio Broadland Norwich 1984–90, gp prog dir East Anglian Radio Group 1990–96 (comprising Broadland FM, SGR FM Ipswich and Bury St Edmunds, SGR Colchester and Amber Radio), md SGR (Suffolk Gp Radio) Ipswich and Bury St Edmunds and SGR Colchester 1996–2002, fndr dir and project mangr Norwich Radio Gp Ltd 2003–06; MInstD 1993; *Recreations* music, badminton, sport, films, food and wine; *Style*— Mike Stewart, Esq; ✉ e-mail mikeatturnpike@aol.com

STEWART, His Hon Judge Neill Alastair; yr s of James Robertson Stewart, CBE, and late Grace Margaret, *née* Kirsop; *b* 8 June 1947; *Educ* Whitgift Sch, Clare Coll Cambridge, Inns of Court Sch of Law; *m* 2000, Tiffany, da of His Hon W L Monro-Davies; 1 s, 1 da; *Career* grad engr Sir Alexander Gibb & Partners 1968–70; practising barr 1975–99; circuit judge (SE Circuit) 1999–; *Style*— His Hon Judge Stewart; ✉ Guildford Crown Court, Bedford Road, Guildford, Surrey GU1 4ST

STEWART, Nicholas John Cameron; QC (1987); s of John Cameron Stewart, and Margaret Mary, *née* Botsford; *b* 16 April 1947; *Educ* Worcester Coll Oxford (open exhibitioner), Cert Dip Accounting and Finance; *m* 1974 (m dis 2000), Pamela Jean, *née* Windham; 1 s (Senan 11 Dec 1981), 2 da (Rosalind 8 Feb 1984, Olivia 3 Aug 1986); *Career* called to the Bar Inner Temple 1971; Queen's Counsel 1987, dep High Court judge (Chancery Div) 1991–; chm Bar Human Rights Ctee of England and Wales 1994–98, pres Union Internationale des Avocats 2001–02; narrator/presenter No Further Questions (BBC Radio 4, two series); FCIArb; *Style*— Nicholas Stewart, Esq, QC

STEWART, Patrick Hewes; s of Alfred Stewart (d 1984), of Mirfield, W Yorks, and Gladys, *née* Barrowclough (d 1979); *b* 13 July 1940; *Educ* Mirfield Secdy Modern, Bristol Old Vic Theatre Sch; *m* 1966 (m dis 1992), Sheila Falconer; 1 s (Daniel b 20 Oct 1968), 1 da (Sophie b 29 June 1973); *Career* actor and dir; ceo Flying Freehold Productions; assoc artist RSC 1967 (now hon artist); chllr Univ of Huddersfield 2004; Hon DLit Pomona Coll, Hon DFA Santa Clara Univ, Hon DFA Julliard Sch NY; GQ Man of the Year (theatre) 1998; *Theatre* roles incl: King John, Shylock, Henry IV, Cassius, Titus Andronicus, Oberon, Othello, Leontes, Enobarbus (SWET Award), Touchstone and Launce, title role in Yonadab (NT) 1986; other credits incl: Who's Afraid of Virginia Woolf? (Young Vic) 1987 (London Fringe Best Actor Award), A Christmas Carol 1993 (Oliver Award Best Entertainment), The Tempest (NY) 1996, Othello (Washington DC) 1997, The Ride Down Mount Morgan (NY) 1998 and 2000 (Drama Desk Nomination), The Master Builder (Albery) 2003, The Caretaker (NY) 2003, A Life in the Theatre (Apollo) 2005; *Television* incl: I Claudius, Tinker Tailor Soldier Spy, Smiley's People, The Mozart Inquest, Oedipus Rex, The Devil's Disciple, Miss Julie, Hamlet, Star Trek: The Next Generation (two Best Actor Awards and a nomination American TV Awards, also dir various episodes of The Next Generation), The Canterville Ghost, Moby Dick (Emmy Best Actor nomination, Golden Globe Best Actor nomination), A Christmas Carol (Screen Actors Guild Nomination), Animal Farm, King of Texas, The Lion in Winter (nomination Best Actor Golden Globe and Screen Actors Guild Awards), Mysterious Island, Eleventh Hour; *Films* incl: Hedda, Dune, Lady Jane, Excalibur, LA Story, Death Train 1993, Robin Hood: Men in Tights 1993, Gun Men 1993, Jeffrey 1996, Star Trek: First Contact 1996, Dad Savage 1997, Conspiracy Theory 1997, Star Trek: Insurrection 1998, The Prince of Egypt 1998, X Men 2000, Jimmy Neutron: Boy Genius 2001, Star Trek: Nemesis 2002, X2 2003, Steamboy 2004; *Recreations* walking, scuba, travel; *Style*— Patrick Stewart; ✉ c/o ICM, Oxford House, 76 Oxford Street, London W1D 1BS (tel 020 7636 6565)

STEWART, Philippa Evelyn; da of Donald Valentine Sebastian Stewart, and Kennette Isabel McAlpin, *née* Ross; *Educ* Lycée Français de Londres, Univ of Sussex; *Career* Wayland Publishers 1971–73, B T Batsford 1973–76, Macdonald & Co Publishers 1976–89, Simon and Schuster International 1989–94, Watts Publishing Group 1995–; *Books* Florence Nightingale (1973), Great Britons: Florence Nightingale (1977), Past into Present: Immigrants (1977), Growing Up in Ancient Greece (1978); *Recreations* country walks, reading, sailing, yoga, friends; *Style*— Miss Philippa Stewart; ✉ Hachette Children's Books, 338 Euston Road, London NW1 3BH (tel 020 7053 6610, e-mail philippa.stewart@hachettechildrens.co.uk)

STEWART, (Col) Sir Robert Christie; KCVO (2002), CBE (1983), TD (1962); s of Maj Alexander C Stewart, MC (d 1927), of Arndean, Scotland, and Florence Hamilton, *née* Lighton (d 1982); *b* 3 August 1926; *Educ* Eton, Univ of Oxford (MA); *m* 21 May 1953, Ann Grizel, da of Air Chief Marshal Hon Sir Ralph Alexander Cochrane, GBE, KCB, AFC (d 1977); 3 s (Alexander (d 2004), John, David), 2 da (Catriona (Countess of Romney), Sara); *Career* Lt Scots Gds 1944–50, 7 Bn Argyll and Sutherland Highlanders TA 1951–65, Lt-Col 1963–66, Hon Col 1/51 Highland Volunteers 1972–75; landowner; HM Lord-Lt Kinross-shire 1966–74, HM Lord-Lt Clackmannanshire 1994–2002; chm Perth and Kinross CC (memb 1953–75), chm and pres Bd of Govrs East of Scotland Coll of Agric 1970–83; *Recreations* shooting, golf, the country; *Clubs* Royal Perth Golfing Soc, County; *Style*— Sir Robert Stewart, KCVO, CBE, TD; ✉ Arndean, Dollar, Clackmannanshire FK14 7NH (tel 01259 742527, fax 01259 743888)

STEWART, Robin Milton; QC (1978); s of Brig Guy Milton Stewart (d 1943), and Dr Elaine Oenone, *née* Earengey (d 2002); *b* 5 August 1938; *Educ* Winchester, New Coll Oxford (MA); *m* 8 Sept 1962, Lynda Grace, da of Arthur Thomas Albert Medhurst (d 1976); 3 s (Andrew Douglas Lorn b 1964, James Milton b 1966, Sholto Robert Douglas b 1969); *Career* called to the Bar: Middle Temple 1963 (bencher 1988), King's Inns Dublin 1975; prosecuting counsel to Inland Revenue (NE Circuit) 1976–78, recorder Crown Court 1978–99; head of chambers 1984–97; dir Bar Mutual Indemnity Fund Ltd 1988–93; memb Professional Conduct Ctee Bar Cncl 1991–93, chm Professional Negligence Bar Assoc 1991–93, former memb Hexham UDC and Tynedale DC; Parly candidate (Cons) Newcastle upon Tyne W 1974; tstee Parkinson's Disease Soc 1999–2002; Freeman City of London, Liveryman Worshipful Co of Glaziers 1966–98; *Recreations* gardens, Scottish family history; *Clubs* Oriental; *Style*— R M Stewart, Esq, QC; ✉ Kilburn House, 96 Front Street, Sowerby, Thirsk, North Yorkshire YO7 1JJ (tel 01845 522922); 199 Strand, London WC2R 1DR (tel 020 7379 9779, fax 020 7379 9481)

STEWART, Roderick David (Rod); CBE (2007); *b* 10 January 1945; *Career* singer and songwriter; apprentice Brentford FC 1961; performed with bands The Five Dimensions, The Hoochie Coochie Men, The Soul Agents, Steampacket, The Shotgun Express; albums: Truth (with Jeff Beck Group, 1967, reached UK no 8), Cosa Nostra - Beck Ola (with Jeff Beck Group, 1969, UK no 39), An Old Raincoat Won't Ever Let You Down (1969), First Step (with The Faces, 1970, UK no 45), Gasoline Alley (1970, UK no 62), Long Player (with The Faces, 1971, UK no 31), Every Picture Tells A Story (1971, UK no 1), A Nod's As Good As A Wink...To A Blind Horse (with The Small Faces, 1971, UK no 2), Never A Dull Moment (1972, UK no 1), Sing It Again Rod (compilation, 1973, UK no 1), Ooh La La (with Small Faces, 1973, UK no 1), Coast to Coast Overture And Beginners (live, with The Faces, 1974, UK no 3), Smiler (1974, UK no 1), Atlantic Crossing (1975, UK no 1), A Night On The Town (1976, UK no 1), The Best of The Faces (compilation, 1977, UK no 24), The Best of Rod Stewart (compilation, 1977, UK no 1), Foot Loose And Fancy Free (1977, UK no 3), Blondes Have More Fun (1978, UK no 3), Rod Stewart's Greatest Hits (1980, UK no 1), Foolish Behaviour (1980, UK no 4), Tonight I'm Yours (1981, UK no 8), Absolutely Live (1982, UK no 35), Body Wishes (1983, UK no 5), Love Touch (1986, UK no 5), Out of Order (1988, UK no 11), The Best of Rod Stewart (1989, UK no 3), Storyteller 1964–90 (box set, 1989), Vagabond Heart (1991, UK no 2), The Best of Rod Stewart (compilation, 1993, UK no 3), Unplugged...and Seated (live, 1993), Spanner in the Works (1995), When We Were the New Boys (1998), Every Beat of My Heart (2000), Human (2000), It Had To Be You...The Great American Songbook (2002), Sweet Little Rock N Roller (2002), As Time Goes By...The Great American Songbook, Vol 2 (2003), Stardust...The Great American Songbook, Vol 3 (2004); recipient of numerous awards, incl Best Traditional Pop Vocal Album (for Stardust...The Great American Songbook, Vol 3) Grammy Awards 2005; *Style*— Rod Stewart, Esq, CBE; ✉ c/o Warner Music, 28 Kensington Church Street, London W8 4EP (tel 020 7937 8844)

STEWART, Roger; QC (2001); s of Martin Neil Davidson Stewart (d 1983), and (Elizabeth) Janet King, *née* Porter; *b* 17 August 1963; *Educ* Oundle, Jesus Coll Cambridge (MA, LLM); *m* 18 June 1988, Georgina Louise, da of Dr Michael Pearce Smith; 2 s (Alexander b 16 Nov 1992, Samuel b 24 July 1995), 1 da (Victoria b 28 Nov 1997); *Career* called to the Bar Inner Temple 1986 (bencher 2003); recorder 2002–; *Books* Jackson & Powell on Professional Negligence (ed 3 edn 1992, ed 4 edn 1997, gen ed 2002); *Clubs* Nat Liberal, Lost Valley Mountaineering Assoc; *Style*— Roger Stewart, Esq, QC; ✉ 4 New Square, Lincoln's Inn, London WC2A 3RJ (tel 020 7822 2000, fax 020 7822 2001, mobile 07973 542981, e-mail r.stewart@4newsquare.com)

STEWART, Roy Irvine; CBE (1985), DL (1992); s of James Irvine Stewart (d 1976), of Tynemouth, and Ida Vera, *née* Pacey (d 1990); *Educ* South Shields Central HS; *Career* co sec to Bellway plc 1966–85, dir Mawson & Wareham (Music) Ltd 1972–, chm J G Windows Ltd 2006–; chm Northumbria Ambulance Serv Nat Health Tst 1990–94; chm Dio of Newcastle Parsonages Bd 1985–2006 (chm emeritus 2006); vice-pres Durham Scout Co Assoc 1997– (co cmmr 1972–91); memb Fairbridge Regnl Ctee 1993–; Tynemouth and Whitley Bay Cons Assoc: hon treas 1980–83, pres 1983–85 and 1996–2000, chm 1985–88, 1993–96 and 2000–03; chm of tstees Great N Air Ambulance Serv Appeal 1991–2006 (hon pres 2006); former JP N Tyneside; High Sheriff Tyne & Wear 1988–89; Freeman City of London 1989, Liveryman Worshipful Co of Chartered Accountants; FCA; *Recreations* music, bridge; *Clubs* Northern Counties; *Style*— Roy I Stewart, Esq, CBE, DL; ✉ Brockenhurst, 2 Broadway, Tynemouth NE30 2LD (tel and fax 0191 257 9791, e-mail roy.stewart8@btopenworld.com)

STEWART, Dr Sir (John) Simon Watson; 6 Bt (UK 1920), of Balgownie; er s of Sir (John) Keith Watson Stewart, 5 Bt (d 1990), and Mary Elizabeth, *née* Moxon; *b* 5 July 1955; *Educ* Uppingham, Charing Cross Hosp Med Sch (MD); *m* 3 June 1978, Catherine Stewart, da of (Henry) Gordon Bond, of Shiplake, Oxon; 1 s ((John) Hamish Watson b 12 Dec 1983), 1 da (Anna Rebecca Watson b 1 May 1987); *Heir* s, Hamish Stewart; *Career* conslt in clinical oncology St Mary's Hosp Paddington; sr lectr Imperial Coll Sch of Med London; Freeman City of London 1980, memb Worshipful Co of Merchant Taylors 1980; FRCP, FRCR; *Recreations* skiing, sail boarding, sailing; *Clubs* Oriental; *Style*— Dr Sir Simon Stewart, Bt; ✉ 8 Chiswick Wharf, London W4 2SR; Department of Oncology, St Mary's Hospital, Praed Street, London W2 1NY (tel 020 7886 1132)

STEWART, Stanley Charles; s of Rev William Henry Hawthorne Stewart (d 2003), of Kingston, Ontario, and Winifred Louise, *née* Ward (d 1994); *b* 14 November 1952, Ahoghill, NI; *Career* writer; Persian Royal Road expdn 1974–75, freelance feature writer Daily Telegraph and Sunday Times 1990–; FRGS 1980, FRSL 2002; *Books* Old Serpent Nile (1991), Frontiers of Heaven (1995, Thomas Cook Travel Book Award 1996), In the Empire of Ghengis Khan (2000, Thomas Cook Travel Book Award 2001, Benjamin Franklin Award 2003); *Clubs* Blacks; *Style*— Stanley Stewart, Esq; ✉ c/o The Sayle Agency, 8A King's Parade, Cambridge CB2 1SJ

STEWART, His Hon Judge Stephen Paul; QC (1996); s of Cyril Stewart (d 1994), and Phyllis Mary, *née* Hough; *b* 9 October 1953; *Educ* Stand GS Whitefield, St Peter's Coll Oxford (MA); *m* 5 July 1980, Dr M Felicity Dyer, da of (Anthony) Martyn Dyer; 1 da (Eleanor Catherine Anne b 3 Oct 1984), 1 s (Peter Edward John b 21 Dec 1989); *Career* called to the Bar Middle Temple 1975 (Harmsworth major exhibitioner and scholar), in practice Northern Circuit, recorder 1999–2003 (asst recorder 1995–99), dep judge of the Technol and Construction Ct 2000–03, designated civil judge and sr circuit judge (Northern Circuit) 2003–; *Recreations* running, music; *Style*— His Hon Judge Stephen Stewart, QC; ✉ Liverpool Combined Court Centre, The Queen Elizabeth II Law Courts, Derby Square, Liverpool L2 1XA

STEWART, Suzy; *b* 7 December 1963, London; *Educ* Wycombe Abbey, Univ of Queensland; *m* 23 March 1991, Andrew Stewart; *Career* slr; ptnr Clifford Chance LLP 2001–; memb: Law Soc of England and Wales, City of London Law Soc; *Style*— Mrs Suzy Stewart; ✉ Clifford Chance LLP, 10 Upper Bank Street, London E14 5JJ (tel 020 7006 4308, e-mail suzy.stewart@cliffordchance.com)

STEWART, Sir William Duncan Paterson; kt (1994); *b* 7 June 1935; *Educ* Dunoon GS, Univ of Glasgow (BSc, PhD, DSc); m; 1 s; *Career* asst lectr Univ of Nottingham 1961–63, lectr Univ of London 1963–68; Univ of Dundee: prof of biology 1968–94, vice-princ 1985–87; chief exec AFRC 1988–90; Cabinet Office: chief scientific advsr 1990–95, head of Office of Science and Technol 1992–95; ind conslt on science and technol; chm Dundee Teaching Hosps NHS Tst 1997–; pres Bioindustry Assoc 1995–; non-exec chm Cyclacel 1998–; non-exec dir Water Research Centre; memb: NERC, AFRC, Advsy Bd for Res Cncls, Advsy Cncl on Science and Technol, Royal Cmmn on Environmental Pollution, NEDO Working Pty on Biotechnology, Cabinet Ctee on Science and Technol, Official Ctee on Science and Technol, MAFF Priorities Bd, Def Scientific Advsy Ctee, DTI Innovation Advsy Bd, Energy Advsy Ctee on R&D, BNSC Res Bd, EC Res Cncl, corp technol Bd SmithKline Beecham; author of over 300 scientific pubns; 20 hon degrees from univs incl Univ of Edinburgh and Univ of Glasgow; CBiol; FRS, FRSE 1973; *Recreations* observing homo sapiens; *Clubs* Athenaeum, Dundee United; *Style*— Sir William Stewart, FRS, FRSE; ✉ Dundee Teaching Hospitals NHS Trust, Ninewalls Hospital, Dundee DD1 9SY (tel 01382 660111)

STEWART, William Gladstone; *b* 15 July 1935; *Educ* Shooters Hill GS London, Woolwich Poly London; *m* 1, 1960 (m dis 1976), Audrey Ann, da of Charles Harrison; 1 s (Nicholas b 1961); 2 other c (Barnaby 1976, Hayley b 1980); m 2, 1997, Laura, da of John Calland; 2 da (Isobel b 1989, Hannah b 1994); *Career* RAEC King's African Rifles 1952–55; Redcoat Butlins 1958, BBC TV 1958–67 (directors' course 1965), freelance prodr, broadcaster and writer 1967–; co-fndr (with Colin Frewin) Sunset and Vine 1976, fndr md Regent Productions 1982 (sold to Pearsons 1999); prodns incl: The Frost Programme, David Frost, Live from London, Father Dear Father, Bless This House, The Price is Right, The Thoughts of Chairman Alf, Tickets for the Titanic, The Lady is a Tramp, The Nineteenth Hole 1988–2003, Fifteen-to-One (also presenter); presenter Georgian Giants - 19th Century Sport (BBC Radio 4) 2005; lectures: on Restitution of the Parthenon Marbles (EP Strasbourg, UNESCO Paris, Smithsonian Inst Washington, NY, Athens and London), Inst of Art and Law Annual Lecture 2000, lecture tour USA and Canada (8 cities) 2003; pres The Media Soc 2003–05; FRTS 1996 (elected to Hall of Fame 2000); *Recreations* the English language, classical history, music, tennis, gardening, riding; *Clubs* Reform; *Style*— William G Stewart, Esq; ✉ PO Box 429, New Malden, Surrey KT3 9AW (tel 020 8942 4280)

STEWART, Prof William James; s of James W Stewart, of Hindhead, Surrey, and Margaret M Stewart; *b* 13 July 1947; *Educ* Blundell's, Imperial Coll London (BSc, MSc); *m* 1976, Dr Jill A Stewart, da of F E Chapman; 2 c (Alexander b 6 June 1983, Antonia b 1 May 1986); *Career* conslt, chief scientist Marconi plc (joined 1971), chm Innos 2004–; visiting prof: UCL, Univ of Southampton; contrib to numerous books and jls; granted numerous patents for inventions in field of optics; memb Editorial Advsy Bd Science; chm ECOC IOOC 1997; Worshipful Co of Scientific Instrument Makers award for achievement; fell Optical Soc of America, MIEEE LEOS, MIEE, MInstD; FREng 1989; *Recreations* woodwork; *Style*— Prof William Stewart, FREng; ✉ Manor House, High Street, Blakesley, Northamptonshire NN12 8RE (mobile 07801 716578, e-mail w.stewart@ieee.org)

STEWART-CLARK, Sir John (Jack); 3 Bt (UK 1918), of Dundas, W Lothian; s of Sir Stewart Stewart-Clark, 2 Bt (d 1971), and Jane Pamela, *née* Clarke (d 1993); *b* 17 September 1929; *Educ* Eton, Balliol Coll Oxford, Harvard Business Sch; *m* 1958, Lydia, da of James William Loudon, of Valkenswaard, The Netherlands; 4 da (Daphne (Mrs Nicholas Stephenson) b 1959, Nadia (Mrs Patrick J Waterfield) b 1963, Zarina (Mrs Richard S Noel) b 1965, Natalie b 1969), 1 s (Alexander Dudley b 1960); *Heir* s, Alexander Stewart-Clark; *Career* late Coldstream Gds; Parly candidate (Cons & Unionist) Aberdeen N 1959; MEP (EDG): E Sussex 1979–94, E Sussex and Kent S 1994–99; treas European Democratic Gp 1979–92, vice-pres European Parliament 1992–97; chm EP Delgn to Canada 1979–82, vice-chm EP Delgn to Japan 1986–89; ctee spokesman on: external affrs 1979–83, institutional affrs 1983–85, youth, culture, educn and media 1989–92, civil liberties 1992–99; md: J & P Coats (Pakistan) Ltd 1961–67, J A Carp's Garenfabrieken (Helmond) Holland 1967–70, Philips Electrical Ltd London 1971–75, Pye of Cambridge Ltd 1975–79; dir: Cope Allman International Ltd 1980–83, Oppenheimer International Ltd 1980–84, Low & Bonar 1982–95, AT Kearney Management Consultants 1985–92, Pioneer Concrete Holdings Ltd 1989–2000; chm Dundas Castle Ltd 1999–; memb Bd Tstee Savings Bank Scotland 1986–89; former memb Cncl RUSI, chm Supervisory Bd European Inst for Security 1984–86, tstee dir European Centre for Work and Soc 1983–; chm: EPIC (European Parliamentarians and Industrialists Cncl) 1984–99, European Action Cncl for Peace in the Balkans 1994–96; pres CRONWE (Conf Regnl Orgns of NW Europe) 1987–93; memb Bd of Govrs European Inst for the Media, memb Bd of Mgmnt European Monitoring Centre for Drugs and Drug Addiction (EMCDDA) 2000–06; jt prodr open air play The Life of Jesus Christ (annually) 2003–06; tstee Mentor Fndn (UK); memb Queen's Bodyguard for Scotland (Royal Co of Archers); *Publications* European Competition Law (jtly), It's My Problem as Well: Drugs Prevention and Education (jtly); *Recreations* golf, tennis, music, travel, vintage cars; *Clubs* Landsdowne; *Style*— Sir Jack Stewart-Clark, Bt; ✉ Dundas Castle, South Queensferry, Edinburgh EH30 9SP (tel 0131 331 1114, fax 0131 331 2670)

STEWART-SMITH, John Ronald; s of Maj James Geoffrey Stewart-Smith (d 1938), of Falcon Hill Kinver, Worcs, and Bertha Mabel Milner, *née* Roberts; *b* 23 February 1932; *Educ* Marlborough, New Zealand; *m* 22 Oct 1955, Catherine May, da of Walter Douglas Montgomery Clarke, JP (d 1948), of Bombay, India; 1 s (Geoffrey b 1958), 2 da (Joanna b 1960, Nicola b 1962); *Career* gp mktg dir Glover Gp Ltd 1976–79, projects dir and co sec Dashwood Finance Co Ltd 1983–, dir Kowloon Shipyard Co Ltd 1983–2003; CEng, MIMechE 1967, MIEx 1974, FIMarE 1989 (MIMarE 1969); *Recreations* bridge, tennis, skiing; *Style*— John Stewart-Smith, Esq; ✉ Dashwood Finance Co Ltd, Georgian House, 63 Coleman Street, London EC2R 5BB (tel 020 7588 3215, fax 020 7588 4818)

STEWARTBY, Baron (Life Peer UK 1992), of Portmoak in the District of Perth and Kinross; Sir (Bernard Harold) Ian Halley Stewart of Stewartby; kt (1991), RD (1972), PC (1989); s of Prof Harold Charles Stewart of Stewartby, CBE, DL (d 2001), and his 1 w Dorothy Irene, *née* Löwen (d 1969); *b* 10 August 1935; *Educ* Haileybury, Jesus Coll Cambridge (MA), Univ of Cambridge (LittD); *m* 8 Oct 1966, Hon Deborah Charlotte Stewart, JP, 2 da of 3 Baron Tweedsmuir (2 s of 1 Baron Tweedsmuir, otherwise known as John Buchan, the author); 2 da (Hon Lydia Barbara Rose Anne Phoebe (Mrs Charles Pretzlik) b 1969, Hon (Dorothy) Louisa Charlotte Amabel (Mrs Andrew Elder) b 1970), 1 s (Hon Henry Ernest Alexander Halley b 1972); *Career* served RNVR 1954–56, Lt-Cdr RNR; with Seccombe Marshall & Campion (bill brokers) 1959–60; chm: The Throgmorton Trust plc 1990–2005, Delian Lloyd's Investment Trust plc 1993–95; dep chm: Standard Chartered plc 1993–2004, Amlin plc 1995–2006; dir: Brown Shipley & Co (merchant bankers) 1971–83, Diploma plc 1990–, Portman Building Society 1995–2002; dir FSA 1993–97; MP (Cons): Hitchin Feb 1974–83, N Herts 1983–92; oppn spokesman Banking Bill 1978–79, PPS to Rt Hon Sir Geoffrey Howe (as Chllr of the Exchequer) 1979–83, under sec MOD (Def Procurement) Jan-Oct 1983, econ sec Treasy with special responsibility for monetary policy and fin instns 1983–87, min of state for the Armed Forces 1987–88, min of state NI 1988–89; memb: Public Expenditure Ctee 1977–79, Public Accounts Ctee 1991–92; former jt sec Cons Parly Fin Ctee, tstee Parly Pension Fund 2000–05; chm Br Acad Ctee for Sylloge of Coins of Br Isles 1993–2003 (memb 1967–), chm Treasure Valuation Ctee 1996–2001, vice-chm Westminster Ctee Protection of Children 1975–92; vice-pres Herts Soc 1974–, vice-pres St John Ambulance Herts 1978–; memb Cncl Haileybury 1980–95 (life govr 1977); tstee Sir Halley Stewart Tst 1978– (pres 2002–); hon fell Jesus Coll Cambridge 1994; FBA 1981, FRSE 1986, FSA, FSA Scot, KStJ 1992 (CStJ 1986); *Books* The Scottish Coinage (1955, 2 edn 1967), Coinage in Tenth-century England (with C E Blunt and C S S Lyon, 1989); *Recreations* history, real tennis; *Clubs* New (Edinburgh), Beefsteak, MCC, Hawks' (Cambridge); *Style*— The Rt Hon Lord Stewartby, PC, RD, FRSE, FSA, FBA; ✉ House of Lords, London SW1A 0PW

STEYN, David Andrew; s of John Hofmeyr Steyn, and Daphne Mary, *née* Nelson; *b* 13 September 1959; *Educ* Robert Gordon's Coll Aberdeen, Univ of Aberdeen (LLB); *m* 9 June 1990, Tanya Susan, da of Elisabeth and Lyon Roussel; 3 da (Elisabeth Daphne b 28 March 1991, Sophie Rebecca b 1 Oct 1996, Emily Charlotte b 10 Oct 1998), 1 s (James Philip b 17 Oct 1992); *Career* global head client serv and mktg, exec vice-pres and memb Exec Ctee Alliance Bernstein LP; *Recreations* theatre, opera, chess; *Clubs* Athenaeum; *Style*— David Steyn, Esq; ✉ 70 Lansdowne Road, London W11 2LR

STEYN, Baron (Life Peer UK 1995), of Swafield in the County of Norfolk; Sir Johan Steyn; kt (1985), PC (1992); *b* 15 August 1932; *Educ* Jan van Riebeeck Sch Cape Town, Univ of Stellenbosch (BA, LLB), UC Oxford (Cape Province Rhodes scholar, MA); *m* Susan Leonore, *née* Lewis; 2 s and 2 da by prev m; *Career* barr South Africa 1958–73 (sr counsel), barr England 1973–, QC 1979, bencher Lincoln's Inn 1985, judge of the High Court of Justice (Commercial Court) 1985–91, Supreme Court Rule Ctee 1985–89, presiding judge Northern Circuit 1989–91, Lord Justice of Appeal 1992–95, Lord of Appeal in Ordinary 1995–2005, memb Essex Court Chambers 2005–; chm: Race Rels Ctee of Bar 1987–88, Departmental Advsy Ctee on Arbitration Law 1990–94, Lord Chllr's Advsy Ctee on Legal Educn and Conduct 1994–96, Cncl Justice 2005–; hon memb: American Law Inst 1999, Soc of Legal Scholars 2002; Hon LLD: Queen Mary & Westfield Coll London 1993–94, UEA 1998; hon fell UCL 2005; *Style*— The Rt Hon the Lord Steyn, PC; ✉ House of Lords, London SW1A 0PW; Essex Court Chambers, 24 Lincoln's Inn Fields, London WC2A 3EG

STIBBON, Gen Sir John James; KCB (1988), OBE (1977); s of Jack Stibbon (d 1939), and Elizabeth Matilda, *née* Dixon (d 1968); *b* 5 January 1935; *Educ* Portsmouth Southern GS, RMA Sandhurst, RMCS (BSc Eng); *m* 10 Aug 1957, Jean Fergusson, da of John Robert Skeggs, of Newquay, Cornwall; 2 da (Jane b 1958, Emma b 1962); *Career* cmmnd RE 1954, Staff Capt War Office 1962–64, Adj 32 Armd Engr Regt 1964–66, instr RAC Centre 1967–68, OC 2 Armd Engr Sqdn 1968–70, DAA md QMG 12 Mech Bde 1971–72, GSO1 (DS) Staff Coll 1973–75, CO 28 Amphibious Engr Regt 1975–77, Asst Mil Sec MOD 1977–79, Cmd 20 Armd Bde 1979–81, RCDS 1982, Cmdt RMCS 1983–85, Asst Chief of Def Staff (operational requirements) MOD 1985–87, Master Gen of the Ordnance 1987–91, Chief Royal Engr 1993–99; Col Cmdt: RAPC 1985–92, RPC 1986–91, RE 1988–99; chm: Royal Star and Garter Home 1991–96, Gordon Sch Fndn 1992–2002; cmmr DYRMS 1993–98; dir Chemring Group plc 1993–2005; chm ITT Defence Ltd 1993–2004; hon vice-pres FA 1987–93, pres Milocarian Athletic Club 1999–; Hon DSc CIT 1989, Hon DSc Univ of Greenwich 2002; CEng, FICE 1989; *Recreations* watercolour painting, association football, palaeontology; *Clubs* Army and Navy; *Style*— Gen Sir John Stibbon, KCB, OBE; ✉ Clifton House, Vicarage Lane, Shrivenham, Swindon, Wiltshire SN6 8DT

STIBY, Robert Andrew; OBE (2007), JP (1976); s of Maj Arthur Robert Charles Stiby, TD, JP (d 1987), and Peggy, *née* Hartley (d 1973); *b* 25 May 1937; *Educ* Marlborough, London Coll of Printing (Dip Printing Mgmnt); *m* 1, 1962 (m dis 1976); 1 s (Jonathan b 10 May 1963), 1 da (Emma b 17 Sept 1965); m 2, 1980 (m dis 1984); m 3, 1986, Julia, da of Sidney Fuller (d 2005), of Canterbury; *Career* Nat Serv 1955–57; md and chm Croydon Advertiser Group of Newspapers 1969–83; chm: Radio Investments Ltd 1972–99, The Local Radio Company Ltd 1996–99, Tindle Radio Ltd 2000–06; dir: Capital Radio 1972–2001, Talk Radio UK 1994–99, Channel 103 2000–06, Midlands Radio 3 (Ireland) 2002–; chm and dir Idyllwild Town Crier (US) 2004–; pres: Newspaper Soc 1983–84, Croydon Boys' Club 1988–93; dir Fairfield Halls 1993–96; chm: Jesse Ward Fndn, Rosetti Fndn; chm of govrs London Coll of Printing 1979, govr Br Sch 2001–07; fell Radio Acad 2001; *Recreations* hill walking, sailing, painting; *Clubs* Reform, MCC; *Style*— Robert Stiby, Esq, OBE; ✉ Priory Barn, Old Standlynch Farm, Downton, Salisbury, Wiltshire SP5 3QR (tel 01722 711959)

STICHBURY, Jane; CBE (2004), QPM (2000); *Career* Met Police Serv 1977–99 (latterly Dep Asst Cmmr Central Area), Chief Constable Dorset 1999–, HM Inspr of Constabulary 2004–; vice-chair Skills for Justice; tstee Streetwise/Police Partnership Tst; memb St John Cncl Dorset; *Style*— Mrs Jane Stichbury, CBE, QPM; ✉ HM Inspectorate of Constabulary South of England Region, White Rose Court, Oriental Road, Woking, Surrey GU22 7PJ

STICKLAND, Prof Neil Charles; s of Henry Frank Stickland (d 1997), of Torquay, Devon, and Audrey Fay, *née* Pinney; *b* 17 October 1949; *Educ* Torquay Boys' GS, Bedford Coll London (BSc), Univ of Hull (PhD), Univ of Edinburgh (DSc); *m* 27 Oct 1973, Margaret Rosamund, da of Arthur Robert Oliver; 3 da (Elizabeth Emma b 28 April 1976, Sarah Caroline b 10 Oct 1978, Rosemary Laura b 20 June 1982); *Career* research asst Zoology Dept Univ of Hull 1970–73; lectr in veterinary anatomy: Univ of Nairobi Kenya 1974–77, Royal (Dick) Sch of Veterinary Studies Univ of Edinburgh 1977–83; RVC Univ of London: sr lectr in veterinary anatomy 1984–94, prof of veterinary anatomy 1994–, head Dept of Veterinary Basic Sciences 1996–2001 and 2003–05, vice-princ research 2002–03; visiting lectr Dept of Veterinary Science Univ of Dar es Salaam Tanzania 1979, visiting assoc prof in anatomy and cellular biology Tufts Univ Boston USA 1982–83; Share-Jones Lecture 1995; author of approx 100 pubns in scientific jls and books (mostly on devpt and growth of skeletal muscle); memb: Anatomical Soc of GB and I 1980 (memb Cncl 1995–99), World Assoc of Veterinary Anatomists 1985, Euro Assoc of Veterinary Anatomists 1990; *Books* Color Atlas of Veterinary Anatomy: Vol 3: The Dog and Cat (jtly, 1996); *Recreations* walking, DIY; *Style*— Prof N C Stickland; ✉ The Royal Veterinary College, Royal College Street, London NW1 0TU (tel 020 7468 5200, fax 020 7468 5204, e-mail nstickland@rvc.ac.uk)

STIGWOOD, Robert Colin; s of late Gordon Stigwood, of Beaumont, Adelaide, and Gwendolyn Burrows; *b* 1934; *Educ* Sacred Heart Coll; *Career* theatre, film, television and record producer; came to England 1956, subsequently held a variety of jobs incl mangr halfway house for delinquents in Cambridge, opened talent agency in London 1962, first independent record prodr in England with release of single Johnny Remember Me (liquidated firm 1965), business mangr Graham Bond Orgn, co-md NEMS Enterprises 1967, fndr Robert Stigwood Orgn 1967, fndr RSO Records 1973, dir Polygram 1976; Int Prodr of Year (ABC Interstate Theatres Inc) 1976; *Stage Musicals* in England and US incl: Oh! Calcutta, The Dirtiest Show in Town, Pippin, Jesus Christ Superstar, Evita, Sweeney Todd, Grease, Saturday Night Fever; *Television* in England and US incl: The Entertainer, The Prime of Miss Jean Brodie (series); *Films* incl: Jesus Christ Superstar, Bugsy Malone, Tommy, Saturday Night Fever, Grease, Sgt Pepper's Lonely Hearts Club Band, Moment by Moment, The Fan, Times Square, Grease 2, Staying Alive, Gallipoli, Evita; *Recreations* sailing, tennis; *Style*— Robert Stigwood, Esq; ✉ Robert Stigwood Organisation Ltd, Barton Manor, East Cowes, Isle of Wight PO32 6LB (tel 01983 280676, fax 01983 293923)

STIHLER, Catherine Dalling; MEP (Lab) Scotland; da of Gordon McLeish Taylor, of Wishaw, and Catherine Doreen, *née* Sanders; *b* 30 July 1973; *Educ* Coltness HS Wishaw, Univ of St Andrews (MA, MLitt); *m* 14 April 2000, David Thomas Stihler, of Salinas, CA; *Career* rep Young Labour Scottish Labour Pty Exec 1993–95, pres Univ of St Andrews Students' Assoc 1994–95, rep Young Labour NEC Labour Pty 1995–97, Parly candidate (Lab) Angus 1997, PA to Anne Begg, MP, *qv*, 1997–99; MEP (Lab) Scotland 1999–, memb Ctees on Environment and Fishing, temp memb Euro Parl Ctee on foot and mouth disease; ed Parliament magazine 2002–; hon pres CAVOC (Lanarkshire based umbrella voluntary organisation); memb: AMICUS, Co-op Pty, Fabian Soc, Euro Movement; *Publications* A Soldier and a Women, chapter in Women and the Military (2000); *Recreations* films, going to the gym, reading and playing backgammon; *Style*— Mrs Catherine Stihler, MEP; ✉ Constituency Office: Music Hall Lane, Dunfermline KY12 7NG (tel 01383 731890, fax 01383 731835, e-mail cstihler@europarl.eu.int, website www.cstihlermep.com)

STILES, George; s of John Leslie Stiles (d 1967), of Haywards Heath, W Sussex, and Joy Irene, *née* Baker (d 1985); *b* 9 August 1961; *Educ* Gresham's, Univ of Exeter (BA); *partner* Hugh Vanstone, *qv*; *Career* composer; memb: BASCA, Musicians Union, Equity, PRS, Mercury Musical Developments; *Theatre* credits with lyricist Anthony Drewe incl: Tutankhamun (Northcott Theatre & Imagination Building London) 1984, Just So (produced by Cameron Mackintosh 1989 and 1990, North Shore Music Theatre 2001, Chichester Festival Theatre 2004) 1985, Honk! (Watermill Theatre 1993, Stephen Joseph Theatre Scarborough 1997, RNT Olivier 1999, UK Tour 2001 (dir Julia McKenzie, *qv*) productions worldwide incl USA, Japan, Far East, South Africa, Israel, Scandinavia), Peter Pan (Copenhagen) 1999 and (Royal Festival Hall, recorded for BBC Radio 3) 2001, Christmas Season at Royal Festival Hall 2002, new songs and additional music Mary Poppins (Prince Edward Theatre and New Amsterdam Broadway) 2004; song contribs incl: The Challenge (Shaw Theatre) 1992, The Mercury Workshop Musical Revue (Jermyn Street) 1994, The Shakespeare Revue (RSC, Barbican, Vaudeville, nat tour); credits with lyricist Paul Leigh incl: Moll Flanders (Lyric Hammersmith 1993, Theatre Royal York 1995 and 1996), Tom Jones (Theatre Royal York 1996 and North Shore Music Theatre 2004), The Three Musketeers (premiere Stadttheater St Gallen Switzerland 2000, San Jose California 2001); other credits incl: composer for Twelfth Night and Uncle Vanya (Sam

S

Mendes' farewell season at Donmar Warehouse) 2002, musical dir and composer for Barry Humphries' Look at me when I'm Talking to You, composer for Habeas Corpus (Donmar Warehouse); musical supervisor for Peter Pan & The Three Musketeers; *Recordings* Honk!, Moll Flanders, The Shakespeare Revue, The Challenge, We Can Be Kind, Musical of the Year, Hey Mr Producer, The Three Musketeers (US cast album), Mary Poppins (London cast album); *Awards* Vivian Ellis Prize (for Just So), TMA Regional Theatre Award for Best Musical (for Moll Flanders) 1995, The Orchestra's Prize and Best Song (for Peter Pan), 2nd Prize Musical of the Year (for The Three Musketeers) 1996, Lawrence Olivier Award for Best New Musical 2000, Elliot Norton Award for Outstanding Musical (for Honk!) 2001; *Publications* Moll Flanders (Samuel French, 1995), Honk! (Weinberger's, 1998), The Three Musketeers (Weinberger's, 1999), Just So (MTI, 2000); *Style*— George Stiles, Esq; ✉ c/o ML2000, 19 Magravine Gardens, London W6 8RL (tel 020 8741 0606, fax 020 8741 7443, e-mail assistant@ml2000.org.uk, website www.stilesanddrewe.com)

STIMPSON, Robin Mackay; WS; *Educ* Dundee HS, Univ of St Andrews (LLB); *Career* admitted slr 1971; specialises in property and charity law; ptnr: Farquharson Craig & Co 1973–74, Anderson Strathern 1975– (currently managing ptnr and head Residential Property Dept); sometime tutor in practical conveyancing and legal practice as a business Univ of Edinburgh Legal Practice Unit; legal advsr Nat Tst for Scot; chm Edinburgh Slrs Property Centre (ESPC) 2002– (dir 1997–2001), dir Investors in People Scotland 2005–; *Style*— Robin Stimpson, Esq, WS; ✉ Anderson Strathern, 1 Rutland Court, Edinburgh EH3 8EY (tel 0131 625 7220, fax 0131 270 7788, e-mail robin.stimpson@andersonstrathern.co.uk)

STIMSON, Theresa Josephine (Tess); da of Michael Stimson, and Jane, *née* Bower (d 2001); *b* 17 July 1966; *Educ* Notre Dame Convent Sch Lingfield, St Hilda's Coll Oxford; *m* 1, 17 July 1993 (m dis 2002), Brent Sadler, *qv*; 2 s (Henry Louis Brent Stimson Sadler b 7 Sept 1994, Matthew Alexander Brent Stimson Sadler b 12 Sept 1997), 1 da (Lily Jane Isabeau Stimson Oliver b 12 Sept 2002); m 2, 23 Dec 2005, Erik Oliver; *Career* prodr ITN 1987–91; assignments incl: King's Cross fire 1987, Purley rail disaster 1988, European elections 1989, Thatcher resignation 1990, Gulf war 1990–91, McCarthy and Mann Beirut hostage releases 1991, Northern Ireland 1987–91; author, freelance journalist and lectr 1991–; assignments incl: Waite release 1991, South Africa 1992–94, Somalia famine 1992–93, Iraq 1992–93, Lebanon 1997–99, UK features and book reviews 2000–; adjunct prof of creative writing Univ of South Florida 2002–05; *Books* Yours Till the End (Sunnie and Jackie Mann biography, 1992); *Novels* Hard News (1993), Soft Focus (1995), Pole Position (1996), The Adultery Club (2007), The Infidelity Chain (2008); *Recreations* scuba diving, rock climbing, tennis, water and snow skiing; *Clubs* Golds; *Style*— Tess Stimson; ✉ 4700 Sunrise Drive South, St Petersburg, Florida 33705, USA (e-mail tessjstimson@aol.com, website www.tessstimson.com)

STING, *né* Gordon Matthew Sumner; CBE (2003); *b* 2 October 1951; *m* 20 Aug 1992, Trudie Styler, *qv*; 2 s, 2 da; 1 s and 1 da from previous m; *Career* musician and actor; teacher St Paul's Primary Sch Cramlington 1971–74, memb The Police 1977–86; Police albums: Outlandos D'Amour (1978, reached UK no 6), Regatta De Blanc (1979, UK no 1), Zenyatta Mondatta (1980, UK no 1), Ghost In The Machine (1982, UK no 1), Synchronicity (1983, UK no 1), Every Breath You Take - The Singles (compilation, 1986, UK no 1), Message In A Box - Complete Recording Sessions (1993), The Police Live (1995); solo albums: Dream Of the Blue Turtles (1985, UK no 1), Bring On The Night (live, 1986), Nothing Like The Sun (1987, UK no 1), The Soul Cages (1991, UK no 1), Ten Summoner's Tales (1993), Demolition Man (1993), Fields of Gold - The Best of Sting 1984–94 (1994), The Living Sea (IMAX movie soundtrack), Mercury Falling (1996), Brand New Day (1999), All This Time (live, 2001), Sacred Love (2003); films: Quadrophenia 1979, Radio On 1980, Brimstone And Treacle 1982, Dune 1984, The Bride 1985, Plenty 1985, Bring On The Night (concert) 1985, Julia and Julia 1987, Stormy Monday 1988, Julia 1988, Mercury Falling 1996, Gentlemen Don't Eat Poets 1997, Lock Stock and Two Smoking Barrels 1999; winner of numerous awards incl: Ivor Novello, BRIT, Grammy (16 awarded in total 1980–2000), BMI (10 awarded in total 1984–2000), Oscar nomination for Best Song for Until (from the film Kate and Leopold) 2002; co-fndr Rainforest Fndn; Hon DMus Univ of Northumbria at Newcastle; *Style*— Sting; ✉ c/o Publicity Department, Polydor Records, 72–80 Black Lion Lane, London W6 9BE

STIRK, Graham; *Educ* Oxford Poly (BA), AA Sch of Architecture (Dip Arch), Kingston Poly; *Career* architect; Richard Rogers Partnership: joined 1983, dir 1988, sr dir 1995; *Projects* incl: Wellcome Fndn HQ Cobham, London Patternoster Sq Competition, Tokyo Forum Competition, Potsdammer Platz Masterplan, Zoofenster Berlin, Lloyds Register of Shipping Liphook, SmithKline Beecham Masterplan, Montevetro apartments Battersea, Padre Pio Pilgrimage Cathedral Foggia Italy, Daiwa II, Rome Congress Hall Competition, Waterside Paddington; *Style*— Graham Stirk, Esq; ✉ Richard Rogers Partnership, Thames Wharf, Rainville Road, London W6 9HA

STIRLING, Sir Angus Duncan Aeneas; kt (1994); s of Duncan Alexander Stirling (d 1990), and Lady Marjorie Stirling (d 2000); *b* 1933; *Educ* Eton, Trinity Coll Cambridge, Univ of London (Dip History of Art); *m* 1959, Armyne Morar Helen, er da of William and Hon Mrs Schofield, of Masham, N Yorks; 1 s, 2 da; *Career* former dep sec Gen Arts Cncl of GB, DG The Nat Tst 1983–95 (dep dir 1979–83), chm ROH Covent Garden 1991–96 (dir 1979–96), sr policy advsr Nat Heritage Meml Fund 1996, chm Greenwich Fndn for the Royal Naval Coll 1996–2003; pres Somerset Branch CPRE 2001–; chm: Friends of Covent Garden 1981–91, Policy Ctee CPRE 1996–2001, Jt Nature Conservation Ctee 1997–2002; memb: Bd of Govrs Byam Shaw Sch of Art 1965–90, Advsy Cncl LSO 1979–, Crafts Cncl 1980–85, Bd of Govrs Courtauld Inst of of Art 1981–83 and 2002–, Live Music Now 1982–89, Theatres' Trust 1983–90, Heritage of London Trust 1983–95, Heritage Educn Trust 1985–96, Samuel Courtauld Trust 1990–, Govt Task Force on Tourism and the Environment 1991, Tourism Ctee Int Cncl on Monuments and Sites (ICOMOS) UK 1993–2002, Cncl Royal Sch of Church Music 1996–98, Fabric Advsy Ctee Wells Cathedral 2001–; Royal Ballet: memb Bd 1979–96 (dep chm 1989–91), govr 1988–96; tstee: World Monuments Fund in Britain 1996–, Stowe House Preservation Trust 1998–; memb Bd of Govrs: Gresham's Sch 1999–2007, City and Guilds of London Art Sch 2003–; pres Friends of Holland Park 2003–, vice-patron Almshouses Assoc 1999–, memb Cncl Kensington Soc 2002–; hon fell Trinity Coll of Music 2004; memb Ct of Assts Worshipful Co of Fishmongers 1991– (Prime Warden 2004–05); Hon DLit: Univ of Leicester 1995, Univ of Greenwich 2002; FRSA; *Clubs* Beefsteak, Garrick, Brooks's, Grillions; *Style*— Sir Angus Stirling; ✉ 25 Ladbroke Grove, London W11 3AY

STIRLING, Prof Charles James Matthew; s of Brig Alexander Dickson Stirling, DSO (d 1961), and Isobel Millicent, *née* Matthew (d 1984); *b* 8 December 1930; *Educ* Edinburgh Acad, Univ of St Andrews (BSc), KCL (PhD, DSc); *m* 1 Sept 1956, Eileen Gibson, da of William Leslie Powell (d 1974), of Bournemouth, Dorset; 3 da (Catherine (decd), Julia, Alexandra); *Career* res fell: Civil Serv Porton 1955–57, ICI Edinburgh 1957–59; lectr in chemistry Queen's Univ Belfast 1959–65, reader in organic chemistry KCL 1965–69, head of dept UCNW 1981–90 (prof of organic chemistry 1969–90), prof of organic chemistry Univ of Sheffield 1990–98 (head Dept of Chemistry 1991–94, prof emeritus 1998–); RSC: pres Perkin Div 1989–91, chm Confs Ctee; pres: Section B (Chemistry) BAAS 1990, Millennium Cmmn Award 1999; chm: Menai Bridge Cncl of Churches 1982–83, Bangor Monteverdi Singers 1974–89; delivered Royal Instn Christmas Lectures (BBC 2) 1992; memb Organic Div Int Union of Pure and Applied Chemistry 1991–95; Hon DSc: Univ of St Andrews 1994, Univ of Aix-Marseille 1999, Univ of Sheffield 2007; public orator Univ of Sheffield 1995–; hon fell Univ of Wales Bangor 2004; hon memb Società Chimica Italiana 2003; FRS 1986, FRSC 1967; *Books* Radicals in Organic Chemistry (1965), Organosulphur Chemistry (ed, 1975), Chemistry of the Sulphonium Group (ed, 1982), Chemistry of Sulphones and Sulphoxides (ed with S Patai and Z Rappoport, 1988); *Recreations* choral music, collection of chiral objects, furniture restoration; *Style*— Prof Charles Stirling, FRS; ✉ Department of Chemistry, University of Sheffield, Sheffield S3 7HF

STIRLING, Prof (William) James; CBE (2006); s of John Easton Stirling (d 1972), and Margaret Eleanor, *née* Norris; *b* 4 February 1953, Belfast; *Educ* Belfast Royal Acad, Peterhouse Cambridge (entrance scholarship, Thomas Parke scholar in mathematics, John Worthington student in mathematics, MA), Univ of Cambridge (Smith's Prize in mathematics, PhD); *m* 30 July 1975, Paula Helene, *née* Close; 1 s (Thomas John b 5 July 1981), 1 da (Helena Rachael b 3 March 1983); *Career* research assoc Physics Dept Univ of Washington Seattle 1979–81, research fell Dept of Applied Mathematics and Theoretical Physics Univ of Cambridge 1981–83; Theory Div CERN Geneva: fell 1983–85, staff memb 1985–86; Univ of Durham: lectr 1986–89, sr lectr 1989–90, reader 1990–92, prof of mathematical sciences and physics 1992–, dir Inst for Particle Physics Phenomenology (IPPP) 2000– (memb Steering Ctee 2000–), memb Senate 2000–, chm Research Ctee Dept of Physics 2003–, chm HEPDATA Database Mgmnt Ctee 2003– (memb 1986–); memb: Ctee Nuclear and Particle Physics Div Inst of Physics 1997–99, Sectional Ctee 2 Royal Soc 2000–03 (chm 2003), Physics Panel Research Assessment Ctee 2001, Research Fellowships Panel A(i) Royal Soc 2002–; PPARC: memb Theory Sub-Ctee 1987–90, memb Particle Physics Ctee 1987–90 and 1998–2001, memb Educn and Trg Ctee 1998–2001, memb CERN Fellowship Panel 1998–2001, memb Panel to Review Sr Research Physicists in the Particle Physics Dept at Rutherford Appleton Lab 2001, chm Science Ctee 2001–03; memb numerous int conf advsy ctees; SERC/PPARC Sr Fellowship 1993–98, Humboldt Research Award 1997; pres Soc of Fells Univ of Durham 2003–, memb Bd of Govrs Royal GS Newcastle upon Tyne 1998–; FInstP 1992, FRS 1999; *Publications* QCD and Collider Physics (1996); numerous research pubns in learned jls; *Recreations* travelling, listening to and playing Irish music; *Style*— Prof James Stirling, CBE; ✉ Institute for Particle Physics Phenomenology, Department of Physics, University of Durham, Science Laboratories Site, South Road, Durham DH1 3LE (tel 0191 334 3811, fax 0191 334 3658, e-mail w.j.stirling@durham.ac.uk)

STIRLING-HAMILTON, Sir Malcolm William Bruce; 14 Bt (NS 1673), of Preston, Haddingtonshire; o s of Sir Bruce Stirling-Hamilton, 13 Bt (d 1989), and Stephanie (who m 2, 1990, Anthony Cole Tinsley), eldest da of Dr William Campbell, of Alloway, Ayrshire; *b* 6 August 1979; *Educ* Stowe, Univ og Loughborough; *Heir* kinsman, Rev Andrew Hamilton; *Style*— Sir Malcolm Stirling-Hamilton, Bt; ✉ The Old Rectory, North Creake, Fakenham, Norfolk NR21 9JJ

STIRLING OF GARDEN, Col Sir James; KCVO, CBE, TD; s of Col Archibald Stirling of Garden, OBE, JP, DL (d 1947); *b* 8 September 1930; *Educ* Rugby, Trinity Coll Cambridge; *m* 1958, Fiona Janetta Sophia, da of Lt-Col D A C Wood Parker, OBE, TD, DL (d 1967), of Keithick, Coupar Angus, Perthshire; 2 s, 2 da; *Career* cmmnd 1 Bn Argyll and Sutherland Highlanders 1950, served Korea (wounded), transferred 7 Bn (TA) 1951, Lt-Col cmdg 1966, CO 3 Bn 1968; hon Col 3/51 Highland Vols TA; Scottish dir Woolwich Building Soc 1977–97, ptnr Kenneth Ryden and Ptnrs (chartered surveyors) 1961–89, dir Scottish Widows Soc 1976–97; pres Highland TAVRA 1991–97 (chm 1982–87); DL Stirlingshire 1969, HM Lord-Lt of Stirling and Falkirk 1983–2005; Hon Sheriff of Stirling 1998; Hon Guild Brother Guildry of Stirling 1995; Hon DUniv Stirling 2004; Prior of the Order of St John of Jerusalem in Scotland 1995; FRICS; GCStJ; *Clubs* New (Edinburgh); *Style*— Col Sir James Stirling of Garden, KCVO, CBE, TD; ✉ Garden, Buchylvie, Stirling (tel 01360 850212)

STIRRAT, Prof Gordon Macmillan; s of Alexander Stirrat (d 1989), and Mary Caroline, *née* Hutchinson (d 1987); *b* 12 March 1940; *Educ* Hutchesons GS Glasgow, Univ of Glasgow (MB ChB), Univ of Oxford (MA), Univ of London (MD); *m* 2 April 1965, Janeen Mary, da of Hugh Brown (d 1983); 3 da (Lorna Margaret b 1966, Carolyn Jane b 1967, Lindsay Ann b 1970); *Career* lectr Univ of London 1970–75, clinical reader Univ of Oxford 1975–82; Univ of Bristol: prof of obstetrics and gynaecology 1982–2000, dean Faculty of Med 1990–93, pro-vice-chllr 1993–97, vice-provost Inst for Advanced Studies 1998–2003, sr res fell Centre for Ethics in Medicine 2000–; memb: South West RHA 1984–90, Bristol & Weston Health Authy 1990–91, Bristol & Dist Health Authy 1991–96, GMC 1993–97, Christian Med Fellowship; FRCOG 1981; *Books* Obstetrics Pocket Consultant: Aids to Obstetrics & Gynaecology, Notes on Obstetrics and Gynaecology; *Recreations* fly fishing, walking, writing, photography; *Style*— Prof Gordon Stirrat; ✉ Malpas Lodge, 24 Henbury Road, Westbury-on-Trym, Bristol BS9 3HJ (tel 0117 950 5310, fax 0117 950 9196, e-mail gstirrat@blueyonder.co.uk)

STIRRUP, Air Chief Marshal Sir Graham Eric (Jock); GCB (2005, KCB 2002, CB 2000), AFC (1983); s of William Hamilton Stirrup, and Jacqueline Brenda, *née* Coulson; *b* 4 December 1949; *Educ* Merchant Taylors', RAF Coll Cranwell, JSDC (1984), RCDS (1993), Higher Command and Staff Course (1994); *m* 4 Sept 1976, Mary Alexandra, da of James Elliott; 1 s (James Elliott b 13 June 1978); *Career* cmmnd RAF 1970, various flying appts UK, Middle East and USA 1971–84, OC 2 Sqn RAF Laarbruch Germany 1985–87, PSO to CAS 1987–90, CO RAF Marham 1990–92, dir Air Force Plans and Progs MOD 1994–97, AOC No 1 Gp RAF 1997–98, Asst Chief of Air Staff 1998–2000, Dep C-in-C Strike Command 2000–02, DCDS (Equipment Capability) 2002–03, CAS 2003–06, CDS 2006–; ADC; DSc 2005; FIMgt 1983, FRAeS 1991; *Recreations* golf, music, history; *Clubs* Commonwealth, RAF; *Style*— Air Chief Marshal Sir Jock Stirrup, GCB, AFC, ADC, DSc

STIRRUPS, David Robert; s of Robert James Stirrups (d 1987), and Eunice Nora, *née* Palmer; *b* 23 June 1948; *Educ* Gillingham GS, Univ of Sheffield (BDS), Open Univ (BA), Sheffield Poly (MSc); *m* 22 July 1971, Anne Elizabeth; 2 da (Kathleen b 1975, Rosemary b and d 1978), 1 s (Robert b 1980); *Career* conslt orthodontist Gtr Glasgow Health Bd 1980–93, currently prof of orthodontics Univ of Dundee; chm Scot Ctee for Hosp Dental Servs 1988–93; memb: Central Ctee for Hosp Dental Servs 1988–93, Dental Cncl RCPS (Glasgow) 1988–92 and 1999–, Gen Dental Cncl 1999–; FDSRCS 1974, RCPS (Glasgow); *Recreations* orienteering; *Clubs* Perth; *Style*— Prof David Stirrups; ✉ Dundee Dental Hospital, Park Place, Dundee DD1 4HN (tel 01382 635961, e-mail d.r.stirrups@dundee.ac.uk)

STIRTON, Prof Charles Howard; s of late Dr Charles Aubrey Stirton, of Natal, South Africa, and Elizabeth Maud, *née* Inglesby; *b* 25 November 1946; *Educ* St Charles's Coll Pietermaritzburg, Univ of Natal (MSc), Univ of Cape Town (PhD, South African Assoc of Botanists Jr Medal), Naval Gymnasium South Africa (Dip Engine Room Mechanics); *m* Jana, da of late Vratislav Žantovsky; 1 da (Elishka Kara Marie); *Career* PRO Natal branch Wildlife Soc of South Africa 1966, lawyers' clerk Paola & Wright 1966, asst mangr Pobana Trading Store 1966–1967, chief professional offr Botanical Research Inst South Africa 1979–82 (sr professional offr 1975–78, South African liaison botanist London 1979–82), B A Krukoff botanist for neotropical legume research Royal Botanic Gardens Kew 1982–87, assoc prof Dept of Botany Univ of Natal 1988–90, freelance writer 1990, author of 124 scientific papers in learned jls; Royal Botanic Gardens Kew: research co-ordinator for economic botany progs 1990–92, dep dir and dep dir of science 1992–95, dep dir and dir of science and horticulture 1995–96; fndr dir National Botanic Garden of Wales 1996–2002, chm Contextua Ltd 2002–05, strategic dir Ouroboros Research and Educn Tst 2005–07 (also tstee); sr res fell Univ of Birmingham 1992–96; hon prof: Univ of Reading 1995–97, Univ of Wales 1997–2005; genera 'Stirtonia' and 'Stirtonanthus' named; dir Galleon Independent Private Client Advisors Ltd; futurist; memb Steering Gp Species Survival Cmmn (IUCN) (chair Plants Sub-Ctee 1994–96), memb Sci Panel Nat Museum and Galleries of Wales; fndr pres and hon life memb Natal Evolutionary Biology Soc; govr Trinity Coll Carmarthen 1997–2000; tstee: ILDIS, Bentham-Moxon Tst 1990–96, Pat Brenan Meml Fund 1990–96, Gateway Gardens Tst 2003–; Hon Dr Univ of Glamorgan 2001; FLS; *Books* Plant Invaders - Beautiful But Dangerous, Advances in Legume Biology, Advances in Legume Systematics 3, Problem Plants of Southern Africa, Weeds in a Changing World; *Recreations* gardening, reading, postal history, postcards, cinema, conservation; *Style*— Prof Charles Stirton; ✉ 4 Nelson Villas, Bath BA1 2BD (tel 01225 425966, e-mail chstirton@tiscali.co.uk)

STOATE, Dr Howard Geoffrey; MP; s of Alvan Stoate, and May, *née* Russell; *b* 14 April 1954; *Educ* Kingston GS, KCL (MB BS, MSc); *m* 1979, Deborah, da of Desmond Dunkerley; 2 s (Thomas b 1984, George b 1987); *Career* GP trg Joyce Green Hosp 1978–81, GP Albion Surgery Bexleyheath 1982–, GP tutor Queen Mary's Hosp Sidcup 1989–, MP (Lab) Dartford 1997–; House of Commons: PPS to Rt Hon John Denham, MP, *qv*, 2001–03, PPS to Rt Hon Estelle Morris, MP (now Baroness Morris of Yardley, PC (Life Peer), *qv*) 2003–05; memb Health Select Ctee 1997–2001 and 2005–, chm All-Pty Gp on Primary Care and Public Health, chm All-Pty Gp on Pharmacy, chm All-Pty Gp on Men's Health; chm Local Research Ethics Ctee Bexleyheath 1995–97, vice-chm Regnl Graduate Educn Bd South Thames 1997; cncllr Dartford BC 1990–99 (chm Fin Ctee 1995–97), vice-pres Dartford Racial Equality Cncl; memb: BMA 1977, Fabian Soc (vice-chm Dartford branch); govr Dartford Boys' GS 1996–2000; FRCGP 1995, DRCOG; *Publications* All's Well That Starts Well. Strategy for Children's Health (with Bryan Jones, 2002), Challenging the Citadel: Breaking the hospitals' grip on the NHS (with Bryan Jones, 2006); *Recreations* running, sailing, reading, music, travelling, spending time with my family; *Clubs* Emsworth Sailing; *Style*— Dr Howard Stoate, MP; ✉ House of Commons, London SW1A 0AA (tel 020 7219 4571, fax 020 7219 6820); consitituency office (tel 01322 343234, fax 01322 343235, e-mail hstoate@hotmail.com)

STOBART, Paul Lancelot; s of George Lancelot Stobart, of La Massana Parc, Andorra, and Elizabeth Carla, *née* Bruxby; *b* 31 May 1957; *Educ* Peterhouse Sch Zimbabwe, Oriel Coll Oxford (BA); *Children* 5 da (Alice Lucy b 14 Dec 1995, Hannah Elizabeth, Grace Georgia (twins) b 6 Jan 2005, Imogen Scarlett, Honor Dulcie (twins) b 2 April 2006); *Career* Price Waterhouse London 1980–84, Hill Samuel London & NY 1984–88; Interbrand Group plc: dir 1988–94, chm Europe 1995–96; Sage Group plc: dir 1996–1997, chief operating offr 1997–2003, md Sage UK and Ireland 2003–; non-exec dir Capital & Regional plc; ACA 1983; *Books* Brand Power (ed, 1994); *Recreations* golf, cricket, theatre; *Clubs* Oxford and Cambridge Golfing Soc, Royal St George's Golf; *Style*— Paul Stobart, Esq; ✉ The Sage Group plc, North Park, Newcastle upon Tyne NE13 9AA (tel 0191 294 3000, fax 0191 294 0001, e-mail paul.stobart@sage.com)

STOCK, Christopher John Robert; s of Dr John Peter Penderell Stock (d 1973), of Newcastle under Lyme, Staffs, and Sybil, *née* Bashford; *b* 1 May 1938; *Educ* Yarlet Hall, Clifton, Univ of St Andrews (BDS), Univ of London (MSc); *m* 12 Oct 1963, Diana Mary, da of Reginald Adolph Lovatt Wenger; 2 da (Corinne Alison b 16 July 1968, Sally Penderell b 18 Nov 1971); *Career* Royal Army Dental Corps 1962–78 (ret Lt-Col as clinical advsr in advanced conservation), currently pt/t in endodontic practice and sr lectr and hon conslt in restorative dentistry Eastman Dental Inst London; memb: Br Endodontic Soc (sec and pres 1982), Fédération Dentaire Internationale; fell Int Coll of Dentists; *Books* Endodontics in Practice (1985, 2 edn 1990), A Colour Atlas of Endodontics (1988), Color Atlas and Text of Endodontics (1995); *Recreations* golf, photography, collecting prints; *Clubs* North Hants Golf, St Enodoc Golf, Royal and Ancient Golf; *Style*— Christopher Stock, Esq; ✉ Heather House, Pines Road, Fleet, Hampshire GU13 8NL (tel 01252 616220); Heath House Endodontic Practice, 52 Fleet Road, Fleet, Hampshire GU13 8PA (tel 01252 811700)

STOCK, Gailene Patricia; AM (1997); da of Roy Keith Stock (d 2002), and Sylvia May, *née* Smith; *b* Ballarat, Victoria, Aust; *Educ* Convent of Mercy Victoria, Royal Ballet Sch (scholar), RMIT Univ Victoria Aust; *m* 31 July 1976, Gary William Norman; 1 da (Lisa Michelle b 12 May 1978); *Career* former ballet dancer; former princ artist: Aust Ballet, Nat Ballet of Canada, Royal Winnipeg Ballet; former dir: Nat Theatre Ballet Sch Victoria Aust, Australian Ballet Sch; currently dir Royal Ballet Sch; memb Exec Ctee Royal Acad of Dance; memb jury various int ballet competitions incl: Prix de Lausanne, Youth America Grand Prix, Diaghilev Int Ballet Competition Moscow, Asian Pacific Ballet Competition Tokyo, Japan Grand Prix Sapporo; Melbourne Achiever Award 1995; ARAD; *Recreations* reading, gardening, theatre; *Style*— Ms Gailene Stock, AM; ✉ The Royal Ballet School, 46 Floral Street, Covent Garden, London WC2E 9DA (tel 020 7836 8899, fax 020 7845 7043, e-mail info@royalballetschool.co.uk)

STOCK, Rt Rev (William) Nigel; *see:* Stockport, Bishop of

STOCKDALE, David Andrew; QC (1995); s of John Ramsden Stockdale (d 1987), and Jean Stewart, *née* Shelley (d 2004); *b* 9 May 1951; *Educ* Giggleswick Sch, Pembroke Coll Oxford (MA); *m* 1 June 1985, Melanie Jane, da of late Anthony Newis Benson; 1 s (William Benson b 1988), 3 da (Verity Katharine b 1989, Grace Elizabeth b 1991, Bridget Claudia b 1994); *Career* called to the Bar Middle Temple 1975 (bencher 2003); in practice Northern Circuit 1976–, recorder of the Crown Court 1993– (asst recorder 1990–93); memb: Professional Negligence Bar Assoc, Personal Injuries Bar Assoc; govr: Giggleswick Sch 1982– (chm 1997–2007), Terra Nova Sch 2000–; *Recreations* family, the outdoors, motorcycling, remote Scotland; *Clubs* Sloane; *Style*— David Stockdale, Esq, QC; ✉ Deans Court Chambers, 24 St John Street, Manchester M3 4DF (Tel 0161 214 6000, fax 0161 214 6001)

STOCKDALE, Dr Elizabeth Joan Noël; *Educ* Bentley GS, Cambridgeshire Coll of Arts and Technol, Univ of Aberdeen Faculty of Med (MB ChB), Univ of London (Dip Med Radiodiagnosis), Univ of Strathclyde Grad Business Sch (MBA); *m* 26 May 1979, Christopher Leo Stockdale; 1 da (Jane Frances b 1981), 2 s (David Leo Andrew b 1983, Alexander James b 1984); *Career* house surgn Aberdeen Royal Infirmary and house physician Woodend Gen Hosp Aberdeen 1972–73, sr house surgn Professorial Surgical Unit Great Ormond St Hosp London 1974, registrar and sr registrar Dept of Diagnostic Radiology St George's Hosp London 1975–79 (with appts to The Royal Nat Orthopaedic Hosp, Atkinson Morley's Hosp, The Royal Marsden Hosp and St James's Hosp), conslt radiologist to Grampian Health Bd 1980–, hon clinical sr lectr Univ of Aberdeen 1980–; BMA: chm Grampian Div 1995–97, memb Scottish Cncl 1997–2000, memb Scottish Ctee for Hosp Med Servs 1997–2000; former pres Aberdeen and NE Branch Med Women's Fedn; memb: Scottish Radiological Soc 1980, European Soc of Paediatric Radiologists 1980, Br Paediatric Assoc 1986, Scottish Surgical Paediatric Soc 1986, Br Inst Radiology 1990, Br Med Ultrasound Soc 1990, Scottish Soc of Paediatric Radiologists 1996, Scottish Medico-Legal Soc 1997, Scottish Standing Ctee RCR 1997–2002, Radiology Section UK Children's Cancer Study Gp (UKCCSG) 1998–; FRCR 1979, FRCPCH 1997; *Style*— Dr Elizabeth Stockdale; ✉ 1 Grant Road, Banchory, Kincardineshire AB31 5UW (tel 01330 823096)

STOCKDALE, Sir Thomas Minshull; 2 Bt (UK 1960), of Hoddington, Co Southampton; er s of Sir Edmund Villiers Minshull Stockdale, 1 Bt, JP (d 1989), and Hon Louise Fermor-Hesketh (d 1994), da of 1 Baron Hesketh; *b* 7 January 1940; *Educ* Eton, Worcester Coll Oxford (MA); *m* 1965, Jacqueline, da of Ha-Van-Vuong, of Saigon; 1 s (John Minshull b 1967), 1 da (Charlotte Fermor b 1970); *Heir* s, John Stockdale; *Career* called to the Bar Inner Temple 1966, bencher Lincoln's Inn 1994; memb Ct of Assts Worshipful Co of Fishmongers (Prime Warden 2001–02); *Recreations* shooting, travel; *Clubs* Turf, MCC; *Style*— Sir Thomas Stockdale, Bt; ✉ Manor Farm, Weston Patrick, Basingstoke, Hampshire RG25 2NT (tel 01256 862841)

STOCKEN, Oliver Henry James; s of Henry Edmund West Stocken (d 1980), and Sheila Guisard, *née* Steele (d 1998); *b* 22 December 1941; *Educ* Felsted, UC Oxford; *m* 1967, Sally Forbes, da of John Dishon, of Aust; 2 s, 1 da; *Career* md Barclays Aust 1982–84; dir: N M Rothschild & Sons 1972–77, Esperanza Ltd 1977–79, Barclays Merchant Bank Ltd 1979–86, Barclays de Zoete Wedd 1986–93 (fin dir 1991–93); fin dir Barclays plc 1993–99; non-exec chm: Home Retail Gp, Stanhope plc, Oval Insurance Ltd; non-exec dir: 3i plc (currently dep chm), Standard Chartered plc; tstee: Nat History Museum (chm), MCC, River and Rowing Museum, Friends of Arundel Cricket Club; memb Cncl RCA; FCA 1967; *Clubs* Brooks's, Garrick, MCC (treas); *Style*— Oliver Stocken Esq; ✉ 3 Burlington Gardens, London W1S 3EP (tel 020 7432 3714, e-mail oliverstocken@yahoo.co.uk)

STOCKHAM, Margaret Jean; da of David Hugh Eveleigh King (d 2001), and Joan Elizabeth Mary, *née* Thompson; *b* 11 December 1954; *Educ* Convent of St Louis Bury St Edmunds, Co Upper Sch Bury St Edmunds, Princess Mary's RAF Hosp Physiotherapy Sch, Univ of Leicester (MSc); *Family* 1 s (James b 13 Jan 1978), 1 da (Danielle b 21 Aug 1986); m, 29 March 1994, Donald Turner; *Career* clinical physiotherapy posts UK and overseas 1978–87, dist physiotherapist Kettering 1987–90, dir Elderly and Therapy Div Priority Services Unit Kettering 1990–94, dir Strategy and Ops Bedford and Shires NHS Tst 1994–98; chief exec: E Berks Community NHS Tst 1998–99, Bedford Primary Care Gp 1999–2001, Bedford PCT 2001–06, Beds PCT 2006–07; md Ptnrs in Practice Ltd 2007–; memb Inst of Dirs, memb Inst of Health Mgmnt 1987; MCSP 1978; *Recreations* reading, cinema, athletics, travel; *Style*— Mrs Margaret Stockham; ✉ Partners in Practice Ltd, 3 Waltham Drive, Abbeyfields, Elstow, Bedfordshire MK42 9FY (tel 01234 293486, e-mail margaret.stockham@ntlworld.com)

STOCKING, Barbara Mary; CBE (2000); da of Percy Frederick Stocking (d 2001), of Rugby, Warwickshire, and Mary, *née* Catling (d 1993); *b* 28 July 1951; *Educ* Univ of Wisconsin Madison (MS), Univ of Illinois Urbana, New Hall Cambridge (BA); *m* 3 Oct 1981, Dr Robert John MacInnes, s of Dr Iain MacInnes, of Maidenhead; 2 s (Andrew Tom b 3 June 1986, Stephen Courtney b 12 Sept 1989); *Career* fell Kings Fund Coll 1983–86, dir Kings Fund Centre for Health Servs Devpt 1987–93; chief exec: Oxford RHA 1993–94, Anglia and Oxford RHA 1994–96; regional dir: Anglia and Oxford NHS Exec 1996–99, South-East NHS Exec 1999–2000; head Modernisation Agency NHS Executive 2000–01; dir Oxfam 2001–; memb: Riverside Health Authy 1985–89, Advsy Ctee UK Harkness Fellowships 1989–95, Central R&D Ctee NHS 1991–96; Hon DSc: Univ of Luton 1998, Oxford Brookes Univ 1999; CIMgt 1996; *Books* The Image and the Reality: A Case Study of the Impacts of Medical Technology (with S L Morrison, 1978), Initiative and Inertia - Case Studies in the Health Service (1985), Expensive Medical Technologies (ed, 1988), A Study of the Diffusion of Medical Technology in Europe (series ed, 1991), Medical Advances (the future shape of acute services, 1992); *Recreations* music; *Style*— Ms Barbara Stocking, CBE; ✉ Oxfam, Oxfam House, John Smith Drive, Cowley, Oxford OX4 2JY (tel 01865 472436)

STOCKPORT, Bishop of 2000–; Rt Rev (William) Nigel Stock; s of Ian Stock, and Elizabeth, *née* Bell; *Educ* Durham Sch, Univ of Durham (BA), Ripon Coll Cuddesdon (DipTh); *Career* ordained: deacon 1976, priest 1977; curate Stockton St Peter Durham 1976–79, priest-in-charge Taraka Lae Papua New Guinea 1979–84, vicar of Shiremoor Newcastle 1985–91, team rector North Shields 1991–98, rural dean of Tynemouth 1992–98, hon canon Newcastle Cathedral 1997–98, canon residentiary Durham Cathedral 1998–2000, chaplain Grey Coll Durham 1999–2000; *Recreations* reading, walking, music, art, history; *Style*— The Rt Rev the Bishop of Stockport; ✉ Bishop's Lodge, Back Lane, Dunham Town, Altrincham, Cheshire WA14 4SG (tel 0161 928 5611, fax 0161 929 0692, mobile 07889 317131, e-mail bpstockport@chester.anglican.org)

STOCKTON, 2 Earl of (UK 1984); Alexander Daniel Alan Macmillan; also Viscount Macmillan of Ovenden; s of Rt Hon Maurice Victor Macmillan, PC, MP (Viscount Macmillan of Ovenden, d 1984), and Katharine, Viscountess Macmillan of Ovenden, DBE; gs of 1 Earl of Stockton (d 1986); *b* 10 October 1943; *Educ* Eton, Ecole Politique Université de Paris, Univ of Strathclyde; *m* 1, 1970 (m dis 1991), Hélène Birgitte (Bitta), da of late Alan Douglas Christie Hamilton, of Stable Green, Mitford, Northumberland; 1 s (Daniel Maurice Alan, Viscount Macmillan of Ovenden b 1974), 2 da (Lady Rebecca Elizabeth b 1980, Lady Louisa Alexandra b 1982); m 2, 1995, Miranda Elizabeth Louise, formerly w of Sir Nicholas Keith Lillington Nuttall, 3 Bt, and previously of late Peter Richard Henry Sellers, CBE, and da of Richard St John Quarry and Diana, Lady Mancroft; *Heir* s, Viscount Macmillan of Ovenden; *Career* book and magazine publisher; journalist Glasgow Herald 1965–66, reporter Daily Telegraph 1967, foreign corr Daily Telegraph 1968–69, chief Euro corr Sunday Telegraph 1969–70; dep chm Macmillan Ltd 1972–80, chm Macmillan Publishers 1980–90, pres Macmillan Ltd 1990–; govr English Speaking Union 1978–84 and 1986–93; chm: Central London TEC 1990–95, London TEC Gp 1991–94, Campaign for Shooting 1996–2000; memb Sec of State's TEC Advsy Gp 1991–94; contested (Cons) Bristol Euro Parly Election 1994, MEP (Cons) SW England 1990–2004; Liveryman Worshipful Co of Merchant Taylors 1972 (memb Ct of Assts 1987, Master 1992–93); Liveryman Worshipful Co of Stationers & Newspaper Makers 1973 (memb Ct of Assts 1996); Hon DUniv Strathclyde 1993; Hon DLitt: De Montfort Univ 1993, Univ of Westminster 1995; hon fell London Inst 2003; FIMgt, FRSA, Hon FISVA 1996, Hon FRICS 1996; *Recreations* shooting, fishing, photography, conversation; *Clubs* Beefsteak, Buck's, Garrick, Pratt's, White's; *Style*— The Rt Hon the Earl of Stockton; ✉ The Macmillan Building, 4–6 Crinan Street, London N1 9XW (tel 020 7833 4000)

STOCKWELL, Anthony Howard (Tony); s of F H C Stockwell, of Enfield, Middx, and G B Stockwell, *née* Colledge; *b* 14 January 1949; *Educ* The Grammar Sch Enfield, Clare Coll Cambridge (exhibitioner, BA); *m* K Richardson; *Career* slr; ptnr Stephenson Harwood (formerly articled clerk and asst slr); memb: Law Soc 1974, City of London Law Soc (memb Banking Law Ctee); winner Daniel Reardon prize (Law Soc); Freeman City of London, Freeman and Liveryman City of London Slrs' Co; *Style*— Tony Stockwell, Esq; ✉ Stephenson Harwood, One St Paul's Churchyard, London EC4M 8SH (tel 020 7329 4422, fax 020 7606 0822)

STOCKWIN, Prof James Arthur Ainscow; s of Wilfred Arthur Stockwin (d 1991), of Sutton Coldfield, and Dr Edith Mary, *née* Ainscow (d 1983); *b* 28 November 1935; *Educ* King Edward's Sch Birmingham, Exeter Coll Oxford (MA), ANU Canberra (PhD); *m* 30 Jan 1960, Audrey Lucretia Hobson, da of Eric Stuart Wood (d 1996); 2 da (Katrina Mary (Mrs Bennett) b 19 Nov 1961, Jane Clare (Mrs Skirrow) b 26 Jan 1964), 2 s (Rupert Arthur b 1 Oct 1966, Timothy James b 20 Dec 1968 d 1987); *Career* lectr, sr lectr, reader ANU Canberra 1964–81, Nissan prof of modern Japanese studies and dir Nissan Inst of Japanese Studies Univ of Oxford 1982–2003, professorial fell St Antony's Coll Oxford 1982–2003 (sub-warden 1999–2001); pres Br Assoc of Japanese Studies 1994–95; *Books* The Japanese Socialist Party and Neutralism (1968), Japan: Divided Politics in a Growth Economy (1975, 2 edn 1982), Dynamic and Immobilist Politics in Japan (ed and part-author, 1988), The Establishment of the Japanese Constitutional System (by Junji Banno, trans 1992), The Story of Tim (1993), Governing Japan: Divided Politics in a Major Economy (1999, 2 edn 2007), Dictionary of the Modern Politics of Japan (2003), Collected Writings of J A A Stockwin (2004), Thirty-Odd Feet Below Belgium: An Affair of Letters in the Great War, 1915–1916 (2005); *Recreations* languages; *Style*— Prof J A

S

A Stockwin; ✉ Nissan Institute of Japanese Studies, 27 Winchester Road, Oxford OX2 6NA (tel 01865 274570, fax 01865 274574, e-mail arthur.stockwin@nissan.ox.ac.uk)

STODDARD, Christopher James; s of Frederick Stoddard, of Congleton, Cheshire, and Millicent, *née* Barnett; *b* 2 June 1947; *Educ* Newcastle HS, Univ of Sheffield (MB ChB, MD); *m* 26 June 1971, Margaret Elizabeth, da of Reginald Bailey (d 1977); 1 da (Emma Louise b 3 Oct 1975), 1 s (James Edward b 12 Oct 1977); *Career* surgical registrar Royal Infirmary Sheffield 1974–76, clinical fell in surgery McMaster Med Centre Hamilton Ontario 1978–79, sr lectr in surgery Liverpool 1981–86, conslt surgn Royal Hallamshire Hosp Sheffield 1986– (lectr in surgery 1977–78), regnl specialty advsr in gen surgery Trent Region 1998–; sec Assoc of Upper Gastrointestinal Surgeons 2001–; memb: Surgical Research Soc, Br Soc of Gastroenterology; FRCS 1976; *Books* Complications of Minor Surgery (1986), Complications of Upper Gastrointestinal Surgery (1987); *Recreations* golf, gardening; *Style*— Christopher Stoddard, Esq; ✉ Blaenwern, 12 Slayleigh Lane, Fulwood, Sheffield (tel 0114 230 9284); Royal Hallamshire Hospital, Glossop Road, Sheffield S10 2JF (tel 0114 271 2126)

STODDART, Christopher West; s of Dr Ian West Stoddart, of Winchester, and Bridget, *née* Pilditch; *b* 10 April 1950; *Educ* Winchester, Churchill Coll Cambridge (open exhibitioner, BA); *m* 1, 1972 (m dis 1977), Deborah, da of John Ounsted; m 2, 1985, Dr Hazel Collins, da of Hon Robert H Grasmere; *Career* graduate trainee Dept of the Environment 1971–75, res sec Centre for Environmental Studies 1976–80, sec ITV Companies Assoc 1981–82 (regnl companies sec 1980–81), dir of resources Tyne Tees Television Ltd 1983–88 (gen mangr 1982–83), md and chief exec Satellite Information Services Ltd 1988–92, md GMTV Ltd 1992–2001, chief exec Go Racing (now attheraces plc) 2001–03; non-exec dir Sterling Publishing Gp plc 1999–2001; chair tstees Changing Faces (charitable tst) 1999–2002; *Recreations* mountaineering, travel, photography; *Style*— Christopher Stoddart, Esq; ✉ e-mail cstoddart@bigfoot.com

STODDART, John Joseph; s of John Stoddart, of Liverpool, and Patricia, *née* Taylor; *b* 6 June 1957; *Educ* St Joan of Arc RC Secdy Modern; *m* 19 July 1980, Deborah Ann, da of Ronald André Lefebvré; *Career* served Grenadier Gds 1972–78 (joined aged 15); photographer 1978– (based Liverpool until 1984, London thereafter); early editorial work for magazines incl The Face and NME, currently working throughout Europe and USA; perm exhbn L'Express (Joseph Sloane Sq); Portrait Photographer of the Year 1989; *Recreations* photography, art; *Style*— John Stoddart, Esq; ✉ 1 Lawrence Mansions, Lordship Place, Chelsea, London SW3 5HU (tel 020 7376 4984)

STODDART, John Maurice; CBE (1995); s of Gordon Stoddart (d 1983), of Wallasey, and May, *née* Ledder (d 1969); *b* 18 September 1938; *Educ* Wallasey GS, Univ of Reading (BA); *Career* head Dept of Econ and Business Studies Sheffield Poly 1970–72, asst dir NE London Poly 1972–76, dir Humberside Coll 1976–83, vice-chllr and princ Sheffield Hallam Univ (previously Sheffield City Poly) 1983–98; dir: Sheffield Sci Park 1988–98, Sheffield TEC 1990–98; memb: CNAA 1980–86, Nat Forum Mgmnt Educn and Devpt 1987–, Cncl for Educn and Trg in Social Work 1989–93, Cncl for Indust and Higher Educn 1990–94; chm: Ctee of Dirs of Polys 1990–93 (vice-chm 1988–90), Higher Educn Quality Cncl 1992–97, Defence Accreditation Bd 1999–2004, Northern General NHS Tst Bd 1999–2001; non-exec dir Sheffield Teaching Hosps Tst Bd 2001–; Hon DEd CNAA 1992, Hon DLitt Coventry 1993, Hon DUniv Middx 1993; hon fell Humberside Coll 1983, companion Br Business Graduates Soc 1984; Hon LLD Univ of Sheffield 1998, Hon DUniv Sheffield Hallam 1998; CIMgt 1990, FRSA 1980; *Publications* author of various articles on education, business education and management; *Recreations* biography, hill walking, rowing; *Clubs* Reform; *Style*— John Stoddart, Esq, CBE; ✉ 6 Tepton Park Gardens, Sheffield S10 3FP (tel 0144 2305467)

STODDART, Patrick Thomas; s of Thomas Stoddart (d 1987), of Leith, Scotland, and Anne Theresa Power (d 1979); *b* 23 November 1944; *Educ* Watford Boys' GS; *m* Nicolette, da of late Gp Capt A D Murray, RAF (ret); *Career* jr reporter Watford Observer 1962, Evening Echo Herts 1967–72, TV columnist London Evening News 1975–80 (joined as reporter 1972); freelance 1980–85 (various TV series as writer/presenter at TVS and Anglia), TV critic Channel 4 Daily 1989–91, broadcasting ed and TV critic Sunday Times 1986–92, freelance writer on broadcasting affrs The Times and Daily Telegraph, conslt ed Broadcast magazine, script conslt various TV cos; ptnr Keighley Stoddart media consultancy until 1998; currently TV critic Express Saturday Magazine; sr lectr in journalism Univ of Westminster 2005– (lectr in cultural journalism 2004–05); media conslt to: Rory Bremner, London Radio, Yorkshire Television, Domaine Productions, Virgin Television, Bronson Knight, LWT and Reuters Television 1993–98; creative conslt to: Talent Television, Paul Knight Productions; editorial dir News World Ltd (conf chair 1997 and 1998); memb RIIA; *Recreations* rugby, cricket, military history, music; *Clubs* Fullerians RFC (chm), Fleet Street Strollers Cricket, Groucho; *Style*— Patrick Stoddart, Esq; ✉ 28 Sherwoods Road, Watford, Hertfordshire WD1 4AZ (tel 01923 229901, fax 01923 351363, e-mail patrick.stoddart@virgin.net)

STODDART, Peter; eld s of Peter Cowe (d 1947), and Amelia McQuillan (d 1985); adopted s of Stanley Stoddart; *b* 23 August 1945, Sunderland; *Educ* Sunderland Tech Coll; *m* 1, 1971 (m dis 1975), Carol Ann, da of late Brian Goodfellow; 1 s (Neil Robert); m 2, 1977 (m dis 1980), Sandie, da of late Wah Loung Yuen; m 3, 2002, Angela Claire Kirton, da of late Frank Reavley; 2 da (Emmeline Claire Kirton, Sarah Ruth); *Career* articled clerk Metcalf McKenzie & Co 1963–68, gp financial accountant T Cowie plc 1968–70, tax mangr Price Waterhouse & Co 1970–74, corporate finance mangr Jennings Johnson & Co 1974–75, co sec Edward Thompson Gp 1975–77, various finance mangr roles 1977–78, various roles British Shipbuilders Corporation 1978–85, finance mangr rising to finance dir Nissan Motor Manfacturing (UK) Ltd 1985–2000 (tstee and latterly dep chm Nissan pension plans 1989–2000), interim ops dir One NE RDA 2000–01, memb Competition Cmmn 2001–; non-exec dir Wirrall C of C 1983–85, memb Cncl and chm Economic Affrs Ctee NE C of C 1996–99; chm: City of Sunderland Common Purpose Forum 1996–2000, NE Euro Forum 1998–2000; dep chm Royal Victoria Infirmary and Associated Hosps NHS Tst 1991–97; chm Wearside Coll of FE 1990–96, dep chm City of Sunderland Coll 1996–97; FCA 1979 (ACA 1969), FRSA 1998; *Recreations* travel, local history studies, books; *Style*— Peter Stoddart, FCA

STODDART, Peter Laurence Bowring; s of Laurence Bowring Stoddart, JP (d 1973), of Cheddington Manor, Leighton Buzzard, Beds, and Gwendolen Mary, *née* Russell; *b* 24 June 1934; *Educ* Sandroyd Sch, Eton, Trinity Coll Oxford; *m* 29 May 1957, Joanna, da of Thomas Adams; 1 s (Clive Laurence Bowring), 2 da (Fiona Gwendolen Jane, Belinda May); *Career* Nat Serv 2 Lt 14/20 King's Hussars 1952–54; with C T Bowring Group 1955–80; dir: C T Bowring & Co Ltd 1967–80, Singer & Friedlander, Crusader Insurance Co Ltd 1967–80, English & American Insurance Co Ltd 1967–80, Fleming Mercantile Investment Trust plc 1976–97; chm Robert Fleming Insurance Brokers 1980–96 (dir 1996–); Capt Bucks CCC 1957–66; Master: Whaddon Chase Hunt 1969–83, Heythrop Hunt 1988–97; memb Ct of Assts Worshipful Co of Salters (Master 1986–87); *Recreations* field sports and countryside, travel; *Clubs* White's, Cavalry and Guards', MCC; *Style*— Peter Stoddart, Esq; ✉ North Rye House, Moreton-in-Marsh, Gloucestershire GL56 0XU (tel 01451 830 636); Robert Fleming Insurance Brokers Ltd, Staple Hall, Stone House Court, London EC3A 7AX (tel 020 7621 1263, fax 020 7623 6175, telex 883 735/6)

STODDART OF SWINDON, Baron (Life Peer UK 1983), of Reading in the Royal County of Berkshire; David Leonard Stoddart; s of late Arthur Leonard Stoddart, and Queenie Victoria, *née* Price; *b* 4 May 1926; *Educ* St Clement Danes GS, Henley GS; *m* 1, 1946 (m dis 1960), Doreen M Maynard; 1 da (Hon Janet Victoria (Hon Mrs Cousins) b 1947); m 2, 1961, Jennifer, adopted da of late Mrs Lois Percival-Alwyn, of Battle, E Sussex; 2 s (Hon Howard David b 1966, Hon Mathwyn Hugh b 1969); *Career* clerical offr CEGB 1957–70 (previous employment in PO Telephones, railways and hosp service); ldr Lab Gp Reading Cncl 1964–72 (ldr Cncl 1967–71), memb Reading CBC 1954–72; Parly candidate (Lab): Newbury 1959 and 1964, Swindon by-election 1969; MP (Lab) Swindon 1970–83; PPS to Min of Housing and Construction 1974–75, asst Govt whip 1975, Lord Cmmr of the Treasury 1976–77, jr oppn spokesman on Industry 1982–83, oppn spokesman on Energy (Lords) 1983–88, oppn whip (Lords) 1983–88; Lab whip withdrawn 2001, now Ind Lab; trade unions: AMICUS (formerly EETPU) 1953–, NALGO 1951–70; memb Nat Jt Cncl Electricity Supply Industry 1967–70; vice-pres Assoc of District Cncls 1994–98; chm: Campaign for an Independent Britain 1991–2007, Alliance Against the European Constitution (AAEC, formerly Anti-Maastricht Alliance) 1992–2004, Global Britain 1998–; memb Cncl Freedom Assoc 2006–; *Style*— The Rt Hon the Lord Stoddart of Swindon; ✉ Sintra, 37A Bath Road, Reading, Berkshire (tel 0118 957 6726); House of Lords, London SW1A 0PW

STOESSL, Susanne Eugenie (Sue); da of Edmund Stoessl (d 1964), of Berkhamsted, Herts, and Olga, *née* Sinreich (d 1945); *b* 28 March 1937; *Educ* Berkhamsted Sch for Girls, Univ of Nottingham; *m* 1968 (sep), Geoffrey William Cleaver; *Career* work study factory mangr C & J Clark 1958–62, prodn mangr British Shoe Corporation 1962–66, statistician Television Audience Measurement 1966–68, head of research and mgmnt servs London Weekend Television 1968–82, head of mktg Channel Four Television 1982–89, freelance media conslt 1989–92, DG Market Research Soc 1992–93, head of broadcast research BBC 1993–97; non-exec dir: Nuclear Electric plc 1990–96, Ealing NHS Trust 1991–99, Magnox Electric plc 1996–98; memb DETR Radioactive Waste Mgmnt Advsy Ctee, memb Duke of Edinburgh Cwlth Study Conf 1962; pres Women's Advtg Club of London 1981–82, chm Find Your Feet 1989–, dep chm Amarant Tst 1993–; memb: Market Research Soc 1973–2000, RTS 1976, Mktg Gp of GB 1982; *Recreations* reading, travel, swimming, farming, tapestry; *Clubs* Reform; *Style*— Ms Sue Stoessl; ✉ 18 Chiswick Staithe, London W4 3TP (tel 020 8995 2957, fax 020 8747 0407)

STOKE-ON-TRENT, Archdeacon of; *see:* Stone, Ven Godfrey

STOKELY, Guy Robert; *b* 30 October 1943; *Educ* Forest Sch, Univ of Oxford (MA); *m* 4 Oct 1968, Wendy Anne; 3 s (Robert b 1970, Tom b 1979, Tim b 1983), 1 da (Sarah b 1973); *Career* fin vice-pres Manufacturers Life Insurance Co 1966–78, gen mangr Saudi Int Bank 1978–91, dir Barclays de Zoete Wedd 1991–97, dir Barclays Capital 1997–; *Recreations* golf, water sports, gardening; *Clubs* RAC; *Style*— Guy Stokely, Esq; ✉ c/o Barclays Capital, 5 North Colonnade, Canary Wharf, London E14 4BB

STOKER, Dr Dennis James; s of Dr George Morris Stoker (d 1949), of Mitcham, Surrey, and Elsie Margaret, *née* Macqueen (d 1986); *b* 22 March 1928; *Educ* Oundle, Guy's Hosp Med Sch Univ of London (MB BS); *m* 1, 22 Sept 1951, Anne Sylvia Nelson (d 1997), da of Norman Forster (d 1962), of Haywards Heath, W Sussex; 2 da (Claire b 1952, Catherine b 1958), 2 s (Philip b 1954, Neil b 1956); m 2, 30 Oct 1999, Sheila Mary Mercer, da of Philip Baines (d 1973), of Wirral, Cheshire; *Career* house physician Guy's Hosp 1951; cmmnd Med Branch RAF 1952: RAF Brampton 1952–53, RAF Bridgnorth 1953–55, RAF Hosp W Kirby 1955–56, Med Div RAF Hosp Wroughton 1956–58, i/c Med Div RAF Hosp Akrotiri Cyprus 1958–61, physician i/c Chest Unit RAF Hosp Wroughton 1961–64, Metabolic Unit St Mary's Hosp London 1964–65, i/c Med Div RAF Hosp Steamer Point Aden 1965–67, i/c Med Div RAF Hosp Cosford Staffs 1967–68, ret Wing Cdr 1968; conslt radiologist: St George's Hosp 1972–87, Royal Nat Orthopaedic Hosp 1972–93 and 1997–2002 (special tstee 1984–2000, chm 1992–98); dean Inst of Orthopaedics 1987–91 (dir of radiological studies 1975–93); ed Skeletal Radiology 1984–96, dean Faculty of Clinical Radiology, vice-pres Royal Coll of Radiologists 1990–91 (memb Faculty Bd 1983–85, memb Cncl 1985–88, Knox medal 1992); Int Skeletal Soc: fndr memb 1974, medal 1993; FRSM 1958, FRCP 1976, FRCR 1975, FRCS 1992; *Books* Knee Arthrography (1980), Orthopaedics: self assessment in radiology (jtly, 1988), Radiology of Skeletal Disorders (jtly, 5 edn 2007); *Recreations* medical history, gardening, genealogy, philology; *Clubs* RAF, Phyllis Court Henley; *Style*— Dr Dennis Stoker; ✉ 3 Pearces Orchard, Henley-on-Thames, Oxfordshire RG9 2LF (tel and fax 01491 575756, e-mail stoker@dj3.demon.co.uk)

STOKER, John Francis; s of Francis Charles Stoker, of Birmingham, and Joyce, *née* Barnwell; *b* 11 September 1950; *Educ* King Edward's Sch Birmingham, Brasenose Coll Oxford (BA); *m* 1982, Julie Mary, *née* Puddicombe; *Career* DOE: admin trainee 1973–76, private sec to Parly Under Sec of State for Housing and Construction 1976–78, princ 1978–85 (posts incl Tenant's Right to Buy 1979–81, Alternatives to Domestic Rates 1981–83, Cabinet Office 1983–85), asst sec 1985–92, Establishments (Organisation) Div 1985–87, Estate Action and Housing Co-op and Tenant's Choice Div 1987–89, project mangr Property Holdings 1989–90, Environment White Paper Div/Environmental Protection Central Div 1990–91, Fin (Housing and General) Div 1992, under sec 1992; dir Merseyside Task Force 1992–94, regional dir Government Office for Merseyside 1994–97, DG National Lottery 1998–99 (dep DG 1997–98), chief charity cmmr 1999–2004, cmmr Compact 2006–; *Recreations* music, books, gardening, food, drink; *Clubs* Travellers, Middx CC; *Style*— John Stoker, Esq

STOKER, Linda Beryl; da of Bernard Alistar Dow, and Beryl Georgina Edith, *née* Taylor; *b* 10 July 1954; *Educ* Goffs GS, NE London Poly; *m* 27 Dec 1993, Gordon Smith; 2 step s (Richard b 1982, Alexander b 1983), 2 da from prev alliance (Emma Kate b 1983, Kimberley Frances b 1984); *Career* publicity offr The Rank Orgn, trg offr Guy's Health Dist 1975, trg mangr EMI Leisure 1977, trg advsr Hotel and Catering Industry Trg Bd 1979, field organiser Manpower Servs Cmmn 1981, md Dow-Stoker Ltd 1983–99, fndr Women Returners Ltd 1990–99; independent conslt, writer and speaker 1999–; special conslt Churchill's Bodyguard (BBC 2) 2007; a Woman of the Year 1990, runner-up Price Waterhouse Rising Stars of 1993 Awards; MIPM, MInstD, FRSA; *Books* Women into Training (1990), Having it All (1991), Women Returners Year Book (1991), Customer Care (1995), Business Counselling (1996), Business Information (1997), Managing Global Diversity (1999), Project Management (2000), Leadership Skills for Women (2001), Beside the Bulldog (2003); *Recreations* gym, tennis, sailing, netball; *Style*— Linda Stoker; ✉ Oak Lodge, The Heath, Hatfield Heath, Bishop's Stortford, Hertfordshire CM22 7AD (tel 01279 730731)

STOKER, Prof Richard; s of Capt Bower Morrell Stoker (d 1983), of Scarborough, N Yorks, and Winifred, *née* Harling (d 2007), of Caslteford, W Yorks; *b* 8 November 1938; *Educ* Breadalbane House Sch Castleford, Huddersfield Sch of Music (with Harold Truscott), Huddersfield Sch of Art, Royal Acad of Music (with Sir Lennox Berkeley), Nadia Boulanger Paris, privately with Arthur Benjamin, Eric Fenby and Benjamin Britten; *m* 1, 1 Sept 1962 (m dis 1985), Jacqueline Margaret Trelfer; m 2, 10 July 1986, Dr Gillian Patricia Watson, da of Kenneth Walter Watson (d 1989), of Littleover, Derby; *Career* composer, actor, conductor, author, painter, pianist and poet; conducting debut Huddersfield Town Hall 1956, broadcasted and performed at Welsh Nat Eisteddfod 1955 and 1956 and Int Eisteddfod 1957; asst librarian LSO 1962–63, prof of composition RAM 1963–87 (tutor 1970–80); visiting prof: Binghamton NY 1970, State Univ of NY 1970; composition teacher: St Paul's Sch 1972–74, Magdalen Coll Cambridge 1974–76; visiting lectr Goldsmiths U3A 1996, 1998 and 2001; adjudicator: Cyprus Orch Composers' Award for Miny of Culture 2001–, RPS Award 2003, BBC Br Composers' Award 2003, 2004 and 2005; compositions incl: Johnson Preserv'd (Opera in 3 acts), Three String Quartets, Three Piano Trios, Polemics (for oboe quartet), Partita (for violin and piano), Music that Brings

Sweet Sleep, Aspects 1 in 3, Aspects of Flight, Canticle 1: Canticle of the Rose, Canticle 2: Make me a Willow Cabin, Canticle 3: Chinese Canticle, A Little Organ Book, Three Improvisations, Organ Symphony, Three Pieces, Organ Partita, Contemporary Organ Technique, Variants, Three Preludes, Sonate Symphonique, Piano Concerto, Piano Variations, Two Piano Sonatas, A York Suite, A Poet's Notebook, Twelve Nocturnes, Duologue, Diversions, Portrait of a Town, Assemblages (4 pianos), Partita for Mandolin and Harp, Three Overtures, Benedictus, Ecce Homo, Proverbs, Three Violin Sonatas, Prelude and Toccata, Monologue, (Guitar) Sonatina, Improvisation, Diversions, Pastoral, Sonata, Concerto (vocal), 5 Songs of Love and Loss, 4 Yeats Songs, 4 Shakespeare Songs, Kristallnächt Monody, Bassoon Quartet, Sonata for Flute, Monody for Mary Magdalene (recorder and strings); featured festival composer at: Buxton 1962, Harlow 1965 and 1968, Camden 1965, Farnham 1964, Cheltenham 1966, 1973 and 1981, Denmark 1980; numerous film and stage credits incl: Troilus and Cressida (Old Vic), Portrait of a Town (Standard), End of the Line (Nat Film Sch), Garden Party (Coliseum), My Friend-My Enemy (The Place), In Control (Movie-craft), The Innocent Sleep (Starlight), Mirror (Lionheart Productions); numerous film and TV credits as actor incl: The Queen, Red Mercury Rising, The Da Vinci Code, The Golden Compass; *Publications* recordings incl: Complete Solo Piano Music (Priory/Parkin), Complete Vocal Music Vol 1 & Piano Duos (ASC CD's), Complete Guitar Music (Vishnick, ASC), Vocal Music Vol 2 (ASC), Tribute to Hoagy Carmichael 2 vols (ACS), Sonatina for clarinet and piano (Chandos), 3 string quartets and string trio (Gaudeamus), Aspects of Flight (Gaudeamus), Piano Variations, Sonata & Concerto for 2 guitars (Gaudeamus), Improvisation (Fonal), Chorale for Strings (Saydisc), Fine and Mellow (JSO), Two Preludes (Royal); composition teacher to: Paul Patterson, *qv*, Joe Jackson, Malcolm Singer, the late Paul Reade, and many others; as artist exhibited at: Lewisham Soc of Arts Summer Exhibition 1992, Lewisham Arts Festival 1992, Blackheath Soc 1993, Laurence House (one-man show) 1992, Social Work: 'Mind' 1989–91, Samaritans 1991–94; magistrate 1995–2003, ed Composer Magazine 1969–80, memb and treas Steering Ctee Lewisham Arts Festival 1990 and 1992; fndr memb RAM Guild (memb Ctee 1994–, hon treas 1995–); Mendelssohn scholar 1962–63, PRS 1962, MCPS 1970, APC 1977– (memb Promotions Ctee 1995–), BASCA 1980 (professional memb), exec memb Composers' Guild 1962– (memb Exec Ctee 1969–80); memb: RSM 1984, Blackheath Art Soc 1988, Public Lending Right Soc 1990–, Lewisham Soc of Arts 1991, Poetry Soc 1992–, European-Atlantic Gp 1993–, U3A (London) 1994–, Magistrates' Assoc 1995–2002, English PEN 1996–, Int PEN 1996–, Crown Court 1998–2003, Br Assoc Composers and Song Writers 1999 (memb Exec Ctee 1999–, memb Legal Affairs Review Cmmn 2000–, memb Gold Badge Awards Cmmn 2002–), Royal Soc of Lit 1999–; fndr memb: Atlantic Cncl 1993, PAMRA 2000, PPL 2000, Creative Rights Alliance 2001–; JP Inner London 1995–2003; finalist Int Poetry Competition Nat Lib of Poetry Maryland USA 1994, Editors' Choice Award 1995, 1996 and 1997; winner of various music awards 1960s, winner Man of the Year Award American Biographical Inst 1997 and 1999; ARCM 1962, FRAM 1978 (ARAM 1971); *Books* Portrait of a Town (1974, film version 1976), Words Without Music (1974), Strolling Players (1978), Open Window-Open Door (1985, film version 1987), Tanglewood (1990, film version 1992), Between the Lines (1991), Diva (1992), Collected Short Stories (1993), Sir Thomas Armstrong - A Celebration (jtly, 1998), Turn Back the Clock (1998), Travellers Tales (1999), A Passage of Time (1999), The Way Of It (2001), A Magic Carpet Ride (2002); poetry anthologised 44 times; stories anthologised 14 times; 8 commissioned contributions Oxford DNB 2004– (advsr 2003–); *Plays*: Screened-Take Five, Super-Mark, Harry Halleluyah (with Lord Meremonth); *Recreations* squash, skiing, tennis, swimming, golf, windsurfing, judo, cricket, rowing, nodding off; *Clubs* Garrick, Debrett Society, RAM Guild; *Style*— Prof Richard Stoker, FRAM; ✉ c/o Ricordi & Co (London) Ltd, 210 New King's Road, London SW6 4NZ (tel 020 7371 7501, fax 020 7371 7270, e-mail gps5@tutor.open.ac.uk, website www.richardstoker.co.uk or www.bmic.co.uk or www.musicweb.uk.net)

STOKES, Dr Adrian Victor; OBE (1983); s of Alfred Samuel Stokes, of London, and Edna, *née* Kerrison; *b* 25 June 1945; *Educ* Orange Hill GS, UCL (BSc, PhD); *m* 3 Oct 1970 (m dis 1978), Caroline Therese, da of Arthur Campbell Miles, of London; *Career* res programmer GEC Computers Ltd 1969–71, res asst/res fell Inst of Computer Sci/Dept of Statistics and Computer Sci UCL 1971–77, sr res fell and sr lectr Sch of Info Sci Hatfield Poly 1977–81, dir computing St Thomas' Hosp 1981–88 (King's Fund fell 1981–84); NHS Info Mgmnt Centre/NHS Info Authy: princ conslt 1989–97, asst dir 1997–99, jt dir 1999–2000; chief exec CAT Ltd 2000–, md Elvis memories (UK) Ltd 2001–; non-exec dir: Barnet Primary Care Tst 2001–, Nat Clinical Assessment Authy 2001–05; special tstee Royal Nat Orthopaedic Hosp NHS Tst 2003–; chm: Euro Workshop for Open Systems Expert Gp Healthcare 1991–97, Disabled Drivers' Motor Club 1972–82, 1991–94 and 1997–2000, BSI Info Systems Technol Assembly 2000–; vice-pres Disabled Drivers' Motor Club 1982–2005, chm Exec Ctee Royal Assoc for Disability and Rehabilitation 1985–92, govr and memb Cncl of Mgmnt Motability 1977–, memb Exec Ctee Assoc for Spina Bifida and Hydrocephalus 1978–85, tstee and memb Cncl of Mgmnt PHAB 1982–90; tstee Ind Living Funds 1993–2002, tstee Mobilise Orgn 2005–; memb: DHSS Working Party on Mobility Allowance 1975, DHSS Working Party on the Invalid Tricycle Repair Serv 1976–80, DHSS Silver Jubilee Ctee On Improving Access for Disabled People 1977–78, DHSS Ctee on Restrictions Against Disabled People 1979–81, Social Security Advsy Ctee 1980–2001, Dept of Tport Panel of Advsrs on Disability 1983–85, Disabled Persons' Tport Advsy Ctee 1986–89, Disability Appeal Tbnl 1993–2003, Cncl on Tbnls 2003–; pres Hendon North Lib Assoc, 1981–83, candidate for London Borough of Barnet Cncl Mill Hill Ward 1968, 1971, 1974 and 1978; hon res fell Dept of Computer Sci UCL 1988–90, hon visiting prof of info mgmnt UC Northampton 1994–1999, hon res fell King Alfred's Coll Winchester 2001–04, govr Univ of Hertfordshire 2005–; Hon DSc Univ of Hertfordshire 1994; Freeman City of London 1988, Liveryman Worshipful Co of Info Technologists 1992 (Freeman 1988); CChem 1976, MRSC 1976, FBCS 1979, MCMI (MIMgt 1986), FInstD 1986, CEng 1990, FRSA 1997, CSci 2004, CITP 2004; *Books* An Introduction to Data Processing Networks (1978), Viewdata: A Public Information Utility (1978, 2 edn 1980), The Concise Encyclopaedia of Computer Terminology (1981), Networks (1981), What to Read in Microcomputing (with C Saiady, 1982), A Concise Encyclopaedia of Information Technology (1982, 3 edn 1986), Integrated Office Systems (1982), Computer Networks: Fundamentals and Practice (with M D and J M Bacon, 1984), Overview of Data Communications (1985), Communications Standards (1986), The A-Z of Business Computing (1986), OSI Standards and Acronyms (1987, 3 edn 1991), The BJHC Abbreviary (with H de Glanville, 1995); *Recreations* philately, science fiction, computer programming, collecting Elvis Presley records; *Style*— Dr Adrian V Stokes, OBE; ✉ 97 Millway, Mill Hill, London NW7 3JL (tel 020 8959 6665, fax 020 8906 4137, mobile 07785 502766)

STOKES, Dr Alistair; *b* 22 July 1948; *Educ* Univ of Wales (BSc, PhD), Univ of Oxford (SRC res fellowship); *m* 22 Aug 1970, Stephanie Mary, da of B H Garland, of Fordingbridge, Hants; 2 da (Charlotte, Samantha); *Career* commercial dir Monsato Co St Louis MO 1980–82 (joined 1976); Glaxo Pharmaceuticals Ltd: int product mangr 1982–83, mktg and sales dir Duncan Flockhart Ltd 1983–85; gen mangr Yorks RHA 1985–87; Glaxo Pharmaceuticals Ltd: dir business devpt 1987–88, md Glaxo Labs Ltd 1988–89, regnl dir Glaxo Holdings plc 1989–90; dir and chief operating offr Porton International 1990–94, chm Ipsen Ltd (formerly Speywood Pharmaceuticals Ltd) 1994–; chm: E Berks Community Health Tst 1992–98, Stowic plc 1998–99; non-exec dir: Octagen Corp 1998–, Quadrant Healthcare plc 1999–2000, Spirogen Ltd 2003–; *Books* Plasma Proteins (1977); *Recreations* reading, walking, music; *Clubs* Naval and Military; *Style*— Dr Alistair Stokes; ✉ Ipsen Ltd, 190 Bath Road, Slough, Berkshire SL1 3XE

STOKES, Baron (Life Peer UK 1969), of Leyland in the County Palatine of Lancaster; Sir Donald Gresham Stokes; kt (1965), TD (1945), DL (Lancs 1968); s of Harry Potts Stokes (d 1954), of Looe, Cornwall, and Mary Elizabeth Gresham, *née* Yates (d 1969); *b* 22 March 1914; *Educ* Blundell's, Harris Inst of Technol Preston; *m* 1, 25 May 1939, Laura Elizabeth Courteney (d 1995), da of late Frederick C Lamb; 1 s (Hon Michael Donald Gresham b 13 June 1947); m 2, 25 June 2000, Mrs Patricia Pascall, *née* Silvester; *Career* cmmnd Royal N Lancs Regt 1938, transferred to REME and served WWII with 8 Army in Middle East and Italy with rank of Lt-Col; student apprentice Leyland Motors Ltd 1930 (export mangr 1946, gen sales and service mangr 1950, dir 1954), md and dep chm Leyland Motor Corp 1963, chm and md British Leyland Motor Corp 1967, chm and chief exec British Leyland Ltd 1973, pres 1975, conslt to Leyland Vehicles 1980, chm and dir The Dutton-Forshaw Motor Group Ltd 1980–90, pres Jack Barclay Ltd 1989–90; dir: Suits 1980–92, The Dovercourt Motor Co 1982–90, KBH Communications 1985–95 (non-exec chm until 1995); pres: CBI 1962, Univ of Manchester Inst of Science and Technol 1972–75, EEF 1967–75; dir: District Bank 1964–69, National Westminster Bank 1969–81, IRC (dep chm 1969–71), EDC for Electronics Industry 1966–68 (chm), London Weekend TV 1967–71; chm: Two Counties Radio 1979–84 (pres 1984–90, chm 1990–94, pres 1994–), GWR Group 1990–94; Cdre Royal Motor Yacht Club 1979–81; Freeman City of London, Liveryman Worshipful Co of Carmen 1964; hon fell Keble Coll Oxford 1968; Hon LLD Lancaster 1967, Hon DTech Loughborough 1968, Hon DSc Southampton 1969, Hon DSc Salford 1971; FIMI (pres 1962), FIRTE (pres 1982–84), MIRA (pres 1966), FIMechE (pres 1972), SAE (USA), FREng 1976 (CEng 1933), FICE 1984; Officier de l'Ordre de la Couronne (Belgium) 1964, Commandeur de l'Ordre de Leopold II (Belgium) 1972; *Recreations* yachting; *Clubs* Royal Motor Yacht, Army and Navy; *Style*— The Rt Hon the Lord Stokes, TD, DL, FREng; ✉ Branksome Cliff, Westminster Road, Poole, Dorset BH13 6JW (tel 01202 763088)

STOKES, Leslie James; s of William James Stokes, and Peggy Florence, *née* Blunsom; *b* 22 May 1951; *Educ* Abbs Cross Tech HS, Sir John Cass Coll, Newcastle upon Tyne Poly (DipAD, RSA travelling bursary prize), RCA (MDes, Braun prize); *m* 1973, Janet Barbara, da of Alfred Johns Victor Hayes; 1 s (William James b 1987), 1 da (Kathryn Louise b 1982); *Career* lectr in 3D design Herts Coll of Art and Design 1976–79, industrial design conslt London and Upjohn 1976–81, ptnr London Associates (industrial design and product devpt) 1981–; Br Design Award 1990; responsible for five Millennium projects; memb various jury panels for Design Cncl Design awards, external examiner Univ of Northumbria 2003; memb Design Business Assoc 1986; FCSD 1989 (MCSD 1981); *Style*— Leslie Stokes, Esq; ✉ London Associates, 105 High Street, Berkhamsted, Hertfordshire HP4 2DG (tel 01442 862631, fax 01442 874354, e-mail office@la-design.co.uk, website www.la-design.co.uk)

STOKES, His Hon Judge Michael George Thomas; QC (1994); s of Michael Philip Stokes (d 1988); *b* 30 May 1948; *Educ* Preston Catholic Coll, Univ of Leeds (LLB); *m* 9 July 1994, Alison H Pollock; 1 da (Anna Elizabeth Hamilton b 19 July 1995), 1 s (Henry James Kerr b 30 May 1999); *Career* called to the Bar Gray's Inn 1971 (Holt scholar, Macaskie scholar); asst lectr Univ of Nottingham 1970–72, in practice Midland & Oxford Circuit 1973–2001, recorder of the Crown Court 1990–2001 (asst recorder 1986–90), circuit judge (Midland Circuit) 2001–, resident judge Leicester Crown Court 2002–; pres Leics and Rutland Magistrates' Assoc 2005–; memb Remuneration and Terms of Work Ctee (formerly Fees and Legal Aid Ctee) Bar Cncl 1996–2000, memb Public Affairs Ctee 2000–01; pres Mental Health Tbnl 1999–; *Recreations* horses, France, travel; *Style*— His Hon Judge Michael Stokes, QC

STOLLER, Anthony David (Tony); CBE (2004); s of Louis Stoller (d 1973), and Pearl, *née* Poster (d 1992); *b* 14 May 1947; *Educ* Hendon Co GS, Gonville & Caius Coll Cambridge (MA, LLB); *m* 1969, Andrea (Andy), *née* Lewisohn; 1 da (Juliette Louise b 1975), 1 s (Timothy b 1976); *Career* grad trainee Thomson Regnl Newspapers 1969–72, mktg mangr Liverpool Daily Post and Echo Ltd 1972–74, sr offr radio then head radio programming IBA 1974–79, dir AIRC 1979–81, md Thames Valley Broadcasting plc 1981–85, md Tyrrell & Green John Lewis Partnership 1985–95, chief exec Radio Authy 1995–2003, external rels dir Ofcom 2003–06; dep chair Joseph Rowntree Fndn 2005–; visiting fell Univ of Bournemouth 2006–; chair Ctee of Reference Friends Provident Stewardship 1999–; *Publications* Wrestling with the Angel (Swarthmore Lecture, 2001); *Recreations* music, cricket, sailing; *Style*— Tony Stoller, Esq, CBE; ✉ 6 Porters House, Porters Lane, Southampton SO14 2AR (e-mail tonystoller@yahoo.co.uk)

STOLLERY, Prof John Leslie; CBE (1994); s of Edgar George Stollery, and Emma Stollery; *b* 21 April 1930; *Educ* E Barnet GS, Imperial Coll of Science and Technol London (BScEng, MScEng, DScEng, DIC); *m* 1956, Jane Elizabeth, da of Walter Reynolds; 4 s; *Career* Aerodynamics Dept De Havilland Aircraft Co 1952–56, reader Aeronautics Dept Imperial Coll London 1962 (lectr 1956); Cranfield Univ (formerly Cranfield Inst of Technol): prof of aerodynamics 1973–95 (emeritus prof 1995–), head Coll of Aeronautics 1976–86 and 1992–95, pro-vice-chllr Faculty of Engrg 1982–85 (dean 1976–79); chm: Aerospace Technol Bd MOD 1986–89, Aviation Ctee DTI 1986–94; pres RAeS 1987–88; memb Airworthiness Requirements Bd 1990–2000; visiting prof: Cornell Aeronautical Labs Buffalo USA 1964, Aeronautical Res Lab Wright Patterson Air Force Base 1971, Nat Aeronautical Lab Bangalore India 1977, Peking Inst of Aeronautics and Astronautics 1979, Univ of Queensland 1983; FRAeS 1975 (Hon FRAeS 1995), FCGI 1984, FAIAA 1988, FREng 1992; *Publications* Shock Tube Research (chief ed, 1971); author of papers in Journal of Fluid Mechanics and other aeronautical jls; *Recreations* watching football, travelling; *Style*— Prof John Stollery, CBE, FREng; ✉ College of Aeronautics, Cranfield University, Cranfield, Bedford MK43 0AL (tel 01234 750111 ext 5089, fax 01234 758207, e-mail j.l.stollery@cranfield.ac.uk)

STOLLIDAY, Ivor Robert; s of Robert Stolliday, and Marie, *née* Winter; *b* 14 September 1946; *Educ* Palmers Sch Grays, UEA (BA, MA); *Career* Dept of Employment 1969–70, British American Tobacco 1970–72, Cmmn on Industrial Relations 1972–75, head Human Resources Dept Anglian Mgmnt Centre 1975–80, ITVA 1980–88 (sec 1982–88), exec dir Television South West 1988–92, chief exec Dartington Hall Trust 1993–2004; chm: Gemini Radio Ltd 1993–95, South West Film and Television Archive 1993–, Sharpham Tst 1998–; dir South West Media Development Agency 1995–2002; visiting prof Calif State Univ Sacramento 1979; tstee Dartington Summer Sch Fndn 1991–; *Recreations* writing, walking; *Style*— Ivor Stolliday, Esq; ✉ Dartington Lodge, Totnes, Devon TQ9 6EN (tel 01803 866998); Dartington Hall Trust, Dartington Hall, Totnes, Devon TQ9 6EJ (tel 01803 847000)

STONE, Maj Gen Anthony Charles Peter; CB (1994); s of Maj Charles Cecil Stone (d 2002), of Somerton, Somerset, and Kathleen Mons, *née* Grogan (d 2003); *b* 25 March 1939; *Educ* St Joseph's Coll, RMA Sandhurst, Staff Coll Camberley; *m* 29 July 1967, (Elizabeth) Mary Eirlys, da of Rev Canon Gideon Davies (d 1987), of Little Comberton, Worcs; 2 s (Guy b 1972, Mark b 1979); *Career* RA: cmmnd 1960, serv in Far East, Middle East, BAOR and UK (light, field, medium, heavy, locating and air def artillery), Battery Cdr Q (Sanna's Post) Battery and 2 i/c 5 Regt RA 1974–75, GSO 2 DASD MOD 1976, DS RMCS 1977, CO 5 Regt RA 1980; founded Special OP Troop 1982, Col GS Def Progs Staff MOD 1983, Mil Dir of Studies RMCS 1985, Dir of Operational Requirements (Land) MOD 1986, Dir Light Weapons Projects MOD 1989, VMGO/DG Policy and Special Projects MOD 1990,

S

DG Land Fighting Systems MOD 1992, DG Land Systems MOD 1994–95, ret Army; Hon Col 5 Regt RA 1990–, Col Cmdt Royal Regt of Artillery 1993–2001, Rep Col Cmdt 1998–99; chm Nash Partnership Ltd 1996–2006, def advsr/ptnr Gracemoor Consultants (UK) 1996–2006, conslt PricewaterhouseCoopers 2006–; memb Ctee UK Defence Forum 1997–, memb Euro-Atlantic Gp 1997–; visiting research fell Dept of Def Studies Univ of York 1996–97; fell RUSI 1997; *Publications* Thoughts on 21st Century Warfare (1999), Trading Freedom for Security (2002), Lessons from Two Gulf Wars (2003), The Numbers Game (2003), The UK's Future Rapid Effects System (2004), Smaller Still & Still Better? Analysis of a reduced army (2005), Prepared or Not Prepared? Is that the question ? (2006); *Recreations* shooting, family, sudoku, writing; *Clubs* Army and Navy; *Style*— Maj Gen Anthony Stone, CB

STONE, Carole; da of Harry A Stone (d 1976), and Kathleen Jacques, *née* Conroy (d 1993); *b* 30 May 1942; *Educ* Ashford County GS for Girls, Southampton Tech Coll; *m* Richard Lindley, s of Lt Col Herbert Guy Lindley, and Penelope Lindley; *Career* joined BBC in 1963 as copy-taker in Newsroom BBC South, asst prodr BBC Radio Brighton 1967–70, gen talks prodr BBC Radio 4 1970, prodr BBC Radio 4's Any Questions? programme 1977–89, freelance TV broadcaster/media conslt 1990–2007; columnist The Church of England Newspaper; dir Lindley Stone Ltd (independent TV prodn co), md YouGovStone Ltd 2007–; pres The Media Soc 1997–99; memb Ctee Women in Journalism 2000–06, dir London Press Club 2001–06; ptnr The Intelligence Squared Debating Forum; tstee The Wallace Collection; patron: Sane, Top UK; *Books* Networking - The Art of Making Friends (2001), The Ultimate Guide to Successful Networking (2004); *Clubs* Reform, Soho House; *Style*— Ms Carole Stone; ✉ Flat 1, 19 Henrietta Street, London WC2E 8QH (tel 020 7379 8664, fax 020 7240 3078, e-mail carole@carolestone.com)

STONE, Clive Graham; s of late Charles Thomas Stone and Frances Lilian Stone; *b* 7 July 1936; *Educ* Northampton Coll of Advanced Technol, City Univ; *m* 1957, Pamela Mary; 3 s; *Career* chm and chief exec Dollond & Aitchison Group plc 1980–93 (gen mgmnt 1968, md 1973, dep chm 1978); dir: Gallaher Ltd 1981–93, Gallaher Pensions Ltd 1984–93, British Retail Consortium 1985–93, Keeler Ltd 1986–93; chm Theodore Hamblin Ltd 1981–93; govr Royal Nat Coll for the Blind 1985–95, vice-pres Fight for Sight 2006– (tstee 1985–, chm 1996–2001), tstee Max Wiseman Meml Fund 1990– (chm 2002–06); Freeman City of London, Master Worshipful Co of Spectacle Makers 1996–97; fell Br Coll of Optometrists; *Recreations* sailing, real tennis, golf; *Clubs* Leamington Tennis Court, Stoneleigh Deer Park Golf, Island Sailing; *Style*— Clive G Stone, Esq; ✉ Abbey Meads, Forrest Road, Kenilworth, Warwickshire CV8 1LT (tel 01926 854553, fax 01926 764324)

STONE, Evan David Robert; QC (1979); s of Laurence George Stone (d 1952), and Lillian Stone (d 1955); *b* 26 August 1928; *Educ* Berkhamsted Sch, Worcester Coll Oxford (MA); *m* 19 Aug 1959, Gisela Bridget Mann; 1 s (Michael David George b 1960); *Career* Nat Serv cmmnd Army, served UK and ME 1947–49; called to the Bar Inner Temple 1954 (bencher 1985); recorder of Crown Courts 1979–98, head of chambers 1988–98; former HM dep coroner Inner W London W Middx and City of London; memb Senate of Inns of Court and the Bar 1985–86; memb Criminal Injuries Compensation Bd 1989–2002; cncllr then alderman London Borough of Islington (dep ldr then ldr of oppn) 1969–74; govr: Moorfields Eye Hosp 1970–79, Highbury Grove Sch 1971–82 (chm of govrs 1978–82); chm City and Hackney HA 1984–92; memb Ctee of Tstees Country Houses Assoc 1994–96; Freeman City of London 1990; *Books* Forensic Medicine (jtly with late Prof Hugh Johnson, 1987); *Recreations* reading, writing, listening to music, sport and games; *Clubs* Garrick, MCC; *Style*— Evan Stone, Esq, QC; ✉ 60 Canonbury Park South, London N1 2JG (tel and fax 020 7226 6820)

STONE, Ven Godfrey Owen; s of William Edward Guy Stone (d 1980), and Shirley Mary, *née* Taylor; *b* 15 December 1949; *Educ* St Bartholomew's GS Newbury, Exeter Coll Oxford (MA), Univ of Birmingham (PGCE), Univ of Sheffield (Diploma in Leadership, Renewal and Mission Studies); *Career* asst curate Rushden-with-Newton Bromswold 1981–86, dir of pastoral studies Wycliffe Hall Oxford 1987–92, rector Bucknall Team Miny 1992–2002, rural dean Stoke-upon-Trent 1998–2002, archdeacon of Stoke-upon-Trent 2002–, hon canon Lichfield Cathedral 2002–; *Recreations* walking, gardening, travel, meteorology, music; *Style*— The Ven the Archdeacon of Stoke-upon-Trent; ✉ Archdeacon's House, 39 The Brackens, Clayton, Newcastle-under-Lyme, Staffordshire ST5 4JL (tel 01782 663066, fax 01782 711165, e-mail archdeacon.stoke@lichfield.anglican.org)

STONE, Prof (Francis) Gordon Albert; CBE (1990); s of late Sidney Charles Stone and late Florence, *née* Coles; *b* 19 May 1925; *Educ* Exeter Sch, Christ's Coll Cambridge (MA, PhD, ScD), Univ of S Calif (Fulbright scholar); *m* 28 June 1956, Judith Maureen, da of late James Hislop, of Sydney, Aust; 3 s (James Francis b 1957, Peter Gordon b 1961, Derek Charles b 1963); *Career* instr then asst prof Harvard Univ 1954–62, reader in inorganic chemistry QMC London 1962–63, prof of inorganic chemistry and head of dept Univ of Bristol 1963–90, Robert A Welch distinguished prof of chemistry Baylor Univ Texas 1990–; visiting prof: Monash Univ Aust 1966, Princeton Univ 1967, Pennsylvania State Univ 1968, Univ of Arizona 1970, Carnegie Mellon Univ 1972, Rhodes Univ 1976; lectures: Boomer Univ of Alberta 1965, Firestone Univ of Wisconsin 1970, Tilden Chemical Soc 1971, Ludwig Mond RSC 1982, Reilly Univ of Notre Dame 1983, Waddington Univ of Durham 1984, Sir Edward Frankland prize lectureship RSC 1987, G W Watt Univ of Texas (Austin) 1988; Royal Soc of Chemistry: memb Cncl 1967–70 and 1981–83, pres Dalton Div 1981–83 (vice-pres 1983–85); SERC: memb Chemistry Ctee 1972–74 and 1982–85, chm Inorganic Chemistry Panel 1982–85, Royal Soc assessor on Science Bd 1986–88; Royal Society: memb Cncl 1986–88, vice-pres 1987–88; chm: 4th Int Conf on Organometallic Chemistry Bristol 1969, Royal Soc of Chemistry Conf on the Chemistry of Platinum Metals Bristol 1981, UGC Review of Chemistry in UK Univs 1988; Awards: Organometallic Chemistry medal 1972, Transition Metal Chemistry medal RSC 1979, Chugaev medal Inst of Inorganic Chemistry USSR Acad of Scis 1978, American Chemistry Soc award in Inorganic Chemistry 1985, Davy medal Royal Soc 1989, Longstaff medal RSC 1990; Hon DSc: Univ of Exeter 1992, Waterloo Univ (Canada) 1992, Univ of Durham 1993, Univ of Salford 1993, Zaragoza Univ (Spain) 1994; FRSC 1970, FRS 1976; *Publications* Inorganic Polymers (ed 1962), Hydrogen Compounds of the Group IV Elements (1962), Advances in Organometallic Chemistry (co-ed 1964–2000, now in 47 volumes), Comprehensive Organometallic Chemistry I and II (ed, 1984 and 1995), Leaving No Stone Unturned (autobiography, 1993); *Recreations* travel; *Style*— Prof Gordon Stone, CBE, FRS; ✉ 88 Hackberry Avenue, Waco, Texas 76706 USA (tel 254 752 3617); Department of Chemistry, Baylor University, Box 7348, Waco, Texas 76798–7348 (tel 254 710 4427, fax 254 710 2403, e-mail gordon_stone@baylor.edu)

STONE, Dr Gordon Victor; s of Victor John Stone (d 1972), of Aberdeen, and Madeleine O'Brien, *née* Imlach; *b* 4 October 1945; *Educ* Aberdeen GS, Univ of Aberdeen (MB ChB, union sec), Univ of Edinburgh (DCM); *m* 16 July 1969, Aileen Susanna, da of James Manson Wilson; 1 da (Joanna Carol b 17 March 1972), 1 s (Euan James Gordon b 10 Dec 1973); *Career* med offr RAF 1970–75, Scottish Health Serv fell in community med 1975–78, specialist in community med Grampian Health Bd Aberdeen 1978–89, sr lectr Univ of Aberdeen 1984–89, chief exec Highland Health Bd Inverness 1994–99 (chief medical offr and dir of public health 1989–94), dir Information and Clinical Effectiveness Highland Health Bd 1999–; FFPHM 1987 (MFCM 1977, MFCM Ireland 1990), FRSA; *Recreations* hill walking, climbing, golf, motor cycling, modern literature; *Style*— Dr Gordon V Stone; ✉ Highland Health Board, Beechwood Park, Inverness IV2 3HG (tel 01463 704887, e-mail gordon.stone@hhb.scot.nhs.uk)

STONE, His Hon Judge Gregory; QC (1994); s of Frederick Albert Leslie Stone, and Marion Gerda, *née* Heller; *b* 12 December 1946; *Educ* Chislehurst and Sidcup GS, L'Université de Rennes, The Queen's Coll Oxford (MA), Univ of Manchester (DipEcon, MA(Econ)); *Children*; 3 da (Rebecca Anne b 18 March 1978, Catherine Marion b 24 Feb 1980, Alexandra Grace b 26 April 1991); *Career* sr economist Morgan Grenfell & Co 1974–76; called to the Bar Inner Temple 1976; standing counsel to DTI 1989–90, practising barr SE Circuit, recorder 2000–01 (asst recorder 1998–2000), circuit judge 2001–; memb Ctee Planning and Environment Bar Assoc 1999–2000; *Books* The Law of Defective Premises (co-author, 1982), The Architect's Journal (co-ed, 2–5 edns); *Recreations* architecture, landscape, travel, walking, music, reading; *Clubs* Athenaeum; *Style*— His Hon Judge Gregory Stone, QC; ✉ Southwark Crown Court, 1 English Grounds, off Battlebridge Lane, London SE1 2HU (tel 020 7522 7200, e-mail gregorystoneqc@btopenworld.com)

STONE, James Hume Walter Miéville; MSP; s of Edward Reginald Stone (d 1986), of Knockbreck, Tain, and Susannah Gladys Hume, *née* Waddell-Dudley; *b* 16 June 1954; *Educ* Tain Royal Acad, Gordonstoun, Univ of St Andrews (MA); *m* 12 Sept 1981, Flora Kathleen Margaret, *née* Armstrong; 2 da (Georgina Margaret Alice b 16 July 1982, Katharine Madeleine Lestrange b 24 Sept 1984), 1 s (Rupert Michael Dudley Maxwell b 24 Sept 1984); *Career* previous jobs incl cleaning, fish-gutting and teaching; site admin Conoco Hutton TLP Project 1984, admin manager Odfjell Drilling & Consulting Co Ltd 1984–86, dir Highland Fine Cheeses Ltd 1986–94; memb Ross & Cromarty DC (vice-chm Policy and Resources) 1986–96, memb Highland Cncl (vice-chm Finance) 1995–99; MSP (Lib Dem) Caithness, Sutherland & Easter Ross 1999–; Lib Dem spokesman: educn and children 1999–2000, fisheries and Highlands 2000–01, equal opportunities 2001–03, finance 2002–03, enterprise, lifelong learning and tourism 2003–07, public health 2007–; Scot Parl: memb Educn, Culture and Sport Ctee 1999–2000, memb Local Govt Ctee 1999–2001, memb Holyrood Progress Gp 2000–04, memb Equal Opportunities Ctee 2001–03, memb Fin Ctee 2002–03, memb Edinburgh Tram (Line One) Ctee 2004–05, memb Enterprise and Culture Ctee 2003–07, chair Art Gp 2002–, dep convenor Communities Ctee 2006–07, convenor Subordinate Legislation Ctee 2007–; memb Exec Ctee (Scotland) Cwlth Parly Assoc; gen cmmr Inland Revenue, memb Cromarty Firth Port Authy 1997–2000, memb (former chm) Tain Community Cncl; dir Highland Festival 1994–2000, govr Eden Ct Theatre 1996–1999, dir Grey Coast Theatre 2000–, dir Scot Parl Business Exchange 2003– (convenor 2004–06); tstee: Tain Museum Tst, Tain Guildry Tst; freelance newspaper columnist for Aberdeen Press & Journal, Ross-Shire Journal and John O'Groat Journal, occasional broadcaster; FRSA; *Recreations* shooting, golf, music, gardening, butterflies, fungi; *Clubs* New (Edinburgh), Armagh; *Style*— Jamie Stone, Esq, MSP; ✉ Sloibcoyle, Edderton, Tain IV19 1LQ (tel 01862 821500); The Scottish Parliament, Edinburgh EH99 1SP (tel 0131 348 5790, fax 0131 348 5807, e-mail jamie.stone.msp@scottish.parliament.uk)

STONE, John Michael; MBE (1991); s of Robert Alfred Stone (d 1983), and Josephine Margery, *née* Sheen (d 2000); *b* 26 April 1941; *Educ* Framlingham Coll; *m* 2 May 1964, Maxine Campbell, da of John Campbell-Lemon (d 1999); 3 da (Karen b 1965, Paula b 1966, Nicola b 1970), 1 s (Timothy b 1974); *Career* md E Russell (West Country) Ltd 1971; chm: E Russell Ltd 1983 (dir 1962), Donald Russell Ltd 1984, Russell Meats Ltd 1984–99, Sims Food Group plc 1988–96 (jt chm 1989); dir: Meat Training Council Ltd 1994–96, Le Riche Gp Ltd 1995–99; Freeman City of London 1964, Worshipful Co of Butchers (Liveryman 1965); fell Inst of Meat; *Books* Meat Buyers' Guide for Caterers (1983), Poultry and Game Buyers' Guide (1995); *Recreations* shooting, golf, cricket; *Clubs* MCC; *Style*— John Stone, Esq, MBE; ✉ Le Courtil a Gots, Rue de la Porte, Castel, Guernsey GY5 7JR

STONE, Joss; *née* Joscelyn Eve Stoker; *b* 1987, Devon; *Educ* Uffculme Comp Cullumpton; *Career* singer and songwriter; face of Gap advtg campaign 2005; Best Br Female and Best Urban Act Brit Awards 2005, nomination: Mercury Music Prize 2004, Best New Artist Grammy Awards 2005; *Singles* Super Duper Love 2004, You Had Me 2004, Right to be Wrong 2005, Spoiled 2005; *Albums* The Soul Sessions 2004, Mind, Body and Soul 2004; *Style*— Ms Joss Stone

STONE, Martin; s of Abraham Stone (d 1971), of Cardiff, S Wales, and Eva Priscilla, *née* Anstee (d 1988); *b* 28 February 1945; *Educ* The Cathedral Sch Llandaff, Canton HS Cardiff, Univ of Liverpool (MB ChB, MD); *m* 4 July 1970, Jane, da of Tudor Lloyd-Williams (d 1978), of Mold, N Wales; 2 s (Andrew Martin b 1971, Robert Charles b 1975), 1 da (Louise Jane b 1980); *Career* jr doctor Liverpool Hosps 1968–72, SHO Torbay Hosp 1972–73, registrar Charing Cross Hosp 1973–75, res registrar MRC 1975–76; sr registrar: St George's Hosp 1976–77, Southampton Hosp 1977–80; conslt gynaecologist Royal Gwent Hosp NHS Trust 1980–; dir Fedn of Ind Practitioner Orgns (FIPO) 2002; memb: Med Advsy Ctee BUPA Hosp Cardiff (chm 1989), London Obstetric and Gynaecological Soc (chm 1992), Med Advsy Ctee St Joseph's Private Hosp (chm 2000–), Welsh Obstetric and Gynaecological Soc (treas 1981–92, pres 2004); pres Caerleon Rotary Club 1992; memb: BMA, Acad of Experts; FRCOG 1986 (MRCOG 1973); *Recreations* skiing, red wine, theatre, golf; *Clubs* Celtic Manor Golf and Country; *Style*— Martin Stone, Esq; ✉ Ye Olde Forge, Llanmartin, Newport, Gwent NP18 2EB (tel 01633 413073, fax 01633 411148, e-mail marjan@globalnet.co.uk); St Joseph's Private Hospital, Harding Avenue, Malpas, Newport, Gwent NPT 6QS (tel 01633 820300); BUPA Hospital, Croescadarn Road, Pentwyn, Cardiff, South Glamorgan CF2 7XL (tel 029 2073 5515)

STONE, Michael John Christopher; DL (Glos 2002); s of Henry Frederick Stone (d 1979), and Joan Barbara, *née* Da Silva; *b* 10 May 1936; *Educ* Bradfield Coll, Hamburg (Language Course); *m* 8 Jan 1966, Louisa, da of Robert Dyson, of Peru; 2 s (Charles b 9 Oct 1966, Andrew b 21 Nov 1970), 1 da (Nicola (Mrs Edward Farquhar) b 11 Jan 1968); *Career* cmmnd RHA 1955–57, served Germany, cmmnd HAC 1957–63; gp chm E D & F Man 1983–2000 (commodity broker 1957); chm: E D & F Man Sugar Ltd, London Sugar Futures Market 1981–84, Wentworth Wooden Jigsaw Co Ltd 1998–, E D & F Man (Holdings) Ltd 2000–03; dir: Alistair Sampson Antiques 1991–, Standard Bank Jersey Ltd 1992–95, Calcot Manor Hotel 1993–, Redhill Aerodrome Ventures Ltd 1995–; chm: Bradfield Fndn 1991–2006, Nat Hosp for Neurology and Neurosurgery Devpt Fndn 1993–98; govr Bradfield Coll 1991–2006; *Recreations* shooting, fishing, skiing; *Clubs* Brooks's, White's; *Style*— Michael Stone, Esq, DL; ✉ Ozleworth Park, Wotton-under-Edge, Gloucestershire GL12 7QA (tel 01453 845591)

STONE, Prof Nicholas James (Nick); s of Frederick James Stone (d 1996), and Edith Mary, *née* Ingham; *b* 1 April 1938, Portsmouth, Hants; *Educ* Portsmouth GS, ChCh Oxford (BA, DPhil); *m* 1, July 1963 (m dis 1984), Mary Christine Gregory; 2 s (Graham Nicholas b 16 Nov 1964, Adrian Richard Ingham b 25 Oct 1969), 1 da (Deborah Frances b 12 Nov 1966); m 2, 30 Nov 1985, Jirina Rikovska; *Career* research physicist Lawrence Berkeley Laboratory 1963–65; Univ of Oxford: research asst Clarendon Laboratory 1965–69, head Low Temperature Nuclear Orientation Research Gp Clarendon Laboratory 1965–2005, lectr in physics 1969–97, prof of physics 1997–2005 (prof emeritus 2005–); tutorial fell in physics St Edmund Hall Oxford 1969–; visiting prof: Univ of Br Columbia 1976–77, Univ of Lyons 1986, Univ of NSW 1987; visiting scientist Los Alamos Nat Laboratory 1977, research assoc CERN Geneva 1990 and 1999, research prof Univ of Tennessee 2002–, research prof Univ of Maryland 2004–05; memb UK nat research ctees SERC, memb Bd Int Research Jls and Int Research Confs; compiler Int Table of Nuclear Moments Brookhaven Nat Nuclear Data Centre 1996–; Pressed Steel Fellowship 1963–65,

DSIR Fellowship 1966–69; *Publications* Low Temperature Nuclear Orientation (1986); over 200 papers on hyperfine interactions and low energy nuclear structure physics; *Recreations* travelling, reading, philately; *Style—* Prof Nick Stone; ✉ Clarendon Laboratory, Department of Physics, Oxford University, Parks Road, Oxford OX1 3PU (tel 01865 272325, fax 01865 272400, e-mail n.stone1@physics.ox.ac.uk)

STONE, Prof Norman; s of Flt Lt Norman Stone, RAF (ka 1942), and Mary Robertson, *née* Pettigrew (d 1991); *b* 8 March 1941; *Educ* Glasgow Acad, Gonville & Caius Coll Cambridge (BA, MA); *m* 1, 2 July 1966 (m dis 1977), Marie Nicole Aubry; 2 s (Nicholas b 1966, Sebastian b 1972); m 2, 11 Aug 1982, Christine Margaret Booker, *née* Verity; 1 s (Rupert b 1983); *Career* Univ of Cambridge: fell Gonville & Caius Coll 1965–71, lectr in Russian history 1968–84, fell Jesus Coll 1971–79, fell Trinity Coll 1979–84; Univ of Oxford: prof of modern history 1984–97, fell Worcester Coll 1984–97; prof of int relations Bilkent Univ Ankara 1997–; *Books* The Eastern Front 1914–1917 (1975, Wolfson Prize 1976), Hitler (1980), Europe Transformed 1878–1919 (1983), The Other Russia (with Michael Glenny, 1990); *Recreations* Eastern Europe, music; *Clubs* Garrick, Beefsteak; *Style—* Prof Norman Stone; ✉ 22 St Margarets Road, Oxford OX2 6RX (tel 01865 439481); Department of International Relations, Bilkent University, 06533 Bilkent, Ankara, Turkey

STONE, Maj-Gen Patrick Philip Dennant; CB (1992), CBE (1984, OBE 1981, MBE 1976); s of Dr Philip Hartley Stone (d 1947), and Elsie Maude, *née* Dennant (d 1993); *b* 7 February 1939; *Educ* Christ's Hosp; *m* 5 June 1967, Christine Iredale, da of Gp Capt Leonard Henry Trent, VC (d 1986); 2 s (Edward Patrick Dennant b 1969, Robert Michael b 1972), 1 da (Celia Elizabeth b 1974); *Career* cmmnd E Anglian Regt 1959, King's African Rifles (Tanzania) 1959–61, Regtl Serv Guyana and Saudi Arabia 1962–64, ADC Govr WA 1965–67, Regt Serv UK W Germany and NI 1967–72, RAF Staff Coll 1972, CO 2 Bn Royal Anglian Regt 1977–80, COS 1 Armd Div 1981–84, Cdr Berlin Bde 1985–87, DG Personnel (Army) 1988, ret 1991; dir of admin Norton Rose slrs 1991–99; Col Royal Anglian Regt 1991–97; *Recreations* country pursuits; *Clubs* Army and Navy; *Style—* Maj-Gen Patrick Stone, CB, CBE; ✉ Home Farm, Hempnall Green, Norwich, Norfolk NR15 2NP (tel 01508 499472)

STONE, Peter John; s of late Dr Thomas Scott Stone; *b* 24 June 1946; *Educ* King's Sch Canterbury, Christ's Coll Cambridge; *m* 1972, Alison, da of Robert Smith Moffett; 2 s, 2 da; *Career* slr, ptnr Clintons 1972–75, banker Close Brothers Ltd 1975–98, dir Stone Alone Ltd 1998–; non-exec dir: Alliance & Leicester plc until 2004, Intermediate Capital Gp, Opus Portfolio Ltd, DTZ Holdings plc; chm Careforce Gp plc until 2007; *Recreations* travel, cricket, tennis, sailing, golf, gardening, music; *Style—* Peter Stone, Esq; ✉ Stone Alone Ltd, 1 Albemarle Street, London W1S 4HA (tel 020 7491 7111, fax 020 7491 8111)

STONE, Philippa Jane; da of (Vivian) Harry George Stubbs (d 1997), of Duston, Northants, and Merle Josephine Mure McKerrell Stubbs, *née* Carver (d 1992); *Educ* Notre Dame HS Northampton, Univ of St Andrews, Univ of Oxford (BSc); *m* (m dis), David Robert Stone, s of Robert Charles Stone (d 2003); 1 da; *Career* business conslt; dir: P J Stone Ltd 1984–2002 and 2006–, Sharepoint Ltd 1984–88, City Child Ltd (chm 1985–86), Children of High Intelligence Ltd 1991–94; tstee Self Esteem Network 1992–96 (chm 1994–95); memb: Redbridge HA 1989–91, European Union of Women (chm London E 1991–95, hon sec Gtr London Area 1992–95), London Cycling Campaign 1996–97; chair Clapham Park West Residents Assoc 2003–04; FMS; *Recreations* art, opera, skiing, tennis; *Clubs* St Andrews Univ Alumni (London, chm 1993–2001, vice-chm 2003–04); *Style—* Mrs Philippa Stone

STONE, Rex; s of Hiram Stone, of Belper, Derbys, and Elsie Lorraine, *née* Taylor; *b* 13 August 1938; *Educ* Herbert Strutt GS; *m* 16 Oct 1965, Anita Kay, da of Albert Arthur Hammond (d 1974), of London; 1 s (Alistair b 7 May 1971), 1 da (Rachel b 23 March 1969); *Career* CA; audit mangr Peat Marwick Mitchell & Co (Jamaica) 1961–65, co sec RB MacMillan Ltd 1965–69; chm: Firestone Investments Ltd 1972–, Alida Holdings plc 1974–92 (fin dir 1969–72, jt md 1972–74), Chevin Holdings Ltd 1975–; dep chm: Derbyshire Building Society 1985–, British Polythene Industries plc 1989–98; FCA 1961; *Recreations* wine, travel, game shooting, golf; *Style—* Rex Stone, Esq; ✉ Firestone Investments Ltd, 29 Bridge Street, Belper, Derby DE56 1AY (tel 01773 827151, fax 01773 829843)

STONE, Richard Anthony; s of Jack Stone (d 1990), and Margaret Elizabeth, *née* Baraclough (d 1983); *b* 3 March 1943; *Educ* Univ of Cambridge (MA); *m* 26 Jan 1975, Susan Joan, da of Ronald James; 2 da (Natasha Louise b 4 Oct 1980, Katrina Elizabeth b 27 June 1984); *Career* Corp Fin Dept Outwich Ltd 1969–72, fin dir Regional Properties Ltd 1972–74; W H Cork Gully & Co (merged with Coopers & Lybrand 1980): articled clerk 1965–68, rejoined 1974, ptnr 1977–, head Insolvency Practice for the Midlands (Birmingham Office) 1982–86, head Corp Fin Div 1987, chm Euro Corp Fin 1992–98, dep chm UK firm 1995–98; memb Global Bd PricewaterhouseCoopers (formerly Coopers & Lybrand) 1998–2000; chm: Shearings Gp Ltd 2001–, Drambuie Ltd; dir: Halma plc 2001–, TR Property Investment Tst 2001–, British Nuclear Fuel plc 2001–05, Agape Ministries Ltd 2001–, Gartmore Global Tst 2002–, Candover Investments plc 2005–; Past Master Worshipful Co of Glaziers (Freeman 1973), Freeman Worshipful Co of CAs; memb City Livery; FCA; *Recreations* opera, ballet, golf, horse racing, travel, gardening; *Clubs* Carlton, IOD; *Style—* Richard A Stone, Esq; ✉ e-mail richard.a.stone@talk21.com

STONE, Richard Frederick; QC (1968); s of Sir Leonard Stone, OBE, QC (d 1978), and Madeleine Marie, *née* Scheffler; *b* 11 March 1928; *Educ* Lakefield Coll Ontario, Rugby, Univ of Cambridge (MA); *m* 1, 1957, Georgina Maxwell, *née* Morris (decd); 2 da (Victoria b 1958, Diana b 1960); m 2, 1964, Susan, *née* van Heel; 2 da (Georgina b 1965, Amelia b 1967); *Career* Lt Worcester Regt 1946–48; called to the Bar Gray's Inn 1952 (bencher 1974, treas 1992); memb: Panel of Lloyd's Arbitrators in Salvage 1968–99, Panel of Wreck Cmmn 1968–98; *Recreations* sailing, windsurfing, diving; *Clubs* Hayling Island Sailing; *Style—* Richard Stone, Esq, QC; ✉ 18 Wittering Road, Hayling Island, Hampshire PO11 9SP (e-mail rrfstone@btinternet.com); Flat N, Rectory Chambers, 50 Old Church Street, Chelsea, London SW3 5DA (tel 020 7351 1719); Stone Chambers, 4 Field Court, Gray's Inn, London WC1R 5EF (tel 020 7440 6900)

STONE, Richard William; s of Leonard William Stone, of Colchester, Essex, and Thelma May, *née* Sparkes; *b* 5 June 1951; *Educ* Colchester Stanway Secdy Sch, Gilberd Sch Colchester; *m* 1, 1975 (m dis 1990), Anthea Margaret, da of Capt Frank Harvey Stephenson, DFC; 2 da (Flavia Xanthe b 28 Oct 1980, Chloe Beatrice b 5 Nov 1984); m 2, 1991, Rhonda Marie, da of Curtis E Miller, MD; 1 s (William Russell b 3 May 1994); *Career* portrait painter; teacher: Copford Glebe School Colchester 1970–71, Colchester Inst 1977–83, Art Centre Pasadena CA 1987–88; delivered numerous invited lectures; subject of many film and TV reports and numerous newspaper articles; vice-pres Colchester Cncl for Voluntary Serv, tstee Minories Art Gallery Colchester 1996, memb Heritage Ctee Royal London Insurance 1998; Paul Harris Fellowship Aust 2001; Freeman City of London 1985, Liveryman Worshipful Co of Painter Stainers; Hon Citizen Austin TX 1989, Hon Texan 1990; *Major Commissions* subjects incl: Sir Arthur Bliss, Sir Adrian Boult, Sir Yehudi Menuhin, HM Queen Elizabeth The Queen Mother, Chief Red Fox, Burmese Nat Dance Co, HRH Princess Margaret, HRH Princess Alice Duchess of Gloucester, HRH Prince Michael of Kent, HRH Princess Michael of Kent, Eric Morecambe, Lord Boothby, Prof Donald Denman, Leo McKern, Viscount De L'Isle, Sir Robert Carswell, Prof Ivor A Richards, Prof Clive Parry, Prof Jeremy Cowan, Prof Stuart Sutherland, Dame Mary Donaldson, Sir Allan Davis, Sir Ralph Perring, Lord Home, Lord Wilson of Rievaulx, Lord Callaghan, US ambass Charles H Price II, Beth Chatto, Dr Marvin Goldberger, HRH The Princess Royal, Ronald Lancaster, Lord Grey of Naunton, Sir James Miskin, Dr James Hooley, HM The Queen, Joseph Maitland Robinson, Neil Foster, Lady Holt, Lady Buck, The Marquess of Tavistock, Lord James Russell, Lord and Lady Robin Russell, Sir Evelyn de Rothschild, William Lese, Bruno Schroder, US ambass William Crowe, Nina Wang, Earl Cadogan, HRH The Duke of York, Michael Pickard, Stanley Booth, HRH The Duke of Edinburgh, HRH The Prince of Wales, the wedding of HRH Prince Edward and Sophie Rhys-Jones, Dame Joan Sutherland, Geng Zhao Jie, Baroness Thatcher, HRH The Duchess of Gloucester, Archbishop Desmond Tutu, Dr James Watson, Richard Wheeler, Gerald Milsom, Luciano Pavarotti, HRH The Countess of Wessex, HRH The Duke of Gloucester, Dame Julie Andrews, Mrs Michael Howard, Lord Sterling of Plaistow, Sir Neil Thorne, Baroness Thatcher (for The Ronald Reagan Library), Rt Hon Michael Howard, Sir Simon Jenkins, Hanabi-ko (Koko), Nancy Reagan, Judy Naake, Michael Grade; *Exhibitions* Plymouth City Art Gallery 1974, Digby Gallery Colchester 1977, QEII (transatlantic liner) 1983–86, Pembroke Coll Cambridge 1984, English Speaking Union of the US 1986 (touring exhbn), Huntington Library and Art Gallery CA 1987, UK/LA Festival Univ of Southern Calif and Woodbury Univ Calif 1988, Laguna Gloria Art Museum Austin TX 1989, Br Consul-Gen's residence LA 1991, Nat Portrait Gall 1992, Faces and Figures (Nassau Co Museum NY) 1997, Westwood Park Colchester 1998, Met Museum of Art NY 2000, Camberwell Rotary Art Show Melbourne 2001, Notable Portraits (Partridge Fine Arts London) 2004, Cold Spring Harbour Lab Long Island NY 2004, Politics of Portraits (J Paul Getty Museum) 2005, LA Regency Club 2005; *Recreations* classical music, gardening; *Style—* Richard Stone, Esq; ✉ West Bergholt Lodge, Colchester, Essex CO6 3EA (tel 01206 241241, fax 01206 240783, e-mail richard.stone@richardstoneuk.com, website www.richardstoneuk.com)

STONE, Terence Reginald Stewart; s of Harry Victor Stone, of Grey Stones, Dawlish, Devon, and Hilda Mary, *née* Western; *b* 18 August 1928; *Educ* Willesden Coll of Technol, Regent St Coll of Architecture, Westminster Univ; *Children* 4 s, 2 da; *Career* sr architect RAF Air Works Sqdn Air Miny 1947–49; chief architect Costain (W Africa) Ltd 1956–60, chm Terence Stone Gp of Companies 1970–, sr ptnr Stewart Stone Design Consits 1988–; md: Terence Stone (Devpt) Ltd 1962–, Terence Stone (Construction) Ltd 1975–; Lord of the Manor Earl Stone Hants; FCIOB, FRSH, FIAS, FCIM, FFB, MRICS; *Recreations* swimming, tennis, badminton, running, motor rallying, skiing, sponsorship and promotion of sport, travel, arts; *Clubs* Rolls Royce Enthusiasts, RROC, Rolls Royce Silver Ghost Assoc (European dir 2000–), RAC; *Style—* Terence Stone, Esq; ✉ Weston House, Hardwick, Plympton, Devon PL7 1UG

STONE, Prof Trevor William; s of Thomas William Stone, and Alice, *née* Reynolds; *b* 7 October 1947; *Educ* Mexborough GS, Univ of London (BPharm, DSc), Univ of Aberdeen (PhD); *m* 1, 1971, Anne, da of Dr Lewis Corina; m 2, 2005, Gail, da of the late William Darlington; *Career* lectr in physiology Univ of Aberdeen 1970–77; Univ of London: sr lectr in neurosciences 1977–83, reader 1983–86, prof of neurosciences 1986–88; prof of pharmacology Univ of Glasgow 1989–; research fell Nat Inst Mental Health Washington DC 1974 and 1977; scientific dir ShinKanco 2002–, dir PharmaLinks 2003–; fell NY Acad of Sci, FRSM, fell Br Pharmacology Soc; *Books* Microiontophoresis (1985), Purines: Basic & Clinical (1991), Adenosine in the Nervous System (1991), Neuropharmacology (1995), Pills, Potions, Poisons (2000); *Recreations* snooker, photography, painting, music; *Style—* Prof T W Stone; ✉ Institute of Biomedical and Life Sciences, West Medical Building, University of Glasgow, Glasgow G12 8QQ (tel 0141 330 4481, e-mail t.w.stone@bio.gla.ac.uk)

STONEFROST, Hilary; da of Maurice Frank Stonefrost, CBE, DL, and Audrey Jean, *née* Fishlock; *b* 12 November 1955; *Educ* LSE (MSc), City Univ (Dip Law), Inns of Court Sch of Law; *m* 1, Aug 1981 (m dis), Nourollah Nourshargh; m 2, Oct 1992, William James Gregory Keegan, *qv*, s of William Keegan (d 1995); 2 da (Caitlin Clare b 5 Sept 1994, Lucinda Grace Julia b 18 Dec 1997), 1 s (James Patrick William (twin) b 18 Dec 1997); *Career* economist Bank of England 1979–89, report for British Bankers Assoc on Euro Central Bank 1990; called to the Bar Middle Temple 1991; visiting tutor in law City Univ 1991–92, ad hoc work for conslts London Economics 1991–92, practising barr and memb Chambers of Michael Crystal QC 3/4 South Square 1992–; *Books* The Law of Receivers and Companies (contrib); *Style—* Ms Hilary Stonefrost; ✉ 3/4 South Square, Gray's Inn, London WC1R 5HP (tel 020 7696 9900, fax 020 7696 9911, e-mail clerks@southsquare.com)

STONEHAM, Prof (Arthur) Marshall; s of Garth Rivers Stoneham (d 1985), and Nancy Wooler, *née* Leslie (d 1997); *b* 18 May 1940; *Educ* Barrow-in-Furness GS for Boys, Univ of Bristol (Merchant Venturers' scholar, BSc, PhD); *m* 25 Aug 1962, Doreen, da of John Montgomery (d 1974), of Barrow-in-Furness; 2 da ((Vanessa) Elise b 2 Sept 1963, (Karen) Nicola b 27 Jan 1966); *Career* Harwell Laboratory UKAEA: res fell Theoretical Physics Div 1964–66, sr scientific offr 1966–70, princ scientific offr 1970–74, gp leader Solid State Materials Gp (later Solid State and Quantum Physics Gp) 1974–89, individual merit promotion to Sr Staff Level 1979 (Band Level 1974), head Tech Area Gen Nuclear Safety Res Prog (Core and Fuel Studies) 1988–89, div head Materials Physics and Metallurgy Div 1989–90, dir Res AEA Industrial Technol 1990–93, AEA chief scientist 1993–97, Massey prof of physics and dir Centre for Materials Research UCL 1995–2005 (emeritus 2005–, hon fell 2006–); dir Oxford Authentication Ltd 1998–; visiting prof Univ of Illinois 1969, Wolfson industrial fell Wolfson Coll Oxford 1985–89 (fell Governing Body 1989–95); visiting prof of chemistry Keele Univ 1988–, visiting prof of physics Univ of Salford 1992–, Lloyd Braga prof Univ of the Minho Portugal 2005; memb Cncl Royal Instn 1992–95; Inst of Physics: ed Jl of Physics C - Solid State Physics 1984–88 (dep ed 1982–84), memb Editorial Bd Semiconductor Sci and Technol 1986–87, chm Books Editorial Advsy Ctee 1988–90, dir Inst of Physics Publishing 1988–2001, memb Cncl 1994–2001, vice-pres 1997–2001, ed-in-chief Jl of Physics - Condensed Matter 2002–06 (memb Exec Editorial Bd 1989–91); memb Cncl Royal Soc 1994–96; chm Hooke Ctee Royal Soc 1992–2000; divnl assoc ed Physical Review Letters (jl of American Physics Soc) 1992–96; memb Polar Solids Gp Ctee RSC; Zeneca Prize Royal Soc 1995, Guthrie Prize Inst of Physics 2006; FInstP 1980, FRS 1989, FIM 1996, fell American Physics Soc 1996; *Books* Theory of Defects in Solids (1975, Russian edn 1978, reprinted 1985, 1996 and 2001), Defects and Defect Processes in Non-Metallic Solids (with W Hayes, 1985), Reliability of Non-Destructive Inspection (with M G Silk and J A G Temple, 1987), Current Issues in Solid State Science (various), Ionic Solids at High Temperatures (1989), Ge Si Strained Layers and their Applications (1995), The Wind Ensemble Sourcebook and Biographical Guide (1997, CB Oldman Prize Int Assoc of Music Librarians 1997), The Wind Ensemble Catalog (1998), Materials Modification by Electronic Excitation (with N Itoh, 2000); *Recreations* music scholarship, orchestral horn playing, reading; *Style—* Prof Marshall Stoneham, FRS; ✉ 14 Bridge End, Dorchester-on-Thames, Wallingford, Oxfordshire OX10 7JP (tel 01865 340066); London Centre for Nanotechnology and Physics Department, University College London, Gower Street, London WC1E 6BT (tel 020 7679 1377 (direct), 020 7679 1308, fax 020 7679 1360 and 020 7679 7145, e-mail ucapams@ucl.ac.uk or a.stoneham@ucl.ac.uk)

STONHOUSE, Rev Sir Michael Philip; 19 (E 1628) and 16 Bt (E 1670), of Radley, Berkshire; s of Sir Philip Allan Stonhouse, 18 and 15 Bt (d 1993), and (Winnifred) Emily, *née* Shield (d 1989); *b* 4 September 1948; *Educ* Medicine Hat Coll, Univ of Alberta (BA), Wycliffe Coll (MDiv); *m* 1977, (Rev) Colleen Eleanor, da of James Albert Coucill (d 1969), of Toronto, Canada; 3 s (Allan James b 1981, David Michael b 1983, Philip Radley b 1987); *Heir* s, Allan Stonhouse; *Career* ordained: deacon 1977, priest 1978 (both Diocese of

Calgary, Canada); asst curate St Peter's Calgary Alberta 1977–80; rector and incumbent: Parkland Parish Alberta 1980–87, St Mark's Innisfail and St Matthew's Bowden Alberta 1987–92, St James Saskatoon Saskatchewan 1992–; *Style*— The Rev Sir Michael Stonhouse, Bt; ✉ 3413–Balfour Street, Saskatoon, Saskatchewan S7H 3Z3, Canada (tel 306 374 4157, e-mail m.stonhouse@sasktel.net); Work tel 306 653 3531, fax 306 653 6547

STONIER, Prof Peter D; s of Frederic Stonier (d 1981), and Phyllis Stonier; *b* 29 April 1945; *Educ* Cheadle Hulme Sch, Univ of Birmingham (BSc), Univ of Sheffield (PhD), Univ of Manchester (MB ChB), Open Univ (BA); *m* 13 May 1989, Elizabeth Margaret, *née* Thomas; 1 s (Thomas William b 10 April 1990), 1 da (Helen Elizabeth b 29 April 1993); *Career* NHS: house offr gen med and gen surgery Manchester Royal Infirmary 1974–75, SHO psychiatry Univ Hosp S Manchester 1975–76, SHO A&E, orthopaedics, gen surgery Leicester Royal Infirmary 1976–77; Hoechst UK Ltd: med advsr 1977–80, head of med services 1980–81, med dir 1982–94; Hoechst Roussel Ltd: med dir 1994–96, bd memb 1994–96; Hoechst Marion Roussel Ltd: med dir 1996–2000, memb Bd 1996–2000, conslt in pharmaceutical med 2000–; visiting prof in pharmaceutical med: Univ of Surrey 1992–, KCL 1998–; chm: Br Assoc of Pharmaceutical Physicians (BrAPP) 1988–90, Walton Manor Research Ethics Ctee 1982–88; memb cncl and treas Tst for Educn and Research in Therapeutics (TERT) 1990–93, memb Cncl Medical Benefit-Risk Fndn 1990–96, memb Cncl RCP 1998–2001, memb Cncl Alternate Medico-Pharmaceutical Forum; memb ABPI Med Ctee 1990–2000, memb Cncl Br Assoc of Psychopharmacology 1993–97, Appeal Panel Nat Inst for Clinical Excellence (NICE); pres: RSM Section of Pharmaceutical Med & Research 1994–96, Int Fedn of Associations of Pharmaceutical Physicians (IFAPP) 1996–98; Faculty of Pharmaceutical Med: memb Educn Ctee 1989–, memb Bd of Examiners 1994–98, convener and chair Task Force for Higher Specialist Trg in Pharmaceutical Med 1995–, chm Fellowship Ctee 1997–2001, vice-pres 1992–96, pres 1997–2001, dir of educn and trg 2003–; Univ of Surrey: course dir MSc in Pharmaceutical Med 1993–2001, med dir Human Psychopharmacology Research Unit (HPRU) 2001–; med dir: Axess Ltd 2001–, Amdipharm plc 2003–; non-exec dir: Phototherapeutics Ltd, Reneuron Ltd 2000–03; memb: Euro Coll of Neuropsychopharmacology (ECNP), Collegium Internationale Neuro-psychopharmacologicum (CINP), Br Pharmacological Soc, Int Med Club; hon research fell Dept Psychology Univ of Leeds 1983–90; MInstD; FFPM 1989, FRCPE 1993, MRCPsych 1994, FRCP 1998, FRSM, FRSA; *Publications* Human Psychopharmacology vol 1–6 (ed, 1987–97), Pharmaceutical Physician (fndr ed, 1989–98), Human Psychopharmacology Clinical and Experimental (ed, 1994–), Clinical Research Manual (ed, 1994–), Careers with the Pharmaceutical Industry (ed, 1994, 2 edn 2003), Medical Marketing Manual (ed, 2001–), Principles and Practices of Pharmaceutical Medicine (ed, 2002); journals: Pharmaceutical Medicine (assoc ed, 1986–97), Pharmaceutical Visions (ed advsr, 1995–2001), IFAPP News (ed, 1996–), Int Jl of Pharmaceutical Med (assoc ed, 1997–); *Recreations* power cruising, hill walking; *Style*— Professor Peter Stonier; ✉ 5 Branstone Road, Kew, Richmond, Surrey TW9 3LB (tel and fax 020 8948 5069, e-mail peterstonier@btinternet.com)

STONOR, Air Marshal Sir Thomas Henry; KCB (1989); s of Alphonsus Stonor (d 1959), and Ann Stonor (d 1994); *b* 5 March 1936; *Educ* St Cuthbert's HS Newcastle upon Tyne, Kings Coll Durham (BSc); *m* 31 March 1964, Robin Antoinette, da of Wilfrid Budd (d 1980); 1 da (Alexandra Clare b 1965), 2 s (Jeremy Thomas b 1966, Giles Wilfrid b 1969); *Career* cmmnd RAF 1959, No 3 Sqdn 2 ATAF 1961–64, CFS, No 6 FTS, RAF Coll Cranwell 1964–67, No 231 OCU 1967–69, RAF Staff Coll 1970, HQ RAF Germany 1971–73, OC 31 Sqdn 1974–76, MA to VCDS 1976–78, OC RAF Coltishall 1978–80, RCDS 1981, Inspr Flight Safety 1982–84, Dir of Control (Airspace Policy) 1985–86, Dep Controller Nat Air Traffic Servs 1987–88, Gp Dir CAA and Controller Nat Air Traffic Servs 1988–91; aviation conslt 1991–2003; FRAeS; *Recreations* music, gardening; *Clubs* RAF; *Style*— Sir Thomas Stonor, KCB; ✉ 213 Woodstock Road, Oxford OX2 7AD (tel 01865 557640, e-mail thomasstonor@clara.co.uk)

STOPPARD, Dr Miriam; da of Sydney Stern, and Jenny Stern; *b* 12 May 1937; *Educ* Newcastle upon Tyne Central HS, Royal Free Hosp Sch of Med London (prize for experimental physiology), King's Coll Med Sch Univ of Durham (MB BS), Univ of Newcastle upon Tyne (MD, MRCP); *Career* Royal Victorian Infirmary King's Coll Hosp Newcastle upon Tyne: house surgn 1961, house physician 1962, SHO in med 1962–63; Univ of Bristol: res fell Dept of Chemical Pathology 1963–65 (MRC scholar in chemical pathology 1963–65), registrar in dermatology 1965–66 (MRC scholar in dermatology), sr registrar in dermatology 1966–68; Syntex Pharmaceuticals Ltd: assoc med dir 1968–71, dep med dir 1971–74, med dir 1974–76, dep md 1976, md 1977–81, dir Syntex Corp 1991–; hon clinical lectr Inst of Dermatology Univ of London; memb: Heberden Soc, Br Assoc of Rheumatology and Rehabilitation; Hon DSc Univ of Durham 2000, Hon LLD Univ of Newcastle upon Tyne 2004; memb RSM, FRCP 1998; *Television* series: Where There's Life (5 series) 1981–, Baby and Co (2 series) 1984–, Woman to Woman 1985, Miriam Stoppard's Health and Beauty Show 1988 and 1992, Dear Miriam 1989, People Today 1991 and 1992; *Publications* Miriam Stoppard's Book of Baby Care (1977), My Medical School (contrib, 1978), Miriam Stoppard's Book of Health Care (1979), The Face and Body Book (1980), Everywoman's Lifeguide (1982), Your Baby (1982), Fifty Plus Lifeguide (1982), Your Growing Child (1983), Baby Care Book (1983), Pregnancy and Birth Book (1984), Baby and Child Medical Handbook (1986), Everygirl's Lifeguide(1987), Feeding Your Family (1987), Miriam Stoppard's Health and Beauty Book (1988), Every Woman's Medical Handbook (1988), 7 lbs in 7 days (1991), Test Your Child (1991), The Magic of Sex (1991), Conception, Pregnancy and Birth (1992), Menopause (1994), A Woman's Body (1994), Complete Baby and Childcare (1995), Questions Children Ask (1997), Sex Education - Growing Up, Relationships and Sex (1997), The New Parent (1999), Teach Your Child (2001), Family Health Guide (2002), Defying Age (2003), New Pregnancy and Birth Book (2004), Toddler Play Series (I Love Shapes, On the Move, My Busy Day, Amazing Colours, 2006), The Grandparents' Book (2006), Baby Play Skills Series (Baby Senses, Baby Talking, Baby Games, Happy Baby, 2007); over 40 publications in med jls, daily column and weekly health page Daily Mirror, monthly page Tesco Magazine and Top Santé; *Recreations* family, skiing, gardening; *Style*— Dr Miriam Stoppard; ✉ Miriam Stoppard Lifetime Ltd, The Media Village, 131–151 Great Titchfield Street, London W1W 5BB

STOPS, Leigh Warwick; s of Dr Denis Warwick Stops, of Kingston, Surrey, and Patricia, *née* Hill; *b* 29 May 1946; *Educ* Latymer Upper Sch, Univ of Sussex (BSc), Lancaster Univ (MA); *m* 3 Dec 1976, Patricia Jane, da of F H J Terry; 2 s (Caspar b 1986, Galen b 1988); *Career* advertising exec; dir: Colman RSCG & Ptnrs 1984–85, research and planning Allen Brady & Marsh Ltd 1985–90, planning Yellowhammer Advertising Ltd 1991–92, conslt The Business Devpt Gp 1992–96, sr lectr Bournemouth Univ 1992–95, dir planning Publicis Ltd 1994–99, sr planner McCann-Erickson 1999–2003, ceo The Blonde Mouse Gp Ltd 2003–, mktg dir Watermans 2006–; *Recreations* sailing, theatre, media, advertisements; *Style*— Leigh W Stops, Esq; ✉ 5 Foster Road, Chiswick, London W4 4NY (tel 020 8742 7332, e-mail leighstops@blueyonder.co.uk)

STORER, Andrew; s of Thomas Storer (d 1978), and Anne, *née* Slimmon; *Educ* Bishop Wand Sch Sunbury-upon-Thames (memb Chapel Royal Choir Hampton Court Palace), Wimbledon Sch of Art (BA); *m* 1985, Jennifer (d 2006), da of Graham Law, and Isobel Drysdale; *Career* ballet and opera designer; worked for various dance and opera cos worldwide incl: Hannover Opera, Stuttgart Ballet, Theatre du Capitole Toulouse, Ballet du Nord, Teatro dell'Opera Rome, Teatro San Carlo Naples, Teatro Regio Turin, Nat Ballet of Portugal, New Jersey Ballet, Nevada Dance Theatre, Ballet de Santiago; work

included in exhbns and pubns incl: Picasso and the Theatre (Brighton Festival) 1982, Design for Dance (Arnolfini Gallery Bristol) 1985, British Theatre Design: The Modern Age 1990, Make Space 1995, 2D-3D Design for Theatre (Soc of British Theatre Designers) 2002; memb Soc of British Theatre Designers; *Productions* London Contemporary Dance Theatre: Songs and Dances, Motorcade, Shadows in the Sun, Unfolding Field; Ballet Rambert: Lonely Town, Lonely Street, Pribaoutki, Colour Moves (with Bridget Riley , qv), Entre Dos Aguas, Light and Shade; Gothenburg Musikteater: Living in America, Love, Life and Death, Russian Story, Eva; other credits incl: Elvira Madigan (Royal Danish Ballet), Romeo and Juliet (Grand Theatre Geneva, Gothenburg Ballet, Arena di Verona and Scottish Ballet), Offenbach (Grand Theatre Geneva, Arena di Verona and Scottish Ballet), Petrouchka (Grand Theatre de Bordeaux), Short Cuts (Arena di Verona), Bach Dances (Semperoper Dresden), The Snowman (Scottish Ballet), Savoy Suite (Eng Nat Ballet), The Fairy Queen (English Consort), Mata Hari (Deutsche Oper Berlin), Bach (Theater Krefeld Möchengladbach), Five: Fifteen (Scottish Opera); *Television and Video* For My Daughter (Danish Royal Ballet/Denmark's Radio/ZDF), Lonely Town, Lonely Street (Ballet Rambert/Denmark's Radio/RM Arts/Virgin Classic Video); lighting designs: Tryst (Scottish Chamber Orch/BBC 1), Sound Bites Two (BBC Scottish Symphony Orch/BBC 2), Red Forecast Orchestral Theatre III (BBC Symphony Orch/BBC 2); *Recreations* walking, painting, Italian cuisine; *Style*— Andrew Storer, Esq; ✉ c/o Valerie West, Donald E Scrimgeour, 49 Springcroft Avenue, London N2 9JH (tel 020 8444 6248, e-mail vwest@dircom.co.uk)

STORER, Prof Roy; s of Harry Storer (d 1980), of Wallasey, and Jessie, *née* Topham (d 1978); *b* 21 February 1928; *Educ* Wallasey GS, Univ of Liverpool (LDS, MSc, FDS, DRD); *m* 16 May 1953, Kathleen Mary Frances Pitman, da of Francis Charles Green; 2 da (Sheila b 26 Feb 1956, Carolyn b 6 May 1958), 1 s (Michael b 10 March 1961); *Career* Capt RADC 1951–52 (Lt 1950–51); sr lectr in dental prosthetics Univ of Liverpool 1962–67 (lectr 1954–61), visiting assoc prof Northwestern Univ Chicago 1961–62, hon conslt dental surgn United Liverpool Hosps 1962–67; Univ of Newcastle upon Tyne: prof of prosthodontics 1968–92, clinical sub-dean Dental Sch 1970–77, dean of dentistry 1977–92, emeritus prof 1992–, formerly memb Senate, Cncl and Ct, chm Physical Recreation Ctee; hon conslt dental surgn United Newcastle Hosps (later Newcastle HA) 1968–92; memb Cncl and sec Br Soc for the Study of Prosthetic Dentistry 1960–69 (pres 1968–69); memb: Gen Dental Cncl 1977–92 (chm Educn Ctee 1986–91), Dental Educn Advsy Cncl (UK) 1978–92, Dental Sub-Ctee of Univ Grants Ctee 1982–89, Bd of Faculty of Dental Surgery RCS 1982–90, EEC Dental Ctee Trg of Dental Practitioners 1986–92, Med Sub-Ctee of Univ Funding Cncl 1989–91; memb Northern Sports Cncl 1973–88; memb Bd of Dirs Durham CCC 1994–98; life memb The Cricket Soc 1976– (sec Durham and NE branch 1995–2003); church warden St Mary the Virgin Ponteland 2000–04; memb BDA 1950; *Recreations* Rugby football, cricket, gardening, vexillology; *Clubs* East India, MCC; *Style*— Prof Roy Storer; ✉ 164 Eastern Way, Darras Hall, Ponteland, Newcastle upon Tyne NE20 9RH (tel and fax 01661 823286, e-mail romapont@aol.com)

STOREY, Christopher Thomas; QC (1995); s of Leslie Hall Storey (d 1974), and Joan, *née* Walsh (d 2003); *b* 13 February 1945; *Educ* Rugby; *m* 1968, Hilary Enid, da of Robert Cushing Johnston; 2 s (Stephen Douglas Edward b 1976, Peter Stuart Desmond b 1978); *Career* chartered accountant 1967–82, barr NE Circuit 1982–, recorder of the Crown Court 2000–; memb Hon Soc Lincoln's Inn 1977; FCA 1967–85; *Recreations* music, classic cars, instructor light aeroplanes, cricket, reading, undergardening; *Style*— Christopher Storey, Esq, QC; ✉ Park Lane Chambers, Westgate, Leeds LS1 2RD (tel 01132 285000)

STOREY, George Anthony (Tony); OBE (1990); s of George William Storey (d 1956), of Haltwhistle, Northumberland, and Edna Mary, *née* Bell (d 2002); *b* 20 February 1939; *Educ* Queen Elizabeth GS Hexham, Univ of Nottingham (BA), Univ of Exeter (DipEd); *m* (m dis), Pamela May, *née* Trapnell; 1 s (Guy Keith b 30 May 1971), 1 da (Anne-Louise b 30 Oct 1972; *Career* Wallasey GS 1961–64, tutor Dept of Educn Univ of Oxford 1964–68, curriculum devpt Bicester Sch 1964–68, warden Cwlth Lodge 1964–68, visiting lectr in education Univ of Botswana Lesotho and Swaziland 1967, asst dir of educn Westmoreland LEA (Kendal) 1968–71, headmaster The Hayfield Sch Doncaster 1971– (currently longest serving secdy head teacher in UK); memb SHA; Lifetime Achievement Award North of England Region Teaching Awards 2004; *Books* Haltwhistle and South Tynedale (1972), Hope of our Sires: QEGS Hexham in the 1950's (1998), Bishop Ridley and the Reiving Ridleys (1999), Altwessel in 1000AD (1999), Ridley and Ridley Hall (2000), Haltwhistle Church (2001), Medieval Haltwhistle (2001), A West End Boy's Own Story (2001), Transport Across the North Pennines from Romans to Railways (2007); also a range of writing on educnl issues; *Recreations* local history, theatre, watching rugby union, Northumberland; *Clubs* The Hayfield Sch; *Style*— Tony Storey, Esq, OBE; ✉ 9 The Paddocks, Lound, Retford, Nottinghamshire DN22 8RR (tel 01777 818627); The Hayfield School, Hurst Lane, Auckley, Doncaster DN9 3HG (tel 01302 770589, fax 01302 770179)

STOREY, Jeremy Brian; QC (1994); s of Capt James Mackie Storey (d 1976), of Harrogate, N Yorks, and Veronica, *née* Walmsley (d 1978); *b* 21 October 1952; *Educ* Uppingham, Downing Coll Cambridge (MA); *m* 19 September 1981, Carolyn, da of Eric Raymond Ansell (d 1996), of Edenbridge, Kent; 2 da (Alexis Erica b 1991, Sasha Louise b 1994); *Career* called to the Bar Inner Temple 1974; recorder of the Crown Court (Western Circuit) 1995– (asst recorder 1990–95), dep judge of the Technology and Construction Ct 1995–, actg deemster (judge) IOM Cts 1999–; asst boundary cmmr for Eng and Wales 2000–; TECBAR approved adjudicator 1999–, MCIArb 1999 (ACIArb 1997); *Recreations* travel, theatre, cricket; *Clubs* MCC, Glamorgan CCC; *Style*— Jeremy Storey, Esq, QC; ✉ 4 Pump Court, Temple, London EC4Y 7AN (tel 020 7842 5555, fax 020 7583 2036)

STOREY, Maurice; CB (2003); s of Albert Henry Storey (d 1984), of Chelmsford, Essex, and Violet Ester, *née* Fisher (d 1984); *b* 14 June 1943; *m* 1, 8 Oct 1966, Hazel (d 1985), da of Joseph F Williams; 1 da (Jennifer b 6 Dec 1973); *m* 2, 30 May 1987, Linda, da of John Mears; 2 s (Shane Thomas b 17 Aug 1987, Karl Alan b 5 April 1989); *Career* apprentice Swan Hunter Shipbuilders 1958–62, ship repair mangr Swan Hunter Ship Repairers 1962–67, asst to marine supt rising to tech supt Shaw Savill Line 1967–72, head Technical Dept Kuwait Oil Tanker Co 1972–76, dir Sea Containers Ltd 1976–90, dir (ship and port mgmnt) Stena Line Ltd 1990–98, chief exec Maritime and Coastguard Agency 1998–2003, chm Hatsu Marine Ltd 2003–; dir: Stena Line Ltd, Stena Line UK Ltd, Stena Line Ports Ltd, Societe du Terminal Transmanche de Dieppe (STTD); pres UK Chamber of Shipping 2006–07 (chm Marine Policy Ctee, vice-chm Cruise Ship and Ferry Section); chm and dir Fishguard and Rosslare Railways and Harbours Co, vice-chm Br Ctee Bureau Veritas, non-exec dir James Fisher plc 2003–; memb of Cncl and Tech Ctees RNLI; Millennium Lecture IMarE 2000; MBA (hc) 2001; memb Soc of Consulting Marine Engrs and Ship Surveyors 1976–; CEng, FRINA 1969, FIMarEst 1972; *Books* The Design, Construction and Introduction of the Stena HSS (1997); *Recreations* swimming, golf, walking; *Style*— Maurice Storey, Esq, CB

STOREY, Michael Gerald; *b* 8 October 1941; *Educ* Queen Elizabeth GS Wakefield, Hosp Admin Staff Coll King Edward's Hosp Fund London, Univ of Chicago (MBA), Inst of Personnel and Development, Inst of Health Care Management; *m*; 2 c; *Career* admin trainee Pinderfields Hosp 1958–61, dep admin York Co Hosp 1961–63, dep admin Royal Orthopaedic Gp of Hosps and admin W Heath Hosp Birmingham 1963–64; vice-pres/int mgmnt conslt Booz Allen 1968–83; City Centre Communications Ltd (cable TV co): co-fndr 1983, variously gen mangr, fndr and md Westminster Cable Ltd; gp dir of corp strategy and public affrs Videotron Corporation Ltd (following takeover of City Centre

Communications) 1990–92, md MFS Communications Ltd 1993–95, pres and ceo MFS Europe 1995–97, exec vice-pres MCI WorldCom Europe (now MCI) 1997–99, pres and chief exec Inmarsat Ventures plc 2000–04, fndr and advsr Immarsat Ventures 2004–; non-exec dir: Hammersmith Royal Post Grad Teaching Hosp 1981–83, Central Blood Laboratories Authy 1982–84, NW Thames RHA 1983–92, chm NW London Mental Health NHS Trust 1993–97; past chm Cable TV Assoc (and past chm Telecommunications Ctee); MHSM 1963, MIPM 1966; *Style*— Michael G Storey, Esq; ✉ 4 St Mark's Crescent, London NW1 7TS (tel 020 7482 2836)

STOREY, Hon Sir Richard; 2 Bt (UK 1960) of Settrington, Co York; CBE (1996), DL; s of Baron Buckton (Life Peer, d 1978), and Elisabeth (d 1951), da of late Brig-Gen W J Woodcock, DSO; *b* 23 January 1937; *Educ* Winchester, Trinity Coll Cambridge (BA, LLB); *m* 1961, Virginia Anne, da of late Sir Kenelm Henry Ernest Cayley, 10 Bt; 1 s, 2 da; *Heir* s, Kenelm Storey; *Career* Nat Serv RNVR 1956; called to the Bar Inner Temple 1962; practised until 1969; chm Portsmouth and Sunderland Newspapers plc 1973–98 (dir 1962–99, chief exec 1973–86); contested (Cons) Don Valley 1966 and Huddersfield W 1970; dir: One Stop Community Stores Ltd 1971–98, Reuters Hldgs plc 1986–92, Press Assoc Ltd 1986–95 (chm 1991–95), The Fleming Mid Cap Investment Tst plc 1989–2002 (chm 1996–2002), Foreign & Colonial Smaller Companies plc 1993–2002, Sunderland plc 1996–2004, Castle Howard Arboretum Tst (CHAT) 1997–, eFinancialNews 2000–06; memb: Regnl Cncl Yorks and Humberside CBI 1974–79, Nat Cncl and Exec Ctee CLA 1980–84 (chm Yorks Exec 1974–76), Press Cncl 1980–86, Cncl Newspaper Soc 1980–98 (pres 1990–91), Cncl INCA-FIEJ Res Assoc 1983–88, CBI Employment Policy Ctee 1984–88, BUPA Assoc 2002–04; fndr chm Regnl Daily Advertising Cncl 1988–90 (dir 1988–91), chm Sir Harold Hillier Gardens and Arboretum Mgmnt Ctee 1989–2005; chm York Health Services NHS Tst 1991–97; tstee: The Royal Botanic Gardens Kew Fndn 1990–2003, Hope & Homes for Children 2002–; rep European Newspaper Publishers' Assoc 1990–96; administers land and woodland; Veitch Meml Medal 2005; High Sheriff N Yorks 1992–93; Supernumary Freeman Worshipful Co of Stationers and Newspapermakers; hon fell Univ of Portsmouth, Hon DLitt Univ of Sunderland; FRSA; *Recreations* sport, silviculture, arboriculture; *Style*— The Hon Sir Richard Storey, Bt, CBE, DL; ✉ 18 Lexham Mews, London W8 6JW (tel 020 7937 2888, fax 020 7937 3888, e-mail storey.london@btinternet.com); 11 Zetland House, Marloes Road, London W8 5LB (tel 020 7937 8823); Settrington House, Malton, North Yorkshire YO17 8NP (tel 01944 768200, fax 01944 768484, e-mail rs@settrington.com)

STOREY, Stuart Ellis; s of Charles Ellis Storey (d 1995), of Holbeach, Lincs, and Kathleen Mary Storey (d 1982); *b* 16 September 1942; *Educ* Spalding GS, Loughborough Coll (Dip PE), Western Kentucky Univ (MA); *m* 28 Nov 1970, Shirley, da of Donald Hugh Godfrey Gardner; 2 s (Benjamin Ellis b 24 Feb 1974, James Stuart b 26 Nov 1976); *Career* TV sports commentator (athletics and other sports); teacher PE and maths Dr Challoner's GS Amersham 1965–67, grad asst coach (swimming, judo, volleyball) Western Univ Kentucky 1967–68, supply teacher in PE Kitwood Sch Boston 1968–69, head of PE Loughton Coll of Further Educn 1969–73 (also dep warden Debden Community Assoc), head of PE Thames Poly 1973 (dir of PE until 1989); with BBC TV Sports Dept 1974–90 and 1991–, with Eurosport 1990–91; covered 8 Olympic Games, 9 World Championships, 7 Cwlth Games and 9 European Championships; athletics career: winner All England Schs 100m hurdles 1959, winner All England Schs 110m hurdles 1961 (runner up 1960), first sr int England v GDR (110m hurdles) 1965, memb GB team Olympic Games Mexico 1968 and European Championships 1969, memb England team Cwlth Games 1970 (all at 110m hurdles); also sometime coach to Geoff Capes (former shot put champion); chm tstees Wodson Park Sport and Recreation Tst, patron SPARKS; *Recreations* golf, gym, cycling; *Style*— Stuart Storey, Esq; ✉ c/o BBC Sport & Events Group, BBC Television Centre, Wood Lane, Shepherds Bush, London W12 7RJ

STORMONTH DARLING, Peter; s of Patrick Stormonth Darling (d 1960), and Edith, *née* Lamb (d 1980); *b* 29 September 1932; *Educ* Winchester, New Coll Oxford (MA); *m* 1, 1958 (m dis), Candis Hitzig; 3 da (Candis Christa b 1959, Elizabeth Iona b 1960, Arabella b 1962); m 2, 1970 (m dis), Maureen O'Leary; *Career* 2 Lt Black Watch 1950–53, served Korean War, Flying Offr RAFVR 1953–56; chm: Mercury Asset Management Group 1979–92, Alta Advisers Ltd, Welbeck Land Ltd; dir: Guardian Capital Group Ltd, Howard de Walden Estates Ltd, LR Global Fund Ltd, Invesco Perpetual Select Tst plc, Galahad plc, Advent Capital Hldgs plc; tstee World Monuments Fund; *Books* City Cinderella, The Life and Times of Mercury Asset Management (1999); *Style*— Peter Stormonth Darling, Esq; ✉ c/o Soditic Limited, 125 Strand, London WC2R 0APW1J 0DS (tel 020 7872 7043)

STORY, Mark Trafford; s of John Story (d 1991), of Co Kildare, and Elaine Story; *b* 10 May 1955; *Educ* Dublin HS, Sch of Law Trinity Coll Dublin (BA, LLB); *Career* prodr RTE Radio 1978–83; sr prodr: Capital Radio 1983–88, BBC Radio 1 1988–90; prog dir: Piccadilly Radio 1990–95, Virgin Radio 1995–97; md Magic 105.4 1998–, md Kiss 100 FM 1999 and Magic 105.4fm; Sony Award winner, New York Radio Gold Medal, Premios Ondos Gold winner; fell Radio Acad 1999; *Recreations* collecting Oriental art; *Style*— Mark Story, Esq

STOTHARD, Sir Peter Michael; kt (2003); s of Wilfred Max Stothard, and Patricia Jean, *née* Savage; *b* 28 February 1951; *Educ* Brentwood Sch, Trinity Coll Oxford (MA); *m* 1980, Sally Ceris, *née* Emerson; 1 da (Anna Ceris b 22 Nov 1983), 1 s (Michael Peter b 20 Dec 1987); *Career* journalist BBC 1974–77, business and political writer Sunday Times 1979–80; The Times: features ed and leader writer 1980–85, dep ed 1985–92, ed 1992–2002; ed TLS 2002–; hon fell Trinity Coll Oxford 2000; *Recreations* ancient and modern literature; *Clubs* Garrick; *Style*— Sir Peter Stothard; ✉ The Times Literary Supplement, Times House, 1 Pennington Street, London E98 1BS

STOTHER, Ian George; s of John Stother, of Lytham, Lancs, and Joan Lilian, *née* Jones; *b* 12 February 1945; *Educ* King Edward VII Sch Lytham, King's Coll Cambridge (MA, MB BChir); *m* 7 April 1969, Jacqueline, da of Alan B Mott, of Heslington, York; 2 da (Lindsay Anne, Clare Jennifer (twins) b 21 April 1972); *Career* clinical dir Orthopaedic Dept Glasgow Royal Infirmary Univ NHS Tst 1995–; hon clinical sr lectr in orthopaedics Univ of Glasgow, orthopaedic advsr Dance Sch for Scotland; fell: Br Assoc for Surgery of the Knee, Int Soc of Arthroscopy, Knee Surgery and Sports Med, Assoc of Surgns of E Africa; FRCSEd 1974, FRCSGlas 1981 (vice-pres surgery 1996–), FBOA; *Recreations* classic cars, ballet; *Style*— Ian Stother, Esq; ✉ Glasgow Nuffield Hospital, 25 Beaconsfield Road, Glasgow G12 0PJ (tel 0141 334 9441, fax 0141 339 1352); Glasgow Royal Infirmary, 10 Alexandra Parade, Glasgow G31 2ER (tel 0141 211 4000)

STOTT, Sir Adrian George Ellingham; 4 Bt (UK 1920), of Stanton, Co Gloucester; s of Sir Philip Sidney Stott, 3 Bt (d 1979), and Cicely Florence, *née* Ellingham (d 1996); *b* 7 October 1948; *Educ* Univ of British Columbia (BSc, MSc), Univ of Waterloo Ontario (MMaths); *Heir* bro, Vyvyan Stott; *Career* dir of planning (county) 1974–77, town planning conslt 1977–80, real estate portfolio mangr 1980–85, mangr of conservation agency 1985, of marketing co 1986–88; mgmnt conslt 1989–; memb: Assoc for Computing Machinery, Canadian Inst of Planners; *Recreations* music, inland waterways, politics; *Clubs* Barge Assoc; *Style*— Sir Adrian Stott Bt; ✉ The Downs, Little Amwell, Hertfordshire SG13 7SA (tel 07956 299966, e-mail stott@sdfg.co.uk)

STOTT, Ian Hood; s of Alan James Stott, and Mae, *née* Hood; *b* 29 January 1934; *Educ* Shrewsbury (1st XV rugby, capt fives); *m* 1, 1957, Gabrielle Mary, da of Rev W S Tuke; 2 s (Robert Ian b 1958, Simon Andrew b 1960 d 1989); m 2, 1979, Patricia Mary, da of Dr M Wynroe; 2 da (Ailsa Jane b 1980, Catherine Mally b 1982); *Career* Nat Serv Green Jackets and Lancs Fus (Lt) 1952–54; James Stott Ltd cotton spinners and weavers Oldham 1954–57, John Bright & Sons Ltd Rochdale 1957–62, proprietor garage gp/caravan park/hotels/property 1962–86, chm and md Oldham Athletic AFC 1986– (chm 1982–); memb: FA Cncl 1986–, Football League Mgmnt Ctee 1986–92 and 1995–, FA Exec 1992–94 and 1999–; vice-chm FA 1999–; *Recreations* cooking, food and drink, bridge, music; *Style*— Ian Stott, Esq; ✉ Oldham Athletic FC, Boundary Park, Oldham, Lancashire OL1 2PA (tel 0161 624 4972, fax 0161 627 5915)

STOTT, Kathryn; da of Desmond Stott, of Nelson, Lancs, and Elsie, *née* Cheetham; *b* 10 December 1958; *Educ* Yehudi Menuhin Sch, Royal Coll of Music (ARCM, Tagore Golden Medal); *Children* 1 da (Lucy b 9 Nov 1984); *Career* pianist; studied under Vlado Perlemuter, Louis Kentner and Kendall Taylor; fifth place Leeds Int Piano Competition 1978, awarded Churchill scholarship 1979; recitals incl: Int Piano Series Wigmore Hall, Michael Nyman Festival South Bank, Gabriel Fauré Festival (artistic leader) Manchester 1995, Britten Concerto with Netherlands Philharmonic Orch Concertgebouw 1995, Beethoven Triple concerto with BBC Scottish Symphony Orch BBC Proms 1995; also played in Germany, Italy, Spain, Czech Republic, Poland, France, Switzerland, Hong Kong, Singapore, Japan, Saudi Arabia, Zimbabwe (USA with Yo-Yo Ma); solo recordings incl: works by Chabrier, Debussy, Liszt, Rachmaninov, Frank Bridge, Fauré complete piano works, Chopin complete Nocturnes; other recordings incl: John Ireland Concerto and Walton Sinfonia Concertante with RPO and Vernon Handley, George Lloyd Concerto No 3 with BBC Philharmonic, Herbert Howells Concerto No 2 with Royal Liverpool Philharmonic Orch and Vernon Handley, Michael Nyman Piano Concerto, Fauré Orchestral Works with Yan Pascal Tortelier and BBC Philharmonic; artistic dir Piano 2000 Festival Manchester (and Piano 2003); Chevalier de l'Ordre des Arts et des Lettres (France) 1995; *Recreations* horse riding, travel, Italian language; *Style*— Ms Kathryn Stott; ✉ c/o Jane Ward, 38 Townfield, Rickmansworth, Hertfordshire WD3 2DD (tel and fax 01923 493903, e-mail ward.music@ntlworld.com)

STOTT, Prof Nigel Clement Halley; CBE (2001); s of Maj Halley Harwin Stott, of Natal, and Joyce, *née* Greathead; *b* 27 November 1939; *Educ* Univ of Edinburgh (BSc, MB ChB); *m* 7 April 1965, (Eleanor) Mary, da of (Townroe) Stephen Collingwood, of Shaftesbury; 1 da (Paula b 4 June 1967), 2 s (Philip b 19 April 1969, Howard b 25 Nov 1971); *Career* registrar Epidemiology Research Unit MRC 1969–70, med offr St Lucy's Hosp Transkei 1970–71, sr lectr Welsh Nat Sch of Med 1972–79, prof of primary med care Southampton 1979–80, prof of gen practice Univ of Wales Coll of Med 1986–99, emeritus prof 2000–; author of numerous chapters and papers; chair: Welsh Scheme Health and Social Research 1999–2005, MRC Topic Review on Research in Primary Care 1997, Reference Gp for Primary Care Strategy for Wales 2001; memb: Welsh Cncl of RCGP 1985–, MRC Health Services and Public Health Research Bd 1998–2002, GMC UK 1999–2004, HE Funding Cncl for Wales 2006–; hon fell Cardiff Univ 2007; FRCPEd 1980, FRCGP 1985, FMedSci 1998; *Books* Primary Health Care: Bridging the Gap between Theory and Practice (1983), Care of the Dying (1984), Health Checks in General Practice (1988), Making Changes (1990), The Nature of General Medical Practice (1995), Oxford Textbook of Primary Medical Care (chapter conslt, 2004), Halley H Stott: Founder of the Valley Trust in Kwazulu Natal (2007); *Recreations* sailing, gardening; *Style*— Prof Nigel Stott, CBE; ✉ Coastguard Cottage, Oxwich, Gower SA3 1LS (tel 01792 390746 or 029 2062 6608)

STOURTON, Edward John Ivo; s of Nigel John Ivo Stourton, OBE, of N Yorks, and Rosemary Jennifer Rushworth Abbott, JP; *b* 24 November 1957; *Educ* Ampleforth, Trinity Coll Cambridge (MA, pres Cambridge Union); *m* 1, 5 July 1980 (m dis), Margaret, da of late Sir James Napier Finney McEwen Bt; 2 s (Ivo b 11 June 1982, Thomas b 28 Sept 1987), 1 da (Eleanor b 1 June 1984); m 2, Nov 2002, Fiona Margaret, *née* Murch (Fiona Stourton, *qv*); *Career* TV journalist 1979–; Washington corr Channel Four News 1986 (fndr memb 1982), Paris corr BBC TV 1988, diplomatic ed ITN 1990–93, presenter BBC One O'Clock News and presenter radio and television documentaries BBC 1993–99, presenter Today Programme (BBC Radio 4) 1999–, presenter Sunday (BBC Radio 4) 2002–; *Books* Absolute Truth: The Catholic Church in the Modern World (1998), In the Footsteps of St Paul (2004), John Paul II: Man of History (2006); *Recreations* reading; *Clubs* Travellers, Hurlingham; *Style*— Edward Stourton, Esq; ✉ c/o BBC, Television Centre, Wood Lane, London W12 7RJ

STOURTON, Fiona Margaret; da of John Edward King, of Llandaff, Cardiff, and Mary Margaret, *née* Beaton; *b* 14 August 1957; *Educ* Godolphin & Latymer Sch, Howells Sch Llandaff, SOAS Univ of London (Rhuvon Guest prize, BA); *m* 1, 1980 (m dis 2002); 1 da (Rosalind Lesley Margaret b 27 Oct 1993); m 2, Nov 2002, Edward Stourton, *qv*; *Career* prodr Hausa/African section BBC World Service 1978–81, trainee BBC News 1981, prodr Newsnight 1985–86 (asst prodr 1981–85); sr prodr: BBC Breakfast Time 1986–87, Newsnight 1987–88, The Late Show 1988–89; political corr and news presenter C4 News/ITN 1992–94 (arts corr and news presenter 1989–92), dep ed Assignment BBC TV 1994–97, ed Correspondent BBC TV 1997–2002, sr exec prodr current affrs BBC Two 2002–; *Recreations* reading, tennis; *Style*— Ms Fiona Stourton; ✉ BBC Television, White City, Wood Lane, London W12 7TS (tel 020 8752 7503)

STOURTON, Hon James Alastair; yr s of 26 Baron Mowbray, 27 Segrave and 23 Stourton, CBE, and Jane Faith, *née* de Yarburgh-Bateson, da of 5 Baron Deramore; *b* 3 July 1956; *Educ* Ampleforth, Magdalene Coll Cambridge (MA); *m* 9 Oct 1993 (m dis 1997), Hon Sophia Ulla Stonor, yst da of 7 Baron Camoys; *Career* Sotheby's: Picture Dept 1979, dir Sotheby's London 1987, dir European Valuations Dept 1990, dir of Euro business devpt 1993, dir Euro Bd 1994, dep chm Sotheby's Europe 1997, chm Sotheby's Inst (Educn) 2002, chm Sotheby's UK 2007; prop The Stourton Press; Knight of Honour and Devotion SMOM; *Books* Great Smaller Museums of Europe (2003), Collectors of our Time: Collecting since 1945 (2007); *Clubs* Roxburghe, Pratt's, White's, Beefsteak; *Style*— The Hon James Stourton; ✉ 21 Moreton Place, London SW1V 2NL; Sotheby's, 34–35 New Bond Street, London W1A 2AA (tel 020 7293 5435, fax 020 7293 5065, e-mail james.stourton@sothebys.com)

STOUT, David Ker; s of Prof Alan Stout (d 1983), and Evelyn Stout (d 1987); *b* 27 January 1932; *Educ* Sydney HS, Univ of Sydney (BA), Magdalen Coll Oxford (BA, Rhodes scholar); *m* 31 July 1956, Margaret, da of William Sugden (d 1951); 2 s (Nigel b 1957, Rowland b 1959), 2 da (Lucy b 1961, Eleanor b 1963); *Career* Mynors fell and lectr in economics UC Oxford 1959–76, economic advsr to various govts (Syria, New Hebrides, Aust, Canada) 1965–76, economic dir NEDO 1970–72 and 1976–80, Tyler prof of economics Univ of Leicester 1980–82, head Economic Dept Unilever 1982–92, dir Centre for Business Strategy London Business Sch 1992–97; author of various papers in books and jls on taxation, growth, inflation and industrial policy, ed Business Strategy Review 1993–98; memb: ESRC 1989–92 (chm Industry Economics and Environment Gp), Biological Science Res Cncl Technol Interaction Bd 1994–98, Mfrg Technol Foresight Panel 1994–99, Advsy Ctee Cambridge DAE; social science advsr to Innovative Mfrg Initiative 1997–2001; govr Cncl NIESR 1972–; hon economics research fell UCL 2002–; FRSA 2000; *Recreations* chess, bivalves, words; *Style*— David Stout; ✉ Nutlands, Ightham, Kent TN15 9DB (tel and fax 01732 780904, e-mail davidkerstout@aol.com)

STOUT, Prof Robert William; s of William Ferguson Stout, CB (d 2005), of Belfast, and Muriel Stout, *née* Kilner (d 2004); *b* 6 March 1942; *Educ* Campbell Coll Belfast (scholar), Queen's Univ Belfast (MD DSc); *m* 31 Dec 1969, Helena Patricia, da of Frederick William Willis (d 1959), of Comber, Co Down; 2 s (Brian b 1971, Alan b 1972), 1 da (Caroline b 1974); *Career* MRC Eli Lilly foreign educn fell Univ of Washington Seattle 1971–73, sr research fell British Heart Fndn 1974–75; Queen's Univ Belfast: sr lectr Dept of Med

S

1975–76, prof of geriatric med Dept of Geriatric Med 1976–2007, dir Sch of Clinical Med 1991–93, dean Faculty of Med 1991–93, provost for med and health sciences 1993–98, dean Faculty of Med and Health Sciences 1998–2001, head Sch of Med 1991–93 and 1998–2001; conslt physician Belfast City Hosp 1975–2007, dir of R&D NI Health and Personal Social Services 2001–07; chm: Specialty Advsy Ctee on Geriatric Med Jt Ctee on Higher Med Trg 1988–92, QAA Benchmarking Gp for Medicine 2000–02 Main Panel B Research Assessment Exercise 2008; pres Ulster Med Soc 1999–2000 (hon treas 1979–83); vice-pres: Age Concern NI 1988–2001 (chm 1986–88), Research Into Ageing 1992–2001; RCP: NI regnl advsr 1984–90, examiner 1990–98; memb Royal Cmmn on Long Term Care 1997–99; Br Geriatrics Soc: memb Cncl 1984–90, memb Exec 1987–90, chm Scientific Ctee 1999–2001, pres 2002–04; memb: Bd UK Clinical Research Collaboration 2004–07; chm: Editorial Bd Age & Ageing 1999–2002, Centre for aAgeing Research and Devpt in Ireland 2003–; memb: Bd of Govrs Methodist Coll Belfast 1983–2002 (hon lay sec 1988–91, chm 1994–97), Southern Health and Social Services Bd 1982–91, NI Health and Social Servs Cncl 1982–85, Eastern Health and Social Services Bd 1992–2002, Health Research Bd Ireland 2002–07; chm Bd of Govrs Edgehill Theological Coll Belfast 2005–; memb GMC 1991–2002; FRCP 1979, FRCPEd 1988, FRCPI 1989, FRCPSG 1995, FMedSci 1998; *Books* Hormones and Atherosclerosis (1982), Arterial Disease in the Elderly (ed, 1984), Diabetes and Atherosclerosis (ed, 1992); *Recreations* golf, gardening, reading; *Clubs* Royal Belfast Golf, RSM; *Style*— Prof Robert Stout; ✉ 3 Larch Hill Drive, Craigavad, Co Down BT18 0JS (tel 028 9042 2253, fax 028 9042 8478, e-mail rwstout@btopenworld.com); Queen's University, Department of Geriatric Medicine, Whitla Medical Building, 97 Lisburn Road, Belfast BT9 7BL (tel 028 9033 5777, fax 028 9032 5839, e-mail r.stout@qub.ac.uk)

STOUTE, Sir Michael Ronald; s of late Maj Ronald Audley Stoute, OBE, of Barbados, and late Mildred Dorothy, *née* Bowen; *b* 22 October 1945; *Educ* Harrison Coll Barbados; *Children* 1 da (Caroline Elizabeth b 23 Jan 1972), 1 s (James Robert Michael b 6 June 1974); *Career* racehorse trainer 1972–, leading flat racing trainer 1981, 1986, 1989, 1994, 1997, 2000, 2003 and 2005, 24 classics won in England and Ireland; trained Derby winners: Shergar 1981, Shahrastani 1986, Kris Kin 2003, North Light 2004; Irish Derby winners: Shergar 1981, Shareef Dancer 1983, Shahrastani 1986; other major races won incl: Breeders Cup (Pilsudski) 1996, Japan Cup (Singspiel) 1996, Dubai World Cup (Singspiel) 1997, Japan Cup (Pilsudski) 1997, Breeders Cup (Kalanisi) 2000, Dubai Sheema Classic (Fantastic Light) 2000, Hong Kong Vase (Daliapor) 2000, Breeders Cup (Islington) 2003; *Recreations* cricket, deep sea fishing; *Style*— Sir Michael Stoute; ✉ Freemason Lodge, Bury Road, Newmarket, Suffolk CB8 7BT (tel 01638 663801, fax 01638 667276)

STOUTZKER, Ian; OBE (1993); s of Aron Stoutzker (d 1968), and Dora Stoutzker (d 1968); *b* 21 January 1929; *Educ* Berkhamstead Sch, Royal Coll of Music (ARCM), LSE (BSc); *m* 3 Sept 1958, Mercedes; 1 da (Riquita (Mrs Wade Newmark) b 1960), 1 s (Robert b 1962); *Career* Samuel Montagu 1952–56, A Keyser and Co (tutor Keyser Ullmann Ltd) 1956–75, chm London Interstate Bank 1971–75, chm Dawnay Day Int 1985–2000; pres Philharmonia Orch 1976–79 (chm 1972–76), vice-pres Royal Coll of Music 1999– (memb Exec Ctee 1968–99); chm: Live Music Now 1980–, Advsy Ctee LSO 1992–2007, Royal Concert Ctee 1999–2001; co-chm Voices Fndn 1994–2003, memb Cncl Musicians' Benevolent Fund 2004– (memb Ctee 1980–2004); FRCM; *Recreations* music, cross country walking; *Style*— Ian Stoutzker, Esq, OBE; ✉ Barrengeppchen 6, Salzburg SO20, Austria

STOW, Mary Frances; da of Montague James Lindsay Stow, of Newbury, Berks, and Colina Mary, *née* Mackintosh; *b* 9 February 1960; *Educ* St Bartholomew's Sch Newbury, Univ of Exeter (BA); *Career* advtg exec; sales and mktg mangr Morris & Verdin wine merchants 1985–88, account planner J Walter Thompson 1989–93, gp planning dir McCann Erickson 1993–95, head of planning/planning dir Collett Dickenson Pearce & Partners March-Aug 1995, ptnr and head of planning HHCL and Partners 1995–; The Charles Channon Award IPA Advtg Effectiveness Awards 1992; memb Women in Advtg and Communications London; *Style*— Ms Mary Stow; ✉ HHCL and Partners, Kent House, 14–17 Market Place, Great Titchfield Street, London W1N 7AJ (e-mail marys@hhcl.com)

STOW, His Hon Judge Timothy Montague Fenwick; QC (1989); s of Geoffrey Montague Fenwick Stow, LVO (d 1990), of Portugal, and Joan Fortescue, *née* Flannery (d 1984); *b* 31 January 1943; *Educ* Eton; *m* 29 May 1965, Alisoun Mary Francis, da of Paul Walter Homberger, OBE (d 1978); 1 s (Richard Montague Fenwick b 15 Dec 1968), 1 da (Emma Mary b 15 Dec 1972); *Career* called to the Bar 1965 (bencher 1998); recorder 1989–, head of chambers 1998–, circuit judge (SE Circuit) 2000–; memb Bar Cncl 1982–85; *Recreations* looking after our country property, sailing, tennis, foreign travel, skiing; *Clubs* Travellers; *Style*— His Hon Judge Stow, QC; ✉ Croydon Crown Court, Altyre Road, Croydon CR9 5AB

STOW, William Llewelyn (Bill); CMG (2002); s of Alfred Frank Stow, of Eastbourne, E Sussex, and Elizabeth Mary Stow; *b* 11 January 1948; *Educ* Eastbourne GS, Churchill Coll Cambridge (MA); *m* 1976, Rosemary Ellen, da of Ernest Burrows (d 1976); 2 s (Daniel William b 24 Sept 1976, Richard Ivan b 28 Nov 1978); *Career* HM Civil Serv: graduate trainee DTI 1971–75, princ Consumer Affrs Div Dept of Prices and Consumer Protection 1975–78, Marine Div Dept of Trade 1978–80, first sec UK Delgn to OECD Paris 1980–83, Int Trade Policy Div DTI 1983–85, first sec UK Perm Rep to EC Brussels 1985–88, Internal Euro Policy Div DTI (i/c policy of the EC single market and Euro economic area) 1988–91, Fin and Resource Mgmnt Div DTI (i/c DTI's budget and negotiations with Treasy) 1991–94, head Euro Community and Trade Rels Div DTI (i/c co-ordination of DTI policy on the EC and for bilateral trade policy rels with all UK's maj trading ptnrs) 1994–96, dep dir gen Trade Policy and Europe DTI 1996–98, dir Employment Rels Directorate DTI 1998, UK dep perm rep to the EU Brussels 1999–; *Recreations* cricket, hill and coastal walking, birdwatching, reading; *Clubs* Mandarins' Cricket; *Style*— Bill Stow, Esq, CMG; ✉ Office of the UK Permanent Representation to the European Union, Avenue d'Auderghem 10, 1040 Brussels, Belgium

STOWE, Grahame Conway; s of Harry Stowe (d 1968), and Evelyn, *née* Pester (d 1990); *b* 22 May 1949; *Educ* Allerton Grange Sch Leeds, Univ of Leeds (LLB); *m* 27 Dec 1981, Marilyn Joyce, da of Arnold Morris; 1 s (Benjamin Harry George b 21 May 1988); *Career* admitted slr 1974, commenced own practice 1981, currently sr ptnr Grahame Stowe Bateson; gained Higher Rights of Audience (Criminal Proceedings) qualification 1996; chm Benefit Appeal Tbnl 1985, pres Mental Health Tbnl 1987; memb Law Soc; *Recreations* squash; *Style*— Grahame Stowe, Esq; ✉ Grahame Stowe Bateson, 5 and 7 Portland Street, Leeds LS1 3DR (tel 0113 246 8163, fax 0113 242 6682, e-mail gcs@gsbsolicitors.com)

STOWELL, Dr Michael James; s of Albert James Stowell (d 1986), of Cardiff, and Kathleen Maud, *née* Poole (d 1996); *b* 10 July 1935; *Educ* St Julian's HS Newport, Univ of Bristol (BSc, PhD); *m* 1, 3 March 1962 (m dis 1990), Rosemary, da of Albert William Allen (d 1962); 1 s (George b 1964), 1 da (Heather b 1966); m 2, 23 Nov 1995, Kerry (d 1998), da of Edward Taif Kern (d 1998); *Career* res mangr TI Res 1978–88 (res scientist 1960, gp ldr 1968), res dir Alcan International Ltd 1990–94 (princ conslt scientist 1989–90); distinguished res fell Dept of Materials Science and Metallurgy Univ of Cambridge 1999–; FInstP 1970, FIM, CEng 1981, FRS 1984; *Recreations* music; *Style*— Dr Michael Stowell, FRS; ✉ 1 Buckingham Drive, Ely, Cambridgeshire CB6 1DR (tel 01353 661305, e-mail stowell290@btinternet.com)

STRABOLGI, 11 Baron (E 1318); David Montague de Burgh Kenworthy; s of 10 Baron Lt-Cdr Hon J M Kenworthy, RN, MP (d 1953), by his 1 w, Doris Whitley (d 1988), only child of Sir Frederick Whitley-Thomson, JP, MP; co-heir to Baronies of Cobham and Burgh; *b* 1 November 1914; *Educ* Gresham's, Chelsea Sch of Art, Académie Scandinave Paris; *m* 1961, Doreen Margaret, er da of late Alexander Morgan, of Ashton-under-Lyne, Lancs; *Heir* n, Andrew Kenworthy; *Career* Maj and Actg Lt-Col RAOC WWII; PPS to Ldr of House of Lords and Lord Privy Seal 1969–70, asst oppn whip House of Lords 1970–74, Capt Queen's Bodyguard of Yeomen of the Guard and dep chief Govt whip 1974–79; oppn spokesman on Arts and Libraries 1979–86; dep speaker House of Lords 1986–2002, elected hereditary peer 1999–; an extra Lord in Waiting to HM The Queen 1998–; memb: Select Ctee for Privileges 1987, Jt Ctee (with Commons) on Consolidation Bills 1987–2002, Ecclesiastical Ctee 1991, Select Ctee on Procedure of the House 1993–96 and 1998–2002, All-Pty Arts and Amenities Gp; hon treas Franco-British Parly Relations Ctee 1991–96; memb Br Section Franco-British Cncl 1981–98; pres Franco-British Soc, memb Cncl Alliance-Française in GB 1970–97; chm Bolton Building Society 1986–87 (dep chm 1983–86); Freeman City of London; Offr de la Légion d'Honneur 1981; *Clubs* Reform; *Style*— The Rt Hon The Lord Strabolgi; ✉ House of Lords, London SW1A 0PW

STRACEY, Sir John Simon; 9 Bt (UK 1818), of Rackheath, Norfolk; s of Capt Algernon Augustus Henry Stracey (d 1940), and Olive Beryl Stracey (d 1972); Sir John Stracey, 1 Bt, was a Recorder of The City of London; suc cous, Sir Michael George Motley Stracey, 8 Bt, 1971; *b* 30 November 1938; *Educ* Wellington, McGill Univ Montreal; *m* 1968, Martha Maria, da of Johann Egger (d 1936), of Innsbruck, Austria; 2 da; *Heir* cous, Henry Stracey; *Career* conslt and designer; *Clubs* Royal St Lawrence Yacht; *Style*— Sir John Stracey, Bt

STRACHAN, Maj Benjamin Leckie (Ben); CMG (1978); s of Charles Gordon Strachan, MC (d 1957), of Crieff, Perthshire, and Annie Primrose, *née* Leckie (d 1972); *b* 4 January 1924; *Educ* Rossall Sch Fleetwood, Univ of Aberdeen (MA); *m* 1, 5 Dec 1946 (m dis 1957), Ellen, *née* Braasch; 1 s (Christian b 1949); m 2, 29 Nov 1958, Lize, da of Tage Lund (d 1985), of Copenhagen, Denmark; 2 s (Robert b 1960, James b 1963); *Career* enlisted 1942, Univ of Durham 1942–43, OCTU Sandhurst 1943–44, 2 Lt Royal Dragoons 1944, Lt served France and Germany (despatches, wounded, POW) 1944–45, Capt instr OCTU 1946–48, Lt 4 QOH serv Malaya (wounded) 1948–51, Capt MECAS 1951–53, Maj GSO2 (int) HQ BT Egypt 1954–55, Capt Sqdn 2 i/c 4 QOH Germany 1955–56 RMSC Shrivenham 1956–58, Maj Sqdn Ldr 10 Royal Hussars 1958–60, GSO2 (int) WO 1960–61, ret to join HM Foreign Serv; FO: first sec Info Res Dept 1961–62, info advsr to Govt of Aden 1962–63, asst head of dept Scientific Relations Dept 1964–66, commercial sec Kuwait 1966–69, cnsllr and chargé d'affaires Amman (Jordan) 1969–71, trade cmmr Toronto 1971–74, consul gen Vancouver 1974–76; HM ambass: Sana'a and Djibouti 1977–78, Beirut 1978–81, Algiers 1981–84; special advsr FCO 1990–91; chm Kincardine and W Aberdeenshire Lib Dems 1994–98, memb Policy Ctee Scottish Lib Dems 1998–; Citoyen D'Honneur Grimaud France 1987; *Books* The Skirts of Alpha: An Alternative to the Materialist Philosophy (2005); *Recreations* sailing, crofting, writing; *Clubs* Lansdowne; *Style*— Maj Ben Strachan, CMG; ✉ Mill of Strachan, Strachan, Banchory, Kincardineshire AB31 6NS (tel and fax 01330 850663)

STRACHAN, (John) Crispian; CBE (2003), QPM (1996), DL (2002); s of late Dr M N Strachan, of Worcestershire, and late Mrs B J Strachan; *b* 5 July 1949; *Educ* King's Sch Macclesfield, Jesus Coll Oxford (MA), Univ of Sheffield (MA); *m* 1974, Denise, da of late Tom Farmer; 3 da, 1 s; *Career* Met Police 1972–93, Sr Cmd Course Police Staff Coll 1992, asst chief constable Strathclyde Police 1993–98, chief constable Northumbria Police 1998–2005; dir OSL 2005–; memb of various community gps in Northumbria; OStJ 2005; *Books* A Guide to Policing in the UK (co-author, 1992); *Recreations* photography, woodwork, country walks; *Style*— Crispian Strachan, Esq, CBE, QPM, DL; ✉ Clifton House, Clifton, Morpeth, Northumberland NE61 6DQ (e-mail crispianstrachan@hotmail.co.uk)

STRACHAN, David John; *b* 24 June 1963, Peterhead, Grampian; *Educ* Elgin Acad, The Queen's Coll Oxford (MA), Wolfson Coll Cambridge (Dip Economics); *Career* early career in banking supervision and market ops with Bank of England; FSA: head of market conduct and infrastructure 1998–2001, dir of deposit-takers 2001–02, dir of insurance firms 2002–04, dir of retail firms and insurance sector ldr 2004–06, dir of maj retail gps and financial stability sector ldr 2006–; *Style*— Mr David Strachan; ✉ Financial Services Authority, 25 The North Colonnade, Canary Wharf, London E14 5HS (tel 020 7066 0900, fax 020 7066 9769, e-mail david.strachan@fsa.gov.uk)

STRACHAN, Prof Hew Francis Anthony; DL (Tweeddale 2006); s of Michael Francis Strachan, CBE, FRSE (d 2000), and Iris Winifred, *née* Hemingway; *b* 1 September 1949; *Educ* Rugby, CCC Cambridge (MA, PhD); *m* 1, 26 June 1971 (m dis 1980), Catherine Blackburn; 2 da (Emily b 1973, Olivia b 1976); m 2, 12 July 1982, Pamela Dorothy Tennant, da of Felix Rowley Symes; 1 s (Mungo b 1990), 1 step s (Jack b 1973), 1 step da (Olivia b 1975); *Career* shipping trainee The Ben Line Steamers Ltd 1971–72; res fell CCC Cambridge 1975–78, sr lectr Dept of War Studies and Int Affairs RMA Sandhurst 1978–79; CCC Cambridge: fell 1979– (life fell 1992–), dean of coll 1981–86, tutor for admissions 1981–88, dir of studies in history 1986–92, sr tutor 1987 and 1989–92; prof of modern history Univ of Glasgow 1992–2001, Chichele prof of the history of war Univ of Oxford 2002–, fell All Souls Coll Oxford 2002–, dir Leverhulme Programme on the Changing Character of War Univ of Oxford 2004–; dir Scottish Centre for War Studies 1996–2001; cncllr Army Records Soc 1990–94 and 2002–06, jt ed War in History jl 1994–; memb Cncl: Soc for Army Historical Res 1980–95, Lancing Coll 1982–90, Nat Army Museum 1994–2003; cmmr Cwlth War Graves Cmmn 2006–; govr: Wellesley House Sch 1983–92, Rugby Sch 1985–, Stowe Sch 1990–2002; memb Queen's Body Guard for Scotland (Royal Co of Archers) (memb Cncl 2003–); Br Acad Thank Offering to Britain fell 1998–99; Hon DUniv Paisley 2005; FRHistS, FRSE 2003; *Books* British Military Uniforms 1768–1796 (1975), History of the Cambridge University Officers Training Corps (1976), European Armies and the Conduct of War (1983), Wellington's Legacy: The Reform of the British Army 1830–54 (1984), From Waterloo to Balaclava: Tactics, Technology and the British Army (1985, Templer Medal), The Politics of the British Army (1997, Westminster Medal), The Oxford Illustrated History of the First World War (ed, 1998), The British Army, Manpower and Society into the 21st Century (ed, 2000), The First World War, Vol I, To Arms (2001), Military Lives (ed, 2002), The First World War: a new illustrated history (2003), Big Wars and Small Wars: The British Army and the Lessons of War in the 20th Century (ed, 2006), Clauswitz on War (2007); *Recreations* shooting, rugby football (now spectating); *Clubs* New (Edinburgh), Hawks' (Cambridge); *Style*— Prof Hew Strachan, DL; ✉ All Souls College, Oxford OX1 4AL (tel 01865 279379)

STRACHAN, Ian Charles; s of Dr Charles Strachan, of Wilmslow, Cheshire, and Margaret, *née* Craig; *b* 7 April 1943; *Educ* Fettes, Christ's Coll Cambridge (MA), Princeton Univ (MPA), Harvard Univ; *m* 1, 29 July 1967 (m dis 1987), Diane Shafer, da of Raymond P Shafer, of Washington DC, USA; 1 da (Shona Elizabeth b 15 Feb 1970); m 2, 28 Nov 1987, Margaret, da of Dr Hugh Auchincloss, of New Jersey, USA; *Career* assoc Ford Fndn Malaysia 1967–69, various positions Exxon Corporation 1970–86, fin dir Gen Sekiyu Tokyo Japan 1979–82, chm and chief exec Esso Hong Kong and Esso China 1982–83, corp strategy mangr Exxon Corpn NY 1984–86, chief fin offr and sr vice-pres Johnson and Higgins NY 1986–87, dep chief exec RTZ Corporation plc London 1991–95 (fin dir 1987–91); BTR plc: dir 1995–99, md July-Dec 1995, chief exec 1996–99; dep chm Invensys plc 1999–2000; non-exec dir: Commercial Union plc 1992–95, Transocean Sedco Forex Inc Houston TX 2000–, Reuters Gp plc 2000–, Instinet Gp 2000–05 (non-exec chm 2003–05), Johnson Matthey plc 2002–, Xstrata plc 2003–; *Recreations* tennis, reading, oriental antiques; *Style*— Ian Strachan

STRACHAN, James Murray; s of Eric Alexander Howieson Strachan, and Jacqueline Georgina, *née* Langoussis; *b* 10 November 1953; *Educ* King's Sch Canterbury, Christ's Coll Cambridge (exhibitioner, BA), London Coll of Printing, London Business Sch; *Career* Chase Manhattan Bank 1976–77; Merrill Lynch: joined 1977, ed Merrill Lynch Int 1982–86, md Merrill Lynch Capital Markets and Merrill Lynch Europe 1986–89; photographer and writer (numerous books published and contribs to Sunday Times, FT and The Times) 1989–97, assoc photographer Getty Images (formerly Tony Stone) 1990–; RNID: tstee and memb Fin Ctee 1994–96, chief exec 1997–2002, chm 2002–07; chm Audit Cmmn 2002–06; non-exec dir: Legal and General Gp 2003–, Bank of England 2006–, Care UK plc 2006–, Welsh Water Ltd 2007–; visiting fell (risk and regulation) LSE 2005–; rotating chair Disability Charities Consortium 1997–2002, co-chair Task Force on Social Services Provision for Deaf and Hard of Hearing People 1998–2002, co-chair NHS Modernising Hearing Aid Services Gp 1999–2002, cmmr Disability Rights Cmmn 1999–2002, chair Task Force on Audiology Services 2000–02; memb: Ministerial Disability Rights Task Force 1997–99, Ministerial Disability Benefits Forum 1998–99, NCVO Advsy Gp on Diversity 2001–03; pres Midland Regnl Assoc for the Deaf 2001–; external memb Transition Gp (Energy) DTI 2001–02; memb Bd and Audit Ctee Office of Gas and Electricity Markets 2000–04, ind memb Business Bd DTI 2002–04; memb Bd Community Fund 2001–03; tstee: Save the Children 1999–2002, Somerset House Tst 2003– (chair Audit and Finance Ctee 2006–); leadership patron Nat Coll of Sch Leadership 2003–; hon fell Univ of the Arts London 2002; *Recreations* photography, film, reading, swimming; *Style*— James Strachan, Esq; ✉ 10B Wedderburn Road, London NW3 5QG (tel 020 7794 9687, fax 020 7794 4593, e-mail james_strachan@btinternet.com)

STRACHAN, John Charles Haggart; s of late Charles George Strachan, and Elsie Strachan; *b* 2 October 1936; *Educ* Univ of London, St Mary's Hosp (MB BS); *m* Caroline Mary, da of John William Parks, MBE, of London; 1 s (James b 1971), 3 da (Alexandra b 1969, Elisabeth b 1972, Cressida b 1983); *Career* conslt orthopaedic surgn New Charing Cross Hosp 1971, surgn to Royal Ballet 1971, surgn Chelsea and Westminster Hosp 1992; Liveryman Worshipful Soc of Apothecaries; FBOA, FRSM, FRCS, FRCSEd; *Recreations* fishing, sailing; *Clubs* Royal Thames Yacht, Royal Southern Yacht, Flyfishers', Garrick; *Style*— John Strachan, Esq; ✉ 28 Chalcot Square, London NW1 (tel 020 7586 1278); 126 Harley Street, London W1N 1AH (tel 020 7935 0142)

STRACHAN, (Douglas) Mark Arthur; QC (1987); s of Flt Lt William Arthur Watkin Strachan (d 1998), and Joyce, *née* Smith; *b* 25 September 1946; *Educ* Orange Hill GS Edgware, St Catherine's Coll Oxford (BCL, MA), Nancy Univ France; *Career* called to the Bar Inner Temple 1969; head of chambers; recorder 1990– (asst recorder 1987–90), dep High Court Judge 1993–; contrib to legal jls: Modern Law Review, New Law Journal, Solicitors Journal; *Recreations* fatherhood, France, food, antiques; *Style*— Mark Strachan, Esq, QC; ✉ 3 Hare Court, Temple, London EC4Y 7BJ (tel 020 7415 7800)

STRACHAN, Dame Valerie Patricia Marie; DCB (1998, CB 1991); *b* 10 January 1940; *Educ* Newland HS, Hull Univ, Manchester Univ; *m* John Strachan; *Career* Customs and Excise: joined as asst princ 1961, seconded to Dept of Economic Affairs, Home Office and Treasury, princ 1966–74, asst sec 1974–80, cmmr (under sec) 1980–87 (also head Treasy/Cabinet Office Jt Mgmnt Unit), dep chm (dep sec) 1987–93, DG Internal Taxation and Customs Gp 1989–93, chm of the Bd 1993–2000, dep chair Community Fund 2000–04; dep chair Big Lottery Fund 2004–06; chair of govrs James Allen's Girls' Sch 2004–, chair Cncl Univ of Southampton 2006–; *Style*— Dame Valerie Strachan, DCB

STRACHEY, (Sir) Charles; 6 Bt (UK 1801), of Sutton Court, Somerset, but does not use title, has not been placed on the Official Roll of the Baronetage; s of Rt Hon Evelyn John St Loe Strachey (d 1963), and cous of 2 Baron Strachie (d 1973); *b* 20 June 1934; *Educ* Westminster, Magdalen Coll Oxford; *m* 1973, Janet Megan, da of Alexander Miller; 1 da; *Heir* kinsman, Henry Strachey; *Career* district dealer rep mangr Ford Motor Co Ltd 1972–75, local govt offr (ret 1993); *Style*— Charles Strachey, Esq; ✉ 31 Northchurch Terrace, London N1 4EB (tel and fax 020 7684 5479)

STRADBROKE, 6 Earl of (UK 1821); Sir (Robert) Keith Rous; 11 Bt (E 1660); also Viscount Dunwich (UK 1821) and Baron Rous (GB 1796); s of 5 Earl of Stradbroke (d 1983, shortly after his brother, 4 Earl) and (1 w) Pamela Catherine Mabell (who d 1972, having obtained a divorce 1941), da of late Capt the Hon Edward James Kay-Shuttleworth (s of 1 Baron Shuttleworth); family motto 'We fight like lions and breed like rabbits'; *b* 25 March 1937; *Educ* Harrow; *m* 1, 1960 (m dis 1977), Dawn Antoinette, da of Thomas Edward Beverley, of Brisbane; 2 s (Robert Keith, Viscount Dunwich b 1961, Hon Wesley Alexander b 1972), 5 da (Lady Ingrid Arnel b 1963, Lady Sophia Rayner b 1964, Lady Heidi Simone b 1966, Lady Pamela Keri b 1968, Lady Brigitte Aylena b 1970); m 2, 1977, Roseanna Mary Blanche, da of Francis Reitman, MD (d 1955), and Susan, *née* Vernon (d 2000); 6 s (Hon Hektor Fraser b 1978, Hon Maximilian Otho b 1981, Hon Henham Mowbray b 1983, Hon Winston Walberswick b 1986, Hon Yoxford Ulysses Uluru b 1989, Hon Ramsar Fyans b 1992), 2 da (Lady Zea Katherina b 1979, Lady Minsmere Matilda b 1988); *Heir* s, Viscount Dunwich; *Career* grazier; dir Sutuse Pty Ltd; landowner (20,000 acres); *Recreations* making babies; *Style*— Keith Rous; ✉ 45–47 Lyndhurst Street, Richmond, Victoria 3121, Australia

STRAFFORD, 8 Earl of (UK 1847); Thomas Edmund Byng; also Baron Strafford (UK 1835), Viscount Enfield (UK 1847); s of 7 Earl of Strafford (d 1984) and his 1 w, late Maria Magdalena Elizabeth, da of late Henry Cloete, CMG, of Alphen, South Africa; *b* 26 September 1936; *Educ* Eton, Clare Coll Cambridge; *m* 1, 1963 (m dis), Jennifer Mary Denise (she m, 1982, Sir Christopher Bland), da of late Rt Hon William Morrison May, MP; 2 s (William, Viscount Enfield b 1964, Hon James b 1969), 2 da (Lady Georgia b 1965, Lady Tara b 1967); m 2, 1981, Mrs Judy (Julia Mary) Howard, yr da of Sir (Charlie) Dennis Pilcher, CBE (d 1994); *Heir* s, Viscount Enfield; *Style*— The Earl of Strafford; ✉ Apple Tree Cottage, Easton, Winchester, Hampshire SO21 1EF (tel 01962 779467)

STRAKER, Nicholas David Barclay; s of Hugh Charles Straker (d 1993), and Elaine Felicia, *née* Peat; *b* 6 May 1952; *Educ* Eton, Durham Agric Coll, Lakeland Agric Coll Alberta; *m* 6 Sept 1980, Victoria Eyre, *née* Gray; 1 s (Sam Charles Barclay), 3 da (Jacquetta Lucy Eyre, Chloë Victoria Piffard, Selina Storm Felicia-Rose); *Career* 9/12 Royal Lancers 1971–75; farmer Little Hutton Farms 1975–76, conslt Towry Law & Co 1978–80; dir: Whitehouse Financial Services Ltd 1980–82, Lycetts Insurance Brokers and Financial Services 1982–; High Sheriff Co Durham 1994–95; ACII, MIMgt; *Recreations* golf, riding, country sports, tennis, gardening; *Clubs* Northern Counties, Eton Vikings; *Style*— Nicholas Straker, Esq; ✉ Lycetts, Milburn House, Dean Street, Newcastle upon Tyne NE1 1PP (tel 0191 232 1151, fax 0191 232 1873)

STRAKER, Timothy Derrick; QC (1996); s of Derrick Straker (d 1976), and Dorothy Elizabeth, *née* Rogers; *b* 25 May 1955; *Educ* Malvern Coll, Downing Coll Cambridge (MA); *m* 17 April 1982 (m dis 2007), Ann, da of late Michael Horton Baylis, of Highgate, London; 2 (Rosemary Elizabeth b 1985, Penelope Ann b 1987); *Career* called to the Bar: Gray's Inn 1977 (bencher 2003), ad eundem Lincoln's Inn 1979, Trinidad and Tobago 2001, NI 2001; asst recorder 1998, recorder 2000–, head of chambers (with Elizabeth Appelby, QC) 2002–; memb: Local Govt and Planning Bar Assoc, Admin Law Bar Assoc, Crown Office Users' Assoc, Admin Court Users' Assoc; *Publications* articles: Judicial Review, Rights of Way Law Review; contrib to Halsbury's Laws of England: Public Health and Environmental Protection, Local Government, Markets; Intelligence Services Act, A Guide to Registration of Political Parties Act, Human Rights and Judical Review: Case Studies in Context (with Ian Goldrein, QC); The Civil Court Practice (conslt ed), Information Rights (contrib); *Recreations* cricket, reading; *Clubs* Royal Over-Seas League, Lansdowne; *Style*— Timothy Straker, Esq, QC; ✉ 4–5 Gray's Inn Square, Gray's Inn, London WC1R 5AH (tel 020 7404 5252, fax 020 7242 7803, e-mail ts@4–5.co.uk)

STRANG, 2 Baron (UK 1954); Colin Strang; s of 1 Baron Strang, GCB, GCMG, MBE (d 1978), and Elsie Wynne Jones (d 1974); mother's ancestor, Col John Jones, signed Charles I's death warrant; *b* 12 June 1922; *Educ* Merchant Taylors', St John's Coll Oxford (MA, BPhil); *m* 1, 1948, Patricia Marie, da of Meiert C Avis, of Johannesburg, South Africa; m 2, 1955, Barbara Mary Hope (d 1982), da of Frederick Albert Carr, of Wimbledon, London; 1 da (Caroline b 1957); m 3, 1984, Mary Shewell, da of Richard Miles, of Thornaby-on-Tees, Cleveland; *Heir* none; *Career* prof of philosophy Univ of Newcastle upon Tyne, ret 1982; *Style*— The Rt Hon the Lord Strang; ✉ Broombank, Lochranza, Isle of Arran KA27 8JF

STRANG, David James Reid; QPM (2002); *Educ* Univ of Durham (BSc), Univ of London (MSc); *Career* with Met Police 1980–98, asst chief constable Lothian and Borders Police 1998–2001, chief constable Dumfries and Galloway Constabulary 2001–07; *Style*— David J R Strang, Esq, QPM

STRANG, Rt Hon Gavin Steel; PC (1997), MP; s of James Steel Strang, of Perthshire; *b* 10 July 1943; *Educ* Morrison's Acad Crieff, Univ of Edinburgh (BSc, PhD), Univ of Cambridge (Dip Agric Sci); *m* 1973, Bettina Smith; 1 s; 2 step s; *Career* memb Tayside Econ Planning Gp 1966–68, scientist with ARC 1968–70; MP (Lab): Edinburgh E 1970–97, Edinburgh E and Mussleburgh 1997–; Parly under sec of state for energy March-Oct 1974, Parly sec to Min for Agric 1974–79, min for Tport 1997–98; oppn front bench spokesman on: agric 1981–82, employment 1987–89; chief oppn spokesperson on food, agric and rural affairs 1992–97; former memb Shadow Cabinet; memb Select Ctee on Science and Technol 1992; chair All Pty Gp for World Govt 2000–; *Style*— The Rt Hon Gavin Strang, MP; ✉ House of Commons, London SW1A 0AA

STRANG, Prof John Stanley; s of William John Strang, CBE, FRS, of Castle Combe, Wilts, and Margaret Nicholas Strang; *b* 12 May 1950; *Educ* Bryanston, Guy's Hosp Med Sch Univ of London (MB BS); *m* 21 April 1984, Jennifer, da of Edwin Austin Campbell Abbey (d 1975); 2 s (Samuel John b 1985, Robert Luke b 1988), 1 da (Jasmine Rebecca b 1991, d 1998); *Career* regnl conslt in drug dependence Manchester 1982–86; Maudsley Bethlem Royal Hosp: conslt psychiatrist in drug dependence 1986–, prof of addiction behaviour and dir of Addiction Research Unit 1995–; conslt advsr on drug dependence to Dept of Health 1986–2003; FRCPsych 1994 (MRCPsych 1977), MD 1995, Hon MRCP 2002; *Books* AIDS and Drug Misuse: the challenge for policy and practice in the 1990s (ed with G Stimson, 1990), Drugs, Alcohol and Tobacco: the science and policy connections (ed with G Edwards and J Jaffe, 1993), Heroin Addiction and Drug Policy: the British system (ed with M Gossop, 1994), Drug Misuse and Community Pharmacy (ed with J Sheridan, 2002), Methadone Matters: Evolving Community Methadone Treatment of Opiate Addiction (ed with G Tober, 2003), Heroin Addiction and the 'British System' (ed with M Gossop, 2005); *Style*— Prof John Strang; ✉ National Addiction Centre, The Maudsley/Institute of Psychiatry, Denmark Hill, London SE5 8AF (tel 020 7848 0438)

STRANG STEEL, Colin Brodie; yr s of Maj Sir (Fiennes) William Strang Steel, 2 Bt (d 1992), of Philiphaugh, Selkirk, and Joan Ella Brodie, *née* Henderson (d 1982); *b* 2 June 1945; *Educ* Eton, RAC Cirencester; *m* 24 Oct 1970, April Eileen, da of Aubrey Fairfax Studd, of Ramsey, IOM; 3 s (James b 1973, Alistair b 1975, Peter b 1977); *Career* chartered surveyor; ptnr Knight Frank & Rutley (now Knight Frank) 1974–2001; chm Scottish Youth Cricket Fndn; FRICS; *Recreations* cricket, football, squash, tennis, wildlife; *Clubs* MCC, Scottish Cricket Union, New (Edinburgh); *Style*— Colin Strang Steel, Esq; ✉ Threepwood, Blainslie, Galashiels, Selkirkshire TD1 2PY (tel 01896 860321)

STRANG STEEL, Malcolm Graham; WS (1973); s of Jock Wykeham Strang Steel (d 1991), of Logie, Kirriemuir, Angus, and Lesley, *née* Graham; *b* 24 November 1946; *Educ* Eton, Trinity Coll Cambridge (BA), Univ of Edinburgh (LLB); *m* 21 Oct 1972, Margaret Philippa, da of William Patrick Scott, OBE, TD, DL (d 1989), of Kierfiold, Stromness, Orkney; 1 s (Patrick Reginald b 1975), 1 da (Laura b 1977); *Career* admitted slr 1973; ptnr: W & J Burness WS 1973–97, Turcan Connell WS 1997–; sec Standing Cncl of Scot Chiefs 1973–83, memb Cncl Law Soc of Scotland 1984–90, tstee Scot Dyslexia Tst 1988–95, sec Scot Agricultural Arbiters and Valuers Assoc 1998–; memb Queen's Body Guard for Scotland (Royal Co of Archers); FRSA; *Recreations* shooting, fishing, skiing, tennis, reading; *Clubs* New (Edinburgh), MCC; *Style*— Malcolm G Strang Steel, Esq, WS; ✉ Greenhead of Arnot, Leslie, Glenrothes KY6 3JQ (tel 01592 840459, fax 01592 841056); Turcan Connell WS, Princes Exchange, 1 Earl Grey Street, Edinburgh EH3 9EE (tel 0131 228 8111, fax 0131 228 8118)

STRANG STEEL, Maj Sir (Fiennes) Michael; 3 Bt (UK 1938), of Philiphaugh, Co Selkirk, CBE (1999), DL; s of Maj Sir (Fiennes) William Strang Steel, 2 Bt, JP, DL (d 1992), and Joan Ella Brodie, *née* Henderson (d 1982); *b* 22 February 1943; *m* 1977, Sarah Jane, da of late J A S Russell, of Mayfield, Lochmaben, Dumfriesshire; 2 s ((Fiennes) Edward b 1978, Sam Arthur b 1983), 1 da (Tara Diana b 1980); *Heir* s, (Fiennes) Edward Strang Steel; *Career* Maj 17/21 Lancers, ret; forestry cmmr 1988–99, memb Deer Cmmn for Scotland; Ensign Queen's Body Guard for Scotland (Royal Co of Archers); *Style*— Sir Michael Strang Steel, Bt, CBE, DL; ✉ Philiphaugh, Selkirk TD7 5LX

STRANGE, 17 Baron (E 1628); Adam Humphrey Drummond; eld s of Capt Humphrey Drummond of Megginch, MC, *qv*, and Lady Strange (16 holder of title, d 2005); *b* 20 April 1953, Dundee; *Educ* Eton, Sandhurst, Heriot Watt Univ (MSc); *m* 14 May 1988, Hon Mary Emma Jeronima, *née* Dewar, eld da of 4 Baron Forteviot, *qv*; 1 da (Hon Sophia Frances b 1991), 1 s (Hon John Adam Humphrey b 1992); *Heir* s, Hon John Drummond; *Career* Grenadier Gds 1973–94, Maj, ret; Perthshire Housing Assoc 1994–; MCIH; *Clubs* Royal Perth Golfing Soc; *Style*— The Lord Strange; ✉ The Mains of Megginch, Errol, Perthshire PH2 7RN

STRANGER-JONES, Anthony John; s of Leonard Ivan Stranger-Jones (d 1983), and Iris Christine, *née* Truscott (d 1991); *b* 30 December 1944; *Educ* Westminster, ChCh Oxford (MA); *m* 19 June 1976, Kazumi, da of Kazuo Matsuo, of Japan; 2 da (Amiko b 1977, Yukiko b 1980), 1 s (David b 1983); *Career* md Amex Finance (Hong Kong) Ltd 1974–76; dir: Amex Bank Ltd 1976–79, Korea Merchant Banking Corporation 1979–82, Barclays Merchant Bank Ltd 1979–86, Barclays de Zoete Wedd Ltd 1986–97 (md Corp and Investment Banking 1995–97); md Corp and Investment Banking Credit Suisse First Boston 1997–98, dir Barclays Private Bank Ltd 1999–2001, chm Essjay Consultants 2002–; ACIB 1971; *Clubs* Asia House, Gloucestershire CCC, IISS, Japan Soc, MCC, Savile; *Style*— Anthony Stranger-Jones, Esq; ✉ 33 Randolph Crescent, London W9 1DP (tel 020 7286 7342, e-mail anthony@stranger-jones.com)

STRANRAER-MULL, The Very Rev Gerald Hugh; s of Capt Gerald Stranraer-Mull (d 1955), and Dolena Mackenzie, *née* Workman (d 1986); *b* 24 November 1942; *Educ* Woodhouse Grove Sch, King's Coll London (AKC); *m* 30 Dec 1967, Glynis Mary, da of Capt David Kempe, of Iden Green, Kent; 1 da (Clare b 1970), 2 s (Michael Paul b and d 1974, Jamie b 1977); *Career* journalist 1960–66; curate: Hexham Abbey 1970–72, Corbridge 1972; rector Ellon and Cruden Bay 1972–, canon Aberdeen Cathedral 1981–, dean of Aberdeen and Orkney 1988–; chm: Ellon Schs Cncl 1982–86, Gordon Health Cncl 1982–86; tstee: Oil Chaplaincy Tst 1993–, Iona Cornerstone Fndn 1994–; *Books* A Turbulent House: The Augustinians at Hexham (1970), View of the Diocese of Aberdeen and Orkney (1977), A Church for Scotland: the story of the Scottish Episcopal Church (2000); *Style*— The Very Rev the Dean of Aberdeen and Orkney; ✉ The Rectory, Ellon, Aberdeenshire AB41 9NP (tel 01358 720366, fax 01358 720256, e-mail gerald.stranraer-mull@virgin.net)

STRATFORD, (Howard) Muir; JP (1978); s of Dr Martin Gould Stratford, VRD (d 1993), of London, and Dr Mavis Winifred Muir Stratford, JP, *née* Beddall (d 1993); *b* 6 June 1936; *Educ* Marlborough; *m* 8 July 1961, Margaret Reid, da of Robert Linton Roderick Ballantine (d 1957); 2 da (Gail b 1964, Fiona b 1967), 1 s (Duncan b 1971); *Career* insurance broker, memb Lloyd's; dir Bowring London Ltd 1980–85 and 1986–91, chief exec Bowring M K Ltd 1985–86; dir Watford FC 1971–90; Liveryman Worshipful Company of Haberdashers 1959, Liveryman Worshipful Company of Insurers 1986; *Recreations* golf, watching football and cricket; *Clubs* MCC, Moor Park Golf; *Style—* Muir Stratford, Esq; ✉ Nobles, Church Lane, Sarratt, Hertfordshire WD3 6HJ (tel 01923 260475, mobile 07836 219412)

STRATFORD, Neil Martin; s of Dr Martin Gould Stratford, VRD (d 1993), of London, and Dr Mavis Winifred Muir Stratford, JP, *née* Beddall (d 1993); *b* 26 April 1938; *Educ* Marlborough, Magdalene Coll Cambridge (MA), Courtauld Inst (BA); *m* 28 Sept 1966, Anita Jennifer (Jenny), da of Peter Edwin Lewis (d 1980); 2 da (Jemima b 1968, Rebecca b 1971); *Career* Coldstream Gds 1956, 2 Lt 1957–58, Lt 1958; trainee Kleinwort Benson Lonsdale 1961–63, lectr Westfield Coll London 1969–75, keeper of medieval and later antiquities British Museum 1975–98 (emeritus 1998–); visiting memb Inst for Advanced Study Princeton 1998–99, visiting prof Paris Ecole Pratique des Hautes Etudes 1999, Appleton prof Univ of Florida Tallahassee 2000, prof de l'histoire de l'art médiéval Paris Ecole Nationale des Chartes 2000–03, visiting sr lecturing fell Duke Univ N Carolina; chm St Albans Cathedral Fabric Advsy Ctee 1995–; Liveryman Worshipful Co of Haberdashers 1959; hon memb Académie de Dijon 1975, foreign memb Soc Nat des Antiquaires de France 1985, correspondant étranger Académie des Inscriptions et Belles-Lettres 2002–; FSA 1976; Officier Ordre des Arts et des Lettres (France) 2006–; *Books* La Sculpture Oubliée de Vézelay (1984), Catalogue of Medieval Enamels in the British Museum, II. Northern Romanesque Enamel (1993), Studies in Burgundian Romanesque Sculpture (1998), La frise monumentale romane de Souvigny (2002), Chronos et Cosmos: Le pilier roman de Souvigny (2005); *Recreations* cricket and football, food and wine, music, particularly opera; *Clubs* Garrick, Beefsteak, MCC, IZ, Cambridge Univ, Pitt, Hawks' (Cambridge); *Style—* Neil Stratford, Esq, FSA; ✉ 17 Church Row, London NW3 6UP

STRATHALMOND, 3 Baron (UK 1955); William Roberton Fraser; o s of 2 Baron Strathalmond, CMG, OBE, TD (d 1976), and Letitia, *née* Krementz; *b* 22 July 1947; *Educ* Loretto; *m* 1973, Amanda Rose, da of Rev Gordon Clifford Taylor, of St Giles-in-the-Fields Rectory, London; 2 s (Hon William b 24 Sept 1976, Hon George b 10 March 1979), 1 da (Hon Virginia b 22 Dec 1982); *Heir* s, Hon William Fraser; *Career* md London Wall Members Agency Ltd 1986–91, dir London Wall Holdings plc 1986–91, chm R W Sturge Ltd 1991–94, dir Gerling at Lloyd's Ltd (formerly Owen & Wilby Underwriting Agency Ltd) 1995–2000; vice-pres RSAS Age Care 1989–; Liveryman Worshipful Co of Girdlers; MICAS 1972; *Style—* The Lord Strathalmond; ✉ Holt House, Elstead, Surrey GU8 6LF

STRATHCLYDE, 2 Baron (UK 1955); Thomas Galloway Dunlop du Roy de Blicquy Galbraith; PC (1995); er s of Hon Sir Thomas Galbraith, KBE, MP (Cons and Unionist) Glasgow Hillhead 1948–82 (d 1982), by his w, Simone Clothilde Fernande Marie Ghislaine (d 1991), eldest da of late Jean du Roy de Blicquy, of Bois d'Hautmont, Brabant, whose marriage with Sir Thomas was dissolved 1974; suc gf, 1 Baron Strathclyde, PC, JP (d 1985); *b* 22 February 1960; *Educ* Sussex House London, Wellington, UEA (BA), Univ of Aix-en-Provence; *m* 27 June 1992, Jane, er da of John Skinner, of Chenies, Herts; 3 da (Hon Elizabeth Ida Skinner b 1 Dec 1993, Hon Annabel Jane Simone Skinner b 15 May 1996, Hon Rose Marie Louise Skinner Galbraith); *Career* insurance broker Bain Clarkson Ltd (formerly Bain Dawes) 1982–88; Lord in Waiting (Govt Whip House of Lords) 1988–89; spokesman for DTI; Parly under sec of state: Dept of Employment (and min for tourism) 1989–90, DOE July-Sept 1990, Scottish Office (min for agric, fish, Highlands and Islands) 1990–92, DOE 1992, DTI 1993; min of state DTI 1994; Capt HM Body Guard of Hon Corps of Gentlemen at Arms (chief Govt whip) 1994–97, oppn chief whip in the Lords 1997–98, oppn spokesman and shadow ldr of the House of Lords 1998–; chm Trafalgar Capital Mgmnt Ltd 2001–, dir Scottish Mortgage Investment Tst plc 2004–; pres Quoted Cos Alliance; memb Bd Cons Fndn, Cons candidate Euro election Merseyside East 1984; patron Pakistan Human Devpt Fund UK; Channel 4 Peer of the Year 2000, Spectator Peer of the Year 2004; *Style—* The Rt Hon Lord Strathclyde, PC; ✉ House of Lords, London SW1A 0PW (tel 020 7219 5353)

STRATHCONA AND MOUNT ROYAL, 4 Baron (UK 1900); Donald Euan Palmer Howard; s of 3 Baron Strathcona and Mount Royal (d 1959), and Hon Diana, *née* Loder (d 1985), da of 1 Baron Wakehurst; *b* 26 November 1923; *Educ* Eton, Trinity Coll Cambridge, McGill Univ Montreal; *m* 1, 1954 (m dis 1977), Lady Jane Mary, da of 12 Earl Waldegrave, KG, GCVO, TD (*see* Howard, Lady Jane); 2 s, 4 da; m 2, 1978, Patricia, da of late Harvey Evelyn Thomas and wid of John Middleton; *Heir* s, Hon Alexander Howard; *Career* sat as Cons in Lords; late Lt RNVR; Urwick Orr and Partners (industrial conslts) 1950–57, pres Steamboat Assoc of GB, a Lord in Waiting to HM (Govt Whip) 1973–74, parly under sec of state for RAF 1974, jt dep leader of oppn House of Lords 1976–79, min of state MOD 1979–81; dir: UK Falklands Island Tst, Coastal Forces Heritage Tst; chm: Bath Festival 1966–73, British Maritime Charitable Fndn, Hales Trophy Tstees; memb: Cncl RHS 1966–73, Cncl SS Great Britain Project 1968–; Warden Worshipful Co of Fishmongers; *Recreations* gardening, sailing; *Clubs* Brooks's, Pratt's, RYS; *Style—* The Rt Hon the Lord Strathcona and Mount Royal; ✉ Townsend Barn, Poulshot, Devizes, Wiltshire SN10 1SD (tel 01380 828329, fax 01380 828738); Kiloran, Isle of Colonsay, Argyll (tel 01951 200301)

STRATHEDEN AND CAMPBELL, 6 Baron (UK 1836 and 1841 respectively); Donald Campbell; o s of 5 Baron Stratheden and Campbell (d 1987), and Evelyn Mary Austen, *née* Smith (d 1989); *b* 4 April 1934; *Educ* Eton; *m* 1, 8 Nov 1957, Hilary Ann Holland (d 1991), da of Lt-Col William Derington Turner (d 1988), of Simonstown, South Africa; 1 s (Hon David Anthony b 13 Feb 1963), 3 da (Hon Tania Ann b 19 Sept 1960, Hon Wendy Meriel b 27 Jan 1969, Hon Joyce Margaret b 25 Feb 1971); m 2, 31 March 2001, Elaine Margaret Fogarty; *Heir* s, Hon David Campbell; *Style—* The Rt Hon the Lord Stratheden and Campbell; ✉ Ridgewood, MS 401, Cooroy, Queensland 4563, Australia

STRATHERN, Prof Andrew Jamieson; s of Robert Strathern (d 1972), and Mary, *née* Sharp (d 1992); *b* 19 January 1939; *Educ* Colchester Royal GS, Trinity Coll Cambridge (major entrance scholar, BA, MA, PhD); *m* 1, 20 July 1973 (m dis 1986), Ann Marilyn Evans; 1 da (Barbara Helen Mary b 1969), 2 s (Alan Leiper b 1975, Hugh Thomas b 1975); m 2, 21 April 1997, Dr Pamela J Stewart; *Career* res fell Trinity Coll Cambridge 1965–68, fell Res Sch of Paufic Studies ANU 1970–72 (res fell 1969–70), prof of social anthropology Univ of Papua New Guinea 1973–76, prof and head of Dept of Anthropology UCL 1976–83, dir Inst of PNG Studies Port Moresby PNG 1981–86, emeritus prof Univ of London 1987–, Andrew W Mellon Distinguished prof of anthropology Univ of Pittsburgh 1987–, dir Center for Pacific Studies James Cook Univ Townsville 1996–; memb Cncl RAI 1977–80, vice-chm Social Anthropology Ctee SSRC 1979–81 (memb 1977–81); Rivers Meml Medal 1976, PNG 10 Anniversary of Ind Medal 1987; memb: Assoc of Social Anthropologists of GB and the Cwlth 1967, Assoc for Social Anthropology in Oceania 1987, European Assoc of Soc Anthropologists 1989, Euro Soc of Oceanists 1993; fell American Anthropological Assoc 1983, FRAI; *Books* The Rope of Moka (1971), Self - Decoration in Mt Hagen (jtly 1971), One Father, One Blood (1972), Ongka (1979), Inequality in Highlands New Guinea Societies (ed, 1982), A Line of Power (1984), The Mi-Culture of the Mt Hagen People (co-ed, 1990), Landmarks (1993), Ru (1993), Voices of Conflict (1993), Migration and Transformations (co-ed, 1994), Body Thoughts (1996), Millennial Markers (co-ed, 1997), Bodies and Persons (co-ed, 1998), Cultural Anthropology, a Contemporary Perspective (co-author 3 edn, 1998), Kuk Heritage: Issues and Debates (co-ed, 1998), Curing and Healing: Medical Anthropology in Global Perspective (jtly, 1999), The Spirit is Coming! A Photographic-Textual Documentation of the Female Spirit Cult in Mt Hagen (jtly, 1999); *Recreations* travel, poetry; *Style—* Prof Andrew Strathern; ✉ 1103 Winterton Street, Pittsburgh, PA 15206, USA (tel 00 1 412 441 5778); Department of Anthropology, University of Pittsburgh, Pittsburgh PA 15260, USA (tel 00 1 412 648 7519, fax 00 1 412 648 7535, e-mail strather@pitt.edu)

STRATHMORE AND KINGHORNE, 18 Earl of (S 1606 and 1677) Michael Fergus Bowes Lyon; also Lord Glamis (S 1445), Earl of Kinghorne (S 1606), Lord Glamis, Tannadyce, Sidlaw and Strathdichtie, Viscount Lyon and Earl of Strathmore and Kinghorne by special charter (S 1677), Baron Bowes (UK 1887), Earl of Strathmore and Kinghorne (UK 1937); s of 17 Earl of Strathmore and Kinghorne (d 1987), and Mary Pamela, *née* McCorquodale; *b* 7 June 1957; *Educ* Univ of Aberdeen (B Land Econ); *m* 1, 14 Nov 1984 (m dis 2004), Isobel Charlotte, da of Capt Anthony Weatherall, of Cowhill, Dumfries; 3 s (Simon Patrick, Lord Glamis b 1986, Hon John Fergus b 1988, Hon George Norman b 1991); m 2, 24 Nov 2005, Dr Damaris Elizabeth Stuart-William; 1 s (Hon Toby Peter Fergus); *Heir* s, Lord Glamis; *Career* a Page of Honour to HM Queen Elizabeth the Queen Mother (his great aunt) 1971–73; Capt Scots Gds; a Lord in Waiting 1989–91; Capt The Queen's Bodyguard of the Yeomen of the Guard (Dep Chief Whip, House of Lords) 1991–94; *Clubs* Turf, Pratt's, Perth; *Style—* The Rt Hon the Earl of Strathmore and Kinghorne, DL; ✉ Glamis Castle, Forfar, Angus DD8 1QJ (website www.glamis-castle.co.uk)

STRATHSPEY, 6 Baron (UK 1884); Sir James Patrick Trevor Grant of Grant; 18 Bt (NS 1625); 33 Chief of the Clan Grant; s of 5 Baron Strathspey (d 1992), and his 1 w, Alice, *née* Bowe (d 2002); *b* 9 September 1943; *Educ* abroad, RAC Cirencester; *m* 1, 1966 (m dis 1984), Linda, da of David Piggott, of Forfar; 3 da (Hon Carolyn Anne Maclean b 1967, Hon Philippa Jane b 1971, Hon Victoria Louise b 1976); m 2, 1985 (m dis 1993), Margaret, da of Robert Drummond, of Fife; *Heir* half-bro, Hon Michael Grant of Grant; *Career* pres Clan Grant Soc; *Style—* The Rt Hon the Lord Strathspey; ✉ The Old Manse, Duthil, Carrbridge, Strathspey PH23 3ND

STRATTON, David; s of Lawrence James William Stratton (d 1989), and Muriel Elizabeth, *née* Hunt (d 2004); *b* 16 May 1947; *Educ* Altrincham GS for Boys, Colwyn Bay GS, Univ of Leeds (LLB); *m* 29 May 1971, Ruth Hazel, da of John Eric Delhanty; 3 s (James Anthony b 1 March 1976, Charles Edward b 21 April 1978, Oliver John b 26 Nov 1979), 3 da (Rachael Joanna b 6 May 1981, Rebecca Alice b 30 March 1987, Jessica Rose b 17 June 1990); *Career* admitted slr 1971; articled clerk to Town Clerk Warrington 1969–71, asst rising to princ asst slr Warrington Borough Cncl 1971–72, gp slr Christian Salvesen Properties Limited 1975–79 (asst gp slr 1972–75), head Commercial Property Dept and dep sr ptnr Halliwell Landau Solicitors Manchester 1979–95, ptnr Field Cunningham & Co Solicitors Manchester 1995–; *Style—* David Stratton, Esq; ✉ Field Cunningham & Co, St John's Court, 70 Quay Street, Manchester M3 3JF (tel 0161 834 4734, fax 0161 834 1772)

STRAUS, Peter Quentin; s of Dr Ronnie Straus, and Graziella Straus, of Wimbledon, London; *b* 10 September 1960; *Educ* KCS Wimbledon, Christ's Coll Cambridge (MA, capt squash and tennis teams); *Career* publisher; Hodder and Stoughton Publishers: graduate trainee 1982–84, sales and marketing asst 1984–86, asst ed New English Library later jr ed, ed then sr ed Hodder and Stoughton Paperbacks 1986–88; editorial dir Hamish Hamilton 1990 (sr ed 1988–90); Macmillan Publishers Ltd: publishing dir and publisher Picador 1990–94, gp literary publisher Macmillan, Picador and Papermac 1994–95, ed-in-chief Macmillan, Pan, Picador, Papermac and Sidgwick & Jackson 1995–96, US scout 1996–97, publisher Picador 1997–, ed-in-chief Pan Macmillan, Macmillan, Pan, Sidgwick & Jackson, Boxtree, Channel 4 Books and Picador 2000–02, literary agent and dir Rogers, Coleridge & White Ltd 2002–; memb Booker Prize Mgmnt Ctee Booker plc 1991–2002, memb Mgmnt Ctee Samuel Johnson Prize 1998–; *Books* 20 Under 35 (ed, 1988); *Recreations* sport, film, theatre, reading; *Clubs* Beerhunters (Player of the Year 1992), Soho House; *Style—* Peter Straus, Esq; ✉ Rogers, Coleridge & White Ltd, 20 Powis Mews, London W1P 1JN (e-mail peters@rcwlitagency.co.uk)

STRAUSS, Derek Ronald; s of Ronald Strauss (d 1990), and Theodora, *née* Instone; *b* 16 May 1939; *Educ* Eton; *m* 26 April 1967, Nicola Mary, da of Gp Capt William Blackwood, OBE, DFC; 2 s (James Digby Ronald b 2 July 1969, Toby Anthony Lavery b 21 Sept 1970); *Career* Lt Cdr RNR (ret); Strauss Turnbull: joined 1957, dir 1961–80, chief exec 1980–83, latterly chm; former: dep chm SG Securities(London) Ltd, chm Mineral Oils and Resources Fund Inc, dir 3i London Smaller Companies Investment Trust plc; currently: jt exec dir Pan Holdings SA, exec dir Ballynahinch Holdings, memb Bd Cayman Real Estate Fund; *Recreations* fishing, shooting, skiing; *Clubs* White's, City of London, Pratt's; *Style—* Derek Strauss

STRAUSS, Toby; s of Peter Strauss (d 1997), and Virginia, *née* Shadwell; *b* 4 October 1959, London; *Educ* St Paul's, Loughborough Univ (BSc); *m* June 1995, Cressida, *née* Spencer; 1 s (Joshua b March 1998), 1 da (Ella b Dec 2000); *Career* IBM 1984–88, Psiax Systems 1988–92, sailed to WI and back 1992–93, assoc princ McKinsey & Co 1993–99, md Charcol/Charcol Online 1999–2002, ceo John Scott & Ptnrs 2003–05, co-fndr and exec chm OrderWork Ltd 2005–; non-exec dir Kensington Gp plc 2005–; *Recreations* sailing, cycling, reading, classical guitar ensemble; *Style—* Toby Strauss, Esq; ✉ OrderWork Ltd, Queens Wharf, Queen Caroline Street, London W6 9RJ

STRAW, Rt Hon John Whitaker (Jack); PC (1997), MP; s of Walter Straw, and Joan Straw; *b* 3 August 1946; *Educ* Brentwood Sch, Univ of Leeds, Inns of Court Sch of Law; *m* 1, 1968 (m dis 1978), Anthea Weston; 1 da (decd); m 2, 1978, Alice Elizabeth Perkins, CB, *qv*; 1 s, 1 da; *Career* called to the Bar Inner Temple 1972 (bencher 1997), barrister 1972–74; pres NUS 1969–71, memb Islington Cncl 1971–78, dep ldr ILEA 1973–74, contested (Lab) Tonbridge and Malling 1974; political advsr to Sec of State for: Social Servs 1974–76, Environment 1976–77, Granada TV (World in Action) 1977–79; MP (Lab) Blackburn 1979–; oppn front bench spokesman on: Treasy and econ affrs 1981–83, environment 1983–87; elected to Shadow Cabinet 1987; chief oppn spokesman on: educn 1987–92, housing and local govt 1992–94, home affrs 1994–97; sec of state Home Office 1997–2001, sec of state FCO 2001–06, ldr House of Commons 2006–07, sec of state for justice and Lord Chllr 2007–; visiting fell Nuffield Coll Oxford 1990–98; chm Pimlico Sch 1995–2000; Hon LLD Univ of Leeds 1999; FRSS 1995; *Style—* The Rt Hon Jack Straw, MP; ✉ House of Commons, London SW1A 0AA

STREAT, Prof Michael; s of George Streat (d 1978), and Lore Streat (d 2000); *b* 23 July 1937; *Educ* UMIST (BSc), Imperial Coll London (PhD, DIC); *m* 3 Dec 1961, Carole Doreen, da of Joseph Bertram Robinson; 1 da (Denise (Mrs Shahar) b 16 June 1963), 1 s (Simon b 12 April 1966); *Career* successively lectr, sr lectr and reader Imperial Coll London 1961–89 (visiting prof 2003–), prof of chemical engrg Loughborough Univ 1989–2002 (now emeritus, head Dept of Chemical Engrg 1992–2000); AMCT; CEng, FIChemE 1973, FREng 2000; *Publications* co-author of numerous articles and papers in learned jls on the application of adsorption and ion exchange technol; *Recreations* antique collecting (especially maps and prints), travelling, armchair sports, family and friends; *Style—* Prof Michael Streat; ✉ 5 Compass Close, Gendale Avenue, Edgware HA8 8HU (e-mail michael.streat@btopenworld.com)

STREATHER, Bruce Godfrey; s of William Godfrey Streather (d 1995), of Staffs, and Pamela Mary, *née* Revell (d 1993); *b* 3 June 1946; *Educ* Malvern, Univ of Oxford (MA); *m* 15 Dec 1973, Geraldine Susan, da of Colin Herbert Clout (d 1995), of San Franciso, USA; 3 da (Charlotte, Annabel, Miranda); *Career* admitted slr 1971; sr ptnr Streathers; memb Law Soc; *Recreations* family, golf; *Clubs* R&A, Sunningdale Golf, Vincent's (Oxford), Littlestone Golf, Moor Hall Golf; *Style*— Bruce Streather, Esq; ✉ Streathers, 128 Wigmore Street, London W1U 3SA (tel 020 7034 4200, fax 020 7034 4301, e-mail bgstreather@streathers.co.uk)

STREATOR, Hon Edward; s of Edward Streator (d 1955), of NY, and Ella, *née* Stout (d 1980); *b* 12 December 1930; *Educ* Princeton Univ (AB); *m* 16 Feb 1957, Priscilla, da of W John Kenney, of Washington; 1 s (Edward b 1958), 2 da (Elinor b 1960, Abigail b 1965); *Career* Lt (JG) USNR 1952–56; joined US Foreign Serv 1956, third sec US Embassy Addis Ababa 1958–60, second sec US Embassy Lomé 1960–62, Office of Intelligence & Research Dept of State 1962–64, staff asst to Sec of State 1964–66, first sec US Mission to NATO Paris and Brussels 1966–69, dep dir rising to dir Office of Nato Affairs Dept of State 1969–75, dep US permanent rep to NATO Brussels 1975–77, min US Embassy London 1977–84, ambass and US rep OECD Paris 1984–87; chm New Atlantic Initiative 1996–; dir The South Bank London 1988–99; govr: Ditchley Fndn 1980–, RUSI 1988–91, ESU 1988–94, British-American Arts Assoc 1989–98; pres American C of C 1989–94, chm European Cncl of American Cs of C 1992–95; memb: Exec Ctee The Pilgrims 1981–2001, Exec Ctee IISS 1988–98, British Museum (Natural History) Int Fndn 1991–2002, Bd Inst of US Studies Univ of London 1993–98, Cncl Oxford Inst for American Studies 1993–1999, Advsy Bd Fulbright Cmmn 1996–2002; Benjamin Franklin Medal RSA 1992; pres and tstee Northcote Parkinson Fndn 2004–, Pilgrims (NY) 2004–; *Recreations* swimming; *Clubs* Metropolitan (Washington), Beefsteak, Garrick, White's, Mill Reef (Antigua), Century Assoc, Knickerbocker (pres, NY); *Style*— Hon Edward Streator; ✉ 535 Park Avenue, New York, NY 10021, USA (tel 00 1 212 486 6688, fax 00 1 212 486 7722, e-mail estreator@nyc.rr.com)

STREET, Dr Andrew Maurice; s of Harry Maurice Street, of Swadlincote, Derbys, and Patricia, *née* Wilson; *b* 30 September 1961; *Educ* Burton-on-Trent GS, St Hild and St Bede Coll Durham (BSc, Univ Prize), Lady Margaret Hall Oxford (DPhil); *m* 14 Oct 2005, Ruth Margaret, *née* Jackson; 1 s (Harry Andrew Alan b 9 Jan 2007); *Career* pt/t researcher AERE Harwell 1986, analyst Baring Brothers & Co Ltd 1986–88, options trader then sr trader Paribas Capital Markets Ltd 1988–91, head of equity derivatives trading Nomura International plc 1991–92, head of equity and commodity risk mgmnt and bd dir Mitsubishi Finance International plc 1992–95 (exec dir/head of arbitrage 1993–95); head of market risk mgmnt and asst dir SFA 1995–98; co-head Traded Risk Dept FSA 1998–2000, md Value Consultants Ltd 2000–; pt/t lectr Thames Valley Univ 2003–; MInstP 1986, MSI; *Publications* Methods of Calculation of Cross Sections for Nuclear Reactors (DPhil thesis, 1987), Handbook of Risk Management and Analysis (2000); articles in Nuclear Science & Engineering magazine and Risk magazine; *Recreations* flying (PPL), theatre, cinema, sailing, reading, tinkering with computers; *Style*— Dr Andrew Street; ✉ Value Consultants Ltd, 36 Elm Grove Road, London W5 3JJ (tel 020 8566 0383, fax 020 8932 2591, e-mail andrew.street@value-consultants.co.uk)

STREET, Prof Sarah; da of D L Street, and C Street; *b* 1 February 1958, Cardiff; *Educ* Univ of Warwick (BA), St Peter's Coll Oxford (DPhil); *Career* archivist Dept of Western Manuscripts Bodleian Library Univ of Oxford 1985–93, Univ of Bristol 1993– (currently prof of film); *Books* Cinema and State (with Margaret Dickinson, 1985), British National Cinema (1997), British Cinema in Documents (2000), Moving Performance (ed with Linda Fitzsimmons, 2000), European Cinema: An Introduction (ed with Jill Forbes, 2000), Costume and Cinema: Dress Codes in Popular Film (2001), Transatlantic Crossings: British Feature Films in the USA (2002), The Titanic in Myth and Memory (ed with Tim Bergfelder, 2004), Black Narcissus (2005); *Style*— Prof Sarah Street; ✉ Department of Drama: Theatre, Film, Television, University of Bristol, Cantocks Close, Woodland Road, Bristol BS8 1UP

STREET, Dame Susan Ruth (Sue); DCB (2005); da of Stefan Galeski, and Anna, *née* Galin; *b* 11 August 1949, London; *Educ* Camden Sch, Univ of St Andrews (MA); *m* 22 July 1972, Richard Street; 1 s (Robin b 6 Dec 1976), 1 da (Rebecca b 22 Sept 1978); *Career* Home Office 1972–74, British Cncl Bogota 1974–81, Home Office 1982–89, dir Top Mgmnt Prog Cabinet Office 1989–92, Price Waterhouse 1992–94, Cabinet Office 1994–96, Fire Serv 1996–99, dir Criminal Policy Gp Home Office 1999–2001, perm sec DCMS 2001–06; advsr Deloitte 2007–; author of articles in Westminster and Whitehall jls; tstee Windsor Leadership Tst; *Recreations* ballet, theatre, family life, poor golf, tennis; *Style*— Dame Sue Street, DCB; ✉ 1 Blenheim Road, London NW8 0LU (tel 020 7624 5920, fax 020 7372 5501, e-mail suestreet2@msn.com)

STREET-PORTER, Janet; *b* 27 December 1946; *Educ* Lady Margaret GS, Architectural Assoc; *m* 1, 1967 (m dis 1975), Tim Street-Porter; m 2, 1975 (m dis 1977), Tony Elliott; m 3, 1979 (m dis 1981), Frank Cvitanovich (d 1988); *Career* journalist, broadcaster and tv prodr; writer for: Petticoat Magazine 1968, Daily Mail 1969–71, Evening Standard 1971–73; contrib to Queen, Vogue, etc; own show LBC Radio 1973; presented numerous series for LWT 1975–81 incl: London Weekend Show, Saturday Night People, Around Midnight, Six O'Clock Show; produced and devised series from 1981 incl: Twentieth Century Box, Get Fresh, Bliss, Network 7; BBC TV: joined 1988, head of Youth and Entertainment Features until 1994, head of Independent Production for Entertainment 1994; md cable channel Live TV for Mirror Group 1994–95; ed The Independent on Sunday 1999–2001; currently ed at large for Independent Newspapers; presented: Design Awards (BBC 2), J'Accuse (C4) 1996, Travels with Pevsner (BBC 2) 1997, Coast to Coast (BBC 2) 1998 (book on same subject 1998), The Midnight Hour (BBC 2) 1998, As the Crow Flies (BBC 2) 1999 (book on same subject 1999), All the Rage (one-woman show, Edinburgh Festival) 2003 and (tour) 2004, So You Think You Can Teach (five) 2004, Street-Porter's Women (Channel 4) 2005, Michael and Me (Sky One) 2005, Janet Saves the Monarchy (Sky One) 2005, The F Word with Gordon Ramsay 2006; winner BAFTA award for originality 1988, Prix Italia for opera The Vampyr 1993; pres: Ramblers' Assoc 1994–96, Globetrotters; assoc FRIBA, FRTS 1994; *Publications* Baggage (autobiography, 2004), Fall Out (memoir, 2006); *Recreations* walking, modern art; *Style*— Ms Janet Street-Porter; ✉ c/o Emma Hardy, Princess Television, Princess Studios, Whiteleys, 151 Queensway, London W2 4SB (tel 020 7985 1917)

STREETER, David Thomas; MBE (2007); s of Reginald David Streeter (d 1976), of East Grinstead, W Sussex, and Dorothy Alice, *née* Fairhurst (d 1994); *b* 20 May 1937; *Educ* Cranbrook Sch, QMC London (BSc); *m* 1, 9 Sept 1967 (m dis 1979), Althea Elizabeth, da of Andrew Haig, of Waldringfield, Suffolk; 1 s (James b 1970); m 2, 5 Jan 1980, Penelope Sheila Dale, da of Gordon Kippax, of Netherfield, E Sussex; 2 da (Katharine b 1981, Olivia b 1987); *Career* Univ of Sussex: lectr in ecology 1965–76, reader in ecology 1976–, dean Sch of Biological Scis 1984–88, pro-vice-chllr 1989–97; lectr and broadcaster; memb: Gen Advsy Cncl BBC 1975–80, Cncl RSNC 1963–83, Advsy Ctee for England Nature Conservancy Cncl 1973–83, Countryside Cmmn 1978–84, SE Regnl Ctee Nat Tst 1989–2001, Nat Park Review Panel 1990–91, Sussex Downs Conservation Bd 1992–2006, Cncl Botanical Soc Br Isles 1994–99, Governing Body Hurstpierpoint Coll 1994–2005, Conservation Panel Nat Tst 1999–, Historic Buildings and Land Panel/Heritage Lottery Fund 1999–2005, Environmental Advsy Panel National Grid plc 2000–03; pres Sussex Wildlife Tst 2004–; FIBiol 1986, FLS 1996; *Books* Discovering Hedgerows (with R Richardson, 1982), The Wild Flowers of The British Isles (with I Garrard, 1983), The Natural History of the Oak Tree (with R Lewington, 1993); *Recreations* natural history, visiting other people's gardens; *Style*— David Streeter, Esq, MBE; ✉ The Holt, Sheepsetting Lane, Heathfield, East Sussex TN21 0UY (tel 01435 862849), The University of Sussex, John Maynard Smith Building, Falmer, Brighton BN1 9QG (tel 01273 877306, fax 01273 678433, e-mail d.t.streeter@sussex.ac.uk)

STREETER, Gary; MP; *Career* MP (Cons): Plymouth Sutton 1992–97, Devon SW 1997–; asst Govt whip 1995–96, Parly sec Lord Chancellor's Department 1996–97; shadow min for Europe 1997–98, shadow sec of state for int devpt 1998–2001, a vice-chm Cons Pty 2001–02, shadow foreign min 2003–04, chm Cons Pty Int Office 2005–; *Style*— Gary Streeter, Esq, MP; ✉ House of Commons, London SW1A 0AA (tel 020 7219 3000)

STREETER, Penny; OBE (2005); da of Peter Stiff, of S Africa, and Marion Hewson, *née* Hammonds; *b* 1 August 1967, Zimbabwe; *Educ* Alberton HS S Africa; *Family* 1 s (Adam b 18 Dec 1986), 2 da (Giselle b 22 Feb 1992, Bonnie b 27 Feb 1994); partner Nick Rea; 1 da (Matilda b 13 March 2001); *Career* owner, fndr and md Ambition 24hours 1996–, owner Nursing Services of S Africa 2006–, fndr QA Calling 2006–; placed first in Virgin Atlantic Fast Track 100 Companies 2002, CBI Entrepreneur of the Year 2003; *Style*— Ms Penny Streeter; ✉ Ambition 24hours, Ambition House, 92–96 Lind Road, Sutton, Surrey SM1 4PL (tel 020 7112 4549, fax 020 8288 8993, e-mail penny.streeter@ambition24hours.co.uk)

STREETS, Paul Richard; OBE (2003); *b* 25 July 1959; *Educ* UCL (BSc), Univ of Reading (MSc), Loughborough Univ (DipCS), Univ of Warwick (MBA); *m* 27 Aug 1993, Alison; 2 c; *Career* field dir Africa Sight Savers 1988–92, head of business and devpt Quantum Care 1993–95, dep dir Amnesty Int UK 1996–98, chief exec Diabetes UK 1998–2003, chief exec Health Devpt Agency 2003–05; chm NHS Modernisation Bd 2000–03; memb ACEVO; *Recreations* my children; *Style*— Paul Streets, OBE

STRETTON, Prof Graham Roy; *b* 22 October 1949; *Educ* Leicester Coll of Art, Trent Poly (Dip ID); *m* Susan Marie, chartered designer; *Career* asst designer Carter Deign Group Ltd 1971–72, designer Howard Sant Partnership 1972–73, designer Lennon and Partners 1973–77, head of interior design section Carter Design Group Ltd 1977–78, co-fndr (with wife) Design & Co 1978, dir Design & Co Consultants Ltd 1987–93, design mangr under contract Interior Consultancy Services Ltd 1989–94; memb Advsy Bd for Interior Design Trent Poly, special project visiting lectr De Montfort Univ; Br Inst of Interior Design (merged with CSD 1988): memb Gen Cncl 1981–86, chm Midland dist 1983–84, chm Publications Ctee until 1986, jr vice-pres 1987, liaison offr with SIAD, Bronze Medal 1988; prof Br Acad of Fencing, sr coach Br Fencing Assoc; FCSD 1980, FBID 1982, FRSA 1987; *Recreations* fencing coach (foil, épée and sabre dips); *Style*— Prof Graham Stretton; ✉ Design & Co, 64 The Ridgeway, Market Harborough, Leicestershire LE16 7HQ (tel 01858 462507, fax 01858 462690, e-mail design.co@btinternet.com)

STRETTON, James; *b* 16 December 1943; *Educ* Laxton GS, Oundle, Worcester Coll Oxford (BA); *m* 20 July 1968, Isobel Christine; *née* Robertson; 2 da (Lynne b 1970, Gillian b 1973); *Career* Standard Life Assurance Co: asst pensions mangr 1974–77, assst investment mangr 1977–84, gen mangr (ops) 1984–88, dep md 1988–94, chief exec UK ops 1994–2002; chm The Wise Gp 2002–; non-exec dir Bank of England 1998–2003, chm Bank of England Pension Fund Trustees Ltd 2001–05; memb: Franchise Bd Lloyd's of London 2003–, Disciplinary Bd of the Actuarial Profession 2004–06; pres Youth Link Scotland 1994–2000, dir Scottish Community Educn Cncl 1996–99, memb Bd Edinburgh Int Festival 1997– (dep chm 2000–07), memb Scottish Business Foum 1998–99; Univ of Edinburgh: memb Ct 1996–2002, rector's assessor 2003–06; tstee Lamp of Lothian Collegiate Tst 2003; FFA 1970; *Style*— James Stretton, Esq

STRETTON, His Hon Peter John; s of William Frank Stretton (d 1978), and Ella Mary Stretton (d 1987); *b* 14 June 1938; *Educ* Bedford Modern Sch; *m* 6 Sept 1973, Annie Stretton; 3 s (Thomas Michael b 15 March 1977, James Peter b 25 Sept 1981, Philip John b 6 Feb 1987), 1 da (Catherine Anne b 8 March 1979); *Career* called to the Bar 1963, recorder 1982–86, circuit judge (Midland & Oxford Circuit) 1986–2003 (dep circuit judge 2003–); *Recreations* squash, golf, running, gardening, family; *Style*— His Hon Peter Stretton

STREVENS, Peter Alan Dawson; s of Stanley Dawson Strevens (d 1966), and Dorothy Victoria, *née* Compson (d 1987); *b* 18 April 1938; *Educ* Eltham Coll London; *m* April 1969, Janet Hyde, da of Lees Hyde Marland (d 1974); 2 s (Nigel Jeremy b 1971, Timothy Maxwell b 1974); *Career* sr asst purser P&O Orient Lines 1955–63, franchise mangr Hertz Int Ltd NY 1963–67; md: United Serv Tport Co Ltd (Hertz Truck Rental) 1969–72 (operations mangr 1967–69), Chatfields-Martin Walter Ltd 1972–91; chm Ford and Slater Ltd 1991–; *Recreations* gardening; *Clubs* RAC; *Style*— Peter Strevens, Esq; ✉ Ford and Slater Ltd, Hazel Drive, Narborough Road South, Leicester LE3 2JG (tel 0116 263 2900, fax 0116 263 0042)

STRICKLAND, Benjamin Vincent Michael (Ben); s of Maj-Gen Eugene Vincent Michael Strickland, CMG, DSO, OBE, CStJ, MM, Star of Jordan (d 1982), and Barbara Lamb, da of Maj Benjamin Lamb, RFA, and gda of Sir J C Lamb; descended from Gen Sir John O'Sullivan, Jacobite cdr at Battle of Culloden; *b* 20 September 1939; *Educ* Mayfield Coll, UC Oxford (MA), Harvard Business Sch (Dip AMP); *m* 1965, Tessa Mary Edwina Grant, da of Rear-Adm John Grant, CB, DSO (d 1996), and gda of Maj-Gen Sir Philip Grant, KCB, CMG; 1 s (Benjamin b 1968), 1 da (Columbine b 1971); *Career* Lt 17/21 Lancers BAOR 1959–60, Lt Inns of Ct and City Yeomanry TA 1964–67; Price Waterhouse & Co 1963–68, dir J Henry Schroder Wagg & Co 1974–91, chief exec Schroders Australia 1978–82, dir and gp md Schroders plc 1983–91; chm Insurance Gp (formerly Iron Trades) 1996–; review of mission and finances Westminster Cathedral 1991, chm Planning and Finance Ctee Westminster Cathedral 1991–96; memb Steering Gp for Vision for London 1991–97; advsr on strategy to leading City law firm 1992–95, advsr on strategic issues to chief execs in service and financial businesses 1994–, mentor to chief execs 2005–; memb Voluntary Reading Help 2004–; FCA, FRSA; *Publications* Bow Group Book on Resources of the Sea (with Lawrence Reed, 1965), chapter on globalisation in Financial Services Handbook (1986); *Recreations* travel, history, films, theatre; *Clubs* Boodle's, Hurlingham; *Style*— Ben Strickland, Esq; ✉ 23 Juer Street, London SW11 4RE (tel 020 7585 2970, fax 020 7924 5269)

STRICKLAND-CONSTABLE, Sir Frederic; 12 Bt (E 1641), of Boynton, Yorkshire; s of Sir Robert Frederick Strickland-Constable, 11 Bt (d 1994), and his 2 w Lettice, *née* Strickland (d 1999); *b* 21 October 1944; *Educ* Westminster, CCC Cambridge (BA), London Business Sch (MSc); *m* 1981, Pauline Margaret, *née* Harding; 1 da (Rose b 1983), 1 s (Charles b 1985); *Heir* s, Charles Strickland-Constable; *Style*— Sir Frederic Strickland-Constable, Bt; ✉ Estate Office, Old Maltongate, Malton YO17 7EG

STRIESSNIG, Herbert; s of Karl Striessnig (d 1938), of Waiern-Feldkirchen, Carinthia, Austria, and Margaret, *née* Steiner (d 1976); *b* 29 August 1929; *Educ* Hotel Mgmnt Sch Bad Gleichenberg Styria Austria; *m* 19 March 1956, Davida Eileen, da of David Hunter Williamson; 1 s (Karl b 22 Aug 1957), 1 da (Suzanne b 18 June 1960); *Career* varied hotel trg/experience Switzerland and Mayfair Hotel London 1949–59, reservations mangr Westbury Hotel London 1959–61, asst gen mangr The Carlton Tower Hotel London 1961–63, co-ordinator devpt of Esso (then Standard Oil of New Jersey) motor hotel chain 1963–64; Metropolitan Hotels London: joined as gen mangr Rembrandt Hotel 1964–66, gen mangr St Ermin's Hotel 1967–68, gen mangr Piccadilly Hotel 1968, gen mangr Europa Hotel 1969–72, gen mangr Mayfair Hotel 1972–83; resident mangr The Churchill Hotel 1984–88, dir and gen mangr The Savoy Hotel 1989–95, ret; Master Innholder; memb: West One Hotel Mangrs' Assoc, Confrèrie de la Chaîne des Rotisseurs, Conseil

Culinaire Français; FHCIMA; *Recreations* swimming, skiing, jogging, watching soccer; *Clubs* Skal; *Style*— Herbert Striessnig, Esq; ✉ The Savoy Hotel, The Strand, London WC2R 0EU (tel 020 7836 4343, fax 020 7240 6040)

STRINGER, Prof Christopher Brian; s of late George Albert Stringer, and late Evelyn Beatrice, *née* Brien, of Horsham; *b* 31 December 1947; *Educ* East Ham GS for Boys, UCL (BSc), Univ of Bristol (PhD, DSc); *m* 2 April 1977 (m dis 2004), Rosemary Susan Margaret, da of late Leonard Peter Frank Lee; 1 da (Katherine Ann b 25 July 1979), 2 s (Paul Nicholas David b 21 Oct 1981, Thomas Peter b 9 April 1986); *Career* temp secdy sch teacher London Borough of Newham 1966; The Natural History Museum (formerly Br Museum (Natural History)): temp scientific offr 1969–70, sr res fell 1973–76, sr scientific offr 1976–86, princ scientific offr (Grade 7) 1986–, head Human Origins Gp 1990–, individual merit promotion (Grade 6) 1993–; visiting lectr Dept of Anthropology Harvard Univ 1979, visiting prof Royal Holloway Coll London 1995–; Br rep Int Assoc for Human Palaeontology 1986–; distinguished lectr Amer Anthropological Assoc 2000; memb: The Primate Soc 1975–, The Quaternary Research Assoc 1975–, American Assoc of Physical Anthropologists 2005–, Palaeoanthropology Soc, AAAS 2005–; Lyell lectureship Br Assoc for the Advancement of Science 1988, Radcliffe lectr Green Coll Oxford 1996, Osman Hill medal 1998, Henry Stopes medal 2000, Mulvaney lectr ANU 2001, Dalrymple lectr Univ of Glasgow 2001, Rivers meml medal RAI; Hon Dr of Laws Univ of Bristol 2000; FRS 2004; *Books* Our Fossil Relatives (with A Gray, 1983), Human Evolution - An Illustrated Guide (with P Andrews, 1989), In Search of the Neanderthals (with C Gamble, 1993), African Exodus (with R McKie, 1996), The Complete World of Human Evolution (with P Andrews, 2005), Homo Britannicus (2006); *Recreations* listening to music, soccer, astronomy, current affairs, travel; *Style*— Prof Christopher Stringer; ✉ Human Origins Programme, Department of Palaeontology, The Natural History Museum, London SW7 5BD (tel 020 7942 5539, fax 020 7942 5546, e-mail c.stringer@nhm.ac.uk)

STRINGER, Graham; MP; *Career* MP (Lab) Manchester Blackley 1997–; a Lord Cmmr to HM Treasy (Govt whip) 2001–02; *Style*— Graham Stringer, Esq, MP; ✉ House of Commons, London SW1A 0AA (tel 020 7219 3000)

STRINGER, Sir Howard; kt (2000); s of Harry Stringer, MBE, and Marjorie Mary, *née* Pook; *b* 19 February 1942, Cardiff (became a US citizen 1985); *Educ* Oundle, Univ of Oxford (MA); *m* 29 July 1978, Dr Jennifer A K Patterson; 1 s (David Ridley), 1 da (Harriet Kinmond); *Career* served US Army Vietnam 1965–67 (US Army Commendation Medal); journalist, prodr and exec CBS Inc 1965–95 (pres 1988–95, numerous awards for progs incl 9 individual Emmys), chm and ceo TELE-TV 1995–97; Sony Corporation: joined 1997, chm Sony Canada 1997–, chm Sony Electronics Ltd 1998–, chm and ceo Sony Corporation of America 1998–, memb Bd 1999–, gp vice-chm 2003–05, corporate head Sony Entertainment Business Gp 2003–, chm and gp ceo 2005–, rep corp exec offr, memb Bd Sony BMG Music, memb Bd Sony Ericsson; chm of tstees American Film Inst 1999–; memb Bd: NY Presbyterian Hosp, American Theater Wing, American Friends of the British Museum, Carnegie Hall, Teach for America, Center for Communication; memb Bd of Tstees Paley Center for Media (formerly the Museum of Television and Radio), memb Corporate Leadership Ctee Lincoln Center for the Performing Arts; hon fell: Merton Coll Oxford 2000, Welsh Coll of Music and Drama 2001; hon dr: London Inst 2003, Univ of Glamorgan 2005; honored Alliance for Lupus Res; *Awards*; Fndn Award Int Radio and TV Soc 1994, memb Broadcasting and Cable Hall of Fame 1996, First Amendment Leadership Award Radio and TV News Directors Fndn 1996, Steven J Ross Humanitarian Award UJA Fedn of NY 1999, memb Welsh Hall of Fame RTS 1999, Communication Award Centre for Communication 2000, Teach for America Annual Award 2001, Phoenix House Award 2002, Int Emmy Fndrs Award 2002, Distinguished Leadership Award NY Hall of Science 2003, Medal of Honor St George's Soc 2004; other honours from: Museum of the Moving Image 1994, Literacy Ptnrs 2002, Nat Multiple Sclerosis Soc 2002, Big Brothers and Big Sisters of NY City 2005, NY Landmarks Conservancy 2005, named one of the World's 100 Most Infulential People Time Magazine 2005, Lincoln Center for the Performing Arts 2006, Visionary Award for Innovative Leadership in Media & Entertainment Paley Center for Media 2007; *Style*— Sir Howard Stringer; ✉ Sony Corporation of America, 550 Madison Avenue, New York, NY 10022, USA (tel 00 1 212 833 6921, fax 00 1 212 833 6932, e-mail stringer_office@sonyusa.com)

STRINGER, Prof Joan K; CBE (2001); da of Frank Bourne, and Doris, *née* Ayres; *b* 12 May 1948, Stoke-on-Trent; *Educ* Univ of Keele (BA, PhD); *Partner* Roel Mali; *Career* Robert Gordon Univ: lectr then sr lectr in public admin 1980–88, head Sch of Public Admin and Law 1988–91, asst princ 1991–96; princ and vice-patron Queen Margaret UC 1996–2002, princ and vice-chllr Napier Univ 2003–; chair Education UK Scotland 2006–, convenor Int Ctee and memb Exec Univs Scotland; memb: Bd of Mgmnt Aberdeen Coll of FE 1992–96, Scottish Ctee Nat Ctee of Inquiry into HE (Dearing Ctee) 1996–97, Human Fertilisation and Embryology Authy 1996–99, Cncl World Assoc Cooperative Educn 1998–2002, Scottish Cncl for Postgrad Medical and Dental Educn 1999–2002, Bd HE Careers Servs Unit 2000–05, Working Gp on the Modernisation of the SHO Dept of Health 2000–02, Advsy Gp Scottish Nursing and Midwifery Educn Cncl (SNMEC) 2000–01, Scottish Health Min's Learning Together Strategy Implementation Gp 2000–01, Equality Challenge Steering Gp Univs UK 2001–03, Bd Quality Assurance Agency for HE 2002–06, Bd HE Statistics Agency 2003–, Bd Leadership Fndn for HE 2005–, Royal Soc Working Gp on HE, Shadow Bd Sector Skills Cncl for Lifelong Learning; former memb Shadow Ministerial Jt Supervisory Gp Careers Scotland; auditor HEQC 1992–97; cmmr for Scotland Equal Opportunities Cmmn 1995–2001, chair NI Equality Cmmn Working Gp 1998–99, chair Scottish Exec's Strategic Expert Gp on Women 2003–04; non-exec dir Grampian Health Bd 1994–96; memb: Govt's Consultative Steering Gp on the Scottish Parl 1998, Exec Ctee Scottish Cncl Devpt and Industry 1998–, Scottish Ctee Br Cncl 2000–, Scottish Selection Ctee Queen's Golden Jubilee Award 2001–, Bd Judicial Appts Bd for Scotland 2002–, Bd Scottish Leadership Fndn, China Forward Planning Gp Scottish Exec 2005–, Br C of C Hong Kong; convener: Product Standards Ctee Scottish Salmon 2001–03, Scottish Cncl for Voluntary Orgns 2002–; memb: Cncl Edinburgh Int Festival Soc 1999–, Devpt Advsy Bd Scottish Opera and Scottish Ballet 2000–02; tstee David Hume Inst, ex-officio tstee Carnegie Tst for the Univs of Scotland; fell 48 Gp Club 2006–; Hon DLitt Univ of Keele 2001; MInstD, CCMI, FRSE, FRSA; hon citizen Shandong China 2007; *Style*— Prof Joan Stringer, CBE; ✉ Napier University, Craighouse Campus, Craighouse Road, Edinburgh EH10 5LG (tel 0131 455 6400, fax 0131 455 6444, e-mail j.stringer@napier.ac.uk)

STRONACH, Prof David Brian; OBE (1975); s of Ian David Stronach (d 1955), of Newstead Abbey, Notts, and Marjorie Jessie Duncan, *née* Minto; *b* 10 June 1931; *Educ* Gordonstoun, St John's Coll Cambridge (MA); *m* 30 June 1966, Ruth Vaadia; 2 da (Keren b 1967, Tami b 1972); *Career* Nat Serv Lt 1 Bn Duke of Wellington's Regt 1950–51; Br Acad archaeological attaché in Iran 1960–61, dir Br Inst of Persian Studies 1961–80, prof of Near Eastern archaeology Univ of Calif Berkeley 1981–2004 (emeritus prof 2004–), curator of Near Eastern archaeology Hearst Museum of Anthropology Univ of Calif Berkeley 1983–2004; fell: Br Sch of Archaeology in Iraq 1957–59, Br Inst of Archaeology at Ankara 1958–59; lectureships incl: Hagop Kevorkian visiting lectr in Iranian art and archaeology Univ of Pennsylvania 1967, Rhind lectr Univ of Edinburgh 1973, Charles Eliot Norton lectr American Inst of Archaeology 1980, visiting prof of archaeology and Iranian studies Univ of Arizona 1980–81, Columbia lectr in Iranian studies Columbia Univ 1986, Charles K Wilkinson lectr Metropolitan Museum of Art NY 1990, Victor M Leventritt lectr in art history Harvard Univ 1991, visiting prof Collège de France 1999; dir of excavations at: Ras al 'Amiya Iraq 1960, Yarim Tepe Iran 1960–62, Pasargadae Iran 1961–63, Tepe Nush-i Jan Iran 1967–78, Shahr-i Qumis/Hecatompylos Iran 1967–78, Nineveh Iraq 1987–90; advsy ed: Iran 1975–, The Jl of Mithraic Studies 1976–79, Iranica Antiqua 1985–, Bulletin of the Asia Institute 1987–, American Journal of Archaeology 1989–96; Ghirshman Prize of Acad des Inscriptions et Belles Lettres Paris 1979, Sir Percy Sykes Medal Royal Soc for Asian Affrs 1980, Gold Medal of the Archaeological Inst of America for Distinguished Archaeological Achievement 2004, Northern California Phi Beta Kappa Excellence in Teaching Award 2006; corr memb German Archaeological Inst 1966–73; first hon vice-pres Br Inst of Persian Studies 1981–; assoc memb Royal Belgian Acad 1988; fell: German Archaeological Inst 1973, Explorers Club NY 1980; FSA 1963; *Books* Pasargadae A Report On The Excavations Conducted By The British Institute of Persian Studies from 1961 to 1963 (1978), Festschrift, Neo-Assyrian, Median, Achaemenian and Other Studies in Honour of D S (1998, 1999), Tepe Nush-i Jan: The Major Buildings of the Median Settlement (with Michael Roaf, 2007); *Recreations* tribal carpets; *Clubs* Hawks' (Cambridge), Explorers (NY); *Style*— Prof David Stronach, OBE, FSA; ✉ Department of Near Eastern Studies, University of California, Berkeley, CA 94720, USA (tel 00 1 510 642 3757, fax 00 1 510 643 8430, e-mail stronach@berkeley.edu)

STRONG, Liam; *Career* with Procter & Gamble 1967–71, various positions with Reckitt & Colman plc 1971–88, dir of mktg and ops British Airways plc 1988–91, ceo Sears plc until 1992–97, ceo MCI Worldcom International 1997–2001, pres and ceo Teleglobe 2003–; govr Ashridge Coll 1995–; *Style*— Liam Strong, Esq

STRONG, Michael John; s of Frank James Strong (d 1987), and Ivy Rose, *née* Fruin (d 1964); *b* 27 December 1947; *Educ* Rutlish Sch Merton, Coll of Estate Mgmnt; *m* 25 April 1970, Anne Mary, da of Rev William Hurst Nightingale (d 1996); 1 s (Jonathan Alexander b 1977); *Career* chartered surveyor; early career with Prudential Assurance Co and Healey & Baker; C B Richard Ellis: joined 1972, ptnr 1977, gp dir 1997, chm Europe 2001, pres EMEA 2005; Freeman: City of London 1981, Worshipful Co of Chartered Surveyors 2002; memb: Royal Acad, RHS; FRICS; *Recreations* golf, tennis, music, travel, gardens; *Style*— Michael Strong, Esq; ✉ The Coolins, Manor House Lane, Little Bookham, Surrey (tel 01372 452196); C B Richard Ellis, Kingsley House, 1A Wimpole Street, London W1G 0RE (tel 020 7182 2000, fax 020 7182 2001, e-mail mike.strong@cbre.com)

STRONG, Richard James; s of John Paterson Strong, OBE, of Tilbrook, Huntingdon, and Margaret St Claire, *née* Ford (d 1982); *b* 5 July 1936; *Educ* Sherborne, Nat Leather Sellers Coll; *m* 1 May 1963, Camilla Lucretia, da of Maj William Walter Dowding (d 1981); 3 da (Melissa b 30 Dec 1965, Amanda b 13 Nov 1968, Samantha b 28 March 1972), 1 s (James b 30 May 1977); *Career* Nat Serv 10 Royal Hussars (PWO); Tanner Strong & Fisher Ltd 1960, md Strong & Fisher (Holdings) plc 1972–91, chm Strong International Ltd 1992–2003; Liveryman Worshipful Co of Grocers; *Recreations* fox hunting, farming, sailing, tennis; *Clubs* Royal Thames Yacht; *Style*— Richard Strong, Esq; ✉ Bletsoe Castle, Bletsoe, Bedfordshire MK44 1QE

STRONG, Sir Roy Colin; kt (1981); yst s of George Edward Clement Strong (d 1984), of Winchmore Hill, London, and Mabel Ada, *née* Smart; *b* 23 August 1935; *Educ* Edmonton Co GS, Queen Mary Coll London, Warburg Inst (PhD); *m* Sept 1971, Julia Trevelyan Oman, CBE (d 2003); *Career* writer, historian, critic (radio, TV and lectures in England and America); Nat Portrait Gallery: asst keeper 1959, dir, keeper and sec 1967–73; dir and sec V&A 1974–87; Ferens prof of fine art Univ of Hull 1972, Walls Lectures Pierpont Morgan Library 1974, Andrew Carnduff Ritchie Lectures Yale Univ 1999; vice-chm South Bank Bd 1986–90; memb: Arts Cncl of GB 1983–87 (chm Arts Panel 1983–87), Fine Arts Advsy Ctee Br Cncl 1974–87, Craft Advsy Cncl, RCA Cncl 1979–87, Br Film Inst Archive Advsy Ctee, Westminster Abbey Architectural Panel 1975–89, Historic Bldgs Cncl Historic Houses Ctee; former tstee: Arundel Castle, Chevening; Shakespeare Prize FVS Fndn Hamburg 1980; pres Garden History Soc 2004–06; High Bailiff and Searcher of the Sanctuary of Westminster Abbey 2000; Liveryman Worshipful Company of Goldsmiths; fell Queen Mary Coll London 1975, sr fell RCA 1983; Hon DLitt: Univ of Leeds 1983, Keele Univ 1984; Hon MA Univ of Worcester 2004; FSA, FRSL 1999; *Television* Royal Gardens (BBC) 1992; *Publications* Portraits of Queen Elizabeth I (1963), Leicester's Triumph (with J A van Dorsten, 1964), Holbein and Henry VIII (1967), Tudor and Jacobean Portraits (1969), The English Icon: Elizabethan and Jacobean Portraiture (1969), Elizabeth R (with Julia Trevelyan Oman, 1971), Van Dyck - Charles I on Horseback (1972), Mary Queen of Scots (with Julia Trevelyan Oman, 1972), Inigo Jones - The Theatre of the Stuart Court (with Stephen Orgel, 1973), Splendour at Court - Renaissance Spectacle and Illusion (1973), An Early Victorian Album, The Hill/Adamson Collection (with Colin Ford, *qv*, 1974), Nicholas Hilliard (1975), The Cult of Elizabeth: Elizabethan Portraiture and Pageantry (1977), And When Did You Last See Your Father? The Victorian Painter and the British Past (1978), The Renaissance Garden in England (1979), Britannia Triumphans: Inigo Jones, Rubens and Whitehall Palace (1980), Designing for the Dancer (contrib, 1981), The English Miniature (contrib, 1981), The New Pelican Guide to English Literature (contrib, 1982), The English Year (with Julia Trevelyan Oman, 1982), The English Renaissance Miniature (1983), Artists of the Tudor Court (catalogue 1983), Art and Power: Renaissance Festivals 1450–1650 (1984), Glyndebourne - A Celebration (contrib, 1984), Strong Points (1985), Henry Prince of Wales (1986), For Veronica Wedgewood These (contrib, 1986), Creating Small Gardens (1986), Gloriana (1987), A Small Garden Designer's Handbook (1987), Cecil Beaton The Royal Portraits (1988), Creating Small Formal Gardens (1989), British Theatre Arts Design (contrib, 1989), Lost Treasures of Britain (1990), England and the Continental Renaissance (contrib, 1990), Sir Philip Sidney's Achievements (contrib, 1990), A Celebration of Gardens (1991), The Garden Trellis (1991), The British Portrait (contrib, 1991), Versace Il Teatro (1991), Small Period Gardens (1992), Royal Gardens (1992), The Art of the Emblem (contrib, 1993), William Larkin (1994), A Country Life (1994), Successful Small Gardens (1994), The Tudor and Stuart Monarchy (3 vols, 1995–97), The Story of Britain (1996), Country Life 1897–1997 - The English Vision (1996), The Roy Strong Diaries 1967–1987 (1997), Happiness (1997), The Spirit of Britain: A Narrative History of the Arts (1999, reissued as The Arts in Britain. A History 2003), Garden Party (2000), The Artist and the Garden (2000), Ornament in the Small Garden (2001), Feast: A History of Grand Eating (2002), The Laskett: The Story of a Garden (2003), Coronation: A History of Kingship and the British Monarchy (2005), A Little History of the English Country Church (2007); *Recreations* gardening, weight training; *Clubs* Garrick, Arts; *Style*— Sir Roy Strong, FSA, FRSL; ✉ The Laskett, Much Birch, Herefordshire HR2 8HZ

STRONGE, Sir James Anselan Maxwell; 10 Bt (UK 1803), of Tynan, Co Armagh; s of late Maxwell Du Pre James Stronge, and 2 cousin of Capt Sir James Matthew Stronge, 9 Bt (assas 1981); *b* 17 July 1946; *Educ* privately; *Style*— Sir James Stronge, Bt

STROUD, Dr Michael (Mike); OBE (1993); s of Victor Stroud, of Ridley, Kent, and Vivienne Richardson, *née* Zelegman; *Educ* Trinity Sch Croydon, UCL (BSc), St George's Hosp Med Sch (MB BS), Univ of London (MD); *m* 1987, Thea, *née* de Moel; 1 s (Callan b 2 Dec 1987), 1 da (Tarn b 17 April 1990); *Career* doctor and explorer; various NHS trg posts 1979–85, NHS registrar in med 1987–89, research in human performance 1989–95 (latterly chief scientist in physiology Defence Research Agency Centre for Human Scis), research fell in nutrition and sr registrar in gastroenterology Southampton Univ Hosps NHS Tst 1995–98, sr lectr in med, gastroenterology and nutrition Southampton Univ Hosps NHS Tst 1998–; Footsteps of Scott Antarctic expdn 1985–86, 5 North Pole expdns 1986–90, crossed Antarctic with Sir Ranulph Fiennes 1992–93 (first unsupported crossing in history), ldr UK team Marathon of the Sands Sahara Desert 1994, Eco-Challenge adventure race 1995 and 1996, first unsupported, non-stop desert crossing of Qatar 2002, seven full marathons on seven continents in seven days with Sir Ranulph Fiennes 2003; various TV and radio appearances incl as endurance expert Are You Tough Enough for the SAS (BBC) and presenter The Challenge (BBC); Polar Medal 1995; memb Physiology Soc 1994; MRCP (UK) 1984, FRCP (London and Edinburgh) 1995; FRGS 1994; *Books* Shadows on The Wasteland (1993), Survival of The Fittest (1998); *Recreations* Polar travel, ultra distance running; *Style—* Dr Mike Stroud, OBE; ✉ c/o Cunningham Management Limited, 271 King Street, London W6 9LZ

STROWGER, Clive; s of Gaston Jack Strowger, CBE, and Kathleen, *née* Gilbert; *b* 4 July 1941; *Educ* Univ Coll Sch Hampstead; *m* 23 Jan 1965, Deirdre Majorie, da of Col Bertram Stuart Trevelyan Archer, GC, OBE; 3 s (Timothy b 26 Aug 1968, Andrew b 18 Dec 1969, Stephen b 29 Sept 1980), 1 da (Louise b 2 June 1975); *Career* various managerial positions Ford Motor Co 1966–71, sr fin mgmnt positions then fin dir BL Int British Leyland Corp 1971–77, Grand Metropolitan 1977–90 (md brewing, chief exec consumer servs, chm and chief exec foods, gp fin dir and chief exec retail and property), chief exec Mountleigh Group plc 1990–91, mgmnt conslt 1991–92, chief exec APV plc 1992–94; chm: London First Centre 1997, Walters Hexagon Ltd 1998, Starpoint Electrics 1998, Focus Central London TEC 1999; chm Advsy Bd Merchant International Gp 1998, memb Bd London First 1995– (treas); advsr and conslt to various companies; non-exec dir deltaDOT Ltd 2005–; Freeman Worshipful Co of Brewers; FCA 1965, ATII 1965, CIMgt 1990; *Recreations* choral singing, family, tennis, skiing; *Style—* Clive Strowger, Esq

STRUDLEY, Brig David; CBE (1991, OBE 1988, MBE 1986); s of Frank Walter Henry Strudley, and Peggy Doris Strudley; *Educ* Portsmouth Sch, RMA Sandhurst (Commandant's Commendation), Army Tech Staff Coll (MSc), Open Univ (MBA), Univ of Leeds (MA); *Career* cmmnd 9/12 Royal Lancers (Prince of Wales's) 1968; CO 2 (Co Armagh) Bn Ulster Defence Regt, directing staff RMCS 1988–89, Dir of Ops HQ NI 1989–91, sr mil advsr Defence Res Agency 1991–93, COS HQ NI 1993–96; Dep Col Royal Irish Regt, pres Royal Br Legion NI, chm Royal Irish Regt Museum Cncl; memb Inst of Counselling 1992, memb IOD 1996; FIMgt 1987 (MIMgt 1982); *Books* Military Technology Handbook (ed, 1988); *Recreations* walking, field sports, furniture restoration; *Clubs* Armagh, Belfast Reform, Naval and Military; *Style—* Brig David Strudley, CBE; ✉ Acorns Children's Hospice Trust, Drake's Court, Alcester Road, Wythall, West Midlands B47 6JR (tel 01564 825009, e-mail david.strudley@acorns.org.uk)

STRUDWICK, Maj-Gen Mark Jeremy; CBE (1990); s of late Ronald Strudwick, and late Mary, *née* Beresford; *b* 19 April 1945; *Educ* St Edmund's Sch Canterbury, RMAS; *m* 1970, Janet Elizabeth Coleridge, da of Lt Col J R Vivers; 1 s, 1 da; *Career* cmmnd The Royal Scots (The Royal Regiment) 1966 (Col 1995–2005), served in UK, BAOR, Cyprus, Canada, India, NI (despatches twice), cmd 1 Bn Royal Scots 1984–87, instr Staff Coll Camberley 1987–88, ACOS G1/G4 HQ NI 1988–90, Higher Command and Staff Course 1989, cmd 3 Inf Bde 1990–91, NDC New Delhi 1992, Dep Mil Sec MOD 1993–95, Dir of Inf 1996–97, ADC to HM The Queen 1996–97, Col Cmdt The Scottish Div 1997–2000, GOC Scotland and Govr Edinburgh Castle 1997–2000; memb Queen's Body Guard for Scotland (Royal Co of Archers) 1994– (Brig 2006); cmmr Queen Victoria Sch Dunblane 1997–2000, govr Royal Sch Bath 1993–2000, govr Gordonstoun 1999–; chief exec The Prince's Scottish Youth Business Tst 2000–, tstee Historic Scotland Fndn 2001–, chm Scottish Veterans Residences 2001–; Cdre Infantry Sailing Assoc 1997–2000; CCMI 2002; *Recreations* golf, shooting, sailing; *Clubs* Army and Navy, The Royal Scots (tstee 1995–); *Style—* Maj-Gen Mark Strudwick, CBE; ✉ Psybt, 15 Exchange Place, Glasgow G1 3AN (tel 0141 248 4999)

STRUTHERS, Prof Allan David; s of Dr David Struthers (d 1987), of Glasgow, and Margaret Thompson, *née* Adams (d 1989); *b* 14 August 1952; *Educ* Hutchesons' Boys' GS Glasgow, Univ of Glasgow (BSc, MB ChB, MD); *m* Julia Elizabeth Anne, da of Robert Diggens (d 1993); 1 da (Kate Lisa b 1980), 1 s (Gordon Allan Benjamin b 1982); *Career* jr then SHO Glasgow Teaching Hosps 1977–80, registrar then research fell Dept of Materia Medica Stobhill Hosp Glasgow 1980–82, sr med registrar Royal Postgraduate Med Sch and Hammersmith Hosp London 1982–85, sr lectr, reader then prof Dept of Clinical Pharmacology Ninewells Hosp and Med Sch Dundee 1985–, prof of cardiovascular med and therapeutics Univ of Dundee; SKB Prize for Research in Clinical Pharmacology (Br Pharmacological Soc) 1990; memb Assoc of Physicians of GB and I 1992; FRCP, FRCPE, FRCPG, FESC 1994; *Books* Atrial Natriuretic Factor (1990); *Recreations* swimming, cycling, travel; *Style—* Prof Allan Struthers

STUART, Alexander Charles; s of Alfred William Noble Stuart, of Sussex, and Eileen Lucy, *née* Winter; *b* 27 January 1955; *Educ* Bexley GS; *m* 1988, Charong Chow; 1 s (Hudson b 23 July 2004); 1 s by Ann Totterdell (Joe Buffalo b 15 Aug 1983 d 1989); *Career* writer; author of film criticism and various screenplays; exec prodr Insignificance (film, dir Nicolas Roeg) 1985; screenwriter: Agatha Christie's Ordeal By Innocence (film, dir Desmond Davis) 1985, The War Zone (film, dir Tim Roth) 1999; writer and presenter TV documentary The End of America (dir Laura Ashton) 1999; prof of film Univ of Miami 1994–97; exhbn Words & Images (Miami Art Museum) 1997; *Books* novels: Glory B (1983), The War Zone (1989, short-listed Whitbread award 1989), Tribes (1992); children's books: Joe, Jo-Jo and the Monkey Masks (1988), Henry and the Sea (with Joe Buffalo Stuart, 1989); non-fiction: Five and a Half Times Three: The Short Life and Death of Joe Buffalo Stuart (with Ann Totterdell, 1990), Life on Mars (1996), The War Zone (published screenplay, 1999); *Recreations* swimming, running, gardening, peace, our dog Stoli; *Clubs* Groucho; *Style—* Alexander Stuart, Esq; ✉ c/o Charles Walker, PFD, Drury House, 34–43 Russell Street, London WC2B 5HA (tel 020 7344 1000, fax 020 7352 7356, e-mail cwalker@pfd.co.uk, website www.alexanderstuart.com)

STUART, Gisela Gschaider; MP; *b* 26 November 1955; *Educ* Realschule Vilsbiburg, Manchester Poly, Univ of London (LLB); *m* (m dis); 2 s; *Career* MP (Lab) Birmingham Edgbaston 1997–; memb House of Commons Social Security Select Ctee 1997–98, PPS to Paul Boateng, MP, *qv*, as min of state at the Home Office 1998–99, Parly under-sec Dept of Health 1999–2001, memb Foreign Affairs Ctee 2001–; ed The House magazine; rep Convention on Future of Europe; tstee: Westminster Fndn, Br Assoc for Central and Eastern Europe; *Publications* The Making of Europe's Constitution (2003); *Style—* Ms Gisela Stuart, MP; ✉ House of Commons, London SW1A 0AA (tel 020 7219 3000)

STUART, Graham; MP; s of Peter Stuart (d 2005), and Joan Stuart; *b* 1962, Carlisle; *Educ* Glenalmond Coll, Selwyn Coll Cambridge; *m* Anne; 2 da (Sophie, Katie); *Career* chm Cambridge Univ Cons Assoc 1985; sole proprietor Go Enterprises 1984–, dir CSL Publishing 1987–; ldr Cons Gp Cambridge CC 2000; Parly candidate (Cons) Cambridge 2001, MP (Cons) Beverley and Holderness 2005–; project dir Cons Pty Yorks and Humberside 2007–; memb Cons Pty Bd 2006–; fndr Beverley and Holderness Pensioners' Action Gp, chm Community Hosps Acting Nationally Together, chm East Riding Health Action Gp 2007; *Style—* Graham Stuart, Esq, MP; ✉ House of Commons, London SW1A 0AA (e-mail graham@grahamstuart.com, website www.grahamstuart.com)

STUART, Sir (James) Keith; kt (1986); s of James Stuart, and Marjorie Stuart; *b* 4 March 1940; *Educ* King George V Sch Southport, Gonville & Caius Coll Cambridge (MA); *m* 1966, Kathleen Anne Pinder, *née* Woodman; 3 s, 1 da; *Career* dist mangr S Western Electricity Bd 1970–72; sec British Transport Docks Bd 1972–75, gen mangr 1976–77, md 1977–82, dep chm 1980–82, chm 1982–83; chm: Associated British Ports Holdings plc 1983–2002, Seeboard plc 1992–96; pres Inst of Freight Forwarders 1983–84, dir Int Assoc of Ports and Harbors 1983–2000 (vice-pres 1985–87); dir: Royal Ordnance Factories 1983–85, BAA plc 1986–92, City of London Investment Tst 1999–, RMC Gp plc 1999–2005, Mallett plc 2005–06; advsr Gas and Electricity Markets Authy 2007– (memb 2000–06); pres Br Quality Fndn 1997–2000; chm UK-South Africa Trade Assoc 1988–93, vice-chm Southern Africa Business Assoc 1995–2002; memb Cncl CIT 1979–88 (vice-pres 1982–83, pres 1985–86); dir Trinity Coll London 1992–; govr: Trinity Coll of Music 1991–2003 (tstee 2001–), Nat Youth Orch of GB 1997–2004; vice-chm Mgmnt Bd and chm Advsy Cncl London Mozart Players 2002–; Freeman City of London 1985, Liveryman Worshipful Co of Clockmakers 1987 (memb Ct of Assts 1998–); FCILT, CIMgt, FRSA, Hon FTCL 1998; *Recreations* music; *Clubs* Brooks's, Oxford and Cambridge (tstee 1989–94); *Style—* Sir Keith Stuart

STUART, (Charles) Murray; CBE; s of Charles Maitland Stuart (d 1984), and Grace Forrester, *née* Kerr (d 1990); *b* 28 July 1933; *Educ* Glasgow Acad, Univ of Glasgow (MA, LLB); *m* 10 April 1963, Netta Caroline, da of Robert Thomson (d 1981); 1 s (David Charles Thomson b 19 Oct 1970), 1 da (Caroline Alison b 29 Dec 1972); *Career* qualified chartered accountant 1961; chief accountant and co sec P & W McLellan Ltd 1961–62, internal auditor and analyst Ford Motor Company 1962–65, fin dir and sec Sheffield Twist Drill & Steel Co Ltd 1965–69, fin dir and asst md Unicorn Industries Ltd 1969–73, fin dir Hepworths Limited (now Next) 1973–74, dep md ICL plc 1977–81 (fin dir 1974–77); MB Group plc (formerly Metal Box): fin dir 1981–83, dir fin planning and admin 1983–86, gp md 1986–87, gp chief exec 1988–89, chm 1989–90; dir and chief fin offr Berisford International plc 1990–91; non-exec chm: Scottish Power plc 1992–2000 (dir 1990–92), Intermediate Capital Group Ltd 1993–2001, Hill Samuel Bank Scotland Ltd 1993–94; exec dir and a vice-chm Hill Samuel Bank Ltd 1992–93; non-exec dir: Hunter Saphir plc 1991–92, Clerical Medical & General Life Assurance Society 1993–96, The Royal Bank of Scotland Group plc 1996–2002, Willis Corroon Group plc 1996–97, CMG Gp plc 1998–2002, Old Mutual plc 1999–2003, National Westminster Bank plc 2000–02; dir St Andrew's Management Institute Ltd 1993–96; dep chm Audit Cmmn 1991–95 (memb 1986–95); memb W Surrey and NE Hants HA 1990–93, chm Hammersmith Hosps NHS Tst 1996–2000; memb: Meteorological Ctee 1994–98, PFI Panel for Scotland 1995–97, Euro Advsy Bd Credit Lyonnais 2000–05, Pres du Comité des Comptes et d'Audit of Supervisory Bd Veolia Environnement SA 2000–; Hon DUniv Paisley 1999, Hon DUniv Glasgow 2001; memb Law Soc Scotland 1957; FCT 1984, CIMgt 1986, FRSA 1988; *Recreations* ballet, theatre, golf; *Clubs* Caledonian; *Style—* Murray Stuart, Esq, CBE; ✉ Longacre, Guildford Road, Chobham, Woking, Surrey GU24 8EA

STUART, Nicholas Willoughby; CB (1990); s of Douglas Willoughby Stuart, of Long Melford, nr Sudbury, Suffolk, and Margaret Eileen, *née* Holms; *b* 2 October 1942; *Educ* Harrow, ChCh Oxford (MA); *m* 1, July 1963 (m dis 1974), Sarah, *née* Mustard; 1 s (Sebastian b 26 Dec 1963 d 1976), 1 da (Henrietta b 21 March 1965); m 2, 30 Dec 1974, Susan Jane Fletcher, *qv*; 1 da (Emily Fletcher b 12 Sept 1983), 1 s (Alexander Fletcher b 1 Feb 1989); *Career* asst princ DES 1964–68, private sec to Min of Arts 1968–69, princ DES 1969–73; private sec to: Head of Civil Serv 1973, PM 1973–76; asst sec DES 1976–79, memb Cabinet of Pres of Euro Cmmn 1979–81, under sec DES 1981–87, dep sec DES 1987–92, dir of resources and strategy Dept of Employment 1992–95, DG for Employment and Lifelong Learning DfEE 1995–2000, DG for Lifelong Learning DfEE 2000–01; chm Nat Inst for Adult Continuing Educn (NIACE) 2003–; memb: Bd Univ for Industry (UFI) 2001–, Cncl Inst of Educn Univ of London 2001–, Curriculum and Qualifications Authy 2002–, CAFCASS 2003–, Cncl GDST 2003–; tstee: Policy Studies Inst 2002–, Harrow Mission 2000–, Specialist Schs and Acads Tst; chair of govrs Edward Wilson Primary Sch 2002–, govr Harrow Sch 1996–; *Style—* Nicholas Stuart, Esq, CB; ✉ 181 Chevening Road, London NW6 6DT (e-mail nwsturt@hotmail.com)

STUART, Sir Phillip Luttrell; 9 Bt (E 1660), of Hartley Mauduit, Hants; s of late Luttrell Hamilton Stuart and nephew of 8 Bt (d 1959); Sir Phillip's name does not, at time of going to press, appear on the Official Roll of Baronets; *b* 7 September 1937; *m* 1, 1962 (m dis 1968), Marlene Rose, da of Otto Muth; 1 da; m 2, 1969, Beverley Claire Pieri; 1 s, 1 da; *Heir* s, Geoffrey Stuart; *Career* Flying Offr RCAF 1957–62; pres Agassiz Industries Ltd; *Style—* Sir Phillip Stuart, Bt; ✉ #50 - 10980 Westdowne Road, Ladysmith, British Columbia, Canada V9G 1X3

STUART-FORBES, Sir William Daniel; 13 Bt (NS 1626), of Pitsligo, and Monymusk, Aberdeenshire; s of William Kenneth Stuart-Forbes (d 1946, 3 s of 10 Bt), and Marjory, *née* Gilchrist (d 1996); suc uncle, Sir Charles Edward Stuart-Forbes, 12 Bt, 1985; *b* 21 August 1935; *m* 1, 1956, Jannette (d 1997), da of Hori Toki George MacDonald (d 1946), of Marlborough, NZ; 3 s (Kenneth Charles b 26 Dec 1956, Daniel Dawson b 1 April 1962, Reginald MacDonald b 3 Oct 1964), 2 da (Catherine Florence (Mrs William Paraha) b 1958, Eileen Jane (Mrs Neil Bertram Brown) b 1960); m 2, 3 March 2001, Betty Dawn Ward, *née* Gibson, wid of Clarence George Ward; *Heir* s, Kenneth Stuart-Forbes; *Style—* Sir William Stuart-Forbes, Bt; ✉ Riverviews, 169 Budge Street, Blenheim, New Zealand

STUART-MENTETH, Sir James Wallace; 6 Bt (UK 1838), of Closeburn, Dumfriesshire, and Mansfield, Ayrshire; s of Sir William Frederick Stuart-Menteth, 5 Bt (d 1952); *b* 13 November 1922; *Educ* Fettes, Univ of St Andrews, Trinity Coll Oxford (MA); *m* 23 April 1949, (Dorothy) Patricia, da of late Frank Greaves Warburton, of Thorrington, Stirling; 2 s (Charles Greaves b 1950, (William) Jeremy b 1953); *Heir* s, Charles Stuart-Menteth; *Career* served WWII Lt Scots Gds (wounded); sometime md Alkali and Paints Div ICI Ltd; memb: Br Limbless Ex-Service Men's Assoc, Royal British Legion (Scotland); *Style—* Sir James Stuart-Menteth, Bt; ✉ Nutwood, Auchencairn, Castle Douglas, Kirkcudbrightshire DG7 1QZ

STUART-MOORE, Hon Mr Justice; Hon Michael Stuart-Moore; s of Kenneth Basil Moore (d 1987), and Marjorie Elizabeth, *née* Hodges; *b* 7 July 1944; *Educ* Cranleigh Sch; *m* 8 Dec 1973, Katherine Ann, da of Kenneth William and Ruth Scott; 1 s (James b 1976), 1 da (Zoe-Olivia b 1978); *Career* called to the Bar Middle Temple 1966; recorder of the Crown Court 1985–, QC 1990, judge of the High Court Hong Kong 1993–97, judge of the Court of Appeal Hong Kong 1997–99, vice-pres of the Court of Appeal Hong Kong 1999–; *Recreations* photography, flute, tennis, travel; *Clubs* Hong Kong; *Style—* The Hon Mr Justice Stuart-Moore

STUART OF FINDHORN, 3 Viscount (UK 1959); Dominic Stuart; s (by 1 m) of 2 Viscount (d 1999); *b* 25 March 1948; *Educ* Eton, Thames Poly (Dip Estate Mgmnt), Ecole Philippe Gaulier (theatre); *m* 1979 (m dis 2002), Yvonne Lucienne, da of Edgar Després, of Ottawa; *Career* actor and writer; *Recreations* metaphysics, psychology, walking, theatre, reading, music; *Style—* The Rt Hon the Viscount Stuart of Findhorn

STUART-SMITH, Rt Hon Sir Murray; kt (1981), PC (1988); s of Edward Stuart-Smith, and Doris, *née* Laughland; *b* 18 November 1927; *Educ* Radley, CCC Cambridge; *m* 1953, Joan; 3 s, 3 da; *Career* called to the Bar Gray's Inn 1952 (bencher 1978, vice-treas 1997–98, treas 1998–99); QC 1970, recorder of the Crown Court 1972–81, judge of the High Court of Justice (Queen's Bench Div) 1981–87, presiding judge Western Circuit 1982–86, a Lord Justice of Appeal 1987–2000; judge Court of Appeal of Gibraltar 2001, judge Court of Appeal of Bermuda 2004; cmmr for Security Service 1989, cmmr for Intelligence Services 1994, chm Proscribed Organisations Appeal Cmmn 2001, chm Pathogens Access Appeal Cmmn 2002; memb Criminal Injuries Compensation Bd 1979–81; hon fell CCC Cambridge 1994; *Recreations* playing cello, shooting, building, playing bridge; *Style—* The Rt Hon Sir Murray Stuart-Smith; ✉ Royal Courts of Justice, Strand, London WC2A 2LL

STUART-SMITH, Stephen James Adrian; s of D M Stuart-Smith, of Leics; *b* 18 August 1954; *Educ* Denstone Coll, KCL (BA), Inst of Educn Univ of London (PGCE), Univ of Reading (MA); *Career* bookseller 1977–78, teacher 1978–85; head History Dept: Lord Wandsworth

Coll Long Sutton 1985–88, Ditcham Park Sch Petersfield 1988–89; md Enitharmon Press 1987–, md Enitharmon Editions Ltd 2001–; administrator Ben Nicholson, David Hockney and Aubrey Beardsley exhibitions for Japan 1992–98; literature assessor London Arts Bd 1994–96, memb Literature Advsy Gp London Arts Bd 1996–2000; memb Ctee Edward Thomas Fellowship 1986–94, memb London Philharmonic Choir 1999–; chair The Poetry Sch 1997–2003, memb Assoc Internationale des Critiques d'Art 1997–; FRSA 1990; *Publications* An Enitharmon Anthology (1990); contrib The Times, The Independent and literary jls; *Recreations* singing, book collecting; *Style*— Stephen Stuart-Smith, Esq; ✉ Enitharmon Press, 26B Caversham Road, London NW5 2DU (tel 020 7482 5697, fax 020 7284 1787, e-mail books@enitharmon.co.uk)

STUART TAYLOR, Sir Nicholas Richard; 4 Bt (UK 1917), of Kennington, Co London; s of Sir Richard Laurence Stuart Taylor, 3 Bt (d 1978), and Lady Stuart Taylor; Sir Frederick Taylor, 1 Bt was pres of RCP; *b* 14 January 1952; *Educ* Bradfield; *m* 1984 (m dis 1999), Malvena Elizabeth Sullivan; 2 da (Virginia Caterina b 1989, Olivia Malvena b 1991); *Heir* none; *Career* slr 1977; *Recreations* skiing and other sports; *Style*— Sir Nicholas Stuart Taylor, Bt; ✉ 30 Siskin Close, Bishops Waltham, Hampshire SO32 1RQ

STUBBS, Dawne Alison; da of William Thomas Telford, of Thrapston, Northamptonshire, and Janet Christine, *née* Smith; *b* 8 June 1967; *Educ* Prince William Sch Oundle, Tresham Coll Kettering, Huddersfield Poly (BSc, awards for design in knitwear); *m* 6 July 1996, Philip Michael Stubbs; 2 s (Elliott Edward b 1 March 1999, Henry William b 19 Sept 2002); *Career* asst designer Lister & Co plc colour yarn spinners 1987–88, designer Pierre Sangan Leicester and CI 1989–92, head of design John Smedley Ltd knitwear design 1992–2001, product/design mangr Sara Lee Courtaulds 2003–05, brand mangr John Smedley Ltd 2005–; winner Br Fashion Award for Classics Royal Albert Hall 1997; *Recreations* dressmaking, languages, knitting, swimming; *Style*— Mrs Philip Stubbs

STUBBS, Imogen Mary; da of Robin Desmond Scrivener Stubbs (d 1974), and Heather Mary, *née* McCracken (d 1986); *b* 20 February 1961; *Educ* St Paul's Girls', Westminster, Exeter Coll Oxford (scholar, BA), RADA (Silver medallist, John Barton Award in Stagefighting); *m* 1994, Sir Trevor Nunn, *qv*; 1 da (Ellie b 1991), 1 s (Jesse b 1996); *Career* actress; numerous contrib book reviews and interviews (incl: The Times, The Observer, The Guardian, Daily Mail, Daily Express); *Theatre* incl: Cabaret (Ipswich) 1985, The Boyfriend (Ipswich) 1985, Two Noble Kinsmen, The Rover and Richard II (all RSC) 1986–87 (Critics' Award for Most Promising Newcomer, nominated Olivier Award for Best Newcomer), Othello (RSC) 1989, Heartbreak House (Yvonne Arnaud Guildford and Haymarket) 1992, St Joan (Strand), Uncle Vanya (Chichester and Albery), A Street Car Named Desire (Haymarket) 1997, Blast From the Past (West Yorkshire Playhouse), Closer (Lyric) 1998, Betrayal (RNT) 1999, The Relapse (RNT) 2001, Three Sisters (Theatre Royal Bath and Southampton) 2002, Mum's the Word (Albert Theatre) 2003; *Television* incl: Deadline (BBC) 1987, The Rainbow (BBC) 1988 (Best Actress in a Series Chicago Film Festival, nominated Best Actress Royal Variety Television Awards), Relatively Speaking (BBC) 1989, Anna Lee (ITV), After The Dance (BBC), Heartbreak House, Mothertime (BBC), Othello (BBC), Blind Ambition (ITV), Big Kids; *Radio* incl: Private Lives, No Way Out, Il Cid, La Bête Humaine, When the Dead Awaken, As You Like It; *Film* incl: Nanou 1985, A Summer Story 1987 (Best Actress Evening Standard Film Awards), Erik The Viking 1988, Fellow Traveller 1989, True Colors 1990, Sandra C'est la Vie 1993, A Pin for the Butterfly 1994, Jack and Sarah 1995, Sense and Sensibility 1995, Twelfth Night 1996, Collusion 2003; *Books* The Undiscovered Road (contrib), Amazonians; *Style*— Miss Imogen Stubbs

STUBBS, Prof Michael Wesley; s of Leonard Garforth Stubbs (d 1987), and Isabella Wardrop, *née* McGavin (d 1991); *b* 23 December 1947; *Educ* Glasgow HS for Boys, King's Coll Cambridge (MA), Univ of Edinburgh (PhD); *Career* lectr in linguistics Univ of Nottingham 1974–85, prof of English in educn Inst of Educn Univ of London 1985–90, prof of English linguistics Univ of Trier 1990–, hon sr research fell Univ of Birmingham 1994–99; chm BAAL 1988–91; *Books* Language, Schools and Classrooms (1976), Language and Literacy (1980), Discourse Analysis (1983), Educational Linguistics (1986), Text and Corpus Analysis (1996), Words and Phrases (2001); *Recreations* mountain walking; *Style*— Prof Michael Stubbs; ✉ FB2 Anglistik, Universität Trier, D-54286 Trier, Germany (tel 00 49 651 201 2278, fax 00 49 651 201 3928, e-mail stubbs@uni-trier.de)

STUBBS, Rebecca; da of James Stuart Stubbs, of Barnsley, S Yorks, and Diane, *née* Rennison; *b* 29 September 1971; *Educ* Darton HS Barnsley, Downing Coll Cambridge (sr Harris scholar, Squire scholar); *Career* called to the Bar: Middle Temple 1994 (Harmsworth entrance exhibitioner, Queen Mother scholar), Supreme Court of Grenada and WI Associated States 2005; jr counsel to the Crown 2000; vice-chm Access to the Bar Ctee of the Bar Cncl 2007; barr rep Insolvency Court Users' Ctee; memb Chancery Bar Assoc 1994, memb Commercial Bar Assoc (COMBAR) 1996; second dan black belt Shotokan karate, represented England JKA Euro Championships Bochum Germany 1997, represented GB ITU age group World Triathlon Championships Edmonton Canada 2001 and Cancun Mexico 2002; FRSA 2004; *Books* Butterworths Practical Insolvency (contrib, 1999), Mithani on Directors Disqualification (contrib, 2002), French on Applications to Wind Up Companies (conslt ed, 2007); *Recreations* cycling, skiing; *Style*— Miss Rebecca Stubbs; ✉ Maitland Chambers, 7 Stone Buildings, Lincoln's Inn, London WC2A 3SZ (tel 020 7406 1200, fax 020 7406 1300, e-mail rstubbs@maitlandchambers.com)

STUBBS, Sir William Hamilton; kt (1994); s of Joseph Stubbs, and Mary, *née* McNicol; *b* 5 November 1937; *Educ* Workington GS Cumberland, St Aloysius Coll Glasgow, Univ of Glasgow (BSc, PhD), Univ of Arizona; *m* 16 April 1963, Marie Margaret, da of Joseph Pierce; 3 da (Nadine Ann b 1964, Hilary Jo b 1966, Fiona Mairi b 1967); *Career* Shell Oil Co California 1964–67, teacher in Glasgow 1967–72, asst dir of educn Carlisle 1972–73 and Cumbria 1973–76, dep dir of educn 1976–77, dep educn offr ILEA 1977–82, educn offr and chief exec ILEA 1982–88, chief exec Polytechnics and Colleges Funding Cncl 1988–92, chief exec FE Funding Cncl 1992–96, rector London Inst 1996–, chm Qualifications and Curriculum Authy 1997–2002; Hon Dr: Open Univ, Sheffield Hallam Univ, Univ of Exeter; hon prof Univ of Warwick; *Style*— Sir William Stubbs; ✉ Locke's Cottage, Manor Road, Adderbury, Oxfordshire OX17 3EL

STUBLEY, Trevor Hugh; s of Frank Stubley (d 1988), of Leeds, and Marie, *née* Ellis; *b* 27 March 1932; *Educ* Leeds Coll of Art, Edinburgh Coll of Art (DA, post dip scholar); *m* 1963, Valerie Ann, *née* Churm; 4 s (Adam b 1964, Justin b 1966, Gabriel b 1970, Nathan b 1974); *Career* artist; vice-pres Royal Soc of Portrait Painters 1994–99; RP 1974, RSW 1990, RWS 1995, RBA 1991; *Portraits* Dame Janet Baker, Lord Boyle of Handsworth, Lord Briggs, Lord Bullock, Sir Zelman Cowen, Lord Dainton of Hallam Moors, Dame Judi Dench, Lord Morris of Grasmere, Sir Patrick Nairne, Lord Porter, J B Priestley, Dorothy Tutin, Lord Wolfenden, HM The Queen 1986, Lord Hailsham 1992; *Work in Collections* National Portrait Gall, Palace of Westminster, British Library, Cranwell RAF Coll, MOD, Royal Inst, IEE, Tower of London, Windsor Castle; illustrator of over 400 children's books 1960–80; *Awards* Andrew Grant Major Travelling Scholar 1955, William Hoffman Wood Gold Medal for Painting 1955, Yorkshire TV Fine Art fell 1981–82, Arts Cncl Award 1982, Hunting Group Art Prize 1986, Singer and Friedlander/Sunday Times Prize 1990; *Style*— Trevor Stubley, RP, RBA, RSW, RWS; ✉ Trevor Stubley Gallery, Greenfield Road, Holmfirth, Huddersfield HD9 3XQ (tel 01484 682026, website www.trevorstubleygallery.co.uk)

STUCHFIELD, Nicolas John (Nic); s of Clifford Roy and Ann Stuchfield; *b* 13 January 1960; *Educ* Forest Sch, Magdalen Coll Oxford (MA); *m* 28 June 1986, Jill, *née* Pendleton; 2 s (Alexander (Sandy) b 2 Feb 1992, James b 12 Aug 1996), 1 da (Lucy b 2 Sept 1993); *Career* ptnr Wedd Durlacher Mordaunt & Co 1985–86, dir BZW Securities 1988–95, chief operating offr BZW Equities 1992–95, chief operating offr and chief investment offr Global Index Investments Barclays Global Investors 1995–97, ceo Tradepoint Financial Networks plc 1997–99, md The Stuchfield Consultancy Ltd 1999–2004, chm Totem Market Valuations Ltd 2002–04, md EDX London Ltd 2003–; London Stock Exchange plc: head of derivative products 2003–, dir for corp devpt 2004–; memb: London Stock Exchange 1983–86, The Securities Inst 1986–; FRSA 1998; *Recreations* opera, walking, travel; *Style*— Nic Stuchfield, Esq; ✉ e-mail nic.stuchfield@stuchfield.com

STUCLEY, Sir Hugh George Coplestone Bampfylde; 6 Bt (UK 1859), of Affeton Castle, Devon, and of Hartland Abbey, N Devon; DL (Devon 1998); s of Sir Dennis Frederic Bankes Stucley, 5 Bt (d 1983), and Hon Sheila Margaret Warwick Bampfylde (d 1996), da of 4 Baron Poltimore; *b* 8 January 1945; *Educ* RAC Cirencester; *m* 1969, Angela Caroline, er da of Richard Toller, of Theale, Berks; 2 s, 2 da; *Heir* s, George Stucley; *Career* Lt RHG; chm Devon Branch CLA 1995–97, pres Devonshire Assoc 1997–98, chm Badgworthy Land Co 1999–2004; High Sheriff Devon 2006–07; *Clubs* Sloane; *Style*— Sir Hugh Stucley, Bt, DL; ✉ Affeton Castle, Worlington, Crediton, Devon

STUDD, Sir Edward Fairfax; 4 Bt (UK 1929), of Netheravon, Wilts; s of Sir Eric Studd, 2 Bt, OBE, and Kathleen Stephana, da of Lydstone Joseph Langmead; suc bro, Sir (Robert) Kynaston Studd, 3 Bt, 1977; *b* 3 May 1929; *Educ* Winchester; *m* 1960, Prudence Janet, da of Alastair Douglas Fyfe, OBE, of Grey Court, Riding Mill, Northumberland; 2 s, 1 da; *Heir* s, Philip Studd; *Career* Subaltern Coldstream Gds, serv Malaya 1948–49; Macneill & Barry Ltd Calcutta 1951–62, Inchcape & Co Ltd 1962–86 (dir 1974–86), chm Gray Dawes Travel Ltd 1987–96; memb Ct of Assts Worshipful Co of Merchant Taylors (Master 1987–88, 1993–94); *Recreations* rural activities; *Clubs* Boodle's, Pratt's; *Style*— Sir Edward Studd, Bt

STUDD, Prof John William Winston; s of Eric Dacombe Studd (d 1941), and Elsie Elizabeth, *née* Kirby (d 1995); *b* 4 March 1940; *Educ* Royal Hosp Sch Ipswich, Univ of Birmingham (MB BS, MD, DSc); *m* 7 May 1980, Dr Margaret Ann Johnson, da of Dr Frederick Johnson, of Hinton Charterhouse, Bath; 1 s (Thomas b 16 Oct 1981), 2 da (Sarah b 7 Dec 1985, Josephine b 18 Feb 1992); *Career* res fell Univ of Birmingham, lectr in obstetrics and gynaecology Univ Coll of Rhodesia 1972, consIt and sr lectr Univ of Nottingham 1974–75, subsequently consIt obstetrician and gynaecologist King's Coll Hosp and Dulwich Hosp London, currently conslt obstetrician and gynaecologist Chelsea and Westminster Hosp London and prof of gynaecology Imperial Coll London; author of papers on: labour, menopause, osteoporosis, premenstrual syndrome, post natal depression, depression in women and infertility, HIV infection in women; ed: Menopause Digest, The Diplomate; memb Editorial Bd: Jl of RSM, British Journal of Obstetrics and Gynaecology, Br Jl of Hosp Med, Int Jl of Gynaecological Endocrinology; memb Cncl and pubns offr RCOG, memb Cncl RSM, chm Nat Osteoporosis Soc, pres Section of Obstetrics and Gynaecology RSM, pres Int Soc of Reproductive Med, chm PMS and Menopause Tst, memb Hosp Conslts and Specialists Assoc; Hon DSc Univ of Birmingham 1994; memb BMA 1962, FRCOG 1982 (MRCOG 1967); *Books* Management of Labour (ed, 1985), Management of the Menopause (ed, 1988), Progress in Obstetrics and Gynaecology (volumes 1–14), Self Assessment in Obstetrics and Gynaecology, The Menopause and Hormone Replacement Therapy (1993, 2 edn 1995), Annual Progress in Reproductive Medicine (1993–94), RCOG Yearbook (1993 and 1994–95), Hysterectomy and HRT (1998), Menopause Annual (1999–2000), Vaginal Hysterectomy (2002), and other undergraduate and postgraduate textbooks; *Recreations* theatre, music, opera, history of medicine; *Style*— Prof John Studd; ✉ 27 Blomfield Road, London W9 1AA (tel 020 7266 0058, fax 020 7266 2663, car 077 7477 4999, e-mail laptop@studd.co.uk); 120 Harley Street, London W1 (tel 020 7486 0497, fax 020 7224 4190, e-mail harley@studd.co.uk); Chelsea and Westminster Hospital, 369 Fulham Road, London SW10 9NH; Fertility & Endocrinology Centre, Lister Hospital, Chelsea Bridge Road, London SW1W 8RH (tel 020 7730 5433, fax 020 7823 6108, telex 21283 LISTER G, e-mail lister@studd.co.uk, website www.studd.co.uk)

STUDHOLME, Sir Henry William; 3 Bt (UK 1956), of Perridge, Co Devon; er s of Sir Paul Henry William Studholme, 2 Bt, DL (d 1990), and Virginia Katherine, *née* Palmer (d 1990); *b* 31 January 1958; *Educ* Eton, Trinity Hall Cambridge (MA); *m* 1 Oct 1988, (Sarah) Lucy Rosita Deans-Chrystall, o da of late Richard S Deans, of Christchurch, NZ, and late Jane R M Deans, of West Wellow, Hants; 1 da (Lorna Jane Virginia b 1 June 1990), 2 s (Joshua Henry Paul b 2 Feb 1992, Jacob Gilfred Richard b 11 June 1993); *Heir* s, Joshua Studholme; *Career* chm SW Regnl Advsy Ctee on Forestry 2000, memb Bd SW RDA 2002–, forestry cmmr 2007–; ACA, CTA; *Style*— Sir Henry Studholme, Bt

STULTIENS, (Alan) Jeffrey; s of Thomas Stultiens (d 1980), of Syresham, Northants, and Kate, *née* Whittaker (d 2000); *b* 12 September 1944; *Educ* Hutton GS, Tiffin Boys' Sch, Kingston Sch of Art, Camberwell Sch of Art and Crafts (DipAD); *m* 4 July 1992, Catherine, da of Martin Knowelden; 2 da (Ellen Alice b 1999, Isobel Kate b 2003); *Career* fine artist; lectr Sir John Cass Sch of Art City of London Poly 1967–73, sr lectr and leader Fndn Course Hertfordshire Coll of Art and Design 1983–87 (sr lectr 1974–83), visiting tutor/assessor Dip in Portraiture Heatherley Sch of Fine Art 1994–2007; first prize John Player Portrait Award Nat Portrait Gallery 1985; RP 1991 (hon sec 1993–96); *Exhibitions* John Player Portrait Award (Nat Portrait Gallery) 1984 and 1985, British Portraiture 1980–85 1985–86, Portraits for the '80s 1986, Royal Soc of Portrait Painters 1990, Women on Canvas 1991, Hunting/Observer Art Prizes 1992, The Portrait Award 1980–89 (Nat Portrait Gallery) 1992, Oriel Ynys Môn 1992, Nikkei Exhibition Tokyo 1993, Royal Coll of Pathologists 1995–96, People's Portraits 2000–01, Di Passagio Venice 2005; *Work in Collections* Nat Portrait Gallery, Merton Coll Oxford, Oriel Coll Oxford, Nat Heart and Lung Inst, Servite Houses, RNLI, Royal Med Fndn, Royal Acad of Music, Royal Coll of Pathologists, Royal Collection Windsor Castle, The Royal Soc, Royal Holloway Coll London, Clan MacLeod, Acad of Med Sciences, Royal Coll of Physicians; *Commissions* incl: Cardinal Basil Hume OSB OM 1987 and 1999, Sir Aaron Klug OM 2001, HM The Queen 2003, numerous private cmmns; *Clubs* Arts; *Style*— Jeffrey Stultiens, Esq, RP; ✉ 26 St George's Close, Toddington, Bedfordshire LU5 6AT (tel 01525 874120, e-mail jeff.stultiens@ntlworld.com)

STUNELL, (Robert) Andrew; OBE (1995), MP; s of late Robert George Stunell, of Powick, Worcs, and Trixie Stunell; *b* 24 November 1942; *Educ* Surbiton GS, Univ of Manchester, Liverpool Poly; *m* 29 July 1967, Gillian Mary Stunell; 2 da (Judith b 1969, Kari b 1970), 3 s (Peter b 1973, Mark b 1974, Daniel b 1979); *Career* architectural asst: various posts 1965–81, freelance 1981–85; cncllrs offr Assoc of Liberal Cncllrs 1985–88; Assoc of Lib Dem Cncllrs: political sec 1989–96, special projects offr 1996–97; cncllr: Chester City Cncl 1979–90, Cheshire CC 1981–91, Stockport MB 1994–2002; memb Assoc of CCs 1985–90 (ldr SLD Gp 1985–90); Parly candidate: Chester 1979–87, Hazel Grove 1992; MP (Lib Dem) Hazel Grove 1997–; Lib Dem spokesperson on energy 1997–2005, Lib Dem chief whip 2001–06, shadow spokesperson for Dept of Communities and Local Govt 2006–; sponsor of Sustainable and Secure Buildings Act 2004; *Books* Guide to Local Government Finance (1985), Success on Balanced Councils (1985), Parish Finance (1986), Success on the Council (1988), Running a Successful Council Group (1990), Budgeting For Real (1991), Open, Active and Effective (1994), Energy: Clean and Green in 2050 (1999), Cleaning up the Mess (2002); *Style*— Andrew Stunell, Esq, OBE, MP; ✉ 84 Lyme Grove, Romiley, Stockport, Cheshire SK6 4DJ; Liberal Democrat Office, 68a Compstall Road, Romiley, Stockport SK6 4DE (tel 0161 406 7070); House of Commons, London SW1A 0AA (tel 020 7219 3000)

STURDEE, Dr David William; s of late Cdr Peter Doveton Sturdee, OBE, of Solihull, W Midlands, and Daphne, *née* Langdon; *b* 13 May 1945; *Educ* Sherborne, St Thomas' Hosp Med Sch London (MB BS, DA), Univ of Birmingham (MD); *m* 4 Sept 1971, Elizabeth Morton, da of Dr John Morton Muir (d 1973); 1 s (Simon William b 1973), 1 da (Claire b 1975); *Career* sr registrar W Midlands rotation 1978–81, conslt obstetrician and gynaecologist Solihull 1981– (past clinical dir), sr clinical lectr Univ of Birmingham 1981– (res fell Dept of Obstetrics and Gynaecology 1975–77); author of many papers in jls, chapters and 4 books on hormone replacement therapy for menopausal symptoms and 2 yearbooks of obstetrics and gynaecology; chm Br Menopause Soc 1995–97, fndr memb Int Menopause Soc (sec-gen 2005–08, pres 2008–); past chm Solihull Div BMA, hon treas Birmingham and Midlands Obstetric and Gynaecological Soc; RCOG: pubns offr and chm Pubns Editorial Ctee 1999–2002, past memb Higher Training and Sub-Specialty Bd Ctees; past ed The Diplomate, co-ed-in-chief Climacteric (Jl Int Menopause Soc) 1998–; FRCOG 1988; *Recreations* singing (St Alphege choir and close harmony, CDs 'Warts and All' and 'Don't Tell the Abbot' by The Surplus Cassocks), golf, fishing; *Clubs* Copt Heath Golf; *Style—* Dr David Sturdee; ✉ 44 Mirfield Road, Solihull, West Midlands B91 1JD (tel 0121 705 1759); Department of Obstetrics and Gynaecology, Solihull Hospital, Lode Lane, Solihull, West Midlands B91 2JL (tel 0121 424 5390, e-mail david.sturdee@btinternet.com)

STURDY, Robert William; MEP (Cons) Eastern England; s of Gordon Sturdy (d 1989), and Kathleen, *née* Wells; *b* 22 June 1944; *Educ* Ashville Coll Harrogate; *m* 12 July 1969, Elizabeth Truus, da of John Hommes; 1 s (Julian), 1 da (Joanna); *Career* accountant; ptnr G E Sturdy and Son; MEP (Cons): Cambridgeshire 1994–99, Eastern England 1999–; dep ldr Br Cons in European Parl 1999–2001, EP (EPP-ED) spokesmen int trade; co-chm Interparly WTO Cmmn; memb EU-ACP JPA; *Recreations* fishing, tennis, skiing, cricket; *Style—* Robert Sturdy, Esq, MEP; ✉ 153 St Neot's Road, Hardwick, Cambridge CB23 7QJ (tel 01954 211790, fax 01954 211786, e-mail rwsturdy@btconnect.com)

STURGEON, Dr David Alexander; s of Flt Lt Alexander Rodger Sturgeon, of Worcs, and Jean, *née* Stansfield; *b* 3 July 1947; *Educ* Hipperholme GS, Univ of Oxford, UCH (BA, MA, BM BCh); *m* 6 Dec 1975, Elizabeth, da of Eric Kurt Lederman, of London; 2 da (Kate b 28 April 1977, Natasha b 29 Aug 1979); *Career* UCH London: Leverhulme jr res fell med sch 1974–75, sr clinical lectr Dept of Mental Health 1977–86, acting head Dept of Mental Health 1981–84, tutor Faculty of Clinical Sciences 1985–87; conslt psychiatrist Camden and Islington NHS Tst and hon sr lectr UCL Hosps 1986–, conslt liaison psychiatrist UCL Hosps 1998–, conslt psychiatrist Student Counselling Serv UCL 2006–; author of various papers on family treatment of schizophrenia, psychophysiology of schizophrenia and psychotherapy; psychiatric advsr to: Br Assoc of Cancer United Patients (Cancer BACUP), Breast Cancer Care; hon psychiatric advsr to Brandon Centre of Counselling and Psychotherapy for Young People; fell and treas Int Coll of Psychosomatic Med; FRCPsych 1986 (MRCPsych 1976); *Books* UCH Textbook of Psychiatry (co-ed, 1990); *Recreations* writing; *Style—* Dr David Sturgeon; ✉ Department of Psychological Medicine, University College Hospital, Grafton Way, London WC1 (tel 020 7387 9300 ext 8585, fax 020 7387 1710)

STURGEON, Nicola; MSP; da of Robert Sturgeon, of Irvine, and Joan, *née* Ferguson; *b* 19 July 1970; *Educ* Greenwood Acad Irvine, Univ of Glasgow (LLB), Dip Legal Practice; *Career* trainee slr McClure Naismith 1993–95, asst slr Bell & Craig 1995–97, assoc slr Drumchapel Law Centre 1997–99; MSP (SNP) Glasgow 1999–, memb Nat Exec, dep ldr SNP and SNP ldr Scottish Parly; *Recreations* theatre, reading; *Style—* Ms Nicola Sturgeon, MSP; ✉ The Scottish Parliament, Edinburgh EH99 1SP (tel 0131 348 5695, fax 0131 348 6475, e-mail nicola.sturgeon.msp@scottish.parliament.uk)

STURGIS, Ann Elisabeth; da of Maj Peter Sturgis (d 1986), and Rachel Sybil, *née* Borthwick (d 1998); *b* 23 October 1945; *Educ* North Foreland Lodge; *Career* estate agent; chm and md Malverns Estate Agents; dir: R H K Seelig Ltd, K A L, Moontron Ltd; fell Incorporated Soc of Estate Agents (FISEA); *Recreations* gardening; *Style—* Miss Ann Sturgis; ✉ Garden Cottage, Dauntsey Park, Chippenham, Wiltshire SN15 4HT; Malverns, Malvern Court, Onslow Square, London SW7 3HU (tel 020 7589 8122, fax 020 7589 4403, e-mail ann@dauntseypark.co.uk)

STURLEY, Air Marshal Philip Oliver; CB (2000), MBE (1985); *Educ* St Ignatius' Coll London, Univ of Southampton, RAF Coll Cranwell, JSDC Greenwich; *m* Micheline; 1 da (Olivia b 15 Feb 1980); *Career* pilot (Phantom) 41 (F) Sqdn RAF Conningsby, pilot (Jaguar) II (AC) Sqdn RAF Laarbruch Germany, Sqdn Leader 1980, Air Staff Offr (Army) HQ 1 (Br) Corps Beilfield, Flight Cdr II (AC) Sqdn, Wing Cdr 1984, leader Strike Cmd Briefing Team RAF High Wycombe 1984–85, Cdr II AC Sqdn Germany 1987–89, memb Air Force Bd Standing Ctee Strategic Support Team MOD 1989–90, Gp Capt 1989, Dir Air Staff Briefing and Co-ordination MOD 1990–92, Cdr Tri-National Tornado Training Estab (TTTE) RAF Cottesmore 1992, Air Cdre 1993; first NATO Liaison Offr UN Force Cdr Former Yugoslavia 1993, sec NATO Mil Ctee 1994–98, Sr Air Staff Offr Strike Command and AOC 38 Gp RAF High Wycombe 1998–2000, Dep Chief Staff Ops Strike Command 2000, ACAS 2000–03, COS AIRNORTH 2003–05; pres RAF Assoc 2005–, specialist advsr to House of Commons Defence Ctee 2006–; QCVSA 1990; FRAeS 1993; *Recreations* gliding (pres RAF Gliding and Soaring Assoc), skiing, golf; *Style—* Air Marshal Philip Sturley, CB, MBE

STURMAN, Jim; QC (2002); s of Gp Capt Roger Sturman, of Exeter, and Anne, *née* Lomas; *b* 19 July 1958; *Educ* Bembridge Sch IOW, Univ of Reading (LLB), Cncl of Legal Educn; *m* 21 Dec 1986, Marcella Convey, da of Dr Cyrus Mineo; 3 s (Michael Edwin Mullaney b 12 Oct 1997, Jonathan James Roger b 4 Nov 1999, Mark Joseph b 22 Sept 2001); *Career* called to the Bar 1982; criminal barr 1983–; specialist criminal and sports law barr acting for the def involved in cases incl: R v Colin Stagg, R v Ian Kay, R v Bowyer and Woodgate, Shipman Inquiry; also specialist advocate in FA disciplinary cases, acted for clubs incl Chelsea FC, West Ham United FC and Tottenham Hotspur FC; memb: Bar of Gibraltar 1986, Criminal Bar Assoc, Int Bar Assoc; memb Ctee Old Bembridgians Assoc; *Style—* Jim Sturman, QC; ✉ 2 Bedford Row, London WC1R 4BU (tel 020 7440 8888, fax 020 7242 1738, e-mail jsturman@2bedfordrow.co.uk)

STURRIDGE, Charles; s of Dr Jerome Sturridge (d 1996), and Alyson Bowman Vaughan, *née* Burke; *b* 24 June 1951; *Educ* Beaumont Coll, Stonyhurst, UC Oxford (BA); *m* 6 July 1985, Phoebe Nicholls, the actress, da of Anthony Nicholls; 3 c; *Career* director and writer; dir and chm Firstsight Films Ltd 2000–; memb BECTU; *Theatre* Hard Times (Belgrade Coventry) 1974, The Seagull (Queens) 1985, Tolomeo (Broomhill Opera) 1998; *Television* incl: World in Action (4 episodes), Coronation Street (16 episodes), Brideshead Revisited (Granada) 1981, Soft Targets (BBC) 1982, The Story Teller - A Story Short 1987, Troubles (writer only, LWT) 1987, A Foreign Field (BBC) 1993, Gullivers Travels (Channel 4) 1996, Longitude (Channel 4) 2000, Shackleton (Channel 4) 2002; *Films* Runners (debut) 1983, Aria (contrib) 1986, A Handful of Dust (co-adaptor) 1988, Where Angels Fear to Tread (co-adaptor) 1991, Fairy Tale - A True Story 1997, Ohio Impromptu (dir) 2000, Lassie 2005; *Awards* for Brideshead Revisited: 17 Awards incl BAFTA for Best Series and Best Actor (Anthony Andrews, *qv*), two Golden Globe Awards, The Grand Award (NY Film & TV Festival), Emmy for Best Supporting Actor (Laurence Olivier); for Runners: Best Film at the Karlovy-Vary Festival, Special Prize Venice Film Festival; for Gullivers Travels: Humanitas Award, Br Television Soc Team Award; 7 Emmy's incl Best Series and Best Special Effects; for Fairy Tale BAFTA Best Children's Film 1998; for Longitude 'Rockie' for Best Mini Series at BANF TV Awards; 6 further BAFTAs incl Best Series; South Bank Show Best TV Drama Award for Ohio Impromptu; for Shackleton: BAFTA Best Drama Serial, Best Costume, Emmy for Outstanding Cinematography, Outstanding Score; *Publications* The Seagull (trans with Tania Alexander, Amber Lane Press, 1983); *Clubs* Groucho; *Style—* Charles Sturridge, Esq; ✉ c/o PFD, Drury House, 34–43 Russell Street, London WC2B 5HA (tel 020 7344 1000, fax 020 7379 6790)

STURROCK, Philip James; s of James Cars Sturrock, of Brighouse, W Yorks, and Joyce, *née* Knowles; *b* 5 October 1947; *Educ* Queen Mary's GS Walsall, Trinity Coll Oxford (MA), Manchester Business Sch (MBA); *m* 1, 5 Aug 1972 (m dis 1995), Susan, da of (William) Horace Haycock, of Walsall, W Midlands; 2 da (Anna b 23 June 1977, Jane b 3 Jan 1983), 1 s (Hugh b 5 May 1981); m 2, 8 Sept 2000, Madeleine Frances Robinson, da of Robert Francis Swift, of St Albans, Herts; *Career* md: IBIS Information Services 1972–80, Pitman Books 1980–83; gp md Routledge and Kegan Paul plc 1983–85, chm and md Cassell plc 1986–99; chm and md The Continuum International Publishing Group Ltd 1999–2006, chm Osprey Publishing Ltd 2007–; Liveryman Worshipful Co of Glaziers; FRSA; *Recreations* walking, reading, travel; *Clubs* Athenaeum; *Style—* Philip Sturrock, Esq; ✉ 62 Benbow House, 24 New Globe Walk, London SE1 9DS

STURROCK, Prof Roger Davidson; *b* 20 October 1946; *Educ* Llanelli Boys' GS, Queen Mary's Sch Basingstoke, King's Coll and Westminster Med Sch London (MB BS, AKC, LRCP, MD); *m*; 3 c; *Career* jt recipient Allessandro Robecchi International Prize in Rheumatology (Euro League Against Rheumatism) 1975, Arthritis and Rheumatism Cncl Anglo-US travelling fell to the USA 1984, currently holds McLeod/ARC chair of rheumatology Univ of Glasgow; past pres Br Soc for Rheumatology; past chair Arthritis Research Campaign; FRCPGlas 1984, FRCP 1985; *Publications* author of numerous articles in learned jls; *Style—* Prof Roger Sturrock; ✉ Centre for Rheumatic Diseases, Medicine - Division of Immunology, Infection and Inflammation, Royal Infirmary, QEB Level 3, Alexandra Parade, Glasgow G31 2ER

STURT, Richard Harry Brooke; s of Horace Holford Sturt (d 1962), of Wimborne, Dorset, and Eveline Frances, *née* Brooke (d 1998); *b* 14 November 1939; *Educ* Marlborough, Peterhouse Cambridge (MA); *m* 3 March 1962, Ann Lesley, da of Brig Charles Leslie Morgan, OBE (d 1982), of Walmer, Kent; 4 s ((Richard) Michael Villiers b 1964, Charles (Patrick) Holford b 1966, (Alexander) Fitzgerald Brooke b 1969, Nicholas (Julian) Holford b 1972); *Career* admitted slr 1966, sr ptnr Mowll & Mowll 1984–2001 (ptnr 1967–84); slr Dover Harbour Bd 1979–2001, slr and clerk to govrs King's Sch Canterbury 1979–91; registrar of Canterbury Dio and legal sec to Bishop in Canterbury 1996–; dep coroner E Kent 1972–79, HM Coroner for Kent (E Kent) 1979–2001; conducted inquests into: Herald of Free Enterprise disaster 1987, Deal Barracks explosion 1990, M2 coach crash 1994, 58 Chinese immigrants 2000; lectr Police Staff Coll 1990–97; memb Bd CAA 1990–96, chm AIRPROX Review 1997–98; memb WaterVoice Nat Cncl 2001–2005, chm WaterVoice Southern Ctee 2001–2005, memb Consumer Cncl for Water 2005– (chm Southern region and lead on European Affrs); dir: Waldershare Park Farms Ltd 1989–, Rubie Estates Ltd 1995–, Grosvenor Lifestyle plc 1996–2001, E Kent Hosps NHS Tst 2001–, Canterbury Festival Fndn 2002– (chm 2006–), Ashford Radio Ltd 2003–; chm: Invicta Sound plc 1984–91, CCU (Medway) Ltd 2004–, Northbourne Park Fndn 2004–; fndr and chm E Kent Holiday Music Tst 1979–; pres St John Ambulance Dover Div 2000–06, memb Cncl St John Kent 2006–; govr: Betteshanger Sch 1978–80, Northbourne Park Sch 1980–85 and 1993– (dep chm 1999–2001, chm 2001–), King's Sch Canterbury 1991–2007, Cumnor House Sch 1996–2001, Canterbury Christ Church UC 2001–05, Canterbury Christ Church Univ 2005–; tstee: Kent Branch Br Red Cross 1991–97, All Saints Waldershare Tst 1978–2001, Cicely Stockmann Memorial Fund 1985–, Canterbury Theatre and Festival Tst 1999–, Rebecca McNie Fndn 2006–; memb Canterbury Cathedral Transitional Cncl 1998–2002; Hon DCL Univ of Kent 2001; FRSA 1990; *Books* Fishery Protection and Foreign Sea Fishing Boats (1973), contrib section on Fisheries, Ports and Harbours, European Communities in Halsbury's Laws of England (4 edn), The Role of the Coroner in Major Disasters (1988), The Collision Regulations (3 edn, 1991), contrib Fisheries section in Vaughan on The Law of the European Communities (2 edn, 1993); *Recreations* cricket, badminton, singing, bridge, genealogy, fly fishing; *Clubs* Athenaeum, Flyfishers', MCC; *Style—* Richard Sturt, Esq; ✉ Kent Cottage, 7 Granville Road, Walmer, Deal, Kent CT14 7LU (tel 01304 240250); Trafalgar House, Gordon Road, Whitfield, Dover, Kent CT16 3PN (tel 01304 873344, fax 01304 873355, e-mail richard.sturt@mowll.co.uk)

STURZAKER, Hugh Gerard; s of George Gerard Sturzaker (d 1971), of Chandlers Ford, Hants, and Gladys Maude, *née* French (d 1990); *Educ* W Buckland Sch Barnstaple, Hertford Coll Oxford (MA), Guy's Hosp Med Sch (BM BCh); *m* 30 March 1968, Ann Elizabeth, da of Ernest Philip Featherstone, of South Croydon, Surrey; 3 s (Robert b 1970, John b 1971, James b 1980), 1 da (Nicola b 1973); *Career* house physician and surgn Guy's Hosp 1966–67, jr lectr in anatomy Guy's Hosp Med Sch 1967–68, surgical registrar Guildford Hosp and Guy's Hosp 1968–73, res fell St Mark's Hosp London 1973–74, sr surgical registrar Guy's Hosp and Gt Ormond St Hosp for Children, conslt gen surgn James Paget Hosp NHS Tst Great Yarmouth 1979–2005, currently hon sr lectr UEA and hon conslt surgn and govr James Paget Hosp; regnl advsr and examiner RCS(Ed); past pres: Oxford Univ Med Soc, Br Med Students' Assoc, E Anglian Surgical Club, Great Yarmouth and Waveney Div BMA; memb: Assoc of Surgns of GB and Ireland, BMA 1966, RSM 1967; FRCSEd 1971, FRCS 1972; *Recreations* gardening, wine and beer making; *Style—* Hugh Sturzaker, Esq; ✉ Hobland House, Hobland, Great Yarmouth, Norfolk NR31 9AR (tel 01493 665287, e-mail hugh@sturzaker.plus.com), James Paget Hospital, Gorleston, Great Yarmouth, Norfolk NR31 6LA (tel 01493 452452)

S

STUTTAFORD, Dr (Irving) Thomas; OBE (1996); s of Dr William Joseph Edward Stuttaford, MC (d 1956), of Horning, Norfolk, and Mary Marjorie Dean, *née* Royden (d 1976); *b* 4 May 1931; *Educ* Gresham's, BNC Oxford, W London Hosp (MRCS, LRCP, DObstRCOG); *m* 1 June 1957, Pamela Christine, da of Lt-Col Richard Ropner, TD (d 1975), of Aldie, Tain, Ross-shire; 3 s (Andrew b 1958, Thomas b 1961, Hugo b 1964); *Career* 2 Lt 10 Royal Hussars (PWO) 1953–55, Lt Scottish Horse TA 1955–59; jr hosp appts 1959–60, gen practice 1960–70, visiting physician BUPA 1970–96 (asst clinical dir 1979–81); clinical asst in venereology: The London Hosp 1974–93, Queen Mary's Hosp for the East End 1974–79, Moorfields Eye Hosp 1975–79; sr med advsr The Rank Orgn 1980–85; private practice in occupational health 1986–; med columnist: The Times 1990– (med corr 1982–90), formerly of ELLE magazine and Options magazine; columnist The Oldie; med advsr: Barclays Bank, Standard Chartered Bank, Rank Hotels and other cos; memb: Blofield and Flegg RDC 1964–66, Norwich City Cncl 1969–71; MP (Cons) Norwich S 1970–74, Parly candidate (Cons) Isle of Ely 1974 and 1979, sec Cons Health and Social Servs Ctee; memb: Cncl Res Def Soc 1970–79, Built Control Campaign 1970–79, Select Ctee on Sci and Technol; *Books* A Birth Control Plan for Britain (with Mr Alistair Service and Dr John Dunwoody, 1972), To Your Good Health - the Wise Drinker's Guide (1997); author of chapters in: Drinking to Your Health (1989), Which Wine Guide (1991), In Your Right Mind (1999); *Recreations* living in the country, conservation of old buildings; *Clubs* Beefsteak, Athenaeum, Reform, Cavalry and Guards', Norfolk (Norwich); *Style—* Dr Thomas Stuttaford, OBE; ✉ 36 Elm Hill, Norwich, Norfolk NR3 1HG (tel 01603 615133); 8 Devonshire Place, London W1N 1PB (tel 020 7486 7166)

STUTTARD, John Boothman; JP (2001); s of Thomas Boothman Stuttard (d 1969), and Helena, *née* Teasdale (d 1969); *b* 6 February 1945; *Educ* Shrewsbury, Churchill Coll Cambridge (MA); *m* 26 Sept 1970, Lesley Sylvia, da of Thomas Geoffrey Daish, of Kenilworth; 2 s (Thomas Henry Boothman (Tom) b 20 Jan 1975, James Midgley (Jamie) b 21 Aug 1976); *Career* VSO teacher SOAS Brunei 1966–67; PricewaterhouseCoopers (formerly Cooper Brothers & Co then Coopers & Lybrand): trainee accountant 1967–70, qualified CA 1970, ptnr 1975–2005, dir of corp mktg and chm of Scandinavian mkt gp 1986–94, formerly sr ptnr global clients PricewaterhouseCoopers China (chm 1994–99), sr ptnr global clients PricewaterhouseCoopers UK 1999–2005, memb Advsy Bd 2005–, conslt 2005–; accounting advsr to CPRS Cabinet Office Whitehall 1982–83; chm Finnish-British C of C 2002–06 (dir 2001–); memb: Univ of Cambridge Appts Bd 1977–81, China-Britain Business Cncl 2000–06, Advsy Ctee E Asia Inst Univ of Cambridge 2001–, Cncl VSO 2006– (memb Advsy Bd VSO Fundraising 2001–06); advsr St Paul's Cathedral Fndn 2005–; chm Totteridge Manor Assoc 2002–05 (dir 1980–2005); govr King Edward's Sch Witley 2002– (chm 450th anniversary appeal 2002–05); tstee: Lord Mayor of London's Disaster Relief Appeal 2002–, Charities Aid Fndn 2002–06 (chm Audit Ctee 2003–06), Morden Coll 2005, Lord Mayor's 800th Anniversary Appeal 2005–; co-chm Br Red Cross City of London Christmas Fayre 2003; pres Lime Street Ward Club 2001–; Alderman City of London 2001–, sponsoring Alderman Guild of Educators 2002–, Sheriff City of London 2005–06, HM Lt City of London 2006–07, Lord Mayor City of London 2006–07, Admiral of the Port of London 2006–07, chief magistrate City of London 2006–07; chllr City Univ London 2006–07; Hon DLitt City Univ 2006; Freeman City of London 1994; Liveryman: Worshipful Co of Glaziers and Painters of Glass 2000 (memb Ct of Assts 2003–), Worshipful Co of Chartered Accountants in Eng and Wales 2002 (memb Ct of Assts 2004–), Worshipful Co of Plumbers 2005 (hon memb Ct of Assts 2005–); hon fell Foreign Policy Assoc 2000; FCA 1979; KJStJ 2006; Commander Order of the Lion of Finland 2004 (Knight (First Class) 1995); *Publications* Peking to Paris in a Pink Rolls-Royce (1998), The New Silk Road - Secrets of Business Success in China Today (2000); *Recreations* travel, vintage and veteran cars, theatre, opera, tennis; *Clubs* China, Rolls-Royce Enthusiasts', 20 Ghost, Automobile de Monaco, GB Veteran Car, Travellers, City Livery, Walbrook; *Style—* John B Stuttard, Esq; ✉ c/o PricewaterhouseCoopers, 1 Embankment Place, London WC2N 6RH (tel 020 7213 4590)

STYLE, Vice-Adm Charles Rodney; CBE (2002); s of Lt Cdr Sir Godfrey Style, CBE, DSC, RN (d 2000), and Sigrid Elisabeth, *née* Carlberg (d 1985); *b* 15 January 1954; *Educ* Eton, Univ of Cambridge (exhibitioner, MA); *m* 31 Jan 1981, Charlotte Amanda, da of Lt Timothy Martin Woodford, RN (d 1966), and Eila Mary, *née* Stirling-Hamilton, step da of George Rudolph Wratislaw Walker; 3 da (Amanda Clare b 24 Nov 1981, Annabel Daisy b 21 Dec 1983, Elizabeth Sigrid b 2 Jan 1990); *Career* joined Royal Navy 1974, trg BRNC Dartmouth (Queen's Sword); served: Antarctic patrol ship HMS Endurance 1977–78, HMS Bacchante 1978–79, HM Yacht Britannia 1980–81, HMS Sandpiper 1981–82 (cmd), HMS Wotton 1982–83 (cmd), HMS Arethusa 1984–85; Flag Lt to C-in-C Fleet, Channel and Eastern Atlantic 1985–87, Cdr 1988, cmd frigate HMS Andromeda 1988–89, Directorate of Naval Plans MOD 1989–92, Staff Offr Ops to Cdr UK Task Gp 1992–93 (incl serv in Adriatic), Capt 1993, cmd frigate HMS Campbeltown 1993–95 (incl Armilla Task Gp cmd Gulf 1993–94), Chief Staff Offr (Ops and Trg) to Flag Offr Sea Trg (FOST) 1995–96, Cdre 1997, Princ Staff Offr to Chief of Defence Staff 1997–98, memb RCDS 1999, cmd aircraft carrier HMS Illustrious 2000–01 (incl serv off Sierra Leone and in the Arabian Sea against terrorism), Rear Admiral 2002, i/c Strategic Deployment and Precision Attack Capability MOD 2002–04, Cdr UK Maritime Force 2004–05, Vice-Adm 2006, DCDS (Commitments) and dir UK Mil Ops MOD 2006–; Naval memb Royal Yacht Sqdn Cowes 2004; advsr Renewal Project St Martin-in-the-Fields 2004; Yr Bro Trinity House 1991, memb Hon Co of Master Mariners 2003; *Recreations* fishing, reading, sailing, music; *Style—* Vice-Adm Charles Style, CBE

STYLE, Christopher John David; QC (2006); s of Maj David Carlyle Willoughby Style, MC, TD (d 1978), of Loweswater, Cumbria, and Dr Anne Marion, *née* Phillips; *b* 13 April 1955; *Educ* St Bees Sch Cumbria, Trinity Hall Cambridge (MA), City of London Poly; *m* 7 April 1990, Victoria Jane, *née* Miles; 3 s (George Alexander b 2 Aug 1991, Charles David b 8 Aug 1993, Peter John b 12 May 1995), 1 da (Catherine Elizabeth b 19 Dec 2000); *Career* Linklaters & Paines 1977–: articled clerk 1977–79, slr 1979, asst slr 1979–85, ptnr 1985–; slr advocate (Higher Cts Civil); memb London Slrs Litigation Assoc; Freeman City of London 1985, memb City of London Slrs Co; FCIArb; *Books* Documentary Evidence (6 edn, 1997); *Recreations* fell walking, rock climbing; *Style—* Mr Christopher Style, QC; ✉ Gainsborough House, 6 Gainsborough Gardens, London NW3 1BJ; Linklaters, One Silk Street, London EC2Y 8HQ (tel 020 7456 2000, fax 020 7456 2222)

STYLE, Montague William; OBE (2007); s of late Cdr Sir Godfrey Style, CBE, DSC, RN, and late Jill Elizabeth, *née* Caruth; *b* 9 October 1943; *Educ* Eton, Ecole des Hautes Etudes Commerciales Paris, INSEAD (MBA); *m* 18 July 1970, Susan Jennifer, da of Peter Wrightson, OBE; 1 da (Sophie Elizabeth b 20 June 1974), 1 s (Oliver Rodney b 6 May 1976); *Career* Morgan Grampian Ltd London 1965–69, The Economist Newspaper Ltd 1969–72, Pharmaceutical Div Ciba-Geigy 1973–96, Novartis 1997–99, md Style Project Partners GmbH Basel 1999–, ptnr Quilt Solutions LLC Witterswil 2006–; chm: Br & Cwlth Soc Mexico 1978–80, Int Sch of Basel 1982–85; pres Br-Swiss C of C 2004–06; MInstD; *Recreations* organist, pianist, walking, fly fishing; *Clubs* Rye Golf, Golf du Rhin Chalampe France; *Style—* Montague Style, Esq, OBE; ✉ 27 rue des Romains, 68480 Bettlach, France (tel 00 33 3 89 07 50 85, mobile 00 41 79 322 57 06, e-mail m.w.style@hrnet.fr)

STYLE, Rodney Hill; s of Col (Rodney) Gerald Style, of Runfold, Farnham, Surrey, and Barbara Hill Style; *b* 25 March 1956; *Educ* Eton; *m* 24 April 1982, Georgina Eve, da of late John Kinloch Kerr of Abbottrule, of Frocester, Glos; 2 s (George b 1985, Hugo b 1985), 1 da (Elizabeth b 1989); *Career* CA; Spicer and Pegler 1976–85, ptnr HW Chartered Accountants 1985–, fin dir HW Fin Servs Ltd 1987–, dir Haines Watts Ltd; Freeman City of London 1981, Liveryman Worshipful Co of Grocers 1991; ACA 1981, CTA 1983; *Recreations* tennis, hunting, shooting, skiing; *Style—* Rodney Style, Esq; ✉ Knowle Farmhouse, North Newington, Oxfordshire OX15 6AN; HW Chartered Accountants, Sterling House, 19/23 High Street, Kidlington, Oxfordshire OX5 2DH (tel 01865 378282, fax 01865 377518)

STYLE, Sir William Frederick; 13 Bt (E 1627), of Wateringbury, Kent; s of Sir William Montague Style, 12 Bt (d 1981), and La Verne, Lady Style (d 2006); *b* 13 May 1945; *Educ* (BSc, MEd); *m* 1, 1968, Wendy Gay, da of Gene and Marjory Wittenberger, of Hartford, Wisconsin, USA; 2 da (Shannon b 1969, Erin b 1973); m 2, 1986, Linnea Lorna, da of Donn and Elizabeth Erickson, of Sussex, Wisconsin, USA; 2 da (McKenna b 1987, McKayla b 1990), 1 s (William Colin b 1995); *Heir* s, William Style; *Career* public sch teacher; *Recreations* yacht (Summer Style); *Clubs* Fond du Lac Yacht; *Style—* Sir William Style, Bt

STYLER, His Hon Judge Granville Charles; s of Samuel Charles Styler (d 1996), of Shipston-on-Stour, Warks, and Frances Joan, *née* Clifford; *b* 9 January 1947; *Educ* King Edward VI Sch Stratford-upon-Avon; *m* 11 Sept 1971, Penelope, da of William Arnold Darbyshire, of Lytham St Annes, Lancs; 3 da (Katie b 1974, Sophie b 1977, Emily b 1979); *Career* called to the Bar Gray's Inn 1970; recorder 1988, circuit judge (Midland & Oxford Circuit) 1992–; *Recreations* tennis, carriage driving, horse racing; *Style—* His Hon Judge Styler

STYLER, Trudie; *m* 20 Aug 1992, Sting, *qv*; 2 s, 2 da; *Career* actress and film producer; fndr Xingu Films; co-fndr (with Sting, *qv*) Rainforest Foundation 1989, ambass UNICEF UK; *Films* actress: Bring on the Night 1985, Mamba 1988, The Grotesque 1995 (also prodr), Me Without You 2001, Confessions of an Ugly Stepsister 2001, Cheeky 2003 (also prodr), Alpha Male 2005 (also prodr); prodr: Boys from Brazil 1993, Moving the Mountain 1994, Lock Stock & Two Smoking Barrels 1998, Snatch 2000, Greenfingers 2001, The Sweatbox 2002, A Kind of Childhood 2002, A Guide to Recognizing Your Saints 2006; *Television* Poldark II 1978, The Body in the Library 1985, The Scold's Bridle 1998, Midsomer Murders 1998, Friends 2001, Love Soup 2005; *Style—* Ms Trudie Styler; ✉ Xingu Films, 12 Cleveland Row, London SW1A 1DH (tel 020 7451 0600, fax 020 7451 0601, e-mail trudie@xingufilms.com)

SUCHET, David; OBE (2002); s Jack Suchet (d 2001), and Joan, *née* Jarché (d 1992); bro of John Suchet, *qv*; *b* 2 May 1946; *Educ* Wellington, LAMDA; *m* 1976, Sheila Anne, da of William Ferris (d 1986), of Stratford-upon-Avon, Warks; 1 s (Robert b 10 May 1981), 1 da (Katherine b 21 July 1983); *Career* actor; began professional career Gateway Theatre Chester 1969; repertory theatres incl: Exeter, Worthing, Birmingham; assoc artiste RSC, memb Cncl LAMDA, govr RSC; visiting prof of theatre Univ of Nebraska 1975; FRSA; *Theatre* incl: Estragon in Waiting for Godot, John Aubrey in Brief Lives, Timon of Athens (Young Vic), This Story of Yours (Hampstead), Separation (Hampstead then Comedy Theatre), Oleanna (Royal Court then Duke of York's Theatre), Mole in Toad of Toad Hall, Sid Field in What a Performance, George in Who's Afraid of Virginia Woolf, Salieri in Amadeus (London, Los Angeles and NY), Gregor in Man and Boy (Duchess Theatre London); RSC incl: Shylock in The Merchant of Venice, Achilles in Troilus and Cressida, Bolingbroke in Richard II, Iago in Othello, Mercutio in Romeo & Juliet, Fool in King Lear, Caliban in The Tempest, Lucio in Measure for Measure; *Television* incl: Edward Teller in Oppenheimer (NNC), Freud in The Life of Freud (BBC), Blott in Blott on the Landscape (BBC), Judge O'Connor in Cause Celebre (Anglia TV), Glougauer in Once in a Lifetime (BBC), Carver in Nobody Here But Us Chickens (Channel 4), Hercule Poirot in Agatha Christie's Poirot (LWT), Joe in Separation (BBC), Verloc in The Secret Agent (BBC), Aaron in Moses (SkyTV and TNT USA), Gen Jacob in Solomon (SkyTV and TNT USA), Seesaw (LWT), John Borne in National Crime Squad, Edward Palmer in Murder in Mind, Baron Stockmar in Victoria and Albert, Augustus Melmotte in The Way We Live Now (BBC), George Carman in Get Carman, Cardinal Wolsey in Henry VIII; *BBC Radio* incl: Ironhand, The Kreuzer Sonata, First Night Impressions, The Shout, Rosenburg in The Trenches, Debussy, Anton Chekov, The Willows in Winter, Letters from Prison, Alpha Course (radio premiere), Isaac Babel Stories, The Gorey Details; *Film* incl: Trouillfou in Hunchback of Notre Dame, Okana in Falcon and The Snowman, Beria in Red Monarch (for Channel 4), Dyer in Song for Europe, Inspector Japp in Thirteen to Dinner, Lafleur in Bigfoot & The Hendersons, Wil in When the Whales Came, Muller in A World Apart, Nagi Hassan in Executive Decision, Vlachos in Deadly Voyage, Oliver in Sunday, A Perfect Murder, RKO, Sabotage, Naji in Live from Baghdad, Thibidoux in The In Laws, Leo in Foolproof; *Awards* nominations for Best Actor incl: Evening Standard Award for Merchant of Venice 1978, SWET Award for The Merchant of Venice 1981, BAFTA Award for Hercule Poirot 1990, 1991 and 1992, Evening Standard Awards for Timon of Athens 1991, Olivier Award for Oleanna 1994, RTA Award for What a Performance 1995; nominations for Best Supporting Actor incl: SWET Award for Once in a Lifetime 1980 and Richard II 1981, ACE Award for The Last Innocent Man 1987; others nominations incl: Actor of the Year in a New Play Award for Separation 1989, Olivier Award 1989, BAFTA Best Actor in a Supporting Role for A World Apart 1989; winner for Best Actor incl: Marseilles Film Festival for Red Monarch 1983, Brit Industry/Scientific Film Assoc Craft Award for Stress 1986; winner 1986 Royal TV Soc Performance Awards for Song for Europe, Freud, Blott on the Landscape; also winner Best Radio Actor Award for Kreutzer Sonata (one man show) 1979 and Variety Club Award for Best Actor for Oleanna; nominations Best Actor for Who's Afraid of Virginia Woolf incl: Evening Standard Award and Olivier Award; winner South Bank Award for Theatrical Achievement and winner Best Actor Critic's Circle Award for Who's Afraid of Virginia Woolf; winner Best Actor Variety Club 1998; Grapevine Award for Lifetime Achievement for Services to the Performing Arts; for Salieri in Amadeus: nomination Best Actor Olivier Awards 1999, Toni Nomination for Best Leading Actor, Drama League Award for Outstanding Performance, Back Stage Award for Best Actor; for Melmotte in The Way We Live Now: BPG Award, RTS Award, TRIC Award, nomination BAFTA; *Publications* author of essays in Players of Shakespeare (on Caliban, Shylock and Iago); *Recreations* photography, clarinet, ornithology; *Style—* David Suchet, Esq, OBE; ✉ c/o Ken McReddie Ltd, 21 Barrett Street, London W1U 1BD (tel 020 7499 7448, fax 020 7408 0886)

SUCHET, John Aleck; eldest s of Jack Suchet (d 2001), and Joan, *née* Jarché (d 1992); bro of David Suchet, OBE, *qv*; *b* 29 March 1944; *Educ* Uppingham, Univ of St Andrews (MA); *m* 1, 1968 (m dis), Moya; 3 s; m 2, 1985, Bonnie Lee; *Career* Reuters News Agency 1967–71, BBC TV News 1971–72, ITN 1972–2004 (reporter, corr, newscaster), five news 2006– (newscaster); TV Journalist of the Year RTS 1986, Newscaster of the Year TRIC 1996; memb Governing Body Royal Acad of Music 2003–07; pres: Friends of the Royal Acad of Music 1998–2006, Hearing Concern 1999–2006; patron Stagetext 2003–06; Hon Dr jur Univ of Dundee 2000; Hon FRAM 2001; *Books* TV News - The Inside Story (1989), The Last Master - Life of Beethoven (Vol 1, 1996, Vol 2, 1997, Vol 3, 1998), The Classic FM Friendly Guide to Beethoven (2006), The Treasures of Beethoven (2007); *Recreations* classical music, exploring the life, times and music of Beethoven; *Style—* John Suchet, Esq; ✉ All-Electric Productions, PO Box 1805, Andover, Hampshire SP10 3ZN

SUCKLING, Prof Colin James; OBE (2006); s of Charles Walter Suckling, CBE, FRS, of Tewin, Herts, and Eleanor Margaret, *née* Watterson; *b* 24 March 1947; *Educ* Quarry Bank HS, Univ of Liverpool (PhD, DSc, Leblanc medal); *m* 19 Aug 1972, Catherine Mary, da of Desmond Patrick Faulkner; 2 s (Christopher Andrew b 5 Nov 1974, Martin Charles b 23 Nov 1981), 1 da (Barbara Janet b 17 May 1977); *Career* Ciba-Geigy res fell Eidgenössische Technische Hochschule Zürich 1970–72; Univ of Strathclyde: lectr in chemistry 1972–80, Royal Soc Smith & Nephew sr res fell 1980–84, personal prof 1984–89, Freeland prof of chemistry 1989–, dean Faculty of Sci 1992–96, dep princ 1996–98 and 2004–05, pro-vice-princ 1998–2000, vice-princ 2000–02; chm Scot Advsy Ctee on Distinction Awards NHS Scot 2003–; memb: Jt Ctee on Higher Surgical Trg 2002–05, Public Liaison Ctee RCPSGlas, Bd Systems Level Integration Ltd 1997–2000, Bd of Mgmnt Bell Coll of Technol 1998–2007, Merchant's House of Glasgow 1998, Court Univ of Paisley 2007–; chm Bd West of Scotland Sch Symphony Orch; dir Glasgow C of C 2001–03; Wolfson Research Award 1989–91; FRSC 1980, FRSE 1987, FRSA 1991, Hon FRCPSGlas 2004, Hon FRCSEd 2005; *Books* Chemistry Through Models (1974), Enzyme Chemistry Impact and Applications (1998); author of over 180 research pubns; *Recreations* music, horn playing and conducting; *Style—* Prof Colin Suckling, OBE, FRSE; ✉ 62 North Grange Road, Bearsden, Glasgow G61 3AF (tel 0141 942 6984); Department of Pure and Applied Chemistry, University of Strathclyde, 295 Cathedral Street, Glasgow G1 1XL (tel 0141 548 2271, fax 0141 548 5743, e-mail c.j.suckling@strath.ac.uk)

SUDBOROUGH, Air Vice Marshal Nigel John; CB (2002), OBE (1989), JP (2004); s of Alexander Sudborough (d 2003), of Northampton, and Beryl, *née* Lynes; *b* 23 March 1948; *Educ* Oundle; *m* 24 July 1971, Anne Marie, da of Lt-Col Kenneth C Brown (d 1994); 1 da (Emma b 31 Oct 1984), 1 s (Charles b 11 Feb 1986); *Career* OC 29 (F) Sqdn 1985–87, OC RAF Leuchars 1993–95, RCDS 1996, Higher Command and Staff Course 2000, Dep COS (Ops) HQ Strike Command 2000–02; DG Winston Churchill Meml Tst 2002–07, dir Sudborough Investments Ltd 2002, non-exec dir Leics Partnership NHS Tst 2007–; Freeman City of London, Liveryman Worshipful Co of Pattenmakers; FCIPD; *Recreations* philately, fly fishing; *Clubs* RAF; *Style*— Air Vice Marshal Nigel Sudborough, CB, OBE; ✉ Knoll House, 5 London Road, Uppingham, Rutland LE15 9TJ (tel 01572 821920)

SUDELEY, 7 Baron (UK 1838); Merlin Charles Sainthill Hanbury-Tracy; s of Capt David Hanbury-Tracy (gs of 4 Baron) and Colline (d 1985), da of Lt-Col Collis St Hill; the 1 Baron was chm of the Cmmn for the Rebuilding of the new Houses of Parliament 1835; suc kinsman (6 Baron) 1941; *b* 17 June 1939; *Educ* Eton, Worcester Coll Oxford; *m* 1, 1980 (m dis 1988), Hon Mrs Elizabeth Villiers, da of late Viscount Bury (s of 9 Earl of Albemarle) and formerly w of Alastair Villiers; m 2, 1999 (m dis 2006), Margarita Kellett; *Heir* kinsman, Andrew Hanbury-Tracy; *Career* introduced debates in the House of Lords on: export of manuscripts 1973, cathedral finance 1980, teaching and use of the Prayer Book in theological colls 1987; cleared the Prayer Book (Protection) Bill on second reading in House of Lords 1981; patron Prayer Book Soc, memb Governing Cncl Manorial Soc of GB, chm Monday Club, past pres Montgomeryshire Soc, vice-chllr Monarchist League, chm Constitutional Monarchy Assoc; occasional lectr: Extra-Mural Dept Univ of Bristol, ESU; contrib to: Contemporary Review, Family History, London Magazine, Monday World, Quarterly Review, Vogue, The Universe, John Pudney's Pick of Today's Short Stories, Montgomeryshire Collections, Salisbury Review, Transactions of the Bristol and Gloucester Archaeological Soc, Die Waage (Zeitschrift der Chemie Grünenthal), London Miscellany, Present Jl of the Monday Club; FSA 1989; *Books* The Sudeleys - Lords of Toddington (jt author); *Recreations* conversation; *Clubs* Brooks's; *Style*— The Rt Hon the Lord Sudeley, FSA; ✉ 25 Melcombe Court, Dorset Square, London NW1 6EP

SUFFIELD, 11 Baron (GB 1786); Sir Anthony Philip Harbord-Hamond; 12 Bt (GB 1745), MC (1950); s of 10 Baron (d 1951), and Nina Annette Mary Crawfuird (d 1955), da of John William Hutchison, of Lauriston Hall, and Edlingham, Kirkcudbrightshire; *b* 19 June 1922; *Educ* Eton; *m* 1952, (Elizabeth) Eve (d 1995), da of late Judge (Samuel Richard) Edgedale, QC, of Field Lodge, Crowthorne, Berks; 3 s, 1 da; *Heir* s, Hon Charles Harbord-Hamond; *Career* Maj Coldstream Gds (ret); served: WWII N Africa and Italy, Malaya 1948–50; memb Hon Corps of Gentlemen-at-Arms 1973–92, Harbinger 1990–92; watercolour artist; *Clubs* Army and Navy, Pratt's; *Style*— The Rt Hon the Lord Suffield, MC; ✉ Gardener's Cottage, Gunton Park, Hanworth, Norfolk NR11 7HL (tel 01263 768423)

SUFFOLK, Archdeacon of; *see:* Arrand, Ven Geoffrey William

SUFFOLK AND BERKSHIRE, Earl of, 21 of Suffolk (E 1603), 14 of Berkshire (E 1626); Michael John James George Robert Howard; also Viscount Andover and Baron Howard of Charlton (E 1622); s of 20 Earl (k on active serv 1941); the 1 Earl was 2 s of 4 Duke of Norfolk; the 9 Earl's w was mistress of George II, who built Marble Hill House, on the Thames between Twickenham and Richmond, for her (the style is Palladian, designed by Lord Pembroke); *b* 27 March 1935; *Educ* Winchester; Nat Serv: Navy; *m* 1, 1960 (m dis 1967), Mme Simone Paulmier, da of Georges Litman, of Paris; m 2, 1973 (m dis 1980), Anita Robsahm, da of Robin Robsahm Fuglesang (d 1991), of Cuckfield, W Sussex; 1 s (Alexander, Viscount Andover b 17 Sept 1974), 1 da (Lady Katharine b 9 April 1976); m 3, 1983, Linda Jacqueline, da of Col Vincent Paravicini and former w of 4 Viscount Bridport; 2 da (Lady Philippa b 1985, Lady Natasha b 28 March 1987); *Heir* s, Viscount Andover; *Style*— The Rt Hon the Earl of Suffolk and Berkshire

SUGAR, Sir Alan; kt (2000); *b* 24 March 1947; *m*; 2 s, 1 da; *Career* Amstrad plc: fndr 1968, chm and md until 2007; chm Tottenham Hotspur plc 1991–2001; dir BETACOM 1996–; appearances as chm of the bd The Apprentice (BBC2) 2005–; Hon DSc: City Univ Business Sch 1988, Brunel Univ 2005; Hon FCGI; *Style*— Sir Alan Sugar

SUGAR, Steven Charles; *Educ* St Peter's Sch York, Peterhouse Cambridge (BA), LSE (MSc), Coll of Law; *married*; *Career* slr and mediator; lectr in economics Univ of Bristol 1972–73, research asst Lib Party 1973–74, tutor LSE 1974–76; Frere Cholmeley Bischoff: articled clerk 1976–78, asst slr 1978–81, ptnr 1981–98, head Corporate Dept 1990–93, managing ptnr 1993–96; fndr ptnr Forsters 1998–2004 (conslt 2004–); CEDR accredited mediator 2004; *Style*— Steven Sugar, Esq; ✉ Forsters LLP, 31 Hill Street, London W1J 5LS (tel 0207 863 8333)

SUGAR, Vivienne; *Career* chief exec City and County of Swansea 1995–2002, memb Richard Cmmn 2002–04, chair Welsh Consumer Cncl 2003–, vice-pres Univ of Swansea 2005–; conslt to local govt and ODPM, ind advsr for Public Appts; Welsh advsr to Joseph Rowntree Fndn (JRF) 2005–; *Style*— Ms Vivienne Sugar; ✉ Welsh Consumer Council, 5th Floor, Longcross Court, 47 Newport Road, Cardiff CF24 0WL (tel 029 2025 5454, fax 029 2025 5464)

SUGDEN, Prof David Edward; s of John Cyril Gouldie Sugden (d 1963), and Patricia, *née* Backhouse; *b* 5 March 1941; *Educ* Warwick Sch, Univ of Oxford (BA, DPhil); *m* 9 Aug 1966, Britta Valborg, da of Harald Stridsberg, of Sweden; 2 s (John Peter, Michael Edward), 1 da (Pauline Charlotta); *Career* scientific offr Br Antarctic Survey 1965–66, lectr then reader Univ of Aberdeen 1966–87; Univ of Edinburgh: prof Dept of Geography 1987–, head Sch of GeoSciences 2003–06, actg dir SAGES (Scottish Alliance for Geoscience, Environment and Society) 2006–07; visiting prof Arctic and Alpine Inst USA; pres Inst of Br Geographers 1995; memb: Royal Scot Geographical Soc, Royal Geographical Soc, Royal Soc (Edinburgh); Polar Medal 2003; FRSE 1990; *Books* Glaciers and Landscape (with B S John, 1976), Arctic and Antarctic (1982), Geomorphology (with S Schumm and R J Chorley, 1986); *Recreations* hill walking, gardening, skiing; *Style*— Prof David Sugden, FRSE; ✉ Institute of Geography, University of Edinburgh, Drummond Street, Edinburgh EH8 9XP (tel 0131 650 7543, fax 0131 556 2524, e-mail des@geo.ed.ac.uk)

SUGDEN, Prof Robert; s of Frank Gerald Sugden (d 1987), and Kathleen, *née* Buckley (d 1999); *b* 26 August 1949; *Educ* Eston GS, Univ of York (BA, DLitt), UC Cardiff (MSc); *m* 26 March 1982, Christine Margaret, da of Leslie Kenneth Upton, of Woking, Surrey; 1 s (Joe b 1984), 1 da (Jane b 1986); *Career* lectr in economics Univ of York 1971–78, reader in economics Univ of Newcastle upon Tyne 1978–85, prof of economics UEA 1985–; FBA 1996; *Books* The Principles of Practical Cost-Benefit Analysis (with A Williams, 1978), The Political Economy of Public Choice (1981), The Economics of Rights, Cooperation and Welfare (1986); *Recreations* walking, gardening; *Style*— Prof Robert Sugden, FBA; ✉ School of Economics, University of East Anglia, Norwich NR4 7TJ (tel 01603 593423, fax 01603 250434, telex 975197, e-mail r.sugden@uea.ac.uk)

SUGGETT, Gavin Robert; s of Kenneth Frederick Suggett (d 1984), of Weybridge, Surrey, and Nancy, *née* Voss-Bark (d 2002); *b* 11 May 1944; *Educ* Felsted, Christ's Coll Cambridge (MA), London Business Sch (MSc); *m* 11 Sept 1971, Louise, da of Hon Lord Migdale (d 1983), of Edinburgh and Sutherland; 2 da (Clare b 1975, Katie b 1980), 1 s (Gordon b 1977); *Career* articled clerk Deloittes Chartered Accountants 1962–66, fin mangr Weir Group Ltd 1971–73; Alliance Trust plc: co sec 1973–89, dir 1987–2003, md 1994–2003, ret 2004; dep chm Assoc of Investment Tst Companies 1999–2001; FCA 1971; *Recreations* organic farming, keep fit, hill walking; *Clubs* New (Edinburgh); *Style*— Gavin Suggett, Esq; ✉ Creich Organic Farm, Mill of Forneth, Blairgowrie, Perthshire PH10 6SP (tel 01350 724220)

SUIRDALE, Viscount; John Michael James Hely-Hutchinson; er s and h of 8 Earl of Donoughmore; *b* 7 August 1952; *Educ* Harrow; *m* 1977 (m dis 2006), Marie-Claire, da of Gerard van den Driessche (d 1985); 2 da (Hon Marie-Pierre Joanna b 1978, Hon Tatiana Louise b 1985), 1 s (Hon Richard Gregory b 1980); *Heir* s, Hon Richard Hely-Hutchinson; *Career* co dir; *Recreations* golf, fishing; *Style*— Viscount Suirdale; ✉ A504, Gilbert Scott Building, Putney, London SW15 3SG

SULLIVAN, Hon Mr Justice; Sir Jeremy Mirth Sullivan; kt (1997); s of late Arthur Brian Sullivan, and Pamela Jean, *née* Kendall; *b* 17 September 1945; *Educ* Framlingham Coll, KCL (LLB, LLM); *m* 1, 1970 (m dis), Ursula Klara Marie, da of late Benno August Friederich Hildenbrock; 2 s (Richard b 1974, Geoffrey b 1976); m 2, 1993, Dr Sandra Jean Farmer, da of late Allan Stuart Fisher; 2 step s; *Career* 2 Lt Suffolk & Cambs Regt (TA) 1963–65; called to the Bar Inner Temple 1968 (bencher 1993); lectr in law City of London Poly 1968–71, in practice Planning & Local Govt Bar 1971–97, QC 1982, recorder 1989–97, dep judge of the High Court 1993–97, judge of the High Court of Justice (Queen's Bench Div) 1997–; attorney-gen to the Prince of Wales 1994–97; chm Tbnls Ctee Judicial Studies Bd 1999–2007, dep chm Parly Boundary Cmmn for England 2004–, memb Parly Bar 1990–97 (hon memb 1997–); memb Cncl RTPI 1983–87, memb Exec Ctee Georgian Gp 1985–89, govr Highgate Sch 1990–2003; LAMTPI 1970, LMRTPI 1976; *Recreations* the Wotton Light Railway; *Style*— The Hon Mr Justice Sullivan; ✉ Royal Courts of Justice, Strand, London WC2A 2LL

SULLIVAN, Michael Francis; s of Sir Richard Benjamin Magniac Sullivan, 8 Bt (d 1977), and Muriel Mary Paget Pineo (d 1988); *b* 4 April 1936; *Educ* St Andrew Coll, Clare Coll Cambridge (MA, MB BChir), St Mary's Hosp London; *m* 1, 22 Aug 1957 (m dis 1978), Inger, da of Arne Mathieson (d 1984); 1 s (Richard b 9 Jan 1961), 1 da (Nicola b 20 Aug 1965); m 2, 22 Dec 1978, Caroline Mary, da of Maj Christopher Griffin (d 1994); 1 da (Lucy b 22 Nov 1980); *Career* spinal surgn Royal Nat Orthopaedic Hosp London 1971–; visiting lectr in spinal surgery: Australia 1985, South Africa 1981, USA 1980, Canada 1982, Japan 1989, most European countries 1989–99; author of numerous articles on spinal surgery; pres European Spinal Surgns 1990–91, sec Int Lumbar Spine Surgns 1975–78; FRCS; *Recreations* cricket, sailing, shooting, golf; *Clubs* MCC, Royal Harwich Yacht, Royal Workington and Newmarket Golf; *Style*— Michael Sullivan, Esq; ✉ 12 Gloucester Crescent, London NW1 7DS (tel 020 7485 4473); The Old Hall, Worlington, Suffolk IP28 8RX (tel 01638 716664)

SULLMAN, Tony Frederick; s of Bernard Frederick Sullman, of Stafford, and Joan, *née* Wells; *b* 7 September 1954; *m* 23 Aug 1985, Freddie, *née* Roberts; 1 s (Andrew Frederick b 13 Nov 1990); *Career* RAF 1971–76, property devpt business 1975–77, serv Sultan of Oman's Air Force (decorated 3 times) 1977–81, franchisee Intacab Ltd 1982–87, purchased KLM Ltd 1987–89, resided Spain 1989–90, fndr franchise gp Somerford Claims plc 1990, fndr franchise gp Claims Direct 1995, fndr Medical Legal Support Services 1996; chief exec: Claims Direct plc (formerly Somerford Claims plc), Medical Legal Support Services; *Recreations* reading law, playing poker, avoiding tax; *Style*— Tony Sullman, Esq; ✉ Claims Direct plc, Grosvenor House, Central Park, Telford TF2 9TU (tel 01952 284800, fax 01952 284801, e-mail tsullman@claims-direct.co.uk)

SULTOON, Jeffrey Alan; s of Maurice Sultoon, of London, and Babette, *née* Braun; *b* 8 October 1953; *Educ* Haberdashers' Aske's, St Edmund Hall Oxford; *m* 11 May 1985, Vivien Caryl, da of Peter Woodbridge, of Guildford, Surrey; 1 s (Hugh); *Career* admitted slr 1978; slr Freshfields 1978–81, ptnr Ashurst Morris Crisp (now Ashurst) 1986– (slr 1981–86); memb Company Law Ctee Law Soc; *Books* Tolley's Company Law (contrib); *Style*— Jeffrey Sultoon, Esq; ✉ Ashurst, Broadwalk House, 5 Appold Street, London EC2A 2HA (tel 020 7638 1111, fax 020 7638 1112, e-mail jeffrey.sultoon@ashursts.com)

SUMBERG, David Anthony Gerald; MEP (Cons) NW England; s of late Joshua Sumberg, and Lorna Sumberg; *b* 2 June 1941; *Educ* Tettenhall Coll Wolverhampton, Coll of Law London; *m* 1972, Carolyn Franks; 1 s, 1 da; *Career* formerly slr; MP (Cons) Bury S 1983–97 (Parly candidate (Cons) Manchester Wythenshawe 1979); PPS to Sir Patrick Mayhew as Attorney-Gen 1986–90; memb Select Ctee: on Home Affairs 1991–92, on Foreign Affrs 1992–97; memb Lord Chllr's Advsy Ctee on Public Records 1992–97; cnsllr Manchester City Cncl 1982–84; MEP (Cons) NW England 1999–; currently dir The Parliamentary Forum Ltd; *Recreations* family and friends; *Style*— David Sumberg, Esq, MEP; ✉ c/o North West Conservatives, 14b Montford Enterprise Centre, Wynford Square, Salford M50 2SN (tel 0161 736 6571, fax 0161 736 5519, e-mail office@northwestconservatives.com)

SUMMERFIELD, Gordon Caleb; CBE (2000); s of Donald Caleb Summerfield (d 1994), and Mary, *née* Ritson (d 1989); *b* 16 December 1939; *Educ* Wellingborough GS; *m* 23 Sept 1961, (Margaret) Anita, da of William Lewis Williams; 1 s (Mark Caleb b 21 Aug 1962), 1 da (Kay b 31 Oct 1964); *Career* mgmnt trainee rising to md Dale Farm Foods Northern Foods plc 1960–86, prodn dir St Ivel plc 1986–89, md Unigate Dairies 1989–91; Unigate plc: md Dairy Gp 1991–94, chief exec Unigate European Foods 1994–2000, non-exec chm Pirtek Europe Ltd 1995–2001, chm Hilton Food Gp plc 2003–; non-exec dir Arla Foods (UK) plc (formerly Express Dairies) 2002–07; pres Dairy Industry Fedn 1996–99, chm Food from Britain 2000–05; tstee Trehane Tst 1995–2007; Prince of Wales Ambassadors Award 1996; *Recreations* aviation, walking, reading, family; *Style*— Gordon Summerfield, Esq; ✉ Hilton Food Group plc, The Interchange, Latham Road, Huntingdon, Cambridgeshire PE29 6YE (tel 01480 383333, fax 01480 387241)

SUMMERFIELD, Linda Victoria (Lin); da of Henry Conrad Fullbrook (d 1952), and Rose Iris, *née* Hollings (d 1991); *b* 24 February 1952; *Educ* Sudbury HS for Girls; *Children* 1 da (Fiona Ruth); *Career* author; works published incl: Count the Days (1989, shortlisted for John Creasey prize), Never Walk Behind Me (1990), Taken by a Stranger (US, 1995); various short stories; *Recreations* reading, walking, sketching, opera, worrying; *Style*— Ms Lin Summerfield; ✉ 24 Butt Road, Great Cornard, Sudbury, Suffolk CO10 0DS; c/o Heather Jeeves, 9 Dryden Place, Edinburgh EH9 1RP (tel and fax 0131 668 3859)

SUMMERFIELD, Spencer Robert; s of Robert Edward Summerfield (d 1991), and Lilian Rose Summerfield; *b* 25 February 1965, Romford, Essex; *Educ* Chigwell Sch, Gonville & Caius Coll Cambridge (MA); *m* 27 August 1994, Karen, *née* Esler; 1 s (Louis Robert b 29 Jan 2001), 1 da (Abigail Catherine b 13 Aug 2002); *Career* Travers Smith Braithwaite (now Travers Smith): joined 1987, ptnr 1997–, head of corp finance 2003–; memb Law Soc 1989; *Publications* Tolley's Company Law (contrib); *Recreations* aerobics, family, cinema; *Style*— Spencer Summerfield, Esq; ✉ Travers Smith, 10 Snow Hill, London EC1A 2AL (tel 020 7295 3229, fax 020 7295 3500, e-mail spencer.summerfield@traverssmith.com)

SUMMERS, Andrew William Graham; CMG (2001); s of Basil Summers (d 1988), and Margaret, *née* Hunt; *b* 19 June 1946; *Educ* Mill Hill Sch (exhibitioner), Fitzwilliam Coll Cambridge, Harvard Business Sch (ISMP); *m* 1971, Frances, *née* Halestrap; 2 da (Sarah b 1974, Kate b 1976), 1 s (Bennet b 1979); *Career* economist CBC Bank Sydney 1968, salesman rising to brand mangr Ranks Hovis McDougall plc 1968–75, md J A Sharwood & Co 1980–85 (mktg mangr then mktg dir 1975–80), md RHM Foods Ltd 1987–90 (commercial dir 1986–87), chief exec Management Charter Initiative 1991–94, chief exec Design Council 1995–2003, chm Brandsmiths 2003–06, chm Design Partners 2004–, chm Companies House 2007–; non-exec dir S Daniels plc 1991–2002, dir Whitybird Ltd 2005–; chm: Euro Trade Ctee DTI 1986–99, RSA Migration Cmmn 2004–06, Int Advsy Bd Hong Kong Design Centre 2004–07; memb: Food from Britain Export Cncl 1982–86, BOTB 1998–99, British Trade International 1999–2003, Advsy Cncl Design Mgmnt Inst USA 1998–, Bd Small Business Serv 2000–07, Advsy Bd VSO 2004–06; dep pres RSA 2003–, Quality Assurance Agency for HE 2005–; adjunct prof Hong Kong Poly Univ 2004–; govr Conservatoire for Dance and Drama 2005–; pres OM Eton Fives Club 2004–, chm Friends of St Mary's Barnes 2000–; Hon DLitt Univ of Westminster; FRSA 1991, CCMI 1997 (memb Bd of Companions 2007–); *Recreations* cooking, theatre; *Style*— Andrew Summers, Esq, CMG; ✉ 114 Station Road, London SW13 0NB (tel and fax 020 8876 6719, e-mail andrew@andrewsummers.co.uk)

SUMMERS, Brian; *b* 1945; *Career* trainee then public finance accountant West Bromwich CBC 1964–73, asst county treas West Midlands CC 1975–84 (chief accountant 1973–75); Birmingham International Airport: joined as commercial dir 1984, financial dir (following company formation) 1987–90, dep md 1990–94, md 1994–2003; chm Tourism West Midlands; memb Cncl/Bd: Birmingham C of C, West Midlands Regnl Assembly, RegencoSandwell, Matthew Boulton Coll; Hon Dr Univ of Central England 2006; *Recreations* West Bromwich Albion FC, sport generally; *Style*— Brian Summers, Esq; ✉ e-mail brian@wal-cott.freeserve.co.uk

SUMMERS, David Lewis; JP (1998); s of Maj Lewis Summers (d 1948), and Beatrice, *née* Greenaway; *b* 25 November 1941; *Educ* Mundella Sch Nottingham, St Edmund Hall Oxford (MA), Univ of Bristol, Harvard Business Sch; *m* 24 Dec 1966, Veronica Yvonne Elizabeth, da of Cyril Clarence King (d 1970); 2 s (Jonathan b 1971, Benjamin b 1973); *Career* RN Lt 1963–66; Longmans 1966–69, Butterworths 1969–97 (sometime dep chm and UK chief exec), dir Royal Society of Medicine Press 1997–2003, publishing conslt 1997–, chm Wilmington plc 2005– (non-exec dir 2001–), former dir Reed Elsevier (UK) Ltd; ed Where to Publish in Law 1998, also contrib various chapters to professional pubns; lay memb Restrictive Practices Court 1999; memb: Competition Cmmn 2000–03, Competition Appeal Tbnl 2003–, Lord Chllr's Advsy Ctee for Kent 2002–; chm of govrs St Bede's Sch Sussex; tstee Kraszna-Krausz Fndn 1998–; Freeman City of London 1988, Liveryman Worshipful Co of Stationers & Newspaper Makers 1989; *Recreations* tennis, learning Finnish; *Clubs* Garrick; *Style*— David Summers, Esq; ✉ Fir Tree Farm, Golford Road, Cranbrook, Kent TN17 3NW (tel and fax 01580 715424)

SUMMERS, Jonathan; *b* 2 October 1946; *Educ* Macleod HS Melbourne Aust, Prahan Tech Coll Melbourne; *m* 29 March 1969, Lesley; 3 c; *Career* baritone; professional debut singing title role in Rigoletto (Kent Opera under Roger Norrington, dir Jonathan Miller) 1975, ENO debut as Tonio in I Pagliacci 1976, Royal Opera House debut as Killian in Der Freischütz 1977; princ Royal Opera Co 1976–86; has performed with: Orchestre de Paris, Berlin Philharmonic, Orchestre Symphonie de Montreal, Sydney Symphony Orch, Melbourne Symphony Orch, most leading Br orchs; Green Room Theatre award for leading male artist (Melbourne Australia) 1988; *Performances* roles incl: title role in Macbeth (ENO) 1990, Figaro in Le Nozze di Figaro (Bavarian Staatsoper) 1990, Marcello in La Bohème (Covent Garden 1990, Chicago Lyric Opera 1993, Nat Theatre Munich 1993, Theâtre du Capitole Toulouse 1995), Grand Prêtre in Samson and Dalila (Covent Garden) 1991 and 1992, Balstrode in Peter Grimes (ENO) 1991, Iago in Otello (Opera Australia Sydney) 1991, Ford in Falstaff (Theâtre du Capitole Toulouse 1991 and 1995, Theâtre Municipale Lausanne 1995), Rodrigo in Don Carlos (ENO) 1992, Don Carlos in The Force of Destiny (ENO) 1992 and 1995, title role in Rigoletto (ENO and Bergen Festival) 1993, Anckarstroem in Un Ballo in Maschera (Opera Australia Melbourne) 1993, Zurga in The Pearl Fishers (ENO) 1994, De Siriex in Fedora (Covent Garden and Chicago Lyric Opera) 1994, Père Germont in La Traviata (Opera Australia Sydney) 1994, Michele in Il Tabarro (Opera Australia Sydney) 1995, title role in Nabucco (WNO 1995 and Opera Australia Melbourne 1996), Kurwenal in Tristan und Isolde (ENO) 1996, title role in Falstaff (Opera Australia Sydney) 1996, Simone Trovai in Korngold's Violanta (Opera North at BBC Proms) 1997, Amonasro in Aida (Opera North) 1997, Iago in Otello (Royal Opera Royal Festival Hall) 1997, Scarpia in Tosca (Spier Festival Cape Town) 1998, Père Germent in La Traviata (WNO & New Israeli Opera Tel Aviv) 1998, title role in Rigoletto (Opera Australia Sydney) 1998, Scarpia in Tosca (Bühnen der Stadt Cologne) 1998, Amfortas in Parsifal (ENO) 1999, Kurvenal in Tristan and Isolde (WNO) 1999, title role in Wozzeck (Opera Australia Sydney) 1999, Balstrode in Peter Grimes (ENO) 1999, title role in Rigoletto (New Israeli Opera Tel Aviv) 2000, Barnaba in La Gioconda (Opera North) 2000, title role in Simon Boccanegra (Opera Australia Sydney) 2000, title role in Wozzeck (Opera Australia Melbourne) 2000 (Opera Male Singer in a Principal Role Green Room Theatre Awards Victoria), Père Germent in La Traviata (WNO) 2001, Balstrode in Peter Grimes (Opera Australia Sydney) 2001, Die Winterreise (Sydney and Melbourne) 2001, Amfortas in Parsifal (State Opera of South Australia Adelaide) 2001 (Best Male Performer in an Opera Helpmann Awards), Pere Germont in La Traviata (New Israeli Opera Tel Aviv) 2001, Balstrode in Peter Grimes (Theatre du Capitole Toulouse) 2002, Prus in Vec Makropulos (Houston Grand Opera) 2002, Scarpia in Tosca (Buhnen der Stadt Cologne) 2002, Alfio in Cavalleria Rusticana, Tonio in I Pagliacci and Scarpia in Tosca (Opera Australia Sydney) 2002 (Best Supporting Male Performer in an Opera Helpmann Awards), Alfio in Cavalleria Rusticana and Tonio in I Pagliacci (WNO) 2003, Kurvenal in Tristan & Isolde (WNO) 2003, Iago in Otello (Opera Australia Sydney) 2003, Scarpia in Tosca (Opera Australia Melbourne) 2003, Hollander in Der Fliegender Hollander (Opera Australia Sydney) 2004, Malatesta in Francesca da Rimini, Michele in Il Tabarro and Tonio in I Pagliacci (all Opera North) 2004, Gunter in Götterdämmerung State Opera of South Australia Adelaide) 2004, Pere Germont in La Traviata and title role in Rigoletto (both WNO) 2005 Klinghoffer in The Death of Klinghoffer (Edinburgh Festival) 2005, Pere Germont in La Traviata (Israeli Opera Tel Aviv) 2005, Ezio in Attila (Chelsea Opera Group) 2006, Renato in Un Ballo in Maschera (The Israeli Opera Tel Aviv) 2006, Alfio in Cavalleria Rusticana (Hamburg Staats Oper) 2006, Tonio in I Pagliacci (Hamburg Staats Oper) 2006, title role in Rigoletto (Opera North) 2006 and 2007 (also Opera Australia Sydney 2006), The Tempest (ROH) 2007; concert repertoire incl: Mendelssohn Elijah, Fauré Requiem, Brahms Requiem, Elgar The Kingdom, The Apostles and The Dream of Gerontius, Orff Carmina Burana, Vaughan Williams Sea Symphony, Mahler Das Knaben Wunderhorn, Delius A Mass of Life, Berlioz L'enfance du Christ, Britten War Requiem; *Recordings* incl: Peter Grimes (Grammy Award 1979), Samson et Dalila, La Bohème (as Leoncavallo), The Bohemian Girl, Carmina Burana, Sea Symphony, Gloriana 1993; videos incl: Samson et Dalila, Der Rosenkavalier, Il Trovatore, Nabucco (with Opera Australia); *Style*— Jonathan Summers, Esq; ✉ website www.jonathansummers.co.uk

SUMMERS, Sue; *Educ* Queen's Coll London, Univ of Bristol (BA); *m* 1, 1979 (m dis 1989), Rod Allen; m 2, Philip Norman; 1 da (Jessica Rose b 22 Nov 1990); *Career* journalist and TV prodr; grad trainee Thomson Regional Newspapers, trainee reporter Reading Evening Post, TV and film corr Screen International, TV ed London Evening Standard, ed screen pages Sunday Times, asst ed (arts) London Daily News, ed 7 Days magazine Sunday Telegraph, freelance writer and broadcaster, co-creative head Finestripe Prodns Ltd; contrib incl: The Observer, Daily Mail, Telegraph Magazine, Radio Times; co-prodr Child of the Death Camps: Truth or Lies, Inside Story (BBC1) 1999, creator Break Up (Channel 4) 1999, prodr Why Men Leave (Channel 4) 2000, co-prodr Touching the Void (winner Best British Film BAFTA 2004), prodr Shrink Rap with Dr Pamela Connelly (More4) 2007; memb: Bafta, Broadcasting Press Guild, Pearson TV Theatre Writers' Award Scheme; *Style*— Ms Sue Summers; ✉ tel 020 7431 6224, fax 020 7433 1666, e-mail sue@finestripe.com

SUMMERTON, Edward James; s of Edward Summerton, of Dundee, and Zenna, *née* Dodds; *b* 9 February 1962; *Educ* Kirkton HS Dundee, Duncan of Jordanstone Coll of Art (BA, MA); *m* Sept 1989, Rosalie, da of Ronald Dow; 1 s (Joseph Daniel b Oct 1991), 1 da (Jasmine Sylvia Zenna b Oct 1993); *Career* lectr in drawing and painting Edinburgh Coll of Art 1990–92, lectr in fine art Duncan of Jordanstone Coll of Art 1993–; visiting artist: Univ of Calif Berkeley, Clermont Ferrand; professional memb Soc of Scottish Artists 1994, ARSA 1996; *Solo Exhibitions* Compass Gallery Glasgow, Clermont Ferrand Art Sch France, RSA Edinburgh, MacRobert Art Centre Stirling, Meffan Inst Forfar, Raw Gallery London, Bird of the Devil (ET4U Art Centre Denmark) 2006, The Rural (Edinburgh Printmakers) 2006; *Group Exhibitions* incl: Lion Rampant (Artspace San Francisco), Metropolis (RAAB Gallery Berlin), Contemporary Scottish Art (Lincoln Art Centre NY), Compass Contribution (Tramway Glasgow), New Contemporaries (Christie's London), Celtic Connections (Glasgow Royal Concert Hall), International Showcase (Limner Gallery NY), Guilding the Summer Town (Royal Scottish Acad Edinburgh) 2005, Blind Sight (Titamk Turku) 2005, Doctor Skin (Perth Museum) 2006; *Awards* Elizabeth Greenshields Award Canada 1986, artists' exchange between Scotland and France 1987, Alistair Salvesen Award 1989, RSA Latimer Award 1993 and 1994, RSA Gillies Bequest 1997; *Publications* Edward Summerton - North of Normal (catalogue, 1996), Line Controller (artist's book, 1998), Guilding the Summer Town (catalogue, 2006), Bird of the Devil (artist's book, 2006); *Recreations* getting lost; *Style*— Edward Summerton, Esq; ✉ Department of Fine Art, Duncan of Jordanstone College of Art, University of Dundee (tel 01382 223261, fax 01382 200983)

SUMMERTON, Dr Neil William; CB (1997); s of Hila Summerton (d 1975), and Nancy Summerton (d 1975); *b* 5 April 1942; *Educ* Wellington GS, KCL (BA, PhD); *m* 1965, Pauline, *née* Webb; 2 s (Ian b 1968, Matthew b 1970); *Career* asst princ Miny of Tport 1966–69, asst sec KCL 1971–74 (PA to princ 1969–71); DOE: princ 1974–78, asst sec 1978–85, under sec Land Use Planning 1985–88, under sec Local Govt Fin Policy 1988–91, under sec Water Directorate 1991–95, dir Water and Land 1996–97; supernumerary fell Mansfield Coll Oxford 1997–2003 (now emeritus), dir Oxford Centre for the Environment, Ethics and Society 1997–2002, dir Oxford Centre for Water Research 1998–2002; Partnership (UK) Ltd: dir 1994–, chm 1997– (exec chm 2005–), exec sec 1997–2002, exec dir 2002–05; non-exec dir: Redland Bricks Ltd 1988–91, North Surrey Water Ltd 1998–2000, Folkestone & Dover Water Services Ltd 1998–, Three Valleys Water plc 2000–; dir and tstee various Christian charities; *Publications* A Noble Task: Eldership and Ministry in the Local Church (revised edn 1994); various articles on historical, ethical, environmental and theological subjects; *Style*— Dr Neil Summerton, CB

SUMNER, Dr Ann Beatrice; da of late Tim Sumner, and Rita Sumner, of Lansdown, Bath; *b* 15 July 1960; *Educ* The Royal Sch Bath, Kingswood Sch Bath, Courtauld Inst London (BA), Newnham Coll Cambridge (PhD); *m* (m dis); 2 da; *Career* archive asst Nat Portrait Gallery London 1984–85, asst curator Holburne of Menstrie Museum Univ of Bath 1985–88, res asst Whitworth Art Gallery Univ of Manchester 1988–89, pt/t curator Museum of Farnham 1991–92, successively keeper then research fell Dulwich Picture Gallery 1992–95, sr curator Harewood House Tst 1994–96, keeper of art Holburne of Menstrie Museum Bath 1996–2000, head of fine art Nat Museum & Gallery of Wales Cardiff 2000–07, dir Barber Inst of Fine Arts Univ of Birmingham 2007–; tstee Methodist Art Collection, memb Ctee Nat Inventory of European Paintings Nat Gallery London; author of numerous art historical articles and pamphlets, regular lectr and contrib to academic seminars and confs; *Exhibition Catalogues* Gainsborough in Bath - A Bicentenary Exhibition (1988), Rembrandt's Girl at a Window (1993), Death, Passion and Politics: Van Dyck and the Digbys (jtly, 1995), Harewood Masterpieces: Watercolours by Turner, Girtin and Varley (jtly), Secret Passion for Noble Fashion: the World of the Portrait Miniature (jtly, 1999), A Classical Vision: the art of Thomas Cromek (jtly, 2000), John Brett A Pre-Raphaelite on the Shores of Wales (jtly, 2001), Thomas Jones (1742–1803): An Artist Rediscovered (jt ed, 2003), Colour and Light: 50 Impressionist Paintings at the National Museum of Wales (2005), Faces of Wales (2006), Things of Beauty (jtly, 2007); *Recreations* tennis,theatre, cinema; *Clubs* Lansdown Lawn Tennis; *Style*— Dr Ann Sumner; ✉ Barber Institute of Fine Arts, University of Birmingham, Edgbaston, Birmingham B15 2TS (tel 0121 414 7333, e-mail a.b.sumner@bham.ac.uk)

SUMNER, Bernard; *b* 4 January 1956; *Educ* Salford GS; *Career* fndr memb and guitarist Joy Division 1978–79, formed New Order (after death of Joy Division singer Ian Curtis) 1980, debut performance The Beach Club Manchester 1980, major tours of the USA 1986, 1987 and 1989; completed solo project alongside Johnny Marr and the Pet Shop Boys with release of album Electronic 1991 (debut performance Electronic 1990); currently involved with Electronic; Blue Monday best selling 12 inch single of all time; *Albums* with Joy Division: Unknown Pleasures (1978), Closer (1979); with New Order: Movement (1981), Power, Corruption and Lies (1983), Low-Life (1985), Brotherhood (1986), Substance (1987), Technique (1989), Republic (1993), Get Ready (2001), Back To Mine (2002); *Recreations* skiing, yachting, clubs; *Style*— Bernard Sumner

SUMNER, Hon Mr Justice; Sir Christopher John Sumner; kt (1996); s of His Hon (William) Donald Massey Sumner, OBE, QC (d 1990), and Muriel Kathleen, *née* Wilson (d 1992); *b* 28 August 1939; *Educ* Charterhouse, Sidney Sussex Coll Cambridge (MA); *m* 24 Sept 1970, Carole Ashley, da of John Ashley Mann (d 1985), and Alison Mann (d 2006); 2 da (Claire Louise (Mrs White) b 6 Sept 1972, Emma Jane (Mrs Jackaman) b 29 Oct 1974), 1 s (William Mark b 30 Nov 1978); *Career* called to the Bar Inner Temple 1961 (bencher 1994); recorder 1983–87, circuit judge (SE Circuit) 1987–96, judge of the High Court of Justice (Family Div) 1996–; memb Judicial Studies Bd 1991–96 and 1999–2005, dir of studies 1995–96; *Clubs* Hurlingham, Burnham Overy Staithe Sailing; *Style*— The Hon Mr Justice Sumner; ✉ The Royal Courts of Justice, Strand, London WC2A 2LL

SUMNER, Christopher Kent; s of George Tomlinson Sumner (d 1979), and Alice Mary Bettley Sumner, *née* Brown (d 1989); *b* 28 September 1943; *Educ* The King's Sch Chester, Univ of Durham (BA, MA); *m* 3 Aug 1967, Marjorie (d 2005), da of George Prince (d 1994); 2 s (Stuart b 1970, Edward b 1974); *Career* slr; HM coroner for Merseyside (Sefton, St Helens and Knowsley districts) 1998–; chm: Social Security Appeal Tbnls 1984–2006, Disability Appeal Tbnls 1992–2006; Parly candidate (Lib) Runcorn 1970; pres Southport and Ormskirk Law Soc 1994; *Recreations* scouting; *Clubs* Rotary, Hillside Golf; *Style*— Christopher K Sumner, Esq; ✉ 4 Mossgiel Avenue, Ainsdale, Southport PR8 2RE (tel 01704 573153, e-mail christopher.sumner@btinternet.com)

SUMNER, Francis Ian; s of Guy Chadwick Sumner (d 1986), and Margaret Hilliard, *née* Wilson (d 1995); *b* 25 October 1942; *Educ* Tonbridge; *m* 29 Dec 1978, Diana Harriman, da of John Ernest Newman; 2 s (Edward John b 18 Nov 1979, Richard William b 12 May 1981), 1 da (Nicola Margaret b 6 Dec 1983); *Career* asst slr Slaughter & May 1966–72 (articled clerk 1961–66); Norton Rose: asst slr 1972–73, ptnr 1973–97, conslt 1997–98; dir: Crown Agents 1992– (dep chm 1998–), Bankers Investment Tst plc 1997–; memb Cncl: City & Guilds of London Inst 1998– (vice-chm 2004–), Assessment and Qualifications Alliance 1998– (vice-chm 2006–); Freeman City of London Solicitors' Co; memb: IOD, Law Soc; Hon FCGI 2003; *Recreations* golf, gardening, fishing, shooting; *Style*— Francis Sumner, Esq; ✉ tel 01732 462337, fax 01732 457419

SUMNERS, Dr David George; s of George William Sumners, of London, and Irene Florence, *née* Kelly; *b* 23 September 1952; *Educ* William Ellis Sch, UCL (BSc, MB BS); *m* 12 June 1976, Susan Mary, da of late Thomas Arthur Bourn; 1 da (Emily Mary b 23 March 1982), 1 s (William David b 28 Feb 1985); *Career* conslt psychiatrist: Edgware Gen Hosp and Napsbury Hosp 1988–92, Grovelands Priory Hosp 1988–; dir NW Thames RHA Brain Injury Rehabilitation Unit 1988–92, med dir Barnet Healthcare NHS Tst 1992–, conslt forensic psychiatrist Kneesworth House Hosp 1992–94, conslt Brain Injury Rehabilitation Tst 1994–, med examiner GMC 2001–; FRCPsych 2001 (MRCPsych 1983); *Style*— Dr David Sumners; ✉ Hertfordshire Partnership NHS Trust, St Albans, Hertfordshire AL3 5JB (tel 01727 834330, fax 01727 834182)

SUMPTION, Jonathan Philip Chadwick; OBE, QC (1986); s of Anthony James Sumption, DSC, and Hedy, *née* Hedigan; *b* 9 December 1948; *Educ* Eton, Magdalen Coll Oxford (MA); *m* 26 June 1971, Teresa Mary, da of Jerome Bernard Whelan; 2 da (Frederique b

1979, Madeleine b 1983), 1 s (Bernard b 1981); *Career* fell Magdalen Coll Oxford 1971–75; called to the Bar Inner Temple 1975 (bencher 1990); judge Courts of Appeal Jersey and Guernsey 1995–, judicial appts cmmr 2006–; tstee Royal Acad of Music 2002–; *Books* Pilgrimage An Image of Medieval Religion (1975), The Albigensian Crusade (1978), The Hundred Years War (vol 1, 1990, vol 2, 1999); *Recreations* music, history; *Style*— Jonathan Sumption, Esq, OBE, QC; ✉ Brick Court Chambers, 7–8 Essex Street, London WC2R 3LD (tel 020 7379 3550, fax 020 7379 3558)

SUNDERLAND, Adam Philip Rothwell; s of Henry Sunderland, of Doncaster, S Yorks, and Marjorie, *née* Rothwell (d 1990); *b* 13 December 1958; *Educ* Oundle, Doncaster GS, The Queen's Coll Oxford (MA); *m* Laura; 1 da (Ella), 1 s (Benjamin); *Career* Ogilvy & Mather Advertising: account exec London 1980–81, account exec NY 1981–84, account supr NY 1984–85, vice-pres/account supr NY 1985–86; vice-pres and memb Exec Ctee Saunders Lubinski and White Advertising Dallas 1986–87, vice-pres/mgmnt supr Ogilvy & Mather Advertising USA 1987–90; Woollams Moira Gaskin O'Malley: bd account dir 1990–92, client servs dir 1992–94, dep md 1994–95; managing ptnr White Door 1997–2004, md Breed Communications Ltd 2005–; *Recreations* golf, tennis, skiing, travel; *Clubs* RAC; *Style*— Adam Sunderland, Esq; ✉ Breed, 67–69 Whitfield Street, London W1T 4HF (tel 020 7462 7888, fax 020 7462 7965, e-mail adam@breedcommunications.com)

SUNDERLAND, Alistair John; s of Dr Robert Slater Sunderland, and Marion, *née* Wilson; *b* 24 March 1949; *Educ* Lewis' Sch for Boys, Liverpool Poly; *m* Glenys, da of Gwylim Thomas; 2 s (Adam Thomas, Geraint John), 2 da (Sian Marion, Rhian Alice); *Career* ptnr Austin-Smith: Lord 1974–; chair Liverpool Urban Design and Conservation Advsy Panel; memb: Bd S Liverpool Housing, Cncl Tate Liverpool, Bd Liverpool Biennial; RIBA: memb 1978–, memb Nat Cncl, memb NW Branch; *Recreations* swimming; *Clubs* Liverpool Architectural Soc (past pres), Long Lane Church; *Style*— Alistair Sunderland, Esq; ✉ Austin-Smith: Lord, Port of Liverpool Building, Pier Head, Liverpool L3 1BY

SUNDERLAND, Prof Eric; CBE (2005, OBE 1999), JP (1999); s of Leonard Sunderland (d 1990), and Mary Agnes, *née* Davies (d 1997); *b* 18 March 1930; *Educ* Amman Valley GS, UCW Aberystwyth (BA, MA), UCL (PhD); *m* 19 Oct 1957, (Jean) Patricia, da of George Albert Watson (d 1972), of Cardiff; 2 da (Rowena, Frances); *Career* res scientist NCB 1957–58; Univ of Durham: lectr in anthropology 1958–66, sr lectr 1966–71, prof 1971–84, pro-vice-chllr 1979–84; princ and vice-chllr UCNW Bangor 1984–95, vice-chllr Univ of Wales 1989–91 (emeritus prof 1995–), pres Univ of Wales Lampeter 1998–2002; sec gen Int Union of Anthropological and Ethnological Scis 1978–98 (pres 1998–2003); chm: Local Govt Boundary Cmmn of Wales 1994–2001, Environment Agency's Advsy Ctee for Wales 1996–2001; chm: Welsh Language Educn Devpt Ctee 1987–94, Wetlands for Wales Project Environment Agency 2001–, CILT Cymru (Centre for Info on Language Teaching and Res); memb: Welsh Language Bd 1988–93, Ct of Govrs Nat Museum of Wales 1991–94, Broadcasting Cncl for Wales (BBC) 1996–2000, Main Bd Br Cncl 1996–2001 (memb Welsh Advsy Ctee 1990–2001 (chm 1996–2001)); chm Gregynog Press Bd 1991–, chm of dirs William Mathias Music Centre 1995–2005, patron Artworks Wales (Cywaith Cymru) 2002–, area pres Scouting Assoc Anglesey Conwy and Gwynedd 2002–,, pres Army Benevolent Fund Gwynedd 2002–, chm Bd Welsh Chamber Orch 2003–, regnl chm Wales The Art Fund 2006– (rep NW Wales branch 1999–), vice-pres Welsh Music Guild 2005–, chm Menai Bridge Community Heritage Tst 2005–, pres Anglesey branch SSAFA 2005–; chief counting offr referendum on Welsh devolution 1997, chm Cmmn on Electoral Arrangements (for Welsh Assembly) 2001–2002, vice-patron Atlantic Cncl of the UK 2002–; pres N Wales Branch Inst of Biology 2005–; chm of tstees Trintiy Fndn Prog Univ of Dublin 2002–; vice-pres Gwynedd Branch Gt Ormond St Hosp Appeal 1988; patron Schizophrenia Assoc GB 1985–; Hrdlička Medal for Anthropological Research 1976, The Mahatma Gandhi Freedom Award (Coll of William & Mary Virginia) 1989; hon memb Gorsedd of Bards Royal Nat Eisteddfod of Wales 1985; hon fell: Croatian Anthropological Soc (Gorjanovic-Krambergeri Medal), Univ of Wales Lampeter 1995 (pres 1998–2002), Univ of Wales Bangor 1996 (pres Bangor Univ Fndn 2000–); Hon LLD Univ of Wales 1997; High Sheriff Gwynedd 1998–99, HM Lord-Lt Gwynedd 1999–2006 (DL 1998); Liveryman Welsh Livery Guild 2001–; Queen's Golden Jubilee Medal 2002; memb: RAI (hon sec 1978–85, hon treas 1985–89, pres 1989–91), SSHB, Biosocial Soc; FIBiol 1975; CStJ 2000; *Books* Genetic Variation in Britain (1973), The Operation of Intelligence: Biological Preconditions for Operation of Intelligence (1980), Genetic and Population Studies in Wales (1986); *Recreations* book collecting, watercolours, gardening, music, travelling; *Clubs* Athenaeum; *Style*— Prof Eric Sunderland, CBE; ✉ Y Bryn, Ffriddoedd Road, Bangor, Gwynedd LL57 2EH (tel 01248 353265, fax 01248 355043)

SUNDERLAND, Sir John Michael; kt (2006); s of Harry Sunderland, and Joyce Eileen, *née* Farnish; *b* 24 August 1945; *Educ* King Edward VII Lytham, Univ of St Andrews (MA); *m* Sept 1965, Jean Margaret, da of Col Alexander Grieve (d 1975); 1 da (Corianne b 1966), 3 s (Jonothan b 1969, Robin b 1972, Ben Alexander b 1978); *Career* Cadbury Schweppes plc: joined 1968, main bd dir 1993–, md Confectionery Stream 1993–96, chief exec 1996–2003, exec chm 2003–; pres: CBI, Food and Drink Fedn 2002–04, Incorporated Soc of Br Advertisers (ISBA) 2002–05; non-exec dir: Rank Organisation 1997–2006, Barclays 2005–; memb Advsy Bd: Ian Jones & Partners, CVC Capital Partners, Marakon Assocs 2006–; dir Financial Reporting Cncl; FRSA, FIGD, CCIMgt; *Style*— Sir John Sunderland; ✉ Three Barrows, Seale Road, Elstead, Surrey GU8 6LF; Cadbury Schweppes plc, 25 Berkeley Square, London W1X 6HT (tel 020 7409 1313, fax 020 7830 5200)

SUNNUCKS, James Horrace George; DL (Essex 1990); s of Stanley Lloyd Sunnucks (d 1953), and Edith Vera Constance, *née* Sendell (d 1979); *b* 20 September 1925; *Educ* Wellington, Trinity Hall Cambridge (MA); *m* 1 Oct 1955, Rosemary Ann (Tessa), da of Col J W Borradaile (d 1946); 4 s (William b 2 Aug 1956, John b 4 March 1959, David b 4 April 1961, Andrew b 3 May 1965); *Career* RNVR 1943–46; called to the Bar Lincoln's Inn 1950 (bencher 1980); memb Parole Review Ctee Chelmsford Prison (later chm) 1970–82, asst Parly boundary cmmr (Wandsworth, Camden, Wilts) 1975–85; Freeman: City of London 1986, Worshipful Co of Gardeners 1986; licensed reader diocese of Chelmsford 1952, pres County of Essex (Eastern Area) OstJ 1990–99, pres Essex Club 1995; memb Inst of Conveyancers 1974 (pres 1988–89); *Books* Williams, Mortimer and Sunnucks on Executors (ed, 15 edn 1970, 18 edn 2000), Halsbury's Laws of England (ed); *Recreations* gardening, local history, sailing; *Clubs* Oxford and Cambridge, Garrick, Norfolk, West Mersea Yacht, Nikaean; *Style*— James Sunnucks, Esq, DL; ✉ East Mersea Hall, Colchester, Essex CO5 8TJ (tel 01206 383 215); 19 Old Buildings, Lincoln's Inn, London WC2; 5 New Square, Lincoln's Inn, London WC2A 3RJ (tel 020 7404 0404, fax 020 7831 6016); Octagon House, Colegate, Norwich

SUNNUCKS, John Lloyd; s of James Sunnucks, and Rosemary Ann, *née* Borradaile; *b* 4 March 1959; *Educ* Wellington, Lincoln Coll Oxford, RMA Sandhurst; *m* Lucinda Jane Frances, *née* Davies; 3 da (Isabel, Miranda, Kitty); *Career* served HM Forces 1981–87, Life Gds; City and Commercial Communications 1987–89, Brunswick Group Ltd 1989– (currently ptnr); *Clubs* Turf; *Style*— John Sunnucks, Esq; ✉ Brunswick Group Ltd, 15–17 Lincoln's Inn Fields, London WC2A 3ED (tel 020 7404 5959)

SUNNUCKS, William; s of James Horace George Sunnucks (d 2005), and Rosemary Anne, *née* Borradaile; *b* 1956; *Educ* Wellington (music scholar), Peterhouse Cambridge (MA), London Business Sch (MBA); *m* 1982, Caroline, *née* Nevill; 2 s (Charlie b 1985, Hugo b 1990), 3 da (Georgina b 1988, Katie b 1993, Annabel b 1999); *Career* Peat Marwick Mitchell 1977–82, Shell Int 1982–85, Union Square plc 1988–91, Securum Int 1992–96, English Welsh & Scottish Railway 1996–2000, Partnerships UK 2000–01, gp finance dir Capital & Regional plc 2002–; chm Land Management Ltd; ACA 1981; *Recreations* sailing (memb Br sailing team 1990–97); *Style*— William Sunnucks, Esq; ✉ Capital & Regional plc, 10 Lower Grosvenor Place, London SW1W 0EN

SUPPERSTONE, Michael Alan; QC (1991); s of Harold Bernard Supperstone (d 1992), of London, and Muriel, *née* Weinstein (d 1978); *b* 30 March 1950; *Educ* St Paul's, Lincoln Coll Oxford (MA, BCL), Harvard Law Sch (visiting scholar); *m* 18 April 1985, Dianne, da of Abe Jaffe, of Surrey; 1 s (Daniel b 1986), 1 da (Laura b 1988); *Career* called to the Bar Middle Temple 1973 (bencher 1999); recorder 1996– (asst recorder 1992–96), dep judge of the High Court 1998–; visiting lectr Nat Univ of Singapore 1981 and 1982; Administrative Law Bar Assoc: sec 1986–90, treas 1991–94, vice-chm 1994–96, chm 1997–98; fell Inst of Advanced Legal Studies 1998; *Books* Judicial Review (1992, 3 edn 2005), Halsbury's Laws of England - Administrative Law Title (4 edn, 1989 and 2001), Immigration and Asylum (1983, 1988, 1994 and 1996), Brownlie's Law of Public Order and National Security (2 edn, 1981), Local Authorities and the Human Rights Act 1998 (1999), Halbury's Laws of England Extradition Law Title (4 edn, 2000), The Freedom of Information Act 2000 (2001), Administrative Court Practice: Judicial Review (2002); *Recreations* tennis; *Clubs* MCC, Garrick, RAC; *Style*— Michael Supperstone, Esq, QC; ✉ 11 King's Bench Walk, Temple, London EC4Y 7EQ (tel 020 7583 0610, fax 020 7583 9123)

SUPRAMANIAM, Paul Atputhakumar Jebarajasingam; er s of Dr James Mark Jeyasabasingam Supramaniam, PPA, Emeritus FCCP, FRCP, of Nonington, Kent and Singapore, and Eunice Princess Jebaranee, *née* Aiyathurai, of Jaffna; *b* 24 March 1957; *Educ* Anglo-Chinese Sch Singapore, Keele Univ (BSocSci), Sidney Sussex Coll Cambridge (Wright Rogers Law scholar, LLM), Trinity Coll of Music London (ATCL, LTCL); *m* 12 Oct 1991, Margaret Rachel Vazeille, *née* Seale, neice of Sir John Seale, 5 Bt; 2 s (James Timothy Bright Aiyathuraisingam b 18 April 1993, Matthew Edward Herring Jeyathuraisingam b 1 Feb 1998); *Career* articled clerk then slr Linklaters & Paines 1984–87, slr Corp Dept Slaughter & May 1988–92, ptnr Holman Fenwick & Willan 1992–98, managing ptnr Lovells Singapore 1998–2002, sr English ptnr (Asia) Latham & Watkins 2002–07, regnl managing ptnr (Asia) Berwin Leighton Paisner 2007–; formerly: pres Singapore UK Assoc, memb Exec Ctee Singapore Indian Devpt Assoc, judicial memb Ct of the Anglican Church of Singapore, memb Gen Synod Singapore, memb Archbishops Advsy Bd, dir Save the Children Singapore; currently: vice-pres British C of C Singapore, dir Singapore Lyric Opera, dir Asian Civilisation Museum Singapore, memb Steering Ctee Nat Art Gallery of Singapore; inf offr Singapore Armed Forces 1976–79, currently head of legal HQ Tradoc (Maj) Singapore, memb HAC 1984; Freeman: City of London, City of London Slrs' Co; memb Law Soc 1986; *Recreations* opera, antiquarian maps, piano playing; *Clubs* HAC, Singapore Polo, Singapore Island Country; *Style*— Maj Paul Supramaniam, SAF; ✉ 2A Victoria Park Close, Singapore 266550; Berwin Leighton Paisner LLP, 63 Market Street, #10–02, Singapore 048942 (e-mail paul.supromaniam@blplaw.com)

SURATGAR, David; s of Prof Lotfali Suratgar (d 1969), of Tehran, and Prof Edith Olive, *née* Hepburn (d 1985); *b* 23 October 1938; *Educ* Silcoates Sch, New Coll Oxford (MA), Columbia Univ NYC (MIA); *m* 1, 6 Aug 1962, Barbara Lita (d 1990), da of Donald Telfer Low, of Wytham, Oxford; 1 da (Roxanne Christina Noelle b 25 Dec 1964), 1 s (Karim Donald Hepburn b 4 Aug 1966); *m* 2, 29 Aug 1994, Wandra Edith, da of Senator Ike Smalley, of Deming, New Mexico; *Career* Legal Dept UN Secretariat 1961–62, Sullivan & Cromwell (lawyers) NYC 1963–64, legal counsel World Bank 1964–73, adjunct prof of law Georgetown 1966–73; Morgan Grenfell & Co Ltd: dir 1973–88, gp dir 1988–97, dep chm Deutsche Morgan Grenfell 1992–97; special legal counsel Bank of England 1976, special advsr European Investment Bank 1994–95, counsel Le Boeuf Lamb Green & MacRae 1995–2001; chm: Fortune Funds Ltd 2001–, Medi Capital Bank plc; dir: BMCE 1995–, Global Alumina Inc; chm: West India Ctee (Royal Charter) 1987–89, Advsy Bd Taylor de Jongh Inc; memb Cncl: Federal Tst 1992–96, Chatham House (RIIA) 1993–2006; memb: Bodleian Library Appeal 1987–2000, Bd UN Cncl on Ageing 2000–03, Bd Lead Int 2003–, Bd Major Projects Assoc Templeton Coll Oxford, Advsy Bd Int Law Inst Washington DC, Int Advsy Bd George Washington Univ, SOASt, Bd Pictet et Cie Water Fund; Oxford Playhouse Tst 1989–2002, Garsington Opera Co 1989–; memb: Gray's Inn, Int Bar Assoc, Br Inst of Int and Comparative Law; *Books* Default and Rescheduling - Sovereign and Corporate Borrowers in Difficulty (1984), International Financial Law (jlty, 1980); *Recreations* shooting, book collecting, theatre, travelling; *Clubs* Travellers, Brooks's, Garrick, Chelsea Arts, Metropolitan (Washington DC); *Style*— David Suratgar, Esq; ✉ 2 Inverness Gardens, London W8 4RN; BMCE Bank, 26 Upper Brook Street, London W1K 7QE (tel 020 7518 8250, fax 020 7629 0596); The Great House, Burford, Oxfordshire OX18 4SN

SURFACE, Richard Charles; *b* 16 June 1948; *Educ* Univ of Minnesota, Univ of Kansas (BA), Harvard Grad Sch of Business Admin (MBA); *m* 1977, Stephanie Maria Josefa Ruth, *née* Hentschel von Gilgenheimb; 2 s, 1 da; *Career* actuarial asst National Life & Accident Insurance Co Tennessee 1970–72; corp treasy analyst Mobil Oil Corp NY 1974–77; dir of Corp Planning Northwest Industries Inc Illinois 1977–81; marketing, strategy, business devpt and gen mngr positions at American Express Co London/Frankfurt 1981–89; gen mangr Corp Devpt Sun Life 1989–91; md: Sun Life International 1991–95, Pearl Gp Ltd 1995–99, AMP (UK) Ltd; md Oliver Wyman 2000–; memb Bd ABI 1998–99; *Recreations* collecting antiquarian books, skiing, opera, theatre; *Clubs* RAC, Groucho; *Style*— Richard Surface; ✉ Mercer Oliver Wyman, 1 Neal Street, Covent Garden, London WC2H 9QL (tel 020 7333 8333, fax 020 7333 8334, e-mail rsurface@mow.com)

SURMAN, Martyn Charles; s of Leslie Charles Surman (d 1970), of Brighton, and Irene Grace, *née* Rogers; *b* 21 November 1944; *Educ* Varndean GS for Boys, Brighton Coll of Technol, Coll of Estate Mgmnt; *m* 1, 1 Oct 1966 (m dis); 2 c (David Keith, Tracey Deborah (twins) b 20 Jan 1968); m 4, 29 May 2007, Sharon Anne Meredith; *Career* trainee bldg surveyor Watney Mann Brewers 1963–69, sr architectural asst and dep to Borough Architect Architect's Dept Hove BC 1974–78 (joined 1969); PSA Services: troubleshooter Bldg Advsy Branch Croydon 1978, area design mangr Portsmouth 1984, gp planning mangr Portsmouth 1986, gp bldg surveyor 1989, acting gp mangr Portsmouth 1989, PSA dep head of profession bldg surveyors 1990, superintending bldg surveyor 1990, PSA head of profession bldg surveyors 1990–91; dir of bldg surveying PSA Specialist Services 1991–92, dir of bldg surveying servs SpS Surveying 1992–93; div dir TBV Consult Ltd 1993–94, div dir TBV Surveying 1995–96, seconded to Burrow Binnie Int Johannesburg 1996 (ldr int team for devpt of strategy policy for future maintenance of state-owned properties in South Africa), dir of mktg Schal Property Services 1996–97, ops dir Kobi Tarmac South Africa 1997–98, md Kobiprop (Pty) Ltd 1998–2002, business ops dir Nkobi Holdings (Pty) Ltd 1998–2002; Parsons Son & Basley: head Building Surveying Dept 2002–05, head Property Mgmnt Dept 2003–, assoc ptnr 2003–; RICS: memb Bldg Surveyors Divnl Exec 1987–91, memb Gen Cncl 1988–91, chm Health and Safety Working Gp 1989–90, memb Bldg Surveyors Divnl Cncl 1987–, pres Bldg Surveyors Div 1990–91; memb Sussex Branch Bldg Surveyors 1991–97 (chm 1992–93); ABE: memb Gen Cncl 1994–97, memb Devpt and Monitoring Ctee 1994–97; memb numerous BSI Cmmns; author and presenter of numerous papers on bldg surveying and construction technol at nat confs seminars and BSI launch, co-author PSA tech guides; external examiner BSc Hons Building Surveying: De Montfort Univ 1993–97, Univ of Brighton 1995–2001; observer memb Sec of State's Bldg Regulations Advsy Ctee (BRAC) 1992–97, memb Buxted PC 1993–97; FRICS 1986 (ARICS 1975), FIAS 1993, FBEng 1993; *Recreations* sport, travelling, golf, theatre; *Clubs* LA Fitness; *Style*— Martyn Surman,

Esq; ✉ Parsons Son & Basley, 32 Queens Road, Brighton BN1 3YE (tel 01273 274017, fax 01273 821224, e-mail martynsurman@psandb.co.uk)

SURMAN, Nancy L; *Educ* Nottingham Trent Univ (BA); *Career* theatre designer; *Productions* Birmingham Repertory Theatre: Johnny Watkins Walks on Water 1995, Bonded 1997, The Road to Hell 1997, Kaahini 1998; SNAP Theatre Co: Tom Jones 1997, Far from the Madding Crowd 1998, Maurice 1998, Rock and Roll and Barbirolli 1999, Sons and Lovers 2001, My Beautiful Launderette 2002, The Buddha of Suburbia 2004; Oxfordshire Touring Theatre Co: Don Quixote de la Mancha 1998, He Said She Said 1999, Beautiful Thing 2000; Gordon Craig Theatre Stevenage: Noel and Gertie 1999 (also nat tour), Aspects of Love 2001 (also at Octagon Theatre Yeovil); Salisbury Playhouse: The Winter's Tale 2000, Rough Crossing 2000 (also at Palace Theatre Watford), The Secret Rapture 2001, The Rivals 2001, The Duchess of Malfi 2002, Barbarians 2003, Waters of the Moon 2004; Jermyn St Theatre: Privates on Parade 2004, Trojan Women 2004, Much Ado About Nothing 2004; other credits incl: The Final Appearance of Miss Mamie Stuart (Torch Theatre Milford Haven), A Stinging Sea (Citizen's Theatre Glasgow) 1993, Talent (Palace Theatre Watford and Mercury Theatre Colchester) 1999, Boudicca's Babes (Eastern Angles Theatre Co tour) 2002, Private Lives (Octagon Theatre Bolton) 2003, Into the Woods (Trinity Coll of Music at Greenwich Theatre) 2003, Get Ken Barlow (Palace Theatre Watford) 2005; *Exhibitions* Costume Drawings 1988, Joseph's Dream: A Century of Civic Achievement 1989, Magic at Mottisfont 1995, Time and Space - Design for Performance 1999, 2D-3D - Designs for Theatre and Performance 2002; *Style—* Ms Nancy Surman; ✉ c/o Karen Baker, Associated Arts, 8 Shrewsbury Lane, London SE16 3JF (tel 020 8856 4958)

SURR, Christopher John; s of (Frederick) Anthony Surr, of Bristol, and Mavis Barbara, *née* Hill (d 1973); *b* 19 September 1957; *Educ* St Brendan's Coll Bristol, UMIST (BSc); *m* 1989, Claire-Marie, da of Kenneth Cyril Attenborough (d 1989); 1 s (Thomas William b 1990); *Career* exec Samuel Montagu & Co 1982–85, dir Barclays de Zoete Wedd 1985–97, md Chase Manhattan Bank 1998–99, global head of mktg CreditTrade 1999–2001, vice-pres business devpt europrospectus.com 2001–05, team md Moody's Investors Service 2005–; fndn govr St Thomas More Sch Chelsea 2002–06; Freeman City of London (by redemption), Liveryman Worshipful Co of Marketors; MCIM 2001; *Recreations* rugby, horse racing, shooting; *Clubs* City Livery; *Style—* Christopher Surr, Esq; ✉ 4 Anderson Street, London SW3 3LU (tel 020 7581 2576); Moody's Investors Service Limited, 2 Minster Court, Mincing Lane, London EC3R 7XB (tel 020 7772 5489, e-mail chris.surr@moodys.com)

SURREY, Christopher Durden (Kit); s of Stephen James Surrey (d 1998), of Southampton, and Frances Vera Talbot, *née* Durden, of Newton Abbot, Devon; *b* 23 June 1946; *Educ* Tauntons GS Southampton, Southampton Art Coll, Wimbledon Sch of Art (DipAD); *m* 19 July 1969, Margaret Jillian, da of Leslie Arnold Grealey; 1 s (Thomas Hamo b 7 May 1973), 1 da (Charlotte Sarah b 18 Sept 1975); *Career* theatre designer and artist; asst designer: Citizens Theatre Glasgow 1968–69, London fringe 1970–72; designer: York Theatre Royal 1972–74, Northcott Theatre Exeter 1974–76; freelance 1976–; GB rep Int Orgn of Scenographers and Theatre Technicians E Berlin 1981 and Moscow 1982; memb Soc of Br Theatre Designers, memb Soc of Graphic Fine Art; nomination Best Designer Barclays/TMA Theatre Awards 2000, winner Best Shakespeare Prodn whatson.com 2001, nomination Best Musical Prodn Laurence Olivier Awards 2002, winner UK Sandford Drawing Prize 2002, winner Derwent Drawing Prize 2004, winner SGFA Drawing Prize 2006; *Theatre* incl: The Master Builder, Jumpers, Death of a Salesman, Toad of Toad Hall (all Theatr Clwyd), One Flew Over the Cuckoo's Nest, Shades of Brown, The Wizard of Oz, Alice in Wonderland, The Turn of the Screw, The Merchant of Venice, The Taming of the Shrew, The Last Yankee, Amadeus, The Grapes of Wrath, Richard IV (premiere), Northanger Abbey (all Northcott), Rosmersholm (Royal Exchange Manchester), Turkey Time, John Bull, The Secret Rapture (all Bristol Old Vic), Peter Grimes, The Queen of Spades (both New Sussex Opera), Troilus and Cressida (Shakespeare Theatre Washington DC) 1992, Othello, Volpone, The Servant, Divine Right (all Birmingham Rep), Blue Remembered Hills (Crucible Sheffield), Cat on a Hot Tin Roof (nat tour), Anna Karenina, Divided Loyalties (premiere), Macbeth, All at Sea (premiere, Gateway Theatre Chester), The Turn of the Screw, Bedevilled (premiere), Bouncers (Theatre Royal York), Trips (premiere, Birmingham Rep), A Midsummer Night's Dream (open-air theatre Regent's Park) 2000, Much Ado About Nothing (open-air theatre Regent's Park) 2000, Queueing for Everest (Sheffield Crucible Theatre) 2000, Love's Labour's Lost (open-air theatre Regent's Park 2001), The Real Thing (nat tour) 2001–02, Oh, What a Lovely War (open-air theatre Regent's Park) 2002, Henry IV part 1, A Midsummer Night's Dream (open-air theatre Regent's Park) 2004, Misconceptions (nat tour) 2004, The Tempest (nat tour) 2004, The Taming of the Shrew (open-air theatre Regent's Park) 2006; prodns for RSC incl: Dingo, Captain Swing, Sore Throats, A Doll's House, The Accrington Pals, Men's Beano, The Suicide, Bond's Lear, Golden Girls, The Comedy of Errors, The Merchant of Venice, Twelfth Night, Cymbeline, The Churchill Play, Playing with Trains, Much Ado About Nothing, The Bright and Bold Design; *Exhibitions* Soc of Br Theatre Designers incl: Central Sch of Art 1976, The Roundhouse 1979, Riverside Studios 1983 and 1987, RCA 1999; also exhibited at: Cleveland International Drawing Biennale 1991, 1st Malvern Open Drawing Competition 1992, Gordon Hepworth Gallery Newton St Cyres 1991, Devon & Exeter Arts Centre 1992, Coopers Gallery Bristol 1992, RA Summer Exhbn 1993 and 2002, Stansell Gallery Taunton 1994, Hawkings Gallery Salisbury 1994, Cheltenham Drawing Competition 1994, Unit 10 Gallery 1995, Taunton Drawing Competition 1995, Dillington House Somerset 1996, The Café Gallery Exeter 1998, Art Haven 2000, SW Acad of Fine Arts 2000, 2001, 2002 and 2003, Royal West of England Acad 2001 and 2003, Soc of Graphic Fine Art 2002, 2003, 2004 and 2006, The Alpine Club London 2006; *Books* Artswest (contrib 1988), British Theatre Design - The Modern Age (contrib 1989), Shakespeare in Performance (contrib, 1995), Time and Space: Design for Performance (1999); *Recreations* walking and climbing; *Clubs* Alpine; *Style—* Kit Surrey, Esq; ✉ Rock Cottage, Balls Farm Road, Alphington, Exeter, Devon EX2 9HZ (tel and fax 01392 270240)

SUSMAN, Peter Joseph; QC (1997); s of Albert Leonard Susman, of London, and Sybil Rebecca, *née* Joseph; *b* 20 February 1943; *Educ* Dulwich Coll, Lincoln Coll Oxford (MA), Law Sch Univ of Chicago (JD); *m* 1, 5 June 1966 (m dis 1996), Peggy Judith Stone; 1 da (Deborah b 16 Nov 1976), 1 s (Daniel b 13 Feb 1979); m 2, 29 July 2006, Belinda Zoe Schwehr; 1 s (Gabriel b 12 Feb 1995); *Career* called to the Bar Middle Temple 1966 (bencher 2006); in practice 1967–70 and 1972– (assoc law firm NYC 1970–72), recorder 1993–; *Recreations* playing the clarinet, windsurfing, skiing, squash; *Style—* Peter Susman, Esq, QC; ✉ Henderson Chambers, 2 Harcourt Buildings, Temple, London EC4Y 9DB (tel 020 7583 9020, fax 020 7583 2686, e-mail psusman@hendersonchambers.co.uk, website www.hendersonchambers.co.uk)

SUSSKIND, Prof Richard Eric; OBE (2000); s of Dr Werner Susskind, of Glasgow, and Shirley, *née* Banks; *b* 28 March 1961; *Educ* Hutchesons' GS Glasgow, Univ of Glasgow (LLB, Dip Legal Practice), Balliol Coll Oxford (Snell exhibitioner, DPhil); *m* 11 Aug 1985, Michelle Dawn, da of Harvey Saul Latter (d 1991); 2 s (Daniel Rex b 10 Oct 1987, Jamie Ross b 28 June 1989), 1 da (Alexandra Lee b 5 Feb 1995); *Career* tutor in law Univ of Oxford 1984–86, head Expert Systems Ernst & Young 1986–89, memb Mgmnt Bd Masons 1994–97 (special advsr 1989–94); ind conslt 1997–; prof The Law Sch Univ of Strathclyde 2001 (visiting prof 1990–2001), Gresham prof of law 2000–04; hon memb Soc for Computers and Law 1992 (chm 1990–92); gen ed Int Jl of Law and IT 1992–, law columnist The Times 1999–; conslt Lord Woolf's inquiry into civil justice system 1995–96; expert consultee: Criminal Courts Review 2000–01, Tribunals Review 2000–01; memb Court of Appeal (Civil Div) Review Team 1996–97; memb ITAC (IT and the Courts) Ctee 1990– (co-chair 2006–), IT advsr to Lord Chief Justice 1998–, IT advsr to Jersey Legal Info Bd 1998–, memb Bd Modernising Govt Project 1999–2001, fndr memb Oxford Internet Inst Advsy Bd 2002–, memb External Advsy Bd AHRC Research Centre for Studies in Intellectual Property and Technol Law Univ of Edinburgh 2002–, memb Freedom of Information Bd 2003–05; chm: Advsy Panel on Crown Copyright 2003–04, Advsy Panel on Public Sector Info 2004–; George and Thomas Hutcheson Award 2001; govr Haberdashers' Aske's Schs Elstree 1998–, memb Balliol Coll Campaign Bd 2000–, memb Cncl Gresham Coll 2002–04; tstee The Lokahi Fndn 2005–; Freeman City of London 1992; Worshipful Co of Info Technologists: Freeman 1992, Liveryman 1993, memb Court of Assts 1994–2003; hon fell Centre for Law and Computing Univ of Durham 2001, hon prof Gresham Coll 2005; FRSA 1992, FRSE 1997, FBCS 1997, CITP 2004; *Books* Expert Systems in Law (1987), Latent Damage Law - The Expert System (1988), Essays on Law and Artificial Intelligence (1993), The Future of Law (1996), Transforming the Law (2000), Essays in Honour of Sir Brian Neill (ed, with M Saville, 2003), The Susskind Interviews: Legal Experts in Changing Times (ed, 2005); *Recreations* running, reading, golf, cinema, skiing; *Style—* Prof Richard Susskind, OBE, FRSE; ✉ 67 Aldenham Avenue, Radlett, Hertfordshire WD7 8JA (tel 01923 469655, fax 01923 469264, e-mail richard@susskind.com)

SUSSMAN, Norman Frederick; CBE (1988, OBE 1981); s of Samuel Sussman (d 1941), of London, and Miriam, *née* Eisen (d 1999); *b* 19 January 1925; *Educ* Univ Coll Sch Hampstead; *m* 8 Feb 1953, Iris (d 1993), da of Maurice Williams; 1 da (Valerie b 21 March 1958); *Career* WWII Capt RA 1943–47; chm of family co L S & J Sussman Ltd until 1996 (joined 1941); memb Clothing Econ Devpt Cncl 1968–88, chm Shirt, Collar and Tie Manufacturers' Fedn 1968 and 1972 (memb Exec Ctee 1962), pres Appeal Textile Benevolent Assoc 1974–75, chm Br Clothing Industry's Jr Cncl 1977–80, fndr chm/Br memb Clothing Industry Assoc 1980–87 (pres 1987–), BCIA rep CBI Cncl 1987–; memb: Devon and Cornwall TEC 1989–95 (chm North Devon Area Bd 1989–97), Bd CAPITB Tst 1990–, Cncl Br Knitting and Clothing Confederation 1991–, Cncl Br Apparel and Textile Confedn, CBI Cncl 1998–2001, Cncl Apparel, Knitting and Textile Alliance; chm: Br Clothing Industry Assoc Pension Fund Mgmnt Ctee, Bill Cole Meml Tst, One in Twelve Appeal, Tstees Action against Breast Cancer; formerly: pres Clothing and Footwear Inst 1980–81, chm Shirley Inst Clothing Ctee, memb Bd Clothing Industry's Productivity Resources Agency, memb Bd Br Clothing Centre, memb Shirt Making Wages Cncl, memb Cncl WIRA; Univ of Bradford: hon visiting fell, chm Steering Ctee for Clothing Degree Course, memb Advsy Ctee Dept of Industrial Technol 1991–95; patron Renaissance Maritime Charitable Tst Ltd; memb Cons Pty (past chm Garden Suburb ward Finchley and Golders Green Constituency); Hon DLitt Univ of Bradford 1995; *Clubs* Hampstead Golf; *Style—* Norman Sussman, Esq, CBE; ✉ Montana, Winnington Road, Finchley, London N2 0TX (tel 020 8455 9394)

SUTCH, Andrew Lang; s of Rev Canon Christopher Lang Sutch, of Stonehouse, Gloucestershire, and Gladys Ethelwyn, *née* Larrington; *b* 10 July 1952; *Educ* Haileybury, Oriel Coll Oxford (MA); *m* 22 May 1982, Shirley Anne, da of Gordon Alger Teichmann, of Wimbledon; 2 s (James b 12 Dec 1983, Francis b 24 Aug 1986); *Career* Lt Intelligence Corps TA 1976–86; admitted slr 1979, ptnr Stephenson Harwood 1984– (joined 1977, sr ptnr 2002–); memb Law Soc 1979; *Recreations* theatre, running; *Style—* Andrew Sutch, Esq; ✉ Stephenson Harwood, One St Paul's Churchyard, London EC4M 8SH (tel 020 7329 4422, fax 020 7329 7100)

SUTCLIFFE, Andrew Harold Wentworth; QC (2001); s of John Harold Vick Sutcliffe, CBE, DL, and Cecilia Mary, *née* Turton (d 1998); *b* 7 September 1960; *Educ* Winchester, Worcester Coll Oxford (pres Oxford Union); *m* 17 Dec 1988, Emma Elisabeth, da of Sir Angus Stirling , *qv*; 3 da (Rose Cecilia b 18 Feb 1990, Helena Tertia Astley b 17 Oct 1993, Laura Mary b 9 June 1995), 1 s (Ralph Andrew Aeneas b 26 June 1991 d 1992); *Career* 2 Lt Royal Scots Dragoon Gds 1978–79; called to the Bar Inner Temple 1983, recorder (NE Circuit) 2000– (asst recorder 1999), dep judge of the High Court (NE Circuit) 2004; govr Fox Primary Sch Notting Hill 1991–; memb: Exec Ctee Zebra Housing Assoc (Zebra Tst) 1985–, Special Projects Ctee Duke of Edinburgh's Award Scheme 1986–96, Ctee Moorland Assoc 1996–, Nat Access Forum; vice-pres Black Face Sheep Breeders Assoc, chm Kildale Agricultural Show Ctee 1988–, tstee Ralph Sutcliffe Fund for Meningitis Res 1993–98; *Clubs* MCC, Kildale Cricket (pres); *Style—* Andrew Sutcliffe, Esq, QC; ✉ Kildale Hall, Whitby, North Yorkshire YO21 2RQ; 3 Verulam Buildings, Gray's Inn, London WC1R 5NT (tel 020 7831 8441, fax 020 7831 8479, e-mail asutcliffe@3vb.com)

SUTCLIFFE, Prof Charles Martin Sydenham; s of Gordon Edward Sutcliffe, and Florence Lillian, *née* Cole; *b* 5 January 1948; *Educ* KCS Wimbledon, Univ of Reading (BA); *Career* International Computers Ltd 1965–68, Unilever 1971–73, lectr Univ of Reading 1973–86, Northern Soc prof of accounting and fin Univ of Newcastle 1986–90, prof of finance and accounting Univ of Southampton 1990–2005, prof of finance Univ of Reading 2005–; dir Univs Superannuation Scheme Ltd 2001–; memb Berkshire CC 1981–85; ACMA 1985, AT11 1968, MInstAM 1968; *Books* The Dangers of Low Level Radiation (1987), Stock Index Futures (1993, 3 edn 2006), Banks and Bad Debts (1995), Management Accounting in Healthcare (1997), Developing Decision Support Systems (1997), Global Tracker Funds (1998), High-Frequency Financial Market Data (1999), Transparency and Fragmentation (2002), Distortion or Distraction: US Restrictions on EU Exchange Trading Screens (2004); *Recreations* cycling; *Style—* Prof Charles Sutcliffe; ✉ The ICMA Centre, University of Reading, PO Box 242, Reading RG6 6BA (tel 0118 931 8239, e-mail c.m.s.sutcliffe@rdg.ac.uk)

SUTCLIFFE, (Charles Wilfred) David; OBE (1995), DL (W Yorks 1991); s of Max Sutcliffe (d 1976), of Shipley, W Yorks, and Mary Doreen Sutcliffe (d 1977); *b* 21 June 1936; *Educ* Uppingham, Univ of Leeds (BA); *m* 6 May 1960, Hanne, da of Carl Olaf Carlsen (d 1967), of Copenhagen, Denmark; 2 s (Charles Peter David b 1961, John Mark Benson b 1963); *Career* Lt 4 Royal Tank Regt; Benson Turner Ltd: jt md 1968–, chm 1978–; chm Benson Turner (Dyers) Ltd 1976–78; dir: Bradford Microfirms Ltd 1981–88, A N Vevers Ltd 1983–2001, Bradford Breakthrough Ltd 1990–99, Bradford TEC 1991–98 (dep chm 1994); fndr chm Bradford Enterprise Agency 1983–89, pres Bradford C of C 1983–85, memb Cncl Lazards W Riding Tst 1985–93; memb High Steward's Cncl York Minster 1980–98; York Minster Fund: tstee 1987–98 and 1999–, chm of tstees 2003–; pres Bradford Textile Soc 1987–88, chm Textiles and Clothing Regnl Innovation Strategy Bd for Yorks and Humberside 1998–2000, memb UK Textiles and Clothing Strategy Gp 1999–2001; High Sheriff Co of W Yorks 1994–95; hon fell Bradford and Ilkley Community Coll 1985; memb Co of Merchants of the Staple of England 1979 (mayor 1996–97), Freeman City of London, Liveryman Guild of Framework Knitters 1983; Hon Freeman and Liveryman Worshipful Co of Clothworkers 1999 (Warden 2001–03, govr and memb Ct of Assts 2003–); CText, FTI; *Recreations* golf, shooting, skiing, sailing, opera; *Clubs* Brooks's, Cavalry and Guards', Bradford; *Style—* David Sutcliffe, Esq, OBE, DL; ✉ Ivy House Farm, Kettlesing, Harrogate, North Yorkshire HG3 2LR (tel 01423 770561); Dakota, The Boat Pool, Rhosneigr, Anglesey LL64 5YZ (tel 01407 811080); Benson Turner Ltd Property & Investment Co, Room 9, 3rd Floor, Parkland Business Centre, Greengates, Bradford BD10 9TQ (tel 01274 623431, fax 01274 391980)

SUTCLIFFE, Gerard (Gerry); MP; s of Henry (Harry) Sutcliffe (d 1985), of Bradford, and Margaret, *née* McCann; *b* 13 May 1953; *Educ* Cardinal Hinsley GS, Bradford Coll; *m* 14 Oct 1972, Maria, da of Eric Holgate; 3 s (Craig Anthony b 17 Aug 1973, Adrian John b 26 Aug 1975, Christopher James 14 May 1989), 1 da (Mary b 29 Dec 1982 d 1983); *Career* retail trainee Brown Muffs dept store, advtg clerk Bradford T&A, printing dept Field Printers; MP (Lab) Bradford S 1994–; PPS to: sec of state for Social Security 1997–98, chief sec to the Treasy 1998–99, sec of state DTI 1999–2001; Parly under sec of state for Employment Relations, Competition and Consumer Affrs; Govt whip 1999, Vice-Chamberlain of HM Household (Govt whip) 2001–06, Parly under sec of state Home Office 2006–; memb Public Accounts Ctee 1996–98, chair PLP Trade Union Gp 1995–2000; Bradford Met Cncl: cncllr 1982–88 and 1990–94, dep ldr 1986–88, ldr 1992–94; chm Parly Football Team; dep sec: SOGAT 1982, GPMU (memb); *Recreations* music, sport, politics; *Style*— Gerry Sutcliffe, Esq, MP; ✉ 76 Kirkgate, Bradford (tel 01274 400007); House of Commons, London SW1A 0AA (tel 020 7219 3247)

SUTCLIFFE, James Harry (Jim); *Educ* Univ of Cape Town (BSc); *Career* Prudential Corporation plc: joined 1976, chief operating offr subsid Jackson National Life 1989–92, dep md Home Service Div 1992–95, main bd dir 1994–97, chief exec Prudential UK 1995–97; exec dir and dep chm Liberty International Holdings plc 1998–99, gp chief exec Old Mutual 2001– (chief exec Life 2000–01); FIA; *Clubs* Pinner Hill Golf; *Style*— Jim Sutcliffe, Esq; ✉ Old Mutual plc, 5th Floor, Old Mutual Place, 2 Lambeth Hill, London EC4V 4GG (tel 020 7002 7000, fax 020 7002 7200)

SUTCLIFFE, Her Hon Linda (Mrs P B Walker); da of James Loftus Woodward (d 1967), and Florence, *née* Brown (d 1990); *b* 2 December 1946; *Educ* Eccles GS, LSE (LLB); *m* 1 (m dis); m 2, 3 Oct 1987, Peter Brian Walker; *Career* lectr in law Univ of Sheffield 1968–81 (pt/t 1976–81); called to the Bar Gray's Inn 1975; practising barr 1976–93, circuit judge (NE Circuit) 1993–2006; pt/t chm Industrial Tbnls 1983–92; *Recreations* music, gardening; *Style*— Her Hon Linda Sutcliffe

SUTCLIFFE, Martin Rhodes; s of John Sutcliffe, JP, DL, of Oldham, Lancs, and Hon Helen, *née* Rhodes; gs of late Lord Rhodes of Saddleworth, KG, DFC, PC, DL; *b* 21 September 1955; *Educ* Hulme GS, Univ of Sheffield (BA, DipArch); *m* 26 July 1980, Gillian Margaret, da of Arthur Price, of Rochdale, Lancs; 1 da (Hannah Sarah Rhodes b 19 April 1982), 1 s (Henry Ellis b 16 April 1987); *Career* architect; Skidmore Owings and Merrill Chicago 1977–78, Montague Assocs Derby 1980–81, Derek Latham and Assocs Derby 1981–85 (assoc 1983–85); projects incl: St Michaels Derby, Heights of Abraham Cable Car Project and Wirksworth Heritage Centre (Civic Tst award commendations); Building Design Partnership (BDP): joined 1985, assoc 1988–90, ptnr 1990–, architect dir (following incorporation) 1997–, co dir 2002–, firm's healthcare sector champion; projects incl: New Romford Hosp, Grimsby Auditorium (RIBA White Rose Regnl Commendation 1996), Sheffield Hallam Univ 'Campus 21' redevelopment programme (RIBA White Rose Regnl Award 1994), Queen Elizabeth Hosp Birmingham; memb Architects for Health; registered architect 1981, RIBA 1981; *Recreations* family and home, visual and performing arts, the built and natural environment, Derbyshire well dressing; *Style*— Martin Sutcliffe, Esq

SUTCLIFFE, Serena; *b* 1945; *m* David Peppercorn, MW, *qv*; *Career* translator UNESCO; author, conslt and expert on wine; dir Peppercorn and Sutcliffe 1988–91, sr dir Sotheby's London, memb European Bd and head of Int Wine Dept Sotheby's 1991–; Master of Wine 1976, chm Inst Masters of Wine 1994–95; memb Académie Internationale du Vin; Inst of Technol NY Professional Excellence Award 2002, Lifetime Achievement Award Bacchus Soc of America 2006; Chevalier dans l'Ordre des Arts et des Lettres (France), Chevalier dans l'Ordre National de la Legion d'Honneur; *Books* Wines of The World, Great Vineyards and Winemakers, The Wine Drinker's Handbook, A Celebration of Champagne (Decanter Book of the Year Award 1988), Bollinger (1994), The Wines of Burgundy (1995, 8 edn 2005); *Style*— Serena Sutcliffe; ✉ Sotheby's, 34–35 New Bond Street, London W1A 2AA (tel 020 7293 5050, e-mail serena.sutcliffe@sothebys.com)

SUTCLIFFE, Thomas Dawson; *b* 12 August 1956; *Educ* Lancaster Royal GS, Emmanuel Coll Cambridge; *m* 3 c; *Career* BBC Radio: joined 1979, sometime researcher Talks and Documentaries, prodr Radio 3 and Radio 4, ed Kaleidoscope 1984–86, presenter A Good Read and Saturday Review (both BBC Radio 4); The Independent: arts ed 1986, currently columnist and assoc ed; contrib Late Review (BBC 2); winner of Peter Black Award for Broadcast Journalism 1995; *Recreations* cooking, reading, sleeping; *Style*— Thomas Sutcliffe, Esq; ✉ The Independent, Independent House, 191 Marsh Wall, London E14 9RS

SUTHERELL, Maj-Gen John Christopher Blake; CB (2002), CBE (1993, OBE 1990, MBE 1982), DL (Suffolk 2006); s of Ernest John Sutherell (d 1999), and Vera Louise, *née* Blake (d 1952); *b* 23 October 1947, Chatteris, Cambs; *Educ* Christ's Hosp, Univ of Durham (BA); *m* 1, 1979, Stephanie Glover (d 1983); m 2, 1987, Amanda Maxwell-Hudson; 1 da (Charlotte Louise b 1989); *Career* cmmnd 2 Lt Royal Anglian Regt 1968, Platoon Cdr RSO and Adj 2 Royal Anglian UK, NI and BAOR 1968–74, Troop and Sqdn Cdr 22 SAS 1974–78, Staff Coll Camberley 1979, DAA and QMG HQ DSAS 1980–82, Co Cdr 1 Royal Anglian UK and Belize 1982–84, directing staff Staff Coll Camberley 1984–87, CO 1 Royal Anglian Gibraltar, UK and NI 1987–90, Divnl Col Staff Coll 1990, cmd 8 Inf Bde NI 1990–92, RCDS 1993, DMS (Army) 1994–96, Dir Special Forces 1996–99, Cmdt RMCS 1999–2002, ret 2002; Col Royal Anglian 2002–07 (Dep-Col 1997–2002), gen sec Offrs Assoc 2003–; pres Royal Norfolk Regt 2001–, cncllr Army Records Soc 2001–05, 2006–; govr Heathfield Sch 2004–06, govr Heathfield St Mary's Sch 2006–; *Recreations* military history; *Clubs* Army and Navy, Special Forces; *Style*— Maj-Gen John Sutherell, CB, CBE, DL; ✉ The Officers' Association, 1st Floor Mountbarrow House, 6–20 Elizabeth Street, London SW1W 9RB (tel 0845 873713, e-mail gs@oaed.org.uk)

SUTHERLAND, Alasdair Douglas Scott; s of R W Sutherland (d Colombo Ceylon 1946), and Audrie, *née* Finch Noyes; *b* 13 October 1945; *Educ* Tonbridge, Trinity Coll Dublin; *m* 1984, Felicity Bosanquet, *née* Fearnley-Whittingstall; *Career* Publicity Dept Metal Box Co 1966–67, Lexington International PR 1967–68, Burson-Marsteller London 1968–72, ptnr in family restaurant business (Small's Cafe, Maunkberry's, etc) 1972–76, vice-pres and divnl dir of mktg communications Burson-Marsteller Hong Kong 1980–82 (joined 1976), dir Good Relations plc and md Good Relations Consumer Ltd 1982–83, jt md Kingsway PR (later Kingsway Rowland, now The Rowland Company) 1983–90; Manning Selvage & Lee Inc: md London and business devpt dir Europe 1990–94, chm London and dir of Euro strategic devpt 1994, chm Paris 1997, exec vice-pres 1998–2003, conslt Int Devpt 2003; pres IPRA 2001, chm IPRA Campaign for Media Transparency; *Recreations* sailing; *Clubs* Foreign Correspondents' (Hong Kong); *Style*— Alasdair Sutherland, Esq; ✉ 12 Earl's Court Square, London SW5 9DP (tel 020 7373 3751)

SUTHERLAND, Donald Gilmour; s of Robert Brayton Sutherland (d 1973), and Annie Brown, *née* Gilmour (d 1988); *b* 15 April 1940; *Educ* George Watson's Coll; *m* 1970, Linda, *née* Malone; 2 s (Hamish b 3 April 1971, Neil b 27 March 1973), 1 da (Polly b 31 Jan 1979); *Career* chartered accountant; apprentice W M Home Cook & Coy 1958–63; Whinney Murray: sr accountant 1963–68 (Glasgow 1966–68), ptnr 1968–73; managing ptnr (Edinburgh) Ernst & Whinney 1985–88 (ptnr 1973–95), regnl managing ptnr (North) Ernst & Young 1988–90, regnl managing ptnr (South) Ernst & Young 1990–95, chm Ernst & Young Trustees Ltd 1996–2005; dir: Standard Life 1990–99, CALA plc 1995–99, Alexander Russell plc 1995–2001 (chm 2000–01), Murray Global Return Tst plc 1995–2005, Quayle Munro Hldgs plc 1995– (chm 1996–99); *Recreations* antique clocks, conservation, golf; *Clubs* New; *Style*— Donald Sutherland, Esq; ✉ Clinton Cottage, 140 Whitehouse Loan, Edinburgh EH9 2AN (tel 0131 447 4621)

SUTHERLAND, (Ian) Douglas; s of Col Francis Ian Sinclair Sutherland, OBE, MC, ED (d 1962), of Moffat and Ceylon, and Helen Myrtle Sutherland (d 1988); *b* 23 October 1945; *Educ* St Bees Sch Cumberland; *m* 1, 11 Oct 1975, Kathryn (d 2000), da of John Henry Wallace (d 1989), of Haltwhistle, Northumberland; 1 da (Iseabail b 13 July 1972), 1 s (Jonathan b 6 Nov 1976); m 2, 27 Dec 2004, Linda Adams, da of Prof Allen Austin Gilmore (d 1985), of Calif, USA; *Career* D M Hall & Son: joined as trainee surveyor 1965, ptnr 1975–2005, managing ptnr 1994–2001, ptnr special projects 2002–05; memb Co of Merchants of the City of Edinburgh; FRICS 1980, MCIArb 1999; *Style*— Douglas Sutherland, Esq; ✉ 9 Rhodes Park, North Berwick, East Lothian EH39 5NA (tel 01620 893406)

SUTHERLAND, Countess of (24 in line, S circa 1235); Elizabeth Millicent Sutherland; also Lady Strathnaver (strictly speaking a territorial style, but treated as a Lordship for purposes of use as courtesy title for heir to Earldom since the end of the sixteenth century); adopted surname of Sutherland under Scots law 1963; Chief of Clan Sutherland; o da of Lord Alistair St Clair Sutherland-Leveson-Gower, MC (d 1921, s of 4 Duke of Sutherland, KG, and Lady Millicent St Clair-Erskine, da of 4 Earl of Rosslyn), and Elizabeth Hélène, *née* Demarest (d 1931); suc to Earldom of Sutherland held by unc, 5 Duke of Sutherland, KT, PC, 1963 (thus came about precisely the contingency that might have caused objection to be made when the Dukedom was so named on its creation 130 years earlier in 1833, *viz* that because the latter was heritable in tail male while the Earldom not only could be held by a female but actually was (by the 1 Duke's wife) at the time of the cr, the two might become separated; the then Countess of Sutherland in her own right (gggg mother of present Countess) was known as the 'Duchess-Countess' in a style analogous to that of the Spanish Count-Duke Olivares of the seventeenth century); *b* 30 March 1921; *Educ* Queen's Coll Harley St, abroad; *m* 5 Jan 1946, Charles Noel Janson, eldest s of late Charles Wilfrid Janson, of London; 2 s (Alistair, Lord Strathnaver, Hon Martin (twins) b 1947), 1 s (Matthew decd), 1 da (Lady Annabel b 1952); *Heir* s, Lord Strathnaver; *Career* serv Land Army 1939–41; hosp laboratory technician: Raigmore Hosp Inverness, St Thomas' Hosp London; chm: Northern Times 1963–88, Dunrobin Sch Ltd 1965–72, Dunrobin Castle Ltd 1972–; *Recreations* reading, swimming; *Style*— The Rt Hon the Countess of Sutherland; ✉ 39 Edwardes Square, London W8 6HJ; Dunrobin Castle, Golspie, Sutherland; House of Tongue, by Lairg, Sutherland

SUTHERLAND, 7 Duke of (UK 1833); Sir Francis Ronald Egerton; 14 Bt (E 1620); also Earl of Ellesmere (UK 1846), Baron Gower (GB 1703), Earl Gower and Viscount Trentham (GB 1746), Marquess of Stafford (GB 1786), Viscount Brackley (UK 1846); s of Cyril Reginald Egerton (d 1992), and Mary, *née* Campbell (d 1949); suc kinsman, 6 Duke of Sutherland, TD, DL, 2000; *b* 18 February 1940, London; *Educ* Eton, RAC Cirencester; *m* 11 May 1974, Victoria Mary, da of late Maj-Gen Edward Alexander Wilmot Williams, CB, CBE, MC, of Herringston, Dorset; 2 s (James Granville, Marquess of Stafford b 12 Aug 1975, Lord Henry Alexander b 28 Feb 1977); *Heir* s, Marquess of Stafford; *Style*— His Grace the Duke of Sutherland

SUTHERLAND, (Robert) James Mackay; s of James Fleming Sutherland (d 1932), and Edith Mary, *née* Meredith (d 1964); *b* 3 November 1922; *Educ* Stowe, Trinity Coll Cambridge (BA); *m* 1, 7 June 1947, Anthea (d 2003), da of John Christopher Hyland (d 1961); 2 da (Chloe Helena Meredith b 15 Sept 1952, Sabina Rachel b 20 Nov 1954); m 2, 19 March 2005, Julia Margaret Hallam Elton, da of Sir Arthur Hallam Rice Elton, Bt (d 1973), of Clevedon, Somerset; *Career* RNVR 1943–46, Lt; asst civil engr: Sir William Halcrow & Partners 1946–56, A J Harris 1956–58; Harris & Sutherland: ptnr 1958–87, active conslt 1987–2002; author of various chapters and papers on engineering and engineering history; memb Royal Fine Art Cmmn 1986–96, former pres Newcomen Soc for the Study of Hist of Sci and Technol 1987–89; memb various ctees of orgns incl: Br Standards Inst, English Heritage; FREng 1986, FICE, FIStructE (vice-pres 1980–82); *Recreations* engineering history, architectural travel; *Clubs* Travellers; *Style*— James Sutherland, Esq, FREng; ✉ 32 Fairfax Road, London W4 1EW (tel 020 8995 7816, e-mail rjmsutherland@lineone.net)

SUTHERLAND, Dame Joan; OM (1991), AC (1975), DBE (1979, CBE 1961); da of William Sutherland, of Sydney; *b* 7 November 1926; *Educ* St Catherine's Waverley; *m* 1954, Richard Bonynge, AO, CBE, *qv*; 1 s; *Career* opera singer; debut Sydney 1947, Royal Opera House Covent Garden 1952; performed in operas at: Glyndebourne, La Scala Milan, Vienna State Opera, Metropolitan Opera NY and many other opera houses worldwide; has made numerous recordings; *Style*— Dame Joan Sutherland, OM, AC, DBE; ✉ c/o Ingpen & Williams Ltd, 7 St Georges Court, 121 Putney Bridge Road, London SW15 2PA

SUTHERLAND, Prof Kathryn; da of Ian Donald Sutherland, and Joyce Bartaby Sutherland; *b* 7 July 1950; *Educ* Bedford Coll London (BA), Somerville Coll Oxford (DPhil); *Career* lectr in English literature Univ of Manchester 1975–93, prof of English Univ of Nottingham 1993–96; Univ of Oxford: professorial fell St Anne's Coll 1996–, reader in bibliography and textual criticism 1996–2002, prof of bibliography and textual criticism 2002–; MA (by incorporation) Univ of Oxford 1996; *Publications* Adam Smith: Interdisciplinary Essays (1995), Electronic Text: Method and Theory (1997), Jane Austen's Textual Lives: From Aeschylus to Bollywood (2005), Digital Technology and the New Republic of Letters (2008); author of numerous critical edns; *Recreations* gardening, music; *Style*— Prof Kathryn Sutherland; ✉ St Anne's College, Oxford OX2 6HS (tel 01865 274893, fax 01865 274899, e-mail kathryn.sutherland@st-annes.ox.ac.uk)

SUTHERLAND, Peter Denis William; Hon KCMG (2004), SC; s of William George Sutherland, of Dublin, and Barbara, *née* Nealon; *b* 25 April 1946; *Educ* Gonzaga Coll, UC Dublin (BCL), Hon Soc of the King's Inns; *m* 18 Sept 1971, Maruja Cabria Valcarcel, da of Paulino Cabria Garcia, of Reinosa, Spain; 2 s (Shane b 1972, Ian b 1974), 1 da (Natalia b 1979); *Career* called to the Bar: King's Inns 1968 (hon bencher), Middle Temple 1976 (bencher); attorney of NY Bar, admitted to practice before the Supreme Court of the US, practising memb Irish Bar 1968–81 (sr counsel 1980); tutor in law UC Dublin 1969–71, memb Cncl of State of Ireland and attorney-gen of Ireland 1981–1982 and 1982–84; Cmmr of EC for Competition and Relations with European Parl 1985–89; visiting fell Kennedy Sch of Govt Harvard Univ 1989, visiting prof UC Dublin 1989–93; chm Allied Irish Banks 1989–93 (non-exec dir 1995–), DG GATT 1993–95, DG World Trade Orgn 1995; British Petroleum plc: non-exec dir 1990–93 and 1995–, dep chm 1995–97, chm 1997–, exec chm 1998–; chm Goldman Sachs International 2002– (chm and md 1995–2002); dir: Investor 1995–2005, Royal Bank of Scotland 2001–; consultor Administration of the Patrimony of the Holy See; chm: Trilateral Cmmn (Europe), Consultative Bd of the DG of the WTO 2002–04; pres The Federal Tst; goodwill ambass UNIDO 2005–, UN special rep for migration 2006–; The David Rockefeller International Leadership Award 1998; Hon LLD: St Louis Univ 1985, Nat Univ of Ireland, Dublin City Univ, Holy Cross Univ, Trinity Coll Dublin, Open Univ, Suffolk Univ MA, Univ of Bath; Grand Cross Order of Leopold II (Belgium), Grand Cross of Civil Merit (Spain), Chevalier of the Legion d'Honneur (France), Centenary Medal (NZ), Euro Parl Gold Medal, Commandeur du Wissam (Morocco), Order of Rio Branco (Brazil), The Grand Cross of the Order of Infante Dom Henrique (Portugal); *Books* 1er Janvier 1993 -çe qui va changer en Europe (1988); *Recreations* tennis, reading; *Clubs* FitzWilliam Lawn Tennis (Dublin), Lansdowne Rugby Football, Royal Irish Yacht, Milltown Golf; *Style*— Peter Sutherland, KCMG, SC; ✉ Goldman Sachs International, Peterborough Court, 133 Fleet Street, London EC4A 2BB (tel 020 7774 1000, fax 020 7774 4001)

SUTHERLAND, Roderick Henry; s of James Alan Sutherland, of Raglan, Monmouthshire, and late Florence Mary Sutherland; *b* 12 November 1965; *Educ* Monmouth Sch, Christ's Coll Cambridge; *m* 22 July 1989, Sophie Louisa, yr da of Sir Clive Whitmore; 2 da (Amelia Zoe Elizabeth, Henrietta Mahalia Anne (twins) b 23 July 2001); *Career* OgilvyOne: joined 1988, creative dir 1997, exec creative dir 1998–, vice-chm 2005; vice-chm Ogilvy UK 2006–; memb Trg and Devpt Cncl IPA 2003–, chm IPA Creative Forum 2005; *Style*— Roderick Sutherland, Esq; ✉ Brasted Place, Brasted, Kent TN16 1JE; Ogilvy, 10 Cabot Square, London E14 4GB (tel 020 7566 7000, fax 020 7566 5111, e-mail rory.sutherland@ogilvy.com)

SUTHERLAND, Stephen William; s of John Stuart Sutherland, of Salisbury, Wilts, and Sylvia Florence, *née* Lock; *b* 15 February 1956; *Educ* Bishop Wordsworth's GS Salisbury, Christ Church Oxford (BA); *Career* Melody Maker: reporter/feature writer 1981–84, reviews ed 1984–86, features ed 1986–88, asst ed 1988–92, former ed Vox Magazine, ed New Musical Express 1992–2000; ed dir: New Musical Express 2000–04, IPC Ignite! 2004–; *Books* 10 Imaginary Years (with Robert James Smith, *qv* of The Cure, 1988); *Recreations* football; *Clubs* Morton's; *Style*— Steve Sutherland, Esq; ✉ IPC Ignite!, 25th Floor, King's Reach Tower, Stamford Street, London SE1 9LS (tel 020 7261 6471, fax 020 7261 5185)

SUTHERLAND, Dame Veronica Evelyn; DBE (1998), CMG (1988); da of Lt-Col M G Beckett, KOYLI (d 1949), and Constance Mary, *née* Cavenagh-Mainwaring; *b* 25 April 1939; *Educ* Royal Sch Bath, Univ of London (BA), Univ of Southampton (MA); *m* 29 Dec 1981, Alex James, s of James Sutherland (d 1969); *Career* HM Dip Serv: third later second sec FCO 1965, second sec Copenhagen 1967, first sec FCO 1970, first sec (devpt) New Delhi 1975, FCO 1978, cnsllr and perm UK delg UNESCO 1981, cnsllr FCO 1984, ambass Abidjan 1987, asst under sec of state (personnel) FCO 1990–95, ambass Dublin 1995–99; dep sec gen i/c economic and social affrs Cwlth Secretariat 1999–2001; pres Lucy Cavendish Coll Cambridge 2001–; Hon LLD Trinity Coll Dublin 1998; *Recreations* painting; *Style*— Dame Veronica E Sutherland, DBE, CMG; ✉ Lucy Cavendish College, Cambridge CB3 0BU

SUTHERLAND OF HOUNDWOOD, Baron (Life Peer UK 2001), of Houndwood in the Scottish Borders; Sir Stewart Ross Sutherland; KT (2002), kt (1995); s of George Arthur Caswell Sutherland (d 1974), of Aberdeen, and Ethel, *née* Masson (d 1995); *b* 25 February 1941; *Educ* Robert Gordon's Coll Aberdeen, Univ of Aberdeen (MA), Corpus Christi Coll Cambridge (MA); *m* 1 Aug 1964, Dr Sheena Sutherland (Lady Sutherland), da of John Robertson (d 1975), of Fraserburgh; 2 da (Hon Fiona Mair b 11 Dec 1966, Hon Kirsten Ann b 20 Aug 1968), 1 s (Hon Duncan Stewart b 9 March 1970); *Career* asst lectr UCNW 1965–68; Univ of Stirling: lectr 1968, sr lectr 1972, reader 1976–77; KCL: prof of history and philosophy of religion 1977–85, fell 1983, vice-princ 1981–85, princ 1985–90; vice-chllr Univ of London 1990–94, princ and vice-chllr Univ of Edinburgh 1994–2002, provost Gresham Coll 2002–, chm Cncl Univ of London 2006–; HM chief inspector of schools HM Inspectorate 1992–94; chm YTL Education (UK) Ltd 2003–; chm Royal Cmmn on Funding of the Long Term Care of the Elderly 1997–99; memb: C of E Bd of Educn 1980–84, UGC Arts Sub-Ctee 1983–85, City Parochial Fndn 1988–90, NW Thames HA 1992–94, Hong Kong Cncl for Academic Accreditation 1992–95, Cncl for Science and Technol 1993–2000, Humanities Research Bd 1994–95, Hong Kong UGC 1995–2004, Higher Educn Funding Cncl 1995–2002; chm: Br Acad Postgrad Studentships Ctee 1987–94, Ethiopian Gemini Tst 1987–92, CVCP Academic Standards Gp 1988–92, Cncl Royal Inst of Philosophy 1988–2006, London Conf on Overseas Students 1989–93, Ctee of Review Scottish Appeals 1994–96, Ctee of Scottish HE Princs 2000–02; vice-chm Ctee of Vice-Chllrs and Princs 1989–92; ed Religious Studies 1984–90; memb Editorial Bd: Scottish Journal of Religious Studies 1980–95, Modern Theology 1984–91; pres: Soc for the Study of Theology 1985 and 1986, Saltire Soc 2002–05, Alzheimer Scotland 2001–, David Hume Inst 2006–; assoc fell Centre for Philosphy and Literature Univ of Warwick 1986–; chm Quarry Products Assoc 2002–05; memb Ct of Assts Worshipful Co of Goldsmiths 2001 (Freeman 1986, Liveryman 1991); Hon LHD: Coll of Wooster Ohio, Cwlth Univ of Virginia 1992, NYU 1996; Hon LLD: Univ of Aberdeen, Nat Univ of Ireland 1992, Univ of St Andrews 2002, McGill Univ Montreal 2003; Hon DUniv Stirling 1993; Hon DLitt: Richmond Coll 1995, Univ of Wales 1996, Univ of Glasgow 1999, Univ of Warwick 2001, Univ of London 2004, Queen Margaret UC Edinburgh 2004; Dr (hc): Uppsala Univ 1995, Univ of Edinburgh 2004; Hon DEd: Robert Gordon Univ Aberdeen 2005, Hong Kong Inst of Educn 2005 hon fell: CCC Cambridge 1989, UC Bangor 1991, Coll of Preceptors 1994, Birbeck Coll London 2003, Inst of Educn Univ of London 2004, RCGP 2005; FRSA 1986, FBA 1992, FRSE 1995 (pres 2002–05), FRCGP 2003, hon fell Faculty of Actuaries 2004; *Books* Atheism and Rejection of God (1977, 2 edn 1980), The Philosophical Frontiers of Christian Theology (ed with B L Hebblethwaite, 1983), God, Jesus and Belief (1984), Faith and Ambiguity (1984), The World's Religions (ed, 1988); author of numerous articles in books and learned jls; *Recreations* Tassie medallions, jazz, theatre; *Clubs* New; *Style*— The Rt Hon the Lord Sutherland of Houndwood, KT; ✉ House of Lords, London SW1A 0PW (e-mail sutherlands@parliament.uk)

SUTHERS, Martin William; OBE (1988), DL (Notts 1999); s of Rev Canon George Suthers (d 1965), of Newcastle upon Tyne, and Susie Mary, *née* Jobson (d 1984); *b* 27 June 1940; *Educ* Dulwich Coll, Christ's Coll Cambridge (Harvey exhibitioner, MA); *m* 1, April 1970 (m dis 1988), Daphne Joan, da of Stuart Glanville Oxland; *m* 2, March 1990, Philippa Leah, da of Denis Ray Melville La Borde; *Career* articled clerk then asst slr Wells & Hind slrs Nottingham 1961–66, conveyancing asst Clerk's Dept Notts County Council 1966–69, asst slr Fishers Burton-on-Trent 1969–70; Messrs J A Simpson, Coulby: asst slr 1970–71, ptnr 1971–, sr ptnr 1992–99; sr ptnr Messrs Hopkins 1999–2000 (conslt 2000–05), conslt Messrs Fraser Brown 2005–; chm: Queen's Med Centre Nottingham Univ Hosp NHS Tst 1993–2000, Rushcliffe PCT 2004–06; cncllr: (Cons) Nottingham City Cncl 1967–69 and 1976–95 (Lord Mayor 1988–89), Notts CC 2000–; Parly candidate (Cons) W Nottingham gen election 1970; chm: W Nottingham Cons Assoc 1974–77, City of Nottingham Cons Fedn 1983–87, Notts Valuation Tbnl 1990– (memb Notts Local Valuation Panel 1976–90), pres Notts Valuation Tbnl 1999–; memb Cncl Univ of Nottingham 1987–99 and 2001–; pres Notts Law Soc 1998–99 (Parly liaison offr 1989–); chm Notts Wildlife Tst (hon sec 1983–2003); memb Law Soc 1965; *Recreations* ornithology; *Style*— Martin Suthers, Esq, OBE, DL; ✉ The Manor House, Main Street, Flintham, Newark, Nottinghamshire NG23 5LA (tel 01636 525554)

SUTTIE, Ian Alexander; *b* 8 June 1945; *Educ* Robert Gordon's Coll Aberdeen, Univ of Aberdeen; *m* 1 Dec 1971, Dorothy Elizabeth; 2 da (Julia b 1974, Fiona b 1976), 1 s (Martin b 1978); *Career* chm: Arnlea plc, First Oil plc, BSW Ltd, Arnlea Systems Ltd, IDJ Properties Ltd, Union Bridge Ltd, Densbridge Ltd, Intercity (Aberdeen) Ltd, Tano Energy Ltd, First Construction, Nautronix plc, First Tech plc, Mooring Systems Ltd, First Whisky Ltd; MICAS; *Recreations* golf, curling; *Clubs* Royal Northern & Univ; *Style*— Ian A Suttie, Esq; ✉ 1 Queen's Terrace, Aberdeen AB10 1XL

SUTTON, Alan John; s of William Clifford Sutton (d 1964), of Abertillery, and Emily, *née* Batten (d 1992); *b* 16 March 1936; *Educ* Hafod-Y-Ddôl GS, Bristol Univ (BSc); *m* 7 Sept 1957, Glenis, da of George Henry (d 1986), of Ebbw Vale; 1 da (Lisa Jayne b 1963 d 1998), 1 s (Andrew Jonathan b 1964); *Career* chief engr English Electric 1957–62, sales mangr Solartron 1962–69, md AB Connectors 1969–76, industrial dir Welsh Office 1976–79, exec dir Welsh Devpt Agency 1979–88, chm and chief exec Anglolink Ltd 1988–, chm A Novo DigiTec Ltd 1998–2003, chm A Novo UK Ltd 2001–05, dir A Novo Holdings Ltd 2001–05, non-exec dir A Novo SA 2003–, chm Conforto Financial Mgmnt 2007–; MIET (MIEE 1962); *Recreations* golf, walking; *Style*— Alan Sutton, Esq; ✉ Brockton House, Heol-y-Delyn, Lisvane, Cardiff CF14 0SR (tel 029 2075 3194, fax 029 2074 7037, e-mail alanjohnsutton@aol.com)

SUTTON, Andrew; s of William Stanley Sutton (d 1998), of Birkenhead, Wirral, and Evelyn Margaret, *née* Kitchin; *b* 27 August 1947; *Educ* Jesus Coll Cambridge (MA); *m* 2003, Jane, *née* Monks; *Career* ptnr PricewaterhouseCoopers (formerly Price Waterhouse before merger) London 1978–2003; memb Cncl Bede House Assoc; govr Birkenhead Sch; Freeman City of London 1988; FCA 1979; *Recreations* walking, opera, music, reading; *Clubs* Brooks's, RAC, Pilgrims; *Style*— Andrew Sutton, Esq; ✉ 7 Court Hill, Chipstead, Surrey CR5 3NQ (tel 01737 552723)

SUTTON, Andrew William; *b* 4 October 1939; *Educ* Brentwood Sch, Univ of Birmingham, Aston Univ; *m* 13 July 1964, Kay, da of Lionel Edge, of Birmingham; 1 da (Rebecca b 6 April 1967), 1 s (Benjamin b 21 Feb 1969); *Career* psychologist: Newport (Mon) 1965–67, Birmingham 1968–84; Univ of Birmingham: hon lectr in educnl psychology 1970–84, assoc Centre for Russian & E Euro Studies 1980–, hon res fell Dept of Psychology 1984–2004; chief exec Fndn for Conductive Educn 1986–2004, pres Fndn for Conductive Educn 2004–; Hon EdD Univ of Wolverhampton 2007; hon conductor Petö Inst Budapest 1990; *Books* jtly: Home, School and Leisure in the Soviet Union (1980), Reconstructing Psychological Practice (1981), Conductive Education (1985), Mária Hári on Conductive Pedagogy (2004); *Recreations* gardening, garden-railways, writing; *Style*— Andrew Sutton, Esq; ✉ 78 Clarendon Street, Leamington Spa, Warwickshire CV32 4PE (tel 01926 311966, e-mail as@nice.ac.uk); The Foundation For Conductive Education, Cannon Hill House Russell Road, Birmingham B13 8RD (tel 0121 449 1569, fax 0121 449 1611, e-mail as@nice.ac.uk)

SUTTON, Dr George Christopher; *b* 4 February 1934; *Educ* Rugby, Corpus Christi Coll Cambridge (MD, MA), UCH Med Sch London; *m* 7 Feb 1959, Angela Elizabeth, *née* Dornan-Fox; 3 da (Sarah-Jane b 1962, Caroline b 1965, Rachel b 1967); *Career* Addenbrooke's Hosp Cambridge 1962–63, med registrar St George's Hosp London 1963–67, fell in cardiology Univ of N Carolina Chapel Hill Med Sch 1965–66, sr registrar in cardiology Brompton Hosp London 1967–71, conslt cardiologist Hillingdon Hosp 1972–98, hon conslt Harefield Hosp 1972–, sr lectr in cardiology Nat Heart and Lung Inst Imperial Coll Sch of Med London 1972–, hon conslt Royal Brompton and Nat Heart and Lung Hosp London 1972–; author of various scientific papers on cardiology; memb: Br Cardiac Soc (Cncl 1982–86), Euro Soc of Cardiology; FRCP 1977, FACC 1977; *Books* Physiological and Clinical Aspects of Cardiac Auscultation, an audio-visual programme (1967), Slide Atlas of Cardiology (1978), An Introduction to Echocardiography (1978), Clinical and Investigatory Features of Cardiac Pathology (1988), Clinical Cardiology - An Illustrated Text (1998); *Recreations* watching cricket, golf, music, photography; *Clubs* MCC; *Style*— Dr George Sutton; ✉ Department of Cardiology, Hammersmith Hospital, Du Cane Road, London W12 0NN (tel 020 8383 3263, fax 020 8740 8373)

SUTTON, Prof John; s of John Sutton, and Marie, *née* Hammond; *b* 10 August 1948; *Educ* Univ Coll Dublin (BSc), Trinity Coll Dublin (MSc(Econ)), Univ of Sheffield (PhD); *m* 1974, Jean, da of Frank Drechsler; 2 da (Gillian b 4 Sept 1979, Katherine b 23 Nov 1981), 1 s (Christopher b 2 Nov 1984); *Career* lectr Univ of Sheffield 1973–77; LSE: lectr 1977–84, reader 1984–88, prof 1988–98, Sir John Hicks prof of economics 1998–; visiting prof: Univ of Tokyo 1981, Univ of Calif San Diego 1986, Harvard Univ 1998–99, Univ of Chicago Grad Sch of Business 2006; Marvin Bower fell Harvard Business Sch 1990–91, William Davidson visiting prof Univ of Michigan 2003; memb Advsy Cncl Access to Japanese Markets (JETRO MITI) Tokyo 1995–2003; memb Gp of Economic Analysis European Union 2002–04, memb Enterprice Policy Gp Ireland 2003–04; pres Royal Economic Soc 2004–07; Franqui medal 1992, Gaston Eyskens prof Leuven Univ 1996; DSc(Econ) (hc) Nat Univ of Ireland 2003, LLD (hc) Univ of Dublin 2004, Docteur ès Sciences Economiques (hc) Université de Lausanne 2004; fell Econometric Soc 1991, FBA 1996, fell European Economic Assoc 2004, foreign hon memb American Economic Assoc 2007; *Books* Protection and Industrial Policy in Europe (jtly, 1986), Sunk Costs and Market Structure (1991), Technology and Market Structure: Theory and History (1998), Marshall's Tendencies: What Can Economists Know? (2000); *Style*— Prof John Sutton, FBA; ✉ London School of Economics and Political Science, Houghton Street, London WC2A 2AE (tel 020 7955 7716)

SUTTON, Air Marshal Sir John Matthias Dobson; KCB (1986, CB 1980); s of Harry Rowston Sutton (d 1990), of Alford, Lincs, and Gertrude, *née* Dobson (d 1979); *b* 9 July 1932; *Educ* Queen Elizabeth GS Alford; *m* 1, 25 Sept 1954 (m dis 1968), Delia Eleanor, *née* Woodward; 1 da (Shenagh b 22 Jan 1957), 1 s (Shaun b 13 Feb 1961); *m* 2, 23 May 1969, Angela Faith, da of Wing Cdr G J Gray, DFC (d 1997), of Fowey, Cornwall; 2 s (Mark b 13 April 1971, Stephen b 8 Oct 1972); *Career* joined RAF 1950, pilot trg (cmmnd) 1951, Fighter Sqdns UK and Germany 1952–61, Staff Coll 1963, CO 249 Sqdn 1964–66, asst sec Chief of Staff's Ctee 1966–69, OC 14 Sqdn 1970–71, asst chief of staff (plans and policy) HQ 2 ATAF 1971–73, staff chief of def staff 1973–74, RCDS 1975, cmdt Central Flying Sch 1976–77, asst chief of air staff (policy) 1977–79, dep Cdr RAF Germany 1980–82, asst chief of def staff (commitments) 1982–84, asst chief of def staff (overseas) 1985, AOC-in-C RAF Support Command 1986–89; Lt-Govr and C-in-C Jersey 1990–95; pres RAF Assoc 2002–05; chm of govrs Nene UC Northampton 1996–2000; KStJ 1990; *Recreations* golf, gardening; *Clubs* RAF, Greetham Valley; *Style*— Air Marshal Sir John Sutton, KCB

SUTTON, Karolina; da of Miroslaw Zawadzki, and Alina, *née* Rudnik; *b* 18 February 1981, Mikolow, Poland; *Educ* Girton Coll Cambridge (MA); *m* 11 July 2002, Robert Sutton; *Career* literary agent International Creative Mgmt 2003–; *Recreations* cinema, walking, cooking, theatre; *Style*— Ms Karolina Sutton; ✉ ICM Books, 4–6 Soho Square, London W1D 3PZ (tel 020 7432 0800)

SUTTON, Linda; *b* 14 December 1947; *Educ* Southend Coll of Technol, Winchester Sch of Art (BA), RCA (MA); *Career* artist; *Solo Exhibitions* Galerij de Zwarte Panter Antwerp 1971, Bedford House Gallery London 1974, L'Agrifoglio Milan 1975, World's End Gallery London 1978, Ikon Gallery Birmingham 1979, Chenil Gallery London 1980, Royal Festival Hall London 1984, Stephen Bartley Gallery London 1986, Beecroft Gallery Westcliff-on-Sea (with Carel Weight, CH, CBE, RA) 1987, Jersey Arts Centre St Helier Channel Islands 1988, Christopher Hull Gallery London 1988, Beaux Arts Bath 1988, Austin/Desmond Fine Art Bloomsbury 1989, Isis Gallery Leigh-on-Sea 1993, Lamont Gallery London 1993 and 1996, Pump House Gallery Battersea Park 1994, Sutton House Hackney 1994, Chappel Galleries Essex 1995 and 2003, Bromham Mill Bedford Arts Festival 1995, Piers Feetham Gallery Fulham London 1995, Emscote Lawn Gallery 1996, Lamont Gallery 1996, John Bloxham Fine Art London 1996, Six Chapel Row Bath 1997, Fosse Gallery Stow-on-the-Wold 1998, Stevenage Arts Centre 1999, UAC Dublin 2000, Workhouse Gallery Chelsea 2000–03, Piers Feetham Gallery London 2002, Chappel Galleries Essex 2003; *Group Exhibitions* incl: Royal Acad Summer Exhibitions 1972–2006, British Painting 1952–77 (Royal Acad) 1977, Bath Festival 1985 and 1988, Jonleigh Gallery Guildford 1987, The Lefevre Gallery London 1988, Business Art Centre Islington 1991–95, Int Art Fair Olympia 1990 and 1991, Directors Choice (New Academy Gallery) 1990, Academia Italia 1990, On Line Gallery Southampton 1992–2001, Isis Gallery Leigh-on-Sea 1992, Chappel Galleries Essex 1993, Fosse Galleries Stow-on-the-Wold 1992–2007, Royal Museum and Art Gallery Canterbury 1993–94, Piers Feetham Gallery 1994–2007; *Awards* prizewinner GLC Spirit of London (Royal Festival Hall) 1979, 1980 and 1981, first prize Contemporary Arts Soc 1981, prize Nat Portrait Gallery 1982, prizewinner Royal Acad Summer Exhibition 1987; *Books* illustrated: ltd edn of poems and etchings (with Brian Patten, 1996), ltd edn The Tempest (2000); Metamorphoses I (2000), Metamorphoses II (2001), Metamorphoses III (2003); *Clubs* Chelsea Arts, Colony Rooms, Arts; *Style—* Miss Linda Sutton; ✉ 192 Battersea Bridge Road, London SW11 3AE

SUTTON, Michael Phillip; s of late Charles Phillip Sutton, of Worksop, Notts, and Maisie, *née* Kelsey; *b* 25 February 1946; *Educ* Haileybury and ISC; *m* 24 July 1971, Susan Margaret, da of John Turner, JP, DL, of Lound, Notts; *Career* chartered accountant 1970; Old Broad Street Securities Ltd 1970–71, md Singer and Friedlander Ltd 1983–98 (joined 1971), dir Creighton's Naturally plc 1994–97; Freeman: City of London 1978, Worshipful Co of Pipe Tobacco Makers and Blenders (memb Ct of Assts 1982); FCA 1976; *Recreations* shooting, fishing, national hunt racing, gardening; *Clubs* Turf, MCC; *Style—* Michael Sutton, Esq; ✉ Singer and Friedlander Ltd, 22a The Ropewalk, The Park, Nottingham NG1 5DT (tel 01159 419721)

SUTTON, Peter John; s of Charles James Sutton (d 1975), and Ruby Ethel, *née* Moorecroft (d 1984); *b* 29 August 1942; *Educ* Brentwood Sch, Clare Coll Cambridge; *m* 12 April 1969, Marjorie, da of Robert Howe; 1 da (Catherine Fiona b 19 Oct 1970), 1 s (David Robert b 22 May 1973); *Career* sr accountant and mangr Deloitte Plender Griffiths & Co 1967–73 (articled clerk 1964–67), mangr Black Geoghegan & Till 1973–74; Spicer and Pegler (name changed to Spicer & Oppenheim 1988, merged to become part of Touche Ross 1990, now Deloitte): mangr 1974–76, ptnr 1976–2000; pres Cambridge Soc of Chartered Accountants 1991–92; treas Cambridgeshire Local Ctee Help the Aged 2001–, tstee and treas Cambridge Family Mediation Service 2002–; hon treas Cambridgeshire Lawn Tennis Assoc 1987–2000; FCA 1968; *Style—* Peter Sutton, Esq; ✉ 2 West Hill Road, Foxton, Cambridge CB2 6SZ (tel 01223 870721, e-mail peterjsutton@btinternet.com)

SUTTON, Philip John; s of Louis Sutton (d 1976), and Ann, *née* Lazarus (d 1980); *b* 20 October 1928; *Educ* Slade Sch of Fine Art UCL; *m* 11 July 1953, Heather Minifie Ellis, da of Arthur Owen Ellis Cooke; 1 s (Jacob b 11 May 1954), 3 da (Imogen b 21 Feb 1956, Saskia b 19 Jan 1958, Rebekah b 30 Sept 1960); *Career* artist; RA 1976 (ARA 1971); *Recreations* running, swimming; *Style—* Philip Sutton, Esq, RA; ✉ 3 Morfa Terr, Manorbier, Tenby, Pembrokeshire SA70 7TH (tel 01834 871474)

SUTTON, Prof Philip (Phil); s of Percy Ronald Sutton (d 1970), and Ivy Nora, *née* Kidgell (d 1960); *b* 28 November 1953, Southampton, Hants; *Educ* Univ of Southampton (BSc, PhD); *m* 14 Sept 1974, Kim, da of Ronald Cummins; 1 s (Richard b 1977), 1 da (Victoria b 1979); *Career* Admiralty Surface Weapons Estab 1975–83, gp ldr Pre-Detector Signal Processing British Aerospace (BAe) Dynamics 1983–85; Above Water Sector DRA: head Special EO Sensors Section 1985–91, dep head then head Special Research Gp 1987–91, business mangr 1992–93, chief scientist 1994; head Battlefield and Vehicles Systems Dept Defence Evaluation and Research Agency (DERA) 1994–98; MOD: dir of corporate research 1998–2001, dir of technol devpt 2001–04, DG research and technol 2004–; visiting prof: Cranfield Univ at Shrivenham 1990, Loughborough Univ of Technol 1992, Imperial Coll London 2006; dir and tstee Cancer Care Soc; FIEE 1996, FInstP 1998, FREng 2006; *Publications* author and co-author of more than 60 tech reports and papers; named inventor on 17 patents and patent applications; *Recreations* science, cycling, sailing, sub aqua diving, snowboarding, expanding limited German language skills, memb local church cncl; *Style—* Prof Phil Sutton; ✉ Ministry of Defence, Main Building, Whitehall, London SW1A 2HB

SUTTON, Prof Richard; s of Dick Brasnett Sutton (d 1980), of Loddon, Norfolk, and Greta Mary, *née* Leadbeter; *b* 1 September 1940; *Educ* Gresham's, KCL, King's Coll Hosp London (MB BS), Univ of London (DSc); *m* 28 Nov 1964 (m dis 1998), (Anna) Gunilla, da of Carl-Axel Cassö (d 1976), of Stockholm, Sweden; 1 s (Edmund b 24 April 1967); *Career* house offr: Plymouth Gen Hosp 1964–65, King's Coll Hosp 1965, St Stephen's Hosp 1966, London Chest Hosp 1966–67; registrar St George's Hosp 1967–68, fell in cardiology Univ of N Carolina USA 1968–69, registrar then sr registrar and temporary conslt Nat Heart Hosp 1970–76, conslt cardiologist Chelsea & Westminster (formerly Westminster Hosp) 1976–, conslt cardiologist Royal Brompton Hosp 1993–; hon conslt cardiologist St Luke's Hosp for the Clergy 1980–; prof of clinical cardiology Imperial Coll London 2003–; chm Cardiology Ctee, chm Specialty Trg Ctee Cardiology London Deanery (NW); regional specialist advsr RCP; ed Europace 1999–2006; Govrs award American Coll of Cardiology 1979 and 1982; co fndr and former pres and sec Br Pacing and Electrophysiology Gp (now Heart Rhythm UK), memb Exec Bd Euro Heart Rhythm Assoc 2002–06, chm Euro Working Gp on Cardiac Pacing Euro Soc of Cardiology 1998–2000; memb: BMA, Royal Soc of Med, Br Cardiac Soc, American Coll of Cardiology, American Heart Assoc, Euro Soc of Cardiology; FRCP 1982 (MRCP 1967), FHRS 2006; *Books* Pacemakers (chapter in Oxford Textbook of Medicine, 1987), Foundations of Cardiac Pacing (Pt 1 1991, Pt 2 1999); *Recreations* opera, tennis, walking; *Style—* Prof Richard Sutton; ✉ 5 Devonshire Place, London W1G 6HL (tel 020 7935 4444, fax 020 7935 6718, telex 263250, e-mail r.sutton@thecondonclinic.co.uk)

SUTTON, Sir Richard Lexington; 9 Bt (GB 1772), of Norwood Park, Notts; s of Sir Robert Lexington Sutton, 8 Bt (d 1981); *b* 27 April 1937; *Educ* Stowe; *m* 1959, Fiamma, da of Giuseppe Marzio Ferrari, of Rome; 1 s (David Robert b 1960), 1 da (Caroline Victoria (Mrs Alexander Gibbs) b 1965); *Heir* s, David Sutton; *Style—* Sir Richard Sutton, Bt

SUTTON, Richard Manners; s of John Charles Ludlow Manners Sutton (d 1992) and Daphne Agnes, *née* Wormald (d 1961); *b* 5 May 1947; *Educ* Charterhouse; *m* 1, 1972 (m dis 1979), Mary, *née* Diebold; m 2, 1979, Penelope Jane, *née* Quinlan; 2 s (William b 1980, Thomas b 1982); *Career* slr; currently managing ptnr Wrigleys; *Style—* Richard Sutton, Esq; ✉ Wrigleys, 19 Cookridge Street, Leeds LS2 3AG

SUTTON, Robert Hiles; s of John Ormerod Sutton, of The Old School House, Tichborne, Hants, and Margaret Patricia, *née* Buckland; *b* 19 January 1954; *Educ* Winchester, Magdalen Coll Oxford (BA); *m* 8 Aug 1981, Carola Jane (Tiggy), da of Sir Anthony Dewey, 3 Bt, of The Rag, Yeovil, Somerset; 2 s (Patrick William b 1984, Jonathan David Ormerod b 1990), 1 da (Joanna Kate b 1987); *Career* Macfarlanes Slrs: joined 1976, ptnr 1983–, sr ptnr 1999–; memb Law Soc; *Recreations* rackets, poker; *Clubs* Boodle's, City; *Style—* Robert Sutton, Esq

SUTTON, Timothy Patrick; s of William Arthur Sutton, of Derby, and Maria Ephigenia, *née* Macronopoulou; *b* 19 June 1958; *Educ* Queen Elizabeth's GS Ashbourne, Magdalen Coll Oxford (MA); *Career* exec chm BSMG Worldwide Europe, vice-chm BSMG Worldwide Inc, currently Weber Shandwick Europe; campaigns incl: long term repositioning prog for British Midland since 1989 (for which recipient PR Week Grand Prix 1991 and IPR Sword of Excellence 1994), defence of brewing indust against MMC recommendations 1989, campaign by independent gas cos to end British Gas plc's domestic monopoly 1993–95, advising int oil industry on the decommissioning of North Sea platforms; memb Superbrands Cncl; speaker at PR indust confs and events; memb Amnesty Int; MIPR 1992, FRSA 1996; *Recreations* flying, cinema, poetry, Derby Co FC; *Style—* Timothy Sutton, Esq; ✉ Weber Shandwick, Fox Court, 14 Gray's Inn Road, London WC1X 8WS

SUZMAN, Janet; da of Saul Suzman, of Johannesburg, South Africa, and Betty, *née* Sonnenberg; *b* 9 February 1939; *Educ* Kingsmead Coll Johannesburg, Univ of the Witwatersrand (BA), LAMDA; *m* 1969 (m dis 1986), Sir Trevor Robert Nunn, *qv*; 1 s (Joshua b 1980); *Career* actress and director; performances incl: The Wars of the Roses 1964, The Relapse 1967, The Taming of the Shrew 1967, A Day in the Death of Joe Egg 1970, Nicholas and Alexandra 1971 (Acad Award nomination), Antony and Cleopatra 1972, Hello and Goodbye 1973 (Evening Standard Award), Three Sisters 1976 (Evening Standard Award), Hedda Gabler 1978, The Greeks 1980, The Draughtsman's Contract 1981, Vassa 1985, Mountbatten-Viceroy of India 1986, The Singing Detective 1987, Andromache 1988, A Dry White Season 1989, Another Time 1989–90, Hippolytus 1991, Nuns on the Run 1991, Leon the Pig Farmer 1992, The Sisters Rosensweig 1994–95, The Retreat From Moscow 1999, The Hollow Crown (Aust tour) 2003, Who's Life is it Anyway 2005; directed: Othello (Market Theatre Johannesburg 1987, Channel 4 TV 1988), A Dream of People (RSC, The Pit) 1990, No Flies on Mr Hunter (Chelsea Centre) 1992, Death of a Salesman 1993 (Liverpool Echo Best Production Award), The Deep Blue Sea (both Theatr Clwyd) 1996, The Good Woman of Sharkville (Market Theatre Johannesburg, and UK tour) 1996, The Cherry Orchard (Birmingham Repertory Theatre) 1997 (Barclays TMA Best Director Award), The Snow Palace 1998 (UK tour, Tricycle Theatre London and Warsaw Festival 1999), The Free State (UK tour) 2000, Hamlet (Baxter Theatre Cape Town and Swan Theatre Stratford-upon-Avon) 2006; vice-pres LAMDA Cncl 1992–; lectr Tanner Lectures BNC Oxford 1995; Hon MA Open Univ 1986; Hon DLitt: Univ of Warwick 1990, Univ of Leicester 1992, Queen Mary & Westfield Coll London 1997, Univ of Southampton 2002, Univ of Middlesex 2003, Kingston Univ 2006; *Publications* Acting with Shakespeare (1997), The Free State - A South African Response to The Cherry Orchard (2000), Commentary on Antony and Cleopatra for Applause Shakespeare Library (2001); *Recreations* yacht 'Chicken Sloop'; *Style—* Miss Janet Suzman; ✉ c/o Steve Kenis & Co, 72–74 Dean Street, London W1D 3SG (tel 020 7534 6001, fax 020 7287 6328)

SVENDSEN, Dr Elisabeth Doreen; MBE (1980); da of Vincent Aubrey Knowles (d 1976), of Elland, W Yorks, and Ileene Hughan, *née* Gowling (d 1978); *b* 23 January 1930; *Educ* Brighouse GS, Rachel McMillen Trg Coll; *m* 20 Oct 1954 (m dis 1982), Niels Denis Svendsen, step s of Svend Iversen; 4 c (Diana Lise b 13 Oct 1955, Paul Andrew b 30 March 1957, Clive Niels b 3 May 1961, Sarah Anna b 28 Jan 1968); *Career* teacher West Vale Sch 1951–53, co sec W T Knowles & Sons Ltd 1953–55; dir: Modern Equipment Co Ltd 1955–61, Branch Thorn Industries 1961–63; business conslt 1963–66 (incl dir Ponsharden Shipyard), dir Salston Hotel Ltd 1966–82; chief exec The Donkey Sanctuary 1977–2007 (fndr and hon administrator 1969–77), fndr and chm of tstees Int Donkey Protection Tst 1976–85 (now amalgamated with The Donkey Sanctuary); fndr and hon administrator: The Slade Centre 1975–97 (now amalgamated with The Elisabeth Svendsen Tst for Children and Donkeys), The Elisabeth Svendsen Tst 1989–2004; hon sec/admin of Welfare Fund for Companion Animals 1999–; memb Br Assoc of Veterinary Parasitology, pres Colaton Raleigh & Dist Ploughing Assoc; Science Pioneer Prize Egyptian Veterinary Assoc 1992, Lord Erskine Award 2001; Hon DVMS Univ of Glasgow 1992; *Books* adult: Down Among the Donkeys (1981), Twelve of My Favourite Donkeys (1982), In Defence of Donkeys (1985), The Professional Handbook of the Donkey (1986, 3 edn 1997), Donkey's Years (1986), A Week in the Life of the Donkey Sanctuary (1988), A Passion for Donkeys (1988), Travels for a Donkey (1990), The Bumper Book of Donkeys (1991), For the Love of Donkeys (1993), Donkey Tales (1995), From Dawn to Dusk at the Donkey Sanctuary (1999), A Donkey Doctor's Diary (2003); for children: The Story of Eeyore - the Naughtiest Donkey in the Sanctuary (1976), Suey the Beach Donkey (1977), More Adventures of Eeyore (1978), Eeyore Helps the Children (1981), The Great Escape (1981), Jacko the Hurricane Donkey (1982), Eeyore and Christmas Crackers (1984), Eeyore Meets a Giant! (1987), The Champion Donkeys (1989), The Story of Blackie and Beauty (1993), The Tale of Naughty Mal and Other Donkey Stories (1994), The Story of Dusty, the Little Ethiopian Donkey (1996), The Story of Joe, the Donkey Who Flew to Jamaica (1997), The Story of Pepe, the Donkey Who Went to Market (1998), Tiny Titch Saves the Day (2000), Bandy and Peanuts Save Little Owl (2001); *Recreations* sailing, gold panning, antique collecting, keeping birds, cookery; *Style—* Dr Elisabeth Svendsen, MBE; ✉ The Donkey Sanctuary, Sidmouth, Devon EX10 0NU (tel 01395 578222, fax 01395 579266, e-mail enquiries@thedonkeysanctuary.com, website www.thedonkeysanctuary.org.uk)

SWAAB, Richard Laing; s of Jack Swaab, of London, and Zena, *née* Urquhart; *b* 7 May 1955; *Educ* KCS Wimbledon, Christ's Coll Cambridge (scholar, MA); *Career* carpenter Harvey Nichols dept store 1976–77; Lintas advtg: prodn controller 1977–79, account exec 1979–82, account dir 1982; planner Benton & Bowles 1982–83, planning ptnr Chuter Morgenthau 1983–87; planner: Ayer Barker 1987, Ogilvy & Mather 1987–90; head of planning Collett Dickenson Pearce 1990–92; WCRS: head of planning 1992–96, strategy dir 1996–98, vice-chm 1998–2001; global planning dir AMV BBDO 2001–03, head of int planning BBDO Europe 2003–04, currently exec vice-chm AMV BBDO; *Recreations* football, swimming, cricket, socialising; *Style—* Richard Swaab, Esq; ✉ AMV BBDO, 151 Marylebone Road, London NW1 5QE (tel 020 7616 3409, fax 020 7616 3600, e-mail swaabr@amvbbdo.com)

SWAAB, Roger Henry; s of Cyril Henry Swaab, of Shrewsbury, and Betty Joan, *née* Moore; *b* 6 June 1944; *Educ* Brewood GS, Birmingham Sch of Arch (DipArch); *m* 18 July 1968, Elizabeth Kay, da of William Edward Smith Penlon, of Staffs; 1 s (Christian b 1973), 1 da (Beth b 1973); *Career* architect; BA Architecture Ltd 1997–, Hickton Madeley Ltd 1998–, Hickton Madeley Architects Ltd 1999–2006, dir SMC Hickton Madeley Architects Ltd 2006–; dir XC2 Creative Computing Ltd; ARIBA, MCIArb; *Recreations* golf; *Clubs* Nefyn and Dist Golf; *Style—* Roger H Swaab, Esq; ✉ Ashley House, Euston Way, Telford TF3 4LT (tel 01952 200002, fax 01952 200001, e-mail rs@hmarchitects.co.uk); Britannia House, 50 Great Charles Street, Birmingham B3 2LT

SWAFFIELD, David Richard; s of Sir James Chesebrough Swaffield, CBE, DL, RD; *b* 11 November 1951; *Educ* Dulwich Coll, Downing Coll Cambridge (MA); *m* 28 March 2002, Carol, da of Roy Howard, of Chichester, W Sussex; 2 s from previous m (James b 1983, Robin b 1988); *Career* investment analysis Rowe & Pitman 1973–75, admitted slr 1979, ptnr Hill Dickinson & Co 1982–89 (slr 1979–82), dir Grayhill Ltd 1984–85; ptnr: Hill Dickinson Davis Campbell 1989–97, Hill Dickinson (Liverpool, London, Manchester and Chester) 1997–; dir Liverpool Law Society Ltd 1991–2003 (hon sec 1997–98, vice-pres 1998–99, pres 1999–2000), mangr Liverpool & London War Risks Insurance Association Ltd 1994–98 (jt mangr 1992–94); govr Birkenhead Sch 1994–2005; 'ambass for Merseyside' 1997–, memb Cncl Professionaliverpool 2001–; *Style—* David Swaffield, Esq; ✉ Ashley Court, Cuddington Green, Malas, Cheshire SY14 7AJ; Hill Dickinson, Pearl Assurance House, Derby Street, Liverpool L2 9UB (tel 0151 236 5400, fax 0151 227 1352, e-mail david.swaffield@hilldickinson.com)

SWAFFIELD, Prof John; *Educ* Univ of Bristol (BSc), City Univ (MPhil, PhD); *Career* responsible for Concorde Fuel System Test Facility Filton 1970–72, head Sch of the Built Environment Heriot-Watt Univ; sometime visiting scientist Nat Bureau of Standards Washington DC; memb Editorial Bd: Building Servs Engrg Research and Technol, Building and Environment; chm Water Regulations Advsy Ctee DEFRA 1996–2003; CEng, MRAeS, FCIBSE, FCIWEM, FRSE; *Books* Pressure Surge in Pipe and Duct Systems (jtly, 1993), Fluid Mechanics (jtly); *Style—* Prof John Swaffield; ✉ School of the Built Environment, Heriot-Watt University, Edinburgh EH14 4AS

SWAIN, Ann; da of late Owen Morris, and Joan Elaine, *née* Collinson; *b* 12 September 1944; *Educ* Eggars GS Alton, Oxford Poly; *m* 1965; 1 da (Pamela Mary b 1 Feb 1973), 1 s (Martin James b 4 Dec 1975); *Career* Radiobiological Laboratory Wantage ARC 1963–65, Rutherford High Energy Laboratory Harwell SRC 1965–68, Forest Sch 1969–71, head of sci and technol Farlington Sch Horsham 1979–91, fndr Links Consultancy 1991–, md SBRC Ltd; non-exec dir S Thames Regnl Health Authy 1994–96, chm W Sussex Family Health Servs Authy 1992–96, ind memb Sussex Police Authy 1995–2007 (vice-chm 2005–07); nat pres UK Fedn of Business and Professional Women 1991–93, exec memb

S

Women's Nat Cmmn 1991–93, exec sec Business and Professional Women International 1999–2002; chm Advsy Panel Police CRR Training 1999–2002; lay advsr to NPT 1999–2003; memb: Women's Advsy Panel RSA 1991–93, Women's Advsy Panel Opportunity 2000 1992–93; chm The 300 Group 1996–99, dir Fair Play SE 1997–; govr Tanbridge House Sch 1993–2005, chm of govrs Arunside Sch; friend WNC 1996–; MRSC; FRSA 1991; *Recreations* swimming; *Clubs* Westminster Dining; *Style*— Mrs Ann Swain; ✉ Links Consultancy, Beeson House, 26 Lintot Square, Southwater, West Sussex RH13 9LA (tel 01403 739373, fax 01403 734432, e-mail ann@horsham.co.uk)

SWAIN, Marilyn Janice; da of Percival Harold Swain (d 1994), and Alice Maud, *née* George (d 1969); *b* 3 May 1931; *Educ* Berkhamsted Sch for Girls, Bartlett Sch of Architecture, UCL; *Career* Phillips auctioneers London 1960–70, Bonhams 1970–73, freelance valuer and lectr 1973–78, head of dept Neales of Nottingham 1978–82, md Fine Art Div William H Brown 1982–92, dir Marilyn Swain Auctions 1992–99; memb Furniture and Works of Art Ctee RICS 1984–95, fndr memb and hon sec Derby Porcelain Int Soc 1985–95, Lincs Rep Nat Art Collections Fund 1996–2003, hon sec Soc of Fine Art Auctioneers 1985–97, ed The Arts Surveyor RICS Faculty Jl 1999; dir: E Midlands Constitutional Convention Ltd 2001–03, Midlands Against Regnl Assemblies; Party candidate (Referendum Pty) Grantham and Stamford 1997 and (UK Ind Pty) Grantham and Stamford 2001; hon memb Soc of Fine Art Auctioneers 2003–; fell Gemmological Assoc of GB 1967–91, FRSA 1972–, FRICS 1981–99, FSVA 1992–95; *Recreations* fair weather sailing and walking, embroidery, giving and receiving dinner parties; *Style*— Miss Marilyn Swain; ✉ 38 Market Place, Folkingham, Lincolnshire NG34 0SF (tel and fax 01529 497440)

SWAINE, Anthony Wells; s of Albert Victor Alexander Swaine (d 1972), of Cornwall, and Hilda May Allen (d 1983); *b* 25 August 1913; *Educ* Chatham House Ramsgate; *Career* architect; in private practice specialising in architectural conservation and repair of historic bldgs; delg to int conferences: ICOMOS (Int Cncl of Monuments and Sites), Confrontation E of Cncl of Europe Avignon 1966, Europa Nostra, Int Conference for Stone Conservation Athens and European Architectural Heritage Year Zurich and Amsterdam; patron Venice in Peril, author of conservation report to UNESCO Il Problema di Venezia; architectural advsr Friends of Friendless Churches, memb Panel of Hon Conslt Architects Historic Churches Preservation Tst, past memb Panel of Architects The Churches Conservation Tst (formerly The Redundant Churches Fund); memb Panel of Architects Almshouses Assoc, former architectural advsr to Faversham Town Cncl now within the Swale BC (responsible for the restoration of historic Faversham, author of Faversham Conserved), former conslt architect for historic bldgs to Thanet DC (responsible for proposed restoration of Margate Old Town, author of conservation report entitled Margate Old Town), former conslt architect for historic bldgs to Tenterden Town Cncl, conslt to other DC; past conslt on repairs to historic bldgs in France and Italy, past pt/t listing of historic bldgs Miny of Housing and Local Govt DOE; memb: Cncl and Tech Panel Ancient Monuments Soc representing the Soc on the Int Cncl of Monuments and Sites, Soc for the Protection of Ancient Bldgs, Georgian Gp, Victorian Soc, Kent and Canterbury Archaeological Socs; fndr memb Canterbury Soc Rochester and other amenity socs; responsible during last war for the Cathedral, the Precincts and King's Sch to the Dean and Chapter of Canterbury; past pt/t teacher of history of architecture and bldg construction Canterbury and Margate Colls of Art; Hon Freeman City of Canterbury; memb IHBC; FRIBA, FSA, FCIOB, AABC; *Recreations* travelling, languages, lecturing (as memb of panel of speakers of Civic Tst), history as applied to architecture, drawing, painting, photography; *Style*— Anthony Swaine, Esq; ✉ The Bastion Tower, 16 Pound Lane, Canterbury, Kent CT1 2BZ (tel 01227 462680, fax 01227 472743); 19 Farrier Street, Deal, Kent CT14 6JR (tel 01304 366369)

SWAINSON, Dr Charles Patrick; s of John Edward Swainson (d 2002), of Winchcombe, Glos, and Diana Patricia, *née* O'Rorke (d 2003); *b* 18 May 1948; *Educ* White Friars Sch Cheltenham, Univ of Edinburgh (MB ChB); *m* 3 July 1981, Marie Adele, da of Charleton Irwin; 1 s (Andrew b 1983); *Career* sr lectr Univ of Otago NZ 1981–86, conslt physician Royal Infirmary 1986–, pt/t sr lectr dept of med Univ of Edinburgh 1986–, med dir Royal Infirmary 1996–99, med dir Lothian Univ Hosps 1999–, med dir NHS Lothian 2003–; FRCP 1984, FFPH 2004, FRCS 2007; *Recreations* wine, singing, skiing, mountaineering; *Style*— Dr Charles Swainson; ✉ NHS Lothian, 148 Pleasance, Edinburgh EH8 9RS (tel 0131 536 9135, fax 0131 536 3302, e-mail charles.swainson@lhb.scot.nhs.uk)

SWALES, Prof Martin William; s of Peter John Swales (d 1978), and Doris, *née* Davies (d 1989); *b* 3 November 1940; *Educ* King Edward's Sch Birmingham, Christ's Coll Cambridge, Univ of Birmingham; *m* 23 Sept 1966, Erika Marta, da of Ernst Meier (d 1988), of Basel, Switzerland; 1 s (Christopher b 1970), 1 da (Catherine b 1973); *Career* lectr in German Univ of Birmingham 1964–70, reader in German KCL 1972–75, prof of German Univ of Toronto 1975–76 (assoc prof 1970–72), prof of German UCL 1976–2003 (dean of arts 1982–85, emeritus prof 2003–), hon dir Inst of Germanic Studies Univ of London 1989–93; FBA 1999; *Books* Arthur Schnitzler (1971), The German Novelle (1977), The German Bildungsroman (1978), Thomas Mann (1980), Adalbert Stifter (with E M Swales, 1984), Goethe - The Sorrows of Young Werther (1987), Buddenbrooks - Family Life as the Mirror of Social Change (1991), Studies of German Prose Fiction in the Age of European Realism (1995), Thomas Mann's Der Zauberberg (2000), Reading Goethe (with E M Swales, 2002); *Recreations* music, theatre, film, amateur dramatics, travel; *Style*— Prof Martin Swales; ✉ 11 De Freville Avenue, Cambridge CB4 1HW (tel 01223 352510); Department of German, University College, Gower Street, London WC1E 6BT (tel 020 7380 7120)

SWAN, Charles; s of Grahame Swan and Rosemary *née* Richmond; *b* 9 November 1956; *Educ* Winchester (exhibitioner), Pembroke Coll Cambridge (exhibitioner, BA), Coll of Law; *m* 1989, Marcia May Morrissy; 2 c (Julia, Tomé); *Career* articled Woodham Smith 1981–83, admitted slr 1983; slr Speechly Bircham 1983–85, ptnr The Simkins Partnership 1985–2005, Swan Turton 2005–; chm Advertising Law Int; memb Law Soc; *Publications* The ABCD of UK Photographic Copyright (co-author), The Advertising Industry (specialist ed), Copinger and Skone James on Copyright (14 edn); *Recreations* hill walking, running; *Style*— Charles Swan, Esq; ✉ Swan Turton, 68A Neal Street, Covent Garden, London WC2H 9PA (tel 020 7520 9560, e-mail charles.swan@swanturton.com)

SWAN, Dr Charles Henry James; s of Matthew Charles Swan, of Wolverhampton, and Kathleen, *née* Downie (d 1992); *b* 5 October 1937; *Educ* Wolverhampton Municipal GS, Univ of Birmingham (MB ChB, MD); *m* 17 June 1961, Ann, da of Robert O'Connor, of Wolverhampton; 1 da (Lindsay Ann b 25 Oct 1967), 1 s (Edward D'Arcy b 12 March 1969); *Career* research fell: Birmingham Gen Hosp 1967–69, NY Med Coll 1969–70; conslt physician N Staffs Hosp 1972–97, med dir Douglas Macmillan Hospice Stoke-on-Trent 1997–2004; memb: Br Soc of Gastroenterology 1967 (pres (endoscopy) 1991–93), Assoc of Physicians 1985, West Midlands Physicians Assoc, N Staffs Med Soc; holder President's Medal Br Soc of Gastroenterology 1996; FRCP 1969, FRCPEd 1994; *Books* Gastrointestinal Endoscopy (1984); *Recreations* golf, horticulture, fell walking, languages; *Clubs* Trentham Golf, Royal St David's Golf; *Style*— Dr Charles Swan; ✉ 9 Sutherland Drive, Westlands, Newcastle-under-Lyme, Staffordshire ST5 3NA (tel 01782 616897); Mencom House, 2 Gower Street, Newcastle-under-Lyme, Staffordshire ST5 1JQ (tel 01782 614174, e-mail charles@norlen.co.uk)

SWAN, Sir Conrad Marshall John Fisher; KCVO (1994, CVO 1986, LVO 1978); s of Dr Henry Swan (*né* Święcicki), of Vancouver Island, BC (whose f, Paul, emigrated from Poland, where the family had long been landed proprietors and from time to time represented in the Senate of pre-Partition Poland); *b* 13 May 1924; *Educ* St George's Coll Weybridge, SOAS Univ of London, Univ of Western Ontario, Peterhouse Cambridge; *m* 1957, Lady Hilda Susan Mary Northcote (d 1995), da of 3 Earl of Iddesleigh; 1 s, 4 da; *Career* Rouge Dragon Pursuivant 1962–68, York Herald of Arms 1968–92, Registrar and Sr Herald-in-Waiting Coll of Arms 1982–92, Garter Principal King of Arms 1992–95, inspr Regtl Colours (UK) 1993–95; lectr; genealogist of Order of Bath 1972–95; conslt to the King of Jordan on orders and decorations 2003–; KStJ (genealogist of Grand Priory Order of St John 1976–95), hon genealogist Order of St Michael & St George 1989–95, Knight Principal Imperial Soc of Knights Bachelor 1995–2001; memb Ct of Assts Worshipful Co of Gunmakers; FSA; Knight of Honour and Devotion SMOM 1979, Cdr Royal Norwegian Order of Merit with Star 1995, Cdr Order of Merit Republic Poland 1995, Knight Cdr Lithuanian Order of the Grand Duke Gediminas 2002, Knight Grand Cross of the Most Distuinguished Order of the Nation (KGCN) (Antigua & Barbuda) 2002; *Books* Canada: Symbols of Sovereignty (1977), The Chapel of the Order of Bath (1978), Blood of the Martyrs (with Peter Drummond Murray of Mastrick, Slains Pursuivant of Arms, 1993), A King from Canada (2005); *Video* The Aboriginal in Heraldry (1996); *Style*— Sir Conrad Swan, KCVO, PhD, FSA; ✉ Boxford House, Suffolk CO10 5JT (tel 01787 210208, fax 01787 211626)

SWAN, Francis Joseph (Frank); s of Robert Ernest Swan, and Margaret Ann, *née* Burg; *b* 26 September 1940; *Educ* De La Salle Sch Marrickville Sydney, Univ of NSW (BSc); *m* 5 Aug 1967, Helen Margaret, da of Clarence Murphy; 3 s (David 14 Aug 1968, Jeffrey, Stephen (twins) b 14 Feb 1971), 1 da (Lianne b 17 March 1974); *Career* Cadbury Schweppes: various mgmnt positions 1964–79 in Aust and NZ, md CSAL Beverage Div Melbourne 1979–88, chief exec CSAL Melbourne 1988–91, md Beverages Stream Cadbury Schweppes plc London 1991–96, ret; dir Fosters Brewing Group Ltd 1996, dir National Foods Ltd 1997, dir Commonwealth Bank of Australia 1997; memb Business Cncl of Australia 1988–91; Fndn fell Australian Inst of Company Dirs 1990, FInstD 1992; *Recreations* tennis; *Clubs* Hawthorn; *Style*— Frank Swan, Esq; ✉ Fosters Brewing Group, 77 Southbank Boulevard, Southbank, Victoria 3106, Australia

SWAN, Richard Roland Seymour; s of Capt Seymour Lankester Swan, RM (d 1988), and Ethel Hayward, *née* Drew; *b* 21 April 1937; *Educ* Cranleigh, Sidney Sussex Coll Cambridge (MA); *m* 1, 16 Sept 1961 (m dis 1967), Penelope Ann, da of Anthony Urling Clark, of Gwelhale, Rock, nr Wadebridge, Cornwall; 2 s (Mark b 1963, Rupert b 1965); m 2, 14 Oct 1967 (m dis 1990), Hedwig Erna Lydia, da of Dr Franz Pesendorfer (d 1944), of Vienna, Austria; 1 s (Michael b 1969), 2 da (Caroline b 1968, Olivia b 1970); *Career* Nat Serv Royal Sussex Regt, 2 Lt 1956, Lt 1959 East Surrey Regt; admitted slr 1963; Notary Public; sr ptnr Heald Nickinson (Milton Keynes) 1979–; non-exec dir Scantronic Holdings plc; dir: Southern Arts, Milton Keynes and N Bucks C of C Trg and Enterprise, Milton Keynes City Orch; memb Norman Hawes Educnl Tst; chm BABC Clubs for Young People 1986–, memb Cncl NABC Clubs for Young People; memb Law Soc 1963; *Recreations* book collecting, reading, walking; *Clubs* Naval and Military, Woburn Golf and Country; *Style*— Richard Swan, Esq; ✉ Ashton House, 95 Silbury Boulevard, Central Milton Keynes MK9 2AH (tel 01908 662277, fax 01908 675667)

SWAN, Rev Preb Ronald Frederick; s of Frederick William Swan (d 1975), of Southampton, and Doris Ann, *née* Tidridge (d 1988); *b* 30 June 1935; *Educ* Taunton's Sch Southampton, St Catharine's Coll Cambridge (MA), Coll of the Resurrection Mirfield; *m* 23 June 1973, Dr Celia Mary Phillips, *qv*, da of Percival Edmund Phillips (d 1989); 1 da (Eleanor Mary Rose b 1974), 1 s (Toby William Barnaby b 1978); *Career* RN 1954–56; curate St John the Baptist Staveley 1961–65; staff: Anglican Chaplaincy to Univ of London, St George's Bloomsbury/Christ the King Gordon Sq 1965–73, St Martin-in-the-Fields 1973–77; vicar: St Barnabas Ealing 1977–88, St Stephen Ealing 1981–88; area dean of Ealing 1984–88, vicar St Mary Harrow on the Hill 1988–98, area dean of Harrow 1990–95, preb St Paul's Cathedral 1998–, master Royal Fndn of St Katharine 1998–; memb: Diocesan Bishop's Cncl 1998–, Cncl St Paul's Cathederal 2000–; govr St Katharine and Shadwell Tst 1998–, tstee All Saints Educnl Tst 1998–; Freeman City of London 1999; *Publications* ed (St Mary's House pubns): Believing in the Church, A Fool for Christ, Advent Readings and Prayers, Travelling Hopefully; *Recreations* walking, theatre, reading, writing, travel; *Clubs* Savile, Nikaean, Zion Coll, Royal Lymington Yacht; *Style*— The Rev Preb Ronald Swan; ✉ The Royal Foundation of Saint Katharine, 2 Butcher Row, London E14 8DS (tel 020 7790 8124, fax 020 7702 7603, e-mail rswan@stkatharine.org.uk)

SWANN, Kate Elizabeth; da of Ian M Prior, and Sheila Prior; *b* 21 December 1964; *Educ* Univ of Bradford (BSc); *m* 1987, Michael Swann; 2 da; *Career* commercial exec then mktg exec Tesco plc 1986–88, brand mangr rising to gp product mangr Homepride Foods 1988–92, mktg mangr rising to gen mktg mangr CocaCola Schweppes Beverages 1992–93, gp mktg controller then mktg dir White Goods Dixons Stores Gp 1993–95, mktg dir Currys 1995–97, md Homebase 1999–2000 (mktg dir 1997–99), md Argos Ltd 2000–03, chief exec WH Smith plc 2003–; non-exec dir British Land 2006–; *Style*— Mrs Kate Swann; ✉ WH Smith plc, 180 Wardour Street, London W1F 8FY (tel 020 7494 1800, fax 020 7851 8847, e-mail kate.swann@whsmith.co.uk)

SWANN, Sir Michael Christopher; 4 Bt (UK 1906), of Prince's Gardens, Royal Borough of Kensington, TD; s of Sir Anthony Charles Christopher Swann, 3 Bt, CMG, OBE (d 1991), and Jean Margaret, *née* Niblock-Stuart (d 2001); *b* 23 September 1941; *Educ* Eton; *m* 1, 1965 (m dis 1985), Hon Lydia Mary Hewitt, da of 8 Viscount Lifford; 2 s (Jonathan Christopher b 1966, Toby Charles b 1971), 1 da (Tessa Margaret b 1969); m 2, 1988, Marilyn Ann, da of Leslie Charles Tobitt, of Montevideo, Uruguay; *Heir* s, Jonathan Swann; *Career* late 60 Rifles; chm Gabbitas Truman and Thring Educnl Tst, gen cmmr of Income Tax; *Style*— Sir Michael Swann, Bt, TD; ✉ 38 Hurlingham Road, London SW6 3RQ

SWANNELL, John; *b* 27 December 1946; *Career* professional photographer; began career as photographic asst Vogue Studios, former asst to David Bailey, fashion photographer (Vogue, Harpers & Queen, Tatler, Ritz newspaper); exhbns incl: several at the Nat Portrait Gallery London (which holds 80 Swannell photographs in their Permanent Collection), fashion photography since 1974 (Royal Photographic Soc Bath) July-Sept 1990; photographer of set of 26 portraits for The Prince Charles Tst 1991 (incl Sir John Gielgud, Lord King, Lord Weatherill, Harvey Goldsmith and David Hockney); other subjects photographed incl: HM The Queen and the Duke of Edinburgh (for the Golden Jubilee 2002), HM Queen Elizabeth the Queen Mother (for her 100th birthday), HRH The Princess Royal, Diana Princess of Wales with her children (private commission), King Hussein of Jordan, King Abdullah and Queen Rania; commissioned to photograph: Royal Family for Royal Mail stamps 2000, Tony and Cherie Blair for Christmas card 2004; portraits for book I'm Still Standing incl: Richard Attenborough, Michael Caine, Bryan Ferry, Norman Foster, Bob Hoskins, Glenda Jackson, Tom Jones, Ken Livingstone, Joanna Lumley; dir over 50 commercials since 1984 specialising in high fashion and beauty; awards incl: Gold award for Best Commercial of the Year 1984 (Boots No 7), Silver award at Cannes for Best 40 Second Commercial (Rimmel Cosmetics), Best Commercial NY 1990 (Johnsons); *Books* Fine Line (1982), Naked Landscape (1982), Twenty Years On (1996), I'm Still Standing (2002); *Style*— John Swannell, Esq

SWANNELL, Robert William Ashburnham; *b* 18 November 1950; *Educ* Rugby, Inns of Ct Sch of Law; *m* Jan 1982, Patricia; 1 s, 1 da; *Career* CA 1973; KPMG 1969–73; called to the Bar Lincoln's Inn 1976; vice-chm J Henry Schroder & Co Ltd 1997– (dir 1985–2000), co-chm Citigroup European Investment Bank 2002–06, vice-chm Citigroup Europe 2006–; non-exec dir British Land Co 1999–; memb Industrial Devpt Advsy Bd DTI; *Style*—

Robert Swannell, Esq; ✉ Citigroup, Citigroup Centre, 33 Canada Square, Canary Wharf, London E14 5LB (tel 020 7986 4000, fax 020 7986 8094)

SWANSEA, 5 Baron (UK 1893); Sir Richard Anthony Hussey Vivian; 5 Bt (UK 1882); s of 4 Baron Swansea (d 2005), and Miriam Antoinette, *née* Caccia-Birch (d 1975); *b* 24 January 1957, Builth Wells, Wales; *Educ* Eton, Univ of Durham (BA, pres Durham Union Soc), City Univ (MBA); *m* 24 Aug 1996, Anna Clementine, *née*, Austin; 1 s (Hon James Henry Hussey Vivian b 25 June 1999), 1 da (Hon Emma Averil Mary Vivian b 8 March 2001); *Heir* s, Hon James Vivian; *Career* fin journalist 1980–98, equity research ed 1998–, WestLB AG 2004–; memb (Cons) Wandsworth BC 1994–2006 (dep mayor 2000–01); memb Cncl Newton Prep Sch Battersea 2002–; Hon Alderman London Borough of Wandsworth 2006; *Publications* China's Metals and World Markets (1992); *Recreations* suduko puzzles, croquet, horse racing; *Clubs* Parson's Green; *Style*— The Rt Hon the Lord Swansea; ✉ 29 Engadine Street, London SW18 5BJ (tel 020 8875 0877, e-mail swanseas@btinternet.com)

SWANSEA AND BRECON, Bishop of 1999–; Rt Rev Anthony Edward Pierce; s of Gwynfor Pierce (d 1990), and Martha Jane Pierce (d 1987); *b* 16 January 1941; *Educ* Dynevor Co Secdy Sch Swansea, Univ of Wales (BA), Linacre Coll Oxford (MA), Ripon Hall Oxford; *Career* curate Swansea St Peter 1965–67, curate Swansea St Mary and Holy Trinity 1967–74, vicar Llwynderw 1974–92, priest-in-charge Swansea St Barnabas 1992–96, canon Brecon Cathedral 1993–5, archdeacon of Gower 1995–99, vicar Swansea St Mary 1996–99; bishops's chaplain to Anglican students UC Swansea 1971–74, chaplain, Singleton Hosp 1980–95, chaplain UC Swansea 1984–88; co-ordinator Hospital Chaplains 1982–95; chm: Social Action Section Bd of Mission 1985–90, Ecumenical Aids Monitoring Gp Wales 1988–95, Social Responsibility Div Provincial Bd of Mission 1990–92; hon ed Welsh Churchman 1972–75; sec Dio Conf and Dio Patronage Bd 1991–95, dio dir of educn 1992–96; sub-prelate Order of St John Priory for Wales 2002; memb: Ct of Govrs UC Swansea 1981, Provincial Selection Panel 1984–95, Cncl Univ of Wales Swansea 1995–; vice-chair Bd Gwalia Housing Assoc; pres Friends of Swansea Festival of Music and the Arts, patron Powys Challenge Tst; *Recreations* reading, painting, theatre, music; *Style*— The Rt Rev the Bishop of Swansea and Brecon; ✉ Ely Tower, Brecon, Powys LD3 9DE (tel 01874 622008, fax 01874 622008, e-mail bishop.swansea&brecon@churchinwales.org.uk)

SWANSON, His Hon Judge John Alexander; s of Sydney Alexander Swanson (d 1997), of Bridlington, E Yorks, and Joan, *née* Webster; *b* 31 May 1944, Leeds; *Educ* Giggleswick Sch Settle, Univ of Newcastle upon Tyne (LLB); *m* 1981 (m dis), Pauline Hearn, *née* Woodmansey; 2 da (Rebecca Jane b 7 Oct 1980, Anna Elizabeth b 5 May 1984); *Career* slr 1970–75, called to the Bar Inner Temple 1975; asst cmmr Boundary Cmmn for Eng 1992–95, recorder 1994–96, circuit judge (North Eastern Circuit) 1996–; *Recreations* fell walking, the American West, 19th and 20th century music, history of railways, malt whisky; *Clubs* Bridlington Yacht, Bridlington Rugby Union; *Style*— His Hon Judge Swanson; ✉ Combined Court Centre, 50 West Bar, Sheffield S3 8PH (tel 0114 281 2400)

SWANSON, Magnus P; *b* 25 April 1958; *Educ* Univ of Edinburgh (LLB); *Career* lawyer; legal apprenticeship Steedman Ramage & Co WS Edinburgh 1980–82, foreign attorney Corp Dept Paul Weiss Rifkind Wharton & Garrison New York 1986–87; Maclay Murray & Spens Glasgow: slr 1982–86, ptnr1987–, chief exec 2003–; dir Scottish Financial Enterprise, chm Homelink Technologies Ltd, dir Law at Work (Hldgs) Ltd; memb: Law Soc of Scotland, Int Bar Assoc; *Publications* Aircraft Finance (co-author Scottish Chapter); *Style*— Magnus P Swanson, Esq; ✉ Maclay Murray & Spens, 151 St Vincent Street, Glasgow G2 5NJ (tel 0141 248 5011, fax 0141 248 5819, e-mail magnus.swanson@mms.co.uk)

SWANSON, Peter Richard; JP; *Educ* Harrow, Wolverhampton Coll of FE, Staffordshire Agricultural Coll; *m*; 2 c; *Career* farmer (600 acres mixed farming), property developer; joined Ansells Brewery Birmingham as mgmnt trainee 1960, seconded to Threlfalls Brewery Liverpool 1961–63, divnl dir of catering Ansells 1967–70 (various supervisory positions 1963–67); farmer 1973–; dir Farmore Farmers (Co-op Farm Requisite Soc) 1973–79; formerly: dir Welsh Quality Lamb Ltd, chm Montgomery Quality Livestock (Mktg Co-operative), ptnr in co mktg animal foodstuffs 1987–92; chm: Coleg Powys 1990–95 (govr 1987–), Powys Health Authy 1993–96, Dyfed Powys Health Authy 1996–; memb: Wales Agricultural Trg Bd 1990–92 (chm Powys Ctee 1980–92), Bd Powys TEC 1990–, NFU (memb Montgomery Co Exec Ctee); *Recreations* scuba diving, cricket, skiing, shooting, wildlife; *Style*— Peter R Swanson, Esq; ✉ Middle Aston, Montgomery, Powys SY15 6TA (tel 01588 638246, fax 01588 630076)

SWANSTON, Andrew Roger; s of James Alexander Swanston (d 1988), and Olive Dora, *née* May, of Great Yarmouth, Norfolk; *b* 15 November 1948; *Educ* Great Yarmouth GS, Brunel Univ (BTech), St Bartholomew's Hosp Med Coll Univ of London (MB BS, MRCS, LRCP); *m* 11 March 1978, Dorothy Jean, da of John Gibson Robson; 1 s (James Andrew b 4 July 1979), 1 da (Kathryn Elizabeth b 18 Jan 1982); *Career* sr registrar in ENT Surgery Royal Nat Throat Nose and Ear Hosp (also Great Ormond Street Hosp for Sick Children, Royal Berkshire Hosp Reading) 1984–87, Janet Nash res fellowship Univ of Zurich 1987, conslt ENT surgn St Bartholomew's Hosp 1987–93, currently conslt ENT surgn and dir The London Otological Centre; VSO Cameroun West Africa 1967–68, memb Cncl Br Assoc of Otolaryngologists 1990–93; FRSM 1980, FRCS in otolaryngology (Eng) 1983; *Books* Otolaryngology volume 4 Rhinology (contrib, 5 edn 1987); *Recreations* trout fishing, classic car restoration; *Style*— Andrew Swanston, Esq; ✉ The London Otological Centre, 66 New Cavendish Street, London W1N 7LD (tel 020 7637 5111)

SWANTON, Dr (Robert) Howard; s of Robert Neil Swanton (d 1976), and Susanne, *née* Baldwin; *b* 30 September 1944; *Educ* Monkton Combe Sch, Queens' Coll Cambridge (fndn scholar, MA, MB BChir, MD), St Thomas' Hosp Med Sch London (exhibitioner, Mead medal in med, Bristowe medal in pathology); *m* Lindsay Ann, da of Arnold Jepson, of Blackburn, Lancs; 1 s (Robert Charles b 24 Feb 1972), 1 da (Josephine Kate b 23 Jan 1975); *Career* house physician St Thomas' Hosp London 1969, house surgn St Peter's Hosp Chertsey 1970; SHO: Hammersmith Hosp 1970–71, Nat Heart Hosp 1971; med registrar Poole Hosp 1971–72, sr med registrar St Thomas' Hosp London 1975–77 (cardiac registrar 1972–74), sr registrar in cardiology Nat Heart Hosp 1977–79; conslt cardiologist: Middlesex Hosp 1979–2001, King Edward VII Hosp for Offrs 1984–, The Heart Hosp UCL Hosps 2001; Br Cardiac Soc: memb 1979–, asst sec 1986–88, sec 1988–90, pres 1998–2001; fell Euro Soc of Cardiology 1994; FRCP 1984 (MRCP 1971), FESC 1994, FACC 2005; *Books* Pocket Consultant in Cardiology (1984, 5 edn 2003); *Recreations* music, photography; *Clubs* St Albans Medical, Arts; *Style*— Dr Howard Swanton; ✉ Kent Lodge, 10 Dover Park Drive, Roehampton, London SW15 5BG (tel 020 8788 6920); Department of Cardiology, The Heart Hospital, 16–18 Westmoreland Street, London W1G 8PH (tel 020 7504 8959, e-mail howard.swanton@uclh.org); 42 Wimpole Street, London W1G 8YF (tel 020 7486 7416)

SWARBRICK, David William; s of Rev John W Swarbrick (d 1973), of Nottingham, and Lydia, *née* Rains (d 1984); *b* 17 January 1927; *Educ* Kingswood Sch Bath, Merton Coll Oxford (MA); *m* 1956, (Joyce Elaine) Margaret; 1 da (Jane Elizabeth b 1957); *Career* ICI plc UK, Europe and SA 1949–85 (latterly chm of cos in SA and dir of other cos); chm: Hillingdon DHA 1986–90, Mount Vernon Hosp NHS Tst 1991–94, Mount Vernon & Watford Hosps NHS Tst 1994–98; Bodley fell Merton Coll Oxford 2002–; pres Merton Soc 1989–92, memb Cncl Brunel Univ 1992–97 (memb Ct 1992–), memb Bd Gray Laboratory Cancer Research Tst Bd 1998–; former rugby player Oxford Univ, Blackheath, Barbarians and England; FInstD; *Clubs* Vincent's (Oxford); *Style*— David Swarbrick, Esq; ✉ Kenwith, Orchehill Avenue, Gerrards Cross, Buckinghamshire SL9 8QL (tel 01753 883307)

SWARBRICK, Dr Edwin Thornton; s of Richard Thornton Swarbrick, and Mary Elizabeth, *née* Cooper; *b* 29 April 1945; *Educ* Pocklington Sch, Wilbraham Acad Mass USA, St George's Med Sch London (MB BS, MD); *m* 3 March 1984, (Angela) Corinne, da of Kenneth Hamer; 2 s (Benjamin Thornton b 8 Jan 1985, Matthew Thornton b 9 Feb 1987), 1 da (Kate Hannah b 31 March 1993); *Career* house physician and surgn St George's Hosp London 1968–69, SHO Brompton Hosp 1970–71, registrar The London Hosp 1971–72, registrar St Mark's Hosp 1972–74, res fell Inst of Child Health London 1974–76, lectr in gastroenterology Bart's 1976–80, conslt physician Wolverhampton 1980–, hon reader in gastroenterology Univ of Wolverhampton 1995; dir of R&D Royal Wolverhampton Hosp Tst; memb: Br Soc for Gastroenterology, BMA; FRCP; *Recreations* equestrian sports, skiing, music, the arts; *Style*— Dr Edwin Swarbrick; ✉ Coppice Green, Shifnal, Shropshire (tel 01952 462226); Nuffield Hospital, Wood Road, Tettenhall, Wolverhampton (tel 01902 754177)

SWARBRICK, Prof James; s of George Winston Swarbrick, and Edith, *née* Cooper; *b* 8 May 1934; *Educ* Sloane GS, Chelsea Coll London (BPharm, PhD, DSc); *m* 1960, Pamela Margaret Oliver; *Career* lectr Chelsea Coll 1964 (asst lectr 1962), visiting asst prof Purdue Univ 1964; Univ of Connecticut: assoc prof 1966, prof and chm Dept of Pharmaceutics 1969, asst dean 1970; dir product devpt Sterling-Winthrop Res Inst NY 1972–75, first prof of pharmaceutics Univ of Sydney 1975–76, dean Sch of Pharmacy Univ of London 1976–78, prof of pharmacy Univ of Southern Calif LA 1978–81, chm Div Pharmaceutics and prof of pharmaceutics Univ of North Carolina 1981–93, vice-pres R&D AAI Inc 1993–99; pres PharmaceuTech Inc 2001–, vice-pres Scientific Affrs aaiPharma Inc 1999–2006; visiting scientist Astra Laboratories Sweden 1971, industry conslt 1965–72 and 1975–93, conslt Aust Dept of Health 1975–76; Food and Drug Admin: chm Generic Drugs Advsy Ctee 1995–97 (memb 1992–97), conslt 1997–; memb Ctee on Specifications Nat Formulary 1970–75, chm Jt US Pharmacopoeia Nat Formulary Panel on Disintegration 1971–75; memb: Ctee on Graduate Programs American Assoc Colls of Pharmacy 1969–71, Practice Trg Ctee Pharmaceutical Soc of NSW 1975–76, Academic Bd Univ of Sydney 1975–76, Collegiate Cncl 1976–78, Educn Ctee Royal Pharmaceutical Soc GB 1976–78, Working Pty on Pre-Registration Training 1977–78; Pharmaceutical Mfrs Assoc Fndn: memb Basic Pharmacology Advsy Ctee 1982–91, chm Pharmaceutics Advsy Ctee 1986–, memb Science Advsy Ctee 1986–; memb Editorial Bd: Jl of Biopharmaceutics and Pharmacokinetics 1973–79, Drug Devpt Communications 1974–82, Pharmaceutical Technol 1978–, Biopharmaceutics and Drug Disposition 1979–; series ed: Current Concepts in the Pharmaceutical Sciences, Drugs and the Pharmaceutical Sciences; fell: Acad of Pharmaceutical Sciences, Royal Pharmaceutical Society of GB 1978 (memb 1961), American Assoc of Pharmaceutical Scientists 1987; CChem, FRSC, FAAS 1966, FRIC 1970; *Publications* Physical Pharmacy (with A N Martin and A Cammarata, 2 edn, 1969, 3 edn, 1983), Encyclopedia of Pharmaceutical Technology (ed), Drugs and the Pharmaceutical Sciences (series ed), contrib to various pharmaceutical books and jls; *Recreations* woodwork, listening to music, golf; *Style*— Prof James Swarbrick; ✉ PharmaceuTech Inc, 180 Doral Drive, Pinehurst, NC 28374, USA (tel 00 1 910 255 3015, e-mail pharmaceutech@earthlink.net)

SWASH, Prof Michael; s of late Edwin Frank Swash, of Milford on Sea, Hants, and Kathleen, *née* Burton; *b* 29 January 1939; *Educ* Forest Sch, London Hosp Med Coll (MD), Univ of Virginia Med Sch, Case-Western Reserve Univ Ohio; *m* 22 Jan 1966, Caroline Mary, da of Edward Payne, of Box, Glos; 3 s (Jesse Edward, Thomas Henry, (Edmond) Joseph); *Career* current positions held: hon conslt neurologist The Royal London Hosp (conslt neurologist 1972–2006), hon conslt neurologist St Mark's Hosp London and St Luke's Hosp for the Clergy London, chief med offr Swiss Reinsurance (UK) Ltd 1985–; sr lectr in neuropathology The London Hosp Med Coll 1981–1994; prof of neurology: Barts and The London NHS Tst, Queen Mary's Sch of Med and Dentistry London 1995–2006 (now emeritus prof); neurologist-adjunct Cleveland Clinic Fndn OH 1980–99, med dir The Royal London Hosp and Assoc Community Servs NHS Tst 1991–94; Spinoza visiting prof Univ of Amsterdam 2000 and various other visiting professorships; hon sec Section of Neurology RSM 1974–77, hon sec NETRHA Advsy Ctee for Neurology and Neurosurgery 1975–78, hon sec Assoc of Br Neurologists 1979–84; chm: Southwark and Camberwell Multiple Sclerosis Soc 1985–1999, Motor Neurone Disease Assoc 1998–2001 (tstee 1994–98), World Fedn of Neurology Research Ctee on Amyotrophic Lateral Sclerosis 1998–; memb Neuroscience Bd MRC 1986–91; memb: NY Acad of Scis, Br Neuropathological Soc, RSM, Br Soc of Clinical Neurophysiology, Assoc of Br Neurologists, American Acad of Neurology, American Neurological Assoc, Australian Neurological Assoc, Pathological Soc of GB, Br Soc of Gastroenterology, American Assoc of Neuromuscular and Electrodiagnostic Medicine; membre d'honneur de la Société Nationale Française de Colo-Proctologie; dir: Medland Int AB, Malvern Arts Press Ltd; memb: Trollope Soc, Anthony Powell Soc; Liveryman Worshipful Soc of Apothecaries 1989; FRCPath, FRCP 1977 (MRCP 1972); *Books* incl: Clinical Neuropathology (jtly, 1982), Muscle Biopsy Pathology (jtly, 1984, 2 edn 1984), Scientific Basis of Clinical Neurology (jtly, 1985), Hierarchies in Neurology (jtly, 1989), Neurology: a concise clinical text (jtly, 1989), Clinical Neurology (2 vols, jtly, 1991), Neuromuscular Diseases (jtly, 3 edn 1995), Colour Guide: Neurology (jtly, 1997, 2 edn 2005), Outcomes in Neurology and Neurosurgery (1998), Amyotrophic Lateral Sclerosis (jtly, 2 edn 2006), Hutchison's Clinical Methods (22 edn 2007); author of more than 400 scientific and medical research papers, founding ed Amyotrophic Lateral Sclerosis 1999–2007; *Recreations* walking, music, rowing, theatre, opera, Morgan Plus 8; *Clubs* London Rowing, Athenaeum, IOD, Rowfant (Cleveland, OH); *Style*— Prof Michael Swash; ✉ Department of Neurology, The London Independent Hospital, London E1 4NL (tel 020 7780 2400, fax 020 7638 4043, mobile 077 6824 2335, e-mail mswash@btinternet.com)

SWATMAN, Philip Hilary; s of late Philip Stenning Swatman, of Parkstone, Dorset, and late Patricia, *née* Meeson; *b* 1 December 1949, Ringwood, Hants; *Educ* St Edward's Sch Oxford, ChCh Oxford (BA); *m* 1972, Rosemary, *née* Cox; 2 da (Elizabeth Harriet b 16 Aug 1978, Rowena Jane b 16 April 1984), 1 s (Richard Oliver b 14 Oct 1981); *Career* KPMG 1971–76, Nat Enterprise Bd 1976–79, N M Rothschild 1979–86 (dir 1986), Chase Property Holdings plc 1987–88; N M Rothschild: rejoined 1987, md 1996, co-head investment banking 1999–2002, vice-chm 2002–; non-exec dir Alfred McAlpine plc 2003–; FCA 1974; *Recreations* sailing, shooting, opera, theatre, golf, fishing, fine wine, travel; *Style*— Philip Swatman, Esq; ✉ N M Rothschild, 1 King William Street, London EC4P 4DU (tel 020 7280 5332, fax 020 7280 5671, e-mail philip.swatman@rothschild.co.uk)

SWAYNE, Desmond Angus; TD, MP; s of George Joseph Swayne, and Elizabeth McAlister, *née* Gibson; *b* 20 August 1956; *Educ* Bedford Sch, Univ of St Andrews (MTheol); *m* 1987, Moira, *née* Teek; 3 c; *Career* schoolmaster 1981–87, systems analyst Royal Bank of Scotland 1988–97, MP (Cons) New Forest W 1997– (Parly candidate Pontypridd 1987 and West Bromwich West 1992); memb Social Security Select Ctee 1997–2001, oppn frontbench spokesman on health until 2001, oppn front bench spokesman on defence 2001–02, oppn whip 2002–04, PPS to Ldr of HM Oppn (Rt Hon Michael Howard then Rt Hon David Cameron) 2004–; *Recreations* Territorial Army (Maj, Pool of Liaison Offrs and Watchkeepers Woolwich), swimming (memb Serpentine swimming club); *Clubs* Cavalry and Guards'; *Style*— Desmond Swayne, Esq, TD, MP; ✉ House of Commons, London SW1A 0AA (tel 020 7219 4886)

S

SWAYNE, Giles Oliver Cairnes; s of Sir Ronald Swayne, MC (d 1991), and Charmian, *née* Cairnes (d 1984); *b* 30 June 1946; *Educ* Ampleforth, Trinity Coll Cambridge; *m* 1, 1972 (m dis 1983), Camilla, *née* Rumbold; 1 s (Orlando b 1974); m 2, 1984 (m dis 2002), Naa Otua, *née* Codjoe; m 3, 2002, Malu, *née* Lin; *Career* composer; studied at RAM 1968–71; dir Gonzaga Music Ltd 2002–; composer in residence Clare Coll Cambridge 2006–; Hon ARAM 1988; *Works* Six Songs of Lust (1966), La Rivière (1966), The Kiss (1967), Sonata for String Quartet (1968), Three Shakespeare Songs (1969), Chamber Music for Strings (1970), Four Lyrical Pieces (1970), The Good-Morrow (1971), String Quartet No 1 (1971), Paraphrase (1971), Trio (1972), Canto for Guitar (1972), Canto for Piano (1973), Canto for Violin (1973), Orlando's Music (1974), Synthesis (1974), Scrapbook (1974), Canto for Clarinet (1975), Charades (1975), Duo (1975), Suite for Guitar (1976), Pentecost Music (1976), Alleluia! (1976), String Quartet No 2 (1977), A World Within (1978), Phoenix Variations (1979), CRY (1979), The Three R's (1980), Freewheeling (1980), Count-down (1981), Canto for Cello (1981), Rhythm-studies 1 and 2 (1982), Magnificat I (1982), Riff-raff (1983), A Song for Haddi (1983), Symphony for Small Orchestra (1984), Le nozze di Cherubino (1984), Naaotwà lála (1984), Missa Tiburtina (1985), Into the Light (1986), Solo (1986), godsong (1986), Nunc dimittis I (1986), O Magnum Mysterium (1986), PP (1987), Tonos (1987), Veni Creator I and II (1987), Songlines (1987), The Coming of Saskia Hawkins (1987), Harmonies of Hell (1988), The Song of Leviathan (1988), A Memory of Sky (1989), No Quiet Place (1990), No Man's Land (1990), Circle of Silence (1991), Zebra Music (1992), The Song of the Tortoise (1992), The Owl and the Pussycat I (1983), String Quartet No 3 (1993), Fiddlesticks (1994), Goodnight, Sweet Ladies (1994), Squeezy (1994), All About Henry (1995), The Tiger (1995), Communion Service in D (1995), A Convocation of Worms (1995), Two Romantic Songs (1996), The Silent Land (1996), Ophelia Drowning (1996), Tombeau (1997), Beatus Vir (1997), Mr Leary's Mechanical Maggot (1997), Chinese Whispers (1997), Petite Messe Solitaire (1997), Echo (1997), Winter Solstice Carol (1998), Groundwork (1998), Merlis Lied (1998), The Flight of the Swan (1999), HAVOC (1999), The Akond of Swat (2000), Peturbèd Spirit (2000), Canto for Flute (2000), Memory Dances (2000), The Akond of Swat (2000), Mancanza (2001), The Murder of Gonzago (2001), Bits and Bobs (2002), Epitaph and Refrain (2002), The Owl and the Pussycat II (2003), Sangre Viva (2003), Midwinter (2003), Stabat Mater (2004), Four Passiontide Motets (2004), Ave verum corpus (2004), Stations of the Cross Books I and II (2004), Magnificat II (2005), Mr Bach's Bottle-bank (2005), Four Christmas Carols (2005), Magnificat II (2005), Nunc dimittis II (2005), Bits of Mrs Bach (2005), Epithalamium (2005), Elegy for a wicked world (2005), Sonata for cello and piano (2006), Sinfonietta concertante (2006), Ten Terrible Tunes (2006), A Clare Eucharis (2006), Creepy-crawlies (2006), Two little motets (2006), There is no rose (2006), Bagatelles 1–3 for piano (2007), Suite for solo celo (2007), Symphony no 1 (2007); *Recordings* CRY (BBC Singers, John Poole, 1985), Magnificat (various), Choral Music of Giles Swayne (BBC Singers, Stephen Cleobury, 1997), Convocation (Nat Youth Choir, Michael Brewer); *Recreations* walking, Racing Demon; *Style*— Giles Swayne, Esq; ✉ c/o Sam Wilcock, Chester Novello, 14–15 Berners Street, London W1T 3LJ (tel 020 7612 7424, e-mail samuel.wilcock@musicsales.co.uk or gs@gonzagamusic.co.uk)

SWAYTHLING, 5 Baron (UK 1907); Sir Charles Edgar Samuel Montagu; 5 Bt (UK 1894); s of 4 Baron Swaythling (d 1998); *b* 20 February 1954; *m* 1996, Hon Angela Lorraine Rawlinson, yst da of Baron Rawlinson of Ewell, PC, QC; 1 da (Hon Delilah Elaine Montagu b 9 Jan 1998); *Style*— The Rt Hon the Lord Swaythling

SWEENEY, Brian Philip; QFSM (2004); s of Philip Sweeney, and Mary, *née* Green; *b* 14 July 1961, Glasgow; *Educ* Holyrood Acad, Glasgow Caledonian Univ, Univ of Coventry (MA), IFireE (Dip); *m* 16 Oct 1994, Pamela Anne, *née* Barrat; 1 s (Ryan Alexander b 12 Jan 1998); *Career* Strathclyde Fire & Rescue: joined 1981, leading firefighter 1983, sub offr 1986, station offr 1989, asst divnl offr 1993, divnl offr 1996, sr divnl offr 1998, asst chief offr and dir of ops 2000, dep chief offr 2003, chief offr/firemaster 2004–; Hon Dr Glasgow Caledonian Univ; Long Serv Good Conduct Medal 2000; memb: Chief Fire Offrs' Assoc, Assoc of Princ Fire Offrs 2000–; MIFireE, MInstD, MCGI; *Recreations* golf, reading; *Style*— Brian Sweeney, Esq, QFSM; ✉ 50 Antonine Road, Dullatur, Glasgow G68 0FE (tel 01236 739581); Strathclyde Fire & Rescue, Headquarters, Bothwell Road, Hamilton, Lanarkshire ML3 0EA (tel 01698 338240, fax 01698 338494, e-mail brian.sweeney@strathclydefire.org)

SWEENEY, Edward (Ed); s of William Sweeney (d 1988), and Louise, *née* Cawley; *b* 6 August 1954; *m* 3 Jan 1987, Janet, da of Cliff Roydhouse; *Career* BIFU: research offr 1976–79, negotiating offr TSB 1979–86, national offr Scotland 1986–89, nat offr insurance 1989–91, dep gen sec 1991–96, gen sec 1996–99; gen sec UNIFI 2000– (jt gen sec 1999–2000); memb: Gen Cncl TUC, Exec Ctee TUC, Bd Investors in People UK Ltd, Mgmnt Bd Employment Tbnl Serv; non-service panel memb for external interviewers for chief fire officers and chief police officers; *Recreations* sport of all kinds, reading, egyptology; *Style*— Ed Sweeney, Esq; ✉ General Secretary, UNIFI, Sheffield House, 1b Amity Grove, London SW20 0LG (tel 020 8946 9151, 020 8879 7916)

SWEENEY, Jeremy Michael; s of Terence Ernest Michael Sweeney, and Dawn Yvonne, *née* Knight; *b* 3 June 1963; *Educ* Epsom Coll; *m* Philippa Sara, da of Maj (ret) Patrick Garway-Templeman; *Career* product devpt Wessex Medical Ltd Midhurst 1982–85, resort mangr Bladon Lines Risoul France 1986–87, crew Schooner Fleurtje Hamilton Bermuda 1987–88, with Mercury Communications 1988–89, subsequently md Ian Greer Associates public affrs conslts until 1996 (joined 1989), with A S Biss & Co 1996–2001 (dep chm), ceo JMS Resources; *Recreations* motorbikes, dogs; *Clubs* Cavalry and Guards'; *Style*— Jeremy Sweeney, Esq; ✉ tel 01730 829222, e-mail jeremy@jmsresources.com

SWEENEY, John Paul; s of Leonard Sweeney, and Barbara, *née* Owen; *b* 7 June 1958; *Educ* Barton Peveril GS, LSE (BSc); *m* 1985, Annie, da of Rex Patterson; 1 s (Sam b 25 November 1988), 1 da (Molly b 18 July 1992); *Career* journalist; with The Sheffield Telegraph 1981–84, freelance 1984–88, with The Observer 1989–; Journalist of the Year What the Papers Say Awards 1997, Paul Foot Award for Investigative Journalism 2005; *Publications* The Life and Evil Times of Nicolae Causescu (1991), Trading With the Enemy: How Britain Armed Iraq (1993), Purple Homicide: Fear and Loathing on Knutsford Heath (1997); *Recreations* poking powerful people with a stick; *Style*— John Sweeney, Esq; ✉ The Observer, 119 Farringdon Road, London EC1R 3ER (tel 020 7713 4252, fax 020 7713 4250)

SWEENEY, Matthew Gerard; s of Clement Sweeney, of Co Donegal, and Josephine, *née* Lavelle; *b* 6 October 1952; *Educ* Franciscan Coll Gormanstown Co Meath, Univ Coll Dublin, Univ of Freiburg (yr abroad), Poly of N London (BA); *m* 14 Sept 1979, Rosemary, da of Benjamin Barber (d 1967); 1 da (Nico Sara b 3 Aug 1980), 1 s (Malvin Leigh b 11 April 1983); *Career* writer; writer in residence Farnham Coll 1984 and 1985, Henfield writing fell UEA 1986, events and publicity asst The Poetry Soc 1988–90, poet in residence Hereford & Worcester 1991, writer in residence The South Bank Centre 1994–95, poet in residence on internet for Chadwyck-Healey 1997–98, poet in residence Nat Library for the Blind 1999, other residencies incl Birmingham Readers & Writers Festival 1993, Salisbury Festival 1994, Aldeburgh Poetry Festival 1998; memb Aosdána 1990; gives regular readings throughout UK and abroad, has reviewed for Telegraph, Sunday Times, Observer, Times supplements and Poetry Review; featured regularly on BBC Radio; awards: Prudence Farmer Prize 1984, Cholmondeley Award 1987, Arts Cncl bursary 1992, Arts Cncl Writer's Award 1999; *Poetry* A Dream of Maps (1981), A Round House (1983), The Lame Waltzer (1985), Blue Shoes (1989), Cacti (1992), The Blue Taps (limited edn pamphlet, 1994), Emergency Kit: Poems For Strange Times (anthology, co-ed with Jo Shapcott, 1996), The Bridal Suite (1997), Penguin Modern Poets 12 (1997), Beyond Bedlam: Poems Written Out of Mental Distress (anthology, co-ed with Ken Smith, 1997), A Smell of Fish (2000); for children: The Flying Spring Onion (1992), Fatso in the Red Suit (1995); *Fiction* for children: The Snow Vulture (1992 and 1994), The Chinese Dressing Gown (1987); *educational*: Writing Poetry (jtly with John Hartley Williams, 1997); *Style*— Matthew Sweeney, Esq; ✉ Rogers, Coleridge & White, 20 Powis Mews, London W11 1JN (tel 020 7221 3717)

SWEENEY, Michael Anthony (Mike); s of Michael Dominick Sweeney (d 1969), of Nottingham, and Madaleine, *née* Beatty (d 1999); *b* 14 October 1944; *Educ* Becket Sch, St John's Coll Cambridge (Rowing blue); *m* 3 August 1968, Tina, *née* Marson; 1 da (Claire Helena 15 April 1970), 1 s (Paul Michael b 29 Nov 1971); *Career* Boat Race: stroke 1965, stroke and pres 1966, umpire 1984, 1986, 1988, 1990, 1996 and 1998; GB eights Euro championships 1967, GB coxless pairs World championships 1970, chm GB Selection Bd 1972–76; team mangr: GB rowing teams 1973–79, Olympic rowing teams 1980 and 1984; elected Henley steward 1974, int (FISA) umpire 1982–, chm of Events Cmmn World Rowing (FISA) Cncl 1990–; chm Henley Royal Regatta 1993–; Henley medals: Ladies' Plate 1966, Visitors' 1966, Wyfold 1967, Stewards' 1968; civil engr construction industry 1967–70, district mangr Severn Trent Water Ltd 1987–95 (river engr 1970–86), project dir Ramesys (e-Business Services) Ltd 1995–; *Recreations* squash, skiing, golf; *Style*— Mike Sweeney, Esq; ✉ 36 The Ropewalk, Nottingham NG1 5DW (tel 0115 947 4690, fax 0115 947 4691)

SWEENEY, Nigel Hamilton; QC (2000); s of Alan Vincent Sweeney, of Dulwich, London, and Dorothy, *née* McKeer; *b* 18 March 1954, London; *Educ* Wellington, Univ of Nottingham (LLB); *m* 1, 1985, Joanna Clair, *née* Slater; 1 s (James Edward Hamilton b 21 Dec 1986), 1 da (Jessica Isabella Clair b 14 Dec 1990); m 2, 2002, Sheila Teresa, *née* Diamond; *Career* called to the Bar Middle Temple 1976 (Winston Churchill Pupillage Prize, Harmsworth scholar, bencher 1997); jr prosecuting counsel to the Crown 1987–91, first jr prosecuting counsel to the Crown 1991–92, sr prosecuting counsel to the Crown 1992–97, first sr prosecuting counsel to the Crown 1997–2000, recorder of the Crown Court 1997–; memb: Criminal Bar Assoc 1977, Health and Safety Bar Assoc 2005; *Recreations* golf, the arts; *Clubs* Garrick, Wisley Golf; *Style*— Nigel Sweeney, Esq, QC; ✉ 6 King's Bench Walk, Temple, London EC4Y 7DR (tel 020 7583 0410, fax 020 7353 8791, e-mail nigel.sweeney@6kbw.com)

SWEENEY, Walter E; *b* 23 April 1949; *Educ* Lawrence Sheriff Sch Rugby, Darwin Coll Cambridge, Univ of Hull; *m* 29 Dec 1992, Dr Nuala Kennan; 3 da (Siobhan, Lucy, Hannah); *Career* admitted slr 1976, in private practice until 1992, practising at Walter Sweeney & Co 1997–2003, practising at Yorkshire Law 2003–; MP (Cons) Vale of Glamorgan 1992–97 (Parly candidate (Cons) Stretford 1983); memb: Welsh Select Ctee 1992–97, Home Affrs Select Ctee 1995–97; vice-chm Legal Affrs Ctee 1994–97 (sec 1992–94); sec: Cons Backbench Home Affrs Ctee 1994–97, Legal Affrs Ctees 1994–96 (vice-chm 1995–97); currently occasional lectr in law Univ of Lincoln, former memb Vale of Glamorgan Community Health Cncl; pres Hull Incorporated Law Soc 2004–05 (vice-pres 2003–04); former cncllr: Rugby BC, Bedfordshire CC; former chm: Rugby YCs, Rugby CPC, Hull Univ FCS; memb N Cave Parish Cncl 2003– (vice chm 2005–), govr N Cave Sch 2003–06; *Recreations* theatre, walking, family; *Style*— Walter Sweeney, Esq

SWEETENHAM, William Francis (Bill); Order of Australia (AM) (1989); s of Vernon Brian Sweetenham, and Ruby Joyce, *née* Johns; *b* 23 March 1950, Rockhampton, Australia; *Educ* Mount Isa HS Queensland; *m* Cheryl Lillian; 2 s (Benjamin Robert, Timothy David), 1 da (Karen Louise); *Career* swimming coach; early career as swimmer then coach, state dir of coaching Queensland, head swimming coach Australian Inst of Sport Canberra until 1991, head swimming coach Hong Kong Sports Inst, nat youth coach Australian Swimming Inc 1995–2000, nat performance dir Br Swimming 2000–07; head coach 5 Olympic Games, coach 8 Cwlth Games, coach 9 World Championships, coach to 9 world record holders and 27 Olympic and World Championship medal winners; memb: American Swim Coaches Assoc, Australian Swim Coaches Assoc, Br Swim Coaches Assoc; Australian Coach of the Year for swimming (three times), Australian Coach of the Year for all sports; Churchill fell 1981; PM's Award (Australia) 1991; *Publications* World Championship Coaching; author of numerous articles; ten World Series videos; *Recreations* sketching; *Style*— Bill Sweetenham, Esq, AM

SWEETING, Adam Raymond Charles; s of Raymond Ernest William Sweeting (d 1966), and Vera Christine, *née* Potts; *b* 3 January 1955; *Educ* Brentwood Sch, Univ of York (BA, MA); *Partner* Gillian Harvey; *Career* feature writer TV & Home Video magazine 1979–80, sub ed Titbits magazine 1980–81, features ed Melody Maker magazine 1984–86 (feature writer 1981–84), freelance writer 1986; currently writer on different types of music for Daily Telegraph and on film and music for Uncut magazine; fndr dir Virtual Television Co (makers of Mr Rock & Roll series (Channel 4) and Pavarotti - The Last Tenor (Arena, BBC2)); regular contrib: Gramophone, Sunday Times, Independent on Sunday, The Times magazine; sometime contrib: Elle (UK and USA), Vogue, Q, You magazine (Mail on Sunday), Radio 4; judge Classical Brit Awards; *Books* Springsteen - Visions of America (1985), Simple Minds (1988), Cover Versions (2004); *Recreations* cricket (playing and watching), cycling, beaches, movies, opera, Formula 1; *Style*— Adam Sweeting, Esq; ✉ e-mail adam.sweeting@btinternet.com

SWEETING, Prof Sir Martin Nicholas; kt (2002), OBE (1995); s of Frank Morris Sweeting (d 1994), and Dorothy May, *née* Skelton (d 2003); *b* 12 March 1951, London; *Educ* Aldenham, Univ of Surrey (BSc, PhD); *m* 1975, Christine; *Career* Marconi Space and Defence Systems; Univ of Surrey: head of research into microsatellite systems (designed two NASA-launched satellites) 1979–85, exec chm Surrey Satellite Technology Ltd (SSTL) 1985– (designed 27 micro/minisatellites); currently: chair Satellite Engineering and dir Surrey Space Centre, chm AMSAT-UK; distinguished prof Univ of Surrey 2006; memb: EU Framework Prog 6 Space Advsy Panel, Aurora Advsy Ctee European Space Agency, Cncl Royal Acad of Engrg, Space Advsy Cncl Br Nat Space Centre 2006–, Space Science Prog Review Bd European Space Agency 2006–; chm of tstees: Nat Space Centre, Radio Communications Fndn; Royal Acad of Engrg Silver Medal 1995, Queen's Award for Technological Achievement (to SSTL) 1998, UK Engineering Cncl Gold Award, Space Achievement Medal Br Interplanetary Soc, Mullard Prize Royal Soc 2000, IAA Malina Medal Space Educn 2002, Industrial Leadership Award American Astronautical Soc 2004, Queen's Award for Innovation and Enterprise 2005, Gold Medal Royal Inst of Navigation, THES Award for Innovavtion (for the Disaster Monitoring Constellation); fell Inst Acad of Astronautics 1999; FIEE, FBIS, FRAeS, MAIAA, MIMgt, FREng 1996, FRS 2000; *Recreations* travelling, photography, amateur radio, cycling; *Style*— Prof Sir Martin Sweeting, OBE, FREng, FRS; ✉ Surrey Space Centre, University of Surrey, Guildford, Surrey GU2 7XH (tel 01483 689888, fax 01483 689503, e-mail m.sweeting@sstl.co.uk)

SWEETMAN, Mrs Ronald; Jennifer Joan; *see:* Dickson, Dr Jennifer

SWEETNAM, Sir (David) Rodney; KCVO (1992), CBE (1990); s of Dr William Sweetnam (d 1970), of Shepperton, Middx, and Irene, *née* Black (d 1967); *b* 5 February 1927; *Educ* Clayesmore, Peterhouse Cambridge, Middx Hosp Med Sch (MA, MB BChir); *m* 23 May 1959, Patricia Ann Staveley, da of A Staveley Gough, OBE; 1 da (Sarah Ann Staveley (Mrs Dawidek) b 20 March 1961), 1 s (David Ian Staveley b 9 May 1963); *Career* Surgn Lt RNVR 1950–52; conslt orthopaedic surgn: The Middx Hosp 1960–92, King Edward VII Hosp for Offrs 1964–97; hon conslt orthopaedic surgn Royal Nat Orthopaedic Hosp 1983–92; hon civil conslt in orthopaedic surgery to the Army 1974–92, orthopaedic surgn to HM The Queen 1982–92; fell UCL 1992–; conslt advsr in orthopaedic surgery to DHSS 1981–90; RCS: fell, memb Cncl 1985–98, vice-pres 1992–94, pres 1995–98; chm: DHSS Advsy Gp on Orthopaedic Implants 1973–81, MRC Working Pty on Bone Sarcoma 1980–85; dir Medical Sickness Annuity and Life Assurance Society 1982–97, dir and dep chm Permanent Assurance Co 1988–95; pres Royal Med Benevolent Fund 1998–2002; tstee: Newman Fndn 1989– (chm 2000–), Hunterian Collection 1999– (chm 2006–); chm Br Editorial Soc of Bone and Joint Surgery 1992–95 (sec and treas 1975–92); vice-pres RSAS Age Care (formerly Royal Surgical Aid Society) 1998–; Hunterian prof RCS 1967, Gordon Taylor meml lectr 1982, Stamford Cade meml lectr 1986, Bradshaw lectr 1992, Robert Jones lectr 1993; Hon Freeman Worshipful Co of Barbers; hon fell Peterhouse Cambridge 2003 (titular scholar); hon fell Br Orthopaedic Assoc (pres 1985–86), memb Combined Servs Orthopaedic Soc (past pres); Hon FACS, Hon FCS of SA, Hon FRCSI, Hon FRCSGlas, Hon FRCSEd, Hon FDSRCS; *Books* The Basis and Practice of Orthopaedic Surgery (jtly), Essentials of Orthopaedics (1970); also author of papers on bone tumours and gen orthopaedic surgery and fractures; *Recreations* garden labouring; *Style*— Sir Rodney Sweetnam, KCVO, CBE; ✉ 25 Woodlands Road, Bushey, Hertfordshire WD23 2LS

SWENSEN, Joseph; s of Anton Swensen, of Pearl River, NY, USA, and Kikue Okamoto Swensen; *b* 4 August 1960; *Educ* Juilliard Sch of Music; *Children* 3 s (David Noah b 17 Aug 1988, Jonathan Algot b 27 Sept 1996, Nicholas b 13 Oct 1999); *Career* conductor, composer, violinist and pianist; debut as pianist 1967, debut as violinist 1968, debut as conductor Juillard Sch 1975, violin recital debut NY 1982, London debut Sibelius Concerto with Royal Philharmonic Orch 1984; violin soloist 1984–88; performed as violinist with orchs incl: The Philharmonia, Cleveland Orch, LA Philharmonic, Pittsburgh Symphony, Bavarian and Stuttgart Radio Symphony Orchs, City of Birmingham Symphony, Bournemouth Symphony; conductor 1988–, princ conductor Scottish Chamber Orch 1996–2005; princ guest conductor: Stockholm Chamber Orch 1995–, Lahti Symphony Orch Finland1995–98, BBC Nat Orch of Wales 2000–03; conducted orchs incl: Royal Danish Symphony Orch, Stockholm Philharmonic, Finnish Radio Symphony Orch, Swedish Radio Symphony Orch (premier of composition 1995), Jerusalem Symphony, Minnesota Orch, Rochester Philharmonic, Kansas City Symphony, Bergen Philharmonic, Bournemouth Symphony, Bournemouth Sinfonietta, London Mozart Players, Helsinki Chamber Orch, Israel Chamber Orch, Aalborg Symphony, New World Symphony, Royal Liverpool Philharmonic Orch, BBC Symphony Orch, Toronto Symphony Orch, BBC Scottish Symphony Orch, City of Birmingham Symphony Orch, Hallé Orch, Ensemble Orchestral de Paris, LA Chamber Orch, Netherlands Symphony Orch, Orchestre Nationale du Capitole de Toulouse, Orquesta de la Ciudad de Granada, Orquestra Nacional do Porto; Leventritt sponsorship award 1978, Avery Fisher career award 1982; *Compositions* incl: Ghazal (for cello, orch and five female voices, premiere Helsinki Choral Orch Inkoo Finland 1993), Seven Last Words (for violin, cello, piano and percussion, premiere March 1993), Mantram (for string orch and amplified chimes, premiere Stockholm Chamber Orch Aug 1994), Elegy (for oboe and orch, premiere Finnish Radio Orch Nov 1994), Latif (for solo cello and low strings, premiere Israel Chamber Orch Dec 1994), Shizue Fantasy for Shakuhachi and String Orch (premiere Swedish Radio Orch Aug 1995), Sinfonia in B; *Style*— Joseph Swensen, Esq; ✉ c/o Victoria Rowsell Artist Management Limited, 34 Addington Square, London SE5 7LB

SWIFT, Prof Cameron Graham; s of Rev Graham Swift (d 1973), and Victoria, *née* Williamson (d 1996); *b* 5 April 1946; *Educ* Lawrence Sheriff Sch Rugby, Univ of London (MB BS), Univ of Dundee (PhD); *m* Margaret Rosemary, da of Henry K Vernon; *Career* MRC res fell in clinical pharmacology Univ of Dundee 1977–80, conslt physician Dept of Med for the elderly N Humberside 1980–84, dir of postgrad med educn N Humberside 1982–84, conslt physician and sr lectr Dept of Geriatric Med Univ of Wales Coll of Med 1984–86; prof of health care of the elderly: Univ of London 1986–2004, Univ of Kent 1986–2004 (emeritus prof 2004–); conslt physician KCH 1986–2004; sec Specialist Advsy Ctee in Geriatric Med Jt Ctee on Higher Med Trg 1992–94; visiting prof Christchurch Sch of Med NZ 1994; Br Geriatrics Soc: chm Trg Ctee 1989–91, chm Pharmacology and Therapeutics Section 1989–93, chm Scientific Ctee 1997–98, pres elect 1998–2000, pres 2000–02; memb Bd: King's Coll Inst of Gerontology 1997–2004, Age Concern; memb Cncl Int Assoc of Gerontology (Europe) 1995–2002; memb: Ctee on Safety of Meds 1987–92, External Reference Gp Dept of Health National Service Framework for Older People 1999–2000, Scientific Advsy Bd Nat Osteoporosis Soc 2001–, UK Medicines Cmmn 2002–05, Scientific Advsy Ctee Assoc of Medical Research Charities 2003–07, Guideline Devpt Gps for Fall Prevention and Osteporosis Nat Inst of Clinical Excellence (NICE) 2003–, Br Pharmacological Soc, Br Geriatrics Soc, Sub-Ctee on Efficacy and Adverse Reactions; chm Editorial Bd Age and Aging 2002–; hon med advsr Research into Ageing 1998–2000; FRCP 1988, FRCPI 1999; *Books* Clinical Pharmacology in the Elderly (ed, 1987); *Recreations* music, ornithology, hill walking, scuba diving; *Style*— Prof Cameron Swift; ✉ Guy's, King's and St Thomas' School of Medicine, Clinical Age Research Unit, Bessemer Road, London SE5 9PJ (tel 020 3299 9000 ext 3420, fax 020 3299 3441, e-mail cameron.swift@kcl.ac.uk)

SWIFT, Hon Mrs Justice; Dame Caroline Jane (Lady Openshaw); DBE (2005); da of Vincent Seymour Swift (d 1979), and Amy Ruth, *née* Johnson; *b* 30 May 1955; *Educ* Lancaster Girls' GS, Univ of Durham (BA, pres Union Soc); *m* 15 Dec 1979, Charles Peter Lawford Openshaw (Hon Mr Justice Openshaw), *qv*, s of late Judge William Harrison Openshaw; 1 da (Alexandra Caroline b 17 July 1984), 1 s (William Henry b 31 Aug 1986); *Career* called to the Bar 1977 (bencher 1997), in practice Northern Circuit 1978–2005, QC 1993, recorder of the Crown Court 1995–2005 (asst recorder 1992–95), dep judge of the High Court 2000–05, leading counsel to the Shipman Inquiry 2001–05, judge of the High Court of Justice (Queen's Bench Div) 2005–; *Recreations* home and family, cooking, theatre, walking; *Style*— The Hon Mrs Justice Swift; ✉ Royal Courts of Justice, Strand, London WC2A 2LL

SWIFT, Clive Walter; *b* 1936; *Educ* Clifton, Gonville & Caius Coll Cambridge (MA); *m* 1960 (m dis 1975), Margaret Drabble, CBE, *qv*; 3 c; *Career* actor, author, initiator The Actors' Centre; dir: LAMDA and RADA 1970s; currently poetry-speaking at The Actor's Centre; hon fell Liverpool John Moores Univ; *Theatre* debut Notts Playhouse 1959, RSC original long-contract artist 1960–68; Prospect prodns 1963 and 1966, Chichester 1966, 1971 and 2000; credits incl: Man and Superman, The Young Churchill, Dear Antoine, Dirty Linen, Inadmissible Evidence, The Potsdam Quartet, Roll on Four O'Clock, Messiah, The Genius, An Enemy of the People, Othello, Mr and Mrs Nobody, An Old Man's Love, Dona Rosita, Higher Than Babel, Richard Bucket Overflows (Cabaret) 2007; *Television* numerous single plays and series; serials incl: Dombey and Son, Dig This Rhubarb!, Waugh On Crime, South Riding, Clayhanger, The Barchester Chronicles, Churchill - The Wilderness Years, The Pickwick Papers, First Among Equals, Keeping Up Appearances (5 series); other credits incl: Peak Practice 1998, Aristocrats 1999, Born and Bred 2001–04; *Radio* debut reading Fielding's Tom Jones 1962, memb BBC Radio Rep 1973; credits incl: Poor Pen 2001, The Right Time 2000–04, The Go-Between 2002, The Old Curiosity Shop 2003, Measure for Measure 2003, Insane Object of Desire 2005, The Radezky March 2005, Much Ado About Nothing 2005, Fridays When It Rains 2006, Fuente Ovejuna 2007; *Film* incl: Catch Us If You Can, Frenzy, The National Health, Deathline, Excalibur, A Passage to India, Gaston's War, Vacuums; *Books* The Job of Acting (1976), The Performing World of the Actor (1981), All Together Now (play, co-author with Peter Buckman, 1981); numerous reviews, articles, poems for Theatre Quarterly, World Medicine, BBC World Service, part-adaptor with Michael Napier Brown and Wilma Holingbery of Anthony Trollope's An Old Mans Love 1996; *Audio Books* incl: The Moonstone, The Canterbury Tales, The History of Mr Polly, The Witch of Exmoor, The Adventures of Robin Hood; *Recreations* watching cricket and soccer, playing piano; *Clubs* Actors' Centre, London Library, Middlesex CC, BAFTA; *Style*— Clive Swift, Esq; ✉ c/o Roxane Vacca Management, 73 Beak Street, London W1R 3LF (tel 020 7734 8085, fax 020 7734 8086)

SWIFT, His Hon Judge David Rowland; s of James Rowland Swift (d 1986), of Heswall, and Iris Julia, *née* Hodson (d 1985); *b* 21 April 1946; *Educ* Kingsmead Sch, Ruthin Sch, Liverpool Coll of Commerce (winner National Mooting Contest 1969, Muir Matthews Prize 1969); *m* 14 Dec 1974, Elizabeth Josephine, da of Joseph Ismay Williamson; 2 s (Anthony b 1975, Robert b 1990), 2 da (Rowena b 1977, Jennifer b 1979); *Career* Percy Hughes & Roberts: articles 1964–69, admitted 1970, ptnr 1971–97; judicial appts: asst recorder 1989–93, recorder 1993–97, circuit judge (Northern Circuit) 1997–; Liverpool Law Soc: memb Ctee 1978–88 and 1992–97, advocacy trg offr 1980–88, parly offr 1992–95, hon treas 1993–94, vice-pres 1994–95, pres 1995–96; memb: Legal Aid Area Ctee 1983–96, Northern Arbitration Assoc 1991–97; chm of govrs Ruthin Sch 1992–99; *Publications* Proceedings Before the Solicitors Disciplinary Tribunal (Sept, 1996); *Recreations* sailing, reading, walking; *Clubs* North West Venturers Yacht, RSA; *Style*— His Hon Judge Swift; ✉ Northern Circuit Office, 15 Quay Street, Manchester M60 9FD

SWIFT, Graham Colin; s of Lionel Allan Stanley Swift, and Sheila Irene, *née* Bourne; *b* 4 May 1949; *Educ* Dulwich Coll, Queens' Coll Cambridge, Univ of York; *Career* author; *Awards* Geoffrey Faber Meml prize, Guardian Fiction prize, RSL Winifred Holtby award 1983, Booker McConnell prize nominee 1983, Premio Grinzane Cavour Italy 1987, Prix du Meilleur Livre Étranger France 1994, Booker prize 1996 (for Last Orders), James Tait Black Meml prize for fiction 1996; DLitt Univ of E Anglia, DUniv York 1998, DLitt Univ of London 2003; hon fell Queens' Coll Cambridge 2005; FRSL 1984; *Books* novels: The Sweet Shop Owner (1980), Shuttlecock (1981), Waterland (1983), Out of this World (1988), Ever After (1992), Last Orders (1996), The Light of Day (2003), Tomorrow (2007); others: Learning to Swim (short stories, 1982, reissued 1993), The Magic Wheel (anthology, ed with David Profumo, *qv*, 1986); *Recreations* fishing; *Style*— Graham Swift, Esq, FRSL

SWIFT, Lionel; QC (1975); s of Harris Swift (d 1971), and Bessie Swift (d 1991); *b* 3 October 1931; *Educ* UCL (LLB), Brasenose Coll Oxford (BCL), Univ of Chicago Law Sch (JD); *m* 1966, Elizabeth (Liz London, fashion conslt), da of Max Herzig, of Montreal; 1 da (Allison (Mrs Jeremy Kanter) b 1968); *Career* called to the Bar Inner Temple 1959, recorder 1979–96, dep High Ct judge Queen's Bench and Family Divisions 1978–96, bencher Inner Temple 1984, head of chambers 1993–2003; jr counsel to Treasy in Probate 1974; chm Institute of Laryngology and Otology 1985–86; *Style*— Lionel Swift, QC; ✉ 4 Paper Buildings, Temple, London EC4Y 7EX (tel 020 7583 0816, fax 020 7353 4979, e-mail clerks@4pb.com, website www.4pb.com)

SWIFT, Malcolm Robin Farquhar; QC (1988); s of late Willie Swift, of Huddersfield, W Yorks, and Heather May Farquhar Swift, OBE, *née* Nield (d 1996); *b* 19 January 1948; *Educ* Colne Valley HS, King's Coll London (LLB, AKC); *m* 1, 20 Sept 1969 (m dis 1993), (Anne) Rachael, da of Ernest Rothery Ayre, of Bolton-by-Bowland, Lancs; 2 da (Joanna b 1972, Catherine b 1975), 1 s (Daniel b 1977); m 2, 1 Aug 2003, Angela, da of Reuben Walters, of Sadberge, Co Durham; *Career* called to the Bar Gray's Inn 1970 (bencher 1998); in practice NE Circuit (ldr 1998–2002), recorder Crown Court 1987; Bar Cncl: co-opted memb Remuneration Ctee 1978–89, elected memb Public Affrs Ctee 1995–2002, elected memb Legal Servs Ctee 1998–99, elected memb Professional Standards Ctee 2000–02; *Recreations* fitness, cycling, music (lead singer Count One and the TIC's); *Style*— Malcolm Swift, Esq, QC; ✉ Park Court Chambers,16 Park Place, Leeds LS1 2SJ (tel 0113 243 3277, fax 0113 242 1285); 9 Lincoln's Inn Fields, London WC2A 3BP (tel 020 7831 4344, fax 020 7831 9945, e-mail malcolm@swiftqc.co.uk)

SWIFT, Dr Peter George Furmston; s of Herbert Swift (d 1988), and Catherine Nell, *née* Edwards (d 1977); *b* 22 January 1943; *Educ* Wyggeston GS for Boys, Downing Coll Cambridge (MA, MB BChir), Guy's Hosp London; *m* 19 Sept 1970, Heather, da of Douglas Hillhouse (d 1970); 3 da (Kate Hazel b 1973, Lucy Jane b 1974, Elizabeth Anne b 1976); *Career* SHO neonatal paediatrics UCH 1971, registrar in paediatrics Sheffield Children's Hosp 1972–74; sr registrar: Royal Hosp for Sick Children Bristol 1974–77, Exeter Hosps 1977–78; conslt paediatrician with special interest in endocrinology and diabetes Leicester Hosps 1979–2006; chm: Children and Young Persons' Advsy Ctee Br Diabetic Assoc 1983–86, Working Pty on Servs for Diabetic Children Br Paediatric Assoc 1987–89; sec Br Soc of Paediatric Endocrinology 1990–93; chm Steering Ctee Hvidore Int Research Gp; sec-gen ISPAD 2002–04 (memb Cncl, ed-in-chief ISPAD Guidelines 2000); memb: Diabetes UK, GMC, BSPED, ESPE; Arnold Bloom lectr Diabetes UK 2003; DCH; FRCPCH, FRCP (MRCP); *Recreations* sports; *Clubs* Leicestershire Golf; *Style*— Dr Peter Swift; ✉ 21 Westminster Road, Leicester LE2 2EH (tel 01162 217376, e-mail peter.swift3@ntlworld.com)

SWIFT, Rebecca Margaret; da of Clive Walter Swift, *qv*, and Margaret Drabble, CBE, *qv*; *b* 10 January 1964; *Educ* New Coll Oxford (BA), Tavistock Clinic (MA); *Career* ed Virago Press 1987–1993, fndr and dir The Literary Consultancy 1996–; tstee: The Maya Centre 2005, The New Writing Partnership 2005; memb Literature House Project Consortium Arts Cncl 2006; shortlisted for Kim Scott Walynn Prize 2004; *Publications* Virago New Poets (1990), Letters from Margaret: The Fascinating Story of Two Babies Swapped at Birth (ed, 1992), Imagining Characters: Conversations about Women Writers - A S Byatt & Ignes Sodré (ed), Poetry in New Writing Six (1995), Spirit Child (libretto, music by J Roditi, 2000), Driftwood Magazine (2006); *Recreations* swimming, walking, talking, eating, karaoke, tennis; *Style*— Ms Rebecca Swift; ✉ c/o The Literary Consultancy, Diorama Arts, 1 Euston Centre, London NW1 3JG (tel and fax 020 7813 4330, e-mail rebecca@literaryconsultancy.co.uk)

SWIFT, Robert; s of Max Swift (d 1960), and Leah Swift (d 1978); *b* 13 August 1941; *Educ* John Marshall HS LA, Univ of London (LLB), Coll of Law; *m* 25 Aug 1963, Hilary, da of Simon Bernard Casson (d 1971); 2 s (Mark b 1969, Simon b 1972); 1 da (Miranda b 1976); *Career* slr; Patent & Trademark Dept EMI Ltd 1967–71, Linklaters & Paines 1971–75, legal asst White and Case NY 1975, ptnr Linklaters & Paines 1976–2001 (head Intellectual Property Dept 1981–94), conslt Linklaters 2001–; vice-chm Intellectual Property Sub-ctee City of London Law Soc; memb: Jt Bar/Law Soc Working Pty on Intellectual Property Law 1986–90, Commercial and Consumer Law Ctee and Intellectual Property Law Sub-Ctee Law Soc; Freeman Worshipful Co of Slrs 1976; memb: Law Soc 1967, Patent Slrs' Assoc, Computer Law Gp; *Recreations* music, books, wine and food; *Style*— Robert Swift, Esq

SWINBURNE, Prof Richard Granville; s of William Henry Swinburne, OBE (d 1994), of Colchester, Essex, and Gladys Edith Swinburne (d 1988); *b* 26 December 1934; *Educ* Exeter Coll Oxford (MA, BPhil); *m* 1960 (sep 1985), Monica; 2 da (Caroline (Mrs David Cope) b 1961, Nicola b 1962); *Career* Fereday fell St John's Coll Oxford 1958–61, Leverhulme res fell Univ of Leeds 1961–63, lectr Univ of Hull 1963–69 (sr lectr 1969–72), visiting assoc prof of philosophy Maryland Univ 1969–70, prof of philosophy Keele Univ 1972–84, Nolloth prof of philosophy of the Christian religion Univ of Oxford 1985–2002; visiting lectureships: Wilde lectr Univ of Oxford 1975–78, Forwood lectr Univ of Liverpool 1976, Marrett meml lectr Exeter Coll Oxford 1980, Gifford lectr Univ of Aberdeen 1982–83 and 1983–84, Edward Cadbury lectr Univ of Birmingham 1987, Wade meml lectr St Louis Univ 1990, Dotterer lectr Penn State Univ 1992, Aquinas lectr

S

Marquette Univ 1997, Paul Holmer lectr Univ of Minnesota 2006; distinguished visiting scholar Univ of Adelaide 1982, visiting prof of philosophy Syracuse Univ 1987; visiting prof: Univ of Rome 2002, Catholic Univ of Lublin 2002, Yale Univ 2003, St Louis Univ 2003; FBA; *Books* Space and Time (1968, 2 edn 1981), The Concept of Miracle (1971), An Introduction to Confirmation Theory (1973), The Coherence of Theism (1977, 1993), The Existence of God (1979, 2 edn 2004), Faith and Reason (1981, 2 edn 2005), Personal Identity (with Sydney Shoemaker 1984), The Evolution of the Soul (1986, 1997), Responsibility and Atonement (1989), Revelation (1991, 2 edn 2007), The Christian God (1994), Is There a God? (1996), Providence and the Problem of Evil (1998), Epistemic Justification (2001), The Resurrection of God Incarnate (2003); ed: The Justification of Induction (1974), Space, Time and Causality (1983), Miracles (1988), Bayes's Theorem (2002); *Style—* Prof Richard Swinburne, FBA; ✉ 50 Butler Close, Oxford OX2 6JG (tel 01865 514406, e-mail richard.swinburne@oriel.ox.ac.uk)

SWINBURNE, Prof Terence Reginald; s of Reginald Swinburne, of Gravesend, Kent, and Gladys Hannah, *née* Shrubsall; *b* 17 July 1936; *Educ* Kent Co GS for Boys Gravesend, Imperial Coll of Sci and Technol Univ of London (BSc, PhD, DSc); *m* 23 Aug 1958, Valerie Mary, da of Daniel Parkes; 2 s (Julian Edward b 25 Sept 1965, Nigel David b 17 Jan 1968); *Career* reader Faculty of Agric Queen's Univ of Belfast 1977 (joined 1960), sr princ sci offr Plant Pathology Res Div Dept of Agric NI 1979–80, head Crop Protection Div E Malling Research Station 1980–85, dir AFRC Inst of Hort Res 1985–90, prof of hort devpt and sr res fell Wye Coll London 1990–98 (emeritus prof of hort 1998–); Govr Hadlow Coll; memb: Br Mycological Soc, Assoc of Applied Biologists, Inst of Biol; FIHort; *Books* Iron, Siderophores and Plant Diseases; *Recreations* sailing; *Clubs* Farmers'; *Style—* Prof Terence Swinburne; ✉ Tan House, Frog Lane, West Malling, Kent (tel 01732 846 090); Wye College, University of London, Kent (tel 01233 812410)

SWINFEN, Prof David Berridge; s of Thomas Berridge Swinfen (d 1973), and Freda Mary Swinfen (d 1990); *b* 8 November 1936; *Educ* Fettes, Hertford Coll Oxford (MA, DPhil); *m* 1960, Ann, da of A B Pettit; 2 s (Michael, Richard), 3 da (Tanya, Katrina, Nicola); *Career* 2 Lt KOSB (Malaya) 1955–57; lectr in modern history Queen's Coll (later Univ of Dundee) 1963–75; Univ of Dundee: sr lectr 1975–90, prof of Cwlth history 1990–, dean Faculty of Arts and Social Sciences 1984–88, head Dept of Modern History 1988–92, dep princ 1992–94, vice-princ 1994–2002; dir Dyslexia Scotland Ltd 2004–; chm Burnwynd History and Art Ltd 2004–; FRHistS, FRSA; *Books* Imperial Control of Colonial Legislation (1970), Ruggles' Regiment - The 122nd New York Volunteers in the American Civil War (1982), Imperial Appeal - The Debate on the Right of Appeal to the Privy Council (1987), The Life and Times of Dundee (1993), The Fall of the Tay Bridge (1994); *Recreations* music, gardening; *Style—* Prof David Swinfen; ✉ 14 Cedar Road, Broughty Ferry, Dundee DD5 3BB (tel 01382 776496, e-mail dswinfen@yahoo.co.uk)

SWINFEN, 3 Baron (UK 1919); Roger Mynors Swinfen Eady; s of 2 Baron Swinfen (d 1977), and his 1 w, Mary Aline (Mary Wesley; d 2002), da of late Col Harold Mynors Farmar, CMG, DSO; *b* 14 December 1938; *Educ* Westminster, RMA Sandhurst; *m* 24 Oct 1962, Patricia Anne, o da of Frank D Blackmore (d 1968), of Dublin; 3 da (Hon Georgina (Hon Mrs Liley) b 1964, Hon Katherine (Hon Mrs Davies) b 1966, Hon Arabella (Hon Mrs Mayo) b 1969), 1 s (Hon Charles b 8 March 1971); *Heir* s, Hon Charles Eady; *Career* Lt The Royal Scots; memb Direct Mail Services Standards Bd 1983–97; chm Parly Gp Video Enquiry Working Party 1983–85; memb: Sub-Ctee C House of Lords Euro Communities Ctee 1990–94, Sub-Ctee B House of Lords Euro Communities Ctee 2004– (also Sub-Ctee C 2006–), Select Ctee on Draft Disability Bill 2004; fell Industry and Parly Tst 1983; pres SE Region Br Sports Assoc for the Disabled 1986–; patron: Disablement Income Gp 1995–, 1 in 8 Gp 1996–2004, Labrador Rescue SE 1996–, World Orthopaedic Concern 2002–; dir The Swinfen Charitable Tst 1998–; JP Kent 1983–85; Liveryman Worshipful Co of Drapers; hon res fell Centre for Online Health Univ of Qld 2001–; ARICS 1970–98; *Style—* The Rt Hon the Lord Swinfen; ✉ House of Lords, London SW1A 0PW

SWINNERTON-DYER, *see:* Dyer

SWINNEY, John Ramsay; MSP; s of Kenneth Swinney, of Edinburgh, and Nancy, *née* Hunter; *b* 13 April 1964; *Educ* Forrester HS Edinburgh, Univ of Edinburgh (MA); *Family* 1 da (Judith b 1994), 1 s (Stuart b 1996); m, 2003, Elizabeth M Quigley; *Career* research offr Scottish Coal Project 1987–88, sr mgmnt conslt Development Options 1988–92, strategic planning princ Scottish Amicable 1992–97; MP (SNP) N Tayside 1997–2001, MSP (SNP) N Tayside 1999–; Scottish Parl: ldr of the Oppn 2000–04, convener Enterprise and Lifelong Learning Ctee 1999–2000, convenor European and External Rels Ctee 2004–05, shadow min for finance and public serv 2005–07, cabinet sec for finance and sustainable growth 2007–; SNP: nat sec 1986–92, vice-convener for publicity 1992–97, Treasy spokesman 1995–99, sr vice-convener 1998–2000, enterprise and lifelong learning spokesman 1999–2000, nat convener (pty ldr) 2000–04, finance and public service reform spokesman 2005–07; *Recreations* hill walking, cycling; *Style—* John Swinney, Esq, MSP; ✉ 35 Perth Street, Blairgowrie PH10 6DL (tel 01250 876576, fax 01250 876991); The Scottish Parliament, Edinburgh EH99 1SP (e-mail john.swinney.msp@scottish.parliament.uk)

SWINSON, Christopher; OBE; s of Arthur Montagu Swinson, of London, and Jean, *née* Dudley; *b* 27 January 1948; *Educ* Wadham Coll Oxford (MA); *m* 9 Sept 1972, Christine Margaret, da of Walter Yeats Hallam (d 1973); 1 s (Timothy b 1987); *Career* mangr Price Waterhouse 1970–78; BDO Binder Hamlyn: sr mangr 1978–81, ptnr 1981–92, nat managing ptnr 1989–92; ptnr BDO Stoy Hayward 1993–2004 (sr ptnr 1997–2004); comptroller and auditor-gen Jersey 2005–; memb: Cncl ICAEW 1985–2001 (vice-pres 1996–97, dep pres 1997–98, pres 1998–99), Financial Reporting Cncl 1990–2000 (dep chm 1998–2000), Financial Reporting Review Panel 1992–98, Bd Pensions Regulator 2005–; audit cmmr 2000–03; tstee Greenwich Fndn for the RNC 1997–2002; hon treas NCVO 1994–97; visiting prof Univ of Bournemouth 2006–; Freeman City of London 1985; memb Worshipful Co of CAs; FCA 1974; *Clubs* Athenaeum; *Style—* Christopher Swinson, Esq, OBE; ✉ Roseheath Wood, Bullbeggars Lane, Potten End, Berkenhamsted HP4 2RS (tel 01442 877564, e-mail cswinson@aol.com)

SWINSON, Jo; MP; *b* 5 February 1980, Glasgow; *Educ* Douglas Acad Milngavie, LSE (BSc); *Career* mktg and PR mangr Viking FM 2000–02, mktg mangr SpaceandPeople Ltd 2002–04, Scottish devpt offr UK Public Health Assoc 2004–05, MP (Lib Dem) E Dunbartonshire 2005– (Parly candidate (Lib Dem) Hull E 2001); memb Lib Dem Fed Exec 2002, vice-chair Lib Dem Gender Balance Task Force 2003–06, chair Lib Dem Campaign for Gender Balance 2007–; cncllr Milngavie Community Cncl 2003–05; memb Amnesty Int; *Style—* Ms Jo Swinson, MP; ✉ House of Commons, London SW1A 0AA (e-mail swinsonj@parliament.uk, website www.joswinson.org.uk)

SWINTON, Katherine Matilda (Tilda); *b* 5 November 1960, London; *Educ* Univ of Cambridge (BA); *Career* actress; *Theatre* RSC season 1984–85, The Tourist Guide (Almeida), Die Massnahme (Almeida), Man to Man (Traverse and Royal Court), Mozart and Salieri (Vienna, Berlin and Almeida), The Long Way Round (RNT); *Television* Zastrozzi (Channel 4), Your Cheatin' Heart (BBC 1); *Film* Caravaggio, Insel Ohne Hoffnung, The Open Universe, Aria, Friendship's Death, The Last of England, L'Ispirazione, Play Me Something, War Requiem, The Garden, The Party - Nature Morte, Edward II, Man to Man, Orlando, Wittgenstein, Blue, Female Perversions, Conceiving Ada, Love Is The Devil, War Zone, The Beach, Possible Worlds, The Deep End, Teknolust, Vanilla Sky, Adaptation, Young Adam, The Statement, Thumbsucker, Constantine, Broken Flowers, The Chronicles of Narnia: The Lion, the Witch and the Wardrobe; *Awards* Best Actress: Boston Film Critics, Las Vegas Film Critics; runner-up Best Actress: NY Film Critics, Toronto Film Critics, Dallas-Fort Worth Film Critics; Best Actress nominations: Golden Globe Awards, Golden Satellite Awards, Online Film Critics, IFP Independent Spirit Awards, London Film Critics, Chicago Film Critics; *Style—* Ms Tilda Swinton; ✉ c/o Hamilton Hodell Ltd, 5th Floor, 66–68 Margaret Street, London W1W 8SR (tel 020 7636 1221, fax 020 7636 1226)

SWIRE, Sir Adrian Christopher; kt (1982), DL (Oxon 1989), AE; yr s of John Kidston Swire, DL (d 1983), of Hubbards Hall, Old Harlow, Essex, by his w Juliet Richenda (d 1981), da of Charles Barclay; bro of Sir John A Swire, CBE, DL, *qv*; *b* 15 February 1932; *Educ* Eton, UC Oxford (MA); *m* 1970, Lady Judith Compton, da of 6 Marquess of Northampton, DSO (d 1978); 2 s, 1 da; *Career* Nat Service Coldstream Gds 1950–52, RAFVR and RAuxAF 1953–61 (Hon Air Cdre RAuxAF 1987–2000); joined Butterfield & Swire Far East 1956; John Swire & Sons Ltd: dir 1961–2004, dep chm 1966–87, chm 1987–97 and 2002–2004, hon pres 2005–; dir: Swire Pacific Ltd, Cathay Pacific Airways 1965–2005, HSBC Holdings plc 1995–2002; memb Int Advsy Cncl China International Trust & Investment Corporation Beijing 1995–2005; dir: Brooke Bond Group 1972–82, NAAFI 1972–86 (dep chm 1982–85); pres Gen Cncl of Br Shipping 1980–81, chm Int Chamber of Shipping 1982–87; memb Gen Ctee Lloyd's Register 1967–99; visiting fell Nuffield Coll Oxford 1981–89 (hon fell 1998); pro-chllr Univ of Southampton 1995–2004; tstee RAF Museum 1983–91, chm RAF Benevolent Fund 1996–2001, pres Spitfire Soc 1996–; memb Cncl Wycombe Abbey Sch 1988–95; Elder Bro Trinity House 1990; Air League Founders Medal 2006; Liveryman: Worshipful Co of Fishmongers 1962, Guild of Air Pilots and Air Navigators 1986; Hon DSc Cranfield Univ 1995, Hon DUniv Southampton 2002; Hon CRAeS 1991; *Clubs* White's, Brooks's, Hong Kong; *Style—* Sir Adrian Swire, DL; ✉ John Swire & Sons Ltd, Swire House, 59 Buckingham Gate, London SW1E 6AJ (tel 020 7834 7717, fax 020 7630 0380)

SWIRE, Hugo George William; MP; s of late Humphrey Swire, and Philippa Sophia, *née* Montgomerie (now Marchioness Townshend); *b* 30 November 1959; *Educ* Eton, Univ of St Andrews, RMA Sandhurst; *m* 1996, Alexandra (Sasha), da of Rt Hon Sir John Nott, KCB; 2 da; *Career* cmmnd 1 Bn Grenadier Guards 1980–83; head Devpt Office Nat Gallery 1988–92, dep dir rising to dir Sotheby's 1992–2001; Parly candidate (Scottish Cons and Unionist) Greenock & Inverclyde 1997, MP (Cons) East Devon 2001–; shadow min for the arts 2004–05, shadow min for culture 2005, shadow sec of state for culture, media and sport 2005–; non-exec dir Photo-Me Int plc 2005–; FRSA 1993; *Recreations* showing my pig; *Clubs* Exmouth Cons Club (pres); *Style—* Hugo Swire, Esq, MP; ✉ House of Commons, London SW1A 0AA

SWIRE, Sir John Anthony; kt (1990), CBE (1977), DL (1996); er s of John Kidston Swire (d 1983); bro of Sir Adrian Swire, DL, *qv*; *b* 28 February 1927; *Educ* Eton, UC Oxford; *m* 1961, Moira Ducharne; 2 s, 1 da; *Career* served Irish Gds (UK and Palestine) 1945–48; joined Butterfield & Swire Hong Kong 1950; John Swire & Sons Ltd: dir 1955–97, chm 1966–87, hon pres 1987–97, life pres 1997; former dir: Royal Insurance Co, British Bank of the Middle East, Ocean Transport & Trading Ltd, James Finlay & Co plc, Shell Transport & Trading Co plc; memb: London Advsy Ctee Hongkong and Shanghai Banking Corp 1969–89, Euro-Asia Centre Advsy Bd 1980–91, Advsy Cncl Sch of Business Stanford Univ 1981–90; dep pro-chllr Univ of Kent at Canterbury 1993–99 (memb Cncl 1989–99); hon fell St Antony's Coll Oxford, hon fell UC Oxford; Hon DL Hong Kong Univ 1989, Hon DCL Univ of Kent at Canterbury 1995; Liveryman Worshipful Co of Fishmongers; *Style—* Sir John Swire, CBE, DL; ✉ Swire House, 59 Buckingham Gate, London SW1E 6AJ (tel 020 7834 7717)

SWIRE, Rhoderick Martin; s of Patrick Douglas Swire, (d 1960), of Salop, and Joan Mary, *née* Allison (d 1970); *b* 27 March 1951; *Educ* Eton, Univ of Birmingham (BSc); *m* 11 June 1977, Georgina Mary, da of Christopher Ronald Thompson, of Salop; 1 s (Hugh b 1979), 2 da (Henrietta b 1981, Camilla b 1985); *Career* Peat Marwick Mitchell 1972–76; John Swire & Sons Ltd: gp accountant Hong Kong 1976–79, asst to chm Aust 1979–81, London 1981; GT Management plc: mangr unquoted investment 1981–88, main bd dir 1987–88; chm: Pantheon Ventures Ltd 1988–, Pantheon Group 1997–; FCA 1980 (ACA 1975); *Recreations* shooting, tennis, gardening; *Clubs* Boodle's; *Style—* Rhoderick Swire, Esq; ✉ Aldenham Park, Bridgnorth, Shropshire WV16 4RN; Pantheon Ventures Ltd, Norfolk House, 31 St James's Square, London SW1Y 4JR (tel 020 7484 6200, fax 020 7484 6201, e-mail rswire@pantheonventures.com)

SWIRE, Sophia; da of Humphrey Swire (d 2004), and Most Hon Marchioness Townshend (formerly Philippa Swire); *Educ* Queensgate Sch London, Univ of Manchester; *Career* fashion designer and entrepreneur; md Sophia Swire London luxury cashmere knitwear and accessories brand 1993–; exhibited: London Fashion Week, NY Fashion Coterie, Accessories Circuit, Premiere Classe Paris, Paris sur Mode, White, Milan; reg rep London Stock Exchange 1987; md Newswire Ltd producing BBC TV documentaries, current affairs and history 1993–, freelance reporter BBC World Service Radio and TV 1993–97; co-fndr Battle Against Narcotics 1990, co-fndr and tstee Learning for Life 1993 (chm Bd of Tstees 1993–2000, tstee 2001–02); memb: UK Fashion Exports 2000, Royal Soc for Asian Affairs, Pakistan Soc, Bhutan Soc; FRGS; *Books* Old Roads, New Highways (contrib, 1997); *Recreations* trekking, elephant polo, skiing, swimming, filming and photography, scuba diving; *Clubs* Frontline; *Style—* Ms Sophia Swire; ✉ tel 020 7370 7342, fax 020 7385 4111, e-mail sophia@sophiaswire.com, website www.sophiaswire.com

SWITHENBANK, Prof Joshua (Jim); s of Joshua Swithenbank (d 1971), and Ethel Eva, *née* Forster (d 1992); *b* 19 October 1931; *Educ* Friend's Sch Wigton, Univ of Birmingham (BSc), Univ of Sheffield (PhD); *m* 29 March 1958, Margaret Elizabeth Anderson, da of Rev James Herbert Manson; 3 da (Elizabeth b 7 May 1960, Christine b 28 March 1965, Shirley Joyce b 20 May 1966), 1 s (Joshua Ross b 11 July 1962); *Career* engr Res and Devpt Dept Rolls Royce Ltd 1953–58, engr Design Dept Canadair 1958, assoc prof Mechanical Engrg McGill Univ Canada 1958–61, prof Dept of Chemical and Process Engrg Univ of Sheffield 1961–; dir Sheffield Univ Waste Incineration Centre (SUWIC) 1992–; author of over 300 articles in scientific jls and books; fndr memb Watt Ctee on Energy Ltd 1975–, memb ACORD 1988–90, gen superintendent res Int Flame Res Fndn 1989–91; Walter Ahlström Prize Finland 2002; Hon Dr Technical Univ of Athens 1997, Hon DEng Univ of Sheffield 2003; FREng 1978, FInstE (pres 1987–88), FIChemE, FIWM; *Recreations* scuba diving, photography, travel, flying (private pilot's licence); *Clubs* British Sub Aqua (advanced diver and instr); *Style—* Prof Jim Swithenbank, FREng; ✉ Department of Chemical and Process Engineering, Sheffield University, Western Bank, Sheffield S1 4DU (tel 0114 222 7502, fax 0114 222 7501, e-mail j.swithenbank@sheffield.ac.uk)

SYCAMORE, His Hon Judge Phillip; s of Frank Sycamore, of Lancaster, Lancs, and Evelyn Martin; *b* 9 March 1951; *Educ* Lancaster Royal GS, Univ of London (LLB); *m* 22 June 1974, Sandra, *née* Cooper; 1 da (Hannah b 1978), 2 s (Thomas b 1980, Jonathan b 1983); *Career* admitted slr 1975, recorder 1999–2001, circuit judge 2001–; memb Criminal Compensation Appeals Panel 2000–01; ptnr Lonsdales slrs Preston and Blackpool 1980–2001; Law Soc: memb Cncl 1991–99, vice-pres 1996–97, pres 1997–98; govr: Lancaster Royal GS; Hon Dr of Laws: Univ of Westminster 1998, Lancaster Univ 1999; *Clubs* Royal Lytham and St Annes Golf, Athenaeum; *Style—* His Hon Judge Sycamore; ✉ c/o Courts Administrators Office, Sessions House, Lancaster Road, Preston, Lancashire PR1 2PDE (tel 01772 821451)

SYKES, Prof Bryan Clifford; s of Frank Sykes, and Irene, *née* Clifford; *b* 9 September 1947; *Educ* Eltham Coll, Univ of Liverpool (BSc), Univ of Bristol (PhD), Univ of Oxford (MA,

DSc); *Children* 1 s (Richard b 1991); *Career* Univ of Oxford: research fell Wolfson Coll 1984–89, lectr in molecular pathology Inst of Molecular Med 1989–97, prof of human genetics 1997–; chm Oxford Ancestors Ltd 2001–; *Publications* The Human Inheritance: Genes, Language and Evolution (1999), The Seven Daughters of Eve (2001), Adam's Curse (2003), Blood of the Isles (2006); also approximately 150 scientific papers; *Recreations* chess, astronomy, croquet, fly fishing; *Clubs* Athenaeum; *Style*— Prof Bryan Sykes; ✉ Wolfson College, Oxford OX2 6UD (e-mail bryan.sykes@wolfson.ox.ac.uk)

SYKES, Sir David Michael; 4 Bt (UK 1921), of Kingsknowes, Galashiels, co Selkirk; s of Michael le Gallais Sykes (d 1981; yr s of Capt Stanley Edgar Sykes, who was yr s of Sir Charles Sykes, 1 Bt, KBE), and his 1 w, Joan, *née* Groome; hp of unc, Sir John Charles Anthony le Gallais Sykes, 3 Bt (d 2001); *b* 10 June 1954; *m* 1974 (m dis 1987), Susan Elizabeth, 3 da of G W Hall; 1 s (Stephen David b 1978); m 2, 1987, Margaret Lynne, da of J T McGreavy; 1 da (Joanna Lauren b 1986); *Style*— Sir David Sykes, Bt

SYKES, Prof Elizabeth Ann Bowen; da of Sir Francis Godfrey Sykes, 9 Bt (d 1990), and Eira Betty, *née* Badcock (d 1970); *b* 17 September 1936; *Educ* Howell's Sch Denbigh, Bedford Coll London (BSc, Gamble Scholar, MSc), Univ of Edinburgh (PhD); *Career* res staff Nat Inst of Industrial Psychology 1959–62, res assoc Dept of Psychological Med Univ of Edinburgh 1962–65, lectr Dept of Psychology UCNW 1965–74; Middx Univ: sr lectr in psychology 1974–87, princ lectr 1987–90, reader 1990–92, prof 1992–, head Sch of Psychology 1993–97 (acting head 1991–93) emeritus prof 2002–; Assoc of Heads of Psychology Depts: memb Ctee 1993–2003, treas 1998–2003; UCL: hon res fell Dept of Pharmacology 1977–79, hon res fell Dept of Psychology 1979–92; author of articles and chapters on psychopharmacology, physical exercise and mental health in books and learned jls, initiator with Prof Hannah Steinberg, *qv*, of Steinberg Principle on new devpts in conservation areas 1989 (Town and Planning Act 1990); memb: Assoc for Study of Animal Behaviour 1963–2002, Br Assoc for Psychopharmacology 1978–, European Behavioural Pharmacology Soc 1986– (fndr memb), European Health Psychology Soc 1992–; sci fell Zoological Soc of London 1975–, assoc fell Br Psychological Soc 1988–; CPsychol 1990; *Style*— Prof Elizabeth A Sykes; ✉ 19 Torriano Cottages, off Leighton Road, London NW5 2TA (tel 020 7267 4783, fax 020 7267 4780, e-mail bowensykes@hotmail.com)

SYKES, Eric; CBE (2005, OBE); s of Vernon Sykes, and Harriet Sykes; *b* 4 May 1923; *m* 14 Feb 1952, Edith Eleanore, da of Bruno Milbrandt; 3 da (Katherine Lee b 6 Sept 1952, Susan Jane b 20 Sept 1953, Julie Louise b 2 July 1958), 1 s (David Kurt b 2 June 1959); *Career* comic actor, writer and director; wireless operator Mobile Signals Unit RAF 1941–47; varied TV and film career (20 feature films); numerous TV appearances incl writing and lead role in Sykes and A... Show for 21 years; silent film writer and dir: The Plank (V), Rhubarb Rhubarb, Mr H is Late, It's Your Move, The Big Freeze; theatre: School for Wives (Piccadilly London) 1997, Caught in the Net (Vaudeville London) 2001, Three Sisters (Playhouse London) 2003, As You Like It (The Peter Hall Co) 2003; film: The Others 2000, Harry Potter and the Goblet of Fire; Freeman City of London; hon fell Univ of Central Lancashire 1999; *Books* UFO's Are Coming Wednesday (1995), The Great Crime of Grapplewick (1996), Smelling of Roses (1997), Eric Sykes' Comedy Heroes (2003), If I Don't Write It Nobody Else Will (autobiography); *Recreations* golf; *Clubs* Royal and Ancient Golf; *Style*— Eric Sykes, Esq, CBE; ✉ 9 Orme Court, Bayswater, London W2 4RL (tel 020 7727 1544)

SYKES, Sir Francis John Badcock; 10 Bt (GB 1781), of Basildon, Berks; o s of Sir Francis Godfrey Sykes, 9 Bt (d 1990), and his 1 w, Eira Betty, *née* Badcock (d 1970); *b* 7 June 1942; *Educ* Shrewsbury, Worcester Coll Oxford (MA); *m* 1966, Susan Alexandra, da of Adm of the Fleet Sir Edward Ashmore, GCB, DSC, by his w Elizabeth, da of Sir Lionel Sturdee, 2 and last Bt, CBE; 3 s (Francis Charles b 1968, Edward William b 1970, Alexander Henry Ashmore b 1974); *Heir* s, Francis Sykes; *Career* admitted slr 1968, conslt legal firm of Thring Townsend, Bath, Swindon and Newbury 2002–05 (ptnr 1972–2002); pres Swindon C of C 1981; govr: Swindon Coll 1982–90, Swindon Enterprise Tst 1982–89; tstee: Roman Research Tst 1990–2002, Merchant's House (Marlborough) Tst 1991–, Wilts Community Fndn 1994–2000, Duchess of Somerset's Hosp 2003–; memb HAC; *Clubs* City Barge (Oxford); *Style*— Sir John Sykes, Bt; ✉ Kingsbury Croft, Kingsbury Street, Marlborough, Wiltshire SN8 1HU

SYKES, Gerard William; s of William Joshua Sykes (d 1987), and Dorothy Lily, *née* Freeman; *b* 3 December 1944; *Educ* Sir Roger Manwoods Sandwich Kent; *m* 1974, Rosalind Mary Louise, da of S Peter Meneaugh; *Career* articled clerk Percy Gore & Co Margate, qualified chartered accountant 1966, mangr Hurdman and Cranstoun 1968–71, ptnr Thornton Baker (now Grant Thornton) 1973– (int mangr 1971–73); Freeman City of London 1977; ACA 1966; *Recreations* vintage cars, skiing; *Clubs* RAC; *Style*— Gerard Sykes, Esq; ✉ Grant Thornton, Grant Thornton House, 22 Melton Street, London NW1 2EP (tel 020 7383 5100)

SYKES, Phillip Rodney; s of Sir Richard Adam Sykes, KCMG, MC (d 1979), and Ann Georgina, *née* Fisher; *b* 17 March 1955; *Educ* Winchester, ChCh Oxford (MA); *m* 26 June 1982, Caroline Frances Gordon, da of Michael Dawson Miller, of Scarsdale Villas, London; 2 s (Richard b 1985, Christopher b 1988), 1 da (Marina b 1991); *Career* Binder Hamlyn: joined 1976, seconded Nat West Bank plc 1985–86, ptnr 1986–94, head Insolvency and Recovery Servs 1991–94; ptnr Global Corp Fin Arthur Andersen 1994–2000; Moore Stephens: sr ptnr Corporate Recovery 2000–, head of corporate advsy services 2004–; ICAEW: vice-chm Investigation Ctee 1997–2003, vice-chm Insolvency Licensing Ctee 2003–, memb Professional Standards Bd 2005–, memb Joint Insolvency Ctee; dist cmmr Garth South Branch Pony Club 2006–; ACA 1986, FABRP 1998, MIPA 2000; *Recreations* riding, skiing, field sports, tennis, theatre; *Clubs* Le Beaujolais; *Style*— Phillip Sykes, Esq; ✉ Moore Stephens LLP, 1 Snow Hill, London EC1A 2DH (tel 020 7334 9191, fax 020 7651 1822, e-mail phillip.sykes@moorestephens.com)

SYKES, Sir Richard Brook; kt (1994); *b* 7 August 1942, Yorks; *Educ* Royds Hall GS Huddersfield, Paddington Tech Coll, Chelsea Coll London, Queen Elizabeth Coll London (BSc), Univ of Bristol (PhD), Univ of London (DSc); *m* Janet Mary Norman; 2 c; *Career* Glaxo Research UK 1972–77; Squibb Inst for Medical Research 1977–86; Glaxo: rejoined as dep chief exec Glaxo Group Research Ltd 1986–87, gp R&D dir Glaxo plc and chm and chief exec Glaxo Group Research Ltd 1987–93, dep chm and chief exec Glaxo plc 1993–97 (GlaxoSmithKline plc since 2000), exec chm 1997–2001, non-exec chm 2001–02; rector Imperial Coll London 2001–; chm Merlion Pharmaceuticals Pte Ltd 2005–; non-exec dir: Rio Tinto plc (formerly RTZ Corporation plc) 1997–, Lonza 2003–, Zeneus Holdings Ltd 2004–05, Metabometrix Ltd 2004–, Abraxis BioScience 2006–; pres: BAAS 1998–99, The R&D Soc 2002–; vice-pres: Nat Soc for Epilepsy 1995–, Br Lung Fndn 1997–; chm: Global Business Cncl on HIV/AIDS 1997–2000, Advsy Cncl to Life Scis Exec Ctee EDB Singapore 2000–, Healthcare Advsy Gp (Apax Partners Ltd) 2002–, Bioscience Leadership Cncl 2004–; dir: Br Pharma Gp 1998–2001, Int AIDS Vaccine Initiative (IAVI) 2000–04; memb: Cncl for Science and Technol 1993–2003, Advsy Cncl Campaign for Science and Technol in the UK 1993–, Fndn for Science and Technol Cncl 1993–, Bd of Mgmnt Ct of Govrs LSHTM 1994–2003, Cncl for Industry and HE 1995–, Trade Policy Forum 1995–2000, Econ Devpt Bd Int Advsy Cncl 1995–, Bd of Tstees Natural History Museum 1996–2005, Advsy Gp on Competitiveness to the President of the Bd of Trade 1997–99, Bd EFPIA 1997–2000, Bd of Tstees Royal Botanic Gardens Kew 2000–05, Cncl Royal Coll of Music 2001–, Cncl RCA 2001–03, Engrg & Technol Bd 2002–05, Strategy Bd DTI 2002–04, HEFCE Bd 2002–; visiting prof: KCL, Univ of Bristol; author of over 100 scientific publications; Hamao Umezawa Meml Award of the Int Soc of Chemotherapy 1999; Hon DSc: Brunel Univ, Univ of Bristol, Univ of Hertfordshire, Univ of Hull, Univ of Leeds, Univ of Newcastle upon Tyne, Univ of Huddersfield, Univ of Westminster, Univ of Edinburgh, Univ of Strathclyde, Univ of Leicester, Univ of Sheffield, Univ of Warwick, Cranfield Univ; Hon DUniv: Surrey, Sheffield Hallam; Hon MD Univ of Birmingham, Hon Dr in Pharmacy Univ of Madrid, Hon LLD Univ of Nottingham; hon fell: Univ of Wales Cardiff, Central Lancashire; Fleming fell Lincoln Coll Oxford; fell: KCL, Imperial Coll Sch of Med London, Imperial Coll London; assoc Inst of Med Laboratory Technologists (AIMLT); hon citizen of Singapore 2004; Hon FRCP, MInstD 1995, FRS 1997, FMedSci 1998, Hon FRPharmS 2001, FCGI 2002, FRCPath 2003, Hon FREng 2004; *Clubs* Athenaeum; *Style*— Sir Richard Sykes, FRS; ✉ Imperial College London, London SW7 2AZ (tel 020 7594 5001, fax 020 7594 5004, e-mail r.sykes@imperial.ac.uk)

SYKES, HE Roger Michael Spencer; OBE (2002); s of Kenneth Sykes (d 1988), and Joan, *née* Wharton (d 2005); *b* 22 October 1948, Grimsby, Lincs; *Educ* Wintringham GS, John Willmott GS, Newport Free GS Essex; *m* 2 May 1977, Anne (Annie), *née* Groves Gidney; 3 s (Adam Nicholas Spencer b 29 Nov 1978, Tristan Charles Spencer b 28 July 1980, Alexander James Spencer b 2 May 1988); *Career* joined FCO 1968; attaché: Caracas 1971–72, Freetown 1972–75, Karachi 1976–78; cultural attaché Valetta 1978–81, press offr FCO 1981–82, attaché Lagos 1982–86, dep high cmmr Port Vila 1986–90, FCO desk offr for India and Nepal 1990–93, political and economic sec Amman 1993–97, head of post Al Khobar 1997–2001, Br Dep High Cmmn Karachi 2001–05, high cmmr to Fiji (concurrently to Tonga, Vanuatu, Tuvalu, Kiribati and Nauru) 2006–; dir St John's Hall Mgmnt Co 2006–, Privy Cncl rep Cncl of Univ of S Pacific 2006–; *Recreations* golf, game fishing, cricket, social history, sampling red wine; *Clubs* Sheringham Golf, Suva Golf, Fiji; *Style*— HE Mr Roger Sykes, OBE; ✉ 47 Gladstone Road, PO Box 1355, Suva, Fiji (tel 0067 9322 9140, fax 0067 9322 9140, e-mail roger.sykes@fco.gov.uk)

SYKES, Rt Rev Prof Stephen Whitefield; *b* 1 August 1939; *Educ* Monkton Combe Sch Bath, St John's Coll Cambridge (MA, Carus Greek Testament prize), Harvard Univ (Joseph Hodges Choate Meml fell), Ripon Hall Oxford (Hulsean essay prize); *Career* St John's Coll Cambridge: fell, dean and dir of studies in theol 1964–74, asst lectr in divinity 1964–67, lectr in divinity 1967–74; van Mildert prof of divinity Univ of Durham and canon of Durham Cathedral 1974–85, regius prof of divinity and fell St John's Coll Cambridge 1985–90, bishop of Ely 1990–99, princ St John's Coll Durham 1999–2006 (pres Cncl 1984–94); chm: N of England Inst for Christian Educn 1980–85, C of E Doctrine Cmmn 1996–2001, Inter-Anglican Theological and Doctrinal Cmmn 2001–; *Books* Friedrich Schleiermacher (1971), Christian Theology Today (1971), Christ, Faith and History (ed, 1972), The Integrity of Anglicanism (1978), Karl Barth: studies in his theological method (ed, 1980), New Studies in Theology (1980), England and Germany, Studies in Theological Diplomacy (ed, 1982), The Identity of Christianity (1984), Authority in the Anglican Communion (ed, 1987), The Study of Anglicanism (1988), Unashamed Anglicanism (1995), The Story of Atonement (1996), Power and Christian Theology (2006); *Recreations* walking; *Style*— The Rt Rev Prof Stephen Sykes; ✉ Ingleside, Whinney Hill, Durham DH1 3BE (tel 0191 384 6465)

SYKES, Sir Tatton Christopher Mark; 8 Bt (GB 1783), of Sledmere, Yorkshire; s of Sir (Mark Tatton) Richard Tatton-Sykes, 7 Bt (d 1978; assumed additional surname of Tatton by deed poll 1977, discontinued at his demise); *b* 24 December 1943; *Educ* Eton, Université d'Aix Marseilles, RAC Cirencester; *Heir* bro, Jeremy Sykes; *Clubs* Brooks's; *Style*— Sir Tatton Sykes, Bt; ✉ Sledmere, Driffield, East Yorkshire YO25 3XG

SYMES, Prof Martin Spencer; s of Oliver Edward Symes (d 2005), and Beatrice Mary, *née* Spencer (d 1997); *b* 19 August 1941; *Educ* Dauntsey's Sch West Lavington, Univ of Cambridge (MA, DipArch), Architectural Assoc (PlanDip), Univ of London (PhD); *m* 23 June 1964, Valerie Joy, da of Harold James Willcox (d 1979); 1 s (Benedick b 1967), 1 da (Francesca b 1971); *Career* architectural asst: London CC 1963, Eero Saarinen Assocs 1964, Yorke Rosenberg Mardall 1965–67; architect Arup Assocs 1968–73, conslt Duffy Eley Giffone Worthington 1975–82, sr lectr UCL 1983–89 (lectr 1973–83), British Gas chair of urban renewal Univ of Manchester 1989–99 (head Dept of Architecture 1991–93), res prof UWE 2000–07; visiting fell Princeton Univ 1980, res fell Univ of Melbourne 1985, visiting prof Tokyo Univ 1990, associated researcher CNRS 1998; sec IAPS Int Assoc for the Study of People and their Physical Surroundings 1984–88, chm RIBA Professional Literature Ctee 1988–93, memb RIBA Validation Panel 2004–; jt ed Journal of Architectural and Planning Research 1984–93; Achievement Award EDRA Environmental Design Research Assoc 1992; Freeman City of London 1995; RIBA 1967, FRSA 1990; *Books* Architects Journal Handbook on the Reuse of Redundant Industrial Buildings (jt ed, 1978), Urban Waterside Regeneration (jt ed, 1993), The Urban Experience (jt ed, 1994), Architects and their Practices (jt author, 1995), Sustainable Urban Development (jt ed, 2005), Changing Professional Practice (jt ed, 2008); *Style*— Prof Martin Symes; ✉ 5 Hallgate, Blackheath, London SE3 9SG (tel 020 8852 6834, e-mail mssymes@aol.com)

SYMES, Robert Alexander (Bob); Baron Symes-Schutzmann von Schutzmannsdorff (cr Austria 1407); s of Dr Herbert Paul Schutzmann von Schutzmannsdorff (d 1937), of Vienna, and Lolabeth (Elizabeth), *née* Bruce Zipser; *b* 6 May 1924; *Educ* Realgymnasium Vienna, Institut am Rosenberg St Gallen, Regent St Poly; *m* 1, 4 Dec 1946, Monica (d 1998), da of Harold Byron James Chapman (ka 1917); 1 da (Roberta Anne b 4 May 1953); m 2, Jan 2007, Dr Sheila Gunn, eld da of James McGlasson, and Ann Millington McGasson; 2 step c (Matthew, Kester); *Career* Br Colonial Serv 1940–41, cmmnd RN 1942, acting Lt Cdr 1942–46 (despatches); freelance broadcaster, writer, film dir, experimental engr, lectr; UK press offr Royal Dutch Airlines 1950–53, BBC Overseas Serv 1953–56, dist offr i/c broadcasting Eastern Region Colonial Office Nigeria 1956–57; BBC: prodr Overseas Servs 1957–58, prog asst German Serv 1958–59, sci prodr and prog co-ordinator Tomorrow's World 1968–74, sci prodr and presenter 1974–80, dir SH Production (Anglo-Austrian bilingual prodn co producing films, documentaries and CD-ROMs); lectured to orgns incl: Br Assoc of Young Scientists, IEE, Chartered Inst of Surveyors, Inst of Engrs, numerous schs and engrg socs, Southern Electric on Tomorrow's World Today, Br Aerospace; ptnr S H Radio Independent Producers; former: pres and chm Inst of Patentees and Inventors, dir County Sound Radio Network plc, chm Border Union Railway, Special Constable Thames Div and Surrey (long service medal and bar), memb E Horsley PC, prospective Euro Parly candidate (Cons); chm of judges Int Railway Film Festivals, pres Sittingbourne and Kemsley Light Railway 2000–, patron Southern Vintage Agricultural Club, life memb Anglo-Austrian Soc; assoc Royal Aeronautical Soc; Knights Cross (First Class) Republic of Austria; *Broadcasts* radio work incl: History of Flying (series, prodr) 1958, History of Surgery (series, prodr)1958, The Ad Hoc Cook (series of cookery progs) 1982, Ad Hoc Living (series) 1983, series of progs on sci for China BBC English by Radio 1987, regular progs on BFBS, LBC and BBC German Serv (in German), film and television work incl: A Bit of an Experience (documentary on brain surgery, prodr) 1963, Model World (series, presenter) 1978, The Model World of Robert Symes 1979, The Line That Refused to Die (documentary, presenter) 1980, The Danube Power Game (documentary, researcher and presenter in Eng and German) 1981, A Lineside Look at Model Railways (presenter, Silver Award Int Film & TV Festival NY) 1984, The Strange Affair of... (series) 1985, Bob's Your Uncle (children's TV series) 1985–88, Tomorrow's World (regular contrib to series) 1986–98, The House That Bob Built (documentary in QED series, presenter), Making Tracks (series on railways, presenter) 1993–, Bahorama International (series of bi-lingual

S

railway films produced in Austria) 1995, two documentaries on the rebirth of the world-famous Austrian Gölsdorf locomotive No 310 1999–2000, The Sierra Madre Express (documentary) 2001, The Fastest Steam Engine in the World (documentary) 2002, The Heyday of the Royal Trains (documentary) 2002, documentary for Austrian and German TV exploring romantic Austria by train and boat 2007; regular science broadcaster BBC Southern Counties Radio 1997–2001, regular guest presenter Two Lochs Radio Garioch; *Publications* Powered Flight (1958), Crikey it Works - Technology for the Young (1992), Young Engineer's Handbook (1993), Eureka - The Book of Inventing (1994), numerous articles in model railway press and on travel and food; *Recreations* model railways, shooting, cooking, travelling, industrial archaeology, preserved trains, trams and steam cars, history and geopolitics; *Style*— Bob Symes, Esq; ✉ Green Dene Cottage, Honeysuckle Bottom, East Horsley, Surrey KT24 5TD (tel 01483 283223)

SYMINGTON, Anita Jane Henderson (Mrs James Longcroft); da of Kenneth Douglas Henderson Self (d 1998), of Norwich, and Hilda Oakley, *née* Cookson (d 1992); *b* 1 October 1950, Altrincham; *Educ* Newcastle upon Tyne Church HS, UEA (BA), Coll of Law; *m* 1, Sept 1977 (m dis 1989), Ian Symington; 1 s (Andrew b 17 June 1982); m 2, Aug 1993, James Longcroft (d 1994); 2 s (Charles b 10 Jan 1990, James b 16 Oct 1991); *Career* admitted slr 1977; Wartnabys 1977–79, full-time farmer Market Harborough 1979–80, legal advsr CLA 1980–83, Lovell White Durrant (latterly Lovells) 1983–91 (ptnr 1989–91), sole practitioner Symington & Co 1991–96, chief legal advsr CLA 1996–99, ptnr and head Agricultural Team Lee & Pembertons Solicitors 1999–; memb Cncl Agricultural Law Assoc; memb: Law Soc 1977, Country Land and Business Assoc (memb Legal and Property Rights Ctee and London Branch Ctee); Liveryman City of London Slrs Co; *Publications* various articles in legal press and in-house magazines; *Recreations* motorboating, skiing, interior decoration; *Clubs* Little Ship, Nelson Boatowners, Bembridge Sailing, Hurlingham, Carnegie; *Style*— Mrs Anita Symington; ✉ Lee & Pembertons, 142 Buckingham Palace Road, London SW1W 9TR (tel 020 7824 9111, fax 020 7824 8804, e-mail a.symington@leepem.co.uk)

SYMMONS, Prof Deborah Pauline Mary; da of late Raymond Keith Symmons, and Betty Symmons; *b* 23 March 1954; *Educ* St Bernard's Convent GS Slough, Univ of Birmingham Med Sch (MB ChB, MD); *Career* house surgn Gen Hosp Birmingham 1977–78, house physician Queen Elizabeth Hosp Birmingham 1978, SHO (communicable and tropical diseases) E Birmingham Hosp 1978–79, SHO (rheumatology and gen med) Hammersmith Hosp 1979, SHO (gen med) Selly Oak Hosp Birmingham 1979–80, registrar (gen med) Selly Oak Hosp Birmingham 1980–81, registrar (rheumatology and gen med) Guy's Hosp 1981–82, locum sr registrar Royal Sussex Co Hosp Brighton 1982–83, clinical res fell Dept of Rheumatology Univ of Birmingham 1983–85, hon sr registrar Queen Elizabeth Hosp Birmingham 1983–85, lectr Dept of Rheumatology Univ of Birmingham 1985–89 (also clinical tutor), hon sr registrar W Midlands RHA 1985–89; hon conslt rheumatologist: Manchester Royal Infirmary and Devonshire Royal Hosp Buxton 1989–94, Norwich NHS Tst 1989–, E Cheshire NHS Tst and Stepping Hill Hosp Stockport 1995–, Macclesfield Dist Gen Hosp; currently prof of rheumatology and musculoskeletal epidemiology and dep dir ARC Epidemiolgy Unit Univ of Manchester; delivered numerous lectures on rheumatology to confs and learned socs in UK and overseas; memb int ctees incl: Int League Against Rheumatism (ILAR) Ctee on Devpt of International Classification of Diseases 10 (ICD 10) to Rheumatology and Orthopedics (R&O), Bone and Joint Decade Monitor Project, Community Oriented Program for Control of Rheumatic Disease (COPCORD) prog (int advsr), EU project on indicators for musculoskeletal health; memb: Steering Ctee nat meeting on Outcome in Rheumatoid Arthritis 1987, BSR Sub-Ctee on computing 1988, BSR Educn Ctee 1989 (jr rep), BSR Heberden Ctee 1989, Arthritis Research Campaign 1992–99 (med sec); current memb: BSR Clinical Affrs Ctee, Rheumatology Specialist Working Gp (chm), RCP Rheumatology Sub-Ctee, NHS Exec Nat Specialised Definitions Working Gp, ARC Clinical Trials Sub-Ctee; memb Editorial Bd Annals of the Rheumatic Diseases; Selly Oak Hosp Jr Dr's Prize 1980, Winthrop Award for best scientific paper Midland Rheumatology Soc 1986, Stephen Whittaker Prize W Midlands Physicians 1986, Michael Mason Prize BSR 1993, Kovacs Travelling Fellowship in Rheumatology RSM 1992; memb: Assoc of Physicians of the UK and Ireland, American Coll of Rheumatology, BSR, Br Soc for Paediatric and Adolescent Rheumatology, RSM, Manchester Medical Soc, NW Rheumatology Club; MFPHM 1999, FRCP 1994 (MRCP 1980); *Publications* Autoimmunity (with W Ollier, 1992), Health Care Needs Assessment for Musculoskeletal Diseases (with C Bankhead, 1994); author of numerous book chapters, case reports, letters, research papers, invited papers and reviews, editorials and science papers; reviewer for various pubns incl: Annals of the Rheumatic Diseases, Arthritis and Rheumatism, Jl of Clinical Epidemiology, Jl of Rheumatology, Jl of Epidemiology and Community Health, Rheumatology, Scandinavian Jl of Rheumatology, The Lancet; *Style*— Prof Deborah Symmons; ✉ ARC Epidemiology Unit, University of Manchester, Stopford Building, Oxford Road, Manchester M13 9PT (tel 0161 275 5044, fax 0161 275 5043)

SYMONS, Christopher John Maurice; QC (1989); s of late Clifford Louis Symons, and late Pamela Constance, *née* Vos; *b* 5 February 1949; *Educ* Clifton, Univ of Kent (BA); *m* 13 July 1974, Susan Mary, da of Gordon Teichmann; 1 s (Nicholas b 1978), 1 da (Samantha b 1980); *Career* called to the Bar: Middle Temple 1972 (bencher 1998), Gibraltar 1985, Ireland 1988, Northern Ireland 1990, Brunei 1999; jr counsel to the Crown (common law) 1985–89, recorder 1993–2004, dep judge of High Court 1998–; *Recreations* hitting balls; *Clubs* Hurlingham, Boodle's, Berkshire Golf, All England Lawn Tennis, Royal Tennis Court, Royal Sotogrande Golf, Valderrama Golf, Jesters; *Style*— Christopher Symons, Esq, QC; ✉ 3 Verulam Buildings, Gray's Inn, London WC1R 5NT (tel 020 7831 8441, fax 020 7831 8479, e-mail csymons@3vb.com)

SYMONS, Mitchell Paul; s of late Alan Stanley Symons, and Louise, *née* Yager; *b* 11 February 1957; *Educ* Mill Hill Sch, LSE (LLB); *m* 1984, Penny Chorlton; 2 s (Jack b 1987, Charles b 1989); *Career* writer and broadcaster; researcher then dir BBC TV 1980–82 (progs incl Friday Night...Saturday Morning, Film 81), TV prodr 1982– (devised: Everybody's Equal 1987–, Your Number Please 1992); a princ writer British & Cwlth edns Trivial Pursuit 1985–86; regular contrib/columnist: Hello! 1988–99, Punch 1989–92, Sunday Magazine 1990–96, Evening Standard 1993–94, Daily Express, Daily Star; conslt: The Mirror 1996, Daily Mail 1996–; also contrib: New Society, The Observer, The Sun, The People, The Sunday Times, The Times, The Guardian, Sunday Express; numerous TV appearances (incl What the Papers Say), regular radio broadcaster; visiting lectr Post Graduate Media Broadcasting Course Highbury Coll Portsmouth 1996–99; If It's In the News Columnist of the Year 2002 (for Daily Express column); *Books* Forfeit! (1986), The Equation Book of Sports Crosswords (1988), The Equation Book of Movie Crosswords (1988), Journolists 1–4 (with John Koski, 1989–92), Movielists (with John Koski, 1992), Hello! Book of Crosswords (1992), Sunday Book of Crosswords (1992), The Chip & Fry Diet (with Penny Symons, 1992), Hello! Crossword Books 1, 2 and 3 (1994), The Book of Criminal Records (1994), The Man Who Short Circuited The Electric Chair (1996), Chris Tarrant's Dangly Bits (with Chris Tarrant, *qv*, 1996), The Lists Book (1997), The Celebrity Lists Book (1998), The Bill Clinton Joke Book (1998), The Celebrity Sex Lists Book (1998), National Lottery Big Draw 2000 (with David Thomas, 1999), All In (2000), The Lot (2002), That Book (2003), This Book (2004), The Other Book (2005), Why Girls Can't Throw (2005), The Sudoku Institute Book (with David Thomas, 2005), How to Avoid a Wombat's Bum (2006), How to Speak Celebrity (2006), Where Do Nudists Keep Their Hankies (2006), My Story (with Penny and Jack Symons, 2007), Don't Get Me Started (2007), Why Eating Bogeys is Good For You (2007); *Recreations* tennis, poker, cricket, bridge, cinema, swimming; *Clubs* Old Millhillians, West Worthing; *Style*— Mitchell Symons, Esq; ✉ e-mail mitchellsymons@columnist.com

SYMONS, Rex Herbert Moss; CBE (1993); s of Herbert Thomas Symons, OBE (d 1959), and Winifred May Symons (d 1999); *b* 10 May 1934; *Educ* Bournemouth Sch, Univ of Southampton (BSc, Fencing colours, pres univ theatre gp); *m* Margaret Gwendoline, da of Henry Charles Everett; 1 s (Paul Rex Charles b 1964); *Career* sales controller phenol Heavy Organic Chemicals Div ICI 1958–61; with British Drug Houses Ltd 1961–68; BDH Ltd (initially subsid of Glaxo, sold to E Merck AG 1973): mktg dir 1968–81, md 1981–89; dep chm Merck Holding Ltd (UK subsid holding co of Merck AG) 1989–91; chm: Dorset Enterprise Agency, E Dorset HA 1989–91, Bournemouth Transport Ltd 1989–, Dorset TEC 1991–97, Poole Hosp NHS Trust 1991–2000, CBI Health and Safety Consultative Ctee 1991–2002, Bournemouth Teaching PCT 2000–; pres Dorset C of C and Industry 1986; memb Health and Safety Cmmn 1989–2002, memb Employment NTO 1997–2002, Cncl Univ of Southampton 2000–, memb Better Regulation Taskforce 2002–; govr Bournemouth and Poole Coll of Art and Design 1996–2001; FRSA, MCIM, FIMgt; *Recreations* theatre, opera, books, gardening, travel; *Style*— Rex Symons, Esq, CBE; ✉ Bournemouth Transport Ltd, Mallard Road, Bournemouth BH8 9PN (tel 01202 636011)

SYMONS OF VERNHAM DEAN, Baroness (Life Peer UK 1996), of Vernham Dean in the County of Hampshire; Elizabeth Conway Symons; PC (2000); da of Ernest Vize Symons, CB (d 1990), of Richmond, and Elizabeth Megan, *née* Jenkins; *b* 14 April 1951; *Educ* Putney HS for Girls, Girton Coll Cambridge (MA); *m* 2001, Philip Alan Bassett, special advsr Strategic Communication Unit PM's Office; 1 s (James Alexander Bassett Symons b 1985); *Career* res Girton Coll Cambridge 1972–74, admin trainee DOE 1974–77, dep gen sec Inland Revenue Staff Fedn (ISRF) 1988–89 (asst sec 1977–88), gen sec Assoc of First Div Civil Servants 1989–96; sits as Labour peer in House of Lords 1996–, Parly under-sec of state FCO 1997–99, min of state MOD 1999–2001, min of state FCO 2001–05, dep ldr House of Lords 2001–05; non-exec dir British Airways plc 2005–; memb: Gen Cncl TUC 1989–96, Civil Serv Coll Advsy Cncl, Cncl Hansard Soc 1993–97, Exec Cncl Campaign for Freedom of Information, Cncl The Industrial Soc, Cncl Open Univ, Panel 2000; cmmr Equal Opportunities Cmmn, govr London Business Sch 1995–97, tstee IPPR 1994–97; hon assoc Nat Cncl of Women 1990–97, co-chm Women's Nat Commn 1997–; FRSA; *Recreations* reading, gardening, entertaining friends; *Style*— The Rt Hon Baroness Symons of Vernham Dean, PC; ✉ c/o Foreign & Commonwealth Office, King Charles Street, London SW1A 2AH

SYMS, Robert Andrew Raymond; MP; s of Raymond Clark Syms, and Mary Elizabeth, *née* Brain; *b* 15 August 1956; *Educ* Colston's Sch Bristol; *m* 1, March 1991 (m dis 1999); m 2, Feb 2000 (sep 2007), Fiona Mellersh, da of late Air Vice Marshall F R L Mellersh, CB, DFC; 1 s, 1 da; *Career* md building and plant hire co based in Chippenham Wilts 1975–; N Wilts DC: cncllr 1983–87, vice-chm and ldr majority Cons Gp 1984–87; Wiltshire CC: cncllr 1985–97, oppn spokesman 1985–90, whip 1990–93, vice-chm Fin Ctee 1990–93; MP (Cons) Poole 1997– (Parly candidate Walsall N 1992); PPS to chm Cons Pty 1999, shadow spokesman DETR 1999–2001, a vice-chm Cons Pty 2001–03, oppn whip March-Nov 2003, shadow spokesman on Local Govt, Housing and Religion 2003–; memb Select Ctee: on Health 1997–2000, on Procedure 1998–2000, on Tport 2001–03; N Wilts Cons Assoc: memb 1979–90, treas 1982–83, dep chm 1983–84, chm 1984–86; fndr chm Calne Devpt Project Tst 1986–97, fndr dir N Wiltshire Enterprise Agency 1986–90; memb: Wessex RHA 1988–90, Bow Gp, Atlantic Cncl, Freedom Assoc; *Recreations* cycling, reading, travel; *Style*— Robert Syms, Esq, MP; ✉ House of Commons, London SW1A 0AA (tel 020 7219 4601, fax 020 7219 6867)

SYNGE, Sir Robert Carson; 8 Bt (UK 1801), of Kiltrough; s of late Neale Hutchinson Synge and n of 7 Bt (d 1942); *b* 4 May 1922; *m* 1944, Dorothy Jean, da of Theodore Johnson, of Cloverdale, BC, Canada; 2 da; *Heir* cous, Neale Synge; *Style*— Sir Robert Synge, Bt

SYNNOTT, Hilary Nicholas Hugh; KCMG (2002, CMG 1997); s of Cdr J N N Synnott, DSC, RN, and Florence England, *née* Hillary; *b* 20 March 1945; *Educ* Beaumont Coll, BRNC Dartmouth (scholar), Peterhouse Cambridge (MA), RN Engrg Coll Manadon; *m* 28 April 1973, Anne Penelope, *née* Clarke; 1 s (decd); *Career* served RN 1962–73 (HM Submarines 1968–73); HM Dip Serv: joined 1973, UK Delgn to OECD Paris 1975–78, Br Embassy Bonn 1978–81, FCO 1981–85, head of chancery Amman 1985–89, head Western Euro Dept FCO 1989–91, head Security Co-ordination Dept FCO 1991–93, min and dep high cmmr New Delhi 1993–96, director (S and SE Asia) and subsequently (Asia-Pacific) FCO 1996–98, high cmmr to Pakistan 2000–03; Coalition Provisional Authy regnl coordinator for Southern Iraq 2003–04, consulting sr fell IISS 2004–; tstee Impact Fndn 2004–; visiting fell Inst of Devpt Studies Univ of Sussex 1998–99; Eric Lane hon fell Clare Coll Cambridge 2007; CEng, MIEE 1970–73; *Books* The Causes and Consequences of South Asia's Nuclear Tests (1999); *Clubs* Oxford and Cambridge; *Style*— Sir Hilary Synnott, KCMG; ✉ e-mail synnott@iiss.org

SYSON, William Watson Cockburn; s of William Cockburn Syson (d 1939), of Edinburgh, and Mary Jane, *née* Watson (d 1983); *b* 12 September 1930; *Educ* Broughton; *Career* Nat Serv Army 1949–51, TA 1951–58; joined Bank of Scotland 1947, sr managerial positions Edinburgh 1969–81, chief mangr Head Office 1981–90, asst gen mangr 1987–90; chm: City Site Estates plc 1990–99, Johnson Fry Second Utilities Tst plc 1993–97, Wiggins Group plc 1993–2002, Aitken Dott Ltd (t/a The Scottish Gallery) 1995–, LeggMason Investors International Utilities Tst plc 2000–03, Graham Tiso Ltd 2001–05, Premier Utilities plc 2003–05; dir: Great Western Resources Inc 1990–94, First International Leasing Corporation Ltd 1990–94, The British Real Estate Group plc 1990–96, Regent Investment Tst Ltd 1991–94, Scottish Value Tst plc 1991–2000; chm Bank of Scotland Edinburgh & District Mangrs and Officials Circle 1978; former lectr Heriot-Watt Coll and Univ, former examiner and moderator Inst of Bankers Scotland, memb Sub-Ctee Bolton Report on Small Businesses 1968; world sen Jr Chamber Int 1970, sr vice-pres Edinburgh and Midlothian Bn Boys' Bde 1970–90 (actg pres 1987–88); chm: City Centre Christian Outreach 1981–82, British Olympic Appeal Scotland 1991–93; hon treas: Victoria League Scotland 1969–75, East of Scotland Branch Br Red Cross 1974–82 (memb Scottish Fin Ctee 1976–81), Scottish Branch Soldiers Sailors and Airmen's Families Assoc 1974–82, Scottish Churches Architectural Heritage Tst 1980–84, UN 50th Anniversary Appeal 1994 (also vice-pres); treas and memb Cncl The Prince's Tst East of Scotland and Borders Area 1978–84; tstee Cattanach Charitable Tst 2000; FCIBS 1979 (memb 1954); *Books* Interpretation of Balance Sheets (1957), Sources of Finance (1973), Forestry (1985); *Recreations* art, music, reading, hill walking, sport; *Clubs* New (Edinburgh), Square, Cronies; *Style*— William Syson, Esq; ✉ Kilrymont, 6A Easter Belmont Road, Edinburgh EH12 6EX (tel 0131 337 1321); Business: 116/4 Hanover Street, Edinburgh EH2 1DR (tel 0131 225 5312, fax 0131 225 5787)

SYSONBY, 3 Baron (UK 1935); John Frederick Ponsonby; s of 2 Baron, DSO (d 1956); *b* 5 August 1945; *Heir* none; *Style*— The Rt Hon the Lord Sysonby

SZÉLL, Patrick John; CMG (2001); s of János Sandor Széll (d 1999), and Vera, *née* Beckett (d 1987); *b* 10 February 1942; *Educ* Reading Sch, Trinity Coll Dublin (MA, LLB, Julian Prize); *m* 1967, Olivia, *née* Brain; 2 s (Redmond b 1969, Thaddeus b 1976), 1 da (Benedicta b 1975); *Career* called to the Bar Inner Temple 1966, legal asst Miny of Housing and Local Govt 1969–70; DEFRA (formerly DOE/DETR): legal asst 1970–73, sr legal asst 1973–85, asst slr 1985–92, dir formerly under sec (legal) 1992–2002; head of the Int Environmental Law Div 1985–2002, legal advsr to UK Delgns at int environmental negotiations 1974–2002; Int Cncl Environmental Law Bonn: memb 1982–, regnl govr 1999–; memb IUCN Cmmn on Environmental Law 1994–2005; UNEP Global Ozone Award 1995, Elizabeth Haub Prize Free Univ of Brussels 1995, US/EPA Stratospheric Ozone Protection Award 2002; *Recreations* travel, hockey, ancient churches; *Style—* Patrick Széll, Esq, CMG

SZIRTES, George Gábor Nicholas; s of László Szirtes, of Budapest, now of Pinner, Middx, and Magdalena Kardos Nussbacher (d 1975); *b* 29 November 1948; *Educ* Kingsbury Co GS, Harrow Sch of Art, Leeds Coll of Art (history of art prize, BA, travelling scholarship), Goldsmiths Coll London; *m* 11 July 1970, Clarissa, da of Rev W S Upchurch; 1 s (Thomas Andrew b 31 Dec 1973), 1 da (Helen Magdalena b 13 Jan 1976); *Career* poet and translator; pt/t teaching jobs until 1975, head of art Hitchin Girls' Sch 1975–80, dir of art and history of art St Christopher Sch Letchworth 1980–89 (pt/t 1989–92), sr lectr in poetry Norfolk Inst of Art and Design 1992–; memb Int PEN 1980–; Br Cncl scholar 1985 and 1989 (latter spent in Budapest), Soc of Authors travelling scholar 2002, Leverhulme research fell 2003; int writer in residence Trinity Coll Dublin 2000; awarded PhD by pubn; FRSL 1982; *Poetry* The Slant Door (1979), November and May (1981), Short Wave (1984), The Photographer in Winter (1986), Metro (1988), Bridge Passages (1991), Blind Field (1994), Selected Poems (1996), The Red All Over Riddle Book (for children, 1997), Portrait of My Father in an English Landscape (1998), The Budapest File (2000), An English Apocalypse (2001), Reel (2004); work incl in various anthologies of modern verse incl: British Poetry Since 1945, The New Poetry, The Firebox; ed: The Collected Poems of Freda Downie (1995), The Colonnade of Teeth, Twentieth Century Hungarian Poetry (jtly with George Gömöri, also trans 1996), An Island of Sound: Hungarian Writing Before and Beyond the Iron Curtain (2004); *Translations* The Tragedy of Man (by Imre Madách, 1989), Through the Smoke (by István Vas, 1989), Anna Édes (by Dezső Kosztolányi, 1992), The Blood of the Walsungs (by Ottó Orbán, 1993), New Life (by Zsuzsa Rakovszky, 1994), The Adventures of Sindbad (by Gyula Krúdy, 1998), The Lost Rider (three centuries of Hungarian poetry, 1998), The Melancholy of Resistance (by László Krasznahorkai, 1999), The Night of Akhenaton:

Selected Poems of Ágnes Nemes Nagy (2003), Conversation at Bolzano (by Sándor Márai, 2004), The Rebels (by Sándor Márai, 2007); *Non-Fiction* Exercise of Power: The Art of Ana Maria Pacheco, New Writing 10 (ed with Penelope Lively, qv, 2001); *Awards* Geoffrey Faber Meml Prize 1980, Cholmondeley Award 1986, shortlisted Whitbread Prize 1992, shortlisted Forward Prize 2000, T S Eliot Prize for Poetry 2005; for translation: Déry Prize 1991, Gold Medal of Hungarian Republic 1991, Euro Poetry Translation Prize 1995, shortlisted George Cushing Prize 2002, Soc of Authors Travelling Scholarship 2002, T S Eliot Prixe 2004, American PEN Translation Award 2005; *Recreations* playing piano, contemporary art and music, football, table tennis, proprietor of Starwheel Press 1976–; *Style—* George Szirtes, Esq, PhD, FRSL; ⌖ 16 Damgate Street, Wymondham, Norfolk NR18 0BQ (tel 01935 603533, e-mail george@georgeszirtes.co.uk, website www.georgeszirtes.co.u); Bloodaxe Books, The Old Signal Box, Falstone, Northumberland NE48 1AB

SZOMBATI, HE Béla; s of Béla Szombati, and Eva Szombati; *b* 16 July 1955, Tel Aviv, Israel; *Educ* Eötvös Loránd Univ Budapest (MA); *m* 1978, Zsuzsa; 2 s (Kristóf, Dániel); *Career* Hungarian diplomat; joined Hungarian Diplomatic Serv 1980, Dept of Int Security Miny of Foreign Affrs 1980–82, third sec Hanoi 1982–85, Dept of Western Europe and N America Miny of Foreign Affrs 1986–88, second sec Washington DC 1988–91, foreign policy advsr Office of the Pres of the Repub 1991–94, ambass Paris 1994–99, dep head of state Secretariat for European Integration Miny of Foreign Affrs 1999–2002, ambass to the Ct of St James's 2002–; Cdr's Cross Polish Order of Merit 2001, Officier de la Legion d'Honneur (France) 2002; *Recreations* music, walking, football; *Clubs* Athenaeum; *Style—* HE Mr Béla Szombati; ⌖ Embassy of the Republic of Hungary, 35 Eaton Place, London SW1X 8BY

SZPIRO, Richard David; *b* 11 August 1944; *Educ* St Paul's Sch, Churchill Coll Cambridge (MA); *m* annulled; 2 s (Toby b 1971, Jamie b 1973); m 2, 1997, Hon Janie Henniker-Major; *Career* merchant banker; Wintrust plc: md 1969–2004, chm 1995–2004; *Recreations* golf, tennis; *Clubs* Mark's, Vanderbilt, Hurlingham; *Style—* Richard Szpiro, Esq

T

TABAKSBLAT, Morris; *Educ* Leiden Univ (Law degree); *m*; 2 s, 1 da; *Career* Unilever: joined 1964, various mktg, sales and gen mgmnt positions in Spain, Brazil and the Netherlands until 1984, joined main Unilever NV and Unilever plc Bds 1984–, personal products coordinator 1984–87, regnl dir N America and chm and chief exec Unilever US Inc 1987–90, chm Foods Exec 1990–93, chm and chief exec Unilever 1994– (chief exec 1992–), also tstee Conf Bd; non-exec chm Reed Elsevier plc 1999–; memb Supervisory Bd: AEGON NV, Royal PTT Nederland NV; memb Euro Round Table of Industrialists; chm Mauritshuis Museum; *Style*— Morris Tabaksblat, Esq; ✉ Unilever NV, Weena 455, 3013 AL Rotterdam, The Netherlands; Unilever plc, Unilever House, London EC4P 4BQ (tel 020 7822 5252, fax 020 7822 5898)

TABAQCHALI, Prof Soad; da of Mahmoud Nadim Tabaqchali, and Munira, *née* Kadri; *b* 15 December 1934; *Educ* English Girls' Coll Alexandria Egypt, Channing Sch Highgate, Univ of St Andrews (MB ChB); *m* 1970 (m dis 1998), Sir Christopher Booth, *qv*; 1 da (Nadya Christina); *Career* house physician Maryfield Hosp Dundee 1959, research fell Royal Free Hosp London 1959–62, asst lectr Royal Postgrad Med Sch London 1965–70; Bart's: lectr, sr lectr then reader 1973–86, prof and head Dept of Med Microbiology 1986–95; prof and head Dept of Med Microbiology Bart's and the Royal London Sch of Med and Dentistry 1995–98 (emeritus prof Dept of Medical Microbiology); hon conslt: NE Thames RHA 1974–94, Royal Hosps NHS Tst London 1994–98; memb Advsy Ctee for Dangerous Pathogens 1986–89, past memb Advsy Ctee MRC; author of over 250 scientific pubns and chapters in int jls and books; past memb Advsy Ctee Prix Galien (UK) Awards; Tulloch Award Univ of Dundee Med Sch; FRCPath 1986 (MRCPath 1984), FRCP 1993 (MRCP 1990); *Recreations* opera, music, travel, charity work; *Style*— Prof Soad Tabaqchali; ✉ 19 Eresby House, Rutland Gate, Knightsbridge, London SW7 1BG (tel 020 7589 2504, e-mail s.tabaqchali@qmul.ac.uk); Wolfson Institute for Preventive Medicine, Charterhouse Square, London EC1M 6BQ

TABNER, Leonard (Len); s of Arthur Leonard Tabner (d 1984), and Thelma, *née* Morten (d 2002); *b* 20 September 1946; *Educ* Victoria St Co Modern Boys South Bank Middlesbrough, Eston GS, Middlesbrough Art Coll, Bath Acad of Art (DipAD), Univ of Reading (MA); *m* 15 May 1971, Helen Lilian, da of Thomas Pitt de Paravicini, and Lillian, *née* Horrocks; 4 s (Isaac Thomas Tabner 22 April 1973, Samuel Leonard 7 Aug 1975, Reuben Frederick b 17 July 1980, Edward Arthur b 24 Jan 1983), 1 da (Kathleen Ella b 6 April 1985); *Career* artist; working on NE coast with British Steel Corp, Cleveland potash mine, Tees & Hartlepool Port Authy and Smith's Dock Shipbuilders 1976–87, offshore oil and gas industry 1987–88; cmmnd by Conoco/DOE/V&A to work in N York Moors Nat Park 1987–88, three month sea voyage to Falkland Islands and S Georgia as guest of RN 1990, two voyages on HMS Exeter N Atlantic 1992 and 1993, cmmnd by Gifu Prefecturial Govt to work in the Haku-San Mountains Japan 1995; worked 1995–: Ireland, arctic Norway, Northern Alaska, Arctic Ocean, Western Isles of Scotland; work in numerous public and private collections in UK and abroad; vice-pres Cleveland Wildlife Tst; *Solo Exhibitions* Middlesbrough Museum and Art Gallery 1973, Stockton Municipal Gallery 1975, Response to the Earth (N Arts Gallery Newcastle upon Tyne and Univ of Durham) 1976, Guisborough, Chapel Beck Museum and Art Gallery and touring 1977, Washington Tyne & Wear 1980, Cleveland and touring 1981, Moira Kelly Gallery London 1982, Univ of Durham 1982, 1985–86 and 1987, Oldham City Art Gallery 1985–86, Cleveland Potash Mine (Sunderland Museum and Art Gallery) 1987, Paintings and Drawings 1970–89 (Agnew's London) 1989, Cowbar Breakwater (Vanessa Devereux Gallery London) 1989, A Voyage to the South London (Broadgate) 1992, Retrospective Exhibition (Laing Art Gallery Newcastle upon Tyne) 1992 (also tour of Scotland and Ulster Museum Belfast 1993), Paintings From Recent Sea Voyages (Agnew's London) 1993, New Paintings (Agnew's London) 1995, 1996, 1997 and 1999, Myles Meehan Gallery Darlington 1998, Hatton Gallery Newcastle upon Tyne 1998, Retrospective Exhibition (North Light Gallery Huddersfield) 2001–02; *Two-Man Exhibitions* Redcar Blast Furnace (with Ian Macdonald) 1983–85, Smiths Dock (with Ian Macdonald, Smiths Dock and touring) 1986–87, V Fields (with Ian Macdonald, touring) 1988, Images of the Tees (with Ian Macdonald, touring) 1989, From the Land and the Sea (with Peter Prendergast, Scarborough Art Gallery and Glynn Vivian Art Gallery Swansea) 1991–92; *Group Exhibitions* numerous since 1970, incl: Artists' Parish Maps (organised by Common Ground, touring) 1986, Artists in National Parks (V&A, and touring UK and USA) 1988–89, Salute to Turner (Agnew's London) 1989, The Broad Horizon (Agnew's London) 1990, The New Patrons (Christie's London) 1992, Centenary Exhibition (Christie's London) 1994; *Books* Len Tabner Drawings - Response to the Earth (1976), Smiths Dock Shipbuilders (with Ian Macdonald, 1987), Images of the Tees (with Ian Macdonald, 1989), Len Tabner - Paintings and Drawings 1970–89 (1989), Inspiration of Landscape (1989), From the Land and the Sea (with Peter Prendergast, 1991), A Voyage to the South (1992), After Japan (1998); *Recreations* building, farming/conservation; *Clubs* Royal Over-Seas League; *Style*— Len Tabner, Esq; ✉ High Boulby, Easington, Saltburn by the Sea, North Riding of Yorkshire TS13 4UT (tel 01287 640948); c/o Thos Agnew & Sons Ltd, 43 Old Bond Street, London W1S 4BS (tel 020 7629 6176, fax 020 7629 4359)

TACKABERRY, John Antony; QC (1982); s of Thomas Raphael Tackaberry (d 1971), and Mary Catherine, *née* Geoghegan (d 1985); *b* 13 November 1939; *Educ* Downside, TCD, Downing Coll Cambridge (MA, LLM), Mountview Theatre Sch (Dip); *m* 1, Penelope (d 1994), da of Seth Holt (d 1971); 2 s (Christopher b 1966, Antony b 1968); m 2, Kate, da of Mark Jones; 1 da (Molly b 2000); *Career* lectr: Chinese Miny of Further Educn 1943–65, Poly of Central London 1965–67; called to the Bar: Gray's Inn 1967, Republic of Ireland 1987, California 1988; recorder of the Crown Court 1988–2005, currently head of chambers; HM Counsel NSW Aust 1990; pres: Soc of Construction Law 1983–85, European Soc of Construction Law 1985–87, Soc of Construction Arbitrators 2007–; memb: Arbitral Panels of Los Angeles Center for Commercial Arbitration 1987–, Singapore Int Arbitration Cncl, Indian Cncl of Arbitration (panel of int arbitrators); chm CIArb 1990 (vice-pres 1988); cmmr UN Compensation Cmmn 1998–2003; chm Street UK 2004–; FCIArb, FFB; *Publications* princ ed Bernstein in Dispute Resolution, author of numerous articles; *Recreations* good food, good wine, good company, photography; *Clubs* Athenaeum; *Style*— John Tackaberry, Esq, QC; ✉ Arbitration Chambers, 22 Willes Road, London NW5 3DS (tel 020 7267 2137, fax 020 7482 1018, e-mail john.tackaberry@arbitration-chambers.com)

TAEL, HE Dr Kaja; *b* 24 July 1960, Tallinn, Estonia; *Educ* Tartu Univ, Acad of Sciences Tallinn; *Career* Estonian diplomat; researcher Dept of Grammar Inst for Language and Literature Acad of Sciences Tallinn 1984–90, guest scholarship Uppsala Univ 1990–91, dir Estonian Inst Tallinn 1991–95 (chm Bd 1995–), foreign policy advsr to Pres of Estonia 1995–98; Miny of Foreign Affrs: joined 1998, exec sec Estonian-Russian Intergovernmental Cmmn 1998–99, DG Policy Planning Dept 1999–2001; ambass to the Ct of St James's 2001–; prof Tallinn Pedagogical Univ 1995–2000; Order of the Polar Star (Sweden) 1995, Order of the Lion (Finland) 1995, Order of the Aztec Eagle (Mexico) 1996, Order of the White Star (Estonia) 2000; *Publications* numerous translations, book contribs, articles and abstracts for int confs; *Style*— HE Dr Kaja Tael; ✉ Embassy of the Republic of Estonia, 16 Hyde Park Gate, London SW7 5DG (tel 020 7589 3428, fax 020 7589 3430)

TAGER, Romie; QC (1995); s of Osias Tager (d 2005), and Minnie Tager (d 1974); *b* 19 July 1947; *Educ* Hasmonean GS Hendon, UCL (LLB); *m* 29 Aug 1971, Esther Marianne, da of Rev Leo Sichel, of Reading; 2 s (Joseph, Simon (twins) b 23 Oct 1980); *Career* called to the Bar Middle Temple 1970; practising barr specialising in commercial, professional negligence and property law; founding head Selborne Chambers 2002–; memb Hon Socs of: Lincoln's Inn, Middle Temple, Inner Temple; memb Int Bar Assoc; chm Greenquest Gp; tstee Jewish Book Cncl; *Recreations* opera, theatre, travel; *Clubs* Peak; *Style*— Romie Tager, Esq, QC; ✉ Selborne Chambers, 10 Essex Street, London WC2R 3AA (tel 020 7420 9500, fax 020 7420 9555, e-mail romie.tager@selbornechambers.co.uk)

TAGGART, Prof David; s of Hugh Taggart, of Coatbridge, Lanarkshire, and Agnes, *née* Graham; *b* 1 July 1958, Glasgow; *Educ* Univ of Glasgow (MB ChB, MD), Univ of Strathclyde (PhD); *Career* sr registrar Brompton Hosp London 1992–95, conslt cardiac surgn John Radcliffe Hosp Oxford 1995–, prof of cardiovascular surgery Univ of Oxford 2004–; author of over 100 peer-reviewed pubns relating to most aspects of adult cardiac surgery especially coronary revascularisation; memb: Soc of Cardiothoracic Surgns of GB and I, European Assoc for Cardio-Thoracic Surgery 1996, American Assoc for Thoracic Surgery 2005; FRCSGlas; *Recreations* snowboarding, windsurfing; *Style*— Prof David Taggart; ✉ Department of Cardiac Surgery, John Radcliffe Hospital, Oxford OX3 9DU (tel 01865 221121, fax 01865 220244, e-mail david.taggart@orh.nhs.uk)

TAGGART, Michael Adrian; s of Michael Taggart (d 1985), and Susan, *née* Duffy; *b* Derry City; *Partner* Jennifer Larrissey; 1 s (Nicholas b 20 Oct 1983); *Career* co-fndr (with bro, John) and md Taggart Homes Ltd 1989–; *Style*— Michael Taggart, Esq; ✉ Taggart Homes Ltd, Unit 1, First Floor, Spencer House, Spencer Road, Londonderry BT47 1AA

TAHIR, Dr Mustapha Mohammed; s of Mohammed Tahir (d 1969), and Sa'adatu, *née* Adamu; *b* 12 September 1960, Sokoto, Nigeria; *Educ* Govt Coll Sokoto Nigeria, Sch of Basic Studies Ahmadu Bello Univ Zaria Nigeria (regnl govt scholar), Univ of Benin Nigeria (MB BS), Royal Coll of Obstetricians and Gynaecologists London (DFFP, Prize for original research presentation), Wessex Deanery (Joint Ctee Cert PG Trg in GP); *m* 2 July 2004, Clare Jane, *née* Murphy; 1 s (Jamal Mustapha Tahir b 25 Aug 2006); *Career* house offr then SHO rotation Univ Teaching Hosp Benin 1985–90, SHO Redruth Hosp, Royal Cornwall Hosp and Hammersmith Hosp London 1991–93, clinical research fell, lectr, clinical asst and registrar in obstetrics and gynaecology Southmead and St Michael's Hosps Bristol 1993–97, SHO Seymour Clinic and Princess Margaret Hosp Swindon 1997–99, GP registrar Old Town Surgery Swindon 1999–2000, specialist registrar Pewsey Surgery 2000–01, locum GP 2001–02, GP Riverview Park Surgery Gravesend and Shrubbery Surgery Northfleet 2003–; memb Cncl and tstee RSM 2005– (London Cncl rep Finance and Exec Ctee 2005–), GP rep for BMA Dartford, Gravesham and Swanley branch 2004–; govr Dover Road East Primary Sch Gravesend 2006–; memb: GMC, MDU, BMA; FRSM; *Recreations* football (Manchester United FC), travel, current affairs, medical law and ethics; *Style*— Dr Mustapha Tahir; ✉ The Riverview Park Surgery, 1 Whinfell Way, Gravesend, Kent DA12 4RX (tel 01474 363020, fax 01474 568861); The Shrubbery Surgery, 65A Perry Street, Northfleet, Kent DA11 8RD

TAIT, Eric; MBE (Mil 1980); s of William Johnston Tait (d 1959), and Sarah, *née* Jones (d 1996); *b* 10 January 1945; *Educ* George Heriot's Sch, RMA Sandhurst, Univ of London (BSc), Univ of Cambridge (MPhil); *m* 1, 29 March 1967 (m dis 1998), Agnes Jane Boag; 1 s (Michael b 1969), 1 da (Eva b 1973); *m* 2, 5 Dec 1998, Stacey Jane, *née* Todd; *Career* Lt-Col RE, served Germany, Middle East, Caribbean, NI (despatches 1976); dir Euro ops Pannell Kerr Forster 1989–92, exec dir PKF International 1992–; ed-in-chief The Accountants Magazine; sec Inst of CAs of Scotland 1984–89; memb Exec Scottish Cncl for Devpt and Industry 1984–89, chm Univ of Nottingham and Trent Euro Advsy Forum 1993–98; FRSA 1997; *Recreations* hill walking, swimming, reading, writing; *Style*— Eric Tait, Esq, MBE; ✉ PKF International Ltd, Farringdon Place, 20 Farringdon Road, London EC1H 3AP (tel 020 7065 0000, fax 020 7065 0650, e-mail eric.tait@pkf.com)

TAIT, Marion Hooper (Mrs Marion Morse); CBE (2003, OBE 1992); da of Charles Arnold Browell Tait, OBE (d 1962), of London, and Betty Maude, *née* Hooper; *b* 7 October 1950; *Educ* Royal Acad of Dancing, Royal Ballet Sch; *m* 9 Oct 1971, David Thomas Morse, s of Thomas Walter Morse (d 1984); *Career* princ dancer with Sadler's Wells Royal Ballet (now The Birmingham Royal Ballet); ballet mistress Birmingham Royal Ballet 1995; worked with leading choreographers and had roles created by: Sir Kenneth MacMillan, Sir Frederick Ashton, David Bintley, Christopher Bruce, Joe Layton; danced all maj classical roles; guest dancer: The Houston Ballet, Munich Ballet, Japan, Aust, Poland (Polich Ballet's Bicentennial medal of Honour); productions for: Hong Kong Ballet, Nat Ballet of Canada; nominated Olivier Award (for Romeo and Juliet) 1994, Dancer of the Year (Dance and Dancers magazine) 1994, Evening Standard Ballet Award (for outstanding performance) 1994, nominated Olivier Award for Outstanding Achievement in Dance (for Pillar of Fire) 1996; *Recreations* needlework; *Style*— Ms Marion Tait, CBE; ✉ c/o Birmingham Royal Ballet, Hippodrome Theatre, Thorp Street, Birmingham B5 4AU

TAIT, Nigel Gordon Thomas Michael; s of Leonard Horsted (d 1977), of Grove, and Teresa Tait; *b* 5 April 1963, London; *Educ* Maidstone Sch for Boys, Worthing Sixth Form Coll, Univ of Nottingham (BA), Trent Poly; *partner* Helen Davis, *née* Greene; 2 s (William James b 18 Sept 1991, Louis Frederick b 15 May 1997), 1 da (Georgia Frances b 9 July 1993); *Career* admitted slr 1988; ptnr Carter-Ruck 1990– (articled clerk 1986–88); memb Law Soc ctees on privacy, defamation, pre-action protocol and 1996 Defamation Act; *Publications* Carter-Ruck on Libel and Slander (contrib, 4 edn and 5 edn); *Recreations* family, supporting Chelsea FC; *Style*— Nigel Tait, Esq; ✉ Carter-Ruck, International Press Centre, 76 Shoe Lane, London EC4A 3JB (tel 020 7353 5005, fax 020 7353 1062, e-mail nigel.tait@carter-ruck.com)

TAIT, Simon John Anderson; s of William Anderson Tait (d 1973), and Alice Mary, *née* Crowther (d 2004); *b* 30 January 1948; *Educ* Hawes Down Secdy Modern Sch, Open Univ (BA); *m* 1979, Ann Sandra, da of George William Hugh Williams (d 1990); 1 s (Adam Anderson b 1988); *Career* journalist; Croydon Advertiser 1966, Brighton Evening Argus 1970, Newham Recorder 1971, Manchester Evening News 1972, writer Government Info Serv 1975, head of PR servs V&A 1980, Telegraph Sunday Magazine 1984, freelance writer 1985, The Times 1988–92, freelance 1992–; co-ed Arts Industry 2003–; *Books* Palaces of Discovery (1989), Times Guide to Museums and Galleries (1989–90 and 1990–91); *Recreations* finding out; *Clubs* Garrick; *Style*— Simon Tait; ✉ 12 Derwent Grove, London SE22 8EA (tel 020 8693 5672)

TALBOT, John Andrew; s of Robert Talbot and Lucy Eileen, *née* Jarvis; *b* 2 August 1949; *Educ* Queen's Sch Wisbech; *m* 1 (m dis), Susan Anne, *née* Hollingberry; 1 s (Martin b 5 March 1969 d 1998), 1 da (Helen b 28 Dec 1970); *m* 2, Jennifer Anne, *née* Crouch; 2 da (Hannah b 7 April 1982, Bethany b 7 Aug 1984), 1 s (George b 25 March 1991); *Career* articled clerk Larking, Larking and Whiting Wisbech 1966 (transferred to Stevenson Smart & Co Peterborough), qualified 1971, various accounting posts 1971–75, joined Spicer and Pegler Nottingham 1975 (ptnr specialising in insolvency and investigation work 1980); Arthur Andersen: ptnr establishing Corp Recovery Practice Birmingham 1983, ptnr responsible for worldwide Corp Fin Gp 1996–99 (ret); ptnr: Talbot Hughes LLP 2001–05, Kroll Talbot Hughes 2005–; chm English National Ballet 2004–; FCA 1971; *Recreations* classical dance, contemporary art, iron age history, natural history; *Style*— John Talbot, Esq; ✉ Kroll Talbot Hughes, 10 Fleet Place, London EC4M 7RB

TALBOT, Prof Michael Owen; s of Prof Alan Talbot (d 1981), and Dr Annelise Talbot, *née* Tømmerup; *b* 4 January 1943; *Educ* Welwyn Garden City GS, Royal Coll of Music (ARCM), Clare Coll Cambridge (open scholar, BA, MusB, PhD); *m* 26 Sept 1970, Shirley Ellen Mashiane-Talbot, da of Jacob Mashiane (d 1975), of SA; 1 s (Stephen b 1975), 1 da (Natasha b 1982); *Career* Univ of Liverpool: asst lectr then lectr in music 1968–79, sr lectr in music 1979–83, reader in music 1983–86, Alsop prof of music 1986–2003, emeritus prof 2003–; memb: Royal Musical Assoc, Società Italiana di Musicologia; memb Editorial Bd: Music and Letters, Istituto Italiano Antonio Vivaldi; corresponding memb Ateneo Veneto 1986, FBA 1990; Cavaliere dell' Ordine Al Merito della Repubblica Italiana 1980; *Books* Vivaldi (1978), Vivaldi (1979), Albinoni: Leben und Werk (1980), Antonio Vivaldi: A Guide to Research (1988), Tomaso Albinoni: The Venetian Composer and His World (1990), Benedetto Vinaccesi: A Musician in Brescia and Venice in the Age of Corelli (1994), The Sacred Vocal Music of Antonio Vivaldi (1995), Venetian Music in the Age of Vivaldi (1999), The Finale in Western Instrumental Music (2001), The Chamber Cantatas of Antonio Vivaldi (2006); *Recreations* chess, reading novels, travel; *Style*— Prof Michael Talbot, FBA; ✉ 36 Montclair Drive, Liverpool L18 0HA (tel 0151 722 3328); Department of Music, University of Liverpool, PO Box 147, Liverpool L69 7WW (tel 0151 794 3095, fax 0151 794 3141, e-mail mtalbot@liv.ac.uk)

TALBOT, Patrick John; QC (1990); s of John Bentley Talbot, MC, of Farnham, Surrey, and Marguerite Maxwell, *née* Townley (d 1995); *b* 28 July 1946; *Educ* Charterhouse, UC Oxford (MA); *m* 1, 8 May 1976 (m dis 1999), Judith Anne, da of David Percival Urwin; 2 da (Sophie Camilla b 28 Nov 1977, Alexandra Claire Maxwell b 8 Nov 1979), 1 s (William Patrick Charles b 2 June 1983); *m* 2, 28 Dec 2000, Elizabeth, da of Ronald Evans; 2 s (Theodore Henry b 16 Sept 1998, Caspar Hugh b 6 May 2001); *Career* called to the Bar Lincoln's Inn 1969 (bencher 1996); in practice Chancery Bar 1970–, recorder 1997–; memb: Senate of Inns of Court and the Bar 1974–77, Cncl of Legal Educn 1977–95 (vice-chm 1992–95), Gen Cncl of the Bar 1993; a judicial chm City Disputes Panel 1997–2000; Lt Bailiff Royal Court of Guernsey 2000–; chm Ripieno Choir 2003–; *Recreations* cricket, skiing, bridge, collecting old toys, choral singing; *Clubs* MCC, Wimbledon Wanderers Cricket; *Style*— Patrick Talbot, Esq, QC; ✉ Serle Court, 6 New Square, Lincoln's Inn, London WC2A 3QS (tel 020 7242 6105, fax 020 7405 4004, e-mail ptalbot@serlecourt.co.uk)

TALBOT, Paul Darius; s of William Ernest Talbot (d 1970), and Winifred May, *née* Mason (d 1991); *b* 9 January 1947; *Educ* Gordon's Sch W End Woking Surrey; *m* May 1970, Pamela; 1 s (Darren William b 12 Feb 1971); *Career* with Hill Samuel 1964–81, sales dir Wardley Unit Trust Managers 1981–83; md: Brown Shipley Unit Trust Managers Ltd 1983–92, Brown Shipley Asset Management Ltd 1989–92; exec dir Fidelity Investment Services Ltd 1992–96, sales dir Portfolio Fund Management Ltd 1996–; memb Exec Ctee Assoc of Unit Tsts and Investment Funds 1987–90 and 1994–95; *Recreations* golf, bridge; *Style*— Paul D Talbot, Esq; ✉ Green Courts, 148 Ember Lane, Esher, Surrey KT10 8EJ (tel 020 8398 4603); Portfolio Fund Management Ltd, 64 London Wall, London EC2M 5TP (tel 020 7638 0808, fax 020 7638 0050)

TALBOT OF MALAHIDE, 10 Baron (I 1831); Reginald John Richard Arundell; DL (Wilts); also Hereditary Lord Adm of Malahide and the Adjacent Seas (a distinction dating by charter from 5 March in the 15 year of the reign of Edward IV). The mother of the 2 and 3 Barons, who was the first holder of the title, was, to use the full designation, cr Baroness Talbot of Malahide and Lady Malahide of Malahide; s of Reginald John Arthur Arundell (changed his surname to Arundell 1945, s of Reginald Aloysius Talbot, ggs of Baroness Talbot of Malahide), and Mabile Arundell, gda of 9 Baron Arundell of Wardour; suc kinsman 9 Baron Talbot of Malahide (d 1987); *b* 9 January 1931; *Educ* Stonyhurst, RMA Sandhurst; *m* 1, 1955, Laura Duff (d 1989), yr da of Gp Capt Edward Tennant, DSO, MC, JP (n of 1 Baron Glenconner), and his 2 w, Victoria Duff, MBE, o da of Sir Robert Duff, 2 Bt; 1 s (Hon Richard John Tennant b 1957), 4 da (Hon Juliet Anne Tennant (Hon Mrs Teakle) b 1959, Hon Catherine Mary Tennant (Hon Mrs Allwood) b 1960, Hon Caroline Rose Tennant (Hon Mrs Peel) b 1962, Hon Lucy Veronica Tennant (Hon Mrs Daniel) b 1965); *m* 2, 1992, Patricia Mary, eldest da of late John Cuthbert Widdrington Riddell, OBE, of Felton Park, and Swinburne Castle, Northumberland, and formerly w of late Maj Geoffrey Thomas Blundell-Brown, MBE; *Heir* s, Hon Richard Arundell, JP; *Career* Vice Lord-Lt Wilts 1996–2006; chm St John Cncl for Wilts 1977–97; memb Chapter Gen 1993–99, KStJ 1988 (CStJ 1983, OStJ 1978); Kt of Honour and Devotion SMOM 1977; hon citizen of State of Maryland; *Style*— The Rt Hon Lord Talbot of Malahide, DL

TALBOT-PONSONBY, Nigel Edward Charles; s of Edward Fitzroy Talbot-Ponsonby (d 1996; ggs of Adm Sir Charles Talbot, KCB, who was s of Very Rev Charles Talbot, Dean of Salisbury, by Lady Elizabeth Somerset, da of 5 Duke of Beaufort; the Dean was n of 3 Baron and 1 Earl Talbot, which two dignities are now held by the Earl of Shrewsbury); *b* 24 September 1946; *Educ* Harrow; *m* 1977, Robina, da of Lt Cdr Henry Bruce, JP, DL, RN, Ret (gs of 9 Earl of Elgin and 13 of Kincardine), of London; 3 s (Henry b 1981, James b 1986, Alexander b 1987); *Career* chartered surveyor and hotelier; exec chm HLL Humberts Leisure chartered surveyors and int leisure business consulting; former memb Recreation and Leisure Mgmnt Ctee RICS; FRICS; *Recreations* sailing, field sports; *Clubs* Royal Thames Yacht; *Style*— Nigel Talbot-Ponsonby, Esq; ✉ Langrish House, Langrish, Petersfield, Hampshire GU32 1RN (tel 01730 263374); HLL Humberts Leisure, 12 Bolton Street, Mayfair, London W1J 8BD (tel 020 7629 6700, fax 020 7409 0475, e-mail ntp@humberts-leisure.com)

TALBOT RICE, Nigel; s of Mervyn Gurney Talbot Rice (d 1979), and Eleanor Butler Adair, *née* Williamson (d 1965); *b* 14 May 1938; *Educ* Charterhouse, ChCh Oxford (MA, DipEd); *m* 20 July 1968, (Rosfrith) Joanna Sarah, da of Air-Cdr F J Manning, CB, CBE, RAF (d

1988); 4 da (Sarah b 24 Oct 1969, Caroline (Mrs Jonathan Bewes) b 26 Sept 1971, Rebecca (Mrs James Nash) b 2 Sept 1973, Helena b 28 Jan 1977); 1 s (Samuel b 17 March 1982); *Career* Nat Serv Coldstream Gds 1957–58; asst master Papplewick Sch Ascot 1961–64, headmaster Summer Fields Sch Oxford 1975–97 (asst master 1965–71, asst headmaster 1971–75); ptnr TR Consultancy 1997–; conslt English Heritage 1997–98; dir Misys Charitable Fndn 1998–; chm: Maclaren Tst, Cancer Research Campaign Oxford Appeal; tstee Oxfordshire Community Fndn; memb Cncl St Luke's Hosp Oxford; govr: Wychwood Sch Oxford, Hordle Walhampton Lymington, St John's Sch Northwood, Cumnor House Sch Danehill; devpt conslt Downe House Sch 1998–2005; hon life memb Macmillan Cancer Care; memb IAPS 1971; *Books* Survey of Religion in Preparatory Schools (1965); *Recreations* golf, gardening, wine; *Style*— Nigel Talbot Rice, Esq; ✉ Yellow Wood House, Ethelred Court, Old Headington, Oxford OX3 9DA; Cool Bawn, Thurlestone, Devon TQ7 3NY

TALLIS, Prof Raymond Courtney; s of Edward Ernest Tallis, and Mary, *née* Burke; *b* 10 October 1946; *Educ* Liverpool Coll, Keble Coll Oxford (open scholar, BA, BM BCh), St Thomas' Hosp Med Sch; *m* 1972, Teresa, *née* Bonneywell; 2 s; *Career* clinical res fell Wessex Neurological Centre 1977–80, sr lectr in geriatric med Univ of Liverpool 1982–87, prof of geriatric med Univ of Manchester 1987–2006, conslt physician Salford Royal Hosps Tst 1987–2006; numerous visiting professorships; memb various med socs; numerous radio talks on topics incl: the meaning of words, the function of art, the political culture of Liverpool; Hon DLitt Univ of Hull 1997, Hon LittD Univ of Manchester 2002; FRCP 1989, FMedSci 2000; *Publications* fiction: Absence (novel, 1999); various short stories; poetry: Between the zones (1985), Glints of Darkness (1989), Fathers and Sons (1993); non-fiction: Not Saussure (1988, 2 edn 1995), In Defence of Realism (1988, 2 edn 1998), The Clinical Neurology of Old Age (1988), The Explicit Animal (1991, 2 edn 1999), Brocklehurst's Textbook of Geriatric Medicine and Gerontology (jt ed, 4 edn 1992, 5 edn 1998, 6 edn 2003), Newton's Sleep (1995), Epilepsy in Elderly People (1996), Enemies of Hope (1997, 2 edn 1999), Theorrhoea and After (1998), Increasing Longevity: medical, social and political implications (1998), On the Edge of Certainty: philosophical explorations (1999), The Raymond Tallis Reader (ed by Michael Grant, 2000), A conversation with Martin Heidegger (2002), The Hand: A Philosophical Inquiry into Human Being 2003, I Am: A Philosophical Inquiry into First Person Being (2004), Hippocratic Oaths: Medicine and its Discontents (2004), Why the Mind is Not a Computer: A Pocket Lexicon of Neuromythology (2004), The Knowing Animal: A Philosophical Inquiry Into Knowledge and Truth (2005); author of: over 200 scientific papers and articles mainly in the field of epilepsy, stroke and the neurological rehabilitation of older people, numerous articles in literary criticism and theory and philosophy; *Recreations* family, Stella Artois, music, thinking; *Clubs* 1942, Athenaeum; *Style*— Prof Raymond Tallis; ✉ 5 Valley Road, Bramhall, Stockport, Cheshire SK7 2NH (tel 0161 439 2548, mobile 07801 834230, fax 0161 440 0434, e-mail raymond@rtallis.wanadoo.co.uk)

TALLON, David Seymour; s of Claude Reginald Tallon (d 2001), of London, and Blanche Mary, *née* Mahony (d 1984); *b* 7 October 1940; *Educ* Rugby; *Children* 3 s (Alastair James b 14 May 1966, Timothy Paul b 6 July 1967, Oliver Mark b 6 July 1967 d 1967), 4 da (Victoria Kate Rebecca b 1 March 1969, Elizabeth Jane Biddy b 16 May 1970, Sarah Georgina b 18 Oct 1994, Louise Christine b 29 May 1999); *m* 2, 9 April 1998, Gillian Lesley, *née* Sandford; *Career* CA 1964; Deloitte Plender Griffiths 1958–67, ptnr Dearden Harper Miller 1969, sr ptnr Dearden Farrow 1986–87; ptnr: BDO Binder Hamlyn 1987–92 (dep sr ptnr 1987–90), Sharp Parsons Tallon 1992–2002, Mercer & Hole 2002–05 (conslt 2005–); chm Children with AIDS Charity 1994–99; Liveryman Worshipful Co of Needlemakers; FCA; *Books* Capital Transfer Tax Planning (2 edn 1976, 3 edn 1978), Inland Revenue Practices & Concessions (1980); *Recreations* golf; *Style*— David Tallon, Esq; ✉ Mercer & Hole, Gloucester House, 72 London Road, St Albans, Hertfordshire AL1 1NS (e-mail davidtallon@mercerhole.co.uk)

TALMAN, Iain James Scott; s of James Maghie Talman (d 1990), and Annie Campbell, *née* Keillor; *b* 18 July 1952, Johnstone, Renfrewshire; *Educ* Gourock HS, Greenock HS, Univ of Glasgow (LLB); *m* 1975, Sheila MacDonald, *née* Pringle; 1 s (James Scott b 1981), 1 da (Eilidh Sheila b 1983); *Career* slr; successively apprentice, asst slr and ptnr Bishop Milne Boyd & Co (then successor firms: Bishop & Co, Bishop and Robertson Chalmers, Morison Bishop) 1974–2002, ptnr Biggart Baillie 2002–; memb: Assoc of Pension Lawyers, Ind Pension Tstees Gp, Scottish Gp Pensions Mgmnt Inst, Assoc of Member-Directed Pension Schemes, Insurance and Actuarial Soc of Glasgow, Scottish Law Agents Soc, Law Soc of Scotland, Royal Faculty of Procurators Glasgow; *Publications* Halliday's Conveyancing Law and Practice (2 edn, Vol 1 1996, Vol 2 1997), Stair Memorial Encyclopaedia (Pensions section, reissue 2004); *Recreations* cinema, travel, saving the planet; *Clubs* Glasgow Art, Nomads; *Style*— Iain Talman, Esq; ✉ Biggart Baillie, Dalmore House, 310 St Vincent Street, Glasgow G2 5QR (tel 0141 228 8000, fax 0141 228 8310, e-mail italman@biggartbaillie.co.uk)

TALVITIE, Tuija Kristiina; da of Juha Talvitie, of Helsinki, and Maire Karlsson; *Educ* Univ of Helsinki (MA); *m* Tuomas Saastamoinen; 2 c (Otso Mikael b 1995, Aarne Tuomas b 1999); *Career* dir British Council Finland 1997–; memb Bd Crisi Mgmnt Initiative 2005–, memb Bd e2; *Recreations* sports, reading, cooking; *Style*— Ms Tuija Talvitie; ✉ British Council, Urho Kekkosen Katu 2C, 00100 Helsinki, Finland (tel 00358 9 7743330, fax 00358 9 7018731, e-mail tuija.talvitie@britishcouncil.fi)

TALWAR, Rana Gurvirendra Singh; s of RS Talwar, and Veera Talwar; *b* 22 March 1948; *Educ* Lawrence Sch Sanawar India, St Stephen's Coll Delhi (BA); *m* 1, 1970 (m dis), Roop Som Dutt; 1 s, 1 da; *m* 2, 1995, Renuka Singh; 1 s; *Career* Citibank: exec trainee for int banking 1969–70, various operational, corp and institutional assignments India 1970–76, gp head Treas and Fin Insts 1976, regnl mangr E India 1977, gp head Treas and Fin Insts Gp Saudi American Bank (Citibank affiliate) Jeddah 1978–80, COS Asia Pacific Div 1981, regnl consumer business mangr Singapore, Malaysia, Indonesia, Thailand and India 1982–88, div exec Asia Pacific 1988–91, exec vice-pres and gp exec (responsible for consumer bank) Asia Pacific, ME and E Europe 1991–95, exec vice-pres Citicorp 1996–97, US and Europe rep 1996–97; Standard Chartered plc: gp exec dir 1997–98, ceo 1997–2001; chm Sabre Capital Worldwide 2002–; non-exec dir Pearson plc 2000–; govr: London Business Sch 1988–, Indian Sch of Business 1999–; *Recreations* golf, tennis, bridge, travel; *Clubs* Tanglin (Singapore), Bengal (Calcutta), Delhi Golf (New Delhi); *Style*— Rana G S Talwar, Esq; ✉ 2nd Floor, Berkeley Square House, Berkeley Square, London W1J 6BD

TAM, Robin Bing-Kuen; QC (2006); s of Sheung Wai Tam, and Arleta Yau-Ling, *née* Chang; *b* 1 June 1964; *Educ* The Leys Sch Cambridge, St John's Coll Cambridge, Inns of Court Sch of Law; *Career* called to the Bar Middle Temple 1986; standing prosecuting jr counsel to the Inland Revenue (SE Circuit) 1993, sr counsel to the Crown 1994–2006 (A Panel 1999–2006), QC 2006; *Style*— Robin Tam, Esq, QC; ✉ 1 Temple Gardens, Temple, London EC4Y 9BB (tel 020 7583 1315)

TAMES, Roger; s of Albert Tames (d 1975), and Phyllis, *née* Amos; *b* 21 September 1951; *m* (m dis); 1 da (Joanne b 1979), 1 s (Ian b 1983); *Career* journalist; reporter Essex & East London Newspapers (Brentwood Argus, Dagenham Post) 1973–75, successively reporter, presenter, football commentator, sports ed and head of sport Tyne Tees Television 1976–2005, head of sports progs filmNova Sports Prodn; progs presented incl: Sportstime, Sporting Chance, Extra Time, The Back Page, Cafe Sport, Football Flashback, North East Match, Soccer Night; memb: NE Sports Bd, Variety Club of GB, Sport Newcastle; *Publications* Steve Cram: The Making of an Athlete (1990), Roker Park:

The Story Video (1997); Official History of Newcastle Utd DVD; *Recreations* squash, running, golf, keeping fit - eating and drinking afterwards; *Style*— Roger Tames, Esq; ✉ filmNova Sports Production, Newcastle House, Albany Court, Monarch Road, Newcastle upon Tyne NE4 7YB

TAMI, Mark Richard; MP; s of Michael John Tami, of Enfield, and Patricia Tami; *b* 3 October 1962; *Educ* Enfield GS, Univ of Wales Swansea; *m* 1992, Sally, da of Arthur Richard Daniels; 2 s (Max Oscar Hugh b 3 March 1998, Oscar Joel Richard b 8 August 2000); *Career* AEEU: head of research 1992–97, head of policy 1999–2001; MP (Lab) Alyn and Deeside 2001–, memb NI Select Ctee 2001–05, currently PPS to John Healey, MP, sec All-Pty Aerospace Gp; memb: Lab Pty Nat Policy Forum 1996–2001, TUC Gen Cncl 1999–2001, League Against Cruel Sports; *Publications* Fabian booklet on the need for compulsory voting; *Recreations* Glamorgan CCC, Norwich City FC, fishing, antiques; *Style*— Mark Tami, Esq, MP; ✉ House of Commons, London SW1A 0AA (tel 020 7219 8174); Constituency Office (tel 01244 819854)

TAMLIN, Keith Maxwell; s of Sydney Thomas Tamlin (d 1946), and Madeline Isabel, *née* Prowse (d 1995); *b* 19 July 1928; *Educ* Ruthin Sch, Univ of Wales (LLB); *m* 21 June 1954, Marian, da of Thomas Roberts; 2 da (Helen Susan b 25 May 1955, Karen Michele b 26 April 1958); *Career* Nat Serv King's (Liverpool) Regt RASC 1947–49 (cmmnd 1947, served ME); slr Supreme Ct of Judicature 1954, ptnr North Kirk & Co Slrs Liverpool 1959 (joined 1954), conslt Cuff Roberts Slrs Liverpool; dir: Everton Football Club Co Ltd 1974–2004 (life vice-pres), H Samuel plc 1979–92 (and other cos within H Samuel Group incl Watches of Switzerland plc), several cos within distributive sector, various cos dealing with racehorses, publications and breeding; pres: Liverpool Jr C of C 1960, Liverpool Round Table 1965; chm Jt Ctees organising Charity Gala Performances at Liverpool Playhouse 1964–65 (to raise funds for Liverpool Central Boys' Club, Liverpool Maternity Hosp and the Br Red Cross and Women's Hosp), memb and slr Ctee Liverpool and Dist Family Servs Unit 1963–82, memb The Mail Order Traders' Assoc of GB (sec 1967, dir 1974); memb: PO Users' Nat Cncl 1970–90, Trg Ctee Distributive Indust Bd 1971–78, Mgmnt Ctee and Cncl Retail Consortium 1973–97, Cncl Advtg Assoc 1982–97, Cncl CBI 1988–92; nominated by HM Govt as a Gp 1 Employers' Rep to Econ and Social Ctee Brussels 1983–93, memb Ctee for Commerce and Distribution Euro Cmmn 1993–99; memb: Liverpool Law Soc, Law Soc (pres 1984); *Recreations* walking, swimming, watching football and professional golf; *Clubs* Athenaeum (Liverpool), East India; *Style*— Keith Tamlin, Esq; ✉ 11 Quickswood Close, Woolton, Liverpool L25 4TT (tel 0151 428 2088, fax 0151 428 2088)

TAMS, John Murray; s of William Murray Tams (d 1976), and Vera, *née* Stone (d 1996); *b* 16 February 1949; *m* 27 June 1992, Sally, da of Stuart Alan Ward; 1 da (Rosie b 30 Aug 1986); *Career* musician, composer and actor; early career: two seasons with Cox's Modern Amusements, hack reporter for various local newspapers Derbys, with BBC Radio Nottingham and BBC Radio Derby, lectr in popular culture WEA, freelance writer NME, Sounds and Melody Maker, involved in record production Topic Records, with E Midlands Mobile Arts theatre gp; also sometime mangr ladies underwear factory, antique dealer, maggot salesman and unrequited teacher of 9 to 13 year olds; former memb bands incl Muckram Wakes, Albion Band and Home Service; estab Rolling Stock Co choir Derbys, co-fndr and prodr No Masters co-op recording label and publisher S Yorks; Hon doctorate Sheffield Hallam Univ 2007; BBC Radio 2 Folk Singer of the Year 2006, Radio 2 Traditional Song of the Year, winner of two Hancock Awards; *Theatre* actor and musical dir under Bill Bryden, *qv*, NT 1977–85, prodns incl Larkrise, The World Turned Upside Down, Dispatches, The Long Voyage Home, The Iceman Cometh, Hughie, Candleford, The Crucible, Cinderella, Golden Boy, A Midsummer Night's Dream, Don Quixote, Glengarry Glen Ross and The Mysteries (and subsequent intermittent Euro tour and revival 2000); musical dir and composer: The Crucible (Birmingham/Salisbury Playhouse), Son of Man (RSC), Uncle Vanya (West End), The Three Sisters (Birmingham Rep), Of Mice and Men (Birmingham Rep); other theatre involvement incl: with United Br Artists Old Vic Theatre, RSC Aldwych Theatre, co-dir Joint Stock theatre co, TUC sponsored tour with 7:84 theatre co during 1984 miner's strike, co-creator The Ship (for Euro City of Culture Festival Glasgow 1990) and The Big Picnic, assoc dir Crucible Theatre Sheffield (incl co-dir and adaptor The Northern Mysteries), assoc dir The Building Co, actor and composer The Good Hope (NT tour); *Television and Film* script assoc, collaborator on musical score and actor (playing the part of Daniel Hagman) Sharpe series ITV; other appearances incl: Sons and Lovers, A Question of Leadership, Clapperclaw, Assembled Memories, The Raggedy Rawney, The Rainbow, God Speed Co-operation, Ill Fares the Land, Back to the Roots, Here We Go A-Wassailing, A Little Night Music, Holy City, The Rainbow, Crimestrike, The Gifted Adult, You Don't Have to Walk to Fly, Albion Market, Floodtide and Travelling Man, No Further Cause for Concern, Ruth Rendell Mysteries, Investigation, The Fool, As You Like It, Six Characters in Search of an Author, Elidor, When Saturday Comes; *Radio* for BBC Radio 4 as composer/studio prodr/ed: Sacco and Vanzetti, Pickwick Papers, Felix Hoult the Radical, HMS Ulysses, The Plutocrat, Volunteers, Daisy Miller, The Nativity, The Passion, Doomsday, Charge of the Light Brigade, From Here to Eternity; music series prodr Radio Ballads 2006 (Sony Gold Radio Award 2007); *Albums* Unity 2000 (Album of the Year and Song of the Year (for Harry Stone) BBC Radio 2 Folk Awards 2001), Home 2002, The Reckoning 2006 (Album of the Year and nominated Best Original Song (for Steelos) BBC Radio 2 Folk Awards); prodr Over the Hills and Far Away (album of music from the Sharpe TV series); singer, musician or prodr on over 50 albums; *Style*— John Tams, Esq; ✉ website www.johntams.co.uk

TAMWORTH, Viscount; Robert William Saswalo Shirley; s and h of 13 Earl Ferrers, PC, DL, *qv*; *b* 29 December 1952; *Educ* Ampleforth; *m* 21 June 1980, Susannah Mary, da of late Charles Edward William Sheepshanks (d 1991), of Arthington Hall, Otley, W Yorks; 1 da (Hon Hermione Mary Annabel b 11 Dec 1982), 2 s (Hon William Robert Charles b 10 Dec 1984, Hon Frederick James Walter b 2 June 1990); *Heir* s, Hon William Shirley; *Career* teaching in Kenya under CMS Youth Service Abroad Scheme 1971–72; articled to Whinney Murray & Co (chartered accountants) 1972–76, asst mangr Ernst & Whinney (now Ernst & Young) 1976–82, gp auditor and sr treasy analyst with BICC plc 1982–86, gp fin controller Viking Property Gp Ltd 1986; dir: Viking Property Gp Ltd 1987–88, Norseman Holdings Ltd (formerly Ashby Securities Ltd) 1987–92 (and assoc cos 1988–92), Derbyshire Student Residences Ltd 1996–2003; md: Ruffer Investment Management Ltd 1999– (dir 1994–), Ruffer LLP 2004–; FCA; Kt SMOM 2005; *Recreations* the British countryside and related activities, the garden; *Clubs* Boodle's; *Style*— Viscount Tamworth; ✉ Ditchingham Hall, Ditchingham, Norfolk NR35 2JX

TAN, Melvyn; s of Tan Keng Hian, of Singapore, and Wong Sou Yuen; *b* 13 October 1956; *Educ* Yehudi Menuhin Sch Surrey, Royal Coll of Music; *Career* fortepianist and harpsichord player, modern piano performer since 1997; interpreter of Baroque, classical and early Romantic works; debut Wigmore Hall 1977, played in all major UK venues; repertoire incl: Weber, Mendelssohn, Chopin; performed with orchs and ensembles incl: Acad of Ancient Music, Eng Chamber Orch, RPO, London Classical Players; US tour playing Beethoven 1985, concert series with Roger Norrington and London Classical Players 1987 and 1988; festivals in 1989 incl: The Beethoven Experience (Purchase NY, with Roger Norrington and London Classical Players), Midsummer Mozart Festival in San Francisco (also Aldeburgh, Bath, Holland and Helsinki); performed in 1990: San Francisco, toured France and Japan, Queen Elizabeth Hall; involved in bringing Beethoven's own fortepiano from Budapest to England for European tour 1992, continues to perform at most major festivals and venues around the world; FRCM; *Recordings* incl: Beethoven's Waldstein, Appassionato and Les Adieux sonatas, Schubert Impromptus, Beethoven Piano Concertos (with Roger Norrington and the London Classical Players), Debussy Preludes Books 1 and 2; *Style*— Melvyn Tan, Esq

TANKERVILLE, 10 Earl of (GB 1714); Peter Grey Bennet; also Baron Ossulston (E 1682); s of 9 Earl of Tankerville (d 1980), and Georgiana Lilian Maude, *née* Wilson (d 1998); *b* 18 October 1956; *Educ* Grace Cathedral Sch San Francisco (chorister), Oberlin Conservatory Ohio (BMus), San Francisco State Univ (MA); *Career* musician San Francisco; *Style*— The Rt Hon the Earl of Tankerville; ✉ 139 Olympia Way, San Francisco, CA 94131, USA (tel 00 1 415 826 6639)

TANLAW, Baron (Life Peer UK 1971), of Tanlawhill in the County of Dumfries; Hon Simon Brooke Mackay; yst s of 2 Earl of Inchcape (d 1939), and Leonora Margaret Brooke (d 1996), da of HH the 3 Rajah of Sarawak (Sir Charles Vyner Brooke (d 1963)); *b* 30 March 1934; *Educ* Eton, Trinity Coll Cambridge (MA); *m* 1, 1959, Joanna Susan, o da of Maj John Henry Hirsch (d 1983); 2 da (Hon Iona Héloïse b 1960, Hon Rebecca Alexandra (Hon Mrs Ayre-Smith) b 1967), 1 s (Hon James Brooke b 1961), and 1 s decd; *m* 2, 1976, Rina Siew Yong, yst da of late Tiong Cha Tan, of Kuala Lumpur, Malaysia; 1 da (Hon Asia Brooke b 1980), 1 s (Hon Brooke Brooke b 1982); *Career* sits as Ind (formerly Lib) in House of Lords; 2 Lt 12 Royal Lancers 1952–54; chm Fandstan Electric Gp Ltd, former dir Inchcape plc; pres Sarawak Assoc 1972–75 and 1998–2001; pres All-Pty Parly Astronomy and Space Environment Gp 1999–, chm Lighter Evenings All-Pty Gp; nat appeal chm Elizabeth FitzRoy Support for People with Learning Disabilities 1985–90; hon fell Univ of Buckingham 1981; Hon DUniv Buckingham 1983; Liveryman: Worshipful Co of Fishmongers, Worshipful Co of Clockmakers; FBHI 1997, FRAS 2003; *Clubs* White's, Oriental, Puffin's; *Style*— The Rt Hon the Lord Tanlaw; ✉ Tanlawhill, By Langholm, Dumfriesshire DG13 0PW

TANN, Prof Jennifer; da of Alfred John Booth, and Frances Booth, of Birmingham; *b* 25 February 1939; *Educ* Badminton Sch Bristol, Univ of Manchester (BA), Univ of Leicester (PhD); *m* 12 Oct 1963, Roger William Tann, s of Richard Henry Tann; 2 s (Edmund John b 8 March 1966, Oliver Richard b 4 June 1974); *Career* research asst Historic Towns Project Oxford 1964–66, pt/t tutor Univ of Hull 1966–69, lectr Aston Univ 1969–73, reader Aston Univ Business Sch 1973–86, dir Centre for Continuing Educn Univ of Newcastle upon Tyne 1986–89, prof of innovation studies Univ of Birmingham 1989– (dean Faculty of Educn and Continuing Studies 1993–96), sr conslt Caret Ltd 1995–, dir Entrepeneurship and Innovation Centre Univ of Birmingham Business Sch 1997–2003, res dir Birmingham Business Sch 1999–2002; visiting prof Dept of Economics Univ of Queensland 1985, visiting prof of mgmnt Univ of Newcastle upon Tyne 1989–94; memb CPPE Stakeholder and User Advsy Bd; bishops' selection advsr, memb Bishop's Cncl Gloucester Dio; tstee: Stroudwater Textile Tst, Educn for Ministry; memb: Newcomen Soc, Cncl Gloucester Cathedral; *Books* Development of the Factory (1971), Selected Papers of Boulton and Watt (1981), Children at Work (1981), Short History of the Stock Exchange Birmingham (1983), Birmingham Assay Office (1993); *Recreations* reading, gardens, music, laughter; *Style*— Prof Jennifer Tann; ✉ Business School, University of Birmingham, Edgbaston, Birmingham B15 2TT (tel 0121 414 5609, fax 0121 414 2982, e-mail j.tann@bham.co.uk)

TANNAHILL, Dr Andrew James; s of Andrew Leckie Tannahill, of Inchinnan, Renfrewshire, and late Elizabeth Johnstone, *née* Preston; *b* 28 April 1954; *Educ* John Neilson Inst Paisley, Univ of Glasgow (MB ChB (with honours), Brunton meml prize), Univ of Edinburgh (MSc); *m* Dr Carol Elizabeth Tannahill, *née* Fyfe; *Career* lectr in pathology Univ of Glasgow and hon registrar in pathology Western Infirmary Glasgow 1981–82, registrar then sr registrar in community med Lothian Health Bd 1982–85, hon clinical tutor Univ of Edinburgh 1984–85, regional specialist in community med E Anglian RHA 1985–88, assoc lectr Univ of Cambridge 1988, sr lectr in public health med Univ of Glasgow and hon conslt in public health med Gtr Glasgow Health Bd 1988–91, chief exec Health Educn Bd for Scotland 1991–2001, hon sr lectr Univ of Dundee 1993–2001, hon fell Univ of Edinburgh 1994–2001; Univ of Glasgow: hon sr lectr 1996–, visiting prof 1997–2001; conslt in public health med NHS Argyll and Clyde 2001–05, interim dir of public health NHS Argyll and Clyde 2004–05, head Evidence for Action and conslt in public health med NHS Health Scotland 2005–; FFPHM 1992 (MFCM 1985), FRCPEd 1996, FRCPGlas 1999; *Books* Health Promotion: Models and Values (1990, 2 edn 1996), Scotland's Health and Health Services (contrib, 2003); also contrib of chapters in other books; *Recreations* photography, digital imaging, painting, music, theatre, birdwatching, countryside, reading; *Style*— Dr Andrew Tannahill; ✉ NHS Health Scotland, Clifton House, Clifton Place, Glasgow G3 7LS (tel 0141 300 1010)

TANNAHILL, Reay; da of James Cowan Tannahill (d 1961), of Glasgow, and Olive Margery, *née* Reay (d 1973); *Educ* Shawlands Acad Glasgow, Univ of Glasgow (MA, CSS); *m* 1958 (m dis 1983), Michael Edwardes (d 1990); *Career* writer; probation offr, advtg copywriter, reporter, historical researcher and graphic designer; occasional contributor to Chicago Tribune, History Today, Sunday Times and The Independent; chm of judges Betty Trask Award 2003; *Non-Fiction* Paris in the Revolution (1966), The Fine Art of Food (1968), Food in History (1973, 3 edn revised and updated 2002, Premio Letterario Internazionale: Chianti Ruffino Antico Fattore), Flesh and Blood (1975, revised and updated edn 1996), Sex in History (1980, revised and updated edn 1989); *Novels* A Dark and Distant Shore (1983), The World, the Flesh and the Devil (1985), Passing Glory (1989, Romantic Novel of the Year Award), In Still and Stormy Waters (1992), Return of the Stranger (1995), Fatal Majesty (1998), The Seventh Son (2001), Having the Builders In (2006); *Recreations* work; *Clubs* Arts, Authors' (chm 1997–2000); *Style*— Ms Reay Tannahill; ✉ c/o MBA Literary Agents Ltd, 62 Grafton Way, London W1P 5LD (tel 020 7387 2076, fax 020 7387 2042, e-mail agent@mbalit.co.uk)

TANNER, Dr Andrea Isobel Duncan; *b* 15 January 1956; *Educ* Notre Dame HS for Girls Dumbarton, Univ of Strathclyde (BA), Univ of Warwick (MA), Birkbeck Coll London (PhD); *m* Dr John Tanner (d 2004); *Career* genealogist to Clarenceaux King of Arms at Coll of Arms 1980–95, freelance researcher; tutor in heraldry, social history, genealogy and family history for WEA, Extra Mural Dept of Birkbeck Coll, Denman Coll, Soc of Genealogists, Elderhostel Fndn; researcher offr Wellcome Tst-funded Mortality in the Metropolis Project at the Inst of Historical Research Senate House 1996–99, currently res fell Kingston Univ; founding hon sec Friends of the Public Record Office 1988–93 (vice-pres 1993–), memb Lord Cncllr's Advsy Cncl on Public Records 1993–99; chair: Users' Section of Archives for London 2005–; memb: Cncl of British Records Assoc 1996–99, Soc for the Study of Social History, Soc of Genealogists, Inst of Historical Research, Archives for London, Friends of Hackney Archives; hon archivist Fortnum & Mason Piccadilly; delivered a variety of seminars and symposium papers in Euro, UK and USA; FSA, FSG; *Publications* Bricks and Mortals; A History of the Kensington Housing Trust (2001); in jls incl: Jl of Medical Biography, Ashmolean Jl of History of Collections, Jl of the Soc for Social History of Medicine, Hygeia Internationalis Historical Jl, The Lancet, The London Jl; *Style*— Dr Andrea Tanner, FSA; ✉ Flat One, 57 Drayton Gardens, London SW10 9RU

TANNER, Prof Brian Keith; s of Sydney Tanner (d 1979), and Gladys, *née* Godwin (d 1994); *b* 3 April 1947, Raunds, Northants; *Educ* Wellingborough GS, Balliol Coll Oxford (Kitchener scholar, MA), Oriel Coll Oxford (Robinson sr scholar, DPhil); *m* 16 Aug 1969, Ruth, *née* Simmonds; 2 s (Robert Edward b 10 Feb 1973, Thomas Matthew b 3 Feb 1975); *Career* jr research fell Linacre Coll Oxford 1971–73; Univ of Durham: univ lectr

1973–83, sr lectr 1983–86, reader 1986–90, prof 1990–, head Dept of Physics 1996–99; chm Durham Scientific Crystals Ltd 2003–; dir: Bede Scientific Instruments Ltd 1978–2000, NE Centre for Scientific Enterprise 2000–; non-exec dir Bede plc 2000–; FInstP 1982, FRSA 1996; *Publications* Introduction to the Physics of Electrons in Solids (1995), X-Ray Metrology (2006); over 300 research papers in int scientific jls; *Recreations* amateur music making (organist, pianist, double bassist), walking; *Style*— Prof Brian Tanner; ✉ Department of Physics, University of Durham, South Road, Durham DH1 3LE (tel 0191 334 3677, fax 0191 334 3551, e-mail b.k.tanner@dur.ac.uk)

TANNER, Brian Michael; CBE (1997), DL (1997); s of Gerald Evelyn Tanner (d 1964), and Mary, *née* Adamson (d 1986); *b* 15 February 1941, Scunthorpe; *Educ* Acklam Hall GS Middlesbrough, Bishops Vesey GS Sutton Coldfield, Univ of Bristol (BA); *m* 15 June 1963, June Ann, *née* Walker; 1 da (Susan Nicola b 29 July 1966), 1 s (Andrew Mark b 9 Jan 1968); *Career* trainee accountant Birmingham CBC 1962–65, gp accountant Coventry CBC 1965–68, chief accountant Teesside CBC 1968–71, asst county treas and asst chief exec Warwickshire CC 1971–75; Somerset CC: county treas 1975–90, chief exec 1990–97; dir Jupiter Int Green Investment Tst 1997–2002; advsr Assoc of CCs 1976–98, princ local authy negotiator 1985–88, pres Soc of County Treasurers 1989–90; memb Accountancy Standards Ctee 1982–84, chm Investment Mgmnt User Gp 1987–90, memb Nat Assoc of Pension Funds 1989–92, cmmr Public Works Loans Bd 1997–; chm: SW Nat Lottery Charities Bd 1997–2003, Taunton and Somerset NHS Tst 1998–2006 (non-exec dir 1997–2006), Taunton Town Partnership 1998–2003, Taunton Vision Cmmn 2003; vice-pres Taunton League of Friends 2006–; dir Somerset Trg and Enterprise Cncl 1990–97; memb: FE Funding Cncl SW Region 1996–99, Wessex Customer Servs Ctee OFWAT 1998–99; tstee: Central Bureau Dept of Educn and Science 1983–94, Avon and Somerset Police Community Fund 1999–, Somerset Crimebeat 2000–06, Somerset Community Fndn 2001–, Somerset St Margaret's Hospice 2005–, Wells Cathedral Cncl 2005–; govr: Millfield Sch 1985–99, Bridgewater Coll of FE 1994–2002, Somerset Coll 2005–; hon treas Relate 1998–2001; High Sheriff Somerset 2003–04; Freeman City of London 1990; memb CIPFA 1965; *Books* Financial Management in the 1990s (co-author, 1990); *Recreations* cricket, rugby, golf, squash, antiques, philateley; *Clubs* Sloane; *Style*— Brian Tanner, Esq; ✉ 8 Broadlands Road, Taunton, Somerset TA1 4HQ (tel 01823 337826, e-mail btanner41@hotmail.com)

TANNER, David Whitlock; OBE (2003); A Douglas Tanner (d 1964), and Connie, *née* Baird; *b* 29 December 1947, London; *Educ* Abingdon Sch, Univ of Bristol (BA), Univ of London (PGCE); *Career* teacher and rowing coach; performance dir GB Rowing (formerly ARA) 1996–, coach men's four Olympic Games 1980, coach men's coxed four Olympic Games 1988, team mangr GB rowing Olympic Games 1992, 1996, 2000 and 2004; dep head Greenford HS 1986–87, headmaster Longford Community Sch 1987–96; FRSA 1992; *Recreations* theatre, classical music, sport, fine food and wine; *Clubs* Leander, London Rowing, Molesley Boat, Remenham; *Style*— David Tanner, Esq, OBE; ✉ International Office, Amateur Rowing Association, 6 Lower Mall, London W6 9DJ (tel 020 8237 6767, fax 020 8563 2265, e-mail david.tanner@gbrowing.org.uk)

TANNOCK, Dr Charles; MEP (Cons) London; s of Robert Tannock, and Ann, *née* England; *b* 25 September 1957; *Educ* Bradfield Coll Berks, Balliol Coll Oxford (MA), Middx Hosp Medical Sch London (MB BS); *m* 1983 (m dis 1988), Rosa Maria Vega Pizarro, da of Sen Ramon Vega Hidalgo, of Santiago, Chile, and Rosa Pizarro de Vega; *Career* MEP (Cons) London 1999–, substitute memb Economic and Monetary Affrs Ctee of European Parl 1999–, substitute memb Environment, Public Health and Consumer Affrs Ctee 1999–2004, memb European Parl-Slovakia Jt Parly Ctee 1999–2004, Cons fin servs spokesman 1999–2002, assistant whip to Cons delgn 2000–02, dep chief whip to Cons delgn 2002–05, memb Foreign Affrs Human Rights and Common Security 2002–, foreign affrs spokesman 2002–; memb European Parl: Russia 2002–, Ukraine 2002–04, Belarus 2002–04, Moldova Delgn 2002–04, Ukraine Delgn 2004– (vice-pres), Human Rights Sub-Ctee 2004–07; house surgn Middlesex Hosp London and house physician Harefield Hosp Harefield 1984–85, psychiatric registrar rotation Charing Cross and Westminster Hospitals W London 1985–88, res fell Charing Cross and Westminster Hosp Med Sch 1988–90, sr registrar rotation UC/Middlesex Hosps 1990–95, conslt psychiatrist and hon sr lectr UCH and Med Sch 1995–; cncllr Royal Borough of Kensington and Chelsea 1998–2000 (former memb of Social Services and Housing Ctee); memb: Chelsea Cons Assoc 1983–, Bow Gp Cncl 1989, Foreign Affairs Forum; vice-chm Kensington Mansions Residents Assoc 1997; fndr memb Concern Against Closure of Long-Stay Mental Hospitals; Freeman City of London 2000; MRCPsych; Commendatore Order of St Maurice and St Lazarus 2000, Presidential Order of Merit of Ukraine 2006; *Publications* Community Care - The Need for Action (1989), AIDS Dementia - A Policy Rethink (1989), A Marriage of Convenience - or Reform of the Community Charge (1991); extensive publications in medical literature; *Recreations* travel, skiing, financial markets; *Style*— Dr Charles Tannock, MEP; ✉ 1A Chelsea Manor Street, London SW3 5RP (tel 020 7349 6946, fax 020 7351 5885)

TANQUERAY, David Andrew; s of David Yeo Bartholomew Tanqueray (d 1944), and Majorie Edith, *née* Macdonald; *b* 23 May 1939; *Educ* Rugby, Clare Coll Cambridge (MA), Univ of Calif Berkeley; *m* 20 Aug 1966, Tamsin Mary, da of Air Cdre Cyril Montague Heard; 2 da (Venetia b 1974, Tabitha b 1977), 1 s (David b 1981); *Career* conslt: Control Data Ltd 1969–84, Floating Point Systems UK Ltd 1985–91, Silicon Graphics UK Ltd 1992–2000, Cray UK Ltd 2000–; awarded Harkness Fellowship 1966; *Recreations* music, amateur dramatics; *Style*— David Tanqueray, Esq; ✉ 27 Cheriton Avenue, Twyford, Berkshire RG10 9DB (tel 0118 934 1544); Cray UK Ltd, 2 Brewery Court, High Street, Theale, Reading RG7 5AH (tel 0118 903 3173, e-mail dt@cray.com)

TANSEY, Rock Benedict; QC (1990); *Educ* Univ of Bristol (LLB, Dip Social Studies); *m* 10 Oct 1964, Wendy Jennifer Ann, *née* Carver; 3 c; *Career* called to the Bar Lincoln's Inn 1966 (bencher 2004), recorder of the Crown Court 1995–2005, head of chambers 25 Bedford Row London; hon chm European Criminal Bar Assoc, chm European Criminal Bar Assoc of Defence Advocates (ECBA) 1996–2003; memb Criminal Bar Assoc; *Recreations* theatre, golf, travel; *Style*— Rock Tansey, Esq, QC; ✉ 25 Bedford Row, London WC1R 4HD (tel 020 7067 1500, fax 020 7067 1507)

TANT, Russell Byron; s of Melvyn John Tant (d 1970), and Sadie Jacobs (d 1989); *b* 20 March 1949; *Educ* Orange Hill Co GS, UCH London (BDS, capt UCH CC); *m* 1, 1981 (m dis 1990), Elizabeth Mary Lorimer; 2 s (Radleigh Lewis Byron b 6 Oct 1983, Sebastian Charles Russell b 5 July 1985); m 2, 29 Oct 1994, Katrina Rushton; 2 da (Emily Charlotte Maris b 3 April 1992, Mollie Bryony b 11 March 1996); *Career* gen dental practice Knightsbridge 1972–76, commenced practice Harpenden Herts 1978, fully private practice Wimpole Street 1985; pres London Dental Study Club 1983; *Recreations* cricket, golf, skiing, squash, music; *Clubs* MCC, Royal Cinque Ports Golf, Harpenden Golf; *Style*— Russell Tant, Esq; ✉ 22 Wimpole Street, London W1 (tel 020 7935 0087)

TANTAM, Prof Digby John Howard; s of Donald Harry Tantam (d 1993), of Cheam, Surrey, and Daphne, *née* Winterbone; *b* 15 March 1948; *Educ* St Paul's, Univ of Oxford (MA, BM BCh), Harvard Univ (MPH), Univ of London (PhD), Open Univ (BA); *m* m 1, 1 s (Robert John Geoffrey b 1978), 1 da (Grace Ruth b 1980); m 2, 1 August 1998, Emma, da of Arie Marinus van Deurzen; *Career* St George's Hosp 1974–75, Harvard Med Sch 1976–77, Maudsley Hosp 1977–83, Dept of Psychiatry Univ of Manchester 1983–90, prof of psychotherapy Univ of Warwick 1990–95, clinical prof of psychotherapy Univ of Sheffield 1995–; memb Inst of Group Analysis; FRCPsych, AFBPsS; *Books* Making Sense of Psychiatric Cases (with M Greenberg and G Szmukler, 1986), A Mind of One's Own (1988, 2 edn 1991), Public Health Impact of Mental Disorder (with D Goldberg, 1990), College Seminars in Psychology and Social Science (with M Birchwood), Psychiatry for the Developing World (with A Duncan and L Appleby), Clinical Topics in Psychotherapy, Psychotherapy and Counselling in Practice; *Recreations* cycling, reading, cooking, gardening, philosophy; *Style*— Prof Digby Tantam; ✉ Dilemma Consultancy, 3 Hollow Meadows Mews, Sheffield S6 6GJ (e-mail dilemma@dial.pipex.com, website www.dilemmas.org)

TAPLEY, (David) Mark; s of John Randolph Tapley (d 1972), of Stafford, and Nancy Doris Rathbone (d 1986); *b* 24 March 1946; *Educ* King Edward VI Sch Stafford, Oriel Coll Oxford (BA), London Business Sch (MBA); *m* April 1970, Judith Ann, da of Basil Wilford, of Stafford; 1 da (Charlotte Emily b June 1977), 1 s (Richard Paul b March 1979); *Career* systems engr ICL 1969–72, investment analyst and portfolio mangr JP Morgan 1974–84 (vice-pres 1982), dir of equities American Express Asset Mgmnt (later Shearson Lehman Global Asset Mgmnt and Posthorn Global Asset Mgmnt) 1984–90, md and chief investment offr WestLB Asset Mgmnt (UK) Ltd 1991–2000; visiting fell Cranfield Sch of Mgmnt 2000–; regular speaker at conferences seminars and trg courses on devpts in investment mgmnt industry; dir: Henderson Eurotrust plc, UK Soc of Investment Professionals; investment advsr Lloyd's Register; Chartered Fin Analyst 1980; AIIMR 1976; *Books* International Portfolio Management (ed and contrib 1986); *Recreations* keeping fit, travel, music; *Style*— Mark Tapley, Esq

TAPNER, (Nicholas) Rory; s of John W Tapner, and Cherry, *née* Moreton; *b* 30 September 1959, London; *Educ* Radley, KCL (LLB); *m* 15 Oct 1988, Alex, *née* Boldero; 2 s (Freddie b 29 Oct 1990, Arthur b 14 July 2000), 2 da (Anna b 6 Sept 1992, Rosie b 16 Oct 1995); *Career* Rowe & Pitman 1983, S G Warburg 1986, global head of equity capital markets SBC 1995; UBS: global head equity capital markets 1998, jt global head of investment banking 1999, chm and ceo Asia Pacific 2004, memb Gp Exec Bd 2006; *Recreations* golf, skiing, collecting clocks and English watercolours; *Style*— Rory Tapner, Esq; ✉ UBS AG, 1 Finsbury Avenue, London EC2M 2PP

TAPP, Richard; *Educ* Univ of Sheffield (LLB), Univ of Leicester (LLM), Nottingham Law Sch (MBA); *Career* trainee slr and asst slr Nat Coal Bd 1981–85, asst slr Imperial Foods Ltd 1985–86; Blue Circle Industries plc: commercial slr 1986–91, princ slr 1992–96, co sec and head of gp legal and secretariat 1996–2001; co sec and dir of legal servs Carillion plc 2001–; MCIArb, FCIS 1992, FRSA; *Style*— Richard Tapp, Esq; ✉ Carillion plc, Birch Street, Wolverhampton WV1 4HP (tel 01902 316334, fax 01902 316340, e-mail rtapp@carillionplc.com)

TAPPER, Prof Colin Frederick Herbert; s of Herbert Frederick Tapper (d 1977), and Florence, *née* Lambard (d 1976); *b* 13 October 1934; *Educ* Bishopshalt GS, Magdalen Coll Oxford (Vinerian scholar); *m* 1 April 1961, Margaret, da of Harold White (d 1978); 1 da (Lucy b 22 Jan 1973); *Career* called to the Bar Gray's Inn 1961; lectr LSE 1959–65; Univ of Oxford: fell Magdalen Coll 1965–2002 (vice-pres 1991–92), reader in law All Souls 1979–92, univ prof of law 1992–2002, emeritus fell 2002–; visiting prof: Univ of Alabama and Univ of NY 1970, Stanford Univ 1976, Monash Univ 1984, Univ of Northern Kentucky 1986, Univ of Sydney 1989, Univ of Western Aust 1991; dir: Butterworth 1979–85, Butterworth Telepublishing 1979–90; conslt: Butterworths 1968–90, Pinsent Masons (Solicitors) 1990–; *Books* Computers and The Law (1973), Computer Law (1978, 4 edn 1990), Cross and Tapper on Evidence (9 edn 1999); *Recreations* reading, writing, computing; *Style*— Prof Colin Tapper; ✉ Corner Cottage, Woodstock Road, Stonesfield, Witney, Oxfordshire OX8 8QA (tel 01993 891284); Magdalen College, Oxford OX1 4AU (tel 01865 276055, fax 01865 276103, e-mail colin.tapper@magd.ox.ac.uk)

TAPPER, Jaimie; *b* British Columbia; *Educ* Nat Ballet Sch Canada; *Career* ballet dancer; first soloist Nat Ballet of Canada 1999 (joined 1994), princ Royal Ballet 2002– (joined 1999); Erik Bruhn Prize 1995; *Performances* with Nat Ballet of Canada incl: Giselle, Juliet, Swanilda, Odette/Odile, Aurora, Lescaut's Mistress, A Month in the Country, The Leaves Are Fading, Spring The Four Seasons (Kudelka); with Royal Ballet incl: Swanilda, Sugar Plum Fairy, Gamzatti, Nikiya, Aurora, Tatiana, Giselle, Manon, Marie Larisch, Terpsichore, Myrtha, M in Carmen, Cinderella, Chlok, L'Hiver in Les Saisons, roles in Triad, Song of the Earth, Agon, The Vertiginous Thrill of Exactitude, Symphonic Variations, Les Biches, Raymonda Act III, Gloria, The Four Temperaments, There Where She Loves; *Style*— Ms Jaimie Tapper; ✉ c/o The Royal Ballet, Royal Opera House, Covent Garden, London WC2E 9DD

TAPPIN, Andrew Brice; s of late Walter Philip Tappin, and late Daphne Mary, *née* Brice; *b* 27 January 1945; *Educ* Willington Sch, Stamford Sch, Tiffin Sch; *m* 4 Sept 1971, Barbara Jane, da of late Clive Edward Midwinter; 1 s (Rupert Clive b 22 Feb 1972), 1 da (Laura Rachel b 22 Oct 1974); *Career* chartered accountant; Annan Dexter & Co 1967–71 (articled clerk 1963–67); ptnr: Dearden Lord Annan Morrish 1972, Dearden Farrow (after merger) 1977, BDO Binder Hamlyn (after merger) 1987–94, conslt Arthur Andersen 1994–98, princ Andrew B Tappin 1999–; dir SLT Training and Resources Ltd; memb Soc of Tst and Estate Practitioners; tstee and dir Suzy Lamplugh Tst; FCA 1977 (ACA 1967); *Books* Capital Transfer Tax Planning (jtly, 1975), Financial Planning for Clients (jtly, 1979); *Recreations* France, squash, running; *Style*— Andrew Tappin, Esq; ✉ 18 East Sheen Avenue, East Sheen, London SW14 8AS (tel 020 8287 8825, fax 020 8287 8747, e-mail andrew.tappin@blueyonder.co.uk)

TAPPIN, Michael; s of Thomas Ernest Tappin (d 2003), of Hendon, and Eileen Sarah, *née* Kitson; *b* 22 December 1946; *Educ* Moat Mount Secdy Modern, Harrow Tech Coll, Univ of Essex, LSE, Univ of Strathclyde; *m* Oct 1971, Angela Florence, da of Douglas Murray Reed; 1 da (Abigail Sarah b 3 September 1977), 1 s (Thomas Edward Michael b 7 Jan 1984); *Career* lectr in American politics Keele Univ 1974–94 and 1999– (pt/t lectr 1994–9); MEP (Lab) Staffordshire W and Congleton 1994–99; Euro Parl: memb Budget Ctee 1994–99, memb Budget Control Ctee 1995–99, substitute memb Economic and Monetary Affrs Ctee 1994–99, substitute memb Delgn with US 1994–99, chm Ceramic Inter-Group 1995–99, PSE co-ordinator Budget Control Ctee 1996–99; Staffordshire CC: memb 1981–97, chm Planning Ctee 1985–89, chm Enterprise and Econ Devpt Ctee 1989–94; chm W Midlands Forum of Local Authorities 1993–94, chm South Stoke Primary Care Tst 2001–06, dep chm Staffordshire Devpt Assoc 1989–94, memb Bd N Staffs Regeneration Zone 2007–; memb: American Political Science Assoc 1974; Stoke-on-Trent Local Strategic Partnership: chair Health Wellbeing Gp 2002–05, chair Employment Gp 2005–, vice chair Resouces Ctee 2005–06; memb Elected Mayors Advsy Panel 2006– (ldr Lab Gp 2007); *Books* American Politics Today (jtly, 1981, 1985, 1989, revised edn 1991); *Recreations* squash, walking, theatre, cinema, reading, music, guitar; *Clubs* Potters; *Style*— Michael Tappin, Esq; ✉ 7 Albert Road, Trentham, Stoke-on-Trent, Staffordshire ST4 8HE (tel and fax 01782 659554, e-mail michaeltappin@yahoo.com)

TAPPS-GERVIS-MEYRICK, Sir George Christopher Cadafael; 7 Bt (GB 1791), of Hinton Admiral, Hampshire; o s of Lt-Col Sir George David Eliott Tapps-Gervis-Meyrick, 6 Bt, MC (d 1988), and Ann, *née* Miller; *b* 10 March 1941; *Educ* Eton, Trinity Coll Cambridge; *m* 14 March 1968, Jean Louise, yst da of Lord William Walter Montagu Douglas Scott, MC (d 1958), 2 s of 7 Duke of Buccleuch; 2 s (George William Owen b 1970, Charles Valentine Llewelyn b 1972), 1 da (Suzannah Daisy b 1978); *Heir* s, George Tapps-Gervis-Meyrick; *Style*— Sir George Meyrick, Bt; ✉ Hinton Admiral, Christchurch, Dorset BH23 7DY

TAPSELL, Sir Peter Hannay Bailey; kt (1985), MP; s of late Eustace Tapsell, and late Jessie, *née* Hannay; *b* 1 February 1930; *Educ* Tonbridge, Merton Coll Oxford (MA); *m* 1, 1963 (m dis 1971), Hon Cecilia, 3 da of 9 Baron Hawke; 1 s (decd); m 2, 1974, Gabrielle, da of

T

late Jean Mahieu, of Normandy, France; *Career* Nat Serv Subaltern The Royal Sussex Regt Middle East 1948–50, hon life memb 6 Sqdn RAF 1971; librarian Oxford Union 1953 (rep on debating tour of USA 1954); Cons Res Dept (Social Servs and Agric) 1954–57 (PA to PM Anthony Eden 1955 Gen Election Campaign), memb London Stock Exchange 1957–90, int investment advsr to several central banks, foreign banks and trading cos; memb Business Advsy Cncl to UNO 2001–; Parly candidate (Cons) Wednesbury by-election 1957; MP (Cons): Nottingham W 1959–64, Horncastle 1966–83, Lindsey E 1983–97, Louth and Horncastle 1997–; oppn front bench spokesman on: foreign and Cwlth affrs 1976–77, Treasy and econ affrs 1977–78; chm Coningsby Club 1957–58, jt chm Br Caribbean Assoc 1963–64; memb: Cncl Inst for Fiscal Studies 1979–2005, Trilateral Cmmn 1979–98, Organising Ctee Zaire River Expedition 1974–75, Ct Univ of Nottingham 1959–64, Ct Univ of Hull 1966–85; hon memb Investment Advsy Bd Brunei Govt 1976–83, Brunei Dato 1971; vice-pres Tennyson Soc 1966–, hon dep chm Mitsubishi Tst Oxford Fndn 1988–, hon fell Merton Coll Oxford 1989 (hon postmaster 1953); *Recreations* travel, walking in mountains, reading history; *Clubs* Athenaeum, Carlton, Hurlingham; *Style*— Sir Peter Tapsell, MP; ✉ House of Commons, London SW1A 0AA (tel 020 7219 3000)

TARBUCK, Jimmy; OBE (1994); *b* 6 February 1940; *Career* comedian, entertainer and after-dinner speaker; started work as garage mechanic, Butlin's Redcoat, TV debut Comedy Box 1962, resident compere Sunday Night at the London Palladium Sept 1965 (following earlier guest appearances), London cabaret debut Talk of the Town, numerous pantomimes and summer seasons; fndr Jimmy Tarbuck Golf Classic (held annually); OStJ; *Television* incl: The Jimmy Tarbuck Show (ATV), Tarbuck's Back (ATV), It's Tarbuck (ATV), Tarbuck's Luck (BBC), Winner Takes All (Yorkshire) 1975–86, Tarby's Frame Game (Yorkshire), reg guest The Parkinson Show, Live From Her Majesty's (LWT) 1983–85, Tarby and Friends (LWT) 1984–86, Live From The Piccadilly (LWT) 1986, Live From The London Palladium (LWT) 1987–88, Tarby After Ten (LWT) 1988, An Audience With Jimmy Tarbuck (LWT) 1994, Tarbuck Late (LWT) 1995; *Awards* Variety Club of Great Britain Award Show Business Personality of the Year; *Books* Tarbuck on Golf, Tarbuck on Showbiz; *Recreations* golf, supporter Liverpool Football Club; *Style*— Jimmy Tarbuck, Esq, OBE; ✉ c/o Peter Prichard International Artistes Ltd, 4th Floor, Holborn Hall, 193–197 High Holborn, London WC1V 7BD (tel 020 7025 0600)

TARENTO, Danielle Claire; da of Jacques Tarento, of Adelaide, Aust, and Julia, *née* Pullen; *b* 31 December 1972, London; *Educ* Sutton HS, Guildhall Sch of Music and Drama (BA); *Career* theatre prodr; actress 1994–2004, co-fndr Menier Chocolate Factory (jt artistic dir 2004–06); Peter Brook Empty Space Award for New Venue 2005, Evening Standard Milton Shulman Award for Outstanding Newcomer 2005, Theatregoers' Choice Award for Best Off West End Production 2005 and 2006; *Recreations* theatre, cinema, eating out; *Style*— Miss Danielle Tarento; ✉ e-mail danielletarento@hotmail.com

TARLETON, Ray Bernard; s of Bernard Tarleton, of Bradford, and Ethel Tarleton; *b* 4 October 1950; *Educ* Belle Vue Boys' GS Bradford, UC Durham (BA, PGCE), UEA (MA); *m* Jacqueline Claire, da of Rev Dr Keith Cripps; 1 da (Alice Emily b 18 Sept 1980), 1 s (Edmund Keith b 2 June 1982); *Career* teacher ODA/Christians Abroad Zambia 1973–75, English teacher Sir Roger Manwood's GS Sandwich 1976–79, second in English North Walsham Girls' HS 1979–80, head of English and drama North Walsham HS 1980–86, dep headmaster Marshland HS Wisbech 1986–89, princ South Dartmoor Community Coll 1989– (specialist sports coll, trg sch, Leading Edge status); on secondment as nat co-ordinator Nat Coll for Sch Leadership (NCSL) Network 2003–; chair Devon Assoc of Secondary Headteachers 2000–02, memb SHA; lectr and teachers' workshop organizer LEA; addressed HMI and RES confs; nat recognition for work on oracy during 1980s; *Books* Learning and Talking - A Practical Guide to Oracy Across the Curriculum (1988); *Recreations* travel, reading, swimming, walking, theatre; *Style*— Ray Tarleton, Esq; ✉ South Dartmoor Community College, Balland Lane, Ashburton, Devon TQ13 7EW (tel 01364 652230, e-mail rtarleton@southdartmoor.devon.sch.uk)

TARN, Prof John Nelson; OBE (1992), DL (Merseyside 1999); s of Percival Nelson Tarn (d 1976), and Mary Isabell, *née* Purvis (d 1972); *b* 23 November 1934; *Educ* Royal GS Newcastle upon Tyne, King's Coll Newcastle (BArch), Gonville & Caius Coll Cambridge (PhD); *Career* architectural asst W B Edwards and Ptnrs Newcastle 1960–63, sr lectr in architecture Univ of Sheffield 1970 (lectr 1963–70), prof of architecture and head of dept Univ of Nottingham 1970–73; Univ of Liverpool: Roscoe prof of architecture 1974–95, head Liverpool Sch of Architecture 1974–86, head Liverpool Sch of Architecture and Building Engrg 1986–90, pro-vice-chllr Univ of Liverpool 1988–91 and 1994–99 (actg vice-chllr 1991–92), emeritus prof 1999–; memb Peak Park Planning Bd 1973–86: chm Planning Control Ctee 1979–97, vice-chm of Bd 1981–86, co-opted memb Planning Control Ctee 1986–97; RIBA: chm Examinations Sub Ctee 1975–97, memb Professional Literature Ctee 1968–77, memb Educn and Professional Devpt Ctee 1978–97; memb: Countryside Cmmn Review Ctee on Nat Parks 1989–90, Technol Ctee UGC 1974–84, Architecture Ctee CNAA 1981–86, Built Environment Ctee 1986–89, Bd Riverside Housing Assoc 1992– (vice-chm 1997–98, chm 1998–2000), The Riverside Gp (chm 2001–), Liverpool Cathedral Fabric Advsy Ctee 1993– (chm 1996–), Patrimony Sub-Ctee Catholic Bishops' Conference of England and Wales 1994–2001, Historic Churches Ctee for RC Diocese of Lancaster, Liverpool, Salford and Shrewsbury 1994–; ARCUK: chm Bd of Educn 1983–86, vice-chm Cncl 1985–86, chm 1987–90; chm: Art and Architecture Dept Liverpool Archdiocese Liturgy Cmmn 1980–, Liverpool Architecture and Design Tst 1996–2007; tstee Nat Museums and Galleries on Merseyside and chm Bldg and Design Ctee 1996–2003, Corp Servs Ctee 2003–; pres Wirral Soc 2001, vice-pres Merseyside Civic Soc 2006; vice-pres CPRE Peak Dist and S Yorkshire Branch 2002–06; Hon DUniv Sheffield Hallam Univ 1997, Hon LLD Univ of Liverpool 1999; hon fell Chinese Univ of Hong Kong 2003; FRIBA, FRHistS, FSA, FRSA; *Books* Working Class Housing in Nineteenth Century Britain (1971), Five Per Cent Philanthropy (1973), The Peak District, Its Architecture (1973); *Clubs* Athenaeum; *Style*— Prof John Tarn, OBE, DL, FSA; ✉ 2 Ashmore Close, Barton Hey Drive, Caldy, Wirral CH48 2JX

TARRANT, Christopher John Charles; s of Dennis Tarrant, of Sidmouth, Devon, and Audrey, *née* Charles; *b* 12 April 1952; *Educ* Brentwood Sch, Pembroke Coll Cambridge (MA), Trinity Coll Bristol (BD London); *m* 10 July 1976, Dr Catherine Joyce Tarrant, da of Derek Lyne; 2 da (Ruth Jennifer b 18 July 1978, Anna Jane b 28 Sept 1981), 1 s (Simon Alastair b 28 Dec 1979); *Career* lectr Ahmadu Bello Univ Zaria Nigeria 1978–80, teacher Whitgift Sch 1980–84, head of geography Aylesbury GS 1984–93 (latterly sr teacher and i/c fin and premises), headmaster Wilson's Sch Sutton 1994–99, headmaster Trinity Sch Croydon 1999–2007; lay reader Anglican Church; FRSA 1997; *Publications* series of six religious educn textbooks for West African O Level syllabus (1979–84); Life in Bible Times (1986); *Recreations* walking, travel, photography, classical music; *Clubs* East India; *Style*— Christopher Tarrant, Esq

TARRANT, Christopher John (Chris); OBE (2004); s of Maj B A Tarrant, MC (d 2005), and Joan Ellen, *née* Cox; *b* 10 October 1946; *Educ* King's Sch Worcester, Univ of Birmingham (BA); *m* 1, 1977 (m dis 1982), Sheila Margaret, da of Maj Ralph Roberton (d 1982); 2 da (Helen Victoria, Jennifer Mary); *m* 2, 1991 (m dis 2007), Ingrid, da of Frederick Henry (Jimmy) Dupré de St Maur (d 1996); 1 da (Samantha Charlotte), 1 s (Toby Charles); *Career* prodr/writer/presenter of TV progs incl: ATV Today 1972, Tiswas 1974, OTT 1981, Everybody's Equal 1989, Tarrant on Television 1989–, The Main Event 1993, Lose a Million 1993, Pop Quiz 1994, Man O Man 1996, Who Wants to be a Millionaire 1998–, Tarrant on Top of the World: In Search of the Polar Bear 2005; presenter of Capital Radio's Breakfast Show 1987–2004; patron: Headway Thames Valley, Phoenix Centre for Handicapped Children, Centrepoint, Milly's Fund; *Awards* incl: Best On-Air Personality Int Radio Festival of NY 1987, TRIC Radio Personality of the Year 1989, Sony Radio Awards Radio Personality of the Year 1990, Variety Club of GB Independent Radio Personality of the Year 1991, Sony Radio Awards Silver Medal 1992 and 1993, Sony Radio Awards Best Breakfast Show 1995, NY World Awards Best Breakfast Show 1996, Variety Club of GB ITV Personality of the Year 1998, Broadcasting Press Guild Television Awards Best TV Performer in a Non-Acting Role 1999, Nat TV Awards Special Recognition Award 2000, TV People's Choice Award Best Game Show 2000, ITV Lifetime Achievement Award 2000, Nat TV Awards Best Game Show 2000, 2001, 2002, 2003 and 2005, GQ Magazine Light Entertainment Show of the Year 2000, TV Quick Light Entertainment Show of the Year 2000, Disney Channel Kids' Award Best Children's TV Show 2000, Sony Radio Industry Gold Award 2001, Radio Acad Lifetime Achievement Award 2002; *Books* Ken's Furry Friends (1986), Fishfriar's Hall Revisited (1987), Ready Steady Go (1990), Rebel Rebel (1991), Tarrant Off the Record (1997), Netty Nutters (1999), Tarrant on Millionaires (1999), Millionaire Moments (2002), Tarrant on Top of the World: In Search of the Polar Bear (2005); *Recreations* fishing, cricket; *Clubs* White Swan Piscatorials, Red Spinners, Lord's Taverners, Variety Club of GB; *Style*— Chris Tarrant, Esq, OBE; ✉ c/o Paul Vaughan, PVA Management Ltd, Hallow Park, Worcester WR2 6PG (tel 01905 640663, fax 01905 641842, e-mail md@pva.co.uk)

TARRANT, Prof John Rex; *b* 12 November 1941; *Educ* Marling GS Stroud, Univ of Hull (BSc, PhD); *m* Biddy, *née* Fisher; *Career* asst lectr Univ Coll Dublin 1966–68; UEA: lectr 1968–74, dean Sch of Environmental Scis 1974–77 and 1981–84, sr lectr 1974–82, reader 1982–94, pro-vice-chllr 1985–88, dep vice-chllr 1989–95, prof 1994–95; vice-chllr Univ of Huddersfield 1995–; visiting prof Dept of Geography Univ of Nebraska USA 1970, visiting lectr Dept of Geography Univ of Canterbury NZ 1973, visiting research assoc Int Food Policy Research Inst Washington DC 1977–78, visiting scholar Food Research Inst Stanford Univ USA 1978, Harris visiting prof Coll of Geosciences Texas A and M Univ USA 1989; memb Assoc of American Geographers 1991; hon fell UEA 1996, Hon DSc Univ of Hull 2000; FRGS 1965; *Books* Agricultural Geography (1974), Food Policies (1980), Food and Farming (1991); also author of 16 book chapters and over 40 articles in professional publications; *Recreations* gliding, motor cycling; *Style*— Prof John Tarrant

TATCH, Brian; s of David Tatch (d 1958), of London and formerly of Glasgow, and Gertrude Tatch (now Gertrude Alper, d 2005); *b* 24 April 1943; *Educ* Central Fndn Grammar, UCL (BSc); *m* 1965, Denise Ann, da of William Eugene Puckett (d 1979), of London and formerly of Louisville, Kentucky; 2 s, 1 da; *Career* consulting actuary; ptnr Clay & Partners 1975–91, chief exec Buck Paterson Consultants Ltd 1991–92, proprietor Brian Tatch & Co 1992–; fndr memb Assoc of Pensioneer Tstees (chm 1981–85); chm: Clay Clark Whitehill Ltd 1987–91 (jt chm 1985–87), The Bridford Group Ltd 1987–91, MCP Pension Tstees Ltd (tstee Maxwell Communication Works Pension Scheme) 1992–96; dir Britain Tstees Ltd 1999–; FIA, FPMI; *Style*— Brian Tatch, Esq; ✉ Brian Tatch & Co, Consulting Actuaries and Trustees, 14 Branscombe Gardens, Winchmore Hill, London N21 3BN (tel 020 8882 6466, fax 020 8882 6866)

TATCHELL, Peter Gary; s of Gordon Basil Tatchell, of Melbourne, Aust, and Mardi Aileen Nitscke, *née* Rhodes; *b* 25 January 1952, Melbourne, Aust; *Educ* Mount Waverley HS Melbourne, West London Coll (Dip), Poly of N London (BSc); *Career* human rights campaigner, co-organiser of gay human rights gp OutRage!, freelance journalist and author; sec Christians for Peace 1970–71, exec Vietnam Moratorium Campaign 1971, activist Gay Liberation Front 1971–73, chair Rockingham Estate Tenants' Assoc 1980–81, sec Southwark and Bermondsey Lab Party 1980–85, co-ordinator UK AIDS Vigil Orgn 1987–89, co-organiser Green & Socialists Confs 1987–89, activist ACT UP London 1989–91; Parly candidate (Lab) Bermondsey (by-election) 1983, London Assembly candidate (Ind Green Left) 2000, Parly candidate (Green) Oxford East 2007–; memb: NUJ 1986–, Republic 2002–, Green Party 2004–; *Publications* The Battle for Bermondsey (1983), Democratic Defence: A Non-Nuclear Alternative (1985), AIDS: A Guide to Survival (1986, 3 edn 1990), Europe in the Pink: Lesbian & Gay Equality in the New Europe (1992), Safer Sexy: The Guide to Gay Sex Safely (1994), We Don't Want to March Straight: Masculinity, Queers & the Military (1995); contrib: Nuclear-Free Defence (1983), Into the Twenty-First Century (1988), Getting There: Steps to a Green Society (1990), Anti-Gay (1996), The Penguin Book of Twentieth Century Protest (1998), Teenage Sex: What Should Schools Teach Children? (2002), The Hate Debate: Should Hate be Punished as a Crime? (2002), Sex & Politics in South Africa (2005); *Recreations* mountain hiking, surfing, art and design, ambushing tyrants and torturers; *Clubs* Heaven; *Style*— Peter Tatchell, Esq; ✉ OutRage!, PO Box 17816, London SW14 8WT (tel 020 8240 0222)

TATE, Catherine; *Educ* Central Sch of Speech and Drama; *Career* writer, actress and comedienne; Best Entertainment Show and Best Comedy Performance RTS Awards 2006, Best Actress Br Comedy Awards 2006; *Theatre* incl: All My Sons (Oxford Theatre Co), The Princes Play (NT), The Way of the World (NT), Catherine Tate Show (Soho Theatre London and Pleasance Theatre Edinburgh), A Servant to Two Masters (RSC, West End and world tour), Some Girl(s) (Gielgud Theatre); *Television* incl: Big Train II (BBC), Wild West (BBC), The Catherine Tate Show (3 series and 2 Christmas specials, BBC), The Bad Mother's Handbook (ITV), Dr Who (Christmas special and regular role 2007–08, BBC); *Film* incl: Mrs Ratcliffe's Revolution, Starter for Ten, Scenes of a Sexual Nature, 66, Love and Other Disasters; *Style*— Ms Catherine Tate; ✉ c/o Dawn Sedgwick Management, 3 Goodwins Court, London WC2N 4LL (tel 020 7240 0404, fax 020 7240 0415, e-mail office@dawnsedgwickmanagement.com)

TATE, David Read; s of Maurice Tate, of Penarth, S Glamorgan, and Florence, *née* Read; *b* 10 February 1955; *Educ* Penarth GS, Jesus Coll Oxford (MA), UCL (MSc), INSEAD Paris (AMP); *Career* Deloitte Haskins & Sells CAs 1977–80 (Mgmnt Consultancy Div 1980–83), Barclays de Zoete Wedd Ltd 1983–90 (dir 1987–90), dir Corporate Fin Div West Merchant Bank Ltd 1990–98, exec dir and head of princ investments WestLB Panmure Ltd 1998–2004, ptnr Nova Capital Gp 2004–06, fndr and managing ptnr Tempo Capital Ptnrs LLP 2006–; FCA 1992 (ACA 1980), FRSA; *Recreations* golf, hill walking, opera, theatre; *Clubs* Royal Porthcawl Golf, Royal Blackheath Golf, Oxford and Cambridge; *Style*— David R Tate, Esq; ✉ Tempo Capital Partners LLP, 52 Jermyn Street, London SW1Y 6LX (tel 020 7255 7510, fax 020 7255 7501, e-mail david.tate@tempo-cap.com)

TATE, Dr Jeffrey Philip; CBE (1990); s of Cyril Henry Tate, of Odiham, Hants, and Ivy Ellen, *née* Naylor; *b* 28 April 1943; *Educ* Farnham GS, Christ's Coll Cambridge (MA, MB BChir), St Thomas' Hosp London; *Career* trained as doctor of med St Thomas' Hosp London 1961–67, left medicine to join London Opera Centre 1969, joined Covent Garden staff 1970, assisted conductors incl Kempe, Krips, Solti, Davies and Kleiber 1973–77; later assisted: Boulez (Bayreuth Ring) 1976–81, Sir John Pritchard (Cologne Opera) 1977; conducted Gothenburg Opera Sweden 1978–80; NY Met Opera debut USA 1979, Covent Garden debut 1982, Salzburg Festival debut 1985; princ conductor English Chamber Orch 1985–; princ guest conductor: French Nat Radio Orch 1989–, Royal Opera House Covent Garden 1991–94 (princ conductor 1986–91), Orchestra Nazionale di RAI Italia 1998–; music dir Rotterdam Philharmonic Orch 1991–94, chief conductor Minnesota Orch Summer Festival 1997–; pres: Assoc for Spina Bifida and Hydrocephalus, Music Space; patron Br Lung Fndn, tstee Firebird Tst; hon fell Christ's Coll Cambridge 1989, hon fell

St Thomas' and Guy's Hosp Med Sch 1994; Hon DMus Univ of Leicester 1993; Officier de l'Ordre des Arts et des Lettres (France) 1990, Chev Ordre Nationale de la Légion d'Honneur 1999; *Recreations* reading, looking at the world going by, a bit of gastronomy; *Style*— Dr Jeffrey Tate, CBE; ✉ c/o English Chamber Orchestra, 2 Coningsby Road, London W5 4HR (tel 020 8840 6565, fax 020 8567 7198)

TATE, (William) John; s of William Kenneth Tate (d 1961), and Dorothy, *née* Pinfold; *b* 12 June 1951; *Educ* Eastcliffe GS Newcastle upon Tyne, KCL (LLB), Inns of Court Sch of Law; *m* 1976, Helen Elizabeth, da of late Alfred Quick; 1 s (Nicholas b 1981), 1 da (Sarah b 1982); *Career* called to the bar Gray's Inn 1974, in practice 1974–76, Flt Lt Legal Dept RAF 1976–78, Slr's Office HM Customs & Excise 1978–88, asst dir Serious Fraud Office 1988–96, dep Parly Cmmr for administration and legal advsr 1996–99, slr to Bloody Sunday Inquiry 1999–2003, dir of legal services Independent Police Complaints Cmmn 2003–; memb Hon Soc of Gray's Inn 1974; *Books* Current Law (delegated legislation ed, 1975–95); *Recreations* rowing, music, modern history, gardening; *Clubs* RAF, Kingston GS Veterans Rowing; *Style*— John Tate, Esq; ✉ The Independent Police Complaints Commission, 90 High Holborn, London WC1V 6BH (tel 020 7166 3038, fax 020 7404 0438)

TATE, Dr (Edward) Nicholas; CBE (2001); s of Joseph Edwin Tate, of Kirklevington, Cleveland, and Eva Elsie, *née* Hopkinson (d 1987); *b* 18 December 1943; *Educ* Huddersfield New Coll, Balliol Coll Oxford (MA), Univ of Liverpool (MA, PhD), Univ of Bristol (PGCE); *m* 1973, Nadya, *née* Grove; 2 da (Emily Sarah b 1974, Harriet Louisa b 1976), 1 s (Oliver Lucian b 1985); *Career* asst master De La Salle Coll Sheffield 1966–71, lectr City of Birmingham Coll of Educn 1972–74, sr lectr Moray House Coll of Educn Edinburgh (joined as lectr) 1974–88, professional offr Nat Curriculum Cncl 1989–91, asst chief exec Sch Examinations and Assessment Cncl 1991–93, chief exec Sch Curriculum and Assessment Authy 1994–97 (asst chief exec 1993–94), chief exec Qualifications and Curriculum Authy 1997–2000, headmaster Winchester Coll 2000–03, DG The Int Sch of Geneva 2003–; Hon DCL Univ of Huddersfield 1998; *Books* Pizarro and the Incas (1982), Modern World History (1988), People and Events in the Modern World (1988), A History of the Modern World (1994); *Clubs* Reform; *Style*— Dr Nicholas Tate, CBE; ✉ Ecole Internationale de Genève, 62 route de Chêne, CH-1208, Geneva, Switzerland

TATE, Sir (Henry) Saxon; 5 Bt (UK 1898), of Park Hill, Streatham, Co London; CBE (1991); s of Lt-Col Sir Henry Tate, 4 Bt, TD, DL (d 1994), and his 1 w, Lilian Nairne, *née* Gregson-Ellis (d 1984); *b* 28 November 1931; *Educ* Eton, ChCh Oxford; *m* 1, 3 Sept 1953 (m dis 1975), Sheila Ann, da of Duncan Robertson; 4 s (Edward Nicholas b 1966, Duncan Saxon b 1968, John William, Paul Henry (twins) b 1969); m 2, 31 Jan 1975, Virginia Joan Sturm; *Heir* s, Edward Tate; *Career* Nat Serv 2 Lt Life Guards 1949–51 (Lt Special Reserve 1951–); Tate & Lyle plc: prodn trainee Liverpool 1952, dir 1956–99, chm Exec Ctee 1973–78, md 1978–80, vice-chm 1980–82; ceo Redpath Industries Ltd Canada 1965–73; also dir: Tate Appointments Ltd 1982–2000 (chm 1991–96), A E Staley Manufacturing Inc 1991–98; chief exec Industrial Devpt Bd for NI 1982–85, chm and chief exec London Future and Options Exchange (London FOX) 1985–91; FIMgt 1975; *Style*— Sir Saxon Tate, Bt, CBE; ✉ 26 Cleaver Square, London SE11 4EA (tel 020 7582 6507)

TATEOSSIAN, Robert; *Educ* Wharton Sch, Univ of Pennsylvania (BA, BSc); *Career* jewellery designer; with Investment Banking Div Merrill Lynch Int 1985–90; prop Tateossian Ltd 1990–; British Export Fashion Award 1995 and 2000; *Style*— Robert Tateossian, Esq; ✉ Suite 3, Fulham Business Exchange, The Boulevard, Imperial Wharf, London SW6 2TL (tel 020 7384 8300, fax 020 7384 8333, mobile 07768 698635, e-mail robert@tateossian.com)

TATHAM, Amanda Jane; da of Christopher Tatham, MW, of Winchester, Hants, and Régine, *née* Legge; *b* 13 March 1953; *Educ* St Paul's Girls' Sch, London Coll of Printing (BA); *m* 1997, Rupert Wollheim; 2 s (Oscar b 1994, Otto b 1998); *Career* graphic designer Pentagram Design 1975–79, designer SMS Design 1979–80, fndr Amanda Tatham Design Ltd 1980–84, fndr ptnr Lambton Place Design 1984–87, co fndr and ptnr Tatham Pearce Ltd 1987–96, fndr Tatham Design Ltd 1996, fndr Designer Breakfasts 2006; graphic design and strategic consultancy incl corp and brand identities, brochures, websites and annual reports for clients incl: AG&G, Architects Benevolent Soc, Aromatherapy Soc, Arthur Brett & Sons, Asda, Asia House, Assoc for Qualitative Research, Barclays, Bentleys Stokes & Lowless, British International Freight Assoc, British & Cwlth Bank, Chetwood Associates, CJ Assocs, Coluga Pictures, Commander Global Hedging Fund, Computer Gym, CS Investments, Cushman & Wakefield Inc, Dalgety, Dept of Employment, Eurotherm, Exec Studio, Framlington, Garry Assoc Consulting Engrs, George Wimpey, GMB, Graseby (formerly Cambridge Electronic Industries), Healey & Baker, Inst of Freight Professionals, Inst of Masters of Wine, James Brett, Just Customer Communcation, Jigsaw Day Nurseries, Joseph Koniak Hair, Lexus, Lloyds Bowmaker, Lloyds TSB, LWT and TVS Sales, Magart Construction, Mitsubishi Finance International, Next, N London Strategic Alliance, Parambe, Portfolio Fund Management, Premier International Trading House, PricewaterhouseCoopers, Prigee International, Rachel Ormrod Qualitative Research, Reckitt & Colman, Renlon Building Preservation, Rosehaugh Stanhope, Royal Mail, Signet Gp (formerly Ratners Gp), Summerdown Pure Mint, Sunesis Communications Strategy, Superior Foods, Superior Packaging, The Broadgate Club, Tomkins, Trigon Mailing Services, Turnstone Research, Tusk Force, WCRS, White Stuff, Woolworths; Communication Arts Award for Design Excellence 1979, Spicer & Oppenheim Effective Finance Communications Award 1988, Stock Exchange & Chartered Accountants' Annual Award for smaller companies' published accounts (Graseby plc) 1995, Business Link for London selected best design project 1999, Design Cncl selected design project for Design in Business Week 2002, nomination D&AD Pencil Award for Royal Mail Magic! stamps 2006; memb: Design Business Assoc (Cncl of Mgmnt 1988–90), D&AD 1978; FCSD 1986 (memb Cncl 1990–93 and 2003–04), FRSA 1992; *Recreations* food, wine, classical and contemporary music, the visual arts; *Style*— Ms Amanda Tatham; ✉ 11 Keith Grove, London W12 9EY (tel 020 8932 2851, fax 020 8746 2419, e-mail amanda@tathamdesign.co.uk, website www.tathamdesign.co.uk)

TATTERSALL, Geoffrey Frank; QC (1992); s of late Frank Tattersall, of Ashton-under-Lyne, and Margaret, *née* Hassall; *b* 22 September 1947; *Educ* Manchester Grammar, ChCh Oxford (exhibitioner, MA), Lincoln's Inn (Tancred studentship in common law); *m* 7 Aug 1971, Hazel, da of late Harold Shaw, and late Alice Shaw; 1 s (Mark b 13 Sept 1976), 2 da (Victoria Louise b 5 April 1979, Hannah Jayne b 12 Nov 1984); *Career* called to the Bar Lincoln's Inn 1970 (bencher 1997), in practice N Circuit 1970–, recorder 1989–, judge of appeal Isle of Man 1997–, dep judge of the High Court 2003–; called to the Bar NSW 1992, sc 1995; lay chm Bolton Deanery Synod 1993–2002, chm House of Laity and vice-pres Manchester Diocesan Synod 1994–2003, memb Gen Synod 1995– (chm Standing Orders Ctee 1999–), hon lay canon Manchester Cathedral 2003, chllr Dio of Carlisle 2003–, dep chllr Dio of Durham 2003–05, chllr Dio of Manchester 2004–, dep vicar-gen Dio of Sodor and Man 2004–; chm Disciplinary Tbnls under Clergy Discipline Measure 2006–; external reviewer of decisions of Dir of Fair Access 2005–; *Recreations* family, music, travel; *Style*— Geoffrey Tattersall, QC; ✉ 12 Byrom Street, Manchester M3 4PP (tel 0161 829 2100); 22 Old Buildings, Lincoln's Inn, London WC2A 3UJ (tel 020 7831 0222)

TATTERSALL, John Hartley; s of Robert Herman Tattersall (d 1958), of Conwy, Gwynedd, and Jean, *née* Stevens (d 1995); *b* 5 April 1952; *Educ* Shrewsbury, Christ's Coll Cambridge (MA); *m* 8 Sept 1984, Madeleine Virginia, da of Robert Edward Hugh Coles, of Caversham, Berks; 2 s (Robert b 1985, Luke 1987), 1 da (Clare b 1990); *Career* ptnr PricewaterhouseCoopers (formerly Coopers & Lybrand before merger) 1985– (joined 1975); chm Risk and Regulation Ctee ICAEW Financial Services Faculty 2007–; memb: Banking Sub-Ctee ICAEW 1989–2007, Capital Ctee Securities and Futures Authy 1993–2001, Prudential Sourcebook Advsy Gp FSA 2000–06; dir: London City Ballet Trust Ltd 1987–96 (dep chm 1995–96), English Touring Opera Ltd 1998–, South Eastern Inst for Theological Educn 2004–; advsy govr St Augustine's Priory Ealing 1995–2002; non-stipendiary min C of E 2007; Freeman Worshipful Co of Horners 1980, Liveryman Guild of Int Bankers 2006; FCA 1989 (ACA 1978); *Books* Towards a Welfare World (jtly, 1973), The Investment Business - Compliance with the Rules (1990), Current Issues in Auditing (contrib, 1997), A Practitioner's Guide to FSA Regulation of Banking (ed, 2002 and 2006), A Practitioner's Guide to the Basel Accord (ed, 2005); *Recreations* walking, opera, ballet; *Style*— John Tattersall, Esq; ✉ 3 St Ann's Villas, Holland Park, London W11 4RU (tel 020 7603 1053, e-mail jhtatters@aol.com); PricewaterhouseCoopers, Southwark Towers, 32 London Bridge Street, London SE1 9SY (tel 020 7212 4689, fax 020 7213 4996, e-mail john.h.tattersall@uk.pwc.com)

TATTERSFIELD, Dr Brian; s of Norman Tattersfield (d 1959), and Marian, *née* Rogers; *b* 12 April 1936; *Educ* Heckmondwike GS, Batley Sch of Art (NDD), RCA (ARCA); *m* 20 April 1963, (Elizabeth) Mary Tindall, da of Richard Newton Wakelin (d 1964), of Richmond, Surrey; 2 da (Jane Charlotte Wakelin b 1964, Emma Louisa Wakelin b 1972); *Career* art dir Young and Rubicam Ltd 1962–63, designer Fletcher Forbes Gill 1963, co-fndr, ptnr and creative head Minale Tattersfield 1964–95, ret; visiting lectr RCA 1978, visiting prof in design Univ of Brighton 1988–; design awards incl: Typomundus Canada 1964, creativity on paper NY 1966, Silver award D&AD 1968 (1970 and 1974–84), Gold award Art Dir Club NY 1975, Poster award Warsaw Biennale 1969, Br Poster Design award 1970, Liderman Gold award for graphic design Madrid 1983, Civic Tst award 1985, D&AD president's award for outstanding contrib to Br design 1987; exhibitions: MOMA NY 1978, London Design Centre 1981, Glasgow Design Centre 1981, MOMA Milan 1983, Cultural Centre of Madrid 1985, Axis Gallery Tokyo 1988; various articles in Br and int jls; memb D&AD; Hon PhD Anglia Poly Univ, Hon DSc Univ of Huddersfield; hon fell RCA, FCSD, FRSA; *Style*— Prof Brian Tattersfield; ✉ Sarisberie Cottage, The Street, West Clandon, Surrey GU4 7ST (tel 01483 222908); 178 High Street, Aldeburgh, Suffolk IP15 5AQ

TAUNTON, Archdeacon of; *see:* Reed, Ven John Peter Cyril

TAUSIG, Peter; s of Dr Walter Charles Tausig (d 1969), and Judith, *née* Morris (d 1995); *b* 15 August 1943; *Educ* Battersea GS, UCL (BSc); *m* 28 June 1987 (m dis 1997); 2 da (Eva Lily Ibolya b 3 April 1988, Katja Francesca b 30 Dec 1990); *Career* economist: Aust Bureau of Census and Statistics 1965–69, CBI 1969, Bank of London and S America 1970–74, International Marine Banking Co 1974–76, S G Warburg/Warburg Securities 1976–88 (dir 1983); exec dir UBS Phillips & Drew 1989–91; dir: Crédit Lyonnais Securities and Crédit Lyonnais Capital Markets 1992–95, Whittingdale Ltd 1996–99; chm Research Ethics Ctee Royal Marsden Hosp 1999–2004, chm Thames Valley Research Ethics Ctee 2004– (vice-chm 2002–03); chm: Kateva Mgmnt 1992–, Ladbroke Square Montessori Sch 1992–, Annemount Sch 1993–96; tstee St Botolphs Project 1999–2004; treas: Heath Hands 2000–03, Br Czech Slovak Assoc 2000–02, Heath and Hampstead Soc 2005–; *Recreations* theatre, literature, music, walking, skiing, travel; *Clubs* Groucho, Oriental; *Style*— Peter Tausig, Esq; ✉ 11 Downshire Hill, Hampstead, London NW3 1NR (tel 020 7435 7099, e-mail peter_tausig@hotmail.com)

TAUSSIG, Andrew John; s of Leo Taussig, and Magda, *née* Szücs; *Educ* Winchester (scholar), Magdalen Coll Oxford (MA), Harvard Univ (PhD); *Career* prodr of various BBC progs incl Talk-In with Sir Robin Day and David Dimbleby 1973–79, special asst to dir news and current affairs BBC 1979–80, dep ed Nationwide prog BBC 1980–81, chief asst TV current affairs BBC 1981–86, controller European services and head of Europe region BBC World Service 1988–96, dir foreign language services BBC World Service 1996–2000; research associate Centre for Socio-Legal Studies Univ of Oxford 2001–, conslt to Br Cncl for World Summit on the Information Soc; memb Cncl Chatham House (RIIA), networking memb Cwlth Prog for Technol Mgmnt (CPTM), dir Vioce of the Listener and Viewer (VLV); *Recreations* photography, antique browsing, travelling; *Clubs* Le Beaujolais; *Style*— Andrew Taussig

TAVENER, Prof Sir John Kenneth; kt (2000); s of Charles Kenneth Tavener (d 1996), and Muriel Evelyn, *née* Brown (d 1985); *b* 28 January 1944; *Educ* Highgate Sch, RAM (scholarship); *m* 1, 17 Nov 1974 (m dis 1980), Victoria, da of Dr Costas Marangopoulos, of Athens; m 2, 8 Sept 1991, Maryanna Elizabeth Malecka, da of Prof Glen Schaefer (d 1986), of Cranfield, Beds; 2 da (Theodora Alexandra b 26 Aug 1993, Sofia Evelyn b 14 Dec 1995); *Career* composer; organist St John's Church London 1960–75, prof of composition Trinity Coll of Music 1968–; memb Russian Orthodox Church; Hon FRAM, Hon FTCL, Hon FRSCM, Hon DMus New Delhi Univ India for services to the Sacred in Art 1990, Hon DMus City Univ London 1995; Apollo Prize Friends of Greek Nat Opera 1993; *Compositions* incl: Cain and Abel (first prize Prince Rainier of Monaco 1965) 1965, The Whale (London) 1968, Celtic Requiem, Ultimos Ritos (Holland Festival) 1974, Akhmatova Requiem 1980 (Edinburgh Festival), Antigone, Thérèse (Covent Garden) 1979, Palintropos (Moscow) 1989, Sappho Fragments, Towards the Son, Mandelion, A Gentle Spirit, Ikon of Light (Tallis Scholars) 1984, Liturgy of St John Chrysostom, Risen!, In Memory of Cats, Let Not the Prince be Silent, Requiem for Father Malachy, Two Hymns to the Mother of God, Kyklike Kinesis, Collegium Regale (King's Coll Cambridge) 1987, Hymn to the Holy Spirit, Acclamation for His All Holiness the Ecumenical Patriarch Demetrios I (Canterbury Cathedral) 1988, Akathist of Thanksgiving (Westminster Abbey) 1988, Ikon of St Seraphim (Truro Cathedral) 1988, The Protecting Veil (Royal Albert Hall) 1989 (The Gramophone award 1992), Resurrection (Glasgow Cathedral) 1990, Apocalypse (BBC Proms cmmn) 1990–92, The Hidden Treasure 1990, The Repentant Thief (LSO cmmn, Barbican) 1991, Mary of Egypt 1992, We Shall See Him as He is 1992, Eternal Memory 1992, Last Sleep of the Virgin 1992, Akhmatova Songs 1993, Song for Athene 1993, The World is Burning (Monteverdi Choir cmmn) 1994, The Myrrh-Bearer (London Symphony Chorus cmmn) 1994, Melina 1994, Innocence 1994, Agraphon 1995, Three Antiphons 1995, Let's Begin Again 1993–95, Svyatuiee 1995, Vlepontas (Delphi cmmn) 1996, Wake Up and Die (Sony cmmn) 1996, The Toll Houses (opera) 1996, Depart in Peace 1997, The Last Discourse 1997, Eternity's Sunrise 1997, Fall and Resurrection (Millennium cmmn, St Paul's Cathedral) 2000, Laila (adapted as Amu by Random Dance Co Sadler's Wells) 2005; *Television and Publications* subject of many TV progs incl: Art and Belief, A Week in the Life of, Making Out, Ultimos Ritos, Celtic Requiem, Glimpses of Paradise 1992, South Bank Show 1998; subject of book by Geoffrey Haydon John Tavener: Glimpses of Paradise (1995); *Recreations* travelling in Greece, house in Greece, collecting icons; *Style*— Prof Sir John Tavener

TAVERNE, Baron (Life Peer UK 1996), of Pimlico in the City of Westminster; Dick Taverne; QC (1965); s of Dr Nicolaas Jacobus Marie Taverne (d 1966), and Louise Victoria, *née* Koch; *b* 18 October 1928; *Educ* Charterhouse, Balliol Coll Oxford; *m* 6 Aug 1955, Janice, da of late Dr Robert Samuel Fleming Hennessey; 2 da ((Hon) Suzanna Taverne, *qv*, b 1960, Hon Caroline b 1963); *Career* called to the Bar 1954; MP (Lab) Lincoln 1962–72: Parly sec Home Office 1966–68, min of state Treasy 1968–69, fin sec 1969–70, resigned Labour Party 1972; re-elected Independent Social Democrat MP Lincoln 1973–74; first dir Inst for Fiscal Studies 1971 (chm 1979–83), chm Public Policy Centre 1984–87, Br memb Spierenburg Ctee to examine working of Euro Cmmn 1979; PRIMA Europe: dir

T

1987–98, chm 1991–94, pres 1994–98; chm AXA Equity & Law Life Assurance Society plc 1998–2001 (dir 1972–97), dir BOC Group plc 1975–95; chm: OLIM Convertible Trust 1989–99, Alcohol and Drug Abuse Prevention and Treatment Ltd 1996–, Sense About Science 2002–, IFG Devpt Ltd 2003–; hon fell Mansfield Coll Oxford 1997; *Books* The Future of the Left (1974), The March of Unreason - Science, Democracy and the New Fundamentalism (2005); *Recreations* sailing; *Style*— The Rt Hon Lord Taverne, QC; ✉ 60 Cambridge Street, London SW1V 4QQ (tel 020 7828 0166)

TAVERNE, (Hon) Suzanna; da of Baron Taverne, QC (Life Peer), *qv*, and Janice, *née* Hennessey; *b* 3 February 1960; *Educ* Pimlico Sch, Westminster, Balliol Coll Oxford (BA); *m* 1993, Marc Vlessing; 1 da (Clara), 1 s (Milo); *Career* SG Warburg & Co Ltd 1982–90, head of strategic planning Newspaper Publishing plc 1990–92, fin dir Newspaper Publishing plc 1992–94, conslt Saatchi & Saatchi 1994–95, dir of strategy and devpt Pearson plc 1995–98, md Br Museum 1999–2001; tstee Nat Cncl for One Parent Families; *Style*— Ms Suzanna Taverne

TAVERNOR, Prof Robert; *b* 19 December 1954, Worcester; *Educ* Chatham House GS Ramsgate, Harvey GS Folkestone, South Bank Poly (BA), PCL (DipArch), Br Sch at Rome (scholar in architecture), St John's Coll Cambridge (PhD); *m* Denise Alexandra, *née* Mackie; 2 da (Joanna b 1984, Faye b 1985), 1 s (James b 1989); *Career* architect; assoc architect Cambridge Design Architects 1983–85, dir Richard Reid Architects 1985–86, founding ptnr Alberti Gp 1988–94, founding dir Design Gp Bath Architects 1990–92; pt/t lectr PCL 1980–82, coll tutor Univ of Cambridge 1980–87 (pt/t lectr 1982–87), lectr in architecture Univ of Bath 1987–92, initiator Centre for Advanced Studies in Architecture Univ of Bath 1991–92, Forbes prof of architecture Univ of Edinburgh 1992–95, prof of architecture Univ of Bath 1995–2005 (head of dept 2003–05), prof of architecture and urban design and dir Cities Prog LSE 2005–; visiting prof Center for Medieval and Renaissance Studies UCLA 1998–99, EU visiting scholar Texas A&M Univ 2002, visiting prof of architecture and urbanism Univ of São Paulo 2004; memb Editorial Bd Architectural Res Quarterly 1994–97 and 1999–; dissertations examiner RIBA 1986–97; awards incl Bath Environmental Award 1992 and 1993; RIBA 1984, ARIAS 1994–96, FRSA 1994; *Publications* L B Alberti On the Art of Building in Ten Books (with J Rykwert and N Leach, 1991), Palladio and Palladianism (1991), Edinburgh (ed, 1995), Andrea Palladio The Four Books on Architecture (ed with R Schofield, 1997, The Architecture Review Architectural Publication of the Year 1997, The Architects' Jl Architectural Publication of the Year 1998), On Alberti and the Art of Building (1998, The Architects' Jl Architectural Publication of the Year 1999), Body and Building: the changing relation of body and architecture (ed with G Dodds, 2002), Smoot's Ear: the measure of humanity (2007); other publications incl: chapters in 11 books, 1 dictionary entry, 10 essays in refereed jls, 15 essays in professional jls, 30 book reviews; *Style*— Prof Robert Tavernor; ✉ London School of Economics and Political Science, Houghton Street, London WC2A 2AE (tel 020 7955 7753, fax 020 7955 7697, e-mail r.tavernor@lse.ac.uk)

TAYAR, Dr René Benedict; s of Oscar Tayar, of Sliema, Malta, and Violet, *née* Riccardi; *b* 3 October 1945; *Educ* St Aloysius' Coll Malta, Royal Univ of Malta (MD); *m* 25 Jan 1971, Margaret Rose, da of Louis Francis Tortell, of Sliema, Malta; 1 s (Benjamin b 8 Sept 1978); *Career* sr registrar in radiology Bristol Royal Infirmary 1977–81 (registrar in radiology 1974–77); conslt radiologist: St Helier Hosp Carshalton 1981–, Nelson Hosp Raynes Park 1981–, Parkside Hosp Wimbledon 1984–, St Helier Hosp NHS Tst (also sec Med Staff Ctee), Atkinson Morley Imaging Centre Wimbledon 1992–96, St Anthony's Hosp N Cheam 1995–; hon sr lectr St George's Hosp Med Sch 1988–; fndr memb: Sir Harry Secombe Scanner Appeal, Secombe Magnet Appeal; hon sec Magnetic Resonance Radiologists Assoc 1998–2003; FRCR; *Recreations* tennis, music, literature; *Clubs* RAC, Pall Mall; *Style*— Dr René Tayar; ✉ 45 Epsom Lane South, Tadworth, Surrey KT20 5TA (tel 01737 813582); Department of Radiodiagnosis, St Helier Hospital, Wrythe Lane, Carshalton, Surrey SM5 1AA (tel and fax 020 8644 4343)

TAYLOR, His Hon Alan Broughton; s of Valentine James Broughton Taylor (d 1992), of Birmingham, and Gladys Maud, *née* Williams (d 1988); *b* 23 January 1939; *Educ* Malvern Coll, Univ of Geneva, Univ of Birmingham (LLB), BNC Oxford (MLitt); *m* 15 Aug 1964, Diana, da of Dr James Robson Hindmarsh (d 1970), of Lytchett Matravers, Dorset; 2 s (Stephen James b 30 Nov 1965, Robert David b 21 Feb 1968); *Career* called to the Bar Gray's Inn 1961; in practice 1962–91, recorder 1979–91; circuit judge: Midland & Oxford Circuit 1991–2001, Midland Circuit 2001–05; a pres Mental Health Review Tbnl 2004–; govr St Matthew's Sch Smethwick 1988–92; FCIArb 1994, chartered arbitrator 2005–; *Books* A Practical Guide to the Care of the Injured (by P S London, contrib 1964), Crime and Civil Society (by Green, Grove and Martin, contrib 2005); *Recreations* philately, fell walking; *Style*— His Hon Alan Taylor

TAYLOR, Alexandra; da of Kenneth Taylor, and Maureen, *née* Bell; *b* 17 February 1959; *Educ* Blaydon Comp, Newcastle upon Tyne Sch of Art (HND, DipAD); *Career* art dir: BBD&O advtg 1981–83, Saatchi & Saatchi 1983–89; sr art dir, gp head and bd dir WCRS 1989; Saatchi & Saatchi: rejoined as gp head and bd dir 1989, head of art 1992–, creative dir 1996–; memb D&AD (memb Exec Ctee 1998–); *Awards* 12 Silver Campaign Press Awards, 1 Gold Campaign Poster Award, 1 Gold Award Creative Circle, 6 Silver Campaign Poster Awards, 5 Silver Br TV Awards, 1 ITVA Award, 4 Silver D&AD Awards, 2 Gold, 1 Silver and 2 Bronze Cannes, 184 entries accepted in Design and Art Direction Annual, 4 Silver nominations D&AD; *Style*— Ms Alexandra Taylor; ✉ Saatchi & Saatchi, 80 Charlotte Street, London W1A 1AQ (tel 020 7636 5060, fax 020 7637 8489)

TAYLOR, Prof Andrew; *b* North Wales; *Educ* Bartlett Sch of Architecture (BSc), Dip Arch RIBA; *Career* architect; MacCormac Jamieson Pritchard, ptnr Patel Taylor Architects 1989–; tutor Bartlett Sch of Architecture, prof Welsh Sch of Architecture Univ of Cardiff 2003–; Civic Tst assessor 1997–99, RIBA Awards assessor, external examiner Univ of Cardiff; memb CABE Enabling Panel; *Competitions* incl: Sainsbury's supermarket 1987, sheltered accomodation Clywd Wales 1989, the city and the river Antwerp Belgium 1990, Choral and Music Centre Rhondda Heritage Park Wales 1990, Europan II Châteauroux France 1991, Peckham London 1991, Ayr Citadel 1993, Europan III Pierre-Bénite France 1994, Thames Barrier Park London 1995, Footbridge Balmaha Scotland 1996, Portland College Nottinghamshire 1998; *Awards* Royal Acad Summer Exhibition Non-Members Award 1988, RIBA Architecture Award (for Arts Centre Wales) 1992, Geoffrey Gribble Conservation Award (for PACE Counselling Centre London) 1995, Glass and Glazing Award (for PACE Counselling Centre London) 1995, Saltire Geddes Planning Award (for Ayr Citadel Scotland) 1995, shortlisted Young Architect of the Year 1997, 4 RIBA Architecture Awards (for Thames Barrier Park, Benslow Music Sch, Peace Park Pavilion and Apartment Battersea) 2001; *Style*— Prof Andrew Taylor; ✉ Patel Taylor Architects, 53 Rawstorne Street, London EC1V 7NQ (tel 020 7278 2323, fax 020 7278 6242, e-mail pta@pateltaylor.co.uk)

TAYLOR, Andrew David; s of Vernon Taylor, of Market Overton, Rutland, and Elizabeth, *née* McGhie (d 1995); *b* 6 March 1952, Leicester; *Educ* Magdalen Coll Sch Oxford, Lincoln Coll Oxford (MA, Hockey blue); *m* 10 Dec 1977, Alison Jane; 1 s (Henry Guy Jonathan b 11 March 1982), 2 da (Julia Poppy b 15 April 1984, Lucy Caroline b 24 Sept 1986); *Career* admitted slr 1980; Richards Butler: joined as articled clerk 1977, ptnr 1983–, chm 2000–05; sec and treas Br Maritime Law Assoc; *Publications* Voyage Charters (3 edn 2007); *Recreations* skiing, hockey, hiking, opera, wine; *Clubs* Travellers, City Univ, City Law, Vincent's (Oxford); *Style*— Andrew Taylor, Esq; ✉ Reed Smith Richards Butler, Beaufort House, 15 St Botolph Street, London EC3A 7EE (tel 020 7247 6555, e-mail adt@richardsbutler.com)

TAYLOR, Andrew John (Andy); s of Thomas Sowler Taylor (d 1986), of Grasmere, Cumbria, and Sarah, *née* McGinley (d 1986); *b* 23 February 1950, Newcastle upon Tyne; *Educ* Rutherford GS Newcastle, Trinity Coll Cambridge (MA); *m* 23 Sept 1985, Elizabeth, *née* Robertson; 2 da (Claire Madderson Sarah b 2 Aug 1985, Louise Frances Anne b 11 Oct 1986); *Career* fndr Sanctuary Gp 1976 (ceo until 2006), currently ceo Phantom Music Mgmnt Ltd and chm Concept Venues Ltd; Music Week Strat award for lifetime contrib to the music industry; FCA 1976, FRSA; *Recreations* wine, fell walking, travel, horse racing; *Clubs* Soho House; *Style*— Andy Taylor, Esq; ✉ Sphere Entertainment Limited, 22–23 Old Burlington Street, London W1S 2JJ (tel 020 7494 5961, fax 020 7494 9445, e-mail andy.taylor@conceptvenues.com)

TAYLOR, Andrew John Robert; s of Rev Arthur John Taylor, of Monmouth, and Hilda Mary, *née* Haines; *b* 14 October 1951; *Educ* The King's Sch Ely, Woodbridge Sch, Emmanuel Coll Cambridge (BA), UCL (MA); *m* 8 Sept 1979, Caroline Jane, da of Ian George Silverwood; 1 da (Sarah Jessica b 9 June 1986), 1 s (William John Alexander b 6 March 1989); *Career* writer; various jobs ranging from boatbuilding to teaching 1973–76, freelance sub ed for London publishers 1975–84, library asst then asst librarian London Borough of Brent 1976–81, self-employed writer 1981–; ed The Author (jl of Soc of Authors) 2004–06; memb: Soc of Authors, Crime Writers' Assoc, Asociación Internacional de Escritores Policiácos; *Awards* John Creasey Meml Award Crime Writers' Assoc 1982 and Edgar nomination from Mystery Writers of America for Caroline Minuscule, Our Fathers' Lies shortlisted for Gold Dagger of Crime Writers Assoc 1985, Snapshot shortlisted for NatWest Children's Book of the Year award 1989, Ellis Peters Historical Dagger of Crime Writers' Assoc 2001 (for The Office of the Dead) and 2003 (for The American Boy); *Books* for children incl: Hairline Cracks (1988), Private Nose (1989), Snapshot (1989), Double Exposure (1990), Negative Image (1992), The Invader (1994); for adults incl: Caroline Minuscule (1982), Waiting for the End of the World (1984), Our Fathers' Lies (1985), An Old School Tie (1986), Freelance Death (1987), The Second Midnight (1988), Blacklist (1988), Blood Relation (1990), Toyshop (1990), The Raven on the Water (1991), The Sleeping Policeman (1992), The Barred Window (1993), Odd Man Out (1993), An Air That Kills (1994), The Mortal Sickness (1995), The Four Last Things (1997), The Lover of the Grave (1997), The Judgement of Strangers (1998), The Suffocating Night (1998), The Office of the Dead (2000), Where Roses Fade (2000), Death's Own Door (2001), Requiem for an Angel (2002), The American Boy (2003), Call the Dying (2004), A Stain on the Silence (2006), Naked to the Hangman (2006); *Clubs* Detection; *Style*— Andrew Taylor, Esq; ✉ c/o Sheil Land Associates Ltd, 52 Doughty Street, London WC1N 2LS

TAYLOR, Annita; da of Romola Piapan (d 1967), of Switzerland, and Rosalia Smak Piapan (d 1984); *b* 21 September 1925; *Educ* Avviamento Professionale Tecnico di Monfalcone Italy; *m* 10 Nov 1946, Alfred Oakley Taylor, s of George Oakley Taylor; 1 da (Ligmoi Hannah b 18 Oct 1947); *Career* md ABBA DG Co Ltd 1983–90 (dir 1978–90); dir: Liglets Co Ltd 1982–, Rosalia Management Services Co Ltd 1989–90; involved with: Riding for the Disabled, Red Cross; *Recreations* racing, polo, shooting; *Clubs* Guards Polo, Jockey, Racehorse Owners' Assoc; *Style*— Mrs Annita Taylor; ✉ Wadley Manor, Faringdon, Oxfordshire SN7 8PN (tel 01367 20556, mobile 07887 803239, e-mail ligmoi@yahoo.com); 19 Millers Court, Chiswick Mall, London W4 2PF (tel 020 8748 2997)

TAYLOR, Baz; s of Alfred William Taylor, of Tankerton, Kent, and Marjorie, *née* Steventon; *b* 30 August 1944; *Educ* Simon Langton GS Canterbury, The Queen's Coll Oxford (MA); *m* 16 May 1970 (m dis 2004), (Marianne) Valerie, da of Eiddfryn James (d 1957), of Caemorgan, Dyfed; 2 da (Alice Jane b 28 May 1971, Katharine Elizabeth b 4 Nov 1972); partner, Hilary Fagg; 1 da (Charlotte b 3 Dec 1994), 1 s (Nico b 3 July 1999); *Career* prodr World in Action Granada TV 1968, dir The Christians 1975 (NY Film and TV Festival Award); memb: Friends of the Earth, Nat Tst, BAFTA 1975; elected memb Cncl Dirs' Guild of GB 1990, memb Advsy Cncl Directors' and Producers' Rights Soc (DPRS) 1995; *Television* dir, prodr and exec prodr numerous series incl: Talent with Julie Walters (NY Film and TV Award), Auf Wiedersehen Pet (Br Press and Broadcasting Award 1983, Drama of the Decade Award 1989), Shine on Harvey Moon, Young Charlie Chaplin (Thames TV, Emmy nomination) 1989, Lovejoy (BBC), Minder (Euston Films) 1992–93, Birds of a Feather 1996, Midsomer Murders (ITV Network) 1997, Broker's Man (BBC) 1998, Unfinished Business (BBC) 1998, My Family (BBC) 2000, The Bill (ITV) 2001–02; *Films* Near Mrs 1991, Shooting Elizabeth 1992, Tattle Tale 1992, Take Three Girls 2004, Lady Godiva - Back in the Saddle 2006, Lovey Dovey 2006; *Books* Cash and Carrie (1986), Love Me, Love My Dog (1987), Donkey Oaty (2000); *Recreations* sailing, golf, walking, skiing; *Clubs* BAFTA, The Stage Golfing Soc; *Style*— Baz Taylor, Esq; ✉ 201 St Margaret's Road, Twickenham TW1 1LU (tel 020 8892 0252, fax 020 8891 1292, mobile 07973 320447, e-mail bazfilms@aol.com, website baztaylor.co.uk)

TAYLOR, Bernard Irvin; s of Albert Ernest Taylor (d 1965), of Swindon, Wilts, and Edna Marion, *née* Tanner; *b* 2 October 1934; *Educ* Swindon Sch of Art, Chelsea Sch of Art (Chelsea Dip, Nat Dip Design), Univ of Birmingham (BA, Art Teacher's Dip); *Career* author and playwright; teacher and book illustrator London 1960–63, teacher and painter of portraits and landscapes, actor New York 1963–70, writer and actor UK 1970–; memb: Actors' Equity, Soc of Authors; *Plays* Daughter of the Apachés (1973), Mice on the First Floor (1974, Thames TV most promising playwright award 1974), Maggie it's Me! (1975); *Novels* The Godsend (1976, translated into 17 languages and filmed), Sweetheart Sweetheart (1977), The Reaping (1980), The Moorstone Sickness (1982), The Kindness of Strangers (1986), Madeleine (1987), Mother's Boys (1988, also made into a film), Saddle the Wind (as Kate Irvine, 1989), Charmed Life (1991), Evil Intent (1994), Since Ruby (1999), So Long at the Fair (as Jess Foley, 2001), Too Close to the Sun (as Jess Foley, 2002), Saddle the Wind (as Jess Foley, 2003), Wait for the Dawn (as Jess Foley, 2005), No Wings to Fly (as Jess Foley, 2006); *Non-Fiction* Cruelly Murdered (1979), Perfect Murder (with Stephen Knight, 1987, Crime Writers' Assoc Gold Dagger award), Murder at the Priory (with Kate Clarke, 1988); has also published numerous short stories; *Style*— Bernard Taylor, Esq; ✉ c/o A M Heath & Co Ltd, 79 St Martin's Lane, London WC2N 4AA (tel 020 7836 4271)

TAYLOR, Bernard John; s of John Taylor (d 1962), and Evelyn Frances Taylor (d 1995); *b* 2 November 1956; *Educ* Cheltenham Coll, St John's Coll Oxford (scholar, MA); *m* 16 June 1984, Sarah Jane, da of John Paskin Taylor, of Paris; 1 s (Henry Bernard Charles b 22 Sept 1992); *Career* dir Med Dív Smiths Industries plc 1983–85 (business planning and acquisitions 1979–82); exec dir: Baring Bros & Co Ltd 1985–94 (mangr and asst dir Corp Fin Dept), Robert Fleming & Co Ltd 1994– (dep chm and chief exec), Robert Fleming Holdings Ltd 1995– (jt chief exec investment banking 1998–2000), Chase Manhattan 2000 (vice-chm EMEA), JP Morgan plc 2001–06 (vice-chm 2001–06); chm and chief exec Braveheart Financial Servs Ltd 2006–, chief exec Evercare Ptnrs Ltd 2007–, vice-chm Evercare Ptnrs Inc 2007–; non-exec dir: New Focus Healthcare 1986–90, ISIS Innovation Ltd 1997– (chm 2001–), Oxford Investments plc 2002–, Ti Automotive plc (dep chm 2001–); memb Cncl Univ of Oxford (chm Audit and Scrutiny Ctee); LRPS (memb 1971), FRSC (memb 1972), CChem; *Books* Photosensitive Film Formation on Copper (I) (1974), Photosensitive Film Formation on Copper (II) (1976), Oxidation of Alcohols to Carbonyl Compounds, Synthesis (1979); *Recreations* photography, gardening, wine; *Clubs* Oxford and Cambridge, Mark's, Brooks's; *Style*— Bernard Taylor, Esq

TAYLOR, Prof Brent William; s of Robert Ernest Taylor (d 1971), of Christchurch, NZ, and Norma Gertrude, *née* Collett; *b* 21 November 1941; *Educ* Christchurch Boys' HS, Univ of Otago (MB ChB), Univ of Bristol (PhD); *m* 17 Jan 1970, Moira Elizabeth, da of Thomas Richard Hall (d 1983), of Palmerston North, NZ; 1 s (Samuel b 1973), 1 da (Katherine b 1975); *Career* jr med posts Christchurch NZ 1967–71, res and trg posts Great Ormond Street and Inst of Child Health London 1971–74, sr lectr in paediatrics Christchurch NZ 1975–81, conslt sr lectr in social paediatrics and epidemiology Univ of Bristol and visiting paediatrician and epidemiologist Riyadh Al Kharj Hosp prog 1981–84, conslt sr lectr in child health St Mary's Hosp Med Sch London 1985–88, prof of community child health Royal Free and Univ Coll Med Sch UCL 1988–; FRACP 1981 (MRACP 1970), FRCP 1985 (MRCP 1971), FRCPCH 1997; *Recreations* opera, walking, London; *Style—* Prof Brent Taylor; ✉ 42 Oakley Road, London N1 3LS (tel 020 7688 9738); General and Adolescent Paediatric Unit, Institute of Child Health, University College London, Guildford Street, London WC1N 1EH (tel 020 7905 2363, e-mail brent.taylor@medsch.ucl.ac.uk)

TAYLOR, Carole; OC (2001); *Educ* Univ of Toronto (BA); *Career* former broadcaster CTV (first female host of W5 and Canada AM), CBC Radio and TV, CKNW and CFTO; chair Canadian Broadcasting Corp (CBC)/Radio-Canada 2001–; currently dir: HSBC Holdings plc, HSBC Bank USA, HSBC North America, Fairmont Hotels and Resorts; former chair: Vancouver Bd of Trade (now govr), Canada Ports Corp, Vancouver Ports Corp; former dir: Canadian Pacific Ltd, CP Rail; numerous appts to bds of public instns; alderman City of Vancouver 1986; Hon LLD Simon Fraser Univ BC 2002, Hon DTech BC Inst of Technol 2003, hon degree in literature BC Open Univ 2004; *Clubs* Vancouver Lawn Tennis and Badminton; *Style—* Ms Carole Taylor, OC; ✉ Office of the Chair, Canadian Broadcasting Corporation, PO Box 3220 Station C, Ottawa, Ontario K1Y 1E4, Canada

TAYLOR, Cavan; s of Albert William Taylor (d 1993), and Muriel, *née* Horncastle (d 1985); *b* 23 February 1935; *Educ* KCS Wimbledon, Emmanuel Coll Cambridge (MA, LLM); *m* 1962, Helen, da of late Everard Tinling; 2 da (Karen b 1963, Camilla b 1970), 1 s (Sean b 1965); *Career* Nat Serv 2 Lt RASC 1953–55; admitted slr 1961; legal dept Distillers Co Ltd 1962–65; ptnr: Piesse & Sons 1966–73, Durrant Piesse 1973–88; sr ptnr Lovell White Durrant 1991–96 (ptnr 1988–96); memb Law Soc; dir: Hampton Gold Mining Areas plc 1979–86, Ludorum Management Ltd 1996–2001, Link Plus Corporation 1999–2003; memb Panel of Adjudicators of the Investment Ombudsman 1996–2000; memb Governing Body KCS Wimbledon 1970–2004 (chm 1973–90 and 2000–04); tstee Sch Fees Charitable Tst 1999–, vice-pres Surrey RFU 2007; Liveryman City of London Solicitors' Co; hon fell KCS Wimbledon 2004; *Recreations* conversation with my children, reading, sailing, gardening; *Clubs* Travellers, KCS Old Boys RFC (pres 1996–2001), Justinians; *Style—* Cavan Taylor, Esq; ✉ Covenham House, 10 Broad Highway, Cobham, Surrey KT11 2RP (tel 01932 864258, fax 01932 865705, e-mail cavan.taylor@btopenworld.com)

TAYLOR, Charles Spencer; s of Leonard Taylor (d 1991), and Phyllis Rose, *née* Emerson (d 1982); *b* 18 January 1952; *Educ* William Fletcher Sch Bognor Regis, Univ of Hull (LLB); *m* 7 Sept 1973, Elizabeth Mary (Liz), da of Ernest Richard Stephens; 2 s (Leo John Julius b 5 June 1987, Jack Michael Marius b 10 Feb 1990); *Career* called to the Bar Middle Temple 1974, in practice SE Circuit; Parl candidate (Lab) Arundel and S Downs 2001; memb Hon Soc of the Middle Temple 1969; *Recreations* gardening; *Style—* Charles Taylor, Esq; ✉ 12 North Pallant, Chichester, West Sussex PO19 1TQ (tel 01243 784538, fax 01243 780861)

TAYLOR, Prof Christopher Malcolm; *b* 15 January 1943; *Educ* KCL (William Siemens prize, Engrg Centenary prize, Jelf medal, BSc Eng), Univ of Leeds (MSc, PhD, DEng); *Career* res engr Lubrication Labs English Electric Co Ltd Whetstone 1967–68; Univ of Leeds: sr engr Industrial Unit of Tribology 1968–71, lectr in mechanical engrg 1971–80, sr lectr in mechanical engrg 1980–86, reader in tribology Dept of Mechanical Engrg 1986–90, dir Inst of Tribology 1987–2001, prof of tribology Dept of Mechanical Engrg 1990–2001, head Dept of Mechanical Engrg 1992–96, dean Faculty of Engrg 1996–97, pro-vice-chllr 1997–2001; vice-chllr Univ of Bradford 2001–07; conf organizer and jt ed Proceedings series of Leeds-Lyon Symposia on Tribology 1974–2000, ed Proceedings Inst of Mechanical Engrs 1993–2002; referee EPSRC and NSF res grants and reports 1986–2001; sr res assoc Nat Res Cncl of America at NASA Res Center Cleveland OH 1976–77; author of numerous articles in scientific jls and pubns; Tribology Silver Medal 1992, IMechE Tribology Gp Donald Julius Groen Prize 1993; CEng, FIMechE (vice-pres 1997–2003, pres 2003–04), CEng, FREng 1995, FCGI 1999; *Style—* Prof Christopher Taylor, FREng

TAYLOR, Dr Christopher Michael; s of Harry Taylor (d 1983), and Margaret Elizabeth, *née* Leigh; *b* 27 July 1952; *Educ* Hutton GS, Christ's Coll Cambridge (MA), King's Coll Hosp Med Sch Univ of London (MB BChir); *m* 4 Nov 1978, Soopamah, da of Arnasalon Munisami (d 1991), of Mauritius; 1 da (Rachel Kevina b 1980), 2 s (Michael Khrishnen b 1983, Andrew James Silven b 1987); *Career* conslt psychiatrist Leeds Mental Health Teaching NHS Tst 1986– (area mangr Gen Psychiatry 1991–95); FRCPsych; *Style—* Dr Christopher Taylor; ✉ Newsam Centre, Seacroft Hospital, York Road, Leeds LS14 6WB (tel 01133 056434)

TAYLOR, Christopher Skidmore; s of S E W Taylor (d 1963), and D Skidmore-Jones (d 1996); *b* 28 May 1941; *Educ* Clifton, Clare Coll Cambridge (exhibitioner, MA), Grad Sch of Business Stanford Univ (Harkness fell, MBA); *m* 1971, Alexandra Nancy, da of Maj Roger Alexander Howard; 2 da (Emily Clare b 1973, Alexia Lucy b 1975), 1 s (Charles Argentine Weston b 1981); *Career* sr fell then lectr Coll of Aeronautics Cranfield (now Cranfield Univ) 1965–67, visiting lectr Grad Sch of Business Harvard Univ 1967–68, corp financier then head of venture capital Hill Samuel & Co Ltd 1968–76, gp treas then asst fin dir Tarmac plc 1976–86; fin dir: Babcock International plc 1986–87, William Collins plc 1988–89, Smiths Industries plc 1989–95; non-exec dir: JBA Holdings plc 1994–99, Hays plc 1995–2004, DBS Mgmnt plc 1999–2001; chm Ctee Country Houses Assoc; FCT 1980; *Recreations* golf, sailing, skiing, opera; *Clubs* Royal Western; *Style—* Christopher Taylor, Esq; ✉ 67 Abbotsbury Road, London W14 8EL (tel 020 7603 6430, e-mail ctyorton@btinternet.com)

TAYLOR, Sir Cyril Julian Hebden; GBE (2004), kt (1989); s of Rev Cyril Eustace Taylor (d 1935), and Marjory Victoria, *née* Hebden (d 1994); *b* 14 May 1935; *Educ* St Marylebone GS London, Roundhay Sch Leeds, Trinity Hall Cambridge (MA), Harvard Business Sch (MBA); *m* 5 June 1965, June Judith (Judy), da of Earl Denman (d 1970); 1 da (Kirsten Livia Hebden b 1970); *Career* Nat Serv 1954–56 (cmmn with E Surrey Regt seconded to 3 Bn King's African Rifles in Kenya during Mau Mau emergency); brand mangr Procter & Gamble Cincinnati OH 1961–64; fndr chm AIFS Inc 1964– (cos incl American Inst for Foreign Study, Camp America, Au Pair in America, American Cncl for Int Studies, AIFS (Aust), AIFS (South Africa) and GIJK); chllr Richmond The American Int Univ London; chair Specialist Schools and Academies Tst 1987–, advsr to sec of state for educn and skills 1987–; Parly candidate (Cons): Huddersfield E Feb 1974, Keighley Oct 1974; Gtr London Cncl for Ruislip Northwood: memb 1977–86, chm Profession and Gen Servs Ctee 1978–81, oppn spokesman for tport, policy and resources 1981–86, dep ldr of the oppn 1983–86; memb Bd of Dirs Centre for Policy Studies 1984–98; pres: Ruislip Northwood Cons Assoc 1986–97, Harvard Business Sch Club of London 1990–93; vice-pres Alumni Cncl Harvard Business Sch 1994–96; chm: Br Friends of Harvard Business Sch, Lexham Gdns Residents' Assoc; High Sheriff Gtr London 1996–97; Hon PhD: New England 1991, Richmond Coll 1997, Open Univ 2001, Brunel Univ 2005; FRSA; *Books and Pamphlets* The Guide to Study Abroad (with Prof John Garraty and Lily von Klemperer), Peace has its Price (1972), No More Tick (1974), The Elected Member's Guide to Reducing Public Expenditure (1980), A Realistic Plan for London Transport (1982), Reforming London's Government (1984), Qualgoes Just Grow (1985), London Preserv'd (1985), Bringing Accountability Back to Local Government (1985), Employment Examined: The Right Approach to More Jobs (1986), Raising Educational Standards (1990), The Future of Britain's Universities (jtly, 1996), Value Added and Educational Outcomes of Specialist Schools (jtly, 1999, 2000, 2001, 2002, 2003, 2004, 2005 and 2006), Excellence in Education: The Making of Great Schools (with Conor Ryan, 2005), Who Will Champion our Vulnerable Children? (2006), Education, Education, Education: 10 Years On (with Tony Blair and Liz Reid, 2007); *Recreations* keen swimmer and gardener; *Clubs* Chelsea Arts, Hurlingham, Carlton, Harvard (New York), Racquet and Tennis (New York); *Style—* Sir Cyril Taylor, GBE; ✉ 1 Lexham Walk, London W8 5JD (tel 020 7370 2081); American Institute for Foreign Study, 37 Queen's Gate, London SW7 5HR (tel 020 7581 7391, fax 020 7581 7388, e-mail ctaylor@aifs.co.uk)

TAYLOR, Dari Jean; MP; da of Daniel Jones (d 1986), and Phylis May Jones (d 1984); *Educ* Burnley Municipal Coll, Univ of Nottingham (BA), Univ of Durham (MA); *m* 1970, David Ernest Taylor; 1 da (Philippa b 11 Nov 1980); *Career* lectr: Basford Coll of FE then Westbridgeford Coll of FE 1970–80, N Tyneside Coll 1986–90; GMB regnl educn offr 1990–97; MP (Lab) Stockton S 1997–; PPS to: Lewis Moonie, MP and Lord Bach 2001–03, Hazel Blears, MP 2003–; memb Intelligence and Security Ctee 2005–; cncllr Sunderland Local Authy 1986–97; chm: Trade Union and Info Gp, Multi Agency on Domestic Violence; *Recreations* opera, walking, classical music, swimming, travel; *Style—* Mrs Dari Taylor, MP; ✉ 109 Lanehouse Road, Thornaby on Tees, Stockton TS17 8AB (tel 01642 604546); House of Commons, London SW1A 0AA (tel 020 7219 4608)

TAYLOR, David; MP; *m* 1969, Pamela; 4 da (Rachel, Sarah, Jessica, Catherine), 1 s (David d 1977); *Career* MP (Lab/Co-op) Leicestershire NW 1997–; memb: Magistrates Assoc, CIPFA; *Style—* David Taylor, Esq, MP; ✉ House of Commons, London SW1A 0AA (tel 020 7219 4567, fax 020 7219 6808, e-mail taylordl@parliament.uk)

TAYLOR, David John; s of late John Robert George Taylor, of Norwich, and Elizabeth Anne Castell, *née* Spalding; *b* 22 August 1960; *Educ* King Edward VI Sch Norwich, St John's Coll Oxford (BA); *m* 22 June 1990, Rachel Elizabeth, da of late Richard Paul Hore; 3 s (Felix John Richard b 29 Oct 1992, Benjamin Anthony Castell b 17 Jan 1996, Leo David Alexander b 13 April 2000); *Career* writer; contrib various papers incl: The Independent, TLS, The Spectator, Private Eye, The Guardian, Sunday Times, The Tablet; FRSL 1997; *Books* Great Eastern Land (novel, 1986), A Vain Conceit: British Fiction in the 1980s (1989), Other People: Portraits From the Nineties (with Marcus Berkmann, 1990), Real Life (novel, 1992), After The War: The Novel and England Since 1945 (1993), W M Thackeray: A Shabby Genteel Story and other writings (ed, 1993), W M Thackeray: The Newcomes (ed, 1994), English Settlement (novel, 1996), George Gissing: New Grub Street (ed, 1997), After Bathing at Baxter's (stories, 1997), Trespass (novel, 1998), Thackeray (biography, 1999), The Comedy Man (novel, 2001), Orwell: The Life (biography, 2003), Kept (novel, 2006), On the Corinthian Spirit: The Decline of Amateurism in Sport (2006), Bright Young People: The rise and fall of a generation 1918–1940 (2007); *Recreations* reading, following Norwich City FC; *Style—* D J Taylor, Esq, FRSL; ✉ c/o Rogers, Coleridge & White Ltd, 20 Powis Mews, London W11 1JN (tel 020 7221 3717, fax 020 7229 9084)

TAYLOR, David Mills; s of Donald Charles Taylor (d 1940), and Elsa Marjorie Taylor (d 1967); *b* 22 December 1935; *Educ* Royal Commercial Travellers' Schs; *m* 1960, Gillian Irene, da of George Edward Washford; 4 da; *Career* gp fin dir: Brooke Bond Oxo Ltd 1968–71, The Guthrie Corporation Ltd 1971–79, Trafalgar House plc 1979–87; fin dir The Fitzroy Robinson Partnership 1987–90, dep dir and dir of fin and servs WWF UK (World Wide Fund For Nature) 1991–96, independent charity conslt 1996–2000, charity cmmr 2000–05; hon treas Nat Cncl for Vol Orgns 1997–2000; chm Royal Pinner Sch Fndn; FCA; *Recreations* golf, travel, gardening; *Style—* David M Taylor, Esq; ✉ Appin Cottage, 2 Beechwood Drive, Cobham, Surrey KT11 2DX (tel and fax 01372 844242)

TAYLOR, David Samuel Irving; s of Samuel Donald Taylor (d 1970), of Pulborough, W Sussex, and Winifred Alice May, *née* Marker (d 2000); *b* 6 June 1942; *Educ* Dauntsey's Sch West Lavington, Univ of Liverpool (MB ChB); *m* 5 July 1969, Anna, da of Air Cdre John Rhys-Jones (d 1972), of Pulborough, W Sussex; 2 s (Matthew Samuel b 1970, Nicholas James b 1972); *Career* res surgn Moorfields Eye Hosp 1971–74, fell in neurophthalmology Univ of Calif San Francisco 1976–77, conslt ophthalmologist Nat Hosp for Nervous Diseases London 1976–89, conslt paediatric ophthalmologist Hosp for Sick Children Gt Ormond St London 1976–, prof Inst Child Health London 2003–; memb Cncl Royal London Soc for the Blind, fndr and organiser Help a Child to See; memb: BMA 1970, RSM 1974, American Acad of Ophthalmology 1976; DSc (Med) UCL 2001; FRCS 1973, FRCP 1984, FCOphth 1988, FRCPCH 1997; *Books* Pediatric Ophthalmology (1990, 3 edn 2005), Practical Paediatric Ophthalmology (jtly, 1996); *Recreations* sailing, tennis, skiing, forestry; *Style—* Prof David Taylor; ✉ 23 Church Road, Barnes, London SW13 9HE (tel 020 8878 0305, e-mail dsit@btinternet.com

TAYLOR, Prof David William; s of Leslie David Taylor (d 1973), of Erith, Kent, and Doris Evelyn, *née* Jarvis; *b* 23 February 1949; *Educ* Picardy Secdy Modern Sch for Boys Erith, Bromley Tech Coll, Univ of Southampton (BSc), Univ of Cambridge (PhD); *m* Susan Miriam, da of Donald Robert Baggett; *Career* lab technician Wellcome Labs for Tropical Med The Wellcome Fndn Beckenham 1967–70, undergraduate Univ of Southampton 1970–73, postgraduate Univ of Cambridge 1973–77, Nat Acad of Sci (USA) postdoctoral fell Nat Naval Med Center Bethesda Maryland 1977–79; Dept of Pathology Univ of Cambridge: research assoc 1979–82, sr research assoc 1982–86, lectr in parasitology 1986–94; Univ of Edinburgh: prof of tropical animal health 1994–, dir Centre for Tropical Veterinary Med 1994–2001, convenor of African studies 1996–2001; dep DG Int Livestock Research Inst Kenya 2000–02; memb: Br Soc for Immunology, Soc of Gen Microbiology, Royal Zoological Soc of Edinburgh; *Recreations* bird watching, painting, cooking, gardening, living in France, DIY; *Style—* Prof David W Taylor; ✉ Centre for Tropical Veterinary Medicine, University of Edinburgh, Easterbush Veterinary Centre, Roslin, Midlothian EH25 9RG (tel 0131 650 6289, e-mail david.w.taylor@ed.ac.uk)

TAYLOR, David William; s of Brig Harry William Taylor, of Croydon, Surrey, and Eva Wade, *née* Day; *b* 10 July 1945; *Educ* Bancroft's Sch (Draper's Co Sch Leaving Award), Worcester Coll Oxford (Open Exhibitioner in Classics, MA), Inst of Educn Univ of London (PGCE distinction, Story-Miller Prize); *m* 1972, Pamela Linda, da of Edward John Taylor, of Coventry; 1 s (Alexander David Nicholas b 11 April 1979), 1 da (Penelope Caroline Louise b 13 May 1983); *Career* Watford Boys' GS: asst classics teacher 1968–73, head of classics 1973–78; chief examiner A Level classics Univ of London 1975–78; HMI Schools: appointed 1978, district inspector Barnet and Newcastle 1978–86, staff inspector secondary and classics 1986–92; OFSTED: joined sr mgmnt 1992, programme mangr 1992–93, head of strategic planning and resources 1993–96, head of teacher educn and training 1996–99, dir of inspection 1999–2004; educnl conslt 2004–, Office of the Schs Adjudicator 2005–; School Teacher Fellowship Merton Coll Oxford 1978; seconded to Touche Ross Mgmnt Consits 1991; memb: Jt Assoc of Classical Teachers (JACT) 1968– (exec sec 1976–78, conslt sec 2005–), London Assoc of Classical Teachers (LACT) 1968– (ed 1970–73, hon treas 1973–76), Strategic Planning Soc 1997–; memb: Nat Tst, Nat Decorative and Fine Arts Soc (NADFAS), IOD; Freeman Guild of Educators 2003– (Lower Warden 2006–07); *Publications* Cicero and Rome (1973), Work in Ancient Greece and Rome (1975), Acting and the Stage (1978), Roman Society (1980), The Greek and Roman Stage (1999); numerous articles in books and professional jls; *Recreations* classical

T

music (especially choral), chess, literature (especially classical), cricket, rookie golf, theatre, travel; *Clubs* Athenaeum, Nizels Golf; *Style*— David Taylor, Esq

TAYLOR, Denise Marilyn; *Educ* Belvedere Sch Liverpool, Liverpool Sch of Dental Surgery Univ of Liverpool (BDS), DipOrth RCS, Cert of Specialist Training in Orthodontics for EC purposes, Cert of Accreditation of Br Soc of Med and Dental Hypnosis; *Career* house offr Liverpool Dental Hosp and Liverpool Royal Infirmary; sr house offr: in oral and maxillofacial surgery Walton Hosp and Liverpool Dental Hosp, in children's dentistry and orthodontics St George's Hosp and Royal Dental Hosp; registrar in orthodontics Southampton Gen Hosp, clinical orthodontist Middx Hosp London and Whipps Cross Hosp Leytonstone, currently specialist in orthodontics Wexham Park Hosp Slough; memb Section of Hypnosis and Psychosomatic Medicine RSM; memb: Br Assoc of Orthodontists, BDA, RSM, Br Soc of Med and Dental Hypnosis (pres), World Fedn of Orthodondists (WFO); *Recreations* ice skating, skiing, tennis, riding, photography, art; *Style*— Ms Denise Taylor; ✉ Wexham Park Hospital, Slough, Berkshire SL2 4HL (tel 01753 633000)

TAYLOR, Donald Leslie; s of Frank St Armand Taylor, of Rustington, W Sussex, and Elizabeth Richmond, *née* Turnbull; *b* 20 September 1948; *Educ* Tollington GS London, RAC Cirencester (DipAgSci, NDA, MRAC); *Career* journalist; trainee Mgmnt Devpt Prog Barclays Bank 1970–73, head office advsr Beechams 1973–74, markets and business corr British Farmer and Stockbreeder 1974–80, dep business ed Farmers Weekly 1980–82, business ed Farming News 1982–91 (also asst ed 1984–91); ed: Farming News 1991–99, Whats New in Farming 1992–96, net-friend.com 1999–2000, www.farmersfriend.co.uk 1999–2000, Cage and Aviary Birds 2000–, Bird Keeper 2000–06, Nat Exhbn of Cage and Aviary Birds 2000–; managing ed: Farming News, Livestock Farming, Spotlight, Farming News Videos 1991–99; dir IPC Media Pension Trustee Ltd 2002–; pres Soc for the Protection of Aviculture 2002–05; sr tstee Morgan Grampian plc Pension Fund 1984–90; memb Guild of Agric Journalists 1974–2001 (memb Cncl 1988–2000); memb British Bird Cncl; *Recreations* stalking, wildfowling, rough shooting, game shooting, gardening, walking, bird keeping; *Clubs* Br Deer Soc, Br Assoc for Shooting and Conservation, East Barnet Shooting; *Style*— Donald Taylor, Esq; ✉ Culblean House, 14 Friary Way, London N12 9PH

TAYLOR, HE Duncan John Rushworth; CBE (2002); *b* 17 October 1958; *m* 1981, Marie-Beatrice (Bebe) Terpougoff; 2 s, 3 step da; *Career* diplomat; entered HM Dip Serv 1982, asst desk offr West African Dept FCO 1982–83, third later second sec Havana 1983–87; FCO: head Japan Section Far Eastern Dept 1987–89, Personnel Ops Dept 1989–90, head Personnel Mgmnt Review Implementation Task Force 1990–9; head Commercial Section Budapest 1992–96, on loan as dir Latin American affrs Rolls Royce 1996–97, head Consular Div FCO 1997–2000, dep consul-gen (press and public affrs) and dep head of mission NY 2000–05, high cmmr to Barbados and Eastern Caribbean States 2005–; *Style*— HE Mr Duncan Taylor, CBE; ✉ c/o Foreign & Commonwealth Office (Bridgetown), King Charles Street, London SW1A 2AH

TAYLOR, Sir Edward Macmillan (Teddy); kt (1991); s of Edward Taylor (d 1962), and Minnie Hamilton Taylor (d 2004); *Educ* Glasgow HS, Univ of Glasgow (MA); *m* 1970, Sheila, da of late Alex Duncan, of Glasgow; 2 s, 1 da; *Career* journalist with Glasgow Herald 1958–59, industrial rels offr with Clyde Shipbuilders' Assoc 1959–64; MP (Cons): Glasgow Cathcart 1964–79, Southend E (by-election) 1980–97, Rochford and Southend E 1997–2005; Parly under sec Scottish Office 1970–71 and 1974 (resigned over decision to join EU); opposition spokesman on: trade 1977, Scottish affrs 1977–79; vice-chm Cons Parly Trade Ctee 1981–83, sec Cons Parly Home Affrs Ctee 1983–95; lost Cons Pty whip over extra Euro funding (one of eight) 1995; delg to Cncl of Europe 2003; *Recreations* golf, chess; *Style*— Sir Teddy Taylor; ✉ 12 Lynton Road, Thorpe Bay, Southend, Essex (tel 01702 586282)

TAYLOR, Prof Eric Andrew; s of Dr Jack Andrew Taylor, of Bruton, Somerset, and Grace, *née* Longley; *b* 22 December 1944; *Educ* Clifton (scholar), Univ of Cambridge (MA, MB BChir, Dean meml prize), Harvard Univ, Middx Hosp Med Sch (med and psychiatry prizes); *m* Dr Anne Patricia Roberts (d 2000); 2 s (Thomas b 1976, Paul b 1980); *Career* hon conslt child and adolescent psychiatry Bethlem Royal Hosp, Maudsley Hosp and KCH 1978–; prof of developmental neuropsychiatry Univ of London 1993– (reader 1987–93), prof of child and adolescent psychiatry Inst of Psychiatry KCL 1998–; ed: Jl of Child Psychology and Psychiatry 1983–95, European Child and Adolescent Psychiatry 2003–; memb scientific staff MRC 1990–2000; memb Cncl Assoc of Child Psychology and Psychiatry 1983–95; sub-dean RCPsych 1996–2000; FRCP 1986, FRCPsych 1988, FMedSci 2000; *Books* The Overactive Child: Clinics in Developmental Medicine No 97 (1986), The Hyperactive Child: A Parent's Guide (1986), The Epidemiology of Childhood Hyperactivity (1991), Child and Adolescent Psychiatry: Modern Approaches (ed jtly, 1993 and 2002); *Style*— Prof Eric Taylor; ✉ Institute of Psychiatry, De Crespigny Park, London SE5 8AF (tel 020 7848 0488)

TAYLOR, Fraser Haxton; *b* 20 February 1960; *Educ* Glasgow Sch of Art (BA), RCA (MA); *Career* artist; fndr memb The Cloth (commercial design studio producing textiles and fashion collections) 1981–87, painting, exhibiting and lecturing in Britain, Europe, USA and the Far East 1987–2001; instr drawing and print on fabric: Glasgow Sch of Art 1984–2001, Edinburgh Coll of Art 1985–2001, Central St Martins Coll of Art and Design 1987–2001, RCA 1992–95, C&G Sch of Art 1997–2001; visiting artist Dept of Fiber and Material Studies Sch of the Art Inst of Chicago 2001–03 (adjunct assoc prof 2003–); resident artist: Aurobora Press San Francisco 2002 and 2003, Mahon and Band Press Melbourne 2005; visiting critic: Univ of Illinois at Chicago 2002, Northern Illinois Univ De Kalb 2003; external examiner Liverpool John Moores University 1991–95; curator: 100% Cotton (Gallery X Sch of the Art Inst of Chicago) 2003, Alternative Constructions (Booster and Seven Chicago) 2004, Again & Again (Open End Gallery Chicago) 2006; Lloyds Young Printmakers Prize 1984; *Solo Exhibitions* incl: The Obscure Objects of Desire (Thumb Gall London) 1985, True to Form (Thumb Gall London) 1987, Land Marks (Jill George Gall London) 1989, Fraser Taylor (Gallery Boards Paris) 1993, Pillar to Post (MacKintosh Museum Glasgow Sch of Art) 1998, Drawing Installation (Gall Aoyama Tokyo) 1998, Even as a Blur (Jill George Gall London) 1998, Out of Place (Tim Olsen Gall Sydney) 1999, Placed Apart (Jill George Gall London) 2000, All So Slippery (Edinburgh Coll of Art) 2000, West Coast Scotland (Gall Aoyama Tokyo) 2000, Paintings (Thomas McCormick Gallery Chicago) 2001, Dialogues Develop, British Art Now (Spica Museum Tokyo) 2001, Between Sundays (Tim Olsen Gallery Sydney) 2001, Amusements: Monotypes (Aurobora Press San Francisco) 2002, Occupation (Thomas McCormick Gallery Chicago) 2003, Edges (Spica Museum Tokyo) 2003, Contours (Aurobora Press San Francisco) 2003, The Assembled Line (Contemporary Art Workshop Chicago) 2004, From Chicago, Paintings and Prints (Jill George Gallery London) 2004, Graft (mn gallery Chicago) 2004, Cul de sac (Bucket Rider Gallery Chicago) 2005, Constraints (Tim Olsen Gallery Sydney) 2005, Reverse Transcriptase (Hyde Park Art Center In The Loop Gallery Chicago) 2006; *Group Exhibitions* incl Beneath the Cloth (RCA London) 1982, The Music Show (Thumb Gall London) 1983, Beneath the Cloth (Oliver and Pink London) 1984, The Cloth (Compass Gall Glasgow) 1985, Human Figure (Royal Acad of Art London) 1986, Two by Eight (Thumb Gall London) 1987, Friends and Contemporaries (John Jones Gall London) 1991, Big Works (Fine Art Consultancy London) 1993, One Hundred Years of Design (RCA London) 1996, Artists of Fame and Promise (Beaux Art Cork Street London) 1997, British Art Now 1998 (Axis Gall Tokyo) 1998, Four Scots (Australian Gall Melbourne) 1999, 2x2 (Tim Olsen Gallery Sydney) 2000, British Art Now (The Music Room London) 2001, Summer Suites (Aurobora Press San Francisco) 2002, Kitchen Sink (Thomas McCormick Gallery Chicago) 2002, Triplex (Sybaris Gallery Michigan) 2003, Evanston Biennial (Evanston Arts Center Illinois) 2004, Exquisite Corpse (Bowdoin College Museum of Art Brunswick) 2004, Black and White (Linda Ross Contemporary Art Projects Michigan) 2004, The Monoprint Show (Jill George Gallery London) 2005, Ukrainian Inst of Modern Art Chicago 2005, Flattened (Evanston Arts Center Illinois) 2006, flowers (de de ce Melbourne) 2006, Optica (Video Art Festival Gojon) 2006; works featured in art fairs incl: Glasgow Art Fair 1996, 1997, 1998 and 1999, Madrid Art Fair 1990, Int Contemporary Air Fair Los Angeles 1986, 1987, 1988 and 1989, Bath Contemporary Art Fair 1984, 1985, 1986, 1987, 1989 and 1990, San Francisco Art Fair 1999 and 2000, Chicago Art Fair 2000; work in public collection at V&A and Art Inst of Chicago; *Style*— Fraser Taylor, Esq; ✉ website www.frasertaylor.com

TAYLOR, Prof Fredric William; s of William Taylor (d 1996), of Swindon, Wilts, and Ena Lloyd, *née* Burns (d 1993); *b* 24 September 1944; *Educ* Duke's Sch, Univ of Liverpool (BSc), Univ of Oxford (DPhil); *m* 28 June 1970, Doris Jean, da of Iver Buer; *Career* sr scientist Jet Propulsion Laboratory Caltech 1970–79; Univ of Oxford: fell Jesus Coll 1979–, head Dept of Atmospheric, Oceanic and Planetary Physics 1979–2000, Halley prof of physics 2000–; medal for exceptional scientific achievement Nat Aeronautics and Space Admin 1981, Rank prize for opto-electronics 1989, special award Worshipful Co of Scientific Instrument Makers 1990; FRMS (vice-pres), FRAS, FRSA; *Books* Cambridge Atlas of the Planets (1982, 3 edn 2001), Remote Sensing of Atmospheres (1984), Titan, the Earthlike Moon (2000), non-LTE in the Atmosphere (2001), Elementary Climate Physics; *Recreations* walking, gardening, history, literature, theatre, sport, gastronomy, railways, poker; *Clubs* Meteorological, Astronomical; *Style*— Prof Fredric Taylor; ✉ Department of Atmospheric, Oceanic and Planetary Physics, Clarendon Laboratory, Parks Road, Oxford OX1 3PU

TAYLOR, Dr George Browne; s of late John Taylor, and Doreen, *née* Browne; *b* 11 May 1949; *Educ* St Aidan's Sch Sunderland, Univ of Newcastle upon Tyne Med Sch (MB BS, EdD); *m* Penelope Rose Anne, *née* Stanford; 2 da (Sarah b 2 Dec 1972, Ruth b 4 May 1979), 2 s (Matthew b 15 Dec 1975, James b 13 Nov 1981); *Career* princ in gen practice Guide Post Northumberland 1976–2001; assoc regnl advsr in gen practice Univ of Newcastle upon Tyne 1986–97, dep dir gen practice Univ of Newcastle upon Tyne 1997–2001; dir of postgrad GP educn and assoc dean Univ of Leeds 2001–; RCGP: memb Examination Bd 1982–89, memb Cncl 1992–94 and 1996–97, chm Quality Network 1995–97; visitor Jt Ctee on Postgrad Trg in Gen Practice 1990–; fndr Northumberland Young Practitioner Educnl Gp 1977; Nuffield visiting scholar Fiji Sch of Med 1970, RCGP visiting scholar The Netherlands 1984; FRCGP 1986 (MRCGP 1976); *Recreations* family, travel, France, wine; *Style*— Dr George Taylor; ✉ Department of Postgraduate Medical and Dental Education, University of Leeds, Willow Terrace Road, Leeds LS2 9JT (tel 0113 343 1501, fax 0113 343 1530, e-mail g.taylor@yorkshiredeanery.com)

TAYLOR, Gordon; s of Alec Taylor (d 1980), of Ashton under Lyne, Lancs, and Mary, *née* Walsh; *b* 28 December 1944; *Educ* Ashton under Lyne GS, Bolton Tech Coll, Univ of London (BSc Econ); *m* 27 July 1968, Catharine Margaret, da of Frederick Johnston, of Bury, Lancs; 2 s (Simon Mark b 1970, Jonathan Peter b 1973); *Career* professional footballer: Bolton Wanderers 1960–70, Birmingham City 1970–76, Blackburn Rovers 1976–78, Vancouver Whitecaps (N American Soccer League) 1977, Bury 1978–80; sec and chief exec PFA 1981– (chm 1978–80), pres Int Body FIF-PRO 1994–; Hon MA Loughborough Univ 1986, Hon DArt De Montfort Univ 1998; *Recreations* theatre, music, reading, watching sport; *Style*— Gordon Taylor, Esq; ✉ Professional Footballers Association, 20 Oxford Court, Bishopsgate, Manchester M2 3WQ (tel 0161 236 0575, fax 0161 228 7229)

TAYLOR, Dr Howard Peter John; s of Ronald Taylor (d 1988), and Winifred Enid, *née* Hedge (d 1996); *b* 17 April 1940; *Educ* The GS Frome, Univ of Manchester (BScTech), City Univ (PhD); *m* Eleanor Stewart, da of Stewart Maloch, of Riverside, California; 2 s (James b 8 Aug 1973, Robert b 24 June 1980); *Career* grad engr Sir Alexander Gibb & Partners 1961–64, dep head (formerly res engr) Design Res Dept Cement & Concrete Assoc 1964–78; chief engr Downmac Concrete Ltd 1978–, former dir of Tarmac Precast Concrete Ltd, now conslt and expert; FICE (memb 1968), FIStructE (memb 1971, pres 1993–94), FREng 1993; *Awards* for published work: American Soc of Civil Engrs, Permanent Way Inst, Inst of Structural Engrs; *Books* Precast Concrete Cladding (1992); *Recreations* tennis, walking, books; *Style*— Dr Howard Taylor, FREng; ✉ Highfield Farmhouse, Pilton, Rutland LE15 9PA (tel 01780 729240, fax 01780 722170, e-mail htaylor@hfpilton.fsnet.co.uk)

TAYLOR, Hugh Henderson; CB (2000); s of Leslie Henderson Taylor (d 1982), and Alison, *née* Brown; *b* 22 March 1950; *Educ* Brentwood Sch, Emmanuel Coll Cambridge (BA); *m* 13 May 1989, Diane Heather, da of Idwal George Bacon; 2 da (Alice Joy b 25 Sept 1991, Madeleine Louise b 6 May 1993); *Career* Home Office: joined 1972, private sec to Min of State 1976–77, Radio Regulatory Dept 1977–81, princ Criminal Policy Dept 1981–83, princ private sec to Home Sec 1983–85, asst sec 1984, head Parole and Lifer Div 1985–88; seconded to Cabinet Office 1988–91, head Personnel Div Prison Service 1992–93, under sec Home Office 1993–96, seconded as head Civil Service Employer Gp Cabinet Office (OPS) 1993–96 (also dir Top Mgmnt Prog 1994–96), dir of services Prison Service 1996–97; Dept of Health: dir of HR NHS Exec 1998–2001, DG (external and corporate affrs, corporate affrs, then departmental mgmnt) 2001–06, perm sec 2006–; *Recreations* reading, watching cricket, rugby and football, music and opera, visiting galleries; *Style*— Hugh Taylor, Esq, CB; ✉ Department of Health, Richmond House, 79 Whitehall, London SW1A 2NS

TAYLOR, Hugh Matthew; s of Derek Taylor, of Hampstead, London, and Diane, *née* Milman; *b* 3 March 1965, London; *Educ* Hasmonean GS Hendon, Middx Business Sch (BA), CIM (Dip), Pennsylvania State Univ (MSc); *m* 2 Jan 1994, Katie, *née* Baum; 1 da (Ellie b 12 Jan 1997), 3 s (Josh b 17 Oct 1998, Sam b 22 Oct 2001, Joe b 11 Oct 2003); *Career* mktg mangr Norfolk Capital Hotels 1989–90, mktg dir Radisson Edwardian Hotels 1990–92, mktg dir Ramada Jarvis Hotels 1992–2001; Hilton Hotels UK: vice-pres mktg 2001–04, regnl vice-pres 2004–; chm: Hotel Mktg Assoc 1995–98, England Mktg Advsy Bd 2003–, Hilton in the Community Fndn; dir VisitBritain 2003–; 15 hotel mktg awards 1998–2004, Caterer and Hotel Keeper (Catey) Award 1996 and 2004; memb Hotel and Catering Int Mgmnt Assoc 1997, fell Tourism Soc 1998, FCIM 1998; *Publications* Hotel and Catering Advertising (1999); *Recreations* tennis, theatre; *Style*— Hugh Taylor, Esq; ✉ 5 Amberden Avenue, London N3 3BJ (tel 020 8343 4392, e-mail hugh.katie@btinternet.com), Hilton Hotels Corporation, Maple Court, Central Park, Reeds Crecent, Watford, Hertfordshire WD24 4QQ (tel 020 7856 8328, e-mail hugh.taylor@hilton.com)

TAYLOR, Ian Colin; MBE (1974), MP; s of late Horace Stanley Taylor, and late Beryl, *née* Harper; *b* 18 April 1945; *Educ* Whitley Abbey Sch Coventry, Keele Univ (BA), LSE (research scholar); *m* 17 June 1974, Hon Carole Alport, da of late Baron Alport (Life Peer); 2 s (Arthur b 1977, Ralph b 1980); *Career* MP (Cons): Esher 1987–97, Esher and Walton 1997–; memb Foreign Affrs Select Ctee 1987–90, memb Sci and Technol Select Ctee 1998–2001, Parly Office of Sci and Technol 1998–, PPS to Rt Hon William Waldegrave MP 1990–94, min for sci and technol DTI 1994–97; vice-chm Parly Information Technol Ctee 2000–, memb Bd Parly Office of Sci and Technol, co-chair Parly Space Ctee, vice-chair Parly IT Ctee 2000–, chair Cons Policy Taskforce on Sciences 2006–; memb Cons Nat Union Exec Ctee 1967–75 and 1990–95, nat chm Fedn of Cons Students

1968–69, chm Euro Union of Christian Democratic and Cons Students 1969–70, hon sec Br Cons Assoc in France 1976–78; chm: Cons Gp for Europe 1985–88, Cwlth Youth Exchange Cncl 1980–84 (vice-pres 1984–), Cons Back Bench Euro Affrs Ctee 1988–89, Cons Foreign and Cwlth Cncl 1990–95, Tory Europe Network 2002–; chm European Movement 2001–, memb Br in Europe Cncl, patron UK Centre for Euro Educn 1991–94; dir: Mathercourt Securities Ltd 1980–91, Radioscape plc 1999– (chm), Petards plc 2000–, Parkmead Gp plc 2001–, Speed-trap Ltd; exec dir: Next Fifteen Gp plc, AXA Framlington Ltd 2005–; dir European Info Soc Gp (EURIM); Freeman Worshipful Co of Information Technologists; ASIP 1972; *Publications* pamphlets: Under Some Delusion (1975), Fair Shares for all the Workers (1988), Releasing the Community Spirit (1990), A Community of Employee Shareholders (1992), The Positive Europe (1993), Escaping the Protectionist Trap (1995), Networking (1996), The Conservative Tradition in Europe (1998), Restoring the Balance (2000), Full Steam Ahead (2001), Europe Our Case (2002), Shaping the New Europe - The British Opportunity (2002), Twin Towers: Europe and America (2003), Corporate Social Responsibility - Should Business Be Socially Aware? (2003); *Recreations* cigars, opera, shooting; *Clubs* Buck's, IOD, Commonwealth; *Style—* Ian Taylor, Esq, MBE, MP; ✉ House of Commons, London SW1A 0AA (tel 020 7219 5221, fax 020 7219 5492, e-mail taylori@parliament.uk, website www.iantaylormp.com)

TAYLOR, Ian Stuart; s of Alan Taylor, of Horsforth, Leeds, and Phyllis, *née* Hutchinson; *b* 21 June 1951; *Educ* Bradford GS, Univ Coll Durham (BA); *m* 1 May 1976, Ann Lynda, da of Harold Sydney Foley; 2 da (Emma Elizabeth b 22 Sept 1980, Katherine Victoria b 11 May 1983); *Career* library asst Shrewsbury BC 1973–74, museum asst Shrewsbuy & Atcham BC 1974–76, dep curator Castle Museum York 1976–81, dir Big Pit Mining Museum Blaenavon Gwent 1981–86, dir NW Museums Serv 1986–2003; convenor Gp of Area Museum Cncl Dirs 1990–98, memb Accreditation Ctee Museums, Libraries and Archives Cncl 2005–; served bds of mgmnt: NW Tourist Bd, NW Arts Bd; memb NW Cultural Consortium 2000–03; memb Ct of Univ of Manchester 1998–2003; tstee Browning Home Family Assessment Centre 2004–, memb Tameside Adoption Panel 2007–; FMA; *Books* Forward Planning - A Handbook to Business (contrib, 1992); *Recreations* museums, music, bookshops, star gazing; *Style—* Ian Taylor, Esq; ✉ 5 Brett Close, Clitheroe, Lancashire BB7 1LN (tel 01200 423001, e-mail iantaylor2000@aol.com)

TAYLOR, Prof Irving; s of Samuel Taylor (d 1992), and Fay, *née* Valcovitch; *b* 7 January 1945; *Educ* Roundhay Sch Leeds, Univ of Sheffield Med Sch (MB ChB, MD, ChM); *m* 31 Aug 1969, Berenice Penelope, da of Dr Henry Brunner, of Slough; 3 da (Justine Samantha b 20 Oct 1971, Tamara Zoe b 5 June 1973, Gabrielle Rivka b 31 Aug 1983); *Career* sr registrar surgery Sheffield 1973–77 (registrar surgery 1971–73, res registrar 1973), sr lectr in surgery Liverpool 1977–81, prof of surgery and head Dept of Surgery Univ of Southampton 1981–93, head Dept of Surgery and chm Bd of Surgery UCL 1993–, vice-dean and dir of clinical studies 2003–; case examiner GMC 2003; Hunterian prof RCS 1981, Jacksonian prof RCS 1996, Stanford Cade lectr RCS 2000; ed sec Assoc of Surgns 1987, ed-in-chief Euro Jl of Surgical Oncology, ed Annals RCS 2004–; pres: Surgical Research Soc 2005– (sec 1985–87), Br Assoc Surgical Oncology, European Soc of Surgical Oncology (ESSO); chm MRC Colorectal Working Party, memb Cncl RCS 2004– sec Assoc of Profs of Surgery 1988; FRCS 1972, memb RSM 1982, memb ILT 2002, FMedSci; *Books* Complications of Surgery of Lower Gastrointestinal Tract (1985), Progress in Surgery 1 (1985), Progress in Surgery 2 (1987), Progress in Surgery 3 (1989), Benign Breast Disease (1989), Recent Advances in Surgery 14–22 (1990, 1992, 1993, 1994, 1995, 1996, 1997, 1998, 1999, 2000, 2001, 2002, 2003, 2004, 2005, 2006 and 2007), Fast Facts in Colorectal Cancer (2000, 2 edn 2002); *Recreations* swimming, bridge, tennis; *Clubs* RSM; *Style—* Prof Irving Taylor; ✉ Department of Surgery, University College London, 74 Huntley Street, London WC1E 6AU (tel 020 7679 6490, e-mail irving.taylor@ucl.ac.uk)

TAYLOR, Sheriff Principal James Alastair; s of Alastair Robert Taylor (d 1983), of Nairn, and Margaret Robertson Fraser; *b* 21 February 1951; *Educ* Nairn Acad, Univ of Aberdeen (BSc, LLB); *m* 1 Nov 1980, Lesley Doig MacLeod; 2 s (Andrew James b May 1983, Robbie MacLeod b June 1985); *Career* apprentice to Brander & Cruickshank and Lefevre & Co Aberdeen 1975–77, asst then ptnr A C Morrison & Richards Aberdeen 1978–86; McGrigor Donald: joined 1987, ptnr 1988–98, head Litigation Dept 1992–98; slr advocate (practising in Court of Session) 1993–98; appointed all Scotland floating sheriff based in the Sheriffdom of Lothian & Borders 1998–99, sheriff princ of Glasgow and Strathkelvin 2005– (sheriff 1999–2005); chm Disciplinary Ctee Inst of Chartered Accountants in Scotland 2001–; *Recreations* golf, jazz, food and wine; *Clubs* Glasgow Golf, Royal Aberdeen Golf, Nairn Golf; *Style—* Sheriff James Taylor; ✉ Sheriff Principal's Chambers, Sheriff Court House, 1 Carlton Place, Glasgow G5 9DA (tel 0141 429 8888, e-mail sheriffp.jtaylor@scotcourts.gov.uk)

TAYLOR, John; MBE (1981); s of Percival Henry Taylor (d 1969), and Florence, *née* Jeffries (d 1981); *b* 4 March 1928; *Educ* Peter Symonds Sch Winchester; *m* 1, 1949, Joyce, da of Harold Hodson (d 1970); 3 s (Patrick b 1950, Ian b 1953, Andrew b 1964), 2 da (Janet b 1956, Jillian b 1960); m 2, 1980, Christiane, da of Capt Edouard Jean Talou (d 1947); *Career* cmmnd RE 1947; chartered architect and designer; fndr: Taylor & Crowther (princ) 1952, John Taylor Architects (sole princ) 1963, Marshman Warren Taylor (jt princ) 1968, MWT Architects (chm) 1972, MWT Planning 1975, MWT Landscapes 1982, MWT Design 1986; fndr and chm The Co of Designers plc 1986–90, fndr and sole princ John Taylor Architects 1991–95, sr ptnr Kensington Taylor Architects 1995–; 7 times Gold medallist DOE Housing Award, 5 times Civic Tst Award; FRIBA, FCSD; *Recreations* sailing, travel; *Style—* John Taylor, Esq, MBE; ✉ Orchard House, Ide Lane, Exeter EX2 8UT (tel 01392 499440); Kensington Taylor Architects (tel 01392 360338)

TAYLOR, John Charles; QC (1984); s of Sidney Herbert Taylor (d 1977), of St Ives, Cambs, and Gertrude Florence, *née* Law; *b* 22 April 1931; *Educ* Palmer's Sch Essex, Queens' Coll Cambridge (MA, LLB), Harvard Univ (LLM); *m* 1964, Jean Aimée, da of William Rankin Monteith (d 1976), late of Purston Manor, Brackley, Northants; 1 da (Victoria Mary Aimée (Mrs Stephen Wolfe-Brown) b 1967); *Career* called to the Bar Middle Temple 1958; memb Stevens Ctee on Minerals Planning Control 1972–74; chm EIP Panel for Leics and Rutland Structure Plan 1985; apptd inspr by Sec of State for the Environment for County Hall London Inquiries 1990 and 1991; owner of Advocate (overall winner Class I (IOK) Cowes Week Regatta) 1991; *Recreations* country pursuits; *Clubs* Athenaeum, Travellers, Royal Ocean Racing; *Style—* John Taylor, Esq, QC; ✉ Clifton Grange, Clifton, Shefford, Bedfordshire

TAYLOR, John Edward; s of Thomas Taylor (d 1962), and Margaret, *née* Renwick; *b* 14 November 1949, Chester-le-Street, Co Durham; *Educ* Chester-le-Street GS, Univ of Durham (BA); *Career* grad trainee Littlewoods Mail Order Stores Wolverhampton 1971–72, exec offr Dept of Employment 1972–75, dep to Ops Mangr ACAS 1975–77 (also sec trade union side), policy analyst Dept of Employment 1977–79, private sec to Min of State for Employment 1979–80, branch head strategy Branch Trg Div Manpower Servs Cmmn 1983–84 (personnel mangr 1980–83), regnl mangr Employment Serv Midlands 1984–86, head Overseas Lab Unit Dept of Employment 1986–88, actg chief exec, dep chief exec and dir of ops Rural Devpt Cmmn 1988–95; chief exec: Devpt Bd for Rural Wales 1995–98, TEC SE Wales 1998–2001, ACAS 2001–; visiting prof in employment rels Univ of Glamorgan 2002– (memb Business Sch Mgmnt Bd 1999–); chm Modis UK Ltd 1999–2001; memb: Industrial Rels Ctee Cabinet Office 2001–05, NHS Partnership Bd 2001–, Bd Learning and Skills Devpt Agency 2004–06, Bd Govt Skills Cncl 2004–, Bd Quality Improvement Agency 2006–, Steering Bd Employment Tbnl System 2006– (memb Task Force 2001–06, memb Nat User Gp 2002–); memb consortium of rural TEC 1990–95, dir Powys TEC 1996–98, dir TEC S E Wales 1998–2001, memb Cncl Welsh TECs 1998–2001, memb Equal Opportunities Gp TEC Nat Cncl 1999–2001, chm Welsh TEC Equal Opportunities Forum 1999–2001; memb: EU Experts Gp on Mobility of Lab 1986–88, UK Tourism Task Force 1991–92, Rural Action for England 1993–95 (sometime chm), Mid-Wales Partnership 1995–98, N Wales Economic Forum 1996–98, SW Wales Economic Forum 1997–98, SE Wales Economic Forum 1998–2001, Wales New Deal Task Force 1998–2001, Youth Enterprise Mgmnt Bd 1998–2001, Youth Task Gp Nat Assembly for Wales 1999–2001, Objective 3 Monitoring Ctee (Wales) 2000–01, Llanwern Task Force (Corus Steel Closure Prog) 2000–01; dir Wales European Centre Brussels 1999–2001; dir Mgmnt Bd Ystrad Mynach Coll 2000–01, govr Thames Valley Univ 2005–; CCMI 2003; *Style—* John Taylor, Esq; ✉ ACAS, Brandon House, 180 Borough High Street, London SE1 1LW

TAYLOR, Prof John Gerald; s of Dr William Taylor (d 1984), and Elsie, *née* Boyd (d 1986); *b* 18 August 1931; *Educ* Lancaster GS, Blackburn GS, Chelmsford GS, Mid Essex Tech Coll (BSc), Christ's Coll Cambridge (BSc, BA, MA, PhD); *m* 1 (m dis); m 2, Pamela Nancy; 2 s (Geoffrey, Robin), 3 da (Frances, Susan, Elizabeth); *Career* Cwlth fell Inst for Advanced Study Princeton 1956–58, res fell Christ's Coll Cambridge 1958–60 (asst lectr Faculty of Mathematics 1959–60); memb: Inst Hautes Études Scientifiques Paris 1960–61, Inst for Advanced Study Princeton 1961–63; sr res fell Churchill Coll Cambridge 1963–64, prof of physics Rutgers Univ 1964–66, lectr in Mathematics Inst and fell Hertford Coll Oxford 1966–67, lectr and reader QMC London 1967–69, prof of physics Univ of Southampton 1969–71; KCL: prof of mathematics 1971–96 (emeritus prof 1996–), dir Centre for Neural Networks 1990–96; guest scientist Inst of Med Res Centre Juelich 1996–98, memb Advsy Bd Brain Scis Inst Tokyo 1998–; chm: Mathematics and Physics Gp Inst of Physics 1981–86 (vice-chm 1988–91), Jt Euro Neural Networks Initiative Cncl 1990–91; Euro ed-in-chief Neural Networks 1990–; convenor Br Neural Network Soc 1988–92; vice-pres European Neural Network Soc 1991–93 and 1994–97 (pres 1993–94), pres Int Neural Network Soc 1995 (memb Governing Bd 1992–), dir NEURONET EC Network of Excellence 1994, co-ordinator EC GNOSYS Cognitive Robot Project 2004–07; fell Cambridge Philosophy Soc; FInstP, fell Soc Arts; *Books* Quantum Mechanics (1969), The Shape of Minds to Come (1971), The New Physics (1972), Black Holes: The End of the Universe? (1973), Superminds (1975), Special Relativity (1975), Science and the Supernatural (1980), The Horizons of Knowledge (1982), Finite Superstrings (1992), The Promise of Neural Networks (1993), When the Clock Struck Zero (1993), The Race for Consciousness (1999), The Mind: A User's Manual (2006); also author of over 500 sci papers and ed of 16 books, numerous radio and TV programmes on popular science; *Recreations* listening to music, theatre, reading; *Style—* Prof John Taylor; ✉ 33 Meredyth Road, Barnes, London SW13 0DS (tel 020 8876 3391); Department of Mathematics, King's College, Strand, London WC2R 2LS (tel 020 7848 2214, fax 020 7848 2017), e-mail john.g.taylor@kcl.ac.uk)

TAYLOR, John Hilton; s of Charles Ronald Taylor, of St Helens, Merseyside, and Brenda, *née* Hilton; *b* 7 May 1958; *Educ* Grange Park Secdy Sch St Helens, Cowley Boys Sch St Helens, Univ of Birmingham (BA, PhD); *m* 24 Sept 1988, Rhona Margaret, da of James Henry Minshull; 1 da (Katherine Sarah Minshull b 29 Aug 1991), 1 s (James Nicholas Minshull b 26 Oct 1994); *Career* Egyptologist; memb Egypt Exploration Soc expedition to Amarna 1981; lectr in Egyptology: Workers Educnl Assoc 1981 and 1985–86, Dept of Extramural Studies Univ of Birmingham 1985–87; curator Dept of Ancient Egypt and Sudan British Museum 1988–; specialist consIt to Gold of the Pharaohs exhbn City Art Centre Edinburgh 1987–88, exhbn organiser Howard Carter - Before Tutankhamun Br Museum 1992–93, exhbn organiser Mummy: The Inside Story Br Museum 2004–05; memb Univ of Cambridge Theban Mission to Luxor 1999–2000; memb Ctee Egypt Exploration Soc 1988–91, 1993–95, 1997–2000 and 2004–06 (hon librarian 1993–98), memb Ctee Assoc for the Study of Travel in Egypt and the Near East 2004–; reviews ed Jl of Egyptian Archaeology 1993–2005, ed Egyptian Archaeology 1994–96; memb Cncl Soc for Libyan Studies 1997–2005; hon fell Inst for Advanced Research in the Humanities Univ of Birmingham 1987–89; *Books* Egyptian Coffins (1989), Egypt and Nubia (1991), Howard Carter - Before Tutankhamun (with Nicholas Reeves, 1992), Unwrapping a Mummy (1995), Death and the Afterlife in Ancient Egypt (2001), The Theban Necropolis: Past, Present and Future (jt ed with Nigel Strudwick, 2003), Mummy: The Inside Story (2004), Mummies: Death and the Afterlife in Ancient Egypt. Treasures from the British Museum (with Nigel Strudwick, 2005); *Recreations* genealogy, English literature, music; *Style—* John Taylor, Esq; ✉ Department of Ancient Egypt and Sudan, The British Museum, Great Russell Street, London WC1B 3DG (tel 020 7323 8330, e-mail jtaylor@thebritishmuseum.ac.uk)

TAYLOR, John Leonard; s of Leonard William Taylor, and Kathleen, *née* Markey; *b* 21 June 1957; *Educ* St Peter's Sch Southbourne; *m* Moyra; 1 da (Verity b 5 Sept 1989), 1 s (Sean b 22 Jan 1992); *Career* media planner/buyer Allen Brady & Marsh Ltd 1975–78; FCB Advertising Ltd: media mangr 1978–86, media dir 1986–90, dep md 1990–92; md Optimedia UK 1992–96, dir of int ops Optimedia International Ltd 1999–2001 (dir Euro ops 1996–2001), chief operating offr Optimedia Worldwide 2001–, dir strategic resources and client service ZenithOptimedia Gp 2002–; *Recreations* triathlon, motorcycling, golf, skiing; *Style—* John Taylor, Esq

TAYLOR, John Mark; s of Wilfred Taylor and Eileen Taylor; *b* 19 August 1941; *Educ* Bromsgrove, Coll of Law; *Career* admitted slr 1966; memb: Solihull Cncl 1971–74, W Midlands CC 1973–86 (ldr 1977–79); Parly candidate (Cons) Dudley E Feb and Oct 1974; MEP (EDG) Midlands E 1979–84, dep chm Cons Gp Euro Parl 1981–82; MP (Cons) Solihull 1983–2005; PPS to Chllr of the Duchy of Lancaster 1987–88, asst Govt whip 1988–89, Lord Cmmr of the Treasy (Govt whip) 1989–90, Vice-Chamberlain of HM Household (sr Govt whip) 1990–92, Parly sec Lord Chllr's Dept 1992–95, Parly under sec of state DTI 1995–97; oppn whip 1997–99, oppn spokesman on NI 1999–2003; memb House of Commons Environment Select Ctee 1983–87; memb Modernisation Select Ctee 2001–02; memb: Parly Assembly of the Cncl of Europe and of the WEU 1997, Home Affrs Select Ctee 2003–05; govr Univ of Birmingham 1977–81; *Recreations* cricket, golf and reading; *Clubs* MCC; *Style—* John M Taylor, Esq; ✉ Apartment 8, Blossomfield Gardens, 34 Blossomfield Road, Solihull, West Midlands B91 1NZ (tel 0121 705 5467)

TAYLOR, Sir John Michael; kt (2004), OBE (1994); s of Eric John Taylor (d 1979), and Dorothy Irene, *née* Spring (d 2000); *b* 15 February 1943; *Educ* King Edward's Sch Birmingham, Emmanuel Coll Cambridge (MA, PhD); *m* 14 Aug 1965, Judith, *née* Moyle; 4 c; *Career* UK Govt 1969–84: supt Computer Applications Div RSRE Malvern 1979–81, head of Command Systems Div Admiralty Surface Weapons Estab 1981–82, head of Command Control and Communications Dept Admiralty Res Estab 1982–84; dir: Info Systems Laboratory Hewlett-Packard Laboratories 1984–86, Bristol Res Centre 1986–90, Hewlett-Packard Laboratories Europe 1990–98 (memb Bd of Dirs Hewlett Packard Ltd 1992–98); DG Research Cncls DTI 1999–2003, chm Roke Manor Research 2004–; non-exec dir Rolls Royce 2005–07; visiting prof Univ of Oxford 2003–; pres IEE (UK) 1998–99, memb Cncl Royal Acad of Engrg 2004–; hon fell Emmanuel Coll Cambridge 2000–; FREng 1986, FRS 1998, FIEE, FBCS, FInstP; *Recreations* family, music, theatre, photography, sailing; *Style—* Sir John M Taylor, OBE, FRS, FREng

TAYLOR, John Russell; s of Arthur Russell Taylor (d 1966), of Dover, Kent, and Kathleen Mary, *née* Picker (d 1991); *b* 19 June 1935; *Educ* Dover GS, Jesus Coll Cambridge (MA), Courtauld Inst of Art London; *Partner* Ying Yeung Li (civil partner, 2006); *Career* The Times: sub ed Educnl Supplement 1959–60, ed asst Literary Supplement 1960–62, film critic 1962–73, American cultural corr 1972–78, art critic 1978–; prof Cinema Div Univ of Southern Calif 1972–78, ed Films and Filming 1983–90; memb: Critics' Circle 1962, Private Libraries Assoc 1967 (pres 1986–88), Assoc Art Historians 1985; AICA 1978; *Books* incl: Anger and After (1962), Cinema Eye Cinema Ear (1964), The Art Nouveau Book in Britain (1966), The Rise and Fall of the Well-Made Play (1967), The Art Dealers (1969), The Hollywood Musical (1971), The Second Wave (1971), Graham Greene on Film (ed 1972), Directors and Directions (1975), Hitch (1978), Impressionism (1981), Strangers in Paradise (1983), Alec Guinness (1984), Edward Wolfe (1986), Orson Welles (1986), Bernard Meninsky (1990), Impressionist Dreams (1990), Ricardo Cinalli (1992), Muriel Pemberton (1993), Igor Mitoraj (1994), Claude Monet (1995), Michael Parkes (1996), Bill Jacklin (1997), The Sun is God (1999), Peter Coker (2002), Philip Sutton (2005), Adrian Henry (2005), Roboz (2006), Donald McGill (2006); *Recreations* buying books, talking to strange dogs; *Style*— John Russell Taylor, Esq; ✉ The Times, 1 Pennington Street, London E1 9XN (tel 020 7782 5000, fax 020 7782 5748)

TAYLOR, Jonathan Francis; CBE (2005); s of Sir Reginald William Taylor (d 1971), of Great Haseley, Oxon, and Lady (Sarah) Ruth, *née* Tyson (d 1993); *b* 12 August 1935; *Educ* Winchester, CCC Oxford (MA); *m* 8 April 1965, (Anthea) Gail, da of Robert Vergette Proctor (d 1985), of Sheffield, S Yorks; 3 s (Luke b 1968, Matthew b 1970, James b 1972); *Career* Nat Serv 2 Lt KAR 1954–56; Booker plc: joined 1959, chm Agric Div 1976–80, dir 1980, chief exec 1984–93, chm 1993–98, chm Booker Prize Mgmnt Ctee 1996–2001; non-exec dir: Tate & Lyle plc 1988–99, MEPC plc 1992–2000, The Equitable Life Assurance Society 1995–2000; chm Ellis & Everard 1993–2000; pres IBEC Inc (USA) 1980–84; dir: Int Agribusiness Mgmnt Assoc 1990–, Arbor Acres Farm Inc USA 1991–98, Winrock Int (USA) 1991–2001; dir and past chm Fndn for the Devpt of Polish Agric 1991–2002; chm: Governing Body SOAS Univ of London 1999–2005 (govr 1988–2005), Paintings in Hospitals 1996–2006, Marshall Cmmn 2000–, Booker Prize Fndn 2001–; memb Advsy Cncl UNIDO 1986–93, curator Bodleian Library 1989–98; govr: RAC Cirencester, Int Inst for the Environment & Devpt, Cwlth Inst 1998–2005; hon fell CCC Oxford; CIMgt 1984, FRSA 1990; *Recreations* travel, collecting watercolours; *Clubs* Brooks's; *Style*— Jonathan Taylor, Esq, CBE; ✉ 48 Edwardes Square, Kensington, London W8 6HH (tel 020 7603 0560, fax 020 7603 3274, e-mail jonathan@jftaylor.com)

TAYLOR, Jonathan Jeremy Kirwan; s of Sir Charles Stuart Taylor, TD, DL; *b* 12 October 1943; *Educ* Eton, St Edmund Hall Oxford (MA); *m* 1966 (sep 1999), Victoria Mary Caroline, da of Hon John Francis McLaren (d 1953); 4 da (Arabella b 1969, Lucinda b 1972, Caroline b 1976, Katherine b 1979); partner, Dominique Vulliamy; 1 da (Coco b 1999); *Career* called to the Bar Middle Temple 1968; dir Baring Asset 1989–97 (formerly Baring Int Investment Mgmnt Ltd) and other Baring Investment Gp Cos; chm: Dragon Partners Ltd, Schroder Japan Growth Fund plc; md Onyx Country Estates Ltd; dir: Greater China Fund Inc, AVK Securities & Finance Ltd (St Petersburg); *Recreations* skiing (Br Olympic Team 1964), golf, tennis, boating; *Clubs* White's, Turf, Hong Kong; *Style*— Jonathan Taylor, Esq; ✉ 41 Burlington Road, London SW6 4NH

TAYLOR, Jonathan McLeod Grigor; s of John Grigor Taylor, and Dorothy Jean, *née* McLeod; *b* 5 March 1955, London; *Educ* Bedales, New Coll Oxford (BA); *m* 1984, Stella, *née* Schimmel; 1 s (James b 1991), 1 da (Venetia b 1995); *Career* HM Treasy 1977–98, cnsllr economics and finance UK Permanent Representation to EU 1994–98, dir macroeconomic policy and int fin HM Treasy 1998–2002, head of public policy UBS AG 2002–05, DG London Investment Banking Assoc (LIBA) 2005–; *Style*— Jonathan Taylor, Esq; ✉ London Investment Banking Association, 6 Frederick's Place, London EC2R 8BT

TAYLOR, Eur Ing Kenneth; JP (1983); s of Kenneth Warburton Taylor (d 1989) and Kathleen, *née* Dilworth; *b* 26 January 1941; *Educ* Accrington Tech Sch, Burnley Coll (HNC), Openshaw Coll (IHVE); *m* 10 June 1960, Jean, da of Dr Staff (d 1956); 1 s (John b 1961), 1 da (Jeanette b 1962); *Career* design engr Burnley Co Borough 1963–71, princ Taylor Marren and Haslam (consltg engrs) 1971–85, chief building serv engr Oldham Met Borough 1985–88, chm Taylor Associates Ltd (consltg forensic engrs) 1988–; expert witness; many pubns in professional jls on legal matters; past chm CIBSE North West; memb Adjudication Soc; Freeman City of London 1999, Liveryman Worshipful Co of Plumbers; CEng, Eur Ing, MAE, FCIBSE, FIPlantE, FSOE, RP, FIPHE, FCMI, memb American Soc of Heating, Refrigerating and Air-Conditioning Engrs (MASHRAE); *Books* A Practical Guide for the Expert Witness, Plant Engineers Reference Book (jt author); *Recreations* music, lectures on building services and health and safety matters; *Clubs* Foreign Travel; *Style*— Eur Ing Kenneth Taylor; ✉ 71 Beaufort Avenue, Bispham, Blackpool, Lancashire FY2 9AG (tel 01253 596308); Taylor Associates Ltd (tel 01253 596818, fax 01253 596818, e-mail forensic.engineer@tiscali.co.uk)

TAYLOR, Kenneth Heywood (Ken); s of Edgar Mason Taylor (d 1931), of Bolton, Lancs, and Helen Agnes, *née* Higgin (d 1978); *b* 10 November 1922; *Educ* Gresham's; *m* 1, 1946 (m dis 1951), Elizabeth Jane, *née* Tillotson; 1 da (Pamela b 1948); m 2, 1953, Gillian Dorothea, da of Harry Erskine Black (d 1971), of Sidmouth, Devon; 1 da (Victoria Mary (Vikki Heywood, *qv*) b 1956), 2 s (Matthew Taylor, MP, *qv* b 1963, Simon b 1964); *Career* TV dramatist; TV plays incl: China Doll, Into the Dark, The Long Distance Blue, The Slaughtermen, The Devil and John Brown, The Seekers, Shoulder to Shoulder, The Poisoning of Charles Bravo; TV adaptions incl: The Melancholy Hussar, The Girls of Slender Means, The Birds Fall Down, Mansfield Park, The Jewel in the Crown, Cause Celebre, The Camomile Lawn, The Peacock Spring; stage plays: The Strange Affair of Charles Bravo, Staying On; BAFTA Writer of the Year Award 1964, Writers' Guild Best Original Teleplay Award 1964, RTS Writers' Award (for The Jewel in the Crown) 1984; memb Writers' Guild of GB; *Publications* Staying On (2001); *Recreations* walking, music; *Style*— Ken Taylor, Esq; ✉ Churchtown House, Gwithian, Hayle, Cornwall TR27 5BX (tel 01736 752287, fax 01736 752536)

TAYLOR, Prof Kenneth MacDonald (Ken); s of Hugh Baird Taylor (d 1996), of Crail, Fife, and Mary, *née* MacDonald (d 1978); *b* 20 October 1947; *Educ* Jordanhill Coll Sch Glasgow, Univ of Glasgow (MB ChB, MD); *m* 14 May 1971, Christine Elizabeth, da of John Buchanan (d 1986), of Ullapool, Ross-shire; 1 s (Iain b 1972), 1 da (Kirstin b 1975); *Career* Hall fell in surgery Western Infirmary Glasgow 1971–72, sr lectr in cardiac surgery Royal Infirmary Glasgow 1980–83 (lectr 1974–79); Imperial Coll Sch of Med at Hammersmith Hosp (Royal Postgrad Med Sch until merger 1997): Br Heart Fndn prof of cardiac surgery 1983–, vice-chm Cardiovascular and Respiratory Div 1997–, memb Principals' Advsy Gp 1997–; clinical dir Cardiac Servs Hammersmith Hosp 2003–; memb: Assoc of Profs of Surgery, Specialist Advsy Ctee in Cardiothoracic Surgery (chm 1992–95), Dept of Health Working Pty on Waiting Times for Coronary Artery Disease 1994–95, Nat Serv Frameworks Reference Panel for Coronary Heart Disease Dept of Health 1998–2002; chm: Database Ctee Euro Assoc for Cardiac Surgery 1994–2002, UK Central Cardiac Audit Steering Ctee 1995–; pres Soc of Perfusionists GB and Ireland 1989– (hon memb 1997); dir Sch of Perfusion Sciences, govr Drayton Manor HS London 1989–94; tstee: Garfield Weston Tst, European Bd of Cardiovascular Perfusion; memb Editorial Bd: Annals of Thoracic Surgery 1990–, Jl of Cardiothoracic and Vascular Anaesthesia 1993–, Jl of Heart Valve Disease 1992–; Br Heart Fndn: memb Cncl 2000–, memb Exec Ctee 2000–, tstee 2006–; hon memb American Acad of Cardiovascular Perfusion; memb: Surgical Res Soc 1977, Soc of Cardiothoracic Surgns of GB and Ireland 1979, British Cardiac Soc 1983, Soc of Thoracic Surgns of America 1986 (memb Database Ctee 1998–), Euro Assoc for Cardiothoracic Surgery 1988, American Assoc for Thoracic Surgery 1989 (honored guest 1998, hon memb 1998); hon alumnus Dept of Cardiovascular and Thoracic Surgery Cleveland Clinic USA; FRCS, FRCSGlas, FESC, fell European Bd of Thoracic and Cardiovascular Surgeons (FETCS); *Books* Pulsatile Perfusion (1982), Handbook of Intensive Care (1984), Perfusion (ed, 1984–), Cardiopulmonary Bypass - Principles and Management (1986), Principles of Surgical Research (1989, 2 edn 1995), Cardiac Surgery and the Brain (1992); *Recreations* family, church, music; *Style*— Prof Ken Taylor; ✉ 129 Argyle Road, Ealing, London W13 0DB; Cardiac Surgery Unit, Hammersmith Hospital, Du Cane Road, London W12 0NN (tel 020 8383 3214, fax 020 8740 7019, e-mail k.m.taylor@imperial.ac.uk)

TAYLOR, Prof Laurence John (Laurie); s of Stanley Douglas Taylor, and Winifred Agnes, *née* Cooper; *Educ* St Mary's Coll Liverpool, Rose Bruford Coll, Birkbeck Univ of London (BA), Univ of Leicester (MA); *m* 1; 1 s (Matthew b 5 Dec 1960); m 2, 16 Dec 1988, Catherine, da of Harold Francis Mahoney; *Career* librarian Liverpool City Cncl 1952–54, salesman British Enka Ltd 1954–57, actor Theatre Workshop Stratford 1960–61, teacher Forest Hill Comp 1961–64; Univ of York: lectr 1965–70, sr lectr 1970–73, reader 1973–75, prof 1975–94; visiting prof: Birkbeck Coll London 1994–, Univ of Westminster 2004–; various radio appearances incl Stop the Week, Speaking as an Expert, The Afternoon Shift, Thinking Allowed, Room for Improvement; Hon DLitt Univ of Nottingham 1992, Hon DPhil Univ of Central England 1993, Hon DLitt Univ of Leicester 2004; fell Birkbeck Coll London; *Books* Psychological Survival (1972), Escape Attempts (1976), In The Underworld (1984), Professor Lapping Sends His Apologies (1986), The Tuesday Afternoon Time Immemorial Committee (1989), Escape Attempts Revisited (1992), Laurie Taylor's Guide to Higher Education (1994), What are Children For? (2002); *Recreations* football, jazz; *Clubs* Groucho; *Style*— Prof Laurie Taylor; ✉ e-mail lolsoc@dircon.co.uk

TAYLOR, Leon; s of Roy Taylor, and Sue Taylor; *b* 2 November 1977; *Career* diver; achievements incl: Bronze medal 10m platform Cwlth Games 1998, Bronze medal 10m synchronised European Championships 1999, fourth place 10m synchronised Olympic Games Sydney 2000, Silver medal 10m platform Cwlth Games 2002, Silver medal 10m synchronised Olympic Games 2004, Bronze medal 10m synchronised World Championships 2005; *Style*— Leon Taylor, Esq

TAYLOR, Margaret Cecilia (Maggie); da of John Marcus Kisch (d 1992), of Dunsfold, Surrey, and Gillian May, *née* Poyser; *b* 31 March 1955; *Educ* Godolphin Sch, St Hilda's Coll Oxford (BA); *m* 30 June 1984, Lee Taylor, s of Edward Thomas Taylor; 1 da (Chloë May b 9 March 1992), 1 s (Henry Thomas b 1 July 1994); *Career* research exec Br Market Research Bureau 1978–80, sr research exec Market Behaviour Ltd 1980–83; Saatchi & Saatchi Advertising: account planner 1983–87, bd dir 1987–90, divnl planning dir 1990; fndr planning ptnr Cowan Kemsley Taylor 1990–97, dir RPM3 (following merger with Butler Lutos Sutton Wilkinson) 1997–2003, fndr dir Kisch Taylor Consulting 2003–; dir Project Tst 1999–; memb: Market Research Soc 1978–, Assoc of Qualitative Research Practitioners 1982, Account Planning Gp 1983–, Women in Advertising and Communication London 1997–; vol Samaritans 2007–; MIPA 1990; *Recreations* skiing, amateur dramatics (memb Cranbourne Amateur Dramatic Soc); *Style*— Mrs Maggie Taylor; ✉ The Old Fox, Winkfield Row, Berkshire RG42 6NG

TAYLOR, Mark; *b* 27 February 1973; *Career* rugby union player (centre); clubs: Pontypool, Swansea, Llanelli Scarlets, Sale Sharks 2005–; Wales: 50 caps, winners Six Nations Championship and Grand Slam 2005, capt touring squad to USA 2005; memb British and Irish Lions touring squad Aust 2001; *Style*— Mr Mark Taylor; ✉ c/o Sale Sharks, Edgeley Park, Hardcastle Road, Stockport SK3 9DD

TAYLOR, Mark Christopher; s of Joseph Norman Taylor, and June Taylor; *b* 24 November 1958; *Educ* Loughborough GS, Univ of Birmingham (BA), Leeds Poly (Dip Hotel Mgmnt); *m* 24 June 1989, Debra June, da of Alan Howes; 2 s (Jack b 1990, Liam b 1994), 1 da (Eleanor b 1991); *Career* hotel mangr Norfolk Capital Hotels 1981–84; chm: Network of Euro Museum Organisations 1998–2001, Campaign for Learning Through Museums 1998–2003, Tourism Heritage Export 2003–05; dir Museums Assoc 1989– (conf mangr 1984–89), memb Bd Nat Campaign for the Arts 1999–; tstee: Bedfordshire Music Tst 2002–, Museum Prize Tst 2002–, Campaign for Museums 2004–; *Recreations* sport, film, food; *Style*— Mark Taylor, Esq; ✉ c/o Museums Association, 24 Calvin Street, London E1 6NW (tel 020 7426 6950, fax 02 7426 6961, e-mail mark@museumsassociation.org)

TAYLOR, Mark R F; *b* 6 December 1943; *Educ* Oriel Coll Oxford (MA), Univ of Manchester (NHS UK Admin Trg Scheme), Canadian Coll of Health Serv Execs (Certified Health Exec); *m*; *Career* lectr/tutor Dip Course in Health Servs Admin Aston Univ Birmingham 1968–70, admin The Aga Khan Hosp Kenya 1971–74 (asst admin 1970), conslt Peat Marwick & Partners Canada 1974–79, exec sec The Aga Khan Fndn Kenya 1979–81, princ Woods Gordon (Ernst & Young) Management Consultants Canada 1981–84, sr vice-pres Toronto Western Hosp Canada 1984–86, chief exec Cromwell Hosp London 1987–89, pres Addiction Research Fndn Toronto 1989–94; chief exec: Royal Devon & Exeter Healthcare NHS Tst 1994–96, Royal Brompton Hosp NHS Tst 1996–98, Royal Brompton and Harefield NHS Trust 1998–2003; non-exec dir NICE 2003– (currently chair Risk Mgmnt Ctee); memb Bd Ind Hosps Assoc 1988–89, fndr memb Bd Crossmatch Health Personnel Agency Ltd 1988–89, chm Toronto Academic Health Scis Cncl 1990–94, hon vice-pres Int Cncl on Alcohol and Addictions 1991– (chair Fin Panel 1992–97), dir CORDA (Heart charity) 1998–; govr Univ of Plymouth 2005–; contrib various learned jls and other pubns; *Clubs* Leander, Athenaeum, Royal Southampton Yacht; *Style*— Mark R F Taylor, Esq

TAYLOR, Martin Gibbeson; CBE (1993); s of Roy Gibbeson Taylor (d 1955), of Worthing, W Sussex, and Vera Constance, *née* Farmer (d 1993); *b* 30 January 1935; *Educ* Haileybury, St Catharine's Coll Cambridge (MA); *m* 18 June 1960, Gunilla Chatarina, da of Nils Bryner (d 1962), of Stockholm, Sweden; 2 s (Thomas b 1963, Seth b 1967); *Career* 2 Lt RA 1953–55; with Mann Judd & Co (CA) 1958–62, co sec Dow Chemical UK 1963–69; Hanson plc: joined 1969, dir 1976–95, vice-chm 1988–95; chm National Westminster Life Assurance Ltd 1992–2000; non-exec dir: Vickers plc, National Westminster Bank plc 1990–2000, Charter plc 1995–2002, Millennium Chemicals Inc 1996–2003; memb: Panel on Takeovers and Mergers until 1995, Cncl CBI until 1996, Companies Ctee CBI (chm 1990–94); govr The Mall Sch 1986–2000; FCA 1961; *Recreations* pictures, books, theatre, sport; *Clubs* MCC, Royal Mid Surrey, Oxford and Cambridge; *Style*— Martin G Taylor, Esq, CBE

TAYLOR, Prof Martin John; s of John Maurice Taylor, of Leicester, and Sheila Mary Barbara, *née* Camacho; *b* 18 February 1952; *Educ* Wyggeston GS, Pembroke Coll Oxford (MA), KCL (PhD); *m* 1 Dec 1973, Sharon Lynn, da of Harold Marlow; 2 da (Rebecca b 28 July 1977, Deborah b 9 May 1979), 2 s (Andrew b 19 March 1981, James b 3 July 1983); *Career* res asst KCL 1976–77, jr lectr Univ of Oxford 1977–78, lectr QMC London 1978–81, professeur associé Besançon 1979–80, fell Trinity Coll Cambridge 1981–85, chair in pure mathematics UMIST (now Univ of Manchester) 1985–; London Mathematical Soc: memb Cncl, jr Whitehead prize 1982, Adams prize 1983, pres 1998–2000, Fröhlich lectr 2003; Royal Soc: Leverhulme sr res fell 1991–92, memb Cncl 2000–01, Wolfson Research Merit Award holder 2002–, vice-pres and physical sec 2004–; chm Bramhall Cncl of Churches; Hon DSc Univ of Leicester 2006; FRS 1996, EPSRC sr fell 1999– (memb Cncl 2004–); *Books* Classgroups of Group Rings (1983), Elliptic Functions and Rings of Integers (with P Cassou-Noguès), Algebraic Number Theory (with A Fröhlich), L-functions and Arithmetic (with J Coates), Group Rings and Class Groups (with K Roggenkamp); *Style*— Prof Martin Taylor, FRS; ✉ Department of Mathematics, University of Manchester, PO Box 88, Manchester M60 1QD (tel 0161 200 3640, e-mail martin.taylor@manchester.ac.uk)

TAYLOR, Matthew Owen John; MP; s of Kenneth Heywood (Ken) Taylor, *qv*, and Gillian Dorothea, *née* Black; bro of Vikki Heywood, *qv*; *b* 3 January 1963; *Educ* St Paul's, Tremorvah Sch, Treliske Sch, Univ Coll Sch, Lady Margaret Hall Oxford (BA); *Career* pres Oxford Univ Students' Union 1985–86, econ research asst Parly Lib Pty 1986–87 (attached to late David Penhaligon, MP for Truro); MP (Lib until 1988, now Lib Dem): Truro (March by-election) 1987–97, Truro and St Austell 1997–; Lib Dem Parly spokesman on: energy 1987–88, local govt, housing and tport 1988–89, trade and industry 1989–90, educn 1990–92, Citizens' Charter and youth issues 1992–94, the environment 1994–97, environment and tport 1997–99, Lib Dem shadow chllr 1999–2003, chm Lib Dem Parly Party 2003–05, Lib Dem shadow for Cabinet Office and social exclusion 2006–07; chm: Lib Dem Communications Ctee 1989–92, Lib Dem Campaigns & Communications Ctee 1992–94; *Style*— Matthew Taylor, Esq, MP; ✉ House of Commons, London SW1A 0AA (tel 020 7219 6686, e-mail taylorm@parliament.uk, website www.matthewtaylor.info)

TAYLOR, Rev Dr Michael Hugh; OBE (1998); s of Albert Taylor and Gwendoline Taylor; *b* 8 September 1936; *Educ* Northampton GS, Univ of Manchester (BD, MA), Union Theological Seminary NY (STM); *m* 1960, Adele May, *née* Dixon; 2 s, 1 da; *Career* Baptist min 1960–69 (North Shields Northumberland, Hall Green Birmingham), princ Northern Baptist Coll Manchester 1970–85, lectr in theology and ethics Univ of Manchester 1970–85, examining chaplain to Bishop of Manchester 1975–85, dir Christian Aid 1985–97, pres Selly Oak Colls Birmingham 1998–; chm Tstees Audenshaw Fndn 1979–92; memb Cncl: VSO 1986–94, Overseas Devpt Inst 1987–; chm Assoc of Protestant Devpt Orgns in Europe (APRODEV) 1991–95; memb WCC Cmmns 1976–91 and 1991–; Fulbright Travel Award 1969, DLitt (Lambeth) 1997; *Books* Variations on a Theme (1973), Learning to Care (1983), Good for the Poor (1990), Christianity and the Persistence of Poverty (1991), Not Angels but Agencies (1995), Jesus and the International Financial Institutions (1997); *Recreations* walking, theatre, cooking; *Style*— The Rev Dr Michael H Taylor, OBE; ✉ Selly Oak Colleges, Birmingham B29 6LQ

TAYLOR, Michael Paul Gordon; s of Gordon Taylor, and Stella, *née* Marsh; *b* 2 March 1949; *Educ* Altrincham GS, St John's Coll Cambridge; *Career* ptnr Norton Rose 1979– (based in Milan office 2000–); Freeman City of London Slrs Co; memb: Int Bar Assoc, Law Soc; MInstEn; *Recreations* sport, theatre, reading; *Clubs* RAC; *Style*— Michael Taylor, Esq; ✉ e-mail michael.taylor@nortonrose.com

TAYLOR, Air Cdre Neil Ernest; s of William Ernest Taylor (d 1999), of Sheffield, and Marjorie, *née* Needes (d 1999); *b* 6 December 1947; *Educ* Central Tech Sch Sheffield, Univ of Sheffield (BSc), Univ of Cambridge (MA); *m* 14 Feb 1976, Angela, da of Bernard Hirst; 3 s (Andrew James b 7 Dec 1976, Richard Jeremy b 17 May 1979, Mark Nicholas b 14 Dec 1982); *Career* cmmnd RAF Coll Cranwell 1971; pilot trg 1971–73, pilot (Lightning, Phantom) 1974–81, Flt Cdr 111 Sqdn and 23 Sqdn 1981–84, personnel offr 1984–85, attended JSDC 1985–86, staff offr MOD 1986–88, OC 23 Sqdn 1988–91, dir of Def Studies (RAF) 1991–94, CO RAF Akrotiri 1994–96, dep dir MOD 1997, sr air advsr HQ Bosnia-Herzegovina 1997–98, dir of personnel RAF 1998–99, asst COS Ops NATO HQ AIRCENT 1999–2000, COS Reaction Force Air Staff Kalkar Germany 2000–01; currently defence conslt; bursar and fell Hughes Hall Cambridge 2002–; dir: Hughes Hall Ltd, TS Defence Consultants Ltd; memb RAF Oxford and Cambridge Soc; FRAeS 1992; *Books* Soviet Forces in Transition (1992), The Gulf War and Some Lessons Learned (1992), The Role of Air Power in Crisis Management (1993), AP3000 Air Power Doctrine (1993), A Short History of the Royal Air Force (1994); *Recreations* pilot RAF Reserves, private pilot, golf, computing, gardening, carpentry; *Clubs* RAF; *Style*— Air Commodore N E Taylor; ✉ Hughes Hall, Cambridge CB1 2EW

TAYLOR, Neil Frederick; *b* 25 May 1951; *Educ* Batley GS, Univ of Sheffield (BA, Dip Architecture); *Career* architect; ptnr FaulknerBrowns; commissions incl: The Dome Doncaster, Civic Offices Chester-le-Street, Claremont Sports Hall, Blackburn Leisure Pool, Perth Waters, Leeds Pedestrianisation; contrib various publications incl: Architects Jl, Architects Review, Domus, Design, Beven Wohnen, Architekt, Architecture d'Aujourd'hui, Sunday Times, Financial Times, Guardian, Telegraph, Economist, Building Design; Summer Exhibition RA (rep UK World Expo Brisbane 1988); *Awards* incl: Civic Tst, RIBA, Europa Nostra, IAKS, Structural Steel, Financial Times; visiting prof Univ of Newcastle 1992–, external examiner Liverpool John Moores Univ (previously for Univ of Newcastle), visiting critic Univ of Sheffield; memb: Urban Design Gp, Validation Ctee Liverpool John Moores Univ, RIBA Visiting Bd of Educn, Higher Educn Funding Cncl Validation Bd, ARCUK; RIBA, MIMgt; *Recreations* involved in local education, architectural history, social evolution of history, football, cricket, riding; *Style*— Neil Taylor, Esq

TAYLOR, (John) Patrick Enfield; s of Arthur Hugh Enfield Taylor, RNVR (d 1983), of Midhurst, W Sussex, and Monica Soames, *née* Cooke (d 2003); *b* 3 April 1948; *Educ* Eton; *m* 1972, Heather Diana, da of Col Roger Barratt, of Haverthwaite, Cumbria (d 2004); 3 da (Melissa b 1976, Pippa b 1980, Hermione b 1983), 1 s (Rupert b 1979); *Career* ptnr Coopers & Lybrand 1980–86 (qualified 1972), fin dir Langdale Group plc 1986–88, dir of fin and business devpt Capital Radio plc 1989–96, chief exec GWR Group plc 2001–03 (non-exec dir 1994–96, dep chief exec and fin dir 1996–2001), chm Nonstopski Ltd, non-exec dir The Future Network plc, non-exec dir Centaur Hldgs plc; FCA; *Recreations* tennis, swimming, sailing, skiing; *Style*— Patrick Taylor, Esq; ✉ e-mail patrick@nonstopski.com

TAYLOR, Prof Peter; s of Peter Taylor (d 1980), and Margaret Alice, *née* Tedman; *b* 21 November 1944, Tring, Herts; *Educ* Henry Mellish GS Nottingham, Univ of Liverpool (BA, PhD); *m* 30 Oct 1965, Enid; 1 s (Carl Richard b 8 June 1966), 1 da (Clare Elizabeth b 6 Dec 1969); *Career* lectr rising to prof of political geography Univ of Newcastle upon Tyne 1970–96, prof of geography Loughborough Univ 1996– (co-dir Globalization and World Cities (GaWC) study gp and network); founding ed: Political Geography 1982–98, Review of Int Political Economy 1992–97; author of more than 300 pubns; FBA 2004; *Publications* The Political Geography of the Twentieth Century (ed, 1992), Political Geography: World-Economy, Nation-State, Locality (1993, 2 edn 1999), Geographies of Global Change: Remapping the World in the Late Twentieth Century (ed with R J Johnston and M W Watts, 1995), World Cities in a World-System (ed with P Knox, 1995), The Way the Modern World Works: World Hegemony to World Impasse (1996), Open the Social Sciences (Gulbenkian Cmmn, 1996), Modernities: A Geohistorical Interpretation (1999), The American Century: Consensus and Coercion in the Projection of American Power (ed with D Slater, 1999), World City Network: a Global Urban Analysis (2004); also author of numerous book contribs, jl papers, reports and reviews; *Style*— Prof Peter Taylor; ✉ 33 Percy Park, Tynemouth NE30 4JZ (tel 0191 259 1113); Department of Geography, Loughborough University, Loughborough LE11 3TU (e-mail p.j.taylor@lboro.ac.uk)

TAYLOR, Peter Cranbourne; s of Maurice Ewan Taylor, OBE (d 1999), of St Andrews, Fife, and Mary Ann, *née* Gorst (d 1993); *b* 11 August 1938; *Educ* Univ of Edinburgh (MA); *m* 27 June 1970, Lois Mary, da of Anthony Godard Templeton, TD (d 1986), of St Andrews, Fife; 1 da (Kerrie b 18 Dec 1972), 1 s (Christopher b 13 Nov 1975); *Career* CA 1962; ptnr: Romanes & Munro Edinburgh 1964–74, Deloitte Haskins & Sells (subsequently Coopers & Lybrand) 1974–95; convenor ICAS, memb Servs Ctee 1984–90, memb Scot Dental Practice Bd 1991–2001; non-exec dir Joint Insolvency Monitoring Unit Ltd 1994–97; chm Scottish Nat Blood Transfusion Assoc 1995– (sec and treas 1981–95); *Recreations* country pursuits; *Style*— Peter Taylor, Esq; ✉ Totleywells House, Winchburgh, West Lothian EH52 6QJ (tel and fax 0131 319 2155)

TAYLOR, Ven Peter Flint; s of late Alan Flint Taylor, of Bristol, and late Josephine Overbury, *née* Dix; *b* 7 March 1944; *Educ* Clifton, Queens' Coll Cambridge (major scholar, MA), London Coll of Divinity (BD); *m* 1971, Joy Marion, da of late Frank Henry Sampson; 1 da (Rebecca Jane b 1974); *Career* ordained: deacon 1970, priest 1971; curate: St Augustine Highbury 1970–73, St Andrew Plymouth 1973–77; vicar Christ Church Ironville Derbyshire 1977–83, priest i/c St James' Riddings Derbyshire 1982–83, rector Holy Trinity Rayleigh Essex 1983–96, pt/t chaplain HM Young Offender Inst & Prison Bullwood Hall 1986–90, rural dean Rochford 1989–96, archdeacon of Harlow 1996–; *Recreations* walking, computing, interest in archaeology of Jerusalem; *Style*— The Ven the Archdeacon of Harlow; ✉ Glebe House, Church Lane, Sheering, Bishop's Stortford, Essex CM22 7NR (tel 01279 734524, fax 01279 734426, e-mail a.harlow@chelmsford.anglican.org)

TAYLOR, (Louis) Philip Chetwynd; s of Philip Hugh Taylor (d 2000), of Newcastle-under-Lyme, Staffs, and Mable Doreen, *née* Bladen (d 1986); *b* 9 October 1950; *Educ* Malvern Coll; *m* 22 May 1976, Odette, da of Thomas Demajo; 2 da (Ruth Doreen Theresa b 21 Nov 1980, Harriet Charlotte Christina b 6 May 1984); *Career* PricewaterhouseCoopers (formerly Price Waterhouse before merger): London 1970–75, Johannesburg 1975–78, London 1978–85, ptnr 1985–, joined Channel Islands firm 1985, sr ptnr 1993–; chm Jersey Branch IoD 1990–93; FCA (ACA 1973); *Recreations* cricket, gardening; *Clubs* United (St Helier); *Style*— Philip Taylor, Esq; ✉ c/o PricewaterhouseCoopers, 22 Colomberie, St Helier, Jersey JE1 4XA (tel 01534 838200, fax 01534 838201)

TAYLOR, Philip (Phil); s of Alexander Taylor (d 1989), and Veronica, *née* Walsh (d 2001); *b* 21 January 1953, Macclesfield; *Educ* All Hallows RC Sch Macclesfield; *m* 5 Jan 1990, Lesley Ann Jenkins; 1 da (Nina Louise b 29 March 1982), 1 s (Alexander James b 5 May 1984); *Career* joined HM Prison Serv 1978; prison offr HMDC Kirklevington and HMP Frankland 1978–88, sr offr HMP Stafford 1989–91 (prison offr 1988–89), princ offr PSC Wakefield and HM Young Offenders Inst Brinsford 1991–93, govr HMP Sudbury, HMP Drake Hall and HMP Birmingham 1993–2000, dep govr HMP Gartree 2000–03, govr HMP Swansea 2003–; *Recreations* hot air ballooning, Formula One motor racing, walking, swimming with dolphins; *Style*— Phil Taylor, Esq; ✉ HMP Bullingdon, PO Box 50, Bicester, Oxon OX25 1WD (tel 01864 353100)

TAYLOR, Philippe Arthur; s of Arthur Peach Taylor, (d 1974), of St Andrews, Fife, and Simone, *née* Vacquin; *b* 9 February 1937; *Educ* Trinity Coll Glenalmond, Univ of St Andrews; *m* 10 Feb 1973, Margaret Nancy, da of Arnold Frederick Wilkins, OBE (d 1985), of Framlingham, Suffolk; 2 s (Rupert Arthur James b 1975, Charles Philip b 1976); *Career* Procter & Gamble 1961–66, Masius Int 1966–70, Br Tourist Authy 1970–75; chief exec: Scottish Tourist Bd 1975–81, Birmingham Convention Bureau 1982–93; chm Br Assoc of Conference Towns 1988–91, vice-chm Ikon Gallery 1988–, Chevalier de l'Ordre des Coteaux de Champagne 1985; FTS 1975; *Books* Captain Crossjack and the Lost Penguin (1969); *Recreations* sailing, painting, tourism, making things; *Clubs* Royal Northumberland YC, Orford Sailing; *Style*— Philippe Taylor, Esq

TAYLOR, Raymond Barry (Ray); s of John Gordon Taylor, of Potters Bar, Herts, and Jean Mary, *née* Hasloch; *b* 26 July 1958; *Educ* Chancellor's Sch; *m* 1982, Sally Patricia, da of Donald Robert Roser; 2 s (Barry b 8 April 1987, Josh b 6 Jan 1992); *Career* set up mktg communications business in 1979 (TPS, renamed Revolution 1995) incorporating Revolution Interactive Ltd (new media based solutions), Revolution Ltd (brand interaction and mktg communications), Revolution Interactive (new media based mktg communications), Revolution Environments (interior design, retail and leisure), Revolution Marketing Logistics Ltd (data capture and fulfilment) and Inc Ltd (print based solutions) 1998–2000, chm Transmission Gp Ltd 2001– (following sale of Revolution to china.com and formation of new gp), chm Co-Incidence Ltd 2003; *Recreations* skiing, sailing, classic cars, family; *Style*— Mr Ray Taylor; ✉ Transmission Group Ltd, RML Suite, Rawmec Business Park, Plumpton Road, Hoddesdon, Hertfordshire EN11 0EE (tel 01992 801953, e-mail ray.taylor@transmissiongroup.com)

TAYLOR, Richard; *b* 6 February 1945; *Educ* Corpus Christi Coll Oxford (MA); *Career* admitted slr 1969; CMS Cameron McKenna (formerly McKenna & Co): articled clerk 1967–69, asst slr 1969–74, on secondment to lawyers' cos in Germany, France and Holland 1973, ptnr 1974–, of counsel 2004; specialist in competition law and EC law, has pleaded before Euro Ct of Justice Luxembourg; former chm of CMS Legal Services; author of various articles on competition and EEC law; past chm Solicitors' Euro Gp; *Style*— Richard Taylor, Esq; ✉ CMS Cameron McKenna, Mitre House, 160 Aldersgate Street, London EC1A 4DD (tel 020 7367 2108, fax 020 7367 2000)

TAYLOR, Richard John; s of William Taylor (d 1993), of Northwich, Cheshire, and Florence Littler, *née* Hough (d 1986); *b* 15 April 1951; *Educ* North Cestrian GS Altrincham, Univ of St Andrews (BSc, capt rowing and United Colls Rugby 1st XV); *m* 2 June 1979, Kay Vivienne, da of Edward Jack Haddon; 1 s (Samuel James b 29 Jan 1983), 1 da (Alice Edwina b 22 Jan 1986); *Career* Spicer and Pegler CAs Manchester 1973–78 (qualified 1976), ptnr Murray Smith & Co CAs 1980– (joined 1978); govr: The Grange Sch Hartford Ltd 1983–, Mid-Cheshire Coll of FE 1993–2001 (chm 1998–2001); chm Chester and N Wales Soc of CAs 1991–92; FCA 1983; *Recreations* sailing (racing a Dart 18 catamaran), golf, waterskiing; *Clubs* Dee Sailing, Sandiway Golf; *Style*— Richard J Taylor, Esq; ✉ Pool Bank, Oulton, Tarporley, Cheshire CW6 9BH (tel 01829 760680); Murray Smith, Chartered Accountants, Grange House, Winsford, Cheshire CW7 2BP (tel 01606 551238, fax 01606 861174, e-mail rjt@murray-smith.co.uk)

TAYLOR, Dr Richard Thomas; MP; s of Thomas Taylor (d 1962), of Lancs, and Mabel, *née* Hickley (d 1992); *b* 7 July 1934; *Educ* The Leys Sch Cambridge, Clare Coll Cambridge (BA), Westminster Hosp (BChir, MB); *m* 1, 1962 (m dis 1986), Ann, da of John Brett; 2 da (Sally b 1 Oct 1964, Caroline b 3 March 1967), 1 s (Stephen b 25 Oct 1968); m 2, 1990, Christine, da of William Miller; 1 da (Georgina b 3 March 1993); *Career* house physician Westminster Hosp 1959, house surgeon Kingston Hosp 1960, house physician London Chest Hosp 1960–61; RAF: gen duties MO 1961–63, SMO Christmas Island 1963, MO RAF Hosp Halton 1963–64; St Stephen's Hosp: sr house physician 1964–65, med registrar 1965–66; Westminster Hosp: med registrar 1966–67, sr med registrar 1967–72; conslt in gen med with special interest in rheumatology Kidderminster Gen Hosp and The Droitwich Centre for Rheumatic Diseases 1972–95; hon clinical tutor Charing Cross and Westminster Med Sch 1985, examiner Birmingham Med Sch 1986–87; chm: Hosp Med Staff Ctee 1975–77 and 1986–90, Kidderminster Hosp League of Friends 1996–2001 (staff rep 1975–90), Cancer Resource Centre Appeal 1997–98, Save Kidderminster Hosp Campaign Ctee 1997–2000, Health Concern 2000–; memb: BMA, Kidderminster Dist Med Ctee 1974–78, Kidderminster DHA 1982–86, Exec Ctee W Midlands Physicians' Assoc 1983–85, Kidderminster Community Health Cncl 1997–98; pres Kidderminster Med Soc 1993; MP (IKHHC) Wyre Forest 2001–, memb Health Select Ctee 2001–; memb: RSPB, Worcs Wildlife Tst, RHS, Nat Tst, English Heritage, Inst of Advanced Motorists, Severn Valley Railway; FRCP 1979 (MRCP 1965); *Recreations* family, wildlife, 1950s and 60s cars, Victorian watercolours; *Clubs* RSM; *Style*— Dr Richard Taylor, MP; ✉ House of Commons, London SW1A 0AA (tel 020 7219 4598, fax 020 7219 1967)

TAYLOR, His Hon Robert Carruthers; s of John Houston Taylor, CBE (d 1983), and Barbara Mary, *née* Carruthers (d 1994); *b* 6 January 1939; *Educ* Wycliffe Coll, St John's Coll Oxford (MA); *m* 16 April 1968, Jacqueline Marjorie, da of Nigel Geoffrey Randall Chambers, of

West Yorks; 1 da (Susannah b 1969), 1 s (John b 1972); *Career* called to the Bar Middle Temple 1961, practised NE Circuit 1961–84, recorder 1976–84, circuit judge (NE Circuit) 1984–2004 (dep circuit judge 2004–); chm Agric Land Tbnl Lancs/Yorks/Humberside) 1979–, memb Mental Health Review Tbnl 2001–; *Recreations* reading, music, gardening, walking; *Style*— His Hon Robert Taylor

TAYLOR, Prof Robert Henry; s of Robert Earl Taylor (d 1985), and Mabel, *née* Warren (d 1995); *b* 15 March 1943; *Educ* Greenville HS Ohio, Ohio Univ (BA), Antioch Coll (MA), Cornell Univ NY (PhD); *m* 1, 1967 (m dis 1999), Joan, da of Edwin Lutton; 1 da (Emily Sara b 1969), 1 s (Edwin Daniel b 1970); m 2, 2000, Ingrid G M Porteous; *Career* social studies teacher Cardozo HS Washington 1965–67, instructor in political science Wilberforce Univ Ohio 1967–69, lectr in govt Univ of Sydney 1974–79; SOAS, Univ of London 1980–96: successively lectr, sr lectr then prof of politics, pro-dir 1992–96; vice-chllr Univ of Buckingham 1997–2000; conslt on Asian affrs 2001–, chm Br Acad S E Asian Studies Ctee, visiting sr research fell Inst of Southeast Asian Studies Singapore 2003–06, memb editorial Bd Asian Affrs; lay memb Asylum and Immigration Tbnl 2003–; *Books* In Search of Southeast Asia (1985), Marxism and Resistance in Burma (1985), The State in Burma (1987), The Politics of Elections in Southeast Asia (1996), Burma: Political Economy under Military Rule (2001), Ideas of Freedom in Asia and Africa (2002), The Emergence of Modern Southeast Asia (2005), Myanmar: Beyond Politics to Societal Imperatives (2005); *Recreations* London, music, wine; *Clubs* Travellers, N Middlesex Golf; *Style*— Prof Robert Taylor; ✉ 13 Baron Close, Friern Village, London N11 3PS (tel 020 8361 4002, e-mail r_h_taylor@btopenworld.com)

TAYLOR, Sir Robert Richard (Bob); KCVO (2006), OBE (1989, MBE (mil) 1972), JP (1994); s of Sydney Arthur Taylor (d 1969), and Edith Alice, *née* Shepherd (d 1961); *b* 14 June 1932; *Educ* Yardley GS Birmingham; *m* 1957, Sheila, *née* Welch; *Career* RAF: joined as trainee pilot 1950, served in Egypt, Germany and Singapore, ret as Sqdn Ldr 1973; Birmingham Airport: asst dir (Admin) 1974–76, airport dir 1976–87, md 1987–94 (ret); dir: Maersk Air (UK) Ltd, Capital Radio plc 1994–2000; chm: Airport Operators' Assoc 1987–88, Birmingham Broadcasting Ltd 1994–2000; pres St John Cncl for the W Midlands; HM Lord-Lt W Midlands 1993–2006 (DL 1985); memb Ct Univ of Warwick, memb Cncl Univ of Warwick 1995–2001; Hon Col Univ of Birmingham OTC 1997–2002; Midlander of the Year 1989, QCVSA 1966, Inst of Mgmnt Silver Medal 1992, Airport Operators' Assoc Silver Medal 1995, Aston Univ Centennial Medal 1995; Freeman City of London; Hon DUniv Univ of Central England 1993, Hon LLD Univ of Birmingham 1998; KStJ 1994; *Recreations* people, books, countryside; *Clubs* RAF; *Style*— Sir Bob Taylor, KCVO, OBE; ✉ Holly Cottage, 43 Fieldgate Lane, Kenilworth, Warwickshire CV8 1BT (tel 01926 853113)

TAYLOR, Dr Robert Thomas; CBE (1990); s of George Taylor (d 1973), of Warrington, Lancs, and Marie Louise, *née* Fidler (d 1986); *b* 21 March 1933; *Educ* Boteler GS, Univ of Oxford (MA, DPhil); *m* 1, 20 Aug 1954 (m dis 1965), Ina, *née* Wilson; 1 s (Timothy b 1959); m 2, 25 Sept 1965, Rosemary Janet, da of Charles Leonard Boileau, of Bexhill-on-Sea, E Sussex; 2 s (Aubrey b 1967, Christopher 1968), 1 da (Alison b 1973); *Career* res assoc Randall Physics Lab Michigan Univ 1957–58, lectr in physics Univ of Liverpool 1959–61 (ICI res fell 1958–59); The Br Cncl: asst regnl rep Madras 1961–64, sci offr Spain 1964–69, dir staff recruitment 1969–73, regnl rep Bombay 1973–77, rep Mexico 1977–81, personnel controller London 1981–86, rep Greece 1986–90, ADG 1990–93; Manchester Business Sch: visiting sr fell 1993–99, chm Mgmnt Interviewing and Research Inst (MIRI) 1993–2004; examiner in physics: Oxford Local Bd 1956–61, Oxford and Cambridge Bd 1957; chief examiner physics NUJMB 1961 (examiner 1960), lay team memb for sch inspections OFSTED 1993–2002; borough cncllr Weald Central Ward Ashford BC 2003–, parish cncllr High Halden Kent 2003–; *Books* contrib Chambers Encyclopaedia (1967); *Recreations* war games, computers; *Style*— Dr Robert T Taylor; ✉ Mark Haven, Ashford Road, High Halden, Kent TN26 3LY (tel 01233 850994, e-mail robert@drrtt.freeserve.co.uk)

TAYLOR, Roger Meddows; s of Michael Meddows Taylor, and Winifred Taylor; *b* 26 July 1949; *Educ* Truro Sch, London Hosp Med Coll, N London Poly (BSc); *m*; 2 s (Felix Luther, Rufus Tiger), 3 da (Rory Eleanor, Tigerlily, Lola Daisy May); *Career* drummer, vocalist and songwriter; co-fndr: Smile 1968, Queen 1970– (with Freddie Mercury (d 1991), Brian May, *qv*, John Deacon, *qv*), The Cross 1987–; Queen albums: Queen (1973, platinum), Queen II (1974, platinum), Sheer Heart Attack (1974, platinum), A Night at the Opera (1975, platinum), A Day at the Races (1976, platinum), News of the World (1977, platinum), Jazz (1978, gold), Live Killers (1979, gold), The Game (1980, platinum), Flash Gordon Original Soundtrack (1980, gold), Greatest Hits (1981, 12 times platinum), Hot Space (1982, gold), The Works (1984, double platinum), A Kind of Magic (1986, double platinum), Live Magic (1986, platinum), The Miracle (1989, platinum), Queen at the Beeb (1989), Innuendo (1991, platinum), Greatest Hits Two (1991, 8 times platinum), Made in Heaven (1995, 4 times platinum); The Cross albums: Shove It (1988), Mad Bad and Dangerous to Know (1990), Blue Rock (1991); other albums: Gettin' Smile (earlier recordings of Smile, 1982), Fun In Space (solo, 1981), Strange Frontier (solo, 1984), Happiness (solo, 1994); number 1 singles: Bohemian Rhapsody 1975 and 1991 (with days of Our Lives), Under Pressure 1981, Innuendo 1991, Somebody to Love (with George Michael), electric fire (solo 1998); produced 1st hit by Jimmy Nail (Love Don't Live Here Any More); numerous tours worldwide, performed at Live Aid Concert Wembley Stadium 1985; voted Best Band of the Eighties ITV/TV Times 1990, Br Phonographic Indust award for Outstanding Contribution to Br Music 1990, Rock and Roll Hall of Fame 2001; Chevalier de l'Ordre des Arts et des Lettres (France) 1997; *Recreations* cars, travel, reading, renovating, working, boating, skiing; *Style*— Roger Taylor, Esq; ✉ c/o Phil Symes, The PR Contact Ltd, Garden Studio, 32 Newman Street, London W1T 1PU

TAYLOR, Roger Miles Whitworth; s of Richard Taylor (d 1965), of Stafford, and Joan Elizabeth, *née* Whitworth; *b* 18 May 1944; *Educ* Repton, Univ of Birmingham (LLB); *m* 1, 26 July 1969 (m dis 2003), Georgina Lucy, da of Francis Tonks (d 1973), of Sark, CI; 2 s (Richard Francis Miles b 1971, Matthew William Roger b 1976), 2 da (Sarah Elizabeth May, Lucy Emily Jane (twins) b 1981); m 2, 19 July 2003, Gabriele Eva, da of Tadeusz Sauter (d 1999), of Wernigerode, Germany; *Career* admitted slr 1968; asst slr: Staffordshire CC 1968–69, Cheshire CC 1969–71; asst co clerk Lincs parts of Lindsey 1971–73, dep co sec Northants CC 1971–73, town clerk and chief exec City of Manchester 1985–88 (dep town clerk 1979–85), chief exec Birmingham City Cncl and sec W Midlands Jt Ctee 1988–94, dir Local Govt Newchurch and Company Strategic Mgmnt Conslts 1994–2000 (chm 1998–2000), md JSS Pinnacle Consulting 2000–, gp dir Pinnacle-psq 2000–04; memb Farrand Ctee on Conveyancing 1983–84, clerk Gtr Manchester Passenger Tport Authy 1986–88; dir Birmingham Training and Enterprise Cncl 1990–93, chm Ofwat Central CSC 2000–02, memb Bd Standards Bd for England 2001–; Mancunian of the Year Manchester Jr C of C 1988; *Recreations* sailing, walking; *Style*— Roger Taylor, Esq; ✉ Pinnacle-psq, Charter House, 2 Farringdon Road, London EC1M 3HN (tel 020 7017 2031, fax 020 7017 2099, e-mail roger.taylor@pinnacle-psq.com)

TAYLOR, Ronald Charles (Ronnie); s of John William Taylor, and Bertha Elanor, *née*, Hoile; *b* 27 October 1924; *Educ* Highgate Sch; *Career* cinematographer; radio offr Merchant Navy 1943–45; camera operator: Gainsborough Studios 1941–42 and 1945–49, then successively Ealing Studios, Pinewood Studios, Vera Cruz Company São Paulo; dir of photography 1980–; pres BSC 1990–92; *Films* as camera operator incl: Lavender Hill Mob (2nd unit), Passport to Pimlico (2nd unit), O Cangercero, Room at the Top, Saturday Night Saturday Morning, The Innocents, Oh What a Lovely War, Young Winston, The Devils, Valentino, Return of a Man Called Horse, The Bobo, Star Wars; as dir of photography incl: The Silent Flute, Tommy, Nairobi, Savage Harvest, Master of the Game, Gandhi, Foreign Body, Popcorn, High Road to China, Chorus Line, The Experts, Cry Freedom, The Champions, Hound of the Baskervilles, Sea of Love, Opera, Rainbow Thief, Unwanted Attentions, The Steal, Redwood Curtain, From Time to Time, Age of Treason, The Good King, Phantom of the Opera, Non Ho Sono; *Awards* for Gandhi: Oscar for Best Cinematography 1982, BSC Award 1982, Eastman Kodak Award 1982, BAFTA nomination for Best Cinematography 1982; for Cry Freedom: BAFTA nomination for Best Cinematography 1987; *Style*— Ronnie Taylor, Esq, BSC

TAYLOR, Prof Samuel Sorby Brittain; s of Samuel Stephen Taylor (d 1970), and Elsie Irene, *née* Chappell (d 1992); *b* 20 September 1930; *Educ* High Storrs GS Sheffield, Univ of Birmingham (MA, PhD); *m* 15 Aug 1956, (Agnes) Nan McCreadie, da of late Peter Ewan, of Dundee; 2 da (Moira Elizabeth b 13 Aug 1959, Dorothy Frances b 1 Feb 1962); *Career* Nat Serv 1956–58, Sub Lt RNVR 1957–; personnel res offr Dunlop Rubber Co 1958–60, res fell (for Voltaire's correspondence vols 66–98, under Theodore Besterman) Institut et Musée Voltaire Geneva 1960–63; Univ of St Andrews: asst 1963, lectr 1964, reader 1972, personal chair 1977–95, prof emeritus 1995–; dir Nuffield Fndn Project on French for Science Students 1991–2000; author of studies of Voltaire, memb Editorial Ctee Voltaire's Complete Works 1967–91; sec gen Soc for Eighteenth Century Studies 1967–68; memb Nat Cncl for Modern Languages 1979– (chm 1981–85), chm Scottish Nat Working Pty on Standard Grade; memb Examinations Bd Inst of Linguists 1986–91; hon sec Scottish Univs French Language Res Assoc 1985–; chm St Andrews Scot Lib Dems 1999–; hon blue St Andrews Univ Athletics Union 2000; Officier dans l'Ordre des Palmes Académiques 1986; *Publications* contrib to: Voltaire's Correspondence (1953–63), Rousseau's Contemporary Reputation in France (1963), New Cambridge Bibliography of English Literature Vol 2 (1971), The Definitive Text of Voltaire's Works: The Leningrad Encadrée (1974), Voltaire's Humour (1979), Re-appraisals of Rousseau: Studies in Honour of R A Leigh (1980), Modern Swiss Literature: Unity and Diversity (1985); Initiator Le Français en Faculté (jtly, 1980), En Fin de Compte (jtly, 1988), Definitive Iconography of Voltaire (1996), Nuffield French for Science Students (jtly, 1999); *Recreations* grade 1 SAF timekeeper for athletics, photography; *Clubs* Fife Athletic, Paris University, Hallamshire Harriers; *Style*— Prof Samuel Taylor; ✉ 11 Irvine Crescent, St Andrews, Fife KY16 8LG (tel 01334 472588)

TAYLOR, Hon Mrs Sarah Lovell; *née* Rippon; 2 da of Baron Rippon of Hexham, PC, QC (Life Peer, d 1997); *b* 10 February 1950; *Educ* Sherborne Sch for Girls Dorset, St Paul's Girls' Sch London, St Anne's Coll Oxford (MA); *m* 1978 (m dis 1988), Michael Taylor; 2 s (James Geoffrey Bethune b 1979, Alexander Edward Yorke b 1982); *Career* admitted slr 1978; called to the NY Bar 1980; Theodore Goddard Solicitors 1974–77, Nixon Hargraves Devans & Doyle NY (Lawyers) 1980–84; dir: Robert Fraser Group Ltd 1986–91, Robert Fraser & Partners Ltd and subsid 1986–91; subsequently ptnr Penningtons and ptnr Woodroffes, currently conslt to Pettman Smith (Knightsbridge); dir: Savoy Asset Mgmnt plc, Jubilee Investment Tst plc; *Style*— The Hon Mrs Sarah Taylor; ✉ 10 Quarrendon Street, London SW6 3SU (tel 020 7736 7843)

TAYLOR, Dr Simon Wheldon; QC (2003); s of Thomas Henry Taylor, of London, and Enid, *née* Wheldon; *b* 4 July 1962, Whitechapel, London; *Educ* Highgate Sch London, Trinity Coll Cambridge (MA), Inns of Court Sch of Law, London Hosp Med Coll (MB, BChir); *m* 24 Nov 1990, Elizabeth Lawes, *née* Paine; 1 s (Harold Thomas Rollinson b 11 July 1994), 2 da (Rosalind Caroline Wheldon b 19 Dec 1995, Isobel Matilda Fawcett b 8 Jan 1998); *Career* barr; house offr London Hosp and Mile End Hosp 1987–88; tenant: 6 Pump Court 1989–98 (pupillage 1988–89), Cloisters 1998–; recorder 2002–; *Style*— Dr Simon Taylor, QC; ✉ Cloisters, 1 Pump Court, Temple, London EC4Y 7AA (tel 020 7827 4000, e-mail st@cloisters.com)

TAYLOR, (Alastair John) Sym; CBE; s of Alastair Anderson Taylor (d 1998), and May Elizabeth, *née* Currie (d 1980); *b* 13 March 1947; *Educ* Kelvinside Acad, Heriot-Watt Univ (BA), JSDC; *m* 14 Aug 1976, Elisabeth Anne, da of Erik Ullman (d 1999); 1 s (James Alastair b 27 April 1978), 1 da (Hannah Elisabeth b 2 Dec 1981); *Career* joined RN 1967, Coy Cdr RMA Sandhurst 1981–82, Capt HMS Zulu 1982–84, HQ SACLANT Norfolk Virginia 1984–87, DA/NA Caribbean 1990–93, Capt HMS Fearless 1993–95, Cdr Br Forces Gibraltar 1997–99; CE Disposal Servs Agency MOD 1999–2005; Freeman: City of London, City of Glasgow; MNI 1987; *Recreations* sport, wine, music; *Style*— Sym Taylor, Esq, CBE; ✉ VT Shipbuilding, Fleet Way, Portsmouth, Hampshire PO1 3AQ (tel 023 9285 7200)

TAYLOR, Terence Thomas; MBE (1980); s of Frederick Taylor (d 1991), and Doreen Taylor (d 1977); *b* 27 August 1939; *Children* 2 da (Justine b 1963, Catherine (Mrs Cotton) b 1965); *Career* mil offr 1960–93, served Def Arms Control Unit MOD 1985–87, cnsllr UK Delgn to Conf on Disarmament Geneva and UN Gen Assembly NY 1988–92, sr mil offr Proliferation and Arms Control Secretariat MOD 1992–93 (also UK rep Panel of Experts UN Register of Conventional Arms), cmmr UN Special Cmmn on Iraq 1993–95, chief inspr Iraq 1993–97, memb Centre for Disarmament Affrs and political affrs offr UN HQ 1994–95, asst dir IISS 1995–, pres and exec dir IISS-US Washington DC 2001–; advsr: Int Ctee Red Cross 1989–95, UK Parly Foreign Affrs Ctee 2000; conslt US Dept of Energy 1993–99; memb: Research Cncl Chemical and Biological Arms Control Inst Washington DC 1995–, UK sec of state for Def's Expert Panel for UK's Strategic Def Review 1998; research fell Center for Int Security and Co-operation Stanford Univ 1993–94; *Publications* incl: The Biotechnology Industry of the United States (with L Celeste Johnson, 1995), Escaping the Prison of the Past (1996), The Military Balance (ed and contrib, 5 edns 1995–2001); author of numerous book chapters and articles; *Recreations* tennis, mountain walking, bird watching; *Style*— Terence Taylor, Esq, MBE; ✉ International Institute for Strategic Studies, Arundel House, 13–15 Arundel Street, London WC2R 3DX (tel 020 7379 7676, fax 020 7836 3108); International Institute for Strategic Studies - US, 1747 Pennsylvania Avenue NW, Suite 700, Washington DC 20006, USA (tel 00 1 202 659 1490, fax 00 1 202 296 1134, e-mail taylor@iiss.org)

TAYLOR, Wendy Ann (Mrs Bruce Robertson); CBE (1988); da of Edward Philip Taylor, and Lilian Maude, *née* Wright; *b* 29 July 1945; *Educ* St Martin's Sch of Art (LDAD); *m* 1982, Bruce Robertson, s of Maurice Robertson; 1 s (Matthew Thomas b 1984); *Career* sculptor; examiner Univ of London 1982–83, memb Ct RCA 1982–, memb Cncl Morley Coll 1985–88, conslt New Town Cmmn Basildon (formerly Basildon Devpt Corp) 1985–88, specialist advsr Fine Art Bd CNAA 1985–93 (memb 1980–85, memb Ctee for Art Design 1987–91), memb Royal Fine Art Cmmn 1981–99, design conslt London Borough of Barking and Dagenham 1989–93 and 1997–2003; memb London Docklands Design Advsy Bd 1989–98; tstee LAMA 1993–; memb PCFC 1989–90; fell Queen Mary & Westfield Coll London 1993; FZS 1989, FRBS 1994, FRSA 2004; *Solo Exhibitions* Axiom Gallery London 1970, Angela Flowers Gallery London 1972, 24 King's Lynn Festival Norfolk and World Trade Centre London 1974, Annely Juda Fine Art London 1975, Oxford Gallery Oxford 1976, Oliver Dowling Gallery Dublin 1976 and 1979, Building Art The Process (Building Centre Gallery) 1986, Nature and Engineering (The Osborne Gp London) 1998–, Austin Desmond & Phipps 1992, Cass Gallery London 2005; shown in over 100 gp exhibitions 1964–82; represented in collections in: GB, USA, Repub of Ireland, NZ, Germany, Sweden, Qatar, Switzerland, Seychelles; *Major Commissions* The Travellers London 1969, Gazebo (edn of 4 London, NY, Oxford, Suffolk) 1970–72, Triad Oxford 1971, Timepiece London 1973, Calthae Leics 1977, Octo Milton Keynes 1979, Counterpoise Birmingham 1980, Compass Bowl Basildon 1980, Sentinel Reigate 1982,

Bronze Relief Canterbury 1981, Equatorial Sundial Bletchley 1982, Essence Milton Keynes 1982, Opus Morley Coll 1983, Gazebo Golder's Hill Park London 1983, Network London 1984, Geo I and Geo II Stratford-upon-Avon 1985, Landscape and Tree of the Wood Fenhurst Surrey 1986, Pharos Peel Park E Kilbride 1986, Ceres Fenhurst Surrey 1986, Nexus Corby Northants 1986, Globe Sundial Swansea Maritime Quarter 1987, Spirit of Enterprise Isle of Dogs London 1987, Silver Fountain Guildford Surrey 1988, The Whirlies E Kilbride 1988, Pilot Kites Norwich Airport 1988, Fire Flow Hamilton Scotland 1988, Armillary Sundial Basildon Essex 1989, Pharos II E Kilbride 1989, Phoenix E Kilbride 1990, Globe Sundial London Zoological Gardens, Continuum Guildford, Sundial Sheffield 1991, Anchorage Salford Quays Manchester, Square Piece Plano Illinois USA, Wyvern Leicestershire 1992, Railings Univ of Sheffield 1993, Stained Glass Window St George's Church Sheffield 1994, Jester Emmanuel Coll Cambridge 1994, Jester II New York 1994, Challenge Stockley Park Middlesex, Equilibrium London 1995, Spirit Vann Surrey, Rope Circle London 1997, Spirit of Barrow Cumbria 1997, Waves London 1998; Dancer Chelsea and Westminster Hosp 1999, Dung Beetles Millennium Conservation Bldg Zoological Soc London 1999, Mariners Astrolabe Brunswick Quay London 1999, Globe View Blackfriars London 2000, Millennium Fountain New River Loop Chase Gardens Enfield 2000, Tortoises With Triangle and Time Holland Park London 2000, Voyager Cinnibar Wharf London 2001, Three Reclining Rope Figures GlaxoSmithKline Middx 2001, Conqueror GlaxoSmithKline Middx 2001, Through the Loop Pacific Place Hong Kong 2002, Around the Square Pacific Place Hong Kong 2002, Chain Piece Warren OH 2002, Knowledge QMC London 2003, Acorn Wall Relief Brunswick Wharf London 2003, Anchor Iron Anchor Iron Wharf Greenwich 2004, Feather Piece Capital East London 2005, Gravesham Heritage 2006, Silver Fountain II Bryn Mawr Pennsylvania; *Awards* Walter Neurath 1964, Pratt 1965, Sainsbury 1966, Arts Cncl 1977, Duais Na Riochta (Kingdom prize), Gold medal Repub of Ireland 1977, winner silk screen Barcham Green Print Competition 1978, Civic Tst Partnership Award Chase Green Enfield 2002, Building of the Year Award Architectural Sculpture 2004; *Recreations* gardening; *Style*— Ms Wendy Taylor, CBE; ✉ 73 Bow Road, Bow, London E3 2AN (tel 020 8981 2037, fax 020 8980 3153, website www.wendytaylorsculpture.co.uk)

TAYLOR, Prof Sir William; kt (1990), CBE (1982); s of Herbert Taylor (d 1969), and Maud Ethel, *née* Peyto (d 1972); *b* 31 May 1930; *Educ* Erith GS, LSE (BScEcon), Westminster Coll London (PGCE), Univ of London Inst of Educn (DipEd, PhD); *m* 30 Dec 1954, Rita, da of Ronald Hague (d 1957); 2 da (Anne Catherine (Mrs Mitchell) b 12 April 1958, Rosemary Caroline (Dr Williams) b 11 March 1960), 1 s (Dr Richard William James b 27 July 1964); *Career* Nat Serv Royal West Kent Regt 1948–49, Intelligence Corps 1950–53, 135 Field Security Section TA; teacher in Kent 1953–59, dep head Slade Green Secdy Sch 1956–59, sr lectr St Luke's Coll Exeter 1959–61, princ lectr and head of Educn Dept Bede Coll Durham 1961–64, tutor and lectr in educn Univ of Oxford 1964–66, prof of educn Univ of Bristol 1966–73, dir Univ of London Inst of Educn 1973–83, princ Univ of London 1983–85, vice-chllr Univ of Hull 1985–91, hon fell Green Coll and visiting prof Univ of Oxford 1991–97, vice-chllr Univ of Huddersfield 1994–95, vice-chllr Thames Valley Univ 1998–99, head Winchester Sch of Art 2004; emeritus fell Univ of London Inst of Educn 1995–; chm of convocation Univ of London 1994–97, academic advsr SE Essex Coll 2000–03, Jersey Scholarship Scheme 2000–05, specialist advsr House of Commons Educn and Skills Ctee 2000–04 and 2007–; chm: Educnl Advsy Cncl of the IBA 1977–83, Univs Cncl for the Educn of Teachers 1976–79, Ctee for Educnl Res Cncl of Europe 1968–71, Nat Fndn for Educnl Res 1984–88, Cncl for the Accreditation of Teacher Educn (CATE) 1984–93, Univs Cncl for Adult and Continuing Educn 1986–90, NFER/Nelson Publishing Co 1988–99, NI Teacher Educn Ctee 1994–2002, Seven Year Review Ctee Univ of Ulster 1998–99, CVCP Higher Educn Funding Options Review Gp 2000–01, IOW Tertiary Strategy Gp 2002–03, Southampton Local Area Review 2002–04, Strategic Area Review of 16+ Educn and Trg in Hants and IOW 2002–05; dir Fenner plc 1988–93; visiting prof Univ of Southampton 1998–; pres: Cncl for Educn in World Citizenship 1980–90, Assoc of Colls of Further and HE 1985–88, Soc for Research into HE 1996–2001 (vice-pres 2004); vice-pres Cncl for International Educn 1992–97; govr: Univ of Glamorgan 1991–2002, Christ Church Coll Canterbury 1996–2004; memb Cncl Hong Kong Inst of Educn 1998–2004; Freeman City of London 1986, Liveryman Worshipful Soc of Apothecaries 1986; Hon DSc Aston Univ 1977, Hon LittD Univ of Leeds 1979, Hon DCL Univ of Kent 1981, Hon DUniv Open Univ 1983, Hon DLitt Loughborough Univ 1984, Hon LLD Univ of Hull 1992; Hon DEd: Univ of Kingston 1993, Univ of Plymouth 1993, Oxford Brookes Univ 1993, Univ of the West of England 1994, Queen's Univ Belfast 1997, Univ of London 1999, Hong Kong Inst of Educn 2004; Hon DScEcon Univ of Huddersfield 1996, Hon DSc(Soc Sci) Univ of Southampton 1998, Hon DUniv Ulster 2000, Hon LLD Univ of Bristol 2001; Hon DLitt: Univ of Leicester 2004, Univ of Glamorgan 2004; Hon DUniv Essex 2004; hon fell Westminster Coll Oxford 1990, centenary fell Thames Poly 1991, fell Christ Church Univ Coll Canterbury 2004; FCP 1977, FCCEA 1978; *Books* The Secondary Modern School (1963), Educational Administration and the Social Sciences (ed jtly 1969, Japanese edn 1970), Society and the Education of Teachers (1969), Towards a Policy for the Education of Teachers (ed, 1969), Policy and Planning in Post Secondary Education (1971), Theory into Practice (1972), Heading for Change (1973), Research Perspectives in Education (ed, 1973), Perspectives and Plans for Graduate Studies (with Downey, Daniels and Baker, 1973), Educational Administration in Australia and Abroad (jt ed with Thomas and Farquhar, 1975), Research and Reform in Teacher Education (1978), Education for the Eighties - the Central Issues (ed with Simon, 1981), New Zealand - OECD Reviews of National Policies for Education (with P H Karmel and Ingrid Eide, 1983), Metaphors of Education (ed, 1984), Universities under Scrutiny (1987); *Recreations* books, music; *Style*— Prof Sir William Taylor, CBE; ✉ 20 Bedford Way, London WC1H 0AL (tel 01962 883485, e-mail william.taylor@btinternet.com)

TAYLOR, William Gibson (Bill); s of John Taylor (d 1983), and Brenda Louise, *née* Gibson; *b* 27 January 1957; *Educ* Rushcliffe Comprehensive Sch Nottingham, Univ of Sheffield (RIBA Nat Students prize, MA, Dip Architecture); *m* 1982, Denise, da of George Roper; 2 s (Robert John Gibson b 1987, Andrew George Gibson b 1989); *Career* worked with Mervyn Awon (architect) on Central Bank of Barbados 1979–80; ptnr Michael Hopkins and Partners 1988– (architect 1982–88); external examiner: Univ of Nottingham, Sheffield Hallam Univ; visiting tutor Queen's Univ Belfast; memb: Br Cncl of Offices, RIBA Sustainable Futures Ctee, Pan European Tensinet Working Gp into Membrane Architecture, Olympic Design Review Panel CABE 2006–; RIBA (assessor), FRSA; *Style*— Bill Taylor, Esq; ✉ Hopkins Architects, 27 Broadley Terrace, London NW1 6LG (tel 020 7724 1751, fax 020 7723 0932, e-mail bill.t@hopkins.co.uk)

TAYLOR, William James; QC (Scot 1986), QC (1998); s of Cecil Taylor (d 1997), of Inverness, and Ellen, *née* Daubney; *b* 13 September 1944; *Educ* Robert Gordon's Coll, Univ of Aberdeen (MA, LLB, pres Aberdeen Univ Union, vice-pres Scottish Union of Students); *Career* admitted Faculty of Advocates 1971, standing jr DHSS 1978–79, standing jr counsel FCO 1979–86, called to the Bar Inner Temple 1990, first person to hold rank QC in Scot and Eng; memb Criminal Injuries Compensation Bd 1997–2000; temp sheriff 1997–99, memb Scot Criminal Cases Review Cmmn 1998–2004; cncllr (Lab) Edinburgh Corporation 1973–75, cncllr (Lab) Lothian Regnl Cncl 1974–82; arbitrator Motor Insurers Bureau; pt/t Sheriff 2003–; chm Scottish Opera 2004–; FRSA; *Recreations* music, theatre, restoring a garden, cooking, Scottish mountains, sailing; *Clubs* Royal Highland Yacht; *Style*— William Taylor, Esq, QC; ✉ Parliament House, Parliament Square, Edinburgh EH1 1RF (tel 0131 226 2881, fax 0131 225 3642, e-mail william.taylor@wanadoo.fr); 2–4 Tudor Street, London EC4Y 0AA (tel 020 7797 7111)

TAYLOR BRADFORD, Barbara; *see:* Bradford, Barbara Taylor

TAYLOR OF BLACKBURN, Baron (Life Peer UK 1978), of Blackburn in the County of Lancaster; Thomas Taylor; CBE (1974, OBE 1969), JP (Blackburn 1960), DL (Lancs 1994); s of James Taylor; *b* 10 June 1929; *Educ* Blakey Moor Higher Grade Sch; *m* 1950, Kathleen, da of John Edward Nurton; 1 s (Hon Paul Nurton b 1953); *Career* memb Blackburn Town Cncl 1954–76 (ldr, and chm Policy and Resources Ctee 1972–76), dep pro-chllr Lancaster Univ 1972–95 (elected life memb Ct), chm Govt Ctee of Enquiry into Mgmnt and Govt of Schs, non-exec dir Grove Ltd 1997– (chm), past chm Juvenile Bench; non-exec dir AES Drax Ltd 2001–04; conslt: BAE Systems plc 1994–, Initial Electronic Security Systems Ltd; advsr: Electronic Data Systems Ltd 1992–, AES Electric Ltd 1999–, Experian 1999–, United Utilities plc 2000–; pres: Free Church Cncl 1962–68, Mill Hill Community Centre Blackburn, Friends of Blackburn Museum and Art Gallery, Assoc of Lancastrians London; patron: Lancashire Wildlife Tst, Friends of Real Lancashire 1999–, Outreach Schools, Holidays for Carers 2000–, Alzheimers Soc (Blackburn, Darwen, Hyndburn and Ribble valley Branch); former memb: Norweb Bd, Select Ctee on Sci and Technol, Cwlth Parly Assoc; Hon LLD Lancaster Univ 1996; Freeman: City of London, Borough of Blackburn; FRGS 1994; *Style*— The Rt Hon the Lord Taylor of Blackburn, CBE, DL

TAYLOR OF BOLTON, Baroness (Life Peer UK 2005), of Bolton in the County of Greater Manchester; (Winifred) Ann Taylor; PC (1997); *b* 2 July 1947; *Educ* Bolton Sch, Univ of Bradford, Univ of Sheffield; *m*; 1 s (b 1982), 1 da (b 1983); *Career* MP (Lab) Bolton W Oct 1974–83 (also contested Feb 1974), Parly candidate Bolton NE 1983, MP (Lab) Dewsbury 1987–2005; PPS to: Sec of State for Defence 1976–77, Sec of State DES 1975–76; Govt whip 1977–79; oppn front bench spokesman: on educn 1979–81, on housing 1981–83, on home affrs 1987–88; memb Shadow Cabinet 1990–97; chief oppn spokesman: on environmental protection 1988–92, on educn 1992–94; shadow chllr of Duchy of Lancaster 1994–95; shadow ldr House of Commons 1994–97, Pres of the Cncl and Ldr of the House of Commons 1997–98, Parly sec to the Treasy (Govt chief whip) 1998–2001; memb Select Ctee on Standards in Public Life (Nolan Select Ctee) 1995, memb Standards and Privileges Ctee 1995–97; chair Select Ctee on Modernisation 1997–98, Intelligence and Security Ctee 2001; dep chair Independent Football Cmmn 2002–; memb Jt Ctee on Parly Privilege 1997–99; former teacher, tutor Open Univ; *Books* Political Action (with Jim Firth, 1978), Choosing Our Future (1992); *Style*— The Rt Hon the Lady Taylor of Bolton, PC

TAYLOR OF HOLBEACH, Baron (Life Peer 2006), of South Holland in the County of Lincolnshire; John Derek Taylor; CBE (1992); s of Percy Otto Taylor (d 2000), and Ethel, *née* Brocklehurst; *b* 12 November 1943, Holbeach, Lincs; *Educ* St Felix Sch Felixstowe, Bedford Sch; *m* 18 April 1968, Julia Aileen, *née* Cunnington; 2 s (Hon Giles Edward Augustus b 15 Feb 1972, Hon Adam Edwin John b 3 May 1975); *Career* dir Taylors Bulbs of Spalding 1968–, chm Springfields Horticultural Soc 2000– (dir 1991–), chm EC Working Pty on European Bulb Industry 1982, chm Bulb Sub-Ctee NFU 1982–87; govr: Glasshouse Crops Research Inst 1984–88, Inst of Horticultural Research 1987–90; memb: Horticultural Devpt Cncl 1986–91, Min of Agriculture's Regnl Panel (Eastern Region) 1990–92 and (East Midlands Region) 1992–96; sits as Cons in House of Lords 2006–, oppn whip and spokesman on environment, work and pensions, and Wales 2006–07, shadow min for DEFRA and oppn whip for work and pensions 2007–; Cons Pty: memb Exec Ctee E Midlands Cncl 1966–98, memb Bd of Finance 1985–89, memb Bd of Mgmnt 1996–98 and 2000–03, pres Nat Union of Cons Assoc and chm Pty Conf 1997–98, dep pty chm 2000–03, chm Nat Cons Convention 2000–03, chair Conservatives Abroad 2001–, chm Candidates Ctee 2002–05, chm Cons Agents Superannuation Fund 2006–; Parly candidate (Cons): Chesterfield (gen election) 1974, Nottingham (European Parl election) 1979; tstee Brogdale Horticultural Tst 1998–2005; chm Holbeach and Elloe Hosp Charitable Tst 1989–2006 (patron 2006–); memb: Lincoln Diocesan Bd of Finance 1995–2001 (memb Assets Ctee 1995–2001 and 2003–), Lincoln Diocesan Synod 1997–2001; FRSA 1994; *Publications* Taylor's Bulb Book (ed, 1994); *Recreations* English landscape and vernacular buildings, travel (particularly in France), literature, arts, music; *Clubs* Farmers'; *Style*— The Lord Taylor of Holbeach, CBE; ✉ House of Lords, London SW1A 0PW (tel 020 7219 3000)

TAYLOR OF WARWICK, Baron (Life Peer UK 1996), of Warwick in the County of Warwickshire; John David Beckett; s of Derief David Samuel Taylor (d 1979), and Enid Maud, *née* Beckett; *b* 21 September 1952; *Educ* Moseley GS, Keele Univ (BA); *m* 1982, Katherine; 2 da (Laura b 29 Oct 1987, Alexandra 16 Feb 1995), 1 s (Mark b 31 Oct 1997); *Career* called to the Bar Gray's Inn 1978 (Advocacy Prize 1978), pt/t judge 1997; legal advsr to: IPC Magazines Ltd 1992–, Kaim Todner Slrs 1992–, BBC 1992–, Teletext Ltd 1992–; md City Technology Colleges Tst 1992–93, non-exec dir North West Regional HA 1992–94, chm Warwick Communications Ltd 1993–; vice-pres: National Small Business Bureau 1998–, British Board of Film Classification 1998–; corp and media advsr 1991–92, media conslt Ashurst Morris Crisp Ltd 1996–97, presenter BBC TV, Carlton TV and Sky TV 1992–97; non-exec chm World Sports Solutions plc 2002–; cncllr Solihull BC 1986–90, Parly candidate Cheltenham 1992; dir Warwick Leadership Fndn (Charity) 1993–; pres African Caribbean Westminster Business Initiative; patron Kidscape Children's Charity 1996–; memb: Variety Club of Great Britain Children's Charity, Ctee Sickle Cell Anaemia Relief Charity (SCAR), Steering Gp for METO (Nat Training Organisation for Mgmnt and Enterprise) DTI 1999–, Independent Football Cmmn 2002–; chllr Bournemouth Univ 2002–; Freedom of London 1999–; fell Industry and Parly Tst 1997, Hon LLD Warwick 1999; MInstD 1997; *Recreations* football (pres Ilford Town FC), cricket, golf, singing; *Style*— The Rt Hon Lord Taylor of Warwick; ✉ House of Lords, London SW1A 0PW (tel 020 7219 0665, fax 020 7219 5979, e-mail taylorjdb@parliament.uk, websites www.lordtaylor.org and www.warwickleadership.org)

TAYLOR-WOOD, Sam; *b* 4 March 1967, London; *Educ* Goldsmiths Coll London; *m* 1997, Jay Jopling, *qv*; 1 da (Angelica b April 1997); *Career* artist; Illy Cafe Prize Most Promising Young Artist Venice Biennale 1997, nominated Turner Prize 1998; *Solo Exhibitions* incl: Killing Time (The Showroom London) 1994, Gallerie Andreas Brändström Stockholm 1995, Travesty of a Mockery (Jay Jopling/White Cube London) 1995–96, Pent-Up (Chisenhale Gallery London, Sunderland City Art Gallery) 1996–97, 16mm (Ridinghouse Editions London) 1996; Sustaining the Crisis (Regen Projects LA) 1997, Five Revolutionary Seconds (Sala Montcada de la Fundacio 'La Caixa' Barcelona) 1997, Kunsthalle Zurich 1997, Louisiana MOMA Humlebaek 1997, Prada Fndn Milan 1998, Donald Young Gallery Seattle 1998, Directions (Hirshorn Museum and Sculpture Garden Washington) 1999, Wüttembergischer Kunstverein Stuttgart 1999, Matthew Marks Gallery NY 2000, Espacio Uno Madrid 2000, Centrum Sztuki Współczesnej Zamek Ujazdowski Warsaw 2000, Photographies et films (Centre Nationale de la Photographie Paris) 2001, Kunstlerverein Malkasten Düsseldorf 2001, Mute (White Cube London) 2001, Shiseido Tokyo 2002, Films and Photographs (Stedelijk Museum Amsterdam) 2002, Hayward Gallery London 2002, Musée d'Art Contemporain de Montréal Quebec 2002, Bawag Fndn Vienna 2003, David (Nat Portrait Gallery London) 2004, Strings (Edinburgh Coll of Art) 2004, Sorrow, Suspension, Ascension (Matthew Marks Gall NY) 2004, New Work (White Cube) 2004, Ascension (Donald Young Gallery Chicago) 2004, Sam Taylor-Wood (State Russian Museum St Petersburg and Museum Contemporary Art Moscow) 2004, Sex and Death and A Few Trees (Galleria Lorcan O'Neill Rome) 2005;

T

Group Exhibitions incl: Showhide Show (Anderson O'Day Gallery London) 1991, Clove Two Gallery London 1992, Close Up (Times Square NY) 1993, Consider the End: Sam Taylor-Wood and PPQ (HQ Redchurch Street London) 1993, Perfect Speed (Toronto, Florida and tour) 1995, Brilliant! New Art from London (Walker Art Centre Minneapolis, Contemporary Art Museum Houston) 1995, Masculin/Feminin (Centre Pompidou Paris) 1995, General Release (Venice Biennale) 1995, Artisti Brittanci a Roma, Festival of Contemporary British Arts (Maggazini d'Arte Moderna Rome) 1996, Contemporary British Art (Toyama Museum) 1996, Full House: Young British Art (Kunstmuseum Wolfsburg) 1996, Speaking of Sofas ICA Biennale of Film and Video (ICA London) 1996, Art & Video in Europe. Electronic Undercurrents (Statens Museum für Kunst Copenhagen) 1996, Sam Taylor-Wood and Pierrick Sorin (Creux de l'Enfer Thiers) 1997, Venice Biennale 1997, Montreal Film Festival 1997, Sensation (Royal Acad of Arts London) 1997, 5th Istanbul Biennial 1997, 2nd Johannesburg Biennale 1997, New British Video Programme (MOMA NY) 1997, Video: Bruce Nauman, Tony Oursler, Sam Taylor-Wood (San Francisco MOMA) 1998, New Photography (MOMA NY) 1998, Turner Prize (Tate Gallery London) 1998, Sam Taylor-Wood, Tracey Emin, Gillian Wearing, Marc Quinn (Galerija DanteMarino Cettina) 1998, Art from the UK: Angela Bulloch, Willie Doherty, Tracey Emin, Sarah Lucas, Sam Taylor-Wood (Sammlung Goetz Munich) 1998, Looking at Ourselves: Works by Women Artists from the Logan Colection (San Francisco MOMA) 1999, Moving Images. Film - Reflexion in der Kunst (Galerie für Zeitgenössische Kunst Leipzig) 1999, The History of the Turner Prize (Artsway Sway) 1999, Imagen em Movimento Image (Chiva São Paulo) 1999, Fourth Wall: Turner on the Thames (Public Arts Devpt Tst South Bank London) 2000, Sincerely Yours. British Art from the 90's (Astrup Fearnely MOMA Oslo) 2000, Making Time: Considering Time as a Material in Contemporary Video & Film (Palm Beach Inst of Contemporary Art) 2000, Out There (White Cube 2 London) 2000, Media City Seoul 2000, Nurture and Desire (in aid of Breakthrough Breast Cancer, Hayward Gallery London) 2000, Contemporary Film and Video (Moderna Museet Stockholm) 2000, Beautiful Productions: Art to Play, art to wear, art to own (Whitechapel Art Gallery London) 2001, A Baroque Party - Moments of Theatrum Mundi in Contemporary Art (Kunsthalle Vienna) 2001, The Body of Art (Valencia Biennial) 2001, Idea Festival Video in the City (Centrum Hedendaagse Kunst Maastrict) 2001, 6 Biennale d'Art Contemporain de Lyon (Musée d'Art Contemporain de Lyon) 2001, Intimacy (Paco des Artes São Paulo) 2002, The Rowan Collection Contemporary British & Irish Art (Irish MOMA Dublin) 2002, Landscape (Saatchi Gallery London) 2002, Embracing the Present: The UBS PaineWebber Art Collection (Portland Art Museum) 2002, Animal, Vegetable, Mineral (Israel Museum Jerusalem) 2002, Social Strategies, Redefining Social Realism (Univ Art Museum Univ of Calif) 2003, Revelation: Representations of Christ in Photography (Israel Museum Jerusalem and Int House of Photography Hamburg) 2003, A Bigger Splash: British Art from Tate 1960–2003 (Pavilhão Lucas Nogueira Garcez São Paulo) 2003, Make Life Beautiful! The Dandy in Photography (Brighton Museum and Art Gallery) 2003, A Century of Artists' Film in Britain (Tate Britain London) 2003, Something More Than Five Revolutionary Seconds (Fondazione Davide Halevim Milan) 2003, Ideal and Reality. A History of the Nude form Neoclassicism to the Present Day (Galleria d'Arte Moderna Bologna) 2004, Contemporary Photography Collection (Fundacion Telefonica Madrid) 2004, Symbolic Space & Repetition (Hudson Valley Centre for Contemporary Art NY) 2004, Other Times British Contemporary Art (City Art Gallery Prague) 2004, Secrets of the 90's (Museum voor Moderne Kunst Arnhem) 2004, Unframed (Standpoint Gallery London) 2004, Some Versions of Light (The Telephone Repeater Station Brompton-on-Swale) 2004, Uproar of Emotions (Museum für Photographie Braunschweig) 2004, The Charged Image (Joseloff Gallery Connecticut) 2004, Hors d'Oeuvre (Cap Musee d'Art Contemporain de Bordeaux) 2004, Canterbury Festival 2004, Perspectives @ 25 (Museum of Contemporary Art Houston) 2004, Masters of Illusion: 150 Years of Trompe 'Oeil in America (Kresge Art Museum MI), The Stuff of Life (City Museum and Art Gallery Bristol and Laing Gallery Newcastle) 2005, Coleccion de Fotografia Contemporanea de Telefonica (MARCO Vigo) 2005, Edvard Munch and the Art of Today (Museum am Ostwall Dortmund) 2005, Between Art and Life (MOMA San Francisco) 2005, Mother and Child (Salvatore Ferragamo NY) 2005, (My Private) Heroes (MARTA Herfod) 2005, Painting on Photography: Photography on Painting (Museum of Contemporary Photography Chicago) 2005, Body: New Art from the UK (Vancouver Art Gallery) 2005, Chronos (CeSAC Caraglio) 2005, Bidibidobidiboo (Turin) 2005; *Works in Collections* incl: New Orleans Museum, Royal Museum of Fine Arts Copenhagen, San Francisco MOMA, Tate Gallery London, Nat Portrait Gallery London, Israel Museum Jerusalem, Fondacio 'La Caixa' Barcelona, Saatchi Collection London, British Cncl London, Samsung Museum, The Robert Shiffler Collection Greenville, Bangkok Museum of Contemporary Art; *Books* Unhinged (1996), Contact (2001), Crying Men (2004); *Style—* Ms Sam Taylor-Wood; ✉ White Cube, 48 Hoxton Square, London N1 6PB (tel 020 7930 5373, fax 020 7749 7480)

TE KANAWA, Dame Kiri Jeanette; DBE (1982, OBE 1973), ONZ (1995), AC; da of late Thomas Te Kanawa, of Auckland, NZ, and late Elanor Te Kanawa; *b* 6 March 1944, Gisborne, NZ; *Educ* St Mary's Coll Auckland, London Opera Centre; *Children* 1 s, 1 da; *Career* opera singer; studied singing under Dame Sister Mary Leo 1959–65; has sung major roles at: ROH, Met Opera (NY), Paris Opera, San Francisco Opera, Sydney Opera, Cologne Opera, La Scala (Milan); sang at Royal Wedding of HRH Prince of Wales to Lady Diana Spencer 1981; appeared on 2000 Today from Gisborne on 1 January 2000; sang at Queen's Jubilee Concert Buckingham Palace 2002; Hon LLD: Univ of Dundee, Warwick 1989; Hon DMus: Univ of Durham 1982, Univ of Oxford 1983, Univ of Cambridge 1997, Univ of Nottingham 1992, Univ of Waikato 1995, Univ of Sunderland 2003, Univ of Bath 2005; *Publications* Land of the Long White Cloud (1989), Opera for Lovers (1997); *Style—* Dame Kiri Te Kanawa, DBE, ONZ, AC

TEAGUE, His Hon Judge (Edward) Thomas Henry; QC (2000); s of Harry John Teague, and Anne Elizabeth, *née* Hunt; *b* 21 May 1954, Weymouth, Dorset; *Educ* St Francis Xavier's Coll Liverpool, Christ's Coll Cambridge (MA); *m* 8 Aug 1980, Helen Mary, da of Daniel Matthew Howard (d 1974); 2 s (Michael b 1983, Dominic b 1985); *Career* called to the Bar Inner Temple 1977; in practice Wales & Chester Circuit 1978–2006, in practice Western Circuit 2002–06, recorder 1997–2006 (asst recorder 1993–97), circuit judge 2006–; legal assessor GMC 2002–06; chm Chester Bar Ctee 2004–06; author of various astronomical papers; FRAS; *Style—* His Hon Judge Teague, QC

TEAR, Robert; CBE (1984); s of Thomas Arthur Tear, of Barry, S Glam, and Edith Marion Tear; *b* 8 March 1939; *Educ* Barry GS, King's Coll Cambridge (MA); *m* 10 Jan 1961, Hilary, da of William Thomas, of Cwmbran, Gwent; 2 da (Rebecca b 22 Nov 1961, Elizabeth b 11 Feb 1966); *Career* opera/concert singer and conductor; regular appearances: throughout America, Covent Garden, Munich, Paris, Salzburg, Brussels and Geneva; holder of Chair of Int Vocal Studies at RAM; hon fell King's Coll Cambridge 1988; Hon DMus RSAMD; RAM, RCM; *Books* Tear Here (1990), Singer Beware (1995); *Recreations* anything interesting; *Clubs* Arts; *Style—* Robert Tear, Esq, CBE; ✉ c/o Askonas Holt, Lonsdale Chambers, 27 Chancery Lane, London WC2A 1PF

TEARE, (Eleanor) Christine; da of James Ralph Teare (d 1990), of the Isle of Man, and Kathleen Mona, *née* Duggan; *b* 21 March 1956, IOM; *Educ* Castle Rushen HS IOM, Royal Acad of Music (two scholarships from Countess of Munster Fndn, DipRAM); *Career* soprano; princ soprano WNO 1985–89, freelance 1989–; roles with WNO incl: Donna Anna in Don Giovanni (debut) 1982, Die Kaiserin in Die Frau ohne Schatten, Amelia in Un Ballo in Maschera, Countess Almaviva in The Marriage of Figaro, Ortlinde and Helmwig in Die Walküre; other opera roles incl: Donna Anna (Opera North) 1986, First Lady in The Magic Flute (ENO) 1986, Helmwig in Die Walküre (ROH debut) 1988 (also Ortlinde, Helmwig and Third Norn in full Ring Cycle 1991), Berta in The Barber of Seville (ENO) 1992, title role in Turandot (ROH) 1996, Flower Maiden in Parsifal (ENO), Donna Anna in Don Giovanni (Opera North), Brünnhilde in Das Ringchen (Pocket Opera Nuremburg), Die Kaiserin in Die Frau Ohne Schatten (Augsburg), Tosca (Augsburg), title role in Elektra (Hagen Opera Dortmund) 2006; concert performances incl: Elgar's The Kingdom, Verdi's Requiem, Haydn's Creation and Schoenberg's Gurrelieder, Marietta in Korngold's Die Tote Stadt (Queen Elizabeth Hall London); ARCM, FTCL, Hon ARAM; *Recreations* theatre, golf, Manx history and culture; *Style—* Miss Christine Teare; ✉ website www.christineteare soprano.co.uk

TEARE, His Hon Judge Jonathan James; s of Prof Donald Teare (d 1979), and Kathleen Agnes Teare; *b* 13 December 1946; *Educ* Rugby, Middle Temple; *m* 1972, Nicola Jill, da of Lt Col Peter Spittall; 2 da (Caroline Clare b 20 December 1974, Joanna Hazel b 6 June 1977); *Career* HAC 1965–69, RRF (TA) 1970–72; called to the Bar Middle Temple 1970; in practice Midland & Oxford Circuit 1971–98, asst recorder 1985–90, recorder 1990–98, circuit judge (Midland & Oxford Circuit) 1998–, presiding sr judge Sovereign Base Areas Cyprus 2007– (dep sr judge 2001–07); memb Mental Health Review Tbnl 2002–; tstee Hollygirt Sch; Freeman City of London 1981, Liveryman Worshipful Soc of Apothecaries 1980; *Recreations* travel, shooting, wine; *Style—* His Hon Judge Teare; ✉ Nottingham Crown Court, 60 Canal Street, Nottingham NG1 7EL (tel 0115 910 3551, e-mail hhjudge.teare@judiciary.gsi.gov.uk)

TEARE, Hon Mr Justice; Sir Nigel John Martin; kt (2006); s of Eric John Teare (d 1980), and Mary Rackham, *née* Faragher (d 1985); *b* 8 January 1952; *Educ* King William's Coll Castletown IOM, St Peter's Coll Oxford (MA); *m* 16 Aug 1975, (Elizabeth) Jane, da of Alan James Pentecost, of Nottingham; 2 s (Roland b 1981, David b 1984), 1 da (Charlotte b 1982); *Career* called to the Bar Lincoln's Inn 1974, jr counsel to treasy in Admty matters 1989–91, QC 1991, recorder 1997–2006 (asst recorder 1993–97), actg deemster IOM High Ct 1998–, judge of the High Court of Justice (Queen's Bench Div) 2006– (dep judge High Court 2002); memb Panel Lloyd's Salvage Arbitrators 1994; arbitrator Lloyd's Salvage Appeal 2000; *Recreations* collecting Manx paintings, golf, squash, tennis; *Clubs* RAC; *Style—* The Hon Mr Justice Teare; ✉ c/o Royal Courts of Justice, Strand, London WC2A 2LL

TEASDALE, Anthony Laurence; s of John S Teasdale, of Beverley, E Yorks, and Pauline, *née* Tomlinson (d 1983); *b* 4 June 1957; *Educ* Slough GS, Balliol Coll Oxford (MA), Nuffield Coll Oxford (MPhil); *m* 2001, Jacqueline Louise Philips; *Career* lectr in politics CCC and Magdalen Coll Oxford 1980–82; policy advsr European Democratic Gp in European Parl Brussels and London 1982–86, asst to DG for Econ and Fin Affrs EC Cncl of Mins Brussels 1986–88; special advsr to: Sec of State for Foreign and Cwlth Affrs 1988–89, Lord Pres of the Cncl and Ldr of House of Commons 1989–90, Chllr of the Exchequer 1996–97; research fell Nuffield Coll Oxford 1992–93; head London office EPP-ED Gp in European Parl Brussels 1993–96 and 1997–2002, sec-gen Cons in European Parl 1999–2002, head of policy strategy EPP-ED Gp in European Parl 2002–07, head of strategy Office of the Pres of the European Parl 2007–; *Recreations* music, reading, travel; *Style—* Anthony Teasdale, Esq; ✉ 2 Queen Anne's Gate, London SW1H 9AA (tel 020 7222 1994, e-mail anthony.teasdale@europarl.europa.eu)

TEATHER, Sarah; MP; *b* 1 June 1974; *Educ* Univ of Cambridge; *Career* former health and social policy advsr Macmillan Cancer Relief; cncllr (Lib Dem) Islington BC 2002–03; MP (Lib Dem) (by-election) Brent East 2003– (Parly candidate (Lib Dem) Finchley and Golders Green 2001); Lib Dem spokesperson: on health 2003–04, for London 2004–05, for community and local govt 2005–, for educn 2006–; *Style—* Ms Sarah Teather, MP; ✉ House of Commons, London SW1A 0AA

TEBBIT, Sir Kevin Reginald; KCB (2002), CMG (1997); *b* 1946; *Educ* Cambridgeshire HS for Boys, St John's Coll Cambridge (sr history scholar); *m*; 2 c; *Career* joined MOD 1969, asst private sec to Sec of State MOD 1972, on secondment HM Dip Serv as first sec UK delegation to NATO Brussels 1979–82; HM Dip Serv: with E Euro and Soviet Dept FCO then head of Chancery Turkey 1982–87, dir of Cabinet to NATO Sec-Gen 1987–88, politico-military cnsllr Washington 1988–91, head Econ Relations Dept subsequently dir of resources and chief inspr FCO 1992–97; dep under sec of state for def and intelligence 1997–98, memb Jt Intelligence Ctee 1997–98, dir GCHQ 1998–, perm under sec of state MOD 1998–2005; strategic conslt and co dir 2006–; visiting prof Queen Mary Coll London 2006–; chm Lifeboat Fund 2004–; *Recreations* music, classical archaeology, walking, West Ham United FC; *Style—* Sir Kevin Tebbit, KCB, CMG

TEBBIT, Baron (Life Peer UK 1992), of Chingford in the London Borough of Waltham Forest; Norman Beresford Tebbit; CH (1987), PC (1981); 2 s of Leonard Albert and Edith Tebbit, of Enfield, Middx; *b* 29 March 1931; *Educ* Edmonton Co GS; *m* 1956, Margaret Elizabeth, da of Stanley Daines, of Chatteris; 2 s (Hon John Beresford b 1958, Hon William Mark b 1965), 1 da (Hon Alison Mary b 1960); *Career* RAF 1949–51, RAuxAF 1952–55; journalist 1947–49, in publishing and advertising 1951–53, airline pilot 1953–70 (memb BALPA and former lay official); MP (Cons): Epping 1970–74, Chingford 1974–92; formerly: memb Select Ctee Science and Technol, chm Cons Aviation Ctee, vice-chm and sec Cons Housing and Construction Ctee, sec New Town MPs; PPS to Min of State for Employment 1972–73, Parly under sec of state for trade 1979–81, min of state for industry 1981, sec of state for employment 1981–83, sec of state for trade and industry 1983–85, chllr of Duchy of Lancaster 1985–87, chm Cons Pty 1985–87; political commentator BSkyB television 1989–97; columnist: The Sun 1995–97, Mail on Sunday 1997–2001; dir: BET plc 1987–96, BT plc 1987–96, Sears plc 1987–99, JCB Excavators Ltd 1987–91, The Spectator (1828) Ltd 1989–2004; Liveryman Guild of Air Pilots and Air Navigators; CRAeS; *Books* Upwardly Mobile, An Autobiography (1988), Unfinished Business (1991); *Style—* The Rt Hon Lord Tebbit, CH, PC; ✉ House of Lords, London SW1A 0PW

TEDDER, 3 Baron (UK 1946); Robin John Tedder; s of 2 Baron Tedder (d 1994), and Peggy Eileen, *née* Growcott; *b* 6 April 1955; *m* 1, 1977, Jennifer Peggy (d 1978), da of John Mangan, of Christchurch, NZ; m 2, 1980, (Rita) Aristea, yr da of John Frangidis, of Sydney, Aust; 2 s (Hon Benjamin John b 1985, Hon Christopher Arthur b 1986), 1 da (Hon Jacqueline Christina b 1988); *Heir* s, Hon Benjamin Tedder; *Career* merchant banker and investor; dir of various cos; *Recreations* sailing, golf; *Clubs* Royal Sydney Yacht Squadron, Royal & Ancient Golf (St Andrews), The Australian Golf; *Style—* The Rt Hon the Lord Tedder

TEDDY, Peter Julian; s of Francis Gerald Teddy, of Te Awamutu, NZ, and Beryl Dorothy Fogg; *b* 2 November 1944; *Educ* Rhyl GS, Univ of Wales (BSc), Univ of Oxford (MA, DPhil, BM BCh); *m* 1, 1 June 1974 (m dis 1988), Fiona Margaret, da of late Richard Edward Millard, CBE, JP; 2 s (Alexander Francis b 1982, William Peter b 1986); m 2, 1989, Rosalee Margaret Elliott; 1 s (Timothy James Elliott b 1990); *Career* former conslt neurosurgeon and clinical dir Dept of Neurological Surgery Radcliffe Infirmary Oxford, conslt neurosurgeon Nat Spinal Injuries Centre, Dept of Spinal Neurosurgery Univ of Oxford, Stoke Mandeville Hosp, currently prof and conslt neurosurgeon Dept of Neurosurgery Royal Melbourne Hospital Parkville Victoria; former clinical dir Oxford Neuroscience Directorate; St Peter's Coll Oxford: sr res fell 1983, emeritus fell; clinical sr lectr (formerly dir of clinical studies) Univ of Oxford Med Sch, examiner Surgical Neurology Intercollegiate Bd; formerly asst ed Br Jl of Neurosurgery; memb: Soc Br

Neurological Surgeons, World Fedn Neurosurgery/American Assoc Neurological Surgery, Neurosurgical Soc Australasia, Soc of Univ Neurosurgeons; *Recreations* tennis, volcanology, foreign travel; *Style—* Peter Teddy, Esq

TEED, Roy Norman; s of Thomas Westcott Teed (d 1983), and Jeannette Sutton (d 1956); *b* 18 May 1928; *Educ* KCS Wimbledon, Royal Acad of Music; *m* 30 Dec 1981, Jennifer Ann, da of Frederick Perry, of Colchester, Essex; 1 s (Paul Lennox Perry b 26 Oct 1982), 2 da (Lucy Charlotte Emily b 16 Sept 1985, Trudy Sarah Jane b 4 March 1988); *Career* composer; Nat Serv RAF 1946–49; student RAM 1949–53, prof RAM 1966–92, many appearances as piano accompanist and church organist 1962–79, pt/t teacher Colchester Sixth Form Coll 1987–99 (ret), pt/t piano teacher Music Sch Colchester Inst 1966–79, external music examiner 1967–92; author of articles in RAM magazine 1983 and 1985, numerous concert programme notes; pres Colchester Symphony Orch and Chamber Ensemble; memb: Performing Right Soc, Br Acad of Composers and Songwriters, Incorporated Soc of Musicians, NATFHE, Royal Soc of Musicians, Friends of MBF; FRAM 1977 (memb RAM Guild); *Compositions* incl: Fanfares and March, Piano Trio, Serenade for 10 Winds, Concertino for Treble Recorder and Strings, Piece for a Special Occasion, A Celebration Overture, Scena for Clarinet and Piano, Toccata for Organ (issued on CD), Elegy and Tarantella for Violin and Piano, Sextet Variations, Overture for Organ, Overture, The Overcoat - An Opera in One Act, Music Fills The Air, Music of the Seasons, Te Deum, Music for a Ballet, A Trip to the Zoo, Elegy Scherzo and Trio, The Pardoner's Tale, Five Funny Songs, Five Epitaphs, Rondo with Variations for Violin and Piano, Two Song Cycles, Sonata for Violin and Piano, Fanfare and Wedding March for Organ, words and music for Jack and the Beanstalk, Theme and Variations for Chamber Orch, Concerto-in-One-Movement for Tenor Trombone and Chamber Orch, Siciliano for Oboe and Piano, The Solitary Reaper for High Voice and Piano (issued on CD), Concert Piece for Tenor Trombone and Piano, Fantasy Quartet for Oboe, Horn, 'Cello and Piano, Come Ye People & Christmas Bells (two carols), Far From My Love (song) for Voice and Piano, Concertino for Trumpet and Strings, Fare Well (song) for High Voice and Piano, Toccata II for Solo Organ, Pastoral Interlude for Solo Organ, King Bounce the First (stage work designed for children), Elegy & Scherzando for String Trio, So Various for Viola and Piano, Introduction & Vivace for Solo Organ, Great Things (poem by Thomas Hardy set as solo song with piano and arranged for vocal and string quartet), A Little Suite (for 2 pianos), Meditation and Dance (piano duet), Dingley Dell (concert overture for orchestra), Six Love Songs (for unaccompanied women's voices, incorporating Your Face), Three Songs of Magic and Mystery (for solo voice and piano), Ploughman Singing (for solo voice and piano), String Trio, Phantasy-Rondo for Flute and Piano (also arranged for flute and strings), The Voices of Children (part song with piano), String Quartet in 4 Movements, Improvisation and Dances (for violin and piano), Three Duos (for flute and oboe), Summer Images (a fantasy for organ), Concert Piece (Chamber Orchestra), Four Lyrical Poems (by Siegfried Sassoon, set to music for solo voice and piano), Aubade (for solo cello, horn and strings), Suswo (variations for a symphonic wind orch), 23 Haiku Verses and A Winter Daybreak (both by James Kirkup, set for voice and piano), The Magic Drum (extracts from ongoing opera, libretto by James Kirkup), Tsunami (a capella choir, adapted poem by James Kirkup), Organ Suite, also several arrangements and sundry solo songs; *Recreations* walking, reading, theatre, swimming, my children's company, cooking; *Clubs* RAM; *Style—* Roy Teed, Esq; ✉ 63 Egret Crescent, Longridge Park, Colchester, Essex CO4 3FP (tel 01206 870839)

TEELING SMITH, Prof George; OBE (1983); s of Herbert Teeling Smith, of Edinburgh, and Jessie Sybil, *née* Dickson (d 1983); *b* 20 March 1928; *Educ* Bryanston, Clare Coll Cambridge (BA), Heriot-Watt Coll; *m* 6 Sept 1967, Diana, *née* St John Stevas; *Career* Nat Serv 1946–48; various pharmaceutical industry appts rising to dep md Winthrop Laboratories 1960–62, dir Office of Health Economics 1962–92, assoc prof Health Economics Research Gp Brunel Univ 1980–94; memb NEDO Pharmaceutical Working Party 1975–77, chm Int Sci Policy Fndn 1988–91, advsr Parly Health Ctee 1993–94; chm BUPA Medical Research and Devpt Ltd 1992–99; MPharm Univ of Bradford 1977; FRPharmS 1978; *Books* How to use the NHS (1970), Health Economics, Prospects for the Future (1987), Measuring Health: A Practical Approach (1989); *Recreations* collecting prints; *Style—* Prof George Teeling Smith, OBE; ✉ 87 Bourne Street, London SW1W 8HF (tel 020 7730 3003, e-mail teelingsmith@btinternet.com)

TELLER, Juergen; *b* Erlangen, Germany; *Educ* Bayerische Staatslehranstalt für Photographie Munich; *Career* photographer; campaigns incl: Anna Molinari, Blumarine, Miu Miu, Comme des Garçons, Helmut Lang, Hugo Boss, Katharine Hamnett, Strenesse, Jigsaw, Yves Saint Laurent, Alberto Biani and Alessandro Dell' Aqua, Zucca, Marc Jacobs, Stüssy, Shisedo, Louis Vuitton, Amex, Italian Telecom, Ungaro, Marc Jacobs Perfume; editorial incl: The Face, ID, Arena, Arena Hommes Plus, Vogues Hommes Int, Vogue (French, Italian, Br, American, Aust), Dazed & Confused, French Glamour, Interview, Details, Suddeustche Zeitung magazine, AbeSea, Per Lui, Marie Claire (Germany), Vibe, Six Magazine, Stern, O3 Tokyo Calling, Jo's Magazine, Visionaire, W magazine, Index, Purple, Liberation, Self Service; record covers: Björk, Elton John, Elastica, Simply Red, Hole, Cocteau Twins, A R Kane, Sinead O'Connor, Everything but the Girl, Scritti Politti, Stereo MCs, PM Dawn, Terry Hall, Herbert Gronemeyer, Babaa Maal, Richie Rich, Neneh Cherry, Soul II Soul, Texas, Supergrass, Terranova, New Order; film projects incl: Calvin Klein Eternity commercial 1996 and 2001, Marc Jacobs (short film) CDFA awards, Can I Own Myself (short film starring Kate Moss) 1998, Go-Sees (short film) 2001; *Solo Exhibitions*: Br Cncl RCA 1990, Festival de la Monde (Deauville 1990, Budapest 1991, Barcelona 1992 (Canon Photographer of the Year), Monaco 1993 (solo exhbn winner Photographer of the Year), Paris 1995, Biarritz 1996), Parco (Tokyo) 1992, Positive View (Saatchi Gallery) 1995, Fashion Exposures 1992–95, exhbn for HIV charity NY Acad of Art, 1 Telford Road London 1996, Der Verborgene Brecht Ein Berliner Stadtrundgang (Cubitt Gallery London and Scalo Gallery Zurich) 1998, The Photographers Gallery (London) 1998, Go-Sees (Pitti Imagine Discovery Gallery Florence) 1999, 90 x 60 x 90 (Museo Jacobo Borges Caracas) 2000, Remake Berlin (Fotomuseum Winterthur, Switzerland) 2000, Lehmann Maupin Gallery (NY) 2000 and 2003, Century Cities (Tate Modern London) 2001, Märchenstüberl (Modern Art London) 2001, Munich Fotomuseum 2002, Folkswang Museum 2002; *Group Exhibitions* Tempo Magazine (Hamburg), 2–Kiss (Paris), Jam (Barbican London) 1996, Biennale di Firenze (Florence) 1996, Mayday communities/communication (The Photographers' Gall London) 1999, Living in the Real World (Museum Dhondt-dhaenens Belgium) 2000; *Books* Juergen Teller (1996), Der Vergorgone Brecht, Ein Berliner Stadtrundgang (1997), Go-Sees (1999), Tracht (2001), More (2001); *Style—* Juergen Teller, Esq

TELTSCHER, Bernard Louis; s of Felix Teltscher (d 1978), of Kingston upon Thames, and Lillie, *née* Knoepfmacher (d 1961); *b* 18 February 1923; *Educ* Czech GS Breclav, UCL (BSc), Trinity Coll Cambridge (MA); *m* 1, 1963 (m dis), Irene Gladys Valerie, da of George Nathaniel Hotten, of Carshalton, Surrey; 1 da (Lisa (decd)); m 2, 1978 (m dis), Jill Patricia, da of Ivor Cooper, of London; 1 s (Mark b 1980), 1 da (Natalie b 1981); m 3, 11 March 1991, Catherine Ann, da of Leslie Frankl (d 1965); *Career* wine importer and property developer; chm: Teltscher Bros Ltd 1978–95 (dir 1958–95), chm Teltscher Estates Ltd 1987–; dir: St James's Bridge Club Ltd 1982–92, Wine & Spirit Assoc of GB & NI 1985–86, Wine Devpt Bd 1985–86, Telco Estates Ltd 1989–, C Hotsu Ltd 1989–; Yugoslav Flag with Gold Star; *Recreations* bridge, travel; *Clubs* Portland, Hurlingham; *Style—* Bernard Teltscher, Esq; ✉ 17 Carlyle Square, London SW3 6EX (tel 020 7351 5091, fax 020 7376 7687); Lutomer House, 100 Prestons Road, London E14 9SB (tel 020 7987 5020, fax 020 7537 2428, e-mail blt@teltscher.co.uk)

TEMIRKANOV, Yuri; *Career* conductor; artistic dir and chief conductor Kirov Opera until 1988, music dir and princ conductor St Petersburg Philharmonic Orch 1988–92, princ conductor Royal Philharmonic Orch 1978–98, princ guest conductor Danish Nat Radio Symphony 1997–, conductor laureate Royal Philharmonic Orch 1998–; music dir Baltimore Symphony Orch 2000–; other orchs conducted incl: Berlin Philharmonic, Vienna Philharmonic, Dresden Staatskapelle, Orchestre National de France, Royal Concertgebouw Orch, all major American orchs; recording contract with BMG/RCA 1988–2002; *Style—* Yuri Temirkanov, Esq; ✉ c/o Christian Thompson, IMG Artists Europe, Lovell House, 616 Chiswick High Road, London W4 5RX (tel 020 8233 5800, fax 020 8233 5801)

TEMKIN, Prof Jennifer (Mrs Graham Zellick); da of late Michael Temkin, of London, and late Minnie, *née* Levy; *b* 6 June 1948; *Educ* South Hampstead HS for Girls, LSE, Univ of London (LLB, LLM, LLD), Inns of Court Sch of Law; *m* 18 Sept 1975, Prof Graham John Zellick, s of Reginald H Zellick, of Windsor, Berks; 1 s (Adam b 1977), 1 da (Lara b 1980); *Career* called to the Bar Middle Temple 1971, lectr in law LSE 1971–89, visiting prof of law Univ of Toronto 1978–79, prof of law and dean Sch of Law Univ of Buckingham 1989–92, prof of law Univ of Sussex 1992– (dir Centre for Legal Studies 1994–97); memb: Editorial Advsy Gp Howard Jl of Criminal Justice 1984–, Scrutiny Ctee on Draft Criminal Code Old Bailey 1985–86, Editorial Bd Jl of Criminal Law 1986–2005, Home Sec's Advsy Gp on Use of Video Recordings in Criminal Proceedings 1988–89, Ctee of Heads Univ Law Schs 1989–92 and 1994–97, Nat Children's Home Ctee on Children who Abuse other Children 1990–92, External Reference Gp Home Office Sex Offences Review 1999–2000, Ctee of Experts on the Treatment of Sex Offenders in Penal Instns and the Community Cncl of Europe 2003–, Expert Gp on Rape and Sexual Assault Victims of Violence and Abuse Prevention Prog Dept of Health 2005–07; govr S Hampstead HS for Girls 1991–99; FRSA 1989; *Books* Rape and the Legal Process (1987, 2 edn 2002), Rape and Criminal Justice (1996); *Style—* Prof Jennifer Temkin; ✉ School of Law, University of Sussex, Arts Building, Falmer, Brighton BN1 9QN (tel 01273 678655, fax 01273 678466, e-mail j.temkin@sussex.ac.uk)

TEMPERLEY, Alice; *b* 1975; *Educ* Central St Martin's Coll of Art, RCA (MA); *m* 2002, Lars von Bennigsen; *Career* fashion designer; launched Temperley London (own label) 2000, concessions worldwide and store NY; official stylist BAFTAs 2005; *Awards* English Print Designer of the Year Indigo Paris 1999, Elle Young Designer of the Year Elle Style Awards 2004, Walpole British Designer of the Year Walpole British Excellence Awards 2004, Most Prominent Designer (in their twenties) American Vogue 2005, Designer of the Year Glamour 2005; *Style—* Ms Alice Temperley; ✉ Temperley London, 6–10 Colville Mews, Lonsdale Road, London W11 2DA (tel 020 7229 7957, fax 020 7243 6538)

TEMPERLEY, Prof Howard Reed; s of Fred Temperley (d 1972), and Eva May Temperley (d 1965); *b* 16 November 1932; *Educ* Royal GS Newcastle upon Tyne, Magdalen Coll Oxford, Yale Univ; *m* 1, 1957 (m dis 1966), Jane Mary, da of William Flambert (d 1993); 1 da (Alison b 1962); m 2, 1966, Rachel Stephanie (d 1990), da of Rowley S Hooper (d 1951); 1 da (Rebecca b 1969), 1 s (Nicholas b 1971); m 3, 1998, Mary Kathryn, da of Lemuel Powe (d 1990); *Career* Nat Serv 2 Lt Armoured Corps 1951–53; asst lectr UCW Aberystwyth 1960–61, lectr Univ of Manchester 1961–67; UEA: sr lectr 1967–81, prof 1981–97, emeritus prof 1997–; chm Br Assoc for American Studies 1986–89; *Books* British Antislavery 1833–1870 (1972), Lieut Colonel Joseph Gubbins's New Brunswick Journals of 1811 and 1813 (ed, 1980), Introduction to American Studies (ed jtly, 1981, 3 edn 1998), White Dreams, Black Africa: The Antislavery Expedition to the Niger 1841 to 1842 (1991), Britain and America since Independence (2002); *Recreations* hill walking; *Clubs* Norfolk; *Style—* Prof Howard Temperley; ✉ 59 Newmarket Road, Norwich NR2 2HW (tel 01603 441403); School of English and American Studies, University of East Anglia, Norwich NR4 7TJ (tel 01603 628497, e-mail h.temperley@uea.ac.uk)

TEMPEST, Henry Roger; DL (N Yorks 1981); yr but only surviving s of Brig-Gen Roger Tempest, CMG, DSO, JP, DL; inherited Broughton Hall Estate on death of elder bro in 1970; *b* 2 April 1924; *Educ* The Oratory, ChCh Oxford; *m* 1957, Janet Evelyn Mary, da of Harold Longton, of Johannesburg; 3 da (Bridget Mary b 1957, Anne Valerie b 1959, Mary Hazel (Mrs Roddy Feilden) b 1961), 2 s (Roger Henry b 1963, Piers b 1973); *Career* Scots Gds 1943–47, serv NW Europe (wounded 1945), apptd to Q Staff HQ Gds Div 1945, Staff Capt 1946; Britannia Rubber Co Ltd 1947–51; emigrated to Lusaka (then in Northern Rhodesia) 1952, incorporated cost accountant (AACWA) South Africa 1959; returned to UK 1961, fin offr Univ of Oxford Dept of Nuclear Physics 1962–72; memb: N Yorks CC 1973–85, Skipton RDC 1973–74, Exec Ctee CLA Yorks 1973–87, Cncl Order of St John N Yorks 1977–87, pres Skipton Branch Royal Br Legion 1974–91; govr: Craven Coll of FE 1974–85, Skipton Girls' HS 1976–85; Lord of the Manors of Broughton, Coleby, Burnsall and Thorpe; memb Pendle Forest and Craven Harriers Hunt Ctee 1973–98; ACIS 1958, FCIS 1971, MBCS 1973; KM; *Clubs* Lansdowne, Pratt's; *Style—* Henry Tempest, Esq, DL; ✉ Broughton Hall, Skipton, North Yorkshire BD23 3AE (tel 01756 692510, e-mail henrytempest@hotmail.com)

TEMPEST-MOGG, Dr Brenden Dayne; s of Alan Reginald Mogg, JP (NSW), Capt RAAF (d 1994), and Ethyl Mavis Tempest-Hay (d 2000); *b* 10 April 1945; *Educ* The Scots Coll Sydney, Univ of NSW (BA), Univ of Essex (MA), Hertford Coll Oxford (MLitt), George Washington Univ Washington DC (EdD), Aust Inst of Professional Counsellors (Dip Counselling); *m* 27 May 1984 (m dis 1990), Galina, da of Ivan Mikhailovich Kobzev (d 1995), of Frunze, Russia; 1 da (Gloria Dela Hay b 27 Feb 1987); *Career* pres: Warnborough Coll 1973–, Warnborough Univ 1997–; visiting overseas lectr 1976–; psychotherapist and clinical counsellor 1985–; conslt on int educn 1988–, conslt on accreditation and quality assurance 1990–, advsr distance learning 1995–; memb: Oxford Business Alumni Univ of Oxford, Br Assoc for Counselling and Psychotherapy, Assoc of Int Educators; JP (NSW) 1967–2005; MInstD 1997; FRSA 1994; *Recreations* sailing, polo, travel, poetry; *Clubs* Cowdray Park Polo, Cirencester Park Polo; *Style—* Dr Brenden D Tempest-Mogg; ✉ e-mail president@warnborough.edu

TEMPLE, Anthony Dominic Afamado; QC; s of Sir Rawden John Afamado Temple, CBE, QC (d 2000), and Margaret, *née* Gunson (d 1980); bro of Victor Bevis Afoumado Temple, QC, *qv*; *b* 21 September 1945; *Educ* Haileybury and ISC, Worcester Coll Oxford (MA); *m* 28 May 1983, Susan Elizabeth, da of Ernst Bodansky (d 1990), of Broadbridge Heath, W Sussex; 2 da (Jessica Elizabeth b 11 Dec 1985, Alexandra Louise b 21 Aug 1988); *Career* called to the Bar Inner Temple 1968; Crown Law Office Western Australia 1968–69; in practice UK 1970–, recorder of the Crown Court 1989– (asst recorder 1982), dep judge of the High Court 1995–; chm Modern Pentathlon Assoc of GB 2004–; *Recreations* modern pentathlon, travel; *Style—* Anthony Temple, QC; ✉ 4 Pump Court, London EC4 (tel 020 7353 2656, fax 020 7583 2036, e-mail atemple@4pumpcourt.com)

TEMPLE, Prof Sir John Graham; kt (2003); s of Joseph Henry Temple (d 2000), and Norah, *née* Selby (d 1987); *b* 14 March 1942; *Educ* William Hulme's GS Manchester, Univ of Liverpool (MB ChB, ChM); *m* 11 April 1966, (Margaret) Jillian Leighton, da of Robert Leighton Hartley (d 1966), of Wigan; 2 s (Robert b 27 Oct 1967, Christopher b 5 July 1972), 1 da (Caroline b 29 Dec 1969); *Career* prof of surgery Univ of Birmingham, consIt surgn Queen Elizabeth Hosp Birmingham 1979–2000; postgrad dean Univ of Birmingham 1991–2000, chair conf of post grad medical deans (COPMed), memb Specialist Trg Authy 1996–2000; regnl advsr in surgery RCS England 1990–94, special advsr to CMO (Calman Training) 1995–, chm Specialist Training Authy Med Royal Coll

T

2000–; memb: BMA 1965, Assoc of Surgns of GB 1974; FMedSci, FRCSEd (memb Cncl 1995–, pres 2000–03), FRCS (now Hon FRCS), FRCSGlas, FRCPEd, FRCP, FACS, FHKCS, Hon FRCGP, Hon FRCSI, Hon FFAEM, FRCA; *Recreations* skiing, sailing; *Style*— Prof Sir John Temple; ✉ Wharncliffe, 24 Westfield Road, Edgbaston, Birmingham B15 3QG (tel 0121 454 2445, e-mail jgtemple@compuserve.com)

TEMPLE, Martin John; CBE (2005); s of John Douglas Temple (d 1982), and Kathleen, *née* Cook; *b* 30 August 1949, Scarborough; *Educ* Bridlington Sch, Univ of Hull (BSc), Newcastle Poly (DipM), INSEAD (AMP); *m* Aug 1972, Lesley, da of James Leonard Imeson; 1 da (Sarah Elizabeth b 7 April 1977), 1 s (Paul James b 11 Feb 1979); *Career* various positions BSC Consett 1970–79, gen mangr British Steel Corp Refractories Gp 1979–85, works dir G R Stein Refractories 1985–87, dir of sales and marketing British Stainless Steel 1987–92; Avesta Sheffield: dir of mktg and sales 1992–95, vice-pres Sales and Distribution Div 1995–98; DG Engineering Employers Fedn (EEF) 1999–, gp chm 600 Gp plc 2007–; chm CEEMET; memb: Bd Women in Science and Engrg (WISE) (former chm), Engrg Technol Bd (ETB), Supervisory Bd Science, Engrg, Technol and Maths Network (SETNET), Bd Sci Engrg Manufacturing Technological Alliance (SEMTA), Bd Nat Metals Technol Centre (NAMTEC); dir Vestry Ct Ltd; Freeman Worshipful Co of Cutlers; *Recreations* rugby, music, countryside, current affairs; *Clubs* Oriental, St Stephens; *Style*— Martin Temple, Esq, CBE; ✉ Churchfield House, Church Lane, Old Ravenfield, Rotherham, South Yorkshire S65 4NG (tel 01709 851973, fax 01709 854989, mobile 07803 187428); Engineering Employers Federation, Broadway House, Tothill Street, London SW1H 9NQ (tel 020 7654 1514, fax 020 7233 1119, e-mail mtemple@eef-fed.org.uk)

TEMPLE, Nicholas John (Nick); s of Leonard Temple (d 1990), and Lilly Irene, *née* Thornton; *b* 2 October 1947; *Educ* Kings Sch Gloucester; *Family* 1 s (Alexander James b 10 Jan 1975), 2 da (Charlotte Elizabeth b 22 July 1977, Rosanna Louise b 12 July 1980); *m*, 14 Oct 2004, Lucinda, *née* Westmacott; *Career* IBM: joined as systems engr 1965, conslt on R&D 1981, estab banking industry products lab Germany 1983, vice-pres systems and product mgmnt IBM Europe 1985–91, chief exec IBM UK Ltd 1991–95, chm IBM UK Ltd 1995–96; mgmnt conslt 1996–; chief exec Armature 1997–99; chm: Retail Business Solutions Ltd 2001–, Blick plc 2002–04, Fox IT 2002–, Tax Computer Systems Ltd, Capula Ltd; non-exec dir: Electrocomponents plc 1997–2007, Datacash plc, Datatec, 4Imprint Gp plc, Tax Computer Systems, Capula, Retail Business Solutions, Fax IT; dep chm Business in the Community 1993–98; *Recreations* rowing, opera, cooking; *Style*— Nick Temple, Esq; ✉ 10 Markham Square, London SW3 4UY (tel 020 77581 2181, fax 020 7584 0644, e-mail mail@nicktemple.co.uk)

TEMPLE, Nina Claire; da of Landon Royce Temple, and Barbara Joan Temple; *b* 21 April 1956; *Educ* Imperial Coll London (BSc); *Children* 1 da (Rebecca 1986), 1 s (Oliver b 1988); *Career* nat sec Communist Pty GB 1990– and led transformation into Democratic Left; co-ordinator Democratic Left 1991–2000; helped found: Unions 21, Make Votes Count (currently dir); *Recreations* rambling, swimming, gardening, movies; *Style*— Ms Nina Temple; ✉ Make Votes Count, 6 Chancel Street, London SE1 0UU (tel 020 7928 2076, e-mail nina@makevotescount.com)

TEMPLE, Ralph; s of Harry Temple (ka 1941), and Julia, *née* Glassman; *b* 15 November 1933; *Educ* Hackney Downs GS; *m* 22 May 1955, Patricia Yvonne, da of Samuel Gould (d 1975), of London; 2 s (Graham Robin b 23 April 1958, Howard Jeremy b 28 March 1960); *Career* managing clerk Wilson Wright and Co CAs 1955–61; Tesco plc: sr exec 1961–73, gp fin dir 1973–83, jt gp md 1983–86; md Temple Consultants (business conslts) 1986–; Freeman City Of London; FCA 1956; *Recreations* golf, travel, bridge, keep fit; *Style*— Ralph Temple, Esq; ✉ 2 Culverlands Close, Stanmore, Middlesex HA7 3AG

TEMPLE, Richard; s of Maurice Victor Temple, and Margaret Temple; *b* 4 September 1962, Stourton, Staffs; *Educ* The Kings Sch Worcester, Univ of Keele (BA), Chester Coll of Law, Univ of Birmingham (LLM); *m* 17 April 1999, Camilla; 1 s, 2 da; *Career* admitted slr 1989; articled clerk then assoc Lovell White Durrant 1987–95, sr assoc Ashurst Morris Crisp 1996–97, ptnr CMS Cameron McKenna 1997–2004, ptnr Hogan & Hartson 2005–; memb: Law Soc 1989, Int Bar Assoc 1996; *Publications* The World Bank Water Sanitation Toolkit (1997 and 2006); *Recreations* tennis, running, Japanese art; *Style*— Richard M Temple, Esq; ✉ Hogan & Hartson, 100 St Paul's Churchyard, London EC4M 8BU (tel 020 7367 0200, fax 020 7367 0220, e-mail rtemple@hhlaw.com)

TEMPLE, Sir Richard Anthony Purbeck; 4 Bt (UK 1876), MC (1941); s of Sir Richard Durand Temple, 3 Bt, DSO (d 1962); *b* 19 January 1913; *Educ* Stowe, Trinity Hall Cambridge; *m* 1, 1936 (m dis 1946), Lucy Geils, da of late Alain Joly de Lotbiniere, of Montreal; 2 s; *m* 2, 1950, Jean, da of late James T Finnie, and widow of Oliver P Croom-Johnson; 1 da; *Heir* s, Richard Temple; *Career* serv WWII (wounded), former Maj KRRC; *Clubs* St James's; *Style*— Sir Richard Temple, Bt, MC

TEMPLE, Victor Bevis Afoumado; QC (1993); s of Sir Rawden Temple, QC, CBE (d 2000), and Margaret, *née* Gunson (d 1980); bro of Anthony Dominic Afamado Temple, QC, *qv*; *b* 23 February 1941; *Educ* Shrewsbury, Inns of Court Sch of Law; *m* 1974, Richenda, *née* Penn-Bull; 2 s (Benjamin, Samuel); *Career* mktg exec: S H Benson 1960–63, J Lyons 1964–65, Beecham Group 1965–68, Alcan Aluminium 1968; called to the Bar Inner Temple 1971 (bencher 1996), sr prosecuting counsel to the Crown 1991–93 (jr prosecuting counsel 1985–91), recorder 1989–; DTI inspr into National Westminster Bank 1992, a chm Police Discipline Appeals Tbnls 1993; *Recreations* rowing, carpentry; *Clubs* Thames Rowing; *Style*— Victor Temple, Esq, QC; ✉ 6 King's Bench Walk, Temple, London EC4Y 7DR (tel 020 7583 0410)

TEMPLE-MORRIS, Baron (Life Peer UK 2001), of Llandaff in the County of South Glamorgan and of Leominster in the County of Herefordshire; Peter Temple-Morris; s of His Honour Sir Owen Temple-Morris (d 1985), and Vera, *née* Thompson (d 1986); *b* 12 February 1938; *Educ* Malvern Coll, St Catharine's Coll Cambridge; *m* 1964, Taheré, er da of H E Senator Khozeimé Alam, of Teheran; 2 s, 2 da; *Career* called to the Bar Inner Temple 1962; Hampstead Cons Political Centre 1971–73, second prosecuting counsel Inland Revenue SE Circuit 1971–74; MP (Cons until Nov 1997 whereafter Independent One-Nation Cons, until 1998, then Lab) Leominster Feb 1974–2001, PPS to Sec of State for Tport 1979; chm: Br Gp Inter-Parly Union 1982–85 (exec 1976–96), Br-Iranian Parly Gp 1983–2005, All-Pty Southern Africa Gp 1992–94, Br-Iranian C of C 2002–04; vice-chm: Cons Parly Foreign Affrs Ctee 1982–90, Cons Parly N Ireland Ctee 1990–92, Cons Euro Affrs Ctee 1990–97, GB-Russia Centre 1992–97, South Africa Gp 1995–2001 (chm 1994–95); vice-pres UN Assoc Cncl; memb: Commons Select Ctee on Foreign Affrs 1987–90; first Br co-chm Br-Irish Inter-Parly Body 1990–97 (memb 1997–2005), exec Commonwealth Parly Assoc (UK Branch) 1993–98 (vice-chm 1994–95); sec Br-Netherlands Parly Gp 2001– (chm 1988–2001), treas Br-Spanish Parly Gp 2001–05 (chm 1992–2001); memb Delegated Powers and Regulatory Reform Ctee House of Lords 2002–06; pres Br-Iranian Business Assoc 1995–2005; admitted slr 1989; memb Academic Cncl Wilton Park (FCO) 1990–97; memb Cncl Malvern Coll 1977–2002, pres Iran Soc 1995–, vice-chm and chm exec Soc of Cons Lawyers 1995–97 (exec 1968–71 and 1990–95); pres St Catharine's Coll Cambridge Soc 2003–04; Liveryman Worshipful Co of Basketmakers; Chevalier du Tastevin (Château de Clos de Vougeot), Jurade de St Emilion; *Recreations* films, books, wine, food, travel; *Clubs* Cardiff and County, Reform; *Style*— The Rt Hon the Lord Temple-Morris; ✉ c/o Moon Beever, Solicitors, 24–26 Bloomsbury Square, London WC1A 2PL (tel 020 7637 0661); House of Lords, London SW1A 0PW (tel 020 7219 4181, e-mail templemorrisp@parliament.uk)

TEMPLE OF STOWE, 8 Earl (UK 1822); (Walter) Grenville Algernon Temple-Gore-Langton; o s of Cdr Hon Evelyn Arthur Grenville Temple-Gore-Langton, DSO, RN (d 1972; yst s of 4 Earl), and Irene, *née* Gartside-Spaight (d 1967); suc his cousin 7 Earl Temple of Stowe 1988; *b* 2 October 1924; *Educ* Pangbourne Coll; *m* 1, 24 July 1954, Zillah Ray (d 1966), da of James Boxall, of Tillington, W Sussex; 2 s (James Grenville, Lord Langton b 1955, Hon Robert Chandos b 1957), 1 da (Lady Anna Clare b 1960); *m* 2, 1 June 1968, (Margaret) Elizabeth Graham, o da of Col Henry William Scarth of Breckness, of Skaill House, Orkney; *Heir* s, Lord Langton; *Style*— The Rt Hon the Earl Temple of Stowe; ✉ The Cottage, Easton, Winchester, Hampshire SO21 1EH; Garth, Outertown, Stromness, Orkney KW16 3JP

TEMPLE-RICHARDS, Charles Leofric Thomas; s of Lt Cdr Leofric Douglas Temple-Richards, RN, of Stibbard, Norfolk (d 1999), and Geraldine Beatrice, *née* Cook; *b* 21 September 1955, Havant, Hants; *Educ* Eton, Magdalene Coll Cambridge; *m* 1986, Virginia Jane, *née* Scott; 2 da (Cornelia b 23 Sept 1989, Juliana b 16 Nov 1991), 1 s (Alec b 30 March 1995); *Career* chartered surveyor Carter Jonas 1977–79; stockbroker: Scrimgeour Kemp-Gee 1979–86, James Capel (later HSBC) 1986–2001, Barratt & Cooke 2001–; MRICS, MSI; *Recreations* shooting, fishing, the countryside, skiing; *Clubs* Millennium, Allsorts, Norfolk; *Style*— C L T Temple-Richards, Esq; ✉ Sennowe Park, Guist, Norfolk NR20 5PB; Barratt & Cooke, 5 Opie Street, Norwich NR1 3DW (tel 01603 624236, e-mail charlietr@barrattandcooke.co.uk)

TEMPLEMAN, Michael; s of Geoffrey Templeman CBE (d 1988), and Dorothy May, *née* Heathcote (d 1996); *b* 6 May 1943; *Educ* King Edward's Sch Birmingham, Selwyn Coll Cambridge (MA); *m* 5 Dec 1970, Jane Margaret Willmer, da of Capt John Kenneth Lee; 4 da (Kathryn Alexandra Joan b 14 Oct 1971, Charlotte Heathcote Mary b 31 Aug 1973, Judith Margaret Elizabeth b 26 Jan 1977, Rosalind Sarah May b 20 June 1981); *Career* Inland Revenue 1965–94: inspr of taxes Maidstone 1965–67 then Canterbury 1967–70, district inspr Cannock 1971–72, tech specialist Oil Taxation 1972–78, district inspr Luton 1978–81, tech specialist Co Taxation 1981–84 then Fin Instns 1984–89, controller Oil Taxation Office 1989–91, dir Fin Instns Div 1992–94; gp taxation dir Schroder plc 1994–; *Recreations* running, music; *Style*— Michael Templeman, Esq; ✉ Schroder Investment Management Ltd, 31 Gresham Street, London EC2 (tel 020 7658 6450)

TEMPLEMAN, Miles Howard; s of Robert James Templeman (d 1990), of London, and Margot Elizabeth, *née* Charlton; *b* 4 October 1947; *Educ* Jesus Coll Cambridge (MA, Capt Rugby first XV), Columbia Univ (Dip Mktg); *m* Janet Elizabeth, da of Lionel James Strang; 2 s (Mark b 1977, James b 1979), 1 da (Sara b 1984); *Career* Young & Rubicam: trainee account mangr Daz 1970–73, product mangr/mktg mangr Lucozade, Ribena and others 1973–78; gen merchandise mangr and mktg dir N Europe Levi Strauss 1978–84; Whitbread plc: md Thresher 1985, gp mktg dir 1988–89, md Whitbread Beer Co 1989, main bd dir 1991, chm Beefeater 1997; chief exec H P Bulmer Holdings plc 2003, pt/t exec chm Eldridge Pope 2004–, non-exec chm YO! Sushi 2004–; non-exec dir: Albert Fisher Gp plc 1994–2000, The Post Office (latterly Consignia plc then Royal Mail Gp plc) 1998–2003, Shepherd Neame 2002–; DG IOD 2004–; memb Ct of Assts Worshipful Co of Brewers; *Recreations* tennis, bridge, cinema; *Style*— Miles Templeman, Esq

TEMPLEMAN, Baron (Life Peer UK 1982), of White Lackington in the County of Somerset; Sydney William Templeman; kt (1972), MBE (1946), PC (1978); s of Herbert William Templeman; *b* 3 March 1920; *Educ* Southall GS, St John's Coll Cambridge; *m* 1, 1946, Margaret Joan (d 1988), da of Morton Rowles; 2 s (Rev the Hon Peter Morton b 1949, Hon Michael Richard b 1951); *m* 2, 12 Dec 1996, Sheila, da of late Frank Templeman, and widow of Dr John Edworthy; *Career* served 4/1 Gurkha Rifles NW Frontier, Arakan, Imphal and Burma 1941–46 (despatches), Hon Major; called to the Bar 1947, QC 1964, memb Middle Temple and Lincoln's Inn, memb Bar Cncl 1961–65, bencher Middle Temple 1969 (treas 1987), High Ct judge (Chancery) 1972–78, Lord Justice of Appeal 1978–82, Lord of Appeal in Ordinary 1982–94; attorney-gen Duchy Lancaster 1970–72; pres Bar Assoc for Commerce Fin & Industry 1982–86; hon fell St John's Coll Cambridge 1982; Hon DLitt Reading 1980; Hon LLD: Univ of Birmingham 1986, CNAA Huddersfield Poly 1990, Univ of Exeter 1991; Hon LLD Nat Law Sch of India Univ Bangalore 1993; visitor Univ of Essex 1990–96; hon memb Canadian & American Bar Assocs; former pres Senate of Inns of Ct and Bar; *Style*— The Rt Hon Lord Templeman, MBE, PC; ✉ Mellowstone, 1 Rosebank Crescent, Exeter EX4 6EJ (tel 01392 275428)

TEMPLETON, Prof (Alexander) Allan; s of Richard Templeton (d 1968), and Minnie, *née* Whitfield (d 2001); *b* 28 June 1946; *Educ* Aberdeen GS, Univ of Aberdeen (MB ChB, MD); *m* 17 Dec 1980, Gillian Constance, da of Geoffrey William John Penney (d 2002), of Eastbourne; 3 s (Richard b 1981, Robert b 1983, Peter b 1987), 1 da (Katherine b 1985); *Career* lectr then sr lectr Univ of Edinburgh 1976–85, regius prof of obstetrics and gynaecology Univ of Aberdeen 1985–; pres RCOG 2004–; author of various pubns on human infertility and gynaecological endocrinology; FRCOG 1987 (MRCOG 1974), FMedSci 2002, FRCPEd 2005, FRCP 2006, FACOG 2007; *Books* The Early Days of Pregnancy (1987), Reproduction and the Law (1990), Infertility (1992), The Prevention of Pelvic Infection (1996), Evidence-Based Fertility Treatment (1998); *Recreations* mountaineering; *Clubs* Royal Northern and Univ; *Style*— Prof Allan Templeton; ✉ Department of Obstetrics and Gynaecology, University of Aberdeen, Foresterhill, Aberdeen AB25 2ZD (tel 01224 550590)

TEMPLETON, Sir John; kt (1987); s of late Harvey Maxwell Templeton, and late Vella, *née* Handly; *b* 29 November 1912; *Educ* Yale Univ (BA), Balliol Coll Oxford (Rhodes scholar, MA); *m* 1, 17 April 1937, Judith Dudley Folk (d 1951); 2 s (John Marks b 1939, Christopher Winston b 1947), 1 da (Anne Dudley (Mrs Zimmerman) b 1941); *m* 2, 31 Dec 1958, Irene Reynolds (d 1993); *Career* vice-pres National Geophysical Co 1937–40; pres: Templeton Dobbrow and Vance Inc 1940–60, Templeton Growth Fund Ltd 1954–85, Templeton Investment Counsel Ltd Edinburgh 1976–83, Templeton World Fund Inc 1978–87; chm Templeton Galbraith and Hansberger Ltd 1986–92; sec Templeton Fndn 1960–; fndr: Templeton Prizes for Progress in Religion 1972, Templeton UK Project Tst 1984; pres Bd of Tstees Princeton Theol Seminary 1967–73 and 1976–85, memb Cncl Templeton Coll (formerly Oxford Centre for Mgmnt Studies) 1983–95, tstee Westminster Abbey Restoration 1993–; hon rector Dubuque Univ 1982–92; hon fell St Edmunds Coll Cambridge 2003; Benjamin Franklin Prize RSA 1995, Robert E Lee Award 1996, Marymount Ethics Award Marymount Univ Virginia, Herman Lay Award 2004; Hon LLD: Beaver Coll 1968, Marquette Univ 1980, Jamestown Coll 1983, Maryville Coll 1984, Babson Coll 1992, Rhodes Coll 1992, Univ of Dubuque 1992, Univ of Rochester 1992, Louisiana Coll 1993, Moravian Coll 1994, Stonehill Coll 1995, Notre Dame Univ 1996, Methodist Coll of NC 1997; Hon DLit: Wilson Coll 1974, Manhattan Coll 1990, Florida Southern Coll 1992; Hon DD Buena Vista Coll 1979, Hon DCL Univ of the South 1984; Hon DHL: Campbell Univ 1993, Brigham Young Univ 1998, Concordia Coll 2000; Hon DH Furman Univ 1995, Hon DBA Methodist Coll of NC 1997, Hon Dr Christian Lit Franciscan Univ of Steubenville 1998; chartered fin analyst 1965, memb Soc of Security Analysts; KStJ 1994; *Books* The Humble Approach (1981), The Templeton Touch (jtly, 1985), The Templeton Plan (1987), Global Investing (1988), The God Who Would be Known (1989), Riches for the Mind and Spirit (1990), Discovering the Laws of Life (1994), Is There Any Reality Except God? (1994), Evidence of Purpose (1994), Future Agenda (1995), Worldwide Laws of Life (1997), Possibilities (2000); *Clubs* White's, Athenaeum, Lansdowne, Royal Over-Seas League, Oxford and Cambridge, Royal Institution, Royal Society of Arts, Lyford Cay (Bahamas); *Style*— Sir John Templeton; ✉ First Trust Bank

Ltd, Lyford Cay, PO Box N-7776, Nassau, Bahamas (tel 00 1 242 362 4904, fax 00 1 242 362 4880)

TEMPLETON, Suzannah Clare (Suzie); da of Ian George Templeton, of Dunbridge, Hants, and Roberta Lambie Mansell, *née* Dearborn; *b* 2 August 1967; *Educ* UCL (BSc), Surrey Inst of Art and Design (BA), RCA (MA); *Career* filmmaker and animator; *Films* Stanley (1999), Inside (2000), Dog (2001), Peter and the Wolf (2006); 42 int film awards incl: McLaren Award 2001, BAFTA 2002, Hiroshima Prize 2002, Br Animation Award 2002, Utrecht Grand Prix 2002, Siena Grand Prix 2002, Melbourne Best Overall Film 2002, Tampere Best Animation 2003, Pulcinella Award 2007, Golden Rose 2007, Annecy Grand Prix 2007; *Style—* Ms Suzie Templeton

TENBY, 3 Viscount (UK 1957) William Lloyd George; JP (Hants); s of 1 Viscount Tenby, TD, PC (d 1967), s of 1 Earl Lloyd George; suc bro, 2 Viscount 1983; *b* 7 November 1927; *Educ* Eastbourne Coll, St Catharine's Coll Cambridge (BA); *m* 1955, Ursula, da of late Lt-Col Henry Edward Medlicott, DSO (d 1948); 2 da (Hon Sara Gwenfron b 1957, Hon Clare Mair b 1961), 1 s (Hon Timothy Henry Gwilym b 1962); *Heir* s, Hon Timothy Lloyd George; *Career* Capt RWF (TA) 1951–61; editorial asst Herbert Jenkins Ltd 1951–54, Advtg Dept Associated Newspapers 1954–57, gp advtg mangr United Dominions Trust Ltd 1957–74, PR advsr to the Chm Kleinwort Benson Ltd 1974–87; crossbencher House of Lords; memb House of Lords and Parly Broadcasting Gps; a pres CPRE (Hants) 1985–2001, chm of tstees Byways Residential Home 2000–; *Style—* The Rt Hon the Viscount Tenby

TENCH, Les; *b* 18 April 1945, St Helens, Merseyside; *Educ* Univ of Nottingham (BSc); *Career* md Twyfords Bathrooms 1976–85, md Steetley Building Products 1985–92, md CRH UK 1992–98, dir Shepherd Building Group 1994–2004, md CRH Europe Building Products 1998–2002, chm SIG plc 2004–; dir Staffs Trg and Enterprise Cncl 1994–97, memb Bd Learning and Skills Cncl 2001–03; govr tertiary colls 1994–97; *Recreations* walking, trekking, visiting unusual places, photography, theatre, music; *Style—* Les Tench, Esq; ✉ SIG plc, Hillsborough Works, Langsett Road, Sheffield S6 2LW (tel 0114 285 6300)

TENNANT, David; s of Alexander McDonald, of Paisley, Strathclyde, and E Helen McDonald; *b* 18 April 1971, Bathgate, Lothian; *Educ* RSAMD; *Career* actor; acted with the 7:84 Theatre Company; *Theatre* incl: Touchstone in As You Like It (RSC) 1996, Romeo in Romeo and Juliet (RSC) 2000, Antipholus of Syracuse in Comedy of Errors (RSC) 2000, Jeff in The Lobby Hero (Donmar Warhouse and New Ambassadors) 2002 (nominated Best Actor Laurence Olivier Theatre Awards 2003); *Television* incl: Casanova in Casanova 2005, The Doctor in Doctor Who 2006 (tenth Doctor); *Films* incl: Bright Young Things 2003, Harry Potter and the Goblet of Fire 2005; *Style—* David Tennant; ✉ c/o ICM, Oxford House, 76 Oxford Street, London W1N 0AX (tel 020 7636 6565, fax 020 7323 0101)

TENNANT, Hon Mrs Emma Christina; da of late 2 Baron Glenconner by his 2 w; *b* 20 October 1937; *Educ* St Paul's Girls' Sch; *m* 1, 1957 (m dis 1962), Sebastian Yorke, s of Henry Yorke and Hon Mrs (Adelaide) Yorke, da of 2 Baron Biddulph; m 2, 1963 (m dis), Christopher Booker, *qv*; m 3, 1968 (m dis 1973), Alexander Cockburn; *Career* novelist (as Emma Tennant); founder ed literary newspaper Bananas; Hon DLitt Univ of Aberdeen 1996; FRSL; *Books* The Bad Sister (1979, reprinted 1999), Wild Nights (1979), The House of Hospitalities (1983), Sisters and Strangers (1989), Frankenstein's Baby (BBC film), Faustine (1992), ABC of Writing (1992), Tess (1993), Pemberley (1994), An Unequal Marriage (1994), Elinor and Marianne (1995), Emma in Love (1996), Strangers: A Family Romance (1998), Girlitude (1999), Burnt Diaries (1999), The Ballad of Sylvia and Ted (2001), A House in Corfu (2001), Felony: a private history of The Aspern Papers (2002), Balmoral (jtly, as Isabel Vane, 2004), Heathcliff's Tale (2005), The Harp Lesson (2005); *Recreations* exploring, walking in Dorset; *Style—* The Hon Mrs Emma Tennant; ✉ c/o Jonathan Cape, Random House, 20 Vauxhall Bridge Road, London SW1V 2SA

TENNANT, Mark Edward; s of Sir Iain Tennant, KT, JP, and the Lady Margaret Tennant; *b* 9 May 1947; *Educ* Eton; *m* 16 Oct 1971, Hermione Rosamond, da of Lt-Col Maurice Howe, OBE; 2 da (Miranda Rosamond Hermione b 15 June 1974, Clementina Margaret Georgina b 21 Nov 1977), 1 s (Edward Iain b 12 May 1983); *Career* vol serv Ockenden Venture India 1965–66, Capt Scots Gds 1966–73; Hambros Bank Ltd: trainee 1973–74, mangr Banking Control Dept 1973–76, mangr International Fixed Interest Dept 1976–81, md Hambro Pacific Ltd Hong Kong 1981–83; dir Fidelity International Ltd 1983–86, chm Bell Laurie White & Co Ltd 1986–91, chm Hill Samuel Unit Trust Managers Ltd and dir Hill Samuel Investment Services Group Ltd 1986–91, md: Chase Global Securities Services (Scotland) 1991–95, Chase Manhattan plc 1995–2001; sr vice-pres JP Morgan 2001–04 (sr advsr 2004–), chm Bluerock Consulting 2004–; non-exec dir: Quality Street Ltd 1993–95, Scotland International 1994–95, JP Morgan Tstees Ltd 1999–2004 (sr advsr 2004–), The Money Portal plc 2005–; memb Int Advsy Bd T Rowe Price 2004–; head of youth leadership St John Ambulance 1973–83, cncllr Surrey Heath DC 1977–79, treas Scottish Cons Pty 1991–; Parly candidate (Cons) Dunfermline E 1992, European Parly candidate (Cons) Highlands and Islands 1994; FRSA 2006; *Recreations* golf, field sports, Scottish music, politics, opera, playing the bagpipes; *Clubs* Boodle's, Pratt's, Swinley Forest Golf; *Style—* Mark Tennant, Esq, FRSA; ✉ Innes House, Elgin, Moray IV30 3NG (tel 01343 842410); JP Morgan plc, 60 Victoria Embankment, London EC4Y 0JP (tel 020 7742 0026, fax 020 7742 0028)

TENNANT, Maj Gen Michael Trenchard (Mike); CB (1994); s of Lt Col Hugh Trenchard Tennant, MC (d 1989), of Jersey, and Mary Isobel, *née* Wilkie (d 1986); *b* 3 September 1941; *Educ* Wellington, RMA Sandhurst, Army Staff Coll; *m* 1, 28 Nov 1964, Susan Daphne (d 1993), da of Lt-Col Frank Maurice Beale, LVO; 3 s (Mark David Trenchard b 27 Aug 1966, Paul Philip b 15 June 1968, Toby Michael James b 21 March 1973); m 2, 8 June 1996, Jacqueline Mary, *née* ap Ellis, wid of David Parish; *Career* Subaltern 7 RHA 1962–67 (served Aden, Bahrain and UK), Adj 32 Regt BAOR 1967–69, Capt 25 Regt 1969–71 (served Hong Kong and Ulster), RMCS 1972, psc 1973, staff offr Mil Ops MOD 1974–75, Battery Cdr 49 Regt BAOR 1976–78, Directing Staff Army Staff Coll 1978–80, CO 1 RHA 1980–83, Cdr BR Trg Team Nigeria 1983–85, Cdr 3 Div RA 1985–87, Cdr RA UKLF 1988–91, Dir Royal Artillery 1991–94, Hon Regt Col 1 RHA 1994–99, Col Cmdt RA 1994–2005, head of external communications Royal Ordnance Div British Aerospace 1994–98, army advsr British Aerospace 1998–2001; chm CCF's Assoc 1996–2003; *Recreations* tennis, golf, bridge; *Clubs* Army and Navy, Fadeaways, Denham Golf, Rye Golf, Senior Golfers; *Style—* Maj-Gen Mike Tennant, CB; ✉ c/o Army and Navy Club, 36 Pall Mall, London SW1Y 5JN (tel 020 7930 9721)

TENNANT OF BALFLUIG, Mark Iain; Baron of Balfluig (cr 1650); s of Maj John Tennant, TD, KStJ (d 1967), of Wittersham, Kent, and Hon Antonia Mary Roby Benson (later Viscountess Radcliffe; d 1982), da of 1 Baron Charnwood; *b* 4 December 1932; *Educ* Eton, New Coll Oxford (MA); *m* 11 Dec 1965, Lady Harriot Pleydell-Bouverie, da of 7 Earl of Radnor, KG, KCVO, JP, DL (d 1968); 1 da (Sophia Roby b 1967), 1 s (Lysander Philip Roby b 1968); *Career* Lt The Rifle Bde (SRO); called to the Bar Inner Temple 1958 (bencher 1984); recorder of the Crown Court 1987, Master of the Supreme Court (Queen's Bench Div) 1988–2005; restored Balfluig Castle (dated 1556) in 1967 being the first to obtain a grant from the Historic Buildings Council for Scotland for a building neither inhabited nor habitable; chm Royal Orchestral Soc for Amateur Musicians 1989; *Recreations* music, architecture, books, shooting; *Clubs* Brooks's; *Style—* Mark Tennant of Balfluig; ✉ 30 Abbey Gardens, London NW8 9AT (tel 020 7624 3200); Balfluig Castle, Alford, Aberdeenshire AB33 8EJ

TENNYSON-d'EYNCOURT, Sir Mark Gervais; 5 Bt (UK 1930), of Carter's Corner Farm, Parish of Herstmonceux, Co Sussex; o s of Sir Giles Gervais Tennyson-d'Eyncourt, 4 Bt (d 1989), and Juanita, *née* Borromeo; *b* 12 March 1967; *Educ* Charterhouse, Kingston Poly (BA); *Heir* none; *Career* fashion designer; Freeman City of London 1989; *Style—* Sir Mark Tennyson-d'Eyncourt, Bt

TEO, HE Michael Eng Cheng; s of late Thian Lai Teo, and late Siew Kheng, *née* Lim; *b* 19 September 1947, Sarawak; *Educ* Auburn Univ, Fletcher Sch of Law and Diplomacy Tufts Univ; *m* 12 June 1977, Sinn Toh Ng; 1 da (Christine b 6 Aug 1969), 1 s (Gabriel b 2 Jan 1995); *Career* Repub of Singapore Air Force (RSAF): joined 1968, distinguished grad USAF War Coll 1985, Cdr 1985, Brig-Gen 1987, Chief of Air Force 1990, ret 1992; Dip Serv: joined 1993, high cmmr to NZ 1994–96, ambass to South Korea 1996–2001, high cmmr to UK and ambass to Ireland 2002–; Gold Singapore Public Admin Medal (Mil) 1989, Outstanding Achievement Award The Philippines 1989, Order of Dip Serv Merit Gwanghwa Medal South Korea 2002; Most Noble Order of the Crown of Thailand 1981, Bintang Swa Bhuana Paksa Utama (Indonesia) 1991, Cdr Legion of Merit (USA) 1991; *Recreations* golf, hiking, reading; *Style—* HE Mr Michael Teo; ✉ High Commission for the Republic of Singapore, 9 Wilton Crescent, London SW1X 8SP (tel 020 7201 5850, fax 020 7245 6583, e-mail info@singaporehc.org.uk)

TEPER, Carl Wolf; s of Joseph Elliot Teper, and Pauline, *née* Mercado (d 1992); *b* 15 June 1955; *Educ* Aylestone Sch, Univ of Warwick (LLB), Cncl of Legal Educn; *Career* called to the Bar Middle Temple 1980; pupillage in chambers of Lord Boston of Faversham, QC 1980–81, head of chambers 1 Gray's Inn Sq 1990– (dep head 1988–90), acting stipendiary magistrate 1999–2000, dep dist judge 2000–, parking adjudicator 2001–; Cncl of Legal Educn: assessor and examiner 1987–97, memb Bd of Examiners 1990–97, memb Bd of Studies 1992–97; memb Bd of Examiners Inns of Court Sch of Law 1997–2000; external examiner: Coll of Law 1997–2001, BPP Law Sch 2003–06; pt/t chm Employment Tbnls 1992–2006, memb Social Security Appeal Tbnl 1992–93; memb: Middle Temple 1977, Gray's Inn 1988; *Recreations* running, studying the Talmud, philanthropy; *Style—* Carl Teper, Esq; ✉ e-mail carl.teper@gmail.com)

TER HAAR, Roger Eduard Lound; QC (1992); s of Dr Dirk ter Haar (d 2002), and Christine Janet ter Haar (d 2005); *b* 14 June 1952; *Educ* Felsted, Magdalen Coll Oxford (BA); *m* 10 Sept 1977, Sarah Anne, da of Peter Leyshon Martyn; 2 s (James b 1978, Harry b 1983), 1 da (Camilla b 1980); *Career* called to the Bar Inner Temple 1974 (bencher 1992); called to the Irish Bar 1997, appointed recorder and dep High Court judge 2003; *Recreations* gardening, golf; *Clubs* Brooks's, Garrick; *Style—* Roger ter Haar, Esq, QC; ✉ Crown Office Chambers, Temple, London EC4Y 7EP (tel 020 7797 8100, fax 020 7797 8101)

TERFEL, Bryn; CBE (2003); *né* Bryn Terfel Jones; s of Hefin Jones, of Garndolbenmaen, Gwynedd, and Nesta, *née* Jones; *Educ* Ysgol Dyffryn Nantlle Gwynedd, Guildhall Sch of Music and Drama (Kathleen Ferrier scholar, Gold Award); *m* 22 August 1987, Lesley, da of George Winston Halliday; 3 s (Tomos b 1 July 1994, Morgan b 10 Oct 1998, Deio Siôn b 28 Jan 2001); *Career* bass baritone; pres: Nat Youth Choir of Wales, Festival of Wales, Welsh Nursery Schs; vice-pres: Cymru A'r Byd, Llangollen Int Eisteddfod, Cymdeithas Owain Glyndwr; patron: Mid Wales Opera, Taunton Choral Soc, Hope House, Cor Meibion Hart, Criccieth Memorial Hall, Aylestone Sch Music Plus Fund, Royal Town of Caernarfon Chamber of Trade and Indust, Ysbyty Gwynedd Kidney Patients Assoc, NW Wales Chambers of Trade and Industry, Usher Hall Appeal; hon fell: Univ of Wales Aberystwyth, Welsh Coll of Music and Drama, Univ of Wales Bangor; Hon Dr Univ of Glamorgan; white robe Gorsedd Eisteddfod Genedlaethol Frenhinol Cymru; *Roles* incl: Guglielmo in Cosi Fan Tutte (WNO) 1990, Figaro in Le Nozze di Figaro (WNO) 1990, Sprecher in Die Zauberflöte (La Monnaie de Brussels) 1991, Figaro in Figaro's Wedding (ENO) 1991, Figaro in Le Nozze di Figaro (Santa Fe) 1991, Spirit Messenger in Die Frau ohne Schatten (Salzburg Easter Festival) 1992, Masetto in Don Giovanni (Covent Garden) 1992, Jochanaan in Salome (Salzburg Festival) 1992 and 1993, Donner in Das Rheingold (Lyric Opera of Chicago) 1993, Ford in Falstaff (WNO) 1993, Figaro in Le Nozze di Figaro (Châtelet, Paris and Lisbon) 1993, 4 male roles in Les Côntes d'Hoffman (Vienna State Opera) 1994, Leporello in Don Giovanni (Salzburg Festival) 1994, 1995 and 1996, Figaro in Le Nozze di Figaro (Metropolitan Opera NY) 1994, Figaro in Le Nozze di Figaro (Covent Garden) 1994, Balstrode in Peter Grimes (Covent Garden) 1995, Leporello in Don Giovanni (Metropolitan Opera and Lyric Opera of Chicago) 1995, Figaro in Le Nozze di Figaro (Saltzburg Festival) 1995, Jochanaan in Salome (Covent Garden) 1995, Nick Shadow in The Rake's Progress (WNO) 1996, Sharpless in Madame Butterfly (New Japan Philharmonic) 1996, 4 male roles in Les Côntes d'Hoffmann (Vienna State Opera) 1996 and 1997, title role in Don Giovanni (Hanover, Köln and London concert performances) 1996, Jochanaan in Salome (Lyric Opera Chicago) 1996, Leporello in Don Giovanni (Ferrara Musica) 1997, Balstrode in Peter Grimes (Vienna State Opera) 1997, Figaro in Le Nozze di Figaro (La Scala Milan and San Francisco) 1997, Wolfram in Tannhäuser (Metropolitan Opera NY) 1997, Figaro in Le Nozze di Figaro (Lyric Opera Chicago and Metropolitan Opera NY) 1998, Jochanaan in Salome (Bayerische Staatsoper) 1998, Scarpia in Tosca (Netherlands Opera) 1998, Falstaff in Falstaff (Australian Opera, Chicago Lyric Opera, Royal Opera Covent Garden) 1999, title role in Don Giovanni (Opera National de Paris) 1999, Leporello in Don Giovanni (Vienna State Opera) 1999, Jochanaan in Salome (Vienna State Opera) 1999, 4 male roles in Les Contes d'Hoffmann (Met Opera NY) 2000, Nick Shadow in The Rakes Progress (San Francisco Opera) 2000, Don Giovanni in Don Giovanni (Metropolitan Opera House NY) 2000, Falstaff in Falstaff (Bayerische Staatsoper Munich and Saltzburg Festival) 2001, Jochanaan in Salome (Vienna Staatsoper) 2001, Don Giovanni in Don Giovanni (Vienna Staatsoper) 2001, Figaro in Le Nozze di Figaro (Munich Festival) 2001, Dulcamara in L'Elisir d'Amore (Netherlands Opera) 2001, Don Giovanni in Don Giovanni (ROH) 2002, Falstaff in Falstaff (Met Opera NY and BayerischeStaatsoper) 2002, 4 male roles in Les Cantes d'Hoffmann (Opera Nationale de Paris) 2002, Sweeney Todd in Sweeney Todd (Lyric Opera of Chicago) 2002, Jochanaan in Salome (Vienna Staatsoper) 2003, Falstaff in Falstaff (Covent Garden and Vienna Staatsoper) 2003, Jochanaan in Salome (Metropolitan Opera) 2004, Méphistophélès in Faust (Covent Garden) 2004, Don Giovanni in Don Giovanni (Lyric Opera of Chicago) 2004, Wotan in Das Rheingold (Covent Garden) 2004 and 2005, Wotan in Die Walküre (Covent Garden) 2005, Falstaff in Falstaff (Houson, LA and Metropolitan Opera) 2005; *Recordings* on Decca, Deutsche Grammophon, L'Oiseau-Lyre, Archiv, Sony Classical, Philips, RCA, Chandos, Hyperion, EMI Classics, BMG Classics, Sain; *Awards* Lieder Prize Cardiff Singer of the World 1989, first winner Br Critics Circle Award (for most outstanding contribution to musical life in GB) 1992, Gramophone Magazine Young Singer of the Year 1992, Newcomer of the Year Int Classic Music Award 1993, Caecilia Prize (for recording of Vagabond) 1995, Grammy Award for Best Classical Vocal Performance (for recording of opera arias) 1996, People's Award Gramophone Awards (for recording of Vagabond) 1996, Britannia Record Club Members Award (for Something Wonderful) 1997, Best Singer 1998–99 Lyric Season Gran Teatre del Liceu Barcelona, Best Opera Recording Grammy Award for The Rake's Progress (Deutsche Grammophon) 1999, John Edwards Meml Award 2000, Prix Caecilia (for recording of Wagner Arias with Claudio Abbado) 2003, Album of the Year (for Bryn) Classical Brit Awards 2004, Male Artist of the Year Classical Brit Awards 2004 and 2005; *Recreations* golf, supporting Manchester United, collecting Fob watches; *Style—* Bryn Terfel, Esq, CBE; ✉ c/o Harlequin Agency Ltd, 203 Fidlas Road, Llanishen, Cardiff CF14 5NA (tel 029 2075 0821, fax 029 2075 5971, e-mail sioned@harlequin-agency.co.uk, website www.harlequin-agency.co.uk)

TERRAS, (Christopher) Richard; s of Frederick Richard Terras (d 1976), and Katherine Joan, *née* Anning (d 1998); *b* 17 October 1937; *Educ* Uppingham, UC Oxford (MA); *m* 1, 27 Oct 1962 (m dis 2003), Janet Esther May, da of Leslie Harold Sydney Baxter (d 1980); 3 da (Clare b 1964, Penelope b 1968, Joanna b 1971), 1 s (Nicholas b 1965); m 2, 11 Nov 2005, Barbara, da of Leslie Bury (d 2004); *Career* chartered accountant; ptnr: Swanwick Terras & Co 1963–65, Abbott & Son 1963–65, Arthur Andersen 1971–99; nat tax dir 1989–99; treas Univ of Manchester 1999–2004; chm NW Kidney Research Assoc 1992–2006; *Recreations* cricket (played for Cheshire); *Clubs* Free Foresters, MCC, Cheshire CCC, Lancashire CCC, Cheshire Gentlemen, Northern Nomads, Leicestershire Gentlemen, Vincent's (Oxford), Forty, St James's (Manchester); *Style*— Richard Terras, Esq; ✉ 21 St Hilary's Park, Alderley Edge, Cheshire SK9 7DA (tel 01625 583832

TERRINGTON, 6 Baron (UK 1918) Christopher Richard James Woodhouse; s of 5 Baron Terrington, DSO, OBE, FRSL (d 2001), and Lady Davidema (Davina) Katharine Cynthia Mary Millicent, *née* Bulwer-Lytton (d 1995), da of 2 Earl of Lytton, KG, GCSI, GCIE, PC (d 1947); *b* 20 September 1946; *Educ* Winchester, Guy's Hosp Med Sch London (MB BS); *m* 27 Feb 1975, Hon Anna Margaret Philipps, da of late Baron Milford; 1 s (Hon Jack b 7 Dec 1978), 1 da (Hon Constance b 1 Jan 1982); *Career* Inst of Urology UCL: sr lectr 1981–97, reader in urology 1997–2005, prof of adolescent urology 2005–; visiting prof: Univ of Pennsylvania Med Sch 2001, Harvard Univ Med Sch 2001; conslt urologist: Royal Marsden Hosp 1981–, St George's Hosp 1985–95; hon conslt urologist: St Peter's Hosp 1981–, Gt Ormond St Hosp for Children 1981–; chm Br Jl of Urology Int 1999–, numerous pubns in learned jls; corresponding memb American Urological Assoc 1985, hon memb Urological Soc of Aust 1999, corresponding memb American Assoc of Genito-Urinary Surgns 2003, hon memb German Urological Soc 2004; Liveryman Worshipful Soc of Apothecaries; FRSM 1981, FRCS 1975, FEBU 1993; *Books* Physiological Basis of Medicine-Urology and Nephrology (1987), Long Term Paediatric Urology (1991), Management of Urological Emergencies (2004); *Recreations* skiing, stalking; *Clubs* Leander; *Style*— Prof the Rt Hon the Lord Terrington; ✉ 31 Eustace Building, 329 Queenstown Road, London SW8 4NT (tel 020 7498 9402, e-mail bjui@ucl.ac.uk)

TERRINGTON, Derek Humphrey; s of late Douglas Jack, of Newmarket, Suffolk, and late Jean Mary, *née* Humphrey; *b* 25 January 1949; *Educ* Sea Point Boys' HS, Univ of Cape Town (MA); *m* 15 July 1978, Jennifer Mary, da of late Leslie Vernon Jones; 1 da (Sarah b 29 Sept 1984), 1 s (William b 18 Nov 1996); *Career* assoc ptnr Grieveson Grant 1984, exec dir Phillips & Drew 1991 (asst dir 1987, dir 1988), dir Kleinwort Benson Securities 1991–96, dir and head of equity research Teather & Greenwood 1996–98, media analyst AXA Investment Managers 1998–2000, media analyst Credit Lyonnais Securities 2000–02, head of pan-European media research Commerzbank Securities 2003–04, sr analyst Blue Oak Capital 2005–; AIIMR, FRSA; *Style*— Derek Terrington, Esq; ✉ 46 Wensleydale Road, Hampton, Middlesex TW12 2LT

TERRY, *see also:* Imbert-Terry

TERRY, Air Marshal Sir Colin George; KBE (1998, OBE 1984), CB (1995); s of George Albert Terry, of Shropshire, and Edna Joan, *née* Purslow; *b* 8 August 1943; *Educ* Bridgnorth GS, RAF Colls Henlow and Cranwell, Imperial Coll London (BSc(Eng), ACGI, hockey colours); *m* 12 March 1966, Gillian, da of late Conrad Glendore Grindley; 2 s (Sarn Conrad b 22 May 1969, Leon Alexander b 24 Jan 1974), 1 da (Adrienne Miya b 24 Nov 1976); *Career* tech cadet RAF Tech Coll Henlow 1961, cmmnd engrg offr 1962, various engrg and instructing appts at tport, trg and fighter stations 1962–69, trg as serv pilot 1969–71, promoted Sqdn Ldr 1971, aircraft project offr Royal Navy Belfast 1971–74, sr engrg offr RAF Phantom sqdns Germany 1974–77, engrg authy for Vulcan, Victor and VC10 propulsion systems HQ Strike Cmd 1977–79, attended RAF Staff Coll Bracknell 1979, promoted Wing Cdr 1979, CO Engrg Wing RAF Coltishall (Jaguars and Sea Kings) 1979–81, engrg authy Lightnings and Phantoms HQ Strike Cmd 1981–82, sr RAF engr and OC Engrg Wing RAF Stanley Falkland Is 1982, promoted Gp Capt 1984, engrg authy Cmd Staff, OC RAF Abingdon (Jaguars, Hawks and Buccaneers), RCDS 1989, promoted Air Cdre 1989, Dir of Support Mgmnt 1989–93, promoted Air Vice-Marshal 1993, DG Support Mgmnt (RAF) 1993–95, COS and Dep C-in-C Logistics Cmd 1995–97, Chief Engr (RAF) 1996–99, promoted Air Marshal 1997, Air Force Bd Memb as Air Memb for Logistics and AOC-in-C Logistics Cmd 1997–99, ret 1999; gp md Inflite Engrg Services Ltd 1999–2001, non-exec chm Meggitt plc 2004– (non-exec dir 2003–); Fg offr RAFVR(T) 1999–; RAeS: memb Cncl 1999–, chm Learned Soc 2003–, pres 2005–; memb Senate Engrg Cncl 1999–2002, chm UK Engrg Cncl, bd memb Engrg & Technology Bd, dir ETB 2002–05; UK advsr to: Aermacchi 2002–, SNECMA 2003–; memb Ctee Queen's Award for Enterprise 2002–, pres CGCA 2002–04; Cdre RAF Sailing Assoc 1994–99, pres Assoc Services Yacht Clubs 1997–99; Freeman City of London; Liveryman Worshipful Co of Engrgs 2004; CEng, FRAeS, FRSA, FILog, FCGI, FREng; *Recreations* sailing, flying, skiing, cooking, music; *Clubs* RAF; *Style*— Air Marshal Sir Colin Terry, KBE, CB; ✉ 6AEF RAF Benson, Wallingford, Oxfordshire OX10 6AA

TERRY, David Robins; s of Joseph Robins Terry (d 1977), of Little Hall, Heslington, York, and Mary Patricia Colston, *née* Douty; *b* 11 November 1942; *Educ* Rishworth Sch Halifax; *m* 19 Nov 1966, Katharine Ruth, da of Amos Eastham, of Selby; 2 s (Nigel Joseph Douty b 15 June 1970, Oliver Stuart Robins b 6 May 1972); *Career* Army Serv 4 and 7 Royal Dragoon Gds 1961; CA 1968; John Gordon Walton & Co Leeds 1962–68; PricewaterhouseCoopers (formerly Price Waterhouse before merger): joined Leeds Office 1969, ptnr 1980, seconded to Budapest office as sr audit ptnr 1992–95, transferred to Sofia office as ptnr i/c Bulgaria, Serbia and Macedonia 1995–98, freelance financial consultant 1998–; pres Cncl of Dudley and Dist C of C 1989–90 (memb 1985–), chm Mgmnt Ctee Dudley Nat Pianoforte Competition 1987–92, govr St Richards Hospice Worcester 1991–92; Merchant Adventurer of Co of Merchant Adventurers of City of York; ATII 1971, FCA 1978; *Recreations* golf, music, family, travel, assistant church organist; *Clubs* Lansdowne; *Style*— David Terry, Esq; ✉ Tapenhall House, Porters Mill, Droitwich, Worcester WR9 OAN; PricewaterhouseCoopers, Sofia 1000, 2 Serdika Street, Bulgaria (tel 00 359 2 9808884, fax 00 359 2 9800404)

TERRY, (Robert) Jeffrey; s of Robert James Terry (d 1996), of Stockport, and Emily, *née* Davison (d 1975); *b* 10 September 1952; *Educ* William Hulme's GS Manchester, King's Coll London (LLB), City Univ (MA (Business Law)); *m* 15 July 1978, Susan Jane, da of Reginald Trevor Kingston Gregory (d 1997), of Bath; 2 da (Sarah Louise b 7 Aug 1983, Anna May Emily b 7 May 1987); *Career* called to the Bar Lincoln's Inn 1976, community lawyer Southend CAB 1976–78; in private practice: London 1978–, Manchester 1989– (chm 8 King St Chambers Business Gp); memb: Northern Circuit Commercial Bar Assoc (fndr memb), Northern Chancery Bar Assoc, Professional Negligence Assoc, American Bar Assoc; CEDR accredited mediator; FCIArb 1997, fell Soc for Advanced Legal Studies 1998; *Recreations* walking, photography, reading, smallholding husbandry; *Style*— Jeffrey Terry, Esq; ✉ 8 King Street, Manchester M2 6AQ (tel 0161 834 9560, fax 0161 834 2733); Lamb Building, Temple, London EC4 (tel 020 7353 6701, fax 020 7353 4686); clerk: Spencer Davis (tel 0161 834 9560)

TERRY, John George; *b* 7 December 1980, Barking, London; *Partner* Toni Poole; 2 c (George John, Summer Rose (twins) b 18 May 2006); *Career* professional footballer; Chelsea FC: joined as apprentice, first team debut 1998, capt 2004–, winners FA Cup 2000 and 2007 (finalists 2002), winners FA Premiership 2005 and 2006 (runners-up 2004 and 2007), League Cup 2005 and 2007; England: 41 caps, capt 2006–, debut v Serbia and Montenegro 2003, capt Under 21s 2001–02, memb squad European Championships 2004 and World Cup 2006; PFA Footballer of the Year 2005; *Style*— Mr John Terry; ✉ c/o Chelsea Football Club, Fulham Road, London SW6 1HS

TERRY, John Victor; s of Norman Victor Terry (d 1981), and Mary Josephine Terry (d 1998); *b* 6 September 1942; *Educ* Leys Sch Cambridge, Jesus Coll Cambridge (MA), Harvard Business Sch (MBA); *m* 3 April 1965, Jane Gillian, da of Donald Pearson, of Cambridge; 2 s (Nicholas b 11 Jan 1969, Simon b 6 May 1971); *Career* gen mangr Herbert Terry and Sons Ltd 1971–75; Anglepoise Lighting Ltd: purchased and formed as independent co 1975, md 1975–88, chm 1988–; pres: Harvard Business Sch Assoc of Midlands 1983–85, Lighting Indust Fedn 1988–89; Freeman Worshipful Co of Lightmongers 1985; sec Frazer Nash Section Vintage Sports Car Club 1990–94; *Recreations* cars, sailing, real tennis; *Clubs* Royal London Yacht, Royal Thames Yacht, Leamington Tennis, British Racing Drivers; *Style*— John Terry, Esq; ✉ Comodore's House, Cowes, Isle of Wight PO31 7AJ (e-mail johnvterry@yahoo.co.uk)

TERRY, Nicholas John; s of John Edmund Terry (d 1978), of Nottingham, and Winifred Nina, *née* White (d 1970); *b* 12 November 1947; *Educ* Peveril Sch Nottingham, Bilborough GS Nottingham, Univ of Bath Sch of Architecture (BSc, BArch); *m* 27 June 1970, Dorothy, da of Leslie Atkins; 1 da (Alexandra Louise Terry b 31 Dec 1977); *Career* architect; Terry Associates Bath 1970, Building Design Partnership Manchester 1972–75, Arthur Erickson Architects Canada 1975–77, J S Bonnington Partnership St Albans 1978–81, Heery Architects and Engineers 1981–89; Building Design Partnership London 1990–: equity ptnr 1995–, company dir Dixon Jones BDP 1995– (chm 1996–), chm BDP Design Ltd 1996–, company dir Building Design Partnership Ltd 1997–, chm Building Design Partnership 2002–06, chm BDP South 2006–; architect dir: Citibank HQ London 1981, Frankfurt 1983, Cribbs Causeway Regional Shopping Centre 1992–98, ROH 1994–2000, Royal Albert Hall 1994–2003, Niketown London 1996–98, Canary Wharf Jubilee Place 1998–2003; vice-chm Int Alliance for Interoperability (IAI) 2005– (chm UK Chapter 2002–), chm European Enterprise Interoperability Centre 2006–; chm BSI (Br Standards) Building and Civil Engrg Sector Policy and Strategy Ctee 2007–; memb: RIBA 1973, AIBC 1976, RAIC 1976, Soc of American Mil Engrs 1985, IOD 1988, Br Cncl of Offices 1990, Br Cncl of Shopping Centres 1995, Int Cncl of Shopping Centres 1995; FRSA 2005; *Exhibitions* Royal Acad Summer Exhibition 1974 and MOMA NY 1979 (Durham Millburngate), Royal Acad Summer Exhibition 1975 (Albert Dock); RIBA, 1982 (Kuwait Stock Exchange); *Awards* incl: Europa Nostra Medal and Civic Tst 1978 (Durham Millburngate), BCSC and ICSC USA 2000 (Cribbs Causeway), RIBA Award, RICS Award, Europa Nostra Dip 2001 (ROH); *Recreations* swimming, walking, gardening, architecture, reading; *Style*— Nicholas Terry, Esq; ✉ Building Design Partnership, 16 Brewhouse Yard, London E1V 4LJ (tel 020 7812 8000, fax 020 7812 8399, e-mail nj-terry@bdp.co.uk)

TERRY, (John) Quinlan; s of Philip John Terry (d 1990), and Phyllis May Whiteman (d 1998); *b* 24 July 1937; *Educ* Bryanston, Architectural Assoc; *m* 9 Sept 1961, Christina Marie-Therese, da of Joachin Tadeusz de Ruttié (d 1968); 4 da (Elizabeth b 1964, Anna b 1965, Martha b 1979, Sophia b 1982), 1 s (Francis Nathanael b 1969); *Career* architect in private practice; works incl: office, retail and housing devpt at Richmond Riverside, 22 Baker Street, Dufours Place Soho, Regent Street Cambridge, Colonial Williamsburg VA, country houses in the classical style in England, Germany and America, New Howard Bldg Downing Coll Cambridge, New Brentwood Cathedral, six villas in Regent's Park for the Crown Estate Cmmrs, New Library Downing Coll, restoration of St Helen's Bishopsgate, restoration of the three state rooms No 10 Downing St; memb Royal Fine Art Cmmn 1994–98; FRIBA 1962; *Recreations* the Pauline Epistles; *Style*— Quinlan Terry, Esq; ✉ Quinlan & Francis Terry, Old Exchange, High Street, Dedham, Colchester CO7 6HA (tel 01206 323186, website www.qftarchitects.com)

TESFAYE, Prof Solomon; s of Ato Tesfaye Ashebir, of Ethiopia, and Weizero Mihret Tsegue; *b* 21 December 1958, Ethiopia; *Educ* Sevenoaks Sch, Univ of Bristol Med Sch (MB ChB, MD); *Career* sr med registrar 1993–96, conslt physician and diabetologist Royal Hallamshire Hosp Sheffield 1997–, currently prof of diabetic medicine Univ of Sheffield; fndr Neuropathic Foot Ulcer Clinic; former assoc ed Diabetologia, author of numerous articles in learned jls incl The Lancet and New England Jl of Med; memb: DH/MRC Diabetes Advsy Gp, Cardiovascular Advsy Gp Medicines and Healthcare Products Regulatory Agency, Advsy Cncl Neuropathy Tst, Bd Quantitative Sensory Testing Soc, Diabetes UK, American Diabetic Assoc, European Diabetic Neuropathy Study Gp; North of England Neurological Assoc Prize 1994; fndr Sheffield Health Action Resource for Ethiopia (SHARE); FRCP 2001 (MRCP 1988); *Recreations* table tennis, Impressionist painting, travelling, music; *Style*— Prof Solomon Tesfaye; ✉ Royal Hallamshire Hospital, Glossop Road, Sheffield S10 2JF (e-mail solomon.tesfaye@sth.nhs.uk)

TESORIERE, HE (Harcourt) Andrew Pretorius; s of Maj Pieter Ivan Tesoriere, and Joyce Margaret, *née* Baxter; *b* 2 November 1950; *Educ* NC Pangbourne, BRNC Dartmouth, UC Wales Aberystwyth (BSc), Ecole Nationale d'Admininistration Paris; *m* 1987, Dr Alma Gloria Vasquez; *Career* RNR 1964–68, offr RN 1969–73; HM Dip Serv: joined FCO 1974, Persian language trg SOAS Univ of London and Iran 1975, oriental sec Kabul 1976–79, third sec Nairobi 1979–81, second sec Abidjan (also accredited to Niamey and Ouagadougou) 1981–84, FCO 1985–87, first sec and head of Chancery then chargé d'affaires Damascus 1987–91, first sec FCO 1991–94, head of field ops UN Office for the Co-ordination of Humanitarian Affrs (OCHA) Afghanistan 1994–95, ambass to Albania 1996–98, on secondment as actg head of mission and sr political advsr UN Special Mission to Afghanistan 1998–2000, chargé d'affaires Kabul 2001–02, ambass to Latvia 2002–05, OSCE electoral advsr for Afghan elections 2004 and 2005, ambass to Algeria 2005–07, sr policy advsr to ISAF Cdr S Afghanistan 2007–; FRGS 1993; *Recreations* travel, sport, foreign languages, art, countryside; *Style*— HE Mr Andrew Tesoriere; ✉ c/o Foreign & Commonwealth Office (Algiers), King Charles Street, London SW1A 2AH

TESTA, Prof Humberto Juan; s of Orestes Miguel Angel Testa (d 1956), of Buenos Aires, Argentina, and Victoria Juana, *née* Vidal; *b* 11 December 1936; *Educ* Sch of Med Buenos Aires Univ (MD), Univ of Manchester (PhD); *m* 18 Dec 1964, Prof Nydia Esther Testa, *qv*, da of Victor Anibal Garcia (d 1982), of Neuquen, Argentina; 1 s (Fernando Julio b 31 Dec 1965), 2 da (Cecilia b 27 Nov 1973, Paula b 2 May 1981); *Career* Manchester Royal Infirmary: res offr 1967–68, res registrar 1968–70, fell in nuclear med 1970–73, conslt in nuclear med 1974–2001; pt/t prof of nuclear med Univ of Manchester 1998–2001, ret; fell: Manchester Med Soc, Br Nuclear Med Soc; miembro honorario nacional Academia De Medicina de Buenos Aires 1988; FRCP 1980, FRCR 1989; *Books* Nuclear Medicine in Urology and Nephrology (ed with O'Reilly and Shields, 1986), Adult Dementias (jtly, 1994), Nephrourology (with M C Prescott) in Clinician's Guide to Nuclear Medicine (series ed P J Ell, 1996); *Recreations* squash, music and reading; *Style*— Prof Humberto Testa; ✉ 27 Barcheston Road, Cheadle, Cheshire SK8 1LJ (tel 0161 428 6873, e-mail titotesta500@hotmail.com)

TESTA, Prof Nydia Esther Garcia; da of Victor Anibal Garcia (d 1981), and Manuela, *née* Barreiros; *b* 15 February 1938; *Educ* Univ of Buenos Aires, Univ of Manchester (PhD); *m* 18 Dec 1964, Prof Humberto Juan Testa, *qv*, s of Orestes Testa (d 1955); 1 s (Fernando b 1965), 2 da (Cecilia b 1973, Paula b 1981); *Career* res fell Cncl of Scientific and Tech Investigations Buenos Aires 1963–67, visiting res fell Paterson Laboratories 1967–74, special appointment scientist Paterson Inst for Cancer Res 1974–2001; author numerous scientific pubns in jls and books; *Style*— Prof Nydia G Testa; ✉ tel 0161 428 6873

TETLOW, His Hon Judge Christopher Bruce; s of George Wilfred Tetlow and Betty Tetlow; *b* 27 February 1943; *Educ* Stowe, Magdalene Coll Cambridge (MA); *m* 1981, Rosalind Jane

Cope; 2 s, 1 da; *Career* called to the Bar Middle Temple 1969, circuit judge (Northern Circuit) 1992–; *Clubs* St James's (Manchester); *Style*— His Hon Judge Tetlow

TETLOW, District Judge Raymond Charles; s of Charles Thomas Tetlow (d 1968), of Pinner, Middx, and Rosa Emily, *née* Milton (d 1972); *b* 15 July 1939; *Educ* Harrow Co GS for Boys; *m* 14 June 1985, Gillian Margaret Simmonite, da of late Wallace Frederick Thomas Aries; 2 step s (Derek Andrew Simmonite b 6 July 1965, Neil James Simmonite b 17 Feb 1968); *Career* articled to David Pritchard town clerk Borough of Harrow, Law Soc finals 1965, admitted slr 1966, asst slr London Borough of Harrow, slr to the cncl Bletchley UDC 1967–73, ptnr Andrew Marchant Solicitors Newport Pagnell 1973–77, sole practitioner in own name Newport Pagnell 1977–92, district judge 1992–2007; hon legal advsr Bucks Assoc of Parish Cncls 1970–91, fndr memb and legal advsr Milton Keynes CAB until 1991; memb Law Soc 1966–98, memb Assoc of District Judges 1992–; memb, treasurer, sec and pres Milton Keynes Dist Law Soc 1970–91; *Clubs* Castle Baynard Ward - City of London; *Style*— District Judge Tetlow

TETTMAR, Victor Stephen Downes; s of Kenneth Gerrard Tettmar (d 2003), and Anita Rosemary, *née* Arnold (d 1995); *b* 8 July 1961, Bridport, Dorset; *Educ* Mountbatten Sch Romsey, Barton Peveril Sixth Form Coll, Univ of Manchester (LLB), Chester Law Sch; *m* 7 July 1984, Amanda Catherine, *née* Wood; 3 da (Anne Rebekah b 10 Dec 1987, Emma Ruth b 6 June 1989, Laura Christine b 11 Sept 1992); *Career* admitted slr 1985; Bond Pearce: slr 1985, ptnr 1991–, memb Bd 2000, managing ptnr 2006–; pres Insolvency Lawyers Assoc 2006–07; memb: Law Soc, Non Admin Receivers Assoc, Lawyer's Christian Fellowship; licensed insolvency practitioner, registered property receiver; past regnl chm Assoc of Business Recovery Professionals; *Publications* Tolley's Insolvency Law (contrib chapter), Jordan's Agricultural Lending: Security and Enforcement (ed, 1999); *Recreations* sailing, mountain walking, skiing; *Clubs* Bristol Corinthian Yacht; *Style*— Victor Tettmar, Esq; ✉ Bond Pearce LLP, 3 Temple Quay, Temple Back East, Bristol BS1 6DZ (tel 0845 415 0000, fax 0845 415 6900, e-mail victor.tettmar@bondpearce.com)

TEVIOT, 2 Baron (UK 1940); Charles John Kerr; s of 1 Baron Teviot, DSO, MC (d 1968, himself ggs of 6 Marquess of Lothian), by his 2 w Angela (d 1979), da of Lt-Col Charles Villiers, CBE, DSO (ggn of 4 Earl of Clarendon) by his w Lady Kathleen Cole (2 da of 4 Earl of Enniskillen); *b* 16 December 1934; *Educ* Eton; *m* 1965, Patricia Mary, da of late Alexander Harris; 1 s (Hon Charles b 1971), 1 da (Hon Catherine b 1976); *Heir* s, Hon Charles Kerr; *Career* genealogist; memb Advsy Cncl on Public Records 1974–82; dir: Debrett's Peerage Ltd 1977–83, Burke's Peerage Research 1983–85, Burke's Peerage Ltd 1984–85; pres Assoc of Genealogists and Record Agents 1997–; FSG 1975; *Recreations* genealogy, walking; *Style*— The Rt Hon the Lord Teviot

TEWKESBURY, Bishop of 1996–; Rt Rev John Stewart Went; s of Douglas Norman Went (d 1970), and Barbara Adelaide, *née* Rand (d 2001); *b* 11 March 1944; *Educ* Colchester Royal GS, CCC Cambridge (MA); *m* 31 Aug 1968, Rosemary Evelyn Amy, da of late Peter Dunn; 3 s (Simon Charles b 28 June 1970, David James b 12 August 1972, Matthew John b 2 June 1975); *Career* asst curate Emmanuel Northwood 1969–75, vicar Holy Trinity Margate 1975–83, vice-princ Wycliffe Hall Oxford 1983–89, archdeacon of Surrey 1989–96; *Publications* Koinonia: Significant Milestone Towards Ecumenical Convergence (1996); contrib to various pubns; *Recreations* music, photography, swimming; *Style*— The Rt Rev the Bishop of Tewkesbury; ✉ Bishops House, Staverton, Gloucester GL51 0TW (e-mail bshptewk@star.co.uk)

TEWSON, Jane; CBE (1999); da of Dr Tim Tewson, of Oxford, and Dr Blue Johnston; *b* 9 January 1958; *Educ* Headington Sch Oxford, Lord William's Sch Thame; *m* 16 May 1992, Dr Charles Lane; 2 s (Charlie, Sam); *Career* project co-ordinator MENCAP 1979–83, fndr and chief exec Charity Projects and Comic Relief 1984–96, fndr PilotLight 1996–99, fndr Timebank 1999, dir PilotLight Australia 2000, dir St James Ethics Centre; tstee Reichstein Fndn; *Recreations* travel, walking, gardening, reading; *Style*— Ms Jane Tewson, CBE; ✉ 35 Cressy Street, Malvern 3144, Melbourne, Australia

TEYNHAM, 20 Baron (E 1616); John Christopher Ingham Roper-Curzon; s of 19 Baron Teynham, DSO, DSC (d 1972), by his 1 w Elspeth (m dis 1956, she d 1976, having m 2, 1958, 6 Marquess of Northampton, DSO); *b* 25 December 1928; *Educ* Eton; *m* 1964, Elizabeth, da of Lt-Col the Hon David Scrymgeour-Wedderburn, DSO (ka 1944) 2 s of 10 Earl of Dundee; 5 s (Hon David b 5 Oct 1965, Hon Jonathan b 27 April 1973, Hon Peter b 20 Nov 1977, Hon William b 27 July 1980, Hon Benjamin b 15 Sept 1982), 5 da (Hon Emma (Hon Mrs Murphy) b 19 Sept 1966, Hon Sophie (Hon Mrs Van Den Bogaerde) b 30 Nov 1967, Hon Lucy (Hon Mrs Fraser) b 23 July 1969, Hon Hermione (Hon Mrs Nixon) (twin) b 27 April 1973, Hon Alice b 18 Dec 1983); *Heir* s, Hon David Roper-Curzon; *Career* late Capt The Buffs (TA) and 2 Lt Coldstream Gds, active serv Palestine 1948, ADC to Govr of Bermuda 1953 and 1955, ADC to Govr of Leeward Islands 1955 (also private sec 1956), ADC to govr of Jamaica 1962; pres Inst of Commerce 1972–, vice-pres Inst of Export, memb Cncl Sail Training Assoc 1964; memb Cncl of l'Orchestre du Monde 1987–; former land agent Hatherop Estate Glos; patron Living of St Mary the Virgin South Baddesley; Lord of the Manor: South Baddesley, Sharpricks; OStJ; *Clubs* Turf, House of Lords Yacht, Ocean Cruising, Puffin's (Edinburgh); *Style*— The Rt Hon the Lord Teynham

THACKARA, John Alexander; s of Alexander Daniel Thackara, of Bath, and Eleanor Hazel, *née* Miller; *b* 6 August 1951; *Educ* Marlborough, Univ of Kent (BA), Univ of Wales (Dip Journalism); *m* 20 April 1989, Hilary Mary, da of late Bowyer Arnold, DFC; 1 da (Kate Eleanor b 1989); *Career* commissioning ed Granada Publishing 1975–79, managing ed NSW Univ Press 1979–80, ed Design Magazine 1981–85, freelance design critic 1985–87, fndr and dir Design Analysis Int 1987, dir of research RCA 1989–92, dir Netherlands Design Inst 1993–99, currently dir Doors of Perception, prog dir Designs of the Time; former chm European Design Industry Summit (EDIS), former memb Co-ordinating Gp Convivio; former memb Virtual Platform (advising Dutch Govt), memb various expert gps advising EC on innovation policy; FRSA 1987; *Books* incl: New British Design (1987), Design after Modernism (1988), Lost in Space: A Traveller's Tale (1995), In the Bubble: Designing In A Complex World (2005); *Recreations* writing; *Clubs* Groucho; *Style*— John Thackara, Esq; ✉ Doors of Perception, 17 Grand Rue, 34190 Ganges, France (e-mail john@doorsofperception.com, website www.doorsofperception.com); website www.thackara.com

THACKER, David Thomas; s of Thomas Richard Thacker, and Alice May, *née* Beaumont; *b* 21 December 1950; *Educ* Wellingborough GS, Univ of York (BA, MA); *m* Margot Elizabeth, *née* Leicester; 3 s (Thomas David b 1984, William Charles b 1986, Edward Arthur b 1989), 1 da (Elizabeth Grace b 1992); *Career* theatre director; York Theatre Royal: asst stage mangr, dep stage mangr then stage mangr 1974–75, asst dir 1975–76; Chester Gateway Theatre: Arts Cncl asst dir 1976–77, assoc dir 1977–78; Duke's Playhouse Lancaster: Arts Cncl assoc dir 1978–79, dir 1980–84; dir Young Vic 1984–93; dir in residence RSC 1993–95; tstee: Hoghton Tower Shakespeare Centre, Shakespeare Nat Tst, Haringey Med Tst; govr Tetherdown Primary Sch; *Theatre* over 100 prodns incl: fifteen plays by William Shakespeare, ten plays by Arthur Miller, seven plays by Samuel Beckett, three plays by Henrik Ibsen, three plays by Eugene O'Neil, Ghosts (Young Vic and West End, London Fringe Award for Best Dir and Olivier Award nomination for Outstanding Achievement 1987), Who's Afraid of Virginia Woolf? (Young Vic, London Fringe Award for Best Prodn 1987), A Touch of the Poet (Young Vic and West End), An Enemy of the People (Young Vic and West End, Olivier Award nomination for Best Dir 1989), The Last Yankee (Young Vic and West End) 1993, Broken Glass (RNT and West End, Olivier Award Play of the Year) 1994, A View From The Bridge (West End) 1994, Death of a Salesman (RNT) 1996; RSC prodns incl: Pericles (Olivier Award Best Dir and Best Revival of a Play 1991), The Two Gentlemen of Verona (also West End), As You Like It, The Merchant of Venice, Julius Caesar, Coriolanus, The Tempest; *Television* over 30 prodns incl: A Doll's House (BAFTA Best Single Drama nomination), Measure for Measure, Death of a Salesman, Broken Glass, The Scold's Bridle, Silent Witness, Waking the Dead, Faith, Murder in Mind, Dalziel and Pascoe; Channel 4 prodns incl Lock Stock; ITV prodns incl: Kavanagh QC, The Vice, Grafters, Foyle's War, The Mayor of Casterbridge; *Recreations* sport, politics, film, reading, family; *Style*— David Thacker; ✉ 55 Onslow Gardens, Muswell Hill, London N10 3JY (tel 020 8444 8436, e-mail davidthacker@blueyonder.co.uk)

THANE, Sarah Ann; CBE (2003), JP (W Suffolk 2005); da of John Arnold Cecil Thane (d 1972), and Winifred Blanche, *née* Wayne (d 2000); *b* 21 September 1951, Birmingham; *Educ* Sutton Coldfield GS for Girls, County HS Stourbridge, City of Birmingham Poly (Dip); *m* 30 March 1996, Peter Robert Wenban; 3 step s, 2 step da; *Career* ITC: dir of public affrs 1990–96, dir of progs and cable 1996–2001, dir of progs and advtg 2001–03; advsr content and standards Ofcom 2003–05; pt/t advsr to: BBC Govrs 2005–06, BBC Tst 2007–; chm RTS 2000–02 (vice-chm 1998–2000); non-exec dir Films of Record 2005–; cmmr Nat Lottery Cmmn 2005–; FRTS 1994; *Recreations* music, visual arts, cooking, gardening, time with friends and family; *Clubs* Reform; *Style*— Ms Sarah Thane, CBE, JP

THANKI, Bankim; QC (2003); s of B D Thanki (d 2004), and Vijayalaxmi Thanki; *b* 19 April 1964; *Educ* Owen's Sch, Balliol Coll Oxford (MA); *m* 21 June 1988, Catherine Jane Margaret, da of James Spotswood (d 2006), of Bangor, Co Down, and Sheila Spotswood; 3 s (Alexander Anand b 15 July 1993, Daniel Rohan b 5 May 1995, Joseph Dev b 26 Dec 2003), 1 da (Olivia Priya b 22 Oct 1998); *Career* called to the Bar Middle Temple 1988 (Harmsworth scholar); memb Fountain Court Chambers 1989–; memb Commercial Bar Assoc; *Publications* Carriage by Air (co-author, 2000), Commercial Court Procedure (jt ed, 2001), Law of Bank Payments (contrib, 2004), Law of Priviledge (ed, 2006); *Recreations* Manchester United FC; *Clubs* RAC; *Style*— Bankim Thanki, Esq, QC; ✉ Fountain Court, Temple, London EC4Y 9DH (tel 020 7583 3335, fax 020 7353 0329)

THATCHER, Anthony Neville; s of Edwin Neville Thatcher (d 1978), and Elsie May, *née* Webster; *b* 10 September 1939; *Educ* Sir John Lawes Sch Harpenden, Univ of Manchester (MSc); *m* 20 Oct 1968, Sally Margaret, da of Henry Joseph Clark, of Norfolk; *Career* Ultra Electronics 1967–77, md Dowty Electronics Controls Ltd 1978–82, gp chief exec Dowty Group plc 1986–91 (md Electronics Div 1982–86, memb Bd 1983), vice-chm Thyssen Bornemisza Group SAM Monaco 1991–; memb: Electronics and Avionics Requirements Bd of DTI 1981–85, Cncl Electronics Engrg Assoc 1983–91 (pres 1986), Cncl Soc of Br Aerospace Cos 1986–91, RARDE Mgmnt Bd (industrial) 1986–91, Engrg Mkts Advsy Ctee DTI 1988–90, Mgmnt Bd Engrg Employers Fedn 1988–91 (vice-pres 1990), Innovation Advsy Bd DTI 1988–91, Bd SW Electricity Bd 1989–91, Engrg Cncl 1989–91; memb Cncl Cheltenham Ladies' Coll 1989–91; Liveryman and tstee Worshipful Co of Glass Sellers; CEng, FIMechE; *Recreations* art, jazz piano, opera, fishing, gardening, bird watching; *Clubs* Athenaeum, Carlton, George Town (Washington DC); *Style*— Anthony Thatcher, Esq; ✉ 12 Gayfere Street, London SW1P 3HP

THATCHER, Baroness (Life Peer UK 1992), of Kesteven in the County of Lincolnshire; Margaret Hilda Thatcher; LG (1995), OM (1990), PC (1970); yr da of Alfred Roberts (d 1970), grocer, of Grantham, Lincs, sometime borough cncllr, alderman and mayor of Grantham, and Beatrice Ethel, *née* Stephenson (d 1960); *b* 13 October 1925; *Educ* Kesteven and Grantham Girls' Sch, Somerville Coll Oxford (MA, BSc); *m* 13 Dec 1951, as his 2 w, Sir Denis Thatcher, Bt (d 2003); 2 c (Hon Mark, Hon Carol (twins) b 15 Aug 1953); *Career* former research chemist; called to the Bar Lincoln's Inn 1954 (hon bencher 1975); Parly candidate (Cons) Dartford 1950 and 1951, MP (Cons) Finchley 1959–92, jt Parly sec Miny of Pensions and National Insurance 1961–64, memb Shadow Cabinet 1967–70 (spokesman on tport, power, Treasury matters, housing and pensions), chief oppn spokesman on educn 1969–70, sec of state for educn and science (and co-chm Women's National Cmmn) 1970–74, chief oppn spokesman on the environment 1974–75, leader of the Opposition Feb 1975–79, prime minister and First Lord of the Treasury (first woman to hold this office) 4 May 1979–28 Nov 1990; minister for the Civil Service Jan 1981–Nov 1990; chllr: Buckingham Univ 1992–98, William and Mary Coll USA 1994–2000; chm of Bd Inst of US Studies Univ of London; vice-pres Royal Soc of St George 1999–; Freedom of Borough of Barnet 1980; Hon Freeman: Worshipful Co of Grocers 1980, Worshipful Co of Poulters; Freedom of Falkland Islands 1983; Donovan Award USA 1981, US Medal of Freedom 1991; hon fell Somerville Coll Oxford 1970; FRS 1983; *Books* The Downing Street Years (1993), The Path to Power (1995); *Style*— The Rt Hon Baroness Thatcher, LG, OM, PC, FRS; ✉ House of Lords, London SW1A 0PW

THEAKSTON, Jamie; *b* 21 December 1970, Sussex; *Educ* BA; *Career* presenter, broadcaster and actor; started as radio travel news reader 1993, former presenter GLR and Radio FiveLive (shows incl Sportscall, Friday Night on 5, Jamie Theakston's Cricket Show), presenter BBC Radio 1 1999–2002, presenter breakfast show Heart 106.2 2005–; presenter of TV shows incl: The O-Zone (BBC 2), Live And Kicking (with Zoe Ball, *qv*, BBC 1) 1996–99, Top Of The Pops (BBC 1) 1999–2002, Holiday (BBC 1), A Question of Pop (BBC 1), The Priory (Channel 4), Beg Borrow or Steal (BBC 2), With A Little Help From My Friends (ITV), The Games (Channel 4), People's Quiz (BBC 1), UK Music Hall of Fame (Channel 4), The Oscars (Sky), The Search (Channel 4); actor: Murder in Mind (BBC TV), Mad About Alice (BBC TV), Linda Green (BBC TV), Art (West End), Home & Beauty (West End), Agatha Christie (ITV), Rock Profile (BBC 2); *Recreations* sport, theatre; *Style*— Jamie Theakston

THELLUSSON, James Hugh; s of Hon Peter Robert Thellusson, of Barnes, London, and Celia Marie, *née* Walsh; *b* 7 January 1961; *Educ* St Paul's, Univ of York (BA), Nat Broadcasting Sch; *m* Dec 1995, Jennifer Louise, *née* Owers; 1 da (Abigail b Feb 1998), 1 s (Ben b 17 June 2002); *Career* reporter on What to Buy for Business 1987–89, dir Paragon Communications 1992–93; Cohn & Wolfe Ltd: jt md 1994–96, int network dir 1997–98, md Europe 1998–2001; ceo Edelman PR 2002–; memb: Friends of the Earth, Shelter, National Trust; winner of numerous PR campaign awards; *Recreations* theatre, poetry, golf, eating out, my daughter; *Clubs* New Zealand Golf; *Style*— James Thellusson, Esq; ✉ Edelman Public Relations, Haymarket House, 28–29 Haymarket, London SW1Y 4SP (tel 020 7344 1210, fax 020 7344 1295, e-mail james.thellusson@edelman.com)

THEMEN, Arthur Edward George; s of Dr Lambert Christian Joseph Themen (d 1945), of Oldham, Lancs, and Ethel Elizabeth, *née* Nadin; *b* 26 November 1939; *Educ* Manchester Grammar, St Catharine's Coll Cambridge (MA), St Mary's Hosp Med Sch Univ of London; *m* 8 Jan 1968 (m dis 1979), Judith Frances Anquetil, da of Frank Alexander Arrowsmith, OBE, of Oxford; 1 da (Justine b 1969), 2 s (Daniel b 1971, Benjamin b 1972); *Career* former house surgn St Mary's Hosp, RPMS; surgical registrar Royal Northern Hosp 1969, sr registrar St Mary's Hosp and Royal Nat Orthopaedic Hosps 1971–74, currently conslt orthopaedic surgn Royal Berks Hosp and assoc surgn Nuffield Orthopaedic Centre Oxford; special interest incl spinal and jt replacement surgery; various articles on joint replacement in professional jls; musical career as jazz musician; memb prize winning Cambridge Univ Jazz Gp 1958 (best soloist 1959), involved with early Br Blues movement; worked with: Mick Jagger, Rod Stewart, Georgie Fame; UK rep in Int Jazz Orch Festival Zurich 1965; began long assoc with Stan Tracey 1974; toured and recorded with: Charlie Parker alumni, Al Haig, Red Rodney; tours incl Chicago and NY Jazz

Festivals; records incl: Captain Adventure 1975, Under Milk Wood 1976, Expressly Ellington 1978 (with Al Haig), Spectrum 1982, Playing in the Yard 1986, Genesis 1987 (with Stan Tracey); memb Contemporary Music Ctee Arts Cncl; FBOA 1974, FRSM; *Recreations* skiing, sailing; *Clubs* Ronnie Scott's; *Style*— Arthur Themen, Esq; ✉ 6 The Blades, Lower Mall, Hammersmith, London W6 9DJ (tel 020 8741 7066); Orthopaedic Department, Royal Berkshire Hospital, London Road, Reading, Berkshire RG1 5AN (tel 0118 958 4711)

THEOBALD, Prof Michael Francis; s of George Charles Theobald (d 1994), of Sanderstead, Surrey, and Elise Dorothy, *née* Baker; *b* 1 September 1946; *Educ* KCL, Univ of Manchester (BSc, MA, PhD); *m* 26 Oct 1972, Pauline Florence, da of Capt Christopher Herbert Harman (d 1989), of St Leonards, nr Ringwood; 1 s (Jonathan Harman b 3 Sept 1978), 1 da (Sarah Pauline b 5 June 1981); *Career* chartered accountant; Price Waterhouse & Co: London 1968–72, Buenos Aires 1972–74; Univ of Manchester 1974–85; prof Univ of Birmingham 1985– (sometime head Dept of Accounting and Finance and dir of research Birmingham Business Sch); former chm: Market Analytical Techniques, Mifranthe and Associates; chm Int Exams Ctee Certified Int Investment Analysts; memb: Trg and Qualifications Cmmn Euro Fedn of Financial Analysts' Socs, various ctees UK Soc of Investment Professionals; conslt to the ESRC and Accounting Standards Bd; dir Euro Capital Markets Inst; tstee and memb Research Advsy Bd Chartered Financial Analysts Research Fndn USA; memb Fin Instruments Task Force; expert witness; academic advsr European Fedn of Financial Analysts' Socs; memb Editorial Bd: Jl of Banking and Finance, Br Accounting Review, Jl of Business Finance and Accounting, Quarterly Int Jl of Finance, Jl of Derivative Accounting; fell UK Soc of Investment Professionals 2000, FCA 1972; *Publications* Research Method and Methodology (co-author); articles published in: Jl of Finance, Jl of Financial and Quantitive Analysis, Jl of Banking and Finance, Jl of Portfolio Mgmnt, Jl of Futures Markets, Jl of Derivatives, Jl of Financial Markets; *Recreations* sport, literature, travel, music, theatre, fine wine and dining; *Style*— Prof Michael Theobald; ✉ Birmingham Business School, University of Birmingham, Edgbaston, Birmingham B15 2TT (tel 0121 414 6540, e-mail m.f.theobald@bham.ac.uk)

THEOBALD, (George) Peter; JP (1974); s of George Oswald Theobald (d 1952), of Surrey, and Helen, *née* Moore (d 1972); *b* 5 August 1931; *Educ* Betteshanger Sch, Harrow; *m* 1955, Josephine Mary, da of Wilfrid Andrew Carmichael Boodle (d 1961); 2 s (Carmichael, Christopher), 3 da (Caroline, Jane, Kate); *Career* cmmnd 5 Regt RHA 1950–52, Lt 290 City of London Regt RA (TA) 1953–59; gp chief exec Robert Warner plc 1953–74; dir: Moran Holdings plc 1977–2005 (chm 1992–2005), Moran Tea Co (India) plc 1981–2005 (chm 1992–2005); memb: Tport Users Consultative Ctee for London 1969–84 (dep chm 1978–79), London Regnl Passengers Ctee 1984–90; church cmmr for England 1978–79, licensed asst Dio of Guildford 1970–; Alderman City of London 1974–79 (common councilman 1968–74); govr: Bridewell Royal Hosp 1974–93, King Edward's Sch Witley 1974–93 (tstee Educn Tst 1977–95), Christ's Hosp 1976–91, St Leonards Mayfield Sch 1982–88; chm St John's Sch Northwood 1989–97; tstee: Nat Flood and Tempest Distress Fund 1977–, Harrow Mission W10 1978–2001; memb Ct of Assts Worshipful Co of Merchant Taylors 1983– (Master 1989–90 and 1991–92); *Recreations* gardening, transport, walking; *Clubs* Oriental, MCC; *Style*— Peter Theobald, Esq

THEOCHAROUS, The Most Rev Archbishop Gregorios; s of Theocharis Hadjittofi, and Maria, *née* Koronou; *b* 2 January 1929; *Educ* HS Lefkonikon Famagusta Cyprus, Pan-Cyprian Gymnasium Nicosia Cyprus, Theol Faculty Univ of Athens Greece; *Career* monk Monastery of Stavrovounion Cyprus 1951; ordained deacon 1953, priest 1959; asst priest then parish priest All Saints' Church Camden Town London 1959–69; consecrated bishop of Tropaeou 1970; Archdiocese of Thyateira and GB: chllr 1965–79, asst bishop 1970–88, archbishop of Thyateira and GB 1988–; orthodox pres: Anglican and Eastern Churches' Assoc, Fellowship of St Alban and St Sergius; co-pres: Soc of St John Chrysostom, Cncl of Christians and Jews; co-patron Religious Educn and Environment Prog; Hon Doctorate Univ of N London 1993; *Recreations* walking, gardening, reading; *Style*— The Most Rev Archbishop Gregorios; ✉ Archdiocese of Thyateira and Great Britain, 5 Craven Hill, London W2 3EN (tel 020 7723 4787, fax 020 7224 9301)

THEROUX, Louis; s of Paul Theroux, and Anne Castle; *b* 20 May 1970, Singapore; *Educ* Westminster, Univ of Oxford; *Career* presenter and journalist; early career as journalist on San Jose Metro and Spy magazine; *Television* incl: TV Nation 1994–95, Weird Weekends 1998–2000, When Louis Met... 2000–02, Louis and the Brothel 2003, Louis, Martin & Michael 2003, Louis and the Nazis 2003, Gambling in Las Vegas 2007, The Most Hated Family in America 2007; *Books* The Call of the Weird: Travels in American Subcultures (2005); *Style*— Louis Theroux, Esq; ✉ c/o Capel & Land Ltd, 29 Wardour Street, London W1D 6PS (tel 020 7734 2414, fax 020 7734 8101)

THETFORD, Bishop of 2001–; Rt Rev Dr David John Atkinson; s of Thomas John Collins Atkinson (d 1986), and Adèle Mary, *née* Cox (d 2000); *b* 5 September 1943; *Educ* Maidstone GS, KCL (BSc, PhD, AKC), Univ of Bristol (MLitt), Univ of Oxford (MA), London Cert in Student Counselling; *m* 1969, Suzan; 1 s (Jonathan b 1972), 1 da (Rachel b 1974); *Career* sci teacher: Maidstone HS 1968–69, Tyndale Hall Bristol 1969–72; ordained: deacon 1972, priest 1973; curate St Peter Halliwell Bolton 1972–74, sr curate St John Harborne 1974–77, librarian Latimer House Oxford 1977–80; Corpus Christi Coll Oxford: chaplain 1980–93, fell and lectr 1984–93; residentiary canon Southwark Cathedral 1993–96, archdeacon of Lewisham 1996–2001; co-fndr Oxford Christian Inst for Counselling, formerly dir Mildmay Mission Hosp, formerly theol conslt Care and Counsel; memb Soc of Ordained Scientists (SOSc); *Books* To Have and to Hold (1979), Homosexuals in the Christian Fellowship (1979), Peace in Our Time? (1985); Bible Speaks Today: Ruth (1984), Genesis 1–11 (1990), Job (1992), Proverbs (1996); Life and Death (1986), Pastoral Ethics (1989, 2 edn 1994), New Dictionary of Christian Ethics and Pastoral Theology (co-ed, 1995), Counselling in Context (1998), Jesus, Lamb of God (1996), God So Loved The World (1999); *Recreations* music, painting, walking; *Style*— The Rt Rev the Bishop of Thetford; ✉ The Red House, 53 Norwich Road, Stoke Holy Cross, Norwich NR14 8AB (tel 01508 491014, fax 01508 492105, e-mail bishop.thetford@4frontmedia.co.uk)

THEWLIS, David; s of Alec Raymond Wheeler, of Blackpool, and Maureen, *née* Thewlis; *b* 20 March 1963; *Educ* Highfield HS Blackpool, St Anne's Coll of FE, Guildhall Sch of Music and Drama; *m* 10 April 1992, Sara Jocelyn, da of Paul Sugarman; *Career* actor; *Theatre* incl: Buddy Holly at the Regal (Greenwich), Ice Cream (Royal Court), Lady and the Clarinet (Netherbow Edinburgh, winner Fringe First, also at King's Head Islington), The Sea (NT); *Television* incl: Dandelion Dead, Valentine Park, Road, Singing Detective, Bit of a Do, Skullduggery, Journey to Knock (Best Actor Rheims Film Festival 1992), Filipina Dreamgirls, Frank Stubbs Promotes, Prime Suspect 3, Endgame (Beckett on Film series), Hamilton Mattress, Dinotopia; *Films* incl: Short and Curlies, Vroom, Resurrected, Afraid of the Dark, Life is Sweet, Damage, The Trial, Naked (Best Actor Cannes Film Festival 1993), Black Beauty, The Island of Dr Moreau, Divorcing Jack, Besieged, Whatever Happened to Harold Smith?, Gangster No1, Goodbye Charlie Bright, Cheeky, Timeline, Harry Potter and the Prisoner of Azkaban; *Books* The Late Hector Kipling (2007); *Recreations* painting; *Style*— David Thewlis, Esq

THEWLIS, Sarah Anne; da of Geoffrey Frank Bennett (d 1996), of Enysford, Kent, and Mollie, *née* Bates; *b* 12 May 1958; *Educ* Dartford GS for Girls, Univ of Hull (BA), Relate Cert in Marital and Couple Counselling; *m* 1983, Rev Dr John Charles Thewlis, s of Dennis Jones Thewlis; *Career* Marks & Spencer plc 1979–91: personnel mangr Marble Arch branch 1984–85, category mangr for store asst personnel mangrs 1985–88, divnl personnel controller for distribution centres 1989–91; dep sec Royal Coll of Physicians 1991–94, co sec and gen mangr Royal Coll of Gen Practitioners 1994–2002, chief exec and registrar Nursing and Midwifery Cncl 2002–; temp conslt in Oman WHO 2006; govr: Deansfield Sch Eltham, Horn Park Sch Eltham; chm Personnel Ctee Southwark Diocese; memb: The Bishop's Equal Opportunities Ctee 2001–, Archbishop's Cncl Ctee on deployment, remuneration and conditions of service 2006; lay memb Employment Tbnl Panel 1999–; FCIPD 1998 (MIPD 1991), FRSA 2001, Hon FRCGP 2002; *Recreations* horses, people, current affairs; *Style*— Sarah Thewlis; ✉ The Rectory, 2 Talbot Road, Carshalton, Surrey SM5 3BS (tel 020 8647 2366, e-mail sat@panicellus.demon.co.uk); Nursing and Midwifery Council, 23 Portland Place, London W1B 1PZ (tel 020 7333 6528, e-mail sarah.thewlis@nmc-uk.org)

THEXTON, Susan Elizabeth Lee; da of John W Thexton, and Dorothy Topham, *née* Lee; *b* 13 September 1960, Newcastle upon Tyne; *Educ* London Coll of Printing (BA); *m* 1 Oct 1994, Peter Worlock; 1 da (Amy b 5 May 1999); *Career* UK sales mangr Software Div Letraset UK Ltd 1984–89, gen mangr Adobe Northern Europe 1989–94, vice-pres Macromedia EMEA 1994–2004, ptnr Thexton Worlock Ltd 2004–05, md ITN Source 2005–; memb Cncl and TV Ctee BAFTA; tstee and non-exec dir NESTA Futurelab; hon visiting prof Middx Univ; FRSA; *Recreations* gardening, drinking good red wine, reading avidly; *Style*— Ms Susan Thexton; ✉ 157 Park Road, Chiswick, London W4 3EX

THIAN, Bob; s of Clifford Peter Thian, of Jersey, and Frances Elizabeth, *née* Stafford-Bird (d 1980); *b* 1 August 1943, South Africa; *Educ* Kenton Coll Nairobi, Oundle, Univ of Geneva; *m* 24 Oct 1964, Liselotte, da of Wilhelm Von Borges; 2 da (Stefanie, Samantha); *Career* called to the Bar Gray's Inn; legal advsr Glaxo Gp Ltd 1968–69, project devpt exec Glaxo-Allenburys Export Ltd 1968–72, md Glaxo Farmaceutica Lda 1972–80, business devpt dir (Europe) Abbott International 1980–82, regnl dir (Europe) Abbott Laboratories 1982–87, vice-pres international ops Pharmaceutical Div Novo Industri A/S 1987–89, gp chief exec North West Water Gp plc 1990–93, fndr and chief exec Renex Ltd 1993–, gp chief exec The Stationery Office Gp 1996–99; chm: IMO Gp Ltd 1999–2000, Tactica Solutions Ltd 1999–2001, Orion Gp Ltd 2001–04, Conseil de Surveillance Expand Santé (Paris) 1999–2001, Astron Gp Ltd 2001–05, Whatman plc 2002–, Southern Water Ltd 2003–, Cardpoint plc 2006–, Equiniti Ltd 2007–; dir: Celltech Gp plc (now Celltech plc) 1992–99, Medeval Ltd 1995–98; *Clubs* Chantilly Golf, Lansdowne; *Style*— Bob Thian, Esq; ✉ 16 Princes Gate Mews, London SW7 2PS (e-mail bob.thian@renex.net)

THIMBLEBY, Prof Harold William; s of Peter Thimbleby, of Rugby, Warks, and Angela Marion, *née* Hodson; *b* 19 July 1955; *Educ* Rugby, Univ of London (BSc, MSc, PhD); *m* 16 Feb 1980, Prudence Mary (Prue), da of Rev Capt Arundel Charles Barker, of Matlock, Derbys; 3 s (William, Samuel, Isaac), 1 da (Jemima); *Career* lectr in computer sci: Queen Mary Coll 1980–82, Univ of York 1982–88; prof of info technol Univ of Stirling (in Dept of Computing 1988–93, Dept of Psychology 1993–94); Univ of Middx: prof of computing research 1994–2001, dir of research 1995–2000, dir Interaction Centre and prof of interaction UCL 2001–05, 28th Gresham prof of geometry Gresham Coll 2001–; co-inventor of Liveware (technique for exploiting computer viruses) 1989, govr St Alban's Sch; Br Computer Soc Wilkes Medal 1987, Toshiba Year of Invention Award; CEng; Freeman: City of London, Worshipful Co of Information Technologists; Hon FRSA; FIEE; *Books* author of over 300 pubns incl: Formal Methods In Human-Computer Interaction (ed with M D Harrison, 1989), User Interface Design (1990), Hyperprogramming (with G F Coulouris, 1993); *Recreations* hill walking, woodwork, electronics; *Style*— Prof Harold Thimbleby; ✉ Swansea University, Swansea SA2 8PP (e-mail h.thimbleby@swansea.ac.uk)

THIN, Dr (Robert) Nicol Traquair; OBE (1995); s of Robert Traquair Thin (d 1990), of Bromley, Kent, and Annie Dempster, *née* Snowball; *b* 21 September 1935; *Educ* Loretto, Univ of Edinburgh Med Sch (MB ChB, MD); *m* 1962, (Agnes) Ann, da of Alexander William Graham, OBE (d 1964), of Inverness; 2 s (Sandy b 1964, Iain b 1968); *Career* cmmnd RAMC 1964, Malaya, Singapore and UK, ret Maj; Maj TA 1974–76; venereologist BMH Singapore 1969–71, conslt venereologist Edinburgh Royal Infirmary 1971–73, conslt in genitourinary med Bart's 1973–81, conslt venereologist St Peter's Hosps London 1975–94 (emeritus conslt UCL Hosps 1994–), civilian conslt in genitourinary med to the Army 1981–2000; hon sr lectr Inst of Urology and conslt in genitourinary med St Thomas' Hosp London 1982–2000; personal conslt advsr in genitourinary med to The CMO at Dept of Health 1994–2000, dir of R&D Guy's and St Thomas' Hosp Tst 1997–2000, emeritus conslt Guy's and St Thomas' Hosp Tst 2001–; pt/t clinical asst and locum conslt in genitounirary med Beckenham Hosp 2001–06; ed British Jl of Venereal Diseases 1975–80, contrib specialist and general textbooks incl Lecture Notes on Sexually Transmitted Diseases; pres Med Soc of Venereal Diseases 1987–89 (memb 1968–), chm Specialist Advsy Ctee on Genitourinary Med of the Jt Ctee on Higher Med Training 1982–83 (memb 1976–81, sec 1981–82), examiner for Dip in Genitourinary Med for Soc of Apothecaries of London 1981–98, pres Soc of Health Advsrs in Sexually Transmitted Diseases 1983–86, memb Expert Advsy Gp on AIDS 1985–87, external examiner of Dip in Venereology for Univ of Liverpool 1987–89, memb Genitourinary Med Sub-Ctee RCP 1987–95 (chm 1995–2002), founding chm Assoc for Genitourinary Med 1992–97, chm Public Health Laboratory Service Ethics Ctee 1997–2003; former postgrad dean Bart's Med Coll; pres Edinburgh Univ Boat Club Alexandra Club (for former rowers) 1998–, former pres pres Edinburgh Univ Boat Club, vice-pres St Thomas' Hosp Boat Club; memb Nat Tst; memb: BMA 1960, Med Soc of Venereal Diseases 1968; FRSM 1988, FRCP, FRCPE; *Recreations* music, reading, overseas travel; *Clubs* City Volunteer Officers; *Style*— Dr Nicol Thin, OBE; ✉ Teratak, 13 Park Avenue, Bromley, Kent BR1 4EF (tel 020 8464 9278)

THIRLWALL, Prof Anthony Philip; s of Isaac Thirlwall (d 1960), and Ivy, *née* Ticehurst (d 1988); *b* 21 April 1941; *Educ* Clark Univ USA (MA), Univ of Leeds (BA, PhD); *m* 26 March 1966 (sep 1986), Gianna, da of Bruno Paoletti (d 1985); 2 s (Lawrence b 1967, Adrian b and d 1975), 1 da (Alexandra 1974); *Career* asst lectr in economics Univ of Leeds 1964; Univ of Kent: lectr in economics 1966, prof of applied economics 1976–2004, emeritus prof 2004–; visiting prof and lectr at several overseas univs; econ advsr Dept of Employment 1968–70; conslt: Pacific Islands Devpt Prog 1989–90 and 1996, African Devpt Bank 1993–94 and 1999, Asian Devpt Bank 2003, UN Conf on Trade and Devpt (UNCTAD) 2005–; memb Editorial Bd: Jl of Devpt Studies, Jl of Post Keynesian Economics, African Devpt Review; memb Action Aid; memb Royal Economic Soc; *Books* Growth and Development: With Special Reference to Developing Economies (1972, 8 edn 2006), Inflation, Saving and Growth in Developing Economies (1974), Regional Growth and Unemployment in the United Kingdom (with R Dixon, 1975), Financing Economic Development (1976), Keynes and International Monetary Relations (ed, 1976), Keynes and Laissez Faire (ed, 1978), Keynes and the Bloomsbury Group (ed with D Crabtree, 1980), Balance of Payments Theory and the United Kingdom Experience (1980, 4 edn 1991), Keynes as a Policy Adviser (ed, 1982), Keynes and Economic Development (ed, 1987), Nicholas Kaldor (1987), Collected Essays of Nicholas Kaldor Volume 9 (ed with F Targetti, 1989), The Essential Kaldor (ed with F Targetti, 1989), European Factor Mobility: Trends and Consequences (ed with I Gordon, 1989), Deindustrialisation (with S Bazen, 1989, 3 edn 1997), The Performance and Prospects of the Pacific Island Economies in the World Economy (1991), Keynes and the Role of the State (ed, 1993), Economic Growth and the Balance of Payments Constraint (with J McCombie, 1994), The Economics of Growth and Development: Selected Essays of A P Thirlwall Vol 1 (1995), Macroeconomic Issues from a Keynesian Perspective: Selected Essays of A P

Thirlwall Vol 2 (1997), Economic Dynamics, Trade and Growth: Essays on Harrodian Themes (ed with G Rampa and L Stella, 1998), The Euro and Regional Divergence in Europe (2000), The Nature of Economic Growth: An Alternative Framework for Understanding the Performance of Nations (2002), Trade, the Balance of Payments and Exchange Rate Policy in Developing Countries (2003), Essays on Balance of Payments Constrained Growth: Theory and Evidence (with J McCombie, 2004); *Recreations* growing geraniums, athletics, tennis, travel; *Clubs* Royal Over-Seas League; *Style*— Prof Anthony Thirlwall; ✉ 14 Moorfield, Canterbury, Kent (tel 01227 769904); Keynes College, University of Kent, Canterbury, Kent (tel 01227 827414, fax 01227 827850, e-mail a.p.thirlwall@kent.ac.uk, website www.kent.ac.uk/economics/staff/at4/)

THISELTON, Prof Rev Canon Anthony Charles; s of Eric Charles Thiselton (d 1979), of Woking, Surrey, and Hilda Winifred, *née* Kevan (d 1969); *b* 13 July 1937; *Educ* City of London Sch, KCL (BD, MTh), Univ of Sheffield (PhD), Univ of Durham (DD); *m* 21 Sept 1963, Rosemary Stella, da of Ernest Walter Harman (d 1979), of Eastbourne, E Sussex; 2 s (Stephen b 1964, Martin b 1969), 1 da (Linda b 1966); *Career* curate Holy Trinity Sydenham 1960–63, chaplain Tyndale Hall Bristol 1963–67, recognised teacher in theology Univ of Bristol 1965–70, sr tutor Tyndale Hall 1967–70, lectr in biblical studies Univ of Sheffield 1970–79 (sr lectr 1979–85), visiting prof and fell Calvin Coll Grand Rapids 1982–83; princ: St John's Coll Nottingham 1985–88, St John's Coll Durham 1988–92 (hon prof in theology 1992); prof of Christian theology and emeritus in residence Dept of Theology Univ of Nottingham 2001– (prof of Christian theology and head of Dept of Theology 1992–2001); canon theologian: Leicester Cathedral 1995–, Southwell Minster 2000–; res prof of Christian theology Chester Coll; memb: C of E Doctrine Cmmn 1976–91 and 1996– (vice-chm 1987–91 and 1996–97), C of E Faith and Order Advsy Gp 1971–81 and 1986–91, CNAA Ctee for Arts and Humanities 1983–87, CNAA Ctee for Humanities 1987–90, Revised Catechism Working Pty 1988–89, C of E Initial Ministerial Educn Ctee 1990–92, Cncl Lincoln Theological Coll 1992–97, Cncl of St John's Nottingham 1992–2001, Human Fertilisation and Embryology Authy 1995–98, Crown Appointments Cmmn of C of E 1998–, C of E Theological Training Ctee 1999–, Clergy Discipline (Doctrine) Gp 1999–2004, Studiorum Novi Testamenti Societas, Soc for the Study of Theology, American Acad of Religion; Gen Synod C of E: rep northern univs 1995–2000, rep Dio of Southwell 2000–; conslt Women in the Episcopate House of Bishops Working Pty 2001–05; memb Editorial Bd: Biblical Interpretation (Leiden) 1992–02, Lund Lectures Chicago 1997, Int Jl of Systematic Theology 1998–, Expository Times (Edinburgh) 2003–; memb: Steering Gp and Revision Ctee C of E Daily Lectionary 2004, Task Gp Theological Educn in the Anglican Communion 2004–; examining chaplain to: Bishop of Sheffield 1976–80, Bishop of Leicester 1979–86 and 1993–2000, Bishop of Southwell 2001–; pres Soc for the Study of Theology 1998–2000; Br Acad Research Award 1995–96; awarded DD by Archbishop of Canterbury at Lambeth 2002; hon fell St John's Coll Durham; *Books* Language, Liturgy and Meaning (1975), The Two Horizons: New Testament Hermeneutics and Philosophical Description (1980, trans into Korean 1990, reprinted 1993), The Responsibility of Hermeneutics (jtly, 1985), New Horizons in Hermeneutics (1992), Interpreting God and the Post-Modern Self (1995), The Promise of Hermeneutics (jtly, 1999), 1 Corinthians: A Commentary in the Greek Text (2000), Concise Encyclopedia of Philosophy of Religion (2002), Thiselton on Hermeneutics: Collected Writings (2 vols, 2005), Reading Luke: Interpretation, Reflection and Formation (jt ed, 2005); contrib: Believing in the Church, We Believe in God, Their Lord and Ours, The Bible the Reformation and the Church, Jesus of Nazareth: Lord and Christ; Cambridge Companion to Biblical Interpretation; *Recreations* organ, choral music, opera; *Style*— Prof the Rev Canon Anthony C Thiselton; ✉ 390 High Road, Chilwell, Nottingham NG9 5EG (tel 01159 176391, fax 0115 917 6392)

THISTLETHWAYTE, (John) Robin; JP; s of Lt Cdr Thomas Thistlethwayte, RNVR (d 1956), of Old Bursledon, Hants, and Hon Eileen Gwladys (d 1955), *née* Berry, eld da of 1 and last Baron Buckland; *b* 8 December 1935; *Educ* Bradfield Coll, RAC Cirencester; *m* 22 Jan 1964, Mary Katharine, da of Lt-Gen Sir (Arthur) Edward Grasett, KBE, CB, DSO, MC, of Adderbury, Oxon; 2 s (Mark b 1964, Hugo b 1967), 1 da (Sophia (Mrs Alexander Davies) b 1972); *Career* chartered surveyor; ptnr Savills 1961–86, conslt to Savills plc 1986–96; mayor of Chipping Norton 1964 and 1965; chm: Chipping Norton Petty Sessional Div 1984 and 1985, N Oxfordshire and Chipping Norton PSD 1989–91; FRICS; *Recreations* shooting, travel; *Clubs* Boodle's, St James's; *Style*— J Robin Thistlethwayte, Esq; ✉ Sorbrook Manor, Adderbury, Oxfordshire OX17 3EG (tel 01295 810203); The Estate Office, Southwick, Fareham, Hampshire PO17 6EA

THOMAS, Dr Adrian Mark Kynaston; s of Prof Peter Kynaston Thomas, of London, and Mary Truscott Cox (d 1977); *b* 1 April 1954; *Educ* Christ Coll Finchley, UCL (MB BS, BSc); *m* 8 July 1978, Susan Margaret, da of Arthur Oliver Viney, of Amersham, Bucks; 2 s (Gareth Kynaston b 1985, Owen Matthew Truscott b 7 July 1990), 1 da (Charlotte Mary Truscott b 1988); *Career* sr registrar Hammersmith Hosp 1981–87; conslt radiologist Bromley Hosps NHS Trust Hosp and Sloane Hosp 1987–; chm Bromley Div BMA 1995–96 and 1998–99; chm Br Soc for the History of Radiology (formerly Radiology History and Heritage Charitable Tst) 2005–; memb: BMA 1976, RSM 1981 (pres Radiology Section 1999–2000), Br Inst of Radiology 1981 (hon sec 1999–2005, hon librarian 2005–), Christian Med Fellowship 1989; FRCR 1984 (MRCR 1982), FRCP 1996; *Books* Self Assessment in Radiology and Imaging: Nuclear Medicine (jt ed, 1989), The Invisible Light, 100 Years of Medical Radiology (jt ed, 1995), Classic Papers in Modern Diagnostic Radiology (jt ed, 2004); *Recreations* history of radiology; *Clubs* Osler (hon sec 2004–); *Style*— Dr Adrian Thomas

THOMAS, Adrian Peter; OBE (1995); s of George Lynn Thomas (d 1998), of Holland-on-Sea, Essex, and Glady Ella Grace, *née* Webster (d 1992); *b* 19 February 1945; *Educ* Forest Sch, Wadham Coll Oxford (MA), SOAS Univ of London (MA); *m* 1977, Robyn Alycon, da of Prof J Laurence Malcolm (d 2001); 1 da (Clare Sally b 1978), 2 s (Hugh Robert, Neil Malcolm (twins) b 1980); *Career* VSO teacher Ihungo Sedy Sch Tanzania 1967–68, various jobs in market res and accountancy 1969–70; British Council: asst rep Sierra Leone 1970–73, regnl offr N Africa 1973–75, Overseas Educnl Appointments Dept 1975–77, Univ of London 1977–78, regnl dir Isfahan 1978–80, asst and dep dir Tech Co-operation Trg Dept 1980–84, regnl rep E Malaysia 1984–88, dep dir Nigeria 1988–91, dir Sudan 1991–95, dir E India 1995–99; sec RAS 2000–03, exec sec Linnean Soc 2004–; memb: Royal Over-Seas League, Amnesty Int, Friends of the Earth; Hon PhD Univ of Gezira Sudan 1995; *Recreations* running, hill walking, history, poetry, natural history; *Style*— Mr Adrian Thomas, OBE; ✉ 30 Warner Road, Crouch End, London N8 7HD (tel 020 8348 4897, e-mail adrianandrobyn@btinternet.com)

THOMAS, Prof Adrian Tregerthen; s of Rev Owen George Thomas, of Cardiff, and Jean Tregerthen, *née* Short; *b* 11 June 1947; *Educ* Kingswood Sch Bath, Univ of Nottingham (BMus), UC Cardiff (MA), Conservatory of Music Kraków Poland; *Career* Queen's Univ Belfast: lectr in music 1972–82, sr lectr 1982–85, Hamilton Harty prof of music 1985–90 and 1993–96; head of music BBC Radio 3 1990–93, prof of music Univ of Wales Cardiff 1996–, chair of music Gresham Coll 2003–06; conductor Br première Lutoslawski's Trois Poèmes d'Henri Michaux 1969, medal Polish Composers' Union for outstanding servs to contemporary Polish music 1989, Order of Merit for Polish Culture 1996, Medal Lutoslawski Soc Warsw 2005; chm Music Ctee Arts Cncl of NI 1986–90, chm BBC Central Music Advsy Ctee 1987–89, memb BBC Gen Advsy Cncl 1988–90; memb Royal Musical Assoc, memb Br Acad of Composers and Songwriters; *Compositions* Intrada (orchestra, 1981), Elegy (violin and piano, 1983), Rau (string octet, 1985), Black Rainbow (a cappella choir, BBC cmmn, 1989); *Books* Grażyna Bacewicz: Chamber and Orchestral Music (1985), Górecki (1997), Polish Music since Szymanowski (2005); *Recreations* hill walking, poetry, Oriental arts; *Style*— Prof Adrian Thomas; ✉ Department of Music, University of Wales, Cardiff CF10 3EB (tel 029 2087 6226, e-mail thomasat@cf.ac.uk)

THOMAS, Sir (John) Alan; kt (1993); s of late Idris Thomas, of Langland, Swansea, and Ellen Constance, *née* Noakes; *b* 4 January 1943; *Educ* Dynevor Sch Swansea, Univ of Nottingham (Richard Thomas & Baldwins Industrial scholar, BSc); *m* 1966, Angela, da of Kathleen Taylor; 2 s (Andrew James b 1971, Alexander Michael b 1974); *Career* chief exec Data Logic Ltd 1973–85, pres and ceo Raytheon Europe 1985–89, vice-pres Raytheon Co (US), dir various Raytheon subsid cos 1978–89, seconded to MOD as head of Def Export Servs Orgn 1989–94; chm: Micro Quoted Growth Trust plc 1997–2001, Chelverton Asset Mgmnt Ltd 1997–2005, Three Valleys Water plc 2000–, Hyder Consltg plc 2002–, Global Design Technologies LLC 2006–; dir: PowerGen plc 1996–99, Radstone Technology plc 2004–06; sr industrial advsr to DG OFWAT 1997–2000; memb: Defence Industries Cncl 1990–94, Engrg Cncl 1994–96; pres Computing Servs & Software Assoc 1980–81; dir Centre for Policy Studies 1996–2003; visiting prof Univ of Westminster 1982, chm Ct of Govrs Univ of Westminster 1999–2005 (govr 1989–, dep chm 1995–98); dir London Welsh RFC 1997–; Liveryman Co of Info Technologists 1988–; CEng, FIEE, FCMA (1st prizewinner); *Recreations* music, sport; *Clubs* Athenaeum; *Style*— Sir Alan Thomas; ✉ 29 Bressenden Place, London SW1E 5DZ (tel 01707 277306, e-mail siralanthomas@aol.com)

THOMAS, Alun; WS; s of Gordon Eric Thomas, of Aust, and Pauline Susan, *née* Hooper; *b* 4 March 1958, Henley; *Educ* George Heriots Edinburgh, Univ of Edinburgh (LLB); *m* 11 Sept 1995, K P Thomas, *née* Philip; 1 s (Lloyd Rhys b 2 July 1997); *Career* admitted slr 1983; ptnr J+F Anderson Strathern (now Anderson Strathern) 1990– (currently head Employment Unit); accredited specialist in employment law Law Soc of Scotland 1996–, CEDR registered mediator; memb: Ctee Scottish Discrimination Law Assoc, Expert and Advsy Panel on Pregnancy Dismissals Equal Opportunities Cmmn; memb: Employment Lawyers Assoc, Law Soc of Scotland 1983; *Style*— Mr Alun Thomas; ✉ Anderson Strathern, 1 Rutland Court, Edinburgh EH3 8EY (tel 0131 625 7245, fax 0131 625 8018, e-mail alun.thomas@andersonstrathern.co.uk)

THOMAS, Andrew Gerald; *b* 19 July 1942; *Educ* Rydal Sch Colwyn Bay; *m* Lesley; 1 da (Helen b 13 May 1967), 1 s (Julian b 3 July 1969); *Career* former chm Greenalls Group plc; currently ptnr Moors Andrew Thomas and Co, chm Greenalls Pension Tst Ltd, non-exec dir: JJB Sports plc, The Restaurant Gp plc; memb Inst of Taxation, memb ICA; *Recreations* theatre, football; *Style*— Andrew Thomas, Esq

THOMAS, Anthony Charles (Tony); s of Charles Derek Thomas (d 1990), and Rosina Miriam, *née* Dukes; *b* 27 May 1952; *Educ* Leamington Coll Leamington Spa, Univ of Manchester (LLB); *m* June 1976, Penelope Bebbington; 2 s (Oliver b 7 Sept 1981, Nicholas b 9 Jan 1987), 1 da (Rebecca b 12 Sept 1983); *Career* Clyde & Co: joined as articled clerk 1974, slr 1976–, ptnr 1980–, currently head Shipping Dept; memb Law Soc; *Recreations* squash, tennis, cricket, rugby (now as spectator), theatre, motor cars; *Clubs* Guildford & Godalming Rugby (vice-pres); *Style*— Tony Thomas, Esq; ✉ Clyde & Co, 51 Eastcheap, London EC3M 1JP (tel 020 7623 1244, fax 020 7623 5427, mobile 07831 866839, e-mail tony.thomas@clydeco.com)

THOMAS, Hon Barbara S; *b* 28 December 1946; *Educ* Univ of Pennsylvania (BA), NY Univ Law Sch (ed NYU Law Review, John Norton Pomeroy Scholar, Jefferson Davis Prize in Public Law, seventeen other prizes in various subjects, JD); *m*; 1 s; *Career* assoc Paul Weiss Rifkind Wharton & Garrison (law firm) 1969–73, ptnr Kaye Scholer Fierman Hays & Handler 1978–80 (joined as assoc 1973), cmmr US Securities and Exchange Cmmn 1980–83 (fndr Int Ctee of Securities Regulators), regnl dir Hong Kong Samuel Montagu & Co Ltd 1984–86, sr vice-pres and head of Int Private Banking Gp Bankers Trust Co 1986–90, md mktg and int Cramer Rosenthal McGlynn Inc 1990–93, exec dir business and legal affrs News International plc 1993–94, chm Whitworths Group Ltd 1995–2000, exec chm Private Equity Investor plc 2000–04, chm UK Atomic Energy Authy 2004–; non-exec chm Axon Gp plc 1998–2003, non-exec dep chm Friends' Provident plc 1998–, non-exec dir Capital Radio 1999–2005, non-exec dir Hardy Underwriting Gp 2004–, chm LIFE 2007–; dep chm Financial Reporting Cncl 2004–; memb: US-Hong Kong Econ Assistance Ctee, Cncl on Foreign Relations, Young Pres's Orgn (London, Hong Kong and Gotham NY chapters), Advsy Cncl Women's Economic Round Table, Forum UK, London and NY chapters Women's Forum; chm Governing Body SOAS 2005–, memb Bd of Govrs Lauder Inst of Mgmnt and Int Studies Wharton Sch Univ of Pennsylvania 1985–; tstee: Royal Acad (memb Special Projects Advsy Ctee 1994–), Wallace Collection 2003–; memb: Bd Int Salzburg Assoc (organisers of Salzburg Festival) 1987–92, Advsy Ctee LSO 1993–; *Clubs* Reform, Cosmopolitan (NY), Economic (NY), River (NY); *Style*— The Honorable Barbara S Thomas; ✉ Eversheds, Senator House, 4th Floor, 85 Queen Victoria Street, London EC4V 4JL; (tel 020 7919 0623, fax 020 7919 0627)

THOMAS, Dr Cedric Marshall; CBE (1991, OBE 1983); s of David John Thomas (d 1958), of Birmingham, and Evis Margaret, *née* Field (d 1946); *b* 26 May 1930; *Educ* King Edward's Sch Birmingham, Univ of Birmingham (BSc, PhD); *m* 1, 12 June 1954, (Dora) Ann (d 1975), da of Walter Pritchard (d 1975), of N Wales; 1 s (Nicholas b 1955), 1 da (Sarah b 1957); *m* 2, 19 Sept 1976, Margaret Elizabeth, *née* Shirley; 3 step da (Carolyn b 1952, Beth b 1959, Helen b 1961), 1 step s (Michael b 1954); *Career* NCB 1954–59, Morgan Crucible Co Ltd 1960–61, chief exec Johnson Progress Gp 1970–77 (joined 1961), business conslt 1977–80, chief exec Benjamin Priest Gp 1983–84 (joined 1980), dir and chief exec Engineering Employers W Midlands Assoc 1984–91, dep chm Thomas William Lench Ltd 1991–2004, dir Jesse Shirley Ltd 1991– (chm 1991–99), non-exec dir Poplars Resource Management Co Ltd 1992–99, non-exec dir Staffs Ambulance Service NHS Tst 1995–2001 (vice-chm 1999–2001); dir Staffordshire Environmental Fund Ltd 1997–2005 (chm 2000–05); EEF: memb Mgmnt Bd 1972–80 and 1981–84, chm Health and Saftey Ctee 1981–84, memb Cncl and Pres's Ctee 1992–95, chm Health Safety and Environment Policy Ctee 1992–95; pres: Minerals Engrg Soc 1969–71, Engrg Employers W Midlands Assoc 1976–78; chm Special Programmes Area Bd 1978–83; memb: Health and Safety Cmmn 1980–90, CBI Health and Safety Policy Ctee 1983–93; chm Area Manpower Bd 1986–88; govr N Staffs Poly 1973–80; CEng, FIMMM, FMES, CCMI, Hon FFOM, FRSA; *Style*— Dr Cedric Thomas, CBE; ✉ Parkfields House, Tittensor, Staffordshire ST12 9HQ (tel and fax 01782 373677, e-mail cemet@parkfields.fsworld.co.uk)

THOMAS, Christopher (Chris); s of Neofitos Theophilou, of London, and Mary, *née* Mouzouris; *b* 1 September 1963; *Educ* Highgate Wood Sch London; *Career* bd dir MJP Carat International 1989–92 (joined as trainee media exec 1980), bd dir MCW Ltd 1992–97, managing ptnr IAG 1997–2000, md Ergonomy Ltd 2000–03, chief operating offr Million-2-1 Ltd 2003–04, dir IMPAQ Group 2005–; dir Int Advertising Assoc (UK Chapter) 1985–92 (joined 1981); accredited mediator London Sch of Psychotherapy 2005; FRGS 1992; *Recreations* cooking, tennis, Arsenal FC; *Style*— Chris Thomas, Esq; ✉ IMPAQ Group, 11 Quarry Street, Guildford, Surrey GU1 3UY (tel 01483 511776, fax 01483 511773, e-mail chris.thomas@impaqgroup.net)

THOMAS, Christopher Peter (Chris); s of Cecil Stevens Thomas, of Highcliffe, Dorset, and Ruth Ela, *née* Roberts; *b* 13 January 1947; *Educ* Latymer Upper Sch, Royal Acad of Music (jr exhibitioner); *m* (m dis); 1 da (Carla b 22 Nov 1971), 1 s (Jan Stevens b 29 Sept 1970); 1 s (Michael James b 15 May 1988), 1 da (Mia b 1 Feb 1991) by another relationship; *Career* pop music producer; credits incl: Climax Blues Band (Climax Chicago

Blues Band, The Climax Blues Band Plays On, A Lot of Bottle, Tightly Knit), Nirvana (Dedicated to Markos III), Procol Harum (Home, Broken Barricades, Live with The Edmonton Symphony Orchestra, Grand Hotel, Exotic Birds and Fruit), Mick Abrahams Band (Mick Abrahams Band, At Last), Christopher Milk (Some People Will Drink Anything), John Cale (Paris 1919), Roxy Music (For Your Pleasure, Stranded, Siren, Viva Roxy Music), Badfinger (Ass, Badfinger, Wish You Were Here), Sadistic Mika Band (Black Ship, Hot! Menu), Kokomo (Kokomo), Bryan Ferry (Let's Stick Together), Krazy Kat (China Seas), Eno (Here Comes The Warm Jets), The Sex Pistols (Never Mind the Bollocks, Filthy Lucre Live), Frankie Miller (Full House), Chris Spedding (Hurt), Tom Robinson Band (Power in the Darkness), Wings (Back to The Egg), The Pretenders (Pretenders, Pretenders II, Learning to Crawl), Pete Townshend (Empty Glass, All The Best Cowboys Have Chinese Eyes, White City), Elton John (The Fox, Jump Up, Too Low For Zero, Breaking Hearts, Reg Strikes Back, Sleeping With the Past, The One, tracks on The Lion King soundtrack album, Live Like Horses (with Luciano Pavarotti), The Big Picture), INXS (Listen Like Thieves, Kick, X), Dave Stewart & The Spiritual Cowboys, Shakespear's Sister (Goodbye Cruel World (prodr), Stay (co-prodr)), Miss World debut album, Marcella Detroit (Jewel), Bryan Adams, Sting and Rod Stewart (All for Love), Pulp (Different Class, This is Hardcore), Paul McCartney (Run Devil Run), Hoggboy, David Gilmour (On an Island), Razorlight (Razorlight); mixing credits incl: Pink Floyd (Dark Side of the Moon, The Division Bell (jtly)), Roxy Music (Country Life), Ronnie Lane (One for the Road); 40 albums produced went silver, gold, platinum; winner: Rolling Stone Critics' Award 1980, Best Single Prodr Billboards 1988, Best Prodr BRIT Awards 1990; md Eddie Jordan's V10; Hon ARAM; *Recreations* travelling, meeting people; *Style*— Chris Thomas; ✉ c/o Geoff Travis, Rough Trade (tel 020 8960 9888)

THOMAS, Dr Christopher Sydney; QC (1989); s of John Raymond Thomas (d 1982), and Daphne May, *née* Thomas; *b* 17 March 1950; *Educ* King's Sch Worcester, Univ of Kent at Canterbury (BA), Faculté International de Droit Comparé (Diplome de Droit Comparé), KCL (PhD); *m* 26 May 1979, Patricia Jane, da of Leslie Heath (d 1994), of Gillingham, Kent; 1 s (Alexander), 1 da (Felicity); *Career* called to the Bar Lincoln's Inn 1973 (Hardwick and Jenkins scholarships); recorder 2000; counsel and arbitrator in building and civil engrg disputes UK and overseas; CEDR accredited mediator 1999; FCIArb 1994; *Recreations* farming, boating; *Style*— Dr Christopher Thomas, QC; ✉ Keating Chambers, 15 Essex Street, London WC2R 3AA (tel 020 7544 2600, fax 020 7544 2700)

THOMAS, David; s of Harold Bushell Thomas (decd), of Bebington, Wirral, and Margaret, *née* Browne (decd); *b* 7 November 1945; *Educ* St Anselm's Coll Birkenhead, Univ of Liverpool (LLB); *m* (m dis); 1 da (Rachel Elenore b 27 Aug 1974), 3 s (Mark Aidan b 10 July 1976, James Matthew, Neil William (twins) b 28 Feb 1980); partner, Jane Bibby; *Career* F S Moore & Price Birkenhead: slr 1969–71, ptnr 1971–85, managing ptnr 1984–85; managing ptnr: Lees Moore & Price Birkenhead 1985–88, Lees Lloyd Whitley Liverpool 1988–93; chm Lees Lloyd Whitley Liverpool and London 1993–96; Banking Ombudsman 1997–2001; Fin Ombudsman Serv: Princ Ombudsman (Banking and Loans) 1999–2004, Princ Ombudsman and corp dir 2004–; pres Liverpool Law Soc 1987–88; Law Soc: memb Cncl 1987–96, chm Specialisation Ctee 1989–92, Practice Devpt Ctee 1992–95, Quality Standards Working Party 1995–96, Research Sub-Ctee 1991–96; memb: Investigation and Discipline Bd Financial Reporting Cncl 2001–, Ctee City of London Law Soc 2004–, Cncl Queen Mary Univ of London 2006–, Audit Advsy Ctee Scottish Public Serv Ombudsman; *Recreations* theatre, modern history, walking; *Style*— David Thomas, Esq; ✉ Financial Ombudsman Service, South Quay Plaza, 183 Marsh Wall, London E14 9SR (tel 020 7964 0692, fax 020 7964 0693, e-mail david.thomas@financial-ombudsman.org.uk)

THOMAS, David; QC (2002); s of Lloyd Thomas (d 2002), and Kathleen, *née* Meanwell; *b* 20 December 1958, Godalming, Surrey; *Educ* Midhurst GS, Wadham Coll Oxford; *m* 1987, Victoria, *née* Cochrane; 1 s (Frederick Roland Charles b 1 Aug 1994), 1 da (Cecily Mary Augusta b 17 Aug 2000); *Career* called to the Bar 1982, called to the Bar Gibraltar 1996; practising barr, currently memb Keating Chambers; accredited mediator 2003; *Publications* Keating on Construction Contracts (contrib, 8 edn); *Recreations* family, gardening; *Clubs* MCC; *Style*— David Thomas, Esq, QC; ✉ c/o John Munton, Keating Chambers, 15 Essex Street, London WC2R 3AU (tel 020 7544 2600, fax 020 7544 2700, e-mail jmunton@keatingchambers.com)

THOMAS, David Arthur; s of David Martell Thomas (d 1960), of Hampton, Middx, and Sybil Elizabeth, *née* Perry; *b* 7 April 1938; *Educ* DES RCA; *m* 1, 8 Aug 1976 (m dis 1986), Georgina Anne Caroline, da of Dr Joseph Linhart, of London; 1 s (Edward b 14 Feb 1977); m 2, 12 Sept 1987, Gillian Mary, da of Norman Duncan Mussett (d 1983); 1 da (Jessica b 5 Jan 1988); *Career* md David Thomas Design Ltd 1965– (designing and producing fine jewellery and silver); one man exhibitions: St Louis and NY USA, Sydney Aust, Tokyo Japan, Goldsmiths' Hall London, Florence Italy; jewellery in perm collections: Worshipful Co of Goldsmiths, De Beers Diamonds, V&A; chm Goldsmiths' Craft Cncl 1986–88; Freeman City of London 1964, Liveryman Worshipful Co of Goldsmiths 1985; FRSA 1964; *Style*— David Thomas, Esq; ✉ 65 Pimlico Road, London SW1 (tel 020 7730 7710, fax 020 7730 5532)

THOMAS, David Gavin; s of Cecil Goring Thomas (d 1974), of Penarth, and Vera Winifred, *née* Wilson (d 1998); *b* 30 January 1943; *Educ* Wycliffe Coll; *m* 14 Aug 1971, Jane Annette, da of John Edward Verdon (d 1984); 2 da (Joanna Louise b 10 April 1975, Laura Anne b 6 July 1979), 1 s (William David b 24 Dec 1976); *Career* qualified CA Peat Marwick Mitchell 1966–68 (articled clerk 1960–66), fin accountant GKN (S Wales) Ltd 1972–73 (mgmnt accountant 1968–72), chief accountant Nova Jersey Knit Ltd 1973–74; Golley Slater & Partners Ltd: co sec 1974–75, fin dir 1976–87, gp fin dir 1987–; FCA; *Recreations* golf, sailing, bridge; *Clubs* Cardiff and County, Glamorganshire Golf, Penarth Yacht, Royal Porthcawl Golf; *Style*— David G Thomas, Esq; ✉ 20 Clinton Road, Penarth, Vale of Glamorgan CF64 3JD (tel 029 2070 5677); Golley Slater Group, Wharton Place, Wharton Street, Cardiff CF10 1GS (tel 029 2038 8621, fax 029 2023 8729)

THOMAS, David Glyndor Treharne; s of Dr John Glyndor Treharne Thomas, MC (Capt RAMC, d 1955), of Cambridge, and Ellen, *née* Geldart (d 1970); *b* 14 May 1941; *Educ* Perse Sch Cambridge, Gonville & Caius Coll Cambridge (MA, MB BChir); *m* 29 Dec 1970, Hazel Agnes Christina, da of William John Cockburn (d 1977), of Paisley; 1 s (William b 1972); *Career* St Mary's Hosp London: house surgn 1966, asst lectr in anatomy 1967–68, SHO in neurology 1969, casualty offr 1969; Royal Postgrad Med Sch Hammersmith Hosp London: SHO in surgery 1970, registrar in cardio-thoracic surgery 1970–71; Inst of Neurological Scis Southern Gen Hosp Glasgow: registrar, sr registrar and lectr in neurosurgery 1972–76; conslt neurosurgn Nat Hosp for Neurology and Neurosurgery and Northwick Park Hosp Harrow 1976–2006, prof of neurosurgery Inst of Neurology 1992–2006 (sr lectr 1976–92), conslt neurosurgn St Mary's Hosp London 1994–2006; numerous invited lectures and visiting professorships worldwide; chm EORTC Experimental Neuro-Oncology Gp 1986–88; memb: Med Acad Staff Ctee BMA 1981–82, Jt Hosp Med Servs Ctee 1981–82; pres Euro Soc for Stereotactic and Functional Neurosurgery, vice-pres European Assoc of Neurosurgical Socs 1991–95, vice-pres World Assoc of Neurosurgical Socs 2001–05; Freeman City of London 1969, Liveryman Worshipful Soc of Apothecaries 1971; MRCS 1966, FRCSEd 1972, FRCPG 1985, FRCP 1994 (MRCP 1970), FRCSEng 1998; *Books* Brain Tumours: Scientific Basis, Clinical Investigation and Current Therapy (ed with D I Graham, 1980), Biology of Brain Tumour (ed with M D Walker, 1986), Neuro-oncology: Primary Brain Tumours (ed, 1989), Stereotactic and Image Directed Surgery of Brain Tumours (ed, 1993), Handbook of Stereotaxy Using the CRW Apparatus (ed with M F Pell, 1994); *Recreations* military and naval history; *Clubs* Athenaeum, RSM; *Style*— Prof David Thomas; ✉ 1 Bryanston Square, London W1H 2DH (tel 020 7724 2614); The National Hospital, Queen Square, London WC1 3BG (tel 020 7829 8755, fax 020 7676 2155)

THOMAS, Prof David John (Dafydd); s of Jack Lloyd Thomas (d 1997), of Fulmer, Bucks, and Rachel, *née* Hunt; *b* 7 December 1943; *Educ* Alleyn's Sch Dulwich, Clare Coll Cambridge (MA, MB BChir), Univ of Birmingham Med Sch (Arthur Thompson scholar, MD); *m* 1966, Celia Margaret, da of Sir Charles Barratt (d 1971), of Kenilworth, Warwicks; 3 da (Dr Rachel b 25 Jan 1970, Eleanor b 13 July 1980, Laura b 3 Feb 1983), 2 s (Dr Charles Lloyd b 18 Aug 1971, George Llewellyn b 26 Jan 1973); *Career* neurological registrar then sr registrar Queen Elizabeth Hosp and Midland Centre for Neurology and Neurosurgery 1972–76, MRC research fell Inst of Neurology and St Thomas' Hosp 1976–78 (Queen Square prize), conslt neurologist and head of dept St Mary's Hosp 1978– and E Berkshire Hosps 1978–2000, sr lectr in neurology and hon conslt neurologist Inst of Neurology and Nat Hosps for Neurology and Neurosurgery 1980–, prof of stroke medicine Imperial Coll Faculty of Medicine 2005–; former chm Special Advsy Ctee on Neurology to Royal Colls, princ neurological investigator MRC Asymptomatic Carotid Surgery Trial 1994–; govr Nat Soc for Epilepsy; memb Cncl Stroke Assoc 1992–; tstee: Assoc of Br Neurologists 1978, Stroke Cncl (American Heart Assoc) 1991, Euro Stroke Cncl 1994, Int Affrs Ctee 1997; FRCP 1985 (MRCP 1972); *Books* Strokes and their Prevention (1988), Neurology, What Shall I Do? (1989, 2 edn 1997), The Eye in Systemic Disease (1990); *Recreations* photography; *Style*— Prof Dafydd Thomas; ✉ Woolletts, Fulmer, Buckinghamshire SL3 6JE (tel 01753 663698, fax 01753 664478)

THOMAS, Sir David John Godfrey; 12 Bt (E 1694), of Wenvoe, Glamorganshire; s of Sir Michael Thomas, 11 Bt (d 2003); *b* 11 June 1961; *Educ* Harrow; *m* 21 Dec 2004, Nicola Jane Lusty; *Career* dir; *Recreations* squash (Eng int), tennis; *Clubs* Hurlingham, MCC, Jesters, Escorts; *Style*— Sir David Thomas, Bt; ✉ 1 Waters Edge, Eternit Walk, London SW6 6QU (tel and fax 020 7381 4078)

THOMAS, Prof David Steven Garfield; s of Frederick Garfield Thomas, of Dover, Kent, and Ruth Muriel, *née* Hopper; *b* 2 October 1958, Dover, Kent; *Educ* Dover GS for Boys, Hertford Coll Oxford (Henry Oliver Becket Meml Prize, BA), Univ of Oxford (PGCE, DPhil); *m* 21 March 1992, Lucy Marie Heath; 2 da (Mair Lucy b 23 Nov 1994, Alice Clara 2 March 1998); *Career* Dept of Geography Univ of Sheffield: lectr 1984–95, prof 1995–2004, dir Sheffield Centre for Int Drylands Research 1995; prof of geography Univ of Oxford 2004–, fell Hertford Coll Oxford 2004–; hon prof Univ of Cape Town 2006; vice-pres RGS 2000–04, pres British Geomorphological Research Gp 2001–02; Dorothy Hodgkin Award BAAS 1994; FRGS 1997; *Books* incl: Arid Zone Geomorphology (1987, 2 edn 1998), The Kalahari Environment (1991), World Atlas of Desertification (1992, 2 edn 1997), Desertification: Exploding the Myth (1994), Dictionary of Physical Geography (2002); *Style*— Prof David Thomas; ✉ Oxford University Centre for the Environment, School of Geography, South Parks Road, Oxford OX1 3QY (tel 01865 285197, fax 01865 285073, e-mail david.thomas@ouce.ox.ac.uk)

THOMAS, Sir Derek Morison David; KCMG (1987, CMG 1977); s of Kenneth Peter David Thomas (d 1982), and Mali McLeod, *née* Morison (d 1972); *b* 31 October 1929; *Educ* Radley, Trinity Hall Cambridge (MA); *m* 1956, Lineke, da of Thijs Van der Mast (d 1988), of Eindhoven, Netherlands; 1 da (Caroline b 1963), 1 s (Matthew b 1967); *Career* Sub Lt RNVR 1955 (Midshipman 1953–55); articled apprentice Dolphin Industry Developments Ltd 1947; entered Dip Serv 1953; served in: Moscow, Manila, Brussels, Sofia, Ottawa, Paris, Washington; dep under sec of state for Europe and political dir FCO 1984–87, ambass to Italy 1987–89; Euro advsr NM Rothschild & Sons 1990–2004; dir: NM Rothschild & Sons 1991–99, Rothschild Italia 1990–97, Rothschild Europe 1991–97, Christow Consultants 1990–99, CDP Nexus 1991–92 (assoc 1990), conslt 2000–04; memb Export Guarantees Advsy Cncl 1991–97, chm Ctee of Liberalisation of Trade in Servs (Br Invisibles) 1992–96; memb Cncl: Univ of Reading 1991–2000, RIIA 1994–97, SOSSAHEL 2000; chm Br Inst of Florence 1996–2002; hon fell Trinity Hall Cambridge 1997; Hon LLD Univ of Leicester 2003; *Style*— Sir Derek Thomas, KCMG; ✉ 12 Lower Sloane Street, London SW1W 8BJ; Ferme de l'Épine, 14490 Planquery, France

THOMAS, Prof (James) Edward; s of James Edward Thomas (ka 1940), of Haverfordwest, Pembrokeshire, and Margaret Elizabeth, *née* Absalom (d 1981); *b* 20 December 1933; *Educ* Haverfordwest GS, Univ of Oxford, Univ of London, Univ of York, Univ of Nottingham (DLitt); *m* 24 Aug 1957, Olwen, da of John Yolland (d 1980); 2 s (Simon b 24 Oct 1958, Philip b 6 June 1961); *Career* Nat Serv RA 1952–54; admin offr Govt of Northern Rhodesia 1957–60, govr HM Prison Serv 1960–67, lectr and sr lectr Univ of Hull 1967–78; Univ of Nottingham: joined as reader 1978, formerly prof Dept of Adult Educn, dean of educn and pro-vice-chllr, currently Robert Peers emeritus prof; bursar Imperial Rels Tst 1970, fell Japan Soc for Promotion of Science, former chm Standing Conf on Univ Teaching and Research in Educn of Adults, vice-chm Univ Cncl on Adult and Continuing Educn; *Books* The English Prison Officer since 1950: A Study in Conflict (1972), Imprisonment in Western Australia: Evolution Theory and Practice (with A Stewart, 1978), The Exploding Prison: Prison Riots and the Case of Hull (with R Pooley, 1980), Radical Adult Education: Theory and Practice (1982), International Biography of Adult Education (with B Elsey, 1985), Learning Democracy in Japan: The Social Education of Japanese Adults (1986), House of Care: Prisons and Prisoners in England 1500–1800 (1988), A Select Biography of Adult Continuing Education (with J H Davis, 5 edn 1988), Radical Agendas? The Politics of Adult Education (with Sallie Westwood, 1991), Making Japan Work (1993), Modern Japan: A Social History since 1868 (1996); *Recreations* music, walking, gardening, cinema; *Style*— Prof J E Thomas; ✉ 100 Mona Road, West Bridgford, Nottingham NG2 5BT (tel 0115 982 0948, e-mail profteddythomas@aol.com)

THOMAS, Prof Edward John; s of John Henry Thomas (d 1958), of Plymouth, Devon, and Lily Elizabeth Jane Thomas; *b* 25 November 1937; *Educ* Devonport HS, Keble Coll Oxford (MA), Univ of London (MSc), Univ of Manchester (PhD); *m* 12 Sept 1964, Erica Jean, da of Eric Distin (d 1977), of Salcombe, Devon; 1 da (Katherine Grace b 1965), 1 s (Gerard William b 1969); *Career* research scientist GEC plc 1962–64, lectr Univ of Manchester 1964–68; Univ of Bristol: staff tutor 1968–80, sr lectr 1980–81, prof of adult educn 1981–92, prof of continuing educn 1992–2003 (emeritus prof 2003–), sometime dir of continuing educn; sec gen Euro Univs Continuing Educn Network 1991–2000; life memb Univs Assoc for Continuing Educn 2000; tstee Friends of WNO 2005–; FRSA 1983; *Books* Type II Superconductivity (1969), From Quarks to Quasars (1977), Lifelong Learning in a Changing Continent (ed, 2003), Adults in Higher Education (ed, 2004); *Recreations* reading, writing, eating, drinking, talking; *Style*— Prof Edward Thomas; ✉ Graduate School of Education, University of Bristol, Bristol BS8 1HH (tel 0117 968 2314, e-mail e.j.thomas@bristol.ac.uk)

THOMAS, Prof Eric Jackson; DL (Bristol); s of Eric Jackson Thomas, of Burnopfield, Co Durham, and late Mary Margaret, *née* Murray; *b* 24 March 1953, Hartlepool, Co Durham; *Educ* Ampleforth, Univ of Newcastle upon Tyne (MB BS, MD); *m* 26 Oct 1976, Narell Marie, *née* Rennard; 1 da (Rachel Frances b 6 Jan 1985), 1 s (David Alexander b 11 June 1986); *Career* lectr in obstetrics and gynaecology Univ of Sheffield 1985–87, sr lectr in obstetrics and gynaecology Univ of Newcastle upon Tyne 1987–90; Univ of Southampton: prof of obstetrics and gynaecology 1991–2001, research co-ordinator Sch of Med 1992–98, head Sch of Med 1995–98, dean Faculty of Med, Health and Biological Sciences 1998–2000; vice-chllr Univ of Bristol 2001–; exec sec Cncl of Heads of Med Schs and Deans of UK Faculties 1999–2000; conslt obstetrician and gynaecologist: Newcastle

Gen Hosp 1987–2000, Southampton Univ Hosps Tst 1991–2001; non-exec dir Southampton Univ Hosps Tst 1997–2000; meds cmmr 2002–03; RCOG: convenor of scientific meetings 1992–95, memb Cncl 1995–2001, chm Scientific Advsy Ctee 1998–; chm: Strategy Bd SW HE RDA 2002–04, DfES Taskforce on Voluntary Giving in HE 2003, Worldwide Univ Network (WUN) 2003–07; memb Bd SW RDA 2003–, memb SW Regnl Sports Bd 2003–07; Hon LLD Univ of Bristol 2004, Hon DSc Univ of Southampton 2006; FRSA 1998, FMedSci 1998, FRCOG 2001 (MRCOG 1983), FRCP 2004; *Recreations* golf, keep fit, reading, Newcastle United; *Clubs* Athenaeum; *Style*— Prof Eric Thomas, DL; ✉ Senate House, Tyndall Avenue, Bristol BS8 1TH (tel 0117 928 7499)

THOMAS, Dr Gareth; s of late Rev Evan George Thomas, and late Nina Mary, *née* Clargo; step s of late Olwen Elizabeth, *née* Jones; *b* 3 November 1945; *Educ* Merchant Taylors', St Mary's Hosp Med Sch (MB BS), Univ of London (MD), LLM (Univ of Wales), MRCS, MRCOG, FRCOG 1987; *m* 20 Sept 1969, Alison Muir, da of late David Muir Kelly, of Haile, Cumbria; 3 s (Mark b 1971, Robert b 1973, James b 1976), 2 da (Anna b 1980, Abigail b 1982); *Career* obstetrician and gynaecologist; house physician St Mary's Hosp London 1969; resident med offr: Queen Charlotte's Hosp London 1970–71, Samaritan Hosp London 1971–72; lectr and hon registrar UCL 1972–75, hon lectr Univ of Oxford 1975–77, sr registrar Oxfordshire RHA 1975–79, conslt Ipswich and East Suffolk 1979–, clinical dir Dept of Gynaecological and Maternity Servs 1991–97, chm Med Staff Ctee The Ipswich Hosp 1997–99, dep med dir Ipswich Hosp NHS Tst 1999–2004; pres Medico-Legal Soc 1998–99, pres East Anglia Obstetrics & Gynaecology Soc 2000–03; RCOG: chm Ethics Ctee 1998–2001: memb Professional Standards Ctee; examiner: Univ of London 1988–, RCOG; Law Soc expert, memb Expert Witness Inst; *Recreations* sailing; *Clubs* Royal Soc of Medicine, Association Broadcasting Doctors; *Style*— Dr Gareth Thomas; ✉ Riverdale, Deben Lane, Waldringfield, Suffolk IP12 4QN (tel and fax 01473 811744)

THOMAS, Gareth; MP; *Career* teacher Willesden HS 1992–95; MP (Lab) Harrow W 1997–; PPS to Rt Hon Charles Clarke, MP until 2003, Parly under sec of state DFID 2003–; chm: Parly Renewables and Sustainable Energy Gp, Co-op Pty; chair All-Pty Olympic Ctee 2003, memb Environment Audit Select Ctee 1997–99; cncllr London Borough of Harrow 1990–97 (spokesperson Health and Social Services 1990–97, chief whip 1996–97); *Recreations* canoeing, Welsh rugby union, running; *Style*— Gareth Thomas, Esq, MP; ✉ House of Commons, London SW1A 0AA (tel 020 7219 3000)

THOMAS, Gareth; *b* 25 July 1974; *m* Jemma; *Career* rugby union player; clubs: Bridgend Cardiff, Celtic Warriors 2003–04, Toulouse 2004– (winners Heineken Cup 2005); Wales: 86 caps (10 as capt), debut v Japan 1995, memb squad World Cup 1995, 1999 and 2003, winners Six Nations Championship and Grand Slam 2005; memb British and Irish Lions touring squad NZ 2005 (capt 2 Test matches); *Style*— Mr Gareth Thomas; ✉ c/o Stade Toulousain, BP 42354, 31022 Toulouse Cedex 2, France

THOMAS, Dr Geoffrey Price; s of Richard Lewis Thomas (d 1983), and Aerona, *née* Price (d 1969); *b* 3 July 1941; *Educ* Maesteg GS, Univ Coll of Swansea (BSc), Churchill Coll Cambridge (PhD); *m* 1965, Judith Vaughan, da of Arsul John Williams; 2 da (Susannah Judith b 1965, Rachel Louise b 1967); *Career* res assoc Cavendish Laboratory 1966–67, staff tutor Univ Coll of Swansea 1967–78; Univ of Oxford: dep dir Dept of External Studies 1978–86, dir Dept for Continuing Educn 1986–, founding pres Kellogg Coll Oxford 1990–; memb Higher Educn Funding Cncl for Wales 2000–; visiting scholar: Smithsonian Inst, Harvard Univ, Univ of Washington, Univ of Calif Berkeley, Northern Illinois Univ, Univ of Georgia; hon fell Linacre Coll Oxford 1990– (fell 1978–90), sr fell Univ of Georgia 2003–, hon fell Trinity Coll Carmarthen 2007–; *Books* The Nuclear Arms Race (jt ed with C F Barnaby, 1982), Science and Sporting Performance (jt ed with B Davies, 1982); *Clubs* Oxford and Cambridge; *Style*— Dr Geoffrey Thomas; ✉ Kellogg College, 62 Banbury Road, Oxford OX2 6dn (tel 01865 270376, fax 01865 270296, e-mail geoffrey.thomas@kellogg.ox.ac.uk)

THOMAS, Harvey; CBE (1990); s of Col John Humphrey Kenneth Thomas (d 1984), of Leamington Spa, and Olga Rosina, *née* Noake (d 2001); *b* 10 April 1939; *Educ* Westminster, Univ of Minnesota, Univ of Hawaii, Northwestern Coll Minnesota; *m* 22 Dec 1978, Marlies, da of Erich Kram, of Wölmersen, Germany; 2 da (Leah Elisabeth b 1984, Lani Christine b 1986); *Career* Billy Graham Evangelistic Assoc 1960–75, int PR conslt 1976–, dir presentation and promotion Cons Party 1985–91, field dir PM's Election Tour 1987, dir The London Cremation Co 1984–, chm Trans World Radio (UK); memb Oakwood Baptist Church N London; fell Chartered Inst of Journalists; FIPR, FRSA; *Books* In the Face of Fear (1985), Making an Impact (1989), If They Haven't Heard It, You Haven't Said It! (1995); *Recreations* family, travel, trains; *Clubs* IOD; *Style*— Harvey Thomas, Esq, CBE; ✉ 23 The Service Road, Potters Bar, Hertfordshire EN6 1QA (tel 01707 649910, fax 01707 662653, e-mail harvey@hthomas.net)

THOMAS, Prof Hilary; da of John Dewi Thomas, of Barnet, Herts, and Maureen Edith, *née* Thomas; *b* 12 November 1959; *Educ* Bishop's Hatfield Girls' Sch, New Hall Cambridge (MA), UCH London (MB BS), Univ of London (PhD); *m* 23 April 1992, Nicholas James Braithwaite, s of Roderick Clive Braithwaite; 2 da (Isobel Angharad Thomas b 18 Feb 1990, Phoebe Clara Thomas b 13 Feb 1993); *Career* SHO: in cardiology Middx Hosp 1986, in med Hammersmith Hosp 1986–87, in neurology Royal Free Hosp 1987; registrar in clinical oncology Hammersmith Hosp 1987–90, clinical res fell ICRF 1990–94, sr lectr in clinical oncology Hammersmith Hosp 1994–98, prof of oncology Univ of Surrey 1998–, lead clinician Macmillan Cancer Network (Surrey, W Sussex, Hants) 2001–04, med dir Royal Surrey County Hosp 2004–07, gp medical dir Care UK 2007–; memb GMC 1994–2003; FRCP 1999 (MRCP 1987), FRCR 1991; *Books* Fight Cancer (with Karol Sikora, 1989), Cancer: A Positive Approach (with Karol Sikora, 1995); *Clubs* Bloomsbury; *Style*— Prof Hilary Thomas; ✉ Care UK, Connaught House, 850 The Crescent, Colchester Business Park, Colchester, Essex CO4 9QB (tel 01206 752552, e-mail hilary.thomas@mercuryhealth.co.uk)

THOMAS, Prof Howard Christopher; s of Harold Thomas (d 1986), and Hilda, *née* Pickering (d 1980); *b* 31 July 1945; *Educ* Thornbury GS, Univ of Newcastle upon Tyne (BSc, MB BS, Phillipson prize in med), Univ of Glasgow (PhD); *m* 31 May 1975, Dilys, da of John Andrew Ferguson (d 1979); 2 s (Robin James b 4 Oct 1978, Oliver b 11 July 1992), 1 da (Lucy b 18 Feb 1980); *Career* lectr in immunology Univ of Glasgow 1971–74; Royal Free Hosp Med Sch London: lectr in med 1974–78, sr Wellcome fell in clinical sci 1978–83, reader in med 1983–84, prof of med 1984–87; prof and chm of med St Mary's Hosp Med Sch/Imperial Coll Sch of Med Univ of London 1987–97, conslt physician and hepatologist St Mary's Hosp 1987–, dep head Div of Med Imperial Coll Sch of Med 1997–, dean (clinical) Faculty of Med Imperial Coll Sch of Med 2001–04; chm: Dept of Health Advsy Gp on Hepatitis 1999–, Dept of Health Steering Gp on Hepatitis C Strategy 2001–, NW Thames Hepatology Clinical Network 2004–, Pan-London Hepatitis Commissioning Gp 2004–; pres: Br Assoc for Study of Liver 1996–98, Euro Soc for Study of Liver 1997; memb: Dept of Health Advsy Panel for Infected Health Care Workers 1994–2000, Cncl and Exec Ctee RCP 2001–, Cncl Br Soc of Gastroenterology 2002–, Nominations Ctee BSG 2002–, Australian Ctee to review Nat Hepatitis C Strategy 2002, Nat Expert Panel on New and Emerging Infections 2003–, Advsy Bd German Network of Competence in Med (Viral Hepatitis) 'Hep-Net' 2003–, Hepatitis Bd Health Protection Agency 2005–, Hepatitis C Action Planc Co-ordinating Gp Health Protection Scotland 2006–; vice-pres Br Liver Tst 2000– (memb Med Advsy Ctee 1990–96); non-exec dir Riotech Pharmaceuticals Ltd 2004–; chm Bd of Tstees Liver Res Tst 1988–; tstee Hepatitis B Fndn 2007–; ed Jl of Viral Hepatitis 1993–; Humphry Davy Rolleston lectr RCP 1986, Cohen lectr Israel 1988, Bushell lectr Aust Soc of Gastroenterology 1990, Hans Popper lectr (SA) 1996, Inaugural Ralph Wright lectr Univ of Southampton 1999, Sheila Sherlock lectr British Soc of Gastroenterology 2005; British Soc of Gastroenterology Res Medal 1984, Hans Popper Int Prize for Distinction in Hepatology 1989, Ivanovsky Medal of Russian Acad of Med Sciences 1997; FRCP, FRCPS, FRCPath, FMedSci; *Books* Clinical Gastrointestinal Immunology (1979), Recent Advances in Hepatology (jt ed Vol 1 1983, Vol 2 1986), Viral Hepatitis (ed, 1993, 1997, 2004); author of various publications on hepatology; *Recreations* tennis and golf; *Clubs* Athenaeum; *Style*— Prof Howard Thomas; ✉ Department of Medicine A, Imperial College School of Medicine at St Mary's Hospital, Praed Street, London W2 1PG (tel 020 7886 6454, e-mail h.thomas@ic.ac.uk)

THOMAS, Hugh; *see*: Thomas of Swynnerton, Baron

THOMAS, (Edward) Hugh Gwynne; s of Dr Edward Gwynne Thomas, OBE, VRD, FRCP (d 1976), and Lisbeth Helen Mair, *née* Thomas (d 1950); *b* 12 December 1938; *Educ* Canford Sch; *m* 1 Dec 1973, Annemary Perry, da of Lawrence Walter Dixon (d 1996), of Poole, Dorset; 3 da (Juliet b 16 Oct 1974, Annabel b 15 May 1977, Louisa b 30 July 1979); *Career* slr 1963, ptnr Keene Marsland 1966–2001; Freeman: City of London 1966, Worshipful Co of Slrs 1966; memb Law Soc 1963; *Recreations* golf, sailing; *Clubs* Beaconsfield Golf; *Style*— Hugh Thomas, Esq; ✉ Orchard Corner, Curzon Avenue, Beaconsfield, Buckinghamshire HP9 2NN (tel 01494 671056)

THOMAS, Hugh Miles; OBE (1995); s of Dr Gwilym Dorrien Thomas, and late Dorothy Gertrude, *née* Jones; *b* 14 October 1944; *Educ* Clifton, Univ of Southampton (BSc); *m* 10 Sept 1966, Alison Mary, da of Lt-Col Richard Ryder Davies (d 1968); 2 s (Simon b 1 July 1970, Ryder b 24 May 1973); *Career* CA 1969; PricewaterhouseCoopers (formerly Price Waterhouse before merger): articled clerk 1966, ptnr 1978–, ptnr i/c Wales 1983–97, sr ptnr for the Baltic States 1997–98, sr ptnr for Lithuania and for Audit and Business Advsy Services for the Baltic States 1998–; pres S Wales Inst of CAs 1987–88; treas Univ Coll of Wales Cardiff 1991–95; memb: Cncl UWIST 1983–88, Cncl UCW Cardiff 1988 and 1991–95, Mgmnt Ctee Cardiff Business Sch, Sports Cncl for Wales 1991–95, Prince of Wales' Ctee (chm Fin and Gen Purposes Ctee) 1984–96; vice-pres: Cardiff Business Club, The Welsh Inst of Int Affrs; FCA 1979; *Recreations* sailing, farming; *Clubs* Cardiff Co; *Style*— Hugh Thomas, Esq, OBE; ✉ The Court, Carrow Hill, St Brides Netherwent, Monmouthshire NP6 3AU (tel 01633 400134, fax 01633 400031); PricewaterhouseCoopers, T Sevcenkos 21, PO Box 620, LT-2009 Vilnius, Lithuania (tel 00 370 2 392300, fax 00 370 2 392301)

THOMAS, Huw George; s of Thomas (Tommy) Thomas, and Phyllis Owen, *née* Lewis; *b* 17 June 1944, Fishguard, Pembrokeshire; *Educ* St Michael's GS Llanelli, Haverfordwest, Birmingham Sch of Architecture (BSc, Dip Arch), Architectural Assoc London (AADip); *m* 1, 1969 (m dis), Priscilla Beatrice, *née* Thomas; 1 s (Nathan Richard 12 March 1975), 2 da (Rebecca Alice Iowri b 27 July 1977, Angharad Bethan b 18 Feb 1979); m 2, 2002, Sarah Louise, da of Bruce Parker, *qv*; 2 s (Milo Conrad, Felix George (twins) b 12 Aug 2003), 1 da (Daisy Ann b 9 Feb 2006); *Career* architect Bank of Uganda 1969–70, sr princ architect Hants CC 1973–80, co-fndr Stevenson and Thomas 1980–1994, fndr Huw Thomas Architects 1994 (specialises in re-use of redundant buildings, incl redeveloping Peninsula Barracks Winchester); hon life memb SAVE, tstee Winchester City Tst, specialist conservation advsr to the Defence Estate; RIBA, RICS and CLA awards for numerous building designs; author of articles for newspapers, magazines and architectural jnls, contrib to TV and radio progs; RIBA 1971; *Recreations* watercolour painting, history, playstations; *Clubs* The Exchange (Winchester); *Style*— Huw Thomas, Esq; ✉ 29 Southgate Street, Winchester SO23 9EB (tel 01962 849292, e-mail hugohuw@mac.com); Huw Thomas Architects, Madoc House, Southgate Street, Winchester SO23 9EB, tel 01962 856169, fax 01962 877752, e-mail mail@huwthomasarchitects.co.uk)

THOMAS, Huw Owen; s of Goronwy Evan Thomas (d 1984), and Morfydd Owen, *née* Jones (d 1993); *b* 11 May 1941; *Educ* Liverpool Coll, WNSM (MB BCh), Univ of Liverpool (MChOrth); *m* 25 Oct 1975, Judith; 2 s (Tom Owen b 11 March 1977, Tristan Goronwy b 26 Jan 1979); *Career* Capt TA RAMC 1970–73; house surgn Cardiff Royal Infirmary 1966, SHO Liverpool 1967–69, prosecutor RCS 1967, sr registrar Liverpool & Wrightington Hosp for Hip Surgery 1974–78, sr conslt orthopaedic surgn Wirral Hosps 1978–96, ret; memb: Medical Appeals Tbnl, Low Friction Soc, BMA, Liverpool Med Instn, Welsh History of Medicine Soc; FRCSEd 1971, FRCS 1972, FBOA, FRSM; *Publications* author of articles on: Metallic Implants from Crematoria, Isolated Dislocation of Scaphoid, Recurrent Dislocation of Patella; *Recreations* family, fishing, shooting, railways and industrial archaeology, classical music; *Style*— Huw Thomas, Esq; ✉ Pinwydden, 18 Pine Walks, Prenton, Wirral CH42 8NE (tel 0151 608 3909, fax 0151 513 2494)

THOMAS, Prof Hywel Rhys; s of Howard Lionel Thomas (d 1976), and Elizabeth Sybil Thomas; *b* Llandovery, Carmarthenshire; *Educ* UC Swansea (BSc, PhD), Imperial Coll London (MSc, DIC); *Partner* Dr Aleksandra Koj; 3 c from previous m (Elizabeth Rose b 21 Feb 1978, Anna Mary b 26 Oct 1979, Matthew Rhys b 12 March 1982); *Career* asst resident engr Scott, Wilson, Kirkpatrick and Partners 1976–78 (grad engr 1973–76), sr research asst UC Swansea 1978–80; Cardiff Sch of Engrg Cardiff Univ: lectr in civil engrg 1980–90, sr lectr 1990–92, reader 1992–95, prof of civil engrg 1995–, dir Geoenvironmental Research Centre 1996–, sr dep head 1999–2002, head Div of Civil Engrg 2002, head 2002–; CEng 1977, FICE 2000 (MICE 1977), FGS 2001, FREng 2003; *Publications* author of 96 articles in learned jls; *Style*— Prof Hywel Thomas; ✉ 184 Adventurers Quay, Cardiff Bay CF10 4NS; Cardiff School of Engineering, Cardiff University, PO Box 925, Newport Road, Cardiff CF24 3AA (tel 029 2087 4965, fax 029 2087 4004, mobile 07788 106499, e-mail thomashr@cardiff.ac.uk)

THOMAS, Ian Mitchell; OBE (1998); s of John Bythell Thomas (d 1977), of Connah's Quay, Clwyd, and Gladys Ethel, *née* Miller (d 1994); *b* 17 May 1933; *Educ* Liverpool Coll, Selwyn Coll Cambridge (MA); *m* 1, 1960 (m dis 1976), Jenifer Diana, da of Dr George Thomas Lance Fletcher Morris (d 1999), of Coggeshall, Essex; 2 s (James b 1961, Mark b 1965), 2 da (Emma b 1963, Victoria b 1969); m 2, 1977 (m dis 1998), Diana Lesley Kathryn, wid of Nicholas Thorne (d 1976); *Career* Nat Serv 4 KORR 1952–54 (2 Lt 1953), PA to COS Br Cwlth Forces Korea 1953, Capt The Liverpool Scottish Queen's Own Cameron Highlanders TA; asst md Hobson Bates and Partners 1965 (dir 1963), jt md Cavenham Foods Ltd 1965–67, md Fabbri and Partners Ltd 1968–70, chm and md Culpeper Ltd 1972–2003, dir Emmetts of Peasenhall 2000–; cncllr (Cons) Islington Cncl 1968–70; vice-pres Herb Soc 1986–87 (memb Cncl 1978–87); pres Old Lerpoolian Soc 1997–99; *Books* Culpeper's Book of Birth (1985), How to Grow Herbs (1988), Culpeper Herbal Notebook (1991); *Recreations* walking Tyson, sailing, skiing, gardening; *Clubs* Royal Temple Yacht, Ramsgate Croquet; *Style*— Ian Thomas, Esq, OBE; ✉ 12 Nelson Crescent, Ramsgate, Kent CT11 9JF (tel 01843 599745, e-mail ianmthomas@aol.com)

THOMAS, James; CBE (1992); s of late David Thomas, of Llysnewydd, Llanybydder, and late Hannah, *née* Morgans; *b* 3 January 1933; *m* 3 Aug 1957, Ann, *née* Roberts; 1 s (David Richard b 24 Aug 1958), 2 da (Dorothy Anna b 12 Jan 1960, Catrin Margaret b 2 July 1967); *Career* farmer; vice-chm RAC 1984– (memb Bd of Mgmnt), dep chm Royal Agric Soc of the Cwlth (hon treas 1971–, memb Advsy Ctee 1971, chm 1990, hon fell 1991); memb: Nat Agric and Countryside Forum, Cncl Royal Assoc of British Dairy Farmers (former), Cncl NFU (former); chm Co Branch British Food and Farming 1988–89; chm E Dyfed HA 1984–95 ret, vice-chm Health Promotion Authy of Wales 1987–95, memb Welsh Health Devpt Int 1991–94 (former chm Jt Staff Consultative Cncl Mgmnt Div); memb Cncl Welsh Sch of Med 1985–88 and 1990–92, fndr memb Standing Ctee Inst of

Health Infomatics UC Aberystwyth, former chm Welsh Health Authorities' Chairmen; govr: Coleg Ceredigion, Llanwenog Primary Sch; former mangr Highmead Residential Sch; sec PCC; *Recreations* photography; *Clubs* Farmers'; *Style*— James Thomas, Esq, CBE

THOMAS, James Robert Graham; s of Cyril John Thomas (d 1987), and Hilary Allcroft, *née* Palins (d 1976); *b* 19 March 1934; *Educ* Whitgift Sch, UCL (state scholar, Bartlett exhibitioner, BA (Arch)), Univ of Westminster (DipTP); *m* 24 Aug 1963, Anne Margaret, da of Thomas Arthur Pawsey (d 1982); 2 da (Joanna Susan (Mrs Weedon) b 1965, Catherine Sara (Mrs Flett) b 1966), 1 s (James William Pawsey b 1968); *Career* architect and town planner; asst architect: with Sir Basil Spence 1957, with Jorn Utzon 1960, with Sir Denys Lasdun 1964–66; dep gp ldr GLC 1966–68, gp planner London Borough of Lewisham 1968–70, princ architect-planner GLC 1972–79 (dep surveyor of historic buildings 1970–72), dep city architect and planning offr City of London 1979–81, dir of devpt London Borough of Tower Hamlets 1981–85, dir of planning and transportation City of Westminster 1985–87, princ Rothermel Thomas 1987–2003, conslt Howard Sharp & Ptnrs 2003–05; memb Structural Advsy Gp Athenaeum 1993–96; pres Soc of Architects Cities of London and Westminster 1986–88; RIBA: vice-pres 1995–97, memb Policy Mgmnt Bd 1995–98, memb Cncl, hon librarian, chm Library Bd; ARCUK: former memb Cncl, memb Bd of Architectural Educn, memb Discipline Ctee; memb: Ctee Soc of Chief Architects in Local Authy 1979–81, Assoc of London Borough Architects 1979–87, Assoc of London Borough Planning Offrs 1979–87, Met Planning Offrs Soc 1979–87, Assoc of London Borough Engrs and Surveyors 1985–; parish clerk St John the Evangelist City of London, memb Southwark Diocesan Advsy Ctee for the Care of Churches 1970–73; Freeman City of London 1979, fndr memb and Liveryman Worshipful Co of Chartered Architects (Master 1987–88), Liveryman Worshipful Co of Fan Makers (Master 2004); brother Worshipful Co of Parish Clerks 1991; FRIBA 1968, FRTPI 1974; *Books* Battle of the Styles (1974), Salisbury Cathedral Close: Conservation and Management (1990); *Recreations* theatre, reading, walking, family, wine; *Clubs* Athenaeum, Chislehurst Golf, Surrey CCC; *Style*— James R G Thomas, Esq; ✉ Brook Cottage, 22A Lower Camden, Chislehurst, Kent BR7 5HX (tel 020 8467 3662)

THOMAS, Jeremy Jack; s of Maj Ralph Thomas, MC (d 2001), and Joy Eveleyn, *née* Spanjer; *b* 26 July 1949; *Educ* Millfield; *m* 1, (m dis 1977), Claudia Frolich; 1 da (Jessica Emily); m 2, 1982, Vivien Patricia, da of Adolph Coughman; 2 s (Jack Felix, Joshua Kit); *Career* film producer; BFI: chm 1992–97, life fell; former pres jury: Tokyo Film Festival, San Sebastian Film Festival, Berlin Film Festival; served on jury Cannes Film Festival 1987; *Film* credits incl: Mad Dog Morgan 1976, The Shout 1977, The Great Rock 'n' Roll Swindle 1979, Bad Timing 1979, Eureka 1982, Merry Christmas Mr Lawrence 1982, The Hit 1983, Insignificance 1984, The Last Emperor (winner of nine Academy Awards incl Best Picture) 1988, Everybody Wins 1989, The Sheltering Sky 1990, Let Him Have It (exec prodr) 1991, Naked Lunch 1991, Little Buddha 1993, Victory (exec prodr) 1994, Stealing Beauty 1995, Crash 1995, Blood and Wine 1996, The Ogre (exec prodr) 1996, The Brave (exec prodr) 1996, All The Little Animals (dir) 1998, The Cup (exec prodr) 1999, Gohatto (exec prodr) 2000, Brother 2000, Sexy Beast 2001, Rabbit-Proof Fence (exec prodr) 2002, Triumph of Love (exec prodr) 2002, Young Adam 2003, The Dreamers 2003, Travellers and Magicians (exec prodr) 2003, Promised Land Hotel (exec prodr) 2004, Dreaming Lhasa (exec prodr) 2004, Heimat 3 (exec prodr) 2004, Don't Come Knocking (exec prodr) 2004, Tideland 2004, Fast Food Nation 2005, Glastonbury (exec prodr) 2005, Joe Strummer: The Future is Unwritten (exec prodr) 2007; *Awards* Best Picture Acad Award (for The Last Emperor) 1987, Michael Balcon BAFTA Award for Contribution to Br Cinema 1991, Evening Standard Lifetime Achievement in Cinema Award 1992, Screen Int Prize for World Cinema Achievement European Film Awards 2006; *Style*— Jeremy Thomas; ✉ The Recorded Picture Co, 24 Hanway Street, London W1T 1UH (tel 020 7636 2251, fax 020 7636 2261)

THOMAS, Jessica D E; *see:* Mann, Jessica D E

THOMAS, Dr John Anthony Griffiths; s of William Thomas (d 1991), of Rhyl, Clwyd, and Bernice Margaret, *née* Griffiths (d 1989); *b* 28 August 1943; *Educ* Alun GS Clwyd, Univ of Leeds (BSc), Keele Univ (PhD); *m* 16 Aug 1965, Sylvia Jean, da of Robert Norman (d 1983); 2 da (Rachel b 1971, Emily b 1974); *Career* Reed Business Publishing Ltd: dir 1970–86, dep md IPC Science and Technology Press Ltd 1977–78, publishing dir IPC Business Press Ltd 1978–84, md Update Gp Ltd 1984–85, md Update-Siebert Ltd 1985–86; BBC Worldwide Ltd (formerly BBC Enterprises Ltd): dir of magazines 1986–93, md 1993–94, md BBC Worldwide Television 1994–95, md BBC Worldwide Learning 1995–97; memb BBC Bd of Mgmnt 1993–95; chm: Redwood Publishing Ltd 1986–93, BBC Frontline Ltd; formerly dir Periodical Publishers Assoc Ltd; FRSA; *Books* Energy Today (1977), The Quest for Fuel (1978), Energy Analysis (ed, 1978); *Recreations* jogging, swimming, reading; *Style*— Dr John Thomas

THOMAS, Air Cdre John Henry Stanley; s of John Russell Thomas (d 1976), and Joan, *née* Heal (d 1994); *b* 13 February 1954, Neath; *Educ* Penistone GS, UCW Aberystwyth (BA); *m* 1978, (Susan) Valerie, *née* Worth; 1 da (Rachel Louise b 24 Nov 1983); *Career* Arthur Andersen 1976–77; RAF: joined 1977, station and cmd HQ appts 1977–92 (incl: HQ Strike Cmd High Wycombe, RAF Mount Pleasant Falkland Is, RAF Hereford and Tongeren Belgium), JSDC 1992, UN coordinator MOD 1992–95, RAF Bruggen Germany 1995–97, dir JSCSC 1997–99, asst dir Air Staff MOD 1999–2001, int mil staff NATO 2001, dep UK mil rep to EU 2002–04, def and air attaché British Embassy Paris 2005–; memb Inst of Linguists 1989; *Recreations* cycling, jazz, wine; *Clubs* RAF, Cercle de L'Union Interalliee (Paris); *Style*— Air Cdre John Thomas; ✉ Defence Section, British Embassy, 35 rue du Faubourg St Honore, 75383 Paris Cedex 08, France (tel 0033 14451 3242, e-mail john.thomas2@fco.gov.uk)

THOMAS, Rt Hon Lord Justice; Rt Hon Sir (Roger) John Laugharne; kt (1996), PC (2003); s of Roger Edward Laugharne Thomas (d 1970), of Cwmgiedd, Ystradgynlais, and Dinah Agnes, *née* Jones (d 1994); *b* 22 October 1947; *Educ* Rugby, Trinity Hall Cambridge (BA), Univ of Chicago Law Sch (JD); *m* 6 Jan 1973, Elizabeth Ann, da of Stephen James Buchanan (d 1984), of Ohio, USA; 1 s (David b 1978), 1 da (Alison b 1980); *Career* teaching asst Mayo Coll India 1965–66; called to the Bar Gray's Inn 1969 (bencher 1992); QC 1984, QC Eastern Caribbean Supreme Court 1986, recorder of the Crown Court 1987–96, judge of the High Court of Justice (Queen's Bench Div Commercial Court) 1996–2003, a presiding judge Wales & Chester Circuit 1998–2001, judge i/c Commercial Court 2002–03, a Lord Justice of Appeal 2003–, sr presiding judge for England and Wales 2003–06; DTI inspr Mirror Group Newspapers plc 1992–2001; cwlth fell Univ of Chicago Law Sch 1969–70, faculty fell Univ of Southampton 1990, Lord Morris of Borth-y-Gest lectr Univ of Wales 2000, fell Univ of Wales Aberstwyth 2002–, fell Univ of Wales Swansea 2003–, hon fell Trinity Hall Cambridge 2004, fell Cardiff Univ 2005; Hon LLD Univ of Glamorgan 2003; *Publications* author of articles and papers on commercial law, devolution in Wales, the Welsh courts and the constitutional position of the judiciary; *Recreations* gardens, travel, walking; *Style*— The Rt Hon Lord Justice Thomas; ✉ Royal Courts of Justice, Strand, London WC2A 2LL

THOMAS, Prof Sir John Meurig; kt (1991); *b* 15 December 1932; *Educ* UC Swansea (BSc), Univ of Wales/QMC London (PhD), Univ of Wales (DSc), Univ of Cambridge (MA, ScD); *m* Margaret (d 2002); 2 da (Lisa Marged (Mrs Oliver Graham), Elen Naomi Fflur); *Career* tech asst Safety in Mines Research Estab Sheffield 1953, scientific offr UKAEA Aldermaston 1957–58; UCNW Bangor: asst lectr in chemistry 1958–59, lectr in physical chemistry 1959–65, reader in chemistry 1965–69; prof of chemistry and head Edward Davies Chemical Lab UCW Aberystwyth 1969–78, head Dept of Physical Chemistry and professorial fell King's Coll Cambridge 1978–86; The Royal Instn of GB: dir 1986–91, dir Davy Faraday Research Lab 1986–91, resident prof of chemistry 1986–88, Fullerian prof of chemistry 1988–95 (now emeritus prof); dep pro-chllr Univ of Wales 1991–94, master Peterhouse Cambridge 1993–2002, currently hon prof Dept of Materials Science Univ of Cambridge, hon distinguished prof Sch of Chemistry Univ of Cardiff 2005–; visiting scientist: Dept of Physics Technol Univ of Eindhoven 1962, Technische Hochschule Karlsruhe 1966, Dept of Organic Chemistry Univ of Florence 1972, IBM Research Lab San José 1977; visiting scholar Pennsylvania State Univ: Dept of Fuel Sci 1963, Coll of Mineral Industries 1967; visiting prof: Dept of Structural Chemistry Weizmann Inst of Science 1969 (memb Governing Body 1981–97, emeritus govr 1997–), Dept of Chemistry Univ of Western Ontario 1971, Centre for Materials Science McMaster Univ Ontario 1978, Northwestern Univ 2004; distinguished visiting prof: American Univ in Cairo 1973, École Nationale Superieure de Chemie de Paris 1991, Jawaharlal Nehru Centre for Advanced Scientific Research Bangalore 1991, in nanoscience Univ of S Carolonia 2005–; distinguished visiting lectr Univ of London 1980; hon visiting prof: Imperial Coll London 1986–91, Queen Mary & Westfield Coll London 1986–91; Baker lectr Cornell Univ 1983, Tetelman fell Yale Univ 1997, Miller prof Univ of Calif Berkeley 1998, Linus Pauling lectureship Caltech 1999; pres: Chemistry Section BAAS 1988–89, London Int Youth Science Fortnight 1989–93, Faraday Div RSC 1999–2001; memb Bd of Tstees: Natural History Museum 1987–91, Science Museum 1990–96; ind memb Radioactive Waste Mgmnt Advsy Ctee 1980–82; memb: Advsy Cncl of Applied Research and Devpt Cabinet Office 1982–85, Governing Body Sci Centre Alexandria Univ 1982–88, Main Ctee UK SERC 1986–90, Chemrawn Ctee Int Union of Pure and Applied Chemistry 1988–93 (chm 1988–91); fndr memb Ctee on the Popularisation of Science (COPUS) Royal Soc Royal Inst and Br Assoc 1986–91; ed-in-chief Catalysis Letters 1988–, memb Editorial Bd Int Review of Physical Chemistry 1989–; pres Llanelli Branch WEA 1994–, vice-pres Cambridge Musical Soc 1995–; hon bencher Gray's Inn 1986; hon professorial fell Academia Sinica 1985, sesquicentenary hon fell Royal Microscopical Soc 1989 foreign hon memb US Acad of Arts and Sciences Boston 1990, hon foreign assoc Engrg Acad Japan 1991, hon foreign memb Russian Acad of Sciences 1994, hon foreign corr memb Nat Acad of Sciences Venezuela 1994, hon assoc Third World Acad of Science 1995; hon foreign fell: American Philosophical Soc 1993 (hon foreign memb 1992), Hungarian Acad of Science 1998, Polish Acad of Science 1998, Royal Spanish Acad of Science, Göttingen Acad of Natural Sciences 2003; Royal Soc: Bakerian Lecture and Prize 1990, Davy Medal 1994, Rutherford Meml Lecture NZ 1996; RSC: Solid State Chemistry Medal 1978, Hugo Müller Medal 1989, Faraday Medal 1989, vice-pres Faraday Div 1989, Longstaff Medal 1996; Chemical Soc London: Corday Medal 1969, Tilden Medal 1973; Messel Gold Medal and Prize Soc of Chemical Industry 1992; American Chemical Soc: Willard Gibbs Medal 1995, first recipient Soc's Award for Creative Research in Catalysis 1999; Linus Pauling Gold Medal for contributions to the advancement of science Stanford Univ, Natta Gold Metal Italian Chemical Soc 2003, Medal of Hon Soc of Cymmrodorion for services to Welsh culture and British public life 2003, Sir George Stokes Gold Medal RSC 2005, Distinguished Achievement Award Int Precious Metal Inst 2007; Hon LLD: Univ of Wales 1984, CNAA 1987; Hon DSc: Heriot-Watt Univ 1989, Univ of Birmingham 1991, Univ of Lyon 1994, Univ of Western Ontario 1995, Univ of Glamorgan 1995, Eindhoven Technol Univ 1995, Univ of Aberdeen 1997, Univ of Surrey 1997, American Univ in Cairo 2003, Univ of Sydney 2005, Clarkson Univ NY 2005; Hon DUniv Open Univ 1991; Dr (hc): Universidad Complutense 1994, Univ of Turin; hon fell: UMIST 1984, UC Swansea 1985, UCNW Bangor 1988, Queen Mary & Westfield Coll London 1990, Univ of Wales Aberystwyth 1996, Univ of Wales Cardiff 1996; memb Academia Europaea 1989; fell: Indian Acad Bangalore 1981, Indian Nat Acad New Dehli 1985, European Acad of Sciences 2006; FRS 1977, Hon FRSE 1993 (Bruce-Preller Prize lectr 1989), Hon FREng 1999, Hon FInstP 1999; *Publications* Introduction to the Principles of Heterogeneous Catalysis (with W J Thomas, 1967, Russian edn, 1969), Surface and Defect Properties of Solids (vols 1–6, contrib and co-ed with M W Roberts, 1972–77), Chemical Physics of Solids and their Surfaces (vol 7 and 8, contrib and co-ed with M W Roberts, 1978–80), Pan Edrychwyf Ar Y Nefoedd, Annual BBC Welsh Lecture (1978), Characterization of Catalysts (contrib and co-ed with R M Lambert, 1980, Russian edn 1983), Proceedings of the Royal Institution of Great Britain (vols 58–63, 1986–91), The Microstructure and Properties of Catalysts (contrib and co-ed with M M J Treacy and J M White, 1988), Catalysis Letters (founding co-ed-in-chief, with G A Somorjai, 1988–), Topics in Catalysis (founding co-ed-in-chief, with G A Somorjai, 1992–), Michael Faraday and his Contemporaries, National Portrait Gallery handlist booklet (with Sir Brian Pippard, 1991), Michael Faraday and the Royal Institution: The Genius of Man and Place (1991), The Legacy of Sir Lawrence Bragg (contrib and co-ed with Sir David Phillips, 1991), Perspectives in Catalysis: Theory and Practice (contrib and co-ed with K I Zamaraev, 1992), Topics in Catalysis (founding co-ed-in-chief, with G A Somorjai, 1992–), New Methods of Modelling Processes Within Solids and on their Surfaces (co-ed with C R A Catlow and A M Stoneham, 1993), Current Opinion in Solid State and Materials Science (founding ed-in-chief 1996–), Heterogeneous Catalysis: Theory and Practice (with W J Thomas, 1997); also author of some 1000 research articles on solid state chemistry and heterogeneous catalysis; *Recreations* ancient civilisations, bird watching, Welsh literature, reading; *Style*— Prof Sir John Meurig Thomas, FRS, FREng; ✉ Department of Materials Science, University of Cambridge, New Museums Site, Cambridge CB2 3QZ (tel 01223 334300, fax 01223 334567)

THOMAS, Kathrin (Kate); CVO (2002), JP, DL (Mid Glamorgan 1989); da of Dillwyn Evans (d 1974), and Dorothy Nelle, *née* Bullock (d 2000); *b* 20 May 1944; *Educ* Cheltenham Ladies' Coll, Sorbonne; *m* 21 Jan 1967, Edward Vaughan Thomas (d 2006), s of Edward Thomas; 2 s (Richard Edward b 7 Feb 1969, Robert Dillwyn b 12 Jan 1971); *Career* dir Penywaun Farms Ltd Nelson Mid Glamorgan; Prince's Tst: chm S Wales 1988–95, chm Prince's Tst Cymru and memb Advsy Cncl 1996–2001; chm: Mid Glamorgan FHSA 1990–94, Mid Glamorgan HA 1994–96, Bro Taf HA 1996–2000; Hon Col 203 (W) Field Hosp (V) 1998–2006; High Sheriff of Mid Glamorgan 1986–87, HM Lord-Lt Mid Glamorgan 2003–; *Recreations* farming and reading; *Clubs* Army and Navy; *Style*— Mrs Edward Thomas, CVO; ✉ Gelli Hir, Nelson, Treharris CF46 6PL

THOMAS, His Hon Judge Keith Garfield; s of (William Geoffrey) Howard Thomas, of Cardiff, and (Dorothy) Shirley Thomas; *b* 10 August 1955; *Educ* Mill Hill Sch, Bristol Poly (LLB), Inns of Court Law Sch; *m* 5 July 2003, Melinda Jane, *née* Vaughan; *Career* called to the Bar Gray's Inn 1977; asst provincial stipendiary magistrate 1995–97, asst recorder 1996–2000, recorder 2000–04, circuit judge 2004–; vice-chm Glamorgan Wanderers RFC; *Style*— His Hon Judge Keith Thomas; ✉ Swansea Crown Court, The Law Courts, St Helen's Road, Swansea SA1 4PF (tel 01792 637000, fax 01792 637049, e-mail hhjudge.thomas2@hmcourts-service.gsi.gov.uk)

THOMAS, Sir Keith Vivian; kt (1988); s of Vivian Jones Thomas (d 1987), and Hilda Janet Eirene, *née* Davies (d 1979); *b* 2 January 1933; *Educ* Barry Co GS, Balliol Coll Oxford (MA); *m* 16 Aug 1961, Valerie June, da of Eric Charles Little, of Beaconsfield, Bucks; 1 da (Emily b 1963), 1 s (Edmund b 1965); *Career* fell: All Souls Coll Oxford 1955–57 and 2001–, St John's Coll Oxford 1957–86 (hon fell 1986); prof of modern history Univ of Oxford 1986 (reader 1978–85), pres CCC Oxford 1986–2000 (hon fell 2000), pro-vice-chllr Univ of Oxford 1988–2000; delg OUP 1980–2000; memb: ESRC 1985–90, Reviewing Ctee on Exports of Works of Art 1990–93, Royal Cmmn on Historical MSS 1992–2002; tstee:

Nat Gallery 1991–98, Br Museum 1999–; chm: Br Library Advsy Ctee for Arts, Humanities and Social Sciences 1997–2002, Supervisory Ctee Oxford Dictionary of National Biography 1992–2004, Advsy Cncl Warburg Inst Univ of London 2000–; Norton Medlicott Medal Historical Assoc 2003; Hon DLitt: Univ of Kent 1983, Univ of Wales 1987, Univ of Hull 1995, Univ of Leicester 1996, Univ of Sussex 1996, Univ of Warwick 1998, Univ of London 2006; Hon LLD Williams Coll Mass 1988, Oglethorpe Univ Georgia 1996; Hon LittD: Univ of Sheffield 1992, Univ of Cambridge 1995; hon fell Balliol Coll Oxford 1984, hon fell Univ of Wales Cardiff 1995; foreign hon memb American Acad of Arts and Sci 1983; FRHistS 1970 (jt literary dir 1970–74, memb Cncl 1975–78, vice-pres 1980–84, hon vice-pres 2001–), FBA 1979 (memb Cncl 1985–88, pres 1993–97), memb Academia Europaea 1993 (tstee 1997–2002); Cavaliere Ufficiale Ordine al Merito della Repubblica Italiana 1991; *Books* Religion and the Decline of Magic (1971), Puritans and Revolutionaries (ed with Donald Pennington, 1978), Man and the Natural World (1983), The Oxford Book of Work (ed, 1999), Roy Jenkins: A Retrospective (ed with Andrew Adonis, 2004); *Recreations* looking for secondhand bookshops; *Style*— Sir Keith Thomas, FBA; ✉ The Broad Gate, Broad Street, Ludlow, Shropshire SY8 1NJ; All Souls College, Oxford OX1 4AL (e-mail keith.thomas@all-souls.ox.ac.uk)

THOMAS, Leslie; *b* 29 April 1965, London; *Educ* Kingston Univ (LLB); *Career* called to the Bar 1988, called to the Cwlth of Dominica Bar 2003; practising barr specialising in human rights and civil rights torts against the police and inquests, memb Garden Court Chambers 1989–; former lectr in employment law and criminal law: Univ of Westminster, Kingston Univ; chm Mgmnt Ctee Central London Law Centre; memb: INQUEST Lawyers Gp, Police Action Lawyers Gp, Liberty; *Publications* INQUESTS: A Practitioner's Guide (co-author); *Recreations* alto saxophone, jazz music, languages, Russian; *Style*— Leslie Thomas, Esq; ✉ Garden Court Chambers Ltd, 57–60 Lincoln's Inn Fields, London WC2A 3LS (tel 020 7993 7600, e-mail lesliet@gclaw.co.uk, website www.gclaw.co.uk)

THOMAS, Leslie John; OBE (2005); s of David James Thomas, MN (ka 1943), and Dorothy Hilda Court Thomas (d 1943); *b* 22 March 1931; *Educ* Dr Barnardo's Kingston upon Thames, Kingston Tech Sch; *m* 1, 1956 (m dis 1970), Maureen, da of Charles Crane; 2 s (Mark, Gareth), 1 da (Lois); m 2, Nov 1971, Diana Miles; 1 s (Matthew); *Career* Nat Serv Singapore, Malaya 1949–51; journalist 1951–63: Exchange Telegraph 1955–57, London Evening News 1957–63; many radio and TV appearances; vice-pres Barnardo's 1998; Hon MA Univ of Wales 1995, Hon DLitt Univ of Nottingham 1998; *Television Plays and Documentaries* incl: Great British Isles (Channel 4 series, also presented) 1989, The Last Detective (adapted from Dangerous Davies novels, ITV) 2003, 2004 and 2005; *Novels* The Virgin Soldiers (1966), Orange Wednesday (1967), The Love Beach (1968), Come to the War (1969), His Lordship (1970), Onward Virgin Soldiers (1971), Arthur McCann and All His Women (1972), The Man with Power (1973), Tropic of Ruislip (1974), Stand Up Virgin Soldiers (1975), Dangerous Davies (1976), Bare Nell (1977), Ormerod's Landing (1978), That Old Gang of Mine (1979), The Magic Army (1981), The Dearest and the Best (1984), The Adventures of Goodnight and Loving (1986), Dangerous in Love (1987), Orders for New York (1989), The Loves and Journeys of Revolving Jones (1991), Arrivals and Departures (1992), Dangerous By Moonlight (1993), Running Away (1994), Kensington Heights (1995), Chloe's Song (1997), Dangerous Davies and the Lonely Heart (1998), Other Times (1999), Waiting for the Day (2003), Dover Beach (2005); *Non-Fiction* Some Lovely Islands (1968), The Hidden Places of Britain (1981), A World of Islands (1983); *Autobiographies* This Time Next Week (1964), In My Wildest Dreams (1984, revised edn 2006); *Recreations* cricket, music, antiques, stamp collecting; *Clubs* MCC, Lord's Taverners, Saints and Sinners; *Style*— Leslie Thomas, Esq, OBE

THOMAS, Prof Lyn Carey; s of William Carey Thomas (d 1994), and Eunice, *née* Morgan (d 1968); *b* 10 August 1946; *Educ* The Lewis Sch Pengam, Jesus Coll Oxford (Dip Mathematics, MA, DPhil); *m* 30 July 1970, Margery Wynn, da of Frederick James Bright; 2 s (Matthew James Carey b 22 June 1974, Stephen Daniel Adam b 10 April 1980), 1 da (Elizabeth Angharad b 29 Sept 1976); *Career* Pilcher sr res fell Dept of Mathematics UC Swansea 1973–74 (res fell 1971–73), lectr then sr lectr in decision theory Univ of Manchester 1974–85, prof of mgmnt sci Univ of Edinburgh 1985–2000, prof of mgmnt sci Univ of Southampton 2000–; NRC sr res assoc Naval Postgrad Sch Montery 1982–83; adjunct prof Monash Univ Melbourne and Edith Cowan Univ Perth; memb: Operational Res Soc 1974 (pres 1994 and 1995), Informs 1979, Edinburgh Mathematical Soc 1985; FIMA 1989, FRSE 1991, FOR 2005; *Books* Games, Theory and Applications (1984, 2 edn 2004), Operational Research Techniques (1986), Credit Scoring and Credit Control (1992), Credit Scoring and its Applications (2002), Readings in Credit Scoring (2004); *Recreations* reading, walking, rugby; *Style*— Prof Lyn Thomas, FRSE; ✉ School of Management, University of Southampton, Highfield, Southampton SO17 1BJ (e-mail l.thomas@soton.ac.uk)

THOMAS, Margaret; da of Francis Stewart Thomas (d 1971), and Grace Darling, *née* Whetherly (d 1978); *b* 26 September 1916; *Educ* privately, Sidcup Sch of Art, Slade, Royal Acad Schs; *Career* artist and painter; solo shows: Leicester Galleries London (1949 and 1951), five shows at Aitken Dotts and Scot Gallery Edinburgh (1952–82), Howard Roberts Cardiff, Canaletto Gallery London, Minories Colchester, Mall Galleries London, Octagon Gallery Belfast, Sally Hunter Fine Arts (1988, 1991, 1995 and 1998), Maltings Concert Hall Gallery Snape, Messum Gallery London 2001 and 2003, Strand Gallery Aldeburgh 2006 and 2007; work in numerous public collections incl: Chantrey Bequest, Miny of Educn, Robert Fleming Holdings Ltd, Lloyd's of London, Exeter Coll Oxford, Univ of Bath, Scot Nat Orchestra, Edinburgh City Corp, Mitsukshi Ltd Tokyo, Warburg & Co; regular exhibitor at Royal Acad and Royal Scot Acad (painting purchased by HRH Prince Philip), portrait of Sir Kyffin Williams RA (purchased by Nat Library of Wales); winner Hunting Gp award Oil Painting of the Year 1982 and 1996; memb: Royal W of Eng Acad, RBA, NEAC; *Recreations* gardening, dogs, vintage cars; *Style*— Miss Margaret Thomas; ✉ Ellingham Mill, Bungay, Suffolk NR35 2EP (tel 01508 518656); 13a North Road, Highgate Village, London N6 4BD (tel 020 8340 2527)

THOMAS, Mark David; *b* 1 March 1967; *Career* trained Fleet Street news agency 1985–88, news reporter The People 1988–94, news reporter then chief reporter News of the World 1994–97, features ed then asst ed Daily Mirror 1997–2001, dep ed Sunday Mirror 2001–03, ed The People 2003–; *Style*— Mark Thomas, Esq; ✉ The People, One Canada Square, London E14 5AP (tel 020 7293 3614, fax 020 7293 3887, e-mail m.thomas@mgn.co.uk)

THOMAS, Martin Robert; s of Philip Anthony Thomas, of Warmington, Oxon, and Joan, *née* Edwards; *b* 2 July 1964; *Educ* N Leamington Sch, Jesus Coll Oxford (BA); *m* 1 April 1995, Alison, da of Derek Field; *Career* account mangr Paragon Communications 1987–89, exec Brunswick Public Relations 1989–90; Cohn & Wolfe: account dir 1990–93, bd dir 1993–94, md 1994–99; worldwide communications dir Media Edge:cia 1999–2004, founding ptnr Nylon 2004–05, head of strategy Media Planning Gp 2005–06; memb Marketing Soc; *Recreations* rugby, beer and other cultural activities; *Style*— Martin Thomas, Esq

THOMAS, Dr Martyn Rhys; *Educ* Bart's Med Coll, King's Coll Hosp Univ of London (MD); *Career* trg in interventional cardiology KCH 1988– (currently also dir of cardiac servs); nat and int trainer in coronary angioplasty, introduced radiation therapy to UK 1998; pres Br Cardiovascular Intervention Soc (BCIS), expert to NICE 1999 and 2005; FRCP 2000 (MRCP 1985); *Recreations* season ticket holder at Crystal Palace FC; *Style*— Dr Martyn Thomas; ✉ King's College Hospital, Denmark Hill, London SE5 9RS (tel 020 7346 3748, fax 020 7346 3489)

THOMAS, Michael David; CMG (1985), QC (1973); s of D Cardigan Thomas and Kathleen Thomas; *b* 8 September 1933; *Educ* Chigwell Sch Essex, LSE; *m* 1, 1958 (m dis 1978), Jane Lena Mary, eldest da of late Francis Neate; 2 s, 2 da; m 2, 1981 (m dis 1986), Mrs Gabrielle Blakemore; m 3, 1988, Baroness Dunn, DBE (Life Peer), *qv*; *Career* called to the Bar Middle Temple 1955 (bencher 1982); jr counsel to Treasury in admiralty matters 1966–73, wreck cmmr and salvage arbitrator Lloyd's 1974–83, attorney-gen Hong Kong 1983–88; memb of Exec and Legislative Cncls Hong Kong 1983–88; *Style*— Michael Thomas, Esq, CMG, QC; ✉ Essex Court Chambers, 24 Lincoln's Inn Fields, London WC2A 3ED (tel 020 7813 8000, fax 020 7813 8080)

THOMAS, Prof Michael Frederic; s of Hugh Frederic Thomas (d 1987), and Kathleen Helena Doris, *née* Phelps (d 1981); *b* 15 September 1933; *Educ* Royal GS Guildford, Univ of Reading (BA, MA), Univ of London (PhD); *m* 29 Dec 1956, (Elizabeth) Anne (d 1992), da of Harry Guest Dadley (d 1955); 1 s (Graham Hugh b 31 Oct 1959), 1 da (Gillian Anne b 31 March 1965); *Career* asst lectr Magee UC Londonderry NI 1957–60, lectr Univ of Ibadan 1960–64, sr lectr in geography Univ of St Andrews 1974–79 (lectr 1964–74), fndn prof of environmental sci Univ of Stirling 1980–2001 (prof emeritus 2001–), Leverhulme Emeritus Fellowship 2002–03; memb: Cncl Royal Scottish Geographical Soc (and convener Research Ctee), Scottish Examinations Bd 1992–97, Scottish Cncl for Nat Parks 1994–96, Exec Ctee Br Geomorphological Research Gp (and hon treas) 2002–06; *Awards* Centenary Medal RSGS 2000, David Linton Award Br Geomorphological Research Gp 2001; FGS 1985, FRSE 1988; *Books* Environment & Land Use in Africa (jtly and jt ed, 1969), Tropical Geomorphology (1974), Land Assessment in Scotland (jt ed, 1980), Evaluation of Land Resources in Scotland (jtly and jt ed, 1990), Geomorphology in the Tropics (1994); jt ed Catena (int jl) 1994–2004, jt reviews ed Environment International 2000–02 (formerly jt ed Progress in Environmental Science 1998–2000), exec ed Transactions RSE 2001–04; *Recreations* listening to classical music, jazz, hill walking, travel; *Style*— Prof Michael Thomas, FRSE; ✉ School of Biological and Environmental Sciences, University of Stirling, Stirling FK9 4LA (tel 01786 467840, fax 01786 467843, e-mail m.f.thomas@stir.ac.uk)

THOMAS, Michael Graham; s of Graham Gerard Thomas, and Dulcie Elizabeth Thomas; *b* 6 January 1960, Porthcawl, S Wales; *Educ* Hornchurch GS, Swayne Sch Rayleigh, SE Essex Sixth Form Coll, Middx Hosp Med Sch (BSc, MB BS, Thomas Yates Prize in Anatomy, ICI Prize in Neuropharmacology), Univ of London (MS); *Career* house surgn Middx Hosp London 1984–85, house physician Orsett Hosp 1984–85; SHO: orthopaedics and traumatology Royal Nat Orthopaedic Hosp Stanmore 1985–86, A&E Edgware Hosp 1986, orthopaedics and traumatology Central Middx Hosp London 1986, gen surgery and renal transplantation Southmead Hosp Bristol 1986–88, Hepatopancreatobiliary Unit Hammersmith Hosp London 1988; surgical registrar KCH London 1988–89, res fell and hon clinical registrar Royal Postgrad Med Sch and St Mark's Hosp London 1989–90; surgical registrar: Hammersmith Hosp 1990–92, Ashford Hosp Middx 1992–93; surgical registrar and locum sr registrar Hammersmith Hosp 1993; lectr in surgery and hon sr surgical registrar: Broadgreen Hosp Liverpool 1993–94, Royal Liverpool Univ Hosp 1994–95; sr lectr and conslt Univ of Bristol 1995–2001, conslt colorectal surgn Bristol Royal Infirmary 1995–; visiting prof Chennai India 2001, visiting lectr All Indian Med Centre New Delhi 2001, Shri Prakash lectr DR N R Res and Digestive Disease Educnl Tst Chennai India 2000; visitor: Nat Cancer Centre Hosp Tokyo 1996, Mt Sinai Hosp NY 1999, Mayo Clinic Rochester, Minneapolis and St Paul's MN 2001; referee: Br Jl of Surgery, Br Jl of Cancer, Res Bd RCS, NW NHS Exec R&D; hon dr Somerset RFU; memb: Surgical Res Soc, Br Soc of Gastroenterology (memb SW Div), Assoc of Surgns, Assoc of Coloproctologists, SW Surgns, Nat Clinical Trials Ctee; admitted Royal Ct of Examiners England; Arris and Gale lectureship RCS 1993 (delivered at Hammersmith Hosp 1994), Ethicon travelling fellowship RCS 1996, res scholarship Fndn for the Promotion of Cancer Research Japan 1996, Continuing Med Educn fellowship RCS(Ed) 1998–2001, travelling fell American Assoc of Colorectal Surgns/Assoc of Coloproctologists GB and I 2001–02; FRCS 1989, FRCSEd 1989, FRCS (Gen) 1996; *Publications* author of numerous articles, abstracts and book reviews published in learned jls; *Recreations* rugby, football, cricket, athletics, swimming, tennis, chess, drama; *Clubs* Birkenhead Park RFC (sometime hon sec), Yatton RFC, Law Soc RFC; *Style*— Michael Thomas, Esq; ✉ 45 Sydenham Hill, Cotham, Bristol BS6 5SL (tel 0117 962 9549, e-mail mgtbristol@aol.com); Department of Surgery, Level 4, Bristol Royal Infirmary, Marlborough Street, Bristol (tel 0117 928 3066, mobile 07876 597388)

THOMAS, Prof Michael James; OBE (1999); *b* 15 July 1933; *Educ* King Edward's Sch Birmingham, UCL (BSc), Graduate Sch of Business Indiana Univ (MBA), De Montfort Univ (DBA); *m* Nancy, *née* Yeoman; 1 s (Huw), 1 da (Helen); *Career* cmmnd Br Army 1952, served Royal Warwickshire Regt, seconded W African Frontier Force Nigeria Regt 1952–53, army res offr 1953–56; market res mangr The Metal Box Co Ltd London 1957–60, Faculty Sch of Mgmnt Syracuse Univ 1960–71 (assoc prof); Lancaster Univ 1971–86: head Dept of Mktg 1972–77, dep chm Sch of Mgmnt 1975–79, memb Univ Cncl 1979–85; prof Univ of Strathclyde 1987–98 (head Dept of Mktg 1988–92, prof emeritus 1999–); visiting prof: Syracuse Univ 1977, Univ of Nigeria 1979, Temple Univ Philadelphia 1980, Univ of Gdansk 1977, Georgetown Univ Washington 1996, Helsinki Sch of Economics 1996, Univ of Karlstad 1999; ldr Strathclyde Consortium (Polish Know-How Fund) 1991–; sr conslt: Silverdale Marketing Consultants, American Marketing Assoc; dep chm Gas Consumers' Cncl for the Northwest 1977–86; chm Mktg Educn Gp of GB and Ireland 1986–90; pres Market Research Soc 1999–2004; nat chm Chartered Inst of Mktg 1995; bd memb Alliance of Univs for Democracy; ed Mktg Intelligence and Planning Jl; memb Editorial Bd: Jl of Marketing Mgmnt, Jl of Int Marketing, Jl of East-West Business, Jl of Brand Mgmnt, Jl of Mktg Practice; chm Jt Parish Ctee Arnside-Silverdale Area of Outstanding Nat Beauty 1975–85; FCIM, FMRS, FAM; Order of Merit (Poland) 1995; *Books* International Marketing Management (1969), Modern Marketing Management (1970–73), International Marketing (1971), Management Sales and Marketing Training (contrib, 1984), The Pocket Guide to Marketing (1986), The Marketing Book (contrib, 1987), The Marketing Digest (1988), The Marketing Handbook (4 edn, 1995), International Marketing (1998), Handbook of Strategic Marketing (1998), How to Prepare a Marketing Plan (5 ed, 1998); *Recreations* book collecting, bird watching, the study of Polish politics; *Clubs* Scottish Ornithologists; *Style*— Prof Michael Thomas, OBE; ✉ Department of Marketing, University of Strathclyde, Stenhouse Building, 173 Cathedral Street, Glasgow G4 0RQ (tel 0141 552 4400, fax 0141 552 2802, telex 77472 UNSLIB G, e-mail michaelt@strath.ac.uk, michael.thomas@mi8.com)

THOMAS, Col Michael John Glyn; s of Glyn Pritchard Thomas (d 1985), and Mary, *née* Moseley (d 1987); *b* 14 February 1938; *Educ* Haileybury and ISC, Univ of Cambridge (MA, MB BChir), Bart's; *m* 23 May 1969, (Sheelagh) Jane, da of Harold Thorpe (d 1979); 1 da (Fleur b 1970); *Career* RMO 2 Bn Para Regt 1964–67, trainee in pathology BMH Singapore 1967–71; specialist in pathology: Colchester MH 1971–74, Singapore 1974–76; sr specialist in pathology and 2 i/c Army Blood Supply Depot (ABSD) 1977–82, exchange fell Walter Reed Army Medical Centre Washington DC 1982–83, offr i/c Leishman Lab 1984–87, CO ABSD 1987–94; private conslt in transfusion medicine and clinical dir The Blood Care Foundation 1995–; memb BMA: Cncl 1973–74 and 1977–82, Central Ethical Ctee 1976–82 (chm 1977–82), Armed Forces Ctee 1971–82 and 1988–93, Jr Membs Forum 1971–78 (chm 1974), Bd of Sci and Educn 1987–93, Rep Body 1972–82 and 1987–93, Expert Ctee on AIDS 1986–, EEC Ctee 1989–93; fell BMA 1995; expert witness on gene mapping ESC, jt patent holder of new method of freezing blood together with special bag in which it is frozen; memb: Br Blood Transfusion Soc 1987 (fndr chm Autologous Transfusion Special Interest Group 1992–98, sec 1998–, memb Cncl 1998–2001), Inst of Medical Ethics 1987, Int Soc of Blood Transfusion 1988 (pres Int Congress 2004), Euro Sch of Transfusion Med (faculty memb) 1993 (faculty memb Slovenia 1997, Italy 1998), American Assoc of Blood Banks 1997; DTM&H 1965, LMSSA 1982, FRCPEd 1997; *Books* co-author: Control of Infection (1989), Nuclear Attack, Ethics and Casualty Selection (1988), Handbook of Medical Ethics (1979 and subsequent edns), Our Genetic Future, Medicine Betrayed, A Code of Practice for the Safe Use and Disposal of Sharps - Dictionary of Medical Ethics (contrib), AIDS and Human Rights a UK Perspective (contrib), Wylie and Churchill Davidson's A Practice of Anaesthesia (contrib chapter on Autologous Transfusion), Cryopreservation and Freeze-Drying Protocols (contrib chapter on Cryopreservation of Human Red Blood Cells), Transfusion in Europe (contrib); *Recreations* DIY, photography, philately; *Clubs* Tanglin (Singapore); *Style*— Dr Michael J G Thomas; ✉ 3 Cholseley Drive, Fleet, Hampshire GU51 1HG (tel 01252 622060, fax 01252 622331, e-mail michaelgj.thomas2@btinternet.com)

THOMAS, Sir (William) Michael Marsh; 3 Bt (UK 1918), of Garreglwyd, Anglesey; s of Major Sir William Eustace Rhyddlad Thomas, 2 Bt, MBE (d 1958), and Enid Helena Marsh (d 1982); *b* 4 December 1930; *Educ* Oundle; *m* 1957, Geraldine, da of Robert Drysdale, of Trearddur Bay, Anglesey; 3 da; *Heir* none; *Career* formerly md Gors Nurseries Ltd; *Style*— Sir Michael Thomas, Bt

THOMAS, Michael Stuart (Mike); s of late Arthur Edward Thomas, and late Mona, *née* Parker; *b* 24 May 1944; *Educ* Latymer Upper Sch, King's Sch Macclesfield, Univ of Liverpool (BA); *m* 31 July 1976, Maureen Theresa, da of late Denis Kelly; 1 s by previous m (Paul b 1973); *Career* pres Liverpool Univ Guild of Undergrads 1965 (formerly memb Nat Exec NUS), head Research Dept Co-op Pty 1966–68, sr research assoc Policy Studies Inst 1968–73, dir The Volunteer Centre 1973–74, MP (Lab and Co-op 1974–81, SDP 1981–83) Newcastle upon Tyne East 1974–83 (Parly candidate: (Lab) Hertfordshire East 1970, (SDP) Newcastle upon Tyne East 1983 and Exeter 1987); PPS to Rt Hon Roy Hattersley MP 1974–76, memb House of Commons Select Ctee on Nationalised Industries 1975–79, chm PLP Trade Gp 1979–81, SDP spokesman on Health and Social Security 1981–83; SDP: memb Policy Ctee 1981–83 and 1984–90, memb Nat Ctee 1981–90, chm Orgn Ctee 1981–88, chm Fin Ctee 1988–89; mgmnt conslt 1978–; dir: Dewe Rogerson Ltd 1984–88, BR Western Region 1985–92, Corporate Communications Strategy 1988–2004, Education 2000 1991–94, Lopex plc 1998–99, Metal Bulletin plc 1998–2002; chm: Burnaby Communications and Information Services Ltd 1978–2005, Media Audits Ltd 1990–2001, Fotorama Ltd 1995–2000, Atalink Ltd 1998–2001, SMF Int Ltd 2000–, Music Choice Europe plc 2000–05, 422 Ltd 2001–02, WAA Ltd 2003–, H K Wentworth Ltd 2005–, UTarget plc 2007–; fndr Parliament's weekly jl The House Magazine 1976, ed The BBC Guide to Parliament 1979 and 1983, author of various articles, reviews and pamphlets; *Recreations* collecting election pottery and medals, gardening, walking, countryside, music, opera, theatre, fine arts and architecture; *Clubs* Reform; *Style*— Mike Thomas, Esq; ✉ Milton Lodge, Iver, Buckinghamshire SL0 0AA (tel 01753 772572, fax 01753 674622, e-mail mike.thomas@hkw.co.uk)

THOMAS, Michael Tilson; s of Ted Thomas, and Roberta Thomas; *b* 21 December 1944; *Educ* Univ of Southern Calif; *Career* conductor, pianist and composer; studied under Ingolf Dahl, John Crown and Alice Ehlers; music dir Young Musicians' Fndn Debut Orch 1963, pianist and conductor Monday Evening Concerts LA 1963–68, asst conductor then principal guest conductor Boston Symphony Orch 1969–74, conductor NY Philharmonic Young People's Concerts 1971–77, music dir Buffalo Philharmonic 1971–79, princ guest conductor LA Philharmonic 1981–85, princ conductor Great Woods Music Festival 1985–88, fndr and artistic dir New World Symphony (trg orch for young musicians USA) 1988–, Pacific Music Festival Sapporo Japan 1990–, princ guest conductor LSO 1995– (princ conductor 1988–95), music dir San Francisco Symphony Orch 1995–; American Music Center Award 2000; recordings incl: Copland orchestral works 1986, Tchaikovsky, Liszt and Rachmaninov Piano Concertos 1986, Mahler Symphony No 3 1987, Kurt Weill Seven Deadly Sins and Little Threepenny Opera 1987, Ravel orchestral works 1988, John McLaughlin Guitar Concerto 1988, Prokofiev Piano Concertos Nos 1 and 2 1988, Steve Reich The Four Sections 1988, Brahms Serenades 1989, Haydn Variations 1989, Tchaikovsky Swan Lake 1990, Janácek Glagolitic Mass 1990, Debussy orchestral works 1991, Tavener Dance Lament of the Repentent Thief 1991, Ives Three Places in New England 1992, Bernstein On the Town 1992, Strauss Lieder 1993, Schumann and Grieg Piano Concertos 1993, Shostakovich Concertos Nos 1 and 2 1993, Bartók Violin Concerto No 2 1993, Copland Quiet City and Emily Dickinson Songs 1994, Barber orchestral works 1994, Villa-Lobos (with New World Symphony Orch, for BMG) 1996, Stravinsky 1996 (with LSO), Copland and Stravinsky 1996, New World Jazz 1998 (with New World Symphony Orch), Mahler Symphony No 7 1999 (with LSO), Stravinsky ballets (Persephone, Firebird, Rite of Spring) 1999 (for San Francisco Symphony Orch, winner of 3 Grammy awards), Mahler Symphony No 6 (with San Fransisco Orch) 2001, Ives Symphony No 4 1999; television: Discovery concerts with LSO (BBC), On the Town 1993 (winner of Gramophone Award for Best Musical Recording), Concerto! (with Dudley Moore, Channel 4/BMG 1993); festivals/tours with LSO (Barbican): Shell LSO UK Tour 1986, The Gershwin Years 1987, The Flight of the Firebird 1989, Steve Reich Series 1989, Childhood 1991, Takemitsu Festival 1991, The Mahler Festival 1994 and 1995, Salzburg Summer Festival 1988 and 1991, USA and Japan 1989, 1991, 1992, Canary Islands 1989, Pacific Music Festival Sapporo Japan 1990, Israel 1991, Salzburg Whitsun Festival 1991 and 1995, USA and several Euro visits 1992, Austria, Germany and USA 1993, Italy and Spain 1994, Japan and Austria 1995 and 1997, Germany 1997, 2001 and 2002; with New World Symphony Orch: Lincoln Center USA 1996, US tour 1997, tour in Monaco 1995; with San Francisco Symphony Orch: 1996 US tour incl American Music Festival, Volkert-Cmmn (world premiere), Adams-Lollapalooza and Penderecki-Violin Concerto no 2 (US premieres), 1997 US tour incl Schubert/Henze-Erlkonig (US premiere), tour in Netherlands, Belgium, France, Germany and Austria 1996, tour in Japan and Hong Kong 1997, tour in Europe 2002 and 2003; opera (with LSO): Rimsky-Korsakov Mlada 1989, L'Enfant et Les Sortilèges 1991, Bernstein On the Town 1992, La Bohème 1994; Robin Holloway Concerto No 3 (world première) 1996; *Awards* Koussevitzky Prize Tanglewood 1968, Ditson Award 1994, Conductor of the Year USA 1994, 3 Grammy awards for Stravinsky ballets with BMG 1999, Grammy Award for Mahler Symphony No 6 2003, Grammy Award for Mahler Symphony No 3 2004; *Style*— Michael Tilson Thomas, Esq; ✉ c/o Van Walsum Management Ltd, 4 Addison Bridge Place, London W14 8XP (tel 020 7371 4343, fax 020 7371 4344, website www.vanwalsum.co.uk)

THOMAS, Neil Philip; s of Simon David Thomas (d 2002), of Stanmore, Middx, and Jessie, *née* Blagborough; *b* 29 April 1950; *Educ* Stowe (scholar), Univ of London (BSc), Middlesex Hosp Med Sch (MB BS); *m* 1, 25 Jan 1974, Mary Josephine Christian (d 1977), da of A V M Patrick Joseph O'Connor, CB, OBE; 1 da (Joanna b 19 June 1977); *m* 2, 29 April 1979, Julia Vera, da of J J Ashken (d 2003); 1 s (James b 17 March 1981), 1 da (Gemma b 15 Oct 1982); *Career* late sr registrar in orthopaedics: Royal Nat Orthopaedic Hosp, UCH and the Westminster Hosp; conslt orthopaedic surgn N Hampshire Hosp Hampshire Clinic and Wessex Knee Unit; instigator of arthroscopic knee courses RCS 1995; memb ACL Study Gp 2002–; pres: Br Assoc of Surgery of the Knee (BASK) 2002–04 (sec 1993–96, chm BASK and Nat Blood Service Allograft Working Gp), European Soc of Knee and Arthroscopic Surgery 2004–06 (vice-pres 2000–04); memb Int Knee Soc; memb Editorial Bd: The Knee 1998–, Knee Surgery Sports Traumatology Arthroscopy Jl (KSSTA) 2000– (chm Bd of Tstees 2006–); assoc ed Jl of Bone and Joint Surgery 2001– (memb Editorial Bd 1998–2002, chm Website Ctee 2000–), memb Cncl Jl of Bone and Joint Surgery 2003– (sec 2006–); visiting prof Perugia Univ 2005, travelling fell European Soc of Sports, Knee Surgery and Arthroscopy (ESSKA)/American Orthopaedic Soc for Sports Med (AOSSM) 2005; Fitton Prize for Orthopaedics 1974, Sir Herbert Seddon Prize and Medal 1986, President's Medal Br Assoc of Surgery of the Knee 1985–86; fell Br Orthopaedic Assoc (memb Cncl 1999–2001); FRCS 1978, FRSM; *Publications* Clinical Challenges in Orthopaedics: The Knee (co-ed, 2000); author various original articles, book chapters and videos on knee surgery; *Recreations* shooting, horticulture, wine; *Clubs* Athenaeum; *Style*— Neil Thomas, Esq; ✉ Little Bullington House, Bullington, Sutton Scotney, Winchester, Hampshire SO21 3QQ (tel 01962 760233); The Hampshire Clinic, Basing Road, Basingstoke, Hampshire RG24 7AL (tel 01256 819222, e-mail neilthomas@wessexknee.co.uk)

THOMAS, (Robert) Neville; QC (1975); s of Robert Derfel Thomas (d 1983), of Clwyd, and Enid Anne, *née* Edwards (d 1990); *b* 31 March 1936; *Educ* Ruthin Sch, Univ of Oxford (MA, BCL); *m* 28 March 1970, Jennifer Anne, da of Philip Henry Akerman Brownrigg, CMG, DSO, OBE, TD (d 1998); 1 s (Gerran b 19 March 1973), 1 da (Meriel b 21 Aug 1975); *Career* Lt Intelligence Corps 1955–57; called to the Bar Inner Temple 1962 (bencher 1985); recorder of the Crown Court 1975–82, head of chambers; *Recreations* fishing, walking, gardening; *Clubs* Garrick; *Style*— Neville Thomas, Esq, QC; ✉ Glansevern, Berriew, Welshpool, Powys SY21 8AH; 3 Verulam Buildings, Gray's Inn, London WC1R 5NT (tel 020 7831 8441, fax 020 7831 8479, e-mail clerks@verulam.co.uk)

THOMAS, (James) Nigel; s of Charles Walter Thomas (d 1956), of Bradford, W Yorks, and Kathleen, *née* Lister; *b* 11 May 1944; *Educ* Bradford GS, St Edmund Hall Oxford (MA), Univ of Oxford Med Sch (BM BCh); *m* 1 April 1968, Gerda, da of Gustav Oelgeklaus (d 1967), of Lengerich, Westphalia; 2 da ((Julia Elizabeth) Kirsten b 22 Sept 1970, (Heide Alicia) Katrin b 28 Aug 1972), 1 s ((Charles Walter) Christian b 31 May 1978); *Career* conslt ENT specialist Groote Schuur Hosp Cape Town SA 1974–76, first asst Radcliffe Infirmary Oxford 1976–79; conslt ENT surgn: King's Coll Hosp London 1979–, Guy's and St Thomas' Hosp; George Herbert Hunt fellowship Univ of Oxford 1978; memb Camberwell Health Authy 1987–92; pres Osler House Club 1967–68; FRCS 1972; *Books* Mawson's Diseases of the Ear (contrib, 1988); *Recreations* rugby, squash, music; *Style*— Nigel Thomas, Esq; ✉ Guy's and St Thomas' Hospital, London SE1 7EH; private sec tel 01689 864047

THOMAS, Prof Noel L'Estrange; s of Richard Gratton Thomas (d 1971), of Sale, Manchester, and Gladys L'Estrange (d 1978); *b* 5 December 1929; *Educ* Sale Co GS for Boys, Univ of Manchester (BA), Univ of Liverpool (MA), Univ of Salford (PhD); *m* 20 Feb 1954, Norma, da of Robert Brown (d 1950), of Manchester; 2 da (Katharine b 1962, Ruth b 1965); *Career* asst Das erste Bundesrealgymnasium Graz 1951–52; asst master: Holt HS for Boys Liverpool 1953–59, Canon Slade GS Bolton 1959–64; Univ of Salford Sch of Modern Languages: lectr in German 1964–73, sr lectr 1973–83, prof 1983–, chm 1984–89; visiting lectr Pädagogische Hochschule Erfurt 1993–94; dir Services for Export and Language; *Books* Modern Prose Passages for Translation into German (with G Weischedel, 1968), Modern German Prose Passages (with G Weischedel, 1972), The Narrative Works of Günter Grass - a critical interpretation (1983), Interpreting as a Language Teaching Technique (ed with Richard Towell, 1985), Grass: Die Blechtrommel (1985), Grass: Katz und Maus (1992); *Recreations* fell walking, choral singing; *Style*— Prof Noel Thomas; ✉ 4 Forest Way, Bromley Cross, Bolton, Lancashire BL7 9YE (tel 01204 591682); School of Modern Languages, University of Salford, Salford M5 4WT (tel 0161 745 7480, fax 0161 295 5110, telex 668680)

THOMAS, Owen John; AM; s of John Owen Thomas (d 1989), and Evelyn Jane, *née* Howells (d 1993), of Cardiff; *b* 3 October 1939; *Educ* Howardian HS, Glamorgan Coll of Educn (CertEd), Univ of Wales Cardiff (MA); *Family* 3 s (John Owen b 1963, Hywel Gwynfor b 1966, Iestyn ab Owen b 1972), 1 da (Eurwen Rhian b 1970); m, Siân Wyn; 2 s (Rhodri, Rhys (twins) b 1987); *Career* tax offr Inland Revenue 1956–61, chemical analyst 1961–68, teacher 1971–78, dep head teacher 1979–99; memb Nat Assembly for Wales (Plaid Cymru) S Wales Central 1999–, memb Shadow Cabinet (Culture, Sport and the Welsh Language), memb Educn and Life-Long Learning, House, Standards and Arts Sub Gp Ctees; memb: Undeb Cenedlaethal Athrawon Cymru 1968–99, Tabernacl Welsh Baptist Chapel Cardiff; govr Ysgol Bro Eirwg Llanrhymney Cardiff; *Publications* Yr Iaith Gymraeg yng Nghaerdydd c.1800–1914 in Iaith Carreg Fy Aelwyd (ed Gerraint Jenkins, 1997), The Welsh Language in Cardiff c.1800–1914 in Language and Community in the Nineteenth Century (ed Gerraint Jenkins, 1998); *Recreations* reading, socialising; *Clubs* Clwb Ifor Bach Cardiff; *Style*— Owen John Thomas, AM; ✉ 4 Llwyn y Grant Place, Penylan, Cardiff CF23 9EX (tel 029 2049 9868, fax 029 2045 4868); National Assembly for Wales, Cardiff Bay, Cardiff CF99 1NA (tel 029 2089 8295, fax 029 2089 8296, mobile 079 7437 4301, e-mail owen.thomas@wales.gsi.gov.uk)

THOMAS, Patricia Eileen; OBE (2003); da of Ieuan Gwynn Thomas (d 1989), and Lovice Eileen, *née* Phillips (d 1998); *b* 3 June 1949; *Educ* St Joseph's Convent Reading, St Hugh's Coll Oxford (MA); *Career* slr; ptnr: Denton Hall Wilde Sapte (formerly Denton Hall & Burgin) 1982–88, SJ Berwin & Co 1988–; chm Planning and Environmental Law Ctee Law Soc, former chm Environmental Law Ctee Int Bar Assoc; memb: Section on Business Law Int Bar Assoc, Planning and Environmental Law Ctee Law Soc; tstee: Theatres Tst, Town and Country Planning Assoc; memb City of London Slrs' Co; *Books* Surveyors Factbook (contrib), Planning Factbook (ed and contrib); *Recreations* architecture, fly fishing, travel; *Style*— Miss Patricia Thomas, OBE

THOMAS, Patrick Anthony; QC (1999); s of Basil Thomas (d 1965), and Marjorie, *née* Tait (d 1977); *b* 30 October 1948; *Educ* Rugby, Lincoln Coll Oxford (BA); *m* 1978, Sheila, da of Reg Jones; 2 da (Victoria b 1980, Rebecca b 1982); *Career* called to the Bar Grays Inn 1973 (bencher 2005), recorder 1992; *Recreations* reading, theatre, walking; *Style*— Patrick Thomas, Esq, QC; ✉ Citadel Chambers, 190 Corporation Street, Birmingham B4 6QD (tel 0121 233 8500, fax 0121 233 8501)

THOMAS, Rear Adm Paul Anthony Moseley; CB (1998); s of late Glyn Pritchard Thomas, and late Mary Thomas, *née* Moseley; *b* 1944; *Educ* Haileybury and ISC; *m* 1972, Rosalyn Patricia, da of John Edgar Lee; 2 da (Briony b 1974, Charlotte b 1982), 1 s (Daniel b 1976); *Career* joined RN 1963, Asst Marine Engr Offr HMS Renown 1971–74, Desk Offr Reactor Design Section 1974–77, Sr Engr Offr HMS Revenge 1977–81, Asst Marine Engr Offr Flag Officer Submarines 1980–81, Staff Offr Shore Support 1981–82, asst dir Nuclear Safety 1982–84, Naval Supt Vulcan Naval Reactor Test Estab Dounreay 1984–87, chm Naval Nuclear Tech Safety Panel 1987–90, dir Nuclear Propulsion 1990–94, Capt RNEC Manadon 1994–95, Chief Strategic Systems Exec MOD (Procurement Exec) 1995–98, ret Rear Adm; dir Strategic Devpt AEA Technology Nuclear Engineering 2000–01, dir Environment, Health, Safety and Quality BNFL 2001–; non-exec dir RSSB Ltd 2005–; Queen's Commendation for Brave Conduct 1980; FREng, MCGI, FIMechE, Hon FINucE; Legion of Merit (US) 1998; *Recreations* cycling, ballooning, walking, anything mechanical; *Style*— Rear Adm Paul Thomas, CB, FREng; ✉ Byway, Chapel Lane Box, Corsham, Wiltshire SN13 8NU (tel 01225 743134); BNFL, Warrington WA4 4GB (tel 01925 835022, e-mail paul.a.thomas@bnfl.com)

THOMAS, Prof Peter David Garner; s of David Thomas (d 1967), and Doris, *née* Davies (d 1965); *b* 1 May 1930; *Educ* St Bees Sch Cumberland, Univ Coll of N Wales (BA, MA), UCL (PhD); *m* 1963 (m dis 1992), Sheila; 2 s (Alan b 1963, Michael b 1965, d 1983), 1 da

(Sally b 1970); *Career* lectr Univ of Glasgow 1959–65 (asst lectr 1956–59); UCW: lectr 1965–68, sr lectr 1968–71, reader 1971–75, prof 1976–97, prof emeritus 1997–; chm: Dyfed LTA 1981–2002, Aberystwyth Lib Democrats 1988–98; awarded Soc of Cincinnati Book Prize 1992; FRHistS 1971; *Books* The House of Commons in the Eighteenth Century (1971), British Politics and the Stamp Act Crisis (1975), Lord North (1976), The American Revolution (1986), The Townshend Duties Crisis (1987), Tea Party to Independence (1991), Revolution in America - Britain and the Colonies 1763–76 (1992), John Wilkes: A Friend to Liberty (1996), Politics in Eighteenth Century Wales (1997), George III: King and Politicians 1760–1770 (2002); *Recreations* lawn tennis; *Style*— Prof Peter Thomas; ✉ 16 Pen-y-Craig, Aberystwyth, Ceredigion SY23 2JA (tel 01970 612053)

THOMAS, Prof Peter Kynaston; CBE; *b* 28 June 1926; *Educ* UCL (scholar, BSc, Trotter medal in clinical surgery), Univ of London (MB BS, MRCP, MD, DSc); *m* 1, 1977, Anita Elizabeth Harding (prof of clinical neurology, d 1995); m 2, 1999, Sawanthana Ponsford (conslt clinical neurophysiologist); *Career* Nat Serv RAMC 1952–54 (sec to Mil Personnel Research Ctee, graded specialist in physiology); jr hosp appts 1950–52 and 1954–61 (UCH, Middx and Nat Hosp Queen Square), asst prof of neurology McGill Univ Montreal, neurologist Montreal Gen Hosp and physician i/c EMG Dept Montreal Neurological Inst 1961–62; conslt neurologist (now hon conslt neurologist): Royal Free Hosp 1962–91, Nat Hosp for Neurology and Neurosurgery 1963–91, Royal Nat Orthopaedic Hosp 1965–74; pt/t sr lectr Univ Dept of Clinical Neurology Inst of Neurology Queen Square 1963–74, prof of neurology (now emeritus prof) Royal Free and Univ Coll Medical Sch and Inst of Neurology Queen Square 1974–91; ed Jl of Anatomy, formerly ed Brain; memb: Assoc of Br Neurologists (past pres), Anatomical Soc of GB and Ireland (memb Cncl), Assoc of Physicians, American Neurological Assoc (hon memb), Australian Neurological Soc (hon memb), Canadian Neurological Soc (hon memb), Euro Neurological Soc (past pres), Spanish Neurological Soc (hon memb), Polish Neurological Soc (hon memb), Austrian Soc of Neurology and Psychiatry (hon memb); Doctor (hc) Mil Med Acad Łódź Poland 1991; fell UCL; FRCP 1967, FRCPath 1990; *Style*— Prof P K Thomas, CBE

THOMAS, Philip Owain; s of Prof James Edward Thomas, and Olwen, *née* Yolland; *b* 6 June 1961; *Educ* Hymers Coll Hull, Plymouth Art Coll; *Partner* Colleen Teresa McDonnell; 1 s (Joseph Matthew McDonnell Thomas b 29 Oct 1991); *Career* photographic asst 1982–84, freelance photographer 1984, writer and features ed Practical Photography magazine 1984–87, features ed then asst ed SLR Photography 1987–88, freelance writer 1988–90, asst ed then ed Empire magazine 1990–93, managing ed Empire and Premier magazines 1994–96, publishing dir 1996–; Writer of the Year PTC 1988, shortlisted Writer of the Year PPA 1988 and 1992, eight awards won with EMAP plc, shortlisted Ed of the Year BSME 1992 and 1993; *Books* Photography in a Week (1992); *Recreations* cooking, talking, drinking wine, attempting to bring up a young family; *Style*— Philip Thomas, Esq; ✉ Empire Magazine, EMAP Metro, Mappin House, 4 Winsley Street, London W1N 7AR (tel 020 7436 1515)

THOMAS, Prof Phillip Charles; s of William Charles Thomas (d 1984), of Abersychan, Gwent, and Gwendolen, *née* Emery (d 1986); *b* 17 June 1942; *Educ* Abersychan GS Gwent, UCNW Bangor (BSc, PhD); *m* 1967, Pamela Mary, da of Leonard Hirst, of Huddersfield, W Yorks; 1 da (Rachel Louise b 9 Aug 1973), 1 s (Adam James b 18 Nov 1975); *Career* lectr Dept of Nutrition and Physiology Univ of Leeds 1966–71, head of Animal Nutrition and Prodn Dept Hannah Res Inst Ayr 1974–87 (res nutritionist 1971–74), prof of agric Univ of Glasgow 1987–99 (visiting prof 1999–2001), princ West of Scotland Coll 1987–90, princ and chief exec Scottish Agric Coll 1990–99 (emeritus prof 1999–), md Artilus Ltd 1999–; chm: Animal Medicines Regulatory Authy 1999–, UK Animal Feedingstuffs Advsy Ctee 1999–2001, Central Scotland Forest Tst 2001–; memb: Scottish Food Advsy Ctee 2000–05, Scottish Natural Heritage Bd 2005–; hon prof Univ of Edinburgh 1991; memb: Nutrition Soc 1969, Biochemical Soc 1970, Br Soc for Animal Prodn 1981; FIBiol 1983 (MIBiol 1981), FRSE 1993, FRAgs 1997 (MRAgs 1995); *Books* Silage for Milk Production (with J A F Rook, 1982), Nutritional Physiology of Farm Animals (with J A F Rook, 1983); *Recreations* watching rugby (formerly rep Caernarfonshire and N Wales); *Clubs* Farmers'; *Style*— Prof Phillip Thomas, FRSE; ✉ Artilus Ltd, 33 Cherry Tree Park, Balerno, Midlothian EH14 5AJ (tel 0131 451 5504, fax 0131 451 5501, e-mail phil.thomas@artilus.co.uk)

THOMAS, Dr Raymond Tudor; OBE (1994); s of Edgar William Thomas (d 1959), and Lilian Phylis, *née* Clift (d 1975); *b* 19 May 1946; *Educ* King's Sch Macclesfield, Jesus Coll Oxford (Meyricke exhibitioner, MA), Univ of the West Indies (Dip Int Relations), Univ of Sussex (DPhil); *m* 23 April 1973, Gloria, da of Bernard Anthony Forsyth; 2 s (Max Richard b 23 July 1975, James Matthew b 28 April 1978); *Career* lectr Inst of Int Relations Trinidad 1970–71; British Council: asst rep Morocco 1974–77, Islamabad 1977–80 and Kuala Lumpur 1980–82, regnl rep Sabah 1982–84, projects offr Science, Technol and Educn Div 1984–86, dir Educnl Contracts Dept 1988–90 (dep dir 1986–88), dir EC Relations 1990–95, regnl dir Middle E and N Africa 1995–2000, dir Turkey 2000–03, dir Brussels 2003–06, ret; dir and treas Lingua Assoc 1990–95, exec sec Euro Fndn for Educnl Capacity Transfer 1993–95, treas Office for Cooperation in Educn 1993–95; *Books* Britain and Vichy: The Dilemma of Anglo-French Relations 1940–42 (1979); *Recreations* family life, travel, reading, fly fishing; *Style*— Dr Ray Thomas, OBE

THOMAS, (Hywel) Rhodri Glyn; AM; s of Thomas Glyn Thomas (d 1973), and Eleanor, *née* Roberts; *b* 11 April 1953; *Educ* Ysgol Morgan Llwyd Wrexham; UCW Aberystwyth (BA), UCW Bangor (BD), UCW Lampeter (MTh); *m* 1975, Marian Gwenfair Thomas; 1 da (Lisa Mererid Glyn b 1982), 2 s (Deian Iorweth Glyn b 1985, Rolant Elidir Glyn b 1988); *Career* minister of religion St Clears area 1978–89 and 1992–; md Cwmni'r Gannwyll Cyf (TV prodn co) 1989–95, Welsh spokesman Forum of Private Business 1992–99, memb Nat Assembly for Wales (Plaid Cymru) Carmarthen East & Dinefwr 1999–; dir 'Sgript' Cyf 1992–, shadow spokesman for Agric and Rural Devpt 1999–2000, memb Euro Affairs Ctee 2000–, spokesman for Plaid Cymru on Sustainable Devpt 2001–, chair SW Wales Regnl Ctee 2001–02, shadow min Agric and Rural Affrs 2002–03, shadow min for Health and Social Services 2003–; Nat Assembly for Wales: chair Agric and Rural Devpt Ctee 2000, chair Culture Ctee 2000–; dep business mangr 2001–; London Marathon 1996 and 2000, memb NSPCC; *Recreations* walking, reading, watching sport; *Style*— Rhodri Glyn Thomas, AM; ✉ Talar Wen, 37 Wind Street, Ammanford, Carmarthenshire SA18 3DN (tel 01269 597677, fax 01269 591334, e-mail rhodri.thomas@wales.gov.uk)

THOMAS, Richard; CMG (1990); s of late Anthony Hugh Thomas, JP, and late Molly Thomas, MBE, *née* Bourne; *b* 18 February 1938; *Educ* Leighton Park Sch Reading, Merton Coll Oxford (MA); *m* 12 Feb 1966, Catherine Jane, da of Daniel Hayes (d 1969), of Richmond, NSW; 2 da (Phoebe Elizabeth b 1967, Corinna Jane b 1971), 1 s (Alexander James b 1969); *Career* Nat Serv 2 Lt RASC 1959–61; HM Dip Serv (ret); asst princ CRO 1961, private sec to Parly Under Sec 1962–63; second sec: Accra 1963–65, Lomé 1965–66; second later first sec: UK Delgn NATO Paris and Brussels 1966–69, FCO 1969–72, New Delhi 1972–75, FCO (asst head of dept) 1976–78; FCO visiting res fell RIIA 1978–79, cnsllr Prague 1979–83, ambass to Iceland 1983–86, overseas inspr 1986–89, ambass to Bulgaria 1989–94, high cmmr to the Eastern Caribbean 1994–98, ret; chm: Friends of Bulgaria 1999–2000, Leonard Cheshire Int 2000–05; tstee Rye Arts Festival 2003– (chm 2005–); *Books* India's Emergence as an Industrial Power: Middle Eastern Contracts (1982); *Recreations* foreign parts, gardening, sketching, skiing; *Clubs* Oxford and Cambridge; *Style*— Richard Thomas, Esq, CMG; ✉ Whole Farm Cottage, Stone-in-Oxney, Tenterden, Kent TN30 7JG (tel 01797 270353, e-mail rica@wholefarm.wanadoo.co.uk)

THOMAS, Richard James; s of late Daniel Lewis Thomas, JP, of Southend-on-Sea, Essex, and Norah Mary, *née* James; *b* 18 June 1949; *Educ* Bishop's Stortford Coll, Univ of Southampton (LLB), Coll of Law Guildford; *m* 18 May 1974, Julia Delicia Thomas, da of late Dr Edward Granville Woodchurch Clarke, MC, of Shurlock Row, Berks; 2 s (Andrew b 1977, Christopher b 1983), 1 da (Gemma b 1979); *Career* articled clerk and asst slr Freshfields 1971–74, slr CAB Legal Serv 1974–79, legal offr and head of resources gp Nat Consumer Cncl 1979–86, dir Consumer Affairs Office of Fair Trading 1986–92, dir Public Policy Clifford Chance 1992–2002, Info Cmmr 2002–; author of reports, articles and broadcasts on a range of legal, consumer and info issues; tstee W London Fair Housing Gp 1976–79; memb: Mgmnt Ctee Gtr London CAB Serv 1977–79, Lord Chllr's Advsy Ctee on Civil Justice Review 1985–88, Mgmnt Ctee Royal Courts of Justice CAB 1992–98, Cncl Banking Ombudsman Scheme 1992–2001, Advsy Ctee Oftel 1995–99, Advtg Advsy Ctee ITC 1996–2002, Direct Mktg Authy 1997–2002, Bd Fin Ombudsman Serv 1999–2002; memb Law Soc; FRSA; *Recreations* family, maintenance of home and garden, travel, sailing; *Style*— Richard Thomas, Esq; ✉ Information Commissioner, Wycliffe House, Water Lane, Wilmslow, Cheshire SK9 5AF (tel 01625 545700)

THOMAS, Richard Stephen; s of Richard Thomas (d 1979), and Leah Mary, *née* Bowen (d 1988); *b* 13 June 1943; *Educ* Pentre GS, UWIST; *m* 23 Sept 1967, Sandra, da of Norman Bishop (d 1990); 1 s (Christopher Richard b 11 Sept 1969), 1 da (Sarah Elizabeth b 7 Sept 1973); *Career* Welsh Hosp Bd 1961–63, admin Cardiff N Hosp Mgmnt Ctee 1963–65, admin Cardiff Royal Infirmary 1965–69, commissioning offr Univ Hosp of Wales 1969–71, commissioning mangr Prince Charles Hosp Merthyr Tydfil 1971–73, project mangr Welsh Health Tech Servs Orgn Cardiff 1974–75, personnel offr West Glamorgan Health Authy 1975–78, area personnel offr Dyfed Health Authy 1978–85, asst gen mangr E Dyfed Health Authy 1986–87, unit gen mangr Carmarthen/Dinefwr Health Unit 1987–92, chief exec Carmarthen & Dist NHS Tst 1992–97, chief exec Morriston Hosp NHS Tst 1997–99, dir Welsh NHS Confedn 1999–2004, ret; past hon sec Welsh Assoc of Health Authorities 1986–88, past chm SW Wales Branch IHSM; MHSM 1966 (DipHSM), MIPD 1971; *Recreations* golf, walking, music, sport spectating; *Clubs* Carmarthen Round Table (pres 1997–98, past chm), Carmarthen Ex Round Tablers (past chm), Towy Carmarthen Rotary (past pres); *Style*— Richard Stephen Thomas, Esq; ✉ Underhill, 7 Llygad-Yr-Haul, Llangunnor, Carmarthen SA31 2LB (tel 01267 231635)

THOMAS, His Honour Judge Roger; QC (2000); s of Donald Thomas (d 1980), of Halifax, Yorks, and Jessie, *née* Attwood (d 2002); *b* 18 August 1954, Halifax, Yorks; *Educ* Worksop Coll Notts, Univ of Hull, Inns of Court Sch of Law; *m* 1 Aug 1981, Vanessa, *née* Van Limburg Stirum; 1 s (George Charles b 3 Feb 1983), 2 da (Laura Jessie b 17 July 1985, Isobel Julia b 16 July 1988); *Career* called to the Bar Inner Temple 1976; practising barr and memb of chambers Broadway House Bradford 1976–2004, circuit judge (Northern Circuit) 2004– (Liverpool Crown Court 2004–05, Manchester Crown Court 2005–); memb Cncl of Circuit Judges; Parly candidate (Lib) Brighouse and Spenborough 1979; *Recreations* sport (playing and watching), cycling; *Style*— His Hon Judge Roger Thomas, QC; ✉ Manchester Crown Court, Minshull Street, Manchester M1 3FS (e-mail rogerthomasqc@zoom.co.uk)

THOMAS, Roger Geraint; OBE (1997); s of Geraint Phillips Thomas (d 1989), and Doreen Augusta, *née* Cooke (d 1975); *b* 22 July 1945; *Educ* Penarth Co Sch, Leighton Park Sch Reading, Univ of Birmingham (LLB); *m* 23 Oct 1971, Rhian Elisabeth Kenyon, da of Erith Kenyon Thomas (d 1975), of Cardigan; *Career* ptnr Eversheds (formerly Phillips & Buck slrs) 1969–2000 (conslt 2000–06); memb: Ct Nat Museum of Wales 1983–2002 (memb Cncl 1985–2002, vice-pres 2000–02), Welsh Cncl CBI 1987–97, 1998–2004 and 2005–, Cncl CBI 1991–97, Gen Advsy Cncl BBC 1992–95, Bd Wales Millenium Centre 1996–98; dep chm Business in Focus Ltd 1998–; vice-chm Techniquest Cardiff 1986–; dir Welsh National Opera Ltd 2000–; business partnership advsr Nat Assembly for Wales 1999–2002; memb Cncl Univ of Cardiff 2000–02, chm and pro-chllr Univ of Glamorgan 2002– (govr 1994–, dep chm 2001–02), dir Univs and Colls Employers Assoc 2004–; memb Law Soc 1969–; CCMI 1996 (chm Cardiff Branch 1988–90, Branch pres 2001–03); FRSA 2000; OStJ 2003; *Recreations* hill walking and music; *Clubs* Cardiff and County, Penarth Yacht; *Style*— Roger G Thomas, Esq, OBE; ✉ e-mail rogergthomas@dsl.pipex.com

THOMAS, Roger Lloyd; QC (1994); s of David Eyron Thomas, CBE, of Cardiff, and Mary Lloyd James; *b* 7 February 1947; *Educ* Cathays HS Cardiff, UCW Aberystwyth (LLB); *m* 10 Aug 1974, Susan Nicola, da of Stuart Ernest Orchard; 1 s (Adam Nicholas Lloyd b 22 Nov 1978), 1 da (Kirsty Nicola Claire b 15 Jan 1981); *Career* called to the Bar Gray's Inn 1969; recorder of the Crown Court 1987–; specialises in criminal law; memb Criminal Bar Assoc; *Recreations* tennis, music, reading; *Clubs* Cardiff Lawn Tennis; *Style*— Roger Thomas, Esq, QC; ✉ 9 Park Place, Cardiff CF1 3DP (tel 029 2038 2731, fax 029 2022 2542); 4 King's Bench Walk, Second Floor, Temple, London EC4Y 7DL (tel 020 7822 7000, fax 0870 429 2781)

THOMAS, Prof (John David) Ronald; s of John Thomas (d 1978), of Gwynfe, Carmarthenshire, and Betty, *née* Watkins (d 1986); *b* 2 January 1926; *Educ* Llandovery GS, Univ of Wales Cardiff (BSc, MSc, DSc, DipEd); *m* 23 Sept 1950, Gwyneth, da of Samuel Thomas (d 1972), of Fishguard, Pembrokeshire; 3 da (Gaenor Ann b 30 June 1953, Lynne Marie b 22 June 1955, Bethan Hâf b 3 July 1962); *Career* blood transfusion trg Clifton Coll and Southmead Hosp Bristol, served RAMC India 1944–47; tech asst Distillers Co Tonbridge 1948, analytical chemist Spillers Ltd Cardiff 1950–51; Glamorgan CC 1951–53; asst lectr Cardiff Coll of Technol 1953–56, lectr SE Essex Tech Coll 1956–58, sr lectr Newport and Monmouthshire Coll of Technol 1958–61, sr lectr and reader UWIST 1961–88, reader then prof Univ of Wales Cardiff 1988–93 (prof emeritus 1994–); visiting prof NEWI Wrexham 1995–96; hon prof Univ Politehnica Bucharest 1996–; hon course advsr Hong Kong Baptist Univ 1991–; RSC: memb Analytical Divnl Cncl 1973– (vice-pres 1974–76, sec 1987–90, pres 1990–92, ed AD News newsletter 1995–2007), memb Cncl 1977–80, 1990–98, 1999–2002 and 2004–05, chm Analytical Editorial Bd 1985–90, schs lectr in analytical chem 1986–87, memb Divnl Affrs Bd 1990–92, memb Professional Affrs and Membership Bd 1993–96, 1997–2000 and 2002–05, memb Educn and Qualifications Bd 1994–2000, advsr for privatisation of UK Lab Govt Chemist 1995–97; memb Cncl: UWIST 1976–79, Univ of Wales Coll of Med 1993–99, Baptist Union of Wales 1994–97; memb Ct: Federal Univ of Wales 1989–2001 and 2002– (memb Cncl 1997–2001, memb Investment Ctee 1998–2001, memb Staffing Ctee 2000–03), Univ of Wales Aberystwyth 1995–; deacon Tabernacl Eglwys y Bedyddwyr Cardiff 1961– (treas 1970–91); sec Baptist Union of Wales Ministerial Superannuation Appeal 1976–78; foreign expert Hunan, North West (Xian) and Shanghai Teachers Univs and Academia Sinica Nanjing 1983 and 1985; visiting prof Japan Soc for the Promotion of Science at Tokyo Inst Technol 1985; T Andrews lectr Queen's Univ Belfast 1973, Commonwealth Fndn lectr CSMC Res Inst Bhavnagar 1976, Moelwyn-Hughes lectr Univ of Cambridge 1988, L S Theobald lectr RSC 2001, Enric Casassas meml lectr Univ of Barcelona 2002; has lectured widely in Europe, Middle and Far East, Aust and USA; memb Govt High Level Mission on Analytical Instrumentation to Japan 1991; RSC medal and award 1981, J Heyrovsky Centenary medal of the Czechoslovak Acad of Sciences 1990; distinguished visiting fell La Trobe (Melbourne) Univ 1989; White Robe Gorsedd of Bards 2000; CChem 1978; FRSC 1960; *Publications* History of the Analytical Division Royal Society of Chemistry (1999); co-author: Calculations in Advanced Physical Chemistry (1962, Hungarian trans 1979), Noble Gases and Their Compounds (1964), Selective Ion-Sensitive Electrodes (1971, Chinese trans 1975, Japanese trans 1978), Dipole Moments in Inorganic

T

Chemistry (1971, Spanish trans 1974), Practical Electrophoresis (1976), Chromatographic Separations and Extractions with Foamed Plastics and Rubbers (1982); Selective Electrode Reviews Vol 1–14 (ed 1979–92); Membrane Electrodes in Drug Analysis (V Cosofret) (trans ed, 1982); over 300 articles in scientific journals on chemical and biosensors, reaction kinetics, separation chemistry and environmental matters; *Recreations* travel, reading (current affairs and history), Wales; *Style—* Prof J D R Thomas; ✉ 4 Orchard Court, Gresford, Wrexham LL12 8EB (tel 01978 856771, e-mail jdrthomas@aol.com)

THOMAS, Simon; *b* 3 February 1960; *Educ* Plymouth Coll of Art & Design (fndn course), Ravensbourne Coll of Art & Design (BA), RCA (MA); *Career* sculptor; asst to: John Maine for Arena on S Bank London 1983–84, Philip King on Docklands Sculpture Project Canary Wharf 1984; work experience: Kemijarvi Int Wood Carving Symposium Kemijarvi Finnish Lapland 1987, Peterborough festival of carving 1988, lecture tour Finnish Lapland centering on Art and Soc Symposium Sarestoniemi Art Museum (for Lappish Summer Univ) 1989, 'Tir Saile' Sculpture Symposium Co Mayo 1993, Rachana Int Sculpture Symposium Lebanon 1995, Third Annual Sculpture Symposium Barichara Santander Columbia 1996, Sixth Int Sculpture Symposium Maalot Galilee Israel 1997, artist in residence School of Maths Univ of Bristol 2002–03; Madame Tussauds Award 1988, pt/t research fell and artist in residence Physics Dept Univ of Bristol 1995–, WBRL funded research project 'Order in Space' Hewlett Packard BRIMS Research Labs Bristol 1997, Morris Singer Casting Prize 1999, winner Gateway to Cornwall/New Celtic Cross competition 2000–01; *Solo Exhibitions* Albermarle Gallery London 1989, Order in Space (Hewlett Packard Research Labs Bristol) 1997–98; *Group Exhibitions* incl: Sculptors of Fame and Promise (Chichester Cathedral) 1988, New Milestones (Dorchester Co Musem) 1988, Concept 88 - Reality 89 (Univ of Essex) 1989, Dartmoor (Plymouth City Art Gallery) 1989, Trees Woods and the Green Man (Craft Cncl Gallery and tour) 1989, Art at Your Fingertips (St Mary Tradescant Museum of Garden History Lambeth) 1990, London Art Fair 1991, 20th C Art Fair (RCA) 1991, British Art Fair (RCA) 1992, Out of Italy (Eagle Gallery London) 1992, Touch (Milton Keynes Exhbn Centre) 1994, Cabinet Pieces (Jason Rhodes Gallery London) 1995, Sculptors of Fame and Promise (Beaux Arts Bath) 1998, inaugural exhbn Spike Island Studio Complex Bristol 1998; *Commissions* New Milestones (Common Ground on Coastal Walk Durdle Moor Dorset) 1985, Three Large Wood Carvings (London Wildlife Tst) 1986, Burning Bush (Louisville Kentucky USA) 1990, Belhus Pole (Essex) 1991, Dryad (Rhinefield House) 1991, two large stone carvings (Louise Steinman Von Hess Museum Penn USA) 1993, three large wood carvings for Leicester Square model farm Norfolk 1994, Hypercone (2m steel sculpture for Nat Tst Gardens Antony House Torpoint Cornwall) 1997, Hypercone 15/15/17 (highly polished 1.2m stainless steel for Hewlett Packard Research Labs Bristol) 1998, Stretching a Point (26m installation for Physics Dept Univ of Bristol) 1998, Inst of Physics Publishing Co (limited edn print) 1999, Small Words (sculpture commemorating Paul Dirac at Expolre Bristol Harbourside) 2000, Tree of Life (tribute to all POWs St Wyllow Lanteglos by Fowey Cornwall) 2002, tribute sculpture to David Green (Gardens of Bristol Sch of Maths) 2003, Spores (collaboration with City Engrg for pirvate coll of Robert Davies) 2003, Star Dust (installation Westbury on Trym Methodist Church) 2004; *Style—* Simon Thomas, Esq

THOMAS, Simon; *b* 1964; *Educ* UCW Aberystwyth (BA), Coll of Librarianship Aberystwyth (Dip Librarianship); *m* Gwen; 1 da, 1 s; *Career* asst curator Nat Library of Wales Aberystwyth 1986–92, policy and res offr Taff-Ely BC 1992–94; Wales Cncl for Voluntary Action 1994–2000: Welsh language devpt offr, anti-poverty devpt offr, mangr Jigso; dir of policy and res Plaid Cymru Nat Exec 1995–98, memb Plaid Cymru Nat Assembly Policy Gp 1997–99, memb Plaid Cymru Policy Forum, policy co-ordinator for the Environment; press mangr (Plaid Cymru) Euro Parl campaign SE Wales 1994, campaign mangr (Plaid Cymru) Gen Election campaign Pontypridd 1997; cncllr Ceredigion CC 1999–2000; MP (Plaid Cymru) Ceredigion 2000–05 (by-election); vice-chair Parly Environment Gp; memb: Environmental Audit Ctee, All-Pty Gp on Volunteering, Parly Catering Ctee, Standards and Privileges Select Ctee; served on standing ctee: Children Leaving Care Bill, Office of Communications Bill; sec All-Pty Wales Campaign against the Poll Tax; vice-chm PRASEG (Parly Renewal Energy Gp); vice-chair: GLOBE (Global Legislators for the Environment), Ct of Govrs Nat Library of Wales, Ct Univ of Wales; fndr memb and sec Radio Ceredigion; *Publications* O'n gwirfodd/As good as our words; Plaid Cymru manifestos: Co Cncls (1992), Unitary Authorities (1995), General Election (1997); National Assembly manifesto (with Cynog Dafis, 1999); numerous articles in Welsh and English language jls; *Recreations* cycling, family life; *Style—* Simon Thomas, Esq; ✉ Constituency Office, Plaid Cymru, 32 Pier Street, Aberystwyth, Ceredigion SY23 2LN (tel 01970 624516, fax 01970 624473)

THOMAS, Stephen Richard; s of Maj Norman Arthur Thomas (d 1974), of E Horsley, and Norah Margaret, *née* Cooke (d 2001); *b* 9 June 1947; *Educ* Elizabeth Coll Guernsey; *m* 17 July 1971, Felicity Ruth, da of Harold Arthur George Quaintance (d 1992), of Rowlstone; 2 s (Daniel b 1973, Peter b 1979), 2 da (Hannah b 1975, Elizabeth b and d 1977); *Career* Deloitte Haskins & Sells: mangr and staff accountant 1965–81, sr accounting advsr seconded to HM Treasy 1981–83, fin servs sector ptnr and Japanese liaison ptnr 1983–90; ptnr and chm Building Socs and Mortgage Lenders Indust Gp Coopers and Lybrand 1990–94; tech advsr Nat Audit Office 1995–96, head Jt Monitoring Unit of the three Insts of CAs 1996–2003; memb Audit Ctee GMC; govr Univ of Winchester; memb St Mary's Church, Basingstoke; FCA 1969; *Recreations* golf, tennis; *Style—* Stephen Thomas, Esq; ✉ Hawthorn House, Tunnel Lane, North Warnborough, Hook, Hampshire RG29 1JT (tel 01256 703254)

THOMAS, Susan Elizabeth Kanter; da of Capt Marvin W Kanter (d 2001), and Miriam Graboys Kanter (d 2002); *b* 29 February 1952; *Educ* Nasson Coll ME (BA); *m* 11 Aug 1974, Stewart Thomas; *Career* personnel dir posts London Borough of Hackney 1976–82, head of personnel South Bank Poly 1982–86; London Borough of Lewisham: asst chief personnel offr 1986–93, dir Personnel and Admin 1993–99; interim dir Corp Servs GLA 1999–2000, DG Corp Servs and Devpt DfES 2000–06 (memb Bd DfES), md ST Partnership Ltd 2006–; pres Soc of Chief Personnel Offrs 1997–98; memb: Editorial Bd People Mgmnt, Bd Government Skills Civil Serv Sector Skills Cncl; FCIPD, FRSA; *Recreations* theatre, reading, golf; *Style—* Mrs Susan Thomas; ✉ ST Partnership Limited, Third Floor, 167 Fleet Street, London EC4A 2EA

THOMAS, Dr Trevor Anthony; s of Arthur William Thomas (d 1981), and Gladys Mary Gwendoline, *née* Hulin (d 1986); *b* 16 March 1939; *Educ* Bristol GS, Univ of St Andrews (MB ChB); *m* 10 July 1965, Yvonne Louise Mary, da of Percival Charles Branch (d 1946); 1 s (Jeremy Simon b 1969); *Career* sr conslt anaesthetist St Michaels Hospital 1975–2002, chm Anaesthesia Div United Bristol Hosp 1977–80 (conslt anaesthetist 1972), South Western regnl assessor in anaesthesia for Confidential Enquiries into Maternal Deaths 1978–2000, central assessor in anaesthesia to the Confidential Enquiry into Maternal Deaths 2000–02, hon clinical lectr Univ of Bristol 1980–2002, chm Hosp Med Ctee Bristol and Weston Health Dist 1988–90, special tstee United Bristol Hosps 1992–99, tstee and cncl of management memb St Peter's Hospice 1996–, med vice-chm Regnl Distinction Awards Ctee 1991–93, dep chm Part 1 Examination for Fellowship of the Royal Coll of Anaesthetists 1991–96 (examiner 1985–96), vice-chm SW Regnl Hosp Med Advsy Ctee 1991–93 (memb 1989–93), emeritus conslt United Bristol Healthcare NHS Tst (chm Med Audit Ctee 1991–94) 2002–; ed Anaesthesia Points West 1976–80; pres: Obstetric Anaesthetists Assoc 1996–99, Soc of Anaesthetists of the South Western Region 1996–97 (hon sec 1985–88); hon sec: Obstetric Anaesthetists Assoc 1981–84 (memb Ctee 1979–81 and 1994–96), Section of Anaesthetics RSM 1993–95 (memb Cncl 1989–96); chm Obstetric Anaesthesia and Analgesia Sub-Ctee World Fedn of Socs of Anaesthesiology 1992–96 (memb Ctee 1988–92); FFARCS 1969, FRCA 1989; *Books* Principles and Practice of Obstetric Anaesthesia and Analgesia (with A Holdcroft, 1999); chapters in: Prescribing in Pregnancy (ed Gordon M Stirrat and Linda Beeley in Clinics in Obstetrics and Gynaecology, 1986), Problems in Obstetric Anaesthesia (ed B M Morgan, 1987), Cardiopulmonary Resuscitation (ed P J F Baskett, 1989), Controversies in Obstetric Anaesthesia 1 & 2 (ed B M Morgan, 1990 and 1992), Handbook of Obstetric Analgesia and Anaesthesia (ed Graham H McMorland and Gertie F Marx, 1992), International Practice of Anaesthesia (ed C Prys-Roberts and B R Brown, 1996), Pain Relief and Anaesthesia in Obstetrics (ed Andre van Zundert and Gerard W Ostheimer, 1996), Clinical Problems in Obstetric Anaesthesia (ed Ian F Russell and Gordon Lyons, 1997), Textbook of Obstetric Anaesthesia (ed David Birnbach, Stephen Gatt and Sanjay Datta, 2000), Regional Analgesia in Obstetrics, A Millennium Update (ed Felicity Reynolds, 2000); *Recreations* Tai Chi, genealogy, scuba diving, swimming, music, theatre; *Style—* Dr Trevor A Thomas; ✉ 14 Cleeve Lawns, Downend, Bristol BS16 6HJ (tel 0117 956 7620); Sir Humphry Davy Department of Anaesthesia, Bristol Royal Infirmary, Maudlin Steet, Bristol BS2 8HW (tel 0117 928 2163)

THOMAS, Vivian Elliott Sgrifan; CBE (1998, OBE 1992); s of William Edward Thomas, and Cicely, *née* Elliott; *b* 13 March 1932; *Educ* Swindon HS, Univ of Southampton; *m* 1962, Valerie Slade; *Career* engrg offr Union Castle Line 1953–58, ceo BP Oil UK Ltd 1989–92 (joined British Petroleum 1959); non-exec dir: Jaguar 1992–, Gowrings 1992–; chm BSI 1992–, memb Nat Cncl CBI; *Recreations* golf, music, theatre; *Clubs* RAC; *Style—* Vivian Thomas, Esq, CBE; ✉ British Standards Institution, 389 Chiswick High Road, London W4 4AL (tel 020 8996 7340)

THOMAS, William Ernest Ghinn; s of Kenneth Dawson Thomas (d 1998), of Sheffield, and Monica Isobel, *née* Markham; *b* 13 February 1948; *Educ* Dulwich Coll, KCL (BSc), St George's Hosp Med Sch London (MB BS); *m* 30 June 1973, Grace Violet, da of Alfred Henry Samways (d 1979), of London; 3 da (Nicola b 1974, Jacqueline b 1979, Hannah b 1983), 2 s (Christopher b 1977, Benjamin b 1985); *Career* Hunterian prof RCS 1987 (Arris and Gale lectr 1982, Bernard Sunley fell 1977), tutor in surgical skills 1995–2003, Moynihan fell Assoc of Surgns 1982, conslt surgn and clinical dir Royal Hallamshire Hosp Sheffield 1986–; exec ed Current Practice in Surgery 1988–97; memb Editorial Bd: Hospital Update, Surgery; memb Ct of Examiners RCS 1992–2000, memb Intercollegiate Court of Examiners, pres Surgical Section RSM 2000; RCS: memb Cncl 2003–, dir of int activities 2003–, chm of educn 2003–; memb: BMA 1974, BSG 1980, SRS 1981, Assoc of Surgns 1986; int tstee Gideons Int 2000– (nat pres 1987–90, vice-pres 1994–96, nat pres 1996–99); Royal Humane Soc Award for Bravery 1974, Dr of the Year Award 1985, European Soc Prize for Surgical Res 1981, Med Mangr of the Year Award 1995; FRCS 1976, MS 1980; *Books* Preparation and Revision for the FRCS (1986), Self-assessment Exercises in Surgery (1986), Nuclear Medicine: Applications to Surgery (1988), Colour Guide to Surgical Pathology (1992), Preparation and Revision for the MRCS and AFRCS (1999 and 2004); *Recreations* skiing, photography, oil painting; *Style—* William Thomas, Esq; ✉ Ash Lodge, 65 Whirlow Park Road, Whirlow, Sheffield S11 9NN (tel 0114 262 0852, fax 0114 236 3695, e-mail wegthomas@btinternet.com, website www.wegthomas.com); Royal Hallamshire Hospital, Glossop Road, Sheffield S10 2JF (tel 0114 271 3142, fax 0114 271 3512, e-mail w.thomas@sth.nhs.uk)

THOMAS, His Hon William Fremlyn Cotter; *b* 18 March 1935; *Career* called to the Bar 1961; circuit judge (SE Circuit) 1990–2005; *Style—* His Hon William Thomas; ✉ Kingston Crown Court, 6–8 Penrhyn Road, Kingston upon Thames, Surrey KT1 2BB

THOMAS, William Gennydd (Bill); s of J Thomas (d 1981), and H Thomas, *née* Riley (d 2001); *b* 4 November 1959, Colne, Lancs; *Educ* Univ of Leeds (BSc), Brunel Univ (MSc), Cranfield Sch of Mgmnt (MBA); *m* 12 Nov 1981, Julie, *née* Stevanovic; 2 da (Katherine b 12 Oct 1987, Elizabeth b 4 July 1993), 1 s (George b 12 July 1989); *Career* R&D systems engr Marconi Co 1981–84, SD-Scicon: systems conslt 1984–88, business mangr 1988–92; EDS: gen mangr Aerospace Gp 1992–94, md UK Mfrg Div 1994–96, global account dir Rolls-Royce account 1996–99, vice-pres and client delivery exec EMEA 1999–2000, vice-pres and gen mangr UK 2000–03, exec vice-pres EMEA 2003–; memb: IT & Telecoms Industry Bd E-Skills UK 2000, Pres's Ctee CBI 2001, Advsy Cncl Business for New Europe 2007; Hon DSc City Univ; *Publications* Competitiveness (2003), Renewing the NHS (2006); *Recreations* rugby, cricket, English sports cars; *Clubs* Sandhurst Cricket; *Style—* Bill Thomas, Esq; ✉ EDS, 2nd Floor, Landsdowne House, Berkeley Square, London W1J 6ER (tel 020 7569 5895, fax 020 7569 5864, e-mail william.thomas@eds.com)

THOMAS, Prof (Meurig) Wynn; OBE (2007); s of William John Thomas (d 1962), and Tydfil, *née* Rees (d 1983); *b* 12 September 1944; *Educ* Gowerton Boys' GS (major state scholar, prize for best arts A-Levels), UC Swansea (Coll scholar, E A Williams jr and sr prizes, major state studentship, BA); *m* 20 Sept 1975, Karen Elizabeth, da of W A Manahan; 1 da (Elin Manahan b 26 Aug 1977); *Career* UC Swansea: asst lectr 1966–69, lectr in English 1969–88, sr lectr 1988–94, prof of English 1994–, dir Centre for Research into the English Literature and Language of Wales 1998–; visiting prof: Harvard Univ 1991–92 (Harvard Summer Sch 1989), Univ of Tübingen 1994–95; Obermann fell Center for Advanced Studies Univ of Iowa 1992; presenter arts progs (BBC Radio Cymru) 1985–88; chm Welsh Books Cncl 2005– (also chm Literature Ctee); vice-chm: Yr Academi Gymreig (Welsh Acad, Welsh language section) 1996–97 (memb 1986–, acting chm 1997–98), Friends of Welsh Books Cncl 1996–2005; sec Univ of Wales Assoc for the Study of Welsh Writing in English 1983–96; memb: Welsh Arts Cncl and chm Literature Ctee 1985–91, Br Library Advsy Ctee for the Arts Humanities and Social Sciences 2000–02, Wales Arts Review 2006; tst memb UK Year of Literature; chm Bd Univ of Wales Press 1999–2003; memb Bd Seren Books 1992–2003, memb Editorial Bd Walt Whitman Quarterly Review, assoc ed Welsh Writing in English: a Yearbook of Critical Essays; nominator The Arts Fndn 1993, adjudicator David Cohen Prize 1996–97; literary executor to late R S Thomas 2000–; hon memb Nat Eisteddfod Gorsedd of Bards 2000; FBA 1996, FEA 2005; *Books* Morgan Llwyd (1984), The Lunar Light of Whitman's Poetry (1987), Llyfr y Tri Aderyn (ed, 1988), A Toy Epic (ed, 1989), Emyr Humphreys (1989), R S Thomas: Y Cawr Awenydd (ed, 1990), Morgan Llwyd: ei gyfeillion a'i gyfnod (1991, Welsh Arts Cncl prize, Vernam Hull Meml prize, Ellis Griffith Meml prize), Wrenching Times: Whitman's Civil War Poetry (ed, 1991), Internal Difference: literature in twentieth-century Wales (1992), The Page's Drift: R S Thomas at Eighty (ed, 1993), Walt Whitman, Dail Glaswellt (trans, 1995), DiFfinio Dwy Lenyddiaeth Cymru (ed, 1995), Walt Whitman and the World (ed British Isles Section, 1996), Annotated Bibliography of English Studies (ed Welsh Studies Section, 1996), John Ormond (1997), Corresponding Cultures: studies in relations between the two literatures of Wales (1999), Gweld Sêr: Cymru a Chanrif America (ed, 2001), Emyr Humphreys, Conversations and Reflections (ed, 2002), Kitchener Davies (2002), Detholion o waith Kitchener Davies (co-ed, 2002), R S Thomas, Residues (ed, 2002), Welsh Writing in English (ed, 2003), Transatlantic Connections: Whitman US-UK (2005); also author of numerous book chapters and articles in learned jls; *Recreations* reading, music, sport (couch-potato style); *Style—* Prof M Wynn Thomas, OBE, FBA; ✉ Department of English, University of Wales Swansea, Singleton Park, Swansea SA2 8PP (tel 01792 295306, fax 01792 295761, e-mail m.w.thomas@swansea.ac.uk)

THOMAS OF GRESFORD, Baron (Life Peer UK 1996), of Gresford in the County Borough of Wrexham; (Donald) Martin Thomas; OBE (1982), QC (1979); s of Hywel Thomas (d 1961), of Wrexham, and Olwen, *née* Jones; *b* 13 March 1937; *Educ* Grove Park GS Wrexham, Peterhouse Cambridge (MA, LLB); *m* 1, 22 July 1961, Nan (d 2000), da of John Kerr, of Fauldhouse, W Lothian; 1 da (Hon Claire b 15 July 1964), 3 s (Hon Andrew b 18 Oct 1965, Hon Gavin b 9 April 1969, Hon Jamie b 18 March 1975); m 2, 21 Oct 2005, Baroness Walmsley (Life Peer), *qv*; *Career* admitted slr 1961, lectr 1966–68; called to the Bar Gray's Inn 1967 (bencher 1989); jr counsel Wales & Chester Circuit 1968–79, recorder of the Crown Court 1976–2002, dep judge of the High Court 1985–; memb Criminal Injuries Compensation Bd 1985–93; chm Marcher Sound Ltd (incl local radio for N Wales and Chester) 1992–2000 (vice-chm 1985–92); pres: Welsh Lib Pty 1978 (chm 1969–71), Welsh Lib Dems 1993–97; Parly candidate (Lib): W Flint 1964, 1968 and 1970, Wrexham 1974, 1979, 1983 and 1987; pres: London Welsh Choral, Sirenien Singers, Friends of Gresford Church; chm Southbank Sinfonia Devpt Cncl; *Recreations* rugby football, rowing, fishing, music making; *Clubs* Reform, Western; *Style*— The Rt Hon Lord Thomas of Gresford, OBE, QC; ✉ Glasfryn, Gresford, Clwyd LL12 8RG (tel 01978 852205, fax 01978 855078); Goldsmith Chambers, Goldsmith Building, Temple, London EC4Y 7BL (tel 020 7353 6802, fax 020 7583 5255, e-mail thomasm@parliament.uk)

THOMAS OF GWYDIR, Baron (Life Peer UK 1987), of Llanrwst in the County of Gwynedd; Peter John Mitchell Thomas; PC (1964), QC (1965); o s of late David Thomas, of Llanrwst, Denbighshire, and Anne Gwendoline, *née* Mitchell; *b* 31 July 1920; *Educ* Epworth Coll Rhyl, Jesus Coll Oxford (MA); *m* 1947, Frances Elizabeth Tessa (d 1985), o da of late Basil Dean, CBE, the theatrical prodr, by his 2 w, Lady Mercy Greville, 2 da of 5 Earl of Warwick; 2 s (Hon David Nigel Mitchell b 1950 d 2002, Hon Huw Basil Maynard Mitchell b 1953 d 2001), 2 da (Hon Frances Jane Mitchell (Hon Mrs Clargo) b 1954, Hon Catherine Clare Mitchell (Hon Mrs Howe) b 1958); *Career* served WWII Bomber Cmd RAF (POW); called to the Bar Middle Temple 1947 (bencher 1971, master emeritus 1991); memb Wales & Chester Circuit, dep chm Cheshire Quarter Sessions 1966–70, Denbighshire Quarter Sessions 1968–70, recorder Crown Court 1974–88, arbitrator ICC Court of Arbitration Paris 1974–88; MP (Cons): Conway 1951–66, Hendon S 1970–87; PPS to Solicitor Gen 1954–59, parly sec Miny of Labour 1959–61, parly under sec of state for Foreign Affrs 1961–63, min of state for Foreign Affrs 1963–64, oppn front bench spokesman on Foreign Affrs and Law 1964–66; chm Cons Pty 1970–72, sec of state for Wales 1970–74; pres Nat Union of Cons and Unionist Assocs 1974–76; fell Jesus Coll Oxford 2001–; *Clubs* Carlton; *Style*— The Rt Hon Lord Thomas of Gwydir, PC, QC; ✉ Millicent Cottage, Elstead, Surrey GU8 6HD (tel 01252 702052); 37 Chester Way, London SE11 4UR (tel 020 7735 6047)

THOMAS OF MACCLESFIELD, Baron (Life Peer UK 1997), of Prestbury in the County of Cheshire; Terence James (Terry) Thomas; CBE (1997); s of William Emrys (d 1993), of Carmarthen, Dyfed, and Mildred Evelyn Thomas (d 2000), of Ammanford, Dyfed; *b* 19 October 1937; *Educ* Queen Elizabeth 1 GS Carmarthen, Univ of Bath Sch of Mgmnt (Postgrad Dip), INSEAD (Advanced Mgmnt Prog); *m* 27 July 1963, Lynda, da of William John Stevens (d 1994); 3 s (Hon Justin b 12 July 1965, Hon Neil b 2 May 1967, Hon Brendan b 9 Jan 1969); *Career* banker; various positions rising to mangr National Provincial Bank then National Westminster Bank, seconded as research mangr then national sales mangr Joint Credit Card Co (Access) 1971–73; Co-operative Bank plc: joined as mktg mangr 1973, subsequently asst gen mangr, jt gen mangr then dir of gp devpt, md 1988–97; former pres Int Co-operative Banking Assoc, former memb Cncl Chartered Inst of Bankers (chief examiner in Mktg of Financial Servs 1983–85); visiting prof Univ of Stirling 1988–91; chm: Venture Technic (Cheshire) Ltd 1984–2000, North West Media Tst Ltd 1998–99, NW Devpt Agency 1998–2002; former chm: NW Partnership, NW Business Leadership Team Ltd, Vector Investments, East Manchester Partnership; former non-exec dir: Stanley Leisure plc, English Partnerships (Central) 1998–99, Cmmn for the New Towns 1998–99; former memb Bd of Tstees: Campaign to Promote the Univ of Salford (CAMPUS), UNICEF; author of various articles in banking and financial jls, has addressed various financial seminars and conventions on banking issues; hon fell Univ of Central Lancashire 2000; Hon DLitt Univ of Salford 1996, Hon Dr Manchester Metropolitan Univ 1998, Hon DUniv Manchester 1999, Hon DUniv UMIST 1999; Mancunian of the Year 1998; FCIB, CIMgt, FRSA 1992; *Style*— The Rt Hon Lord Thomas of Macclesfield, CBE; ✉ House of Lords, London SW1A 0PW

THOMAS OF SWYNNERTON, Baron (Life Peer UK 1981), of Notting Hill in Greater London; Hugh Swynnerton Thomas; s of Hugh Whitelegge Thomas, CMG (d 1960; s of Rev T W Thomas and sometime of the Colonial Serv, sec for Native Affairs in the Gold Gold Coast; chief commissioner Ashanti 1932 and UK rep to League of Nations *re* Togoland Mandate Report 1931 and 1934), and Margery Angelo Augusta, *née* Swynnerton; *b* 21 October 1931; *Educ* Sherborne, Queens' Coll Cambridge (MA); *m* 1962, Hon Vanessa Mary Jebb, da of 1 Baron Gladwyn (d 1996); 2 s (Hon Charles Inigo Gladwyn b 1962, Hon (Henry) Isambard Tobias b 1964), 1 da (Hon Isabella Pandora b 1966); *Career* sits as cross-bencher in House of Lords; historian; with Foreign Office 1954–57, sec to UK Delgn to UN Disarmament Sub-Ctee 1955–56, lectr RMA Sandhurst 1957, prof of history Univ of Reading 1966–76, visiting prof Sch of Hispanic American Studies Seville 2000; chm Centre for Policy Studies 1979–91; King Juan Carlos I prof of Spanish civilisation NYU 1995–96, univ prof Boston Univ 1996; co pres Hispano-British Tertulias 1987–93; Somerset Maugham Prize 1962, Arts Cncl Prize for History (first Nat Book Awards) 1980; Knight Grand Cross Order of Isabel la Católica (Spain) 2001 (Cdr 1987), Order of the Aztec Eagle (Mexico) 1995; *Publications* as Hugh Thomas: The World's Game (1957), The Spanish Civil War (1961, revised edn 1977, revised and illustrated edn Spain 1979), The Story of Sandhurst (1961), The Suez Affair (1967), Cuba, or the Pursuit of Freedom (1971), The Selected Writings of José Antonio Primo de Rivera (ed, 1972), Goya and the Third of May 1808 (1972), Europe, the Radical Challenge (1973), John Strachey (1973), The Cuban Revolution (1977), An Unfinished History of the World (1979, revised edn 1989, published in the US as A History of the World 1979), The Case for the Round Reading Room (1983), Havannah (novel, 1984), Armed Truce (1986), A Traveller's Companion to Madrid (1988), Klara (novel, 1988), The Conquest of Mexico (1993, US title Conquest 1994), The Slave Trade (1997), Who's Who of the Conquistadors (2000), Rivers of Gold (2003), Barreiros: Motor of Spain (2007), Letter from Asturias (2007), Baumanchais in Seville (2007); *Clubs* Athenaeum, Beefsteak; *Style*— The Rt Hon Lord Thomas of Swynnerton; ✉ House of Lords, London SW1A 0PW

THOMAS OF WALLISWOOD, Baroness (Life Peer UK 1994), of Dorking in the County of Surrey; Susan Petronella Thomas; OBE (1989), DL (Surrey 1996); da of John Arrow, and Ebba Fordham, *née* Roll; *b* 20 December 1935; *Educ* Univ of Oxford; *m* 1958 (sep), David Churchill Thomas, CMG, o s of late David Bernard Thomas; 1 s, 2 da; *Career* Parly candidate (Lib Dem) Mole Valley 1983 and 1987, Euro Parly candidate Surrey constituency 1994, Lib Dem frontbench spokesperson on tport 1994–2001, Lib Dem frontbench spokesperson on women 2001–; former pres Women Lib Dems; Surrey CC: memb 1985–97, served on various ctees, vice-chair Cncl and chair Highways and Tport Ctee 1993–96, chair of CC 1996–97; Surrey CC rep ACC, Airports Policy Consortium and SERPLAN until 1997; former memb E Surrey Community Health Cncl, non-exec dir E Surrey Hosp and Community Healthcare Tst 1993–97, memb Surrey Probation Ctee 1997–2001, memb Surrey Probation Bd 2001–; *Recreations* gardening, reading, ballet, theatre, travel; *Style*— The Rt Hon Baroness Thomas of Walliswood, OBE, DL; ✉ House of Lords, London SW1A 0PW (e-mail thomass@parliament.uk)

THOMAS OF WINCHESTER, Baroness (Life Peer 2006), of Winchester in the County of Hampshire; Celia Marjorie Thomas; MBE (1985); da of David Leslie Roberts Thomas (d 1973), of Winchester, and Marjorie, *née* Best (d 1983); *b* 14 October 1945, Winchester, Hants; *Educ* St Swithun's Sch Winchester; *Career* administrator Winchester Diocesan Bd of Finance 1964–66, fundraiser Winchester Cathedral 1966–67, administrator Pilgrims' Sch Winchester 1967–72, administrator Christ Church Cathedral Sch Oxford 1972–74, Office of Rt Hon Jeremy Thorpe MP 1975–76, head Lib Dem Whips office House of Lords 1977–2006; chair Keynes Forum (formerly Lib Summer Sch) 2001–; *Recreations* music, gardening, theatre; *Clubs* 2 Brydges Place; *Style*— The Baroness Thomas of Winchester, MBE; ✉ House of Lords, London SW1A 0PW (tel 020 7219 3586)

THOMASON, Prof Harry; s of (Joseph) Alfred Thomason (d 1982), of Croston, and Edna, *née* Penwarden (d 1994); *b* 29 February 1940; *Educ* Hutton GS, Chester Coll, Loughborough Univ of Technol (DLC, PhD), Univ of Salford (MSc); *m* 3 Aug 1966, Marie, da of Herbert Flintoff (d 1975), of Newburgh; 1 s (Timothy Simon b 26 Jan 1968); *Career* lectr Royal Coll of Advanced Technol Salford 1963–66, sr lectr Univ of Salford 1974–77 (lectr 1966–74); Loughborough Univ of Technol: founding prof and head Dept of Physical Educn and Sports Sci 1977–87, pro-vice-chllr 1985–87, sr pro-vice-chllr 1987–91, pro-vice-chllr External Rels 1991–2003; dir Nat Inst of Sport and Med 1991–96; Br Assoc of Sport and Med: memb Cncl and treas, memb Exec Ctee 1964–80 and 1987–2003, vice-pres 2003–; Miny of Sports rep E Midlands Region 1983–89; memb Med Sub-Ctee BOA, assessor Assoc of Cwlth Univs Scholarship Scheme 1984–93; dir: Loughborough Consultants Ltd 1989–2003, T&S Philosophies 2006–, Monarch Technols 2006–; advsr to: Miny of Educn Singapore 1983–87 and 1990–, BAe plc, Telekom Malaysia, Min of Educn Malaysia; memb Bd: DfEE/DTI Educn & Trg Export Ctee, DfEE/DTI/Br Cncl British Training International, BAe Virtual Univ; dir Ford Design Inst Detroit 1995–; Churchill fell 1976 (chm); govr Kirkham GS 1998–2005, chm Leicester GS 2001; memb of Ct Univ of Lancaster 2007–; Hon DSc Loughborough Univ; FRSM 1970, FRSA 1990; *Books* Sports Medicine (contrib, 1976), Basic Book of Sports Medicine (contrib, 1978), Science and Sporting Performance (contrib, 1982); extensive number of papers on educn and trg requirements for individual govts and cos 1984–2007; *Recreations* skiing, hill walking, learning to sail, golf; *Clubs* Athenaeum, Royal Windemere Yacht, Royal Dornoch Golf; *Style*— Prof Harry Thomason; ✉ Heaton Grange, Longtail Hill, Bowness-on-Windermere, Cumbria LA23 3JD (tel 01539 443557, e-mail harry.thomason@btopenworld.com)

THOMASON, (Kenneth) Roy; OBE (1986); s of Thomas Roger Thomason (d 1989), and Constance Dora, *née* Wilcox (d 1998); *b* 14 December 1944; *Educ* Cheney Sch Oxford, Univ of London (LLB); *m* 6 Sept 1969, Christine Ann, da of William Richard Parsons (d 1985); 2 s (Richard b 1972, Edward b 1974); 2 da (Julia b 1978, Emily b 1981); *Career* admitted slr 1969, sr ptnr Horden & George Bournemouth 1979–91; MP (Cons) Bromsgrove 1992–97, Cons ldr Environment Select Ctee 1994–97; vice-chm Cons Environment Ctee 1992–97, jt chm All Pty Export Gp 1995–97; Cons Pty: constituency chm Bournemouth West 1981–82, chm Wessex Area Local Govt Advsy Ctee 1981–83, memb Nat Local Govt Advsy Ctee 1981–97 (vice-chm 1989–91), memb Nat Union Exec 1989–91; ldr Bournemouth BC 1974–82 (memb 1970–92, hon alderman 1993); Assoc of Dist Cncls: memb Cncl 1979–91, Cons gp ldr 1981–87, chm Housing and Environmental Health Ctee 1983–87, chm 1987–91; chm: Charminster Estates Ltd and other property cos 1998–, London Strategic Housing 2002–06 (dir 2001–06); fell Industry and Parly Tst; FRSA; *Recreations* family, reading, architectural history, local church and village activities; *Style*— Roy Thomason, Esq, OBE; ✉ Fockbury House, Fockbury Dodford, Bromsgrove, Worcestershire B61 9AP (tel 01527 880578)

THOMPSON, Adrian Richard; s of Harold Albert Thompson, of London, and Daphne Yvonne, *née* Shrimpton (d 1990); *b* 28 July 1954; *Educ* Wandsworth Sch, Guildhall Sch of Music & Drama; *m* 30 July 1977, Judith Mary, da of John William Panes (decd); 2 s (George Harold Gwilym b 16 Oct 1982, Samuel John b 17 June 1985); *Career* tenor; opera performances incl: title role Peter Grimes, Skuratov in The House Of The Dead (Oper Frankfurt), Canio I Pagliacci (Oper Frankfurt), Monostatos in Die Zauberflöte (ROH), Arv in Nielson's Maskarade (ROH), Valzacchi in Der Rosenkavalier (ROH), Florestan in Fidelio (WNO), Albert Gregor in The Makropoulos Case (Opera Zuid), Erik in Der Fliegende Holländer (Opera Zuid), Laca in Jenufa (Opera Zuid), the title role Janacek's The Diary of One who Disappeared (Brussels and Aix-en-Provence Festivals), Zivny in Janacek's Osud (Garsington Opera), Midas in Die Liebe Der Danae (Garsington Opera), Grigory in Boris Godunov (Brighton Festival), Bacchus in Ariadne Auf Naxos (Barbican); other performances incl: Lutoslawski's Paroles Tisées (London Sinfonietta), Janacek's Glagolitic Mass (Hallé Orch), Elgar's Dream of Gerontius (Czech Philharmonic Orch); repertoire incl: Beethoven 9th Symphony, Verdi Requiem and Mahler Das Lied von der Erde, Bach St John and St Matthew Passions; performed with: Glyndebourne Festival Opera, ENO, Scottish Opera, Opera du Rhin, Badisches Staatstheater, Karlsruhe, Oper de Stadt Köln, Staatstheater Stuttgart, Staatstheater Darmstadt, Théâtre des Champs Elysées, New Israeli Opera, Netherlands Opera, LSO, London Philharmonic, The Philharmonia, London Mozart Players, Eng Chamber Orch, BBC Symphony Orch, Northern Sinfonia, RTE Symphonia Orch; *Recreations* walking, trams, touring; *Style*— Adrian Thompson, Esq

THOMPSON, His Hon Anthony Arthur Richard; QC (1980); s of William Frank McGregor Thompson (d 1934), and Doris Louise, *née* Hill (d 1988); *b* 4 July 1932; *Educ* Latymer Upper Sch, UC Oxford (MA), Sorbonne; *m* 1958, Francoise Alix Marie, da of Joseph Justin Reynier (d 1981); 2 s (Richard, Mark), 1 s decd, 1 da (Melissa); *Career* called to the Bar Inner Temple 1957 (bencher 1986); chm Bar Euro Gp 1984–86, recorder of the Crown Court 1985–92; avocat of the Paris Bar 1988; circuit judge: SE Circuit 1992, Western Circuit 1993–2003 (dep circuit judge 2003–); liaison judge for Cornwall 1993–99, resident judge for Cornwall 1996–99, designated civil judge for Winchester 1999–2003; vice-pres Cornwall Magistrates' Assoc 1994–2004; FCIArb 1991; *Publications* The Second Banking Directive of the European Community (1991); *Recreations* food and wine, theatre, cinema, lawn tennis; *Clubs* Roehampton; *Style*— His Hon Anthony Thompson, QC

THOMPSON, Bruce Kevin; s of Keith Thompson, of Cheltenham, Glos, and Kathleen, *née* Reeves; *b* 14 November 1959, Bath; *Educ* Newcastle HS, New Coll Oxford; *m* 23 Oct 1993, Fabienne, *née* Goddet; 2 da (Séverine b 13 Feb 1995, Aurélie b 19 June 1997); *Career* head of classics Cheltenham Coll 1986–94, dep rector Dollar Acad 1994–2000, headmaster Strathallan Sch 2000–; govr Craigclowan Sch, dir New Park Tst, memb HMC 2000– (memb Sports Ctee); *Recreations* indoor rowing, weight training, literature; *Clubs* Leander; *Style*— Bruce Thompson, Esq; ✉ Coventrees, Forgandenny, Perth PH2 9HP (tel and fax 01738 815002); Strathallan School, Forgandenny, Perth PH2 9EG (tel 01738 815000, fax 01738 815001, e-mail headmaster@strathallan.co.uk)

THOMPSON, Dr Catriona; da of John MacIntosh (d 1938), and Kate Ann, *née* Mackinnon (d 1975); *b* 29 May 1937; *Educ* Portree HS Isle of Skye, Univ of Edinburgh (MB ChB); *m* 16 July 1964, Douglas Theophilus Thompson, s of George Batchin Thompson, MBE (d 1958); 2 s (Hal b 1 Sept 1968, Andrew b 20 Jan 1975); *Career* hon lectr Dept of Anaesthetics Univ of Zimbabwe 1972–76; conslt anaesthetist: Harare Central Hosp Zimbabwe 1967–77, Parirenyatwa Gp of Hosps Harare Zimbabwe 1970–82, Ayrshire and Arran Health Bd Crosshouse Hosp 1988–2002; first nat pres Zimbabwe Assoc of Univ Women 1980–82, pres Glasgow Assoc of Women Graduates 1995–98, memb Br Fedn of Women Graduates 1986–, pre convener Membership Ctee Int Fedn of Univ Women

T

1989–92, pres Edinburgh Assoc of Women Graduates 2005–, chm Presidents Fund Edinburgh Assoc of Univ Women 2005–, first pres Scottish Fedn of Univ Women 2006–; procedural advsr: 79 and 80 Cncls 25 Conf of Int Fedn of Univ Women Japan 1995, 81 Cncl of Int Fedn of Univ Women Geneva 1997; constitutional and procedural advsr Int Fedn Univ Women 1999–2005; co-ordinator International Relations for Br Fedn of Women Graduates 1999–2005; chm Scottish Standing Ctee 1997–98; memb: NW Regnl Pain Soc 1986–93, North British Pain Assoc 1993–; FFARCS 1970; *Recreations* golf, badminton, walking, bridge; *Style*— Dr Catriona Thompson; ✉ 101/2 Greenbank Drive, Edinburgh EH10 5GB (e-mail catriona@shamwari-25.freeserve.co.uk)

THOMPSON, Sir Christopher Peile; 6 Bt (UK 1890), of Park Gate, Guiseley, Yorks; s of Lt-Col Sir Peile Thompson, OBE, 5 Bt (d 1985), and his wife, Barbara Johnson (d 1993), da of late Horace Johnson Rampling; *b* 21 December 1944; *Educ* Marlborough, RMA Sandhurst, Staff Coll; *m* 1, 1969 (m dis 1997), Anna Elizabeth, da of late Maj Arthur George Callander, of Avebury, Wilts; 1 da (Alexandra Lucy (Hon Mrs Piers Portman) b 1973), 1 s (Peile Richard b 1975); m 2, 2001, Penelope, Viscountess Portman, *née* Allin, wid of 9 Viscount Portman (d 1999); *Heir* s, Peile Thompson; *Career* 11 Hussars (PAO), then Royal Hussars (PWO), cmmnd 1965, CO Royal Hussars 1985–87, ret 1990; private sec to HRH Prince Michael of Kent 1990–92 (equerry 1989–); dir: The Hyde Park Appeal 1991–96, Nuclear Decommissioning Ltd 1994–2000 (non-exec chm 1995–2000), Logical Security Limited 1996–98, Falcon Security Control (Overseas) Ltd 2000–04; memb Standing Cncl of the Baronetage 2001–07; patron: Earth 2000 1997–2000, Tusk Tst; *Recreations* shooting, fishing, golf, tennis, reading; *Clubs* White's, Cavalry and Guards', Mill Reef (Antigua), Woodroffes; *Style*— Sir Christopher Thompson, Bt

THOMPSON, Clive Hepworth; CBE (1998); s of Sidney Hepworth Thompson (d 1956), and Vera, *née* Wynne (d 1981); *b* 9 July 1937; *Educ* Holywell GS, Univ of Manchester (BSc, MSc), Harvard Univ (Dip Mgmnt); *m* 1962, Joan Mary, da of Henry Kershaw; 2 s (David Stuart b 28 Aug 1965, Graham John b 1 Feb 1969); *Career* British Resin Products (pt of BP Chemicals): trainee 1961, various positions rising to gen mangr Barry 1975–78, gen mangr Baglan Bay 1978–82; dir Petrochemicals and Mfrg BP Chemicals 1983–90, vice-pres (ops and supply) ARCO Chemical Europe 1990–95; sec of state for Wales nominee Welsh Water Authy 1980–82, memb IMMAC DTI 1986–88; Audit Cmmn: memb 1991–97, dep chm 1995–97, acting chm 1995; company dir 1997–; chm various industrial reorganisation initiatives; non-exec dir Frimley Park Hosp NHS Tst 1999–2002, chm Ashford St Peter's NHS Tst 2002–; author various articles for chemical industry; memb Ct of Assts Worshipful Co of Horners 1995 (Liveryman 1989); *Recreations* hill walking (mainly Scotland), opera, watching cricket and rugby, golf, reading; *Clubs* Harvard Business, Windlesham Golf; *Style*— Clive Thompson, Esq, CBE; ✉ Dwr Golau, 13 Herons Court, Lightwater, Surrey GU18 5SW (tel and fax 01276 476410, mobile 07836 787602, e-mail thompson@heronscourt.fsnet.co.uk)

THOMPSON, Sir Clive Malcolm; kt (1996); *b* 4 April 1943; *Educ* Clifton, Univ of Birmingham (BSc); *Career* formerly exec Royal Dutch Shell Group, Boots Co plc and Cadbury Schweppes plc; Rentokil Initial plc (formerly Rentokil Gp plc): gp chief exec 1982–2003, non-exec chm 2003–04; non-exec dir: Caradon plc 1986–96, Wellcome plc 1993–95, Seeboard plc 1995–96, BAT Industries plc 1995–98, J Sainsbury plc 1995–2001; non-exec chm European Home Retail plc 2000–06; pres CBI 1998–2000 (dep pres 1997–98 and 2000–01), vice-pres CIM, dep chm Financial Reporting Cncl 1999–2001, memb Ctee on Corp Governance 1996–98; Hon DSc Univ of Birmingham 1999; *Style*— Sir Clive Thompson

THOMPSON, Damian Mark; s of Leonard Gilbert Thompson (d 1985), and Pamela Mary, *née* Benbow; *b* 24 January 1962; *Educ* Presentation Coll Reading, Mansfield Coll Oxford (MA), LSE (PhD); *Career* reporter The Reading Chronicle 1984–88; religious affairs correspondent The Daily Telegraph 1991–95, currently ed-in-chief The Catholic Herald; author of reviews and articles in: Daily Telegraph, Sunday Telegraph, The Times, The Spectator; *Books* The End of Time: Faith and Fear in the Shadow of the Millennium (1996, 1999); *Recreations* playing the piano; *Clubs* Athenaeum; *Style*— Damian Thompson, Esq; ✉ 19 Moorhouse Road, London W2 5DH (tel 020 7229 1948)

THOMPSON, (John) Daniel; CBE (1997), DL (Co Armagh); s of Eric McCrea Thompson (d 1987), of Portadown, and Betty Georgina, *née* Brown (d 1986); *b* 31 August 1944; *Educ* Portadown Coll, Trinity Coll Dublin (MA); *m* 15 March 1973, Joan Evelyn, da of Ernest Elkin; 2 s (Hugo Charles Daniel b 10 April 1975, Rory James William b 18 June 1977); *Career* slr of the Supreme Court NI 1970–2004, pt/t chm Appeals Serv NI 1973–, NP 1975–2004, HM coroner for S Down 1987–2005; chm: Southern Health and Social Servs Bd 1990–94, Eastern Health and Social Servs Bd 1994–2000; memb: NI Advsy Ctee on Telecoms 1989–97, PO Users' Cncl NI 1989–2000, Historic Bldgs Cncl NI 1991–97 (vice-chm 1995–97), Senate of Queen's Univ of Belfast 1995–2000 (Equal Opportunities, Nominations, Health, Audit and SU Resources and Devpt Ctees), Exec Ctee Nexus Inst 2000–06 (chm 2005–06), Bd Irish Assoc of Suicidology 2001–06 (vice-chm 2003–06); chm and tstee Armagh Nat History and Philosophical Soc 1991–, chm Charles Sheils Charity Armagh 2005–; High Sheriff Co Armagh 1991; MCIArb 1999, FRSA 1999 (memb Irish Ctee 2003–); *Publications* commentary on HPSS 1995–2000, guide to Greencastle Co Down 1999; articles on the built heritage; *Recreations* cottage in South Down, sailing, pétanque (memb Irish team 1990 and 1991); *Clubs* Royal Over-Seas League, The Armagh (tstee and pres); *Style*— J Daniel Thompson, Esq, CBE, FRSA, DL; ✉ Ardress Cottage, Annaghmore, Co Armagh BT62 1SQ (tel and fax 028 3885 1347)

THOMPSON, David; s of Bernard Thompson, of Castleford, W Yorks, and Violet, *née* Laidler; *b* 28 October 1944; *Educ* King's Sch Pontefract; *m* 24 Oct 1970, Glenys, da of Harry Colley, of Badsworth, W Yorks; 2 s (Anthony David b 24 Aug 1972, Richard Martin b 17 Feb 1976); *Career* John Gordon Walton CAs until 1975, sr ptnr Buckle Barton 1981– (ptnr 1978–81); fin dir: European Concert Orchestra Ltd 1991– (also co sec), Campbells Leisure (Bradford) Ltd 1996–2001; chm: Omnis Associates Ltd 1986–95, DT Financial Consultants Ltd 1986–, Buckle Barton Pensioneer Trustees Ltd 1988–97; dir: Tong Garden Centre plc 2001–, Dermatology.co.uk Ltd 2004–05, Trilogy Records Ltd 2006– (also co sec), Marshall Minerals Ltd 2006– (also co sec), Great Northern Solutions Ltd 2007– (also co sec), Xperience GB Ltd 2007–, Mr Yorkshire Ltd 2007–; co sec: Anthony Thompson (Trumpet) Ltd 1998–, Goodprofit Ltd 2005–, Vision Chemicals Ltd 2005–, Aquados Ltd 2006–07, Jack Burton Enterprises Ltd 2006–; Bradford City AFC Ltd: fin dir 1986–2001, vice-chm 1990–2001, vice-pres 2001–05; dep songster ldr Castleford Corps Salvation Army, memb Advsy Bd Salvation Army (Yorks Div) 1998–; govr Leeds Coll of Music 1998–2006 (chm of govrs 2000–06); FCA 1979 (ACA 1969); *Recreations* football, most sports; *Clubs* The Leeds; *Style*— David Thompson, Esq; ✉ Stone Lea, Badsworth Court, Badsworth, Pontefract, West Yorkshire WF9 1NW (tel 01977 645467, e-mail dt25@aol.com); Buckle Barton, Sanderson House, Station Road, Horsforth, Leeds LS18 5NT (tel 0113 258 8216/258 0464, fax 0113 239 0270, mobile 07836 265365, e-mail dt@bucklebarton.biz)

THOMPSON, David Anthony Roland; *Career* The Boots Company plc: joined 1966, fin dir Retail Div 1980–89, gp fin controller 1989–90, gp fin dir 1990–2002, jt gp md and fin dir 1997–2000, dep chief exec and fin dir 2000–02; memb Bd: Cadbury Schweppes plc 1998–, Nottingham Building Society 2002– (chm 2004–); FCA; *Style*— David Thompson, Esq; ✉ Cadbury Schweppes plc, 25 Berkeley Square, London W1J 6HB (tel 020 7409 1313)

THOMPSON, David John; s of Cyril Thompson, and Doris, *née* Savage; *b* 22 November 1951; *Educ* Beverley GS, Univ of Manchester (BA Econ), LSE (MSc Econ); *Career* economist Dept of Environment and Dept of Tport 1973–83, economist Monopolies and Mergers Cmmn 1984–, dir of res on regulation Inst for Fiscal Studies 1984–86, econ advsr Dept of Tport 1987–88, sr res fell London Business School and economist HM Treasy 1989–91, sr econ advsr Dept for Educn 1992–98, dir Economics Plus 1996–98; currently dir of Economics and Statistics DEFRA (formerly MAFF); *Publications* various contributions to books and articles in academic jls; *Recreations* watching soccer, rugby league, and the Tour de France; rock and roll; *Style*— David Thompson, Esq; ✉ Director of Economics and Statistics, DEFRA, Whitehall Place (West Block), London SW1A 2HH (tel 020 7270 8539, fax 020 7270 8536, e-mail david.thompson@defra.gsi.gov.uk)

THOMPSON, David M; *Educ* Univ of Cambridge; *Career* documentary prodr Open University Productions 1975, prodr Everyman and Shadowlands (winner BAFTA and Emmy awards) 1979; BBC: creator and exec prodr Screenplay series, exec prodr single drama (incl Woman in White and A Rather English Marriage) head of films and single drama 1997–; films for cinema and TV incl: Perfect Strangers, The Lost Prince, Conspiracy, Mrs Brown, The Gathering Storm, Out of Control, Ratcatcher, Tomorrow La Scala!, Captives, Face, Billy Elliot, Dirty Pretty Things, In This World, Morvern Callar, I Capture the Castle, The Mother, Iris, The Heart of Me, Sylvia, Last Resort, The Life and Death of Peter Sellers, Code 46, The Mighty Celt, Mrs Henderson Presents, Red Dust, Millions, My Summer of Love, Stage Beauty, Sweet Sixteen, In This World, Bullet Boy, The History Boys, Red Road, Starter for 10, Miss Potter, Notes on a Scandal; *Awards* 3 BAFTAS, Primetime Emmy, Golden Globe Awards, Int Emmy, Monte Carlo Nymphe D'Or, Prix Europa, Prix Futura, Euro Television Programme of the Year, RTS Awards, Gold Medal New York Film and TV Festival, Evening Standard Br Film Award, Banff Festival Best Drama; *Style*— David M Thompson, Esq; ✉ BBC Head of Film, First Floor, 1 Mortimer Street, London W1T 3JA

THOMPSON, Derek Paul; s of Stanley Moorhouse Thompson (d 1985), and Lilian, *née* Forster; *b* 31 July 1950; *Educ* Fyling Hall, Guisborough GS; *m* 1996, Julie; 2 s from previous m (Alexander McLaren b 5 June 1982, James Gordon b 5 Nov 1984), 1 da (India Elizabeth b 14 Dec 1997), 1 s (Hugo Stanley Peter b 16 July 2002); *Career* horce-racing commentator and presenter; BBC Radio Sport 1972–81, ITV Sport 1981–85, Channel 4 Racing 1985–; racecourse commentator UK and Dubai Racing Club; *Recreations* tennis, golf, jogging; *Style*— Derek Thompson, Esq; ✉ Channel Four Racing, Teddington Studios, Teddington, Middlesex TW11 9NT (tel 020 8781 2770, fax 020 8781 2762)

THOMPSON, (Ila) Dianne; CBE (2006); da of Ronald Wood, of Thornhill Lees, W Yorks, and Joan, *née* Pinder (d 1985); *b* 31 December 1950; *Educ* Batley Girls' GS, Manchester Poly (Univ of London external BA), Inst of Mktg (sr exec dip); *m* 9 Aug 1972 (m dis 1992), Roger Paul Thompson, s of William Thompson; 1 da (Joanna Rachel b 29 Aug 1984); *Career* product and gp product mangr Cooperative Wholesale Soc 1972–74, export and UK mktg mangr ICI Paints Div 1974–79, md Thompson Maud Jones (Advertising) Ltd 1981–86, mktg dir Sterling Roncraft 1986–88, md Sandvik Saws and Tools Ltd 1988–92, dir of mktg Woolworths plc 1992–94, mktg dir Signet Group plc (formerly Ratners) 1994–97, chief exec Camelot Gp plc 2000– (commercial ops dir 1997–1999); non-exec dir: RAC Gp plc 2002–05, Wyevale Garden Centres 2005, Domino's Pizza 2006–; sr lectr in strategic planning and marketing Manchester Poly 1979–86, sr conslt Business and Technol Centre 1985–86; pres CIM 2000–04; memb: Mktg Gp, Women's Advtg Club of London; Veuve Clicquot Business Woman of the Year 2000, Press Complaints Cmmn; Marketer of the Year 2001, Gold Medal CMI 2006; Companion Inst of Mgmnt 2002; Hon DBA Manchester Metropolitan Univ, Hon DCL Univ of Huddersfield, Hon DL Middlesex Univ; fell Mktg Soc 2001; FCIM 2000, FRSA 2000, FCAM 2003; *Recreations* theatre, entertaining, dining out, travel, reading; *Style*— Mrs Dianne Thompson, CBE; ✉ Camelot Group plc, Tolpits Lane, Watford, Hertfordshire WD18 9RN (tel 01923 425000)

THOMPSON, Dr Dorothy Joan; da of Frank William Walbank, and Mary Woodward, *née* Fox (d 1987); *b* 31 May 1939; *Educ* Birkenhead High Sch GPDST, Girton Coll Cambridge (William Menzies exhibitioner in classics, Thérèse Montefiore and Alfred Zimmern prizes, MA, PhD), Univ of Bristol (CertEd), Br Sch of Archaeology Athens; *m* 1 (m dis 1979), Michael Hewson Crawford; m 2, 1982, John Alexander Thompson; *Career* Henry Carrington and Bentham Dumont Koe studentship Univ of Cambridge 1962–64; Girton Coll Cambridge: Eugénie Strong research fell and lectr in classics 1965–68, official fell and lectr in classics and history 1968–2006, grad tutor (arts) 1971–81 and 1995–96, sr tutor 1981–92, dir of studies in classics 1983–2006, life fell 2006–; lectr in classics Clare Coll Cambridge 1973–2006 (bye fell 2006–), Isaac Newton Tst lectr in classics Univ of Cambridge 1992–2005; visiting memb Inst for Advanced Study Princeton (Fulbright Travel award and scholarship, Volkswagenstiftung award) 1982–83; Princeton Univ: visiting prof Dept of Classics 1986, visiting sr fell Cncl of the Humanities and Old Dominion fell 1986; Josephus Daniels fell Research Triangle Fndn Nat Humanities Center NC 1993–94; major res fell Leverhulme Tst 2002–04; pres Assoc Internationale de Papyrologues 2001–07; memb: Classical Assoc 1961, Hellenic Soc 1963, Fondation Égyptologique Reine Elisabeth Bruxelles 1964, Roman Soc 1977, American Soc of Papyrologists; Br Cncl and Flemish Nationaal Fonds voor Wetenschappelijk Onderzoek award (jtly) 1993–94; FBA 1996; *Books* Kerkeosiris: an Egyptian village in the Ptolemaic period (1971), Studies on Ptolemaic Memphis (jtly, 1980), Memphis under the Ptolemies (1988, James H Breasted prize American Historical Assoc 1989), Counting the People in Hellenistic Egypt (jtly, 2006); also author of numerous book chapters and articles in learned jls; *Recreations* reading, walking; *Style*— Dr Dorothy J Thompson, FBA; ✉ Girton College, Cambridge CB3 0JG (tel 01223 338999, fax 01223 338896, e-mail djt17@cam.ac.uk)

THOMPSON, Dudley Stuart; s of Joel Percy Thompson (d 1964), and Joan Evelyn, *née* Anstey (d 1984); *b* 4 November 1942; *Educ* Whitgift Sch; *m* 27 June 1970, Anne Elizabeth, da of John Egerton Coope (d 1964); 2 da (Karen Juliette b July 1973, Hazel Joan b Sept 1978), 1 s (Paul Dudley Fitzgerald b April 1975); *Career* sr mangr Touche Ross & Co 1969–78, gp chief accountant Imperial Continental Gas Assoc 1978–87, gp fin dir Goode Durrant plc 1988–98; dir: Northgate Motor Hldgs Ltd 1988–98, Laidlaw Gp plc 1988–93, Rawlings Brothers Ltd 1988–95, Ravenstock Tam (Hldgs) Ltd 1991–2002 (chm 1998–2002); chm: Raven Hire Ltd 1998–2002, Tudorgrade (Container Repairs) Ltd 1998–2001; non-exec dir Baldwins Industrial Services plc 1998–2002; chm Merstham Village Tst; FCA 1965, FCT 1982, MIMgt 1985; *Recreations* golf, theatre, gardening; *Clubs* Walton Heath Golf, Hunstanton Golf; *Style*— Dudley Thompson, Esq; ✉ 3 The Beeches, Fetcham, Leatherhead, Surrey KT22 9DT (tel 01372 370021, fax 01372 362590)

THOMPSON, Edward Henry; OBE (2005); s of John Alfred Thompson (d 1963), and Anne, *née* Graham (d 1994); *b* 16 July 1940, Glasgow; *Educ* Hyndland Sr Secdy Sch; *m* 30 Sept 1964, Cath, *née* Fitzpatrick; 1 s (Stephen b 1 April 1966), 1 da (Justine b 18 April 1969); *Career* early career as apprentice accountant Paterson & Benzie Glasgow then co sec and office mangr Duthie Shaw; Watson & Philip: accountant then gen mangr 1972, memb Bd 1976, jt md 1986; chm and chief exec Morning Noon & Night 1991–2004; chm and owner Dundee United FC; memb Bd Scottish Premier League; Lifetime Achievement Award Scottish Grocery Trade 2003, fell Scottish Grocers Fedn 2006; fell: CIMA, ACCA; *Style*— Edward Thompson, Esq, OBE; ✉ Dundee United Football Club, Tannadice Park, Tannadice Street, Dundee DD3 7JW (tel 01382 833166, fax 01382 815610)

THOMPSON, Ernest Victor; s of Ernest Arthur Thompson (d 1964), and Victoria, *née* Harrup (d 1949); *b* 14 July 1931; *Educ* Burford GS; *m* 1, 1952 (m dis 1972), Elizabeth Spiller; 2 da (Carol b 1954, Virginia b 1957); m 2, 1972, Celia Carole, da of Nelson Burton;

2 s (Nathan Wyatt b 1977, Luke Adam b 1980); *Career* RN 1947–56; Bristol Constabulary 1956–63, investigator BOAC 1963–64, chief security offr Dept of Civil Aviation Rhodesia 1964–70, various Civil Serv appts 1970–75, author 1975–; Bard of the Cornish Gorsedd; pres Cornish Lit Guild, vice-pres West Country Writers' Assoc; memb: Royal Inst of Cornwall 1977, Missouri Supreme Ct Historical Assoc 1983, RSL 1992; *Books* incl: Chase the Wind (1977, Best Historical Novel), Harvest of the Sun (1978), Music Makers (1979), Ben Retallick (1980), The Dream Traders (1981), Singing Spears (1982), The Restless Sea (1983), Cry Once Alone (1984), Polrudden (1985), The Stricken Land (1986), Becky (1988), God's Highlander (1989), Lottie Trago (1990), Cassie (1991), Homeland (as James Munro, 1991), Wychwood (1992), Blue Dress Girl (1992), Mistress of Polrudden (1993), The Tolpuddle Woman (1994), Ruddlemoor (1995), Lewin's Mead, Moontide (1996), Cast No Shadows; Mud Huts and Missionaries (1997), Fires of Evening (1998), Here, There and Yesterday (1999), Somewhere a Bird is Singing (1999), Winds of Fortune (2000), Seek a New Dawn (2001), The Lost Years (2002), Paths of Destiny (2003), Tomorrow is For Ever (2004), The Vagrant King (2005), Brothers in War (2006), Though the Heavens May Fall (2007); *Recreations* travel, historical research, music; *Style*— E V Thompson, Esq; ✉ The Gwern, Wormbridge, Herefordshire HR2 9DT (tel and fax 01981 570400, e-mail thompsonev@hotmail.com)

THOMPSON, Estelle Margaret; *b* 8 June 1960; *Educ* Sheffield City Poly (BA), RCA (MA); *Career* artist; pt/t lectr: St Martin's Sch of Art, Christie's Fine Art Course, Ruskin Sch of Art, RCA, Slade Sch of Fine Art; sr research fell De Montfort Univ 1995–99; *Solo Exhibitions* incl: Pomeroy Purdy (now Purdy Hicks) Gallery 1989, 1991, 1992, 1993 and 1996, Eastbourne Clarke Gallery Florida 1989 and 1990, Castlefield Gallery Manchester 1992, Purdy Hicks Gallery London touring to Winchester Gallery Winchester Sch of Art, Towner Art Gallery Eastbourne and Darlington Arts Centre 1993, Galerie Helmut Pabst Frankfurt 1996, Usher Gallery Lincoln 1998, Mead Gallery Warwick 1998, South Hill Park Bracknell 1998, NY Print Fair 1998, Purdy Hicks Gallery London 1998, 1999, 2000, 2001, 2002, 2003 and 2005, Galerie Helmut Pabst Frankfurt 1999, Angel Row Gallery Nottingham, The New Art Gallery Walsall, Wetterling Gallery Stockholm 2004; *Group Exhibitions* incl: Three Painters from the RCA (Paton Gallery) 1985, Women and Water (Odette Gilbert Gallery) 1988, Homage to the Square (Flaxman Gallery) 1989 and 1990, The Theory and Practice of the Small Painting (Anderson O'Day Gallery) 1990, Whitechapel Open 1990 and 1992, Art in Worship (Worcester Cathedral and Tewkesbury Abbey) 1991, (dis)parities (Mappin Art Gallery Sheffield and Pomeroy Purdy Gallery) 1992, Bruise - Paintings for the 90's (Ikon Gallery Birmingham) 1992, BDO Binder Hamlyn Art Collection London 1993, Moving into View: Recent British Painting (Royal Festival Hall London touring to Darlington Arts Centre, Chapter Cardiff, Oriel Gallery Mold, Newlyn Orion Gallery Penzance, Univ of Northumbria Newcastle upon Tyne, Drumcroon Arts Centre Wigan, Harrogate Museum and Art Gallery and Victoria Art Gallery Bath) 1993–96, Castlefield Gallery 10th Anniversary (Whitworth Art Gallery Univ of Manchester) 1994, Six British Painters (Galerie Helmut Pabst Frankfurt), Shadow of Life Art 97, The Printshow (Flowers Graphics and Purdy Hicks Gallery) 1997, Etchings from Hope (Sufferance Press Marlborough Graphics) 1998, News Works (Purdy Hicks Gallery) 1998, Works on Paper (Purdy Hicks Gallery) 1999, Blue (The New Art Gallery Walsall) 2000, British Abstract Painting (Flowers East London, Rosenburg & Kaufman Fine Art NY) 2001, Ols & Co (Jane Deering Gallery Boston) 2003, Drawing Two Hundred (The Drawing Room London) 2005; *Collections* Arts Cncl, Br Cncl, Br Museum, Towner Art Gallery Sussex, Arthur Andersen Collection, The Contemporary Art Soc, County NatWest, Reed International, Unilever plc, Coopers & Lybrand, De Beers, Pearl Assurance, New Hall Cambridge, Oldham Art Gallery Greater Manchester, Univ of Warwick, De Montfort Univ Leicester, Chelsea & Westminster Hosp, Ferens Art Gallery Hull, Deutsche Bank, Economist Gp, Reynolds Porter Chamberlain, TI Group plc, New York City Library, Goldman Sachs, Pearson plc New York, The New Art Gallery Walsall; *Commissions* Quaglino's Restaurant 1989, Milton Keynes Theatre 1999 *Awards* Royal Over-Seas League Travel Award 1988, Prudential awards for the arts/Arts Cncl special award 1990; *Style*— Ms Estelle Thompson; ✉ c/o Purdy Hicks Gallery, 65 Hopton Street, London SE1 9GZ (tel 020 7401 9229, fax 020 7401 9595, e-mail estelle_thompson@hotmail.com, website www.purdyhicks.com)

THOMPSON, Gabriel Piers; s of James Thompson, of Kings Norton, Birmingham, and Mary Josephine, *née* McAndrew; *b* 8 March 1962; *Educ* The Reading Bluecoat Sch Sonning-on-Thames Berks; *m* 16 Nov 1991, Sonia Horler, da of Joseph Spiteri; 2 da (Katrina, Felicity); *Career* Reading Evening Post: trainee reporter 1981, sub-ed 1982, passed NCTJ proficiency test 1983, sr reporter 1983; sub-ed: Middlesbrough Evening Gazette 1984, Newcastle Journal 1985; The Independent: layout sub-ed 1986, foreign sub-ed 1987, foreign prodn ed 1989; prodn ed The Independent on Sunday 1990 (chief sub-ed 1990); The Independent: dep night ed 1992, prodn ed 1996, formerly design ed; *Recreations* smoking, drinking, arguing, grouting; *Style*— Gabriel Thompson, Esq

THOMPSON, Prof George Edward; OBE (2000); s of John Henry Thompson (d 1994), of Liverpool, and Elsie May, *née* Serridge (d 1983); *b* 7 March 1946; *Educ* Alsop High Sch Liverpool, Univ of Nottingham (BSc, PhD); *m* 1971, Marilyn Judith, da of Norman Lucas Wright; 1 s (James Robert b 18 Sept 1975), 1 da (Sarah Louise b 6 April 1979); *Career* postdoctoral res assoc Univ of Nottingham 1970–73, section ldr rising to princ scientist Howson-Algraphy Leeds 1973–78, UMIST (now Univ of Manchester): successively lectr, sr lectr and reader 1978–90, prof of corrosion science and engrg 1990–; author of over 700 pubns in int jls and confs; Beilby Medal 1987, T P Hoar Award 1997, selected to class of fells of the Electrochemical Soc 1998, U R Evans Award 2000, Sainte-Claire Deville Medal 2001, Jim Kape Meml Medal 2001, 2002 and 2006, Cavallero Medal 2006; Hon DSc Victoria Univ of Manchester 1998; FIMF, FICorrST, FIMMM, FREng; *Recreations* gardening, football, travel; *Style*— Prof George Thompson, OBE; ✉ Corrosion and Protection Centre, School of Materials, University of Manchester, PO Box 88, Manchester M60 1QD (tel 0161 200 4859, fax 0161 200 4865, e-mail george.thompson@manchester.ac.uk)

THOMPSON, Prof Gilbert Richard; s of Lt-Col Richard Louis Thompson (d 1976), and Violet Mary, *née* Harrison (d 1955); *b* 20 November 1932; *Educ* Downside, St Thomas' Hosp Med Sch (MB BS), Univ of London (MD); *m* 14 June 1958, Sheila Jacqueline Mary, da of Melchior Deurvorst (d 1977); 2 da (Anna b 1959, Jennifer b 1977), 2 s (Mark b 1961, Philip b 1971); *Career* Lt RAMC Royal Army Med Coll Millbank 1957–58; Capt RAMC mil hosp: Accra Ghana 1959–61, Millbank 1961–63; registrar and sr registrar in med Hammersmith Hosp 1963–66, research fell Harvard Med Sch and Mass Gen Hosp Boston 1966–67, lectr in med Royal Postgrad Med Sch and conslt physician Hammersmith Hosp 1967–72, asst prof Baylor Coll of Med and Methodist Hosp Houston 1972–73, sr lectr in med Royal Postgrad Med Sch 1972–74, conslt MRC Lipid Metabolism Unit Hammersmith Hosp 1975–83, visiting prof Royal Victoria Hosp Montreal 1981–82, conslt MRC Lipoprotein Team Hammersmith Hosp 1984–98, currently emeritus prof of clinical lipidology Imperial Coll Faculty of Med Hammersmith Hosp; former chm Br Atherosclerosis Soc, former chm Br Hyperlipidaemia Assoc; FRCP 1973 (MRCP); *Books* A Handbook of Hyperlipidaemia (1989, 2 edn 1994), Coronary Risk Factors and their Detection (1992), Hammersmith Marathon (1999), Dyslipidaemia in Clinical Practice (2002, 2 edn 2006); *Recreations* hill walking, skiing, fly fishing; *Clubs* Flyfishers; *Style*— Prof Gilbert Thompson; ✉ Metabolic Medicine, Imperial College Faculty of Medicine, Hammersmith Hospital, Du Cane Road, London W12 0NN (tel and fax 020 8994 6143, e-mail g.thompson@imperial.ac.uk)

THOMPSON, Guy Charles Wallace; s of Cdr John Lionel Wallace Thompson (d 1987), and Patricia June, *née* Etchells (d 1997); *b* 23 November 1952; *Educ* Sutton Valence, Univ of Newcastle upon Tyne (BA, BArch); *m* 2 Aug 1975 (m dis 2003), Gillian Edna, da of P R Brown; 1 da (Amy Charlotte b 21 Nov 1982), 1 s (Joel Henry Xavier b 31 Dec 1991); *Career* architectural asst PSA Edinburgh 1974–75, design conslt Planning Dept Tyne & Wear Cncl (Highways and Environmental Works Team Section) 1977; Norman & Dawbarn: architectural asst 1977, assoc 1983, ptnr/dir 1988–2005, md 1994–99, chief exec 1999–2005; projects incl: operating theatres RAF Hosp Ely 1978, Mil Works Force accommodation Chilwell 1984, Southwood Business Park Farnborough, Consulate and Cultural Centre Queensgate Kensington, Wembley Community Care Centre; dir Capita Norman and Dawbarn 2005–06, head of architecture and housing The Concrete Centre 2006–; RIBA: chm W Surrey Branch 1994–96, regnl lottery advsr 1996–98, chm SE Regn 1998–2000 (vice-chm 1995–97), memb Nat Cncl 1998–2004, dir RIBA Enterprises 2002–05, memb Housing Gp 2007–; chm Construction Industry Cncl SE region 2002–03; dir The Wren Insurance Association Ltd 1990–2005; dir and vice-pres Thames Valley C of C and Industry 1995–96; pres: Guildford and Dist C of C 1995–97, Surrey C of C 1997–99; dir Surrey Business Link 1997–99, chm Surrey Economic Partnership 2006–; govr St Nicholas C of E Infant Sch 1997–2005; memb ARCUK 1978, ARIBA 1978, Ordre des Architectes 1993; *Awards* Northern Brick Fedn Design Award 1977, competition winner Hawth Centre for the Performing Arts 1986, Civic Design Award Best Office Building 1991, Downlands Prize The Church 1999, NHS Best Primary Care Premises Devpt Wembley Centre for Health and Care 2000, Downlands Prize Southfields Community Learning Centre 2001; *Recreations* wine, walking, architecture; *Clubs* Reform; *Style*— Guy Thompson, Esq; ✉ The Bumpers, Seale Lane, Putenham, Surrey GU3 1AX (tel 01483 810696); The Concrete Centre, 4 Riverside House, 4 Meadows Business Park, Station Approach, Blackwater, Camberley, Surrey GU17 9AB (tel 01276 606831)

THOMPSON, James Craig; s of Alfred Thompson, of Newcastle upon Tyne, and Eleanor, *née* Craig; *b* 27 October 1933; *Educ* Heaton GS, Rutherford Coll Newcastle upon Tyne; *m* 4 Sept 1957, Catherine, da of James Warburton, of Newcastle upon Tyne; 1 s (Roderic b 1959), 1 da (Fiona b 1963); *Career* commercial exec 1960–76: Belfast Telegraph, Newcastle Chronicle and Journal, Scotsman Publications, Liverpool Post and Echo; md South Eastern Newspapers 1975–79, advtg and mktg mangr/dep md Kent Messenger Gp 1976–79 (dir 1972–79); chm and md: Maidstone United Football Club Ltd 1970–92, Adverkit International Ltd 1979–90, Harvest Publications 1983–95, Presscom Ltd 1998–; chm North Kent Land Holdings Ltd 1992–94; chief exec: Maidstone and District C of C and Industry 1994–2000 (policy dir 2001–03), Business Point Maidstone 1996–2003, Maidstone Enterprise Agency 1998–2003; md: Dartford Football Club plc 1991–93, Maidstone Invicta FC Ltd 1993–94; dir MLO Ltd 1999–2002, dir Associated C of C 2000–03, policy dir Kent Gateway C of C 2001–03, cncllr Otham PC 2003– (chm 2005–); pres: Eastern Professional Floodlight League 1976–94, Maidstone Minor League 1976–2003, Kent League 1984–89, Football Conf 1989– (pres 1990–); chm: Southern Football League 1977–79 (life memb 1985), Alliance Premier Football League 1979–89; memb Cncl Football Assoc 1980–90, life govr Kent County Agric Soc, hon life memb Kent CCC; memb: Catenian Assoc (pres Maidstone Circle 1974–75), MCC; Liveryman Worshipful Co of Stationers & Newspaper Makers; MCIM, MIMgt, FInstD; *Recreations* walking, Northumbrian history; *Clubs* Maidstone (pres 1997); *Style*— James Thompson, Esq; ✉ Prescott House, Otham, Maidstone, Kent ME15 8RL (tel 01622 861606)

THOMPSON, James Francis (Paddy); s of John Cherry Watson Thompson (d 1967), and Gladys Jessie, *née* Taylor (d 1989); *b* 11 March 1939; *Educ* Loretto; *m* 30 March 1967, Alison Margaret, da of John Burnet Maitland Cowan; 3 da (Heather Alison b 5 Oct 1970, Jennifer Isabel b 11 July 1972, Patricia Jean b 13 Oct 1975); *Career* stockbroking trainee Glasgow 1957–62, journalist Financial Times 1962–65, business ed Glasgow Herald 1965–70, dir Portfolio Management (Scotland) Ltd 1970–75, local dir Singer and Friedlander 1975–81; dir: James Finlay Investment Management Ltd 1981–96, James Finlay Nominees Ltd 1981–96, James Finlay Bank Ltd 1986–96, Bell Lawrie Investment Management 1996–99, ret; *Recreations* golf, reading; *Clubs* West of Scotland FC, London Scottish RFC, Buchanan Castle Golf; *Style*— Paddy Thompson, Esq; ✉ Woodrising, Buchanan Castle Estate, Dryman, Glasgow G63 0HX (tel 01360 660426)

THOMPSON, Prof (John) Jeffrey; CBE (1989); s of John Thompson (d 1968), of Southport, Lancs, and Elsie May, *née* Wright (d 2005); *b* 13 July 1938; *Educ* King George V Sch Southport, St John's Coll Cambridge (MA), Balliol Coll Oxford (MA), Hatfield Poly (PhD); *m* 6 April 1963, Kathleen Audrey, da of Francis Arthur Gough (d 1989), of Southport, Lancs; 3 da (Karen b 1965, Alison b 1966, Lynda 1971); *Career* schoolmaster Blundell's Sch 1961–65, head of chemistry Watford GS 1965–69, lectr KCL 1968–69, Shell fell UCL 1969–70, lectr and tutor Dept of Educnl Studies Univ of Oxford 1970–79, lectr in chemistry Keble Coll Oxford 1970–76, emeritus prof of educn Univ of Bath (prof of educn 1979–2005, pro-vice-chllr 1986–89); chm Examining Bd Int Bacc 1984–89, dep chm Sch Examinations and Assessment Cncl 1988–92, vice-pres and gen sec BAAS 1984–91 (chm Cncl 1991–96, vice-pres 1996–99); dir for int educn Int Bacc Organisation (IBO) 2000–02, academic dir IBO 2002–03, head of Int Bacc Research Unit 2000–05, chair Int Primary Curriculum Advsy Bd 2004–, dir United World Colls Int Bd 2006–; dep chm Examinations Appeals Bd DfEE 1999–2002, chm DfES 2002–; chm Assoc for Sci Educn 1981; memb: Cncl Wildfowl and Wetlands Tst, Royal Soc Educn Ctee, Assoc for Sci Educn, Nat Cmmn for Educn, English Nat Bd for Nursing Midwifery and Health Visiting 1993–2002; tstee Bath Royal Literary and Scientific Inst 1992–2001; dir Wessex Int 1999–2001; Outstanding Contribution to Int Educn Award European Cncl of Int Schs 2005, Lifetime Contribution to Int Educn Award Int Schs Assoc Geneva 2006; Hon DLitt Univ of Hertfordshire 2000; Freeman City of London 1992, Liveryman Worshipful Co of Goldsmiths 1992; hon memb: Assoc for Science Educn, Br Assoc for Advancement of Science (BAAS); FRSC, FRSA 1984; *Books* An Introduction to Chemical Energetics (1967), Study of Chemistry Programmes (1972), Modern Physical Chemistry (1982), A Foundation Course in Chemistry (1982), Dimensions of Science (ed, 1986), The Chemistry Dimension (1987), International Education: Principles and Practice (ed 1998), International Schools and International Education (ed, 2000), International Education in Practice (ed, 2002), Handbook of Research in International Education (ed, 2007); *Recreations* N country art and music, collecting sugar wrappers, 4 granddaughters and 2 grandsons; *Style*— Prof Jeffrey Thompson, CBE; ✉ Department of Education, University of Bath, Claverton Down, Bath BA2 7AY

THOMPSON, Jeremy Gordon; s of Gordon Alfred Thompson, and Edna Betty, *née* Illman; *b* 23 September 1947; *Educ* Sevenoaks Sch, King's Sch Worcester; *m* 1, 1970 (m dis 1980), Nichola Wood; 2 s (James Spencer b 1971, Adam Redvers b 1972); m 2, 1986, Lynn Patricia Bowland; *Career* foreign affairs correspondent; trainee chartered surveyor then trainee account exec with advtg agency London 1965–67; reporter: Cambridge Evening News 1967–71, BBC Radio Sheffield 1971–74, Look North (BBC TV Leeds) 1974–77; N of England corr BBC TV News 1977–82; ITN: chief sports corr 1982–86, Asia corr (setting up new bureau in Hong Kong) 1987–90, corr covering Gulf War and Yugoslavia 1990–91, Africa corr 1991–93; Sky Television plc: Sky News sr Africa corr 1993–95, Sky News US corr 1995–98, presenter Sky News 'Live at Five'; sporting stories: Olympic Games LA 1984, Seoul 1988 and Atlanta 1996, England cricket tours to Aust, W Indies, India and Pakistan, football World Cup Spain 1982, rugby World Cup South Africa 1995, numerous other sporting events; news stories: assassination of Indira Gandhi 1984, Bhopal tragedy India 1984, student political uprising Tiananmen Square China 1989,

T

democracy riots in South Korea, Benazir Bhutto's election in Pakistan, child labour scandal in India, Sri Lankan war, Phillipine and Fiji coups, Vietnamese pull out from Cambodia, famine in Somalia, end of apartheid and election of President Nelson Mandela, genocide in Rwanda, civil wars in Sudan, Mozambique and Angola, O J Simpson trial, re-election of President Bill Clinton 1996, the Lewinsky scandal, Kosovo campaign, Iraq war 2003, Asian tsunami 2004, death of Pope John Paul II 2005, London bombings 2005, Israel/Lebanon war 2006; memb: NUJ 1967–, Cricket Writers Club 1982–, Rugby Writers Club 1982–, Hong Kong Foreign Correspondents Assoc; winner Outstanding Coverage of a Single Breaking News Story EMMY for report on Bisho massacre South Africa 1992 (first News EMMY won by a British network), Gold Award for Best Corr NY TV Festival 1994 and 1995, RTS News Event Award for Kosovo liberation day 1999–2000, RTS News Channel of the Year Award 2001/02, BAFTA News Award for coverage of Sept 11 attacks 2001/02, RTS News Event Award for coverage of Soham murder case 2002/03, BAFTA News Award for coverage of Soham murders 2002/03, RTS News Channel Award for coverage of Iraq War 2003, TRIC Digital/Satellite TV Personality of the Year 2004, RTS TV News Presenter of the Year 2005, RTS News Channel Award 2006–07; appeared in films Volcano (as TV news reporter), Shaun of the Dead and The Bourne Ultimatum; *Recreations* cricket, golf, swimming, walking, game and bird watching; *Style*— Jeremy Thompson, Esq; ✉ tel (work) 020 7705 3000, e-mail jeremy.thompson@bskyb.com

THOMPSON, Jeremy Sinclair; s of late Norman Sinclair Thompson, CBE, of Burton Bradstock, Dorset, and Peggy, *née* Sivil; *b* 6 April 1954; *Educ* Durham Sch, Keble Coll Oxford (MA); *m* 12 June 1982, Lucy Jane Thompson, da of Peter Joseph Wagner (d 1983); 2 da (Victoria b 1986, Poppy b 1989), 1 s (Samuel b 1995); *Career* Peat Marwick Mitchell 1976–80, dir accounting servs Air Florida Europe Ltd 1980–82, conslt Coopers & Lybrand Associates 1982–84; md: Sinclair Thompson Associates 1985–86, Tranwood Earl & Co Ltd 1986–91; dir: Tranwood plc 1987–91, Filofax Group plc 1990–92; gp md Vaile Sinclair Ltd 1991–97, md Contessa Investments Ltd 1998–, chm Futures Training 2001–; ACA 1980; *Recreations* rowing, sailing, flying; *Clubs* Leander, Royal Ocean Racing; *Style*— Jeremy Thompson, Esq; ✉ Milton Manor, Milton Abbas, Dorset DT11 0AZ (tel 01258 880857, fax 01258 881043, e-mail jeremysthompson@aol.com)

THOMPSON, Sir (Thomas d'Eyncourt) John; 6 Bt (UK 1806), of Hartsbourne Manor, Hertfordshire; s of Sir Lionel Tennyson Thompson, 5 Bt (d 1999); *b* 22 December 1956; *Educ* Eton, King's Coll London; *m* 2002, Tanya, da of Michael Willcocks, of Chideock, Dorset; 1 da (Arabella Grace b 22 May 2004), 1 s (Thomas Boulden Cameron b 31 Jan 2006); *Career* dir Rockspring Iberia Madrid; professional associate RICS; *Style*— Sir John Thompson, Bt; ✉ Covarrubias 3, 1D, 28010 Madrid, Spain (tel 0034 91 4482253, fax 0034 91 4468474)

THOMPSON, John; MBE (1975); s of late Arthur Thompson, and late Josephine, *née* Brooke; *b* 28 May 1945; *Educ* St Nicholas GS, Central London Poly (DMS); *m* 9 July 1966, Barbara, da of late Ernest Hopper; 1 da (Ailsa b 1967); *Career* FCO: vice-consul Düsseldorf 1966–69, Abu Dhabi 1969–72, Phnom Penh 1972–74; DTI 1975–77; FCO: first sec, consul and head of Chancery, Luanda 1979–82; consul São Paulo 1982–85; asst head: South Pacific Dept, Aid Policy Dept; high cmmr to Vanuatu 1988–92, dep consul-gen and dir of trade NYC 1992–97, head Information Systems Dept and Library and Records Dept FCO 1997–99, head Information Mgmnt Gp FCO Services 1999–2002, ambass to Angola 2002–05 (concurrently non-resident ambass to São Tomé and Principe); *Recreations* philately, reading, walking, bridge; *Style*— John Thompson, Esq, MBE; ✉ c/o Foreign & Commonwealth Office, King Charles Street, London SW1A 2AH

THOMPSON, Air Vice-Marshal John Hugh; CB (2000), QCVSA (1981); s of late Thomas Thompson, and late Dulcie, *née* Matthews; *b* 18 September 1947; *Educ* RAF Coll Cranwell, Army Staff Coll Camberley, RCDS; *m* 20 Dec 1969, Mary Elizabeth, da of George Emerson; 1 da (Samantha Joy b 12 June 1973), 2 s (Matthew Robert b 2 Sept 1974, George Hugh b 18 April 1986); *Career* RAF; Pilot Offr trg 1965–69, fighter pilot Bahrain 1970–71, qualified weapons instr Germany 1971–75, Harrier Operational Conversion Unit later Staff Offr Gp HQ 1975–82, Cdr 3 (Fighter) Sqdn Germany 1982–85, Staff Offr Air Plans MOD 1985–89, Cdr RAF Wittering 1989–91, Sr Staff Offr HQ 2 Gp Rheindalen 1992–96 (incl 3 months as NATO liaison offr HQ UNPROFOR Zagreb), mil advsr to Carl Bildt Brussels and Sarajevo 1996–97, AOC and Cmdt RAF Coll Cranwell 1997–98, AOC 1 Gp 1998–2000, defence attaché and head Br Defence Staff Washington 2000–; *Recreations* golf, skiing, reading, Balkan watching; *Clubs* RAF; *Style*— Air Vice-Marshal J Thompson, CB; ✉ British Embassy, 3100 Massachusetts Avenue NW, Washington DC 20008, USA (tel 202 588 6700, fax 202 588 7887, e-mail jthompso@moduk.org)

THOMPSON, John Michael; s of Arthur Leslie Thompson (d 1972), of Eastbourne, E Sussex; *b* 15 July 1944; *Educ* Stationers' Co's Sch, London Business Sch; *m* 21 Dec 1968, Farzie; 1 da (Sarah Elizabeth b 1 Jan 1973), 1 s (Neil John b 23 May 1974); *Career* articled clerk Wilkins Kennedy & Co CAs London 1961–66, Thornton Baker & Co London 1966–68; PricewaterhouseCoopers (formerly Coopers & Lybrand before merger): Tehran 1968–72, London 1972–73, ptnr Tehran 1974–79, ptnr London 1980–2001, ptnr i/c Insolvency Div London 1987–96, ptnr i/c IT 1988–96, UK head of business recovery services 1996–2001; dir Melli Bank plc 2003–; memb: Ctee for ME Trade (COMET) 1992–93, Insolvency Licensing Ctee ICAEW 1991–2000, Review Ctee ICAEW 2001–; memb: Insolvency Practitioners' Assoc 1986, Soc of Practitioners in Insolvency 1990; FCA 1966; *Recreations* music, piano, travel, theatre, running, walking; *Style*— John Thompson, Esq; ✉ Suite 408, Butlers Wharf Building, 36 Shad Thames, London SE1 2YE (tel 020 7357 0394)

THOMPSON, John Michael Anthony; s of George Edward Thompson (d 1982), of Deganwy, Gwynedd, and Joan, *née* Smith; *b* 3 February 1941; *Educ* William Hulme's GS Manchester, Univ of Manchester (BA, MA); *m* 24 July 1965, Alison Sara, da of Walter Bowers, of Cheadle Hulme, Gtr Manchester; 2 da (Hannah Jane b 19 March 1973, Harriet Mary b 13 Feb 1976); *Career* res asst Whitworth Art Gallery 1964–66, keeper Rutherston Collection Manchester City Art Gallery 1966–68; dir: NW Museum and Gallery Serv 1968–70, Arts and Museums Bradford 1970–75, Tyne & Wear Co Museums and Galleries 1975–86, Tyne & Wear Jt Museums Serv 1986–91; museums and heritage conslt 1991–, dir: Museums and Galleries Consultancy 1992–95, Jarrow 700AD Ltd 1993–; fndr memb and hon sec Gp of Dirs of Museums in Br Isles, pres Museums North 1990–91; advsr Assoc of Met Authorities 1983–91; chm Gosforth Adult Educn Assoc 1993–, tech advsr Heritage Lottery Fund 1996–2000, external verifier for Museums Trg Inst 1996–99, external verifier for QFI (Qualifications for Industry) 1999–2006, advsr UNESCO 2001–05, professional reviewer Museums Assoc 2004–, learning and access expert advsr Heritage Lottery Fund 2004–; conslt Prince Research Consultants 1993–2007; memb: Standards Steering Ctee Museums Trg Inst 1990–93 (chair Curatorship Gp 1990–93), Assoc of Independent Museums; govr Gosforth HS 1993–; FMA 1977 (AMA 1970), MIMgt 1994; *Books* Manual of Curatorship, A Guide to Museum Practice (1984, new edn 1992); *Recreations* running, travel, visiting exhibitions; *Style*— John Thompson, Esq; ✉ 21 Linden Road, Gosforth, Newcastle upon Tyne NE3 4EY (tel and fax 0191 284 7304)

THOMPSON, (Charles Arthur) Jonathan; s of William Arthur Lisle Thompson, of Liverpool and Anglesey, and Margaret Elizabeth; *b* 27 May 1954; *Educ* Liverpool Coll, Blackpool Coll (HND); *m* 4 Oct 1986, Caroline Jane, da of John Albert Howard; 2 da (Elizabeth Jane b 3 March 1989, Emily Louise b 25 Sept 1990); *Career* Historic House Hotels 1983– (gen mangr Bodysgallen Hall 1983–88, dir and gen mangr Hartwell House 1989–); past memb Overseas Mktg Intelligence Ctee; chm Thames and Chilterns Div BHA; memb: Hotel Catering and Institutional Mgmnt Assoc, Restaurateurs Assoc of GB, Confrérie des Chevalliers de Tastevin; Master Innholder 1990–; AA Red Stars 1983–, RAC Blue Ribbons 1988, Hotel of the Year Andrew Hayer's Hideaway Report 1985–87 and 1992, Welsh Tourist Bd award for services to tourism 1986–, Queen's award for export achievement 1987, Good Hotel Guide César award for outstanding restoration and first class hotel mgmnt 1988–, Good Food Guide Buckinghamshire County Restaurant of the Year 1989, Which? Hotel Guide Buckinghamshire County Hotel of the Year 1996; MHCIMA; *Recreations* sailing, history and heritage, my family; *Style*— Jonathan Thompson, Esq; ✉ Awelfor, Ffordd Llechi, Rhosneigr, Isle of Anglesey, Gwynedd LL64 5JY (tel 01407 810289); Historic House Hotels, Hartwell House, Oxford Road, Aylesbury, Buckinghamshire HP17 8NL (tel 01296 747444, fax 01296 747450)

THOMPSON, (Rupert) Julian de la Mare; s of Rupert Spens Thompson (d 1952), and Florence Elizabeth de la Mare; *b* 23 July 1941; *Educ* Eton, King's Coll Cambridge (MA); *m* 6 March 1965, Jacqueline Mary, da of John William Linnell Ivimy; 3 da (Rebecca b 1966, Sophia b 1968, Cecilia b 1971); *Career* Sotheby's: dir 1969–97, chm 1982–86, chm Sotheby's Asia 1992–97 (non-exec chm 1997–2003); *Style*— Julian Thompson, Esq; ✉ Crossington Farm, Upton Bishop, Ross-on-Wye, Hereford HR9 7UE (tel 01989 780471, e-mail rjdlmthompson@hotmail.com)

THOMPSON, Linda (Linda Kenis); da of Charles Pettifer (d 1973), and Betty, *née* Meechan (d 1999); *b* 23 August 1947; *Educ* Queens Park GS Glasgow; *m* 1, 1972 (m dis 1982), Richard Thompson; 3 c (Maimuna b 20 Oct 1973, Teddy b 19 Feb 1976, Kami b 28 Feb 1982); m 2, 10 April 1983, Stephen M Kenis; *Career* folk-rock singer and songwriter; worked with many folk singers incl Richard Thompson, Bob Dylan, Nick Drake and Sandy Denny; songwriter for many people incl Emmylou Harris; has written and performed for theatre, notably Bill Bryden's Mysteries trilogy RNT; patron NSPCC; *Albums* incl: I Want to See the Bright Lights Tonight (with Richard Thompson) 1974, Shoot Out The Lights (with Richard Thompson) 1982, One Clear Moment 1985, Dreams Fly Away (compilation) 1996, Fashionably Late 2002; *Awards* incl: Best Female Singer Rolling Stone magazine 1982, Grammy nomination 1982, numerous songwriting awards; *Recreations* reading, reviewing books; *Style*— Linda Thompson; ✉ c/o Jake Guralnik, 217A Wyckoff Street, Brooklyn, New York, NY 11217, USA (tel 001 218 222 1591, fax 001 718 852 9519, e-mail 2jakes@2jakes@usa.net)

THOMPSON, Dr (Ian) McKim; s of John William Thompson (d 1976), of Solihull, and Dr Elizabeth Maria, *née* Williams (d 1998); *b* 19 August 1938; *Educ* Epsom Coll, Univ of Birmingham (MB ChB); *m* 8 Sept 1962 (m dis 1988), Dr (Veronica) Jane, da of John Dent Richards (d 1987), of Fladbury; 2 s (David b 1966, Peter b 1969), 1 da (Suzanne b 1972); *Career* lectr in pathology Univ of Birmingham 1964–67, conslt forensic pathologist to HM Coroner City of Birmingham 1966–97, dep sec BMA 1969–96, memb GMC 1979–95, lectr Dept of Adult Educn Keele Univ 1985–, vice-pres BMA 1998–, pres Birmingham Med Inst 2003–, fndr memb AMEC; pres Sands Cox Soc Univ of Birmingham 2006; hon memb Collegiate Med Coll of Spain 1975; BMA 1961, FRSM 1988–98; *Books* The Hospital Gazetteer (ed, 1972), BMA Handbook for Trainee Doctors in General Practice (ed 1985), BMA Handbook for Hospital Junior Doctors (ed, 1985); *Recreations* inland waterways, rambling; *Style*— Dr McKim Thompson; ✉ Canal Cottage, Hinksford Lane, Kingswinford DY6 0BH

THOMPSON, Mark; s of Owen Edgar Thompson (d 1997), and Barbara Adele, *née* Lister; *b* 12 April 1957; *Educ* Radley, Univ of Birmingham; *Partner* Anthony Ward, *qv*; *Career* set and costume designer; *Theatre* rep incl: Worcester, Exeter, Sheffield, Leeds; for Royal Manchester Exchange credits incl: Jumpers, The Country Wife, Mumbo Jumbo (also Hammersmith Lyric), The School for Scandal; for Almeida credits incl: Volpone, Betrayal, Party Time, Butterfly Kiss; for RSC credits incl: Measure for Measure, The Wizard of Oz, Much Ado About Nothing, The Comedy of Errors, Hamlet; for RNT credits incl: The Wind in the Willows, The Madness of George III, Arcadia (also Haymarket West End, Lincoln Centre New York), Pericles, What the Butler Saw, The Day I Stood Still, Henry IV part 1 and 2, Once in a Lifetime, The Alchemist, The Rose Tattoo; for Royal Court credits incl: Six Degrees of Separation (also Comedy Theatre), Hysteria (also Mark Taper Forum LA), The Kitchen, WildEast, The Woman Before, Piano/Forte; other credits incl: Owners (Old Vic), Good (Brussels), The Scarlet Pimpernel (Chichester and Her Majesty's), Cabaret (Strand), The Sneeze (Aldwych), Ivanov, Much Ado About Nothing (both Strand), A Little Night Music (Piccadilly), Shadowlands (Queen's and Broadway), Joseph and the Amazing Technicolor Dreamcoat (Palladium and Canadian/Aust/USA tours), Insignificance, Company (both Donmar Warehouse and Albery), Art (Wyndhams), The Unexpected Man (RSC and NYC Duchess), Doctor Dolittle (Hammersmith Apollo), The Blue Room (Donmar Warehouse and New York), Mamma Mia! (Prince Edward, Broadway and Australian, US, Canadian and World tours), Blast! (Hammersmith Apollo and Broadway), Bombay Dreams (Apollo Victoria and Broadway), Kean (Apollo); *Opera* credits incl: Falstaff (Scottish Opera), Peter Grimes (Opera North), Ariadne Auf Naxos (Salzburg), Il Viaggio A Reims (ROH), Hänsel and Gretel (Sydney Opera House), The Two Widows (ENO), Queen of Spades (Met, New York), Montag Aus Licht (costume only, La Scala, Milan); *Ballet* Don Quixote (Royal Ballet); *Films* costumes for The Madness of King George; *Awards* for Wind in the Willows: Olivier Award 1991, Plays and Players Award 1991, Critics' Circle Award 1991; other awards incl: Olivier Award for Set Design and Costume Design for Joseph and the Amazing Technicolor Dreamcoat and The Comedy of Errors 1992, Olivier Award for Set Design for Hysteria 1994, Critics' Circle Award for The Kitchen 1995; *Style*— Mark Thompson

THOMPSON, Mark John Thompson; s of Duncan John Thompson Thompson (d 1986), of Preston, and Sydney Columba, *née* Corduff (d 2002); *b* 31 July 1957; *Educ* Stonyhurst (scholar), Merton Coll Oxford (postmaster, MA, Violet Vaughan Morgan English prize, ed Isis); *m* 20 Sept 1987, Jane Emilie, da of Prof Baruch Samuel Blumberg, former master Balliol Coll Oxford; 2 s, 1 da; *Career* BBC: joined as res asst trainee 1979, researcher Everyman and Nationwide 1979–80, asst prodr Nationwide 1980–82, prodr Breakfast Time 1982–84, output ed London Plus 1984–85, output ed Newsnight 1985–87, ed Nine O'Clock News 1988–90, ed Panorama 1990–92, head of Features Dept 1992–94, head of Factual Progs 1994–96, controller of BBC2 1996–98, dir of national and regnl broadcasting 1998–2000, dir of television 2000–02; chief exec Channel Four Television Corp 2002–04, DG BBC 2004–; visiting fell Nuffield Coll Oxford 2005, hon fell Merton Coll Oxford 2006; chair Edinburgh Int TV Festival 1996; Monte Carlo TV Festival Golden Nymph Award for Panorama film Drowning in Blood 1991, RTS Home Current Affrs Award for Panorama film The Max Factor 1992; FRTS 1998, FRSA 2000; *Recreations* walking, cooking; *Clubs* Reform; *Style*— Mark Thompson, Esq; ✉ c/o BBC Media Centre, 201 Wood Lane, London W12 7TQ

THOMPSON, Martin William; s of John William Thompson (d 1968); *b* 8 May 1946; *Educ* Deacons Sch Peterborough, Goldsmiths' Sch of Art (DipAD); *m* 1972, Lynda Mia Minka, da of Sir John Peel; 3 s (Ansel b 7 Feb 1977, Robbie b 5 Jan 1980, Murray b 24 July 1982); *Career* photographer; asst to John S Clarke 1969–72, freelance 1972–74, carpenter and gen builder 1974–78, advtg photography 1978–; currently co-prop All Your Prey Ltd; campaigns incl: Volvo, Sainsbury's, Benson & Hedges, Sherwoods, COI; winner 4 Campaign Silver Awards; *Recreations* sailing, keeping a small flock of sheep; *Clubs* Haven Ports, Cruising Assoc; *Style*— Martin Thompson, Esq

THOMPSON, Michael; s of Eric Thompson, of Menston, W Yorks, and Mary, *née* Shuttleworth; *b* 18 June 1954; *Educ* Bradford GS, Trinity Coll Cambridge (MA); *m* Linda, *née* Adapoe; 2 s (Christopher, Luke), 1 da (Bethany); *Career* RAF Reservist 1973–76; Freshfields: articled clerk 1977–79, asst slr 1979–85, ptnr Corporate Tax Dept 1985–2005, conslt 2005–; chm Law Soc's Revenue Law Sub-Ctee on Petroleum Taxation, memb UK Oil Industry Tax Ctee Steering Gp; Freeman City of London Slrs' Co 1987; memb Law Soc; *Recreations* sailing, fell walking; *Style*— Michael Thompson, Esq; ✉ Freshfields Bruckhaus Deringer, 65 Fleet Street, London EC4Y 1HS (tel 020 7936 4000, fax 020 7832 7001)

THOMPSON, Michael Reginald; s of Frederick John Thompson (d 2000), of Bramcote, Notts, and Dorothy, *née* Greensmith (d 1987); *b* 19 July 1943; *Educ* High Pavement GS, Univ of Sheffield (MB ChB, MD); *m* 3 Jan 1970, Judith Ann, da of John Hatchett Glover (d 1987), of Stratford-upon-Avon, Warks; 3 da (Hannah Louise b 28 April 1972, Emma Judith b 14 Nov 1975, Victoria Jillian b 24 March 1977); *Career* Nuffield travelling fell 1963, lectr in surgery Univ of Manchester Med Sch 1972–75, Harkness fell Dept of Physiology Univ of Michigan Ann Arbour and VA Centre Wadsworth UCLA 1973–75, sr registrar Bristol Hosps 1975–81, conslt surgn Portsmouth and SE Hants 1981–; chm Nat Audit of Bowel Cancer Ctee (NDOCAP); Assoc of Coloproctology of GB and I: treas 1995–98, sec 1999–2002, pres 2005–06; pres Coloproctology Section RSM (memb Cncl, sec 1996–97), sec Surgical Sub-Section Ctee Br Soc of Gastroenterology 1996–99; pres: Portsmouth and SE Hants Div BMA 1995–96, St Marks Assoc 2005; chm Guidelines Ctee for Bowel Cancer Dept of Health 1999–2000; memb: Br Soc of Gastroenterology, Assoc of Surgns of GB and I, BMA (treas of local branch 1984–2000), RSM; FRCS 1971; *Recreations* sailing, theatre; *Clubs* 83 Surgical Travelling (sec); *Style*— Michael Thompson, Esq; ✉ 5 Teapot Row, Clocktower Drive, Southsea, Hampshire PO4 9YA; The Barn, Sandisbury Lane, Steep, Petersfield, Hampshire GU32 2DP; Queen Alexandra Hospital, Cosham, Portsmouth PO6 3LY (tel 023 9228 6710); BUPA Hospital, Havant, Portsmouth PO9 5NP (tel 023 9245 6000)

THOMPSON, (John) Michael Strutt; s of John Thompson (d 1951), of Weald, Kent, and Donnie Agnes Beatrice, *née* Strutt (d 1979); *b* 14 December 1931; *Educ* Felsted; *m* 24 Oct 1959, Fiona Mary, da of Wing Cdr Malcolm Glassford Begg, MC (d 1969), of Alresford, Hants; 1 s (Marcus Peter Strutt b 1961), 1 da (Julia Mariette (Mrs Gallagher) b 1963); *Career* Nat Serv 2 Lt cmmnd Rifle Bde 1956–58; res sub agent RH & RW Clutton Hursley Estate Hants 1958–65, agent and sec Ernest Cook Tst Fairford Glos 1965–73, chief agent Fitzwilliam Estates Milton Park Peterborough Cambs 1974–97, sec Earl Fitzwilliam Charitable Tst 1997–2007; gen cmmr Income Tax Peterborough 1981–2006; pres: local Cons branch 1981–97, Land Agency and Agric Div RICS 1985–86; chm Landowners' Gp 1987–91; pres: Cambs CLA 1994–96, Longhorn Cattle Soc 1998–2000; FRICS 1956, FAAV 1986; *Recreations* fishing, shooting, golf; *Clubs* Farmers; *Style*— Michael Thompson, Esq; ✉ Top House, Thorpe Langton, Market Harborough, Leicestershire LE16 7TS (tel 01858 545342, fax 01858 545887)

THOMPSON, Sir Michael Warwick; kt (1991); s of Kelvin Warwick Thompson (d 1985), and Madeleine, *née* Walford; *b* 1 June 1931; *Educ* Rydal Sch, Univ of Liverpool (BSc, DSc, Oliver Lodge prizewinner); *m* 1, 1954, Sybil Noreen (d 2000), da of John Rosser Spooner (d 1959); 2 s (Andrew Warwick b 5 Dec 1957, Dr Paul Warwick Thompson, *qv*, b 9 Aug 1959); m 2, Jennifer Ann, da of C Douglas Mitchell; *Career* res scientist AERE Harwell 1953–65, prof of experimental physics Univ of Sussex 1965–80 (pro-vice-chllr 1972–78), vice-chllr UEA 1980–86, vice-chllr and princ Univ of Birmingham 1987–96; tstee Barber Inst of Fine Art 1987–2007; non-exec dir: Alliance & Leicester Building Society (now Alliance & Leicester plc) 1979–2000 (dep chm 1995–99), Cobuild Ltd 1987–96, W Midlands RHA 1990–96 (memb 1987–90, dep chm 1995–96); author of one book, edited works and numerous papers in sci jls; scientific interests incl radiation damage and atomic collisions in solids, nuclear power, its civil applications and energy policy; Inst of Physics C V Boys prizewinner 1972; memb: E Sussex Educn Ctee 1973–78, E Sussex AHA 1973–80, Physics Ctee SRC 1972–79 (sometime chm), Cncl Ctee of Vice-Chllrs and Princs 1989–93 and 1994–96, Cncl Assoc of Commonwealth Univs 1990–95, Cncl Queen Mary & Westfield Coll London 1996–2000; tstee Bart's Med Coll 1998–2000; pres: Bodmin Decorative and Fine Arts Soc 2000–, Fowey River Assoc 2001–07; Hon LLD Univ of Birmingham 1997, Hon DSc Univ of Sussex 1998; FInstP 1964; Grosserverdienst Kreuz (German Federal Republic) 1997; *Recreations* the Arts, sailing, fly fishing, gardening, walking; *Clubs* Athenaeum, Royal Fowey Yacht; *Style*— Sir Michael Thompson; ✉ Readymoney Cottage, 3 Tower Park, Fowey, Cornwall PL23 1JD (tel 01726 833420)

THOMPSON, Nicholas; s of Eric Thompson (d 1975), of Kilmington, Devon, and Dorothy, *née* Lake (d 1982); *b* 25 February 1936; *Educ* Christ's Hosp, Oxford Sch of Architecture (DipArch, Fourth Year Travel bursary), Architects Journal Travel bursary, RIBA Goodwin & Wimperis bursary and medal; *m* Alice Clare, da of Rev Canon Heneage Ferraby; 2 s (Mark b 1968, Paul b 1971); *Career* architect; with Norman and Dawbarn architects 1957–59; 2 Lt RE Hong Kong and Sabah 1960–61; subsequently joined Andrew Renton & Associates, sr ptnr RHWL (Renton Howard Wood Levin Partnership) 1974–, ptnr Arts Team RHWL 1998–; specialises in building design for the performing arts incl: Crucible Theatre Sheffield (Civic Tst & RIBA awards) 1971, Univ of Warwick Arts Centre (RIBA award) 1973, Theatre Royal and Royal Concert Hall Nottingham (both RIBA awards) 1978–82, Duke of York's Theatre London 1979, The Old Vic London (RIBA commendation, Civic Tst award) 1984, Alhambra Theatre Bradford (RIBA regnl award) 1986, Towngate Theatre Basildon 1987, Theatre Royal Newcastle (RIBA regnl award) 1988, New Theatre Cardiff (Civic Tst commendation) 1988, Lyceum Theatre Sheffield (RIBA regnl award and Sheffield City Cncl design award) 1990, New Victoria Theatre Woking 1992, Donmar Warehouse 1992, BBC Radio Drama Studio 1992, Prince Edward Theatre London 1993, Haymarket Theatre Basingstoke 1993, Anvil Concert Hall Basingstoke (RIBA Regnl award) 1994, Chicken Shed Children's Theatre N London 1994, Camberley Hall 1995, Musik Theater Stuttgart 1995, Musik Theater Duisburg 1996, Bridgewater Concert Hall Manchester 1996, refurbishment of Palladium Theatre London, The Dome Concert Hall and Museum Brighton, Greshams Sch Theatre, study for Opera North and Grand Theatre Leeds, study for RSC Stratford, Collins Theatre Islington 1997, Malvern Festival Theatre and Sadler's Wells Theatre 1999, masterplan and boarding houses for Christ's Hospital Sch 1998–2001, renovation of London Coliseum for ENO 1999–2004, Wells Cathedral Sch 2000, masterplan for Central Business District Liverpool 2001; theatre renovation for Sir Cameron Mackintosh, *qv*, incl Prince of Wales, Queen's and Geilgud; refurbishment of Wigmore Hall and Strand Theatre 2003–06; overseas projects incl: theatre consultancy to Shah of Iran, design of Concert Hall and Acad of Music for Sultan of Oman, Nat Theatre Damascus (int competition winner), TV studios for Hutchvision Hong Kong 1991, design concept St James Theatre Wellington NZ 1995, design concept Theatre Royal Sydney and Crown Theatre Melbourne 1996, design conslt Lazaristes Theatre and art gall Thessalonika 1996, conslt Athens Opera House 1997–2004, conslt Gennardius Lecture Theatre American Sch of Classical Studies Athens 2000, designer for reinstatement Fine Arts Building Chicago 2004–; ARIBA 1961, FRSA 1997; *Recreations* outdoors and active by day (travel, sailing, painting, gardening), watching performances by night, collecting modern art; *Clubs* Garrick; *Style*— Nicholas Thompson, Esq; ✉ Arts Team at RHWL, 133 Long Acre, London WC2 (tel 020 7379 7900, fax 020 7836 4881, e-mail nthompson@rhwl.co.uk)

THOMPSON, Sir Nicholas Annesley Marler; 2 Bt (UK 1963), of Reculver, Co Kent; s of Sir Richard Hilton Marler Thompson, 1 Bt (d 1999); *b* 19 March 1947; *Educ* King's Sch Canterbury, Univ of Kent at Canterbury (BA); *m* 1982, Venetia Catherine, yr da of John Horace Broke Heathcote, of Conington House, nr Peterborough; 3 s (Simon William b 1985, Charles Frederick b 1986, David Jonathan b 1990), 1 da (Emma Louise b 1991); *Heir* s, Simon Thompson; *Career* admitted slr 1973, currently sr lawyer CMS Cameron McKenna LLP; memb Westminster City Cncl 1978–86, dep Lord Mayor of Westminster 1983–84; Parly candidate (Cons) Newham South 1983; memb Exec Ctee Standing Cncl of the Baronetage 2003–; *Recreations* foreign travel, walking, theatre, reading, cycling; *Clubs* Carlton; *Style*— Sir Nicholas Thompson, Bt; ✉ Maxgate, George Road, Kingston upon Thames, Surrey KT2 7NR (tel 020 8942 7251); CMS Cameron McKenna, Mitre House, 160 Aldersgate Street, London EC1A 4DD (tel 020 7367 3000, fax 020 7367 2000, e-mail nicholas.thompson@cms-cmck.com)

THOMPSON, Paul; *see:* Warwick Thompson, Dr Paul

THOMPSON, Sir Paul Anthony; 2 Bt (UK 1963), of Walton-on-the-Hill, City of Liverpool; s of Sir Kenneth Pugh Thompson, 1 Bt (d 1984), MP (Cons) for Walton Liverpool 1950–64, Asst PMG 1957–59, and Nanne, Lady Thompson, JP (d 1994), *née* Broome; *b* 6 October 1939; *m* 1971, Pauline Dorothy, da of Robert Orrell Spencer, of Tippett House, Smithills, Bolton, Lancs; 2 s (Richard, David), 2 da (Karena, Nicola); *Heir* s, Richard Thompson; *Career* co dir; *Style*— Sir Paul Thompson, Bt; ✉ Woodlands Farmhouse, Ruff Lane, Ormskirk, Lancashire L39 4UL

THOMPSON, Paul Hungerford; s of Dr A H Thompson (d 1974), and B D Thompson (d 1972); *b* 26 March 1954, London; *m* 1979, Jacqueline; 2 s; *Career* ptnr Bircham Dyson Bell (and predecessor firms) 1982–; *Books* Parliaments and Assemblies of the United Kingdom (1999); *Style*— Paul Thompson, Esq; ✉ Bircham Dyson Bell, 50 Broadway, London SW1H 0DY (tel 020 7227 7064, fax 020 7233 1351, e-mail paulthompson@bdb-law.co.uk)

THOMPSON, Prof Paul Richard; *b* 1935; *Educ* Bishop's Stortford Coll, CCC Oxford, The Queen's Coll Oxford (MA, DPhil), Univ of Aberdeen (DLitt); *m* 1, Thea, *née* Vigne; 1 s (Stephen), 1 da (Sarah); m 2, Natasha Burchardt; 1 da (Esther); m 3, Elaine Bauer; *Career* jr research fell The Queen's Coll Oxford 1961–64; Univ of Essex: lectr in sociology 1964–69, sr lectr 1969–71, reader 1971–88, research prof of social history 1988–; sr research fell Nuffield Coll Oxford 1968–89, visiting prof of art history Johns Hopkins Univ 1972, Hoffman Wood prof of architecture Univ of Leeds 1977–78, Benjamin Meaker prof Univ of Bristol 1987; dir: Nat Life Story Collection 1987–96, Qualidata 1994–2001; sr research fell Inst of Community Studies 2002–; ed: Victorian Soc Conf Reports 1965–67, Oral History 1970–, Life Stories 1985–89, Int Yearbook of Oral History and Life Stories 1992–96, Memory and Narrative 1996–2002; *Books* History of English Architecture (jtly, 1965, 2 edn 1979), The Work of William Morris (1967, new edns 1977 and 1991), Socialists Liberal and Labour: The Struggle for London 1880–1914 (1967), William Butterfield (1971), The Edwardians: The Remaking of British Society (1975, new edn 1992), Living the Fishing (1983), The Voice of the Past: Oral History (3 edn, 2000), I Don't Feel Old (1990), The Myths We Live By (jtly, 1990), The Nineties: Personal Recollections of the 20th Century (1993), Listening for a Change: Oral Testimony and Development (jtly, 1993), Between Generations: Family Models, Myths and Memories (jtly, 1993), City Lives (with Cathy Courtney, 1996), Pathways to Social Class (jtly, 1997), Growing Up in Step Families (jtly, 1997), Narrative and Genre (jtly, 1998), On Living through Soviet Russia (jtly, 2004), Jamaican Hands Across the Atlantic (with Elaine Bauer, 2006); *Recreations* cycling, drawing, music, friendship, travel; *Style*— Prof Paul Thompson; ✉ 5 West Street, Wivenhoe, Essex CO7 9DE (tel 01206 824644, e-mail paulth@youngfoundation.org)

THOMPSON, His Hon Judge Peter John; s of Eric Thompson (d 1967), and Olive Ethel, *née* Miskin (d 1996); *b* 30 December 1943, Ripon, N Yorks; *Educ* Glyn GS Epsom, St Catherine's Coll Oxford (MA), Coll of Law; *m* 23 Aug 1969, Elisabeth Anne Granger, *née* Rees; 2 da (Victoria Jane b 11 Oct 1973, Georgina Kaye b 6 March 1975), 1 s (Oliver Eric b 1 May 1977); *Career* admitted slr England and Wales 1970, slr and barr Supreme Court of Victoria Aust 1972; ptnr: Turner Martin & Symes 1976–91, Eversheds 1991–97; recorder 1993–98 (asst recorder 1988–93), circuit judge 1998–; pres Suffolk and N Essex Law Soc 1995, memb Law Soc 1970; chair Relate Ipswich and Suffolk 1990–96; chair Melton Sports Soccer Club 1979–95; *Recreations* 6-a-side soccer, tennis, jogging, literature, theatre, visiting France and Australia; *Style*— His Hon Judge Thompson; ✉ Ipswich Crown Court, Russell Road, Ipswich, Suffolk IP1 2AG (tel 01473 228585)

THOMPSON, Dr Peter John; s of George Kenneth Thompson (d 1982), and Gladys Pamela, *née* Partington (d 1987); *b* 17 April 1937; *Educ* Chance Tech Coll, Aston Univ (BSc, MSc), CNAA (DTech); *m* 9 Sept 1961, (Dorothy) Ann, da of Frank Smith (d 1969); 1 s (Mark b 1965), 2 da (Nicola b 1968, Louise b 1988); *Career* student apprentice Tube Investments Birmingham 1953–61, lectr and sr lectr Harris Coll Preston 1961–65 and 1968–70, sr sci offr UKAEA Preston 1965–68, princ lectr in prodn engrg Sheffield City Poly 1970–77, dean and head Dept of Engrg Trent Poly Nottingham 1977–83, dep rector Poly of Central London 1983–86, chief exec NCVQ 1986–91, educn and trg conslt 1991–; visiting prof Open Business Sch 1992–96; conslt City & Guilds Sr Awards 1992–94; memb: Mfrg Mech and Prodn Engrg Bd CNAA 1978–85, Ctee for Engrg in Polys 1981–85, Engrg Scis Divnl Bd IMechE 1982–84, Further Educn Unit 1989–91, Cncl Open Coll 1987–89; CEng, FIEE 1979, FIPD 1987; *Recreations* golf, genealogy; *Style*— Dr Peter Thompson; ✉ tel 01442 865127

THOMPSON, Peter John Stuart (Nimble); s of late Douglas Stuart Thompson, and Irene Agnes, *née* Laird, OBE; *b* 28 September 1946; *Educ* Rossall Sch, Univ of Leeds (LLB); *m* 18 July 1970, Morven Mary, da of late Guy Hanscomb; 2 s (Angus Iain Stuart b 1973 d 1988, Archibald Fergus Stuart b 1992), 1 da (Siona Catherine Stuart b 1975); *Career* admitted slr 1971; Eversheds: ptnr 1973–99, managing ptnr 1989–94, sr ptnr Leeds and Manchester 1994–99, dep chm 1995–98; chm: N G Bailey Ltd, TEP Electrical Distributors Ltd; non-exec dir: S Lyles plc 1994–99, Rushbond plc, Scarborough Building Soc, and other companies; chm of govrs Leeds Metropolitan Univ 2000–06, vice-chm of govrs Giggleswick Sch; chm of tstees EUREKA! museum for children, tstee Yorkshire Children's Hosp Fund; chm IoD Yorkshire Region; former chm: Royal Armouries Business Partnership, CIArb NE Branch; memb Law Soc; Hon Dr of Laws Leeds Met Univ; MCIArb, FInstD; *Recreations* fishing, walking and talking; *Clubs* RAC; *Style*— Nimble Thompson, Esq; ✉ The Grange, Kirkby Malzeard, Ripon, North Yorkshire HG4 3RY (tel 01765 658398, e-mail nimble@nimble.entadsl.com)

T

THOMPSON, Rhodri; QC (2002); s of Ralph Thompson (d 1989), and Dilys, *née* Hughes; *b* 5 May 1960, Farnborough, Kent; *Educ* Eastbourne Coll, UC Oxford (MA, BPhil), City Univ (Dip Law); *m* 5 Aug 1989, Paula, *née* Donaghy; 2 da (Oonagh b 17 Oct 1993, Fionnuala b 27 Nov 1999), 1 s (Patrick b 24 Oct 1995); *Career* called to the Bar Middle Temple 1989; practising barr, memb Monckton Chambers 1990–2000, memb Matrix 2000– (chair Mgmnt Ctee 2004–06); memb: Bar European Gp, UK Assoc for European Law; chair of tstees Westgate Chapel Lewes 2004–, tstee Tom Paine Project 2005–; *Publications* Single Market for Pharmaceuticals (1994), EC Law of Competition (contrib, 4, 5 and 6 edns); *Recreations* music, tennis, badminton, golf, walking; *Style*— Rhodri Thompson, Esq, QC; ✉ Matrix, Griffin Building, Gray's Inn, London WC1R 5LN (tel 020 7611 9316, fax 020 7404 3448, e-mail rhodrithompson@matrixlaw.co.uk)

THOMPSON, Richard Henry; s of Lt-Col Richard Louis Thompson (d 1976), and Violet Mary, *née* Harrison (d 1955); *b* 6 August 1936; *Educ* Downside, St Catharine's Coll Cambridge (county major scholarship, MA); *m* 14 July 1962, Cynthia Joan, da of Col

Nicholas Hurst, MC; 2 da (Emma Catharine b 16 April 1963, Lucinda Mary b 20 Aug 1966); *Career* Nat Serv cmmnd RE 1954–56; qualified with Sir Alexander Gibb & Partners 1959–63, exec dir P E Consulting Group Ltd 1964–75, chief exec New Court & Partners Ltd 1976–77; co-fndr and chm: Thompson Clive & Partners Ltd 1978–, Pantheon Hldgs 1988–96, Solon Ventures Ltd 2005–; CEng, MICE 1963, FIMC 1975; *Publications* Real Venture Capital; *Recreations* literature, music, fishing, tennis, golf; *Clubs* Brooks's, Hawks' (Cambridge), Lansdowne, Queen's; *Style*— Richard Thompson, Esq; ✉ Thompson Clive & Partners Ltd, 24 Old Bond Street, London W1S 4AW (tel 020 7535 4900, fax 020 7493 9172)

THOMPSON, Sir Richard Paul Hepworth; KCVO (2003); s of Stanley Henry Thompson (d 1966), and Winifred Lilian Collier (d 2002); *b* 14 April 1940; *Educ* Epsom Coll, Univ of Oxford (MA, DM), St Thomas's Hosp Med Sch; *m* 1974, Eleanor Mary, da of Timothy Noel Joseph Hughes (d 1979); *Career* conslt physician: St Thomas' Hosp 1972–2005, King Edward VII Hosp for Offrs 1982–2005; physician: to the Royal Household 1982–93, to HM The Queen 1993–2005; examiner: in med Soc of Apothecaries 1976–80, Faculty of Dental Surgery RCS 1980–87; govr Guy's Hosp Med Sch 1980–82; memb: Mgmnt Ctee Inst of Psychiatry 1981–95, Mgmnt Ctee King Edward VII's Fund for London 1985–89 and 1992–96, Cncl Royal Med Fndn of Epsom Coll 2003–; vice-chm Cncl Br Heart Fndn 2001–, tstee Thrive 2001–, treas RCP 2003–; Liveryman Worshipful Soc of Apothecaries; FRCP; *Recreations* gardening; *Style*— Sir Richard Thompson, KCVO; ✉ 36 Dealtry Road, London SW15 6NL (tel 020 8789 3839); St Thomas' Hospital, London SE1 7EH (tel 020 7188 2504)

THOMPSON, Robert; *Educ* Lancaster Univ, Keele Univ; *Career* civil servant; former: chief exec of an NHS Tst, dir Strategic Devpt NHS; head Public and Patient Involvement Dept of Health; AIPM, AHSM; *Style*— Robert Thompson, Esq

THOMPSON, (Peter) Robin; s of Robert Leslie Thompson (d 1967), of Bristol, and Ellen Mabel, *née* Gibbons (d 1966); *b* 30 September 1941; *Educ* Farmor's Sch, Hinckley Sch; *m* 27 March 1965, Pauline Ann, da of Frederick Box; 2 s (Julian Guy b 25 July 1967, Dominic Giles b 23 Jan 1971); *Career* chief reporter Wiltshire and Gloucestershire Standard 1963 (joined 1958), sr journalist Bristol Evening Post 1967–73 (acted as corr for most nat media, subsequently specialised in Glos region), first PR offr Reading BC 1973–78 (work incl promotion of the Hexagon Centre), PR mangr to six cos under Vickers Ltd 1978–80, sr practitioner design consultancy 1980–81, founding ptnr Contact Marketing Services (now Earl & Thompson Marketing Ltd) 1981 (chm and jt md until 1996), dep chm The Marketing Services Group plc 1996–97, md Thompson and Wilson Communications 1997, currently mktg conslt; formerly memb SW Regnl Cncl CBI, chm Glos Prince's Tst (presented with commemorative certificate by HRH The Prince of Wales in appreciation of work for the Prince's Tst and volunteers), chm Glos Crimestoppers 1995, dir Business Link Advsy Bd, Pied Piper Appeal for Children's Hosps (children's room named Robin Thompson Room in new Pied Piper funded children's hosp), Cirencester AFC; MIPR 1979, memb PRCA 1989; *Recreations* music, theatre, travel, reading, football, my business; *Clubs* Cirencester Rotary; *Style*— Robin Thompson, Esq; ✉ 8 Morestall Drive, Cirencester, Gloucestershire GL7 1TF (tel 01285 654106, mobile 07966 495908, e-mail pollybox@hotmail.com)

THOMPSON, Simon Robert; s of Robert Sydney Thompson, and Patricia Thompson; *b* 16 June 1959; *Educ* Manchester Grammar, University Coll Oxford (MA); *m* 5 April 1986, Anne Fiona, *née* Graham-Bryce; *Career* Lloyds Bank International 1981–85, NM Rothschild & Sons Ltd 1985–94, dir SG Warburg & Co Ltd 1994–95, head of project finance Minorco SA 1995–97, pres Minorco Brasil 1997–99; Anglo American plc: ceo Zinc 1999–01, ceo Base Matals 2003–04, chm Exploration Div 2003–07, non-exec dir Anglogold Ashanti Ltd 2004–07, chm Tarmac 2004–07, exec dir 2005–07; *Recreations* mountaineering, skiing, reading, cooking; *Clubs* Athenaeum, Alpine Club; *Style*— Simon Thompson, Esq

THOMPSON, Sophie; da of Eric Norman Thompson, and Phyllida Law; *Educ* Camden Sch for Girls, Bristol Old Vic Theatre Sch; *Career* actress; *Theatre* Bristol Old Vic: Perdita in The Winter's Tale, Dulgrett and Ange in Top Girls, Chorus in The Bacchae, Violet in The Merry Gentlemen, Lavinia in Androcles and the Lion, In Times Like These, The Fourth of July; Renaissance Theatre Co: Margaret in Much Ado About Nothing, Celia in As You Like It, Ophelia in Hamlet; RSC: Rosalind in As You Like It, Helena in All's Well That Ends Well, Marcie Banks in Wildest Dreams; other credits incl: The Daughter in The Real Thing (Strand Theatre London), Lika in The Promise (Latchmere Theatre London), Dog in The Garden Girls (Bush Theatre London), Rita in A Prayer for Wings, The Daughter in Laburnum Grove (Palace Theatre Watford), The Maid in A Month in the Country (Cambridge Theatre Co), Laurel in The Chalk Garden (Chichester Festival Theatre), Juliet in Romeo and Juliet (NT Studio), Amy in Company (Albery Theatre London), Baker's Wife in Into the Woods (Donmar Warehouse London), A Period of Adjustment (Palace Theatre Watford), The Schoolmistress (Royal Exchange Theatre Manchester), A Midsummer Night's Dream (NT Studio); *Television* BBC: Clare in Nelson's Column, Gillian Player in A Message to Posterity, A Traveller in Time, The Crucible; other credits incl: Aggie in The Master Blackmailer (Granada), Val in The Complete Guide to Relationships (Kudos Prodns/Carlton), Secret Orchards (Granada), Blind Men (LWT), Mrs Perks in The Railway Children (Carlton); guest appearances on The Phil Cool Show and So What Now with Lee Evans; *Film* credits incl: Mission Girl in The Missionary, Francesca in 21, Lydia in Four Weddings and a Funeral, Mary Musgrave in Persuasion, Miss Bates in Emma, Rose in Dancing at Lughnasa, Moxie in Relative Values, Dorothy in Gosford Park; *Awards* Clarence Derwent Award 1996 (for Company), Best Actress in a Musical Olivier Awards 1999 (for Into the Woods); nominated: Best Supporting Actress Olivier Awards 1994 (for Wildest Dreams), Best Supporting Actress in a Musical Olivier Awards 1996 (for Company), Best Supporting Actress London Film Critics' Circle Awards 2001 (for Relative Values); *Style*— Ms Sophie Thompson; ✉ c/o ICM (tel 020 7636 6565)

THOMPSON, Suki Frances Allison; da of Barry Bunker, of Wales, and Alison Harris, *née* Hayman; *b* 7 March 1967, Wimbledon, London; *Educ* Truro HS, St Austell Coll, Univ of Leeds (BA), Kingston Business Sch; *m* 7 Oct 1995, Alan Thompson; 2 c (Jazmyn b 14 Jan 1998, Sam b 13 Oct 1999); *Career* various communications and advtg agencies incl TBWA, FCA and Rapp Collins 1991–95, md Kendall Tarrant Hong Kong 1996–97; md and fndr: Club Spirit (Bunker Gin) 1998–2000, Haystack Gp 2001–; bd dir Mktg Soc; memb Women in Advtg and Communications London (WACL); *Recreations* running, theatre, cooking, shopping, my children; *Clubs* Morton's (Ambassador); *Style*— Mrs Suki Thompson; ✉ Tylers Green House, School Road, Penn, Buckinghamshire HP10 8EF (tel 01494 814043); The Haystack Group, 8 Hanover Street, London W1 17E, e-mail suki@thehaystackgroup.com)

THOMPSON, Terence James; s of James Andrew Thompson (d 1984), of Burton upon Trent, Staffs, and Irene, *née* Smith (d 1974); *b* 19 January 1928; *Educ* Birmingham Sch of Music; *m* 18 Aug 1951 (m dis 1957); *Career* Band of 1 Bn S Staffs Regt 1946–48; music master West Bromwich Tech HS 1950–59, clarinet tutor Birmingham Sch of Music ca 1955, clarinet teacher Sch of St Mary and St Anne Abbots Bromley 1957–95, head of music March End Sch Wednesfield 1960–66, lectr W Midlands Coll of Higher Educn 1965–89, sr teacher Wolverhampton Music Sch 1968–93; professional clarinettist and saxophonist, numerous published works listed in catalogue of Br Music Info Centre and www.bl.uk; publishers: Chappell & Co Ltd, Schott & Co Ltd, Studio Music; memb: Br Acad of Composers and Songwriters, Schs Music Assoc, Clarinet and Saxophone Soc, Central Composers' Alliance, Black Country Soc, Performing Rights Soc, Mechanical Copyright Protection Soc, Light Music Soc, NUT, Musicians' Union, Br Assoc of Symphonic Bands and Wind Ensembles, Birmingham Conservatoire Assoc; Man of the Year American Biographical Inst 2006; *Recreations* motoring, philately, the canal scene; *Style*— Terence Thompson, Esq; ✉ 58 Willenhall Road, Bilston, West Midlands WV14 6NW (tel 01902 495646, website www.composersalliance.com)

THOMPSON, Prof William; s of William Thompson (d 1969), and Amelia Thompson; *b* 2 February 1937; *Educ* Wallace HS Lisburn, Queen's Univ Belfast (BSc, MB BCh, BAO, MD); *m* 8 July 1961, Anne Elizabeth, da of Professor James Morrison, OBE (d 1987); 3 da (Christine Louise (Mrs Gordon) b 1963, Gillian Claire (Mrs Gordon) b 1967, Karen Anne b 1968), 1 s (Andrew James b 1964); *Career* lectr in obstetrics and gynaecology Univ of Singapore 1968–69, sr lectr and conslt obstetrician and gynaecologist Royal Maternity Hosp Belfast 1970–80, prof and head Dept of Obstetrics and Gynaecology Queen's Univ of Belfast 1980–, conslt obstetrician and gynaecologist Royal Maternity and Royal Victoria Hosps Belfast 1980–; treas Int Fedn of Fertility Socs, chm Med Staff Ctee Royal Maternity Hosp Belfast; memb: Br Med Soc, Gynaecological Visiting Soc; FRCOG; *Books* Fertility and Sterility (1986), Perinatal Medicine (1988); *Recreations* gardening, travelling, photography; *Style*— Prof William Thompson

THOMSON, Alan Matthew; s of George Kerr Thomson (d 1991), and Jean Lees, *née* Gemmell, of Renfrewshire; *b* 6 September 1946; *Educ* Eastwood HS Renfrewshire (capt Scottish Schs football team), Univ of Glasgow (MA); *m* 8 Aug 1973, Linda Mary, da of Peter Hamilton, of W Lothian; 2 da (Jennifer b 5 March 1976, Victoria b 27 June 1987), 2 s (Paul b 26 Sept 1977, Richard b 2 Aug 1983); *Career* professional footballer Glasgow Rangers FC 1962–66, trainee chartered accountant Fleming and Wilson Glasgow 1967–70, auditor Arthur Andersen & Co Glasgow 1970–71, audit mangr Price Waterhouse Paris 1971–75; Rockwell International: fin dir Paris 1975–78, treasy mangr Pittsburgh 1978–79, fin dir UK 1979–82; chief fin offr Raychem Ltd Swindon 1982–84, fin controller Courtaulds Textiles plc 1984–87; fin dir: Courtaulds Coatings 1987–92, The Rugby Group plc 1992–95, Smiths Group plc 1995–2006; non-exec dir Johnson Matthey plc 2002–; MICAS 1970; *Recreations* golf, tennis; *Clubs* Copt Heath Golf; *Style*— Alan Thomson, Esq

THOMSON, Alexander James (Alex); s of Archie Thomson, and Marjorie Thomson; *Educ* Cranbourne Comp Basingstoke, Queen Mary's Coll Basingstoke, UC Oxford, Univ of Cardiff (Dip Journalism); *Children* 2 s (George, Henry (twins) b 2000); *Career* with BBC TV Cardiff 1984, trainee BBC London 1985–86, reporter Spotlight BBC TV Belfast 1986–88, reporter Channel 4 News 1988–98, presenter and chief corr Channel 4 News 1998–; external examiner Cardiff Journalism Sch Univ of Wales 2005; RTS Awards 1990, 1994 and 1998, BAFTA Award 1996, BAFTA Award 2004, series of awards for int war reporting NY Festival and Monte Carlo Festival; hon fell UC Falmouth Sch of Journalism 2006; *Books* Ram Ram India (1985), Smokescreen: The Media and the Gulf War (1991); *Recreations* surfing, natural history, Newcastle United FC; *Style*— Alex Thomson

THOMSON, Andrew Edward; s of Andrew Thomson, of Leven Fife, Scotland, and Margaret Gordon Cairns, *née* Trainer; *b* 26 November 1955; *Educ* Kirkland HS; *m* 18 Sept 1982, Linda June, da of Tony Gerald Leeves; 2 s (Edward Thomas b 24 Aug 1986, David Andrew b 27 Sept 1990); *Career* bowls player; memb Cyphers Indoor Bowling Club, first tournament win Buckhaven Bowls Club Championship 1972; titles: Thames Cockney Classic 1986, Ely Masters Singles 1988 and 1991, Tennants Welsh Classic 1989, UK Singles 1991 and 1992, World Indoor Pairs champion 1993, World Indoor Singles champion 1994 and 1995, Mazda International Singles winner 1994, Woolwich Scottish Master winner 1994, World Outdoor Fours champion 1996, World Indoor Singles runner-up 1997, World Indoor Pairs runner-up 2000; represented Scotland 1979; represented England 1981–: sixth place singles Cwlth Games Edinburgh 1986, fifth place pairs Cwlth Games Auckland 1990, bronze medal pairs Cwlth Games Victoria 1994; records: nat singles indoor 1989, 1990 and 1991 (outdoor 1981), pairs indoor 1986 and 1991, triples indoor 1981, fours indoor 1983, 1984, 1988, 1989 and 1990; *Recreations* football, cricket; *Style*— Andrew Thomson, Esq; ✉ 20 Telford Road, New Eltham, London SE9 3RD; Cyphers Indoor Bowling Club, Kingshall Road, Beckenham, Kent BR3 1LP (tel 020 8778 3889)

THOMSON, Prof Andrew James; s of Andrew Henderson Thomson (d 1997), of Shoreham-by-Sea, W Sussex, and Eva Frances Annie Thomson (d 1979); *b* 31 July 1940; *Educ* Steyning GS, Wadham Coll Oxford (state scholar, BA), Univ of Oxford (DPhil, MA); *m* Anne, da of Jack Marsden; 2 s (Mark Andrew b 29 May 1967, Neil Henderson b 25 March 1969); *Career* research asst prof Dept of Biophysics Michigan State Univ 1965–67; Sch of Chemical Sciences (later Sch of Chemical Sciences and Pharmacy) UEA: sr demonstrator 1967–68, lectr 1968–77, sr lectr 1977–83, reader 1983–84, head Inorganic Chemistry Sector 1984–93, prof of chemistry 1985–, dean 2002–04; dean Faculty of Science UEA 2004–; jt dir UK Centre for Metallobiology 1988–; Silver Medal for analytical spectroscopy RSC 1991, Hugo Müller lectr RSC 1997, Interdisciplinary Award RSC 2002, Chatt lectr RSC 2003; memb: British Biophysical Soc, Biochemical Soc, RSC; FRS 1993; *Recreations* hill walking; *Style*— Prof Andrew Thomson, FRS; ✉ 12 Armitage Close, Cringleford, Norwich NR4 6XZ (tel 01603 504623); School of Chemical Sciences and Pharmacy, University of East Anglia, Norwich NR4 7TJ (tel 01603 593051, e-mail a.thomson@uea.ac.uk)

THOMSON, (Hon) Caroline Agnes Morgan; da of Lord Thomson of Monifieth, KT, PC, DL, FRSE (Life Peer), *qv*, and Grace, *née* Jenkins; *b* 15 May 1954; *Educ* Mary Datchelor Girls' Sch Camberwell London, Univ of York (BA); *m* 1, 12 Nov 1977 (m dis 1981), Ian Campbell Bradley; m 2, 30 July 1983, Roger John Liddle; 1 s (Andrew b 29 Oct 1989); *Career* BBC: trainee BBC News 1975–77, parly reporter 1977–78, sr prodr various radio and TV progs incl Analysis and Panorama 1978–82, dir Policy and Legal 2000–, dir Strategy and Distribution 2005–06, chief operating offr 2006–; political asst to Rt Hon Roy Jenkins MP 1982–83; Channel 4 TV: commissioning ed 1984–90, head of corp affrs 1990–95; BBC World Service: dir of strategy and corp affairs 1995–96, dep md 1996–98, dep chief exec 1998–2000; dir Edinburgh Film Festival 1994–95; chm World Service Tst 1998–2001; non-exec dir: Digital UK, The Pensions Regulator; memb: fell RTS 2007, BAFTA 1988; *Recreations* domesticity; *Style*— Miss Caroline Thomson; ✉ BBC Media Centre, 201 Wood Lane, London W12 7TQ (tel 020 8008 1801, fax 020 8222 6969, e-mail caroline.thomson@bbc.co.uk)

THOMSON, Charles Grant; s of William Eddie Spalding Thomson (d 2000), of Bearsden, Glasgow, and Helen Donaldson, *née* Campbell (d 1994); *b* 23 September 1948; *Educ* Jordanhill Coll Sch, Univ of Glasgow (BSc); *m* 11 July 1970, Pamela Anne, da of Frederick Simpson Mackay (d 1987), of Bearsden, Glasgow; 1 da (Susan b 1975), 1 s (Richard b 1979); *Career* Scottish Mutual Assurance plc (t/o by Abbey National plc 1992): joined 1969, actuary 1990, dir and dep chief exec Scottish Mutual Group 1992–94, dir and actuary Abbey National Life plc 1993–95, dir and actuary Scottish Mutual Assurance plc 1994–95; dir and appointed actuary Scottish Widows Fund and Life Assurance Society 1997–2000 (exec bd dir 1995–2000), dir and actuary Direct Line Life 1997–99, dir and actuary Tesco Personal Finance Life 1998–2000, dir, dep chief exec and actuary Scottish Widows plc 2000, chief exec Equitable Life 2001–; Faculty of Actuaries: memb Cncl 1983–86, 1989–92 and 1997–2000, chm Faculty Examinations Bd 1989–92 (memb 1982–92, sec 1985–89); chm Life Bd of Faculty and Inst of Actuaries 1998–2000; FFA 1973; *Recreations* golf, travel, fine wine; *Clubs* Glasgow Golf, Windyhill Golf, Caledonian; *Style*— Charles Thomson, Esq; ✉ London House, Aldersgate Street, London

THOMSON, Sir (Frederick Douglas) David; 3 Bt (UK 1929), of Glendarroch, Co Midlothian; s of Sir (James) Douglas Wishart, 2 Bt (d 1972), and Bettina, er da of late Lt Cdr David William Shafto Douglas, RN; *b* 14 February 1940; *Educ* Eton, UC Oxford (BA); *m* 1, 1967 (m dis 1994), Caroline Anne, da of late Maj Timothy Stuart Lewis, Royal Scots Greys; 2 s, 1 da; m 2, 2003 Hilary Claire, da of late Sidney Paul Youlden, MC; *Heir* s, Simon Thomson; *Career* dir Ben Line Steamers Ltd 1964–89; chm: Britannia Steamship Insurance Assoc Ltd (dir 1965–), Through Transport Mutual Insurance Assoc Ltd (dir 1973–), S A Meacock & Co Ltd 1996–, The Investment Co plc 2005–; memb Queen's Body Guard for Scotland (Royal Co of Archers); *Clubs* Boodle's; *Style*— Sir David Thomson, Bt; ✉ Holylee, Walkerburn, Peeblesshire EH43 6BD (tel 01896 870673, fax 01896 870461)

THOMSON, David Paget; s of late Sir George Thomson, FRS, Nobel Laureate; *b* 19 March 1931; *Educ* Rugby, Trinity Coll Cambridge; *m* 1959, Patience Mary, da of late Sir Lawrence Bragg, CH, MC, FRS, Nobel Laureate; 2 s, 2 da; *Career* Lt Cdr RNR, joined Lazard Bros & Co Ltd 1956, md 1966, seconded HM Foreign Service 1971–73, economic counsellor Bonn, Lazards 1973–86; chm: Jufcrest Ltd 1985–88, F & C German Investment Tst plc 1990–98, Dresdner RCM Emerging Markets plc 1993–2001; memb Monopolies and Mergers Cmmn 1984–94, DG Br Invisible Exports Cncl 1987–89, dir Wesleyan Assurance Ltd 1997–2000; chm: Cncl The Royal Instn 1985–87, Portsmouth Naval Base Property Tst 1992–98, Fitzwilliam Museum Tst Cambridge 1988–93, Med Sickness Soc 1995–97; dir F & C Eurotrust plc 1998–2001, tstee Lucy Cavendish Coll Cambridge 1987–98; Past Master Co of Plumbers; *Clubs* Athenaeum (chm 1995–98); *Style*— David Thomson, Esq; ✉ Little Stoke House, Wallingford, Oxfordshire OX10 6AX (tel 01491 837161, fax 01491 826795)

THOMSON, Maj-Gen David Phillips; CB (1993), CBE (1989), MC (1965); s of Cyril Robert William Thomson (d 1957), and Louise Mary, *née* Phillips (d 1984); *b* 30 January 1942; *Educ* Eastbourne Coll, RMA Sandhurst (Earl Wavell Meml Prize, Brian Philpott Mil History Prize); *Career* cmmnd Argyll and Sutherland Highlanders 1962, Bde Maj 6th Armoured Bde 1975, instr Staff Coll 1980, CO 1st Bn The Argyll and Sutherland Highlanders 1982, COS RMCS 1985, COS 1st Armoured Div 1986, Cdr 1st Infantry Bde/UK Mobile Force 1987, sr Army memb RCDS 1992–95; Col The Argyll and Sutherland Highlanders, Capt of the Royal Castle of Tarbert 1992–2000; despatches 1968 and 1992; chm Sussex Combined Services Museum Tst 1997–2007; chm Carlisle Grange Residents Co Ltd 1997–; FRGS; *Recreations* golf, historical research; *Style*— Maj-Gen D P Thomson, CB, CBE, MC; ✉ c/o Home Headquarters, The Argyll and Sutherland Highlanders, The Castle, Stirling FK8 1EH (tel 01786 475165)

THOMSON, Elizabeth Mary; da of Frederick William Charles Thomson, and Catherine Edna, *née* Fardell (d 1999); *b* 12 September 1957; *Educ* East Barnet Sch, Univ of Liverpool (BA); *Career* publishing asst Arabian Publications 1980, music ed Music Sales and Omnibus 1980–82, freelance ed 1983; Publishing News: editorial asst rising to feature writer 1984–97, assoc ed 1998–2003, ed 2003–; ed Books 1995–2003; visiting fell Open Univ Sixties Res Gp 1999–2002; memb: Soc of Bookmen, Soc of Authors, PEN, NUJ; *Publications* Conclusions on the Wall: New Essays on Bob Dylan (1980), Folk Songs and Dances of England (1982), Folk Songs and Dances of Scotland (1982), The Lennon Companion (co-ed, 1987 and 2004), The Dylan Companion (co-ed, 1990, revised edn 2001), The Bowie Companion (co-ed, 1993); book contrib: Turning On: Rock in the Late Sixties (1985), Whitaker's Almanack (1996), The New Grove Dictionary of Music & Musicians (revised edn, 2001); newspaper and magazine contrib: The Times, Sunday Telegraph, The Independent, The Listener, Books & Bookmen, New Statesman & Society, Bulletin, Chic (literary ed 1993–94), Classical Music, Mojo; *Recreations* music, travel, photography; *Clubs* London Press; *Style*— Ms Elizabeth Thomson; ✉ Birchwood Mansions, 133 Fortis Green Road, London N10 3LX (e-mail lizthomson@publishingnews.co.uk)

THOMSON, Gordon; s of John Thomson, and Kate Beveridge; *b* 13 January 1972, Falkirk; *Educ* St Katherine's Sch Bristol, Univ of Glasgow (MA); *m* 12 Sept 2003, Lydia, *née* Chambers; 1 s (Charlie b 1 Feb 1999), 2 da (Grace b 19 Oct 2000, Ava b 24 June 2004); *Career* contributing ed Goal 1997–98, freelance writer 1997–99, asst prodr Sky Sports News 1999; Maxim (UK): commisioning ed 1999–2000, sr ed 2000–02; dep ed Observer Sport Monthly 2002–04, ed Time Out 2004–; shortlisted New Ed of the Year BSME Awards 2005; *Books* The Man in Black (1998); *Recreations* cooking, eating out, squash, cinema, music, golf, exploring London with family, the arts; *Clubs* Groucho, Scotch Malt Whisky Soc; *Style*— Gordon Thomson, Esq; ✉ Time Out Magazine, Universal House, 251 Tottenham Court Road, London W1T 7AB (tel 020 7813 6118, e-mail gordonthomson@timeout.com)

THOMSON, Grant Hugh; s of Albert Edward Thomson (d 1976), and Muriel Frances, *née* Craggs (d 1986); *b* 11 November 1935; *m* 1, 1959 (m dis), Vera Anne, da of H Cibula; 1 da; m 2, 1985, Mary Rayleigh, da of Harold Stanfield Strutt; *Career* served HM Forces RAF photographer II 1954–60, photographer Guided Weapons and Aircraft Divs BAC 1960–64, photographic mangr BKS Surveys Ltd 1964–67, tech servs product specialist (aerial) Ilford Ltd 1967–72, lectr Int Inst for Aerospace Survey and Earth Scis (ITC) Enschede The Netherlands 1972–74; photographic mangr: Hunting Technical Services Ltd, Hunting Surveys and Consultants Ltd 1974–95; convener RPS Aerospace Imaging Section 1987–2004; independent conslt to commercial and govt remote sensing orgns in the UK and overseas; author of numerous pubns relating to aerospace photography in various photographic jls; hon memb Photogrammetric Soc 1998; FRPS 1985, FBIPP 1987, FRAS 1997, FBIS 1998; *Clubs* Medmenham (assoc memb); *Style*— Grant H Thomson, Esq; ✉ 57 Winslow Field, Great Missenden, Buckinghamshire HP16 9AR

THOMSON, Ian; s of John Murray Thomson (d 2002), and Ingrid, *née* Haugas; *b* 24 June 1961, London; *Educ* Dulwich Coll, Univ of Cambridge (MA); *m* 1991, Laura, da of Dr John Fleminger, and Dr Ruth Jackson; *Career* freelance writer and journalist 1983–; RSL W H Heinemann Award 2003; affiliate London Haiti Support Gp; FRSL 2004; *Books* Southern Italy (1989), Bonjour Blanc: A Journey Through Haiti (1990), Primo Levi: A Life (2002); *Clubs* The Academy; *Style*— Ian Thomson, Esq; ✉ c/o PFD, Drury House, 34–43 Russell Street, London WC2B 5HA (tel 020 7344 1000, fax 020 7836 9539, e-mail postmaster@pfd.co.uk)

THOMSON, James Phillips Spalding; s of Dr James Laing Spalding Thomson, and Peggy Marion, *née* Phillips; *b* 2 October 1939; *Educ* Haileybury and ISC, Middx Hosp Med Sch London (MB BS, LRCP, DObstRCOG, MS); *m* 1968, Dr Anne Katharine Thomson, MRCP, da of Richard Derek Richards, FRCS; 1 s (James Richards Phillips b 2 Feb 1971), 3 da (Rebecca Jane Katharine b 21 Aug 1973, Sally Anne Charlotte b 9 Feb 1979, Georgina Mary Caroline b 22 Jan 1985); *Career* jr med and surgical appts: Kettering Gen Hosp 1962, Middx Hosp 1963, 1968, 1969 and 1971–74, Cheltenham Gen Hosp 1966–67, Central Middx Hosp 1970, St Mark's Hosp 1970–71; demonstrator Dept of Anatomy Middx Hosp Med Sch 1964–66, pt/t hon conslt surgn St John's Hosp for Diseases of the Skin 1973–75; conslt surgn: St Mark's Hosp 1974–99 (clinical dir 1990–97, now emeritus conslt surgn), Royal Northern Hosp 1975–77, Hackney and Homerton Hosps 1977–90, Central Middlesex Hosp 1999; hon conslt surgn St Luke's Hosp for the Clergy 1976–99 (vice-chm Cncl 1992–2003), hon conslt surgn St Mary's Hosp 1982–99; civil conslt in surgery RAF 1984–99 (now hon conslt surgn), civilian conslt in colorectal surgery RN 1986–99 (now emeritus conslt in surgery), hon conslt advsr in surgery Ileostomy Assoc of GB and Ireland 1986–99, hon sr lectr in surgery Bart's Med Coll 1977–94, hon sr clinical lectr in surgery Imperial Coll Sch of Med 1994–99; memb RCS Ct of Examiners, examiner in surgery at Univs of Cambridge, Liverpool and London; convenor Gatherings for Holders of Lambeth Degrees 1990–; administrator The Priory Church of St Bartholomew the Great W Smithfield 2000–02, master Sutton's Hosp in Charterhouse 2001–; Liveryman: Worshipful Soc of Apothecaries, Worshipful Co of Barbers; memb: Travelling Surgical Soc (sec 1982–90, pres 1999–2002), Surgical Research Soc, Br Soc of Gastroenterology (memb Ctee Surgical Section 1986–88), Assoc of Coloproctology of GB and Ireland (sec 1989–90), NE Thames Metropolitan Surgical Soc, BMA, Med Soc for the Study of Venereal Disease, RN Med Club, Military Surgical Soc; associate memb Br Assoc of Clinical Anatomists; Section of Coloproctology RSM: memb Cncl 1983–, vice-pres 1986–88 and 1990–94, hon sec 1988–90, pres 1994–95, Frederick Salmon Medal 1996; pres: Friends of St mark's Hosp 2005–, Haileybury Soc 2006–07; tstee: Rev Dr George Richards Charity 2001–, Medical Coll of St Bartholomew's Hosp Tst 2002–, St Andrew's (Holborn) Fndn 2003–; DM (Lambeth) 1987; fell Queen Mary Univ of London 2006–; fell Assoc of Surgns of GB and Ireland (memb Cncl 1983–86), fell Hunterian Soc (memb Cncl 1994–97, pres-elect 2000–01, pres 2001–02), patron and fell Burgon Soc 2003–; FRCS 1969 (MRCS 1962); *Books* Colorectal Disease - An Introduction for Surgeons and Physicians (jtly, 1981), Frontiers in Colorectal Disease (jtly, 1986), Updates in Coloproctology (jtly, 1992), Familial Adenomatous Polyposis (jtly, 1994); also author of pubns and chapter contribs to books mainly on colon and rectal surgery; *Recreations* church music, railways and canals; *Clubs* Athenaeum, RSM; *Style*— James P S Thomson, Esq, DM, MS, FRCS; ✉ Master's Lodge, Charterhouse, Charterhouse Square, London EC1M 6AN (tel 020 7253 0272, mobile 07801 648802, e-mail jamespsthomson@aol.com); St Martin's House, The Street, Hindringham, Norfolk NR21 0PR (tel 01328 822093)

THOMSON, Sir John Adam; GCMG (1985, KCMG 1978, CMG 1972); s of Sir George Paget Thomson, FRS (d 1975), sometime Master CCC Cambridge, and Kathleen Buchanan, *née* Smith (d 1941); *b* 27 April 1927; *Educ* Phillips Exeter Acad USA, Univ of Aberdeen, Trinity Coll Cambridge; *m* 1, 1953, Elizabeth Anne McClure (d 1988); 3 s, 1 da; m 2, 1992, Judith Ogden Bullitt; *Career* joined FO 1950, head of Planning Staff FO 1967, on secondment to Cabinet Office as chief of Assessments Staff 1968–71, min and dep perm rep N Atlantic Cncl 1972–73, head UK Delgn MBFR Exploratory Talks in Vienna 1973, asst under sec FCO 1973–76, high cmmr to India 1977–82, UK perm rep UNO NY and UK rep Security Cncl (with personal rank of ambass) 1982–87, chm CSCE rapporteur mission to Bosnia-Hercegovina 1992, memb CSCE mission to Albania 1994; dir ANZ Grindlays Bank 1987–96 (int advsr 1996–), chm Fleming Emerging Markets Investment Trust plc 1991–; princ dir 21 Century Trust London 1987–90, memb Howie Ctee on Sch Educn in Scot, tstee Nat Museums of Scot 1990–, memb Cncl Int Inst of Strategic Studies 1987–96, chm Minority Rights Gp International 1991–; tstee: Univ of Aberdeen Devpt Tst 1989–, Indian Nat Tst for Art and Cultural Heritage (UK) 1989–, Inst for Advanced Studies in the Humanities Edinburgh 1991–; memb Governing Body: Inst of Devpt Studies, Overseas Devpt Inst, 21 Century Tst; dir's visitor Inst for Advanced Study Princeton USA 1995–96; assoc memb Nuffield Coll Oxford 1987–91; *Books* Crusader Castles (co-author with R Fedden, 1956); *Recreations* hill walking; *Clubs* Athenaeum, Century (New York); *Style*— Sir John Thomson, GCMG; ✉ Fleming Emerging Markets Investment Trust plc, 25 Copthall Avenue, London EC2R 7DR

THOMSON, John K; s of Sir Ian Thomson, KBE, CMG, of Edinburgh, and Nancy, *née* Kearsley (d 1988); *b* 17 February 1950; *Educ* St Kentigern Coll Auckland, Edinburgh Acad, Univ of Strathclyde (BA), Univ of Oxford (Dip Econ Devpt); *m* July 1973, Lorna, da of Allan White; 1 s (Alastair b Aug 1991); *Career* research economist South Pacific Bureau for Economic Co-operation Fiji 1973–75, research offr Scottish Cncl (Devpt and Industry) Edinburgh 1976–80, analyst Scottish Investment Trust Edinburgh 1980–82; Standard Life: investment mangr 1982–94, asst gen mangr (Devpt) 1994–96, chief investment mangr 1996–97; md Stewart Ivory 1998–2000, md Ailsa Capital Mgmnt 2001–03, chm RIA Capital Markets 2004–; MSI 1993; *Recreations* gardening, walking; *Style*— John K Thomson

THOMSON, Brig John Reid; QVRM (2003), TD (1988); s of Alexander Patrick Thomson (d 2001), and Helen, *née* Reid; *b* 17 August 1953; *Educ* Dalry HS Ayrshire, RMA Sandhurst, Univ of Southampton (BA), Strathclyde Grad Business Sch (MBA), CIM (DipM), Inst of Direct Mktg (Dip Direct Mktg); *Career* cmmnd RA 1973; HM Armed Forces (Army) 1971–76, TA 1976– (dep inspr gen 2000–03); accountant then fin dir then md London 1979–86, business devpt dir Edinburgh 1987–91, dir of open learning (MBA prog) and sr lectr in marketing Napier Univ Business Sch 1991–, non-exec dir Imumed International Germany 2000–02; int mgmnt conslt; completed major projects in: Switzerland, Belarus, Germany, UK; ADC to HM The Queen 1997–2003; conslt and friend Hopetoun House Preservation Tst, supporter and friend RA Heritage Appeal, past chm and memb Scottish Vol Offrs' Charity Ball Ctee; chm: City of Edinburgh Artillery Offrs Assoc 2000–05, Nat Artillery Assoc 2003–, Scottish Artillery Historical Soc 2005–; Hon Col Glasgow & Strathclyde Univs OTC 1998–, Hon Col Cmdt Royal Regt of Artillery 2001–, Hon Col 105 Regt RA (Volunteers) 2004–; Freeman City of London 1985; MILT 2001, FCIM 2007; *Recreations* equestrian, tennis, swimming, walking, gardening, arts; *Clubs* Royal Scot (Edinburgh); *Style*— Brig John Thomson, QVRM, TD; ✉ Napier University Business School, Craiglockhart Campus, Edinburgh EH14 1DJ (tel 0131 455 4406, fax 0131 455 4540, e-mail jo.thomson@napier.ac.uk)

THOMSON, Prof Joseph McGeachy; s of James Thomson, of Campbeltown, and Catherine Morrans, *née* McGeachy; *b* 6 May 1948; *Educ* Keil Sch Dumbarton, Univ of Edinburgh (LLB); *m* 1999, Annie Iverson; *Career* lectr: Univ of Birmingham 1970–74, KCL 1974–84; prof of law Univ of Strathclyde 1984–90, regius prof of law Univ of Glasgow 1991–2005; Scottish law cmmr 2000–, dep gen ed Stair Meml Encyclopaedia of the Laws of Scotland 1985–96; FRSE 1996, FRSA 1996, Hon FSALS 2001; *Books* Contract Law in Scotland (with Hector L McQueen, 2000, 2 edn 2007), Delictual Liability (3 edn, 2004), Scots Private Law (2006), Family Law in Scotland (5 edn, 2006); *Recreations* opera, ballet, food and wine; *Clubs* Scottish Art; *Style*— Prof Joseph Thomson, FRSE; ✉ 27 Howe Street, Edinburgh EH3 6TF (tel 0131 652 3870); Scottish Law Commission, 140 Causewayside, Edinburgh EH9 1PR (tel 0131 668 2131, e-mail joseph.thomson@scotlawcom.gov.uk)

THOMSON, Malcolm George; QC (Scot 1987); s of George Robert Thomson, OBE (d 1987), and Daphne Ethel, *née* Daniels; *b* 6 April 1950; *Educ* The Edinburgh Acad, Univ of Edinburgh (LLB); *m* 18 March 1978 (m dis 2001), Susan Gordon, da of Gordon Aitken (d 1997); 2 da (Victoria b 1982, Jacqueline b 1989); *Career* advocate at the Scottish Bar 1974, barr Lincoln's Inn 1991; standing jr counsel 1982–87: Dept of Agriculture and Fisheries for Scotland, The Forestry Cmmn Scotland; temp judge Court of Session Scotland 2002–; Scottish case ed Current Law 1977–96, ed Scots Law Times Reports 1989–2003, chm NHS Tbnl (Scotland) 1995–2005, memb Scottish Legal Aid Bd 1998–2006; *Recreations* sailing, skiing; *Clubs* New (Edinburgh); *Style*— Malcolm Thomson, Esq, QC; ✉ 12 Succoth Avenue, Edinburgh EH12 6BT (tel 0131 337 4911); Advocates Library, Parliament House, Edinburgh EH1 1RF (tel 0131 226 5071)

THOMSON, Sir Mark Wilfrid Home; 3 Bt (UK 1925), of Old Nunthorpe, Co York; s of Sir Ivo Wilfrid Home Thomson, 2 Bt (d 1991), and his 1 w, Sybil Marguerite, *née* Thompson; *b* 29 December 1939; *m* 1976 (m dis 1996), Lady Jacqueline Rosemary Margot Rufus Isaacs, o da of 3 Marquess of Reading; 1 da (Daisy Jacqueline Carol b 1977), 3 s (Albert Mark Home b 1979, Jake Michael Alfred, Luke Ivo Charles (twins) b 1983); *Heir* s, Albert Thomson; *Style*— Sir Mark Thomson, Bt; ✉ 148 Oakwood Court, Abbotsbury Road, London W14 8JS

THOMSON, Neil Alexander; s of Alexander and Irene Thomson; *b* 17 May 1959; *Educ* Aberdeen HS, Aberdeen Coll of Commerce (Scot HND), Middlesex Business Sch (MBA);

T

m 29 June 1985, Karen Ann, da of George McGregor; 1 da (Cassia b 3 June 1991); *Career* CA 1983; roles at PPHN, Courtalds Coatings, PA Consulting, and Deloittes Haskins & Sells, chief operating offr St Lukes Communications Ltd 1995–; dir Job Ownership Ltd; ACMA 1985, MBIM 1987; *Recreations* running half marathons, fitness training, chess; *Style—* Neil Thomson, Esq; ✉ St Lukes Communications Ltd, 22 Dukes Road, London WC1H 9AD (tel 020 7380 8888, fax 020 7380 8899)

THOMSON, Prof Neil Campbell; s of late Prof Adam Simpson Turnbull Thomson, of Ayr, and late Margaret Campbell, *née* Templeton; *b* 3 April 1948; *Educ* Spiers Sch Beith, Univ of Glasgow (MB ChB, MD); *m* 16 Aug 1973, Lorna Jean, da of late William Sim Walker Fraser, of Perth; 2 s (David Fraser b 10 July 1976, Andrew Campbell b 8 May 1978), 1 da (Jennifer Lorna b 22 May 1985); *Career* jr hosp doctor Glasgow Teaching Hosps 1972–80, res fell McMaster Univ Ontario Canada 1980–81, conslt physician Western Infirmary Glasgow 1982–, hon prof Univ of Glasgow 1996–, prof of respiratory med Univ of Glasgow 2001; chm Res Ctees: Br Lung Fndn, The Nat Asthma Campaign; memb: Advsy Bd MRC, Ctee on the Safety of Med 1999–2001; memb: Assoc of Physicians (memb Exec 2003–06), Br Thoracic Soc (former hon sec), American Thoracic Soc, Scot Soc of Physicians, Br Soc for Allergy and Clinical Immunology; FRCP; *Books* Handbook of Clinical Allergy (1990), Asthma: Basic Mechanisms and Clinical Management (1988, 3 edn 1998), Manual of Asthma Management (1995, 2 edn 2001), Astham and COPD: Basic Mechanisms and Clinical Management (2002); *Recreations* fishing, gardening, hill walking; *Style—* Prof Neil Thomson; ✉ Department of Respiratory Medicine, University of Glasgow and Western Infirmary, Glasgow G11 6NT (tel 0141 211 3241, fax 0141 211 3464, e-mail n.c.thomson@clinmed.gla.ac.uk)

THOMSON, Robert James; s of Henry James Thomson, of Wangaratta, Aust, and Gen Amelda Gaffy; *b* 11 March 1961; *m* 25 April 1992, Ping Wang; 2 s (Luke Qiao-Rui b 21 Jan 2000, Jack Hong-Yi b 8 Jan 2002); *Career* fin and gen affrs reporter then Sydney corr The Herald (Melbourne) 1979–83; Sydney Morning Herald: sr feature writer 1983–85 (nomination Aust Journalist of the Year), Beijing corr (jtly writing for FT) 1985–89; FT: Tokyo corr 1989–94, foreign news ed 1994–96, ed Weekend FT and asst ed FT 1996–98, managing ed US edn of FT 1998–2002; ed The Times 2002–; dir US Advsy Bd FTSE 2000–02, dir and chm Arts International 2000–02; dir Soc of American Business Eds and Writers 2001–02, memb Bd Knight-Bagelot Fellowship Columbia Univ; US Business Journalist of the Year The Journalist and Financial Reporting (TJFR) 2001; *Publications* The Judges - A Portrait of the Australian Judiciary (1986), The Chinese Army (co-author, 1990), True Fiction (ed, 1998); *Recreations* reading, tennis, cinema; *Style—* Robert Thomson; ✉ The Times, Times House, 1 Pennington Street, London E98 1TT (tel 020 7782 5000)

THOMSON, Dr Wendy; CBE (2005); da of Shirley Basil Thomson (d 1970), and Grace, *née* Frazer; *b* 28 October 1953; *Educ* Verdun HS, McGill Univ Montreal (Dip Collegial Studies, Batchelor of Social Work, Master of Social Work), Univ of Bristol (PhD); *Children* 1 adopted da (Mia Xiu Zhi Thomson b 14 Oct 2001), 2 step s (Samuel Dorne b 11 Feb 1983, Jack Dorne b 12 Feb 1985); *Career* pt/t sessional lectr McGill Univ Montreal 1977–81, exec dir Head and Hands (Montreal) 1976–80, exec dir West Island Association for People with Learning Disabilities (Quebec) 1981–82, sr programmes offr GLC 1985–86, head of fin and programmes London Strategic Policy Unit (LSPU) 1986–87, asst chief exec Islington Cncl 1987–93, chief exec Turning Point 1993–96, chief exec London Borough of Newham 1996–99, dir of inspection Audit Cmmn 1999–2001, head OPSR 2001–05, seconded as chief exec Local Government Leadership Centre 2004–05, prof and dir Sch of Social Work McGill Univ Montreal 2005–; *Books* incl: Bureaucracy and Community (contrib, 1990), Citizen's Rights in a Modern Welfare System (contrib, 1992), Management for Quality in Local Government (contrib, 1992), Fitness for Purpose: Shaping new Patterns for Organisations and Management (co-author, 1993); also contrib to various other publications and author numerous conf papers; *Recreations* reading, gardening, shopping; *Style—* Dr Wendy Thomson, CBE

THOMSON OF MONIFIETH, Baron (Life Peer UK 1977), of Monifieth in the District of the City of Dundee; George Morgan Thomson; KT (1981), PC (1966), DL (1992); s of late James Thomson, of Monifieth, Angus; *b* 16 January 1921; *Educ* Grove Acad Dundee; *m* 1948, Grace, da of Cunningham Jenkins, of Glasgow; 2 da (Caroline Agnes Morgan Thomson, *qv* (Hon Mrs Liddle) b 1954, Hon Ailsa Ballantine (Rev Lady Newby) b 1956); *Career* on staff of Dandy rising to chief sub ed 1930s; asst ed then ed Forward 1946–53; MP (Lab) Dundee East 1952–72; min of State FO 1964–66, chllr of Duchy of Lancaster 1966–67 and 1969–70, joint min of state FO 1967, sec of state for Cwlth Affrs 1967–68, min without portfolio 1968–69, shadow def min 1970–72; EEC cmmr 1973–77; chm: Euro Movement in Br 1977–80, Advertising Standards Authy 1977–80; dir: ICI plc 1977–90, Woolwich Equitable Building Soc 1979–91, Royal Bank of Scotland Group 1977–90, English National Opera 1987–93, Value and Income Tst 1986–2000; First Crown Estate cmmr 1978–80, chm IBA 1981–88, vice-pres Royal TV Soc 1982–88, vice-chm Euro Inst of Media 1989–94; pres: History of Advertising Tst 1985–99, Voice of Listener and Viewer 1990–; chllr Heriot-Watt Univ 1977–91; tstee: Pilgrim Tst, Thomson Fndn; chm of tstees Leeds Castle Fndn 1994–2001; memb Nolan Ctee 1994–97; Lib Dem spokesman foreign affrs and broadcasting House of Lords 1989–98; chm Scottish Peers Assoc 1996–98; Gold medal Euro Assoc of Advtg Agencies 1994; Hon LLD Dundee 1967, Hon DLitt Heriot-Watt 1973, Hon DSc Aston 1976, Hon DLitt New Univ of Ulster 1984, Hon DCL Kent 1989, FRSE 1985; *Style—* The Rt Hon the Lord Thomson of Monifieth, KT, PC, FRSE; ✉ House of Lords, London SW1A 0PW (tel 020 7219 6718)

THORBEK, Erik; s of Kai Birch (d 1988), and Dr Agro Grete Thorbek; *b* 10 January 1941; *Educ* Billum Coll Denmark; *m* 6 April 1963, Susan Margaret, da of Sidney Gair (d 1977); 2 s (Alexander b 1964, Nikolas b 1973), 2 da (Francesca b 1966, Natasha b 1975); *Career* chm and chief exec H & T Walker Ltd 1963–; *Recreations* fine dining, travel, sailing, skiing, golf, horse racing, shooting; *Clubs* Turf, Helford River Sailing, Mullian Golf, Marks, Harry's Bar, Annabel's; *Style—* Erik Thorbek; ✉ Landewednack House, Church Cove, The Lizard, Cornwall TR12 7PQ

THORBURN, Andrew; s of James Beresford Thorburn (d 1972), and Marjorie Clara Thorburn (d 1987); *b* 20 March 1934; *Educ* Bridport GS, Univ of Southampton (BSc); *m* 1957, Margaret Anne, da of Reginald Crack (d 1964); 1 s (Edward), 2 da (Jenny, Anna); *Career* dir Notts/Derbys Sub-Regnl Study 1968–70, county planning offr of E Sussex 1973–83, chief exec English Tourist Bd 1983–85, head of tourism and leisure Grant Thornton 1986–90, princ Thorburns (leisure planning consultancy) 1990–, chm Bow Street Partners Ltd 1999–2005; pres Royal Town Planning Inst 1982; memb: Int Soc of City and Regnl Planners, Town and Country Planning Assoc; fell Tourism Soc; FRTPI; *Books* Planning Villages (1971), The Missing Museum (2006); *Recreations* sailing; *Style—* Andrew Thorburn, Esq; ✉ 1 Mill House, Lower Quay, Fareham, Hampshire PO16 0RH (tel 01329 825251)

THORBURN, Dr Samuel; CBE (2004, OBE 1987); s of Samuel Thorburn, MBE (d 1984), of Strathclyde, and Isabella Thorburn (d 1983); *b* 15 October 1930; *Educ* Hamilton Acad, Royal Technical Coll (now Univ of Strathclyde); *m* 1953, Margaret Elizabeth May; 1 s (David John b 1958), 1 da (Lynne Margaret b 1967); *Career* design and construction engr Colvilles Ltd 1951–58, chief engr Whatlings Foundations Ltd 1958–61; engrg dir: Caledonian Foundations Ltd 1961–64, GKN Foundations Ltd 1964–66; Thorburn Gp: fndr 1966, dir Thorburn Associates 1966–90, dir Thorburn plc 1990–92, gp conslt 1992–99; tstee and visiting prof Univ of Strathclyde; pres IStructE 1997–98; chm: Certification Advsy Cncl for the Service Sector, Int Ctee on Professional Practice Int Soc of Soil Mechanics and Fndn Engrg, Ctee responsible for Govt Guide to Safety at Sports Grounds, Ctee responsible for Guidance on Temporary Demountable Structures, Building Standards Advsy Ctee Scottish Exec, Scottish Registration Bd for Certifiers of Design (Building Structures), Advsy Ctee David Livingstone Centre for Sustainability 2007–; memb: Cncl and Exec Ctee ICE, Football Licensing Authy, Standing Ctee on Structural Safety; conslt Dept of Energy, specialist advsr to Home Office and Defence Ctees House of Commons, advsr Br design and construction of bridge fndns; former memb Tech Advsy Ctee: BSI, CIRIA, Science and Research Cncl, DOE, Dept of Energy; former chm Tech Ctee: IStructE, ICE; Oscar Faber award IStructE 1970, Rear Adm John Garth Watson medal 1993, Gold medal IStructE 2003; Freeman Citizen of Glasgow; FICE 1967, FIStructE 1970, FASCE 1971, FREng 1984; *Publications* Underpinning (1985), Underpinning and Retention (1992), author of numerous papers and contribs to publications on engrg; *Recreations* golf, painting, gardening; *Style—* Dr Sam Thorburn, CBE, FREng; ✉ 32 Lochbroom Drive, Newton Mearns, East Renfrewshire G77 5PF (tel 0141 639 2724, fax 0141 616 0223)

THORLEY, Simon Joe; QC (1989); s of Sir Gerald Bowers Thorley, TD (d 1988), and Beryl Preston, *née* Rhodes (who m 2, Sir David Lancaster Nicolson (d 1996)); *b* 22 May 1950; *Educ* Rugby, Keble Coll Oxford (MA); *m* 7 May 1983, Jane Elizabeth, da of Frank Cockcroft, of Saltburn by Sea, Cleveland; 2 s (Matthew b 1984, Nicholas b 1985), 1 da (Francesca b 1988); *Career* called to the Bar Inner Temple 1972 (bencher 1999); barr specialising in patent matters; appointed to hear Trade Mark Appeals 1996–2003, dep chm Copyright Tbnl 1997–2006, dep judge of the High Court 1998–; chm Intellectual Property Bar Assoc (formerly Patent Bar Assoc) 1995–99, memb Bar Cncl 1995–99; *Books* Terrell on Patents (jt ed, 13, 14, 15 and 16 edn); *Recreations* family, shooting, opera; *Style—* Simon Thorley, Esq, QC; ✉ 3 New Square, Lincoln's Inn, London WC2A 3RS (tel 020 7405 1111, fax 020 7405 7800)

THORN, Jeremy Gordon; s of James Douglas Thorn (d 1999), of Appleton, Cheshire, and Daphne Elizabeth, *née* Robinson; *b* 23 March 1948; *Educ* Mill Hill Sch, Univ of Leeds (BSc), European Coll of Marketing (Dip), Cranfield Sch of Mgmnt, London Business Sch, Oxford Psychologists; *m* 24 July 1971 (m dis 1997), Èilis Anne, da of Christopher Maurice Coffey, of Street, Somerset; 4 da (Jessica b 1977, Rachel b 1982, Alicen b 1984, Stephanie b 1987); *Career* dir of sales and mktg: Baugh & Weedon Ltd 1978–81, Bradley & Foster Ltd 1981–83, Spear & Jackson Ltd 1984–86, British Ropes Ltd 1986–89, Bridon Fishing Ltd 1989–93; chm Bristol Wire Rope Ltd 1988–93, md Bridon Ropes Ltd 1989–93; Bridon Ropes Ltd awarded Investor in People Award 1992 and 1993, Design Award 1993, Prince Michael of Kent Award for Road Safety 1993, Queen's Award for Technol 1993; chm Fedn of Wire Rope Manufacturers of GB 1989–92, UK spokesman Euro Wire Rope Info Serv 1986–93; chm: QED Consltg 1998–2007 (md 1993–98), Thorn Hinton Ltd 1998–2007 (dir 1993–98), LightWork Design Ltd 2000–06, Navis Works Ltd 2002–06, Office Works Ltd 2003–06, Machine Works Ltd 2003–06; dir: Barnsley/Doncaster TEC (dep chm) 1989–93, Quantum Generation Ltd 1993–95, Spawforth Planning and Urban Regeneration Ltd 2004–; pres Doncaster Branch Inst of Mgmnt 1989–, chm Judging Panel Nat Trg Awards 1998–2000 (memb 1993–98); CEng, MIM, CCMI, FRSA; *Books* How to Negotiate Better Deals (1989), The First Time Sales Manager (1990), Developing Your Career in Management (1992), Effective Presentations (2000), Pricing Strategy (2001), Recruitment Practice (2002); *Recreations* music, sport (former chm W Midlands Region Amateur Fencing Assoc, sometime fencing team capt Univ of Leeds, Warks, W Midlands and Yorks, former Warks épée and sabre champion and W Midlands and Yorks sabre champion); *Style—* Jeremy Thorn, Esq; ✉ Longridge, Silver Street, Fairburn, Knottingley, West Yorkshire WF11 9JA (e-mail jeremy@yorkshireuk.net)

THORN, His Hon Roger Eric; QC (1990); s of James Douglas (Pat) Thorn, of Appleton, Cheshire, and Daphne Elizabeth, *née* Robinson; *b* 23 March 1948; *Educ* Mill Hill Sch London, Univ of Newcastle upon Tyne (LLB); *m* 2005, Clare Lillywhite; 2 step da; *Career* called to the Bar Middle Temple 1970 (Harmsworth scholar and major exhibitioner, bencher 1999); in practice NE Circuit, recorder 1999–2004 (asst recorder 1996–99), dep judge of the High Court 2000, circuit judge (NE Circuit) 2004–; memb Bar Cncl Panel of Arbitrators 1999, memb Restricted Patient's Panel Mental Health Review Tbnl2000; head Mission to Kosova Bar Human Rights Ctee 2000; memb Middle Temple Faculty of Advocacy; memb Senate Univ of Hull (liaison judge Law Sch), life govr Mill Hill Sch; *Books* A Practical Guide to Road Traffic Accident Claims (1987), Road Traffic Accident Claims (1990), Negotiating Better Deals (legal contrib, 1988), Kosova 2000: Justice not Revenge (jtly, 2000); *Recreations* theatre, music, walking, bridge; *Clubs* National Liberal, Durham County, Old Millhillians; *Style—* His Hon Judge Thorn, QC; ✉ Hull Combined Court Centre, Lowgate, Hull HU1 2EZ

THORNBER, Iain; JP (1988), DL (Lochaber, Inverness and Badenoch and Strathspey); s of James Thornber (d 1982), of Morvern, Argyll, and Jeannie Easton Campbell, *née* Stenhouse (d 2003); *b* 3 February 1948; *Educ* Glenhurich Public Sch; *Career* company factor Glensanda Estate Morvern (Foster Yeoman Ltd) 1980; tstee W Highland Museum Fort William; memb: Forestry Cmmn local advsy panel, Morvern Red Deer Mgmnt Gp; rep memb Royal Soc for Nature Conservation Rahoy Hills Nature Reserve; memb Lochaber JP Advsy Ctee; pres Lochaber Sea Cadets; Hon Sheriff Grampian, Highland and Islands 2007; FSA Scot 1973, FRSA 1987, FSA 1990; *Books* The Castles of Morvern, Argyll (1975), The Sculptured Stones of Cill Choluimchille Morvern, Argyll (1975), The Gaelic Bards of Morvern (1985), Rats (1989), Bronze Age Cairns in the Aline Valley, Morvern, Argyll (in Proceedings of the Society of Antiquaries of Scotland Vol 106, jt author, 1974–75), The Gaelic Bards of Morvern (1985), Cairn 3, Acharn, Morvern, Argyll (in Proceedings of the Society of Antiquaries of Scotland Vol 118, jt author, 1988), Moidart, or Among the Clanranalds (ed 1989 edn), 1793–1993 - The Story of the 79th Cameron Highlanders (Seaforth & Camerons) (1993); *Publications* Glenshian and Inverailort Deer Forest (1999), Dail na Cille, the Field of the Church (2001), Morvern-A Highland Parish by Norman MacLeod (ed, 2002); *Recreations* deer stalking, photography, local history research; *Style—* Iain Thornber, JP, DL; ✉ Knock House, Morvern, Oban, Argyll PA34 5UU (tel 01967 421651, fax 01967 421638, e-mail iain@iainthornber.co.uk); Glensanda Estate, Morvern, Argyll (tel 0163 173 415, fax 0163 173 460, telex 777792)

THORNBERRY, Emily; MP; da of Cedric Thornberry, and Sallie, *née* Bone; *b* 27 July 1960, London; *Educ* Univ of Kent at Canterbury; *m* Christopher Nugee, QC, *qv*; 3 c; *Career* called to the Bar Grays Inn 1983; memb Tooks Court 1985–; MP (Lab) Islington S and Finsbury 2005–; *Style—* Ms Emily Thornberry, MP; ✉ House of Commons, London SW1A 0AA

THORNE, Clive Duncan; s of late Desmond Clive Thorne, of East Dean, E Sussex, and May, *née* Davey; *b* 21 January 1952; *Educ* Eastbourne GS, Trinity Hall Cambridge (MA); *m* 1, 11 Oct 1975 (m dis 1982), Catherine Sykes; m 2, 12 July 1986, Alison Mary Healy, da of Cdr Michael Healy, MBE, of Beaulieu sur Mer, France; *Career* articled clerk Clifford-Turner 1975–77; admitted slr England 1977, slr Hong Kong 1984, barr and slr Victoria Aust 1985; ptnr Denton Hall (later Denton Wilde Sapte) 1987–2004, currently ptnr Arnold and Porter London office; memb: Arbitrators Panel Patents County Court, World Intellectual Property Orgn (WIPO), ICC, and Nominet ICANN domain name disputes panels, Working Gp on High Court Intellectual Property Protocol; author of numerous articles on intellectual property incl Euro Intellectual Property Review and other jls; associate: Chartered Inst of Trade Mark Agents, Chartered Inst of Patent Agents; memb: Law Soc, AIPPI, Int Bar Assoc (formerly vice-chm Ctee R (Computer and Technol Law)); fndr memb and dir: The Intellectual Property Lawyers Orgn (TIPLO),

Computer Law Gp; FCIArb; *Books* Sony Guide to Home Taping (contrib, 1983), Intellectual Property - The New Law (1989), User's Guide to Copyright (jtly, 2006); *Recreations* English music, opera, reading, walking, flute playing; *Style—* Clive Thorne, Esq; ✉ Arnold and Porter (UK) LLP, Tower 42, 25 Old Broad Street, London EC2N 1HQ (tel 020 7786 6100, fax 020 7786 6299, e-mail clive_thorne@aporter.com)

THORNE, Maj George; MC (1945), ERD, DL (Oxon 1961); 2 s of Gen Sir (Augustus Francis) Andrew Nicol Thorne, KCB, CMG, DSO, DL (d 1970), of Knowl Hill House, nr Reading (*see* Burke's Landed Gentry, 18 edn, vol II, 1969), and Hon Margaret Douglas-Pennant (d 1967), 10 da of 2 Baron Penrhyn; *b* 1 July 1912; *Educ* Eton, Trinity Coll Oxford; *m* 18 April 1942, Juliet Agnes, o da of Hon (Arthur) George Villiers Peel, JP, DL (d 1956), 2 s of 1 Viscount Peel, and Lady Agnes Lygon, da of 6 Earl Beauchamp; 2 s (Robert George (Robin), Ian David Peel), 1 da (Viola Georgina Juliet (Mrs Nicholas Halsey)); *Career* Maj late Grenadier Gds (SR), serv WWII, ADC to GOC 1 Div (Maj-Gen Hon Harold Alexander) 1939–40, OC No 3 Co 1 Bn Grenadier Gds 1941–45, Capt The King's Co 1 Bn Grenadier Gds 1945 (despatches); memb sales staff McVitie & Price Ltd 1934–39 and 1946–67; farmer 1950–; Peppard Branch Royal Br Legion 1946–99, Dunkirk Veterans Assoc (Henley); *Recreations* country pursuits; *Style—* Maj George Thorne, MC, ERD, DL; ✉ Chilton House, Chilton, Aylesbury, Buckinghamshire HP18 9LR (tel 01844 265219)

THORNE, Lesley Karen; da of Lt-Col James Shaw, of Hereford, and Catherine, *née* Barrie; *b* 19 November 1973, Rinteln, Germany; *Educ* Royal Sch Bath, Univ of Warwick (BA); *m* 17 July 2004, Matthew David Jon Thorne; 1 s (Luke David James); *Career* PA to md Fourth Estate 1996–97, editorial asst to Publisher Hamish Hamilton then editorial dir Viking 1997–99, asst to md rising to agent Aitken Alexander Associates Ltd (formerly Gillon Aitken Associates) 1999– (currently managing literary client list and handling film and TV); *Recreations* film, music, walking, literature; *Style—* Mrs Lesley Thorne; ✉ Aitken Alexander Associates Ltd, 18–21 Cavaye Place, London SW10 9PT (tel 020 7373 8672, fax 020 7373 6002, e-mail lesley@aitkenalexander.co.uk)

THORNE, Matthew Wadman John; s of Robin Horton John Thorne, CMG, OBE (d 2004), of Old Heathfield, E Sussex, and Joan Helen, *née* Wadman (d 2000); *b* 27 June 1952; *Educ* Dragon Sch, King's Sch Canterbury, Trinity Coll Oxford (MA); *m* 1978, (Sheila) Leigh, da of Col Hon Robert George Hugh Phillimore, OBE (d 1984), 3 s of 2 Baron Phillimore, MC, DL; 2 da (Aelene b 17 June 1981, Marini b 4 Aug 1992), 3 s (Robin b 15 Feb 1983, Andrew b 27 Feb 1986, Edward b 16 July 1989); *Career* Price Waterhouse 1975–78, County Natwest 1978–83, Beazer plc 1983–91 (dir 1984–91); dir Ricardo International plc 1991–92, gp fin dir McCarthy & Stone plc 1993–; non-exec dir: BM Group plc 1991–93, UMECO plc 1992–2002, Bournemouth Univ 1996–2002; FCA 1978; *Style—* Matthew Thorne, Esq; ✉ The Mount, Bannerdown Road, Batheaston, Bath BA1 8EG

THORNE, Prof Michael Philip; *b* 19 October 1951, Chelmsford, Essex; *Educ* QMC London (BSc), Univ of Birmingham (PhD); *m* 1975, Val, *née* Swift; 3 s (Jonathan Mark b 1976, William James b 1987, Edward Alexander 1994); *Career* lectr: SE Derbyshire Coll 1973–75, UCL 1978–79, UC Cardiff 1979–88; head Sch of Computing Univ of Sunderland 1989–93, pro-vice-chllr Univ of Sunderland 1993–97, vice-princ Napier Univ 1998–2001, vice-chllr Univ of E London 2001–; memb Bd: London Thames Gateway Urban Devpt Corp 2004–, Learning and Skills Network 2006–; non-exec dir Scottish Univ for Industry, chair Open Learning Fndn, former chair Lead Scotland; memb Bd: Northern Sinfonia, Northern Jr Philharmonic, Broadway Theatre 2006–; FIMA, FBCS, FRSA; *Publications* author and co-author of 11 books and numerous academic papers, articles and radio and TV progs; *Recreations* music (bassoon and conducting), theatre, hill walking, reading funding council circulars; *Clubs* Reform; *Style—* Prof Michael Thorne; ✉ University of East London, Longbridge Road, Dagenham, Essex RM8 3PS (tel 020 8223 4001, mobile 07768 542697)

THORNE, Dr Napier Arnold; s of Arnold Thorne (d 1959), of Cape Town, South Africa, and Wilhelmina Rosa, *née* Ayson (d 1970); *b* 26 December 1920; *Educ* Eastbourne Coll, Bart's Med Coll London (MB BS, MD); *m* 16 May 1953, Pamela Joan (d 2003), da of Robert Thomas Frederick Houchin, of Ruckinge, Kent; 3 da (Susan b 1954, Jane b 1957, Katherine b 1959), 1 s (Robert Napier b 1959); *Career* conslt dermatologist: Prince of Wales Hosp 1955–85, Royal London Hosp 1968–81; hon conslt dermatologist: Italian Hosp London 1969–89, Hosp of St John and St Elizabeth 1976–; sen Univ of London 1970–80, pres Inst of Trichologists 1972–98, tstee Chichester Festival Theatre 1976–2001, tstee and chm Philological Fndn 1982–95; Freeman City of London; Liveryman: Worshipful Co of Farriers 1965, Worshipful Soc of Apothecaries 1978; MRCS 1945, memb BMA 1945, fell Hunterian Soc 1947, FRSM 1949, fell Br Assoc of Dermatologists 1959, fell Med Soc of London 1961, FRCP 1972 (LRCP 1945, MRCP 1949), FRSA 1983; *Recreations* music, reading; *Clubs* RSM; *Style—* Dr Napier Thorne; ✉ 3 Rosewood, 11 Park Road, Haslemere, Surrey GU27 2NJ (tel 01428 644224, mobile 07768 583220)

THORNE, Sir Neil Gordon; kt (1992), OBE (1980), TD (1969), DL (Gtr London 1991); s of Henry Frederick Thorne (d 1964); *b* 8 August 1932; *Educ* City of London Sch, Univ of London; *Career* TA 1952–82, Col ex RA, CO Univ of London OTC 1976–80; memb Metropolitan Special Constabulary (HAC) 1983–92; chartered surveyor 1961–, sr ptnr Hull & Co 1962–77; Borough of Redbridge: cncllr 1965–68, alderman 1975–78; memb GLC and chm Central Area Bd 1967–73; MP (Cons) Ilford S 1979–92; memb House of Commons Defence Ctee 1983–92, sponsored 22 private Parly Bills for public tport 1988–92; chm: Anglo Nepalese All-Pty Parly Gp 1979–92, Nat Cncl for Civil Def 1982–86, Armed Forces Parly Scheme 1987–, Lord Mayor's Appeal for St Paul's Cathedral 1993–94, Police Serv Parly Scheme 1994–, Cons One Nation Forum 1995–98; memb Military Educn Ctee Univ of Leeds 1994–; pres: London Dist St John Ambulance 1992–2003, Redbridge Chamber of Commerce 1992–, Redbridge Age Concern 1993–, Inst of Civil Defence and Disaster Studies 1996–, N and E London REME Assoc 2000–; vice-pres Britain Nepal Soc 1998– (chm Britain Nepal Soc 1992–98); tstee: Children in Distress 1986–, Memorial Gates Tst 1999–2007; patron Benevolent Fund for W Essex Hospices 2001–; memb Lloyd's of London 1975–; memb Court of Referees 1987–92; Hon Col Leeds Univ OTC 1999–; rep DL London Borough of Brent 2001–2007; fndr memb Royal Artillery Firepower Museum; Freeman City of London 1966, Prime Warden Worshipful Co of Blacksmiths 2000–01; FICDDS 1996; FCGI 1997; Almoner Order of St John 1995–97, KStJ 1995 (OStJ 1988, CStJ 1992); *Publications* A Study of Pedestrian Shopping Streets (1973), Highway Robbery in the Twentieth Century - policy reform for compulsory purchase (1990); *Recreations* tennis, mountain walking, riding and music; *Clubs* HAC; *Style—* Sir Neil Thorne, OBE, TD, DL; ✉ 13 Cowley Street, London SW1P 3LZ (tel 020 7222 0480)

THORNE, Peter Geoffrey; s of Ernest Geoffrey Thorne (d 1976), of Duncliffe, Saunton, N Devon, and Edwina Mary, *née* Wilkinson; *b* 2 June 1948; *Educ* Clifton; *m* Jane Frances, da of John David Henson, MC, OBE; 1 s (Benjamin David Geoffrey b 11 July 1981), 1 da (Lucy Frances Alice b 18 Jan 1984); *Career* articles Messrs Sargent & Probert Slrs of Exeter 1965–70, admitted slr 1971 (Sir George Fowler prize for best qualifier from Devon); Norton Rose (formerly Norton Rose Botterell & Roche): joined 1971, specialist in asset fin (particularly ship and aircraft), ptnr 1977–, Hong Kong office 1981–83; memb: City of London Slrs Co, Law Soc, Int Bar Assoc, RAeS, GAPAN; *Recreations* flying, fishing, philately, skiing; *Style—* Peter Thorne, Esq; ✉ c/o Ann Cheyne, Norton Rose, 3 More London Riverside, London SE1 2AQ (tel 020 7283 6000, fax 020 7283 6500)

THORNE, Robert George (Robin); s of Maj George Thorne, MC, DL; *b* 7 February 1943; *Educ* Eton, RAC Cirencester; *m* Feb 1990, Sarah, da of J F Priestley, MC; *Career* local dir Barclays Bank Ltd: Bristol 1973–76, Newcastle upon Tyne 1977–80, London Northern 1980–83, Pall Mall 1983–94; dir Phillips Auctioneers and Valuers 1994–97, assoc dir Tangible Securities Ltd 1997–, chm Cole & Son (Wallpapers) Ltd 2001–04; dir Ridgeway Grain Ltd 2001; tstee: Phillimore Estates 1991, The Royal Green Jackets Museum 2002; memb Fin Ctee Worshipful Co of Cordwainers 1990–2004; *Recreations* country pursuits; *Clubs* Brooks's, Pratt's; *Style—* Robin Thorne, Esq; ✉ Ovington House, Ovington, Alresford, Hampshire SO24 0RB

THORNE, Rosemary Prudence; da of Arnold Rex Bishop, of Clevedon, Avon, and Brenda Prudence, *née* Withers; *b* 12 February 1952; *Educ* Univ of Warwick (BSc); *Career* accountant BOC Ltd 1974–77, chief accountant Mothercare plc 1977–82, gp financial controller Habitat Mothercare plc 1982–85, gp financial controller Storehouse plc 1986, finance dir and co sec Harrods Ltd (House of Fraser plc) 1986–90, gp financial controller Grand Metropolitan plc 1990–92, gp financial dir J Sainsbury plc 1992–99, gp finance dir Bradford & Bingley 2000–06, gp finance dir Ladbrokes plc 2006–07; non-exec dir: Royal Mail Hldgs 2002–04, Cadbury Schweppes 2004–; The Hundred Gp of Fin Dirs: memb Main Ctee, chm Tech Ctee; memb: Financial Reporting Cncl, Financial Reporting Review Panel, Cncl Univ of Warwick; FCMA, FCT, CCMI; *Style—* Miss Rosemary P Thorne

THORNEWILL, Fiona Susan; MBE (2006); da of Ralph Cowling, of Upton, Notts, and Jean Cowling; *b* 10 July 1966, Upton, Notts; *Educ* Rodney Sch Kirklington; *m* 26 May 1996, Mike Thornewill, s of Peter Leslie Graham Thornewill (d 1983); *Career* explorer; first Br female to: walk to Geographic S Pole 2000, walk to Geographic N Pole 2001 (first female to walk to both geographic poles), walk solo and unsupported to Geographic S Pole 2004 (also fastest person to do so: 41 days and 8 hours); formerly prop of ladies gym, currently recruitment conslt Harpers; pt/t polar guide; motivational speaker; supporter: NSPCC, Macmillan Cancer Care; Pride of Britain Award 2000, RADAR Award for Human Achievement 2001, European Woman of the Year 2004; *Recreations* running, cycling, sailing, the great outdoors, socialising; *Style—* Mrs Fiona Thornewill, MBE; ✉ Bluebell Barn, Thurgarton, Nottinghamshire NG14 7FW (tel 07979 538772, e-mail fiona@polarchallenge.org); c/o Jan Jenkins, Pinewood Studios, Pinewood Road, Iver, Buckinghamshire SL0 0NH (tel 01753 651700, e-mail jan@speakerscorner-pinewood.co.uk)

THORNEYCROFT, Hon John Hamo; LVO (1992); s of Baron Thorneycroft, CH, PC (Life Peer, d 1994), and his 1 w Sheila Wells, *née* Page; *b* 24 March 1940; *Educ* Eton, Univ of Cambridge, UWIST (DipArch); *m* 1971, Delia, da of Arthur William Lloyd (d 1977), of Penallt, Gwent; 1 da (Eleanor b 1974), 1 s (Richard b 1977); *Career* architect Dept of Ancient Monuments and Historic Buildings DoE 1974–84; English Heritage: architect 1984–, head Central Govt and Palaces Branch London Region 1992–96, head Govt Historic Estates Unit (GHEU, formerly Government Historic Buildings Advisory Unit) 1996–2005; memb Int Cncl on Monuments and Sites (ICOMOS); RIBA 1988, Hon FSA 2005; memb Order of Orange Nassau 1982; *Style—* The Hon John Thorneycroft, LVO, FSA, RIBA; ✉ The Gatehouse, 11 Monk Street, Monmouth NP25 3NZ

THORNHILL, Andrew Robert; QC (1985); s of Edward Percy Thornhill, of Bristol, and Amelia Joy Thornhill; *b* 4 August 1943; *Educ* Clifton, CCC Oxford; *m* 5 Aug 1971, Helen Mary, da of George William Livingston, of Gainsborough; 2 da (Emily Mary b 12 June 1972, Eleanor Clare b 19 June 1980), 2 s (George Percy b 1 Dec 1973, Henry Robert b 26 May 1977); *Career* called to the Bar Middle Temple 1969, joined chambers of H H Monroe 1969, bencher 1995, head of chambers, recorder (Western Circuit) 1997–; *Recreations* sailing, walking, education; *Clubs* Oxford and Cambridge, Tamesis, Ban Yacht, Royal Thames Yacht; *Style—* Andrew Thornhill, Esq, QC; ✉ Pump Court Tax Chambers, 16 Bedford Row, London WC1R 4EB (tel 020 7414 8080, fax 020 7414 8099)

THORNHILL, Richard John; s of Richard Norwood Thornhill, and Eleanor Louise, *née* Hoey; *b* 13 November 1954; *Educ* Malvern, St John's Coll Oxford (MA); *m* 30 Aug 1980, Nicola, da of Peter John Dyke, of Derby; 3 s (Hugo b 1989, Frederick b 1992, Rafe b 1997); *Career* admitted slr 1979, admitted slr of the Supreme Court Hong Kong 1982; Slaughter & May: articled clerk 1977–79, asst slr Hong Kong Office 1982–84, ptnr 1986–, sr ptnr Slaughter & May Hong Kong 1991–; memb Law Soc; *Recreations* walking, water skiing, theatre, opera; *Style—* Richard Thornhill, Esq; ✉ Slaughter and May, 47th Floor, Jardine House, One Connaught Place, Central, Hong Kong

THORNTON, Andrew Robert; *Career* national hunt jockey; several winners incl: The Ritz Club Chase 1996, The Pertemps King George VI 1997, The Tote Cheltenham Gold Cup 1998, Royal and Sun Alliance Novice Hurdle 1998, The Sun King of the Punters' Tolworth Hurdle 1998, The Racing Post Trophy 1998, The Betterware Cup Steeplechase 1998, The Emblem Chase 1998; other races incl: Pertemps Christmas Hurdle 1998, Prix la Barka 1999, Rehearsal Chase 1999, Agfa Chase 1999, Rehearsal Chase Chepstow 1999, 2002 and 2003, Scottish Grand National 2001, Hennessey Cognac Gold Cup 2002, Badger Beer Chase 2002 and 2003, Edward Mamner Grade 2 Chase 2003, EBF Mares Hurdle Final 2004, Noel Novice Chase 2004 and 2005, The Reynoldstown Chase 2005, Dipper Novices Chase 2006, Cotswold Chase 2006, The Great Yorkshire Chase 2006 and 2007; winner Lester Award Jockey Assoc of GB 1996 and 1997, Jump Ride of the Year on Kingscliff 2003; *Recreations* football, golf, cricket; *Style—* Andrew Thornton, Esq

THORNTON, His Hon Judge Anthony Christopher Lawrence; QC (1988); s of Maj Richard Thornton (d 1983), and Margery Alice Clerk, CBE (d 1993); *b* 18 August 1947; *Educ* Eton, Keble Coll Oxford (MA, BCL); *m* 1, 18 Feb 1983 (m dis), Lyn Christine, da of Laurence Thurlby, of Cambridge; 1 s (Matthew James b 12 June 1983); m 2, 24 June 2006, Dawn Elisabeth; *Career* called to the Bar Middle Temple 1970 (bencher 1992); recorder 1992–94, official referee 1994–98, judge of Technol and Construction Court 1998–; memb Gen Cncl of the Bar 1988–94 (treas 1990–92, chm Professional Standards Ctee 1992–93); Freeman City of London 1976, memb Ct of Assts Worshipful Co of Leathersellers 1976; MIArb 1987; *Books* Halsbury's Laws Vol 4: Building Contracts (jt ed and contrib, 1972, reissue 1992), Construction Law Review (jt ed), Burns - The Expert Witness (contrib, 1989); *Recreations* opera, football, legal history; *Clubs* RAC; *Style—* His Hon Judge Thornton, QC; ✉ Technology and Construction Court, St Dunstan's House, 133–137 Fetter Lane, London EC4A 1HD (tel 020 7947 6022)

THORNTON, Frank, *né* Frank Thornton Ball; s of William Ernest Ball (d 1978), Rosina Mary, *née* Thornton; *b* 15 January 1921, London; *Educ* Alleyn's Sch Dulwich, London Sch of Dramatic Art (scholarship); *m* 5 June 1945, Beryl Jane Margaret, da of Thomas Evans; 1 da (Jane Thornton); *Career* formerly insurance clerk 1937–1939; RAFVR 1943–47; actor; Actors Benevolent Fund: memb Cncl 1971–, vice-pres 1982–90; *Theatre* roles incl: Mosca in Ben Jonson's Volpone, Hassan, Don't Shoot - We're English, Meals On Wheels (Royal Court), Empton QC in Alibi for a Judge (Savoy), Minnit and Procurio in The Young Visiters, Cncllr Parker in When We Are Married, Eeyore in Winnie-The-Pooh, Sir Andrew Aguecheek in Twelfth Night, Duncan in Macbeth, Sir Patrick Cullen in The Doctor's Dilemma, Shut Your Eyes and Think Of England (Apollo), Bedroom Farce (Theatre Royal Windsor), George in Jumpers, The Chairs (Royal Exchange), Dr Wicksteed in Habeas Corpus, Dr Sloper in The Heiress, Sir Joseph Porter in HMS Pinafore, DCI Hubbard in Dial M for Murder, Barney Cashman in Last of the Red-Hot Lovers, Sir John Tremayne in Me and My Girl (Adelphi), John of Gaunt in Richard II, Maj Gen in The Pirates Of Penzance, The Cabinet Minister, Gen de Gaulle in Winnie, Count Shabelsky in Ivanov, Leonato in Much Ado About Nothing, The Reluctant Debutante, George Bernard Shaw in The Best of Friends, Spread a Little Happiness, It Runs in The Family (Playhouse), Music In The Air (Barbican), Strike Up The Band, A Patriot for Me (RSC Barbican), Hobson in Hobson's Choice (Lyric), Of Thee

I Sing, Cash on Delivery, Jubilee, The Jermyn Street Revue; *Television* credits incl: It's a Square World, The World of Beachcomber, HMS Paradise, Gremio in The Taming of The Shrew, Capt Peacock in Are You Being Served? and Grace and Favour, Truly in Last Of The Summer Wine; *Films* over 60, incl: The Bed-Sitting Room, A Funny Thing Happened on the Way to the Forum, A Flea in Her Ear, Great Expectations, The Old Curiosity Shop, Gosford Park; *Radio* several plays and sitcoms incl: The Embassy Lark, The Big Business Lark and Mind Your Own Business; *Clubs* Garrick; *Style*— Frank Thornton, Esq; ✉ c/o Daly Pearson Associates, 586a Kings Road, London SW6 2DX (tel 020 7384 1036, fax 020 7610 9512)

THORNTON, Baroness (Life Peer UK 1998), of Manningham in the County of West Yorkshire; (Dorothea) Glenys Thornton; da of Peter Thornton, and Jean, *née* Furness; *b* 16 October 1952; *Educ* Thornton Secdy Sch Bradford, LSE (BSc(Econ)); *m* Feb 1977, John Carr, s of Henry Carr; 1 s (Hon George Carr b 4 Aug 1986) 1 da (Hon Ruby Carr b 10 March 1988); *Career* nat organiser Gingerbread 1976–78, projects dir Inst of Community Studies 1979–81, political sec Royal Arsenal Co-op Soc 1981–86, public and political affrs advsr CWS 1986–92, gen sec Fabian Soc 1993–94 (dir of devpt 1994–96); dir Emily's List 1993–; chair Pall Mall Conslts; chm Gtr London Lab Pty 1986–91, chair Social Enterprise Coalition 2001–; govr LSE 2002–; FRSA; *Recreations* canoeing, hill walking, Star Trek; *Style*— The Rt Hon the Baroness Thornton; ✉ House of Lords, London SW1A 0PW (tel 020 7219 8502, fax 020 7263 0157, e-mail thorntong@parliament.uk)

THORNTON, James Michael (Jim); s of Dr Michael Thornton, of Audlem, Cheshire, and Margaret, *née* Hastie; *b* 19 January 1963, Nantwich, Cheshire; *Educ* Malvern Coll, Royal Holloway Coll Univ of London (BA), Watford Coll; *m* 2 Sept 1989, Melanie, *née* Hoare; 1 da (Ellerie b 19 Jan 1994), 1 s (Oliver b 7 May 1996); *Career* advtg agency copywriter: JWT (J Walter Thompson) 1986–95, GGT 1995–97; copywriter/creative dir TBWA 1997–99, creative dir Mother 1999–2003, exec creative dir Leo Burnett Ltd 2003–; gardening corr Marmalade Magazine 2003–04; memb D&AD 1997; *Recreations* being a dad; *Clubs* Stoke City London Supporters, Sussex CCC, Century, Hurst House; *Style*— Jim Thornton, Esq; ✉ Leo Burnett Ltd, Warwick Building, Kensington Village, Avonmore Road, London W14 8HQ (tel 020 7751 1800, fax 020 7071 1415, e-mail jim.thornton@leoburnett.co.uk)

THORNTON, Prof Janet Maureen; CBE (2000); da of James Stanley McLoughlin, of Dorset, and Kathleen, *née* Barlow; *b* 23 May 1949; *Educ* Univ of Nottingham (BSc), KCL and Nat Inst for Med Research (PhD); *m* 25 July 1970, Alan David Thornton, s of David Thornton; 1 s (Alexander b 29 Oct 1975), 1 da (Hazel b 7 Dec 1977); *Career* research asst Lab of Molecular Biophysics Univ of Oxford 1973–78; tutor Open Univ 1976–83; research scientist Molecular Pharmacology Nat Inst for Med Research 1978; Birkbeck Coll London: SERC advanced fell Crystallography Dept 1979–83, lectr 1983–89, sr lectr 1989–90, head Jt Research Sch in Biomolecular Sciences 1996–, Bernal chair Crystallography Dept 1996–, dir BBSRC Centre for Structural Biology 1998–2001; prof of biomolecular structure UCL 1990–2001, dir European Bioinformatics Inst 2001–, fell Churchill Coll Cambridge 2002–; Wellcome visiting prof Rutgers State Univ 1995; chm BBSRC Bioinformatics Ctee 1995–98, chm Br Biophysical Soc 1995–98; memb: SERC Biochemistry/Biophysics Sub-Ctee for grant peer review 1989–92, Protein and Peptide Research Gp Ctee Biochemical Soc 1989–92, Ctee Br Biophysical Soc 1992–94, Advsy Bd Brookhaven Protein Structure Databank 1992–, MRC Molecular and Cellular Med Bd B 1993–97, Chemicals and Pharmaceuticals Directorate BBSRC 1994–97, BBSRC Strategy Bd 1999–, EPSRC Life Sciences Peer Review Coll 1999–, Cncl Protein Soc 1999–; memb Editorial Bd: Protein Engineering, Current Opinion in Structural Biology, Structure, Folding and Design, Molecular Recognition, Jl of Molecular Biology; memb Scientific Advsy Bd Oxford Molecular Ltd 1990–97; conslt Euro Bioinformatics Inst; Ronald Tress Prize for Research 1986, Pfizer Academic Award for Excellence in Research 1991, Federation of European Biochemical Societies lectr 1993, Han Neurath Award Protein Soc 2000–; foreign assoc memb Nat Acad of Scientists USA; FRS 1999; *Publications* author of 200 papers in scientific and learned jls; *Recreations* reading, music, walking, gardens; *Style*— Prof Janet Thornton, CBE, FRS; ✉ European Bioinformatics Institute, The Wellcome Trust Genome Campus, Cambridge CB10 1SD (tel 01223 494648, fax 01223 494000, e-mail director@ebi.ac.uk)

THORNTON, Kate Louise; da of Dennis Thornton, and Sandra, *née* Parker; *b* 7 February 1973; *Career* television and radio presenter; feature writer/entertainment columnist Daily Mirror and Sunday Mirror 1993–95, ed Smash Hits 1995–96, contributing ed Marie Claire 1997–2003, writer Sunday Times 1997–2004; guest and documentary presenter Radio 2 2002–; television incl: presenter Top of the Pops 1998–99, entertainment reporter This Morning (ITV) 1998–2000, The Ideal Home Show 2001–02, Holiday (BBC 1) 2001–03, Holiday - You Call the Shots (BBC 1) 2001–03, Pop Idol Extra (ITV 2) 2001–03; *Recreations* music; *Style*— Ms Kate Thornton; ✉ Talkback Management, 20–21 Newman Street, London W1T 1PG

THORNTON, Prof (Robert) Kelsey Rought; s of Harold Thornton (d 1975), and Mildred, *née* Brooks (d 1995); *b* 12 August 1938; *Educ* Burnley GS, Univ of Manchester (BA, MA, PhD); *m* 1, 3 Aug 1961 (m dis 1976), Sarah Elizabeth Ann, da of Hendri Griffiths; 2 s (Jason b 1965, Ben b 1968); m 2, 22 Sept 1989 (m dis 2003), Eileen Valerie, da of Maurice Davison; 1 da (Amy b 1979), 1 s (Thomas b 1982); m 3, 28 Feb 2004, Hilary Marchant, da of Francis Thompson; *Career* Univ of Newcastle upon Tyne: lectr 1965–75, sr lectr 1975–84, prof 1984–89, visiting prof 2001–; prof Sch of Eng Univ of Birmingham 1989–2000 (head of Sch 1989–96); chm John Clare Soc 1987–90; pres Friends of the Dymock Poets; FRSA; *Books* incl: John Clare: The Midsummer Cushion (1978), John Clare: The Rural Muse (1982), The Decadent Dilemma (1983), Gerard Manley Hopkins: The Poems (1973), All My Eyes See: The Visual World of Gerard Manley Hopkins (1975), Ivor Gurney Collected Letters (1991), Ivor Gurney: Best Poems and the Book of Five Makings (1995), Poetry of the 1890s (1997), Ivor Gurney: 80 Poems or So (1997), Ernest Dowson: Collected Shorter Fiction (2003), Ernest Dowson: Collected Poems (2003); ed jls: The Ivor Gurney Soc Jl (1995–), 28 vols in the series Decadents, Symbolists, Anti-Decadents (1993–96); *Recreations* water colour painting, book collecting; *Style*— Prof Kelsey Thornton; ✉ 2 Rectory Terrace, Gosforth, Newcastle upon Tyne NE3 1XY (tel 0191 284 3083, e-mail rkrthornton@btinternet.com)

THORNTON, Kevin Nicholas; s of Edmond Thornton (d 2005), and Rita, *née* Landy; *b* 26 April 1958, Cashel, Co Tipperary, Ireland; *Educ* Christian Bros Sch Cashel, Regnl Tech Coll Galway, Nat Coll of Art and Design (Dip), Dublin Inst of Technol Coll of Catering; *m* Muriel, *née* O'Connor; 2 s (Edward, Conor); *Career* chef and restaurateur; jr chef positions Galway, London, Switzerland, Dublin, and Toronto 1974–87, sous chef Marcel's Bistro Toronto 1985, chef sausiere Shelbourne Hotel Dublin 1986, chef de partie Restaurant Paul Bocuse Lyon 1987 (3 Michelin Stars), sous chef Shelbourne Hotel Dublin 1988, chef de cuisine Adare Manor Co Limerick 1989; chef and prop: The Wine Epergne Dublin 1990, Thornton's Restaurant Dublin 1994– (2 Michelin Stars 2001 (Michelin Star 1995), 4 AA Rosettes 2000 (3 Rosettes 1998); Restaurant of the Year: Egon Ronay 1996, Jameson Good Food Guide 1997 and 2003, AA Good Food Guide 2000, Food and Wine Magazine 2001); lectr Coll of Catering Dublin 1992; 2 Gold medals and Silver medal Chef Ireland 1991 (Silver and Bronze medals 1989), Hotelympia Silver medal 1992 (Bronze medal 1990), Bocuse D'Or 1992, Gilbeys Gold medal 1996; Chef of the Year: Egon Ronay 1995, Wedgwood 1997, Food and Wine Magazine 2001 (runner-up 2003 and 2004); *Publications* Food for Life; *Style*— Kevin Thornton, Esq; ✉ Thornton's Restaurant, 128 St Stephens Green, Dublin 2, Ireland (tel 00 353 1 478 7008, fax 00 353 1 478 7009, e-mail thorntonsrestaurant@eircom.net, website www.thorntonsrestaurant.com)

THORNTON, Sir (George) Malcolm; kt (1992); s of George Edmund Thornton by his w Ethel; *b* 3 April 1939; *Educ* Wallasey GS, Liverpool Nautical Coll; *m* 1, 1962; 1 s; m 2, 1972, Sue Banton (d 1989); m 3, 1990, Rosemary, *née* Hewitt; *Career* former River Mersey pilot; memb: Wallasey County Borough Cncl 1965–74, Wirral Metropolitan Cncl 1973–79 (ldr 1974–77); chm Merseyside Dists Liaison Ctee 1975–77; vice-pres: Assoc of Met Authorities, Burnham Ctee 1978–79; chm: AMA Educn Ctee 1978–79, Cncl of Local Educn Authorities 1978–79; MP (Cons): Liverpool Garston 1979–83, Crosby 1983–97; PPS to Rt Hon Patrick Jenkin: as Industry Sec 1981–83, as Environment Sec 1983–84; memb Select Ctee on: Environment 1979–81, Educn and Employment 1985–97 (chm 1988–97); sec: Cons Parly Shipping and Shipbuilding Ctee 1979–81, Cons Parly Educn Ctee; chm: Keene Public Affairs Conslts Ltd 1997–, Broadskill Ltd (formerly Intuition Gp Ltd) 2002–, Value Based Solutions 2006–; non-exec dir: Stack Computer Solutions Ltd 2001–, Adviserplus Business Solutions Ltd; chm Bd of Tstees Mersey Mission To Seafarers 2002–; pro-chllr and chm Bd Liverpool John Moores Univ 2001– (chm Audit Ctee 2003–); fell Industry and Parliament Tst; Hon Col 156 (NW) Tport Regt the Royal Logistic Corps (V) 2000–05, Hon DEd De Montfort Univ; FRSA; *Recreations* golf, home entertaining, word games; *Style*— Sir Malcolm Thornton, FRSA; ✉ Meadow Brook, 79 Barnston Road, Heswall, Wirral CH60 1UE

THORNTON, Margaret Barbara; da of Cyril Arthur Wales (d 1983), and Anna Margaret Wales, MBE, *née* Chang; *b* 28 January 1940; *Educ* Burgess Hill PNEU Sussex, Mary Wray Secretarial Coll Sussex; *m* 1972, Adrian Heber Thornton, s of Nigel Heber Thornton, Croix de Guerre (d 1941); 2 da (Emily Harriet b 1973, Rebecca Louise b 1980), 1 s (Jasper Hamilton b 1975); *Career* md Redfern Gallery; artists represented: Sarah Armstrong-Jones, Frank Avray Wilson, Elizabeth Butterworth, Paul Emsley, Paul Feiler, Annabel Gault, William Gear, RA, Danny Markey, Brendan Neiland, RA, Bryan Organ, Patrick Procktor, David Tindle, RA, Paul Wunderlich; *Recreations* visiting galleries, museums and antique markets; *Style*— Mrs Margaret Thornton; ✉ The Redfern Gallery, 20 Cork Street, London W1 (tel 020 7734 1732, 020 7734 0578, fax 020 7494 2908, e-mail art@redfern-gallery.demon.co.uk, website www.redfern-gallery.com)

THORNTON, Peter Anthony; s of Robert Thornton (d 1990), and Freda, *née* Willey (d 2000); *b* 8 May 1944; *Educ* Bradford GS, Univ of Manchester (BSc); *m* 1, 1969 (m dis 1987); 2 da (Victoria Jane b 1973, Charlotte Sarah b 1974), 1 s (James William b 1976); m 2, 1997, Susan, da of Herbert Harris, of Maidstone, Kent; *Career* chartered surveyor and engineer; chief exec Greycoat Estates Ltd; Liveryman Worshipful Co of Chartered Surveyors; FRICS, FICE; *Recreations* tennis, water skiing, cars, golf; *Clubs* Harbour; *Style*— Peter Thornton, Esq; ✉ Van Buren Cottage, Queen's Ride, Barnes Common, London SW13 0JF (tel 020 8788 1969); Greycoat Estates Ltd, 9 Savoy Street, London WC2E 7EG (tel 020 7379 1000, fax 020 7379 8708, mobile 07768 152584, e-mail pthornton@greycoat.co.uk)

THORNTON, Peter Ribblesdale; QC (1992); s of Robert Ribblesdale Thornton, of Winterborne Whitechurch, Dorset, and Ruth Eleanor, *née* Tuckson; *b* 17 October 1946; *Educ* Clifton, St John's Coll Cambridge (BA); *m* 13 June 1981, Susan Margaret, da of Maneck Ardeshir Dalal; 1 s (Daniel Richard Dalal b 14 July 1990), 1 da (Amy Christina Dalal b 30 June 1992); *Career* called to the Bar Middle Temple 1969 (bencher 2001); recorder 1997– (asst recorder 1994–97), dep judge of the High Court 2003–; jt head Doughty Street Chambers 2005– (fndr memb, dep head 1990–2005); chm: NCCL 1981–83, Civil Liberties Tst 1991–95; *Books* Public Order Law (1987), Decade of Decline: Civil Liberties in the Thatcher Years (1989), The Penguin Civil Liberty Guide (co-ed, 1989), Archbold: Criminal Pleading, Evidence and Practice (contrib ed, 1992–); *Style*— Peter Thornton, Esq, QC; ✉ Doughty Street Chambers, 10–11 Doughty Street, London WC1N 2PL (tel 020 7404 1313, fax 020 7404 2283)

THORNTON, Richard Chicheley; s of Capt Edward Chicheley Thornton, DSC, RN (d 1959), of Titchfield, Hants, and Margaret Noel, *née* Terry (d 1970); *b* 5 July 1931; *Educ* Stowe, Keble Coll Oxford; *m* 1, 1958 (m dis 1987); 2 da (Mary b 1959, Lucy b 1960), 1 s (Henry b 1963); m 2, 1989, Susan, da of Dudley Middleton (d 1986); *Career* Nat Serv cmmnd 2 Lt Royal Signals 1950, Capt Royal Signals TA 1952–58; called to the Bar Gray's Inn 1957; co-fndr GT Management 1969, fndr Thornton & Co 1985 (pres 1991–94), chm The Establishment Investment Tst plc 2002–05 (dir 2005–); a vice-pres The Marine Soc 1992; Freeman City of London 1987, memb Worshipful Co of Watermen and Lightermen 1987; hon fell Keble Coll Oxford 1986; *Recreations* golf, opera, sailing; *Clubs* Beefsteak, Garrick, Royal Thames Yacht, Sorrento Golf (Aust); *Style*— Richard Thornton, Esq; ✉ 25 Pelham Place, London SW7 2NQ (tel 020 7589 7878, fax 020 7591 3929)

THORNTON, Robert Thomas; s of Tom Devlin, of California, and Ethel Thornton, *née* Conroy; *b* 8 July 1951; *Educ* Sharston Secdy Sch, Hollings Coll Manchester (City & Guilds), Westminster Coll (City & Guilds); *m* 12 July 1981, Susan Elizabeth, da of Brian Steer; 2 da (Rachel b 28 Oct 1983, Jennifer b 30 Sept 1985); *Career* apprentice chef Grosvenor House Park Lane 1969–71, commis saucier Bayerischerhof Hotel München 1971–72, garde mangr Hotel Schweizerhof Davos Platz Schweiz 1972–73, fndr Moss Nook 1973, sous chef Montreux Palace 1974–76, head chef Moss Nook 1976–90, exec chef Underscar Manor Cumbria 1990–; appeared on Kids in the Kitchen 1993; fndr memb Chefs Culinary Circle of NW England; fundraiser for various charities; *Awards* Cheshire Life Restaurant of the Year (Moss Nook) 1992, Lancashire Life Magazine Top Twelve Chefs of NW 1992, Underscar Manor recommended in various pubns 1992–, Lancashire Life Magazine Small Hotel of the Year (Underscar Manor) 1993, Harpers & Queen 100 Best Restaurants 1996; *Recreations* marathons, cricket, football, golf, swimming, fell walking, guitar playing; *Clubs* Keswick Golf; *Style*— Robert Thornton, Esq; ✉ Underscar Manor, Applethwaite, Keswick, Cumbria CA12 4PH (tel 017687 75000, fax 017687 74904)

THORNTON, Stephen; CBE (2002); s of Harry Thornton, and Alice, *née* Ainsworth; *b* 23 January 1954; *Educ* Paston Sch North Walsham, Univ of Manchester (BA); *m* Lorraine; 2 c; *Career* joined NHS nat grad mgmnt trg prog 1979, subsequently held various NHS operational mgmnt appts running servs for mental health, learning disability, community health servs and health promotion, exec dir E Anglian RHA (incl period of secondment to Dept of Health) then chief exec Cambridge and Huntingdon HA until 1997, chief exec NHS Confedn 1997–2001, chief exec The Health Fndn 2002–; cmmr Healthcare Cmmn 2003–06, non-exec dir Monitor (ind regulator of NHS fndn tsts) 2006–; writer and regular speaker on health and health serv issues in UK and abroad; dir Christian Blind Mission (UK) 2002–05, memb Cncl Open Univ 2002–06; FHSM (DipHSM), FRSM; *Clubs* Commonwealth; *Style*— Stephen Thornton, Esq, CBE; ✉ The Health Foundation, 90 Long Acre, London WC2E 9RA (tel 020 7257 8000, fax 020 7257 8001)

THOROLD, Sir (Anthony) Oliver; 16 Bt (E 1642); s of Sir Anthony Thorold, 15 Bt, OBE, DSC (d 1999); *b* 15 April 1945; *Educ* Winchester, Lincoln Coll Oxford; *m* 1977, Prof Genevra Richardson, *qv*, da of John L Richardson (d 2002), of Broadshaw, W Lothian; 1 s (Henry b 1981), 1 da (Lydia b 1985); *Heir* s, Henry Lowry; *Career* barr Inner Temple 1971; *Style*— Sir Oliver Thorold, Bt

THORP, James Noble; s of Arthur Thorp (d 1953), and Annie, *née* Rollinson (d 1975); *b* 27 October 1934; *Educ* Rothwell GS, Leeds Coll of Art Sch of Architecture (DipArch); *m* 18 Jan 1958, Jean, da of Arthur Brown (d 1972); 2 s (Ian James b 1958, Julian Alexander b 1969), 2 da (Sally Ann b 1961, Jayne Stella b 1964); *Career* architect, estab private practice 1961 (specialised in ecclesiastical design); lectr in design Leeds Coll of Art, Leeds Poly and Univ of Sheffield 1964–87; Civic Tst assessor; Leeds Gold Medal 1964, DOE Award for Design 1976, Civic Tst Commendation 1987, Wakefield MDC Design Award 1996, RIBA White Rose Design Awards, EASA Presidents Design Award 1999; ARIBA; *Publications* Church Building, Chiesa Oggi (Italy); *Recreations* skiing, amateur theatre, scenic design, music; *Style*— James Thorp, Esq, ARIBA; ✉ 73 Church Street, Woodlesford, Leeds 26 (tel 0113 282 6303); James Thorp, The Studio, 73 Church Street, Woodlesford, Leeds LS26 8RE (tel 0113 282 6303, e-mail james@thorp1934.freeserve.co.uk)

THORP, Jeremy Walter; CMG (2001); s of Walter Thorp (d 1977), of Dublin, and Dorothy Bliss (d 1989); *b* 12 December 1941; *Educ* King Edward VII Sch Sheffield, CCC Oxford (MA); *m* 15 Sept 1973, Estela Maria, da of Alberto Lessa (d 1968), of Montevideo, Uruguay; *Career* HM Treasy 1963–78: asst private sec to Sec of State for Econ Affrs 1967–69, financial attaché HM Embassy Washington 1971–73; FCO: joined 1978, first sec head of Chancery and consul-gen Lima 1982–86, dep head of mission Dublin 1988–92, head Res and Fin Dept FCO 1993–97; with Unilever plc 1997–98; ambass to Colombia 1998–2001 (ret), dir Br Bankers' Assoc 2002–06, sec Jt Money Laundering Steering Gp 2002–06; memb Advsy Cncl Inst Briefing and Conf Centre Farnham Castle 2002–06; tstee Children of the Andes, memb Bd Br-Colombian C of C, chm Anglo-Colombian Soc; *Recreations* music, walking, swimming, travel, reading, modern Irish history; *Style*— Jeremy Thorp, Esq, CMG; ✉ 9 Coutts Crescent, St Albans Road, London NW5 1RF (e-mail jerestelathorp@aol.com)

THORPE, *see also:* Gardner-Thorpe

THORPE, Adam Naylor; s of Bernard Naylor Thorpe, and Sheila Grace, *née* Greenlees (d 2003); *b* 5 December 1956; *Educ* Marlborough, Magdalen Coll Oxford (BA); *m* 23 Nov 1985, Joanna Louise Wistreich; 2 s (Joshua, Sacha), 1 da (Anastasia); *Career* co fndr Equinox Travelling Theatre 1980, drama and mime teacher City and E London Coll Stepney 1983–87, lectr in English PCL 1987–90, poetry critic The Observer 1989–95, currently book critic The Guardian; author and poet; winner: Eric Gregory award 1985, second prize Nat Poetry Competition 1986; *Poetry* Mornings in the Baltic (1988, shortlisted Whitbread Prize for Poetry 1988), Meeting Montaigne (1990), From the Neanderthal (1999), Nine Lessons from the Dark (2003), Birds with a Broken Wing (2007); *Novels* Ulverton (1992, Winifred Holtby Prize for best regnl novel), Still (1995), Pieces of Light (1998), Nineteen Twenty-One (2001), No Telling (2003), The Rules of Perspective (2005), Between Each Breath (2007); *Plays* The Fen Story (Monday play Radio 4, 1991), Offa's Daughter (Sunday play Radio 3, 1993), Couch Grass and Ribbon (stage play, 1996), Devastated Areas (Saturday play Radio 4, 2006); *Short Story Collections* Shifts (2000), Is This The Way You Said? (2006); *Recreations* walking, swimming, music, theatre; *Style*— Adam Thorpe

THORPE, Adèle Loraine; da of Lionel Raphael Lewis (d 2005), and Bettie Louise, *née* Frome; *b* 29 September 1952, London; *Educ* Henrietta Barnett; *m* 16 April 1982, Simon Peter Thorpe, s of Stanley Thorpe; 1 da (Katy Elizabeth b 1987); *Career* northern Euro accountant Amdahl (UK) Ltd 1978–81, fin dir Tandem Computer Ltd 1981–87, dir Sybase Software Ltd 1987–91, Western Europe controller Control Data 1991–93, self-employed 1993–; dir Cortex Corp 1993–95, dir and co sec of several small cos; chm Slough Branch BIM 1985–87; memb: Cncl ICSA, Thames Water Customer Servs Ctee 1988–93, IT Scheme Ctee City & Guilds; Master Worshipful Co of Chartered Secretaries and Administrators 2007–08, Liveryman and Hon Offr Worshipful Co of World Traders; FICSA (memb 1977); *Style*— Mrs Adèle Thorpe

THORPE, Prof Alan John; s of Jack Fielding Thorpe (d 1987), and Dorothy Kathleen, *née* Davey (d 2003); *b* 15 July 1952, Newcastle upon Tyne; *Educ* Univ of Warwick (BSc), Imperial Coll London (PhD); *m* 17 February 1979, Helen Elizabeth, *née* Edgar; 1 da (Alison Mary b 16 May 1980), 1 s (David Leslie b 16 Dec 1982); *Career* postdoctoral research asst Imperial Coll London 1976–81, scientist Met Office 1981–82, lectr, reader then prof of meteorology Univ of Reading 1982–99, dir Hadley Centre Met Office 1999–2001, dir NERC Centres of Atmospheric Science 2001–05, chief exec NERC 2005–; visiting prof Univ of Reading; RMS L F Richardson Prize 1979; author of over 100 papers in peer-reviewed jls; L F Richardson Prize 1976, RMS Buchan Prize 1992; *Recreations* art history and appreciation; *Style*— Prof Alan Thorpe; ✉ Natural Environment Research Council, Polaris House, North Star Avenue, Swindon SN2 1EU (e-mail hqpo@nerc.ac.uk)

THORPE, Amelia Jane; da of Robert Barrie Thorpe, of Boxford, Suffolk, and Margaret, *née* Davenport; *b* 1 July 1961; *Educ* Beaconsfield HS; *m* 23 Dec 1991, Adam Russell, s of Peter Caton Russell; 2 da (Evelina b 28 March 1994, Edie b 4 May 1996); *Career* publishing dir Merehurst Ltd 1983–89, md Ebury Press (responsible for Ebury Press, Vermilion, Rider, Fodor's) and memb Exec Mgmnt Ctee Random House Gp 1989–2002, publishing, editorial conslt and writer 2002–; FRSA; *Recreations* food and wine, art and antiques; *Style*— Ms Amelia Thorpe; ✉ 4 Lyndhurst Square, London SE15 5AR (tel and fax 020 7701 9336, e-mail ameliathorpe@hotmail.com)

THORPE, His Hon Judge Anthony Geoffrey Younghusband; s of Lt Cdr G J Y Thorpe, MBE; *b* 21 August 1941; *Educ* Highgate Sch, BRNC Dartmouth, Inns of Court Sch of Law (Treas's prize for Inner Temple), King's Coll London; *m* 15 Jan 1966, Janet Patricia; 1 da (Madeleine Louise b 12 Dec 1967), 1 s (Simon Francis Younghusband b 27 Sept 1969); *Career* RN: Cdr 1978, served HMS Hermes, Ark Royal, Vidal and Blake, Capt and Chief Naval Judge Advocate 1984, sec to Adm Sir John Woodward, GBE, KCB (C in C Naval Home Cmd) 1987, ret 1990; called to the Bar Inner Temple 1972, recorder Crown Court 1989–90 (asst recorder 1984–89), circuit judge (SE Circuit) 1990–, resident judge Chichester Crown Court; pres: Social Security Appeal Tribunals, Medical Appeal Tribunals and Disability Appeal Tribunals 1992–94, Vaccine Damage Appeal Tribunals 1992–94, Child Support Appeal Tribunals 1992–94; author of treatise Mine Warfare at Sea (Ocean Devpt and Int Law, 1987); *Recreations* sailing; *Clubs* Naval and Military, Hill Street, Mayfair; *Style*— His Hon Judge Thorpe; ✉ The Crown Court, Southgate, Chichester, West Sussex PO19 1SX (tel 01243 787590)

THORPE, David Allan; s of Albert David Thorpe (d 1979), of Upton-upon-Severn, Worcs, and Gertrude Kathleen, *née* Wilkins; *b* 7 August 1949, Stourport-on-Severn, Worcs; *Educ* Hanley Castle GS Worcs; *m* 1, 1971 (m dis 1989), Maureen June Adams; m 2, 22 March 2003, Sheila, *née* York; 2 da (Karen Julie, Andrea Louise); *Career* early career as accountant in local govt Worcs, Essex and London (latterly asst treas London Borough of Havering), subsequently in sales and mktg Honeywell; EDS: joined 1994 (i/c developing govt business), ceo UK 1995, chief operating offr EMEA 1996, pres European business until 2003; currently chm: Tunstall Gp Holdings, CAS Service Ltd; currently non-exec dir: VT Gp plc, Innovation Gp, iSoft plc; former non-exec dir: Torex plc, Staffware plc, Anite plc (interim ceo 2003); chm Racecourse Assoc 2004–, dir BHB, dir Horserace Betting Levy Bd; memb Worshipful Co of Info Technologists; memb Chartered Inst of Public Finance Accountancy 1971; *Recreations* horses (breeding and racing), walking, wine and food; *Clubs* RAC; *Style*— David A Thorpe, Esq

THORPE, Denis; s of Thomas Thorpe (d 1995), of Mansfield, Notts, and Laura Thorpe (d 1995); *b* 6 August 1932; *Educ* High Oakham Sch Mansfield; *m* 30 March 1959, Patricia Ann, *née* Fiddes; 3 da (Josephine Mary b 8 May 1960, Jane Elizabeth b 17 Oct 1961, Lucy Ann b 28 Aug 1964), 3 s (Peter John b 11 Feb 1963, Robert James b 18 Nov 1966, David Gerard b 23 Aug 1971); *Career* photographer; Nat Serv RAF 1950–52; Mansfield Reporter (weekly newspaper) 1948, Northampton Chronicle & Echo 1954–55, Lincolnshire Echo 1955, Birmingham Gazette & Dispatch 1955–57, Daily Mail 1957–74, The Guardian 1974–96; subject of BBC TV Film Worth A Thousand Words 1983; Hon MA Univ of Manchester 1995; life memb NUJ 1996; FRPS 1990 (ARPS 1974), FBIPP 1994 (ABIPP 1992); *Exhibitions* The World of Denis Thorpe (Portico Gallery Manchester) 1982, Russia Through the Lens (Barbican) 1986, Denis Thorpe - Guardian Photographer (Victoria Theatre Stoke-on-Trent) 1990, Denis Thorpe - Photojournalist 1998–99 (The Potteries Museum Art Gallery), On Home Ground: Photographs by Denis Thorpe (The Lowry) 2001, Denis Thorpe Photographs 1950–2000 (Guardian Archive Centre London) 2004; *Awards* Br Press Pictures Awards: Br Regnl Press Photographer of the Year 1971, Picture Essay of the Year 1975–77, Photokina Obelisk (Cologne) 1974, FIAP (Fédération Internationale des Associations de Photographes) Medals 1974–76, UN Special Award 1976, Worlds Press Photo Fndn Gold Medal 1979, Ilford Photographer of the Year 1988, UK Picture Ed's Guild Business and Indust Photographer of the Year 1995; *Books* The Shepherds Year (1979), Pictorial Group Monograph (1994), Denis Thorpe on Home Ground (2001), Denis Thorpe Photographs 1950–2000 (2004); *Recreations* hill walking, playing ragtime piano; *Style*— Denis Thorpe, Esq; ✉ c/o The Guardian, Editorial Department, 164 Deansgate, Manchester M60 2RR

THORPE, Geoffrey Digby; s of late Gordon Digby Thorpe, and Agnes Joyce Saville, *née* Haines; *b* 24 September 1949; *Educ* Windsor GS for Boys, Architectural Assoc Sch of Architecture (AA Dip); *m* 29 Sept 1973, Jane Florence, da of late James Hay McElwee, of Havant, Hampshire; 1 da (Holly b 1980); *Career* indust gp architect; Milton Keynes Devpt Corp 1974–78, asst co architect East Sussex 1978–80, chm Thorpe Architecture Ltd 1980–, princ Thorpe Architecture 1993–2006, princ Thorpe Wheatley Ltd 2006–; chm Prospace Ltd; memb Br Cncl for Offices; RIBA 1975; memb: ARCUK 1975, AA; *Recreations* fly and game fishing, boating; *Style*— Geoffrey Thorpe, Esq; ✉ Thorpe Wheatley Ltd, Sparks Yard, Tarrant Street, Arundel, West Sussex BN18 9SB (tel 01903 883500, fax 01903 882188, e-mail geoff@twarch.co.uk, website www.thorpearchitecture.com)

THORPE, Graham Paul; *b* 1 August 1969, Farnham, Surrey; *Career* professional cricketer with Surrey CCC; England: 100 test matches, 82 one-day ints, test debut v Australia 1993, memb team touring WI 1993–94, SA 1995–96, Zimbabwe and NZ 1996–97, WI 1998, SA 1998, Emirates Trophy 1998, Pakistan and Sri Lanka 2000–01, Zimbabwe, India and NZ 2001–02, Bangladesh and Sri Lanka 2003, WI 2004 and SA 2004–05, ret from int cricket 2005; Wisden Cricketer of the Year 1998; *Style*— Graham Thorpe, Esq; ✉ c/o Surrey CCC, The Oval, Kennington, London SE11 5SS

THORPE, John Frederick; OBE (2003); s of Thomas Alfred Thorpe (d 1983), of Blisworth, Northants, and Edith Rosamund, *née* Ashby; *b* 17 October 1939; *Educ* Oundle, Law Soc Sch of Law; *m* 4 May 1963, Susan Margaret, da of Andrew Roy Banham; 1 da (Joanna Margaret b 8 Sept 1967), 2 s (Michael Jonathan b 6 Nov 1968, Roger James Thomas b 19 June 1975); *Career* solicitor; articles with Phipps & Troup Northampton 1957–62, admitted as slr 1963, slr Boyes, Turner & Burrows Reading 1963–64; Shoosmiths & Harrison: joined as ptnr 1964, managing ptnr 1986–89, sr ptnr 1989–98; pres Northampton Law Soc 1984–85; chm: Nene Fndn 1992–2002, Northants C of C TEC 1996–98, Moulton Coll 1998–2006; Freeman City of London, memb Ct of Assts Worshipful Co of Farmers (jr Warden 2006–07); High Sheriff Northants 2004; *Recreations* cricket, tennis, walking, golf, rugby supporter; *Style*— John Thorpe, Esq, OBE; ✉ The Manor House, Everdon, Daventry, Northamptonshire NN11 3BN (tel 01327 361286)

THORPE, Rt Hon Lord Justice; Rt Hon Sir Mathew Alexander; kt (1988); yr s of late Michael Alexander Thorpe, of Petworth, W Sussex, and Dorothea Margaret, *née* Lambert; *b* 30 July 1938; *Educ* Stowe, Balliol Coll Oxford; *m* 1, 30 Dec 1966, Lavinia Hermione, da of Maj Robert James Buxton (d 1968); 3 s (Gervase b 1967, Alexander b 1969, Marcus b 1971); m 2, 3 Aug 1989, Mrs Carola Millar; *Career* called to the Bar Inner Temple 1961 (bencher 1985); QC 1980, recorder of the Crown Court 1982, judge of the High Court of Justice (Family Div) 1988–95, a Lord Justice of Appeal 1995–, head of int family justice 2005–, dep head of family justice 2005–; *Style*— The Rt Hon Lord Justice Thorpe; ✉ Royal Courts of Justice, Strand, London WC2A 2LL

THORPE, Phillip A; *Career* barr and slr Wellington NZ 1976–79, public prosecutor Republic of Nauru 1979–81, various appts Securities Cmmn Hong Kong 1981–87, chief exec Hong Kong Futures Exchange 1987–89, chief exec Assoc of Futures Brokers and Dealers (AFBD) UK 1989–91, dep chief exec Securities and Futures Authy (SFA) following merger of AFBD and Securities Assoc 1991–93 (seconded as chief exec London Commodity Exchange Ltd 1991–92, seconded to SIB working on review of Financial Services Act regulatory system 1992–93), chief exec Investment Management Regulatory Organisation Ltd (IMRO) 1993–98, md FSA 1998–2001, pres Inst for Financial Markets Washington DC 2001–; *Style*— Phillip Thorpe, Esq; ✉ IFM, 2001 Pennsylvania Avenue, Washington DC 20006 USA (tel 202 223 1528, fax 202 296 3184)

THOURON, Sir John Rupert Hunt; KBE (1976, CBE 1967); s of John Longstreth Thouron, and Amelia Thouron; *b* 10 May 1908; *Educ* Sherborne; *m* 1 (m dis); 1 s; m 2, 1953, Esther duPont, da of Lammot duPont; *Career* Br Army Offr, served WWII Major Black Watch; (with Lady Thouron) fndr Thouron Univ of Pennsylvania Fund for British-American Student Exchange 1960; *Recreations* horticulture, racing, hunting, fishing, golf; *Clubs* Vicmead, Seminole, Jupiter Island, The Brook (all US), White's, Sunningdale, Royal St George's; *Style*— Sir John Thouron, KBE; ✉ Summer: DOE RUN, Unionville, Chester County, Pa 19375, USA (tel 00 1 610 384 5542); Winter: 416 South Beach Road, Hobe Sound, Florida 33455, USA (tel 00 1 407 546 3577); office: 5801 Kennett Pike, Greenville, Delaware 19807, USA (tel 00 1 302 652 6350)

THREADGOLD, Andrew Richard; s of Stanley Dennis Threadgold, of Brentwood, Essex, and late Phyllis Ethel, *née* Marsh; *b* 8 February 1944; *Educ* Brentwood Sch, Univ of Nottingham (BA), Univ of Melbourne (PhD); *m* 1, 1966 (m dis), Rosalind; 2 s (Richard b 1967, Matthew b 1971); m 2, 1994, Deirdre; 1 da (Zoe b 1995); *Career* mangr econ info Int Wool Secretariat 1971–74, advsr Econ Div Bank of England 1974–84, on secondment chief economist Postel Investment Management Ltd 1984–86, head fin supervision Gen Div Bank of England 1986–87, chief exec and dir securities investment Postel Investment Management Ltd 1987–93, with AMP 1993–98 (latterly chief investment offr); non-exec dir: Equitable Life 2001–, Inflexion 2004–; *Style*— Andrew Threadgold, Esq

THRIFT, Prof Nigel John; s of Leonard John Thrift (d 1997), and Joyce Mary, *née* Wakeley; *b* 12 October 1949, Bath; *Educ* Nailsea Sch, UCW Aberystwyth (BA), Univ of Bristol (PhD, DSc); *m* 6 May 1978, Lynda Jean Thrift; 2 da (Victoria Caroline Jane b 29 April 1979, Jessica Abigail b 26 May 1982); *Career* research offr Martin Centre for Architectural and Urban Studies Univ of Cambridge 1975–76, research fell Dept of Geography Univ of Leeds 1976–78, sr research fell Dept of Human Geography ANU 1981–83 (research fell 1979–81); Dept of Geography St David's UC Lampeter: lectr 1984–86, Univ of Wales reader 1986–87; Univ of Bristol: lectr Dept of Geography 1987–88, reader Dept of Geography 1988–90, prof Sch of Geographical Sciences 1990–2003 (emeritus prof 2003–), head Sch of Geographical Sciences 1995–99, chair Univ Research Ctee 2001–03; head Div of Life and Environmental Sciences and prof Sch of Geography Univ of Oxford 2004–05, student ChCh Oxford, pro-vice-chllr (research) Univ of Oxford 2005–06, vice-chllr Univ of Warwick 2006–; hon memb of faculty Dept of Geography UCLA 1984, hon memb of faculty Geographical Inst ETH Zürich 1987, hon research scholar Sch of Earth Sciences Macquarie Univ Sydney 1989, visiting prof Grad Sch of Architecure and Urban Planning UCLA 1992, fell Netherlands Inst of Advanced Study Wassenaar 1993, guest prof Institut für Geographie Univ of Vienna 1998, fell Swedish Collegium for Advanced Study in the Social Sciences Uppsala 1999, distinguished visiting prof Nat Univ of Singapore 2002, visiting prof Univ of Oxford 2006–; memb: Research Assessment Exercise 2001 Panel for Geography HEFCE 1999–2001, Geography Panel Leverhulme Prize Fellowship 2000–, Research Priorities Bd ESRC 2001–05; chair Research Assessment Exercise 2008 Main Panel H HEFCE 2005–07; ed: Environment and Planning A, Society and Space; author, co-author, ed or co-ed of 35 books and 200 papers in jls and edited collections, memb 10 editorial bds; RGS Heath Award 1988, RSGS Newbigin Prize 1998, Univ of Helsinki Medal 1999, RGS Victoria Medal 2003, Distinguished Scholarship Honours Assoc of American Geographers 2007; MA (by incorporation) Univ of Oxford 2004; AcSS 2000, FBA 2003; *Style*— Prof Nigel Thrift; ✉ University House, University of Warwick, Kirby Corner Road, Coventry CV4 8UW (tel 024 7642 3630, mobile 07920 533140, e-mail vc@warwick.ac.uk)

THRING, Jeremy John; DL (Avon 1988–96, Somerset 1997–); o s of late Christopher William Thring, MBE, TD, of Upton Lovell, Wilts, and Joan Evelyn, *née* Graham; *b* 11 May 1936; *Educ* Winchester; *m* 30 June 1962, Cynthia Kay, da of late Gilbert Kirkpatrick Smith, of Bath; 2 da (Lucinda Katharine (Mrs Edward St J Hall) b 8 Aug 1963, Candida Sara (Mrs David Pilkington) b 11 May 1965); *Career* Nat Serv cmmnd 3 Kings Own Hussars 1955; admitted slr 1962, NP 1962, in practice Thring Townsend Bath; local dir Coutts Bank 1989–2004; chm Royal Nat Hosp for Rheumatic Diseases NHS Trust 1991–99; chm Cncl Univ of Bath 1994–2003 (pro-chllr 2001–); tstee: R J Harris Charitable Tst, The Pixiella Tst; memb: Law Soc, Soc of Provincial Notaries; Hon LLD Univ of Bath; *Recreations* stalking, shooting, fishing; *Style*— Jeremy Thring, Esq, DL, LLD (Hon); ✉ Belcombe House, Bradford-on-Avon, Wiltshire (tel 01225 862295); Thring Townsend, Midland Bridge, Bath BA1 2HQ (tel 01225 340099, fax 01225 319735, e-mail jthring@ttuk.com)

THROWER, Keith Rex; OBE (1986); s of Stanley Frank Thrower (d 1966), of London, and Ellen Amelia Thrower (d 1963); *b* 26 December 1934; *Educ* St Dunstan's Coll London, Reading Coll of Advanced Technol (HNC Electronic Engrg, HNC Endorsements); *m* 1, 1958, Janice Barbara, *née* Brooks; 3 da (Sarah Jane b 10 Nov 1959, Marianne Judith b 7 March 1965, Margaret Louise b 17 July 1966); m 2, 1984, Alma, *née* Heath; *Career* technician: Cinema Television Ltd 1955–56, New Electronics Products 1956–58; electronic engr Dynatron Radio Ltd 1958–60; Racal Electronics plc: sr electronic engr 1960–64, princ electronic engr 1964–66, chief engr/gen mangr Radio Div 1966–68, tech dir Racal Instruments Ltd 1968–73, dir of advanced devpt 1973–78, dep chm Racal Research Ltd 1985–95 (md 1978–85), tech dir Racal Chubb Ltd 1985–91, res dir Racal Radio Group Ltd 1985–95; fndr Kalma Ltd 1995–99; FIERE 1984 (MIERE 1964, pres 1986–87), FIEE 1988, FREng 1992; *Books* History of the British Radio Valve to 1940 (1992), British Radio Valves, The Vintage Years: 1904–1925 (1999); *Recreations* reading, writing, philately, history of science and technology; *Style*— Keith Thrower, Esq, OBE, FREng; ✉ 4 Mapledene, Caversham, Reading, Berkshire RG4 7DQ (tel 0118 947 4813, fax 0118 948 3730)

THROWER, (James) Simeon; s of Derek Bert Thrower, MBE, of Woldingham, Surrey, and Mary, *née* O'Connor; *b* 24 May 1950; *Educ* Royal GS High Wycombe, Univ of Leeds (LLB); *m* 21 June 1980, Alexandra Mary Elizabeth, da of late George Reginald Lanning, MC; 3 da (Justine Victoria b 15 Aug 1982, Catherine Georgina b 22 April 1985, Eleanor Juliet b 19 Nov 1990); *Career* called to the Bar Middle Temple 1973 (ad eundem Lincoln's Inn 1983), head of chambers 1985–, bencher 1998–; *Recreations* golf, sailing, travel; *Clubs* Wentworth Golf, Rosslyn Park RFC; *Style*— Simeon Thrower, Esq; ✉ 11 Old Square, Lincoln's Inn, London WC2A 3TS (tel 020 7242 5022, fax 020 7404 0445, e-mail simlaw@11oldsquare.com)

THRUSH, Prof Brian Arthur; s of Arthur Albert Thrush (d 1963), of Hampstead, London, and Dorothy Charlotte, *née* Money (d 1983); *b* 23 July 1928; *Educ* Haberdashers' Aske's, Emmanuel Coll Cambridge (BA, MA, PhD, ScD); *m* 31 May 1958, Rosemary Catherine, da of George Henry Terry (d 1970), of Ottawa, Canada; 1 s (Basil Mark Brian b 1965), 1 da (Felicity Elizabeth b 1967); *Career* conslt to US Nat Bureau of Standards 1957–58; Univ of Cambridge: demonstrator in physical chemistry 1953–58, asst dir of res 1959–64, lectr 1964–69, reader 1969–78, prof of physical chemistry 1978–95, vice-master Emmanuel Coll 1986–90 (fell 1960–), head of Chemistry Dept 1988–93; visiting prof Chinese Acad of Sci 1980–; memb: Lawes Agric Tst Ctee 1979–89, Natural Environment Res Cncl 1985–90, Cncl of the Royal Soc 1989–91; Tilden lectr Chemical Soc 1965, Michael Polanyi medallist Royal Soc of Chemistry 1980, awarded Rank Prize for Opto-Electronics 1992; memb Academia Europaea 1990 (memb Cncl 1992–98); FRS 1976, FRSC 1977; *Recreations* wine, walking; *Style*— Prof Brian Thrush, FRS; ✉ Brook Cottage, Pemberton Terrace, Cambridge CB2 1JA (tel 01223 357 637); University of Cambridge, Department of Chemistry, Lensfield Road, Cambridge CB2 1EW (tel 01223 336 458, fax 01223 336 362, e-mail bat1@cam.ac.uk); Emmanuel College, Cambridge CB2 3AP

THUBRON, Colin Gerald Dryden; CBE (2007); s of Brig Gerald Ernest Thubron, DSO, OBE (d 1992), of Piltdown, E Sussex, and Evelyn Kate Mary, *née* Dryden; *b* 14 June 1939; *Educ* Eton; *Career* on editorial staff: Hutchinson & Co 1959–62, Macmillan Co NY 1964–65; freelance film-maker 1962–64; author; RSGS Mungo Park Medal 2000, RSAA Lawrence of Arabia Memorial Medal 2000; Hon DLitt Univ of Warwick; FRSL 1969 (vice-pres 2003); *Books* Mirror to Damascus (1967), The Hills of Adonis (1968), Jerusalem (1969), Journey Into Cyprus (1975), The God in the Mountain (1977), Emperor (1978), Among the Russians (1983), A Cruel Madness (1984, Silver Pen Award), Behind the Wall (1987, Hawthornden Prize, Thomas Cook Award), Falling (1989), Turning Back the Sun (1991), The Lost Heart of Asia (1994), Distance (1996), In Siberia (1999), To the Last City (2002), Shadow of the Silk Road (2006); *Style*— Colin Thubron, Esq, CBE, FRSL; ✉ 28 Upper Addison Gardens, London W14 8AJ

THURLEY, Dr Simon John; s of late Thomas Manley Thurley, and Rachel, *née* House; *b* 29 August 1962; *Educ* Kimbolton Sch, Bedford Coll London (BA), Courtauld Inst (MA, PhD); *Career* inspector of ancient monuments Crown Bldgs and Monuments Gp English Heritage 1981–89, curator of the Historic Royal Palaces 1989–97, dir Museum of London 1997–2002, chief exec English Heritage 2002–; visiting prof of medieval London history Royal Holloway Coll London 2000; pres Huntingdonshire Local History Soc, vice-pres NADFAS, chm Soc for Ct Studies, memb St Paul's Cathedral Cncl; hon fell Royal Holloway Univ of London 2003; memb Inst of Field Archaeologists; FSA; *Publications* Henry VIII - Images of a Tudor King (jtly, 1989), The Royal Palaces of Tudor England - Architecture and Court Life 1460–1547 (1993), Whitehall Palace - An Architectural History (1999), Hampton Court - An Architectural and Social History (2003), Lost Buildings of Britain (2004); contrib many volumes, magazines and jls; *Style*— Dr Simon Thurley; ✉ English Heritage, 1 Waterhouse Square, 138–142 Holborn EC1N 2ST (tel 020 7973 3222, e-mail simon.thurley@english-heritage.org)

THURLOW, Dr Alexander Cresswell; s of Maurice Cresswell Thurlow (d 1940), and Despina Alexandra, *née* Evangelinou; *b* 13 April 1940; *Educ* Brighton Hove E Sussex GS, St Mary's Hosp Med Sch (MB BS); *m* 29 June 1963, Joanna, da of Stefan Woycicki, of Wilts; 2 da (Susan Kristina b 1965, Jane b 1966); *Career* sr registrar in anaesthesia St Thomas' Hosp and Hosp For Sick Children 1969–72; conslt anaesthetist: St George's Hosp 1972–, Royal Dental Hosp 1972–82; asst prof of anaesthesia Stanford Univ 1975–76, tutor and lectr in anaesthesia Royal Coll of Anaesthetists 1977–; chm Southern Soc of Anaesthetists, memb Assoc of Anaesthetists, memb Assoc of Dental Anaesthetists; memb BMA, FRCA 1968; *Books* contrib: Clinics In Anaesthesiology (1983), Anaesthesia and Sedation in Dentistry (1983), A Practice of Anaesthesia (1984); *Recreations* swimming, travel, opera, theatre; *Style*— Dr Alexander Thurlow; ✉ Department of Anaesthesia, St George's Hospital, Blackshaw Road, London SW17 0QT (tel 020 8672 1255)

THURLOW, Prof David George; OBE (1987); s of Frederick Charles Thurlow (d 1986), of Bury St Edmunds, Suffolk, and Audrey Isabel Mary, *née* Farrow; *b* 31 March 1939; *Educ* King Edward VI Sch Bury St Edmunds, Dept of Architecture Cambridge Coll of Art, Sch of Architecture Canterbury Coll of Art, Univ of Cambridge (MA); *m* 19 Dec 1959, Pamela Ann, da of Percy Adolphous Rumbelow; 3 da (Suzanne Elizabeth, Jane Ann, Emma Louise); *Career* architect; fndr ptnr: Cambridge Design Group 1970, Cambridge Design Architects 1975, Design Group Cambridge 1988, Thurlow, Carnell & Curtis 1991, David Thurlow Partnership 2002; Faculty of Architecture Univ of Cambridge 1970–77, Sch of Architecture Univ of Nottingham 1991–96, emeritus prof of architecture South Bank Univ 1998– (head Architecture Div 1996–97), dir MA in architectural design Univ of Bath 2001–05; exhibitor Royal Acad Summer Exhibition 1983–; awards incl: RIBA Award 1976, 1984, 1986 and 1990, Civic Tst Award 1978 and 1986, DOE Housing Award 1985; assessor: RIBA Awards 1979, 1984, 1986 and 1990, Civic Tst Awards 1979–97; fndr memb: Granta Housing Soc, Cambridge Forum for the Construction Industry 1981 (chm 1985–86); memb PSA Design Panel 1987–89; pres Assoc of Conslt Architects (ACA) 1991–93, Surveyors Club 2004; ARIBA 1965; *Recreations* cricket, golf, food; *Clubs* Athenaeum, MCC, Surveyors (pres); *Style*— Prof David Thurlow, OBE; ✉ The Studio, Chillswood, Church Lane, Limpley Stoke, Bath BA2 7GH (tel 01225 720114, fax 01225 720118, e-mail dt@davidthurlowconsultancy.co.uk, website www.davidthurlowconsultancy.co.uk)

THURLOW, 8 Baron (GB 1792); Francis Edward Hovell-Thurlow-Cumming-Bruce; KCMG (1961, CMG 1957); 2 s of Rev 6 Baron Thurlow (d 1952), and Grace Catherine, *née* Trotter (d 1959); suc bro, 7 Baron Thurlow, CB, CBE, DSO (d 1971); *b* 9 March 1912; *Educ* Shrewsbury, Trinity Coll Cambridge (MA); *m* 13 Aug 1949, Yvonne Diana (d 1990), da of late Aubyn Harold Raymond Wilson, of St Andrews, Fife, and formerly w of Mandell Creighton Dormehl; 2 s, 2 da; *Heir* s, Hon Roualeyn Hovell-Thurlow-Cumming-Bruce; *Career* Dept of Agric for Scotland 1935–37; HM Dip Serv: sec NZ 1939–44 and Canada 1944–45, private sec to Sec of State for Commonwealth Relations 1947–49, cnsllr New Delhi 1949–52, advsr to Govr of Gold Coast 1955, dep high cmmr Ghana 1957 and Canada 1958, high cmmr to NZ 1959–63 and Nigeria 1963–66, dep under sec FCO 1964, govr and C-in-C of Bahamas 1968–72; KStJ; *Recreations* gardening; *Clubs* Travellers; *Style*— The Rt Hon the Lord Thurlow, KCMG; ✉ 102 Leith Mansions, Grantully Road, London W9 1LJ (tel 020 7289 9664, e-mail fthurlow@btinternet.com)

THURNHAM, Peter Giles; s of Giles Rymer Thurnham (d 1975), and Marjorie May, *née* Preston (d 1994); *b* 21 August 1938; *Educ* Oundle, Peterhouse Cambridge, Harvard Business Sch, Cranfield Inst of Technol; *m* 1963 (m dis 2004), Sarah Janet, da of Harold Keenlyside Stroude (d 1974); 1 s, 3 da, 1 s adopted; *Career* professional engr running own business WR Group (employing over 600 people) 1972–2002; memb S Lakeland Dist Cncl 1982–84; MP (Cons until Oct 1996, Lib Dem thereafter) Bolton NE 1983–97; PPS to: Rt Hon Norman Fowler as Sec of State for Employment 1987–90, Eric Forth and Robert Jackson as jt Parly Under-Secs of State Dept of Employment 1991–92, Rt Hon Michael Howard as Sec of State DOE 1992–93; memb: Social Security Select Ctee 1993–95, Public Accounts Ctee 1995–97; sec Cons Employment Ctee 1986–87; vice-chm: All-Pty Parly Gp for Children 1987–97, All-Pty Parly Gp for Disability 1992–97 (former chm Cons Disability Gp); vice-chm Cons Small Business Ctee 1985–87; dir Rathbone 1997–2001; pres: Campaign for Inter Country Adoption, Croft Care Tst Barrow, Adoption Forum; FIMechE; *Recreations* country life; *Style*— Peter Thurnham, Esq; ✉ Fourstones House, Bentham, Lancaster LA2 7DL (tel 01524 264876, fax 01524 264877, e-mail peter@fourstoneshouse.co.uk)

THURSBY, Peter Lionel; s of Lionel Albert Thursby (d 1967), and Florence Bessie, *née* Macey (d 1973); *b* 23 December 1930; *m* 30 Aug 1956, Maureen Suzanne, da of late Donald Newton Aspden; *Career* Nat Serv 1949–51; head of art Heles GS Exeter 1960–71, head of Sch of Art and Design Exeter Coll 1971–89; practising sculptor; 20 solo exhibitions nationally, 13 public commissions in UK and USA incl 10 ft bronze fountain in Dallas; pres Royal West of England Acad Bristol (first sculptor pres) 1995–2000; Hon Dr Art UWE 1995; FRBS (awarded silver medal for bronze sculpture 1986); *Recreations* genealogy, wildlife, swimming, music, theatre, cinema; *Clubs* Chelsea Arts, Exeter Golf and Country; *Style*— Peter Thursby, Esq; ✉ Oakley House, 28 Oakley Close, Pinhoe, Exeter, Devon EX1 3SB (tel and fax 01392 467931, website www.peterthursbysculptor.co.uk)

THURSBY-PELHAM, Brig (Mervyn) Christopher; OBE (1986); s of Nevill Cressett Thursby-Pelham (d 1950), of Danyrallt Park, Carmarthenshire, and Yseulte, *née* Peel (d 1982); *b* 23 March 1921; *Educ* Wellington, Merton Coll Oxford; *m* 16 Jan 1943, Rachel Mary Latimer, da of Sir Walter Stuart James Willson (d 1952), of Kenward, Kent; 1 da (Philippa Rachel Mary b 1943), 1 s (David Thomas Cressett b 1948); *Career* cmmnd Welsh Gds 1941, serv 3 Bn N Africa, Italy and Austria 1943–45, serv 1 Bn Palestine and Egypt, grad Staff Coll Camberley 1950, GSO2 (Ops) 6 Armd Div BAOR 1951–53, Regtl Adj Welsh Gds 1956–57, DS Staff Coll Camberley 1957–60, Cmdt Gds Depot Pirbright 1960–63, GSO1 (Ops) Allied Staff Berlin 1963–64, Regtl Lt-Col cmdg WG 1964–67, COS Br Forces Gulf 1967–69, COS London Dist 1969–72, Dep Fortress Cdr Gibraltar 1972–74, Dep Cdr Midwest Dist UK 1974–76; ADC to HM The Queen 1972–76; DG Br Heart Fndn 1976–86 and 1988–90 (memb Cncl 1990–93), co pres Royal Br Legion Berks 1985–91 (vice-pres 1991–), pres Welsh Gds Assoc Monmouthshire branch 1987–99, Gds Assoc Reading branch 1991–99; *Recreations* reading, travel; *Clubs* Cavalry and Guards', Royal Yacht Sqdn; *Style*— Brig Christopher Thursby-Pelham, OBE; ✉ Thorpe Hall Stables, Thorpe Morieux, Bury St Edmunds, Suffolk IP30 0NW

THURSBY-PELHAM, Douglas Thomas Harvey; s of Col Donald Hervey Thursby-Pelham, of Bagshot, Surrey, and Chantal Jeanne Marie Anne, *née* Walsh de Serrant; *b* 27 September 1956; *Educ* Wellington, KCL (BA); *m* 9 Aug 1986, Zoë Anne, da of late David Stanley Joseph Moseley; 2 da (Alexandra Anne b 10 Aug 1988, Victoria Alice b 26 July 1993), 1 s (Charles David Harvey b 13 Dec 1989); *Career* Londsdale Advertising Ltd: grad trainee 1979–81, account exec 1981–83, account mangr 1983–84; account dir Allen Brady and Marsh Ltd 1985–86 (joined 1984), bd dir BMP DDB Needham (formerly known as Reeves Robertshaw Needham then DDB Needham Worldwide) 1988–89 (joined 1986), client servs dir Publicis Ltd 1994–97 (gp account dir 1990–94), md Clark and Taylor 1997–98, account md Young & Rubicam EMEA 1998–; IPA Advertising Effectiveness Award 1992, Advtg and Mktg Effectiveness Award New York Festival 1995; *Style*— Douglas Thursby-Pelham, Esq; ✉ Littledean, Bramdean, Alresford, Hampshire SO24 0JU (tel 01962 771358, e-mail dthursbypelham@aol.com)

THURSO, 3 Viscount (UK 1952); Sir John Archibald Sinclair; 6 Bt (GB 1786), MP; s of 2 Viscount Thurso (d 1995), and Margaret Beaumont, *née* Robertson; *b* 10 September 1953; *Educ* Eton, Westminster Tech Coll; *m* 12 June 1976, Marion Ticknor, da of Louis D Sage, of Connecticut, USA, and Constance Cluett Ward, *qv*, of Dunkeld, Perthshire; 1 da (Hon Louisa Ticknor Beaumont b 15 March 1980), 2 s (Hon James Alexander Robin b 14 Jan 1984, Hon George Henry MacDonald b 29 Oct 1989); *Heir* s, Hon James Sinclair, yr of Ulbster; *Career* mgmnt trainee Savoy Hotel plc 1972–77, reception mangr Claridge's 1978–81, gen mangr Hotel Lancaster Paris (part of the Savoy Gp) 1981–85, dir SA Lancaster 1982–85, vice-chm Prestige Hotels 1984–89, fndr gen mangr Cliveden Bucks for Blakeney Hotels 1985–92; dir Cliveden House Ltd 1987–94, chief exec Granfel Holdings Ltd 1992–95; md Fitness and Leisure Holdings Ltd 1995–2001; non-exec chm:

Lochdhu Hotels Ltd, Thurso Fisheries Ltd, Sinclair Family Trust Ltd, Int Wine and Spirit Competition 1999–; vice-chm Prestige Hotels 1983–90; non-exec dir: Savoy Hotel plc 1993–98, Walker Greenbank 1997–99, Millennium & Copthorne plc 2002–; sat as Lib Dem in House of Lords 1995–99; MP (Lib Dem) Caithness, Sutherland & Easter Ross 2001–; spokesman for Scottish affrs 2001–06, spokesman for transport 2003–05; chm: Game Conservancy Bucks 1990–92, Clubs Panel BHA 1992–95, Scrabster Harbour Tst 1996–2001, Walker Greenbank 1999–2002; patron: HCIMA 1997–2003, Inst of Mgmnt Services 1998–; pres: Licensed Victuallers Schs 1996–97, Acad of Food and Wine Service 1998–; Hon DBA Oxford Brookes Univ 2004; Freeman City of London 1991; FHCIMA 1991, FInstD 1997, Master Innholder 1991 (chm 1995–97); *Recreations* fishing, shooting, food, wine; *Clubs* New (Edinburgh), Brooks's; *Style*— The Rt Hon the Viscount Thurso, MP; ✉ House of Commons, London SW1A 0AA; Thurso East Mains, Thurso, Caithness KW14 8HW (tel 01847 893134, e-mail thursoj@parliament.uk)

THURSTON, Dr John Gavin Bourdas; s of Gavin Leonard Bourdas Thurston (d 1980), and Ione Witham, *née* Barber (d 1967); *b* 8 April 1937; *Educ* Haileybury, Guy's Hosp Med Sch London (MB BS); *m* 1, Felicity, *née* Neal; 1 da (Georgette Margaret (Mrs McCready) *b* 1959), 1 s (Gavin *b* 1962); *m* 2, Joy Elizabeth, *née* Leech; 3 s (Gareth *b* 1966, John *b* 1969, Andrew *b* 1972); *m* 3, Stephanie Sarah, *née* Mayo; *Career* house physician and surgn: Guy's Hosp 1961–62, Lewisham Hosp 1962; house physician Brompton Hosp 1962–63, registrar Westminster Hosp 1964–66, res sr registrar Br Heart Fndn 1967–68, sr cardiology registrar Westminster Hosp 1968–78, conslt A&E Dept Queen Mary's Hosp Roehampton 1979–97, clinical dir A&E Dept Darent Valley Hosp 1997–; disaster doctor RFU Twickenham 1990–2006; MO: Surrey Co RFC, Rosslyn Park RFC; med companion Grand Order of Water Rats; pres A/E Section RSM 1988–90, hon sec Br Assoc of A/E Med 1984–90; Freeman City of London 1965, Liveryman Worshipful Soc of Apothecaries 1963; memb: BMA 1962, Br Assoc of A/E Med 1979; FRSM 1986, FRCP 1992, fell Int Fedn for Emergency Med (FIFEM) 2004, FCEM (fndr fell and hon registrar); *Books* Scientific Foundations of Anaesthesia (co-author, 1976), Hyperbaric Medicine (co-author, 1977); *Recreations* eating, drinking, rugby, humour, after-dinner speaking, study of good English; *Clubs* Rosslyn Park RFC; *Style*— Dr John Thurston; ✉ Vessels, Bessels Green Road, Sevenoaks, Kent TN13 2PT (tel 01732 458367); Darent Valley Hospital, Dartford, Kent DA2 8DA (tel 01322 428160, fax 01322 42816, mobile 07850 597913, e-mail johnthurston@btinternet.com)

THURSTON, Julian Paul; s of Ronald Thurston, of Dunstable, Beds, and Eileen Joyce Thurston, *née* Salmon; *b* 11 May 1955; *Educ* Bedford Sch, Merton Coll Oxford (MA), Coll of Law London; *m* 11 July 1981, Julia Sarah, da of Thomas George Kerslake (d 1966); 1 da (Sarah *b* 1987), 1 s (Thomas *b* 1989); *Career* admitted slr 1979; ptnr: CMS Cameron McKenna (formerly McKenna & Co) 1986–99 (latterly head Technology Gp and Commercial Practice Gp), Arnold & Porter 1999–2003, Morrison & Foerster LLP 2003–; non-exec dir Cancer Research Campaign Technology (then Cancer Research Ventures) 1988–2002; *Style*— Julian Thurston, Esq; ✉ Morrison & Foerster LLP, 21 Garlick Hill, London EC4V 2AU

THWAITE, Ann Barbara; da of A J Harrop (d 1963), and Hilda Mary, *née* Valentine (d 1990); *b* 4 October 1932; *Educ* Marsden Sch Wellington NZ, Queen Elizabeth Girls' GS Barnet, St Hilda's Coll Oxford (MA, DLitt); *m* 4 Aug 1955, Anthony Thwaite, OBE, FRSL, *qv*; 4 da (Emily *b* 1957, Caroline *b* 1959, Lucy *b* 1961, Alice *b* 1965); *Career* writer; occasional reviewer: TLS 1963–85, The Guardian, TES, Washington Post, Daily Telegraph, Times; visiting prof Tokyo Joshi Daigaku 1985–86 and 2005, Helen Stubbs lectr Toronto Public Library 1991, Ezra Jack Keats lectr Univ of Southern Mississippi 1992; govr: St Mary's Middle Sch Long Stratton 1990–2002, Hapton VC Primary Sch 1994–2006; vice-pres Tennyson Soc; Churchill fell 1993, Gladys Krieble Delmas fell British Library 1998, hon fell Univ of Surrey 2001; FRSL; *Books* children's books incl: The Camelthorn Papers (1969), Allsorts 1–7 (ed, 1968–75), Tracks (1978), Allsorts of Poems (ed, 1978), The Ashton Affair (1995), The Horse at Hilly Fields (1996); other publications: Waiting for the Party: The Life of Frances Hodgson Burnett (1974, reissued 1994), My Oxford (ed, 1977), Edmund Gosse: A Literary Landscape (1984, Duff Cooper Meml Award 1985), A A Milne: His Life (1990, Whitbread Biography Prize 1990), Portraits from Life: Essays by Edmund Gosse (ed, 1991), The Brilliant Career of Winnie-the-Pooh (1992), Emily Tennyson, the Poet's Wife (1996), Glimpses of the Wonderful: the life of Philip Henry Gosse (2002); *Recreations* other people's lives, punting on the Tas; *Clubs* Soc of Authors, Royal Over-Seas League, Children's Books History Soc; *Style*— Ann Thwaite; ✉ The Mill House, Low Tharston, Norfolk NR15 2YN (tel 01508 489569); c/o Curtis Brown, 28/29 Haymarket, London SW1Y 4SP (tel 020 7396 6600)

THWAITE, Anthony Simon; OBE (1990); s of Hartley Thwaite, JP (d 1978), and Alice Evelyn, *née* Mallinson (d 1998); *b* 23 June 1930; *Educ* Kingswood Sch, ChCh Oxford (MA); *m* 4 Aug 1955, Ann Barbara Thwaite, *qv*, da of Angus John Harrop (d 1963), of NZ and London; 4 da (Emily *b* 1957, Caroline *b* 1959, Lucy *b* 1961, Alice *b* 1965); *Career* Nat Serv Sgt Instr Rifle Bde and RAEC 1949–51; lectr English lit Univ of Tokyo 1955–57, prodr BBC radio 1957–62, literary ed The Listener 1962–65, asst prof English Univ of Libya Benghazi 1965–67, literary ed New Statesman 1968–72, co-ed Encounter 1973–85, Japan Fndn fell 1985–86, dir André Deutsch Ltd 1986–92 (editorial conslt 1992–95), writer in residence Vanderbilt Univ Nashville USA 1992; Richard Hillary Meml Prize 1968, Cholmondeley Award for Poetry 1983, chm of judges Booker Prize 1986; former memb: Ctee of Mgmnt Soc of Authors, Lit Panel Arts Cncl of GB, Lit Advsy Ctee Br Cncl; current memb: Cncl RSL, Soc of Authors, Soc for Post-Medieval Archaeology, Medieval Pottery Research Gp, Soc for Libyan Studies, Philip Larkin Soc (pres); Ctee RLF; hon lay canon Norwich Cathedral 2005; Hon LittD Univ of Hull 1989; FRSL 1978, FSA 2000; *Books* incl Poems 1953–83 (1984), Six Centuries of Verse (1984), Poetry Today (1985, revised edn 1996), Letter From Tokyo (1987), Philip Larkin: Collected Poems (ed, 1988), Poems 1953–88 (1989), Philip Larkin: Selected Letters 1940–1985 (ed, 1992), The Dust of the World (1994), Selected Poems 1956–96 (1997), Penguin Book of Japanese Verse (co-ed revised edn, 1998), Anthony Thwaite in Conversation with Peter Dale and Ian Hamilton (1999), A Different Country (2000), Philip Larkin, Further Requirements (ed, 2001), A Move in the Weather (2003), The Ruins of Time (ed, 2006), Collected Poems (2007); *Recreations* archaeology, travel; *Style*— Anthony Thwaite; ✉ The Mill House, Low Tharston, Norfolk NR15 2YN (tel 01508 489569, fax 01508 489221)

THWAITES, (John Gilbert) Hugh; s of Dr John Gilbert Thwaites (d 1990), and Enid Joan, *née* Baker; *b* 24 September 1935; *Educ* St Andrew's Sch Eastbourne, Winchester; *m* 17 Nov 1961, Valerie Norwood, da of Norman Oscar Wright; 2 s (James Nicholas Gilbert *b* 30 Aug 1962, Peter Hugh *b* 11 Dec 1968), 1 da (Louise Catherine *b* 4 March 1964); *Career* Nat Serv as 2 Lt RA 1954–56; mangr Harrisons & Crosfield Ltd in India and Indonesia 1956–64; Brooke Bond Group plc: mangr Calcutta 1964–67, dir Brooke Bond Ceylon 1967–72, gen mangr Brooke Bond Kenya 1972–77, md Brooke Bond Pakistan 1977–80, dir Brooke Bond Oxo Ltd 1981–85; chm Lipton Ltd (subsid of Unilever plc) 1986–95; non-exec dir Croydon Health Authy 1990–92, chm Mayday Healthcare NHS Trust Croydon 1993–97; pres UK Tea Buyers' Assoc 1983, chm UK Tea Assoc 1988–89; *Recreations* music, history, golf, sailing; *Clubs* Oriental, MCC; *Style*— Hugh Thwaites, Esq; ✉ Chailey End, Newick, East Sussex BN8 4RA (tel 01825 722933, e-mail hugh@thwaitefamily.com)

THWAITES, Ronald; QC (1987); s of Stanley Thwaites, of Stockton-on-Tees, and Aviva, *née* Cohen; *b* 21 January 1946; *Educ* Richard Hind Secdy Tech Sch Stockton, Grangefield GS Stockton, Kingston Coll of Technol (LLB); *m* 7 Aug 1972, Judith Adelaide Foley, da of late Barry Baron Myers; 3 s (George *b* 1973, David *b* 1976, Harry *b* 1981), 1 da (Stephanie *b* 1980); *Career* called to the Bar Gray's Inn 1970 (ad eundem Inner Temple 1981); head of chambers Ely Place Chambers 2000–; *Recreations* lighting bonfires; *Style*— Ronald Thwaites, Esq, QC; ✉ Ely Place Chambers, 30 Ely Place, Holborn Circus, London EC1N 6TD (tel 020 7400 9600, fax 020 7400 9630)

TIBBUTT, Dr David Arthur; s of Sidney Arthur William Tibbutt (d 1955), of Wadhurst, E Sussex, and Dorothy Ellen, *née* Lay (d 1994); *b* 8 March 1941; *Educ* The Skinners' GS Tunbridge Wells, St Peter's Coll Oxford (MA, BM BCh, DM); *m* 26 Nov 1966, Jane, da of Air Vice-Marshal Sir George David Harvey, KBE, CB, DFC (d 1969), of Over Worton, Oxon; 2 s (Mark David *b* 1968, William George *b* 1970); *Career* jr hosp doctor United Oxford Hosp 1968–76; Worcester Royal Infirmary NHS Tst: conslt physician 1976–98, clinical dir 1994–96; coordinator and advsr for continuing medical educn Miny of Health of Republic of Uganda and Tropical Health and Educn Tst 1998–, visiting conslt physician to Kitovu Hosp Masaka Uganda 2003–; various pubns on thromboembolic disease 1974–, visiting lectr and external examiner Makerere Univ Med Sch Kampala Uganda 1965–97, post grad clinical tutor (Worcester Dist) 1987–92, RCP tutor for Worcester Dist 1987–93; ed Charles Hastings Postgraduate Jl 1991–98, pres Worcester Dist Br Heart Fndn 1984–98, tstee Worcestershire Hosp Charitable Tst 1987–; memb bd Worcester Citizens' Advice Bureau 2002–, chm Worcester Cons Assoc Policy Forum 2002–04, memb Worcester Dist Community Health Cncl 2001–03, memb Patient and Public Involvement in Health Forum Worcester Acute Hosp Tst 2003–06; cncllr Worcester City Cncl 2004– (memb Cabinet 2006–); tstee: Worcester Municipal Charities 2003–, Worcester Racial Equality Cncl 2004–; memb: BMA 1968, W Midlands Physicians Assoc 1976, Br Cardiac Soc 1993; FRCP 1983 (MRCP 1971), FRSM 1992–98; *Books* Pulmonary Embolism: Current Therapeutic Concepts (1977); *Recreations* watercolour painting, gardening, philately; *Style*— Dr David Tibbutt; ✉ Kitovu, 8, Stuart Rise, Red Hill Lane, Worcester WR5 2QQ (tel and fax 01905 355451, e-mail david@tibbutt.co.uk)

TICEHURST, His Hon Judge David Keith; s of Frederick John Ticehurst, of Bryher, Isles of Scilly, and Barbara Elisabeth, *née* Hyde; *b* 1 May 1950; *Educ* Taunton's Sch Southampton, Keynsham GS Bristol, Kingston Poly (BA); *m* 25 March 1972, Gillian, da of Reginald Colston Shepherd, and Daphne, *née* Sapey; *Career* articled clerk Lawrence & Co Bristol 1972–74, admitted slr 1975, Lawrence & Co Bristol 1975–78, Osborne Clarke 1978–80 (ptnr Osborne Clarke 1980–98), asst recorder 1991–94, recorder 1994–98, circuit judge (Western Circuit) 1998–; Higher Court advocate (all proceedings) 1994; lectr in law and broadcast journalism UWE 1990–94; memb Law Soc 1975, fndr memb Employment Lawyers Assoc (SW region rep); govr Sidcot Sch 1999–2007; *Recreations* cricket, watching rugby, painting, reading; *Clubs* Gloucestershire CCC (life memb), Bristol RFC, Winscombe RFC (vice-pres), Old Herpesians CC; *Style*— His Hon Judge Ticehurst; ✉ The Law Courts, Small Street, Bristol BS1 1DA

TICKELL, Clare; *Educ* Univ of Bristol (CQSW); *m* 15 March 1987, Edward Andres; 2 s (Finn *b* 20 March 1989, Luke *b* 14 March 1991); *Career* asst warden Avon Probation Service 1982–84, dep dir Centrepoint 1986–89, dir Riverpoint 1989–1992; chief exec: Phoenix House 1991–97, Stonham Housing Assoc 1997–2004, NCH 2004–; memb Mgmnt Bd Information Cmmn 2003–; FRSA; *Recreations* swimming, reading, art; *Style*— Ms Clare Tickell; ✉ NCH, 85 Highbury Park, London N5 1UD

TICKELL, Sir Crispin Charles Cervantes; GCMG (1989), KCVO (1983, MVO 1958); s of Jerrard Tickell (d 1966), and Renée Oriana, *née* Haynes (d 1992); *b* 25 August 1930; *Educ* Westminster (King's scholar), ChCh Oxford (Hinchliffe and hon scholar, Gladstone Meml exhibitioner, MA); *m* 1, 1954 (m dis 1976), Chloë, da of Sir James Gunn, RA; 2 s, 1 da; *m* 2, 1977, Penelope Thorne Thorne, da of Dr Vernon Thorne Thorne; *Career* Coldstream Gds 1952–54; joined British Dip Serv 1954, served FO 1954–55, The Hague 1955–58, Mexico 1958–61, FO Planning Staff 1961–64, Paris 1964–70; private sec to Mins responsible for British entry into Euro Community 1970–72, head Western Orgns Dept FCO 1972–75, fell Center for Int Affairs Harvard Univ 1975–76, chef de cabinet to Pres of Cmmn of Euro Community 1977–81, visiting fell All Souls Coll Oxford 1981, British ambass to Mexico 1981–83, dep under sec of state (Economic) FCO 1983–84, permanent sec Overseas Devpt Admin 1984–87, British permanent rep to UN 1987–90; warden Green Coll Oxford 1990–97, dir Green Coll Centre for Environmental Policy and Understanding 1992–2006, dir Policy Foresight Prog James Martin Inst for Science and Civilisation Oxford 2006–; dir BOC Fndn for the Environment 1990–2003; non-exec dir: IBM UK Hldgs Ltd 1990–95 (memb Advsy Bd 1995–2000), Govett Mexican Horizons Investment Co Ltd 1992–96, Govett American Smaller Companies Trust 1996–98, Govett Enhanced Income Investment Tst 1999–2004; chm: Climate Inst Washington DC 1990–2002, Int Inst for Environment and Devpt 1990–94, Earthwatch Europe 1991–97, Advsy Ctee Darwin Initiative for the Survival of Species 1992–99, St Andrews/Conoco Phillips Prize for the Environment 2000–; pres: Royal Geographical Soc 1990–93 (Patron's Medal 2000), Marine Biological Assoc 1990–2001, The National Society for Clean Air 1997–99, The Gaia Society 1998–2001; tstee: Natural History Museum 1992–2001, WWF (UK) 1993–99, Royal Botanic Garden Edinburgh 1997–2001; convenor of the Govt Panel on Sustainable Devpt 1994–2000, memb Task Force on Urban Regeneration 1998–99, memb Task Force on Potentially Hazardous Near Earth Objects 2000; sr visiting fell Harvard Univ Center for the Environment 2002–03; chllr Univ of Kent 1996–2006; advsr-at-large to the pres Arizona State Univ 2004–; Hon LLD: Univ of Massachusetts USA 1990, Univ of Birmingham 1991, Univ of Bristol 1991, Univ of Kent at Canterbury 1996, Univ of Nottingham 2003; Hon DUniv Stirling 1990; Hon DSc: UEA 1990, Univ of Sussex 1991, Cranfield Univ 1992, Loughborough Univ 1995, Sheffield Hallam Univ 1996, Univ of East London 1998, Univ of Exeter 1999, Univ of Hull 2001; Hon DLitt: PCL (now Univ of Westminster) 1990, Univ of Plymouth 2001, Univ of St Andrews 2002, Univ of Southampton 2002, Oxford Brookes Univ 2002, Univ du Littoral Cote d'Opale 2002; hon fell: Westminster Sch 1993, St Edmund's Coll Cambridge 1995, Green Coll Oxford 1997, Royal Instn of GB 2002; Hon FRIBA 2000; hon memb: Academia Mexicana de Derecho Internacional 1983, Orden Academica de Derecho, de la Cultura, y de la Paz 1989; Offr Order of Orange Nassau (Netherlands) 1958, Order of the Aztec Eagle with sash (Mexico) 1994; *Books* The Evacuees (contrib, 1968), Life After Death (1976), Climatic Change and World Affairs (Harvard Univ 1977, Pergamon 1978, jt revised edn 1986), The United Kingdom-The United Nations (1990), Sustaining Earth (1990), Science for the Earth (contrib, 1995), The Changing World (contrib, 1996), Mary Anning of Lyme Regis (1996), Remaking the Landscape (contrib, 2002), Managing the Earth (contrib, 2002), Johannesburg Summit 2002 (contrib, 2002), Roy Jenkins: A Retrospective (contrib, 2004); *Recreations* climatology, palaeohistory, art (especially pre Columbian), mountains; *Clubs* Brooks's, Garrick; *Style*— Sir Crispin Tickell, GCMG, KCVO; ✉ Ablington Old Barn, Ablington, Cirencester, Gloucestershire GL7 5NU

TICKLE, Geraldine Ellen; da of Michael Casey (d 1994), and Johanna, *née* Abbott (d 1996); *b* 11 February 1951, Bromley, Kent; *Educ* Holy Trinity Convent, KCL (LLB), Cncl of Legal Educn; *m* 8 Nov 1980 (m dis); 2 da (Victoria Alexandra *b* 9 Dec 1982, Olivia Catherine *b* 10 Dec 1986); *Career* called to the Bar Gray's Inn 1973, admitted slr 1982; pupil then tenant barr's chambers London 1973–76, HM Customs and Excise Legal Office 1976–83, Wragge and Co Solicitors 1984–95 (joined as legal researcher, later commercial lawyer then competition ptnr), ptnr Martineau Johnson 1995–; vice-chm Competition Law Assoc 2003– (chm Working Party on Competition Law), vice-pres Ligue International du Droit de la Concurrence, memb Jt Working Party Law Socs and Bars of GB and NI

1999–, memb Advsy Ctee Inst of European Law Birmingham Univ; *Publications* contrib to numerous pubns incl Remedies for Breach of EC Law, International Intellectual Property Law, Structuring International Contracts, European Community Law, Antitrust Between EC Law and National Law; articles for periodicals including PFI Intelligence, Utility Week and Motor Law; *Recreations* boating, travel, reading, cinema, theatre, skiing; *Clubs* Royal Dart Yacht; *Style*— Mrs Geraldine Tickle; ✉ Martineau Johnson, 35 New Bridge Street, London EC4V 6BW (tel 0870 763 1529, fax 0870 763 1929, e-mail geraldine.tickle@martjohn.com)

TIDBALL, Paul William; s of Trevor James Tidball, of Rhiwbina, Cardiff, and Brenda, *née* Cross; *b* 14 April 1950, Cardiff; *Educ* Cardiff HS; *m* 20 Dec 1972, Jean, *née* Munro; 1 s (Matthew b 19 Nov 1974), 1 da (Jessica b 2 Aug 1977); *Career* trainee and mgmnt positions with nat cos 1970–76, joined HM Prison Serv as asst govr 1976, asst govr HM Borstal Hewell Grange Redditch 1976–80, asst govr HMP Cardiff 1980–88, dep govr HMP Featherstone Wolverhampton 1988–91, Prison Serv Trg and Devpt Gp 1991–97 (latterly head of activities and servs trg); govr HMP Drake Hall Staffs 1997–2003, govr HMP Cardiff 2003–06; pres Prison Govrs Assoc 2006–; *Recreations* travel, music, concert goer, theatre, comedy, conservation (memb Woodland Tst), outdoor pursuits, historic tport (Severn Valley Railway), rugby (Wales and Llanelli), cooking and entertaining, CAMRA life memb; *Style*— Paul Tidball, Esq; ✉ Prison Governors Association, 217 Cleland House, Page Street, London SW1P 4LN (e-mail paul.tidball@hmps.gsi.gov.uk)

TIDE-FRATER, Susanne; *b* Germany; *Educ* Sorbonne, Institut Français de la Mode Paris; *Career* early career with German Mktg Inst and Peclers Paris; head Design Mgmnt Dept and head int rels Institut Français de la Mode; Selfridges: joined creative dept 1996, head creative direction 2002–04; creative dir Harrods 2004–06, brand conslt 2006–; *Style*— Ms Susanne Tide-Frater; ✉ 154 Cholmley Gardens, London NW6 1AD

TIDMARSH, James Napier (Jay); MBE (1989), JP (1977); yr s of late Edward and Madeline Tidmarsh; *b* 15 September 1932; *Educ* Taunton Sch; *m* Virginia Tidmarsh; 2 s (Mark b 1969, Toby b 1971); *Career* Nat Serv cmmnd 1 Bn DCLI, TA 4/5 Som LI 1952–54; factory mangr/dir/md in footwear industry UK and Australasia 1955–72; md Dycem Ltd 1972–96, fndr dir GWR Radio plc 1985–89; dir: Bristol C of C 1992–, Learning Partnership West 1995–99; pres Avon and Bristol Fedn of Clubs for Young People 1994–98 (chm 1982–94), vice-chm Nat Assoc Prison Visitors 1966–69, memb Cncl Univ of Bristol 1994–2000; patron, pres and memb of many local and regnl tsts; memb Soc of Merchant Venturers (Master 1994–95); High Sheriff Avon 1995–96, HM Lord-Lt County and City of Bristol 1996–2007; Hon Col RMR Bristol 1998–2005; Hon LLD: Univ of Bristol 2002, UWE 2003; FRSA 2000; KStJ 1997; *Clubs* Royal Commonwealth Soc, Army and Navy, Saintsbury, Clifton (Bristol); *Style*— Jay Tidmarsh, Esq, MBE; ✉ 8 Prince's Buildings, Clifton, Bristol BS8 4LB (tel 0117 973 0462, fax 0117 970 6649)

TIDY, William Edward (Bill); MBE (2001); *b* 9 October 1933; *m* 1960, Rosa; 2 s (Nick, Robert), 1 da (Sylvia); *Career* Mil Serv RE 1952–56, worked within advtg agency 1956–57, professional cartoonist 1957–; cartoon strips incl: Chelm of Tryg (Punch) 1966–67, The Cloggies (Private Eye) 1967–81, (The Listener) 1985–86, Doctor Whittle (General Practitioner) 1970–2001, Grimbledon Down (New Scientist) 1970–94, The Fosdyke Saga (The Daily Mirror) 1971–85, Kegbuster (What's Brewing) 1976–, The Sporting Spagthorpes (Titbits) 1976–79, Intergalactic Mirror (The Mirror Group) 1979–81, The Last Chip Shop (Private Eye) 1981–85, The Crudgingtons (Today) 1986–87, Billy Bucket (Private Eye) 1988–89, Savage Sports (The Mail On Sunday) 1988–89, God's Own County (Yorkshire Post) 1989–90, String King (Punch) 1996–97; TV presenter: Weekend (Granada), Three Days Last Summer (BBC 2), Tidy Up Walsall (BBC 1), Tidy Up Naples (BBC 2), It's My City (BBC 1), Draw Me (BBC 2); numerous radio and TV guest appearances incl This Is Your Life 1975; radio presenter Tidy Answers (BBC Radio 4); after-dinner speaker for numerous orgns incl pub cos; designer of stage sets and costumes; produces range of greetings and christmas cards; Granada TV's What The Papers Say Cartoonist of the Year 1974, The Soc of Strip Illustrators Award 1980; *Publications* playwright: The Great Eric Ackroyd Disaster (Oldham Coliseum), The Cloggies (Theatre Clwyd), The Fosdyke Saga (Bush Theatre and Arts Cncl tour); writer and illustrator: Laugh with Bill Tidy, Tidy's World, The Fosdyke Saga (15 vols), The World's Worst Golf Club, Robbie And The Blobbies, A Day At Cringemound School, The Incredible Bed, Draw Me 387 Baked Beans, Save Daring Waring with a Pencil?, Is There Any News of the Iceberg? (autobiography, 1995), Kegbuster Remembers (1997), The Tidy Book of Quotations (1998), Disgraceful Archaeology (with Dr Paul Bahn, 1999); illustrator: The Exploding Present (by John Wells), Napoleon's Retreat From Wigan (by Mike Harding), The Book of Heroic Failures (by Stephen Pile), Everbody's Doing It (by Max Hodes), Fisherman's Friend (with Derrick Geer), Rosa Tidy's Pasta Book (by Rosa Tidy), Fine Glances (by Mike Seabrook), Golfing Anthology (by Mike Seabrook), Food For All The Family (by Magnus Pike), Service Banking (by Michael Hanson), F U C Smith The Greatest Cricketer of Them All; *Recreations* supporting Everton FC, cultivating peas and beans, watching ships and aircraft, playing cricket, looking after various dependants, furry friends and masses of goldfish; *Clubs* Cartoonists' Club of GB, Lord's Taverners, Armed Forces Benevolent Fund; *Style*— Bill Tidy, Esq, MBE; ✉ Terry Meadow Farm, Boylestone, Derbyshire DE6 5AB (tel and fax 01335 330 858, e-mail bill@billtidy.com, website www.broadband.co.uk/billtidy)

TIERNAN, John Patrick; s of Joseph Anthony Tiernan, of Dublin, and Bridget, *née* Keogh; *b* 30 April 1958; *Educ* Trinity Coll Dublin (BDSc, BA, Sheldon Friel meml prize), RCS (DGDP); *m* 27 Oct 1978, Maire Eilis, da of Lt Col Alphonsis Igoe; 2 s (Mark John b 5 April 1979, David Raymond b 23 March 1982); *Career* asst in dental practice Sheerness Kent 1980–81; princ in practice: Waterlooville 1981–84, Portsmouth 1983–94; clinical asst Queen Alexandra Hosp Portsmouth 1988–90; Dental Protection: pt/t 1993–94, dento-legal advsr 1994–97, sr dento-legal advsr 1997–99, head of Practitioner Serv 1999–2004, asst dental dir 2004–; conslt John Thompson Production 1985–94; dir: Petrie Tucker Ltd 1991–93, Domas Ltd 1992–94; non-exec dir Integrated Dental Holdings Ltd 1998–2004; GDC: memb 1991–2001, memb Professional Conduct Ctee 1991–93, memb Special Purposes Ctee 1991–94, memb Oral Health Educn Ctee 1991–94, memb Dental Auxiliaries Ctee 1994–95, chm Specialist Review Gp 1995–98, memb Educn Ctee 1995–2001, memb Postgraduate Educn Ctee 1995–98, memb Specialist Training Advsy Ctee 1999–2000, GDC advsr SCOPME 1997–98, vice-chm Fin Ctee 2001– (memb 1999–2001); BDA: memb 1981–, memb Representative Bd 1990–94, memb Cncl 1992–94, memb Wessex Branch Cncl 1990–94; Br Dental Health Fndn: memb 1983–99, memb Cncl 1985–95, chm 1986, media spokesperson 1986–98, dir of PR 1989–91; pres London Irish Dental Soc 1985–87 (vice-pres 1984–85), chm Caring Dental Gp 1992–93, memb Exec Ctee Medical Protection Soc; memb Editorial Bd The Dentist 1988–; lectures extensively in the UK and internationally on both dental and after-dinner occasions; *Recreations* sailing, skiing, swimming, golf, formerly running (rep Ireland cross-country); *Style*— John Tiernan, Esq; ✉ e-mail jptiernan@btinternet.com

TIFFIN, Simon; *Career* journalist; early career chief sub ed and sports ed GQ, ed GQ Active 1998–2001 (dep ed 1996–98), dep ed Harpers & Queen 2001–03, ed Esquire 2003–; Ed of the Year (Men's Magazines) BSME Awards 2003; *Style*— Simon Tiffin, Esq; ✉ Esquire, National Magazine House, 72 Broadwick Street, London W1F 9EP

TIGHE, Anthony Rodger; s of Brian Anthony Michael Tighe, of Bickerstaff, Lancs, and Paula Angela, *née* Capper; *b* 9 March 1951; *Educ* St Edward's Coll Liverpool, Univ of Greenwich; *m* 1991 (m dis), Rachel Suzanne, *née* Pearson; 2 c; *Career* with Berger Paints 1972–74, in family business 1974–76; Wilsons Brewery Manchester: sales force 1976–78, area sales mangr 1978–80, sales promotion mangr 1980–82, PR mangr 1982–83; head of PR Grand Metropolitan Brewing North 1983–84; Greenwood Tighe Public Relations (now part of Euro RSCG Group): fndr md 1984–88, chief exec 1988–93; fndr Mere Communication Ltd 1993–; dir Lake Design (UK) Ltd 1998, non-exec dir Tameside Acute NHS Tst 1993–98; non exec dir Capt Mere Golf and Country Club 2007 (Capt 2003–); MIPR 1984; *Awards* first winner Inst of PR Sword of Excellence for product relations 1984; *Recreations* golf, Everton FC; *Clubs* Mere Golf and Country, RAC; *Style*— Anthony Tighe, Esq; ✉ Mere Communication Ltd, Campaign House, 8 Cecil Road, Hale, Cheshire WA15 9PA (tel 0161 928 8700, e-mail tony@mere.co.uk)

TILEY, Prof John; CBE (2003); s of William Arthur Tiley (d 1965), Audrey Ellen Tiley (d 1974); *b* 25 February 1941; *Educ* Winchester, Lincoln Coll Oxford (Winter Williams law scholar, MA, BCL); *m* 1964, Jillinda Millicent, da of William Bryan Draper; 3 c (Nicholas John b 19 Dec 1966, Christopher George b 17 June 1968, Mary Isobel b 13 Aug 1971); *Career* lectr Lincoln Coll Oxford 1963–64, lectr in law Univ of Birmingham 1964–67; Univ of Cambridge: fell Queens' Coll 1967– (vice-pres 1988–96), asst lectr in law 1967–72, lectr 1972–87, reader in law of taxation 1987–90, prof of law of taxation 1990–, chm Faculty Bd of Law 1992–95; visiting prof: Dalhousie Univ 1972–73, Univ of Auckland 1973, Univ of Western Ontario 1978–79, Case Western Reserve Univ 1985–86, 1996 and 2002, Univ of Paris IX 1992–97, Univ of Paris I 1998–2000; called to the Bar Inner Temple 1964, hon bencher 1993; recorder 1989–99 (asst recorder 1984–88); gen ed: Butterworth's UK Tax Guide (Tiley and Collison's UK Tax Guide since 1997) 1982–; pres Soc of Public Teachers of Law 1995–96 (vice-pres 1994–95); author of numerous articles in pubns; LLD Univ of Cambridge 1995; *Books* A Casebook on Equity and Succession (1968), Beattie's Elements of Estate Duty (ed, 7 edn 1970, 8 edn 1974), Elements of Capital Transfer Tax (with Hayton, 1975, 2 edn 1978), Revenue Law (1976, 5 edn 2005); *Recreations* walking, listening to music, travel, visiting art galleries and museums; *Style*— Prof John Tiley, CBE; ✉ Queens' College, Cambridge CB3 9ET (tel 01223 335511)

TILEY, Timothy Francis Thornhill; s of Rev George Edward Tiley (d 1985), and Cecilia Frances Mystica Thornhill (d 1982); descended from ancient family of Thornhill, of Thornhill in Yorks, which can trace continuous line of descent from saxon theign Eisulf de Thornhill (1080–1165), membs of the family of Jordan de Thornhill (s of Eisulf) are portrayed in a group of the most famous of the 13th century miracle windows in the Trinity chapel of Canterbury Cathedral; *b* 6 June 1949; *Educ* Malvern Coll, St Peter's Coll Oxford (MA); *m* 12 Oct 1990, Margaret Reid; *Career* fndr and md Tim Tiley Ltd (publishers of philosophical and religious prints) 1978–; co-fndr of Brass Rubbing Centres: Oxford 1973, Bristol 1974, Stratford-upon-Avon 1974, London 1975, Edinburgh 1976, Bath 1976, Glastonbury 1977, Washington DC 1977; FInstD 1992; *Recreations* piano, reading, travelling, historical studies; *Style*— Timothy Tiley, Esq; ✉ 12 Salisbury Road, Redland, Bristol BS6 7AW (tel 0117 942 3397, e-mail tim@timtiley.com)

TILL, David Richard; s of Henry Rheid Till (d 1998), and Dorothy, *née* Smith (d 1975); *b* 27 April 1942; *Educ* Univ of Oxford (BA), Univ of London (MSc); *m* Elizabeth Mary, da of Ralph Ambrose Kekwick, FRS; 2 da (Corinna Ruth b 1970, and Isabel Sarah b 1973); *Career* maths teacher Latymer Upper Sch Hammersmith 1964–68, lectr then sr lectr in computer science Westfield Coll then King's Coll London 1970–89; City Univ: sr lectr then reader 1989–2002, head Dept of Computer Science 1991–95; *Books* Principles of Functional Programming (jtly, 1984), An Introduction to Formal Specification and Z (jtly, 1991, 2 edn 1996); *Recreations* music a consuming passion, playing piano, organ and violin, singing in and conducting choirs, composing a little, languages (Spanish, French and German); *Style*— David Till, Esq; ✉ 7 Kempe Road, London NW6 6SP (tel 020 8960 1904, e-mail davidtill@beeb.net)

TILL, Prof Jeremy William; s of Barry Till, of London, and Shirley, *née* Phillipson (d 1991); *b* 5 April 1957; *Educ* Univ of Cambridge (MA), Poly of Central London (DipArch), Middlesex Univ (MA); *Partner* Prof Sarah Wigglesworth; *Career* architect and academic; architect Alex Gordon Partnership 1984–87, architect David Gibson Architects 1987–88, Peter Currie Architects 1988–93, ptnr Sarah Wigglesworth Architects 1993–; sr lectr Kingston Poly Sch of Architecture 1986–92, Univ of Pennsylvania Philadelphia 1991, Bartlett Sch of Architecture UCL 1991–98: lectr 1992–93, sub-dean of faculty and faculty tutor 1993–96, sr lectr in architecture 1996–98; prof of architecture and head of sch Univ of Sheffield Sch of Architecture 1999–; visiting prof Tech Univ Vienna 1996, external examiner Manchester Sch of Architecture 1997–, Eva Maddox Distinguished Lectr Univ of Illinois at Chicago 1998; invited critic and lectr 1987–; RIBA: memb 1995, memb Educn and Professional Devpt Bd 1996–98, chm review gp 1997, memb Educn Strategy Ctee 1998–2001, curriculum advsr 1999, chair RIBA Awards Gp 2004–; UK entry Venice Architecture Biennale 2006; *Awards* incl Bannister Fletcher Prize for dissertation 1983, Fulbright Arts Fell 1990, EAAE Biennial Award for Architectural Writing 1995, Civic Tst Award 2002, RIBA Sustainability Award 2004, RIBA Award 2004; *Publications* The Everyday and Architecture (with Sarah Wigglesworth, 1998), Architecture and Participation (2005); numerous book chapters, jl articles and published conf papers on architecture and urban devpt; *Recreations* cooking and eating; *Style*— Professor Jeremy Till; ✉ School of Architecture, Western Bank, Sheffield S10 2TN (tel 0114 222 0347, fax 0114 279 8276, e-mail j.till@sheffield.ac.uk)

TILL, Stewart; CBE (2000); *b* 24 April 1951; *Career* early career in advtg: Leo Burnett, Saatchi & Saatchi; TV project mangr and mktg dir WEA Records 1979–83, regnl dir for N Europe and vice-pres CBS/Fox Video 1983, dep md Sky TV 1988–90, head of movies BSkyB 1990–92, with PolyGram Filmed Entertainment 1992–99 (latterly pres), pres Universal Pictures International 1999–2000, pres Signpost Films 2000–02, chm and ceo United International Pictures 2002–; co-chair Film Policy Review Gp DCMS 1997–99, chm Film Cncl 2004– (dep chm 1999–2004), vice-chm Skillset; tstee Nat Film and TV Sch Fndn; govr Dulwich Coll; *Style*— Stewart Till, Esq, CBE; ✉ United International Pictures, 45 Beadon Road, London W6 0EG

TILLER, Ven John; s of Harry Maurice Tiller (d 1992), and Lucille Tiller (d 2004); *b* 22 June 1938; *Educ* St Albans Sch, ChCh Oxford (MA), Univ of Bristol (MLitt); *m* 5 Aug 1961, Ruth Alison, da of Charles Arthur Watson (d 1966); 2 s (Andrew b 1964, Jonathan b 1967), 1 da (Rachel b 1965); *Career* lectr Trinity Coll Bristol 1967–73, priest in charge Christ Church Bedford 1973–78, chief sec Advsy Cncl for the Church's Miny 1978–84, chllr and canon residentiary of Hereford Cathedral 1984–2004, dir of trg Diocese of Hereford 1991–2000, archdeacon of Hereford 2002–04 (emeritus 2004–); *Books* A Strategy for the Church's Ministry (1983), The Gospel Community (1987), Hereford Cathedral: a History (2000); *Style*— The Ven John Tiller; ✉ 2 Pulley Lane, Bayston Hill, Shrewsbury SY3 0JH (tel 01743 873595, e-mail canjtiller@aol.com)

TILLETT, Michael Burn; QC (1996); s of Cyril Vernon Tillett (d 1997), and Norah Phyllis Tillett (d 1986); *b* 3 September 1942; *Educ* Marlborough, Queens' Coll Cambridge (MA); *m* 2 April 1977, Kathryn Ann, da of Dr J K Samuel; 2 da (Alexandra b 15 Nov 1978, Kirsty b 12 Aug 1980); *Career* called to the Bar Inner Temple 1965, recorder of the Crown Ct 1989–, chm of Mental Health Review Tribunals 2000–; *Recreations* riding, mountaineering, skiing, sailing; *Clubs* Hurlingham, RAC, Downhill Only; *Style*— Michael Tillett, Esq, QC; ✉ 39 Essex Street, London WC2R 3AT (tel 020 7832 1111, fax 020 7353 3978, e-mail michael.tillett@39essex.co.uk)

TILLEY, Andrew Raymond; s of Raymond Hugh Tilley, of Tettenhall, Wolverhampton, and Carrie, *née* Lucas; *b* 22 September 1956; *Educ* Regis Comp Tettenhall, Univ of Southampton (BSc, PhD); *m* 16 Nov 1990, Olwen Mary, da of James Anthony Rice, of Rugeley, Staffs; 1 da (Grace Elizabeth b 27 June 1995); 2 c from prev m (Laura Anne b

18 Sept 1983, Mark Thomas b 14 Aug 1985); *Career* water quality controller Essex Water Co 1978–79, postgrad res 1979–82; Boase Massimi Pollitt advtg: joined as trainee media planner 1982, assoc dir 1984–86, bd dir 1986–89, md BMP Solutions in Media (subsid) 1987–89; Delaney Fletcher Slaymaker Delaney & Bozell (formerly Delaney Fletcher Delaney): media planning dir 1989, exec media dir 1989–91, dep md 1991; Zenith Media: dir of strategic planning 1991–94, dep md 1994–95, md 1995–97; fndr managing ptnr Unity independent communications consultancy 1997–2003, founding ptnr The Ingram Partnership 2003–; chm Media Circle 1995–99; dir Prince's Tst 2001–; MIPA 1990; *Recreations* football, cricket, photography, horse racing, collecting old maps; *Style*— Andrew Tilley, Esq

TILLMAN, Harold Peter; s of late Jack Tillman, of London, and late Frances, *née* Cornbloom; *b* 15 October 1945, London; *Educ* Balham Co GS, Pitman's Coll, London Coll of Fashion; *m* 1969, Stephanie, *née* Ogus; 1 s (Mitchell b 2 Aug 1975), 1 da (Meredith b 9 March 1982); *Career* fndr and md Lincroft Kilgour plc 1966–74, vice-chm Sumrie Clothes plc 1980–83, chm Honorbilt Group plc 1986–90, chm BMB Group 1999–2004, chm Jaeger 2003–; *Recreations* gym, tennis, golf; *Clubs* Annabel's; *Style*— Harold Tillman, Esq; ✉ Jaeger, 57 Broadwick Street, London W1F 9QS (tel 020 7200 4000, e-mail harold.tillman@jaeger.co.uk)

TILLMANN, Prof Ulrike Luise; da of Ewald Tillmann, and Marie-Luise Tillmann; *Educ* Gymnasium Georgianum Vreden, Brandeis Univ (BA summa cum laude, Volleyball blue letter), Stanford Univ (MA, PhD), Bonn Univ; *Career* SERC res asst Univ of Cambridge 1990–92, jr res fell Clare Hall Cambridge 1990–92; Univ of Oxford: fell and tutor in mathematics Merton Coll 1992–, univ lectr in mathematics 1992–, titular prof 2000–; visiting prof: Trondheim Univ 2001; EPSRC Advanced Fellowship 1997–2003; conference organiser: Br Topology Meeting 1997, New Developments in K-Theory (Quillen's 60th) 2001, Topology, Geometry and Quantum Field Theory (Segal's 60th) 2002; invited speaker: Br Mathematical Colloquium 2000 and 2002, Int Congress of Mathematics 2002; delivered numerous conference talks; ed Topology 2002–06, founding ed Jl of Topology 2007–; memb Editorial Bd: Oxford QJM 2000–, Algebraic and Geometric Topology 2000–, London Mathematical Soc jls 2004–07; memb EPSRC Coll 1997–; Whitehead Prize London Mathematical Soc 2004, Chaire de la Vallée Poussin 2006–07, L M S Cartwright lectr 2006; *Publications* author of book reviews and numerous papers in mathematical jls; *Recreations* singing; *Style*— Prof Ulrike Tillmann; ✉ Mathematical Institute, 24–29 St Giles, Oxford OX1 3LB

TILLYARD, Stella; da of Stephen Tillyard, and Margot Tillyard; *b* 16 January 1957; *Educ* St Anne's Coll Oxford (BA), Harvard Univ (Knox fell), Linacre Coll Oxford (Domus student, PhD); *m* Prof John Brewer; 2 c (Grace b 1987, Fox b 1995); *Career* lectr Harvard Univ and UCLA until 1992; sometime writer: New York Times, The Times, The Guardian, Esquire, Traveller; contrib radio and TV progs; author of numerous articles and reviews; memb Soc of Authors *Awards* Nicolaus Pevsner Prize 1987, History Today Book of the Year 1994, Fawcett Prize 1995; *Books* The Impact of Modernism (1987), Aristocrats: Caroline, Emily, Louisa & Sarah Lennox (1994), Citizen Lord: Edward Fitzgerald 1763–98 (shortlisted Whitbread Biography Award 1997), A Royal Affair (2006); *Recreations* swimming, architecture, reading, sleep; *Clubs* YMCA, Tropos (Florence); *Style*— Miss Stella Tillyard; ✉ Gillon Aitken, 18–21 Cavaye Place, London SW10 9PT (tel 020 7373 8672, fax 020 7373 6002)

TILLYER, William; *b* 25 September 1938; *Educ* Middlesbrough Coll of Art, Slade Sch of Fine Art, Atelier 17 Paris; *Career* artist and lectr; Central Sch of Art 1964–70, Bath Acad of Art 1964–72, Watford Sch of Art 1970–73, Goldsmiths Coll London 1975–76, Loughborough Sch of Art 1975–76; visiting prof Rhode Island Sch of Brown Univ 1975–76; visiting lectr: Reading Coll of Art 1975–76, St Martin's Sch of Art 1980; artist in residence: Univ of Melbourne 1981–82, David and Sarah Kowitz Program Bedford Hills NY 2001, Cill Rialaig Project Co Kerry 2001; *Solo Exhibitions* incl: Arnolfini Gallery Bristol 1970–73, Serpentine Gallery 1971, Galerie Theodor Hoss Stuttgart 1974, Museum of Contemporary Art Utrecht 1975, ICA 1975, Sunderland Arts Centre 1975–79, Melbourne Univ Gallery 1982, Jan Turner Gallery LA 1987, Smith Anderson Gallery Calif 1989, Bernard Jacobson Gallery 1989, 1991 and 1993, Wildenstein & Co 1991 and 1994, Adelson Galleries NY 1993, Andre Emmerich Gallery NY 1994, Galerie Miya Tokyo 1995, The Fluxion Paintings (Bernard Jacobson Gallery) 1996, William Tillyer 1956–1996 (The Cleveland Gallery Middlesbrough 1996 and Whitworth Art Gallery Manchester 1997), Bernard Jacobson Gallery 1999 and 2000, Annandale Galleries Sydney Aust 1996, Annandale Galleries 2002, Bernard Jacobson London and NY 2002, The Encounter Works (Bernard Jacobson Gallery) 2002, In the South (works on paper, Bernard Jacobson Gallery) 2003, The Farrago Constructs (Bernard Jacobson Gallery) 2004, Five Larger Paintings 1990–2003 (Eton Coll) 2004, The Revisionist Wire Works (Bernard Jacobson Gallery) 2006; *Group Exhibitions* incl: Young Contemporaries (ICA) 1959 and 1961, Forty Christmas Trees (Arnolfini Gallery) 1972, Recent Acquisitions (V&A) 1973, Le Jeune Gravure Contemporaine (Musée d'Art Madame Paris) 1974, British Painting 1952–77 (RA, New Dehli, touring) 1977, British Art since 1960 (Kunsthalle, Lund Univ) 1979, Eight British Artists (Bernard Jacobson Gallery NY) 1980, Four British Artists (Jan Turner Gallery LA) 1988, Cleveland Gallery 1994, Jerwood Painting Prize 1998, New Acquisitions (UCL Art Collections) 2006; *Work in Collections* V&A, Arts Cncl of GB, The Br Cncl, Tate, Manchester City Art Gallery, Univ of Reading, MOMA NY, Brooklyn Art Museum NY, Boston Museum of Art, Fort Worth Art Museum TX, Northern Arts Assoc, Museum of Contemporary Art Friedrickstad, Museum of Art Łódź, Museum of Contemporary Art Utrecht, Westminster Bank London, Bank of America, Univ of Melbourne, Federal Savings Bank LA, The Art Gallery of Western Aust, Broadgate Collection London, Cleveland Gallery, Whitworth Gallery Manchester; *Publications* subject of monograph William Tillyer: Against the Grain (by Prof Norbert Lynton, 2000), Hardware: Variations on a theme of encounter (catalogue essay, 2002); *Style*— William Tillyer, Esq, FRSA; ✉ Bernard Jacobson Gallery, 6 Cork Street, London W1S 3EE (tel 020 7734 3431, e-mail william@tillyer.com, website www.tillyer.com or www.jacobsongallery.com)

TILSON, Jake; s of Joe Tilson, *qv*, of Wilts, and Jos, *née* Morton; *b* 14 February 1958; *Educ* Holland Park Sch, Chippenham GS, Chelsea Sch of Art (BA), Royal Coll of Art (MA); *m* Jennifer Elizabeth Lee, *qv*, da of Ernest McLean Bovelle Lee; 1 da (Hannah Lee Tilson b 26 May 1995); *Career* artist; lectr in communication design RCA 1987–2000, lectr Painting Dept Ruskin Sch of Art Oxford; Erna Plachte artist in residence The Laboratory Ruskin Sch of Drawing and Fine Art 1994–96; ed and publisher: Cipher magazine 1979–81, Atlas magazine 1985–; designer Jake Tilson Studio, clients incl Haworth Tompkins, Claudio Silvestrin, Childnet, Arts Cncl and Fontshop International; creator website www.thecooker.com 1994; *Solo Exhibitions* Xerographies 1977–83 (Galerie J et J Donguy Paris) 1983, Excavator-Barcelona-Excavator (Nigel Greenwood Gallery) 1986, One World (Warehouse London & Liverpool) 1987, Collages 1986–89 (Stylt Göteborg Sweden) 1989, How Far is an Hour (Nigel Greenwood Gallery) 1989, How Far is an Hour (Galleria Cavallino Venice Italy) 1990, The Terminator Line (Nigel Greenwood Gallery) 1990, The Terminator Line Outtakes (Printed Matter at Dia, NY) 1991, Investigations in Cities 1977–97 (retrospective exhibition, Museo Internacional de Electrografia Cuenca Spain) 1997; *Group Exhibitions* Northern Young Contemporaries (Whitworth Gallery Manchester) 1977, Ecritures (Fondation National des Arts Graphiques et Plastiques Paris) 1980, Ars Machina (La Maison de la Culture de Rennes) 1982, Paris Bienale 1982, New Media 2 (Malmö Konsthall Sweden) 1984, Copyart Biennale Barcelona 1985, Br Art & Design (Vienna) 1986, Artist as Publisher (Crafts Cncl) 1986, Rencontres Autour de la Revue Luna-Park (Centre Georges Pompidou) 1987, Br Artists' Books (Centre for the Book Arts NY) 1987, Art in Production (Manchester City Art Gallery) 1988 and 1989, Exhibition Road - 150 Years (RCA) 1988, 20 Years of Br Art from the Sackner Archive (BASS Museum Miami Florida) 1988, Atlas 3 (Nigel Greenwood Gallery) 1988, Echtzeit (Kasseler Kunstverein) 1988, Paper (Amics Tokyo) 1988, Original Copies (MOMA Kyoto Tokyo, RCA) 1990, Self Image (Design Museum) 1991, Langu(im)age (Nigel Greenwood Gallery) 1992, John Moores Exhbn Liverpool 1992, Work and Turn (Tokyo and Sweden) 1992, Stylt Germany 1993, John Moores 18 Liverpool 1993, Whitechapel Open London 1994, Looking At Words Reading Pictures London 1994, tidsvag Göteborg 1994, Artists Books Tate Gallery 1995, Networks 95, Airport (The Photographers Gallery) 1997, European Echoes (Goteborg) 1998, Eye Was A Child (Saatchi Gallery) 1998, La Biennale De Montréal 1998, Sound (Refusalon San Francisco) 1998, Not There (Rena Bransten Gallery San Francisco) 1999, Net Conditions (ZKM) 1999, Art Journeaux (Kassel Kunstverein) 2000, The Year Dot, Black Box (Aspex Gallery) 2000, Over The Ocean (Roda Sten) 2000, Independence (South London Gallery) 2003, Ways of Saying (Loman Street Studio) 2003; *Film, Video and Audio* Jour et Nuit (Atlas Films, 1989), Jeff and Jake Get Married (Atlas Films, 1990), Put the Message in the Box (World Party, Ensign Records, 1990), Thankyou World (World Party, Ensign Records, 1991), Outtakes (Atlas Films, 1991), Dry Signals (Atlas Films, 1992), Gate 23 (Atlas audio, 1993), Foundsounds CD (Atlas, 1994), City Picture Fiction (Atlas Audio, 1996), Vulture Reality (Atlas Films, 1999), Hannah Sleeps (Atlas Audio, 1999), Hungerford Bridge (Atlas Audio, 1999); *Awards* London Arts Assoc Literature grant 1980, Art Cncl Arts Publishing subsidy 1981, Unilever prize 1983, Major Travelling scholarship RCA 1983, first prize Royal Over-Seas League Exhibition 1988, nominated Andre Simon Award 2007; *Books* artists' books incl: Light and Dark (1979), Exposure (1980), 8 Views of Paris (1980), The V Agents (1980), Excavator-Barcelona-Excavador (1986), Breakfast Special (1989), The Terminator Line (1991), Wallphone (1994), How to Make a Tortilla Press (2003), 3 Found Fonts (2003), Independence Lunch (2003), A Tale of 12 Kitchens (2006); *Style*— Jake Tilson, Esq; ✉ 16 Talfourd Road, London SE15 5NY

TILSON, Joseph Charles (Joe); s of Frederick Arthur Edward Tilson (d 1973), and Ethel Stapeley Louise, *née* Saunders (d 1982); *b* 24 August 1928; *Educ* St Martin's Sch of Art, RCA, Br Sch at Rome; *m* 2 Aug 1956, Joslyn, da of Alistair Morton (d 1963); 1 s (Jake, *qv*, b 1958), 2 da (Anna Jesse b 1959, Sophy Jane b 1965); *Career* RAF 1946–49; painter, sculptor, printmaker; worked in Italy and Spain 1955–57; visiting lectr 1962–63: Slade Sch of Art, King's Coll London, Univ of Durham; teacher Sch of Visual Arts NY 1966, visiting lectr Staatliche Hochschule für Bildende Künste Hamburg 1971–72; memb Arts Panel and Cncl 1966–71; exhbns incl Venice Biennale 1964; work at: Marlborough Gallery 1966, Waddington Galleries; retrospective exhbns: Boymans Van Beuningen Museum Rotterdam 1973, Vancouver Art Gallery 1979, Volterra 1983, Palazzo Pubblico Siena 1995, Sackler Galleries Royal Acad of Arts 2002; Biennale prizes Kraków 1974 and Ljubljana 1985, subject of TV films 1963, 1968 and 1974; memb Accademia Nazionale di San Luca Rome; ARCA 1955, RA 1991 (ARA 1985); *Recreations* planting trees; *Style*— Joe Tilson, Esq, RA; ✉ c/o Gio Marconi, Via Tadino, 15 20124 Milan, Italy (tel 02 29404373, fax 02 294 05573, e-mail giomarconi@mclink.it); Alan Cristea Gallery, 31 Cork Street, London W1X 2NU (tel 020 7439 1866, fax 020 7734 1549, e-mail info@alancristea.com, website www.alancristea.com); Waddington Galleries, 11 Cork Street, London W1S 3LT (tel 020 7851 2200, fax 020 7734 4146, e-mail mail@waddington-galleries.com, website www.waddington-galleries.com)

TILT, Sir (Robin) Richard; kt (1999); s of Francis Arthur Tilt (d 1988), of Malvern, Worcs, and Mary Elizabeth, *née* Ashworth; *b* 11 March 1944; *Educ* King's Sch Worcester, Univ of Nottingham (BA), Open Univ (Dip); *m* 22 Oct 1966, Kate, da of Thomas Henry and Mabel Busby; 2 s (Jonathan Richard b 12 Nov 1967, Matthew Edward b 3 Jan 1970), 1 da (Rachel Gwynedd b 20 June 1974); *Career* with HM Prison Service; asst govr HM Borstal Wellingborough 1968–71, tutor Prison Serv Staff Coll Wakefield 1971–74, govr HM Borstal Pollington 1974–75; dep govr: HM Prison Ranby 1975–78, HM Prison Gartree 1978–80; govr HM Prison Bedford 1980–82, head Manpower Section HQ 1982–84, govr HM Prison Gartree 1984–88, dep regnl dir Midlands 1988–89, head of industrial rels HQ 1989–92, head of fin Police Dept 1992–94; Prison Serv: dir of servs 1994, dir of security 1994–95, DG 1995–99; cmmr Social Fund 2000–; chm Leics, Northants and Rutland SHA 2002–06; memb Sentencing Advsy Panel 1999–2002, chm Social Security Advy Ctee 2004–; Churchill fell 1991; *Recreations* theatre, reading, walking; *Style*— Sir Richard Tilt; ✉ Independent Review Service, 4th Floor Centre City Podium, 5 Hill Street, Birmingham B5 4UB (tel 0121 6062106)

TIMBERS, Brig Kenneth Alan; s of Capt Arthur Robert Timbers (d 1942), of Woodbridge, Suffolk, and Nancy Gwendoline, *née* Smith (d 1984); *b* 11 July 1935; *Educ* Harvey GS Folkestone, RMA Sandhurst; *m* 21 Sept 1957, (Ursula) Bridget, da of Canon Eric Arthur Newman (d 1970); 1 da (Tricia b 1959), 2 s (Stephen b 1961, Michael b 1962); *Career* cmmnd RA 1956, gunnery staff course 1963–64, army staff course 1966–68, promoted Maj 1967, Lt-Col 1974, cmd 47 Field Regt RA 1976–78, GSO1 (W) HQ DRA 1978–81, promoted Col 1981, project mangr 155mm Systems 1981–85, promoted Brig 1985, dir Quality Assurance 1985–88, ret 1988; history sec RA Instn 1988–99, ret 1999; chm: RA Hist Tst 2001–06, RA Hist Soc 2001–, Friends Nat Army Museum 2002–; dir RA Museums Ltd 2001–06, dep chm Friends of RA Museum 2001–; conslt on history of artillery; FCMI (FIMgt 1985); *Recreations* fine arts, photography, travel; *Clubs* Army and Navy; *Style*— Brig K A Timbers; ✉ 32 Strongbow Road, Eltham, London SE9 1DT (tel 020 8850 8397, e-mail katim@btinternet.com)

TIMMINS, Dr Derek John; s of Ronald Timmins (d 1979), and Ann, *née* Mulville; *b* 7 October 1953; *Educ* UP Holland GS, Univ of Liverpool (BM, MB BS, ChB); *Career* appointed conslt physician Liverpool Health Authy 1988; FRCP, MRCGP, DRCOG; *Recreations* music, gardening, sports, walking, photography; *Style*— Dr Derek Timmins

TIMMINS, Col Sir John Bradford; KCVO (2002), OBE (1973), TD (1968 and bar 1974), JP (1987); s of Capt John James Timmins (d 1972); *b* 23 June 1932; *Educ* Dudley GS, Aston Univ (MSc); *m* 1956, Jean, *née* Edwards; 5 s, 1 da; *Career* Col TA; ADC to HM The Queen 1975–80; Cdr 75 Engr Regt 1971–73, Dep Cdr 30 Engr Brigade 1973–75; Hon Col: 75 Engr Regt 1980–90, Manchester & Salford UOTC 1990–98, Gtr Manchester ACF 1991–; former civil engr and chartered builder, chm Warburton Properties Ltd 1973–; vice-pres TA & VRA for NW England and IOM 1987– (pres 1994–99); co pres Order of St John 1988–, pres Royal Soc of St George Gtr Manchester 1988–; HM Lord-Lt Gtr Manchester 1987– (High Sheriff 1986–87); Hon DSc Univ of Salford 1990, Hon LLD Univ of Manchester 2001; Hon RNCM 1994; KStJ 1988; *Recreations* gardening; *Clubs* Army and Navy, Manchester Literary and Philosophical; *Style*— Col Sir John Timmins, KCVO, OBE, TD

TIMMS, Rt Hon Stephen Creswell; PC (2006), MP; s of Ronald James Timms (d 1991), and Margaret Joyce, *née* Johnson; *b* 29 July 1955; *Educ* Farnborough GS, Emmanuel Coll Cambridge (exhibitioner, sr scholar, MA, MPhil); *m* 26 July 1986, Hui-Leng, da of C C Lim; *Career* conslt Logica Ltd 1978–86, mangr telecommunications reports Ovum Ltd 1994 (princ conslt 1986–94); MP (Lab): Newham NE 1994–97, East Ham 1997–; memb Treasy Select Ctee 1995–97, PPS to Min of State for Employment 1997–98 and to Sec of State for NI 1998, Parly under sec DSS 1998–99, min of state DSS 1999, fin sec to the Treasy 1999–2001, min of state for school standards 2001–02, min of state for e-commerce, communications and competitiveness 2002–03, min of state for energy,

T

e-commerce and postal services 2003–04, financial sec to HM Treasy 2004–05, min of state for pensions DWP 2005–06, chief sec to the Treasy 2006–07; sec: Little Ilford branch Lab Pty 1979–81, Newham NE CLP 1981–84; London Borough of Newham: cncllr 1984–97, chm Planning Ctee 1987–90, ldr 1990–94; memb: E London Business Alliance Newham Area Bd 1990–, Stratford Devpt Partnership Bd 1992–94; hon pres Telecommunications Users' Assoc 1995–98; vice-chm Christian Socialist Movement 1996–98; memb: Ramblers' Assoc, Plaistow Christian Fellowship; Hon DEd Univ of E London 2002; *Books* Broadband Communications: The Commercial Impact (with Richard Kee, 1986), ISDN: Customer Premises Equipment (with Richard Kee, 1988), Broadband Communications: Market Strategies (with Iain Stevenson, 1992); *Recreations* walking and cycling; *Style*— The Rt Hon Stephen Timms, MP; ✉ House of Commons, London SW1A 0AA (tel 020 7219 4000, e-mail stephen@stephentimms.org.uk, website www.stephentimms.org.uk)

TIMOTHY, Christopher Hugh; s of Eifion Andrew Comber Timothy (d 1990), and Gwladys Marian, *née* Hailstone; *b* 14 October 1940; *Educ* Priory GS, Central Sch of Speech and Drama (John Gielgud scholar, Laurence Olivier Award); *m* 1; 4 s (Simon Jon, Nicholas Eifion, Robin James, David), 2 da (Tabitha Jane, Kate Elizabeth); m 2; 1 da (Grace Jane); *Career* actor; various radio plays and voice-overs for both radio and TV; *Theatre* weekly rep Worthing, 3 years with NT; roles incl: MP in Chips with Everything (NY), Petruchio in Taming of the Shrew (Farnham), Brian in A Day in the Death of Joe Egg (Haymarket Leicester), Fanny in Charlie's Aunt (Theatre Royal Plymouth), Rassendyl and The King in The Prisoner of Zenda (Bromley and Chichester), Trofimov in The Cherry Orchard (Chichester); West End incl: Chesney Allen in Underneath the Arches, Hibbert in Journey's End, Bernard in Happy Birthday, Rosencrantz in Rosencrantz and Guildenstern Are Dead, Walter Plinge in The Actor's Nightmare, Clive in See How They Run, Dangerous Corner; nat tours incl: The Cure For Love, The Real Thing, Moment of Weakness, Confusions, Darling Buds of May, Barbara Taylor-Bradford's Dangerous To Know, Mindgame, Heroes 2006, Hay Fever 2007; various pantomime roles incl Robinson Crusoe (also prodr/dir, Theatre Royal Brighton) 1990–91; *Television* James Herriot in All Creatures Great and Small (series, BBC), Murder Must Advertise (Lord Peter Wimsey series, BBC), Julius Caesar, Much Ado About Nothing, Twelfth Night, Ladykillers, Galton and Simpson Playhouse, The Ronnie Barker Playhouse, Murder Most English (Flaxborough Chronicles), The Moon Shines Bright on Charlie Chaplin, Take Three Girls, Take Three Women, The Fenn Street Gang, Z-Cars, The Liver Birds, Return of the Saint, Doctors (also dir) 2000–06, Casualty 2004; other appearances incl: Celebrity Squares, Give Us a Clue, The Two Ronnies, Call My Bluff; *Films* Othello, Here We Go Round The Mulberry Bush, The Virgin Soldiers, Alfred the Great, The Mind of Mr Soames, Spring and Port Wine, Up the Chastity Belt; co-produced and presented James Herriot's Yorkshire...the film (1993); *Awards* Outstanding Male Personality of the Year Screenwriters' Guild 1978, BBC Personality of the Year Variety Club of GB (jtly) 1979; *Style*— Christopher Timothy, Esq

TIMPERLEY, Prof Walter Richard; s of Capt Walter Alonzo Timperley, RAMC (d 1965), and Rosalie Mary, *née* Randles (d 1967); *b* 16 June 1936; *Educ* Oundle, Univ of Oxford (MA, BM BCh, DM); *m* 1 April 1961, Rosalind Marjorie, da of late Frederick Norman Baron; 2 da (Jane Clare b 8 Feb 1964, Anne Louise b 29 June 1965); *Career* lectr in neuropathology Univ of Manchester 1967–71 (now emeritus), conslt neuropathologist Sheffield Health Authy 1971–, hon clinical lectr Univ of Sheffield 1971–, hon prof Univ of Sheffield 1999–; sec-gen World Assoc of Socs of Pathology 1993– (sometime chm Constitution and Bye-Laws Ctee), pres Assoc of Clinical Pathologists 1994 (memb Cncl 1984–, chm Cncl 1990–93), pres N of England Neurological Assoc 1994–95, cncl memb RCPath 1987–90 and 1993–96; memb: BMA, Br Neuropathological Assoc, Int Neuropathological Soc, World Assoc of Socs of Pathology, Assoc of Br Neurologists; *Books* Neurological Complications in Clinical Haematology (1980); *Recreations* walking, photography, reading, ornithology; *Style*— Dr Walter Timperley

TIMSON, Mrs Rodney; Penelope Anne Constance; *see:* Keith, Penelope Anne Constance

TINDALE, Gordon Anthony; OBE (1983); s of late George Augustus Tindale, and late Olive Sarah, *née* Collier; *b* 17 March 1938; *Educ* Highgate Sch, Trinity Coll Oxford (BA), Birkbeck Coll London (MA); *m* June 1960, Sonia Mary, da of late Arthur Bertram Spencer Soper; 1 da (Helen Frances b Nov 1960), 1 s (Stephen Christopher b March 1963); *Career* Nat Serv 1956–58, 2 Lt Royal Signals, Lt reserve serv 23 SAS; language training MECAS serv in Amman, Baghdad and London 1961–71, Br Cncl rep Lesotho, Botswana and Swaziland 1975–78, dir ME Dept 1978, Br Cncl rep Lusaka Zambia 1979–83, head Mgmnt Div 1983–87, Br Cncl rep Cairo Egypt 1987–89 (asst cultural attaché 1971–74), cultural cnsllr Washington DC USA 1989–94, dir Govt and Public Affairs WH Smith (USA) Inc 1994–99; *Recreations* golf, music, theatre; *Clubs* Hendon Golf (capt 2002–03), West Heath Tennis; *Style*— Gordon Tindale, Esq, OBE; ✉ 26 Oppidans Road, London NW3 3AG (tel 020 7722 9343)

TINDALL, Gillian Elizabeth; da of D H Tindall; *b* 4 May 1938; *Educ* Univ of Oxford (MA); *m* 1963, Richard G Lansdown; 1 s; *Career* novelist, biographer, and historian; freelance journalist; occasional articles and reviews for: The Observer, The Guardian, New Statesman, New Society, London Evening Standard, The Times, Encounter, Sunday Times, The Independent, Daily Telegraph, New York Times; occasional broadcaster BBC, plays for Radio 4; JP Inner London Area 1980–98; FRSL; Chevalier de l'Ordre des Arts et des Lettres (France) 2001; *Books* novels: No Name in the Street (1959), The Water and the Sound (1961), The Edge of the Paper (1963), The Youngest (1967), Someone Else (1969, 2 edn 1975), Fly Away Home (1971, Somerset Maugham Award 1972), The Traveller and His Child (1975), The Intruder (1979), Looking Forward (1983), To the City (1987), Give Them All My Love (1989), Spirit Weddings (1992); short stories: Dances of Death (1973), The China Egg and Other Stories (1981), Journey of a Lifetime (1990); biography: The Born Exile: George Gissing (1974); other non-fiction: A Handbook on Witchcraft (1965), The Fields Beneath (1977), City of Gold: the biography of Bombay (1981), Rosamond Lehmann: an appreciation (1985), Architecture of the British Empire (contrib, 1986), Countries of the Mind: the meaning of place to writers (1991), Célestine: Voices from a French Village (1995, Franco-British Soc Award), The Journey of Martin Nadaud (1999), The Man Who Drew London: Wenceslaus Hollar in reality and imagination (2002), The House by the Thames (2006); *Recreations* keeping house, foreign travel; *Style*— Ms Gillian Tindall, FRSL; ✉ c/o Curtis Brown Ltd, 4th Floor, Haymarket House, 28–29 Haymarket, London SW1Y 4SP (tel 020 7393 4400, fax 020 7393 4401)

TINDALL, Justin Matthew Robert; s of David Tindall, of Pewsey, Wilts, and Brenda May, *née* Randall; *b* 17 August 1965, Taplow, Berks; *Educ* Stubbington House Ascot, Seaford Coll Sussex, Goldsmiths Coll Univ of London (BA); *partner* Susan McKellar Cameron Cooper; 1 da (Misty May b 27 Sept 1998); *Career* art dir SMI Advertising 1991–96, art dir FCA! 1996–99; DDB London: joined 1999, creative dir and head of art 2004–, memb Exec Bd 2005–; *Awards* incl: 1 Gold and 9 Silver Campaign Poster Awards, 2 Gold, 3 Silver and 1 Bronze Campaign Press Awards, 2 Gold, 9 Silver and 3 Bronze Creative Circle Awards, 5 Silver Pencil D&AD Awards, 3 Gold, 1 Silver and 1 Bronze Lions Cannes Awards, 7 Gold, 5 Silver and 3 Bronze Clio Awards, 3 Gold, 3 Silver and 1 Bronze One Show Awards, 1 Gold and 1 Silver CIMTG Awards, 2 Gold Epica Awards, 4 Gold Eurobest Awards, Gold Br TV Award, Gold London Int Awards; *Recreations* tennis, golf, painting; *Clubs* Royal Automobile; *Style*— Justin Tindall, Esq; ✉ The Red Brick Road, 50–54 Beak Street, London W1F 9RN (tel 020 7575 7600, e-mail justin.tindall@theredbrickroad.com)

TINDALL, Michael James (Mike); MBE (2004); *b* 18 October 1978, Wharfedale; *Educ* Queen Elizabeth GS Wakefield; *Career* rugby union player (centre); clubs: Bath until 2005, Gloucester 2005–; England: 49 caps, debut v Ireland 2000, winners Six Nations Championship 2000, 2001 and 2003 (Grand Slam 2003), ranked no 1 team in world 2003, winners World Cup Aust 2003; *Style*— Mike Tindall, Esq, MBE

TINDLE, David; s of Ernest Edwin Cook (d 1975), and Dorothy, *née* Smith (who m 2, 1946, William Tindle, and d 1974); assumed surname of Tindle 1946; *b* 29 April 1932; *Educ* Coventry Secdy Modern Sch, Coventry Sch of Art; *Career* artist; visiting tutor many art schs 1956–, tutor RCA 1972–83; Ruskin Master of Drawing and Fine Art Oxford 1985–87 (MA 1985); currently lives and works in Italy; many one man exhibitions incl: Piccadilly Gallery 1954–83, Coventry City Art Gallery 1957, Galerie du Tours San Francisco 1964, Northern Art Gallery 1972, Fischer Fine Art 1985, 1989 and 1992, Gallery XX Hamburg 1974, 1977, 1980 and 1985, St Edmund Hall Oxford 1994, Redfern Gallery 1994, 1996, 2000, 2001, 2003, 2005 and 2007, Redfern Gallery work from 1987–97; represented in exhibitions: Royal Acad 1954, 1968, 1970 and 1972– (annually), Salon de la Jeune Peinture (Paris) 1967, Internationale Biennale of Realist Art (Bologna) 1967, Eros in Albion - Six English Painters (Florence) 1989; work represented at: The Tate Gallery, The Arts Cncl, Chantrey Bequest DOE, London Museum, De Beers Collection, Royal Acad, Nat Portrait Gallery, Ashmolean Museum Oxford; designed stage set for Tchaikovsky's Iolanta (Aldeburgh Festival) 1988; Johnson Wax Award Royal Acad 1983; hon fell St Edmund Hall Oxford 1988; ARA 1973, RA 1979, FRCA 1981, Hon FRCA 1983; *Style*— David Tindle, Esq, RA; ✉ c/o The Royal Academy, Burlington House, Piccadilly, London W1V 0DS; The Redfern Gallery, 20 Cork Street, London W1X 2HL

TINDLE, Sir Ray Stanley; kt (1994), CBE (1987, OBE 1974), DL (Surrey); s of John Robert Tindle (d 1975), and Maud, *née* Bilney (d 1952); *b* 8 October 1926; *Educ* Torquay GS, Strand Sch; *m* 8 Oct 1949, Beryl Julia, da of David Charles Ellis (d 1968); 1 s (Owen Charles b 1956); *Career* Capt Devonshire Regt 1944–47, served Far East; chm: Farnham Castle Newspapers Ltd 1969–, Tindle Newspapers Ltd, Farnham Herald, Cornish Times, Cornish & Devon Post, Mid Devon Advertiser, Tenby Observer, Cambrian News, 166 other titles, and 12 radio stations; memb MMC Newspaper Panel 1987–93; fndr Tindle Enterprise Centres for the Unemployed 1984, treas Newspaper Soc 1988–2002 (pres 1971–72), memb Cncl Cwlth Press Union, vice-pres Newspaper Press Fund; life patron Small Business Bureau 1995; chm Project Planning Sub Ctee Univ of Surrey 1964–69; memb Ct of Assts Worshipful Co of Stationers and Newspaper Makers (Master 1985–86); Hon DLitt Univ of Buckingham; FCIS, FCIArb, FCIJ; *Style*— Sir Ray Tindle, CBE, DL; ✉ Tindle Newspapers Ltd, The Old Court House, Farnham, Surrey GU9 7PT (tel 01252 735667, fax 01252 734007)

TINER, John Ivan; s of Kenneth Ivan Tiner, of Surrey, and Joan, *née* Benham; *b* 25 February 1957, Guildford, Surrey; *Educ* St Peter's Sch Guildford, Kingston Univ (accountancy fndn course); *m* 1978, Geraldine Marion Alison, da of James Henry Kassell; 2 s (Mark Andrew James b 1981, Matthew Paul Ivan b 1984), 1 da (Annabelle Elizabeth Mary b 1987); *Career* chartered accountant Tansley Witt (merged with Arthur Andersen) 1976–79; Arthur Andersen: joined 1979, mangr 1982, ptnr 1988–2001, head of fin markets 1993–99, managing ptnr UK Financial Markets 1995–99, managing ptnr Worldwide Financial Service Industry 1997–2001, managing ptnr UK Business Consulting 1998–2001; FSA: md Consumer, Investment and Insurance Directorate 2001–03, chief exec 2003–07; ldr Bank of England review of UK banking supervision 1996; ACA 1980, memb ICAEW; *Books* Accounting for Treasury Products (jtly, 1988, 2 edn 1991); *Recreations* tennis, golf, sailing; *Clubs* Mosimann's; *Style*— John Tiner, Esq

TINKER, Prof Anthea Margaret; CBE (2000); da of James Collins (d 1991), and Margaret, *née* Herring (d 1999); *b* 24 October 1932; *Educ* Convent of Our Lady of Compassion Olton, Univ of Birmingham (BCom, William Morton meml prize), City Univ London (PhD); *m* 29 Dec 1956, Rev Prebendary Eric Tinker, OBE, s of Frank Stanley Tinker (d 1923); 2 s (Jonathan Hugh b 27 March 1959, Andrew Michael b 14 May 1960), 1 da (Rachel Mary b 4 May 1964); *Career* asst then buyer Boxfoldia Ltd Birmingham 1953–54, HM inspr of factories 1954–58; pt/t lectr and res: Univ of Birmingham and Birmingham Sch of Planning 1958–65, Dept of Extra Mural Studies Univ of London and other London colls 1965–75 (full time res Royal Cmmn on Local Govt 1967); res fell City Univ London 1975–77, sr then princ res offr DOE 1977–88, dir Age Concern Inst of Gerontology KCL 1988–98, prof of social gerontology Univ of London 1988–, visiting Tower res fell Victoria Univ of Wellington NZ 2001; memb C of E Synod Working Pty on Ageing 1987–90, govr Centre for Policy on Ageing 1988–94, conslt OECD Paris 1989–94 and 2000, memb Joseph Rowntree Fndn Inquiry into the Costs of Continuing Care 1994–96, expert Euro Union 1991–, conslt WHO 2003–04; chair and memb various nat advsy ctees on ageing, scientific advsr to various Govt Depts; chm Research Ethics Ctee KCL; vice-pres Section Gerontology/Geriatrics RSM 2000–02 (pres 1998–2000); FKC 1998, founding AcSS 1999; memb: Br Soc of Gerontology, Social Res Assoc, Social Policy Assoc, Assoc for Educnl Gerontology, Royal Soc of Arts, Br Assoc, Cncl Int Soc of Gerontechnology 1999–2003; FRSM; *Books* The Non-Specialist Graduate in Industry (1954), The Inner London Education Authority (1968), Housing the Elderly: How Successful are Granny Annexes? (1976), Housing the Elderly near Relatives: Moving and Other Options (1980), Women in Housing: Access and Influence (with Marion Brion, 1980), Elderly People in Modern Society (1981, 2 edn 1984, 3 edn 1992, 4 edn 1997), Families in Flats (with Judith Littlewood, 1981), Staying at Home: Helping Elderly People (1984), The Telecommunication Needs of Disabled and Elderly People (1989), An Evaluation of Very Sheltered Housing (1989), A Review of Research on Falls Among Elderly People (jtly, 1990), Falls and Elderly People: a Study of Current Professional Practice in England and Innovations Abroad (jtly, 1991), Medication in Sheltered Housing (jtly, 1992), Caring: The Importance of Third Age Carers (jtly, 1992), Life after Sixty - A Profile of Britain's Older Population (jtly, 1992), Homes and Travel: Local Life in the Third Age (jtly, 1992), The Information Needs of Elderly People (jtly, 1993), Loneliness in Old Age (ed, 1993), The Care of Frail Elderly People in the UK (jtly, 1994), Difficult to Let Sheltered Housing (jtly, 1995), Getting Around After Sixty (jtly, 1996), Alternative Models of Care for Older People: Research Vol 2 Royal Cmmn on Long Term Care (jtly, 1999), Home Ownership in Old Age: financial benefit or burden? (jtly, 1999), To Have and to Hold: the bond between older people and the homes they own (jtly, 1999), Eighty-five not out (jtly, 2001), University Research Ethics Committees: The role, remit and conduct (jtly, 2004), Facts and Misunderstandings about Pensions and Retirement Ages (jtly, 2005), Improving the Provision of Information about Assistive Technology (jtly, 2005); *Recreations* social policy, family, visiting France; *Style*— Prof Anthea Tinker, CBE; ✉ 35 Theberton Street, London N1 0QY (tel 020 7359 4750); Institute of Gerontology, King's College London, 5th Floor, Melbourne House, 46 Aldwych, London WC2B 4LL (tel 020 7848 3033, e-mail anthea.tinker@kcl.ac.uk)

TINKER, Prof (Philip) Bernard Hague; OBE (2000); s of Philip Tinker (d 1978), and Gertrude, *née* Hague (d 1977); *b* 1 February 1930; *Educ* Rochdale HS, Univ of Sheffield (BSc, PhD), Univ of Oxford (MA, DSc); *m* 27 Aug 1955, Maureen, da of Joseph Ellis (d 1952); 1 s (John Philip b 1956), 1 da (Amanda Jane b 1960); *Career* Overseas Res Serv 1955–62, Rothamsted Experimental Station 1962–65, lectr in soil sci Univ of Oxford 1965–71, prof of agric botany Univ of Leeds 1971–77, head of Soils Div and dep dir Rothamsted Experimental Station 1977–85, dir of sci NERC 1985–92, sr visiting fell Plant Sci Dept

Univ of Oxford 1992–; sr res fell St Cross Coll Oxford 1987–95, visiting prof Imperial Coll of Sci and Technol London 1992–95; Francis New medal Fertilizer Soc 1991, Busk medal RGS 1994; memb Norwegian Acad of Sci 1987, hon memb Int Union of Soil Sci 2002; FIBiol 1976, FRSC 1985, Hon FRAgS 1990, FLS 1992; *Publications* Ninth Symposium of British Ecological Society (ed, 1969), Solute Movement in the Soil-Root System (1977), Endomycorrhizas (ed, 1977), Soil and Agriculture: Critical Reviews (1980), Advances in Plant Nutrition (ed, vol I 1984, vol II 1985, vol III 1988), Solute Movement in the Rhizosphere (2000), Shades of Green - a review of UK farming systems (ed, 2000), The Oil Palm (2003); *Recreations* gardening, map collecting; *Clubs* Farmers'; *Style*— Prof Bernard Tinker, OBE; ✉ The Glebe House, Broadwell, Gloucestershire GL7 3QS (tel 01367 860436, e-mail bernard.tinker@btinternet.com)

TINNISWOOD, Peter; s of Maurice Tinniswood, of Thames Ditton Surrey, and Anne, *née* Matchett; *b* 30 May 1951; *Educ* Charterhouse, Magdalen Coll Oxford (MA, PGCE), INSEAD (MBA); *m* 1975, Catharina, *née* Oeschger; *Career* asst master: Repton Sch 1974–76, Marlborough Coll 1976–80; sec-gen Franco-Br C of C and Indust 1981–83; asst master, head of Dept and housemaster Marlborough Coll 1983–91, master Magdalen Coll Sch Oxford 1991–98, head master Lancing Coll 1998–2005; tstee: Cambridge Business Studies Project Tst 1991–2001, Choir Schools' Assoc Bursary Tst 1994–98; govr: Dorset House Sch 2000–, Mowden Sch 2002–05; *Publications* Marketing Decisions (1981), Marketing and Production Decisions (1991); *Clubs* East India, Lansdowne; *Style*— Peter Tinniswood, Esq; ✉ Samvara, Les Girvaysses, 81170 Noailles, France

TINSON, Dame Susan (Sue); DBE (1990); *Career* assoc ed Independent Television News; former ed News at Ten; non-exec dir: Freeserve 1999–, Yorkshire Building Soc 1999–; tstee Nat Heritage Lottery Fund 1995–; memb Int Press Inst; FRSA, FRTS (vice-pres); *Style*— Dame Sue Tinson, DBE

TINSTON, Robert Sydney; CBE (2001); s of Sydney James Tinston (d 1985), of Margaret Hester, *née* Jardine (d 2001); *b* 29 March 1951; *Educ* Stockport Sch, Univ of Edinburgh (BSc); *m* 1975, Catherine Mary, da of John Joseph Somers; 1 da (Helen Catherine b 8 Feb 1978), 1 s (James Robert b 11 Sept 1979); *Career* asst sector admin: Withington Hosp Manchester 1976–78, KCH London 1978–79; hosp sec Cookridge Hosp Leeds 1979–83, gen mangr General Infirmary Leeds 1986–89 (commissioning offr 1983–86), chief exec Royal Liverpool Univ Hosp 1989–91, dep chief exec Mersey RHA 1991–93, chief exec NW RHA 1993–96, regnl dir NHS Exec North West 1996–2002; visiting prof Univ of Manchester; vice-chair Western Cheshire PCT 2006; MHSM (DipHSM) 1979; FRSA 1994, CIMgt 1997; *Recreations* astronomy, genealogy, Stockport County FC, pure breed poultry keeping; *Style*— Robert Tinston, Esq, CBE; ✉ The Thatched Cottage, Utkinton, Tarporley, Cheshire CW6 0LL

TIPPING, Simon Patrick (Paddy); MP; s of late John Tipping, and late Joan Tipping; *b* 24 October 1949; *Educ* Hipperholme GS, Univ of Nottingham (BA, MA); *m* 8 Jan 1970, Irene Margaret, *née* Quinn; 2 da; *Career* social worker Notts 1972–79, project ldr Church of England Children's Soc Nottingham 1979–83, cncllr Notts CC 1981–93 (sometime chm Fin Ctee); Parly candidate (Lab) Rushcliffe 1987, MP (Lab) Sherwood 1992–; PPS to Rt Hon Jack Straw, MP 1997–98 and 2005–07, Parly under-sec of state Privy Cncl Office 1998–2001, dep ldr of the House of Commons 2007–; dir: Notts Co-operative Devpt Agency 1983–93, Nottingham Devpt Enterprise; memb: UNISON, Co-op Pty; *Recreations* family, gardening, running; *Clubs* Clipstone Miners' Welfare; *Style*— Paddy Tipping, Esq, MP; ✉ House of Commons, London SW1A 0AA

TIPTAFT, David Howard Palmer; CBE (1992), JP (1972); s of C Paxman Tiptaft, MC, JP (d 1984), of Wentworth, S Yorks, and Irene, *née* Palmer (d 1968); *b* 6 January 1938; *Educ* Shrewsbury; *m* 1 June 1963, Jennifer Cherry, da of Gerald Richard Millward (d 1967); 2 da (Elgiva b 10 March 1964, Genovefa b 20 Dec 1966), 2 s (Justyn b 30 Sept 1965, Quintin b 19 June 1970); *Career* qualified CA 1962, Arthur Young 1961–64, princ Tiptaft Smith & Co 1966–; chm Don Valley Cons Assoc 1964–75, treas Rother Valley Cons Assoc 1976–83, chm Wentworth Cons Assoc 1983–92, chm Yorks Area Conservatives 1993–96 (treas 1988–93), chm S Yorks Area Conservatives 2006–; treas Yorks Gardens Tst; FCA 1973; *Recreations* flying, tennis, opera, Wagner; *Clubs* Carlton; *Style*— David Tiptaft, Esq, CBE; ✉ Ashcroft House, Wentworth, South Yorkshire (tel 01226 742972); Tiptaft Smith and Co, Montagu Chambers, Montagu Square, Mexborough, South Yorkshire (tel 01709 582991)

TIRAMANI, Jennifer Jane (Jenny); da of Fredo Paulo Tiramani, and Barbara Doreen, *née* King; *Educ* Dartford GS for Girls, Central Sch of Art and Design, Trent Poly; *Career* theatre designer and dress historian; designer 7:84 England and 7:84 Scotland theatre companies 1978–84, assoc designer Theatre Royal Stratford E 1980–97, designer Renaissance Theatre Co 1988–90; Shakespeare's Globe: assoc designer 1997–2002 (designs incl: Hamlet 2000, Twelfth Night 2002), dir of theatre design 2003– (designs incl The Tempest 2005); dress advsr and contrib to Searching for Shakespeare exhbn Nat Portrait Gallery 2006; West End prodns incl: Steaming (Comedy Theatre) 1981, The Big Life (Apollo Theatre) 2005; Laurence Olivier Award for Costume Design (for Twelfth Night) 2003; *Publications* Janet Arnold and the Globe Wardrobe: Handmade Clothes for Shakespeare's Actors (in Costume (vol 34), 2000), The Sanders Portrait (in Costume (vol 39), 2005); *Style*— Ms Jenny Tiramani; ✉ 47 Charles Square, London N1 6HT (tel and fax 020 7490 0987, e-mail jennyt@ruff.co.uk)

TISHLER, Gillian; da of Harry Tishler, of Ponteland, Northumberland, and Joyce, *née* Andrews; *b* 27 March 1958; *Educ* St Anne's Coll Oxford (BA); *m* 8 June 1991, Richard Wood; *Career* fast stream trainee rising to private sec to jr min MAFF 1979–87, Parly offr rising to head of public affrs RNIB 1987–93, chief exec YWCA of GB 1993–; *Style*— Ms Gillian Tishler; ✉ YWCA (England & Wales), Clarendon House, 52 Cornmarket Street, Oxford OX1 3EJ (tel 01865 304209)

TITCHMARSH, Alan Fred; MBE (2000), VMH (2004), DL (Hants 2001); s of Alan Titchmarsh (d 1986), of Ilkley, W Yorks, and Bessie, *née* Hardisty (d 2002); *b* 2 May 1949; *Educ* Shipley Art and Tech Inst, Hertfordshire Coll of Agriculture and Horticulture (Nat Cert Horticulture), Royal Botanic Gardens Kew (Dip Horticulture, Sir Joseph Hooker Prize, Keith Jones Cup for public speaking); *m* 1975, Alison Margaret, da of Geoffrey Herbert Needs; 2 da (Polly Alexandra b 1980, Camilla Rose b 1982); *Career* freelance writer, presenter, interviewer and broadcaster 1979–; apprentice gardener Parks Dept Ilkley Urban District Cncl 1964–68, staff training supervisor Royal Botanic Gardens Kew 1972–74, asst ed Gardening Books Hamlyn Publishing Group 1974–76, dep ed Amateur Gardening magazine 1978–79 (asst ed 1976–78); gardening corr: Woman's Own 1982–85, Daily Mail 1986–99, Radio Times 1996–2001 and 2004–, Daily Express and Sunday Express 1999–; gardening ed Homes and Gardens 1985–89; pres: Gardening for Disabled Tst 1989–, Telephones for the Blind 1993–; vice-pres: Wessex Cancer Tst 1988–, Butterfly Conservation 2000–; patron Rainbow Tst 1993–, vice-patron Jubilee Sailing Tst 1999–, tstee Nat Maritime Museum 2005–; Freeman City of London 1989, Liveryman Worshipful Co of Gardeners 1989; Hon DSc Univ of Bradford 1999; Hon DUniv: Essex 1999, Leeds Met Univ 2004, Winchester 2007; FIHort, FCGI 2000; *Radio* BBC Radio progs: You and Yours 1975–82, Down to Earth 1982–89, A House In A Garden 1987–91, Radio 2 Arts Prog 1990–97, Melodies for You 2007–; *Television* presenter BBC TV progs: Nationwide (gardening expert) 1980–83, Breakfast Time (gardening expert) 1983–86, The Chelsea Flower Show 1983–97 and 2001–, Open Air 1986–87, Daytime Live 1987–90, Grow Biz Quiz 1989, Songs of Praise 1989–94, More Than Meets The Eye 1990, Scene Today 1990, Pebble Mill 1991–96, Titchmarsh's Travels 1991, Titchmarsh On Song 1992, Sweet Inspiration 1993–94, Gardeners' World 1996–2002, Ground Force 1997–2002, Ask the Family 1999; presenter: Down by the River (Meridian) 1994–95, Relative Knowledge (Meridian) 1997, How to be a Gardener 2002–03, The Royal Gardeners 2003, BBC Proms 2004–, British Isles: A Natural History 2004, 20th Century Roadshow 2005, The Gardener's Year 2005, Britain's Best (UKTV) 2007, The Great British Village Show 2007, Saving Planet Earth 207, The Nature of Britain 2007, The Alan Titchmarsh Show (ITV) 2007; *Awards* Gardening Writer of the Year 1980 and 1983, Royal Horticultural Soc's Gold Medal Chelsea Flower Show 1985, Yorkshireman of the Year 1997, Variety Club of Great Britain TV Personality of the Year 1999 (for the Ground Force team), Special Award Inst of Horticulture 2004, Special Award TRIC 2004; *Books* incl: Gardening Under Cover (1979), Climbers and Wall Plants (1980), Gardening Techniques (1981), The Allotment Gardener's Handbook (1982), The Rock Gardener's Handbook (1983), Supergardener (1983), Alan Titchmarsh's Avant-Gardening (1984 and 1994), Daytime Live Gardening Book (1990), The English River (1993), Alan Titchmarsh's Favourite Gardens (1995), Mr MacGregor (novel, 1998), Alan Titchmarsh's Complete Book of Gardening (1999), Ground Force Weekend Workbook (conslt ed, 1999), The Last Lighthouse Keeper (novel, 1999), Animal Instincts (novel, 2000), Only Dad (novel, 2001), How to be a Gardener: The Basics (2002), Trowel and Error (2002), How to be a Gardener: Secrets of Success (2003), The Royal Gardeners (2003), Rosie (novel, 2004), British Isles: A Natural History (2004), Fill My Stocking (anthology, 2005), The Gardener's Year (2005), Love and Dr Devon (novel, 2006), Nobbut a Lad (2006), England Our England (2007), The Nature of Britain (2007); *Recreations* boating; *Clubs* Lord's Taverners, Royal London Yacht; *Style*— Alan Titchmarsh, Esq, MBE, VMH, DL; ✉ c/o Caroline Mitchell, Colt Hill House, Odiham, Hampshire RG29 1AL (tel 01256 702839)

TITCOMB, Hugh Harrison; s of Francis William Titcomb, of Newbury, and Margaret Ann, *née* Bright; *b* 21 December 1959, Newbury, Berks; *Educ* Univ of Warwick (BA); *m* 10 Sept 1994, Karen Jane, *née* Basson; 1 s (Christopher b 5 Feb 1997), 1 da (Anna b 25 Feb 1999); *Career* dir Robert Fleming 1994–2002, md Bank of New York 2002–03, ceo Ansbacher Gp 2003–; FCIB 2003; *Style*— Hugh Titcomb, Esq; ✉ Ansbacher & Co, Two London Bridge, London SE1 9RA (tel 020 7089 4950, e-mail hugh.titcomb@ansbacher.com)

TITCOMB, (Simon) James; s of Geoffrey Cowley Baden Titcomb (d 1960), of Brighton, E Sussex, and Molly Gwendolyn Titcomb (d 1985); *b* 10 July 1931; *Educ* Brighton Coll; *m* 1957, Ann Constance, da of Gerald Bernard Vokins (d 1987); 2 s (Clive b 1958, Mark b 1962), 1 da (Clarissa b 1965); *Career* Lt Nat Serv 1955–57; memb Stock Exchange 1962, ptnr de Zoete & Bevan (Stockbrokers) 1962–86 (sr ptnr 1976–86); dir of various public and private cos; FCA, CIMgt; *Recreations* golf, bridge, travel, wildlife; *Clubs* Brooks's, City of London, Piltdown Golf; *Style*— James Titcomb, Esq; ✉ Buttonwood House, Maresfield Park, East Sussex TN22 2HA (tel 01825 763909)

TITE, Prof Michael Stanley; s of Arthur Robert Tite (d 1985), and Evelyn Francis Violet, *née* Endersby (d 1971); *b* 9 November 1938; *Educ* Trinity Sch of John Whitgift Croydon, ChCh Oxford (exhibitioner, MA, DPhil); *m* 10 June 1967, Virgina Byng, da of Rear Adm Gambier John Byng Noel, CB (d 1995), of Haslemere, Surrey; 2 da (Sarah Beatrice b 1970, Alice Evelyn Byng b 1972); *Career* ICI res fell Univ of Leeds 1964–67, lectr Univ of Essex 1967–75, keeper Res Lab British Museum 1975–89, Edward Hall prof of archaeological science Univ of Oxford 1989–2004 (emeritus prof 2004–), fell Linacre Coll Oxford 1989–2004 (emeritus fell 2004–); fell Int Inst for Conservation (FIIC) 1990–2004; FSA 1977; *Books* Methods of Physical Examination in Archaeology (1972); *Recreations* walking, gardening, travel; *Style*— Prof Michael Tite, FSA; ✉ Research Laboratory for Archaeology and the History of Art, Dyson Perrins Building, South Parks Road, Oxford OX1 3QY

TITE, Nicholas William Spencer (Nick); s of William Timpson Tite (d 1970), and Stephanie Frances, *née* Spencer; *b* 29 July 1950; *Educ* Wellingborough Sch, Northampton Sch of Art (travelling scholar), Winchester Sch of Art (DipAD, first year painting prize); *Career* Studio Prints Queen's Crescent London 1974–76, etching technician Central Sch of Art 1976–78, Editions Alecto (working on Tom Phillips's Dante's Inferno) 1978, creation of Talfourd Press (prodn controller Tom Phillips's Dante's Inferno) 1980–83, ed RA Magazine 1983–2001, head of publishing operations RA Publications 2007– (ed dir 1998–2006); responsible for exhibitions in Friends' Room at Royal Acad incl: Ghika, Bryan Kneale, Carel Weight, S W Hayter, Leonard McComb, RAs Through the Lens, Etchings by Academicians 1985–98; *Recreations* tennis; *Style*— Nick Tite, Esq; ✉ RA Publications, Royal Academy Enterprises, Royal Academy of Arts, Burlington House, London W1J 0BD (tel 020 7300 5659, fax 020 7300 5881, e-mail nick.tite@royalacademy.org.uk)

TITLEY, Gary; MEP (Lab) North West England; s of late Wilfred James Titley, and Joyce Lillian Titley; *b* 19 January 1950; *Educ* Univ of York (BA, PGCE); *m* 1975, Maria (Charo) Rosario; 1 s (Adam), 1 da (Samantha); *Career* various positions until 1973 incl: bus conductor, delivery driver, postman, security guard, labourer and barman; TEFL Bilbao 1973–75, history teacher Earls High Sch Halesowen 1976–84; campaign mangr to Terry Pitt, MEP (and later John Bird, MEP) 1983–89; Parly candidate (Lab): Bromsgrove 1983, Dudley W 1987; memb Bolton W CLP; memb W Midlands CC 1981–86: vice-chm Econ Devpt Ctee 1981–84, vice-chm Consumer Servs Ctee 1984–86; MEP (Lab): Greater Manchester W 1989–99, NW England 1999–; leader EP Labour Gp 2002–; former memb: Environment, REX, Econ and Monetary, and Tport Ctees; pres Jt Parly Ctee with: Finland 1991–93, European Economic Area 1993–94 (vice-pres 1994–97), Slovenia 1997–; vice-pres delgn to Czech, Slovak and Slovenian Parliaments 1994–97; pres EP Jt Parly Ctee with Lithuania; rapporteur on: Finland's accession to EU, Future of the Euro Defence Industries; dir W Midlands Enterprise Bd 1982–89, vice-chair Euro Parly Delgn for Rels with Czech Republic, rapportuer on Finland's accession to EU 1995; chm: W Midlands Co-op Finance Co 1982–89, Black Country Co-op Development Agency 1982–88; Cdr Order of the White Rose of Finland, Austrian Gold Cross, Order of Lithuanian Grand Duke Gediminas; *Recreations* family, reading, sport; *Style*— Gary Titley, Esq, MEP; ✉ 16 Spring Lane, Radcliffe, Manchester M26 2TQ (tel 0161 724 4008)

T

TITTERINGTON, David Michael; s of Geoffrey Bridge Titterington, of Beverley, E Yorks, and Claire Elizabeth, *née* Parsons; *b* 10 January 1958; *Educ* Northern Sch of Music, Pembroke Coll Oxford (organ scholar, MA), Conservatoire Rueil-Malmaison Paris; *Career* organist; debut Royal Festival Hall 1986; concert and concerto performances at major festivals and venues worldwide incl: Bicentennial Festival of Sydney 1988 and festivals of Hong Kong, New Zealand, Istanbul, Schleswig-Holstein, Cheltenham, Adelaide and Israel; BBC Proms debut 1990; orchestras played with incl: BBC Symphony, BBC Scottish Symphony, Bournemouth Sinfonietta, English Sinfonia, Berlin Symphony, Lahti Symphony; has given masterclasses internationally; numerous recordings made incl complete works of César Franck (for BBC), also recorded for Hyperion Records, Multisonic and ASV; world premiere performances incl: Petr Eben's Job 1986, Naji Hakim's Rubaiyat 1990, Diana Burrell's Arched Forms with Bells (Proms cmmn) 1990, Henze Symphony No 9 (BBC Proms) 2000, Stephen Montague's Toccare Incandescent (South Bank cmmn, Royal Festival Hall) 2004, Giles Swayne's 14 Stations of the Cross (25th Cambridge Festival cmmn, King's Coll Cambridge); organ consIt: Pembroke Coll Oxford 1995, Chapel Royal HM Tower of London 2000, St Catherine's Coll Cambridge 2002, Sidney Sussex Coll Cambridge 2007–, Canterbury Cathedral 2007–; artistic dir Euro Organ Festival 1992; Royal Acad of Music: prof of organ 1990–, head of organ studies 1996–; visiting prof Ferenc Liszt Acad Budapest 1997–; gen ed organ repertoire series United Music Publishers London 1987–97; Ian Fleming award 1983, French Government

Scholarship 1983–84, Arts Council Bursary 1984, Premier Prix 1984, Prix d'Excellence 1985 (Rueil-Malmaison Conservatoire, Paris); memb: Royal Soc of Musicians of GB 1996; elected to SCR Pembroke Coll Oxford 1999; hon fell Univ of Bolton 1992, hon prof and Hon DMus Liszt Ferenc Univ Budapest 2000; Hon ARAM 1994, Hon FRCO 1999; *Clubs* Athenaeum; *Style*— David Titterington, Esq; ✉ c/o Royal Academy of Music, Marylebone Road, London NW1 5HT (tel 020 7873 7339, fax 020 7873 7439, e-mail d.titterington@ram.ac.uk)

TITTERRELL, Andrew James (Andy); s of Charles Titterrell, and Carol Titterrell; *b* 10 January 1981, Dartford, Kent; *m* 17 July 2005, Delyth; *Career* rugby union player (hooker); clubs: Saracens, Waterloo, Sale Sharks 2001–07, Gloucester 2007– (winners Parker Pen Shield 2002, European Challenge Cup 2005); England: 5 caps, debut v NZ 2004; memb British and Irish Lions touring squad NZ 2005; *Style*— Mr Andy Titterrell; ✉ c/o Gloucester Rugby Football Club, Kingsholm, Kingsholm Road, Gloucester GL1 3AX

TOALSTER, John Raymond; s of Chief Petty Offr John Edward Toalster, RNVR (ka 1944), and Adeline Enid, *née* Smith; *b* 12 March 1941; *Educ* Kingston HS Hull N Humberside, LSE (BSc); *m* 21 Sept 1963, Christine Anne, da of Edward Percy Paget (d 1970); 1 s (Quentin Simon Edward b 1966), 2 da (Rachel Jane b 1969, Bethan Claire b 1981); *Career* lectr in economics Univ of Sierra Leone 1964–67, corp planner Mobil Oil 1967–69, sr analyst (oils) stockbroking 1970–77, corporate fin mangr Kuwait International Investment Co 1977–81, energy specialist stockbroking 1982–90; dir: Hoare Govett 1982–90, Security Pacific, Société General Strauss Turnbull 1990–; FInstPet 1988; private circulation to clients; *Recreations* swimming, sailing, badminton; *Style*— John Toalster, Esq; ✉ Fig St Farm, Sevenoaks, Kent (tel 01732 453357); Société General Strauss Turnbull, Exchange House, Primrose Street, London EC2A (tel 020 7638 5699, fax 020 7588 1437)

TOASE, Philip (Phil); CBE (2004); *b* 26 September 1953, Wakefield; *Educ* Queen Elizabeth GS Wakefield, South Bank Univ/Fire Serv Coll (BSc); *m* Lorraine; 1 s (James), 1 da (Anna), 1 step s (Greig); *Career* West Yorkshire Fire and Rescue Service: joined 1974, station offr Dewsbury Fire Station 1981–90, sr divnl offr 1990–95, asst chief fire offr 1995–99, dep chief fire offr 1999–2000, chief fire offr and chief exec 2000–; pres Chief Fire Offrs Assoc 2006–07; W L Gore technol scholar 1996; FIFireE, memb C&G; *Recreations* golf, walking, supporting Manchester United; *Style*— Phil Toase, Esq, CBE; ✉ West Yorkshire Fire Service, Oakroyd Hall, Birkenshaw, West Yorkshire BD11 2DY (tel 01274 655701, fax 01274 655776, e-mail phil.toase@westyorksfire.gov.uk)

TOBIAS, Prof Jeffrey Stewart; s of Gerald Joseph Tobias, of Bournemouth, Dorset, and Sylvia, *née* Pearlberg; *b* 4 December 1946; *Educ* Hendon GS, Gonville& Caius Coll Cambridge (MA, MD), Bart's Med Coll; *m* 16 Nov 1973, Dr Gabriela Jill Jaecker, da of Hans Jaecker, of Crowborough, E Sussex; 1 da (Katharine Deborah b 1978), 2 s (Benjamin Alexander b 1980, Max William Solomon b 1983); *Career* SHO Bart's, UCH and Hammersmith Hosp 1972–73, fell in med (oncology) Harvard Med Sch 1974–75, sr registrar Royal Marsden Hosp and Inst of Cancer Research 1976–80, conslt clinical oncology UCH and Middlesex Hosps London 1981–, clinical dir Meyerstein Inst of Oncology 1992–97, prof of cancer med UCL Med Sch 2002–; hon sec Br Oncological Assoc 1985–90, chm UK Co-ordinating Ctee for Cancer Research Head and Neck Working Pty 1989–, pres Assoc of Head and Neck Oncologists of Great Britain 1995–97; memb: MRC Working Pty in Gynaecological and Brain Tumors, Cancer Research Campaign Working Pty in Breast Cancer (chm New Studies Sub-Gp), Cncl Royal Coll of Radiologists 1991–95; chair Cancer Research Campaign Educn Ctee; tstee and memb Cancer Research UK; Cncl fell American Soc for Therapeutic Radiology; FRCP, FRCR; *Publications* Primary Management of Breast Cancer (1985), Cancer and its Management (with R L Souhami, 1986, 5 edn 2005), Cancer - A Colour Atlas (1990), Cancer: What Every Patient Needs to Know (1995), Current Radiation Oncology Vols 1 - 3 (1994–98), Breast Cancer: New Horizons in Research and Treatment (2000), Informed Consent in Medical Research (with L Doyal, 2001); author of original articles in med jls, features and editorials in BMJ and The Lancet; *Recreations* music, writing, theatre, cycling, walking; *Clubs* Garrick, RSM; *Style*— Prof Jeffrey Tobias; ✉ 48 Northchurch Road, London N1 4EJ (tel 020 7249 2326); Department of Oncology, University College Hospital, London NW1 2EB (tel 020 7380 9214, fax 020 7380 9055, e-mail j.tobias@uclh.org)

TOD, Alison Jane; da of Robin Tod, of Abergavenny, and Jacqueline Rendall, *née* Davies; *b* 24 September 1963; *Educ* St David's Ursuline Convent Brecon, Alsager Coll, Univ of Lampeter (BA); *Partner* Neil Thomas; *Career* fashion designer; designs for: Kangol, Harpers & Queen A list for Millinery, London Fashion Week; exhibited at: V&A, Museum of Hatting; shows: Hay-on-Wye (for pres Bill Clinton), Clothes Show Live; Welsh Designer of the Year (fashion and accessories) 1995 and 1996; memb Br Hat Guild; memb: NSPCC (Full Stop Campaign), Cancer Research Campaign, Soroptomists, Save the Children, Stroke Assoc, Lady Taverners, Variety Club of GB, Br Heart Fndn, NHS Tst St David's Fndn, Carers' Assoc (Prince's Royal Tst for Carers); *Recreations* art galleries, travel, collecting antiques, horses, charity work; *Style*— Miss Alison Tod; ✉ Hatherleigh Place, Merthyr Link Road, Abergavenny, Monmouthshire NP7 7RL (tel 01873 855923, fax 01873 856891)

TODD, Dr (William Taylor) Andrew; s of James McArthur Todd, of Edinburgh, and Jean Morley, *née* Smith; *b* 14 July 1953; *Educ* George Heriot's Sch, Univ of Edinburgh (BSc, MB ChB); *m* 1 July 1978, Morag Jennifer, da of Trevor John Ransley, of Edinburgh; 3 da (Jennifer b 1980, Rachel b 1983, Anna b 1987); *Career* Royal Infirmary Edinburgh: res house offr 1977, SHO in med 1978, registrar 1979–82; sr registrar City Hosp Edinburgh 1984 (registrar 1979–81); visiting lectr Univ of Zimbabwe 1983, conslt physician and postgrad tutor Monklands Hosp 1985–, specialty advsr communicable diseases; memb: Speciality Advsy Ctee (infectious diseases/tropical med), jt ctee on higher med training; elder Church of Scotland; trg and manpower co-ordinator Cncl Br Infection Soc 1997–2002; FRCPE, FRCPG; *Publications* Principles and Practice of Medicine (contrib to infection/tropical med section); *Recreations* curling, hill walking; *Style*— Dr Andrew Todd; ✉ 17 Crosshill Drive, Rutherglen, Glasgow G73 3QT (tel 0141 647 7288, e-mail wtat@ntlworld.com); Infectious Diseases Unit, Monklands Hospital NHS Trust, Airdrie, Lanarkshire ML6 0JS (tel 01236 746120)

TODD, HE Damian Roderic (Ric); s of George Todd, and Annette, *née* Goodchild; *b* 29 August 1959; *Educ* Lawrence Sherriff GS Rugby, Worcester Coll Oxford; *m* 23 May 1987, Alison, *née* Digby; 1 s (Oliver b 2 March 1989), 2 da (Anya b 23 Sept 1992, Sally b 2 Feb 1999); *Career* joined HM Dip Serv 1980; FCO 1980–81, third later second sec Pretoria and Cape Town 1981–84, FCO 1984–87, consul and first sec Prague 1987–89, FCO 1989–91, first sec (economic) Bonn 1991–95, on secondment HM Treasy 1995–97, FCO 1997–98, on secondment HM Treasy 1998–2001, head EU Communication and Strategy (EUCS), ambass to Slovakia 2001–04, finance dir FCO 2004–07, ambass to Poland 2007–; *Recreations* history, family life, looking at buildings; *Style*— HE Mr Ric Todd; ✉ c/o Foreign & Commonwealth Office (Warsaw), King Charles Street, London SW1A 2AH (tel 020 7270 3000)

TODD, Daphne Jane; OBE (2002); da of Frank Todd (d 1976), of Whitstable, and Annie Mary, *née* Lord; *b* 27 March 1947; *Educ* Simon Langton GS for Girls Canterbury, Slade Sch of Fine Art (DFA, Higher Dip Fine Art); *m* 31 Aug 1984, Lt-Col (Patrick Robert) Terence Driscoll; 1 da (Mary Jane b 12 Nov 1977); *Career* artist specialising in portraits incl: HRH the Grand Duke of Luxembourg, Lord Adrian, Dame Janet Baker, Spike Milligan, Sir Neil Cossons, Baron Klingspor, Sir Kirby and Lady Laing, Christopher Ondaatje, Dame Anne Mueller, Lord Sainsbury of Preston Candover, Dame Marilyn Strathern, Lord Sharman, Sir Tom Stoppard, Lord Ashburton, Lord Deedes, Lord Tugendhat, Lord Fellowes, Lord Armstrong of Ilminster; dir of studies Heatherley Sch of Art 1980–86; govr: Thomas Heatherley Educnl Tst 1986–, Fedn of Br Artists 1994–2000; pres Royal Soc of Portrait Painters 1994–2000 (hon sec 1990–91); hon memb Soc of Women Artists 1995; *Exhibitions* incl retrospective exhibition Morley Gallery 1989, solo exhbn Messum Gall 2001 and 2004; work in numerous collections incl: Royal Acad (Chantrey Bequest), Regtl HQ Irish Guards, London, Cambridge, Oxford, Wales and De Montfort Univs, Royal Holloway Museum and Art Gallery, Bishop's Palace Hereford, BMA, Instn of Civil Engrs, Ondaatje Hall, Nat Portrait Gallery, Science Museum, Royal Collection Windsor, People's Portraits Girton Coll Cambridge; David Murray Award for Landscape Painting 1971, Br Inst Award for Figurative Painting 1972, second prize John Player Portrait Award Nat Portrait Gallery 1983, first prize Oil Painting of the Year Hunting Group Nat Art Prize Competition 1984, GLC Prize 1984, Ondaatje Prize for Portraiture 2001, RP Gold Medal 2001; Hon Dr of Arts De Montfort Univ 1998; ambass for East Suusex 2004; Freeman: City of London 1997, Worshipful Co of Painter-Stainers 1997 (Hon Liveryman 2004); NEAC 1984, RP 1985, FRSA; *Clubs* Arts, Chelsea Arts; *Style*— Miss Daphne Todd, OBE, PPRP, NEAC; ✉ Salters Green Farm, Mayfield, East Sussex TN20 6NP (tel and fax 01892 852472)

TODD, Dr Gillian Bees; da of Dr David Joseph Davies, MBE (d 1987), of Johnston, Pembs, and Beti Mary Davies (d 1977); *b* 29 September 1942; *Educ* Taskers Sch for Girls, Welsh Nat Sch of Med (Elizabeth Pipe prize in med); *m* 1981, Dr John Neild Todd; 2 s; *Career* med GP 1967–70, trainee in public health med 1970–79, conslt in public health med Trent Regnl HA 1979–83, dist gen mangr Central Nottinghamshire 1983–91; chief exec: S Birmingham Acute Unit 1991–94, S Glamorgan HA 1994–96, Bro-Taf HA 1996–99; dir Specialised Health Service Cmmn for Wales 1999–2002, med dir Powys Local Health Bd 2002–; memb BMA; MIMgt, MHSM, FFPHM 1987; *Recreations* walking, embroidery, knitting; *Style*— Dr Gillian Todd; ✉ Powys Local Health Board, Mansion House, Bronllys, Brecon, Powys LD3 0LS

TODD, (Thomas) Keith; CBE (2004); s of Thomas William Todd, and Cecilie Olive Francis, *née* Hefti; *b* 22 June 1953; *m* 19 May 1979, Anne Elizabeth, da of Hilson Adam Hendrie, of Edinburgh; 2 da (Fiona Elizabeth b 1980, Nicola Anne b 1982), 2 s ((Thomas) Christopher b 1984, Andrew Adam Paul b 1986); *Career* chief fin offr Cincinnati Electronics 1981–86, fin dir The Marconi Co 1986–87, chief exec ICL plc 1996–2000 (fin dir 1987–96); dir Camelot Group plc 1994–2000, chm and ceo Dexterus Jan-Oct 2001; chm: Knotty Green Consultant Ltd 2000–, ECSoft plc 2002–03 (dir 2001), Easynet plc 2002–06, Broadband Stakeholder Gp 2002–05, FFastfill plc 2002–, Magic Lantern Prodns 2006–, Aminotech plc 2007–; memb Cncl Open Univ 1992–2000 (hon treas 1992–97); Hon DUniv Open Univ; FCMA, FRSA; *Recreations* golf, tennis; *Style*— Keith Todd, Esq, CBE; ✉ e-mail todd@knottygreen.com

TODD, Prof Malcolm; s of Wilfrid Todd (d 1980), of Durham, and Rose Evelyn, *née* Johnson (d 1996); *b* 27 November 1939; *Educ* Henry Smith Sch, Univ of Wales (BA, DLitt), BNC Oxford (Dip); *m* 2 Sept 1964, Molly, da of Alexander John Tanner (d 1987), of London; 1 da (Katharine Grace b 1965), 1 s (Malcolm Richard b 1966); *Career* res asst Rheinisches Landesmuseum Bonn 1963–65, reader Univ of Nottingham 1977–79 (lectr 1965–74, sr lectr 1974–77), prof of archaeology Univ of Exeter 1979–96, princ Trevelyan Coll Durham 1996–2000; visiting fell: All Souls Coll Oxford 1984, BNC Oxford 1990–91; sr res fell Br Acad 1990–91; vice-pres Roman Soc 1984–; tstee: Roman Res Tst 1994–99, Trevelyan Tst 1996–; memb: Royal Cmmn on Historical Monuments 1986–93, Cncl Nat Tst 1986–92, German Archaeological Inst 1977; *Books* The Northern Barbarians (1975, 2 edn 1987), Roman Britain (1981, 1985 and 1999), The South-West To AD 1000 (1987), Britannia (ed, 1984–89), Research on Roman Britain: 1960–89 (ed, 1989), Les Germains aux Frontières de l'Empire Romain (1990), The Early Germans (1992), I Germani (1996), Die Germanen (2000), Migrants and Invaders (2001), Die Zeit der Völkerwanderung (2001), A Companion to Roman Britain (ed, 2004), Roman Mining in Somerset (2007); contrib: Cambridge Ancient History (revised edn, 1998), Oxford Dictionary of National Biography (2004); *Recreations* reading, writing; *Style*— Prof Malcolm Todd

TODD, Mark; MP; *Educ* Emmanuel Coll Cambridge; *Career* MP (Lab) Derbyshire S 1997–; *Style*— Mark Todd, MP; ✉ House of Commons, London SW1A 0AA (tel 020 7219 3549, e-mail markwtodd@btconnect.com, website www.marktodd.org.uk)

TODD, Michael Alan; QC (1997); s of Charles Edward Alan Todd, and Betty, *née* Bromwich (d 1997); *Educ* Kenilworth GS, Keele Univ (BA); *m* 1976, Deborah, da of Harold Thomas Collett (decd); *Career* called to the Bar Lincoln's Inn 1977, jr counsel to the Crown (Chancery) 1992–97; memb Hon Soc of Lincoln's Inn; *Recreations* equestrianism; *Style*— Michael Todd, Esq, QC; ✉ Erskine Chambers, 33 Chancery Lane, London WC2A 3EN (tel 020 7242 5532, fax 020 7831 0125)

TODHUNTER, Michael John Benjamin; DL (2005); s of Brig Edward Joseph Todhunter (d 1976), and Agnes Mary, *née* Swire (d 1975); *b* 25 March 1935; *Educ* Eton, Magdalen Coll Oxford (MA); *m* 1959, Caroline Francesca, da of Maj William Walter Dowding (d 1980); 1 s (Charles), 2 da (Nicola (Mrs James Denoon Duncan), Emily (Mrs E J (Manoli) Olympitis)); *Career* 2 Lt 11 Hussars (PAO) 1953–55; banker; Jessel Toynbee & Co Ltd 1958–84 (dir 1962, dep chm 1977), chief exec Alexanders Discount plc 1984–86, dir Mercantile House Holdings plc 1984–86, md PK English Trust Co Ltd 1986–89, London advsr Yasuda Trust Banking Co Ltd 1989–98; chm Clyde Shipping Co Ltd 1978–2000; dir: James Finlay Ltd 1977– (chm 2002–), Newbury Racecourse plc 1983–2004, Kleinwort Capital Trust plc 1989–2005 (chm 1999–2005); tstee: Great Ormond Street Hosp 1979–96, Missions to Seamen 1980–96, The Gift of Thomas Pocklington 1990–99; hon fell Inst of Child Health; High Sheriff Royal Co of Berkshire 1999; *Recreations* travel, shooting; *Clubs* White's, Pratt's; *Style*— Michael Todhunter, Esq, DL; ✉ The Old Rectory, Farnborough, Wantage, Oxfordshire OX12 8NX (tel 01488 638298, fax 01488 638091); The Studio, 4 Lowndes Street, London SW1X 9ET (tel 020 7235 6421); office: Swire House, 59 Buckingham Gate, London SW1E 6AJ (tel 020 7834 7717, fax 020 7630 5534, e-mail m_todhunter@btinternet.com)

TOFT, Dr Anthony Douglas; CBE (1995); s of William Vincent Toft (d 1982), and Anne, *née* Laing; *b* 29 October 1944; *Educ* Perth Acad, Univ of Edinburgh (BSc, MB ChB, MD); *m* 23 July 1968, Maureen Margaret, da of John Darling (d 1986); 1 s (Neil b 1970), 1 da (Gillian b 1972); *Career* conslt physician gen med and endocrinology Royal Infirmary Edinburgh 1978–, chief MO Scottish Equitable Life Assurance Society 1988–; Royal Coll of Physicians of Edinburgh: memb Cncl 1985–88, vice-pres 1990–91, pres 1991–94; memb Assoc of Physicians of GB and I 1984, chm Scottish Royal Colleges 1992–94, vice-chm UK Conf of Med Royal Colleges 1993–94, chm Jt Ctee on Higher Med Trg 1994–96, memb Health Advsy Appts Ctee 1994–2000; memb GMC 1996–2003; physician to HM The Queen in Scotland 1996–; chm Professional and Linguistic Assessments Bd (PLAB) 2000–06, pres Br Thyroid Assoc 1996–99; FRCPEd 1980, FRCP 1992, FRCPGlas 1993, FRCPI 1993, FRCSEd ad hominem 1994; Hon: FCPS (Pakistan) 1990, FRACP 1993, FACP 1993, FRCP (Canada) 1994, FRCGP 1994, FCPS (Bangladesh) 1994, FFPM 1994, MAM (Malaysia) 1994, FAM (Singapore) 1994, FFAEM 1997; *Books* Diagnosis and Management of Endocrine Diseases (1982); *Recreations* golf, gardening, hill walking; *Style*— Dr Anthony Toft, CBE; ✉ 41 Hermitage Gardens, Edinburgh EH10 6AZ (tel 0131 447 2221); Endocrine Clinic, Royal Infirmary, Edinburgh EH16 5SA (tel 0131 242 1480)

TOGHILL, Dr Peter James; s of John Walter Toghill (d 1991), and Lena Mary, *née* Jow (d 1985); *b* 16 June 1932; *Educ* Watford GS, Univ Coll Hosp Med Sch (MB BS), Univ of

London (MD); *m* 25 April 1964, Rosemary Anne, da of Alfred Samuel Cash, of Whatton, Nottinghamshire; 3 da (Claire Elizabeth b 1966, Helen Louise b 1969, Joanna Mary b 1972); *Career* Capt RAMC 1956–58; British Empire Cancer Campaign res fell and med registrar Univ Coll Hosp London 1960–64, sr med registrar King's Coll Hosp 1964–68, conslt physician Gen Hosp Nottingham and Univ Hosp Nottingham 1968–93, emeritus conslt physician QMC Nottingham 1993–, clinical dean Univ of Nottingham Med Sch 1977–80, dir of educn RCP London 1993–98; pres: Nottingham Med/Chirurgical Soc 1987–88, Nottinghamshire Medico-Legal Soc 1990–91; cncllr, pro-censor and censor RCP London 1990–93; Simms lectr RCP 1994, Samuel Gee lectr RCP 1996; FRCP, FRCPE, MRCS; *Books* Examining Patients (1990), Essential Medical Procedures (1996), Introduction to the Symptoms and Signs in Medicine (2000), Four Pieces of Luck: A Physician's Journey; author of numerous pubns on medical education, and diseases of the liver and spleen; *Recreations* Nottinghamshire cricket, painting, growing roses; *Style*— Dr Peter Toghill; ✉ 119 Lambley Lane, Burton Joyce, Nottingham NG14 5BL (tel 0115 931 2446, e-mail ptoghill@dialstart.net)

TOKSVIG, Sandi Birgitte; da of Claus Bertel Toksvig (d 1988), and Julie Anne, *née* Brett, of Surrey; *b* 3 May 1958; *Educ* Mamaroneck HS NY, Tormead Sch Guildford, Girton Coll Cambridge (MA, Therese Montefiore Meml Award); *Career* actress, comedienne and writer; Channel 4 Political Humourist of the Year 2007, Radio Broadcaster of the Year Broadcast Press Guild 2007; *Theatre* Nottingham Rep 1980–81, New Shakespeare Co (Open Air Theatre Regents Park) 1981, with The Comedy Store Players 1987–93; plays incl: The Pocket Dream (co-writer with Elly Brewer, Nottingham Playhouse then Albery Theatre) 1991–92, Big Night Out At The Little Sands Picture Palace (writer, Nottingham Playhouse) 1993, Big Night Out At The Little Palace Theatre (co-writer, Palace Theatre Watford) 2002; *Television* incl: Number 73 (co-writer) 1982–87, Toksvig (co-writer), Whose Line Is It Anyway?, Behind The Headlines, The Big One (co-writer), Sindy Hits Thirty, The Talking Show, Call My Bluff, Island Race (co-writer), Great Journeys; *Radio* reg contrib to Loose Ends (BBC Radio 4), Pick of the Week (BBC Radio 4) 1993, presenter Sound Company (BBC Radio 4) 1995, host Darling You Were Marvellous (BBC Radio 4) 1996, presenter Excess Baggage (BBC Radio 4) 2002–, presenter The Sandi Toksvig Show (LBC) 2003, chair The News Quiz (Radio 4) 2006–, reg on I'm Sorry I Haven't A Clue; also co-writer: Kin of the Castle, Cat's Whiskers; *Film* Paris By Night, Sweet Nothings; *Books* Island Race: Improbable Voyage Round the Coast of Britain (with John McCarthy, 1996), Supersaver Mouse (1998), Suspersaver Mouse to the Rescue (1999), Unusual Boy (1996), Whistling for the Elephants (1999), The Troublesome Tooth Fairy (2000), Flying Under Bridges (2001), The Gladys Society (2002), The Travels of Lady Bulldog Burton (2002), Hitler's Canary (2005), Melted into Air; *Recreations* skiing, arboreal activities; *Clubs* 2 Brydges Place, Univ Women's; *Style*— Ms Sandi Toksvig; ✉ c/o PFD, Drury House, 34–43 Russell Street, London WC2B 5HA (tel 020 7344 1000, fax 020 7379 6790)

TOLAND, Prof John Francis; s of Joseph Toland (d 1986), and Catherine, *née* McGarvey (d 2001); *b* 28 April 1949; *Educ* St Columb's Coll Derry, Queen's Univ Belfast (BSc), Univ of Sussex (MSc, DPhil); *m* 2 July 1977, Susan, *née* Beck; *Career* Battelle Advanced Studies Centre 1973, Fluid Mechanics Research Inst Univ of Essex 1973–79, lectr UCL 1979–82, prof Univ of Bath 1982–, dir Int Centre for Mathematical Sciences Edinburgh 2002–; memb: London Mathematical Soc (pres 2005–07), Edinburgh Mathematical Soc; Berwick Prize London Mathematical Soc 2000; hon prof of mathematics: Univ of Edinburgh, Heriot-Watt Univ; Hon DSc: Queen's Univ Belfast 2000, Univ of Edinburgh 2007, Heriot-Watt Univ 2007; FRS 1999, FInstP 2000, FRSE 2003; *Books* Analytic Theory of Global Bifircation (with B Buffoni, 2003); *Recreations* dogs, horses; *Style*— Prof John Toland; ✉ 15 Lansdown Park, Bath BA1 5TG (tel 01225 330996); Department of Mathematical Sciences, University of Bath, Bath BA2 7AY (tel 01225 386188, fax 01225 323436, e-mail jft@maths.bath.ac.uk)

TOLKIEN, Tracy; da of Mark Steinberg and Anne, *née* Taraski; *b* 26 January 1962; *Educ* Clayton HS St Louis Missouri, Smith Coll Mass, Courtauld Inst; *m* Simon Mario Reuel Tolkien; 1 s (Nicholas b 20 Aug 1990), 1 da (Anna b 24 Feb 2002); *Career* co-founded Steinberg and Tolkien with Mark Steinberg in 1992, since then has become one of the largest and most famous vintage fashion shops in the world specialising in couture and antique originals incl Schiaparellia and Balenciaga; voted one of London's top 20 fashion shops The Evening Standard 1997, voted one of Vogue's top five fashion shops worldwide 1998; *Books* A Collector's Guide to Costume Jewellery (1998), Vintage: The Art of Dressing Up (2000), Handbags (2001), Costume Jewellery (2001); *Recreations* writing poetry, reading, talking to my son Nicholas, digging through auctions, antique shops, flea markets and junk heaps, listening to Bob Dylan, walking on beaches, champagne, thought, Simon; *Clubs* Bluebird; *Style*— Mrs Tracy Tolkien; ✉ 193 Kings Road, Chelsea, London SW3 5EB (tel 020 7376 3660, fax 020 7376 3630)

TOLLEMACHE, Sir Lyonel Humphry John; 7 Bt (GB 1793), JP (Leics), DL (Leics); s of Maj-Gen Sir Humphry Thomas Tollemache 6 Bt, CB, CBE, DL (d 1990), and Nora Priscilla, *née* Taylor (d 1990); *b* 10 July 1931; *Educ* Uppingham, RAC Cirencester; *m* 6 Feb 1960, Mary Joscelyne, da of Col William Henry Whitbread, TD; 2 da (Katheryne Mary b 1960, Henrietta Joscelyne (Mrs David Chubb) b 1970), 2 s (Lyonel Thomas b 23 Jan 1963 d 1996, Richard John b 4 May 1966); *Heir* s, Richard Tollemache, JP; *Career* cmmnd Coldstream Gds, Maj; High Sheriff Leics 1978–79, cncllr Melton RDC/BC 1969–87 (Mayor 1976–77), cncllr Leics CC 1985–97; Liveryman Worshipful Co of Grocers; FRICS; *Style*— Sir Lyonel Tollemache, Bt, JP, DL; ✉ Buckminster Park, Grantham, Lincolnshire NG33 5RU (tel 01476 860349)

TOLLEMACHE, Hon Michael David Douglas; s of 4 Baron Tollemache (d 1975); *b* 23 August 1944; *Educ* Eton, Trinity Coll Cambridge (MA); *m* 1, 5 Feb 1969 (m dis 2000), Thérèsa, da of Peter Bowring; 2 s (twins), 1 da; m 2, 15 Feb 2002, Clare, da of David Lawman; *Career* dir: Michael Tollemache Ltd 1967–2000, Artemis SA 1985–93, Partridge Fine Arts plc 1997–2000, Nevill Keating Tollemache Ltd 2002–07; chm Soc of London Art Dealers 1995–98, vice-pres Confédération Internationale des Négociants en Oeuvres d'Art 2000–; *Clubs* White's; *Style*— The Hon Michael Tollemache; ✉ Michael Tollemache Fine Art, 43 Duke Street, St James's, London SW1Y 6DD (tel 020 7930 9883)

TOLLEMACHE, 5 Baron (UK 1876); Timothy John Edward Tollemache; JP (2003); s of 4 Baron Tollemache, MC, DL (d 1975); *b* 13 December 1939; *Educ* Eton; *m* 1970, Alexandra Dorothy Jean, da of Col Hugo Meynell, MC, JP, DL (d 1960); 1 da (Hon Selina b 1973), 2 s (Hon Edward b 1976, Hon James b 1980); *Heir* s, Hon Edward Tollemache; *Career* cmmnd Coldstream Gds 1959–62; dir Fortis (UK) Ltd 1980–, and other companies; farmer and landowner; pres: Suffolk Assoc of Local Cncls 1978–96, Friends of Ipswich Museums 1980–96, Suffolk Family History Soc 1988–2003, Suffolk Agric Assoc 1988, Ipswich and District CAB 1998–2003, Suffolk Scout Cncl 2003–, St John Cncl for Suffolk 2003–, Music for Country Churches (Suffolk) 2003–, Army Benevolent Fund (Suffolk) 2003–, Royal Life Saving Soc (Suffolk) 2003–, Friends of Suffolk Record Office 2003–, Britain-Australia Society (Suffolk) 2003–; chm: HHA (E Anglia) 1979–83, Cncl St John (Suffolk) 1982–89, St Edmundsbury Cathedral Appeal 1986–90, Suffolk Branch CLA 1990–93, Suffolk Historic Churches Tst 1996–2003; vice-pres: Cheshire BRCS 1980–, Suffolk Preservation Soc; patron: Suffolk Accident Rescue Services 1983–, Suffolk Preservation Soc 2003–, NSPCC (Suffolk) 2003–, BRCS (Suffolk) 2003–, Disability Care Enterprise 2003–, Debenham Bowls Club 2003–, Suffolk Historic Churches Tst 2003–, Gainsborough's House Museum 2003–, Magistrates Assoc (Suffolk) 2003–, Friends of St Edmundsbury Cathedral 2003–, Suffolk Wildlife Tst 2003–, Suffolk Acre 2003–, Help the Aged (Suffolk) 2003–, SSAFA - Forces Help (Suffolk) 2003– (pres 1996–2003), East Anglia Children's Hospice 2005–, St Nicholas Hospice Bury St Edmunds 2006–, Friends of Royal Hosp Sch 2006–; HM Lord-Lt Suffolk 2003– (DL 1984, Vice Lord-Lt 1994–2003); KStJ 2004 (CStJ 1988); *Recreations* shooting, fishing; *Clubs* White's, Pratt's; *Style*— The Lord Tollemache, JP; ✉ Helmingham Hall, Stowmarket, Suffolk IP14 6EF

TOLLEY, Prof Arnold Trevor; s of Arthur William Tolley (d 1970), and Dorothy Letty Tolley, *née* Freeman (d 1987); *b* 15 May 1927, Birmingham; *Educ* King Edward's Sch Birmingham, The Queen's Coll Oxford (BA); *m* 2 June 1974, Dr Glenda Mary Patrick; *Career* admin asst and admin offr NCB 1951–55; lectr in English Univ of Turku Finland 1955–61, lectr then sr lectr in English Monash Univ Victoria Aust 1961–65; Carleton Univ Ottawa Canada: asst prof of English 1965–67, assoc prof of English 1967–72, dean Faculty of Arts 1969–74, prof of English 1972–96 (now emeritus), Marston Lafrance fell 1978, chm Comparative Lit 1984–90; chm Bd of Tstees SAW Gall Ottawa 1977–80 (fndr memb 1973–80); New Democratic Pty (NDP): pres Prov Riding Assoc Stormont/Dundas (formerly Stormont, Dundas and Glengarry) 1977–2002, memb Small Business Ctee Ontario 1990–96, memb Prov Exec Ontario 1991–96, chm Municipal Ctee Ontario 1991–96; cncllr Williamsburg Township Cncl 1988–94, pres Dundas County Assoc for the Mentally Retarded 1990–93, pres Williamsburg Non-Profit Housing Corp 1992–; pres Montreal Vintage Music Soc 1984–; FRSL 1998; *Publications* as author: The Early Published Poems of Stephen Spender: A Chronology (1967), The Poetry of the Thirties (1975), The Poetry of the Forties (1985), My Proper Ground: A Study of the Work of Philip Larkin and its Development (1991), Larkin at Work (1997); as ed: John Lehmann: A Tribute (1987), Roy Fuller: A Tribute (1993), The Literary Essays, by John Heath-Stubbs (1998), Early Poems and Juvenilia, by Philip Larkin (2005), British Literary Periodicals of World War II and Aftermath: A Critical Hsitory (2007); guest ed several issues Aquarius 1985–2003; contrib to various reference works; *Recreations* collecting jazz records, collecting antique oriental rugs, cooking; *Style*— Prof A T Tolley; ✉ Seven Willows, 13075 County Road 18, Williamsburg, Ontario K0C 2H0, Canada (tel 00 1 613 535 2011, e-mail tolleysevenwillows@w3connex.ca)

TOLLEY, David Anthony; s of Frank Stanley Tolley, of Sale, Cheshire, and Elizabeth, *née* Dean; *b* 29 November 1947; *Educ* Manchester Grammar, King's Coll Hosp Med Sch (MB BS); *m* 4 July 1970, Judith Anne, da of Wing Cdr Dennis Martin Finn, DFC (d 1983), of Salisbury, Wilts; 3 s (Nicholas, Christopher, Jeremy), 1 da (Felicity Jane); *Career* conslt urological surgeon: Royal Infirmary Edinburgh 1980–91, Western Gen Hosp 1991–; dir the Scottish Lithotriptor Centre Western Gen Hosp Edinburgh 1991–; prog dir East of Scotland Trg Prog in Urology 1996–2001; memb: Urological Cancer Working Pty MRC 1983–94, Editorial Bd Br Jl of Urology 1994–99, Jt Ctee on Higher Surgical Trg in Urology 1995–2001, Editorial Ctee Jl of Endourology, Cncl RCSEd 2000–, Jt Intercollegiate Examination Bd Urology 2000– (examiner 1995–2000), Bd European Soc for Urotechnology, Bd Minimal Access Therapy Trg Unit Scotland, various ctees Br Assoc of Urological Surgns (also memb Cncl), various ctees Royal Coll of Surgns Edinburgh, Cncl RCS Edinburgh, Cncl Br Assoc Urological Surgns (BAUS); pres: Br Soc of Endourology 1995–98, European Intrarenal Surgery Soc 2003–04; chm: Specialty Advsy Bd in Urology RCS(Ed) 1997–2002, Section of Endourology BAUS, Urology Specialist Trg Ctee East of Scotland; chm Quincentenary Executive RCSEd; ed BAUS Today 2000–01; FRCS 1974, FRCSEd 1983; *Recreations* golf, countryside, music; *Clubs* New (Edinburgh), Luffness New Golf; *Style*— David Tolley, Esq; ✉ Murrayfield Hospital, Corstorphine Road, Edinburgh (tel 0131 334 0363)

TOLMAN, Jeffery Alexander Spencer; s of Gerald James Spencer, of Cornwall, and Doris Rosaline, *née* Lane (d 1966); *b* 12 July 1950; *Educ* St Clement Danes GS, Univ of Wales Sch of Int Politics; *Career* product mangr Birds Eye Foods (Unilever) 1971–73, account exec Ogilvy & Mather 1973–74; McCann Erickson 1974–79: account supervisor, account dir, assoc dir then dir; fndr ptnr Grandfield Rork Collins 1979–85; Saatchi & Saatchi Advertising: gp account dir 1985–86, dep chm 1987–91, chief exec (strategy) 1987–91, non-exec dep chm 1991–93; Tolman Cunard Ltd: chm (strategy and corp communication specialists) 1992–2004, advsr and thought leader on contemporary strategy, sustainability and stakeholder engagement 2004–; non-exec dep chm Forward Publishing 1991–97, non-exec dir RAC Holdings Ltd 1995–99; memb Euro Advsy Bd Masai SA 2000–02; alumnus British-American Project; Liveryman Worshipful Co of Coachmakers and Coach Harness Makers; *Recreations* walking, eating, drinking, politics; *Clubs* RAC; *Style*— Jeffery Tolman, Esq; ✉ e-mail jt@tolman-cunard.co.uk

TOLSTOY-MILOSLAVSKY, Count Nikolai Dmitrievich; s of (Count) Dimitry Tolstoy, QC (d 1997), and his 1 w, Frieda Mary, *née* Wicksteed; *b* 23 June 1935; *Educ* Wellington, Trinity Coll Dublin (MA); *m* 1971, Georgina Katherine, da of Maj Peter Brown, of Southmoor, Berks; 3 da (Alexandra b 1973, Anastasia b 1975, Xenia b 1980), 1 s (Dmitri b 1978); *Heir* s, (Count) Dmitri Tolstoy-Miloslavsky; *Career* author, historian, biographer; has appeared on numerous TV and radio progs and delivered lectures at univs and int academic confs worldwide; Int Freedom Award US Industrial Cncl Educnl Fndn 1987; appointed Capt in the Cossack Army 1993; chllr Monarchist League, hon memb Russian Heraldry Soc; life memb: Royal Stuart Soc, Royal Martyr Church Union, Forty-Five Assoc; memb: Cncl for Christians and Jews, Irish Texts Soc, Roman Soc, Int Arthurian Soc; FRSL; *Books* The Founding of Evil Hold School (1968), Night of The Long Knives (1972), Victims of Yalta (1978), The Half-Mad Lord (biography of Thomas Pitt, 1978), Stalin's Secret War (1981), The Tolstoys - Twenty-Four Generations of Russian History (1983), The Quest for Merlin (1985), The Minister and the Massacres (1986), States, Countries, Provinces (1986), The Coming of the King - The First Book of Merlin (1988); author of numerous articles and reviews on Celtic studies in learned jls; *Recreations* second-hand and academic bookshops, walking, tennis, drinking in inns; *Style*— Count Tolstoy-Miloslavsky; ✉ Court Close, Southmoor, Abingdon, Oxfordshire OX13 5HS (tel 01865 820186)

TOLVAS-VINCENT, Christina Elisabeth; da of Ilpo Tolvas, of Turku, Finland, and Riitta, *née* Haahdenniemi; *b* 7 September 1964, Turku, Finland; *Educ* Katedralskolan i Åbo Finland, Univ of Turku (LLM); *m* 10 Aug 1991, Dr Jonathan David Vincent; *Career* memb Finnish Bar 1994, admitted slr Eng and Wales 1995; reporter Radio Åboland Finnish Broadcasting Co 1988–90, lectr and acting grad asst in business law Univ of Tampere 1988–90; Hepherd Winstanley & Pugh: paralegal 1991–95, slr then sr slr 1995–97, ptnr 1997; ptnr Bond Pearce (following merger) 1998– (currently local head of employment team); author of numerous articles on employment law issues; memb: Law Soc, European Employment Lawyers' Assoc, Employment Lawyers Assoc, Finnish Bar Assoc, Finnish Lawyers' Assoc; *Recreations* classical music (formerly harpsichordist, pianist, clarinetist and singer, now mainly listener), travel; *Style*— Mrs Christina Tolvas-Vincent; ✉ Bond Pearce LLP, Oceana House, 39–49 Commercial Road, Southampton SO15 1GA (tel 0845 415 0000, fax 0845 415 8200, e-mail christina.tolvas-vincent@bondpearce.com)

TOM, Peter William Gregory; CBE (2006); s of John Gregory Tom (decd), of Bardon Hill, Leicester, and Barbara, *née* Lambden; *b* 26 July 1940; *Educ* Hinckley GS; *m* 1; 1 s (John b 1966 (decd)), 2 da (Saffron b 1972, Layla b 1975); m 2, April 2002, Kay, *née* Shires; 1 s (Joseph b 2004); *Career* joined Bardon Hill Quarries Ltd 1956, chief exec Bardon Gp plc until 1997, non-exec chm Aggregate Industries Ltd 2006– (chief exec 1997–2005); non-exec dir AGA Foodservice Gp plc 2004–; chm Leicester Football Club plc (Leicester Tigers rugby club), dir England Rugby Ltd; Hon DTech De Montfort Univ; CIMgt; *Recreations* tennis, theatre, cycling; *Style*— Peter W G Tom, Esq, CBE; ✉ Aggregate

Industries Limited, Bardon Hall, Copt Oak Road, Markfield, Leicestershire LE67 9PJ (tel 01530 816600)

TOMALIN, Claire; da of Emile Delavenay (d 2003), and Muriel Emily, *née* Herbert (d 1984); *b* 20 June 1933; *Educ* Lycée Français de Londres, Girls GS Hitchin, Dartington Hall Sch, Newnham Coll Cambridge (MA); *m* 1, 17 Sept 1955, Nicholas Osborne Tomalin (d 1973), s of Miles Ridley Tomalin (d 1983); 3 da (Josephine Sarah b 1956, Susanna Lucy b 1958 d 1980, Emily Claire Elizabeth b 1961), 2 s (Daniel b and d 1960, Thomas Nicholas Ronald b 1970); m 2, 5 June 1993, Michael Frayn, *qv*; *Career* writer; publishers ed, reader, journalist 1953–67; literary ed: New Statesman 1974–78 (dep literary ed 1968–70), Sunday Times 1980–86; vice-pres English PEN and Soc of Authors 1999, vice-pres Royal Literary Fund 2000– (tstee 1975–99, registrar 1984–2000); memb: Mgmnt Ctee Soc of Authors 1996–99 (memb London Library Ctee 1997–2000), Advsy Ctee for the Arts, Humanities and Social Sciences British Library 1997–2002, Cncl Royal Soc of Literature 1997–2000; tstee Nat Portrait Gallery 1992–2002; fell Wordsworth Tst 2003– (tstee 2001–03); Samuel Pepys Award 2003, Rose Mary Crawshay Prize 2003; hon fell: Lucy Cavendish Coll Cambridge 2003, Newnham Coll Cambridge 2003; Hon LittD: UEA 2005, Univ of Birmingham 2005, Univ of Greenwich 2006, Univ of Cambridge 2007; FRSL 1974; *Books* Life and Death of Mary Wollstonecraft (1974, reissued 1993), Shelley and His World (1980), Katherine Mansfield: A Secret Life (1987), The Invisible Woman: The Story of Nelly Ternan and Charles Dickens (1990), Mrs Jordan's Profession (1994), Jane Austen: A Life (1997), Maurice (ed, 1998), Several Strangers (1999), Samuel Pepys: The Unequalled Self (2002, Whitbread Book of the Year 2002), Thomas Hardy: The Time-torn Man (2006), Selected Poems of Thomas Hardy (ed, 2006), Selected Poems of Milton (ed, 2008); *Plays* The Winter Wife (1991); *Style*— Mrs Claire Tomalin, FRSL

TOMALSKI, Bob; s of Felix Stanislaus Tomalski (d 1964), and Gladys Nora, *née* Russell (d 1988); *b* 7 February 1953; *Educ* Holy Family Sch Morden, Carshalton Tech Coll, Merton Tech Coll; *Career* shop asst Davis Photographic New Malden 1971–78, tech sales mangr Unilet HiFi New Malden 1978–87, tech ed CD Review and ed Making Better Movies 1987–90, gp tech ed WV Publications (publishers of What Video magazine and others) 1990–; freelance broadcaster on technology and science incl BBC Radio 5 (Five Aside, Formula Five, AM Alternative, The Big Byte), BBC Radio 4 (The Parts, You and Yours), London News Radio phone-ins, Talk UK, BBC TV (Homewise, People Today, Breakfast News, 9 O'Clock News), ITV (Video View, Amazing Science), Channel Four (The Big Breakfast) Sky News; regular writer for: What Video, What Satellite, What Camcorder, Camcorder User, What Cellphone, Home Cinema Choice, World Radio and TV Handbook, Theatre Living Tokyo; memb Moving Image Soc; *Recreations* amateur radio (call sign G6CQF), internet, videography, computing, reading, homebrew real ale; *Style*— Bob Tomalski, MBKS; ✉ WV Publications, 57–59 Rochester Place, London NW1 9JU (tel 020 7331 1000, e-mail bob@medianet.demon.co.uk)

TOMBS, Baron (Life Peer UK 1990), of Brailes in the County of Warwickshire; Sir Francis Leonard Tombs; kt (1978); s of Joseph Tombs; *b* 17 May 1924; *Educ* Elmore Green Sch Walsall, Birmingham Coll of Technol, Univ of London (BSc); *m* 1949, Marjorie Evans; 3 da (Hon Catherine Barbara b 22 April 1950, Hon Elisabeth Jane b 18 Dec 1952, Hon Margaret Clare b 25 Nov 1958); *Career* trained with: GEC Ltd Birmingham 1939–45, Birmingham Corp Electricity Supply Dept 1946–47, Br Electricity Authy 1948–57; gen mangr GEC Ltd Kent 1958–67, dir and gen mangr James Howden & Co Glasgow 1967–68; South of Scotland Electricity Bd: dir of engrg 1969–73, dep chm 1973–74, chm 1974–77; chm: Electricity Cncl for England and Wales 1977–80, Weir Group plc 1981–83, Turner & Newall plc 1982–89, Rolls-Royce plc 1985–92, The Engineering Cncl 1985–88, The Advsy Cncl on Sci and Technol 1987–90, Molecule Theatre Co 1985–92; dir: N M Rothschild & Sons Ltd 1981–94, Rolls-Royce Ltd 1982–92, Turner & Newall International Ltd 1982–89, Turner & Newall Welfare Trust Ltd 1982–89, Shell-UK Ltd 1983–94; pro-chllr and chm Cncl Cranfield Inst of Technol 1985–91, chllr Univ of Strathclyde 1991–97; vice-pres Engrs for Disaster Relief 1985–93; Freeman City of London, Liveryman and Prime Warden Worshipful Co of Goldsmiths 1994–95; Hon DUniv and Hon LLD Univ of Strathclyde; Hon DSc: Aston Univ, Łódź Univ (Poland), Cranfield Inst of Technol, City Univ London, Univ of Bradford, Queen's Univ Belfast, Univ of Surrey, Univ of Nottingham, Univ of Cambridge, Univ of Warwick; Hon DTech Loughborough Univ of Technol, Hon DEd CNAA; FREng 1977 (past vice-pres), Hon FIEE (past pres), Hon FIMechE, Hon FICE, Hon FIChemE, Hon FRSE 1996, Hon FCGI; hon memb Br Nuclear Energy Soc; *Style*— The Rt Hon the Lord Tombs, FREng; ✉ Honington Lodge, Honington, Shipston-upon-Stour, Warwickshire CV36 5AA

TOMBS, Sebastian; s of David Martineau Tombs (d 1986), and Jane Burns, *née* Parley (d 2000); *b* 11 October 1949; *Educ* Bryanston, Corpus Christi Coll Cambridge (choral exhibitioner, DipArch); *m* Eva, da of Leo Heirman (d 1983); 2 s (Michael b 1985, Leonardo b 1988), 1 da (Rowena b 1987); *Career* on staff in architectural/planning office N Philadelphia USA 1972–73 (yr practical trg from CCC Cambridge), RMJM Partnership Edinburgh 1975–76, Roland Wedgwood Associates Edinburgh 1976–77, Fountainbridge Housing Assoc 1977–78, area architect Housing Corp 1978–81, private sector work Housing Dept Edinburgh DC 1981–86, sec and treas RIAS 1995– (dep sec and dir of practice 1986–94), chief exec Architecture and Design Scotland 2005–; chm: Edinburgh Gp Anthroposophical Soc 1986–89, Scottish Ecological Design Assoc (co-fndr) 1994–97, Assoc of Planning Suprs (co-fndr) 1995–97; memb City of Edinburgh's Lord Provost's Cmmn on Sustainable Devpt 1997–98; Parly candidate (Scot Lib Dem) Edinburgh N and Leith: Scot 1999 and 2003, UK 2001; ARCUK 1977, FRIAS 1990 (ARIAS 1978), MCIArb 2002 (ACIArb 1991); *Publications* Tracing the Past, Chasing the Future (2000); *Recreations* sketching, reverse cycling, composing songs and doggerel; *Style*— Sebastian Tombs, Esq; ✉ Architecture and Design Scotland, Bakehouse Close, 146 Canongate, Edinburgh EH8 8DD (tel 0131 556 6699, fax 0131 556 6633, e-mail sebastian.tombs@ads.org.uk)

TOMISON, Maureen; da of Andrew Learmonth Tomison (d 1954), and Maureen, *née* Miskimmin; *b* 31 May 1941; *Educ* Univ of St Andrews, London Guildhall Univ (MA), Eng Gardening Sch (Dip); *m* 1, 1970 (m dis 1983), Maurice Trowbridge (decd); 1 s (Andrew b 30 Sept 1971); m 2, 1994, Lt Cdr David Sandford, RN; *Career* with Bristol Evening Post 1963–65, with The Sun 1965–68 (first female political corr for a nat newspaper), with Daily Sketch 1968–71; political advsr State of the Nation Granada TV; Parly candidate (Cons): Dundee W Feb 1974, Norwich S Oct 1974; advsr Cons front bench Yes to Europe Vote 1975; currently prospective Parly candidate (Lab) Folkestone & Hythe; ceo and fndr Politics Europe, ceo and fndr Decision Makers (int political and PR consultancy), ceo EMU Consltts; corp communications dir IOD, public affrs dir Hill and Knowlton 1982–84, corporate communications dir Sea Containers 1984–87, sec-gen EFPA 1988–95 (pan European mfrg gp); chair UK Women of Europe 1999–, memb Cncl Br in Europe, life memb European Movement, fell Br Assoc of Women Entrepreneurs, MIPR; FCMI; *Awards* honoured by Women of Scot 1988 and 1992, European Business Woman of Achievement 1991, Best Political Campaign PR Week 1991 (runner-up 1992), nomination UK Women of Europe 1991 and 1992; *Books* English Sickness (1971), Thatcherism: A Fundamental Departure (1983); *Recreations* skiing, gardening, music, water sports, singing Gaelic songs, history, fencing, bridge; *Clubs* Ski Club of GB, Cwlth Soc; *Style*— Ms Maureen Tomison; ✉ Elinlegh Court, Stone Street, Stelling Minnis, Kent CT4 6DF; Politics Europe (e-mail mtomison@politicseurope.com)

TOMKINS, Prof Cyril Robert; s of Charles Albert Tomkins (d 1955), of Southampton, and Gladys Rose Silvester (d 1993); *b* 27 May 1939; *Educ* Price's Sch, Univ of Bristol (BA), LSE (MSc); *m* 10 Aug 1963, Dorothy, da of Sydney Parker (d 1988), of Portsmouth; 2 s (Neil b 1967, Stephen b 1969); *Career* accountant for four years, lectr Univ of Hull 1969–70, sr res offr and lectr UCNW 1970–73, sr lectr Univ of Strathclyde 1973–75, emeritus prof Univ of Bath 2001– (prof of accounting and finance 1975–2001, pro-vice-chllr 1993–96); funded research projects incl work on local govt financial control, comparison of investment decision making in UK and German cos, developing financial mgmnt in central govt and fin control in the construction industry; memb Editorial Bd: Auditing and Accountability, Financial Management and Accountability; chm Br Accounting Assoc 1989; elected to Br Accounting Assoc Hall of Fame 2004; CIPFA 1967, FCCA; *Publications* books incl: Financial Planning in Divisionalised Companies (1974), Achieving Economy Efficiency and Effectiveness in the Public Sector (1987), Corporate Resources Allocation - Strategy and Finance (1991), Strategic Investment Decisions: a comparison of UK and German investments in the motor components industry (1994), Governance Processes for Public Services (1998), Cost Management and its Interplay with Business Strategy and Context (1999); numerous journal articles, govt reports and other papers incl: The Everyday Accountant and Researching his Reality (1983), Making Sense of Cost-Plus Transfer Prices (1990), Can Target Costing and Whole Life Costing be Applied in the Construction Industry? (2000), Interdependencies, Trust and Information in Relationships, Alliances and Networks (2001), Cost Management and Accounting Methods to Support Clean Aerospace (2003); various reviews; *Recreations* travel, golf, gardening, reading, rugby, walking; *Style*— Prof Cyril Tomkins; ✉ e-mail cyril.tomkins@3disp.co.uk

TOMKINS, Patrick (Paddy); *b* 20 August 1960; *Educ* Hastings GS, KCL (Bramshill scholar, BA), RCDS; *m* Susan; 1 da, 1 s; *Career* joined Sussex Police 1979; Met Police: Chief Supt 1993, Cdr 1997, seconded as Dep Asst Cmmr to HM Inspectorate of Constabulary 1999–2002; Chief Constable Lothian and Borders Police 2002–; *Recreations* history, cycling, reading, fishing; *Clubs* New (Edinburgh); *Style*— Paddy Tomkins, Esq; ✉ Lothian and Borders Police Headquarters, Fettes Avenue, Edinburgh EH4 1RB (tel 0131 311 3086, e-mail chief.constable@lbp.pnn.police.uk)

TOMKINS, Prof Peter Maurice; s of Rowland Maurice Tomkins, of Leeds, W Yorks, and Gwendoline Mary, *née* Dunkley; *b* 29 November 1941; *Educ* Leeds Modern Sch, Univ of Bradford (BTech), Univ of Leeds (PhD); *m* 14 May 1988, Rosemary Anne, da of John Gale Harrison, of Stockport, Cheshire; 1 da (Amber Lauren b 17 Oct 1990), 1 s (Sebastian Rowan Matt b 19 August 2004); *Career* R&D scientist Albright & Wilson plc 1963–64, univ demonstrator then fell Univ of Leeds 1964–67, dept mangr (mfrg, R&D devpt, brands) Mars Confectionery Ltd 1967–69, mangr then princ consllt Arthur Young & Co 1969–71, vice-pres and gen mangr Encyclopaedia Britannica International Ltd 1971–73, chief exec and dir D M Management Consultants Ltd (strategic relationship mktg consultancy) 1973–; memb Advsy Bd Cass Business Sch 2004–; author of mgmnt and mktg articles in various jls; memb Lloyd's 1978–; memb: Bd BDMA 1979–91, Cncl Inst of Mgmnt Consltts 1986–98 (pres 1995–96); tstee Int Cncl of Mgmnt Consulting Insts (ICMCI) 1995–2000; vice-chm Bd of Tstees Chartered Inst of Mktg 2001–; pres European Mktg Confedn 2003–; chm Community Industry Bd (Nat Assoc of Youth Clubs) 1975–78, vice-pres UK Youth 1982– (former dep chm), fndr tstee CAF Cert 1984–93, tstee Bd Volunteer Centre UK 1992–96, chm and tstee National Confederation of Parent Teacher Assocs 1997–2005; chm Schoolympics Ltd 2006–; memb SW Thames RHA 1986–90, non-exec dir Bath Royal United Hosp NHS Tst 2006–; Freeman City of London; Liveryman Worshipful Co of Marketors 1996–; memb RSC 1968, CChem 1970, CCMI (FIMgt 1972), FInstD 1980, FIMC 1982, memb DMA 1992 (fndr memb), FCIM 1992, FIDM 1994, chartered marketer 1998, CSci 2004; *Recreations* squash, skiing, jogging, charity work; *Clubs* IOD; *Style*— Prof Peter Tomkins; ✉ D M Management Consultants Ltd, 19 Clarges Street, London W1Y 7PG (tel 020 7499 8030, mobile 07802 484789, e-mail pmt@dmmc.co.uk)

TOMKINSON, Robert Charles; s of William Robert Tomkinson (d 1980), and Helen Mary Tomkinson, MBE, *née* Blane (d 2000); *b* 14 July 1941; *Educ* Marlborough, Univ of Oxford (MA); *m* 15 June 1968, Joanna Sally, da of Maj William Philip Stuart Hastings (d 2003); 2 s (James Robert b 1970, Simon William b 1972); *Career* mangr Peat Marwick Mitchell & Co 1966–75, dep md Scrimgeour Hardcastle & Co Ltd 1975–79, fin dir Intercontinental Fuels Ltd 1979–81; gp fin dir: Automotive Products plc 1982–86, Electrocomponents plc 1986–97; chm: Hutchinson Smith Ltd 1997–99, Pittards plc 1997–2004, Univ of Buckingham 1998–2005, KIG Ltd 2000–06; non-exec jt dep chm Jardine Lloyd Thompson Gp plc 1987–2001; non-exec dir: The Unipart Gp of Cos, Barloworld plc, Barloworld Ltd SA; FCA 1966, FCT 1985; *Recreations* salmon fishing, riding, skiing; *Clubs* Boodle's; *Style*— Robert Tomkinson, Esq; ✉ Home Farm, Wappenham, Towcester, Northamptonshire NN12 8SJ (tel 01327 860939, fax 01327 860839, e-mail robert.tomkinson@easynet.co.uk)

TOMKYS, Sir (William) Roger; KCMG (1991, CMG 1984), DL (Cambs 1996); s of William Arthur Tomkys (d 1973), of Harden, W Yorks, and Edith Tomkys (d 1984); *b* 15 March 1937; *Educ* Bradford GS, Balliol Coll Oxford (MA); *m* 1963, Margaret Jean, da of Norman Beilby Abbey (d 1964), of Barrow-in-Furness; 1 s, 1 da; *Career* HM Foreign Serv 1960–92; seconded to Cabinet Office 1975, head Near East and N Africa Dept FCO 1977–80, head of Chancery and cnsllr Rome 1980–81, ambass and consul-gen to Bahrain 1981–84, ambass to Syria 1984–86, princ fin offr FCO 1986–89, dep under sec of state 1989–90, high cmmr to Kenya 1990–92; also served: Athens, Benghazi, Amman; studied MECAS; master Pembroke Coll Cambridge 1992–2004, chm Arab-British C of C 2004–; Commendatore Dell'Ordine Al Merito Italy 1980, Order of Bahrain (first class) 1984; *Style*— Sir Roger Tomkys, KCMG, DL; ✉ Croydon House Farm, Croydon, Royston, Hertfordshire SG8 0EF

TOMLINS, Christopher David Corbett; s of Maj David Corbett Tomlins (d 2001), of Bosham, West Sussex, and Pamela Gertrude, *née* Steele; *b* 15 August 1940; *Educ* Bradfield, Guy's Hosp Med and Dental Sch BDS, MB BS (London), LRCP, MRCS, FDSRCS; *m* 28 Oct 1972, Gillian Joan, da of Spencer Charles Cawthorn (d 1974); 4 s (David b 1974, Julian b 1976, Roger b 1976 (twin), Michael b 1979); *Career* dental house surgn Edgware Gen Hosp and Guy's Hosp 1964, orthopaedic house surgn Guy's Hosp 1970, house physician St Luke's Hosp Guildford 1970; registrar: Eastman Dental Hosp 1971–72, Westminster and Queen Mary's Roehampton 1972–73; sr registrar Westminster, Queen Mary's and UCH 1973–76, visiting registrar Univ of Witswatersrand Johannesburg 1976, consllt oral and maxillofacial surgn Royal Berks Hosp Reading 1976–2007, locum consllt until 2007, ret; hon treas BMA 1988 (chm 1984, vice-chm W Berks dist 1986), chm Reading Section BDA 1986, chm Oxford Regnl Ctee Hosp Dental Servs 1991–96; memb: Central Ctee Hosp Dental Servs 1991–96, Central Manpower Ctee (Dental) 1991–96; regnl advsr in oral surgery 1996–2003; memb Reading Pathological Soc (pres 2003–04); fell BAOMS 1976; *Recreations* sailing, skiing, walking, photography; *Style*— Christopher Tomlins, Esq; ✉ Hazeldene, Wolverton Common, Tadley, Hampshire RG26 5RY (tel 01635 298719, e-mail tomlins@rg265ry.fsnet.co.uk); 13 Bath Road, Reading, Berkshire RG1 6HH (tel 0118 955 3461)

TOMLINSON, Prof (Alfred) Charles; CBE (2001); s of Alfred Tomlinson, DCM (d 1973), of Stoke-on-Trent, and May, *née* Lucas (d 1972); *b* 8 January 1927; *Educ* Longton HS, Queens' Coll Cambridge (BA, MA), Univ of London (MA); *m* 23 Oct 1948, Brenda, da of Edwin Albert Raybould (d 1977), of Stoke-on-Trent; 2 da (Justine, Juliet); *Career* visiting prof Univ of New Mexico 1962–63, O'Connor prof Colgate Univ NY 1967–68 and 1989–90, visiting fell of humanities Princeton Univ 1981, prof of Eng lit Univ of Bristol 1982–92, sr research fell 1996– (lectr 1956–68, reader 1968–82, prof emeritus 1992), Lamont prof Union Coll NY 1987; numerous public lectures and poetry readings throughout the world 1960–; graphics exhibited at Gimpel Fils and Leicester Galleries, one man shows at OUP London 1972 and Clare Coll Cambridge 1975, Arts Cncl touring exhibition The Graphics and Poetry of Charles Tomlinson opened at the Hayward Gallery London then toured England, Canada and the USA 1978; hon fell Queens' Coll Cambridge 1976; Hon DLitt: Keele Univ 1981, Colgate Univ NY 1981, Univ of New Mexico 1986, Univ of Bristol 2004; hon prof Keele Univ 1989–92, hon fell Royal Holloway and Bedford New Coll London 1991; foreign hon fell American Acad of Arts and Sciences 1998, hon fell Modern Language Assoc 2003; FRSL 1975–94; *Books* incl: Selected W C Williams (ed, 1976), Selected Octavio Paz (ed, 1979), Oxford Book of Verse in English Translation (ed, 1980), Some Americans (1981), Poetry and Metamorphosis (1983), Collected Poems (1987), The Return (1987), Annunciations (1989), Renga and Airborn (with Octavio Paz), Selected George Oppen (ed, 1990), The Door in the Wall (1992), Eros English'd, Erotic Classical Poems (ed, 1992), Selected Attilio Bertolucci (ed and trans, 1993), Jubilation (1995), Selected Poems 1955–1997 (1997), The Vineyard Above the Sea (1999), American Essays: Making it New (2001), Skywriting (2003), Metamorphoses (2003), Selected John Dryden (ed, 2004), Cracks in the Universe (2006); *Graphics* incl: Eden (1985); *Recreations* music, gardening, walking, travel; *Style*— Prof Charles Tomlinson, CBE; ✉ c/o Carcanet Press, 30 Cross Street, Manchester M2 7AQ

TOMLINSON, Claire Janet; da of Lascelles Arthur Lucas (d 1988), and Ethel Barbara, *née* Daer (d 1997); *b* 14 February 1944; *Educ* Wycombe Abbey, Millfield, Somerville Coll Oxford (MA, Polo, Fencing and Squash half blues); *m* 16 March 1968, (George) Simon Tomlinson, s of George Antony Tomlinson (d 1954); 1 da (Emma b 30 Oct 1974), 2 s (Luke b 27 Jan 1977, Mark b 25 March 1982); *Career* polo player; first woman to play against Cambridge, capt Oxford Univ team 1966, pioneered breakthrough for women to be allowed in high-goal polo 1978, memb winning team Queen's Cup 1979, capt English Team who were winners of the first worldwide Ladies' Int Polo Tournament 1991; highest rated woman polo player in the World, has achieved higher handicap than any other woman (5 goals in 1986, currently 2 goals), memb team that set up professional coaching in polo; currently HPA sr coach at both Pony Club and Int level, also active player; England team coach: World Cup 2001–07 (finalists 2004), test series Argentina 2002; fencing: memb England under-21 team 1962–63, capt Oxford ladies' team 1965–66; *Style*— Mrs Claire Tomlinson; ✉ Down Farm, Westonbirt, Tetbury, Gloucestershire GL8 8QW (tel 01666 880214)

TOMLINSON, Geoffrey Ralph (Geoff); s of Ralph Gardner Tomlinson, of Preston, Lancs, and Dorothy, *née* Porter (d 2003); *b* 14 March 1954, Preston, Lancs; *Educ* Kirkham GS, Univ of Durham (BA), Coll of Law Chester; *m* 12 Dec 1983, Mrs Christine Mary Clement, *née* Seddon; 1 s (Andrew Ralph b 3 Dec 1984), 1 step s (Daniel b 10 June 1978); *Career* slr; Napthens: trainee slr 1976–78, asst slr 1978–80, ptnr 1980–; memb: Law Soc 1978, Gideons Int; past govr Fulwood HS; past tstee: Age Concern, Saltmine Tst, Deafway; *Recreations* golf, fell walking, watching rugby and football (Preston North End); *Clubs* Preston Grasshoppers RFC (vice-pres), Preston Golf; *Style*— Geoff Tomlinson, Esq; ✉ Napthens, 7 Winckley Square, Preston PR1 3JD (tel 01772 883883, fax 01772 257805, e-mail geoff.tomlinson@napthens.co.uk)

TOMLINSON, Canon Dr Howard Charles; s of Arthur Tomlinson (d 1987), and Amy, *née* Morley (d 1999); *b* 3 April 1948; *Educ* Ashville Coll Harrogate, Bedford Coll London (BA), Univ of Reading (PhD, Julian Corbett Prize in Naval History, Royal Historical Soc Alexander Prize); *m* 1970, Dr Heather, *née* Morcumb; 2 da (Clare Victoria b 22 April 1976, Sarah Elizabeth b 27 May 1979), 2 s (Michael James b 1 Oct 1977, Edward Alexander b 26 Oct 1981 d 2006); *Career* research fell Univ of Wales 1974–76, head of history and tutor Wellington Coll 1977–87, headmaster Hereford Cathedral Sch 1987–2005; memb HMC 1987–2005, memb Choir Schs' Assoc 1987–2005 (chm 2002–04); lay canon Hereford Cathedral; life memb Nat Tst; FRHistS 1974; *Books* Guns and Government: The Ordnance Office Under the Later Stuarts (1979), Before the English Civil War (ed, 1983), Politics, Religion and Society, 1640–60 (ed, 1989), A History of Hereford Cathedral (contrib, 2000); *Recreations* cricket, choral singing, golf, history; *Clubs* MCC, Scarborough CC, Herefordshire CC; *Style*— Canon Dr Howard Tomlinson; ✉ 34 Park Street, Hereford HR1 2RD (tel 01432 341010, e-mail howardtomlinson@ukonline.co.uk)

TOMLINSON, Baron (Life Peer UK 1998), of Walsall in the County of West Midlands; John Edward Tomlinson; *Career* MP (Lab) Meriden 1974–79, PPS to PM Harold Wilson 1975–76, Parly under sec of state FCO 1976–79; MEP (Lab/Co-op) Birmingham W 1984–99; memb Parly Assembly: Cncl of Europe, WEU; House of Lords rep Convention on the Future of Europe, memb EU Select Ctee on Foreign and Secuirty Policy; memb Cncl Britain in Europe; pres of tstees Industry and Parliament Tst; pres Br Flouridation Soc; chm Assoc of Ind HE Providers, chm Advsy Bd London Sch of Commerce; *Style*— The Lord Tomlinson; ✉ House of Lords, London SW1A 0PW

TOMLINSON, Sir John Rowland; kt (2005), CBE (1997); s of Rowland Tomlinson (d 1994), and Ellen, *née* Greenwood (d 1969); *b* 22 September 1946; *Educ* Accrington GS, Univ of Manchester (BSc), Royal Manchester Coll of Music; *m* 9 Aug 1969, Moya, *née* Joel; 2 da (Abigail 27 Aug 1971, Ellen Tamasine 15 Feb 1973), 1 s (Joseph b 3 March 1976); *Career* operatic bass; princ: Glyndebourne Festival 1971–74, ENO 1974–80; also roles with: Royal Opera, Opera North, Scottish Opera; major roles incl: Boris in Boris Godunov (ENO Manchester) 1982, Don Basilio in Il Barbiere di Seville (Covent Garden) 1985, Moses in Moses (ENO) 1986, Fiesco in Simone Boccanegra (ENO) 1988, Wotan/The Wanderer in The Ring (Bayreuth) 1988–98, Wanderer in Siegfried (Bologna) 1990, Mefistofeles in Faust (Santiago, Chile) 1990, Attila in Attila (Opera North) 1990, Filippo II in Don Carlos (Opera North) 1992, Konig Marke in Tristan & Isolde (Bayreuth Festival) 1993, Mefistofeles in Damnation de Faust (La Fenice Venice) 1993, Hans Sachs in Die Meistersinger (Covent Garden) 1993 and 1997, Gurnemanz in Parsifal (Staatsoper Berlin) 1992–94, Claggart in Billy Budd (Covent Garden) 1995, Hans Sachs in Die Meistersinger (Staatsoper Berlin) 1995, Kingfisher in Midsummer Marriage (Covent Garden) 1996, Bluebeard in Bluebeard's Castle (Berlin Philharmonic) 1996, 4 Villains in Tales of Hoffman (ENO) 1998, Moses in Moses and Aron (NY Met) 1999, Golaud in Pelleas and Melisande (Glyndebourne Festival) 1999, Mefistofeles in Faust (Staatsoper Munich) 2000, Hagen in Gotterdammerung (Bayreuth Festival) 2000, Baron Ochs in Rosenkavalier (Staatsoper Dresden) 2000, Borromeo in Palestrina (Covent Garden) 2001, Gurnemanz in Parsifal (NY Met) 2001, Wotan/Wanderer in The Ring (Munich) 2003, title role in Boris Godunov (Covent Garden) 2003, title role in Flying Dutchman (Bayreuth Festival) 2003–04, Balstrode in Peter Grimes (Salzburg Festival) 2005, Wanderer in Siegfried (Covent Garden) 2005, Fiesco in Simone Boccanegra (Hamburg) 2006, Hagen in Götterdämmerung (Covent Garden) 2006; numerous appearances at international venues incl: ROH Covent Garden (debut 1976), Paris Opera, Berlin, Vienna, Amsterdam, Geneva, NY, Tokyo, Salzburg, Lisbon, Madrid, Santiago, Milan, Bologna, Florence, Copenhagen, Stuttgart, Bayreuth, Dresden, Munich, Bordeaux, Avignon, Aix-en-Provence, Orange, San Diego, Pittsburgh, Chicago, Vancouver and San Francisco; awards incl Royal Philharmonic Soc singing award 1991 and 1998, Wagner Soc Reginald Goodall Award 1996, South Bank Show Award 1998, Evening Standard Opera Award 1998; Hon FRNCM 1996, Hon DMus: Univ of Sussex 1997, Univ of Manchester 1998, Univ of Birmingham 2004, Univ of Nottingham 2004; *Recreations* tennis; *Style*— Sir John Tomlinson, CBE; ✉ c/o Music International, 13 Ardilaun Road, Highbury, London N5 2QR (tel 020 7359 5183)

TOMLINSON, Lindsay; OBE (2005); *Educ* Univ of Cambridge (MA); *m*; 1 da, 4 s; *Career* with Commercial Union plc 1974–76, conslt pensions actuary Metropolitan Pensions Assoc 1976–81, sr investment mangr Provident Mutual 1981–87; BZW Investment Management Ltd: joined 1987, md UK business 1990–92, dep chief exec 1992–94, chief exec 1994–96; chief exec Europe Barclays Global Investors 1996–2003, vice-chm Barclays Global Investors 2003–; *Style*— Lindsay Tomlinson, Esq, OBE; ✉ Barclays Global Investors, Murray House, 1 Royal Mint Court, London EC3N 4HH (tel 020 7668 8866, fax 020 7668 6866, e-mail lindsay.tomlinson@barclaysglobal.com)

TOMLINSON, Sir Michael John; kt (2005), CBE (1997); s of Jack Tomlinson (d 1993), of Rotherham, S Yorks, and Edith, *née* Cresswell (d 1988); *b* 17 October 1942; *Educ* Oakwood Tech HS Rotherham, Bournemouth Sch, Univ of Durham (BSc), Univ of Nottingham (PGCE); *m* 17 July 1965, Maureen Janet, da of Wilfred Ernest Tupling; 1 s (Philip John b 3 Jan 1968), 1 da (Jane Louise 23 March 1970); *Career* chemistry teacher Henry Mellish GS Nottingham 1965–69, head of chemistry Ashby-de-la-Zouch GS 1969–78, seconded to ICI Ltd 1977, chief inspr of schs HM Inspectorate of Schs 1989–92 (joined 1978), dir of inspection OFSTED 1995–2000 (dep dir 1992–94), HM's chief inspr of schs OFSTED 2000–02, chair tst bd responsible for Hackney Educn Services 2002–07; dir Nat Science Year 2002–03, pres Assoc for Science Educn 2005; chair Govt's working gp on 14–19 reform 2003–04; non-exec dir RM plc; tstee: Comino Fndn 2002, Industrial Tst 2003, Business Dynamics 2004, Trident 2005; author of various pubns for BP Ltd 1974–78; Hon Dr Univs of: Wolverhampton 2004, Middx 2005, East Anglia 2005, Northumbria 2005, Nottingham Trent 2005, De Montfort 2005, Leicester 2006, Durham 2007; Chemical Soc Educn Bronze Medal 1975; Queen's Silver Jubilee Medal 1977; FRSA (hon life fell 2006); *Books* New Movements in the Study and Teaching of Chemistry (1975), Organic Chemistry: A Problem-Solving Approach (1977), Mechanisms in Organic Chemistry: Case Studies (1978); *Recreations* gardening, fishing, reading, food and drink; *Style*— Sir Michael Tomlinson, CBE; ✉ Brooksby, Mayhall Lane, Chesham Bois, Amersham, Buckinghamshire HP6 5NR (tel 01494 726967, fax 01494 727338)

TOMLINSON, Prof Richard Allan; s of James Edward Tomlinson (d 1963), and Dorothea Mary, *née* Grellier (d 1983); *b* 25 April 1932; *Educ* King Edward's Sch Birmingham, St John's Coll Cambridge (MA); *m* 14 Dec 1957, Heather Margaret, da of Ernest Fraser Murphy (d 1965); 3 s (Nicholas John b 1959, Peter Brian b 1962, Edward James b 1965), 1 da (Penelope Ann b 1961); *Career* asst Dept of Greek Univ of Edinburgh 1957–58; Univ of Birmingham: asst lectr 1958–61, lectr 1961–69, sr lectr 1969–71, prof of ancient history and archaeology 1971–95; vice-pres Br Sch at Athens 2001– (dir 1995–96); memb: Victorian Soc, Hellenic Soc; FSA; *Books* Argos and the Argolid (1972), Greek Sanctuaries (1976), Epidauros (1980), Greek Architecture (1989), The Athens of Alma Tadema (1991), From Mycenae to Constantinople (1992), Greek and Roman Architecture (1994); *Recreations* walking; *Style*— Prof Richard Tomlinson, FSA; ✉ c/o Institute of Archaeology and Antiquity, University of Birmingham, Birmingham B15 2TT (tel 0121 414 5497, fax 0121 414 3595)

TOMLINSON, Prof Sally; da of Clifford Gilmore Entwistle (d 1966), and Alice Nora, *née* Stubbs (d 1974); *b* 22 August 1936; *Educ* Macclesfield HS, Univ of Liverpool (BA), Univ of Birmingham (MSocSci), Univ of Warwick (PhD); *m* 31 Aug 1957, Sqdn Ldr Brian Joseph Tomlinson (RAF ret); 2 da (Susan b 1960, Joanna b 1963), 1 s (Simon b 1962); *Career* lectr and sr lectr W Midlands Coll of Educn 1969–73, sr res fell Univ of Warwick 1974–77, prof of educn Lancaster Univ 1984–91 (lectr and sr lectr 1978–84), prof of educn UC Swansea 1991–92; Goldsmiths Coll London: Goldsmith prof of policy and mgmnt in educn 1992–98 (emeritus prof 1998–), dean Faculty of Educn 1993–95, pro-warden 1994–97; sr research fell Dept of Educational Studies Univ of Oxford 1998–2000; sr assoc memb St Antony's Coll Oxford 1984–85; memb: Univ Cncl for Educn of Teachers 1984–, Cmmn of the Future of Multi-ethnic Britain 1998–2000, Ct Univ of Bradford 2001–04, Cncl Univ of Gloucestershire 2001–; chair of tstees Africa Educn Tst 2005– (tstee 1992–); res assoc: Inst for Public Policy Res 1990–92; FRSA; *Books* Colonial Immigrants in a British City - A Class Analysis (with John Rex, 1979), Education Subnormality - A Study in Decision Making (1981), Special Education: Policy Practices and Social Issues (jt ed, 1981), A Sociology of Special Education (1982), Ethnic Minorites in British Schools: A Review of the Literature 1960–1982 (1983), Home and School in Multicultural Britain (1984), Special Education and Social Interests (ed with Len Barton, 1984), Affirmative Action and Positive Policies in the Education of Ethnic Minorities (ed with Abraham Yogev, 1989), The School Effect: A Study of Multi-Racial Comprehensives (with David Smith, 1989), Multi-Cultural Education in White Schools (1990), The Assessment of Special Educational Needs: Whose Problem? (with David Galloway and Derrick Armstrong, 1994), Educational Reform and its Consequences (1994), Ethnic Relations and Schooling (ed with Maurice Craft, 1995), Education 14–19: Critical perspectives (1997), School Effectiveness for Whom? (ed with Slee R and Weiner G, 1998), Hackney Downs: The School that Dared to Fight (with M O'Connor, E Hales, and J Davis, 1999), Education in a Post-Welfare Society (2001, 2 edn 2005), Selection Isn't Working (with T Edwards, 2002), Race and Education: Politics and Policy (2008); *Style*— Prof Sally Tomlinson; ✉ Department of Educational Studies, University of Oxford, 15 Norham Gardens, Oxford OX2 6PY (tel 01865 274024)

TOMLINSON, Prof Stephen; CBE (2007); s of Frank Tomlinson, of Bolton, Lancs, and Elsie, *née* Towler; *b* 20 December 1944; *Educ* Hayward GS Bolton, Univ of Sheffield (MB ChB, MD); *m* 14 Oct 1970, Christine Margaret, da of George Hope, of Sheffield, S Yorks; 2 da (Rebecca b 1974, Sarah b 1977); *Career* Wellcome Tst sr lectr 1980–85 (sr res fell 1977–80), reader in med Univ of Sheffield 1982–85; Univ of Manchester Med Sch: prof of med 1985–2001, dean Med Sch and Faculty of Med 1993–97, dean Faculty of Med Dentistry and Nursing 1997–99, vice-chllr Univ of Wales Coll of Med 2001–2004, provost Cardiff Univ 2004–; author of pubns on mechanisms of hormone action, and intracellular signalling and orgn of health care in diabetes; exec sec Cncl Heads of Med Schs & Faculties of Med in the UK 1997–99; chm Assoc of Clinical Profs of Med 1996–99 (sec 1994–96), chm Fedn Assoc of Clinical Profs 1997–2000, pres Assoc of Physicians of GB and I 2002–03 (sec 1988–93, treas 1993–98); chm Tropical Health and Educn Tst 2007–; chm ASH Wales 2007–; FRCP, FMedSci; *Style*— Prof Stephen Tomlinson, CBE; ✉ Tŷ Gwyn, St Andrews Major, Dinas Powys CF64 4HD (tel 029 2051 2041); Office of the Provost, Cardiff University, Cardigan House, Heath Park, Cardiff CF4 4XN (tel 029 2074 2029, e-mail tomlinsons@cf.ac.uk)

TOMLINSON, Hon Mr Justice; Sir Stephen Miles Tomlinson; kt (2000); s of Capt Enoch Tomlinson, and Mary Marjorie Cecelia, *née* Miles; *b* 29 March 1952; *Educ* King's Sch Worcester, Worcester Coll Oxford (MA); *m* 15 March 1980, Joanna Kathleen, da of Ian Joseph Greig; 1 s, 1 da; *Career* called to the Bar Inner Temple 1974 (bencher 1990); QC 1988, judge of the High Court of Justice (Queen's Bench Div) 2000–; memb of governing body Shrewsbury Sch 2003–; *Recreations* cricket, gardening, walking, family; *Clubs* Garrick, MCC; *Style*— The Hon Mr Justice Tomlinson; ✉ Royal Courts of Justice, Strand, London WC2A 2LL

TOMS, Michael Rodney (Mike); s of Walter Toms (d 2005), of Hebden Bridge, W Yorks, and Anne Brown (d 1957); *b* 1 July 1953, Stoke-on-Trent, Staffs; *Educ* Rotherham GS, UC Durham (BA), Univ of Nottingham (MA); *m* 26 June 1976, Jane Rosemary, *née* Moss; 2 da (Natalie b 15 Oct 1981, Hannah b 11 March 1985), 1 s (Matthew b 17 Nov 1989); *Career* various positions Br Airports Authy 1978–87; BAA plc: various sr positions incl chief economist and strategy dir 1987–2002, memb Bd and gp planning dir 2002–06; dir: Viridian Gp plc, UK Coal plc, Oxera Consulting; memb Governing Bd Airports Cncl Int (ACI) 2002–06; MRTPI 1978, MRICS 1980, FRAeS 2001; *Style*— Mike Toms, Esq

TOMS, Dr Rhinedd Margaret; da of David Peregrine Jones (d 1983), of Llanelli, Carmarthenshire, and Margaret Edith, *née* Davies (d 1996); *b* 18 June 1942; *Educ* Howells Sch Denbigh, Girton Coll Cambridge (MA), Westminster Med Sch (MB BChir); *m* 19 Oct 1968, Brian Frank Toms (d 1985), s of Harold Frank Toms (d 1989), of Rushden, Northants; 1 da (Eleanor b 1969), 1 s (David b 1971); *Career* clinical MO London Borough of Southwark 1968–71, SMO Lambeth Lewisham and Southwark AHA 1973–75, trg posts in psychiatry 1976–84, conslt psychiatrist NE Essex Mental Health Tst 1984–2005; hon conslt St Luke's Hosp for the Clergy 1990–2004, clinical tutor in psychiatry Br Postgrad Med Fedn 1988–92, Tst med advsr 1993–96; second opinion appointed dr Mental Halth Act Cmmn 1987–; memb Exec Ctee Phoenix Gp Homes; memb BMA; *Recreations* gardening, music, craft, choral singing; *Style*— Dr Rhinedd Toms; ✉ 45 Oaks Drive, Colchester, Essex CO3 3PS (tel 01206 549547)

TOMSETT, Alan Jeffrey; OBE (1974); s of Maurice Jeffrey Tomsett (d 1987), and Edith Sarah, *née* Mackelworth (d 1953); *b* 3 May 1922; *Educ* Trinity Sch of John Whitgift Croydon, Univ of London (BCom); *m* 1948, Joyce May, da of Walter Albert Hill (d 1959); 1 s (Ian), 1 da (Ann); *Career* served WWII 1941–46 with RAF (Middle East 1942–45); Hodgson Harris & Co Chartered Accountants London 1938, Smallfield Rawlins & Co 1951, Northern Mercantile & Investment Corporation 1955, William Baird & Co Ltd 1962–63; fin dir British Transport Docks Bd 1974–83 (chief accountant and fin controller 1964–73), dir Associated British Ports Holdings plc 1983–92 (fin dir 1983–87); churchwarden St John's Shirley 1988–92; FCA, FCMA, CPFA, JDipMA, FCIS, FCILT (vice-pres 1981–82, hon treas 1982–88), FRSA; *Recreations* gardening; *Clubs* Victory Services; *Style*— Alan Jeffrey Tomsett, Esq, OBE; ✉ 14 Colts Bay, Craigwell on Sea, Bognor Regis, West Sussex PO21 4EH

TONBRIDGE, Bishop of 2002–; Rt Rev Dr Brian Colin Castle; s of Ernest Castle, and Sarah, *née* Shepherd; *b* 7 September 1949; *Educ* Wilson's GS London, UCL (BA), Univ of Oxford (MA), Grad Sch of Ecumenical Studies Bossey Switzerland (Cert Ecumenical Studies), Univ of Birmingham (PhD), Cuddesdon Theol Coll; *m* Jane; 1 s (Jamie), 2 da (Sarah, Bethan); *Career* social worker Lambeth 1972–74, teacher Lesotho (through USPG) 1974; ordained: deacon 1977, priest 1978; curate St Nicholas' Sutton 1977, curate St Peter's Limpsfield 1977–81, priest-in-charge Chingola, Chililabombwe and Solwezi Northern Zambia (through USPG) 1981–84 (also lay trg offr, memb Diocesan and Provincial Synod, memb Bishop's Cncl), tutor Grad Sch Ecumenical Inst Bossey Switzerland 1984–85, vicar of North Petherton and Northmoor Green 1985–92, vice-princ and dir of pastoral studies Ripon Coll Cuddesdon 1992–2001 (actg princ 1993 and 1996), hon canon Rochester Cathedral 2002–; Archbishop's advsr in alternative spiritualities and new religious movements; Univ of Oxford: memb Faculty of Theology, examiner (BTh and MTh), chair of examiners for MTh, chm Supervisory Ctee for BTh and MTh, memb Faculty of Theology Ctee preparing for Dept of Educn Teaching Quality Assessment; PhD examiner Univ of Birmingham, external examiner (BTh) Univ of Wolverhampton 1999–2004; memb: Steering Gp Oxford Partnership for Theol Educn and Trg, Miny Ctee Dio of Oxford, Mission Theology Advsy Gp (Sub-Ctee of Archbishops' Cncl Bd of Mission); delivered various lectures and talks, conducted ordination retreats, invited preacher Boston Univ; *Publications* Hymns: The making and shaping of a theology for the whole people of God (1990), Sing a New Song to the Lord (1994), Unofficial God? Voices from Beyond the Walls (2004); various articles and book reviews published in Christian jls; *Recreations* music, fly fishing, cross-country skiing, photography; *Style*— The Rt Rev the Bishop of Tonbridge; ✉ Bishop's Lodge, 48 St Botolph's Road, Sevenoaks, Kent TN13 3AG (tel 01732 456070, fax 01732 741449, e-mail bishop.tonbridge@rochester.anglican.org)

TONG, Chee Hwee; s of Hong Hoe Tong, of Ipoh, Malaysia, and Ah Looi Chong; *b* 28 May 1963; *Educ* Sungei Pari HS Malaysia; *m* 26 March 1996, Sow Fun Ho; 2 s (Kah Yin Tong b 13 Feb 1999, Kah Weng Tong b 9 Oct 2000); *Career* trained Happy Valley Restaurant Singapore 1982–84, third fryer chef Happy Valley Restaurant Malaysia 1985–87, third fryer chef Carlton Hotel Singapore 1988–89, second fryer chef Sheraton Towers Singapore 1989–95, first fryer chef Marriott Hotel Singapore 1995–96, sr fryer chef Ritz Carlton Singapore 1996–2001, head chef Hakkasan London 2001– (1 Michelin Star 2003–, Oriental Restaurant of the Year 2003 Carlton Restaurant Awards); *Style*— Mr Tong Chee Hwee; ✉ Hakkasan, 8 Hanway Place, London W1P 9DH (tel 020 7927 7000, fax 020 7907 1889)

TONGE, Baroness (Life Peer UK 2005), of Kew in the London Borough of Richmond upon Thames; Dr Jennifer Louise (Jenny) Tonge; da of Sidney Smith (d 1958), of W Midlands, and Violet Louise, *née* Williams (d 1991); *b* 19 February 1941; *Educ* Dudley Girls' HS, UCL, UCH (MB BS); *m* 1964, Dr Keith Angus Tonge, s of Kenneth Gordon Tonge; 2 s (Hon David b 1968, Hon Richard b 1976), 1 da (Mary b 1970 d 2004); *Career* sr family planning doctor 1974–97, sr med offr Women's Servs Ealing HA 1983–88, mangr Community Health Servs West London Healthcare Tst 1992–97; MP (Lib Dem) Richmond Park 1997–2005 (Parly candidate Richmond and Barnes 1992); int devpt spokesperson for Lib Dems 1997–2003; memb Select Ctee on Int Devpt 1997–99; memb Lib Dem Federal Policy Ctee, chair Lib Dem Health Panel 1992–97; chair Richmond and Barnes Lib Assoc 1978–80 (chair Social Servs Ctee 1983–87), memb London Borough of Richmond upon Thames Cncl (Kew Ward) 1981–90; chair of govrs Waldegrave Sch 1988–92; hon fell Faculty of Family Planning (RCOG) 1999; fell Royal Soc of Public Health and Hygiene 1996; *Style*— The Rt Hon the Lady Tonge

TONGE, Michael (Mike); QPM (2005); s of Alan Tonge, and Joan Tonge; *b* 12 May 1957, Bolton; *Educ* Stand GS for Boys Manchester, Padgate Coll of HE Warrington, Victoria Univ of Manchester (BA), Fitzwilliam Coll Cambridge (Dip); *m*; 2 da; *Career* with Lancashire Constabulary 1978–99; Merseyside Police: Asst Chief Constable 1999–2001, Dep Chief Constable 2001–04; Chief Constable Gwent Police 2004–; led Review of Omagh Bomb Enquiry Policing Bd of NI 2002; *Recreations* golf, climbing, walking, sports generally, wine, music; *Style*— Mike Tonge, Esq, QPM; ✉ Gwent Police Headquarters, Croesyceiliog, Cwmbran, Gwent NP44 2XJ

TONGUE, Carole; da of Walter Archer Tongue, of Lausanne, Switzerland, and Muriel Esther, *née* Lambert; *b* 14 October 1955; *Educ* Brentwood Co HS, Loughborough Univ of Technol (BA); *m* 28 Dec 1990, Chris Pond, MP, *qv*; 1 da (Eleanore Christabel b 20 Dec 1992); *Career* asst ed Laboratory Practice 1977–78, courier for Sunsites Ltd in France 1978–79, Robert Schumann scholarship for res in social affrs Euro Parliament 1979–80, sec and admin asst in Socialist Gp Secretariat of Euro Parliament 1980–84; MEP (Lab) London East 1984–99; spokesperson on media/culture policy for Pty of the Gp of Euro Socialists Euro Parliament 1995–99 (memb Temporary Ctee on Employment and Industry, memb Youth, Media and Culture Ctee, substitute memb Social Affairs Ctee); sr visiting fell Dept of Euro Studies Loughborough Univ; vice-chm: AMA, SERA; memb: RIIA, MSF, GMB, CND, END, One World, Friends of the Earth, Greenpeace, Fabian Soc; *Recreations* piano, cello, tennis, squash, riding, cinema, theatre, opera; *Style*— Ms Carole Tongue; ✉ London East European Constituency Office, Coventry House, 1 Coventry Road, Ilford, Essex IG1 4QR (tel 020 8554 3236, fax 020 8518 2783)

TONGUE, Christopher Hugh; s of Francis James Tongue (d 1998), of Bath, and Edith May, *née* Laver (d 1977); *b* 2 April 1943; *Educ* Kingswood Sch Bath, Jesus Coll Cambridge, Makerere Coll Univ of E Africa; *m* 3 Jan 1976, Chelsia, da of Rev E Gordon Hitchings; 2 s (Craig James b 23 Aug 1977, Giles Hendrik b 19 July 1980); *Career* teacher: Kagumo HS 1966–68, Felsted Sch 1968–84, Diocesan Coll Cape Town 1975–76; headmaster: Keil Sch 1984–92, St John's Sch Leatherhead 1993–2004; currently educn conslt, charity and fundraising appts; memb Ctee HMC 2001–04 (memb Professional Devpt Sub-Ctee 1996– (chm 2001–04)); govr: Danes Hill Sch, Shrewsbury House Sch, Sutton Valence Sch, St George's Sch Ascot; *Recreations* cricket, rugby, golf, hill walking, classic music; *Style*— Christopher Tongue, Esq; ✉ 21 Kilmaine Road, Fulham, London SW6 7JU (tel 020 7381 5507, e-mail tongue.chris@gmail.com)

TONKING, His Hon Judge (Russel) Simon William Ferguson; DL; s of Lt-Col John Wilson Tonking, MBE, TD (d 1992), and Mary Oldham Tonking, *née* Ferguson (d 1971); *b* 25 March 1952; *Educ* The King's Sch Canterbury, Emmanuel Coll Cambridge (MA); *m* 10 July 1976, (Sylvia) Mithra, da of Colin Ian McIntyre; 1 da (Flora b 1984), 1 s (William b 1988); *Career* called to the Bar Inner Temple 1975; recorder 1994–97 (asst recorder 1991–94); circuit judge: Midland & Oxford Circuit 1997–2001, Midland Circuit 2001–; resident judge Stafford Combined Court 2006–; steward Lichfield Cathedral (head steward 1984–86, pres 2003–04), dep chllr Dio of Southwell 1997–2005; memb Criminal Ctee Judicial Studies Bd 2005–; *Style*— His Hon Judge Tonking; ✉ Stafford Combined Court Centre, Victoria Square, Stafford ST16 2QQ (tel 01785 610730)

TONKS, John; s of late John Henry Tonks, of Brewood, Staffs, and late Gladys Mary, *née* Maddocks; *b* 14 August 1927; *Educ* Dudley GS, Birmingham Coll of Art (maj scholar, NDD Sculpture, art teacher's Dip); *m* 14 July 1951, Sylvia Irene, da of Thomas William Taylor; 1 s (Julian Matthew John b 19 April 1953), 1 da (Caroline Louise Sylvia Mary b 12 April 1956); *Career* specialist art teacher in secdy schs 1952–65, lectr rising to sr lectr and princ lectr in sculpture W Midlands Coll of Higher Educn 1965–82, freelance sculptor 1982–; solo exhibitions incl: V B Gallery St Louis USA 1981, Oriel 31 Welshpool 1983, Ombersley Gallery Worcs 1983, Britain Salutes New York (Poole Willis Gallery NY) 1983, Helias Gallery Birmingham 1984, Univ of Birmingham 1984, Liverpool Int Garden Festival 1984, Garden Festival Wales 1992; public cmmns: Statue of Virgin Mary (St Mary's Church, Enville, Staffs), Sculpture of the Risen Christ (Wombourne Parish Church Staffs), The Family (Alexander Hosp, Redditch, Worcs), St Cecilia (Gardens of Pendrell Hall, Staffs), Girl Awakening (Gretna Museum/Tourist Centre), Roman Woman (Birmingham Botanical Gardens), The Runaway Lovers (Gretna Museum/Tourist Centre); fell RSBS 1978 (assoc 1967, vice-pres 1990); *Recreations* walking and work; *Style*— John Tonks, Esq; ✉ 11 Pedmore Court Road, Pedmore, Stourbridge, West Midlands DY8 2PH (tel 01384 390698)

TONKS, Julian Matthew John; s of John Tonks, of Comhampton, Worcs, and Sylvia Irene, *née* Taylor; *b* 19 April 1953; *Educ* Dudley GS, Trinity Coll Oxford (MA, MLitt); *m* 14 Aug 1980, Ann Miles, da of James Miles Henderson, of Granite City, Illinois; 1 s (Henry Miles James); *Career* admitted slr 1982; asst slr Freshfields 1982–86; Pinsent Curtis (formerly Pinsent & Co): tax ptnr 1987–, dep sr ptnr 1993–94, sr ptnr 1994–2001; sr ptnr Pinsent Masons (formerly Pinsents) 2001–; chm Birmingham Common Purpose 1994–2001, tstee Birmingham Royal Ballet Tst 1996–2002, Midlands CBI Regnl Cncl 1998–; *Recreations* reading modern novels and medieval history, swimming, castles, collecting photographs, wine; *Style*— Julian Tonks, Esq; ✉ 17 Ampton Road, Edgbaston, Birmingham B15 2UJ; Pinsent Masons, Dashwood House, 69 Old Broad Street, London EC2M 1NR (tel 020 7418 7000, fax 020 7418 7050)

TONRY, Prof Michael; *b* 7 June 1945, Martinsburg, WV; *Educ* Univ of N Carolina Chapel Hill (AB), Yale Law Sch (LLB); *Career* in private practice Sonnenschein Carlin & Nath Chicago 1970–71, research assoc Center for Studies in Criminal Justice Univ of Chicago 1971–73, lectr in law Faculty of Law Univ of Birmingham 1973–74, in private practice Dechert Price & Rhoads Philadelphia 1974–76, prof of law Univ of Maryland Sch of Law 1976–83, private solo law practice Castine ME 1983–90, Sonosky prof of law and public policy Univ of Minnesota 1990–, dir Inst of Criminology and prof of law and public policy Univ of Cambridge 1999–; sr research fell Netherlands Inst for the Study of Crime and Law Enforcement Leiden 2003–; visiting prof: Univ of Leiden 1996–98, Max-Planck Inst for Int and Comparative Criminal Law 1998–99, Univ of Lausanne 2001–; visiting fell All Souls Coll Oxford 1994–95; dir MacArthur Fndn/US Dept of Justice Prog on Human Devpt and Criminal Behavior 1986–90; ed: Crime and Justice - A Review of Research 1977–, The Castine Patriot 1987–90 (also publisher), Overcrowded Times 1989–2000, Studies in Crime and Public Policy 1992–, Readers in Crime and Justice 1993–; Humboldt-Stiftung Forschungspreisträger 1997–2002; *Publications* Research on Sentencing: The Search for Reform (co-ed and contrib, 1983), Reform and Punishment - Essays on Criminal Sentencing (co-ed, 1983), Hypnotically Refreshed Testimony: Enhanced Memory or Tampering with the Evidence? (jtly, 1985), Communities and Crime (co-ed, 1986), The Sentencing Commission - Guidelines for Criminal Sanctions (jtly, 1987), Sentencing Reform Impacts (1987), Prediction and Classification (co-ed, 1987), Managing Appeals in Federal Courts (jtly, 1988), Family Violence (co-ed, 1989), Drugs and Crime (co-ed, 1990), Between Prison and Probation - Intermediate Punishments in a Rational Sentencing System (jtly, 1990), Human Development and Criminal Behaviour (jtly, 1991), Modern Policing (co-ed, 1992), Beyond the Law: Crime in Complex Organizations (co-ed, 1993), Intermediate Sanctions in Overcrowded Times (co-ed, 1995), Building a Safer Society (co-ed, 1995), Malign Neglect - Race, Crime, and Punishment in America (1995), Sentencing Matters (1996), Sentencing Reform in Overcrowded Times - A Comparative Perspective (co-ed, 1997), Ethnicity, Crime, and Immigration - Comparative and Cross-national Perspectives (ed, 1997), Intermediate Sanctions in Sentencing Guidelines (1997), Youth Violence (co-ed, 1998), The Handbook of Crime and Punishment (ed, 1998), Prisons (co-ed, 1999), Sentencing and Sanctions in Western Countries (co-ed, 2001), Penal Reform in Overcrowded Times (ed, 2001), Reform and Punishment: The Future of Sentencing (co-ed, 2002), Ideology, Crime and Criminal Justice: A Symposium in Honour of Sir Leon Radinowicz (co-ed, 2002), Youth Crime and Youth Justice: Comparative and Cross-national Perspectives (co-ed, 2003), Confronting Crime: Crime Control under New Labour (ed, 2003), Cross-national Studies of Crime and Justice (co-ed, 2003), Thinking about Crime: Sense and Sensibility in American Penal Culture (2004), Punishment and Politics: Evidence and Emulation in the Making of English Crime Control Policy (2004); author of numerous articles in learned jls; *Style*— Prof Michael Tonry; ✉ Institute of Criminology, University of London, 7 West Road, Cambridge CB3 9DT (tel 01223 335381, fax 01223 335356, e-mail director@crim.cam.ac.uk)

TOOBY, Michael Bowen; s of Leslie and Jill Tooby, of Long Itchington, Warks; *b* 20 December 1956; *Educ* King Henry VIII Sch Coventry, Magdalene Coll Cambridge; *Career* asst curator Kettles Yard Cambridge 1978–80, exhbns organiser Third Eye Centre Glasgow 1980–84, keeper Mappin Art Gallery Sheffield 1984–92, curator Tate Gallery St Ives 1992–2000, dir Nat Museum and Gall Cardiff 2000–06, dir progs and learning Amgueddfa Cymru/Nat Museums Wales 2006–; chm Engage (Nat Orgn for Gallery and Visual Arts Educators) 1999–2004, memb Stabilisation Advsy Panel Arts Cncl of England 1999–2004, memb Museums and Galleries Ctee AHRC 2005–; *Style*— Michael Tooby, Esq; ✉ National Museum Wales, Cathays Park, Cardiff CF10 3NP (tel 029 20 573 206)

TOOGOOD, John; QPM (1977); s of James Waller Giddings Toogood (d 1964), of Chippenham, Wilts, and Katherine Mary, *née* Winter (d 1956); *b* 19 August 1924; *Educ* Chippenham GS, King's Coll London (LLB, LLM); *m* 1, 19 Oct 1946 (m dis 1949), June, da of Leslie Llewellyn Rowlands (d 1970), of Plymouth, Devon; m 2, 20 Dec 1951, Josephine, *née* Curran (d 1984); 1 da (Katherine b 3 Sept 1962); m 3, 23 July 1986 (remarried), June Martin *née* Rowlands (d 2001); *Career* RM 1942–46; Met Police 1946–83 (ret as Cdr); called to the Bar Gray's Inn 1957, in practice 1983–; memb Medico-Legal Soc 1955–99; SBStJ 1984; *Recreations* family; *Style*— John Toogood, Esq, QPM; ✉ 4 King's Bench Walk, Temple, London EC4V 7DL (tel 020 7822 8822)

TOOKEY, Christopher David; s of Alan Oliver Tookey, and Winifreda, *née* Marsh; *b* 9 April 1950; *Educ* Tonbridge, Exeter Coll Oxford (MA, ed Isis, pres Oxford Union); *m* 2 Sept 1989, Frances Anne, da of Henry Robert Heasman; 1 s (Daniel b 12 April 1991); *Career* writer, broadcaster, director, producer and composer of musicals; prodns incl: Hard Times 1973, Room with a Revue 1974, Retrogrim's Progress 1974, Hanky Park 1975, Dick Whittington 1975 and 1976, An Evening with Noel and Gertie 1975 and 1976, The Resurrection of the British Musical 1977, Him 'n' Her 1979, Ladies and Jurgen 1980, Hard Times - The Musical 1998 and 2000; asst theatre dir Belgrade Theatre Co 1973–74, Haymarket and Phoenix Theatre Leicester 1974–75, TV prodr and dir Associated Television 1975–82, weekend ed and assoc features ed TV-am 1982–83, freelance TV dir 1983–89; credits incl: Revolver, After Dark, Network 7, various rock videos; as freelance journalist: Books and Bookmen 1983–86, film critic Sunday Telegraph 1989–92 (freelance feature writer 1986, TV critic 1987–89), TV critic and feature writer Daily Telegraph 1986–93, film critic, feature writer and occasional theatre critic Daily Mail 1993–, theatre critic Mail on Sunday 1993; also freelance journalist for Prospect, Applause, The Sunday Times, The Observer, The European, The Literary Review, Drama, and National Review (US); freelance broadcaster 1989– (progs incl Sky News, The Arts Prog (BBC Radio 2), What the Papers Say (BBC 2), Book Choice (Channel 4), Meridian (BBC), First Edition (BSB), Open House (Channel 5), presenter Back Row and The Film Programme (BBC Radio 4)); presenter ALFS Awards Ceremony (London Film Critics) 1994–99; chm Film Critics' Circle 1994–98; *Publications* The Critics' Film Guide (1994), Tookey's Movie Guide (internet pubn, 2002–); *Style*— Christopher Tookey, Esq; ✉ 4 Alwyne Villas, London N1 2HQ (tel 020 7226 2726, fax 020 7354 2574)

TOOLEY, Dr Peter John Hocart; s of Dr Patrick Hocart Tooley (d 1991), of Vale, Guernsey, and Brenda Margaret, *née* Williams (d 1939); *b* 28 February 1939; *Educ* Elizabeth Coll Guernsey, St George's Sch Harpenden, Univ of London, London Hosp Med Coll (MRCS, LRCP, MB BS, MRCGP, DObst RCOG, DMJ), Dip of the Faculty of Family Planning (DFFP), LLM; *m* 1, 1966 (m dis 1983), Elizabeth Monica, da of Percy Roche (d 1991), of Twyford, Berks; 2 da (Lucy b 1967, Josephine b 1971), 1 s (Patrick b 1969); m 2, 1987, Diana Edith, *née* Sturdy; *Career* sr ptnr gen med practice Twyford 1974–90 (princ 1966, trainer 1977–81), asst dep coroner Borough of Reading 1984–89; Janssen-Cilag Ltd (formerly Janssen Pharmaceutical Ltd): med conslt gen practice affrs 1986–90, sr med advsr 1990–93, head of med affrs 1993–98, med dir Ireland 1996–98; med dir Daiichi Sankyo UK Ltd (formerly Sankyo Pharma UK Ltd) 1998–, med dir Alliance Pharmaceuticals 1998–2007, conslt medical dir A Menarini Pharma UK SRL; conslt pharmaceutical physician 1998–; MO: Oxfordshire RFU 1970–97, Henley RFC 1970–97, Marks & Spencer plc Reading 1980–90; memb: Berks Local Med Ctee 1978–86, Reading Pathological Soc, memb Bolam Soc 1995– (hon sec); chm Reading Med Club 1980–83 and 1987–90 (fndr memb), vice-chm Polehampton Charities 1986–90 (tstee 1975); Freeman City of London, Liveryman Worshipful Soc of Apothecaries 1965 (memb Livery Cmmn 1994–2005, chm 2002–04); memb: Medico-Legal Soc; BMA, Br Acad of Forensic Sciences, Br Assoc of Pharmaceutical Physicians; FRSM; *Recreations* sports, gardening, travel; *Style*— Dr Peter Tooley; ✉ Les Mielles, L'Ancresse, Vale, Guernsey GY3 5AZ (tel 01481 244543, fax 01481 242505 e-mail tooleyp@guernsey.net); PT Pharma Consultancy (Guernsey) Ltd, Les Mielles, L'Ancresse, Vale, Guernsey GY3 5AZ (tel 01481 242607, fax 01481 242505)

TOONE, Dr Brian Kenneth; s of Donald Freer Thomas (d 1979), and Mary Mable Ethel, *née* Downing; *b* 1 July 1937; *Educ* St Laurence Coll Ramsgate, King's Coll and St George's Hosp Med Sch London (MB BS, MPhil); *m* 1, 28 Sept 1965 (m dis 1979), Megan Reece; m 2, 20 March 2002, Ann Klotz; *Career* conslt: Dept of Psychological Med KCH 1980–2003 (hon conslt 2003–), The Maudsley and Bethlem Royal Hosp 1991–2003 (hon conslt 2003–); hon sr lectr Inst of Psychiatry London 1986– (sub-dean 1984–87), currently recognised teacher Univ of London; author of chapters and scientific articles on organic psychiatry and psychiatric aspects of epilepsy; FRCP 1988 (MRCP 1967), FRCPsych 1988 (MRCPsych 1973); *Recreations* tennis, squash; *Style*— Dr Brian Toone; ✉ 4 Grove Park, London SE5 8LT (tel 020 7733 3499, fax 020 77378192, e-mail brian.toone@btinternet.com)

TOOP, Alan James; s of James Cecil Toop (d 1973), of London, and Elsie Ada, *née* Lavers (d 1993); *b* 25 February 1934; *Educ* Highbury GS, UCL (BA); *m* 12 Sept 1964, Tessa Peggy Elaine, da of Richard Eric Widdis (d 1966), of Kenton, Middx; 1 s (Adam b 1965), 2 da (Annie b 1968, Rosie b 1972); *Career* brand mangr Wall's Ice Cream 1958–61, mktg mangr Lever Bros 1961–65, account dir J Walter Thompson 1967–70, chm The Sales Machine International Ltd 1970–99, chm Adam Phones Ltd 1999–; FCIM, FISP; *Books* Choosing The Right Sales Promotion (1966), Crackingjack! Sales Promotion Techniques (1991), European Sales Promotion (1992), Sales Promotion in Postmodern Marketing (1994); *Recreations* exercise; *Style*— Alan Toop, Esq; ✉ 93 Riverview Gardens, London SW13 8RA; Adam Phones Ltd, 2–3 Dolphin Square, Edensor Road, London W4 2ST (tel 020 8742 0101, fax 020 8742 3679)

TOOP, David; s of Leslie John Toop, of Waltham Cross, Herts, and Doris Ada May, *née* Purver; *b* 5 May 1949; *Educ* Broxbourne GS, Hornsey Coll of Art, Watford Coll of Art; *m* 1, 30 May 1987, Kimberley (d 1995), da of Les Leston; 1 da (Juliette Angelica b 13 Feb 1990); m 2, 11 Oct 2003, Eileen, da of John Peters; *Career* musician, author, curator; played with Paul Burwell 1970–80, gave three illustrated music talks BBC Radio 3 1971–75, recorded three pieces for The Obscure Label 1975, launched record label Quartz 1978, recorded with Flying Lizards 1979, publisher and co-ed Collusion magazine 1981–83, pop music critic The Sunday Times 1986–88, monthly music columnist and feature writer The Face 1984–96, music critic The Times 1988–96; contrib to Arena, Wire, GQ, Bookforum, NY Times, Gramophone, and various books; composed soundtrack to Lisbon Expo Acqua Matrix night show spectacular 1998; curator Sonic Boom sound art exhbn (Hayward Gallery) 2000, sound curator Radical Fashion exhbn (V&A) 2001, curator Not Necessarily English Music (2 CD compliation for Leonardo Music Jl/MIT Press), composed and performed Siren Space Thames Festival 2002; sound installations: Tokyo ICC 2000, Bruges WAV Festival 2002, Charles Fort Kinsale 2005, Beijing Zhongshan Park 2005, Beijing Capital Museum 2006, Stourhead Garden 2006; curator Playing John Cage (Arnolfini Bristol) 2006; London Coll of Communication: visiting research fell and visiting lectr Sch of Media 2000–05, AHRC research fell in creative and performing arts 2004–07, sr research fell 2007–; visiting prof Univ of the Arts London 2005–; memb: Sonic Arts Network, Electronic Music Fndn, Japanese Garden Soc, Takemitsu Soc; *Recordings* Buried Dreams (with Max Eastley) 1994, Screen Ceremonies (solo album) 1995, Pink Noir (solo album) 1996, Spirit World (solo album) 1997, Museum of Fruit (solo album) 1999, Hot Pants Idol (solo album) 1999, Needle in the Groove (with Jeff Noon) 2000, 37th Floor at Sunset (solo album) 2000, Black Chamber (solo album) 2003, Doll Creature (with Max Eastley) 2004, Sound Body (solo album) 2007; *Books* The Rap Attack (1984), The Rap Attack 2 (1991), Ocean of Sound (1995), Exotica (1999), Rap Attack 3 (1999), Haunted Weather (2004); *Style*— David Toop, Esq; ✉ website www.davidtoop.com

TOOTAL, Christopher Peter; s of Charles Stanley Albert Tootal, of Plaxtol, Kent, and Patricia Mary, *née* Swanson; *b* 10 March 1936; *Educ* Repton, The Queen's Coll Oxford (Robert Styring scholar, BA, BSc); *m* 20 April 1968, Alison Jane, da of late Archibald James Forbes; 1 s (Alastair James David b 22 April 1970), 1 da (Joanna Helen Natacha b 13 March 1974); *Career* tech asst Frank B Dehn & Co 1958–60, chartered patent agent Gill Jennings & Every 1962–64 (tech asst 1960–62); Herbert Smith: articled clerk 1964–67, asst slr 1967–68, ptnr 1968–2001, chm Copyright Tbnl 1998–2006; Liveryman Worshipful Co of Tallow Chandlers 1965– (Master 2001–02); *Books* The Law of Industrial Design - Registered Designs, Copyright and Design Right (1990); *Recreations* music, sailing, photography; *Clubs* Royal Harwich Yacht; *Style*— Christopher Tootal, Esq; ✉ Herbert Smith, Exchange House, Primrose Street, London EC2A 2HS (tel 020 7374 8000, fax 020 7374 0888)

TOPE, Baron (Life Peer UK 1994), of Sutton in the London Borough of Sutton; Graham Norman; CBE (1991), AM; s of Leslie Norman Tope (d 1983), of Sutton, and Winifred Sophia, *née* Merrick (d 1972); *b* 30 November 1943; *Educ* Whitgift Sch; *m* 22 July 1972, Margaret, da of Frank East; 2 s (Hon Andrew b 3 July 1974, Hon David b 21 June 1976); *Career* with Unilever Group 1961–69, insurance mangr Air Products Ltd 1970–72, MP (Lib) Sutton and Cheam 1972–74, dep gen sec Voluntary Action Camden 1975–90; London Borough of Sutton: cncllr (Lib/Lib Dem) 1974–, ldr 1986–99, cncl spokesman on libraries and heritage, community safety and economic devpt 1999–2006, spokesman on community, safety, leisure and libraries 2006–; pres London Lib Dems 1991–2000; Assoc of London Govt: Lib Dem ldr 1997–2000, Lib Dem Int and Euro spokesman 1997–2000; UK memb EU Ctee of the Regions 1994–, ldr ELDR (Lib gp) Ctee of the Regions 1996–2002; first vice-chair Constitutional Affairs Cmmn 2004–06 (chair 2002–04); spokesperson on educn House of Lords 1994–2000; memb London Assembly GLA (Lib Dem) 2000–, ldr Lib gp, chair Fin Ctee on Met Police Authy 2000–, memb Mayor of London's Advsy Cabinet 2000–04; chair Local Govt Gp for Europe 2005–; *Recreations* politics, history, reading, walking, gardening; *Style*— The Rt Hon the Lord Tope, CBE, AM; ✉ Greater London Authority, City Hall, The Queen's Walk, London SE1 0AA (tel 020 7983 4413, fax 020 7983 4344, e-mail graham.tope@london.gov.uk)

TOPOLSKI, Daniel; s of Feliks Topolski (d 1989), the artist, of London, and Marion Everall Topolski (d 1985); *b* 4 June 1945; *Educ* French Lycée London, Westminster, New Coll Oxford; *m* Susan Gilmore, da of James Gilbert; 2 da (Emma Sheridan b 30 Jan 1987, Tamsin Lucy Gilbert b 17 Nov 1990), 1 s (Lucien Sinclair Feliks b 21 May 1997); *Career* prodr BBC TV 1969–73, expdn leader Iran and Turkey 1973–74; writer on travel and sport, TV and radio commentator, journalist, photographer, motivational speaker; memb: London Rowing Club 1964–, Leander Club 1965–; Henley Royal Regatta: competitor 1962–93, winner 1969–70 and 1976–77, Henley steward 1991–; major championships incl: second place lightweight coxless fours World Championships (Nottingham) 1975, Gold medal lightweight eights World Championships (Amsterdam) 1977; participant Oxford v Cambridge Boat Race 1967 (winner) and 1968, chief coach to Oxford Univ for Boat Race 1973–87 (won 12, longest ever Oxford winning sequence (10), 3 course records 1974, 1976 and 1984 (16 mins 45 secs)), coach: Nat Women's Rowing Squad 1978–80, Women's VIII Olympic Games Moscow 1980, Men's Pair Olympic Games LA 1984: winner Travel Radio Prog of Year Award 1994; Churchill fell, FRGS; *Books* Muzungu: One Man's Africa (1976), Travels with My Father: South America (1983), Boat Race: The Oxford Revival (1985), True Blue: The Oxford Boat Race Mutiny (1989, sports book of the year, filmed 1996), Henley the Regatta (1989); *Style*— Daniel Topolski, Esq; ✉ 69 Randolph Avenue, London W9 1DW (tel 020 7289 8939, fax 020 7266 1884, e-mail dtopo35410@aol.com)

TORA, Brian Roberto; adopted s of Ernest Carlo Tora (d 2005), and Betty Lilian, *née* Squires (d 1971); *b* 21 September 1945; *Educ* Bancroft's Sch; *m* 1, 4 July 1975 (m dis 1988), Jennifer, da of (Julius) Dennis Israel Blanckensee (d 1951); 2 s (Matthew b 26 Dec 1977, Thomas b 5 June 1979); m 2, 20 Oct 1989, Elizabeth Mary, *née* Edgecombe; *Career* Grieveson Grant 1963–74, investment mangr Singer & Friedlander 1974–79, investment dir van Cutsem & Assocs 1979–82, investment dir Touche Remnant Fin Mgmnt 1982–85, head of retail mktg James Capel & Co 1985–91; Gerrard Investment Mgmnt Ltd (formerly Greig Middleton): mktg dir 1991–98, head of asset mgmnt 1998–2000, head Intermediary Div 2002–05, investment communications dir 2005–06; regular broadcaster, columnist in Fund Strategy, Money Marketing and others; FSI; *Publications* The Second Financial Services Revolution (1995); contrib articles on investment to several jls; *Recreations* bridge, reading, food and wine, travel; *Style*— Brian Tora, Esq; ✉ Enniskillen Lodge, Little Waldingfield, Suffolk CO10 0SU (tel 01787 247783)

TORDOFF, Baron (Life Peer UK 1981), of Knutsford in the County of Cheshire; Geoffrey Johnson Tordoff; s of late Stanley Acomb Tordoff, of Marple, Cheshire; *b* 11 October 1928; *Educ* Manchester Grammar, Univ of Manchester; *m* 1953, Mary Patricia, da of Thomas Swarbrick, of Leeds; 3 da (Hon Mary Catherine b 1954, Hon Frances Jane b 1956, Hon Paula Mary b 1960), 2 s (Hon Nicholas Gregory b 1958, Hon Mark Edmund b 1962); *Career* contested (Lib) Northwich 1964, Knutsford 1966 and 1970; Lib Party: chm Assembly Ctee 1974–76, memb Nat Exec 1975–84, chm 1976–79, pres 1983–84, chm Campaigns and Elections Ctee 1980 and 1981; House of Lords: dep Lib chief whip 1983–84, Lib chief whip 1984–88, Lib Dem chief whip 1988–94, a dep speaker 1994–, princ dep chm of ctees 1994–2001, chm Select Ctee on the European Communities 1994–2001, chm of ctees 2001–02; memb PCC 1995–2002; extra Lord in Waiting 2004–; *Clubs* National Liberal; *Style*— The Rt Hon the Lord Tordoff; ✉ House of Lords, London SW1A 0PW

TORNBOHM, (Peter) Noel; s of Eric Anthony Tornbohm (d 1986), of Darlington, and May, *née* Barrow (d 1969); *b* 11 January 1943; *Educ* Queen Elizabeth GS Darlington, UCL (LLB); *m* 1, 29 May 1965 (m dis 1982), Yvonne Hamilton, da of Wilfred Vincent Miller, of Darlington; 1 da (Catherine b 16 June 1969), 1 s (Paul b 28 March 1971); m 2, 13 Feb 1983 (m dis 1997), Maureen Roberta (Mo), da of Frank Griffin, of Mickleover, Derby; *Career* admitted slr 1967; ptnr Smith Roddam & Co 1968–71 (joined 1967), ptnr then sr ptnr Gadsby Coxon & Copestake (now Nelsons) 1973–2002 (conslt 2002–05), ret; former memb City of Derby 126 Round Table, chm Derby 41 Club 1990–91 (memb); memb Law Soc, Slrs Benevolent Assoc; *Recreations* playing and listening to music, dog walking, English local history; *Style*— Noel Tornbohm, Esq; ✉ 84 Church Road, Quarndon, Derby DE22 5JA (tel 01332 553376)

TORO-HARDY, HE Alfredo; s of Fernando Toro, and Ofelia, *née* Hardy; *b* 22 May 1950, Caracas, Venezuela; *Educ* Central Univ of Venezuela, Univ of Paris II, Int Inst of Public Admin Paris, Univ of Pennsylvania; *m* 1, 1972 (m dis 1998), Dinorah, *née* Carnevali; 1 da (Daniela b 1973), 2 s (Alfredo b 1980, Bernardo b 1984); m 2, 2001, Gabriela, *née* Gaxiola; *Career* Venezuelan diplomat; advsr Presidential Cmmns for Border Affrs 1991–92, advsr to Min of Foreign Affrs 1992–94, dir (with rank of ambass) Diplomatic Acad Foreign Affrs Miny 1992–94; ambass: Brazil 1994–97, Chile 1997–99, USA 1999–2001 (concurrently ambass to Bahamas), Ct of St James's 2001– (concurrently ambass to Ireland); memb: Consultative Bd Nat Security and Def Cncl 1988–2000, Inter-American Dialogue Washington DC, Justice Cmmn Santiago, Chairman's Club, RIIA, Windsor Energy Gp; visiting scholar/sr Fulbright scholar Princeton Univ 1986–87, assoc prof Simón Bolívar Univ Caracas 1989– (co-ordinator Latin American Studies Inst and dir N American Studies Centre 1989–91), ad honorem prof Univ of Brasilia 1996–97, prof and guest speaker at several univs and academic instns worldwide; memb Editorial Bd: Economía Hoy 1990–91, Política Internacional 1992–2002; weekly columnist and contrib: Visión 1989–90, El Diario de Caracas 1989–94, El Globo 1989–97, Gazeta Mercantil 1994–97, El Universal 1994–2002, Folha de São Paulo 1995–97, El Mercurio 1997–99; host weekly TV prog Radio Caracas Televisión 1992–94; *Books* author or co-author of 26 published books on foreign affrs and int trade relations; *Style*— HE Señor Alfredo Toro-Hardy; ✉ Venezuelan Embassy, 1 Cromwell Road, London SW7 2HR (tel 020 7584 5375)

TORPHICHEN, 15 Lord (S 1564); James Andrew Douglas Sandilands; s of 14 Lord Torphichen (d 1975); *b* 27 August 1946; *Educ* King's Sch Canterbury, Univ of Birmingham, Napier Coll Edinburgh; *m* 1976, Margaret Elizabeth, da of William Alfred Beale (d 1967), of Boston, Mass; 4 da (Margaret b 1979, Mary b 1981, Anne b 1985, Alison b 1990); *Heir* kinsman, Robert Powell (Robin) Sandilands; *Career* electronics engr; *Style*— The Rt Hon the Lord Torphichen; ✉ Calder House, Mid-Calder, West Lothian EH53 0HN

TORPY, Air Chief Marshal Sir Glenn Lester; KCB (2005), CBE (2000), DSO (1991), ADC (2006); s of Gordon Torpy, of Carterton, Oxon, and Susan, *née* Linsey (d 1972); *b* 27 July 1953; *Educ* Imperial Coll London (BSc); *m* 16 April 1977, Christine, *née* Jackson; *Career* OC 13 Sqdn 1989–92, personal staff offr to AOC in Chief Strike Cmd 1992–94, Station Cdr RAF Brüggen 1994–96, RCDS 1997, ACOS (Ops) Perm Jt HQ 1998–99, dir Air Ops MOD 1999–2000, ACDS (Ops) 2000–01, AOC No 1 Gp 2001–03, Dep C-in-C Strike Command 2003–04, Chief Jt Ops 2004–06, CAS 2006–; Freeman Worshipful Co of Haberdashers; FRAeS 2003, FCEI 2007; *Recreations* golf, hill walking, military history, cabinet making; *Style*— Air Chief Marshal Sir Glenn Torpy, KCB, CBE, DSO, ADC; ✉ Level 5, Zone I, Ministry of Defence, Main Building, Whitehall, London SW1A 2HB

TORRANCE, (David) Andrew; s of James Torrance (d 2005), and Gladys, *née* Riley (d 1995); *b* 18 May 1953; *Educ* Merchant Taylors' Sch Crosby, Emmanuel Coll Cambridge (MA), London Business Sch (MSc); *m* 30 Dec 1983, Ann Lesley, da of George Tasker (d 1972), of Bebington, Wirral; 1 da (Lucy b 1984), 1 s (James b 1987); *Career* The Boston Consulting Group Ltd: joined 1976, mangr 1981, vice-pres and dir until 1992; chm and chief exec ITT London & Edinburgh Insurance Group 1995–98 (joined 1992), chief exec Allianz Insurance plc 2003– (joined 1999–); chm The Motor Insurance Repair Research Centre (Thatcham) 2000–05; memb Worshipful Co of Insurers; *Recreations* cars, tennis, food, wine; *Style*— Andrew Torrance, Esq; ✉ 117 Lansdowne Road, London W11 2LF (tel 020 7727 9019, fax 020 7221 6541); Allianz Insurance plc, 57 Ladymead, Guildford, Surrey GU1 1DB (tel 01483 552700, fax 01483 532904, e-mail andrew.torrance@allianz.co.uk)

TORRANCE, Prof John Steele (Jack); s of Robert Torrance (d 1941), of Belfast, NI, and Charlotte Robinson Torrance (d 1982); *b* 11 January 1926; *Educ* Belfast Coll of Technol; *m* 8 Sept 1948, Rosetta Fitz-Simons, da of Thomas Patterson Shepherd (d 1980), of Donaghadee, NI; 4 da (Sharon Rose b 1952, Cheryl Sara b 1954, Candida Eleanor b 1956, Dara Rosetta b 1960); *Career* trainee Harland & Wolfe Belfast 1941–50 (seconded DNC Bath 1946), sr engr G N Haden and J R W Murland 1950–60, sr ptnr Steensen Varming Mulcahy & Partners Edinburgh 1972–85 (associate then ptnr 1960–72); involved in design for major projects incl: hosps, univs, banks, insurance cos, commercial offices, swimming and leisure complexes; ret, now specialises in litigation, arbitration, adjudication and Dispute Review Bd matters; visiting prof: Univ of Strathclyde 1988–94, Caledonian Univ 1994–2001; industrial prof Heriot-Watt Univ 1989–; contrib numerous articles in tech jls; cmmr Scot Cncl fot Int Arbitration; CEng, Hon FCIBSE (nat pres 1985–86), Hon FRIAS, FCIArb, FConsE, memb Expert Witness Inst; *Recreations* music, reading, golf; *Style*— Prof Jack Torrance; ✉ 1 Southbank Court, Easter Park Drive, Edinburgh EH4 6SH (tel 0131 312 6923, fax 0131 539 7038, e-mail johnstorrance@talk21.com)

TORRANCE, Samuel Robert (Sam); OBE (2003, MBE 1990); s of Robert Torrance, of Largs, Ayrshire, and June Torrance; *b* 24 August 1953; *m* Suzanne Danielle; 1 s (Daniel b 4 Aug 1988), 2 da (Phoebe b 29 June 1992, Anouska b 19 June 1995); *Career* professional golfer; *Tournament Victories* under 25 Match Play Radici Open 1972, Zambian Open 1975, Piccadilly medal Martini Int 1976, Scottish PGA Championship 1980, 1985, 1991 and 1993, Australian PGA Championship 1980, Irish Open 1981 and 1995, Spanish Open 1982, Portuguese Open 1982 and 1983, Scandinavian Open 1983, Tunisian Open 1984, Benson & Hedges Int 1984, Sanyo Open 1984, Monte Carlo Open 1985, Italian Open 1987 and 1995, German Masters 1990, Jersey Open 1991, Kronenbourg Open 1993, Catalan Open 1993, Honda Open 1993, French Open 1998; capt Asahi Glass Four Tours 1991 (winners); memb Ryder Cup team: 1981, 1983, 1985 (winners), 1987 (winners), 1989 (winners), 1991, 1993 and 1995 (winners), capt 2002 (winners); memb Dunhill Cup team: 1976, 1978, 1982, 1984, 1985, 1987, 1989, 1990, 1991, 1993 and 1995 (winners); memb World Cup team: 1976, 1978, 1982, 1984, 1985, 1987, 1989, 1990, 1991, 1993 and 1995; memb Hennessy Cognac Cup: 1976, 1978, 1980, 1982 and 1984; memb Double Diamond team: 1973, 1976 and 1977; finished 2nd Order of Merit 1995 (3rd 1993); *Recreations* family, snooker, cards, gambling; *Style*— Sam Torrance, Esq, OBE; ✉ c/o Katrina Johnston, Carnegie Sports International, 4th Floor, The Glasshouse, 1 Battersea Bridge Road, London SW11 3BZ (tel 020 7924 4882, fax 020 7924 4883)

TORRANCE, Prof Victor Brownlie; CBE (1991); s of Thomas Brownlie Torrance (d 1969), and Mary King Torrance, MBE, *née* Miller (d 1992); *b* 24 February 1937; *Educ* Wishaw High Sch, Heriot-Watt Univ (BSc, MSc), Univ of Edinburgh (PhD); *m* 1 (m dis 1982), Mary McParland; 2 da (Adrienne Joan b 20 Sept 1964, Deirdrie Ann b 15 March 1967), 1 s (Andrew Brownlie b 19 March 1968); m 2, (m dis 1992); m 3, 1999, Madinah, *née* Hussin; *Career* sr lectr i/c Bldg Div Sch of Architecture and Bldg Singapore Poly Singapore 1966–68, assoc prof and head Dept of Bldg and Estate Mgmnt Faculty of Architecture and Bldg Nat Univ of Singapore 1968–72, William Watson prof of bldg Dept of Bldg Engrg and Surveying Heriot-Watt Univ 1972–91, prof of bldg Dept of Civil and Bldg Engrg Loughborough Univ 1991–92, London Master Builders' prof of bldg Bartlett Sch of the Built Environment UCL 1992–96; prof of construction mgmnt Mara Univ of Technol 1996–; ptnr Building and Design Consultants 1976–91; memb: Bd of Govrs Edinburgh Coll of Art 1973–88, Civil Engrg and Transport Ctee and Bldg Sub-Ctee Science Res Cncl 1975–80, CNAA Bldg Bd 1978–81, CNAA Technol Res Ctee 1982–85, Scot Bldg Standards Advsy Ctee Res Sub-Ctee 1982–85; chm RIAS Res Steering Ctee 1982–85, memb Panel of Visitors to the Bldg Res Estab 1985–89, co-ordinator CIB Working Cmmn 71 1986–92, conslt of Bldg Investigation Centre 1987–91, dir Lloyds Surveyors 1989–96, dir Unihectare Sdn Bhd 1997–; chm Cncl of Profs of Bldg 1987–92, pres Chartered Inst of Bldg 1988–89; chm: Advsy Bd of Wimlas Testing Servs, Geo Wimpey Laboratories 1988–96; chm CIOB Environment Ctee 1990–96; FCIOB 1972, FIMgt 1972, FRSA 1973, Hon MRICS 1986; *Style*— Prof Victor Torrance, CBE; ✉ Faculty of Architecture, Planning and Surveying, Mara University of Technology, 40450 Shah Alam, Selangor, Malaysia (direct tel 00 603 5544 4364, fax 00 603 5880 4652, e-mail jvbtorrance@yahoo.com)

TORRE DIAZ, 7 Conde (Count; cr of 1846 by Queen Isabel II of Spain); Paul Gerald de Zulueta; only s of Maj Peter Paul John de Zulueta (Welsh Gds, d 1982; whose mother, Dora, m as her 2 husband, 5 Marquess of Bristol), by his w Tessa, who m as 2 husb, 2 Viscount Montgomery of Alamein, er da of late Lt-Gen Sir Frederick Browning, GCVO, KBE, CB, DSO, and Daphne du Maurier, the novelist; *b* 12 April 1956; *Educ* Ampleforth, RMA Sandhurst; *m* 18 June 1988, Susan, o da of Dr G J Pritchard, of Stanwell Moor; 2 s (Guy Peter b 26 Aug 1990, Hugh Philip b 1 Aug 1993); *Career* Welsh Gds 1977–87, Adj 1983–85; Robert Fleming & Co 1987–89; ptnr MaST International plc 1990–; Knight of Honour and Devotion SMOM; *Recreations* reading, family and fitness; *Clubs* Pratt's, Bath and Racquets, Anglo-Chilean, Anglo-Argentine, Anglo-Peruvian; *Style*— P G de Zulueta; ✉ e-mail paul.dezulueta@mast.co.uk

TORRINGTON, 11 Viscount (GB 1721); Sir Timothy Howard St George Byng; 11 Bt (GB 1715); Baron Byng of Southill (GB 1721); s of Hon George Byng, RN (d on active service 1944, himself s of 10 Viscount, whom present Viscount suc 1961), and Anne Yvonne Bostock, *née* Wood; *b* 13 July 1943; *Educ* Harrow, St Edmund Hall Oxford (BA); *m* 1973, Susan Honor, da of Michael George Thomas Webster, of Dummer, Hants; 3 da (Hon Henrietta Rose b 1977, Hon Georgina Isabel b 1980, Hon Malaika Anne b 13 April 1982); *Heir* kinsman, John Cranmer-Byng, MC; *Career* md Anvil Petroleum plc 1975–85, exec dir Flextech plc 1988–93, md Heritage Petroleum Corp (Canada) 1995–2000, dir Lansdowne Oil & Gas plc; chm Sub-Ctee F House of Lords Select Ctee on European Community 1984–87; *Recreations* travel and field sports; *Clubs* White's, Pratt's, Muthaiga (Nairobi); *Style*— The Rt Hon the Viscount Torrington

TORRY, HE Peter James; GCVO (2004), KCMG (2003); *b* 2 August 1948; *Educ* Dover Coll, New Coll Oxford; *m* 1979, Angela Wakeling, *née* Wood; 3 da; *Career* diplomat; entered HM Dip Serv 1970, third sec Havana 1971–74, second sec (economic) Jakarta 1974–77, first sec FCO 1977–81, first sec (political) Bonn 1981–85, first sec then cnsllr FCO 1985–89, cnsllr Washington DC 1989–93, dir for personnel and security FCO 1993–98, ambass to Spain 1998–2003, ambass to Germany 2003–07; *Recreations* golf, walking, ski-ing, books, antique furniture; *Style*— HE Sir Peter Torry, GCVO, KCMG; ✉ c/o Foreign & Commonwealth Office (Berlin), King Charles Street, London SW1A 2AH

TOSH, (Neil) Murray; MBE (1987), MSP; s of Neil Ferguson Tosh, of St Boswells, Roxburghshire, and Mary, *née* Murray; *b* 1 September 1950; *Educ* Kilmarnock Acad, Univ of Glasgow (MA), Jordanhill Coll of Educn (secdy teaching qualification in history); *m* Sept 1970, Christine; 2 s (Christopher b 1974, Nicholas b 1980), 1 da (Caroline b 1976); *Career* princ teacher of history: Kilwinning Acad 1977–84, Belmont Acad Ayr 1984–99; Parly candidate Glasgow Hillhead 1983; district cncllr Kyle & Carrick 1987–96 (convenor Housing Ctee, vice-convenor Planning & Devpt Ctee 1992–96); MSP (Cons): Scotland South 1999–2003, West of Scotland 2003–; Scot Parl: Cons spokesman on tport and the environment 1999–2001 and on tport and planning 2001, dep presiding offr 2001–, convenor Procedures Ctee 1999–2003, memb Subordinate Legislation Ctee 2003–; chm: Central Ayrshire Cons Unionist Assoc 1980–83, Ayr Cons & Unionist Assoc 1985–90; *Recreations* hill walking, reading (history, politics and biography), watching football, touring, visiting historic towns, castles, cathedrals and country houses; *Style*— Murray Tosh, Esq, MBE, MSP; ✉ The Scottish Parliament, Edinburgh EH99 1SP (tel 0131 348 5000, fax 0131 348 5932, e-mail murray.tosh.msp@scottish.parliament.uk)

TOSSWILL, (Timothy Maurice) Stephen; s of Timothy Dymond Tosswill (d 1991), and Sigrid, *née* Bohn (d 1985); *b* 28 April 1949; *Educ* Rugby, St Paul's, Univ of London (LLB, LLM); *Career* criminal lawyer, admitted slr 1976; princ Tosswill & Co 1985– (ptnr 1976–85), author of articles in legal periodicals and on the internet; MRIN; *Recreations* masterly inactivity; *Style*— Stephen Tosswill, Esq; ✉ 260 Brixton Hill, London SW2 1HP (tel 020 8674 9494, fax 020 8671 8987, e-mail tmst@criminallaw.co.uk)

TOTMAN, Edward Bartram; s of Edward Bartram Totman (d 1989), of Sutton, Surrey, and Joan Cecilia Mary, *née* McCamley; *b* 28 June 1942; *Educ* Wimbledon Coll, KCL (LLB); *m* 25 July 1970, Colette Maria, da of Vincent Aloysius Jackson (d 1962), of Cheam, Surrey; 1 s (Julian b 1971), 3 da (Marissa b 1973, Siobhan b 1976, Carmel b 1979); *Career* admitted slr 1970; articled clerk then slr GLC 1965–72, Abbey National Building Society 1972–74, Mercantile Credit Co Ltd 1974–79, ptnr D J Freeman 1981–2003 (joined 1979), conslt Olswang 2003–; memb Law Soc 1970; *Recreations* tennis, swimming, photography, reading; *Style*— Edward Totman, Esq; ✉ 21 St Margaret Drive, Epsom, Surrey KT18 7LB (tel 01372 739029); Olswang, 90 High Holborn, London WC1V 6XX (tel 020 7067 3636, fax 020 7067 3999, e-mail ted.totman@olswang.com)

TOUCHE, Sir Rodney Gordon; 2 Bt (UK 1962), of Dorking, Surrey; s of Rt Hon Sir Gordon Cosmo Touche, 1 Bt (d 1972); *b* 5 December 1928; *Educ* Marlborough, UC Oxford; *m* 30 April 1955, Ouida Ann, er da of late Frederick Gerald MacLellan, of Moncton, New Brunswick, Canada; 1 s, 3 da; *Heir* s, Eric Touche; *Style*— Sir Rodney Touche, Bt; ✉ 1100 8th Avenue (Apt 2403), Calgary, Alberta T2P 3T9, Canada (tel 00 1 403 233 8800, fax 00 1 403 233 8801, e-mail rtouche@telusplanet.net)

TOUHIG, Rt Hon (James) Donnelly (Don); PC (2006), MP; s of Michael Touhig (d 1982), and Agnes Catherine, *née* Corten; *b* 5 December 1947; *Educ* St Francis Sch, E Monmouth Coll; *m* 21 Sept 1968, Jennifer, da of Clifford Hughes; 2 s (Matthew b 24 Jan 1972, James b 19 April 1978), 2 da (Charlotte b 3 May 1975, Katie b 27 Sept 1983); *Career* apprentice radio and TV engr, journalist then ed; gen mangr newspaper gp, business devpt gp and printing company; MP (Lab) Islwyn 1995–; PPS to Chllr of the Exchequer 1997–99, govt whip 1999–2001, Parly under sec of state Wales Office 2001–05, Parly under sec MOD 2005–06; memb Select Ctee for: Welsh Affrs 1996–97, Public Accounts 2006; memb Leadership Campaign Team (responsible for devolution campaign in Wales) 1996–97; memb Lab Pty Departmental Ctee for: Home Affrs 1997–2001, Trade and Industry 1997–2001, Treasury 1997–2001, Health 1997–2001; hon sec Welsh Regnl Gp of Lab MPs 1995–99; memb Co-operative Pty, chair Co-operative Parly Gp 1999; *Recreations* reading, cooking for family and friends; *Style*— The Rt Hon Don Touhig, MP; ✉ Danydderwen, Aspen Avenue, Blackwood, Gwent NP12 1WW; Constituency Office, 6 Woodfieldside Business Park, Penmaen Road, Pontllanfraith, Blackwood, Gwent NP12 2DG (tel 01495 231990, fax 01495 231959); House of Commons, London SW1A 0AA (tel 020 7219 6435)

TOULMIN, His Hon Judge John Kelvin; CMG (1994), QC (1980); s of late Arthur Heaton (Mike) Toulmin (d 1994), of Reigate, Surrey, and late B Toulmin, *née* Fraser (d 1989); *b* 14 February 1941; *Educ* Winchester, Trinity Hall Cambridge (MA), Univ of Michigan Law Sch (LLM); *m* 13 May 1967, Carolyn Merton, da of Merton Gullick (d 1953); 1 s (Geoffrey b 1969), 2 da (Alison b 1972, Hilary b 1975); *Career* called to the Bar Middle Temple 1965 (bencher 1986); Western Circuit memb Bar Cncl/Senate 1971–77, 1978–81 and 1986–93, chm Young Barrs' Ctee 1973–75, chm Bar Int Practice Ctee 1987, memb Supreme Court Rules Ctee 1976–80, recorder of the Crown Court 1984–97, called to the Bar NI 1989, called to the Bar Irish Repub 1991, official referee 1997–98, judge of the Technol and Construction Court 1998–; UK delgn to Cncl of the Bars and Law Socs of Europe (CCBE) 1983–90 (ldr of the UK delgn 1987–90), pres CCBE 1993 (vice-pres 1991–92); tstee: ProCorda 1992–97, Europäische Rechtsakademie Trier 1993– (vice-chm 1994–97, chm of tstees 1997–); memb: CPR Int Arbitration and Conciliation Panel NY 1993–98, Disputes Settlement Panel WTO 1996–; chm Temple Music Tst 2002– (memb 1991–); govr The Maudsley and Bethlem Royal Hosps 1979–87, memb Ctee of Mgmnt Inst of Psychiatry 1982–2002 (chm 1999–2002); Univ of Michigan Law Sch: W W Bishop fell 1993, memb Bd of Visitors 1996–2006; memb Cncl KCL 1997–, FKC 2006; hon memb Law Soc of England and Wales 1994; Austrian Great Decoration for Merit 1995; *Books* DHSS report into Unnecessary Dental Treatment in NHS (co author, 1986), author of articles on rights of estab and recognition of diplomas in Europe, Butterworths Banking Encyclopaedia (ed European Law Section), Butterworths European Community Legal Systems (conslt ed, 1992), EFTA Legal Systems (conslt ed, 1993); *Recreations* cricket, listening to music, theatre, Burgundy; *Clubs* MCC, Pilgrims; *Style*— His Hon Judge John Toulmin, CMG, QC; ✉ Royal Courts of Justice, Technology and Construction Court, St Dunstan's House, 133–137 Fetter Lane, London EC4 1HD

TOULSON, Alan Kilsha; s of Stanley Kilsha Toulson (d 1992), of Redhill, Surrey, and Lilian Mary, *née* Picknell (d 1985); *b* 27 August 1942; *Educ* Mill Hill Sch, KCL (LLB); *m* 28 June 1969, Sarah, da of Noel Stanley Farrow; 2 da (Katie b 5 June 1971, Bonnie b 2 March 1980), 2 s (Sam b 27 Jan 1973, Luke b 17 Oct 1976); *Career* slr; Reynolds Porter Chamberlain: articled clerk 1964–66, ptnr 1966–2004, sr ptnr 1991–2004; memb Law Soc

1966–2004; chm Swedish C of C for UK 1996–99; chm of govrs St Clement Danes Sch 1985–95, tstee George Adamson Wildlife Preservation Tst 1988–; AKC; *Recreations* skiing, sailing, walking, school mgmnt; *Style—* Alan Toulson, Esq; ✉ Doggetts, Chipperfield, Hertfordshire WD4 9DJ (tel 01923 263413)

TOULSON, Lady; Elizabeth; CBE (1999); da of Henry Bertram Chrimes (d 1997), and Suzanne Corbett-Lowe (d 2000); *b* 10 November 1948; *Educ* Univ of Liverpool (LLB), Univ of Cambridge (Dip Comparative Law); *m* April 1973, Rt Hon Lord Justice Toulson, *qv*, s of Stanley Kilsha Toulson; 2 da (Susanna Jane b 4 Feb 1975, Rachel Elizabeth b 26 Feb 1977), 2 s (Henry Alexander b 4 Nov 1979, Thomas Grenfell b 8 April 1984); *Career* called to the Bar 1974; WRVS: tstee 1981, vice-chair 1989–93, chm 1993–99; govr: Charterhouse 1998–, Sutton's Hosp Charterhouse 2004–; dir Queen Elizabeth Fndn for the Disabled 1999–; chm: Children's Soc 2001–, Nykia-Vwaza Tst 2004, Time for Families 2006; FRSA 2006; *Recreations* skiing, tennis, walking, swimming, classical music; *Style—* Lady Toulson, CBE; ✉ Billhurst Farm, White Hart Lane, Wood Street Green, Surrey GU3 3DZ (tel 01483 235246, fax 01483 235347, mobile 07977 489256, e-mail elizabeth@toulsonfamily.co.uk); 201 Rowan House, 2 Greycoat Street, London SW1P 2QD (tel 020 7630 5325)

TOULSON, Rt Hon Lord Justice; Rt Hon Sir Roger Grenfell Toulson; kt (1996), PC (2007); s of Stanley Kilsha Toulson (d 1992), of Redhill, Surrey, and Lilian Mary Toulson (d 1985); *b* 23 September 1946; *Educ* Mill Hill Sch, Jesus Coll Cambridge (MA, LLB); *m* 28 April 1973, Elizabeth (Lady Toulson, CBE), *qv*, da of Henry Bertram Chrimes (d 1997), of Wirral, Merseyside; 2 da (Susanna b 1975, Rachel b 1977), 2 s (Henry b 1979, Thomas b 1984); *Career* called to the Bar Inner Temple 1969 (bencher 1995); QC 1986, recorder of the Crown Court 1987–96, judge of the High Court of Justice (Queen's Bench Div) 1996–2007, presiding judge Western Circuit 1997–2002, a Lord Justice of Appeal 2007–; chm Law Cmmn 2002–06, memb Judicial Appts Cmmn 2007–; Hon LLD UWE 2002; *Books* Confidentiality (with C M Phipps, 1996, 2 edn 2006); *Recreations* skiing, tennis, gardening; *Style—* The Rt Hon Lord Justice Toulson; ✉ Billhurst Farm, Wood Street Village, Surrey GU3 3DZ (tel 01483 235 246, fax 01483 235 347); Royal Courts of Justice, Strand, London WC2A 2LL

TOWERS, Dr David Anthony; s of George Thomas Towers (d 1970), of Winsford, Cheshire, and Joyce Leigh, *née* Sadler; *b* 27 May 1947; *Educ* Verdin GS Winsford Cheshire, Univ of Newcastle upon Tyne (BSc), Univ of Leeds (PhD); *m* 1, 8 Sept 1973 (m dis 1991), Lorna Mary, da of Samuel Hoole (d 1954), of Winsford, Cheshire; 2 s (Martin b 1968, Timothy b 1974), 1 da (Ailsa b 1976); m 2, 22 Oct 1994, Sandra Marie, da of Hubert Bott, of Ravensthorpe, Northamptonshire; *Career* temp lectr Univ of Sheffield 1973–74 (jr res fell 1971–73); Lancaster Univ: lectr 1974–88, sr lectr 1988–, head of mathematics 1989–95, assoc dean Faculty of Applied Sciences Undergraduate Training; res assoc Univ of Calif Berkeley 1978–79, various papers on algebra and mathematical educn; ed: Proceedings of Undergraduate Mathematics Teaching Conf Univ of Nottingham, Palgrave Guides Series in Mathematics; memb London Mathematical Soc 1972; *Books* Guide to Linear Algebra (1988); *Recreations* singing, opera, theatre, reading, DIY; *Style—* Dr David Towers; ✉ Department of Mathematics, Lancaster University, Lancaster LA1 4YF (tel 01524 593944, fax 01524 841710, telex 65111 LANCUL G, e-mail d.towers@lancaster.ac.uk)

TOWERS, John; CBE (1995); *b* 30 March 1948; *Educ* Durham Johnston Sch, Univ of Bradford (BTech(MechEng)); *m* Bethanie, *née* Williams; 1 da (Laura b 23 Sept 1980), 1 s (Michael b 30 Aug 1982); *Career* gen mangr Perkins Engines Ltd Peterborough 1985–86 (joined 1970), vice-pres Varity Corporation Ltd Toronto (formerly Massey-Ferguson, parent co of Perkins Engines) 1986–87, md Massey-Ferguson Tractors Ltd Coventry 1987–88; Rover Group: dir of mfrg and acting md Land Rover Ltd Solihull 1988–89, dir of product devpt Rover Group Ltd Coventry 1989–91, md product supply 1991–92, gp md 1992–94, chief exec 1994–96; chief exec Concentric plc 1996–, fndr dir HatWel Ltd (mgmnt consltss) 1996–, chm Serck Heat Transfer Group 1998–2000, chm MG Rover Group 2000–05; non-exec dir: Honda UK Ltd 1989–94, Midland Bank plc 1994–96, B Elliott plc 1996–98; memb Design Cncl; FIMechE, CEng, FIIM, FREng 1992; *Recreations* golf, squash, tennis, music; *Style—* John Towers, Esq, CBE, FREng

TOWERS, Jonathan Henry Nicholson; s of John Richard Hugh Towers, of Lund House, Harrogate, N Yorks, and Gwyneth Helen Marshall, *née* Nicholson; *b* 5 April 1939; *Educ* Radley, Clare Coll Cambridge (MA); *m* 29 Sept 1979, Vanessa Catherine, da of Francis John Milward, of Barlow Woodseats Hall, Derbys; 2 s (Edward b 1982, Harry b 1988); *Career* ptnr Grays slrs York 1967–98, sole practitioner 1998–; under sheriff Yorks and Hallamshire 1988–, hon treas Under Sheriffs' Assoc 1991–, hon treas The Shrievalty Assoc 2002–06 (hon sec 1995–2001); hon sec Nat Crimebeat 1997–2001 and 2004– (hon treas 2005–), past chm York Area Appeals Ctee for Mental Health; memb Law Soc 1966; pres The Yorkshire Law Soc 1996–97; *Recreations* golf, shooting, walking, reading, skiing; *Clubs* Leander (assoc), Bradford; *Style—* Jonathan Towers, Esq; ✉ West House, Nun Monkton, York YO26 8ER (tel 01423 330643, fax 01423 330264)

TOWERS, (William) Lennox; s of John Maxwell Towers (d 2001), and Betty, *née* Moody (d 1977); *b* 24 September 1946, Lennoxtown, Strathclyde; *Educ* Hutchesons' Boys' GS Glasgow, Leeds GS, Univ of Exeter (LLB); *m* 1972, Jan, *née* Morrill; 2 s (Alex b 1977, Edmund b 1985), 1 da (Frankie b 1980); *Career* ptnr Booth & Co Slrs Leeds (later Addleshaw Booth & Co) 1974–2003 (managing ptnr 1993–94), conslt Addleshaw Goddard LLP 2004–; NP 1979–; memb Law Soc; *Recreations* sailing, walking, family pursuits; *Style—* Lennox Towers, Esq; ✉ Addleshaw Goddard LLP, Sovereign House, Sovereign Street, Leeds LS1 1HQ (tel 0113 209 2026, e-mail lennox.towers@addleshawgoddard.com)

TOWILL, Prof Denis Royston; *b* 28 April 1933; *Educ* Univ of Bristol (BSc), Univ of Birmingham (MSc, DSc); *m* 27 March 1961, Christine Ann Forrester; 1 da (Rachel b 22 Dec 1962), 2 s (Jonathan b 2 Dec 1964, Edwin b 17 May 1970); *Career* engr; dynamic analyst Br Aerospace Weston/Filton 1957–59, conslt Norris Consultants Bristol 1959–62; subsequently: sr lectr RMCS Shrivenham, prof and head of dept UWIST Cardiff (reader 1966–69, prof 1970–87); prof and head Sch of Electrical, Electronic and Systems Engrg Univ of Wales Coll of Cardiff 1988–92, Univ of Wales Lucas research prof 1992–; memb Exec Cmmn to oversee formation of Univ of Wales Coll of Cardiff 1987–88; served on various SERC, Technol Foresight, IFAC and Royal Acad of Engrg ctees, memb IEE Cncl (chm IEE Mgmnt and Design Bd 1990–91); distinguished overseas scientist fell of Eta Kapa Nu 1978; Clerk Maxwell Langham Thompson and McMichael premiums IERE, Lord Hirst premium IEE; MIProdE 1964, FIEE 1972, FREng 1988; *Books* Transfer Function Techniques for Control Engineers (1970), Coefficient Plane Models for Control System Analysis and Design (1981), Systems Approach to AMT Deployment (1993); *Recreations* music, sport; *Clubs* Bristol Rovers Presidents, Glamorgan CC, Radyr CC (vice-pres); *Style—* Prof Denis R Towill, FREng; ✉ Logistics Systems Dynamics Group, Cardiff Business School, Cardiff University, Aberconway Building, Colum Drive Cardiff CF10 3EU (tel 029 2087 6083, fax 029 2084 2292)

TOWLE, Bridget Ellen; CBE (2001); da of William Henry Towle (d 2001), of Barrow upon Soar, Leics, and Marjorie Louisa, *née* Hardstaff (d 1987); *b* 19 April 1942; *Educ* Westonbirt Sch, Univ of Exeter (BA), Leicester Poly/de Montfort Univ (post grad courses in Textile Technol and Business Mgmnt); *Career* teacher VSO Uganda 1965–66; Towles plc: mgmnt trainee 1966–67, mktg mgmnt roles 1967–94, dir 1972–94, jt md 1980–94; The Guide Assoc: various local appts incl county cmmr Leics 1985–92, chief cmmr of the Cwlth 1996–2001, the chief guide 1996–2001; vice-pres Girlguiding UK 2003–; memb Cncl: Univ of Leicester 2000–, Coll of Optometrists 2004–; tstee RAF Benevolent Fund 2005–; Hon LLD Univ of Exeter 2000, Hon DLitt Loughborough Univ 2002; FRSA 1999; *Recreations* decorative arts, walking; *Style—* Miss Bridget Towle, CBE

TOWLER, Peter Jeremy Hamilton; s of Stuart Hamilton-Towler, MBE (d 2002), and Betty Irene, *née* Hardwidge; *b* 21 March 1952; *Educ* Peter Symonds Sch (now Peter Symonds Coll) Winchester, Clare Coll Cambridge (MA); *m* 15 Sept 1979, Dr Martha Crellin, da of Norman Langdon-Down (d 1991), of Shepperton-on-Thames, Middx; 1 s, 1 da; *Career* called to the Bar Middle Temple 1974 (Harmsworth scholar); recorder (Western Circuit) 1997–; memb: Western Circuit 1976– (memb Circuit and Wine Ctee 1990–96), Planning and Environment Bar Assoc 1988–; legal examiner Diocese of Winchester 1994–; fndr memb and chm Ampfield Conservation Tst 1988–92 (pres 1992–99); chm Stroud Sch Assoc 1993–95, memb Ctee Hants CCC 1999–, chm Rose Bowl Appeal 2001–02, chm Howzat Appeal 2003–; Freeman City of London 1982, Liveryman Worshipful Co of Weavers 1982; FCIArb 1994 (ACIArb 1984); *Recreations* cricket, reading, conservation; *Clubs* MCC, Hants CCC; *Style—* Peter Towler, Esq; ✉ 17 Carlton Crescent, Southampton SO15 2XR (tel 023 8032 0320, fax 023 8032 0321)

TOWNEND, James Barrie Stanley; QC (1978); s of Frederick Stanley Townend (d 1967), of Deal, Kent, and Marjorie Elizabeth, *née* Arnold (d 1991); *b* 21 February 1938; *Educ* Tonbridge, Lincoln Coll Oxford (MA); *m* 20 June 1970 (m dis 2005), Airelle Claire, da of Hermann Dail Nies, of Wimbledon; 1 step da (Pascale Jéhanne Lucie Howe); *Career* Nat Serv in BAOR and UK 1955–57, Lt RA; called to the Bar Middle Temple 1962 (bencher 1987), recorder of the Crown Court 1979–2003, head of chambers 1982–99; memb: Kingston and Esher DHA 1983–86, Senate of the Inns of Court and Bar 1984–86, Gen Cncl of the Bar 1984–88; chm: Family Law Bar Assoc 1986–88, Supreme Court Procedure Ctee 1986–88; legal assessor to: GMC 1999–, GDC 1999–, GCC 2001–; asst boundary cmmr 2000–; *Recreations* fishing, sailing, writing verse; *Style—* James Barrie Stanley Townend, QC; ✉ 1 King's Bench Walk, Temple, London EC4Y 7DB (tel 020 7936 1500, fax 020 7936 1590, e-mail jtqcdeal@aol.com)

TOWNEND, John Coupe; s of Harry Norman Townend (d 1988), of Sherborne, Dorset, and Joyce Dentith, *née* Coupe; *b* 24 August 1947; *Educ* Liverpool Inst, LSE (BSc, MSc); *m* 15 March 1969, Dorothy, da of David William Allister (d 1971); 3 s (Andrew, Jonathan, Christopher); *Career* Bank of England: joined 1968, head of Wholesale Mkts Supervision Div 1986–90, head Gilt-Edged and Money Mkts Div 1990–94, dep dir 1994–98, dir for Europe 1999–, ed Practical Issues Arising from the Euro; former contrib articles to various economic jls; *Recreations* running, fell walking, opera, birds; *Style—* John Townend, Esq; ✉ Bank of England, Threadneedle Street, London EC2R 8AH

TOWNEND, Richard Frank Stuart; s of Col H Stuart Townend (d 2002), and Beatrice May, *née* Lord; *b* 15 July 1942; *Educ* Westminster, Univ of Lausanne, Royal Coll of Music, Academie d'Orgue Romainmôtier Switzerland; *m* 1970, Janet Elaine, da of James Gibson; 2 s (William b 19 Jan 1974, Edmund b 4 March 1977); *Career* organist; resident recitalist St Margaret Lothbury, specialising in Renaissance and Baroque repertoire; given recitals throughout Europe incl Int Organ Festival Switzerland (first English musician so invited), numerous broadcasts and recordings; headmaster and owner Hill House Int Junior Sch; sometime visiting lectr Int Organ Acad St Vith Belgium, Fachakademie für Evangelische Kirchenmusik Bayreuth Germany; fell Lancashire Sch of Music, fell Guild of Musicians and Singers, hon fell Acad of St Cecilia; memb Royal Soc of Musicians; Master Worshipful Co of Parish Clerics 2007–08; *Clubs* Savage, National; *Style—* Richard Townend, Esq; ✉ Hill House, 17 Hans Place, London SW1X 0EP (tel 020 7584 1331, fax 020 7589 1206, e-mail r.townend@orange.net)

TOWNSEND, (John) Anthony Victor; s of John Richard Christopher Townsend (d 1996), of Kintbury, Berks, and Carla Hillerns, *née* Lehmann (d 1990); *b* 24 January 1948; *Educ* Harrow, Selwyn Coll Cambridge (MA); *m* 16 April 1971, Carolyn Ann, da of Sir Walter Salomon (d 1987); 1 s (Christopher b 26 Feb 1974), 1 da (Alexandra b 26 Feb 1976); *Career* with Brown Shipley & Co Ltd bankers 1969–74, Rea Brothers Ltd bankers 1974–78, John Townsend & Co (Holdings) Ltd 1979–87, Finsbury Asset Management Ltd (investment banking) 1988–98; chm: British and American Investment Tst plc, Iimia Investment Tst plc, Ukraine Opportunity Tst plc until 2007; dir: Finsbury Technology Tst plc, Finsbury Growth Tst plc, Finsbury Worldwide Pharmaceutical Tst plc, BRIT Insurance Holdings plc, F&C Global Smaller Cos plc; chm Assoc of Investment Tst Cos 2001–03; chm of govrs Cranleigh Sch, chm of tstees Harrow Mission; Past Master Worshipful Co of Pattenmakers; FRSA; *Recreations* tennis, shooting, skiing; *Clubs* City of London, RAC; *Style—* Anthony Townsend, Esq; ✉ The Coach House, Winterfold, Barhatch Lane, Cranleigh, Surrey GU6 7NH (tel 01483 271366); 22 Donne Place, London SW3 2NH (tel 020 7589 9856, fax 020 7589 2144, e-mail anthonytownsend@dsl.pipex.com)

TOWNSEND, Brig Ian Glen; CBE (2005); s of Kenneth Townsend, of Leamington Spa, Warks, and Irene Dorothy, *née* Singleton; *b* 7 February 1941; *Educ* Dulwich Coll, RMA Sandhurst, Staff Coll; *m* 1, 19 Sept 1964 (m dis 1988), Loraine Jean, da of William A H Birnie (d 1978), of USA; 2 da (Lucie, Helen (twins) b 1966); m 2, 17 Feb 1989, Susan Natalie, da of Cdr Frank A L Heron-Watson (d 1990), of Scotland; 2 step s (Anthony b 1965, Ben b 1969); *Career* regtl and staff appts in UK, Germany, NI, Belgium 1961–91 incl: mil asst to UK Mil Rep NATO HQ 1979–81, CO 27 Field Regt RA 1981–83, Col operational requirements MOD 1983–86, Cdr artillery 1 Armd Div 1986–88, ACOS (Trg) HQ UKLF 1988–91, ret 1991; dir mktg and sales VSEL 1991–93, md Townsend Associates 1993–96, dir Legion Enterprise Ltd 1999–2001, dir NMA Enterprise 2003–; dir Tidworth Coll 1999–2001, govr Salisbury Coll 2001–03; DG Royal Br Legion 1996–2006, dir 7 Armd Div Memorial Ltd 2000, dir Nat Memorial Arboretum 2003–, tstee Armed Forces Memorail Tst 2003–; chm: Confedn Serv and Ex-Service Orgns 2002–03, World Veterans Fedn Europe 2002–; vice-pres World Veterans' Fedn 2006–; Freeman City of London 1999; CCMI (FIMgt 1988), FRSA 2006; *Recreations* gardening, golf, painting, music, wine; *Clubs* Army and Navy, Royal Over-Seas League; *Style—* Brig Ian Townsend, CBE; ✉ Airleywight, Stapleford, Wiltshire SP3 4LJ

TOWNSEND, Jonathan Richard Arthur; s of David Charles Humphrey Townsend (d 1997), and Honor Stobart, *née* Hancock (d 1967); *b* 30 November 1942; *Educ* Winchester, CCC Oxford (BA); *m* Sarah Elizabeth, da of Cdr Gordon Chalmers Fortin, RN, of Lavenham, Suffolk; 2 da (Honor Sarah b 2 Sept 1968, Louise Rosamond b 12 March 1971); *Career* prodn mangr DRG plc 1961–62 and 1965–68; ptnr: Laing and Cruickshank 1972–73 (joined 1968), de Zoete and Bevan 1973–86; md Barclays de Zoete Securities 1986–90, dir i/c business devpt Kleinwort Benson 1990–93, vice-chm ABN AMRO Hoare Govett Corporate Finance Ltd 1993–98, ind conslt 1998–2003, dir John East and Partners 2004–; *Recreations* my girls, Italy, opera, shooting, bridge, cricket; *Clubs* Brooks's, MCC, Vincent's (Oxford); *Style—* Jonathan Townsend, Esq; ✉ Buxhall Vale, Buxhall, Stowmarket, Suffolk IP14 3DH (tel 01449 736032, e-mail jrat@btopenworld.com)

TOWNSEND, Lady Juliet Margaret; *née* Smith; LVO (1981); da of 2 Earl of Birkenhead, TD (d 1975); *b* 9 September 1941; *Educ* Westonbirt Sch, Somerville Coll Oxford; *m* 1970, John Richard Townsend, s of Lt-Col Clarence Henry Southgate Townsend, OBE, MC, TD, MRCVS (d 1953); 3 da; *Career* lady-in-waiting to HRH The Princess Margaret, Countess of Snowdon 1965–71, extra lady-in-waiting 1971–2002; High Sheriff of Northamptonshire 1991–92, HM Lord-Lt Northamptonshire 1998– (DL 1990); *Style—* The Lady Juliet Townsend, LVO; ✉ Newbottle Manor, Banbury, Oxfordshire OX17 3DD (tel 01295 811295)

T

TOWNSEND, Michael; s of Edgar Maurice Townsend (d 1985), and Agnes, *née* Pearson (d 1988); *b* 10 June 1941; *Educ* Harrogate GS, Sidney Sussex Coll Cambridge (minor scholar, MA); *m* 1966, Gillian Maryska, da of Wilfred Dorrien Wickson (d 1992); 3 s (Alistair John b 3 Sept 1970, Christopher James b 1 Dec 1972, Jonathan Mark b 13 Nov 1975); *Career* articled clerk Blackburns Robson Coates CAs (now Robson Rhodes) Leeds 1963–69, various posts rising to fin controller Sperry Gyroscope Ltd Bracknell 1969–75, fin controller Plessey Radar Ltd 1975–79, gp fin controller Smiths Industries plc 1988–90 (fin controller Smiths Industries Aerospace Defence Systems 1979–88); Rolls-Royce plc: gp fin controller 1990–91, fin dir 1991–99; non-exec chm Spirax-Sarco Engineering plc 2005– (non-exec dir 1997–); non-exec dir Northern Electric plc 1992–97; sec Irish Setter Assoc England 1995–2001, chm of tstees Kennel Club Charitable Tst 2002– (tstee 1998–, memb Gen Ctee 2002–); FCA 1976 (ACA 1966); *Recreations* cricket, all ball games, dogs (especially Irish Setters), canals; *Clubs* Kennel; *Style*— Michael Townsend, Esq; ✉ Hawthorns, Oakley Road, Cheltenham, Gloucestershire GL52 6NZ (tel and fax 01242 521872, e-mail townsend@waitrose.com)

TOWNSEND, Michael John; OBE (2003); s of John Townsend, of Herefords, and Kathleen, *née* Barnes; *b* 12 July 1957; *Educ* Lord Williams Sch Thame, Univ of North Wales Bangor (BSc); *m* 15 June 1991, Amanda Rosina, da of Peter Adkins; 2 s (George Frederick James b 25 March 1993, Henry John Peter b 6 Feb 1995); *Career* project leader Christian Children's Fund Sponsorship Programme Kenya 1980–83, regnl mangr Economic Forestry Gp UK 1986–92, Michael Townsend Forestry & Landscapes 1992–95; Woodland Tst: ops dir 1995–97, chief exec 1997–2004, currently special advsr; FICFor 1986; *Recreations* cooking, walking, gardening; *Style*— Michael Townsend, Esq, OBE; ✉ The Woodland Trust, Autumn Park, Dysart Road, Grantham, Lincolnshire NG31 6LL (tel 01476 581111, fax 01475 590808)

TOWNSEND, Prof Peter Brereton; s of Flt Lt Philip Brereton Townsend (d 1991), of Scotton, N Yorks, and Alice Mary, *née* Southcote (d 1995); *b* 6 April 1928; *Educ* Univ Coll Sch, St John's Coll Cambridge (BA), Free Univ Berlin; *m* 1, 18 June 1949 (m dis 1974), Ruth, *née* Pearce; 4 s (Matthew b 1952, Adam b 1953, Christian b 1957, Benjamin b 1962); m 2, 14 June 1976 (m dis 1980), Joy, *née* Skegg; 1 da (Lucy b 1976); m 3, 4 Jan 1985, Baroness Corston, PC (Life Peer), *qv*, da of Laurie Parkin, of Yeovil; *Career* RASC and RAEC 1946–48; res sec Political and Econ Planning 1952–54, res offr Inst of Community Studies Bethnal Green 1954–57, res fell (later lectr) LSE 1957–63, prof of sociology Univ of Essex 1963–81 (pro-vice-chllr 1975–78), prof of social policy Univ of Bristol 1982–93 (emeritus 1993–); distinguished visiting Michael Harrington prof of social science (International Poverty) City Univ of NY 1991–92, visiting prof of Int Social Policy LSE 1998–99, prof Int Social Policy 1999–, acting dir Centre for the Study of Human Rights 2001–02; conslt to: UN 1993–95, UN Devpt Prog 1994–96, EU 1998; min Foreign Affairs Denmark 1997–2000; chm: Child Poverty Action Gp 1969–89 (pres 1989–), Disability Alliance 1974–99 (pres 1999–), Channel 4 Poverty Cmmn 1996, Nat Steering Gp Review of Allocation of NHS Resources Nat Assembly for Wales 2000–01, chair Standing Ctee on the Allocation of NHS Resources Nat Assembly for Wales 2002–; former pres Psychiatric Rehabilitation Assoc 1967–85, pres Mencap SW region 1990–93, pt/t govt advsr and consl t; memb: Exec Ctee Fabian Soc 1958–89 (chm 1965–66, vice-pres 1989–), Chief Scientist's Ctee DHSS 1976–79, Res Working Gp on Inequalities in Health 1977–80, Br Sociological Assoc 1961–, Social Policy Assoc 1978–; Hon DUniv Essex 1990, Hon DLitt Univ of Teesside 1994, Hon Dr Open Univ 1995, Hon DSci Univ of Edinburgh 1996, Hon DArts Univ of Lincolnshire and Humberside 1997, Hon DUniv York 2000, Hon DUniv Stirling 2002, Hon DSocSci Baptist Univ of Hong Kong 2005, Hon DLitt Nat Univ of Ireland 2006; AcSS 1999, sr fell Br Acad 2004; *Books* incl: Cambridge Anthology (ed, 1952), The Family Life of Old People (1957), The Last Refuge: A Survey of Residential Institutions and Homes for the Aged in England and Wales (1962), The Poor and Poorest (with Brian Abel-Smith, 1965), The Aged in the Welfare State (with Dorothy Wedderburn, 1965), Old People in Three Industrial Societies (with Ethel Shanas and others, 1968), The Concept of Poverty (ed, 1970), The Social Minority (1973), Disability Rights Handbook (jtly, 1976–84), Sociology and Social Policy (1975), Poverty in the United Kingdom (1979), Inequalities in Health (with Sir Douglas Black and others, 1980), Disability in Britain (with Alan Walker, 1982), Responses to Poverty: Lessons from Europe (with Roger Lawson and Robert Walker, 1984), Health and Deprivation: Inequality and the North (with Peter Phillimore and Alastair Beattie 1987), Poverty and Labour in London (with Paul Corrigan and Ute Kowarzik, 1987), Inequalities in Health: The Black Report and the Health Divide (ed with Margaret Whitehead and Nick Davidson, 1982, revised 1988 and 1992), The International Analysis of Poverty (1993), A Poor Future: Can We Counter Growing Poverty in Britain and Across the World? (1996), Poverty and Social Exclusion in Britain (jtly, 2000), Breadline Europe: The Measurement of Poverty (with David Gordon, 2000), Targeting Poor Health (2001), World Poverty: New Policies to Defeat an Old Enemy (2002), Child Poverty in the Developing World (report to UNICEF, jtly, 2003), Inequalities in Health: The Welsh Dimension (2005), Social Security: Building Decent Societies (ed, 2007); *Recreations* athletics, gardening; *Style*— Prof Peter Townsend; ✉ Department of Social Policy, London School of Economics and Political Science, Houghton Street, London WC2A 2AE (tel 020 7955 6632); c/o School for Policy Studies, University of Bristol, 8 Priory Road, Bristol BS8 1TZ (tel 0117 954 6771)

TOWNSEND, Dr Ralph Douglas; s of Harry Douglas Townsend, of Perth, Aust, and Neila Margaret, *née* McPherson; *b* 13 December 1951, Perth, Aust; *Educ* Scotch Coll Aust, Univ of Western Aust (Cwlth scholar, BA), Univ of Kent (MA), Keble Coll Oxford (sr scholar, DPhil); *m* 25 Aug 1973, Cathryn Julie, *née* Arnold; 1 da (Elspeth Mary b 24 March 1983), 1 s (Francis Harry b 12 Dec 1984); *Career* asst master Dover Coll 1975–77, asst master Abingdon Sch 1977–78, warden St Gregory's House Oxford 1978–82, research fell and dean of degrees Lincoln Coll Oxford 1982–85, asst master and head of Eng Eton Coll 1985–89, headmaster Sydney GS 1989–99, headmaster Oundle 1999–2005, headmaster Winchester Coll 2005–; author of two books on Christian spirituality and of numerous articles and reviews, gen ed Studies in Early Australian History and Letters 1995–99; Hon Liveryman Grocers' Co 2005; *Recreations* music, reading, fell walking; *Clubs* Australian (Sydney), East India; *Style*— Dr Ralph Townsend; ✉ Witham Close, 62 Kingsgate Street, Winchester, Hampshire SO23 9PF (fax 01962 832865); Winchester College, College Street, Winchester, Hampshire SO23 9NA (tel 01962 621105, e-mail hm@wincoll.ac.uk)

TOWNSEND, Susan (Sue); *b* 2 April 1946; *Educ* South Wigston Girls' HS; *Career* author and playwright; joined Writers Group Phoenix Arts Centre 1978 (winner Thames Television Bursary as writer in residence for Womberang); FRSL 1993; *Books* The Secret Diary of Adrian Mole aged 13 3/4, The Growing Pains of Adrian Mole, The True Confessions of Adrian Albert Mole, Margaret Hilda Roberts and Susan Lilian Townsend (1989), Rebuilding Coventry (1988), The Secret Diary of Adrian Mole aged 13 3/4 - The Play, Bazaar and Rummage, Groping for Words, Womberang: Three Plays by Sue Townsend, Great Celestial Cow (1984), Mr Bevan's Dream, The Queen and I (1992), Adrian Mole: The Wilderness Years (1994), Ghost Children (1997), Adrian Mole: The Cappucino Years (1999), Number Ten (2002), Queen Camilla (2006); *Plays* Womberang (Soho Poly) 1979, The Ghost of Daniel Lambert (Phoenix Arts Centre and Leicester Haymarket Theatre) 1981, Dayroom (Croydon Warehouse Theatre) 1981, Captain Christmas and the Evil Adults (Phoenix Arts Centre) 1982, Bazaar and Rummage (Royal Court Theatre Upstairs) 1982, Groping for Words (Croydon Warehouse Theatre) 1983, The Great Celestial Cow (Royal Court Theatre and tour) 1984, Ten Tiny Fingers, Nine Tiny Toes (Library Theatre Manchester) 1989, Ear Nose and Throat (Arts Theatre Cambridge) 1988, Disneyland it Ain't (Royal Court Theatre Upstairs) 1989, Queen and I (Vaudeville Theatre London) 1994; *Television* incl: contrib Revolting Women (BBC, 1981), Bazaar and Rummage (BBC, 1983), The Secret Diary of Adrian Mole (Thames TV, 1985), The Growing Pains of Adrian Mole (Thames TV, 1987), The Refuge (Channel 4, 1987); *Recreations* reading, looking at pictures, canoeing; *Style*— Ms Sue Townsend, FRSL

TOWNSHEND, Prof Alan; s of Dr Stanley Charles Townshend (d 2000), of Ammanford, Carms, and Betsy, *née* Roberts (d 2001); *b* 20 June 1939; *Educ* Pontadawe GS, Univ of Birmingham (BSc, PhD, DSc); *m* 11 Aug 1962, Enid, da of Harold Horton (d 1990), of South Kirkby, W Yorks; 3 s (Robert Michael b 1966, Peter Charles b 1967, Gareth Richard b 1970); *Career* lectr in chemistry Univ of Birmingham 1964–80; Univ of Hull: sr lectr then reader in analytical chemistry 1980–84, prof 1984–2004, dean Sch of Chemistry 1989–92 and 1997, dir Inst for Chemistry in Industry 1993–96 and 1999–, dep dean Faculty of Sci and the Environment 1997–2000, dep dean Faculty of Sci 2000–01, emeritus prof 2004–; Royal Soc of Chemistry Silver medal 1975 (Gold medal 1991), AnalaR Gold medal 1987, Geoff Wilson medal Deakin Univ Aust 2003; Theophilus Redwood lectr 1988; memb Analytical Div Ctee Int Union of Pure and Applied Chemistry 1991–95, pres Analytical Div Royal Soc of Chemistry 1996–98; CChem, FRSC 1978; *Books* Inorganic Reaction Chemistry: Systematic Chemical Separation (1980), Inorganic Reaction Chemistry: Reactions of the Elements and their Compounds Part A: Alkali Metals to Nitrogen (1981), Inorganic Reaction Chemistry: Reactions of the Elements and their Compounds Part B: Osmium to Zirconium (1981), Dictionary of Analytical Reagents (1993), Flame Chemiluminescence Analysis by Molecular Emission Cavity Detection (1994), Encyclopedia of Analytical Science (10 vols, ed-in-chief, 1995, 2 edn 2004), Analytica Chimica Acta (sr ed); *Recreations* walking, food and wine; *Style*— Prof Alan Townshend; ✉ Department of Chemistry, University of Hull, Hull HU6 7RX (tel 01482 465457, fax 01482 470225, e-mail a.townshend@hull.ac.uk)

TOWNSHEND, Lady Carolyn Elizabeth Ann; da of 7 Marquess Townshend, *qv*; *b* 27 September 1940; *Educ* Univ of Florence; *m* 13 Oct 1962 (m dis 1971), Antonio Capellini; 1 s (Vincenzo Charles Capellini Townshend); *Career* international special event mgmnt; md Carolyn Townshend & Associates; FRSA, FInstD; *Recreations* theatre, painting, film, music; *Style*— The Lady Carolyn Townshend; ✉ 73 Cranmer Court, Whiteheads Grove, Chelsea, London SW3 3HJ (tel 020 7584 3542, e-mail carolyn.townshend@btopenworld.com, website www.ladycarolyntownshend.co.uk)

TOWNSHEND, Hon Charlotte Anne; DL (Dorset 1999); da of 9 Viscount Galway (d 1971), and Lady Teresa Agnew, *née* Fox-Strangways (d 1989); *b* 16 April 1955, London; *m* 1, 1983 (m dis 1987), Guy Martin James Morrison; 1 s (Simon George Strangways b 1984); m 2, 1995, James Reginald Townshend; 1 da (Melissa Susan Charlotte b 1996); *Career* High Sheriff Dorset 2005–06; *Style*— The Hon Mrs Townshend; ✉ Melbury House, Melbury Sampford, Dorchester, Dorset DT2 0LF (tel 01935 83231, fax 01935 83959, e-mail melbury.house@ilchester-estate.co.uk)

TOWNSHEND, 7 Marquess (GB 1787); Sir George John Patrick Dominic Townshend; 11 Bt (E 1617); also Baron Townshend of Lynn Regis (E 1661) and Viscount Townshend of Raynham (E 1682); s of 6 Marquess (d 1921) whose forebear, 1 Marquess and Field Marshal commanded the field of Quebec after the death of Gen Wolfe; *b* 13 May 1916; *Educ* Harrow; *m* 1, 1939 (m dis 1960), Elizabeth Pamela Audrey (d 1989), da of Maj Thomas Luby; 1 s, 2 da (one of whom Lady Carolyn Townshend, *qv*); m 2, 1960, Ann Frances (d 1988), da of late Arthur Pellew Darlow; 1 s, 1 da; m 3, 2004, Mrs Philippa Sophia Swire, da of Col George Jardine Kidston-Montgomerie of Southannan, DSO, MC, DL; *Heir* s, Viscount Raynham; *Career* Norfolk Yeomanry 1936–40, Scots Gds 1940–45; chm: Anglia TV Ltd 1958–86, Anglia TV Group plc 1976–86, Survival Anglia Ltd 1971–86, AP Bank Ltd 1975–87, London Merchant Securities plc 1964–95, Raynham Farm Co Ltd 1957–, Norfolk Agric Station 1973–87 (pres 1987–); dir: Norwich Union Life Insurance Society Ltd 1950–86 (vice-chm 1973–86), Norwich Union Fire Insurance Society Ltd 1950–86 (vice-chm 1975–86), Riggs National Corporation 1987–89; pres Morley Agricultural Fndn 1987; DL Norfolk 1951–61; Hon DCL UEA 1989; FRSA 1990; *Clubs* White's, MCC, Norfolk, Pilgrims; *Style*— The Most Hon the Marquess Townshend; ✉ Raynham Hall, Fakenham, Norfolk NR21 7EP (tel 01328 862133)

TOWNSHEND, Peter (Pete); s of Cliff Townshend; *b* 19 May 1945; *Educ* Acton Co GS, Ealing Art Coll; *m* 1968, Karen Astley; 1s, 2 da; *Career* musician; memb: The Detours 1961–63, The High Numbers (released single I'm The Face 1964) 1963–64, The Who 1964–89, solo 1979–; albums with The Who: My Generation (1965, reached UK no 5), A Quick one (1966, UK no 4), The Who Sell Out (1968, UK no 13), Tommy (1969, UK no 2, Broadway musical 1993, winner 5 Tony awards, revived London 1996), Live At Leeds (live, 1970, UK no 3), Who's Next (1971, UK no 1), Meaty Beaty Big And Bouncy (compilation, 1971, UK no 9), Quadrophenia (1973, UK no 2), Odds And Sods (compilation, 1974, UK no 10), Tommy (soundtrack, 1975, UK no 14), The Who By Numbers (1975, UK no 7), The Story Of The Who (compilation, 1976, UK no 2), Who Are You? (1978, UK no 6), The Kids Are Alright (compilation, 1979, UK no 26), Quadrophenia (soundtrack, 1979, UK no 23), Face Dances (1981, UK no 2), It's Hard (1982, UK no 11), Who's Last (1984, UK no 48), Who's Better, Who's Best (1988, UK no 10), Joined Together (1990), 30 Years of Maximum R&B (1994); solo albums: Who Came First (1972, UK no 30), Rough Mix (with Ronnie Lane, 1977, UK no 44), Empty Glass (1980, UK no 11), All The Best Cowboys Have Chinese Eyes (1982, UK no 32), Scoop (1983), White City (1985, UK no 70), Scoop II (1987), The Iron Man (1989, London musical at Young Vic 1993), Psychoderelict (1993), Best of Pete Townshend (1996); appearances at festivals incl: National Jazz and Blues Festival 1965, 1966 and 1969, Monterey Pop Festival 1967, Rock at the Oval 1972, Farewell Tour 1982–83, Live Aid Wembley 1985, Who Reunion Tour 1989; films incl: Tommy, Quadrophenia, The Kids Are Alright; publisher; owner Eel Pie Recording Ltd 1972–; fndr: Eel Pie (bookshops and publishing) 1972–83, Meher Baba Oceanic (UK archival library) 1976–81; ed Faber & Faber 1983–; *Awards* Ivor Novello Award for Contribution to Br Music 1982, Br Phonographic Industry Award 1983, BRIT Lifetime Achievement Award 1983, BRIT Award for Contribution to Br Music 1988, Living Legend Award Int Rock Awards 1991, Tony Award for Tommy score 1993, Grammy Award for Tommy 1993, Dora Mavor Moore Award for Tommy in Toronto 1994, Olivier Award for Tommy in London 1997, Q Award for Lifetime Achievement 1997, Ivor Novello Lifetime Achievement Award 2001, BMI President's Award 2002, PRS Awards for CSI and CSI Miami 2004, Silver Clef 30th Anniversary Award for The Who 2005; *Books* Horses Neck (1985); *Style*— Pete Townshend, Esq; ✉ c/o Trinifold Management, 12 Oval Road, London NW1 7DH (tel 020 7419 4300, fax 020 7419 4325, website www.petetownshend.com and www.eelpie.com)

TOWNSLEY, Barry Stephen; CBE (2004); s of Dr William Townsley; *b* 14 October 1946; *Educ* Hasmonean GS; *m* 3 Nov 1975, Hon Laura Helen, da of Baron Wolfson of Marylebone (Life Peer); 3 da (Alexandra Jane Wolfson b 3 May 1977, Georgina Kate Wolfson b 26 May 1979, Isabella Edith Wolfson b 22 June 1994), 1 s (Charles Ralph Wolfson b 2 June 1984); *Career* W Greenwell & Co 1964–69; dir Astaire & Co 1969–76; fndr and sr ptnr Townsley & Co 1976–99, chm Insinger Townsley 1999–2004, dir Bank Insinger de Beaufort plc 1999–2004, chm Dawnay, Day Capital Markets 2006–; vice-pres Weizmann Inst Fndn, fndr memb and princ sponsor Stockley Acad; vice-chm and tstee Serpentine Gallery London; *Recreations* contemporary art, golf; *Style*— Barry Townsley,

Esq, CBE; ✉ Dawnay, Day Capital Markets, 8–10 Grosvenor Gardens, London SW1W 0DH (e-mail barry.townsley@dawnayday.com)

TOY, Carol Margaret (Maggie); da of Dr Mark Toy, and Patricia Beryl Toy; *Educ* Marple Hall Co HS Cheshire, Portsmouth Poly (BA, Postgrad Dip); partner Tim Forster; 2 s (Hector Cavanagh Forster-Toy b 8 Oct 2002, Arthur Cavanagh Forster-Toy b 7 Dec 2004); *Career* architectural asst Moxham Clark Partnership Manchester 1982, architectural asst Derek Arend Associates London 1986–87; asst Academy Editions 1988; Academy Gp Ltd: house ed Architectural Design Magazine 1989–92 (ed 1993–2002), commissioning and managing ed 1993–97, sr publishing ed of Architecture 1997–2003; fndr The Toy Factory 2006; delivered numerous lectures and chaired architecture debates; exhibitions curated incl: Theory and Experimentation 1991, Architecture on the Horizon 1996; co-fndr Magpip; *Publications* Deconstruction: A Pocket Guide (jtly, 1990), Free Spirit in Architecture (jtly, 1992), Los Angeles (1994), Educating Architects (jt ed, 1995), Building Sights (jt ed, 1995), Practically Minimal (2000), The Architect (2001); author of articles and reviews in architecture journals; *Recreations* designing and sewing wedding, bridesmaid and ball dresses, opera, music, theatre, cinema, cycling, swimming; *Style—* Ms Maggie Toy; ✉ 60 Torbay Road, London NW6 7DZ (mobile 07803 906146, e-mail maggietoy@tiscali.co.uk)

TOYE, Bryan Edward; JP; s of Herbert Graham Donovan Toye (d 1969), and Marion Alberta, *née* Montignani (d 1999); *b* 17 March 1938; *Educ* St Andrews, Eastbourne, Stowe; *m* 8 Oct 1982, Fiona Ann, da of Gordon Henry James Hogg, of Wellington, NZ; 3 s (Charles Edward Graham b 16 Dec 1983, Frederick b 6 Jan 1988, Guy b 15 Sept 1997), 1 da (Elisabeth Fiona Ann b 27 July 1985); *Career* joined Toye & Co 1956, dir Toye Kenning & Spencer 1962–, dir Toye & Co 1966, chm Toye and Co plc and 23 assoc subsid cos 1969–, dep chm Futurama Sign Gp Ltd 1992–96; memb: Cncl DMA, Clothing Interest Gp (CLING); memb Cncl NCPCC London 1966–69; chm Greater London Playing Fields Assoc 1988–90, memb Cncl London Playing Fields Soc 1990–92; memb Ctee King George's Fund for Sailor's Policy and Resources 1990–92; tstee: Queen Elizabeth Scholarship Tst (also founder memb) 1990–96, NED Trehaven Tst Ltd 1990–97, Britain-Australia Bicentennial Tst (until 2007), Black Country Museum (London Gp) 1991–97, British Red Cross (London Branch, vice-pres); memb stewards enclosure Henley Royal Regatta 1980–; govr: King Edward's Sch Witley 1988–93, Bridewell Royal Hosp 1989–96, Christ's Hosp 1989–96, City of London Freemen's Sch 1993–96; hon memb Ct of Assts Hon Artillery Co 1983–96, Hon Col 55 Ordnance Co ROAC (V) 1988–93, Hon Col 124 Havering Petroleum Sqdn (V) RLC 1994–2000; Hon Ordnance Offr Tower of London 1994–; memb Territorial Aux & Vol Reserve Assoc for Greater London 1992–99, memb City of London Territorial Aux & Vol Reserve Assoc 1992–99; NED HR (Navy) 1999–2005; memb: City of London Royal Soc of St George 1981–, Ct RCA 1983–86, Huguenot Soc 1985–, Ctee Old Stoic Soc 1985–92, Advsy Bd House of Windsor Collection Ltd 1994–95; pres Royal Warrant Holders Assoc 1991–92 (memb Cncl 1982–, Hon Auditor 1998–); memb Lloyd's 1985–91; Alderman The Ward of Lime St 1983–97, pres City Livery Club 1988–89; memb Ct of Assts: Worshipful Co of Gold & Silver Wyre Drawers (Master 1984), Worshipful Co of Broderers (Master 1996–97), Guild of Freemen of the City of London; Prime Warden Worshipful Co of Goldsmiths 2004 (Liveryman 1985, Warden 2001); FInstD 1966, FIMgt 1983, FRSA 1985; OStJ 1980; *Recreations* rugby, cricket, squash, shooting, swimming, tennis, gardening, classical music, entertaining; *Clubs* Leander, RAC, Middx Co RFC, Wasps RFC (tstee and vice-pres, chm Exec Ctee 1992–93), British-American Armed Forces Dining, MCC, Broadway Cricket (vice-pres); *Style—* Bryan Toye, Esq; ✉ Toye & Co plc, Regalia House, Newtown Road, Bedworth, Warwickshire CV12 8QR (tel 024 7684 8800, fax 024 7684 8847)

TOYE, Col (Claude) Hugh; OBE (1962, MBE 1947); s of Rev Percy Sheffield Toye (d 1968), and Sarah, *née* Griffiths (d 1966); *b* 28 March 1917; *Educ* Kingswood Sch Bath, Queens' Coll Cambridge (exhibitioner, MA); *m* 1958, Betty (d 1999), da of Lionel Hayne (d 1932), of Oulton Broad, Suffolk; 1 s (decd); *Career* enlisted Private RAMC (TA) 1938, Field Ambulance France 1940 (despatches), cmmnd RA 1941, Capt Instr Intelligence Sch Karachi 1943–44, Maj CSDIC (India) 1944–46, GSO2 (Intelligence) HQ ALFSEA 1946–47, acting GSO1 (Intelligence) Burma Cmd May-Sept 1947, Staff Coll Camberley 1948, 14 Fd Regt RA Hong Kong 1949–51 (Adj), DAA and QMG HQ 56 Armd Div (TA) 1951–53, GSO II Political Office MEF Cyprus 1956–58, Cmd 36 Battery RA Cyprus 1958 (UK 1959), Lt-Col Mil Attaché Vientiane 1960–62, GSO I (SD) SHAPE Paris 1962–64, Gwilym Gibbon res fell Nuffield Coll Oxford (DPhil) 1964–66, Col UK mil advsr's rep HQ SEATO Bangkok 1966–68, def advsr UK Mission to UN NY 1969–70, Dep Cdr Br Army Staff Washington 1970–72, ret 1972; treas Cuddesdon Theol Coll Oxford 1974–75; local SSAFA rep 1975–85; *Books* The Springing Tiger, a study of the Indian National Army and Subhas Chandra Bose (1959), Laos: Buffer State or Battleground (1968, revised 1971); *Recreations* war history, music; *Clubs* Army and Navy; *Style—* Col Hugh Toye, OBE; ✉ Westgate House, Millington Road, Wallingford, Oxfordshire OX10 8FE

TOYE, Prof John Francis Joseph; s of John Redmond Toye (d 1997), and Adele, *née* Francis (d 1972); *b* 7 October 1942; *Educ* Christ's Coll Finchley, Jesus Coll Cambridge (MA), Harvard Univ, SOAS Univ of London (MSc, PhD); *m* 18 March 1967, Janet, da of late Richard Henry Reason, of Harrow, London; 1 s (Richard b 1973), 1 da (Eleanor b 1970); *Career* asst princ HM Treasy 1965–68, res fell SOAS London 1970–72, fell (later tutor) Wolfson Coll Cambridge 1972–80 (asst dir of devpt studies 1977–80); dir: Commodities Research Unit Ltd 1980–82, Centre for Devpt Studies UC Swansea 1982–87, Inst of Devpt Studies Univ of Sussex (dir and professorial fell) 1987–97, UN Conf on Trade and Devpt Geneva 1998–2000; visiting prof Univ of Oxford 2000–03; memb: Wandsworth Community Rels Cncl 1968–72, Cambridge Cncl of Community Rels 1972–80, W Glamorgan Equal Opportunities Gp 1983–87; pres Devpt Studies Assoc of GB and I 1994–96; *Books* Taxation and Economic Development (1978), Trade and Poor Countries (1979), Public Expenditure and Indian Development Policy (1981), Dilemmas of Development (1987), Does Aid Work in India? (1990), Aid and Power (1991), Keynes on Population (2000), The UN and Global Political Economy (2004); *Recreations* music, walking, theatre; *Style—* Prof John Toye; ✉ Room 20.10, Department for International Development, University of Oxford, Mansfield Road, Oxford OX1 3TB

TOYE, Wendy; CBE (1992); da of Ernest Walter Toye and Jessie Crichton, *née* Ramsay; *b* 1 May 1917; *Educ* privately; *m* (m dis) Edward Selwyn Sharp; *Career* choreographer, actress, director and dancer; studied dancing as a child and first appeared at the Royal Albert Hall in 1921, winner numerous dancing awards incl the Charleston championship (Albert Hall) 1929, produced a ballet at the Palladium when only ten years of age, made her first professional appearance on the stage at the Old Vic as Cobweb in A Midsummer Night's Dream 1929, Marigold in Toad of Toad Hall, choreographer Mother Earth (Savoy) 1929, numerous roles with Ninette de Valois Vic-Wells Ballet Co 1930, princ dancer in The Golden Toy, toured with Anton Dolin 1934–35; choreographed and princ dancer: Markora Dolin Co, Rambert Ballet Co; arranged the dances for George Black's prodns 1937–44 (incl Black and Blue, Black Velvet, Black Vanities, Strike a New Note and Strike It Again), Gay Rosalinda (Palace) 1945–48, starred opposite Arthur Askey in Follow the Girls (Her Majesty's) 1945; directed prodns of Big Ben, Bless the Bride and Tough at the Top for Sir Charles B Cochran (Adelphi) 1946, played princ girl in the pantomime Simple Simon (Birmingham) 1947, Winnie Tate in Annie Get Your Gun (London Coliseum), sent her co Ballet-Hoo de Wendy Toye to Paris for a season 1948; dir numerous prodns incl: Virtue in Danger, Robert & Elizabeth, On The Level, As You Like It, Show Boat, She Stoops to Conquer, Soldiers Tale (Young Vic), The Great Waltz and Cowardy Custard, Follow the Star (Chichester), The Mikado (Opera House Ankara Turkey); other prodns incl: This Thing Called Love (Ambassadors) 1984, Noel and Gertie (Princess Grace Theatre Monte Carlo) 1984, assoc prodr Barnum (Victoria Palace) and Singin' in the Rain (London Palladium), Gala tribute to Joyce Grenfell 1985; Shaw Festival Theatre Canada: Celemare, Mad Woman of Chaillot; assoc prodr Torvill & Dean Ice Show World Tour 1985, dir and choreographer Kiss Me Kate (Copenhagen) and Unholy Trinity (Stephenville Festival) 1986, Laburnham Grove (Watford Palace) 1987, Miranda (Chichester Festival Theatre) 1987, Songbook (Watermill Theatre) 1988, Ziegfeld (London Palladium) 1988, Mrs Dot (Watford Palace) 1988, Family and Friends (Sadler's Wells) 1988, Last Night Gala (Old Sadler's Wells), When That I Was (Manitoba Theatre Center) 1988, Oh (Coward Playhouse Hong Kong) 1989, Cinderella (Palace Waterford), Till We Meet Again Concert (Festival Hall) 1989, Retrospective Season of Films Directed by Wendy Toye (Festival de Films des Femmes International, Paris) 1990, Penny Black (Wavendon) 1990, Moll Flanders (Watermill Theatre) 1990, Captain Beaky's Heavens Up (Playhouse) 1990, 2 Operas (Aix en Provence Festival) 1991, The Drummer (Watermill Theatre) 1991, Sound of Music (pre London Nat Tour and Sadler's Wells) 1992/93, See How They Run (Watermill Theatre), The Kingfisher (Vienna's Eng Theatre) 1993, Under Their Hats (King's Head) 1994, Anastasia File (Watermill Theatre) 1994, Lloyd George knew my Father (Watermill Theatre) 1995, Warts and All, Rogues to Riches (Watermill Theatre) 1996, Under Their Hats (Northcott Exeter, Yvonne Arnard Theatre and London) 1996, Finale 1996, Cast Night (Sadlers Wells) 1996, 30 Not Out (30th anniversary gala, Watermill) 1997; ENO prodns incl: Bluebeards Castle, The Telephone, Russalka, La Vie Parisienne, Orpheus In The Underworld, Italian Girl in Algiers, Fledermaus; Opera de Chambre Menton prodns incl: Der Apothoker 1994, Serva Padrona 1994; Seraglio, The Impresario For Yehudi Menuhin's Bath Festival (with Menuhin conducting); dir films: The Stranger Left No Card (first prize Cannes Film Festival), On The Twentieth Day, Raising A Riot, We Joined The Navy, Three Cases of Murder, The Teckman Mystery, All For Mary, True As A Turtle, The King's Breakfast; Br Film Inst: A Restrospective (NFT) 1995; lectured in Australia 1977, memb Cncl LAMDA, original memb Accreditation Bd instigated by NCDT for Acting Courses 1981–84, served Equity Cncl as first dirs rep 1974 (dirs Sub-Ctee 1971); examiner LAMDA, guest of hon Tokyo Int Film Festival 1992; memb: Grand Cncl Royal Acad of Dancing, Ctee for Wavendon All Music Scheme, Vivian Ellis Award Scheme, Richard Stillgoe Award Scheme; Queen's Silver Jubilee Medal 1977; Hon DLitt City Univ 1996; *Recreations* embroidery, gardening; *Style—* Dr Wendy Toye, CBE; ✉ c/o Jean Diamond, London Management, 2–4 Noel Street, London W1V 3RB

TOYNBEE, Polly; da of Philip Toynbee (d 1981), and Anne Barbara Denise, *née* Powell (d 2004); *b* 27 December 1946; *Educ* Badminton Sch Bristol, Holland Park Comprehensive, St Anne's Coll Oxford (John Gamble scholar); *m* 28 Dec 1970, Peter George James Jenkins (d 1992), s of Kenneth E Jenkins, of Norfolk; 2 da (Millicent (Milly) b 5 Dec 1971, Flora b 17 Dec 1975), 1 s (Nathaniel b 10 Jan 1985), 1 step da (Amy b 29 Oct 1964); *Career* journalist; reporter The Observer 1968–71, ed The Washington Monthly USA 1971–72, feature writer The Observer 1972–77, columnist The Guardian 1977–88, social affrs ed BBC 1988–95, assoc ed and columnist The Independent 1995–97, political and social commentator The Guardian 1997–; columnist Radio Times 1992–; dir Political Quarterly; pres Social Policy Assoc 2005–; Catherine Pakenham Award for Journalism 1975, Columnist of the Year British Press Awards 1986 and 2007, Writer of the Year (Consumer Mags) PPA Awards 1997, George Orwell Prize 1997, Columnist of the Year Nat Press Awards 2006; memb NUJ; Parly candidate (SDP) Lewisham E 1983–; chair Brighton Dome and Festival 2006–; *Books* Leftovers (1966), A Working Life (1972), Hospital (1979), The Way We Live Now (1981), Lost Children (1985), Did Things Get Better? (with David Walker, 2001), Hard Work: Life in Low Pay Britain (2003), Better of Worse? Has Labour Delivered? (2005); *Recreations* children; *Style—* Ms Polly Toynbee; ✉ The Guardian, 119 Farringdon Road, London EC1R 3ER (tel 020 7278 2332)

TOYNBEE, Simon Victor; yst s of Ralph Victor Toynbee (d 1970), and Bridget, *née* Monins (d 2005); *b* 30 January 1944; *Educ* Winchester; *m* 12 Aug 1967, Antoinette Mary (d 2003), da of John Walter Devonshire (d 2006); 3 da (Georgina (Mrs James Colquhoun) b 1969, Elizabeth (Mrs Anthony Lang) b 1971, Susannah b 1980); *Career* 2 Lt The RB 1963–65; Jessel Toynbee and Co Ltd 1966–72, Singer and Friedlander Ltd 1973–82 (dir Investment Dept 1977–82), Henderson Administration Ltd 1982–90 (dir 1986–90), investment dir Mercury Fund Managers Ltd 1990–92, investment mangr PPP 1992–94, sr investment mangr Majedie Investments plc 1995–99, dir Majedie Investment Trust Mgmnt Ltd 1995–99, exec chm Progressive Value Mgmnt Ltd 1999–2007, dir Progressive Asset Mgmnt Ltd 1999–2007; chm Investment Ctee Royal Green Jackets Funds; hon treas for Kent Nat Gardens Scheme; *Recreations* gardening, golf; *Clubs* Green Jackets, MCC, Boodle's, Rye Golf; *Style—* S V Toynbee, Esq; ✉ Old Tong Farm, Brenchley, Kent TN12 7HT (tel 01892 723552, e-mail toynbeea@aol.com); Progressive Focus Management Ltd, 145–157 St John Street, London EC1V 4RU (tel 020 7566 5551, fax 020 7336 0865, e-mail stoynbee@pro-asset.com)

TOYNE SEWELL, Maj-Gen Timothy Patrick; DL (Greater London); s of Brig Edgar Patrick Sewell, CBE (d 1956), and Elizabeth Cecily Mease, *née* Toyne, MBE; *b* 7 July 1941; *Educ* Bedford Sch, RMA Sandhurst; *m* 7 Aug 1965, Jennifer, *née* Lunt; 1 s (Patrick b 1967), 1 da (Melanie b 1969); *Career* cmmnd KOSB 1961; served: Aden, Malaysia, BAOR, NI; Staff Coll 1973, CO 1 KOSB 1981–83, COS HQ British Forces Falkland Island 1983–84, Cdr 19 Inf Bde 1985–87, RCDS 1988, Cdr BMATT Zimbabwe 1989–91, Cmdt RMA Sandhurst 1991–94, head Recruiting Implementation Team 1994–95; dir Goodenough Coll 1995–2006, chair Int Bd United World Colls 2006–; govr Haileybury Sch 1994–, govr Lambrook Haileybury Sch 2003– (chm 2003–), memb Cncl Queen Mary & Westfield Coll London; tstee: Bill Marshall Tst, Med Coll of St Bartholomew's Hosp Tst 1996–2005; Col KOSB 1996–2001; pres Army Tennis & Rackets Assoc 1994–2001; chm: Benjamin Britten Int Violin Competition 2003–, Kyiv Festival 2003–; Freeman City of London 2006; *Recreations* music, tennis, golf, fishing; *Clubs* Royal Over-Seas League (memb Cncl 2002–); *Style—* Maj-Gen T P Toyne Sewell, DL; ✉ United World Colleges, 17–21 Emerald Street, London WC1N 3QN (e-mail timtoynesewell@googlemail.com)

TOZZI, Keith; s of Edward Thomas Tozzi (d 1995), and Winifred, *née* Killick (d 2005); *b* 23 February 1949; *Educ* Dartford GS, City Univ (BSc), Univ of Kent (MA), Harvard Business Sch (ISMP); *m* Maria Cecilia; 1 da (Sarah b 24 Aug 1975), 2 s (Matthew b 23 Nov 1977, Alexander b 7 Sept 1998); *Career* div dir Southern Water 1988–92, gp tech dir Southern Water plc 1992–96, chief exec British Standards Institution 1996–2000, gp chief exec Swan Gp plc 2000–03, non-exec dir Legal & General UK Select Investment Tst plc 2000–03, non-exec chm RSVP.com 2000–, non-exec dir Seal Analytical Ltd 2004–, non-exec chm Inspicio plc 2005–, non-exec chm Concateno plc 2006–; chm: National Joint Utilities Gp 1993–96, IOD (Sussex) 1995–97; Liveryman Worshipful Co of Water Conservators; FICE 1975, FIWEM 1976, CIMgt 1979, FRSA 2002; *Recreations* classic cars, gardening; *Clubs* Athenaeum; *Style—* Keith Tozzi, Esq; ✉ Littleworth House, Littleworth, West Sussex RH13 8JF (tel 01403 710488, fax 01403 711219, e-mail keithtozzi@aol.com)

TOZZI, Nigel Kenneth; QC (2001); s of Ronald Kenneth Tozzi (d 2001), and Doreen Elsie Florence, *née* Baddams (d 2002); *b* 31 August 1957; *Educ* Hitchin Boys' GS, Univ of Exeter (LLB), Cncl of Legal Educ; *m* 7 May 1983, Sara Louise Clare, da of Derek Charles Cornish; 2 s (Adam Thomas Edward b 15 Feb 1987, Matthew Charles William b 4 Oct 1990), 1 da (Alice Kathleen Clare b 24 Oct 1988); *Career* called to the Bar Gray's Inn

T

1980 (Holt scholar); memb: Commercial Bar Assoc, Professional Negligence Bar Assoc, Bar Insurance Law Assoc, London Common Law and Bar Assoc, Justice; *Recreations* playing hockey, watching cricket and rugby, theatre, cinema; *Clubs* Sevenoaks Hockey, MCC; *Style*— Nigel Tozzi, Esq, QC; ⊠ 4 Pump Court, Temple, London EC4Y 7AN (tel 020 7842 5555, fax 020 7583 2036, e-mail ntozzi@4pumpcourt.com)

TRACE, Anthony John; QC (1998); s of Commander Peter Trace, RD (and bar), RNR (d 1981); and Anne, *née* Allison-Beer; *b* 23 October 1958; *Educ* Uppingham, Magdalene Coll Cambridge (MA, Bundy Scholarship, Master's Reading Prize); *m* 1986, Caroline Tessa, da of His Hon Anthony Durrant; 4 c (Charlotte, Oliver (twins) b 13 May 1988, Hugo b 18 April 1991, Rupert b 27 July 1993); *Career* called to the Bar Lincoln's Inn 1981 (bencher 2006), winner Crowther Advocacy Shield 1981, jt winner Observer Mace Debating competition 1981; memb: Chancery Bar Assoc 1982– (hon sec 1997–2001, vice-chm 2001–04), COMBAR 1997–, ACTAPS 1997–; fndr memb: Campaign for Real Gin 1978–, Friends of Turkey 2006; memb: St Luke's (Kew) Parochial Church Cncl 1987–90 and 1996–97, St Luke's House Ctee 1988–89, Queen's Sch (Kew) PTA 1996–97; tstee Uppingham Sch 1999–; Freeman City of London, Liveryman Worshipful Co of Musicians; *Publications* Butterworths European Law Service Company Law (contrib, 1992), dep managing ed Receivers, Administrators and Liquidators Quarterly 1993–2002, Butterworths Practical Insolvency (contrib, 1999); *Recreations* stalking, shooting, fishing, the Turf, music, messing about in boats, socialising with friends; *Clubs* Pitt (Cambridge), Athenaeum, Garrick; *Style*— Anthony Trace, Esq, QC; ⊠ Maitland Chambers, 7 Stone Buildings, Lincoln's Inn, London WC2A 3SZ (tel 020 7406 1200, fax 020 7406 1300, e-mail clerks@maitlandchambers.com)

TRACEY, Eric Frank; s of late Allan Lewis Tracey, of Auckland, NZ, and late Marcelle Frances, *née* Petrie; *b* 3 July 1948; *Educ* Mount Albert GS Auckland, Univ of Auckland (BCom, MCom); *m* 16 May 1970, Patricia, da of late G S (Bill) Gamble, of Hatch End, Middx; *Career* Inland Revenue NZ 1965, lectr Univ of Auckland 1970–72, with Touche Ross (now Deloitte & Touche LLP) London 1973–2004 (ptnr 1980–2004), actg finance dir Amey 2002–03, finance dir Wembley plc 2005; chm Yellow Culture Ltd; non-exec dir Chloride Gp 2005–; master Worshipful Co of World Traders 2003–04; FCA 1975 (ACA 1970), ACIS 1972; *Recreations* walking, rugby, cricket, cooking, creative gardening, NZ plants; *Clubs* MCC, Pythouse Players; *Style*— Eric Tracey, Esq

TRACEY, Prof Ian Graham; s of William Tracey (d 1994), and Helene Mignon, *née* Harris; *b* 27 May 1955; *Educ* Trinity Coll of Music, St Katharine's Coll Liverpool (PGCE); *Career* organist and master of the choristers Liverpool Cathedral 1980–; prof, fell and organist Liverpool John Moores Univ (formerly Liverpool Poly) 1988–; chorus master Royal Liverpool Philharmonic Soc 1985–, organist City of Liverpool (formerly conslt organist) 1986–; pres Inc Assoc of Organists 2001–03; memb: Jospice Int, Cambridge Soc of Musicians, Int Contemporary Music Awards; Award for Classical Music NW Arts 1994; Hon DMus Univ of Liverpool 2006; FTCL 1976, FRSA 1988, Hon FRCO 2002; *Recreations* cookery, fine wines, canal boating, fell walking; *Clubs* Artists' (Liverpool); *Style*— Prof Ian Tracey; ⊠ Mornington House, Mornington Terrace, Upper Duke Street, Liverpool L1 9DY (tel and fax 0151 708 8471, website www.iantracey.org.uk)

TRACEY, Stanley William; OBE (1986); s of Stanley Clark Tracey (d 1957), and Florence Louise, *née* Guest (d 1984); *b* 30 December 1926; *m* 1, 1946 (m dis), Joan Lower; m 2, 1957 (m dis 1960), Jean Richards; m 3, 24 Dec 1960, Florence Mary (Jackie), da of Douglas Richard Buckland (d 1970), of London; 1 s (Clark b 1961), 1 da (Sarah b 1962); *Career* served RAF 1946–48; composer of over 500 titles incl: Under Milkwood Suite 1965, Genesis and some 50 albums; resident pianist Ronnie Scotts Club London 1960–66, ptnr (with wife) Steam Record Co 1975–91; toured ME 1982, S America 1980 with own quartet, pianist/leader quartet, quintet, sextet (Hexad), octet and 15 piece orchestra, signed to Blue Note record label 1992; subject of Godfather of British Jazz (BBC documentary) 2003; composer/arranger BT Jazz Awards 1997 and 1999; winner: piano section Br Jazz Awards 1992, composer/arranger Br Jazz Awards 1993 and 1995, composer/arranger BBC Radio 2 Award 1993, Octet album Portraits Plus shortlisted for Mercury Music Prize 1993, small gp Br Jazz Awards 1995, Lifetime Achievement Awards BBC Jazz Awards 2002; Hon DLitt Univ of Herts 1997; memb RSM & JB, fell City of Leeds Coll of Music; Hon RAM; *Style*— Stanley Tracey, Esq, OBE; ⊠ 19 St Augusta Court, Batchwood View, St Albans, Hertfordshire AL3 5SS (tel 01727 852595)

TRAFFORD, Roger Samuel; s of Jack Trafford (d 2001), of St Cleer, Cornwall, and Sylvia, *née* Holmwood (d 1979); *b* 12 February 1939; *Educ* Forest Sch, Hertford Coll Oxford (MA); *m* 24 July 1971, Cheryl Anne, da of Gordon Robert Ellis Norbrook, of Barnes, London; 2 s (James Richard Ellis b 11 Nov 1973, George Roger Ellis b 21 April 1976); *Career* English teacher The Fessenden Sch Boston Mass 1962–65, housemaster and head of English St Paul's Prep Sch London 1965–73; headmaster: King's Coll Prep Sch Taunton 1973–82, Clifton Coll Prep Sch Bristol 1982–93, Dragon Sch Oxford 1993–2002; educn offr Cognits Schs Gp; Walter Hines Page scholarship to USA 1987; vice-chm ISIS South and West 1977–82, chm Nat ISIS 1996–2000; vice-pres IAPS (memb Cncl 1982–84, 1987–89, 1990–92, 1994–97 and 1997–2000, chm 1991–92); dep chm ISC 1999–2003; govr: Gordonstoun Sch, Millfield Sch, Clifton Coll, Port Regis, The Perse Sch Cambridge, Beaudesert Park; *Recreations* rackets, real tennis, skiing, education, rugby; *Clubs* Lansdowne, Boasters, Unicorn; *Style*— Roger Trafford, Esq; ⊠ Greystones, Alvescot, Bampton, Oxfordshire OX18 2QA (e-mail rogertrafford@btinternet.com)

TRAHAR, Anthony John; s of Thomas Walter Trahar, and Thelma, *née* Ashmead-Bartlett; *b* 1 June 1949; *Educ* St John's Coll Johannesburg, Univ of the Witwatersrand (BCom); *m* Patricia Jane; 1 s (Andrew), 1 da (Frances); *Career* CA (SA) 1973; Anglo American Corp of SA Ltd: mgmnt trainee 1974, PA to chm 1976–77; exec chm Mondi Paper Co 1989–2002, exec dir Anglo American Corp 1991, chm Mondi Europe 1993–2003, chm South African Motor Corp (Pty) Ltd 1996–2000, chm AECI Ltd 1999–2001, chm Anglo Forest Products 1999–2003, chm Anglo Industrial Minerals Div 1999–2004, ceo Anglo American plc 2000–07; chm Palaeo Anthropological Scientific Tst 1999–2007; memb SA Inst of Chartered Accountants 1975, MInstD (SA) 1982; Knight Cdr Gold Cross with Star (First Class) (Austria); PhD (hc) Univ of Pretoria; *Recreations* trout fishing, shooting, classic cars, music; *Clubs* RAC, Rand (Johannesburg), River (Johannesburg); *Style*— Tony Trahar, Esq

TRAILL, Sir Alan; GBE (1984), QSO (1990); s of George Traill, and Margaret Eleanor, *née* Matthews; *b* 7 May 1935; *Educ* St Andrew's Sch Eastbourne, Charterhouse, Jesus Coll Cambridge (MA); *m* 1964, Sarah Jane, *née* Hutt; 1 s (Philip); *Career* dir Morice Tozer & Beck 1960–73; chm: Traill Attenborough Ltd 1973–81, Lyon Holdings 1981–86; dir: Lyon Traill Attenborough (Lloyd's Brokers) 1981–86, PWS Holdings 1986–87, Aegis Insurance Brokers 1987–89, Medex Assistance (Europe) plc 1993–98; md: Colburn Traill Ltd 1989–96, Colburn French & Keen Ltd 1994–96; div dir: First City Insurance Brokers 1996–2000, Pathfinder Team Consulting Ltd 1996–; dir Int Disputes Resolution Centre Ltd 1999–; dir Monetary Authy Cayman Is 2003–06; currently at Arbitrator & Expert Witness; memb: Lloyd's 1964–89, Ct of Common Cncl City of London 1970–2005, London Ct of Int Arbitration 1981–86; memb Cncl Br Insurance Brokers' Assoc 1978–79 (chm Reinsurance Brokers' Ctee 1978), memb Ctee ARIAS (UK) 1998–; Alderman Langbourn Ward 1975–2005, Sheriff 1982–83, Lord Mayor of London 1984–85; dir City Arts Tst 1980–, govr Christ's Hosp Fndn 2003– (almoner 1980–2003); vice-pres King Edward's Sch Witley 2003–05, govr St Paul's Cathedral Choir Sch Fndn 1987–95, chm govr Yehudi Menhuin Sch 2000–, patron Lord Mayor Treloar Coll 2002–; tstee RSC 1982–2004, memb Advsy Bd and Educn Ctee London Symphony Orchestra 1996–; chllr City Univ 1984–85 (Hon DMus 1984); chm: UK-NZ 1990 Ctee, Friends of Waitangi Fndn; memb Ct of Assts: Worshipful Co of Cutlers (Master 1979–80), Master Worshipful Co of Musicians (Master 1999–2000); *Recreations* DIY, music and opera, assisting education; *Style*— Sir Alan Traill, GBE, QSO; ⊠ Wheelers Farm, Thursley, Surrey GU8 6QE (tel 07714 328204, fax 01252 703271, e-mail atraill.granary@btinternet.com)

TRAINOR, Prof Richard Hughes; s of late William Richard Trainor, and Sarah Frances, *née* Hughes; *b* 31 December 1948; *Educ* Calvert Hall HS, Brown Univ (BA), Princeton Univ (MA), Merton Coll Oxford (MA), Nuffield Coll Oxford (DPhil); *m* 28 June 1980, Dr Marguerite Wright Dupree, da of Prof A Hunter Dupree; 1 s (Richard Hunter b 1987), 1 da (Marguerite Sarah b 1992); *Career* jr research fell Wolfson Coll Oxford 1977–79, lectr Balliol Coll Oxford 1978–79; Univ of Glasgow: lectr in economic history 1979–89, sr lectr in economic and social history 1989–95, prof of social history 1995–2000, dir Design and Implementation of Software in History Project 1985–89, co-dir Computers in Teaching Initiative Centre for History, Archaeology and Art History 1989–99, dean and head Planning Unit Faculty of Social Sciences 1992–96, vice-princ 1996–2000; vice-chllr and prof of social history Univ of Greenwich 2000–04, princ and prof of social history KCL 2004–; pres: Glasgow and West of Scotland Branch Historical Assoc 1991–93, Universities UK 2007– (memb Bd 2002–05, treas 2006–07); memb: Jt Information Systems Ctee 2001–05, HEFCE Quality Assurance, Learning and Teaching Ctee 2003–06, London Higher Steering Ctee Bd 2003–06, US/UK Fulbright Cmmn 2003–, HE Acad Bd 2004–07, Leadership, Governance and Mgmnt Ctee HEFCE 2006–07, Cncl AHRC 2006–; convenor: Steering Gp Learning and Teaching Support Network 2000–04, Steering Gp UUK/DfES Review of Student Servs 2002, Steering Gp Nat Teaching Fellowship Scheme 2005–07; chair Advsy Cncl Inst of Historical Research 2004–, hon sec Econ History Soc 1998–2004; chair London Met Network 2002–06, memb Exec Ctee then Membership Ctee The Pilgrims 2004–; govr Henley Mgmnt Coll 2003–05; hon fell: Trinity Coll of Music 2003, Merton Coll Oxford 2004; FRHistS 1990, FRSA 1995, AcSS 2001; *Books* Historians, Computers and Data: Applications in Research and Teaching (ed with E Mawdsley et al, 1991), Towards an International Curriculum for History and Computing (ed with D Spaeth et al, 1992), The Teaching of Historical Computing: An International Framework (ed with D Spaeth et al, 1993), Black Country Elites: The Exercise of Authority in an Industrialised Area 1830–1900 (1993), Urban Governance: Britain and Beyond Since 1750 (ed with R Morris, 2000), University, City and State: The University of Glasgow since 1870 (with M Moss and J F Munro, 2000); also author of numerous articles in books and jls; *Recreations* parenting, observing politics, tennis; *Clubs* Athenaeum; *Style*— Prof Richard Trainor; ⊠ Office of the Principal, King's College London, James Clerk Maxwell Building, 57 Waterloo Road, London SE1 8WA (tel 020 7848 3434, fax 020 7848 3430, e-mail principal@kcl.ac.uk)

TRANTER, Jane; da of Donald Tranter, and Joan, *née* Gay; *b* 17 March 1963; *Educ* Kingswood Sch Bath, King's Coll London (BA English Lit); *m* David Attwood; *Career* asst floor mangr BBC 1986–88, script ed Casualty BBC Drama Dept 1988, script ed BBC Films Dept 1989–92 (TV credits incl award-winning Alive and Kicking, The Last Romantics, The Kremlin Farewell and Bad Girl, feature films credits The Hour of the Pig and Sarafina); Carlton TV: commissioning ed Drama 1992–93, head of drama 1993–95; exec prodr Carlton UK Productions 1995–97, re-joined BBC as exec prodr Films and Single Drama 1997–98, series exec prodr BBC 1 Drama Serials and Single Films 1998–2000, controller Drama Commissioning BBC 2000–06, controller BBC Fiction 2006–; memb Lab Pty; *Style*— Ms Jane Tranter

TRAPP, Deirdre; *b* 21 September 1961, Ipswich, Suffolk; *Educ* St Hilda's Coll Oxford; *m* Roger; 3 da (Georgia b 24 Jan 1992, Olivia b 4 Jan 1994, Lucinda b 28 May 1997); *Career* slr; specialises in EU and UK competition law; ptnr Freshfields Bruckhaus Deringer 1995– (co-head Antitrust, Competition and Trade Gp 2000–); non-governmental advsr to European Cmmn; memb: Competition Task Force Business and Industry Advsy Ctee OECD, Structural Transaction Review Task Force American Bar Assoc; *Style*— Mrs Deirdre Trapp; ⊠ Freshfields Bruckhaus Deringer, 65 Fleet Street, London EC4Y 1HS (e-mail deirdre.trapp@freshfields.com)

TRAVERS, Andrew Keith Buchanan (Andy); *b* 3 January 1962; *Career* well-logging engr 1982–83, IC design engr National Semi Conductor, ASIC design engr/conslt Dectroswiss Switzerland 1986–89, sr design engr/conslt IBM PC Company UK 1989–94, dir CIPD (IBM) UK 1994–96, ceo Scottish Design Ltd 1996–99, ceo Virtual Component Exchange Ltd 1999–2003, ceo VCX Software Ltd 2003–; *Recreations* rugby, tennis, sailing, skiing; *Clubs* Hillhead Sports; *Style*— Andy Travers, Esq

TRAVERS, David; s of George Bowes Travers (d 1966), and Gertrude Colbert, *née* Churnside; *b* 19 March 1957; *Educ* Spennymoor Secdy Sch, KCL (LLB, AKC, LLM), Inns of Court Sch of Law; *m* 13 Oct 1984, Sheila Mary, da of Martin Killoran, CBE, QFSM; 2 da (Rosamond Mary b 11 Oct 1988, Jennifer Claire b 15 April 1991), 1 s (James David b 28 July 1992); *Career* called to the Bar Middle Temple 1981 (Harmsworth scholar), formerly in practice Manchester (memb Exec Northern Circuit 1985–87), in practice Midland & Oxford Circuit 1988–, accredited mediator 2000; legal advsr: Professional Conduct Ctee GMC 2002–, Professional Conduct Ctee General Dental Cncl; pt/t lectr Accountancy Tuition Centre Manchester and Liverpool until 1983, occasional lectr Dept of Mgmnt Scis UMIST 1986–87, occasional libel reader Express newspapers 1987–88, occasional tutor Dept of Biomedical Sci and Biomedical Ethics Univ of Birmingham 1995–96; lectr at professional conferences; after dinner speaker; exec ed King's Counsel 1979 (ed 1978); Royal Inst sci scholar 1975, memb Delegacy Governing Body KCL 1977–78, sabbatical pres KCL Union of Students 1979–80 (hon life memb 1980), pres Middle Temple Students' Assoc 1980–81; participant Warwick Int Workshop on Corporate Control and Accountability 1991; memb: Bar Cncl 1995–2000, Birmingham Law Soc IT Ctee 1995–97, Law Reform Ctee Bar Cncl 1996–98, Bar Services & IT Ctee Bar Cncl 1996–99, Planning and Environment Bar Assoc, UK Enviromental Law Assoc, Bar European Gp, Admin Law Bar Assoc, Food Law Gp, Hon Soc of the Middle Temple 1978; *Recreations* family, language, music, running; *Style*— David Travers, Esq; ⊠ 6 Pump Court, Temple, London EC4Y 7AR (tel 020 7797 8400, fax 020 7797 8401, e-mail davidtravers@6pumpcourt.co.uk)

TRAVERS, Harry Anthony; s of Sidney Travers, and Marice, *née* Berger; *b* 7 November 1963, Manchester; *Educ* Manchester Grammar, St Edmund Hall Oxford (open scholar, BCL, MA); *m* 1 Sept 2002, Miriam Farbey; 1 s (William Nicholas Louis b 11 Jan 2004); *Career* called to the Bar Middle Temple 1990; admitted slr 1990; specialises in law relating to white collar crime; Berwin Leighton 1987–91, BCL Burton Copeland 1991– (ptnr 1995–); memb: Law Soc, London Criminal Courts Slrs Assoc, Assoc of Regulatory and Disciplinary Lawyers, Int Bar Assoc; *Recreations* golf, Manchester United FC, music; *Style*— Harry Travers, Esq; ⊠ BCL Burton Copeland, 51 Lincoln's Inn Fields, London WC2A 3LZ (tel 020 7430 2277, fax 020 7430 1101, e-mail htravers@burtoncopeland.co.uk)

TRAVERSE-HEALY, Kevin Timothy; DL (2001); s of Prof Tim Traverse-Healy, OBE, *qv*, and Joan, *née* Thompson; *b* 30 November 1949; *Educ* Xaverian Coll Brighton, Redrice Coll, Lewes Tech Coll, Coll of Law London, Univ of Leicester (MA); *m* 12 Jan 1974, Sarah-Jane (Sally), *née* Magill; 1 da (Alexia Claire b 9 Aug 1979), 1 s (James Timothy Brendan b 16 May 1983); *Career* articled clerk Duchin & Co and Berwin & Co 1969–72; exhibitions offr (later PR exec) British Oxygen Co and PR exec BOC International (Southern Africa) 1972–76, dir Traverse-Healy Ltd 1976–92, fndr md Traverse-Healy & Regester Ltd 1980–87, md Charles Barker Traverse-Healy Ltd 1987–91, chief exec (ops) Charles Barker Ltd 1991–92, md Centre for Public Affairs Studies 1992–2005, ind mgmnt conslt 1992–, advsr National Commercial Bank of Saudi Arabia 1995–96; dir e.g. Ltd 1996–98, conslt Communication Skills Europe Ltd 1998–2005; ptnr Traverse-Healy Consult 1996–; strategic conslt COI 2006–; dir Rainbow Rovers Ltd (charity) 1989–98; advsr ACFA 1998–2005 (ed Army Cadet magazine), Lt Col ACF 1998–; chm Advsy Bd Astrolabe Communications Ltd 2002–, memb Vice-Pres's Steering Gp on Communications Strategy European Cmmn 2004–06; vice-patron Atlantic Cncl of the UK 2003–04; visiting prof Univ of Lugano 1998–, memb PR Advsy Bd Ball State Univ 1997–; lectr and contrib to various PR handbooks; first recipient CERP (Centre European de Relations Publique) medal for contrib to European PR 1985; tstee IPR Benevolent Fund 1995–2000; FCIPR (pres 1985); *Recreations* communication, cadets, countryside; *Clubs* London Flotilla; *Style—* Kevin Traverse-Healy, Esq, DL; ✉ tel 020 7582 7475, mobile 07778 021720, e-mail kevinth@dial.pipex.com

TRAVERSE-HEALY, Prof Tim; OBE (1989); s of John Healy, MBE, and Gladys, *née* Traverse; *b* 25 March 1923; *Educ* Stonyhurst, St Mary's Hosp Med Sch London (DipCAM); *m* 8 March 1946, Joan, da of Sidney Thompson (d 1968), of London and Sussex; 2 s (Sean b 1947, Kevin, *qv*, b 1949), 3 da (Sharon (Mrs Butterfield) b 1951, Corinne (Mrs Russell) b 1953, Jeannine b 1954); *Career* WWII RA Territorial Res, RM Commandos and Special Forces 1941–46; memb Public and Social Policy Ctee Nat Westminster Bank 1952–92, sr ptnr Traverse-Healy Ltd Corporate Affrs Counsel 1947–93, dir Centre for Public Affrs Studies 1969–; chm (UK) PR Educn Tst 1990–92; visiting prof: Univ of Stirling, Univ of Wales, Baylor Univ Texas USA 1988–97, Ball Univ Indiana USA 1998–2001; vice-pres Euro PR Confedn 1965–69, memb Professional Practices Ctee (UK) PR Conslts Assoc 1988–92; Int PR Assoc: fndr sec 1950–61, cncl memb 1961–68, pres 1968–73, emeritus memb 1982, Presidential Gold medal 1985, pres World PR congress Tel Aviv 1970 and Geneva 1973; PR congress fndr lectures: Boston 1976, Bombay 1982, Melbourne 1988, Istanbul 2005; chm Coll Emeriti 2006; pres: Int Fndn for PR Res and Educn 1983–85, Int Fndn for PR Studies 1986–87 (tstee 1987–88); memb (US) Public Affairs Cncl 1975–91 (US); PR News award (UK) 1983, PR Week award 1987, (US) Page Soc award 1990, (US) Ball Univ award 1997; Hon FIPR 1988 (Tallents Gold medal 1985); memb: RM Officers' Assoc, Commandos Assoc, London Flotilla; MIPR 1948, FIPR 1956 (pres 1967–68), FIPA 1957, FRSA 1953; *Recreations* Irish Soc, French politics; *Clubs* Athenaeum, Philippics; *Style—* Prof Tim Traverse-Healy, OBE; ✉ 2 Henman Close, Devizes, Wiltshire SN10 1HD (e-mail proftim@compuserve.com)

TRAVIS, (Ernest Raymond) Anthony; s of Ernest Raymond Travis, and Constance Mary Travis; *b* 18 May 1943; *Educ* Harrow; *m* 1, 1967 (m dis 1977), Hon Rosemary Gail, da of Baron Pritchard (d 1995), of Haddon; m 2, 1978, Jean Heather, da of John MacDonald (d 1983); m 3, 1987, Peta Jane, da of Sir Peter Foster; *Career* called to the Bar Inner Temple 1965; chm and chief exec Travis Perkins plc 1981–2001, chm Anglia Maltings (Holding) Ltd 2005–; chm of tstees Constance Travis Charitable Tst 1988–, tstee ESCP/EAP European Sch of Mgmnt 2002–, govr Royal Acad of Music 2006–; dir Northampton Saints plc 2000–06; *Recreations* opera, tennis, ruby union (touchline); *Style—* Anthony Travis, Esq; ✉ 86 Drayton Gardens, London SW10; Pitters Farm, Naish Hill, Chippenham, Wiltshire

TRAVIS, John Anthony; s of Leonard Kirkbride Travis (d 2000), of Brighton, E Sussex, and Elsie Travis (d 1961); *b* 18 August 1945; *Educ* Brighton Sch of Music & Drama, Doris Isaacs Sch of Dancing, Royal Ballet Sch, Univ of Manchester (Dip Theatre Archives); *Career* dancer Covent Garden Opera Ballet; London Festival Ballet (English Nat Ballet): dancer then leading soloist 1966–77, created London Festival Ballet Archive 1979, prog presenter and head Educn Dept 1980–87; on secondment to study at V&A 1977, studied at Lincoln Centre NY 1978; teaching: annually at Nat Festivals of Youth Dance classes and repertoire at all levels, at community centres, theatres, schs; five Brazilian Cities 1982 and first Summer Sch in Dominica 1990; teacher of classical ballet and coordinator for all performances and projects Northern Sch of Contemporary Dance Leeds 1989–95; guest teacher Northern Ballet Sch Manchester 1985–88; lectr on history of dance; artistic co-ordinator Dance Advance 1988–89 (touring mangr for China visit 1989), dir of 3 Youth Dance Spectaculars for Greater London Arts and Opening Gala of Northern Sch of Contemporary Dance 1988; dir: Bd Phoenix Dance Co 1985–93, British Ballet Organization 1995; patron: East London Regnl Dance Cncl, Harehills Dance Umbrella; memb: Exec Ctee Nat Organization for Dance and Mime (Dance UK) 1984–89, Cncl of Mgmnt Br Ballet Orgn 1991–95, Bd Northern Ballet Theatre (chm Educn Ctee) 1990–93, Bd Dance UK 1998–, Bd Mark Baldwin Dance Co 1999–2002; memb Dance Panel: SE Arts 1982–87, Eastern Arts 1983–87, Gtr London Arts Assocs 1980–86, Laurence Olivier Awards (Dance Panel) 1998–99; tstee: Dancers Resettlement Fund 1989–93, Dance Teachers' Benevolent Fnd 1995–, Cncl for Dance Educn and Trg 1995–99 and 2002–; *Style—* John Travis, Esq; ✉ The British Ballet Organization, Woolborough House, 39 Lonsdale Road, London SW13 9JP (tel 020 8748 1241, fax 020 8748 1301, e-mail info@bbo.org.uk)

TRAYHURN, Prof Paul; s of William George Trayhurn (d 1975), and Eileen Ella, *née* Morphew (d 1986); *b* 6 May 1948; *Educ* Colyton GS, Univ of Reading (BSc), Univ of Oxford (DPhil, DSc); *m* 12 July 1969, Deborah Hartland, *née* Gigg; 3 s (Theo William b 24 Dec 1977, Hanno Edmund b 9 March 1983, Felix Timothy b 13 May 1985), 1 da (Venetia Harriet b 24 Aug 1980); *Career* NATO Euro res fell Centre de Neurochimie CNRS 1972–73, post-doctoral fell Univ of Oxford 1973–75, MRC scientific staff Dunn Nutrition Laboratory 1975–86, prof and heritage scholar Nutrition and Metabolism Res Gp Univ of Alberta 1986–88; head Div of Biochemical Sciences Rowett Research Inst 1988–2000 (asst dir Academic Affrs 1997–2000), prof of nutritional biology Univ of Oslo Norway 2000–01, prof of nutritional biology Univ of Liverpool 2001–; hon prof Depts of Biomedical Sciences and Molecular and Cell Biology Univ of Aberdeen 1992–2000; Evelyn Williams visiting prof Univ of Sydney 1992; chm: Scientific Ctee 8th Euro Congress on Obesity (Dublin), Exec Cncl Korean Collaboration Centre for Biotechnology and the Biological Sciences 1995–2000, BBSRC Agri-Food Directorate Ctee 1997–99, MRC Advsy Bd 1997–2003, Awards Ctee Int Assoc for the Study of Obesity 1998–; ed-in-chief Br Jl of Nutrition 1999–2005; author of over 400 scientific pubns; memb: Biochemical Soc 1970, Nutrition Soc 1975 (chm Scottish section 1993–95), Physiological Soc 1993, American Assoc for the Advancement of Science; FRSE 1997; *Recreations* listening to classical music, bemoaning the decline of scientific culture; *Style—* Prof Paul Trayhurn, FRSE; ✉ School of Clinical Sciences, University of Liverpool, University Clinical Departments, Liverpool L69 3GA (tel 0151 706 4033, fax 0151 706 5802, e-mail p.traynhurn@liv.ac.uk)

TREACY, Hon Mr Justice; Sir Colman Maurice Treacy; kt (2002); s of Dr Maurice Colman Treacy, and Mary Teresa, *née* Frisby; *b* 28 July 1949; *Educ* Stonyhurst, Jesus Coll Cambridge (open scholar, MA); *m* 1 (m dis); 1 s, 1 da; m 2, 2002, Jane Ann, da of Edwin Hooper and Maureen Hooper; 1 step da; *Career* called to the Bar Middle Temple 1971 (bencher 1999); in practice Midland & Oxford Circuit, QC 1990, recorder of the Crown Court 1991–2002, head of chambers 1994–2000, asst boundary cmmr 2000–02, judge of the High Court (Queen's Bench Div) 2002–, presiding judge Midland Circuit 2006–; memb: Mental Health Review Tbnl 1999–2002, Warwickshire Criminal Justice Strategy Ctee 2000–02; *Style—* The Hon Mr Justice Treacy; ✉ Royal Courts of Justice, Strand, London WC2A 2LL (tel 020 7947 6000)

TREACY, Philip Anthony; s of James Vincent Treacy (d 1978), and Katie Agnes Treacy (d 1993); *b* 26 May 1967; *Educ* St Cuan's Coll Castle Blakeney Co Galway, Regional Tech Coll Galway, Nat Coll of Art and Design Dublin (BA), RCA (MDes); *Career* milliner; estab Philip Treacy Ltd 1990; hat mfr to designers incl: Karl Lagerfeld at Chanel (Paris), Gianni Versace (Milan), Valentino (Rome), Rifat Ozbek (London), Givenchy (Paris); design dir for interiors G W County Galway (Monogram's Hotel) 2005, luxury sports wear range for Umbro 2006; Accessory Designer of the Year (British Fashion Awards) 1991, 1992, 1993, 1996 and 1997, Haute Couture Paris 2000, 2001 and 2003, Design of the Year China Fashion Awards 2004; hon dr NUI; *Style—* Philip Treacy, Esq; ✉ Philip Treacy Ltd, 69 Elizabeth Street, London SW1W 9PJ (tel 020 7730 3992, fax 020 7824 8262)

TREANOR, Frances Mary Elizabeth; da of George Francis Treanor (d 1978), of London, and Biddy, *née* Maunsell (d 1964); *b* 16 April 1944; *Educ* Convent of the Sacred Heart HS for Girls Hammersmith, Goldsmiths Coll London (NDD), Hornsey Coll of Art (ATC); *m* 1, 9 Oct 1965 (m dis 1969), Francis John Elliott, s of Aubrey Elliott (d 1988), of Wales; 1 da (Lizzie Taylor b 1966); m 2, 30 Oct 1969 (m dis 1982), (Thomas) Anthony Taylor, s of Thomas Taylor (d 1984), of Cornwall; *Career* artist; ILEA teacher DES 1966, pt/t teacher of art ILEA 1967–87, sessional lectr in art and design at American Coll in London 1979–87; vice-chm Blackheath Art Soc 1974, memb Steering Gp Greenwich Lone Parent Project 1984, memb Ctee Women in Docklands 2004, first artist-in-residence Greenwich Park 2005–06; memb Cncl Pastel Soc, FBA 1982 and 1986; *Commissions* Volvo purchase 1987, Govt purchase Art of Govt Scheme Derry's Gift 1987, Govt print purchase Inland Revenue and Custom & Excise 1988, set design OUDS prodn of Shakespeare's As You Like It summer tour Japan, USA and England 1988, 3i Commercial Property 1988, Capital & Counties 1988, Dean Witter International 1989, Woolwich 1989, Japan Development Bank 1990, Bruce McGaw Graphics NY 1990, NBJ Brokers (Insurance) 1991, Collyer-Bristow (Solicitors) purchase 1992, UNICEF 1992, Camden Graphics 1993, Broomfield Hosp Mid-Essex NHS Tst Arts Project 2001; *Exhibitions* Greenwich and Docklands Festival 1996, University of Central England 1997, Century Gallery Datchet 1997, Chelsea Town Hall Gall 1994, Alexandra Palace 1994, Bonham's Salerooms 1994, The Second CBI Art Initiative Receptions 1994, Woodlands Art Open 1995, Marks and Spencer (c/o Coram Gall) 1995, Alrsford Gall 1995, AIM Show NEC Birmingham 1995, Making a Mark Mall Galleries 1995, Contemporary Art Group 1996, House and Garden Show Olympia 1996–99, Gallery at Architecture Ltd Greenwich (solo) 1997–99, Royal West of England Acad 1997, Artifex Flora and Erotica 1998, Innocent Fine Art Bristol 1998, Woodlands' Open Exhibition 1999, Great Wyrley HS 1999, The Pastel Society 2000, English Heritage Rangers House 2000, St Alfege Church 2000, Greenwich and Docklands 2000; *Awards* L'Artiste Assoifée 1975, George Rowney Pastel 1982, Frank Herring Award for Merit 1984, Willi Hoffman-Guth Award 1988; *Books and Publications* Pastel Painting Techniques (with Guy Roddon, 1987), The Medici Society (1987), Choosing & Mixing Colours (with J Galton, 1988), Drawing With Colour (with J Martin, 1990), Women Artists Diary (contrib, 1988), Pastel Masterclass (contrib, ed by Judy Martin, 1993), Vibrant Flower Painting (1995); contrib to The Artist, Artists' and Illustrators' Magazine and various other pubns; *Recreations* TV, conversation, antique markets, gardening; *Style—* Miss Frances Treanor; ✉ 121 Royal Hill, Greenwich, London SE10 8SS (tel 020 8692 3239, website www.francestreanor.com)

TREASURE, Prof Tom; s of Wilfrid Samuel Treasure, of Cheltenham, Glos, and Rita, *née* Luanaig (d 1991); *b* 12 August 1947; *Educ* St Boniface's Coll Plymouth, Guy's Hosp Med Sch Univ of London (MB BS, MRCS, LRCP, MS, MD); *m* 25 June 1977, Prof Janet Linda Treasure, da of Peter Burden; 1 s (Samuel Wilfrid b 17 Dec 1981), 1 da (Jean Dorothy b 6 Nov 1983); *Career* surgical trg Addenbrooke's Hosp, Hammersmith Hosp, Charing Cross Hosp, St Thomas' Hosp and Kent & Canterbury Hosp 1972–77, specialist trg The London Chest Hosp, The Brompton Hosp and Univ of Alabama 1978–81; res trg: Anatomy Dept Univ of Newcastle upon Tyne 1971–72, Sherrington Sch of Physiology St Thomas' Hosp Med Sch 1976–77, Dept of Surgery Univ of Alabama 1981; currently prof of cardiothoracic surgery Guy's Hosp London; memb Ed Advsy Bd BMJ; Hunterian prof RCS 1983; memb: Cncl Br Cardiac Soc 1986–90, Specialist Advsy Ctee in Cardiothoracic Surgery RCS 1989–96, Cncl Euro Assoc of Cardiothoracic Surgery 1989–92, Br Cardiac Soc, Br Assoc of Clinical Anatomists, BMA, Br Thoracic Soc, Euro Assoc for Cardiothoracic Surgery, MRS, RSM (memb Cncl 1996), Soc of Thoracic and Cardiovascular Surgns of GB and I, Surgical Res Soc; FRCS 1975, fell Fellowship of Postgrad Med 1991; *Books* A Pocket Examiner in Surgery (with J M A Northover, 1984), Belcher's Thoracic Surgical Management (5 edn with M F Sturridge, 1985), Current Surgical Practice Vol 5 (ed with J Hadfield and M Hobsley, 1990), Current Surgical Practice Vols 6 & 7 (ed with M Hobsley and A Johnson, 1993), Disorders of the Cardiovascular System (with David Patterson, 1994); *Style—* Prof Tom Treasure; ✉ Guy's Hospital, London SE1 9RT

TREBILCOCK, Peter James; s of James Charles Trebilcock, of Chorley, and Joan, *née* Craig; *b* 19 June 1957; *Educ* Liverpool Poly (BA Arch, DipArch, Sch of Architecture Prize for Architecture); *m* 7 Jan 1989, Elizabeth Ann, da of Robert Alfred Stanton; 2 s (Aaron Robert James b 15 Sept 1996, Joel Peter b 14 April 1999); *Career* architect; Austin-Smith Lord Warrington 1983–85, assoc Building Design Partnership Preston and Manchester offices 1989–96 (joined 1985), head of architecture AMEC Group Ltd 2000– (joined 1996); conslt architect to Steel Construction Inst and British Steel 1990–2003; pres N Lancs Soc of Architects 1995–97; RIBA: memb Nat Cncl 1997–2003, chm NW Regn 1998–2000, vice-pres membership 2001–03, memb Holdings Bd 2001–03, chair Professional Services Bd 2003; author of several publications; judge Young Architect of the Year Awards 1998 and 1999; jt first prize RIBA/British Gas Energy Mgmnt Competition (hosp design) 1982, Charles Reynolds bursary Concrete Soc 1983, finalist Apple Computers/Designers Jl Design Competition 1990, first prize Cynamid European Architectural Competition 1981 (teenage bedroom design), two RIBA Awards 2006, Civic Tst Award 2006; RIBA 1985, MaPS 1995; *Recreations* travel, writing, church activities (The Church of Jesus Christ of Latter-day Saints); *Style—* Peter Trebilcock, Esq; ✉ AMEC Design & Project Services, AMEC House, 410 Birchwood Boulevard, Birchwood, Warrington WA3 7WD (tel 01925 281800, fax 01925 281799, e-mail peter.trebilcock@amec.com, website www.amec.com)

TREDINNICK, David; MP; s of Stephen Victor Tredinnick (d 1995) and Evelyn Mabel, *née* Wates; *b* 19 January 1950; *Educ* Eton, Mons Offr Cadet Sch, Grad Business Sch Univ of Cape Town (MBA), St John's Coll Oxford (MLitt); *m* 7 July 1983, Rebecca, da of Roland Shott; 1 da (Sophie b 22 Feb 1987), 1 s (Thomas b 6 July 1989); *Career* Grenadier Gds 1968–71; sales and mktg computer industry 1976–79; MP (Cons) Bosworth 1987–, jt sec Cons Backbench Defence and Foreign Affrs Ctees 1990, PPS to Rt Hon Sir Wyn Roberts as min of state for Wales 1990–94; chm: Anglo-East Euro Trading Co, Br Atlantic Gp of Young Politicians 1989–91, Future of Europe Tst 1991–95, Ukraine Business Agency 1992–97; chm Parly Gp for Integrated and Complementary Health Care 2006– (treas 1989–, co-chm 2002–06); chm: Jt Ctee on Statutory Instruments 1997–2005, Select Ctee on Statutory Instruments 1997–2005; co-chm Br Meml Garden Tst UK Ltd 2003–05; *Recreations* golf, skiing, windsurfing, tennis; *Style—* David Tredinnick, Esq, MP; ✉ House of Commons, London SW1A 0AA (tel 020 7219 4514, e-mail davidtredinnickmp@parliament.uk)

TREDINNICK, Noël Harwood; s of Harold James Tredinnick (d 2003), of Beckenham, Kent, and Nola Frewin, *née* Harwood; *b* 9 March 1949; *Educ* St Olave's GS for Boys, Southwark Cathedral, Guildhall Sch of Music and Drama, Inst of Educn Univ of London (Dip Ed); *m* 3 July 1976, Fiona Jean, da of James Malcolm Couper-Johnston, of Beckenham, Kent; 1 da (Isabel Jane b 1983), 1 s (James Alexander Johnston b 24 Aug 1994); *Career* school master Langley Park Sch for Boys Beckenham 1971–75, prof and memb Acad Bd Guildhall Sch 1975–, organist and dir of music All Souls Church Langham Place London

T

1972–, artistic dir Langham Arts 1987–, prof of conducting Guildhall Sch of Music 1993–; composer, orchestrator and conductor: Beckenham Chorale 1971–72, All Souls Orch 1972–, BBC Concert Orch 1985–89, BBC Radio Orch 1988–90; musical dir: BBC Radio (Religious Dept), Songs of Praise BBC TV; writer and broadcaster radio series; fndr and conductor Prom Praise, conductor Palm Beach Opera Orch 1994–95, musical dir Billy Graham Mission Toronto 1995 and Ottawa 1998; vice-chm Jubilate Hymns Ltd; numerous recordings and performances incl Cliff Richard, Mary O'Hara, Harry Secombe, Lesley Garrett, Ben Heppner and Amy Grant; dir music for HM Queen Elizabeth II St James's Palace 1996, Balmoral 2000 and Golden Jubilee celebrations 2002; memb Archbishop's Cmmn on Church Music; DMus (Lambeth) 2002; *Recreations* theatre, architecture, country walking; *Clubs* ACG; *Style*— Dr Noël Tredinnick; ✉ 2 All Souls Place, London W1U 3HW (tel 020 7935 7246, fax 020 7935 7486, e-mail noeltredinnick@hotmail.com)

TREDRE, Roger Ford; s of Dr Alec Ford Tredre, and Angela Joyce, *née* Morris; *b* 9 March 1962; *Educ* Epsom Coll, Sidney Sussex Coll Cambridge (scholar, MA); *m* Aug 2004, Feier Chen; 1 da (Olivia Chen b 20 Jan 2005), 1 s (Nicholas Ford b 10 May 2006); *Career* journalist; staff writer The Bulletin Brussels 1984–86, dep ed Fashion Weekly 1989 (news ed 1987–88), fashion and design corr The Independent 1989–93, news and features writer The Observer 1993–97, arts corr The Observer 1997–99, ed-in-chief Worth Global Style Network 1999–2006, assoc lectr fashion MA course Central St Martins Sch of Art & Design 1999–; *Recreations* Dartmoor walking; *Style*— Roger Tredre, Esq; ✉ 18 Stronsa Road, London W12 9LB (tel 020 8811 2572, e-mail r.tredre@gmail.com)

TREDWELL, Paul Philippe; s of Ronald Jean Tredwell, of Dudley, W Midlands, and Rita May, *née* Pugh; *b* 23 February 1956; *Educ* Queen Mary's GS, Queens' Coll Cambridge (MA, LLB); *m* 31 Oct 1987, Melanie Barbara Alice, da of Robin Stuart Brown; 1 da (Rosanna Elise b 4 Nov 1989), 1 s (Rory Luc b 11 Nov 1992); *Career* account mangr Young & Rubicam advtg 1980–83 (joined as graduate trainee 1979); Abbott Mead Vickers BBDO Ltd: joined 1983, account dir 1984–93, bd dir 1987–93; client gp dir Euro RSCG Ltd (now Euro RSCG Wnek Gosper) 1993–96, client servs dir Leagas Delaney Partnership 1998–99 (bd account dir 1996–97), dir Saatchi & Saatchi 1999–; memb Mktg Soc, MIPA; *Recreations* Rugby Union, golf; *Style*— Paul Tredwell, Esq; ✉ Saatchi & Saatchi, 80 Charlotte Street, London W1A 1AQ (tel 020 7462 7010, e-mail paul.tredwell@saatchi.co.uk)

TREES, Prof Alexander John (Sandy); *b* 12 June 1946; *Educ* Univ of Edinburgh (BVMS, PhD); *m* 1970, Frances Ann, *née* McAnally; 1 da (Katherine Lucy b 15 Oct 1977); *Career* research Univ of Edinburgh expdn to Kenya 1969–70, asst in gen vet practice Derby 1970–71, research assoc Centre for Tropical Vet Med (CTVM) Univ of Edinburgh 1971, memb CTVM/Vom Collaboration Project Nat Inst for Vet Research Vom Nigeria 1974–76; Elanco Products Co Rome: vet advsr for ME 1977–79, vet advsr ME, Turkey and Africa 1979–80, head Animal Science ME and Africa 1980; Faculty of Vet Science Univ of Liverpool: appointed lectr Dept of Vet Parasitology 1980 (tenure granted 1983), head Dept of Vet Parasitology 1992–2001, prof of vet parasitology (personal chair) 1994–, dean 2001–; Liverpool Sch of Tropical Med: head Parasite and Vector Biology Div 1994–97, memb Cncl 1995–2004; MRC visiting sr scientist MRC Lab Bo Sierra Leone 1984–88; memb Vet Med Interest Gp Wellcome Tst 1998–2003; memb Editorial Bd: Research in Vet Science 1991–2001, Trends in Parasitology (formerly Parasitology Today) 1992–; author of numerous book chapters, reviews, articles and other contribs to learned jls, invited speaker at confs and symposia worldwide; Assoc of Vet Teachers and Research Workers (AVTRW): memb 1980–, jr vice-pres 1995–96, memb Cncl 1995–2001, pres 1996–97, Selborne Medal for vet research 2005; memb: Br Soc of Parasitology 1980–, BVA 1980– (chair Educn Gp and memb Vet Policy Gp 1997–2001), Royal Soc of Tropical Med and Hygiene 1986– (memb Cncl and Medals Ctee 1997–2000); Birrel-Grey Travelling Scholarship Univ of Edinburgh 1971, Cwlth Fndn Fellowship 1982, founding diplomate European Vet Parasitology Coll (DipEVPC) 2003; MRCVS 1969 (memb Cncl and Educn Ctee 2000–); *Style*— Prof Sandy Trees; ✉ Veterinary Parasitology, School of Tropical Medicine, Liverpool L3 5QA (tel 0151 705 3235, fax 0151 705 3373, e-mail trees@liverpool.ac.uk)

TREFETHEN, Prof Lloyd N; *b* 30 August 1955; *Educ* Phillips Exeter Acad, Harvard Univ (AB), Stanford Univ (MS, PhD); *m*; 2 c; *Career* NSF post-doctoral fell and adjunct asst prof Courant Inst of Mathematical Scis New York Univ 1982–84, assoc prof of applied mathematics MIT 1987–91 (asst prof 1984–87), prof of computer sci Cornell Univ 1994–97 (assoc prof 1991–93), prof of numerical analysis Univ of Oxford 1997–; ed: SIAM Jl on Numerical Analysis 1984–99, Numerische Mathematik 1988–99, SIAM Review 1989–, Calcolo 1998–; assoc ed: Jl of Computational and Applied Mathematics 1987–, Japan Jl of Industrial and Applied Mathematics 1991–96; FRS 2005; *Books* Numerical Conformal Mapping (ed, 1986), Finite Difference and Spectral Methods for Ordinary and Partial Differential Equations (1996), Numerical Linear Algebra (with David Bau, 1997), Spectral Methods in MATLAB (2000), Schwarz-Christoffel Mapping (with Tobin Driscoll, 2002); also author of numerous articles in learned jls; *Style*— Prof Lloyd Trefethen; ✉ Balliol College, Oxford OX1 3BJ (tel 01865 273886, fax 01865 273839, e-mail lnt@comlab.ox.ac.uk)

TREFGARNE, 2 Baron (UK 1947); David Garro Trefgarne; PC (1989); s of 1 Baron Trefgarne (d 1960), and Elizabeth (who m 2, 1962 (m dis 1966), Cdr Anthony Tosswill Courtney, OBE (d 1988); and 3, 1971, Hugh Cecil Howat Ker (d 1987)), da of late Charles Edward Churchill, of Ashton Keynes, Wilts; *b* 31 March 1941; *Educ* Haileybury, Princeton Univ; *m* 1968, Rosalie, er da of Baron Lane of Horsell (Life Peer), *qv*; 2 s (Hon George b 1970, Hon Justin b 1973), 1 da (Hon Rebecca b 1976); *Heir* s, Hon George Trefgarne; *Career* oppn whip House of Lords 1977–79, a Lord in Waiting (govt whip) 1979–81; under sec of state: Dept of Trade 1981, FCO 1981–82, DHSS 1982–83, MOD (for armed forces) 1983–85; min of state for def support 1985–86, min of state for def procurement 1986–89, min for trade DTI 1989–90; elected memb of the House of Lords 1999–; dir and conslt various cos; non-exec dir Siebe plc 1991–98; pres: Mech and Metal Trades Confedn 1990–, Popular Flying Assoc 1992–2003, British Assoc of Aviation Consultants 1995–; hon pres Instn of Incorporated Engrs 2003–06, pres Welding INst 2006–, dep pres Instn of Engrg and Technol 2006–; chm: Engrg & Marine Trg Authy (now Science, Engrg and Mfrg Technologies Alliance (SEMTA)) 1994–, Brooklands Museum Tst 2002–; life govr Haileybury 1992–, govr Guildford Sch of Acting 1992–2000, tstee Mary Rose Tst 1994–2000; Royal Aero Club Bronze medal (jtly) for flight from UK to Aust and back in light aircraft 1963; Hon Dr Staffordshire Univ 2004, hon fell Univ of Central Lancashire 2004; Hon FIIE; *Recreations* flying, photography; *Style*— The Rt Hon the Lord Trefgarne, PC; ✉ House of Lords, London SW1A 0PW

TREFGARNE, Hon Trevor Garro; 2 s of 1 Baron Trefgarne (d 1960), and Elizabeth, *née* Churchill; *b* 18 January 1944; *Educ* Cheltenham Coll, Cranfield Sch of Mgmnt; *m* 1, 1967 (m dis 1979), Diana Elizabeth, da of late Michael Gibb, of Taynton, Oxon, by his w Ursula; 2 s (Rupert b 1972, Oliver b 1974), 1 da (Susannah b 1976); m 2, 1979, Caroline France, da of Michael Gosschalk, of Monte Carlo; 1 s (Mark b 1982), 1 da (Camilla b 1988); *Career* dir Pentos plc 1972–75, chm Nesco Investments plc 1976–87; dir: Templeton Emerging Markets Investment Trust plc 1989–2002, EFG plc 1992–94, Templeton Central & Eastern European Investment Co 1996–98, Global Yatirim Holding AS 2002–, Garro Securities Ltd, Franklin Templeton Investment Funds 2002–, Gartmore High Income Tst plc; chm: Recovery Tst plc 2001–, Enterprise Insurance Co Ltd Ghana; *Style*— The Hon Trevor Trefgarne; ✉ 30 Kimbell Gardens, London SW6 6QQ

TREGGIARI, Prof Susan Mary; da of Walter Howard Franklin (d 1987), of Great Rissington, Glos, and Elizabeth Mary, *née* Washbourn; *b* 11 March 1940, Moreton-in-Marsh, Glos; *Educ* Cheltenham Ladies' Coll (scholar), Lady Margaret Hall Oxford (scholar, MA), Univ of Oxford (BLitt, DLitt); *m* 1964, Arnaldo Treggiari; 2 da (Joanna b 1965, Silvia b 1967); *Career* pt/t lectr Goldsmiths Coll London 1965–66, lectr North-Western Poly London 1966–69; Dept of Classical Studies Univ of Ottawa: asst prof 1970–71, assoc prof 1971–79, prof 1979–84, chm 1981–82; Stanford Univ: prof Dept of Classics 1982–2001 (chm 1987–90, 1992–93), Anne T and Robert M Bass prof Sch of Humanities and Sciences 1992–2001; memb Sub-Faculty of Ancient History Univ of Oxford 2001–; visiting prof: Sweet Briar Coll VA 1969–70, Dept of Classics and History Yale Univ 1993–94; visiting fell: BNC Oxford 1976–77, All Souls Coll Oxford 1995–96; jt ed Classical News and Views/Echos du monde classique 1974–81 (actg ed 1973–74), gen ed (jtly) Clarendon Ancient History Series 1994–, co-ed Ancient History Bulletin 1996–2003; memb Editorial Bd: Phoenix 1972 and 1975–78, Florilegium 1979–98; pres: Assoc of Ancient Historians 1981–84, American Philological Assoc 1997; Charles J Goodwin Award of Merit American Philological Assoc 1993, John Simon Guggenheim Meml Fndn Fellowship 1995–96; fell American Acad of Arts and Sciences 1995; *Books* Roman Freedmen during the Late Republic (1969, reissued 2000), Cicero's Cilician Letters (1973, 2 edn 1997), Roman Marriage (1991), Roman Social History (2002), Terentia, Tullia and Publilia (2007); *Style*— Prof Susan Treggiari

TREGLOWN, Prof Jeremy Dickinson; s of late Rev Geoffrey Leonard Treglown, MBE, Hon CF, of Cheltenham, Glos, and Beryl Miriam Treglown; *b* 24 May 1946; *Educ* Bristol GS, St Peter's Coll Saltley, St Peter's Coll Oxford (MA, BLitt), UCL (PhD); *m* 1, 1970 (m dis 1982), Rona Mary Bower; 1 s, 2 da; m 2, 1984, Holly Mary Belinda Eley, *née* Urquhart; *Career* lectr in English Lincoln Coll Oxford 1973–76, lectr UCL 1976–79, ed TLS 1982–90 (asst ed 1980–82), prof of English Univ of Warwick 1993– (chair Dept of English and Comparative Literature Studies 1995–98); contrib to jls incl: FT, TLS, New Yorker; visiting fell All Souls Coll Oxford 1986, Mellon visiting assoc Caltech, fell Huntington Library San Marino 1988, Ferris prof Princeton Univ 1992, Jackson Brothers fell Beinecke Library Yale Univ 1999, Leverhulme res fell 2001–03, Mellon fell Humanities Res Center Univ of Texas Austin 2002, Margaret and Herman Sokol fell Center for Scholars and Writers NY Public Library 2002–03; hon res fell UCL 1991–; chm of judges: Booker Prize 1991, Whitbread Book of the Year Award 1997; FRSL 1989 (memb Cncl); *Publications* The Letters of John Wilmot, Earl of Rochester (ed, 1980), Spirit of Wit: Reconsiderations of Rochester (ed, 1982), The Lantern-Bearers: Essays by Robert Louis Stevenson (ed, 1988), Roald Dahl: A Biography (1994), Grub Street and the Ivory Tower: Literary Journalism and Literary Scholarship from Fielding to the Internet (ed with Bridget Bennett, 1998), Romancing: The Life and Work of Henry Green (2000), V S Prichett: A Working Life (2004), Essential Stories by V S Pritchett (ed, 2005), The Complete Short Stories of Roald Dahl (ed, 2006); gen ed Plays in Performance series 1981–85; *Style*— Prof Jeremy Treglown; ✉ Department of English and Comparative Literary Studies, University of Warwick, Coventry CV4 7AL

TREGONING, Christopher William Courtenay; 3 and yst s of Lt-Col John Langford Tregoning, MBE, TD (d 1976), of Inkpen, Newbury, and Sioned Georgina Courtenay, *née* Strick (d 1994); bro of Julian George Tregoning, *qv*; *b* 15 June 1948; *Educ* Harrow, Fitzwilliam Coll Cambridge (MA); *m* 15 Sept 1973, Antonia Isabella Mary, da of Maj John Albert Miles Critchley-Salmonson, of Great Barton, Suffolk; 3 s (Harry John William b 28 Jan 1976, Daniel Christopher Leonard b 30 Dec 1977, Thomas Anthony Cecil b 26 Jan 1982); *Career* Thomson McLintock & Co 1970–74, Barclays Bank Ltd 1974–79, dep md Den Norske Bank plc (formerly Nordic Bank plc) 1986– (joined 1979); FCA 1974; *Recreations* field sports, racing, sporting paintings; *Style*— Christopher Tregoning, Esq; ✉ Den Norske Bank plc, 20 St Dunstan's Hill, London EC3R 8HY (tel 020 7621 1111, fax 020 7626 7400)

TREGONING, Julian George; 2 s of Lt-Col John Langford Tregoning, MBE, TD (d 1976), and Sioned Georgina Courtenay, *née* Strick (d 1994); bro of Christopher William Courtenay Tregoning, *qv*; *b* 24 October 1946; *Educ* Harrow, BRNC Dartmouth; *m* Tessa Jane, da of Cdr Norman Lanyon, DSC** (d 1982); 2 s (Oliver b 1973, Guy b 1975); *Career* RN 1965–68; dir: Save & Prosper Group Ltd 1985–95 (joined 1968), Robert Fleming & Co Ltd 1995–98, Mellon International Ltd 2000–, New Star Financial Opportunities Fund Ltd 2001–; chm Assoc of Unit Tst and Investment Funds 1993–95 (int rep 1993–99); dep chm Univ of London Pension Scheme 1999–; pres Fédération Européene des Fonds et Sociétés d'Investissement 1997–98; treas Royal UK Beneficent Assoc (Rukba) 1990–2003, chm City of London Club 2000–03; memb Ct of Assts Worshipful Co of Grocers (Master 2001–02); govr Oundle Sch; MSI; *Recreations* messing about in boats, opera, watercolours, wine; *Clubs* Boodle's, City of London, MCC, St Moritz Tobogganing; *Style*— Julian Tregoning, Esq

TREGONING, Marcus Philip Norris; s of Peter Norris Tregoning, MC, and Anne Katherine, *née* Fitzgeorge-Parker; *b* 31 July 1959, Birmingham; *m* 7 March 1998, Arabella Julia, *née* Wright; 2 s (George b 11 Sept 1998, Peter b 29 Sept 2003), 2 da (Jessica b 23 Oct 1999, Alice b 4 Aug 2004); *Career* racehorse trainer; formerly asst trainer to Major W R Hern, trainer Kingwood House Stables 1998–; horses trained incl Sir Percy (winner Epsom Derby 2006); Flat Trainer of the Year Horserace Writers and Photographers Assoc 2006; *Recreations* shooting, fishing; *Style*— Marcus Tregoning, Esq; ✉ Kingwood House, Kingwood House Stables, Lambourn, Hungerford, Berkshire RG17 7RS (tel 01488 73300, fax 01488 71728, e-mail enquires@kingwood-stables.co.uk)

TREGUNNA, Brian John; s of Frederick Charles Tregunna (d 1997), and Gladys, *née* Hambly; *b* 1 June 1959, Truro, Cornwall; *Educ* Falmouth Sch, Univ of Central Lancs (BSc), Univ of Coventry (MA); *m* 7 March 1981, Gail, *née* Bartle; 3 da (Beth b 19 Feb 1985, Mary b 6 June 1986, Alice b 3 Feb 1988); *Career* firefighter Cornwall County Fire Brigade 1978; Hereford & Worcester Fire & Rescue Service: divnl offr 1997, deputy chief fire offr 2001; chief fire offr and chief exec Derbys Fire & Rescue Service 2005–; memb: IFireE 1985, Chief Fire Offrs Assoc 2001; *Recreations* hiking, rugby, reading; *Style*— Brian Tregunna, Esq; ✉ 9 Hardwick Drive, Mickleover, Derby DE3 9BN (tel 01332 232730, e-mail brian@btregunna.wanadoo.co.uk); Derbyshire Fire & Rescue Service, The Old Hall, Burton Road, Littleover, Derby DE23 6EH (tel 01332 777001, fax 01332 270360, e-mail btregunna@derbys-fire.gov.uk)

TREHEARNE, Ian Richard; s of Edward Brian Geoffrey Trehearne, of Keyhaven, Hants, and Mary Violet, *née* Blake; *b* 17 May 1950, Birmingham; *Educ* Felsted, Univ of Durham (BA); *m* 1975, Madeleine Elizabeth, *née* Epstein; 1 da (Ghislaine Florence b 1984); *Career* slr; called to the Bar 1980; local govt (Newham, Islington, Westminster, Camden) 1972–84; ptnr Berwin Leighton Paisner 1988– (joined 1985); memb Planning Ctee Br Cncl of Offices; supporter Planning Aid Tst; MRTPI; *Recreations* sailing, theatre, books; *Style*— Ian Trehearne, Esq; ✉ 20 New End Square, London NW3 1LN (tel 020 7435 6310, fax 020 7794 8816); Berwin Leighton Paisner, Adelaide House, London Bridge, London EC4R 9HA (tel 020 7760 4259, fax 020 7760 1111, e-mail ian.trehearne@blplaw.com)

TREITEL, Prof Sir Guenter Heinz; kt (1997), QC (1983); s of Theodor Treitel (d 1973), and Hanna, *née* Levy (d 1951); *b* 26 October 1928; *Educ* Kilburn GS, Magdalen Coll Oxford (MA, BCL, DCL); *m* 1 Jan 1957, Phyllis Margaret, da of Ronald Cook (d 1990); 2 s (Richard James b 1958, Henry Marcus b 1960); *Career* called to the Bar Gray's Inn 1952, hon bencher 1982; asst lectr LSE 1951–53; Univ of Oxford: lectr Univ Coll 1953–54, fell Magdalen Coll 1954–79 (emeritus fell 1979), All Souls reader in Eng law 1964–79, Vinerian prof of Eng law 1979–96 (emeritus prof 1996), fell All Souls Coll 1979–96 (emeritus fell 1996); visiting lectr/prof 1963–2003 Univs of: Chicago, Houston, Southern Methodist, Virginia, Santa Clara, W Aust; visiting scholar Ernst von Caemmerer Stiftung 1990; tstee Br Museum 1983–98, memb Cncl Nat Tst 1984–93; FBA 1977; *Books* The Law of Contract (1962, 11 edn 2003), An Outline of the Law of Contract (1975, 6 edn 2004), Remedies for Breach of Contract, A Comparative Account (1988), Unmöglichkeit, 'Impracticability' und 'Frustration' im anglo-amerikanischen Recht (1991), Frustration and Force Majeure (1994, 2 edn 2004), Some Landmarks of Twentieth Century Contract Law (2002); jt ed of: Benjamin's Sale of Goods (1975, 7 edn 2006), Chitty on Contracts (23 edn 1968 - 29 edn 2004), Dicey (& Morris) Conflict of Laws (7 edn 1958, 8 edn 1967), English Private Law (2000), Carver on Bills of Lading (2001, 2 edn 2005); *Recreations* reading, music; *Style*— Prof Sir Guenter Treitel, QC, FBA; ✉ All Souls College, Oxford OX1 4AL (tel 01865 279379, fax 01865 279299)

TRELAWNY, Sir John Barry Salusbury-; 13 Bt (E 1628), of Trelawny, Cornwall; s of Sir John William Robin Maurice Salusbury-Trelawny, 12 Bt (d 1956), by his 1 w, Glenys Mary, da of John Cameron Kynoch; *b* 4 September 1934; *Educ* HMS Worcester; *m* 1958, Carol Knox, yr da of C F K Watson, of The Field, Saltwood, Kent; 1 s, 3 da; *Heir* s, John Salusbury-Trelawny; *Career* Nat Serv RNVR; dir: Martin Walter Group Ltd 1971–74, Korn/Ferry International 1977–83, Morris & Blakey plc 1978–79; chm Goddard Kay Rogers & Associates mgmnt conslts until 1995 (dir 1984); pres: Folkstone, Hythe and District Scouts Assoc 1975–, London Cornish Assoc 1997–2005; JP Kent 1973–78; FInstM; *Clubs* Royal Naval Sailing Assoc, Royal Cinque Ports Yacht; *Style*— Sir John Trelawny, Bt; ✉ Beavers Hill, Saltwood, Hythe, Kent CT21 4QA (tel 01303 266476)

TRELFORD, Prof Donald Gilchrist; s of late Thomas Staplin Trelford, of Coventry, and late Doris, *née* Gilchrist; *b* 9 November 1937; *Educ* Bablake Sch Coventry, Selwyn Coll Cambridge (MA); *m* 1, 1963, Janice Ingram; 2 s, 1 da; m 2, 1978, Katherine Louise Mark; 1 da; m 3, 2001, Claire Elizabeth Bishop; *Career* ed Times of Malawi 1963–66; corr in Africa: The Observer, The Times, BBC; The Observer: dep ed 1969–75, ed and dir 1975–93, chief exec 1992–93; sports columnist Daily Telegraph 1993–, prof of journalism studies Univ of Sheffield 1994–2000 (visiting prof 2000–); regular broadcasts on radio and TV, regular speaker at int media confs; pres Media Soc 1999–2002, vice-pres Br Sports Tst; chm London Press Club 2002–, chm of judges Br Press Awards 2002–05; memb: Br Exec Ctee Int Press Inst, Defence Press and Broadcasting Ctee 1984–93, Olivier Awards Ctee 1985–93, MCC Ctee 1988–91, Advsy Bd London Choral Soc; chm Soc of Gentlemen Lovers of Musick 1995–2002; memb: Competition Cmmn 1999–2006, Exec Bd Nat Acad of Writing 1999–2003; memb Cncl Advtg Standards Authy 2002–; Hon DLitt Univ of Sheffield; Freeman City of London, Liveryman Worshipful Co of Stationers & Newspaper Makers; FRSA; *Publications* County Champions (contrib, 1982), Sunday Best (annual anthology, ed, 1981–83), Siege (jt author, 1980), Snookered (1986), Child of Change (with Garry Kasparov, 1987), Saturday's Boys (contrib, 1990), Fine Glances (contrib, 1990), Len Hutton Remembered (1992), The Observer at 200 (ed, 1992), W G Grace (1998); *Recreations* golf, tennis, snooker; *Clubs* Garrick, MCC; *Style*— Prof Donald Trelford; ✉ 15 Fowler Road, London N1 2EP (tel 07850 131742, e-mail donaldtrelford@yahoo.co.uk); Apartado 146, 07460 Pollenca, Mallorca, Spain

TREMAIN, Rose; CBE (2007); da of Keith Nicholas Thomson, and Viola Mabel, *née* Dudley; *b* 2 August 1943; *Educ* Sorbonne, UEA (BA); *m* 1, 7 May 1971 (m dis 1976), Jon Tremain; 1 da (Eleanor Rachel b 16 July 1972); m 2, 2 Aug 1982 (m dis 1991), Jonathan Dudley; *Career* author; FRSL 1983; *Awards* Dylan Thomas Prize 1984, Giles Cooper Award 1985, Angel Prize 1985 and 1989, Sunday Express Book of the Year Award 1989, James Tait Black Meml Prize 1992, Prix Femina Étranger 1994, Whitbread Novel Prize 1999; *Books* Sadler's Birthday (1975), Letter to Sister Benedicta (1978), The Cupboard (1980), The Colonel's Daughter (1982), The Swimming Pool Season (1984), The Garden of The Villa Mollini (1986), Restoration (1989), Sacred Country (1992), Evangelista's Fan (1994), Collected Short Stories (1996), The Way I Found Her (1997), Music and Silence (1999), The Colour (2003), The Darkness of Wallis Simpson (2005), The Road Home (2007); *Recreations* gardening, yoga; *Style*— Ms Rose Tremain, CBE; ✉ 2 High House, South Avenue, Thorpe St Andrew, Norwich NR7 0EZ (tel 01603 439682, fax 01603 434234)

TRENCHARD, 3 Viscount (UK 1936); Sir Hugh Trenchard; 3 Bt (UK 1919); also Baron Trenchard (UK 1930); s of 2 Viscount Trenchard, MC (d 1987), and of Patricia, da of Adm Sir Sidney Bailey, KBE, CB, DSO; *b* 12 March 1951; *Educ* Eton, Trinity Coll Cambridge; *m* 1975, Fiona Elizabeth, da of 2 Baron Margadale, TD, DL (d 2003); 2 s (Hon Alexander Thomas b 1978, Hon William James b 1986), 2 da (Hon Katherine Clare b 1980, Hon Laura Mary b 1987); *Heir* s, Hon Alexander Trenchard; *Career* Capt 4 Royal Green Jackets, TA 1973–80; Kleinwort Benson Ltd 1973–96: chief rep in Japan 1980–85, dir 1986–96; Kleinwort Benson International Inc: gen mangr Tokyo 1985–88, pres 1988–95, dep chm 1995–96; rep in Japan of Kleinwort Benson Group plc 1993–95; dir: Dover Japan Inc 1985–87, ACP Holdings Ltd 1990–94, Robert Fleming & Co Ltd 1996–98, Robert Fleming International Ltd 1998–2000, Berkeley Technology Ltd 1999–, Westhall Capital Ltd 2001–03, Dryden Wealth Mgmnt Ltd 2004–05, Stratton Street PCC Ltd 2006–; chm The Dejima Fund Ltd 2001–, sr advsr Prudential Financial Inc 2002–; DG European Fund and Asset Mgmnt Assoc 2006; European Business Community in Japan: chm Securities Ctee 1993–95, vice-chm Cncl 1995; dir: Japan Securities Dealers Assoc 1994–95, Bond Underwriters Assoc of Japan 1994–95; memb: Japan Assoc of Corp Execs 1987–95, Cncl Japan Soc 1992–93 and 1995– (vice-chm 1996–2000, jt chm 2000–04); hon treas House of Lords All-Pty Defence Study Gp 1992–93, vice-chm Br-Japanese Parly Gp 1997–99 and 2004–, memb Jt Ctee on Fin Servs and Markets 1999, elected hereditary peer House of Lords 2004–; pres NE Herts Cons Assoc 2001–; chm RAF Benevolent Fund 2006– (memb Cncl 1991–2003); Hon Air Cdre 600 (City of London) Sqdn RAuxAF 2006–; *Clubs* Brooks's, Cavalry and Guards, Pratt's, Tokyo; *Style*— The Rt Hon the Viscount Trenchard; ✉ Standon Lordship, Ware, Hertfordshire SG11 1PR (tel 01920 823785, fax 01920 823802, e-mail trenchardh@aol.com)

TREND, Hon Michael St John; CBE (1997); er s of Baron Trend, GCB, CVO, PC (Life Peer, d 1987), and Patricia Charlotte, *née* Shaw; *b* 1952; *Educ* Westminster, Oriel Coll Oxford, in Athens (Greek Govt scholarship); *m* 28 Feb 1987, Jill E, er da of L A Kershaw; 1 s, 2 da; *Career* journalist, editor and broadcaster; ed: History Today 1981–84, House of Commons Magazine 1984–86; home ed The Spectator 1986–90, latterly chief leader writer Daily Telegraph; MP (Cons): Windsor and Maidenhead 1992–97, Windsor 1997–2005; memb Select Ctee on Health 1992–93; PPS: Dept of Environment 1993–94, Dept of Health 1994, Dept of Tport 1994–95; dep chm Cons Party 1995–98, oppn frontbench spokesman foreign and Cwlth affrs 1998–99, spokesman on pensions 1999, chm Conservative Int Office 1999–; govr Westminster Fndn for Democracy; *Style*— The Hon Michael Trend, CBE

TRENOUTH, Dr Michael John; s of John Trenouth, of Grange-over-Sands, and Marjorie Trenouth; *b* 2 June 1946; *Educ* Friend's Sch Lancaster, Univ of Manchester (BSc, BDS, MDS, PhD, DOrth, DDO, FDS, RCPS); *Career* Manchester Dental Hosp: house offr 1971–72, lectr in oral surgery 1972–75, lectr in dental anatomy and hon registrar orthodontics 1975–78, lectr in orthodontics and hon sr registrar orthodontics 1978–85; conslt orthodontist Preston Royal Hosp 1985–, dental post graduate tutor Lancaster, Preston, Chorley and Blackpool Dists 1991–98; treas Manchester and Region Orthodontic Study Gp 1980–85; chm NW Regnl Ctee Hosp Dental Servs 2003– (hon sec 1996–2003); *Recreations* skiing, sailing, fell walking, ice skating; *Style*— Dr Michael Trenouth; ✉ Royal Preston Hospital, Sharoe Green Lane, Preston PR2 9HT (tel 01772 522597, e-mail karen.pool@lthtr.nhs.uk)

TRESCOTHICK, Marcus Edward; MBE (2006); *b* 25 December 1975, Keynsham, Somerset; *m* Hayley; 1 da (Ellie Louise b 2005); *Career* professional cricketer; with Somerset CCC 1993–; England: 76 test matches, 123 one-day ints, test debut v West Indies 2000, one day int debut v Zimbabwe 2000, memb team touring Pakistan and Sri Lanka 2000–01, Zimbabwe, India and NZ 2001–02 (capt one-day int v Zimbabwe 2001), Bangladesh and Sri Lanka 2003, West Indies 2004, South Africa 2004–05 and Pakistan 2005; *Style*— Marcus Trescothick, Esq, MBE; ✉ c/o Somerset CCC, The County Ground, Taunton, Somerset TA1 1JT

TRETHOWAN, (Henry) Brock; s of Michael Trethowan, OBE (d 1968), of Hants, and Phyllis Franklin, *née* Miles (d 1981); *b* 22 June 1937; *Educ* Sherborne; *m* 11 April 1970, Virginia, da of Lt-Col Geoffrey Charles Lee, of Farnham, Surrey; 2 da (Rebecca b 1966, Henrietta b 1977); *Career* solicitor; recorder of the Crown Court 1990–2003; full time immigration judge 1997–2003 (pt/t 2003–07); *Style*— Brock Trethowan, Esq; ✉ 32 Pilgrims Mead, Bishopdown Farm, Salisbury, Wiltshire SP1 3GX (tel 01722 332017, e-mail brock.trethowan@btopenworld.com)

TREUHERZ, Julian Benjamin; s of late Werner Treuherz (d 1999), and Irmgard, *née* Amberg (d 2001); *b* 12 March 1947; *Educ* Manchester Grammar, ChCh Oxford (MA), UEA (MA); *Career* Manchester City Art Gallery: trainee 1971, asst keeper of fine art 1972, keeper of fine art 1974; keeper of art galleries National Museums Liverpool 1989–2007; memb: Museums Assoc 1971, Victorian Soc 1971 (hon sec Manchester Group 1972–79, chm Manchester Group 1980–83); memb Ctee: Contemporary Art Soc 1990–94, Liverpool Univ Fine Arts Advsy Gp 1990–2000, NACF Merseyside Gp 1991–2007, Whitworth Art Gallery 1993–2005, Burlington Magazine Consultative 2003–; tstee Lakeland Arts Tst 1997–; *Publications* Pre-Raphaelite Paintings from the Manchester City Art Gallery (1981), Hard Times - Social Realism in Victorian Art (1987), Country Houses of Cheshire (jtly with Peter de Figueiredo, 1988), Victorian Painting (1993), Dante Gabriel Rossetti (jtly, 2003); various articles in art-historical jls; *Recreations* playing the piano, cooking, opera; *Style*— Julian Treuherz, Esq; ✉ 1 Ingestre Road, Oxton, Wirral CH43 5TZ

TREVAIL, Charles; s of Donald Charles Trevail (d 1986), and Lois Mary, *née* Rowse (d 2003); *b* 22 August 1960; *Educ* Plymouth Coll, Univ of Durham (BA), Postgrad Dip Mktg; *m* 1995, Imelda Primrose; 2 da (Florence Lois Kate b 15 Sept 1996, Martha Elizabeth b 8 May 1999); *Career* formerly: various mktg posts LDDC and Acco Rexel, business conslt Strategy International; Sampson Tyrrell Enterprise (Enterprise Identity Group t/a Enterprise IG since 1998): account dir 1988–91, bd dir 1991–95, md 1995–99; ceo FutureBrand (brand consultancy of Interpublic) 1999–2003, memb Bd McCann Europe, fndr Promise Corp plc (business consultancy) 2004; reg speaker at confs on branding and commentator in media, occasional advsr to New Labour on strategy; memb Marketing Soc; FRSA; *Recreations* football, tennis, sailing, hill walking, bird watching, politics, family; *Style*— Charles Trevail, Esq

TREVELYAN, Sir Geoffrey Washington; 11 Bt (E 1662), of Nettlecombe, Somerset (claim to the senior baronetcy has been accepted by the College of Arms); 5 Bt (UK 1874), of Wallington, Northumberland; s of Rt Hon Sir Charles Philips Trevelyan, 3 Bt (d 1958); s bro, Sir George Lowthian Trevelyan, 4 Bt (d 1996); *b* 4 July 1920; *Educ* Oundle, Trinity Coll Cambridge (MA); *m* 3 May 1947, Gillian Isabel Trevelyan, MBE (d 2000), eldest da of late Alexander Louis Sandison Wood, OBE, of Whelpley Hill, Bucks; 1 s (Peter John b 11 Sept 1948), 1 da (Sandra Mary (Mrs David Bradley) b 5 Aug 1951); *Heir* s, Peter Trevelyan; *Career* de Havilland AC Co Ltd 1941–61; dir: Chatto & Windus Ltd, Hogarth Press Ltd 1962–78, Chatto, Bodley Head and Jonathan Cape Ltd 1970–78; chm Thames North Region of Abbeyfield Soc 1985–94, hon treas Family Planning Assoc 1975–90; dir: The Lake Hunts Ltd 1978–97, Family Planning Sales Ltd 1985–90; *Style*— Sir Geoffrey Trevelyan, Bt; ✉ Lower Silkstead, 3 Abbey Mill End, St Albans, Hertfordshire AL3 4HN (tel 01727 864866)

TREVELYAN KEE, Hon Mrs (Catherine Mary); OBE (1977); da of Baron Trevelyan (Life Peer, d 1985), and Violet Margaret, *née* Bartholomew; *b* 1943; *Educ* St Mary's Sch Calne, Univ of St Andrews; *m* 10 Dec 1990, Robert Kee; *Career* exec dir New York City Cultural Cncl and Cultural Cncl Fndn 1969–73, admin Windsor Festival 1974–76, dep sec-gen London Celebrations Ctee for the Queen's Silver Jubilee 1976–77, exhbn organiser 1978–80, Carlton Cleeve Ltd, md The Burlington Magazine 1980–, dir The Burlington Magazine Fndn Inc 1986–; govr Int Students House Univ of London until 1997, memb Cncl Br Museum Friends, tstee Public Catalogue Fndn 2006–; *Style*— The Hon Mrs Trevelyan Kee, OBE

TREVERTON-JONES, Ronald; s of Dennis Ford Treverton-Jones (d 1950), of Newport, Gwent, and Alison Joy Bielski, *née* Morris-Prosser; *b* 1 August 1949; *Educ* Malvern Coll, Univ of Wales Swansea (BSc); *m* 1, 31 July 1970 (m dis 1985), Margaret Jean, da of Donald John Purser, of Northfield, Birmingham; 2 s (Peter b 1976, Michael b 1978); m 2, 17 Oct 1987, Jacqueline Diane, da of James Leslie Beckingham Welch (d 1974), of Quinton, Birmingham; *Career* grad trainee National Westminster Bank 1970–72, trainee N Lea Barham & Brooks 1970–74, sr ptnr Harris Allday 1992–2006 (ptnr 1976–), md EFG Harris Allday 2006–, dir EFG Private Bank Ltd 2006–; vice-chm The Bow Group London 1979–80, chm Birmingham Bow Group 1979–80; chm Birmingham Stock Exchange Assoc 1995–99; memb Stock Exchange 1975; *Books* Financing our Cities (with Edwina Currie and Peter McGauley, 1976), Right Wheel - A Conservative Policy for the Motor Industry (1977); *Recreations* country pursuits, woodland management, travel; *Style*— Ronald Treverton-Jones, Esq; ✉ Ravenhill Court, Lulsley, Knightwick, Worcestershire WR6 5QW (tel 01886 821242); La Bartelle Basse, Pont De Russac, 46170, Castelnau-Montratier, France; EFG Harris Allday, 33 Great Charles Street, Birmingham B3 3JN (tel 0121 214 2221, fax 0121 236 2587, e-mail ronald.treverton-jones@efgha.com)

TREVES, Vanni Emanuele; s of Giuliano Treves (ka 1944), and Marianna, *née* Baer; *b* 3 November 1940; *Educ* St Paul's (fndn scholar), Univ of Oxford (MA), Univ of Illinois (res fell, Fulbright scholar, LLM); *m* 7 Jan 1971, Angela Veronica, da of Lt-Gen Sir Richard Fyffe, DSO, OBE, MC (d 1971); 2 s (Alexander b 1973, William b 1975), 1 da (Louise b 1983); *Career* slr; ptnr Macfarlanes Slrs 1970–2002 (sr ptnr 1987–99); dir: Oceonics Group plc 1984–95, Saatchi & Saatchi Co plc 1987–90, Fiskars Ltd 1989–, Amplifon 2000–; chm: BBA Group plc 1989–2001, McKechnie plc 1991–2000, Dennis Group plc 1996–99, Channel Four Television Corporation 1998–2003, Equitable Life Assurance Society 2001–, Intertek Group plc 2001–, Korn/Ferry International UK 2004–; tstee: J Paul Getty Jr Charitable Tst, 29th May 1961 Charitable Tst, Fledgeling Equity and Bond Funds (chm 1992–2000); vice-pres London Fedn of Boys' Clubs; chm: NSPCC Justice for Children Appeal, Bd of Patrons Nat Portrait Gallery; slr to the Royal Acad of Arts; chm: London Business Sch 1998–2006, Nat Coll for Sch Leadership 2004–; govr Sadler's Wells Fndn; hon fell London Business Sch; *Recreations* walking, eating, watercolours; *Clubs* Boodle's, City of London; *Style*— Vanni Treves, Esq

TREVETHIN, Baron ; *see:* Oaksey, Baron

TREVETT, Peter George; QC (1992); s of George Albert Trevett (d 1995), of Surbiton, Surrey, and Janet, *née* Ayling (d 1992); *b* 25 November 1947; *Educ* Kingston GS, Queens' Coll Cambridge (MA, LLM); *m* 8 July 1972, Vera Lucia; 2 s (Thomas b 1973, Philip b 1978), 1 da (Jessica b 1982); *Career* called to the Bar Lincoln's Inn 1971 (bencher), practising revenue barr 1973–; author of various articles in professional jls; *Recreations* golf, collecting succulent plants, gardening, book collecting, reading; *Style*— Peter Trevett, Esq, QC; ✉ 11 New Square, Lincoln's Inn, London WC2A 3QB (tel 020 7242 4017, fax 020 7831 2391)

TREVITT, William James Piper; s of William John Maskell Trevitt, of Hereford, and Jane Valerie, *née* Piper; *b* 8 April 1969; *Educ* Royal Ballet Schs; *m* 9 Aug 1992, Rebecca, *née* Holmes; 3 s (Joseph Zebulon b 15 April 1994, Zachary George b 25 Aug 1996, Elijah Ben b 4 April 2002); *Career* Royal Ballet: joined 1987, first artist 1989–90, soloist 1990–93, first soloist 1993–94, princ 1994–99; fndr memb K Ballet; perfs incl: Siegfried in Swan Lake, Solor in La Bayadère, Count Albrecht in Giselle, the Prince in Cinderella, the Prince in Sleeping Beauty, Colas in La Fille Ma Gardee, Oberon in The Dream, the Rake in The Rake's Progress, lead in Push Comes to Shove, Mr Jeremy Fisher in Tales of Beatrix Potter, Mercutio in Romeo and Juliet, Lescaut in Manon, the Friend in The Judas Tree, Mr Wordly Wise in Mr Worldly Wise, leading man in Ballet Imperial; other perfs incl: Agon, Stravinsky Violin Concerto (Aria I), Symphony in C (Third Movement), Duo concertant, La Ronde, Herman Schmerman; co-founded George Piper Dances with Michael Nunn , *qv*; perfs with George Piper Dances incl: Steptext, Sigue, Truly great thing, Critical Mass, Torsion, other mens wives, Approximate Sonata I, V, Mesmerics, restaged Halleloo, choreographed Tangoid and Moments of Plastic Jubilation; also with Michael Nunn: co-filmed and co-directed Ballet Boyz and Ballet Boyz II - The Next Step (Channel 4), presented 4Dance (Channel 4) 2003 and 2004, created Critic's Choice ***** (featuring Matthew Bourne, *qv*, Michael Clark, Akram Khan, *qv*, Russell Maliphant, *qv* and Christopher Wheeldon) 2004, Broken Fall (commissioned by Russell Malipahnt, premiered ROH) 2004, dir and choreographer of Naked (premiered at Sadler's Wells) 2005; *Awards* nominated South Bank Show Dance Award 2001 and 2003, nomination (for Memerics) Best New Dance Production Laurence Olivier Award 2004, winner (for Broken Fall) Best New Dance Production Laurence Olivier Award 2004; *Recreations* photography, cinema; *Style*— William Trevitt, Esq; ✉ George Piper Dances, Sadler's Wells, Rosebery Avenue, London EC1R 4TN (tel 020 7863 8238, e-mail william@gpdances.com)

TREVOR, John Clyfford; s of Clyfford Trevor (d 1970), and Louisa Ryder, *née* Airey (d 2002); *b* 16 August 1932; *Educ* USA, Millfield; *m* 14 Sept 1957, Jane Carolyn, da of Capt Charles Houstoun-Boswall (d 1946), Royal Scots Greys (*see* Baronetage); 2 da (Carolyn b 1959, Emma b 1963), 2 s (Mark b 1961, Richard b 1969); *Career* Nat Serv 2 Lt 1 Bn East Surrey Regt 1952–53, served Libya and Egypt; J Trevor & Sons (merged with Gooch & Wagstaff): sr ptnr 1972–88, chm 1988–96, sr exec 1996–99; chm J Trevor Mortleman and Poland Ltd Lloyd's brokers 1985–88; RICS: chm Gen Practice Div of the Central London Branch 1973–74, chm Central London Branch 1978–79, chm Working Pty on Conveyancing 1986–92; memb Gen Practice Divnl Gen Cncl 1985–91; chm London Branch CIArb 1999–2000; FRICS, MCIArb; *Recreations* furniture restoration, gardening; *Clubs* Naval and Military, MCC; *Style*— John Trevor, Esq; ✉ Northborough Manor, Northborough, Peterborough, Cambridgeshire PE6 9BJ (tel 01733 252134)

TREVOR, William; Hon KBE (2002, Hon CBE 1977); *b* 24 May 1928; *Educ* St Columba's Coll Dublin, Trinity Coll Dublin; *m* 1952, Jane, da of C N Ryan; 2 s; *Career* writer; Allied Irish Banks' Prize 1976, Hudson Review Prize 1990, David Cohen Prize 1999, Ireland Fund Literary Prize 2005; Hon DLitt: Univ of Exeter 1984, Trinity Coll Dublin 1986, Queen's Univ Belfast 1989, Nat Univ of Ireland Cork 1990; memb Irish Acad of Letters; CLit 1994; *Books* The Old Boys (1964, Hawthornden Prize), The Boarding House (1965), The Love Department (1966), The Day We Got Drunk on Cake (1967), Mrs Eckdorf in O'Neill's Hotel (1969), Miss Gomez and the Brethren (1971), The Ballroom of Romance (1972), Elizabeth Alone (1973), Angels at the Ritz (1975, Royal Soc of Literature Award), The Children of Dynmouth (1976, Whitbread Award), Lovers of Their Time (1978), The Distant Past (1979), Other People's Worlds (1980), Beyond the Pale (1981), Fools of Fortune (1983, Whitbread Award), A Writer's Ireland (1984), The News from Ireland (1986), Nights at the Alexandra (1987), The Silence in the Garden (1989, Yorkshire Post Book of the Year), Family Sins (1990), Two Lives (1991), Juliet's Story (1991), Collected Stories (1992), Excursions in the Real World (1993), Felicia's Journey (1994, Sunday Express Book of the Year, Whitbread Book of the Year), After Rain (1996), Death in Summer (1998), The Hill Bachelors (2000, Macmillan/PEN Award, Irish Time Literature Prize), The Story of Lucy Gault (2002, Listowel Prize for Irish Fiction); *Style*— William Trevor, KBE

TREW, Anthony Leslie Gwynn; OBE (2001); s of Howel Douglas Gwynne Trew (d 2003), of Burwash, E Sussex, and Madeline Louisa, *née* Daniel (d 1987); *b* 20 March 1942; *Educ* Haileybury and ISC; *m* 1, 24 April 1976 (m dis 1994), Angela Rosalind Drury, da of late Gerald Drury Culverwell; 3 da (Cressida b 1981, Annabel b 1985, Felicity b 1986), 1 s (Charles b 1989); m 2, 25 Sept 2002, Sheila, da of George W Gray (d 2003), of Yeovil, Somerset; *Career* admitted slr 1968, ptnr Richards Butler 1974–2000, conslt 2000–06; govr The British Sch Al Khubairat Abu Dhabi 1987–2002, chm Br Business Gp Abu Dhabi 1996–2000; Freeman City of London 1976; *Recreations* swimming, walking, talking, reading; *Clubs* Reform; *Style*— Anthony Trew, Esq, OBE; ✉ Pleasure House, Ashburnham, Battle, East Sussex TN33 9PE (tel 01435 830524)

TREWAVAS, Prof Anthony James; s of Clifford John Trewavas (d 1986), of Penzance, Cornwall, and Phyllis Mary, *née* Timms (d 1993); *b* 17 June 1939; *Educ* Roan GS, UCL (BSc, PhD); *m* 29 Aug 1963, Valerie, da of Ivor John Leng; 2 da (Seren Angharad b 6 Jan 1969, Eira Siobhan b 14 Feb 1970), 1 s (Joseph Jonathan Christopher b 16 July 1979); *Career* postdoctoral fell UEA; prof of plant biochemistry Univ of Edinburgh 1990– (lectr 1970–84, reader 1984–90); visiting prof: Michigan State Univ 1973, Nat Acad of Sciences Poland 1979, Univ of Illinois 1980, Univ of Alberta 1983, Univ of Calif Davis 1985, Univ of Bonn 1987, Univ of N Carolina 1988, Nat Univ of Mexico 1989, Univ of Milan 1996; memb Editorial Bd Plant Physiology 1989–; elected memb American Soc of Plant Physiologists 1999, memb Academia Europaea 2002; FRSE 1993, FRSA 1995, FRS 1999; *Recreations* music, reading, bonsai growing; *Style*— Prof Anthony Trewavas, FRS, FRSE, FRSA; ✉ Institute of Cell and Molecular Biology, King's Buildings, University of Edinburgh, Edinburgh EH9 3JH (tel 0131 650 5328, fax 0131 651 3331, e-mail trewavas@ed.ac.uk)

TREWBY, John Allan; CB (1999); s of late Vice Adm Sir Allan Trewby, KCB, of Henley-on-Thames, Oxon, and Lady Sandra Trewby, *née* Stedham; *b* 17 September 1945; *Educ* Marlborough, Trinity Coll Cambridge (MA); *m* 1971, Belinda Mary, *née* Boving; 3 c (Penny b 1973, Alexander b 1975, Alice b 1984); *Career* RN: joined 1963, memb Jt Serv Expdn to the Sahara Desert 1969, Cdr HMS Collingwood 1979, weapon engrg offr HMS Illustrious (Falklands War) 1982, Capt 1984, Cdre Clyde Submarine Base 1992–94, Rear Adm 1994, chief exec Naval Bases and Supply Agency 1996–99, chief naval engr offr 1997–99; naval advsr BAE Systems 1999–; govr West Hill Park Sch, special cmmr Duke of York's Royal Military Sch Dover; Liveryman Worshipful Co of Engrs 2000, Freeman City of London 2000; MInstD, FIEE 1985, FREng 1999; *Recreations* golf, tennis, skiing; *Clubs* Army and Navy; *Style*— Rear Adm John Trewby, CB, FREng; ✉ Lancaster House PO Box 87, Farnborough Aerospace Centre, Farnborough, Hampshire GU14 6YU (tel 01252 384726, fax 01252 384855, e-mail john.trewby@baesystems.com)

TREWIN, Ion Courtenay Gill; s of John Courtenay Trewin, OBE (d 1990), the theatre critic and author, and Wendy Elizabeth, *née* Monk (d 2000); *b* 13 July 1943; *Educ* Highgate Sch; *m* 7 Aug 1965, Susan Harriet, da of Walter Harry Merry (d 1953), of Highgate, London; 1 s (Simon, *qv*, b 1966), 1 da (Maria b 1971); *Career* reporter: The Independent & South Devon Times Plymouth 1960–63, The Sunday Telegraph 1963–67; The Times: ed staff 1967–79, ed The Times Diary 1969–72, literary ed 1972–79; ed Drama Magazine 1979–81; publisher: Hodder & Stoughton 1979–92 (sr ed 1979–85, editorial dir 1985–91, publishing dir 1991–92), Orion Publishing Gp 1992–2006 (publishing dir Weidenfeld & Nicolson imprint 1992–96, dir 1994–2006, md Weidenfeld & Nicolson div 1996–2002, ed-in-chief 2001–06); chm: Library Ctee Highgate Literary and Scientific Inst 1974–90, Soc of Bookmen 1986–88, Cheltenham Festival of Literature 1997–; chm of judges Booker Prize for Fiction 1974; memb: Lit Panel Arts Cncl of GB 1975–78, Arts and Library Ctee MCC 1988–98, Advsy Ctee Man Booker Prize (formerly Booker Prize) 1989–; administrator Man Booker prizes 2006–; author of introductions to new edns of classic thrillers (for Leslie Charteris, Sapper and Dornford Yates); *Books* Journalism (1975), Norfolk Cottage (1977), Alan Clark's Diaries: Into Politics (ed, 2000), Alan Clark's The Last Diaries (ed, 2002); *Recreations* indulging grandsons, watching cricket, gossip, gardening; *Clubs* Garrick, MCC; *Style*— Ion Trewin, Esq; ✉ 44 Cholmeley Lodge, Cholmeley Park, Highgate, London N6 5EN (tel 020 8374 3964); Beck House, 88 Chapel Road, Dersingham, King's Lynn, Norfolk PE31 6PL (tel 01485 544089, e-mail ion.trewin@orionbooks.co.uk)

TREWIN, Simon Courtenay; s of Ion Trewin , *qv*, and Susan Harriet, *née* Merry; *Educ* Highgate Sch, Univ of Kent at Canterbury (BA); *m* 1992, Helen Adie; 1s (Jack Courtenay b 1993); *Career* as memb Equity: Chichester Festival Theatre 1984–85, Birmingham Rep 1985–86, Duncan Weldon Ltd 1985–93; literary agent Sheil Land Associates 1993–99; PFD (formerly Peters, Fraser and Dunlop Ltd): dep head Literary Dept 1999–2006, dir 2006–, jt head Literary Dept 2006–; sec Assoc of Authors' Agents 2001–04; *Publications* Rock and Pop Elevens (jtly, 2004), Live8: The Official Book (jtly, 2005), The Encyclopaedia of Guilty Pleasures (jtly, 2006), Shopping While Drunk (jtly, 2007), The Complete Bigot (jtly, 2007); *Recreations* cats, theatre-going, trying to keep pace with wife and son, book collecting; *Clubs* Old Cholmelians Soc, The Hospital; *Style*— Simon Trewin, Esq; ✉ PFD, Drury House, 34–43 Russell Street, London WC2B 5HA (tel 020 7344 1002, fax 020 7836 9541, e-mail strewin@pfd.co.uk, website www.pfd.co.uk)

TRIBE, Elisabeth Jane; da of Michael Tribe, and Wendie, *née* Farley; *Educ* N London Collegiate Sch, Emmanuel Coll Cambridge (MA); *m* Martin Gammon; 1 s (Oscar), 1 da (Lydia); *Career* successively sec, editorial asst, jr ed and commissioning ed Routledge 1987–93, sr commissioning ed then publisher Hodder & Stoughton 1993–96, ed dir rising to dir schools publishing Hodder Headline 1996–, md Schs Div Hodder Educn 2007–; former chair WHSmith Link-Up Charities Tst, former govr S Camden Community Sch; *Recreations* gardening, reading, walking, cycling; *Style*— Mrs Elisabeth Tribe; ✉ Hodder Education, 338 Euston Road, London NW1 3BH (tel 020 7873 6287, e-mail elisabeth.tribe@hodder.co.uk)

TRIBE, John Edward; s of George Edward Tribe (d 1996), of March, Cambs, and Gwendoline, *née* Morton; *b* 24 March 1946; *Educ* Oundle, Univ of Reading (BSc); *Career* dir family farming businesses 1969–97; dir Marcam & MDS Supplies Ltd 1978–2004, chm United Farmers Trading Agency 1990–95 (dir 1989–95); first chm March and Chatteris Trg Gp 1978–80; chm: March Branch NFU 1985–86, Cambs Area Trg Ctee Agric Trg Bd (ATB) 1987–90, Fenland Crime Prevention Panel 1988–89, Cambs Co NFU 1990; E of England Agric Soc: chm Safety Ctee 1990–93, memb Cncl 1990–, memb Fin Ctee 1998–2003, chm Dog Show Ctee 1999–2002, chm Flower Show Ctee 2003–; memb: Bd ATB W Anglia (LATB9) 1990–93, Corp Cambs Coll of Agric and Horticulture until merger 1998; dir Cambs TEC (Central and Southern Cambs Trg and Enterprise Cncl) 1990–97, first chm Consortium of Rural TEC's 1991–97; *Recreations* shooting, classic cars, wine, historic buildings, travel; *Style*— John Edward Tribe, Esq; ✉ Stapleford Grange, Stapleford, Cambridge CB2 5ED; 321 Chancery Circle, Naples, FL 34110–4404, USA (e-mail jetribe@btinternet.com)

TRICKETT, Jon; MP; s of Laurence Thomas Trickett, of Leeds, and Rose Trickett; *b* 2 July 1950; *Educ* Univ of Hull (BA), Univ of Leeds (MA); *m* 1994, Sarah, da of Thomas Balfour, of Carlisle; 1 s (Daniel Paul b 1975), 1 da (Emma Rachel b 1975); *Career* leader Leeds City Cncl 1989–96 (cncllr 1984–96); MP (Lab) Hemsworth 1996–, PPS to Min Without Portfolio 1997–98, PPS to Sec of State DTI 1998–99; *Recreations* cycling; *Style*— Jon Trickett, Esq, MP; ✉ House of Commons, London SW1A 0AA (tel 020 7219 5074)

TRICKETT, Lynn; da of Dr Jack Fishman, of London, and Eileen, *née* Slonims; *b* 19 May 1945; *Educ* St Martin in the Fields HS for Girls, Chelsea Sch of Art; *m* 8 March 1968, Terence Wilden Trickett; 1 s (Alexander Wilden b 9 Aug 1973), 2 da (Polly Kate b 4 Nov 1977, Rosey Anna b 22 Dec 1983); *Career* designer: Planning Unit 1966–67, Wiggins Teape 1967–69, FFS Advertising Agency NY 1969–70; fndr ptnr Trickett & Webb 1971–2003, Trickett Associates 2003–; work exhibited and published throughout the world, winner of numerous awards in Europe, Asia and USA; regular jury memb D&AD and RSA Bursaries and other European and American design competitions, external examiner various BA and MA graphic design courses, memb Graphic Design Ctee CNAA 1986–87, past memb Cncl Chartered Soc of Designers; tstee and memb Br Design and Art Direction Exec Ctee 2001–04; chm Nat Graphic Design & Print Awards 1990, chm and co fndr Donside Student Awards, chm Loerie Design Awards SA 2003, chm Consort Royal Student Awards 2004–05, foreman Br Design and Art Direction Graphics Jury 2004, chm Howard Smith Paper Student Awards 2006–07; lectures given on graphic design and stamp design in Europe, USA and Australia; FCSD, FRSA; *Publications* contrib to and featured in numerous books on graphic design incl: A Smile in the Mind, The Graphics Book, International Women in Design, Graphic Design and Designers, Who's Who in Graphic Design, Media Careers/Design First Choice; *Recreations* Russian avant garde art, British art of the 1930s-1950s, British poster design of the 1940s; *Style*— Mrs Lynn Trickett; ✉ 9 Hamilton Terrace, London NW8 9RE (tel 020 7286 5209)

TRIESMAN, Baron (Life Peer UK 2004), of Tottenham in the London Borough of Haringey; David Maxim Triesman; s of Michael Triesman (d 1992), of London, and Rita, *née* Lubran (d 1986); *b* 30 October 1943; *Educ* Stationers' Company's Sch London, Univ of Essex (BA, MA), King's Coll Cambridge; *m* 2004, Lucy, da of Ben Hooberman, and Ellen Hooberman; *Career* research offr in addictions Inst of Psychiatry Univ of London 1970–74, seconded to ASTMS 1974–75, sr lectr and co-ordinator of postgrad research in social sciences South Bank Poly (now London South Bank Univ) 1975–84, dep gen sec Nat Assoc of Teachers in Further and Higher Educn 1984–93, gen sec Assoc of Univ Teachers 1993–2001; chm Teacher's Panel Burnham FHE Ctee 1980–84; non-exec chm: Mortgage Credit Corp 1980–2000, Victoria Management Ltd 1999–2001; chm Usecolour Fndn 2001; memb: Kensington, Chelsea and Westminster AHA 1976–82, Univ Entrance and Schs Examinations Bd for social science 1980–84, Home Office Consultative Ctee on Prison Educn 1980–83, Greater London Manpower Bd (additional memb GLC) 1981–86, TUC Public Servs Ctee 1984–1990, Highgate Literary and Scientific Inst 1990, Independent Review of Higher Educn (Bett Ctee) 1998–99, Panel on Public Appts DTI 1997–2001, HEFCE Standing Ctee on Business and the Community 1999–2001, Br North American Ctee 1999–, Public Management Fndn 2000–01, Cncl Ruskin Coll Oxford 2000–02, Better Regulation Task Force (Cabinet Office) 2000–02, Public Service Productivity Panel (HM Treasy) 2000–02, Charles Rennie MacKintosh Soc; visiting prof in social economics S Lawrence Univ 1977, visiting scholar in economics Wolfson Coll Cambridge 2000–, sr visiting fell Univ of Warwick 2003–, visiting fell in govt LSE 2004–; gen sec Lab Pty 2001–03, Lord in Waiting (Govt whip) 2004–05, Parly sec FCO 2005–; hon fell Univ of Northampton; FSS 1984, FRSA 1992; *Books* The Medical and Non-Medical Use of Drugs (1970), Football Mania (with G Vinai, 1972), Football in London (1985), College Administration (1988), Managing Change (1991), Can Unions Survive? (1999); *Recreations* football (memb Tottenham youth team 1961–63), walking, fine art and print collecting, blues guitar; *Clubs* Tottenham Hotspur Supporters', Middlesex CCC, Reform; *Style*— The Rt Hon the Lord Triesman

TRIGG, Prof Roger Hugh; s of Rev Ivor Trigg, of Taunton, Somerset, and Muriel Grace, *née* Collins; *b* 14 August 1941; *Educ* Bristol GS, New Coll Oxford (MA, DPhil); *m* 12 July 1972, Julia, da of Wilfred Gibbs, of Taunton, Somerset; 1 s (Nicholas b 10 May 1973 d 1990), 1 da (Alison b 26 Jan 1977); *Career* Univ of Warwick: lectr 1966–74, sr lectr 1974–78, reader 1978–87, chm Dept of Philosophy 1984–91 and 1994–95, founding dir Centre for Res in Philosophy and Literature 1985–91, prof of philosophy 1987–2007; interim dir Ian Ramsay Centre Univ of Oxford 2006–; visiting fell: St Cross Coll Oxford 1986–87, 1991–92 and 2006–07, Harris Manchester Coll Oxford 1996; Stanton lectr in philosophy of religion Univ of Cambridge 1997; visiting fell Center of Theol Inquiry Princeton 2002; pres: British Soc for the Philosophy of Religion 1993–96, Mind Assoc 1997–98; chm Nat Ctee for Philosophy 1998–2003, founding chm Br Philosophical Assoc 2003–04; JP Warks 1981–91; *Books* Pain and Emotion (1970), Reason and Commitment (1973), Reality at Risk (1980, revised edn 1989), The Shaping of Man (1982), Understanding Social Science (1985, 2 edn 2000), Ideas of Human Nature (1988, 2 edn 1999), Rationality and Science (1993), Rationality and Religion (1998), Philosophy Matters (2001), Morality Matters (2004), Religion in Public Life (2007); *Style—* Prof Roger Trigg; ✉ Ian Ramsay Centre, University of Oxford, 11 Bevington Road, Oxford OX2 6NB (tel 01865 274548, e-mail roger.trigg@theology.ox.ac.uk)

TRIGGER, His Hon Judge Ian James Campbell; s of Lt Walter James Trigger (d 1961), and Mary Elizabeth, *née* Roberts (d 1984); *b* 16 November 1943; *Educ* Ruthin Sch, UCW Aberystwyth (LLB), Downing Coll Cambridge (MA, LLM); *m* 28 Aug 1971, Jennifer Ann, da of Harry Colin Downs (d 1986); 2 s (Ieuan Mungo Campbell b 12 Oct 1973, Simon Huw Campbell b 21 April 1977); *Career* lectr in law UWIST 1967–70; called to the Bar Inner Temple 1970 (major scholar 1968); in practice Northern Circuit 1970–93, asst recorder 1986–90, recorder 1990–93, circuit judge (Northern Circuit) 1993–; pres Mental Health Review Tbnl 1995–; pt/t chm: Social Security Appeal Tbnl 1983–93, Med Appeal Tbnl 1989–93, Disability Appeal Tbnl 1992–93, Immigration Appeal Tbnl 1998–2005; immigration judge 2005–; churchwarden: St Saviour's Oxton 1986–88, St Garmon's Llanarmon-yn-Iâl 2005–07; licensed lay reader Church in Wales 2005–, judge Provincial Court Church in Wales 2005–, chm St Asaph Diocesan Conf 2005–; *Recreations* preserving the countryside from the ravages of greed and the Church from mediocrity; *Style—* His Hon Judge Trigger; ✉ Queen Elizabeth II Law Courts, Derby Square, Liverpool L2 1XA (tel 0151 473 7373)

TRIGGS HODGE, Andrew; s of Peter Triggs Hodge, and Liv Triggs Hodge; *b* 3 March 1979; *Educ* Upper Wharfedale Sch Skipton, South Craven Sch Keighley, Staffs Univ (BSc), Univ of Oxford (MSc); *Career* rower; joined Molesey Boat Club 2000; winner (pair) GB Trials 2004, 2005 and 2006; ninth (eights) Olympic Games Athens 2004, Gold medal (coxless fours) World Championships 2005 and 2006 (Bronze medal (eights) 2003), memb winning Oxford crew Oxford and Cambridge Boat Race 2005; BOA Athletes of the Year (jtly, as memb coxless fours); *Style—* Andrew Triggs Hodge, Esq; ✉ tel 07887 775991, e-mail andrew@andrew-hodge.com, website www.andrew-hodge.com; c/o Tim Sice, CSS Stella Sports, 3rd Floor, 11 Maiden Lane, London WC2E 7NA (tel 020 7078 1427, fax 020 7078 1402, e-mail tim.sice@css-stellar.com)

TRIMBLE, Baron (Life Peer 2006), of Lisnagarvey in the County of Antrim; (William) David Trimble; PC (1998); s of William Trimble (d 1968), and Ivy, *née* Jack; *b* 15 October 1944; *Educ* Bangor GS, Queen's Univ Belfast (LLB); *m* 1978, Daphne Elizabeth, da of Gerald Montgomery Orr (d 1981); 2 s (Richard David b 1982, Nicholas James b 1986), 2 da (Victoria Claire b 1984, Sarah Elizabeth b 1992); *Career* called to the Bar of NI 1969; sr lectr Faculty of Law Queen's Univ Belfast 1977–90 (lectr 1968–77), ed NI Law Reports 1975–90; MP (UUP) Upper Bann 1990–2005, MLA (UUP) Upper Bann; ldr UUP 1995–2005; elected NI Forum 1996–98, first min NI Assembly 1998–2002; winner Nobel Peace Prize 1998, Parliamentarian of the Year Zurich/Spectator Parly Awards 2001; *Books* Housing Law in Northern Ireland (co-author, 1984), Human Rights and Responsibilities in Britain and Ireland (co-author, 1986); *Recreations* music, opera, history, reading; *Style—* The Rt Hon the Lord Trimble, PC; ✉ 2 Queen Street, Lurgan BT66 8BQ (tel 028 3832 8088, fax 028 3832 2343)

TRIMLESTOWN, 21 Baron (I 1461); Raymond Charles Barnewall; s of 19 Baron Trimlestown (d 1990), and Muriel, *née* Schneider (d 1937); suc bro, 20 Baron Trimlestown, 1997; *b* 29 December 1930, Epsom, Surrey; *Educ* Ampleforth; *Career* Br Army NI 1949–51, apple farmer family business Co Waterford 1952–56, dairy farmer 1956, ret 1988; formerly with Somerset Cattle Breeding Centre Dartington Hall (progeny testing bulls for artificial insemination); supporter WWF, RNLI; *Recreations* tennis, gardening, antiques, all aspects of wildlife, small ship cruising (zodiacs); *Style—* The Lord Trimlestown; ✉ Autumn Cottage, Pockford Road, Chiddingfold, Surrey GU8 4TP (tel 01428 684106)

TRINH, HE Duc Du; *b* 1949, Phu Tho Province, Vietnam; *m* Ta Kim Son; 2 s; *Career* Vietnamese diplomat; desk offr Miny of Foreign Affrs 1974, min cnsllr Paris 1989–91, chargé d'affaires Paris 1992, DG Northwest European Dept 1994–95 and 2000–03 (dep dir 1993–94), ambass to Francophone Community and UNESCO Paris 1996–99 (chm Francophone Community 1997), ambass to the Ct of St James's 2003–; *Style—* HE Mr Trinh Duc Du; ✉ Embassy of the Socialist Republic of Vietnam, 12–14 Victoria Road, London W8 5RD

TRINICK, Anthony Graham Kyle (Tony); s of Alexander Leslie Trinick (d 1983), and Jean Edna Kyle, *née* Ferrier (d 1983); *b* 26 October 1943; *Educ* St Dunstan's Coll Catford, Borough Poly London (ONC, Dip H&V Engrg, HNC); *m* 1967, Clare Elisabeth, da of Dr Paul Freeman; 2 s (Mark David Kyle b 21 Sept 1973, Andrew Timothy Kyle b 5 April 1977); *Career* G N Haden & Sons Ltd: apprentice 1962–66, engr 1966–73, design mangr Lloyds Computer Centre 1973–77, project mangr Haden International 1977–81, project dir Torness NPS 1981–84, project dir Aldermaston AWRE 90 Building 1984–87, HQ dir 1987–91, dir Haden Young Ltd 1987–92, dir Haden Building Services Ltd and Haden International Ltd 1992–95; princ TriTone Partnership 1995–, visiting prof Dept of Architecture and Building Technol Univ of Nottingham 1995–98; devpt dir: Fox Linton Assoc (interior design and architecture) 1996–, Panel-Built Environment HEFCE RAE 2001 1999–2002; special prof Sch of the Built Environment Univ of Nottingham 2000–; memb: American Soc for Heating, Refrigeration and AC Engrs 1970–2000, Assoc of Project Mangrs 1979; Freeman City of London, Liveryman Worshipful Co of Fan Makers; CEng 1990; MCIA 1996; FCIBSE 1989 (MCIBSE 1966), FREng 1994; *Recreations* sailing, swimming, walking, bee keeping (memb Kent Beekeepers' Assoc); *Clubs* IOD, Castle Baynard Ward; *Style—* Tony Trinick, Esq, FREng; ✉ TriTone Partnership, 5 Little Thrift, Petts Wood, Orpington, Kent BR5 1NQ (tel and fax 01689 820838, e-mail tonytrinick@trinick.com)

TRINICK, (George) Marcus Arthur; s of George Edward Michael Trinick, OBE, DL (d 1994), and Maud Elizabeth Lyon, *née* Hutchinson (d 1998); *b* 11 June 1952, Surrey; *Educ* Haileybury and ISC, Queen's Univ Belfast (BA); *m* 3 Nov 1978 (m dis); 1 s (John Michael Robert b 11 Dec 1980), 1 da (Loveday Jessica Mary b 4 Oct 1983); partner, Geraldine Mortimore; *Career* admitted slr 1983 (rights of audience in higher courts 2007); slr specialising in energy, planning and environmental law; ptnr: Coodes 1985–90 (joined 1983), Bond Pearce 1990– (trainee then slr 1979–83, rejoined 1990); memb Bd Br Wind Energy Assoc, memb American and European Wind Energy Assocs, memb Scottish Renewables Forum; runner-up Ptnr of the Year The Lawyer magazine 2004; memb Law Soc 1983, legal memb RTPI 2003; *Recreations* shooting, walking, travel, reading, Roman history, cricket; *Clubs* Lobsters Cricket, Trevithick Soc, Nat Tst; *Style—* Marcus Trinick, Esq; ✉ Bond Pearce LLP, 3 Temple Quay, Temple Back East, Bristol BS1 6DZ (tel 0845 415 000, e-mail mtrinick@bondpearce.com)

TRIPP, Rt Rev Howard George; s of Basil Tripp (d 1981), and Alice, *née* Haslett (d 1985); *b* 3 July 1927, Croydon; *Educ* John Fisher Sch Purley, St John's Seminary Wonersh; *Career* asst priest: St Mary Blackheath 1953–56, E Sheen 1956–62; diocesan covenant organiser 1958–68, asst fin sec 1962–68, parish priest E Sheen 1965–71, sec Southwark Catholic Childrens' Soc 1971–80, auxiliary bishop in Southwark 1980–2004, titular bishop of Newport 1980–; *Recreations* vegetable gardening; *Style—* The Rt Rev Howard Tripp; ✉ 8 Arterberry Road, London SW20 8AJ (tel 020 8946 4609, e-mail htripp@tiscali.co.uk)

TRIPPIER, Sir David; kt (1992), RD, JP (Rochdale 1975), DL (Lancashire 1994); s of Maj Austin Wilkinson Trippier, MC (d 1993), of Norden, Rochdale, Greater Manchester, and Mary Trippier (d 1974); *b* 15 May 1946; *Educ* Bury GS; *m* 1975, Ruth Worthington, barr; 3 s; *Career* cmmnd Offr Royal Marines Reserve 1968; MP (Cons): Rossendale 1979–83, Rossendale and Darwen 1983–92; PPS to Kenneth Clarke as min of state for health DHSS 1982–83; Parly under sec of state: for trade and industry 1983–85, Dept of Employment 1985–87, Dept of the Environment 1987–89; min of state DOE 1989–92; sec Cons Parly Def Ctee 1980–82; ldr Cons Gp Rochdale Cncl 1974–76 (cncllr 1969–78); nat vice-chm Assoc of Cons Clubs 1980, dep chm Cons Pty May-Dec 1990; chm: W H Ireland Ltd Stockbrokers, Sir David Trippier & Associates Ltd; dir Granada TV Ltd; govr Manchester GS 1993–2004; fndr: Rossendale Enterprise Trust, Rossendale Groundwork Trust; pres: Manchester Chamber of Commerce and Industry 1999–2000, Royal Lancs Agric Soc 1999–2000; Hon Col Royal Marines Reserve Merseyside 1996–; High Sheriff Lancs 1997–98; memb Stock Exchange 1968; FRSA 2006; *Publications* Lend me Your Ears (autobiography, 1999); *Style—* Sir David Trippier, RD, JP, DL

TRITTON, Maj Sir Anthony John Ernest; 4 Bt (UK 1905); s of Maj Sir Geoffrey Ernest Tritton, 3 Bt, CBE (d 1976); *b* 4 March 1927; *Educ* Eton; *m* 1957, Diana, da of Rear Adm St John Aldrich Micklethwait, CB, DSO; 1 s (Jeremy), 1 da (Clarissa); *Heir* s, Jeremy Tritton; *Career* Maj (ret) The Queen's Own Hussars; farmer; *Recreations* shooting, fishing; *Clubs* Cavalry and Guards'; *Style—* Maj Sir Anthony Tritton, Bt; ✉ River House, Heytesbury, Warminster, Wiltshire BA12 0EE

TRITTON, (Elizabeth) Clare (Mrs McLaren-Throckmorton); QC (1988); da of Prof A L d'Abreu, CBE (d 1976), of Coughton Court, Alcester, Warks, and Elizabeth Throckmorton (d 1970); *b* 18 August 1935; *Educ* Convent of The Holy Child, Mayfield St Leonards, Univ of Birmingham (BA); *m* 1 (m dis 1971), Alan George Tritton, DL; 1 da (Christina Margaret (Mrs Williams) b 24 Sept 1960), 2 s (Guy b 18 Nov 1963, Charles b 12 May 1965); m 2, 21 Dec 1973, Andrew McLaren; *Career* called to the Bar 1968; chm The Bar European Gp 1982–84, UK rapporteur to FIDE Sept 1988, vice-chm Int Practice Ctee Bar Cncl 1988–90, memb Cmmn on the Legislative Process of the Hansard Soc for Parly Govt 1991–93; dir and memb FIMBRA 1991–97, cmmr Monopolies and Mergers Cmmn 1993–97, chm Primary Immuno Deficiency Assoc 2002–; memb Euro Ctee Br Invisible Exports Cncl 1989–93; chief exec Throckmorton Estates, non-exec dir Severn Trent plc 1991–2003; tstee dir Birmingham Royal Ballet 1996–2000; fndr Bar European News, author of numerous legal articles; memb CLA Warwickshire Ctee 2002; *Books* Towards A Community Air Transport Policy (contrib, 1989); *Recreations* travelling, gardening, reading; *Style—* professional: Mrs Clare Tritton, QC; otherwise: Mrs Clare McLaren-Throckmorton; ✉ Coughton Court, Alcester, Warwickshire B49 5JA (tel 01789 400777, fax 01789 765544, e-mail secretary@throckmortons.co.uk); Molland Estate, South Molton, Devon EX36 3ND (tel 01769 550325, fax 01769 550524)

TRITTON, (Robert) Guy Henton; s of Alan George Tritton, of Great Leighs, Essex, and Elizabeth Clare, of Coughton Court, Alcester; *b* 18 November 1963; *Educ* Eton, Univ of Durham (BSc); *m* 30 Aug 1995, Ursula Jane, da of Carl Pycraft; 1 da (Lara Ursula b 6 Sept 1996), 2 s (Luke Charles Henton b 16 Oct 1998, Jocelyn Raphael Malet b 5 April 2002); *Career* barrister; called to the Bar Inner Temple 1987, Pegasus scholar 1990; practising in intellectual property; chm Rhino Ark (UK); chm Cwm Dulas; *Books* Intellectual Property in Europe (1996, 3 edn 2007); *Recreations* piano playing, shooting, windsurfing, music; *Style—* Guy Tritton, Esq; ✉ Hogarth Chambers, 5 New Square, London WC2A 3RJ (tel 020 7404 0404, fax 020 7404 0505, e-mail guy.tritton@btinternet.com)

TRITTON, Peter Robert Jolliffe; s of Lt-Col J H Tritton, MBE (d 1988), and Pamela, *née* Skewes-Cox (d 2004); *b* 22 May 1951; *Educ* Charterhouse; *m* 9 Sept 1975, Hon Sally Louise Nelson, yr da of 2 Baron Nelson of Stafford (d 1995); 1 s (Jonathan James Hedley b 1981), 1 da (Emma Pamela Louise b 1986); *Career* dir Alexander Howden Insurance Brokers 1980–85; dir of PR: Alexander Howden Gp 1985–97, Alexander & Alexander Services UK plc 1988–97; exec dir corp affrs Aon Gp Ltd 1997–2001; *Recreations* good food; *Style—* Peter Tritton, Esq; ✉ Weasel Cottage, Brent Pelham, Hertfordshire SG9 0HH (tel 01279 777584)

TROLLOPE, Andrew David Hedderwick; QC (1991); s of Arthur George Cecil Trollope, of Overton, Hants, and Rosemary, *née* Hodson; *b* 6 November 1948; *Educ* Charterhouse, Univ of Nancy; *m* 1978, Anne Forbes; 2 s (Harvey Evelyn b 16 Jan 1980, Francis Henry b 2 Nov 1981); *Career* called to the Bar Inner Temple 1971 (bencher 2002); recorder of the Crown Court 1989– (asst recorder 1984), head of chambers; memb: Criminal Bar Assoc Ctee 1991–2002, SE Circuit Ctee 1990–93, 1994–97 and 2006–; chm: N London Bar Mess 1998–2001, Int Rels Ctee Bar Cncl, Advsy Cncl Br Inst of Int and Comparative Law; fell Soc of Advanced Legal Studies (FSALS) 1998; *Recreations* opera, jazz, travel, tennis, sailing; *Clubs* Garrick, Hurlingham; *Style—* Andrew Trollope, Esq, QC, FSALS; ✉ 187 Fleet Street, London EC4A 2AT (tel 020 7430 7430, fax 020 7430 7431, e-mail chambers@187fleetstreet.com)

TROLLOPE, Sir Anthony Simon; 17 Bt (E 1642), of Casewick, Co Lincoln; o s of Sir Anthony Owen Clavering Trollope, 16 Bt (d 1987), and Joan Mary Alexis, *née* Gibbes; *b* 31 August 1945; *Educ* Univ of Sydney (BA); *m* 1969, Denise, da of Trevern Thompson, of N Sydney, Australia; 2 da (Kellie Yvette b 1970, Analese Christine b 1972); *Heir* bro, Hugh Trollope; *Style—* Sir Anthony Trollope, Bt; ✉ Churinga Lodge, 28 Midson Road, Oakville, NSW 2765, Australia

TROLLOPE, Joanna; OBE (1996), DL (Glos 2000); da of Arthur George Cecil Trollope, of Overton, Hampshire, and Rosemary, *née* Hodson; *b* 9 December 1943; *Educ* Reigate Co Sch For Girls, St Hugh's Coll Oxford (MA); *m* 1, 14 May 1966 (m dis 1984), David Roger William Potter, *qv*, s of William Edward Potter, of Durweston, Dorset; 2 da (Louise (Mrs Paul Ansdell) b 15 Jan 1969, Antonia (Mrs Jonathan Prentice) b 23 Oct 1971); m 2, 12 April 1985 (m dis 1999), Ian Bayley Curteis, *qv*, s of John Richard Jones, of Lydd, Romney Marsh; *Career* writer; Info Res Dept FO 1965–67, English teacher in various schs, feature writer Harpers and Queen, freelance work for maj newspapers; chair Dept of Nat Heritage Advsy Ctee on Nat Reading Initiative 1996–97, memb Govt Ctee for Nat Year of Reading 1997–; fndr and co-tstee Joanna Trollope Charitable Tst; memb Campaign Bd St Hugh's Coll Oxford 1996–; memb: Soc of Authors (memb Cncl), Trollope Soc, Romantic Novelists' Assoc, West Country Writers' Assoc; patron: Mulberry Bush Sch Standlake; *Books* Parson Harding's Daughter (Historical Novel of the Year, 1980), The Taverners' Place (1986), Britannia's Daughters (non-fiction, 1983), The Choir (1988), A Village Affair (1989), A Passionate Man (1990), The Rector's Wife (1991), The Men and the Girls (1992), A Spanish Lover (1993), The Best of Friends (1995), A Country Habit - An Anthology (ed and introduction, 1993), Next of Kin (1996), Other People's Children (1998), Marrying the Mistress (2001), Girl From the South (2002), Brother and Sister (2004), The Book Boy (2006), Second Honeymoon (2006); under pseudonym Caroline Harvey: Legacy of Love

(1992), A Second Legacy (1993), A Castle in Italy (1993), Parson Harding's Daughter (reissue, Corgi, 1995), The Steps of the Sun (1996), The Brass Dolphin (1997); *Style*— Miss Joanna Trollope, OBE, DL; ✉ c/o PFD, Drury House, Russell Street, London WC2B 5HA (website www.joannatrollope.com)

TROMANS, District Judge Christopher John; s of Percy Tromans (d 1979), and Phyllis Eileen, *née* Berryman (d 1991); *b* 25 November 1942; *Educ* Truro Sch, St Edmund Hall Oxford (MA); *m* 31 May 1969, Gillian, da of John Delbridge Roberts (d 1966); 1 da (Sarah b 1970), 1 s (Andrew b 1972); *Career* admitted slr 1968; ptnr: Sitwell Money and Murdoch Truro 1971–79, Murdoch Tromans and Hoskin Truro and Redruth 1979–88, Murdoch Tromans Truro 1988–92; NP 1970; memb No 4 SW Legal Aid Area Ctee and Appeals Panel 1982–92, dep High Court and County Court registrar Western Circuit 1987–90, dep district judge 1991–92, jt district judge Plymouth District Registry of High Court and Plymouth County Court 1992–, nominated care district judge 1996–, district bench sec Western Circuit 1999–, Judicial Studies Bd trg judge 2001–; Univ of Plymouth: visiting lectr 1995–, conslt law degree course validation 2001; memb Lions Club of Tavistock, govr Truro Sch 1975–2005 (dep chm 1978–91), memb Cncl Coll of St Mark and St John Plymouth 2001, govr Kelly Coll 2007–; memb Royal Inst of Cornwall; hon memb Western Circuit 1992; ACIArb 1978, FRSA 1990; *Recreations* country life, travel, military history; *Clubs* East India, Plymouth Athenaeum, West Devon (Tavistock); *Style*— District Judge Christopher Tromans; ✉ The Law Courts, Armada Way, Plymouth, Devon PL1 2ER (tel 01752 208284, fax 01752 208286, e-mail districtjudge.tromans@judiciary.gsi.gov.uk)

TROMPETER, Dr Richard Simon; s of Nysen Trompeter, and Betty, *née* Rubin; *b* 27 January 1946; *Educ* Orange Hill Co GS for Boys London, Guy's Hosp Med Sch (MB BS, ed Guy's Hosp Gazette 1969–70); *m* 26 March 1978, Barbara Ann, da of Ervin Blum; 2 da (Sara b 1973, Rebecca b 1986), 2 s (Alexander b 1979, Nicholas b 1981); *Career* house surgn Guy's Hosp and house physician St Mary Abbots Hosp 1970–71; SHO 1971–74: Renal Unit Royal Free Hosp, paediatrics Guy's Hosp and The London Hosp, neonatal paediatrics John Radcliffe Hosp, Gt Ormond St Hosp; registrar Hosp for Sick Children Gt Ormond St 1975–77, research fell Dept of Immunology Inst of Child Health 1977–78, hon sr registrar and lectr in paediatrics Guy's Hosp Med Sch 1979–84, sr lectr in paediatrics Royal Free Hosp Sch of Med 1984–87, conslt paediatric nephrologist The Royal Free Hosp 1986–89 (Sch of Med: hon sr lectr, memb Academic Staff Assoc 1984–87, memb Educn Cncl 1984–89, memb Sch Cncl 1986–87, memb Library Ctee 1988–89); Hosp for Sick Children Great Ormond St: conslt paediatric nephrologist 1986–89, princ appt 1989–, clinical dir Medical Unit and Urology Directorate 1991–97, clinical dir Int and Private Patient Directorate 1997–2000, memb Div of Physicians 1987–, memb Clinical Ethics Forum 1995–2000, chm BMA Local Negotiating Ctee 1996–97, chm Clinical Ethics Ctee 2000–05; hon reader in paediatric nephrology UCL 2006–; memb Advsy Bd Novartis Pharmaceuticals UK Ltd 2000–05; memb Editorial Bd: Paediatric Transplantation 2000–, Paediatric Nephrology 2004–; examiner (MRCP) RCP 1996–2000, sr examiner (MRCPCH) RCPCH 2004–; memb RCP Standing Ctee of Membs 1976–78, jr staff rep Br Paediatric Assoc Cncl 1982–83, clinical rep Conf of Med Academic Reps 1982–83, govr ILEA Royal Free Hosp Sch 1985–89, memb Bd of Studies in Med Univ of London 1986–89, chm Div of Child Health Hampstead Authy 1987–89 (memb Div of Physicians 1984–89, memb Exec Ctee 1988–89), memb Exec Ctee and Cncl Renal Assoc 1989, sec Assoc of Paediatricians N Thames (East) 1995–97, memb Finance Ctee RCPCH 1998–2002, memb Clinical Ethics Ctee Br Transplantation Soc 2003–, cncllr Int Paediatric Transplant Assoc 2005–07, treas Br Assoc for Paediatric Nephrology 2006–, treas and sec Int Pediatric Transplant Assoc 2006–; FRCP 1989 (MRCP 1973), FRCPCH 1997; *Recreations* literature, theatre; *Style*— Dr Richard Trompeter; ✉ Hospital for Sick Children, Great Ormond Street, London WC1 3JH (tel 020 7405 9200, fax 020 7829 8841, e-mail trompr@gosh.nhs.uk)

TROOSTWYK, David Koos; s of Joseph Koos Troostwyk (d 1976), and Beatrice Isobel, *née* Thornborough (d 1978); *b* 5 August 1929; *Educ* Royal Coll of Art (travelling scholar, ARCA); *Career* artist; head of painting Winchester Sch of Art 1964–67, head of sculpture Sydney Coll of Arts 1977–79, former visiting lectr Slade and Chelsea Sch of Arts; work in collections incl Arts Cncl, Tate Gallery and privately; *Solo Exhibitions* Univ of Southampton 1966, Gulbenkian Gallery 1969, Kasmin Ltd 1971, ICA 1974, Felicity Samuel Gallery 1977, Inst of Modern Art Brisbane 1979, Matt's Gallery 1979, Akumulatory Gallery Poznan 1980, Matt's Gallery 1981, 1984 and 1994, Robert Sandelson Gallery London 1999, Tate Britain Birthday Exhibit 1999, Succession Manufacturing Ltd 2000, Tate Britain Birthday Exhibit 2004; *Group Exhibitions* incl: Kursaal Ostende 1968, Galerie 20 Amsterdam 1968, Annely Juda Gallery 1969, Axiom Gallery 1970, Alfred Schmela Düsseldorf 1972, Int Poezie Rotterdam 1974, Int Art Fair Basle 1975, Biannual Sydney 1976, ICA LA 1978, Tate Gallery (books) 1982, Barcelona (books) 1983, Artspace Sydney 1984, Backspace (Matt's Gallery) 1999, Whitechapel 2000; *Publications* incl: Imitation (1977), Private Act (1999); *Style*— David Troostwyk, Esq; ✉ Apartment 4, 3 Chester Way, London SE11 4UT (tel and fax 020 7735 9278); Agent: Matt's Gallery, 42–44 Copperfield Road, London E3 4RR (tel 020 8983 1771, fax 020 8983 1435)

TROSS, Jonathan Edward Simon; CB (2004); s of Francis Gisbert Tross, and Audrey, *née* Payne; *b* 21 January 1949; *Educ* Chislehurst and Sidcup GS, UC Oxford (BA); *m* 17 June 1972, Ann Elizabeth, da of John Leslie Humphries; 1 s (David Edward b 29 Dec 1978), 1 da (Ruth Ellen b 22 Aug 1981); *Career* teacher in Kenya 1971; DHSS: grad trainee 1972–77, princ 1977–84, asst sec Supp Benefit Review 1984–87; asst dir Corp Div Barclays Bank 1987–90, head Pharmaceutical Industry Branch Dept of Health 1990–91, head Fininace Div DSS (formerly DHSS) 1991–94, dir of corp mgmnt Gp Dept of Work and Pensions (formerly DSS) 1994–99, head of constitution secretariat Cabinet Office 1999–2001, actg chief exec then chief exec Children and Family Court Advsy and Support Serv (Cafcass) 2001–04; *Recreations* football, theatre, books, allotment; *Clubs* Fulham FC; *Style*— Jonathan Tross, Esq, CB

TROTMAN, Andrew Frederick; s of Campbell Grant Trotman, and Audrey, *née* Simpson (d 1974); *b* 9 December 1954; *Educ* Alleyne's GS Stevenage, Balliol Coll Oxford (MA, PGCE, Greyhounds XV Rugby, Coll 1st VIII Rowing); *m* 1980, Mary Rosalind, da of Dr Phillip Spencer (d 1961), and Joan, *née* Vickers; 1 da (Eleanor Mary b 1989), 1 s (Jack William Andrew b 1991); *Career* asst master Radley Coll 1978–84, housemaster Abingdon Sch 1984–90, dep rector Edinburgh Acad 1991–95, headmaster St Peter's Sch York 1995–2004, warden St Edward's Sch Oxford 2004–; memb HMC; JP City of York 1997–2003; MInstD; *Recreations* music, rowing, walking, bagpiping; *Clubs* East India, Lansdowne; *Style*— Andrew Trotman, Esq; ✉ 289 Woodstock Road, Oxford OX2 7NY (tel 01865 319289)

TROTT, John Francis Henry; s of Francis Herbert Trott (d 1969), and Ellen Jane, *née* Tilbury; *b* 23 January 1938; *Educ* Whitgift Sch, Merton Coll Oxford (BA); *m* 24 April 1965, Averil Margaret, da of Harold Charles Milestone, of Caterham, Surrey; 2 s (Christopher John b 1966, Jeremy Charles b 1973), 1 da (Nicola Margaret b 1968); *Career* merchant banker; dir Kleinwort Benson Ltd 1972–86, chm and chief exec Kleinwort Benson International Investment Ltd 1986–92, exec vice-pres Bessemer Trust Co NA 1992–98, chm Standard Life Assurance Co 1998–2003 (dir 1974–2003), chm Brunner Investment Trust 1998–2005 (dir 1978–2005), chm Murray International Tst 2002–; *Recreations* golf, tennis; *Style*— John Trott, Esq; ✉ Odstock, Castle Square, Bletchingley, Surrey RH1 4LB (tel 01883 743100)

TROTT, Philip David Anthony; s of Sqdn Ldr Sydney Harold Trott (d 1985), of Fareham, and Ruth, *née* Neubauer (d 2001); *b* 5 June 1952; *Educ* Oxford Poly, UCL (LLB); *Career* admitted slr 1979; Dale Parkinson & Co 1977–78; Lawford & Co: articles 1978–79, asst slr 1979–82, ptnr 1982–89; ptnr: Thomson Snell & Passmore 1989–92, Bates Wells & Braithwaite 1992–; lectr and speaker at various legal conferences and seminars; hon legal advsr Holborn Cross CAB 1979–96, advsr to Art Law 1983–84, joint chm Sub-Ctee Immigration Law Practitioners' Assoc (ILPA) 1988– (chm 1986–88, memb Exec 1984–90, 1994–95 and 2001–02); occasional author of legal articles on immigration and employment law, occasional speaker on immigration issues on radio and TV; lectr UWE; memb: Law Soc, Industrial Law Soc 1978–89, Employment Lawyers' Assoc 1993, American Immigration Lawyers' Assoc 1993–, memb Advsy Panel to Office of Immigration Servs Cmmr 2001–; *Publications* Immigration & International Employment Law (ed, 1999–2001), McDonald's Immigration Law and Practice (chapter author, 6 edn), Jackson's Immigration Law and Practice (chapter author, 3 edn); *Recreations* sailing, swimming, hill walking, flying, travel; *Style*— Philip Trott, Esq; ✉ Bates Wells & Braithwaite, Scandinavian House, 2–6 Cannon Street, London EC4M 6YH (tel 020 7551 7777, fax 020 7551 7800, e-mail p.trott@bateswells.co.uk)

TROTTER, Maj Alexander Richard; JP; s of Maj H R Trotter (d 1962), of Duns, Berwicks, and Rona M, *née* Murray; *b* 20 February 1939; *Educ* Eton, City of London Tech Coll; *m* 1 June 1970, Julia Henrietta, da of Sir Peter McClintock Greenwell, 3 Bt (d 1979); 3 s (Henry b 1972, Edward b 1973, Rupert b 1977); *Career* served Royal Scots Greys 1958–68; mangr Charterhall Estate and Farm 1969, chm Meadowhead Ltd (formerly Mortonhall Park Ltd) 1973–, memb Cncl Scot Landowners' Fedn 1975–2004 (convener 1982–85, vice-pres 1986–96, pres 1996–2001), dir Timber Growers GB Ltd 1977–82, vice-chm Border Grain Ltd 1984–2003; memb Berwickshire CC 1969–75 (chm Roads Ctee 1974–75), memb Dept of Agric Working Party on the Agric Holding (Scotland) Legislation 1981–82, chm Scottish Ctee of Nature Conservancy Cncl 1985–90, memb UK Ctee for Euro Year of the Environment 1986–88; Brig Queen's Body Guard for Scotland (Royal Co of Archers); chm Thirlestane Castle Tst 1996–; DL Berwicks 1987, HM Lord-Lt Berwicks 2000–; FRSA 1987; OStJ 2005; *Recreations* skiing, country sports, golf; *Clubs* New (Edinburgh), Pratt's; *Style*— Maj Alexander Trotter; ✉ Charterhall, Duns, Berwickshire TD11 3RE (tel 01890 840210, office 01890 840301, fax 01890 840651, e-mail alex@charterhall.net)

TROTTER, Andrew James; s of Geoffrey Trotter (d 1999), and Mella, *née* Sanger; *b* 5 August 1954, London; *Educ* Lancing Coll (scholar), Merton Coll Oxford (MA, exhibitioner); *m* 21 Dec 1985, Jilly, *née* Edge; 1 da (Sarah b 5 Oct 1987), 1 s (Luke b 29 May 1989); *Career* admitted slr 1981; grad trainee Surrey CC 1975–77, Withers 1978–83, Norton Rose 1983–85, ptnr Donne Mileham and Haddock 1987–97 (joined 1985), ptnr and head of corporate Shadbolt & Co LLP 1997–; memb Law Soc 1981; *Recreations* golf, football, tennis, travel; ✉ Shadbolt & Co LLP, Chatham Court, Lesbourne Road, Reigate RH2 7LD (tel 01737 226277, fax 01737 226165, e-mail andrew_trotter@shadboltlaw.com)

TROTTER, Prof David; *Career* King Edward VII prof of English Univ of Cambridge, fell Gonville & Caius Coll Cambridge; FBA 2004; *Style*— Prof David Trotter; ✉ Gonville & Caius College, Trinity Street, Cambridge CB2 1TA

TROTTER, Dame Janet Olive; DBE (2001, OBE 1991), DL (Glos 2006); da of Anthony George Trotter, of Canterbury, and Joyce Edith, *née* Patrick; *b* 29 October 1943; *Educ* Tech HS for Girls Maidstone, Derby Diocesan Coll of Educn, Univ of London (BD, MA), Brunel Univ (MSc); *Career* teacher: Hythe Secdy Sch Kent 1965–67, Chartham Secdy Sch Kent 1967–69, Rochester GS for Girls 1969–73; lectr: King Alfred's Coll of HE Winchester 1973–85, St Martin's Coll of HE Lancaster 1985–86; dir Univ of Glos (formerly Cheltenham and Gloucester Coll of HE) 1986–2006; memb: HE Funding Cncl 1992–96, Teacher Trg Agency 1994–99; memb and chair Gloucester Health 1993–96, chair S and West NHS Exec 1996–2001, chair Glos Hosps NHS Fndn Tst 2006–; contrib to various pubns on religious educn and curriculum devpt; involvement with various church orgns incl Fndn for Church Leadership, chair Winston's Wish (charity for bereaved children); hon fell King Alfred's Coll 1999, hon fell Canterbury Christchurch UC 2001; Hon DTech PECS Univ Hungary, Hon LLD Univ of Bristol; Hon DEd: UWE 2001, Brunel Univ 2004, Univ of Leicester 2006; CCMI 2002; *Recreations* walking, cycling and music; *Style*— Dame Janet Trotter, DBE, DL; ✉ Gloucestershire Hospitals NHS Foundation Trust, 1 College Lawn, Cheltenham GL53 7AG

TROTTER, John Geoffrey; *b* 13 July 1951; *Educ* Lancing, Worcester Coll Oxford (Open exhibitioner, BA), Coll of Law London; *Career* Lovells: qualified in 1977, based New York 1980–82, ptnr London 1983–; chm Insurance Ctee Int Bar Assoc 2002–04; memb: Law Soc, London Slrs' Litigation Assoc, City of London Slrs' Co; *Books* Liability of Lawyers and Indemnity Insurance (co-ed); *Recreations* golf, tennis, ornithology, theatre, gardening; *Clubs* Roehampton; *Style*— J G Trotter, Esq; ✉ Lovells, Atlantic House, Holborn Viaduct, London EC1A 2FG (tel 020 7296 2000, fax 020 7296 2001)

TROTTER, Sir Neville Guthrie; kt (1997), JP (Newcastle upon Tyne 1973), DL (Tyne & Wear 1997); s of Capt Alexander Trotter (d 1941), and Elizabeth, *née* Guthrie (d 1992); *b* 27 January 1932; *Educ* Shrewsbury, Univ of Durham (BCom); *m* 1983, Caroline, da of Capt John Darley Farrow, OBE, RN (d 1999), and Oona, *née* Hall; 1 da (Sophie b 1985); *Career* RAF (short serv cmmn) 1955–58; CA, ptnr Thornton Baker & Co 1962–74, conslt Grant Thornton 1974–2005; MP (Cons) Tynemouth 1974–97 (stood down); former memb: Select Ctees on Tport and Defence, Trade & Industry Sub-Ctee of Expenditure Ctee, House of Commons Armed Forces Parly Scheme (RAF); pres Northern Defence Industries Ltd 2000–; dir: NE Chamber of Commerce, Trade and Industry, Northern Business Forum; vice-pres: Soc of Maritime Institute 1996– (former Parly conslt), Soc for Prevention of Solvent Abuse 1996–; fndr chm British American C of C in the North East of England 1999–; Cons Parly Ctees: sec Military Aviation Ctee 1976–79, chm Shipping and Shipbuilding Ctee 1979–85 and 1994–97 (vice-chm 1976–79), sec Industry Ctee 1981–83, sec Tport Ctee 1983–84; former Parly conslt to: British Transport Police Federation, Bowrings plc, Go Ahead Gp; former dir: MidAmerican Energy Holdings Co (parent co of Northern Electric plc), Wm Baird plc, Darchem Ltd, Romag plc; private bills passed on Consumer Safety, Licensing Law, Glue Sniffing; memb: Newcastle City Cncl 1963–74 (Alderman 1970–74, chm Fin Ctee, Traffic, Highways and Tport Ctee, Theatre Ctee), Cncl European Atlantic Gp 1997–; formerly: memb Tyne & Wear Met Cncl, memb CAA Airline Users Ctee, vice-chm Northumberland Police Authy; pres: Northern Area Cons Pty 1996–2003, Tyneside branch Royal Marine's Assoc until 2001; former memb: Northern Econ Planning Cncl, Tyne Improvement Cmmn, Tyneside Passenger Tport Authy, Industrial Relations Tbnl; currently memb: UK Defence Forum, Parly Maritime Gp Steering Ctee, UK Atlantic Cncl, US Naval Inst, RUSI (former memb Cncl), Air League, Railway Studies Assoc, NE Reserve Forces and Cadets Assoc (formerly TAVRA) 1997–, Cncl US Navy League in the UK, US Air Force Assoc, Great North Eastern Railway Business Forum; Hon Col: Royal Marines Reserve 1998–2003, Durham Army Cadet Force 2003–05; High Sheriff Co of Tyne & Wear 2004–05; memb Cncl: High Sheriff's Assoc of England and Wales 2005–, Northumbria Order of St John; Liveryman Worshipful Co of Chartered Accountants; FCA, FRAeS, FCIT; *Recreations* aviation, military history, gardening, fell walking, defence, study of foreign affrs; *Clubs* RAF, Northern Counties, Newcastle upon Tyne; *Style*— Sir Neville Trotter, DL; ✉ Northern Counties Club, Hood Street, Newcastle upon Tyne NE1 6LH

TROTTER, Thomas Andrew; s of His Hon Richard Stanley Trotter (d 1974), of Heswall, Merseyside, and Ruth Elizabeth, *née* Pierce (d 1982); *b* 4 April 1957; *Educ* Malvern Coll, RCM, Univ of Cambridge (MA); *Career* concert organist; scholar RCM 1974; organ scholar: St George's Chapel Windsor 1975–76, King's Coll Cambridge 1976–79; organist:

St Margaret's Church Westminster 1982–, to the City of Birmingham 1983–; debut Royal Festival Hall 1980, Prom Royal Albert Hall 1986, Mozart's Fantasia in F minor (BBC Proms) 1997; festival performances in UK and Europe; tours to: USA, Aust, and the Far East; recording artist for Decca 1989–; first prize winner: Bach Prize, St Albans Int Organ Competition 1979, Prix de Virtuosité, Conservatoire Rueil-Malmaison Paris 1981, Franz Liszt Grand Prix du Disque 1995; Instrumental Award Royal Philharmonic Soc 2002; Hon Dr: Univ of Central Eng 2003, Univ of Birmingham 2006; ARCM, FRCO; *Style—* Thomas Trotter, Esq; ✉ c/o Symphony Hall, Broad Street, Birmingham B1 2EA (tel 0121 200 2000)

TROTTER, Timothy Hugh Southcombe; s of Antony Stuart Trotter (d 1976), of Brandsby, N Yorks, and Marie Louise, *née* Brook; *b* 7 January 1959; *Educ* Wellington, Thames Valley Univ (BA, capt of Tennis, capt of Rugby); *m* 31 May 1986, Caroline, da of Peter Edney Brewer; 2 s (Alexander Antony Stuart b 16 May 1989, Oliver Peter Hugh b 3 Sept 1991); *Career* ptnr and dep md Hill Murray Ltd 1985–91, fndr and chm Ludgate Communications Ltd 1991–98; Ludgate Group Ltd: md 1991–98, chm 1997–98; dep chm Weber PR Worldwide 1997–98, chm Trotter & Co 1998–; FIPR 1998 (MIPR 1986), FCIM 2005 (MCIM 1984), FInstD 2006 (MInstD 1993); *Recreations* tennis, skiing, shooting, backgammon, equestrianism, theatre; *Clubs* City of London, Queen's, Harlequins RFC, RAC; *Style—* Timothy Trotter, Esq; ✉ h2glenfern, 161 New Bond Street, London W1S 2UD

TROUBRIDGE, Sir Thomas Richard; 7 Bt (GB 1799); s of Sir Peter Troubridge, 6 Bt (d 1988), and Hon Venetia (now Hon Mrs (Derick) Forbes), da of 1 Baron Weeks; *b* 23 January 1955; *Educ* Eton, Univ Coll Durham; *m* 1984, Hon Rosemary Douglas-Pennant, da of 6 Baron Penrhyn, DSO, MBE (d 2003); 1 da (Emily Rose b 1987), 2 s (Edward Peter b 1989, Nicholas Douglas St Vincent b 1993); *Heir* s, Edward Troubridge; *Career* ptnr PricewaterhouseCoopers (formerly Price Waterhouse before merger); FCA; *Recreations* sailing ('Spreadeagle'), skiing; *Clubs* Hurlingham, Itchenor Sailing, White's; *Style—* Sir Thomas Troubridge, Bt; ✉ 96 Napier Court, Ranelagh Gardens, London SW6 3XA; PricewaterhouseCoopers, 1 Embankment Place, London WC2N 6RH

TROULLIDES, Andrew John (Andy); s of Joannis Panayis Troullides, of London, and Mirianthi, *née* Stylianou; *b* 1 September 1957; *Educ* Archbishop Tenison's GS London; *m* Sept 1991, Clare Jane, da of Richard E Little; 2 da (Lydia b 29 July 1993, Celia b 20 Dec 1999), 1 s (William b 21 Aug 1995); *Career* Ulster TV 1974–77, Anglia TV 1978–79, J Walter Thompson 1979–82, dir Lowe Howard-Spink 1982–90, media dir Burkitt Weinreich Bryant 1990–93, md MediaCom UK Ltd (part of WPP Group) 1994–99 (gen mangr 1993–94), jt gp md MediaCom TMB (part of WPP Group) 1999, md Optimad Media Systems 1999–2006, chief media officer Independent Media Distribution plc 2007–; fndr chm Blandford St Soc; MIPA 1993; *Style—* Andy Troullides, Esq

TROUP, (John) Edward Astley; s of Vice Adm Sir Anthony Troup, KCB, DSC, and Lady Cordelia Mary; *b* 26 January 1955; *Educ* Oundle, CCC Oxford (MA, MSc); *m* 16 Dec 1978, Siriol Jane, da of Lt-Col John Samuel Martin, OBE; 3 s (Lawrence b 18 May 1985, Madoc b 19 May 1989, Galen b 23 Feb 1991), 1 da (Mabyn b 9 April 1987); *Career* admitted slr 1981; ptnr Simmons & Simmons 1984–95, special advsr (on tax matters) HM Treasury 1995–97, head of tax strategy Simmons & Simmons 1997–2004, dir business and indirect tax HM Treasy 2004–; Freeman: Worshipful Co of Grocers, City of London 1980; ATII; *Recreations* cinema, cycling, bird-watching, Beethoven; *Style—* Edward Troup, Esq; ✉ HM Treasury, One Horse Guards Road, London SW1A 2HQ (tel 020 7270 6006)

TROUP, Prof Malcolm; s of William John Troup (d 1971), of Toronto, and Wendela Mary, *née* Seymour Conway (d 1960); *b* 22 February 1930; *Educ* Royal Conservatory of Music Toronto (ARCT), Saarlandisches Konservatorium, Univ of York (DPhil Mus), Guildhall Sch of Music and Drama (FGSM); *m* 24 Feb 1962, Carmen Lamarca-Bello Subercaseaux, da of Arturo Lamarca-Bello (d 1963), of Paris, Santiago and San Francisco; 1 da (Wendela (Mrs Christopher Lumley) b 1963); *Career* concert pianist 1954–70; toured worldwide; int festivals incl: Prague, Berlin, York, Belfast, Montreal Expo, CBC Toronto, Halifax, Cwlth Arts Festival London; played with leading orchestras incl: LSO, Hallé, Berliner-Sinfonie, Hamburg, Bucharest, Warsaw, Oslo Philharmonic, Bergen Harmonien, Toronto, Winnipeg, São Paulo, Lima, Santiago; first performances of important modern works, numerous recordings; dir of music Guildhall Sch of Music and Drama 1970–75, prof of music and head of dept City Univ London 1975–93, emeritus, founder and visiting prof 1995; judge: CBC Nat Talent Competition, Eckhard-Grammaté Piano Competition, Young Musicians of the Year, Chopin Competition of Aust 1988, 1st Dvořák Int Piano Competition 1997, Int Piano Competition Rome 1997, 1st EPTA Int Piano Competition Zagreb 1999, Reykjavik 2000, Cyprus 2001 and Rome 2002, 1st Claudio Arrau Int Piano Competition Santiago and Chillan 2003, Gina Bachauer Int Piano Competition Salt Lake City; pres Oxford Int Piano Festival, vice-pres World Piano Competition, fndr and vice-pres Asociación Latinoamericana de Profesores de Piano (ALAPP/Chile), govr Music Therapy Charity Tst, chm Euro Piano Teachers Assoc, chm Beethoven Piano Soc of Europe, tstee Jewish Music Inst; ed Piano Journal 1987–; external examiner: KCL, Univ of York, Keele Univ; music advsr: Royal Netherlands Govt, Br Cncl, Canada Cncl, Leverhulme Tst; Cwlth medal 1955, Harriet Cohen Int award, Medal of the American Liszt Soc 1998; Freeman City of London 1971, Liveryman Worshipful Co of Musicians 1973 (memb Ct of Assts 1991–, Sr Warden 1997–98, Master 1998–99); memb RSM 1988; hon prof Univ of Chile 1966, Hon LLD Meml Univ of Newfoundland 1985, Hon DMus City Univ London 1995; FRSA 1986; *Books* Serial Strawinsky in 20 Century Music, Orchestral Music of the 1950s and 1960s in The Messiaen Companion (1994), 'The Piano' in Science & Psychology of Music Performance (jtly, 2002); author of various articles in: Composer, Music and Musicians, Music Teacher, Piano Journal, Revista Universitaria de Chile; *Style—* Prof Malcolm Troup; ✉ Department of Music, City University, Northampton Square, London EC1V 0HB (tel 020 7477 8284, fax 020 7477 8576)

TROWELL, Dr Joan Mary; da of Gordon Watson Trowell (d 1969), and Vera, *née* Kilham (d 1969); *b* 2 January 1941; *Educ* Walthamstow Hall Sevenoaks, Royal Free Hosp Med Sch London (MB BS); *m* 31 Oct 1970, John Percy Perry (d 1985), s of Percy Perry (d 1964); 1 s (Mark b 1972), 1 da (Helen b 1974); *Career* house physician London: Royal Free Hosp 1964, Royal Northern Hosp 1965, Brompton Hosp 1967, Hammersmith Hosp 1967; med registrar: Addenbrooke's Hosp Cambridge 1968, Hammersmith Hosp 1969; emeritus fell Nuffield Dept of Clinical Med Oxford 1971, hon conslt physician John Radcliffe Hosp Oxford 1981, dep dir of Clinical Studies Oxford 1995–98; exec of Oxon Cncl for Alcohol and Drug Use; Med Cncl on Alcoholism: dep chm, regnl and univ rep, memb Educn Ctee, memb Nat Exec Ctee 1998–; memb and vice-chm Bd of Visitors Oxford Prison 1987–96, memb Ind Monitoring Bd (formerly Bd of Visitors) HM Prison Grendon & Springhill 1996–; memb local review ctee Parole Bd; Hon MA Oxford 1971; Med Women's Fedn: pres Oxford Region 1991–93, memb Nat Cncl 1993–, memb Nat Exec Ctee 1994–, nat vice-pres 1997–98, pres 1998–99; GMC: memb (representing Univs of Oxford and Cambridge) 1998–2003, memb Educn Ctee 1999–2003, elected med memb 2003–, chm Fitness to Practise Ctee 2003–06; memb: BMA (pres Oxford Div 1992–93), Nat Clinical Advsy Bd and Info Standards Bd NHS Nat Prog for IT; chm of tstees Royal Medical Benevolent Fund; FRCP 1987; *Books* Topics in Gastroenterology (1975), Oxford Textbook of Medicine (contrib, 1986), Oxford Textbook of Pathology (contrib, 1991), Medical Woman (ed, 1999–2001); *Clubs* Reform, Oxford and Cambridge; *Style—* Dr Joan Trowell; ✉ Camp Corner Cottage, Old London Road, Milton Common, Thame, Oxfordshire OX9 2JR; John Radcliffe Hospital, Headington, Oxford OX3 9DU (e-mail joan.trowell@ndm.ox.ac.uk)

TROWER, William Spencer Philip; QC (2001); s of late Anthony Gosselin Trower, of Stanstead Bury, Herts, and Catherine Joan, *née* Kellett; *b* 28 December 1959; *Educ* Eton, ChCh Oxford (MA), City Univ (Dip Law); *m* 30 Aug 1986, Mary Louise, da of Gerard Nicolas Pyemont Chastel de Boinville; 4 da (Emily Katherine b 18 Aug 1987, Alice Charlotte b 29 Jan 1989, Lucy Harriet b 14 May 1992, Rosanna Mary b 20 Dec 1993); *Career* called to the Bar 1983; *Books* Corporate Administrations and Rescue Procedures (jtly, 1994, 2 edn 2004); *Clubs* Garrick; *Style—* William Trower, Esq, QC; ✉ Walkern Bury Farm, Bassus Green, Stevenage, Hertfordshire SG2 7JH (tel 01438 861004); 3–4 South Square, Gray's Inn, London WC1R 5HP (tel 020 7696 9900, fax 020 7696 9911, mobile 07968 764453, e-mail williamtrower@southsquare.com)

TROWSDALE, Prof John; s of Roy R Trowsdale, and Doris, *née* Graham; *b* 8 February 1949; *Educ* Beverley GS, Univ of Birmingham (BSc, PhD); *m* 1971, Susan Price; 3 c (Sam A b 1975, Jodie L b 1977, Alice R Z b 1989); *Career* Euro fell Biochemical Soc France 1973–75, research fell Scripps Clinic and Research Fndn La Jolla Calif 1975–78, SRC research fell Univ of Oxford 1978–79; ICRF London: fell 1979–82, research scientist 1982–85, sr scientist 1986–90, princ scientist 1990–97; prof of immunology Univ of Cambridge 1997–; FMedSci 2000; *Publications* author of articles in scientific jls; *Recreations* rock, jazz and classical music, painting; *Style—* Prof John Trowsdale; ✉ Immunology Division, Department of Pathology, Tennis Court Road, Cambridge CB2 1QP (tel 01223 330248, fax 01223 333875)

TRUDGILL, Prof Peter John; s of John Trudgill (d 1986), of Norwich, and Hettie Jean, *née* Gooch; *b* 7 November 1943; *Educ* City of Norwich Sch, King's Coll Cambridge (MA), Univ of Edinburgh (MA, PhD); *m* 15 Feb 1980, Jean Marie, da of Wade F Hannah; *Career* successively lectr, reader then prof Univ of Reading 1970–86, reader then prof Univ of Essex 1986–92, prof of English language and linguistics Univ of Lausanne Switzerland 1993–98, prof of English linguistics Univ of Fribourg Switzerland 1998–; Dr (hc) Uppsala Univ Sweden 1995, Dr (hc): UEA 2002, La Trobe Aust; fell Norwegian Acad of Arts and Sciences 1995, fell Norwegian Acad of Sciences and Letters 1996, FBA 1989; *Books* academic: The Social differentiation of English in Norwich (1974), Sociolinguistics: an introduction (1974, reprinted 17 times, 3 edn 1995), Accent dialect and the school (1975), Sociolinguistic patterns in British English (ed, 1978), English accents and dialects: an introduction to social and regional varieties of British English (with A Hughes, 1979, 3 edn 1996), Dialectology (with J K Chambers, 1980), International English: a guide to varieties of Standard English (with J Hannah, 1982), On dialect: social and geographical perspectives (1982), Language in the British Isles (ed, 1984), Applied sociolinguistics (ed, 1984), A grammar of English dialect (with V Edwards and B Weltens, 1984), Dialects in contact (1986), Dialects of England (1990), Bad language (with L G Andersson, 1990), English dialects: Studies in grammatical variation (ed with J K Chambers, 1991), Introducing language and society (1992), Dialects (1994), Language Myths (ed with L Bauer, 1998), New-dialect Formation (2004); non academic: Coping with America: A beginners guide to the USA (1982, shortlisted Thomas Cook Travel Book Prize 1983, 2 edn 1985); *Style—* Prof Peter J Trudgill, FBA; ✉ School of Language, Linguistics and Translation Studies, University of East Anglia, Norwich NR4 7TJ (e-mail peter.trudgill@unifr.ch)

TRUE, Nicholas Edward; CBE (1992); s of Edward Thomas True (d 1991), and Kathleen Louise; *b* 31 July 1951; *Educ* Nottingham HS, Peterhouse Cambridge (MA); *m* 7 July 1979, Anne-Marie Elena Kathleen Blanco, da of Robin Adrian Hood (d 1993); 2 s (James Alexios Edward b 26 Aug 1981, Thomas-Leo Richard b 30 May 1984), 1 da (Sophia Miriam Marie-Louise Blanco b 10 Aug 1992); *Career* memb Cons Res Dept 1976–82, PA to Lord Whitelaw 1978–82, special advsr to Sec of State DHSS 1982–86, dir of Public Policy Unit Ltd 1986–90, dep head Prime Minister's Policy Unit 1990–95, ministerial nominee English Sports Cncl 1996–97, special advsr PM's Office 1997, private sec to Ldr of the Oppn House of Lords 1997–; cncllr Richmond-upon-Thames 1986–90, 1998– (dep ldr 2002–06, ldr of the oppn 2006–); tstee: Sir Harold Hood's Charitable Tst 1996–, Richmond Civic Endowment Tst 2006–; *Recreations* books, cricket, Italy, opera, Byzantium; *Clubs* Travellers, Beefsteak; *Style—* Nicholas True, Esq, CBE; ✉ 114 Palewell Park, London SW14 8JH (tel 020 8876 9628, fax 020 8876 3096, e-mail truen@parliament.uk)

TRULUCK, (Maj-Gen) Ashley Ernest George; CB (2001), CBE (1997); s of Maj George William Truluck, of Ely, Cambs, and Elizabeth, *née* Kitchener (d 1986); *b* 7 December 1947; *Educ* RMA Sandhurst, Open Univ (BA), Staff Coll Camberley, RMCS Shrivenham, RCDS; *m* 21 Feb 1976, Jennifer Jane, *née* Bell; 1 da (Cherry Louise b 25 July 1981), 1 s (Laurence James George b 13 March 1985); *Career* regtl duty Bde of Gurkhas 1970–74, ADC to Cdr Land Forces Far East 1974–75, communications offr Gds Armd Bde 1976–77, staff offr MOD 1980–81, Sqdn Cdr BAOR UK 1982–84, memb Directing Staff RMCS Shrivenham 1984–86, Regtl Cdr BAOR 1986–88, Col Army Staff Duties 1989–90, cdr Royal Sch of Signals and Blandford Garrison 1991–92, Brig Gen Staff UK Land Command 1994–96, dir Attack Helicopter 1997–98, ACOS SHAPE 1998–2000; Col Cmdt Royal Corps of Signals 2001–07, chm Royal Signals Benevolent Fund 2003–; chm Defence Housing Review 2000, chief exec London Magistrates Courts 2001–03, chm London Criminal Justice Bd 2001–03, md Ashley Truluck Associates Ltd 2003–, nat project dir Fire and Rescue Servs Communications Project 2005–; Adm Royal Signals Yacht Club 2004–; FCMI, FInstD; *Recreations* offshore sailing, hill walking, country pursuits, history and the arts, family; *Clubs* Army and Navy, Ocean Cruising, Int Assoc of Cape Horners; *Style—* Ashley Truluck, CB, CBE; ✉ e-mail ashley.truluck@broadchalke.co.uk

TRUMAN, Prof Aubrey; s of Edwin Truman (d 1966), of Wolstanton, Newcastle-under-Lyme, Staffs, and Nellie, *née* Nixon (d 1972); *b* 9 December 1943, Staffordshire; *Educ* Wolstanton CGS, Univ of Oxford (open exhibitioner, open scholar, MA, Dip, DPhil); *m* 24 July 1965, Jane, da of Harold Pratt; 2 da (Rachel b 12 Nov 1968, Emma b 26 July 1970), 1 s (Thomas b 29 Aug 1977); *Career* sr lectr Dept of Maths Heriot-Watt Univ 1978–82 (lectr 1969–78); Univ of Wales Swansea: prof of maths 1982–, head Dept of Maths 1985–, dean Faculty of Sci 1989–92; visiting prof Univ of Maryland 2002; sec Int Assoc of Mathematical Physics 1991–; organiser of confs incl IX Int Congress on Mathematical Physics 1988; mathematical physics ed Europhysics Letters 1989–92, an ed Proceedings A of the Royal Soc of Edinburgh 1993–97; FRSE 1983, FIMA; *Books* incl: Stochastic and Quantum Mechanics (jt ed, 1992), Stochastic Analysis and Applications, (jt ed, 1996); author of numerous pubns in learned jls; *Recreations* walking and bridge; *Style—* Prof Aubrey Truman, FRSE; ✉ Department of Mathematics, University of Wales Swansea, Singleton Park, Swansea SA2 8PP

TRUMPINGTON, Baroness (Life Peer UK 1980), of Sandwich in the County of Kent; Dame Jean Alys Barker; DCVO (2005), PC (1992); da of late Maj Arthur Edward Campbell-Harris, MC, and Doris Marie, *née* Robson; *b* 23 October 1922; *Educ* privately in England and France; *m* 1954, William Alan Barker (d 1988); 1 s (Hon Adam Campbell Barker, *qv* b 1955); *Career* sits as Cons peer in House of Lords; Cons cncllr Cambridge City Cncl Trumpington Ward 1963–73 (Mayor of Cambridge 1971–72, Dep Mayor 1972–73), Cons co cncllr Cambs Trumpington Ward 1973–75, hon cncllr City of Cambridge 1975–; JP: Cambridge 1972–75, S Westminster 1976–82; UK delegate to UN Status of Women Cmmn 1979–81; Baroness in Waiting to HM The Queen 1983–85; Parly under-sec of state: DHSS 1985–87, MAFF 1987–89; min of state MAFF 1989–92; Baroness in Waiting 1992–97, Extra Baroness in Waiting to HM The Queen 1998–; hon fell Lucy Cavendish Coll Cambridge 1980, Hon FRCPath, Hon ARCVS; Officier de l'Ordre Nationale du Mérite; *Recreations* bridge, racing, antique hunting; *Style—* The Rt Hon the Baroness Trumpington, DCVO, PC; ✉ House of Lords, London SW1A 0PW

T

TRURO, Bishop of 1997–; Rt Rev William Ind; *Educ* Duke of York's Sch Dover, Univ of Leeds (BA), Coll of the Resurrection Mirfield; *m* 1967, Frances Isobel, *née* Bramald; 3 s (Michael Jonathan b 19 Feb 1970, Martin William b 12 Nov 1972, Philip Robert b 7 Dec 1974); *Career* asst curate St Dunstan's Feltham 1966–70, priest i/c St Joseph The Worker Northolt 1970–74, team vicar Basingstoke (St Gabriel's Popley) 1974–87, examining chaplain to Bishop of Winchester 1975–82, dir of ordinands Dio of Winchester 1980–86, hon canon Winchester Cathedral 1985–87, bishop of Grantham 1987–97, dean of Stamford 1988–97; memb House of Lords 2002–; pt/t vice-princ Aston Trg Scheme 1977–82, memb C of E Doctrine Cmmn 1980–86, currently memb Cncl Grubb Inst; *Recreations* cricket, bird watching; *Style*— The Rt Rev the Lord Bishop of Truro; ✉ Lis Escop, Truro, Cornwall TR3 6QQ (tel 01872 862657, fax 01872 862037, e-mail bishop@truro.anglican.org)

TRUSCOTT, Baron (Life Peer UK 2004), of St James's in the City of Westminster; Peter Derek Truscott; s of late Derek Truscott, of Newton Abbot, Devon; *b* 20 March 1959; *Educ* Newton Abbot GS, Exeter Coll Oxford (MA, DPhil); *m* 1991, Svetlana, da of late Col Prof Nicolai Chernicov, of St Petersburg, Russia; *Career* memb Colchester BC 1988–92, MEP (Lab) Herts 1994–99, Lab Pty spokesman on Foreign Affrs and Defence 1997–99; vice-pres Ctee on Security and Disarmament 1994–99; departmental liaison peer MOD 2004–05; memb: TGWU 1986–, Co-op Pty 1987–, Foreign Affrs Ctee 1994–99, Foreign Affrs, Def and Devpt Select Ctee Sub-Ctee C 2005–; assoc fell: IPPR 2000– (visiting research fell 1999–2000), RUSI 2005–; *Books* Russia First (1997), European Defence (2000), Kursk (2002), Putin's Progress (2004); *Style*— The Lord Truscott

TRUSCOTT, Prof Terence George; s of Leonard Truscott (d 1979), of Bargoed, and Doris, *née* Lloyd (d 1994); *b* 8 May 1939; *Educ* Bargoed GS, Univ of Wales Swansea (BSc, PhD, DSc); *m* 1962, Marylin, da of Idris Evans; 1 da (Caroline Siân b 1971); *Career* post-doctoral research fell Univ of Minnesota 1964–65, sr scientist J Lyons & Co 1965–66, lectr in chemistry Univ of Bradford 1966–71, project ldr International Nickel Company of Canada 1971–73, prof and head of chemistry Univ of Paisley 1974–90, head Dept of Chemistry Keele Univ 1993– (prof of physical chemistry 1990–93); The Dr Lee's visiting fell ChCh Oxford 1993–94; fndr pres Euro Soc of Photobiology; FRSC 1974, FRSE 1988; *Books* Flash Photolysis and Pulse Radiolysis: Chemistry of Biology and Medicine (contrib, 1983, Russian edn 1987), Excited States and Free Radicals in Biology and Medicine (1993), also ed of three text-books; *Recreations* golf, bridge; *Clubs* Trentham Golf; *Style*— Prof Terence Truscott, FRSE; ✉ Department of Chemistry, Keele University, Staffordshire ST5 5BG (tel 01782 583038, fax 01782 712378, e-mail cha31@keele.ac.uk)

TRUSLER, Colin Harold; s of Harold Sidney Trusler (d 1973), and Alice Joan, *née* Angell; *b* 11 July 1942; *Educ* Loughborough GS, Wadham Coll Oxford (scholar, MA), Harvard Business Sch; *m* 1, 1965, Jill Vivienne, *née* Bullen; 2 s (Rupert Charles b 1969, Simon Edward b 1973), 1 da (Philippa Sarah b 1971); m 2, 1982, Fiona Innes, *née* Parsons; 2 s (Felix Colin Innes b 1986, Barnaby Colin Innes b 1991); *Career* graduate trainee Public Relations Partnership 1963–66, conslt Brook Hart Ruder & Finn International 1966–69; Lloyds Bank: PR advsr 1969–72, mktg mangr 1972–78, head of mktg 1978–86; Shandwick Consultants: dir 1986–88, md 1988–90, chm and chief exec 1990–93, chm 1993–97; md Shandwick UK 1993–98, fndr dir The Senior Executive Network Ltd 1998–2004, non-exec dir MORI Ltd 2005–06, interim mktg dir Ipsos MORI 2006–; magistrate City of London 2003–; chm of govrs St Thomas's Sch 2000–; FRSA 1992; *Recreations* tennis, family life; *Style*— Colin Trusler, Esq; ✉ e-mail colin_trusler@yahoo.co.uk

TRUSS, Lynne; da of Ernest Edward Truss (d 1991), and Joan Dorothy, *née* Sellar; *b* 31 May 1955, Kingston upon Thames; *Educ* Tiffin Girls' GS Kingston upon Thames (Gamble Prize), UCL (BA, Morley Medal Award, George Smith Prize, Rosa Morrison scholar); *Career* dep literary ed Times Higher Education Supplement 1978–1986, literary ed The Listener 1986–90, columnist, critic and sportswriter The Times 1991–2000; many plays, series, comedies and talks for BBC Radio; Columnist of the Year 1996; memb Soc of Authors 2005, FRSL 2005; *Publications* With One Lousy Free Packet of Seed (1994), Making the Cat Laugh (1995), Tennyson's Gift (1996), Going Loco (1999), Tennyson and his Circle (1999), Eats, Shoots and Leaves (2003, Book of the Year Br Book Awards 2004), Talk to the Hand (2005); *Recreations* theatre, travel; *Clubs* Groucho; *Style*— Lynne Truss; ✉ c/o Anthony Goff, David Higham Associates Ltd, 5–8 Lower John Street, London W1F 9HA (tel 020 7434 5900, e-mail anthonygoff@davidhigham.co.uk); website www.lynnetruss.com

TRUST, Howard Bailey; *b* 6 October 1954; *Educ* Gonville & Caius Coll Cambridge (MA); *m* (m dis); 4 c; *Career* slr: Lovell, White & King London 1980–85, Morgan Grenfell & Co Ltd London 1985–87; co sec Morgan Grenfell plc London 1987–89, gp legal dir Barclays de Zoete Wedd Holdings Ltd London 1989–95, gp gen counsel and sec Barclays plc 1995–2003; memb: Int Bar Assoc, Law Soc, City of London Slrs' Co; *Style*— Howard Trust, Esq; ✉ Schroders plc, 31 Gresham Street, London EC2V 7QA (tel 020 7658 6444, e-mail howard.trust@schroders.com)

TRUSWELL, Paul Anthony; MP; s of John and Olive Truswell; *b* 17 November 1955; *Educ* Firth Park Comp Sch, Univ of Leeds (BA); *m* 1981, Suzanne Clare, da of Desmond Evans; 2 s (Richard b 27 Nov 1989, Michael b 25 June 1992); *Career* journalist Yorkshire Post Newspapers 1977–88, local govt offr Wakefield MDC 1988–97, MP (Lab) Pudsey 1997–; cncllr Leeds City Cncl 1982–97; memb: Leeds Eastern HA 1982–90, Leeds Community Health Cncl 1990–92, Leeds Family Health Servs Authy 1992–96; *Recreations* playing various sports with my children, photography, cinema, cricket; *Clubs* Guiseley Factory Workers' Social; *Style*— Paul Truswell, Esq, MP; ✉ House of Commons, London SW1A 0AA (tel 020 7219 3504, fax 020 7219 2252); constituency office: 10A Greenside, Pudsey, West Yorkshire LS28 8PU (tel 0113 229 3553)

TRYNKA, Paul; s of Kazimierz Trynka, of Beverley, E Yorks, and Maureen, *née* Castle; *b* 17 October 1960; *Educ* Hymers Coll Hull, Hull Coll of FE, Univ of Hull (BSc); *Partner* Lucy Wise; 1 s (Curtis b 16 Sept 2000); *Career* ed Int Musician magazine 1989 (features ed 1986–89), ed Radio & Music magazine 1990, ed-in-chief Guitar magazine, Rock CD magazine and Soul CD magazine 1991–96, ed-in-chief MOJO magazine (features ed 1996), editorial dir Q magazine; friend of Christ Church Spitalfields; *Books* incl: The Electric Guitar (1993), Portrait of the Blues (with Val Wilmer, 1996), From Cowboys to Catwalks - A History of Denim (2002); *Style*— Paul Trynka, Esq; ✉ MOJO, Emap, 4 Winsley Street, London W1W 8HF (tel 020 7436 1515, fax 020 7312 8296)

TRYON, 3 Baron (UK 1940); Anthony George Merrik Tryon; OBE (2001), DL (Wilts 1992); s of 2 Baron Tryon, GCVO, KCB, DSO, PC (d 1976), and Etheldreda (d 2002), da of Sir Merrik Burrell, 7 Bt, CBE; *b* 26 May 1940; *Educ* Eton; *m* 1973, Dale Elizabeth (d 1997), da of Barry Harper, of Melbourne, Aust; 2 da (Hon Zoë b 1974, Hon Victoria b 1979), 2 s (Hon Charles b 1976, Hon Edward (twin) b 1979); *Heir* s, Hon Charles Tryon; *Career* page of honour to HM The Queen 1954–56; Capt Royal Wilts Yeo; dir Lazard Bros & Co Ltd 1976–83, chm English & Scottish Investors Ltd 1977–87; Liveryman Worshipful Co of Gunmakers; *Recreations* fishing, shooting; *Clubs* White's, Pratt's; *Style*— The Rt Hon the Lord Tryon, OBE, DL; ✉ Fordie Lodge, Comrie, Perthshire PH6 2LT (tel 01764 679060, fax 01764 679063)

TSUNEMATSU, Samuel Ikuo (Sammy); s of Takashi Tsunematsu (d 1966), of Satsuma, Japan, and Toyono, *née* Nakanoue; *b* 4 October 1951; *Educ* Obirin Univ Tokyo (BA); *m* 15 Feb 1985, Yoshiko, da of Kiyoshi Yorifuji, of Hokkaido, Japan; *Career* dir Gendai Travel Ltd 1980, md Soseki Museum London 1984, dir Y & S Co; prof of English Sojo Univ Japan 2005–; *Books* Soseki in London (1985), The World of Yoshio Markino (1989), Yoshio Markino - A Japanese Artist in London (1990), Chuzo Matsuyama - A Japanese Artist in London (1991), The Colour of London-Markino Yoshio Gashu (1992), Alone in this World (1992), London no oishii Itadaki-Kata (1996), The Painter of Mist - The Story of Yoshio Markino (1997), Travels in Manchuria and Korea (2000), Eikoku Oshitsu Goyo-tashi (2001), Tatsujin no London Annai (2002); Japanese translations: Watashino London Paris Rome Inshoki (1990), Waga Riso no Eikokujosei Tachi (1990), Kirino London (1991), Jutsukai Nishi (1991), Seiyo to Toyo no Hikaku Shisoron (1992), My Fair London (1993), Kochira London Soseki Kinenkan (1994); English translations: Travels in Manchuria and Korea (1999), Inside My Glass Doors (2002), The 210th Day (2002), Spring Miscellany and London Essays (2002), Records of Chips and and Shavings (2004), My Individualism (2004), The Heredity of Taste (2004); other translations: Un artista japonés en Londres (Spanish, 1993), Un artiste japonais à Londres (French, 1993); *Recreations* reading the ancient Chinese, Latin and Greek classics in order to forget the modern civilisation; *Clubs* National Liberal; *Style*— Sammy Tsunematsu, Esq; ✉ 3F Kuhonji-Daini Building, 5–4, 4–Chome, Kuhonji, Kumamoto-City, Japan 862–0976; Soseki Museum in London, 80 The Chase, London SW4 0NG (tel 020 7720 8718, e-mail nsoseki@hotmail.com)

TUCK, Sir Bruce Adolph Reginald; 3 Bt (UK 1910), of Park Crescent, St Marylebone; s of Major Sir (William) Reginald Tuck, 2 Bt (d 1954, s of Sir Adolph Tuck, 1 Bt, who was gs of Raphael Tuck, fine art publisher and chm and md of Raphael Tuck and Sons); *b* 29 June 1926; *Educ* Canford; *m* 1, 1949 (m dis in Jamaica 1964), Luise, da of John C Renfro, of San Angelo, Texas, USA; 2 s; m 2, 1968, Pamela Dorothy, da of Alfred Michael Nicholson, of London; 1 da; *Heir* s, Richard Tuck; *Career* Lt Scots Gds 1945–47; with Miller-Carnegie; *Clubs* Lansdowne; *Style*— Sir Bruce Tuck, Bt; ✉ Montego Bay, PO Box 274, Jamaica

TUCK, (Anne) Victoria (Vicky); *Educ* Univ of Kent (BA), Inst of Educn Univ of London (PGCE), Univ de Lille et de Paris (Dip Supérieur de Droit et de Français des Affaires), South Bank Univ (MA); *Career* teacher Putney HS 1976–81, head of modern languages Bromley HS 1981–86, lectr Inst of Educn Univ of London 1991–94, dep head City of London Sch for Girls 1994–96, princ Cheltenham Ladies' Coll 1996–; external examiner KCL until 1999; govr: Mount House Sch 2004–, St Hugh's Farringdon 2004–; pres GSA 2008; MIL 1999; *Style*— Mrs Vicky Tuck; ✉ The Cheltenham Ladies' College, Bayshill Road, Cheltenham, Gloucestershire GL50 3EP (tel 01242 520691, fax 01242 227882, e-mail principal@cheltladiescollege.org)

TUCKER, Alistair John James; s of James Charles Henry Tucker (d 1982), and Mary Hannah, *née* Featherstonehaugh (d 1975); *b* 17 February 1936; *Educ* Southend HS, Keble Coll Oxford (MA); *m* 2 Sept 1967, Deirdre Ann Forster, da of George Moore, of Amersham, Bucks; 1 s (Alistair b 1976), 1 da (Hannah b 1972); *Career* Subaltern The Green Howards 1958–60; exec dir within Transport Holding Co 1967–70, md Alistair Tucker Halcrow and Assoc 1970–91, dir Air Tport Practice Price Waterhouse Management Consultants 1991–95, princ Alistair Tucker Associates 1995–; special advsr UK House of Commons Tport Ctee 1992–97; visiting prof Univ of Surrey 1987–93; MCIT 1972, MRAeS 1980; *Recreations* walking, travel, archaeology; *Clubs* Athenaeum; *Style*— Alistair Tucker, Esq; ✉ 50 Primrose Gardens, London NW3 4TP (tel 020 7483 4061, e-mail alistairtucker@googlemail.com)

TUCKER, Clive Fenemore; CB (1996); s of William Frederick (d 1992) and Joan Tucker; *b* 13 July 1944; *Educ* Cheltenham GS, Balliol Coll Oxford (BA); *m* Caroline; 2 da (Elisabeth, Fiona); *Career* Min of Labour, Dept of Employment: joined 1965, private sec to perm sec 1969–70, princ Trg Policy 1970–74, sabbatical USA/Canada 1974, sec Manpower Services Cmmn 1975–78, asst sec Employment and Industrial Relations 1978–87, under sec Grade 3 1987–, Top Mgmnt Prog 1989, under sec Grade 3 Industrial Relations 1990–95; dir Int Affairs DfEE 1995–2001; non-exec dir RTZ Chemicals 1987–90, Fulbright cmmr 1998–; pres EU Employment Ctee 2001–03; dir Jt DWP/DFES Int Unit 2001–06; *Recreations* music, theatre, literature, the countryside; *Style*— Clive Tucker, CB; ✉ DWP/DFES, Caxton House, Tothill Street, London SW1H 9NF

TUCKER, Derek Alan; s of Gwynne Tucker (d 1989), and Sheila Elizabeth, *née* Lynch, of Codsall, Staffs; *b* 31 October 1953; *Educ* Quarry Bank GS Liverpool, Municipal GS Wolverhampton; *m* 1 (m dis 1991); 1 s (Paul), 1 da (Elizabeth); m 2, 8 June 2000, Marilyn Lyla Sclater; *Career* journalist; Express & Star 1972–92: trainee reporter, reporter, chief reporter, news ed, news ed and dep ed; ed Press & Journal Aberdeen 1992–; chm Eds' Ctee Scottish Daily Newspaper Soc 2003–05, memb Code of Practice Ctee 2002–; former offr RAF (volunteer reserve) 1988–94; *Recreations* golf, travel, any sport not involving horses; *Clubs* Royal Northern & Univ; *Style*— Derek Tucker, Esq; ✉ Aberdeen Journals, Lang Stracht, Mastrick, Aberdeen AB15 6DF (tel 01224 343300, fax 01224 344114, e-mail d.tucker@ajl.co.uk)

TUCKER, Prof John Barry; *b* 17 March 1941; *Educ* Queen Elizabeth GS Atherstone, Peterhouse Cambridge (state scholar, Kitchener nat meml scholar, MA, PhD); *m* 1975, Janet, *née* Murray; 2 c; *Career* Fulbright scholar and research assoc Dept of Zoology Indiana Univ 1966–68, SRC post-doctoral research fell Dept of Zoology Univ of Cambridge 1968–69; Univ of St Andrews: lectr in zoology 1969–78, reader 1978–90, prof of cell biology 1990–, memb Ct (Senate assessor 1993–97); memb Editorial Bd Development (formerly Jl of Embryology and Experimental Morphology) 1979–88; FRSE 1996; *Publications* author of numerous book chapters, papers and articles in learned jls; *Style*— Prof John Tucker, FRSE; ✉ School of Biology, Bute Medical Building, University of St Andrews, St Andrews, Fife KY16 9TS (tel 01334 463560, fax 01334 463600, e-mail jbt@st-and.ac.uk)

TUCKER, John Channon; s of John Basil Laurence Tucker, and Ursula Thackeray, *née* Hill (d 2001); *b* 31 July 1958, Brisbane, Aust; *Educ* South Aust Inst of Technol (BA), Univ of Adelaide (LLB); *m* 24 Sept 1983, Madeleine Jane Penn, *née* Boucaut; 3 s (Sam b 30 Jan 1985, Joshua b 19 Sept 1986, Michael b 8 Feb 1989), 1 da (Rebecca b 2 Aug 1992); *Career* barr and slr S Aust 1980, admitted slr Eng and Wales 1988; ptnr Finlaysons Adelaide 1984–89, ptnr Linklaters London 1990– (global head of banking 1999–); tstee Sir Robert Menzies Meml Tst; memb Glyndebourne Festival Soc; memb Law Soc 1988; assoc Aust Soc of Certified Practising Accountants 1984; *Recreations* family, sailing, golf, diving, tennis, skiing, opera; *Clubs* Adelaide, Royal S Aust Yacht Sqdn, RORC, Hurlingham, MCC, Surrey CCC, Wimbledon Park Golf; *Style*— John Tucker, Esq; ✉ Linklaters, 1 Silk Street, London EC2Y 8HQ (tel 020 7456 2000, fax 020 7456 2222, e-mail john.tucker@linklaters.com)

TUCKER, (John) Keith; s of Reginald John Tucker (d 1976), and Nancy, *née* Harker (d 1993); *b* 24 March 1945; *Educ* Haberdashers' Aske's, Charing Cross Hosp Med Sch (MB BS); *m* 4 Oct 1975, Jill Margaret, da of Dr Thomas Oliphant McKane (d 1972), of Greater Easton, Essex; 3 s (Timothy b 1977, Alexander b 1979, Ian b 1981); *Career* house surgn Charing Cross Hosp 1969, registrar Addenbrooke's Hosp Cambridge 1971–73, sr registrar St Bartholomew's Higher Orthopaedic Training Scheme 1973–77, conslt orthopaedic surgn Norfolk and Norwich Hosp 1977–; hon clinical tutor in med Univ of Cambridge; author of various scientific papers, co-designer of Hip Replacements System 1982–; external examiner in surgery Univ of Cambridge 1994–97; chm Orthopaedic Data Evaluation Panel Nat Inst for Clinical Excellence (NICE); memb: The Br Hip Soc (hon sec 1998–2005, vice-pres 2005, pres 2007–08), Br Orthopaedic Assoc (memb Cncl 1993–96), BMA, National Joint Registry Steering Ctee 2007–; hon MD Univ of Murcia Spain 1985; FRCS (MRCS), LRCP; *Recreations* family; *Style*— Keith Tucker, Esq; ✉ 77 Newmarket Road, Norwich (tel 01603 614016, fax 01603 766469)

TUCKER, Paul M W; s of B W Tucker, and late H M Tucker, *née* Lloyd; *b* 24 March 1958; *Educ* Codsall HS, Trinity Coll Cambridge (MA); *m* Sophie Dierick; *Career* Bank of England: bank supervisor and corp financier (seconded) at merchant bank 1980–87, advsr (seconded) to Hong Kong Securities Review Ctee Hong Kong Govt 1987–88, Bank of England Markets Area (reviewing UK's wholesale payments system) 1988–89, private sec to Govr 1989–92, Gilt-Edged and Money Markets Div 1993–96 (head of div 1994–96), head Monetary Assessment and Strategy Div 1997–98, dep dir Fin Stability and Mgmnt Ctee 1999–2002, exec dir Markets 2002–, memb Monetary Policy Ctee Secretariat 1997–2002, memb Monetary Policy Ctee 2002–; *Clubs* Athenaeum; *Style*— Paul Tucker, Esq; ✉ Bank of England, Threadneedle Street, London EC2R 8AH (tel 020 7601 4444)

TUCKER, Sir Richard Howard; kt (1985); s of His Hon Judge Howard Archibald Tucker (d 1963), and Margaret Minton, *née* Thacker (d 1976); *b* 9 July 1930; *Educ* Shrewsbury, The Queen's Coll Oxford (MA); *m* 1, 1958 (m dis 1974), Paula Mary Bennett Frost; 1 s (Stephen), 2 da (Anneli, Gemma); m 2, 1975, Wendy Kate Standbrook (d 1988); m 3, 16 Sept 1989, Mrs Jacqueline S R Thomson, wid of William Thomson; *Career* called to the Bar Lincoln's Inn 1954 (bencher 1979, treas 2002); QC 1972, recorder 1972–85, judge of the High Court of Justice (Queen's Bench Div) 1985–2000, presiding judge Midland & Oxford Circuit 1986–90; memb: Employment Appeal Tbnl 1986–2000, Parole Bd 1996–2003 (vice-chm 1998–2000); cmmr Royal Court of Jersey 2003–; qualified mediator 2004–; hon fell The Queen's Coll Oxford 1992; *Recreations* gardening, shooting, sailing, model railways; *Clubs* Garrick, Leander, Bar Yacht; *Style*— Sir Richard Tucker; ✉ Treasury Office, Lincoln's Inn, London WC2A 3TL

TUCKER, Dr Sam Michael; s of Harry Tucker (d 1970), and Ray Tucker (d 1982); *b* 15 October 1926; *Educ* Benoni HS, Univ of the Witwatersrand (MB BCh); *m* 13 Dec 1953, Barbara Helen, da of M Kaplan; 1 da (Dana b 1956), 2 s (Mark b 1957, Trevor b 1962); *Career* conslt paediatrician Hillingdon Hosp Uxbridge and 152 Harley St London, clinical tutor and examiner RCP; memb Hillingdon Dist HA, chm Med Advsy Ctee Portland Hosp 1987–88; assoc prof Brunel Univ Uxbridge 1988–; RSM: pres Section of Paediatrics 1987–88 and 2005–06, memb Cncl 1996, sr hon treas 2000–; tstee: Child Bunns Tst, Friends of Russian Children; *Recreations* football, golf; *Style*— Dr Sam Tucker; ✉ 65 Uphill Road, Mill Hill, London NW7 4PT (tel 020 8959 0500, e-mail samtucker@btinternet.com); 152 Harley Street, London W1 (tel 020 7935 1859, fax 020 8906 2406)

TUCKEY, Andrew Marmaduke Lane; s of Henry Lane Tuckey (d 1982), and Aileen Rosemary, *née* Newsom-Davis; *b* 28 August 1943; *Educ* Plumtree Sch Zimbabwe; *m* 24 June 1967 (m dis 1998), Margaret Louise, da of Dr Clive Barnes (d 1979); 1 s (Jonathan b 1970), 2 da (Clara b 1972, Anna b 1982); m 2, 27 August 1998, Tracy Elisabeth, da of Stanley Long; 2 da (Eleanor b 1999, Florence b 2002); *Career* chm Baring Bros & Co Ltd and dir various Baring subsids 1968–95, conslt ING Barings 1995–96; sr advsr: Donaldson Lufkin & Jenrette 1996–2000, Credit Suisse First Boston 2000–01, Bridgewell 2001–; *Recreations* music, tennis; *Clubs* White's; *Style*— Andrew Tuckey, Esq; ✉ 11 Horbury Mews, London W11 3NL; Bridgewell, Old Change House, 128 Queen Victoria Street, London EC4

TUCKEY, Rt Hon Lord Justice; Rt Hon Sir Simon Lane Tuckey; kt (1992), PC (1998); s of Henry Lane Tuckey (d 1982), and Aileen Rosemary, *née* Newsom-Davis; *b* 17 October 1941; *Educ* Plumtree Sch Zimbabwe; *m* 1964, Jennifer Rosemary, da of Sir Charles Edgar Matthews Hardie (d 1998); 1 s (William b 1966), 2 da (Camilla (Mrs Richard Parsons) b 1965, Kate b 1970); *Career* called to the Bar Lincoln's Inn 1964, QC 1981, recorder of the Crown Court 1984, judge of the High Court of Justice (Queen's Bench Division) 1992–98, presiding judge Western Circuit 1995–97, judge i/c Commercial List 1997–98, a Lord Justice of Appeal 1998–; chm Review Panel Fin Reporting Cncl 1990, co-chm Civil and Family Ctee Judicial Studies Bd 1993–95; *Recreations* sailing, tennis; *Style*— The Rt Hon Lord Justice Tuckey; ✉ Royal Courts of Justice, Strand, London WC2

TUDOR, Dr (Fiona) Philippa; da of (James) Brian Tudor, and late Rosaleen, *née* O'Connor; *Educ* Sch of Saints Mary and Anne Abbots Bromley, Somerville Coll Oxford (MA, DPhil); *m* 30 Sept 1989, David Beamish, *qv*; 1 da (Amelia May Tudor b 31 May 1994); *Career* House of Lords: clerk 1982, sr clerk 1986, chief clerk 1993, Clerk of Private Bills 1997–2001; head Parly and Constitutional Div Scotland Office 2001–03, head of HR House of Lords 2003–; author of articles on history and parliamentary procedure; FCIPD, DipCG; *Recreations* running; *Style*— Dr Philippa Tudor; ✉ Human Resources Office, House of Lords, London SW1A 0PW (tel 020 7219 3186)

TUDOR-CRAIG, Dr Pamela (Pamela, Lady Wedgwood); da of Herbert Wynn Reeves, of London, and Madeleine Marian, *née* Brows; *Educ* Courtauld Inst; *m* 1, (Algernon) James Riccarton Tudor-Craig, FSA (d 1969), o s of Maj Sir Algernon Tudor Tudor-Craig, KBE, FSA (d 1943); 1 da (Elizabeth Jocelyn); m 2, as his 2 w, Sir John Hamilton Wedgwood, 2 Bt, TD (d 1989); *Career* art historian; prof of art history: Univ of Evansville at Harlaxton Coll 1979–89 (fndr Annual Int Symposium on Inter-disciplinary Eng Medieval Studies 1984), Grinnell London 1990–95; speaker in confs at Poitiers, Regensburg and Landegg; lecture tours of America: Kalamazoo, Smithsonian and Nat Gallery Washington, Harvard Univ, Metropolitan Museum NY (twice), Univ Museum in Philadelphia, Stanford Univ; TV work incl: Richard III with Barlow and Watt 1976, Light of Experience 1976, Round Table at Winchester (Horizon) 1977, Richard III for Timewatch 1983, The Trial of Richard III for ITV (nominated as programme of the year) 1984, The Secret Life of Paintings BBC2 1986; many radio progs; memb ctee to advise on conservation: West Front at Wells Cathedral 1973–85, Exeter Cathedral 1979–86; chm and vice-chm Paintings Ctee Cncl for the Care of Churches 1975–96; memb: DAC St Edmundsbury and Ipswich 1966–69, DAC London 1970–73, Cathedrals Advsy Cmmn for Eng 1976–91, Architectural Advsy Panel Westminster Abbey 1979–98, Ctee Fabric Southwell Minster 1984–2001, Ctee Fabric Lincoln Cathedral 1986–92, Ctee Fabric Peterborough Cathedral 1987–96, Cncl Soc of Antiquaries 1989–92, Cultural Affrs Ctee ESU 1990–2000; fndr Cambridgeshire Historic Churches Tst 1982; chm Friends of Sussex Historic Churches 2002–; judge of History Today annual History Prize 1993–98; FSA; *Publications* incl: Richard III (1973), The Secret Life of Paintings (with Richard Foster, 1986), New Bell's Cathedral Guide to Westminster Abbey (jtly, 1986), Old St Paul's (2004), Harlaxton Symposium Volumes; author of numerous articles, regular contrib to Arts Page of Church Times, History Today and Resurgence; *Recreations* walking with my dogs and swimming in the sea; *Style*— Dr Pamela Tudor-Craig, FSA; ✉ 9 St Anne's Crescent, Lewes, East Sussex BN7 1SB (tel 01273 479564)

TUDOR JOHN, William (Bill); DL (Herts 2006); s of Tudor John (d 2001), of Castle House, Llantrisant, Mid Glamorgan, and Gwen, *née* Griffiths (d 1969); *b* 26 April 1944; *Educ* Cowbridge Sch, Downing Coll Cambridge; *m* 25 Feb 1967, Jane, da of Peter Clark, of Cowbridge, Mid Glam; 3 da (Rebecca b 1971, Katherine (Mrs Alexander Turner) b 1974, Elizabeth (Mrs Nicholas Atkinson) b 1980); *Career* Allen & Overy: articled clerk 1967–69, asst slr 1969–70; banker Orion Bank Ltd 1970–72; Allen & Overy: ptnr 1972–2001, managing ptnr 1992–94, sr ptnr 1994–2000; md and chm Euro Commitment Ctee Lehman Brothers 2000–; non-exec chm: Suttons Seeds Ltd 1978–93, Horticultural and Botanical Holdings Ltd 1985–93, The Portman Building Soc 2006– (non-exec dir 2001–); non-exec dir: Woolwich plc 2000, Nat Film and Television Sch 2000–, Sun Bank plc 2001–03, Grainger Trust plc 2005–; vice-chm Financial Markets Law Ctee 2002– (memb 1996–); chm Advsy Cncl Oxford Univ Law Fndn 1998–2003; memb Devpt Bd: Univ of Oxford 1999–, Nat Museum of Wales 2006–; chm Wales in London 2001–06; appeal steward Br Boxing Bd of Control 1980–; assoc fell Downing Coll Cambridge 1986–92 and 1997–; Freeman City of London, memb City of London Slrs' Co 1972, Liveryman Worshipful Co of Gunmakers 1994; memb: Law Soc 1969, Int Bar Assoc 1976; High Sheriff Herts 2006–07; *Recreations* shooting, rugby football, reading, music; *Clubs* Justinians, Cardiff and County, City, City of London; *Style*— Bill Tudor John, Esq, DL; ✉ Willian Bury, Willian, Hertfordshire SG6 2AF (tel 01462 683532, e-mail tjwillian@btinternet.com); Lehman Brothers, 25 Bank Street, London E14 5LE (tel 020 7102 1035, fax 020 7067 8303, e-mail btjohn@lehman.com)

TUDOR-WILLIAMS, Dr Robert; s of David Tudor-Williams, LDS RCS (d 1990), of Haverfordwest, and Nanette *née* Llewellin; *b* 4 November 1945; *Educ* Haverfordwest GS, Guy's Hosp (BDS, LDS, RCS); *m* 1971, Margaret Ann, da of Alfred Hector Morris (d 1998); 2 s (Laurence b 6 April 1973, Dylan b 8 April 1974), 1 da (Rebecca b 16 Jan 1979); *Career* asst house surgn Guy's Hosp 1970, house surgn KCH 1970–71, sr hosp dental offr Eastman Dental Hosp 1972, gen practice in City and West End 1970–72, princ of gp practice Fulham 1972–80, clinical asst in oral surgery Charing Cross Hosp 1974–87; in private practice: Esher 1980–, Harley St 1988–2005; special interests: cosmetic and restorative dentistry, headaches, migraines and disorders of the TMJ 1988–; lectr Hammersmith and W London Coll: to dental surgery assts 1977–88, to med secs 1978–87; lectr and course dir to dental surgery assts BDA 1988–94; radio dentist: LBC 1989–94, London Newstalk 1152 AM 1994–96; memb Panel of Examiners: RCS(Ed) 1988–, Examining Bd for Dental Surgery Assts 1982–94; external examiner RCS 1991–93; memb: BDA 1970– (chm Kingston and Dist Section 1983–84), Ealing Hammersmith and Hounslow LDC 1975–90, Br Soc of Periodontology 1985–, L D Pankey Assoc 1985–, Br Dental Migraine Study Gp 1985–, Br Soc of Gen Dental Surgery 1986–, Br Dental Health Fndn 1988–, Fédération Dentaire Internationale 1990–, Faculty of Gen Dental Practice UK 1992–, American Equilibration Soc 1996–, Assoc of Broadcasting Doctors and Dentists 1995–, Exec Ctee Central London Private Practitioners' Forum; Freeman City of London 1997; Liveryman: Worshipful Soc of Apothocaries, Worshipful Co of Blacksmiths; MGDS RCSEd 1986, FRSM 1986; *Recreations* sailing, gardening, theatre, swimming, cycling, shooting, fishing; *Clubs* Royal Soc of Med, IOD, Esher 41; *Style*— Dr Robert Tudor-Williams; ✉ The Birches, 50 Grove Way, Esher, Surrey KT10 8HL (tel 020 8398 5953, e-mail info@tudorwilliamsdentistry.co.uk, website www.tudorwilliamsdentistry.co.uk)

TUFFREY, Michael William (Mike); AM; *b* 30 September 1959; *Educ* Douai Sch Woolhampton, Univ of Durham (BA); *m*; 1 s, 2 da; *Career* accountant KPMG London 1981–84, research and parly offr Lib/SDP Whips Office House of Lords 1984–87, memb GLC/ILEA for Vauxhall 1985–86, dir of Fin and Admin Action Resource Centre London 1987–90, community affrs conslt Prima Europe London 1990–97, elected memb Lambeth Cncl 1990–2002 (Lib Dem ldr 1990–98, de facto jt cncl ldr 1994–98), dir The Corporate Citizenship Co London mgmnt consultancy 1997– (ed Corporate Citizenship Briefing 1991–); GLA: memb London Assembly (Lib Dem) London (list) 2002–, ldr Lib Dem Gp 2006–, memb Budget Ctee, memb Environment Ctee, memb London Fire and Emergency Planning Authy; memb Assoc of London Govt Leaders Ctee (dep Lib Dem ldr 1994–2000); Lambeth rep AMA and LGA; memb bd various regenerative initiatives incl: Brixton Challenge, Business Link London, London Devpt Partnership, Cross River Partnership, Central London Partnership, South Bank Partnership; memb: Lib Dem Pty (formerly Lib Pty) 1978–, Friends of the Earth, Amnesty Int, Natural Childbirth Tst; parish memb St Mary's Clapham; assoc ICAEW; *Recreations* licensed radio amateur (G8LHQ); *Style*— Mike Tuffrey, Esq, AM; ✉ 50 Lynette Avenue, London SW4 9HD (tel 020 8673 1684, e-mail mike.tuffrey@london.gov.uk)

TUFNELL, Col Greville Wyndham; CVO (2002), DL (Glos 1994); s of Maj K E M Tufnell, MC (d 1976) and E H Dufaur (d 1979); *b* 7 April 1932; *Educ* Eton, RMA Sandhurst; *m* 1, 1962, Hon Anne Rosemary Trench (d 1992), da of 5 Baron Ashtown, OBE (d 1979), and wid of Capt Timothy Patrick Arnold Gosselin, Scots Guards (d 1961); 3 da (Caroline, Belinda (Mrs Benjamin Wright), Georgina (Mrs Edward Way)), 1 step da (Nicola (Mrs Angus Ward)); m 2, 1994, Susan Arnot, da of Edward Gordon Heath, and formerly w of David Burrows (d 1993); *Career* 2 Lt Grenadier Gds 1952, Adj 2 Bn 1959–61, GSO 3 WO (MO2) 1962–63, Staff Coll 1964, Maj 1965, DAQMG London Dist 1966–67, GSO 2 HQ Div 1969–71, Lt-Col 1971, cmdg 1 Bn Grenadier Gds 1971–73 (despatches 1972), Bde Maj Household Div 1974–76, Col 1976, cmdg Grenadier Gds 1976–78; Yeomen of the Guard: Exon 1979, Ensign 1985, Clerk to the Cheque and Adjutant 1987, Lieutenant 1993–2002; life vice-pres Grenadier Gds Assoc 1980–; devpt offr Nat Star Centre for Disabled Youth 1982–94; Freeman City of London, Liveryman Worshipful Co of Grocers; *Clubs* Cavalry and Guards', MCC, Pitt, Sloane; *Style*— Col G W Tufnell, CVO, DL; ✉ The Manor House, Ampney St Peter, Cirencester, Gloucestershire GL7 5SH (tel 01285 851065, fax 01285 850314)

TUGE-ERECIŃSKA, HE Barbara; *b* 24 March 1956, Gdańsk, Poland; *Educ* Univ of Gdańsk (MA); *m* (m dis); 1 s; *Career* Polish diplomat; expert Solidarity (ind self-governing trade union) nat HQ 1981–, hon sec Consular Agency Gdynia 1987–90, bd's plenipotentiary City of Gdańsk Office 1990–91, ambass extraordinary and plenipotentiary to Sweden 1991–97, sr counsel to the Minister and Dir Europe (West Dept) Miny of Foreign Affrs 1997–99, dir European Policy Dept 1999, undersec of state Miny of Foreign Affrs 1999–2001, ambass extraordinary and plenipotentiary Copenhagen 2001–05, sec of state Miny of Foreign Affrs 2005–06, ambass extraordinary and plenipotentiary to the Ct of St James's 2006–; *Style*— HE Ms Barbara Tuge-Erecińska; ✉ Polish Embassy, 47 Portland Place, London W1B 1JH

TUGENDHAT, Baron (Life Peer UK 1993), of Widdington in the County of Essex; Sir Christopher Samuel Tugendhat; kt (1990); er s of Dr Georg Tugendhat (d 1973), of London, and Máire, *née* Littledale (d 1994); bro of Sir Michael George Tugendhat, QC (Hon Mr Justice Tugendhat), *qv*; *b* 23 February 1937; *Educ* Ampleforth, Gonville & Caius Coll Cambridge; *m* 1967, Julia Lissant, da of Kenneth D Dobson, of Keston, Kent; 2 s (Hon James Walter b 1971, Hon Angus George Harry b 1974); *Career* leader and feature writer Financial Times 1960–70; MP (Cons): Cities of London and Westminster 1970–74, City of London and Westminster South 1974–76; Br EEC cmmr (responsible for budget, fin control, personnel and admin) 1977–81, vice-pres Cmmn of Euro Communities (responsible for budget, fin control, fin insts and taxation) 1981–85; chm: CAA 1986–91, Royal Inst of Int Affrs Chatham House 1986–95, Abbey National plc 1991–2002, Blue Circle Industries plc 1996–2001; non-exec chm European Advsy Bd Lehman Brothers, Europe 2002–; dep chm Nat Westminster Bank 1990–91 (dir 1985–91); non-exec dir: The BOC Group plc 1985–96, Commercial Union Assurance Co plc 1988–91, LWT (Holdings) plc 1991–94, Eurotunnel plc 1991–2003, Rio Tinto plc (formerly RTZ Corporation plc) 1997–2004; chllr Univ of Bath 1998–; hon fell Gonville & Caius Coll Cambridge 1998; Hon LLD Univ of Bath 1998, Hon DLitt UMIST 2002; *Publications* books incl: Oil: The Biggest Business (1968), The Multinationals (1971), Making Sense of Europe (1986), Options for British Foreign Policy in the 1990's (with William Wallace, 1988); pamphlets incl: Britain, Europe and the Third World (1976), Conservatives in Europe (1979), Is Reform Possible? (1981); *Recreations* conversation, reading, being with my family; *Clubs* Athenaeum; *Style*— The Rt Hon Lord Tugendhat; ✉ 35 Westbourne Park Road, London W2 5QD; Lehman Brothers, 25 Bank Street, London E14 5LE

TUGENDHAT, Hon Mr Justice; Sir Michael George Tugenhat; kt (2003); s of Dr Georg Tugendhat (d 1973), and Máire, *née* Littledale (d 1994); bro of Baron Tugendhat (Life Peer), *qv*, *b* 21 October 1944; *Educ* Ampleforth, Gonville & Caius Coll Cambridge (MA),

Yale Univ; *m* 6 June 1970, Blandine Marie, da of Comte Pierre-Charles Menche de Loisne, of France, 4 s (Charles b 1972, Thomas b 1973, Gregory b 1977, Henry b 1986); *Career* called to the Bar Inner Temple 1969 (bencher); QC 1986; judge of the High Court of Justice (Queen's Bench Div) 2003–; fell Inst of Advanced Legal Studies; *Books* The Law of Privacy and the Media (jt ed, 2002); *Clubs* Brooks's; *Style*— The Hon Mr Justice Tugendhat; ✉ Royal Courts of Justice, Strand, London WC2A 2LL

TUITE, Sir Christopher Hugh; 14 Bt (I 1622), of Sonnagh, Westmeath; s of Sir Dennis George Harmsworth Tuite, 13 Bt, MBE (d 1981, descended from the Sir Richard de Tuite or Tuitt, who was one of Strongbow's followers in his invasion of Ireland in 1172); *b* 3 November 1949; *Educ* Wellington, Univ of Liverpool (BSc), Univ of Bristol (PhD); *m* 1976, Deborah Ann, da of A E Martz, of Punxutawny, USA; 2 s (Thomas Livingstone b 1977, Jonathan Christopher Hannington b 1981); *Heir* s, Thomas Tuite; *Career* res offr The Wildfowl Tst 1978–81; pres Spirutec Inc (Arizona) 1982–86, controller Nature Conservancy Washington DC 1987–99, controller Int Fund for Animal Welfare 1999– (latterly dir wildlife and habitat protection); *Style*— Sir Christopher Tuite, Bt

TUKE, Peter Godfrey; s of Dr Reginald Godfrey Tuke (d 1973), of Bournemouth, Dorset, and Dorothy Beatrice, *née* Underwood (d 1948); *b* 14 June 1944; *Educ* Radley, Keble Coll Oxford (MA, Rowing blue), Poly of Central London (BA, DipArch); *m* 21 June 1975, Susan, da of Edward Albert Hamilton Lawrence (d 1978), of Handcross, W Sussex; 2 s (Edward b 1978, William b 1980); *Career* corporate planning BP 1967–71, architect and ptnr Tuke Manton Architects LLP (formerly Prior Manton Tuke Powell) 1981–; responsible for acute healthcare work incl major projects at BMI Clementine Churchill Hosp, Hampshire Clinic, Kings Oak Hosp, HCA Int Princess Grace Hosp and Portland Hosp for Women and Children, also responsible for new boathouse for Oxford Univ Boatclub Wallingford; pres Radley Mariners 1993–96; memb Bd Royal Hosp for Neuro-Disablity 2006–; Freeman City of London 2004, Freeman Worshipful Co of Watermen and Lightermen of the River Thames; RIBA 1979; *Recreations* theatre, sailing, walking; *Clubs* Vincent's (Oxford), Leander, Newport (Pembs) Boat; *Style*— Peter Tuke, Esq; ✉ 48 Brodrick Road, London SW17 7DY (tel 020 8672 8678); Tuke Manton Architects LLP, 20 Prescott Place, London SW4 6BT (tel 020 7627 8085, fax 020 7627 2658, e-mail ptuke@tukemanton.co.uk, website www.tukemanton.co.uk)

TULLO, Carol Anne; da of Edward Alan Dodgson, of Woolton, Liverpool, and late Patricia, *née* Masterson; *b* 9 January 1956; *Educ* Holly Lodge, Univ of Hull (LLB), Inns of Court Sch of Law; *m* 5 May 1979, Robin Brownrigg Tullo, s of James Francis Swanzy Tullo, of London; 1 da (Alice Sophia b 1986), 1 s (Luke Edward Swanzy b 1991); *Career* called to the Bar Inner Temple 1977; dir Stevens 1985–96, publishing dir Sweet & Maxwell Ltd 1988–96, dir ESC Publishing Ltd 1990–96, dir Legal Information Resources Ltd 1994–96, publishing conslt 1996–97, controller Her Majesty's Stationery Office, Queen's Printer and Govt Printer for N Ireland 1997–, Queen's Printer for Scotland 1999–, dir Office of Public Sector Information 2005–, dir Nat Archives 2006–; chm Law Publishers' Exec Publishers' Assoc 1995–2004; memb Bd Cncl of Academic and Professional Publishers 1995–2004; hon visiting prof Dept of Information Science City Univ 2000–; *Style*— Mrs Carol Tullo; ✉ OPSI, Admiralty Arch, The Mall, London SW1A 2WH (tel 020 7276 2660, fax 020 7276 2661, e-mail carol.tullo@opsi.x.gsi.gov.uk)

TULLOCH, Alastair Robert Clifford; s of James Richard Moore Tulloch (d 1998), and Heather Netta (d 1989); *b* 1 October 1955; *Educ* St Andrew's Coll, Magdalen Coll Oxford; *m* 15 Aug 1987, Hilary, da of Rev Alasdair Macdonell, of St Mary's Haddington, Scotland; 1 da (Emma Heather b 1988), 4 s (Robin b and d 1989, Hugh Gordon b 1991, Iain Alastair, Angus James (twins) b 1992); *Career* asst slr: Lovell White and King 1980–82 (articled 1978–80), McNeil and Co Dubai 1982–84, Clifford Turner 1984–86; ptnr: Frere Cholmeley Bischoff 1987–98, Eversheds (following merger) 1998; sole princ Tulloch & Co 1999–; memb Law Soc; *Recreations* DIY, skiing, sailing, hill walking; *Style*— Alastair Tulloch, Esq

TULLOCH, Clive William; s of Ewan William Tulloch (d 2001), of Richmond, Surrey, and Sylvia Phoebe, *née* Mott; *b* 21 June 1948; *Educ* Winchester; *m* Tessa Celia Geraldine, da of Prof Harry Frederick Trewman; 1 da (Caroline Sylvia Geraldine b 2 Dec 1982), 1 s (James Harry William b 23 Aug 1985); *Career* Coopers & Lybrand 1967–79, ptnr Morison Stoneham & Co 1980–81 (joined 1979), PricewaterhouseCoopers (formerly Coopers & Lybrand before merger 1998) 1981–2006 (ptnr 1983–2006, ptnr responsible for risk mgmnt in UK tax and HR consulting practice 1997–2006); chief exec Free Representation Unit 2006–; memb ICAEW Working Pty on Practice Assurance for Tax 2002; London C of C: chm Taxation Ctee 1994–97 (memb 1987–2001), memb Cncl 1994–2001; tstee: Tax Advsrs' Benevolent Fund 2000–, Tax Advsrs' Charitable Tst 2000–, TaxAid UK 2001–04; govr St Nicholas Primary Sch Chislehurst 1989–95; hon treas The Bach Choir 1997–2006; memb Worshipful Co of Tax Advsrs (memb Ct of Assts 1998–, Master 2004–05); FCA 1976 (ACA 1971), CTA (fell) (FTII 1994); *Books* The CCH Company Car Tax Guide 1999–2000 (jt author and princ ed (and on previous edns)), Car or Cash? (2 edn), Employee Share Schemes in Practice; *Recreations* choral singing, walking; *Clubs* Lansdowne, RSA, National Liberal, Aldrich Catch; *Style*— Clive W Tulloch, Esq; ✉ Lamorna, Sleeper's Hill, Winchester, Hampshire SO22 4NB; Free Representation Unit, 289–293 High Holborn, London WC1V 7HZ (tel 020 7611 9567, e-mail chief.exec@freerepresentationunit.org.uk)

TULLOCH, Iain William Patrick; s of Maj William Alexander Tulloch, (d 1988), of Monkton, Ayrshire, and Margaret Edith Phyllis, *née* Farquhar (d 1968); *b* 12 December 1940; *Educ* Rugby, Brown Univ USA; *m* 5 Oct 1967, Charmian Mary, da of Michael Anthony Callender, of Alton, Hants; 1 da (Leesa b 1969), 1 s (Gillen b 1971); *Career* Lt Ayrshire Yeomanry 1966; qualified CA 1966; exec dir: Murray Johnstone Ltd 1987–98, Murray Ventures 1992–98; non-exec dir: American Opportunity Trust 1989–, Galtres Foods Ltd (chm 1998–2001) until 2001, IFC Group 1990–92, Mining (Scotland) Ltd 1995–2000, Murray VCT plc 1995–, Ward Packaging Ltd 1994–2000; current appointments: Msele Nedventures 2000–, chm Swiss Technol Venture Capital Fund 2000–; memb Cncl Br Venture Capital Assoc 1988–94; *Recreations* royal tennis, squash, golf, gardening; *Clubs* Prestwick Golf, Western; *Style*— Iain Tulloch, Esq; ✉ Swallow Ha', Symington, Ayrshire KA1 5PN

TULLY, David John; s of William Scarth Carlisle Tully, CBE (d 1987), and Patience Treby, *née* Betts (d 2005); *b* 13 March 1942; *Educ* Twyford, Sherborne; *m* 7 May 1965, Susan Patricia, da of (James) Geoffrey Arnott; 1 s (James Herbert b 1967), 2 da (Louise Patience b 1969, Clare Jane b 1972); *Career* slr; sr ptnr Addleshaw Goddard (formerly Addleshaw Sons & Latham Manchester) 1994–97 (ptnr 1969–99); chm Joseph Holt Ltd 2000, non-exec dir Cheshire Building Society 2000–07; former chm: Manchester Young Slrs, Nat Young Slrs, Cransley Sch; former pres Manchester Law Soc; govr Manchester GS; *Recreations* shooting, fishing, golf; *Clubs* St James's (Manchester, former chm and pres), Manchester Tennis and Racquets, Ringway Golf; *Style*— David Tully, Esq; ✉ The Cherries, 5 Greenside Drive, Hale, Altrincham, Cheshire WA14 3HX (tel 0161 928 3029)

TULLY, Sir (William) Mark; KBE (2002, OBE 1985); s of late William Scarth Carlisle Tully, CBE, and Patience Treby, *née* Betts; *b* 24 October 1935; *Educ* New Sch Darjeeling India, Twyford Sch Winchester, Marlborough, Trinity Hall Cambridge (MA); *m* 13 Aug 1960, (Frances) Margaret, da of late Frank Howard Butler; 2 da (Sarah b 1961, Emma b 1963), 2 s (Sam b 1965, Patrick b 1967); *Career* Nat Serv 2 Lt 1 Royal Dragoons 1954–56; regnl dir Abbeyfield Soc for housing old people 1960–64; BBC: Personnel Dept 1964–65, asst then acting rep BBC Delhi 1965–69, Hindi prog organiser External Servs London 1969–70, chief talks writer External Servs 1970–71, chief Delhi Bureau 1972–93, S Asia corr 1993–94 (resigned from the BBC); currently freelance journalist and broadcaster, presenter Something Understood (Unique Broadcasting Ltd for BBC Radio 4) 1995–; hon fell Trinity Hall Cambridge 1994; Hon DUniv Bradford 1992, Hon DLitt Univ of Strathclyde 1997, hon dr Richmond Univ in London 1999, Hon DUniv Central England 2002; *Awards* Dimbleby Award BAFTA 1984, Radio and Critics Broadcasting Press Guild Radio Award 1984, Sony Award for Radio Documentary 1994; *Books* Amritsar Mrs Gandhi's Last Battle (with Satish Jacob, 1985), Raj to Rajiv (with Zareer Masani, 1988), No Fullstops in India (Viking, 1991), The Heart of India (Viking, 1995), The Lives of Jesus (BBC, 1996), India in Slow Motion (2002); *Recreations* reading, fishing, bird watching; *Clubs* Oriental, Press and Gymkhana (Delhi), Travellers; *Style*— Sir Mark Tully, KBE; ✉ 1 Nizamuddin East, New Delhi 110013, India (tel and fax 00 91 11 462 9687, 00 91 11 460 2878)

TUNBRIDGE, Dr (William) Michael Gregg; s of Sir Ronald Ernest Tunbridge, OBE (d 1984), of Leeds, and Dorothy, *née* Gregg (d 1999); *b* 13 June 1940; *Educ* Kingswood Sch Bath, Queens' Coll Cambridge (MA, MD), UCH; *m* 28 Aug 1965, Felicity Katherine Edith, da of Arthur Myers Parrish (d 1987), of Bangor; 2 da (Clare b 1968, Anne b 1970); *Career* conslt physician Newcastle Gen Hosp 1977–94, sr lectr in med Univ of Newcastle upon Tyne until 1994, dir of postgrad med educn and trg Univ of Oxford and Region 1994–2003, conslt physician Oxford Radcliffe Hosps NHS Tst 1994–2005, emeritus physician Nuffield Dept of Medicine 2005–; professorial fell Wadham Coll Oxford 1994–2003 (emeritus fell 2003–); memb: Diabetes UK, Br Thyroid Assoc, Soc for Endocrinology; FRCP 1979; *Recreations* walking, golf; *Clubs* Athenaeum; *Style*— Dr Michael Tunbridge; ✉ Coppermill, Church Lane, Weston on the Green, Bicester, Oxfordshire OX25 3QS (tel and fax 01869 350691, e-mail tunbridge@coppermill.fsnet.co.uk)

TUNNACLIFFE, Paul Derek; *b* 13 April 1962; *Career* co sec Hanson plc 1997– (asst sec 1987–97); FCIS 1993; *Style*— Paul Tunnacliffe, Esq; ✉ Hanson plc, 1 Grosvenor Place, London SW1X 7JH (tel 020 7245 1245, fax 020 7235 3455)

TUNNICLIFFE, Baron (Life Peer UK 2004), of Bracknell in the County of Berkshire; Denis Tunnicliffe; CBE (1993); *b* 17 January 1943; *Educ* Henry Cavendish Sch Derby, UCL (State scholar, BSc), Coll of Air Trg Hamble; *m* 1968, Susan, *née* Dale; 2 s (Hon Alan Dale b 29 Sept 1971, Hon Richard Dale b 1 March 1973); *Career* British Airways: co-pilot VC10 then B747 1966–72, various personnel and industrial rels roles BOAC (latterly Overseas Div BA) 1972–77, head of planning Flight Ops 1977–80, controller of fuel 1980–82, gen mangr Caribbean 1982, head of consultancy servs 1982–83, sr gen mangr Market Centres 1983–84, dir of marketplace performance 1984–86; chief exec Aviation Div International Leisure Group 1986–88, md London Underground Ltd 1988–98, chief exec London Transport 1998–2000 (memb Bd 1993–2000); non-exec chm: UKAEA 2002–04, Rail Safety and Standards Bd 2003–; non exec memb Bd Def Logistics Orgn 2006–07, non-exec memb Bd Def Equipment and Support 2007–; cncllr: New Windsor BC 1971–75, Berks CC 1974–77, Bracknell DC 1979–83; FCIT 1990, CIMgt 1991, FRSA 1992; *Recreations* boating, church, flying; *Clubs* RAF, RAC; *Style*— The Rt Hon the Lord Tunnicliffe, CBE; ✉ House of Lords, London SW1A 0PW

TUNNICLIFFE, Michael John (Mike); s of Brian Tunnicliffe, of London, and Dorothy Anne Baxendale, *née* Richardson; *b* 19 January 1961; *Educ* Bramhall HS; *m* 24 Aug 1990, Elaine Clare, *née* Jackson; 1 da (Ava Talullah Grace b 14 Jan 1994), 1 s (Milo Oscar Jack b 17 Jan 1997); *Career* advtg sales exec Link House Publications 1979–80, advtg sales mangr Burke House Periodicals 1980–81, media exec, media mangr then dep gp dir Saatchi and Saatchi Advertising 1981–83, media mangr Leagas Delaney Partnership 1983–84, media mangr, assoc dir then dir HDM: Horner Collis and Kirvan 1984–90; CIA Group plc: dir CIA Media UK 1990, dep md CIA Media UK 1993, dir CIA UK Holdings 1994–97, md CIA Medianetwork UK 1994–97, dir CIA Medianetwork Europe Holdings 1995–97; Interpublic Gp: md Western International Media 1998–2000, exec vice-pres Initiative Media 2000–05, chief strategic offr Initiative North America 2005–06, global client and network devpt dir Initiative 2006–07; IPA Advertising Effectiveness Award 1988; memb: Media Circle 1981, Mktg Soc 1994; *Recreations* sailing, golf, tennis; *Clubs* RAC; *Style*— Mike Tunnicliffe, Esq

TUNSTALL-PEDOE, Prof Hugh David; s of Prof Dan Pedoe (d 1998), and (Bessie Maude) Mary, *née* Tunstall (d 1965); *b* 30 December 1939; *Educ* Haberdashers' Aske's Hampstead Sch, Dulwich Coll, King's Coll Cambridge, Guy's Hosp Med Sch (MB BChir, MA, MD); *m* 24 June 1967, Jacqueline Helen, da of Kenneth B Burbidge (d 1991), of Felmersham, Beds; 2 s (William b 1969, Oliver b 1973), 1 da (Susan b 1971); *Career* house physician 1964–66: Guy's, Brompton Hosp, Nat Hosp for Nervous Diseases; jr registrar Guy's 1967, clinical scientific staff Social Med Unit MRC 1969–71, lectr in med London Hosp 1971–74 (registrar in gen med 1968–69); St Mary's Hosp 1974–81: sr lectr in epidemiology, conslt physician, hon community physician; Univ of Dundee Ninewells Med Sch 1981–: dir Cardiovascular Epidemiology Unit, prof of cardiovascular epidemiology, sr lectr in med; conslt cardiologist and conslt in public health Tayside Health Bd 1981; various pubns in jls; chm Working Gp on Epidemiology and Prevention Euro Soc of Cardiology 1983–85, memb Resuscitation Cncl of UK; inventor Dundee Coronary Risk-Disk (Toshiba Year of Invention award 1991); winner of first BUPA Epidemiology award 1996; FRCP 1981, FFPH 1981, FRCPE 1985, FESC 1988; *Books* Multiple Choice Questions in Epidemiology and Community Medicine (with W C S Smith, 1987), MONICA Monograph and Multimedia Sourcebook (ed, 2003); *Recreations* golf, bee-keeping, jogging; *Style*— Prof Hugh Tunstall-Pedoe; ✉ 4 Hill Street, Broughty Ferry, Dundee DD5 2JL (tel 01382 477358, fax 01382 731942); Cardiovascular Epidemiology Unit, Ninewells Hospital and Medical School, Dundee DD1 9SY (tel 01382 644255, fax 01382 641095, e-mail h.tunstallpedoe@dundee.ac.uk)

TUOHY, Denis John; s of John Vincent Tuohy (d 1976), of Scariff, Co Clare, and Anne Mary, *née* Doody; *b* 2 April 1937; *Educ* Clongowes Wood Coll Ireland, Queen's Univ Belfast (BA, Blayney exhibition prize, Peel prize, debating medal); *m* 1, 1960 (m dis 1988), Eleanor Moya, da of Felix Charles McCann; 2 s (Mark b 12 June 1962, Christopher b 3 April 1964), 2 da (Eleanor b 14 July 1969, Catherine b 21 Oct 1974); m 2, 1998 (m dis 2007), Elizabeth Moran; *Career* TV reporter, presenter and writer and radio presenter: BBC NI 1960–64 (also actor), Late Night Line Up (BBC 2) 1964–67, 24 Hours (BBC 1) 1967–71 (also prodr), Man Alive (BBC 2) 1971–72, Panorama (BBC 1) 1974–75, This Week (Thames) 1972–74 and 1986–92, TV Eye (Thames) 1979–86, People and Politics (Thames) 1973, Midweek (BBC 1) 1974, Tonight (BBC 1) 1975–79, Reporting London (Thames) 1981–82, The Garden Party (BBC 1) 1990–91, Central Weekend (Central) 1993, Classic FM 1993, Something Understood (BBC Radio 4) 1995–, The Jimmy Young Programme (BBC Radio 2) 1996, The World Tonight (BBC Radio 4) 2001, The Sunday Show (RTE Radio 1) 2003, A Living Word (RTE Radio 1) 2003, The Midnight Court (RTE TV) 2003; prodr Southern Eye (BBC South) 1993, newscaster ITN 1994–2001; many documentaries as presenter, writer and narrator incl: Lord of the Rings (BBC 1) 1974, A Life of O'Reilly (BBC 1) 1974, Mr Truman Why Did You Drop the Second Bomb? (BBC 1) 1975, Do You Know Where Jimmy Carter Lives? (BBC 1) 1977, To Us a Child (Thames, UNICEF) 1986, The Blitz (Thames) 1990, The Longest Walk (BBC 2) 1994, Secret History: Dad's Army (Channel 4) 1998, Secret History: The Real Saatchi Brothers Masters of Illusion (Channel 4) 1999, The Law and the Lunatic (BBC 1) 1999, Vets on the Wild Side (Discovery) 1999–2001, Cards of Identity (RTE Radio 1) 2002; actor: Fair City (RTE TV), The Clinic (RTE TV) 2003, Fallout (RTE TV) 2006, The Tempest (Cork Midsummer Festival) 2006, Killinaskully (RTE TV) 2007, Strength and Honour (2007); Eisenhower travelling fellowship (survey of public TV in USA) 1967; contrib: Irish Times, Sunday Independent, Belfast Telegraph, The Tablet, The Independent, New Statesman, The Scotsman, The Irish News, British Poetry Review; memb NUJ 1970–; *Publications* Wide-eyed in Medialand (memoirs, 2005); *Recreations* watching rugby and cricket, theatre, cinema, walking; *Clubs* London Irish RFC; *Style*— Denis Tuohy, Esq; ✉ 16 Avrora na Mara, Shore Road, Rostrevor, Co Down BT34 3UP (tel 02841 739945)

TUPPER, Sir Charles Hibbert; 5 Bt (UK 1888), of Armdale, Halifax, Nova Scotia; s of Sir James Macdonald Tupper, 4 Bt (d 1967), and Mary Agnes Jean, *née* Collins; Sir Charles, 1 Bt (d 1915), was PM of Nova Scotia 1864–67 (encompassing date of Union), PM of Canada 1896, ldr of oppn 1896–1900; *b* 4 July 1930; *m* 1959 (m dis 1975); 1 s (Charles Hibbert b 1964); *Heir* s, Charles Tupper; *Style*— Sir Charles Tupper, Bt; ✉ Suite 1101, 955 Marine Drive, West Vancouver, British Columbia V7T 1A9, Canada (tel 00 1 604 926 5734)

TURBERFIELD, Dr Alan Frank; CBE (1990); s of Frank Turberfield (d 1993), and Agnes, *née* Jackson (d 1970); *b* 24 September 1930; *Educ* Ashby de la Zouch Boys' GS, St John's Coll Oxford (open scholar, MA), Harris Manchester Coll Oxford (DPhil); *m* 4 Aug 1956, Gillian Doris, da of Leonard William George Markwell (d 1973), of Bexhill, and Doris, *née* Stone (d 1990); 1 s (Paul b 1961), 1 da (Alison b 1963); *Career* RAEC 1952–54; asst master: King Edward VII Sch Sheffield 1954–58, Birkenhead Sch 1958–63; head of classics Portsmouth GS 1963–68, HM Inspectorate of Schs 1968–90, staff inspr for secdy educn 1977–90 (with classics 1977–83), official visits to Sweden, Holland, Austria, Bonn, Strasbourg, China and Malaysia, dir sch and coll awards Royal Anniversary Tst 1990–91; postdoctoral fell Harris Manchester Coll Oxford 1998–2003; Methodist local preacher 1953–2004; memb Ct Oxford Brookes Univ 1999–2007; memb: Hub Club (DES), Assoc HMI, Jt Assoc of Classical Teachers, Wesl Hist Soc; FRSA 2000–07; *Books* Voyage of Aeneas (with D A S John, 1968), John Scott Lidgett, Archbishop of Methodism? (2003); *Recreations* ancient Greek, theatre, travel, theology, Ecumenism, watching cricket; *Style*— Dr Alan Turberfield, CBE; ✉ 80 The Cloisters, Pegasus Grange, White House Road, Oxford OX1 4QQ

TURCAN, Henry Watson; s of Henry Hutchison Turcan, TD (d 1977), of Newburgh, Fife, and Lilias Cheyne (d 1975); *b* 22 August 1941; *Educ* Rugby, Trinity Coll Oxford (MA); *m* 18 April 1969, Jane, da of Arthur Woodman Blair, WS, of Dunbar, E Lothian; 1 da (Chloë b 1972), 1 s (Henry b 1974); *Career* called to the Bar Inner Temple 1965 (bencher 1992); legal assessor Gen Optical Cncl 1982–2002, recorder of the Crown Court 1985–, special adjudicator immigration appeals 1998–2005, immigration judge 2005–; *Recreations* shooting, fishing, golf; *Clubs* Royal and Ancient Golf (St Andrews), Hon Co of Edinburgh Golfers (Muirfield); *Style*— Henry Turcan, Esq; ✉ 4 Paper Buildings, Temple, London EC4Y 7EX (tel 020 7353 3420)

TURCAN, Robert Cheyne; s of H H Turcan (d 1977), of Lindores, Fife, and Lilias, *née* Cheyne (d 1975); *b* 28 May 1947; *Educ* Rugby, Trinity Coll Oxford, Univ of Edinburgh; *m* 1974, Elizabeth Catherine, da of John Carslake, DL, of Preston Bagot, Warwicks; 2 s, 2 da; *Career* apprentice Shepherd & Wedderburn 1970–72; Dundas & Wilson: joined 1973, ptnr 1973–97, head of Private Client Dept 1989–97; jt sr ptnr Turcan Connell (slrs and asset mangrs) 1997–; dir of several private cos; jt master Fife Foxhounds; *Recreations* foxhunting, gardening, stalking; *Clubs* New (Edinburgh), Royal & Ancient Golf; *Style*— Robert Turcan, Esq; ✉ Lindores House, Cupar, Fife (tel 01337 840369); Turcan Connell WS, Princes Exchange, 1 Earl Grey Street, Edinburgh EH13 9EE (tel 0131 228 8111, fax 0131 228 8118)

TURING, Sir John Dermot; 12 Bt (NS 1638), of Foveran, Aberdeenshire; s of John Ferrier Turing (d 1983), and his 2 w, Beryl Mary Ada, *née* Hann; suc kinsman Sir John Leslie Turing, 11 Bt, MC (d 1987); *b* 26 February 1961; *Educ* Sherborne, King's Coll Cambridge (MA), New Coll Oxford (DPhil); *m* 26 July 1986, (Dr) Nicola Jane, da of Malcolm Douglas Simmonds, of Wimborne Minster, Dorset; 2 s (John Malcolm Ferrier b 5 Sept 1988, James Robert Edward b 6 Jan 1991); *Heir* s, John Turing; *Career* admitted slr 1991; *Style*— Sir John Dermot Turing, Bt

TURLIK, Piotr (Peter) Zbigniew Vincent de Paulo; s of Zbigniew Tomasz Turlik (d 1943 in Majdanek Concentration Camp), of Warsaw, Poland, and Teresa Zofia, *née* Majewska (d 2003); *b* 15 January 1943; *Educ* The John Fisher Sch Purley, Coll of Estate Mgmnt London; *m* 9 Sept 1967, Marie-Madeleine, da of Theodor Radosky (d 1947), of Beauvoir sur Niort, France; *Career* asst dir Gtr London Cncl (Docklands Jt Ctee) 1978–80, asst sec seconded to Dept of Environment 1980–81, dir of strategic affairs London Docklands Devpt Corp 1989–98 (dir of industrial devpt 1981–84, dir of business devpt 1984–89); vice-pres Docklands Business Club 1989 (jt chm 1984–89), govr Hackney Coll 1984–90, memb Working Party on Urban Regeneration RICS 1988–98; ARICS 1971; *Recreations* travel, reading (biographies, history), small scale gardening; *Clubs* East India, Ognisko (Polish Hearth); *Style*— Peter Turlik, Esq; ✉ 12 Wincott Street, Kennington, London SE11 4NT (tel 020 75823045), 4 Chemin du College, Clavette-la Jarrie, France 17220

TURNAGE, Mark-Anthony; *b* 10 June 1960; *Educ* Royal Coll of Music, Tanglewood USA (Mendelssohn scholar); *Career* composer; studied with Oliver Knussen, John Lambert, Gunther Schuller, Hans Werner Henze; composer in assoc CBSO 1989–93, composer in assoc ENO 1995–2000, assoc composer BBC Symphony Orch 2000–; artistic conslt Contemporary Opera Studio, composer in residence at Winnipeg New Music Festival and Avanti Summer Sounds 1998, composer in residence Cheltenham Festival 1999; subject of retrospective South Bank Centre 1998; *Compositions* orchestral works incl: Night Dances 1981, Three Screaming Popes 1989, Momentum 1991, Drowned Out 1993, Your Rockaby 1993, Dispelling the Fears (2 trumpets and orch, cmmnd by Philharmonia Orch) 1995, Four-Horned Fandango (CBSO) 1995–96, Silent Cities (cmmnd by Tokyo Philharmonic Orch for UK 98 Japan Festival) 1999, Another Set To (BBC Symphony Orch) 2000, Dark Crossing 2001, Etudes and Elegies 2001–02; voice and ensemble: Lament for a Hanging Man 1983, Greek Suite 1989, Some Days 1989, Twice Through the Heart (Aldeburgh) 1997; various ensembles: On All Fours 1985, Release 1987, Three Farewells 1990, This Silence 1993, Blood on the Floor (cmmnd by Ensemble Modern) 1994, Bass Inventions (Dave Holland/Asko) 2001; other compositions incl: Sarabande (soprano saxophone and piano) 1985, Greek (2 Act opera, cmmnd by Munich Biennale, televised 1990) 1988, Kai (solo cello and ensemble) 1990, Sleep On (cello and piano) 1992, Two Elegies Framing a Shout (soprano saxophone and piano) 1994, The Silver Tassie (opera, cmmnd by ENO, televised) 2000; *Recordings* labels: EMI Classical, Universal, NMC Recordings, Black Box; *Awards* winner Yorkshire Arts Young Composers' Competition (Entranced) 1982, Munich Biennale Prize for Best Score and Best Libretto 1988, RPS/Charles Heidsieck Music Award for best television prog (Greek) 1990, South Bank Show Award (The Silver Tassie) 2000, Olivier Award for Outstanding Achievement in Opera (The Silver Tassie) 2001; recording of Your Rockaby with Night Dances and Dispelling the Fears nominated for 1997 Mercury Music Prize; *Style*— Mark-Anthony Turnage, Esq

TURNBERG, Baron (Life Peer UK 2000), of Cheadle in the County of Cheshire; Prof Sir Leslie Arnold; kt (1994); s of Hyman Turnberg (d 1985), and Dora, *née* Bloomfield; *b* 22 March 1934; *Educ* Stand GS, Univ of Manchester (MB ChB, MD); *m* 30 Jan 1968, Edna, da of Berthold Barme (d 1981); 1 s (Daniel b 1970), 1 da (Helen b 1971); *Career* lectr Royal Free Hosp 1966–67, research fell Univ of Texas Dallas 1967–68, prof of med Univ of Manchester 1973–97 (sr lectr 1968–73, dean of Faculty of Med 1986–89); pres: RCP 1992–97, Assoc of Physicians of GB 1996, Medical Protection Soc (MPS) 1997–2007, Med Cncl on Alcoholism 1998–2002, Br Soc of Gastroenterology 1999–2000; chm: Conf of Med

Royal Colls 1994–96, Specialist Trg Authority of Medical Royal Colls 1996–98, Bd of Public Health Laboratory Service (PHLS) 1997–2002, Bd of Health Quality Serv 1999–2004, UK Forum on Genetics and Insurance 1999–2002, National Centre for the Replacement, Refinement and Reduction of Animals in Research 2004–07, Medical Advsy Bd Nations Healthcare 2005–07; vice-pres Acad of Med Sci 1998–2004; scientific advsr Assoc of Medical Research Charities (AMRC) 1997–; former memb: GMC, Med Advsy Ctee of Ctee of Vice-Chllrs and Principals, MRC; currently memb: Br Soc of Gastroenterology, Assoc of Physicians of GB, Select Ctee on Science and Technology House of Lords 2001–05, Bd Renovo plc 2006–; Hon DSc: Univ of Salford 1997, Univ of Manchester 1998, Univ of London 2000; FRCP 1973, FRCPS 1995, FRCPEd 1996, FRCOG 1996, FRCOphth 1997, FRCS 1997, FRCPsych 1997, FMedSci 1998; *Books* Intestinal Transport (1981), Electrolyte and Water Transport Across Gastro-Intestinal Epithelia (1982), Clinical Gastroenterology (1989); *Recreations* reading, chinese ceramics, walking; *Style*— The Rt Hon the Lord Turnberg; ✉ House of Lords, London SW1A 0PW

TURNBULL, (Charles Colin) Andrew; s of Charles Elliot Turnbull, of Ilkley, W Yorks, and Vera Mavis, *née* Clarke; *b* 10 May 1950; *Educ* Leeds GS, Coll of Estate Management Univ of Reading, Univ of Liverpool (BA Econ), Univ of Birmingham (MSc); *m* 31 July 1976, Una Jane, da of Arnold Raymond Humphrey; 3 da (Hannah Elizabeth b 24 Sept 1981, Holly Katherine b 13 March 1984, Lydia Helen b 13 June 1988); *Career* British Airways: joined 1973, cargo marketing offr 1974, passenger traffic forecasts offr 1975, sr forecasts offr 1977–78; project work in: Ecuador, Venezuela, USA, Ghana, Ivory Coast, Sudan, SA, Saudi Arabia, Abu Dhabi, Dubai; Poulter plc: joined as res mangr 1979, head of res 1981, dir of res and planning 1983, ptnr 1985, dep md 1992–98; independent market res conslt 1998–; awarded Communications, Advertising and Marketing Dip 1979, Kelliher Cup (Communications Advertising and Marketing Fndn) for paper on int advtg 1979; memb: Market Res Soc 1980, Account Planning Group 1989, Mktg Soc 1995; *Recreations* sailing, tennis, music, three daughters; *Style*— Andrew Turnbull, Esq; ✉ Low Rigg, 15 Clifton Road, Ben Rhydding, Ilkley, West Yorkshire LS29 8TU (tel 01943 609367)

TURNBULL, Baron (Life Peer UK 2005), of Enfield in the London Borough of Enfield; Sir Andrew Turnbull; KCB (1998, CB 1990), CVO (1992); s of Anthony Turnbull, and Mary, *née* Williams; *b* 21 January 1945; *Educ* Enfield GS, Christ's Coll Cambridge (BA); *m* 1967, Diane Elizabeth, da of Roland Clarke, and Elizabeth Clarke; 2 s (Hon Adam b 1974, Hon Benet b 1977); *Career* economist Govt of Zambia 1968–70; HM Treasy: joined 1970, seconded to IMF Washington 1976–78, asst sec 1978–83, under sec 1985–88; private sec of econ affrs to the PM 1983–85, princ private sec to the PM 1988–92; HM Treasy: dep sec of public fin 1992–93, second perm sec of public expenditure 1993–94; perm sec: DOE 1994–97, DETR 1997–98, HM Treasy 1998–2002; Sec to the Cabinet and Head of the Home Civil Service 2002–05; sr advsr Booz Allen Hamilton 2006–; non-exec dir: British Land 2006–, Prudential 2006–, Arup Gp 2006–, Frontier Economics 2006–; Cdre Civil Service Sailing Assoc 1996–05, chm Civil Service Sports Cncl 2001–05; vice-patron Disabled Sailing Assoc; *Recreations* walking, opera, golf; *Style*— The Lord Turnbull, KCB, CVO

TURNBULL, (George) Anthony Twentyman; s of Stuart John Twentyman Turnbull (d 1991), and Hilda Joyce, *née* Taylor (d 1983); *b* 26 June 1938; *Educ* Charterhouse, ChCh Oxford (MA); *m* 14 June 1962, Petronel Jonette Rene Turnbull, JP, da of Maj James Williams Thursby Dunn (d 1969), of Clewer, Berks; 1 da (Victoria Jonette b 1963), 2 s (Robert Edward Twentyman b 1965, Timothy William John b 1970); *Career* called to the Bar 1962; Debenham Tewson & Chinnocks: joined 1962, ptnr 1965, chief exec 1987; chief exec DTZ Debenham Thorpe 1993–95 (int conslt 1995–96); non-exec dir: Greycoat plc 1996–99, Oriental Restaurants plc 1996–2000, Property Intelligence plc 1996–2002 (chm 1997–2002), Lend Lease Europe GP Ltd 1999–; md Beachfield Productions Ltd 2001–, chm Intelligent Addressing (Holdings) Ltd 2003–; chm of tstees Oglander Brading Roman Villa Tst; Freeman Worshipful Co of Fruiterers (hon asst 1992, Renter Warden 2000, Upper Warden 2001, Master 2002); FRICS; *Recreations* theatre, conversation, playing games; *Clubs* Savile, Royal London Yacht; *Style*— Anthony Turnbull, Esq; ✉ Beachfield, Beachfield Road, Sandown, Isle of Wight PO36 8LT (tel and fax 01983 403533, e-mail mail@beachfieldproductions.com)

TURNBULL, Christopher James; s of Rev Capt James Turnbull, of Glastonbury, and Rosemary Erskine Turnbull; *b* 15 April 1950; *Educ* Haileybury, Queens' Coll Cambridge (MA, MB BChir), Westminster Med Sch; *m* 5 Jan 1974, Susan Mary, da of Roger Avery Lovelock, Horsell, Woking; 2 s (James Edward b 1979, Luke Christopher b 1985), 1 da (Claire Elizabeth b 1982); *Career* GP vocational trainee Sandhurst Berks 1976–79, registrar in med Wellington Hosp NZ 1979–81, sr registrar in geriatric med Liverpool rotations 1981–83, conslt physician geriatric med Wirral 1983–, clinical dir for the elderly 1988–89 and 1995–96; sec Specialist Advsy Ctee in Geriatric Med RCP 2005–; chm: Wirral Assoc for Care of the Elderly 1983–91, Wirral Planning GP for the Elderly 1988–91, Special Interest Gp in Diabetes 1992–95; prog dir and regnl speciality advsr Geriatric Med Mersey 2001–04; author of articles on: glaucoma in the elderly, postural hypotension in the elderly, Parkinsons Disease in the elderly, diabetes in the elderly, fractures in the elderly; memb: Br Geriatrics Soc, Br Assoc for Serv to the Elderly; FRCP, MRCGP; *Recreations* dinghy sailing, renaissance music; *Style*— Christopher Turnbull, Esq; ✉ Arrowe Park Hospital, Arrowe Park Road, Upton, Wirral, Merseyside CH49 5PE (tel 0151 678 5111, e-mail sjturn@liv.ac.uk)

TURNBULL, John Neil; s of John Smith Turnbull (d 1941), of South Shields, and Kathleen Bernadette Higgins; *b* 13 February 1940; *Educ* St Cuthbert GS Newcastle upon Tyne, King's Coll Durham (BSc); *m* 1966, Aloysia, *née* Lindemann; 2 s (John Michael b 13 Oct 1968, David Stephen b 11 Dec 1970); *Career* British Petroleum: technologist BP Research Centre 1961–64, commissioning engr BP refinery Dinslaken W Germany 1964–66, project ldr BP Res Centre 1966–70, commissioning engr BP Chemicals Baglan Bay W Glamorgan 1970–74, prodn control mangr BP Baglan Bay 1974–76, tech devpt mangr BP Baglan Bay 1976–77, asst works mangr BP Baglan Bay 1977–79, gen mangr polyethylene BP Chemicals Geneva 1979–84, dir polymers BP Chemicals London 1984–86, dir technol petrochemicals and polymers BP Chemicals London 1986–89, dep chief exec nitrogen/nitriles BP Chemicals America 1989–91, dep chief exec mfrg technol BP Chemicals London 1991–93, ret; conslt 1994–; dir International Forum Stowe Vermont USA 1995–; FIChemE, FREng 1992, FRSA 2006; *Recreations* skiing, music, reading, walking, theatre; *Style*— John Turnbull, Esq, FREng, FRSA; ✉ Mulberry House, Vineyard Drive, Bourne End, Buckinghamshire SL8 5PD (tel 01628 850768, e-mail jnt@turnbull.org)

TURNBULL, (Wilson) Mark; *b* 1 April 1943; *Educ* George Watson Coll, Edinburgh Coll of Art Sch of Architecture (DipArch with Distinction in Design), Univ of Pennsylvania (MLA); *Career* teaching asst Dept of Landscape Architecture and Regional Planning Univ of Pennsylvania 1968–70, asst prof of architecture Univ of Southern Calif 1970–74, assoc then ptnr W J Cairns and Partners environmental conslts 1974–82, ptnr Design Innovations Research 1978–82, princ Turnbull Jeffrey Partnership 1982–99 (chm 1999–2001), chm TJP Envision Ltd 1999–, princ Mark Turnbull Landscape Architect 1999–; external examiner Dept of Landscape Architecture Heriot-Watt Univ 1984–88; Edinburgh Corp Medal for Civic Design 1968, Andrew Grant scholarships Edinburgh Coll of Art Sch of Architecture 1964, 1965, 1967 and 1968, Fulbright travel scholarship 1968, faculty medal Dept of Landscape Architecture Univ of Pennsylvania 1970; memb: Cncl Cockburn Assoc 1986–95, Countryside Cmmn for Scotland 1988–92, Royal Fine Art

T

Cmmn for Scotland 1996–2005; chm Edinburgh Green Belt Initiative 1988–91, dir and vice-chm Edinburgh Green Belt Tst 1991–; RIBA 1977, MBCS 1986, FLI 1989 (ALI 1975), FRIAS 1991 (ARIAS 1977); *Recreations* sailing; *Style*— Mark Turnbull, Esq; ✉ Mark Turnbull Landscape Architect, Creag an Tuirc House, Balquhidder, Perthshire FK19 8NY (tel 01877 384728, fax 01877 384764, mobile 07774 685970, e-mail mark@mtla.co.uk)

TURNBULL, Peter John; s of John Colin Turnbull, of Rotherham, S Yorks, and Patricia, *née* O'Brien; *b* 23 October 1950; *Educ* Oakwood Secdy Modern Sch Rotherham, Richmond Coll of FE, Cambs Coll of Arts & Technol (BA), Univ of Huddersfield (MA), UC Cardiff (CQSW); *Career* offr Regnl Cncl Public Serv of Strathclyde 1978–92, Leeds City Cncl 1992–95; crime writer 1981–; *Books* Deep and Crisp and Even (1981), Dead Knock (1982), Fair Friday (1983), Big Money (1983), The Claws of the Gryphon (1986), Two Way Cut (1988), Condition Purple (1989), The Justice Game (1990), And Did Murder Him (1991), Long Day Monday (1992), The Killing Floor (1994), The Killer Who Never Was (1996), Embracing Skeletons (1996), The Man With No Face (1998), Death Trap (2000), The Return (2001), Perils and Dangers (2001), Dark Secrets (2002), Reality Checkpoint (2004), Chill Factor (2005), The Trophy Wife (2005), Sweet Humphrey (2005), False Knight (2006), Once a Biker (2007); *Recreations* relaxing in the company of good friends; *Style*— Peter Turnbull, Esq; ✉ c/o PFD (tel 020 7344 1035)

TURNBULL, Rev Dr Richard Duncan; s of Alan Turnbull, of Doncaster, Yorks, and Kathleen, *née* Ormston (d 1978); *b* 17 October 1960, Manchester; *Educ* Moseley GS, Normanton HS W Yorks, Univ of Reading (BA), St John's Coll Univ of Durham (BA, PhD), Univ of Oxford (MA); *m* Caroline, *née* Andrew; 3 da (Sarah b 7 May 1989, Kathryn b 12 Jan 1992, Rebecca b 4 Nov 1996), 1 s (Matthew b 2 Dec 1993); *Career* CA 1985; trainee rising to mangr Ernst & Young 1987–90; curate Highfield 1994–97, vicar Chineham 1998–2005 (also memb various Dio of Winchester ctees incl chm House of Clergy and memb Standing Ctee Bishops Cncl 2000–05), princ Wycliffe Hall Oxford 2005–; C of E appts incl: memb Gen Synod 1995–2005 (chm Business Ctee 2004–05), memb Inter-Diocesan Finance Forum 1997–2005, chm Clergy Stipends Review 1999–2001, memb Archbishops' Cncl 2003–05 (memb Finance Ctee 1997–2005); advsr on ethical investment Ecclesiastical Insurance Gp 2002–; author of articles in academic jls and on the subject of evangelicals and the ecumenical movement; chair of govrs Portswood Primary Sch Southampton 1995–97; *Publications* Anglican and Evangelical? (2007); *Recreations* reading, walking, family, friends; *Clubs* Oxford and Cambridge; *Style*— The Rev Dr Richard Turnbull; ✉ Wycliffe Hall, 54 Banbury Road, Oxford OX2 6PW (tel 01865 274209, fax 01865 557866, e-mail richard.turnbull@wycliffe.ox.ac.uk)

TURNBULL, Steven Michael; s of Philip Peveril Turnbull (d 1987), of Rock, Cornwall, and Dorothy June Turnbull; *b* 24 October 1952; *Educ* Monkton Combe Sch, UC Oxford (BA); *m* 22 Sept 1985, Mary Ann, da of David M Colyer, of Cheltenham, Glos; 1 s (Matthew b 11 July 1987), 1 da (Clare b 21 Aug 1988); *Career* Linklaters: joined 1975, slr 1978, joined Corporate Dept, ptnr 1985; memb Law Soc, memb City of London Slrs' Co; *Recreations* golf, tennis, family; *Clubs* Oxford and Cambridge Golfing Soc, Royal Wimbledon Golf; *Style*— Steven Turnbull, Esq; ✉ Linklaters, One Silk Street, London EC2Y 8HQ (tel 020 7456 2000, fax 020 7456 2222, e-mail steven.turnbull@linklaters.com)

TURNBULL, William; *b* 11 January 1922; *Educ* Slade Sch of Art; *Career* artist; *Solo Exhibitions* Hanover Gallery 1950 and 1952, ICA 1957, Molton Gallery 1960 and 1961, Marlborough-Gerson Gallery NY 1963, Art Inst Detroit 1963, Bennington Coll Vermont 1965, Galerie Muller Stuttgart 1965 and 1974, Pavilion Gallery Balboa Calif 1966, Waddington Galleries 1967, 1969, 1970, 1976, 1981, 1985, 1987, 1991, 1998, 2001 and 2004, IX Bienal Sao Paolo Brazil touring 1967–68, Hayward Gallery 1968, Tate Gallery 1973, Scottish Arts Cncl 1974, Waddington and Tooth Galleries 1978, The Scottish Gallery Edinburgh 1981, Waddington and Shell Fine Art Toronto 1982, Theo Waddington Fine Arts NY 1982, Galerie Kutter Luxembourg 1983, Nat Museum Art Gallery Singapore 1984, Galerie Folker Skulima W Berlin 1987, Terry Dintenfass Inc NY 1986–88, John Berggruen Gallery San Francisco 1988–89, Arnold Herstand Gallery NY 1989, Sculpture on the Close (Jesus Coll Cambridge) 1990, Galeria Freites Caracas 1992, Galerie Michael Haas Berlin 1992, Galerie Neuman Düsseldorf 1993, Galerie Von Braunbehrens Munich 1993, Galerie Vander Darmstadt 1994, Serpentine Gallery 1995, Barbara Mathes Gallery NY 1998 and 2002, Galerie Thomas Munich 2002, Yorkshire Sculpture Park 2005; *Selected Group Exhibitions* Venice Biennale (Br Pavilion, Venice) 1952, Pittsburgh Int (Carnegie Inst Pittsburg PA) 1958, 1961 and 1962, Situation (RBA Galleries) 1960, Second Int Exhbn of Sculpture (Musee Rodin Paris) 1961, Hirshhorn Collection (Guggenheim Museum NY) 1962, Seventh Int Art Exhibition Tokyo 1963, Guggenheim Int NY 1964, Br Sculpture in the Sixties (Tate Gallery) 1965, First Int Exhibition of Modern Sculpture (Hakone Open Air Museum Japan) 1969, McAlpine Collection (Tate Gallery) 1971, Art Inglese Oggie (Palazzo Reale Milan) 1976, Tate 79 (Tate Gallery) 1979, Br Sculpture in the twentieth century: part 2 symbol and imagination 1951–80 (Whitechapel Art Gallery 1982, Forty Years of Modern Art 1945–85 (Tate Gallery) 1986, Br Art in the Twentieth Century: The Modern Movement (Royal Acad and touring) 1987, Britannica: Trente Ans de Sculpture 1960–88 (Musee de Beaux Arts, Le Havre) 1988, Modern Br Sculpture from the Collection (Tate Liverpool) 1988, Scottish Art Since 1900 (Scottish Nat Gallery of Modern Art Edinburgh and Barbican Art Gallery) 1989, The Independent Group: Postwar Britain and the Aesthetics of Plenty (ICA) 1990–91, Here and Now (The Sepentine Gallery) 1995, From Blast to Pop: Aspects of Modern British Art 1915–65 (The Smart Museum of Art Univ of Chicago) 1997, Transition: The London Art Scene in the Fifties (Barbican AA Galleries Londn (2002); works in the collections of: Albright - Knox Art Gallery Buffalo, Arts Cncl of GB, Art Gallery of Ontario, Br Cncl, Contemporary Arts Soc, Dundee Museum and Art Gallery, Franklin P Murphy Sculpture Garden UCLA, Glasgow Museum and Art Gallery, Hirshorn Museum and Sculpture (Smithsonian Inst) Washington DC, Univ of Hull, McCrory Corp NY, Museum of Contemporary Art Tehran, Nat Gallery of Art Washington DC, Scottish Nat Gallery of Modern Art Edinburgh, Stadtisches Museum Leverkusen Germany, Sydney Opera House, Tate Gallery, V&A, Westfalisches Landesmuseum Munster; *Style*— William Turnbull, Esq; ✉ c/o Waddington Galleries Ltd, 11 Cork Street, London W1S 3LT (tel 020 7851 2200, fax 020 7734 4146)

TURNER, Amédée Edward; QC (1976); s of Frederick William Turner (d 1945), and Ruth Hempson (d 1970); mother's side Huguenot Swiss; *b* 26 March 1929; *Educ* ChCh Oxford; *m* 1960, Deborah Dudley, da of Dr Philip Owen; 1 s, 1 da; *Career* called to the Bar Inner Temple 1954; in practice Patent Bar 1954–57, assoc Kenyon & Kenyon patent attorneys NY 1957–60, in practice London 1960–; Parly candidate (Cons) Norwich N gen elections 1964, 1966 and 1970; MEP (EDG 1979–92, EPP 1992–94): Suffolk and Harwich 1979–84, Suffolk and SE Cambs 1984–94; vice-chm Legal Ctee 1979–84; memb: Econ and Monetary Ctee 1979–84, ACP Jt Assembly 1979–94, Tport Ctee 1981–84, Energy and Technol Ctee 1983–89; chief whip European Democratic Gp 1989–92, chm Ctee on Int Affrs and Civil Rights 1992–94; hon memb European Parl 1994–, memb Exec Ctee European League for Economic Co-operation 1996–; sr counsel to: Oppenheimer, Wolff & Donnelly (US lawyers) 1994–2002, APCO Europe (Brussels) 1995–99, Worldspace Ltd 1999–2001; assisted Macedonian Parl to play fuller part in political system and its rules of procedure 2001–02; memb Advsy Cncl Anglican Observer UN 2002–06, organiser and author of report of Anglican, Episcopalian and Muslim discussions on attitudes of lay Muslims to democracy, human rights and rule of law throughout USA and Britain 2005–06; *Publications* The Law of Trade Secrets (1962, supplement 1968), The Law of the New European Patent (1979), Manual for the Macedonian Parliament (2002); author of over 40 European Parly reports, reports on patent litigation for the European Cmmn 2003 and 2006, and numerous Cons Pty study papers on defence, oil and Middle East; *Recreations* garden designs, painting; *Clubs* Coningsby, United and Cecil, Twenty; *Style*— Amédée Turner, Esq, QC; ✉ Penthouse 7, Bickenhall Mansions, Bickenhall Street, London W1W 6BS (tel 020 7935 2949, fax 020 7935 2950, e-mail amedee.turner@btinternet.com); The Barn, Westleton, Saxmundham, Suffolk; La Combe de la Boissière, St Maximin, Uzès, France

TURNER, Andrew Charles; s of Ralph Turner, of Leeds; *b* 1956; *Educ* Leeds GS, Christ's Coll Cambridge (MA); *m* 1982, Janice Helen, da of Albert Charles Minker; 3 s (Nicholas b 1987, William, Jonathan (twins) b 1990); *Career* PricewaterhouseCoopers (formerly Coopers & Lybrand): London office 1977–85 and 1988–2003, Tokyo office 1985–88, audit and consulting ptnr 1990–2003, ptnr-in-charge Banking and Capital Markets Regulatory Consulting Gp 1999–2003; compliance dir Abbey (formerly Abbey National) 2003–05, gp compliance offr Zurich Financial Servs 2006–; FCA 1990 (ACA 1980); *Recreations* genealogy, photography, Jimi Hendrix (music and memorabilia); *Style*— Andy Turner; ✉ e-mail aturner447@aol.com

TURNER, Andrew John; MP; s of Eustace Albert Turner (d 2001), and Joyce Mary, *née* Lowe (d 1994); *b* 24 October 1953; *Educ* Rugby, Keble Coll Oxford (MA), Univ of Birmingham, Henley Mgmnt Centre; *Partner* Carole Ann Dennett; *Career* teacher Lord Williams's Sch Oxon 1978–84, educn desk then trade and indust desk Cons Res Dept 1984–86, special advsr to sec of state for Social Servs 1986–87, dir Grant Maintained Schs Fndn 1988–97, educn conslt 1997–2001, head of Minerva project GDST 1999–2000, head of educn policy and resources London Borough of Southwark 2000–01, MP (Cons) IOW 2001– (Parly candidate: Hackney S and Shoreditch 1992, IOW 1997; Euro Parl candidate Birmingham E 1994); memb Educn and Skills Select Ctee, memb Exec 1922 Ctee 2001–03, a vice-chm (campaigning) Cons Pty 2003–05, shadow min for charities 2005–; memb Oxford City Cncl 1979–96; Sheriff Oxford 1994–95; FRSA; *Recreations* walking, countryside, avoiding gardening; *Style*— Andrew Turner, Esq, MP; ✉ House of Commons, London SW1A 0AA (e-mail mail@islandmp.com)

TURNER, Brian James; CBE (2002); s of late Lawrence Turner, of Morley, Leeds, and late Lily, *née* Riley; *b* 7 May 1946; *Educ* Morley GS, Leeds Coll of Food Technol, Borough Poly, Ealing Hotel Sch; *m* Denise, da of Alan Parker, of Rothwell, W Yorks; 2 s (Simeon James b 18 Nov 1974, Benjamin Jon b 5 July 1977); *Career* chef/restaurateur; Simpsons on the Strand London 1964–66, Savoy Hotel London 1966–69, Beau-Rivage Palace Lausanne-Ouchy Switzerland 1969–70, Claridges Hotel London 1970–71, Capital Hotel London 1971–86, Turners of Walton Street London 1986–2001, ptnr Foxtrot Oscar restaurant chain 2001–03, opened Brian Turner Restaurant Crowne Plaza Hotel NEC Birmingham 2002 (closed 2005), opened Brian Turner Mayfair 2003, opened Turner's Grill Copthorne Hotel Slough 2005, opened Turner's Grill Copthorne Hotel Birmingham 2006; pres Acad of Culinary Arts 2004– (chm 1993–2004); Good Food Guide Special Award 1996; FHCIMA 1988 (MHCIMA 1980–88); *Books* Ready Steady Cook (with Antony Worrall-Thompson, 1996), Brian Turner: A Yorkshire Lad (2000), Brian Turner's Favourite British Recipes (2003); *Style*— Brian Turner, Esq, CBE; ✉ Millennium Hotel, London Mayfair, Grosvenor Square, London W1K 2HP (tel 020 7495 0220, fax 020 7495 0440, e-mail turnerrest@aol.com, website www.brianturner.co.uk)

TURNER, Prof Bryan Stanley; s of Stanley William Turner (d 1974), and Sophia, *née* Brooks (d 1995); *b* 14 January 1945; *Educ* George Dixon GS Birmingham, Univ of Leeds (BA, PhD), Univ of Cambridge (MA); *m* 1996, Eileen Richardson; *Career* lectr Univ of Aberdeen 1969–82, prof Flinders Univ Adelaide Aust 1982–86, prof Univ of Utrecht Netherlands 1986–89, prof Univ of Essex 1989–92, prof Deakin Univ Aust 1992–98, prof Univ of Cambridge 1998–2005, professorial fell Fitzwilliam Coll Cambridge 2002–05, prof Nat Univ of Singapore 2005–; memb: Br Sociological Assoc 1970–, Aust Acad of Social Sciences 1987–, American Sociological Assoc 1990–; involved with Ismaili Inst London; Hon DLitt Flinders Univ Aust; FRSA 2002; *Publications* Cambridge Dictionary of Sociology (2006), Vulnerability and Human Rights (2006), Pragmatism in European Social Theory (jt ed, 2007); *Recreations* gardening, travel, collecting books; *Style*— Prof Bryan Turner; ✉ Asia Rearch Institute, Tower Block, Bukit Timah Campus, National University of Singapore, Singapore 259770 (tel 00 65 6516 3810, e-mail aribst@nus.edu.sg)

TURNER, David Andrew; QC (1991); s of James Turner (d 1986), and Phyllis, *née* Molyneux (d 2006); *b* 6 March 1947; *Educ* King George V Sch Southport, Queens' Coll Cambridge (MA, LLM); *m* 18 March 1978, Mary Christine, da of Eric Herbert Moffatt, of Douglas, IOM; 2 s (James b 1981, Charles b 1982), 1 da (Helen b 1984); *Career* called to the Bar Gray's Inn 1971 (bencher 2001); recorder of the Crown Court 1990–; *Recreations* squash, music; *Style*— David Turner, QC; ✉ Exchange Chambers, Pearl Assurance House, Derby Square, Liverpool L2 9XX (tel 0151 236 7747)

TURNER, His Hon Judge David George Patrick; QC (2000); s of George Patrick Turner (d 1988), of Londonderry, and Elsie Bamford, *née* McClure; *b* 11 July 1954; *Educ* Foyle Coll Londonderry, KCL (LLB, AKC), Coll of Law London; *m* 4 March 1978, Jean Patricia, da of Gerald William Hewett, of Carleton Rode, Norfolk; 2 s (Robert b 7 Oct 1980, Richard b 30 Oct 1982); *Career* called to the Bar Gray's Inn 1976; in practice South Eastern Circuit 1976–2004, recorder 2000–04 (asst recorder 1997–2000), circuit judge (South Eastern Circuit) 2004–; chllr Dio of Chester 1998–, dep chllr Dio of Liverpool 2001–02, dep chllr Dio of London 2002–; lay reader All Souls' Langham Place (churchwarden 1983–2006), memb Legal Advsy Cmmn C of E 2006–, a chm Clergy Discipline Tbnls 2007–; tstee: Langham Partnership, St Paul's Tst (Portman Square), London Lectures Tst; memb: Ecclesiastical Law Soc, Ecclesiastical Judges Assoc; *Recreations* reading, swimming, family; *Style*— His Hon Judge David Turner, QC; ✉ c/o The Crown Court, New Street, Chelmsford, Essex CM1 1EL (tel 0245 603000, fax 01245 603011); e-mail dgptqc@hotmail.com

TURNER, David John; s of Frederick Turner, of Prenton, Merseyside, and Sheila Margaret, *née* Collinson; *b* 7 February 1945; *Educ* Birkenhead Sch; *m* Julia Anne, *née* Thompson; 3 da (Sarah Frances b 28 Feb 1970, Catherine Margaret b 19 Feb 1974, Alice Elsie b 5 May 2001), 2 s (Jonathon Frederick b 22 March 1978, Archie David (twin) b 5 May 2001); *Career* chartered accountant: Cook & Co Liverpool 1963–67, Touche Ross & Co London 1967–69; mgmnt auditor Mobil Oil Corpn 1969–71, chief accountant Mobil Servs Ltd 1971–73, special projects co-ordinator Mobil Europe Inc 1973–74; fin dir: Booker Agriculture 1975–84, Booker plc (formerly Booker McConnell Ltd) 1984–93, GKN plc 1993–2001; Brambles Industries UK and Australia: chief fin offr 2001–203, chief exec 2003–07; non-exec dir Whitbread plc 2001–06; *Recreations* tennis, skiing; *Clubs* Boodle's; *Style*— David J Turner, Esq

TURNER, Prof Denys Alan; s of Alan, and Barbara Turner; *Educ* Mount St Mary's Coll Spinkhill, UC Dublin (BA, MA), Univ of Oxford (DPhil); *Career* UC Dublin: coll lectr in philosophy 1967–74, univ lectr in philosophy 1974–76; Univ of Bristol: lectr in the philosophy of religion 1977–89, sr lectr 1989–95; H G Wood prof of theology Univ of Birmingham 1995–99, Norris-Hulse prof of divinity Univ of Cambridge 1999– (fell Peterhouse); Exec Ctee Catholic Inst for Int Rels: 1982–86, chm 1986–94; memb: Catholic Theological Assoc of GB 1986–, Eckhart Soc 1989–, Editorial Bd Reviews in Religion and Theology; chm Newman Fellowships Tst 1989–96, tstee St Mary's Hospice Birmingham 1996–99; *Books* The Philosophy of Karl Marx (1969), Marxism and Christianity (1983), Eros and Allegory (1995), The Darkness of God (1995), Faith Seeking (2002); *Recreations* classical music from Dufay to Mahler, digging; *Style*— Prof Denys

Turner; ✉ Faculty of Divinity, University of Cambridge, West Road, Cambridge CB3 9BS (tel 01223 763020, e-mail dat25@cam.ac.uk)

TURNER, Derek; CBE (2003); *b* 8 May 1953, Surbiton, Surrey; *Educ* Hinchley Wood Co Secdy Sch, Univ of Sheffield (BEng); *m* (m dis); 1 da, 1 step s; *Career* asst engr Herts CC 1974–80, professional offr Transportation and Devpt Dept GLC 1980–82, princ engr Directorate of Technical and Contract Servs London Borough of Hackney 1982–85, gp planner Highways Planning and Transportation Planning Dept London Borough of Islington 1985–86, dep borough engr Technical Servs Dept London Borough of Wandsworth 1988–90 (asst borough engr 1986–88), borough engr and surveyor Technical Servs Directorate London Borough of Haringey 1990–91, traffic dir for London 1991–2000 (prog dir London Bus Initiative 1999–2000, established Red Routes and bus lane enforcement cameras), md Street Mgmnt Transport for London 2000–03 (devised, designed and implemented Central London Congestion Charging, created London Traffic Control Centre and responsible for pedestranisation of Trafalgar Square London), princ Derek Turner Consltg Ltd 2003–04, dir Colin Buchan and Partners 2004–05, nat traffic dir for motorways and trunk roads in England Highways Agency 2005– (memb Bd Highways Agency 2005–); non-exec dir Infocell Hldgs Limited 2003–05; visiting prof in civil and environmental engrg UCL 2003–; chm Transport Bd ICE 1999–2000; former memb: London Area Traffic Survey Steering Gp, Assoc of London Authorities/London Boroughs Assoc Transport Jt Working Party, London Transportation Study Steering Gp, Assoc of London Borough Engrs and Surveyors (gp chm 1991), Transport for London Implementation Gp, London Bus Initiative (chm Strategy Gp), Road Pricing Working Party, Millennium Access Co-ordination Gp, London Bus Priority Steering Gp, Urban Traffic Mgmnt and Control (UTMC) Steering Gp, Traffic Control Systems Unit (TCSU) Mgmnt Liaison Ctee; former chair: World Squares for All Steering Gp, London Sustainable Distribution Partnership; currently: memb Degree Prog Advsy Panel UCL, memb Road Capacity and Congestion Charging Forum; author of conf papers and int lectures on traffic and highway engrg, transportation policy and mgmnt, gives professional evidence to Transport Select Ctee House of Commons; Bus Industry Innovation Award for Bus Lane Enforcement Cameras 1998, AA Award 2000, Transport Planner of the Year Transportation Planning Soc 2003, European Transport Planner of the Year 2003; CEng, memb Inst of Municipal Engrs 1979, MCMI 1985, FIHT 1991 (MIHT 1978), FICE 1991 (MICE 1980), FCILT 1995, FRSA, FILT, FREng 2005; *Style*— Derek Turner, Esq, CBE

TURNER, Dr Desmond Stanley; MP; s of Stanley Turner (d 1956), and Elsie, *née* Morris (d 2002); *Educ* Luton GS, Imperial Coll London (BSc), UCL (MSc), Univ of London (PhD), Univ of Brighton (PGCE); *m* 1, 1966 (m dis 1987), Lynette, *née* Gwyn-Jones; 1 da (Oliviab 1969); m 2, 1997, Lynn, *née* Rogers; *Career* various research positions 1963–78: Royal Free Hosp Sch of Med, St Mary's Hosp Sch of Med, Guy's Hosp Sch of Med, Univ of Surrey, Univ of Sussex; chm and md Martlet Brewery 1979–83, science teacher 1984; MP (Lab) Brighton Kemptown 1997–; cncllr: E Sussex CC 1985–97, Brighton BC 1994–97, Brighton & Hove Cncl 1996–99; R D Lawrence Meml fell Br Diabetic Assoc; *Recreations* sailing, fencing; *Style*— Dr Desmond Turner, MP; ✉ House of Commons, London SW1A 0AA (tel 020 7219 4024, fax 020 7219 0264, e-mail turnerd@parliament.uk)

TURNER, Frank; s of Frank Turner (d 1977), of Earby, Lancs, and Marion, *née* Robinson (d 2005); *b* 7 June 1943; *Educ* Keighley Tech Coll, Univ of Salford (BSc), Columbia Univ Business Sch NY (long distance running trophy); *m* 1967, Byrnece, da of Jack Crawshaw; 1 da (Suzanne Nicola b 5 Feb 1972), 1 s (Julian Mark b 4 July 1977); *Career* Rolls-Royce Ltd: apprentice 1959, grad apprentice 1963–67, machine tool devpt engr 1967–69, tech asst and prog mangr RB211 1969–72, fin controller Rolls Royce 1971 Ltd Barnoldswick 1972–73, prodn products mangr Barnoldswick 1973–75, product centre mangr Derby 1975–78, gen mangr prodn 1978–80, dir mfrg 1980–83, dir mfrg engrg 1983–85, dir industrial and marine Ansty 1985–87, chm Cooper Rolls Inc 1985–87, dir Civil Engines Rolls-Royce plc 1987–92, dir International Aero Engines AG 1987–92, memb Bd Rolls-Royce Inc 1987–90, appointed to Main Bd Rolls-Royce plc 1988, chm Sawley Packaging Co 1990–92; md Aerospace Lucas Industries plc 1992–96, chief exec BM Aviation Services Ltd 1996–2000; dir: British Midland plc 1997–2000, British Regional Airlines Holdings Ltd 1997–98; non-exec dir: ASW plc 1995–2002, Wagon Industrial Holdings plc 1996–2002, AeroInventory plc 2000–05 (chm), Material Logistics plc 2000–04, Mott MacDonald 2000–05; chm: Potenza Gp Ltd 2000–, Mettis Gp Ltd 2001–03, SRTechnics Holding 2002–06, Symmetry Medical Inc 2006–, GCAT (Global & Commerical Aviation Training) Ltd 2006–, Westfield Sports Cars Ltd 2006–; chm of engrg BAAS 1993–94, pres Aviation Trg Assoc 1994–98; prof Univ of Warwick 1993–; memb Cncl: RAeS 1998–2004, British Aerospace Cos 1998–2000; Mensforth Gold Medal IProdE (for contrib to Br mfrg technol) 1985, James Clayton Award IMechE (for contrib to design, devpt and mfr of aero gas turbines); FREng 1986, FIEE 1986, FIMechE 1986, FRAeS 1989, FInstD 2000; *Recreations* family, sailing, running, windsurfing, keep fit, music; *Style*— Frank Turner, Esq, FREng; ✉ Potenza Ltd, 46 Main Street, Kings Newton, Derbyshire DE73 8BX (tel 01332 862179, fax 01332 865463, e-mail f.turner@potenzaenterprises.com)

TURNER, Prof Grenville; s of Arnold Turner, of Todmorden, and Florence Turner; *b* 1 November 1936; *Educ* Todmorden GS, St John's Coll Cambridge (MA), Balliol Coll Oxford (DPhil); *m* 8 April 1961, Kathleen, da of William Morris (d 1986), of Rochdale; 1 s (Patrick b 1968), 1 da (Charlotte b 1966); *Career* asst prof Univ of Calif Berkeley 1962–64, res assoc Caltech 1970–71, prof of physics Univ of Sheffield 1980–88 (lectr 1964–74, sr lectr 1974–79, reader 1979–80), prof of isotope geochemistry Univ of Manchester 1988–2002 (research prof 2002–); memb Ctees: SERC, Br Nat Space Centre PPARC; Rumford Medal Royal Soc 1996, Leonard Medal Meteoritical Soc 1999, Urey Medal European Assoc of Geochemistry 2002, Gold Medal Royal Astronomical Soc 2004; fell Geochemical Soc and European Assoc of Geochemistry 1996, fell Meteoritical Soc 1980, fell American Geophysical Union 1998; FRS 1980 (memb Cncl 1990–92); *Recreations* photography, walking, theatre; *Style*— Prof Grenville Turner, FRS; ✉ 42 Edgehill Road, Sheffield S7 1SP; School of Earth, Atmosphere and Environmental Sciences, The University of Manchester M13 9PL (tel 0161 275 0401, fax 0161 275 3947, e-mail grenville.turner@manchester.ac.uk)

TURNER, James; QC (1998); s of James Gordon Melville Turner, GC (d 1967), and Peggy Pamela, *née* Masters; *b* 23 November 1952; *Educ* Bexhill GS, Univ of Hull (LLB); *m* 7 July 1979 (sep), Sheila, da of John Barclay Green, OBE, of Woking, Surrey (d 1994); 3 s (George b 27 Jan 1981, Roderick b 1 Nov 1986, Felix b 31 Jan 1991), 2 da (Phoebe b 23 Nov 1983, Poppy b 11 Nov 1992); *Career* called to the Bar Inner Temple 1976 (master of the bench 2006), memb Supplementary Panel of Treasy Counsel (common law) 1995–98; memb: Criminal Bar Assoc, Family Law Bar Assoc, Administrative Law Bar Assoc, Howard League for Penal Reform, Justice; *Publications* Archbold's Criminal Pleading, Evidence & Practice (jt ed); *Recreations* eating, reading, cinema, soul music, theatre; *Style*— James Turner, Esq, QC; ✉ 1 King's Bench Walk, London EC4Y 7DR (tel 020 7936 1500, fax 020 7936 1590, e-mail jturner@1kbw.co.uk)

TURNER, James Alan; s of Dr David Charles Turner, and Elizabeth Abbott, *née* Eglington; *b* 16 July 1971, London; *Educ* Loughborough Univ (BA), Univ of Middx (CPE), Nottingham Trent Univ (LPC); *Partner* Wendy Rainbow; *Career* admitted slr; trainee Wilson Browne 1995–97, assoc slr Criminal Law Dept Toller Hales & Collcutt 1997–2000, ptnr Tuckers Slrs' 2000–; memb: Law Soc, Criminal Law Slrs' Assoc, London Criminal Courts Slrs Assoc; *Recreations* motorbikes, guitars, poker; *Style*— James Turner, Esq; ✉ Tuckers Solicitors, 210 Corporation Street, Birmingham B4 6QB (tel 0121 236 4324, fax 0121 236 4364, e-mail turnerj@tuckerssolicitors.com)

TURNER, John; s of Arnold Turner, of Thorpe Willoughby, N Yorks, and Winifred Mary, *née* Goodrum; *b* 4 April 1945; *Educ* Otago Boys's HS NZ, King's Sch Pontefract, Leeds Coll of Technol; *m* 1, Joy Mary Cousins; 1 da (Mary Elizabeth b 12 Feb 1974); m 2, Jennifer Anne, da of late William Shakespeare Clark; 1 da (Eve b 13 Dec 1980); *Career* advtg photographer specialising in still-life and automotive photography; asst to Gene Vernier and Peter Alexander 1964–67, freelance 1967–; pictures featured in Campaign Press & Poster, AFAEP, D&AD, Clio, Creative Circle and other related awards; memb Assoc of Photographers (judge The Tenth Awards); *Recreations* photography; *Style*— John Turner, Esq

TURNER, Prof John Derfel; s of Joseph Turner (d 1962), and Dorothy Winifred, *née* Derfel (d 1979); *b* 27 February 1928; *Educ* Manchester Grammar, Univ of Manchester (BA, MA, DipEd); *m* 6 June 1951, Susan Broady, da of Robert Baldwin Hovey, MC, OBE (d 1974); 2 s (Stephen b 1953, Leigh b 1959); *Career* Educn Offr RAF 1948–50; teacher Prince Henry's GS Evesham 1951–53, sr lectr in educn Nigerian Coll of Arts Science and Technol 1956–61 (lectr in English 1953–56), lectr in educn Inst of Educn Univ of Exeter 1961–64, prof of educn and dir Sch of Educn Univ of Botswana Lesotho and Swaziland 1964–70 (pro-vice-chllr 1966–70, emeritus prof 1970); Univ of Manchester: prof of educn and dir Sch of Educn 1970–76, prof of adult and higher educn Univ of Manchester 1976–85, dir Sch of Educn, dean Faculty of Educn 1985–91, pro-vice-chllr 1991–94, emeritus prof of educn 1994; rector UC of Botswana Univ of Botswana and Swaziland 1981–82 (vice-chllr 1982–84); patron Coll of Teachers (formerly Coll of Preceptors) 2004– (pres 1994–2004); memb: UK Nat Cmmn UNESCO 1975–81, IUC Working Parties on E and Central Africa and on Rural Devpt 1975–81, Educn Sub-Ctee UGC 1980–81, Working Pty on Academic Devpt of Univ of Juba 1977–78; pres Cmmn on Educn, Culture and Trg in Namibia 1999–; chm: Cncl Social Studies Advsy Ctee Selly Oak Colls 1975–81, Univs' Cncl for Educn of Teachers 1979–81 and 1988–91 (vice-chm 1976–79), Bd Govrs Abbotsholme Sch 1980–98, Cncl of Validating Univs 1990–94, Pres's Cmmn on HE in Namibia 1991–92; chm Editorial Bd Int Jl of Educn and Devpt 1978–81, ed Jl of Practice in Educn for Devpt 1994–99; methodist local preacher; Hon LLD Ohio Univ 1982, Hon DLitt Univ of Botswana 1995; hon fell Bolton Inst of Technol 1988; Hon FCP 1985, FRSA 1999; *Recreations* reading, music, theatre, walking; *Style*— Prof John Turner; ✉ 13 Firswood Mount, Gatley, Cheadle, Cheshire SK8 4JY (tel 0161 283 8429, fax 0161 282 1022, e-mail johndturner@ntlworld.com)

TURNER, Prof John Richard George; s of George Hugh Turner (d 1983), of Liverpool, and Elsie Ellen, *née* Booth (d 2002); *b* 11 September 1940; *Educ* Quarry Bank HS Liverpool, Univ of Liverpool (BSc), Univ of Oxford (DPhil, DSc); *m* 3 April 1967, Sandra Fordyce, da of Alexander Thomson Millar (d 1994), of Dundee; 1 s (Richard b 1970), 1 da (Lois b 1977); *Career* research asst NY Zoological Soc Trinidad and Tobago 1964, lectr in biology Univ of York 1965–72, assoc prof of biology Stony Brook Campus NY State Univ 1971–77, princ scientific offr Rothamsted Experimental Station Harpenden 1977–78; Univ of Leeds: lectr in genetics 1978–81, reader in evolutionary genetics 1981–87, prof of evolutionary genetics 1987–2000, research prof 2000–03, hon fell 2003–; memb: Race and Intelligence Ctee Genetics Soc of America 1976, Animal Procedures Ctee Home Office 1997–2000; memb Editorial Bd: Heredity, Evolution, Entomologist, Evolutionary Ecology; Scott Holland lectr KCL 1989; various radio and TV appearances; fndr memb Conservation Soc, jt sec Cncl for Academic Autonomy; memb: Lepidopterists' Soc, Yorkshire Wildlife Tst, Yorkshire Naturalists Union, Br Dragonfly Soc, Plantlife, American Soc of Naturalists 1971; exhibition of drawings Fairbairn House Leeds 1991; Liverpool Biological Soc Prize 1960; FRES 1962, FRSA 1993; *Publications* incl: Rimbaud translations in Poetry and Audience (1989), translation of Verlaine's She and Her Cat (commendation Times Stephen Spender Prize 2005); author of over 100 papers in scientific jls and book reviews for Spectator, TLS and NY Times; contrib to books on: evolution, ecology, behaviour, genetics, butterflies, biogeography, history of science; *Recreations* opera, swimming, collecting things, wildlife, drawing, translating poetry, spoonerising; *Style*— Prof John Turner; ✉ Faculty of Biological Sciences, University of Leeds, Leeds LS2 9JT (tel 0113 343 2828, fax 0113 343 2835, e-mail j.r.g.turner@leeds.ac.uk)

TURNER, John Warren; CBE (1988); s of Thomas Henry Huxley Turner, CBE (d 1973), of Cardiff, and Phebe Elvira, *née* Evans; *b* 12 October 1935; *Educ* Shrewsbury, St John's Coll Cambridge; *m* 8 Oct 1966, Jillian Fiona Geraldine, da of Thomas Ouchterlony Turton Hart (d 1995); 1 s (Gavin b 1972); *Career* 2 Lt RE Middle East 1957–59, TA 1959–66, ret Capt; construction conslt 1989–2004; former chm and md E Turner and Sons Ltd (dir 1964–89), dir Principality Building Society 1985–97, dir Peter Alan Ltd 1991–98, chm Principality Property Sales Ltd 1991–97, dir BSI 1994–2000; chm: Bldg Regulations Advsy Ctee BRAC 1985–91 (memb 1971–91), Cncl Bldg and Civil Engrg BSI 1985–91, Technical Sector Bd Building and Civil Engrg BSI 1991–98, Standards Bd BSI 1997–2004; perm UK rep Technical Sector Bd Construction Comité Européen de Normalisation (CEN) 1990–98, chm Construction Mandates Forum CEN 1991–2000; memb: Wales Cncl CBI 1980–86, Cncl Br Bd of Agrément BBA 1980–98; pres: Concrete Soc 1976–77, Wales Div IOD 1981–86 (memb Employment Ctee IOD 1982–97), Bldg Employers' Confedn 1985–86; memb Nat Jt Cncl for the Building Industry (ldr Employers' Side 1981–84) 1980–99, UK delg XII and XIII Construction Industry Confs ILO Geneva 1983 and 1987; memb TAVR Assoc for Wales 1974–91; govr Christ Coll Brecon 1981–84; IAAS Peter Stone Award (for contrib to devpt of building regulations) 1985; JP 1979–85; *Recreations* golf; *Clubs* Cardiff and County, Royal Porthcawl Golf, R&A; *Style*— John Turner, Esq, CBE; ✉ 12 Fulmar Road, Porthcawl, Mid Glamorgan CF36 3UL (tel 01656 782418)

TURNER, Jon Lys; s of Edward Turner (d 1976), and Anne, *née* Telfer; *b* 14 June 1959; *Educ* Felsted, Newport Art Sch (BA), RCA (MA); *Career* trained as graphic designer; proprietor Jon Lys Turner Ltd 1984–88 (clients incl Liberty and Virgin), divnl dir (retail) Fitch RS 1988–90 (clients incl Dillons the Bookstore), gp creative head Imagination Ltd 1990–94 (clients incl MTV and Ford), head of global design The Body Shop International plc 1994–2000, exec creative dir Enterprise IG WPP Gp 2000–02, creative dir Boots plc 2002–; other design projects incl murals for Soho Soho Restaurant and RNT London; contrib TV progs: Business Matter (BBC) 1994, Winning by Design (BBC) 1995; speaker for Speakers for Business on The Power of Design 1995; Marketing Week/Design Business Assoc Design Effectiveness Own Brand Packaging Award 1998, Design Cncl Millennium Award for the design of 'Eau No!' product range 1999, Marketing Week/Design Business Assoc Design Effectiveness Campaign Award 2000; FCSD 1995, FRSA 1998; *Books* The Retail Future (creator and designer, 1990); *Style*— Jon Turner, Esq; ✉ tel 0115 959 5109, e-mail jon.turner@boots.co.uk

TURNER, Jonathan David Chattyn; s of Maxwell Turner, and Naomi, *née* Myers; *b* 13 May 1958; *Educ* Rugby, Corpus Christi Coll Cambridge (BA, MA), Université Libre de Bruxelles (Lic Sp Dr Eur), Queen Mary Coll London; *m* 23 Nov 1986, Caroline Frances Esther, da of Lawrence Sam Berman, CB; 2 s (Jacob b 1988, Gabriel b 1992), 1 da (Camilla b 1990); *Career* called to the Bar Gray's Inn 1982, pupillage in chambers of Leonard Hoffmann QC, Robin Jacob QC and Alastair Wilson QC 1982–83, in private practice as barr specialising in intellectual property and competition law 1983–95 and 1997–, head of IP and IT law Coopers and Lybrand 1995–97; assoc memb: Chartered Inst of Patent Agents, Inst of Trade Mark Agents; domain name panelist World Intellectual Property

Orgn and Czech Arbitration Court; *Books* Halsbury's Laws of England, EC Competition Law (1986), European Patent Office Reports (1986–1995), Forms and Agreements on Intellectual Property and International Licensing (1979–89), Law of the European Communities, Competition Law (1986–2006), Countdown to 2000 - A Guide to the Legal Issues (1998), European Patent Infringement Cases (1999), Domain Names - A Practical Guide (2002); *Recreations* walking, theatre, music; *Style*— Jonathan D C Turner, Esq; ✉ Thirteen Old Square, Lincoln's Inn, London WC2A 3AU (tel 020 7831 4445, fax 020 7841 5825, e-mail mail@jonathanturner.com, website www.jonathanturner.com)

TURNER, Prof Kenneth John; s of Graham Leslie Turner (d 1970), of Glasgow, and Christina McInnes, *née* Fraser; *b* 21 February 1949; *Educ* Hutchesons Boys' GS, Univ of Glasgow (BSc), Univ of Edinburgh (PhD); *m* 15 Sept 1973, Elizabeth Mary Christina, da of Rev William James Hutton, of Glasgow; 2 s (Duncan b 1979, Robin b 1981); *Career* data communications conslt 1980–86, prof of computing sci Univ of Stirling 1986–; memb: Int Fedn for Info Processing; *Books* Formal Description Techniques (ed, 1988), Using Formal Description Techniques (ed, 1993), Service Provision (ed, 2004); *Recreations* choral activities, handicrafts, sailing; *Style*— Prof Kenneth Turner; ✉ Department of Computing Science and Mathematics, University of Stirling, Stirling FK9 4LA (tel 01786 467423, fax 01786 464551, e-mail kjt@cs.stir.ac.uk)

TURNER, Lawrence Frederick; OBE (1982); s of Frederick Thomas Turner (d 1967), of Warks, and Edith Elizabeth Turner (d 1975); *b* 28 January 1929; *Educ* Moseley GS, Aston Univ (BSc, CEng); *m* 5 June 1954, Jeanette (d 2006), da of Wilfred Edwin Clements (d 1967), of Warks; 2 s (Adrian Richard Lawrence b 1957, (Anthony) Christopher b 1959), 1 da (Susan Kathryn b 1965); *Career* chartered electrical engr; chm Static Systems Gp plc 1964–; dep chm Dudley Health Tst 1994–98; pres Inst of Hosp Engrg 1979–81; Freeman City of London 1986, Past Master Worshipful Co of Fan Makers, Past Master Worshipful Co of Engrs; FIEE, FCIBSE; *Recreations* sailing (yacht Tarantella), music, opera, rowing; *Clubs* Athenaeum, Royal Dart Yacht; *Style*— Lawrence Turner, Esq, OBE; ✉ Damsells Cross, The Park, Painswick, Gloucestershire GL6 6SR (tel 01452 814384, e-mail lawrence@lfturner.com); 381 Shakespeare Tower, Barbican, London EC2Y 8NJ (tel 020 7638 5393); Static Systems Group plc, Heath Mill Road, Wombourn, Staffordshire WV5 8AN (tel 01902 895551)

TURNER, Mark George; QC (1998); s of Jeffrey Farrar Turner, of Kendal, Cumbria, and Joyce, *née* Barkas; *b* 27 August 1959; *Educ* Sedbergh, The Queen's Coll Oxford (BA); *m* 23 Jan 1988, Caroline Sophia, da of George Haydn Bullock, of Richmond, Surrey; 3 da (Alice Elizabeth b 29 Oct 1989, Fiona Maud b 6 June 1991, Lydia Sophia b 20 May 1993); *Career* called to the Bar Gray's Inn 1981 (bencher), tenant Deans Ct Chambers Manchester 1982–, called to the Bar Northern Circuit 1982, recorder 2000– (asst recorder 1998–2000); memb Personal Injury Bar Assoc; *Publications* Occupational Asthma, Mucous Membrane Disease-Industrial Diseases Litigation (2003), Occupational Stress (2006); *Recreations* classical music, history, general knowledge quizzes; *Clubs* Mastermind (semi finalist 1988); *Style*— Mark Turner, QC; ✉ Deans Court Chambers, 24 St John Street, Manchester M3 4DF (tel 0161 214 6000, fax 0161 214 6001, e-mail mturnerqc@aol.com, turner@deanscourt.co.uk)

TURNER, Martin Paul; s of Fredrick William Harold Turner, of Llanfoist, Gwent, and Magaret Mary, *née* Downey; *b* 28 February 1951; *Educ* Tredegar GS, Harvard Business Sch; *m* 8 Aug 1970, Elizabeth Jane, da of Haydn Hedworth Houlding; 2 da (Kathryn Louise b 17 Aug 1976, Carys Elizabeth b 1 Nov 1987), 2 s (David Martyn b 15 Jan 1980, Peter John b 17 Aug 1990); *Career* finance trainee N Monmouthshire Health Authy 1969, chief internal auditor Hosp Mgmnt Ctee 1974; Gwent Health Authy: asst treas 1976–77, finance offr 1977–81, sr asst treas 1981–, dep treas 1982–86, gen mangr Community Servs 1986–90, gen mangr (Hosp Servs) 1990–92; chief exec: Gwent Healthcare NHS Tst (formerly Glan Hafren NHS Tst) 1993–99, Gwent Healthcare NHS Tst; FCCA, MHSM, MCMI; *Recreations* golf, travel, gardening; *Style*— Martin Turner, Esq; ✉ Maescoed, Bettws Newydd, Usk, Gwent NP15 1EQ (tel 01873 880841); Gwent Healthcare NHS Trust, Grange House, Llanfrechfa Grange, Cwmbran, Torfaen NP44 8YN (tel 01633 623483, fax 01633 623817, e-mail martin.turner@gwent.wales.nhs.uk)

TURNER, Michael John; s of Geoffrey Maurice Turner (d 1993), and Peggy Patricia Dora, *née* Brookes; *b* 8 February 1950; *Educ* King Edward VI Sch Southampton; *m* 7 July 1975, Kazue, da of Goro Shimada; 2 da (Anna-Marie Namie b 2 Jan 1977, Louisa-Jane Kei b 4 March 1981); *Career* articled clerk Hamilton and Rowland CA's Southampton 1968–72; Touche Ross (now Deloitte & Touche): joined 1972, ptnr 1979–, ptnr i/c Japanese Business 1983, gp ptnr Audit Dept London 1984–94, ptnr Chinese Business 1992–94, ptnr i/c Korea Desk 1998–2000, ptnr i/c Company Secretarial Div; Deloitte Touche Tohmatsu: dep chm European Japanese Exec, chm Finance Ctee; govr Hampton Sch; FCA 1980 (ACA 1972); *Recreations* golf, hockey, tennis; *Clubs* Teddington Hockey (vice-pres), Burhill Golf; *Style*— Michael Turner, Esq; ✉ Miyabi, 92 Burwood Road, Walton on Thames, Surrey KT12 4AP (tel 01932 223679, fax 01932 223679); Deloitte & Touche, Hill House, 1 Little New Street, London EC4A 3TR (tel 020 7303 3552, fax 020 7583 8517)

TURNER, Michael John; s of Gerald Mortimer Turner, of Ashtead, Surrey, and Joyce Isobel Marguerite, *née* Healy; *b* 12 June 1951; *Educ* Eton; *m* 17 July 1982, Diana Mary St Clair, da of David Michael St Clair Weir; 4 s (Freddie b 1985, Munchie b 1987, Harry b 1989, Tom b 1992); *Career* Fuller Smith & Turner plc: dir 1985–, md 1992–2002, chief exec 2002–; chm: Leonard Tong 1986–87 (dir 1982–91), George Gale and Co Ltd 2006–; Liveryman Worshipful Co of Vintners, Liveryman Worshipful Co of Brewers; FCA; *Recreations* skiing, shooting, golf, tennis, motor racing, travel; *Clubs* Aldeburgh Golf, Eton Vikings, Berkshire Golf, Hurlingham; *Style*— Michael Turner, Esq; ✉ 5 Bowerdean Street, London SW6 3TN; Fuller Smith & Turner plc, Griffin Brewery, Chiswick, London W4 2QB

TURNER, Michael John (Mike); CBE (1999); s of Thomas Albert Turner, of Stockport, Cheshire, and Hilda, *née* Pendlebury; *b* 5 August 1948; *Educ* Didsbury Tech HS Manchester, Manchester Poly (BA); *m* 1, 1972 (m dis 1984), Rosalind, *née* Thomas; 2 s (Andrew Richard b 14 Sept 1976, Nicholas James b 5 July 1978); m 2, 1985, Jean Crotty; 2 step da (Johanna Crotty b 17 Jan 1969, Victoria Crotty (Mrs Morley) b 25 May 1971); *Career* BAE Systems plc (and predecessor cos): contracts officer Hawker Siddeley Aviation Manchester 1970 (undergrad apprentice 1966–70), contracts mangr (military) Manchester Div British Aerospace Aircraft Gp 1978–80, admin mangr 1980–81, exec dir admin 1981–82, divnl admin dir 1982–84 (concurrently ldr Advanced Turboprop Project), divnl dir and gen mangr Kingston 1984–86, dir and gen mangr Weybridge, Kingston and Dunsfold 1986–87, dir of mktg and product support Mil Aircraft Div 1987–88, exec vice-pres defence mktg 1988–92, chm and md British Aerospace Regional Aircraft Ltd and chm Jetstream Aircraft 1992–94, chm British Aerospace Airbus Ltd 1994–, main bd dir 1994–, gp md British Aerospace plc 1997–98, exec dir 1998–99, chief operating officer 1999–2002, chief exec 2002–; pres: Soc of Br Aerospace Cos 1996 (vice-pres 1995–96), AeroSpace and Defence Industries Assoc of Europe (ASD) 2003–04; jt chm Aerospace Innovation and Growth Team; Br Inst of Mgmnt Young Mangr of the Year 1973; Hon Dr Manchester Met Univ 2006; ACIS 1973, FRAeS 1991; *Recreations* golf, cricket, rugby, Manchester United; *Style*— Mike Turner, Esq, CBE; ✉ BAE Systems plc, Stirling Square, 6 Carlton Gardens, London SW1Y 5AD (tel 01252 383928, fax 01252 383906)

TURNER, Dr Michael Skinner; s of Sir Michael William Turner, CBE (d 1980), of London, and Lady Wendy, *née* Stranack (d 1999); *b* 12 August 1947; *Educ* Marlborough, Univ of London and St Thomas' Hosp (MB BS, MRCS, LRCP), Washington USA (MD); *Children* 3 da (Lucinda b 6 Dec 1974, Camilla b 3 July 1980, Alexia b 29 Jan 1984); *Career* chief med advsr: Horseracing Regulatory Authy, British Ski and Snowboard Fedn 1973–99; dir of med services Br Olympic Assoc 1992–94; med advsr 1980–97: Texaco, P&O, Vickers, Barclays de Zoete Wedd, ANZ/Grindlays Bank, Hongkong & Shanghai Banking Group, Hoare Govett; Br team doctor Winter Olympics: Calgary 1988, Albertville 1992, Lillehammer 1994; memb Med Ctee Int Ski Fedn 1989–99, LTA 1994–2007; memb Editorial Bd Br Jl of Sports Med; fell: RCSI and RCPI Faculty of Sports and Exercise Med, Faculty of Sport and Exercise Medicine (FSEM) (UK); Desborough Award for Services to Olympic Sport 1994, Sir Robert Atkins Award for Services to Sports Medicine 2006; Freeman City of London 1971, Liveryman Worshipful Co of Skinners; *Recreations* skiing, racing, tennis, watersports; *Style*— Dr Michael Turner; ✉ 30 Devonshire Street, London W1G 6PU (fax 020 7228 7495, e-mail uksportdoc@aol.com)

TURNER, Hon (Edward) Neil; OBE (2002), DL; s of 1 Baron Netherthorpe (d 1980), and Margaret Lucy, *née* Mattock; *b* 27 January 1941; *Educ* Rugby, RAC Cirencester, Univ of London; *m* 12 Oct 1963, Gillian Mary, da of Christopher John King (d 1963); 1 s (Charles b 3 May 1966), 1 da (Sara b 4 Feb 1971); *Career* chm: Edward Turner and Son Ltd 1971–, Lazard Smaller Equities Investment Tst plc 1994–96, INVESCO Enterprise Tst plc 1996–2002; pres: Sheffield C of C 1996–97, Assoc of Yorks and Humber Cs of C 1997–99; dep chair Regnl Assembly for Yorks and Humberside 1998–99; vice-chm Yorks and Humberside Devpt Assoc 1989–92; memb: Yorks and Humberside Econ Planning Cncl 1975–79, Residuary Body for S Yorks 1985–89, Nat Cncl CBI 1993–98, RASE Cncl 1999–2002; chm Rural Div Cmmn S Yorks and W Yorks 1983–91; gen cmmr of Taxes 1973–; High Sheriff S Yorks 1983–84; master Co of Cutlers in Hallamshire 2003–04; Hon Col 212 (Yorks) Field Hosp (V) 1998–2003; chm The Broomgrove Tst 1976–2006; Liveryman The Worshipful Co of Farmers; Dip FBA (London); FRICS; *Recreations* shooting, golf; *Clubs* Lindrick Golf, Farmers'; *Style*— The Hon Neil Turner, OBE, DL; ✉ The Limes, Crowgate, South Anston, Sheffield, South Yorkshire S25 5AL (tel 01909 550097, fax 01909 550544)

TURNER, Neil; MP; *b* 16 September 1945; *Educ* Carlisle GS; *m* Susan Beatrice; 1 s (James Timothy); *Career* quantity surveyor 1963–92; MP (Lab) Wigan 1999– (by-election); cncllr Wigan BC 1972–74, cncllr Wigan MBC 1975–2000; chm: Highways 7 Works Ctee 1980–97, Best Value Review Panel 1998–2000, AMA Public Services Ctee 1995–97, LGA Quality Panel 1997–99; memb Lab Pty 1964–; *Recreations* Wigan RLFC, Wigan Athletic FC, WWII (particularly naval); *Clubs* St Thomas's Labour (Marsh Green Wigan); *Style*— Neil Turner, Esq, MP; ✉ Gerrard Winstanley House, Crawford Street, Wigan WN1 1NG (tel 01942 242047, fax 01942 828009); House of Commons, London SW1A 0AA

TURNER, Nicola Mary (Niki); da of Alan John Turner, and Mary Frances, *née* Sawbridge; *Educ* Wadhurst Coll, Reigate Sch of Art, Central St Martins Coll of Art (BA); *m* Alfred Theodore Coles; 1 da (Iona Evelyn b 31 March 2003), 1 s (Arthur Neill b 21 April 2005); *Career* set and costume designer; art dir Inside Out (film); memb Tate Gallery; *Productions* Oxford Stage Co: A Midsummer Night's Dream, Johnny Blue, The Comic Mysteries; Derby Playhouse: The Glass Menagerie, Grapevine, Lips Together Teeth Apart, Extremities, Danny Bouncing, Watching the Sand from the Sea; W Yorks Playhouse: Spend Spend Spend, The World Goes 'Round, Pilgermann, The Snow Queen; Salisbury Playhouse: Wallflowering, The Rover, The Banished Cavaliers, The Crucible; Eastern Angles tour: A Bad Case of Love, Inheritance, Boats; Mercury Theatre Colchester: Romeo and Juliet, A View From the Bridge, Shirley Valentine, Grounded, The Aspern Papers; Gate Theatre Notting Hill: The False Servant, Talking Tongues, The Gentleman from Olmedo (costumes); RSC: As You Like It (co-designer), Oroonoko, Brixton Stories, The Island Princess; other credits incl: Things Fall Apart (Royal Court and W Yorks Playhouse, also US and UK tour), Henceforward (New Victoria Stoke), Maddie (West End and Salisbury Playhouse), Adam Bede (Derby Playhouse and York Theatre Royal), Time and the Conways (Salisbury Playhouse and Mercury Theatre Colchester), The Beatification of Area Boy (W Yorks Playhouse, Brooklyn Acad and Euro tour), The Winslow Boy (Birmingham Rep and W Yorks Playhouse), Artemisia (mixed media project for Turtle Key Prodns), Our Boys (Derby Playhouse and Donmar Warehouse), Carmen (Regency Opera tour and Holland Park Opera), Great Expectations (Derby Playhouse and Philadelphia), La Traviata (English Touring Opera), Tender (Birmingham Rep and Hampstead Theatre), Further than the Furthest Thing (RNT, Tricycle Theatre, Tron Theatre and Traverse Theatre), The External (Theatre Royal Bath and Greenwich Theatre touring co-prodn), Soul Train (Turnstyle No 1 tour), Speaking in Tongues (Hampstead Theatre and Derby Playhouse), L'Amore Industrioso (Holland Park Opera), Junk (Oxford Stage Co and Den Nationale Scene Norway), Othello (New Victoria Stoke), On the Piste (Tivoli Theatre Dublin), A Passage to India (Shared Experience), Gone to Earh (Shared Experience), Embryonic Dreams (Edinburgh Festival), Yerma (Edinburgh Festival), Sarka (Garsington Opera), Osud (Garsington Opera), Rusalka (Opera North and Sydney Opera House), Cherevichki (Garsington Opera), A Midsummer Night's Dream (ROH); *Awards* McColl Arts Fndn Travel Bursary 1990, Fringe First Award Edinburgh Festival (for Further than the Furthest Thing); *Recreations* walking, gardening, house restoration, visiting exhibitions (especially contemporary and installation art); *Style*— Niki Turner; ✉ c/o Clare Vidal Hall, 57 Carthew Road, London W6 0DU (tel 020 8741 7647, fax 020 8741 9459)

TURNER, Prof Raymond; s of Mrs Winifred Howe; *b* 28 April 1947; *Career* prof of computer sci Univ of Essex 1985– (lectr 1973–85, dean Grad Sch 1999–); Sloan fell in cognitive sci Univ of Mass 1982 (sr res fell 1986 and 1989), visiting prof Univ of Rochester NY 1982, visiting fell Centre for Study of Language and Information Stanford Univ Calif 1984 (conslt in sci 1982), visiting prof Univ of Texas Austin 1987; *Books* Logics for Artificial Intelligence (1984), Truth and Modality for Knowledge Representation (1990), Constructive Foundations for Functional Languages; *Style*— Prof Raymond Turner; ✉ Department of Computer Science, University of Essex, Colchester, Essex CO4 3SQ (e-mail turnr@essex.ac.uk)

TURNER, Raymond Edward; *b* 3 August 1946; *Educ* Fairfax HS Southend, Braintree and Chelmsford Tech Coll (HNC), Leeds Coll of Art (BA), Guildhall Univ (Dr Technol); *m* 16 Aug 1969, Sandra Rosemary; 2 da (Alice b 27 Feb 1971, Coral b 6 April 1973); *Career* sr creative designer Gillette Industries 1974–77; Kilkenny Design - Nat Design Authy of Ireland: ind design mangr 1978–80, mangr of design 1980–83, head of design consultancy and asst chief exec 1983–85; design dir London Regnl Transport 1985–88; Wolff Olins: divnl md 1988–90, dir and princ 1990–92; design mgmnt conslt to Eurotunnel and IBM-UK; gp design dir BAA plc 1995– (design dir 1993–95); memb: Advsy Bd Bank of England, Design Mgmnt Inst Boston; chm Bd of Govrs Design Dimension; FCSD, FRSA; *Recreations* outdoor pursuits and the arts; *Style*— Raymond Turner, Esq; ✉ Group Design Director, BAA plc, 130 Wilton Road, London SW1V 1LQ (tel 020 7932 6758, fax 020 7932 6811, e-mail Raymond_Turner@baa.co.uk)

TURNER, Richard Keith; OBE (2007); s of Richard Louis Turner, and Queenie Kate Turner; *b* 2 October 1944, London; *Educ* E Barnet GS, Univ of Leeds (BSc, MSc); *m* 1968, Jenny Georgina, *née* Whitehead; 2 s (Richard, Simon (twins) b 1969), 1 da (Julie b 1973); *Career* grad engr Herts CC 1965–67, sr engr Leeds CC 1967–73; Freight Transport Assoc: highways and traffic advsr 1973–83, dir of planning 1983–95, dep DG 1995–2000, ceo 2001–; memb Cmmn for Integrated Transport 2004–; CEng 1972, MICE 1972, FIHT 1980, FILT 1993; *Recreations* big DIY, cycling, swimming; *Clubs* RAC; *Style*— Richard Turner, Esq, OBE; ✉ Freight Transport Association, Hermes House, St John's Road, Tunbridge Wells, Kent TN4 9UZ (tel 01892 552281, fax 01892 552371, e-mail rturner@fta.co.uk)

TURNER, Richard Timmis; CMG (2002), OBE (1978); s of Dr John Richard Timmis Turner (d 2003), and Alison Elizabeth, *née* Bythell (d 2003); *b* 17 August 1942; *Educ* Shrewsbury, Univ of Manchester (BA); *m* 11 Sept 1982, Margaret Rose Mary, da of Dr Ivor Corbett (d 1982); 2 da (Catherine b 1983, Rebecca b 1985); *Career* joined Rolls-Royce Ltd 1965, commercial mangr Rolls-Royce Inc NY 1971–74, mktg exec civil engines Rolls-Royce Ltd 1977, commercial dir civil engines Rolls-Royce plc 1989–91 (gp mktg dir 1988–91), dir Rolls-Royce plc 1992–2002 (re-joined as gp mktg dir 1991); non-exec dir: Corus Gp plc 1994–2004, Senior plc 1996–2004; memb: Cncl Soc of Br Aerospace Companies 1992–2002 (pres 1994–95), Bd Br Trade Int 1999–2003 (chm Business Advsy Panel 1999–2003), Bd Nat Campaign for the Arts 2006–; MInstD, FRAeS; *Recreations* opera, music, rugby; *Clubs* Athenaeum; *Style*— Richard Turner, Esq, CMG, OBE; ✉ 45 Clarendon Road, London W11 4JD (tel and fax 020 7727 7697, e-mail richardturner45@yahoo.co.uk)

TURNER, Robert Lockley; s of Capt James Lockley-Turner, OBE (d 1954), and Maud Beatrice, *née* Hillyard (d 1993); *b* 2 September 1935; *Educ* Clifton, St Catharine's Coll Cambridge (MA); *m* 5 Oct 1963, Jennifer Mary, da of Alan Guy Fishwick Leather, TD, of Tarporley, Cheshire; 1 s (Guy Lockley b 1967), 1 da (Claire Henrietta b 1969); *Career* barr (bencher Gray's Inn 2000); cmmnd Gloucestershire Regt 1959, Army Legal Serv 1959–66 (Maj 1962); in practice Midland & Oxford Circuit 1967–84, recorder of the Crown Court 1981–84, Sr Master Queen's Bench Div of Supreme Court 1996– (Master 1984–), Queen's Remembrancer 1996–; assessor Access to Justice Inquiry 1994–96; prescribed offr for election petitions 1996–; advsr to Law Reform Cmmn Malta 1993; pres High Court Enforcement Offrs Assoc; memb: Notarial Bd, Judges Cncl 2002–; hon sr steward Westminster Abbey 1985–; tstee Soldiers of Gloster Museum; Hon DLL UWE; Freeman City of London 1997, Liveryman Worshipful Co of Scriveners 1997, Liveryman Worshipful Co of Goldsmiths; Hon FICM (also pres); *Publications* The Office and Functions of Queen's Bench Masters (1990), Chitty and Jacobs Queen's Bench Forms (ed jtly, 1992), High Court Litigation Manual (conslt ed, 1992), The Annual Practice (ed, 1995), Supreme Court Practice (ed jtly, 1997), Atkin's Court Forms (chief advsy ed, 1997–), Civil Procedure (2000–07); *Recreations* anglo-saxons, granddaughters; *Clubs* Army and Navy; *Style*— Robert Turner, Esq; ✉ Royal Courts of Justice, Strand, London WC2A 2LL

TURNER, Roger Burton; s of late Jack Burton Turner, of Soham, Cambs, and Jean, *née* Trevor; *b* 28 July 1947; *Educ* Hawes Down Co Secdy Sch, KCL (BD, MTh), Inst of Educn Univ of London (PGCE), Univ of Kent (MA), Inns of Court Sch of Law, Coll of Law, Birkbeck Coll Univ of London; *m* 13 April 1998, Jennifer, da of late Dr Harry Bound, of Guernsey; *Career* asst master Ashford GS 1972–77, lectr in New Testament studies La Sainte Union Coll of Higher Educn Southampton 1977–80, called to the Bar Gray's Inn 1982, in practice SE Circuit 1983–99, admitted slr 1999, slr-advocate (higher courts criminal) 1999, conslt Wainwright Cummins 1999–2000, conslt Foreman Young 2000–03, conslt Dalton Holmes Gray 2003–; visiting research fell Inst of Historical Research Univ of London 1995–96; art critic Guernsey Press and Star 2005–; contrib: New Dictionary of National Biography (articles on Jacobites and eighteenth century lawyers); contrib symposium The Earl of Burlington and His Politics 1995; pres W London Law Soc 2003–04; memb Catholic Writers' Guild; *Publications* Manchester and the '45: a study of Jacobitism in context (1996), Chaplains in the Household of Lord Burlington 1715–53, in Lord Burlington - The Man and His Politics: Questions of Loyalty (1998); author of various articles about exhbns; *Recreations* watercolour painting, history of art (esp 17th and 18th Century), reading, composing light verse; *Clubs* Lansdowne; *Style*— Roger Turner, Esq; ✉ 26 Evesham Road, London N11 2RN (tel 020 8368 1430, fax 020 8368 6144, e-mail roger.turner@ukonline.co.uk)

TURNER, Simon Andrew; s of Ernest Neville Turner (d 1982), of Grimsby, Lincs, and Joyce, *née* Frow; *b* 9 October 1954; *Educ* Brigg GS, Sidney Sussex Coll Cambridge (BA, dep pres Student Union, Cncl of the Senate student rep); *m* 9 June 1984, Nancy Katherine, da of James Baird, of Tuscaloosa, Alabama; 2 s (Christopher James b 15 April 1985, John Michael b 10 Sept 1986), 1 da (Lindsay Katherine b 4 May 1990); *Career* trainee accountant George Angus Ltd fluid seals factory Wallsend 1978–79; Procter & Gamble: brand asst UK 1979–82, brand mangr Switzerland 1982–84, brand mangr Holland 1985–86, assoc advtg mangr Belgium 1986–87; bd mktg dir Coca-Cola GB 1988–90, mangr New Product Devpt The Coca-Cola Co Atlanta 1990–93, mktg dir Van Den Bergh Foods Ltd 1993–97, md Philips Consumer Electronics UK Ltd 1997–99, md PC World 1999–2004 (dep md 1999), gp md computing and communications Dixons Gp plc 2004–; *Recreations* family, church, creative writing (none published); *Style*— Simon Turner, Esq

TURNER LAING, Sophie; da of Graham Turner Laing, of Goring-on-Thames, Berks, and Gilly Drummond, *née* Clark; *b* 7 September 1960; *m* 30 May 1987, Carlo Comninos, s of Michael Comninos; 1 s (Alexander b 5 March 1989), 1 da (Marina b 14 Oct 1992); *Career* broadcaster; events co-ordinator Variety Club of GB 1979–80, asst to md K M Campbell Pty Melbourne 1980–82, sales dir Henson Int Television 1982–89, jt fndr, dep md and bd dir HIT Entertainment plc 1989–95, vice-pres broadcasting Flextech Television 1995–98, controller programme acquisition BBC Broadcasting 1998–2003, dir Film Channels and Acquisitions BSkyB 2003–04, dep md Sky Networks 2004, md Entertainment BSkyB 2007; tstee BAFTA, govr Nat Film and Television Sch 2004–; *Clubs* Variety, Mark's; *Style*— Ms Sophie Turner Laing; ✉ Grant Way, Isleworth, Middlesex TW7 5QD (tel 020 7805 8271, fax 020 7805 8130, e-mail sophie.turner-laing@bskyb.com)

TURNER OF ECCHINSWELL, Baron (Life Peer UK 2005), of Ecchinswell in the County of Hampshire; (Jonathan) Adair Turner; s of Geoffrey Vincent Turner, and Kathleen Margaret, *née* Broadhurst (d 1977); *Educ* Hutchesons' GS Glasgow, Glenalmond Sch, Gonville & Caius Coll Cambridge (scholar, MA, chm Cambridge Univ Cons Assoc, pres Cambridge Union); *m* 4 May 1985, Orna Ni Chionna; 2 da (Eleanor Catherine b 18 Nov 1988, Julia Christine b 1 Sept 1991); *Career* Corp Planning Dept BP 1979, Chase Manhattan Bank NA 1979–82; McKinsey & Co (strategic consltts): joined 1982, princ (ptnr) 1988, dir (sr ptnr) 1994; DG CBI 1995–99; vice-chm Merrill Lynch Europe 2000–06; non-exec dir: United Business Media plc 2000–, Netscalibur Ltd 2000–01, Siemens plc 2006–, Standard Chartered plc 2006–; ind advsr HM Govt's Forward Strategy Unit 2001–, chm Ind Pensions Cmmn 2002–06, chm Low Pay Cmmn 2003–06; chair ESRC 2007– (memb 2003–07), memb Mgmnt Cncl NIESR; ESU debating tour of USA 1979; visiting prof: LSE, Cass Business Sch, City Univ; tstee: WWF UK, SCF UK; hon degree City Univ; *Books* Just Capital: The Liberal Economy (2001); *Recreations* theatre, opera, skiing; *Style*— The Lord Turner of Ecchinswell

TURNER-WARWICK, Dr Richard Trevor; CBE (1991); s of William Turner-Warwick, FRCS (d 1949), and Dr Joan Margaret Warwick (d 1990); *b* 21 February 1925; *Educ* Bedales, Oriel Coll Oxford (DM, pres OUBC and 1946 Crew), Middlesex Hosp (Broderip scholarship); *m* 21 Jan 1950, Prof Dame Margaret Turner-Warwick, DBE, da of W Harvey Moore, QC (d 1965); 2 da (Gillian (Mrs Bathe) b 1953, Lynne (Prof Turner-Stokes) b 1955); *Career* surgn; Hunterian prof RCS 1957 and 1977; conslt surgn Middlesex Hosp 1960, conslt urologist Royal Nat Orthopaedic Hosp 1962, St Peter's Hosp 1964, King Edward VII Hosp for Officers 1964, Royal Prince Alfred Hosp Sydney 1978, Robert Luff Fndn fell in reconstructive urology 1990–, numerous scientific pubns and contrib to urological and reconstructive surgical texts; memb: Cncl RCS 1978–92, Cncl RCOG 1990–92; Freeman City of London, Liveryman Worshipful Soc of Apothecaries; Hon DSc NY 1985, Hon FRACS 1986, Hon FACS 1997; memb American Assoc of Genito-Urinary Surgns 1978, fell Australasian Urological Soc 1987; Hon FRSM 2003; FRCS 1952, FACS 1978, FRCP 1987, FRCOG 1990; *Recreations* family, fishing, gardening; *Clubs* Vincent's (Oxford), Leander, The Houghton; *Style*— Dr Richard Turner-Warwick, CBE; ✉ Pynes House, Thorverton, Exeter EX5 5LT (tel 01392 861173)

TURNOR, Richard William Corbet; s of Maj Anthony Richard Turnor, CBE, DL, and Joyce Winnifred, *née* Osborn; *b* 15 March 1956; *Educ* Maidwell Hall Sch, Eton, Keble Coll Oxford (BA); *m* 31 Dec 1985, Louisa Mary, da of Andrew Garden Duff Forbes; 1 s (William Michael Francis b 1988), 2 da (Elizabeth Beatrice b 1990, Rosalind Mary b 1993); *Career* admitted slr 1980; Allen & Overy: joined 1979, ptnr 1985–2007, memb Private Client Dept and Commercial Tst and Partnerships Gp; chm Assoc of Partnership Practitioners 2001–04, memb Law Soc Regulations Review Working Pty 1999–2003; memb Law Soc 1981; tstee Royal Marsden Cancer Campaign 2002–07; *Recreations* conservation, growing trees, field sports, skiing; *Style*— Richard Turnor, Esq; ✉ Allen & Overy LLP, One Bishops Square, London E1 6AO (e-mail richard.turnor@allenovery.com)

TUROK, Prof Neil Geoffrey; s of Ben Turok, of Cape Town, South Africa, and Mary, *née* Butcher; *b* 16 November 1958, Johannesburg, South Africa; *Educ* Churchill Coll Cambridge (BA), Imperial Coll London (PhD); *m* 1992, Corinne Squire; 1 da (Ruby b 24 Sept 1992); *Career* postdoctoral fell Inst for Theoretical Physics Santa Barbara 1983–85; Imperial Coll London: advanced research fell 1985–87, reader in theoretical physics 1991–92; assoc scientist Fermilab Chicago 1987–88; Princeton Univ: asst prof of physics 1988–91, assoc prof 1992–94, full prof 1994–96; prof of mathematical physics Univ of Cambridge 1997–; extraordinary prof of physics Univ of Stellenbosch South Africa 2003; fndr African Inst for Mathematical Sciences 2003; author of over 150 scientific papers and ed of several books; James Clerk Maxwell Medal 1992; FInstP 1992; *Recreations* nature, jazz; *Style*— Prof Neil Turok; ✉ Centre for Mathematical Sciences, Cambridge CB3 0WA (tel 01223 337872, fax 01223 766883, e-mail n.g.turok@damtp.cam.ac.uk)

TURTON, Eugenie Christine (Genie); CB (1996); da of Arthur Turton (d 1973), and Georgina, *née* Fairhurst (d 2005); *b* 19 February 1946; *Educ* Nottingham Girls HS (GPDST), Girton Coll Cambridge (MA); *Career* princ private sec to Sec of State for Tport 1978–80, memb Channel Link Financing Group Midland Bank 1981–82, head Machinery of Govt Div Cabinet Office 1982–85, dep sec DOE 1991–94 (under sec 1986–91), dir Citizen's Charter Unit Cabinet Office 1994–97, dir Govt Office for London 1997–2000; DG: DETR/DTLR 2000–02, ODPM 2002–04; non-exec dir: Woolwich Building Soc 1987–91, Wates Gp 2004–, Rockpools Ltd; memb Cncl City Univ 2001–04; tstee: Pilgrim Tst 1991–, Horniman Museum 2002–, Dulwich Picture Gallery 2004–, Historic Houses Assoc 2004–, AA Motoring Tst 2005–07; *Recreations* music, books, painting; *Style*— Mrs Genie Turton, CB

TURVEY, Peter James; s of late Douglas Ronald Turvey, of Croydon, and late Kathleen Mildred, *née* Smith; *b* 9 May 1943; *Educ* Whitgift Sch, BNC Oxford (MA); *m* 23 Oct 1965, (Norah) Louise, da of late Dr Peter O'Flynn, of Croydon; 3 da (Marie-Louise b 1967, Caroline b 1972, Fiona b 1975), 1 s (Andrew b 1968); *Career* asst gen mangr Swiss Re (UK) 1972–87, princ William M Mercer 1987–94, md Gerling Global Re 1995–2004; vice-pres Inst of Actuaries 1988–91 (hon sec 1984–86), chm Staple Inn Actuarial Soc 1988–90; memb Ct of Assts Worshipful Co of Actuaries (Master 1990–91); FIA 1968; *Recreations* skiing, bridge, travelling; *Style*— Peter Turvey, Esq; ✉ mobile 07785 244937, e-mail peterturvey@waitrose.com

TURVEY, Timothy John (Tim); s of Raymond Hilton Turvey, of Oxford (d 1995), and Mary, *née* Drown; *b* 13 October 1947, London; *Educ* Monkton Combe Sch Bath, UC Cardiff (BSc), Univ of Bath (DipEd); *m* 1 May 1993, Dr Janet Hilary Webster; 1 s (James Christopher Corke-Webster b 18 May 1987); *Career* asst master The Edinburgh Acad 1970–75, head of biology and dir of studies Monkton Combe Sch 1975–90; The Hulme GS Oldham: dep head 1990–95, headmaster 1995–2000; headmaster The King's Sch Chester 2000–07; chief examiner Assessment and Qualifications Alliance, conslt ed Longmans, chm Ind Schs Cncl Teacher Induction Panel; memb: Common Entrance Sci Panel, Cncl SHA (chm NW area), Ctee HMC, Ct Univ of Manchester; CBiol 1978, FIBiol 1993 (MIBiol 1978), FLS 1984; *Publications* Gas Exchange and Transport in Plants (ed, 1985), Biology Study Guide I (ed, 1985), Biology Teachers' Guide I (ed, 1985), Inheritance (1986), GCSE Dual Award Balanced Science (1988), Nuffield Co-ordinated Sciences: Biology (ed, 1988), Nuffield Co-ordinated Sciences: Teachers' Guide (contrib, 1988), Biology Course Guide (ed, 1994), Biology Projects and Investigations (ed, 1994), Biology Foundation Unit (ed, 1994), The Entitlement Curriculum in Independent Schools (1995); *Recreations* theatre, cooking; *Clubs* Cheshire Pitt, East India, Chester Business, Leander; *Style*— Tim Turvey, Esq; ✉ 5 Plowley Close, Didsbury, Manchester M20 2DB (tel 07771 801054, e-mail timturvey@btinternet.com)

TURZYNSKI, Gregory Michael Stefan (Greg); s of Leon Dominik Turzynski, of Piltdown, E Sussex, and Olivia Lilian, *née* Ball (d 2002); *b* 16 June 1959; *Educ* St Mary's RC Sch, St Ignatius Coll, Bedford Coll London (BSc); *m* 25 June 1993, Kim, da of Sidney Burgess; *Career* Young & Rubicam advtg: joined 1982, gp buying mangr 1986–90, broadcast dir 1990–92, dep media dir 1992–94, media dir 1994–96; md Optimedia 2002– (managing ptnr 1996–2002); *Style*— Greg Turzynski, Esq

TUSA, Sir John; kt (2003); s of John Tusa, OBE (d 1994), and Lydia, *née* Sklenarova (d 1997); *b* 2 March 1936; *Educ* Gresham's, Trinity Coll Cambridge (BA); *m* 1960, Ann Hilary, da of Stanley Dowson, of Lancs; 2 s (Sash, Francis); *Career* BBC: presenter Newsnight (BBC 2) 1980–86, presenter Timewatch (BBC 2) 1982–84, md BBC World Service 1986–92, presenter One O'Clock News 1993–95; md Barbican Centre 1995–2007; pres Wolfson Coll Cambridge 1993; chm Advsy Ctee Govt Art Collection until 2003, a vice-chm London Int String Quartet Competition 1995–, chm Univ of the Arts London 2007–, chm Victoria and Albert Museum 2007–; memb Bd: English National Opera 1996–2003, Design Museum 1998–2000; tstee: Nat Portrait Gallery 1988–2000, Br Museum 2000– (dep chm 2004–), Somerset House 2004–06, Turquoise Mountain Tst 2006–; former tstee: Thomson Fndn, Wigmore Hall Tst (chm 1999–); hon memb Royal Acad of Music and the Guildhall Sch of Music and Drama 1999; Freeman City of London 1997; Hon LLD Univ of London 1993, Hon DUniv Heriot-Watt 1994, Hon DLitt City Univ 1997, Hon DUniv Essex 2006; Hon ISM 2001, Hon FRIBA 2001; Knight First Class Order of the White Rose of Finland 1997; *Awards* RTS Journalist of the Year 1984, BAFTA Richard Dimbleby Award 1984, Harvey Lee Award BPG Radio Awards 1991, RTS Presenter of the Year 1995; *Books* The Nuremberg Trial (co-author with Ann Tusa, 1984), The Berlin Blockade (co-author with Ann Tusa, 1988), Conversations with the World (1990), A World in Your Ear (1992), Art Matters: Reflecting on Culture (1999), On Creativity - Interviews Exploring the Process (2003), The Janus Aspect: Artists in the Twenty-First Century (2005), Engaged with the Arts@ Writings from the Frontline (2007); *Recreations* tennis, opera, listening; *Style*— Sir John Tusa; ✉ 16 Canonbury Place, London N1 2NN (tel 020 7704 2451); Barbican Arts Centre, Silk Street, London EC2Y 8DS (tel 020 7382 7001)

TUSHINGHAM, Rita; da of John Tushingham, of Liverpool, and Enid Ellen, *née* Lott; *b* 14 March 1942; *Educ* La Sagesse Convent Liverpool; *m* 1, 1 Dec 1962 (m dis 1976), Terence William Bicknell; 2 da (Dodonna b 1 May 1964, Aisha b 16 June 1971); *m* 2, 27 Aug 1981 (m dis 1996), Ousama Rawi, s of Najib El-Rawi, of Geneva, Switzerland; *Career* actress; began career Liverpool Repertory Theatre 1958; *Television* incl: Bread 1988, Dante and Beatrice in Liverpool 1989, Sunday Pursuit 1990, Dieter Gütt ein Journalist 1991, The Stretford Wives 2002, New Tricks 2005, Miss Marple - The Sittaford Mystery

T

2005, Angel Cake 2006; *Radio* Patty and Chip's with Scrap's 1997, Margo Beyond the Box 2003; *Film* A Taste of Honey (first film) 1961, The Girl with Green Eyes 1965, The Knack 1965, Doctor Zhivago 1966, The Trap 1967, The Guru 1968, Bedsitting Room 1969, A Judgement in Stone 1986, Resurrected 1988, Hard Days Hard Nights 1989, Paper Marriage 1991, The Rapture of Deceit 1991, Desert Lunch 1992, Hamburg Poison (for TV) 1992, An Awfully Big Adventure 1994, The Boy From Mercury 1995, Under the Skin 1996, A Night with Joan (for TV) 1997, Swing 1998, Out of Depth 1998, Home Ground 2000, Shadow Play (for TV) 2001, Being Julia 2003, Loneliness and the Modern Pentathalon 2004, Puffball 2006, The Hideout 2006, There For Me 2007; *Awards* incl: Cannes Film Festival Award for Best Actress, New York Film Critics' Award, Golden Globe Award (for A Taste of Honey); Variety Club of GB Best Actress Award (for The Girl with Green Eyes), Mexican Film Festival Award for Best Actress (for The Knack); *Recreations* incl: care and protection of animals, cooking, painting, gardening; *Style*— Miss Rita Tushingham; ✉ c/o Triona Adams, International Artistes, 4th Floor, Holborn Hall, 193–197 High Holborn, London WC1V 7BD (tel 020 7025 0600, fax 020 7404 9865)

TUTSSEL, Glenn Gifford; s of J H Tutssel, of Barry, Glamorgan, and C I Tutssel (d 1992); *b* 2 May 1951; *Educ* Barry Boys Comp, W of England Coll of Art, London Coll of Printing (BA); *m* 1976, Jane Alison, da of P Bowles; 1 da (Lauren May b 1982), 1 s (Leon Paul b 1988); *Career* designer/dir Lock Pettersen 1974–84; creative dir Michael Peters plc 1984–92, Tutssels 1993– (estab holding co The Brand Union with Lambie-Nairn & Co 1997); external examiner: Univ of Dundee 1990–95, Univ of Plymouth 1995–; memb Exec Ctee D&AD; D&AD Silver Awards 1984, 1987, 1990 and 2001, Communication Arts Awards (USA) 1981, 1984, 1985, 1990, 1991, 1992, 1996 and 1998, Clio Awards (USA) 1988, 1989, 1990 and 1997, Br Design Effectiveness Awards (for brands and literature) 1995, Gold Studio Awards (Canada) 1989 and 1990 and Silver Studio Awards 1990 and 1991; memb: Sportsman's Assoc, Nat Small-Bore Rifle Assoc, Br Western Soc, Nat Bit Spur and Saddle Collectors' Assoc (USA), Royal Mail Stamp Advsy Ctee; *Recreations* formerly judo (First Dan aged 16); *Clubs* Teddington Cricket, Ham and Petersham Rifle; *Style*— Glenn Tutssel, Esq; ✉ Tutssels, 42 Cross Deep, Strawberry Hill, Middlesex TW1 4RA (tel 020 8892 1379, fax 020 8288 9719, e-mail tutsells@macunlimited.net)

TUTSSEL, Mark Christopher; s of Stanley Ernest Tutssel, of Barry, S Wales; *Educ* Barry Boys' Comp Sch, Cardiff Coll of Art & Design (DipAD, Harrison Cowley advtg fell); *m* Julie Elizabeth, da of Dennis James Cripps; 1 s (Lewis James); *Career* jr art dir Saatchi & Saatchi advtg 1980, art dir MWK/Aspect 1981–85; Leo Burnett Ltd: art dir 1986–89, creative gp head 1989–91, assoc creative dir 1992–93, bd creative dir 1994–98, jt exec creative dir 1998–2002, vice-chm/dep chief creative offr Leo Burnett USA 2002–05, vice-chm and dep chief creative offr Leo Burnett Worldwide 2005–06, chief creative offr Leo Burnett Worldwide 2006–; winner various advtg industry awards incl: The Cannes Grand Prix, 30 Cannes Lions, 2 Eurobest Grand Prix, 20 Eurobest Golds, 5 D&AD Silvers, 7 Campaign Press Silvers, Art Dirs' Club of Europe Gold, 2 Art Dirs' Club of NY Golds, 2 Int Clio Grand Prix, 22 Clio Golds, The British Television Grand Prix, The Int Andy Award of Excellence Grand Prix, 20 Andy Awards, 2 International Addy Grand Prix, 30 Gold Addys, USA Communication Arts Award of Excellence; MSIAD 1980, FRSA; *Recreations* modern art, sport (former Welsh schoolboys champion football and basketball), music, my son; *Clubs* Design and Art Direction, NY One, Soho House; *Style*— Mark Tutssel, Esq; ✉ e-mail mark.tutssel@leoburnett.com

TUTT, Leo Edward; s of Leo Edward Tutt (d 1975), of Sydney, Aust, and Dorothy, *née* McAdam (d 1988); *b* 6 April 1938; *Educ* Knox GS NSW; *m* 26 May 1961, Heather Elphinstone, da of Charles Walter Coombe (d 1965), of Sydney, Aust; 2 s (Leo, James), 1 da (Katherine); *Career* chartered accountant in public practice 1966–73; chm Tutt Bryant Ltd 1973–96 (jt md 1973–74), dir and chief exec Escor Ltd 1974–78, chm and chief exec Bowater Industries Aust 1974–96, dir and chief exec Aust and Far East Rexam plc (formerly Bowater plc) 1978–96; non-exec dep chm Bundaberg Sugar Company Ltd (Aust Listed Co) 1984–91, non-exec dir Friends Provident Life Office 1987–93; dir: State Rail Authy NSW 1989–94, Metway Bank Ltd (Aust Listed Co) 1992–96, Suncorp-Metway Ltd 2007–; chm: MIM Holdings Ltd (Aust Listed Co) 1991–2003, Detroit Diesel-Allison Aust Pty Ltd 1996–2001, Promina Gp Ltd 1996–, Pirelli Cables Aust Ltd 1999–, Internet Travel Gp Ltd 2001–02, Crane Gp Ltd (Aust Listed Co) 2001–; dir Aust Graduate Sch of Business 1999–2004; hon fell Univ of Sydney 1996; FCA 1966, FAIM 1966, FCPA 1994, FAICD 2001; *Recreations* sailing, golf; *Clubs* American, Avondale Golf, Elanora Country, Royal Motor Yacht, Royal Prince Alfred Yacht, Royal Sydney Yacht Squadron, Union (Sydney); *Style*— Leo Tutt, Esq; ✉ Sedlescombe, 58 Prince Alfred Parade, Newport, NSW 2106, Australia (tel 00 61 2 9979 5744, e-mail leo_tutt@promina.com.au)

TUTT, Dr Leslie William Godfrey; s of Charles Leslie Tutt, of London, and Emily Ditcham, *née* Wiseman; *b* 13 October 1921; *Educ* RMCS (pac), Univ of London (MSc, PhD); *Career* actuary and mathematical statistician in private practice; business advsr and conslt to a number of companies; lectures widely to professional bodies and universities in UK, USA, Central and Eastern Europe; contrib numerous res papers and tech articles to actuarial, statistical and fin jls 1950–; Inst of Statisticians: memb Cncl 1968–74 and 1975–81, vice-chm 1981–84, chm 1984–87, vice-pres 1987–93; memb: Exec Ctee Pensions Res Accountants Gp 1976–85, Cncl Nat Assoc Pension Funds 1979–83; Faculty of Actuaries: tutor 1951–98, memb Cncl 1975–78, memb Bd of Examiners 1980–90; examinations assessor CII 1980–2005; Liveryman: Worshipful Co of Loriners 1975, Worshipful Co of Actuaries 1979; awarded Lectureship Dip Dept of Mathematics Moscow State Univ 1997; FFA 1949, FSS 1951, FIS 1951, assoc Soc of Actuaries USA 1968, fell Soc of Actuaries in Ireland 1972, FPMI 1976; *Books* Private Pension Scheme Finance (1970), Pensions and Employee Benefits (contrib, 1973), Pension Schemes, Investment, Communications and Overseas Aspects (1977), Pension Law and Taxation (1985), Financial Aspects of Pension Business (1986), Financial Aspects of Life Business (1987), Financial Services Marketing and Investor Protection (1988), Life Assurance (1988), Pensions (1988), Financial Advisers' Competence Test (jtly, 1989), Taxation and Trusts (1990), Personal Investment Planning (1990), Corporate Investment Planning (1991), Pensions and Insurance Administration (1992), Personal Financial Planning (1995), Pension Law, Administration and Taxation (jtly, 1998), Financial Aspects of Long Term Business (2002); *Recreations* running, bobsleighing, riding the Cresta Run, golf; *Clubs* Athenaeum, City Livery, New (Edinburgh); *Style*— Dr L W G Tutt; ✉ 21 Sandilands, Croydon, Surrey CR0 5DF (tel 020 8654 2995)

TUTT, Sylvia Irene Maud; da of Charles Leslie Tutt, of London, and Emily Ditcham, *née* Wiseman; *Career* chartered sec and administrator in private practice; author of numerous technical articles in professional and financial journals; Inst of Chartered Secs and Administrators: memb Benevolent Fund Mgmnt Ctee 1975–90, memb Cncl 1975–76 and 1980–82, memb Educn Ctee 1980–82, memb Pubns and PR Ctee 1980–82, rep memb Crossways Tst 1977–2003, pres Women's Soc 1975–76 (memb Ctee 1968–71 and 1976–87, hon sec 1971–74, vice-pres 1973–75), chm London Branch 1984–85 (memb Ctee 1974–82 and 1985–87, vice-chm 1982–84); sr examiner: CII 1975–2005, Soc of Financial Advisers 1992–2005; pres: Soroptimist Int of Central London 1976–78 (vice-pres 1974–76), United Wards Club of the City of London 1998–99 (vice-pres 1996–98), Farringdon Ward Club 1999–2000 (vice-pres 1997–99); vice-pres Royal Soc of St George City of London 2003– (vice-chm 2000–01, chm 2001–03); memb Ct City Univ London 2003–; Worshipful Co of Scriveners: Liveryman 1978, memb Ct of Assts 1999–2005, Renter Warden 2005–06, Upper Warden 2006–07, Master 2007–; Freeman Guild of Freemen City of London 1976; Worshipful Co of Chartered Secs and Administrators: Liveryman 1977, memb Ct of Assts 1977–, Jr Warden 1981–82, Sr Warden 1982–83, Master 1983–84, managing tstee Charitable Tst 1978–, memb Fin and Gen Purposes Ctee 1995–2004; FCIS, FRSA, FSS; *Books* Private Pension Scheme Finance (jtly, 1970), Pensions and Employee Benefits (contrib, 1973), Pension Law and Taxation (jtly, 1985), Financial Aspects of Pension Business (jtly, 1986), Financial Aspects of Life Business (jtly, 1987), A Mastership of a Livery Company (1988), Financial Aspects of Long Term Business (1991), Pension Law, Administration and Taxation (jtly, 1998); *Recreations* horse riding, golf, winter sports; *Clubs* City Livery (vice-pres 2000–02, pres 2002–04), Royal Over-Seas League; *Style*— Sylvia I M Tutt; ✉ 21 Sandilands, Croydon, Surrey CR0 5DF(tel 020 8654 2995)

TWEED, Jill (Mrs Hicks); da of late Maj Jack Robert Lowrie Tweed, and Kathleen Janie, *née* Freeth; *b* 7 December 1935; *Educ* Slade Sch of Art (BA); *m* Philip Lionel Sholto Hicks, s of Brig P Hicks; 1 da (Nicola b 1960), 1 s (David b 1971); *Career* sculptor; solo and gp exhibitions incl: Royal Acad 1979, Poole-Willis Gallery NYC 1984, Barbican Centre 1990, Flowers East Gallery 1991, Bruton Street Gallery London 1997–, Messum's London 2004–; cmmns incl: HM Queen Elizabeth Queen Mother 1980, HRH Prince Charles and Lady Diana Spencer 1981, HE The Governor of Guernsey, Hampshire Sculpture Tst 1991; 4m bronze purchased by Hants CC for Caen Normandy (D-Day Remembrance) 1994, other work incl 3m high bronze (The Railwayman) Eastleigh 1995, 3m high bronze (The Bargeman) Sittingbourne Kent 1996, public sculpture (The Maltmaker) Ware Herts 1998, public sculpture (War Meml) for Eastleigh Hants 2000; FRBS, FRSA; *Recreations* horse riding; *Style*— Ms Jill Tweed; ✉ tel 01993 850347; c/o Messum's, 8 Cork Street, London

TWEED, (David) John; s of William Tweed (d 1989), and Margaret, *née* Gittus (d 1984); *b* 14 December 1946; *Educ* The King's Sch Chester, Univ of Manchester (BA, BArch); *m* 26 April 1980, Helen Elspeth Hamilton, da of Dr Frank Hamilton-Leckie, MC, TD, of Monklands, Uddingston, Glasgow; 2 da (Hilary b 1986, Anna b 1994); *Career* currently ptnr Tweed Nuttall Warburton chartered architects Chester (founded as John Tweed Assocs); cmmns incl: masterplanning phase 1 Old Port of Chester Regeneration Programme, major housing schemes for Wainhomes, Crosby Homes, Taylor Woodrow Devpts and Bellway Homes, Scout HQ Chester (Civic Award) 2000; RIBA: memb Cncl NW Region 1983–87 and 1994–98, memb NW Educn Cee 1987–, chm NW Practice Ctee 1994–98; chm Mgmnt Ctee Architects Benevolent Soc Claverton Ct Chester 1985–89, pres Cheshire Soc of Architects 1985–86, memb Cncl The Architects Benevolent Soc 1986–; chm: Chester Historic Bldgs Preservation Tst 1991–92, Chester Sustainable Environmental Educn Network 1997–; tstee Chester Civic Tst 2000–; RIBA 1974, ACIArb 1983, FRSA 1995; *Recreations* family, rowing, sailing, gardening, boatbuilding; *Clubs* Royal Chester Rowing; *Style*— John Tweed, Esq; ✉ Ivy House, Hob Hill, Tilston, Malpas, Cheshire SY14 7DU (tel 01829 250301); Duncraig House, Salen, Argyll PH36 4JN; Tweed Nuttall Warburton, Chartered Architects, Chapel House, City Road, Chester CH1 3AE (tel 01244 310388, fax 01244 325643, e-mail john.tweed@tnw-architecture.co.uk)

TWEED, Paul; s of William Park Tweed (d 2003), and Mary Elizabeth, *née* Loudon (d 2004); *b* 6 June 1955, Belfast; *m* 11 July 2003, Selena Mary, *née* Kerins; 1 s (Conor Duncan b 22 March 1983), 1 da (Shannon Julia b 9 March 1987); *Career* admitted slr: NI, England and Wales, Repub of Ireland; slr specialising in defamation and defence litigation; sr ptnr Johnsons Slrs; clients incl: Liam Neeson, Britney Spears, Jennifer Lopez, Van Morrison, Whitney Houston, Steve Bing, Chris de Burgh, Patrick Kielty and The Corrs; acted in the case B J Eastwood v Barry McGuigan resulting in highest libel award in Northern Irish legal history (£450,000); memb: Law Soc of NI 1978, Law Soc of England and Wales 1992, Law Soc of Ireland 1999; *Recreations* running, tennis, squash, boxing; *Style*— Paul Tweed, Esq; ✉ Johnsons, Johnson House, 50–56 Wellington Place, Belfast BT1 6GF (tel 028 9024 0183, fax 028 9023 3266)

TWEEDIE, Prof Sir David Philip; kt (1994); s of Aidrian Ian Tweedie, of Doncaster, and Marie Patricia, *née* Phillips; *b* 7 July 1944; *Educ* Grangemouth HS, Univ of Edinburgh (BCom, PhD); *m* 6 June 1970, Janice Christine, da of George Haddow Brown; 2 s (Ross Steven b 10 June 1976, Mark David b 25 May 1977); *Career* apprentice Mann Judd Gordon & Co Chartered Accountants Glasgow 1969–72, CA 1972; Univ of Edinburgh: lectr Dept of Accounting and Business Methods 1973–78, dir of studies 1973–75, assoc dean Faculty of Social Scis 1975–78; tech dir Inst of Chartered Accountants of Scotland 1978–81, nat res ptnr KMG Thomson McLintock 1982–87, nat tech ptnr KPMG Peat Marwick McLintock 1987–90; chm: Accounting Standards Bd 1990–2000 (ex officio memb Fin Reporting Cncl), Urgent Issues Task Force 1990–2000, Int Accounting Standards Bd 2001–, Standards Advsy Cncl 2001–05; Lancaster Univ: visiting prof of accounting Int Centre for Res in Accounting (ICRA) 1978–88, tstee ICRA 1982–93, dep chm Bd of Tstees ICRA 1986–93; visiting prof of accounting Dept of Economics Univ of Bristol 1988–2000, visiting prof of accounting Mgmnt Sch Univ Edinburgh 2000–; memb Cncl ICAEW 1989–91 (memb Auditing Res Fndn 1988–90), chm CCAB Auditing Practices Ctee 1989–90 (vice-chm 1986–88, memb 1985–90), UK and Irish rep Int Auditing Practices Ctee 1983–88, UK and Irish rep International Accounting Standards Ctee 1995–2000; awarded ICAEW Founding Societies Centenary Award 1997; CIMA Award 1998; Hon DSc(Econ) Univ of Hull 1993, Hon DSc(SocSci) Univ of Edinburgh 2001; Hon LLD: Lancaster Univ 1993, Univ of Exeter 1997, Univ of Dundee 1998; Hon DLitt Heriot-Watt Univ 1996; Hon DBA: Napier Univ 1999, Oxford Brookes Univ 2004; Hon FIA 2000, FRSE 2001, Hon FSIP 2004, Hon FCCA 2005; *Books* The Private Shareholder and The Corporate Report (with T A Lee, 1977), Financial Reporting Inflation and The Capital Maintenance Concept (1979), The Institutional Investor and Financial Information (with T A Lee, 1981), The Debate on Inflation Accounting (with G Whittington, 1984); *Style*— Prof Sir David Tweedie; ✉ International Accounting Standards Board, 30 Cannon Street, London EC4M 6XH (tel 020 7246 6410, fax 020 7246 6411)

TWEEDSMUIR, 3 Baron (UK 1935), of Elsfield, Co Oxford; William James de l'Aigle Buchan; s of 1 Baron Tweedsmuir, GCMG, GCVO, CH, PC (d 1940; the author John Buchan), and Susan Charlotte (d 1977), da of Capt Hon Norman de l'Aigle Grosvenor; suc bro, 2 Baron Tweedsmuir, CBE, CD (d 1996); *b* 10 January 1916; *Educ* Eton, New Coll Oxford; *m* 1, 1939 (m dis 1946), Nesta Irene, da of Lt-Col C D Crozier; 1 da (Hon Perdita Caroline (Hon Mrs Connolly) b 1940); m 2, 1946 (m dis 1960), Barbara Howard (d 1969), da of Ernest Nash Ensor; 3 da (Hon Deborah Charlotte (Baroness Stewartby) b 1947, Hon Laura Mary Clare (Hon Mrs David Crackanthorpe), Hon Ursula Margaret Bridget (Hon Mrs Wide) (twins) b 1953), 3 s (Hon John William Howard de l'Aigle (Toby) b 1950, Hon (Charles Walter) Edward Ralph) b 1951, Hon James Ernest Buchan b 1954); m 3, 1960, Sauré Cynthia Mary, da of late Maj G E Tatchell, Royal Lincs Regt; 1 s (Hon Alexander Edward b 1961); *Heir* s, Hon Toby Buchan; *Career* Sqdn Ldr RAF Vol Reserve; *Books* John Buchan, a Memoir (biography of father, 1982), The Rags of Time (autobiography, 1990), three novels; *Clubs* Travellers; *Style*— The Rt Hon the Lord Tweedsmuir

TWEEDY, Colin David; LVO (2003), OBE (2000); s of Clifford Harry Tweedy, of Abbotsbury, Dorset, and Kitty Audrey, *née* Matthews; *b* 26 October 1953; *Educ* City of Bath Boys' Sch, St Catherine's Coll Oxford (MA); *Career* mangr Thorndike Theatre Leatherhead 1976–78, corp fin offr Guinness Mahon 1978–80, asst dir Streets Financial PR 1980–83, chief exec Arts & Business (Assoc for Business Sponsorship of the Arts (ABSA)) 1983–; chm Comité Européen pour le Rapprochement de l'Economie et de la Culture (CEREC); memb: UK Nat Ctee Euro Cinema and TV Year 1988–89, Cncl Japan Festival 1991, Cncl for Charitable Support, Global Advsy Bd of the Mariinsky Theatre under the patronage of The Prince of Wales, Cncl NMSO (Nat Musicians Symphony Orch); memb Advsy Panel Whitbread Book Awards; judge: PR Week Awards, Art & Work Awards 2002; tstee: The Ideas Fndn, Serpentine Gallery, Next Generation Fndn; dir: Covent Garden Int Festival 1995–2001, Oxford Stage Co, Mariinsky Theatre Tst; former dir Crusaid; selector Discerning Eye 2000 exhibition; Hollis Sponsorship Personality of the Year 2003; Freeman City of London 1978; CCMI 2002, FRSA; *Books* A Celebration of Ten Years' Business Sponsorship of the Arts (1987); *Recreations* the arts in general, opera, theatre and contemporary art in particular, food, Italy and travel; *Clubs* Groucho, Home House, Hospital; *Style*— Colin Tweedy, Esq, LVO, OBE; ✉ Arts & Business, Nutmeg House, 60 Gainsford Street, Butlers Wharf, London SE1 2NY (tel 020 7378 8143, fax 020 7407 7527, e-mail head.office@aandb.org.uk)

TWEMLOW, William Antony (Tony); s of Richard Lawrence Twemlow (d 1994), of West Kirby, Wirral, and Sylvia Doreen Twemlow (d 1991); *b* 2 December 1943; *Educ* Calday Grange GS, Downing Coll Cambridge (MA); *m* 12 Oct 1968, Margaret, da of William Thompson Scollay (d 1979); 2 s (Roy William b 15 Dec 1971, James Antony b 28 Sept 1982), 1 da (Laura Jane b 6 July 1973); *Career* Cuff Roberts: articled clerk 1965–68, asst slr 1968–71, ptnr 1971–, managing ptnr 1986–93; licensed insolvency practitioner 1987; chm: Liverpool Young Slrs Gp 1969–70, Young Slrs Gp Law Soc 1978–79, Liverpool Bd of Legal Studies 1988–91; dir Slrs' Benevolent Assoc 1980–91, memb: Law Soc 1968, Liverpool Law Soc 1968, Remuneration and Practice Devpt Ctee Law Soc 1980–92, Insolvency Lawyers Assoc 1989, Insolvency Practitioners Assoc 1990; pres Liverpool Law Soc 1994–95; memb Royal Liverpool Philharmonic Choir 1965–94, dep vice-chm Royal Liverpool Philharmonic Soc 1988–91 (memb Bd 1986–93); dir Hoylake Cottage Hosp Tst Ltd 1989–92; *Recreations* music, tennis; *Style*— Tony Twemlow, Esq

TWIGG, Derek; MP; *b* 9 July 1959; *Educ* Bankfield Sch Widnes, Halton Coll of FE; *Career* former civil servant until 1996; MP (Lab) Halton 1997–; PPS to: min of state for Energy and Euro Competitiveness 1999–2001, Rt Hon Stephen Byers, MP, *qv*, 2001–02; asst Govt whip 2002–04, Parly under sec of state DfES 2004–05, Parly under sec of state Dept of Tport 2005–; chm Halton Constituency Lab Pty 1985–96, chm NW Gp of Labour MPs 1999–2000; memb Public Accounts Ctee 1998–99; cnclr Cheshire CC 1981–85; Halton BC: cnclr 1983–97, chm housing 1987–93, chm fin 1993–96; *Recreations* various sporting activities, hill walking, reading military history; *Style*— Derek Twigg, Esq, MP; ✉ House of Commons, London SW1A 0AA (tel 020 7219 3000, e-mail twiggd@parliament.uk)

TWIGG, Stephen; *b* 25 December 1966; *Educ* Southgate Sch, Balliol Coll Oxford (BA, pres NUS 1990–92); *Career* Amnesty Int, NCVO, research asst to Margaret Hodge, MP, lobbyist Rowland Gp, gen sec Fabian Soc until 1997; MP (Lab) Enfield Southgate 1997–2005; Parly sec Privy Cncl Office 2001–02, Parly under sec of state DfES 2002–04, min of state for schs 2004–05; dir Foreign Policy Centre 2005–; special projects dir Aegis Tst; chair: Progress, Young People Now Fndn; memb: Amicus, Holocaust Educnl Tst; tstee Workers Educn Assoc; cnclr Islington BC 1992–97 (chief whip 1994–96, dep ldr 1996); govr Jubilee Primary Sch; *Style*— Stephen Twigg

TWIGGER, Terry; *b* 21 November 1949; *Educ* Univ of Bristol (BSc); *m*; 2 da; *Career* early career with: Deloitte & Touche, Lucas Aerospace (latterly finance dir); Meggitt plc: dir of finance 1993–95, gp finance dir 1995–2001, memb Bd 1995–, chief exec 2001–; dir: Society of British Aerospace Companies, Phoenix Travel (Dorset) Ltd; FCA, MRAeS; *Recreations* shooting, fishing, sailing; *Style*— Terry Twigger, Esq; ✉ Meggitt plc, Farrs House, Cowgrove, Wimborne, Dorset BH21 4EL (tel 01202 847847, fax 01202 842478)

TWIGGY, *see:* Lawson, Lesley

TWINCH, Richard William; s of Richard Herbert Twinch, of Whitchurch, Salop, and Roma Bayliss, *née* Silver; *b* 29 October 1950; *Educ* Wellington, Clare Coll Cambridge (MA), AA Sch of Architecture (AADipl); *m* Hazel Cecilia, da of James Herbert Merrison (d 1987); 1 s (Oliver b 1975), 2 da (Jemila b 1977, Anna b 1981); *Career* architect and special technol conslt; lectr and tutor Prince of Wales's Inst of Architecture 1992–95, lectr in architecture Oxford Brookes Univ 1996–2000; author of tech software for architects incl: Condensation Control 1981–92, Heat Loss Performance 1983–91; dir: Richard Twinch Design, Chisholme Inst Beshara Sch of Esoteric Educn 1985–2001; commentator to Beshara Magazine 1986–90, lectr and conslt in CAD; MA external examiner Visual and Traditional Arts Unit RCA 1990 and 1991; computer columnist to Building Design magazine 1985–96, author of numerous articles on CAD in architectural press, papers incl Thermal Insulation and Condensation and Building Materials (1988); sign conslt Crowne Plaza Hotel Heathrow 1998; external examiner to Prince's Fndn 2000–01, expert validation assessor Univ of Wales 2000–; projects incl house extensions and conversions in Oxford; finalist Downland Prize 1999; RIBA; *Recreations* listening to music, walking, tennis; *Style*— Richard Twinch, Esq; ✉ 7 Hill Top Road, Oxford OX4 1PB (tel 01865 202108, e-mail twinch@community.co.uk, website www.twinchdesign.co.uk)

TWINE, Derek Milton; CBE (2007); s of Edward Montague Twine (d 1976), of Horley, Surrey, and Winifred May, *née* Milton (d 1993); *b* 1 May 1951; *Educ* Reigate GS, UC of N Wales Bangor (BA); *m* 7 Sept 1974, Rhoda, da of Very Rev R J N Lockhart; 1 da (Nicola b 11 April 1977), 1 s (Paul b 12 Jan 1979); *Career* lectr Univ of Wales 1975–76 (res 1973–75); The Scout Assoc: dir Venture Scout Trg 1976–79, dir of prog 1979–85, exec cmmr (prog and trg) 1985–96, chief exec 1996–; memb Mgmnt Ctee and chm Educn and Standards Nat Youth Agency (NYA) 1991–95; Nat Cncl for Vol Youth Servs (NCVYS): memb Exec Ctee and chm Devpt Project 1979–82, chm Trg Mangrs' Gp 1989–97; memb Youth Panel Nat Tst 1978–85, tstee Whitechapel Fndn, govr Davenant Fndn Sch; author of various articles in youthwork and educnl press; FITD 1987, FIPD 1994, FRSA 2002; *Recreations* church activities, theatre, cooking, cross-country running; *Style*— Derek Twine, Esq, CBE; ✉ The Scout Association, Gilwell Park, Chingford, London E4 7QW (tel 020 8433 7105, fax 020 8433 7108, e-mail derek.twine@scout.org.uk)

TWINING, Prof William Lawrence; Hon QC (2002); s of Baron Twining (Life Peer, d 1967); *b* 1934; *Educ* Charterhouse, BNC Oxford (DCL), Chicago Univ (JD); *m* 1957, Penelope Elizabeth, da of Richard Wall Morris; 1 s, 1 da; *Career* prof of jurisprudence Queen's Univ Belfast 1965–72, prof of law Univ of Warwick 1972–82, Quain prof of jurisprudence UCL 1983–96 (research prof of law 1996–2004, Quain prof of jurisprudence emeritus 2004–); pres Soc of Public Teachers of Law 1978–79, chm Cwlth Legal Educn Assoc 1983–93; Hon LLD: Victoria Univ BC Canada 1980, Univ of Edinburgh 1994, Queen's Univ Belfast 1999, Southampton Inst 2000, York Univ Toronto 2002; foreign hon memb Ammerican Acad of Arts and Sciences 2007; *Books* Karl Llewellyn and the Realist Movement (1973), How to do Things with Rules (jtly, 4 edn 1999), Theories of Evidence - Bentham & Wigmore (1985), Rethinking Evidence (1990, 2 edn 2006), Analysis of Evidence (jtly, 1991, 2 edn 2005), Legal Records in the Commonwealth (jtly), Blackstone's Tower: The English Law School (1994), Law in Context: Enlarging a Discipline (1997), Globalisation and Legal Theory (2000), The Great Juristic Bazaar (2002), Evidence and Inference in History and Law (jt ed, 2003); *Style*— Prof William Twining, QC; ✉ 10 Mill Lane, Iffley, Oxford OX4 4EJ; University College London, Faculty of Laws, Bentham House, 4 Endsleigh Gardens, London WC1H 0EG

TWINN, Dr Ian David; s of David Twinn (d 2005), of Cambridge, and Gwynneth Irene, *née* Ellis; *b* 26 April 1950; *Educ* Netherhall Secdy Modern Sch Cambridge, Cambridge GS, UCW Aberystwyth (BA), Univ of Reading (PhD); *m* 28 July 1973, Frances Elizabeth, da of Godfrey Nall Holtby (d 1988); 2 s (David b 1983, John b 1986); *Career* sr lectr in town planning Poly of the South Bank 1975–83; MP (Cons) Edmonton 1983–97, dir of public affrs ISBA 1998–, MEP (Cons) London 2003–04 (Euro Parly candidate 1999 and 2004); PPS to: Rt Hon Sir Peter Morrison 1985–90, David Trippier as Min of State DOE 1990–92, Sir John Cope as Paymaster-Gen at the Treasy 1992–94; currently vice-chm Br-Caribbean Assoc; Freeman City of London 1981; FRGS (MIBG 1972), FRSA 1989; Cdr Order of Honour (Greece) 2000; *Recreations* antique furniture restoration, collecting second-hand books, bookcase building; *Clubs* RAC; *Style*— Dr Ian Twinn; ✉ 85 Calton Avenue, London SE21 7DF (tel 020 8299 4210, fax 020 8299 4088)

TWISK, Russell Godfrey; *b* 24 August 1941; *Educ* Salesian Coll Farnborough; *m* 1965, Ellen Elizabeth Bambury; 2 da; *Career* writer and journalist; Harmsworth Press: dep ed Golf Illustrated 1960, sub ed Sphere; freelance journalist 1962; BBC: joined Editorial Staff Radio Times 1966, dep ed Radio Times 1971, devpt mangr 1975, ed The Listener 1981–87, ed numerous BBC pubns; ed-in-chief British Reader's Digest 1988–2002 (ed-at-large 2002–06); dir: The Reader's Digest Assoc Ltd 1989–2004, RD Publications 1990–2004; radio critic The Observer 1989–94, writer daily birthday column The Times 2003–; publisher BBC Adult Literacy Project, deviser Radio Times Drama Awards; govr London Coll of Printing 1967–87 (chm 1974 and 1978); chm: The Reader's Digest Tst 1988–98, BSME 1989, Nat Leadership Ctee Charities Aid Fndn 1991; pres Media Soc 1993–95; dir Greenwich and Docklands Int Festival 1997–2002, tstee Christian Responsibility in Public Affairs 1998–; memb PCC 1999–2002; *Recreations* running, map reading, golf; *Clubs* Garrick; *Style*— Russell Twisk, Esq; ✉ The Old Barn, East Harting, Petersfield, Hampshire GU31 5LZ (tel 01730 825769, fax 01730 825725, e-mail rtwisk@aol.com)

TWIST, Stephen John; s of late James Twist, of Darlington, Co Durham, and Kathleen Twist; *b* 26 September 1950; *Educ* Queen Elizabeth GS Darlington, Univ of Liverpool (LLB), Inns of Court Sch of Law London; *m* 4 May 1990, Ann, *née* Stockburn; 1 s (Miles Henry b 16 March 1993); *Career* called to the Bar Middle Temple 1979; in practice: London 1979–88, York 1988–; memb: Hon Soc of Middle Temple, Hon Soc Gray's Inn, North Eastern Circuit, Family Law Bar Assoc, Assoc of Northern Mediators; advsr to constabularies and public authorities on admin law, professional standards, ethics, human rights and firearms; public sector arbitrator and mediator; sometime broadcaster on deafness issues and the law BBC and Channel 4; registered and panel mediator CEDR (former memb Public Sector Working Party), FCIArb 2000; *Publications* ADR Management and Resolution of Complaints in Relation to Police Disputes and Misconduct (1999), A Guide for Panels under the Police (Conduct) Regulations (2004); *Recreations* early music, environmental conservation; *Style*— Stephen Twist, Esq; ✉ York Chambers, 14 Toft Green, York YO1 6JT (tel 01904 620048, fax 01904 610056, website www.yorkchambers.co.uk); Rotterdam House, 116 The Quayside, Newcastle, NE1 3DY (tel 0191 206 4677, fax 0191 206 4172, e-mail suttonbank@btinternet.com, website www.suttonbank.btinternet.co.uk)

TWISTON DAVIES, David James; s of Mervyn Peter Twiston Davies (d 2002), of Somerset, and Isabel Anne, *née* Fox (d 2002), of Montreal, Canada; *b* 23 March 1945; *Educ* Downside; *m* 10 June 1970, Margaret Anne (Rita), da of Francis Gerard Montgomery (d 1978); 3 s (Benedict, James, Huw), 1 da (Bess); *Career* journalist; East Anglian Daily Times 1966–68, Winnipeg Free Press 1968–70; The Daily Telegraph: news sub ed 1970–77, asst literary ed 1977–86, dep obituaries ed 1986–87, letters ed 1987–88, ed Peterborough column 1988–89, letters ed 1989–2001, chief obituary writer 2001–; Freeman City of London; *Books* Canada from Afar: The Daily Telegraph Book of Canadian Obituaries (ed, 1996), The Daily Telegraph Book of Letters (ed, 1998), The Daily Telegraph Book of Military Obituaries (ed, 2003), The Daily Telegraph Book of Naval Obituaries (ed, 2004); *Recreations* defending the reputation of the British Empire; *Clubs* Travellers; *Style*— David Twiston Davies, Esq; ✉ 20 Warwick Park, Tunbridge Wells, Kent TN2 5TB (tel 01892 528292); The Daily Telegraph, 1 Canada Square, Canary Wharf, London E14 5DT (tel 020 7538 7121, fax 020 7538 7166)

TWITCHETT, John Anthony Murray; s of Joseph Ernest James Twitchett (d 1959), of Chigwell, Essex, and Olive Jessie, *née* Lidford (d 1986); *b* 26 July 1932; *Educ* Chigwell Sch; *m* 1, 30 March 1960, Doricka Edith (d 1963), da of late Henry Edmund Palfreman, of London; m 2, 25 Jan 1964 (m dis 1972), Rosemary, da of Joseph Hallam, of Torquay, S Devon; 2 da (Elizabeth Anne b 23 Nov 1964, Caroline Mary b 11 June 1966); *Career* former landowner Woodeaton Oxon; ptnr David John Ceramics 1970–97, curator Royal Crown Derby Museum 1972–97, dir The Antique Ceramic Bureau 1996–; int lectr at venues incl: V&A, Canadian Nat Gallery Ottawa, Royal Ontario Museum Toronto, Musée des Beaux Arts Montréal; first Charles Norman lecture 1996; chm Derby Porcelain Int Soc 1997–2000; life tstee The Royal Crown Derby Museum Trust 1988, tstee The Raven Mason Bd Keele Univ; former memb Ctee Burford and Dist Refugee Aid Soc (resigned 2001); memb: Nat Tst, NFU (resigned 2000); FRSA 1975; *Books* Royal Crown Derby (1976), Derby Porcelain (1980), Landscapes on Derby and Worcester (with Henry Sandon, 1984), Painters and the Derby China Works (with John Murdoch, 1987), London - World City 1800–1840 (contrib exhbn catalogue Essen, 1992), In Account with Sampson Hancock (1996), Derby Porcelain: The Guide (2002); *Recreations* walking; *Style*— John Twitchett, Esq; ✉ Filkins Hall, Filkins Lechlade, Gloucestershire GL7 3JJ

TWIVY, Paul Christopher Barstow; s of Dr Samuel Barstow Twivy (d 2004), of Dunstable, Beds, and Sheila, *née* Webster (d 1993); *b* 19 October 1958; *Educ* Haberdashers' Aske's, Magdalen Coll Oxford (BA); *m* 1, 31 July 1982 (m dis), Martha Mary Ball; 2 s (Samuel b 1985, Joshua b 1988); m 2, 27 Oct 1991, Gabrielle Ruth Guz; 1 s (Max b 1994), 2 da (Eve b 1995, Clara b 1999); *Career* bd dir Hedger Mitchell Stark 1982–83, md Still Price Court Twivy D'Souza Lintas 1985–92, dep chm J Walter Thompson 1992–93, gp chief exec Bates Dorland 1994–96; mktg advsr: BBC 1997–99, New Millennium Experience Co 1997; chm Circus Communications Ltd 1998–2002, chief strategic planning offr McCann-Erickson 2002, dir Twivy Consultancy Ltd 2002–; author; memb Comic Relief; tstee Pilotlight, spokesman for advtg indust; memb Mktg Soc; FIPA; *Recreations* freelance comedy writer, playwright, poetry, reading, swimming, music (guitar and piano); *Clubs* Oxford Union, Groucho; *Style*— Paul Twivy, Esq; ✉ 46 Pattison Road, London NW2 2HJ (tel and fax 020 7794 1610, e-mail paul.twivy@btconnect.com)

TWYMAN, Prof Michael Loton; s of Lawrence Alfred Twyman (d 1980), and Gladys Mary, *née* Williams (d 2001); *b* 15 July 1934; *Educ* Sir George Monoux GS, Univ of Reading (BA, PhD), Trinity Coll Cambridge; *m* 31 July 1958, Pauline Mary, da of Edward Frank Andrews; 2 s (Jeremy James b 9 Oct 1960, Daniel John Soulby b 9 Oct 1966), 1 da (Nicola Clare b 25 Jan 1963); *Career* Univ of Reading: asst lectr in typography and graphic art 1959–62, lectr 1962–71, sr lectr in typography & graphic communication 1971–76, prof and head Dept of Typography & Graphic Communication 1976–98, dir Centre for Ephemera Studies 1993–, prof emeritus 1998–; visiting fell Mellon Center for British Art Yale 1981; chm: ICOGRADA (Int Cncl of Graphic Design Assocs) Working Gp on Graphic Design History 1984–88, Curatorium Int Inst for Information Design Vienna 1989–2002; Assoc Typographique Internationale: chm Ctee for Educn in Letterforms 1974–77, chm Res and Educn Ctee 1991–95, memb Bd of Dirs 1994–99; Printing Historical Soc: memb Ctee 1964–, asst ed Jl 1969–84, chm 1991–2004, vice-pres 2004–; memb Graphic Design Panel Nat Cncl for Diplomas in Art & Design 1971–74; Cncl for Nat Academic Awards: memb Ctee of Art & Design 1978–81, vice-chm Graphic Design Bd 1972–80, memb Sub-Ctee for Res Degrees 1978–83; tstee: Fndn for Ephemera Studies (pres 1999–), Printing Heritage Tst (chm 1999–); Samuel Pepys Medal for Outstanding Contribution to Ephemera Studies 1983, American Printing History Assoc Individual Award for Distinguished Achievement 2007; fell Inst of Printing (FIOP); *Books* John Soulby, printer, Ulverston (1966), Lithography 1800–1850: the techniques of drawing on

T

stone in England and France and their application in works of topography (1970), Printing 1770–1970: an illustrated history of its development and uses in England (1970, reprinted 1998), A Directory of London Lithographic Printers 1800–1850 (1976), Henry Bankes's Treatise on Lithography (1976), The Landscape Alphabet (1986), Early Lithographed Books (1990), Early Lithographed Music (1996), The British Library Guide to Printing: History and Techniques (1998), The Encyclopedia of Ephemera (ed and completed, 2000, reprinted 2001), Breaking the Mould: The First Hundred Years of Lithography (2001), L'Imprimerie: Histore et Techniques (2007); numerous articles in professional jls; *Style*— Prof Michael Twyman; ✉ Department of Typography & Graphic Communication, The University of Reading, 2 Earley Gate, Whiteknights, Reading, Berkshire RG6 6AU (tel 0118 931 8081, fax 0118 935 1680, e-mail lithomn@totalise.co.uk)

TWYMAN, Paul Hadleigh; s of late Lawrence Alfred Twyman, and late Gladys Mary, *née* Williams; *Educ* Chatham House Sch Ramsgate, Univ of Sheffield (BA), LSE (MSc Econ); *Career* schoolmaster 1963–64; Civil Serv: asst princ Bd of Trade 1967–71, memb Secretariat Cmmn on the Third London Airport 1969–71, private sec to sec of state for Trade and Industry 1971–73, princ Anti-Dumping Unit DTI 1976–78, asst sec and head Overseas Projects Gp DTI 1978–81, Civil Aviation Div 1981–83, Dept of Tport 1983, Cabinet Office 1984, under sec and dir Enterprise and Deregulation Unit Dept of Employment 1985–87; econ advsr to chm of Cons Pty and head Econ Section Cons Res Dept 1987, exec chm Political Strategy Ltd 1988–; corp strategy dir Bates UK 1996–99; non-exec dir: Nationwide Building Society 1987–2002 (dir Anglia Building Society 1983 until merger 1987), D'Arcy Masius Benton and Bowles (DMB&B) 1990–96, Connex Rail Ltd 1999–2001; memb Bd Connex Transport UK Ltd 2001–02; Euro Parly candidate Greater Manchester West 1989, cncllr Thanet DC 1991–95; memb Thanet Dist Police Advsy Ctee 1989–99, vice-chair Lambeth Community Police Consultative Gp 2000–02 (hon comptroller 1999–2000); assoc memb Kensington & Chelsea and Westminster HA 1996–2002; tstee Opportunity Int UK 1996–2002; memb: Royal African Soc, African Studies Assoc, Public Mgmnt and Policy Assoc; govr: City of Westminster Coll 1999–2003, London Central LSC 2001–; FIMgt, MCIT, MCIB, FRSA; *Recreations* hill walking, gardening, family and friends, observing gorillas; *Style*— Paul Twyman, Esq

TYDEMAN, John Peter; OBE (2003); s of George Alfred Tydeman (d 1960), of Cheshunt, Herts, and Gladys Florence Beatrice, *née* Brown (d 1982); *b* 30 March 1936; *Educ* Hertford GS, Trinity Coll Cambridge (MA); *Career* 2 Lt 1 Singapore Regt RA 1954–56, served Malaya; drama director; head of drama radio BBC 1986–94 (radio drama prodr 1960–79, asst head radio drama 1979–86); awarded: Prix Italia 1970, Prix Futura 1979 and 1983, Broadcasting Press Guild Award for outstanding radio prodn 1983, Sony Special Award for Servs to Radio 1994; stage prodns incl: Objections to Sex and Violence (Royal Court) 1975, The Bells of Hell (Garrick Theatre) 1977, Falstaff (Fortune Theatre) 1984, Night Must Fall (Haymarket) 1996; *Recreations* swimming, foreign places, theatre; *Clubs* Garrick; *Style*— John Tydeman, Esq, OBE; ✉ 88 Great Titchfield Street, London W1W 6SE (tel and fax 020 7636 3886)

TYDEMAN, Prof William Marcus; s of Henry Marcus Tydeman, MBE (d 1975), of East Malling, Kent, and Elizabeth Mary, *née* Shepherd (d 1988); *b* 29 August 1935; *Educ* Maidstone GS, UC Oxford (MA, MLitt); *m* 29 July 1961, Jacqueline Barbara Anne, da of Robert Lewis Jennison (d 1957); 2 da (Josephine b 1963, Rosalind b 1966); *Career* RCS 1954–56, cmmnd 2 Lt 1955; Univ of Wales Bangor: asst lectr in English 1961–64, lectr 1964–70, sr lectr 1970–83, reader 1983–86, prof 1986–97 (emeritus 1997–), head Dept of English 1983–89, head Sch of English and Linguistics 1989–92; *Books* English Poetry 1400–1580 (ed, 1970), The Theatre in the Middle Ages (1978), Four Tudor Comedies (ed, 1984), Dr Faustus: Text and Performance (1984), English Medieval Theatre 1400–1500 (1986), The Welsh Connection (ed, 1986), The State of the Art: Christopher Marlowe (jtly, 1989), Two Tudor Tragedies (ed, 1992), Christopher Marlowe: the plays and their sources (jtly, 1994), The Bancrofts at the Prince of Wales's Theatre (1996), Oscar Wilde: Salome (jtly, 1996), Medieval European Stage 500–1550 (ed, 2001); *Recreations* theatre, local history; *Style*— Prof William Tydeman; ✉ School of English & Linguistics, University of Wales, Bangor, Gwynedd LL57 2DG (tel and fax 01248 382102)

TYE, Alan Peter; *b* 18 September 1933; *Educ* Regent St Poly Sch of Architecture (DipArch); *m* 1, 1960; 1 da (Helen Elna b 1962), 1 s (Martin Anders b 1964); m 2, 1966, Anita Birgitta Goethe-Tye; 1 da (Madeleine b 1967), 2 s (Nicolas b 1969, Kevin b 1973); *Career* Alan Tye Design 1962–; visiting tutor RCA 1978–83 (external assessor 1987–), guest prof Royal Acad of Fine Arts Copenhagen 1996; inaugural RDI lecture LA 1998; memb Selection Ctee Cncl of Industrial Design 1967, Civic Tst Award assessor 1968 and 1969, fndr Healthy Industrial Design process 1977, specialist advsr on ind design CNAA 1980, London regnl assessor RIBA 1981, RSA Bursary judge 1983–2003, chm Product Liability Seminar CSD 1987, awards assessor RIBA 1988, external assessor RCA degrees 1989, chm RSA New for Old EEC Bursary 1993–2003, external examiner Guildhall Univ MA Design for Disability 2000; founder memb Product Innovation in Architecture Soc of RIBA 1999; RIBA 1959, RDI 1986; *Awards* Int Design Prize Rome 1962, Cncl of Ind Design Award 1965, 1966 and 1981, Br Aluminium Design Award 1966, first prize GAI Award 1969, Observer (London) Design Award 1969, Ringling Museum of Art (Fla) Award 1969, Gold Medal Graphic Design 1970, first prize GAI Award Int Bldg Exhibition 1971, British Aluminium Eros Trophy 1973, 4 awards for design excellence Aust 1973, commendation for architecture 1977, Inst of Business Designers Int Award (NY) 1982, Int Bldg Exhibits top design award 1983 (1985), ROSCOE Design Award NY 1988, finalist Prince Philip Designer of the Year Award 1993 and 1999, RIBA Regnl Design Award 1995; RDI 1986; *Recreations* tai chi, aikido; *Style*— Alan Tye, Esq; ✉ Great West Plantation, Tring, Hertfordshire HP23 6DA (tel 01442 825353, fax 01442 827723, website www.tyedesign.co.uk)

TYERS, Anthony Gordon; s of Arthur Tyers, of Sunbury on Thames, Surrey, and Marion Joan, *née* Cheal; *b* 14 September 1944; *Educ* Hampton Sch, Charing Cross Hosp Univ of London (MB BS); *m* 7 Oct 1983, Renée Constance Barbara, da of Frits De Waard, of Waalre, Netherlands; 2 s (Jonathan b 30 July 1986, Richard b 30 April 1989), 2 da (Johanna b 19 May 1991, Rebecca b 9 Nov 1993); *Career* registrar Univ Coll Hosp London 1973–76, sr registrar Moorfields Eye Hosp 1978–81, fell Massachusetts Eye and Ear Infirmary Boston USA 1981–82, sr registrar Moorfields Eye Hosp and Middx Hosp London 1982–86; conslt ophthalmic surgn: Salisbury Gen Hosps 1986–, Moorfields Eye Hosp 1997–99; former pres Br Oculo-Plastic Surgery Soc; tstee Salisbury Hosps Fndn, Euro Soc of Ophthalmic Plastic and Reconstructive Surgery; memb: BMA, RSM, Southern Ophthalmological Soc; FRCS 1974, FRCSEd 1980, FRCOphth 1989; *Books* Basic Clinical Ophthalmology (contrib, 1984), Colour Atlas of Ophthalmic Plastic Surgery (jtly, 1994, 2 edn 2001), Eyetext.net (contrib, 2000), Plastic and Orbital Surgery (contrib, 2001), Maxillo-Facial Trauma and Esthetic Reconstruction (contrib, 2002); *Recreations* sailing, skiing, campanology; *Style*— Anthony Tyers, Esq; ✉ Salisbury District Hospital, Salisbury SP2 8BJ (tel 01722 336262, fax 01722 425155); New Hall Hospital, Salisbury SP5 4EY (tel and fax 01722 439680)

TYLER, Antony Nigel (Tony); s of Maj-Gen Sir Leslie Tyler, KBE, CB (d 1992), and Sheila, *née* Field (d 2003); *b* 27 April 1955, Moascar, Egypt; *Educ* Worth Sch, BNC Oxford (BA); *Children* 2 s, 1 da; *Career* joined Swire Gp 1977; Cathay Pacific Airways: joined 1978, dir of serv delivery 1994–96, dir of corp devpt 1996–2004, chief operating offr 2005–07, chief exec 2007–; chm Dragonair; memb Hong Kong Logistics Devpt Cncl, memb Bd Asian Youth Orch; *Recreations* tennis, hiking, rock and folk guitar; *Clubs* Hong Kong Country (vice-chm), Hong Kong, RAC; *Style*— Tony Tyler, Esq; ✉ Cathay Pacific Airways Limited, 8 Scenic Road, Hong Kong International Airport, Hong Kong (tel 00 852 2747 5151, e-mail tonytyler@cathaypacific.com)

TYLER, David; s of Ronald Julian Meek, of Stoke-on-Trent, and Ruth Hannah, *née* Sewell, of Wembley; *b* 24 June 1961; *Educ* Haberdashers' Aske's, Clare Coll Cambridge (fndn scholar, MA); *Children* 2 s, 2 da; *Career* prodr; toured UK, Edinburgh Festival and Australia with Cambridge Footlights (prodns incl Hawaiian Cheese Party, Feeling the Benefit and Get Your Coat Dear, We're Leaving) 1983–85; stand-up comedian and writer (Week Ending and News Huddlines) 1985; prodr/dir 1986–: Radio Active, Week Ending, Cabaret Upstairs, The Big Fun Show, Dial M for Pizza, Unnatural Acts, At Home With the Hardys, Live on Arrival, The Woody Allen Reader, Jeremy Hardy Speaks to the Nation series 1 - 7 (BBC Radio 4), King Stupid, The Very World of Milton Jones, Crown Jewels, The 99p Challenge, Giles Wembley-Hogg Goes Off, Deep Trouble, Armando Iannucci's Charm Offensive; prodr/writer: Spitting Image series 6 and 7, The Sound of Maggie 1989 (ITV), Coogan's Run, The Paul and Pauline Calf Audio Experience, The Tony Ferrino Phenomenon, Introducing Tony Ferrino - Who and Why? A Quest 1995–96 (BBC); prodr: Up Yer News 1990 (BSB), And Now in Colour, It's A Mad World World World World, The Paul Calf Video Diary, The Imaginatively-Titled Punt & Dennis Show, Three Fights Two Weddings and a Funeral, Angus Deayton's End of the Year Show, Paul Merton - The Series (series 1 and 2), Dead at Thirty, Absolutely, Cows, tlc, Gash, The Strategic Humour Initiative, The Comic Side of 7 Days Music Hall Meltdown 1996 (Channel 4); exec prodr The Marriage of Figaro 1994 (BBC), exec prodr dinnerladies (BBC1), exec prodr/writer The Big Snog 1995 (Channel 4), series prodr The Jack Docherty Show 1997 (Channel 5), co-dir The Man Who Thinks He's It (national and West End tour), formed Pozzitive TV (with prodr/dir Geoff Posner) 1993–; author of articles in The Independent and The Guardian and regular contrib to New Moon and Nexus magazines; memb: Equity 1984, Labour Party; *Awards* BAFTA Best Comedy Award for Three Fights Two Weddings and a Funeral 1994, Sony (Bronze) Award for Jeremy Hardy Speaks to the Nation series 2 1995, Silver Rose of Montreux for The Tony Ferrino Phenomenon 1996, Sony (Bronze) Award for Crown Jewels 1996, Sony (Bronze) Award for The Very World of Milton Jones 2000, Sony (Silver) Award for The 99p Challenge 2004, Sony Award (Bronze) for Armando Iannucci's Charm Offensive 2006, Sony Award (Silver) for Giles Wemmbley Hogg Gent Zum Fussball Weltmeisterschaft Weg 2006; *Recreations* spotting dumped cars in Crouch End; *Clubs* The British Interplanetary Society; *Style*— David Tyler, Esq; ✉ c/o Pozzitive Television, Paramount House, 162–170 Wardour Street, London W1V 4AB (tel 020 7734 3258, fax 020 7437 3130, e-mail david@pozzitive.co.uk)

TYLER, David; *b* 23 January 1953; *Educ* Rendcomb Coll, Trinity Hall Cambridge (MA); *Career* Unilever plc 1974–86, County Natwest Ltd 1986–89, Christie's Int plc 1989–96, fin dir GUS plc 1997–2006, chm 3i Quoted Private Equity Ltd 2007–; non-exec dir: Burberry Gp plc 2002–, Experian Gp plc 2006–, Reckitt Benckiser plc 2007–; FCMA 1978, MCT 1991; *Style*— David Tyler, Esq; ✉ Experian Group plc, 80 Victoria Street, London SW1E 5JL (tel 020 3042 4302, fax 020 3042 4250)

TYLER, Ian Paul; s of Ray Lindley Tyler (d 2002), and Peggy May, *née* Boreham; *b* 7 July 1960, Wells, Somerset; *Educ* Ringwood Comp Sch, Univ of Birmingham (BCom); *m* 25 June 1983, Janet Lynn, *née* Kempson; 2 da (Amy Rebecca b 6 Oct 1993, Lucy Charlotte b 17 Nov 1995); *Career* Arthur Anderson & Co 1982–88, gp treas and financial comptroller Storehouse plc 1988–91, gp financial comptroller Hanson plc 1991–93, finance dir Arc Ltd 1993–96; Balfour Beatty plc: finance dir 1996–2002, chief operating offr 2002–04, chief exec 2005–; pres Construction Industry Charity for the Homeless (CRASH); CA 1985; *Recreations* flying, fitness; *Style*— Ian Tyler, Esq; ✉ Grasslands, The Ridge, Woldingham, Surrey CR3 7AL (tel 01883 652264); Balfour Beatty plc, 130 Wilton Road, London SW1V 1LQ (tel 020 7216 6825, e-mail ian.taylor@balfourbeatty.com)

TYLER, Leonard Charles; s of Sydney James Tyler, and Elsie May, *née* Reeve; *b* 14 November 1951; *Educ* Southend HS, Jesus Coll Oxford (open exhibitioner, MA), City Univ (MSc); *m* 22 Sept 1984, Ann Wyn, da of William Evans; 1 s (Thomas Huw b 11 Oct 1985), 1 da (Catrin Victoria b 13 Feb 1987); *Career* DOE 1975–78; British Council: asst rep Malaysia 1978–81, asst rep Sudan 1981–84, regnl offr S E Asia 1984–86, trg City Univ 1986–87, Information Technology Gp 1987–93, dir Nordic Countries Copenhagen 1993–98; chief exec RCPCH 1998–; *Books* The Herring Seller's Apprentice (novel, 2007); *Recreations* skiing, hill walking, reading, memb Mensa; *Style*— Leonard Tyler, Esq; ✉ RCPCH, 50 Hallam Street, London W1W 6DE (tel 020 7307 5604); 31 Lonsdale Square, Islington, London N1 1EW; Findon Farmhouse, Findon, West Sussex BN14 0TF2

TYLER, Baron (Life Peer UK 2005), of Linkinhorne in the County of Cornwall; Paul Archer Tyler; CBE (1985), DL (Cornwall 2006); s of Oliver Walter Tyler (d 1957), and (Ursula) Grace Gibbons, *née* May; *b* 29 October 1941; *Educ* Sherborne, Exeter Coll Oxford (MA); *m* 27 June 1970, Nicola Mary (Nicky), da of Michael Warren Ingram, OBE, of South Cerney, Glos; 1 da (Hon Sophie Grace Auriol b 1972), 1 s (Hon Dominick Michael Archer b 1975); *Career* dep dir then dir of public affrs RIBA 1966–73, regnl organiser and bd memb Shelter 1975–76, md Courier Newspaper Group 1976–81, dir then sr conslt Good Relations Ltd 1982–92, dir Western Approaches PR Ltd 1987–2000; MP: (Lib) Bodmin Feb-Oct 1974, (Lib Dem) N Cornwall 1992–2005; Lib Dem shadow ldr House of Commons 1997–2005; Lib Dem chief whip 1997–2001; Lib Dem Parly spokesman on: agriculture and rural affrs 1992–97, food 1997–2000; shadow min for constitutional affrs House of Lords; memb Jt Ctee on House of Lords Reform 2002–03; memb Select Ctee: on Procedure 1992–97, on Parly Privilege 1997–99, on Modernisation of House of Commons 1997–2005; memb Jt Ctee on Lords/Commons Conventions 2006–; chm All-Pty Coastal Gp 1992–97, chm All-Pty Organophosphate Gp 1992–2005, treas All-Pty Tourism Gp 1992–97, hon sec All-Pty Water Gp 1992–97; cncllr Devon CC 1964–70, memb Devon and Cornwall Police Authy 1965–70, vice-chm Dartmoor Nat Park 1965–70; vice-pres: Br Resorts Assoc, YHA; MIPR 1987; *Publications* Power to the Provinces (1968), A New Deal for Rural Britain (1978), Country Lives, Country Landscapes (1996), Britain's Democratic Deficit (2003), House of Lords Reform: Breaking the Deadlock (2005); *Recreations* sailing, walking, Cornish ancestry; *Style*— Lord Tyler, CBE, DL; ✉ House of Lords, London SW1A 0PW (website www.paultyler.libdems.org)

TYLER, Richard Herbert (Dick); s of Peter Anthony Tyler, of Winchcombe, Glos, and Barbara Margaret, *née* Wilson; *b* 19 February 1959, Cheltenham, Glos; *Educ* Cheltenham GS, Fitzwilliam Coll Cambridge (MA); *m* 28 Sept 1985, Ann Christine; 2 da (Alice Jemima b 22 Jan 1989, Laura Ellen b 7 March 1991); *Career* McKenna & Co Slrs: articled clerk 1983–85, asst slr 1985–92, ptnr 1992–97; CMS Cameron McKenna: ptnr 1997–2000, managing ptnr 2000–; memb: Law Soc, City of London Slrs' Co; memb London Legacy 2020 Culture Bd 2006–; pres Old Patesians Rugby Football Club (Nat League 3 (South)) 2006–; *Style*— Dick Tyler, Esq; ✉ CMS Cameron McKenna, Mitre House, 160 Aldersgate Street, London EC1A 4DD (tel 020 7367 3000, e-mail dick.tyler@cms-cmck.com)

TYNAN, Bill; *b* 18 August 1940; *Educ* St Mungo's Acad, Stow Coll; *Career* trade union official, memb numerous ctees AEU; joined Lab Pty 1969, MP (Lab) Hamilton S 1999–2005 (by-election), pt/t researcher for John Robertson, MP 2005–; currently special advsr to All Pty Parly Nuclear Energy Gp; political interests incl Europe and NI, employment law, social security, int devpt, equal opportunities and social inclusion; dir: Lanarkshire Voluntary Sector (SoLVE) 2006–, Trade Unions for Safe Nucelar Energy (TUSNE) 2007–; *Recreations* golf, gardening, DIY, watching football; *Clubs* Colville Park

Golf; *Style*— Bill Tynan, Esq; ✉ 6 East Scott Terrace, Hamilton ML3 6LL (tel and fax 01698 421660)

TYRE, Colin Jack; QC (1998); s of James Tyre, of Dunoon, Argyll (d 1993), and Lilias, *née* Kincaid; *b* 17 April 1956, Dunoon, Argyll; *Educ* Dunoon GS, Univ of Edinburgh (LLB, Lord Pres Cooper Mem Scholarship Prize), Univ of Aix-Marseille (Dip); *m* 18 Sept 1982, Elaine, *née* Carlin; 2 da (Kirsty b 8 Aug 1986, Catriona b 1 Jan 1989), 1 s (Euan b 18 May 1992); *Career* called to Scottish Bar 1987; apprentice Shepherd and Wedderburn 1977–79, lectr in law Univ of Edinburgh 1980–83, tax ed CCH Editions Ltd 1983–86, advocate 1987–, pt/t cmmr Scottish Law Cmmn 2003–; pres Cncl of Bars and Law Socs of Europe 2007 (head UK delgn 2004); memb Faculty of Advocates 1987; *Publications* CCH Inheritance Tax Reporter (1984), Tax for Litigation Lawyers (co-author, 2000), contrib to Stair Mem Encyclopedia (contrib, 1986–); *Recreations* mountain walking, golf, orienteering, popular music; *Style*— Colin Tyre, QC; ✉ Advocates Library, Parliament House, Edinburgh EH1 1RF (tel 0131 226 5071, fax 0131 225 3642)

TYRER, His Hon Judge Christopher John Meese; s of late Jack Meese Tyrer, of Rhiwbina, Cardiff, and Margaret Joan, *née* Wyatt; *b* 22 May 1944; *Educ* Wellington, Univ of Bristol (LLB); *m* 9 Feb 1974, (Monica) Jane Tyrer, JP, da of Peter Beckett, of Pontefract, W Yorks; 1 da (Rebecca b 1979), 1 s (David b 1981); *Career* called to the Bar Inner Temple 1968; dep judiciary 1979 (dep judge 1979–82), asst recorder 1982–83, recorder 1983–89, circuit judge (SE Circuit) 1989–; vice-chm St John's Sch Lacey Green 1989–90 (govr 1984–92), chm Speen Sch 1989–90 and 1995–96 (govr 1984–96), memb Bucks Assoc of Govrs of Primary Schs 1989–90 (chm High Wycombe Div 1989–90), govr The Misbourne Sch 1993– (vice-chm 1995–2000, chm 2000–), patron Bucks Chilterns UC Student Law Soc; chm English Baroque Choir 1998–99; *Recreations* music, reading, photography, growing things, supporting Wycombe Wanderers FC; *Style*— His Hon Judge Christopher Tyrer; ✉ Randalls Cottage, Loosley Row, Princes Risborough, Aylesbury, Buckinghamshire HP27 0NU (tel 01844 344650); Aylesbury Crown Court, Market Square, Aylesbury, Buckinghamshire HP20 1XD (tel 01296 40401)

TYRIE, Andrew; MP; *Educ* Felsted, Trinity Coll Oxford (MA), Coll of Europe Bruges, Wolfson Coll Cambridge (MPhil); *Career* with British Petroleum at Group Head Office; full time advsr to Rt Hon Nigel Lawson, MP and then Rt Hon John Major, MP as Chllrs of the Exchequer 1986–90; contested Houghton and Washington 1992; former sr economist EBRD; MP (Cons) Chichester 1997–, shadow financial sec 2003–04, shadow paymaster gen 2004–05; memb: House of Commons Select Ctee on Public Admin 1997–2001, Public Accounts Cmmn 1997–, Treasy Select Ctee 2001–03, Exec Ctee of 1922 Ctee 2005–06, Constitutional Affrs Select Ctee 2005–; Woodrow Wilson Scholar 1990, fell Nuffield Coll Oxford 1990–91; *Publications* The Prospects for Public Spending (1996), Reforming the Lords: A Conservative Approach (1998), Leviathan at Large: The New Regulator for the Financial Markets (2000), Mr Blair's Poodle: An Agenda for Reviving the House of Commons (2000), Back from the Brink (2001), The New Statism (2002), Axis of Instability: America, Britain and the New World Order after Iraq (2003), Pruning the Politicians: The Case for a Smaller House of Commons (2004), Mr Blair's Poodle Goes to War: The House of Commons, Congress and Iraq (2004), The Conservative Party's proposals for the funding of political parties (2006), One Nation Again (2006); *Style*— Andrew Tyrie, Esq, MP; ✉ House of Commons, London SW1A 0AA

TYRRELL, Alan Rupert; QC (1976); *b* 27 June 1933; *Educ* LSE (LLB); *m* 1960, Elaine Eleanor, *née* Ware; 1 s (Simon), 1 da (Alison); *Career* called to the Bar Gray's Inn 1956 (bencher

1986), recorder of the Crown Court 1972–98, dep judge of the High Court (Queen's Bench Div) 1990–98; chm: Bar European Gp 1986–88, Int Practice Ctee Bar Cncl 1988; Lord Chancellor's legal visitor 1990–, memb Cncl Medical Protection Soc 1990–98, memb Criminal Injuries Compensation Bd and Appeal Panel 1999–; ICC Arbitrator 1999–2006; dir Papworth Hosp NHS Tst 1993–2000, chm (employment affrs) Fedn of Small Businesses 2003–; MEP (EDG) London East 1979–84; FCIArb 1993; *Books* The Legal Professions in the New Europe (ed, 1992, 2 edn 1996), Public Procurement in Europe: Enforcement and Remedies (ed, 1997); *Clubs* Athenaeum; *Style*— Alan Tyrrell, Esq, QC; ✉ 15 Willifield Way, Hampstead Garden Suburb, London NW11 7XU; Tanfield Chambers, 2–5 Warwick Court, London WC1R 5DJ (tel 020 7421 5300, e-mail alantyrrell@ntlworld.com)

TYRRELL, Prof Robert James; *b* 6 June 1951; *Educ* Univ of Oxford (MA), LSE (MSc); *Career* chm The Henley Centre 1995–96 (chief exec 1986–95), non-exec dir New Solutions Ltd 1997–2000, non-exec devpt ptnr Cognosis strategic consultancy 1998–, chm RISC Futures Paris 1999–2000, chm Sociovision UK 2001–, Euro chm Global Futures Forum 2001–; visiting prof City Univ Business Sch 1994–; memb: Advsy Cncl Demos 1993– (tstee 2001–), Cncl Cons Pty Policy Forum 1999–; *Style*— Prof Robert Tyrrell

TYRWHITT, Sir Reginald Thomas Newman; 3 Bt (UK 1919), of Terschelling, and of Oxford; s of Adm Sir St John Reginald Joseph Tyrwhitt, 2 Bt, KCB, DSO, DSC (d 1961), and Nancy Veronica, da of Charles Newman Gilbey (gn of Sir Walter Gilbey, 1 Bt); gs of 1 Bt Adm of the Fleet Sir Reginald York Tyrwhitt, GCB, DSO; Sir St John's gf's gf, Richard, was 3 s of Capt John Tyrwhitt, RN (d 1812), of Netherclay House, Somerset, by his w Katherine (paternal gda of Lady Susan Clinton, da of 6 Earl of Lincoln (a dignity now subsumed in the Duchy of Newcastle); Richard's er bro was (Sir) Thomas, *née* Tyrwhitt, who assumed (1790) the name of Jones (although subsequent holders of the Btcy appear to have been known as Tyrwhitt) and was cr a Bt 1808; Sir Thomas's ggs, Sir Raymond Tyrwhitt, 4 Bt, inherited his mother's Barony of Berners; John Tyrwhitt of Netherclay was seventh in descent from Marmaduke Tyrwhitt, yr s of Sir William Tyrwhitt, of Kettilby; *b* 21 February 1947; *Educ* Downside; *m* 1, 1972 (m dis 1980, annulled 1984), Sheila Gail, da of late William Alistair Crawford Nicoll, of Liphook, Hants; *m* 2, 1984, Charlotte, o da of Capt Angus Jeremy Christopher Hildyard, DL, RA (d 1995); 1 s (Robert St John Hildyard b 1987), 1 da (Letitia Mary Hildyard b 1988); *Heir* s, Robert Tyrwhitt; *Career* served Royal Artillery 1966–69; subsequent career with cos associated with UK paper industry; *Recreations* drawing, fishing, shooting; *Style*— Sir Reginald Tyrwhitt, Bt

TYZACK, His Hon Judge David Ian Heslop; QC (1999); s of Ernest Rudolf Tyzack, MBE (d 1973), and Joan Mary, *née* Palmer (d 1993); *b* 21 March 1946; *Educ* Allhallows Sch, St Catharine's Coll Cambridge (MA); *m* 27 Jan 1973, Elizabeth Anne, da of Maj Henry Frank Cubitt, TD (d 1991); 1 da (Anna b 6 April 1981), 1 s (William b 12 June 1983); *Career* called to the Bar Inner Temple 1970, in practice Western Circuit, head of chambers 1988–2000, asst recorder of the Crown Court 1995–2000, recorder 2000, dep judge of High Court of Justice 2000–, circuit judge (Western Circuit) 2000–; chm Devon & Cornwall Branch Family Law Barristers' Assoc, memb The Hon Soc of the Inner Temple 1970; *Books* Essential Family Practice (2000); *Recreations* gardening, walking, skiing, church; *Style*— His Hon Judge Tyzack, QC; ✉ Southernhay Chambers, 33 Southernhay East, Exeter, Devon (tel 01392 255777, fax 01392 412021)

T

U

UCHIDA, Mitsuko; da of Fujio Uchida, of Tokyo, Japan, and Yasuko Uchida; *b* 20 December 1948; *Educ* Hochschule für Musik und Davstellende Kunst Vienna; *Career* pianist; artist in residence Cleveland Orch 2002–, co-dir (with Richard Goode) Marlboro Music Festival; has played with most major int orchs (repertoire ranges from Mozart to Schönberg, Messiaen and Birtwistle); gave US première of Harrison Birtwistle's piano concerto Antiphonies with Los Angeles Philharmonic Orch and Pierre Boulez; opened Harrods Int Piano Series commemorating 150th anniversary of Chopin's death at Royal Festival Hall 2000; performed Mitsuko Uchida: Vienna Revisited series Carnegie Hall 2003; *Recordings* incl: complete Mozart piano sonatas, all Mozart piano concertos, Mozart quintet for piano and winds, Chopin Piano Sonatas 2 and 3, Debussy 12 Études, R Schumann Carnaval, Beethoven piano concerto series, various Schubert sonatas and impromptus, Schoenberg Piano Concerto; *Awards* first prize Int Beethoven Competition Vienna, second prize Int Chopin Competition Warsaw; numerous record prizes incl: The Gramophone Award 1989, Edison prize (Holland), Gramophone Award 2001, Royal Philharmonic Soc Instrumentalist Award 2004; *Recreations* music; *Style—* Miss Mitsuko Uchida; ✉ c/o Victoria Rowsell Artist Management, 34 Addington Square, London SE5 7LB (tel and fax 020 7701 3219, e-mail ch@victoriarowsell.co.uk)

UDDIN, Wali Tasar; MBE (1995), JP (1984); *b* 17 April 1952, Moulvibazar, Bangladesh; *Educ* Moulvibazar Govt HS, Putney Coll (HNC); *m* 1975, Syeda; 2 s (Shahan, Ahsan), 3 da (Hafiza, Suhaly, Ruhaly); *Career* chm and chief exec Universal Koba Corp Ltd and Britannia Spice Scot Ltd 2000–, also conslt The Verandah and Lancers Brassiere; estab Travel Link Worldwide Ltd, chm and chief exec Frontline Int Air Services UK Ltd 1997–; conslt in restaurant and travel trade sectors; hon consul-gen of Bangladesh in Scot 1993–98 and 2002–, chief co-ordinator Indian Earthquake Disaster Appeal Fund Scot 2001, chief co-ordinator Bangladesh Flood Victim Appeal Fund Scot, chm Bangladesh-Br C of C, founding dir Edinburgh Mela (Asian Festival) Ltd, fndr and chm Bangladesh Samity (Assoc) Edinburgh; co-ordinator Expo Bangladesh 2005; chm: Cwlth Soc Edinburgh, Bangladeshi Cncl in Scot, Scot Bangladeshi Int Humanitarian Tst, Bangla Scot Fndn, Ethnic Enterprise Centre Edinburgh; dir Edinburgh C of C 2002–; patron: Bangladesh Cyclone Disaster Appeal Fund, Royal Hosp for Sick Children Edinburgh, Scot Sch of Asian Cuisine Fife Coll; dir Sylhet Women's Med Coll and Hosp 2005, advsr Atish Dipankar Univ of Science and Technol 2004; chm Advsy Bd Univ of E London Business Sch 2004–; patron Lion Children's Hosp Sylhet 1997; tstee: Bangladesh Female Acad 2004, Shahajalal Mosque Edinburgh; memb Edinburgh Merchant Co, bd memb Cncl for Foreign C of C and Industries; exec memb Royal Cwlth Soc Edinburgh; Young Scot Award Int Jr C of C 1992, Lifetime Achievement Award Asian Jewel Awards 2006; DBA (hc) Queen Margaret UC 2000, Hon DLitt Heriot-Watt Univ 2007; MInstD, MCMI, FInstSMM; *Recreations* supporting Heart of Midlothian FC and the Bangladesh cricket team, football, family, working with the televisual media (ethnic, national and international); *Clubs* Rotary Int; *Style—* Dr Wali Tasar Uddin, MBE, JP; ✉ Universal Koba Corporation Ltd, Britannia Spice Restaurant, 150 Commercial Street, Ocean Drive, Leith, Edinburgh EH6 6LB (e-mail waliuddin@aol.com, website www.britanniaspice.co.uk); Frontline International Air Services Ltd, 22 Chalton Street, London NW1 1JH

UFF, Prof John Francis; CBE (2002), QC (1983); s of Frederick Uff (d 1981), and Eva Uff (d 1969); *b* 30 January 1942; *Educ* Stratton Sch, KCL (BSc, PhD); *m* 29 July 1967, Diana Muriel, da of Prof Ronald Graveson, CBE; 2 s (Alexander John b 1973, Christopher Edward b 1975), 1 da (Leonora Meriel b 1977); *Career* civil engr 1966–70, called to the Bar 1970, practised in chambers of Donald Keating QC, head of chambers 1992–97; bencher of Gray's Inn 1993, recorder of Crown Court 1998; appointed arbitrator in many UK and foreign commercial disputes (mostly engrg and construction), chm Ind Cmmn of Inquiry into Yorkshire Water 1996, chm Public Inquiry into Southall rail accident 1997, jt chm Public Inquiry into Train Protection Systems 1999; dir Centre of Construction Law and Mgmnt KCL 1987–99, Nash prof of engrg law Univ of London 1991–2003, emeritus prof of engrg law 2003–; Inst of Civil Engrgs Gold Medal 2002; FKC 1997; FICE 1982, FCIArb 1982, FREng 1995; *Books* ICE Arbitration Practice (1985), Construction Contract Policy (1989), International and ICC Arbitration (1991), Legal Obligations in Construction (1992), Construction Law (9 edn 2005), Keating on Building Contracts (contrib), Chitty on Contracts (contrib); *Recreations* fiddling with violins, farming; *Clubs* Athenaeum; *Style—* Prof John Uff, CBE, QC, FREng; ✉ 15 Essex Street, Outer Temple, London WC2R 3AU (tel 020 7544 2600); Pale Farm, Chipperfield Hertfordshire WD4 9BH

UFLAND, Richard Mark; s of Bertram Ufland, and Shirley, *née* Gross; *b* 4 May 1957; *Educ* St Paul's, Downing Coll Cambridge (MA); *m* 20 Oct 1985, Jane Camilla, da of Louis Rapaport; 2 s (James b 1987, William b 1990), 1 da (Olivia b 1994); *Career* ptnr: Stephenson Harwood 1986–98, Lovells 1998–; Freeman: City of London, Worshipful Co of Slrs of the City of London; memb Law Soc (memb Company Law Ctee); *Recreations* opera, bridge, theatre, skiing; *Style—* Richard Ufland, Esq; ✉ Brambers, The Grove, Radlett, Hertfordshire WD7 7NF (tel 01923 854378, e-mail richard@ufland.com); Lovells, Atlantic House, Holborn Viaduct, London EC1A 2FG (tel 020 7296 2000, fax 020 7296 2001, e-mail richard.ufland@lovells.com)

ULIJASZEK, Prof Stanley Jan; *b* 3 July 1954; *Educ* Victoria Univ of Manchester (BSc), Queen Elizabeth College Univ of London (MSc), KCL (PhD); *m* Pauline; 2 s (Michael, Peter), 1 da (Alexandra); *Career* Univ of Cambridge: memb Faculty of Biology 1986–, asst lectr, univ lectr then research assoc Dept of Biological Anthropology 1986–97, MA (by incorporation) 1990, memb CCC 1994–99; assoc prof and head Dept of Nutrition Curtin Sch of Public Health Aust 1997–99; Univ of Oxford: MA (by incorporation) 1999, univ lectr Inst of Biological Anthropology 1999–2001, univ lectr Inst of Social and Cultural Anthropology 2001–04, sr research assoc Oxford Inst of Ageing 2002–, sr research assoc Centre for Devpt Studies Queen Elizabeth House 2003–, prof of human ecology Inst of Social and Cultural Anthropology 2004–, fell St Cross Coll; Japan Soc for the Promotion of Science fell and visiting prof Univ of Tokyo 1994, visiting assoc prof Univ of Pennsylvania 1994, research assoc PNG Inst of Medical Research 2001, visiting fell ANU 2004 and 2005, fell Univ of Melbourne 2005– (visiting fell 2002, 2004 and 2005); ed Jl of Comparative Human Biology (Homo) 2002–, assoc ed Economics and Human Biology 2003–04; memb Editorial Bd: Jl of Biosocial Science 1991– (book review ed 1996–), Anthropologischer Anzeiger 1997–, Annals of Human Biology 1998–2004, American Jl of Human Biology 2003–; author of numerous articles in peer-reviewed jls and chapters in books; foreign co-op researcher Kagoshima Univ Research Center for the Pacific Islands 1993–, UK rep Int Assoc of Human Biologists 1994–97, memb Review Panel Wenner-Gren Fndn for Anthropological Research 2005–; memb: Soc for the Study of Human Biology 1983– (memb Ctee 1989–99 and 2000–, prog sec 1991–96 and 2002–), Nutrition Soc 1986–, Int Cmmn on the Anthropology of Food 1987– (cmmr Asia-Pacific region 1997–2003), Biosocial Soc 1988– (memb Ctee 1990–99 and 2000–04, treas 1992–96), Human Biology Assoc USA 1990–, American Assoc of Physical Anthropologists 1991–, Australasian Soc for Human Biology 1993– (memb Ctee 1998–99), European Anthropological Assoc 1994– (memb Cncl 1995–98), American Anthropology Assoc 1994–, American Soc for Nutritional Sciences 1997–, NY Acad of Science 1997–, Int Union of Anthropological and Ethnological Sciences 1998–; *Books* Nutritional Anthropology: Prospects and Perspectives (jtly, 1993), Seasonality and Human Ecology (jt ed, 1993), Anthropometry: the Individual and the Population (jt ed, 1994, 2 edn 2005), Health Intervention in Less Developed Nations (ed, 1995), Human Energetics in Biological Anthropology (1995, 2 edn 2005), Long-term Consequences of Early Environment: Growth, Development and the Lifespan Developmental Perspective (jt ed, 1996), Human Adaptability, Past, Present, and Future (jt ed, 1997), Cambridge Encyclopedia of Human Growth and Development (jt ed, 1998), Urbanism, Health and Human Biology in Industrialised Countries (jt ed, 1999); *Recreations* cycling, swimming, painting; *Style—* Prof Stanley Ulijaszek; ✉ Institute of Social and Cultural Anthropology, 51 Banbury Road, Oxford OX2 6QS

ULLATHORNE, Peter Lindley; JP (SW London 1994); s of Philip Stanley Ullathorne (d 1990), and Mary Lindley, *née* Burland (d 1996); *b* 6 August 1948; *Educ* Chesterfield GS, City of Leicester Poly, AA Sch of Architecture (AADipl); *Career* architect; Richard Rogers Partnership 1971–74, Louis De Soissons Partnership 1974–77, GMW Partnership 1977–80, YRM Architects 1980–83, DEGW Architects 1983–86, md First Architecture Group plc 1986–89, gp dir McColl Gp Ltd 1989–91, dir Chanin Hartland Ullathorne 1991–94, vice-pres Gensler and Associates/Architects 1994–2002, vice-pres HOK International 2002–04, currently dir Navigant Consulting Inc; RIBA client design advsr; memb Assoc Parly Design Gp; visiting prof Univ of Cincinnati 1985; Freeman City of London 1990, Liveryman Worshipful Co of Chartered Architects; memb AA 1971, RIBA 1974, FRSA 1989, AIA 1995, FRSH 1997; *Recreations* reading, architecture, music, seaside life; *Clubs* RAC, London Library, Lord's Taverners, Reform; *Style—* Peter Lindley Ullathorne, Esq; ✉ 136 Somerset Road, Wimbledon, London SW19 5HP (tel 020 8879 1208, e-mail peter@ullathorne.com)

ULLMAN, Tracey; da of Anthony John Ullman (d 1966), and Dorin, *née* Cleaver; *b* 30 December 1959; *Educ* The Italia Conti Stage Sch Brixton; *m* 27 Dec 1983, Allan McKeown, *qv*; 1 da (Mabel Ellen b 2 April 1986), 1 s (John Albert Victor b 6 Aug 1991); *Career* comedy actress and singer; *Dancer* Gigi (Theatre des Westerns Berlin) 1976, Second Generation (Blackpool and Liverpool) 1977; musicals: Elvis (Astoria) 1978, Oh Boy (Astoria) 1978, Rocky Horror Show (Comedy Theatre) 1979; *Theatre* Talent (Everyman Liverpool) 1980, Dracula (Young Vic) 1980, Four in a Million (Royal Court) 1981, She Stoops to Conquer (Lyric Hammersmith) 1982, The Taming of the Shrew (NY Shakespeare Festival Broadway) 1990, The Big Love (one woman show) 1991; *Television* incl: Three of a Kind 1981–83, A Kick up the Eighties 1981 and 1983, The Young Visitors 1984, Girls on Top 1985, The Tracey Ullman Show 1987–90, Tracey Takes On 1996, Ally McBeal 1998–99, Visible Panty Lines 2001; *Film* Plenty 1984, I Love You to Death 1989, Panic 2000, Small Time Crooks 2000, C-Scam 2000, A Dirty Shame 2004; *Recordings* various top ten singles 1981–84, You Broke my Heart in Seventeen Places (album, Gold record); *Awards* Most Promising New Actress London Theatre Critics Award 1981, Best Light Entertainment Performance BAFTA 1983, five American comedy awards 1988–90, Best Female Comedy Performance Golden Globe Awards USA 1988; Emmy Awards (USA): Best Variety Show TV 1989, Best Writing 1990, Best Performance in a Variety Music or Comedy Show 1990, 1994 and 1997; *Recreations* hiking, riding, finding unspoilt areas of the earth and being quiet; *Style—* Miss Tracey Ullman

ULLMANN, (Frederick) Ralph; s of Prof Walter Ullmann, FBA (d 1983), of Cambridge, and Elizabeth, *née* Knapp (d 2001); *b* 29 July 1945; *Educ* Cambs HS for Boys, Trinity Coll Cambridge (open scholar, MA), Dept of Educn Univ of Cambridge (PGCE); *m* Alison, da of Derek Kemp; 2 s (Thomas b 12 April 1981, Alexander b 14 June 1985), 1 da (Penelope b 8 Feb 1984); *Career* second i/c history and head of gen studies Bishop's Stortford Coll 1968–72; Bloxham Sch: head of history 1972–76, housemaster and sr housemaster 1974–85; headmaster: Ruthin Sch 1986–93, Wellingborough Sch 1993–2004; examiner A Level history London Bd 1978–85; memb: SHA 1985 (memb Nat Cncl and Professional Ctee 1997–), SHMIS 1986 (chm Professional Devpt Ctee 1990–93), HMC 1993–2004, (memb Community Service Sub-Ctee 1995–2001, Professional Devpt Ctee 1997–2004, sec Midland Div 1998 (chm 1999), memb Ctee 1998 and 1999), GTC 2001 (chair Policy Servs Gp, memb Cncl, memb Coordinating, Professional and Audit Ctees); memb Educn Ctee Chester C of C and Industry 1989–93, founding memb Bd Castle Theatre Wellingborough 1994–98, chm Rudolf Kempe Soc; FCP 1985 (ACP 1984); *Recreations* music, photography, wine, cricket, dog walking, fiction and history; *Clubs* Cambridge Union, East India, Leicestershire CCC; *Style—* Ralph Ullmann, Esq; ✉ 7 School Lane, Braybrooke, Market Harborough, Leicestershire LE16 8LS

ULLSTEIN, Augustus Rupert Patrick Anthony; QC (1992); s of Frederick Charles Leopold Ullstein (d 1988), of Chiswick, London, and Patricia, *née* Guinness (d 2002); *b* 21 March 1947; *Educ* Bradfield, LSE (LLB); *m* 12 Sept 1970, Pamela Margaret, da of Claude Wells (d 1974), of Woodford, Essex; 2 da (Elizabeth b 1 June 1977, Caroline b 28 Oct 1978), 2 s (William b 3 July 1980, George b 29 April 1983); *Career* called to the Bar Inner Temple 1970; dep registrar Family Div 1987, recorder 1999– (asst recorder 1994–99); memb Cncl Acad of Experts 1995–; dir Saxon Radio 1980–87; Freeman City of London 1982, Worshipful Co of Bowyers 2002; *Books* The Law of Restrictive Trade Practices and Monopolies (second supplement to second edn, 1973), Matrimonial and Domestic Injunctions (1982), Compensation for Personal Injury in English, German and Italian Law (with Sir Basil Markesinis, QC); *Recreations* after dinner speaking, my children; *Style—* Augustus Ullstein, Esq, QC; ✉ 39 Essex Street, London WC2R 3AT

ULLSWATER, 2 Viscount (UK 1921); Nicholas James Christopher Lowther; LVO (2002), PC (1994); s of Lt John Arthur Lowther, MVO, RNVR (d 1942); suc ggf, 1 Viscount Ullswater, GCB (s of late Hon William Lowther, bro of late 3 Earl of Lonsdale), 1949; *b* 9 January 1942; *Educ* Eton, Trinity Coll Cambridge; *m* 1967, Susan, da of James Howard Weatherby, of Salisbury, Wilts, by his w Mary (4 da of Sir Hereward Wake, 13 Bt, CB, CMG, DSO, JP, DL); 2 da (Hon Emma (Hon Mrs Stewart-Smith) b 1968, Hon Clare (Hon Mrs Flawn-Thomas) b 1970), 2 s (Hon Benjamin b 1975, Hon Edward b 8 Oct 1981); *Heir* s, Hon Benjamin Lowther; *Career* Capt Royal Wessex Yeo TAVR 1973–78; a Lord in Waiting 1989–90; Parly under-sec of state Dept of Employment 1990–93, Capt HM Body Guard of Hon Corps of Gentlemen at Arms (Chief Govt Whip) 1993–94, min of state DOE 1994–95; private sec to HRH The Princess Margaret, Countess of Snowdon 1998–2002; elected to House of Lords 2003; *Style*— The Rt Hon the Viscount Ullswater, LVO, PC; ✉ The Old Rectory, Docking, King's Lynn, Norfolk PE31 8LJ (tel 01485 518822)

UNDERHILL, Prof John Richard; s of Edward James William Underhill, of Havant, Hants, and Kathleen Ivy, *née* Thorn; *b* 5 January 1961, Portsmouth; *Educ* Portsmouth GS, Univ of Bristol (BSc), Univ of Wales (PhD); *m* 25 Sept 1985, Rosemary Anne, *née* Gigg; 1 da (Laura Kathleen Anne b 5 Oct 1993), 1 s (Matthew Robert Edward b 31 March 1995); *Career* exploration geoscientist Shell International 1985–89, prof of stratigraphy Grant Inst of Earth Science Univ of Edinburgh 1989–, assoc prof Dept of Petroleum Engrg Heriot-Watt Univ; memb All Pty Parly Gp for Earth Sciences 2003–; memb Cncl Geological Soc of London; Distinguished Lectr Award European Assoc of Petroleum Geoscientists Meeting Berlin 1989 and Paris 1992, Pres's Award Geological Soc 1990, Matson Award for Excellence in Presentation American Association of Petroleum Geologists Annual Meeting Calgary 1992, American Association of Petroleum Geologists Distinguished Lectr US and Canada tour 1998–99, Wollaston Fund Geological Soc 2000; AAPG 1984, FGS 1984, FRSE 2004; *Recreations* squash, football refereeing, running; *Style*— Prof John Underhill; ✉ Grant Institute of Earth Sciences, School of Geosciences, University of Edinburgh, The King's Buildings, West Mains Road, Edinburgh EH9 3JW (tel 0131 650 1000, fax 0131 668 3184, e-mail jru@glg.ed.ac.uk)

UNDERHILL, Hon Mr Justice; Sir Nicholas Edward Underhill; kt (2006); s of Michael Thomas Ben Underhill (d 1987), and Rosalie Jean Beaumont, *née* Kinloch; *b* 12 May 1952; *Educ* Winchester, New Coll Oxford (MA); *m* 1987, Nina Charlotte Margarete, *née* Grunfeld; 2 s (b 1987 and 1998), 2 da (b 1990 and 1992); *Career* called to the Bar Gray's Inn 1976 (bencher 2000); QC 1992, recorder of the Crown Court 1994–2006, judge of the High Court of Justice (Queen's Bench Div) 2006– (dep judge1998–2006); judge Employment Appeal Tbnl 2000–03; Attorney-Gen to HRH The Prince of Wales 1998–2006; chair Bar Pro Bono Unit 2002–05; *Books* The Lord Chancellor (1976); *Style*— The Hon Mr Justice Underhill; ✉ Royal Courts of Justice, Strand, London WC2A 2LL

UNDERHILL, Nicholas Peter; s of Kenneth Underhill, and Evelyn Ellen, *née* Barnard; *b* 15 January 1955; *Educ* William Ellis Sch; *m* 28 July 1973, Julie Ann Evelyn, da of Wilfred Augustus Michael Chard, of London; 4 s (Matthew, James, Julian, Oliver), 1 da (Lyndsey); *Career* property advtg mangr Evening Standard 1974–75, ptnr Druce & Co 1978–81, equity ptnr Hampton & Sons 1986–87, md Hamptons (estate agents) 1988–89, chm Underhill Group of Companies 1989–92; dir: Keith Cardale Groves 1992–96, Hamptons International 1996–98, Stirling Ackroyd Hong Kong and Dublin 1998–2003; md Stirling Ackroyd 1998–2003, currently md City and Mayfair Properties; chm Mayfair Media Marketing 1998–2002; memb Land Inst; *Recreations* shooting, rugby, skiing, opera, real tennis; *Clubs* Carlton, MCC, Saracens RFC, Lord's Taverners, Annabel's; *Style*— Nicholas Underhill, Esq; ✉ e-mail nick@cityandmayfair.com

UNDERHILL, (Christopher) William Youard; s of Christopher James Avery Underhill, and Frances Mary Underhill; *Educ* LSE (LLB); *Career* slr; Slaughter and May: joined 1981, ptnr 1990–; memb Law Soc, memb City of London Solicitors' Co; *Style*— William Underhill, Esq; ✉ Slaughter and May, One Bunhill Row, London EC1Y 8YY (tel 020 7090 3060, e-mail william.underhill@slaughterandmay.com)

UNDERWOOD, Ashley Grenville; QC (2001); s of Dennis William Underwood (d 1995), and Brenda Stephenson, *née* Witts; *b* 28 December 1953, Kent; *Educ* LSE (LLB); *m* 28 Aug 1982, Heather, *née* Legget; 1 da (Sally Davina b 22 July 1986); *Career* called to the Bar Gray's Inn 1976; head of chambers 2 Field Court 1999–2006, memb Landmark Chambers 2006–; *Style*— Ashley Underwood, Esq, QC; ✉ Landmark Chambers, 180 Fleet Street, London EC4A 2HG (tel 020 7430 1221, fax 020 7421 6060, e-mail aunderwood@landmarkchambers.co.uk)

UNDERWOOD, Prof Geoffrey; s of Stanley Underwood (d 1978), of Hull, E Yorks, and Marjorie, *née* Hulme (d 2003); *b* 16 May 1947, Hull, E Yorks; *Educ* Kelvin Hall Hull, Bedford Coll London (BSc), Univ of Sheffield (PhD); *m* 1 Aug 1969, Jean Dianne Marina, *née* Strange; *Career* Univ of Nottingham: lectr in psychology 1972–86, sr lectr in psychology 1986–88, reader in cognitive psychology 1988–90, prof of cognitive psychology 1990–, head Sch of Psychology 1998–2001; asst prof of psychology Univ of Waterloo Canada 1974–75; ed Br Jl of Psychology 2000–05; Hon DSc Univ of London 1995; FBPsS 1994, FRSA 2002; *Books* Computers and Learning (with Jean Underwood, 1990), Eye Guidance in Reading and Scene Perception (ed, 1998), Oxford Guide to the Mind (ed, 2001); *Recreations* skiing, mountain walking, supporting Hull City FC; *Style*— Prof Geoffrey Underwood; ✉ School of Psychology, University of Nottingham, University Park, Nottingham NG7 2RD (tel 0115 951 5313, fax 0115 951 5311, e-mail geoff.underwood@nottingham.ac.uk)

UNDERWOOD, Grahame John Taylor; s of Wing Cdr Shirley Taylor Underwood, OBE, of Elston, nr Newark, and Joyce Mary, *née* Smith; *b* 1 July 1944; *Educ* Ashby de la Zouch GS, Poly of N London (DipArch); *m* 4 May 1968, Christine Elva, da of Sqdn Ldr Cecil Reginald Long, MBE, DSM (d 1972); 2 s (Christopher Taylor b 1971, Toby Grahame b 1972), 1 da (Lucy Jane b 1974); *Career* Watkins Gray International: architect and planner 1969–72, assoc 1972–83, ptnr and dir 1983–, gp chm 2003–07; dir: Watkins Gray Peter Jones 1983–90, Watkins Gray International Ltd 1983–2007, Watkins Gray Ho & Partners 1989–2000, WGI Interiors Ltd 1997–2007, WGI Sports and Leisure Ltd 1997–2007, WGI Education Ltd 1998–2000, WGI Housing Ltd 1999–2002, WGI Leeds Ltd 1999–2007, GGA WatkinsGray Ltd 2001–07, WGI Halliday Meecham Ltd 2003–07, Wren Insurance Assoc Ltd 2003–06; memb Watkins Gray International LLP 2002–07 (conslt 2007–); princ designs incl: Royal Masonic Hosp, Nat Heart and Chest Hosps London and Baghdad, Dammam and Unayzah Hosps Saudi Arabia, Bromley Hosp, Orpington Hosp, Ekaterinburg Cardiology Hosp and Oncology Hosp, Togliatti Maternity Hosp, Belfast Children's Hosp (design competition winner), Altnagelvin Hosp, Joyce Green Hosp, health planning for govts of Syria and Indonesia, Kwong Wah Hosp Hong Kong, Mater Infirmorum Belfast (design competition winner), Downpatrick Community Hosp (design competition winner), Ambulatory Care Centre Birmingham, Sha Tin Dementia Centre Hong Kong, E Kent Hosps Master Plan, Peterborough Hosps Master Plan, Dundonald Hosp Belfast, St George's Hosp London, Cork Univ Hosp, Kent Cardiac Centre, master plan Antrim Hosp, Craigavon Hosp, Ulster Hosp, Shropshire Community Care, Enniskillen and Omagh Hosps, Northampton Mental Health Hosp, 3 Shires Community Hosp Prog; fndr memb Care Health Planning; memb NHS Design Review Panel 2007–; chm Edgbaston Round Table 1984, dir Kent Gliding Club (chm 1998–2003); Freeman Guild of Air Pilots and Air Navigators 1993 (Liveryman 2006); RIBA 1973, MRIN 1996; *Books* Architects Jl Handbook of Ironmongery (1979), The Security of Buildings (1984); author of numerous tech articles; *Recreations* flying, gliding; *Style*— Grahame Underwood, Esq; ✉ 10 Wents Wood, Weavering, Kent ME14 5BL (tel 01622 631734, e-mail gu@gjtu.com)

UNDERWOOD, Prof Ian; s of Robert Underwood, of Airdrie, and Mary, *née* O'Connor; *b* 24 June 1959, Airdrie; *Educ* Univ of Glasgow (BSc), Univ of Strathclyde (MSc), Univ of Edinburgh (PhD); *m* 11 Sept 2002, Muriel June; 1 da (Victoria Joy), 1 s (James Robert); *Career* Univ of Edinburgh: lectr 1989, reader 1999, prof 2005; Microemissive Displays Ltd: co-fndr 1999, dir of product devpt 2001, dir of strategic mktg 2003; design authy for the world's smallest colour TV screen Guinness Book of Records 2004; Fulbright fell 1991; Ben Sturgeon Award Soc for Information Display 1999, Ernst & Young Emerging Entrepreneur of the Year 2003, Gannochy Prize for Innovation RSE 2004; memb Soc of Information Display; MIEEE, FRSE 2004; *Style*— Prof Ian Underwood; ✉ Scottish Microelectronics Centre, West Mains Road, Edinburgh EH9 3BU

UNDERWOOD, Kerry; s of Ernest Albert Underwood, of Harrow, Middlesex, and Jeanie, *née* Barr; *b* 4 June 1956, South Ruislip, London; *Educ* Trent Poly, Coll of Law; *Career* admitted slr 1981; ptnr Tilley Underwood 1986–90, sr ptnr Underwoods Slrs 1991–, sr ptnr Underwoods South Africa 2003–; chm Employment Tbnls 1993–2000; conslt LexisNexis, conslt to various Cwlth countries; memb Panel of Slrs: Disability Rights Cmmn, Equal Opportunities Cmmn; memb working party on fixed costs Civil Justice Cncl, chief exec Law Abroad Ltd; involved with: Victim Support (former local chm Herts), Toynbee Hall (vol memb legal advice team); lectr, writer and broadcaster; cncllr (Lab) London Borough of Harrow 1978–82, Parly candidate (Lab) Worthing 1979; FCIArb; KStJ; *Books* No Win, No Fee, No Worries (1998, revised edn 2000), Fixed Costs (2004, 2 edn 2006), Butterworths Personal Injury Litigation Service (ed Costs, Funding and Referral Fees Section); *Recreations* cricket, football, travelling, photography, literature, gardening, Elvis Presley, T S Eliot; *Clubs* Queen's Park Rangers FC, Cricketers, Bovingdon CC; *Style*— Kerry Underwood, Esq; ✉ Underwoods Solicitors, 79 Marlowes, Hemel Hempstead HP1 1LF (tel 01442 430900, fax 01442 239861, e-mail kerryunderwood@underwoods-solicitors.com)

UNDERWOOD, Susan Lois; OBE; da of John Ayton Underwood, of St Andrews, and Sheila Lois, *née* Rankin; *b* 6 August 1956; *Educ* Kilgraston Sch, Allhallows Sch, Univ of St Andrews (MA), Univ of Leicester (grad cert mus studies), TEFL; *Children* 1 da (Mitya Susan Underwood b 16 July 1983), 1 s (Callum John Underwood b 17 June 1987); *Career* res supvr Yorkshire & Humberside Museums Cncl 1981–82, volunteer Yorkshire Museum of Farming 1982–83, curator Nat Railway Museum York 1983–84, keeper of local history Scunthorpe Museum and Art Gall 1985–88, dir NE Museums 1990–2001 (dep dir 1988–90), chief exec NE Museums Libraries and Archives Cncl 2001–05, dir Sharjah Museums Dept UAE 2005–; pres Museums North 1992–93; chair: Social History Curators Gp 1990–91, East End Carers (Newcastle) 1996–97; Bd memb: Northern Centre for Contemporary Art 1990–92, Northern Arts 1992–98, Live Theatre Co Ltd 1992–97; memb Nat Tst Regnl Ctee 1996–2003; memb Cncl Univ of Newcastle 1998–; tstee Baltic Flour Mills Visual Arts Tst 1998–2004; cmmr English Heritage 1997–2004; examiner Mus Assoc dip 1990–92, external examiner Museum Studies Univ of Leicester 1998–; FMA 1993 (AMA 1985); *Recreations* walking, tennis, the arts, spending time with my children; *Clubs* St Rules Golf (St Andrews); *Style*— Miss Susan Underwood, OBE

UNMACK, Timothy Stuart Brooke; s of Randall Carter Unmack (d 1978), and Anne Roberta, *née* Stuart (d 1972); *b* 5 August 1937; *Educ* Radley, Christ Church Oxford (MA); *m* 21 May 1966, Eleanor Gillian, da of George Aidan Drury Tait (d 1970); 2 s (Guy Douglas b 13 March 1975, Neil Alexander b 29 July 1977); *Career* Nat Serv RN; admitted slr 1965, sr ptnr Beaumont and Son 1987–97 (ptnr 1968–97), Shadbolt & Co: conslt 1998–2000, ptnr 2000–04; conslt Clyde & Co 2004–; chm Central Asia and Transcaucasia Law Assoc; memb Int Law Assoc's Ctee on Legal Aspects of Air Traffic Control; dir HealthProm; former chm Royal Philanthropic Soc Redhill; memb Worshipful Co of Barbers; memb: Law Soc 1965, Royal Soc for Asian Affairs 1987, fell Royal Aeronautical Soc 2004; *Books* Civil Aviation: Standards and Liabilities; *Recreations* sailing, languages; *Clubs* Oxford and Cambridge; *Style*— Timothy Unmack, Esq; ✉ 51 Eastcheap, London EC3M 1JP (tel 020 7623 1244, fax 020 7623 5427, e-mail tim.unmack@clydeco.com)

UNSWORTH, Prof Anthony; s of James Unsworth (d 1984), and Annie, *née* Halliwell (d 2000); *b* 7 February 1945; *Educ* Worsley Coll, Warrington Tech Coll, Univ of Salford (BSc Mechanical Engrg (1st class)), Univ of Leeds (MSc, Samuel Denison Prize, Tribology Silver Medal IMechE, PhD, DEng); *m* 22 Dec 1967, Jill, da of late Kenneth Chetwood; *Career* apprentice David Brown Corp 1961, research engr David Brown Gear Industries 1967–69, ARC lectr in bioengineering Univ of Leeds 1971–76 (ARC research fell 1969–71); Univ of Durham: lectr 1976–79, sr lectr 1979–83 (visiting research scientist Mechanical and Aerospace Engrg Cornell Univ NY 1981), reader 1983–89, prof of engrg 1989–, chm Sch of Engrg and Applied Sci 1989–94 and 2000–2006, dean of science and dir Centre for Biomedical Engrg 1994–2000, dir of research Faculty of Science, memb Senate 1984–87, 1990–94 and 1996–2006, memb Cncl 1993–2003, also memb or chm numerous univ ctees; memb Ctee Engrg in Med Gp IMechE 1984– (chm 1989–92), memb Ctee ACTION Research 1989–95 (chm Bioengineering Advsy Panel 1992–95); memb Bd of Govrs Univ of Teesside (formerly Poly) 1986–2000, dir ACTION (charity) 1992–95, memb S Durham HA 1993–96; chm: S Durham Research Ethics Ctee 1993–96, Northern Regnl Research Ethics Ctee 1995–96; memb Editorial Bd: Jl of Orthopaedic Rheumatology 1987–98, Current Orthopaedics 1988–98; ed Engrg in Med Newsletter IMechE 1988–90, ed Proceedings of Instn of Mech Engrs Part H Engrg in Med 1993– (memb Editorial Bd 1988–); scientific referee for papers submitted to various learned jls; author of over 270 publications; deliverer of over 150 lectures to learned socs (incl 60 overseas); Donald Julius Groen Prize IMechE 1991, James Clayton Prize IMechE 1999, James Alfred Ewing Medal ICE 2005; memb Br Orthopaedic Research Soc 1975; FIMechE 1984 (MIMechE 1972), FREng 1996, FICE 2003; *Recreations* singing operetta and sacred music; *Style*— Prof Anthony Unsworth, FREng; ✉ School of Engineering, University of Durham, South Road, Durham DH1 3LE (tel 0191 334 2521, fax 0191 334 2512, e-mail tony.unsworth@durham.ac.uk)

UNSWORTH, Barry Forster; s of Michael Unsworth (d 1949), and Elsie, *née* Forster (d 1954); *b* 10 August 1930; *Educ* Stockton-on-Tees GS, Univ of Manchester (BA); *m* 1, 1959 (m dis 1991), Valerie Irene, *née* Moore; 3 da (Madeleine b 1961, Tania b 1964, Thomasina b 1968); m 2, 1992, Aira, *née* Pohjanvaara-Buffa; *Career* novelist; Arts Cncl literary fell Charlotte Mason Coll Ambleside 1978–79, Northern Arts literary fell Univs of Durham and Newcastle upon Tyne 1982–84; writer in residence: Univ of Liverpool 1984–85, Lund Univ 1988–; Hon LittD Univ of Manchester 1998; memb Soc of Authors; FRSL 1974; *Books* The Partnership (1966), The Greeks Have a Word for It (1967), The Hide (1970), Mooncranker's Gift (1973, Heinemann prize 1973), The Big Day (1976), Pascali's Island (1980, shortlisted for Booker Prize, filmed 1988), The Rage of the Vulture (1982), Stone Virgin (1985), Sugar and Rum (1988), Sacred Hunger (1992, co-winner Booker Prize), Morality Play (1995, shortlisted for the Booker Prize, filmed as The Reckoning 2003), After Hannibal (1996), Losing Nelson (1999), The Songs of the Kings (2002), The Ruby in her Navel (2006); *Style*— Barry Unsworth, Esq, FRSL; ✉ c/o Vivien Green, Sheil Land Associates, 52 Doughty Street, London WC1N 2LS (tel 020 7405 9351, fax 020 7831 2127)

UNSWORTH, Michael Anthony; s of Lt Cdr John Geoffrey Unsworth, MBE, of Hayling Island, Hants, and Joan Rhyllis, *née* Clemes; *b* 29 October 1949; *Educ* St John's Coll Southsea, Enfield Coll of Technol (BA); *m* 1 Dec 1973, Masa, da of Prof Zitomir Lozica, of Orebic, Croatia; 2 da (Tania Elizabeth b 10 Oct 1978, Tessa Joanna b 27 June 1981);

Career res analyst Grieveson Grant & Co 1972–79; Scott Goff Hancock & Co: sr oil analyst 1979–81, ptnr 1981–86, co merged with Smith Bros to form Smith New Court plc 1986, dir i/c energy res 1986–95, dir i/c res 1989–95, Bd dir 1991–95, md Capital Markets 1994–95; dep chief exec Smith New Court Far East Ltd 1995, head of research Asia Pacific Region Merrill Lynch 1995–98, co-ceo Merrill Lynch Phatra Securities Co 1998–2000; pres Supervisory Bd Jadran Capital dd; dir: Smart City People (Thailand) Recruitment Co Ltd, R M Asia Gp; *Recreations* sailing, opera, theatre; *Clubs* Royal Bangkok Sports, British Bangkok, Little Ship; *Style*— Michael Unsworth, Esq

UNSWORTH, Dr Philip Francis; s of Stephen Unsworth (d 1959), of Manchester, and Teresa *née* McElin (d 1997); *b* 18 September 1947; *Educ* St Bede's Coll, Univ of Manchester (BSc, MB ChB); *Career* house surgn and physician Manchester Royal Inf 1971–72; lectr: Middlesex Hosp 1972–75, St Thomas' Hosp 1975–76; microbiologist Colindale 1977–79; undergraduate clinical tutor Tameside Hosp 1980–2003; conslt microbiologist: Tameside and Glossop DHA 1979–94, Tameside and Glossop Acute Services NHS Tst 1994–; hon clinical lectr in Med Microbiology Manchester Med Sch 1999–; memb Hospital Infection Soc 1981–, Assoc of Med Microbiologists, Br Soc of Antimicrobial Chemotherapy; FRCPath 1989 (MRCPath 1978); *Recreations* reading, sports, walking, music, languages; *Style*— Dr Philip Unsworth; ✉ 1 Pine Road, Didsbury, Manchester M20 6UY; Department of Microbiology, Tameside General Hospital, Ashton-under-Lyne, Lancashire OL6 9RW (tel 0161 331 6500, fax 0161 344 6496, e-mail philip.unsworth@tgh.nhs.uk)

UNWIN, Sir (James) Brian; KCB (1990); s of Reginald Unwin (d 1975), and Winifred Annie, *née* Walthall (d 1989); *b* 21 September 1935; *Educ* Chesterfield Sch, New Coll Oxford (MA), Yale Univ (MA); *m* 5 May 1964, Diana Susan, da of Sir David Aubrey Scott, GCMG; 3 s (Michael Alexander, Christopher James, Nicholas Edward); *Career* HM Civil Serv: asst princ CRO 1960, private sec to High Cmmr Fedn of Rhodesia and Nyasaland 1961–64, first sec Accra 1964–65, FCO 1965–68, HM Treasy 1968–81 (private sec to chief sec 1970–72, asst sec 1972, under sec 1976, seconded to Cabinet Office 1981–83, dep sec 1983–85), UK dir European Investment Bank 1983–85, dep sec Cabinet Office 1985–87, chm of the Bd HM Customs & Excise 1987–93, pres European Investment Bank 1993–99 (hon pres 2000–), govr European Bank for Reconstruction and Development 1993–99, chm Supervisory Bd European Investment Fund 1994–99; chm Asset Trust Housing Ltd 2003–; memb: Bd of Dirs ENO 1993–94 and 2000– (hon sec 1987–93), Bd Centre d'Etudes Prospectives (CEPROS) 1996–2000, Bd Fondation Pierre Werner Luxembourg 1998–2000, Bd of Dirs Dexia 2000–, Cncl Federal Tst for Educn and Research 2003–; chm: Civil Serv Sports Cncl 1989–93, Customs Co-operation Cncl 1991–92; pres European Centre for Nature Conservation (ECNC) 2001–; chm European Task Force on Banking and Biodiversity 2003–; hon fell New Coll Oxford 1997, pres New Coll Soc 2004–; CIMgt 1988; Médaille d'Or Fondation du Mérite Européen 1995, Grand Offr L'Ordre de la Couronne (Belgium) 2001, Grand Croix de l'Ordre Grand Ducal de la Couronne de Chêne (Luxembourg) 2001, Cdr Order of Ouissam Aloui (Morocco) 1998; *Recreations* bird watching, opera, Wellingtoniana, Trollope; *Clubs* Reform; *Style*— Sir Brian Unwin, KCB; ✉ c/o Reform Club, 104 Pall Mall, London SW1Y 5EW

UNWIN, David Charles; QC (1995); s of Peter Charles Unwin (d 1991), and Rosemary Gwendolen Winifred, *née* Locket (d 2005); *b* 12 May 1947; *Educ* Clifton, Trinity Coll Oxford (BA); *m* 16 Aug 1969, Lorna, da of Richard Frank Bullivant; 1 da (Catherine b 1974), 1 s (James b 1978); *Career* called to the Bar Lincoln's Inn 1971, Treasy jr counsel in charity matters 1987–95; charity cmmnr 2002–; *Recreations* music, mountaineering, windsurfing; *Style*— David Unwin, Esq, QC

UNWIN, Eric Geoffrey (Geoff); s of Maurice Doughty Unwin, and Olive Milburn, *née* Watson; *b* 9 August 1942; *Educ* Heaton GS Newcastle upon Tyne, Kings Coll Durham (BSc); *m* 1 July 1967, Margaret Bronia, *née* Element; 1 s (b 1 May 1973), 1 da (b 25 April 1975); *Career* with Cadbury 1963–68; Hoskyns Group plc (computer servs gp): joined John Hoskyns & Co 1968, md Hoskyns Systems Development 1978, dir Hoskyns Group plc 1982–93, md 1984–88 (incl Stock Exchange flotation 1986), exec chm 1988–93; chief operating offr Cap Gemini Sogeti 1993–2000, ceo Cap Gemini Ernst & Young 2000–02, memb of Bd Cap Gemini Gp (formerly Cap Gemini Ernst & Young) 2000– (non-voting memb 2002–); non-exec dir United News & Media plc 1995–2002, chm United Business Media 2002–07; chm: Trigenix Ltd (formerly 3G Lab) until 2002, Halma plc 2003– (dep chm 2002), Liberata plc 2003–, Omnibus Systems Ltd 2005–, The Cloud Networks Ltd 2005–06, Taptu Ltd 2006–; pres UK Computing Servs Assoc 1987–88, memb Info Technol Advsy Bd 1988–91; Freeman City of London 1987, fndr memb and Liveryman Worshipful Co of Information Technologists 1987; CIMgt 1987 (memb Bd of Companions 1990–93); *Recreations* golf, skiing, the Arts, theatre, gardening, riding; *Clubs* RAC, Hendon Golf, Hunstanton Golf, Royal North West Norfolk Golf, Morfontaine Golf (France); *Style*— Geoff Unwin, Esq; ✉ e-mail geoff.unwin@gunwin.co.uk

UNWIN, Julia; CBE (2006, OBE 2000); da of P W Unwin, and Monica Unwin; *b* 6 July 1956; *Educ* Univ of Liverpool (BA), Open Univ (Dip Effective Mgmnt), LSE (MSc); *Partner* Patrick Kelly; 2 da; *Career* health and social services field worker Liverpool Cncl for Voluntary Service 1978–80, community liaison offr Social Services Dept London Borough of Southwark 1980–82, head Voluntary Sector Liaison Team Gr London Cncl 1982–86, dir Homeless Network 1986–92, memb Bd Housing Corp 1992–2002 (chair Investment Ctee 1992–2001), cmmr Charity Commission 1998–2003, dep chair Food Standards Agency 2003–; freelance conslt work 1993–: sr assoc and chair Cmmn of Inquiry into Care Market Kings Fund, ind advsr Natwest Gp Charitable Tst 1995–2000, policy advsr Baring Fndn and Nat Lottery Charities Bd, ind memb Cabinet Office Peer Reviews of Govt Depts; ind adjudicator Audit Cmmn 2001–04; DTI: ind memb Mgmnt Bd Fair Markets Gp 2002–, memb Audit Ctee 2002–; memb: Bd QUEST 1999–2002, Ctee of Reference and Ethical Investment Ctee Friends Provident 2000– (chair 2004–), Bd Nat Consumer Cncl 2001–; chair Refugee Cncl 1995–98, tstee Public Mgmnt Fndn 1997–2001, memb Public Interest Gen Cncl Office for Public Mgmnt 2003–; *Publications* Who Pays for Core Costs? (1999), The Grant Making Tango (2004); *Style*— Ms Julia Unwin, CBE; ✉ Food Standards Agency, Aviation House, 125 Kingsway, London WC2B 6NH

UNWIN, Vicky; da of Thomas Michael Unwin, of Milverton, Somerset, and Sheila Margaret Findlay Mills; *b* 3 November 1957; *Educ* Wycombe Abbey, Oxford HS, Girton Coll Cambridge (BA); *m* 18 June 1983, Ross Brett Cattell, s of Dr William Ross Cattell, of London; 1 s (Thomas William b 21 Jan 1988), 1 da (Louise Ann b 7 Dec 1989); *Career* dir Heinemann Educnl Boleswa 1987–, publishing dir Heinemann Educnl Books 1987–90 (graduate traineeship 1979–80), md Heinemann International Literature and Textbooks 1990–93, ptnr Specialist Advsy Gp on Africa 1993–96, mangr Telegraph Books 1996–97, dir of Enterprises Telegraph Gp Ltd 1997–99, md PRNewswire Europe 1999–2003, md World Publications Ltd 2003–05, chief exec Third Millennium Information Ltd 2005, media dir Aga Khan Fund for Econ Devpt 2006–, non-exec dir Art First Ltd; sec Int Charity Assoc for Teaching Caribbean and African Literature 1984–87; *Recreations* skiing, walking, riding, gardening, reading, diving; *Style*— Ms Vicky Unwin; ✉ 4 Parkhill Road, London NW3 2YN (tel 020 7424 9423)

UPSHON, Laurence Marshall (Laurie); s of Lt-Col Hector Llewellyn Marshall Upshon (d 1957), and Hilda Winifred, *née* Southgate; *b* 21 June 1950; *Educ* St Peter's Sch Merrow; *m* 18 July 1970, Heide Maria, da of Gustav Hawlin, of Salzburg, Austria; 1 da (Claire b 1976), 2 s (Rupert b 1977, Robin b 1979); *Career* asst gp ed Stratford Express Gp 1974–76, Southern TV 1976–87 (features ed 1980); TVS Television: exec prodr news and current affairs 1982–84 (sr prodr 1981), ed Coast to Coast 1984–85; controller of news and operations ITV Central (formerly Carlton Broadcasting Central Region) 1995– (ed Central News 1985, controller of news Central Television 1989–95); chm Media Archive for Central England; dir: Central Independent Television, Digital Media Centre Univ of Central England; life vice-pres Newspaper Press Fund 1999–; memb RTNDA(US); FRTS 1997; *Recreations* sport (cricket), painting, reading, music; *Style*— Laurie Upshon, Esq; ✉ Willow Court, Kemerton, Tewkesbury, Gloucestershire GL20 7JN (tel 01386 725428); Carlton Broadcasting, Gas Street, Birmingham B1 2JT (tel 0121 643 9898, fax 0121 634 4712)

UPTON, Prof Graham; s of late William Upton, of Sydney, Aust, and Edna May, *née* Groves; *b* 30 April 1944; *Educ* Univ of Sydney (MA, DipEd), Univ of NSW (MEd), Univ of Wales (PhD); *m* 1 (m dis 1984), Jennifer Ann; 1 s (Stuart Ingham b 10 Jan 1969), 1 da (Sonja Cape b 13 March 1970); m 2, Elizabeth Mary Hayward, da of Jack Speed; 1 s (James Llewellyn b 20 Dec 1986), 1 da (Hermione Catherine b 19 Jan 1988); *Career* schoolteacher NSW 1966–71, lectr in special educn Leeds Poly 1972–74; UC Cardiff 1974–88: lectr, sr lectr, reader, head Dept of Educn, dean Faculty of Educn; pro-vice-chllr Univ of Birmingham 1993–97 (prof of educn and head Sch of Educn 1988–93), vice-chllr Oxford Brookes Univ 1997–2007; chair Oxfordshire Community Partnership 2002–; memb Cncl Headington Sch Oxford 1999–2007, chair Oxford Playhouse 2005– (memb Bd 2001–); FBPsS 1996, FRSA 1999, AcSS 2000; *Books* Physical & Creative Activities for the Mentally Handicapped (1979), Educating Children with Behaviour Problems (1983), Staff Training and Special Education Needs (1991), Special Educational Needs (1992), Emotional and Behavioural Difficulties (1994), Voice of the Child (1996), Effective Schooling for Pupils with Emotional and Behavioural Difficulties (1998); *Style*— Prof Graham Upton

UPTON, Paul David; s of John Clement and Deidre Joy Upton, of Bexleyheath; *b* 19 August 1960; *Educ* Bexley & Erith Tech HS for Boys, Univ of Sussex (BA); *m* 1986, Esther Helen Eva, da of Eric Slade; 3 s (Samuel b 1987, Alexander b 1989, William b 1995); *Career* Lloyd's underwriter; marine underwriter Cigna Re (UK) Co Ltd 1983–87; former reinsurance underwriter and active underwriter Kingsmead Underwriting Agency Ltd (formerly Claremount Underwriting Agency Ltd), former active underwriter Advent Syndicate 780; underwriter marine and energy Endurance Worldwide Insurance Ltd 2004–; ACII 1995; *Recreations* most sports, classical music, Chelsea FC; *Style*— Paul Upton, Esq

URBAN, Mark; s of Harry Urban, and Josephine Urban; *Educ* KCS Wimbledon, LSE; *m* 1993; 1 s, 2 da; *Career* asst prodr BBC 1983–86, def corr The Independent 1986–90, reporter Newsnight (BBC) 1990–93, ME corr BBC 1993–94, dip ed Newsnight (BBC) 1995–; *Publications* Soviet Land Power (1983), War in Afghanistan (1987), Big Boys' Rules (1992), UK Eyes Alpha (1996), The Illegal (1996), The Linguist (1998), The Man Who Broke Napoleon's Codes (2001), Rifles: Six Years with Wellington's Legendary Sharpshooters (2003); *Style*— Mark Urban, Esq; ✉ Newsnight, BBC TV Centre, London W12 7RJ

URBAN, Stuart; s of Dr Garri Urban, of Caracas, Venezuela, and Josephine Maureen, *née* Johnson; *b* 11 September 1958; *Educ* KCS Wimbledon, Balliol Coll Oxford (exhibitioner, MA); *m* 12 July 1987, Dr Dana Bežanov, da of Ilija Bežanov; 1 da (Leah Jessie Rebeccah b 13 Sept 1988), 1 s (David Alexander b 2 March 1991); *Career* writer and director; made two as teenager (The Virus of War 1972 and Spaghetti Special 1974) since preserved in Nat Film Archive; professional debut as dir Pocketful of Dreams (BBC Playhouse) 1981; dir many series incl: Bergerac, The Bill; dir Our Friends in the North (BBC) 1994/95, writer and dir An Ungentlemanly Act (BBC/Union Pictures); writer Deadly Voyage (HBO/BBC) 1996, writer/prodr/dir Preaching to the Perverted (feature film) 1997, prodr/dir/co-writer (with Harold Pinter) Against the War (BBC2 documentary) 1999, writer/prodr/dir Revelation (feature film) 2001, writer/prodr/dir Tovarisch, I Am Not Dead (documentary feature film) 2006; *Awards* winner BAFTA Award for Best Single Drama 1992, The Indy (best overall prodn) and Best Drama Awards at The Indies Awards 1993, Gold Plaques (best TV movie, best direction) and Silver Plaque (screenplay) at Chicago Film Festival 1992, BAFTA Award for Best Drama Serial and RTS Best Drama Serial (Our Friends in the North) 1996, Monte Carlo Silver Nymph for Best Screen Play (Deadly Voyage) 1997; *Recreations* snow and water skiing; *Clubs* Annabel's, Tramp; *Style*— Stuart Urban, Esq; ✉ c/o Linda Seifert Management, 91 Berwick Street, London W1F 0NE (tel 020 7292 7390, fax 020 7292 7391)

URE, Alan Willis; CBE (1984), RD (1969); s of Colin McGregor Ure (d 1963), and Edith Hannah Eileen Willis Swinburne (d 1945); *b* 30 March 1926; *Educ* Kelvinside Acad, Merchiston Castle Sch Edinburgh, Pembroke Coll Cambridge; *m* 1, 1953 (dis 2000), Mary Christine, da of late John C Henry; 2 da (Fiona b 1954 d 1995, Alison b 1959), 1 s (John b 1956); m 2, 2001, Lorraine Elizabeth, da of late John H Evers, OBE, and wid of John Dymoke White; *Career* RNVR 1944–58, RNR 1958–81 (Lt Cdr); memb Construction Industry Trg Bd 1982–85, pres Nat Fedn of Bldg Trades Employers 1981–82, memb Royal Cmmn on Civil Liability and Compensation for Personal Injury 1974–78; chm Nat Jt Cncl for the Bldg Industry 1989–91, formerly dep md Trollope and Colls Holdings, formerly md Trollope and Colls Ltd and Trollope and Colls Management Ltd; vice-pres Fedn Internationale Européenne de Construction 1982–85; Freeman: City of London, City of Glasgow; Liveryman Worshipful Co of Bakers, memb Incorporation of Bakers; *Recreations* reading, sailing; *Clubs* Naval, RNSA, RNVR Yacht (Cdre 1992–93); *Style*— Alan Ure, Esq, CBE, RD; ✉ The Counting House, Cavendish, Suffolk CO10 8AZ

URE, David; *Career* Reuters Group plc: joined Reuters as journalist 1968, i/c ops in Europe 1983–92 (also i/c Middle E and Africa 1989–92), main bd dir 1989–2000, chm Radinz Ltd 2000–04, strategic advsr on gp strategy, mktg and business devpt 2001–04, former chair Reuters Fndn; chm: Iris Financial 2004–, NetEconomy 2006–; non-exec dir: Woolwich plc 1998–2000, Blackwell Publishing 2004–, ITN 2004–; *Style*— David Ure, Esq

URE, James (Midge); OBE (2005); *b* 10 October 1953; *Career* singer, songwriter, prodr and video dir; with bands: Slik (number one single Forever and Ever 1976), The Rich Kids, Thin Lizzy (for USA tour 1979), Visage (Visage and Anvil albums), Ultravox 1979–86; albums with Ultravox: Vienna 1980, Rage in Eden 1981, Quartet 1982, Lament 1984, The Collection 1984, U Vox 1986, If I Was - The Very Best of Ultravox 1993; solo albums: The Gift 1985, Answers 1988, Pure 1991; co-writer and prodr Band Aid's Do They Know It's Christmas? 1984 (UK's biggest selling single); composer film music: Max Headroom (C4), Turnaround (Major Film Prodns), Playboy Late Night Theme (Playboy Channel); has produced records and directed videos for various other artists; tstee Band Aid; musical dir: Prince's Tst 1986–88 (3 times), Nelson Mandela Concert 1988; *Style*— Midge Ure, Esq, OBE

URE, Jean Ann; da of William Ure (d 1969), of Croydon, and Vera Primrose, *née* Belsen (d 1988); *b* 1 January 1943; *Educ* Croydon HS, Webber-Douglas Acad of Dramatic Art; *m* 12 Aug 1967, Leonard Gregory; *Career* writer; memb Soc of Authors; Redbridge Book Award 2004; *Books* incl: Dance for Two (children's book, publ while at sch), See You Thursday (1980), A Proper Little Nooryeff (1981), Plague 99 (1989, Lancs Book Award 1990), Skinny Melon and Me (1996), Becky Bananas (1997), Whistle and I'll Come (1997, Stockton Children's Book Award), Just 16 (1999), Fruit and Nutcase (1999), Secret Life of Sally Tomato (2000), Shrinking Violet (2002), Bad Alice (2003), Secret Meeting (2004), Is Anybody There? (2004), Sugar and Spice (2005); *Recreations* animals, walking, reading, music; *Style*— Ms Jean Ure; ✉ 88 Southbridge Road, Croydon CR0 1AF (tel 020 8760 9818, fax 020 8688 6565, e-mail jean.ure@btopenworld.com); c/o Caroline Sheldon Literary Agency, Thorley Manor Farm, Thorley, Yarmouth PO41 0SJ (tel 01983 760205)

UREN, (John) Michael Leal; OBE (1999); s of Arthur Claude Uren (d 1977), of Rickmansworth, Herts, and Doris May, *née* Leal (d 1983); *b* 1 September 1923; *Educ* Sherborne, Imperial Coll London (BSc, ACGI); *m* 26 Nov 1955, Serena Anne, da of Edward Raymond Peal, of Salisbury; 2 s (David Richard b 1960, (Robert) Mark b 1962); *Career* RN 1943–46; cmmnd Sub-Lt RNVR, air engr offr Fleet Air Arm; chartered civil engr: Sir Alexander Gibb & Partners Persia 1946–51, sr engr The Cementation Co Scot 1951–53, Holland & Hannen and Cubitts NZ 1953–55, Industrial Complex for Pressed Steel Co Swindon 1955–56, British European Airways Base Heathrow 1956–58, Dowsett Engineering Construction Ltd (dir 1958, md 1961); fndr and developer Civil and Marine Ltd 1955 (played a major part in devpt of UK offshore marine aggregates indust and pioneered devpt of blast furnace slag as a special cement to enhance the durability of concrete whilst reducing emission of carbon dioxide gases by over 90% compared with standard cement production, in the interest of global warming); former chm: Civil and Marine (Holdings) Ltd, Civil and Marine Slag Cement Ltd, The Appleby Group Ltd, Calumite Ltd, Calumite sro (Czech Repub), Civil and Marine Inc (USA); pres Cementitious Slag Makers Assoc; vice-pres Royal London Soc for the Blind (memb Cncl 1974–94, chm 1981–94), memb Cncl Quarry Products Assoc 1993–2003; Freeman City of London 1958, Master Worshipful Co of Cordwainers 1990–91 (Liveryman 1958–); CEng, MICE, MIStructE, MCIWEM, FRICS; *Recreations* 15th and 16th century timber framed buildings, country pursuits, farming (pedigree Romney sheep); *Clubs* Naval and Military, Naval; *Style*— Michael Uren, Esq, OBE; ✉ Priory Farm, Appledore Road, Tenterden, Kent TN30 7DD (tel 01580 765779)

URLEZAGA, Iñaki; *b* Buenos Aires; *Educ* Teatro Colón Ballet Sch, Sch of American Ballet; *Career* ballet dancer; princ Royal Ballet 2000– (joined 1995); *Performances* with Teatro Colón incl: Siegfried, Poet in Eugene Onegin, Basilio in Don Quixote, Prince in The Nutcracker, James in Pierre Lacotte's La Sylphide, Le Corsaire pas de deux; with Royal Ballet incl: Siegfried, Romeo, Albrecht, Colas, Prince Florimund, Basilio, Prince in The Nutcracker, Prince in Cinderella, Jean de Brienne in Raymonda Act III, Solor, Kschessinska's partner, Officer in Anastasia, Palemon in Ondine, Des Grieux, Her Lover in Lilac Garden, Vershinin in Winter Dreams, Symphony in C, Concerto, Rhapsody, Amores, Jeux, Les Biches, Monotones II, Towards Poetry in Dance Bites, Remanso, Gloria, The Leaves Are Fading, Song of the Earth, The Four Temperaments, This House Will Burn; *Style*— Iñaki Urlezaga, Esq; ✉ c/o The Royal Ballet, Royal Opera House, Covent Garden, London WC2E 9DD

URQUHART, Linda Hamilton; WS (1985); da of Douglas Hamilton Urquhart, of Edinburgh, and Ina Allan, *née* Priest (d 1991); *b* 21 September 1959, Edinburgh; *Educ* James Gillespie's HS Edinburgh, Univ of Edinburgh (LLB, DipLP); *m* 20 Aug 1988, David Spencer Burns; 2 da (Isla b 2 July 1991, Joanna b 20 March 1994); *Career* trainee slr Steedman Ramage & Co WS 1981–83; Morton Fraser: slr 1983–85, ptnr 1985–, chief exec 1999–; memb Cncl CBI Scotland 2004– (vice-chm 2007–); co-ed Greens Property Law Bulletin; memb Edinburgh and Lothians Bd Prince's Tst Scotland, unit helper Girl Guiding UK; The Insider Elite Readers' Award 2003; *Recreations* skiing, sailing, walking; *Style*— Miss Linda H Urquhart, WS; ✉ Morton Fraser, 30–31 Queen Street, Edinburgh EH2 1JX (tel 0131 247 1020, fax 0131 247 1007, e-mail lhu@morton-fraser.com)

URQUHART, Peter William; s of Maj-Gen Ronald Walton Urquhart, CB, DSO, DL (d 1968), of Tibberton, Glos, and Jean Margaret, *née* Moir; *b* 10 July 1944; *Educ* Bedford Sch, Pembroke Coll Cambridge (MA); *m* 1 May 1976 (m dis 1998), Hon Anne Serena, da of Baron Griffiths, MC, PC (Life Peer), of Kensington, London; 3 da (Katherine b 1978, Flora b 1981, Serena b 1984), 1 s (James b 1980); *Career* RMA Sandhurst 1963–64, Lt RE 1964–69; stockbroker: James Capel 1969–75, Gilbert Elliot 1975–76, Sheppards & Chase 1976–79, Mercury Asset Management (formerly Warburg Investment Management) 1981–96 (dir 1984–96); non-exec dir Phase Eight 1996–2002; tstee Henry Smith charity 1996–2006; FSI 1992; *Recreations* field sports, horses, golf, gardening; *Style*— Peter Urquhart, Esq; ✉ Fisherton de la Mere House, Warminster, Wiltshire BA12 0PZ

URQUHART, Hon Ronald Douglas Lauchlan; yr s of Baron Tayside, OBE (Life Peer, d 1975), and Hilda Gwendoline, *née* Harris; name of Lauchlan derives from ancestor in 1745 rebellion nicknamed 'the Big Sword' or 'Lauchlan'; *b* 20 February 1948; *Educ* Fettes, Univ of Edinburgh (LLB); *m* 1975, Dorothy May Jackson; *Career* chartered accountant; gp fin dir BMS Associates Gp 1999–; Liveryman Worshipful Co of Needlemakers; *Recreations* golf, backgammon; *Clubs* Caledonian, Hong Kong, Betchworth Park Golf; *Style*— The Hon Ronald Urquhart; ✉ Brockham Park House, Betchworth, Surrey RH3 7BS

URSELL, Bruce Anthony; s of Stuart Ursell (d 2005), of Edgware, London, and Nancy, *née* Fallowes; *b* 28 August 1942; *Educ* William Ellis Sch Highgate; *m* 19 Feb 1966, Anne Carole, da of John Pitt (d 1970); 1 s (Piers John b 1971), 2 da (Philippa Anne b 1972, Virginia Anne b 1974); *Career* mangr Standard Chartered Bank 1961–68, gen mangr Western American Bank 1968–74; chief exec: Guinness Mahon & Co Ltd 1984–87 (dir 1974–84), British & Commonwealth Merchant Bank plc 1987–90; chm Lockton Developments Plc 1985–95; dir: Surrey Broadcasting (USA) 1986–93, British & Commonwealth Holdings plc 1987–90, Oppenheimer Fund Management (USA) 1989–90, Standard Bank London Ltd 2000– (conslt 1998–); chm Mgmnt Bd Pannell Kerr Forster 1994–98; *Recreations* theatre, cinema, reading, mountain walking; *Clubs* East India; *Style*— Bruce Ursell; ✉ 1 The Crescent, Hartford, Cheshire (tel 01606 781219, fax 01606 781528); MGR Ltd, PO Box 28, Northwich, Cheshire CW8 1QY (e-mail b@bigglesgb.com)

URWIN, Rt Rev Lindsay Goodall; *see:* Horsham, Bishop of

USBORNE, (Thomas) Peter; s of Thomas George Usborne (d 1993), and Gerda, *née* Just (d 1998); *b* 18 August 1937; *Educ* Summerfields Sch, Eton, Balliol Coll Oxford, INSEAD (MBA); *m* 30 Oct 1964, Cornelie, da of Alfred Tücking, of Munich; 1 s (Martin b 3 May 1973), 1 da (Nicola b 12 Dec 1969); *Career* 2 Lt Rifle Brigade, seconded VI KAR 1956–58; co-fndr and md Private Eye Magazine 1962–65, sr scientist Metra Sigma Martech Management Consultancy, publishing dir Macdonald Educational 1968–73, fndr and md Usborne Publishing Ltd; *Recreations* flying, sailing, France; *Clubs* Garrick, Groucho; *Style*— Peter Usborne, Esq; ✉ Usborne Publishing Limited, Usborne House, 83–85 Saffron Hill, London EC1N 8RT (tel 020 7430 2800)

USDEN, Arline; da of Leslie Usden (d 1966), of Manchester, and Jane, *née* Hewitt (d 1970); *m* 1963 (m dis), Swavek Pogorzelski, s of late Antony Pogorzelski, of Warsaw, Poland; 2 da (Anya b 1967, Janina b 1971); *Career* reporter: Ellesmere Port News and Advertiser, Doncaster Gazette, Yorkshire Evening News; asst fashion ed Honey, ed Beauty Plus, PR offr (consumer affrs) Food Manufacturers' Fedn, beauty ed Woman, ed Successful Slimming, ed The Lady 1991– (eighth ed since 1885); *Books* incl: In Great Shape, The Body Beautiful, Beauty Works: How to Look 10 Years Younger; *Recreations* opera, classical music, travel, bridge, gardening; *Style*— Ms Arline Usden; ✉ The Lady, 39–40 Bedford Street, London WC2E 9ER (tel 020 7379 4717, fax 020 7836 4620)

USHER, Sir Andrew John; 8 Bt (UK 1899), of Norton, Ratho, Midlothian, and of Wells, Hobkirk, Roxburghshire; s of Sir John Usher, Bt (d 1998); *b* 8 February 1963; *Educ* Hilton Coll SA; *m* 1987, Charlotte Louise Alexandra, da of Robert Eldridge (d 1999); 2 s (Rory James Andrew b 1991, Callum b 1994); *Heir* s, Rory Usher; *Style*— Sir Andrew Usher, Bt

USHERWOOD, Nicholas John; s of Stephen Dean Usherwood, of London and Hazel, *née* Weston (d 1968); *b* 4 June 1943; *Educ* Westminster, Courtauld Inst of Art London (BA); *m* 1, 1979 (m dis 1990), Henrietta Mahaffy; 1 s (Theodore Patrick John b 1981), 1 da (Constance Hazel Kate b 1985); m 2, 1991, Jilly Szaybo; *Career* lectr in art history Portsmouth and Wimbledon Colls of Art 1965–68, res under Sir Nikolaus Pevsner on Pelican History of Art 1966–68; Royal Acad of Arts: admin 1969–74 (admin Turner Bicentenary Exhibition 1974), exhibitions sec 1974–77; dep keeper i/c exhibitions and PR British Museum 1977–78; freelance writer, critic, lectr and exhibition organiser and curator 1978–; curator and cataloguer of exhibitions incl: David Inshaw (Brighton Gallery and Museum) 1978, Algernon Newton RA (Sheffield and Royal Acad of Arts) 1980, The Ruralists (Arnolfini Bristol and Camden Arts Centre) 1981, Tristram Hillier (Bradford and Royal Acad of Arts) 1983, Julian Trevelyan (Watermans Art Centre) 1985, Peter Blake - Commercial Art (Watermans Art Centre Brentford) 1986, Alfred Munnings 1878–1959 (Manchester City Art Galleries) 1986, Mass Observation (Watermans Art Centre Brentford) 1987, Richard Eurich War Paintings (Imperial War Museum) 1991, Sir Sidney Nolan 75th Birthday Retrospective (Terrace Gallery Harewood House) 1992, Richard Eurich Retrospective (Southampton Art Gallery) 1994, Sir Sidney Nolan (Agnews, London) 1997, Julian Trevelyan Retrospective (Royal Coll of Art) 1998, Feliks Topolski Collections 2001–02, Joash Woodrow Retrospective 2005, Discerning Eye 2005, Leonard McComb (Agnew's) 2006, Norman Adanes Retrospective (Univ Art Gallery Newcastle-upon-Tyne) 2007; exhibitions organized: Athena Art Awards 1985–88, Images of Paradise 1989, New Generation (Bonhams London) 1990, Painting Today (Bonhams London) 1991, 1992 and 1993, Endangered Spaces (CPRE/Christies) 1996; regular contrib to: Daily Telegraph, The Guardian, Galleries (features ed 1998–); regular lectr at regnl art schs; Picker fell and critic in residence Kingston Poly (now Kingston Univ) 1990–91 and 1992–93, tstee Evelyn Williams Tst 1995–; memb: CNAA 1976–78, Int Assoc of Art Critics (sec Br section 1995–99, pres Br Section 2000–02); Chevalier Order of Leopold II of Belgium 1972; *Recreations* maps (new), music, poetry, new places (town and country), cricket, talking to painters; *Style*— Nicholas Usherwood, Esq; ✉ 82 High Street, Hampton Wick, Surrey KT1 4DQ (tel 020 8973 0921, e-mail nicholasusherwood@hotmail.com)

USSHER, Kitty; MP; da of Patrick David Lance Ussher, and Susan Margaret Whitfield, *qv*; *b* 18 March 1971; *Educ* Birkbeck Coll London, Balliol Coll Oxford; *m*; 1 da; *Career* Parlimentary researcher 1993–97, Economist Intellegence Unit 1997–98, Centre for European Reform 1998–2000, chief economist Britain in Europe 2000–01; Lambeth Cncl: cncllr 1998–2002, chair Environment Scrutiny Ctee 2000–01, chair Fin Scrutiny Ctee 2001–02; special adviser to The Rt Hon Patricia Hewitt, MP Sec of State for Trade and Industry 2001–04; MP (Lab) Burnley 2005–, memb Public Accoutns Ctee 2005–; memb Amicus, Fabian Soc, Co-operative Pty, Socialist Environmental Research Assoc; *Style*— Kitty Ussher, MP; ✉ House of Commons, London SW1A 0AA

UTTLEY-MOORE, William James (Bill); CBE (1988); s of William Uttley-Moore (d 1973), and Louisa Clara, *née* Dixon; *b* 19 July 1944; *Educ* Erith Tech Sch, SE London Tech Coll, Borough Poly (BSc); *m* 4 June 1966, Jennifer, da of late Henry James Benger; 1 s (William Daren b 4 April 1972); *Career* student apprentice and devpt engr Cintel Ltd 1960–68, project ldr Molins Machine Co Ltd 1968–69; Computing Devices Co Ltd: chief engr 1969–75, tech dir 1975–79, md 1979–85, chm and md 1985–2000; fndr chm Conqueror Broadcasting Ltd 1996–; chm E Sussex Economic Partnership 1998–2001; fndr dir: Sussex Trg and Enterprise Cncl, Southern Sound Local Radio; dir: Southdown TV, 1066 Country Devpt Panel, Castleham Industries, Hastings Economic Devpt Company; chm: Sussex Inst of Dirs, Indust Section Hastings C of C; memb: Chancellor's Advsy Gp Univ of Sussex, Defence Scientific Advsy Cncl; govr William Parker Secdy Sch; CEng, FREng 1993, FIEE, FRAeS; *Recreations* practical engineering, running, walking, nature, classical music, charities; *Style*— Bill Uttley-Moore, Esq, CBE, FREng; ✉ Tilekiln Farm, Ore, Hastings, East Sussex TN35 5EL (tel 01424 426322, e-mail billuttley-moore@freeserve.co.uk)

U

V

VADGAMA, Prof Pankaj; s of Maganlal Premji Vadgama (d 1963), and Champaben, *née* Gajjar; *b* 16 February 1948; *Educ* King's Sch Harrow, Orange Hill GS, Univ of Newcastle upon Tyne (MB BS, BSc, PhD); *m* 1977, Dixa, da of Mohanlal Bakrania; 2 da (Reena b 10 March 1978, Preeya b 1 May 1988), 1 s (Rooshin b 2 Nov 1979); *Career* house physician Newcastle Gen Hosp 1971–72, demonstrator in histopathology 1972, sr registrar in clinical biochemistry Royal Victoria Infirmary Newcastle 1977–78 (registrar 1973–77), MRC trg fell Univ of Newcastle upon Tyne 1978–81, sr registrar in clinical biochemistry Newcastle Gen Hosp 1981–83; Univ of Newcastle upon Tyne: princ res assoc 1983–87, dir of Biosensor Gp 1987–88; Univ of Manchester: prof of clinical biochemistry 1988–2000, head Dept of Med Hope Hosp 1992–98 (hon chemical pathologist 1988–2000), memb of staff Manchester Materials Science Centre 1999–2000; currently dir Interdisciplinary Research Centre in Biomedical Materials Queen Mary Univ of London, hon conslt chemical pathologist and head of science Royal London Hosp, memb: Med Engrg & Sensors Ctee EPSRC 1987–92, Molecular Sensors Ctee LINK/EPSRC 1989–96, Project Mgmnt Gp EC Concerted Action on In Vivo Sensors 1988–96, MEDLINK 1995–, EPSRC Med Engrg Coll 1994–; memb Editorial Bd: Physiological Measurement, Analyst 1990–2003, Medical Engineering and Physics; sec UK Heads of Academic Depts of Clinical Biochemistry 1992–96; IEE Engineering Sci and Educn Jl Prize 1994, Sandoz lectr Br Geriatrics Soc 1989, invited lectr to numerous other meetings and confs; invited organiser of scientific meetings for: Br Biophysical Soc, IEE, Assoc of Clinical Biochemists, American Chemical Soc, etc; awarded £4m of grants for res into biosensors since 1989; memb Assoc of Clinical Biochemists 1988; FRCPath 1989, FRSC 1996, CPhys, FInstP 2000, fell Inst Materials; *Publications* author of numerous original articles and reviews in scientific jls on biosensors; *Recreations* reading, walking; *Style*— Prof Pankaj Vadgama; ✉ 16 Wellfield Loughton, Essex IG10 1NX; IRC in Biomedical Materials, Queen Mary, University of London, Mile End Road, London EN4 4NS (tel 020 7882 5285, e-mail p.vadgama@qmul.ac.uk)

VAISEY, David George; CBE (1996); s of William Thomas Vaisey (d 1992), and Minnie, *née* Payne (d 1987); *b* 15 March 1935; *Educ* Rendcomb Coll, Exeter Coll Oxford (MA); *m* 7 Aug 1965, Maureen Anne, da of August Alfred Mansell (d 1939); 2 da (Katharine b 1968, Elizabeth b 1969); *Career* Nat Serv 1954–56, 2 Lt Glos Regt, seconded KAR 1955–56 serv Kenya; archivist Staffs CC 1960–63, asst (later sr asst) librarian Bodleian Library Oxford 1963–75, dep keeper Univ of Oxford Archives 1966–75, keeper of western manuscripts Bodleian Library Oxford 1975–86, Bodley's librarian 1986–96 (emeritus 1997–), keeper Univ of Oxford Archives 1995–2000; professorial fell Exeter Coll Oxford 1975–2000 (emeritus 2000–), hon fell Kellogg Coll Oxford 1996–; visiting prof library studies UCLA 1985, memb Royal Cmmn on Historical Manuscripts 1986–98, hon res fell Sch of Library Archive and Info Studies UCL 1987–, chm Nat Cncl on Archives 1988–91; visiting prof Texas Christian Univ Fort Worth Texas 1991; pres Soc of Archivists 1999–2002; vice-pres Br Records Assoc 1998–2006; tstee Kraszna Krausz Fndn 1991–2003; FRHistS 1973, FSA 1974; Encomienda Order of Isabel la Católica (Spain) 1989; *Books* Staffordshire and the Great Rebellion (jtly, 1964), Probate Inventories of Lichfield and District 1568–1680 (1969), Victorian and Edwardian Oxford from Old Photographs (jtly, 1971), Oxford Shops and Shopping (1972), Art for Commerce (jtly, 1973), Oxfordshire, A Handbook for Local Historians (jtly, 1973, 2 edn 1974), The Diary of Thomas Turner 1754–65 (1984, revised 1985 and 1995); *Style*— David Vaisey, Esq, CBE, FSA; ✉ Bodleian Library, Oxford OX1 3BG (tel 01865 277165, fax 01865 277187, e-mail david.vaisey@bodley.ox.ac.uk)

VAIZEY, Hon Edward Henry Butler (Ed); MP; s of John Ernest Vaizey (Baron Vaizey (Life Peer), d 1984), and Marina Alandra Vaizey (Lady Vaizey), *qv*; *b* 5 June 1968; *Educ* St Paul's, Merton Coll Oxford (MA), City Univ (Dip), Inns of Court Sch of Law; *m* 2005, Alexandra Mary Jane Holland; 1 s (b 2006); *Career* called to the Bar Middle Temple 1993; desk offr Cons Research Dept 1989–91, practising barr 1993–96, dir Public Policy Unit 1996–97, dir Politics Int 1997–98, dir Consolidated Communications 1998–2003, chief speech writer to Ldr of the Oppn 2004, MP (Cons) Wantage 2005– (Parly candidate (Cons) Bristol E 1997); shadow min for the arts 2006–; memb Consumer Credit Bill Standing Ctee 2005, Modernisation Select Ctee 2005, Environmental Audit Select Ctee 2006, numerous All Pty Gps; dep chm Cons Globalisation and Global Poverty Policy Gp 2006; memb Armed Forces Parly Scheme, Cons Friends of Israel, Industry and Parl Tst; non-exec dir Edexcel Ltd 2007–; tstee Trident Tst, vice-chm Home Farm Tst; patron: Friends of St Mary's Church Buckland, Friends of Israel Fndn, Wantage Choral Soc, CHANT (Community Hosp Acting Nationally Together), Hansard Soc; govr Cholsey Primary Sch; *Publications* ed Blue Books series: A Blue Tomorrow (jtly, 2001), The Blue Book on Transport (jtly, 2002), The Blue Book on Health (2002); *Recreations* riding, watching Chelsea FC and Didcot Town FC; *Clubs* Garrick, Soho House, Didcot Cons; *Style*— The Hon Ed Vaizey, MP; ✉ House of Commons, London SW1A 0AA (tel 020 7219 6350, e-mail vaizeye@parliament.uk)

VAIZEY, Lady; Marina Alandra; o da of late Lyman Stansky, of New York, USA, and late Ruth Stansky; *b* 16 January 1938; *Educ* Brearley Sch New York, Putney Sch Vermont, Radcliffe Coll Harvard Univ (BA), Girton Coll Cambridge (MA); *m* 1961, Baron Vaizey (Life Peer, d 1984); 1 da (Hon Polly (Hon Mrs McAndrew) b 1962), 2 s (Hon Thomas b 1964, Hon Edward, *qv* b 1968); *Career* art critic: Financial Times 1970–74, Sunday Times 1974–92; dance critic Now! 1979–81; ed Nat Art Collections Fund Publications 1991–94, conslt Nat Art Collections Fund 1994–98; memb Visual Arts Advsy Ctee Br Cncl 1987–2002; tstee: Arts Cncl 1975–79, Nat Museums and Galleries on Merseyside 1986–2001, Crafts Cncl 1988–94, Geffrye Museum London 1990–, Imperial War Museum 1991–2003, South Bank Centre 1993–2003, 20th Century Soc 1995–98, London Open House 1996–2008, Int Rescue Ctee UK 1998–2007, Assoc for Cultural Exchange 1998–, Nat Army Museum 2001–; memb Cncl: Friends of the V&A 2001– (chm 2008–), Friends of the Nat Army Museum 2002–06, Friends of the Imperial War Museum 2003–; memb Governance Forum Museums Assoc 2003–; author, broadcaster, exhibition organiser, lecturer, ctee memb; judge Turner Prize 1997; *Books* 100 Masterpieces of Art (1979), Andrew Wyeth (1980), The Artist as Photographer (1982), Peter Blake (1985), Christo (1990), Christiane Kubrick (1990), Picasso's Ladies (1998), Sutton Taylor (1999), Felim Egan (1999), Great Women Collectors (with Charlotte Gere, 1999), Art: The Critics' Choice (ed, 1999), Magdalene Odundo (2001), The British Museum Smile (2002), Colin Rose (2003), Wendy Ramshaw (2004); *Recreations* arts, travel; *Style*— The Lady Vaizey; ✉ 24 Heathfield Terrace, Chiswick, London W4 4JE (tel 020 8994 7994, e-mail marina@vaizey.demon.co.uk)

VAJDA, Christopher Stephen; QC (1997); *b* 6 July 1955; *Educ* Winchester, CCC Cambridge, Institut D'Etudes Européens, Université Libre de Bruxelles; *Career* called to the Bar Gray's Inn 1979 (bencher), called to the Bar Northern Ireland 1996; memb Supplementary Panel of Treasury Counsel 1993–97, arbitrator Sports Dispute Resolution Panel; *Publications* Bellamy & Child's European Community Law of Competition (contrib), Competitive Litigation in the UK (contrib); *Recreations* architecture, opera, tennis, theatre; *Clubs* RAC; *Style*— Christopher Vajda, Esq, QC; ✉ Monckton Chambers, 1 Raymond Buildings, Gray's Inn, London WC1R 5WR (tel 020 7405 7211, fax 405 2084, webiste www.monckton.com)

VALDINGER, Jan Robin; s of late Maj Stefan Valdinger-Vajda, MC, of Chertsey, Surrey, and Peggy, *née* Chadwick; *b* 28 September 1945; *Educ* Univ of Newcastle upon Tyne (LLB); *m* 28 Sept 1974, Rosemary Jane, da of late Brendan O'Conor Donelan; 1 s (Stefan b 1975), 2 da (Anna b 1977, Juliet b 1980); *Career* slr Clifford Turner & Co 1970–74, corp fin exec Morgan Grenfell & Co 1974–79; Standard Chartered Merchant Bank Ltd: chief exec Merchant Banking Div India 1979–83, md Hong Kong 1983–87, dir Advsy Servs London 1987–91; dir of corp servs TI Group plc 1991–92, ptnr Jaques & Lewis 1992–94; chief-exec PPF Investment Company 1996–2003, ptnr Superbrands, managing ptnr Change Partnership for Czech and Slovak Republics; memb Bd Br C of C; memb Law Soc; *Clubs* Hong Kong, Hong Kong Jockey, Burhill Golf, Karlstejn Golf; *Style*— Jan Valdinger, Esq; ✉ Fairway sro, Slezska 63, 130 00 Prague 3, Czech Republic (tel 00 420 242 454 750, fax 00 420 242 454 741, e-mail valdinger@fairway.cz)

VALE, Dr (John) Allister; s of John Richard Vale (d 1994), of Grappenhall, Cheshire, and Ellen, *née* Warburton; *b* 13 June 1944; *Educ* Co GS Altrincham, Guy's Hosp London (MB BS, MD); *m* 4 Sept 1971, Elizabeth Margaret Hastings, da of Brig Leonard Walter Jubb (d 1979), of Chislehurst, Kent; 2 da (Fiona b 1974, Katherine b 1975); *Career* conslt clinical pharmacologist and dir Nat Poisons Info Service (Birmingham Unit) and W Midlands Poisons Unit City Hosp Birmingham 1982–, dir Centre for Chemical Incidents 1996–99; sr clinical lectr Dept of Med Univ of Birmingham 1982–; censor RCP 2002–04; chm MRCP(UK) Part 1 Examining Bd 1995–2003 (sec 1982–95), chm MRCP(UK) Policy Ctee 2002–03 (sec 1994–2002), med dir MRCP(UK) Examination and Central Office 2003–06, chm MRCP(UK) Mgmnt Bd 2003–06; examiner: RCP (MRCP(UK) and AFOM), Univ of Birmingham (med and toxicology), Univ of London (clinical pharmacology); conslt to: DOH, DOT, DOE, MOD, CEC, WHO/IPCS; chm W Midlands Advsy Ctee on Chemical Incidents 1990–99; ed-in-chief Toxicological Reviews 2003–06, dep ed Clinical Toxicology 2001–04; memb Editorial Bd: Medicine (chm), Drugs; memb: W Birmingham HA 1985–90, Poisons Bd Home Office 1985–99; Euro Assoc of Poisons Centres and Clinical Toxicologists (EAPCCT): pres 1992–98, memb Scientific Ctee 1992– (chm 1992–2000); pres Br Toxicology Soc 2004–06 (memb Exec 1997–), memb Br Pharmacological Soc; FRSM, FRCP 1984, fell American Acad of Clinical Toxicology 1988 (tstee 1991–97), FFOM (by distinction) 1992, FRCPEd 1994, FRCPGlas 1997, fell Br Toxicology Soc 2006, Hon FRCPS Glas 2007; *Books* Poisoning - Diagnosis and Treatment (with T J Meredith, 1979), A Concise Guide to the Management of Poisoning (with T J Meredith, 1981), Our National Life (ed, 1998); *Recreations* reading, travel, photography; *Clubs* National; *Style*— Dr Allister Vale; ✉ National Poisons Information Service (Birmingham Unit), City Hospital, Birmingham B18 7QH (tel 0121 507 4123, fax 0121 507 5580, e-mail allistervale@npis.org)

VALENTINE, Dr Donald Graham; s of Rev Cyril Henry Valentine (d 1957), and Ada Grace, *née* Herington (d 1982); *b* 5 November 1929; *Educ* East Grinstead Co GS, Trinity Coll Cambridge (BA, MA, LLB), Utrecht Univ Netherlands (Dr Jur); *m* 25 March 1961, Vera Ruth, da of Robert Klinger (d 1954); 2 da (Tessa, Jill); *Career* asst lectr LSE 1954, called to the Bar Lincoln's Inn 1956, lectr LSE 1957, practising barr 1958–2002, prof of law Univ of Nigeria 1966–67, reader in law LSE 1967–81; chartered arbitrator, memb Cncl CIArb 1994–2001 (chm London Branch CIArb 1991–93); Master Worshipful Co of Arbitrators 2007, Freeman City of London 1988; FCIArb; *Books* The Court of Justice of the European Coal and Steel Community (1956), The Court of Justice of the European Communities (2 vols, 1966); *Recreations* greenhouse gardening; *Clubs* Garrick; *Style*— Dr D G Valentine; ✉ 1 Atkin Building, Gray's Inn, London WC1R 5AT (tel 020 7404 0102, fax 020 7405 7456, e-mail clerks@atkinchambers.law.co.uk)

VALENTINE, Baroness (Life Peer UK 2005), of Putney, in the London Borough of Wandsworth; Josephine Clare (Jo) Valentine; da of Michael Valentine, of Putney, London, and Shirley, *née* Hall; *b* 8 December 1958, Putney, London; *Educ* St Paul's Girls' Sch, Univ of Oxford; *m* 30 Aug 1990, Simon Acland; 2 da (Hon Eloise Anne b 22 Oct 1991, Hon Isabel Agnes b 6 Nov 1993); *Career* corp finance Man Barings plc 1981–88, ceo The Blackburn Partnership 1988–90, head of corp finance and planning BOC Gp plc 1990–95, ceo Central London Partnership 1995–97; London First: chief operating offr 1997–2003, ceo 2003–; cmmr Nat Lottery 2001–05; tstee Teach First 2005–; *Recreations* bridge, travel, piano; *Style*— The Lady Valentine; ✉ London First, 1 Hobhouse Court, Suffolk Street, London SW1Y 4HH (tel 020 7665 1500, fax 020 7665 1501, e-mail jvalentine@london-first.co.uk)

VALIOS, Nicholas Paul; QC (1991); *b* 5 May 1943; *Educ* Stonyhurst; *m* 2 Sept 1967, Cynthia Valerie; 1 da (Natalie b 6 Aug 1969), 1 s (Mark b 11 Sept 1973); *Career* called to the Bar Inner Temple 1964; recorder of the Crown Court 1986– (asst recorder 1981), head of chambers; *Recreations* windsurfing, computing; *Style*— Nicholas Valios, Esq, QC; ✉ 4 Breams Buildings, Temple, London EC4 1AQ

VALLANCE, Air Vice Marshal Andrew George Buchanan; CB (2003), OBE (1987); s of George Charles Buchanan Vallance, and Dorothy Mabel, *née* Wootton; *Educ* RAF Coll Cranwell, Queens' Coll Cambridge (MPhil); *m* 1972, Katherine Ray, *née* Fox; 1 da (Sophie Clare b 25 Nov 1974), 1 s (Marcus Gregory Buchanan b 21 Aug 1979); *Career* cmmnd RAF 1969, sqdn pilot 9, 617 and 27 Sqdns, Flight Cdr 50 Sqdn 1977–79, RAF Staff Coll 1980, personal staff offr to Air Memb for Personnel 1981, OC 55 Sqdn 1982–84, personal staff offr to Chief of Air Staff 1984–87, dir Defence Studies 1988–90, chief Mil Co-operation SHAPE 1991–93, OC RAF Wyton 1993–95, dep dir Nuclear Policy MOD 1995, chief Special Weapons Br SHAPE 1996–98, COS Reaction Forces Air Staff NATO 1998–2000, COS and Dep C-in-C RAF Personnel and Trg Command 2000, Exec Asst to COS (EACOS) Cmd Structure Implementation Supreme HQ Allied Powers Europe

(SHAPE) 2001–04, sec Def Press and Broadcasting Advsy Ctee 2005–; memb IISS 1988, MRUSI 1988, FRAeS 1999; *Books* Air Power (1989), RAF Air Power Doctrine (1990), The Air Weapon (1995); *Recreations* military history, classical music, structural gardening, strategic studies; *Clubs* RAF; *Style*— Air Vice Marshal Andrew Vallance, CB, OBE; ✉ Defence Press and Broadcasting Advisory Committee, Main Building, Whitehall, London SW1A 2HB (tel 020 7218 2206, fax 020 7218 5857, e-mail andrew.vallance352@mod.uk)

VALLANCE, Charles Alexander Bester; s of Julian Vallance, of Follifoot, N Yorks, and Sylvia, *née* Wright; *b* 23 September 1964; *Educ* Sedbergh, Univ of Nottingham (MA); *m* 31 Jan 1993, Irina, da of late Mikhail Corcashvilli; *Career* advtg exec: BWBC, BBH, WCRS; founding ptnr VCCP 2002–; major clients incl: O2, ING Direct, Coca-Cola, Dyson, Hyundai, five; awards incl: Boxbuster's CC Cafeteria Award 1996, VCCP Fndrs' Day Flask 2003, 2004, 2005 and 2006; *Recreations* very amateurish cricket, golf and riding; *Clubs* The Academy, Moortown Golf (Yorks), Boxbusters' CC (Soho), London County CC, MCC; *Style*— Charles Vallance, Esq; ✉ VCCP, Greencoat House, Francis Street, London SW1P 1DH

VALLANCE, Dr Elizabeth Mary (Lady Vallance of Tummel); JP (Inner London); da of William Henderson McGonnigill, and Hon Jean, da of 1 Baron Kirkwood of Bearsden; *b* 8 April 1945; *Educ* Univ of St Andrews (MA), LSE (MSc), Univ of London (PhD); *m* 5 Aug 1967, Baron Vallance of Tummel (Life Peer), *qv*; 1 da (Hon Rachel Emma Jane (Hon Mrs William Densham) b 1972), 1 s (Hon Edmund William Thomas b 1975); *Career* Queen Mary & Westfield Coll London: univ lectr, reader in politics, head Dept of Political Studies 1985–88, visiting prof 1990–97, hon fell 1997; dir: HMV Group 1990–97, Norwich Union plc 1995–2000, Charter European Tst plc 1998–2002, CGNU plc 2000–02, Aviva plc 2002–, Charter Pan-European Tst plc 2002–, Medical Protection Society 2005–; chm: St George's Healthcare NHS Tst 1993–99, Inst of Education Univ of London 2000, NHS Advsy Ctee on Distinction Awards 2000–03, Advsy Ctee on Clinical Excellence Awards 2003–05; vice-chm Health Fndn 2000–, memb Ctee on Standards in Public Life 2004–; fndr and chm Me Too 1999; Sloan fell London Business Sch; author; FRSA 1990, FCGI 2004; *Books* The State, Society and Self-Destruction (1975), Women in the House (1979), Women of Europe (1985), Member of Parliament (jtly, 1987, 2 edn 1990), Business Ethics in a New Europe (jtly, 1992), Business Ethics at Work (1995); *Style*— Dr Elizabeth Vallance; ✉ Institute of Education, Bedford Way, London WC1H 0AL

VALLANCE, Philip Ian Fergus; QC (1989); s of Aylmer Vallance (d 1955), and Helen, *née* Gosse (d 1952); *b* 20 December 1943; *Educ* Bryanston, New Coll Oxford (scholar, BA); *m* 23 June 1973, Wendy Lee, da of J D Alston, CBE, of Diss, Norfolk; 1 s (Henry b 6 Dec 1979), 1 da (Lucy b 10 April 1981); *Career* called to the Bar Inner Temple 1968; *Clubs* Travellers; *Style*— Philip Vallance, Esq, QC; ✉ Berrymans Lace Mawer, Salisbury House, London Wall, London EC2M 5QN (tel 020 7638 2811)

VALLANCE, Richard Anthony; s of Tony Vallance, of Oxford, and Jean Vallance; *b* 26 January 1947, Wells, Somerset; *Educ* King's Sch Bruton; *m* 6 April 1974, Robyn; 2 s (Barnaby Thomas b 29 Aug 1978, Sebastian James b 15 Sept 1980); *Career* admitted slr 1970; ptnr Compton Carr 1972; Charles Russell: ptnr 1996, head Clinical Negligence and Personal Injury Gp 1996–, head of litigation 1998–2002; assessor Clinical Negligence Specialist Panel Law Soc, chm Claimant Clinical Negligence Practitioners' Gp; memb: Medico-Legal Soc, Richard Grant Soc, Assoc of Personal Injury Lawyers (APIL), Assoc of Victims of Med Accidents (AVMA); author of chapters in specialist legal pubns; memb Law Soc 1970; *Recreations* gardening, squash, tennis, theatre; *Style*— Richard Vallance, Esq; ✉ The Old Bell, Langley Upper Green, Saffron Walden, Essex CB11 4RU (tel 01799 550474); Charles Russell, 8–10 New Fetter Lane, London EC4A 1RS (tel 020 7203 5169, fax 020 7203 0207, e-mail richard.vallance@charlesrussell.co.uk)

VALLANCE OF TUMMEL, Baron (Life Peer UK 2004), of Tummel in Perth and Kinross; Sir Iain David Thomas Vallance; kt (1994); s of Edmund Thomas Vallance, CBE, ERD; *b* 20 May 1943; *Educ* Edinburgh Acad, Dulwich Coll, Glasgow Acad, BNC Oxford (BA), London Business Sch (MSc); *m* 5 Aug 1967, Dr Elizabeth Mary Vallance, JP, *qv*; 1 da (Hon Rachel Emma Jane b 1972), 1 s (Hon Edmund William Thomas b 1975); *Career* joined GPO 1966; British Telecommunications (BT) plc: dir (following separation from GPO) 1981–2001, chief of operations 1985–86, chief exec 1986–95, chm 1987–2001, pres emeritus 2001–02; non-exec vice-chm Royal Bank of Scotland Group plc 1994– (dir 1993–); pres CBI 2000–02, vice-pres Princess Royal Tst for Carers, chm European Services Forum 2003–; memb: Pres's Ctee CBI, Allianz Int Advsy Bd, Euro Advsy Ctee NYSE (chm 2000–02), Int Advsy Bd Br-American C of C 1991–2002, Pres's Ctee and Advsy Cncl Business in the Community 1998–2002, Supervisory Bd Siemens AG 2003–, European Advsy Cncl Rothschild Group 2003–; memb Bd of Dirs Mobil Corp 1996–99; fell London Business Sch, hon govr Glasgow Acad; Liveryman Worshipful Co of Wheelwrights, Freeman City of London; Hon DSc: Univ of Ulster, Napier Univ, City Univ; Hon DTech: Loughborough Univ of Technol, Robert Gordon Univ; Hon DEng Heriot-Watt Univ, Hon DBA Kingston Univ; hon fell BNC Oxford; *Recreations* walking, playing the piano, listening to music; *Style*— The Lord Vallance of Tummel

VALLANCE-OWEN, Dr Andrew John; s of Prof John Vallance-Owen, *qv*, of Cambridge, and Renée, *née* Thornton; *b* 5 September 1951; *Educ* Epsom Coll Surrey, Univ of Birmingham Med Sch (MB ChB), Open Univ (MBA); *m* 1977, Frances Mary, da of Albert William Glover (d 1990); 2 s (Anthony Ian b 20 April 1983, Simon Huw b 10 Sept 1985), 1 da (Nicola Louise b 4 July 1988); *Career* surgical trg: Newcastle upon Tyne 1977–80 and 1981–83, Melbourne Aust 1980; BMA: provincial sec N of England 1983–85, Scottish sec 1986–89, head of central servs and int affrs London 1989–94, sec BMA charitable tsts 1989–94; BUPA: med dir BUPA Health Servs 1994–95, group med dir 1995–; non-exec dir: Health Dialog Servs Corp Boston USA 1997–2006, Outcome Technologies Ltd 2002–; vice-chm Cncl Royal Medical Fndn of Epsom Coll; fndn govr and chm Fund-raising Appeal Ctee The Latymer Sch Edmonton, govr and chm Devpt Bd Queenswood Sch Herts 2001–; Freeman City of London, Liveryman Worshipful Soc of Apothecaries; memb BMA 1976; FRSCEd 1982, FRSM 1989, FRSA 1992; *Recreations* music, sailing, gardening, photography, family; *Style*— Dr Andrew Vallance-Owen; ✉ 13 Lancaster Avenue, Hadley Wood, Hertfordshire EN4 0EP (tel 020 8440 9503, fax 020 8364 8770); BUPA House, 15–19 Bloomsbury Way, London WC1A 2BA (tel 020 7656 2037, fax 020 7656 2708, mobile 07836 750252, e-mail vallanca@bupa.com)

VALLANCE-OWEN, Prof John; s of Edwin Augustine Owen (d 1973), of Bangor, N Wales, and Julia May, *née* Vallance (d 1974); *b* 31 October 1920; *Educ* Friars Sch Bangor N Wales, Epsom Coll Surrey, St John's Coll Cambridge, The London Hosp (MA, MD); *m* 24 June 1950, Renee, da of Harold Thornton (d 1952), of Stanmore, Middx; 2 s (Andrew, *qv*, b 1951, Colin b 1963), 2 da (Sarah b 1954, Catherine b 1961); *Career* ROC 1939–43; various appts incl pathology asst and med first asst to Sir Horace Evans London Hosp 1946–51, Rockefeller travelling fell Univ of Pennsylvania Philadelphia USA 1955–56, sr med registrar to Prof Russell Fraser Royal Postgrad Med Sch London Hammersmith Hosp 1951–55 and 1956–58 (liaison physician Obstetric Dept 1953–55); Royal Victoria Infirmary Newcastle upon Tyne: conslt physician and lectr in med Univ of Durham 1958–64, conslt physician and reader in med Univ of Newcastle upon Tyne 1964–66; conslt physician and prof of med Queen's Univ Royal Victoria Hosp Belfast NI 1966–82, dir of med servs Maltese Islands 1981–82; Prince of Wales Hosp Shatin NT Hong Kong: fndn prof and chm Dept of Med Chinese Univ of Hong Kong 1983–88, currently emeritus prof; assoc dean Faculty Med Chinese Univ of Hong Kong, hon conslt med to Hong Kong Govt 1984–88, hon conslt med Br Army Hong Kong 1985–88, conslt physician London Ind Hosp 1988–99, med advsr on clinical complaints NE Thames RHA 1989–96 and NW Thames RHA 1994–96 conslt physician London Ind Hosp 1988–99, conslt physician The Wellington Hosp 1999–2003; currently visiting prof ICSTM Hammersmith Hosp 1988–; memb Northern Health and Social Servs Bd DHSS NI 1973–82 (memb Standing Med Advsy Ctee 1969–73); cncllr: RCP London 1976–79 (regnl advsr NI 1970–75), RCP Ireland 1976–82; life memb RSM; FRCP, FRCPI, FRCPath; *Books* Essentials of Cardiology (1961, 2 edn 1968), Diabetes: Its Physiological & Biochemical Basis (1975); *Recreations* tennis, golf, music; *Clubs* E India, United Servs Recreation (Hong Kong); *Style*— Prof John Vallance-Owen; ✉ 10 Spinney Drive, Great Shelford, Cambridge CB2 5LY (tel 01223 842767); 17 St Matthews Lodge, Oakley Square, London NW1 1NB (tel 020 7388 3644); Cuildochart, Killin, Perthshire (tel 015672 337)

VALLAT, Prof Sir Francis Aimé; GBE (1981), KCMG (1962, CMG 1955), QC (1961); s of Col Frederick Vallat, OBE (d 1922); *b* 25 May 1912; *Educ* UC Toronto, Gonville & Caius Coll Cambridge; *m* 1, 1939 (m dis 1973), Mary Alison, da of F H Cockell; 1 s, 1 da; m 2, 1988, Patricia Maria (d 1995), da of Capt Hamish Morton Anderson, MB ChB, RAMC; m 3, 1996, Joan Olive, wid of Adm Sir F R Parham, GBE, KCB, DSO; *Career* served WWII as Flt Lt RAFVR; called to the Bar Gray's Inn 1935 (bencher 1971); joined FO 1945, legal advsr Perm UK Delegation to UN 1950–54, dep legal advsr FO 1954–60, legal advsr 1960–68, visiting prof McGill Univ Montreal 1965–66; dir Int Law Studies King's Coll London 1968–76, reader Int Law Univ of London 1969–70 (prof 1970–76, prof emeritus 1976–); memb: Int Law Cmmn 1973–81 (chm 1977–78), Permanent Court of Arbitration 1981–92, Curatorium Hague Acad of Int Law 1982–98 (vice-pres 1993–98), Inst of Int Law 1965–99 (vice-pres 1989–91, memb emeritus 1999–); Dr en dr (hc) Univ of Lausanne 1979; *Clubs* Hurlingham, Sloane; *Style*— Prof Sir Francis Vallat, GBE, KCMG, QC; ✉ The Coach House, Church Road, West Lavington, Midhurst, West Sussex GU29 0EH

VALLINGS, Robert Ross; s of Lt Cdr Robert Archibald Vallings, DSC, RNVR (d 1969), of Perth, Scotland, and Alice Mary Joan, *née* Bramsdon (d 1964); *b* 18 November 1943; *Educ* Rugby; *m* 12 May 1973, Penelope Claire, da of Dr Thomas Parham Lalonde (d 1982), of Romsey, Hants; 1 s (Timothy b 1974), 1 da (Claire b 1975); *Career* admitted slr 1969; Radcliffes: ptnr 1970–, managing ptnr 1992–96, sr ptnr 1998–2004; *Recreations* sport; *Clubs* Naval and Military, Richmond FC, Hurlingham, Royal Mid-Surrey Golf; *Style*— Robert Vallings, Esq; ✉ RadcliffesLeBrasseur, 5 Great College Street, Westminster, London SW1P 3SJ (tel 020 7222 7040, fax 020 7222 6208, e-mail robert.vallings@rlb-law.com)

VALLO, (Maria) Ambra; da of Gianni Vallo, of Naples, Italy, and Lucia Acquaviva; *b* Naples, Italy; *Educ* Royal Ballet Sch of Flanders Antwerp; *Career* ballet dancer; former soloist Royal Ballet of Walloons and Royal Ballet of Flanders, with Eng Nat Ballet 1993–96 (latterly sr soloist), with Birmingham Royal Ballet 1996– (princ 2001–); repertory incl: Giselle in Giselle, Juliet in Romeo and Juliet, Odette/Odile in Swan Lake, Aurora in The Sleeping Beauty, Sugar Plum Fairy in The Nutcracker, Swanhilda in Coppélia, Kitri in Don Quixote, Lise in La Fille Mal Gardée, Lead Girl in Etude, Young Girl in The Two Pigeons, Polka and Girl in Solitaire, Bathsheba in Far from the Madding Crowd, Isabella in Edward II, Guinevere in Arthur, Roxane in Cyrano, Belle and wild girl in Beauty and the Beast, Annunciation in The Protecting Veil, Maggie, Vicky and Salvation Army in Hobson's Choice, Lover Girl in Carmina Burana, Titania and Desdemona in The Shakespeare Suite, Spring in The Seasons, princ in Powder, Calliope Rag in Elite Syncopations, La Capricciosa in Lady and the Fool, Sanguine Variation in The Four Temperaments, Graduation Ball, Voices of Spring, The Walk to the Paradise Garden, Symphonic Variations, Serenade, Symphony in Three Movements, Concerto Barocco, Tarantella, Square Dance, Violin Conerto No 2 Mouvement, Tchaikovsky pas de deux Apollo, princ girl 2nd movement in Western Symphony, Chorus, Dance House, In the Upper Room, That's Life in Sinatra Songs, Five Tangos; first prize Luxembourg Int Grand Prix, Gold medal Rieti Int Competition, Silver medal Houlgate France, Most Talented Up-and-Coming Dancer Positano Critics Circle Award 1991, Best Female Dancer Danza & Danza Critics Circle Award 2004, Best Performance Positano Critics Circle Award 2002; *Recreations* engine-free hang gliding, travel, country walking, cinema, reading; *Style*— Miss Ambra Vallo

VALMAN, Dr (Hyman) Bernard; s of Samuel Valman, and Lillian, *née* Schwoltz; *b* 10 February 1934; *Educ* Charterhouse, Univ of Cambridge (MA, MD); *m* 24 May 1964, Thea, da of Maj Weiss (d 1958); 1 da (Nadia Deborah b 11 Jan 1968), 1 s (Martin David b 29 Dec 1969); *Career* Nat Serv Capt RAMC 1959–61; sr registrar The Hosp for Sick Children Gt Ormond St 1969–72, conslt paediatrician Northwick Park Hosp and Clinical Res Centre Harrow 1972–; RCP: sec to Paediatric Ctee 1981–91, chm Examining Bd for Dip in Child Health 1990–95; ed Archives of Disease in Childhood 1982–94; memb Soc of Authors; FRSM, FRCP, FRCPCH (hon archivist); *Books* ABC of The First Year (5 edn, 2002), When Your Child Is Ill (2 edn, 2002); *Recreations* gardening, editing, writing; *Style*— Dr Bernard Valman; ✉ Northwick Park Hospital, Harrow, Middlesex HA1 3UJ (tel 020 8864 3232)

VALNER, Nicholas Edmund; *b* 14 September 1953; *Educ* Stonyhurst, Univ of Oxford (MA); *m*; 3 c; *Career* Frere Cholmeley Bischoff: articled clerk (admitted 1979), ptnr 1985–98, head of Media; ptnr Eversheds (following merger) 1998– (head of Int Arbitration and London Commercial Litigation); chair numerous confs on arbitration law Inst of Arbitrators, frequent speaker IBA, Inst of Civil and Comparative Law and American Bar Assoc; memb: IBA, London Slrs' Litigation Assoc; ACIArb; *Style*— Nicholas Valner, Esq; ✉ Eversheds, Senator House, 85 Queen Victoria Street, London EC4V 4JL (tel 020 7919 4500, fax 020 7919 4919)

VAN ALLAN, Richard; CBE (2002); s of Joseph Arthur Jones, of Mansfield, Notts, and Irene Hannah, *née* Taylor; *b* 28 May 1935; *Educ* Brunts GS Mansfield, Worcester Coll of Educn (DipEd), Birmingham Sch of Music; *m* 1, 1963 (m dis 1974), Elizabeth Mary, da of Bib Peabody (d 1973), of Leamington Spa, Warks; 1 s (Guy Richard b 1967); m 2, 1976 (m dis 1987), Elisabeth Rosemary, da of Richard Pickering, DM, of Cape Town, South Africa; 1 s (Robert Tristan b 1979 d 1999), 1 da (Emma Mary b 1983); *Career* operatic bass; former police offr (Sgt Special Investigation Branch, RMP police constable 1953–56) and sch teacher, professional singer 1964–; dir Nat Opera Studio until 2001, memb Bd of Dirs ENO 1995–98 (resigned); principal bass at: Glyndebourne, WNO, ENO, Scottish Opera, Royal Opera House Covent Garden, Nice, Bordeaux, Paris, Marseille, Bruxelles, Madrid, San Diego, Miami, Boston, Seattle, Metropolitan NY, Buenos Aires, Victoria State Opera Melbourne, Houston; awarded Sir Charles Santley Meml Gift 1995; Hon RAM, hon fell Birmingham Conservatoire (formerly Birmingham Schs of Music); *Recordings* incl: Don Alfonso in Cosi Fan Tutte (Grammy award), Leporello in Don Giovanni (Grammy nomination), Sir Walter Raleigh in Gloriana (Grammy nomination); *Recreations* cricket, golf, shooting; *Style*— Richard Van Allan, Esq, CBE; ✉ 18 Octavia Street, London SW11 3DN (tel 020 7228 8462, fax 020 7228 4367, e-mail rvanallan@aol.com)

van ANDEL, Prof Tjeerd Hendrik; s of Dr Jacobus Cornelis van Andel (d 1980), and Olga Marie Louise van Andel-Ripke (d 1971); *b* 15 February 1923, Rotterdam, Netherlands; *Educ* Gymnasium Leeuwarden, Univ of Groningen (BSc, MSc, PhD); *Family* 4 da (Charlotte (Mrs Bialek) b 10 Oct 1951, Barbara (Mrs Caselli) b 1 Aug 1953, Jessica (Mrs Jenkel) b 26 Jan 1955, Carol (Mrs Cobb) b 8 Dec 1957), 2 s (Jacob Christopher b 30 Sept 1966, Jeffery Paul b 7 Nov 1968); m, 12 Feb 1988, Dr Katharine Bridget (Kate) Pretty, *qv*; *Career* lectr in geology Univ of Wageningen 1949–50, sedimentologist and head Central Sediment Lab Bataafse Petroleum Maatschappij Amsterdam 1950–53, sedimentologist Cia Shell de Venezuela Maracaibo 1953–56, research geologist Scripps

V

Instn of Oceanography Calif 1957–68, prof of oceanography and head of marine geosciences Grad Sch of Oceanography Oregon State Univ Corvallis 1968–76, Wayne Lowell prof of ocean sciences Stanford Univ 1976–88 (emeritus 1988–), hon prof of earth history, quaternary science and geo-archaeology Univ of Cambridge 1988–, sr research fell Dept of Archaeology Boston Univ 1989–; memb Clare Hall Cambridge; ldr of research projects, chief scientist on expeditions in Pacific and Atlantic Oceans; fell: Geological Soc of America 1958, Royal Netherlands Acad of Sciences 1975, American Geophysical Union 1980, AAAS 1981, Calif Acad of Sciences 1983 (hon fell 1988); founding memb Int Assoc of Sedimentologists 1954; memb: Assoc for Environmental Archaeology 1989, Quaternary Research Assoc 1991, Soc for Archaeological Science 1992; Royal-Dutch Shell Distinguished Grad Fellowship 1946–50, Francis P Shepard Medal for Marine Geology 1978, First Norman Watkins Award in Oceanography Univ of Rhode Island 1980, Van Waterschoot van der Gracht Medal Royal Netherlands Geological Soc 1984, Award for Excellence in Teaching Sch of Earth Sciences Stanford Univ 1984, Archaeological Geology Award Geological Soc of America 1997; *Publications* 15 books and edited vols incl: Tales of an Old Ocean (1977), New Views on an Old Planet - Continental Drift and the History of the Earth (1985, 2 edn 1994, Award for Best Scholarly Book in Physical Sciences in 1985 American Assoc of Publishers), Neanderthals and Modern Humans in the European Landscape of the Last Glaciation - Archaeological Results of the Stage 3 Project (with W Davies, 2003); also author of 161 papers in scientific jls and 49 miscellaneous papers; *Recreations* gardening, reading (mostly historical), travel; *Style*— Prof Tjeerd H van Andel; ✉ Department of Earth Sciences, University of Cambridge, Downing Street, Cambridge CB2 3EQ (tel 01223 333440, fax 01223 333540, e-mail vanandel@esc.cam.ac.uk)

van CUTSEM, Geoffrey Neil; yr s of Bernard van Cutsem (d 1975), and Mary (d 1989), da of Capt Edward Compton, JP, DL (s of Lord Alwyne Compton, 2 s of 4 Marquess of Northampton, KG), of Newby Hall, Ripon; yr bro of Hugh van Cutsem, *qv*; *b* 23 November 1944; *Educ* Ampleforth; *m* 1, 30 Oct 1969 (m dis 2003), Sarah, only da of Alastair McCorquodale; 2 da (Sophie b 5 Aug 1975, Zara b 11 Dec 1978); m 2, 2006, Mrs Lucy Price; *Career* served RHG (Blues and Royals) 1963–68, Capt 1967; exec dir Savills 1987–2006 (joined 1969); former tstee Cancer Res UK; chm of tstees St Mary's Sch Ascot Berks; FRICS 1973; *Clubs* White's, Pratt's; *Style*— Geoffrey van Cutsem, Esq; ✉ The Old Vicarage, Well, Bedale, North Yorkshire DL8 2PX (tel 01677 470448)

van CUTSEM, Hugh Bernard Edward; s of Bernard van Cutsem (d 1975), and Mary, da of Capt Edward Compton, JP, DL (himself s of Lord Alwyne Compton, 2 s of 4 Marquess of Northampton, KG), of Newby Hall, Ripon; er bro of Geoffrey van Cutsem, *qv*; *b* 21 July 1941; *Educ* Ampleforth; *m* 1971, Jonkvrouwe Emilie Elise Christine, da of Jonkheer Pieter Quarles van Ufford (Netherlands cr of Willem I 1814), of Westgate House, Thetford; 4 s; *Career* Lt Life Gds; bloodstock breeder, farmer; vice-pres Game Conservancy, chm Norfolk Branch Country Land and Business Assoc; memb: Cncl Nat Tst 1998–, Cncl English Nature 2002; pres SW Norfolk Cons Assoc; Sec-Gen and Knight of Honour and Devotion Br Assoc SMOM; *Clubs* Jockey, White's, Pratt's; *Style*— Hugh van Cutsem, Esq; ✉ Hilborough House, Thetford, Norfolk IP26 5BQ

van de VEN, Prof Johan Jacob (Hans); s of Henricus Morius Gerardus Johannes van de Ven, and Reinera Johanna Liduina, *née* Jonker Roelants; *b* 10 January 1958, The Hague, Netherlands; *Educ* Leiden Univ (BA), Harvard Univ (PhD); *m* 16 July 1983, Susan Elizabeth, *née* Kerr; 3 s (Johan Malcolm, Derek Marius (twins) b 10 Oct 1991, Willem Andrew b 8 Nov 1997); *Career* Faculty of Oriental Studies Univ of Cambridge: lectr 1988, sr lectr 2000, reader 2002, prof 2004; chm Ivonne van de Ven Fndn; Philip Lilienthal Prize 1991; Br Acad research reader 1996–98; memb: Assoc of Asian Studies, European Assoc of Asian Studies; *Publications* From Friend to Comrade: The Founding of the Chinese Communist Party (1991), War and Nationalism in China (2001); *Recreations* tennis, camping, sailing; *Style*— Prof Hans van de Ven; ✉ Faculty of Asian and Middle Eastern Studies, University of Cambridge, Sidgwick Avenue, Cambridge CB3 9DA (tel 01223 338331, e-mail jjv10@cam.ac.uk)

VAN DE WALLE, Leslie; s of Philippe Van de Walle, of Paris, France, and Luce, *née* Beaubien; *b* 27 March 1956; *m* 22 June 1982, Domitille; 2 da (Stephanie b 1 May 1984, Philippine b 17 July 1986); *Career* product mangr Danone France 1980–84; Cadbury Schweppes plc: md France 1984–1990 and 1992–93, md Benelux 1990–92, md Iberia 1993–94; United Biscuits plc: md European Snacks 1994–96, chief exec European Snacks and Biscuits 1996–98, chief exec McVities Gp 1998–99, gp chief exec 1999–2002; successively pres Shell S America and Africa Shell Int, pres Shell Europe Oil Products then exec vice-pres global retail Royal Dutch Shell 2001–07, chief exec Rexam plc 2007–; non-exec dir Aegis Gp plc 2003–; memb: Golf Mgmnt Bd, Food and Drink Fedn, Food and Drink Assoc; *Recreations* golf, movies, reading, tourism; *Clubs* Foxhills Golf, Chantilly Golf, Chairman's; *Style*— Leslie Van de Walle, Esq; ✉ Rexam plc, 4 Millbank, London SW1P 3XR

van den BERGH, Maarten Albert; s of Sidney James van den Bergh, and Maria, *née* Mijers; *b* 19 April 1942, NY (holds Dutch nationality); *Educ* Univ of Groningen Netherlands; *m* Marjan Désirée, *née* Kramer; 2 da; *Career* Royal Dutch/Shell Gp: joined 1968, co-ordinator East and Australasia Area 1981–83, dep gp treas Shell Int 1983–87, chm Shell Cos Thailand 1987–89, regnl co-ordinator Western Hemisphere and Africa Shell Int 1989–92, gp md 1992–2000, vice-chm Ctee of MDs and pres Royal Dutch Petroleum Co 1998–2000; chm: Lloyds TSB Gp plc 2001–06 (dep chm 2000–01), Akzo Nobel NV 2006– (memb Supervisory Bd 2005–); non-exec dir: Royal Dutch Shell plc, BT Gp plc 2000– (dep chm 2006–), British Airways plc 2002–; memb Steering Bd and Dutch co-chm Apeldoorn Conf 2003–; memb: Chief Exec's Cncl of Int Advsrs of the Hong Kong Special Admin Region 1998–2002, Pres of the Philippines Special Bd of Advsrs 2001–05, Advsy Cncl Amsterdam Inst of Fin 2001–05; memb Guild of Int Bankers until 2006; advsr Rembrandt Soc 2001–05; FCIB 2001–06 (vice-pres), CCMI 2001–06; *Recreations* European history, Asian antiques; *Clubs* Soc De Witte (The Hague); *Style*— Maarten van den Bergh, Esq

VAN DER BIJL, His Hon Judge Nigel Charles; s of late Nicholas Alexander Christian Van der Bijl, and Mollie Van der Bijl; *b* 28 April 1948; *Educ* Trinity Coll Dublin (BA, LLB); *m* 1974, Loba, *née* Nassiri; 1 s, 1 da; *Career* called to the Bar Inner Temple 1973; co sec Int Div Beecham Pharmaceutical 1973–74, legal mangr Shahpur Chemical Co Ltd and Nat Iranian Oil Co Tehran 1974–77, barr in private practice 1977–2001, recorder 1996–2001, circuit judge (SE Circuit) 2001–, hon recorder City of Canterbury 2004–; friend Br Sch of Athens 1996–; *Recreations* cycling; *Clubs* Bar Cycling (pres); *Style*— His Hon Judge Van der Bijl; ✉ c/o The Law Courts, Chaucer Road, Canterbury, Kent CT1 1ZA

van der WERFF, His Hon Jonathan Ervine; s of James van der Werff (d 1960), of London, and Clare Poupart, *née* Ervine (d 2006); *b* 23 June 1935; *Educ* Harrow, RMA Sandhurst; *m* 17 Sept 1968, Katharine Bridget, da of Maj James Colvin (d 1993), of Withypool, Somerset; 2 da (Olivia b 1971, Claudia b 1976); *Career* joined Coldstream Gds 1953, RMA Sandhurst 1954–55, cmmnd 1955, Adj 1 Bn 1962–64, Maj 1967, ret 1968; called to the Bar Inner Temple 1969, recorder 1986, circuit judge (SE Circuit) 1986, resident judge Croydon Combined Court Centre 1989–93, sr circuit judge 1993, resident judge Inner London Crown Court 1993–2007; *Clubs* Pratt's, Boodle's, Bembridge Sailing, Something; *Style*— His Hon Jonathan van der Werff; ✉ Inner London Crown Court, The Sessions House, Newington Causeway, London SE1 6AZ

van der WYCK, Jonkheer Herman Constantyn; s of Jonkheer Hendrik Lodewyk van der Wyck, OBE (d 1986), Col Royal Netherlands Artillery, and Berendina Johanna van Welderen, Baroness Rengers (d 1963); *b* 17 March 1934; *Educ* Inst for Int Studies Univ of Geneva (MA), Rotterdam and Ann Arbour Business Sch (MA); *m* 1, 1959 (m dis 1969), Danielle Mourgue d'Algue; 1 da (Edina Nathalie b 8 Aug 1960), 1 s (Patrick Henri Louis b 5 Dec 1962); m 2, 1977 (m dis 1988), Jonkvrouwe Viviana Olga Paulina van Reigersberg Versluys; 2 s (Edzard Lorillard b 10 Oct 1980, Alexander Lodewyk b 5 Aug 1985); *Career* Capt Royal Dutch Cavalry, ret; vice-chm and md UBS Warburg, ret; dir: Compagnie Internationale de Placements et de Capitalisation, Wilken USA Select Fund; chm Hermes Focus Asset Management Europe; *Recreations* skiing, water skiing, swimming, tennis, reading, music; *Style*— Jonkheer Herman C van der Wyck; ✉ 27 South Terrace, London SW7 2TB (tel 020 7584 9931)

van GELDER, Peter Samuel; s of Joseph van Gelder (d 1988), and Sylvia, *née* Cornberg; *b* 12 August 1953; *Educ* Westmount HS Montreal, Aston Univ (BSc), UC Cardiff (Postgrad Dip Journalism); *m* Mary-Jane, da of Hugh Campbell Drummond; 1 s (Joseph Robert b 22 Jan 1989), 1 da (Katharine Elizabeth b 12 Feb 1992); *Career* news asst BBC Wales Cardiff 1977–78, news prodr and political corr BBC Radio Leeds 1978–81, asst prodr Newsnight BBC TV London 1981–82; TV-am: asst prodr Michael Parkinson Show 1982–84, news reporter 1984–86, prodr Good Morning Britain 1986–88, ed Children's Progs 1988–89, asst managing ed 1989–91, managing ed 1991–93; md Teletext Ltd 1993–97, md British Interactive Broadcasting 1997–98, principal and md Informed Sources 1999–2002, dir Westminster Forum Projects (Westminster Media Forum, Westminster eForum, Westminster Nutrition Forum, Westminster Health Forum, Westminster Educn Forum) 2002–; *Books* Offscreen Onscreen (1991); *Recreations* music, writing, pinball; *Style*— Peter van Gelder, Esq

van HEYNINGEN, Prof Veronica; da of Laszlo Daniel (d 1973), and Anne, *née* Eisler; *b* 12 November 1946, Hungary; *Educ* Humphrey Perkins Sch, Girton Coll Cambridge (MA), Northwestern Univ IL (MS), Lady Margaret Hall Oxford (DPhil); *m* 1968, Simon van Heyningen, s of William E van Heyningen; 1 s (Paul b 5 July 1975), 1 da (Eleanor b 25 Dec 1976); *Career* Beit Memorial fell: Oxford Genetics Laboratory 1973–74, MRC Mammalian Genome Unit Edinburgh 1974–76; MRC Human Genetics Unit Edinburgh: MRC postdoctoral scientist 1977–81, appt of unlimited tenure 1981–86, appt to sr scientist grade 1986–91, special appt grade 1991–, head Cell Genetics Section 1992–; Howard Hughes Int Research Scholar 1993–98; hon treas Genetical Society 1994–98; Human Genome Organisation (HUGO): memb, memb Human Genome Mapping Committee 1994, chm 1996; pres European Soc of Human Genetics 2003; memb: Human Genetics Cmmn 2000–05, European Molecular Biology Organisation 2002–; memb Editorial Bd: British Journal of Cancer 1990–97, Human Molecular Genetics 1996–2003, PLOS Genetics 2005–; tstee National Museums of Scotland 1993–2000; hon prof Faculty of Medicine Univ of Edinburgh 1995, FRSE 1997, FMedSci 1999, FRS 2007; *Publications* author of over 200 articles in learned jls; *Recreations* museums, theatre, travel, cooking; *Style*— Prof Veronica van Heyningen, FRS; ✉ MRC Human Genetics Unit, Western General Hospital, Edinburgh EH4 2XU (tel 0131 467 8405, fax 0131 467 8456, e-mail v.vanheyningen@hgu.mrc.ac.uk)

VAN ORDEN, Brig Geoffrey Charles; MBE (1973), MEP (Cons) Eastern England; s of late Thomas Henry Van Orden, and late Mary Van Orden; *b* 10 April 1945; *Educ* Sandown Sch, Mons Officer Cadet Sch, Univ of Sussex (BA), Indian Defence Services Staff Coll; *m* 1974, Frances; 3 da; *Career* cmmnd Intelligence Corps 1964, operational service in Borneo, NI etc, directing staff Führungs Akademie der Bundeswehr Hamburg 1985–88, COS and ACOS G2 Berlin (Br Sector) 1988–90, Assessment Staff Cabinet Office 1990, res assoc IISS and service fell Dept of War Studies KCL 1990–91, head Int Military Staff Secretariat NATO HQ 1991–94, transferred to Reg Res 1994; sr official EC Directorate-General External Relations 1995–99; MEP (Cons) Eastern England 1999–, Cons spokesman on def, memb Foreign Affrs, Human Rights and Def Ctee European Parl (vice-chm 2001–06), memb delgns to NATO and to Turkey, Parly rapporteur on Bulgaria; memb: IISS 1991–, Friends of the Union 1997–, Countryside Alliance 1999–, Bow Gp 1999–; fndr memb Anglo-German Officers Assoc 1991–; Freeman: City of London 1991, Worshipful Co of Painter-Stainers 1991; FIMgt 1993; *Publications* various articles on foreign and security policy issues; *Clubs* Army and Navy; *Style*— Mr Geoffrey Van Orden, MBE, MEP; ✉ 88 Rectory Lane, Chelmsford, Essex CM1 1RF (tel 01245 345141, fax 01245 269757, e-mail gvanorden@europarl.eu.int)

VAN OUTEN, Denise; *b* 1974, Basildon, Essex; *Career* television personality and actress; *Theatre* Chicago (London) 2001–02, Chicago (Broadway) 2002, Tell Me On A Sunday (Gielgud Theatre) 2003; *Television* appearances incl: Crossbow 1986, Kappatoo 1990, Operation Good Guys 1997, The Young Person's Guide to Becoming a Rock Star 1998, Jack and the Beanstalk 1998; presenter: The Big Breakfast 1995–99 and 2000–01, Something for the Weekend 1999, Prickly Heat 2000–; starred in Babes in the Wood 1998; *Film* appearances incl: Tube Tales 1999, Love Honour And Obey 2000; *Style*— Ms Denise Van Outen; ✉ c/o PFD, Drury House, 34–43 Russell Street, London WC2B 5HA

van PRAAG, Lucas; s of Louis van Praag, CBE (d 1993), and Angela, *née* McCorquodale; *b* 12 January 1950; *Educ* Frensham Heights Sch, Sch of Navigation Warsash, Univ of Durham (BA); *m* 1996, Miranda, da of Richard Allan; 2 s (Joe b 27 March 1997, Sam b 6 Nov 1998), 1 da (Lola b 2 Aug 2000); *Career* Bankers Trust Company 1975–85, Sabre International Group Ltd 1986–89, John Brown Publishing Ltd 1989–92, ptnr Brunswick Group Ltd 1992–2000; md Goldman Sachs & Co 2000–; *Recreations* reading, sailing, skiing, friends; *Clubs* Groucho; *Style*— Lucas van Praag, Esq; ✉ Goldman Sachs & Co, 85 Broad Street, New York, NY 10004, USA (tel 212 902 7712, e-mail lucas.vanpraag@gs.com)

VAN REENEN, Prof John; s of L Van Reenen and A Van Reenen, *née* Williams; *b* 26 December 1965, Carlisle; *Educ* Queens Coll Cambridge (Joshua King Prize, BA), LSE (MSc), UCL (PhD); *m* 20 May 2001, Sarah Chambers; *Career* research fell Inst for Fiscal Studies 1992–99, prof Dept of Economics UCL 1994–2003, currently dir Centre for Economic Performance and prof Dept of Economics LSE; visiting prof Dept of Economics Univ of California 1998–99; policy advsr on educn, enterprise and tax 10 Downing St 1999–2000, sr policy advsr to Sec of State for Health 2000–01, advsr to Chief Economist of DG Competition EC 2003–, academic assoc HM Treasy 2003–, memb Strategy Bd on Productivity ONS; chief coordinator EU TSER Network R&D Innovation and Productivity project 1996–99; memb Editorial Bd: Review of Economic Studies 1997–2003, European Economic Review 1999–2003, Jl of Industrial Economics 1999– (assoc ed 1996–), Editorial Policy 2000–03; author of numerous articles in learned jls incl American Economic Review, Br Jl of Industrial Relations and Quarterly Jl of Economics; ptnr Lexecon Ltd 2001–02; memb: Econometric Soc, American Economic Assoc; *Clubs* Blacks; *Style*— Prof John Van Reenen; ✉ Centre for Economic Performance, London School of Economics, Houghton Street, London WC2A 2AE (tel 020 7955 6976)

van RIJSBERGEN, Prof Cornelis Joost; s of Jacob Adam van Rijsbergen (d 1987), and Gerritdina, *née* Verheij; *b* 17 October 1943; *Educ* Univ of W Aust (BSc), Univ of Cambridge (PhD); *m* 22 May 1965, Juliet Hilary, da of Ernest Arthur Clement Gundry, of Perth, Aust; 1 da (Nicola b 1973); *Career* tutor in mathematics Univ of W Aust 1966–68, lectr Monash Univ 1973–75, Royal Soc res fell Univ of Cambridge 1975–79 (sr res offr King's Coll 1969–72); prof of computer sci: Univ Coll Dublin 1980–86, Univ of Glasgow 1986–; ed-in-chief The Computer Jl 1993–2000; Tony Kent Strix Award 2004; Fell BCS 1971, FIEE 1987, FRSE 1994, FREng 2004, FACM 2004; *Books* Information Retrieval (2 edn, 1979), The Geometry of Information Retrieval (2004); *Recreations* swimming, cinema, travel, fiction; *Clubs* Oxford and Cambridge; *Style*— Prof Cornelis van Rijsbergen, FRSE; ✉ 14 Park Parade, Cambridge CB5 8AL (tel 01223 360318); 18A Westbourne Gardens, Glasgow G12 9XD (tel 0141 339 8331); Department of Computing Science, University of Glasgow, Glasgow G12 8QQ (tel 0141 330 4463, fax 0141 330 4913, telex 777070 UNIGLA, e-mail keith@dcs.gla.ac.uk)

van WALSUM, Joeske; s of Hans van Walsum, of Amsterdam, Holland, and Lies, *née* Schuurman-Stekhoven; *b* 26 May 1949; *Educ* Robert Gordon's Coll Aberdeen, RCM London; *m* 10 July 1969 (m dis 2002), Elizabeth Ann, da of Ronald Charles Marsh; 2 da (Georgiana b 27 Feb 1976, Abigail b 16 Dec 1977); m 2, 17 April 2003, Rachel, da of Mark Bostock; *Career* freelance musician and flute teacher 1971–74, chm Van Walsum Management (int mangrs of conductors, composers, musicians, singers and orchs and promoters of concert series and tours) 1975–; chm Br Assoc of Concert Agents 1989–92; organiser and chm Musicians for Armenia benefit concert 1988; *Recreations* white water canoeing, long distance walking, roller blading, cycling; *Style—* Joeske van Walsum, Esq; ✉ Van Walsum Management, The Tower Building, 11 York Road, London SE1 7NX (tel 020 7902 0521, fax 020 7902 0530, e-mail jvw@vanwalsum.co.uk, website www.vanwalsum.com)

VANCE, Charles Ivan; s of E Goldblatt; *b* 1929; *Educ* Royal Sch Dungannon, Queen's Univ Belfast; *m* 1966, Hon Imogen Moynihan, da of 2 Baron Moynihan, OBE, TD (d 1965); 1 da (Jacqueline); *Career* actor, theatrical director, producer, publisher and editor; acting debut with Anew MacMaster Co (Gaiety Dublin) 1949, directing debut The Glass Menagerie (Arts Cambridge) 1960, fndr Civic Theatre Chelmsford 1962, i/c rep cos Tunbridge Wells, Torquay, Whitby and Hastings 1962–, fndr dir Charles Vance Prodns (created Eastbourne Theatre Co 1969), purchased Leas Pavilion Theatre Folkestone 1976 (HQ until 1985); mangr: Floral Hall Theatre Scarborough 1984–86, Beck Theatre Hillingdon 1986–90, Grand Opera House York 1988–89, Summer Theatre Manor Pavilion Sidmouth 1987–; dir and vice-chm Festival of Britain Theatre 1975–; numerous prodns as dir incl Witness for the Prosecution (revival) 1979 and 1992; numerous prodns as dir and prodr incl: Daisy Pulls it Off 1991, Gaslight 1991, Time and Time Again 1991, My Cousin Rachel 1992, Witness for the Prosecution 1992, Godspell 1994, Brideshead Revisited 1995, Jane Eyre 1996, Lettice & Lovage 1997, Kind Hearts & Coronets 1998, The 39 Steps 1998, The Ladykillers 1999, What the Butler Saw 1999, Passport to Pimlico 2000, Oh What a Lovely War 2000, The Lady Vanishes 2001, Bedside Manners 2001, Lavender Hill Mob 2002, Who Killed Agatha Christie? 2002, Edge of Darkness 2003, The musical Celebration of Heartbeat 2004; fndr Vance Offord (Publications) Ltd (publishers of Br Theatre Directory, Br Theatre Review and Municipal Entertainment) 1971, chm and fndr Platform Publications Ltd 1987–, ed-in-chief Team Publishing 1986–87, ed Amateur Stage 1987–; ed All I Want for Christmas 1995; dir: Theatres Investment Fund 1975–83, Entertainment Investments Ltd 1980–82, International Holiday Investments 1980–87, Southern Counties Television 1980–87, Channel Radio 1981–86, Gateway Broadcasting Ltd 1982; chm Prestige Plays Ltd (dir 1987–93); ops dir Contemporary Theatres Ltd 1992–94, chm Charles Vance Productions 1994–; patron Voluntary Arts Network; Theatrical Mgmnt Assoc: memb Cncl 1969, pres 1971–73 and 1973–76, exec vice-pres 1976–; tstee dir Folkestone Theatre Co 1979–85; chm: Provincial Theatre Cncl 1971–87, Standing Advsy Ctee on Local Authy and the Theatre 1977–90 (vice-chm 1975–77), Gala and Fund-raising Ctee Br Theatre Assoc 1986–90, Standing Advsy Ctee on Local Authy and the Performing Arts 1990–95; vice-chm Theatres Advsy Cncl responsible for theatres threatened by devpt 1974–2002; memb: Theatres Nat Ctee 1971–, Drama Advsy Panel SE Arts Assoc 1974–85, Prince of Wales's Jubilee Entertainments Ctee 1977, Entertainment Exec Ctee Artists' Benevolent Fund 1980–; vice-pres E Sussex RSPCA 1975–; memb CBI; Chambellan de L'ordre des Coteaux de Champagne; FRSA, FInstD; *Books* British Theatre Directory (1972, 1973, 1974 and 1975), Amateur Theatre Yearbook (ed, 1989, 1991, 1992, 1994, 1997 and 1999), Community Theatre Directory 2003 and 2004, Agatha Christie, the Theatrical Celebration (1990); published plays: Wuthering Heights (adaptation, 1992), Jane Eyre (adaptation, 1996); *Recreations* travel, cooking, sailing (in 1956 single handed crossing Atlantic), dog breeding; *Clubs* RAC, Wig and Pen, Kennel (memb Ctee 1989–), Hurlingham, Groucho, Home House, Variety Club of GB, Rotary Club of London, Lord's Taverners; *Style—* Charles Vance, Esq; ✉ Hampden House, 2 Weymouth Street, London W1W 5BT (tel 020 7636 4343, fax 020 7636 2323, e-mail cvpersonal@aol.com)

VANDERSTEEN, Martin Hugh; s of William Martin Vandersteen (d 1983), and Dorothy Margaret, *née* Leith (d 1994); *b* 9 August 1935; *Educ* Harrow Co GS, Open Univ (BSc); *m* 3 April 1967, Catherine Susan Mary, da of John Cansdale Webb (d 1992), and Kathleen Anna, *née* Smith; 2 s (Anthony b 1970, William b 1973); *Career* Andersen Consulting (now Accenture): joined 1957, ptnr 1968, UK managing ptnr 1973–86, managing ptnr regnl 1989–94, managing ptnr resources and quality 1994–97; chm: UK Mgmnt Consulting Assoc 1981, Kingston Hosp NHS Tst 1999–2000, Barts and the London Hosp NHS Tst 2001–03; FCA; *Recreations* sailing, fishing, golf, swimming; *Clubs* Arts, Royal Ocean Racing, Royal Southern Yacht, Royal Wimbledon Golf, Otter Swimming; *Style—* Martin Vandersteen, Esq; ✉ 2 Bristol Gardens, Putney Heath, London SW15 3TG (tel 020 8788 9026, e-mail mvanderstn@aol.com)

VANE PERCY, Christopher David; s of Kenneth Vane Percy (d 1998), and Jean Farquharson; *b* 15 March 1945; *Educ* Bedford Sch; *m* 17 May 1973, Lady Linda Denise Grosvenor, da of 5 Baron Ebury, DSO (d 1957); 1 s (Maximilian Egerton b 1979), 2 da (Grace Dorothy Denise b 1981, Tryce Mary Susanne b 1991); *Career* interior designer; pres Int Interior Design Assoc (London chapter), chm Br Interior Designers Assoc (BIDA); patron Cambridge Gardens Tst; memb Godmanchester Town Cncl 1985–; *Books* The Glass of Lalique - A Collector's Guide (1977); *Style—* Christopher Vane Percy, Esq; ✉ Island Hall, Godmanchester, Cambridgeshire PE29 2BA (tel 01480 459676); CVP Designs Ltd, The Old Dairy, 7 Hewer Street, London W10 6DU (tel 020 8960 9026, fax 020 8969 3589, e-mail cvp@cvpdesigns.com)

VANEZIS, Prof Peter Savvas; OBE (2001); *b* 11 December 1947; *Educ* Univ of Bristol (MB ChB, MD), Soc of Apothecaries (DMJ (Path)), Univ of London (PhD); *Career* Univ of Glasgow: regius prof of forensic med and science 1993–2003, dir Human Identification Centre 1994–2003, visiting prof 2003–; visiting prof South Bank Univ 2001–, DG Centre for Int Forensic Assistance 2001–03, chief forensic med offr and head of Dept of Forensic Medical Scis Forensic Sci Serv London 2003–06, dir Cameron Forensic Medical Sciences Queen Mary Sch of Medicine and Dentistry Univ of London 2006–; advsr in forensic medicine to Int Ctee of the Red Cross; FRCPath 1990, FRCPGlas 1998, FFFLM 2006; *Style—* Prof Peter Vanezis, OBE

VANN JONES, Prof John; s of John Jones (d 1975), and Elizabeth, *née* Kelly; *b* 8 May 1945; *Educ* Hyndland Sch Glasgow, Univ of Glasgow (MB ChB, PhD); *m* 23 Sept 1970, Anne Margaret, da of Andrew Abercrombie, of Glasgow; 2 s (Richard John, Simon Andrew), 2 da (Kerstin Anne, Caroline Patricia); *Career* lectr in cardiology Univ of Glasgow 1972–77 (res fell 1969–72), MRC travelling fell Univ of Gothenburg 1975–76, reader in cardiovascular med Univ of Oxford 1980–81 (lectr 1977–80), conslt cardiologist Bristol 1981–; memb: Br Cardiac Soc, Br Hypertension Soc; hon prof Univ of Bristol 1993; FRCP 1987; *Books* Scientific Foundations of Cardiology (1983), Outline of Cardiology (1983 and 1992), Essential Medicine (1993 and 1998); *Recreations* golf, table tennis, swimming; *Clubs* Bristol Clifton Golf; *Style—* Prof John Vann Jones; ✉ Park House, Chew Lane, Chew Magna BS40 8QA (tel 01275 332164); Cardiology Department, Royal Infirmary, Bristol BS2 8HW (tel 0117 923 0000)

VANNER, Michael John; s of Walter Geoffrey Vanner (d 1933), of Winkfield, Berks, and Doris Ellen, *née* Hall (d 1977); *b* 6 December 1932; *Educ* Blundell's, Sidney Sussex Coll Cambridge (MA); *m* 1 July 1961, Myra, da of William John Sharpe (d 1982), of Fetcham, Surrey; 2 s (Luke b 1967, Guy b 1970); *Career* res engr Electrical Res Assoc 1955–64, chief devpt engr BICC Construction Co Ltd 1964–75, engrg conslt Balfour Beatty Power Construction Ltd 1981–86 (engrg mangr 1975–81), princ Construction and Material Servs (int consulting) 1986–, princ engr Ewbank Preece Ltd 1989–92, transmission engr AMEC Power Ltd 1992–94, OHL engr Merz & McLellan 1994–; chm IEE PG Power Cables and Overhead Lines 1988–91, chm BSI PEL/11 Overhead Lines 1991–, chm CIGRE SC22-07 Overhead Lines 1995–2002; CEng, FIEE 1994 (MIEE 1984), CPhys, MInstP 1962, MBGS 1961; *Books* The Structure of Soil and A Critical Review of The Mechanisms of Soil Moisture Retention And Migration (1961); *Recreations* walking, sailing; *Style—* Michael Vanner, Esq; ✉ 15 Pensford Court, Newcastle upon Tyne NE3 2RA (tel 0191 271 2546); Construction and Material Services, 11 West Avenue, Redhill, Surrey RH1 5BA (tel 01737 762729)

VANSITTART, Peter; s of Edwin Vansittart (d 1920), and Mignon Therese Vansittart (d 1987); *b* 27 August 1920; *Educ* Haileybury, Worcester Coll Oxford (maj scholarship); *Career* novelist, historian, critic; author 50 books since 1942; hon fell Worcester Coll Oxford; FRSL; *Recreations* walking, gardening; *Clubs* Beefsteak; *Style—* Peter Vansittart, Esq; ✉ Little Manor, Kersey, Suffolk IP7 6DZ

VANSTONE, Hugh; s of J R B Vanstone, of Exeter, and M L Vanstone; *b* 8 August 1965; *Educ* Exeter Sch; *Partner* George Stiles, composer, *qv*; *Career* lighting designer; trained Northcott Theatre Exeter 1980–86, conslt Imagination 1986–, freelance 1989–, assoc to Andrew Bridge, *qv* (lighting designer) 1989–94; memb Assoc of Lighting Designers 1983–; *Theatre* credits RSC incl: Antony & Cleopatra, Hamlet (nominated for Olivier Award 1997), The Winter's Tale; RNT incl: The Cherry Orchard, The Homecoming, Closer, The Day I Stood Still, The Pillowman; other recent credits incl: Peter Pan (West Yorkshire Playhouse), Tanz der Vampire (Vienna and Stuttgart), The Front Page, Howard Katz, The Pillow Man, Life x3, Howard Katz, The Philadelphia Story (Old Vic); Donmar Warehouse incl: Pacific Overtures (Olivier Award 2003), Uncle Vanya, Twelfth Night, The Blue Room, Juno and the Paycock, The Front Page, Orpheus Descending, Insignificance, Mary Stuart; Almeida incl: The Lady From the Sea, Butterfly Kiss; West End credits incl: The Lady in the Van, The Graduate (Olivier Award 2001), Blast!, The Caretaker, Art (Wyndham's, nominated for Olivier Award 1996), Doctor Dolittle, The Unexpected Man, Closer, Copacabana, Once on this Island, Bombay Dreams, The Breath of Life, Tell Me On A Sunday; Broadway credits incl: Art, The Blue Room, Closer, The Unexpected Man, The Graduate, Follies, Life x3, Blast!, Spamalot (nomination Tony Award for Best Lighting 2005); *Opera* credits incl: Macbeth (ROH), The Rake's Progress (WNO), La Bohème, Dialogues of the Carmelites (ENO), Die Fledermaus (Scottish Opera), Carmen (Opera North), The Bartered Bride (Glyndebourne); *Ballet* Alice in Wonderland (English Nat Ballet); *Awards* Olivier Award for Best Lighting Designer 1999 and 2001, Best Visual Presentation Lighting Design Nat Broadway Theatre Awards 2002; *Style—* Hugh Vanstone, Esq; ✉ Simpson-Fox Associates, 52 Shattesbury Avenue, London W1V 7DE (tel 020 7434 9167, e-mail cary@simpson-fox.demon.co.uk)

VARA, Shailesh Lakhman; MP; s of Lakhman Arjan Vara, and Savita, *née* Gadher; *b* 4 September 1960, Uganda; *Educ* Aylebury GS, Brunel Univ (LLB); *m* 2002, Beverley, *née* Deanne; 2 s; *Career* slr; articled Richards Butler 1988–90 (in Hong Kong 1989–90), Crossman Block 1991–92, Payne Hicks Beach 1992–93, CMS Cameron McKenna 1994–2001; vice-chm Cons Pty 2001–05; MP (Cons) Cambridgeshire NW 2005– (Parly candidate (Cons): Birmingham Ladywood 1997, Northampton S 2001), memb Select Ctee on Environment, Food and Rural Affrs 2005–06, shadow dep ldr House of Commons 2006–, treas BBC All Pty Gp 2005–, jt sec Cons Backbench Gp on Foreign Affrs 2006, memb Standing Ctee on Company Law Reform Bill 2006, jt vice-chm All Pty Parly Gp on Trafficking of Women and Children 2006–, jt vice-chm All Pty Parly Gp for Legal and Constitutional Affrs 2007–; vice-pres Small Business Bureau 1998–, vice-chm Business Ctee Soc of Cons Lawyers 2006– (treas 2001–04); govr Westminster Kingsway Coll 2002–05 (memb Audit Ctee 2002–05); memb Campaign Exec Gp Great Fen Project 2005–; vice-pres Huntingdonshire CCC 2007–; Asian Jewel Award 2004; *Recreations* travel, cricket, Tae Kwon Do; *Style—* Shailesh Vara, Esq, MP; ✉ House of Commons, London SW1A 0AA (tel 020 7219 3000, e-mail varas@parliament.uk, website www.shaileshvara.com)

VARAH, Dr (Edward) Chad; CH (2000), CBE (1995, OBE 1969); s of Canon William Edward Varah (d 1945), and Mary, *née* Atkinson (d 1965); *b* 12 November 1911; *Educ* Worksop Coll, Keble Coll Oxford (MA), Lincoln Theological Coll (renamed Chad Varah House); *m* 1940, (Doris) Susan, OBE (d 1993), da of Harry Whanslaw (d 1961); 4 s (Michael, Andrew, David, Charles), 1 da (Felicity (Mrs John Harding)); *Career* staff scriptwriter Eagle and Girl 1950–62; C of E clerk in holy orders 1935; rector Lord Mayor's Parish Church of St Stephen Walbrook 1953–2003, prebendary St Paul's Cathedral 1975–2003; fndr: The Samaritans 1953, Befrienders International 1974, Men Against Genital Mutilation of Girls 1999; chm: The Samaritans Inc 1963–66, Befrienders Int 1974–83 (pres 1983–86); conslt: Forum Magazine 1962–2002, Nat Assoc of Crisis Intervention People's Republic of China 1994–2002; patron: Outsiders Club 1984–2001, Terrence Higgins Tst 1987–99; pres Ctee Publishing Russian Church Music 1960–80; Romanian Patriarchal Cross 1968, Albert Schweitzer Gold Medal 1972, Louis Dublin Award American Assoc Suicidology 1974, Prix de l'Inst de la Vie 1977, Pride of Britain Lifetime Achievement Award 2000; Hon Liveryman Worshipful Co of Grocers, Hon Liveryman Worshipful Co of Carmen; Hon LLD: Univ of Leicester 1979, Univ of St Andrews 1982, Univ of Leeds 1985; Hon DSc City Univ 1993; Hon DLitt De Montfort Univ 1998, Hon DA Univ of Lincoln 2000; hon citizen of Lincoln 2000; hon fell Keble Coll Oxford 1981; *Books* The Samaritans, Befriending the Suicidal (1988), Before I Die Again (autobiography, 1992); *Recreations* reading, music, watching TV nature programmes; *Clubs* Athenaeum, Oxford Union; *Style—* Dr Chad Varah, CH, CBE

VARCOE, Jeremy Richard Lovering Grosvenor; CMG (1989); s of Ronald Arthur Grosvenor Varcoe, TD (d 1993), and Zöe Elizabeth, *née* Lovering (d 1971); *b* 20 September 1937; *Educ* Charterhouse, Lincoln Coll Oxford (MA); *m* 1, 30 Dec 1961, Wendy Anne (d 1991), da of Robert F Moss, MBE (d 1973); 2 da (Francesca b 1964, Lucy b 1966); m 2, 8 July 1995, Ruth S Murdoch, *née* Wallis; *Career* Nat Serv 2 Lt 4 RTR 1956–58; dist offr HMOCS Swaziland 1962–65, called to the Bar 1966, asst legal advsr GKN Ltd 1966–67, lectr in law Univ of Birmingham 1967–70; HM Dip Serv: first sec FCO 1970–71, dep sec-gen Pearce Cmmn on Rhodesian Opinion 1971–72, first sec Ankara 1972–74, head of Chancery Lusaka 1974–78, first sec FCO 1978–79, cnsllr (commercial) Kuala Lumpur 1979–82, head Southern Africa Dept FCO 1982–84, cnsllr Ankara 1984–85, Standard Chartered Bank Istanbul (unpaid leave from FCO) 1985–86, ambass to Somalia 1987–89, min and dep high cmmr Lagos 1989–90, asst under-sec co-ordinator London Economic Summit 1991, ret; dir General United World Colleges 1992–94, dep dir Oxford Univ Devpt Office 1995–96; pt/t immigration judge 1995–; *Books* Legal Aid In Criminal Proceedings - A Regional Survey (with Prof G F Borrie, 1970); *Recreations* sailing, public affairs; *Clubs* St Enodoc Golf; *Style—* Jeremy Varcoe, Esq, CMG; ✉ Lemail Quinnies, Egloshayle, Wadebridge, Cornwall PL27 6JQ (tel and fax 01208 895127, e-mail varcoeuk@aol.com)

VARCOE, (Christopher) Stephen; s of Philip William Varcoe, OBE (d 1980), and Mary Northwood, *née* Mercier (d 2004); *b* 19 May 1949; *Educ* King's Sch Canterbury, King's

Coll Cambridge (MA), Guildhall Sch of Music; *m* 22 April 1972, Melinda, da of William Arthur Davies; 2 da (Flora b 22 Nov 1975, Oriana b 9 April 1988), 3 s (Josiah b 6 March 1979, Amyas b 16 Nov 1982, Leander b 26 March 1986 d 1986); *Career* baritone; freelance concert and opera singer 1970–; Calouste Gulbenkian Fndn Fellowship 1977; prof Royal Coll of Music 2003–; *Publications* Cambridge Companion to Singing (contrib), Sing English Song; *Recreations* building, painting, gardening; *Style*— Stephen Varcoe, Esq

VARDY, Prof Alan Edward; s of John Moreton Vardy (d 1990), and Margaret, *née* Thompson; *b* 6 November 1945; *Educ* High Storrs GS Sheffield, Univ of Leeds (BSc, PhD, DEng, Heseldin Graduation Prize, Yorks Union of Insts Prize), Univ of Dundee (DSc); *m* 5 Oct 1991, Susan Janet, *née* Upstone; 2 s (Hamish b 1970, Malcolm b 1972), 1 da (Jennifer b 1971); *Career* lectr Univ of Leeds 1972–75 (research offr 1971–72), Royal Soc Warren research fell Univ of Cambridge 1975–79; Univ of Dundee: prof of civil engrg 1979–95, dep princ and vice-princ 1988–89 (dep princ 1985–88), pt/t research prof in civil engrg 1995–; dir Dundee Tunnel Research 1995–; chm and ed of ten int confs; founder memb Tport Sector Panel Technology Foresight, tstee Dundee Univ Students' Assoc (DUSA); memb: Int Assoc for Hydraulic Research 1991; FRSA 1982, FICE 1989 (MICE 1975), FASCE 1995 (MASCE 1980), FRSE 2002, FHEA 2007, FREng 2007; *Publications* Fluid Principles (1990); author of numerous jl papers and refereed conf papers; *Recreations* wine, walking, wife, house-building; *Style*— Prof Alan Vardy; ✉ Civil Engineering Division, University of Dundee, Dundee DD1 4HN (tel 01382 384342, fax 01382 384816)

VARLEY, Baron (Life Peer UK 1990), of Chesterfield in the County of Derbyshire; Eric Graham Varley; PC (1974), DL; s of Frank and Eva Varley; *b* 11 August 1932; *Educ* Ruskin Coll Oxford; *m* 1955, Marjorie Turner; 1 s; *Career* worked in engineering and mining industry; branch sec NUM 1955–64 (memb Derbys Area Exec Ctee 1956–64); MP (Lab) Chesterfield 1964–84, asst govt whip 1967–68, PPS to Harold Wilson as PM 1968–69, min of state Technology 1969–70; energy sec 1974–75, industry sec 1975–79; chief oppn spokesman Employment 1979–83, treas Lab Pty 1981–83, oppn front bench spokesman Employment 1981–83; chm and chief exec Coalite Gp 1984–89 (dep exec chm 1983–84); non-exec dir: Cathelco Ltd, Laxgate Ltd 1991–92; memb: Thyssen (GB) Advsy Cncl, House of Lords Euro Communities Ctee 1992–96; steward and bailiff of the Manor of Northstead 1984–85; *Style*— The Rt Hon Lord Varley, PC, DL; ✉ House of Lords, London SW1A 0PW

VARLEY, John Christian; TD (1991, and bar 1997); s of Maurice Varley, of Northallerton, N Yorks, and Audrey, *née* Whitfield; *b* 5 October 1960, Leeds, W Yorks; *Educ* Univ of Leeds (BA), McGill Univ Montreal (MBA); *m* 25 Aug 1995, Rebecca, *née* Warner; 2 da (Helena b 1 Nov 1997, Rosanna b 10 May 2000), 1 s (Thomas b 10 July 2002); *Career* mktg exec Dunlop Holdings 1982–84, asst product mangr Gestetner Int 1984–86; Br Telecom: mktg mangr IDD 1986–90, mangr IDD Strategy Products & Services Div 1990–92, mangr Int Telephony Products & Services Div 1992–95, sr customer and field ops mangr Networks and Systems Div Scotland South 1995–98, gen mangr customer serv Corporate Clients 1998, prog dir AT&T/BT Global Venture 1998–99, dir Project Heritage 1999–2000; ceo Clinton Devon Estates 2000–; memb Bd: Countryside Agency 2002–06 (chm Audit and Risk Mgmnt Ctee 2003–06), Cmmn for Rural Communities 2006– (chm Audit and Risk Ctee 2006–); dir SW Chamber of Rural Enterprise 2003–; memb: SW Sustainable Food and Farming Steering Gp 2002–05, SW Regnl Assembly 2003–05, Govt's Digital Inclusion Panel 2003–04, Land Use and Access Panel Nat Tst 2005–, SW Regnl Forestry Framework Steering Gp 2004–; chm of tstees David Arnold-Forster Tst 2003–, tstee E Devon Pebblebed Heaths Conservation Tst 2006–; Offr Cadet Leeds Univ OTC 1978, cmmnd 2 Lt 1980; Herts & Beds Yeomanry: Lt 1982–87, Capt (also Capt RHQ 100 Field Regt RA) 1987–93, Maj and Batty Cdr 1993–96; Maj and Dep Pres Territorial Cmmns Bd Scotland 1996–2000, RARO 2000–; FCIM; *Recreations* theatre, horse riding, outdoor pursuits; *Clubs* Cavalry & Guards, Farmers; *Style*— John Varley, Esq, TD; ✉ Clinton Devon Estates, Rolle Estate Office, East Budleigh, Budleigh Salterton, Devon EX9 7DP (tel 01395 441144, e-mail john.varley@clintondevon.com)

VARLEY, John Silvester; *b* 1 April 1956; *Educ* Downside, Oriel Coll Oxford (MA), Coll of Law; *m* 1981, Carolyn Thorn, da of Sir Richard Thorn Pease, Bt, *qv*; 1 da (Emma b 1989), 1 s (George b 1994); *Career* slr Commercial Law Dept Frere Cholmeley Slrs 1979–82, asst dir Corporate Fin Dept Barclays Merchant Bank (renamed latterly as Barclays De Zoete Wedd (BZW)) 1982–89, md BZW Asia 1989–91, dep chief exec BZW Global Equities Div 1991–94, dir Odey Asset Mgmnt 1994–95, chm BZW Asset Mgmnt 1995–96, chm BZW Property Investment Mgmnt 1995–96, chm BZW Investment Mgmnt 1995–96, dir Barclays Private Bank 1995–2000, dir Barclays Global Investors 1995–2000, memb Gp Exec Ctee Barclays 1996–, chm Barclays Asset Mgmnt Gp 1996–98, dir Barclays and Barclays Bank plc 1998–, chief exec Barclays Retail Financial Services 1998–2000, gp fin dir Barclays 2000–03, gp chief exec Barclays 2004–; non-exec dir AstraZeneca plc 2006–; *Recreations* fishing; *Clubs* Brooks's; *Style*— John Varley, Esq; ✉ Barclays Bank plc, 1 Churchill Place, London E14 5HP (tel 020 7116 3000, e-mail john.varley@barclays.com)

VARLEY, Rosemary Margaret (Rosie); OBE (2007); da of Ratcliffe Bowen Wright (d 1998), and Dr Margaret Bowen Wright, *née* Davies Williams; *b* 22 December 1951; *Educ* New Hall Chelmsford, St Mary's Coll Durham (BA), Univ of Manchester (MA); *m* 1976, Andrew Iain Varley (d 2005), s of William Thomas Varley; 1 s (Hugo Benedict Tancred George b 23 Oct 1980), 1 da (Beatrice Mary Annunciata b 24 Oct 1984); *Career* Univ of Manchester: research asst Health Servs Mgmnt Unit 1977–80, lectr in social admin 1980–81, lectr in health servs mgmnt 1981–83 (concurrently tutor to the NHS Nat Admin Trg Scheme); ind sch mgmnt Moreton Hall 1983–93, memb W Suffolk HA 1984–92 (vice-chm 1988–92), memb NHS Nat Trg Authy 1989–91, chm Mid Anglia Community Health NHS Tst 1992–97; regnl chm: NHS Exec Anglia and Oxford 1997–98, NHS Exec Eastern Regn 1999–2001; regnl cmmr NHS Appts Cmmn 2001–06, chm Gen Optical Cncl 1999–, chm Skills for Health Eastern Region 2006–, chm Public Guardian Bd 2007–; lay memb: Mental Health Review Tbnl 1995–, Ind Tbnl Serv (Disability Benefit Panel) 1997–; pres W Suffolk MIND, fndr chm W Suffolk Young NSPCC 1984–92, memb Cncl of Mgmnt St Nicholas' Hospice 1985–96, memb Jt Br Advsy Ctee on Children's Nursing 1995–97, vice-chm NAHAT 1995–97; memb Anglia and Oxford Multi Centre Research Ethics Ctee 1997–99; govr Priory Sch Bury St Edmunds 2007–; Freeman City of London 2005; Liveryman Worshipful Co of Spectacle Makers 2006; FRSM; *Recreations* walking, sailing, family; *Style*— Mrs Rosie Varley, OBE; ✉ e-mail rosievarley@btinternet.com

VARMA, Dr Alakh Niranjan; s of Phulan Prasad Varma (d 1957), and Karorpati Varma (d 1989); *b* 27 February 1932; *Educ* Patna Univ of India (BSc, MB BS, DPM), Univ of Edinburgh (DPM); *m* 17 Nov 1959, Dr Sashi Bala Varma, MD, DCP, da of Anjani Bir Prasad (d 1960), of Lucknow, India; 2 s (Dr Niraj Varma b 1 Oct 1960, Anu Ranjan b 14 June 1964); *Career* asst MO India 1957–60, sr MO Ghana Africa 1961–68, conslt in child and adolescent psychiatry 1973–2000, psychiatrist BC Canada 1981–82; MRCPsych; *Recreations* travelling, photography; *Style*— Dr Alakh Varma; ✉ 149 Grantham Road, Sleaford, Lincolnshire NG34 7NR (tel 01529 303681)

VARMA, Moni; s of Pooran Chand Varma, and Chanan Devi Varma; *b* 21 January 1949, Ludhiana, India; *m* Shobha, *née* Sharma; 1 da (Priya b 24 June 1983), 1 s (Rajiv b 18 Sept 1985); *Career* early career as salesman printing firm Malawi, fndr then md steel co (bought out by President of Malawi 1971), worked in steel industry UK 1980, fndr Veetee Rice 1986; hon consul for Malawi; *Recreations* golf, cricket; *Clubs* Reform; *Style*— Moni Varma, Esq; ✉ Aston House, 23 Russell Road, Moor Park, Northwood, Middlesex HA6 2LP (tel 01923 822352, fax 01923 824843); Veetee Rice Ltd, Veetee House, 21 Neptune Close, Medway City Estate, Rochester, Kent ME2 4LT (tel 01634 292819, fax 01634 717792, e-mail moni@veetee.com)

VARNEY, Sir David Robert; kt (2006); s of Robert Kitchener Frederick Varney, and Winifred Gwendoline, *née* Williams; *b* 11 May 1946; *Educ* Brockley Co GS, Univ of Surrey (BSc), Manchester Business Sch (MBA); *m* 31 July 1971, Dr Patricia Ann, *née* Billingham; 1 s (Justin Sinclair b 12 June 1975), 1 da (Meredith Louise b 25 Feb 1978); *Career* personnel asst Shell Refining Co 1968; Shell Co of Aust: strategic planning mangr 1974, islands mangr 1974–77; euro prods trading mangr Shell Int Petroleum Maatschapi (SIPM) 1977–79, business devpt dir Shell Coal 1979–83, chief exec Svenska Shell 1987–90, head of mktg Branding and Product Devpt Dept Shell Int Petroleum Co (SIPCO) 1990–92, md Downstream Oil Shell UK 1992–95, dir Oil Products SIPCO Europe 1996, chief exec BG plc 1996–2000, chm mmO2 plc 2001–04, exec chm HM Revenue and Customs 2004–06, sr advsr on transformational govt strategy to Chllr of the Exchequer 2006–07, non-exec dir HM Treasy 2004–; non-exec dir Cable and Wireless plc 1999–2000; pres UK Petroleum Industry Assoc 1993–94, pres Inst of Petroleum 1994–96, vice-pres Combined Heat and Power Assoc 1996–2000, memb Bd of Oil & Gas Projects and Supplies Office (OSO) 1996–99, chm Business in the Community 2002–04, pres Inst for Employment Studies 2003–; memb: President's Cncl CBI 1997–2000 and 2001–04, Food and Farming Cmmn 2001–02, Advsy Cncl Nat Consumer's Assoc 2002–, Cncl Royal Soc of Med 2003–05, Advsy Cncl Demos; Alumnus of the Year Univ of Manchester 2005; memb Cncl Univ of Surrey 1994–2002; Hon DTechMet Univ 2006, Hon LLD Univ of Bath 2006, Hon DUniv Surrey 2007; CIMgt (pres 2005–06), CIGE, FRSM, FInstE; *Recreations* opera, rugby, formula one motor racing, sailing; *Clubs* Royal Soc of Med, Upper Thames Sailing; *Style*— Sir David Varney; ✉ River Thatch, The Abbotsbrook, Bourne End, Buckinghamshire SL8 5QU (tel 01628 521077, e-mail david@varney.uk.com)

VARNISH, Peter; OBE (1982); s of John Varnish (d 1985), and Hilary Ilma Ada, *née* Godfrey (d 1982); *b* 30 May 1947; *Educ* Warwick Sch, UCNW (BSc); *m* 10 Aug 1968, Shirley Anne, da of George Bertram Bendelow; 2 s (Jason b 7 March 1973, David b 8 May 1975); *Career* SERL: memb Res Gp on High Power Lasers 1968–70, memb Res Gp on High Power Travelling Wave Tubes 1970–72; head Electron Bombarded Semiconductor Res RSRE 1972–75, scientific advsr to MOD British Embassy Washington 1975–79; MOD: UK electronic warfare co-ordinator ARE Portsdown 1979–81, head Antenna Section and offr i/c ARE Funtington 1981–84, head Radar Div ARE Portsdown 1984, head Signature Control Div ARE Funtington 1984–89, head Electronic Warfare and Weapons Dept ARE 1989–90, dir Above Water Warfare ARE 1990, Business Sector dir Above Water Systems DRA 1991–92, RCDS 1992, dir Strategic Defence Initiative Participation Office 1993, dir Science Ballistic Missile Defence 1994–95; dir Business Devpt Defence Evaluation and Research Agency (DERA), dir of Technol (DERA) 2000–01; chm: Stealth Conf 1988 and 2002, Military Microwaves 1990–97, Asia DEF EX, IDEX 1995–99, 2001, 2003 and 2005, IMDEX-ASIA 1997–99, Gulf Def Conference Abu Dhabi 2001, 2003 and 2005, Int Geopolitical Technol Solutions (London) 2001–, Air Launched Weapons 2002–03 and 2005, Stealth 2003–2005, Interoperability 2003–04 and 2005, Aviation Repair and Maintenance 2004–05, Homeland Defence and Asymmetric Warfare 2004–05, Homeland Defence Symposium Dubai 2005, Global Security Singapore 2007 (vice-chm 2005); Technol Transfer and Offset GOCA NY 2006, Technol for C-Terrorism City Forum 2006, ID Cards and Terrorism City Forum 2007; chief exec: S3T Ltd 2001–06, Consols Ltd 2006–; dir: Closed Solutions Ltd 2002–, CMB Technol 2003–05, CMB Inc 2003–, CMBIE Ltd 2003–04, Sparks Technol Ltd 2003–05, Geopolitical Solutions Ltd 2004–, Table 27 Ltd 2004–, QTEL Europe plc 2005–06; chm: Definition Int Ltd 2002–, Wrightson Gp 2003–; advsr to: Evesham Ltd, Radiation Watch Ltd, Rolatube Ltd, Strategic Communications Laboratory Ltd; defence advsr to Cons Pty shadow min for defence procurement; lectr Higher Staff Course Bracknell 2000; memb: Sensors Ctee Defence Scientific Advsy Cncl, Stealth Working Pty Defence Scientific Advsy Cncl, Jt MOD Industry Liaison Ctee of Guided Weapons, MOD Faraday Initiative 2005–, Mgmnt Bd ARE, Cncl ERA Ltd, Advsy Ctee Dept of Electrical and Electronics Engrg Univ of Surrey, Faraday Initiative; author of numerous scientific and defence papers and patents; TV appearances on Discovery channel and Horizon; SMIEEE 1976, CEng 1988, FIET (FIEE 1988), MIMgt 1989, FREng 1995, FRSA 1997; *Recreations* watching rugby football, being a grandfather, hill walking, computer engineering, photography; *Clubs* Army and Navy, Brooks's, Savage; *Style*— Peter Varnish, Esq, OBE, FREng; ✉ Four Corners, 1 Greatfield Way, Rowlands Castle, Hampshire PO9 6AG (tel 023 9241 2440, fax 023 9241 2940, e-mail peter.varnish@btopenworld.com); Consols Ltd, 1 High Street, Guildford, Surrey GU2 4HP

VARVILL, Michael; s of Robert Varvill, DSC (d 2003), of West Wittering, W Sussex, and Rachel, *née* Millar; *b* 21 October 1950, Calabar, Nigeria; *Educ* Gordonstoun, Schule Schloss Salem Germany, Univ of London (LLB), Coll of Law; *m* 1, 1978 (m dis 1990), Margrete Lynner; 2 s (Wilfrid Halfdan b 28 Aug 1982, John Fitzadam b 11 April 1987), 1 da (Celia Anemone b 29 June 1984); m 2, 1998, Sarah Jane Pelham Harker, da of Capt JWF Briggs and Mrs BN Briggs; *Career* admitted slr 1974; ptnr: Lane & Partners London 1981– (asst slr 1974–81), Marks & Murase (formerly Wender, Murase & White) Park Avenue NY 1984–97; Freeman City of York; memb Law Soc, memb Inst of Trade Mark Attorneys (MITMA), MCIArb; *Recreations* sport, the arts; *Clubs* Itchenor Sailing, Hurlingham, Royal Thames Yacht; *Style*— Michael Varvill, Esq; ✉ Lane & Partners, 15 Bloomsbury Square, London WC1A 2LS (tel 020 7242 2626, fax 020 7242 0387)

VASSAR-SMITH, Sir John Rathborne; 4 Bt (UK 1917), of Charlton Park, Charlton Kings, Co Gloucester; s of Sir Richard Rathborne Vassar-Smith, 3 Bt, TD (d 1995), and Dawn Mary, *née* Woods (d 2001); *b* 23 July 1936; *Educ* Eton; *m* 1971, Roberta Elaine, da of Wing Cdr Norman Williamson; 2 s (Richard Rathborne b 1975, David Rathborne b 1978); *Heir* s, Richard Vassar-Smith; *Career* ran St Ronan's Prep Sch (rtd); *Style*— Sir John Vassar-Smith, Bt; ✉ 24 Haywards Close, Wantage, Oxfordshire OX12 7AT (tel 01235 765147)

VASUDEV, Dr Kadaba Srinath; DL (Lancs); s of Dr Kadaba Vedanta Srinath, and Lalitha Srinath; *b* 5 May 1943; *Educ* Univ of Bangalore (MB BS); *m* 28 June 1972, Pratibha, da of Mandyam Dhati Narayan; 2 s (Naveen Srinath, Chetan Srinath), 1 da (Archana Srinath); *Career* conslt histopathologist/cytopathologist Dept of Pathology Victoria Hosp Blackpool 1977–2005 (clinical dir Pathology Directorate 1993–96), undergrad tutor Univ of Manchester 1982–94 (postgrad clinical tutor 1982–93), ret; memb: Int Acad of Pathology, Ethnic Minority Liaison Gp and Standing Advsy Ctee for Religious Educn (SACRE), Blackpool BC, Bd of Govrs St George's Church of England HS Blackpool, Ind Advsy Gp Lancs Constabulary Western Div; panel memb Lancashire Youth Offending Team; tstee: Handicapped Aid Tst Lytham, Life Educn Centres for Lancs (memb S West Support Gp); Rotary Club of Blackpool, Palatine: pres 1995–96, chm Int Cmmn 1992–93 and 1993–94, chm Vocational Serv Ctee 1997–98, chm Community and Vocational Serv Ctee 1999–2001, District 1190 drug awareness advsr 1998–2001; memb Bharatiya Vidya Bhavan Manchester; Worshipful Master Lodge Amounderness Preston 2001–02; FRCPath 1988; *Recreations* photography, music appreciation, theatre; *Style*— Dr Kadaba Vasudev, DL; ✉ 10 Silverdale Road, St Annes, Lancashire FY8 3RE (tel 01253 720747, fax 01253 720747)

VAUGHAN, Dr Caroline Lesley; da of Frederick Alan Vaughan (d 1970), and Helen Mary, *née* Brackett (d 1983); *b* 5 February 1941; *Educ* Croydon HS, Univ of Manchester (BSc), Chelsea Coll London (PhD); *Career* post doctoral fell: MD Anderson Hosp Houston TX

1965–68, King's Coll London 1968–69; fin analyst and mktg mangr WR Grace Euro Consumer Products Div Paris 1969–74, commercial planner Tube Investments (Domestic Appliances Div and Head Office) 1974–78, divnl exec Nat Enterprise Bd 1978–80, dir of business devpt Celltech Ltd 1980–84, chief exec Newmarket Venture Capital plc 1984–94, dep chm: London Catalyst 1993–2006, Home Grown Cereals Authy 1994–2000; non-exec dir: Hammersmith Hosps Tst 1994–2002, Sterix Ltd 1999–2001, Riotech Pharmaceuticals Ltd 2002–06; memb: Advsy Bd Korda Seed Capital Fund 1990–2002, Food and Drink Panel Technology Foresight Prog 1994–98, Ownership Bd Veterinary Labs Agency 1995–2003, Wine Guild of UK 1998–, Research Ethics Ctee Hammersmith Hosp NHS Tst 2002–; cmmr Royal Cmmn for the Exhbn of 1851 1998–; govr Imperial Coll London 1997–2005; Freeman Co of World Traders 1999–; MInstD, FRSA; *Recreations* theatre, opera, travel; *Style—* Dr Caroline Vaughan; ✉ 8 Park Lane, Reigate, Surrrey RH2 8JX (tel and fax 01737 210145)

VAUGHAN, Prof David John; s of Samuel John Vaughan (d 1982), of Newport, Gwent, and Esther Ruby, *née* Edwards (d 1984); *b* 10 April 1946; *Educ* Newport HS, UCL (BSc), Imperial Coll London (MSc), UC Oxford (DPhil, DSc); *m* 31 Dec 1971 (m dis 1993), Heather Elizabeth, da of Alan Marat Ross (d 1979), of Christchurch, Hants; 1 s (Emlyn James b 1979); *Career* res assoc Dept Earth and Planetary Sci MIT 1971–74, reader mineralogy Aston Univ 1979–88 (lectr geological scis 1974–79), visiting prof Virginia Poly Inst and State Univ 1980, prof mineralogy Univ of Manchester 1988–; pres: Mineralogical Soc (GB & Ireland) 1988–89, European Mineralogical Union 2000–; RSC Award in Geochemistry 2005, Schlumberger Medal Mineralogical Soc 2006; FIMM 1984, fell Mineralogical Soc of America, fell Geochemical Soc; *Books* Mineral Chemistry of Metal Sulfides (with J Craig, 1978), Ore Microscopy and Ore Petrography (with J Craig, 1981), Resources of The Earth (with J Craig and B Skinner, 1988), Sulfide Mineralogy and Geochemistry (2006); *Recreations* painting, walking; *Style—* Prof David Vaughan; ✉ c/o School of Earth, Atmospheric and Environmental Sciences, University of Manchester, Manchester M13 9PL (tel 0161 275 3935, e-mail david.vaughan@man.ac.uk)

VAUGHAN, Dr Elizabeth; da of William Jones (d 1974), and Mary Ellen Morris (d 1987); *b* 12 March 1937; *Educ* Llanfylin GS, RAM London; *m* 1, June 1968, Raymond Peter Brown, s of Stanley Kitchener Brown (d 1980); 1 s (Mark b 21 Oct 1970), 1 da (Sarah b 5 Aug 1974); *Career* opera singer (soprano and latterly mezzo-soprano); Royal Opera House princ soprano roles: Butterfly, Traviata, Leonora, Gilda, Abigaille, Elettra, Donna Elvira, Teresa, Liu, Musetta, Alice, Princess Suor' Angelica, Herodias, witch, Madame de Croissay; ENO guest artist: Aida, Butterfly, Fidelio; Scottish Opera, WNO and Opera North: Lady Macbeth, Abigaille, Butterfly, Traviata; performed worldwide incl in: Paris Opera, Metropolitan NY, Florence, Vienna, Japan, S America, Canada, Aust, Miami, Houston, Berlin, Athens; numerous TV and radio performances; Hon DMus Univ of Wales; FRAM (licentiate and assoc), FRWCMD; *Recreations* needlepoint, antiques fairs; *Style—* Dr Elizabeth Vaughan; ✉ c/o IMG Artists, Lovell House, 616 Chiswick High Road, London W4 5RX

VAUGHAN, Johnny; *b* 1966; *Educ* Uppingham; *Career* formerly employed as: grill chef, jewel courier, sales asst, video shop mangr; launched Two's A Crowd Theatre Co 1984; TV presenter: Moviewatch (Channel Four), Naked City (Channel Four), Talking About Sex (Channel Four), Late Licence (Channel Four), The Good Sex Guide International (Carlton), Win, Lose or Draw (STV), Coca Cola Hit Mix (Sky TV), The Fall Guy (BBC), Here's Johnny (Channel Four), The Big Breakfast (Channel Four), Johnny Vaughan Tonight (BBC); *Awards* Best Entertainer TV Quick 1998, GQ Man of the Year 1998, TRIC Best TV Entertainer on Independent TV, Sun Best TV Entertainer 1998, Loaded Magazine Best TV Presenter, GQ Magazine Best TV Presenter 1999, winner RTS Best Presenter Award 1999–2000, runner-up Richard Dimbleby BAFTA for best news features presenter 2000, Creative Freedom Award for Best Entertainer, Butlins Favourite Entertainer 2000 (hon Red Coat); *Style—* Johnny Vaughan, Esq; ✉ c/o Duncan Heath, ICM, Oxford House, 76 Oxford Street, London W1D 1BS (tel 020 7636 6565, fax 020 7323 0101)

VAUGHAN, Michael Paul; OBE (2006); *b* 29 October 1974, Manchester; *Career* professional cricketer with Yorkshire CCC; England: 70 test matches (highest test score 197 v India 2002), 86 one-day ints, 2 Twenty20 appearances, capt 2003– (ret as one-day capt 2007), toured with under-19 team, capt England A team 1998–99, test debut v South Africa 1999–2000, memb team touring Pakistan and Sri Lanka 2000–01, India and NZ 2001–02, Australia 2002–03, Bangladesh and Sri Lanka 2003, West Indies 2004, Zimbabwe 2004, South Africa 2004–05 and Pakistan 2005; Professional Cricketers' Association Player of the Year 2002; Freeman City of Sheffield 2005; *Style—* Michael Vaughan, Esq, OBE; ✉ c/o Yorkshire CCC, Headingley Cricket Ground, Leeds LS6 3BU

VAUGHAN, Oliver John; s of Maj Joseph Herbert Vaughan (d 1972), and Mary Lavender, *née* Holroyd Smith (d 1989); *b* 28 July 1946; *Educ* Dominican Schs of Llanarth & Laxton, Univ of Neuchâtel; *m* June 1984, Diana Frances Elizabeth (Boo), da of Cdr Philip Richard Martineau, RN, of Moses Hill Farm, Marley Heights, Surrey; 2 s (Jamie Joseph b 12 July 1986, Jeremy Philip b 22 Oct 1988), 1 da (Tara Megan b 1 Aug 1991), 1 foster da (Joanna Eu b 2 Jan 1970 (d 1 Oct 1998)); *Career* co fndr Juliana's 1966, subsequently opened offices in London, Hong Kong, Singapore and NY, obtained Stock Exchange listing 1983, sold to Wembley plc 1989; chm: Blue Oar plc, Albany Capital plc, Sailing Adventures Ltd; *Recreations* sailing, skiing, shooting, fishing; *Clubs* Garrick, Royal Thames Yacht; *Style—* Oliver Vaughan, Esq; ✉ 20 Phillimore Gardens, London W8 7QE; Blackbrook, Skenfrith, Monmouthshire NP7 8UB

VAUGHAN, Dr Roger; s of Benjamin Frederick Vaughan (decd), and Marjorie, *née* Wallace (decd); *b* 14 June 1944; *Educ* Manchester Grammar, Univ of Newcastle upon Tyne (BSc, PhD); *m* 1; 3 s (Adam John b 1973, Benjamin Nicholas Gray b 1974, Thomas Peter b 1976), 2 da (Ellen Kate b 1979, Anna Cecilia b 1980); m 2, Valerie; 2 step s (James Maxwell Phillpott b 1973, Jonathan Peter Phillpott b 1975 d 1998); *Career* student apprentice Vickers Group 1962, shipbuilding devpt engr Swan Hunter Shipbuilders Ltd 1970–71, md A & P Appledore Ltd (joined 1971), dir Performance Improvement and Productivity Br Shipbuilders 1981–86, dir Swan Hunter Ltd, chm and chief exec Swan Hunter Shipbuilders Ltd until 1993, conslt 1993–95, chief exec Sch of Mgmnt Univ of Newcastle upon Tyne 1995–99 (visiting prof 2000–01 and 2005–); non-exec dir Newcastle City Health NHS Tst 1996–2001; dir Northern Sinfonia Concert Soc Ltd 1996–2002; chm Safinah Ltd 1999–; pres Shipbuilders and Shiprepairers Assoc 1991–93; memb Nat Curriculum Council (NCC) 1992–93; Shipbuilding Gold Medal NE Coast Inst of Engrs and Shipbuilders 1969; FRINA (MRINA 1963), FREng 1990, FRSA 1993; *Recreations* music, theatre, ballet, opera, sailing, walking, reading; *Style—* Dr Roger Vaughan, FREng; ✉ Correslaw, Netherwitton, Morpeth, Northumberland NE61 4NW (tel and fax 01670 772686, e-mail roger.vaughan@correslaw.co.uk)

VAUX OF HARROWDEN, 11 Baron (E 1523); Anthony William Gilbey; s of 10 Baron (d 2002), by his 1 cous Maureen Gilbey; *b* 25 May 1940; *Educ* Ampleforth; *m* 4 July 1964, Beverley, o da of Charles Alexander Walton, of Cooden, E Sussex; 2 s (Hon Richard b 1965, Hon Philip b 1967), 2 da (Hon Victoria b 1969, Hon Elizabeth b 1989); *Heir* s, Hon Richard Gilbey; *Career* accountant, farmer; Liveryman Worshipful Co of Vintners; *Recreations* walking, fishing, shooting; *Style—* The Rt Hon the Lord Vaux of Harrowden; ✉ Rusko, Gatehouse of Fleet, Kirkcudbrightshire

VAVALIDIS, Barabara Joan; *see:* Donoghue, Barbara Joan

VAVASOUR, Sir Eric Michel Joseph Marmaduke; 6 Bt (UK 1828); s of Hugh Bernard Moore Vavasour (d 1989), and Monique Pauline Marie Madeleine, *née* Beck (d 1982); suc kinsman, Sir Geoffrey William Vavasour, 5 Bt, DSC (d 1997); *b* 3 January 1953; *Educ* BSc; *m* 1976, Isabelle Baudouin Françoise Alain Cécile Cornelie Ghislaine, da of André van Hille, of Brussels; 2 s (Joseph Ian Hugh André b 1978, Thomas Bernard André Hugh b 1984), 1 da (Emilie Isabelle Marguerite Monique b 1980); *Heir* s, Joseph Vavasour; *Career* dir: Faraday Technol Hldgs Ltd, BAL Broadcast Ltd 2001; MIEE; *Style—* Sir Eric Vavasour, Bt; ✉ 15 Mill Lane, Earl Shilton, Leicestershire LE9 7AW

VAVER, Prof David; s of Ladislav Vaver (d 1996), and Pola, *née* Komito (d 2003); *b* 28 March 1946; *Educ* Univ of Auckland (BA, LLB), Univ of Chicago (JD), Univ of Oxford (MA); *m* 30 Nov 1978, Maxine, *née* McClenaghan; 1 s (Daniel Alexander b 1 Sept 1986), 1 da (Amy Louise b 25 Feb 1990); *Career* called to the Bar NZ 1970; visiting asst prof of law Univ of Br Columbia 1971–72, lectr rising to sr lectr in law Univ of Auckland 1972–78, assoc prof of law Univ of Br Columbia 1978–85, prof Osgoode Hall Law Sch York Univ Toronto 1985–98, prof of intellectual property and IT law Univ of Oxford 1998–, dir Oxford Intellectual Property Research Centre 1998–, fell St Peter's Coll Oxford; memb Royal Soc Working Gp on Intellectual Property 2001–03, memb Intellectual Property Advsy Ctee 2001–05; ed Intellectual Property Jl 1984–98; academic memb Intellectual Property Inst of Canada 1986, assoc memb Chartered Inst of Patent Agents 1999; *Publications* Intellectual Property Law (1997), Copyright Law (2000), Intellectual Property Rights: Critical Concepts in Law (5 vols, 2006); numerous articles in UK and int legal periodicals; *Recreations* music, art, reading; *Style—* Prof David Vaver; ✉ St Peter's College, Oxford OX1 2DL (tel 01865 278919, fax 01865 278959, e-mail david.vaver@spc.ox.ac.uk)

VAZ, Rt Hon (Nigel) Keith Anthony Standish; PC (2006), MP; s of late Tony Vaz, and Merlyn Verona Rosemary, *née* Pereira; *b* 26 November 1956; *Educ* Latymer Upper Sch, Gonville & Caius Coll Cambridge (MA); *m* 3 April 1993, Maria Fernandes; 1 s (Luke Swraj b 2 March 1995), 1 da (Anjali Olga Verona b 4 April 1997); *Career* slr Richmond upon Thames Cncl 1982, sr slr London Borough of Islington 1982–85, slr Highfields & Belgrave Law Centre Leicester 1985–87; called to the Bar 1990; contested Euro elections: Richmond & Barnes 1983, Surrey West 1984; MP (Lab) Leicester E 1987–; memb: Home Affrs Select Ctee 1987–92, Constitutional Affrs Select Ctee 2003–; memb Standing Ctees on: Immigration Bill 1987–88, Legal Aid Bill 1988, Children Bill 1989, Football Spectators Bill 1989, NHS and Community Care Bill 1989–90, Cts and Legal Servs 1990–, Armed Forces Bill 1991; chm: Lab Party Race Action Gp 1983–, Unison Gp 1990–99, Lab Pty Regnl Exec 1994–96; chair: Parly Nupe Gp, All-Pty Parly Footwear and Leather Industry Gp; jt vice-chair Lab Pty Dept Ctee for Int Devpt 1997–2000, memb Lab Pty Dept Ctee for Home Affrs 1997–2001; treas All-Pty Race and Community Gp 2003–, chair All-Pty Yemen Gp, vice-chair All-Pty Chinese in Br Gp 2003–; treas Tribune Gp (vice-chair 1992); sec: Legal Servs Campaign, Indo-Br Parly Gp, Lab Educn Gp, Parly Lab Party Wool and Textiles Gp; co-ordinator BCCI Parly Gp 1991–, shadow jr min for environment (with responsibilities for inner city and local govt) 1992–94, shadow min for planning and regeneration 1994–97, PPS to the Attorney Gen 1997–99, Parly sec Lord Chancellor's Department 1999, min for Europe 1999–2001; memb Exec Ctee Inter-Parly Union; vice-chair Br Cncl 1998–99; pres: Thurnby Lodge Boys Club 1987–1997, Leicester and S Leicestershire RSPCA 1988–2000, Hillcroft Football Club 1988–2000, Leicester & South Leicestershire RSPCA 1988, India Devpt Gp (UK) 1992–, Nat Orgn of Asian Businesses; govr: Hamilton Community Coll Leicester 1987–91, St Patrick's Sch Leicester 1985–89, Regent Coll 1998; patron: Ginger Bread 1990–99, Leicester Rowing Club 1992–99, Asian Business Club 1998–99; columnist: Tribune, Catholic Herald; memb Nat Advsy Bd Crime Concern; memb: UNISON, Lab Party; memb Clothing and Footwear Inst 1988, memb Bd Br Cncl 1999; *Style—* The Rt Hon Keith Vaz, MP; ✉ 144 Uppingham Road, Leicester (tel 0116 212 2028, fax 0116 2122121); House of Commons, London SW1A 0AA

VEAL, Sheriff Kevin Anthony; s of George Algernon Veal (d 1985), of Dundee, and Pauline Grace, *née* Short (d 1992); *b* 16 September 1946; *Educ* Lawside Roman Catholic Acad Dundee, Univ of St Andrews (LLB); *m* 29 Oct 1969, Monica, da of James Flynn (d 1976), and Mary, *née* Breslin (d 2004); 4 c (Mary Pauline b 8 Sept 1970, Matthew Gerard b 23 April 1974, Dominic Joseph b 18 March 1978, Bridget Ann b 17 July 1987); *Career* apprentice slr Dickie, McDonald, Gray & Fair WS Dundee 1966–68, asst to Gilruth Pollock & Smith Dundee 1968–71, Notary Public 1971, ptnr Burns Veal & Gillan Dundee 1971–93, sheriff of Tayside Central and Fife (at Forfar) 1993– (temp sheriff 1984–93); pt/t tutor Dept of Law Univ of Dundee 1978–85, dean Faculty of Procurators and Solicitors Dundee 1991–93; musical dir Cecilian Choir Dundee 1975–, hon pres Dundee Operatic Soc 2003–; memb Ct Univ of Abertay Dundee 1998–; Knight Cdr of Equestrian Order Holy Sepulchre of Jerusalem 1998 (Knight 1989), Knight of St Gregory the Great 1993; *Recreations* choral and classical music, organ playing, hill walking; *Style—* Sheriff Kevin Veal; ✉ Sheriff Court House, Market Street, Forfar DD8 3LA (tel 01307 462186)

VEEDER, Van Vechten (Johnny); QC (1986); s of John Van Vechten Veeder (d 1976), and Helen, *née* Townley; *b* 14 December 1948; *Educ* Neuilly Paris, Clifton, Jesus Coll Cambridge (MA); *Career* called to the Bar Inner Temple 1971; gen ed Arbitration International; *Publications* The ICCA National Report on England (1988 and 1996), The Final Report on the Independent Inquiry into the Capital Market activities of the London Borough of Hammersmith and Fulham (with Barratt and Reddington, 1991); *Recreations* sailing, reading, travelling; *Clubs* Aldeburgh Yacht, Orford Sailing, Little Ship, Garrick; *Style—* V V Veeder, Esq, QC; ✉ Essex Court Chambers, 24 Lincoln's Inn Fields, London WC2A 3ED (tel 020 7813 8000, fax 020 7813 8080, e-mail vvveeder@compuserve.com)

VEITCH, Prof (George) Bryan Austin; s of late Michael Veitch, and Evelyn, *née* Davis; *b* 18 April 1935; *Educ* Houghton-le-Spring GS, Rutherford Tech Coll (HNC), Sch of Pharmacy Sunderland Tech Coll (Pharmaceutical Chemist Qualifying Exam), Royal Victoria Infirmary Newcastle (MR Pharm S), Univ of London (ext deg, BSc), Aston Univ (PhD); *m* 16 Dec 1967, Annette, da of John Lee (d 1979); 1 s (Angus John Martin b 20 May 1969), 1 da (Catriona Helen b 29 June 1972); *Career* scientific technician NCB 1951–55, res technician Univ of Durham 1955–56, pre-registration student Royal Victoria Infirmary 1959–60, locum pharmacist 1960; Aston Univ: asst lectr in phytochemistry 1960–64, lectr in medicinal chemistry 1964–76, organiser Continuing Educn Courses 1971–83, sr lectr and MSc course tutor 1976–83; regnl pharmaceutical offr Oxford RHA 1983–87, chief pharmaceutical advsr to Sec of State for Wales Welsh Office 1987–95; visiting sr lectr Aston Univ 1983–89, visiting prof Univ of Wales 1990–95; external examiner: Natural Products Al Faateh Univ Tripoli 1980–83, Clinical Pharmacy to Undergrad Course UWIST 1984–87, res degrees Univ of Bradford, Univ of Wales, Sunderland Poly 1984–87, Univ of Portsmouth 1990–94, Univ of Leeds 1995–99, Univ of Manchester, Queen's Univ Belfast; fndr memb Coll of Pharmacy Practice 1981; chm Coll of Pharmacy Practice 1999–2001 (govr Bd 1989–2001, vice-chm 1997–99); vice-chm Welsh Executive RPSGB 1998–; advsr Parkinson's Disease Soc, memb Govt Panel Standards for Advertising Medicines; memb: Soc of Drug Res 1968, Phytochemical Soc Europe 1972, American Soc of Pharmacognosy 1975, UK Clinical Pharmacy Assoc 1981, European Clinical Pharmacy Assoc 1986, W Midlands Region Pharmaceutical Educn Ctee 1976–83; chm: Lichfield Sci and Med Soc 2001, Lichfield Festival Assoc 2001; author of books and articles in med jls; Charter Silver Medalist RPSGB 1999; CChem 1985, FRSC 1985, FLS 1985, FRPharmS 1988, FCPP 1997; *Recreations* fell walking, photography, railways, music; *Style—* Prof Bryan Veitch

VELARDE, (Peter) Giles; s of F X Velarde, OBE, FRIBA (d 1960), of Liverpool; *b* 12 February 1935; *Educ* Ampleforth, Chelsea Sch of Art; *m* 1967, Celia Mary, *née* Heddy; 1 s, 2 da; *Career* Nat Serv Sub Lt RN; museum and heritage exhbn designer, author of books and

V

articles, lectr in English and French; estab Giles Velarde Associates creative consultancy; maj design projects incl: exhibits for Natural History Museum (British Fossils 1980, Treasures of the Earth 1985, Britain's Offshore Oil and Gas 1988), creative conslt/designer Musee du Marbre Boulogne 1989, designer and conslt for new museum in the 18th century Manor House restoration project Bury St Edmunds 1990–93, design of new Musicology Gallery Horniman Museum and Gardens 1993, concept designer for phase II of Museum of Liverpool Life 1993–, concept designer for phase III - the King's Regiment Galleries Nat Museums and Galleries on Merseyside 1994–, concept for new Ulster/American Gallery on the History of Emigration NI 1994, concept designer for Manchester Museum HLF Bid 1997, designer of Rye Museum East Street & Rye Castle Museum 1998–99; visiting lectr for annual museum exhbn project Kingston Poly Sch of 3D Design 1985–92; Univ of Humberside: visiting lectr 1985–, outside advsr for Museum and Exhbn Design degree course and external examiner 1991–95; visiting lectr: Inst of Archaeology Univ of London 1990–, Univ of Essex Faculty of Fine Arts 1998–, Univ of Salford Heritage Design Course 1999–; memb: Bullough Ctee on Graphic Communication Zoological Soc of London 1983, Design Advsy Ctee MOMI 1986–87, Panel of Judges for new Museum of Evolution Natural History Museum Paris 1987; past chm Museum Designers' Gp Museums Assoc; occasional contrib: Design Week, Museums Jl; FCSD 1981–97, fell Museums Assoc 1983, FRSA 1993; *Books and Publications* Did Britain Make It? Part 1: Exhibition Design (1986), Designing Exhibitions (1988, revised 2 edn 2001); Manual of Curatorship (contrib Section 3, 1984), Manual of Heritage Management (contrib, 1995), Manual of Touring Exhibitions (contrib, 1995); *Recreations* cooking, walking, English market towns; *Style*— Giles Velarde, Esq; ✉ Fir Trees Studio, Cliff End Lane, Pett Level, East Sussex TN35 4EF (tel 01424 813445, e-mail gilesvelarde@onetel.com)

VELJANOVSKI, Dr Cento; s of Gavril Veljanovski, of Macedonia, and Margaret, *née* Wagenaar; *b* 19 February 1953; *Educ* Monash Univ (BEc, MEc), Univ of Oxford (DPhil); *m* 1990, Annabel, da of Col William Fazakerley, of Sherborne, Dorset; 1 da (Lydia Rose b 17 Oct 1992), 1 s (Tomas Cento b 6 July 1995); *Career* jr res fell Wolfson Coll Oxford 1978–84, visiting prof Univ of Toronto 1980–81, lectr UCL 1984–87, res and ed dir Inst of Econ Affairs 1987–91; dir Lexecon Ltd 1990–94, non-exec dir Flextech plc 1993–95, managing ptnr Case Associates 1996–; econ advsr Republic of Macedonia 1991–94; memb: Int Bar Assoc, CIArb, IOD, Competition Law Assoc; Freeman City of London, Liveryman Worshipful Co of Glass Sellers; ACIArb; *Books* Selling the State - Privatisation in Britain (1987), Privatisation and Competition (1989), Freedom in Broadcasting (1989), The Media in Britain Today (1990), Regulators and the Market (1991), Pay TV in Australia (1999), The Economics of Law (2006), Economic Principles of Law (2007); *Recreations* rowing, art, television, walking; *Clubs* Oxford and Cambridge, Chelsea Arts, Annabel's, Commonwealth; *Style*— Dr Cento Veljanovski

VELLACOTT, Keith David; MBE (2007); s of Hugh Douglas Sempill Vellacott (d 1987), of Tavistock, and Lorraine Freda Vellacott; *b* 25 February 1948; *Educ* Kelly Coll, The London Hosp Med Coll, DM (Nottingham); *m* 17 March 1973, Jinette, da of Godfrey Herbert Gibbs, of Teignmouth; 2 s (Darren Adrian b 1975, d 1986, Guy Neil b 1977), 1 da (Adele Fiona b 1980); *Career* res fell Univ of Nottingham 1977–81, surgical sr registrar Bristol Royal Infirmary 1981–86, conslt gen surgn Royal Gwent Hosp 1986–; memb: Assoc of Coloproctology, Assoc of Surgns of England and Ireland; FRCS 1976 (examiner 2000–); *Style*— Keith Vellacott, MBE; ✉ Royal Gwent Hospital, Cardiff Road, Newport, South Wales NP20 2UB

VELMANS, Marianne H; da of Loet A Velmans, of Sheffield, MA, and Edith, *née* van Hessen; *b* 5 July 1950; *Educ* Int Sch of Geneva, Univ of Sussex (BA); *m* Paul A Sidey; 1 s (Jack b 18 Oct 1984), 1 da (Saskia b 23 April 1990); *Career* Penguin Books 1973–80, head of London office Doubleday & Co Inc 1980–87, publishing dir Doubleday (Transworld Publishers Ltd) 1987–; *Books* Working Mother - A Practical Handbook (with Sarah Litvinoff, 1987, revised edn 1993); *Style*— Ms Marianne Velmans; ✉ Doubleday, 61–63 Uxbridge Road, London W5 5SA (tel 020 8579 2652, fax 020 8579 5479, e-mail m.velmans@transworld-publishers.co.uk)

VENABLES, (Harold) David Spenser; CB (1993); s of Maj Cedric Venables TD (d 1976), of Warborough, Oxon, and Gladys, *née* Hall (d 1973); *b* 14 October 1932; *Educ* Denstone Coll; *m* 18 July 1964, Teresa Grace, da of James Cornelius Watts (d 1960), of Hove, E Sussex; 1 da (Louise b 1965), 1 s (Julian b 1967); *Career* Pilot Offr Central Reconnaissance Estab RAF 1957–58; admitted slr 1956; entered Official Slr's Office 1960, memb Lord Chllr's Ctee on Age of Majority 1965–67, asst official slr 1977–80, official slr to the Supreme Ct 1980–93; *Books* A Guide to the Law Affecting Mental Patients (1975), Halsbury's Laws of England (contrib to 4 edn), The Racing Fifteen-hundreds: A History of Voiturette Racing 1931–40 (1984), Napier: The First to Wear the Green (1998), First Among Champions: The Alfa Romeo Grand Prix Cars (2000), Bugatti: A Racing History (2002), Brooklands: The Official Centenary History (2007); *Recreations* vintage motor cars, military and motoring history; *Style*— David Venables, Esq, CB; ✉ 11 Onslow Road, Hove, East Sussex BN3 6TA (tel 01273 502374)

VENABLES, Robert; QC (1990); s of Walter Edwin Venables, MM, of Wath upon Dearne, Rotherham, and Mildred Daisy Robson, *née* Taylor; *b* 1 October 1947; *Educ* Wath upon Dearne Co GS, Merton Coll Oxford (MA), LSE (LLM); *Career* lectr: Merton Coll Oxford 1972–75, UCL 1973–75; Univ of Oxford: official fell and tutor in jurisprudence St Edmund Hall 1975–80 (fell by special election 1992), CUF lectr; called to the Bar Middle Temple 1973 (bencher 1999), in practice 1976–; chm Revenue Bar Assoc 2001–; consltg ed The Offshore Tax Planning Review, The Personal Tax Planning Review and The Corporate Tax Review, chm Advsy Editorial Bd The Charity Law and Practice Review; treas CRUSAID 1991–96 (pres Cncl 1996–2000, memb Cncl 1996–), dir Yves Guihannec Fndn 1992–, tstee Temple Music Tst 2001–; FTII 1983 (memb Cncl 1999–); *Books* Inheritance Tax Planning (3 edn, 1996), Tax Planning Through Trusts (1990), National Insurance Contribution Planning (1990), Tax Planning and Fundraising for Charities (2 edn, 1994, 3 edn, 2001), Non-Resident Trusts (7 edn, 1998, 8 edn, 2001); *Recreations* music making; *Clubs* Travellers; *Style*— Robert Venables, Esq, QC; ✉ 61 Harrington Gardens, London SW7 4JZ; Chambers, 24 Old Buildings, Lincoln's Inn, London WC2A 3UR (tel 020 7242 2744, fax 020 7831 8095)

VENABLES, Robert Michael Cochrane; s of Cdr Gilbert Henry Venables, DSO, OBE, RN (d 1986), and Muriel Joan, *née* Haes (d 1990); *b* 8 February 1939; *Educ* Portsmouth GS; *m* 13 May 1972, Hazel Lesley, da of Wilfred Keith Gowing (d 1990); 2 da (Caroline b 1973, Hermione b 1987), 2 s (Gilbert b 1974, John b 1977); *Career* admitted slr 1962, in private practice London, Petersfield and Portsmouth 1962–70; Treasy Slr's Dept: legal asst 1970–73, sr legal asst 1973–80, asst Treasy slr 1980–89; charity cmmr 1989–97, admin dir and sec Cobbe Collection Tst 1997–2000, conslt Bircham Dyson Bell (formerly Bircham & Co) 1997–; Bircham Dyson Bell visiting prof of charity law London South Bank Univ 2005–; memb: Petersfield UDC 1968–71, Int Nuclear Law Assoc 1976–91 (memb Bd 1981–83), First Div Assoc (Exec Ctee 1980–82 and 1987–92, chm Legal Section 1981–83), Law Soc (memb Cncl 1993–2001), City of Westminster Law Soc 1976–2001, City of Westminster and Holborn Law Soc 2001– (pres 1997–98); tstee: Law Care (formerly SolCare) 1997– (chm 1998–2003 and 2004–), Incorporated Cncl of Law Reporting for England and Wales 1998–, Law Soc Charity 1999–, Vision Aid Overseas 2003–; co-opted memb E Hants DC 2001 and 2003– (chm Standards Ctee); FRSA 1995; *Recreations* opera, theatre, collecting domestic anachronisms; *Style*— Robert Venables, Esq; ✉ c/o Messrs Bircham Dyson Bell, 50 Broadway, London SW1H 0BL (tel 020 7227 7000)

VENABLES, Terence Frederick (Terry); *b* 6 January 1943; *Educ* Dagenham HS; *m* Yvette; 2 da (Nancy, Tracy); *Career* former professional footballer, now coach; clubs as player: Chelsea 1958–66 (capt 1962), Tottenham Hotspur 1966–68 (winners FA Cup 1967), Queens Park Rangers 1968–73; clubs as manager: Crystal Palace 1976–80 (coach 1973–76) and 1998–99, Queens Park Rangers 1980–84 (winners Second Div 1980, runners up FA Cup final 1982), Barcelona 1984–87 (winners Spanish Championship 1984, finalists European Cup 1985), Tottenham Hotspur 1987–91 (winners FA Cup 1991); chief exec Tottenham Hotspur plc 1991–93, coach England nat team 1994–96, coach Australia nat team 1996–98 chm Portsmouth FC 1996–98, coach Middlesbrough FC 2000–01, coach Leeds United FC 2002–03, asst coach England nat team 2006–; only player to have represented England at all levels; regular appearances on various TV football progs; co-author TV detective series Hazell; *Books* They Used to Play on Grass (1971), Terry Venables: Autobiography (1994), Venables' England (1996), Terry Venables: The Best Game in the World (1996); *Style*— Terry Venables, Esq

VENABLES-LLEWELYN, Sir John Michael Dillwyn-; 4 Bt (UK 1890), of Penllergaer, Llangyfelach and Ynis-y-gerwn, Cadoxton juxta Neath, Glamorganshire; s of Brig Sir (Charles) Michael Dillwyn-Venables-Llewelyn, 3 Bt, MVO (d 1976), and Lady Delia Mary Hicks-Beach, sister of 2 Earl St Aldwyn; *b* 12 August 1938; *Educ* Eton, Magdalene Coll Cambridge; *m* 1, 1963 (m dis 1972), Nina, da of late J S Hallam; 2 da (Georgina Katherine (Mrs Antony H Mead) b 1964, Emma Susan b 1967); m 2, 1975, Nina Gay Richardson Oliver (d 1995); *Heir* none; *Career* farmer; *Style*— Sir John Venables-Llewelyn, Bt

VENKITARAMAN, Prof Ashok; *Educ* Christian Medical Coll Vellore India (MB, BS, Kutumbiah Gold Medal in Medicine, Carman Prize in Surgery, Chandy Gold Medal for Clinical Studies), UCL (PhD), Univ of Cambridge (MA); *m* 24 June 1984, Dr Rajini, da of Col PV Ramana; *Career* house physician Christian Medical Coll Hosp Vellore India 1983–84, fell Lady Tata Meml Tst UCL & Charing Cross & Westminster Med Sch 1985–88; MRC Laboratory of Molecular Biology Cambridge: fell Beit Meml Tst 1988–91, memb Scientic Staff 1991–98; Ursula Zoellner prof of cancer research Sch of Clinical Medicine Univ of Cambridge 1998–; dep-dir MRC Cancer Cell Unit 2001–; memb EMBO European Acad 2004; professorial fell New Hall Cambridge, FMedSci; *Publications* numerous articles in scientific and medical jls (1982–); *Style*— Prof Ashok Venkitaraman; ✉ Department of Oncology/CCU, Hutchison/MRC Research Centre, Hills Road, Cambridge CB2 2XZ (tel 01223 336901, fax 01223 763374)

VENNER, Rt Rev Stephen Squires; *see:* Dover, Bishop of

VENNING, Philip Duncombe Riley; OBE (2003); s of Roger Riley Venning, MBE (d 1953), and Rosemary Stella Cenzi, *née* Mann; *b* 24 March 1947; *Educ* Sherborne, Principia Coll IL, Trinity Hall Cambridge (MA); *m* 4 April 1987, Elizabeth Frances Ann, da of late Michael Anthony Robelou Powers; 2 da (Laura Rosemary Ann b 28 May 1993, Grace Merlyn Frances b 14 July 1995); *Career* journalist Times Educnl Supplement 1970–81 (asst ed 1978), freelance writer 1981–84; sec: Soc for the Protection of Ancient Buildings 1984–, William Morris Craft Fellowship Ctee 1986–96; memb: Westminster Abbey Fabric Cmmn 1998–, Cncl Nat Tst 1992–2001, Expert Advsy Panel Heritage Lottery Fund 2005–; tstee: Historic Churches Preservation Tst 1995–2005 (vice-pres 2006–), Heritage Link 2002–03; FSA 1989, FRSA 1990; *Recreations* visiting old buildings, book collecting; *Style*— Philip Venning, Esq, OBE, FSA; ✉ 17 Highgate High Street, London N6 5JT; Society for the Protection of Ancient Buildings, 37 Spital Square, London E1 6DY (tel 020 7377 1644)

VENTRY, 8 Baron (I 1800); Sir Andrew Wesley Daubeny de Moleyns; 8 Bt (1797); assumed by deed poll 1966 the surname of Daubeny de Moleyns; s (by 2nd w) of Hon Francis Alexander Innys Eveleigh-Ross-de-Moleyns (d 1964), s of 6 Baron Ventry, and his 2 w Joan (later Mrs Nigel Springett; d 1993), eldest da of Harold Wesley, of Surrey; suc uncle, 7 Baron, 1987; *b* 28 May 1943; *Educ* Aldenham; *m* 1, 20 Feb 1963 (m dis 1979), Nelly Edouard Renée, da of Abel Chaumillon, of Loma de los Riseos, Villa Angel, Torremolinos, Malaga, Spain; 2 da (Hon Elizabeth-Ann b 1964, Hon Brigitte b 1967), 1 s (Hon Francis b 1865); m 2, 1983, Jill Rosemary, da of Cecil Walter Oram; 1 da (Hon Lisa b 1985); *Heir* s, Hon Francis Daubeny de Moleyns; *Career* farmer 1961–, in electronics 1986–; dir: Burgie Lodge Farms Ltd 1970–, C & R Briggs Commercials 1986–87, Glenscott Motor Controls Inc 1987–88 (vice-pres), Glenscott Motor Controls Inc 1988–94 (pres); European mktg mangr Unico Int 1994–; *Recreations* travel, photography, sailing, skiing; *Style*— The Rt Hon the Lord Ventry

VENUGOPAL, Dr Sriramashetty; OBE; s of Satyanarayan Sriramashetty (d 1962), and Manikyamma, *née* Akkenapalli; *b* 14 May 1933; *Educ* Osmania Med Coll Hyderabad (BSc, MB BS), Madras Univ (DMRD); *m* 22 May 1960, Subhadra (Meena), da of Raja Bahadur Sita Ramachander Rao (d 1949); 1 da (Anu b 1962), 1 s (Arun b 1964); *Career* med posts Osmania Hosp, state med servs Hyderabad Singareni Collieries 1959–65, registrar in radiology Selly Oak Hosp Birmingham 1965–66, registrar in chest med Springfield Hosp Grimsby 1966–67, princ in gen practice Aston Birmingham 1967–2001, hosp practitioner in psychiatry All Saints Hosp Birmingham 1972–96; contrib jls on medico-political subjects; fndr memb and chm Link House Cncl 1975–92, memb Local Review Ctee for Winson Green Prison 1981–83, fndr memb Osmania Grad Med Assoc in UK 1984–; memb: W Birmingham HA 1984–89, Working Gp DHSS 1984–89 (Local Med Ctee 1975–2001, Dist Med Ctee 1978–93), GMC 1984–99, Birmingham Community Liaison Advsy Ctee 1985; vice-chm: Hyderabad Charitable Tst 1985, Birmingham Div BMA 1980 (chm 1985–86); Overseas Doctors' Assoc: fndr memb 1975–, dep treas 1975–81, nat vice-chm 1981–87, chm info and advsy serv 1981–99, nat chm 1987–93, nat pres 1993–99; since retirement involved with Rotary charity work, aided Tsunami affected fishermen families at Cuddalore India, coordinator annual eye camps in India (enabled over 1000 eye operations); memb and former pres Aston Branch Rotary Club; FRSM 1986, FRIPHH 1988, FRCGP 1997 (MRCGP 1990), MFPHM 1998; *Recreations* medical politics, music, gardening; *Clubs* Aston Rotary; *Style*— Dr Sriramashetty Venugopal, OBE

VENVILLE, Malcolm Frank; s of Barry Venville (d 1978), of Birmingham, and Catherine Louise, *née* May; *b* 5 September 1962; *Educ* Lighthall Comp, Solihull Tech Coll, Poly of Central London (BA); *Career* engrg apprenticeship British Leyland 1980–81, Art and Design foundation course Solihull Tech Coll 1981–83, BA(Hons) in Film, Video and Photographic Arts Poly of Central London 1983–86, photographic asst 1987–90, freelance photographer 1990–; *Awards* Creative Circle Advtg Awards: bronze Most Promising Beginner for Photography 1992, silver Most Promising Beginner for Direction 1993, various gold and silvers; Assoc of Photographers: 3 merits and 1 silver Tenth Awards 1993, 2 silvers and 1 merit Eleventh Awards 1994, 1 merit 1995; 1 silver and inclusions D&AD; *Style*— Malcolm Venville, Esq

VERCOE, David James; s of Henry Frank Vercoe, of Kegworth, nr Derby, and Lillian Joy, *née* Surrage, of Kegworth; *b* 15 September 1949; *Educ* Loughborough GS, Univ of Manchester (BA); *m* 26 April 1976 (m dis), Elizabeth Anne, *née* Latta; m 2, Feb 1995, Madeleine Louise, *née* Cuming; 2 s (Oliver Henry b 24 June 1996, Harry Girard b 22 Nov 1998); *Career* head of Music Dept BBC Radio Two 1991–93 (ed progs 1988–90, managing ed 1990–91), managing ed BBC Radio Two 1994–97, project dir Brand Marketing BBC Corp Affrs 1997–2000, head Relationship Devpt BBC Technology Ltd 2001–02, freelance project mangr and conslt 2002–; *Recreations* sailing, skiing; *Style*— David Vercoe, Esq; ✉ e-mail david@davidvercoe.com

VERDIN, Anthony; s of Jack Arthur Verdin (d 1997), and Doris Hilda Verdin (d 1995); *b* 16 November 1932; *Educ* Christ's Hosp, Merton Coll Oxford (MA, MSc); *m* 1, 1958, Greta; 2 da (Julia b 1962, Annemarie b 1963), 1 s (John b 1965); m 2, 1986, Araminta, da of Michael Henry Carlile Morris; 2 da (Aurelia b 1986, Agatha b 1991), 1 s (Arthur b 1987); *Career* managing ptnr Cherwell Boathouse 1968–; dir: Chelart Ltd 1978–, Chelsea Arts Club Ltd 1987–, Morris & Verdin Ltd 1981–2004; md: Analysis Automation Ltd 1971–90, Verdin Ltd 1990–2004; chm: first Sch on Process Analytical Instrumentation Warwick Univ 1972, Cncl of Gas Detection Equipment Manufacturers 1987–90; toured USA and W Indies with Golden Oldies and Miami Rugby Club 1976–1981; Freeman City of London 1989, Liveryman Worshipful Co of Scientific Instrument Makers; CEng, MInstMC; *Publications* books incl: Gas Analysis Instrumentation (1973), and numerous articles and lectures on instrumentation techniques and air pollution; *Recreations* family, rugby football, tennis (lawn and real), cricket, music, reading, wine tasting; *Clubs* Chelsea Arts, Henley Wanderers RFC, QI Oxford; *Style*— Anthony Verdin, Esq

VERE HODGE, Dr (Richard) Anthony; s of Rev Preb Francis Vere Hodge, and Eleanor Mary, *née* Connor; *b* 27 December 1943; *Educ* Radley, Trinity Coll Dublin (BA), Worcester Coll Oxford (DPhil); *m*; 1 s, 2 da; *Career* joined Beecham Pharmaceuticals (then SmithKline Beecham Pharmaceuticals, now GlaxoSmithKline) 1969, worked on Interferon Inducers then Human Interferon (project mangr 1974–76), transferred to Antiviral Chemotherapy Project (which discovered Penciclovir 1983, and Famiclovir 1985); princ author of first publication with named antiherpesvirus compounds Famciclovir and Penciclovir (1989) and other articles on subject; seconded to Worldwide Strategic Product Devpt SmithKline Beecham 1993, assoc dir Anti-infectives Section 1995–96; dir Vere Hodge Antivirals Ltd 1996–, conslt Pharmasset Inc 2000–05; reviews ed Antiviral Chemistry and Chemotherapy (AVCC) 2005–; memb: The Chromotographic Soc 1989, Int Soc for Antiviral Research 1990 (memb Pubn Ctee 2006–), American Soc for Microbiology 1997; MRSC 1968; *Books* Integration of Pharmaceutical Discovery and Development: Case Studies (1998, contrib a chapter); *Recreations* bell ringing, gardening, hill walking; *Style*— Dr Anthony Vere Hodge

VERE-LAURIE, Lt-Col George Edward; DL (1993 Notts); o s of Lt-Col George Halliburton Foster Peel Vere-Laurie, JP, DL (d 1981), of Carlton Hall, Notts, and (Caroline) Judith, *née* Francklin (d 1987); *b* 3 September 1935; *Educ* Eton, RMA Sandhurst, Univ of London (BSc); *Career* cmmnd 9 Lancers 1955, cmd 9/12 Royal Lancers (PWO) 1974–77; md Trackpower Transmissions Ltd 1979–91, chm Central Notts Healthcare (NHS) Tst 1992–98; Lord of the Manors of Carlton-on-Trent and Willoughby-in-Norwell Notts; High Sheriff Notts 1991–92; Freeman City of London, memb Ct of Assts Worshipful Co of Saddlers (Master 1989–90); FIMgt 1981; *Recreations* horses, fox hunting, country life; *Style*— Lt-Col George Vere-Laurie, DL; ✉ Carlton Hall, Church Lane, Carlton-on-Trent, Newark, Nottinghamshire NG23 6LP (tel 01636 821421)

VEREKER, Sir John Michael Medlicott; KCB (1999, CB 1992); s of Cdr Charles William Medlicott Vereker (d 1995), and Marjorie Hughes, *née* Whatley (d 1984); *b* 9 August 1944; *Educ* Marlborough, Keele Univ (BA); *m* 7 Nov 1971, Judith, da of Hobart Rowen, of Washington, DC; 1 da (Jennifer b 1973), 1 s (Andrew b 1975); *Career* asst princ: ODM 1967–69, World Bank Washington 1970–72; princ ODM 1972, private sec to successive Mins at ODM, asst sec 1978, PM's Office 1980–83, under sec FCO ODA 1983–88 (princ fin offr 1986–88), dep sec (teachers) DES 1988, dep sec (further and higher educn and science) DES 1988–94, permanent sec ODA 1994–97, permanent sec Dept for Int Devpt 1997–2002, govr and C-in-C Bermuda 2002–07; chm Student Loans Co Ltd 1989–91; *Style*— Sir John Vereker, KCB

VEREKER, Rupert David Peregrine Medlicott; s of John Stanley Herbert Medlicott Vereker, and Valerie Ann Virginia, *née* Threlfall; *b* 31 July 1957; *Educ* Radley, Univ of Bradford (BA); *m* 9 Aug 1986, Philippa Janet, da of Geoffrey Stocks; 2 s (Frederick James Herbert Medlicott b 30 June 1990, Jack Rupert William Medlicott b 30 Jan 1992); *Career* advertising exec; Benton & Bowles (now DMB & B) 1980–85 (graduate trainee then account mangr), Doyle Dane Bernbach (now BMP DDB Needham) 1985–87 (account mangr then dir), md BV Gp plc 1987–2003, md Sonic Network 2004–; *Style*— Rupert Vereker, Esq

VEREY, David John; CBE (2004); s of Michael John Verey (d 2000), and Sylvia Mary, *née* Wilson; cous of (Henry) Nicholas Verey (d 1996); *b* 8 December 1950; *Educ* Eton, Trinity Coll Cambridge (MA); *m* 1, 1974 (m dis 1990), Luise, *née* Jaschke; 2 s, 1 da; m 2, 1990, Emma Katharine Broadhead, da of Sir Christophor Laidlaw, *qv*; *Career* Lazard Brothers & Co: joined 1972, dir 1983–2001, dep chief exec 1985–90, chief exec 1990–2000, chm 1992–2001; dep gp chm Cazenove Gp plc 2001–02, chm The Blackstone Gp UK; non-exec dir: Pearson plc 1996–2000, Daily Mail and General Trust plc 2004–; chm of tstees Tate Gallery 1999–2004 (tstee 1992–2004), chm Nat Art Collections Fund 2004–; fell Eton Coll 1997–, hon fell St Hugh's Coll Oxford; *Recreations* stalking, bridge, gardening, travel; *Style*— David Verey, Esq, CBE

VERITY, Dr Christopher Michael; s of Rev Harry William Verity (d 1988), of Cambridge, and Gladys, *née* Banks; *b* 18 February 1946; *Educ* Merchant Taylors' Sch Crosby, Leeds GS, Keble Coll Oxford (MA, BM BCh), St Thomas' Hosp Med Sch; *m* 5 May 1984, Dorothy Bowes (Kelly), da of Clifford Claud Jupp, of Br Columbia; *Career* MO Save The Children Fund Phnom Penh Cambodia 1974, med registrar St Thomas' Hosp 1974–75, house physician Hosp For Sick Children Gt Ormond St 1977, fell Dept of Paediatric Neurology Univ of Br Columbia Canada 1980–81, lectr Dept of Child Health Bristol Royal Hosp For Sick Children 1982–85, conslt paediatric neurologist Addenbrooke's Hosp Cambridge 1985–, assoc lectr Univ of Cambridge Med Sch 1985–; chair: MacKeith Meetings Ctee 1992–97, Br Paediatric Surveillance Unit Exec Ctee 1995–2001; vice-pres RCPCH 2003–; memb Ctee Br Branch International League against Epilepsy 1996–2003, med advsr Roald Dahl Fndn 1997–; author papers on: the Polle syndrome, follow up after cerebral hemispherectomy, hereditary sensory neuropathies, febrile convulsions in a nat cohort, variant Creutzfeldt-Jakob disease in UK children; memb: Br Paediatric Neurology Assoc, Assoc of Br Neurologists; FRCP 1990, FRCPCH 1997; *Recreations* windsurfing, skiing, golf, painting; *Style*— Dr Christopher Verity; ✉ Child Development Centre, Box 107, Addenbrooke's Hospital, Hills Road, Cambridge CB2 2QQ (tel 01223 216662, fax 01223 242171, e-mail christopher.verity@addenbrookes.nhs.uk)

VERJEE, Rumi; *Educ* Downing Coll Cambridge; *Career* chm Thomas Goode & Co; Wilkins fell Cambridge 2003; *Style*— Rumi Verjee, Esq; ✉ Thomas Goode & Co Ltd, 19 South Audley Street, London W1K 2BN (tel 020 7499 2823, fax 020 7629 4230)

VERMES, Prof Geza; s of Ernö Vermes (d 1944), and Terezia, *née* Riesz (d 1944); *b* 22 June 1924; *Educ* Gymnasium of Gyula Hungary, Budapest Univ, Univ of Louvain, Coll St Albert of Louvain; *m* 12 May 1958, (Noreen) Pamela, *née* Hobson (d 1993); m 2, 29 Nov 1996, Margaret Unarska; *Career* lectr (later sr lectr) in biblical studies Univ of Newcastle upon Tyne 1957–65; Univ of Oxford: prof of Jewish Studies 1989–91 (reader 1965–89, prof 1989–91, now emeritus prof), professorial fell Wolfson Coll 1965–91 (now emeritus); ed Jl of Jewish Studies 1971–; govr Oxford Centre for Hebrew Studies 1972–92, dir Oxford Forum for Qumran Research 1991–, chm Oxford Cncl of Christians and Jews 1980–86; W Bacher Medallist Hungarian Acad of Sciences 1996; Hon DD: Edinburgh 1989, Durham 1990; Hon DLitt Univ of Sheffield 1994; FBA 1985, fell European Acad of Arts, Sciences and Humanities 2001; *Books* Discovery in the Judean Desert (1956), Scripture and Tradition in Judaism (1961), Jesus the Jew (1973), Post-Biblical Jewish Studies (1975), Jesus and the World of Judaism (1983), History of the Jewish People in the Age of Jesus by E Schürer (jt reviser with F Millar and M Goodman, 1973–87), The Religion of Jesus the Jew (1993), The Dead Sea Scrolls - Qumran in Perspective (1994), The Dead Sea Scrolls in English (1995), The Complete Dead Sea Scrolls in English (1997, revised edn 2004), Discoveries in the Judaean Desert XXVI (with P S Alexander, 1998), Providential Accidents: An Autobiography (1998), An Introduction to the Complete Dead Sea Scrolls (1999), The Dead Sea Scrolls (2000), The Changing Faces of Jesus (2000), Jesus In His Jewish Context (2003), The Authentic Gospel of Jesus (2003), The Passion (2005), Who's Who in the Age of Jesus (2005), The Nativity: History and Legend (2006), The Resurrection (2008); *Recreations* watching wildlife; *Style*— Prof Geza Vermes, FBA; ✉ West Wood Cottage, Foxcombe Lane, Boars Hill, Oxford OX1 5DH (tel 01865 735 384, fax 01865 735 034, e-mail geza.vermes@orinst.ox.ac.uk)

VERMONT, David Neville; s of Leon Vermont (d 1949), and Anne MacDonald, *née* Hardy (d 1972); *b* 13 February 1931; *Educ* Mercers' Sch, Christ's Coll Cambridge (MA); *m* 1, 16 March 1957, Ann Marion (d 1992), da of late Lloyd Wilson; 2 s (Christopher b 1959, Charles b 1961), 1 da (Rachel b 1964); m 2, Grizelda, da of late Alexander d'Agapeyeff; *Career* Cadet Bn HAC 1947–50, Nat Serv 2 Regt RHA 1950–52 (served Germany BAOR, cmmnd 1951), 1 Regt HAC RHA 1952–62 (cmmnd 1956); Sedgwick Group plc 1955–88, dep chm gp reinsurance subsid E W Payne Cos Ltd 1975–87, dir Sumitomo Marine & Fire Insurance Co (Europe) Ltd 1975–90, dir City Fire Insurance Co Ltd and Bimeh Iran Insurance Co (UK) Ltd, London rep Compagnie de Réassurance d'Ile de France (Corifrance) 1988–2001; memb Lloyd's 1969–99; chm: Reinsurance Brokers' Assoc 1976–77, Brokers' Reinsurance Ctee 1977–78; vice-pres Argentine Dio Assoc (chm 1973–88), dir London Handel Society Ltd (chm 1992–97); govr: St Paul's Schs (chm 1981–82), Corp of the Sons of the Clergy (and memb Ct); memb: Ct City Univ, Cncl Gresham Coll 1981–2005 (chm 1988–93); tstee Whitechapel Art Gallery Fndn 1984–97; Freeman City of London 1952, Master Worshipful Co of Mercers 1981–82; hon memb Faculty of Divinity Univ of Cambridge 1998–, hon fell Gresham Coll 2000–, Dr of Humane Letters Schiller Univ 2006; FRSA; Cross of St Augustine 2005; *Books* A Brief History of Gresham College (with Richard Chartres); *Recreations* walking, opera, chamber music; *Clubs* Garrick, MCC, Oxford and Cambridge, City Livery, Nikaean, Beefsteak; *Style*— David Vermont, Esq; ✉ Coombe House, Uley, Gloucestershire GL11 5AQ (tel 01453 860287, fax 01453 861037, e-mail dnvermont@aol.com)

VERNEY, Sir Edmund Ralph; 6 Bt (UK 1818), of Claydon House, Buckinghamshire; s of Sir Ralph Verney, 5 Bt (d 2001); *b* 28 June 1950; *Educ* Harrow, York Univ; *m* 1982, Daphne Fausset-Farquhar, of Lovelocks House, Shefford Woodlands, Hungerford; 1 s (Andrew Nicholas b 1983), 1 da (Ella b 1985); *Heir* s, Andrew Verney; *Career* High Sheriff of Bucks 1998–99; Prime Warden Worshipful Co of Dyers 2001–02; FRICS; *Clubs* Brooks's; *Style*— Sir Edmund Verney, Bt; ✉ Claydon House, Middle Claydon, Buckingham MK18 2EX

VERNON, 11 Baron (GB 1762); Anthony William Vernon-Harcourt; s of Col William Ronald Denis Vernon-Harcourt, OBE (d 1999), and Nancy Everil, *née* Leatham; suc kinsman, 10 Baron Vernon, 2000; *b* 29 October 1939, Richmond, N Yorks; *Educ* Eton, Magdalene Coll Cambridge (MA); *m* 3 Dec 1966, Cherry Stanhope, *née* Corbin; 1 da (Hon Charlotte Lucy (Hon Mrs Kaye) b 1968), 3 s (Hon Simon Anthony b 1969, Hon Edward William b 1973, Hon Oliver Thomas b 1977); *Heir* s, Hon Simon Vernon-Harcourt; *Career* fndr and chm Monks Partnership 1980–2002, dir PricewaterhouseCoopers 2000–02; ed Charterhouse Top Management Remuneration 1978–88; chm Cambridge Advanced Motorcyclists; involved with: Home-Start, C of E; sometime memb: IPM, IOD; *Publications* incl: Executive and All-Employee Share Schemes (1981), Company Car Policy Guide (1981–87), Boardroom Pay and Incentives in Growth Companies (1984), Performance Related Bonuses for Senior Management (1989), Archibald Sturrock: Pioneer Locomotive Engineer (2007); *Recreations* motorcycling, railway history, gardening; *Style*— The Rt Hon the Lord Vernon

VERNON, Dr Clare Christine; da of Stephen Vernon, 12 Willows Ave, Lytham St Annes, Lancashire, and Mary, *née* Dewhirst; *b* 23 October 1951; *Educ* Queen Mary Sch Lytham, Girton Coll Cambridge (MA, MB BChir), Bart's; *m* 17 July 1976 (m dis 1988), George, s of Herbert Evans (d 1984); *Career* registrar in radiotherapy: Royal Free Hosp 1979, Middx Hosp 1982; sr registrar in radiotherapy Mount Vernon Hosp 1984, conslt clinical oncologist Hammersmith Hosp 1986–; prof in radiation oncology Hong Kong, Alexandria and Lahore; memb: BMA 1976, GMC 1976, 1951 Club 1986; FRCR 1984, MPS 1989; *Recreations* sports, music, archaeology; *Clubs* 1951; *Style*— Dr Clare C Vernon; ✉ 18 Brookfield Avenue, Ealing, London W5 1LA (tel 020 8997 1786); Department of Clinical Oncology, Hammersmith Hospital, Du Cane Road, London W12 0HS (tel 020 8383 3177, fax 020 8383 1789, e-mail clarecvernon@hotmail.co.uk)

VERNON, Diana Charlotte; da of Roderick W P Vernon, of Chobham, Surrey, and Jennifer F F, *née* Tyrrell; *b* 30 April 1961; *Educ* St Michael's Burton Park, St Mary's Coll Durham (BA), KCL (PGCE); *Career* editorial asst John Wiley & Sons Ltd 1982–84, account exec Business Image PR 1984–85, Grayling PR 1985–87, Thorn EMI plc 1987–89, LIG plc 1989–93; Downe House Sch Newbury 1994–2000, headmistress Woldingham Sch Caterham 2000–; govr: Lilian Baylis Sch London 1985–2002, Flexlands Sch Chobham 1994–2004, Princes Mead Sch Winchester 1999–2001, Conifers Sch Midhurst 2003–06, Stoke Brunswick East Grinstead 2003–06, Cumnor House Danehill 2003–05, St Christopher's Hampstead 2003–; *Recreations* theatre, travel, cookery, swimming; *Style*— Miss Diana Vernon; ✉ Woldingham School, Marden Park, Caterham, Surrey CR3 7YA (tel 01883 349431, fax 01883 348653)

VERNON, Sir Nigel John Douglas; 4 Bt (UK 1914), of Shotwick Park, Co Chester; s of Sir (William) Norman Vernon, 3 Bt (d 1967); *b* 2 May 1924; *Educ* Charterhouse; *m* 29 Nov 1947, Margaret Ellen (d 1999), da of late Robert Lyle Dobell, of Waverton, Chester; 2 s (1 s decd), 1 da; *Heir* s, James Vernon; *Career* Lt RNVR 1942–45; dir Aon Risk Services UK Ltd Insurance Brokers 1984–99, ret; *Recreations* gardening, shooting, golf; *Clubs* Naval, Army and Navy; *Style*— Sir Nigel Vernon, Bt

VERNON, Dr Stephen Andrew; s of Alan Vernon (d 1979), of Alderley Edge, Cheshire, and Phyllis Mary Vernon; *b* 10 February 1955; *Educ* King's Sch Macclesfield, Univ of Bristol Med Sch (MB ChB), Univ of Nottingham (DM); *m* 1 Sept 1985, Alison Elizabeth Mary, da of Claude Walton (d 1990), of Mansfield, Notts; 1 da (Olivia Katherine b 2 Dec 1989), 1 s (Simon Alexander Alan b 5 Feb 1992); *Career* house physician Bristol Royal Infirmary 1978–79, house surgn Frenchay Hosp Bristol 1979, demonstrator and lectr in anatomy Bristol Med Sch 1979–80, SHO and registrar in ophthalmology Bristol Eye Hosp 1980–83, sr registrar Oxford Eye Hosp 1983–86, sr lectr and founding head Academic Unit of Ophthalmology Univ of Nottingham and hon conslt ophthalmologist Nottingham HA 1986–94, conslt ophthalmologist Univ Hosp NHS Tst Nottingham 1994–; author of academic pubns on ophthalmic epidemiology, diabetic retinopathy and glaucoma detection and mgmnt; memb: Euro Glaucoma Soc, Midlands Ophthalmic Soc (treas 1992–99, pres 2000–01), UK and Eire Glaucoma (memb Cncl 2000–05, chm 2005–); FRCS 1982, FRCOphth 1989; *Books* Ophthalmology (1988), Passing Postgraduate Examinations in Ophthalmology (1992), Differential diagnosis in Ophthalmology (1998); *Recreations* golf, skiing, music and drama; *Style*— Dr Stephen Vernon; ✉ Department of Ophthalmology, University Hospital, Nottingham NG7 2UH (tel 0115 924 9924 ext 63200, e-mail stephen.vernon@nuh.nhs.uk)

VERRILL, John Rothwell; s of Dr Peter John Verrill, of Aldeburgh, and Christine Mary, *née* Rothwell; *b* 25 March 1954; *Educ* Univ Coll Sch, UCL (LLB); *m* 1980; 4 s; m 2, 23 Dec 2002, Louise Verrill, *qv*; *Career* admitted slr 1981; Lawrence Graham: asst slr 1982–86, ptnr 1986–, head of Corp Recovery Gp; Licensed Insolvency Practitioner 1990–; Freeman

V

Worshipful Co of Slrs 1988; memb: Law Soc, City of Westminster Law Soc, Int Bar Assoc (UK Energy Lawyers Gp), Insolvency Practitioners Assoc, Cncl and pres Assoc of Business Recovery Professionals, R3; memb Insolvency Lawyers Assoc, dir INSOL Int; *Books* Butterworth's Insolvency Meetings Manual (1995); *Recreations* rowing, shooting, opera; *Clubs* Leander, Travellers; *Style*— John Verrill, Esq; ✉ Lawrence Graham, 190 Strand, London WC2R 1JN (tel 020 7379 0000, fax 020 7379 6854, e-mail john.verrill@lg-legal.com)

VERRILL, Louise; da of Geoffrey Gay, of Amesbury, Wilts, and Ann, *née* Rickman; *b* 29 March 1955, London; *Educ* Benenden, UWE (DipLP); *m* 23 Dec 2002, John Verrill, *qv*; 1 da (Catherine Elisabeth Fox b 15 Dec 1981), 1 s (William Marcus St Vigor Fox b 17 Aug 1984), 4 step s; *Career* admitted slr 1997; slr specialising in insolvency and corporate restructuring; ptnr and head of London Business Support and Restructuring team Addleshaw Goddard; memb Exec Ctee INSOL Europe 2004–, co-chm G36 INSOL Int 2004–07 (tech chair Int European Regnl Conf Prague 2004); memb: Ctee Int Bar Assoc, Investigation Ctee ICAEW 2001–04; former ed Eurofenix, memb Editorial Bd INSOL World, author of articles for legal and accountancy press; pres: Insolvency Practitioners Assoc 2005–06, Insolvency Lawyers Assoc 2007–; memb: American Bankruptcy Inst, Assoc of Business Recovery Professionals, Assoc of Partnership of Practitioners Law Soc; licensed insolvency practitioner; *Recreations* gardening, tennis, skiing, sailing, shooting; *Style*— Mrs Louise Verrill; ✉ Addleshaw Goddard LLP, 150 Aldersgate Street, London EC1A 4EJ (tel 020 7160 3113, fax 020 7160 3333, e-mail louise.verrill@addleshawgoddard.com)

VERTUE, Beryl; OBE (2000); *Career* chm and prodr Hartswood Films Ltd; chm PACT 1999–2001; credits incl: Men Behaving Badly (six series and two Christmas specials, BBC, exec conslt US version), Wonderful You (ITV), Is it Legal? (three series), In Love With Elizabeth (documentary, BBC1), Officers and Gentlemen (documentary, BBC2), The Red Baron (documentary, BBC2), Border Café (BBC1), The War behind the Wire (BBC2), The Savages (BBC1), Coupling (four series, BBC2), Carrie and Barry (two series, BBC1); BAFTA Award for Outstanding Creative Contribution to Television 2004; FRTS; *Style*— Ms Beryl Vertue, OBE; ✉ Hartswood Films Ltd, Twickenham Studios, The Barons, St Margarets, Twickenham, Middlesex TW1 2AW (tel 020 8607 8736, fax 020 8607 8744)

VERULAM, 7 Earl of (UK 1815); Sir John Duncan Grimston; 14 Bt (E 1629); also Lord Forrester (S 1633), Baron Dunboyne and Viscount Grimston (I 1719), Baron Verulam (GB 1790), Viscount Grimston (UK 1815); s of 6 Earl of Verulam (d 1973); *b* 21 April 1951; *Educ* Eton, Christ Church Oxford; *m* 1976, Dione Angela, da of Jeremy F E Smith, of Balcombe House, E Sussex; 3 s (James Walter, Viscount Grimston b 1978, Hon Hugo Guy Sylvester b 1979, Hon Sam George b 1983), 1 da (Lady Flora Hermione b 1981); *Heir* s, Viscount Grimston; *Career* dir Baring Brothers & Co Ltd 1987–96, md ABN-Amro Bank NV 1996–2000, vice-chm Kleinworth Benson Private Bank 2004– (dir 2001–03); *Recreations* country pursuits; *Clubs* Beefsteak, White's; *Style*— The Rt Hon the Earl of Verulam; ✉ Gorhambury, St Albans, Hertfordshire AL3 6AH (tel 01727 855000)

VESSEY, Prof Martin Paterson; CBE (1994); s of Sydney James Vessey (d 1988), of Mill Hill, London, and Catherine, *née* Thomson (d 2000); *b* 22 July 1936; *Educ* UCS Hampstead, UCL, UCH Med Sch (MD, MA Oxon); *m* 21 May 1959, Anne, da of Prof Benjamin Stanley Platt, CMG (d 1969); 2 s (Rupert b 1964, Ben b 1967), 1 da (Alice b 1970); *Career* prof of public health Univ of Oxford 1974–2000, fell St Cross Coll Oxford 1974–; memb: Oxford Preservation Tst, Nat Tst, Campaign to Protect Rural England, BMA, Soc for Social Med; author of 3 books and over 400 scientific papers; FRS 1991; *Recreations* fine arts, motoring, Victorian engineering, conservation; *Style*— Prof Martin Vessey, CBE, FRS; ✉ Clifden Cottage, Burford Road, Fulbrook, Oxfordshire OX18 4BL (tel 01993 824985); Department of Public Health, University of Oxford, Old Road Campus, Headington, Oxford (tel 01865 227030, e-mail martin.vessey@dphpc.ox.ac.uk)

VESTEY, Edmund Hoyle; DL (Essex 1978, Suffolk 1991); only s of Ronald Vestey, DL; *b* 1932; *Educ* Eton; *m* 1960, Anne Moubray (d 2007), yr da of Gen Sir Geoffry Scoones, KCB, KBE, CSI, DSO, MC; 4 s (Timothy b 1961, James b 1962, George b 1964, Robin b 1968); *Career* served as 2 Lt Queen's Bays 1951–52; chm: Albion Insurance Co 1970, Blue Star Line 1971–95, Union International plc 1988–96, Star Offshore Services plc 1989–95, Vestey Group Ltd 1993–95 (dir 1995–2000); pres: Gen Cncl Br Shipping 1981–82, Chamber of Shipping 1992–94; jt master Thurlow Foxhounds 1966–, chm MFHA 1992–96; pres: Suffolk Agric Soc 1976, E of England Agric Soc 1995, Essex County Scouts Cncl 1979–87; High Sheriff Essex 1977–78; Lt City of London Yeomanry 1952–60; Liveryman: Worshipful Co of Butchers, Worshipful Co of Shipwrights, Worshipful Co of Farmers; *Clubs* Cavalry, Carlton; *Style*— Edmund Vestey, Esq, DL; ✉ Iolaire Lodge, Lochinver, Sutherland IV27 4JY; Sunnyside Farmhouse, Hawick, Roxburghshire; Little Thurlow Hall, Haverhill, Suffolk CB9 7LQ

VESTEY, 3 Baron (UK 1922); Sir Samuel George Armstrong Vestey; 3 Bt (UK 1913), DL (Glos 1982); s of Capt the Hon William Howarth Vestey, Scots Gds (ka Italy 1944, only s of 2 Baron Vestey), and Pamela, da of George Nesbitt Armstrong, s of Charles Nesbitt Frederick Armstrong and Dame Nellie Melba, GBE, the opera singer; suc gf 1954; *b* 19 March 1941; *Educ* Eton; *m* 1, 1970 (m dis 1981), Kathryn Mary, da of John Eccles, of Moor Park, Herts; 2 da (Hon Saffron Alexandra (Hon Mrs Idiens) b 1971, Hon Flora Grace b 1978); m 2, 1981, Celia Elizabeth, yr da of Maj (Hubert) Guy Broughton Knight, MC (d 1993), of Lockinge, Oxon, and Hester, sis of Countess (w of 6 Earl) of Clanwilliam; 2 s (Hon William Guy b 1983, Hon Arthur George b 1985), 1 da (Hon Mary Henrietta b 1992); *Heir* s, Hon William Vestey (page of honour to HM The Queen 1995–98); *Career* Lt Scots Gds; chm Vestey Group plc and associated cos; pres: London Meat Trade and Drovers' Benevolent Assoc 1973, Inst of Meat 1978–83, Royal Bath & W of England Soc 1994, Br Horse Soc 1994–; chm: Meat Trg Cncl 1992–95, Steeplechase Co Cheltenham, Royal Agricultural Soc of the Cwlth; Master of the Horse 1999–; Liveryman Worshipful Co of Butchers; patron of one living; patron Gloucestershire CCC; GCStJ, Lord Prior of the Order of St John 1991–2001; *Clubs* White's, Jockey (Newmarket), Melbourne (Melbourne), I Zingari; *Style*— The Rt Hon the Lord Vestey, DL; ✉ Stowell Park, Northleach, Gloucestershire GL54 3LE (tel 01285 720308, fax 01285 720360)

VETTRIANO, Jack; OBE (2003); *b* 1951, Fife; *Career* artist; *Solo Exhibitions* incl: Lovers and Other Strangers (Portland Gall London and Kirkcaldy Museum & Art Gall Fife) 2000, Affairs of the Heart (Portland Gall London) 2004, Love, Surrender and Devotion (Portland Gall London and Kirkcaldy Museum & Art Gall Fife) 2006; also in Edinburgh, London, Hong Kong, NY and Johannesburg; *Group Exhibitions* incl: Royal Scottish Acad Annual Exhbn 1989, Royal Acad Summer Exhbn 1990, Int 20th Century Arts Fair (The Armory NY) 1999, artLONDON 2002; work in permanent collection of Kirkcaldy Art Gall; Hon DLitt Univ of St Andrews 2003; *Books* subject of: Fallen Angels: Paintings by Jack Vettriano (ed W Gordon Smith, 1999), Lovers and Other Strangers: Paintings by Jack Vettriano (ed Anthony Quinn, 2002), Jack Vettriano (Anthony Quinn, 2004); *Style*— Jack Vettriano, Esq, OBE; ✉ c/o Karen Swan, 12 Braehead House, Victoria Road, Kirkcaldy, Fife KY1 2SD

VICARI, Andrew; s of Cavaliere Vittorio Vicari, and Italia, *née* Bertani; *b* 20 April 1938, Port Talbot, W Glamorgan; *Educ* Neath GS for Boys, Slade Sch of Fine Art London; *Career* artist; official painter: king and govt of Saudi Arabia, Interpol, Compagnie Republicaine de Securite (CRS); European Parl and Cncl of Europe Beaux Arts Prize 1995; world patron Millennium Tst, hon memb European Hotel Mangrs Assoc; Hon Col US 6 Cavalry, hon memb Rotary Int; pres Carwyn James Rugby Sch Wales, hon vice-pres Neath Male Voice Choir; Freeman City of London 2002, memb Guild of Freemen of the City of London, memb Worshipful Co of Firefighters, Liveryman of Wales; FZS; Brig d'Honneur CRS (France), Brig d'Honneur de la Police Nationale (France), Commanduer Confrerie des Chevaliers des Tastevins (France), Chevalier Order of Merit (Monaco); *Major Exhibitions* incl: New Burlington Galleries London 1955, Redfern Gallery London 1956, Obelisk Gallery London 1956, Exhibitions Grand Palais des Champs Elysées Societe des Artistes Français Paris 1957, RBA Galleries London 1957, United Soc of Artists 1957, Grand Palais des Champs Elysées Paris 1959, Faces in Wales (Temple of Peace Civic Centre Cardiff) 1960, The Last Supper (Foyle's Art Gallery London) 1960, Thomson House Cardiff 1960, Vicari Exhibition of Paintings and Drawings (Leicester Sq London) 1961 (in aid of ICRF), Kalamazoo Museum of Art MI 1962, Columbus Museum of Art OH 1963, Harrison Library NY 1963, Contemporary Art Soc of GB Vicari Retrospective (UC Wales) 1963, Bath Festival 1964, Circolo Della Stampa Rome 1965, The Virgin and the Gypsy (London Screenplays) 1970, Archer Gallery London 1972, Madden Galleries London 1973, Galerie Vendome Beirut 1974, The Triumph of the Bedouin (King Faisal Conf Centre Riyadh) 1974–78, Romantic Realism of Vicari (8th Int Art Fair Basle) 1977, Chevy Chase Art Center Washington DC 1978, Salle Empire Hotel de Paris Monte Carlo 1981, Galerie du Carlton Cannes 1981, The Majesty of King Faisal (King Faisal Fndn Riyadh) 1984, Petit Palais MOMA Geneva 1984, Les Vigonades de la Concorde (Hotel de Crillon Paris) 1988, Interpol World HQ Lyons 1989, Siege Credit Lyonnais Bank Lyons 1989, The Majesty of King Fahd (Rashid Engrg Museum Riyadh) 1989, Palais Amerique-Latin Monaco 1991, La Guerre du Golfe (Les Invalides Paris) 1991, Hotel Meurice Paris 1991, CRS Versailles 1994, Palais des Beaux Arts Beijing 1995, Governor's Palace St Petersburg 1995, La Vigonade des Motards de la Police Nationale (Miny of the Interior Paris) 2000, The Vicari Collection of Paintings and Drawings Produced in the Kingdom of Saudi Arabia 1998–2001 (Royal Suite Riyadh Intercontinental Hotel) 2001, An Essex Celebration of Constable & Gainsborough (10 landscapes) 2003, Parable of Majesty & Reconciliation (retrospective, Abu Dhabi and The Palace One & Only Royal Mirage Dubai) 2005, 4 Carvaggios and 1 Vicari (Sardinia, Malta and Minorca) 2006, portraits of iconic figures of the 20th Century (Dubai Community Theatre and Arts Centre) 2006, The Enigma: A Retrospective Exhibition of Paintings and Drawings 1956–2006 (Grosvenor House Dubai) 2006; *Commissions* incl: The Children of Tymorfa four panels for Glamorgan Educn Authy 1956, Cyclorama: Harlequins, Colombines & Children for Nat Eisteddfod Llandudno 1964, Bath Festival Exhibition 1964, The Vigonade of the Millennium Stadium mural for S dressing room (to remove notorious jinx) Millennium Stadium Cardiff 2002, Triptych of Sir Alex Ferguson 2003 for Manchester United Carrington Training Ground 2003; *Work in Collections* incl: Dallas Museum of Fine Arts, Nat Library of Wales, Museum of Tel Aviv, Contemporary Arts Soc of GB, Tate Gallery, Columbus Museum of Fine Arts, Pezzo Pozzoli Museum Milan, Petit Palais MOMA Geneva, David Lloyd Kreeger Collection Washington DC, IBM Collection Armonk, Palais Princier Monaco, Musée des Timbres et Monnaie Monaco, Hermitage Museum St Petersburg, King Faisal Conf Centre Riyadh, Chinese Miny of Culture Beijing, King Faisal Fndn Museum Riyadh, Rashid Engrg Museum Riyadh, Collection National Library of Riyadh, Credit Lyonnais Bank Lyons and Paris, Tournament Identity for Celtic Manor Wales Open Golf Championship 2007, series of landscape paintings as official artist to the Ryder Cup Course at Celtic Manor 2007; *Publications* Triumph of the Bedouin (1978), Ghazi A Al Ghosaibi: From the Orient and the Desert (illustrations, 1984), The Mystery of Memory: The Truth is Not Enough (vol 1 of autobiography, 2007); *Recreations* cinema, squash, food and wine; *Clubs* MCC, East India and Public Schools, Cardiff and County, Bristol Channel Yacht; *Style*— Maitre Andrew Vicari; ✉ e-mail a.vicari@andrew-vicari.com, website www.andrew-vicari.com; c/o Philip Oag (manager) e-mail p.oag@andrew-vicari.com

VICK, Graham; *b* 30 December 1953; *Career* artistic dir City of Birmingham Touring Opera, dir of prodns Glyndebourne Festival Opera; hon prof of music Univ of Birmingham; Chevalier de l'Ordre des Arts et des Lettres (France); *Style*— Graham Vick, Esq; ✉ c/o Ingpen & Williams Ltd, 7 St George's Court, 131 Putney Bridge Road, London SW15 2PA (tel 020 8874 3222, fax 020 8877 3113)

VICK, Laurence; s of Alfred Spencer Vick (d 1996), and Patricia Mae, *née* Eyles (d 1987); *b* 14 December 1952, Birmingham; *Educ* King Edward VI Camp Hill Sch Birmingham, Lanchester Poly Coventry (LLB), Coll of Law Guildford; *m* 11 March 1983, Josie, *née* Gale; 3 s (Andrew b 2 April 1985, Alex 10 April 1989, Harry 19 Dec 1992), 1 da (Hannah b 8 Oct 1987); *Career* admitted slr 1981, chartered insur practitioner 1999; slr specialising in clinical negligence; ptnr: Haxby Jarvis Coventry 1981–91, Brindley Twist Tafft and James Coventry 1991–94, Tozers Exeter 1994–99, Michelmores Exeter 1999–; memb Law Soc 1981, chartered insurance practitioner 1999; lead slr Bristol Heart Children Action Gp at Bristol Heart Inquiry); assoc Chartered Insur Inst; *Recreations* family, guitar, garden, Aston Villa FC; *Style*— Laurence Vick, Esq; ✉ Karelia House, Hillside Road, Sidmouth, Devon EX10 8JF (tel 01395 513081); Michelmores Solicitors, Pynes Hill, Exeter EX2 5WR (tel 01392 688688, fax 01392 360563, e-mail lnv@michelmores.com)

VICKERMAN, Andrew; s of Ferdinand Vickerman (d 1992), and Joyce, *née* Hill (d 1979); *b* 30 October 1954; *Educ* Solihull Sch, Queens' Coll Cambridge (MA, PhD); *m* 1, 31 Oct 1987 (m dis), Eva, da of Cecil Uwedo; 2 da (Jody Sarah b 27 Feb 1981 (decd), Michelle Andaya b 20 Aug 1989), 1 s (David Gareth b 25 Sept 1986); m 2, 29 July 2005, Maria Evangeli; *Career* various academic appts 1977–85, econ advsr to PM of PNG 1985–89, economist UN Study Mission Vietnam 1989–90, sr econ advsr to Govt of PNG (secondment from World Bank) 1989–91, commercial advsr Rio Tinto plc 1991–93, fin dir Lihir Gold Ltd 1993–98; Rio Tinto plc: head of external affrs 1998–2002, head of communication and sustainable devpt 2003–06, global head of communications and external relations 2006–; *Books* The Fate of the Peasantry (1986); also author of numerous articles and contribs; *Recreations* skiing, sailing, travel; *Style*— Andrew Vickerman, Esq; ✉ Rio Tinto plc, 6 St James's Square, London SW1Y 4LD (tel 020 8080 1142, e-mail andrew.vickerman@riotinto.com)

VICKERMAN, Prof Keith; s of Jack Vickerman, and Mabel, *née* Dyson; *b* 21 March 1933; *Educ* King James GS Almondbury, UCL (BSc, PhD, DSc), Univ of Exeter; *m* 16 Sept 1961, Moira, da of Wilfrid Dutton, MC; 1 da (Louise Charlotte b 1973); *Career* Royal Soc tropical res fell UCL 1963–68 (Wellcome lectr 1958–63); Univ of Glasgow: reader 1968–74, prof 1974–84, regius prof of zoology 1984–98, head of dept 1979–85; Leeuwenhoek lectr Royal Soc 1994, Linnean Soc Gold Medal for Zoology 1996; served on various ctees of WHO, ODA, NERC and SERC; fell UCL 1985; FRSE 1970, FRS 1984, FMedSci 1998; *Books* The Protozoa (with F E G Cox, 1967); author numerous articles and res papers in learned jls; *Recreations* sketching, gardening; *Style*— Prof Keith Vickerman, FRS, FRSE; ✉ Division of Environmental and Evolutionary Biology, University of Glasgow, Kerr Building, Glasgow G12 8QQ (tel 0141 330 4433, e-mail k.vickerman@bio.gla.ac.uk)

VICKERMAN, Prof Roger William; s of William Vickerman (d 1965), and Gertrude Ethel, *née* Passingham (d 1996); *b* 31 August 1947; *Educ* Clare Coll Cambridge (MA), Univ of Sussex (DPhil); *m* 1973, Christine Ann, *née* Wragg; 2 s (Stephen Roger b 10 Nov 1979, Thomas John b 15 March 1986), 2 da (Jennifer Ann b 10 Nov 1979, Karen Elizabeth b 21 June 1984); *Career* jr res fell in tport economics Univ of Sussex 1972, lectr in economics Univ of Hull 1972–76; Univ of Kent at Canterbury: lectr in economics 1977–79, sr lectr in economics 1979–87, dir Channel Tunnel Res Unit 1986–93, prof of regnl and tport economics 1989–98, dir Centre for Euro Regnl and Tport Economics 1993–, head Dept of Economics 1993–99 and 2005–, Jean Monnet prof of Euro economics 1998–; visiting res scholar Universität Münster Germany 1980, visiting assoc prof Dept of Economics

Univ of Guelph Ontario Canada 1984, visiting prof Inst for Tport Studies Univ of Sydney Australia 1999; SSRC/ESRC: memb Study Gp on Environmental Economics 1974–76, Regnl and Urban Economics 1975–, Sports Cncl Panel on Recreation and Leisure Res 1977–87, Res Training Bd Sub-Gp on Human Geography and Planning 1990, Mid Term Review Panel Tport Studies Unit 1998–99, Commissioning Panel on Res Centre Gps and Priority Networks 1999–2000; memb: Planning Res Advsy Gp DOE 1994–95, Kent Economic Forum 1992–97, Infrastructure Gp East Kent Initiative 1992–98, Standing Advsy Ctee on Trunk Road Assessment DETR 1996–99; memb Ed Bd: Regional Studies, Papers in Regional Science, les Cahiers Scientifiques du Transport, Transport Policy; churchwarden St Cosmus and St Damian in the Blean; Hon Dr Univ Marburg 2002; FRSA 1989, FCILT 1996, AcSS 2001; *Publications* The Channel Tunnel: Public Policy, Regional Development and European Integration (with I M Holliday and G Marcou, 1991), Infrastructure and Regional Development (ed, 1991), The Single European Market: Prospects for Economic Integration (1992), Convergence and Divergence among European Regions (ed with H W Armstrong, 1995), The Econometrics of Major Transport Infrastructures (ed with Emile Quinet, 1997), Principles of Transport Economics (with Emile Quinet, 2004); also 74 chapters in edited books and 60 articles in learned jls; *Recreations* music, travel and transport, photography; *Style—* Professor Roger Vickerman; ✉ Department of Economics, Keynes College, University of Kent, Canterbury, Kent CT2 7NP (tel 01227 823495, fax 01227 827784, e-mail r.w.vickerman@kent.ac.uk)

VICKERS, Adrian Michael; s of Hugh Anthony Vickers (d 1970), of Greasby, Cheshire, and Margaret, *née* Rae (d 1989); *b* 24 September 1938; *Educ* Beaumont Coll, Merton Coll Oxford (MA); *m* 1, 1977 (m dis), Andrea Tyminski; 2 s (Matthew b 29 Jan 1979, Dominic b 25 May 1983), 1 da (Sophie b 8 Nov 1981); m 2, 1998, Emma Dinwoodie; *Career* trainee S H Benson 1962–63, dir Robert Sharp & Partners 1963–76, dep chm Abbott Mead Vickers BBDO 1976–99; pres IAA (UK Chapter); FIPA; *Recreations* golf, skiing; *Clubs* Royal Mid-Surrey, Minchinhampton Golf; *Style—* Adrian Vickers, Esq; ✉ Abbott Mead Vickers BBDO Ltd, 151 Marylebone Road, London NW1 5QE (tel 020 7616 3500, fax 020 7616 3800)

VICKERS, Hugo Ralph; s of Ralph Cecil Vickers, MC (d 1992), and Dulcie, *née* Metcalf (d 1992); nephew of Baroness Vickers, DBE (d 1994); *b* 12 November 1951; *Educ* Eton, Strasbourg Univ; *m* 23 Sept 1995, Elizabeth Anne Blyth, yr da of Michael Vickers, of Montaillac, France; 2 s (Arthur Hugo Blyth b 12 March 1999, George Henry Edward b 1 Feb 2001), 1 da (Alice Elizabeth Margaret (twin) b 1 Feb 2001); *Career* author, reviewer, broadcaster, lectr; worked with London Celebrations Ctee for Queen's Silver Jubilee 1977, admin Great Children's Pty 1979; literary executor to the late Sir Charles Johnston and the late Sir Cecil Beaton; lay steward St George's Chapel Windsor Castle 1970– (dep vice-capt 1996–); chm Jubilee Walkway Tst 2002– (tstee 2000–); memb: Prince of Wales's Royal Parks Tree Apeal 1987–2003, Cncl of Windsor Festival 1999–, Cncl of Friends of St George's 2001–04 and 2005–; Liveryman Worshipful Co of Musicians; *Books* We Want The Queen (1977), Gladys, Duchess of Marlborough (1979, reissued 1987), Debrett's Book of the Royal Wedding (1981), Cocktails and Laughter (ed, 1983), Cecil Beaton - The Authorised Biography (1985, reissued 1986, 1993, 2002 and 2003), Vivien Leigh (1988, reissued 1990), Royal Orders (1994), Loving Garbo (1994, reissued 1995), The Private World of the Duke and Duchess of Windsor (1995), The Kiss: The Story of an Obsession (1996, reissued 1997, Stern Silver Pen Award for Non-Fiction 1997), Alice, Princess Andrew of Greece (2000, reissued 2001), The Unexpurgated Beaton (ed, 2002), Beaton in the Sixties (ed, 2003), Alexis: The Memories of the Baron de Redé (ed, 2005), Elizabeth, The Queen Mother (2005); *Recreations* photography, reading, music, travel; *Style—* Hugo Vickers, Esq; ✉ Wyeford, Ramsdell, Hampshire RG26 5QL (tel 01256 850044); 62 Lexham Gardens, London W8 5JA

VICKERS, Jeffrey; s of Edward Vickers (d 1984), and Rose, *née* Soloman (d 2001); *b* 3 June 1937; *Educ* Harold Co Sch Stratford; *m* 1 (m dis 1982), Angela Vickers; 1 da (Joanne b 1 May 1965), 1 s (Andrew b 11 Feb 1967); m 2, 22 July 1982, Barbara, da of James Ebury Clair May, DSM, RN (d 1986); *Career* chm: DPM Gp of Cos 1959–, Chromacopy 1979– (name changed to C2 Media, fndr and ptnr Chromacopy of America 1979–), Helicopter Grafix Ltd 1992–, Genix Imaging Ltd, Mission Control EFX Ltd, Flawless Media Ltd, Creative Resource Ltd; chm, dir and co-fndr Chancerygate Gp of Cos (finalists Property Week Developer of the Year Awards 2001), European dir Safe Habor Holdings (USA), mktg conslt to Empire Property Gp Ltd; Prince of Wales Award for Industrial Innovation and Prodn; memb Fulham Cons Assoc; works with and supports: Prostate Research Campaign UK, Heart Cells Fndn; tstee Empire Schizophrenia Tst; licentiate Master Photographers' Assoc (LMPA) 2004; FInstD 1983, FRPS 1997; *Recreations* photography, skiing, sailing, swimming, classical music and opera; *Clubs* Hurlingham; *Style—* Jeffrey Vickers, Esq; ✉ DPM Design Consultants Ltd, 32 Broadwick Street, London W1F 8JB (tel 020 7439 7786, fax 020 7437 2201)

VICKERS, Prof Sir John Stuart; kt (2005); s of Aubrey and Kay Vickers, of Eastbourne, E Sussex; *b* 7 July 1958; *Educ* Eastbourne GS, Oriel Coll Oxford (BA), Univ of Oxford (MPhil, DPhil); *m* 1991, Maureen Emily, da of David and Dorothy Freed; 1 s (James Alexander b 19 Oct 1994), 2 da (Zoë Elizabeth, Hannah Rose (twins) b 26 Nov 1996); *Career* fin analyst Shell UK 1979–81; Univ of Oxford: fell All Souls 1979–84 and 1991–, Roy Harrod fell in the economics of business and public policy Nuffield Coll 1984–90, Drummond prof of political economy 1991–; exec dir and chief economist Bank of England and memb Monetary Policy Ctee 1998–2000; OFT: DG 2000–03, chm 2003–05; visiting scholar Princeton Univ 1988, visiting lectr Harvard Univ 1989 and 1990, visiting prof London Business Sch 1996; pres: Inst for Fiscal Studies 2003–07, Royal Economic Soc 2007–; delg Oxford Univ Press 2006–; Rhodes tstee 2006; Hon DLitt UEA 2001; hon fell Oriel Coll Oxford 2005; FBA 1998, fell Econometric Soc 1998; *Books* Privatization - An Economic Analysis (with George Yarrow, 1988), Regulatory Reform (with Mark Armstrong and Simon Cowan, 1994); author of articles on industrial orgn, regulation and competition in jls; *Style—* Prof Sir John Vickers, FBA; ✉ All Souls College, Oxford OX1 4AL (tel 01865 279379, fax 01865 279299)

VICKERS, Prof Michael; *Educ* UCNW Bangor (BA), CCC Cambridge (Dip Classical Archaeology), Univ of Wales (DLitt); *Career* asst lectr in ancient history and classical archaeology UC Dublin 1966–69, lectr in archaeology Univ of Libya Benghazi 1969–70; Ashmolean Museum Oxford: asst keeper 1971–88, tenure 1976, actg keeper 1987, 1992, 1996, 2000–01 and 2002, sr asst keeper 1988–; sr research fell Jesus Coll Oxford 1996– (garden master 2001–, dean of degrees 2002–), prof of archaeology Univ of Oxford 2002– (reader 1996–2002) visiting prof: Scuola di Specializzazione in Archeologia Università di Catania 2002, Dept of Classics Univ of Boulder Colorado 2003; visiting lectr Univ of Texas at Austin 1979–80; visiting memb: UC Cambridge 1970–71, Inst for Advanced Study Princeton 1976, Inst for Advanced Studies Hebrew Univ of Jerusalem 1993; George Tait Meml lectr Eton Coll 1987, Kress lectr Archaeological Inst of America 2002–03; corresponding memb German Archaeological Inst 1978, hon memb Vani Expdn Centre for Archaeological Studies Georgian Acad of Sciences 1995; FSA 1978, FRSA 1993; *Books* The Roman World (1977, 2 edn 1989), Hellas (with K Branigan, 1980), Artful Crafts: Ancient Greek Silverware and Pottery (with David Gill, 1994), Pericles on Stage: Political Comedy in Aristophanes' Early Plays (1997), Pichvnari 1: Results of Excavations Conducted by the Joint British-Georgian Expedition 1998–2002 (with Amiran Kakhidze, 2004); *Style—* Prof Michael Vickers; ✉ Jesus College, Oxford OX1 3DW

VICKERS, Paul Andrew; s of John Frederick Vickers, of Chislehurst, Kent, and Daphne Rosemary, *née* Reed; *b* 20 January 1960; *Educ* Alleyn's Sch Dulwich, Univ of Southampton (LLB); *m* 21 May 1988, Eileen Anne, da of John Danial MacDonald; *Career* called to the Bar Inner Temple 1983, in practice 1983–86, legal mangr London Daily News 1986–87; TV-am plc: co lawyer 1987–88, co sec 1988, exec dir 1991, asst md 1992–93; dir Independent Music Radio Ltd (Virgin Radio Ltd) 1992–93, sec and gp legal dir Mirror Group Newspapers plc 1992–94, exec dir Mirror Group plc 1994–99, sec and gp legal dir Trinity Mirror plc 1999–; *Recreations* food, wine, reading, films; *Style—* Paul Vickers, Esq; ✉ Trinity Mirror plc, One Canada Square, Canary Wharf, London E14 5AP (tel 020 7293 3358)

VICKERY, Benedict Simon; s of late Alan Vane Vickery, of Baylham, Suffolk, and Heather Felicity Ann Vickery; *b* 23 June 1959; *Educ* Univ of Bristol (BA), Univ of Sheffield (BArch); *m* 24 April 1996, Susan Marjorie, *née* Hoyal; 1 da (Sophie Rebecca Hoyal); *Career* architect; Frederick Gibberd Coombes & Partners 1984–88, YRM Architects 1988–93; HOK Sport (formerly Lobb Partnership): joined 1993, work on Stadium Australia 1996–98, managing architect Wembley Stadium 1998–, currently princ; memb ARB 1985, RIBA 1985; *Style—* Benedict Vickery, Esq; ✉ HOK Sport, 14 Blades Court, Deodar Road, Putney, London SW15 2NU (tel 020 8874 7666, fax 020 8874 7470, e-mail ben.vickery@hok.com)

VICKERY, Philip; s of Robert Edmund Vickery, of Densole, Kent, and Theresa Mary, *née* Billington; *b* 2 May 1961; *Educ* St Edmund's RC Secdy Sch Dover, S Kent Coll of Technol Folkestone; *m* 25 Aug 1990 (m dis), Sarah Ann, da of William Brian Lock; *Career* apprentice chef Burlington Hotel Folkestone 1978–79; chef: Michael's Nook Country House Hotel Grasmere 1979–84, Gravetye Manor East Grinstead 1985–86 and 1987–88, Restaurant 74 Winchen Canterbury 1986–87, Mount Somerset Country House Hotel Taunton 1989–90, Castle Hotel 1990–99 (company dir until 2000, shareholder); awards for Castle Hotel: Michelin star, Egon Ronay star, Egon Ronay Dessert Chef of the Year 1995, four out of five Good Food Guide 1996 and 1997, eight out of ten Good Food Guide 1998, West Country Restaurant of the Year 1998, Egon Ronay Chef of the Year 1998, AA Restaurant Guide 2000 four rossettes 1996–99; memb Académie Culinaire de France 1992; former memb Int Squad Amateur Judo Assoc; *Books* Just Food (1999), The Proof of the Pudding (2003), Britain: The Cookbook (2007); *Style—* Philip Vickery, Esq; ✉ c/o John Rush, Lacey Associates, Lacey Farm, Low Street, Sloley, Norfolk NR12 8HD (tel 01692 538032, website www.vickery.tv)

VICKERY, Philip John (Phil); MBE (2004); *b* 14 March 1976, Barnstaple; *Educ* Bude Haven Secdy Sch Cornwall; *Career* rugby union player (prop); clubs: Bude RUFC, Redruth RUFC, Gloucester RFC (capt), London Wasps RFC (winners Heineken Cup 2007); England: 56 caps, debut v Wales 1998, capt 2007–, winners Six Nations Championship 2000 and 2001, ranked no 1 team in world 2003, winners World Cup Aust 2003, memb squad World Cup France 2007; memb squad Br Lions tour to Aust 2001; *Style—* Phil Vickery, Esq, MBE

VICTOR, Ed; s of Jack Victor (d 1987), of Los Angeles, CA, and Lydia Victor (d 2000); *b* 9 September 1939; *Educ* Dartmouth Coll NH (BA), Pembroke Coll Cambridge (MLitt); *m* 1, 1963, Michelene Dinah, da of Avram Samuels (d 1985); 2 s (Adam b 1964, Ivan b 1966); m 2, 1980, Carol Ryan, da of Clifton Boggs (d 1992), of San Diego, CA; 1 s (Ryan b 1984); *Career* editorial dir: Weidenfeld & Nicolson 1965–67, Jonathan Cape Ltd 1967–70; sr ed Alfred A Knopf Inc NY 1971–72, dir John Farquharson Ltd 1973–77, chm and md Ed Victor Ltd 1977–; *Books* The Obvious Diet (2001); *Recreations* opera, golf, tennis, travel; *Clubs* Beefsteak, Garrick; *Style—* Ed Victor, Esq; ✉ 10 Cambridge Gate, Regents Park, London NW1 4JX (tel 020 7224 3030); Ed Victor Ltd, 6 Bayley Street, Bedford Square, London WC1B 3HB (tel 020 7304 4100, fax 020 7304 4111, e-mail ed@edvictor.com)

VIDLER, Andria; da of Trevor Vidler, and Carol Vidler; *b* 12 May 1966; *Educ* Tunbridge Wells Girls' GS, Sevenoaks Sch, Cambridge Poly (BA), Univ of Bradford (MBA); *m* 20 April 1996, Adrian Gibb; 2 da (Tabitha, Imogen); *Career* grad mgmnt trainee Coats Viyella 1987–90, business dir Still Price Lintas 1992–94 (business mangr 1990–92), mktg mangr BBC Radio 5 Live 1994–96, head mktg BBC News 1996–98, head mktg and business devpt BBC Sport 1998–2001 (temporarily overseeing mktg and communications BBC Radio and Music Div), md Capital Radio and Capital Gold 2001–02, md Capital FM Network 2002–03, md Magic FM 2005–; dir Capital Charities Ltd, memb Mktg Soc; *Recreations* swimming, theatre; *Style—* Mrs Andria Vidler

VIDLER, Cedric Graham (Ced); *b* 20 June 1944; *m*; *Career* with Doyle Dane Bernbach advtg NY 1966–67, subsequently with KMP later Davidson Pearce advtg, then fndr of creative consultancy Lippa Newton, fndr ptnr Carl Ally London (became Pincus Vidler Arthur FitzGerald following MBO) 1974–82, creative dir rising to exec creative dir and chm BBDO London (following takeover) 1982–89, exec creative dir Lintas:London 1989, subsequently Euro creative dir Lintas Worldwide until 1996 (currently conslt); Annistone Ltd; numerous awards won for creative work throughout career; MIPA; *Recreations* driving a very fast boat, classic cars, Prince's Youth Tst; *Style—* Ced Vidler, Esq; ✉ Annistone Ltd, 39 Colcokes Road, Banstead, Surrey SM7 2EJ

VIGGERS, Peter John; MP; s of John Sidney Viggers (d 1969), of Gosport, Hants; *b* 13 March 1938; *Educ* Alverstoke Sch, Portsmouth GS, Trinity Hall Cambridge (MA); *m* 1968, Jennifer Mary, da of Dr R B McMillan (d 1975); 1 da, 2 s; *Career* RAF pilot 1956–58, TA 1963–70; co slr Chrysler (UK) Ltd 1968–70; dir: Edward Bates & Sons Ltd 1970–75, Richardson Smith Ltd (chm), Gough Hotels Ltd and other cos 1970–76, Premier Consolidated Oilfields Ltd 1973–86, Sweetheart International Ltd 1982–86, Nynex Group of Cos 1991–95, Tracer Petroleum Corporation 1996–98; MP (Cons) Gosport Feb 1974–, PPS to Slr Gen 1979–83, delegate to N Atlantic Assembly 1980–86 and 1992– (vice-chm Political Ctee 1995–2000, chm 2000–05), PPS to Chief Sec to Treasy 1983–85, Parly under sec of state for NI (indust min) 1986–89, chm British-Japanese Parly Gp 1992–99 (vice-chm 2000–); memb Select Ctee on: Membs' Interests 1991–93, Defence 1992–97 (vice-chm 2000–05), Treasy 2005–; underwriting memb of Lloyd's 1973–2002 (memb Cncl 1992–96), chm tstees Lloyd's Pension Fund 1996–; memb Nat Ctee RNLI 1980– (vice-pres 1990–); *Clubs* Boodle's, Gosport Cons (pres); *Style—* Peter Viggers, Esq, MP; ✉ House of Commons, London SW1A 0AA

VILJOEN, His Hon (Theo) Leon; s of Robert Bartlett Viljoen (d 1974), and Cecilia Jacoba, *née* van der Walt; *b* 25 August 1937; *Educ* Afrikaanse Hoër Seunskool Pretoria, Univ of Pretoria; *m* 25 Feb 1967, Dorothy Nina, da of Prof S G Raybould; 2 da (Nina Cecilia b 5 Nov 1979, Tessa Eleanor b 14 April 1981); *Career* called to the Bar Middle Temple 1972; legal assessor to UK Central Cncl for Nursing, Midwifery and Health Visitors 1988–92, recorder of the Crown Court 1991–92, circuit judge (SE Circuit) 1992–2007; memb Parole Bd 1997–2003, appraiser to Parole Bd 2004–; *Recreations* house in France, gardening, wine; *Style—* His Hon Leon Viljoen; ✉ 2 Harcourt Buildings, Temple, London EC4Y 9DB (e-mail lviljoen@lix.compulink.co.uk)

VILLAGE, Peter Malcolm; QC (2002); s of Malcolm Rowland Village (d 1987), and Margaret Village; *b* 3 February 1961; *Educ* Repton, Univ of Leeds (LLB), Inns of Court Sch of Law; *m* 28 March 1992, Alison Helen, da of Herbert Wallis; 1 s (Thomas b 2 March 1993), 2 da (Alice, Emily (twins) b 21 June 1994); *Career* called to the Bar: Inner Temple 1983, NI 1997; specialist in planning and compulsory purchase; memb: Planning and Environmental Law Bar Assoc, Compulsory Purchase Assoc; govr Repton Sch 1998–; *Recreations* shooting, fly fishing, skiing, walking the dog; *Clubs* Brooks's; *Style—* Peter

Village, Esq, QC; ✉ 4–5 Grays Inn Square, London WC1R 5JP (tel 020 7404 5252, fax 020 7242 7803, e-mail pvillage@4–5.co.uk)

VILLAR, Richard Neville; s of George Roger Villar, DSC, RN, and Diana Mary, *née* Thomas; *b* 24 April 1953; *Educ* Marlborough, St Thomas' Hosp Medical Sch (BSc, MB BS), Univ of Cambridge (MA), Univ of Southampton (MS); *m* 4 June 1983, (Barbara) Louise Bell, da of Patrick George Arthur Ross Lobban; 2 s (Ruairidh b 1985, Angus b 1988), 1 da (Felicity b 1995); *Career* RAMC 1979–84; conslt Addenbrooke's Hosp Cambridge 1988–2004 (sr registrar 1985–88), clinical dir Cambridge Hip and Knee Unit; memb World Orthopaedic Concern; memb: Euro Hip Soc, Br Assoc for Surgery of the Knee; Lord of the Manor of: Twineham Benfield, Eltisley, Guilden Morden; FBOA 1989, FRCS; *Recreations* fell running, mountaineering, cross country skiing; *Style—* Richard Villar, Esq; ✉ The Wellington Hospital (tel 020 7483 5270, fax 020 7483 5271 e-mail rvillar@uk-consultants.co.uk)

VILLAS-BOAS, Manuel de Magalhães e Menezes; s of Augusto de Magalhães e Menezes Villas-Boas, and Maria Luisa, *née* Ribeiro de Sá Ramos Chaves Bessone Basto; *b* 29 May 1945; *Educ* Economics Inst Lisbon Univ (BA); *m* 20 April 1985, Christine Marie Françoise, da of Michael Julien Gudefin, Chev Legion d'Honneur, of Greenwich, Connecticut, USA; 2 s (António b 1986, Alexandre b 1990); *Career* asst mangr Banco Espírito Santo e Comercial de Lisboa Lisbon 1972–76, sr mangr Manufacturers Hanover Ltd London 1976–79; exec dir 1979–83: The Royal Bank of Canada, Orion Royal Bank Ltd London; sr vice-pres and London rep Espirito Santo International Holding London 1983–; dir: Espírito Santo Financial Gp SA 1990–, Banco Espírito Santo e Comercial de Lisboa Lisbon 1992–, Banco Espírito Santo de Investimento 1992–; Knight of Honour and Devotion Sovereign and Military Order of Malta, Knight Cdr Order of Infante D Henrique; *Books* Os Magalhães (1998), João Jacinto de Magalhães, um Empreendedor Cientifico na Europa do Século XVIII (2000); *Recreations* art, music, sport; *Clubs* IOD, Turf (Lisbon); *Style—* Manuel de Magalhães e Menezes Villas-Boas, Esq; ✉ 73 Harrington Gardens, London SW7 4JZ; Espírito Santo Financial Group, 33 Queen Street, London EC4R 1ES (tel 020 7332 4350, fax 020 7332 4355)

VILLIERS, Charles Nigel; s of Capt Robert Alexander Villiers, CBE, RN (d 1990), and Elizabeth Mary, *née* Friend (d 1985); *b* 25 January 1941; *Educ* Winchester, New Coll Oxford (MA); *m* 7 Aug 1970, Sally Priscilla, da of Capt David Henry Magnay, RN (d 1968); 1 da (Caroline b 1974), 1 s (Christopher b 1976); *Career* Arthur Andersen 1963–67, Industrial & Commercial Finance Corporation 1967–72; County Bank (subsid of National Westminster Bank): dir 1974, dep chief exec 1977, chm and chief exec 1984–86; dir National Westminster Bank 1985–88, chm County NatWest 1986–88, chief exec NatWest Investment Bank 1986–88, dir and md Corp Devpt Div Abbey National plc 1989–99; pres Abbey National France 1993–96, chm First National Bank 1996–99 (dep chm 1995–96), exec dep chm Abbey National plc 1999–2001, chm Scottish Mutual 2000; non-exec dir DTZ Holdings (formerly Debenham Tewson & Chinnocks Holdings) 1997–2004; treas East Thames Housing Gp 2001–; FCA 1976 (ACA 1966); *Recreations* opera, skiing, tennis; *Clubs* Reform; *Style—* Charles Villiers, Esq

VILLIERS, Jane Hyde; da of John Hyde Villiers, and Ursule Louise, *née* Collins; *Educ* West Heath Sch, Coaching Inn Southover Manor Lewis; *Career* self-employed in fashion industry 1980–89, literary agent Sheil Land 1989–94 (clients incl: Peter Ackroyd, Vikram Seth, Barry Unsworth), ptnr and md Sayle Screen 1994– (clients incl: Sue Townsend, Chris Monger, Marc Evans, Santosh Sivan, William Corlett, Gitta Sereny); prodr My Little Eye (Working Title feature film) 2001; patron: Amnesty, Red Cross, Crisis; *Recreations* travelling, swimming, cinema; *Style—* Ms Jane Villiers; ✉ Sayle Screen Ltd, 11 Jubilee Place, London SW3 3TD (tel 020 7823 3883, e-mail jane@saylescreen.com)

VILLIERS, Theresa; MP; *Educ* Sarum Hall Sch, Francis Holland Sch, Univ of Bristol (LLB), Jesus Coll Oxford (BCL), Inns of Court Sch of Law; *m* June 1999, Sean Wilken; *Career* barr Lincoln's Inn 1993–95, lectr in law KCL 1995–99; MEP (Cons) London 1999–2005, Cons dep chm European Parl 2001–03; MP (Cons) Chipping Barnet 2005–, shadow chief sec to the Treasy 2005–07, shadow sec of state for tport 2007–; House of Commons: memb Select Ctee on Environmental Audit 2005–, vice-chair All-Pty Israel Gp 2005–; *Publications* Waiver, Variation and Estoppel (co-author with Sean Wilken), European Tax Harmonisation: the impending threat; author of various legal texts; *Style—* Mrs Theresa Villiers, MP; ✉ House of Commons, London SW1A 0AA

VINCE, Dr Frank Peter; s of Dr Rupert James Vince (d 1987), of Doncaster, and Olive Myra Vince (d 1985); *b* 19 June 1937; *Educ* Doncaster GS, Sidney Sussex Coll Cambridge (BA), The London Hosp Med Sch (MB BChir); *m* 7 Jan 1967, Sheila, da of Dr Laurence Cleveland Martin (d 1981), of Cambridge; 1 da (Joanna b 1968), 1 s (Richard James Martin b 1970); *Career* med registrar Addenbrooke's Hosp Cambridge 1964–66, lectr and sr registrar The London Hosp Whitechapel 1967–71 (house offr 1962–63), conslt physician Coventry Hosp 1971–2002, chief med offr Axa Sun Life (previously Axa Equity and Law Insurance Soc) 1982–, sr lectr in postgrad med Univ of Warwick 1985–1997; various pubns in med jls on subjects of diabetes, endocrinology and problems of growth and development; pres elect Assurance Medical Soc; tstee Home Farm Tst (chm 1997–2000), former co-opted memb Coventry City Cncl; former memb Coventry HA; memb: Coventry Educn Authy 1981–90, Soc for Endocrinology, Cncl Assurance Med Soc (AMS); memb Worshipful Co of Worsted Weavers of Coventry; FRSM, FRCP 1979; *Recreations* music; *Style—* Dr Frank Vince; ✉ 42 Kenilworth Road, Coventry CV3 6PG (tel 024 7641 0347, e-mail shvince@globalnet.co.uk)

VINCENT, Alan Henry; MBE (2001); *b* 12 February 1939; *Educ* Univ of Exeter (BSc); *m* Dec 1967, Wendy, *née* Andrews; 2 s (Timothy b 1969, Peter b 1974), 1 da (Alison b 1970); *Career* GKN Westland Helicopters Ltd (formerly Westland Aircraft): dynamicist Fairey Aviation Div 1960–64, dynamicist Yeovil 1964–73, sometime chief dynamicist, head Advanced Rotor Design, chief mech engr, chief engr, chief designer, head of engrg 1988–2001, conslt; dir GKN Westland Design Servs; memb: Airworthiness Requirements Bd, SBAC Technical Bd, RAeS Rotorcraft Ctee; Society Silver Medal RAeS 2003; FREng, FRAeS; *Style—* Alan Vincent, Esq, MBE, FREng, FRAeS; ✉ Westland Helicopters Ltd, Box 3, Yeovil, Somerset BA20 2YB (tel 01935 702502, fax 01935 704015)

VINCENT, Prof Angela Carmen; da of Sir Joseph Molony, KCVO, QC (d 1978), and Carmen, *née* Dent (d 2003); *b* 30 September 1942, Woking, Surrey; *Educ* St Mary's Convent Ascot, Westminster Hospital Medical Sch (MB, BS), UCL (MSc); *m* 1967, Philip Vincent; 2 da (Dr Antonia (Tonia) Vincent (Mrs Hilary Davan Wetton) b 24 May 1968, Dr Katherine Sleeman b 22 July 1974), 2 s (Patrick b 27 May 1970, Bruno b 29 March 1979); *Career* UCL: research asst 1969–72, research assoc 1972–77; research fell and hon sr lectr Royal Free Hospital Sch of Medicine 1977–88; Univ of Oxford: research fell 1988–92, lectr in clinical neuroimmunology 1992–98, prof of neuroimmunology 1998–, head Dept of Clinical Neurology 2005–; fell Somerville Coll Oxfrod 1992– (Janet Vaughan lectr in biomedical sciences 1998); visiting prof of neuroimmunology Univ of Liverpool 2000–03, visiting prof and Moskovitz lectr London Ontario 2003; memb: Steering Ctee Medical Gp Amnesty Int (Br Section) 1990–98, Assoc of Br Neurologists 1994–, Int Soc for Neuroimmunology (vice-pres 1996–2001, pres 2001–04), American Neurological Assoc 1997, Br Soc for Immunology (chair Neuroimmunology Gp 1998–2000), Scientific Ctee Patrick Berthoud Fndn 1998– (chair 2006–), Scientific Bd European Sch of Neuroimmunology 1999–; Guarantor of Brain 1999– (memb Travel Grants Ctee 1997–, memb Bd of Mgmnt 2003–), Myasthenia Gravis Fndn of America (Scientific Programme Ctee 2000–03), Soc for Neuroscience 2002–, MRC Neurosciences and Mental Health Bd 2004–08; Dr (hc) Bergen Norway 2004, MRCS, LRCP, FRCPath 1997 (MRCPath 1991), FMedSci 2002; *Publications* Neuromuscular Transmission: Basic and Applied Aspects (ed with Dennis Wray, 1990), Autoantibodies in Neurological Diseases (ed with G Martino, 2001), Clinical Neuroimmunology (ed with J Antel, G Birnbaum and H-P Hartung, 2006); 207 peer reviewed publications, over 50 chapters and reviews; *Recreations* tennis, opera particularly Wagner, children and grandchildren; *Clubs* RSM; *Style—* Prof Angela Vincent; ✉ Taverners, Woodeaton, Oxford OX3 9TH; Neurosciences Group, Weatherall Institute of Molecular Medicine, John Radcliffe Hospital, Oxford OX3 9DS (tel 01865 222321, fax 01865 222402, e-mail angela.vincent@imm.ox.ac.uk)

VINCENT, Rev Dr John James; s of David Vincent (d 1976), and Ethel Beatrice, *née* Gadd (d 2001); *b* 29 December 1929; *Educ* Manchester Grammar, Richmond Coll London (BD), Drew Univ (STM), Univ of Basel (DTheol); *m* 4 Dec 1958, Grace Johnston, da of Rev Wilfred Stafford; 2 s (Christopher b 1961, James b 1966), 1 da (Faith b 1964); *Career* Sgt RAMC 1947–49; min Manchester and Salford Mission 1956–62; supt min: Rochdale Mission 1962–69, Sheffield Inner City Ecumenical Mission 1970–97; dir Urban Theol Unit Sheffield 1970–97 (dir emeritus 1997–), supervisor Doctoral Prog in Contextual, Urban and Liberation Theologies Univ of Sheffield 1993–, Univ of Birmingham 2003–; visiting prof of theol: Univ of Boston Autumn 1969, NY Theol Seminary Spring 1970; visiting prof of theol Drew Univ NJ 1977; chm NW CND 1957–65; founding memb and leader Ashram Community Tst 1967–, chm Urban Mission Training Assoc of GB 1976–77 and 1984–91, memb Cncl Christian Orgns for Social, Political and Economic Change 1981–89, exec Assoc Centres of Adult Theol Educn 1984–90, memb Studiorum Novi Testamenti Societas 1961–, pres Methodist Church GB 1989–90, hon lectr Biblical Studies Dept Univ of Sheffield 1990–, co-ordinator British Liberation Theology Institute 1990–, hon lectr Theol Dept Univ of Birmingham 2003–; Centenary Achievement Award Univ of Sheffield 2005; fell St Deiniol's Library 2003; *Books* Christ in a Nuclear World (1962), Christ and Methodism (1965), Secular Christ (1968), The Race Race (1970), The Jesus Thing (1973), Alternative Church (1976), Starting All Over Again (1981), OK, Let's be Methodists (1984), Radical Jesus (1986, revised edn 2004), Britain in the 90's (1989), Discipleship in the 90's (1991), Liberation Theology UK (ed, 1995), Gospel From the City (ed, 1997), The Cities: A Methodist Report (jtly 1997), Liberation Spirituality (ed, 1999), Hope from the City (2000), Bible and Practice (ed, 2001), Journey: Explorations into Discipleship (2001), Faithfulness in the City (ed, 2003), Methodist and Radical (jt ed, 2004), Mark: Gospel of Action (ed, 2006), Primitive Christianity (ed, 2007); *Recreations* writing, jogging; *Style—* The Rev Dr John Vincent; ✉ 178 Abbeyfield Road, Sheffield, S4 7AY (tel 0114 243 6688); Urban Theology Unit, 210 Abbeyfield Road, Sheffield S4 7AZ (tel and fax 0114 243 5342, e-mail john@utu-sheffield.demon.co.uk)

VINCENT, Robin Anthony; CMG (2006), CBE (2001); s of John Kenneth Vincent (d 1991), and Ivy Elizabeth Anne, *née* Grayer (d 1996); *b* 27 February 1944; *Educ* King's Sch Worcester; *m* 12 June 1971, Hazel Ruth, da of Frederick John Perkins; 2 s (Mark Christian b 4 Aug 1972, Stephen Peter b 30 June 1974); *Career* clerk Worcestershire Quarter Sessions 1962–70, sr asst then dep clerk to Worcester Co Justices 1970–72; higher exec offr: Worcester Crown Court 1972–76, Worcester Co Court 1976–77; sr exec offr (Personnel) Circuit Administrator's Office Birmingham 1977–80, chief clerk Worcester Crown Court 1980–82, princ chief clerk Manchester Crown Court 1982–86; head of div: Court Serv Devpt Div London 1986–91, Personnel Mgmnt Div London 1991–93, Judicial Appointments Div London 1993; circuit administrator Northern Circuit Manchester 1993–2001, conslt Int Court Mgmnt (working with UN and BR Cncl) 2001–, asst sec gen UN 2002–05, registrar of the Special Ct (War Crimes) for Sierra Leone 2002–05, sr conslt on int criminal and transitional justice issues 2006–; *Recreations* cricket, soccer, gardening; *Clubs* Eggington CC, Old Vigornians, Stockport Georgians; *Style—* Robin Vincent, Esq, CMG, CBE; ✉ The Moorings, 33 Grange Road, Bramhall, Stockport SK7 3BD (tel 0161 440 9526, e-mail r.vincent@hotmail.co.uk)

VINCENT, Sir William Percy Maxwell; 3 Bt (UK 1936), of Watton, Co Norfolk; s of Sir Lacey Vincent, 2 Bt (d 1963), and Helen, Lady Vincent (d 2000); *b* 1 February 1945; *Educ* Eton, New York Inst of Finance; *m* 1976, Christine Margaret, da of Rev Edward Gibson Walton (d 1989), of Petersfield, Hants; 3 s; *Heir* s, Edward Vincent; *Career* late 2 Lt Irish Gds, served Malaya; dir Save & Prosper Investment Management 1980–85, Touche Remnant & Co 1985, md and investment dir Touche Remnant Co 1986, dir Société Générale Touche Remnant 1989–92, dir M & G (North America) Ltd 1992–95, md Cambridge Associates (UK) Ltd 1995–; *Recreations* sailing, skiing; *Clubs* Household Div Yacht; *Style—* Sir William Vincent, Bt; ✉ Thieves Lane Barn, nr Clanfield, Hampshire PO8 0PY

VINCENT OF COLESHILL, Baron (Life Peer UK 1996), of Shrivenham in the County of Oxfordshire; Field Marshal the Lord Richard Frederick Vincent; GBE (1990), KCB (1984), DSO (1972); s of late Frederick Vincent, and late Frances Elizabeth, *née* Coleshill; *b* 23 August 1931; *Educ* Aldenham, RMC of Sci Shrivenham; *m* 1955, Jean Paterson, da of late Kenneth Stewart; 1 s, 1 da (and 1 s decd); *Career* Cmdt RMC of Sci 1980–83, Master Gen of the Ordnance MOD 1983–87, Chief of the Def Staff 1991–92 (Vice-Chief 1987–91), chm Mil Ctee NATO 1993–96; Col Cmdt: REME 1983–87, RA 1983–2000; Hon Col: 100 (Yeo) Field Regt RA (Volunteers) TA 1982–91, 12 Air Def Regt 1985–91; Master Gunner St James's Park 1996–2001; chm: Hunting Engineering Ltd 1998–2001 (dir 1996–1998), Hunting-BRAE Ltd 1998–2003 (dir1997–98), Hunting Defence Ltd 1996–2003; pres Defence Manufacturers Assoc 2000–05 (vice-pres 1996–2000); dir: Vickers Defence Systems Ltd 1996–2002, INSYS Ltd 2002–; non-exec dir Royal Artillery Museums Ltd 1996–2000, memb Cmmn on Britain and Europe (RIIA) 1996–; Kermit Roosevelt lectr USA 1988, visiting fell Aust Coll of Def and Strategic Studies 1995–99; pres: Combined Servs Winter Sports Assoc 1983–90, Army Skiing Assoc 1983–87, Cncl of Univ Military Educn Ctees 1999–2006, Cranfield Tst 1999–; memb Ct Cranfield Inst of Technol 1981–83, govr Aldenham Sch 1987–, chm of Govrs Imperial Coll of Sci, Technology and Med 1996–2004 (govr 1995), memb Ct Univ of Greenwich 1997–2001, chllr Cranfield Univ 1998–; patron INSPIRE Charity Fndn 1997–; fell Imperial Coll London 1995, fell City and Guilds of London Inst 1999; Jordanian Order of Merit (First Class), USA Legion of Merit (Degree of Cdr); Freeman: City of London (memb Guild of Freemen), Worshipful Co of Wheelwrights 1997; Hon DSc Cranfield 1985; FIMechE 1990, FRAeS 1990, FCGI 1991; *Recreations* establishing a second career, seven grandchildren; *Clubs* Pilgrims, Army and Navy, Cavalry and Guards; *Style—* Field Marshal The Lord Vincent of Coleshill, GBE, KCB, DSO; ✉ House of Lords, London SW1A 0PW

VINCENZI, Penny; da of Stanley George Hannaford (d 1985), of New Milton, Hants, and Mary Blanche, *née* Hawkey (d 1987); *b* 10 April 1939; *Educ* Notting Hill and Ealing HS; *m* 27 May 1960, Paul Robert Vincenzi, s of Dr Julius Vincenzi (d 1996), of Earls Colne, Essex; 4 da (Polly b 1963, Sophie b 1965, Emily b 1975, Claudia b 1979); *Career* freelance journalist and author; formerly first fashion ed Nova Magazine; *Books* The Complete Liar (1979), There's One Born Every Minute (1985), Old Sins (1989), Wicked Pleasures (1992), An Outrageous Affair (1993), Another Woman (1994), Forbidden Places (1995), The Dilemma (1996), Windfall (1997), Almost a Crime (1999), No Angel (2000), Something Dangerous (2001), Into Temptation (2002); *Recreations* family life, talking, eating and drinking; *Style—* Mrs Penny Vincenzi

VINCZE, Ernest Anthony; *b* 1942; *Career* director of photography; started in the field of documentaries; past head of dept Cinematography Nat Film Sch; features and TV series incl: Mystic Masseur, The Dance, Macbeth, Sea of Souls, Shooting the Past, A Very British Coup, A Woman of Substance, Kennedy, Roseland, The Camomile Lawn, Jeeves and Wooster, Nightmare Years, A Perfect Hero, Heavy Weather, Stone Scissors Paper, Scrubbers, Shanghai Surprise, Winstanley, Biggles; *Documentary Awards* incl: Flaherty Award, Prix Italia, Golden Gate San Francisco, BAFTA; *Awards* nominated Br Acad Award for Best Cinematography 1984 and 1989, winner Emmy (for A Very British Coup) 1988, winner Best Cinematography Festival Internacional de Cinema de Troia (for The Dance) 1999; memb BSC, fell Moving Image Soc, memb Cncl BAFTA; *Style*— Ernie Vincze, BSC

VINE, Barbara; *see:* Rendell of Babergh, Baroness

VINE, Deirdre Ann; da of Paul Ashley Lawrence Vine, of Pulborough, W Sussex; *b* 21 September 1953; *Educ* UCL (BA); *Career* ed-in-chief Womans Journal 1988–97, editorial conslt and writer 1998–, launch ed (with Eve Pollard, *qv*) Aura, ed Theatregoer; memb: Br Guild of Travel Writers 1978, BSME 1986, Women in Journalism 1996, PEN 2001; *Books* Boulogne (1983), Paris and Ile De France (1992); *Recreations* opera, theatre, cinema, wine and food; *Clubs* Oxford and Cambridge; *Style*— Ms Deirdre Vine; ✉ 7 Porchester Terrace, London W2 3TH (e-mail dvine@mixedweb.com)

VINE, Dennis; s of Harold Edward Vine (d 1966), of Ealing, London, and Mary Maud Vine (now Nicholls); *b* 24 April 1937; *Educ* Penyrenglyn Treherbert, Drayton Manor GS Ealing, Regent St Poly (now Univ of Westminster); *m* 12 June 1965, Anne, da of H S Hawley; 1 s (Richard Edward b 9 March 1967), 1 da (Joanna b 6 March 1969); *Career* surveyor; Ealing BC 1954, Westminster City Cncl 1960; Vigers Chartered Surveyors (now GVA Grimley): joined 1962, ptnr responsible for building surveying 1969, jt sr ptnr 1983, sr ptnr 1990, ptnr of new merged practice 1991–98, conslt to GVA Grimley; RICS: memb 1962–, pres Building Surveyors Div 1987–88; memb Bd Br Home & Hosp for Incurables (BHHI); tstee and memb Bd Royal Masonic Benevolent Inst (RMBI); Freeman City of London 1987, Liveryman Worshipful Co of London Surveyors 1987; hon fell Coll of Estate Mgmnt 1997; FRICS 1971; *Recreations* tennis, golf; *Clubs* RAC, West Surrey Golf; *Style*— Dennis Vine, Esq; ✉ GVA Grimley, 10 Stratton Street, London W1X 6JR (tel 020 7911 2131, fax 020 7911 2426, e-mail dzv@gvagrimley.co.uk, mobile 07836 773049, home tel and fax 01483 422200)

VINE, Jeremy Guy; s of Guy Vine, of Cheam, Surrey, and Diana, *née* Tillett; *b* 17 May 1965; *Educ* Epsom Coll, Univ of Durham (BA); *m* 14 Sept 2002, Rachel Katherine; 1 da (Martha b 16 March 2004); *Career* journalist; reporter Coventy Evening Telegraph 1986–87; BBC: news trainee 1987–89, reporter Today prog 1989–93, lobby corr 1993–97, Africa corr 1997–2000; presenter: Newsnight 1999–2002, The Politics Show (BBC 1) 2003–05, Jeremy Vine Show (Radio 2) 2003–, Election Swingometer 2006–, Panorama (BBC 1) 2007–; Stendhal Award for European coverage 1995, Amnesty International Radio Award for Sierra Leone reports 1999, Monte Carlo Silver Nymph for exposé on South African Police 1999, Speech Broadcaster of the Year Sony Awards 2005 (Silver Award 2006); *Clubs* Soho House, Reform, Chelsea FC; *Style*— Jeremy Vine, Esq; ✉ Radio 2, BBC Western House, London W1A 1AA (tel 020 7765 2129, e-mail jeremy.vine@bbc.co.uk)

VINE, John; CBE (2007), QPM (2002); *Educ* North Staffs Poly (BA), Univ of Abertay (MSc); *Career* joined W Yorks Police 1981, uniform patrol and community constable then sargeant Bradford and Leeds, selected for special course Police Staff Coll Bramshill, patrol sargeant Halifax 1985–87, Toller Lane and Manningham Sub Divs Bradford: 1987–90, Chief Constable's staff offr in rank of Chief Inspr 1990–92, Supt 1992–95; strategic command course 1995, Asst Chief Constable Lancashire Constabulary 1996–2000 (ops, personnel and training, latterly corp devpt), Chief Constable Tayside Police 2000–; responsible for policing arrangements for G8 World Ldrs Summit 2005; ACPO Scotland: pres 2003–04, currently chm Road Policing Business Area and Operational Policing Business Area; FCIPD; *Style*— John Vine, Esq, CBE, QPM; ✉ Tayside Police HQ, West Bell Street, Dundee DD1 9JU

VINE, Brig (Martin) Spencer; OBE (1995); s of Francis Vine; *b* 29 March 1953; *Educ* King Edward's Sch Bath, RMA Sandhurst, Army Staff Coll Camberley; *m* 10 May 1975, Miranda Frances, *née* King; 1 da (Pippa b 20 May 1981), 1 s (Charlie b 19 July 1983); *Career* regtl duty 1 Glosters 1973–89, chief instr RMA Sandhurst 1990–92, CO 1 Glosters 1992–94 (last CO of Regt), Cdr Battle Gp Trg Unit 1994–95, Dep Cdr Br Forces Former Yugoslavia 1995–96, US Army War Coll 1996–97, Asst Mil Attaché Br Embassy Washington DC 1997–2000, COS HQ Infantry 2000–02, Dep Cdr London District 2002–05, Cdr Multinational Force (NW) Bosnia 2005, def advsr to Br High Cmmr Islamabad 2005–07; int fell US Army War Coll; memb Friends of the Regts of Gloucestershire Regt Museum; Meritorious Service Medal USA 2000; *Recreations* field sports; *Clubs* Army and Navy; *Style*— Brig M S Vine, OBE; ✉ Regimental Office, The Rifles, Custom House, 31 Commercial Road, Gloucester GL1 2HE

VINE-LOTT, Anthony Keith; s of Keith Miles Vine-Lott, of Hyde, Cheshire, and Jessie, *née* Meadowcroft; *b* 24 October 1947; *Educ* King Edward VI Macclesfield, Sheffield Poly; *m* 1, 13 Dec 1969 (m dis 1980), Barbara Elaine; 1 da (Anne Marie Elizabeth b 4 Jan 1974); m 2, 18 June 1982 (m dis 1998), Dr Ailsa Vine-Lott; m 3, 10 July 1999, Catherine Rosemary Reid (Kate) Avery, *qv*; *Career* engrg scholarship Wimpey UK Ltd 1966–70, mktg mangr UK computer software co's 1970–76, md Surlodge Ltd 1976–78, field servs mangr Honeywell Network Information Systems Ltd (taken over by General Electric USA) 1978–81, mktg servs dir WANG UK Ltd 1981–86, chm The Cleaver Co; md Barclays Stockbrokers Ltd 1988–96, dir Barclays Financial Services Ltd 1993–96, chm Barclays Bank Trust Co Ltd 1995–96, chm Barclays Insurance Services Co Ltd 1995–96; head Fin Servs and Business Transformation Consultancy Robson Rhodes CA 1997–2000; currently DG PEP and ISA Managers Assoc, dir Jt Money Laundering Steering Gp; Lord of the Manor of Beckett; FCIM 1990, FRSA 1991, FSI 2006; *Recreations* yachting, gardening, golf; *Style*— Anthony Vine-Lott, Esq; ✉ Broom House, Crabtree Lane, Headley, Epsom, Surrey KT18 6PS (tel 01372 374728, fax 01372 363176)

VINES, Prof David Anthony; s of Robert Godfrey Vines, and Vera Frances Vines; *b* 8 May 1949; *Educ* Scotch Coll Melbourne, Univ of Melbourne (BA), Univ of Cambridge (MA, PhD); *m* 1, 1979, Susannah Lucy Robinson (m dis 1992); 3 s; m 2, 1995, Jane Elizabeth Bingham; 2 step s; *Career* Univ of Cambridge: fell Pembroke Coll 1976–85, research offr and sr research offr Dept of Applied Economics 1979–85; research fell Centre for Economic Policy Research London 1985–, Adam Smith prof of political economy Univ of Glasgow 1985–92, adjunct prof of economics Research Sch of Pacific and Asian Studes ANU 1991–; Univ of Oxford: fell and tutor in economics Balliol Coll 1992–, reader in economics 1997–2000, prof of economics 2000–; memb Bd: Channel 4 Television 1987–92, Glasgow Devpt Agency 1990–92; economic conslt to Sec of State for Scotland 1987–92, conslt IMF 1988 and 1989; memb ESRC: Economic Affairs Ctee 1985–87, Research Progs Bd 1992–93; dir Research Prog on Global Economic Instns 1994–2000, memb Academic Panel HM Treasy 1986–1995, memb Cncl Royal Economic Soc 1988–92; memb Bd: Analysys 1989–2002, Scot Early Music Consort 1990–; cmmr BFI Enquiry into the Future of the BBC 1992; *Publications* Stagflation Vol II: Demand Management (jtly, 1983), Macroeconomic Interactions Between North and South (jtly, 1988), Macroeconomic Policy: inflation, weath and the exchange rate (jtly, 1989), Deregulation and the Future of Commercial Television (jtly, 1989), Information, Strategy, and Public Policy (jtly, 1991), North South and International Macroeconomic Policy (jtly, 1995), Europe, East Asia and APEC (jtly, 1998), The Asian Financial Crises (jtly, 1999), The World Bank: structure and policies (jtly, 2000), The IMF and its Critics: Reform of Global Financial Architecture (jtly, 2004); papers on international macroeconomics and macroeconomic policy in professional jls; *Recreations* hill walking, music; *Style*— Prof David Vines; ✉ Balliol College, Oxford OX1 3BJ (tel 01865 271067, fax 01865 271094, e-mail david.vines@economics.ox.ac.uk)

VINK, *see:* de Vink

VINSON, Baron (Life Peer UK 1985), of Roddam Dene in the County of Northumberland; Nigel Vinson; LVO (1979), DL (1990); s of Ronald Vinson (d 1976), of Wateringbury, Kent, and his 2 w, Bettina Myra Olivia (d 1966), da of Dr Gerald Southwell-Sander; *b* 27 January 1931; *Educ* RNC Pangbourne; *m* 10 June 1972, Yvonne Ann, da of Dr John Olaf Collin, of Forest Row, E Sussex; 3 da (Hon Bettina Claire (Mrs Witheridge) b 1974, Hon Rowena Ann (Mrs Cown) b 1977, Hon Antonia Charlotte (Mrs Bennett) b 1979); *Career* Lt Queen's Royal Regt 1949–51; fndn donor Martin Mere Wildfowl Tst; fndr Plastic Coatings Ltd (chm 1952–72); dir: Sugar Bd 1968–75, British Airports Authority 1973–80, Centre for Policy Studies 1974–80; dep chm: Electra Investment Trust 1975–98, Barclays Bank UK 1982–88; memb Cncl King George V Jubilee Tst 1974–78, hon dir Queen's Silver Jubilee Tst 1974–78: dep chm CBI Smaller Firms Cncl 1979–84, chm: Cncl for Small Industries in Rural Areas 1980–82, Newcastle Technol Centre 1985–88, Rural Devpt Cmmn 1980–90, Bd of Tstees Inst of Econ Affrs 1989–96 (memb 1971–, chm 1987–95, life vice-pres 1996–); Industrial Participation Assoc: chm 1971–78, pres 1979–90; pres NE Civic Tst 1996–2000, chm Prince's Tst NE Region 1997–2000; tstee: St George's House Windsor Castle 1990–96, CIVITAS 2004–; FIMgt, FRSA; *Books* Personal and Portable Pensions for All (1985), Take Upon Retiring (1997); *Recreations* horses, objets d'art, crafts, farming; *Clubs* Boodle's, Pratt's; *Style*— The Rt Hon Lord Vinson, LVO, DL

VINTER, Graham David; s of Alan James Vinter (d 1993), and Lilian Ann Esther, *née* Brown (d 1985); *b* 4 March 1956; *Educ* Chichester HS for Boys, BNC Oxford (BA), Ludwig-Maximilians-Universität Munich; *m* 22 Sept 1990, Anne Elizabeth, da of Alec Baldock; 1 da (Rebecca Jane Alexandra b 28 July 1991), 2 s (William Oliver James b 9 Sept 1993, Edward Thomas Adam b 19 Oct 1997); *Career* Allen & Overy: articled clerk 1980–82, assoc 1982–88, ptnr 1988–, head Projects Gp 1996–; memb Law Soc 1980; cncllr Mole Valley DC 1998–2000; *Books* Project Finance: A Legal Guide (1995, 3 edn 2006); *Recreations* tennis, golf, skiing, chess; *Style*— Graham Vinter, Esq; ✉ Allen & Overy LLP, Level 32, 40 Bank Street, Canary Wharf, London E14 5NR (tel 020 3088 0000, fax 020 3088 0088, e-mail graham.vinter@allenovery.com)

VINTON, Alfred Merton; *b* 1938, Argentina; *Educ* Choate Sch CT, Harvard Univ (BA); *m* Anna (-Maria) Vinton, *qv*; 1 da (Isabel Anousha b 3 Dec 1985), 1 s (George Oliver b 21 Oct 1987); *Career* J P Morgan: dir Banco Frances del Rio de la Plata Argentina 1968–73, responsible for Latin American business 1973–77, gen mangr Saudi International Bank London 1977–80, sr vice-pres and gen mangr Morgan Guaranty's London Branch 1980–86, vice-chm Morgan Guaranty Ltd and chm Morgan Guaranty Sterling Securities Ltd London 1986–87; chief operating offr N M Rothschild & Sons Ltd 1988–92; ceo Entreprises Quilmes SA and Three Cities Holdings Ltd 1992–94; chm Electra Partners Ltd 1995–; non-exec dir: Sand Aire Investments plc 1995–, Sagitta Investment Advisers Ltd 1996–2001, Unipart Gp 1998–, Amerindo Internet Fund plc 2000–; chm Lambert Howarth Gp plc 2000–; chm American Banks Assoc of London 1984–85; memb Exec Ctee BBA 1984–85; memb Advsy Ctee London Symphony Orch; tstee: American Museum in Bath, Oundle Fndn; *Style*— Alfred Vinton, Esq; ✉ Stoke Albany House, Stoke Albany, Market Harborough, Leicestershire LE16 8PT (tel 01858 535227, fax 01858 535482, e-mail freddy115@aol.com)

VINTON, Anna (-Maria); da of Charles Dugan-Chapman, and Mary Elizabeth Chapman; *b* 17 November 1947; *Educ* Chatelard Sch Les Avants Switzerland, Guildhall Sch of Music and Drama; *m* 1 (m dis), Anthony Greatrex Hawser; m 2, Alfred Merton Vinton, *qv*; 1 da (Isabel Anusha b 3 Dec 1985), 1 s (George Oliver b 21 Oct 1987); *Career* theatre agent: Cochrane Theatrical Agency 1967–68, Norma Skemp Agency 1969–70; private property co 1970–72; fndr and mangr: The Reject Linenshop Beauchamp Place London 1972, The Reject Shops plc 1973 (jt chm 1973–94); chm: Saxon Foods Ltd 1997–2001, Rap Ltd 1997–2003, Rap Spiderweb Ltd 2003–, Wilton Antiques Ltd 2002–; dir: Prepco Ltd 1998–2000, Printing Hldgs Co Ltd 2000–; non-exec dir: Cadbury Schweppes plc 1991–97, Courtaulds Textiles plc 1992–98, Thomas Jourdan plc 1996–97, WEW Group 1997–99, Remploy Ltd 2000–06, Bibendum Wine Ltd 2002–; tstee: Marie Curie Fndn (patron Leics), Winged Fellowship Tst (now Vitalise) 1998; memb: School Teachers' Review Body 1992–96, Covent Garden Market Authy 1992–98, FE Funding Cncl 1999–2001, Royal Parks Advsy Bd 1999–2002; *Recreations* skiing, riding, gardening, theatre, reading; *Style*— Mrs Anna Vinton; ✉ Stoke Albany House, Market Harborough, Leicestershire LE16 8PT; Pelham Cottage, 24 Pelham Street, London SW7 2NG

VIRDI, Prof Kuldeep Singh; s of Gurdial Singh Virdi, of Faridabad, India, and Sital Kaur, *née* Hoogan; *b* 19 May 1944; *Educ* Univ of Agra (BSc), IIT Bombay (BTech), Univ of Roorkee (ME), Univ of London (PhD, DIC); *m* 24 March 1975, Anne Margaret, da of Raymond Robert Pope, of Sydney, Aust; 1 da (Nina b 1979); *Career* res fell and scientist Structural Engrg Res Centre Roorkee 1965, asst engr Engineers India Ltd New Delhi 1970, Constrado res fell Dept of Civil Engrg Imperial Coll London 1973 (res asst 1970), lectr in structural engrg Dept of Civil Engrg Univ of Melbourne 1976; Sch of Engrg and Mathematical Sciences City Univ London: lectr in civil engrg 1979, reader 1983, head of dept 1986–91, prof of structural engrg 1988–, assoc dean 2003– (dep dean 1988–93, asst dean 2001–03), currently dir Engrg Structures Res Centre; external examiner MSc in structural engrg Heriot-Watt Univ; hon award foreign memb Royal Soc Arts and Scis Göteborg 1999, Gold Medal Brno Univ of Technol 1999; author of 75 articles in jls and int conference proceedings and ed 2 books; Dr (hc) Univ of Architecture, Civil Engrg and Geodesy Sofia 2003; FICE 1982, FIStructE 1982, FHEA 2007; *Recreations* theatre, music, badminton, travel; *Style*— Prof Kuldeep S Virdi

VIRGILS, Katherine Ruth; da of Russell Virgils, of San Marcos, Texas, and Shirley, *née* Koppen; *b* 28 August 1954; *Educ* Brighton Art Coll, Ravensbourne Art Coll (BA), RCA (MA); *m* 1989, Peter Raymond Camp, s of Maurice Raymond Camp; 2 s (Louis Elliot Virgils Camp b 4 July 1990, Maurice Emil Linwell Camp b 28 Sept 1995); *Career* artist; memb: Royal Coll of Art Soc 1982, Crafts Cncl 1983, Ranthamhore Soc 1989, Tibet Soc 1991; FRGS 1991; *Solo Exhibitions* Head Faces Elevations (Camden Arts Centre) 1983, Spirit Syntax Structure (Thumb Gallery London) 1986, Moguls Myths Minatures (Thumb Gallery) 1988, Ruth Segel Gallery NY 1988, Tales of Tigers and Temples (Jill George Gallery London) 1989, The Latitude of Ruins (Jill George Gallery) 1995, Echoes of Pilgrimage (The Orangery Holland Park) 2001; *Group Exhibitions* V&A 1981, Hayward Annual London 1982, LA Int Art Fair 1987–90; important works in the collections of: Contemporary Art Soc, Sainsbury Collection, Crafts Cncl Collection, Merrill Lynch, Calvin Klein, Glaxo Export HQ, IBM, BR, Herbert Smith, Lloyds Bank HQ (Cannons Marsh Bristol), Prudential Insurance Co, Harlech TV, Honeywell, Sir Terence Conran, Mitsui, Royal Caribbean, Private Residence of the Ruling Family of the Gulf States; *Awards*: Crafts Cncl grant 1982, Oxford Arts Cncl award 1984, Sainsbury prize (Chelsea Fair) 1985; *Books* The Latitude of Ruins (1992); *Recreations* travel in India, Mayan architecture and ruins; *Style*— Ms Katherine Virgils; ✉ The Bowling Hall, 346 Kennington Road, London SE11 4LD (tel 020 7840 0454, e-mail kvirgils@freenet.co.uk, website www.katherinevirgils.com)

VIS, Dr Rudolf Jan (Rudi); MP; s of Laurens Vis (d 1951), and Helena Vis (d 1981); *b* 4 April 1941; *Educ* High Sch The Netherlands, Univ of Maryland (BSc), LSE (MSc), Brunel Univ (PhD); *m* 1, 1968 (m dis), Joan Nancy Hanin; 1 s; m 2, 8 March 2001 (partner since 1988), Jacqueline Ruth Suffling; 2 s; *Career* lectr Univ of East London 1971–97, MP (Lab) Finchley and Golders Green 1997–; cncllr London Borough of Barnet 1986–98; memb:

V

Cncl of Euro 1997–, WEU 1997–; *Recreations* walking through London; *Style*— Dr Rudi Vis, MP; ✉ House of Commons, London SW1A 0AA (tel 020 7219 4956, fax 020 7219 0565)

VITEZ, Charles Oscar; s of Samuel Thomas Vitez (d 1972), and Suzanne Vitez; *b* 24 October 1948; *Educ* Westminster City Sch; *Career* CA 1972, ptnr KPMG 1987–93 (joined as taxation specialist 1973), ptnr Charles Vitez & Co 1993–; *Books* Taxation of UK Life Assurance Business (1986), Taxation of Unit Trusts (1994), MacLeod & Levitt, Taxation of Insurance Business (contrib, 1999); *Style*— Charles Vitez, Esq; ✉ 37 Preston Road, Wembley, Middlesex HA9 8JZ (tel 020 8904 5996, fax 020 8908 3207, e-mail vitez@btinternet.com)

VITORIA, Mary Christine; QC (1997); *Educ* Univ of London (BSc, PhD, LLB); *m* Prof Clive Ashwin; *Career* called to the Bar Lincoln's Inn 1975 (Lincoln's Inn and Buchanan Prizes); lectr in law law Queen Mary Coll London 1975–78, in practice 1978–; *Publications* Modern Law of Copyright and Designs (jtly, 1994, 3 edn 2000), Halsbury's Laws of England: Copyright; Patents and Registered Designs; ed Reports of Patent Cases and Fleet Street Reports; *Recreations* opera, bird watching; *Style*— Dr Mary Vitoria, QC; ✉ 8 New Square, Lincoln's Inn, London WC2A 3QP (tel 020 7405 4321, fax 020 7405 9955)

VIVIAN, 7 Baron (UK 1841), of Glynn, and of Truro, Co Cornwall; Sir Charles Crespigny Hussey Vivian; 7 Bt (UK 1828); s of 6 Baron Vivian (d 2004), and Catherine Joyce, *née* Hope (now Countess of Mexborough); *b* 20 December 1966, Durham; *Educ* Milton Abbey; *Career* Henderson Administration 1987–92, Club Mediterrane 1992–96, Citigate Dewe Rogerson 1996–2002, founding dir Pelham PR; *Recreations* waterskiing, rugby, cricket, shooting, theatre, travel; *Clubs* White's, Greenhouse; *Style*— The Rt Hon the Lord Vivian; ✉ 28 Walpole Street, London SW3 4QS (tel 020 7823 4561, mobile 07977 297903, e-mail charles.vivian@pelhampr.com)

VOAK, Jonathan Russell Saunders; s of Capt Allan Frederick Voak, of St Brelade, Jersey, and Annette Mary, *née* Langlois; *b* 25 October 1960; *Educ* Victoria Coll Jersey, Leicester Poly (now De Montfort Univ) (BA); *m* 1 (m dis 1994); m 2, 1995, Colette Louise, *née* Townsend; 2 da (Bethany Lillie Rose b 10 March 1997, Bella Summer Céleste b 27 July 1998), 2 s (Joshua Jacques Louis b 21 Nov 2000, Benjamin Jean Pierre b 16 July 2003); *Career* curatorial asst to dir of V&A (Sir Roy Strong) 1984–87 (museum asst Metalwork Dept 1983–84), curator Apsley House Wellington Museum 1987–95 (also curator Ham House and Osterley Park House 1989–90); dir: Hunt Museum 1996, Atelier Ltd 1997–; conslt The Osborne Gp 1998–99; publications ed V&A Museum Report of the Bd of Tstees 1983–86 and 1986–89; co-ed: (with Sir Hugh Casson) V&A Album Gold Edition 1987, John Le Capelain exhbn catalogue Jersey 1988; contrib: Wellington in Spain exhbn catalogue Madrid 1988, Baixella da Victoria - Portugal's Gift of Silver to the Duke of Wellington 1992, London - World City exhbn catalogue Essen 1992; co-author and ed Apsley House, The Wellington Collection at Apsley House, Wellington Museum 1995, ed Atelier Ltd Catalogues 1997–, author of numerous articles; Eighth Wellington lectr Univ of Southampton 1996; memb: BADA, LAPADA, CINOA (Int Assoc of Art and Antique Dealers), La Société Jersiaise (memb Exec Ctee), Attingham Soc; tstee: Jersey Heritage Tst, Chantrey Tst; chef tenant Du Fief De La Reine Grouville; *Recreations* motor racing, painting; *Style*— Jonathan Voak, Esq; ✉ Atelier Ltd, Le Bourg Farm, Le Grand Bourg, Grouville, Jersey JE3 9UY (tel 01534 855728, fax 01534 852099, e-mail art@atelierlimited.com)

VOGENAUER, Prof Stefan; s of Dieter Vogenauer, of Eutin, Germany, and Brigitte Maria, *née* Franz; *b* 4 August 1968, Eutin, Germany; *Educ* Kiel Univ, Univ of Paris, Trinity Coll Oxford (MJur, Clifford Chance prize, Herbert Hart prize); *m* 3 May 1997, Jutta; 2 s (Johannes Benedikt, David Nikolaus), 1 da (Veronika Elisabeth); *Career* research asst Law Faculty Regensburg, research fell Max Planck Inst for Foreign Private Law and Private Int Law, pt/t lectr Bucerius Law Sch, qualified as German Rechtsanwalt, fell BNC Oxford 2003–, prof of comparative law Univ of Oxford 2003–, dir Oxford Inst for European and Comparative Law 2004–; *Style*— Prof Stefan Vogenauer; ✉ Brasenose College, Oxford OX1 4AJ (e-mail stefan.vogenauer@iecl.ox.ac.uk)

VOGT, (Susan) Harriet; da of Richard Vogt, of Washington DC, and Joan, *née* Davis; *b* 31 July 1954; *Educ* Sidwell Friends Sch Washington DC, Westonbirt Sch, Univ of Sussex (BAPsych); *Partner* common law husband, Philip Gallagher; 2 s (Matthew Patrick Pierce Gallagher b 20 March 1991, James Conor Osmond Gallagher b 18 March 1993); *Career* dir of planning Ayer Advertising 1985–91 (dir 1984–91), corp cnsllr and strategist 1992–93, dir Portman Communications 1993–, dir Techmedia 1997–2001, ptnr Two Brains Brand Planning and Qualitative Res; *Recreations* consuming books, films, clothes, Italian food and culture; *Style*— Ms Harriet Vogt; ✉ East Grange, Steeple Aston, Oxfordshire OX25 4SR

VOLES, Prof Roger; s of Bertram Richard Edward Voles (d 1978), and Winifred Mabel, *née* Barnes (d 1988); *b* 20 July 1930; *Educ* Archbishop Tenison's Sch, Univ of London (BSc, MTech, DTech, DSc(Eng)); *m* 24 Sept 1966, Vida Margaret Murray, da of Alec Riley (d 1973); *Career* tech dir Thorn EMI Electronics 1989–91 (chief scientist 1974–89); ind conslt 1991–; visiting prof UCL 1993–; contributed 44 papers to jls of IEE and IEEE; granted over 100 patents; organised 10 int confs; former chm: AGARD Avionics Panel, EEA Res Advsy Ctee, IEE Electronics Divnl Bd; Freeman Worshipful Co of Engrs 1984, Freeman Worshipful Co of Scientific Instrument Makers 2004; FIEE 1971, FInstP 1971, FREng 1983, FIMA 1989, FIEEE 1999; *Recreations* mountain walking, genealogy, travel; *Style*— Prof Roger Voles, FREng; ✉ 49 Park Road, Chiswick, London W4 3EY

VOLK, Stephen Geoffrey; s of Dilwyn Mills Volk, of Pontypridd, S Wales, and Marion, *née* Hartnell; *b* 3 July 1954; *Educ* Coventry Sch of Art (BA), Univ of Bristol (postgrad cert in radio, film and TV studies); *m* Patricia; *Career* advtg copywriter 1977–85; writer; BBC ASIFA ICOGRADA (Int Cncl of Graphic Design Assocs) Prize for Animation 1976, London Advtg Award (for COI film 'Mark') 1979, D&AD Awards 1984 and 1985, Best Short Film Galway Film Festival and Celtic Film Festival 1997, BAFTA Award (for The Deadness of Dad), nomination HWA Bram Stoker Award (for 31/10); *Screenplays* incl: Gothic (directed by Ken Russell), The Kiss (jtly), The Guardian (jtly, directed by William Friedkin), Ghostwatch (BBC), Massage (BBC), I'll Be Watching You (BBC), The Deadness of Dad (short), Cyclops (Channel 4), Superstition (jtly), Octane, Afterlife (TV series); *Plays* Answering Spirits; *Publications* Gothic (novel), Dark Corners (story collection); *Style*— Stephen Volk, Esq; ✉ 9 Coppice Hill, Bradford-on-Avon, Wiltshire BA15 1JT; c/o Linda Seifert Management, 22 Poland Street, London W1F 8QQ (tel 020 7292 7390, fax 020 7292 7391, e-mail contact@lindaseifert.com)

VOLTERRA, Robert Gustavo; s of Vito Volterra, of Toronto, Canada, and Gail, *née* Gnaedinger; *b* 20 September 1964, Toronto, Canada; *Educ* Univ of Western Ontario (Lt-Govr of Ontario scholar, BA), York Univ Toronto (LLB), Trinity Hall Cambridge (Cwlth scholar, LLM); *Career* barr and slr Upper Canada, slr advocate Eng and Wales; slr specialising in public int law and int dispute resolution; slr with law practice of Prof Sir Elihu Lauterpacht, CBE, QC, *qv*, 1994–96, head Public Int Law Gp Freshfields Bruckhaus Deringer 1996–2001, ptnr and head Public Int Law Gp Herbert Smith 2001–05, ptnr Latham & Watkins LLP 2005– (also global chair Int Dispute Resolution Practice and head Public Int Law Gp); Faculty of Law Osgoode Hall Law Sch York Univ Toronto 1992–94, research fell Research Centre for Int Law Univ of Cambridge 1994–96, Faculty of Law Univ de Paris X 1996–99, Geopolitics and Boundaries Research Centre Univ of London 1998–, visiting prof Faculty of Law UCL 2000–; jt sec Br branch Int Law Assoc, memb Latin American Arbitration Ctee Int C of C, memb Expert Panel for States UNCTAD Prog on Dispute Settlement in Int Trade, Investment and Intellectual Property, memb Mgmnt Bd Forum on Int Investment Law Br Inst of Int and Comparative Law, legal expert Legal Advsy Task Force Energy Charter Secretariat; First Class Order of Bahrain 2001; *Style*— Robert Volterra, Esq; ✉ Latham & Watkins LLP, 99 Bishopsgate, London EC2M 3XF (tel 020 7710 1090, fax 020 7374 4460, e-mail robert.volterra@lw.com, website www.lw.com)

von DOHNÁNYI, Christoph; *b* Berlin; *Educ* Munich Acad of Music (Richard Strauss Prize), Florida State Univ; *Career* conductor and repetiteur Frankfurt Opera 1953, gen music dir Lübeck, chief conductor Westdeutsche Rundfunk Sinfonie Orchester Cologne, gen music dir and opera dir Frankfurt Opera, intendant and chief conductor Hamburg Opera, music dir Cleveland Orch 1984–2002 (music dir designate 1982, music dir laureate 2002), princ conductor Philharmonia Orch 1997– (princ guest conductor 1994–97), chief conductor NDR Symphony Orch Hamburg 2004–; guest conductor: ROH Covent Garden, La Scala Milan, Met Opera NY, Lyric Opera Chicago, Zurich Opera, Vienna State Opera, Berlin Philharmonic, Vienna Philharmonic, Israel Philharmonic, Orchestre de Paris, Royal Concertgebouw Orch, NY Philharmonic, Pittsburgh Symphony Orch, Philadelphia Orch, Chicago Symphony Orch, Boston Symphony Orch; recordings with Cleveland Orch incl: complete symphonies of Beethoven, Brahms and Schumann, symphonies by Bruckner, Dvorák, Mahler, Mozart, Schubert and Tchaikovsky, works by Adams, Bartók, Berlioz, Birtwistle, Busoni, Ives, Ravel, Richard Strauss, Varèse and Webern; prodns with Vienna Philharmonic incl: Der Rosenkavalier, Salome, Cosi fan Tutte, Erwartung, Duke Bluebeard's Castle, Die Zauberflöte, Ariadne auf Naxos, Die Bassariden, Baal; prodns with Philharmonia Orch incl: Die Frau ohne Schatten, Moses und Aron, Oedipus Rex, Hänsel und Gretel, Die Schweigsame Frau, Arabella (all at Chatelet Theatre Paris), Edinburgh Festival 2002, BBC Proms 2002, Luzern Festival 2002; *Style*— Christoph von Dohnányi, Esq; ✉ Philharmonia Orchestra, First Floor, 125 High Holborn, London WC1V 6QA

von ETZDORF, Georgina Milagra; da of Roderick Rudiger von Etzdorf (d 1996), of Devizes, Wilts, and Audrey, *née* Catterns; *Educ* Downe House, St Martin's Sch of Art, Camberwell Sch of Art (BA); *Career* freelance textile designer 1978–79, freelance designer developing designs from paper work and silk screens on to fabric 1979–80, fndr Georgina von Etzdorf Partnership designing printing and selling wool, silk and velvet designs 1981, artistic dir in team producing biannual collections of clothing and accessories for men and women 1991–; lectures and teaching appointments: Cooper Hewitt Museum NYC, Nova Scotia Sch of Art and Design, Glasgow Coll of Art, St Martin's Sch of Art, Royal Coll of Art, The Crafts Cncl; hon fell London Inst 2003, Hon Dr of Design Winchester Sch of Art Univ of Southampton 1996; RDI 1997; *Exhibitions* Smithsonian Instn's Nat Museum of Design Washington, Cooper Hewitt Museum NY, V&A London, 25 year retrospective Manchester City Art Gallery 2006; *Awards* BBC 4 Radio Enterprise Award for Small Businesses 1984, British Apparel Export Award 1986, British Gas Award Manchester Prize for Art and Industry 1988, highly commended Int Textile and Fashion Competition (Design Centre Stuttgart) 1988, finalist Export Awards (British Knitting and Clothing Export Cncl in conjunction with The Clothes Show) 1989; *Recreations* singing, dancing, playing the ukelele; *Clubs* Chelsea Arts; *Style*— Ms Georgina von Etzdorf; ✉ Craigleath, Bowerchalke, Salisbury, Wiltshire SP5 5DB (e-mail gve@gve.co.uk)

VON MALLINCKRODT, George W; Hon KBE (1997); s of Arnold Wilhelm von Mallinckrodt, and Valentine, *née* von Joest; *b* 19 August 1930; *Educ* Salem; *m* 31 July 1958, Charmaine, da of Helmut Schroder; 2 da (Claire b 11 Aug 1960, Sophie b 8 Aug 1967), 2 s (Philip b 26 Dec 1962, Edward b 29 June 1969); *Career* merchant banker; Agfa AG (Munich) 1948–51, Münchmeyer & Co (Hamburg) 1951–53, Kleinwort Sons & Co (London) 1953–54, J Henry Schroder Banking Corp (NY) 1954–55, Union Bank of Switzerland (Geneva) 1956–57; Schroders plc: rejoined J Henry Schroder Banking Corp NY 1957, joined J Henry Schroder & Co Ltd 1960, dir 1977–, chm 1984–95, chm Schroder & Co Bank AG Zurich 1984–2003, chm Schroder US Holdings Inc NY 1984–, dir Schroders Australia Holdings Ltd Sydney 1984–2001, dir Schroder & Co Inc NY 1986–2000, dir Schroder International Merchant Bankers Ltd Singapore 1988–2000, dir Schroder Polska Sp zoo 1993–2000, pres 1995–; also dir: Allianz of America Inc (NY) 1978–84, Banque Privée de Gestion Financière (Paris) 1980–83, Euris SA (Paris) 1987–98, Siemens plc 1989–2000, Foreign and Colonial German Tst 1992–98; chm Cncl World Economic Forum 1995–97; advsr Bain & Company 1997–2005; memb: Euro Advsy Ctee McGraw-Hill Inc 1986–89, City Advsy Gp CBI 1990–, Ct of Benefactors Univ of Oxford 1990–, Circle of Patrons 1995–, Br N American Ctee, Supervisory Bd Trader.com 2000–01, Cncl John F Kennedy Sch of Govt Univ of Harvard 2005–; pres: German YMCA London 1962–, German Chamber of Industry & Commerce UK 1992–95 (vice-pres 1995–); Hon DCL Bishop's Univ Quebec 1994; Freeman City of London 2004; FRSA, CIMgt; Cross of the Order of Merit FRG 1986, Offr's Cross of the Order of Merit FRG 1990, Cdr's Cross of the Order of Merit FRG 2001; *Recreations* shooting, skiing; *Style*— George W von Mallinckrodt, KBE; ✉ Schroders plc, 31 Gresham Street, London EC2V 7QA (tel 020 7658 6370, fax 020 7658 2211)

von OTTER, Anne Sofie; *Educ* in Stockholm, Guildhall Sch of Music and Drama London; *Career* mezzo-soprano; studied with Vera Rozsa; appeared at venues incl: Royal Opera House Covent Garden, Chicago, Vienna, Paris, Met Opera NY, La Scala Milan, Opera Houses of Berlin, Munich, Geneva, Lyon and Stockholm, BBC Proms; worked with conductors incl: Sir Colin Davis, John Eliot Gardiner, Carlo Maria Giulini, James Levine, Riccardo Muti, Claudio Abbudo, Giuseppe Sinopoli, Sir Georg Solti; *Performances* incl: Oktavian in Der Rosenkavalier (with Met Opera under Carlos Kleiber and in Chicago, London, Paris, Vienna, Stockholm and Munich), Orfeo (Geneva), Dorabella in Cosi fan Tutte (London, Paris, Frankfurt and Cologne), title role in La Cenerentola (Covent Garden), Idamantes in Idomeneo (Met Opera and Vienna), Romeo in I Capuleti (Covent Garden), title role in Alceste (Opera de la Bastille), title role in Ariodante (Opera de la Bastille), title role in Carmen (Glyndebourne Festival Opera); *Recordings* incl: Cosi fan Tutte (with Sir Georg Solti), Orfeo (with John Eliot Gardiner), Hänsel and Gretel (with Jeffrey Tate), Der Rosenkavalier and Bluebeard's Castle (with Bernard Haitink), Le Nozze di Figaro (with James Levine), Ariadne auf Naxos (with Giuseppe Sinopoli), Bach B Minor Mass (with Sir Georg Solti), Lieder recitals of Grieg, Mahler and Brahms; *Style*— Ms Anne Sofie von Otter; ✉ IMG Artists Europe, Lovell House, 616 Chiswick High Road, London W4 5RX (tel 020 8233 5800, fax 020 8233 5801)

von SIMSON, David; s of Prof Dr Werner von Simson (d 1996), of Freiburg, Germany, and Kathleen, *née* Turner (d 1996); bro of Piers von Simson, *qv*; *b* 19 September 1950; *Educ* Lancing, New Coll Oxford (BA); *Children* 2 da (Alice b 5 June 1982, Rachel b 15 May 1984); *Career* mangr Samuel Montagu & Co Ltd 1976–79; dir: Hill Samuel Securities Ltd 1982–84, Hill Samuel & Co Ltd 1984–85; memb Supervisory Bd Bank von Ernst & Cie 1984–85, exec dir Swiss Bank Corporation International Ltd 1985–95, chief exec then chm SBC Warburg France 1993–97, former md Warburg Dillon Read, currently ptnr Europa Partners Ltd; formerly: chm In Technology plc, non-exec dir Gardner Merchant Ltd; *Style*— David von Simson, Esq

von SIMSON, Piers; s of Prof Werner von Simson (d 1996), of Freiburg, Germany, and Kathleen Aimee, *née* Turner (d 1996); bro of David von Simson, *qv*; *b* 23 September 1946; *Educ* Lancing, New Coll Oxford (BA), Univ of Calif Berkeley (LLM); *m* 1, 6 Aug 1977, Lindsay, da of late Prof E J H Corner; 2 da (Cara Isabel Camilla b 15 June 1978, Isabel Victoria b 17 April 1982), 1 s (James Francis Louis b 16 April 1983); m 2, 17 April 1996, Sarah, da of David Phillips, of Prisk, S Glamorgan; 3 s (Thomas Maximilian b 25 July 1996, Felix, Charles (twins) b 22 Aug 1997), 1 da (Florence Lily b 17 Dec 2001); *Career* called to the Bar Middle Temple 1969, dir S G Warburg & Co Ltd 1979–95 (joined 1972), dir S G Warburg Group plc 1989–95, md SBC Warburg 1995–96, dir Soditic Ltd 1996–; *Recreations* opera, books, sailing, winter sports; *Style—* Piers von Simson, Esq; ✉ Soditic Ltd, Wellington House, 125 Strand, London WC2R 0AP (tel 020 7872 7000, fax 020 7872 7102)

von WESTENHOLZ, Piers Patrick Frederick; Baron; s of Baron Henry Frederick Everard von Westenholz (d 1984), of Crackney, Widford, Herts; *b* 10 December 1943; *Educ* Downside; *m* 1, 1964 (m dis 1969), Sarah, da of Raimund von Hofmannstahl (s of the poet Hugo von Hofmannstahl) by his 2 w, Lady Elizabeth Paget (da of 6 Marquess of Anglesey, GCVO); m 2, 1979, Jane, da of Arthur Leveson, of Hall Place, Ropley, Hants; 1 s, 2 da; *Career* antique dealer and decorator; memb Br Olympic ski team Innsbruck 1964; *Recreations* shooting, fishing, skiing; *Style—* Baron von Westenholz; ✉ 76 Pimlico Road, London SW1W 8PL

VOORSANGER, Jessica; *Educ* Parson Sch of Design, Brooklyn Museum Art Sch, Tyler Sch of Art Temple Univ, Rhode Is Sch of Design (BFA), Goldsmiths Coll London (MA); *Career* artist; fndr (with Bob Smith, *qv*) Leytonstone Centre for Contemporary Art; *Solo Exhibitions* Romance Novels (Freud's Bar London) 1991, Travel Tips (Travellers Bookshop London) 1991, Birthday Party (Peter Doig's Studio London) 1994, Baby Shower (Camden Arts Centre) 1995, Star Sightings (Modern Culture NY) 1996, The Retrieval Series: Bob Geldof (Modern Culture Project Space NY) 1996, Let's Go Rangers (Modern Culture Project Space NY) 1997, Art Stars (Anthony Wilkinson Gallery London), 1998, Stinky Village (Virgin Megastore London) 1999, Bono & Sting Wouldn't Be Anything Without: Jessica Voorsanger's The David's (The International 3 Manchester) 2001; *Group Exhibitions* Sex Salon (Epoche Gallery NY) 1990, China June 6 1989 (PS1) 1990, The Capsule (Tower Bridge Piazza) 1991, Bingo Bongo (Tower Bridge Piazza) 1992, Relative Values (Smith Art Gallery & Museum Stirling) 1993, The Pet Show (63 Union St London) 1993, Blood Brothers: Jessica Voorsanger meets David & Shaun Cassidy (installation, Nosepaint Performance Art Gp) 1993, Fete Worse than Death (Hoxton Square London) 1994, Something's Wrong (The Tannery London) 1994, Candyman II (Unit 7 Bermondsey London) 1994, The Curator's Egg (Anthony Reynolds Gallery London) 1994, Sarah Staton's Supastore (Laure Genillard Gallery London) 1994, Art Unlimited: Multiples of the 1960s and 1990s from the Arts Cncl Collection (Glasgow Contemporary Arts and Royal Festival Hall) 1994–95, Hit & Run (1–4) (various venues incl Miny of Sound London) 1994–95, Miniatures (The Agency London) 1995, Dad (Gasworks London) 1995, Life of its Own (Zivot Sam O Sobe) (Br Cncl Window Gallery Prague) 1995, Lost Property (W-139 Amsterdam and Great Western Studios London) 1995, Supastore (Middlesbrough) 1995, Imprint 93 (City Racing Gallery London) 1995, The Hanging Picnic (Factual Nonsense in Hoxton Square London) 1995, 10 Years of Student Exhibitions (Economist Plaza London) 1995, Gang Warfare (London & McKinney Contemporary Arts Dallas) 1995, Cocaine Orgasm (Bank Space @ Burbage House London) 1995, My Darling Cicciolina (Last Orders London) 1995, Glass Shelf Show (ICA) 1995–97, Kiss This (Focal Point Gallery Southend-on-Sea) 1996, Yer Self is Steam (85 Charlotte St London) 1996, Gol'96 (Sam's Salon London) 1996, Live/Life (Musee d'Arte Moderne de la cite de Paris) 1996, BANK TV, Video Myths (Dog Gallery London) 1996, Club Shiop (Sam's Salon London) 1996, 100 Per Cent Love (Coin Copy Store London) 1996, It's A Stitch Up! (Dog Gallery London) 1997, Big Blue (Coin Copy Store London and tour) 1997, Imprint 93 (Norwich Gallery) 1997, Posture: An Assessment of Figuration (David Klein Gallery Birmingham MI) 1997, The Meltdown Festival (Royal Festival Hall) 1997, Double Life (Waiting Room Univ of Wolverhampton and Art Coll Wolverhampton) 1997, BANK TABLOID (ICA London) 1997, Networking (Arts Cncl touring exhbn) 1997–99, Date With an Artist (NGCA Sunderland) 1998, Again Again (Galerie Carbone & Alberto Peola Arte Contemporanae Turin) 1998, Fame (Firstdraft Sydney) 1998, Global Housewarming (1st Floor Gallery Melbourne) 1998, Host (Tramway Glasgow) 1998, Cloth-Bound (Laure Genillard Gallery London) 1998, Show Me the Money 1 (8 Duke Mews London) 1998, Channel 3 (Team Gallery NY) 1998, Feeringbury VIII Cultivated (Feeringbury Manor Essex) 1998, Show Me The Money 3 (8 Duke Mews London) 1998, Vauxhall Gardens (Norwich Gallery) 1998, homel (home London) 1998, My Eye Hurts (Thread Waxing Space NY and Green Room Manchester) 1999, 48 Hours (The Tablet London) 1999, Reciprocity (The Sun & Dove London) 1999, Cab Gallery London 1999 (exhibited on the inside and outside of a London taxi), MuSEUM MAgOgO (Glasgow Project Space) 1999, Liverpool Biennial 1999–, Tectonic (La Panderia Mexico City) 2000, Crush (Hoax London) 2000, Drawing of Lots (The Gallery Univ of Central Lancashire) 2000, Combi (Stavanger Norway) 2000, Playmaker (Galerie Paula Boettcher Berlin) 2000, Family Art Project (with Bob Smith, SITE Kunstverein Dusseldorf) 2000, Realm of the Senses (with Bob Smith, Turku Art Museum) 2000, In the City (Modern Culture at the Gershwin Hotel NY) 2000, Then there is no mountain, then there is (Generator Dundee) 2001, Porta-Project (Goldsmiths Coll London) 2001, Century City (Tate Modern London) 2001, Ecole de Bob Smith & David Burrows (Trade Apartment London) 2001, CRYlawn (Goldman Tevis Gallery LA) 2001, Record Collection (VTO Gallery London), Sally Barker Gallery at 291 Gallery London 2001, Teeth & Trousers (Cell Project Space Ideal House London) 2001, Across the Pond (The Practice Space LA) 2001; *Style—* Ms Jessica Voorsanger; ✉ c/o Anthony Wilkinson Gallery, 242 Cambridge Heath Road, London E2 9DA (tel 020 8980 2662)

VORA, Dr Jiten; *b* 3 April 1954; *Educ* St John's Coll Cambridge (Humphry Davy exhbn, scholarship and studentship, coll prize, Rolleston travel exhbn, Wright prize, MA, MB BChir, MD); *m* Cerys; 2 s; *Career* house surgn New Addenbrooke's Hosp Cambridge 1979, house physician Ipswich Hosp 1979–80, SHO Leicester Hosps 1980–82, registrar Leicester Royal Infirmary 1982–84, res fell Dept of Med Univ of Wales Coll of Med 1984–87, lectr and hon sr registrar in med, gen med, diabetes and endocrinology Univ of Wales Coll of Med 1987–91, Fulbright sr res scholar and visiting prof Dept of Med (Div of Nephrology and Hypertension) Oregon Health Sciences Univ 1991–93, conslt physician Royal Liverpool Univ Hosp and hon sr lectr Univ of Liverpool 1993–, examiner Univ of Liverpool; regular lectr at univs and learned socs; pres Local Charter Br Diabetic Assoc; chm Diabetes Working Sub-Gp Dist Med Advsy Ctee (also Royal Liverpool Univ Hosp rep); organiser: WHO Multi City Action Plan in Diabetes, Regnl HA Study Day - Diabetes and Renal Disease, Nat/Int Meeting - Renal Disease in Type II Diabetes; regnl co-ordinator and organiser Soc for Endocrinology; Royal Liverpool Univ Hosp rep Regnl Med Ctee Speciality Sub-Ctee for Diabetes and Endocrinology; memb: S Sefton HA Diabetes Advsy Gp, Liverpool Diabetes Register/Shared Care Gp, Diabetes UK Strategic Review Gp, S Sefton Diabetes Register Working Gp, Regnl Diabetes Care Devpt Panel, Regnl Diabetes Services Accreditation Panel, Advsy Panel Med Devices Agency, Working Party RC Opthalmologists (memb Guidelines Gp for treatment of diabetic retinopathy), NHS R&D Screening Ctee (Sub-Gp on Diabetic Retinopathy), Renal and Retinopathy Gps Nat Service Framework - Diabetes; assoc ed Diabetic Med (jl of Br Diabetic Assoc); memb: Med Res Soc, RSM, Soc of Endocrinology, Diabetes UK, Euro Assoc for the Study of Diabetes, Euro Diabetic Nephropathy Study Gp, Nat Kidney Fndn, Br Hypertension Soc; FRCP 1996 (MRCP 1981); *Publications* author of numerous articles published in learned jls and papers presented to learned societies; regular reviewer for jls incl: Diabetes, Diabetes Care, Diabetologia, Diabetic Medicine, J Diab Complications, BMJ, New England Jl of Medicine, The Lancet, Nutrition; *Recreations* cooking, cricket, squash, skiing, mountain cycling, golf; *Style—* Dr Jiten Vora; ✉ Royal Liverpool University Hospital, Prescot Street, Liverpool L7 8XP (tel 0151 706 3470, fax 0151 706 5871, e-mail jiten.vora@rlbuh-tr.nwest.nhs.uk)

VORDERMAN, Carol Jean; MBE (2000); *b* 24 December 1960; *Educ* Ysgol Mair Rhyl, Blessed Edward Jones HS Rhyl, Sidney Sussex Coll Cambridge (MA); *Family* 1 da (Katie), 1 s (Cameron); *Career* broadcaster and author; civil engr Sir Alfred McAlpine 1981; columnist: Daily Telegraph 1996–98, Daily Mirror 1998–2004; memb DTI Task Force Action into Engrg 1995; tstee Nat Endowment for Science, Technology and the Arts (NESTA) 1998–2001; memb Home Office Internet Task Force 2001–02; patron: Express Link Up, CLAPA (Cleft Lip and Palate Assoc); hon fell Univ of Wales (Bangor), Hon MA Univ of Bath, Hon D Univ Leeds Metropolitan Univ; Assoc MICE; FRSA; *Television* progs incl: Countdown (first woman to appear on Channel 4) 1982–, World Chess Championship Kasparov v Short (Channel 4) 1993, educn corr GMTV 1993–94, Tomorrow's World (BBC1) 1994–95, Computers Don't Bite (BBC 2) 1997, National Lottery Live (BBC 1) 1997, Carol Vorderman's Better Homes (ITV) 1999–2003, Find a Fortune (ITV) 1999–2000, Star Lives 1999–2000, Pride of Britain Awards Ceremony 2000–, Britain's Brainiest (ITV) 2001–02; host various confs and awards ceremonies; *Books* incl: How Mathematics Works (1996), Carol Vorderman's Guide to the Internet (1998, 2 edn 2001), Maths Made Easy (1999), Science Made Easy (2000), English Made Easy (2000), Carol Vorderman's Detox For Life (with Ko Chohan, 2001), Carol Vorderman's Summer Detox (2003), Carol Vorderman's Detox Recipes (2004), How To Do Sudoku (2005), Super Brain (2007); *Style—* Carol Vorderman; ✉ c/o John Miles Organisation, Cadbury Camp Lane, Clapton-in-Gordano, Bristol BS20 9SB (tel 01275 854675, fax 01275 810186)

VOREMBERG, Rhoderick Peter Grosvenor (Rhoddy); s of Dato' Rudolf Peter Voremberg, DKDS, PJK, and Rosella, *née* Bartelot; *b* 19 November 1954, Trowbridge, Wilts; *Educ* Cumnor House Sch Sussex, Rugby, Magdalene Coll Cambridge (MA); *m* 15 March 1980, Susan Mary, *née* Burnet; 2 da (Jessica b 14 March 1983, Olivia b 30 Nov 1987), 1 s (Rupert b 17 April 1985); *Career* slr; articled clerk then asst slr Burges Salmon Bristol 1978–82; Wilsons: joined 1982, ptnr 1985–, sr ptnr 2003–06; tstee: Stanley Picker Tst, Wilts Community Fndn 1998–2006, Salisbury Almshouse and Welfare Charities 1999–; chm Salisbury Arts Centre 2006–; memb Soc of Tst and Estate Practitioners 1991; *Recreations* amateur silversmith, match rifle shooting (capt English Eight 1996–2001), fishing, books, typography, fine art; *Clubs* Hawks' (Cambridge), English Eight (Bisley), Commonwealth; *Style—* R P G Voremberg, Esq; ✉ Glebe House, Odstock, Salisbury, Wiltshire SP5 4JB; Wilsons, Steynings House, Summerlock Approach, Salisbury SP2 7RJ (tel 01722 412412, fax 01722 427520, e-mail rv@wilsonslaw.com)

VOS, Geoffrey Charles; QC (1993); s of Bernard Vos (d 1974), of London, and Pamela Celeste Rose, *née* Heilbuth; *b* 22 April 1955; *Educ* UCS, Gonville & Caius Coll Cambridge (MA); *m* 31 March 1984, Vivien Mary, da of Albert Edward Dowdeswell (d 1982), of Birmingham; 1 da (Charlotte b 1985), 2 step da (Maria b 1965, Louise b 1965), 1 step s (Carl b 1973); *Career* called to the Bar Inner Temple 1977, bencher Lincoln's Inn; judge Courts of Appeal of Jersey and Guernsey 2005–; chm: Chancery Bar Assoc 1999–2001 (hon sec 1994–97, vice-chm 1997–99), Bar Cncl 2007 (vice-chm 2006, chm Fees Collection Ctee 1995–2004, chm Professional Standards Ctee 2004– (vice-chm 2001–03)); ex officio memb Gen Cncl of the Bar 1999–2001 and 2004–; *Recreations* farming, wine, photography; *Clubs* Oxford and Cambridge, Worcs Golf; *Style—* Geoffrey Vos, Esq, QC; ✉ 3 Stone Buildings, Lincoln's Inn, London WC2A 3XL (tel 020 7242 4937, fax 020 7405 3896)

VOSS, Prof Christopher Arnold; s of Dr H J Voss, of Cottingham, Northants, and Matthew, *née* Arnold (d 1989); *b* 23 December 1942; *Educ* Bedford Sch, Imperial Coll London (BSc), London Business Sch (MSc, PhD); *m* 14 Dec 1977, Carolyn Jill, da of Sir Richard Kingsland, DFC, of Canberra, Aust; 1 da (Georgina b 1978), 1 s (Barnaby b 1981); *Career* mangr Stuarts & Lloyds Ltd 1960–67, conslt Harbridge House Europe 1970–75, visiting prof Univ of Western Ontario 1975–77, lectr London Business Sch 1977–84, Alan Edward Higgs prof of mfrg strategy and policy Univ of Warwick 1984–90, dir Centre for Operations Mgmnt London Business Sch 1990–; dep dean London Business Sch 1999–2002; dir European Case Clearing House 2002–; chm European Ops Mgmnt Assoc 1989–2001; MBICS 1971, FRSA 1989, fell Br Acad of Mgmnt 1995, FIMechE 2001, fell Prodn and Ops Mgmnt Soc 2005, fell Decision Science Inst 2005; *Books* Operation Management in Service Industries and the Public Sector (1985), Just-In-Time Management (1988), Performance Measurement in Service Industries (1992), Manufacturing Strategy - Process and Content (1992), Made in Europe (1994), International Manufacturing Strategies (1998); *Recreations* skiing, violin, book collecting; *Style—* Prof Christopher Voss; ✉ London Business School, Sussex Place, Regents Park, London NW1 4SA (tel 020 7000 8812, fax 020 7000 7001)

VRANCH, Richard Leslie; s of Leslie William Frank Vranch (d 1991), of Somerset, and Rea Helen Vranch (d 2005); *b* 29 June 1959; *Educ* Bristol GS, Trinity Hall Cambridge (MA, PhD); *Career* actor, writer and former musician; writing incl: films for NatWest, Boots, AA, Harper Collins, Ryman and the Sheik (play for Tamasha Theatre Co) 2002, articles, comedy sketches, feature film script Sole Representation 1999; Plessey res fell St John's Coll Oxford 1984–85; *Theatre* work incl: Aftertaste (with Tony Slattery, *qv*) 1981–, The Comedy Store Players 1986–, English Teaching Theatre (tour to Europe, ME and Mexico) 1988–94, Secret Policeman's Biggest Ball (Cambridge Theatre) 1990, Hysteria 2 and Hysteria 3 1991, Clive in The Dead Set 1992, Paul Merton Show (London Palladium) 1994, Lifegame (West Yorkshire Playhouse), Mexico (one-man show) 1999; *Television* appearances incl: Whose Line Is It Anyway? (Channel 4) 1988–97, The Secret Policeman's Biggest Ball 1990, Jackanory (BBC) 1993 and 1994, The Music Game (Channel 4) 1993, Cue the Music 1994–96, Beat That Einstein (Channel 4) 1994, Paul Merton at the Palladium (BBC) 1994, Mind Games (BBC) 2005, Celebrity Weakest Link (BBC) 2005; various animations and voice overs; writer Smack the Pony 1999–2002; *Radio* for BBC Radio 4 incl: The Hot Club 1989, Wordly Wise 1997, Cross Questioned 1997, Just a Minute 1999, Puzzle Panel 2005; Jammin (BBC Radio 2, team capt) 2001–04; *Film* Balloon Seller in The Suicidal Dog; *Publications* Defects in Irradiated MOS Structures (PhD thesis); 'Spin-dependent and localisation effects at Si/SiO2 device interfaces' in Semi-conductor Science and Technol, vol 4, 1999; Cartoons in Punch, Maxim (with Lucy Allen), The Spectator; *Recreations* travel in Europe and Latin America; *Clubs* Century; *Style—* Richard Vranch; ✉ e-mail richard@richardvranch.com; c/o Sue Terry Voices (tel 020 7434 2040); c/o Michele Milburn, International Artistes (tel 020 7025 0600)

V

VYVYAN, Sir (Ralph) Ferrers Alexander; 13 Bt (E 1645), of Trelowarren, Cornwall; s of Sir John Stanley Vyvyan, 12 Bt (d 1995), and his 3 w, Jonet Noel, *née* Barclay; *b* 21 August 1960; *Educ* Charterhouse, Sandhurst, AA Sch of Architecture; *m* 1986, Victoria Arabella, yst da of M B Ogle, of Buckfastleigh, Devon; 5 s (Joshua Drummond b 10 Oct 1986, Frederick George b 21 Dec 1987, Rowan Arthur b 23 Oct 1989, Inigo Valentine b 14 Feb 1994, Gabriel Francis b 6 Feb 1999); *Heir* s, Joshua Vyvyan; *Style—* Sir Ferrers Vyvyan, Bt

W

WAAGE, Prof Jeffrey King; OBE (2007); s of Prof Karl Mensch Waage, of Connecticut, USA, and Elizabeth, *née* King; *b* 15 March 1953; *Educ* Hopkins GS, Princeton Univ (AB, Phi Beta Kappa), Imperial Coll London (Marshall fell, PhD, DIC); *m* 18 March 1983, Cynthia, da of Dr Charles Day Masters (m dis); 1 da (Hannah b 23 Nov 1984), 3 s (Alexander b 26 Sept 1986, Nicholas b 29 March 1989, Theodore b 27 Feb 1994); *Career* postdoctoral work in entomology Univ of Texas Austin 1978, lectr in insect ecology Imperial Coll London 1978–86, dir Int Inst of Biological Control 1992–98 (joined as chief research offr 1986, subsequently dep dir), chief exec CABI Bioscience 1998–2001, head Dept of Agric Sciences Imperial Coll London 2001–; pres Int Orgn of Biological Control 1996–2000, chair Global Invasive Species Prog 2000–03; has worked extensively in tropical America, Africa and Asia on aspects of ecology and pest mgmnt since 1975; memb: Br Ecological Soc 1978, Royal Entomological Soc of London 1978, Entomological Soc of America 1980; MIBiol 2001; *Recreations* walking; *Style*— Prof Jeffrey Waage, OBE; ✉ Centre for Environmental Policay, Imperial College, London SW7 5BD

WACE, Rupert; s of Rodney Sant Wace, and Heather Mary Wace; *Educ* Marlborough; *Children* 3 s (Timothy, Oliver, Arthur); *Career* formerly with: Sotheby's London, Christie's; prop Rupert Wace Ancient Art Ltd 1988–; supporter: KIDS, Br Museum, Chelsea Physic Gdn; memb: BADA 1999, IADAA 1995, ADA 1989; *Books* Celtic Sculpture (1989), Egyptian, Greek and Roman Antiquities (1991), Pharoah's Creatures: Animals from Ancient Egypt (2004), Eternal Woman: The Female Form in Antiquity (2005); *Recreations* salmon fishing, tennis, horse racing; *Style*— Rupert Wace, Esq; ✉ Rupert Wace Ancient Art, 14 Old Bond Street, London W1S 4PP (tel 020 7495 1623, fax 020 7495 8495, e-mail rupert@rupertwace.co.uk)

WADDELL, Bruce; s of Ken Waddell, and Christina Ann Waddell; *b* 18 March 1959, Bo'ness, W Lothian; *m* 15 Oct 1994, Cathy, *née* Cullis; 1 s (Daniel b 24 Dec 1995); *Career* with Johnston Newspapers 1977–87, sub ed then chief sub ed Scottish Sun 1987–90, dep ed Sunday Scot 1990–91, mktg and sales exec Murray Int 1991–93, dep ed Scottish Sun 1993–98, ed Scottish Sun 1998–2003, ed Daily Record 2003–; memb: Newspaper Press Fund, Scottish Daily Newspaper Soc; *Recreations* football, classic cars, cinema, golf; *Style*— Bruce Waddell, Esq; ✉ Daily Record, One Cental Quay, Glasgow G3 8DA (tel 0141 309 3000, fax 0141 309 3340)

WADDELL, Heather; yr da of Robert (Roy) Waddell (d 1980), of Hughenden, Glasgow, and Maureen, *née* Buchanan, MBE (d 2006); *b* 11 July 1950; *Educ* Westbourne Sch Glasgow, St Leonard's Sch St Andrews, Univ of St Andrews (MA), Byam Shaw Sch of Art London (Dip Fine Art, Leverhulme bursary), Univ of London (CertEd); *Partner* 1974–78, Roger Wilson (d 1999), Australian artist; *Career* author, art critic, artist, photographer and publisher; lectr in English and gen studies Paddington Coll London 1978, researcher Int Artists Exchange Prog in Aust and NZ (Gulbenkian scholarship awarded 1979), London corr Vie des Arts 1979–89, int admin artists' exchange programe ACME Gallery London 1980, Central Bureau for Educational Visits and Exchanges grant to set up art sch exchange links in Belgium and Holland 1980, fndr and md Art Guide Publications Ltd 1980–87 (art guides to London, NY, Paris, Berlin, Amsterdam, Madrid, Glasgow, Aust and UK), publisher Art Guide Publications imprint A&C Black 1987–90, arts ed élan arts magazine The European 1990–91, visual arts ed Time Out Publications 1989–93, lectr in art history American Univ Summer Sch Paris 1995; freelance art critic: The Evening Standard 1974, The Artist 1974–75, TES 1977, The Glasgow Herald 1994– (London art critic 1980–84), Artnews USA 1986, New Art International Paris 1986, Artline UK 1985–92, The Independent 1988–89, Independent on Sunday 1993, visual arts ed Chic magazine 1994–98, The Times 1996, BBC World Servs 1998, ITV News 2000; co-organiser New Scottish Prints Exhbn as part of Britain Salutes NY (toured USA) 1983, conslt Int Contemporary Art Fair London 1984–90, organiser Henri Goetz Exhibition London 1986, chm of judges The Art Show 1994; judge: Bernard Denvir AICA Art Critics' Prize 1994, 2003 and 2006, Royal Over-Seas League Open 1998, Art for the Millennium Guernsey 2000; artist and photographer: Battersea Arts Centre 1979, 5 + 1 Aust photos exhibition NSW House Art Gallery London 1980, Morley Gallery (IAA exhbn) 1984), Art Guides (London and Glasgow), Blue Guides (London and Paris), The Independent, The European, Time Out Publications, National Portrait Gallery London (4 photographs 20th Century Collection); 27 Holland Park Avenue Ltd: company dir 1987–, company sec 1992–; Int Assoc of Art Critics (AICA): memb 1980–, memb Exec Ctee 1982–97 and 2001–06, treas 1984–86, PR 1990–97, creating AICA UK archives (now in Tate archives), organiser BD AICA Award 1995, 2003 and 2006; mentor to St Andrews Univ arts students 2003–; memb: Exec Ctee Int Assoc of Artists 1978–84, Soc of Young Publishers 1980–86, Ind Publishers' Guild 1980–89 and 2002–, Map and Guide Book Ctee and Art Book Publishers' Ctee Publishers' Assoc 1983–87, Soc of Authors 2003–; hon memb Royal Over-Seas League; *Books* author of: London Art and Artists Guide (1979, 10 edn 2006), The London Art World 1979–99 (2000), The Artists' Directory (1981, 3 edn 1989), Henri Goetz: 50 Years of Painting (1986); contrib: Encyclopaedia of London (Macmillan, 1986), L'Ecosse: pierre, vent et lumière (1988), Blue Guide to Spain (1988), Londres (Editions Autrement Paris, 1997 and 2000); visual arts section in Time Out: London Guide, New York Guide, Visitor's Guide, Shopping Guide 1987–92; British Figurative Art 1980–92: Paintings of Hope and Despair (1992); artist catalogues/statements: Kenneth Lauder, Victoria Achache, Natahsa Kissell and Peter Harrap, Denis Clarke, Peter Griffin and Mim Hain; *Recreations* travel, swimming, friends and their children, contemporary literature and films, enjoying life; *Style*— Heather Waddell; ✉ 27 Holland Park Avenue, London W11 3RW (e-mail hw.artlondon@virgin.net, website www.hwlondonartandartistsguide.com)

WADDELL, Martin; s of Martin Mayne Waddell, and Alice, *née* Duffell; *b* 10 April 1941, Belfast; *Educ* Eaton House Sch London, St Clement Danes Sch London, Down HS Downpatrick; *m* Dec 1969, Rosaleen Margaret, da of Thomas Arthur Carragher; 3 s (Thomas Mayne (Tom) b 1970, David Martin b 1972, Peter Matthew b 1975); *Career* writer (also writes as Catherine Sefton) 1966–; former work experience incls bookselling and junk-stalling; memb: Soc of Authors, Irish Writers' Union, Children's Literature Assoc of Ireland; *Books include* Starry Night (The Other Award, runner-up Guardian Young Fiction Award), Can't You Sleep Little Bear (Smarties Prize, Sheffield Book Award, Prix de Critiques de Livres pour Enfants de la Communauté Française de Belgique, Prix Verselle), The Park in the Dark (Emil/Kurt Maschler Award), The Hidden House (Emil/Kurt Maschler Award short list), Rosie's Babies (Best Book for Babies Award), Squeak-a-Lot, Grandma's Bill (runner-up Bisto Book of the Year Award, Acorn Award short list), Farmer Duck (Smarties Prize, Emil/Kurt Maschler Award short list), Owl Babies (Hans Christian Andersen Award 2004); *Style*— Martin Waddell, Esq; ✉ c/o David Higham Associates, 5–8 Lower John Street, Golden Square, London W1R 4HA (tel 020 7437 7888, fax 020 7437 1072)

WADDINGTON, Baron (Life Peer UK 1990), of Read in the County of Lancashire; Sir David Charles Waddington; GCVO (1994), PC (1987), QC (1971), DL (Lancashire 1991); s of late Charles Waddington, JP, of Read, Lancs, and Minnie Hughan Waddington; *b* 2 August 1929; *Educ* Sedbergh, Hertford Coll Oxford; *m* 1958, Gillian Rosemary, da of Alan Green, CBE, of Sabden, Lancs; 3 s (Hon James Charles b 1960, Hon Matthew David b 1962, Hon Alistair Paul b 1965), 2 da (Hon Jennifer Rosemary b 1965, Hon Victoria Jane b 1971); *Career* 2 Lt 12 Royal Lancers 1951–53; called to the Bar Gray's Inn 1951, recorder of the Crown Court 1972; former dir: J J Broadley Ltd, J and J Roberts Ltd, Wolstenholme Rink Ltd; Parly candidate (Cons): Farnworth 1955, Nelson and Colne 1964, Heywood and Royton 1966; MP (Cons): Nelson and Colne 1968–74, Clitheroe March 1979–83, Ribble Valley 1983–90; Lord Cmmr of the Treasy 1979–81, Parly under sec employment 1981–83, min of state Home Office 1983–87, govt chief whip 1987–89, home sec 1989–90; Lord Privy Seal and Leader of the House of Lords 1990–92, govr and C-in-C Bermuda 1992–1997; *Style*— The Rt Hon Lord Waddington, GCVO, PC, QC, DL; ✉ Old Bailiffs, South Cheriton, Templecombe, Somerset BA8 0BH

WADDINGTON, Prof David James; s of Eric James Waddington (d 1958), and Marjorie Edith, *née* Harding (d 1995); *b* 27 May 1932; *Educ* Marlborough, Imperial Coll London (BSc, ARCS, DIC, PhD); *m* 17 Aug 1957, Isobel, da of Ernest Hesketh (d 1994); 2 s (Matthew b 1963, Rupert b 1964), 1 da (Jessica b 1970); *Career* head Sci Dept Wellington Coll 1961–64 (teacher 1956–64); York Univ 1965–: prof of chemical educn 1978–2000, head dept 1983–92, pro-vice-chllr 1985–91, emeritus prof 2000–; visiting prof Univ of Kiel 2000–; pres Educn Div Royal Soc Chem 1981–83, chm Ctee Teaching Chemistry Int Union Pure and Applied Chem 1981–85, sec Ctee Teaching Sci Int Cncl Sci Unions 1985–89 (chm 1989–94); hon prof Mendeleev Univ of Chemical Technology Moscow; Nyholm medal Royal Soc Chem 1985, Brasted Award American Chem Soc 1988; Liveryman Worshipful Co of Salters 2001; Brazilian Grand Cross National Order of Merit 1997; *Books* Kinetics and Mechanism: Case Studies (1977), Modern Organic Chemistry (1985), Chemistry, The Salters' Approach (1989), Salters' Advanced Chemistry (1994, new edn 2000); ed: Teaching School Chemistry (1984), Chemistry in Action (1987), Education Industry and Technology (1987), Bringing Chemistry to Life (1992), Science for Understanding Tomorrow's World: Global Change (1994), Global Environmental Change: Science Education and Training (1995), Partners in Chemical Education (1996), Salters' Higher Chemistry (1999), The Essential Chemistry Industry (1999), Evaluation as a Tool for Improving Science Education (2005), Context Based Learning of Science (2005); *Recreations* golf; *Style*— Prof David Waddington; ✉ Department of Chemistry, University of York, Heslington, York YO10 5DD (tel 01904 433467, fax 01904 434078, e-mail djw1@york.ac.uk)

WADDINGTON, Leslie; s of late Victor Waddington, and Zelda, *née* Levine; *b* 9 February 1934; *Educ* Portora Royal Sch, Sorbonne, Ecole du Louvre Paris (Dip); *m* 1, 1967 (m dis 1983), Ferriel, *née* Lyle; 2 da; m 2, 1985, Clodagh Frances, *née* Fanshawe; *Career* chm and jt fndr Waddington Galleries 1957– (md 1966–); chm: Pictura Maastricht Art Fair 1996–2000, Modern Section Maastricht Art Fair 1996–2004; sr FRCA 1993; *Recreations* reading, walking; *Style*— Leslie Waddington, Esq; ✉ Waddington Galleries, 11 Cork Street, London W1S 3LT (tel 020 7851 2200)

WADDINGTON, Prof Peter Anthony James; s of James William Harker Waddington (d 1980), and Patricia Ann, *née* Nil; *b* 6 March 1947; *Educ* Moseley Road Sch of Art, Matthew Boulton Tech Coll, Univ of London (external BSc), Univ of Leeds (MA, PhD); *m* 1968, Diane Anita, da of George Atherley; 1 s (Daniel Bevan b 15 Nov 1978), 1 da (Claire Shelley b 9 April 1980); *Career* Univ of Leeds: SSRC studentship 1969–70, res offr/fell Dept of Adult Educn 1970–74, lectr in sociology 1974–76; Univ of Reading: lectr in sociology 1976–92, reader in police studies 1992–95, prof of sociology 1995–99, prof of political sociology 1999–2006; prof of social policy and dir Policy Research Inst Univ of Wolverhampton 2006–; *Books* The Training of Prison Governors (1983), Arming an Unarmed Police (1988), The Strong Arm of the Law (1991), Calling the Police (1993), Liberty and Order (1995), Policing Citizens (1999), Violent Workplace (2006); *Style*— Prof Peter Waddington; ✉ School of Humanities, Social Sciences and Languages, University of Wolverhampton, Wulfruna Street, Wolverhampton WV1 1SB (tel 01902 321000, e-mail p.a.j.waddington@wlv.ac.uk)

WADDINGTON, Robert; s of George Waddington (d 1967), and Mary Gwendoline, *née* Briggs (Mrs Renwick); *b* 20 January 1942, Haslingden, Lancs; *Educ* Uppingham; *m* 24 Jan 1976, Jennifer Ann, da of late Sir Anthony Banks Jenkinson, 13 Bt (d 1989); 2 s (Thomas Anthony b 10 May 1977, Guy George b 6 Sept 1979); *Career* CA; Peat Marwick Mitchell 1960–64, Hambros Bank Ltd 1971–97 (dir 1984); non-exec dir: Stanley Leisure plc 1998–, Elvaston Investments Ltd 1999–; *Recreations* shooting, golf, gardening; *Clubs* Turf; *Style*— R Waddington, Esq

WADDINGTON, Susan (Sue); *Educ* Blyth GS Norwich, Univ of Leicester (BA, MEd); *Career* early career as community project ldr and lectr in social policy; asst dir of educn: Derbys CC 1988–90, Birmingham CC 1990–94; MEP (Lab) Leicestershire and S Lincolnshire 1994–99, European devpt offr Nat Inst of Continuing Educn 2000–; memb (Lab) Leics CC 1973–91 and 2003–; Parly candidate Leics NW 1987, European Parly candidate E Midlands 1999; vice-pres European Assoc for the Educn of Adults 2001; *Style*— Ms Sue Waddington

WADE, Dr John Philip Huddart; s of Dr Edward Geoffrey Wade (d 1999), of Cheadle Hulme, Cheshire, and Mary Ward Pickering, *née* Huddart; *b* 19 April 1950; *Educ* Cheadle Hulme Sch, Univ of Cambridge (BA), Manchester Med Sch (MB BChir), Univ of Cambridge (MD); *m* 26 April 1976, Charlotte, da of Dr Elozor Leslie Feinmann (d 1983) and Sylvia Feinmann (d 1989); 1 da (Jessica Alice Feinmann), 1 s (Charles Louis Feinmann); *Career* registrar St Thomas' Hosp 1978, sr registrar Nat Hosp for Nervous Disease London and St Bartholomew's Hosp 1984–85, res fell Cerebrovascular Disease Univ of Western Ontario 1985–86, currently conslt neurologist Charing Cross Hosp and conslt neurologist Wexham Park Hosp Slough; present research interests incl: role of functional neuroimaging in neurology, early diagnosis of dementia, evaluation of individual patients with severe extracranial occlusive vascular disease; memb Assoc Br Neurologists 1986, fell Stroke Cncl American Heart Assoc 1988, FRCP 1992; *Publications* papers incl: Reactivity of the cerebral circulation in patients with occlusive carotid disease (with M M Brown, R W Ross Russell and C Bishop, 1986), CBF and vasoreactivity in patients with arteriovenous malformations (with J K Farrar and V C Hachinski, 1987); various invited chapters in books; abstract papers incl: Cerebral blood flow in subjects with high oxygen affinity haemoglobin at Euro Conf of Haemorheology London (with T C Pearson), Impact of contra lateral ICA stenosis on outcome of symptomatic ICA occlusion at Associates of Br Neurologists Glasgow (with V Hachinski and H J M Barnett, 1989); *Recreations* sailing; *Style*— Dr John Wade; ✉ 11 Gardnor Road, Hampstead, London NW3 (tel 020 7431 2900); Department of Neurosciences, Charing Cross Hospital, Fulham Palace Road, London W6 (tel 020 8846 1303, fax 020 8846 1187)

WADE, Keith Martin; s of Alec Raymond Wade, of Freshwater, Isle of Wight, and Maureen Briggs; *b* 5 October 1961; *Educ* Bosworth Coll Desford, LSE (BSc, MSc); *m* 20 Jan 1990; 1 s, 1 da; *Career* res offr Centre for Economic Forecasting London Business Sch 1984–88; Schroders: joined 1988, UK economist 1988–91, chief economist 1992–; memb Addenbrookes Investment Ctee 2006–; memb: Soc of Business Economists, Soc of Investment Professionals; *Books* Macroeconomics (co-author, 1995); *Recreations* gardening, golf; *Style*— Keith Wade, Esq; ✉ Schroders plc, 31 Gresham Street, London EC2V 7AS (tel 020 7658 6000, e-mail keith.m.wade@schroders.com)

WADE, Prof Kenneth; s of Harry Kennington Wade (d 1983), of Sleaford, Lincs, and Anna Elizabeth, *née* Cartwright (d 1992); *b* 13 October 1932; *Educ* Carre's GS Sleaford, Univ of Nottingham (BSc, PhD, DSc); *m* 14 July 1962, Gertrud Rosmarie (Trudy), da of Willy Hetzel (d 1965), of Grenchen, Switzerland; 1 s (Alan b 1963), 2 da (Marianne b 1965, Julia b 1968); *Career* postdoctoral res fell: Univ of Cambridge 1957–59, Cornell Univ 1959–60; lectr in chemistry Derby Coll of Technol 1960–61; Univ of Durham: lectr in chemistry 1961–71, sr lectr 1971–77, reader 1977–83, prof 1983–2001, emeritus prof 2001–, chm Dept of Chemistry 1986–89; pres Dalton Div RSC 1995–97; FRSC; FRS 1989; *Books* Organometallic Compounds: The Main Group Elements (with G E Coates, 1967), Principles of Organometallic Chemistry (with G E Coates, M L H Green and P Powell 1968), Electron Deficient Compounds (1971), Chemistry of Aluminium, Gallium, Indium and Thallium (with A J Banister 1976), Hypercarbon Chemistry (with G A Olah, G K S Prakash, R E Williams, and L D Field 1987), Electron Deficient Boron and Carbon Clusters (with G A Olah and R E Williams, 1990), Contemporary Boron Chemistry (with M G Davidson, A K Hughes and T B Marder, 2000); *Recreations* walking; *Style*— Prof Kenneth Wade, FRS; ✉ Chemistry Department, University of Durham Science Laboratories, South Road, Durham DH1 3LE (tel 0191 334 2122, fax 0191 384 4737, e-mail kenneth.wade@durham.ac.uk)

WADE, Martyn John; s of Albert R Wade (d 1979), of Birmingham, and Nancy Joan, *née* Exon (d 1980); *b* 24 March 1955, Birmingham; *Educ* King Edward IV Five Ways GS Birmingham, Newcastle Poly (BA), Univ of Wales Aberystwyth (MLib); *m* 1978, Anne Rosemary, *née* Patterson; *Career* trainee librarian Northumberland CC 1976–78, branch librarian Sunderland MBC 1978–81, branch librarian and librarian in charge Sutton LBC 1981–87, librarian Northumberland CC 1987–91, area librarian Leicestershire CC 1991–93, area library offr Cambridgeshire CC 1994–99, head of libraries, info and learning Glasgow City Cncl 1999–2002, nat librarian Nat Library of Scotland 2002–; MCLIP 1978, FRSA 2006; *Recreations* motorcycling, reading, the arts, cooking; *Clubs* Waverley Motor Cycle; *Style*— Martyn Wade, Esq; ✉ National Library of Scotland, George IV Bridge, Edinburgh EH1 1EW (tel 0131 623 3700, fax 0131 623 3702)

WADE, Michael John; s of Peter Wade (d 2005), and Lorna A M Harris; *b* 22 May 1954; *Educ* Royal Russell, N Staffs Coll; *m* 1997, Dr Caroline Sarah Dashwood, da of Sir Francis Dashwood, Bt (d 2000); 1 s (Alexander Francis Neville b 1 Jan 1998); *Career* fndr and chm Holman Wade Ltd 1980–93, dir Horace Clarkson plc 1986–93, fndr and chief exec Rostrum Gp Ltd 2000–; memb Lloyd's 1980–, memb Cncl and Ctee Lloyd's 1987–92, chm Lloyd's Community Prog 1988–94, memb Lloyd's Taskforce 1991, fndr Corporate Lloyd's Membership Ltd 1993, chief exec CLM Insurance Fund plc (appointed dep chm on merger with SVB Holdings plc 1999); chm: Opera Interludes Ltd 1990–, Bowood Holdings Ltd 2005–; dir: Rostrum Gp Ltd 2000–, Paterson Martin Ltd 2006–; non-exec dir BRIT Holdings plc 2002–03; treas Cons Pty 2000– (memb Economic Competitiveness Policy Gp 2006–) tstee Salisbury Cathedral Girl Choristers' Tst 2003–, patron Salisbury Arts Centre; *Recreations* music, shooting, flying, architectural restoration; *Clubs* Turf; *Style*— Michael J Wade, Esq; ✉ Trafalgar Park, nr Salisbury, Wiltshire SP5 3QR (website www.trafalgarpark.com); 87 Vincent Square, London SW1P 2PQ (tel 020 7821 0675, fax 020 7821 0676, e-mail michaeljwade@hotmail.com or michael.wade@rostrumgroup.com)

WADE, Mike; s of James Edward Wade, and May, *née* Wakefield; *Educ* Royal Liberty GS, Coll for Distributive Trades (HNC); *Career* grad trainee Unilever, mktg dir Ciba-Giegy Consumer Products, ptnr Owen Wade Delmonte, md Chetwyn Haddons, md Index Advtg, ceo FCA! Ltd, dir of strategy Publicis UK; lectr IPA and Inst of Mktg; MIPA 1971, MMRS 1985; *Publications* Wolfe (Tamla Motown album, 1969), Dear God (1979); *Recreations* music, photography, nature, travel, literature; *Style*— Mike Wade, Esq; ✉ Publicis, 82 Baker Street, London W1U 6AE (tel 020 7935 4426, mobile 07831 289239, e-mail mike.wade@publicis.co.uk)

WADE, Neville Edward Henry; JP (Herts); *b* 5 February 1945; *Educ* Caludon Castle Sch Coventry, Coventry Tech Coll, Coventry Coll of Art, CAM (DipPR); *m*; 2 c; *Career* PR conslt; clerical offr Coventry Corporation 1961–64, PR offr Coventry Climax Engines Ltd 1965–69, PR mangr Lansing Limited 1970–79, dir/ptnr Zaxhurst Limited Winchester 1979–85, dir Welbeck Golin/Harris Communications Ltd 1985–91, ind conslt 1991–; dir: Ilex Court Management Ltd 1992–99, Strategic Partnership (London) 1994–2005; moderator: CAM PR Dip, Watford Int PR Dip; memb: Qualifications and Awards Bd CIPR 2005–, PR Degrees Advsy Panel London Coll of Communication 2005–; vice-chm Qualifications and Awards Bd CIPR; memb Herts Area Bd Nat Probation Serv 1996–2007; past appts incl: chm IPR Disciplinary Ctee, memb Bd and chm Educn & Trg Ctee PRCA, chief examiner CAM Dip in PR, pres Winchester Jr Chamber, dep pres Winchester C of C, fndr chm Basingstoke Publicity Club, memb New Alresford PC, jt fndr Alresford Pigs Assoc, chm of Govrs Sun Hill Schs, chm Electric Vehicle Assoc of GB; first IPR CAM Dip Award, Sir Stephen Tallent's Medal (for servs to IPR and practice of PR) 1994, IPRA Golden World Award 1995; FCIPR (pres 1983, Hon FCIPR 1998), fell CAM Fndn, FRSA 2004; *Style*— Neville Wade, Esq; ✉ PO Box 544, Berkhamsted, Hertfordshire HP4 3WA (tel 01442 866656, fax 01442 870839, e-mail neville.wade2@btinternet.com)

WADE, Nicholas James; s of William John Wade, and Sarah Ellen, *née* Ostick; *b* 27 March 1942; *Educ* Queen Elizabeth's GS Mansfield, Univ of Edinburgh (BSc), Monash Univ (PhD); *m* 1965, Christine, *née* Whetton; 2 da (Rebecca Jane b 1971, Helena Kate b 1972); *Career* postdoctoral fell Max-Planck Inst for Behavioural Physiology Seewiesen Germany 1969–70; Univ of Dundee Dept of Psychology: lectr 1970–78, reader 1978–91, prof of visual psychology 1991–; memb Experimental Psychology Soc 1974; FRSE 1997; *Publications* Brewster and Wheatstone on Vision (1983), Visual Allusions: Pictures of Perception (1990), Visual Perception: An Introduction (1991, new edn 2001), Psychologists in Word and Image (1995), A Natural History of Vision (1998), Purkinje's Vision: The Dawning of Neuroscience (2001), Destined for Distinguished Oblivion: The Scientific Vision of William Charles Wells 1757–1817 (2003), Perception and Illusion: Historical Perspectives (2005), The Moving Tablet of the Eye: The Origins of Modern Eye Movement Research (2005), Insegne Ambigue Percorsi Obliqui tra Storia, Scienza e Arte, de Galileo a Magritte (2007), Circles: Science, Sense and Symbol (2007); *Recreations* golf, cycling, hill walking; *Clubs* Scotscraig Golf, New Golf (St Andrews), The Newport; *Style*— Prof Nicholas Wade, FRSE; ✉ School of Psychology, University of Dundee, Dundee DD1 4HN (tel 01382 384616, fax 01382 229993, e-mail n.j.wade@dundee.ac.uk)

WADE, Paul Francis Joseph; s of Rosemary Wade (d 1997); *b* 19 March 1953, Derby; *Educ* Queen Margaret's Acad Ayr, Univ of Glasgow (LLB); *m* 1, 28 Aug 1976 (m dis), Kirstine; 1 s (David b 20 Nov 1985); m 2, 24 June 1994, Gillian; 2 da (Katherine b 31 Jan 1996, Charlotte b 12 June 2000); *Career* admitted slr 1976; specialises in defence of prosecutions arising from serious or fatal accidents; trainee slr then slr Biggart Baillie 1974–78, slr then ptnr Cochran Sayers & Cook 1979–93, ptnr and head of Glasgow office Simpson and Marwick 1993–; author of various articles and papers on corporate killing and health and safety prosecutions; memb: Law Soc of Scotland 1976, Soc of Slr Advocates 1993; *Recreations* walking, reading, travel, cooking; *Style*— Paul Wade, Esq; ✉ 87 Springkell Avenue, Glasgow G41 4EJ; Simpson and Marwick, 91 West George Street, Glasgow G2 1PB (tel 0141 248 2666, fax 0141 248 9590, e-mail paul.wade@simpmar.com)

WADE, Rebekah; da of late Robert Wade, and Deborah Wade; *b* 27 May 1968; *Educ* Appleton Hall, Sorbonne; *Career* features ed, then assoc ed rising to dep ed News of the World 1989–98, dep ed The Sun 1998–2000, ed News of the World 2000–02, ed The Sun 2003–; fndr memb and pres Women in Journalism; *Style*— Ms Rebekah Wade; ✉ The Sun, 1 Virginia Street, London E98 1SN

WADE, Richard Samuel Marlar; s of Neil Wade, of Mayfield, East Sussex, and Jane, *née* Marlar; *b* 28 February 1968, Brighton, Sussex; *Educ* Brighton Coll, Univ of Birmingham (LLB), Coll of Law; *m* 6 Aug 1994, Denise, *née* Jones; 2 da (Kira Josephine b 17 Feb 2004, Juliet Clare b 22 July 2006); *Career* trainee slr then slr Denton Wilde Sapte (formerly Wilde Sapte) 1992–97; Blake Lapthorn Tarlo Lyons: slr 1997–2000, ptnr 2000–, head of construction 2004–; author of articles in Accountancy and QS Week; memb: Law Soc 1994, Soc of Construction Law (Oxford regnl coordinator), TECSA (Technology and Construction Court Slrs Assoc) 1999; *Recreations* sport, music (contemporary and classical), travel, wine; *Clubs* Primary, Wooden Spoon Soc; *Style*— Richard Wade, Esq; ✉ Blake Lapthorn Tarlo Lyons, Seacourt Tower, West Way, Oxford OX2 OFB (tel 01865 254244, fax 01865 244983, e-mail richard.wade@bllaw.co.uk)

WADE-GERY, Sir Robert Lucian; KCMG (1982), KCVO (1983); o s of late Prof Henry Theodore Wade-Gery, MC, FBA, and Vivian, *née* Whitfield; *b* 22 April 1929; *Educ* Winchester, New Coll Oxford; *m* 16 June 1962, Sarah, da of Adam Denzil Marris, CMG (d 1983); 1 da (Laura Katharine b 1965), 1 s (William Richard b 1967); *Career* entered Foreign Serv 1951; served: London, Bonn, Tel Aviv, Saigon; under sec Central Policy Review Staff 1971–73; min: Madrid 1973–77, Moscow 1977–79; dep sec of the Cabinet 1979–82, high cmmr to India 1982–87; vice-chm: Barclays de Zoete Wedd Ltd 1994–97 (exec dir 1987–93), Barclays Capital 1997–99; dir Barclays Bank Spain 1990–2001, India Index Fund 1993–2004; sr conslt Br Invisibles 1999–2001, Barclays Private Bank 1999–2002; fell All Souls Coll Oxford 1951–73, 1987–89 and 1997–; chm of govrs SOAS Univ of London 1990–98, chm Anglo-Spanish Soc 1995–98 (dep chm 1993–95), hon treas Int Inst for Strategic Studies 1993–2005; *Recreations* walking, sailing, history, travel; *Clubs* Boodle's, Beefsteak; *Style*— Sir Robert Wade-Gery, KCMG, KCVO; ✉ The Old Vicarage, Cold Aston, Cheltenham, Gloucestershire GL54 3BW (tel 01451 821115, fax 01451 822486); 14 Hill View, 2 Primrose Hill Road, London NW3 3AX (tel 020 7722 4754, fax 020 7586 5966)

WADE OF CHORLTON, Baron (Life Peer UK 1990), of Chester in the County of Cheshire; Sir (William) Oulton Wade; kt (1982), JP; s of Samuel Norman Wade, of Chester, and Joan Ferris, *née* Wild; *b* 24 December 1932; *Educ* Birkenhead Sch, Queen's Univ Belfast; *m* 1959, Gillian Margaret, da of Desmond Leete, of Buxton; 1 s (Hon Christopher James Oulton b 1961), 1 da (Hon Alexandra Jane b 1964); *Career* farmer and cheesemaker; pres CHPA; chm: NIMTECH, Midas Capital Partners Ltd, Rocktron Ltd; dir: Murray Vernon Ltd, Murray Vernon (Holdings) Ltd, Rising Stars Growth Fund Ltd; former memb Cheshire CC, chm City of Chester Cons Assoc 1973–76, jt hon treas Cons Pty 1982–90; chm: English Cheese Export Cncl 1982–84, Rural Economy Gp, Chester Heritage Tst, Historic Cheshire Churches Preservation Tst; chm Children's Safety Educn Fndn, tstee John Beckett Fndn, tstee Tony Vernon Fndn; Freeman City of London, Liveryman Worshipful Co of Farmers; *Clubs* Chester City, St James's (Manchester), Portico Library (Manchester); *Style*— The Rt Hon Lord Wade of Chorlton

WADHAM, John; s of Ernest George Wadham (d 1997), and Unity Winifred, *née* Errington (d 2003); *b* 24 January 1952, Croydon, Surrey; *Educ* Stanley Tech Sch London, LSE (BSc), Univ of Surrey (MSc, Cert), Coll of Law; *m* 8 April 2004, Alison Macnair; *Career* admitted slr 1989; social worker London Borough of Richmond 1975–77, legal advsr Wandsworth Law Centres 1976–86; Liberty: legal advsr 1990–95, dir 1995–2003; dep chair IPCC 2003–; memb Editorial Bd European Human Rights Law Review; hon lectr: Sch of Law Univ of Kent, Law Sch and Scarman Centre Univ of Leicester; memb: Liberty, Amnesty Int, Legal Action Gp, Soc of Lab Lawyers, Law Soc, First Div Assoc; *Publications* Blackstone's Guide to the Freedom of Information Act (2 edn 2005), Blackstone's Guide to the Identity Cards Act (2006), Blackstone's Guide to the Human Rights Act (4 edn 2007); *Recreations* flying (private pilot); *Style*— John Wadham; ✉ Independent Police Complaints Commission, 90 High Holborn, London WC1V 6BH (tel 020 7166 3000)

WADHAM, Julian Neil Rohan; *b* 7 August 1958; *Educ* Ampleforth, Central Sch of Speech and Drama; *Career* actor; *Theatre* RNT incl: That Face, Tartuffe, Once in a While The Odd Thing Happens, The Changeling, Mountain Language, The Madness of King George III, The Winter's Tale; Royal Court incl: Falkland Sound, The Recruiting Officer, Our Country's Good, Serious Money; other credits incl: Another Country (Queen's), Our Country's Good (Garrick), When We Were Married (Whitehall), A Letter of Resignation (Comedy), Plenty (Albery), The Good Samaritan (Hampstead); *Television* Ghostboat, Egypt, Justice in Wonderland, Middlemarch, Goodbye Cruel World, Blind Justice, The Guest, After The War, Bright Eyes, Baal, The Gentle Touch, Me and My Girl, Hot Metal, Chancer, Bergerac, Poirot, Casualty, Growing Pains, Between the Lines, Stay Lucky, Full Stretch, The Wingless Bird, Lucan - The Trial, A Dance to the Music of Time, Gypsy Woman, A Touch of Frost, Wallis and Edward, Sherlock Holmes, The Government Inspector, Tom Brown's Schooldays, The Alan Clarke Diaries, Island at War, Christopher Wren, Foyle's War; *Film* Goya's Ghosts, Maurice, Mountbatten - The Last Viceroy, The Madness of King George, The Secret Agent, The English Patient, Keep the Aspidistra Flying, High Heels and Low Lifes, Exorcist - The Beginning, A Different Loyalty, Wah Wah; *Style*— Julian Wadham; ✉ c/o Gilly Sanguenetti, Ken MrReddie Associates Ltd, 36–40 Glasshouse Street, London W1B 5DL (tel 020 7439 1456, fax 020 7734 6530, e-mail email@kenmcreddie.com)

WADHAMS, Prof Peter; s of Frank Cecil Wadhams (d 1971), and Winifred Grace, *née* Smith (d 2001); *b* 14 May 1948; *Educ* Palmer's Sch Grays, Churchill Coll Cambridge (coll scholar, MA), Scott Polar Res Inst Univ of Cambridge (PhD), Univ of Cambridge (ScD); *m* 11 Oct 1980, Maria Pia, da of Renato Casarini, of Milan, Italy; *Career* research scientist Bedford Inst of Oceanography Dartmouth NS (participant in Hudson-70, first expedition to circumnavigate Americas) 1969–70; postdoctoral fell Inst of Ocean Sciences Victoria BC 1974–75; Scott Polar Research Inst Univ of Cambridge: research assoc 1976–81, asst dir of research 1981–88, dir 1988–92, reader in Polar studies 1992–2001, prof of ocean physics 2001–02; prof of ocean physics Dept of Applied Maths and Theoretical Physics (DAMTP) Univ of Cambridge 2002–, sr fell Scottish Assoc for Marine Science

W

Dunstaffnage Marine Lab Oban 2003–04; sr res fell Churchill Coll Cambridge 1983–93; visiting prof of arctic marine science US Naval Postgrad Sch Monterey CA 1980–81, Green scholar Scripps Inst of Oceanography La Jolla CA 1987–88, Walker-Ames prof Univ of Washington Seattle 1987–88, visiting prof Nat Inst of Polar Research Tokyo 1995 and 1996–97, professeur associé Université Pierre et Marie Curie Paris 2005 and 2007; co-ordinator: Int Prog for Antarctic Buoys, World Climate Research Prog; UK delg Arctic Ocean Sciences Bd, pres Cmmn for Sea Ice IAPSO; memb: Scientific Ctee European Environment Agency, SCAR Gp of Specialists on Climate Change, Working Gp on Global Change Int Arctic Science Ctee; awarded: W S Bruce Prize (Royal Soc of Edinburgh) 1977, Polar Medal 1987, Italgas Prize for Environmental Sciences (Italy) 1990; memb: Int Glaciological Soc 1970, American Geophysical Union 1976, Challenger Soc 1983, Remote Sensing Soc 1984; fell: Arctic Inst of N America 1983, Explorers' Club 1998; FRGS 1989; *Books* Ice Technology for Polar Operations (co-ed, 1990), Advances in Ice Technology (co-ed, 1992), Marine, Offshore and Ice Technology (co-ed, 1994), The Arctic and Environmental Change (co-ed, 1996), The Freshwater Budget of the Arctic Circle (co-ed, 2000), Ice in the Ocean (2000); *Recreations* painting, sailing; *Style*— Prof Peter Wadhams; ✉ Department of Applied Mathematics and Theoretical Physics (DAMTP), University of Cambridge, Centre for Mathematical Sciences, Wilberforce Road, Cambridge CB3 0WB (tel 01223 760372, fax 01223 760493, e-mail p.wadhams@damtp.cam.ac.uk); Laboratoire D'Océanographie de Villefranche, BP28, Villefranche-sur-Mer 06230, France (tel 00 33 06 93 76 38 02, e-mail wadhams@obs-vlfr.fr)

WADHWANI, Dr Sushil; CBE (2002); *b* 7 December 1959; *Educ* LSE (BSc, MSc, PhD); *Career* economist; reader/lectr LSE 1984–91, dir Equity Strategy Goldman Sachs Int 1991–95, dir of res Tudor Proprietary Trading 1995–99; external memb Monetary Policy Ctee 1999–2002; fund mangr Keynes Fund; visiting prof: City Univ Business Sch, LSE; *Style*— Dr Sushil Wadhwani, CBE; ✉ Wadhwani Asset Management, Warwick Court, 5 Paternoster Square, London EC4M 7DX (tel 020 7663 3400, fax 020 7663 3410, e-mail sushilw@waniasset.com)

WADIA, Jim; *Educ* Switzerland; *m* Joelle; 1 da (Jane), 1 s (Daniel); *Career* called to the Bar 1969, articled clerk Chalmers Impey (now Kidsons Impey), qualified CA 1973; Arthur Andersen: joined 1977, mangr 1978–82, ptnr 1982–, head of London Tax Practice 1989–93, managing ptnr UK practice 1993–97, memb Bd of Ptnrs Andersen Worldwide 1993–, worldwide managing ptnr 1997–2000; memb Royal Soc of Arts; *Recreations* sport (especially watching and playing tennis), theatre; *Style*— Jim Wadia, Esq; ✉ Worldwide Managing Partner, Arthur Andersen, 1 Surrey Street, London WC2R 2PS (tel 020 7438 3000, fax 020 7831 1133)

WADIA, Nina; da of Minoo Wadia, and Homai Wadia; *Educ* Island Sch Hong Kong, London Theatre Sch (Dip classical acting); *Career* comedienne and actress; supporter of numerous charities; *Theatre* credits incl: Romeo and Juliet (Theatre Royal, Stratford East), Macbeth (Globe Theatre), Alice in Wonderland, Vagina Monologues (West End); *Television* credits incl: Goodness Gracious Me (nomination Int Emmy Awards), Sita Gita (nomination Best Performance by a TV Actress Emma Awards), New Tricks, Waking the Dead, All About Me (shortlist Golden Rose Award 2004), Murder In Mind, Perfect World, Chambers, White Teeth, The Barftas, The Vicar of Dibley, Kiss Me Kate, The Stangerers, Holby City, The Bill, Casualty, Gandhi vs Gandhi, Freedom's Daughter; *Film* credits incl: Code 46, Sixth Happiness, Such a Long Journey, Flight, Cup & Lip, Gran, Shooting Cupid, Delivering Mina; *Radio credits* incl: The Tempest (BBC Radio 3), The Taming of the Shrew (BBC Radio 3), Westway (BBC World Serv); *Awards* Greatest Achievement by an Actress Soc for the Black Arts in Br 1994, Sony award 1997 and 1998, Br Comedy award 1998, Into Leadership Diversity award 2000, Cmmn for Racial Equality (CRE) award 2000 and 2001, Comic Heritage award 2000, Woman of Achievement Cosmopolitan Magazine 2000, BBC Asia 2001, Women in Film and Television, Asian Women of Achievement; *Recreations* sports, interior design, cooking, my husband; *Style*— Ms Nina Wadia; ✉ c/o Sarah MacCormick, Curtis Brown Ltd, Haymarket House, 28–29 Haymarket, London SW1Y 4SP (tel 020 7393 4474, fax 020 7393 4401, e-mail maccormick@curtisbrown.co.uk)

WADLEY, Veronica; da of Neville John Wadley, and Anne Hawise Colleton, *née* Bowring; *b* 28 February 1952; *Educ* Francis Holland Sch London, Benenden; *m* 1 June 1985, Tom Bower, s of George Bower; 1 da (Sophie b 18 April 1986), 1 s (Alexander b 4 Oct 1990); *Career* journalist; Condé Nast Publications 1971–74, Sunday Telegraph Magazine 1978–81, Mail on Sunday 1982–86; Daily Telegraph: features ed 1986–89, asst ed 1989–94, dep ed 1994–95; Daily Mail: assoc ed 1995–98, dep ed (features) 1998–2002; ed Evening Standard 2002–; *Style*— Miss Veronica Wadley; ✉ The Evening Standard, Northcliffe House, 2 Derry Street, Kensington, London W8 5EE

WADSWORTH, Brian; s of George and Betty Wadsworth; *b* 18 January 1952; *Educ* Univ of Br Columbia (BA); *m* 1987, Anne Jacqueline; *Career* princ BA, BAA, NBC privatisations 1986–89, sec BA plc 1989–91, sec Br Oxygen plc 1995; Dept of Tport: dir of finance 1995–97, dir Logistics and Maritime Tport 1999–2007, dir Strategic Roads, Planning and Nat Networks 2007–; chm: Consultative Shipping Gp 1999–, European Maritime Safety Agency 2003–, advsr on railway restructuring and privatisation World Bank; memb Glyndebourne Festival Soc; Liveryman: Worshipful Co of Carmen, Worshipful Co of Shipwrights; Freeman City of London 1997, FCILT, FRSA; *Books* Best Methods of Railway Restructuring and Privatisation (contrib, 1995); *Recreations* travel, opera, sailing; *Style*— Brian Wadsworth, Esq

WADSWORTH, David Grant; s of Fred Wadsworth (d 1960), and Lona, *née* Booth (d 1970); *b* 30 December 1944; *Educ* Hipperholme GS, Oriel Coll Oxford (MA), Univ of Newcastle upon Tyne (MPhil); *m* Marcia Armour, *née* Lyles; 1 step s (Robert James b 1980), 1 step da (Susanne Jane b 1984); *Career* teacher Glos and Blackpool 1966–73, admin posts Educn Dept Leeds City Cncl 1973–85, dep dir of educn Northumberland 1985–89, chief educn offr Beds 1989–96, chief exec Service Children's Educn 1997–; memb: Yorks CCC and RFU, Cambridge Univ RUFC, Army RFU; Hon DEd De Montfort Univ 1996; Chevalier de l'Ordre des Palmes Académiques 1992, Cavaliere dell'Ordine Al Merito della Repubblica Italiana 1994; *Recreations* rugby and cricket (passively), epicurean delights; *Clubs* Oxford and Cambridge; *Style*— David G Wadsworth, Esq; ✉ HQ SCE, BFPO 40

WADSWORTH, His Hon Judge James Patrick; QC (1981); s of Francis Thomas Bernard Wadsworth (d 1940), of Newcastle, and Geraldine Rosa, *née* Brannan (d 1953); *b* 7 September 1940; *Educ* Stonyhurst, Univ Coll Oxford (MA); *m* 1963, Judith, da of Morrison Scott, of Newport on Tay; 1 da (Katharine (Mrs Ousterman) b 1964), 1 s (Francis b 1967); *Career* called to the Bar Inner Temple 1963, bencher 1988, recorder of the Crown Ct 1980–, circuit judge (SE Circuit) 2000–; *Style*— His Hon Judge Wadsworth, QC; ✉ The Crown Court, English Grounds, London SE1 2HU

WADSWORTH, Roger Leonard; s of Leonard Wadsworth (d 1985), and Irene Nellie, *née* Hughes (d 2001); *b* 2 May 1950; *Educ* Hurstpierpoint Coll, Kingston Poly (BA); *m* 1988, Sandra Anne, da of R A Carney, of Barry County, MO; *Career* chm and md Wadsworth Holdings Ltd 1979–; chm: Wadsworth Electronics Ltd 1979–, Blazepoint Ltd 2000, Wadsworth Rugged Systems Ltd 2003; fndr and sec Knoydart Deer Mgmnt Gp 1988–93, nat tstee dir and vice-chm British Deer Soc 2002–; *Recreations* wildlife management, game and habitat conservation, stalking, shooting, Lusitano horses; *Clubs* RAC, Home House, Outrigger; *Style*— Roger Wadsworth, Esq; ✉ Wadsworth Holdings Ltd, Central Avenue, West Molesey, Surrey KT8 2QB (tel 020 8268 6500)

WAGNER, Erica; da of Arthur Malcolm Wagner, of NYC, and Ellen Franklin Wagner; *b* 24 September 1967; *Educ* The Brearley Sch NYC, St Paul's Girls' Sch, CCC Cambridge (BA), UEA (MA); *m* 23 Jan 1993, Francis Jonathan Gilbert, s of Peter Gilbert; 1 s (Theodore Malcolm b 24 July 2000); *Career* journalist; freelance ed, researcher and book reviewer 1992–95; The Times: asst to literary ed 1995–96, literary ed 1996–; judge Man Booker Prize 2002; *Books* Gravity: Stories (1997), Ariel's Gift: Ted Hughes, Sylvia Plath and the Story of Birthday Letters (2000), Seizure (novel, 2007); *Recreations* family life, stories, walking, fencing, bridges; *Style*— Ms Erica Wagner; ✉ The Times, 1 Pennington Street, London E98 1TT (tel 020 7782 5000, fax 020 7782 5126, e-mail erica.wagner@thetimes.co.uk)

WAGNER, Lady; Dame Gillian Mary Millicent; DBE (1994, OBE 1977); eldest da of Maj Henry Archibald Roger Graham (d 1970), and Hon Margaret Beatrice Lopes (d 1984), 3 da of 1 Baron Roborough; *b* 25 October 1927; *Educ* Cheltenham Ladies' Coll, Geneva Univ (Licence ès Sciences Morales), LSE (Dip Social Admin), Univ of London (PhD); *m* 26 Feb 1953, Sir Anthony Richard Wagner, KCB, KCVO (d 1995); 1 da (Lucy Elizabeth Millicent (Mrs Richard McCarraher) b 22 Oct 1954), 2 s (Roger Henry Melchior Wagner, *qv* b 28 Feb 1957, Mark Anthony b 18 Dec 1958); *Career* chm: Barnardo's 1978–84 (memb Cncl 1969–97), Review into Residential Care 1985–88, Thomas Coram Fndn 1990–95; pres: SKILL Nat Bureau for Students with Disabilities 1978–91, IAPS 1984–90, Nat Centre for Volunteering 1993– (chm 1984–89), Abbeyfield Soc 1996–2002, Abbeyfield UK 2003–; chm: Felixstowe Coll 1978–87, Leche Tst 1991–97, Carnegie UK Tst 1995–2000 (tstee 1980–2002); govr: Nat Inst for Social Work 1988–96, LSE 1991–96; tstee Princess Royal Tst for Carers 1992–2002; Freeman City of London; Hon DSocSc Univ of Bristol 1989, Hon LLD Univ of Liverpool 1990; *Books* Barnardo (1979), Children of the Empire (1982), The Chocolate Conscience (1987), Thomas Coram, Gent (2004); *Recreations* gardening, travelling; *Clubs* Athenaeum; *Style*— Dame Gillian Wagner, DBE; ✉ Flat 31, 55 Ebusy Street, London SW1W 0PA (tel 020 7730 0040)

WAGNER, Dr Nicholas Alan Giles; s of Thomas Donald Wagner, of Croydon, Surrey (d 1980), and Valerie Jacqueline Cameron Peers, *née* Kemp (d 2003), of Marlow, Bucks; step s of Roger Ernest Peers, CBE (sec of the King's Fund, d 1968), of London W11; *b* 17 January 1945; *Educ* Whitgift Sch, Bart's Med Coll London (MB BS); *m* Linda Iris, da of James Halstead (d 1999), of Brentford, Middx; 1 s (Alexander Jonathan Halstead); *Career* conslt psychiatrist W Middx Univ Hosp 1978–88, conslt in mental health for older people Herefords Primary Care NHS Tst 1988–2001; hon sr lectr Charing Cross and Westminster Med Sch 1984–88; med memb Mental Health Review Tbnl 2000–, second opinion appointed dr Mental Health Act Cmmn 2000–; chm Herefords Alzheimer's Soc 2003– (fndr chm 1989), chm W Midlands Assoc of Old Age Psychiatrists 1997–2001; DPM; FRCPsych; *CD-ROM* Depression and Dementia in Older People (academic contrib, 2004); *Recreations* food, gardening, motoring, wine; *Clubs* Porsche GB, 2CV GB, Jaguar Enthusiasts'; *Style*— Dr Nicholas Wagner, FRCPsych; ✉ Alzheimer's Society, Herefordshire Branch, 49 Breinton Road, Hereford HR4 0JY (tel 01432 371137)

WAGNER, Roger Henry Melchior; s of Sir Anthony Richard Wagner, KCB, KCVO (d 1995), and Dame Gillian Wagner, DBE, *qv*; *b* 28 February 1957; *Educ* Eton, Lincoln Coll Oxford (open scholar, MA), Royal Acad Schs; *m* 24 Oct 1998, Anne, da of Dr Towy Myrddin-Evans; *Career* artist; *Solo Exhibitions* incl: Anthony Mould Ltd 1985, 1988, 1995, 1999, 2000 and 2004, 42nd Aldeburgh Festival 1989, Ashmolean Museum Oxford 1994 (retrospective), Out of the Whirlwind: illustrations to the Book of Job (Bartlemas Chapel Oxford) 1995, touring exhbn to Ely Cathedral, Norwich Cathedral, St Edmundsbury Cathedral, Southwark Cathedral, Wells Cathedral, Chester Cathedral, The Chapel Royal Brighton, Mirfield Abbey and the Ark-T Centre 1997–2004, The Prince's Fndn 2001, Lady Margaret Hall Oxford 2004; *Group Exhibitions* incl: New Icons (Mead Gallery Univ of Warwick, The Royal Albert Museum Exeter and The Usher Gallery Lincoln) 1989–90, Images of Christ (Albermarle Gallery) 1991, Images of Christ (Northampton Museum and Art Gallery and St Paul's Cathedral) 1993, Europe: Art et Passages (Paris) 1999, The Light of the World (Edinburgh City Art Gallery) 1999–2000, The Salutation (Oxford) 2000, Blake's Heaven (Scholar Fine Art) 2000, Roads to Damascus (Eton Coll) 2002, Thomas Gibson Fine Art 2002, St Paul's Cathedral 2004, Art-T Centre 2004, Loughborough Univ 2004, The Queen's Coll Oxford 2006 and 2007; *Publications* Fire Sonnets (1984), In a Strange Land (1988), The Book of Praises (1994), A Silent Voice (1996), Out of the Whirlwind (1997); *Clubs* Reynolds; *Style*— Roger Wagner, Esq; ✉ e-mail rhmwagner@aol.com, website www.rogerwagner.co.uk; c/o Anthony Mould Ltd, 173 New Bond Street, London W1Y 9PB (tel 020 7491 4627, fax 020 7355 3865)

WAINE, David Michael; s of Capt Leslie Arthur Waine (d 1984), and Linda, *née* Pridmore; *b* 12 June 1944; *Educ* Reading Collegiate Sch; *m* 23 April 1966, Elizabeth Ann, da of John Halls (d 1967); 1 da (Nicola Frances b 1969); *Career* sports ed Newbury Weekly News 1960–64; BBC TV and radio reporter: Radio 4 Today prog, World at One, World Serv, TV news and current affrs, South Today, Points West 1964–67; BBC mgmnt: prog organiser Radio Brighton 1967–70, mangr Radio Bristol 1970–78, regnl TV mangr South West (Plymouth) 1978–83, head Network Prodn Centre Pebble Mill 1983–86, head of broadcasting Midlands 1986–92, head of broadcasting Midlands and East 1992–94; dir: Devpt Non-Metropolitan Radio 1994–2001, Television and Radio Trg Unit Ltd 2001–; ptnr David Waine Associates 1994–2003; pres Birmingham Press Club 1988–94; chm Birmingham Repertory Theatre Co 1996–2000 (dir 1993–96), chm Birmingham Media Devpt Agency/Screen Cmmn 1995–98; memb Birmingham C of E Diocesan Communications Advsy Gp 1995–; FRTS; *Recreations* sport, arts, gardening; *Style*— David Waine, Esq

WAINE, Peter Edward; s of Dr Theodore Edward Waine, of Bilton, Warks, and Mary Florence, *née* Goodson; *b* 27 June 1949; *Educ* Bilton Grange, Worksop Coll, Univ of Bradford (BSc); *m* 21 June 1973, Stefanie Dale, da of Philip Albert Snow, OBE, JP, of Angmering, W Sussex, and niece of late Baron Snow of Leicester, CBE (C P Snow, the author); 1 da (Philippa Wigmore b 21 May 1981); *Career* personnel mangr: GEC 1970–74, Cape Industries 1974–79, Coopers & Lybrand 1979–83; dir: CBI 1983–88, Blue Arrow 1988–90, W R Royle & Sons (non-exec) 1988–96, SSK Ltd 1994–98; co-fndr Hanson Green 1990–; non-exec chm: Corecare Ltd 1990–92, Arkley House Finance Ltd 1990–92, The Sales Training Co 1994–97; non-exec dir Quarto Gp 1998–; visiting fell Bradford Business Sch 1994; nat vice-chm The Bow Group 1972 (chm Birmingham Gp 1971), cncllr Rugby DC 1973–77, Parly candidate (Cons) Nottingham North 1979; non-exec dir: East Herts Dist Health Authy 1990–92, East Herts Tst 1994–96; memb Int Cricket Cncl 1994–2005; tstee: Royal Opera House 1999–2001; formerly: memb Current Affairs Ctee ESU, chm Brogdale Tst 2001–06, The Tree Cncl, Welwyn Garden City Soc, memb Cncl Euro Business Sch; visiting prof: Cass Business Sch London 2004–, Warwick Business Sch; Freeman: City of London 1978, Worshipful Co of Carmen; FIMgt (former memb Cncl); *Publications* Spring Cleaning Britain (1974), Withering Heights (1976), The Independent Board Director (with Dr David Clutterbuck, 1993), Takeover (with Mike Walker, 2000, trans 5 languages), The Board Game (2002); weekly columnist under pseudonym for London newspaper (1984–87); *Recreations* gardening, walking, tennis; *Clubs* MCC, Savile, Housman Soc; *Style*— Peter Waine, Esq; ✉ Hanson Green, 110 Park Street, London W1K 6NX (tel 020 7493 0837, fax 020 7355 1436)

WAINSCOAT, Prof James Stephen; s of Arnold John Wainscoat (d 2004), and Mary Hilda, *née* Bateman (d 1989); *b* 7 May 1949; *Educ* Holme Valley GS, Univ of Liverpool (MB ChB), Univ of Birmingham (MSc); *m* 14 Aug 1971, Beverly Susan, da of Walter Hannah (d 1987); 1 s (Luke), 2 da (Emma, Nancy); *Career* conslt haematologist Oxford Radcliffe Hosp 1985–, prof Univ of Oxford 1998– (sr lectr 1986–98), hon dir Molecular Haematology Unit Leukaemia Res Fund Univ of Oxford 1988–; FRCP 1991 (MRCP 1976),

FRCPath 1992 (MRCPath 1980); *Recreations* music, sport; *Style—* Prof James Wainscoat; ✉ Department of Haematology, Oxford Radcliffe Hospital, Headington, Oxford OX3 9DU (tel 01865 220330)

WAINWRIGHT, Dr (Anthony) Christopher; yr s of Robert Everard Wainwright, CMG (d 1990), of Shaftesbury, Dorset, and Bridget Doris, *née* Alan-Williams (d 2001); *b* 25 October 1943; *Educ* Marlborough, St Thomas' Hosp Univ of London (MB BS); *m* 6 Sept 1968, Ursula, da of Ernest Herbert Jeans (d 1977), 1 s (James b 1972 d 1998), 1 da (Sophie b 1975); *Career* sr registrar Univ Hosp Wales 1971–72, lectr in anaesthesia Univ of Bristol 1972–75, conslt anaesthetist Univ of Southampton Hosps and hon clinical teacher Univ of Southampton 1975–2006; memb: BMA, RSM; co fndr Wig and Scalpel Soc, former chm Copythorne Parish Cncl, memb New Forest Advsy Ctee Nat Tst; FRCA 1971; *Books* chapters in Lee's Synopsis of Anaesthesia, Anaesthesia Review 4 and Co2 Lasers in Otolaryngology; author of papers on ophthalmic anaesthesia; *Recreations* horses, music, medieval architecture; *Style—* Dr Christopher Wainwright; ✉ Ashton Cottage, Kewlake Lane, Cadnam, Southampton SO40 2NT

WAINWRIGHT, Faith Helen; da of Cdr Brian Hebden Wainwright, RN, and Anne Vera, *née* Temple; *b* 25 May 1962, Dunfermline, Fife; *Educ* Queen Anne's Caversham, St Edmund Hall Oxford (BA); *m* 2 July 1988, Kieran J Glynn, s of Brian J Glynn; 1 s (Brian b 17 July 1993), 2 da (Finola, Eleanor (twins) b 9 Aug 1995); *Career* structural engr; Arup: joined 1983, dir 1998–, skills network dir; memb Extreme Events Mitigation Task Force 2001–; memb: Standing Ctee on Structural Safety 2001–07, Cncl IStructE 2003–06, Jt Bd of Moderators 2004–, Ctee for Safety in Tall Buildings, Advsy Cncl Br Library 2004–; juror: BBC Design Awards 1996, OASYS Design Awards 2001; MInstD, FIStructE 2003 (MIStructE 1987), FREng 2003, FICE 2003; *Projects* incl: ITN London, Lycée Albert Camus Frejus, Western Morning News Plymouth, American Air Museum Duxford, Tate Modern London, Hongkong and Shanghai Banking Corp HQ Canary Wharf London, London Bridge Tower; *Style—* Ms Faith Wainwright; ✉ Arup, 13 Fitzroy Street, London W1T 4BQ (tel 020 7755 2051, fax 020 7755 2150, e-mail faith.wainwright@arup.com)

WAINWRIGHT, Geoffrey John; MBE; s of Frederick Wainwright, and Dorothy, *née* Worton; *b* 19 September 1937; *Educ* Pembroke Docks Sch, Univ of Wales, Univ of London; *m* 23 Dec 1977, Judith; 2 da (Rhiannon b 1961, Sarah b 1963), 1 s (Nicholas b 1966); *Career* prof of environmental archaeology Univ of Baroda India 1961–63, princ inspector of ancient monuments DOE 1980–89 (inspector 1963–80), chief archaeologist English Heritage 1989–99, fndr Bluestone Partnership 1999; visiting prof: Univ of Southampton 1991–, Inst of Archaeology UCL 1995–; Soc of Antiquaries: dir 1984–90, vice-pres 1997–2001, treas 2001–07, pres 2007–; vice-chm Royal Cmmn on Ancient Monuments (Wales) 1987–2002, pres Prehistoric Soc 1981–85, pres Cambrian Archeological Assoc 2002–03, chm Bd of Dirs Wessex Archaeology 2004–, memb Cncl Cambria Archaeology 2004–; hon memb European Archaeology Cncl 2000–; hon MIFA; fell Univ of Wales Coll of Cardiff 1985, hon fell Univ of Wales Lampeter 1996; FSA, FRSA; *Books* Coygan Camp (1967), Stone Age in India (1967), Durrington Walls (1971), Mount Pleasant (1979), Gussage All Saints (1979), The Henge Monuments (1989), Balksbury Camp Hampshire (1995); *Recreations* rugby, food and drink, walking; *Style—* Geoffrey Wainwright, Esq, MBE, FSA; ✉ Bluestone, 13 Park Cottages, Crown Road, Twickenham TW1 3EQ (tel 020 8891 2429, e-mail geoff@bluestone.eu.com)

WAITE, Charlie; s of Air Cdre R N Waite (d 1974), and Jessamy, *née* Lowenthal (d 2001); *b* 18 February 1949; *Educ* Salisbury Coll of Art; *m* 1974, Jessica, *née* Benton; 1 da (Ella Bahama b 8 Oct 1975); *Career* landscape photographic artist; early career in Br theatre and TV; over 250 lectures on landscape photography in UK; Hon FBIPP 2000; *Exhibitions* incl: London (five times), Tokyo (twice), Centre for Photographic Art Carmel CA 1999, Broadway NY 2002, OXO Gallery London 2002, 2003 and 2004; *Publications* National Trust Book of Long Walks (1982), Long Walks in France (1983), Landscape in Britain (1983), David Steel's Border Country (1984), English Country Towns (1984), The Loire (1985), Provence (1985), Languedoc (1985), Dordogne (1985), Villages in France (1986), Tuscany (1987), The Rhine (1987), Landscape in France (1988), Scottish Islands (1989), Charlie Waite's Venice (1989), Charlie Waite's Italian Landscapes (1990), Andalusia (1991), Lombardy (1991), Charlie Waite's Spanish Landscapes (1992), The Making of Landscape Photographs (1992), Seeing Landscapes (1999), In My Mind's Eye (2003); *Recreations* looking at river banks; *Style—* Charlie Waite, Esq; ✉ PO Box 1558, Gillingham, Dorset SP8 5RE (e-mail landscape@charliewaite.com, website www.charliewaite.com)

WAITE, (Winston Anthony) John; s of John Clifford Waite (d 1989), of Gawsworth, Cheshire, and Margaret Ada, *née* Van Schuyk-Smith; *b* 26 February 1951; *Educ* Wilmslow GS, Univ of Manchester (BA); *m* 13 July 1984, Cate Anne Valerie, da of Stuart-Campbell, of Islington, London; 2 s (Gulliver b 1994, Diggory b 1996), 2 da (Flossie b 1990, Jessica b 1991); *Career* BBC: graduate trainee 1973–76, TV and radio presenter 1976–; radio progs incl: Face the Facts (formerly, BBC Radio 4), You and Yours (BBC Radio 4); TV progs incl: On the Line (BBC 2), Wildlife Showcase (BBC 2); *Recreations* music, reading, wine; *Style—* John Waite, Esq; ✉ BBC Radio 4, Broadcasting House, London W1A 1AA

WAITE, Rt Hon Sir John Douglas Waite; kt (1982), PC (1993); s of Archibald Waite; *b* 3 July 1932; *Educ* Sherborne, CCC Cambridge; *m* 1966, Julia Mary, da of Joseph Tangye; 3 s and 2 step s; *Career* 2 Lt RA 1951–52; called to the Bar Gray's Inn 1956 (bencher 1981); QC 1975, judge of the High Court of Justice (Family Div) 1982–92, Lord Justice of Appeal 1993–97; pres Employment Appeal Tribunal 1983–85, presiding judge NE Circuit 1990–92; judge Court of Appeal Gibraltar 1997–2000; chm: UNICEF (UK) 1997–2004, UCL Hosp Charities 1997–2004; co-chair Ind Asylum Cmmn 2006–; *Style—* The Rt Hon Sir John Waite

WAITE, Jonathan Gilbert Stokes; QC (2002); s of Capt Henry David Stokes Waite, RN (d 2005), of Reigate, Surrey, and Joan Winifred, *née* Paull; *b* 15 February 1956; *Educ* Sherborne, Trinity Coll Cambridge (MA); *Career* called to the Bar Inner Temple 1978; in practice in common law SE Circuit 1979–; hon sec Bar Golfing Soc 1987–93; *Recreations* golf, bridge, wine, skiing; *Clubs* Woking Golf, Aldeburgh Golf, Rye Golf, Royal St George's Golf; *Style—* Jonathan Waite, Esq, QC; ✉ 76 Forthbridge Road, Battersea, London SW11 5NY (tel 020 7228 4488); Crown Office Chambers, 2 Crown Office Row, Temple, London EC4Y 7HJ (tel 020 7797 8100, fax 020 7797 8101, e-mail waite@crownofficechambers.com)

WAKE, Maj Sir Hereward; 14 Bt (E 1621), of Clevedon, Somerset, MC (1942), DL (Northants 1955); s of Maj-Gen Sir Hereward Wake, 13 Bt, CB, CMG, DSO, JP, DL (d 1963, himself tenth in descent from the 1 Bt; the latter was in turn fifteenth in descent from Hugh Wac or Wake, feudal Baron by tenure of Bourne and Deeping *temp* King Stephen; this family's descent from Hereward the Wake, albeit in the female line, seems probable although not proven); *b* 7 October 1916; *Educ* Eton, RMC; *m* 1952, Julia Rosemary, JP, DL, da of Capt Geoffrey W M Lees, of Falcutt House, nr Brackley, Northants; 1 s, 3 da; *Heir* s, Hereward Charles Wake; *Career* served 1937–46 with 1, 2, 7 and 9 Bns 60 Rifles (Burma, Egypt, N Africa, NW Europe and Greece), Maj, ret 1947; studied agric and land agency; High Sheriff Northants 1955, Vice Lord-Lt Northamptonshire 1984–91; pres: Northamptonshire Record Soc, Northamptonshire Normany Veterans Assoc; patron: Northamptonshire Assoc of Youth Clubs, Northamptonshire GS; fell Univ of Northampton; Liveryman Worshipful Co of Merchant Taylors; *Style—* Maj Sir Hereward Wake, Bt, MC, DL

WAKE-WALKER, David Christopher; s of Capt Christopher Baldwin Hughes Wake-Walker, RN (d 1998), and Lady Anne, da of 7 Earl Spencer; 1 cous to Diana, Princess of Wales (d 1997); *b* 11 March 1947; *Educ* Winchester, Univ of St Andrews (MA); *m* 1979, Jennifer Rosemary, only da of Capt Patrick Vaulkhard (d 1995); 2 s (Frederic b 1981, Nicholas b 1985); *Career* dir Kleinwort Benson Ltd 1981–1995 (joined 1969), md Kleinwort Benson (Hong Kong) Ltd 1983–86, dir Kleinwort Benson Gp plc 1990–95, dir Dentons Pension Management Ltd 2001–06, dir Meridian Petroleum plc 2006–, chm Delsol Ltd 2001–; chm Orwell Park Sch 1997–; chm SFCorp Ltd 2004–; ACIB 1972; *Clubs* Wanderers, Aldeburgh Yacht, Hong Kong, Shek O Country, Hurlingham; *Style—* David Wake-Walker Esq; ✉ 82 Royal Hill, London SE10 8RT (tel and fax 020 8691 4666); 7 Trebeck Street, London W1J 7LU (tel 020 7409 7233, fax 020 7408 0783, e-mail david@wake-walker.com)

WAKEFIELD, Her Hon Anne Prudence; da of John Arkell Wakefield (d 1995), of Burford, Oxon, and Stella Adelaide, *née* Rees; *b* 25 May 1943; *Educ* Burford Sch, LSE (LLB), Newnham Coll Cambridge (LLM, Dip Criminology); *m* 1974 (m dis 2002), Robert Reid, s of John Reid; 2 s (Edward James b 1976, David Robert b 1978), 1 da (Sarah Anne b 1980); *Career* called to the Bar Gray's Inn 1968; asst recorder 1991, recorder 1995, circuit judge (SE Circuit) 1999–2005; assoc Newnham Coll Cambridge; FRSA; *Style—* Her Hon Anne Wakefield

WAKEFIELD, Dean of; *see:* Nairn-Briggs, Very Rev George Peter

WAKEFIELD, Sir (Edward) Humphry Tyrrell; 2 Bt (UK 1962), of Kendal, Co Westmorland; s of Sir Edward Birkbeck Wakefield, 1 Bt, CIE (d 1969, himself yr bro of 1 Baron Wakefield of Kendal); *b* 11 July 1936; *Educ* Gordonstoun, Trinity Coll Cambridge (MA); *m* 1, 1960 (m dis 1964), Priscilla, da of (Oliver) Robin Bagot; m 2, 1966 (m dis 1971), Hon Elizabeth Sophia Sidney, da of 1 Viscount De L'Isle, VC, KG, GCMG, GCVO, PC; 1 s; m 3, 1974, Hon Katherine Mary Alice Baring, da of 1 Baron Howick of Glendale, KG, GCMG, KCVO (d 1973); 1 s (and 1 s decd), 1 da; *Heir* s, Capt Maximilian Wakefield, Royal Hussars (PWO); *Career* Capt 10 Royal Hussars; fndr Stately Homes Collection, exec vice-pres Mallett America Ltd 1970–75, former dir Mallett & Son (Antiques) Ltd; chm: Tyrrell & Moore Ltd 1975–91, Sir Humphry Wakefield & Partners Ltd; former dir Spoleto Festival, dir Tree of Life Fndn (UK charity), chm Wilderness Fndn, memb Standing Cncl of the Baronetage; pres: Northumberland Mountain Rescue Services, Avison Tst, Tibetan Spaniel Assoc; patron: Actors Centre (North), Medicine and Chernobyl, Shadow Dance; memb: Soc of the Dilettante, Surtees Soc; tstee Chillingham Wild Cattle Assoc; joined membs of NZ Everest Expedition on their first ascent of Mt Wakefield NZ 1992 (and subsequently on Everest Expedition), memb Mt Vaughan Antarctic Expedition 1994; fell Pierrepont Morgan Library USA; FRGS; Freedom of Kansas City, hon citizen Cities of Houston and New Orleans, Hon Col Louisiana; *Publications* author of numerous articles on antique furniture and architecture; *Clubs* Harlequins, Beefsteak, Cavalry and Guards', Turf, Scott Polar; *Style—* Sir Humphry Wakefield, Bt; ✉ Chillingham Castle, Chillingham, Northumberland NE66 5NJ; c/o Barclays Bank, St James's Street, Derby DE1 1QU

WAKEFIELD, His Hon Judge Robert; *b* 14 February 1946; *Educ* Univ of Birmingham (LLB), Brasenose Coll Oxford (BCL); *Career* called to the Bar Middle Temple 1969, recorder 1993–96, circuit judge (SE Circuit) 1996–; *Style—* His Hon Judge Wakefield; ✉ Inner London Crown Court, Sessions House, Newington Causeway, London SE1 6AZ (tel 020 7234 3100)

WAKEFIELD, Bishop of 2003–; Rt Rev Stephen George Platten; s of Capt George Henry Platten, RM (d 1969), of Enfield, Middx, and Marjory Agnes, *née* Sheward (d 2000); *b* 17 May 1947; *Educ* Stationers' Co's Sch, Univ of London (BEd), Trinity Coll Oxford (DipTh, BD), Cuddesdon Theol Coll; *m* 1 April 1972, Rosslie, da of David Robert Thompson, of Newbury, Berks; 2 s (Aidan Stephen George b 1976, Gregory Austin David b 1978); *Career* with Shell International Petroleum Co Ltd 1966–68; ordained: deacon 1975, priest 1976; asst curate St Andrew Headington Oxford 1975–78, chaplain and tutor Lincoln Theol Coll 1978–82, diocesan dir of ordinands and canon residentiary Portsmouth Cathedral 1983–89, dir of post-ordination trg and continuing ministerial educn Dio of Portsmouth 1984–89, hon canon Canterbury Cathedral 1990–95, Archbishop of Canterbury's sec for ecumenical affairs 1990–95, anglican sec Anglican-RC International Cmmn (II) 1990–95, dean of Norwich 1995–2003; min provincial Euro Province 3 Order Soc of St Francis 1991–96; chm C of E Liturgical Cmmn 2005–; chm Soc for Study of Christian Ethics 1983–88, guestmaster Nikaean Club 1990–95, dir SCM Press 1990–, chm SCM-Canterbury Press 2001–; memb Cncl Hymns Ancient and Modern 1998–; Hon DLitt UEA 2003; *Books* Deacons in the Ministry of the Church (contrib, 1987), Ethics - Our Choices (sr ed, 1989), Say One for Me (contrib, ed A W Carr, 1992), Pilgrims (1996), Spirit and Tradition: An Essay on Change (with George Pattison, 1996), Augustine's Legacy: Authority and Leadership in Anglicanism (1997), New Soundings (ed with Graham James and Andrew Chandler, 1997), Flagships of the Spirit (ed with Christopher Lewis, 1998), Seeing Ourselves (ed and contrib, 1998), The Pilgrim Guide to Norwich (1998), The Retreat of the State (ed and contrib, 1999), Ink and Spirit (ed and contrib, 2000), Runcie: On Reflection (2002), Open Government (ed, 2003), Anglicanism and the Western Christian Tradition (ed and contrib, 2003), Dreaming Spires: Cathedrals and a New Age (ed and contrib); author of contribs to theol and educnl jls; *Recreations* reading, music, walking, Northumberland; *Clubs* Athenaeum, Norfolk; *Style—* The Rt Rev the Bishop of Wakefield; ✉ Bishop's Lodge, Woodthorpe Lane, Wakefield, West Yorkshire WF2 6JL (tel 01924 255349, fax 01924 250202, e-mail bishop@bishopofwakefield.org.uk)

WAKEFORD, Richard; *Educ* KCL (BSc); *m* 1976; 3 s; *Career* various posts DOE 1975–87; Nuffield and Leverhulme fell Woodrow Wilson Sch of Public and Int Affairs Princeton Univ 1987–88; DOE: princ mangr Water Bill (privatisation) 1988–89, memb team on Environment White Paper This Common Inheritance 1989–90, last chief exec Crown Suppliers 1990–91, head Devpt Plans and Policies Div 1991–94; asst sec Econ and Domestic Affairs Secretariat Cabinet Office 1994–96; chief exec Countryside Agency (formerly Countryside Cmmn) 1996–2005, head Environment and Rural Affrs Dept Scottish Exec 2005–; memb UK Sustainable Devpt Cmmn 1999–2004; Hon Dr Univ of Glos 2002; FRSA, Hon MRTPI 2002; *Publications* Speeding Planning Appeals: Report of an Efficiency Scrutiny into Written Representations Planning Appeals (1986), American Development Control: Parallels and Paradoxes from an English Perspective (1990); author of articles for Urban Lawyer; *Recreations* gardens, walking, cycling, taking pictures; *Style—* Richard Wakeford, Esq

WAKEHAM, Baron (Life Peer UK 1992), of Maldon in the County of Essex; John Wakeham; PC (1983), JP (Inner London 1972), DL (Hants 1997); s of Maj Walter John Wakeham (d 1965), of Godalming, Surrey; *b* 22 June 1932; *Educ* Charterhouse; *m* 1, 1965, Anne Roberta (k 1984), da of late Harold Edwin Bailey; 2 adopted s (Jonathan Martin b 1972, Benedict Ian b 1975); m 2, 1985, Alison Bridget, MBE, da of Ven Edwin James Greenfield Ward, LVO; 1 s (Hon David Robert b 1987); *Career* CA; contested (Cons): Coventry East 1966, Putney Wandsworth 1970; MP (Cons): Maldon 1974–83, Colchester S and Maldon 1983–92; asst Govt whip 1979–81, a Lord Cmmr to the Treasy (Govt whip) 1981, under sec of state for Industry 1981–82, min of state Treasy 1982–83, Parly sec to the Treasy and chief whip 1983–87, Lord Privy Seal 1987–88, Lord Pres of the Cncl 1988–89, ldr of the House of Commons 1987–89, sec of state for Energy 1989–92, responsible for devpt of presentation of Govt policies 1990–92, Lord Privy Seal and ldr of the House of Lords 1992–94; chair Royal Cmmn on the reform of House of Lords 1999; chm: PCC 1995–2002, British Horseracing Bd 1996–98 (memb 1995); chllr Brunel Univ 1997–; tstee HMS Warrior 1860 1997–; pres GamCare 1997–2002; chm Alexandra Rose Day 1998–; govr: Sutton's Hosp Charterhouse 1992, St Swithun's Sch 1994–2002; *Recreations* sailing, racing, reading; *Clubs* Buck's, Carlton (chm 1992–98), Garrick, Royal

Yacht Squadron, St Stephen's Constitutional; *Style*— The Rt Hon Lord Wakeham, PC, DL, FCA; ✉ House of Lords, London SW1A 0PW (tel 020 8767 6931)

WAKEHAM, Prof William Arnot; s of Stanley William Wakeham (d 1969), of Bristol, and Winifred Gladys, *née* Crocker (d 1946); *b* 25 September 1944; *Educ* Bristol Cathedral Sch, Univ of Exeter (BSc, PhD, DSc); *m* 1, 1969 (m dis 1978), Christina Marjorie, da of Kenneth Stone, of Weymouth, Dorset; 1 s (Leigh b 1974); m 2, 23 Dec 1978, Sylvia Frances Tolley; 2 s (Russell Jon b 1983, Nicholas Ashley b 1986); *Career* research assoc Brown Univ USA 1969–71; Imperial Coll London: lectr dept of chemical engrg 1971–79, reader in chemical physics of fluids 1979–85, prof of chemical physics 1985–2001, head Dept of Chemical Engrg 1988–96, pro-rector (research) 1996, pro-rector (resources) 1999, dep rector 1997–2001; vice-chllr Univ of Southampton 2001–; memb: SEEDA 2004–, EPSRC 2005–; Touloukian medal American Soc of Mechanical Engrs, Rossini lectr, Ared Cezairliyan lectr; Hon DSc: Lisbon Univ, Univ of Exeter; Hon DEd Southampton Solent Univ; CEng, CPhys; FIChemE, FInstP, FIEE, FCGI, FIC, FREng 1997; *Books* Intermolecular Forces: Their Origin and Determination (1981), The Forces Between Molecules (1986), The Transport Properties of Fluids (1989), International Thermodynamic Tables of the Fluid State: Vol 10 - Ethylene (1989), Measurement of the Transport Properties of Fluids (1991), Status and Future Developments in the Study of Transport Properties (1992), Measurement of the Thermodynamic Properties of Single Phases (2003); *Recreations* waterskiing; *Clubs* Athenaeum; *Style*— Prof William Wakeham, FREng; ✉ University of Southampton, Highfield, Southampton SO17 1BJ (tel 023 8059 2801, fax 023 8059 3159, e-mail vice-chancellor@soton.ac.uk)

WAKEHURST, 3 Baron (UK 1934); (John) Christopher Loder; s of 2 Baron Wakehurst, KG, KCMG (d 1970), and Margaret, Lady Wakehurst, DBE, *née* Tennant (d 1994); *b* 23 September 1925; *Educ* Eton, King's Sch Sydney, Trinity Coll Cambridge (MA, LLB); *m* 1, 27 Oct 1956, Ingeborg (d 1977), da of Walther Krumbholz; 1 s (Hon Timothy Walter b 28 March 1958), 1 da (Hon Christina Anne b 13 Dec 1959); m 2, 10 Sept 1983, (Francine) Brigid, da of William Noble, of Cirencester, Glos; *Heir* s, Hon Timothy Loder; *Career* serv WWII RANVR and RNVR; called to the Bar 1950; chm: Anglo & Overseas Tst plc until 1996, The Overseas Investment Tst plc until 1995, Morgan Grenfell Equity Income Tst plc until 1995; dep chm London and Manchester Gp plc until 1995; dir Morgan Grenfell Latin American Companies Tst plc until 1996; *Clubs* Chelsea Arts; *Style*— The Rt Hon the Lord Wakehurst; ✉ Trillinghurst Oast, Ranters Lane, Goudhurst, Kent TN17 1HL (tel 01580 211502)

WAKELEY, Amanda Jane; da of Sir John Cecil Nicholson Wakeley, 2 Bt, *qv*; *b* 15 September 1962; *Educ* Cheltenham Ladies' Coll; *Career* fashion designer; early career experience working in fashion indust NY 1983–85, in business working for private cmmns 1987–90, fndr Amanda Wakeley label 1990; collections sold in England, Europe, USA, Far East and Middle East, opened flagship shop Chelsea Sept 1993; co-chair Fashion Targets Breast Cancer Appeal 1996– (raised over £5 million); winner Glamour category British Fashion Awards 1992, 1993 and 1996; *Recreations* water-skiing, snow-skiing, driving, horseback riding, travel, photography; *Style*— Miss Amanda Wakeley; ✉ 7 Old Park Lane, London W1K 1QR (tel 020 7529 0933, e-mail ajw@amandawakely.com)

WAKELEY, Sir John Cecil Nicholson; 2 Bt (UK 1952), of Liss, Co Southampton; s of Sir Cecil Pembrey Grey Wakeley, 1 Bt, KBE, CB, FRCS (d 1979), and Dr Elizabeth Muriel Wakeley, *née* Nicholson-Smith (d 1985); *b* 27 August 1926; *Educ* Canford, Univ of London (MB BS); *m* 10 April 1954, June, o da of Donald Frank Leney; 2 s (Nicholas, Charles), 1 da (Amanda Wakeley, *qv*); *Heir* s, Nicholas Wakeley; *Career* past appts: chief inspr City of London Special Constabulary, sr consulting surgn W Cheshire Gp of Hosps; formerly memb: Liverpool Regional Hosp Bd, Mersey RHA, Cncl Royal Coll of Surgns of Eng; hon conslt advsr (civilian) to RAF; Liveryman: Worshipful Co of Barbers, Worshipful Soc of Apothecaries; FRCS, FACS; CStJ 1957; *Recreations* photography, music, model railway; *Style*— Sir John Wakeley, Bt; ✉ Croxton Green Cottage, Croxton Green, Cholmondley, Malpas, Cheshire SY14 8HG (tel 01829 720530)

WAKELEY, Robin Anthony Wade; GSM (1955); s of Leslie Stuart Pembrey Wakeley (d 1961), of Welwyn Garden City, Herts, and Mary Louise Lloyd, *née* Wade; *b* 1 March 1937; *Educ* Hitchin GS for Boys, King's Coll London, King's Coll Hosp (BDS, Prosthetics prize); *m* 1, 1964 (m dis 1980), Pamela Margaret, da of Trevor James; 1 s (Roderick Stuart James b 15 Oct 1965), 2 da (Annabel Jane b 29 June 1967, Sophie Louise Wade b 1 Nov 1971); m 2, 1987, Carolyn, da of Frank Dakin; *Career* Nat Serv; res house surgn King's Coll Hosp 1964, pt/t lectr Guy's Hosp 1967–71 (pt/t registrar 1965–67), in private practice Harley Street 1971– (pt/t private practice 1965–71); Freeman City of London, Liveryman Worshipful Soc of Apothecaries 1976; *Recreations* golf, walking, collecting antiques; *Clubs* Reform; *Style*— Robin Wakeley, Esq

WAKELEY, Timothy Grey (Tim); s of late William Grey Pembury Wakeley, Fitzalan Court, Rustington, W Sussex, and Daisy Lillian, *née* Poole; *b* 13 December 1943; *Educ* Carshalton Coll; *m* 29 April 1967, Anne Caroline Duyland, da of Adm Sir John Fitzroy Duyland Bush, GCB; 2 s (Oliver Grey b 20 Aug 1969, Adam Grey b 2 Oct 1978), 2 da (Fenella Duyland b 8 April 1971, Melissa Emily (twin) b 2 Oct 1978); *Career* ptnr W Greenwell & Co 1972–86 (trainee 1961), md Greenwell Montagu Stockbrokers 1986–92, md James Capel & Co 2001–03 (investment mgmnt dir 1993–2001); assoc memb Soc of Investment Analysts, MSI; *Recreations* tennis, fly fishing, skiing, vintage cars; *Clubs* City of London; *Style*— Tim Wakeley, Esq; ✉ Little Green, Thursley, Godalming, Surrey GU8 6QE (tel 01252 702320); 14 Arnold Mansions, Queen's Club Gardens, London W14 9RD (tel 020 7381 4948)

WAKELIN, Dr (Alexander) Peter; s of Richard Langford Wakelin (d 1987), and Rosemary Margaret, *née* Culley (d 1998); *b* 13 February 1962, Swansea; *Educ* Olchfa Comp Sch Swansea, Swansea Coll of Art, Keble Coll Oxford (BA, proxime accessit Henry Oliver Beckitt Dissertation Prize), Ironbridge Gorge Museum/Univ of Birmingham (MSocSci), Wolverhampton Poly (PhD); *partner* Clive Hicks-Jenkins; *Career* Wolverhampton Poly: res asst Sch of Humanities and Cultural Studies 1984–88, dir and ESRC named res fell Portbooks Prog Faculty of Arts Wolverhampton Poly 1988–90; inspr of ancient monuments and historic bldgs Cadw 1990–2003, head Regeneration Unit Communities Directorate Welsh Assembly Govt 2003–05, sec Royal Cmmn on the Ancient and Hist Monuments of Wales 2005–; memb: Cncl Assoc for Industrial Archaeology 1986–95, UK Ctee Assoc for History and Computing 1987–90; Cncl for British Archaeology: memb Res and Conservation Ctee 1995–2000, memb Pubns Ctee 2000–; ed Industrial Archaeology News 1988–95, memb Editorial Bd Industrial Archaeology Review 1995–; Contemporary Art Soc for Wales: memb Exec Ctee 1998–, purchaser 2002; advsr Richard and Rosemary Wakelin Purchase Award Glynn Vivian Art Gallery Swansea 1999–, memb Advsy Bd Planet: The Welsh Internationalist 2004–; hon fell Univ of Wales Sch of Art Aberystwyth 2004–; FSA 2002; *Publications* incl: The Encyclopaedia of Industrial Archaeology (contrib, 1992), The Gloucester Coastal Port Books 1575–1765: A summary (co-author, 1995, database on CD-ROM 1998), Collieries of Wales: Engineering and Architecture (co-author, 1995), Creating an Art Community: 50 Years of the Welsh Group (1999), Glenys Cour: Paintings and Works on Paper 1980–2003 (co-author, 2003), An Art-Accustomed Eye: John Gibbs and Art Appreciation in Wales 1945–1996 (2004), A Guide to Blaenavon Ironworks and World Heritage Site (2006), The Painter's Quarry: The Art of Peter Prendergast (co-author, 2006); author of articles in jls and newspapers and chapters in books incl New Dictionary of National Biography, Industrial Archaeology Review, Archaeologica Cambrensis, The Local Historian, Landscape History, Design History, Art Review, The Guardian and Heritage in Wales; *Recreations* writing, sea-kayaking; *Style*— Dr Peter Wakelin; ✉ Royal Commission on the Ancient and Historical Monuments of Wales, Crown Building, Plas Crug, Aberystwyth, Ceredigion SY23 1NJ (tel 01970 621202)

WAKELING, Richard Keith Arthur; s of late Eric George Wakeling, and late Dorothy Ethel Wakeling; *b* 19 November 1946; *Educ* Enfield GS, Churchill Coll Cambridge (prize scholar, MA); *m* 9 Oct 1971, Carmen; 3 s (Simon, David, Nicholas); *Career* called to the Bar Inner Temple 1971; gp treas BOC Group plc 1977–83, fin dir John Brown plc 1983–86; Charter Consolidated plc: fin dir 1986–88, acting chief exec 1988–89; Johnson Matthey plc: dep chief exec 1990, chief exec 1991–94; chm Polar Capital Technology Tst plc, dep chm Celtic Group Holdings Ltd 1994–97; non-exec dir: Costain Group plc 1992–96, Laura Ashley Holdings plc 1994–95, Staveley Industries plc 1995–99, Logica plc 1995–2002, Oxford Instruments plc 1995–2001, Bain Hogg Group plc 1996–97, MG plc 1999–2000, Henderson Geared Income and Growth Tst plc 1995–2003, Brunner Investment Tst plc; FCT; *Recreations* medieval history and architecture, golf, gardening; *Style*— Richard Wakeling, Esq; ✉ 46 The Bourne, Southgate, London N14 6QS (tel and fax 020 8886 8143)

WAKEMAN, Sir Edward Offley Bertram; 6 Bt (UK 1828), of Perdiswell Hall, Worcestershire; s of Capt Sir Offley Wakeman, 4 Bt, CBE (d 1975), and his 2 w, Josceline Etheldreda, *née* Mitford (d 1996, in her 103rd year); suc his half-bro Sir (Offley) David Wakeman, 5 Bt 1991; *b* 31 July 1934; *Heir* none; *Style*— Sir Edward Wakeman, Bt

WAKEMAN, Eur Ing Prof Richard John; s of Ronald Wakeman, of Exmouth, Devon, and Kathleen, *née* Smith; *b* 15 April 1948; *Educ* King Edward VI GS Bury St Edmunds, UMIST (BSc, MSc, PhD); *m* 24 July 1971, Patricia Joan, da of Jack Morris; 2 s (Simon Richard b 24 June 1976, Mark Andrew b 4 April 1979); *Career* Lennig Chemicals Ltd: chemical engr 1970, conslt engr 1972–; research asst UMIST 1972–73; Univ of Exeter: lectr 1973–86, reader in particle technol 1986–90, prof of process engrg 1990–95; Loughborough Univ: prof of chemical engrg 1995– (assoc dean of engrg 1997–2000), head of chemical engrg 2000–; visiting engr Univ of Calif Berkeley 1980, visiting prof Univ of Pardubice 2004–; Filtration Soc: memb Cncl 1982–89, chm 1987–89, tstee 1989–, hon sec 2000–; chm Working Party Euro Fedn of Chemical Engrs 1996– (memb 1984–); exec ed The Transactions of the Institution of Chemical Engrs 1999–; non-exec dir: The Filtration Society Ltd 1983–89 and 2000–, Exeter Enterprises Ltd 1987–90; author of over 450 research articles, patents and books/book contribs 1971–; Suttle Award Filtration Soc 1971, Moulton Medal IChemE 1991 and 1995 (Jr Moulton Medal 1978), Gold Medal Filtration Soc 1993, 2003 and 2005, Chemical Weekly Award Indian Inst of Chemical Engrs 2004; CEng 1977, FIChemE 1989 (MIChemE 1977), Eur Ing 1989, FREng 1996, CSci 2004; *Recreations* philately, antiquities, industrial archaeology; *Style*— Eur Ing Prof Richard Wakeman, FREng; ✉ 5 Henry Dane Way, Newbold, Coalville, Leicestershire LE67 8PP (tel and fax 01530 223124); Department of Chemical Engineering, Loughborough University, Loughborough, Leicestershire LE11 3TU (tel 01509 222500, fax 01509 223923, mobile 0779 706021, e-mail r.j.wakeman@lboro.ac.uk)

WALBRAN, Sandra; *née* Holdsworth; *b* 25 July 1965, Bradford, W Yorks; *Educ* Univ of Salford (BSc), Univ of Humberside (MSc), Univ of Bradford (Cert), Huddersfield Poly (Cert); *m* 2 Sept 2005, Robin Moore; *Career* Bradford MDC: environmental health offr 1987–92, environmental health mangr 1992–2002; South Lakeland DC: food and safety mangr 2002–04, improvement mangr 2004–05, head of strategy and performance 2005–, corp change mangr 2007–; memb Bd Food Standards Agency 2002–; memb Lacors Food Hygiene Gp and Policy Forum 1992–2002; memb Chartered Inst of Environmental Health 1987; *Recreations* outdoor pursuits incl fell walking, running, mountain biking, skiing and sailing; *Clubs* Achille Ratti Climbing; *Style*— Mrs Sandra Walbran; ✉ South Lakeland District Council, South Lakeland House, Lowther Street, Kendal, Cumbria LA9 4UD (tel 01539 797589, e-mail s.walbran@southlakeland.gov.uk)

WALCOTT, Theodore (Theo); *b* 16 March 1989, London; *Career* professional footballer; clubs: Southampton 2004–06, Arsenal 2006–; England: 1 cap, debut v Hungary 2006 (youngest player to represent England), memb squad World Cup 2006; *Style*— Theo Walcott, Esq; ✉ c/o Arsenal FC, Arsenal Stadium, Highbury, London N5 1BU

WALD, Prof Nicholas John; s of Adolf Max Wald, of London, and Frieda Shatsow (d 1986); *b* 31 May 1944; *Educ* Owen's Sch, UCH (MB BS), Univ of London (DSc); *m* 2 Jan 1966, Nancy Evelyn, *née* Miller; 1 da (Karen b 1966), 3 s (David b 1968, Richard b 1971, Jonathan b 1977); *Career* MRC Epidemiology and Med Care Unit 1971– (memb sci staff), ICRF Cancer Epidemiology and Clinical Trials Unit Oxford 1972–83, prof and head of Centre for Environmental and Preventive Med Bart's 1983– (dir Wolfson Inst of Preventive Medicine 1992–95 and 1997–); ed-in-chief Jl of Medical Screening (inaugural ed) 1994–; hon dir Cancer Research Campaign Screening Gp 1986–2000, hon conslt East London & City and Oxford RHA's; Advsy Cncl on Sci and Technol: memb Med Res and Health Ctee 1991–92; MRC: memb Steering Ctee of the MRC Study on Multivitamins and Neural-Tube Defects 1982–92, chm Smoking Review Working Gp 1986–90, chm Study Monitoring Ctee of the MRC Randomised Clinical Trial of Colo-Rectal Cancer Screening 1986–, chm Steering Ctee for Multicentre Aneurysm Screening Study 1997–; Dept of Health: memb Advsy Ctee on Breast Cancer Screening 1986–99, memb Ind Sci Ctee on Smoking and Health 1983–91, Central Research and Devpt Ctee 1991–96, memb Chief Medical Offr's Health of the Nation Working Gp 1991–97, memb Chief Medical Offr's Advsy Gp on Folate Supplementation in the Prevention of Neural Tube Defects 1991–92, memb Scientific Ctee on Tobacco and Health 1993–2002, memb Advsy Ctee on Cervical Screening 1996–99, memb Medicines Control Agency Expert Advsy Panel 1996–, Population Screening Panel 1993–1998, Ctee on Med Aspects of Food and Nutrition Policy, Working Gp of Nutritional Status of Population, Folic Acid Subgroup 1996–2000, Ctee Nat Screening, Antenatal Subgroup 1997, HPV/LBC Pilots Steering Gp 2000–03, Advsy Gp for the Evaluation of UK Colorectal Cancer Screening Pilot 2000–03; Royal Coll of Physicians: memb Ctee on Ethical Issues in Medicine 1988–, memb Sub-Ctee on Ethical Issues in Clinical Genetics 1988–91, memb Special Advsy Gp to Med Info Technol Ctee 1984–94; NE Thames RHA: memb Clinical Genetics Advsy Sub-Ctee 1984–1992, memb Dist Res Ethics Ctee 1990–95, memb Cncl Coronary Prevention Gp 1993–94; memb: Action on Smoking and Health Res Ctee 1982–91, Wellcome Trust Physiology and Pharmacology Panel 1995–2000, Nuclear Test Veterans Advsy Gp Nat Radiological Bd 2000–04, Faculty of Public Health Info Sub-Ctee 2001–05, Lung Cancer Gp Nat Cancer Res Network 2001–05, WHO Working Gp on Methodologies of Non-Communicable Disease Screening 2001–, Bd of Dirs Int Soc of Prenatal Diagnosis; Nat Ctee for Clinical Lab Standards (NCCLS), Sub-Ctee on Maternal Serum Screening 2001–; memb Editorial Bd Prenatal Diagnosis; FFPH 1982, FRCP 1986, FRCOG 1992, FMedSci 1998, CBiol, FIBiol 2000, FRS 2004; *Awards* William Julius Mickle Fellowship 1990, Kennedy Fndn Int Award in Scientific Research 2000, US Public Health Service and Centers for Disease Control Award (jtly with Richard Smithells) 2002; *Books* Alpha-Fetoprotein Screening - The Current Issues (ed with J E Haddow, 1981), Antenatal and Neonatal Screening (ed, 1984, 2 edn (ed with I Leck) 2000), Interpretation of Negative Epidemiological Evidence for Carcinogenicity (ed with R Doll, 1985), The Epidemiological Approach (1985, 4 edn 2004), UK Smoking Statistics (jt ed, 1988 and 1991), Nicotine Smoking and the Low Tar Programme (ed with P Froggatt, 1989), Smoking and Hormone Related Disorders (ed with J Baron, 1990), Passive Smoking: A Health Hazard (jt ed, 1991), International Smoking Statistics (co-author, 1994); *Recreations* boating, economics; *Clubs* Athenaeum; *Style*— Prof Nicholas Wald; ✉ Centre for Environmental and Preventive Medicine, Wolfson Institute of Preventive Medicine, Bart's and The London,

Queen Mary School of Medicine and Dentistry, Charterhouse Square, London EC1M 6BQ (tel 020 7882 6269, fax 020 7882 6270, e-mail n.j.wald@qmul.ac.uk)

WALDEGRAVE, Lady (Linda Margaret) Caroline; OBE (2000); da of Maj Richard Burrows, of Tunbridge Wells, Kent, and Molly, *née* Hollins; *b* 14 August 1952; *Educ* Convent of the Sacred Heart Woldingham, Cordon Bleu Sch of Cookery; *m* 1977, Baron Waldegrave of North Hill, PC (Life Peer), *qv*, s of 12 Earl Waldegrave, KG, GCVO, TD (d 1995); 3 da (Katharine Mary b 15 Sept 1980, Elizabeth Laura b 27 Oct 1983, Harriet Horatia b 28 Jan 1988), 1 s (James Victor b 12 Dec 1984); *Career* joined Leith's Catering as jr cook 1972; proprietor: Leiths Sch of Food and Wine 1994– (estab with Prue Leith 1975); dir Waldegrave Farms Ltd 1994–; memb Health Educn Authy 1985–88; pres: Portobello Tst 1987–2000, Hosp Caterers Assoc; tstee Nat Life Story Collection; *Books* Leith's Cookery School (with Prue Leith, 1985), The Healthy Gourmet (1986), Sainsbury's Low Fat Gourmet (1987), Leith's Cookery Bible (with Prue Leith, 1991), Leith's Complete Christmas (jtly, 1992), Leith's Fish Bible (jtly, 1995), Leith's Easy Dinner Parties (jtly, 1995), Leith's Healthy Eating (jtly, 1996); *Recreations* tennis, bridge; *Style*— Lady Waldegrave, OBE; ✉ Leiths School of Food and Wine Ltd, 21 St Albans Grove, Kensington, London W8 5BP (tel 020 7229 0177, fax 020 7937 5257, e-mail info@leiths.com)

WALDEGRAVE, 13 Earl (GB 1729); Sir James Sherbrooke Waldegrave; 17 Bt (E 1643), of Hever Castle, Co Kent; also Baron Waldegrave (E 1686) and Viscount Chewton (GB 1729); s of 12 Earl Waldegrave, KG, GCVO, TD (d May 1995), and Mary Hermione, *née* Grenfell (d Nov 1995); *b* 8 December 1940; *Educ* Eton, Trinity Coll Cambridge; *m* 12 April 1986 (m dis 1996), Mary Alison Anthea, da of Sir Robert Allason Furness, KBE, CMG (d 1954); 2 s (Edward Robert, Viscount Chewton b 1986, Hon Arthur Riversdale b 1989); *Heir* s, Viscount Chewton; *Clubs* Beefsteak, Garrick, Leander, HLYC; *Style*— The Rt Hon Earl Waldegrave; ✉ Chewton House, Chewton Mendip, Radstock, Somerset BA3 4LL

WALDEGRAVE OF NORTH HILL, Baron (Life Peer UK 1999), of Chewton Mendip in the County of Somerset; William Arthur Waldegrave; PC (1990); 2 s of 12 Earl Waldegrave, KG, GCVO, TD (d 1995), and Mary Hermione, *née* Grenfell (d Nov 1995); *b* 15 August 1946; *Educ* Eton, CCC Oxford, Harvard Univ; *m* 1977, (Linda Margaret) Caroline (Lady Waldegrave, OBE, *qv*), da of Maj Richard Burrows, of Tunbridge Wells, Kent; 3 da (Hon Katharine Mary b 15 Sept 1980, Hon Elizabeth Laura b 27 Oct 1983, Hon Harriet Horatia b 28 Jan 1988), 1 s (Hon James Victor b 12 Dec 1984); *Career* distinguished fell All Souls Oxford; CPRS 1971–73, on political staff 10 Downing St 1973–74, head Political Office of Rt Hon Edward Heath (as ldr of the oppn) 1974–75; with GEC Ltd 1975–81, memb IBA Advsy Cncl 1980; MP (Cons) Bristol W 1979–97, jt vice-chm Fin Ctee to Sept 1981, under sec of state DES (for Higher Educn) 1981–83, chm Ctee for Local Authy Higher Educn 1982–83, under sec of state DOE 1983–85, min of state DOE 1985, min of state FCO 1988, sec of state for Health 1990–92, Chancellor of the Duchy of Lancaster (with responsibility for the Citizen's Charter and Sci) 1992–94, min for agriculture fisheries and food 1994–95, chief sec to the Treasy 1995–97; pres Parly and Sci Ctee 2001; JP Inner London 1975–79; md Corp Fin Dresdner Kleinwort Wasserstein 1998–2003; vice-chm Investment Banking Div UBS 2003–; dir: Bristol & West plc, Finsbury Life Sciences Investment Tst (now Finsbury Emerging Biotechnology Tst), Sotherans Ltd, Waldegrave Farms Ltd; tstee: Rhodes Tst 1992– (chm 2002–), Beit Memorial Fellowships for Med Res; chm Nat Museum of Sci and Indust 2002–, chm of tstees Bristol Cathedral Tst; *Books* The Binding of Leviathan - Conservatism and the Future (1977), Changing Gear - What the Government Should Do Next (pamphlet, co-author, 1981), various other pamphlets; *Clubs* Beefsteak, Pratt's, White's; *Style*— The Rt Hon the Lord Waldegrave of North Hill, PC

WALDEN, David Peter; s of Gerald Isaac Walden, of Newcastle upon Tyne, and Shirley Betty, *née* Rothfield (d 1981); *b* 23 September 1954; *Educ* Royal GS Newcastle upon Tyne, St John's Coll Oxford (BA, Gibbs Prize for modern history); *m* 1981, Janet Rosamund, da of Harry Day, MBE; 1 s (Jonathan Paul b 2 Aug 1985), 1 da (Rachel Sarah b 23 Nov 1987); *Career* DHSS: admin trainee 1977, princ Nurses' Pay 1982–85, private sec to dep chm NHS Mgmnt Bd 1985–86, asst sec Doctors' Pay and Conditions 1989–90, on secondment as personnel dir Poole Hosp NHS Tst 1991–93, head Community Care Branch Dept of Health 1993–96, under sec and head Health Promotion Div Dept of Health 1996–99, head Social Care Policy Dept of Health 1999–2001, seconded as exec dir of health servs devpt Anchor Tst 2001–03, transition dir Ind Regulator of NHS Fndn Tsts 2003–04, dir of strategy Cmmn for Social Care 2004–; *Style*— David Walden, Esq; ✉ Commission for Social Care Inspection, 33 Greycoat Street, London SW1P 2QF (tel 020 7979 2050)

WALDIE, Ian Michael; s of George Alistair (Ted) Waldie, of Queensland, Aust, and Dulcie Michel, *née* Clark; *b* 21 January 1970; *Educ* Burnside HS Nambour Aust, Queensland Coll of Art Brisbane Aust (Assoc Dip of Arts in Applied Photography); *Career* news photographer; cadet photographer The Sunshine Coast Daily (Maroochydore Queensland) 1988–89, photographer The Brisbane Courier Mail (Brisbane Queensland) 1989–92, freelance photographer Scotland 1992–93 (working for The Herald, The Scotsman, The Daily Record, The Sunday Mail, Take-A-Break and Rex Features), stringer photographer (covering Scotland for the Reuters UK and int serv) Reuters Ltd 1993–96, staff photographer Reuter UK Pictures (based London) 1996–2002, sr photographer EMEA Getty Images 2002–; notable assignments since 1993 incl: numerous royal visits and functions, state visits by John Major, Mikhail Gorbachov, Nelson Mandela, Paul Keating, The Dalai Lama, Mother Theresa, the PM of Finland and The King and Queen of Norway, Scottish Cup Finals 1993 and 1994, Rugby Five Nations Tournament 1992, 1993, 1994 and 1995, Scottish Open Golf Championships 1993, 1994 and 1995, Alfred Dunhill Cup Golf Championships 1993, 1994 and 1995, Cons Pty Conf 1994 and 1995, Lab Pty Conf 1995 and 1997, Rugby World Cup South Africa 1995, World Championships in Athletics 1995 and 1997, conflict in NI over Protestant marching season in Portadown, Belfast, Londonderry, Inniskillen and Bellaghy 1997, Boris Yeltsin and Bill Clinton summit meeting in Helsinki 1997, followed Tony Blair on campaign bus in run-up to the general election 1997, Wimbledon Championships 1997, Br Open Golf Championships 1997, funeral of Diana, Princess of Wales 1997, Scottish Devolution vote and count 1997, HM The Queen's Golden Wedding Anniversary 1997, Sharjah Champions Trophy UAE 1997, Peace Referendum in Ireland 1998, World Cup Football France 1998, Omagh bombing in NI 1998, Lab Pty Conf 1998, Euro Cup Winners Cup Final (Chelsea v Stuttgart) 1998, FA Cup Final (Arsenal v Newcastle) 1998, England Cricket Tour Australia 1998–99, Cricket World Cup 1999, Wimbledon Tennis Championships 1999, Royal Wedding of Prince Edward and Sophie Rhys Jones 1999; memb: Australian Journalists Assoc (AJA) 1988–93, NUJ 1992; *Awards* Best Sports Picture (Scottish Sports Photography Awards) 1994, Best News Picture (Scottish Airports Press Photography Awards) 1994, Photographer of the Year, Young Photographer of the Year and Best News Photographer of the Year (Br Picture Eds Guild) 1994, Nikon UK Press Photographer of the Year 1997, Fujifilm Photographer of the Year 2002, British Press Photographer of the Year 2002, Guinness Best Black and White Photographer of the Year (Picture Editor's Awards) 2003; *Recreations* surfing (in Australia), music (ex-drummer), squash, rally driving, various other sports; *Style*— Ian Waldie, Esq

WALDMAN, Guido; s of Milton Waldman, and Marguerite, *née* David; *Educ* Downside (exhibitioner), BNC Oxford (open scholarship, BA); *m* Lalage; 2 da (Nicola, Zoë Axelle); *Career* subsid rights manager, ed, dir The Bodley Head 1958–88, contracts dir The Bodley Head and Jonathan Cape 1985–88; The Harvill Press: ed 1988–2000, editorial dir and head of contracts 1995–2000; Weidenfeld (translation) Prize 1998; *Books* A Fogazzaro: A House Divided (trans, 1963), The Penguin Book of Italian Short Stories (ed, 1969), L Ariosto: Orlando Furioso (trans, 1974), I Went to School One Morning (1978), The Late Flowering of Captain Latham (1979), G Greene and M F Allain: The Other Man (trans, 1983), G Boccaccio: The Decameron (trans, 1993), A Baricco: Silk (trans, 1997) La Fontaine: Forbidden Fruit (trans, 1998), J Echenoz: Lake (trans, 1998), La Fontaine: The Complete Tales in Verse (trans, 2000), Publishing Agreements (contrib, 3 edn), J Echenoz: I'm Off (trans, 2001), A Buzzi: The Perfect Egg (trans, 2005); *Recreations* piano, Spanish guitar, cartoon-drawing, translating; *Style*— Guido Waldman, Esq; ✉ 9 Elia Street, London N1 8DE (tel 020 7837 9656, fax 020 7837 9677)

WALDMAN, Simon; *b* 26 January 1966; *Educ* Liverpool Coll Liverpool, Univ of Bristol (BA); *Career* journalist; reporter Shoe & Leather News 1988–89, reporter Drapers Record 1989, dep ed Media Week 1990–93, freelance journalist 1993–96; The Guardian: joined 1996, head of Guardian Unlimited (award-winning network of websites) 1999–, dir of digital publishing 2001–, memb bd Guardian Newspapers Ltd 2001–06, gp dir of digital strategy and devpt Guardian Media Gp 2006–; *Style*— Simon Waldman, Esq; ✉ Guardian Media Group, 60 Farringdon Road, London EC1R 3GA (tel 020 7278 2332, fax 020 7242 0679, e-mail simon.waldman@gmgplc.co.uk)

WALDMANN, Dr Carl; s of Leon Waldmann (d 1970), and Rene, *née* Schafer; bro of Prof Herman Waldmann, *qv*; *b* 25 March 1951; *Educ* Forest Sch, Sidney Sussex Coll Cambridge (BA), London Hosp (MA, MB BChir, DA); *m* 27 July 1980, Judith; 1 da (Anna b 1981); *Career* Flt-Lt Unit MO RAF Brize Norton 1977–78, Sqdn Ldr 1981–82, sr specialist anaesthetics RAF Ely 1980–82 (specialist 1978–80); sr registrar in intensive care Whipps Cross Hosp 1982–83; sr registrar in anaesthetics: London Hosp 1984–85 (houseman 1975–76, sr house offr in anaesthetics 1976–77, lectr in anaesthetics 1983–84), Great Ormond St Hosp 1985–86; conslt in anaesthetics and dir of intensive care Royal Berks and Battle Hosps Reading 1986–; European dip in Intensive Care Med 1993; ed Care of the Critically Ill 2000– (dep ed 1997); Intensive Care Soc: elected to Cncl 1998, ed jl 1999, treas 2003, pres 2007; memb European Soc of Intensive Care Medicine 1993 (chm Technol Assesment Section 2002) FFARCS 1980; *Books* Pocket Consultant Intensive Care (1985), Respiration: The Breath of Life (1985), Hazards and Complications of Anaesthesia (1987), Kaufman, Anaesthesia Reviews, Intensive Care Manual, Intensive Care Aftercare; *Recreations* fencing, squash, skiing, water-skiing; *Clubs* Hanover Int (Reading), Berkshire Raquets; *Style*— Dr Carl Waldmann; ✉ 2 Dewe Lane, Burghfield, Reading RG30 3SU (tel 0118 957 6381, e-mail cswald@aol.com); Intensive Therapy Unit, Royal Berkshire Hospital, Reading (tel 0118 322 7250, fax 0118 322 7250)

WALDMANN, Prof Herman; s of Leon Waldmann (d 1970), and Rene, *née* Schafer; bro of Dr Carl Waldmann, *qv*, and David Waldmann; *b* 27 February 1945; *Educ* Sir George Monoux GS Walthamstow, Sidney Sussex Coll Cambridge (exhibitioner, hon scholar, MA, PhD), London Hosp Med Sch (open scholar, MB BChir, Hutchinson prize for clinical res); *m* 1971, Judith Ruth; *Career* house physician and surgeon London Hosp 1969–70, MRC jr res fell 1970–73; Dept of Pathology Univ of Cambridge: demonstrator 1973–76, lectr 1975–76, reader in therapeutic immunology 1985, Kay Kendall prof of therapeutic immunology 1989–94; King's Coll Cambridge: res fell 1973–78, side tutor 1975–76, fell 1985–94; prof of pathology Sir William Dunn Sch of Pathology Univ of Oxford 1994–, fell Lincoln Coll Oxford 1994–; visiting scientist with Dr C Milstein Laboratory of Molecular Biology Cambridge 1978–79, SHO Dept of Med Royal Postgrad Med Sch London 1982, Eleanor Roosevelt fell Stanford Univ 1987; memb Advsy Ctee MRC Cell Bd 1986–91; invited speaker at numerous symposia in the areas of immunology, haematology and transplantation; Graham Bull prize RCP 1989–90; hon fell Queen Mary & Westfield Coll London 1996; founding fell Acad of Med Sci; MRCP, FRCPath (MRCPath), FRS 1990; *Publications* author of numerous articles in learned jls; *Recreations* family, friends, food, travel, music, tinnitus; *Style*— Prof Herman Waldmann, FRS; ✉ 4 Apsley Road, Oxford OX2 7QY; Sir William Dunn School of Pathology, South Parks Road, Oxford OX1 3RE (tel 01865 275500)

WALDUCK, (Hugh) Richard; OBE (2001), JP (Middx, Haringey 1974–2003, City of London 2003–), DL (Herts 2000); s of Hugh Stanley Walduck (d 1975), of Hatfield, Herts, and Enid Rosalind (Wendy) Walduck; *b* 21 November 1941; *Educ* Harrow, St Catharine's Coll Cambridge (MA); *m* 1, 1969 (m dis 1980); 2 s (Alexander b 1971, Nicholas b 1972), 2 step s (Richard b 1966, Simon b 1968), 1 step da (Nicola b 1971); m 2, 1981, Susan Marion Sherwood; *Career* dir and sec Imperial London Hotels Ltd 1964–; county pres St John Ambulance Herts 1990–2005; pres Royal Br Legion N Mymms 1998–; memb: Action on Addiction Cncl 1993–2000, Devpt Ctee Univ of Herts; dir Nat Crimebeat 1998–, vice-pres Herts Community Fndn 2000; tstee: Br Humane Assoc 2001–, Royal Engrs Museum Fndn; patron: St Alban's Cathedral, Isabel Hospice, HAPAS, Herts Agric Soc, Caribbean Women's Equality Forum, Herts Action on Disability; memb Cncl Shrievalty Assoc 1999–2001; signatory to Leadership Challenge for Racial Equality; Chapter Gen Order of St John 1990–99, Chapter Priory of England Order of St John 2002–03; High Sheriff Herts 1997; Liveryman Worshipful Co of Basketmakers 1968 (Prime Warden 2007), Alderman of the City of London (Ward of Tower) 2003–07; Hon DLitt Univ of Herts 2001; KStJ 2000 (OStJ 1989, CStJ 1997); *Recreations* history, skiing, beekeeping; *Clubs* City Livery, United Guilds, Royal Soc of St George, Pilgrims, Cooks, Tower Ward; *Style*— Richard Walduck, Esq, OBE, DL; ✉ c/o Director's Office, Imperial Hotel, Russell Square, London WC1B 5BB (tel 020 7837 3655, fax 020 7278 0469, e-mail hr.walduck@imperialhotels.co.uk)

WALES, Anthony Edward; s of Albert Edward Wales, of Collingham, Nottinghamshire, and Kathleen May, *née* Rosenthal; *b* 20 December 1955; *Educ* Stamford Sch, Worcester Coll Oxford (MA); *m* 1 Sept 1984, Lynda, da of Leonard Page (d 1987); 2 s (Edward b 1987, Thomas b 1989), 1 da (Victoria b 1993); *Career* slr; ptnr Turner Kenneth Brown 1986–94 (joined 1979), gen counsel The Economist Newspaper Ltd 1994–2001, sr vice-pres and gen counsel AOL Europe 2002–; memb: Law Soc 1981, Law Soc Hong Kong 1986; *Style*— Anthony Wales, Esq; ✉ AOL Europe, 200 Hammersmith Road, London W6 7DL (tel 020 7348 8770, fax 020 7348 8663)

WALES, Archbishop of 2003–; Most Rev Dr Barry Cennydd Morgan; s of Rhys Haydn Morgan (d 1983), and Mary Gwyneth, *née* Davies (d 1988); *b* 31 January 1947; *Educ* UCL (BA), Selwyn Coll Cambridge (MA), Westcott House Cambridge (Powis exhibitioner), Univ of Wales (PhD); *m* Aug 1969, Hilary Patricia, da of Ieuan Lewis; 1 s (Jonathan Rhodri b 19 July 1975), 1 da (Lucy Rachel Angharad b 4 Feb 1977); *Career* ordained (Llandaff): deacon 1972, priest 1973, bishop 1993; curate St Andrew's Major Dinas Powis 1972–75, chaplain Bryn-y-Don Community Sch 1972–75, chaplain and lectr St Michael's Coll Llandaff 1975–77, lectr UC Cardiff 1975–77, warden Church Hostel Bangor, Anglican chaplain and lectr in theol UCNW 1977–84, ed Welsh Churchman 1975–82; examining chaplain: to Archbishop of Wales 1978–82, to Bishop of Bangor 1983; in-serv trg offr 1979–84, warden of ordinands Dio of Bangor 1982–84, canon of Bangor Cathedral 1983–84, rector Rectorial Parish of Wrexham 1984–86, archdeacon of Merioneth and rector of Criccieth 1986–93, bishop of Bangor 1993–99, bishop of Llandaff 1999–; chm: Archbishop's Doctrinal Cmmn 1983–93 (memb 1982, chm 1990–93), Div of Stewardship Provincial Bd of Mission 1988–94; vice-pres Bible Soc 1999, vice-chm Nat Soc 1999; memb: Central Ctee World Cncl of Churches 1996–2006, Primates Standing Ctee 2003; pres Welsh Centre for Int Affrs 2004; pro-chllr Univ of Wales 2006; hon fell: UCW Bangor, Univ of Wales Cardiff, Univ of Wales Lampeter, Univ of Wales Inst Cardiff (UWIC); *Publications* O Ddydd i Ddydd, Pwyllgor Darlleniadau Beiblaidd Cyngor Eglwysi Cymru (1980), History of the Church Hostel and Anglican Chaplaincy at

University College of North Wales Bangor (1986), Concepts of Mission and Ministry in Anglican University Chaplaincy Work (1988), Strangely Orthodox: R S Thomas and his Poetry of Faith (2006); *Recreations* golf; *Style—* The Most Rev the Archbishop of Wales; ✉ Llys Esgob, The Cathedral Green, Llandaff, Cardiff CF5 2YE (tel 029 2056 2400, fax 029 2056 8410, e-mail archbishop@churchinwales.org.uk)

WALES, Gregory John; s of A J Wales, of Guildford, Surrey, and B Wales, *née* Read; *b* 17 May 1949; *Educ* Guildford Royal GS; *m* 29 July 1972, Jennifer Hilary, da of E Brown, of St Albans, Herts; 2 s (Nicholas b 1978, Andrew b 1981); *Career* CA 1974; sr lectr City 1976–79, mgmnt conslt 1976–80, mangr Arthur Andersen & Co 1980–82, ptnr Coombes Wales Quinnell 1982–90; dir Sherbourne Fndn, sr conslt CeEx Inc (strategic consultancy); pres Action Sociale pour la RDC; Freeman City of London; FCA; *Recreations* cricket, squash, real tennis; *Style—* Gregory Wales, Esq

WALEY-COHEN, Robert Bernard; 2 s of Sir Bernard Waley-Cohen, 1 Bt (d 1991), and Hon Joyce (Hon Lady Waley Cohen, JP, decd), da of 1 Baron Nathan (d 1963); *b* 10 November 1948; *Educ* Eton; *m* 1975, Hon Felicity Ann, da of 3 Viscount Bearsted, TD, DL (d 1986); 3 s (Marcus Richard b 1977, Sam Bernard b 1982, Thomas Andrew b 1984 d 2004), 1 da (Jessica Suzanna b 1979); *Career* exec Christie's 1969–81 (gen mangr USA 1970–73); chm and ceo Alliance Imaging Inc 1983–88, chm Bd Point-to-Point 2005–, dep chm Alliance Medical Ltd 2006– (chief exec 1989–2006), chm Pony Racing Authy 2007–; memb Cncl Countryside Alliance 1998–2002, memb Cncl Nat Tst 2001–; tstee: Countryside Fndn for Educn 1997–2001, Animal Health Tst 2007–, Place 2 Be 2007–; steward of the Jockey Club 1995–2000; *Recreations* the arts, conservation, racing (racehorses include: Rustle, The Dragon Master, Katarino, Makounji, Libertine); *Clubs* Jockey; *Style—* Robert Waley-Cohen, Esq; ✉ tel 020 7244 6022, e-mail rwc@alliance.co.uk

WALEY-COHEN, Sir Stephen Harry; 2 Bt (UK 1961), of Honeymead, Co Somerset; s of Sir Bernard Nathaniel Waley-Cohen, 1 Bt (d 1991), and Hon Lady Waley-Cohen; *b* 22 June 1946; *Educ* Eton, Magdalene Coll Cambridge (MA); *m* 1, 1972 (m dis 1986), Pamela Elizabeth, yr da of J E Doniger, of Knutsford, Cheshire; 2 s (Lionel Robert b 7 Aug 1974, Jack David b 7 Sept 1979), 1 da (Harriet Ann b 20 June 1976); m 2, 1986, Josephine Burnett, yr da of Duncan M Spencer, of Bedford, New York; 2 da (Tamsin Alice b 4 April 1986, Freya Charlotte b 20 Feb 1989); *Heir* s, Lionel Waley-Cohen; *Career* fin journalist Daily Mail 1968–73, ed Money Mail Handbook 1972–74, dir and publisher Euromoney Publications Ltd 1969–83, chief exec Maybox Group plc (theatre and cinema owners and managers) 1984–89; dir Publishing Holdings plc 1986–88, chm Willis Faber & Dumas (Agencies) Ltd 1992–99 (dir 1988), dir St Martin's Theatre Ltd 1989–, md Victoria Palace 1989–; chm: Thorndike Holdings ltd 1989–1998, Policy Portfolio plc 1993–98, First Call Group plc 1996–98, Portsmouth & Sunderland Newspaper plc 1998–99 (dir 1994–98); dir: Stewart Wrightson Members Agency Ltd 1987–98, Exeter Preferred Capital Investment Trust plc 1992–2003, Savoy Theatre Ltd 1996–98, Ambassadors Theatre 2007–; md: Mousetrap Productions Ltd 1994–, Vaudeville Theatre 1996–2001, Savoy Theatre Management Ltd 1997–2005; advsy dir Theatres Mutual Insurance Co 1995–; chm RADA 2007– (memb Cncl 2004–); memb Fin Ctee UCL 1984–89, chm JCA Charitable Fndn (formerly Jewish Colonisation Assoc) 1992– (memb Cncl 1984–), memb Soc of London Theatres 1984– (memb Bd 1993–, pres 2002–05), chm Exec Ctee Br American Project for the Successor Generation 1989–92; tstee The Theatres Tst 1998–2004; govr Wellesley House Sch 1972–97; Liveryman Worshipful Co of Clothworkers; *Clubs* Garrick; *Style—* Sir Stephen Waley-Cohen, Bt; ✉ 1 Wallingford Avenue, London W10 6QA

WALFORD, Dr Diana Marion; CBE (2002); da of late Lt-Col Joseph Norton, of Beckenham, and Thelma, *née* Nurick; *b* 26 February 1944; *Educ* Calder HS for Girls Liverpool, Univ of Liverpool (George Holt scholarship, BSc, MB ChB, MD, George Holt medal, J Hill Abram prize), Univ of London (MSc, N and S Devi prize); *m* 9 Dec 1970, Arthur David Walford, s of Wing Cdr Adolph A Walford (decd), of Bushey Heath, Herts; 1 da (Sally b 8 Aug 1972), 1 s (Alexander b 5 May 1982); *Career* house surgn Liverpool Royal Infirmary March–Aug 1969 (house physician 1968–69); SHO: St Mary's Hosp 1969–70, Northwick Park Hosp 1970–71; sr registrar rotation 1972–75, N London Blood Transfusion Centre MRC res fell and hon sr registrar Clinical Res Centre Northwick Park Hosp 1975–76, hon conslt haematologist Central Middx Hosp 1977–87; Dept of Health: sr med offr Medicines Div 1976–79, princ med offr Sci Servs Equipment Building Div 1979–83, sr princ med offr and under sec Med Manpower and Educn Div 1983–86, sabbatical LSHTM 1986–87, sr princ med offr and under sec Int Health Microbiology of Food and Water and Communicable Disease Div 1987–89, dep chief med offr and med dir NHS Mgmnt Exec 1989–92, dir Public Health Laboratory Service 1993–2002, princ Mansfield Coll Oxford 2002–; contrib to various med books and jls; govr Ditchley Fndn 2001–; MA (by incorporation) Univ of Oxford 2002; FRSM 1972, FRCPath 1986 (MRCPath 1974), FRCP 1990 (MRCP 1972), FFPHM 1994 (MFPHM 1989), FRSA 2002; *Style—* Dr Diana Walford, CBE; ✉ Mansfield College, Oxford OX1 3TF (tel 01865 282894, e-mail diana.walford@mansfield.ox.ac.uk)

WALFORD, Prof Geoffrey; *b* 30 April 1949, London; *Educ* Univ of Kent (BSc, PhD), Open Univ (BA, MSc, MBA), Univ of Oxford (PGCE, MA, MPhil), Univ of London (MA); *Career* SSRC conversion fell St John's Coll Oxford 1976–78; Aston Univ: lectr in sociology of educn 1979–83, lectr in educn policy and mgmnt 1983–90, sr lectr in sociology and educn policy 1990–94; Univ of Oxford: fell Green Coll 1995–, lectr in educnl studies 1995–97, reader in educn policy 1997–2000, prof of educn policy 2000–, jr proctor 2001–02; series ed Studies in Educnl Ethnography 1997–, jt ed Br Jl of Educnl Studies 1999–2002 (memb Editorial Bd 1998–2002), ed Oxford Review of Educn 2004– (memb Editorial Bd 2001–), dep ed Ethnography and Educn 2005–; memb Editorial Bd: Jl of Educn Policy 1995–, Br Educnl Research Jl 1996–99 and 2004–, Int Jl of Research and Method in Educn 2004–, Diaspora, Indigenous and Minority Educn 2005–; author of more than 100 academic articles and book chapters; memb Br Educnl Research Assoc 1985; *Books* Life in Public Schools (1986), Restructuring Universities: Politics and Power in the Management of Change (1987), Privatization and Privilege in Education (1990), City Technology College (jtly, 1991), Doing Educational Research (ed, 1991), Choice and Equity in Education (1994), Researching the Powerful in Education (ed, 1994), Educational Politics: Pressure Groups and Faith-Based Schools (1995), Affirming the Comprehensive Ideal (jt ed, 1997), Doing Research About Education (ed, 1998), Policy, Politics and Education: Sponsored Grant-Maintained Schools and Religious Diversity (2000), Doing Qualitative Educational Research (2001), Private Schooling: Tradition and Diversity (2005), Markets and Equity in Education (2006); *Recreations* reading, travel, walking; *Style—* Prof Geoffrey Walford; ✉ Department of Education, University of Oxford, 15 Norham Gardens, Oxford OX2 6PY (tel 01865 274141, e-mail geoffrey.walford@education.ox.ac.uk)

WALFORD, His Hon Judge John de Guise; s of Edward Wynn Walford (d 1989), of Norton-on-Tees, Cleveland, and Dorothy Ann, *née* Bouchier; *b* 23 February 1948; *Educ* Sedbergh, Queens' Coll Cambridge (MA); *m* 30 July 1977, Pamela Elizabeth, da of Dr Peter Russell; 1 da (Caroline Louise b 6 May 1978), 1 s (Charles de Guise b 17 Sept 1979); *Career* called to the Bar Middle Temple 1971, in practice NE Circuit 1974–93, recorder of the Crown Court 1989–93 (asst recorder 1985–89), standing counsel (Criminal) DSS NE Circuit) 1991–93, circuit judge (NE Circuit) 1993–; chllr Diocese of Bradford 1999–; *Recreations* cricket, tennis, opera, watching Middlesbrough FC; *Clubs* Hawks' (Cambridge), Free Foresters CC; *Style—* His Hon Judge Walford; ✉ The Law Courts, Russell Street, Middlesbrough TS1 2AE (tel 01642 340000)

WALKER, *see also:* Forestier-Walker

WALKER, Adam Christopher; s of Terence Jolley, and Sheila, *née* Baron; *b* 26 September 1967, Leicester; *Educ* Uppingham (top entrance scholar), Univ of Newcastle (BA); *m* 3 Nov 1995, Yvonne, *née* Leckie; 3 s (Sebastian Charles b 31 May 1997, Frederick Alexander b 18 May 1999, Samuel Joseph b 18 Sept 2004), 1 da (Eloise Rose b 18 Dec 2006); *Career* corp fin mangr Touche Ross & Co 1989–94, assoc dir corp fin NatWest Markets 1994–98, dir Arthur Andersen 1998–2000, jt md GorillaPark 2000–01, gp fin dir Nat Express Gp plc 2003– (head of corp devpt 2001–03); ACA 1992; *Recreations* cricket, rugby, opera, theatre; *Style—* Adam Walker, Esq; ✉ National Express Group plc, 75 Davies Street, London W1K 5HT (fax 020 7529 2147, e-mail awalker@natex.co.uk)

WALKER, Alan Edward; s of Ben Walker, of Fort Worth, TX, and Hilda, *née* Roberts (d 2002); *b* 13 November 1965, Bury, Lancs; *Educ* Bury GS, Magdalene Coll Cambridge (BA, Norah Dias Prize, scholar (hc), LLM), Guildford Law Sch; *Career* slr; Addleshaw Booth & Co 1989–2000, Cobbetts LLP 2000–; memb: Property Litigation Assoc, Law Soc; *Style—* Alan Walker, Esq; ✉ Cobbetts LLP, Ship Canal House, King Street, Manchester M2 4WB (tel 0845 165 5413, fax 0845 166 6631, e-mail alan.walker@cobbetts.co.uk)

WALKER, Prof Andrew Charles; s of Maurice Frederick Walker, of Harrow, Middx, and Margaret Florence, *née* Rust; *b* 24 June 1948; *Educ* Kingsbury County GS, Univ of Essex (BA, MSc, PhD); *m* 2 April 1972, Margaret Elizabeth, da of Arthur Mortimer, of Heckmondwike, W Yorks; 2 c (Edmund, Abigail (twins) b 1978); *Career* Nat Res Cncl of Canada postdoctoral fell Ottawa Canada, Sci Res Cncl fell Dept of Physics Univ of Essex 1974–75, sr scientific offr UK AEA Culham Laboratory 1975–83; Heriot-Watt Univ: lectr in physics 1983–85, reader then prof of physics 1985–88, chair of modern optics 1988–, dir of postgrad studies 1998–2001, dep princ (resources) 2001–06, vice princ 2006–; memb Ctee: Quantum Electronics Gp Inst of Physics 1979–85 (hon sec 1982–85), Scottish Branch Inst of Physics 1985–88; memb: SERC/DTI Advance Devices and Materials Ctee 1992–94, EPSRC Coll 1994–2005; chm Scottish Branch Inst of Physics 1993–95 (vice-chm 1991–93, past chm 1995–97); dir: Terahertz Photonics Ltd 1998–2000 (chm of Bd), Edinburgh Business Sch 2001– (memb Bd), Technology Ventures Scotland 2002–05; tstee RSE Scotland Fndn 2003–05 (chm 2004–05); author of over 200 scientific articles and letters in the field of optoelectronics; FInstP 1987, FRSE 1994 (memb Cncl and sec for meetings 1998–2001, vice-pres 2001–04, fellowship sec 2005–); *Recreations* music (piano, guitar), sailing; *Style—* Prof Andrew Walker, FRSE; ✉ Heriot-Watt University, Riccarton, Edinburgh EH14 4AS (tel 0131 451 3036, fax 0131 451 3744, e-mail a.c.walker@hw.ac.uk)

WALKER, (Hon) Anna; CB (2003); er da of Baron Butterworth, CBE (Life Peer, d 2003); *b* 5 May 1951; *Educ* Oxford HS, Benenden, Bryn Mawr Coll USA (ESU scholarship), Lady Margaret Hall Oxford (MA); *m* 1983, Timothy Edward Hanson Walker, *qv*, s of Harris Walker; 3 da (Sophie (adopted) b 1975, Beth b 1984, Polly b 1986); *Career* Br Cncl 1972–73, CBI 1973–74; HM Civil Serv: ME Div DTI 1975–76, Post and Telecommunications Div DTI 1976–77, private sec to Sec of State for Industry 1977–78, princ Shipping Policy Div DTI 1979–83, princ Fin Div DTI 1983–84, interdepartmental review of budgetary control 1985–86, Cabinet Office 1986–87, Personnel Div 1987–88, asst sec Competition Policy Div DTI 1988–91, dir of competition Office of Telecommunications (Oftel) 1991–94, dep DG Oftel 1994–97, dep DG Energy DTI 1998, DG Energy DTI 1998–2001, DG (land use and rural affrs) DEFRA 2001–03; chief exec Healthcare Cmmn 2004–; *Recreations* theatre, travel, cycling; *Style—* Mrs Anna Walker, CB; ✉ Healthcare Commission, Finsbury Tower, 103–105 Bunhill Row, London EC1Y 8TG (tel 020 7488 9200, fax 020 7448 9222, e-mail anna.walker@healthcarecommission.org.uk)

WALKER, Catherine Marguerite Marie-Therese; da of Remy Baheux, and Agnes Lefèbvre; *b* 27 June 1945; *Educ* Univs of Lille and Aix-en-Provence (Maitre-es-Lettres Philosophy); *m* 1969, John David Walker (decd); 2 da (Naomi Carolyn b 1971, Marianne Emily b 1972); *Career* fashion designer; dir Film Dept French Inst London 1970, memb Lecture Dept French Embassy 1971; dir and proprietor: The Chelsea Design Co Ltd 1977–, Catherine Walker Ltd 2003–; Catherine Walker Twenty-Five Years British Couture 1977–2002 display V&A 2002; Br Fashion Awards Designer of the Year for Couture 1990–91, Br Fashion Awards Designer of the Year for Glamour 1991–92; fndr sponsor Breast Cancer Haven Catherine Walker Tree of Life, donor patron Gilda's Club 1999; FRSA 2000; *Books* Catherine Walker, An Autobiography (1998), Catherine Walker, Twenty-Five Years British Couture, 1977–2002 (2002); *Style—* Mrs Catherine Walker; ✉ Catherine Walker Ltd, 65 Sydney Street, Chelsea, London SW3 6PX (tel 020 7352 4626, e-mail catwalk@catherinewalker.com)

WALKER, Charles; MP; *Educ* Univ of Oregon; *m* Fiona; 2 s (Alistair, James), 1 da (Charlotte); *Career* former dir Blue Arrow; cncllr Wandsworth BC 2002–06; MP (Cons) Broxbourne 2005– (Parly candidate (Cons) Ealing N 2001); *Style—* Charles Walker, Esq, MP; ✉ House of Commons, London SW1A 0AA

WALKER, Christine; *b* 1953; *Educ* Rhodesia, Ireland, Univ of Exeter; *Career* initial career in publishing, subsequently with Media Unit Benton & Bowles advtg agency 1976–85, fndr memb Ray Morgan & Partners ind media co 1985 (sold to Saatchi & Saatchi plc 1988); Zenith Media (Saatchi & Saatchi media arm): fndr head of broadcast rising to md, chief exec until 1997; jt managing ptnr Walker Media (jt venture with M&C Saatchi) 1998–; dir: Meridian Outdoor Advertising Ltd 1993–97, The National Film and Television School Ltd 1993–97, Equinox Communications Ltd 1994–97; Adwoman of the Year 1990, voted amongst UK's top business women (Options and Cosmopolitan magazines) 1992; memb: Cncl IPA, Women's Advtg and Communications London, Mktg Gp of GB; *Style—* Ms Christine Walker

WALKER, (Louis) David; MBE, TD; s of Louis Charles Walker, MBE (d 1981), and Margaret Ann, *née* Phillips (d 1988); *b* 4 July 1932; *Educ* Chipping Sodbury GS, Merchant Venturers' Coll, Univ of Bristol; *m* 1, 29 Feb 1964 (m dis 1995); 1 da (Sarah b 3 Jan 1965); m 2, 8 July 2000, Sue; *Career* Nat Serv 2 Lt RA 1953, Lt (later Capt) Royal Aust Artillery (CMF) 1956, Lt RA (TA) 1959, Capt 4 Bn Wiltshire Regt 1963–67; Union International Group Aust 1955–58 (London 1958–62), Marsh Harris Group Calne 1962–65, G Brazil & Co Ltd 1965–68, Unilever Group London 1968–71, dir Robert Wilson & Sons (1849) Ltd Scot 1971–78; McKey Food Service Ltd: md 1978–90, chm 1990–2000, ret; chm: McKey Holdings (Europe) Ltd 1990–2000, McKey Wholesale Ltd 1991–92, Key Meats Ltd 1991–2000, Key Country Foods Ltd 1991–2000, Key Country Bacon Ltd 1992–2000, Key Country Provisions Ltd 1992–2000, Mollington Properties 2000–; dir Holmesterne Foods 2001–04; watch offr Sail Trg Assoc; BMMA: memb Cncl 1981–, pres 1994–2000; formerly chm McDonald's Euro Meat Prods Quality Control Ctee; cmmr for Meat and Livestock Cmmn 1994–2002, memb Cncl, Exec and Food Policy & Resources Ctee Food and Drink Fedn 1995–2000; dir Assured Br Meat 1999–2001; underwriter Lloyd's 1990–2002; Freeman and Liveryman: Worshipful Co of Tallow Chandlers 1963–, Worshipful Co of Butchers 1985; memb Inst of Meat 1959; FRSH 1985 (MRSH 1959); *Recreations* sailing, game shooting, military history, vintage car rallying; *Clubs* Royal Thames Yacht, Royal Artillery Yacht, Royal Dart Yacht, Bentley Drivers; *Style—* L David Walker, Esq, MBE, TD; ✉ The Grange, Mollington, Banbury, Oxfordshire OX17 1AP (tel 01295 758657, fax 01295 758887, mobile 07850 936929)

WALKER, David; s of John Walker, and Irene, *née* Connor; *b* 8 November 1950; *Educ* Corby GS, St Catharine's Coll Cambridge (scholarship, Figgis Prize, sr scholarship, MA), Univ of Sussex/Ecole Pratique des Hautes Etudes (MA); *m* 9 Feb 1974 (m dis 1997), Karen; 1

s (Michael b 7 Dec 1982); *Career* sr reporter Times Higher Educn Supplement 1973–77, Harkness fell, congressional fell and visiting scholar Graduate Sch of Public Policy Univ of Calif Berkeley 1977–79, journalist Britain section The Economist 1979–81, local govt corr and ldr writer The Times 1981–86, chief ldr writer London Daily News 1987, public admin corr The Times 1987–90, chief ldr writer The Independent 1996–98, writer and section ed The Guardian 1998–, ed Guardian Public magazine 2004–; presenter Analysis (BBC Radio) 1988–; RICS Radio Journalist of the Year 1993; non-exec dir Places for People Gp 1999–2003; memb Cncl ESRC 2007–; tstee: National Centre for Social Res 2002–, Nuffield Tst 2007–; memb Franco-Br Cncl (Br Section) 2001–; hon memb CIPFA; *Books* Media Made in California (1981), Municipal Empire (1983), Sources Close to the Prime Minister (1984), The Times Guide to the State (1995), Public Relations in Local Government (1997), Did Things Get Better (with Polly Toynbee, 2001), Better or Worse (with Polly Toynbee, 2005); *Recreations* tennis, clarinet, running; *Clubs* Reform; *Style—* David Walker, Esq; ✉ 1 Crescent Grove, London SW4 7AF (tel 020 7498 9740); The Guardian, 119 Farringdon Road, London EC1R 3ER (tel 020 7713 4668, e-mail david.walker@guardian.co.uk)

WALKER, David; s of Francis Allen Walker (d 1994), of Tibshelf, Derbys, and Dorothy, *née* Buck; *b* 23 October 1947; *Educ* Tupton Hall GS, Hertford Coll Oxford (BA, 4 times Soccer blue, capt Univ XI); *m* 1972, Elizabeth Grace, *née* Creswell; 2 s (Simon David, Mark Jonathan (twins) b 17 Aug 1975), 1 da (Kathryn Elizabeth b 25 Feb 1978); *Career* graduate trainee Marley Buildings Ltd 1970–72; E J Arnold & Son Ltd: area mangr 1972–74, product mangr 1974–77, merchandise mangr 1977–79, divnl dir 1979–84; Lex Volvo (subsid of Lex Service plc): gen mangr 1984–86, ops dir 1987–89, divnl dir 1990–94; md Hyundai Car (UK) Ltd (now subsid of RAC plc) 1994–; MCIM; *Recreations* walking, cycling; *Style—* David Walker, Esq; ✉ Hyundai Car (UK) Ltd, St Johns Court, Easton Street, High Wycombe, Buckinghamshire HP11 1JX (tel 01494 428600, fax 01494 428699)

WALKER, Sir David Alan; kt (1991); *b* 31 December 1939; *Educ* Chesterfield Sch, Queens' Coll Cambridge (MA); *m* 20 April 1963, Isobel, *née* Cooper; 2 da (Elspeth b 4 June 1966, Penelope b 12 April 1970), 1 s (Jonathan b 29 Jan 1968); *Career* HM Treasy: joined 1961, private sec to Jt Perm Sec 1964–66, seconded Staff IMF Washington 1970–73, asst sec 1973–77; Bank of England: chief advsr then chief Econ Intelligence Dept, asst dir 1980, exec dir fin and indust 1982–88; chm: Johnson Matthey Bankers Ltd (later Minories Finance Ltd) 1985–88, Securities and Investments Bd 1988–1992; chm The Agricultural Mortgage Corp plc 1993–94, dep chm Lloyds Bank plc 1992–94, dir Morgan Stanley Inc 1994–97, exec chm Morgan Stanley Group (Europe) plc (latterly Morgan Stanley Dean Witter (Europe) Ltd) 1994–2006 (sr advsr 2006–), exec chm Morgan Stanley International Inc 1995–2001 (currently sr adviser); chm RVC Europe Ltd; non-exec dir: Bank of England until 1993, National Power plc 1993–94, British Invisibles 1993–, Reuters Holdings plc 1994–2000, Legal & General 2002– (vice-chm 2004–); chm Financial Markets Gp LSE 1987–94, pt/t memb Bd CEGB 1987–89, nominated memb Cncl Lloyd's 1988–92; chm Exec Ctee Int Orgn of Securities Cmmns 1990–92; govr: Henley Mgmnt Coll 1993–99, LSE 1993–95; memb and treas Gp of Thirty 1993–; co-chm Cambridge Univ 800th Anniversary Campaign 2005–; hon fell Queens' Coll Cambridge, Hon LLD Univ of Exeter 2002; *Recreations* music, long-distance walking; *Clubs* Reform; *Style—* Sir David Walker

WALKER, Air Vice-Marshal David Allan; OBE (1995), MVO (1992); s of Allan Walker (d 1999), and Audrey, *née* Brothwell; *b* 14 July 1956; *Educ* City of London Sch, Univ of Bradford (RAF cadet, BSc), RAF Coll; *m* 1983, Jane Alison, *née* Calder; *Career* equerry to HM The Queen 1989–92, loan serv South Africa 1994, Cmd RAF Halton 1997–98, dir Corp Communications RAF 1998–2002, dir Personnel and Trg Policy RAF 2002–03, AOC RAF Trg Gp and chief exec Trg Gp Defence Agency 2003–04, Master HM Household 2005–, Extra Equerry to HM The Queen 2005; vice-pres Royal Int Air Tatoo; Liveryman Worshipful Co of Bakers 1991; MCIPD; *Recreations* walking dogs, keeping fit(ish), old cars, shooting; *Clubs* RAF, Royal Over-Seas League; *Style—* Air Vice-Marshal David Walker, OBE, MVO; ✉ Buckingham Palace, London SW1A 1AA

WALKER, Prof David Maxwell; CBE (1986), QC (Scot 1958); s of James Mitchell Walker (d 1934), of Bishopbriggs, Glasgow, and Mary Paton Colquhoun, *née* Irvine (d 1971); *b* 9 April 1920; *Educ* Glasgow HS, Univ of Glasgow (MA, LLB, LLD), Univ of Edinburgh (PhD, LLD), Univ of London (LLB, LLD); *m* 1 Sept 1954, Margaret Walker, OBE, MA, da of Robert Knox (d 1970); *Career* WWII: NCO Cameronians (Scottish Rifles) 1939, 2 Lt HLI 1940, transferred to RIASC 1941, served India 1941–42 and N Africa 1942–43, 8 Indian Div Italy 1943–46 (Bde Supply and Tport Offr HQ 21 Indian Inf Brig); advocate Scottish Bar 1948, in practice Scottish Bar 1948–53, called to the Bar Middle Temple 1957; Univ of Glasgow: prof of jurisprudence 1954–58, dean Faculty of Law 1956–59, regius prof of law 1958–90, convenor Sch of Law 1984–88, sr res fell 1990–; dir Scottish Univs' Law Inst 1974–80; chm: HS of Glasgow Educn Tst 1980–2002, Hamlyn Tst 1988–93; hon pres Friends of Glasgow Univ Library; Hon LLD Univ of Edinburgh 1974; FBA 1976, FRSE 1980, FSA Scot 1966, FRSA 1991; *Books* Law of Damages in Scotland (1955), The Scottish Legal System (1959, 8 edn 2001), Law of Delict in Scotland (1966, 2 edn 1981), Principles of Scottish Private Law (2 vols 1970, 4 edn 4 vols 1988–89), Law of Prescription and Limitation in Scotland (1973, 6 edn 2002), Law of Civil Remedies in Scotland (1974), Law of Contracts and Related Obligations in Scotland (1979, 3 edn 1994), The Oxford Companion to Law (1980), Stair's Institutions of the Law of Scotland (ed 1981), Stair Tercentenary Studies (ed 1981), The Scottish Jurists (1985), A Legal History of Scotland (7 vols 1988–2004); author of numerous papers in legal journals; *Recreations* book-collecting, Scottish history; *Style—* Prof David M Walker, CBE, QC, FRSE, FBA; ✉ 1 Beaumont Gate, Glasgow G12 9EE (tel 0141 339 2802)

WALKER, Rt Rev David Stuart; *see:* Dudley, Bishop of

WALKER, Rt Rev Dominic Edward William Murray; *see:* Monmouth, Bishop of

WALKER, Dorothy; da of John Walker (d 1982), and Dorothy, *née* Reid; *b* 18 July 1957; *Educ* Montrose Acad, Inst of Archaeology Univ of London (BA); *m* 1985, William Newlands of Lauriston, *qv*; *Career* conslt Comshare 1981–87, mktg mangr Digital Equipment Corp 1987–94, ed-in-chief Boston Morgan London 1994–; writer; columnist Times Educational Supplement; contrib: The Times, Sunday Times, Mail on Sunday, Evening Standard, Daily Telegraph, The Guardian, The Independent, The Scotsman, Saga Magazine; Technology Writer of the Year BT Technology Awards 1997; memb Soc of Authors; FSA Scot; *Books* Education in the Digital Age (1998); *Clubs* Bluebird; *Style—* Ms Dorothy Walker; ✉ Alliance Press Features, Suite 435, 405 Kings Road, London SW10 0BB (tel 020 7351 6468); Lauriston Castle, St Cyrus, Kincardineshire DD10 0DJ (tel 01674 850488, e-mail mail@dorothywalker.com)

WALKER, Geoffrey Hurst; s of Raymond Bennet Walker, of Perth, Scotland, and Joan Edith Agnes, *née* Michie; *b* 7 February 1956; *Educ* Bell Baxter HS Cupar, Univ of Edinburgh (BCom); *m* 1995, Rosaleen, da of John Fay (d 1992); *Career* audit mangr Arthur Young 1978–87; fin dir: Serif Cowells plc 1987–89, DPS Typecraft Ltd 1990–99; currently chief financial offr Digital Technol Int; Liveryman Worshipful Co of Gold & Silver Wyre Drawers; CA 1981, FRSA 2001; *Recreations* walking, philately; *Style—* Geoffrey Walker, Esq; ✉ 15 Colburn Avenue, Caterham, Surrey CR3 6HW (tel 01883 343576); Brentwood House, 169 King's Road, Brentwood, Essex CM14 4EG (tel 01277 246000, fax 01277 228767)

WALKER, Graham Edwards; s of late Eric Walker, of N Wales, and late Mary, *née* Edwards; *b* 6 July 1939; *Educ* Wallasey GS; *m* Annabel; 2 s (Max b 1 Aug 1966, Jago b 20 Aug 1972), 1 da (Abbey b 15 Feb 1964); *Career* yachtsman; memb Br Admiral's Cup team 1983, 1985, 1987, 1989, 1993 and 1997 (capt 1983, 1987 and 1993), capt Br Southern Cross team 1983, world 3/4 ton champion 1986, chm Br Americas Cup challenge 1986–87; dir: Argyll Group 1983–89, Broad Street Group 1989–90; chm Europa Aviation 1995–2001; *Recreations* yachting, shooting, rugby, vintage cars; *Clubs* Crusade Yacht, Royal Thames, Yacht Club of Monaco, NBFC (RU), Harelquins, RAC; *Style—* Graham Walker, Esq; ✉ 3rd Floor, Residence Le Castellara, 9 Avenue President Kennedy, 98000, Monaco (e-mail grahamworldwide@hotmail.com)

WALKER, Sir Harold Berners; KCMG (1991); s of Adm Sir Harold Walker, KCB, RN (d 1975), and Olive Marjory, *née* Berners (d 1991); *b* 19 October 1932; *Educ* Winchester, Univ of Oxford (MA); *m* 1, 1960, Jane, *née* Bittleston; 2 da (Caroline Jane b 7 Sept 1961, Katherine Baker b 26 Jan 1965), 1 s (Christopher Harold b 3 Sept 1963); m 2, 2004, Anne Savage, *née* Gourlay; *Career* HM Dip Serv 1955–92; served FO, ME Centre for Arab Studies, Dubai, Cairo, Damascus, Washington, Jedda, FCO; ambass: Bahrain 1979–81, UAE 1981–86, Ethiopia 1986–89, Iraq 1990–91; memb Cwlth War Graves Cmmn 1992–97, chm Bahrain Soc 1993–98, chm Jerusalem and the East Mission Tst 1996–2000 (vice-chm 1994–96), chm Royal Soc for Asian Affairs 2002–; pres: Friends of the Imperial War Museum 1992–97, CARE International 1997–2001, Br Soc of Middle Eastern Studies 2006–; memb Corp Woking Sixth Form Coll 1996–99; assoc fell RUSI 1992–97; *Clubs* Oxford and Cambridge; *Style—* Sir Harold Walker, KCMG; ✉ 39 Charlwood Street, London SW1V 2DU (e-mail walker.turaco@btinternet.com)

WALKER, Dr Ian Robert; s of Robert Douglas Walker, and Rhoda Walker; *Educ* Bankers' Inst of Australasia (ABIA), Melbourne Theol Coll (LTh), Univ of Bristol (BA), Univ of Wales Swansea (PhD); *Career* head of religious studies Badminton Sch 1977–79, tutor Univ of Wales Swansea 1978, head of religious studies Dulwich Coll 1979–86, headmaster King's Sch Rochester 1986–; memb HMC 1986; lay canon and memb Chapter Rochester Cathedral; Freeman City of London, Liveryman Worshipful Soc of Apothecaries; FCP 1988, FRSA 1992; Knight Cdr Order of St George (Hungary) 2004; *Publications* Plato's Euthyphro (1984), Christ in the Community (1990), Classroom Classics (1991), Faith and Belief: A Philosophical Approach (1994); numerous academic articles on philosophy; *Recreations* writing, oil painting, cricket, martial arts, Egyptology; *Clubs* Athenaeum, East India; *Style—* Dr Ian Walker; ✉ King's School, Satis House, Boley Hill, Rochester, Kent ME1 1TE (tel 01634 888555, fax 01634 888505, e-mail walker@kings-school-rochester.co.uk)

WALKER, Prof Isobel Deda; da of Dr Thomas Alfred Christie, of Auchterarder, Perthshire, and Edith Anderson, *née* Young; *b* 4 October 1944; *Educ* Jordanhill Coll Sch Glasgow, Univ of Glasgow (MB, ChB, MD); *m* 13 April 1966, Dr Colin Alexander Walker; 2 s (Jason b 1969, Lewis b 1975), 3 da (Nicola b 1972, Emily b 1979, Abigail b 1982); *Career* conslt haematologist Glasgow Royal Infirmary 1978–, hon prof Univ of Glasgow 2003–; dir UK Nat External Quality Assurance Scheme (NEQAS) in Blood Coagulation 2005–; pres Br Soc for Haematology 1999–2000, pres Scottish Haematology Soc 2002–, chair Scottish Regnl Cncl RCPath 2004–; FRCPath 1984, FRCPEd 1985; *Recreations* French language, needlework, opera; *Style—* Prof Isobel Walker; ✉ Department of Haematology, Glasgow Royal Infirmary, Castle Street, Glasgow G40 1SF (tel 0141 552 5692, fax 0141 211 4919)

WALKER, James Michael; s of Alan Walker, and Pamela, *née* Senior; *b* 24 May 1965; *Educ* Allerton Grange Sch Leeds, LSE (BSc(Econ)); *m* 11 Sept 1992, Siân, *née* Salt; 1 s (George Hubert b 1994), 1 da (Olivia Grace b 1997); *Career* dir of media consultancy Henley Centre 1995–97, jt md J Walter Thompson & Co London 1997–98, worldwide chm ATG MindShare 1998–, fndr Edge Marketing 1999–2003, chm Brand Science 1999–2003, EMEA md Accenture Marketing Sciences (AMS)/Accenture 2003; *Style—* James Walker, Esq

WALKER, Janet Sheila; da of David Walker, of Chew Magna, Bristol, and Sheila, *née* Rapps; *b* 21 April 1953; *Educ* Keynsham GS, Somerville Coll Oxford (MA), L'Institut des Hautes Études Internationales Univ of Nice; *Career* Price Waterhouse 1976–80 (qualified ACA), chief accountant Handmade Films 1980–81, cost controller Channel 4 1981–82, head of prog fin Thames TV 1982–84, London Films and Limehouse 1984–87, fin dir British Screen Finance 1987–88, dep dir of fin Channel 4 1988–94 (concurrently UK rep EURIMAGES film funding orgn), fin controller for regnl broadcasting BBC 1994–96, fin dir Granada Media Group 1996–98, dir of fin and business affrs Channel 4 1998–2003, commercial and fin dir Ascot Racecourse 2003–; non-exec dir: Design Council, Pizza Express plc 1999–2003, Henderson High Income Trust plc 2007–; ACA 1979; *Style—* Miss Janet Walker; ✉ Ascot Racecourse, Ascot, Berkshire SL5 7JX (tel 01344 878522)

WALKER, Janey P W; da of Brig Harry Walker (d 1968), and Patsy, *née* Iuel-Brockdorff; *b* 10 April 1958; *Educ* Brechin HS, Benenden Sch, Univ of York (BA), Univ of Chicago Illinois (Benton fell); *m* 26 July 1997, Hamish Mykura; 2 da (twins b 2000); *Career* prodr: BBC News and Current Affrs 1982–87, The Late Show BBC TV 1989–91, Edge WNET New York City 1991–92; BBC New York 1992–95, series ed Wired World Wall to Wall TV 1995–96, commissioning ed arts and music Channel Four Television Corp 1996–99, managing ed commissioning Channel Four Television Corp 1999– (also head of educn 2006–); *Recreations* visual arts, modern fiction, walking; *Style—* Ms Janey Walker; ✉ Channel 4 Television, 124 Horseferry Road, London SW1P 2TX (tel 020 7396 4444, fax 020 7306 8360, e-mail jwalker@channel4.co.uk)

WALKER, Jeremy; s of Raymond St John (Henry) Walker (d 1980), and Mary, *née* Dudley; *b* 12 July 1949; *Educ* Brentwood Sch, Univ of Birmingham (BA, Barber Prize for local history); *m* 1968, June, da of Robert Lockhart; 2 s (Patrick b 1968, Toby b 1974), 1 da (Tamsin b 1969); *Career* civil servant; admin trainee Dept of Employment 1971–73, private sec to chm MSC 1974–76, princ Health & Safety Executive 1976–77, Economic Secretariat Cabinet Office 1977–79, princ Employment Service MSC 1979–82, asst sec Australian Dept of Employment & Indust Rels Canberra 1982–84, regnl employment mangr for Yorks & Humberside MSC 1984–86, head of community progs and new job trg scheme MSC 1986–88, regnl dir Yorks & Humberside Dept of Employment 1988–94 (ldr Leeds/Bradford City Action Team 1990–94), regnl dir Govt Office for Yorkshire and the Humber 1994–99, chief exec North Yorks CC 1999–2005; public policy conslt 2005–; chm Yorks Regnl Flood Defence Ctee 2005–; *Recreations* gardening, hobby farming; *Style—* Jeremy Walker, Esq

WALKER, Malcolm Conrad; CBE (1995); s of Willie Walker (d 1960), and Ethel Mary, *née* Ellam (d 1987); *b* 11 February 1946, Huddersfield, W Yorks; *Educ* Mirfield GS; *m* 4 Oct 1969, (Nest) Rhianydd, da of Benjamin Jones (d 1976); 3 c; *Career* trainee mangr F W Woolworth & Co 1964–71, jt fndr and exec chm Iceland Frozen Foods plc 1970–2001, fndr Cooltrader 2001, chief exec Iceland Foods Ltd 2005–; *Recreations* deer stalking, skiing, family, home; *Style—* Malcolm Walker, Esq, CBE; ✉ Iceland Foods Ltd, Second Avenue, Deeside Industrial Park, Deeside, Flintshire CH5 2NW

WALKER, Prof Martin; *Educ* Univ of Newcastle upon Tyne (BA, PhD); *Career* reader in accounting and finance LSE, prof of accounting and business computing Univ of Dundee; Univ of Manchester: prof of finance and accounting 1989–, head of accounting and finance 1990–94, dean Faculty of Social Sciences and Law 2000–03; jt ed Jl of Business Finance and Accounting; *Books* Information and Capital Markets (with Norman Strong, 1987); *Style—* Prof Martin Walker; ✉ Manchester Business School, The University of Manchester, Booth Street West, Manchester M15 6PB

WALKER, Michael Giles Neish; CBE (1985); s of Sir William Giles Newsom Walker (d 1989), and Mildred Brenda, *née* Nairn (d 1983); *b* 28 August 1933; *Educ* Shrewsbury, St John's Coll Cambridge (MA); *m* 27 Jan 1960, Margaret Ruby, da of Lt-Col John D Hills, MC (d 1975); 2 s (Simon Giles David b 1961, Geordie Michael b 1966), 1 da (Nicola

Margaret b 1965); *Career* chm Sidlaw Group plc 1988–99 (joined 1957, chief exec 1976–88); non-exec dir: Scottish and Southern Energy plc (formerly Scottish Hydro-Electric plc) 1982–98, Dunedin Smaller Companies Investment Trust plc 1982–2004, Ivory & Sime Smaller Companies Trust plc 1990–2004 (chm 1992–2004); *Clubs* Cavalry and Guards', Royal & Ancient, Hon Co of Edinburgh Golfers; *Style—* Michael Walker, Esq, CBE; ✉ Shanwell House, Kinross KY13 0RG

WALKER, Dr Michael John; s of Stephen Thomas Walker, of Mount Bures, Suffolk, and Sheila, *née* Ereaut; *b* 24 November 1955; *Educ* Colchester Royal GS, CCC Cambridge (BA, PhD, Manners scholarship), Univ of Cambridge (PGCE, coll award); *Family* 1 s (David Alexander b 5 July 1985), 2 da (Sarah Frances b 29 March 1987, Anna Bridget Grace b 13 May 1995); *Career* visiting lectr Birmingham-Southern Coll AL 1977–78, supervisor Univ of Cambridge 1978–82; Dulwich Coll: asst history master 1982–86, housemaster 1983–86; head history Gresham's Sch 1986–89; King Edward VI GS Chelmsford: sr teacher 1989–92, second dep head 1992–94, first dep head 1994–99, headmaster 1999–; memb SHA 2002–, fndr and memb Steering Gp Consortium for Sch Improvement in Essex, chm Consortium of Selective Schs in Essex 2003–04 (vice-chair 2000–03), memb Nat Leading Edge Steering Gp 2003–04, lead memb Nat Heads' Gp Innovation Unit DfES 2005–07, Next Practice project Higher Level Teaching Skills 2006, Core Gp memb UK ARIA project on assessment 2007–08; vice-pres Helen Rollason Cancer Care Tst, memb Bd Tom Clark Appeal (Teenage Cancer Tst); memb Old Chelmsfordians Assoc; *Recreations* art, design, set design, reading, walking, photography, painting, squash, tennis; *Style—* Dr Michael Walker; ✉ King Edward VI Grammar School, Broomfield Road, Chelmsford, Essex CM1 3SX (tel 01245 353510, fax 01245 344741, e-mail office@kegs.org.uk)

WALKER, Nigel Keith; DL (S Glamorgan 2003); s of Frank George Walker, and Joyce Merle, *née* Foster; *b* 15 June 1963; *Educ* Rumney HS, Open Univ, Univ of Glamorgan; *m* Mary; 3 da (Rebecca b Aug 1993, Eleanor b March 1995, Abigail b 18 Dec 1997); *Career* former athlete and rugby player; with Cardiff Athletics Club; honours at 110m hurdles: UK champion 1983, AAA champion 1984, semi-finalist Olympic Games LA 1984, Bronze medal Euro Indoor Championships France and World Indoor Championships USA 1987; 26 UK int appearances 1983–92 (jr int 1980–82); ret from athletics 1992; debut for Cardiff RFC 1992, debut for Wales 1993 v Ireland; ret from rugby 1998; civil servant 1982–93, devpt offr Sports Cncl for Wales 1993–97, fitness conslt Cardiff RFC 1996–97; presenter: HTV 1996–2000, Channel Four Athletics 1998–99, commentator Eurosport 1999–2001; player devpt mangr Welsh Rugby Union 2000–01, head of sport BBC Wales 2001–; memb Bd UK Sport 2006–; *Recreations* DIY, journalism; *Style—* Nigel Walker, Esq, DL; ✉ c/o BBC Wales, Broadcasting House, Llandaff, Cardiff CF5 2YQ

WALKER, Sir (Baldwin) Patrick; 4 Bt (UK 1856), of Oakley House, Suffolk; also hereditary Pasha of the Ottoman Empire; s of late Cdr Baldwin Charles Walker (d 1927; himself s of Sir Francis Elliot Walker, 3 Bt (d 1928), in his turn 2 surviving s of Adm Sir Baldwin Wake Walker, 1 Bt, KCB, who was Comptroller of the (Royal) Navy and sometime Adm in the Turkish service, whereby he was cr a Pasha), and Mary, *née* Barnett (d 1991); *b* 10 September 1924; *Educ* Gordonstoun; *m* 1, 1948 (m dis 1954), Joy Yvonne, da of Sir Arrol Moir, 2 Bt (d 1957); m 2, 1954, Sandra Stewart; m 3, 1966, Rosemary Ann, da of late Henry Hollingdrake; 1 s, 1 da; m 4, 1980, Vanessa Joyce, da of Dr Alan Clay; *Heir* s, Christopher Walker; *Career* served RN 1942–58; Planned Music Ltd 1958–62, emigrated to South Africa 1962, with Findlays 1962–64, Uniswa Insurance 1964–68, farmer 1969–74, various solar energy cos 1975–83, Pennypinchers 1983–87, propr PW Marketing (mktg heat pumps, pool heating, solar energy, water purification pumps and filters, fuel cells, photovoltaics and airblasters) 1988–; *Style—* Sir Patrick Walker, Bt; ✉ PO Box 7322, Blanco 6531, South Africa

WALKER, Dr Paul Crawford; JP; s of Dr Joseph Viccars Walker (d 1986), of Northants, and Mary Tilley, *née* Crawford (d 1984); *b* 9 December 1940; *Educ* Queen Elizabeth GS Darlington, Downing Coll Cambridge (MA, MB BChir); *m* 1962, Barbara Georgina, da of Albert Edward Bliss, of Cambs; 3 da (Kate, Victoria, Caroline); *Career* Capt RAMC(V) 1975–78; regnl med offr NE Thames RHA 1977–85, gen mangr Frenchay HA 1985–88, hon conslt in community med Bristol and Weston HA 1988–89, dir public health Norwich HA 1989–93, dir Centre for Health Policy Res UEA 1990–93, sr lectr Univ of Wales Coll of Med 1993–1994; dir Independent Public Health 1993–, dir of public health Powys Local Health Bd 2003–, dir of public health Ceredigion Local Health Bd 2004–05; chm CAER Consortium 1985–89; memb: Exec Ctee Gtr London Alcohol Advsy Service 1978–85, Mgmnt Ctee Kings Fund Centre 1980–84, NHS Computer Policy Ctee 1984–85, Advsy Ctee on Misuse of Drugs 1984–87, Bristol and District Community Health Cncl 1996–99, Avon Probation Ctee 1997–99, Avon and Somerset Police Authy 1998–99; Essex Cmmn for the Peace 1980–85, Avon Cmmn for the Peace 1985–89 and 1995–; vice-chm Professional Advsy Gp NHSTA 1987–88, pres Socialist Health Assoc 2003– (vice-pres 1999–2003), chm Welsh Food Alliance 1998–2000, chm Welsh Public Health Assoc 2004– (sec 1998–2004), tstee UK Public Health Assoc; Powys Alliance for Health 1999–2003, Ceredigion Local Health Gp 2001–03; hon treas Transform Drug Policy Fndn; hon sr lectr LSHTM 1983–85, visiting prof QMC London 1985, hon sr lectr UEA 1990–93; visiting fell: UWE 1999–, Univ of Glamorgan 2004–; cncllr City and Co of Bristol 1995–99; *Recreations* railway history, anthropology; *Style—* Dr Paul Walker; ✉ Chagford, 8 Church Avenue, Stoke Bishop, Bristol BS9 1LD (tel and fax 0117 968 2205, e-mail paul@crawfordwalker.freeserve.co.uk)

WALKER, Paul Mackenzie; s of David Gordon Mackenzie Walker (d 2001), and Jean Mackenzie Walker (d 2006); *b* 26 August 1960; *Educ* The High Sch Glasgow, Univ of Glasgow (MA), Strathclyde Graduate Business Sch (MBA), Univ of Northumbria (Dip Law, BVC, LLM); *m* 2006, Alison Johnston, da of Alistair Lindsay, of Dalry and Balmaclellan; 1 da (Emily b 2007); *Career* civil servant 1977–81; researcher House of Commons 1986–87; special advsr Corp Policy Dept Cumbria County Cncl 1987–92; asst regnl dir (Scotland and N England) CBI 1993–96, exec search conslt 1996–98; dir gen Fertiliser Manufacturer's Assoc 1998–2000; portfolio of writing, lecturing,consulting and mediation work 2000–; called to the Bar Lincoln's Inn 2004; Parly candidate (Scottish Cons & Unionist) gen elections of 1983 and 1987; vol business mentor for Prince's Scottish Youth Business Tst 2001–; Elder Church of Scotland 1993–; CEDR accredited 2006; MCIArb, FRSA, FSA Scot; *Recreations* Royal Naval Reserve, skiing, sailing (cruising), walking, DIY; *Clubs* Army and Navy, Farmers'; *Style—* Paul Mackenzie Walker, Esq; ✉ Wynncote, Canonbie, Dumfriesshire DG14 0TD

WALKER, Raymond Augustus; QC (1988); s of Air Chief Marshal Sir Augustus Walker, GCB, CBE, DSO, DFC, AFC, (d 1986), and Dorothy Brenda, *née* Brewis; *b* 26 August 1943; *Educ* Radley, Univ of Cambridge (MA); *m* 2 Sept 1976, June Rose, da of Thomas Wisby; 1 s (James b 19 June 1979); *Career* called to the Bar Middle Temple 1966; recorder 1993; *Recreations* golf, tennis, skiing, sailing, opera; *Clubs* Garrick, Royal West Norfolk Golf, Sunningdale Golf; *Style—* Raymond Walker, Esq, QC; ✉ Lombard Chambers, 1 Sekforde Street, Clerkenwell, London EC1R 0BE (tel 020 7107 2100)

WALKER, His Hon Richard; s of Edwin Roland Walker (d 1980), of Epsom, Surrey, and Barbara Joan, *née* Swann (d 1985); *b* 9 March 1942; *Educ* Epsom Coll, Worcester Coll Oxford (MA); *m* 29 March 1969, Angela Joan, da of John Robert Hodgkinson, of Minehead, Somerset; 2 da (Rosemary b 1972, Sarah b 1974); *Career* called to the Bar Inner Temple 1966; asst cmmr: Parly Boundary Cmmn 1978–89, Local Govt Boundary Cmmn 1982–89; recorder 1989, circuit judge 1989–2006; commissary gen City and Diocese of Canterbury 1995–; chm Pathfinders (Anglican Youth Movement) 1978–84, vice-chm Church Pastoral-Aid Soc 1978–85; *Books* Carter-Ruck on Libel and Slander (jt ed 3 edn, 1985, 4 edn 1992); *Style—* His Hon Richard Walker

WALKER, Richard John; OBE; s of George Walker (decd), and Gwendolen, *née* Clarke (decd); *b* 1952, Reading, Berks; *Educ* Woolverstone Hall Ipswich, Guildford Coll, St Peter's Coll Oxford (MA), Univ of Manchester (Dip, PGCE); *m* 1978, Lauren Michaela; 1 da (Rowan Frances b 1979), 1 s (William George Arthur b 1986); *Career* English teacher: Spain 1976–77 and 1980–81, Kuwait 1977–78; lectr Univ of Manchester 1979–80, sr lectr Coll of St Mark and St John 1989–92; Br Cncl: advsr to Thai govt 1983–85, dep dir literature Arts Dept 1985–87, asst dir of arts, culture and English Lagos Nigeria 1987–89, first sec (cultural) New Delhi India 1994–98, dir São Paulo Brazil 1998–2000, regnl dir East Asia 2000–05, dir Cyprus 2005–; *Publications* Language for Literature, A Curious Child; reviews, articles in THES and Literary Review; *Recreations* travel, other cultures, arts especially literature, visual arts, history, sport: tennis, walking, football; *Style—* Richard Walker, Esq, OBE; ✉ British Council, 10 Spring Gardens, London SW1A 2BN

WALKER, Sir Rodney Myerscough; kt (1996); s of Norman Walker (d 1943), of Wakefield, W Yorks, and Lucy, *née* Kitchen (d 1987); *b* 10 April 1943; *Educ* Thornes House GS Wakefield; *m* 16 March 1974, Anne Margaret, da of Walter Aspinall (d 1972), of Leeds; 2 s (Alexander b 1976, Timothy b 1977); *Career* currently controlling shareholder Myerscough Holdings Ltd; chm: The Rugby Football League 1993–2002, UK Sports Cncl 1997–2003, Wembley National Stadium Tst 2000–02, Empire Interactive plc 2000–06, Donington Park Estates 2000–05, Manchester 2002 Commonwealth Games until 2001, Leicester City plc until 2002, Goals Soccer Centres plc 2002–, Spice Holdings plc 2002–, Titanic Exhibitions 2003–04, World Snooker 2003–, Healthcare Communications plc 2004–06, SMC Gp plc 2004–, Skin Health Spa plc 2005–06; former chm and pres Wakefield Round Table; pres: Wakefield Theatre Tst, Yorks Cancer Research 2002–, The Myerscough Charitable Tst 2003–, Amateur Athletics Assoc of England 2004–; vice-pres Hospital Heartbeat Appeal 2004–; vice-chm: NSPCC Full Stop Appeal 1998–; tstee: St Oswald Charitable Tst, The Rowland St Oswald (1984) Charitable Tst, The Clarke Hall Farm Tst Ltd, Sports Aid Fndn; Hon DUniv; FRSA; *Recreations* golf, charity work; *Style—* Sir Rodney Walker; ✉ Tower House, Bond Street, Wakefield, West Yorkshire WF1 2QP (tel 01924 374349, fax 01924 374358, mobile 07802 252281, e-mail mail@sirrodneywalker.uk.com)

WALKER, Sarah Elizabeth Royle (Mrs R G Allum); CBE (1991); da of Alan Royle Walker, and Elizabeth Brownrigg; *Educ* Pate's GS for Girls Cheltenham, RCM; *m* 1972, Graham Allum; *Career* mezzo-soprano; maj appearances in Br, America, Aust, NZ, Europe; operatic debuts incl: Coronation of Poppea (Kent Opera 1969, San Francisco Opera 1981), La Calisto (Glyndebourne 1970), Les Troyens (Scottish Opera 1972, Wienstaatsoper 1980), princ mezzo-soprano ENO 1972–77, Die Meistersinger (Chicago Lyric Opera 1977), Werther (Covent Gdn 1979), Giulio Caesare (Le Grand Theâtre Genève 1983), Capriccio (Brussels 1983), Teseo (Siena 1985), Samson (NY Metro Opera 1986); Marcellina in Le Nozze di Figaro (Covent Garden) 1995; numerous recordings and videos incl title role in Britten's Gloriana; Prince Consort prof of singing RCM 1993–; vocal performance conslt GSMD 1999–; pres Cheltenham Bach Choir 1986–; FRCM 1987, LRAM, FGSM 2000; *Recreations* interior design, encouraging husband with gardening; *Style—* Miss Sarah Walker, CBE; ✉ c/o Askonas Holt Ltd, Lonsdale Chambers, 27 Chancery Lane, London WC2A 1PF (tel 020 7400 1700, fax 020 7400 1799, e-mail info@askonasholt.co.uk, website www.sarahwalker.com)

WALKER, Simon Edward John; s of Louis Charles Vivian Walker (d 1997), of London, and Joan Wallace, *née* Keith (d 1979); *b* 28 May 1953, South Africa; *Educ* South African Coll Sch Cape Town, Balliol Coll Oxford (pres Oxford Union); *m* Mary Virginia Strang; 1 s (Jeremy b 26 Oct 1985), 1 da (Gini b 3 June 1992); *Career* TV journalist NZ 1975–79, professional journalism fell Stanford Univ 1979–80, dir of communications/dir Parly Oppn Research Unit NZ 1980–84, concurrently presenter Fair Go (TVNZ); dir: Communicor Public Relations Wellington NZ 1984–89, NZ Centre for Independent Studies 1987–89; Hill & Knowlton: dep head of public affrs London 1989–90, dir of Euro public affrs and md Brussels 1990–94; ptnr Brunswick Group Ltd 1994–98 (special advsr to the PM No 10 Policy Unit 1996–97), dir of communications British Airways plc 1998–2003, dir of corporate mktg and communications Reuters plc 2003–; communications sec to HM The Queen 2000–02; dir Comair Ltd (SA) 2000–01; memb: NZ Broadcasting Tbnl 1987–88, Better Regulations Cmmn 2006–; tstee: NZ-UK Link Fndn 2003–, Reuters Fndn, Jamestown UK Fndn; PR Professional of the Year 2002; *Books* Rogernomics: Economic Reform in New Zealand 1984–1989 (ed, 1989); *Recreations* reading, politics; *Clubs* Athenaeum; *Style—* Simon Walker, Esq; ✉ 86 Brook Green, London W6 7BD (tel 020 7602 3883, e-mail simon.walker@communicormedia.com or simon.walker@reuters.com)

WALKER, Simon Jeremy; s of Alan William Walker, of Oxon, and Shirley Ann Lillian, *née* Fremel; *b* 2 April 1967; *Educ* Abingdon Sch, Trent Poly (BA); *m* 11 Aug 1990, Frances Mary, da of William Godfrey Townsend; 1 da (Daisy Megan b 28 Dec 1996), 1 s (Benjamin John William b 13 May 1998); *Career* photographer; freelanced for various Br newspapers and magazines 1988–89, The Independent 1989, Sunday Telegraph 1990 (joined 1989), Sunday Express 1990–91, Sunday Times 1991; The Times: freelance 1993–95, joined staff 1995, news picture ed 2004–; contrib Gamma Press Agency 1991–; David Hodge/Observer Young Photojournalist of the Year 1987, Nikon Press Photographer of the Month July 1989, runner-up Most Promising Newcomer Category Br Press Photographer of the Year Awards 1990 (commended 1989), highly commended Nikon Royal Photographer of the Year 1998; FRSA 2002; *Books* Para - Inside the Parachute Regiment (1993); *Recreations* tennis, golf, walking the dog; *Style—* Simon Walker, Esq; ✉ 8 Fairlawn Grove, London W4 5EH (tel 020 8995 9029, e-mail simon.walker@thetimes.co.uk)

WALKER, (Brian) Stuart; s of William Walker (d 1975), and Annie, *née* Jackson (d 1990); *b* 5 March 1932; *Educ* Blackpool Sch of Art (NDD), Royal Acad Schs London (David Murray scholar, Dip, Bronze Medal for painting, Silver Medal for drawing); *m* 1, 1961 (m dis), Adrienne Elizabeth Atkinson; 2 da (Anna b 5 April 1963, Lucy b 27 July 1965); m 2, 2000, Francesca Elizabeth Boyd; 1 s (Jack b 13 Sept 1995); *Career* sr designer BBC Television 1968–84 (designer 1961–68), prodn designer Handmade Films 1984, sr designer BBC Television 1984–90, freelance prodn designer working on TV film prodns and feature films 1990–; maj prodns since 1974 incl: The Love School, The Chester Mystery Cycle, Divorce - a Trilogy, Bet Your Life, Private Lives, Exiles, Danton's Death, Romeo and Juliet, Measure for Measure, School Play, St Joan, Arabian Nights, Hot House, The Combination, Life After Death, Last Love, Minor Complications, Winnie, James Joyce, An Englishman Abroad (BAFTA Award for TV Design 1984), Desert of Lies, The Dog it Was, The Big H, In the Secret State, Private Function (feature film), Shoot for the Sun, Inappropriate Behaviour, Border, Road (RTS Prodn Design Award 1988), Deadline, Mountain Language, Mountain and the Molehill, Portrait of a Marriage (BAFTA Award for TV Design 1991), London Kills Me (feature film), The Camomile Lawn, The Clothes in the Wardrobe, Captives (feature film), Absence of War, Hollow Reed, The Revengers' Comedies, Heart, Features, Talking Heads; RDI 1989; *Style—* Stuart Walker, Esq; ✉ stuartswalk@aol.com

WALKER, Tim Philip Buchanan; s of W L B Walker, and Claudine Ella, *née* Mawby; *b* 23 June 1963; *Educ* Millfield; *Career* journalist; Evening Echo Bournemouth 1983–85, Evening Argus Brighton 1985–87, The Observer 1987–90, The European 1990–93, Tatler 1993–94, Daily Mail 1994–2002 (dep diary ed 1998–2002, Mail on Sunday); Sunday

Telegraph: diary ed 2002–, theatre critic 2005–; freelance presenter: LBC London 1989–94, Channel 4 2000, Sky 2002–, BBC 2002–, ITN 2002–05; Young Journalist of the Year Br Press Awards 1987; *Books* Norma - A Biography (1993); *Style—* Tim Walker, Esq; ✉ Sunday Telegraph, 1 Canada Square, Canary Wharf, London E14 5DT (tel 020 7538 7417, e-mail tim.walker@telegraph.co.uk)

WALKER, Timothy Alexander; AM (2000); s of Keith James Walker, of Launceston, Tasmania, and Elaine, *née* Edwards (d 2002); *b* 23 November 1954, Hobart, Tasmania; *Educ* Riverside HS, Launceston Matriculation Coll, Univ of Tasmania (BA, Dip Ed, AMusA), Univ of New England (Dip Fin Mgmnt); *Career* teacher The Don Coll 1978–81, concerts mangr Canberra Sch of Music Aust Nat Univ 1981–87, public progs mangr Nat Film and Sound Archive 1987, gen mangr Aust Chamber Orchestra 1989–99 (marketing and devpt mangr 1987–89); ceo World Orchestras 1999–2003, chief exec and artistic dir LPO 2003–; involved with Henry Wood Hall Tst; memb: Int Soc for the Performing Arts 1989, Royal Philharmonic Soc 2003; *Style—* Timothy Walker, Esq, AM; ✉ London Philharmonic Orchestra, 89 Albert Embankment, London SE1 7TP (tel 020 7840 4218)

WALKER, Timothy Edward Hanson; CB (1998); s of Harris and Elizabeth Walker; *b* 27 July 1945; *Educ* Tonbridge, Brasenose Coll Oxford (MA, DPhil); *m* 1, 1969, Judith, *née* Mann (d 1976); 1 da; m 2, 1983, Anna Walker, CB, *qv*, *née* Butterworth; 2 da; *Career* res fell UC Oxford and exhibitioner of Royal Cmmn of 1851 Oxford and Paris 1969–71; Harkness fell: Commonwealth Fund of New York 1971, Univ of Virginia 1971, Northwestern Univ 1972; strategic planner GLC 1974–77, princ DTI 1977–83, Sloan fell London Business Sch 1983; DTI: asst sec 1983–85, head of Policy Planning Unit 1985–86, princ private sec to Secs of State for Trade and Indust 1986–87, under sec and dir Inf Engrg Directorate/dir Alvey Prog 1987–89, head of Atomic Energy Div 1989–95; dep sec and DG Immigration and Nationality Dept Home Office 1995–98, dep chm and cmmr HM Customs and Excise 1998–2000, DG Health and Safety Exec 2000–05; non-exec dir: ICI Chemicals and Polymers Ltd 1988–89, Govt Div UKAEA 1994–95, Inland Revenue 1998–2000, London Strategic Health Authy 2006–; hon vice-pres Inst of Occupational Safety and Health 2002–, govr IAEA (UK) 1989–94, chm Assembly of Donors EBRD Nuclear Safety Account 1993–95; memb: Cncl Inst of Employment Studies 2001–05, Science and Technol Ctee Int Risk Governance Cncl 2004–; contrib to scientific jls; memb Cncl Univ of Warwick 2000–06; tstee Prostate Cancer Charity 2006–; Hon DSc Cranfield Univ 2003, hon fell Warwick Mfrg Gp 2005; FRSA 2000, CEng 2003, FInstP 2003, FIEE 2004; *Recreations* African tribal art, gardening, cookery; *Style—* Timothy Walker, Esq

WALKER, William Connell (Bill); OBE (1998); s of Charles and Willamina Walker; *b* 20 February 1929; *Educ* Dundee: Logie and Blackness Schs, Trades Coll, Coll of Arts; Coll of Distributive Trades London; *m* 1956, Mavis Lambert, 3 da; *Career* Sqdn-Ldr RAFVR; md Retail Stores Gp; MP (Cons) Perth and E Perthshire 1979–83, Tayside N 1983–97 (Parly candidate (Cons) Dundee E Oct 1974); former memb: Select Ctee on Scottish Affrs, Select Ctee on Parly Cmmn for Admin; former jt sec Aviation Ctee, jt vice-chm Cons Backbench Euro Affrs Ctee 1982–97; sec: Scottish Cons Ctee, RAF Parly Gp, Cons Defence Ctee; former chm: Scottish Cons Back-Bench Ctee, Cons Aviation Ctee 1993–97, Cons Pty Orgn Ctee 1993–97, All-Pty Scout Gp; former vice-chm: All-Pty Scotch Whisky Gp, All-Pty Scottish Sports Gp, World Parly Scout Union; treas Br-Zimbabwe Parly Gp; dep chm Scottish Cons and Unionist Pty 2000–02, memb Bd Cons Pty 2000–02; pres Walker Associates; dir: Stagecoach Int Servs Ltd 1982–94, Stagecoach Malawi Ltd 1984–94; hon pres Air Cadet Gliding 1996–, vice-pres Br Gliding Assoc 1991–; *Clubs* RAF; *Style—* Bill Walker, Esq, OBE

WALKER-ARNOTT, Edward Ian; s of Charles Douglas Walker-Arnott (d 1980), of Woodford, Essex, and Kathleen Margaret, *née* Brittain (d 2000); *b* 18 September 1939; *Educ* Haileybury, Univ of London (LLB), UCL (LLM); *m* 11 Sept 1971, (Phyllis) Jane, da of Lt-Col J M Ricketts, MC (d 1987), of Weston, Devon; 2 da (Emily b 7 April 1974, Hannah b 9 July 1979), 1 s (William b 9 Nov 1981); *Career* admitted slr 1963, ptnr Herbert Smith 1968–2000 (sr ptnr 1993–2000), conslt 2000–; non-exec dir: Sturge Holdings plc 1989–95, Hanover Acceptances 2000–; memb: Cork Ctee on Review of Insolvency Law 1977–82, Insolvency Practitioners Tbnl; memb Cncl: Lloyd's 1983–88 (hon memb 1988), Haileybury Coll (treas 1977–88), Benenden Sch 1988–93; visiting prof UCL 2000–; dir RNT 2000–; govr: South Bank Centre 1999–, Wellcome Tst 2000–; Freeman Worshipful Co of Slrs, hon memb Ct of Assts Worshipful Co of Loriners; memb Law Soc; hon fell UCL 1999; *Recreations* cricket, walking, gardening; *Clubs* City of London; *Style—* Edward Walker-Arnott, Esq; ✉ Manuden Hall, Manuden, Bishop's Stortford, Hertfordshire CM23 1DY; Herbert Smith, Exchange House, Primrose Street, London EC2A 2HS (tel 020 7374 8000)

WALKER-ARNOTT, (Brian) Richard; DL (Gtr London 2001); s of (Charles) Douglas Walker-Arnott (d 1980), and Kathleen Margaret, *née* Brittain (d 2000); *b* 8 September 1937; *Educ* Haileybury (scholar), Trinity Hall Cambridge (exhibitioner, MA); *m* 23 Jan 1988, Deborah Clare, da of John Ounsted; 1 s (Charles Laurence b 12 Oct 1989), 1 da (Harriet Rose b 8 July 1992); *Career* PR Dept Procter & Gamble Limited (Newcastle upon Tyne) 1960–68, Charles Barker 1968–73, FJ Lyons 1974–76; dir Charles Barker 1976–91; chief exec Assoc of Recognised English Language Servs 1992–99; RBK&C: cncllr 1974–2006, former chm various ctees and chief whip Majority Pty, dep ldr Majority Pty 1991–2000, mayor 2000–01, memb Cabinet 2001–06; chm Kensington Cons Assoc 1980–83, rep DL for Royal Borough of Kensington and Chelsea 2006–; Master Worshipful Co of Loriners 1990 (memb Ct of Assts); MIPR 1968, DipCAM 1978; *Recreations* mountain walking; *Clubs* Tyne Rowing; *Style—* Richard Walker-Arnott, Esq, DL; ✉ 27 Finstock Road, London W10 6LU (tel 020 8968 4448)

WALKER OF GESTINGTHORPE, Baron (Life Peer UK 2002), of Gestingthorpe in the County of Essex Robert Walker; kt (1994), PC (1997); s of late Ronald Robert Antony Walker, and late Mary Helen, *née* Welsh; *b* 17 March 1938; *Educ* Downside, Trinity Coll Cambridge (BA); *m* 3 Sept 1962, Suzanne Diana, *née* Leggi; 1 s (Hon Robert Thomas b 1963), 3 da (Hon Penelope Mary b 1966, Hon Julian Diana b 1968, Hon Henrietta Solveig b 1972); *Career* 2 Lt Nat Serv RA 1959–61; barr in practice at Chancery Bar 1961–94, QC 1982–94, judge of the High Court of Justice (Chancery Div) 1994–97, Lord Justice of Appeal 1997–2002, Lord of Appeal in Ordinary 2002–; bencher Lincoln's Inn 1990; hon fell Trinity Coll Cambridge 2006; *Style—* The Rt Hon the Lord Walker of Gestingthorpe, PC; ✉ House of Lords, London SW1A 0PW

WALKER OF WORCESTER, Baron (Life Peer UK 1992), of Abbots Morton in the County of Hereford and Worcester; Peter Edward Walker; MBE (1960), PC (1970); s of Sydney Walker, and Rose, *née* Dean; *b* 25 March 1932; *Educ* Latymer Upper Sch, NYU (LLD); *m* 22 Feb 1969, Tessa Joan, da of Geoffrey Ivan Pout; 3 s (Hon Jonathan Peter b 1970, Hon Timothy Rupert b 1975, Hon Robin Caspar b 1978), 2 da (Hon Shara Jane b 1971, Hon Marianna Clare b 1985); *Career* memb Cons Party National Exec Ctee 1956, nat chm Young Cons 1958–60, Parly candidate (Cons) Dartford 1955 and 1959, MP (Cons) Worcester 1961–92; PPS to Ldr of the House of Commons 1963–64; oppn spokesman: on fin and economics 1964–66, on tport 1966–68, on local govt, housing and land 1968–70; min for housing and local govt 1970; sec of state: for the environment 1970–72, for trade and industry 1972–74; oppn spokesman: on trade and industry and consumer affrs Feb-June 1974, on def 1974–75; minister for agric, fisheries and food 1979–83, sec of state for energy 1983–87, sec of state for Wales 1987–90; chm Kleinwort Benson Group plc 1996–98, currently vice-chm Dresdner Kleinwort Wasserstein; chm: Cornhill Insurance plc 1992–2003, Allianz Cornhill Insurance plc 2003–06; non-exec dir: LIFFE Holdings plc, ITM Power; vice-pres German-Br Chamber of Industry and Commerce 2002– (pres 1999–2002); Freeman City of Worcester 2003; Cdr's Cross of Order of Merit of Federal Republic of Germany 1994, Chilean Order of Bernardo O'Higgins Degree Gran Official 1995, Grand Offr Order of the May of the Argentine Republic 2003; *Books* The Ascent of Britain (1976), Trust the People (1987), Staying Power (autobiography, 1991); *Recreations* tennis, reading, music; *Clubs* Carlton; *Style—* The Rt Hon Lord Walker of Worcester, MBE, PC; ✉ Abbots Morton Manor, Gooms Hill, Abbots Morton, Worcestershire

WALKER-SMITH, Prof John Angus; s of Dr Angus Buchanan Walker-Smith (d 1975), of Sydney, Australia, and Alexandra Buckingham, *née* Trindall (d 1970); *b* 1 December 1936; *Educ* Sydney C of E GS, Univ of Sydney (MB BS, MD); *m* 29 Aug 1969, Elizabeth Cantley, da of late George Blaikie, of Edinburgh; 2 da (Louise b 13 Aug 1970, Laura b 17 March 1975), 1 s (James b 15 July 1978); *Career* house physician: Hammersmith Hosp 1963, Brompton Hosp 1963; res fell: (gastroenterology) Royal Prince Alfred Hosp Sydney 1964–66 (res med offr 1960–61), Kinderklinik Zurich Switzerland 1968; student supervisor and hon assoc physician Royal Alexandra Hosp for Children 1969–72 (res med offr 1962–67, professorial registrar 1967–69), conslt paediatrician St Bartholomew's Hosp 1973–95 (prof of paediatric gastroenterology 1985–95), prof Univ Dept of Paediatric Gastroenterology Royal Free and Univ Coll Med Sch 1995–2000 (emeritus prof 2000–), research assoc Wellcome Tst Centre for History of Medicine UCL 2000–; memb St Barnabas C of E Woodford; Freeman City of London, Liveryman Worshipful Soc of Apothecaries; FRACP, FRCP (London and Edinburgh); memb: BMA, Br Paediatric Assoc, Br Soc of Gastroenterology; *Books* Diseases of Small Intestine in Childhood (4 edns 1975, 1979, 1988, 1999), Practical Paediatric Gastroenterology (with J R Hamilton and W A Walker 1983, 2 edn 1995), Enduring Memories: A Paediatric Gastroenterologist Remembers (2003); *Recreations* swimming, photography, painting, philately; *Style—* Prof John Walker-Smith; ✉ 16 Monkham's Drive, Woodford Green, Essex IG8 0LQ (tel 020 8505 7756)

WALKER-SMITH, (Hon) Sir (John) Jonah; 2 Bt (UK 1960), of Broxbourne, Co Herts; o s of Baron Broxbourne, TD, PC, QC (Life Peer and 1 Bt, d 1992), and Dorothy, *née* Etherton; *b* 6 September 1939; *Educ* Westminster, ChCh Oxford; *m* 1974, Aileen Marie, o da of late Joseph Smith; 1 da (Charmian Lucinda b 23 Aug 1977), 1 s (Daniel Derek b 26 March 1980); *Heir* s, Daniel Walker-Smith; *Career* called to the Bar Middle Temple 1963; *Clubs* Garrick; *Style—* Sir Jonah Walker-Smith, Bt; ✉ De Montfort Chambers, 45 Princess Road East, Leicester LE1 7DQ

WALKINGTON, Alexander Stuart Burnett (Sandy); s of Capt Ian Alexander Greet Walkington, of Tavistock, Devon, and Shelagh Winnifred Mary Mackenzie, *née* Munro (d 1994); *b* 5 December 1953; *Educ* Cheltenham Coll (scholar), Trinity Hall Cambridge (Dr Cooper law student, MA), Coll of Law London, Tulane Univ New Orleans; *m* 1988, Francesca Mary, da of Francis Weal; 2 s (Edward Alexander Alban b 1 Nov 1988, Thomas Francis Pageant b 12 Oct 1990), 1 da (Dora Clementine Bianca b 25 Dec 1995); *Career* called to the Bar Gray's Inn 1976 (Gerald Moody scholar); Tulane Univ 1977–78, Parly asst to Emlyn Hooson, QC, MP (now Baron Hooson, QC (Life Peer), *qv*) 1978–79, head of research Parly Lib Pty 1979–81, various positions rising to mangr of external affrs Texaco Ltd 1981–91, mangr of int PR Texaco Inc NY 1991–92, dir of public affrs BT Group plc 1992–2005, dir general election communications Lib Dem Pty 2005, dir gp public affrs Transport for London 2005–06, public policy advsr 2006–; memb Advsy Bd Editorial Intelligence 2006–; Parly candidate (Lib/SDP Alliance) St Albans 1983 and 1987, memb St Albans City Cncl 1984–91, memb Nat Cncl CBI 1998–2002; fell Industry and Parliament Tst; MIPR, FRSA; *Recreations* family, walking, studying architecture; *Clubs* Welwyn Sports and Social; *Style—* Sandy Walkington, Esq; ✉ 6 Hobbs Hill, Welwyn, Hertfordshire AL6 9DS

WALKLEY, Geoffrey; s of Alexander Joseph Charles Walkley, of Winwick, Cambs, and Vera Cecilia Walkley; *b* 25 July 1944; *Educ* East Ham GS for Boys, Univs of Durham and Newcastle (LLB); *m* 18 Jan 1969, Barbara Eunice, da of Ernest Dunstan; 1 s (Richard Andrew b 21 Dec 1970 d 2006), 1 da (Sarah Elizabeth b 29 April 1973); *Career* admitted slr 1968; Bartlett & Gluckstein: articled 1966–68, asst slr 1968–71, ptnr 1971–78; ptnr Bartlett & Gluckstein Crawley & De Reya (later Bartletts, De Reya) 1978–88, ptnr Nabarro Nathanson 1988–93, ptnr Penningtons 1993–2004 (conslt 2004–); memb: Law Soc, Slrs' Benevolent Assoc, Soc for Computers and Law, RYA, RHS; assoc memb RSC; *Recreations* sailing, books, gardening, carpentry; *Clubs* Maylandsea Bay Sailing (hon sec and hon auditor); *Style—* Geoffrey Walkley, Esq; ✉ Penningtons, Bucklersbury House, 83 Cannon Street, London EC4N 8PE (tel 020 7457 3000, fax 020 7457 3240, e-mail walkleyg@penningtons.co.uk)

WALKLING, (Anthony) Kim; s of William Charles Walkling (d 1989), and Vida Karina, *née* Beare; *b* 27 September 1957; *Educ* Sutton HS Plymouth, UCL (LLB); *m* 20 Sept 1986, (Margaret Caroline) Deirdre, *née* Moore, da of Samuel James Moore (d 2006), of Purley, Surrey; 1 s ((James) Christopher Charles b 1990), 1 da (Katherine Sophie Olivia b 1994); *Career* articled clerk Slaughter and May 1980–82, asst slr Watson, Farley & Williams 1982–87; ptnr: SJ Berwin & Co 1987–92, Theodore Goddard 1992–97, Simmons & Simmons 1998–; memb: Law Soc 1982, European Air Law Assoc 1989; *Recreations* photography, music, good food and wine; *Style—* Kim Walkling, Esq; ✉ Simmons & Simmons, CityPoint, One Ropemaker Street, London EC2Y 9SS (e-mail kim.walkling@simmons-simmons.com)

WALL, David Richard; CBE (1985); s of Charles Wall, and Dorothy Irene, *née* Barden; *b* 15 March 1946; *Educ* Haliford House Shepperton, Royal Ballet Sch White Lodge Richmond, Royal Ballet Sch Upper Sch; *m* 1 Aug 1967, Alfreda, da of Edward Thorogood (d 1966); 1 da (Annaliese b 15 Oct 1971), 1 s (Daniel b 12 Dec 1974); *Career* Royal Ballet 1963–: soloist 1964, princ dancer 1966–84; danced all major classical roles incl: Rakes Progress 1965, Swan Lake (with Margot Fonteyn) 1966, Giselle (Peter Wright prodn) 1968, Walk to the Paradise Garden 1972, Manon 1974, Dancers at a Gathering 1974, Romeo and Juliet 1975, La Bayadère 1975, Rituals 1975, Mayerling 1977; dir and gen sec Royal Acad of Dancing 1985–91, lectr and teacher Rambert Sch 1991–, dance conslt Remedial Dance Clinic 1991–, dir Boys' Classical Graduates Course London Studio Centre 1992, guest repetiteur London City Ballet Co 1992–95, ballet master English National Ballet Co 1995–; *Style—* David Wall, Esq, CBE

WALL, Geoffrey; s of Frank Wall, and Gwyneth, *née* Chadwick; *Educ* Wallasey GS, Univ of Sussex (BA), Sorbonne, St Edmund Hall Oxford (BPhil); *Career* Univ of York: lectr 1975–97, sr lectr 1997–, reader 2002–; ed Cambridge Quarterly 1998–; freelance journalist and travel writer; literary biographer; memb: Greenpeace, Amnesty Int; *Books* Flaubert: A Life (2001, shortlisted Whitbread Award for Biography); *Recreations* cycling, rock climbing, going to Paris; *Style—* Geoffrey Wall, Esq; ✉ c/o David Higham Associates, 5–8 Lower John Street, Golden Square, London W1R 4HA; e-mail gw2@york.ac.uk

WALL, Prof Jasper V; s of Philip Errington Wall (d 1973), and Lilian Margaret, *née* Blackburn (d 1980); *b* 15 January 1942; *Educ* Vankleek Hill Collegiate Inst, Queen's Univ at Kingston (BSc), Univ of Toronto (MSc), Australian Nat Univ (PhD); *m* 1969, Jennifer Anne, da of Prof Stanley D Lash (d 1994); 1 da (Kristina b 1965), 1 s (Matthew b 1976); *Career* res sci Australian Nat Radio Astronomy Observatory Parkes NSW 1970–74, RAS Leverhulme Fell Cavendish Lab 1974–75, Royal Soc Jaffé Donation Fell Cavendish Lab 1975–79, head Astrophysics and Astrometry Div Royal Greenwich Observatory 1979–87, offr-in-charge Isaac Newton Gp of Telescopes La Palma Canary Islands 1987–90; Royal Greenwich Observatory: head Technol Div 1990–91, head Astronomy Div and dep dir 1991–93, head Royal Greenwich Observatory and head Astronomy Div Royal

Observatories 1993–95, dir Royal Greenwich Observatory 1995–98; visiting reader Univ of Sussex 1980–90, visiting prof Dept of Astrophysics Univ of Oxford 1998–, adjunct prof Dept of Physics and Astronomy Univ of British Columbia 2003–; chm Editorial Bd Astronomy & Geophysics 1999–2002; FRAS 1975 (memb Cncl 1992–96, vice-pres 1996), FRSA 1998; *Publications* Modern Technology and its Influence on Astronomy (ed with A Boksenberg, 1986), Optics in Astronomy (1993), The Universe at High Redshifts (with A Aragón-Salamanca and N Tanvir, 1997), Practical Statistics for Astronomers (with C Jenkins, 2003); author 150 papers in professional jls; *Recreations* hiking, skiing, music; *Style*— Prof J V Wall

WALL, Malcolm Robert; s of Maj Gen Robert P W Wall, of Essex, and Patricia, *née* O'Brien, of York; *b* 24 July 1956; *Educ* Allhallows Sch Dorset, Univ of Kent (BA); *m* Elizabeth; 3 da (Emma b 4 Aug 1985, Josephine b 10 March 1987, Rebecca b 28 June 1991); *Career* sales exec Southern Television 1978–80, sales exec rising to sales dir Anglia Television Ltd 1980–87, sales and mktg dir Granada Television 1988–92, dep ceo Meridian Broadcasting 1992–94, md Anglia Television Ltd 1994–96; dep dir United Broadcasting & Entertainment Ltd 1996–98, md of HTV Group 1997–99, chief exec United Broadcasting and Entertainment Ltd 1999–2000, ceo United Business Media plc 2001–05, currently chief exec Content Div Virgin Media; non-exec dir: Five, Creston plc 2007–, ITE Gp plc; chm Harlequin FC Ltd 1997–2000; *Clubs* Harlequin FC, MCC, RAC; *Style*— Malcolm Wall, Esq

WALL, Michael Charles; s of James Wall, and Joan Margaret Wall; *Educ* Trinity Sch of John Whitgift, Univ of Sussex (UAU rugby, tennis capt); *Career* bd dir Simons Palmer, ptnr and fndr Fallon Ltd (managing ptnr London until 2004) pres int ops Fallon Worldwide 2004–; MIPA 2000; *Recreations* tennis, golf; *Clubs* Brocket Hall Golf; *Style*— Michael Wall, Esq

WALL, Rt Hon Lord Justice; Rt Hon Sir Nicholas Peter Rathbone; kt (1993), PC (2004); s of Frederick Stanley Wall (d 1978), of London, and Margaret Helen, *née* Woods (d 1998); *b* 14 March 1945; *Educ* Dulwich Coll, Trinity Coll Cambridge (scholar, MA, pres Cambridge Union 1967); *m* 31 August 1973, Margaret Diana Wall, JP, da of Norman Sydee (d 1992), of London; 4 c (Imogen b 1975, Emma b 1977, Rosalind b 1980, Simon b 1983); *Career* called to the Bar Gray's Inn 1969; QC 1988, recorder of the Crown Court 1990–93, judge of the High Court of Justice (Family Div) 1993–2004, Family Div liaison judge Northern Circuit 1996–2001, judge Employment Appeal Tbnl 2001–, judge of the Administrative Court 2003–04, a Lord Justice of Appeal 2004–; hon memb Northern Circuit 2001; *Books* Rayden and Jackson on Divorce (jt ed 16 edn, 1991, 17 edn 1997), Rooted Sorrows (Psychoanalytic perspectives on child protection, assessment, therapy and treatment) (ed and contrib, 1997), Divided Duties: care planning for children within the Family Justice System (contrib, 1998), A Handbook for Expert Witnesses in Children Act Cases (2000), Family Law: Essays for the New Millennuim (contrib, 2000), Delight and Dole (contrib, 2002); *Recreations* collecting and binding books, opera, walking, composing clerihews; *Style*— The Rt Hon Lord Justice Wall; ✉ Royal Courts of Justice, Strand, London WC2A 2LL

WALL, Prof (Charles) Terence Clegg; s of Charles Wall (d 1976), of Woodfield, Dursley, and Ruth, *née* Clegg (d 1998); *b* 14 December 1936; *Educ* Marlborough, Trinity Coll Cambridge (BA, PhD); *m* 22 Aug 1959, Alexandra Joy, da of Prof Leslie Spencer Hearnshaw (d 1991), of West Kirby; 2 s (Nicholas b 1962, Alexander b 1967), 2 da (Catherine b 1963, Lucy b 1965); *Career* fell Trinity Coll Cambridge 1959–64, Harkness fell 1960–61, univ reader and fell St Catherine's Coll Oxford 1964–65, prof of pure mathematics Univ of Liverpool 1965–99, Royal Soc Leverhulme visiting prof Mexico 1967, sr fell SERC 1983–88, sr fell Univ of Liverpool 1999–; treas: Wirral area SDP 1985–88, West Wirral Lib Dems 1988–, Hoylake Chamber Concert Soc 2000–; fell Cambridge Philosophical Soc 1958–, memb American Mathematical Soc 1961–, pres London Mathematical Soc 1978–80 (memb 1961–, memb Cncl 1973–80 and 1992–96); foreign memb Royal Danish Acad 1990–; FRS (memb Cncl 1974–76); *Books* Surgery on Compact Manifolds (1970), A Geometric Introduction to Topology (1970), The Geometry of Topological Stability (with Andrew du Plessis, 1995), Singular Points of Plane Curves (2004); *Recreations* reading, walking, gardening, home winemaking; *Style*— Prof C T C Wall, FRS; ✉ 5 Kirby Park, West Kirby, Wirral, Merseyside CH48 2HA (tel 0151 625 5063); Department of Mathematical Sciences, University of Liverpool, PO Box 147, Liverpool L69 3BX (tel 0151 794 4060, fax 0151 794 4061, telex 627095, e-mail ctcw@liverpool.ac.uk)

WALLACE, Prof (William) Angus; s of Dr William Bethune Wallace (d 1981), of Dundee, Scotland, and Dr Frances Barret, *née* Early (d 1992); *b* 31 October 1948; *Educ* Dundee HS, Univ of St Andrews (MB ChB); *m* 2 Jan 1971, Jacqueline Vera Studley, da of Dr George William Eglinton Studley (d 1995), of East Finchley, London; 1 da (Suzanne b 1973), 2 s (Malcolm b 1975, Andrew b 1979); *Career* jr house offr Dundee Royal Infirmary and Maryfield Hosp 1972–73, demonstrator in anatomy Univ of Nottingham 1973–74; SHO: Nottingham 1974–75, Derby 1975; basic surgical trg registrar Newcastle and Gateshead Hosps 1975–77, orthopaedic registrar Nottingham Hosps 1978–81, res fell MRC 1979, lectr in orthopaedic surgery Univ of Nottingham 1981–84, visiting res fell Toronto W Hosp Canada 1983, sr lectr in orthopaedic surgery Univ of Manchester 1984–85, med dir North Western Orthotic Unit and med advsr Dept of Orthopaedic Mechanics Univ of Salford 1984–85, prof of orthopaedic and accident surgery Univ of Nottingham 1985–, med dir MSc Course in Sports Med Univ of Nottingham 1995–2001, chm Inter Collegiate Specialty Bd in Trauma and Orthopaedic Surgery 2002–05; memb Cncl RCS(Ed) 1990–2000 and 2005– (vice-pres 1997–2000), dean Faculty of Med Informatics RCS(Ed) 2000–05; pres: Br Orthopaedics Sports Trauma Assoc 1997–99, Br Elbow and Shoulder Soc 2001–03; chm: Clinical Curriculum Ctee Nottingham Med Sch 1992–95, Nat Osteoporosis Soc 1996–98, Nat Sports Medicine Inst of the UK 1999–2003; co-chair Research Gp Health Technologies (Faraday) and Knowledge Transfer Network 2002–, memb Exec Ctee European Soc for Surgery of the Shoulder and Elbow 2003–06, memb Cncl Faculty of Sport and Exercise Medicine UK 2006–; tstee AA Motoring Tst 2003–; Sir Walter Mercer Gold Medal RCS(Ed) 1985, Weigelt-Wallace Award for Med Care 1995; memb RSM; FRCSEd 1977, FRCSEd (orthopaedic) 1985, FRCS 1997; *Recreations* narrowboat cruising, jogging, woodwork; *Style*— Prof W Angus Wallace; ✉ University Hospital, Queen's Medical Centre, Nottingham NG7 2UH (tel 0115 823 1121, fax 0115 823 1118, e-mail angus.wallace@rcsed.ac.uk)

WALLACE, (Robert) Ben Lobban; s of Robert L Wallace, of Perthshire, and Christine, *née* Aitchison; *b* 15 May 1970; *Educ* Millfield, RMA Sandhurst; *m* Dec 2001, Liza, *née* Cooke; *Career* Scots Guards Offr 1990–98: Platoon Cdr 1992 (mentioned in despatches 1991), Ops Offr 1993, Intelligence Offr 1994, Co Cdr 1997; ski instructor Austria Nat Ski Sch 1988–89; MSP (Cons) Scotland North East 1999–2003, shadow spokesman for Health, memb European Ctee, memb Rifkind Policy Cmmn; overseas dir QinetiQ 2003–05; MP (Cons) Lancaster and Wyre 2005–; memb Royal Co of Arches 2007; *Recreations* skiing, sailing, diving, horse racing; *Clubs* Third Guards, Carlton; *Style*— Ben Wallace, Esq, MP; ✉ Constituency Office, The Great Eccleston Village Centre, 59 High Street, Great Eccleston, Lancashire PR3 0YB (e-mail wallaceb@parliament.uk); House of Commons, London SW1A 0AA

WALLACE, Brian Godman; s of James Alexander Gaul Wallace, and Phyllis May, *née* Godman; *b* 1 March 1954; *Educ* Royal High Sch Edinburgh, Univ of St Andrews (MA); *Children* 1 da (Fiona b 11 March 1984), 1 s (Callum James b 27 April 1986); *Career* mangr Price Waterhouse CAs Dubai 1980–82 (asst mangr London 1976–80); Schlumberger: chief accountant Dubai 1982–84, European financial controller London 1984–85, Middle E financial controller Dubai 1985–87, Eastern Hemisphere finance dir Paris 1987–89; gp financial controller APV plc London 1989–91, gp finance dir Geest plc 1991–95, gp financial dir Hilton Group plc 1995–2006 (dep gp chief exec 2000–06), finance dir Ladbrokes plc 2007–; non-exec dir: Hays plc 2001–, Scottish & Newcastle plc 2006–; ACA; *Recreations* golf, tennis, theatre; *Style*— Brian Wallace, Esq

WALLACE, Lt-Gen Sir Christopher Brooke Quentin; KBE (1997, OBE 1983, MBE 1978), DL (Hants 2004); s of late Major Robert Quentin Wallace, and Diana Pamela Wallace, *née* Galtrey, of Thorpeness, Suffolk; *b* 3 January 1943; *Educ* Shrewsbury, RMA Sandhurst; *m* 6 Dec 1969, Delicia Margaret Agnes, da of Gerald Curtis; 1 s (Wyndham b 4 July 1971), 1 da (Suzannah b 16 Feb 1974); *Career* cmmnd 1962, CO 3 Bn Royal Green Jackets 1983–85, Cdr 7 Armd Bde 1986–88, dir Public Relations (Army) 1989–90, Cdr 3 Armd Div 1990–93, Cmdt Staff Coll Camberley 1993–94, team ldr Permanent Joint HQ Implementation 1994–96, Chief of Jt Ops Perm Jt HQ (UK) 1996–99, ret Army 1999; Cmdt RCDS 2001–04; memb Cncl RUSI 1996–2000; rep Col Cmdt: Royal Green Jackets 1995–98, Light Div 1998–99; pres Army Golf Assoc 1995–2000; chm Royal Green Jackets Museum Tstees 1999–, dep chm Imperial War Museum 2006– (tstee 1999–); *Books* A Brief History of The King's Royal Rifle Corps, 1755–1965 (2005), Focus on Courage: The 59 Victoria Crosses of The Royal Green Jackets (2006), Rifles and Kukris: Delhi 1857 (2007); *Recreations* golf, bird watching, military history; *Clubs* Sunningdale Golf, Army and Navy; *Style*— Lt-Gen Sir Christopher Wallace, KBE, DL; ✉ c/o RHQ The Rifles, Peninsula Barracks, Winchester, Hampshire SO23 8TS

WALLACE, Prof Sir David James; kt (2004), CBE (1996); s of Robert Elder Wallace, and Jane McConnell, *née* Elliot; *b* 7 October 1945; *Educ* Hawick HS, Univ of Edinburgh (BSc, PhD); *m* 1970, Elizabeth Anne Yeats; 1 da; *Career* Harkness fell Dept of Physics Princeton Univ 1970–72, reader Dept of Physics Univ of Southampton 1978–79 (lectr 1972–78), Tait prof of mathematical physics Univ of Edinburgh 1979–93 (head of physics 1984–87), vice-chllr Loughborough Univ 1994–2006, master Churchill Coll Cambridge 2006–, dir Isaac Newton Inst for Mathematical Sciences and J N M Rothschild & Sons prof of mathematical sciences Univ of Cambridge 2006–; dir: Edinburgh Concurrent Supercomputer 1987–89, Edinburgh Parallel Computing Centre 1990–93; author of pubns in research and review jls in various areas of theoretical physics and computing; memb Cncl and chm Science Bd SERC 1990–94 (chm Physics Ctee 1987–90), memb Cncl and chm Tech Opportunities Panel EPSRC 1994–98, pres Physics Section Br Assoc for the Advancement of Science 1994; Office of Science and Technol: memb Link and TCS Bds 1995–2001, chm TCS quinquennial review 2001, chm e-Science Steering Ctee 2001–06; memb numerous panels in science, info and communication technols European Cmmn, memb European Science and Technol Assembly 1997–98; memb Scottish Higher Educn Funding Cncl 1993–97, chm CVCP/SCOP Task Force on Sport in Higher Educn 1995–97, chm Value for Money Steering Ctee HEFCE 1997–2003; non-exec dir: Scottish Life Assurance Co 1999–2001, Taylor & Francis Gp plc 2000–04; pres Inst of Physics 2002–04, vice-pres and treas Royal Soc 2002–07; DL Leics 2001–06; Maxwell Medal Inst of Physics 1980; Hon DEng Heriot-Watt Univ 2002; Hon DSc Univs of: Edinburgh 2003, Leicester 2005, Loughborough 2006, Southampton 2006; CIMgt 2001; FRS 1986, FRSE 1982, FREng 1998, FInstP; *Recreations* exercise, eating well, mycophagy; *Style*— Prof Sir David Wallace, CBE, FRS, FREng

WALLACE, Prof Helen Sarah; CMG (2000); da of Edward Rushworth (d 1975), of Leicester, and Joyce, *née* Robinson (d 2002); *b* 25 June 1946; *Educ* Univ of Oxford (MA), Coll of Europe Bruges (Dip European Studies), Univ of Manchester (PhD); *m* 24 Aug 1968, Baron Wallace of Saltaire (Life Peer) , *qv*, s of William Edward Wallace (d 1995); 1 da (Hon Harriet Katherine b 1 Sept 1977), 1 s (Hon Edward William Joseph b 5 May 1981); *Career* admin offr Dept of Extra-Mural Studies Univ of Manchester 1968–69, res assoc Dept of Govt Univ of Manchester 1972–73, lectr UMIST 1974–78, lectr and sr lectr Civil Service Coll 1978–85, on secondment Planning Staff FCO 1979–80, sr res fell and dir W European Prog RIIA 1985–92, prof of contemporary European studies and dir then co-dir Sussex European Inst Univ of Sussex 1992–2001, prog dir One Europe or Several? Prog ESRC 1998–2001, dir Robert Schuman Centre Euro Univ Inst Florence 2001–06; visiting prof Coll of Europe 1976–; hon Jean Monnet chair of contemporary Euro studies 1997; FBA 2000; Chevalier dans l'Ordre National du Mérite 1996; *Publications* Interlocking Dimensions of European Integration (2001), Policy-Making in the European Union (with Mark Pollack and William Wallace, 2005); author of numerous essays and articles in learned jls; *Style*— Prof Helen Wallace, CMG, FBA

WALLACE, Prof Ian; s of Francis Jardine Wallace, and Edith, *née* Reay; *b* 8 December 1942; *Educ* Carlisle GS, Univ of Oxford (Cutlers scholar, DAAD scholar, MA, BLitt); *m* 8 July 1967, Trudy, da of Paul Johann Breitenmoser; 1 s (Daniel Frederick b 16 Nov 1976); *Career* asst prof in German Univ of Maine USA 1969–72 (instr 1967–69), lectr in German Univ of Dundee 1972–84; Loughborough Univ: prof of modern languages 1984–91, head Dept of European Studies 1987–90; Univ of Bath: prof of German 1991–2003, head Sch of Modern Languages and Int Studies 1992–95; fndr ed German Monitor 1979–; chm of tstees Bath Royal Literary and Scientific Inst 1996–2000, pres Int Feuchtwanger Soc; *Books* The Writer and Society in the GDR (ed, 1984), Volker Braun (1986), East Germany (1987), The German Revolution of 1989 (co-ed, 1992), Berlin (1993), Aliens (ed, 1994), Anna Seghers in Perspective (ed, 1998), Heiner Müller (co-ed, 2000), Fractured Biographies (ed, 2003); *Recreations* sport, music; *Style*— Prof Ian Wallace

WALLACE, Rt Hon James Robert; PC (2000), QC (Scot 1997), MSP; s of John Fergus Thomson Wallace, of Annan, Dumfriesshire, and Grace Hannah, *née* Maxwell; *b* 25 August 1954; *Educ* Annan Acad, Downing Coll Cambridge (MA), Univ of Edinburgh (LLB); *m* 9 July 1983, Rosemary Janet, da of late William Grant Paton Fraser, OBE, TD, of Milngavie, Glasgow; 2 da (Helen b 1985, Clare b 1987); *Career* admitted Faculty of Advocates 1979; memb Scottish Lib Pty Nat Exec 1976–85 (vice-chm 1982–85), ldr Scottish Lib Dems 1992–2005; MP (Lib until 1988, now Lib Dem) Orkney and Shetland 1983–2001 (Parly candidate (Lib) Dumfries 1979, Euro Parly candidate (Lib) S Scotland 1979); Lib Parly spokesman on defence and dep whip 1985–87, Alliance election spokesman on tport 1987, Lib chief whip and defence spokesman 1987, Lib Dem chief whip 1988–92; Lib Dem spokesman: on employment and fisheries 1988–92, on Scotland 1992, on maritime affairs and fishing 1992–97; MSP Orkney (Lib Dem) 1999–; Scottish Exec: dep first minister 1999–2005 (acting first min 2000 and 2001), min for Justice 1999–2003, min for Enterprise and Lifelong Learning 2003–05; Elder of Church of Scotland; *Recreations* music, horseriding, golf, travel; *Clubs* Caledonian, Scottish Liberal; *Style*— The Rt Hon James Wallace, QC, MSP; ✉ Northwood House, Tankerness, Orkney KW17 2QS (tel 01856 861383); The Scottish Parliament, Edinburgh EH99 1SP (tel 0131 348 5815, e-mail jim.wallace.msp@scottish.parliament.uk)

WALLACE, Joanna J (Mrs David Crowley); da of Joseph Barry Wallace (d 1998), and Margaret, *née* Barnes; *b* 3 September 1965; *Educ* UCL (BSc), Univ of Calif (MBA), Keele Univ (Dip); *m* 17 Feb 2001, David Crowley; 1 da (Erin b 24 Dec 2001); *Career* mgmnt conslt: BUS Ltd 1987–89, Breuer Conslts San Francisco 1989–91; regnl planning mangr N Calif and health services planner San Francisco Med Centre Kaiser Permanente 1991–95, dir of business mgmnt E Cheshire NHS Tst 1995–97, chief exec St Helens and Knowsley HA 1997–2000, chief exec Christie Hosp NHS Tst 2000–05, UK ceo Aptium Cancer Care Ltd 2006–; memb Nat Sentencing Advsy Panel; *Recreations* running, windsurfing, reading, supporting Bolton Wanderers FC; *Style*— Ms Joanna J Wallace; ✉ Aptium Cancer Care, Booths Park, Chelford Road, Knutsford WA16 8QZ

WALLACE, John Williamson; OBE (1995); s of Christopher Kidd Wallace, of Glenrothes, Fife, and Ann Drummond, *née* Allan; *b* 14 April 1949; *Educ* Buckhaven HS, King's Coll Cambridge (MA); *m* 3 July 1971, Elizabeth Jane, da of Prof Ronald Max Hartwell, of Oxford; 2 s (Cosmo b 1979, Esme b 1982); *Career* asst princ trumpet LSO 1974–76, princ trumpet Philharmonia 1976–95, artistic dir brass RAM 1992–2001, princ RSAMD 2002–; performed obligato trumpet at Royal Wedding 1981, performed first performance Malcolm Arnold Concerto 1982, Sir Peter Maxwell Davies trumpet concerto Hiroshima 1988, Tim Souster Trumpet Concerto 1988, Robert Saxton, Dominic Muldowney, James Macmillan Trumpet Concerto 1993, Sir Peter Maxwell Davies Trumpet Quintet 1999; trumpet duets: Prime Number (1990), Odd Number (1991), Even Number (1991); soloist Last Night of the Proms 1996; formed Wallace Collection Brass Ensemble 1986 (19 solo and gp recordings); hon memb RCM 1982, FRAM, FRSAMD; *Books* First Book of Trumpet Solos (1985), Second Book of Trumpet Solos (1985), The Cambridge Companion to Brass Instruments (co-ed); *Style*— John Wallace, Esq, OBE

WALLACE, Keith; *b* 5 June 1945; *Educ* Mill Hill Sch, KCL (Postgrad Cert); *Career* admitted slr 1971; ptnr Bird & Bird 1972–84, clerk Richard Cloudesley's Charity 1976–, ed Pension Lawyer 1984–99, ptnr and now conslt Richards Butler 1985–; memb Takeover Panel 1994; chm: Maldon Unit Trust Managers Ltd 1987–2000, Independent Pension Trustee Ltd 1990–2000, London Endowed Charities Forum 2002–, Beaufort Trust Corporation Ltd (dir 1985–); ed/commentator (Pensions) Television Educn Network 1992–98; vice-pres Holborn Law Soc 1983–84; memb: Ctee Assoc Pension Lawyers 1984–89, NAPF Investment Ctee 1991–96, Cncl Occupational Pensions Advsy Serv (now Pensions Advsy Serv) 1992–, UK Soc of Investment Professionals; tstee Wishbone Tst 2000–03, Cncl The Assoc of Corporate Tstees (TACT), memb English Chamber Choir 1993–2000, cancellarius English Chantry Choir 2002–; *Books* Tomorrow's Lawyers: Computers and Legal Training (1981), Trust Deed and Rules Checklist (1993), Banking Litigation (1999); *Style*— Keith Wallace, Esq; ✉ Richards Butler, Beaufort House, 15 St Botolph Street, London EC3A 7EE (tel 020 7247 6555, fax 020 7247 5091)

WALLACE, Marjorie Shiona (Countess Skarbek); MBE; da of William Wallace (d 1975), and Doris Gertrude, *née* Tulloch (d 1989); *b* 10 January 1945, Kenya; *Educ* Rodean Sch Johannesburg, Parsons Mead, UCL (BA); *m* Count Andrzej Skarbek; 3 s (Sacha b 29 May 1972, Stefan b 2 March 1976, Justin Maximillian b 3 October 1979), 1 da (Sophia Augusta b 23 January 1984); *Career* writer and researcher Frost Programme ITV 1966–69, reporter and film dir Nationwide and Midweek BBC 1969–72; Sunday Times: reporter Insight team 1972–89, social services corr 1974–89, sr feature writer; conslt Earth Year 2050 TVS 1983–84, fndr SANE 1986– (chief exec 1989–), fndr Prince of Wales Int Centre for SANE Research Oxford 2003–; awards: Campaigning Journalist of the Year Br Press Awards 1982 and 1986, John Pringle Meml Award 1986, Oddfellow Prize Book Tst 1987, Snowdon Special Award 1988, Medical Journalist of the Year 1988, Evian Health Award 1991 and 1995, European Woman of Achievement 1992, Br Neuroscience Public Voice Award 2003, shortlisted Lifetime Achievement Award UK Charity Awards 2002 and Beacon Awards 2003; research fell Nuffield Coll Oxford 1989–91; regular lectr and tv/radio guest; memb: Mgmnt Advsy Ctee Inst of Psychiatry 1989–2002 (memb Advsy Ctee 2003–), Ethical Research Ctee Inst of Psychiatry 1991–2002, BUPA 1997–, National Disability Cncl 1998–2002; chm Friends of the Open Air Theatre Ctee 1991–, patron Hay Literary Festival 2002; fell Univ of London; Hon DSc City Univ 2001; Hon FRCPsych 1997; *Publications* On Giant's Shoulders (1976), Suffer the Children, the Thalidomide Campaign (co-author, 1978), The Superpoison (1979), The Silent Twins (1986), Campaign and Be Damned (1991); screenplays: On Giant's Shoulders (1978, Int Emmy), The Silent Twins (1986); documentaries: Whose Mind Is It? (BBC, 1988), Circles of Madness (BBC, 1994); *Recreations* poetry, opera, piano, Victorian ballads, dining out, friends; *Clubs* Groucho, Athenaeum; *Style*— Marjorie Wallace; ✉ SANE, 1st Floor, Cityside House, 40 Alder Street, London E1 1EE (tel 020 7375 1002, fax 020 7375 2162)

WALLACE, Rt Rev Martin William; *see:* Selby, Bishop of

WALLACE, (George) Roger; *b* 20 April 1946; *m* 28 June 1969, Susan (Sue); 2 c (Mark, Helen (twins) b 25 July 1975); *Career* Coalite Group Ltd (formerly Coalite Group plc): gp accountant 1976–80, gp fin controller 1980–82, fin dir 1982–89; dir CTC Fisheries Ltd 1986–; fin dir: Anglo United plc 1990– (chief fin offr 1989–90), Falkland Islands Holdings plc 1997–; MCIMA; *Style*— Roger Wallace, Esq; ✉ Anglo United plc, PO Box 149, Buttermilk Lane, Bolsover, Chesterfield, Derbyshire S44 6YU (tel 01246 822122)

WALLACE, (Wellesley) Theodore Octavius; s of Dr Caleb Paul Wallace (d 1981), of Whitecroft, West Clandon, Surrey, and Dr Lucy Elizabeth Rainsford, *née* Pigott (d 1968); *b* 10 April 1938; *Educ* Charterhouse, Christ Church Oxford (MA); *m* 23 Jan 1988, Maria Amelia, o da of Sir Ian George Abercromby, 10 Bt (d 2003); 1 s (James Abercromby Octavius b 18 Jan 1989), 1 da (Lucy Mary Diana b 4 Nov 1991); *Career* 2 Lt RA 1958, Lt Surrey Yeomanry TA 1959; called to the Bar Inner Temple 1963; memb Lloyd's; govr Inner London Sch 1966–86, chm Chelsea Cons Assoc 1981–84, chm VAT and Duties Tribunal 1992– (pt/t chm 1989–92); special cmmr 1999– (dep special cmmr 1992–99); hon sec Taxation Sub-Ctee Soc of Cons Lawyers 1975–92; Cons candidate: Pontypool Feb 1974, South Battersea Oct 1974 and May 1979; *Recreations* tennis, racing, skiing; *Style*— Theodore Wallace, Esq; ✉ Whitecroft, West Clandon, Surrey GU4 7TD (tel 01483 222574); 46 Belleville Road, London SW11 6QT (tel 020 7228 7740); Combined Tax Tribunals, 15–19 Bedford Avenue, London WC1B 3AS

WALLACE, Vivien Rosemary Lumsdaine; da of late Capt James Edward Lumsdaine Wallace, and late Gwynne Wallace, *née* Jones; *b* 11 February 1944; *Educ* St Martin's Sch Solihull, Emma Willard Troy NY (ESU scholarship), Arts Cncl of GB bursary to study theatre admin; *m* 1, 2 Sept 1964, Anthony Thomas Etridge; m 2, 27 June 1981, Terence Francis Frank Coleman, *qv*; 1 da (Eliza b 1983), 1 s (Jack b 1984); *Career* press offr London Festival Ballet 1969–71, first ever press offr Royal Ballet Covent Garden 1972–74, chief press offr National Theatre 1975–77; Granada Television International: NY mangr 1979, head of sales 1981, dir of sales 1983, chief exec 1987–92; md Lippin-Wallace (television mktg co based London and LA) 1993–96, head of public affairs National Theatre 1996–2003, mktg dir Old Vic Theatre Co 2004–; dir: Granada Television Ltd 1987–92, Nat Assoc of TV Production Execs USA 1988–92; chm TBA Films and Television Hamburg 1989–92; FRSA; *Style*— Miss Vivien Wallace

WALLACE-HADRILL, Prof Andrew Frederic; OBE (2004); s of John Michael Wallace-Hadrill (d 1985), of Oxford, and Anne, *née* Wakefield; *b* 29 July 1951; *Educ* Rugby (scholar), CCC Oxford (Charles Oldham scholar, Hertford and da Paravicini scholar, Craven and Ireland scholar, BA, DPhil); *m* 31 July 1975, Josephine Claire, da of John Temple Forbes Braddock; 1 da (Sophie Margaret Anne b 22 Sept 1980), 1 s (Michael Sutherland b 9 June 1984); *Career* fell and dir of studies in classics Magdalene Coll Cambridge 1976–83, jt lectr in classics Jesus Coll Cambridge 1979–83, lectr in ancient history Univ of Leicester 1983–87, prof of classics and head of dept Univ of Reading 1987–95, dir British Sch at Rome 1995–; ed Jl of Roman Studies 1990–95; memb Soc for the Promotion of Roman Studies 1973–; dir Herculaneum Conservation Project 2001–; FSA 1998; *Books* Suetonius: the scholar and his Caesars (1983), Ammianus Marcellinus - The Later Roman Empire AD 354–378 (1986), Patronage in Ancient Society (ed, 1989), City and Country in the Ancient World (jt ed, 1991), Augustan Rome (1993), Houses and Society in Pompeii and Herculaneum (1994), Domestic Space in the Roman World: Pompeii and Beyond (jt ed, 1997), The British School at Rome: One Hundred Years (2001); *Style*— Prof Andrew Wallace-Hadrill, OBE, FSA; ✉ The British School at Rome, via Gramsci 61, 00197 Rome, Italy (tel 00 39 6 3264939)

WALLACE OF SALTAIRE, Baron (Life Peer UK 1995), of Shipley in the County of West Yorkshire; William John Lawrence Wallace; s of William Edward Wallace, and Mary Agnes, *née* Tricks; *b* 12 March 1941; *Educ* Westminster Abbey Choir Sch, St Edward's Sch Oxford, King's Coll Cambridge (BA), Cornell Univ (PhD); *m* 25 Aug 1968, Helen Sarah, da of Edward Rushworth (d 1975); 1 da (Hon Harriet Katherine b 1 Sept 1977), 1 s (Hon Edward William Joseph b 1981); *Career* lectr in govt Univ of Manchester 1966–77, dir of studies RIIA 1978–90, Hallstein fell St Antony's Coll Oxford 1990–95, prof of int relations LSE 1999–2005 (currently emeritus prof, reader in int relations 1995–99); visiting prof of int studies Central European Univ 1994–97; memb various Lib Pty and SDP Lib Alliance Nat Ctees 1973–88; Parly candidate Lib Pty: Huddersfield West 1970, Manchester Moss Side 1974, Shipley 1983 and 1987; Lib Dem spokesman on foreign affairs House of Lords, memb Euro Union Ctee House of Lords 1996–2001; *Books* The Transformation of Western Europe (1990), The Foreign Policy Process in Britain (1976), Policy Making in the European Community (1983, 5 edn 2005), Regional Integration: the West European Experience (1994); *Style*— The Rt Hon Lord Wallace of Saltaire; ✉ House of Lords, London SW1A 0PW

WALLER, Gary Peter Anthony; s of John Waller (d 1965), and Elizabeth Waller (d 2000); *b* 24 June 1945; *Educ* Rugby, Lancaster Univ (BA), Open Univ Business Sch (MBA); *Career* contested (Cons) Rother Valley Feb and Oct 1974; MP (Cons): Brighouse and Spenborough 1979–83, Keighley 1983–97; memb House of Commons Select Ctee on Tport 1979–82, PPS to Rt Hon David Howell as Sec of State for Tport 1982–83; chm: All-Pty Wool Textile Gp 1984–89, House of Commons Information Select Ctee 1992–97 (memb 1991–97); vice-chm Cons Parly Tport Ctee 1992–97; dir Which? Ltd 2002–04 and 2006–; memb Cncl Consumers' Assoc 1995–; *Recreations* music, sport, photography, cycling, classic cars; *Clubs* Carlton; *Style*— Gary Waller, Esq; ✉ Monksfield, Sawbridgeworth Road, Hatfield Heath, Bishop's Stortford CM22 7DR (tel 01279 739345, e-mail gary.waller@which.net)

WALLER, Guy de Warrenne; s of Desmond de Warrenne (d 1978), and Angela Mary, *née* Wright; *b* 10 February 1950; *Educ* Hurstpierpoint Coll, Worcester Coll Oxford (MA), Wolfson Coll Oxford (MSc); *m* 30 Aug 1980, Hilary Ann, da of Rt Rev D J Farmbrough; 4 c (Becky b 11 Nov 1982, Lottie b 27 May 1984, Lucy b 13 April 1988, Jocelyn b 4 Dec 1989); *Career* Radley Coll: asst master 1974–93, head of chemistry 1982–88, housemaster 1988–93, master i/c hockey 1975–78, coach 1st XV backs 1979–86, master i/c cricket 1983–92; headmaster Lord Wandsworth Coll 1993–97, headmaster Cranleigh Sch 1997–; FRSA 1993; *Publications* Thinking Chemistry (1980), Advancing Chemistry (1982), Condensed Chemistry (1985), Teach Yourself GCSE Chemistry (1987); *Recreations* music, sport (two hockey blues, and a cricket blue), chess, family, British motorcycles; *Clubs* MCC, Free Foresters, Vincent's (Oxford), Ladykillers; *Style*— Guy Waller, Esq; ✉ Cranleigh School, Cranleigh, Surrey GU6 8QQ (tel 01483 273666, fax 01483 273696, e-mail gw@cranleigh.org)

WALLER, Jane Ashton; da of Charles Ashton Waller, of Bucks, and Barbara Mary *née* Batt; *b* 19 May 1944; *Educ* Ladymede Sch Little Kimble, Croham Hurst Sch Croydon, Hornsey Art Sch (BA), Royal Coll of Art (MA); *m* 11 June 1983, Michael Hugh Vaughan-Rees, s of Lyle Vaughan-Rees (d 1962); *Career* since 1982: exhibited ceramics and life-drawings in London and many other parts of the country also in Kuwait, collections in LA, Chicago and Miami; work is sold at Bonhams and Sothebys; author of articles in Ceramic Review; started successful one woman campaign to save the Oxo Tower on the South Bank; involved in Coin St Orgn; *Books* A Stitch in Time (1972), Some Things for the Children (1974), A Man's Book (1977), The Thirties Family Knitting Book (1981), The Man's Knitting Book (1984), Women in Wartime (jt 1987), Women in Uniform (jt 1989), Handbuilt Ceramics (1990), Blitz (jtly 1990), Colour in Clay (1998), The Human Form in Clay (2001), Knitting Fashions of the 1940s (2006); *For Children* Below the Green Pond (1982), Saving the Dinosaurs (1994), The Sludge-Gulpers (1997); *Recreations* reading, gardening, knitting, writing, conservation, cooking, ceramics, walking in the country; *Style*— Ms Jane Waller; ✉ e-mail janewaller@metronet.co.uk, website www.janewaller.co.uk

WALLER, Jonathan Neil; s of Douglas Victor Waller (d 2007), and Kristine Daphne Desmond Rieley (d 1982); *b* 16 April 1956; *Educ* Cherry Orchard HS Northampton, Northampton GS, Nene Coll Northampton, Coventry (Lanchester) Poly, Chelsea Sch of Art (BA, MA); *Career* artist; painting fellowship S Glamorgan Inst of HE Cardiff 1985–86, full time artist London 1987–; pt/t sr lectr Coventry Univ; grants incl: Welsh Arts Cncl 1986, British Cncl 1990; first prize Midland View 3 1984, Mark Rothko Meml Tst travelling scholarship to USA 1988; *Solo Exhibitions* Paton Gallery London 1986 and 1988, Flowers East London 1990, 1992, 1993 and 1994, Doncaster Museum and Art Gallery 1994, New End Gallery London 1997, New End Gallery London 1998, Axiom Centre for the Arts Cheltenham, Transcriptions (Art at Glebe House Leamington Spa) 2000, Lanchester Gallery Coventry 2003, Jonathan Waller's True Adventures (Nat Maritime Museum Cornwall Falmouth) 2005, Jonathan Waller's True Adventures (Arlington Gallery London) 2006; *Group Exhibitions* New Contemporaries (ICA) 1984, Midland View 3 (Nottingham and tour) 1984, Four New Painters (Paton Gallery) 1986, Royal Over-Seas League London 1986, London Glasgow New York (Met Museum NY) 1988, The New British Painting (Cincinnati and tour) 1988, Pacesetters (City Art Gallery Peterborough) 1988, The Thatcher Years: An Artistic Retrospective (Flowers East) 1989, Confrontation: Three British Artists (Joy Emery Gallery Detroit) 1989, Angela Flowers Gallery 1990 Barbican 1989, Flowers at Moos (Gallery Moos NY) 1990, This Sporting Life (Flowers East) 1990, Kunst Europa (Badischer Kunstverein Karlsruhe) 1991, Nudes (Waterman's Arts Centre Brentford) 1991, Artists Choice (Flowers East) 1992, Human Form (Parnham House) 1992, Heads (Royal Museum and Art Gallery Canterbury) 1993, But Big is Better... (Flowers East) 1993, New Figurative Painting (Salander-O'Reilly Galleries/Fred Hoffman Beverly Hills) 1993, By Underground to Kew (London Transport Museum and Kew Gardens Gallery) 1994, Six Gallery Artists (Angela Flowers Gallery) 1994, After Redoute (Flowers East) 1994, Twenty-fifth Anniversary (Flowers East) 1995, The Discerning Eye (Mall Galleries London) 1995, Naked (Flowers East) 1997, Angela Flowers Gallery 1997, Taboo (New End Gallery) 1997, Provocative Prints (New End Gallery) 1998, Cheltenham Open Drawing Exhibition 1998, Cheltenham & Gloucester College of HE, Künstlerwerkstalt Banhof Westend Berlin, Univ of Lincolnshire and Humberside 1998–99, Modern Portraits: Expressions of Intimacy (Golden Gate Univ San Francisco) 1998, Love Religion Explosives (St Margaret's Church Norwich) 1999, Small is Beautiful (Flowers East) 1999, The Comfort of Strangers (Waterman's Art Centre Brentford) 1999, Drawing Parallels (Lanchester Gallery Coventry) 2000, Small is Beautiful (Flowers East) 2002, Sun and Moon (Falmouth Art Gallery) 2004, We can work it out (Three Colts Gallery London) 2004, Paintings from the Nineties (Flowers Central London) 2005, The Circus Show (Three Colts Gallery London) 2005, Through the Looking Glass (Three Colts Gallery London) 2006, Ctrl, Alt, Delete (Lanchester Gallery Coventry) 2006), The Great Exhibition Room (Arlington Gallery London) 2006–07; *Commissions* poster for London Underground on subject of Kew Gardens 1994, two paintings for Terminal 3 Heathrow Airport on subject of London parks 1995; work in the collections of: Metropolitan Museum NY, Contemporary Art Soc, Unilever plc, Dept of the Environment, Bankers Trust, Readers Digest London and NY, London Underground, Br Airports Authy, Tate Gallery, Basildon Hosp; *Style*— Jonathan Waller, Esq; ✉ 35 Campbell Road, Walthamstow, London E17 6RR (tel 020 8509 0537, e-mail j.waller@coventry.ac.uk)

W

WALLER, Rt Hon Lord Justice; Rt Hon Sir (George) Mark; kt (1989), PC (1996); s of The Rt Hon Sir George Stanley Waller, OBE (d 1999) (a former Lord Justice of Appeal), and Hon Lady Elizabeth Margery Waller, *née* Hacking; *b* 13 October 1940; *Educ* Oundle, Univ of Durham (LLB); *m* 1967, Rachel Elizabeth, da of His Hon Christopher Beaumont, MBE (d 2002), of Boroughbridge, N Yorks; 3 s (Charles b 1968 d 1997, Richard b 1969, Philip b 1973); *Career* called to the Bar Gray's Inn 1964, QC 1979, recorder of the Crown Court 1986–89, judge of the High Court of Justice (Queen's Bench Div) 1989–96, presiding judge (NE Circuit) 1992–95, judge i/c Commercial List 1995–96, a Lord Justice of Appeal 1996–, chm Judicial Studies Bd 1999–2003, pres Cncl of the Inns of Ct 2003–06, vice-pres Court of Appeal (Civil Div) 2006–; *Recreations* tennis, golf; *Clubs* Garrick, MCC, Huntercombe; *Style*— The Rt Hon Sir Mark Waller; ✉ c/o Royal Courts of Justice, Strand, London WC2A 2LL

WALLER, Rev Dr Ralph; *b* 11 December 1945; *Educ* John Leggot GS Scunthorpe, Univ of Oxford (MA), Richmond Coll Divinity Sch Univ of London (BD, Westcott New Testament Greek Prize, Hodson Smith Church History Prize), Univ of Nottingham (MTh), Univ of London (PhD); *m* 28 Dec 1968, Carol, *née* Roberts; 1 da (Elizabeth b 24 June 1983); *Career* VSO teacher and house master Shri Shivajh Mil Sch Poona India 1967–68; teacher Riddings Comp Sch Scunthorpe 1968; student Richmond Coll Divinity Sch Univ of London 1969–72; Methodist min Melton Mowbray Circuit 1972–75 (ordained 1975); min of Elvet Methodist Church Durham City and Methodist chaplain Univ of Durham 1975–81; chaplain St Mary's Coll and St Aidan's Coll Durham 1979–81; chaplain Westminster Coll Oxford (also tutor in theology and res tutor) 1981–88; princ and tutor in theology Harris Manchester Coll Oxford 1988–, chm Theology Faculty Univ of Oxford 1995–97, memb Hebdomadal Cncl Univ of Oxford 1997–2000, dir Fndn for the Study of Christianity and Soc 1990–98, dir Farmington Inst 2001–; Alfred North Whitehead distinguished visiting lectr Univ of Redlands CA 1992, Judge Russell distinguished visiting lectr on mgmnt Menlo Coll CA; select preacher Univ of Oxford 1992, 1997 and 2006; individual winner Templeton UK Award 1994; govr: St Mary's Coll Durham 1979–81, Kingswood Sch 1994–2006, Rydal Sch 2002–07; memb: Dr Barnardo's Adoption Ctee 1979–81, Ecclesiastical History Soc, Manchester Acad Tst, Mary Humphrey Churchill Tst 1993–2005; chm Joan Crewdson Tst; Hon DLitt Menlo Coll CA 1995, Hon DLitt Ball State Univ IN 1997, Hon DTheol Uppsala Univ 1999, Hon DH St Olaf Coll MN 2001, Hon DD Hartwick Coll NY 2003, Hon DHL Christopher Newport Univ 2005, Hon DH Univ of Indianapolis 2006; *Publications* Truth, Liberty and Religion (contrib, 1986), Grace and Freedom (contrib, 1988), Studies in Church History (contrib to vol 25, 1988), Christian Spirituality (1999), John Wesley: A Personal Portrait (2003), Joy of Heaven (2003); *Recreations* walking, swimming, browsing round second-hand bookshops; *Style*— The Rev Dr Ralph Waller; ✉ The Farmington Institute, Harris Manchester College, Oxford OX1 3TD (tel 01865 271965)

WALLER, His Hon Judge Stephen Philip; s of Ronald Waller, and Susannah Waller; *b* 2 January 1950; *Educ* Mill Hill Sch, UCL (LLB); *m* 1, 1972 (m dis), Anne Brooksbank; 1 s, 1 da; m 2, 1986, Jennifer Welch; 1 da; *Career* called to the Bar Inner Temple 1972; circuit judge (SE Circuit) 1996–; *Recreations* music; *Style*— His Hon Judge Waller; ✉ c/o Croydon Crown Court, Altyre Road, Croydon CR9 5AB

WALLERSTEINER, Dr Anthony Kurt; *b* 7 August 1963; *Educ* King's Sch Canterbury, Trinity Coll Cambridge (MA, open scholar, Crawford travelling scholar), Univ of Kent (PhD); *m* 1994, Valerie Anne, *née* MacDougall-Jones; 2 da (Isabella b 22 April 1995, Imogen b 12 July 1996), 1 s (Caspar b 1 June 1999); *Career* asst master: Bancroft Sch Woodford Green 1986, Sherborne 1986–89, St Paul's Sch 1989–92; Tonbridge Sch: head of history 1992–2000, housemaster 1999–2003; headmaster Stowe Sch 2003–; govr: Ashfold Sch 2004–, Winchester House Sch 2004–, Summerfields Prep Sch 2006–; contrib various reviews for Burlington Magazine; memb: Cncl Tate St Ives, HMC 2003–; *Recreations* Cornish art, music, travel, family; *Clubs* East India, Lansdowne; *Style*— Dr Anthony Wallersteiner; ✉ Kinloss, Stowe, Buckingham MK18 5EH (tel 01280 818240, fax 01280 818182); Stowe School, Buckingham MK18 5EH (tel 01280 818000, fax 01280 818181, e-mail awallersteiner@stowe.co.uk)

WALLEY, Joan Lorraine; MP; da of Arthur Simeon Walley (d 1968), and Mary Emma, *née* Pass (d 1991); *b* 23 January 1949; *Educ* Biddulph GS, Univ of Hull (BA), Univ Coll of Swansea (Dip); *m* 2 Aug 1980, Jan Ostrowski, s of Adam Ostrowski; 2 s; *Career* local govt offr NACRO, memb Lambeth Cncl 1982–86, MP (Lab) Stoke-on-Trent N 1987–; oppn front bench spokesman on: environment 1988–90, transport 1990–95; memb: Environment Audit Ctee, All-Pty Parly Football Ctee, All-Pty Parly Street Lighting Gp; pres: West Midlands Home and Water Safety Cncl, Stoke on Trent Primary Sch Sports Assoc; vice-pres: Inst of Environmental Health Offrs, SERA; *Recreations* swimming, walking, music, German language; *Style*— Joan Walley, MP; ✉ House of Commons, London SW1A 0AA

WALLIAMS, David; *b* 20 August 1971; *Educ* Reigate GS, Univ of Bristol; *Career* comedian, actor, writer; acted with Nat Youth Theatre, collaborated with comedy ptnr Matt Lucas, *qv* 1995–; *Theatre* incl: Sir Bernard Chumley and Friends (Edinburgh Festival) 1995, 1996 and 1997, Little Britain Tour 2005–07; *Television* incl: Rock Profile 1999–2000, Sir Bernard's Stately Homes 1999, Attachments 2000 and 2001, Spaced 2001, Randall and Hopkirk (Deceased) 2002, Little Britain 2003, 2004, 2005 and 2006, Hustle 2003, Cruise of the Gods 2003, Agatha Christie's Miss Marple: The Body in the Library 2004, Waking the Dead 2004, French and Saunders 2005, Stoned 2006, A Cock and Bull Story 2006, Virgin Territory 2007, Stardust 2007, Capturing Mary 2007, Hotel Babylon 2007; *Radio* incl Little Britain (BBC Radio 4) 2001 and 2002; *Awards* for Little Britain: Silver Sony Radio Acad Award 2003, Gold Best Comedy Spoken Word Publisher Awards 2004, Best Comedy Performance and Best Entertainment RTS Awards 2004, Best Comedy Nat TV Awards 2004, 2005 and 2006, Best Comedy South Bank Show Awards 2005, Best Comedy Broadcast Magazine Awards 2005, Best TV Show NME Awards 2005, Best Comedy TRIC Awards 2005, Best Comedy Golden Rose TV Awards 2006, Best Comedy Int Emmy 2006; British Comedy Awards: Best Newcomer 2003, People's Choice Award 2004, Best Comedy Actor (jtly with Matt Lucas) 2004, Best Br Comedy 2004, Best TV Comedy 2005, Ronnie Barker Writer's Award 2005; BAFTA Awards: Best Comedy Series 2004 and 2005, Best Comedy Performance 2005; for swimming the English Channel: Sports Personality of the Year Special Award 2006, Special Recognition Nat TV Awards 2006, Inspiration Award Pride of Britain 2006; *Style*— David Walliams; ✉ c/o Troika Talent, 3rd Floor, 74 Clerkenwell Road, London EC1M 5QA (tel 020 7336 7868)

WALLINGER, John David Arnold; s of Sir Geoffrey Arnold Wallinger, GBE, KCMG (d 1979), and Diana, *née* Peel Nelson (d 1986); *b* 1 May 1940; *Educ* Winchester, Clare Coll Cambridge (BA); *m* 16 Feb 1966, Rosamund Elizabeth, da of Jack Philip Albert Gavin Clifford Wolff, MBE; *Career* ptnr: Panmure Gordon & Co 1972–75, Rowe & Pitman 1975–86; dir S G Warburg Securities 1986–95, vice-chm S G Warburg International 1994–95; exec dir SBC Warburg Dillon Read (UBS Warburg) 1995–98; dir: Spring Pond Farming 1998, Jupiter European Opportunities Tst plc 2000–, JEOT Securities Ltd 2001–, Attica Int Portfolio Ltd 2003–; chm: General & Oriental Holdings 1999–2001, Attica Inst Multi-Manager plc 2000–, Attica 360 Funds plc, Zebedee European Fund Ltd 2001–, Zebedee Capital Int Ltd 2001–, Greenfield Ventures Ltd 2001–03, Kingsbridge Capital Ltd 2002–, Kingsbridge Capital Advsrs Ltd 2003–; conslt: UBS AG 1998–, TSI, IMRS; *Recreations* golf, fishing, racing; *Clubs* White's, Swinley Forest Golf, New Zealand Golf, Holyport Tennis, Le Cercle de Deauville, Jockey; *Style*— John Wallinger, Esq; ✉ UBS AG, 1 Curzon Street, London W1Y 7FN (tel 020 7567 5757, fax 020 7567 5621)

WALLIS, Prof David Ian; s of Leonard Stephen Wallis (d 1974), Stevenage, Herts, and Kathleen Muriel, *née* Culpin (d 1991); *b* 12 March 1934; *Educ* Alleynes GS Stevenage, Downing Coll Cambridge (MA, PhD); *m* 30 April 1960 (sep), Mary Elizabeth, da of John Cecil Ford (d 1985), of Soham, Cambs; 1 da (Naomi Natasha b 1963), 2 s ((David) Stephen b 1965, Dominic John b 1966); *Career* NATO research fell Univ of Pennsylvania 1959–61, sr research fell in physiology Aberdeen 1961–67; Univ of Wales Coll Cardiff: lectr in physiology 1967–71, sr lectr 1971–76, reader 1976–83, personal chair and prof 1983, head of dept 1987–94, established chair and prof of physiology 1989, emeritus prof of physiology 2000; memb Editorial Bd Br Jl of Pharmacology 1981–88; chm Ctee of Br Pharmacological Soc 1993–95; memb: Physiological Soc, Brain Research Assoc; hon fell Br Pharmacological Soc; *Books* Cardiovascular Pharmacology of 5HT: Prospective Therapeutic Applications, If I Were a Blackbird: Recollections of Old Stevenage; *Recreations* painting, music; *Style*— Prof David Wallis; ✉ Unit of Physiology, School of Biosciences, University of Wales, College of Cardiff, PO Box 911, Cardiff CF1 3US (tel 029 2087 4036, fax 029 2087 4094, e-mail wallisdi@cardiff.ac.uk)

WALLIS, Diana Paulette; MEP; *b* 28 June 1954; *Career* slr in private practice 1983–99; MEP (Lib Dem) Yorks and the Humber 1999–; European Parl: vice-pres 2007–, ldr Lib Dem European Parly Pty 2001–04 and 2006–, memb Legal Affrs Ctee (European Lib Dem spokesperson), memb Petitions Ctee, subst memb Internal Market Ctee, pres delgn to Iceland, Norway and Switzerland EEA Jt Parly Ctee 2004– (first vice-pres of delgn 1999–2004); cncllr Humberside Cncl 1994–95, dep ldr E Riding Unitary Cncl 1995–99, memb Regnl Assembly Ldr's Gp 1995–99; pt/t lectr in European business law Univ of Hull 1995–99; pres Inst of Translation and Interpreting 2002–; memb Law Soc (and EU Ctee 2002–), Campaign for Yorks; *Clubs* National Liberal; *Style*— Ms Diana Wallis, MEP; ✉ PO Box 196, Brough, East Yorkshire HU15 1UX (tel 01482 666898, e-mail diana@dianawallismep.org.uk, website www.dianawallismep.org.uk)

WALLIS, Prof Kenneth Frank; s of Leslie Wallis (d 1982), of Wath upon Dearne, S Yorks, and Vera Daisy, *née* Stone (d 1993); *b* 26 March 1938; *Educ* Wath upon Dearne GS, Univ of Manchester (BSc, MScTech), Stanford Univ (PhD); *m* 26 July 1963, Margaret Sheila, da of William Harold Campbell (d 2003), of Churchill, Somerset; *Career* lectr and reader LSE 1966–77, professor of econometrics Univ of Warwick 1977–2001 (emeritus prof 2001–), dir ESRC Macroeconomic Modelling Bureau 1983–99; exec memb NUS 1961–63; memb Cncl: RSS 1972–76, Royal Econ Soc 1989–94, Econometric Soc 1995–97, Br Acad 2002–05; chm HM Treasy Acad Panel 1987–91 (memb 1980–2001), memb Nat Statistics Methodology Advsy Ctee 2001–; Hon DUniv Groningen 1999, fell Econometric Soc 1975, FBA 1994, fell Inst of Forecasters 2003; *Books* Introductory Econometrics (1972, 1981), Topics in Applied Econometrics (1973, 1979), Models of the UK Economy 1–4 (1984–87), Econometrics and Quantitative Economics (ed with D F Hendry, 1984), Macroeconometric Modelling (1994), Time Series Analysis and Macroeconometric Modelling (1995), Advances in Economics and Econometrics, vols I-III (ed with D M Kreps, 1997); *Recreations* travel, music, gardening, swimming; *Style*— Prof Kenneth F Wallis, FBA; ✉ Department of Economics, University of Warwick, Coventry CV4 7AL (tel 024 7652 3055, fax 024 7652 3032, e-mail k.f.wallis@warwick.ac.uk)

WALLIS, Maria; QPM (2002); *Educ* Univ of Bristol (BSc); *m*; *Career* served Met Police (S London) 1976–87; chief inspr: Community Relations Policy Unit New Scotland Yard 1987–89, West End Central Police Station London 1989–91; detective supt SE London 1991, ACPO Crime Ctee Secretatiat 1992–93; Sussex Police: Asst Chief Constable (crime) 1994–98, Asst Chief Constable (ops) 1998–99 (responsible for 9 divs and organisational services 1999–2000), Dep Chief Constable 2000–01, Acting Chief Constable 2001–02; Chief Constable Devon and Cornwall 2002–; chair Local Criminal Justice Bd, patron Cornwall Domestic Violence Forum, patron Network for Surviving Stalking, memb Br Soc of Criminology; *Recreations* reading, gardening, walking; *Style*— Mrs Maria Wallis, QPM; ✉ Devon and Cornwall Constabulary, Middlemoor Headquarters, Exeter EX2 7HQ (tel 08452 777444)

WALLIS, Neil John; *b* 4 October 1950; *m* 16 August 1975, Gaye Martine, *née* Ramsden; 1 da (Amy Claire b 28 January 1984), 1 s (Charlie Elliot b 7 January 1994); *Career* journalist Daily Star until 1986; The Sun: joined 1986, assoc ed 1990–93, dep ed 1993–98; ed Sunday People 1998–03, dep ed News of the World 2003–; *Recreations* family, birdwatching, Manchester United; *Style*— Neil Wallis, Esq

WALLS, (William) Alan; s of Harold Walls, of Sedgefield, Cleveland, and Marjorie, *née* Orton; *b* 18 September 1956; *Educ* Trinity Hall Cambridge (MA); *m* 29 July 1978, Julie, da of John Brown; 2 s (Thomas William b 4 Sept 1985, Adam Edward b 11 Feb 1991), 1 da (Rachel Hannah Louise b 8 June 1987); *Career* slr; Linklaters: articled 1979–81, slr 1981–87, ptnr 1987–, licensed insolvency practitioner 1990–; memb: Int Bar Assoc, London Slrs Litigation Assoc, Assoc Européenne des Practiceans de Procedures Collectives, City of London Slrs Co 1987, Law Soc; *Recreations* walking, sailing; *Style*— Alan Walls, Esq; ✉ Linklaters, One Silk Street, London EC2Y 8HQ (tel 020 7456 2000, fax 020 7456 2222, e-mail awalls@linklaters.com)

WALLS, (John) Russell Fotheringham; *Career* successively gp fin dir: Coats Viyella plc, Wellcome plc, BAA plc 1995–2002; non-exec chm Delphic Europe Ltd; non-exec dir: Hilton Gp plc 1996–2003, Stagecoach Gp plc 2000–06, Signet Gp 2002–, Aviva plc 2004–; fell Assoc of Chartered Certified Accountants.; *Style*— Russell Walls, Esq

WALLWORK, John; s of Thomas Wallwork, and Vera, *née* Reid; *b* 8 July 1946; *Educ* Accrington GS, Univ of Edinburgh (BSc, MB ChB); *m* 1973, Elizabeth (Ann), da of John Selwyn Medley (d 1988), of New Plymouth, NZ; 2 da (Sarah b 18 April 1977, Alice b 9 May 1989), 1 s (Nicholas b 25 March 1982); *Career* surgical registrar Royal Infirmary Edinburgh 1975–76; sr registrar: Royal Infirmary Glasgow 1978–79, Bart's 1979–81, Adelaide Hosp 1977–78; chief res in cardiovascular and cardiac transplant surgery Stanford Univ 1980–81, currently prof of cardiothoracic surgery Papworth Hosp Cambs; memb: Br Transplant Soc, Cardiac Soc, Int Soc for Heart and Lung Transplantation, Scot Thoracic Soc, Soc of Thoracic and Cardiovascular Surgns of GB and Ireland, Euro Assoc for Cardio-Thoracic Surgery, Transplant Soc, Euro Soc for Organ Transplantation; past pres Int Soc for Heart and Lung Transplants; Lister Professorship RCSEd 1985–86, hon chair in cardiothoracic surgery Univ of Cambridge 2002; Hon MA Univ of Cambridge 1986; fellowships ad eundem: FRCS 1992, FRCPEd 1999, FRCP 2001; FRCSEd, FMedSci 2002; *Books* Heart Disease: What it is and How it is Treated (1987), Heart and Heart-Lung Transplantation (1989); *Clubs* Caledonian; *Style*— John Wallwork, Esq; ✉ Papworth Hospital, Papworth Everards, Cambridgeshire CB23 3RE (tel 01480 364418, fax 01480 831281, e-mail john.wallwork@papworth.nhs.uk)

WALMSLEY, Andrew; *Educ* Kingston Univ (MBA); *m*; 1 s, 1 da; *Career* TV buyer BMP 1988, co-fndr BMP Interaction (now Tribal DDB) 1995, head of digital media Bartle Bogle Hegarty 1997, co-fndr (with Charlie Dobres, *qv*) i-level 1998– (chief operating offr 1998–2007, dep chm 2007–); first chm Digital Mktg Gp (now part of IPA), chair Jt Industry Ctee on Web Measurement; judge: Revolution Awards, New Media Age Effectiveness Awards; *Style*— Andrew Walmsley, Esq; ✉ i-level, 26–30 Strutton Ground, London SW1P 2HR (tel 020 7340 2700, fax 020 7340 2701)

WALMSLEY, Claire; da of John Patrick Slavin (d 1971), and (Margaret) Mabel, *née* Reader; *b* 6 May 1944; *Educ* Convent of the Holy Child Jesus Blackpool, Royal Coll of Music; *m* 1964 (m dis 1982), Christopher Roberts Walmsley (d 1995); 2 da (Frances b 18 Nov 1964, Jennie b 13 April 1968), 1 s (Alexis b 14 April 1971); *Career* broadcaster, TV prodr and documentary film maker; BBC 1976–90, md Boxclever Productions Ltd (ind TV prodn co) and Boxclever Communication Training 1990–, media conslt and communication coach 2000–; memb: BAFTA, RTS, IOD, Forum; FRSA; *Books* Assertiveness - The Right to be You (1991), Letting Go (1993); *Recreations* family, theatre, sailing, travel; *Style*— Ms Claire Walmsley; ✉ 602 Peninsula Apartments, 4 Praed Street, London W2 1JJ (e-mail claire@clairewalmsley.co.uk)

WALMSLEY, Prof Ian Alexander; s of Richard Melville Walmsley, and Hazel Florence, *née* Wilkinson; *b* 13 January 1960, Hyde, Cheshire; *Educ* Imperial Coll London (BSc), Univ of Rochester (PhD); *m* 17 May 1986, Katherine Frances Pardee; 2 s (Alexander Pardee Walmsley b 22 May 1992, Nathaniel Pearre Walmsley b 27 Feb 1994), 1 da (Penelope Clair Walmsley b 25 April 1997); *Career* postdoctoral research assoc Cornell Univ 1986–87; Inst of Optics Univ of Rochester: asst prof 1988–93, assoc prof 1994–97, prof 1998–2002, interim dir 2000–01, adjunct prof 2002–06; visiting prof Universität Ulm Germany 1995; Univ of Oxford: prof 2001–05, head Sub-Dept of Atomic and Laser Physics 2002–, Hooke prof of experimental physics 2005–; sr visiting fell Princeton Univ 2002–; memb: Optics Express Implementation Ctee 1997, NRC Visiting Ctee for JILA 2000–02, Inst of Physics QEP Gp Ctee 2005–07, EPSRC Technical Opportunities Panel 2006–, EPSRC Physics Strategic Advsy Team 2006–, QIPC '06 Program Ctee, IQEC '07 Sub-Ctee (chair); topical ed Jl of the Optical Soc of America B 1999–2005, advsy ed: Jl of Physics B 1999–2004, Jl of Modern Optics 2000–06; memb Convocation Univ of London; fell Optical Soc of America 1997 (dir at large 2006–), fell American Physical Soc 2000, FInstP 2004; *Awards* National Science Fndn Presidential Young Investigator Award 1990, Sch of Engineering and Applied Science Undergraduate Teaching Award 1995, Goergen Award for Undergraduate Teaching 1999, Leibinger Innovationspreis 2006; *Publications* Ultrafast Optics IV (jt ed, 2004), Proceedings of the Conference on Coherence and Quantum Optics (jt ed, 2004); numerous articles in scientific jls; *Style*— Prof Ian Walmsley; ✉ Department of Physics, University of Oxford, Clarendon Laboratory, Parks Road, Oxford OX1 3PU (tel 01865 272 205, fax 01865 272 375, e-mail walmsley@physics.ox.ac.uk)

WALMSLEY, Baroness (Life Peer UK 2000), of West Derby in the County of Merseyside; Joan Margaret Walmsley; da of Leo John Watson, and Monica *née* Nolan; *Educ* Notre Dame HS Liverpool, Univ of Liverpool (BSc), Manchester Metropolitan Univ (PGCE); *m* 21 Oct 2005, Baron Thomas of Gresford, OBE, QC (Life Peer), *qv*; *Career* cytologist Christie Hosp Manchester 1966–67, teacher Buxton Coll 1979–86, PR conslt Intercommunication 1987–89, PR conslt Hill & Knowlton UK Ltd 1989–95, prop JWPR and Walmsley Jones Communications 1995–2003; Lib Dem educn spokesman in House of Lords; memb Cncl Mgmnt of Alcohol and Drug Addiction Prevention and Treatment; chm Botanic Gardens Conservation Int; patron: SKCV Childrens Tst, Helena Kennedy Tst, Family Planning Assoc; NSPCC Parly ambass, tstee UNICEF UK; *Recreations* music, theatre, gardening; *Style*— The Rt Hon the Lady Walmsley; ✉ House of Lords, London SW1A 0PW (tel 020 7219 6047, fax 020 7219 8602, mobile 07979 528488, e-mail walmsleyj@parliament.uk)

WALMSLEY, Dr Katharine Mary (Kate); da of David Robert Walmsley (d 2004), of Ickleford, Herts, and Muriel Jean, *née* McKelvie (d 1990); *b* 5 May 1948; *Educ* Hitchin Girls' GS, Univ of Bristol (MB ChB); *m* 23 Sept 1972 (m dis 1991), Dr (John) Roy Davies; 2 da (Claire Louise b 18 July 1980, Angharad Caroline Mary b 6 Nov 1984); *Career* conslt radiologist: UCLH 1979–, Royal Free Hosp 1979–92, King Edward VII's Hosp 1986–; FRCR 1977; *Recreations* theatre, art, travel; *Style*— Dr Kate Walmsley; ✉ Specialist X-Ray Reception, 2nd Floor Interventional Department, UCH, 235 Euston Road, London NW1 2BU (tel 020 7380 9015, e-mail katewalmsley@uclh.org)

WALMSLEY, Nigel Norman; s of Norman Walmsley (d 1996), and Ida Walmsley; *b* 26 January 1942; *Educ* William Hulme Sch Manchester, Univ of Oxford (BA); *m* Jane, author and broadcaster; 1 da (Katie b 8 Sept 1977); *Career* asst sec Dept of Industry 1975–77, dir of mktg Post Office 1979–82, md Capital Radio Gp 1982–91; Carlton Communications plc: exec dir 1991–2001, chm Carlton TV 1994–2001 (chief exec 1991–94); chm: GMTV 2000–2001, Tourism South East 2002–, BARB 2002–; Eagle Rock Entertainment 2002–; non-exec dir: Energis plc 1997–2002, De Vere Gp plc 2001–06; vice-chm Advtg Assoc 1992–2003; memb Cncl: ASA 2004–, Passenger Focus 2005–, Postwatch 2006–; former chm: GLAA, Ind Radio Industry Res Ctee, Wren Orch of London; govr South Bank Centre; *Recreations* theatre, walking; *Style*— Nigel Walmsley, Esq; ✉ BARB Ltd, 18 Dering Street, London W1S 1AQ

WALMSLEY, Dr Thomas (Tom); s of late Prof Robert Walmsley, of St Andrews, Fife; *b* 15 August 1946; *Educ* Fettes, Univ of Dundee (MB ChB), Univ of Edinburgh (DPM); *m* 1, 1973 (m dis 1981), Jane Walsh, of Edinburgh; 1 da (Anna); m 2, 1981, Linda Hardwick, of Arbroath, Scotland (d 2003); 2 s (William George, Christopher Robert (Kit)); m 3, 2004, Sally Westaway, of Port Elizabeth, SA; *Career* lectr in psychiatry Univ of Edinburgh 1975–77, conslt psychiatrist Royal Edinburgh Hosp 1977–81, conslt psychiatrist Wessex RHA 1981–; regnl advsr in psychiatry 1998–2003; memb RSM; visiting prof Univ of Kuwait 1994; MRCPsych 1974, FRCPsych 1997; *Recreations* reading, walking, maps; *Style*— Dr Tom Walmsley; ✉ Longcroft, Botley Road, Shedfield, Southampton SO32 2HN; Osborn Centre, Fareham, Hampshire PO16 7ES (tel 01329 288331)

WALPOLE, 10 Baron (GB 1723); Robert Horatio Walpole; JP (Norfolk); also 8 Baron Walpole of Wolterton (GB 1756); patron of 6 livings; s of 9 Baron Walpole, TD (d 1989); *b* 8 December 1938; *Educ* Eton, King's Coll Cambridge (MA, Dip Agric); *m* 1, 30 June 1962 (m dis 1979), (Sybil) Judith (d 1993), yr da of late Theodore Thomas Schofield, of Harpenden, Herts; 2 da (Hon Alice Louise b 1 Sept 1963, Hon Emma Judith b 10 Oct 1964), 2 s (Hon Jonathan Robert Hugh b Nov 16 1967, Hon Benedict Thomas Orford b 1 June 1969); m 2, 1980, Laurel Celia, o da of Sidney Tom Ball, of Swindon, Wilts; 2 s (Hon Roger Horatio Calibut b 1980, Hon Henry William b 1982), 1 da (Hon Grace Mary b 1986); *Heir* s, Hon Jonathan Walpole; *Career* sits as crossbencher in House of Lords (elected 1999); memb: Agric Sub-Ctee of Select Ctee on European Communities 1991–94, Environment Sub-Ctee of Select Ctee on European Communities 1995–99, Select Ctee on Euro Communities 1996–99, EU Sub-Ctee Environment Agriculture and Consumer Protection 2001–03, EU Sub-Ctee Energy, Industry and Tport 2003–; hon fell St Mary's UC Strawberry Hill; *Style*— The Rt Hon the Lord Walpole; ✉ Mannington Hall, Norwich, Norfolk NR11 7BB

WALPORT, Dr Mark Jeremy; *b* 25 January 1953; *Educ* St Paul's, Clare Coll Cambridge (MA, MB BChir, Harrison-Watson student, PhD), Middx Hosp Med Sch; *m*; 4 c; *Career* jr hosp appts Middx, Hammersmith, Guy's and Brompton Hosps 1977–82, MRC trg fell MRC Centre Cambridge and hon sr registrar Addenbrooke's Hosp Cambridge 1982–85 (dir of studies in pathology Clare Coll Cambridge 1984–85); Royal Postgrad Med Sch Hammersmith Hosp: head Rheumatology Unit Dept of Med 1985–97, sr lectr in rheumatology 1985–90, reader in rheumatological med 1990–91, prof of med 1991–97, vice-dean (research) 1994–97; dir R&D Hammersmith Hosps Tst 1994–98, prof of med and chm Div of Med Imperial Coll Sch of Med Hammersmith Hosp (following merger) 1997–2003, dir The Wellcome Tst 2003– (govr 2000–03); fell Imperial Coll 2006; Br Soc for Rheumatology: memb Cncl 1989–95, memb Heberden Ctee 1990–95 (chm 1993–95); memb: Scientific Co-ordinating Ctee Arthritis and Rheumatism Cncl 1992–99, Working Ctee on Ethics of Xenotransplantation Nuffield Bioethics Cncl 1995–96, Molecular and Cell Panel Wellcome Tst 1995–2002 (chm 1998–2002), Health Ctee Br Cncl 1998–2002, Cncl for Science and Technol 2004–; fndr fell, memb Cncl and registrar Acad of Med Sciences 1998–2003; asst ed Br Jl of Rheumatology 1981–86, advsy ed Arthritis and Rheumatism 1996–2001, series ed Br Medical Bulletin 1998–2003, ed-in-chief Clinical and Experimental Immunology 1998–2000; memb Assoc of Physicians 1990, hon memb American Assoc of Physicians 2001; Roche Rheumatology Prize 1991, Graham Bull Prize in Clinical Sci RCP 1996; Philip Ellman Lecture RCP 1995; Hon DSc Univ of Sheffield 2006; FRCP 1990, FRCPath 1997, FMedSci 1998; *Books* Clinical Aspects of Immunology (jt ed, 5 edn 1993), Immunobiology (jtly, 6 edn 2005); author of numerous scientific papers; *Style*— Dr Mark Walport; ✉ The Wellcome Trust, 215 Euston Road, London NW1 2BE (tel 020 7611 8888)

WALSH, Amanda (Mrs Brian Stewart); da of David Joseph Walsh, of Thurlestone, S Devon, and Eileen Julia Frances Walsh; *b* 27 November 1955; *Educ* St Mary's Convent Worcester, Kingston Univ (BA); *m* 28 Sept 1989, Brian Stewart; 1 step da (Sophie b 25 Sept 1982); *Career* sales and mktg exec Tek Translation Ltd 1978–80, account exec Wasey Campbell Ewald Advertising 1980–83; WCRS: joined 1984, bd dir 1987–89, client servs and new business dir 1990–93, md 1993–95; ptnr and ceo Walsh Trott Chick Smith 1995–2003, European ceo United Gp (formerly Red Cell Network) 2004–06, ceo Lowe London 2006–; memb Bd UK Film Cncl 2006–; pres Women's Advertising and Communications Club London 2002, memb Mktg Soc 1991; tstee Brain and Spine Fndn; MIPA (memb Bd 1993–2003); *Style*— Ms Amanda Walsh

WALSH, Andrew Geoffrey; s of Dr Geoffrey Parkin Walsh, of Blackburn, Lancs, and Dorothy, *née* Baldwin; *b* 26 July 1954; *Educ* Westholme Sch Blackburn, Queen Elizabeth GS Blackburn, Magdalen Coll Oxford (MA), Trinity Hall Cambridge (LLB); *m* 2, Sept 1989, Emma Belmonte; 1 da (Flora b 20 Jan 1997); *Career* admitted slr 1979; ptnr: Pinsent Masons (London office) 1993–2005, Shadbolt & Co LLP 2005–; memb City of London Slrs' Co; *Books* Bus Company Privatisation (1992), Privatisation of London Buses (1993), Privatisation of Next Step Agencies (1994), Rail Privatisation (1994–95), Trust Ports Privatisation (1995), Public/Private Partnership for London Underground (1997), Accounting for PFI (1999), A Legal Perspective on Risk Management in PPP Projects (2001–02); *Recreations* gym, cycling, Blackburn Rovers FC, historic buildings, theatre; *Clubs* Reebok Sports, MCC; *Style*— Mr Andrew Walsh; ✉ Shadbolt & Co LLP, Old Change House, 128 Queen Victoria Street, London EC4V 4HR

WALSH, Barbara Ann; da of late James Walsh, of Chelford, Cheshire, and Audrey, *née* Dean; *b* 1 March 1955; *Educ* Manchester HS, Univ of Birmingham (BSc); *m* 1; 1 da (Emma Jane b 29 Oct 1981), 1 s (James Nicholas b 26 Aug 1984); m 2, Peter Charles Wozencroft; 2 s (William George b 23 Dec 1996, Daniel Charles b 9 Nov 1999); *Career* gen mangr Hillingdon HA 1985–88, chief exec Riverside Mental Health NHS Tst 1988–93, chief exec Community Health Sheffield NHS Tst 1993–2001, chief exec S Yorks Workforce Confedn 2001–05; dir Change Through Partnership, dir Homestart Sheffield; chair FFW Ltd 2003–; chair Governing Body Phillimore Community Primary Sch 2001–; MHSM 1981; *Recreations* family, walking, cooking, reading; *Style*— Ms Barbara Walsh; ✉ FFW Ltd, 760 Ecclesall Road, Sheffield S11 8TB (tel 07976 280 379, e-mail barbarawalsh@fastmail.fm)

WALSH, Campbell; s of Isaac Walsh, of Stirling, Scotland, and Shelagh, *née* Campbell; *b* 26 November 1977, Glasgow; *Educ* Univ of Nottingham (MSc, Dip IT); *Career* canoeist; Silver medal K1 slalom Olympic Games Athens 2004, champion K1 slalom World Cup 2004; BBC E Midlands Sportsman of the Year 2004; *Clubs* CR Cats Canoe; *Style*— Campbell Walsh, Esq; ✉ c/o British Canoe Union, John Dudderidge House, Adbolton Lane, West Bridgford, Nottingham NG2 5AS

WALSH, Colin Stephen; *b* 26 January 1955; *Educ* Portsmouth GS, ChCh Oxford (MA); *Career* asst organist Salisbury Cathedral 1978–85, organist and master of the music St Albans Cathedral 1985–88, organist and master of the choristers Lincoln Cathedral 1988–, organist laureate 2003–; has given many organ recitals in UK and overseas: French organ music from Salisbury 1985, French organ music from St Albans 1987, Great European Organ Series Lincoln Cathedral 1989, Vierne 24 Pieces en Style Libre 1991, English organ music 1992, Vierne Symphonies 2 and 3 1993, Popular Organ Music 1993, 1898!, Two Willis Organs 1998, French organ music from Lincoln 2004; ARCM 1972, FRCO 1977; *Recreations* walking, dining out, travel, theatre, steam trains; *Style*— Colin Walsh, Esq; ✉ Lincoln Cathedral, 12 Minster Yard, Lincoln LN2 1PJ (tel 01522 544544)

WALSH, John Henry Martin; s of Martin Walsh (d 1986), of Galway, Eire, and Anne, *née* Durkin (d 1998); *b* 24 October 1953; *Educ* Wimbledon Coll, Exeter Coll Oxford (BA), Univ Coll Dublin (MA); *Partner* Carolyn Hart; 2 da (Sophie Matilda Hart-Walsh b 11 Aug 1987, Clementine Hart-Walsh b 5 July 1995), 1 s (Max Henry Thomas Hart-Walsh b 30 Aug 1991); *Career* journalist 1978–; Advtg Dept The Tablet, Gollancz publishers 1977–78, assoc ed The Director Magazine 1978–82; lit ed then features and lit ed Evening Standard 1986–88, lit ed and feature writer The Sunday Times 1988–93, ed Independent Magazine 1993–95; The Independent: lit ed 1995–96, feature writer 1996–, asst ed 1998–; freelance feature writer and reviewer for various newspapers and magazines incl: The Times, Time Out, Tatler, Harpers, Q, Mojo, Word, New Yorker; broadcaster: Books and Company (Radio 4), The Write Stuff (Radio 4); script ed Book Choice (Channel 4) 1995–; dir Cheltenham Literary Festival 1997 and 1998; *Books* Growing Up Catholic (1989), The Falling Angels: An Irish Romance (1999), Are You Talking To Me?: A Life Through the Movies (2003), Sunday at the Cross Bones (2007); *Recreations* drinking, talking, music; *Clubs* Groucho; *Style*— John Walsh, Esq; ✉ The Independent, Independent House, 191 Marsh Wall, London E14 9RS (tel 020 7005 2000, e-mail j.walsh@independent.co.uk)

WALSH, Jonathan George Michael; s of Charles Arthur Walsh (d 1978), of India, and Surrey, and Joan Violet Braidwood, *née* Allen (d 1969); *b* 21 April 1944; *Educ* Eton, Sorbonne Univ; *m* 24 Feb 1968, Angela Mary, da of Rear-Adm Sir Anthony Cecil Capel Miers, VC, KBE, CB, DSO (d 1985); 4 s (David b 1969, William b 1971, James b 1974, Harry b 1981); *Career* admitted slr 1969; ptnr: Joynson-Hicks London 1972, Taylor Joynson Garrett 1989, Stephenson Harwood 1991–2004, conslt Charles Russell 2004–; Freeman City of London 1982, Liveryman Worshipful Co of Tin Plate Workers 1982; memb Law Soc 1969; *Recreations* real tennis, lawn tennis, shooting; *Clubs* Boodle's, Queen's, MCC; *Style*— Jonathan Walsh, Esq; ✉ The Old Vicarage, Enford, Pewsey, Wiltshire SN9 6AX (tel 01980 671424); Charles Russell LLP, 8–10 New Fetter Lane, London EC4A 1RS (e-mail jonathan.walsh@charlesrussell.co.uk)

WALSH, Michael Jeffrey; s of Kenneth Francis Walsh, of Alford, Lincs, and Edith, *née* Hudson; *b* 1 October 1949; *Educ* Hulme GS Oldham, Univ of Durham; *m* Sally, da of Rev Ronald Forbes Shaw; 1 s, 1 da; *Career* advertising exec; Young & Rubicam: grad trainee 1972, account exec 1972–74, account mangr 1974–78, account dir 1978–80, bd dir 1980, new business dir 1981–82, memb UK Exec Ctee; Ogilvy & Mather: dir Bd and mgmnt supervisor 1983–84, head of account mgmnt 1984–85, dir of client service 1985–86, md 1986–89, elected to Worldwide Bd 1989, chm 1989–90, UK gp chm 1990–99, ceo EMEA 1994–; tstee British Red Cross 1994–2004 (vice-chm 1994–2000, then hon vice-chm), worldwide tstee WWF 1996–99, chm UK Disaster Emergency Ctee 2005–; chm Alkrington Young Conservatives 1966–67; *Recreations* collecting Victorian and Edwardian children's books, antiques, tennis, sailing, golf; *Clubs* RAC, Hunstanton Golf, Highgate Golf, Marks, Annabel's, Royal West Norfolk Golf; *Style*— Michael Walsh, Esq; ✉ Ogilvy & Mather, 10 Cabot Square, Canary Wharf, London E14 4QB (tel 020 7345 3000)

WALSH, Michael Ravell; s of Lt-Col John Mainwaring Walsh, MC, RA (ret), and Dr Wendy Felicitée Walsh, *née* Storey; *Educ* Wellington (exhibitioner), Trinity Coll Dublin, Clare Coll Cambridge (exhibitioner, MA); *m* 1975, Nei Rotee Katarina Tekee; 1 s, 2 da; *Career* econ advsr Govt of Gilbert and Ellice Islands 1971–76, civil servant 1976–78, dir planning and info servs Crown Agents 1978–86; various posts: PA Consulting Gp 1986–95,

W

SchlumbergerSema 1995–2001, Xansa plc 2001–03; dir MAANA Ltd 2003–; hon consul Republic of Kiribati; chm Pacific Islands Soc of the UK and Ireland; Liveryman Worshipful Co of Mgmnt Conslts; memb Inst of Mgmnt Conslts 1984, MInstD; *Publications* A Guide to Programme Management; *Recreations* gardening, country pursuits, traditional Irish, Scottish and Appalachian music; *Style—* Michael Walsh, Esq; ✉ Kiribati Consulate, The Great House, Llanddewi Rhydderch, Monmouthshire NP7 9UY (tel and fax 01873 840375, e-mail mravellwalsh@btopenworld.com)

WALSH, (Mary) Noelle (Mrs Heslam); da of late Thomas Walsh, and Mary Kate, *née* Ferguson; *b* 26 December 1954; *Educ* UEA (BA); *m* 15 Oct 1988, David Howard Heslam, s of late Capt James William Heslam; 1 da (Ciara b 15 Aug 1989), 1 s (Calum b 17 May 1991); *Career* news ed Cosmopolitan Magazine 1979–85, ed Good Housekeeping Magazine 1987–91 (dep ed 1985–87), journalist Daily Telegraph 1991–92, dir The Value for Money Co Ltd 1992–, dir websites www.gooddealdirectory.co.uk, www.gooddealhouse.com and www.ukgrandsales.co.uk; memb 300 Gp; FRSA; *Books* Hot Lips - The Ultimate Kiss and Tell Guide (1985), Ragtime to Wartime - The Best of Good Housekeeping 1922–1939 (1986), The Home Front - The Best of Good Housekeeping 1939–1945 (1987), Good Housekeeping - The Christmas Book (1988), Food Glorious Food - Eating and Drinking with Good Housekeeping 1922–42 (1990), Things My Mother Should Have Told Me - The Best of Good Housekeeping 1922–40 (1991), Childhood Memories - Growing Up with Good Housekeeping 1922–1942 (1991), The Good Deal Directory (annually 1994–2005), The Home Shopping Handbook (1994), Baby on a Budget (1995), Wonderful Weddings (1996), Factory Shopping and Sightseeing Guide (1996), The Good Mail Order Guide (1996); *Recreations* bargain hunting, antiques, sailing; *Clubs* Network, Forum UK; *Style—* Miss Noelle Walsh; ✉ Cottage by the Church, Filkins, Lechlade, Gloucestershire GL7 3JG (tel 01367 860017, fax 01367 860177, e-mail nheslam@aol.com)

WALSH, Most Rev Patrick Joseph; *see:* Down and Connor, Bishop of (RC)

WALSH, Paul S; *Educ* Royton & Compton Sch Oldham, Manchester Poly; *Career* Grand Metropolitan: joined 1982, finance dir Brewing Div 1986, subsequently with InterContinental Hotels, chief exec Pillsbury 1992–99; ceo Diageo plc 2000– (chief operating offr 2000); non-exec dir: Federal Express Corp, Centrica plc 2003–; vice-chm Scotch Whisky Assoc 2006– (memb Cncl 2001–); *Style—* Mr Paul S Walsh; ✉ Diageo plc, 8 Henrietta Place, London W1G 0NB (tel 020 7927 5361, fax 020 7927 4641)

WALSH, Stephen John; s of C A Walsh, LLM, of Winchester, Hants, and E B Walsh, *née* Boardman; *b* 14 September 1945; *Educ* Lancing, Coll of Law Guildford, Royal Coll of Art (MA); *m* 22 Feb 1975, Georgina Elizabeth, da of George William Stott; 3 da (Jessica Anne Elizabeth b 18 Oct 1980, Antonia Sarah Georgina b 29 May 1982, Clarissa Rachel Emily b 20 Jan 1989); *Career* articled clerk to Messrs Arnold Cooper and Tompkins Slrs 1965–67, designer Apple Corps (The Beatles co) 1967–68, postgrad student RCA 1969–72, pt/t creative dir Scenses Art Gallery London 1972–73, design conslt DI Design and Development Consultants Inc 1974–78, regnl dir (Middle East) Fitch & Co 1978–82, md Fitch (International) Ltd 1982–84, fndr and chief exec Crighton Ltd 1984–90, md Crighton McColl 1990–92, dir Business Design Group McColl 1992–95, dir Hanseatica Project Design and Development 1995–2003; dir ARC Airport Retail Consultants 1999–; dir ARCH 1995–; FCSD; *Recreations* sailing, skiing, drawing; *Clubs* Durban Country (Natal); *Style—* Stephen Walsh, Esq; ✉ 64 Cranbury Road, London SW6 2NJ (tel 020 7736 8991, e-mail sw@hanseat.demon.co.uk)

WALSHAM, Prof Geoff; s of Harry Walsham (d 1976), and Charlotte, *née* Wood (d 2006); *b* 10 June 1946, Manchester; *Educ* Manchester Grammar, Univ of Oxford (MA), Univ of Warwick (MSc); *m* 7 March 1970, Alison, *née* Evans; 1 da (Jenny b 17 Oct 1973), 3 s (Peter b 16 Jan 1976, Matthew b 18 July 1978, Thomas b 22 Feb 1980); *Career* lectr in mathematics Mindanao State Univ Philippines 1966–67, operational res analyst BP Chemicals Int London 1968–72, lectr in operational res Univ of Nairobi 1972–75, lectr in mgmnt studies Engineering Dept Univ of Cambridge 1975–94, prof of info mgmnt Lancaster Univ 1994–96; Univ of Cambridge: assoc dir of exec educn Judge Inst of Mgmnt Studies 1996–98, res prof of mgmnt studies 1998–2001, prof of mgmnt studies (info systems) Judge Business Sch 2001–; *Publications* Interpreting Information Systems in Organizations (1993), Making a World of Difference: Information Technology in a Global Context (2001); author of over 100 other pubns; *Recreations* mountain walking, travel, gardening, reading; *Style—* Prof Geoff Walsham; ✉ Judge Business School, University of Cambridge, Trumpington Street, Cambridge CB2 1AG (tel 01223 339606, e-mail g.walsham@jbs.cam.ac.uk, website www.jbs.cam.ac.uk)

WALSHAM, Sir Timothy John; 5 Bt (UK 1831), of Knill Court, Herefordshire; o s of Rear Adm Sir John Scarlett Warren Walsham, 4 Bt, CB, OBE (d 1992), and Sheila Christina, *née* Bannerman; *b* 26 April 1939; *Educ* Sherborne; *Heir* kinsman, Gerald Walsham; *Style—* Sir Timothy Walsham, Bt; ✉ Beckford Close, Tisbury, Wiltshire

WALSINGHAM, 9 Baron (GB 1780); John de Grey; MC (1951); s of 8 Baron Walsingham, DSO, OBE, JP, DL (d 1965, half-n of 6 Baron, FRS); *b* 21 February 1925; *Educ* Wellington, Univ of Aberdeen, Magdalen Coll Oxford (MA), Royal Mil Coll of Science (now Cranfield Univ); *m* 30 July 1963, Wendy, er da of Edward Sidney Hoare; 2 da (Hon Sarah b 1964, Hon Elizabeth b 1966), 1 s (Hon Robert b 1969); *Heir* s, Hon Robert de Grey; *Career* Army 1942–47 (cmmnd 1944), Foreign Serv 1950, Lt-Col RA; co dir; fndr and md: Merton Farming Co Ltd 1972, Anglian Processors Ltd (now AP (East Anglia) Ltd) 1974; hon life memb Mark Twain Soc (for contributions to world peace); FInstD; *Publications* www.ontheoriginsofspeaking.com (online, 2006); *Recreations* etymology; *Style—* The Rt Hon the Lord Walsingham, MC; ✉ The Hassocks, Merton, Thetford, Norfolk IP25 6QP (tel and fax 01953 885385, office 01953 883370, e-mail hassocks@lineone.net)

WALTER, Harriet Mary; CBE (2000); da of Roderick Walter (d 1996), of London, and Xandra Carandini, *née* Lee (later Lady de Trafford; d 2002); *b* 24 September 1950; *Educ* Cranborne Chase Sch, LAMDA; *Career* actress; debut Duke's Playhouse Lancaster 1974; nat tours 1975–78 with: 7:84, Joint Stock, Paines Plough; assoc artist RSC 1987; memb: Amnesty Int, Friends of the Earth, PEN; Hon DLitt Univ of Birmingham 2001; *Theatre* Royal Court Theatre 1980–81 incl: Cloud Nine, The Seagull, Ophelia in Hamlet; RSC incl: Helena in All's Well That Ends Well (toured Broadway 1983), The Castle 1985 (nomination Olivier Award for Best Actress), Twelfth Night, The Duchess of Malfi, Macbeth 1999–2000, Much Ado About Nothing 2002, Antony and Cleopatra 2006–07; RNT incl: Dinner (also at Wyndhams), Life x 3 (also at Old Vic, nomination Olivier Award for Best Actress), Arcadia, The Children's Hour; other work incl: The Possessed (Almeida), Three Birds Alighting on a Field (Royal Court and Manhattan Theatre Club NY), Old Times (Wyndhams), Hedda Gabler (Chichester Festival Theatre), Ivanov (Almeida), The Late Middle Classes (Watford), The Royal Family (Theatre Royal Haymarket), Us and Them (Hampstead), Mary Stuart (Donmar Warehouse and Apollo Theatre); *Television* incl: The Imitation Game, Harriet Vane in the Lord Peter Wimsey Mysteries, The Price, The Men's Room, Ashenden, Unfinished Business, Dance to the Music of Time, George Eliot: A Scandalous Life; *Film* incl: Turtle Diary 1985, The Good Father 1985, Milou en Mai 1990, Sense and Sensibility 1995, Keep The Aspidistra Flying 1997, The Governess 1998, Bedrooms and Hallways 1998, Onegin 1999, Villa des Roses 2002, Bright Young Things 2003, Chromophobia 2005, Babel 2006, Atonement 2007; *Awards* Olivier Award (for The Three Sisters, Twelfth Night and A Question of Geography) 1988, Sony Radio Award 1988 and 1992, Evening Standard Award (for Mary Stuart) 2005, Pragnell Shakespeare Award 2007; *Books* Other People's Shoes (1999), Macbeth (Actors on Shakespeare series, 2002); contributions to other books incl: Clamorous Voices - Shakespeare's Women Today (1988), Players of Shakespeare Vol 3 (1993), Mother's Reflections by Daughters (1995); *Style—* Ms Harriet Walter, CBE; ✉ c/o Conway van Gelder Ltd, 18–21 Jermyn Street, London SW1Y 6HP (tel 020 7287 0077, fax 020 7287 1940)

WALTER, Jeremy Canning (Jerry); s of Richard Walter, OBE, and Beryl, *née* Pugh; *b* 22 August 1948; *Educ* King's Sch Canterbury, Sidney Sussex Coll Cambridge (MA, LLB); *m* 1, 24 Aug 1973 (m dis 1985), Judith Jane, da of Dr Denton Rowlands, of Tamworth, Staffs (d 1987); 2 da (Emma b 1976, Alison b 1979); *m* 2, 17 Oct 1992, Dawna Beth, da of Sidney Rosenberg (d 1965), of Lawrence, Mass, USA; *Career* Ellis Piers & Young Jackson 1971–73, admitted slr 1973; Simmons & Simmons: asst slr 1973–76, ptnr 1976–, head Corp Dept 1996– (also responsibility for activities in Middle East), head Energy Gp 1998–; conslt ed (Company Law) Jl of Soc for Advanced Legal Studies 1998–; memb: Law Soc, Exec Ctee Br Polish Legal Assoc 1992–, Int Bar Assoc (Arab Regnl Forum Cncl 1998– (vice-chair 2000–03), East-West Forum), American Bar Assoc (Int Law and Practice Section), Int C of C Fin Servs Cmmn, The Securities Inst, Soc of Advanced Legal Studies, Ctee of City of London Law Soc 1999–; Freeman City of London Slrs Co; *Recreations* sport, travel; *Clubs* MCC; *Style—* Jerry Walter, Esq; ✉ Simmons & Simmons, CityPoint, One Ropemaker Street, London EC2Y 9SS (tel 020 7628 2020, fax 020 7628 2070)

WALTER, Michael; s of Leonard Walter (d 1990), and Anne, *née* Rue; *b* 6 May 1956; *Educ* The King's Sch Chester, Christ's Coll Cambridge (MA); *m* 27 Nov 1982, Joan Margaret, da of Arthur Colin Hubbard (d 1978); 1 da (Helen Margaret b 1984), 1 s (Matthew Michael b 1987); *Career* admitted slr 1981 (England and Wales, Hong Kong); Stephenson Harwood: articled clerk 1979–81, asst slr 1981–86, ptnr 1986–97; Herbert Smith: ptnr 1997–, head of corporate 2005–; memb: Law Soc, Law Soc of Hong Kong; Freeman: City of London 1987, Worshipful Co of Slrs 1987; *Recreations* orienteering, trekking, sailing, reading, music, skiing, scuba diving; *Clubs* Royal Hong Kong Yacht, Royal Hong Kong Jockey, Hong Kong FC, Harlequins RFC, Oriental; *Style—* Michael Walter, Esq; ✉ Herbert Smith, Exchange House, Primrose Street, London EC2A 2HS (tel 020 7374 8000, e-mail michael.walter@herbertsmith.com)

WALTER, Natasha; da of late Nicolas Walter, and Ruth Walter; *b* 20 January 1967; *Educ* N London Collegiate Sch, St John's Coll Cambridge, Harvard Univ; *Children* 1 da (Clara Lattimer Walter b 16 Dec 2000); *Career* journalist; jr teaching fell Harvard Univ 1989, dep literary ed The Independent 1993–94; currently contrib: Newsnight Review (BBC 2), Front Row (BBC Radio 4), The Guardian, The Observer, The Independent; *Books* The New Feminism (1998), On the Move: Feminism for a new generation (ed, 1999); *Style—* Ms Natasha Walter; ✉ c/o Lutyens & Rubinstein, 231 Westbourne Park Road, London W11 1EB

WALTER, Robert John; MP; s of Richard Walter (d 2001), of Warminster, Wilts, and Irene Walter; *b* 30 May 1948; *Educ* Warminster, Aston Univ (BSc); *m* 1, 28 Aug 1970, Sally (d 1995); 1 da (Elizabeth b 1974), 2 s (Charles b 1976, Alexander b 1977); *Career* former investment banker and farmer; dir: FW Holst (Europe) Ltd 1984–86, TV-UK Ltd 1988, Silver Apex Films Ltd 2003–06; vice-pres Aubrey G Lanston & Co Inc 1986–97; visiting lectr Univ of Westminster; farmer in West Country; MP (Cons) N Dorset 1997– (Parly candidate (Cons) Bedwellty 1979); oppn front bench spokesman on constitutional affairs (Wales) 1999–2001; memb: Health Select Ctee 1997–99, Int Devpt Select Ctee 2001–03, European Scrutiny Ctee 1998–99, Treasury Select Ctee 2003–05; memb Exec 1922 Ctee 2002–05; vice-chm: All-Pty Gp on Lupus, Free Trade Gp, Human Rights Gp 2003–, Prison Health Gp 2005–; treas: Br-Japanese Parly Gp 1997–, Br-Caribbean Parly Gp 1997–, All-Pty Gp on Charities 1997–; chm: Aston Univ Cons Assoc 1967–69, W Wilts Young Cons 1972–75, Euro Democrat Forum 1979–84, Foreign Affrs Forum 1985–87, Cons Gp for Europe 1992–95 (vice-chm 1984–86, dep chm 1989–92), Positive European Gp of Cons MPs and Peers; memb: Assembly of WEU 2001– (chm Defence Ctee, pres Federated Gp of Christian Democrats and European Democrats), Parly Assembly of the Cncl of Europe 2002– (chm Media Sub-ctee); chm Bd of Govrs Tachbrook Sch 1980–2000; Vice Cdre House of Commons Yacht Club 2006– (hon sec 1998–99, Rear Cdre 2001); Freeman City of London 1983, Liveryman Worshipful Co of Needlemakers 1983; AMIIMR, MSI; *Recreations* sailing, shooting; *Style—* Robert Walter, Esq, MP; ✉ House of Commons, London SW1A 0AA (tel 020 7219 6981, fax 020 7219 2608, e-mail walterr@parliament.uk, website www.bobwaltermp.com)

WALTERS, Eric; *b* 3 August 1944; *Educ* Bablake Sch Coventry, Selwyn Coll Cambridge (MA); *m* 12 Aug 1967, Katharina; 1 da (Katya b 25 May 1973), 1 s (Eric Andrew b 28 Sept 1976); *Career* res offr British Petroleum Co plc 1965–67, conslt Cape Industries plc 1967–69, sr conslt International Systems Research Ltd 1969–72, divnl mangr Lex Service Group plc 1976–80 (planner 1972–76); Grand Metropolitan plc: md CC Soft Drinks Ltd 1980–82, chm Soft Drinks and Overseas Brewing 1982, chief exec Retailing Div 1984; gp md Dominion International Group plc 1986–87; md Kundert Int Ltd; ptnr: Schroder Ventures 1987–97, Alchemy Partners 1997–2000, Englefield Capital 2001–; non-exec dir Capita Gp plc 2001–; CIMgt; *Recreations* skiing, hiking, swimming; *Clubs* Athenaeum, Carlton, RAC; *Style—* Eric Walters, Esq; ✉ 60 Montagu Mansions, London W1U 6LD (e-mail ericfishwalters@hotmail.com)

WALTERS, John Latimer; QC (1997); s of John Paton Walters (d 1993), and Charlotte Alison, *née* Cunningham (d 1994); *b* 15 September 1948; *Educ* Rugby, Balliol Coll Oxford (MA); *m* 2, 1990, Caroline Elizabeth, *née* Byles; 2 da (Isolde, Susanna), 1 step s (Alexander Bain); *Career* chartered accountant: Arthur Andersen & Co 1970–73, Josolyne Layton-Bennett & Co 1973–75, Peat Marwick Mitchell & Co 1975–76; legal career: called to the Bar Middle Temple 1977, in practice Gray's Inn 1978–; dep special cmmr and pt/t chm of VAT and Duties Tbnl 2002–; local preacher in Methodist Church (Diss Circuit); FCA 1974, ATII 1974; *Books* VAT and Property (with David Goy, QC, 1989, 2 edn 1993); *Recreations* gardening, genealogy, painting, tapestry; *Style—* John Walters, QC; ✉ Gray's Inn Tax Chambers, Gray's Inn, London WC1R 5JA (tel 020 7242 2642, fax 020 7831 9017, e-mail jw@taxbar.com)

WALTERS, Julie; OBE (1999); *b* 22 February 1950; *Career* actress; *Theatre* incl: seasons at Everyman Theatre Liverpool and Bristol Old Vic, Educating Rita (RSC Warehouse and Piccadilly Theatre), Having a Ball (Lyric), Jumpers (Royal Exchange), Fool for Love (NT and Lyric), When I was a Girl I Used to Scream and Shout (Whitehall), Frankie and Johnnie, Serafina in The Rose Tattoo (dir Sir Peter Hall), All My Sons (NT, Olivier Award for Best Actress), Acorn Antiques the Musical (Theatre Royal Haymarket); *Television* incl: The Birthday Party, Secret Diary of Adrian Mole, Victoria Wood - As Seen on TV (BAFTA nomination), Boys From the Blackstuff (BAFTA nomination), She'll Be Wearing Pink Pyjamas, Say Something Happened (by Alan Bennett, BAFTA nomination), Intensive Care (by Alan Bennett), Talking Heads (by Alan Bennett), GBH (by Alan Bleasdale), Julie Walters & Friends (TV special Christmas 1991, 2 BAFTA nominations), Wide Eyed and Legless (Screen One, BBC, BAFTA nomination), Bambino Mio (Screen One), Pat and Margaret (Screen One), Jake's Progress (by Alan Bleasdale, Channel 4), Little Red Riding Hood and the Wolf (by Roald Dahl, BBC), Bathtime (short film, BBC), Brazen Hussies (BBC Screen Two film), Melissa (BBC), Green Card, Dinner Ladies (with Victoria Wood, BBC), Jack and the Beanstalk, My Beautiful Son (ITV, BAFTA Award for Best Actress), Murder (BAFTA Award for Best Actress), The Wife of Bath (BAFTA Award for Best Actress), The Return (Broadcasting Press Guild TV Awards Best Actress), Ruby in the Smoke (BBC); *Film* incl: Rita in Educating Rita (Oscar nominee, BAFTA Award, Golden Globe Award), Buster, Personal Services (BAFTA nomination),

Joe Orton's mother in Prick Up Your Ears, Killing Dad, Steppin' Out (Variety Club Award, BAFTA nomination) Just Like a Woman, Clothes in the Wardrobe, Sister My Sister, Intimate Relations, Girls' Night, Titanic Town, Billy Elliot (BAFTA Award, Oscar nomination), Harry Potter and the Philosopher's Stone, Before You Go, Harry Potter and the Chamber of Secrets, Calendar Girls, Harry Potter and the Prisoner of Azkaban, Wah-Wah, Driving Lessons, Becoming Jane, Mamma Mia; *Books* Maggie's Tree (novel, 2006); *Style—* Ms Julie Walters, OBE; ✉ c/o ICM Ltd, Oxford House, 76 Oxford Street, London W1N 0AX (tel 020 7636 6565, fax 020 7323 0101)

WALTERS, Prof Kenneth; *b* 14 September 1934; *Educ* Dynevor GS Swansea, UC Swansea (state scholar, BSc, MSc, PhD), Univ of Wales (DSc); *m*; 3 c; *Career* res assoc Brown Univ RI and asst prof San Diego State Coll CA 1959–60; Univ of Wales Aberystwyth: lectr in applied mathematics 1960–65, sr lectr 1965–70, reader 1970–73, prof 1973–; pres Br Soc of Rheology 1974–76, pres European Soc of Rheology 1996–2000, chm Int Ctee on Rheology 2000–04; memb Editorial Bd: Rheologica Acta 1972–, Jl of Rheology 1988–2002; exec ed Jl of Non-Newtonian Fluid Mechanics 1975–2001; Gold Medal Br Soc of Rheology 1984, Weissenberg Award European Soc of Rheology 2002; Hon Dr Université Joseph Fourier Grenoble 1998; hon fell Univ Coll Swansea 1992, foreign assoc Nat Acad of Engrg USA 1995; FRS 1991; *Books* Rheometry (1975), Rheometry: Industrial Applications (ed, 1980), Numerical Simulation of non-Newtonian Flow (with M J Crochet and A R Davies, 1984), An Introduction to Rheology (with H A Barnes and J F Hutton, 1989), Rheological Phenomena in Focus (with D V Boger, 1993), Rheology: An Historical Perspective (with R I Tanner, 1998), The Way it Was (2003); *Style—* Prof Kenneth Walters, FRS; ✉ Institute of Mathematical and Physical Sciences, University of Wales, Aberystwyth, Ceredigion SY23 3BZ (tel 01970 622750, fax 01970 622777, e-mail kew@aber.ac.uk)

WALTERS, Minette Caroline Mary; da of Samuel Henry Doddington Jebb (d 1960), and Minette Colleen Helen, *née* Paul; *b* 26 September 1949; *Educ* Godolphin Sch Salisbury, Univ of Durham (BA); *m* 1978, Alexander Hamilton Walters, s of Dr F J H Walters; 2 s (Roland Francis Samuel b 13 Dec 1979, Philip Gladwyn Hamilton b 12 Jan 1982); *Career* sub ed then ed IPC Magazines 1972–76, freelance writer 1976–; prison visitor; DLitt: Bournemouth Univ, Southampton Solent Univ; *Books* The Ice House (1992, Crime Writers' Assoc John Creasey Award), The Sculptress (1993, Edgar Allen Poe Award, Macavity Award), The Scold's Bridle (1994, Crime Writers' Assoc Gold Dagger Award), The Dark Room (1995), The Echo (1997), The Breaker (1998), The Shape of Snakes (2000, Pelle Rosenkrantz Award Denmark), Acid Row (2001), Fox Evil (2002, Crime Writers' Assoc Gold Dagger Award), Disordered Minds (2003), The Devil's Feather (2005), Chickenfeed (2006); *Recreations* DIY, sailing, books, Radio 4, films, tv, theatre, crossword puzzles; *Style—* Mrs Minette Walters; ✉ c/o Gregory & Company, 3 Barb Mews, London W6 7PA (tel 020 7610 4676, fax 020 7610 4686)

WALTERS, Nicholas McIndoe; s of Sir Dennis Walters, MBE, of London, and Vanora, *née* McIndoe; *b* 16 May 1957; *Educ* Downside, Univ of Exeter; *m* 1 Aug 1987, Emma Mary, yr da of David Blamey; 2 s (Benedict McIndoe b 15 Jan 1992, Alexander Bowman b 2 April 1994); *Career* legislative asst to Howard Baker, majority ldr The Senate Washington DC 1980–81; exec: The Marconi Company 1981–82, Paul Winner Marketing Ltd 1982–83; dir Good Relations Ltd 1983–88, md GCI Group 1999–2003 (dep md 1997–99), chm GCI Group Asia Pacific 2000–03, md Manning Selvage and Lee 2003–; Parly candidate (Cons) Merthyr Tydfil 1987; MIPR; *Recreations* skiing, tennis; *Clubs* Annabel's, Raffles, Hurlingham; *Style—* Nicholas Walters, Esq; ✉ Manning Selvage and Lee, Pembroke Building, Kensington Village, Avonmore Road, London W14 8DG (tel 020 7878 3000)

WALTERS, Philip; s of Moss Walters (decd), and Eileen Walters (decd); *Educ* Highgate Sch, Keble Coll Oxford (BA); *Career* Hodder and Stoughton: joined as grad trainee 1976, various posts rising to md Educational Div 1997; md Hodder Educn 2001–; former chair Educnl Publishers Cncl; memb: Cncl Book Aid Int, World Book Day Ctee; *Recreations* golf, film, watching Spurs, watching England play cricket; *Style—* Philip Walters, Esq; ✉ Hodder Education, Hodder Headline plc, 338 Euston Road, London NW1 3BH (tel 020 7873 6236, fax 020 7873 6299, mobile 07778 709534, e-mail philip.walters@hodder.co.uk)

WALTERS, Rhodri Havard; s of late Havard Walters, of Merthyr Tydfil, and Veigan, *née* Hughes; *b* 28 February 1950; *Educ* Cyfarthfa Castle GS Merthyr Tydfil, Jesus Coll Oxford (exhibitioner, MA, DPhil); *Career* clerk Parliament Office House of Lords 1975–, clerk Select Ctee on Overseas Trade 1984–85, seconded to Cabinet Office as private sec to Ldr of the House and Govt Chief Whip 1986–89, Civil Service Nuffield and Leverhulme travelling fell (attached to US Congress) 1989–90, clerk to Select Ctee on Science and Technol House of Lords 1990–93, establishment offr (clerk to Fin, Staff and Refreshment Sub-ctees) House of Lords 1993–2000, clerk of Public Bills 2000–02, clerk of Ctees and clerk of the Overseas Office 2002–07, reading clerk 2007–; sec Ecclesiastical Ctee 2000–03; *Publications* How Parliament Works (1987, 6 edn 2006), 'The House of Lords' in the British Constitution in the Twentieth Century (2003); various articles in Economic History Review, Welsh History Review and Government and Opposition; *Recreations* rowing, gardening, skiing, church music; *Style—* Rhodri Walters, Esq; ✉ Committee Office, House of Lords, London SW1A 0PW (tel 020 7219 3187, e-mail waltersrh@parliament.uk)

WALTERSON, Inga Ruth; da of Francis Sinclair Walterson, of W Burrafirth, Shetland, and Mary Olive, *née* Bowie; *b* 27 May 1964; *Educ* Univ of Aberdeen (MA); *m* Ian James Douglas Anderson, s of John Robertson Anderson (d 1987), of Lerwick, Shetland, and Ella, *née* Morrison (d 1986); 2 s (Bo Ellis b 1998, Finn Erik b 2002); *Career* md Shetland Islands Broadcasting Company Ltd; *Style—* Ms Inga Walterson; ✉ Shetland Islands Broadcasting Company Ltd, Market Street, Lerwick, Shetland ZE1 0JN (tel 01595 695299, fax 01595 695696, e-mail info@sibc.co.uk)

WALTHER, Robert Philippe; s of Prof David Philippe Walther (d 1973), and Barbara, *née* Brook; *b* 31 July 1943; *Educ* Charterhouse, ChCh Oxford (MA); *m* 21 June 1969, Anne, da of Lionel Wigglesworth, of Woldingham, Surrey; 1 da (Julie Clare b 1973), 1 s (Luke b 1978); *Career* Clerical Medical Investment Group: joined 1965, dep investment mangr 1972, investment mangr 1976, asst gen mangr (investments) 1980, dir 1985–2001, gp chief exec 1994–2001; memb Exec Ctee Halifax plc 1999–2001; chm: Fleming Claverhouse 1997–2005, Fidelity European Valuers 2001–, Investment Ctee Assoc of Br Insurers; dir: Nationwide Building Soc 2002– BUPA 2004–; AIIMR 1969, FIA 1970; *Recreations* hockey, golf, bridge, sailing; *Clubs* Oxford and Cambridge; *Style—* Robert Walther, Esq; ✉ Ashwell's Barn, Chesham Lane, Chalfont St Giles, Buckinghamshire HP8 4AS (tel 01494 875575, fax 01494 876518, e-mail rob_walther@hotmail.com)

WALTHO, Lynda; MP; *b* 22 May 1960; *Educ* Keele Univ, Univ of Central England (PGCE); *m*; 2 c; *Career* sometime teacher, advsr Neena Gill MEP; MP (Lab) Stourbridge 2005–; memb GMB; *Style—* Ms Lynda Waltho, MP; ✉ House of Commons, London SW1A 0AA

WALTON, Alastair Henry; s of Sir Raymond Henry Walton (d 1988), of Wimbledon, London, and Helen Alexandra, *née* Dingwall; *b* 26 August 1954; *Educ* Winchester, Balliol Coll Oxford (BA); *m* 28 July 1984, Hon Mary Synolda, *née* Butler, da of 28 Baron Dunboyne (d 2004), of Chelsea, London; 4 da (Alexandra Mary b 1985, Christina Frances b 1986, Stephanie Katherine b 1988, Florence Lucy b 1992); *Career* called to the Bar Lincoln's Inn 1977, in practice 1978–; *Recreations* lawn tennis; *Style—* Alastair Walton, Esq; ✉ 26 Paradise Walk, Chelsea, London SW3 4JL (tel 020 7376 5304); Maitland Chambers, 7 Stone Buildings, Lincoln's Inn, London WC2A 3SZ (tel 020 7406 1200, fax 020 7406 1300)

WALTON, Dr Bryan; s of Henry Walton (d 1985), and Helen, *née* Pincus (d 1989); *b* 29 August 1943; *Educ* City of London Sch, London Hosp Med Coll (MB BS); *m* 1, 7 July 1968 (m dis), (Sarah) Ruth, da of Philip Levitan (d 1989); 1 da (Anna b 1973), 1 s (Jonathan b 1976); m 2, 9 Nov 2002, Heather Teresa, da of Eric Ball; *Career* conslt anaesthetist London Hosp 1974–95, advsr in anaesthesia and intensive care Princess Grace Hosp London 1984–; memb: Med Prof Soc, Assoc of Anaesthetists 1972, Anaesthetic Res Soc 1980, Hunterian Soc 1985, Chelsea Clinical Soc 1989; FRCA; *Books* chapters: Adverse Reactions to Anaesthetic Drugs (1981), Scientific Foundations of Anaesthesia (3 edn 1982, 4 edn 1990), Hazards and Complications of Anaesthesia (1987, 2 edn 1993), Medicine in the Practice of Anaesthesia (1989); many pubns on anaesthesia and the liver, and anaesthesia and immunology; *Recreations* classical music; *Style—* Dr Bryan Walton; ✉ 9 Loom Lane, Radlett, Hertfordshire WD7 8AA (tel 01923 853923, fax 01923 853570)

WALTON, Christopher Henry; s of Frank Pearson Walton (d 1966), of Eastbourne, E Sussex, and Marion Ada Beasley (d 1989); *b* 20 June 1930; *Educ* Stockport GS, Gonville & Caius Coll Cambridge (MA); *m* 25 April 1959, Judith Vivien, da of Ernest Leslie Philp (d 1950), of Alexandria, Egypt; *Career* 2 Lt Lancs Fus 1949–51, Capt Royal Fus TA 1951–59; Cwlth Devpt Corp 1954–65, initiator and dir Kenya Tea Devpt Authy 1959–65; exec and dir: Kyle Products Ltd Gp 1965–67, Eastern Produce Ltd Gp 1967–69; div chief Projects Dept Eastern and Western Africa World Bank Washington 1969–87; Wolfson Coll Oxford: bursar 1987–95, emeritus fell 1995–; fin advsr Oxford Union Soc 1995–2000, hon sec Oxford Literary and Debating Soc 1996–; on Cons Party Candidates List 1966–69, dep chm Cons Party Overseas Devpt Ctee 1967–68; govr: Pusey House Oxford 1990–2004 (vice-pres 2004–), Stowe Sch 1992–2005; chm Oxfordshire Historic Churches Tst; *Recreations* ecclesiastical architecture, conservative politics, rowing; *Clubs* Oriental, Leander; *Style—* Christopher Walton, Esq; ✉ The Corner House, Foxcombe Lane, Boars Hill, Oxford OX1 5DH (tel 01865 735179, fax 01865 736604, e-mail chris.walton@wolfson.oxford.ac.uk)

WALTON, Field Laurence Joseph; s of Joseph Field Horace Walton (d 1982), and Marie Joan, *née* Lennard (d 1984); *b* 17 April 1940; *Educ* Loughborough Univ (BTech, MSc, played rugby for Eng Univs 1st XV); *m* 26 May 1965, Susan Thompstone, da of Basil Rowe; 1 da (Virginia Mary Spencer b 15 Dec 1966), 1 s (Francis Joseph Field b 1 Feb 1968); *Career* electrical apprentice then project engr Hawker Siddeley 1958–67, project mangr John Laing plc 1968–70, planning mangr Plessey plc 1970–71, engrg analyst Cazenove & Co 1971–74, engrg analyst Quilter Hilton Goodison 1974–77, investment mangr Electra Funds and md Temple Bar Fund Managers 1977–85, md Guinness Mahon Fund Managers 1985–89, chm Guinness Mahon Asset Managers 1989–92; chm: Eleco Holdings plc 1983–97 (ind dir 1997), Henry Cooke Group plc 1993–95, Biofuels Corp plc 2003–06; independent dir: Temple Bar Investment Trust 1983–, Martin International Holdings plc 1994–2004, Romney, Hythe & Dymchurch Railway plc 1995–; dir: Macarthur & Co Ltd 1997– (assoc 1995–97), Rocktron Ltd 1998–2004, Peter Peregrinus Ltd 1998–2005; Freeman: City of London, Worshipful Co of Glass Sellers; CEng, FIEE, FCMI, FSI; *Recreations* golf; *Clubs* Leicester FC, Harewood Downs Golf, Beaconsfield Golf; *Style—* Field Walton, Esq; ✉ Christow Cottage, Seer Green Lane, Jordans, Buckinghamshire HP9 2ST (tel 01494 874971, fax 01494 876426)

WALTON, Ven Geoffrey Elmer; s of Maj Harold Walton (d 1978), and Edith Margaret, *née* Dawson (d 1983); *b* 19 February 1934; *Educ* West Bridgford GS, Univ of Durham (BA), Queen's Coll Birmingham (Dip Theol); *m* 9 Sept 1961, Edith Mollie, da of John Patrick O'Connor (d 1970); 1 s (Jeremy Mark b 1968); *Career* vicar of Norwell Notts and Dio Youth chaplain 1965–69, recruitment and selection sec Advsy Cncl for the Church's Min London 1969–75, rural dean of Weymouth 1980–82, hon canon Salisbury Cathedral 1981, archdeacon of Dorset 1982–2000 (archdeacon emeritus 2000–); incumbent: Holy Trinity Weymouth 1975–82, Witchampton with Long Crichel and Moor Crichel 1982–2000; chm: Dorset Co Scouts, E Dorset Housing Assoc 1992–2003, Synergy Housing Gp 2003–05; *Recreations* religious drama, conjuring, walking; *Style—* The Ven Geoffrey Elmer; ✉ Priory Cottage, 6 Hibberds Field, Cranborne, Wimborne, Dorset BH21 5QL (tel 01725 517167)

WALTON, John Cannell; *b* 26 January 1946; *Educ* King Edward VI, Norwich Sch, UCL (BSc Econ); *Career* investment analyst then head of investment res Hill Samuel & Co 1968–72, acquisitions analyst Sterling Land 1972–74, investment mangr then dir of investments Imperial Life Assurance 1975–85, investment dir British Empire Securities & General Trust plc 1985–2004, chm Asset Value Investors Ltd 2004– (md 1985–2004); ASIP; *Style—* John Walton, Esq; ✉ Asset Value Investors Ltd, Bennet House, 54 St James' Street, London SW1A 1JT (tel 020 7647 2900, fax 020 7647 2901, e-mail john.walton@assetvalueinvestors.com)

WALTON, Prof John Christopher; s of W G C Walton, and R M Walton, *née* Wheeler; *b* 4 December 1941, St Albans, Herts; *Educ* Watford GS for Boys, Univ of Sheffield (BSc, DSc), St Andrews Univ (PhD); *m* 28 July 1971, Jane, *née* Lehman; 1 s (Christopher), 1 da (Emma); *Career* asst lectr Univ of Dundee 1966–69; St Andrews Univ: lectr 1969–80, sr lectr 1980–86, reader 1986–96, prof of reactive chemistry 1997–; chm Electron Spin Resonance Gp RSC 2001–04; govr Newbold Coll; memb Seventh-Day Adventist Church; RSC Silver medal and Award for organic reaction mechanisms 1994; CChem 1991, FRSC 1991, FRSE 1995; *Publications* Free Radical Chemistry (1974), Radicals (1979); author of over 250 articles and reviews in sci jls; *Recreations* origins science, fitness classes; *Style—* Prof John Walton; ✉ 14 Irvine Crescent, St Andrews, Fife KY16 8LG (tel 01334 474244); University of St Andrews, School of Chemistry, North Haugh, St Andrews, Fife KY16 9ST (tel 01334 463864, fax 01334 463808, e-mail jcw@st-and.ac.uk)

WALTON, John Victor; s of Eric Roscoe Walton (d 1961), of Radlett, Herts, and Ethel Marjorie, *née* Addinsell (d 1983); *b* 5 December 1925; *Educ* Aldenham, Ruskin Sch of Drawing Oxford, Slade Sch of Fine Art, UCL (Dip Fine Art); *m* 1, 1950 (m dis 1970), Annette Rolande Francoise D'Exea; 2 s (James Andre b 1950, Roland Dominic b 1966), 1 da (Victoria Ann b 1953); m 2, 1989, Alice Ellsworth, *née* Low; *Career* portrait painter; princ Heatherley Sch of Fine Art 1974–; exhibitions incl: Royal Acad, Royal Soc of Portrait Painters, Paris Salon (hon mention), Institut de France, Académie des Beaux Arts; paintings in national instns and private collections in GB & abroad; co sec Thomas Heatherley Educnl Tst 1976–, chm Fedn of Br Artists 1990–97 (govr 1982–97); RP 1976 (memb Cncl 1979–81 and 1983–90, hon treas 2000–03); *Recreations* painting, cycling, history; *Clubs* Chelsea Arts; *Style—* John Walton, Esq; ✉ 30 Park Road, Radlett, Hertfordshire WD7 8EQ; The Heatherley School of Fine Art, 80 Upcerne Road, Chelsea SW10 0SH (tel 020 7351 4190)

WALTON, Col Peter Sinclair; s of late Col William Patrick Everard Walton, CBE, and Ruby Marcella Bloomfield, *née* Maffett, of Tenterden, Kent; *b* 3 January 1939; *Educ* St John's Sch Leatherhead; *m* 1, July 1971 (m dis 1997), Michelle Frances, da of late Philip Edward Aldous, OBE, of Cape Province, South Africa; 1 s (David Sinclair b 1972), 1 da (Victoria Louise b 1978); m 2, Sept 2000, Gilly, da of late Maj Gordon Edwards, of Frinton-on-Sea, Essex; *Career* served Army (Logistics and Staff 1957–89, Col 1985), Hon Col RLC TA 1993–99; tstee and designer RAOC Museum 1976–93; memb Cncl: Assoc of Independent Museums 1990–95, Friends of Nat Army Museum 1991–95, Br Assoc of Friends of Museums 1996–97; sec Army Museums Ogilby Tst 1989–96, memb Standing Conf on Archives and Museums 1993–95, project leader BAFM Heritage Volunteer Training Project 1997–2004, conslt military antecedents to Bonham's 1998–, int conslt MOD

Defence Logistics Orgn 2000–02, memb Professionalisation Advsy Gp Nat Volunteer Mangrs Forum 2001–03; vice-pres: Victorian Mil Soc, Corps of Drums Soc; tstee RLC Museum 2000–04; memb: Museums Assoc, HAC, SAHR; Freeman City of London, Liveryman Worshipful Co of Farriers; Sultan of Oman's Distinguished Service Medal 1975; *Books* Simkin's Soldiers - The British Army in 1890 (vol I 1982, vol II 1986), A Celebration of Empire (1997), A Handbook for Heritage Volunteer Managers and Administrators (1999); *Style*— Col Peter Walton; ✉ 1 Walkhurst Cottages, Benenden, Kent TN17 4DS (tel and fax 01580 242855, e-mail walton@scarletgunner.com)

WALTON JONES, Howard; s of Alfred (Freddie) Hayter Walton Jones (d 1996), of Majorca, and Carmen Mary, *née* Rowlands; ggf A Jones founded A Jones & Sons 1857 London; *b* 18 February 1945; *Educ* Monkton Combe Sch Bath; *m* 20 July 1968, Susan Dorothy Ann, da of John Brian Edwards Penn (d 1980); 2 da (Emma b 1972, Katy b 1975); *Career* md A Jones & Sons plc (shoe retailers) 1976–; dir: Church & Co plc (shoe mfrs) 1976–, Babers of Oxford St (shoe retailers) 1976–; *Recreations* tennis; *Style*— Howard Walton Jones, Esq; ✉ A Jones & Sons plc, 18 Maple Road, Eastbourne, East Sussex BN23 6NZ (tel 01323 730532, fax 01323 738272)

WALTON OF DETCHANT, Baron (Life Peer UK 1989), of Detchant in the County of Northumberland; Sir John Nicholas Walton; kt (1979), TD (1962); s of Herbert Walton; *b* 16 September 1922; *Educ* Alderman Wraith GS, King's Coll Med Sch Univ of Durham (MD), Univ of Newcastle upon Tyne (DSc); *m* 1946, Elizabeth (Betty) Harrison (d 2003); 1 s, 2 da; *Career* Col (late RAMC) CO I (N) Gen Hosp (TA) 1963–66, Hon Col 201 (N) Gen Hosp (T & AVR) 1968–73; conslt neurologist Univ of Newcastle Hosps 1958–83, prof of neurology Univ of Newcastle upon Tyne 1968–83 (dean of med 1971–81); chm Hamlyn Nat Cmmn on Educn 1991–93; memb GMC 1971–90 (chm Educn Ctee 1975–82, pres 1982–89); pres BMA 1980–82, ASME 1982–94, RSM 1984–86, ABN 1987–88; first vice-pres World Fedn of Neurology 1981–89 (pres 1989–97), life pres Muscular Dystrophy Gp GB 2000– (chm 1970–95); warden Green Coll Oxford 1983–89; Hon DUniv Aix Marseille, Laurea (hc) Genoa, Hon MD Univ of Sheffield, Hon MD Mahidol Univ Thailand; Hon DSc: Univ of Leeds, Univ of Leicester, Univ of Hull, Oxford Brookes Univ, Univ of Durham; Hon DCL Univ of Newcastle upon Tyne; hon fell: Inst of Educn Univ of London, Norwegian Acad of Arts and Science; FRCP, Hon FRCPE, FRCPath, FRCPsych, FRCPCH, FMedSci; *Books* incl: Subarachnoid Haemorrhage, Polymyositis (with R D Adams), Essentials of Neurology, Disorders of Voluntary Muscle (ed), Brain's Diseases of the Nervous System (ed), The Spice of Life (autobiography); *Recreations* cricket, golf, music, walking; *Clubs* Athenaeum, Oxford and Cambridge, MCC, Bamburgh Castle Golf (pres 1987–); *Style*— The Rt Hon Lord Walton of Detchant, TD; ✉ The Old Piggery, Detchant, Belford, Northumberland NE70 7PF (tel 01668 213374, fax 01668 213012, e-mail waldetch@aol.com)

WALZER, Stephen; *b* 19 March 1943; *Educ* Univ of Bristol (LLB); *Career* admitted slr 1969; legal advsr BP Chemicals Ltd 1970–73, various posts in Legal Dept British Petroleum Co plc 1973–92 (latterly mangr int legal affrs), asst gen counsel int governmental affrs British American Tobacco plc (formerly BAT Industries plc) 1992–2005; memb Competition Cmmn, chm UK Competition Law Ctee Int C of C, rapporteur to Paris Int C of C Competition Cmmn, acting dir Br Inst of Int and Comparative Law until 2005; memb: Slrs Regulation Authy (also memb Educn and Trg and Quality Assurance Sub-Ctees), Devpt Ctee Br Inst of Int and Comparative Law (also fndr memb Competition Law Forum), Competition Law Ctee UNICE, Industrial Relations and Competition Gps European Round Table, Company Law and Int Investment Panels CBI, Jt Working Pty on Competition Law Bar Cncl/Law Soc; public interest memb Audit Review Ctee Inst of Chartered Accountants in England and Wales; memb: Int Law Assoc, Competition Law Assoc, UK Assoc for European Law, RIIA; accredited mediator; *Style*— Stephen Walzer, Esq

WAN, Dr Horatio Ho-Hee; s of Cheuk-ming Wan (d 1988), of Hong Kong, and Shun-Hing, *née* Au (d 1979); *b* 24 June 1935; *Educ* Ling-nan Middle Sch Hong Kong, Univ of Hong Kong (MB BS), Univ of Manchester (MSc); *m* 24 Feb 1960, Octavia Huang Iong-Iong, da of Chen-Ying Huang, of Hong Kong; 1 da (Valeria Jit-Wing Wan Ricci b 1961), 1 s (Dennis Jit-Yin b 1971); *Career* MO Nethersole Hosp Hong Kong, sr house offr Aberdeen Teaching Hosps 1972–74, med registrar SE Kent 1974–75, res fell and med registrar Christie Hosp Manchester 1975–77, lectr and sr med registrar Univ Hosp of S Manchester 1977–78, clinical dir Tameside Gen Hosp 1996–2002 (conslt physician in geriatric med 1979–); pres Manchester Chinatown Lions Club Int 1987–88; FRCP (London) 1992 (MRCP 1975); *Publications* author of articles in various med jls incl: Jl of Human Hypertension (Level of Blood Pressure in People of Chinese Origin Living in Britain, 2003), British Jl of Cancer, Postgraduate Medical Jl, Int Jl of Immunopharmacology; *Recreations* travel, reading, investment, walking; *Style*— Dr Horatio Wan; ✉ 2nd Floor, 16 Nicholas Street, Manchester M1 4EJ (tel 0161 228 2548)

WAN, Joseph Sai Cheong; *b* 27 February 1954; *Educ* in Hong Kong; *m* Flora Mei Yee; 2 da (Samantha Anne b 1986, Stephanie Eve b 1988); *Career* Peat Marwick (latterly KPMG Peat Marwick): joined as CA Hong Kong 1978, in London 1985–86, associate Hong Kong 1986–87; gp fin dir Dickson Concepts Ltd Hong Kong 1987–92 (responsible for acquisition of S T Dupont France 1987 and Harvey Nichols 1991), md Harvey Nichols & Co Ltd 1992–96, chief exec Harvey Nichols Gp plc 1996–; FCA (ACA 1978), FCIArb, FInstD, FRSA; *Clubs* Hong Kong Jockey; *Style*— Joseph Wan, Esq; ✉ Harvey Nichols & Co Ltd, 67 Brompton Road, London SW3 1DB (tel 020 7201 8564, fax 020 7823 1571, e-mail joseph.wan@harveynichols.com)

WANAMAKER, Zoë; CBE (2001); da of Sam Wanamaker, CBE (d 1993), and Charlotte Holland (d 1997); *Educ* King Alfred Sch, Sidcot Sch, Hornsey Coll of Art, Central Sch of Speech and Drama; *m* 7 Nov 1994, Gawn Grainger; *Career* actress; tstee and hon pres Globe Theatre; vice-pres Voluntary Euthanasia Soc; Hon DLitt: Southbank Univ 1995, Richmond American Int Univ 1999; *Theatre* Manchester 69 Co incl: A Midsummer Night's Dream 1970, Guys and Dolls 1972; Edinburgh Lyceum Theatre incl: The Cherry Orchard 1971 (also at the Stables Theatre Club 1970), Dick Whittington 1971–72; Young Vic 1974 incl: Tom Thumb, Much Ado About Nothing; Nottingham Playhouse 1975–76 incl: A Streetcar Named Desire, Pygmalion, The Beggar's Opera, Trumpets and Drums; Piccadilly Theatre incl: Wild Oats 1977, Once in a Lifetime 1979–80 (RSC 1978–79, SWET Award 1979); RSC Stratford and London 1976– incl: The Devil's Disciple, Wild Oats (also West End), Ivanov, The Taming of the Shrew, Captain Swing, Piaf (also West End and Broadway, Tony nomination 1981), A Comedy of Errors, Twelfth Night and The Time of Your Life 1983–85 (all Olivier Award nominations), Mother Courage (Drama Award 1985), Othello (Olivier Award nomination 1989); NT incl: The Importance of Being Earnest 1982–83, The Bay at Nice and Wrecked Eggs 1986–87, Mrs Klein (also West End, Olivier Award nomination) 1988–89, The Crucible 1990–91 (Olivier Award nomination), Battle Royal 1999–2000; other credits incl: Twelfth Night (Leeds Playhouse 1971, Cambridge Theatre Co 1973–74), Cabaret (Farnham) 1974, Kiss Me Kate (Oxford Playhouse) 1974, The Taming of the Shrew (New Shakespeare Co Round House) 1975, Loot (Manhattan Theatre Club, Music Box Theatre Broadway, Tony nomination 1986), Made in Bangkok (Mark Taper Forum LA) 1988, The Last Yankee (Young Vic (Olivier Award nomination)) 1993, Dead Funny (Hampstead and West End (Variety Club Best Actress Award)) 1994, The Glass Menagerie (Donmar and Comedy (Olivier Award nomination for Best Actress 1996)) 1995, Sylvia (Apollo) 1996, Electra (Chichester Festival and Donmar (Olivier Award for Best Actress 1998, Variety Club Award for Best Actress 1998)) 1997, The Old Neighbourhood (Royal Court) 1998, Electra (McCarter Theatre Princeton, Barrymore Theatre Broadway (Tony nomination Best Actress 1999)) 1998, Boston Marriage (Donmar Warehouse and New Ambassadors (Olivier Award nomination Best Actress 2002)) 2001, His Girl Friday (RNT) 2003, Awake & Sing! (Belasco Theatre NY) 2006 (NY City Drama Desk Award for Outstanding Ensemble Performance, Calloway Award, nomination Tony Award for Best Performance), The Rose Tattoo (RNT) 2007; *Television* Sally For Keeps 1970, The Eagle Has Landed 1972, Between the Wars 1973, The Silver Mask 1973, Lorna and Ted 1973, The Confederacy of Wives 1974, The Village Hall 1975, Danton's Death 1977, Beaux Strategem 1977, The Devil's Crown 1978–79, Strike 1981, Baal 1981, All the World's A Stage 1982, Richard III 1982, Enemies of the State 1982, Edge of Darkness 1985, Paradise Postponed 1985, Poor Little Rich Girl 1987, Once in a Lifetime 1987, The Dog it was that Died 1988, Ball Trap on the Côte Sauvage 1989, Othello 1989, Prime Suspect (BAFTA nomination) 1990, Love Hurts (BAFTA nomination) 1991, 1992 and 1993, Dance to the Music of Time 1997, Gormenghast 1999, David Copperfield (BBC) 1999, Adrian Mole, The Cappuccino Years 2000, My Family (BBC series) 2002–07 (2 BAFTA nominations, Best Actress Rose d'Or 2005), Marple: A Murder is Announced 2004, Dr Who: The End of the World 2005, Johnny and the Bomb (BBC) 2005, A Waste of Shame (BBC) 2005, Poirot: Cards on the Table 2006, Dr Who: New Earth (BBC) 2006; as narrator: Testimony Films, Veterans - 'Last Survivors of the Great War' (BBC) 1998 (Gold Hugo Award); *Radio* incl: The Golden Bowl, Plenty 1979, Bay at Nice 1987, A February Morning 1990, Carol (book reading) 1990, Such Rotten Luck 1991 (series I & II 1989); *Films* incl: Inside the Third Reich 1982, The Raggedy Rawney 1987, Wilde (BAFTA nomination) 1997, Swept From The Sea, Harry Potter and the Philosopher's Stone 2001, Five Children and It 2004; TV films: The Blackheath Poisonings (Central) 1991, Memento Mori (BBC) 1991, Countess Alice (BBC) 1991, The English Wife 1994, The Widowing of Mrs Holroyd (BBC) 1995, Leprechauns (Hallmark) 1999; *Style*— Ms Zoë Wanamaker, CBE; ✉ c/o Conway van Gelder Ltd, 18–21 Jermyn Street, London SW1Y 6HP (tel 020 7287 0077, fax 020 7287 1940)

WANLESS, Sir Derek; kt (2005); s of Norman Hall Wanless (d 1980), and Edna Mary, *née* Charlton; *b* 29 September 1947; *Educ* Royal GS Newcastle upon Tyne, King's Coll Cambridge (MA), Harvard Univ (PMD); *m* 25 Sept 1971, Vera, da of William West; 4 da (Marie Clare b 26 Aug 1974, Helen Kathryn b 24 Feb 1976, Rachael Louise, Christine Ruth (twins) b 20 Feb 1979), 1 s (Steven William b 7 Jan 1985); *Career* National Westminster Bank plc: with Statistics Section Market Intelligence 1970–73, PA to Gen Mangr Financial Control 1973–75, planning mangr Domestic Banking Div 1975–78, asst mangr 15 Bishopsgate Branch 1978–79, sr project mangr Domestic Banking Div 1979–80, mktg mangr Domestic Banking Div 1980–82, area dir NE Area 1982–85, area dir W Yorks Area 1985–86, dir of personal banking servs 1986–88, gen mangr UK Branch Business 1989–90, chief exec UK Financial Servs 1990–92, gp main bd dir 1991–99, dep gp chief exec and gp head NatWest Markets Feb-March 1992, gp chief exec March 1992–99; dir MasterCard International and vice-chm Eurocard International 1989–90, chm MasterCard and Eurocard Members (UK and Republic of Ireland) Forum Ltd 1989; non-exec Northumbrian Water Gp plc 2006– (non-exec dir 2003–), non-exec dir Northern Rock plc; vice-chm Statistics Cmmn 2004–; author of reports: Securing our Future Health: Taking a Long-Term View for Chllr of the Exchequer 2002, Securing Good Health for the PM, Chllr and Sec of State for Health 2004; advsr on health issues Welsh Assembly 2002–03; sometime chm: Advsy Ctee on Business and the Environment, Nat Advsy Cncl for Educn and Trg Targets, Financial Servs Trg Orgn; pres: Chartered Inst of Bankers, Institut International d'Etudies Bancaires; tstee NESTA; Freeman City of London 1992; Hon DSc City Univ 1995; MIS 1973, AIB 1978, FCIB 1990, FRSA 1991, CIMgt 1992, Hon FFPH 2004; *Recreations* all sports, chess, music, walking, gardening; *Clubs* Reform; *Style*— Sir Derek Wanless

WAPSHOTT, Nicholas Henry; s of Raymond Gibson Wapshott (d 1995), of Hereford, and Olivia Beryl, *née* Darch (d 1970); *b* 13 January 1952; *Educ* Rendcomb Coll, Univ of York; *m* Louise Nicholson, da of (Royden) Joseph Nicholson; 2 s (William Henry Joseph Nicholson b 5 Aug 1988, Oliver Evelyn Samuel Nicholson b 4 July 1990); *Career* journalist, broadcaster and author; The Scotsman 1973–76, The Times 1976–83, political ed The Observer 1988–92 (features ed 1983–88), ed The Times Magazine (formerly The Saturday Review) 1992–97, ed Saturday Times 1997–2001, N American corr The Times 2001–05, nat and foreign ed NY Sun 2006–; Liveryman Worshipful Co of Leathersellers; *Books* Peter O'Toole (1982), Thatcher (with George Brock, 1983), The Man Between: A Biography of Carol Reed (1990), Rex Harrison (1991), Older: A Biography of George Michael (with Tim Wapshott, 1998), Ronald Reagan and Margaret Thatcher: A Political Marriage (2007); *Recreations* watching films, travelling, elephants; *Clubs* Garrick; *Style*— Nicholas Wapshott, Esq; ✉ c/o Kathy Robbins, The Robbins Office, 405 Park Avenue, New York, NY 10022, USA (e-mail krobbins@robbinsoffice.com)

WARBURG, (Christina) Clare Barham; da of Dr (Alan) Barham Carter (d 1995), of Weybridge, Surrey, and Mollie Christina, *née* Sanders (d 1995); *Educ* St Michael's Sch, Université de Poitiers; *m* 1, 8 June 1968 (m dis 1975), Andrew Oscar Warburg, s of late Brig Thomas Raphael Warburg, CBE, of Maidstone, Kent; 2 s (Mark b 9 Jan 1971, Daniel b 2 Dec 1972); *m* 2, 28 Feb 1983 (m dis 1987) Peter Brian Adie; m 3, 13 May 1995, Dr Stuart St Pierre Slatter; *Career* paper conservator and watercolour restorer; fine art dealer 1975–: Kensington Park Galleries 1975–78, freelance 1978–; memb: Kensington Ctee Save The Children Fund, Avenues Youth Project Ctee; *Recreations* gardening, antiques, photography; *Style*— Mrs Clare Warburg; ✉ Tarrant Abbey, Near Blandford, Dorset DT11 9HU

WARBURTON, David; s of Harold Warburton, (d 1988), of Shipley, W Yorks, and Ada, *née* Sinfield (d 1960); *b* 10 January 1942; *Educ* St Walburgas Sch Shipley, Cottingley Manor Sch Bingley, Coleg Harlech; *m* 15 Oct 1966, Carole Anne Susan, da of Frank Tomney (d 1984), of Rickmansworth, Herts, and former MP for Hammersmith; 2 da (Sara Anne b 25 Sept 1968, Caroline Susan b 28 July 1970); *Career* GMWU educn offr 1965–67 (regnl offr 1967–73), nat industrial offr GMBATU 1973–90, sr nat offr GMB and APEX 1990–95; vice-pres Int Fedn Chemical and Energy Workers 1986–92, sec UK Chemical Unions Cncl 1978–85, chm TUC Gen Purpose Ctee 1984–95; memb: NEDC 1973–86, Cwlth Devpt Corp 1979–87, MOD Industrial Cncl 1988–91, Civil Air Tport Nat Jt Cncl 1992–95, Industrial Tbnl 1995–, Construction Task Force 1997–98, Employment Tbnls 1998–; dir Friends of the Speaker 1996–2002; sec Friends of Palestine 1983–; memb: Upper Wharfedale Museum Soc 1978–, Yorkshire Soc 1983–, Assoc for Int Cancer Research 1989–, Amnesty Int 1990–, Crazy Horses Investment Tst; ed People First! 2002–; memb Chorleywood PC 2002–06; *Books* Pharmaceuticals for the People (1973), Drug Industry (1975), UK Chemicals: The Way Forward (1977), Economic Detente (1980), The Case for Voters Tax Credits (1983), Forward Labour (1985), Facts Figures and Damned Statistics (1987), Breakthrough in Legal Aid (1998); contrib numerous articles to leading jls; *Recreations* hill climbing, music, 1930–50 film memorabilia; *Clubs* Victoria (Westminster); *Style*— David Warburton, Esq; ✉ 47 Hill Rise, Chorleywood, Rickmansworth, Hertfordshire WD3 7NY (tel 01923 778726)

WARBY, Mark David John; QC (2002); s of David James Warby, of Almondsbury, Bristol, and Clare Shirley, *née* Hodgson; *b* 10 October 1958, Berkeley, Glos; *Educ* Bristol GS, St John's Coll Oxford (scholar, MA); *m* 3 Aug 1985, Ann, *née* Kenrick; 2 da (Isabel b 7 Sept 1989, Rachel b 17 July 1996), 1 s (Milo b 28 Jan 1991); *Career* barr specialising in media, entertainment and sport law 1983–; *Books* The Law of Privacy and the Media (contrib, 2002); *Recreations* surfing, tennis, guitar, food, wine and family; *Clubs* Crackington Haven Surf, Butterfly Tennis (chair 1997–2003); *Style*— Mark Warby, Esq, QC; ✉ 5 Raymond

Buildings, Gray's Inn, London WC1R 5BP (tel 020 7692 5120, fax 020 7831 2686, e-mail markwarby@5rb.com)

WARCHUS, Matthew; *b* 24 October 1966; *Educ* Univ of Bristol (BA Music and Drama, special commendation for practical work in drama); *Career* director; dir Nat Youth Theatre of GB 1989 and 1990, Bristol Old Vic 1991, asst dir RSC 1991–92, assoc dir W Yorkshire Playhouse 1993; also freelance dir; *Theatre* for RSC (as dir) incl: Henry V 1995, The Devil is an Ass (The Swan & Pit) 1995, Hamlet 1997; for West Yorkshire Playhouse: Life is A Dream (nominated TMA Best Dir), Who's Afraid of Virginia Woolf, Fiddler on the Roof, The Plough and the Stars, Death of a Salesman, Betrayal, True West; other prodns incl: The Life of Stuff (Donmar), True West (Donmar) 1994, Volpone (RNT) 1995, Art (Wyndhams) 1996, The Unexpected Man (Duchess) 1998, Our House (Cambridge), Tell Me On A Sunday (Gielgud); *Opera* Troilus and Cressidi (Opera North), The Rake's Progress (WNO), Falstaff (Opera North and ENO); *Awards* Shakespeare's Globe Award for Most Promising Newcomer 1994, The Sydney Edward's Award for Best Director (for Volpone and Henry V) 1995, Evening Standard Award for Best Dir (for Volpone and Henry V); Olivier Award nomination for Best Director (for Volpone, Henry V, Art and Hamlet) 1996; *Style*— Matthew Warchus, Esq

WARD, Dr Adam Anthony; s of Dennis Harold Ward, of Mark Cross, E Sussex, and Margaret Maud, *née* Record; *b* 15 June 1947; *Educ* Tonbridge, Springhill Sch, King's Coll London, Westminster Med Sch Univ of London (MB BS), LSHTM (MSc), Hotel Dieu Univ of Paris (DipOrthMed); *Career* clinician, lectr and broadcaster; ed Broadway Magazine 1970, lectr and hon sr registrar (epidemiology) Westminster Med Sch 1978–79; physician: Dept of Orthopaedic Med Hotel Dieu Paris 1982–83, Dept of Musculoskeletal Medicine Royal London Homoeopathic Hosp 1983–, UCL Hosps NHS Tst; dir and conslt orthopaedic and musculoskeletal physician and specialist in complementary med; memb: British Inst of Musculoskeletal Med, Faculty of Homoeopathy London (fell), British Med Acupuncture Soc, Editorial Bd Acupuncture in Medicine jl; examiner Soc of Apothecaries London; *Recreations* walking, skiing and relaxing; *Style*— Dr Adam A Ward; ✉ 41 Frankfield Rise, Tunbridge Wells, Kent TN2 5LF (tel 01892 525799)

WARD, Rt Hon Lord Justice; Rt Hon Sir Alan Hylton; kt (1988), PC (1995); s of Stanley Victor Ward (d 1974), and Mary, *née* Whittingham; *b* 15 February 1938; *Educ* Christian Bros Coll Pretoria, Univ of Pretoria (BA, LLB), Pembroke Coll Cambridge (MA, LLB); *m* 1, 1963 (m dis 1982); 2 da (Wendy b 1965, Emma b 1966), 1 s (Mark b 1968); m 2, 1983 Helen Madeleine, da of Keith Gilbert, and Ruth Gilbert; 2 da (Amelia b 1984 d 2001, Katharine (twin) b 1984); *Career* attorney Supreme Court South Africa 1959–61; called to the Bar Gray's Inn 1964 (bencher 1988, treas 2006); QC 1984, judge of the High Court of Justice (Family Div) 1988–95, Lord Justice of Appeal 1995–; former liaison judge Midland & Oxford Circuit; hon fell Pembroke Coll Cambridge 1998; Hon LLD UEA; *Recreations* when not reading and writing boring judgements, trying to remember what recreation is; *Clubs* Garrick, MCC; *Style*— The Rt Hon Lord Justice Ward; ✉ Royal Courts of Justice, Strand, London WC2A 2LL (tel 020 7936 6752)

WARD, Anthony John; s of John George Ward (d 1995), and Joyce Finlay, *née* Ford; *b* 23 September 1962, Winchester, Hants; *Educ* Downside, SSEES Univ of London (BA), Coll of Law; *m* 1 July 1991, Hilary Jane; 2 s (Henry b 17 Sept 1992, Archie b 23 Sept 1996), 2 da (Kate b 25 March 1994, Charlotte b 8 Sept 2000); *Career* slr; ptnr: Ashurst Morris Crisp 1996–98, Shearman & Sterling 1998–; *Style*— Anthony Ward, Esq; ✉ Shearman & Sterling LLP, Broadgate West, 9 Appold Street, London EC2A 2AP (tel 020 7655 5959)

WARD, Anthony Robert; s of Stanley Roy Ward, of Worcestershire, and Jeanette, *née* Mantle; *b* 6 January 1957; *Educ* Wrekin Coll, Wimbledon Sch of Art (BA); *Partner* Mark Thompson, *qv*, theatre designer; *Career* costume and set designer; worked extensively in rep incl: Royal Exchange Manchester, Bristol Old Vic, Derby Playhouse, Haymarket Theatre Leicester, Nottingham Playhouse, Theatre Royal Plymouth, Theatre Royal York; *Theatre* for RSC incl: A Midsummer Night's Dream, King Lear, The Tempest, Artists & Admirers, The Winter's Tale, The Alchemist, The Virtuoso, Troilus & Cressida, Cymbeline, Twelfth Night, The Lion, The Witch and the Wardrobe, The Secret Garden; for RNT incl: Sweet Bird of Youth, Napoli Milionaria, The Way of the World, La Grande Magia, John Gabriel Borkman, Othello, The Invention of Love, Oklahoma! (Lyceum Theatre and Broadway), Remember This, My Fair Lady (also Theatre Royal); other credits incl: Chitty Chitty Bang Bang (London Palladium and Broadway), Oliver! (London Palladium and nat tour), The Magic Flute (Glyndebourne), Gypsy (Broadway), The Rehearsal, A Hard Heart, Dona Rosita, The Novice (all Almeida), Assassins, Nine, To The Green Fields Beyond, Uncle Vanya, Twelfth Night (all Donmar Warehouse), Burning Issues (Hampstead Theatre), The Royal Family (Theatre Royal), Mary Stuart (Donmar Warehouse and Apollo Theatre), The Night of the Iguana (Lyric Theatre), The Royal Hunt of the Sun (NT); *Opera* for Opera North incl: La Bohème, Yolande, The Nutcracker, L'Étoile, Gloriana (also ROH), Peter Grimes; other credits incl: The Makropulos Case (Metropolitan Opera, NY), Tosca (De Vlaamse Opera, Antwerp), Manon Lescaut (Opera de Paris, Bastille & De Vlaamse Opera), Macbeth (Bastille), Dialogues of the Carmelites (ENO and WNO), Il Ritorno d'Ulisse (Aix-en-Provence Festival); *Ballet* The Nutcracker (Adventures in Motion Pictures, Sadlers Wells), Masquerade, Les Rendezvous, Dance Variations (all Royal Ballet); *Film* A Midsummer Night's Dream (RSC prodn, dir Adrian Noble, *qv*), Gloriana - A Film (BBC); *Awards* Olivier Award nominations incl: Best Costume & Set Design (for A Winter's Tale) 1994, Best Set Design (for Sweet Bird of Youth and The Tempest) 1995, Best Set Design (for A Midsummer Night's Dream, La Grande Magia and The Way of the World) 1996; Tony Award nomination for Scenic Design (for A Midsummer Night's Dream) 1995–96, Best Costume & Set Design My Fair Lady 2002, Best Set Design Chitty Chitty Bang Bang 2003; winner Olivier Award Best Costume Design (for A Midsummer Night's Dream, La Grande Magia and The Way of the World) 1996, winner Olivier Award Best Set Design (for Oklahoma!) 1999, winner OBIE for set design (for Uncle Vanya) 2002–03; *Style*— Anthony Ward, Esq; ✉ c/o agent, Harriet Cruickshank, 97 Old South Lambeth Road, London SW8 1XU (tel 020 7735 2933, fax 020 7820 1081)

WARD, Bernard Leonard; s of Leonard Ward (d 1968), of W Midlands, and Louisa Elizabeth, *née* Knock; *b* 18 July 1934; *Educ* Holyhead Rd Secdy Modern Wednesbury; *m* 26 July 1958, Shiela Mary, da of Thomas Maguire (d 1948); 2 da (Karen Lesley b 1958, Stephanie Ann b 1966); *Career* served with N Staffs Regt Korea; photographer; began career Far East, apprenticed to world's leading photographers, in sole practice (specialising in portraits of people and animals) 1979–; recipient of numerous awards from BIPP, Master Photographic Assoc, Kodak and London Portrait Gp; memb MPS; FBIPP, FRPS, FMPA, FRSA; *Recreations* tennis, sailing, skating, golf, fly fishing, horse riding; *Clubs* Telford Racquet; *Style*— Bernard Ward, Esq; ✉ Bernard's Gallery, 70 Lucknow Road, Willenhall, West Midlands WV12 4QG (tel 01902 602985)

WARD, Christopher John; s of late John Stanley Ward, and Jacqueline Law Hume, *née* Costin (d 1996); *b* 25 August 1942; *Educ* KCS Wimbledon; *m* 1 (m dis 1987); 2 da (Sadie b 13 Aug 1973, Martha b 6 April 1976), 1 s (William b 18 April 1979); m 2, 1991, Nonie Niesewand; *Career* reporter: Driffield Times 1959, Newcastle Evening Chronicle 1960–63; reporter, columnist and sub-ed Daily Mirror 1963–76, asst ed Daily and Sunday Mirror 1976–81, ed Daily Express 1981–83, jt fndr and chm Redwood Publishing Ltd 1983–; non-exec dir Acorn Group plc (formerly Acorn Computer Group plc) 1983–99; tstee WWF 1994–2000, chm WWF-UK 2002–; Mark Boxer Award BSME 1995; *Books* How to Complain (1974), Our Cheque is in the Post (1980); *Recreations* walking in the Scottish Borders; *Clubs* Savile, Garrick; *Style*— Christopher Ward, Esq; ✉ Glenburn Hall, Jedburgh, Roxburghshire TD8 6QB (tel 01835 865801, fax 01835 865803, e-mail cj.ward@btinternet.com); Redwood Publishing Ltd, 7 St Martin's Place, London WC2N 4HA (tel 020 7747 0705)

WARD, Claire Margaret; MP; da of Frank Ward, and Catherine, *née* McClure; *b* 9 May 1972; *Educ* Loreto Coll (RC Girls) St Albans, Univ of Hertfordshire (LLB), Brunel Univ (MA), Coll of Law London; *Career* various pt/t clerical positions 1985–92, PA to Lab Gp Hertsmere BC 1992–95, trainee slr Pattinson & Brewer Slrs London 1995–97, qualified slr 1998; MP (Lab) Watford 1997–; asst Govt whip 2005–06, a Lord Cmmr of HM Treasy (Govt whip) 2006–; sec All-Pty Film Industry Gp 1997–2005, chair House of Commons Select Ctee for Culture, Media and Sport 2002– (memb 1997–), chair All-Pty Parly Youth Affrs Gp 2001–05; memb: T&GWU, Fabian Soc, Co-op Pty, Lab NEC 1991–95; winner S East TUC Mike Perkins Meml Award for Young Trade Unionist 1989, winner T&GWU Nat Youth Award 1990; hon vice-pres Watford FC; *Recreations* cinema, watching football, dining out; *Style*— Claire Ward, MP; ✉ House of Commons, London SW1A 0AA (tel 020 7219 4910, fax 020 7219 0468)

WARD, Clive Richard; s of William Herbert Ward (d 1982), and Muriel, *née* Wright; *b* 30 July 1945; *Educ* Sevenoaks Sch, Univ of Cambridge (MA); *m* 9 Sept 1972, Catherine Angela, da of Lt Cdr Godfrey Joseph Hines (d 1999), of Droxford, Hants; 3 da (Joanna b 1975, Diana b 1977, Emily b 1979); *Career* CA 1971, asst sec Take Over Panel 1975–77, ptnr Ernst and Young 1979–90 (head corp fin London 1987), corp devpt dir Shandwick plc 1990–91, dir The Capita Group plc 1992–94, ptnr Ernst & Young 1994–2006, dir EY Trustees Ltd 2006–; treas Nat Assoc of Victims Support Schemes 2002–; Freeman: Worshipful Co of Barbers 1985, Worshipful Co of Tobacco Pipe Makers and Tobacco Blenders 1975; FCA 1979; *Books* Guide to Company Flotation (1989); *Recreations* golf, fishing, music, gardening; *Clubs* RAC; *Style*— Clive Ward, Esq; ✉ Market Heath House, Brenchley, Tonbridge, Kent TN12 7PA (tel 01892 722172); Ernst & Young LLP, 1 More London Place, London SE1 2AF (e-mail cward5@uk.ey.com)

WARD, Constance Cluett; da of George Bywater Cluett, II (d 1957), of NY, and Marion, *née* Ticknor (d 1980); *b* 25 October 1928; *Educ* Knox Sch NY, Emma Willard Sch NY, Finch Coll NY; *m* 1, 1949 (m dis 1963), Louis D Sage; 3 da (Deborah Sage Rockefeller b 1951, Marion (The Viscountess Thurso) b 1954, Martha (Mrs Martha D Berry) b 1959); m 2, 1975, Alexander Reginald (Reggie) Ward (d 1987); *Career* hotelier; prop Kinnaird Dunkeld 1987–; AA Country House Hotel of Year 1992, RAC Blue Ribbon 1995–98, RAC Gold Ribbon 1999–2006, Gallivanter's Guide Award for Excellence and Editor's Choice Awards 2002, 3 AA rosettes and three stars 2003–06, 4 red roofs Michelin Guide 2004; memb Relais et Châteaux, memb Chevaliers de Tastevin 1990–; *Recreations* music, books, grandchildren; *Clubs* The Colony (NYC); *Style*— Mrs Constance Cluett Ward; ✉ Balmacneil House, Kinnaird Estate, Dunkeld, Perthshire PH8 0LB (tel and fax 01796 482254, e-mail conniekinnaird@aol.com); Kinnaird, Kinnaird Estate, Dunkeld, Perthshire PH8 0LB (tel 01796 482440, fax 01796 482289, e-mail enquiry@kinnairdestate.com)

WARD, Dr David; s of Ernest Ward, and Hilda Grace Ward; *Educ* Old Swinford Hosp, Guy's Hosp (BSc, MB BS, Gowland Hopkins Prize), Univ of London MD; *Career* trained in cardiology St Bart's, conslt St George's Hosp 1986–; memb: Br Cardiac Soc 1981, Apothecaries Soc 1985, Liszt Soc, Albania Soc, Piano Player Gp; Freeman City of London 1979; FACC 1981, FRCP 1989; *Publications* Clinical Electrophysiology of the Heart (1987); *Recreations* music, boating, squash; *Style*— Dr David Ward; ✉ 84 Harley Street, London W1G 7HW (tel 020 7079 4290, fax 020 7079 4294)

WARD, David James; s of Leslie Edward Ward, of Egham, Surrey, and Margaret, *née* Cook; *b* 1 May 1946; *Educ* Manor Croft Sch Egham, Brookland Tech Coll, Richmond Coll of Technol; *m* 10 April 1971, Glenora Ann, da of late Robert Gordon Tott; 2 da (Joanna Louise b 1 March 1980, Sarah Michele b 30 July 1982); *Career* freelance photographer 1978–; press photographer, work published in various magazines papers and books, photographer of Royalty, show business people and actors, specialist in portraiture; winner of many merits and awards incl: Press Photographer of the Year, Kodak Photographer of the Year, Panorama Photographer of the Year, Kodak Gold Award for Portrait Photography 1993, UK Portrait Photographer of the Year 1996; BIPP Press Photographer of the Year 1997; Br Photographers' Assoc 1990; FBIPP 1994; *Books* Wonderful World Series (1985); *Recreations* jogging, squash, cycling; *Clubs* Roundtable (Egham); *Style*— David Ward, Esq; ✉ Latchets, Harpesford Avenue, Virginia Water, Surrey GU25 4RE (tel 01344 843421); The Studio, Latchets, Harpesford Avenue, Virginia Water, Surrey GU25 4RE (tel 01344 843421)

WARD, Dr Dermot Joseph; s of Richard Ward (d 1985), of Dublin, and Margaret, *née* Whitty (d 1962); *b* 7 June 1933; *Educ* St James Secdy Sch Dublin; *m* 3 Aug 1961, Ruth Eva, da of George Nathaniel Stedmond (d 1978), of Dublin; 2 s (Jonathan Dermot b 1965, Simon Richard b 1969); *Career* sr registrar in psychiatry Bath Clinical Area 1965–68, med dir St Lomans Hosp Dublin 1979–86 (conslt psychiatrist 1969–86); conslt psychiatrist: Graylingwell Hosp Chichester 1986–88, St Davids Hosp Carmarthen 1988–; pubns in: Br Med Jl, Irish Med Jl, Br Jl of Psychiatry; memb Inst of Economic Affrs 1983; LRCPI, LRCSI, LM, FRCPI, FRCPsych, DPM, memb BMA 1961, FRSM 1983; *Recreations* writing, literature, theatre, films and travel; *Style*— Dr Dermot Ward; ✉ 4 Jubilee Terrace, Chichester, West Sussex PO19 7XT

WARD, Gerald John; CBE, DL (Berks 2000); s of Col Edward John Sutton Ward, LVO, MC (d 1990); *b* 31 May 1938; *Educ* Eton, RMA Sandhurst, RAC Cirencester; *m* 1, 1967 (m dis 1983), Rosalind Elizabeth, da of Hon Richard Lygon (d 1972); 2 da; m 2, 1984, Amanda, da of Sir Lacey Vincent, 2 Bt (d 1963); *Career* Capt RHG; industrialist and farmer; chm: UK Solenoid Ltd, Public Service Broadcasting Tst; Extra Equerry to HRH The Prince of Wales 1987; *Clubs* White's; *Style*— Gerald Ward, Esq, CBE, DL; ✉ Chilton Park Farm, Hungerford, Berkshire RG17 0SY (tel 01488 682329)

WARD, Graham Norman Charles; CBE (2004); s of Ronald Charles Edward Ward (d 1999), and Hazel Winnifred, *née* Ellis (d 2002); *b* 9 May 1952; *Educ* Dulwich Coll, Jesus Coll Oxford (MA, Boxing blue); *m* 1, 1975 (m dis 1981), Ingrid Imogen Sylvia, da of Hubert Edward Philip Peter Baden-Powell (d 1994); 2 s (Peter Ronald Norman b 15 June 1978, Andrew Charles Richard b 16 Sept 1980); m 2, 1993, Ann, da of Joseph Mistri; 1 s (Alexander Christopher Edward b 14 Feb 1996); *Career* PricewaterhouseCoopers (formerly Price Waterhouse before merger): articled clerk 1974–77, personal tech asst to chm Account Standards Ctee 1978–79, seconded to HM Treasy 1985, ptnr 1986–, dir Electricity Services Europe 1990–94, dir Business Devpt 1993–94, chm World Utilities Gp 1994–96, dep chm World Energy Gp 1996–98, World Utilities ldr Global Energy and Mining Gp 1998–2000, sr ptnr Global Energy and Utilities Gp 2000–; chm: Young Chartered Accountants Gp 1980–81, London Soc of Chartered Accountants 1989–90 (memb Ctee 1983–91), Chartered Accountants in the Community 1996–2002, Consultative Ctee of Accountancy Bodies 2000–01, Power Sector Advsy Gp UK Trade & Investment 2001–04; membership sec Pensions Res Accountants Gp 1985–90; memb: Cncl Soc of Pension Conslts 1988–90, Cncl ICAEW 1991–2003 (vice-pres 1998–99, dep pres 1999–2000, pres 2000–01), Ctee Br Energy Assoc 1997–2004 (vice-chm 1998–2001, chm 2001–04), Takeover Panel 2000–01, Financial Reporting Cncl 2000– (dep chm 2000–01), Bd Int Fedn of Accountants 2000–06 (pres 2004–06), Auditing Practices Bd 2001–04 (vice-chm 2003–04), Bd Indo British Partnership Network 2005–, Financial Servs Sector Advsy Bd UK Trade & Investment 2006–; pres: Jesus Coll Assoc 1990–91, Chartered Accountants Students' Soc of London 1992–96 (vice-pres 1987–92); vice-pres Univ of Oxford Amateur Boxing Club 1990–, Soc of Cons Accountants 1992–, Epilepsy Research Fndn 1997–; govr Goodenough Coll 2004–; Freeman: City of London 1994, Worshipful

Co of Chartered Accountants 1994 (memb Ct of Assts 1997, Jr Warden 2007–); FCA 1983 (ACA 1977), CIGEM, FEI, FRSA; *Books* The Work of a Pension Scheme Actuary (1987), Pensions: Your Way Through The Maze (1988), A Practitioner's Guide to Audit Regulation in the UK (consIt ed, 2004); *Recreations* boxing, rugby, opera, ballet; *Clubs* Carlton, Vincent's (Oxford); *Style*— Graham Ward, Esq, CBE; ✉ PricewaterhouseCoopers, 1 Embankment Place, London WC2N 6RH (tel 020 7804 3101, fax 020 7804 3134, e-mail graham.n.ward@uk.pwc.com)

WARD, Ian; s of Alan Ward (d 1990), of Washington, Tyne and Wear and Ann, *née* Anderson; *b* 12 May 1959, Newcastle upon Tyne; *Educ* Washington Sch, Univ of Durham (BA); *m* 5 April 1991, Andrea Helen, *née* Wilson; 2 da (Antonia b 20 June 1994, Emilia b 4 June 1997); *Career* slr; ptnr: Eversheds 1989–97 (joined as articled clerk 1981), Dickinson Dees 1997– (currently head Property Dept); memb Law Soc; *Recreations* travel, skiing; *Style*— Ian Ward, Esq; ✉ Dickinson Dees, 1 Trinity Gardens, Broad Chare, Newcastle upon Tyne (tel 0191 279 9244, fax 0191 230 8920, e-mail ian.ward@dickinson-dees.com)

WARD, Prof Ian Macmillan; *b* 9 April 1928; *Educ* Royal GS Newcastle upon Tyne, Magdalen Coll Oxford (MA, DPhil); *m*; 3 c; *Career* tech offr Fibres Div ICI Ltd Harrogate 1954–61, res assoc Div of Applied Mathematics Brown Univ USA 1961–62, head Basic Physics Section ICI Fibres 1962–66 (ICI res assoc 1965–66), sr lectr in physics of materials H H Wills Physics Laboratory Univ of Bristol 1966–70; Univ of Leeds: prof of physics 1970–94, chm of dept 1975–78 and 1987–89, Cavendish prof 1987–94, dir Interdisciplinary Res Centre in Polymer Sci and Technol 1989–94, research prof 1994–; chm: Br Polymer Physics Gp Inst of Physics 1971–75 (sec 1967–71), Macromolecular Physics Section Euro Physical Soc 1976–81; pres Br Soc of Rheology 1984–86; memb Advsy Bd Jl of Macromolecular Science (Physics) 1966–, jt ed Solid State Science Series Cambridge Univ Press 1966–, ed Polymer 1974–; memb Editorial Bd: Jl of Materials Science 1974–, Plastics and Rubber Processing and Applications 1981–, Jl of Applied Polymer Science 1989–; A A Griffiths Silver Medal Inst of Materials 1982, S G Smith Meml Medal Textile Inst 1984, Swinburne Medal Inst of Materials 1988, Charles Vernon Boys Medal and Prize Inst of Physics 1993, Glazebrook Medal Inst of Physics 2004, Netlon Medal Inst of Materials 2004; hon degree Univ of Bradford 1993; FRS 1983, FInstP, FIM; *Publications* Mechanical Properties of Solid Polymers (1971, 2 edn 1983), Structure and Properties of Oriented Polymers (ed, 1975, 2 edn 1997), Ultra High Modulus Polymers (ed jtly, 1979), Advances in Oriented Polymers - 1 (ed, 1982), Advances in Oriented Polymers - 2 (1987), An Introduction to the Mechanical Properties of Solid Polymers (with D W Hadley, 1993, 2 edn with J Sweeney, 2004), Solid Phase Processing of Polymers (ed jtly, 2000); around 600 papers in polymer science; *Style*— Prof Ian M Ward, FRS; ✉ IRC in Polymer Science and Technology, University of Leeds, Leeds LS2 9JT (tel 0113 343 3808, fax 0113 343 3846, e-mail i.m.ward@leeds.ac.uk)

WARD, (William) Ian Roy; s of William Gerald Roy Ward (d 1977), of St Leonards-on-Sea, and Ellinor Ward, *née* Ostergaard (d 1964); *b* 17 September 1936; *Educ* Bembridge Sch, Thames Nautical Trg Coll HMS Worcester; *m* 21 Nov 1964, Vivienne, da of George Edward Garton Watson (d 1971), of Cape Town, South Africa; 2 da (Michele b 4 Sept 1967, Alison b 31 Aug 1975), 1 s (Duncan b 30 Sept 1969); *Career* Lt RNR until 1965; Merchant Navy 1954–58 and 1962–64, called to the Bar 1962, Admiralty Chambers 1964–75, ptnr (specialising in shipping) Lovell White Durrant 1976–95, consIt Holman Fenwick & Willam 1996–2000, pt/t immigration judge 1999–; dir British & International Sailors' Soc; Freeman Worshipful Co of Solicitors; memb Law Soc 1976; FCIArb 1972; *Recreations* sailing, walking; *Clubs* East India; *Style*— Ian Ward, Esq; ✉ 67 The Avenue, Kew, Richmond, Surrey TW9 2AH (tel 020 8940 0260); Castle Hill, Newport, Dyfed SA42 OQD (tel 01239 820263)

WARD, Sir John MacQueen; kt (2003), CBE (1995); s of Marcus Waddie Ward (d 1963), of Edinburgh, and Catherine, *née* MacQueen (d 1996); *b* 1 August 1940; *Educ* Edinburgh Acad, Fettes; *m* Barbara MacIntosh; 3 da (Marsali, Mhairi, Morag); 1 s (Marcus); *Career* IBM: plant controller 1966–75, dir of info systems Euro 1975–79, manufacturing controller 1979–81, dir Havant Manufacturing Plant 1982–90 (first Br Quality Award, Wills Faber Award, two Queen's Awards for export and technol), dir UK Govt and Public Serv Business 1991–95, res dir Scotand & N England 1991–97; chm 1990–94: Scottish Electronics Forum, Quality Scotland Fndn, Advsy Scottish Cncl for Educn and Trg Targets, CBI; chm: Euro Assets Tst 1995–, Scottish Homes 1996–2002, Scottish Post Office Bd 1997–2001, Scottish Qualification Authy 2000–04, Scottish Enterprise 2004–; non-exec chm: Macfarlane Gp plc 1995–2003 (chm 1998–2003), Dunfermline Bldg Soc 2002–07; memb: Sec of State's Scottish Econ Cncl 1990–94, Sec of State's Scottish Business Forum 1998–99; chm of govrs Queen Margaret UC 2000–04; tsee Nat Museums of Scotland; visiting prof Heriot-Watt Univ; Hon DSc Napier Univ, Hon DBA Univ of Strathclyde, Hon DL Glasgow Caledonian Univ, Hon DUniv Heriot-Watt; hon fell SCOTVEC; MICAS, MIEE, FRSA, FRSE; *Recreations* walking, DIY, reading; *Clubs* New (Edinburgh); *Style*— Sir John Ward, CBE; ✉ Barnton Brae, Edinburgh EH4 6DG

WARD, John Streeton; OBE (1989), DL; s of Charles Eric Ward, of Stamford, Lincs, and Agnes Anne, *née* Streeton; *b* 28 September 1933; *Educ* Stamford Sch; *m* 1, 28 Sept 1957 (m dis 1998), Dorothy Sheila; 2 s (Graham b 1960, Richard b 1966); m 2, 1999, Eileen McCabe; *Career* Barclays Bank: joined 1950, local dir Preston 1974–79, sr local dir Newcastle upon Tyne 1983–88 (local dir 1979–83), regnl dir Barclays Bank plc 1988–93 (chm Barclays Northern Regnl Bd); dir and dep chm North England Building Society 1993–94, dir and jt dep chm Northern Rock plc (following merger) 1994–2002; chm: Stobo Castle Health Spa Ltd 2000–, Stainton Metal Co Ltd 2002–, Warmseal Windows Ltd 2004–; non-exec dir: Tyne & Wear Enterprise Trust Ltd (ENTRUST) 1981–90, Northern Investors Company plc 1984–2004, Tyne & Wear Development Corp (dep chm) 1987–98, The Newcastle Initiative 1988–94 (chm 1990–93), Theatre Royal Trust Ltd 1988– (vice-chm), Northumbrian Water Group plc 1989–99 (dep chm 1993–96), Grainger Trust plc 1994–2004, Arriva plc (formerly Cowie Gp) 1994–2002; non-exec chm Waters & Robson Ltd 1996–99; dir Church Schools Co 1998–2003, tstee Northern Rock Fndn 2002–05; memb: Bd Business in the Community Tyne & Wear & Northumberland (chm 1985–90), Bd of Govrs Newcastle upon Tyne Poly until 1992, Cncl Univ of Durham 1993–2001, N of England Industrial Devpt Bd 1995–2000 (chm 1999–2000), Newcastle upon Tyne West End Partnership City Challenge Bd 1992–96, Appeal Ctee Marie Curie Cancer Care; vice-chm Tyneside Stables Project Ltd St Thomas St Workshops; tstee and treas Sunderland Univ Devpt Tst 1999–, tstee and dir W Harton Action Station 2005–; chm: Cruddas Park Community Tst Newcastle upon Tyne, British Olympic Appeal NE Region 1984 and 1988, Cncl Sunderland HS 1999–2005, Bubble Fndn 2006–; High Sheriff Tyne & Wear 1998–99; ACIB; *Recreations* golf, theatre-going, tennis, Sunderland AFC supporter; *Clubs* R&A, Northumberland Golf; *Style*— John S Ward, Esq, OBE, DL; ✉ tel 0191 529 3036, fax 0191 529 5741, e-mail eastfieldsjohn@aol.com

WARD, (Christopher) John William; s of Gp Capt Thomas Maxfield Ward, CBE, DFC (d 1969), and Peggy, *née* Field (d 2004); *b* 21 June 1942; *Educ* CCC Oxford (BA Lit Hum), Univ of E Anglia (DipEcon); *m* 1971 (m dis 1988), Diane, *née* Lelliott; partner, Susan Corby; *Career* Bank of England 1965–74; gen sec: Bank of England Staff Organisation 1974–80, Assoc First Div of Civil Servants 1980–88; head of devpt Opera North 1988–94, dir of corp affairs West Yorkshire Playhouse 1994–97, dir of devpt ENO 1997–2002, dir of devpt Crafts Cncl 2003–04, devpt advsr Welsh Nat Opera 2003–; chm Swindon Supporters in London 1987–88; *Style*— John Ward, Esq; ✉ Welsh National Opera, Wales Millennium Centre, Cardiff Bay, Cardiff CF10 5AL (tel 029 2063 5042)

WARD, Sir Joseph James Laffey; 4 Bt (UK 1911), of Wellington, New Zealand; s of Sir Joseph George Davidson Ward, 3 Bt (d 1970), and Joan Mary Haden, *née* Laffey (d 1993); *b* 11 November 1946; *m* 1968, Robyn Allison, da of William Maitland Martin, of Rotorua, NZ; 1 s (Joseph James Martin b 1971), 1 da (Theresa Jane b 1972); *Heir* s, Joseph Ward; *Style*— Sir Joseph Ward, Bt; ✉ 3 Regal Place, Milford, Auckland, New Zealand

WARD, Rev Prof (John Stephen) Keith; s of John Ward (d 1983), of Hexham, Northumberland, and Evelyn, *née* Simpson; *b* 22 August 1938; *Educ* Hexham GS, Univ of Wales (BA), Linacre Coll Oxford (BLitt, DD), Trinity Hall Cambridge (MA, DD); *m* 21 June 1963, Marian, da of Albert Trotman (d 1942), of Ystrad Rhondda, S Wales; 1 s (Alun James b 1968), 1 da (Fiona Caroline b 1966); *Career* lectr in logic Univ of Glasgow 1964–69, lectr in philosophy Univ of St Andrews 1969–71, lectr in philosophy of religion King's Coll London 1971–76, ordained priest C of E 1972, fell and dean Trinity Hall Cambridge 1976–83, F D Maurice prof of moral and social theology Univ of London 1983–86, prof of history and philosophy of religion King's Coll London 1986–91, regius prof of divinity Univ of Oxford and canon of Christ Church 1991–2003; pres World Congress of Faiths, memb Cncl Royal Inst of Philosophy; FBA 2001; *Books* Kant's View of Ethics (1972), The Concept of God (1974), Rational Theology and the Creativity of God (1982), The Living God (1984), Images of Eternity (1987), Divine Action (1990), A Vision to Pursue (1991), Religion and Revelation (1994), Religion and Creation (1996), God Chance and Necessity (1996), Religion and Human Nature (1998), God Faith and the New Millennium (1998), Religion and Community (2000), A Short Introduction to Christianity (2000), God: A Guide for the Perplexed (2002), The Case for Religion (2004); *Recreations* music, walking; *Style*— The Rev Prof Keith Ward; ✉ Church View, Abingdon Road, Cumnor, Oxford OX2 9QN (tel 01865 865513)

WARD, Dr Keith Douglas; s of Thomas Derek Ward, of Malvern, Worcs, and Doreen, *née* Johnson; *Educ* Univ of Cambridge (MA), Univ of Birmingham (PhD); *m* 1978, Hilary Janet, da of Frederick Stubbs; *Career* research scientist on radar Def Research Agency Malvern 1977–95, dir T W Research Ltd (radar systems) 1995–; author of over 70 papers and reports; winner: Electronics Letters Premium IEE 1980, Mountbatten Prize 1990; MIEEE (USA) 1989, FIEE 1996 (MIEE 1989), FREng 1997; *Recreations* travel, walking, photography, music, gardening, DIY; *Style*— Dr Keith Ward, FREng; ✉ T W Research Ltd, Harcourt Barn, Harcourt Road, Malvern, Worcestershire WR14 4DW (tel 01684 563882, fax 01684 566748, e-mail keith.ward@ieee.org)

WARD, Maxwell Colin Bernard; s of Maj Bernard Maxwell Ward, LVO (d 1991), and Margaret Sunniva, *née* Neven-Spence (d 1962); *b* 22 August 1949; *Educ* Harrow, St Catharine's Coll Cambridge (MA); *m* 17 April 1982, Sarah, da of Lt-Col Peter William Marsham, MBE (d 1970); 2 da (Laura Sunniva b 2 April 1984, Antonia Hersey b 27 Sept 1993), 2 s (Charles Bernard Maxwell b 27 Feb 1986, Frederick Peter Neven b 15 Feb 1989); *Career* ptnr Baillie Gifford & Co 1975–2000 (investment trainee 1971–74); dir: Scottish Equitable Life Assurance Society 1988–94, Scottish Equitable plc 1995–98, Aegon UK plc 1999–, Foreign & Colonial Investment Tst plc 2000–; md The Independent Investment Tst plc 2000–, chm Dunedin Income Growth Investment Tst plc 2001–06, main bd memb Capability Scotland 1981–, memb General Cncl The King's Fund 1998–; *Recreations* tennis, squash, bridge, country pursuits, golf; *Clubs* New (Edinburgh), Cavalry and Guards; *Style*— Maxwell Ward, Esq; ✉ Stobshiel House, Humbie, East Lothian EH36 5PD (tel 01875 833646); The Independent Investment Trust plc, 11 Charlotte Square, Edinburgh EH2 4DR (tel 0131 220 4167, fax 0131 220 4168)

WARD, (Charles John) Nicholas; *b* 1 August 1941; *Educ* Charterhouse, INSEAD (MBA); *m* 1967, Deirdre Veronica, *née* Shaw; 2 da; *Career* early career spanned several cos engaged in textiles, venture capital, overseas trading, retail, distribution, healthcare, leisure and property sectors, since 1990s chm or non-exec dir of numerous cos in retail, textile, healthcare, tport, stockbroking and fund mgmnt, coal mining, student accomodation, agric and environmental sectors; chm: Ryan Group Ltd 1995–2004, ADAS Holdings Ltd 1998–, UPP Projects Ltd 2006–07; dep chm Albert E Sharp Hldgs 1996–98; ind memb Steering Bd Insolvency Service (agency of DTI) 2004–06; non-exec dir Anglia & Oxford RHA 1990–96, chm NHS Supplies Authy 1995–98; chm Govt advsy gps on volunteering: Make a Difference Team 1994–96, Volunteering Partenrship 1995–96, Volunteering Partnership Forum for England 1996–97; pres Independent Custody Visiting Assoc (formerly Nat Assoc for Lay Visiting) 1996–2006 (chm 1992–96), chm Lay Visiting Charitable Tst 1995–; chm: The British Liver Tst 1999–2004, CORGI Tst 2005; memb Devpt Cncl City of London Sch for Girls 2003–07; fell Soc of Turnaround Professionals 2001–; Liveryman Worshipful Co of Tylers and Bricklayers (Master 1991–92); FCA 1964; *Clubs* RSM; *Style*— C J Nicholas Ward, Esq; ✉ Bacon House, Greatworth, Banbury, Oxfordshire OX17 2DX (tel 01295 712732, fax 01295 713550, e-mail nicholasward@variouscompanies.com); Flat 12, 77 Warwick Square, London SW1V 2AR (tel 020 7834 9175, fax 020 7630 1323)

WARD, Peter Terry; *b* 8 October 1945; *m*; 1 da, 1 s; *Career* Standard-Triumph Motor Co: service liaison offr 1967–69, area mangr field service engrg and parts 1969–71, parts sales supervisor 1971–72, seconded to British Leyland France 1972, parts sales mangr Jaguar Rover Triumph Ltd (following gp reorganisation) 1973–75; Unipart Ltd: commercial mangr 1975–76, mangr distributor devpt 1976–77, sales dir 1977–79; dir parts ops Talbot Motor Co (and md subsid Motaquip Ltd) 1979–83; Rolls-Royce Motor Cars Ltd: dir sales and mktg 1983–84, md Sales and Mktg Div 1984–86, md 1986, md and chief exec 1987, chief exec Rolls-Royce Motors Holdings Ltd 1990, exec dir Vickers plc (parent co of Rolls-Royce) 1991–95, chm and chief exec Rolls-Royce Motor Cars Ltd 1991–94 (chm only 1995, resigned Feb), md ops Vickers plc 1993–94; former chm and chief exec Cunard Line and exec dir Trafalgar House plc (taken over by Kvaerner ASA 1996), exec chm TG21 plc (formerly TOAD Gp plc) 2002– (non-exec chm 2001–02), chm Raymarine plc 2005–; non-exec dir Bridon plc 1994–, dir European Advsy Bd Harley-Davidson Inc; pres Soc of Motor Manufacturers and Traders 1994–95 (also chm SMMT Int Trade Ctee), bd memb Association des Constructeurs European d'Automobiles, chm Crewe Economic Devpt Exec, vice-pres Motor and Allied Trades Benevolent Fund (BEN); Liveryman Worshipful Co of Coachmakers & Coach Harness Makers; *Style*— Peter Ward, Esq

WARD, Philip; s of Albert Edwin Ward, of Doncaster, and Mildred, *née* Elsey; *Educ* Haberdashers' Aske's Sch Hampstead, Perugia, Coimbra, MECAS (Lebanon); *m* 4 April 1964, Audrey Joan, da of Lawrence Monk, and Ellen Monk, of Newport, Essex; 2 da (Carolyn b 1966, Angela b 1968); *Career* coordinator Library Servs Libya 1963–71, Unesco expert Library Servs and Documentation Egypt 1973, Unesco dir of Nat Library Serv Indonesia 1973–74, professional writer 1974–; fndr Private Libraries Assoc 1956–, FRGS, FRSA, ALA; *Books* The Oxford Companion to Spanish Literature 1978, A Dictionary of Common Fallacies (2 vols, 1978–80), A Lifetime's Reading (1982), Contemporary Designer Bookbinders (1995); novels: Forgotten Games (1984), The Comfort of Women (2002); poetry: Impostors and their Imitators (1978), Lost Songs (1981), His Enamel Mug (2003); plays: Garrity (1970); travel books incl: Japanese Capitals (1985), Travels in Oman (1986), Finnish Cities (1987), Polish Cities (1988), Bulgaria (1989), Wight Magic (1990), South India (1991), Western India (1991), Bulgarian Voices: Letting the People Speak (1992), Sofia (1993), Bahrain: a Travel Guide (1993), Gujarat, Daman, Diu: a Travel Guide (1994); *Recreations* meditative basketball (following the teachings of Hirohide Ogawa) and reading; *Style*— Philip Ward, Esq

WARD, Phillip David; s of Frederick William Ward, of E Retford, Notts, and Phyllis Mavis, *née* Hawker; *b* 1 September 1950; *Educ* Sir John Talbot's GS, Univ of Sheffield (BJur);

m 1974, Barbara Patricia, da of Wilfred Taylor; 2 da (Joanna Claire b 23 April 1980, Justine Nichola b 15 Nov 1982); *Career* DOE: joined 1973, seconded to Hackney/Islington Inner City Partnership 1978–80, head Local Govt Fin Taxation Div 1985–88, Nuffield/Leverhulme scholar 1988–89, head Global Atmosphere Div 1989–90, princ private sec to Sec of State 1990–92, dir Construction Sponsorship 1992–97, dir Energy, Environment and Waste 1997–2001, dir of fin 2001–02, dir local govt performance 2002–; FInstE; *Recreations* cinema, sailing, travel; *Style—* Phillip Ward, Esq

WARD, Rear Adm Rees Graham John; CB (2002); s of John Walter Ward, and Helen Burt, *née* Foggo; *Educ* Dunfermline HS, Plympton GS, Queens' Coll Cambridge (MA), Cranfield Univ (MSc 1981, MSc 2001); *Career* served HMS Russel 1972–73 (Queen's Sword 1972), served HMS Brighton 1977–79, Seawolf Project MOD PE 1981–83, promoted Cdr 1983, served HMS Ark Royal 1984–87, mil asst to Controller of the Navy 1988–89, promoted Capt 1990, asst dir Surface Weapons DOR (Sea) 1990–92, mil asst to Chief of Defence Procurement 1992–94, memb Cncl RUSI 1994–98, promoted Cdre 1995, DOR (Sea) 1995–97, promoted Rear Adm 1999, Asst Chief of Defence Staff (Operational Requirements) 1999, Capability Mangr (Strategic Deployment) 1999–2002, chief exec Defence Communication Services Agency 2002–07, dir gen Defence Manufacturers Assoc 2007–; represented GB and Scotland at athletics and cross-country running 1972–77, pres RN Athletics Assoc; FIEE 1997; *Publications* Allies in Conflict - European Defence Industry (paper, 1998); *Recreations* reading, running marathons; *Clubs* Hawks' (Cambridge); *Style—* Rear Adm Rees Ward, CB; ✉ HQ DCSA, Basil Hill Site, Corsham, Wiltshire SN13 9NR (tel 01225 814785, fax 01225 814966, e-mail dcsa-ce@defence.mod.uk)

WARD, Dr Richard Churchill; s of Alan Ward (d 2004), and Margaret, *née* Reynolds (d 1999); *b* 6 March 1957, Sunninghill, Berks; *Educ* Wellington Coll, Univ of Exeter; *m* 2 Oct 1990, Carol, *née* Cole; 2 s (Christopher (Kit) b 3 March 1992, Sebastian b 3 Nov 2003); *Career* scientist SERC 1982–88, sr mangr BP Research 1988–91, head of business devpt BP Oil Trading Int 1991–94, head of mktg Tradition Financial Services 1994–95; Int Petroleum Exchange: dir product devpt and research 1995–96, exec vice-pres 1996–99, chief exec 1999–2005, vice-chm 2005–06; chief exec Lloyd's of London 2006–; MRI, FRSA; *Recreations* dinghy sailing, hockey, skiing, tennis; *Style—* Dr Richard Ward; ✉ Lloyd's of London, One Lime Street, London EC3M 7HA (tel 020 7327 6930, fax 020 7327 6512, e-mail richard.ward@lloyds.com)

WARD, Prof Richard Samuel; s of Walter John Ward (d 1986), and Eileen, *née* Phillips; *b* 6 September 1951, South Africa; *Educ* Rhodes Univ SA (BSc, MSc), Univ of Oxford (DPhil); *m* 30 June 1991, Rebecca Nora, *née* Barlow; 1 s (Michael James b 15 Feb 1993), 1 da (Susanna Naomi b 18 June 1997); *Career* jr research fell Merton Coll Oxford 1977–79, lectr and fell TCD 1979–82; Univ of Durham: lectr 1983–, prof 1991–; Jr Whitehead Prize London Mathematical Soc 1989; FRS 2005; *Publications* Twistor Geometry and Field Theory (jtly, 1990); *Recreations* family, music, reading; *Style—* Prof Richard Ward; ✉ Department of Mathematical Sciences, University of Durham, South Road, Durham DH1 3LE (tel 0191 334 3118, e-mail richard.ward@durham.ac.uk)

WARD, Maj-Gen Robert William; CB (1989), MBE (1972), DL (2000); s of Lt-Col William Denby Ward (d 1973), and Monica Thérèse, *née* Collett-White (d 1985); *b* 17 October 1935; *Educ* Rugby, RMA Sandhurst; *m* 16 April 1966, Lavinia Dorothy, da of Col (Alexander James) Henry Cramsie, OBE, DL, JP (d 1982); 2 s (Thomas b 1968, James b 1973), 1 da (Gemma b 1970); *Career* cmmnd The Queen's Bays (later 1 The Queen's Dragoon Gds) 1955; served: Jordan, Libya, Germany and Borneo 1955–64 and NI 1976; student RN Staff Coll 1967, GSO2 Intelligence Bahrain 1968–69, Cdr A Squadron, QDG Berlin 1970–72, Nat Def Coll 1972–73, MA to C in C BAOR 1973–75, CO 1 Queen's Dragoon Gds 1975–77, Col GS Army Staff Coll 1977–78, cmd 22 Armoured Bde 1979–82, student Nat Def Coll Canada 1982–83, asst COS Northern Army Gp 1983–86, GOC Western District 1986–89; Col 1 Queen's Dragoon Gds 1991–97, Hon Col Royal Mercian & Lancastrian Yeo 1995–2001; landscape and garden design conslt 1992–; sec Game Conservancy (Shropshire) 1993–2000, pres SSAFA - Forces Help Shropshire 1994–; chm: Nat Meml Arboretum 1995–98, Shropshire Historic Parks and Gardens Tst 1996–2002; *Recreations* gardening, outdoor sports, country pursuits, food, wine, travel; *Clubs* Army and Navy, MCC, I Zingari; *Style—* Maj-Gen Robert Ward, CB, MBE, DL

WARD, Prof Roy Charles; s of Charles Henry Ward (d 1996), and Hilda May, *née* Norris (d 1987); *b* 8 July 1937; *Educ* Reading Sch, Univ of Reading (BA, PhD); *m* 2 April 1966, (Georgina) Kay, da of Percy Frederick Kirby (d 1962); 2 da (Katie b 1970, Sally Ann b 1973); *Career* Univ of Hull: lectr 1960, sr lectr 1972–77, reader 1977–1981, prof 1981–92 (emeritus prof 1992), dean of Sci Faculty 1986–87, pro-vice-chllr 1987–91; visiting prof: McMaster Univ Canada 1968, Univ of Maryland USA 1968–69, Univ of Br Columbia Canada 1971, Univ of Lagos Nigeria 1974, Univ of New England Aust 1982, Waikato Univ New Zealand 1993; chm GEOWISE (environmental consultancy); MAFF/DEFRA: chm Minister's NE Regnl Advsy Panel 1996–97, appointee to Yorkshire Regional Flood Defence Ctee, chm Bd of UK Register of Organic Food Standards 1999–2003, chm Yorkshire Regnl Flood Defence Ctee 2000–05 (memb 1999–2000); memb Rural Devpt Cmmn Humberside Ctee 1987–95; chm of Govrs Scarborough Coll 1992–95; *Books* Principles of Hydrology (1967, 4 edn 1999), Floods: A Geographical Perspective (1975), Floods: Physical Processes and Human Impacts (jtly, 1998); *Recreations* music, bowls, walking, wine; *Style—* Prof Roy Ward; ✉ 2 Pinfold Garth, Castle Howard Road, Malton, North Yorkshire YO17 7XQ (e-mailroycward@tiscali.co.uk)

WARD, Simon Charles Vivian; s of Maj Vivian Horrocks Ward (d 1998), and Leila Penelope, *née* Every; *b* 23 March 1942; *Educ* Shrewsbury, Trinity Coll Cambridge (MA); *m* 18 Sept 1965, Jillian Eileen, da of Thomas Roycroft East (d 1980), of Dublin; 3 da (Victoria Penelope Jane (Mrs Matthew Doull) b 1969, Antonia Lisa (Mrs Charles Crawshay), Lucinda Fiona (The Hon Mrs Nicholas Napier) (twins) b 1971); *Career* trainee stockbroker Govett Sons & Co 1963–65; ptnrs' asst: Hedderwick Hunt Cox and Co 1965–67, Hedderwick Borthwick and Co 1967–70; ptnr Montagu Loebl Stanley and Co 1972–86; dir: Fleming Montagu Stanley Ltd 1986–89, Fleming Private Asset Management Ltd 1989–2000; chm: Fleming Private Fund Management Ltd 1989 (dir 1975–2000), The Conduit Mead Company Ltd 2003– (dir 2001–); MSI (memb Int Stock Exchange 1968); *Recreations* skiing, tennis, shooting, gardening, opera, ballet; *Clubs* Boodle's; *Style—* Simon Ward, Esq; ✉ The Dower House, Bulmer, Sudbury, Suffolk CO10 7EN (tel 01787 373257, office 01787 319707, e-mail dowerhouse@talk21.com)

WARD, Tony; OBE (1998); *Educ* Univ of Leeds (BSc); *Career* various personnel positions Grand Metropolitan plc until 1992, dir of human resources Kingfisher plc 1992–97; BAA: gp human resources 997–99, gp services dir 1999–; non-exec dir SThree plc; dep chair Cmmn for Racial Equality 1993–95 (cmmr 1990–95); memb CBI Employment Ctee 1995–2004; FIPD, FRSA; *Style—* Tony Ward, Esq, OBE

WARD THOMPSON, Prof Catharine Joan; da of Peter Michaeljohn Ward, of Croxley Green, Herts, and Janet Mary, *née* Bruce (*see* Debrett's Peerage, Bruce, Bt cr 1628); *b* 5 December 1952; *Educ* Holy Cross Convent Chalfont St Peter, Rickmansworth GS, Univ of Southampton (BSc), Univ of Edinburgh (DipLA); *m* 30 Dec 1983, Henry Swift Thompson, s of Henry Swift Thompson (d 2004), of Grass Valley, CA, and Hancock Point, ME, USA; 2 da (Emma b 27 Sept 1985, Joanna b 19 Sept 1991), 1 s (James b 21 Nov 1987); *Career* landscape asst Justice and Webb Landscape Architects Vancouver BC Canada 1974–75, landscape architect and sr landscape architect W J Cairns & Ptnrs 1976–81, princ LDS Assocs Landscape Architects and Landscape Scientists 1986–90; Edinburgh Coll of Art: lectr 1981–88, head Dept of Landscape Architecture 1989–2000, prof 1999–, dir of research Environmental Studies 2000–02, research prof of landscape architecture 2002–; hon prof Univ of Edinburgh 2007–; dir OPENspace Research Centre 2001–; visiting research scholar Univ of Pennsylvania, Harvard 1994–95; landscape advsr Forestry Cmmn 1998–; memb: Amnesty International, World Devpt Movement; FLI, Chartered Landscape Architect (Design); FRSA; *Recreations* dance, choreography, theatre; *Style—* Prof Catharine Ward Thompson; ✉ 11 Douglas Crescent, Edinburgh EH12 5BB (tel 0131 337 6818); Hancock Point, Maine 04640, USA; OPENspace Research Centre, Edinburgh College of Art, Lauriston Place, Edinburgh EH3 9DF (tel 0131 221 6176, fax 0131 221 6157, e-mail c.ward-thompson@eca.ac.uk)

WARDELL, Gareth Lodwig; s of John Thomas Wardell, and Jenny Ceridwen Wardell; *b* 29 November 1944; *Educ* Gwendraeth GS, LSE (BSc, MSc); *m* 1967, Jennifer Dawn Evans; 1 s (Alistair); *Career* former teacher, princ lectr in geography Trinity Coll Carmarthen 1997–2000 (sr lectr in geography 1973–82); election agent then research asst to Dr Roger Thomas as MP for Carmarthen 1979–82, MP (Lab) Gower 1982–97, chm Select Ctee on Welsh Affrs 1984–97; dir The Industry Tst; non-exec dir Milford Docks Co 2003–; memb: Bd Environment Agency 1997–, Forestry Cmmn 1999–, Cmmn for Wales; lay memb GMC 1995 (memb 1994); FRGS, hon fell Inst for Waste Mgmnt 2001; *Recreations* swimming, cross-country running; *Style—* Gareth Wardell, Esq; ✉ 67 Elder Grove, Carmarthen, Dyfed SA31 2LH

WARDEN-OWEN, Edward (Eddie); s of Norman Warden-Owen, of Trearddur Bay, Gwynedd, and Gwladys Elinor, *née* Jones; *b* 25 June 1949; *Educ* Holyhead Co Secdy Sch, Cardiff Coll of Educn; *m* 18 Aug 1989, Susan Virginia, da of Thomas Henry Alexander Gill, of Havant, Hants; 2 s (Myles Elliot b 1991, Marcus Lloyd b 1994); *Career* teacher of physical educn 1972–74, began career in sailmaking 1974, dir of Bruce Banks Sails Ltd 1984–97, currently md Warden Owen Associates; sporting highlights in yachting; 470 class rep Olympic Games 1980, helmsman of Phoenix, memb Br Admirals Cup Team 1985 (top scoring boat overall), Skipper of Indulgence V, winner 3/4 Ton Cup 1986, navigator of White Crusader in Br challenge for America's Cup 1986–87, Silk Cut Helmsman of the Year 1987, winner Congressional Cup 1987, Nippon Cup 1988 and Omega Gold Cup 1991, skipper of Crusader in 12 Metre World Championships 1988 (winner Midnight Sun Cup Race), skipper of Indulgence VII, memb British Admirals Cup winning team 1989, runner up One Ton Cup 1989, coach to NZ Team America's Cup Challenge 1991–92, coach to Spanish Americas Cup Challenge 1995 and 1999, skipper Indulgence winner of Fastnet Race 1993, skipper Mumm a Mia winner of Mumm 36 Euro Championships 1994 and Fastnet Race (Mumm 36 class) 1995, memb winning Italian team Admirals Cup 1995, skipper Babbalaas winner of Southern Ocean Racing Circuit 1996, skipper Highland Fling winner Key West Race Week 2000; *Recreations* squash, tennis, skiing, golf, horse riding; *Clubs* Royal Ocean Racing, Royal Thames Yacht, Holyhead Sailing, Trearddur Bay Sailing; *Style—* Eddie Warden-Owen, Esq; ✉ Warden Owen Associates, 24 Shore Road, Warsash, Hampshire SO31 9FU (tel 01489 574625, fax 01489 577766, e-mail eddiewo@dial.pipex.com)

WARDINGTON, 3 Baron (UK 1936), of Alnmouth, Co Northumberland; William Simon Pease; s of 1 Baron Wardington (d 1950), and Dorothy Charlotte (d 1983), da of 1 Baron Forster (d 1936, when title became extinct); suc bro, 2 Baron Wardington (d 2005); *b* 15 October 1925, London; *Educ* Eton (capt Oppidans, chm Pop), New Coll Oxford (MA, steward JCR), St Thomas' Hosp Medical Sch (MB BS); *m* 26 Oct 1962, Hon Elizabeth Jane, *née* Ormsby Gore (d 2004), da of 4 Baron Harlech, KG, GCMG, PC (d 1964); *Heir* none; *Career* Capt Grenadier Gds 1944–47; conslt ENT surgn Central Middx and Northwick Park Hosps 1969–85; FRCS 1960; *Recreations* gardening; *Clubs* Royal Yacht Sqdn, Island Sailing; *Style—* The Lord Wardington; ✉ 45 Elizabeth Court, Milmans Street, London SW10 0DA (tel 020 7351 0954); Lepe House, Exbury, Southampton SO45 1AD (tel 023 8089 3724)

WARDLAW, Prof Alastair Connell; s of Prof Claude Wilson Wardlaw (d 1985), of Bramhall, Cheshire, and Jessie, *née* Connell (d 1971); *b* 20 January 1930; *Educ* Manchester Grammar, Univ of Manchester (BSc, MSc, PhD, DSc); *m* 1 July 1954, Jacqueline Shirley, da of Reginald Ormsby Jones, of Durrus, Ireland; 2 da (Joanna b 1958, Valerie b 1961), 1 s (Malcolm b 1963); *Career* res fell: Western Reserve Univ Cleveland OH 1953–55, St Mary's Hosp Med Sch London 1955–58; res memb Connaught Med Res Laboratories Toronto 1958–66; prof of microbiology: Univ of Toronto 1966–70, Univ of Glasgow 1970–96 (emeritus prof 1996–); pres Br Pteridological Soc 2001–04; memb: Marshall Aid Scholarship Cmmn, American Soc for Microbiology 1978; FRSE 1972; *Books* Sourcebook of Experiments for the Teaching of Microbiology, Practical Statistics for Experimental Biologists, Pathogenesis and Immunity in Pertussis; *Recreations* cultivation of ferns (holder of the NCCPG nat collection of Br ferns); *Style—* Prof Alastair Wardlaw, FRSE; ✉ 92 Drymen Road, Bearsden, Glasgow G61 2SY (tel 0141 942 2461, e-mail a.wardlaw@tiscali.co.uk)

WARDLAW, Sir Henry John; 21 Bt (NS 1631), of Pitreavie, Fifeshire; s of Sir Henry Wardlaw, 20 Bt (d 1983), and Ellen, *née* Brady (d 1977); *b* 30 November 1930; *Educ* Univ of Melbourne (MB, BS); *m* 1962, Julie-Ann, da of late Edward Patrick Kirwan; 5 s ((Henry) Justin b 10 Aug 1963, Edward Patrick b 1 July 1964, Simon John b 19 June 1965, Anthony James b 1 Oct 1968, Adrian Stewart b 2 April 1971), 2 da (Janet Montgomerie b 7 Sept 1967, Marie Ellen b 29 Sept 1977); *Heir* s, Justin Wardlaw; *Style—* Sir Henry Wardlaw, Bt; ✉ Mandalay, 75–77 Two Bays Road, Mount Eliza 3930, Victoria, Australia

WARDLE, Anthony Peter; s of Peter John Wardle, of Minehead, Somerset, and Caroline Mina Gertrude, *née* Salter; *b* 9 August 1948; *Educ* Hertford GS, Thames Nautical Training Coll, Univ of Southampton Sch of Navigation; *m* 24 June 1972, Susan Margaret, *née* Lewis; 2 da (Jessica Ann b 3 June 1979, Eleanor Katherine b 18 June 1981); *Career* navigating apprenticeship Peninsular & Oriental Steam Navigation Co 1966–69, mktg consultancy 1970–, Mann Wardle Group Ltd (acquired by Saatchi & Saatchi plc 1987), chm Saatchi & Saatchi subsids 1987–93, ptnr Wardle & Associates 1987–93; *Recreations* shooting, fishing, scribbling; *Style—* Anthony Wardle, Esq; ✉ Hassage House, Hassage nr Faulkland, Bath, Somerset BA3 5XG (tel 01373 834456)

WARDLE, Peter; s of late Alec Wardle, and Patricia, *née* Haker; *b* 3 July 1962; *Educ* Emanuel Sch, Merton Coll Oxford (MA); *m* 19 Feb 2005, Jo Gray; *Career* private sec to Min for Higher Educn and Sci Dept of Educn and Sci 1987–90; Inland Revenue: admin trainee 1985–87, princ 1990–94, asst dir 1994–98, dir of strategy and planning 1998–2000; dir of corporate servs Cabinet Office 2000–03, chief exec Electoral Cmmn 2004–; *Recreations* walking, climbing; *Style—* Peter Wardle, Esq; ✉ Electoral Commission, Trevelyan House, Great Peter Street, London SW1P 2HW

WARE, Robert; s of Dr M Ware, and W E Ware, *née* Boyce; *b* 1951; *Educ* Bryanston; *m* 2005, Diane, *née* Spencer; *Career* mgmnt trainee Dunlop (asst advtg mangr Dunlop Sports Co Ltd) 1969–72, transferred as account mangr to Sharps (now part of Saatchi & Saatchi) 1971–74, account dir then assoc dir Winship Webber & Co (advtg agency, later merged with Vernon Stratton Ltd) 1974–78, account dir DPP (creative consultancy) 1978–79, UK md JPP International 1979, md (Hitchin) then gp bd dir Bartlett Ray & Jarvis Ltd (advtg agency) 1979–85, chm and chief exec Ware Anthony Rust Ltd 1985–2005; winner ISP awards for New Berry Fruits and Toblerone (with Bartlett Ray & Jarvis Ltd); chm Mktg Ctee: Children's Haven Appeal, Cambridge Arts Theatre appeal; memb Worshipful Soc of Apothecaries; MIPA; *Recreations* golf, cricket, wining and dining; *Clubs* Gog Magog Golf; *Style—* Robert Ware, Esq; ✉ website www.warecambridge.com

WAREING, Robert Nelson; MP; s of Robert Wareing (d 1960), and Florence Patricia, *née* Mallon (d 1964); *b* 20 August 1930; *Educ* Ranworth Square Sch, Alsop HS Liverpool, Bolton Coll of Educn, Univ of London (BSc, external degree); *m* 1962, Betty (d 1989), da of Thomas Coward (d 1964); *Career* local govt offr 1946–48, LAC RAF 1948–50, local govt offr 1950–56, coll lectr 1957–83, chm Merseyside Econ Devpt Co Ltd 1981–86; Parly candidate (Lab): Berwick-upon-Tweed 1970, Liverpool Edge Hill March 1979 (by-election) and May 1979; MP (Lab) Liverpool West Derby 1983–; asst opposition whip 1987–92, memb Select Ctee on Foreign Affrs 1992–97; chm Br-Yugoslav Parly Gp 1994–97, sec Br-Russian Parly Gp 1997– (vice-chm 1992–97), treas Br-Azerbaijan Gp 1997–, treas Br-Ukraine All-Pty Gp 1999–, vice-chm Br-Serbia-Montenegro Gp 2003–, vice-chm Br-Macedonia Gp 2003–, vice-chm Br-Armenia Gp 2004–, treas Br-German Parly Gp 2005–; Merseyside CC: cncllr 1981–86, chief whip Lab Gp 1981–83; memb: Hansard Soc, Br-Russia Centre, Br-East West Centre; *Recreations* concert-going, soccer, travel; *Clubs* Royal Navy Kirkby; *Style*— Robert Wareing, Esq, MP; ✉ House of Commons, London SW1A 0AA (tel 020 7219 3482, fax 020 7219 6187, constituency office: tel 0151 256 9111, fax 0151 226 0285)

WARENIUS, Prof Hilmar Meek; s of Tor Adolph Warenius (d 1971), and Ruby Gwendoline, *née* Meek; *b* 12 January 1942; *Educ* Penzance GS, Downing Coll Cambridge (MA, PhD), Middlesex Hosp Med Sch London (MB BChir (Cantab), DMRT); *m* 19 Aug 1972, Rosamund Jean Talbot, da of Leopold Edward Hill (d 1957); 1 s (Christopher b 1976), 2 da (Eleanor b 1979, Fleur b 1985); *Career* sr house offr Royal Marsden Hosp 1970–71, registrar in radiotherapy Middlesex Hosp 1972–74; first asst to Prof Mitchell at Addenbrooke's Hosp Cambridge 1974–75, MRC clinical res fell Univ of Cambridge 1975–79, first asst to Mr William Ross Univ of Newcastle and Newcastle Gen Hosp 1979–80, conslt in radiotherapy and oncology in Newcastle 1980–82, CRC prof of radiation oncology Univ of Liverpool 1982–90, MRC hon clinical coordinator Fast Neutron Studies 1982–89, currently prof and dir Oncology Res Unit Dept of Med Univ of Liverpool; chief med offr and dir of R&D TheRyte Ltd 1998–; visiting prof and hon conslt Dept of Clinical Oncology Hammersmith Hosp London 1995–97; Cardiff Univ accredited expert witness 2005; FRCR, FRCP; *Recreations* swimming, guitar, choral society, cooking; *Style*— Prof Hilmar Warenius; ✉ 14 Delavor Road, Heswall, Wirral, Merseyside (tel 0151 342 3034); Oncology Research Unit, Department of Medicine, The University of Liverpool, University Clinical Departments, The Duncan Building, Danlby Street, Liverpool L69 3GA (tel 0151 706 4530, fax 0151 706 5802, e-mail warenius@liverpool.ac.uk)

WARHAM, Mark Francis; s of Joseph Warham, of Leeds, and Eileen, *née* Northover; *b* 2 January 1962, Leeds; *Educ* St Thomas Aquinas GS Leeds, St Catherine's Coll Oxford (BA); *m* 12 Feb 2000, Olivia, *née* Dagtoglou; 3 da (Eleanor, Francesca (twins) b 5 July 2002, Anna b 23 April 2004); *Career* investment controller 3i 1982–86, J Henry Schroder & Co Ltd 1986–2000 (dir 1995), md Morgan Stanley & Co Ltd 2000–, seconded as DG Takeover Panel 2005–07; *Publications* Mergers and Acquisitions: Guide to Principles and Practice (ed, 1998–99); *Recreations* mountaineering, ornithology, photography; *Clubs* Alpine; *Style*— Mark Warham, Esq; ✉ The Takeover Panel, 10 Paternoster Square, London EC4M 7DY (tel 020 7382 9026)

WARHURST, Pam; CBE (2005); *Career* ldr Calderdale Cncl W Yorks 1995–99, Yorks and Humberside rep Ctee of the Regions EC 1995–99, vice-chair Regnl Assembly Yorks and Humberside 1998–1999, dep chair Countryside Agency 1999–2006; chair: Bear Wholefood Co-operative, National Countryside Access Forum, Penine Prospects, Calderdale Healthcare NHS Trust 2000–01; memb: Bd Yorkshire Forward 1998–2002, Rural Affrs Forum for England, MOD Advsy Gp on Environment, Bd Natural England; FRSA; *Style*— Ms Pam Warhurst, CBE; ✉ Countryside Agency, John Dower House, Crescent Place, Cheltenham, Gloucestershire GL50 3RA (tel 01242 521381)

WARIN, Dr Andrew Peter; s of Dr John Fairbairn Warin, OBE (d 1990), of Iffley, Oxford, and Dr Kathleen Warin (d 1999); *b* 16 January 1945; *Educ* Radley, Guy's Hosp Med Sch London (MB BS); *m* 1, 3 Sept 1966 (m dis 1987), Dr Judith M Warin, da of V D H Rutland, of Farnborough, Hants; 2 da (Fiona b 11 Nov 1969, Joanna b 10 Nov 1970), 1 s (Benjamin b 2 Jan 1974); m 2, 21 April 1993, Stella, *née* Purcell; *Career* conslt dermatologist and sr lectr St John's Hosp for Diseases of Skin 1976–80, conslt dermatologist Exeter 1980–; author of articles on psoriasis, mycosis, fungoides and glucagonoma syndrome; FRSM, FRCP, memb Br Assoc of Dermatologists; *Recreations* swimming, running, tennis, skiing, clarinet; *Style*— Dr Andrew Warin; ✉ The Gables, Priory Close, East Budleigh, Devon EX9 7EZ; Royal Devon and Exeter Hospital, Barrack Road, Exeter, Devon EX2 5DW (tel 01392 402613, e-mail andrew@warin505.fsnet.co.uk)

WARING, Sir (Alfred) Holburt; 3 Bt (UK 1935); s of Sir Alfred Waring, 2 Bt (d 1981), and Winifred, Lady Waring; *b* 2 August 1933; *Educ* Rossall; *m* 1958, Ana, da of Valentine Medinilla; 1 s, 2 da; *Heir* s, Michael Waring; *Career* dir: SRM Plastics, Waring Investments, Property Realisation Co Ltd; *Recreations* tennis, golf, squash, swimming; *Clubs* Moor Park Golf; *Style*— Sir Holburt Waring, Bt; ✉ 30 Russell Road, Moor Park, Northwood, Middlesex HA6 2LR

WARING, Prof Michael John; s of Frederick Waring (d 1998), and Kathleen Waring (d 1999); *b* 8 November 1939, Lancaster; *Educ* Friends' Sch Lancaster, Downing Coll Cambridge (MA), Univ of Cambridge (PhD, ScD); *m* 1973 (m dis 1979), A J Milner; 1 s (Christian Stephen Milner b 7 March 1974); *Career* fell Dept of Terrestrial Magnetism (DTM) Carnegie Instn of Washington 1964–65; Univ of Cambridge: demonstrator in biochemistry 1965–67, lectr in pharmacology 1967–90, reader in chemotherapy 1990–, prof of chemotherapy 1999–; fell and lectr in biochemistry Jesus Coll Cambridge 1965– (also tutor, dir of studies in biological sciences and med, librarian and steward); hon visiting conslt Cancer Research Laboratory Auckland 1975–; visiting prof: H C Ørsted Inst Copenhagen 1983, Université du Québec Montreal 1985, Institut Pasteur Paris 1989, Université de Paris 1991, Univ of Texas at Austin 1998, Caltech 2003 and 2005 (visiting scientist 1992, visiting assoc in chemistry 1999); memb Steering Ctee Int Soc for the Study of Drug-Nucleic Acid Interactions 1997; memb: Biochemical Soc 1965–, Br Pharmacological Soc 1968–, Cambridge Centre for Molecular Recognition 1995–; memb advsy panels for orgns incl: Human Frontier Science Prog, Danish Nat Research Fndn, Australian Research Cncl, US Nat Science Fndn, NZ MRC, Auckland Med Research Fndn, Minority Biomedical Research Support Prog NIH, Israel Science Fndn, Health Research Bd of Ireland, Stoke Mandeville Burns and Reconstructive Surgery Research Tst, Center for Molecular Med and Drug Devpt Karachi, Institut National de la Santé et de la Recherche Médicale (INSERM); organiser for int meetings, plenary and guest lectr at symposia and confs worldwide; series ed Cancer Biology & Medicine Kluwer Academic Publishers; memb Editorial Bd: Biochemical Jl 1974, Antimicrobial Agents & Chemotherapy 1978–91, Molecular Pharmacology 1979–98, Oncology Research 1984–, Jl of Molecular Recognition 1987– (ed 1991–98), Biochimica et Biophysica Acta 1996–2004, Current Medicinal Chemistry - Anti Cancer Agents 2000–, The Open Cancer Jl 2007–, Drug Design, Devpt and Therapy 2007–; Br Cncl exchange fell Consejo Superior de Investigaciones Cientificas (CSIC) Spain 1975 and 1978, EMBO res fell Madrid 1977, Royal Soc exchange fell Spain 1979 and 1982, Royal soc exchange fell Poland 1984; Rex Williamson lectr Deakin Univ Geelong; memb Monumental Brass Soc 1965–, memb Cambridge Philosophical Soc 1967–; memb Bd of Govrs: Witan Hall Reading 2002, Sevenoaks Sch 2005; fell Int Union Against Cancer 1977, membre correspondant Muséum National d'Histoire Naturelle Paris 1995; FRSC 2006; *Publications* European Brasses (jtly, 1967), The Molecular Basis of Antibiotic Action (jtly, 1972), Molecular Aspects of Anti-Cancer Drug Action (jt ed, 1983), Biology of Carcinogenesis (jt ed, 1987), The Science of Cancer Treatment (jt ed, 1990), The Search for New Anti-Cancer Drugs (jt ed, 1991), Molecular Aspects of Anticancer Drug-DNA Interactions (jt ed, vol 1 1993, vol 2 1994), The Genetics of Cancer (jt ed, 1995), Methods in Enzymology, vol 340: Drug-Nucleic Acid Interactions (jt ed, 2001), Topics in Current Chemistry, vol 253: DNA Binders and Related Subjects (jt ed, 2005), Sequence-Specific DNA Binding Agents (2006); also author of 300 pubns in learned jls; *Recreations* music (organ, choral), monumental brasses, aviation; *Style*— Prof Michael Waring; ✉ Jesus College, University of Cambridge, Cambridge CB5 8BL (tel 01223 339441); Department of Pharmacology, University of Cambridge, Tennis Court Road, Cambridge CB2 1PD (tel 01223 334003, fax 01223 334100, e-mail mjw11@cam.ac.uk)

WARK, Kirsty; *b* 3 February 1955; *Educ* Univ of Edinburgh; *m* Alan Clements; 1 s, 1 da; *Career* BBC Radio 1976–83: researcher, prodr (Good Morning Scotland, Order Order, World at One); BBC TV 1983–; fndr ptnr Wark Clements & Co (later IWC Media) 1990–2005, dir Black Pepper Media Ltd; presenter: General Election Night 1987, 1992, 1997 and 2001 (BBC TV), The Late Show 1990–93 (BBC TV), One Foot in the Past 1993–2000 (BBC TV), Newsnight 1993– (BBC TV), Newsnight Review (BBC TV), Scottish Referendum 1997 (BBC TV), Turning into Children 1998– (BBC Radio), Vote '99 - Scotland Decides (BBC TV), Rough Justice (BBC TV) 1999–, Restless Nation (BBC TV), The Kirsty Wark Show 1999–2001 (BBC TV), Building a Nation (BBC TV), Lives Less Ordinary 2002 (BBC TV) and 2003 (BBC Scotland), Scottish Parliamentary Elections 2003 (BBC Scotland), Tales from Europe (BBC TV) 2004, 2005 and 2006; Hon FRIBA; *Publications* Restless Nation (jtly); *Recreations* family, tennis, swimming, cooking, beachcombing, architecture, reading; *Style*— Ms Kirsty Wark

WARKENTIN, Juliet; da of John and Germaine Warkentin, of Toronto, Canada; *b* 10 May 1961; *Educ* Univ of Toronto (BA); *m* Andrew Lamb; *Career* former ed: Toronto Life Fashion, Drapers Record, marie claire; md Mktg and Internet Devpt Arcadia Gp plc, former ptnr The Fourth Room, currently editorial dir Redwood Gp; Canadian Nat Magazine Award 1989, Business and Professional Magazine Editor of the Year PPA Awards 1995; FRSA; *Style*— Ms Juliet Warkentin

WARLAND, Philip John; s of Ernest Alfred Henry Warland (d 1998), and Winifred Mary, *née* Poyntz-Owen (d 1991); *b* 25 December 1945; *Educ* KCS; *m* 1 (m dis); 3 s (David b 1972, Richard b 1973, John b 1978); m 2, 2003, Sheila Anne Nicoll; *Career* head Info Div Bank of England 1985–89, gp personnel resources mangr Standard Chartered Bank 1989–90, dir gen Assoc of Unit Tsts and Investment Funds 1991–2001, advsr Euro regulatory consulting PricewaterhouseCoopers 2001–06, Halsey Consulting 2006–; chm Oasis Charitable Tst 1986–2006; *Recreations* golf, cricket, walking; *Style*— Philip Warland, Esq; ✉ Halsey Consulting, 20 Ironmonger Lane, London EC2V 8EP

WARLOW, Prof Charles Picton; s of Charles Edward Picton Warlow (d 1988), and Nancy Mary McLellan, *née* Hine (d 1987); *b* 9 September 1943; *Educ* Univ of Cambridge (BA, MB BChir, MD), St George's Hosp Med Sch London; *Children* 2 s (Benjamin b 1 Aug 1980, Oliver b 27 Oct 1984), 2 da (Margaret b 25 March 1982, Lucy b 17 Feb 2004); *Career* clinical reader in neurology Univ of Oxford 1977–86, fell Green Coll Oxford 1979–86, prof of med neurology Univ of Edinburgh 1987–; memb: Assoc of Br Neurologists (pres 2001–03), Br Assoc of Stroke Physicians, Euro Neurological Soc, American Neurological Assoc; FRCP, FRCPEd, FRCPGlas, FMedSci, FRSE; *Books* Transient Ischaemic Attacks (1982), Dilemmas in the Management of the Neurological Patient (1984), More Dilemmas in the Management of the Neurological Patient (1987), Stroke and Living with Stroke (with Barbara Woodhouse, 1987), Handbook of Neurology (1991), Transient Ischaemic Attacks of the Brain and Eye (jtly, 1994), Stroke - a practical guide to management (jtly 1996, 2 edn 2000), Practical Neurology (ed), The Lancet Handbook of Treatment of Neurology (ed); *Recreations* sailing, photography, mountains; *Style*— Prof Charles Warlow; ✉ Department of Clinical Neurosciences, Western General Hospital, Crewe Road South, Edinburgh EH4 2XU (tel 0131 537 2082, e-mail cpw@skull.dcn.ed.ac.uk)

WARMAN, Alister Seager; s of Mark Warman, and Zillah Warman; *Educ* Harrow, Courtauld Inst of Art London; *Career* lectr Poly of Newcastle upon Tyne 1970–74, Art Dept Arts Cncl of GB 1975–85, dir Serpentine Gallery London 1985–91, princ Byam Shaw Sch of Art Central St Martins Coll of Art and Design Univ of the Arts London 1991–; *Style*— Alister Warman, Esq; ✉ Byam Shaw School of Art, 2 Elthorne Road, London N19 4AG (tel 020 7281 4111, fax 020 7281 1632)

WARMINGTON, Anthony Marshall; s of Sir Marshall Warmington, 3 Bt (d 1995), of Swallowfield Park, Reading, Berks, and Eileen Mary, *née* Howes (d 1969); *b* 1 July 1946; *Educ* Charterhouse, Univ of Grenoble; *m* 1, 1973 (m dis 1987), Carolyn Patricia (d 1993), da of late Micky Simonds; 1 s (Oliver Marshall Simonds b 30 Sept 1974), 1 da (Katherine Louise b 22 Feb 1977); m 2, 2007, Edwina Dyson, da of Gp Capt R S Ryan, CBE; *Career* Lt Queen's Dragoon Gds, served NI Aden Germany; investment mangr various city instns 1965–77; dir: Streets Financial PR 1980–87 (joined 1977), Manning Selvage & Lee 1987–89; dir: Burson-Marsteller 1989–91, Burson-Marsteller Financial 1989–91 (head int investor rels); dir Financial Public Relations Ltd 1991–2005; advsr to: Lithuania 1994, Macedonia 1995–96, Estonia 1997, Bulgaria 1997–98 and 2005–06, Ukraine 1997–98, Uzbekistan 1997–98, Romania 1998 and 2006, West Indies 1998, Egypt 1998–99, Armenia 1998–99, Vietnam 1999, Guyana 1999, Latvia 1999, Ethiopia 2000, Montenegro 2001, Ghana 2002, Malawi 2002, 2004 and 2005, Jamaica 2003, Turkey 2003, Jordan 2005–06, Libya 2007; memb Mensa 1990; *Recreations* golf, shooting, theatre, tennis; *Clubs* MCC, Cavalry and Guards; *Style*— Anthony Warmington, Esq; ✉ e-mail awarmington@hotmail.com

WARMINGTON, Neil; s of Terrence Clifford Warmington, and Rita Mary, *née* Lankester; *Educ* Boswells Sch Chelmsford, Braintree Coll of FE, Maidstone Coll of Art (BA), Motley Theatre Design Sch (MA); *Career* artist and designer; *Theatre* set and costume designs: I Put a Spell On You (Leicester Haymarket), Coriolanus (Tramway Glasgow), Arsenic & Old Lace (Royal Lyceum Edinburgh), Initmate Exchanges (Duke's Playhouse Lancaster), Merlin (Part 2) (Royal Lyceum Edinburgh), Comedians (Royal Lyceum Edinburgh), Fiddler on the Roof (West Yorkshire Playhouse), Life is a Dream (West Yorkshire Playhouse), Merlin (Tankred Däcrst) (Royal Lyceum Edinburgh), Much Ado About Nothing (Liverpool Everyman Theatre), Waiting for Godot (Liverpool Everyman Theatre), The Life of Stuff (Donmar Warehouse London), Blithe Spirit (York Theatre Royal), Henry V (RSC), Troilus and Cressida (Grand Theatre Leeds and ROH), Desire Under the Elms (Shared Experience Theatre and Tricycle Theatre London), Angels in America (7:84 Theatre Co), The Tempest (Contact Theatre Manchester), Women Laughing (Watford Palace and Duke of York's Theatre), Passing Places (Traverse Theatre Edinburgh), Dissent (Traverse Theatre), The Duchess of Malfi (Bath Theatre Royal), The Glass Menagerie (Royal Lyceum Edinburgh), Glasgow 1999 Year of Architecture launch (Scottish Exhibition and Conference Centre (SECC)), Jane Eyre (Shared Experience Theatre and Young Vic), Don Juan (English Touring Theatre), Family (Traverse Theatre), The Taming of the Shrew (English Touring Theatre), Riddance (Paines Plough), The Drowned World (Paines Plough), The Straits (Paines Plough and tour to NY), Splendour (Paines Plough and Traverse Theatre), The Marriage of Figaro (Garsington Opera Festival), Prada (Milan), Solemn Mass for a Full Moon (Barbican and Traverse Theatre), King of the Fields (Traverse Theatre), Love's Labour Lost (English Touring Theatre), Gagarin's Way (Traverse Theatre, RNT, West End and NY), Wiping My Mother's Arse (Traverse Theatre), Woyzeck (Royal Lyceum Edinburgh), Ghosts (English Touring Theatre), King Lear (Old Vic/English Touring Theatre), Helmet

(Traverse Theatre and Paines Plough), Slab Boys Trilogy (Traverse Theatre), Playhouse Creatures (West Yorkshire Playhouse), Dumbstruck (Dundee Rep), Scenes from an Execution (Dundee Rep, nominee Best Design and Best Prodn Ctitic's Awards for Theatre in Scotland), Lie of the Mind (Dundee Rep), Knives in Hens (Tag), The Birthday Party (Tag); *Solo Exhibitions* Hutcheson Hall Glasgow, GFT Glasgow, Swanston Street Studios Glasgow, Donmar Warehouse London, King Street Gallery Glasgow, 23 Edinburgh Billboards Glasgow Year of Architecture, The Connecticut Gallery USA; *Group Exhibitions* Leicester Haymarket, Almeida Theatre London, Theatre Museum London, Coventry Gallery London, Leith Open Edinburgh, Pacesetters (Peterborough Art Gallery), RNT, CCA Glasgow, Sandra Drew Gallery Canterbury, John Moores Liverpool, Serpentine Gallery London; *Awards* Linbury Prize for Stage Design, 3 awards for Best Design TMA, 5 Edinburgh Fringe Festival awards, Sir Alfred Munnings Florence Prize for Painting, Noel Machin Painting Prize; *Recreations* galleries, theatre, chess; *Style*— Neil Warmington, Esq; ✉ c/o Michael McCoy, ICM Ltd, Oxford House, 76 Oxford Street, London W1D 1BS (tel 020 7636 6565, e-mail michael_mccoy@icmlondon.co.uk)

WARNER, Alan; s of Frank Warner (d 1996), of Oban, Argyll, and Patsy, *née* Bowman (d 2000); *b* 5 August 1964; *Educ* Oban HS, Ealing Coll of HE (BA), Univ of Glasgow (MPhil); *m* 6 Aug 1996, Hollie Cleak; *Career* novelist and screenwriter; *Novels* Morvern Callar (1995, Somerset Maugham Award, Whitbread First Book Award, IMPAC shortlist, film 2000), These Demented Lands (1997, Encore Award), The Sopranos (1998, Saltire Scottish Book of the Year Award), The Man Who Walks (2002, nominated Saltire Scottish Book of the Year Award), The Worms Can Carry Me to Heaven (2006); *Recreations* searching for that innocent hobby; *Clubs* Tesco Club Card; *Style*— Alan Warner, Esq; ✉ c/o David Godwin Associates, 55 Monmouth Street, London WC2H 9DG (tel 020 7240 9992, fax 020 7395 6110)

WARNER, Deborah; CBE (2006); da of Roger Harold Metford Warner, of Oxon, and Ruth Ernestine, *née* Hurcombe; *b* 12 May 1959; *Educ* Sidcot Sch, St Clare's Coll, Central Sch of Speech and Drama London; *Career* artistic dir Kick Theatre Co 1980–86, res dir RSC 1987–89, assoc dir RNT 1990–98, assoc dir Abbey Theatre Dublin 2000–04; Officier de l'Ordre des Arts et des Lettres (France) 2000 (Chevalier 1992); *Productions* Kick Theatre Co: The Good Person of Szechwan 1980, Woyzeck 1981 and 1982, The Tempest 1983, Measure for Measure 1984, King Lear 1985, Coriolanus 1986; RSC: Titus Andronicus (Best Dir Olivier Awards, Best Dir Evening Standard Awards 1989) 1987, King John 1988, Electra 1988 and 1990; RNT: The Good Person of Sichuan 1989, King Lear 1990, Richard II 1995–96, The PowerBook 2002–03, Happy Days 2006; other credits incl: Hedda Gabler 1991 (Abbey Theatre Dublin and Playhouse Theatre London, Best Director and Best Prodn Olivier Awards 1992 (TV version 1992)), Wozzeck (Opera North) 1993 and 1996, Coriolan (Salzburg Festival) 1993–94, Footfalls (The Garrick) 1994, Don Giovanni (Glyndebourne Festival Opera and Channel 4) 1994 and 1995, The Waste Land (Fitzroy Prodns) 1995–99, The St Pancras Project and The Tower Project (LIFT Festival) 1995 and 1999, Une Maison de Poupée (Odéon, Paris) 1997, Honegger's Joan of Arc at the Stake (BBC Proms) 1997, The Turn of the Screw (ROH, Evening Standard and South Bank Awards 1998) 1997 and 2001, Bobigny 1998, The Diary of One Who Vanished (ENO/Bobigny/NT and New York) 1999, The Angel Project (Perth Int Art Festival) 2001 (Lincoln Center Festival) 2003, Medea (Abbey Theatre Dublin, Queens Theatre London) 2000–01 (BAM/USA tour and Broadway) 2002–03, St John Passion (ENO) 2000 and 2003, Fidelio (Glyndebourne Festival Opera) 2001 and 2002, The Rape of Lucretia (Munich) 2004, Julius Caesar (Barbican, Chaillot Paris, Madrid and Luxembourg) 2005, Dido and Aeneas (Vienna) 2006, Fidelio (Glyndebourne) 2006, La Voix Humanire (Opera North) 2006, Death in Venice (ENO) 2007; *Film* The Last September 1999; *Recreations* travelling; *Style*— Ms Deborah Warner, CBE; ✉ c/o Leah Schmidt, The Agency, 24 Pottery Lane, Holland Park, London W11 4LZ (tel 020 7727 1346, fax 020 7727 9037)

WARNER, Dr Francis Robert Le Plastrier; s of Canon Hugh Compton Warner (d 1955), vicar of Epsom, Surrey, and Nancy Le Plastrier, *née* Owen (d 1992); *b* 21 October 1937; *Educ* Christ's Hosp, London Coll of Music, St Catharine's Coll Cambridge (choral exhibitioner, MA), Univ of Oxford (MA, DLitt); *m* 1, 1958 (m dis 1972), Mary, *née* Hall; 2 da (Georgina b 1962, Lucy b 1967); m 2, 1983, Penelope Anne, da of John Hugh Davis, of Blagdon, nr Bristol; 1 da (Miranda b 1985), 1 s (Benedict b 1988); *Career* poet and dramatist; Univ of Cambridge: supervisor in English St Catharine's Coll 1959–65, staff tutor in English, memb Bd of Extramural Studies 1963–65, hon fell St Catharine's Coll 1999–; Univ of Oxford: Lord White fell in English literature and sr English tutor St Peter's Coll 1965–99, fell librarian 1966–76, univ lectr 1966–99, dean of degrees 1984–2006, vice-master 1987–89, pro-proctor 1989–90, 1996–97 and 1999–2000, emeritus fell St Peter's Coll 1999–; conductor Honegger's King David in King's Coll Chapel 1958 (CD issued 2003); Messing Int Award (USA) for Distinguished Contribs to Literature 1972, Silver Medal Benemerenti of the Constantinian Order of St George (Italy) 1990, elected academico correspondente estrangeiro Portuguese Academia de Letras e Artes 1993; memb Southern Arts Drama Panel Arts Cncl of GB 1976–80 (chm 1978–79 and 1979–80); *Poetry* Perennia (1962), Early Poems (1964), Experimental Sonnets (1965), Madrigals (1967), The Poetry of Francis Warner (USA, 1970), Lucca Quartet (1975), Morning Vespers (1980), Spring Harvest (1981), Epithalamium (1983), Collected Poems 1960–84 (1985), Nightingales: Poems 1985–96 (1997), Cambridge (2001), Oxford (2002), By the Cam and the Isis (2005); *Plays* Maquettes, a trilogy of one-act plays (1972); Requiem: Pt 1 Lying Figures (1972), Pt 2 Killing Time (1976), Pt 3 Meeting Ends (1974); A Conception of Love (1978), Light Shadows (1980), Moving Reflections (1983), Living Creation (1985), Healing Nature: The Athens of Pericles (1988), Byzantium (1990), Virgil and Caesar (1993), Agora: an Epic (1994), King Francis 1st (1995), Goethe's Weimar (1997), Rembrandt's Mirror (1999); *Editor* Eleven Poems by Edmund Blunden (1965), Garland (1968), Studies in the Arts (1968); *Recreations* children and grandchildren, cathedral music, travel; *Clubs* Athenaeum; *Style*— Dr Francis Warner; ✉ St Peter's College, Oxford OX1 2DL (tel 01865 278 900); St Catharine's College, Cambridge CB2 1RL (tel 01223 338300)

WARNER, James Royston; s of Peter John Warner, of Broadway, Worcs, and Joan Emily May, *née* Hodge; *b* 27 August 1948; *Educ* Prince Henry's GS Evesham, Gonville & Caius Coll Cambridge (MA); *m* 23 May 1992, Melissa, da of Ronald Brooks, of Tollerton; 1 da (Chloe Jane Brooks-Warner b 15 July 1985); *Career* industrial engr British Leyland 1970–73; Mars Ltd: mgmnt servs mangr 1973–75, distribution mangr 1975–78, materials and purchasing mangr 1978–80, factory mangr 1980–82; PricewaterhouseCoopers (formerly Coopers & Lybrand before merger): conslt 1982–85, ptnr 1985–, practice ldr Manufacturing and Logistics (Europe) 1990 (head (UK) 1988), worldwide ldr Supply Chain Management Practice 1993; fell: Inst of Logistics, Br Inst of Operations Mgmnt; *Recreations* music, walking on Dartmoor, cooking, spending time with my family; *Style*— James Warner, Esq; ✉ mobile 07802 201741, e-mail james.r.warner@uk.pwcglobal.com

WARNER, Jeremy; s of Jonathan Warner, and Marigold, *née* Brayshaw; *b* 23 September 1955; *Educ* Magdalen Coll Sch Oxford, UCL; *m* 17 May 1988, Henrietta, *née* Franklin; 1 s (Sam b 17 Dec 1987), 2 da (Florence b 17 July 1992, Emma b 22 June 2000); *Career* reporter The Scotsman 1978–82; The Times: business reporter 1982–84, business corr 1984–86; The Independent: business corr 1986–88, assoc business ed 1988–92, city ed (The Independent on Sunday) 1992–94, business and city ed 1994–; tstee The Independent pension scheme; *Awards* Br Press Award Specialist Writer of the Year 1992, Wincott Award Fin Journalist of the Year 1993, Wincott Award Fin Jl of the Year 1997 and 2005, Special Guild of Br Newspaper Eds Award for outstanding contribution in defense of the freedom of the press 1997; *Recreations* walking, running; *Style*— Jeremy Warner, Esq; ✉ The Independent, Independent House, 191 Marsh Wall, London E14 9RS (tel 020 7005 2696, fax 020 7005 2098, e-mail j.warner@independent.co.uk)

WARNER, Prof John Oliver; s of Henry Paul Warner (d 1992), and Ursula, *née* Troplowitz, of London; *b* 19 July 1945; *Educ* The Lawrence Sheriff Sch Rugby, Univ of Sheffield Med Sch (MB ChB, MD, DCH, Pleasance prize in paediatrics); *m* 1990, Dr Jill Amanda Warner, da of Maurice Halliday; 2 da (Olivia b 26 May 1991, Abigail b 21 Aug 1994); *Career* jr hosp posts Sheffield 1968–72; Hosp for Sick Children Great Ormond St: registrar 1972–74, res fell 1974–77, sr registrar 1977–80; conslt paediatric chest physician Royal Brompton Nat Heart and Lung Hosp (jt hosp and acad appt with Nat Heart and Lung Inst) 1980, subsequently sr lectr then reader in paediatrics Univ of London until 1990, prof of child health Univ of Southampton 1990–2006, prof of paediatrics and head Dept of Paediatrics Imperial Coll London; ed-in-chief Paediatric Allergy and Immunology; memb Editorial Bd: Paediatric Pulmonology; pres Int Paediatric Respiratory Allergy and Immunology Soc 2004–; memb: RSM 1976, Br Soc for Allergy and Clinical Immunology 1979 (former sec and chm Paediatric Sub-Ctee), Br Thoracic Soc 1983, American Thoracic Soc 1992, Euro Respiratory Soc 1991 (head of Paediatric Assembly 1993–97), Advsy Ctee for Novel Foods and Processes FSA 1998–2007; fndr chm Cystic Fibrosis Holiday Fund Charity 1986–90; tstee Anaphylaxis Campaign; int fell Acad of American Allergy, Asthma and Immunlogy 2001; FRCP 1986, FRCPCH 1997, FMedSci 1999; *Publications* Childhood Asthma: a guide for parents and children (with S J Goldsworthy, 1981, 1982 and 1983), Scoliosis: Prevention (proceedings of Phillips Zorab symposium, 1983), British Medical Bulletin (scientific ed, 1992), A Colour Atlas of Paediatric Allergy (with W F Jackson, 1994), Textbook of Pediatric Asthma: An international perspective (jt ed, 2001); also author of over 300 published scientific papers; *Recreations* cricket, horse riding; *Clubs* MCC; *Style*— Prof John Warner; ✉ Navaho, Hurdle Way, Compton, Winchester SO21 2AN; Department of Paediatrics, Imperial College, St Mary's Campus, Wright-Fleming Institute, Norfolk Place, London W2 1PG (tel 020 7594 3990, e-mail j.o.warner@imperial.ac.uk)

WARNER, Marina Sarah; da of Col Esmond Pelham Warner, TD (d 1982), of Cambridge, and Emilia, *née* Terzulli; *b* 9 November 1946; *Educ* Lady Margaret Hall Oxford (MA); *m* 1, 31 Jan 1972 (m dis 1980), (Hon) William Hartley Hume Shawcross, *qv*, s of Baron Shawcross (Life Peer, d 2003); 1 s (Conrad Hartley Pelham b 1977); m 2, 16 Dec 1981 (m dis 1998), John Piers Dewe Mathews, s of Denys Cosmo Dewe Mathews (d 1986), of London; partner, 2002–, Graeme Segal; *Career* writer; Getty Scholar Getty Center for the History of Art and the Humanities 1987–88, Tinbergen prof Erasmus Univ Rotterdam 1991, Reith lectr 1994; visiting prof: Queen Mary & Westfield Coll London 1994–, Univ of Ulster 1994–95, Mellon prof of history of art Univ of Pittsburgh 1997, Univ of St Andrews, Stanford Univ 2000; prof Univ of Essex 2004; Whitney J Oates fell Princeton Univ 1996, fell commoner Trinity Coll Cambridge 1998, fell All Souls Coll Oxford 2001, hon research fell Birkbeck Coll London 1999; Clarendon lectr Univ of Oxford 2001, Tanner lectr Yale Univ 1999, Robb lectr Auckland NZ 2004; memb: Exec Ctee Charter 88 1993–97, Advsy Bd Royal Mint to 1993, Mgmnt Ctee Nat Cncl for One Parent Families 1992–2000, Ctee London Library 1996–2000, Advsy Cncl Br Library 1997–99, Arts Cncl Literature Panel 1997–2000; tstee Artangel 1999–2004; contrib: Times Literary Supplement, Washington Post Book World, London Review of Books, Independent, Independent on Sunday, New York Times Book Review, Times Higher Educn Supplement; Aby-Warburg Prize 2004, Warburg Prize 2005; Hon DLitt: Univ of Exeter 1995, Sheffield Hallam Univ 1995, Univ of York 1997, Univ of North London 1997, Univ of St Andrews 1998, Tavistock Inst Univ of East London 1999, Royal Coll of Art London 2004, Univ of Kent 2005, Univ of Oxford 2006, Univ of Leicester 2006; hon fell Lady Margaret Hall Oxford 2000; FRSL 1985, FBA 2005; Chevalier de l'Ordre des Arts et des Lettres (France) 2004, Commendatore de la Stella della Solidareità (Italy) 2005; *Books* The Dragon Empress (1972), Alone of All Her Sex: The Myth and the Cult of the Virgin Mary (1976), Queen Victoria's Sketchbook (1980), Joan of Arc: The Image of Female Heroism (1981), Monuments and Maidens: The Allegory of the Female Form (1985), Into the Dangerous World: Childhood and its Costs (1991), L'Atalante (1993), Managing Monsters: Six Myths of Our Time (Reith lectures, 1994), Wonder Tales (ed, 1994), From the Beast to the Blonde: On Fairy Tales and Their Tellers (1994), The Inner Eye (catalogue, 1996), No Go the Bogeyman: Scaring, Lulling and Making Mock (1998), Fantastic Metamorphoses, Other Worlds (Clarendon lectures, 2002), Phantasmagoria (2006); fiction: In A Dark Wood (1977), The Skating Party (1983), The Lost Father (1988), Indigo (1992), The Mermaids in the Basement (short stories, 1993), The Leto Bundle (2001), Murderers I Have Known (short stories, 2002), Signs and Wonders: Essays on Literature (2003); children's books: The Impossible Day (1981), The Impossible Night (1981), The Impossible Bath (1982), The Impossible Rocket (1982), The Wobbly Tooth (1984); juvenile: The Crack in the Teacup (1979); libretti: The Queen of Sheba's Legs (1994), In the House of Crossed Desires (1996); *Recreations* travel, looking at pictures; *Style*— Miss Marina Warner; ✉ c/o Rogers, Coleridge and White, 20 Powis Mews, London W11 1JN (tel 020 7221 3717)

WARNER, Baron (Life Peer UK 1998), of Brockley in the London Borough of Lewisham; Norman Reginald Warner; PC (2006); s of Albert Henry Edwin Warner, and Laura Edith, *née* Bennett; *b* 8 September 1940; *Educ* Dulwich Coll, Univ of Calif Berkley (MA, Harkness fell), Nuffield Coll Oxford (Gwilym Gibbon fell); *m* 1 (m dis 1981), Anne Lesley; 1 s (Hon Andrew Simon b 1967), 1 da (Hon Justine Emma b 1969); m 2, Suzanne Elizabeth; 1 s (Hon Joel James Stephen b 1981); *Career* DHSS: various posts concerned with NHS 1960–74, princ private sec to Sec of State for Social Services 1974–76, asst sec Supplementary Benefit 1976–79, asst sec Operational Planning 1979–81, regnl controller Wales and SW Region 1981–83, under sec Supplementary Benefit and Housing Benefit 1984–85; dir Social Services Kent County Cncl 1985–91, chm City and E London Family Services Authy 1991–94, md Warner Consultancy and Training Services 1991–97, chm National Inquiry into Children's Homes 1992, memb Local Govt Cmmn 1995–96, sr policy advsr to Home Sec 1997–98; Parly under sec of state (Lords) Dept of Health 2003–05, min of state (NHS reform) Dept of Health 2005–06; sr research fell in European social welfare and chm European Inst of Social Services Univ of Kent; chm: The Residential Forum 1993–97, Royal Philanthropic Soc 1993–98 (vice-chm 1998–99), Youth Justice Bd for England and Wales 1998–2003, London Sports Bd 2003, Provider Devpt Agency NHS London 2007–; former chm NCVO; tstee Leonard Cheshire Fndn and MacIntyre Care 1994–97, former memb Assoc of Dirs of Social Services; *Recreations* walking, sport, reading, cinema, theatre; *Style*— The Rt Hon the Lord Warner, PC

WARNER, Peter Mark; s of late Dr Marcel Mark Warner, of Weybridge, Surrey, and late Birthe Johanna Warner; *b* 21 June 1959; *Educ* Woking County GS, Kingston Poly Business Sch (BA); *m* Carolyn Frances, *née* Rice; 3 da (Charlotte Emily (Lottie) b 30 Nov 1997, Abigail Leah (Abbie) b 11 April 2000, Henrietta Eve Warner b 7 Jan 2003); *Career* account exec Tim Arnold and Associates (sales promotion agency) 1981–83, client services dir IMP Ltd 1989–93 (joined as account exec 1983), ptnr HHCL and Partners 1993–99; entrepreneur; *Recreations* gardening, fell walking, rare breed sheep, motorcycling, canal restoration; *Clubs* Goodwood Road Racing; *Style*— P Warner, Esq; ✉ Rodgate, Rodgate Lane, Haslemere, Surrey GU27 2EW (tel 01428 708093, fax 01428 708085, e-mail peterwarner@rodgate.com)

WARNER, Philip Courtenay Thomas; s and h of Sir (Edward Courtenay) Henry Warner, 3 Bt, and Jocelyn Mary Beevor; *b* 3 April 1951; *Educ* Eton; *m* 1982, Penelope Anne, yr da of John Lack Elmer (d 1973); 1 s, 4 da; *Career* barr; chm Warner Estate Hldgs plc 1993–

(memb Bd 1979–); non-exec dir Stonemartin plc, dir of private cos; *Recreations* fishing; *Style*— Philip Warner, Esq

WARNER, Simon Metford; s of Roger Harold Metford Warner, of Burford, Oxford, and Ruth Ernestine, *née* Hurcombe; *b* 12 January 1951; *Educ* Downs Sch Colwall, Leighton Park Sch Reading, Churchill Coll Cambridge (MA), Univ of Bristol; *m* 1974, Judith, da of Capt W Adams; 1 s (Leo b 1980); *Career* staff photographer Sotheby's 1973–75, theatre and landscape photographer and lens-based artist 1975–; touring exhbn Airedale - a Changing Landscape (Bradford Museums) 1998, installation and performance The Daguerre Project 2000, video installation Follow a Shadow (Impressions Gallery York) 2003, video A Guide to Yorkshire Rivers (Cartwright Hall Art Gallery Bradford) 2003, High Tide (touring exhbn) 2004, video installation Leaving Home (Brontë Parsonage Museum Haworth) 2005, performance Lavater - The Shadow of History 2006–07; NESTA research fell 2006–08; *Publications* Pennine Landscapes (with J Warner, 1978), Discovering West Yorkshire 1999, The Brontës at Haworth (with Ann Dinsdale, 2006); contribs incl: National Trail Guides to the Pennine Way and Peddars Way, Country Life, Telegraph Magazine, Radio Times; *Recreations* cycling, theatre; *Style*— Simon Warner, Esq; ✉ Whitestone Farm, Stanbury, Keighley, West Yorkshire BD22 0JW (tel and fax 01535 644644, e-mail photos@simonwarner.co.uk, website www.simonwarner.co.uk)

WARNER, Val; da of Alister Alfred Warner (d 1987), and Ivy Miriam Warner, *née* Robins (d 1985); *b* 15 January 1946, Middx; *Educ* Harrow County Sch for Girls, Somerville Coll Oxford (BA); *Career* pt/t teacher 1968–71, freelance proof-reader and copy ed 1971–77, writer in residence Univ of Swansea 1977–78, writer in residence Univ of Dundee 1979–81, freelance writer 1981–; memb Writers in Prison Ctee English PEN 1998–; Gregory Award for Poetry 1975; FRSL 1999; *Publications* poetry: These Yellow Photos (1971), Under the Penthouse (1973), Before Lunch (1986), Tooting Idyll (1998); The Centenary Corbière (trans, 1975, reissued 2003), The Collected Poems and Prose of Charlotte Mew (ed, 1981), The Collected Poems and Selected Prose of Charlotte Mew (ed, 1997, reissued 2003); *Recreations* reading, walking; *Clubs* PEN; *Style*— Ms Val Warner; ✉ 7 Rushmore Road, London E5 0ET (tel 020 8985 3942, e-mail valwarner@etce.freeserve.co.uk)

WARNICK, Marilyn Karen; da of Edward Stephen Warnick, of State College, PA, and Mary Kozel Warnick; *b* 20 June 1950; *Educ* Pennsylvania State Univ (BA, MA); *Career* ed Quartet Books 1978–80, mangr NY office Quartet Books 1980–85, sr ed Penguin 1986–88, publishing dir Telegraph Books 1988–96, commissioning ed (features) Daily Mail 1996–97, features ed Good Housekeeping 1997–99, books ed Mail on Sunday 1999–; memb Women in Journalism; *Recreations* travel, opera, gardening, family; *Clubs* The Academy; *Style*— Ms Marilyn Warnick; ✉ 56 The Avenue, London NW6 7NP; The Mail on Sunday, Northcliffe House, 2 Derry Street, London W8 5TS (tel 020 7938 6393, fax 020 7937 6882, mobile 07720 412145, e-mail marilyn.warnick@mailonsunday.co.uk)

WARNOCK, Hon Felix Geoffrey; er s of Sir Geoffrey Warnock (d 1995), and Baroness Warnock (Life Peer), *qv*; *b* 18 January 1952; *Educ* Winchester, Royal Coll of Music (ARCM); *m* 27 Aug 1975, Juliet, da of Arthur Robert Lehwalder, of Seattle, Washington, USA; 1 s (Daniel Arthur Richard b 1985), 2 da (Eleanor Denise b 1982, Polly Patricia b 1986); *Career* bassoonist: Acad of St Martin-in-the-Fields 1975–89, Albion Ensemble 1980–92, Acad of Ancient Music 1981–89; prof of bassoon Trinity Coll of Music 1985–90; gen mangr Orchestra of the Age of Enlightenment 1989–94, dir of early music RAM 1993–95, gen mangr The English Concert 1995–; chm Dr John Radcliffe Tst 2003–; *Recreations* bridge, golf; *Style*— The Hon Felix Warnock; ✉ 5 Kingsbridge Road, London W10 6PU (tel 020 8969 5738, fax 020 8964 4670); The English Concert, 8 St George's Terrace, London NW1 8XJ (tel 020 7911 0905, fax 020 7911 0904, e-mail ec@englishconcert.co.uk)

WARNOCK, Baroness (Life Peer UK 1985), of Weeke in the City of Winchester; Dame (Helen) Mary Warnock; DBE (1984); da of Archibald Edward Wilson (d 1924), of Winchester, and Ethel Mary (d 1952), eldest da of Sir Felix Otto Schuster, 1 Bt; *b* 14 April 1924; *Educ* St Swithun's Sch Winchester, Lady Margaret Hall Oxford (MA, BPhil); *m* 1949, Sir Geoffrey Warnock (d 1995), s of James Warnock, OBE, MD (d 1953), of Leeds; 2 s (Hon Felix Geoffrey, *qv*, b 1952, Hon James Marcus Alexander b 1953), 3 da (Hon Kathleen (Kitty) b 1950, Hon Stephana (Fanny) (Hon Mrs Branson) b 1956, Hon (Grizel) Maria (Hon Mrs Henriques) b 1961); *Career* fell and tutor in philosophy St Hugh's Coll Oxford 1949–66, former headmistress Oxford HS; former memb SSRC, chm Ctee of Enquiry into Human Fertilisation, former memb IBA; chm: Advsy Ctee on Animal Experiments, Ctee of Enquiry into Education of Handicapped; chair Planning Aid Tst; memb Royal Cmmn on Environmental Pollution 1979–85; Albert Medallist RSA; Talbot Res fell LMH until 1976, FCP; mistress Girton Coll Cambridge 1985–91 (life fell); hon degrees: Open Univ, Essex, Melbourne, Bath, Exeter, Manchester, Glasgow, York, Warwick, Liverpool, London, St Andrews; hon fell: St Hugh's Coll Oxford, Lady Margaret Hall Oxford, Hertford Coll Oxford; Hon FBA, Hon FRCP; *Books* Ethics Since 1900, Existentialism, Imagination, Schools of Thought, What Must We Teach? (with T Devlin), Education: A Way Forward, Memory, A Common Policy for Education, The Uses of Philosophy, Imagination and Time, Women Philosophers, An Intelligent Person's Guide to Ethics, A Memoir: People and Places, Making Babies, Nature and Mortality: A Philosopher in Public Life; *Recreations* gardening, music; *Style*— The Lady Warnock, DBE; ✉ 60 Church Street, Great Bedwyn, Marlborough, Wiltshire SN8 3PF; House of Lords, London SW1A 0PW (tel 020 7219 8619)

WARNOCK, His Hon Judge (Alastair) Robert Lyon; s of Alexander Nelson Lyon Warnock (d 2001), and Anobel Forest Lyon, *née* Henderson (d 1974); *b* 23 July 1953; *Educ* Sedbergh, UEA (BA); *m* 20 March 1993, Sally Mary, *née* Tomkinson; *Career* called to the Bar Lincoln's Inn 1977 (Tancred scholar); pupillage with Her Hon Judge Downey 1977–78, practising barr specialising in common law Northern Circuit 1977–2003 (memb Chambers of His Hon Judge D Forster Liverpool), recorder 2000–03 (asst recorder 1993–2000), circuit judge 2003–; memb Family Law Bar Assoc, pres SW Lancs Magistrates Assoc; pres Royal Liverpool Golf Club Village Play; vice-pres Artisan's Golf Assoc; *Recreations* golf, wine, travel; *Clubs* Royal Liverpool Golf, Artists' (Liverpool), Bar Golf Soc; *Style*— His Hon Judge Warnock; ✉ Bolton Combined Court, Blackhorse Street, Bolton BL1 1SU (tel 01204 392881, fax 01204 363204)

WARNOCK-SMITH, Shbn; QC (2002); da of Thomas John Davies (d 1983), and Denise Dorothy, *née* Newman (d 2003); *b* 13 September 1948, Portsmouth; *Educ* Westlake HS Auckland, Portsmouth HS, KCL (LLB, LLM); *Partner* Andrew de la Rosa; 1 s (Henry John b 25 Oct 1983), 1 da (Harriet Shân b 5 Sept 1985); *Career* called to the Bar 1979; practising barr Chancery Bar 1979–; memb Editorial Bd Wills and Trust Law Reports; bencher Hon Soc of Lincoln's Inn; tstee Eric Anker-Petersen Charity 2004–; memb: Soc of Trust and Estate Practitioners, Association of Contentious Trust and Probate Specialists, Chancery Bar Assoc; *Publications* Heywood & Massey on Court of Protection Practice (ed); *Recreations* Chicago, travel, interior design, architecture; *Style*— Mrs Shbn Warnock-Smith, QC; ✉ 5 Stone Buildings, Lincoln's Inn, London WC2A 3XT (tel 020 7242 6201, fax 020 7831 8102, e-mail swarnocksmith@5sblaw.com)

WARRELL, Prof David Alan; s of Alan Theophilus Warrell, ISO, of Abingdon, and late Mildred Emma, *née* Hunt; *b* 6 October 1939; *Educ* Portsmouth GS, ChCh Oxford (MA, DM, BCh, DSc), St Thomas' Hosp Med Sch London; *m* 11 Oct 1975, Mary Jean, da of George Prentice, of London; 2 da (Helen b 1981, Clare b 1985); *Career* lectr and consit physician Royal Postgrad Med Sch London 1974–75, conslt physician Radcliffe Infirmary Oxford 1975–79, fell St Cross Coll Oxford 1977–2006 (hon fell 2007–), hon conslt physician Oxfordshire HA 1979–, founding dir Wellcome-Mahidol Univ Oxford Tropical Med Prog Bangkok 1979–86, hon clinical dir Alistair Reid Venom Res Unit Liverpool Sch of Tropical Med 1983–; Univ of Oxford: prof of tropical med and infectious diseases 1987–2006 (emeritus prof of tropical med 2006–), dir Centre for Tropical Med 1987–2001 (founding dir emeritus 2001–), head Nuffield Department of Clinical Med 2002–04; visiting prof Faculty of Tropical Med Mahidol Univ Bangkok 1997–, princ fell Aust Venom Res Unit Univ of Melbourne 1998–; sr advsr in tropical medicine MRC 2001–, chm AIDS Therapeutic Trials Ctees MRC 1987–93, chm MRC China UK Research Ethics Ctee 2007–; hon conslt in malariology to the Army 1989–, hon med advsr RGS 1994– (also memb Cncl), memb FCO Pro Bono Medical Panel 2002–; pres Br Venom Gp 1992–, pres Int Fedn for Tropical Med 1996–2000, pres Royal Soc of Tropical Med and Hygiene 1997–99; WHO: conslt on malaria, rabies and snake bites, memb Steering Ctee for Chemotherapy of Malaria 1986–91, memb Expert Advsy Panel on Malaria 1989–; tstee Tropical Health and Educn Tst 1988–2004, patron Cambodia Tst 1991–2003, delegate OUP 1999–2006; Chalmer's Medal Royal Soc 1981, Ambuj Nath Bose Prize RCP 1994, Harveian orator RCP 2001, Busk Medal RGS 2003, Guthrie Medal RAMC 2994, Mary Kingsley Centenary Medal Liverpool Sch of Tropical Med 2005; profesor honorario Universidad Nacional Mayor de San Marcos Lima 2005; hon fell: Ceylon Coll of Physicians, Australasian Coll of Tropical Med, Australasian Soc for Infectious Diseases, Assoc of Physicians of GB and I, American Soc of Tropical Med and Hygiene (ASTMH); FRCP, MRCS, FRCPEd, FZS 1967, FRGS 1989, FMedSci 1998; Knight Commander Order of the White Elephant (Thailand) 2004; *Books* Rabies - The Facts (1986), Oxford Textbook of Medicine (1987, 4 edn 2003), Essential Malariology (1993, 4 edn 2002), Expedition Medicine (1998, 2 edn 2002), Concise Oxford Textbook of Medicine (2000); *Recreations* music, hill walking, natural history, book collecting; *Style*— Prof David Warrell; ✉ Nuffield Department of Clinical Medicine, University of Oxford; John Radcliffe Hospital, Headington, Oxford OX3 9DU (tel 01865 220968, fax 01865 220984, e-mail david.warrell@ndm.ox.ac.uk)

WARREN, Dr Graham Barry; s of Charles Graham Thomas Warren, and Joyce Thelma, *née* Roberts; *b* 25 February 1948; *Educ* Willesden Co GS, Pembroke Coll Cambridge (MA, PhD); *m* 18 June 1966, Philippa Mary Adeline, da of Alexander Edward Temple-Cole (d 1981), of Shoreham, Kent; 4 da (Joanna b 5 Nov 1966, Eleanor b 20 Aug 1969, Katya b 13 Nov 1979, Alexandra b 7 Dec 1980); *Career* MRC jr res fell Nat Inst for Med Res London 1972–74, res fell Gonville & Caius Coll Cambridge and Stothert res fell of the Royal Soc Biochemistry Dept Univ of Cambridge 1975–77, sr scientist Euro Molecular Biology Lab Heidelberg W Germany (formerly gp ldr) 1977–85, prof and head of Dept of Biochemistry Univ of Dundee 1985–88, princ scientist Imperial Cancer Res Fund 1988–99, prof of cell biology Yale Univ Med Sch until 2006, scientific dir Max F Perutz Labs Vienna 2007–; memb EMBO; FRS; *Style*— Dr Graham Warren, FRS; ✉ Max F Perutz Laboratories, Dr Bohr-Gosse 9, A-1030 Vienna, Austria (tel 00 43 664 60277 24001, e-mail graham.warren@mfpl.ac.at)

WARREN, John Anthony; *b* 11 June 1953; *Educ* Tiffin Sch, Univ of Bristol (BSc); *m* 1975, Anna; 2 s; *Career* Ernst & Young 1974–81; United Biscuits (Holdings) plc: chief accountant rising to fin dir UK, Int Sr Mgmnt Programme Harvard Business Sch 1990, gp fin dir (main bd) 1990–2000, chief exec Asia Pacific 1995–96; gp fin dir WH Smith plc 2000–05; non-exec dir: Rexam plc 1994–2003, RAC plc 2003–05, Rank Gp 2005–, Arla Foods UK plc 2006–07, Bovis Homes Group plc 2006–, Spectris plc 2006–, BPP Holdings plc 2006–, Uniq plc 2007–; ACA 1977; *Style*— John Warren, Esq

WARREN, Prof Lynda May; da of Leonard Warren, of Croydon, and Peggy, *née* Tatnell (d 1984); *b* 26 April 1950, Croydon; *Educ* Croydon HS for Girls, Univ of London (BSc, PhD), Croydon Coll (LLB), Univ of Wales Cardiff (MSc); *m* 1, 3 June 1973 (m dis), Christopher Tydeman; m 2, 19 July 1986, Barry Thomas; 1 s (Marc b 26 July 1986); *Career* postgrad res asst Univ of London 1975–81, sr lectr in biology Poly of Central London 1981–84, lectr in biology Goldsmiths Coll London 1984–87, lectr then sr lectr in law Univ of Wales Cardiff 1987–95, prof of environmental law Univ of Wales Aberystwyth 1996–2003; memb: Countryside Cncl for Wales 1992–2003, Radioactive Waste Mgmnt Advsy Ctee 1994–2004, Bd Environment Agency 2000–06, Ctee on Radioactive Waste Mgmnt 2003–, Royal Cmmn on Environmental Pollution 2005–, Jt Nature Conservation Ctee 2006–; chair Salmon and Freshwater Fisheries Review Gp 1998–2000; ed: Environmental Law Review, Law, Science and Policy; author of over 100 scientific and legal papers; tstee: WWF-UK 2002–04, W & SW Wales Wildlife Tst 2004–, Assoc of River Tsts 2004–, Field Studies Cncl 2005–; FIBiol 1990; *Recreations* travel especially in the Middle East, fashion; *Style*— Prof Lynda Warren; ✉ Ynys Einion, Eglwys Fach, Machynlleth SY20 8SX (tel 01654 781344, fax 01654 781276, e-mail lm.warren@btopenworld.com)

WARREN, Martin Hugh; s of Frederick Michael Warren, of Devon, and Anne, *née* Phillips; *b* 12 February 1961, Bideford, Devon; *Educ* Univ of Bristol (LLB, Sweet and Maxwell Prize); *m* (sep); 2 da (Katie, Sarah), 1 s (Thomas); *Career* admitted slr 1985; slr specialising in employment law; articled Osborne Clarke; Eversheds: joined 1985, asst slr 1985–86, assoc 1986–89, ptnr 1989–, currently head of labor law, head of dept 2004–06, head of HR practice gp 2006–; employment advsr CBI; memb Law Soc 1985; *Recreations* diving, cycling, walking; *Clubs* Reform; *Style*— Martin Warren, Esq; ✉ Eversheds LLP, 1 Callaghan Square, Cardiff CF10 5BT (tel 029 2047 7570, fax 029 2046 4347, e-mail martinwarren@eversheds.com)

WARREN, Michael Christopher; s of Joseph Henry Warren (d 1971), and Helen, *née* Ashworth (d 1946); *b* 30 December 1944; *Educ* Palmers Sch for Boys Thurrock, Central Sch of Speech and Drama; *m* 1, 1969 (m dis 1978), Kathleen Mary, *née* Reindorp; m 2, 1992 Lindsay Kathlyn, da of William Heathcote Roberts; 1 da (Rebecca Roberts-Warren b 19 Aug 1983); *Career* journalist Essex and Thurrock Gazette 1963–65, various theatre work (incl 69 Theatre Co Manchester) 1969–71, res exec and assoc dir Research Services Ltd 1971–81, head of Survey Unit Consumers' Assoc 1981–86, dir of res COI 1986–93, DG Market Research Soc 1993–97 (memb Professional Standards Ctee 1988–91, memb Educn Ctee 1992–93), assoc dir Market Research Solutions Ltd 1997–98, research conslt/author 1998–; memb Research Resource Bd ESRC 1994–98; visiting prof Sch of Human Sciences Univ of Surrey 2000–06; exec ed Int Jl of Market Res 2000–05; author of various articles on research techniques and mgmnt; dir Acad of Social Sciences 2002–04, fndr memb Social Research Assoc, memb Market Research Soc 1975, FRSA 1995; *Recreations* jazz, cricket, theatre, rugby, competitive model aviation; *Clubs* Ronnie Scott's, Harlequins; *Style*— Michael Warren, Esq; ✉ 30 Cole Park Road, Twickenham, Middlesex TW1 1HS (tel 020 8891 3130, fax 020 8891 1970, e-mail michael.c.warren@btinternet.com)

WARREN, Hon Mr Justice; Sir Nicholas Roger Warren; kt (2005); s of Roger Warren (d 1991), and Muriel, *née* Reeves (d 1998); *b* 20 May 1949; *Educ* Bryanston, UC Oxford (scholar, BA); *m* 1, 1978 (m dis 1989); 2 s, 1 da; m 2, 1994; *Career* called to the Bar Middle Temple 1972 (Astbury scholar); QC 1993, recorder 1999–2005 (asst recorder 1995–99), judge of the High Court of Justice (Chancery Div) 2005– (dep judge of the High Court 1999–2005); chm Chancery Bar Assoc 2001–03; *Recreations* music, sailing; *Style*— The Hon Mr Justice Warren; ✉ Royal Courts of Justice, Strand, London WC2A 2LL

WARREN, Prof Peter Michael; s of Arthur George Warren (d 1947), and Alison Joan, *née* White (d 1942); *b* 23 June 1938; *Educ* Sandbach Sch, Llandovery Coll, UCNW Bangor (BA), CCC Cambridge (MA, PhD); *m* 18 June 1966, Elizabeth Margaret, da of Percy Halliday, of Beaconsfield, Bucks; 1 da (Diktynna b 1979), 1 s (Damian b 1984); *Career* reader in Aegean archaeology Univ of Birmingham 1976 (lectr 1972–74, sr lectr 1974–76);

Univ of Bristol: prof of ancient history and classical archaeology 1977–2001 (emeritus prof 2001–), dean Faculty of Arts 1988–90, pro-vice-chllr 1991–95, fell 1995–96, sr res fell 2001–; visiting prof Univ of Minnesota 1981, Geddes-Harrower prof of Greek art and archaeology Univ of Aberdeen 1986–87, Félix Neubergh lectr Univ of Göteborg 1986, foreign fell Onassis Fndn Greece 2007; pres: Wotton-under-Edge Historical Soc 1986–90, Bristol Anglo-Hellenic Cultural Soc 1987–98, Birmingham and Midlands Branch Classical Assoc 1996–97, Bristol and Glos Archaeological Soc 2000–01 (memb Cncl 1977–, vice-chm 1980–81, chm 1981–83, vice-pres 1989–93); Br Sch Athens: chm Managing Ctee 1979–83 (memb 1973–77, 1978–79, 1986–90 and 1994–98), memb Cncl 1999–2003, acting chm 2000, chm 2003–04, vice-pres 2005–; memb Cncl Soc for the Promotion of Hellenic Studies 1978–81; hon fell Archaeological Soc of Athens 1987, corresponding fell Soc for Cretan Historical Studies 1992, corresponding memb Austrian Acad of Scis 1997; Dr (hc) Univ of Athens; FSA 1973, FBA 1997; *Books* Minoan Stone Vases (1969), Myrtos An Early Bronze Age Settlement in Crete (1972), The Aegean Civilizations (1975 and 1989), Minoan Religion as Ritual Action (1988), Aegean Bronze Age Chronology (with V Hankey, 1989), The Early Minoan Tombs of Lebena, Southern Crete (with St Alexiou, 2004); *Recreations* Manchester United, history of Mediterranean botany, growing Cistaceae (national collection); *Style*— Prof Peter Warren, FSA, FBA; ✉ Claremont House, 5 Merlin Haven, Wotton-under-Edge, Gloucestershire GL12 7BA (tel 01453 842 290); Department of Archaeology and Anthropology, University of Bristol, 43 Woodland Road, Bristol BS8 1UU (tel 0117 954 6084/954 6060)

WARREN, Dr Peter Tolman; CBE (1998); s of late Hugh Alan Warren, OBE, of Sanderstead, Surrey, and late Florence Christine, *née* Tolman; *b* 20 December 1937; *Educ* Whitgift Sch S Croydon, Queens' Coll Cambridge (BA, MA, PhD); *m* 9 Sept 1961, Angela Mary, da of late Thomas Henry Curtis, of Sanderstead, Surrey; 2 s (Simon b 1965, Timothy b 1970), 1 da (Katherine b 1967); *Career* princ scientific offr Br Geological Survey (previously Inst Geological Sci/Geological Survey & Museum) 1962–72 (formerly scientific offr), princ scientific offr Cabinet Office Whitehall 1972–76, safety advsr NERC 1976–77, exec sec Royal Soc of London 1985–97 (dep exec sec 1977–85), dir World Humanity Action Trust 1997–99; chm Cambridge Soc (Surrey Branch) 2000–05; vice-pres: Geological Soc 1992–96, Parly and Scientific Ctee 1995–98 and 2001–04, Br Assoc Adv Sci 1997–2002; memb: Cncl GDST 1989–2005, Ct of Govrs and Cncl of Nat Museums and Galleries of Wales 2000–06, Exec Ctee Stakeholder Forum for Our Common Future 2001–05; memb Ct of Assts Guild of Educators 2002– (Master 2007–08), administrator Livery Schs Link 2004–06; govr Sheffield HS for Girls 1999–2005; FGS, C.Geol; *Books* Geology of the Country around Rhyl and Denbigh (jtly, 1984); *Recreations* gardening, geology; *Clubs* Athenaeum; *Style*— Dr Peter Warren, CBE; ✉ 34 Plough Lane, Purley, Surrey CR8 3QA (tel 020 8660 4087, fax 020 8668 7640)

WARREN, Robert John; s of Dr John Nettleton Warren, of Arundel, W Sussex, and Mary, *née* Clayton; *b* 29 December 1935; *Educ* Lancing, Brighton Coll of Tech and Arts; *m* 1962, Madeline Lee, da of Fred Redfearn; 1 da (b 4 July 1965), 1 s (b 4 Jan 1968); *Career* schoolmaster 1955, Nat Serv RNVR Sub Lt 1955–57, reporter Hampshire Chronicle 1957–58, reporter Coventry Evening Telegraph 1958–60, reporter/sub ed Chronicle Herald Halifax Canada 1960–61, sub ed Montreal Star 1961–63; News of the World: reporter 1963–71, dep news ed 1971–74, news ed 1974–93, asst ed 1985–93, assoc ed 1993–95, exec ed 1995–, ombudsman 2000–; chm The Journalists' Charity 2007; *Recreations* golf, gardening; *Clubs* National Liberal, Wig and Pen; *Style*— Robert Warren, Esq; ✉ The News of the World, 1 Virginia Street, London E98 1NW (tel 020 7782 4410)

WARREN, Dr Roderic Ellis; s of Ronald Thomas Warren (d 1970), of Tadworth, Surrey, and Mabel Elsie Warren; *b* 24 October 1948; *Educ* Whitgift Sch Croydon, Gonville & Caius Coll Cambridge (MA, MB BChir), Westminster Hosp Med Sch; *m* 6 Sept 1976, Pamela Rose, da of Frederick John Taft (d 1976), of Canterbury; 1 s (Charles), 2 da (Elizabeth, Eleanor); *Career* conslt microbiologist Addenbrooke's Hosp 1976–93, dir Public Health Laboratory Royal Shrewsbury Hosp 1993–95 and 2001–, conslt microbiologist Shrewsbury and Telford Hosp NHS Tst 2003–; gp dir Public Health Laboratory Service Midlands 1995–2002; hon sr lectr Univ of Birmingham 1977–93; FRCPath 1989; *Recreations* occasional; *Style*— Dr Roderic Warren; ✉ Microbiology Laboratory, Royal Shrewsbury Hospital, Mytton Oak Road, Shrewsbury SY3 8XQ (tel 01743 261161)

WARREN-GASH, HE Haydon; s of Alexis Patrick Warren-Gash (d 1997), and Cynthia June, *née* Phillips; *b* 1949, Kenya; *Educ* Marlborough, Sidney Sussex Coll Cambridge (MA); *m* 1973, Caroline, *née* Leather; 1 s (Alexander b 1975), 1 da (Vanessa b 1977); *Career* HM Dip Serv 1971–: Latin American Desk FCO 1971–72, Turkish language student Univ of London 1972–73, third sec Ankara 1973–77, second then first sec Political Section Madrid 1977–81, staff Perm Under Sec's Dept rising to private sec to Min of State (Sir Cranley Onslow then Sir Richard Luce) FCO 1981–85, first sec Commercial Section Paris 1985–89, dep head Southern Euro Dept FCO 1989–91, dep high cmmr Nairobi 1991–94, head Southern Euro Dept FCO 1994–97, ambass to the Ivory Coast (concurrently accredited to Liberia, Burkina Faso and Niger) 1997–2001, ambass to Morocco 2002–05 (concurrently accredited to Mauritania), ambass to Colombia 2005–; *Clubs* Muthaiga; *Style*— HE Mr Haydon Warren-Gash; ✉ c/o Foreign & Commonwealth Office (Bogotá), King Charles Street, London SW1A 2AH

WARRINGTON, Bishop of 2000–; Rt Rev David Willfred Michael Jennings; s of Rev Willfred Jennings (d 1970), of Kensington, London, and Nona Janet, *née* de Winton; *b* 13 July 1944; *Educ* Radley, KCL (AKC); *m* 11 Oct 1969, Sarah Catherine, da of Dr Robert Fynn, of Harare, Zimbabwe; 3 s (Andrew Willfred Mark b 1971, Peter Timothy John b 1974, Michael Robert James b 1978); *Career* asst curate: Walton PC Liverpool 1967–69, Christ Church Hants 1969–73; vicar: of Hythe Southampton 1973–80, of Romford St Edward 1980–92; rural dean of Havering 1985–92, non-residentiary canon of Chelmsford Cathedral 1987–92, archdeacon of Southend 1992–2000; *Recreations* exploring the buildings of the British Isles; *Style*— The Rt Rev the Bishop of Warrington; ✉ 34 Central Avenue, Eccleston Park, Prescot L34 2QP (tel 0151 426 1897, fax 0151 493 2479)

WARRY, Dr Peter Thomas; s of Vivian Warry, of Dorset, and Pamela, *née* Lane; *b* 31 August 1949; *Educ* Clifton, Merton Coll Oxford (open exhbn, MA), Univ of London (LLB), Univ of Reading (PhD); *m* 1981, Rosemary Olive, *née* Furbank; 1 da (Sarah b 1987); *Career* various positions 1968–79: MoD, Electricity Cncl, British Leyland; md Self-Changing Gears Ltd 1979–82, gp md Aerospace Engineering plc 1982–84, special advsr and dep head PM's Policy Unit 1984–86, dir of planning and business devpt Plessey Telecoms 1986–87, dir and chm Building Products Div Norcros plc 1988–94, bd dir British Energy plc 1996–98; chief exec Nuclear Electric 1995–98; chm: Victrex plc 1999–, BSS Gp plc 2004– (non-exec dir 1999–2003), Kier Gp plc 2004– (non-exec dir 1998–2003); non-exec dir: Heatherwood and Wexham Park Hospitals Tst 1992–95, PTS Gp plc 1995–99, Office of the Rail Regulator 1999–2003, Thames Water Utilities Ltd 2001–05; chm Economic Impact Gp Office of Sci and Innovation 2006; industrial prof Univ of Warwick 1993–; chm: PPARC 2001–07, STFC 2007–; memb Cncl Univ of Reading 2006–; CEng, FCMA 1983, FIET 1995, FIMechE 1995, FREng 2006; *Publications* A New Direction for the Post Office (1991), Efficiency in Price-Control Reviews (2000), Tegulae: Manufacture, Typology and Use in Roman Britain (2006); *Recreations* archaeology, squash, walking, tennis; *Style*— Dr Peter Warry, FREng; ✉ Coxhorne, London Road, Cheltenham, Gloucestershire GL52 6UY (tel 01242 518552)

WARWICK, Archdeacon of; *see:* Paget-Wilkes, Ven Michael Jocelyn James

WARWICK, 9 Earl Brooke (GB 1746) and of (GB 1759); Guy David Greville; also Baron Brooke (E 1621); s of 8 Earl of Warwick (d 1996), and Sarah Anne Chester, *née* Beatty; *b* 30 January 1957; *Educ* Eton, Ecole des Roches; *m* 1, 1981 (m dis 1992), Susan (Susie) McKinley, da of George William McKinley Wilson, of Melbourne, Australia, and formerly w of Nicholas Sydney Cobbold; 1 s (Charles Fulke Chester, Lord Brooke b 27 July 1982), 2 step c; m 2, Oct 1996, Louisa, yr da of Dr Peter Heenan, of Perth, Western Australia; *Heir* s, Lord Brooke; *Recreations* golf, surfing; *Clubs* White's; *Style*— The Rt Hon the Earl of Warwick; ✉ 4 Walter Street, Claremont, Perth, Western Australia 6010

WARWICK OF UNDERCLIFFE, Baroness (Life Peer UK 1999), of Undercliffe in the County of West Yorkshire; Diana Warwick; *b* 16 July 1945; *Educ* Univ of London (BA); *m* 1969, Sean Terence Bowes Young; *Career* tech asst NUT 1969–72, asst sec Civil and Public Servs Assoc 1972–83, gen sec Assoc of Univ Teachers 1983–92, first chief exec Westminster Fndn for Democracy (all-pty advsy gp for newly democratised countries) 1992–95, chief exec Universities UK (formerly Ctee of Vice-Chllrs and Principals) 1995–; chm Tstees Ctee VSO 1994–2004; memb: Bd British Cncl 1985–95, Employment Appeals Tbnl 1987–99, Exec Bd Industrial Soc 1987–93, Gen Cncl TUC 1989–92, Nolan/Neill Ctee 1995–99, Technol Foresight Steering Gp 1998–; govr Cwlth Inst 1988–95; Hon DLitt Univ of Bradford, Hon Dr Open Univ; *Style*— Baroness Warwick of Undercliffe; ✉ Universities UK, Woburn House, 20 Tavistock Square, London WC1H 9HQ (tel 020 7419 5402, fax 020 7380 0137)

WARWICK THOMPSON, Dr Paul; s of Prof Sir Michael Warwick Thompson, *qv*, and Sybil, *née* Spooner; *b* 9 August 1959; *Educ* Bryanston, Univ of Bristol (BA), UEA (MA, PhD); *m* 1985, Adline, da of Max Finlay; 1 da (Roberta Beatrice b 1987), 1 s (Oscar Leo b 1990); *Career* English teacher St Bede's Sch Eastbourne, scriptwriter/researcher The Design Cncl London 1987–88; Design Museum London: curator contemporary design 1988–90, curator 1990–92, curatorial dir 1992–94, dir 1994–2001; dir Smithsonian Cooper-Hewitt Nat Design Museum NY 2001–; FRSA; *Books* Review 1 New Design (1989), Review 2 New Design (1990); *Style*— Dr Paul Warwick Thompson; ✉ Smithsonian Cooper-Hewitt National Design Museum, 2 East 91st Street, New York NY 10128–0669 USA (tel 00 1 212 849 8373)

WASHINGTON, Joan; *Educ* Central Sch of Speech and Drama (distinction), Univ London (Dip); *m* 1 Nov 1986, Richard E Grant *qv*; 1 da (Olivia b 4 Jan 1989); *Career* accent/dialogue coach; began career teaching in remand homes, comprehensive schs, RCN; taught over 320 accents, has taught regularly at RADA and Central; *Theatre* West End prodns incl: Anything Goes, Orpheus Descending (Broadway), Crazy for You, City of Angels, She Loves Me, Sunset Boulevard, Whistle Down the Wind, The Iceman Cometh, Plenty, The King and I, Calico, Suddenly Last Summer, The Goat or Who is Sylvia?, Death of a Salesman, Guys and Dolls, Evita; RNT: Guys and Dolls, Beggar's Opera, Brighton Beach Memoirs, A View from the Bridge, Cat on a Hot Tin Roof, The Shaughraun, The Crucible, After the Fall, Pygmalion, Carousel, Sweeney Todd, Angels in America, The Children's Hour, Sweet Bird of Youth, Broken Glass, Guys and Dolls, Oklahoma, Our Lady of Sligo, EdMOND, Mourning Becomes Electra, The Dark Materials, Once in a Lifetime, The Reporter; RSC: The Merchant of Venice, The Jew of Malta, Across Oka, Great Expectations; Royal Court: Rat in the Skull, The Edward Bond Season, Serious Money, The Queen and I, The Weir, A Really Classy Affair, A Dublin Carol; *Television* incl: The Singing Detective, Lorna Doone, Old Times, Top Girls, Roots, Suddenly Last Summer, Middlemarch, Scarlett, Our Friends from the North, Tom Jones, The Russian Bride, Daniel Deronda, May 33rd, Jane Eyre; *Films* incl: Yentl, The Bounty, Greystoke, Plenty, Prick up your Ears, A World Apart, The Trial, Damage, Second Best, Carrington, Jane Eyre, Jude, French Kiss, Fierce Creatures, The Borrowers, 101 Dalmations, My Life So Far, Eugene Onegin, 102 Dalmations, Captain Corelli's Mandolin, Charlotte Gray, In My Country, Stage Beauty, Goal, Wah-Wah, River Queen, Breaking and Entering, Notes on a Scandal, A Mighty Heart, Miss Pettigrew Lives for a Day; *Animations* The Miracle Maker, The Canterbury Tales; *Broadcasts* How the Edwardians Spoke (BBC4); *Style*— Ms Joan Washington

WASINONDH, HE Kitti; *b* 23 November 1951; *Educ* Chulalongkorn Univ Bangkok, Nat Inst of Devpt Admin Bangkok (MPA); *m* 1980, Nutchanart; *Career* Thai diplomat; attaché then third sec Southeast Asia Div Dept of Political Affrs Miny of Foreign Affrs 1978–79, third sec then second sec Belgrade 1982–83; Dept of Economic Affrs: second sec Div of Economic Rels and Cooperation 1985, second sec Div of Int Economic Affrs 1986, first sec Div of Economic Rels and Cooperation 1987, seconded to Ops Center Royal Thai Army 1988–90, chief of secretariat 1991; min cnsllr Brussels 1993, dir Commerce and Industry Div Dept of ASEAN Affrs 1997, dep DG Dept of Info 1998, dep DG Dept of East Asian Affrs 1999, consul-gen Sydney 2000, DG Dept of ASEAN Affairs 2002, DG Dept of Info 2006, ambass extraordinary and plenipotentiary to the Court of St James's 2007–; Knight Grand Cross (First Class) Most Exalted Order of the White Elephant 2002 (Knight Cdr (Second Class) 1996, Cdr (Third Class) 1988), Chakrabarti Mala Medal 2003, Knight Grand Cordon (Special Class) Most Noble Order of the Crown of Thailand 2005 (Knight Grand Cross (First Class) 1999, Knight Cdr (Second Class) 1991, Cdr (Third Class) 1985); *Style*— HE Mr Kitti Wasinondh; ✉ Royal Thai Embassy, 29–30 Queen's Gate, London SW7 5JB (tel 020 7225 5500, fax 020 7823 9695, e-mail thaiembassy.info@btconnect.com and thaiembassy.econ@btconnect.com)

WASON, (Robert) Graham; s of Cathcart Roland Wason, and Margaret Ogilvie, *née* Lamb; gs of Rear Adm Cathcart Romer Wason, CMG, CIE (d 1941), ggs of Rt Hon Eugene Wason, MP (Liberal MP and Chm Scottish Liberal Party), gggs of P R Wason, MP for Ipswich, Promoter of Reform Bill 1832 and co-fndr of Reform Club; *b* 6 January 1951; *Educ* Alleyne's GS Stevenage, Univ of Surrey (BSc); *Career* ptnr Deloitte Conslting 1983–98, md Greenwich Gateway 1998–99; dir All Being Well Ltd 2002–; formerly in tourism and hotels ops in Europe and Africa and 'Holiday Which?'; dir The Tourism Soc 1997– (vice-chm 1997–99, chm 1999–2004); vice-pres of Strategy and Devpt World Travel and Tourism Cncl 1999–2003; chm Tourism Leisure Sports and Recreation Ctee Br Conslts Bureau until 1995; memb Advsy Bd: Sch of Mgmnt Univ of Surrey, Inst of Tourism Guiding; fell Hotel and Catering Int Mgmnt Assoc, fell Tourism Soc; FRSA; *Publications* The Luxury Country House Hotel Survey (1987), The European Incentive Travel Survey (1993), European Golf Facilities (1995), Tourism Taxation: Striking a Fair Deal (1999), Corporate Social Leadership in Travel and Tourism (2002); *Recreations* tennis, travel, cultural exchange and Making a Difference missions; *Style*— Graham Wason, Esq; ✉ Cossington Park, Bridgwater, Somerset TA7 8LH (e-mail rgwason@gmail.com)

WASS, Alexandra (Sasha); QC (2000); da of Sir Douglas Wass, GCB, and Dr Milica Pavicic; *b* 19 February 1958; *Educ* Wimbledon HS, Univ of Livepool; *m* 31 May 1986, Nigel Ronald Adrian Hall; 1 s (Adam Edward b 19 Nov 1986), 1 da (Harriet Grace b 25 Feb 1989); *Career* called to the Bar Gray's Inn 1981 (bencher 2003); asst recorder 1997–2000, recorder (SE Circuit) 2000–; Criminal Bar Assoc: memb Ctee 1992–, treas 1997–2000, dir of educn 2002–; *Style*— Miss Sasha Wass, QC; ✉ 6 King's Bench Walk, Temple, London EC4Y 7DR (tel 020 7583 0410, fax 020 7353 8791)

WASS, Prof John Andrew Hall; s of Samuel Hall Wass (d 1970), and June Mary Vaudine, *née* Blaikie (d 1992); *b* 14 August 1947; *Educ* Rugby, Guy's Hosp Med Sch London (MB BS, MD); *m* 1, 1970 (m dis 1997), Valerie *née* Vincent; 1 da (Katherine b 1974), 1 s (Samuel b 1979); m 2, 1998, Sally, da of Guy Smith (d 1998), and Diana Smith (d 2000); *Career* registrar: KCH London 1973–74, Guy's Hosp London 1974–75; sub-dean of Med Coll and prof of clinical endocrinology Bart's London 1989–95 (univ lectr 1976–81, sr lectr

1982–85, reader 1985–89), conslt in endocrinology Radcliffe Infirmary and Churchill Hosp Oxford 1995–, prof of endocrinology Univ of Oxford 1998–; advsr to Cancer-BACUP 1985–, med dir Bart's City Life Saver 1993–; Linacre fell RCP 1994–98; ed Clinical Endocrinology jl 1991–94; vice-chm Ctee of Mgmnt Royal Med Benevolent Fund 1990–94 (memb 1982–94 and 1996–2000); pres: Euro Fedn of Endocrine Socs 2001–03 (memb Exec Ctee 1994–2001, vice-pres 1998–2001), Endocrine Section RSM 1997–98 (sec 1988–92); chm Soc for Endocrinology 2005– (sec 2002–05); sec: Assoc of Clinical Profs Univ of London 1993–95, Clinical Endocrinology Tst 1996–2005; memb Exec Ctee Int Soc of Endocrinology 1996–2000; admissions tutor fell Green Coll Oxford 2001–03; co-fndr The Pituitary Fndn 1994 (tstee 1999–2006); chm Bart's Choral Soc 1992–95; govr Purcell Sch 2000–; memb: American Endocrine Soc, Assoc of Physicians; Freeman City of London 1983, Liveryman Worshipful Co of Barbers; fell Green Coll Oxford (MA) 1995; FRSM, FRCP 1986 (MRCP 1973); *Publications* Neuroendocrine Perspectives (1987), Clinical Endocrine Oncology (ed, 1997), Oxford Textbook of Endocrinology (ed, 2002), Handbook of Acromegaly (2002); also author of articles and chapters on: acromegaly, pituitary tumours, growth hormone, growth factors, osteoporosis; *Recreations* music, theatre, wine, Scotland; *Clubs* Garrick; *Style—* Prof John Wass; ✉ Holmby House, Sibford Ferris, Banbury, Oxfordshire OX15 5RG (tel 01295 780589); Department of Endocrinology, Churchill Hospital, Old Road, Headington, Oxford OX3 7LE (tel 01865 227621, fax 01865 742348, e-mail john.wass@noc.anglox.nhs.uk)

WASTELL, David John; s of Ian Wastell, of London, and Audrey, *née* Overton; *b* 3 January 1957; *Educ* Latymer Sch Edmonton, New Coll Oxford (MA); *Partner* Fiona Turner; 3 da (Kirsty b 27 Dec 1993, Catriona b 7 June 1996, Eilidh b 2 May 1998); *Career* Tavistock Times and Sunday Independent (Mirror Group Newspapers Grad Trainee Scheme) 1979–81, feature writer Scottish Daily Record 1981–86; Sunday Telegraph: reporter/feature writer 1986–88, political corr 1988–92, political ed 1992–98, Washington corr 1998, dep foreign ed until 2005, foreign ed 2005–; *Recreations* mountaineering, walking, sailing, skiing; *Style—* David Wastell, Esq

WATERFORD, 8 Marquess of (I 1789); Sir John Hubert de la Poer Beresford; 12 Bt (I 1665); also Baron of Le Poer (I 1375), Viscount Tyrone, Baron Beresford (both I 1720), Earl of Tyrone (I 1746), and Baron Tyrone (GB 1786, in which title he sat in House of Lords); s of 7 Marquess of Waterford (d 1934); *b* 14 July 1933; *Educ* Eton; *m* 23 July 1957, Lady Caroline Olein Geraldine Wyndham-Quin, da of 6 Earl of Dunraven and Mount-Earl (d 1965); 3 s (Henry Nicholas de la Poer, Earl of Tyrone b 1958, Lord Charles Richard de la Poer b 1960, Lord James Patrick de la Poer b 1965), 1 da (Lady Alice Rose de la Poer b 31 July 1970); *Heir* s, Earl of Tyrone; *Career* Lt RHG Supp Reserve; *Clubs* White's; *Style—* The Most Hon the Marquess of Waterford; ✉ Curraghmore, Portlaw, Co Waterford (tel 00 353 51 387102, fax 00 353 51 387481)

WATERHOUSE, Keith Spencer; CBE (1991); s of Ernest Waterhouse, and Elsie Edith Waterhouse; *b* 6 February 1929; *Educ* Osmondthorpe Cncl Sch Leeds, Leeds Coll of Commerce; *m* 1 (m dis); 1 s, 2 da; m 2, 1984 (m dis); *Career* writer and journalist 1950–; columnist: Daily Mirror 1970–86, Daily Mail 1986–; contrib to various pubns; hon fell Leeds Metropolitan Univ; FRSL 1986; *Awards* Granada Columnist of the Year 1970, IPC Descriptive Writer of the Year 1970, IPC Columnist of the Year 1973, British Press Awards Columnist of the Year 1978, Granada Special Quarter Century award 1982, British Press Awards Columnist of the Year 1990, Press Club Edgar Wallace Trophy 1997, Gerald Barry Lifetime Achievement Award 2000; *Plays* Mr & Mrs Nobody 1986, Jeffrey Bernard is Unwell 1989 (Evening Standard Comedy of the Year award 1990), Bookends 1990, Our Song 1992, Good Grief 1998; plays (with Willis Hall) incl: Billy Liar 1960, Celebration 1961, England Our England (revue, music by Dudley Moore), Squat Betty & the Sponge Room, All Things Bright and Beautiful 1963, Say Who You Are 1965, Children's Day 1969, Who's Who 1972, Saturday Sunday Monday and Filumena (adaptions from plays by Eduardo de Filippo) 1973, The Card (musical adaption from novel by Arnold Bennett, music and lyrics Tony Hatch and Jackie Trent) 1973, Worzel Gummidge (music Denis King), Budgie (musical, lyrics Don Black, music Mort Schuman); *Screenplays* (with Willis Hall) incl: Whistle Down the Wind, Billy Liar, A Kind of Loving, Man in the Middle, Pretty Polly, Lock up your Daughters; *TV Films* incl: There is a Happy Land, The Warmonger, Charlie Muffin (from Brian Fremantle's novel) 1983, This Office Life (from own novel) 1985, The Great Paper Chase (from the book Slip Up by Anthony Delano) 1986; *TV Series* incl: The Upchat Line, West End Tales, The Happy Apple, Charters and Caldicott, Andy Capp; TV series with Willis Hall: Queenie's Castle, Budgie, The Upper Crusts, Billy Liar, Worzel Gummidge (character created by Barbara Euphan Todd); *Novels* incl: There is a Happy Land (1957), Billy Liar (1959), Jubb (1963), The Bucket Shop (1968), Billy Liar on the Moon (1975), Office Life (1978), Maggie Muggins (1981), In the Mood (1983), Thinks (1984), Our Song (1988), Bimbo (1990), Unsweet Charity (1992), Good Grief (1997), Soho (2001), Palace Pier (2003); *General* The Passing of the Third Floor Buck (anthology of Punch pieces, 1974), Mondays, Thursdays (Daily Mirror columns 1976), Rhubarb, Rhubarb (1979), Fanny Peculiar (1983), Mrs Pooter's Diary (1983), Waterhouse at Large (1985), The Collected Letters of a Nobody (1986), The Theory and Practice of Lunch (1986), The Theory and Practice of Travel (1988), Waterhouse on Newspaper Style (1989, revised and expanded from Daily Mirror Style 1980), English Our English (1991), City Lights (memoirs, 1994), Streets Ahead (memoirs, 1995); *Clubs* Garrick, Pen, Chelsea Arts; *Style—* Keith Waterhouse, Esq, CBE, FRSL; ✉ 84 Coleherne Court, London SW5 0EE; agent: Nick Quinn, The Agency, 24 Pottery Lane, London W11 4LZ (tel 020 7727 1346); literary agent: David Higham Associates, 5–8 Lower John Street, London W1R 3PE (tel 020 7437 7888)

WATERHOUSE, Norman; s of Norman Waterhouse, and Jean Gardner Hamilton Reid; *b* 13 October 1954; *Educ* Salesian Coll Farnborough, Univ of Birmingham Med Sch (MB ChB); *m* Elizabeth Clare; 2 da (Suki, Imogen); *Career* plastic surgn trg: Frenchay Hosp Bristol, Hospital Tondu Bordeaux, South Australian Craniofacial Unit Adelaide, Mount Vernon Hosp Northwood, Tokyo Metropolitan Hosp; former conslt in plastic and reconstructive surgery: St Bart's Hosp and The London Hosp Whitechapel 1989–91, Charing Cross Hosp, St Mary's Hosp Paddington, Westminster Hosp; currently conslt in craniofacial, aesthetic and reconstructive plastic surgery Chelsea & Westminster Hosp; pres Royal Soc of Med (plastic surgery section); memb European Craniofacial Soc; FRCS 1982, FRCSEd 1982, FRCS (plastic surgery) 1988; *Recreations* rock climbing, mountaineering, Wado-ryu karate (2nd Dan); *Style—* Norman Waterhouse, Esq; ✉ 55 Harley Street, London W1N 1DD (tel 020 7636 4073, fax 020 7636 6417, e-mail wtrhouse@globalnet.co.uk)

WATERHOUSE, Prof Roger William; s of Ronald and Dorothy May Waterhouse; *b* 29 April 1940; *Educ* King Edward VII Sch Sheffield, CCC Oxford (MA); *m* 1, 1962 (m dis), Mania, *née* Jevinsky; 2 da, 1 s; m 2, 1979, Jaqueline Mary, *née* Dymond; 1 da, 1 s; *Career* lectr Shoreditch Coll of FE 1961–62, teacher Kibbutz Ma'abarot 1962–64, head of economics Myers Grove Comp Sch 1964–66, subsequently asst lectr, lectr, sr lectr and princ lectr Hendon Coll of Technol 1966–73, head Dept of Humanities and dean of humanities Middx Poly 1973–86, dep dir academic planning Wolverhampton Poly 1986–89, dir Derbys Coll of HE 1989–92, fndr vice-chllr Univ of Derby 1992–; chm: Interfaculty Studies Bd CNAA, Derbyshire Careers Service Ltd, Derbyshire Lifelong Learning Partnership, Highpeak Rural Action Zone; memb: Philosophy Panel CNAA, Working Pty on Credit Accumulation and Transfer Scheme (CATS), Ctee for Arts and Social Sciences CNNA, Derby Educn Ctee, Derby and Derbys Econ Partnership, E Midlands Tourism Bd; fndr and first chair SE England Consortium for CATS (SEEC), fndr and first pres Trans-European Exchange and Transfer Consortium (TEXT); Hon DUniv Middx; FRSA; *Recreations* wood-turning; *Style—* Prof Roger Waterhouse; ✉ University of Derby, Kedleston Road, Derby DE22 1GB (tel 01332 591000)

WATERHOUSE, Sir Ronald Gough Waterhouse; GBE (2002), kt (1978); s of Thomas Waterhouse, CBE (d 1961), and Doris Helena Gough (d 1993); *b* 8 May 1926; *Educ* Holywell GS, St John's Coll Cambridge (MA, LLM); *m* 1960, Sarah Selina, da of Capt Ernest Augustus Ingram (d 1954), of Bletchley Park Stud; 1 s, 2 da; *Career* RAFVR 1944–48; called to the Bar Middle Temple 1952 (bencher 1977, treas 1995), QC 1969; dep chm: Cheshire QS 1964–71, Flintshire QS 1966–71; recorder of the Crown Court 1972–77, judge of the High Court of Justice (Queen's Bench Div) 1988–96 (Family Div 1978–88), ret; judge of Employment Appeal Tbnl 1979–88, presiding judge Wales & Chester Circuit 1980–84; chm Tbnl of Inquiry into Child Abuse in N Wales 1996–2000; chm Local Govt Boundary Cmmn for Wales 1974–78, vice-pres Zoological Soc of London 1981–84 and 1991–92 (sometime memb Cncl 1972–92), chm Ind Supervisory Authy for Hunting 2000–05, memb City Disputes Panel 2002–; pres: Llangollen Int Musical Eisteddfod 1994–97, St John's Wood Soc 1994–97; Hon LLD Univ of Wales 1986; *Recreations* golf, watching cricket, music; *Clubs* Garrick, MCC, Cardiff and County, Pilgrims; *Style—* Sir Ronald Waterhouse, GBE; ✉ Greystone House, Walford, Ross-on-Wye, Herefordshire HR9 5RJ

WATERLOW, Sir Christopher Rupert; 5 Bt (UK 1873), of London; s of (Peter) Rupert Waterlow (d 1969), of Knightsbridge, London, and Jill Elizabeth, *née* Gourlay (d 1961); gs of Sir Philip Alexander Waterlow, 4 Bt (d 1973), and 3 cous twice removed of Sir Thomas Waterlow, 3 Bt, CBE, of Harrow Weald; *b* 12 August 1959; *Educ* Stonyhurst, Ravensbourne Coll of Design & Communication; *m* 17 Sept 2003, Nicola Louise, yr da of Robert McDonald, of Petts Wood Kent; *Heir* kinsman, Nicholas Waterlow; *Career* camera operator QVC The Shopping Channel; memb: Stonyhurst Assoc, Berchman Soc, Guild of Television Cameramen; fell Inst of Videography (also assessment offr); *Recreations* music, good food; *Style—* Sir Christopher Waterlow, Bt; ✉ 78 Portland Road, Bromley, Kent BR1 5AZ (e-mail chris_waterlow@qvc.com or crownproductions@hotmail.com)

WATERLOW, Sir (James) Gerard; 4 Bt (UK 1930), of Harrow Weald, Middlesex; s of Sir Thomas Waterlow, 3 Bt, CBE (d 1982); *b* 3 September 1939; *Educ* Marlborough, Trinity Coll Cambridge; *m* 1965, Diana Suzanne, yr da of Sir Thomas Skyrme, KCVO, CB, CBE, TD, JP, and Hon Mrs Suzanne Skyrme, *née* Lyle; 1 da (Amanda Jane (Mrs Jason Howard) b 1968), 1 s (Thomas James b 1970); *Heir* s, Thomas Waterlow; *Clubs* Lansdowne; *Style—* Sir Gerard Waterlow, Bt; ✉ Rushall Lodge, Pewsey, Wiltshire SN9 6EN (tel 01980 630300)

WATERMAN, Clive Adrian; s of Harvey Waterman (d 1967), of Hendon, London, and Hannah, *née* Spector (d 1995); *b* 13 August 1949; *Educ* Haberdashers' Aske's Sch Elstree, London Hosp Med Coll (BDS), Royal Dental Hosp of London (MSc); *Career* clinical asst London Hosp 1973–75 (house surgn 1973), registrar Eastman Dental Hosp 1976–77, pt/t clinical asst Guy's Hosp 1977–84, gen and specialist practice 1977–, pt/t lectr King's Coll 1985–2002, specialist in periodontics 1998–; chm GP Section Br Soc of Periodontology 1990–94, asst sec BSP 1994–95; memb: Kingston and Richmond Local Dental Ctee 1988–, Cncl BSP 1990–95, memb BDA Scientific Programme Sub-Ctee 1990–; *Recreations* cricket, skiing, squash, wine, dining; *Clubs* Riverside, Reform, MCC; *Style—* Clive Waterman, Esq; ✉ 4 Elm Grove Road, Barnes, London SW13 0BT (tel 020 8878 8986, fax 020 8878 9755, e-mail clive@c4gum.co.uk)

WATERMAN, Dr Dame Fanny; DBE (2005, CBE 2000, OBE 1971); da of Myer Waterman (d 1984), of Leeds, and Mary, *née* Behrmann (d 1978); *b* 22 March 1920; *Educ* Chapel Allerton HS Leeds, RCM; *m* Dr Geoffrey de Keyser (d 2001); 2 s; *Career* concert pianist and teacher of int repute; chm and artistic dir Leeds Int Pianoforte Competition, jury memb of prestigious piano competitions incl: the Tchaikovsky, Rubinstein (vice-pres), First Chinese Int Piano Competition, and Leeds Int (pres); fndr (with Marion Harewood) Leeds Int Pianoforte Competition 1961; vice-pres: European Piano-Teachers Assoc 1975–, Harrogate Int Festival 1999– (govr 1983–99), World Fedn of Int Music Competitions 1992–2000; tstee Edward Boyle Meml Tst 1981–96; regular broadcaster tv and radio, author of over thirty books on piano-playing and teaching; ISM Distinguished Musician Award 2000, Lifetime Achievement Award World Fedn of Int Competitions 2002, Yorkshire Soc Lifetime Achievement Award 2003; Hon Freeman City of Leeds 2004; Hon DMus Leeds 1992, Dr Univ of York 1995; FRCM 1972; *Books* incl: Me and My Piano Repertoire, Duets Books 1 & 2, The Young Pianist's Dictionary; *Recreations* travel, reading, voluntary work, cooking; *Style—* Dr Dame Fanny Waterman, DBE, FRCM; ✉ Woodgarth, Oakwood Grove, Leeds LS8 2PA (tel 0113 265 5771, fax 0113 265 0754)

WATERMAN, Howard John; *b* 23 May 1953; *Educ* Univ of Southampton (LLB), Coll of Law; *m* 1 Nov 1981, Sharon; 1 da (Lauren b 1 Sept 1988), 1 s (Craig b 31 Dec 1992); *Career* admitted slr 1977; ptnr Cameron Markby Hewitt 1984–94, ptnr Sidley Austin 1994–; memb Law Soc 1977; *Recreations* chess, bridge, sports; *Style—* Howard Waterman, Esq; ✉ The Folly, 2 Newgate Street Village, Hertfordshire SG13 8RA (tel 01707 875338); Sidley Austin (tel 020 7360 3600, e-mail hwaterman@sidley.com)

WATERMAN, Peter Alan (Pete); OBE (2005); s of John Edward Waterman (d 2002), of Coventry, and Stella, *née* Lord (d 1978); *b* 15 January 1947; *Educ* Frederick Bird Secdy Modern Coventry; *m* 1, 1970, Elizabeth Reynolds; 1 s (Paul Andrew b 1972); m 2, 1980, Julie Reeves; 1 s (Peter Alan b 1981); m 3, 1991, Denise Gyngell; 2 da (Toni Tuesday b 1990, Charlie Ella b 1991); *Career* record producer; former disc jockey at local pubs and Mecca dancehall, former Arts and Repertoire man for various record cos; formed Loose Ends Productions with Peter Collins working with artists incl Musical Youth and Nick Kershaw until 1983, fndr ptnr Stock Aitken Waterman (with Mike Stock and Matt Aitken) 1984–93; has won numerous Silver, Gold and Platinum Discs since 1985 for writing and/or producing artists incl: Princess, Hazell Dean, Dead or Alive, Bananarama, Mel and Kim, Sinitta, Rick Astley, Kylie Minogue, Brother Beyond, Jason Donovan, Donna Summer, Sonia, Big Fun, Cliff Richard, Westlife, Steps; involved with charity work incl SAW Goes to the Albert (Royal Marsden Hosp) and records: Let it Be (Ferry Aid), The Harder I Try (Young Variety Club of GB), Help (Comic Relief), Lets All Chant, I Haven't Stopped Dancing Yet and Use It Up and Wear It Out (Help a London Child), Ferry 'Cross the Mersey (Mersey Aid), Do They Know It's Christmas? (Ethiopia Famine Appeal), You've Got a Friend (Childline), Especially For You (Children In Need), Thank Abba for the Music (Brits School); judge: Pop Idol (ITV) 2001 and 2003, Popstars: The Rivals (ITV) 2002; ldr of consortium that purchased the first passenger part of BR to be privatised 1993; Hon DBA Coventry Univ 2001, Hon DMus Univ of Liverpool 2004; *Awards* BPI Best British Producers 1988; Music Week Top Producers for: Singles (1st) and Albums (3rd) 1987, Singles (1st) and Albums (1st) 1988 and 1989; Ivor Novello awards (UK): Songwriters of the Year 1987, 1988 and 1989, Writers of Most Performed Works 1987, 1988 and 1989; BMI awards (USA) Writers of Most Performed Works 1987, 1988 and 1989, Jasrac awards (Japan) and Cash awards (Hong Kong) Writers of Most Performed Foreign Works 1989, Music Week Award for Outstanding Achievement in the Music Industry 1999; *Recreations* steam railways, model railways; *Style—* Dr Peter Waterman, Esq, OBE

WATERMAN, Prof Peter George; s of George Leonard Waterman (d 1992), and Queenie Rose Waterman (d 1988); *b* 28 April 1946; *Educ* Judd GS Tonbridge, Univ of London (BPharm, DSc), Univ of Strathclyde (PhD); *m* 1968, Margaret, da of Carl Humble; *Career* Univ of Strathclyde: asst lectr 1969–72, lectr 1972–83, sr lectr 1983, reader 1983–87, personal prof 1987, prof of phytochemistry Dept of Pharmaceutical Sciences 1990; dir Centre for Phytochemistry Southern Cross Univ NSW 1999–2003, currently emeritus prof of phytochemistry; formerly dir of natural products prog Strathclyde Inst for Drug Research 1991–99; sr res Nat Museums of Kenya 1983–85; founding ceo Australian Phytochemicals Ltd, formerly dir BioProspect Ltd; conslt: Forestry Res Inst of Malaysia, Western Australian Herbarium, Australian Nat Herbarium, ODA; Tate and Lyle award Phytochemical Soc of Europe 1983; author of 6 books and numerous papers in scientific jls; former ed-in-chief Biochemical Systematics and Ecology; Hon Dr Université de Franche-Comte 1994; memb: Phytochemical Soc of Europe, American Soc for Pharmacognosy, Linnean Soc, Int Soc for Chemical Ecology; FRSE 1991; *Recreations* ornithology, conservation of rainforest remnants; *Style*— Prof Peter G Waterman, FRSE; ✉ Centre for Phytochemistry and Pharmacology, Southern Cross University, PO Box 157, Lismore, NSW 2480, Australia (tel 61 2 6622 3211, fax 61 2 6622 3459, e-mail pwaterma@scu.edu.au)

WATERPARK, 7 Baron (I 1729); Sir Frederick Caryll Philip Cavendish; 8 Bt (GB 1755); s of Brig-Gen Frederick Cavendish, bro of 6 Baron and 6 in descent from William Cavendish, natural s of 3 Duke of Devonshire; suc unc 1948; *b* 6 October 1926; *Educ* Eton, RMC Medal of Honour; *m* 17 April 1951, Danièle, da of Roger Guirche, of Paris; 1 s, 2 da; *Heir* s, Hon Roderick Cavendish; *Career* served: Grenadier Gds, Kenya Police Reserve; md Spartan Air Services 1955–60; dir: Handley Page Ltd 1968–70, Airborne Group plc 1990–93; CSE Aviation Ltd: sales dir 1962, dep chm 1984, chief exec 1989–90; dep chm and md CSE Int 1984–90; dir D T Dobie (East Africa) Ltd 1995–; tstee RAF Museum 1994–; *Clubs* Cavalry and Guards', The Air Squadron; *Style*— The Rt Hon Lord Waterpark

WATERS, Brian Richard Anthony; s of late Montague Waters, QC, of London, and late Jessica Freedman; *b* 27 March 1944; *Educ* City of London Sch, St John's Coll Cambridge (MA), Univ of Cambridge (DipArch), PCL (DipTP); *m* 1 Nov 1974, Myriam Leiva, da of José Ramon Leiva Alvarez, of Bogotá, Colombia; *Career* chartered architect and town planner; princ The Boisot Waters Cohen Partnership (design), ptnr Studio & Gallery Crown Reach; dir Land Research Unit Ltd; pres Cities of London and Westminster Soc of Architects 1980–82, vice-pres RIBA 1988–89 and 1991–92 (memb Cncl 1987–92); chm Nat Architecture Conf London 1991, London Planning Devpt Forum 1990–; memb Cncl Assoc of Consultant Architects 1997– (vice-pres 2003–06, pres 2007–); jt publishing ed Planning in London; town planning corr Architects' Jl 1997–, ed Architectural Journalist of the Year commendation 1979, 1982, 1984 and 1986; pres John Carpenter Club (Old Citizens' Assoc) 2004–05; Freeman: City of London, Co of Chartered Architects (memb Ct 1991–, Master 2002); RIBA, MRTPI; *Books* author of books, articles and reviews for various architectural pubns, Inst Economic Affairs and CPC; *Recreations* tennis, dressage, painting (exhbn of work at Leighton House 2002), pots, Siberian huskies, growing lavender in Cataluña; *Clubs* RAC, Hurlingham; *Style*— Brian R A Waters, Esq; ✉ Studio Crown Reach, 149A Grosvenor Road, London SW1V 3JY (tel 020 7828 6555, fax 020 7834 9470, e-mail brian@bwcp.co.uk, website www.bwcp.co.uk)

WATERS, Brian Wallace; s of Stanley Wallace Waters (d 1993), of Harpenden, Herts, and Kathleen, *née* Thake (d 2002); *b* 24 November 1936; *Educ* City of London Sch, Harvard Business Sch; *m* 1 April 1961, Gillian, da of Herbert William Harris (d 1976); 4 s (Andrew b 1963, James b 1965, Richard b 1967, Mark b 1975); *Career* Ernst & Young: ptnr 1968, exec vice-chm (Europe) 1979–82, chm (Europe) 1982–85, managing ptnr East Anglia 1985–92, managing ptnr Ernst & Young Birmingham 1992–96, managing ptnr Midlands Region 1994–97; chm London Soc of Chartered Accountants 1976–77, memb Cncl ICAEW 1983–87, memb Exec Ctee Union Européennes des Experts Comptables 1983–87; memb: Horserace Betting Levy Appeal Tbnl 1986–, The Evelyn Tst 1997–; MFH United Hunt Club Co Cork 1998–; Worshipful Co of Drapers; FCA 1960, FCMA 1962; *Recreations* cricket, hunting, horse racing, fishing; *Clubs* MCC, Lord's Taverners; *Style*— Brian Waters, Esq; ✉ The Chequers, Preston, Hitchin, Hertfordshire SG4 7TY

WATERS, Donald Henry; OBE (1994); s of Henry Lethbridge Waters (d 1978), of Edinburgh, and Jean Manson, *née* Baxter (d 1987); *b* 17 December 1937; *Educ* George Watson's Coll Edinburgh, Inverness Royal Acad; *m* 5 May 1962, June Leslie, da of Andrew Hutchison (d 1984), of Forres, Moray; 2 da (Jennifer Dawn b 1963, Gillian Claire b 1966), 1 s (Andrew Henry Lethbridge b 1969); *Career* Grampian Television plc: dir 1979–97, chief exec 1987–97, dep chm 1993–97; dir: John M Henderson Ltd 1972–75, Glenburnie Properties Ltd 1976–97 (chm 1993–97), Scottish Television and Grampian Sales Ltd (STAGS) 1980–98, Blenheim Travel Ltd 1981–91, Moray Firth Radio Ltd 1982–97, Independent Television Publications Ltd 1987–90, Cablevision Scotland plc 1987–91, Central Scotland Radio Ltd Scot FM 1994–96 (chm 1995–96), GRT Bus Group plc 1994–95, British Linen Bank Group Ltd 1995–99, Scottish Media Group plc 1997–2005, Digital 3 and 4 Ltd 1997–98, James Johnston & Co of Elgin Ltd 1999–, Aberdeen Asset Mgmnt plc 2000–; memb: Ct British Linen Bank Ltd 1994–98, Consignia Advsy Bd for Scotland (formerly Scottish Post Office Bd) 1996–2003, North of Scotland Bd Bank of Scotland 1999–2001; visiting prof of film and media studies Univ of Stirling 1991, memb Cncl Cinema and Television Benevolent Fund 1986–99, chm Celtic Film and TV Assoc 1994–96 (tstee Scotland 1990–97), memb Independent Television Association Ltd 1994–97; chm Police Dependent Tst Grampian Region 1991–96, dir Aberdeen Royal Hosps NHS Tst 1996–99 (chm New Aberdeen Royal Children's Hosp Project Steering Gp), jt chm Grampian Cancer Macmillan 1999–2004; memb: RTS 1988–, BAFTA UK 1980 (Scottish vice-chm 1992–97), Cncl SATRO, CBI Scotland Cncl 1994–2001, Grampian Initiative, Grampian and Islands Family Tst (GIFT) 1988–2006; govr Univ of Aberdeen 1998–99; a Burgess of Guild Aberdeen 1979– (assessor 1998–2001); MICAS 1961, FRSA 1990; *Recreations* gardening, travel, hill walking; *Clubs* Royal Northern and Univ Aberdeen (past chm); *Style*— Donald Waters, Esq, OBE, CA; ✉ Balquhidder, 141 North Deeside Road, Milltimber, Aberdeen AB13 0JS (tel 01224 867131, e-mail waters@rsc.co.uk)

WATERS, Malcolm Ian; QC (1997); s of Ian Power Waters (d 2003), of Purley, Surrey, and Yvonne, *née* Mosley (d 2004); *b* 11 October 1953; *Educ* Whitgift Sch, St Catherine's Coll Oxford (MA, BCL); *m* 2002, Setsu Sato; *Career* called to the Bar Lincoln's Inn 1977; memb: Chancery Bar Assoc 1978, Professional Negligence Bar Assoc 1992, Charity Law Assoc 1996; *Publications* Wurtzburg and Mills Building Society Law (jtly, 15 edn, 1989), The Building Societies Act 1986 (jtly, 1987), The Law of Investor Protection (jtly, 3 edn, 2003), Halsbury's Laws of England Vol 19 (1): Friendly Societies (conslt ed, 2007 reissue); contrib: Standard Conditions of Sale (1 to 4 edn), Standard Commercial Property Conditions (1 and 2 edns), Halsbury's Laws of England (const ed, 4 edn, 2007; *Recreations* music, gardening; *Style*— Malcolm Waters, Esq, QC; ✉ Radcliffe Chambers, 11 New Square, Lincoln's Inn, London WC2A 3QB (tel 020 7831 0081, fax 020 7405 2560, e-mail mwaters@radcliffechambers.com)

WATERS, Sarah; *b* 1966, Pembrokeshire; *Educ* Univ of Kent, Lancaster Univ, Univ of London; *Career* writer; former assoc lectr Open Univ; *Publications* Tipping the Velvet (1998, TV adaptation 2002, Betty Trask Award 1999, Library Jl's Best Book of the Year 1999, Mail on Sunday/John Llewellyn Rhys Prize 1999, NY Times Notable Book of the Year Award 1999, Lambda Literary Award for Fiction 2000), Affinity (1999, American Library Assoc GLBT Roundtable Book Award 2000, Ferro-Grumley Award for Lesbian and Gay Fiction 2000, Somerset Maugham Award 2000, Sunday Times Young Writer of the Year Award 2000, shortlist Lambda Literary Award for Fiction 2000, shortlist Mail on Sunday/John Llewellyn Rhys Prize 2000), Fingersmith (2002, TV adaptation 2005, British Book Awards Author of the Year 2002, Crime Writers' Assoc Ellis Peters Historical Dagger 2002, shortlist Man Booker Prize for Fiction 2002, shortlist Orange Prize for Fiction 2002), The Night Watch (2006, shortlist Man Booker Prize for Fiction 2006, shortlist Orange Prize for Fiction 2006); *Style*— Ms Sarah Waters; ✉ c/o Nick Harrop, Greene & Heaton, 37 Goldhawk Road, London W12 8QQ (tel 020 8749 0315, fax 020 8749 0318)

WATERSON, Prof Michael John; s of Geoffrey Waterson, of Burton Joyce, Notts, and Christine Mary Waterson; *b* 29 July 1950, Meriden, Warks; *Educ* Bude GS, Univ of Warwick (BA, PhD), LSE (MSc); *m* 1972, Sally Ann, *née* Davis; 1 s (Thomas Philip b 16 Nov 1984), 1 da (Alice Jane b 11 July 1989); *Career* Univ of Newcastle upon Tyne: lectr in economics 1974–86, reader in economics 1986–88; visiting lectr in economics Univ of Sydney 1987–88, prof of economics Univ of Reading 1988–91, prof of economics Univ of Warwick 1991–; chm Utilities Appeal Panel Guernsey 2002–, memb Competition Cmmn 2005–, specialist advsr Sub-Ctee B House of Lords Select Ctee 2005–06; FRSA 1989; *Publications* Economic Theory of the Industry (1984), Regulation of the Firm and Natural Monopoly (1988), Buyer Power and Competition in European Food Retailing (jtly, 2002); *Recreations* walking, playing musical instruments; *Style*— Prof Michael Waterson; ✉ Department of Economics, University of Warwick, Coventry CV4 7AL (tel 024 7652 3427, fax 024 7652 3032, e-mail michael.waterson@warwick.ac.uk)

WATERSON, Nigel Christopher; MP; s of late James Waterson, and Katherine Mahon; *b* 12 October 1950; *Educ* Leeds GS, The Queen's Coll Oxford; *m* Dr Barbara Judge; *Career* slr and barr; pres Oxford Univ Cons Assoc 1970, res asst to Sally Oppenheim MP 1972–73, chm Bow Gp 1986–87 (hon patron 1993–95); MP (Cons) Eastbourne 1992– (Parly candidate (Cons) Islington S and Finsbury 1979); PPS to: Gerald Malone as Min for Health 1995–96, to Rt Hon Michael Heseltine as Dep PM 1996–97; oppn whip 1997–99, shadow min DETR 1999–2001, oppn frontbench spokesman on trade and industry 2001–02, shadow pensions min 2003–, memb Work and Pensions Select Ctee 2003–05; formerly: vice-chm All Pty Head Injuries Gp, vice-chm Cons Backbench Tport Ctee, vice-chm Cons Backbench Tourism Ctee, sec Cons Backbench Shipping and Shipbuilding Ctee; currently: co-chm All Pty Parly Gp for Older People, All Pty Disablement Gp, Br-American Parly Gp, Parly Maritime Gp, Lords and Commons Solicitors Gp, All Pty Br-Caribbean Gp, All Pty Czech and Slovak Gp, Inter-Parly Union, Parly Advsy Cncl for Tport Safety, All Pty Cricket Gp, vice-chm All Pty Br-Greek Gp, sec Br-Cyprus Cwlth Parly Assoc Gp; memb IPU; cncllr London Borough of Hammersmith and Fulham 1974–78; chm: Hammersmith Cons Assoc 1987–90, Hammersmith and Fulham Jt Mgmnt Ctee 1988–90; memb Mgmnt Ctee Stonham Housing Assoc Hostel for Ex-Offenders 1988–90, vice-pres Eastbourne Branch BLESMA; *Recreations* reading, music; *Clubs* Eastbourne Constitutional, Coningsby; *Style*— Nigel Waterson, Esq, MP; ✉ House of Commons, London SW1A 0AA (e-mail watersonn@parliament.uk)

WATERSTONE, Timothy John Stuart; s of Malcolm Stuart Waterstone, MBE (d 1977), of Maresfield, E Sussex, and Sylvia Catherine, *née* Sawday (d 1967); *b* 30 May 1939; *Educ* Tonbridge, St Catharine's Coll Cambridge (MA); *m* 1, Oct 1962 (m dis 1971), Patricia Harcourt-Poole; 2 s (Richard b 1963, Martin b 1965), 1 da (Sylvie b 1969); m 2, Oct 1972 (m dis 1990), Clare Perkins; 2 da (Amanda b 1975, Maya b 1977), 1 s (Oliver b 1980); m 3, Feb 1991, Mary Rose Alison; 2 da (Lucy Rose b 1992, Daisy Alison b 1994); *Career* Carritt Moran & Co Calcutta 1962–64, Allied Breweries plc 1965–73, W H Smith Group plc 1973–81, fndr chm and chief exec Waterstone & Co 1982–93; fndr chm HMV Media Gp plc (merged business of Waterstone's, Dillons and HMV) 1998–2001; fndr and chm Chelsea Stores Ltd (incl Daisy & Tom, and Early Learning Centre 2004) 1996–; chm Priory Investments Ltd 1990–95, dep chm Sinclair-Stevenson Publishers Ltd 1989–92; memb Bd: Futurestart (BT Venture Capital Fund) 1992–, Hill Samuel UK Emerging Cos Investment Tst plc 1996–2001, Yale Univ Press 1992–, Virago Publishers 1995–96; chm DTI Working Gp on Smaller Quoted Companies and Private Investors 1999; tstee International House 1986–92, memb Ctee Booker Prize 1986–93; chm: Princes Youth Business Tst Awards 1990, Shelter 25th Anniversary Appeal 1991–92, London Int Festival of Theatre 1990–92, The Elgar Fndn 1992–98, KCL Library Bd 1999–2002; co-fndr Bookaid 1992; dir: The Academy of Ancient Music 1990–95, The London Philharmonic Orchestra 1990–97; memb: Bd Downing Classic VCT 1998–2003, National Gallery Co 1996–2003; *Fiction* Lilley & Chase (1994), An Imperfect Marriage (1995), A Passage of Lives (1996); *Non-Fiction* Swimming Against The Stream (2006); *Recreations* being with Rosie Alison; *Clubs* Garrick; *Style*— Timothy Waterstone, Esq; ✉ Burdett House, 15 Buckingham Street, London WC2N 6DU

WATERWORTH, Sir Alan William; KCVO (2007); s of late James William Waterworth, and late Alice Waterworth; *b* 22 September 1931; *Educ* Uppingham, Trinity Coll Cambridge (MA); *m* 1955, Myriam Baete; 4 c (Richard b 1956, Shirley (Mrs Duncan) b 1958, Andrew b 1961, Nigel b 1963); *Career* Waterworth Bros Ltd: sometime dir and md, chm 1954–69; Skelmesdale Devpt Corporation: memb 1971–85, dir and dep chm 1979–85; chm Liverpool City Magistrates 1985–89; pres Merseyside IoD 1974–77, dir Everton FC 1970–93 (chm 1974–77); chm: Liverpool Boys Assoc 1965–75, Merseyside Youth Assoc 1971–75, Merseyside Police Authy 1984–92; tstee National Museums and Galleries on Merseyside 1994–2004; Hon Col Merseyside ACF 1994–2007; High Sheriff of Merseyside 1992, HM Lord-Lt Merseyside 1993–2006; Hon LLD Univ of Liverpool 2001, hon fell Liverpool John Moores Univ; KStJ 1994; *Clubs* Athenaeum (Liverpool), Artists (Liverpool), Army and Navy; *Style*— Sir Alan Waterworth, KCVO; ✉ Crewood Hall, Kingsley, Cheshire WA6 8HR (tel 01928 788316)

WATES, Andrew Trace Allan; DL (Surrey 2006); s of Sir Ronald Wallace Wates (d 1986), and Lady Phyllis Mary, *née* Trace (d 2006); *b* 16 November 1940; *Educ* Oundle, Emmanuel Coll Cambridge (BA); *m* 19 June 1965, Sarah Mary de Burgh Wates, *née* Macartney; 5 s (Timothy Andrew de Burgh b 3 June 1966, Jonathan Giles Macartney b 16 June 1967, Richard James Alexander b 1 Feb 1971, Simon David Sam b 17 March 1975, William Ronald James b 11 April 1977 (decd)); *Career* joined Wates Gp 1964, dir sales and mktg Wates Construction 1972–73, chm Wates Leisure 1973, chm Wates Gp 2000–06, currently chm Wates Family Holdings; chm: United Racecourses 1996–2003, Leisure & Media VCT 2002–, Gambado Ltd 2004–; dir Jockey Club Racecourses (formerly Racecourse Holdings Trust) 1994–; dir: Inst for Family Business 2004–, International Family Business Network 2004–; patron and tstee various Surrey charities; FNAEA; *Recreations* horse racing, golf, shooting, fishing; *Clubs* White's, Turf; *Style*— Andrew Wates, Esq, DL; ✉ Henfold House, Beare Green, Surrey RH5 4RW (tel 01306 631324, fax 01306 631794); Wates Group Limited, Wates House, Station Approach, Leatherhead, Surrey KT22 7SW (tel 01372 861051, fax 01372 861053, e-mail andrew.wates@wates.co.uk)

WATHEN, Rev Mark William Gerard; TD (1946); s of Gerard Anstruther Wathen, CIE (d 1958), and Melicent Louis, *née* Buxton (d 1984); *b* 18 September 1912; *Educ* Gresham's; *m* 1940, Rosemary (d 2006), da of Charles Hartridge, of W Sussex, and his w Kathleen, er da of Sir Fortescue Flannery, 1 Bt; 2 s (Roderick b 1940, Jonathan b 1951), 2 da (Primula b 1946 d 1991, Erica (Mrs Jonathan Strange) b 1949); *Career* served WWII 11 (HAC) Regt RHA North Africa and Italy 1939–45; dir Barclays Bank (City, Ipswich, Norwich) 1948–72; High Sheriff Norfolk 1968; memb Gen Synod C of E 1970–80, church cmmr 1973–78, ordained deacon and priest 1982, priest i/c St Columba's Church Isle of Skye 1982–92; Master Worshipful Co of Mercers 1963; *Recreations* the church, reading and writing; *Clubs* Brooks's, MCC; *Style*— The Rev Mark Wathen, TD; ✉ Tollgate Cottage, Marsham, Norwich NR10 5PX (tel 01263 732673)

WATKIN, Dr Bernard Curtis; s of Harold Victor Watkin (d 1989), and Mary Curtis (d 1965); *b* 29 August 1931; *Educ* Hymers Coll, Tiffin Sch, Univ of London (MB BS), St Bartholomew's Hosp (DPhysMed); *m* 21 Oct 1967, Jennifer Ann, da of Dr Edward Street; 2 da (Eleanor Curtis b 5 April 1971, Jessica Kate b 5 Feb 1973); *Career* hon clinical asst in rheumatology St Stephen's Hosp London; registrar Arthur Stanley Inst of Rheumatology Middx Hosp London, registrar in physical med St Thomas' Hosp London, scientific advsr in orthopaedics ICI Ltd, sports injury conslt to IMG (International Management Group); med offr to BCU at Olympic Games Munich 1972; memb: Br Assoc of Manipulative Med, Soc of Orthopaedic Med; FRSM; *Books* contrib to various books on lumbar disorders; paper on Tempero-Mandibula Joint in Rheumatoid Arthritis (1969); *Style*— Dr Bernard Watkin; ✉ 30A Wimpole Street, London W1G 8YA (tel 08700 760211, fax 020 7935 8269)

WATKIN, (Francis) David; s of John Wilfrid Watkin, and Beatrice Lynda Dadswell; *b* 23 March 1925; *Career* director of photography; served Army 1944–47; American Academy Award 1985, Br Academy Award 1986; *Film* incl: The Knack, Help, Marat Sade, The Charge of the Light Brigade, Catch 22, The Devils, The Boyfriend, Jesus of Nazareth, Chariots of Fire, White Nights, Out of Africa, Moonstruck, Memphis Belle, Hamlet, This Boy's Life, Jane Eyre, Bogus, Tea with Mussolini; *Documentary* films incl The England of Elizabeth; *Books* Why Is There Only One Word For Thesaurus? (autobiography); *Recreations* music, reading; *Style*— David Watkin; ✉ 6 Sussex Mews, Brighton BN12 1GZ

WATKIN, Prof David John; s of Thomas Charles Watkin (d 2006), and Vera Mary, *née* Saunders (d 1996); *b* 7 April 1941; *Educ* Farnham GS, Trinity Hall Cambridge (MA, PhD, LittD); *Career* Univ of Cambridge: fell Peterhouse 1970–, lectr in history of art 1972–, head Dept of History of Art 1989–92 and 2007–07, prof of history of architecture 2001– (reader 1993); memb: Historic Bldgs Advsy Ctee, Historic Bldgs and Monuments Cmmn 1980–95, vice-chm Georgian Gp; Hon Dr of Arts De Montfort Univ 1996; Hon FRIBA 2001; FSA 1979; *Books* Thomas Hope 1769–1831 and The Neo-Classical Idea (1968), The Life and Work of CR Cockerell RA (1974), Morality and Architecture (1977), English Architecture: A Concise History (1979, 2 edn 2000), The Rise of Architectural History (1980), Neo-Classical and Nineteenth Century Architecture (with Robin Middleton, 1980), Athenian Stuart: Pioneer of the Greek Revival (1982), The English Vision: The Picturesque in Architecture, Landscape and Garden Design (1982), A History of Western Architecture (1986, 4 edn 2005), German Architecture and the Classical Ideal: 1740–1840 (with Tilman Mellinghoff, 1987), Sir John Soane: Enlightenment Thought and the Royal Academy Lectures (1996), The Age of Wilkins: The Architecture of Improvement (2000), Sir John Soane: The Royal Academy Lectures (2000), Morality and Architecture Revisited (2001), Alfred Gilbey: A Memoir by Some Friends (ed, 2001), John Simpson: The Queen's Gallery Buckingham Palace and other Works (with Richard John, 2002), The Architect King: George III and the Culture of the Enlightenment (2004), Radical Classicism: The Architecture of Quinlan Terry (2006); *Clubs* Brooks's, Beefsteak; *Style*— Prof David Watkin; ✉ Peterhouse, Cambridge CB2 1RD (tel 01223 338200); Albany, Piccadilly, London W1J 0AU

WATKINS, Maj-Gen Guy Hansard; CB (1986), OBE (1974); s of Col Alfred Norman Mitchell Watkins (d 1970), and Sylvia Christine, *née* Downing (d 1988); *b* 30 November 1933; *Educ* The King's Sch Canterbury; *m* 15 Feb 1958, Sylvia Margaret, da of William Lawrence Grant, of Walton-on-the-Hill, Surrey; 2 s (Michael b 1959, Peter b 1971), 2 da (Anne-Marie b 1961, Carol b 1965); *Career* cmmnd RA 1953, CO 39 Regt RA (BAOR) 1973, Task Force Cdr (BAOR) 1977, Dir Public Relations (Army) 1980, Cmd Artillery Div (BAOR) 1982, Dir Gen Army Manning and Recruiting 1985, ret 1986; chief exec The Royal Hong Kong Jockey Club 1986–96, chm Hong Kong Breeders Club Int Advsy Bd 2005–; dir: British Bloodstock Agency plc 1996, Racecourse Holdings Trust 1996; chm Sportal Racing 1999; hon racing conslt Macau Jockey Club 1999–2001; Liveryman Worshipful Co of Farriers; *Recreations* racing, golf, fishing; *Clubs* Hong Kong Jockey, West Sussex Golf, Oriental; *Style*— Maj-Gen Guy Watkins, CB, OBE

WATKINS, Prof Hugh Christian; *b* 7 June 1959; *Educ* Gresham's, St Bartholomew's Med Coll London (BSc, MB BS, Brackenbury and Bourne prize in gen med), Univ of London (PhD, MD), Univ of Oxford (MA); *Career* house physician Professorial Med Unit St Bartholomew's Hosp London 1984–85, SHO John Radcliffe Hosp Oxford 1985–87, registrar in gen med and cardiology Thomas' Hosp London 1988–89; Harvard Med Sch: research fell in med 1990–94, instr in med 1994–95, asst prof of med 1995–96; concurrently: assoc physician Brigham and Women's Hosp Boston 1994–96, hon sr lectr Dept of Cardiological Scis St George's Hosp Med Sch London 1995 (lectr 1990–94); Field Marshal Alexander prof of cardiovascular med (head Dept of Cardiovascular Med) Univ of Oxford 1996–, professorial fell Exeter Coll Oxford 1996–, hon conslt in cardiology and gen med John Radcliffe Hosp Oxford 1996–; Young Research Worker Prize Br Cardiac Soc 1992, Goulstonian lectr RCP 1998, Graham Bull Prize RCP 2003; memb Editoral Bd: Br Med Jl, Circulation, Heart; author of original reports, reviews, editorials and book chapters; FMedSci 1999, fell American Heart Assoc (FAHA) 2001, FRCP; *Style*— Prof Hugh C Watkins; ✉ Department of Cardiovascular Medicine, Level 5, John Radcliffe Hospital, Oxford OX3 9DU (e-mail hugh.watkins@cardiov.ox.ac.uk)

WATKINS, James Arthur; s of William Arthur Watkins (d 2001), of York, and Mary Lilian Chapman; *b* 26 September 1945; *Educ* Archbishop Holgate's Sch York, Univ of Leeds (LLB); *m* 1, 4 March 1967 (m dis), Ursula Barbara; 2 da (Philippa Jane Langford b 1975, Victoria Joanne Langford b 1977); m 2, 7 Jan 1993, Lisa, *née* Cattermole; 1 s (Oscar George James b 6 Sept 1995), 2 da (Cosima Amelia Clementine b 6 Nov 1996, Scarlett Adelaide b 10 Jan 2001); *Career* Linklaters & Paines: articled clerk 1967, asst slr 1969, ptnr 1975–94; legal dir Trafalgar House plc 1994–96, legal dir Schroders plc 1996–97, dir and gp gen counsel Jardine Matheson Group 1997–2003; Freeman City of London 1976, memb Worshipful Co of Solicitors 1976; memb: Law Soc 1969, Int Bar Assoc 1978, Union Internationale des Avocats 1980; *Recreations* golf, reading, music, food and wine; *Clubs* Hurlingham, Annabel's, RAC, Coombe Hill Golf, Hong Kong, Hong Kong Jockey, Shek-O Country; *Style*— James Watkins, Esq; ✉ 63 Royal Castle, 23 Pik Sha Road, Clearwater Bay, Hong Kong (tel 852 2809 2338, fax 852 2809 2182, e-mail jaw@jamesawatkins.com)

WATKINS, Prof Jeffrey Clifton; s of Colin Hereward Watkins (d 1983), and Amelia Miriam Watkins (d 1981); *b* 20 December 1929; *Educ* Perth Modern Sch, Univ of Western Aust (MSc, Hackett travelling studentship award), Univ of Cambridge (PhD); *m* 1973, Beatrice Joan, da of Morton Thacher, and Enid Elizabeth; 1 s (Timothy Douglas b 10 Sept 1973), 1 da (Katherine Helen b 9 Oct 1975); *Career* postdoctoral research fell: Univ of Cambridge (Rockefeller fell) 1954–55, Yale Univ 1955–57, ANU 1958–65 (fell 1961–65); scientific offr ARC Inst of Animal Physiology Babraham 1965–67, memb Scientific Staff MRC Neuropsychiatry Unit Carshalton 1968–73; Univ of Bristol Sch of Med: sr research fell Depts of Physiology and Pharmacology 1973–83, hon sr research fell Dept of Pharmacology 1983–89, hon prof of pharmacology 1989–99, prof emeritus 1999–; dir: Tocris Neuramin Ltd 1985–94, Tocris Cookson Ltd 1994–2006; Wakeman Award (USA) for outstanding achievement in neuroscience 1992, Dana Award (USA) for pioneering achievement in health 1994, Bristol-Myers Squibb Award (USA) for distinguished achievement in neuroscience research 1995, Thudichum Medal for distinguished contributions to neuroscience 2000, Wellcome Gold Medal in Pharmacology 2001; memb: Int Brain Research Orgn 1969, Br Pharmacological Soc 1974 (hon fell), Br Physiological Soc 1975, (American) Soc for Neuroscience 1988; memb Academia Europaea 1989; FRS 1988, FIBiol 1998, FMedSci 1999; *Books* The NMDA Receptor (ed with G L Collingridge, 1989, 2 edn 1995); *Recreations* the countryside; *Style*— Prof Jeffrey Watkins, FRS; ✉ 8 Lower Court Road, Lower Almondsbury, Bristol BS32 4DX (tel 01454 613829, e-mail jeffwatkins@onetel.com)

WATKINS, John; s of Charles Watkins, and Kathleen Myrtle, *née* Cullis (d 1969); *b* 16 December 1943; *Educ* Yeovil Sch; *m* 2 Sept 1967, Diane Mary, da of Cyril Charles Hooper; 2 s (James Charles Cullis b 24 Oct 1969, Alastair John Cullis b 2 Aug 1972), 2 da (Philippa Louise b 11 Sept 1974, Gemma Kate b 7 Sept 1978); *Career* articled clerk Howard Howes & Co 1962–68; ptnr: Mazars Neville Russell (formerly Neville Russell) 1972–89, Ernst & Young 1989–97; dir: Trustee Services Company Ltd, Lisunqwe plc, Red Rock Resources plc, Regency Mines plc, Starvest plc, Greatland Gold plc, Franchise Investment Strategies plc; sole tax practitioner and business advsr; FCA (ACA 1968); *Clubs* RAC; *Style*— John Watkins, Esq; ✉ 67 Park Road, Woking, Surrey GU22 7DH (tel 01483 771992, fax 01483 772087, e-mail john@jwca.co.uk)

WATKINS, Paul Alan; s of John Llewellyn Watkins (decd), and Patricia Frances Watkins; *b* 5 February 1946; *Educ* King Henry VIII GS Abergavenny, Univ of Manchester Sch of Architecture (BA, BArch); *Career* Tripe & Wakeham Partnership 1972–74; Sheppard Robson (architects, planners and interior designers) London: joined 1974, assoc 1979–88, ptnr 1988–2006, conslt 2006–; projects incl: Royal Mint Court London EC3 (offices, residential and community use) 1985–90, 103 Wigmore St London W1 (major office refurbishment) 1993–96, 1 Silk St London EC2 (major HQ office renovation) 1994–96, 1 St James's Sq London SW1 (HQ office redevelopment) 1995–98, 70 Grosvenor Sq London W1 (HQ office redevelopment) 1997–99, 10 Aldermanbury London EC2 (HQ Office redevelopment) 1997–2000, 95 Queen Victoria St London EC4 (office and leisure redevelopment) 2000–03, One Hanover Square London W1 (retail, office and residential redevelopment) 2002–04, Abford House London SW1 2004–; RIBA; *Recreations* running, badminton, tennis; *Style*— Paul Watkins, Esq; ✉ Sheppard Robson, 77 Parkway, London NW1 7PU (tel 020 7504 1700, fax 020 7504 1701, e-mail paul.watkins@sheppardrobson.com)

WATKINS, Paul Rhys; s of John Watkins, of Argoed, Gwent, and Esther Elizabeth Picton Evans; *b* 4 January 1970; *Educ* Pontllanfraith Comp, Yehudi Menuhin Sch of Music, St Catharine's Coll Cambridge; *m* 28 Aug 1993, Jennifer Alexandra, da of Jaime Laredo; *Career* cellist; studied under William Pleeth, Melissa Phelps and Johannes Goritzki; former memb EC Youth Orch; winner string section BBC Young Musician of the Year 1988, award winner for best performance of a cmmnd work Scheveningen Int Music Competition Holland 1991, winner Leeds Conductors' Competition 2002; princ cellist BBC Symphony Orch 1990–98; memb Nash Ensemble; conductor Yehudi Menuhin Sch Orch 1994–98; prof Royal Acad of Music; guest princ: LSO, Eng Chamber Orch, RPO, LPO, London Sinfonietta, Bournemouth Symphony Orch; memb World Orch for Peace (at invitation of Sir Georg Solti, 50 anniversary of UN); numerous television and radio appearances, incl subject of Statements (BBC series), featured soloist Elgar Cello Concerto Masterworks (BBC 2); featured artist Young Artists New Year Series (presented by Park Lane Gp) 1993; memb: Musicians Union, RSA, Advsy Cncl Violoncello Soc of London; hon fell Welsh Coll of Music and Drama; FRSA, Hon ARAM; *Performances* incl: Elgar Concerto (with BBC Symphony Orch under Andrew Davis) BBC Proms 1993, Strauss' Don Quixote (with BBC Symphony Orch under Alexander Lazarev) Royal Festival Hall 1994, Lutoslawski's Cello Concerto (with BBC Symphony Orch under Tadaaki Otaka) BBC Proms 1997, Sullivan Concerto (BBC Symphony Orch with Sir Charles Mackerras) BBC Proms 2000, Tour of China with BBC Scottish Orch 2000; as soloist with: Philharmonia Orch, BBC Nat Orch of Wales, BBC Philharmonic, Bournemouth Symphony Orch, BBC Scottish Symphony Orch, City of Birmingham Symphony Orch; other recitals incl: Metropolitan Museum of Art NY (with Ruth Laredo 1995 and as pianist and cellist 1997), Gardner Museum Boston 1995, Marlboro Music Festival USA, Int Musicians' Seminar Prussia Cove, Gstaad Festival, Schweitzer Festival, BBC Proms 1999, Wigmore Hall 2001; as conductor with: BBC Symphony Orch, BBC Philharmonic, Scottish Chamber Orch, City of Birmingham Symphony Orch, Philharmonia Orch, Royal Liverpool Philharmonic Orch, Britten Sinfonia; *Recordings* Haydn's Concerto in C maj (with BBC Symphony Orch under Mark Wigglesworth), Tchaikovsky's Variations on a Rococo Theme (with BBC Symphony Orch under Andrew Davis), Toru Takemitsu's Orion and Pleiades (with BBC Nat Orch of Wales under Tadaaki Otaka), French chamber music (with Britten-Pears Ensemble), Poulenc Cello Sonata (with Ian Brown), Tobias Picker Cello Concerto, Britten Solo Suites, Britten, Bridge, Goehr & Watkins Recital, Britten/Berg Violin Concertos (with BBC Symphony Orch); *Style*— Paul Watkins, Esq; ✉ c/o Sullivan Sweetland Limited, 1 Hillgate Place, Balham Hill, London SW12 9ER (tel 020 8772 3470, fax 020 8673 8959, e-mail es@sullivansweetland.co.uk)

WATKINS, Dr Peter John; s of Kenneth Harold Watkins (d 1938), and Irmgard Madeleine, *née* Herrmann (d 1989); *b* 6 February 1936; *Educ* Ampleforth, Gonville & Caius Coll Cambridge and Bart's London (MA, MB BChir, MD); *m* 1, 1970, Gillian Barbara (d 1985), da of Eric Fowler; 2 da (Julia Rachel b 7 Feb 1971, Sara Helen b 12 Dec 1972), 1 s (Benedict Kenneth b 27 Nov 1974); m 2, 1993, Valerie Joan Brown; 2 step s (Thomas Dominic Brown b 31 Oct 1974, Adam Robert Brown b 29 Sept 1976); *Career* jr resident appts Bart's London 1961–65; Gen Hosp Birmingham: SHO 1965–66, research fell 1966–68, sr registrar 1968–71; KCH London: conslt physician 1971–2000, ret, dir of postgrad educn 1989–98; hon sr lectr King's Coll Sch of Med and Dentistry (now GKT) 1987–2000, ret; ed Jl of the Royal Coll of Physicians of London 1998–2005; visiting prof Amsterdam Med Centre 1985; Br Diabetic Assoc: chm Med Advsy Ctee 1980–83, chm Med and Scientific Section 1990–93; chm: Clinical Autonomic Research Soc 1986–87, Specialist Advsy Ctee on Endocrinology and Diabetes 1987–90; hon sec and treas Assoc of Physicians of GB and I 1983–93, hon sec Choosing Priorities in the NHS RCP 1994–95; pres Euro Diabetic Nephropathy Study Gp 1996–99; Castelli-Pedroli Prize and Golgi Lecture Euro Assoc for the Study of Diabetes 1990, Charles Best Lecture Toronto Diabetes Assoc 1996, Banting Lecture Br Diabetic Assoc 1997; govr Elmgreen Sch W Norwood 2005–; memb: Assoc of Physicians of GB and I, RSM; professional memb Diabetes UK; FRCP, FRSA 2004; *Books* Long-term Complications of Diabetes (ed, 1986), ABC of Diabetes (5 edn, 2003), Diabetes and its Management (6 edn, 2003); *Recreations* hill walking, music; *Style*— Dr Peter J Watkins; ✉ 31 Lancaster Avenue, London SE27 9EL (tel 020 8761 8086, e-mail peter-val.watkins@tiscali.co.uk)

WATKINS, Richard Valentine; *b* 23 September 1950; *Educ* Wellington, Loughborough Univ of Technol (BSc); *m* 1978, Charlotte, *née* de Laszlo; 2 s, 1 da; *Career* Phillips & Drew Inc 1972–77, mangr and overseas rep Kleinwort Benson 1977–83, md Phillips & Drew Inc (NY) 1983–86, pres Hoare Govett Inc (NY) 1986–88, chm Burns Fry Hoare Govett Inc (NY) 1988, exec dir J Henry Schroder Wagg & Co Ltd 1988–92, former chief exec Schroder Securities Ltd and dir of related cos in SE Asia, Japan, Korea, Switzerland; fndr dir and chief exec BBV LatInvest Securities and dir related cos 1992–98, dir LatInvest Holdings 1992–2000, chm Deutsche Latin American Companies Tst plc 1999–2004, fndr dir and chief exec Liability Solutions 1999–; memb Advsy Cncl Inst of the Americas 1996–; *Recreations* skiing; *Style*— Richard Watkins, Esq; ✉ 7 Chesham Mews, London SW1X 8HS (tel 020 7235 2434)

WATKINS, Prof (Eric) Sidney (Sid); OBE (2002); s of Wallace Watkins (d 1962), of Liverpool, and Jessica Burkey Watkins (d 1979); *b* 6 September 1928; *Educ* Prescot GS, Univ of Liverpool (Br Calendar Cables scholar, John Rankin exhibitioner in anatomy, Neurophysiology scholar, BSc, MB ChB, MD), MD (NY); *Career* Nat Serv Capt RAMC, served as specialist physiologist W Africa MRC 1953–56; gen surgical, orthopaedic and neurosurgical trg and research Bristol, Oxford and London 1956–62; prof of neurosurgery: SUNY 1962–70, Univ of London 1971–93 (emeritus prof 1993–); chief MO Formula One Racing; Fédération Internationale de l'Automobile: pres Med Cmmn 1981–, pres FIA Inst of Motor Sport Safety 2004–; Labatt's Safety Award for Motor Racing (London) 1991, Motor Mfr Industries Award (London) 1996, Mario Andretti Award for High Achievement (Detroit) 1996, Prince Michael Centenary Award of Merit RAC for contribution to safety in motor racing (London) 1997, Br Racing and Sport Car Club Gold Trophy for services to motor racing (London) 1998, Autosport Gregor Grant Award for major contributions to safety in motor racing 1999; tstee: Br Brain and Spine Fndn, Health Unlimited, Grand Prix Mechanics' Tst; Hon DSc Univ of Liverpool; FRCSEd; *Books* Stereotaxic Atlas of Thalamus (1969), Stereotaxic Atlas of Cerebellum and Brain Stem (1978), Life at the Limit (1996), Beyond the Limit (2000); *Recreations* fly fishing, game fishing, deep sea fishing, golf; *Clubs* Athenaeum, RAC; *Style*— Prof Sid Watkins, OBE; ✉ Princess Grace Hospital, Nottingham Place, London W1M 3FD (tel 020 7486 1234, fax 020 7935 2198)

WATKINS, Dr Stephen John; s of Norman Watkins (d 1975), and Lois Watkins (d 1995); *b* 2 July 1950, Nelson, Lancs; *Educ* Nelson GS, Univ of Manchester (Haworth maj entrance scholar, BSc, MB ChB, MSc); *m* 2 Nov 1985, Elizabeth Watkins; *Career* hosp dr trg Manchester and Macclesfield 1974–79, gen medical practitioner Macclesfield 1979, public health trg posts Blackburn, Salford, Manchester and Oldham 1979–84, specialist in community medicine Oldham 1984–90, dir of public health for Stockport 1990–, lectr in public health and epidemiology Univ of Manchester 1991–; lead dir of public health Gtr Manchester: transport and land planning 2002–, research 2004–, cancer 2005–06, corporate citizenship 2006–; lead dir of public health NW Region: sustainable devpt 2007–, community cohesion (jtly) 2007–; pres Medical Practitioners' Union 1988–98, memb Cncl and dir BMA 1991–, chm Transport and Health Study Gp Manchester Medical Soc 1997– (pres Public Health Forum 2004–05); James Preston Meml Award 2000; FFPH 1993 (MFPH 1984), MILT 2002, Hon FFFP 2004; *Publications* Medical Manpower and Career Structure (1980), Medicine and Labour: The Politics of a Profession (1987), Health on the Move (ed, 1991), Conviction by Mathematical Error (2000), A Country City (2001); Annual Public Health Reports of Stockport (1991–2006); author of papers on unemployment and health, work and health, and economic policy and health in WHO and other pubns 1984–94; *Recreations* rambling, railway enthusiast; *Style*— Dr Stephen Watkins; ✉ Stockport Primary Care Trust, Regent House, Heaton Lane, Stockport SK4 1BS (tel 0161 426 5031, e-mail stephen.watkins@stockport-pct.nhs.uk)

WATKINSON, Angela; MP; *b* 1941; *Educ* Wanstead Co HS, Anglia Poly Univ; *Children* 1 s, 2 da; *Career* early career in banking, former local govt offr; former cncllr (Cons): Havering BC, Essex CC; MP (Cons) Upminster 2001–; oppn whip 2002–04, shadow min for educn 2004–05, shadow min for local govt affrs and communities 2005–; treas All Pty Sweden Gp 2002, treas All Pty Isle of Man Gp 2004, jt chair All Pty Breast Cancer Gp 2005; memb UK Cncl of Europe 2005; former chm Upminster Cons Assoc (Emerson Park Branch); *Style*— Angela Watkinson, MP; ✉ House of Commons, London SW1A 0AA

WATKINSON, David Robert; s of late Robert Douglas Watkinson, of Woking, Surrey, and Muriel Winifred, *née* Reeves; *b* 6 October 1947; *Educ* Woking GS for Boys, Clare Coll Cambridge (MA, LLB); *Partner* Suzanne Eve Tarlin; 1 da (Eva Rose b 1 July 1980); *Career* called to the Bar Middle Temple 1972; fndr memb chambers Wellington St London 1974–88 (committed to working in social welfare areas of law), specialist in housing law and law relating to gypsies/travellers including planning; memb: Exec Ctee Family Squatting Advsy Service 1972–75, N Islington Law Centre 1974–78; memb and legal advsr to campaign against criminal trespass laws 1974–78, occasional legal advsr Advsy Serv to Squatters 1975–, concerned with publicity for campaign of limitation of rights of defence in W Germany late 1970s, campaigned to extend grant of Legal Aid in particular to Magistrates' Courts 1979–80, memb Stop the Criminal Trespass Law Campaign 1983–84, teacher of housing law Univ of Warwick 1984 and occasional expert witness/course ldr 1997–2004, observer on behalf of Haldane Soc for Socialist Lawyers and Agric Allied Workers Branch TGWU at trial of agric day labourers in Spain 1986, lectures on legal aspects of housing South Bank Poly and other instns 1988, assoc dir Nat Housing Law Serv 1991–93, memb Legal and Parly Ctee SQUASH (Squatters Action for Secure Homes) 1993–94; vice-chm Housing Law Practitioners Assoc 1994–2000 (memb Exec Ctee 1994–2007), vice-chair Housing and Land Ctee Civil Justice Cncl 2002–; exec memb Ctee Admin Law Bar Assoc 1999–2006, memb Civil Justice Cncl (appointed by Lord Chllr) 2000–02; occasional lectr Local Govt Gp Law Soc 1995, 1997, 1998 and 1999; training course leader Administrative Law Bar Assoc 1996–; author of reviews and articles on housing 1974– (Legal Action, Roof, Law Soc's Gazette, Haldane Soc Bulletin, All England Legal Opinion, Solicitor's Journal from the Lawyers Collective Mumbai); memb: Haldane Soc Socialist Lawyers Legal Action Gp, Admin Law Bar Assoc, Housing Law Practitioners' Assoc, Nicaragua Solidarity Campaign; Barr of the Year Award Legal Aid Practitioners Gp 2005; *Books* Law in a Housing Crisis (1975), NCCL Civil Rights Guide (1978), Squatting - The Real Story (1980), Critical Lawyers Handbook (1992); Squatting Trespass and Civil Liberties (jtly, 1976), Gypsy and Traveller Law (2004); *Recreations* travel, theatre, cinema, ethnic music, history, archaeology, fiction, swimming; *Style*— David Watkinson, Esq; ✉ Garden Court Chambers, 57–60 Lincoln's Inn Fields, London WC2A 3LS (tel 020 7993 7600, fax 020 7993 7700, e-mail davidw@gclaw.co.uk)

WATKINSON, Douglas Arthur; s of Raymond Arthur Watkinson (d 1947), and Joan Lilian, *née* Crawley (d 1972); *b* 5 July 1945; *Educ* Haberdashers' Aske's, East Fifteen Acting Sch; *m* 20 June 1972, Lesley Moira, da of Stanley Thompson; 2 da (Fenella Laurie b 31 May 1978, Ailsa Morag b 2 Nov 1983), 2 s (Callum Neil b 21 Aug 1979, Duncan Clyde b 23 Feb 1981); *Career* freelance writer; began as actor, script ed BBC 1972–75, freelance writer 1975–; contrib to TV series/serials incl: Z Cars, The Brothers, Owen MD, Duchess of Duke Street, Spy Trap, Onedin Line, Juliet Bravo, The Bill, Boon, Maybury, Lovejoy, Poirot, Anna Lee, Midsomer Murders, Kavanagh, QC, Heartbeat; sole writer of series: For Maddie With Love, Strange True Stories, The New Statesman, Forever Green, Land of Promise; stage plays: Let's Do It My Way, The Dragon's Tail, Caesar and Me; Haggard Hawk (novel); memb Writers' Guild; *Recreations* travel, photography, bonsai, reading; *Clubs* National Liberal; *Style*— Douglas Watkinson, Esq; ✉ c/o David Higham Associates, 5–8 Lower John Street, Golden Square, London W1F 9HA

WATKINSON, Ernest Cooper; s of John Ernest Watkinson (d 1960), and Margaret Hannah, *née* Cooper (d 1971); *b* 4 September 1937; *Educ* Skerry's Coll, Sch of Architecture King's Coll Durham (H B Saint Meml Prize, Br Paints Prize, Dip Arch); *m* 1961, Sheila Joan (d 1994), da of Victor Ernest Strong (d 1974); 2 s (Neil b 1964, Simon b 1966); *Career* Williamson Faulkner Brown & Partners (amalgamation of W H Williamson and H F Brown 1962): joined 1960, assoc 1963, ptnr 1965; practice became Faulkner-Brown Hendy Watkinson Stonor 1972 then FaulknerBrowns 1986; practice has won over 50 awards incl: RIBA Architecture Awards, Civic Tst Awards, Structural Steel Awards, Concrete Soc Awards; external examiner Sch of Architecture Univ of Newcastle upon Tyne 1986–88; Freeman City of London 1985, memb Guild of Freemen City of London 1986, Liveryman Worshipful Co of Chartered Architects 1989; FRIBA 1962, memb Assoc of Conslt Architects 1988; *Recreations* travel, theatre, gardening, Rotary; *Clubs* East India; *Style*— Ernest Watkinson, Esq; ✉ FaulknerBrowns, Dobson House, Northumbrian Way, Killingworth, Newcastle upon Tyne NE12 0QW (tel 0191 268 3007, fax 0191 268 5227, e-mail ernie.watkinson@btopenworld.com)

WATLING, His Hon the Rev (David) Brian Watling; QC (1979); s of Russell Watling and Stella, *née* Ridley; *b* 18 June 1935; *Educ* Charterhouse, King's Coll London; *m* 1964, Noelle Bugden, WRNS; *Career* called to the Bar 1957; Treasy counsel Central Criminal Court 1972–79, recorder of the Crown Court 1979–81, circuit judge (SE Circuit) 1981–2001, resident judge Chelmsford Crown Court 1997–2001, judicial memb Parole Bd 2002–; legal assessor GMC 2002–; Univ of Buckingham: visiting lectr 1977–80, prof in law 1980–84; C of E: reader 1985, ordained deacon 1987, priest 1988; non-stipendary min Dio of St Edmundsbury and Ipswich 1987–; *Clubs* Garrick; *Style*— His Hon the Rev Brian Watling, QC; ✉ Howe's House, 5 High Street, Nayland, Suffolk CO6 4JE

WATNEY, (John) Adrian; s of Maj John Douglas Watney, RA (d 1983), of Dorking, Surrey, and Barbara Ann, *née* Smith (d 2001); *b* 3 October 1943; *Educ* Sherborne; *m* 9 Sept 1967, Angela Winifred, da of Dudley Partridge (d 1982), of Horsley, Surrey; 3 da (Katherine b 1970, Sarah b 1972, Victoria b 1976), 1 s (Christopher b 1981); *Career* admitted slr 1968; currently conslt Pinsent Masons Solicitors; dir and chm: Alzheimer Research Tst, Longacre Estates Ltd, Long Martin Estates Ltd, Portman Settled Estates Ltd; chm Leaftree Ltd; tstee and chm Classical Road Show; tstee: Aplastic Anaemia Tst, Portman Family Trusts, Barts Fndn for Research and Devpt, Med Coll St Barts Hosp Tst; govr Walsall City Acad; hon memb Faculty of Divinity Univ of Cambridge; hon fell QMC London; memb Law Soc; Freeman: City of London 1964, Worshipful Co Mercers (Master 1990–91), Merchant Adventureres of York 1990–; *Recreations* golf, cricket, rugby, opera; *Clubs* Home House, Royal and Ancient Golf (St Andrews), MCC, Rye Golf, Walton Heath Golf, Hon Co of Edinburgh Golfers, City Livery, Arts; *Style*— Adrian Watney, Esq; ✉ Pinsent Masons, 30 Aylesbury Street, London EC1R 0ER (tel 020 7490 4000, fax 020 7490 2545)

WATSON, *see also:* Inglefield-Watson, Milne-Watson

WATSON, Adrian Keith; s of Keith Watson, and Stella, *née* Crippin; *b* 20 November 1952, Birmingham; *Educ* Dudley GS, Univ of Sheffield (BA); *m* 24 Sept 1977, Joanna, *née* Round; 1 s (James b 11 June 1985); *Career* slr; ptnr: Rigbey Loose & Mills 1979–82 (joined 1976), Pinsent & Co 1983–86 (joined 1982), Anthony Collins Slrs 1986–95, Garrett & Co 1995–99, DLA 1999–2005, Cobbetts 2005–; tstee Living Springs; memb Law Soc 1978; released music album Hostage to Fortune 2006; *Recreations* music (piano, singing), golf, skiing; *Clubs* Stourbridge Golf; *Style*— Adrian Watson, Esq; ✉ Cobbetts, One Colmore Square, Birmingham B4 6AJ (tel 0845 404 2264, fax 0845 166 6515, e-mail adrian.watson@cobbetts.co.uk)

WATSON, Alan Carlos; s of William Carlos Watson (d 1990), and Doris May, *née* Putwain; *b* 26 October 1940; *Educ* Willesden Tech Coll (HNC); *m* 12 Sept 1964, Sandra Mary, da of John Bruce Garner; 1 s (Ashley b 8 April 1966), 1 da (Martine b 11 Dec 1968); *Career* student apprentice Matthew Hall Mechanical Services Ltd, ptnr Building Design Partnership 1988– (joined 1972); expert witness for House of Commons Select Ctee Channel Tunnel Hybrid Bill; FCIWEM; *Recreations* golf; *Style*— Alan Watson, Esq; ✉ 17 Silver Close, Harrow, Middlesex HA3 6JT

WATSON, Professor Alan Rees; *Educ* Univ of Edinburgh Med Sch (BSc, MB ChB); *Career* surgical house offr Princess Margaret Hosp Nassau Bahamas 1973, med house offr Eastern Gen Hosp Edinburgh 1974, neonatal house offr Elsie Inglis Maternity Hosp Edinburgh 1974–75, SHO in paediatrics Royal Hosp for Sick Children Edinburgh 1975, SHO in gen med Eastern Gen Hosp Edinburgh 1975–76, locum GP Muswellbrook NSW and Deputising Serv Sydney Aust 1976, locum casualty offr Lyell McEwin Hosp Adelaide S Aust 1976, registrar in paediatrics King Edward VIII Hosp Durban SA 1977, locum lectr/consIt Dept of Child Health Univ of Natal Durban SA 1978, tutor in child health Univ of Manchester (hon registrar) 1979, lectr in child health Royal Manchester Children's Hosp Univ of Manchester (hon sr registrar) 1979–82, clinical fell (subspeciality res) in paediatric nephrology Hosp for Sick Children Toronto 1982–83, staff nephrologist and asst prof Hosp for Sick Children Toronto and Univ of Toronto Canada 1983–85, conslt paediatric nephrologist and unit dir Children and Young People's Kidney Unit City Hosp NHS Tst Nottingham 1985–; Univ of Nottingham: clinical teacher 1985–, special sr lectr Div of Child Health Sch of Human Devpt 1999–2005, special prof of paediatric nephrology 2005–; inaugural chm City Hosp Ethics of Clinical Practice Ctee 1994–2004, chair UK Clinical Ethics Network 2003–; fndr and organiser: Trent and Anglia Paediatric Nephro-urology Gp 1994–, Trent Paediatric Nephrology Gp 1999–, Trent and Anglia Paediatric Haemofiltration Gp 2000–; fndr and gp co-ordinator Euro Paediatric Peritoneal Working Gp 1999–; advsr: Nat Kidney Res Fund Helpline 2000–, Nat Kidney Fund 2003–; memb Scientific Ctee Int Soc for Peritoneal Dialysis Montreal 2001, memb Cncl European Soc of Paediatric Nephrology 2003–06 (chm Scientific Ctee 2006); memb: Manchester Paediatric Club 1980–83, Br Paediatric Assoc 1980–99, Assoc for Paediatric Educn in Europe 1981–83, Paediatric Res Soc 1981–99, American Soc of Nephrology 1983–, Int Soc of Nephrology 1984–, Int Paediatric Nephrology Assoc 1984–, Br Assoc of Paediatric Nephrology 1985–, Renal Assoc UK 1986–, Euro Soc of Paediatric Nephrology 1986–, Int Soc for Peritoneal Dialysis 1986–, Nottingham Medico-Chirurgical Soc 1986–, Nottingham Medico-Legal Soc 1988–92, Int Soc of Nutrition and Metabolism in Renal Disease 1992–; B Merit Award NHS 1998; Licentiate Med Cncl of Canada 1983; MRCP 1976, FRCPEd 1988, FRCPCH 1997; *Publications* author of 175 papers and 25 chapters in books; *Style*— Prof Alan R Watson; ✉ Children and Young People's Kidney Unit, City Hospital, Nottingham NG5 1PB (tel 0115 962 7961, fax 0115 962 7759, e-mail alan.watson@nuh.nhs.uk)

WATSON, Alastair Alexander Linton; s of Maj-Gen Andrew Linton Watson, CB, and Mary Elizabeth, *née* Rigby; *b* 15 February 1953, Wüppertal, Germany; *Educ* Eagle House Sandhurst Camberley, Wellington, New Coll Oxford (MA), Staff Coll Camberley; *m* 28 Sept 1980, Selina, *née* Mather; 2 da (Sophia, Alice), 1 s (Harry); *Career* Black Watch Br Army 1975–91, sales dir then central ops dir Fired Earth plc and Fired Earth Ltd 1991–2003, private sec to HRH The Duke of York 2003–; *Recreations* country pursuits, choral music; *Clubs* Pitt, Vincent's (Oxford); *Style*— Alastair Watson, Esq; ✉ Park Farm House, Cornwell, Chipping Norton, Oxfordshire OX7 6TY (tel 01608 658569, e-mail aalwatson@hotmail.com); Buckingham Palace, London SW1A 0AA

WATSON, Prof (George) Alistair; s of George Arthur Watson (d 1972), and Grace Ann, *née* MacDonald (d 2006); *Educ* Breadalbane Acad, Univ of Edinburgh (BSc, MSc), Australian Nat Univ (PhD); *m* 6 April 1971, (Margaret) Hilary, da of Robert Whitton Mackay (d 1971); 1 da (Kirsty b 1989); *Career* Univ of Dundee: lectr 1970–82, sr lectr 1982–84, reader 1984–88, prof 1988–, head Dept of Mathematics and Computer Sci 1992–97, head Dept of Mathematics 1997–98 and 2004–06; FIMA 1972; FRSE 1996; *Books* Computational Methods for Matrix Eigenproblems (with A R Gourlay, 1973), Approximation Theory and Numerical Methods (1980); *Recreations* opera, photography, gardening; *Style*— Prof Alistair Watson, FRSE; ✉ 7 Albany Road, Broughty Ferry, Dundee DD5 1NS (tel 01382 779473); Department of Mathematics, University of Dundee, Dundee DD1 4HN (tel 01382 344472, e-mail gawatson@maths.dundee.ac.uk)

WATSON, Sir (James) Andrew; 5 Bt (UK 1866), of Henrietta Street, Cavendish Sq, St Marylebone, Co Middx; s of Sir Thomas Watson, 4 Bt (d 1941), and Ella, Lady Watson (d 1996); *b* 30 December 1937; *Educ* Eton; *m* 1965, Christabel Mary, eldest da of Maj Kenneth Ralph Malcolm (Peter) Carlisle (d 1983), and sis of Sir Kenneth Carlisle, *qv*; 2 s, 1 da; *Heir* s, Roland Watson; *Career* Lt Life Gds; called to the Bar Inner Temple 1966;

W

recorder of the Crown Court 1985–2003; govr RSC 1989–2002; *Style*— Sir Andrew Watson, Bt

WATSON, Dr (Nicholas) Andrew; s of Phillip Charles Watson, of Brundall, Norfolk, and Venetia Madeline Le Poer, *née* Wyon; *b* 25 August 1952; *Educ* Boston GS, Univ of Nottingham Med Sch (BMedSci, MB BS, DCH); *m* 18 Nov 1977, Elaine Alma, da of late Jack Attack; 1 da (Helen Ruth b 5 Jan 1983), 1 s (Edward Phillip b 29 Oct 1984); *Career* jr house offr Derby Royal Infirmary and Nottingham City Hosp 1975–76; SHO in Depts of: Geriatric Med City Hosp 1976–77, Med City Hosp 1977, Traumatology Queens Med Centre 1978, Paediatrics Queen's Med Centre 1978–79; postgrad traineeship in gen practice Nottingham 1977–78 and 1979, princ in gen practice Keyworth 1979–82, specialist in orthopaedic med 1982–; lectr in USA and UK with Soc of Orthopaedic Med 1982–; author of numerous published papers letters and articles on orthopaedic med; pres Soc of Orthopaedic Med 1992–2001 (elected to Cncl 1982, chm 1988–92); MRCGP 1979, fell Soc of Orthopaedic Med 1982 (memb 1981); *Recreations* music (has played piano, viola, mandolin and crumhorn), plays jazz guitar in a jazz band; *Style*— Dr Andrew Watson; ✉ 10 Golf Course Road, Stanton on the Wolds, Nottinghamshire NG12 5BH (tel 0115 937 3603); 30A Wimpole Street, London W1G 8YA (tel 07000 781687)

WATSON, Prof Andrew; *Educ* Imperial Coll London (BSc), Univ of Reading (PhD); *Career* postdoctoral studies Dept of Atmosphere, Oceanic and Space Sciences Univ of Michigan 1978–81, scientist Marine Biological Assoc then Plymouth Marine Lab 1982–95, prof Sch of Environmental Sciences UEA 1996–; Fridtjof Nansen Medal European Geosciences Union 2004; FRS 2003; *Style*— Prof Andrew Watson; ✉ School of Environmental Sciences, University of East Anglia, Norwich NR4 7TJ

WATSON, Prof Andrew James; s of Leslie John Watson (d 1996), of Steyning, W Sussex, and Ena Florence, *née* Bence (d 2000); *b* 30 November 1952, Worthing, W Sussex; *Educ* Steyning GS, Imperial Coll London (BSc), Univ of Reading (PhD); *m* 1978, Jacqueline Elizabeth, *née* Pughe; 2 s (Adam Richard b 1982, James Geraint Robert b 1985); *Career* research scientist: Dept of Atmosphere, Ocean and Space Sciences Univ of Michigan 1978–81, Marine Biological Assoc 1981–88, Plymouth Marine Lab 1989–95; prof of environmental science UEA 1996–; author of numerous papers and articles in scientific jls; memb Challenger Soc for Marine Science 1994; Nansen medallist European Geosciences Union 2004; FRS 2003; *Style*— Prof Andrew Watson; ✉ School of Environmental Sciences, University of East Anglia, Norwich NR4 7TJ (tel 01603 592560, e-mail a.watson@uea.ac.uk)

WATSON, Andrew Stewart; s of Leslie Donald Watson, of Malvern, Worcs, and Joan Beatrice, *née* Everton; *b* 29 March 1950; *Educ* King's Sch Worcester, St John's Coll Oxford; *m* 11 Dec 1976, Lea Karin, da of Eino Arvid Nordberg (d 1963); *Career* admitted slr 1975; Thomson Snell and Passmore: articled clerk 1973, ptnr 1981, head Litigation Dept 1986; memb Law Soc (memb specialist clinic negligence panel); *Recreations* running, reading, music, cooking; *Style*— Andrew Watson, Esq; ✉ 3 Lonsdale Gardens, Tunbridge Wells, Kent TN1 1NX (tel 01892 510000, fax 01892 549884)

WATSON, Anthony; s of Lt Cdr Andrew Patrick Watson, RNR, and Harriet, *née* Hewardine (d 1981); *b* 2 April 1945; *Educ* Campbell Coll Belfast, Queen's Univ Belfast (BSc); *m* 29 July 1972, Heather Jane, da of Lt Cdr Wilfred Norman Dye, RNR (d 1988); 2 s (Edward b 1975, Tom b 1976), 1 da (Tilly b 1980); *Career* called to the Bar Lincoln's Inn (bencher 2002); dir: Touche Remnant & Co 1978–85, Touche Remnant Hldgs 1978–85; chief investment offr Citibank NA 1985–90, chm Citifunds Ltd 1985–90, chm Citicare Ltd 1985–90; AMP Asset Management plc: dir int investment 1991–95, md 1996–98; Hermes Pensions Mgmnt: chief investment offr 1998–2001, chief exec 2002–06; chm: Asian Infrastructure Fund Ltd 1999– (dir 1994–), MEPC Ltd 2004–06 (dir 2000–), Marks & Spencer Pension Tst 2006–; dir: Cathay Holdings Ltd 1992–96, Virgin Direct Financial Services Ltd 1996–98, Innisfree plc 1997–98, Edinburgh Fund Managers plc 2001–02, Botts & Co Holding Ltd 2001–03, Securities Inst 2001–, Investment Mgmnt Assoc Ltd 2002–05, Hermes Equity Ownership Services Ltd 2005–, Vodafone Gp plc 2006–, Witan Investment Trust plc 2006–, Hammerson Gp plc 2006–; chm Strategic Investment Bd for NI 2003–, memb Fin Reporting Cncl 2004–; dir Fndn Bd Queen's Univ Belfast 2002–; played for London Irish RFC first XV 1967–68; AIIMR 1971, Hon FSI 2006; *Clubs* RAC; *Style*— Anthony Watson, Esq

WATSON, Anthony Gerard (Tony); s of George Maurice Watson, JP, of Market Deeping, Lincs, and Anne, *née* McDonnell; *b* 28 May 1955; *Educ* St John Fisher Peterborough, North Staffs Poly (BA); *m* 1, 17 Sept 1982, Susan Ann, da of Malcolm Gutteridge, of Stockton on Tees; 2 s (Samuel John b 3 Sept 1983, Tom b 10 Jan 1985), 1 da (Emily Anne b 7 Feb 1987); m 2, 1994, Sylvie Helen, *née* Pask; 1 s (Daniel James b 6 Sept 1993), 1 da (Sabrina Helen b 23 April 1997); *Career* reporter Stamford Mercury 1978–79, news ed Evening Despatch Darlington 1983–84 (reporter 1979–81), reporter Yorkshire Post 1984–86, researcher World in Action Granada TV 1986–88, ed Yorkshire Post 1989–2003 (dep ed 1988–89); Press Assoc: head of business devpt 2003–04, editorial dir 2004–07, ed-in-chief and dir 2007–; awarded Br Press Awards 1986 and 1987, YTV Journalist of the Year 1986; memb Bd Soc of Eds; *Style*— Tony Watson, Esq

WATSON, Antony Edward Douglas; QC (1986); s of William Edward Watson, of Hanchurch, Staffs, and Margaret Douglas; *b* 6 March 1945; *Educ* Sedbergh, Sidney Sussex Coll Cambridge (MA); *m* 15 Sept 1972, Gillian Mary, da of Alfred John Bevan-Arthur, of Bramishall, Staffs; 2 da (Edwina b 1978, Willa b 1981); *Career* called to the Bar Inner Temple 1968; specialising in Intellectual Property Law; head of chambers 2004–; dep chm Copy Right Tbnl 1994–98; *Recreations* country pursuits, wine, opera; *Style*— Antony Watson, Esq, QC; ✉ 3 New Square, Lincoln's Inn, London WC2A 3RS (tel 020 7405 1111)

WATSON, Charles Basil Lucas; s of Capt Basil Watson, RN, of Hampshire, and Heather, *née* McMullen; *Educ* Sherborne, KCL (BA); *m* Fiona, da of Alan Mitchell; 1 s (Jack b 4 June 1992), 1 da (Rosie b 4 Feb 1996); *Career* communications conslt Good Relations Group 1983–87, investor rels conslt Valin Pollen Group 1987–89, transatlantic sailing expdn to Orinoco Delta (on sabbatical) 1989–90 (Royal Cruising Club Exploration Award), chief exec Financial Dynamics 2001–, led MBO of Fin Dynamics Int 2003; *Recreations* skiing, fishing, sailing, modern history; *Clubs* Royal Cruising; *Style*— Charles Watson, Esq; ✉ Financial Dynamics Ltd, Holborn Gate, 26 Southampton Buildings, London WC2A 1PB (tel 020 7831 3113, fax 020 7405 8007, mobile 07887 787508, e-mail charles.watson@fd.com)

WATSON, Christopher Ian (Chris); s of Philip James Watson, of Weybridge, Surrey, and Freda Ethel, *née* Duerre; *b* 2 May 1957, Swansea; *Educ* Marlborough (scholar), New Coll Oxford (MA); *m* 1, 1984; 1 da (Emma Charlotte Duerre (plays Hermione in Harry Potter films) b 15 May 1990), 1 s (Alexander Sebastien Luesby b 1 Dec 1992); m 2, 11 Dec 1999, Elizabeth Ann, *née* Green; 1 s (Toby Philip Lowell b 25 Jan 2003), 2 da (Nina Islay Emily, Lucy Eireann Ruth (twins) b 10 Sept 2004); *Career* admitted slr Eng and Wales 1981, avocat Paris Bar 1993; ptnr: Simmons and Simmons 1988–99 (trainee slr 1981–83, asst slr 1983–88), Allen and Overy LLP 2000–05, Dechert LLP 2006–; memb Communications Law Ctee Int Bar Assoc 2007; memb Law Soc 1983; *Clubs* Oxford and Cambridge, Lowtonian Soc, Order of the Knights of the Round Table; *Style*— Chris Watson, Esq; ✉ Dechert LLP, 160 Queen Victoria Street, London EC4V 4QQ (tel 020 7184 7610, fax 020 7184 6610, e-mail chris.watson@dechert.com)

WATSON, Christopher John; s of Allan John Watson (d 1965), of Uxbridge, and Dorothy C, *née* Perry (d 2005); *b* 21 June 1940; *Educ* Leighton Park Sch Reading, Univ of Bristol (BA); *m* 20 July 1963, Mary, da of Andrew Warden Vincent (d 1986), of Hereford; 1 da (Clare b 1967), 2 s (Angus b 1969, Peter b 1972); *Career* KCL 1962–63, Northumberland CC 1963–65, Univ of Sussex 1966–68, res offr Scottish Devpt Dept 1968–72; Centre for Urban and Regional Studies Univ of Birmingham: res fell 1972–79, lectr 1979–83, sr lectr 1983–, dir of int affrs 1984–94, head of dept 1988–93, sr fell 2002–; dir The Japan Centre Univ of Birmingham 1994–2002; regnl co-ordinator (Midlands) Japan 2001, project dir (W Midlands) W Midlands Region-Shizuoka Prefecture Link 2003–; memb Bd of Mgmnt Mercian Housing Assoc Ltd 1984–2006 (chm 1999–2005), memb Bd FRC Gp 2003–, co sec Housing Vision Consultancy 2007–; *Publications* Housing in Clydeside 1970 (with J B Cullingworth, 1971), Housing Policy and the Housing System (with Alan Murie and Pat Niner, 1975), Housing and the New Welfare State: Perspectives on East Asia and Europe (with Richard Groves and Alan Murie, 2007), contrib to various books and jls; *Recreations* music, travel; *Style*— Christopher Watson, Esq; ✉ Centre for Urban and Regional Studies, The University of Birmingham, Edgbaston, Birmingham B15 2TT (tel 0121 414 5026, fax 0121 414 3279)

WATSON, David Alan; s of John Watson, of Ledsham, N Yorks, and Elizabeth, *née* Bentley; *b* 29 April 1950; *Educ* Nottingham HS, St John's Coll Cambridge (exhibitioner, MA); *m* 21 July 1984, Christine Elizabeth, da of Victor Hutchinson; *Career* asst account exec Pressmark 1972; Infopress: joined as account exec 1972, successively account dir, assoc dir, dir then md, chief exec 1992–99; int dir Key Communications 1999 (md London 1999–2001), dir Surrey House 2002–06, princ Campaignteam 2006–; FIPR 1998 (MIPR 1981); *Recreations* fly fishing; *Style*— David Watson, Esq; ✉ Campaignteam, 37 Shirleys, Ditchling, West Sussex BN6 8UD (tel 01273 845462)

WATSON, Prof Elaine Denise; da of Alexander Watson (d 1987), and Isabella, *née* Petticrew; *b* 8 September 1955, Ayrshire; *Educ* Univ of Glasgow (BVMS, MVM), Univ of Bristol (PhD), Univ of Edinburgh (DSc), European Coll of Animal Reproduction (Dip); *m* 9 Sept 1989, Christopher Clarke; 1 s (Marcus b 13 Sept 1996); *Career* res offr MAFF Cattle Breeding Centre Sheffield 1979–82, vet res offr ARC Inst for Res on Animal Disease 1982–84, res assoc Univ of Bristol Sch of Veterinary Science 1984–87, asst prof of equine reproduction Univ of Pennsylvania 1987–91; Royal (Dick) Sch of Veterinary Studies: sr lectr 1991–95, reader 1995–99, prof of veterinary reproduction 1999–, dean 2003–; pres European Coll of Animal Reproduction; memb: Scientific Advsy Ctee, Scot Agricultural Coll, Cncl RCVS (chair Fellowship Sub-Ctee); Richard Hartley Clinical Prize Equine Veterinary Jl 1988; FRCVS 1990; *Books* Equine Medicine, Surgery and Reproduction (jtly, 1997); contrib: The Equine Manual (1995), Diagnostic Techniques in Equine Medicine (1997), Self Assessment Colour Review of Equine Internal Medicine (1997), Equine Practice 3 (1998); *Recreations* cycling, walking, horseriding, travel, theatre, films; *Style*— Prof Elaine Watson; ✉ Royal (Dick) School of Veterinary Studies, University of Edinburgh, Easter Bush, Midlothian EH25 9RG (tel 0131 650 6102, e-mail elaine.watson@ed.ac.uk)

WATSON, Graham Forgie; s of George William Forgie Watson (d 1982), and Margaret Kinlay, *née* Hogg (d 1983); *b* 14 January 1958; *Educ* George Heriot's Sch Edinburgh, Univ of Edinburgh (LLB); *m* 3 May 1983, (Elspeth) Margaret, da of Alexander Brewster (d 1983); 2 da (Rebecca b 1989, Sally b 1991); *Career* CA 1982; KPMG 1979–83, dir Noble Grossart Ltd 1984–91, md The Carnegie Partnership Ltd 1991–93, ptnr Deloitte & Touche 1994–2003, md MacFarlane Gray Corp Finance 2004–, dir Scottish Inst of Sport Fndn 2005–; dir N Lanarkshire Leisure Tst 2006–; FRSA; *Recreations* golf, squash, skiing; *Clubs* New (Edinburgh), Loch Lomond Golf, Bruntsfield Links Golf, Golf House Club Elie; *Style*— Graham F Watson, Esq; ✉ MacFarlane Gray Corporate Finance, 6 Chester Street, Edinburgh EH3 7RA (tel 0131 226 4264, fax 0131 225 7112, e-mail gfw@mgcf.co.uk)

WATSON, Graham Robert; MEP; s of Gordon Graham Watson (d 1991), and Stephanie, *née* Revill-Johnson; *b* 23 March 1956; *Educ* City of Bath Boys' Sch, Heriot-Watt Univ (BA); *m* 5 Sept 1987, Dr Rita Giannini, da of Dr Mario Giannini; 1 da (Frederica b 26 Jan 1992), 1 s (Gregory b 27 April 1995); *Career* freelance interpreter and translator 1979–80, administrator Paisley Coll of Technology (now Paisley Univ) 1980–83, head private office ldr Lib Pty (Rt Hon (now Sir) David Steel MP) 1983–87, sr press offr TSB Gp plc 1987–88; HSBC Holdings plc: sr public affairs mangr 1993–94 (public affairs mangr 1988–93, seconded to EBRD 1991); MEP: Somerset and N Devon 1994–99, SW England 1999–, leader Euro Lib Dem MEPs 2002–; fndr memb Euro Community's Youth Forum 1980, gen sec Int Fedn of Liberal and Radical Youth 1979–81 (vice-pres 1977–79), memb Governing Bd Euro Youth Centre 1980–82, chm Euro Parl Ctee on Justice and Home Affairs 1999–2001, ldr UK Lib Dem Pty Euro Parl 1999–2001; MIL, MIPR; *Books* The Liberals in the North-South Dialogue (ed, 1980), To the Power of Ten (ed, 2000), Liberalism and Globalisation (ed, 2001), Liberal Language (2003), EU've Got Mail (2004), Liberal Democracy and Globalisation (2006), Liberalism: Something to shout about (2006), The Power of Speech (2006); *Recreations* sailing, choir singing, writing; *Clubs* Royal Commonwealth; *Style*— Graham Watson, Esq, MEP; ✉ The European Parliament, Rue Wiertz, 1047 Brussels, Belgium; South West England Liberal Democrats, Bagehot's Foundry, Beard's Yard, Langport, Somerset TA10 9PS (website www.grahamwatsonmep.org)

WATSON, Maj Gen Henry Stuart Ramsay; CBE (1973, MBE 1954); s of Maj Henry Angus Watson, CBE, MVO (d 1952), and Dorothy Bannerman Watson, OBE, *née* Ramsay (d 1968); *b* 9 July 1922; *Educ* Winchester; *m* 1965, Susan, o da of Col William Hall Jackson, CBE, DL, of Barford, nr Warwick; 2 s (Angus b 1967, William b 1969), 1 da (Edwina b 1971); *Career* cmmnd 2 Lt 13/18 Royal Hussars 1942, Lt 1943, Capt 1945, Adj 13/18 H 1945–46 and 1948–50; psc 1951, GSO2 HQ 1 Corps, 1952–53, instr RMA Sandhurst 1955–57, instr Staff Coll Camberley 1960–62, CO 13/18 Royal Hussars 1962–64 Col GS, SHAPE 1965–68, Col Def Policy Staff MOD 1968, IDC 1969, BGS HQ BAOR 1970–73, dir Def Policy Staff MOD 1973–74, sr Army Directing Staff RCDS 1974–76, Col 13/18 Royal Hussars 1979–90; dep dir gen IOD 1985–88 (exec dir 1977–85), dir Treasurer's Dept Cons Central Office 1992–94 (dep dir 1989–92); *Recreations* golf, gardening; *Clubs* Cavalry and Guards', Huntercombe Golf, St Enodoc Golf; *Style*— Maj Gen H S R Watson, CBE; ✉ The White Cross, Askett, Princes Risborough, Buckinghamshire HP27 9LR (tel and fax 01844 347601, e-mail sands@gotadsl.co.uk)

WATSON, Ian; *b* 20 April 1943, St Albans; *Educ* Tynemouth Sch, Balliol Coll Oxford (scholar, BA); *m* 1 Sept 1962, Judith, *née* Jackson (d 2001); 1 da (Jessica b 1973); *Career* author; Eng and French lit res Oxford 1963–65 (res degree 1965), lectr in lit UC Dar es Salaam Tanzania 1965–67, lectr in Eng lit Tokyo Univ of Educn 1967–70 (pt/t Keio Univ Tokyo and Japan Women's Univ), lectr then sr lectr in complementary studies Sch of History of Art Birmingham Poly and course teacher in sci fiction and futures studies 1970–76; memb Cncl Sci Fiction Fndn London 1974–91; features ed Foundation - The Review of Science Fiction 1974–91 (reg contrib sci fiction criticism), Euro ed SFWA Bulletin 1983–; memb Towcester and Dist Lab Pty 1980–, CND 1980–; CC candidate (Lab): Helmdon Div Northamptonshire 1981, Towcester Div Northamptonshire 1984, Middleton Cheney Div Northamptonshire 1989; *Books* incl: Japan - A Cat's Eye View (1969), The Embedding (1973, Prix Apollo 1975, Premios Zikkurath for best foreign novel in Spanish trans 1978), The Jonah Kit (1975, Br Sci Fiction Orbit award 1976, Br Sci Fiction Assoc award 1977), Orgasmachine (1976), The Martian Inca (1977), Japan Tomorrow (1977), Alien Embassy (1977), Miracle Visitors (1978), The Very Slow Time Machine - Science Fiction Stories (1979, finalist World Sci Fiction Achievement (Hugo) award), God's World (1979), The Gardens of Delight (1980), Under Heaven's Bridge (with Michael Bishop, 1981), Deathhunter - Pictures at an Exhibition (ed, 1981), Sunstroke and

Other Stories (1982), Chekhov's Journey (1983), Changes (ed, 1983), The Book of the River (1984), Converts (1984), The Book of the Stars (1984), The Book of Being (1985), The Book of Ian Watson (1985), Slow Birds and Other Stories (1985), Afterlives (ed, 1986), Queenmagic Kingmagic (1986), Evil Water and Other Stories (1987), The Power (1987), The Fire Worm (1988), Whores of Babylon (1988), Meat (1988), Salvage Rites and Other Stories (1989), The Flies of Memory (1990), Inquisitor (1990), Stalin's Teardrops (1991), Space Marine (1993), Lucky's Harvest: the first book of Mana (1993), The Coming of Vertumnus and other stories (1994), The Fallen Moon: the second book of Mana (1994), Harlequin (1994), Chaos Child (1995), Hard Questions (1996), Oracle (1997), The Lexicographer's Love Song (2001), The Great Escape (2002), Mockymen (2003), The Butterflies of Memory (2006); screen credit for screen story for Steven Spielberg's AI Artificial Intelligence 2001; *Style—* Mr Ian Watson; ✉ Daisy Cottage, Moreton Pinkney, Daventry, Northamptonshire NN11 3SQ (e-mail ianwatson@cix.co.uk, website www.ianwatson.info)

WATSON, Ven Jeffrey John Seagrief; s of John Cole Watson (d 1987), and Marguerite Freda Rose, *née* Seagrief, of Histon, Cambs; *b* 29 April 1939; *Educ* Univ Coll Sch Hampstead, Emmanuel Coll Cambridge (minor scholar, MA), Clifton Theol Coll Bristol; *m* 20 Sept 1969, Rosemary Grace, da of Harold Arnold John Lea; 1 da (Rachel Helen b 16 Jan 1971), 1 s (David John Seagrief b 18 April 1973); *Career* curate: Christ Church Beckenham (Dio of Rochester) 1965–69, St Jude Southsea (Dio of Portsmouth) 1969–71; vicar Christ Church Winchester (Dio of Winchester) 1971–81, examining chaplain to the Bishop of Winchester 1976–93, vicar of Bitterne (Dio of Winchester) 1981–93, rural dean of Southampton 1983–93, proctor in convocation 1985–95, hon canon of Winchester Cathedral 1991–93, archdeacon of Ely 1993–2004 (archdeacon emeritus 2004–), hon canon of Ely Cathedral 1993–2004; chm C of E Vocations Advsy Sub-Ctee 1991–99, chm C of E Miny Candidates' Panel 1999–; *Recreations* photography, travel, walking, friends, singing barbershop; *Style—* The Ven Jeffrey Watson; ✉ 7 Ferry Road, Hythe, Southampton, Hampshire SO45 5GB (tel 023 8084 1189)

WATSON, Jenny; *Career* dir Global Ptnrs and Assocs; chair Equal Opportunities Cmmn 2005– (cmmr 1999–, dep chair 2000–05); dep chair: Ctee on Radioactive Waste Mgmnt, Banking Code Standards Bd; memb: Advertising Advsy Ctee CAP (Broadcast), Cncl Women's Library London Met Univ; *Style—* Ms Jenny Watson; ✉ Equal Opportunities Commission, 36 Broadway, London SW1H 0BH

WATSON, Dr John David; *b* 7 February 1946; *Educ* The Acad Omagh, Trinity Coll Dublin (BA, MB BCh, BAO), LM (Rotunda Hosp), Univ of Edinburgh (DipSocMed); *m*; 3 c; *Career* house offr Adelaide Hosp Dublin 1971–72, dir of public health Northern Health and Social Servs Bd 1989– (chief admin med offr 1981–89); author of published papers in learned jls; memb Bd Faculty of Public Health Med; visiting prof of public health Univ of Ulster 2000–05; fell Ulster Med Soc; DObstRCOG, FFCM London 1986 (MFCM 1977), FFPHM 1989, MFPHMI 1997, FRCP 1999; *Clubs* Tyrone County; *Style—* Dr John Watson; ✉ 2 The Old Mill, Dunadry Road, Dunadry, Co Antrim BT41 4QF

WATSON, John Grenville Bernard; OBE (1998); s of Norman Victor Watson (d 1969), of Leeds, and Ruby Ernestine, *née* Hawker (d 1962); *b* 21 February 1943; *Educ* Bootham Sch York, Coll of Law; *m* 12 June 1965, Deanna, da of Jack Wood (d 1970), of Sheffield; 1 s (Alexander b 1973), 2 da (Melinda b 1975, Sophie b 1975); *Career* asst slr Hepworth & Chadwick 1967–69, mgmnt trainee John Waddingtons Ltd 1969–73, md Waddingtons Games Ltd 1976–79 (mktg dir 1973–76), dir Main Bd John Waddingtons plc 1979–89; MP (Cons): Skipton 1979–83, Skipton and Ripon 1983–87; PPS 1981–86; dir Goddard Kay Rogers (Northern) Ltd 1989–93; memb Leeds Devpt Corp 1988–93, chief exec Bradford City Challenge Ltd 1992–97, chm Heritage Lottery Fund for Yorkshire 2005–; non-exec dir Yorkshire Building Society 1995–2004; chm Bradford Community NHS Tst 1996–2002; memb N Yorks CC 2005–; nat chm Young Cons 1970–72, chm Cons Candidates Assoc 1975–79, pres Br Youth Cncl 1979–83, Freeman City of London, memb Ct of Assts Worshipful Co of the Makers of Playing Cards; memb Law Soc; *Books* Home from Home (1973), Changing Gear (contrib, 1982), View From The Terrace (contrib, 1986); *Recreations* walking, bungee jumping, travel; *Style—* John Watson, Esq, OBE; ✉ Evergreen Cottage, Main Street, Kirk Deighton, Wetherby LS22 4DZ (tel 01937 588273, e-mail johnwatson@ukonline.co.uk)

WATSON, (Joseph) John Henderson; s of Charles Henderson Watson, and Elsie Mary Watson; *Educ* Univ of Leeds; *Career* project engr ICI 1962–67, prodn and tech mangr DIO Factory 1967–72, personnel and industrial rels mangr Boots Gp 1972–85, personnel dir Boots Pharmaceuticals 1985–91, md Boots Contract Manufacturing 1991–2001, gp bd dir Boots Co plc 1996–2001; chm: Boots Pensions Ltd, Boots Charitable Tst; currently chm Nottingham Development Enterprise; govr Nottingham Trent Univ; FIMechE, FIPD; *Recreations* bridge, golf, political issues; *Style—* John Watson, Esq

WATSON, John Henry; OBE (2001); s of Henry William Watson (d 1963), and Rose Hannah, *née* Abley (d 1982); *b* 25 January 1944; *Educ* Wolverhampton GS; *m* 1966, Marigold Anne, da of Rev William Young Milne, Rector of Malvern Wells; 1 s (decd), 3 da; *Career* qualified as CA 1966, mgmnt conslt Touche Ross & Co 1968–71, fin dir Pillsbury UK Ltd 1975–85, sr vice-pres Pillsbury Canada Ltd 1985; vice-pres int fin The Pillsbury Co USA; chief fin offr and exec vice-pres Rank America 1989–2000; pres Br American Business Gp of Atlanta 1999–2000; exec vice-pres and chief admin offr MFI America Inc 2001–; FCA; *Recreations* various; *Style—* John Watson, Esq, OBE, FCA; ✉ 110 Spalding Mill, Dunwoody, Georgia 30350, USA

WATSON, John Michael (Mike); s of (George) Ian Watson, and Caroline Murray, *née* Gilchrist; *Educ* Clifton, CCC Cambridge; *m* 1997, Liz, *née* Andrews; 3 c from previous m; *Career* various roles rising to tech dir Europe Honeywell Inc 1968–82, dir mktg and tech strategy ICL plc 1982–88, md BICC Technologies Ltd (part of BICC Gp plc) 1988–91, non-exec chm Signal Processors Ltd 1992–94, non-exec dir OSI Gp plc 1992–95, dir business devpt OASiS Gp plc 1992–94, exec dir mktg and sales AEA Technology plc 1994–98, chief exec Tertio Ltd 1998–99, chm NWP Communications Ltd 2001–04, regnl chm Vistage Int Ltd 2002–, chm FWL Technologies Ltd 2002–04; non-exec dir: Spectrum Interactive plc 2005–, Zamano plc 2006–; lead lecturer IEE Faraday Lecture 1986–87, presented BCS-sponsored lecture RSA 1990; Liveryman Worshipful Co of Information Technologists; memb Br Computer Soc; FRSA, FIEE, FREng (past memb Cncl); *Recreations* skiing, golf, gardening, theatre; *Style—* Mike Watson, Esq; ✉ Bank House, High Street, Shipton-under-Wychwood, Oxfordshire OX7 6BA (tel 01993 832624, e-mail mike@jmw-enterprises.fsbusiness.co.uk)

WATSON, Mervyn Edward Robert; s of Robert George Watson, of Darlington, Co Durham, and Beryl May, *née* Lord; *b* 23 August 1945; *Educ* Queen Elizabeth GS Darlington, Univ of Nottingham (BSc), Univ of Sask Canada (BA); *Career* trainee mangr BSC 1963–68, res metallurgist Hudson Bay Mining and Smelting Co Manitoba Canada 1968–70, actor Coventry Theatre in Educn Co 1972–75, actor and assoc dir Humberside Theatre Hull 1975–77, assoc dir Alan Ayckbourn's Theatre in the Round Scarborough, playwright and freelance theatre dir 1979–80, sr prodr Granada TV 1980–91, dep head of drama series BBC TV Drama Group 1991–94, dep controller of drama Yorkshire Television 1994–98, md Red Rooster Film and Television 1998–2000, exec prodr BBC Drama Series 2000–; *Television* prodr/exec prodr progs for Granada TV incl: Coronation Street 1982–84 and 1989–91, First Among Equals (by Jeffrey Archer) 1985–86, Floodtide (by Roger Marshall) 1987, Wipe Out (by Martin Stone and Ric Maher) 1988; for BBC TV incl: Harry, Pie in the Sky, Casualty, Down to Earth; for Yorkshire TV incl Emmerdale 1994–98; *Plays* (written) incl: Big Deal (stage play for 9 to 11 year olds) 1975, Reversed Charges (stage and radio) 1978, Hands (with Rosemary Leach, TV play) 1980, Family Man (with Julie Walters and John Duttine, TV play) 1983, Coronation Street 1991–; *Recreations* DIY, hill walking, skiing; *Style—* Mervyn Watson, Esq; ✉ e-mail mervyn.watson@bbc.co.uk

WATSON, Dr Michael Leonard; s of Col Edgar Stewart Watson, OBE, of Bridlington and Dorothy, *née* Mansfield; *b* 29 March 1949; *Educ* Merchiston Castle Sch Edinburgh, Univ of Edinburgh (BSc, MB ChB, MD); *m* 1, 27 March 1971, Penelope Ann, da of William H A Bartlett, of Elvanfoot; 1 da (Fiona Jane b 15 Oct 1976), 1 s (James Stuart Michael b 31 Jan 1979); m 2, 6 Sept 1992, Marion, da of R T Emond, of London; *Career* travelling fell MRC 1981–82, conslt physician Royal Infirmary Edinburgh 1984–, head of Med Services Royal Infirmary Edinburgh 1996–2001; med dir NHS Educn Scotland 2005–; chair Symposium Ctee RCP Edinburgh; FRCP 1986–90; *Recreations* mountaineering; *Style—* Dr Michael L Watson; ✉ 44 Ann Street, Edinburgh EH4 1PJ (tel 0131 332 2205); NHS Education Scotland, 66 Rose Street, Edinburgh EH2 2NN (tel 0131 220 8695)

WATSON, Mike; *see:* Rt Hon Lord Watson of Invergowrie

WATSON, Moray Robin Philip Adrian; s of Capt Gerard Arthur Watson (ka 1940), and Jean, *née* MacFarlane (d 1969); *b* 25 June 1928; *Educ* Eton, Webber-Douglas Acad for Singing and Dramatic Art; *m* 28 June 1955, Pamela Phyllis, da of Percy Garfield Marmont (d 1977); 1 da (Emma Kate b 1957), 1 s (Robin Guy Stewart b 1959); *Career* actor; cmmnd 5 Bn Northamptonshire Regt 1948, served Austria; London debut Small Hotel (St Martin's) 1955; *Theatre* incl: A River Breeze, Plaintiff in a Pretty Hour, The Grass is Greener, The Bad Soldier, Smith (title role), The Doctor's Dilemma (with Wilfred Hyde White and Anna Massey) 1963, The Public Eye (Broadway) 1963–64, You Never Can Tell (with Ralph Richardson and Harry Andrews) 1965, The Rivals (with Ralph Richardson and Margaret Rutherford) 1966, Hay Fever (with Penelope Keith), Lettice and Lovage (with Geraldine McEwan), Under Their Hats (Flanders and Swann Revue, dir by Wendy Toye); Fools Rush In (by Ray Cooney) 1996, Super-Beasts (Emlyn Williams' adaptation of Saki Short Stories) 1997, Col Pickering in Pygmalion (Albery), The Chiltern Hundreds (Vaudeville Theatre) 2000, Nobody's Perfect (two nat tours); one person show Sir Max Beerbohm Remembers (based on the writings of Sir Max Beerbohm), Ancestral Voices (Hugh Massingberd's one person show based on the writings of James Lees-Milne), Looking Back and Dropping Names 2007; *Television* incl: The Quatermass Experiment 1961, Compact 1962–63, Pride and Prejudice, The Pallisers, Nobody's Perfect, Rumpole of the Bailey, Seal Morning, The Body in the Library, The Darling Buds of May, Midsomer Murders, Perfect World, Bertie and Elizabeth; *Films* incl: The Grass is Greener, The Valiant, Operation Crossbow, The Sea Wolves, Every Home Should Have One; *Clubs* The Garrick; *Style—* Moray Watson, Esq; ✉ 81 Elm Grove Road, Barnes, London SW13 0BX; c/o Lesley Duff, 31 Percy Street, London W1T 2DD

WATSON, Dr Peter; OBE 1987; *b* 9 January 1944; *Educ* Univ of Leeds (BSc), Univ of Waterloo Canada (MSc, PhD); *Career* sci offr II rising to princ sci offr BR Research 1971–76; GKN plc 1976–91: mangr Materials Engrg then dir Product Engrg GKN Technology Ltd 1976–82, chm GKN Technology Ltd 1982–87, gen mangr Product Devpt GKN Gp 1982–87, memb GKN Gp Mgmnt Ctee 1984–87, dir Assa Stenman AB Sweden 1984–87, chm GKN Axles Div 1986–91, dir Product & Business Devpt GKN Automotive Div 1987–91, chm GKN Composites Ltd 1987–91, supervisory bd memb Uni Carden AG Germany 1987–90, pres GKN Technology Inc USA 1987–90, chm GKN Powder Metallurgy Div 1990–91, chm GKN Suspensions Div 1990–91; Bd memb Engrg BR 1991–94 (also chm BR Maintenance Ltd, dir BR Telecommunications Ltd and chm Procurement Ctee), exec chm AEA Technology plc 2002–05 (chief exec 1994–2001); non-exec dir: Spectris plc 1997–2003, Martin Currie Enhanced Income Tst plc 2000–05, HSL Ltd 2006–, SVL Ltd 2007–; chm Porterbrook Leasing Co 1996, chm Engrg Policy Ctee Sheffield Hallam Univ, chm Lontra Ltd 2006–; pres Engrg Integrity Soc; visiting prof Imperial Coll London 2005–; memb Bd Univ of Wolverhampton; FIMechE, FCIPS, FREng 1998; *Style—* Dr Peter Watson; ✉ 49 Suckling Gren Lane, Codsall, Wolverhampton WV8 2BT (tel 01902 845252, fax 01902 847356)

WATSON, Peter Frank Patrick; s of Frank Patrick Watson (d 1963), of Birmingham, and Lilian Ethel, *née* Hopwood (d 1993); *b* 23 April 1943; *Educ* Cheltenham GS, Univ of Durham (Psychology prize), Univ of London, Univ of Rome; *m* 1 (m dis), Nichola Theodas; m 2 (m dis), Lesley Rowlatt; *Career* intern Tavistock Clinic 1966–68; dep ed New Society 1968–71, Sunday Times 1971–81, The Times 1981–83, The Observer 1985–97, research assoc McDonald Inst for Archaeological Research Univ of Cambridge 1997; regular contrib New York Times; Italian Govt music scholarship 1964, US Govt bursary 1970, Crime Writers of Britain Gold Dagger 1982, SAFE Beacon Award 2006; memb: PEN 1988, Br Psychological Soc; *Books* War on the Mind: the Military Uses and Abuses of Psychology (1973), Twins (1980), The Caravaggio Conspiracy (1982), Wisdom & Strength: the Biography of a Renaissance Masterpiece (1990), From Manet to Manhattan: the Rise of the Modern Art Market (1992), Nureyev: a Biography (1994), The Death of Hitler (with Ada Petrova, 1995), Sotheby's: Inside Story (1997), A Terrible Beauty: the People and Ideas that Shaped the Modern Mind (2000), Ideas: A History from Fire to Freud (2005), The Medici Conspiracy: Organized Crime, Looted Antiquities, Rogue Museums (with Cecilia Todeschini, 2006); author of 5 novels set in the art world; books translated into 20 languages; *Recreations* opera, cricket, fishing; *Clubs* Garrick; *Style—* Peter Watson, Esq

WATSON, Prof (John) Richard; s of Reginald Joseph Watson, and Alice Mabel, *née* Tennant; *b* 15 June 1934; *Educ* Magdalen Coll Oxford (MA), Univ of Glasgow (PhD); *m* 21 July 1962, Pauline Elizabeth, *née* Roberts; 1 s (David James b 1966), 2 da (Elizabeth Emma b 1968, Rachel Clare b 1971); *Career* 2 Lt RA 1953–55; lectr: Univ of Glasgow 1962–66, Univ of Leicester 1966–78; Univ of Durham: prof of English 1978–99, public orator 1989–99, emeritus prof 1999–; gen ed Dictionary of Hymnology Research Project 2001–; memb Archbishops' Cmmn on Church Music 1988–92, chm Modern Humanities Research Assoc 1990–99; pres Int Assoc of Univ Profs of English 1995–98, pres Charles Lamb Soc 2003–, vice-pres Charles Wesley Soc 1994–2003; *Books* Wordsworth's Vital Soul (1982), Everyman's Book of Victorian Verse (ed, 1982), English Poetry of the Romantic Period 1789–1830 (1985), The Poetry of Gerard Manley Hopkins (1987), Companion to Hymns and Psalms (with K Trickett, 1988), A Handbook to English Romanticism (with J Raimond, 1992), The English Hymn (1997), An Annotated Anthology of Hymns (2002), Romanticism and War (2003), Awake My Soul (2004); *Recreations* playing the cello, bookbinding, cycling, hill walking; *Style—* Prof Richard Watson; ✉ Stoneyhurst, 27 Albert Street, Western Hill, Durham DH1 4RL (tel 0191 384 5716); University of Durham, English Department, Hallgarth House, 77 Hallgarth Street, Durham DH1 3AY (e-mail j.r.watson@durham.ac.uk)

WATSON, Sheila; da of Ron Watson (d 2000), of Sunderland, and Sheila Watson; *b* 21 December 1965; *Educ* Univ of Oxford (BA), Univ of London (MSc); *m* Andrew Trigg; 3 s (George b 23 June 1998, Tom b 11 Dec 2001, Jack b 17 April 2004); *Career* res offr Inst for Fiscal Studies 1988–90, econ advsr to Rt Hon Margaret Beckett, MP, *qv*, 1990–94, dep dir and conslt economist Centre for Local Econ Strategies 1994–97, special advsr to Pres of the Bd of Trade 1997–2001, special advsr to Leader of the House 1998–2001, special advsr to sec of state for Environment, Food and Rural Affrs 2001–06, sr special advsr to Foreign Sec 2006–; *Publications* Economic Policy and the division of income within the family (1990), Modelling the effects of prescription charge rises (in Fiscal Studies, 1990), What should count as public expenditure? (in Public Expenditure, ed D Corry, 1997), The Role of Development Trusts (1997), The consequences of the abolition of the Inner London Education Authority (in Fiscal Studies, 1988); *Style*— Ms Sheila Watson; ✉ Foreign and Commonwealth Office, King Charles Street, London SW1A 2AH (tel 020 7008 2117, fax 020 7008 2336, e-mail sheila.watson@fco.gov.uk)

WATSON, Sheila Mary; da of Joseph Herbert Watson, OBE, MC (d 1990), and Evelyn Ada, *née* Patching (d 1993); *b* 8 March 1931; *Educ* The Warren Worthing, King's Coll London, Univ of Bordeaux (BA); *m* 1, 2 Sept 1961 (m dis), Neil Francis Elliot Blackmore, s of late William Blackmore, MD; 2 da (Karen Anne b 30 May 1964, Laura b 10 Sept 1967); m 2, 15 April 1972, David Hugh Arthur Christie-Murray; *Career* dir David Higham Associates (authors' agents) 1955–71, dir and sec Bolt & Watson Ltd 1971–83, currently chair Watson Little Ltd (md 1983–2003); *Recreations* reading, walking; *Style*— Ms Sheila Watson; ✉ Capo Di Monte, Windmill Hill, London NW3 6RJ (tel 020 7431 6819); Watson Little Ltd (tel 020 7431 0770, e-mail sw@watsonlittle.com)

WATSON, Shirley; da of Andrew Johnson, of Hexham, Northumberland, and Adella, *née* Cowen; *b* 24 May 1955; *Educ* Queen Elizabeth GS, Univ of Bradford (BSc); *m* 22 Sept 1979, David Alan Watson, s of Harold Roy Watson (d 1971); *Career* articled clerk rising to asst mangr Ernst & Young CAs 1984–88, mgmnt accountant rising to fin dir Marketing Solutions Ltd 1988–89, UK fin controller Boase Massimi Pollitt advtg agency 1988–89, fin dir BMP DDB 1989–; ACA 1981, MIPA 1990; *Style*— Mrs Shirley Watson; ✉ 68 Games Road, Ludgrove Hall, Barnet EN4 9HW (tel 020 8441 7169); BMP DDB Ltd, 12 Bishop's Bridge Road, London W2 6AA (tel 020 7258 4856, fax 020 7723 9846)

WATSON, Simon John; s of John Charles Watson, of Reigate, Surrey, and Lorna Kathleen, *née* Whitehouse; *b* 13 May 1958; *Educ* Maidstone GS, St Catherine's Coll Oxford (MA); *Career* admitted slr 1983; ptnr Simmons & Simmons 1988– (articled clerk 1981–83, asst slr 1983–88); memb Law Soc; *Recreations* opera, bridge; *Style*— Simon Watson, Esq; ✉ City Point, One Ropemaker Street, London EC2Y 9SS (tel 020 7628 2020, fax 020 7628 2070)

WATSON, Prof Stephen Roger; s of John Cole Watson, MBE (d 1987), of London, and Marguerite Freda Rose, *née* Seagrief; *b* 29 August 1943; *Educ* UCS Hampstead, Emmanuel Coll Cambridge (MA, PhD); *m* 26 July 1969, Rosemary Victoria, da of Rt Rev Cyril James Tucker, CBE (d 1992), of Cambridge; 1 s (Oliver b 5 Feb 1972), 1 da (Emily b 18 Feb 1975); *Career* planning asst Shell International Petroleum Co 1970–71; Univ of Cambridge: fell Emmanuel Coll 1971– (res fell 1968–70), lectr Engrg Dept 1971–86, Peat Marwick prof of mgmnt studies 1986–94, dir Judge Inst of Mgmnt Studies 1990–94; dean Management Sch Lancaster Univ 1994–2001, princ Henley Management Coll 2001–05; dir: Cambridge Decision Analysts 1984–94, Environmental Resources Management 1989–95; *Books* Decision Synthesis (with D M Buede, 1988); *Recreations* overseas development, singing; *Style*— Prof Stephen Watson; ✉ 33 De Freville Avenue, Cambridge CB4 1HW (tel 01223 319527, e-mail srw12@cam.ac.uk)

WATSON, Tom; MP; *b* 1967; *Educ* King Charles I Sch Kidderminster; *Career* dep gen election co-ordinator Lab Pty until 1997, political offr AEEU 1997–2001; MP (Lab) West Bromwich E 2001–, PPS to Rt Hon Dawn Primarolo MP 2003–04, asst govt whip 2004–05, lord cmmr to HM Treasy 2005–06, Parly under sec of state MOD 2006–; *Style*— Tom Watson, Esq, MP; ✉ House of Commons, London SW1A 0AA

WATSON-GANDY OF MYRTON, Professor Mark; s of James Alastair Christian Campbell Watson-Gandy, and Barbara Jadwiga Theresa, *née* Madry; *b* 8 November 1967; *Educ* Dr Challoner's GS, Univ of Essex (LLB), Inns of Court Sch of Law, ICAEW; *m* 1997, Emanuella Johanna Christina, *née* Giavarra; 1 s (James b 2002); *Career* called to the Bar Inner Temple 1990; practising barrister, one of the prosecuting counsel to the DTI 1999–2002, jr counsel to the Crown 2000; accountant, memb Professional Advsy Panel Inst of Fin Accountants; visiting prof Univ of Westminster 1999–; memb Panel of Arbitrators: ICAEW, World Intellectual Property Orgn, Alternative Dispute Resolution Services (ADRS); chm Ctee of Tstees Inst of Heraldic and Genealogical Studies; head of professional standards and hon fell Inst of Certified Bookkeepers 1997; memb Guild of Freeman; Freeman City of London 1995, Liveryman Worshipful Co of Scrivener's 1996; KM; *Publications* books incl: Beyond the Peradventure, Thomson Tax Guide (co-ed), Watson-Gandy on the Law Relating to Accountants; jls incl: Justice of the Peace (local govt ed, 1993–99), Family Court Reporter (asst ed, 1993–99), Litigation (ed, 1994–98), European Current Law (contributing ed, 1998–2000); *Style*— Professor Mark Watson-Gandy; ✉ 13 Old Square, Lincoln's Inn, London WC2A 3UA (tel 020 7831 4445, fax 020 7841 5825, e-mail mwg@13oldsquare.com)

WATSON OF INVERGOWRIE, Baron (Life Peer UK 1997), of Invergowrie in Perth and Kinross; Michael Goodall (Mike) Watson; s of Clarke Carter Watson (d 1995), and Agnes Hope, *née* Goodall (d 1991); *b* 1 May 1949; *Educ* Dundee HS, Heriot-Watt Univ (BA); *Career* devpt offr and tutor Mid-Derbyshire Workers Educnl Assoc 1974–77, trade union official ASTMS (now Amicus) 1977–89 (divnl offr 1977–87, regnl offr 1987–89), MP (Lab) Glasgow Central (by-election) 1989–97; memb: Select Ctee on Parly Cmmr for Admin 1990–95, Public Accounts Ctee 1995–97, Leadership Campaign Team (with responsibility for foreign affairs) 1995–97; chm PLP Ctee on Overseas Devpt Aid 1991–97, sec PLP Trade Union Gp 1990–97; dir P S Communication Consultants Ltd 1997–99; MSP (Lab) Glasgow Cathcart 1999–2005; min for tourism, culture and sport 2001–03; memb Exec Ctee Lab Pty Scot Cncl 1987–90; *Books* Rags to Riches - The Official History of Dundee United Football Club (1985), Year Zero: An Inside View of the Scottish Parliament (2001); *Recreations* running, watching Dundee United FC, reading; *Style*— The Lord Watson of Invergowrie; ✉ House of Lords, London SW1A 0PW (tel 020 7219 8731, e-mail watsonm@parliament.uk)

WATSON OF RICHMOND, Baron (Life Peer UK 1999), of Richmond in the London Borough of Richmond upon Thames; Alan John Watson; CBE (1985); s of Rev John William Watson (d 1980), of Bognor Regis, and Edna Mary, *née* Peters (d 1985); *b* 3 February 1941; *Educ* Kingswood Sch Bath, Jesus Coll Cambridge (MA); *m* 1965, Karen, da of Hartwig Lederer (d 1966), of Frankfurt-on-Main; 2 s (Hon Stephen b 1966, Hon Martin b 1968); *Career* history scholar and res asst to regius prof of modern history Cambridge 1962–64; broadcaster; presenter The Money Programme (BBC 2) and Panorama (BBC 1) 1964–76, head of radio & TV EEC Cmmn 1976–80; presenter: You and 92 (BBC 1) 1990, The Germans (Channel 4) 1992, Key Witness (BBC Radio 4) 1996; chief exec Charles Barker City Ltd 1980–83, dep chm Sterling PR Ltd 1985–86; chm: City and Corporate Counsel Ltd 1987–93, Corporate Vision Ltd 1989–98, Threadneedle Publishing Group plc 1989–94, CTN (Corporate Television Networks) Ltd 1992–, Burson-Marsteller Europe 1996– (chm Burson-Marsteller UK 1994–96), Coca-Cola European Advsy Bd 2004–, Raisin Social Ltd 2005–; visiting fell Louvainium Business Sch Brussels 1990–94, Erasmus visiting prof Catholic Univ of Louvain 1990–, hon prof German Studies Univ of Birmingham 1997–, memb Bd GB Studies Centre Humboldt Univ Berlin 1999–, visiting fell Oriel Coll Oxford 2003–; pres Lib Pty 1984–85, vice-chm European Movement 1995–2001; memb: House of Lords Select Ctee on the EU 2000–04 and 2006–, Exec Bd UNICEF 1985–92, Exec Jesus Coll Cambridge Soc 1987–94, Bd Prince of Wales Int Business Leaders' Forum 1996–, BT Bd Community and Charities Ctee 1996–2004; chm: Royal Television Soc 1992–94, British-German Assoc 1992– (chm 1992–2000, pres 2001), Royal Acad Devpt Bd 1999–2001, Cncl of Cwlth Socs 2003–; pres Heathrow Assoc for the Control of Aircraft Noise 1991–95; chm: Bd of Govrs Westminster Coll Oxford 1988–94, Richmond Theatre Appeal 1990–91, Father Thames Tst 1998–, Cambridge Univ Chemistry Advsy Bd 2000–, The Cambridge Fndn 2005–; govr: Kingswood Sch 1984–90, ESU 1993– (dep chm 1995–99, chm 2000, int chm 2002–06, int chm emeritus 2006–); tstee Richmond Univ; Hon Doctorate St Lawrence Univ 1992; hon prof of int studies Univ of St Petersburg 2003–, hon fell Jesus Coll Cambridge 2004, hon prof Korea Univ 2004; Int Award Manila Univ 2005; German Order of Merit 1995 (Grand Cross 2002), Grand Cross Romanian Order of Merit 2004; FRTS 1992, FIPR 1999, FIVCA 2000; *Books* Europe at Risk (1974), The Germans (1992, 1994 and 1995); *Recreations* travel, wines, boating; *Clubs* Brooks's, RAC, Kennel; *Style*— The Rt Hon the Lord Watson of Richmond, CBE; ✉ Cholmondeley House, 3 Cholmondeley Walk, Richmond, Surrey; Somerset Lodge, Nunney, Somerset; Burson-Marsteller, 24–28 Bloomsbury Way, London WC1A 2PX (tel 020 7300 6320, fax 020 7242 1520)

WATT, *see also:* Harvie-Watt

WATT, Alison; da of James Watt, and Annie (Nancy), *née* Sinclair; *b* 11 December 1965; *Educ* Glasgow Sch of Art (BA, postgrad studies, first prize Glasgow Competition, Armour prize for still life painting); *Career* artist; assoc artist Nat Gallery London 2006–; *Solo Exhibitions* One Woman Show (The Scottish Gallery, London) 1990, One Woman Show - Contemporary Art Season (Kelvingrove Art Gallery and Museum Glasgow) 1990, Flowers East Gallery London 1993 and 1995, Charles Belloc Lowndes Fine Art Chicago 1996, Monotypes (Flowers East Gallery London) 1997, Fold (The Fruitmarket Gallery Edinburgh) 1997, Aberdeen Art Gallery 1998, Leeds Metropolitan Univ Gallery 1998, Scottish Nat Gallery of Modern Art Edinburgh 2000, Dulwich Picture Gallery London 2001, Still (installation, Old St Paul's Church Edinburgh) 2004, Nat Gallery 2008; *Group Exhibitions* incl: British Inst Fund (Royal Acad of Arts London) 1986, Nat Portrait Competition (Nat Portrait Gallery London) 1987, Six Women Artists (Scottish Gallery Edinburgh) 1988, London Opening (Scottish Gallery London) 1989, Royal Scottish Portrait Award (Royal Scottish Acad Edinburgh) 1989, The Compass Contribution (Tramway Glasgow) 1990, Scottish Art in the 20th Century (Royal West of England Acad Bristol) 1991, The Portrait Award (Nat Portrait Gallery London) 1992, Plymouth City Museum & Art Gallery 1992, LA Art Fair 1992, Art '93 London 1993, Decouvertes (Paris Art Fair) 1993, Fred Hoffman Gallery LA 1993, Inner Visions (Flowers East Gallery London) 1994, The Twenty Fifth Anniversary Exhibition (Flowers East at London Fields) 1995, The Power of Images (Martin Gropius Bau Berlin) 1996, Four British Painters (John McEnroe Gallery NY) 1996, Bad Blood (Glasgow Print Studio) 1996, Paintings (Mendenhall Gallery Pasadena) 1996, Treasures For Everyone (Nat Art Collections Fund Christie's London) 1997, Von Kopf Bis Fuss (Ursula Buckle Stiftung Kraichtal) 1997, Body Politic (Wolverhampton Art Gallery) 1997, Londres, Glasgow (Galerie Rachlin Lemarie Paris) 1998, Human Figure (Gallerie de Belle Feuille Montreal) 1999, Narcissus (Nat Portrait Gallery London) 2001, Fold (City Art Gallery Leicester) 2002, Jerwood Painting Prize Exhbn (Jerwood Space London) 2003; *Commissions* HRH Queen Elizabeth The Queen Mother (Nat Portrait Gallery London), Kelvingrove Art Gallery and Museum Glasgow, The Observer, EMI Records, News Scotland Ltd, Mirror Gp Newspapers, Collins Publishers, numerous private cmmns; *Works in Collections* Nat Portrait Gallery, Glasgow Art Gallery and Museum, BBC, Robert Fleming Holdings Ltd London, Robert and Susan Kasen Summer NY, Aberdeen Art Gallery, National Westminster Bank plc, McMaster Univ Art Gallery, The Freud Museum London, Ferens Art Gallery Hull, Christie's Corporate Art Collection, Scottish Nat Gallery of Modern Art, Deutsche Bank, Southampton City Art Gallery, Scottish Parliament; *Awards* first prize for painting Br Inst Fund (Royal Acad of Arts) 1986, winner John Player Portrait Award (Nat Portrait Gallery) 1987, Elizabeth Greenshields Fndn Award Montreal Canada 1989, special commendation Morrison Scottish Portrait Award (Royal Scottish Acad) 1989, The Lord Provost's Prize 1993, Artist's Award Scottish Arts Cncl 1996, shortlisted Jerwood Painting Prize 2003, Creative Scotland Award 2004; *Style*— Ms Alison Watt; ✉ c/o Ingleby Gallery, 6 Carlton Terrace, Edinburgh EH7 5DD

WATT, Prof Graham Charles Murray; s of Alan Crombie Robertson Watt (d 1989), of Skene, Aberdeenshire, and Helen, *née* Hughes; *b* 3 January 1952; *Educ* Aberdeen GS, Univ of Aberdeen (BMedBiol, MB ChB, MD, Cardno prize in anatomy, McWillie prize in biochemistry and physiology, Durno prize and Lizard medal in anatomy, Munday and Venn prize, Watt prize in social med); *m* 29 Dec 1983, Elizabeth Anne, da of John Munro; 2 da (Nuala Catherine Morley b 12 Dec 1984, Vari Helen Munro b 29 May 1986); *Career* med house officer City Hosp Aberdeen 1976–77, surgical house officer Gilbert Bain Hosp Lerwick 1977, registrar in histopathology and morbid anatomy Leicester General Hosp 1977–78, surgical house officer in general med Aberdeen Hosps 1978–80, registrar in geriatric med Dept of Health Care of the Elderly Sherwood Hosp Nottingham 1980, res registrar MRC Epidemiology and Med Care unit Northwick Park Hosp 1980–82, paediatric vocational trainee in general practice Ladywell Med Centre and Sch of Community Paediatrics Univ of Edinburgh 1982–83, head MONICA Project Centre and res fell Dept of General Practice Univ of Glasgow 1983–86, hon lectr Cardiovascular Epidemiology Unit Univ of Dundee 1983–86, trainee GP Townhead Health Centre Glasgow 1986, trainee in community med Greater Glasgow Health Bd 1986–87, sr med offr Chief Scientist Office Scottish Home and Health Dept 1987–89, prof of general practice Univ of Glasgow 1994– (sr lectr in public health 1990–94); currently hon conslt in public health med Greater Glasgow Health Bd; memb: BMA, Soc of Social Med, Assoc of Univ Depts of General Practice; MRCP 1979, MRCGP 1986, FRCPGlas 1991, FFPHM 1994 (MFPHM 1987), FMedSci 2000; *Publications* author of numerous research pubns and invited scientific presentations on epidemiology of cardiorespiratory disease in families, inequalities in health, environmental health and health servs research; *Clubs* Kettle; *Style*— Prof Graham Watt; ✉ University Department of General Practice, 1 Horselethill Road, Glasgow G12 9LX (tel 0141 330 8345, fax 0141 330 8331)

WATT, Iain Alasdair; s of Dr Andrew Watt (d 1999), of Edinburgh, and Margaret Fawns, *née* Brown (d 1967); *Educ* Edinburgh Acad, Univ of Hull (BSc); *m* 30 June 1971, Lynne Neilson, da of Harold Livingston (d 1984), of Kirkcaldy; 3 s (Nicholas b 15 Feb 1973, Christopher Nial b 25 April 1975, Oliver Noel b 10 July 1980), 1 da (Gemma Stephanie Margaret b 12 April 1985); *Career* joined Bank of Scotland Gp 1964, dir British Linen Bank Ltd (subsid) 1986–, former chief exec Edinburgh Fund Managers Gp plc; dir other cos incl Edinburgh Dragon Trust; bd tstee Nat Museums Scotland, tstee Nat Museums Scotland Charitable Tst; memb Cncl Queens Nursing Inst in Scotland; FCIB; *Recreations* tennis, golf; *Clubs* Golf House Elie, Bruntsfield Golf, N Berwick Golf, Mid Ocean Bermuda, Aberdour Tennis; *Style*— I A Watt, Esq; ✉ Sycamore Bank, North Queensferry, Fife (tel 01383 413645)

WATT, HE James Wilfrid; CVO (1997); s of Anthony James MacDonald Watt, and Sona Elvey, *née* White; *b* 5 November 1951, Carlisle, Cumbria; *Educ* Ampleforth, The Queen's Coll Oxford (BA); *m* 1, 1980, Elizabeth Ghislaine, *née* Villeneuvre (decd); 1 s (Louis b 1981), 1 da (Clelia b 1986); m 2, 2004, Amal Saad; *Career* diplomat; entered HM Dip Serv 1977, FCO 1977–78, language trg 1978–80, second then first sec (Chancery) Abu Dhabi 1980–83, FCO 1983–85, first sec (Chancery) UKMIS NY 1985–89, dep head UN Dept FCO 1989–92, dep head of mission Amman 1992–96, dep high cmmr Islamabad 1996–98, career devpt attachment SOAS Univ of London 1999–2000, dir of consular services FCO 2000–03, ambass to Lebanon 2003–06, ambass to Jordan 2006–; *Recreations* languages, travel, archaeology, the outdoors; *Clubs* Athenaeum; *Style*— HE Mr James Watt, CVO; ✉ c/o Foreign & Commonwealth Office (Amman), King Charles Street, London SW1A 2AH (e-mail james.watt@fco.gov.uk)

WATT, Dr Jean Barbara; da of Capt Douglas Maxwell Watt, MM (d 1967), of Kingsheath, Birmingham, and Barbara Gwenllian Havard, *née* Jones; *b* 15 December 1948; *Educ* Howells Sch Llandaff, King Edward VI Sch for Girls Kings Heath Birmingham, Univ of Birmingham (MB ChB); *m* 15 July 1978, Gavin Neil McKenzie, s of Roderick Charles

McKenzie (d 1969), of Warlingham, Surrey; 2 da (Molly b 1980, Charlotte b 1985); *Career* SHO Univ Hosp of Wales Cardiff 1973–76, registrar The Hosp for Sick Children Great Ormond Street London 1976–79, sr registrar in paediatrics St Mary's Hosp Paddington London 1982–87, conslt paediatrician Royal Shrewsbury Hosp 1987–, former clinical dir Community Children's Directorate; hon sr lectr in paediatrics Univ of Birmingham; W Midlands Regnl Advsr RCPCH 2000–06; FRCP 1994 (MRCP 1975), FRCPCH 1997; *Recreations* gardening; *Style—* Dr Jean Watt; ✉ Meole Cottage, Mill Road, Meolebrace, Shrewsbury SY3 9JT

WATT, John Gillies McArthur; QC (Scot 1992); s of Peter Julius Watt (d 1978), and Nancy, *née* McArthur (d 1998); *b* 14 October 1949; *Educ* Clydebank HS, Univ of Glasgow, Univ of Edinburgh (LLB); *m* 1 (m dis 1988), Catherine, yr da of Robert Russell, of Toronto; 2 da (Rowan b 5 Nov 1976, Harriet b 27 Dec 1979); m 2, Nov 1988, Susan, o da of Dr Tom C Sparks Jr, of Ardmore, Oklahoma and Breckenridge, Colorado; *Career* law apprentice Messrs Mackenzie Roberton Glasgow, admitted slr 1974, ptnr Stewart & Bennett, Argyll 1975–78, admitted Faculty of Advocates 1979, advocate depute 1989, temp sheriff 1991, called to the English Bar Middle Temple 1992; memb Incorporation of Coopers of Glasgow 1976–; *Recreations* shooting, sailing, skiing, opera; *Clubs* Lansdowne, Royal Western Yacht (Glasgow); *Style—* John Watt, Esq, QC

WATT, Laurence Johnstone (Laurie); s of Alexander D J Watt (d 1991), and Rosalind Chris, *née* Valentine; *b* 30 March 1946; *m* 13 Sept 1975 (m dis 2002), Lyndal Joan; 2 s (Alexander b 1977, Theo b 1980); *Career* admitted slr Hong Kong 1978, admitted barr and slr Supreme Ct of Victoria Aust 1983; Cole and Cole: articled clerk 1964–70, admitted slr 1970; Charles Russell: joined 1972, ptnr 1974, sr ptnr until 2006, sr counsel 2006–, specialising in int commercial litigation, public int law and music law; dir ALFA Int (formerly American Law Firm Assoc); memb: Law Soc, Royal Philharmonic Soc (memb Hon Cncl of Mgmnt), Int Bar Assoc, Cwlth Law Assoc; tstee: London Philharmonic Orch Tst, Assoc of Br Orchestras Tst, Salzburg Festival Tst, Schubert Ensemble Tst; *Publications* various articles on musico-legal and musical subjects; *Recreations* music (performing and listening), photography, popular science, reading; *Clubs* Garrick; *Style—* Laurie Watt, Esq; ✉ c/o Charles Russell, 8–10 New Fetter Lane, London EC4A 1RS (tel 020 7203 5145, fax 020 3023 5525, mobile 07831 633088, e-mail laurie.watt@charlesrussell.co.uk)

WATTERS, James Andrew Donaldson; s of Andrew James Watters (d 2003), of Dumfriesshire, and Elsa Donaldson, *née* Broatch; *b* 16 March 1948; *Educ* KCS Wimbledon, Pembroke Coll Oxford (BA); *m* 21 July 1973, Lesley Jane Aves, da of Cyril Joseph Churchman (d 1963); 2 s (Alexander b 4 March 1978, Rupert b 11 June 1980), 1 da (Flora b 16 May 1985); *Career* admitted slr 1972, articled clerk and slr Stephenson Harwood 1970–75, slr Norton Rose 1976–79, sr legal advsr Investors in Industry plc 1980–82; ptnr: Goodwille & Co 1982–85, Stephenson Harwood 1985–92, Watson Farley & Williams 1992–; Freeman City of London; memb Law Soc 1972; *Style—* James Watters, Esq; ✉ 59 de Beauvoir Road, London N1 5AU (tel 020 7503 9080); Watson Farley & Williams, 15 Appold Street, London EC2A 2HB (tel 020 7814 8000, fax 020 7814 8141/2, e-mail jwatters@wfw.com)

WATTIS, Prof John Philip; s of Philip William Wattis, of Leeds, and (Elizabeth) Joan, *née* Nickson; *b* 4 February 1949; *Educ* St Joseph's Coll Blackpool, Univ of Liverpool Med Sch (MB ChB); *m* 12 July 1969, Florence Elizabeth (Libby), da of David John Roberts (d 1980); 2 s (Mark b 1980, Peter b 1985), 2 da (Sharon b 1982, Ruth b 1988); *Career* house offr The Royal Infirmary Liverpool 1972–73, med supt Amudat Mission Hosp Uganda 1973–75, registrar in psychiatry John Conolly Hosp Birmingham 1975–78, lectr in health care of the elderly Univ of Nottingham 1978–81, sr lectr and conslt in old age psychiatry St James's Univ Hosp Leeds 1986–2000 (conslt 1981–86); Leeds Community and Mental Health NHS Trust: med dir 1995–99, assoc dir R&D 1999–2000; visiting prof in psychiatry of old age Univ of Huddersfield 2000–, conslt in psychiatry of old age and actg R&D dir Calderdale and Huddersfield NHS Tst 2001–02, conslt in psychiatry of old age and assoc med dir SW Yorks NHS Tst 2002–05; Section for Psychiatry of Old Age RCPsych (past chm, hon sec and public educn offr), chm Gen and Old Age Psychiatry Specialty Advsy Ctee RCPsych 1997–2001; memb Dementia Gp Christian Cncl on Ageing (past chm); former chm and fndr Leeds Branch Alzheimer's Disease Soc; self-employed coach and mentor to health service staff; FRCPsych 1991 (MRCPsych 1978); *Books* Psychological Assessment of Old People (ed with I Hindmarsh, 1988), Confusion in Old Age (1989), Practical Management of Depression in Old Age (ed with S Curran and S Lynch, 2001), Practical Management of Dementia: A Multidisciplinary Approach (ed with S Curran, 2004), Practical Psychiatry of Old Age (4 edn with S Curran, 2006); *Recreations* mountain biking, photography; *Style—* Prof John Wattis; ✉ Harold Wilson Building, University of Huddersfield, Queensgate, Huddersfield HD1 3DH (tel 01484 343451, e-mail j.wattis@hud.ac.uk or johnwattis@aol.com)

WATTS, Sir Arthur Desmond; KCMG (1989, CMG 1977), QC (1988); s of Col Arthur Edward Watts (d 1958), and Eileen May, *née* Challons (d 1981); *b* 14 November 1931; *Educ* Haileybury, RMA Sandhurst, Downing Coll Cambridge (MA, LLB, Whewell scholar in Int Law); *m* 1957, Iris Ann Collier; 1 s (Christopher), 1 da (Catherine); *Career* called to the Bar Gray's Inn 1957 (bencher 1996); HM Dip Serv: legal asst FO 1957–59, legal advsr Br Property Cmmn (later Br Embassy) Cairo 1959–62, asst legal advsr FO 1962–67, legal advsr Br Embassy Bonn 1967–69, asst slr Law Offrs Dept 1969–70, legal cnsllr FCO 1970–73, cnsllr (legal advsr) Office of UK Permanent Rep to EEC 1973–77, legal cnsllr FCO 1977–82, dep legal advsr FCO 1982–87 and legal advsr 1987–91, ret; in practice at the Bar 1991–; special negotiator for succession issues in former Yugoslavia 1996–2001; memb: Panel of Arbitrators UN Law of the Sea Convention 1998–, Eritrea-Ethiopia Boundary Cmmn 2001–, Ireland-UK Arbitration Tbnl 2002–, Malaysia-Singapore Arbitration Tbnl 2003–05, UK Nat Gp Permanent Court of Arbitration 2003–, Barbados-Trinidad and Tobago Artitration Tbnl 2004–06; pres or memb of various int foreign investment arbitrational tbnls; counsel before Int Court of Justice for France, Slovak Repub, Nigeria, Indonesia, Colombia, Ukraine, and Jordan; memb: Bd of Mgmnt Br Inst of Int and Comparative Law 1987–2006 (memb Advsy Cncl 2006–), Bd Inst of Advanced Legal Studies 1988–91, Advsy Bd Institut für Internationales Recht Kiel 1989–2002, Editorial Ctee Br Year Book of Int Law 1991–, Sussex Heritage Tst 2001– (chm 2006–), Advsy Cncl Liechtenstein Inst for Self-Determination Princeton Univ 2003–07; memb Institut de Droit International 1997– (assoc memb 1991–97); hon pres Br Branch Int Law Assoc 1998– (pres 1992–98); hon fell Downing Coll Cambridge 1999; Order of Independence (Jordan) 2007; *Books* Legal Effects of War (4 edn with Lord McNair, 1966), Encyclopaedic Dictionary of International Law (jt ed, 1986), Oppenheim's International Law (vol 1, 9 edn with Sir Robert Jennings, 1992), International Law and the Antarctic Treaty System (1992), Self Determination and Self Administration (with Danspeckgruber 1997), The International Law Commission 1949–98 (3 vols 1999); contribs to int legal pubns incl British Year Book of International Law and International and Comparative Law Quarterly; *Style—* Sir Arthur Watts, KCMG, QC; ✉ 20 Essex Street, London WC2R 3AL (tel 020 7583 9294, fax 020 7583 1341)

WATTS, Prof Cedric Thomas; s of Thomas Henry Watts (d 1964), of Cheltenham, Glos, and Mary Adelaide, *née* Cheshire (d 1965); *b* 19 February 1937; *Educ* Cheltenham GS, Pembroke Coll Cambridge (MA, PhD); *m* 3 Jan 1963, Judith Edna Mary, da of Charles Edward Hill (d 1974); 2 da (Linda b 1964 d 1985, Sarah b 1972), 1 s (William b 1967); *Career* Nat Serv RN 1956–58; asst lectr Cambs Coll of Arts and Technol 1964–65, prof English and American Sch Univ of Sussex 1983– (lectr 1965–79, reader 1979–83); *Books* Conrad's Heart of Darkness: A Critical and Contextual Discussion (1977), Cunninghame Graham: A Critical Biography (jtly, 1979), A Preface to Conrad (1982), R B Cunninghame Graham (1983), The Deceptive Text (1984), A Preface to Keats (1985), William Shakespeare: Measure for Measure (1986), Hamlet (1988), Joseph Conrad: A Literary Life (1989), Literature and Money (1990), Joseph Conrad: Nostromo (1990), Romeo and Juliet (1991), Thomas Hardy: Jude the Obscure (1992), Joseph Conrad (1994), A Preface to Greene (1997), Henry V, War Criminal? and Other Shakespeare Puzzles (jtly, 2000), Joseph Conrad: The Secret Agent (2007); *Style—* Prof Cedric Watts; ✉ University of Sussex, Brighton, East Sussex BN1 9QN (tel 01273 606755, e-mail c.t.watts@sussex.ac.uk)

WATTS, Charles Robert (Charlie); *b* 2 June 1941; *m* 14 Oct 1964, Shirley Anne, *née* Shepherd; 1 da; *Career* drummer; joined Rolling Stones 1963; signed recording contracts with: Impact Records/Decca 1963, London Records/Decca 1965, Rolling Stones Records, CBS 1983, Virgin 1992; albums with Rolling Stones: The Rolling Stones (1964, reached UK no 1), The Rolling Stones No 2 (1965, no 1), Out of Our Heads (1965, UK no 2), Aftermath (1966, UK no 1), Big Hits (High Tide and Green Grass) (compilation, 1966, UK no 4), got LIVE if you want it! (live, 1967), Between The Buttons (1967, UK no 3), Flowers (US compilation, 1967, US no 3), Their Satanic Majesties Request (1967, UK no 3), Beggars Banquet (1968, UK no 3), Through The Past Darkly (Big Hits Volume 2) (compilation, 1969, UK no 2), Let It Bleed (1969, UK no 1), Get Yer Ya-Ya's Out! (live, 1970, UK no 1), Stone Age (compilation, 1971, UK no 4), Sticky Fingers (1971, UK no 1), Hot Rocks 1964–71 (US compilation, 1972, US no 9), Goats Head Soup (1973, UK no 1), It's Only Rock'N'Roll (1974, UK no 2), Made In The Shade (compilation, 1975, UK no 14), Rolled Gold - The Very Best of The Rolling Stones (compilation, 1975, UK no 7), Black and Blue (1976, UK no 2), Love You Live (live, 1977, UK no 3), Some Girls (1978, UK no 2), Emotional Rescue (1980, UK no 1), Tattoo You (1981, UK no 2), Still Life (American Concert 1981) (live, 1981, UK no 4), Undercover (1983, UK no 3), Rewind 1971–84 (compilation, 1984, UK no 23), Dirty Work (1986, UK, no 4), Steel Wheels (1989, UK no 2), Flashpoint (live, 1991, UK no 6), Voodoo Lounge (1994, UK no 1), Bridges to Babylon (1997, UK no 6), Forty Licks (2002); has toured with The Charlie Watts Orchestra 1985–86; solo albums: Charlie Watts Orchestra - Live at Fulham Town Hall 1986, From One Charlie (with book Ode to a High Flying Bird) 1992, A Tribute to Charlie Parker 1992, Warm & Tender 1993, From One Charlie 1995, Long Ago & Far Away 1996; concert films: Sympathy For The Devil (dir Jean Luc Godard) 1969, Gimme Shelter 1970, Ladies and Gentleman, The Rolling Stones 1977, Let's Spend The Night Together (dir Hal Ashby) 1983, Flashpoint (film of 1990 Steel Wheels Tour) 1991; *Books* Ode To A High Flying Bird (1965); *Recreations* jazz; *Style—* Charlie Watts, Esq; ✉ c/o Munro Sounds, 5 Church Row, Wandsworth Plain, London SW18 1ES

WATTS, Prof Colin; s of George Watts (d 1982), and Kathleen Mary, *née* Downing; *b* 28 April 1953, London; *Educ* The Friends Sch Saffron Walden, Univ of Bristol (BSc), Univ of Sussex (DPhil); *m* 21 Dec 1979, Susan Mary, *née* Light; 2 da (Helen Mary b 12 Sept 1981, Emily Rose b 14 Sept 1984), 1 s (Simon James b 26 Feb 1989); *Career* EMBO fell UCLA 1980–82, Beit meml fell MRC Lab of Molecular Biology Cambridge 1982–85; Univ of Dundee: lectr 1992–98, reader 1992–98, prof of immunobiology 1998–; E de Rotschild & Y Mayent fell Inst Curie Paris 1999; contrib to various scientific jls; memb: Basel Inst for Immunology 1991, European Molecular Biology Orgn 1996; Tenovus Scotland Margaret Maclellan Prize 2000, Descartes Prize EU 2002; FRSE 1999, FRS 2005; *Recreations* music, cities, armchair sport; *Style—* Prof Colin Watts; ✉ Wellcome Trust Biocentre, School of Life Sciences, University of Dundee DD1 5EH (tel 01382 344233, fax 01382 345783, e-mail c.watts@dundee.ac.uk)

WATTS, David Leonard (Dave); MP; s of late Leonard Watts, and late Sarah, *née* Rowe; *b* 26 August 1951; *Educ* Seel Road Secdy Sch; *m* 1972, Charmaine Avril, da of O P Davies; 2 s (Paul, David); *Career* full time cncllr 1989–92, regnl organiser Lab Pty 1991–92; researcher to: Angela Eagle, MP, *qv*, 1992–93, The Rt Hon Lord Evans of Parkside, *qv*, 1993–97; MP (Lab) St Helens N 1997–; PPS to: Rt Hon John Spellar, *qv*, Rt Hon John Prescott, *qv*, 2003–05; Govt whip 2005–; sometime UK pres Euro Gp of Industrial Regions; chm St Helens FE Coll; vice-chm AMA; *Style—* Dave Watts, Esq, MP; ✉ House of Commons, London SW1A 0AA (tel 020 7219 3000); constituency office: Ann Ward House, 1 Milk Street, St Helens, Merseyside WA10 1PX (tel 01744 623416, fax 01744 623417)

WATTS, Edward (Ted); s of Edward Samuel Window Watts (d 1975), of Hornchurch, Essex, and Louise, *née* Coffey (d 2000); *b* 19 March 1940; *Educ* East Ham GS for Boys, SW Essex Tech Coll; *m* 18 June 1960, Iris Josephine, da of Edward John Frost, MBE; 2 s (Mark Edward b 3 March 1963, Paul Jonathan b 27 June 1968), and 1 da decd; *Career* Cotton Ballard & Blow Architects 1959–62, E Wookey & Co General Practice Surveyors 1962–64, chief surveyor Ian Fraser & Assoc (Architects & Town Planners) 1964–66, team leader Housing Devpt Br GLC 1966–67, fndr Edward Watts & Co 1967–99 (now Watts & Partners); dir: RICS Journals Ltd 1982–88 (chm 1986–88), Surveyors Holdings 1983–88, People Need Homes plc 1991–96, WASP plc 1994–98, Buildingcare Ltd 1994–98, Avilla Developments Ltd 1999–; non-exec dir: WSP Group 1993–2002, Thamesmead Town 1994–2000; fndr chm Hyde Housing Assoc 1967–70 (memb until 1985), chm: Tech Ctee Building Conservation Tst 1984–86, Empty Homes Agency 1997–2002, Tilfen Ltd 1999–2002, Blackheath Preservation Tst 2001– (dir 2000–), Cedar Rydal Ltd; memb: Gen Cncl RICS 1982–95 (pres 1991–92), ARCUK 1991–97, Urban Villages Group 1992–96, Bd Coll of Estate Mgmnt 1994–97, Ministerial Advsy Bd PACE 1995–2000, Home Office Steering Gp on strategy for Central London accommodation 1995–97; Freeman City of London; Hon DSc South Bank Univ 1992; MInstD; FRICS 1971 (ARICS 1962), FIMgt 1982; *Recreations* sailing, cruising, racing; *Clubs* Royal Cruising, Royal Lymington Yacht; *Style—* Ted Watts, Esq; ✉ Flexford Farm, South Sway Lane, Sway, Lymington, Hampshire SO41 6DP (tel 01590 681053, fax 01590 681170, e-mail ted.watts@virgin.net)

WATTS, (Edward) Jonathan; s of Albert Edward Watts (d 1972), of Blackpool, and Joan Mary Watts (d 1972); *b* 5 December 1954, Blackpool, Lancs; *Educ* Arnold GS Blackpool, Univ of Hertfordshire; *m* 10 Aug 1996, Lisa Mary, *née* Gernon; *Career* sales and mktg mangr Control Dataset Ltd 1977–82, gen mangr Control Data UK Data Services 1982–84, md Datapoint Corp (NZ) Ltd 1984–87, gp mktg and business devpt dir Sintrom plc 1987–90, gp md BellSouth Europe/Air Call Communications Ltd 1990–94, md NB3/Dolphin Telecommunications 1994–97, md COLT Telecommunications 1998–2002, pres Hutchison Network Services; non-exec dir Alliance & Leicester plc; *Recreations* golf, property renovation, travel, public speaking; *Style—* Jonathan Watts

WATTS, Kevan Vincent; s of late Spencer Frederick Watts, and late Olive Mary Watts; *Educ* Kent Coll Canterbury, Univ of Oxford (BA, Philosophy prize, BPhil); *m* Prudence Mary, *née* Lloyd Vine; 2 da (Lucinda, Elizabeth), 1 s (Henry); *Career* with HM Treasy 1974–81; Merrill Lynch: joined 1981, subsequently various roles in corp finance and M&A NY and London offices until 1993, head of investment banking EMEA 1993–97, sr vice-pres Merrill Lynch & Co Inc 1997–, exec chm Asia Pacific region 1997–2000, co-head of global investment banking 2000–02, chm EMEA and Pacific rim 2002–04, chm int 2004–; memb: Devpt Ctee Nat Gallery, Cncl Int Business Leaders Forum, Advsy Bd Opportunity Now, Advsy Bd Heart of the City; *Style—* Kevan Watts, Esq; ✉ Merrill Lynch (Asia Pacific) Ltd, 15/F Citibank Tower, 3 Garden Road, Central, Hong Kong

WATTS, Sir Philip Beverley; KCMG (2003); s of late Samuel Watts, and late Edith Philippa, *née* Wale; *b* 25 June 1945; *Educ* Wyggeston GS Leicester, Univ of Leeds (BSc, MSc); *m* 1966, Janet Edna, *née* Lockwood, da of Cephas William Lockwood; 1 da (Sarah b 1969), 1 s (Jonathan b 1972); *Career* science teacher Methodist Boys High Sch Freetown

Sierra Leone 1966–68; Shell International: joined 1969, seismologist Indonesia 1970–74, geophysicist 1974–77, exploration mangr Norway 1978–81, div head Malaysia, Brunei, Singapore, London 1981–83, exploration dir UK 1983–85, head EP Liaison Europe The Hague 1986–88, head EP Economics & Planning The Hague 1989–91, md Nigeria 1991–94, regnl co-ordinator Europe The Hague 1994–95, dir Planning, Environment & External Affairs London 1996–97, gp md Royal Dutch/Shell Gp 1997–2004, md Shell Transport and Trading 1997–2004 (chm 2001–04); memb: Governing Body ICC UK 1997– (chm 1998–2004), Exec Bd ICC (Worldwide) 1997–2000, Exec Ctee World Business Cncl for Sustainable Devpt 1998–2004 (chm 2002–03); FEI, FInstPet, FRGS, FGS; *Recreations* travel, gardening, reading; *Style*— Sir Philip Watts, KCMG

WATTS, Dr Richard Arthur; s of Richard W E Watts, FRCP, and Joan E M Lambert, FRCOG; *Educ* Highgate Sch London, Hertford Coll Oxford (MA, DM); *Career* conslt rheumatologist Ipswich Hosp NHS Tst 1994–, hon sr lectr UEA 1998; ed Rheumatology 2002–; hon clinical advsr Arthritis Res Campaign; memb Assoc of Physicians of the UK and Ireland 2005; fell American Coll of Rheumatology 1990, fell Br Soc of Rheumatology 1995, FRCP 1999; *Publications* Autoimmune Rheumatic Diseases (jtly, 2 edn, 1999); author of numerous academic papers relating to rheumatology; *Recreations* skiing, gardening, Central Asian travel; *Style*— Dr Richard Watts; ✉ Ipswich Hospital NHS Trust, Heath Road, Ipswich IP5 5PD (tel 01473 702362, fax 01473 702039, e-mail richard.watts@ipswichhospital.nhs.uk)

WATTS, Serena Margaret (Mrs Robert Sexton); da of James Cooper Tully (d 2001), Martha Madeline Patricia (d 1997), *née* Howell; *b* 23 May 1952, Isleworth, Middx; *Educ* Lourdes Mount Convent Sch, Digby Stuart Teacher Trg Coll W London Inst (CertEd, Dip); *m* 4 Oct 1986, Robert Anthony Sexton; 2 s (Joseph Stanford James Watts b 2 July 1973, Anthony Mark Watts b 2 Dec 1974); *Career* probation offr Middlesex Probation Serv 1984–99, joined HM Prison Serv 1999, jr govr HMP Erlestoke 2000–03 (head of residence 2003), dep govr HMP Shepton Mallet 2003–04, dep govr HMP Bristol 2004–05, govr HMP Dartmoor 2005–; memb Kingston Branch Soroptimist; *Recreations* reading, listening to music, theatre and my passion - my two red setters who keep me active!; *Style*— Mrs Serena Watts; ✉ HMP Dartmoor, Princetown, Yelverton, Devon PL20 6RR (tel 01822 892000, fax 01822 892005, e-mail serena.m.watts@hmps.gsi.gov.uk)

WATTS, Prof Simon; MBE (1996); s of Peter Annesley Watts (d 1976), and Valerie, *née* Kennard (d 1997); *b* 18 December 1949; *Educ* Blundell's (scholar), St John's Coll Oxford (hon scholar, MA), Univ of Birmingham (MSc), CNAA (PhD); *m* 1977, Elizabeth Stewart, da of Arthur Maurice Stewart-Wallace; 2 s (Thomas Annesley b 1979, Edward Stewart b 1981); *Career* student apprentice EMI Electronics 1967; chief scientist: Sensors Gp Thorn EMI Electronics 1987–95, Radar and Electronic Warfare Div Racal Defence Electronics 1995–2000, Thales Sensors 2000–05, vice-pres and dep scientific dir Aerospace Div Thales UK 2005–; chm: Radar Research Consultative Ctee FEI/DERA 1990–96, Fedn of the Electronics Industry (FEI) Res and Technol Ctee 1996–98, Radar 97 (int radar conf) 1997; visiting prof Dept of Electronic and Electrical Engrg UCL 2003–; lectr on annual radar short courses: Univ of Birmingham 1988–93, Univ of Surrey 1994–; guest ed IEE Proceedings (Radar, Sonar & Navigation) 1991 and 2001; memb local C of E church; Freeman City of London 2005, Liveryman Worshipful Co of Engrs 2006; FIEE 1992, FREng 2000, FIEEE 2003 (SMIEEE 1993); *Publications* Sea Clutter: Scattering, the K-distribution and Radar Performance (jtly, 2006); 30 papers published in jls and conferences, five patents; *Recreations* amateur radio, gardening, cooking, listening to music; *Style*— Prof Simon Watts, MBE, FREng; ✉ Thales UK, Aerospace Division, Crawley, West Sussex RH10 9PZ (tel 01293 644674)

WATTS, Timothy; DL (West Midlands, 2005); s of late Walter Watts, and Constance, *née* Daniels (d 1998); *b* 30 September 1948, Birmingham; *m* 6 Aug 2004, June, *née* Hunt; 2 da (Amy b 25 May 1980, Fay b 9 July 1983); *Career* Pertemps Gp of Cos: joined Pertemps family business 1970, early career Wolverhampton office, employment conslt in commercial and tech divs, became Pertemps Recruitment Partnership 1994, resigned as chm 2002; ambass Advantage West Midlands 2005–, former memb W Midlands Cncl CBI, founding sponsor Tomorrow's People; vice-pres Spinal Injuries Assoc 2005–; lifetime pres of Birmingham Fndn; memb Beta Gamma Sigma Soc Aston Univ 2006–; Daily Telegraph/British Telecom Award for Customer Service 1995, Business of the Year (Pertemps) 1997, Businessman of the Year 1997, Master Entrepreneur of the Year Central England 2002, included in Sunday Times Top 100 Companies (Pertemps); Hon DSc Aston Univ 2007; fell Inst of Employment Conslts; *Style*— Timothy Watts, Esq, DL; ✉ Pertemps Investments Ltd, Meriden Hall, Main Road, Meriden CV1 7PT (tel 01676 525000, fax 01676 525109, e-mail tim.watts@pertemps.co.uk)

WATTS-ROBERTSON, John; s of Joseph Watts-Robertson, of Warwickshire, and Romaine, *née* Howell; *b* 3 May 1957; *Educ* Alcester GS, West Bromwich Coll of Commerce and Technol, London Coll of Printing (NCTJ proficiency certificate); *m* 3 May 1980, Susan Margaret, *née* Field; 1 da (Sarah Louise b 24 May 1984); *Career* photographer: Stratford-upon-Avon Herald 1974–75, Wellingborough News Echo 1975–77, Northants Evening Telegraph 1977–93; freelance photographer: The Guardian 1993– (part time 1989–93), The Sunday Telegraph 1993– (part time 1992–93); *Awards* News Photographer of the Year E Midlands Allied Press 1985 and 1986, Press Photographer of the Year UK Press Gazette 1989, British Regnl Press Photographer of the Year 1989, News Photographer of the Year Birmingham Press Club 1989, winner Ilford Nat Photo of the Month Aug 1991, winner (Features) Ilford Nat Awards 1991; ARPS; *Recreations* cinema, theatre, reading, swimming, ice skating; *Style*— John Watts-Robertson, Esq; ✉ 1 Nansen Close, Rothwell, Kettering, Northamptonshire NN14 6TZ (tel 078 5093 1219, e-mail jr.photos@freeuk.com); Picture Desk, The Guardian, 119 Farringdon Road, London EC1R 3ER

WAUGH, Andrew Peter; QC (1998); *Educ* Brighton Coll, City Univ London (BSc, Dip Law); *Career* called to the Bar 1982; practising barr specialising in intellectual property law; currently memb of chambers Three New Square; memb: Intellectual Property Bar Assoc, Chancery Bar Assoc, Int Assoc for the Protection of Intellectual Property (AIPPI); *Style*— Andrew Waugh, Esq, QC; ✉ Three New Square, Lincoln's Inn, London WC2A 3RS

WAUGH, Dr Michael Anthony; s of Anthony Lawrence Waugh, of Richmond, Surrey, and Nancy Genevieve, *née* Vernon; *b* 19 September 1943; *Educ* St George's Coll Weybridge, Charing Cross Hosp Med Sch London (MB BS); *Career* conslt physician genito-urinary medicine Gen Infirmary Leeds 1975–2004, pt/t secondment Aids Unit Dept of Health 1992–93; pres Med Soc for Study of Venereal Diseases 1989–91 (hon sec 1981–89); Int Union Against Sexually Transmitted Infections: sec gen 1984–95, pres 1995–99, sr cnsllr 2001; founding dep ed Int Jl of STD and Aids 1993; memb Editorial Bd: Skin Med 2002–, Community Dermatology 2005–; observer Venereology and Dermatovenereology Specialists Ctee Union of Euro Med Specialists 1984–92; hon sr lectr Univ of Leeds 1985–2004 (Soc of Apothecaries lectr in history of med 1984–2000); hon librarian, offr and memb Cncl RSM 1995–99; extra memb of Cncl RSM 1999–2001; corresponding memb Austrian Soc for Dermatology and Venereology 1990, conslt Thai Training Insts Postgrad Course on STDs 2000–, memb Bd European Acad of Dermatology and Venereology 1994–2000 (hon life memb 2001, sec Ethical Cmmn 2004), conslt advsr Dept of Disease Control Thailand 2006; Lifetime Achievement Award International Union Against Sexually Transmitted Infections 2005, Distinguished Serv Award European Acad of Dermatology and Venereology 2006; fell The Netherlands Soc for Dermatology and Venereology 1996, hon fell Hungarian STD Soc 2000, hon memb Deutsche STD Gesellschaft 2005, hon sub-dean RSM (Northern and Yorkshire branch) 2005; Liveryman Worshipful Soc of Apothecaries 1970; DHMSA 1970, Dip Venereology 1974; fell Australasian Coll of Sexual Health Physicians 1996, fndn fell Australasian Chapter of Sexual Health Medicine (FAChSHM) 2004; FRCPI 1994 (MRCPI 1993), FRCP 1995; *Books* Sexually Transmitted Diseases (contrib, 2 edn, 1990), History of Sexually Transmitted Diseases (1990), Sex, Disease and Society (jt ed, 1997), Oxford Illustrated Companion to Medicine (venereology section, 2001), Dictionary of National Biography (contrib 3 sections, 2004); *Recreations* gardening, travelling; *Style*— Dr Michael Waugh; ✉ Wellfield House, 151 Roker Lane, Pudsey, Leeds LS28 9ND (tel 0113 256 5255, e-mail mike@mawpud.fsnet.co.uk); Nuffield Hospital Leeds, 2 Leighton Street, Leeds LS1 3EB (tel 0113 388 2000)

WAUGH, Simon John; s of Peter Waugh (d 2001), and Christine Waugh; *b* 24 April 1958, London; *Educ* Sevenoaks Sch; *m* 11 March 2000, Refilwe, da of Arthur Maimane; 2 da (Amy b 4 Feb 1989, Ella b 22 July 2001), 4 s (Peter b 24 Oct 1990, Stuart, Matthew (twins) b 5 Feb 1992, Zachary b 23 March 2003); *Career* UK sales and mktg dir American Express 1976–88, commercial dir Lloyds Bank Insurance 1988–93, md Saga 1993–97; Centrica plc: gp mktg dir 1997–2004, md Centrica Financial Servs 1997–2002, dep md British Gas 2002–04; chm AWD Chase De Vere 2005–, non-exec dir Johnston Press 2003–; dep chm Sparks Children's Charity; hon life fell: Mktg Soc, DMA; *Recreations* sport (rugby, football, golf), politics, reading; *Clubs* Drift Golf; *Style*— Simon Waugh, Esq; ✉ AWD Chase De Vere, 10 Paternoster Square, London EC4M 7DY (tel 020 7029 9451, fax 020 7236 8341, e-mail simon.waugh@awdplc.com)

WAUGH, Lady Teresa Lorraine; da of 6 Earl of Onslow, KBE, MC, TD (d 1971); sis of 7 Earl of Onslow, *qv*; *b* 1940; *m* 1961, Auberon Waugh (d 2001); 2 s, 2 da; *Career* translator and novelist; *Books* Painting Water (1984), Waterloo Waterloo (1986), An Intolerable Burden (1988), Song at Twilight (1989), Sylvia's Lot (1994), The Gossips (1995), A Friend Like Harvey (1999), The House (2002); *Style*— Lady Teresa Waugh; ✉ Combe Florey House, Combe Florey, Taunton, Somerset TA4 3JD (tel 01823 432297)

WAVERLEY, 3 Viscount (UK 1952); John Desmond Forbes Anderson; o s of 2 Viscount Waverley (d 1990), and Lorna Myrtle Ann, *née* Ledgerwood; *b* 31 October 1949; *Educ* Malvern; *Heir* s, Hon Forbes Anderson; *Career* elected hereditary peer House of Lords 1999–; advsr CCC Gp; memb RIIA; Grand Cross Order of San Carlos (Colombia) 1998, Jubilee Medal (Kazakhstan) 2002; *Recreations* golf, walking; *Clubs* Rye Golf; *Style*— The Rt Hon the Viscount Waverley; ✉ House of Lords, London SW1A 0PW

WAX, Ruby; da of Edward Wax, and Berta, *née* Goldmann; *b* 19 April 1953; *Educ* Evanston Township HS, Univ of Denver, Univ of Calif Berkeley, RSAMD (Gold Medal in acting); *m* 16 May 1988, Edward Richard Morison Bye; 1 s (Maximillian b 11 Nov 1988), 2 da (Madeline b 10 Dec 1990, Marina b 5 Nov 1993); *Career* actor and comedienne; Performer of the Year British Comedy Awards 1993; *Theatre* Crucible Theatre 1976, RSC 1978–82, Wax Acts (one woman show, UK tour and West End) 1992, Stressed (one woman show, UK, Aust and NZ tour) 2000, The Witches (Wyndhams Theatre) 2005; *Television* Not The Nine O'Clock News (writer) 1983, Girls On Top 1984–85, Don't Miss Wax 1985–87, Hit and Run 1988–89, Full Wax 1989–94, Ruby Wax Meets... 1996–98, Ruby 1997–99 and 2000, Ruby's American Pie 1999–2000, Hot Wax 2001, The Waiting Game 2001–02, Life with Ruby 2002, Commercial Breakdown 2002, Ruby Wax with... 2003; documentaries incl: Miami Memoirs 1987, East Meets Wax 1988, Ruby Takes a Trip 1992; *Publications* How Do You Want Me? (autobiography, 2002); *Style*— Miss Ruby Wax; ✉ c/o PFD, Drury House, 34–43 Russell Street, London WC2B 5HA

WAXMAN, Prof Jonathan; s of David Waxman, and Shirley, *née* Friedman; *b* 31 October 1951; *Educ* Haberdashers' Aske's, UCL (BSc, MB BS, MD); *Children* 1 da (Thea Millie b 22 Dec 1993), 1 s (Frederick Merlin b 24 April 1996); *Career* trained in med UCH London, registrar in med St Mary's Hosp London 1979–81, sr registrar in oncology Bart's 1981–86, conslt oncologist Hammersmith Hospital 1986–; fndr and chm Prostate Cancer Charity; memb: Assoc of Physicians, Assoc of Cancer Physicians, American Soc of Clinical Oncology; FRCP; *Books* The New Endocrinology of Cancer (jtly, 1988), The Molecular Biology of Cancer (jtly, 1989), Urological Oncology (jtly, 1992), Interleukin II (jtly, 1992), Molecular Endocrinology of Cancer (1996), Cancer Chemotherapy Treatment Protocols (1998), Cancer and the Law (1999), The Prostate Cancer Book (2001), Treatment Options in Urological Oncology (2001), Lecture Notes in Oncology (2006); *Style*— Prof Jonathan Waxman; ✉ Department of Oncology, Hammersmith Hospital, Imperial College, Du Cane Road, London W12 0NN (tel 020 8383 4651, fax 020 8383 4653)

WAY, Adam Gerald Richmond (Bertie); s of Col A G Way, MC; *b* 29 February 1952; *Educ* Eton; *m* Susanna, *née*, Nicholas; *Career* short serv cmmn Grenadier Gds 1972–75; dir i/c gp business devpt Chime Communications plc (formerly Lowe Bell Communications Ltd) 1991– (joined 1986); non-exec chm The Blomfield Group (exec search and recruitment conslts); memb Cncl WellBeing (health research charity for women and babies), chm Starlight Fndn; *Recreations* country pursuits; *Style*— A G R Way, Esq; ✉ Chime Communications plc, 14 Curzon Street, London W1Y 8LP (tel 020 7861 8543, fax 020 7861 8520)

WAY, Andrew Mark; s of Maxwell Andrew Way (d 1975), and Jane Kathleen, *née* Palliser; *b* 27 February 1959, Bournemouth, Dorset; *Educ* Bournemouth Sch, Bristol Sch of Nursing (SRN), Thomas Guy Sch of Nursing (RMN), Charles West Sch of Nursing (RSCN), City Univ (BSc), Keele Univ (MBA); *Career* gen mangr St George's Hosp Tooting 1992–95, gen mangr and chief operating offr Hammersmith Hosps NHS Tst 1995–2002, chief exec Heatherwood & Wrexham Hosps NHS Tst 2002–05, chief exec Royal Free Hampstead NHS Tst 2005–; *Recreations* swimming, skiing, travel, bridge; *Style*— Andrew Way, Esq; ✉ Royal Free Hospital, Pond Street, London NW3 2QG (tel 020 7830 2176, fax 020 7830 2961, e-mail andrew.way@royalfree.nhs.uk)

WAY, John Stanley; s of Stanley George Godwin Way (d 1985), and Margaret Jean, *née* Edwards; *b* 18 December 1946; *Educ* St John's Sch Leatherhead; *m* 1 Feb 1975, (Diana) Jayne, da of Maj Thomas Herbert Sills, MBE, TD, DL (d 1988), of Sandy, Beds; 2 s (Robert b 1979, Duncan b 1986); *Career* Coopers & Lybrand 1969–73; Continental Illinois Nat Bank & Tst Chicago: Far East regnl auditor 1974–79, Euro/Latin America regnl auditor London 1979–83, int auditor 1983–87; int auditor worldwide Prudential Insurance Co of America 1987–90, sr conslt The Bank Relationship Consultancy 1991–92, dir audit and risk mgmnt Inchcape plc 1992–99, gp internal auditor ICI plc 1999–2004, chief internal auditor Abbey National plc 2004–05, dir of business assurance Centrica plc 2006–; FCA 1969, FHKSA 1977, MIMgt 1978, IIA 1978; *Recreations* golf, tennis, cricket; *Clubs* Surrey CCC, IOD; *Style*— John Way, Esq; ✉ Passworth, School Lane, Ockham, Surrey GU23 6PA

WAY, Patrick Edward; s of John Francis Way (d 1996), of Solihull, and Margaret Helen Laura, *née* Ewins (d 2000); *b* 6 February 1954; *Educ* Solihull Sch, Univ of Leeds (BA); *m* 10 June 1978, Judith Anne, da of Dr Peter Orchard Williams, CBE, of Bletchingdon; 3 s (Oliver Christopher Patrick b 16 Dec 1983, Frederick William Patrick b 6 Feb 1987, Dominic Hugo Patrick b 29 Nov 1988); *Career* admitted slr 1979, asst slr Lawrence Graham 1979–82, tax ptnr Nabarro Nathanson 1985–87 (asst 1982–85), ptnr and head of Corp Tax Dept Gouldens 1987–94, called to the Bar Lincoln's Inn 1994, tax barr Gray's Inn 1994–; founding ed Trusts and Estates 1985, tax ed The BES Magazine 1986; memb Revenue Bar Assoc; *Books* Death and Taxes (1985), Maximising Opportunities under the BES (1986), The BES and Assured Tenancies - The New Rules (1988), Tax Advice for Company Transactions (ed and contrib, 1992), The Enterprise Investment Scheme (1994), Joint Ventures (ed and contrib, 1994), Tolley's Tax Planning (contrib, 2006–07); *Recreations* rugby, contemporary art; *Clubs* Travellers; *Style*— Patrick Way,

Esq; ✉ Gray's Inn Tax Chambers, Gray's Inn, London WC1R 5JA (tel 020 7242 2642, e-mail pw@taxbar.com)

WAY, Philip John Robert; s of Philip William Frederick Way (d 1969), of Enfield, Middx, and Ellen Gladys, *née* Wallace (d 1981); *b* 16 March 1940; *Educ* Higher Grade Sch, Ealing Tech Coll; *m* 29 May 1965, Joan Dawn, da of Alfred Richard Maclannan; 1 s (Duncan Edward b 6 Dec 1971), 1 da (Alison Ruth b 15 Dec 1975); *Career* actively engaged in industrial photography for the electricity supply industry 1962–92 (latterly mangr), ptnr in visual resource mgmnt consultancy 1992–95, prop Philip Way Photography 1995–; hon photographer: St Paul's Cathedral 1982–95, 'Not Forgotten' Assoc; winner Black and White Photography category Financial Times Photographic Awards, twice winner Martini Royal Photographic Annual Awards; pres BIPP 1995–96 (variously memb Regional Ctee/regional treas and regional chm, memb Nat Cncl/nat treas), currently chm BIPP Benevolent Soc; ARPS, Hon FBIPP; *Style—* Philip Way, Esq; ✉ 2 Green Moor Link, Winchmore Hill, London N21 2ND (tel 020 8360 5876, business tel and fax 020 8360 3034, e-mail pwphotography1@btinternet.com)

WAYNE, Prof Richard Peer; s of Arthur W Wayne, and Stella B, *née* Lloyd; *b* 5 December 1938; *Educ* Worthing HS, Trinity Coll Cambridge (open scholar, sr scholar, research scholar, MA, PhD, Mathison prize), Univ of Oxford (MA); *m* 6 April 1963, Brenda, da of Richard Tapp; 1 da (Carol Elisabeth b 17 Aug 1969), 1 s (Andrew Richard b 30 April 1971); *Career* res asst Univ of Liverpool 1963–65, dept demonstrator Physical Chemistry Lab Univ of Oxford 1965; ChCh Oxford: elected tutor and coll lectr 1965, elected official student 1966, elected Dr Lee's reader in chemistry 1973, tutor for graduates 1988–92; Univ of Oxford: appointed lectr 1967, chm Sub-Faculty of Chemistry 1986–88 (sec 1978–79), dir of graduate studies physical sciences 1988–90, chm Faculty Bd of Physical Sciences 1990–92 (vice-chm 1988–90), memb Ctee to review Robert Hooke Inst 1990–91, memb advsy ctee on Encaenia hon degrees 1991–94, chm co-ordinating ctee for first year course in physical sciences 1991–92, memb Telecommunications Ctee 1993–, examiner in natural sciences, doctoral examiner and res supervisor, prof of chemistry 1996–; visiting prof of photochemistry Univ of Calif Riverside 1968–69, visiting sr scientist Nat Bureau of Standards Washington DC 1973, visiting sr scientist Centre de Recherches en Physique de l'Environnement Orléans 1975–76, conseiller scientifique Centre National d'Etudes des Télécommunications 1976–80, guest scientist Universität Wuppertal 1984 and 1986, visiting scientist UCLA, professeur invité Université de Bordeaux 1993, visiting prof and prof honorario Univ of Córdoba Argentina 1996; memb: Ctee on the Meteorological Effects of Stratospheric Aircraft (COMESA), Working Gp (ii) Br Nat Ctee for Solar Terrestrial Physics, Atmospheric Neutral Chemistry Study Gp of Middle Atmospheric Prog, Co-ordinating Ctee for Res in Atmospheric Chemistry (CCRAC), Science Panel on Stratospheric Ozone Cmmn of Euro Communities, Mgmnt Panel Atmospheric Chemistry Initiative Science and Engrg Res Cncl, EUROTRAC Applications Project 1993–, Electoral Bd Chair of Atmospheric Physics Univ of Stockholm 1994–95, Scientific Steering Gp Lab Studies in Atmospheric Chemistry NERC 1995–, Electoral Bd Chair of Atmospheric Chemistry Univ of Copenhagen 1999, Conseil de l'École Doctorale Sciences et Technologie Université d'Orléans 2000–; conseillor scientifique l'Institut Français du Pétrole 1991–, co-opted memb LACTOZ Steering Ctee 1994–, memb local organising ctee XVIIth Int Photochemistry Conf 1994–95; ed-in-chief Jl of Photochemistry (now Jl of Photochemistry and Photobiology) 1972–, memb Comité Éditorial Revue de l'Institut Français du Pétrole 1996–; doctoral examiner Univ of Cambridge and numerous univs in UK, France Germany, Ireland, Sweden; external examiner Univ of Plymouth 2000–; lectures and addresses incl: BAAS 1986, plenary lectr autumn meeting RSC 1993, Bedson lectr Univ of Newcastle 1991, Iddles Millennium lectr Univ of New Hampshire 2000, Irvine lectr Univ of St Andrews 2002; RSC award for Reaction Kinetics 2000; Dr (hc) Univ Castilla-La Mancha Spain 2002; *Publications* Photochemistry (1970), Chemistry of Atmospheres (1985, 3 edn 2000), Principles and Applications of Photochemistry (1988), The Nitrate Radical: Physics, Chemistry and the Atmosphere (sr exec ed, 1991), Chemical Instrumentation (1994), Halogen Oxides: Radicals, Sources and Reservoirs in the Laboratory and in the Atmosphere (sr exec ed, 1995), Photochemistry (with C E Wayne, 1996); author of over 250 research papers, reviews and chapters in books in fields of reaction kinetics, photochemistry, and atmospheric chemistry; *Style—* Prof Richard Wayne; ✉ Physical and Theoretical Chemistry Laboratory, South Parks Road, Oxford OX1 3QZ (tel 01865 275434, fax 01865 275410, e-mail wayne@physchem.ox.ac.uk)

WEAIRE, Prof Denis Lawrence; *b* 17 October 1942; *Educ* Belfast Royal Acad, Clare Coll Cambridge (BA), Univ of Calif Berkeley, Univ of Chicago, Univ of Cambridge (PhD); *Career* res fell Harvard Univ 1969–70, J W Gibbs instr Yale Univ 1970–72 (asst prof 1972–73, assoc prof 1973–74), sr lectr Heriot-Watt Univ 1974–77 (reader 1977–79, prof 1979), prof of experimental physics UC Dublin 1980–84 (head of dept 1983–84 and 2003–05), Erasmus Smith's prof of natural and experimental philosophy Trinity Coll Dublin 1984– (head of dept 1984–89, fell 1987–, dean of sci 1989–92); ed-in-chief Jl of Physics 1994–97, pres Euro Physical Soc 1997–99 (vice-pres 1996–97 and 1999–2000), chm Solid State Physics Sub-Ctee Inst of Physics 1981–84 (memb 1979–81); sec/treas Euro Assoc of Deans of Sci 1990–92, dir Magnetic Solutions Ltd 1994–; vice-pres Royal Irish Acad 2001–02; memb: Advsy Ctee Inst for Amorphous Studies Michigan USA 1983–, Irish Nat Ctee for Physics (Royal Irish Acad) 1984–, MRS Euro Ctee 1984–86, Jt Res Centre EEC Scientific Cncl 1985–88, Advsy Bd Physics Bulletin 1985–88, Bd DIAS Sch of Cosmic Studies 1985–90, Editorial Bd Jl of Physics 1986–88 (hon ed 1994–98), EEC Evaluation Panel on Non-Nuclear Energies 1985–86, Royal Irish Acad delegate Cncl of the Euro Physical Soc 1986–88, Royal Irish Acad/RDS Ctee on Historic Scientific Instruments 1986, Semiconductors and Insulators Section Ctee EPS 1988–94, Ed Panel Modern Physics B World Scientific Co 1988–92, Royal Irish Acad Ctee on History and Philosophy of Sci 1987–, Editorial Advsy Bd Forma 1988–, Cncl Royal Irish Acad 1989–93 and 2000–, Advsy Ctee Hitachi Res Ireland 1989–94, Bd of Birr Sci and Heritage Tst 1990–99, Ed Advsy Ctee Materials Res Bulletin 1991–95, CODAS 1993–, Physics Panel EC Human Capital and Mobility Prog 1992–94; vice-pres Academia Europaea 2003– (memb 1998–, memb Cncl 1999–2002); EPS Cecil Powell Medal 2002, Cunnigham Medal Royal Irish Acad 2005; Dr (hc) Tech Univ of Lisbon 2001; FRS 1999; *Books* Introduction to Physical Mathematics (with P G Harper, 1985), The Physics of Foams (with S Hutzler, 1999), The Pursuit of Perfect Packing (with T Aste, 2000); Tetrahedrally Bonded Amorphous Semi-conductors (ed with S Kirkpatrick and M H Brodsky, 1974), The Recursion Method (ed with D Pettifor, 1985), Solid State Science - Past, Present and Predicted (ed with C Windsor, 1987), Tradition and Reform: Science and Engineering in Ireland 1800–1930 (ed with N McMillan, J R Nudds, S P McKenna Lawlor, 1988), Epioptics (ed with J F McGilp and C Patterson, 1995), The Kelvin Problem (ed, 1997); *Style—* Prof Denis Weaire, FRS; ✉ Physics Department, Trinity College, Dublin, Ireland (tel 3531 608 1055, fax 3531 671 1759, e-mail dweaire@tcd.ie)

WEALE, Prof Albert Peter; s of Albert Cecil Weale (d 1978), of Brighton, and Elizabeth Margaret, *née* Granger (d 1975); *b* 30 May 1950; *Educ* Varndean GS for Boys Brighton, Clare Coll Cambridge (MA, PhD); *m* 1, 17 Sept 1976 (m dis 1985), Jane, *née* Leresche; m 2, 28 Jan 1994, Jan, *née* Harris; *Career* Sir James Knott res fell Dept of Politics Univ of Newcastle upon Tyne 1974–76, lectr in politics 1976–85, asst dir Inst for Res in the Social Sciences Univ of York 1982–85, prof of politics UEA 1985–92, prof of govt Univ of Essex 1992–; chm: Nuffield Cncl of Bioethics Working Party on Ethics of Xenotransplantation 1996, Grants Ctee The King's Fund 1996–2001; memb Nuffield Cncl on Bioethics 1998–2004; co-ed Br Jl of Political Science 1992–; FRSA 1993, FBA 1998; *Books* Equality and Social Policy (1978), Political Theory and Social Policy (1983), Lone Mothers, Paid Work and Social Security (co-author, 1984), Cost and Choice in Health Care (ed, 1989), Controlling Pollution in the Round (co-author, 1991), Innovation and Environmental Risk (co-ed, 1991), The New Politics of Pollution (1992), Environmental Standards in the European Union in an Interdisciplinary Framework (co-ed, 1995), Citizenship, Democracy and Justice in the New Europe (co-ed, 1997), Political Theory and the European Union (co ed, 1998), Democracy (1999), Environmental Governance in Europe (co-authored 2000), Risk, Democratic Citizenship and Public Policy (ed, 2002), Democratic Citizenship and the European Union (2005); *Recreations* walking, music, company of friends, visual arts; *Style—* Prof Albert Weale, FBA; ✉ Department of Government, University of Essex, Wivenhoe Park, Colchester, Essex CO4 3SQ (tel 01206 872127, fax 01206 873234, e-mail weala@essex.ac.uk)

WEALE, Dr Martin Robert; CBE (1999); *b* 4 December 1955; *Educ* Highgate Sch, Clare Coll Cambridge (BA), Univ of Cambridge (ScD); *Career* ODI fell Nat Statistical Office Malawi 1977–79, research offr Dept of Applied Economics Cambridge 1979–87, lectr Faculty of Economics and Politics Univ of Cambridge 1987–95, dir NIESR 1995–; memb: HM Treasy Ind Panel of Economic Forecasting Advsrs 1996–97, Statistics Cmmn 2000–, Bd of Actuarial Standards 2006–; treas Alzheimer's Research Tst; Hon DSc City Univ 2007; hon fell Inst of Actuaries 2001; *Books* British Banking (1986), Macroeconomic Policy - Inflation, Wealth and the Exchange Rate (1989), Reconciliation of National Income and Expenditure (1995); *Clubs* Athenaeum; *Style—* Dr Martin Weale, CBE; ✉ National Institute of Economic and Social Research, 2 Dean Trench Street, London SW1P 3HE (tel 020 7222 7665, e-mail mweale@niesr.ac.uk)

WEALE, Timothy Donald; TD; s of Donald Jones Weale (d 1971), and Freda Jessy, *née* Gardiner (d 1991); *b* 10 April 1951; *Educ* Magdalen Coll Sch Oxford, Coll of Estate Mgmnt Reading; *m* 12 Oct 1974, Pamela Anne, da of Gerard Gordon Moore (d 1972); 1 s (Edward b 15 April 1981), 1 da (Alice b 21 April 1983); *Career* TA, ret; Wessex Regt (Rifle Vols) 1979–86, Inns of Ct and City Yeo 1986–94 (tstee 1995–); vice-pres Royal Yeomanry Band 1992–2004; ptnr Pearsons 1984–86, dir Prudential Property Services 1986–89, ptnr Healey and Baker (now Cushman & Wakefield) 1989–, ceo Healey and Baker Al Bourj Dubai UAE 2001–02, ceo Cushman & Wakefield, Healey & Baker Gulf Operations 2002–04, ptnr C&W Capital Markets Gp UK 2004–; pres NE Hants Div St John Ambulance 1996–, memb Cncl Order of St John Hants 2006–; adsvy memb BYFC 1985–95; Freeman City of London 1996; FSVA, FRVA, IRRV, FRICS, FRGS; *Recreations* sailing, skiing, vintage cars, gardening, field sports, music, antiques, design; *Clubs* VSCC, Cavalry and Guards', Greywell Flyfishers, Leander, 1918 Auctioneers, Dubai International Marine; *Style—* Timothy Weale, Esq, TD, FRICS, FRGS; ✉ Thackham Court, Hartley Wintney, Basingstoke, Hampshire RG27 8JG (tel 01252 843900, mobile 07834 825197); C&W 43–45 Portman Square, London W1A 3BG (tel 020 7152 5583)

WEARE, Dr (Trevor) John; OBE (1990); s of Trevor Leslie Weare, and Edna Margaret, *née* Roberts; *b* 31 December 1943; *Educ* Aston Tech Coll, Imperial Coll London (Granville studentship prize in physics); *m* 20 June 1964, Margaret Ann, da of Harry Wright; 2 s (Michael John b 1969, Stuart Martin b 1972); *Career* post-doctoral res fell Dept of Theoretical Physics: McGill Univ Montreal Canada 1968–70, Univ of Oxford 1970–72; Hydraulics Res Station: sr scientific offr 1972–75, princ scientific offr 1975–78, sr princ scientific offr 1978–81, chief scientific offr 1981–82; chief exec HR Wallingford Group Ltd (formerly Hydraulics Research Ltd) 1982–99 (chm 1999–), chm S Oxfordshire Housing Assoc 1987–; FRSA 1987, FIWEM 1989; *Style—* Dr John Weare, OBE; ✉ HR Wallingford Group Ltd, Howbery Park, Wallingford, Oxfordshire OX10 8BA (tel 01491 835381, fax 01491 825430, e-mail tjw@hrwallingford.co.uk)

WEARING, Gillian; *b* 1963; *Educ* Chelsea Sch of Art (BTech), Goldsmiths Coll London (BA); *Career* artist; subject of profile South Bank Show (LWT) 1998, guest ed Documents sur L'art 1996; tstee Tate 2000–; BT Young Contemporaries 1993, Turner Prize 1997, Phaidon Press Award 1999; *Solo Exhibitions* City Racing London 1993, Maureen Paley Interim Art London 1994, 1996, 1997 and 1999, Valentina Moncada Br Cncl Rome 1996, Br Cncl Prague 1996, Le Consortium Dijon 1996, Wish You Were Here (Amsterdam) 1996, Emi Fontana Milan 1997, Bloom Gallery Amsterdam 1997, Kunsthaus Zurich 1997, 10–16 Chisenhale Gallery London 1997, Kunstler Wiener Secession Vienna 1997, Jay Gorney Modern Art NY 1997, Galerie Drantmann Brussels 1997, Centre d'Art Contemporain Geneva 1998, Gallery Koyanagi Tokyo 1998, Maureen Paley Interim Art London 1999 and 2003, Serpentine Gallery 2000, Gorney, Bravin & Lee NY 2000, Regen Projects LA 2000, Angel Row Gallery Nottingham 2001, Unspoken (Kunstverein München) 2001, Museo do Chiado Portugal 2001, Sous Influence (Musée d'Art Moderne de la Ville de Paris) 2001, la Caixa (Madrid) 2001, Centro Galego de Arte Contemporánea (Santiago Spain) 2001, Trilogy (Vancouver Art Gallery) 2002, Mass Observation (MCA Chicago and tour) 2002, Kunsthaus Glarus Switzerland 2002, Album (Maureen Paley Interim Art London and Gorney Bravin & Lee NY) 2003 and (Regen Projects LA) 2004, Kiasma/Museum of Contemporary Art Helsinki 2004, Frans Hals Museum Haarlem 2004, Snapshot (Bloomberg Space London) 2005, Family History (Maureen Paley London) 2006, Living Proof (Australian Centre for Contemporary Art Melbourne) 2006, Elsewhere? (Galleria Emi Fontana Milan) 2007, Family Monument (Galleria Civica di Arte Contemporanea Trento) 2007; *Collections* Arts Cncl of GB, Br Cncl London, Contemporary Art Soc London, Govt Art Collection GB, Irish MOMA, Kunsthaus Zurich, Peter & Eileen Norton Family Fndn LA, Saatchi Collection, Simmons & Simmons London, Southampton City Cncl, South London Gallery, Südwest LB Stuttgart, Tate Gallery; *Style—* Ms Gillian Wearing; ✉ c/o Maureen Paley, 21 Herald Street, London E2 6JT (tel 020 7729 4112, fax 020 7729 4113)

WEATHERALL, Prof Sir David John; s of Harry Weatherall (d 1973), and Gwendoline Charlotte Miriam, *née* Tharme (d 1985); *b* 9 March 1933; *Educ* Calday Grange GS, Univ of Liverpool (MB ChB, MD); *m* 20 June 1962, Stella Mayorga Isobel, da of Rev Campo Mayorga, of Bogotá, Colombia; 1 s (Mark b 1968); *Career* regius prof of med Univ of Oxford 1992–2000 (Nuffield prof of clinical med 1974–92); hon dir: MRC Molecular Haematology Unit 1980–2000, Inst of Molecular Med Univ of Oxford (latterly Weatherall Inst of Molecular Medicine) 1989–2000; chllr Keele Univ 2002–; Hon MD: Leeds, Sheffield, Nottingham, Oxford Brookes, South Bank; Hon DSc: Manchester, Edinburgh, Leicester, Aberdeen, London, Keele, Mahidol Univ (Thailand), South Bank, Exeter, Cambridge; Hon LLD: Liverpool, Bristol; overseas memb Nat Acad of Sciences USA 1990, vice-pres Royal Soc 1990–91 (Royal medal 1990, Buchanan medal 1994), pres Int Soc Haematology 1992, pres Br Assoc Advancement Sci 1995; hon fell Imperial Coll London, Hon FRCOG, Hon FRACP, Hon FACP; FRCP, FRCPath, FRCPEd, FRS; *Books* The Thalassaemia Syndromes (with J B Clegg, 1965, 4 edn 2001), Blood and Its Disorders (with R M Hardisty, 1974, 2 edn 1982), The New Genetics and Clinical Practice (1982, 3 edn, 1991), The Oxford Textbook of Medicine (with J G G Ledingham and D A Warrell, 1983, 3 edn 1995), Science and the Quiet Art (1995); *Recreations* music, oriental food; *Style—* Prof Sir David Weatherall, FRS; ✉ 8 Cumnor Rise Road, Cumnor Hill, Oxford OX2 9HD

WEATHERALL, Vice Adm Sir James Lamb (Jim); KCVO (2001), KBE (1989), DL (Hants 2004); s of Lt Cdr Alwyne Thomas Hirst Weatherall, RNR (d 1939), and Olive Catherine Joan, *née* Cuthbert (d 1977); *b* 28 February 1936; *Educ* Gordonstoun; *m* 12 May 1962, Jean Stewart, *née* Macpherson, da of 1 Baron Drumalbyn, KBE, PC; 2 s (Niall b 1967, Ian b 1976), 3 da (Sarah b 1968, Annie b 1974, Elizabeth b 1976); *Career* cadet BRNC Dartmouth, HMS Triumph 1954, midshipman HMS Albion 1955–56; Sub Lt: HMS

Scotsman 1956, HM Yacht Britannia 1958; Lt: HMS Lagos 1959–60, HMS Wizard 1960–61, Long Navigation Course 1961–62, HMS Houghton 1962–64, HMS Tartar 1964, HMS Eastbourne 1965–66; Lt Cdr Advanced Navigation Course 1966, HMS Soberton 1966–67 (i/c), HMS London 1968–70; Lt Cdr/Cdr HMS Ulster 1970–72 (i/c); Cdr: MOD 1972–74, HMS Tartar 1975–76 (i/c), Cdr Sea Trg 1976–77, HMS Ark Royal 1978; Capt: Nato Def Coll 1979, MOD-Naval Plans 1979–81, HMS Andromeda (i/c), and 8 Frigate Sqdn 1982–84 (incl Falklands), RN Presentation Team 1984–85, HMS Ark Royal (i/c) 1985–87; ADC HM The Queen 1986–87; Rear Adm Staff of Supreme Allied Cdr Europe 1987–89; Vice Adm Dep Supreme Allied Cdr Atlantic 1989–91, HM Marshal of the Diplomatic Corps 1992–01, extra equerry to HM The Queen 2001–, HM Lt for the City of London 2001–; chm: Sea Cadet Assoc 1992–98, Sea Cadet Cncl 1992–98, Lord Mayor of London's Charity 1997–98; tstee Marwell Preservation Tst 1992–2007 (chm 1999); pres Int Social Service (UK) 1996–2001; tstee and warden Box Hill Sch 2003– (govr 1992–2003, chm 1993–2003), warden Gordonstoun Sch 2004 (govr 1993–2003, chm 1996–2003); tstee WWF (UK) 2001–; Freeman City of London 1985, Liveryman Worshipful Co of Shipwrights 1985 (memb Ct of Assts 1989, Prime Warden 2001–02), Younger Brother Trinity House 1986; *Recreations* fishing, stamp collecting; *Clubs* RN of 1765 and 1785, Royal Over-Seas League; *Style—* Vice Adm Sir James Weatherall, KCVO, KBE, DL; ✉ Craig House, Bishop's Waltham, Southampton SO32 1FS (tel 01489 892483)

WEATHERILL, (Hon) Bernard Richard; QC (1996); s of Baron Weatherill, PC, DL (Life Peer), and Lyn, *née* Eatwell; *b* 20 May 1951; *Educ* Malvern, Principia Coll Illinois (int scholar), Univ of Kent (BA); *m* 1, 1977 (m dis 2001), Sally Maxwell, da of late John Ronald Fisher; 1 da (Julia Rosemary b 12 April 1982), 1 s (Thomas Bernard b 3 March 1984); m 2, 2005, Clare, da of late Peter W de B Forsyth; *Career* called to the Bar Middle Temple 1974 (bencher 2002); asst recorder 1998–2000, recorder 2000–; memb Gen Cncl of the Bar 1990–92 and 1993–95; memb: Chancery Bar Assoc, Professional Negligence Bar Assoc, Assoc of Business Recovery Professionals, Assoc of Contentious Tst and Probate Specialists (ACTAPS), Property Bar Assoc; chm Bar Services Co Ltd 2001–, non-exec dir A Cohen & Co plc 1989–2000; ACIArb 1997, mediator 2002; *Recreations* wine, lawn tennis, real tennis, bridge, golf, avoiding gardening, cultivating friendships; *Clubs* All England Lawn Tennis and Croquet, Hurlingham, Royal Tennis Court, Jesters, Royal Wimbledon Golf; *Style—* Bernard Weatherill, QC; ✉ Enterprise Chambers, 9 Old Square, Lincoln's Inn, London WC2A 3SR (tel 020 7405 9471, fax 020 7242 1447)

WEATHERILL, Prof Stephen Robson; *b* 21 March 1961; *Educ* Queens' Coll Cambridge (MA), Univ of Edinburgh (MSc); *Career* research asst Brunel Univ 1985, lectr Univ of Reading 1986–87, lectr Univ of Manchester 1987–90; Univ of Nottingham: lectr 1990–93, reader 1993–95, prof of European law 1995–97; Jacques Delors prof of EC law Univ of Oxford 1998–; *Style—* Prof Stephen Weatherill; ✉ Somerville College, Oxford OX2 6HD (tel 01865 270600, fax 01865 270620, e-mail stephen.weatherill@law.oxford.ac.uk)

WEATHERUP, Hon Mr Justice; Sir Ronald Eccles Weatherup; kt (2001); s of Rev Samuel Weatherup (d 1953), and Meta, *née* Reaney; *Educ* Methodist Coll Belfast, Queen's Univ Belfast; *m* Muriel, *née* Stewart; 1 s (Colin), 2 da (Clare, Diane); *Career* called to the Bar NI 1971, QC (NI) 1993, judge of the High Court of Justice in NI 2001–; *Style—* The Hon Mr Justice Weatherup; ✉ c/o Royal Courts of Justice, Chichester Street, Belfast BT1 3JF

WEAVER, Barrie Keith; s of James Richard Weaver (d 1977), of Corton, Norfolk, and Theresa, *née* Cooper; *b* 10 December 1946; *Educ* Wallington Sch, Central Sch of Art (BA); *m* 15 Nov 1996, Angela Wendy, da of Stephen Douglas Hawksley, of Davenham, Cheshire; 1 da (Honor Georgina May b 28 June 2003); *Career* designer: Conran Assocs 1971–73, Pentagram Design 1973–76; fndr Roberts Weaver Design 1977, chm Weaver Associates 1990–98, dir Weaver Design Ltd 1999–; cmmns incl: TI Group 1978–80, British Telecom 1982–84, Herman Miller, STC 1984–85, Applied Materials USA 1985–87, Plessey 1985–87, Nixdorf 1986–88, Hitachi, Matsushita Japan 1988–89, Qualcast, Nissan Japan 1990–91, LG, Samsung Korea 1991–92, BICC 1991–92, Airbus 1992, Stiga 1992, Whirlpool 1993, Universal Pictures, Mizuno Japan 1994, British Telecom 1995, Braun Germany 1996, Medison Korea 1996, Ransomes UK 1996, Antonov Ukraine 1997–98, Netas Turkey, Tunstall UK 1998–99, Subaru Japan 2001–02, nxt audio 2003; recipient: four Br Design Awards, Industrie Form Germany 1988 and 1996, Prince Philip Award, Designer of the Year 1990, Good Design Award Norway 1993, Design Innovations Award Germany 1994 and 1995; judge Sony Design Bursaries 1998–2002; memb Design Cncl 1989–95; FRSA 1984, FCSD 1982; *Recreations* antiques, paintings, gardening, looking at buildings; *Clubs* Lansdowne; *Style—* Barrie Weaver, Esq; ✉ 70 Lilyville Road, London SW6 5DW (tel 020 7736 1631, e-mail barrie@weaver.co.uk); Le Moutier, Aubry le Panthou, 61120, France (tel 0033 02 33 35 99 99)

WEAVER, (Christopher) Giles Herron; s of Lt-Col John Frederick Herron Weaver (d 1993), and Ursula Priscilla Marie Gabrielle, *née* Horlick (d 1997); *b* 4 April 1946; *Educ* Eton, London Business Sch (MSc); *m* 30 July 1974, Rosamund Betty, da of Lionel Mayhew (d 1992), of Alton, Hants; 2 da (Flora b 1975, Johanna b 1983), 2 s (Freddy b 1977, Jack b 1986); *Career* CA; articles with Arthur Young 1966–71; asst to chm: Jessel Securities 1973–75, Berry Wiggins 1975–76; i/c pension funds Ivory and Sime plc 1976–86, md pensions mgmnt Prudential Portfolio Mangrs 1986–90; Murray Johnstone Ltd: investment dir 1990–93, md 1993–99, chm 1999–2000; chm: Helical Bar plc, Charter European Tst plc, European Kenmore Industrial Property Fund Ltd, AH Medical Properties plc 2007–; former chm Murray Emerging Growth and Income Tst plc; dir: Aberdeen Asset Mgmnt plc, James Finlay Ltd, Anglo and Overseas Tst plc, Isis Property Tst II Ltd; prop Greywalls Hotel Gullane 1976–; former chm Historic Houses Assoc in Scotland, former dep chm of tstees Nat Galleries of Scotland; FCA 1977 (ACA 1970); *Recreations* skiing, golf, tennis, stalking, bridge; *Clubs* New (Edinburgh), Boodle's, HCEG (Muirfield), Hurlingham, Denham; *Style—* Giles Weaver, Esq; ✉ Greywalls, Gullane, East Lothian EH31 2EG (tel 01620 842144); 47 Glebe Place, London SW3 5JE (mobile 07774 896471, e-mail giles.weaver@aberdeen-asset.com)

WEAVER, (Richard) Irving; s of John Weaver (d 1991), and Joyce, *née* Roebuck (d 1997); *b* 15 March 1949, Doncaster, Yorks; *Educ* Mexborough GS, Sheffield Poly; *m* 5 July 1972, Dorothy, *née* Crowcroft; 2 s (Andrew Richard b 24 Aug 1973, Simon Daniel b 20 Dec 1977), 1 da (Helen Jayne b 14 Nov 1975); *Career* Strata Gp Ltd (formerly Weaver Building Gp Ltd (founded by gf, Oscar Weaver)): surveyor 1968, md 1978, chm 1989–, sole shareholder 2002–; majority shareholder Strata Construction Ltd 2005–; Entrepreneur of the Year IOD Yorks region 2005; *Clubs* sailing, golf, theatre, travel; *Style—* Irving Weaver, Esq; ✉ Strata, Quay Point, Lakeside, Doncaster DN4 5PL (website www.homesbystrata.com)

WEAVER, Karl; s of Max and Enid Weaver; *b* 21 July 1972; *Educ* Woodbridge HS, Bancroft's Sch, Queen Mary & Westfield Coll London (BSc, MSc); *m* 3 May 1997, Fiona *née* Harvey; *Career* analyst OHerlihy Associates Ltd 1994–95, sr conslt The Henley Centre London 1995–99, managing ptnr Advanced Techniques Gp (ATG) Worldwide MindShare 1999–2003, dir Data2Decisions Ltd 2003–; Freeman City of London (by redemption); memb Worshipful Co of Marketors; *Recreations* trumpet playing; *Style—* Karl Weaver; ✉ tel 020 8502 9160, e-mail karl.weaver@d2dlimited.com

WEAVER, Prof Lawrence Trevelyan; s of Sir Toby Weaver, CB (d 2001), and Marjorie (Lady Weaver, d 2003), da of Rt Hon Sir Charles Trevelyan, 3 Bt (d 1958); *b* 13 October 1948; *Educ* Clifton, CCC Cambridge (exhibitioner, MA, MB BChir), DObstRCOG, DCH (London), Univ of Cambridge (MD, Lionel Whitby medal), Univ of Glasgow (DSc); *m* Camilla, *née* Simmons; 1 s, 1 da; *Career* MRC trg fell Dunn Nutrition Lab and hon sr registrar Dept of Paediatrics Addenbrooke's Hosp Cambridge 1984–86, clinical res fell (Fulbright travel scholar) Harvard Med Sch Depts of Pediatric Gastroenterology and Nutrition Children's Hosp and Massachusetts Gen Hosp Boston 1987–88, memb MRC Scientific Staff Dunn Nutrition Lab and hon conslt paediatrician Addenbrooke's Hosp and Univ of Cambridge 1988–94, hon conslt paediatrician Royal Hosp for Sick Children Yorkshill Glasgow 1994–, Samson Gemmell prof of child health Univ of Glasgow 1996– (reader in human nutrition 1994–96); FRSA, FRCPCH, FRCP, FRCPGlas; *Recreations* being outdoors; *Style—* Prof Lawrence Weaver; ✉ Department of Child Health, University of Glasgow, Royal Hospital for Sick Children, Yorkhill, Glasgow G3 8SJ (tel 0141 201 0236, fax 0141 201 0837, e-mail lweaver@clinmed.gla.ac.uk)

WEAVER, Oliver; QC (1985); s of Denis Weaver, and Kathleen Nesville, *née* Lynch; *b* 27 March 1942; *Educ* Friends' Sch Saffron Walden, Trinity Coll Cambridge (MA, LLM); *m* 3 Oct 1964, Julia Mary, *née* MacClymont; 2 da (Lucy (Mrs Piers Moreau) b 1967, Mary-Ann (Mrs Christopher Middleton) b 1970), 1 s (James b 1969); *Career* pres Cambridge Union Soc 1963; called to the Bar: Middle Temple 1965, Lincoln's Inn 1969; memb: Bar Cncl 1981–84, Panel of Chairmen of Authorisation and Disciplinary Tribunals of the Securities and Futures Assoc 1988–93, Cncl of Law Reporting 1986–93; *Recreations* fishing, racing, gun dogs; *Style—* Oliver Weaver, Esq, QC; ✉ Kennel Farm, Albury End, Ware, Hertfordshire SG11 2HS (tel 01279 771 331); Erskine Chambers, 30 Lincoln's Inn Fields, London WC2A 3PF (tel 020 7242 5532)

WEBB, Prof Sir Adrian Leonard; kt (2000); s of Leonard Webb, of Melksham, Wilts, and Rosina, *née* Staines; *b* 19 July 1943; *Educ* St Julian's HS Newport Gwent, Univ of Birmingham (BSocSci), LSE (MSc), Loughborough Univ (DLitt); *m* 1, (m dis); 2 s (Rhicert b 20 April 1967, Geraint b 17 July 1971); m 2, 1996, Monjulee, da of Dass, of Kuala Lumpur, Malaysia; *Career* lectr LSE 1966–74, res dir Personal Social Servs Cncl 1974–76; Loughborough Univ: prof of social policy 1976–93, dir Centre for Res in Social Policy 1982–91, pro-vice-chllr 1988–93; vice-chllr Univ of Glamorgan 1993–2005; chm: Bd of Govrs Volunteer Centre 1978–84, Ctee on Workforce Planning and Trg in Social Servs 1987–88, Dept of Health Task Force on Nursing Research 1992–93, Heads of HE in Wales 2000–03, Pontypridd and Rhondda NHS Tst 2005–; memb: DHSS Res Liaison Gps 1975–90 (sci advsr Chief Scientist's Departmental Res Ctee DHSS 1987–90), Sociology and Social Admin Ctee SSRC 1976–80, Cncl on Tbnls 1985–91, Eng Nat Bd on Nursing Midwifery and Health Visiting 1988–93, CBI Cncl Wales 1993–98, Dearing Ctee of Enquiry on Higher Educn 1996–97, Public Servs Productivity Panel HM Treasy 2000–06; non-exec dir: Nat Cncl Education and Learning Wales (ELWa) 2001–06, Nat Assembly for Wales 2003–, E Glamorgan NHS Tst; advsr on social policy and social work: Univ Funding Cncl 1989–92, Leics DHA 1992–93, NHS Wales R&D Forum 1993–; vice-pres Leics Regnl Cncl Guideposts Tst Ltd 1988–93; chm Social Admin Assoc 1977–80; memb: Social Policy Assoc, Br Sociological Assoc, Political Studies Assoc; FRSA 1987; *Books* numerous articles and books on social policy incl (jtly): Change Choice and Conflict in Social Policy (1975), Planning Need and Scarcity - Essays on the Personal Social Services (1986), The Economic Approach to Social Policy (1986), Social Work Social Care and Social Planning (1987), Joint Approaches to Social Policy - Rationality and Practice (1988); *Recreations* walking, painting (water colour), ornithology; *Clubs* Nat Liberal; *Style—* Prof Sir Adrian Webb; ✉ Pontypridd and Rhondda NHS Trust, Pontypridd, Mid Glamorgan CF38 1UY (tel 01443 443845, e-mail adrian.webb@pr-tr.wales.nhs.uk)

WEBB, Dr Andrew Roy; s of Michael Edward John Webb, of Oundle, Northants, and Carol Janice, *née* Finlay; *b* 6 February 1958, Croydon; *Educ* Sponne Sch Towcester, Northampton GS, WNSM (MB, BCh), Univ of Wales (MD); *m* 27 March 1999, Suzanne Elizabeth, *née* Gunn; 5 s (Matthew James Andrew b 25 Feb 1983, Adam Mark Richard b 5 Jan 1985, Tomas Michael Roy b 12 Nov 2002, James Robert Dylan b 31 Aug 2004, Alexander Samuel Ieuan b 12 Dec 2006); *Career* UCL Hosps NHS Fndn Tst: conslt physician in intensive care medicine 1990–, clinical dir intensive care services 1992–2001, clinical dir cardiac services 1997–2001, med dir clinical services 2001–06, med dir Acute Hosp 2006–; Intensive Care Soc: memb Cncl 1997–2003, hon treas 2000–03, memb Higher Awards Ctee 2004–; chm All Wales Critical Care Devpt Ctee 2001–; asst ed and memb Editorial Bd Intensive Care Medicine jl 1990–95 (memb Editorial Advsy Bd 1995–2003), section ed for health technol assessment Jl of Critical Care 2001–; FRCP 1997 (MRCP 1984); *Publications* Critical Care Algorithms (jtly, 1991), Medical Emergencies Algorithms (jtly, 1994), The Oxford Handbook of Critical Care (jtly, 1997, 2 edn 2005), The Oxford Textbook of Critical Care (jtly, 1999); numerous book chapters and articles; *Style—* Dr Andrew Webb; ✉ UCL Hospitals NHS Foundation Trust, 2nd Floor East, 250 Euston Road, London NW1 2PG (tel 020 7380 9613, fax 020 7380 9110, e-mail a.webb@uclh.nhs.uk)

WEBB, His Hon Judge Anthony Ronald; s of late Ronald Alfred Webb, of Tenterden, Kent, and Muriel Dorothy, *née* Empleton; *b* 17 July 1947; *Educ* Chislehurst and Sidcup GS, Univ of Bristol (LLB); *m* 29 Sept 1979, Sarah Lynette, da of Denzil Edward Kieft, of Lagos, Portugal; 1 da (Camilla b 1986), 2 s (Guy b 1989, Piers b 1994); *Career* called to the Bar Inner Temple 1970; recorder of the Crown Court 1993–99 (asst recorder 1989–93), circuit judge (SE Circuit) 1999–, resident judge Canterbury Crown Court 2001–; chm Kent Criminal Justice Strategy Ctee 2000–02, memb Mental Health Review Tbnl 2002–; memb Cncl Univ of Kent 2003–; *Recreations* equestrian, travel, conservation, gardening; *Clubs* Kent CCC; *Style—* His Hon Judge Webb; ✉ Canterbury Combined Court Centre, The Law Courts, Chaucer Road, Canterbury, Kent CT1 1ZA (tel 01227 819200, fax 01227 819329)

WEBB, Brian James; s of Frederick William Webb (d 1972), and Esther, *née* Foxall; *b* 15 January 1945; *Educ* Brookfield Sch Liverpool, Liverpool Coll of Art, Canterbury Coll of Art (DipAD); *m* 1969, Gail Elizabeth, da of George Henderson Barker (d 1986); 1 da (Holly Katharine b 4 Feb 1976), 1 s (James William Robin b 4 Jan 1980); *Career* asst graphic designer Michael Tucker Assocs 1967–69, graphic designer Derek Forsyth Partnership 1969–71; designer and dir: Trickett & Webb Ltd 1971–2003, Webb & Webb 2003–; visiting prof Univ of the Arts London 1999–, visiting lectr numerous colls in UK, USA and Asia; work has been exhibited and published throughout the world; contrib Penrose Annual, Best of British Packaging, Best of British Corporate Identity and other jls; winner of numerous awards D&AD, Donside and Nat Calendar Awards for work on clients incl: Thames TV, Midland Bank, Royal Mail; pres CSD 2003–; memb: Cncl CSD 1980–87 and 1989– (chm Graphics Gp 1980–85), Exec Ctee D & AD 1987–89; memb juries: D&AD 1975–, Design Bursary RSA 1980–; external assessor CNAA UK; fell UC of the Creative Arts 2004; memb D&AD 1972, FCSD 1972, FRSA 1980, FSTD 1994; *Publications* For Shop Use Only - Eric Ravilious, Curwen and Dent stock blocks and devices (1994), Submarine Dream - Eric Ravilious, lithography (1996–7), Austerity to Affluence - British Art and Design 1945–62 (graphic design and typhography section, 1997), A thousand years, a thousand words - a celebration of the Royal Millennium Stamp Project (2000), Design: Edward Bawden and Eric Ravilious (2005), Design: Paul Nash and John Nash (2006), Design: E McKnight Kauffer (2007); *Recreations* walking, working; *Style—* Brian Webb, Esq; ✉ Webb & Webb Design Limited, H16 Perserverence Works, 38 Kingsland Road, London E2 8DD (tel 020 7739 7895)

WEBB, Christine; da of Horace John Webb, of Hythe, Kent, and Marjorie Alice, *née* Spurgeon; *b* 28 March 1945; *Educ* Waterloo Park Co GS Liverpool, Univ of Manchester (BA), Univ of London (MSc, PhD); *Career* staff nurse Middx Hosp 1968, night sister Northwick Park Hosp 1971–72, ward sister Royal Free Hosp 1972–73, pupil midwife Whittington Hosp 1973; nurse tutor: Middx Hosp 1975 (unqualified nurse tutor 1973–74),

Miny of Health Mozambique 1975–78; sr nurse tutor UCH 1978–80, research asst Chelsea Coll London 1980–82, pt/t clinical teacher Royal Free Hosp 1981–82, lectr Dept of Nursing Univ of Manchester 1982–84, princ lectr in nursing Bristol Poly 1984–89; Univ of Manchester: prof of nursing 1989–96, head Sch of Nursing Studies 1990–95; prof of health studies Univ of Plymouth 1996–; ed: Jl of Clinical Nursing 1996–2002, Jl of Advanced Nursing 2001–; *Books* Sexuality, Nursing and Health (1985), Feminist Practice in Women's Health Care (ed, 1986), Women's Health - Midwifery and Gynaecological Nursing (ed, 1986), Textbook of Adult Nursing (jt ed, 1992), Working Together? Interprofessional Relations in Health Care (jtly, 1994); book reviews for various learned jls; *Recreations* walking, dogs, reading; *Style*— Prof Christine Webb; ✉ Faculty of Health and Social Work, University of Plymouth, Exeter EX2 6AS (tel 01392 475147)

WEBB, Prof Colin; s of Sidney Joseph Webb (d 1985), and Stella Taylor, *née* Botten (d 1976); *b* 11 October 1954; *Educ* Leominster GS, Aston Univ (BSc, PhD); *m* 14 April 1984, Ann Elizabeth, da of Charles Edward Kelly; 1 s (Richard Hereford b 11 Oct 1985), 1 da (Kate Elizabeth b 24 April 1989); *Career* UMIST (now Univ of Manchester): research assoc 1979–83, lectr in chem engrg 1983–91, sr lectr chem engrg 1991–94, Satake prof of grain process engrg 1994–, head Dept of Chemical Engrg 2000–; visiting academic Monash Univ Australia 1988, CEC fell Hungarian Acad of Sciences Veszprém 1993, guest researcher Nat Inst of Bioscience and Human Technol Tsukuba Japan 1993, examiner Inst of Brewing 1998–; founding fell Int Acad of Food Science and Technol 1999, memb American Assoc of Cereal Chemists 1995; FIChemE 1992; *Publications* Plant and Animal Cells: Process Possibilities (1987), Studies in Viable Cell Immobilisation (1996), Cereals: Novel Uses and Processes (1997), Bubbles in Food (1999); *Recreations* cycling, walking, badminton; *Style*— Prof Colin Webb; ✉ Department of Chemical Engineering, University of Manchester, PO Box 88, Sackville Street, Manchester M60 1QD (tel 0161 200 4379, fax 0161 200 4399, e-mail colin.webb@manchester.ac.uk)

WEBB, Prof Colin Edward; MBE (2000); s of Alfred Edward Webb (d 1985), and Doris, *née* Collins (d 1966); *b* 9 December 1937; *Educ* Erith GS, Univ of Nottingham (Ford (Dagenham) Trust scholar, BSc), Univ of Oxford (DPhil, Prize in Waverley Gold Medal Competition for Scientific Essay); *m* 1, 6 June 1964, Pamela Mabel Cooper (d 1992), da of Maj Wilfred Alan Cooper White (d 1984); 2 da (Susan Patricia (Mrs S Steel) b 17 March 1967, Julie Diane (Mrs T Pottle) b 28 August 1970); m 2, 25 July 1995, Margaret Helen Marshall, da of Gordon Dewar (d 1968); *Career* memb tech staff Bell Telephone Labs Murray Hill NJ 1964–68; Clarendon Lab Univ of Oxford: AEI res fell in physics 1968–71, lectr 1971–90, reader in physics 1990–92, prof of laser physics 1992–2002; Jesus Coll Oxford: official tutorial fell 1973–88, sr res fell in physics 1988–2005, emeritus fell 2005–; visiting prof Dept of Physics Univ of Salford 1988–2004, visiting prof dept of mechanical engr Cranfield Univ 1999–; chm and fndr Oxford Lasers Ltd 1977– (Achievement Award of Worshipful Company of Scientific Instrument Makers 1986, Queen's Award for Export 1987, Queen's Award for Technol 1989 and 1991), Clifford Patterson Lecture & Medal Royal Soc 1998; Optical Soc of America: memb 1960–88, fell 1988–, dir-at-large 1991–94; pres UK Consortium for Photonics and Optics (UKCPO) 1998–2002; FInstP 1985 (memb 1968–85, Duddell Medal and Prize 1985, Glazebrook Medal and Prize 2001), FRS 1992; *Publications* over 100 papers in scientific jls and numerous chapters in books; *Recreations* music, photography, travel, reading; *Clubs* Royal Society; *Style*— Prof Colin Webb, MBE, FRS; ✉ Oxford Lasers Ltd, Unit 8, Moorbrook Park, Didcot, Oxfordshire OX11 7HP (tel 01235 810088, fax 01235 810060); Department of Atomic and Laser Physics, University of Oxford, The Clarendon Laboratory, Parks Road, Oxford OX1 3PU (tel 01865 272254, fax 01865 272375, e-mail c.webb1@physics.ox.ac.uk)

WEBB, Prof David John; s of Alfred William Owen Webb, of London, and Edna May, *née* Parish; *b* 1 September 1953; *Educ* Dulwich Coll (Kent scholar), The Royal London Hosp (MB BS, MD), Univ of Edinburgh (DSc); *m* 23 June 1984, Dr Margaret Jane Cullen, da of Dr Archibald Skinnider Cullen; 3 s (David Matthew b 29 July 1992, Matthew Owen Cullen b 28 Aug 1995, Mark Ewen b 11 May 1999); *Career* MRC clinical research fell MRC Blood Pressure Unit Glasgow 1982–85, lectr in clinical pharmacology Dept of Pharmacology and Clinical Pharmacology St George's Hosp Med Sch London 1985–89; Univ of Edinburgh: sr lectr Dept of Med and dir Clinical Research Centre 1990–95, Christison prof of therapeutics and clinical pharmacology Clinical Pharmacology Unit and Research Centre 1995–, head Dept of Med Western Gen Hosp 1997–98, head Dept Med Sciences 1998–2001, ldr Wellcome Tst Cardiovascular Initiative 1997–2001, ldr Wellcome Tst Clinical Research Facility Educn Prog 1998–, head Centre for Cardiovascular Science 2000–04; hon conslt physician Lothian Univ Hospitals NHS Tst Edinburgh 1990–; hon tstee and jt research dir High Blood Pressure Fndn 1991–; chm: Lothian Area Drug and Therapeutics Ctee 1998–2005, Coll Ctee on Clinical Pharmacology and Therapeutics, RCP 1999–2000, RCP(Ed) Symposium Ctee 1999–; chair: Scottish Exec's New Drugs Ctee 2001–04, Project Grants Ctee Br Heart Fndn 2004–, Profs and Heads CPT 2004; chair Scottish Medicines Consortium 2004–; memb: MRS 1982, Scottish Soc for Experimental Med 1982 (memb Cncl 1994–97), Br Hypertension Soc 1985 (memb Exec Ctee 1991–94), Euro Soc of Hypertension 1987, Int Soc of Hypertension 1988, Scottish Cardiac Soc 1992, Faculty of Pharmaceutical Med RCP UK 1992, Research Defence Soc 1992, American Heart Assoc 1994, Euro Network of Therapeutics Teachers (assoc) 1994, Assoc of Physicians of GB and I 1994, Scottish Soc of Physicians 1995, Assoc of Clinical Profs of Med 1996, Soc for Meds Research 1996, Advsy Bd MRC 1997–98, Wellcome Tst Physiology & Pharmacology Panel 1997–2000, Scottish Exec's Scottish Medical and Scientific Advsy Ctee 2001; Br Pharmacological Soc: memb 1988, memb Exec 1994–96, hon sec, dir and tstee 1996–99, memb Cncl and dir 2004–; Biennial SmithKline Beecham Fndn Prize for Research Br Pharmacological Soc 1994, Lilly Biennial Prize and Gold Medal for Research in Clinical Pharmacology Br Pharmacological Soc 2003; memb: Scottish Malt Whisky Society; FRCP, FRSE, FESC, FFPM, FMedSci, fell Br Pharmacology Soc; *Books* The Molecular Biology and Pharmacology of the Endothelins (Molecular Biology Intelligence Unit Monograph Series, with G A Gray, 1995), The Endothelium in Hypertension (ed with P J T Vallance, 1996), Vascular Endothelium in Human Physiology and Pathophysiology (ed with P J T Vallance, 1999), The Year in Therapeutics Vol 1 (2005); *Recreations* summer and winter mountaineering, scuba diving, opera, bridge, chess; *Clubs* Scottish Mountaineering; *Style*— Prof David Webb; ✉ 73 Great King Street, Edinburgh EH3 6RN (tel 0131 556 7145); Clinical Pharmacology Unit, Centre for Cardiovascular Science, Queen's Medical Research Institute, Room E3.22, 47 Little France Crescent, Edinburgh EH16 4TJ (e-mail d.j.webb@ed.ac.uk)

WEBB, Iain Andrew; s of Eric Webb, of York, and Oris, *née* Dyson; *b* 30 March 1959; *Educ* Scalby Secdy Sch Scarborough, Joseph Rowntree Secdy Sch York, Rambert Sch of Ballet London, The Royal Ballet Sch London; *m* 30 July 1982, Margaret, da of Ettore Barbieri; 1 s (Jason Alexander b 29 July 1987); *Career* Sadlers Well's Royal Ballet (now The Birmingham Royal Ballet) 1979–89; princ roles: Oberon in Ashton's The Dream, The Young Man in Ashton's The Two Pigeons, Franz in Wright's Coppélia, Colas and Alain in Ashton's La Fille mal Gardée, Prince Siegfried and Benno in Wright's Swan Lake, Pas de Quatre in Nureyev's Raymonda Act III, Blue Bird and Pas de Quatre in Wright's Sleeping Beauty, The Poet in Les Sylphides; Balanchine's The Prodigal Son, Van Manen's 5 Tango's, Kay in Bintley's The Snow Queen; created roles in: Bintley's Polonia, Night Moves, Choros The Swan of Tuonela, Flowers of the Forest; performed Petrushka 1988/89 season; joined The Royal Ballet at Covent Garden 1989; debut as the King of the South in MacMillan's The Prince of the Pagodes, Mercury in Bintley's The Plants, danced in first performances of Balanchine's Violin Concerts and Page's Bloodline, Alain in Ashton's La Fille mal Gardée, guest appearances in Spain and SA 1989 and 1992, received sponsorship to study with Royal Danish Ballet March 1992, prog organiser and conslt for the Celebration of Classical Dance evening Harrogate Festival 1992; 1992–93 season: Bottom in The Dream, Mrs Tiggywinkle and Alexander Bland Pig in The Tales of Beatrix Potter, the small ugly sister (Ashton's Role) in Ashton's Cinderella, Sancho Panza in Mikhail Barysnikov's Don Quixote and the Pas de Quatra in MacMillan's Gloria; 1993–94 season: The Doctor in MacMillan's Different Drummer, Gallison in Anthony Dowell's Sleeping Beauty; prod and dir Patrick Armand and Friends Gala for 1993 Harrogate Int Festival, co-prodr an evening with principals and soloists of the Stuttgart Ballet 1994, prodr gala performance for the 150th anniversary of the Shaftesbury Homes at the Banqueting House 1994; co-dir The Dance Agency 1993–, fndr Dance Cares 1994, memb Bd of Dirs Adventures in Motion Pictures 1994, asst dir K Ballet Japan 2003–, tutor London Studio Centre; *Recreations* history of ballet, collecting ballet memorabilia, music, photography; *Style*— Iain Webb, Esq; ✉ London Studio Centre, 42–50 York Way, London N1 9AB

WEBB, Justin Oliver; s of Charles Webb (d 1983), and Gloria, *née* Crocombe (d 2006); *b* 3 January 1961; *Educ* Friends' Sch Sidcot, LSE (BSc(Econ)); *m* 30 Aug 1996, Sarah Louise, da of Charles G A Gordon; 3 c (Martha Sarah, Samuel Oliver (twins) b 28 March 2000, Clara Jayne b 1 Feb 2004); *Career* BBC: news trainee 1984–86, reporter BBC Radio Ulster 1986–87, reporter Today prog Radio 4 1987–88, news reporter and foreign affrs corr BBC Radio and Television 1988–93 (assignments incl: Gulf War, Russia, USA, Middle E, India, Western and Eastern Europe, South Africa, Bosnia), full-time presenter Breakfast News 1994–99 (occasional presenter 1993–94), Europe corr 1999–2002, chief Washington corr 2002–; *Style*— Justin Webb, Esq; ✉ c/o BBC News, BBC Television Centre, Wood Lane, London W12 7RJ (tel 020 8743 8000)

WEBB, Keith Stewart; s of Arthur Saunders Webb, of Walsall, and Doris Martha, *née* Cheadle; *b* 19 March 1947; *Educ* Joseph Leckie Sch Walsall, Matthew Boulton Coll Birmingham, Sch of Art and Design Walsall; *m* 13 Aug 1972, Gillian, da of Anthony Anson; 2 da (Nicola Lucy b 5 Aug 1978, Amy Francesca b 27 Dec 1984); *Career* Lucas Industries: in trg Group Advertising Facility 1964–67, prodn controller 1967–68, press offr Lucas Electrical 1968–69, chief press offr 1969–70, dep gp PR mangr 1970–72; Edson Evers and Associates: joined 1973, assoc ptnr 1974–85, ptnr 1985–; MIPR 1974, Dip in Communication and Mktg 1976; *Recreations* swimming, yachting; *Style*— Keith Webb, Esq; ✉ Yew Tree House, 366 Birmingham Road, Walsall, West Midlands WS5 3NX (tel 01922 21032); Edson Evers & Associates, New Garden Street, Stafford ST17 4AG (tel 01785 255146, fax 01785 211518, e-mail pr@edsonevers.co.uk)

WEBB, Patrick John Ryall; s of Kenneth Edmund Ryall Webb, of Tadworth, Surrey, and Marjorie Eveline Ryall, *née* Nuthall; *b* 31 March 1944; *Educ* St Edward's Sch Oxford, Trinity Hall Cambridge; *m* 22 March 1969, Dr Joanna Webb, da of Thomas Gilbert Burton (d 1976), of Hull; 1 s (Edward b 1970), 2 da (Georgina b 1971, Elly b 1975); *Career* articled clerk Ernst and Young 1965–69, mangr Peat Marwick McLintock 1969–81; co sec: Touche Remnant and Co 1981–85, James Capel and Co 1986–91; dir James Capel Unit Trust Mgmnt Ltd 1989–91; md G W Hutton & Co (Underwriting Agency) Ltd 1991–95, fin dir CLM Managing Agency Ltd 1994–97; dir St Martin-in-the-Fields Enterprise Ltd 1998–2004, chm and dir Kinetic Insurance Brokers 2001–, chm St Martin's Centurions 2005–; conslt Hampden plc 1998–; dir Walton Heath Golf Club 1985–93, chm and govr Bramley Sch 1975–95; affiliate Securities Inst (ASI); FCA 1970, FRSA; *Recreations* golf, music, tennis; *Style*— Patrick Webb, Esq; ✉ 17 Tower Road, Tadworth, Surrey KT20 5QY (tel 01737 814606, e-mail spiderw@globalnet.co.uk)

WEBB, Richard; s of Lt-Col Richard Webb (d 1988), and Iris Webb (d 1996); *b* 26 July 1943; *Educ* Marlborough; *m* 25 Feb 1992, Gillian Blane, *née* Jenkins; *Career* Condé Nast Publications Ltd 1966–70, dir Michael Joseph Ltd publishers London 1970–74; co-fndr and md: Webb & Bower (Publishers) Ltd, Country Diary of an Edwardian Lady Ltd, RW.UK Ltd, Richard Webb, Publisher 1975–; *Clubs* Royal Dart Yacht; *Style*— Richard Webb, Esq; ✉ Driftwood Quay, Warfleet, Dartmouth, Devon TQ6 9BZ (tel 01803 835525, e-mail rwukltd@btconnect.com, website www.dartmouthbooks.co.uk)

WEBB, Robert Stopford; QC (1988); s of R V B Webb, MC, of Styal, Cheshire, and Isabella Raine, *née* Hinks; *b* 4 October 1948; *Educ* Wycliffe Coll, Univ of Exeter (LLB); *m* 1 April 1975, Angela Mary, da of Bernard Bruce Freshwater (d 1978); 2 s (Alfred b 1978, William b 1980); *Career* called to the Bar: Inner Temple 1971 (bencher 1998), Lincoln's Inn 1996; head of chambers 5 Bell Yard 1988–98, recorder 1993–98; general counsel Br Airways 1998–, chm Air Law Ctee Royal Aeronautical Soc 1988–92, chm Int Practice Ctee Bar Cncl, vice-chm Air Law Ctee Int Bar Assoc 1990–92; dir London Stock Exchange 2001–; non-exec dir BBC 2007–; memb: Bd Int Acad of Trial Lawyers, Chllr's Advsy Cncl Univ of Exeter; membre de la Commission d'Arbitrage Aérien et Spatial (Paris) 1994; FRAeS; *Recreations* golf, fly fishing; *Clubs* Reform, RAC, Royal Wimbledon Golf, Royal Lytham St Anne's Golf, Prestbury Golf; *Style*— Robert Webb, Esq, QC; ✉ British Airways, HBB3, PO Box 365, Harmondsworth UB7 0GB (tel 020 8738 6870, fax 020 8738 9964)

WEBB, Rodney Anson John; JP; s of Ernest Herbert Webb (d 1983), of Norwich, Norfolk, and Irene Maud, *née* Gotts (d 2003); *b* 24 April 1944; *Educ* Bracondale Sch Norwich; *m* 1, 8 Nov 1969 (m dis), Angela Delys, da of Frederick Lukies (d 1981), of Salhouse, Norfolk; 3 da (Alison b 1971, Victoria b 1977, Hannah b 1986); m 2, 15 Sept 2001, Dr Annalisa Sartori, da of Alfonso and Lina Sartori of Padova, Italy; 2 da (Antonia b 2002, Lavinia b 2004); *Career* md: Bowater Flexible Packaging 1978, Bowater Cartons 1980, Crest Packaging 1985–2003; memb Ctee Br Carton Assoc 1980–81, pres Flexible Packaging Assoc 1983–84; vice-pres: Euro Flexible Packaging Assoc 1984–86, UK spokesman Euro Aluminium Foil Assoc 1988–91, pres Euro Aluminium Foil Assoc Converters 1992; FCA; *Recreations* golf, tennis, skiing, water skiing; *Style*— Rodney Webb, Esq; ✉ Shirrenden, Horsmonden, Kent TN12 8DN (tel 01892 722 889)

WEBB, Simon; CBE (1991); s of Canon Bertie Webb, of Worcester, and Jane, *née* Braley; *b* 21 October 1951; *Educ* Kings Sch Worcester, Hertford Coll Oxford; *m* 1975, Alexandra Jane, da of Gerald Henry Hobart Culme-Seymour; 1 s (Rowland Henry b 1978), 1 da (Clementine Evelyn b 1982); *Career* MOD: admin trainee 1972–75, asst private sec to Min of State 1975–77, princ 1977–82; with HM Treasury 1982–85, dir Resources and Progs (Warships) Dept MOD 1985–88, with Rand Corp Santa Monica California 1988–89; MOD: private sec to Sec of State 1989–92, min (defence materiel) British Embassy Washington DC 1992–96, DG Resources Procurement Executive 1996–98, team leader Smart Procurement Implementation 1998–99, asst under sec of state (Home and Overseas) 1999, policy dir 2001–; *Publications* Defense Acquisition and Free Markets (1990); *Recreations* gardens, opera, cycling; *Clubs* Reform; *Style*— Simon Webb; ✉ Ministry of Defence, Metropole Building, Northumberland Avenue, London WC2N 5BP (tel 020 7218 9000)

WEBB, Steven; MP; *Career* economist Inst of Fiscal Studies 1986–95, prof of social policy Univ of Bath 1995–97; MP (Lib Dem) Northavon 1997–; Lib Dem shadow min for work and pensions 1999–2005, Lib Dem shadow min for health 2005–; *Style*— Steve Webb, MP; ✉ House of Commons, London SW1A 0AA (tel 020 7219 3000)

WEBB, Prof William; s of Christopher Webb, of Woking, Surrey, and Genebeth, *née* Mooring; *b* 4 May 1967, Hersham, Surrey; *Educ* Univ of Southampton (BEng, PhD), Southampton Univ Mgmnt Sch (MBA); *m* 17 June 1995, Alison, *née* Porter; 2 da (Katherine b 17 Dec 1997, Hannah b 23 Feb 2001); *Career* engr; Multiple Access

Communications Ltd 1989–93 (dir 1992–93), Smith System Engrg Ltd 1993–97 (head of spectrum mgmnt 1995–97), head of wireless local loop div Netcom Conslts 1997–98, Motorola 1998–2001 (dir of corp strategy 2000–01), mgmnt conslt in wireless technol practice PA Consulting 2001–03, head of R&D and sr technologist Ofcom 2003–; visiting prof: Centre for Communications Systems Research (CCSR) Univ of Surrey 2003–, De MOntfort Univ 2007–; memb: Judging Panel Wall St Jl Innovation Awards 2002–, Bd of Tstees IET 2006–; vice-pres IEE 2004–06; CEng 1992, SMIEEE 1995, FIEE 2001, FREng 2005; *Publications* Modern Quadrature Amplitude Modulation (1994, 2 edn 2004), Introduction to Wireless Local Loop (1998, 2 edn 2000), Understanding Cellular Radio (1998), The Complete Wireless Communications Professional (1999), Single and Multi-Carrier QAM (2000), The Future of Wireless Communications (2001), Wireless Communications: The Future (2007), Essentials of Modern Spectrum Management (2007); *Recreations* cycling, music, reading; *Style—* Prof William Webb; ✉ Ofcom, Riverside House, 2A Southwark Bridge Road, London SE1 9HA (e-mail william.webb@ofcom.org.uk)

WEBBER, John Anthony; s of Walter James Webber (d 1972), of Birmingham, and Edith, *née* Lloyd (d 1964); *b* 15 February 1951; *Educ* Birmingham Secdy Sch, Birmingham Coll of Food and Domestic Arts (City & Guilds), Westminster Coll of Food London (City & Guilds); *m* 5 Aug 1987, Caroline Isobel, da of Ian Jackson, of Appin, Argyll; 1 s (Nigel John b 10 Feb 1989), 2 da (Chloe Caroline b 4 Jan 1992, Abigail Louise b 14 Feb 1995); *Career* chef; first commis chef rising to chef de partie Park Lane Hotel Piccadilly 1969–73; Dorchester Hotel Park Lane: second commis chef 1973–75, first commis chef 1975–76, chef de partie 1976–79, sous chef 1979–80; head chef: Gidleigh Park Hotel Chagford 1980–85 (Michelin rosette 1982), Clivedon 1985–88; exec chef 'Kinnaird' Kinnaird Estate 1988–98 (Michelin rosette 1992, 4/5 Good Food Guide 1996), culinary dir Drambuie Scottish Chefs National Cookery Centre 1998–, culinary dir Nairns Cook Sch 2000–; Cert of Merit (Salon Culinaire de Londres) 1976, Silver Medal (City of Truro Festival of Culinary Arts) 1980, Gold Medal (Torquay Gastronomic Festival) 1981; Master Craftsman Craft Guild of Chefs, Master Chef Master Chefs Inst; *Recreations* fishing, eating out, music; *Style—* John Webber, Esq; ✉ Sonas, 22 Vennacher Avenue, Callander, Stirlingshire FK17 8JQ (tel and fax 01877 339552)

WEBER, Prof Richard Robert; s of Richard Robert Weber (d 1988), and Elizabeth, *née* Bray; *b* 25 February 1953; *Educ* Walnut Hills HS, Solihull Sch, Downing Coll Cambridge (MA, Mayhew Prize, PhD); *Career* Univ of Cambridge: research fell Queens' Coll 1977–78, tutor and dir of studies in mathematics, manufacturing engrg and management studies Queens' Coll 1978–92, lectr Dept of Engrg 1984–92 (asst lectr 1978–84), reader in management science 1992–94, Churchill prof of mathematics for operational research Dept of Pure Mathematics and Mathematical Statistics 1994–, vice-pres Queens' Coll 1996–; memb: Operational Research Soc, Operations Research Soc of America; FRSS; *Recreations* hiking, fitness training, travel; *Style—* Prof Richard Weber; ✉ Queens' College, Cambridge CB3 9ET (tel 01223 335570); Department of Pure Mathematics and Mathematical Statistics, Statistical Laboratory, University of Cambridge, Wilberforce Road, Cambridge CB3 0WB (tel 01223 337944, fax 01223 337956, e-mail rrw1@cam.ac.uk)

WEBSTER, Prof Alec; s of Richard Webster (d 1979), and Gladys, *née* Hargreaves (d 1997); *b* 5 June 1950, Accrington, Lancs; *Educ* Accrington GS, Keele Univ (BA), UCL (MSc), Univ of Leicester (PGCE), Univ of Nottingham (PhD), Univ of Bristol (MPhil); *m* 1, 1972 (m dis 1987), Anne Isobel, da of Jack Hindmoor; 3 s (Joseph b 26 Nov 1977, Rick b 1 Dec 1979, Robin b 10 Aug 1987), 1 da (Elizabeth b 26 March 1982); m 2, 1995, Valerie Joy, da of Dennis Crome; *Career* teacher 1973–76, educnl psychologist ILEA 1976–77, educnl psychologist Bucks LEA 1977–80, sr specialist educnl psychologist for language and hearing-impaired children Berks LEA 1980–86, sr educnl psychologist Clwyd LEA 1986–88, memb Advsy Team Clwyd LEA 1988–90, area sr educnl psychologist Avon LEA 1990–92 (mangr Bristol Psychology Serv team); Univ of Bristol: lectr Grad Sch of Educn and dir Centre for Literacy Studies 1993–96, reader in educn 1997, co-ordinator Centre for Psychology and Language Studies 1997–99, dir Professional Trg in Educnl Psychology 1998, co-ordinator Centre for Applied Educnl Psychology 1999, co-ordinator EdD in educnl psychology 1999, prof of educnl psychology 2000–; secondment as lectr in special educn then research fell Bulmershe Coll of FE 1984–86; visiting lectr: Univ of Reading, Bracknell Coll of HE, UCL, Univ of Southampton, Univ of Birmingham, Med Sch Univ of Cambridge, Inst of Educn Univ of London, Univ of Manchester, Univ of Sheffield; conslt psychologist Mary Hare Sch for the Deaf 1980–86, memb Deafness Research Gp Univ of Nottingham 1985–91, memb Policy Review Forum Royal Coll of Speech and Language Therapists 1995–; memb Editorial Bd: Br Jl of Special Educn 1988–91, Br Jl of the Assoc of Teachers of the Deaf 1995–, Deafness and Educn Int 1997–, Educnl and Child Psychology 2000–02; delivered numerous addresses and conf presentations; FBPsS 1988, CPsychol 1992; *Publications* The Hearing-Impaired Child in the Ordinary School (jtly, 1984), Deafness, Development and Literacy (1986), Children with Speech and Language Difficulties (jtly, 1987), Children with Hearing Difficulties (jtly, 1989), Profiles of the Hearing-Impaired (jtly, 1990), Profiles of the Language-Impaired (jtly, 1991), Start-Right Profile: A Good Start to School (jtly, 1991), The Essential Evaluation Toolkit (1991), Literacy and Hearing-Impaired Children: A Distance Learning Course for Teachers (1991), School Marketing (jtly, 1992), Profiles of Development: Planning for Individual Progress within the National Curriculum (jtly, 1992), Supporting Learning: Hearing-Impairment (jtly, 1993), Managing Change through a Consortium: An Evaluation of TVEI (jtly, 1994), Supporting Learning in the Primary School: Meeting Individual Needs under the new Code of Practice (jtly, 1994), Managing the Literacy Curriculum: How Schools can become Communities of Readers and Writers (jtly, 1995), Supporting Learning in the Secondary School: Raising Individual Achievement under the New Code of Practice volume 1 - Management and Co-ordination (jtly, 1995), Supporting Learning in the Secondary School: Meeting Individual Needs under the New Code of Practice volume 2 - Issues for Practitioners (jtly, 1995), Behaviour Education: Teaching Positive Behaviour in the Primary School (jtly, 1996), Raising Achievement in Hearing-Impaired Pupils (jtly, 1997), Children with Visual Impairments: Social Interaction, Language and Learning (jtly, 1998, shortlised 1999 Book of the Year Award Nat Assoc of Special Educnl Needs/TES), Addressing the Literacy Needs of Offenders under Probation Supervision (jtly, 1998), Supporting Learning in the Early Years (jtly 1998); ed of numerous books and jls, author of book contribs and papers in refereed academic and professional jls; *Recreations* playing cello and violin, drawing and painting; *Style—* Prof Alec Webster; ✉ Graduate School of Education, University of Bristol, 35 Berkeley Square, Bristol BS8 1JA (tel 0117 928 7028, fax 0117 925 1537, e-mail alec.webster@bris.ac.uk)

WEBSTER, Alistair Stevenson; QC (1995); s of His Hon Ian Webster (d 2002), of Rochdale, Lancs, and Margaret, *née* Sharples; *b* 28 April 1953; *Educ* Hulme GS Oldham, BNC Oxford (BA); *m* 4 June 1977, Barbara Anne, da of Dr Donald Longbottom (d 1961); 2 da (Elizabeth b 1982, Alexandra b 1985); *Career* called to the Bar Middle Temple 1976 (bencher 2004); hon sec Northern Circuit 1988–93, recorder 1996– (asst recorder 1992); memb Gen Cncl of the Bar 1994–95; memb Legal and Judicial Ctees Lancs and Gtr Manchester Local Criminal Justice Bds; *Recreations* skiing, cricket, tennis; *Clubs* Rochdale Racquets; *Style—* Alistair Webster, Esq, QC; ✉ Lincoln House Chambers, 1 Brazenose Street, Manchester M2 5EL (tel 0161 832 5701, fax 0161 832 0839, e-mail websterqc@aol.com)

WEBSTER, David Gordon Comyn; s of Alfred Edward Comyn Webster (d 1998), and Meryl Mary, *née* Clutterbuck (d 1970); *b* 11 February 1945; *Educ* Glasgow Acad, Univ of Glasgow (LLB); *m* 12 Feb 1972, (Pamela) Gail, da of Dr Dennis Frank Runnicles, of Sevenoaks, Kent; 3 s (Michael Gordon Comyn b 25 Sept 1974, Nicholas Gordon Comyn b 9 Jan 1978, Jonathan Hugo Comyn b 27 Feb 1983); *Career* Lt RNR, ret 1970; admitted slr 1968, corp fin Samuel Montagu & Co 1969–72, Wm Brandts 1972–73, fin dir Oriel Foods Ltd 1973–76; Safeway plc (formerly Argyll Group plc): fndr dir 1977–2004, fin dir 1977–89, exec dep chm 1989–97, exec chm 1997–2004; chm: Makinson Cowell Ltd 2004–, InterContinental Hotels Gp plc 2004– (non-exec dir 2003–); non-exec dir: Reed International plc 1992–2002, Reed Elsevier plc 1993–2002 (non-exec chm 1998–99), Elsevier NV 1999–2002; dir Nat Life Story Collection 2005–; pres Inst of Grocery Distribution 2001–02; memb: Nat Employers' Liaison Ctee 1992–2002, Corp Advsy Gp Tate Gallery 1997–2004; *Recreations* military history, gardening, skiing; *Style—* David Webster, Esq; ✉ InterContinental Hotels Group plc, 67 Alma Road, Windsor, Berkshire SL4 3HD (tel 01753 410100)

WEBSTER, Rev Prof John Bainbridge; *b* 20 June 1955; *Educ* Clare Coll Cambridge (MA, PhD); *Career* Stephenson fell Univ of Sheffield 1981–82, tutor in systematic theology St John's Coll Durham 1982–86, prof of systematic theology Wycliffe Coll Univ of Toronto 1986–96, Lady Margaret prof of divinity Univ of Oxford and canon of Christ Church Oxford 1996–2003, prof of systematic theology Univ of Aberdeen 2003–; FRSE 2005; *Books* Eberhard Jüngel (1986), The Possibilities of Theology (1994), Barth's Ethics of Reconciliation (1995), Barth's Moral Theology (1998), Theology after Liberalism (ed, 2000), The Cambridge Companion to Karl Barth (ed, 2000), Barth (2000), Word and Church (2001), Holiness (2002), Holy Scripture (2002), Confessing God (2005), Barth's Earlier Theology (2005); also author of various articles in learned jls; *Style—* The Rev Prof John Webster; ✉ King's College, Aberdeen AB24 3UB

WEBSTER, Prof (Anthony) John Francis; s of Flt Lt John Terence Webster, DFC (ka 1940), and Lilian Hypatia, *née* Mogg; *b* 24 August 1938; *Educ* Wellingborough Sch, St John's Coll Cambridge (MA, Vet MB), Univ of Glasgow (PhD); *m* 1, 31 Aug 1964, Maureen Anne Sanderson (d 1997), da of Joseph Blair (d 1959); 1 s (Mark b 1965), 1 da (Joanne b 1967); m 2, 4 Aug 2000, Elizabeth Anne, da of Charles Jenvey (d 1981); *Career* assoc prof Univ of Alberta Canada 1966–70, princ vet res offr Rowett Research Inst Aberdeen 1970–77, prof of animal husbandry Univ of Bristol 1977–2004 (head Sch of Vet Sci 1993–2004, emeritus prof 2004–); pres: Br Soc of Animal Prodn 1991, Nutrition Soc 1992–95; MRCVS 1963 (memb Cncl 1993–97); *Books* Understanding the Dairy Cow (1987), Animal Welfare: A Cool Eye towards Eden (1995), Animal Welfare: Limping towards Eden (1995); *Recreations* sailing, music, gardening; *Style—* Prof John Webster; ✉ Old Sock Cottage, Mudford Sock, Yeovil, Somerset BA22 8EA (e-mail john.webster@bris.ac.uk)

WEBSTER, John Vernon; s of Dr (Francis) Vernon Webster, CBE, of Maidenhead, Berks, and Jill Mary, *née* Archer; *b* 27 May 1961, Maidenhead, Berks; *Educ* Maidenhead GS (now Desborough Sch), Univ of Manchester (LLB), Coll of Law London; *m* 9 Aug 1986, Karen Ann, *née* Campbell-Trotter; 1 da (Eleanor Charlotte b 14 May 2003); *Career* slr Blandy & Blandy 1985–88 (articled clerk 1983–85); Veale Wasbrough Lawyers: slr 1988–94, ptnr 1994–, head Personal Injury Dept (now branded Augustines Injury Law) 1996–; memb Glos Courts Bd 2004–, SW regnl coordinator Assoc of Personal Injury Lawyers (APIL) 2003–06, accredited memb Personal Injury Panel Law Soc 1995–, chm Bristol Civil Courts Ctee 1998–; memb: Law Soc 1985–, Bristol Law Soc (memb Cncl 1998–2005); fell Coll of Personal Injury Lawyers 2000; *Publications* APIL Personal Injury: Law, Practice and Precedents (2006); *Recreations* skiing, football, walking, travel, gardening, family; *Style—* John Webster, Esq; ✉ Augustines Injury Law, St Augustines Yard, Orchard Lane, Bristol BS1 5DE (tel 0117 314 5400, fax 0117 314 5405, e-mail jwebster@vwl.co.uk)

WEBSTER, Maj (Richard) Michael Otley; s of Brig Frederick Richard Webster, of Winchester, Hants, and Beryl Helena Sellars, *née* Otley; *b* 11 August 1942; *Educ* Charterhouse, RMA Sandhurst, Army Staff Coll Camberley; *m* 12 June 1971, Joanna Gay Enid, da of Lt Col Richard Henry Oothout Simpson, DSO; 2 s (Jonathan Richard b 4 July 1972, Rupert James b 21 June 1974); *Career* cmmnd RA, served Germany, Aden and UK, cmd The King's Troop RHA 1962–79; rode in amateur steeplechases 1967–77; with United Racecourses Ltd 1979–96; clerk of the course: Kempton Park 1980–96 (gen mangr 1981–94), Lingfield Park 1986–87, Epsom Downs 1988–95, Bangor-on-Dee 1996–2003 (also mangr), Chester 2001–03; memb Horseracing Advsy Cncl 1987–90; dist cmmr Garth South Pony Club 1987–90; sec Royal Hants Regt Tst 2004–06; memb Hon Corps of Gentlemen at Arms (HM Body Guard) 1993–; memb Nat Jt Pitch Cncl 2000–03; *Recreations* shooting, cricket, racing; *Clubs* Army and Navy; *Style—* Maj Michael Webster; ✉ Coopers Farm, Hartley Wespall, Hook, Hampshire RG27 0BQ (tel 01256 882413, e-mail michaelwebster@hartleycoopers.co.uk)

WEBSTER, Prof Nigel Robert; s of Derek Stanley Webster, of Walsall, and Sheila Margaret Flora, *née* Squire; *b* 14 June 1953; *Educ* Univ of Leeds (BSc, MB ChB, PhD); *m* 2 July 1977, Diana Christina Shirley, da of Brian Robert Galt Hutchinson, of York, 2 da (Lorna Elizabeth b 1984, Lucy Anne b 1987), 1 s (Oliver James b 1986); *Career* memb Scientific Staff Div of Anaesthesia MRC Clinical Res Centre 1986–88, conslt in anaesthesia, dir of transplant anaesthesia and co-dir of intensive care St James' Univ Hosp Leeds 1988–94, prof Dept of Anaesthesia and Intensive Care Univ of Aberdeen and hon conslt Aberdeen Royal Infirmary 1994–; memb: Intensive Care Soc, Euro Soc of Intensive Care Med, Soc for Free Radical Res, Elgar Soc; FFARCS, FRCP; *Books* Research Techniques in Anaesthesia (1988), Intensive Care: Developments and controversies (1992); *Recreations* flying, music, gardening; *Style—* Prof Nigel Webster; ✉ Aberdeen Royal Infirmary, Forester Hill, Aberdeen AB25 2ZD (tel 01224 681818, e-mail n.r.webster@abdn.ac.uk)

WEBSTER, Norman; s of George Wyndham Webster (d 1974), of Dover, and Naomi, *née* Wardill (d 1969); *b* 6 May 1924; *Educ* Dover GS, Tunbridge Wells Sch of Art, Royal Coll of Art (royal exhibitioner ARCA); *m* 1947, Joan Winifred, da of James Tristram Augustus Simpson; 3 s (Matthew Norman b 14 Aug 1953, Simon Julian b 10 July 1956, Mark Wardill b 23 Aug 1960); *Career* lectr in drawing and engraving College of Art Leeds 1949, then sr lectr in printmaking Fine Art Dept Leeds Poly (following amalgamation) until 1985; solo exhbns: Northern Artists Gallery Leeds 1969, Goosewell Gallery Menston 1977, Northern Artists Gallery Harrogate 1978, The Hart Holes Studios Holmfirth 1978, Manor House Gallery Ilkley 1980; exhbns incl: Bankside Gallery Blackfriars, Royal Academy, New English Art Club, Yorkshire Printmakers America, Canada, Israel and Germany; collections: Arts Council of GB, Ashmolean Museum, FA, Univ of Salford, DOE, Leeds City Art Gallery, Wakefield City Art Gallery, Harrogate Art Gallery; sr fell RE 1994 (fell 1973, ARE 1951), sr fell RWS 1994 (fell 1975, ARWS 1966); *Recreations* reading, classical music, walking the dog; *Style—* Norman Webster, Esq

WEBSTER, Paul; *b* 19 September 1952; *Career* co-dir Osiris Film London 1979–81, fndr Palace Pictures 1982–88, launched Working Title Film LA 1990–92, head of prodn Miramax Films 1995–97 (responsible for films incl The English Patient, Welcome to Sarajevo, Wings of the Dove), chief exec Film Four Ltd 1998–2002; prodr: The Tall Guy (1988), Drop Dead Fred (1990), Bob Roberts (exec prodr, 1992), Romeo Is Bleeding (1993), Little Oddessa (Silver Lion Venice Film Festival, 1994), The Pallbearer (1995), Gridlock'd (1996), The Yards (1998), Buffalo Soldiers (2001), The Warrior (2001), Dog Eat Dog (2001), Charlotte Gray (2001), Miranda (2002), Once Upon a Time in the Midlands (2002), It's All About Love (2003), The Priniciples of Lust (2003), The Actors (2003), To Kill a King

(2003), The Motorcycle Diaries (2004); memb: BAFTA Cncl, BAFTA Film Cncl; *Style—* Paul Webster, Esq

WEBSTER, Prof (John) Paul Garrett; s of Leonard Garrett Webster (d 1976), and Dorothy Agnes, *née* White (d 1991); *b* 16 July 1942, Ripon, N Yorks; *Educ* The Leys Sch Cambridge, Univ of Reading (BSc), Univ of London (Dip Farm Business Admin, PhD); *m* 1972, Amanda Jane, *née* Hetigin; 1 s (Michael Garrett b 1974), 1 da (Lucy Jean b 1976); *Career* Dept of Agric Sciences Imperial Coll London (merged with Wye Coll 2000): asst lectr 1965–67, lectr 1967–76, sr lectr 1976–81, reader 1981–91, prof of agric business mgmnt 1991–2005,, dep head and dir of fin 2001–04, emeritus prof 2005–; Wye Coll London: head Farm Business Unit 1989–2002, head Dept of Agric Economics 1991–94, vice-princ 1996–98, dean of grad studies 1998–99; lectr in rural economy Makere Univ Uganda 1970–71, Drapers' Co lectr Univ of New England Armidale Aust 1974, visiting prof Lincoln Univ NZ 1999–2000; economist Engrg Dept Int Rice Research Inst Philippines 1980–81; pres Agric Economics Soc 1999–2000 (chm Exec Ctee 1991–96), chm Educn Ctee Int of Agric Mgmnt 1991–95, ind memb Advsy Ctee on Pesticides MAFF 1992–99; tstee Frank Parkinson Agricultural Tst 2005–; author of various book contribs and papers in learned jls; Hon Freeman Worshipful Co of Farmers 2000 (memb Educn and Research Ctee 1988–); fell Royal Agric Socs 2002; FBIM 1980, FRSA 1987, FIAgrM 1996; *Style—* Prof Paul Webster; ✉ Imperial College London, Wye Campus, Ashford, Kent TN25 5AH

WEBSTER, Richard Joseph; s of Peter Joseph Webster, of Dulwich, London; *b* 7 July 1953; *Educ* Dulwich HS, Harvard Business Sch; *m* 1980, Patricia Catherine, da of Gerald Stanley Edwards, of East Grinstead, W Sussex; 1 da (Victoria Catherine b Sept 1983), 1 s (James Joseph b April 1985); *Career* insurance underwriting with Brit Insurance; *Recreations* family, golf, watching rugby; *Clubs* various; *Style—* Richard J Webster, Esq; ✉ Brit Insurance, 55 Bishopsgate, London EC2N 3AS (tel 020 7984 8954, e-mail richard.webster@britinsurance.com)

WEBSTER, Sue; da of Ray and Linda Webster; *b* 1967; *Educ* Leicester Poly, Nottingham Poly (BA); *Career* artist; collaborator with Tim Noble, *qv*; residency Dean Clough Halifax 1989–92; *Two-Person Exhibitions* British Rubbish (Independent Art Space London) 1996, Home Chance (Rivington St London) 1997, Vague Us (Habitat London) 1998, WOW (Modern Art London) 1998, The New Barbarians (Chisenhale Gallery London) 1999, I Love You (Deitch Projects NY) 2000, British Wildlife (Modern Art London) 2000, Masters of the Universe (Deste Fndn, Athens) 2000, Instant Gratification (Gagosian Gallery Beverly Hills) 2001, Ghastly Arrangements (Milton Keynes Gallery) 2002, Black Magic (MW Projects London) 2002, Real Life is Rubbish (Statements at Art Basel Miami) 2002, PS1/MoMA (Long Island City NY) 2003, Modern Art is Dead (Modern Art London) 2004, Noble & Webster (MFA Boston) 2004, The New Barbarians (CAC Malaga) 2005, The Joy of Sex (Kukje Gallery Seoul) 2005, The Glory Hole (Bortolami Dayan NY) 2005; *Group Exhibitions* incl: Lift (Brick Lane London) 1993, Hijack (NY London and Berlin) 1994, Fete Worse Than Death (Hoxton Square London) 1994, Absolut Art (RCA London) 1994, Self Storage (Artangel London) 1995, Hanging Picnic (Hoxton Sq London) 1995, Fools Rain (ICA London) 1996, Turning the Tables (Chisenhale Gallery London) 1997, Livestock Market (London) 1997, Sex and the British (Galerie Thaddaeus Ropac Salzburg and Paris) 2000, Man-Body in Art from 1950 to 2000 (ARKEN Copenhagen) 2000, Apocalypse (Royal Acad of Art London) 2000, Tattoo Show (Modern Art London) 2001, Form Follows Fiction (Castello di Rivoli Turin) 2001, Casino 2001 (SMAK Ghent) 2002, 2001 A Space Oddity (A22 Projects London) 2001, Shortcuts (Nicosia Municipal Arts Centre Cyprus) 2001, Art Crazy Nation (Milton Keynes Gallery) 2002, State of Play (Serpentine Gallery London) 2004, New Blood (Saatchi Gallery London) 2004, Monument To Now (Dakis Joannou Collection Athens) 2004, Masquerade (MCA Sydney) 2006; *Recreations* DJing; *Clubs* Colony Room; *Style—* Miss Sue Webster; ✉ c/o Modern Art, 10 Vyner Street, London E2 9DG (tel 020 8980 7742, e-mail info@modernartinc.com)

WEBSTER, Trevor; s of Samuel Webster (d 1982), and Winifred, *née* Chapman (d 1977); *b* 1 November 1937; *Educ* Leeds GS, Univ of Leeds (LLB); *m* (m dis); *Career* customs offr Rhodesia and Nyasaland 1956–57, reporter 1960–64 (Financial World, Investors Review, Stock Exchange Gazette), reporter Daily Express 1966; The Scotsman city ed 1970–86 (dep city ed 1964–70), dep city ed Daily News 1987, Questor ed Daily Telegraph 1987–88, city ed Daily Express 1989–91 (dep city ed 1988–89), freelance for Daily Mail, Daily Express and Evening Standard 1991–; *Books* Corfu and the Ionian Isles (1986), Athens and Greek Mainland (1987), Rhodes and the Dodecanese (1988), Crete and the Cyclades (1989), Greek Island Delights (1990), Where To Go In Greece (1995); *Recreations* tennis, skiing, travel, wine, theatre, cinema; *Clubs* National Liberal, Hunters, City Golf; *Style—* Trevor Webster, Esq

WEDDERBURN, Prof Dorothy; da of Frederick C Barnard (d 1953), and Ethel C, *née* Lawrence (d 1969); *b* 18 September 1925; *Educ* Walthamstow HS For Girls, Girton Coll Cambridge (MA); *Career* res offr Dept of Applied Economics Univ of Cambridge 1950–65; Imperial Coll of Sci and Technol London: lectr in industrial sociology 1965–70, reader 1970–77, prof 1977–81, dir Industrial Sociology Unit 1973–81, head Dept of Social and Econ Studies 1978–81; princ: Bedford Coll London 1981–85, Royal Holloway and Bedford New Coll London 1985–90; sr res fell Imperial Coll of Sci and Technol London 1990–, emeritus prof of industrial sociology Univ of London 1990–; hon pres Fawcett Soc 1986–2002, pt/t memb Royal Cmmn on the Distribution of Income and Wealth 1974–78; non-exec dir Kensington, Chelsea and Westminster Dist HA 1992–2002; memb: Cncl Advsy Conciliation and Arbitration Serv 1976–82, ESRC 1976–82, Bd Anglo-German Fndn 1987–2004, Cncl Loughborough Univ 1990–93, Medical Manpower Standing Advsy Ctee Dept of Health 1991–96, Ct City Univ 1992–, Cncl Goldsmiths Coll London 1994–2000; govr London Guildhall Univ 1989–99; Hon DLitt: Univ of Warwick 1984, Loughborough Univ 1989; Hon DUniv Brunel 1990, Hon LLD Univ of Cambridge 1991, Hon DSci City Univ 1991, Hon DSocSci Univ of Southampton 1999; fell Ealing Coll of Higher Educn 1985; hon fell: Imperial Coll London 1986, Royal Holloway and Bedford New Coll London 1991, Goldsmiths Coll London; *Books* White Collar Redundancy (1964), Redundancy and the Railwaymen (1964), The Aged in the Welfare State (with P Townsend, 1965), Workers' Attitudes and Technology (1972); *Recreations* politics, walking, cooking; *Style—* Prof Dorothy Wedderburn; ✉ Flat 5, 65 Ladbroke Grove, London W11 2PD (tel 020 7229 3136)

WEDDERBURN OF CHARLTON, Baron (Life Peer UK 1977), of Highgate in Greater London; Prof Kenneth William Wedderburn; QC (1990); s of Herbert John Wedderburn; *b* 13 April 1927; *Educ* Aske's (Hatcham) GS, Whitgift Sch, Queens' Coll Cambridge (MA, LLB, Chancellor's Medal for English Law); *m* 1, 1951 (m dis 1962), Nina, da of Dr Myer Salaman; 2 da (Hon Sarah Louise b 1954, Hon Lucy Rachel b 1960), 1 s (Hon David Roland b 1956); m 2, 1962 (m dis 1969), Dorothy Enid, da of Frederick C Barnard and formerly w of William A Cole; m 3, 1969, Frances Ann, da of Basil F Knight; 1 s (Hon Jonathan Michael b 1972); *Career* served RAF 1949–51; sat as Lab peer in House of Lords until 2006 (Lab employment spokesman 1980–1993), crossbench peer 2006–; called to the Bar Middle Temple 1953; fell Clare Coll and lectr Faculty of Law Univ of Cambridge 1952–64, Cassel prof of commercial law LSE 1964–92 (prof emeritus 1992–, hon fell 1998–), hon fell Clare Coll Cambridge 1997–; visiting prof: UCLA Law Sch 1967, Harvard Law Sch 1969–70; chm: London and Provincial Theatre Cncls 1973–92, Ind Review Ctee 1976–; ed Modern Law Review 1970–88, memb Editorial Bd Int Labour Law Reports 1975–; hon pres Ind Law Soc 1997–; vice-pres Haldane Soc; Hon Dott Giur Univ of Pavia 1987, Hon Dott Econ Univ of Siena 1991, Hon Dott Law Univ of Stockholm; FBA 1981; *Publications* Clerk and Lindsell on Torts (jt ed 1961–2001), The Worker and the Law (1965, 3 edn 1986), Cases and Materials on Labour Law (1967), Employment Grievances and Disputes Procedures (with P L Davies, 1969), Labour Law and Industrial Relations (with R Lewis and J Clark, 1982), Employment Rights in Britain and Europe (1991), Labour Law and Freedom (1995), I Diritti del Lavoro (1998); *Recreations* Charlton Athletic FC; *Style—* Prof the Rt Hon the Lord Wedderburn of Charlton, QC, FBA; ✉ 29 Woodside Avenue, Highgate, London N6 4SP (tel 020 8444 8472, e-mail bill.wedderburn@btinternet.com)

WEDDLE, Stephen Norman; s of Norman Harold Weddle, of Sutton Coldfield, W Midlands, and Irene, *née* Furniss; *b* 1 January 1950; *Educ* Fairfax High Sch Sutton Coldfield, NE London Poly (BSc), Bedford Coll London; *m* July 1977 (m dis 1980), Brigid, da of late Edward Couch; *Career* grad trainee journalist Birmingham Post and Mail 1972–75, reporter BBC Radio Stoke-on-Trent 1975–76; BBC TV: prodr Cool It 1985–90, ed Daytime Live 1987–90, ed Daytime UK 1990–91, ed Pebble Mill 1991–94 (researcher, dir and prodr 1976), ed Special Projects 1994–2001; dir Invisible Inc (prodn co) 2001–; RTS Best Original TV Achievement Award 1987, Variety Clubs International Media Award 1993, RTS Midland Centre Award; *Recreations* supporting Tottenham Hotspur FC, cinema, travel, reading novels, comedy and politics, eccentric dancing; *Style—* Stephen Weddle, Esq; ✉ Invisible Inc, 52 Binswood Avenue, Leamington Spa, Warwickshire CV32 5RX (tel 01926 314036, e-mail info@invisibleinc.tv, website www.invisibleinc.tv)

WEDEL, Claus Viggo; *b* 1 April 1940; *Educ* Denmark; *m* Judi; 1 s (Anders), 3 da (Susse, Anna, and Harriett); *Career* fndr chm and md Anglo-Norden Ltd 1966–, chm JMC Timber Ltd 1980–; *Recreations* shooting, sailing; *Style—* Claus Wedel, Esq; ✉ Anglo-Norden Ltd, Eagle Wharf, Helena Road, Ipswich IP3 0BT

WEDGWOOD, Antony John; s of Dr John Wedgwood, CBE (d 2007), and Margaret Webb Mason (d 1995); *b* 31 January 1944; *Educ* Marlborough, Trinity Coll Cambridge (MA); *m* 18 July 1970, Angela Margaret Mary, da of Dr E D Page; 2 da (Elizabeth b 15 July 1975, Caroline b 7 July 1981), 1 s (Tom b 20 April 1978); *Career* Peat Marwick Mitchell & Co (now KPMG): articled 1966 (qualified 1969), ptnr 1981–2001; memb: various professional ctees and working parties Auditing Practices Bd, ICAEW, Br Bankers' Assoc, Financial Reporting Review Panel 2001–07; tstee and treas Historic Churches Preservation Tst 2002–; FCA (ACA 1969); *Publications* A Guide to the Financial Services Act 1986 (jtly 1986), author of numerous articles on accounting and banking; *Recreations* reading, old cars and wirelesses, travel; *Clubs* Athenaeum; *Style—* Antony Wedgwood, Esq; ✉ 10 Milner Place, London N1 1TN (tel 020 7607 2954)

WEDGWOOD, Pamela, Lady; *see:* Tudor-Craig, Dr Pamela

WEDGWOOD, 4 Baron (UK 1942); Piers Anthony Weymouth Wedgwood; s of 3 Baron Wedgwood (d 1970, 5 in descent from Josiah Wedgwood, first MP for the newly enfranchised Stoke-on-Trent 1832–34 and s of Josiah Wedgwood, FRS, who founded the pottery), by his 2 w, Jane Weymouth, *née* Poulton; *b* 20 September 1954; *Educ* Marlborough, RMA Sandhurst; *m* 30 May 1985, Mary Regina Margaret Kavanagh, da of late Edward Quinn, of Philadelphia, USA; 1 da (Hon Alexandra Mary Kavanagh b 3 Oct 1987); *Career* late Capt Royal Scots (The Royal Regt); dir Waterford Wedgwood plc; FRSA; *Clubs* RAC; *Style—* The Rt Hon the Lord Wedgwood; ✉ Waterford Wedgwood plc, Barlaston, Stoke-on-Trent ST12 9ES

WEDLAKE, William John; s of late William John Wedlake, of South Zeal, Devon, and Patricia Mary, *née* Hunt; *b* 24 April 1956; *Educ* Okehampton GS, Exeter Coll of Educn, Univ of Warwick (BSc); *m* 4 July 1987, Elizabeth Kessick, da of late Brian Kessick Bowes; 3 s (Joshua William b 2 May 1989, James Henry b 29 Aug 1990, George Oliver b 5 December 1999), 1 da (Sophie Elizabeth b 16 April 1992); *Career* chartered accountant; formerly with: Arthur Andersen Bristol, Price Waterhouse USA and London; fin dir Schroders 1987–93, fin dir Guardian Insurance (Guardian Royal Exchange) 1993–96, chief fin offr Terra Nova (Bermuda) Holdings 1996–2000, ceo NextPharma Technologies Holding Ltd 2000–; FCA; *Recreations* horse riding, walking, motor racing; *Style—* William J Wedlake, Esq; ✉ NextPharma Technologies Holding Ltd, Connaught House, Portsmouth Road, Send, Surrey GU23 7JY (tel 01483 479120, fax 01483 479135, e-mail bill.wedlake@nextpharma.com)

WEEKS, Wilfred John Thomas (Wilf); OBE (2006); s of William Weeks, of Launceston, Cornwall, and Kathleen, *née* Penhale; *b* 8 February 1948; *Educ* Shebbear Coll, KCL (BD); *m* 10 June 1981, Anne Veronica, da of late Arnold Harrison; 3 s (Orlando b 8 Aug 1983, Matthew b 20 May 1985, Caspar b 10 Jan 1988); *Career* youth and community offr/educn offr and sec Fedn of Cons Students 1974–76, head of the private office of Rt Hon Sir Edward Heath 1976–80, fndr chm GJW Government Relations 1980–2000, chm European Public Affrs Weber Shandwick 2002–; chm Friends of the Tate Gallery 1990–99, memb Cncl Tate Britain 1999–2002, chm Bd of Tstees Dulwich Picture Gallery 2000–, chm Heritage Educn Tst 2005– (tstee 2002–), non-exec dir Helical Bar 2005–; chm Devpt Appeal and memb Exec Bd LAMDA 2001–; hon treas Hansard Soc 1999–; winner Goodman Award 2004; *Recreations* gardening, collecting; *Clubs* Garrick; *Style—* Wilf Weeks, Esq, OBE; ✉ Weber Shandwick GJW, Fox Court, 14 Gray's Inn Road, London WC1X 8WS (tel 020 7067 0302, fax 0870 0990 5441)

WEETMAN, Prof Anthony Peter; s of Kenneth Weetman (d 1991), and Evelyn, *née* Healer; *b* 29 April 1953; *Educ* Univ of Newcastle upon Tyne Med Sch (BMedSci, MB, MD, DSc); *m* 20 Feb 1982, Sheila Lois, da of John Seymour Thompson, OBE, (d 1985); 1 s (James b 1986), 1 da (Chloe b 1989); *Career* MRC trg fell 1981–83, MRC travelling fell 1984–85, Wellcome sr res fell 1985–89, lectr in med Univ of Cambridge and hon conslt physician Addenbrooke's Hosp 1989–91, dean of the medical sch and prof of med Univ of Sheffield and hon conslt physician Northern General Hosp 1991–; Goulstonian lectr RCP 1991, Merck Prize European Thyroid Assoc 2002, Bradshaw lectr RCP 2006, Clinical Endocrinology Tst lectr 2006; FRCP 1990 (MRCP 1979), FMedSci 1998, FRCPEd 2004; *Publications* author of original papers on thyroid disease and autoimmunity; *Recreations* fell walking; *Style—* Prof Anthony Weetman; ✉ School of Medicine and Biomedical Sciences, Beech Hill Road, Sheffield S10 2RX (tel 0114 271 2570, fax 0114 271 3960, e-mail a.p.weetman@sheffield.ac.uk)

WEGENEK, Robert Jan; s of Boleslaw Wegenek, of Wolverhampton, and Celina, *née* Nowakowska; *b* 12 August 1966, Wolverhampton; *Educ* Wolverhampton GS, St Aidan's Coll Durham (BA), Coll of Law Chester; *m* 28 Sept 2002, Suzi, *née* Sherlock; 1 s (Alek Leo b 27 April 2004), 1 da (Molly Izabela b 4 Jan 2006); *Career* admitted slr 1991; ptnr: Edge Ellison 1998–2000 (nat head of commercial servs 1999–2000), Hammonds 2000– (head of London office 2006–); trg princ Law Soc 2001; memb Law Soc 1991; *Publications* E-Commerce: A Guide to the Law of Electronic Business (ed-in-chief, 2002), Vertäge in der Werbebranche (2007); *Recreations* mountain biking, football, horse racing, cooking; *Style—* Robert Wegenek, Esq; ✉ Hammonds, 7 Devonshire Square, Cutlers Gardens, London EC2M 4YM (tel 0870 839 1534, fax 0870 458 2926, e-mail robert.wegenek@hammonds.com)

WEIDENFELD, Baron (Life Peer UK 1976), of Chelsea in Greater London; (Arthur) George Weidenfeld; kt (1969); s of Max and Rosa Weidenfeld; *b* 13 September 1919; *Educ* Piaristen Gymnasium Vienna, Vienna Univ, Konsular Akademie; *m* 1, 1952, Jane, da of J Edward Sieff; 1 da (Hon Laura Miriam Elizabeth (Hon Mrs Barnett) b 1953); m 2, 1956 (m dis 1961), Barbara (d 1996), da of Maj George Skelton and former wife of Cyril Connolly; m 3, 1966 (m dis 1973), Sandra, da of Charles Shipman Payson; m 4, 14 July 1992, Annabelle, da of late Cdr Nicholas Whitestone; *Career* served WWII BBC Monitoring Serv 1939–42, news commentator with BBC 1942–45; fndr Contact Magazine

W

and Books 1945, columnist News Chronicle 1945–46, fndr chm Weidenfeld & Nicolson Ltd 1948–; spent 1 year as political advsr and chief of cabinet to Chaim Weizmann (Pres of Israel 1948–52); chm Cheyne Capital; hon chm Bd of Govrs Ben Gurion Univ of Negev Beer-Sheva 2004– (chm 1996–2004); govr: Univ of Tel Aviv, Weizmann Inst of Sci, Jerusalem Fndn, Diplomatic Coll Vienna 2000–; memb Bd: South Bank 1986–99, English Nat Opera 1988–98; tstee: Nat Portrait Gallery 1988–95, Herbert Quandt Stiftung (Bad Homburg) 1998–, Alfred Herrhausen Soc for Int Dialogue 2004; hon fell: St Peter's Coll Oxford, St Anne's Coll Oxford 1994; vice-chm Oxford Univ Devpt Campaign 1992–99; Hon Senator of Bonn Univ 1996; conslt: Bertelsmann Fndn (Ger) 1995–, Burda Medien (Munich) 1995–; conslt and columnist Axel Springer Verlag (Ger); Hon DLitt Univ of Exeter 2001; Chevalier de l'Ordre National de la Legion d'Honneur 1990; Knight Cdrs Cross (Badge and Star) of the Order of Merit of the Fed Republic of Germany, holder Golden Knight's Cross with Star of the Austrian Order of Merit, Charlemagne Medal for European Media Aachen Germany 2000, Austrian Cross of Merit First Class of Science and the Arts; *Recreations* opera, travel; *Clubs* Garrick; *Style*— The Rt Hon Lord Weidenfeld; ✉ 9 Chelsea Embankment, London SW3 (tel 020 7351 0042)

WEIL, Prof Daniel; s of late Dr Alfredo Leopoldo Weil, and Mina, *née* Rosenbaum; *b* 7 September 1953; *Educ* Universidad Nacional de Buenos Aires (Arquitecto FAU UMBA), RCA (MA); *Career* industrial designer and lectr; unit master Dip Sch Architectural Assoc 1983–86, external examiner MA design Glasgow Sch of Art 1987–90; visiting lectr: RCA, Middx Poly, Kingston Poly, Sch of Architecture Univ of Milan, Bezalel Sch of Art Jerusalem; md Parenthesis Ltd 1982–90, fndr and ptnr Weil and Taylor (design consultancy for major clients) 1985–91, ptnr Pentagram design conslts 1992–, prof of industrial design RCA; exhibitions incl: Memphis Milan 1982, 100 Designers Trienale of Milan 1983, Design Since 1945 (Philadelphia Museum of Art) 1983, Heavy Box (Architectural Assoc) 1985, Contemporary Landscape (MOMA Kyoto) 1985, British Design (Kunstmuseum Vienna) 1986, Inspiration (Tokyo, Paris, Milan) 1988, Metropolis (ICA London) 1988, The Plastic Age (V&A) 1990; work in public collections incl The Bag Radio (MOMA NY); memb Design Sub-Ctee D&AD, juror BBC Design Awards 1990; sr fell RCA 2002; FCSD 1989; *Style*— Prof Daniel Weil; ✉ Pentagram Design Ltd, 11 Needham Road, London W11 2RP (tel 020 7229 3477)

WEIL, Peter Leo John; s of Robert Weil of Berlin, Germany, and Renate Scheyer; *b* 7 September 1951; *Educ* Methodist Coll Belfast, Queens' Coll Cambridge (BA); *Career* researcher Granada TV 1973–77 (Granada Reports, World in Action); BBC: prodr BBC TV Current Affairs 1977–84 (Nationwide, Newsnight, Panorama), head of Youth Progs BBC NI 1984–86 (actg dep head of progs 1986), ed Open Air BBC NW 1986–88, exec prodr Wogan 1988–89, head of topical features 1989–90, head of network TV BBC North 1990–92; head of progs Barraclough Carey North Productions 1992–98, exec news ed London News Network 1998; Discovery Networks Europe: vice-pres (content) Discovery UK until 2003, gen mangr and sr vice-pres Animal Planet Int 2003–; exec prodr: People's Parliament, The Other Side of Midnight, First Edition; *Recreations* cinema, walking, good food; *Style*— Peter Weil, Esq; ✉ Discovery Networks Europe, 160 Great Portland Street, London W1W 5QA (tel 020 7886 8300, fax 020 7886 8312)

WEINBERG, Prof Felix Jiri; s of Victor Weinberg (d 1988), and late Nelly, *née* Altschul; *Educ* Univ of London (BSc, DIC, PhD, DSc); *m* 24 July 1954, Jill Nesta (d 2006), da of Jack Alfred Piggott (d 1970); 3 s (John Felix, Peter David (twins) b 27 April 1958, Michael Jonathan b 8 Jan 1969); *Career* Dept of Chemical Engrg and Chemical Technol Imperial Coll London: res asst 1951–54, asst lectr 1954–56, lectr 1956–60, sr lectr in combustion 1960–64, reader in combustion 1964–67, prof of combustion physics 1967–93, emeritus prof of combustion physics and sr research fell 1993–; visiting prof at various univs and insts across the world; fndr and first chm Combustion Physics Gp Inst of Physics 1974–, chm Br Section Combustion Inst 1975–80, cncl memb Inst of Energy (formerly Inst of Fuel) 1976–79; conslt to numerous scientific establishments; prolific contrib to scientific literature and memb editorial bds of various specialist jls; foreign assoc American Acad of Engineering 2001; Silver Combustion medal The Combustion Inst Pittsburgh 1972, Bernard Lewis Gold medal Univ of Waterloo 1980, Rumford medal Royal Soc 1988, Italgas prize for research and innovation in energy science Turin Acad 1991, Smolenski medal Polish Acad of Sci 1999; Hon DSc Technion Israel 1990; FInstE 1974, CEng 1974, FInstP 1960, FRS 1983, FCGI 1998; *Publications* author and co-author of books on electrical and optical aspects of flames; *Recreations* travel, Eastern philosophies, archery; *Style*— Prof Felix Weinberg, FRS; ✉ Imperial College London, Department of Chemical Engineering, South Kensington Campus, London SW7 2AZ (tel 020 7594 5580, fax 020 7594 5604, e-mail f.weinberg@imperial.ac.uk)

WEINBERG, Sir Mark Aubrey; kt (1987); s of Philip Weinberg (d 1933); *b* 9 August 1931; *Educ* King Edward's Johannesburg, Univ of the Witwatersrand, LSE; *m* 1980, Anouska (Anouska Hempel, the fashion designer), da of Albert Geissler (d 1980); *Career* md Abbey Life Assurance 1961–70, chm Allied Dunbar Assurance 1971–90, dir BAT Industries 1985–89, dep chm SIB 1986–90; chm: J Rothschild Assurance plc 1991–2002, St James's Place Capital 1991–2004 (currently pres), Life Assurance Holding Corp 1995–2003, Pension Insurance Corp 2006–, Synergy Insurance Services 2006–; jt chm The Per Cent Club 1985–97, chm Stock Exchange Ctee on Private Share Ownership 1995–, tstee Tate Gallery 1985–92; *Books* Take-overs and Mergers (5 edn, 1989); *Recreations* skiing, bridge; *Clubs* Portland; *Style*— Sir Mark Weinberg; ✉ St James's Place, Spencer House, 27 St James's Place, London SW1A 1NR (tel 020 7514 1909)

WEIR, Arabella; da of Sir Michael Weir, KCMG, and Alison, *née* Walker; *b* 1957, San Francisco CA; *Career* comedienne, actress, writer; columnist The Guardian 2001–04; *Television* incl: The Corner House 1987, Les Girls 1988, The All New Alexei Sayle Show (also writer) 1994, The Fast Show (also writer) 1994–2003, Ted & Ralph 1998, My Summer with Des 1998, She's Gotta Have It (presenter) 1998, The Creatives 1998, Posh Nosh (also writer) 2003; appearances incl: Loose Women 2004, Grumpy Old Women 2006; *Film* incl Shooting Fish 1997; *Radio* Smelling of Roses (BBC Radio 4) 2000–03; *Books* Does My Bum Look Big in This? (1997), Onwards and Upwards (1999), Stupid Cupid (2002); *Style*— Ms Arabella Weir; ✉ c/o Roxane Vacca Management, 73 Beak Street, London W1F 9SR (tel 020 7734 8085, fax 020 7734 8086)

WEIR, Hon Lord; David Bruce; s of James Douglas Weir (d 1981), of Argyll, and Kathleen Maxwell, *née* Auld (d 1975); *b* 19 December 1931; *Educ* The Leys Sch Cambridge, Univ of Glasgow (MA, LLB); *m* 1964, Katharine Lindsay, da of Hon Lord Cameron (decd); 3 s (Donald b 1965, Robert b 1967, John b 1971); *Career* admitted to Faculty of Advocates 1959, QC (Scot) 1971, advocate depute 1979–82, senator of the Coll of Justice in Scotland 1985–97; justice Ct of Appeal Repub of Botswana 2000–02; chm: Med Appeal Tbnl 1972–77, Pension Appeals Tbnl for Scotland 1978–84 (pres 1984–85), NHS Tbnl Scotland 1983–85; memb: Criminal Injuries Compensation Bd 1974–79 and 1984–85, The Parole Bd for Scotland 1988–91; govr Fettes Coll 1986–95 (chm 1989–95), vice-chm S Knapdale Community Cncl 1997–2005, memb Bd Scottish Int Piano Competition 1997–; memb Cncl RYA 2005–; hon sheriff North Strathclyde at Campbeltown; *Recreations* sailing (Tryad), music; *Clubs* New (Edinburgh), Royal Cruising, Royal Highland Yacht; *Style*— The Hon Lord Weir; ✉ c/o Parliament House, High Street, Edinburgh EH1 1RQ (tel 0131 225 2595)

WEIR, Prof Donald MacKay; s of Dr Henry James Weir, of Dumbartonshire, and Gwendoline, *née* MacKay (d 1981); *b* 16 September 1928; *Educ* Edinburgh Acad, Univ of Edinburgh (MB ChB, MD); *m* 1, 1956, Dr Sylvia Eva Leiman (m dis 1976); 3 s (Michael b 1957, David b 1959, Philip b 1961); m 2, 6 July 1976, Dr (Cecelia) Caroline Blackwell, da of Cecil Blackwell (d 1986), of Texas; *Career* res fell Rheumatism Res Unit MRC Taplow 1957–61, personal chair in microbiology and immunology Univ of Edinburgh 1983– (lectr Bacteriology Dept 1961–67, sr lectr and hon conslt 1967–78, reader 1978–83), prof emeritus and hon fell Univ of Edinburgh 1994–; hon visiting prof Inst Pasteur Athens Greece 1989–92; memb: Br Soc of Immunology, Br Soc of Cell Biology; FRCPEd; *Books* Weir's Handbook of Experimental Immunology (1967, 1973, 1983, 1986 and 1997), Immunology (1970, 1971, 1973, 1977, 1983, 1988, 1993 and 1997), Principles of Infection and Immunity in Patient Care (1981), Aids To Immunology (1986); *Recreations* sailing; *Clubs* Royal Forth Yacht; *Style*— Prof Donald Weir; ✉ 36 Drummond Place, Edinburgh EH3 6PW (tel 0131 556 7646); University of Edinburgh Medical School, Department of Medical Microbiology, Teviot Place, Edinburgh EH8 9AG (tel 0131 650 3170, fax 0131 650 6531)

WEIR, Dame Gillian Constance; DBE (1996, CBE 1989); da of Cecil Alexander Weir (d 1941), of Martinborough, NZ, and Clarice Mildred Foy, *née* Bignell (d 1965); *b* 17 January 1941; *Educ* Wanganui Girls Coll, Royal Coll of Music; *m* 1, 1967 (m dis 1971), Clive Rowland Webster; m 2, 1972, Lawrence Irving Phelps (d 1999), s of Herbert Spencer Phelps (d 1979), of Somerville, MA; *Career* int concert organist 1965–; concerto appearances incl: all leading Br orchs, Boston Symphony Orch, Seattle Symphony Orch, Aust ABC Orchs, Euro orchs; regular performer at int festivals incl: Edinburgh, Bath, Flanders, Proms, Europhalia, Aldeburgh; performed in major int concert halls and cathedrals incl: Royal Albert Hall, Royal Festival Hall, Sydney Opera House, Palais des Beaux Arts, Lincoln Center, Kennedy Center; frequent nat and int radio and TV appearances (incl own 6 part series The King of Instruments (BBC), and 60 Minutes documentary on life/career), adjudicator int competitions, artist in residence at major univs, lectures and master classes held internationally; Prince Consort prof Royal Coll of Music 1999–, distinguished visiting lectr Peabody Inst of Music Baltimore 2005–06; recordings for: Priory, Virgin Classics, Argo, Chandos, Koss Classics, Decca, Collins Classics (Complete Works of Olivier Messiaen released 1994 (rereleased on Priory 2002), Complete Works of César Franck released 1997), Priory, Linn; prizes incl: St Albans Int Organ Competition 1964, Countess Munster Award 1965, Int Performer of the Year American Guild of Organists NY USA 1981, Musician of the Year Int Music Guide 1982, Turnovsky Fndn Award 1985, Silver Medal Albert Schweitzer Assoc 1998, Evening Standard Award for Outstanding Solo Performance 1998, Lifetime Achievement Award NZ Soc (later Link Soc) London 2005; subject of South Bank Show documentary 2000; first woman pres: Incorporated Assoc of Organists 1981–83, Royal Coll of Organists 1994–96; pres: Incorporated Soc of Musicians 1992–93, Soloists' Ensemble 1997–; co-opted to Cncl Royal Philharmonic Soc 1995–2001 (elected memb); tstee Eric Thompson Tst; memb Royal Soc of Musicians of GB 1996–; patron: Oundle Int Festival, Friends of Young Artists' Platform, Cirencester Early Music Festival; Hon DMus: Univ of Victoria Wellington NZ 1983, Univ of Hull 1999, Univ of Exeter 2001, Univ of Leicester 2003, Univ of Aberdeen 2004; Hon DLitt Univ of Huddersfield 1997, Hon DUniv Central England 2001; hon memb RAM, Hon FRCO 1975, hon fell Royal Canadian Coll of Organists 1983, Hon FRCM 2000; *Publications* Grove's International Dictionary of Music and Musicians (contrib), The Messiaen Companion (contrib); frequent contrib to professional jls; *Recreations* theatre; *Style*— Dame Gillian Weir, DBE; ✉ e-mail gillianweir@gillianweir.com

WEIR, Dr Hugh William Lindsay; s of Maj Terence John Collison Weir (d 1958), and Rosamund Suzanne, *née* Gibson (d 2001); *b* 29 August 1934; *Educ* Ireland and abroad, DLitt; *m* 1973, Hon Grania Rachel O'Brien, da of 16 Baron Inchiquin (d 1968); *Career* teacher, illustrator, journalist, author and publisher; md: Weir Machinery Ltd 1965–75, Ballinakella Press, Bell'Acards; memb Nat Cncl CARE; Irish heritage historian 1980–, lectr Inst of Irish Studies; pres: Young Environmentalist Fedn, Clare Young Environmentalists 1980–; vice-pres Clare Archeological and Historical Soc, Nat Monuments advsr Clare Co Cncl 1995–2000, chm Clare Heritage Forum 2003–07; memb Editorial Ctee The Other Clare 1996–97, environment corr The Clare Champion and regular contrib Church of Ireland Gazette, Oidhreacht Award 1990 for journalism and environmental promotion; diocesan lay preacher Limerick and Killaloe; memb: Killaloe Diocesan Synod 1970–99, Gen Synod Church of Ireland 1974–99 (memb Standing Ctee 1980–86), Church of Ireland Representative Body 1980–89, Cncl of Reference Christian Trg Inst 1999–2000 and 2004– (dir 2000–04); dir Hunt Museums Tst 2000–; dir Post Polio Syndrome Gp Ireland 2006–; fndr memb Assoc of Teachers of Foreign Students in Ireland; FRGS; *Books* O'Brien - People and Places (1984), Houses of Clare (1986), Ireland - A Thousand Kings (1988), Trapa - An Adventure in Spanish and English (1990), O'Connor - People and Places (1994), CYE: A Social, Educational and Environmental Exercise (1999), One of Our Own - Memoirs of Change (2001), Brian Boru - High King of Ireland, 941–1014 (2003); *Recreations* writing, art, boating and angling, travel; *Style*— Dr Hugh Weir; ✉ Ballinakella Lodge, Whitegate, Co Clare, Ireland (tel 00 353 61 927030, fax 00 353 61 927418, e-mail weirgroup@hotmail.com)

WEIR, Judith; CBE (1995); *b* 1954; *Educ* King's Coll Cambridge, Tanglewood Summer Sch (Koussevitsky fellowship); *Career* composer; studied under John Tavener, Robin Holloway and Gunther Schuller; sometime memb Nat Youth Orch; composer in residence Southern Arts Assoc 1976–79, lectr Music Dept Univ of Glasgow 1979–82, creative arts fell Trinity Coll Cambridge 1983–85, Guinness composer in residence RSAMD 1988–91, Fairbairn composer-in-assoc City of Birmingham Symphony Orch 1995–98, artistic dir Spitalfields Festival 1995–2000; winner Critics' Circle Music Section Award for most outstanding contribution to Br musical life 1994, hon doctorate Univ of Aberdeen 1995; *Operas* A Night at the Chinese Opera (cmmnd BBC for Kent Opera) 1987, Heaven Ablaze in His Breast (opera and dance collaboration with Ian Spink and Second Stride, screened BBC, winner Int Opera Screen Festival Helsinki 1991) 1989, Blond Eckbert (cmmnd ENO) 1994; *Orchestral works* Scipio's Dream (BBC 2) 1991, Music Untangled, Heroic Strokes of the Bow, Combattimento II 1993, music for Sir Peter Hall's The Gift of the Gorgon (RSC), music for Caryl Churchill's The Skriker (RNT) 1994, Musicians Wrestle Everywhere 1995, Moon and Star (premiere BBC Proms) 1995, Piano Concerto 1997, We are Shadows 1999; *Other* Sanctus (choral work, British premiere last night of the Proms 1997); *Style*— Ms Judith Weir

WEIR, Michael Fraser (Mike); MP; *b* 24 March 1957; *Educ* Arbroath HS, Univ of Aberdeen (LLB); *Career* slr 1981–2001; MP (SNP) Angus 2001–; dean Soc of Procurators and Slrs in Angus 2001; memb: SNP, Law Soc of Scotland; *Style*— Mike Weir, Esq, MP; ✉ 16 Brothock Bridge, Arbroath, Angus DD11 1NG (tel 01241 874522, fax 01241 879350, e-mail weirm@parliament.uk)

WEIR, Peter James; MLA; s of James Weir, of Bangor, Wales, and Margaret, *née* Maxwell; *b* 21 November 1968; *Educ* Bangor GS, Queen's Univ Belfast (MSocSci, LLB); *Career* barr-at-law NI Bar 1992–98, lectr in constitutional and admin law Univ of Ulster Jordanstown 1993, public rep 1996–; memb NI Forum (N Down) 1996–98, memb UUP Talks Team 1996–98, vice-chm Forum Educn Ctee 1997–98; MLA (DUP) N Down 1998–; memb NI Assembly: Standing Orders Ctee 1998–99, Finance and Personnel Ctee 1998–, Environment Ctee 2007–, Business Ctee 2007–; cncllr N Down 2005–; vice-pres NI Local Govt Assoc 2006–; former chm: Queen's UU, UU Students Orgn, Ulster Young Unionist Cncl; memb: Orange Order and Royal Black Preceptory, Hamilton Road Presbyterian Church, 3rd Bangor Boys' Bde 1974–87, Senate Queen's Univ Belfast, Cncl for Legal Educn, SE Educn and Library Bd 2005–, NI Police Bd 2006–; ed Ulster Review 1998–2000; *Publications* The Anglo Irish Agreement - Three Years On (co-author, 1998),

Unionism, National Parties and Ulster (co-author, 1991), UUP Submission on Electoral Reform (1997); *Recreations* football, cricket, history, books, music; *Style—* Peter Weir, Esq, MLA; ✉ Northern Ireland Assembly, Parliament Buildings, Stormont Estate, Belfast BT4 3XX

WEIR, Sarah Jane St Clair; da of David Michael St Clair Weir, of Devon, and Marion Baldwin Cox, *née* Miller, of London; *b* 9 October 1958, Edinburgh; *Educ* St Agnes and St Michael's Convent East Grinstead, Birkbeck Coll London (BA); *Partner* Louise Mary Hide; *Career* md Aldgate Gp Brokers 1992–94 (joined 1979), asst Purdy Hicks Gallery London 1994–95; dep DG Arts & Business 1995–97, fundraising dir Royal Acad of Arts 1997–2001, exec dir Almeida Theatre 2001–03, exec dir Arts Cncl London 2003–; FRSA 2003; *Recreations* the arts, walking, reading, contemplating; *Style—* Ms Sarah Weir; ✉ 2 Pear Tree Court, London EC1R 0DS (tel 020 7608 6157, fax 020 7608 4100, e-mail sarah.weir@artscouncil.org.uk)

WEIR, 3 Viscount (UK 1938); William Kenneth James Weir; also Baron Weir (UK 1918); s of 2 Viscount Weir, CBE (d 1975), of Montgreenan, Kilwinning, Ayrshire, and his 1 w, Lucette Isabel, *née* Crowdy (d 1972); *b* 9 November 1933; *Educ* Eton, Trinity Coll Cambridge (BA); *m* 1, 1964 (m dis 1972), Diana Lucy, da of late Peter Lewis MacDougall of Ottawa, Canada; 1 s (Hon James William Hartland b 6 June 1965), 1 da (Hon Lorna Elizabeth b 17 May 1967); m 2, 6 Nov 1976 (m dis), Mrs Jacqueline Mary Marr, da of late Baron Louis de Chollet, of Fribourg, Switzerland; m 3, 24 Nov 1989, Marina, da of late Marc Sevastopoulo; 1 s (Hon Andrew Alexander Marc b 1989); *Heir* s, Hon James Weir; *Career* Nat Serv with RN 1955–57; chm: Great Northern Investment Trust Ltd 1975–82, Weir Group plc 1983–98 (vice-chm 1981–83, chm and chief exec 1972–81, chm 1983–99); co-chm RIT and Northern plc 1982–83, vice-chm St James's Place Capital plc; dir: British Steel Corporation 1972–76, Balfour Beatty plc (formerly BICC plc) 1977– (chm 1996–2003), Br Bank of the Middle East 1977–79, Canadian Pacific Ltd 1989–2001, CP Ships (chm 2001–04), L F Rothschild Unterberg Towbin 1983–85; memb: Ct of Bank of England 1972–84, Scottish Econ Cncl 1972–84, Engrg Industries Cncl 1975–80, London Advsy Ctee of Hongkong and Shanghai Banking Corp 1980–92; chm: Engrg Design Res Centre 1988–91, Patrons of Nat Galleries of Scotland 1984–94, Major British Exporters 1994–99, British Water 1998–2000; pres BEAMA 1988–89 and 1993–95; Hon DEng Univ of Glasgow 1993; FIBF 1984, MIES 1985, FRSA 1987, Hon FREng 1993; *Recreations* golf, shooting; *Clubs* White's; *Style—* The Rt Hon the Viscount Weir; ✉ Rodinghead, Mauchline, Ayrshire KA5 5TR (tel 01563 884233)

WEISMAN, Malcolm; OBE (1997); s of David Weisman (d 1969), and Jeanie Pearl Weisman (d 1980); *Educ* Parmiter's Sch, Harrogate GS, LSE, St Catherine's Coll Oxford (MA); *m* 1958, Rosalie, da of Dr A A Spiro (d 1963), of St John's Wood; 2 s (Brian b 1959, Daniel b 1963); *Career* Jewish chaplain RAF 1956, hon chaplain Univ of Oxford 1971–, sr chaplain HM Forces 1972–, sec-gen Allied Air Forces Chiefs of Chaplains Ctee 1980–92 (hon pres 1993), sec Former Chiefs of Air Forces Chaplains Assoc 1994; called to the Bar Middle Temple 1961, asst cmmr Parly Boundaries 1976–88, dep circuit judge 1976–80, recorder of the Crown Court 1980, head of chambers 1982–90, special immigration adjudicator 1998, memb Bar Disciplinary Tbnl; memb: MOD Advsy Ctee on Mil Chaplaincy, Cabinet of Chief Rabbi of Cwlth, Nat Exec Cncl of Christians and Jews, Three Faiths Forum Working Pty; ed Menorah magazine; vice-pres and religious advsr Cwlth Jewish Cncl, religious advsr to small Jewish communities and Hillel cnsllr to Oxford and New Univs; memb Cts of Univs of East Anglia, Sussex, Kent, Lancaster, Essex and Warwick; memb SCR Univs of Kent, East Anglia and Lancaster; fell Univ of Essex Centre for Study of Theol; govr and tstee Parmiter's Sch, former govr Carmel Coll and Selly Oak Coll of Christian Jewish Relations; tstee: Multi-Faith and Int Multi-Faith Chaplaincy Centre Univ of Derby, Jewish Music Heritage Tst; patron Jewish Nat Fund; hon chaplain to Lord Mayor of Westminster 1992–93, chaplain to Mayor of Barnett 1994–95, chaplain to Mayor of Redbridge 2005–06, chaplain to Mayor of Montgomery 2006–07; Blackstone Pupillage Award 1961, Man of the Year Award 1980, Chief Rabbi's Award for Excellence 1993, USA Mil Chaplaincy Award for Outstanding Serv 1998, Gold Medal Int Cncl of Christians and Jews 2002, United Synagogue Rabbinic Cncl Award for Work and Leadership 2005; hon fell Univ of Lancaster 2006; *Recreations* reading, walking, doing nothing; *Style—* Malcolm Weisman, Esq, OBE; ✉ 1 Gray's Inn Square, London WC1R 5AA (tel 020 7405 8946, fax 020 7405 1617)

WEISS, Prof Bernard Lawson; s of Joseph Joshua Weiss, and Frances Sonia, *née* Lawson; *b* 9 July 1948; *Educ* Univ of Newcastle upon Tyne (BSc, PhD, DEng), Univ of Surrey (DSc); *m* 12 Dec 1982, Sheila Margaret, *née* Hermiston; 1 s (Oliver Joseph b 23 Sept 1987), 1 da (Jessica Anne b 18 May 1989); *Career* Univ of Newcastle upon Tyne: SRC ad hominem postdoctoral research fell 1975–76, Wolfson Fndn research fell 1977; SRC research fell UCL 1977–79; Univ of Surrey: lectr 1979–86, sr lectr 1986–93, reader 1993–96, prof of microelectronics 1996–, head Sch of Electronics and Physical Sciences 2001 (dep head 1996–2001), pro-vice-chllr 2005–; visiting scholar Univ of Berkeley California 1980; visiting prof: Univ of Cincinnati 1991, Technische Hochschule Darmstadt Germany 1994–95, Univ of Michigan Ann Arbor 2000; hon prof Univ of Hong Kong 1996–2000 (reader 1994–96, William Mong visiting research fell 1997); non-exec dir Surrey Satellite Technol 2003–05; memb Governing Body Frensham Heights Sch Surrey, memb Governing Body St Mary's Univ Coll; 150th Anniversary Medal Warsaw Univ of Technol 1993, Achievement Medal IEE 2004; Leadership Fndn fell 2006; FIEE 1989, FInstP 1994, FREng 2005; *Publications* over 125 articles in professional jls and 50 in published conference proceedings; *Recreations* walking, cycling, collecting antique maps; *Style—* Prof Bernard Weiss; ✉ University of Surrey, Guildford, Surrey GU2 7XH (tel 01483 689128, e-mail b.weiss@surrey.ac.uk)

WEISS, John Roger; CB (2004); s of Ernst Weiss (d 1983), of Basel, Switzerland, and Betsy, *née* Hallam (d 1989); *b* 27 December 1944; *Educ* St Helen's Coll Thames Ditton Surrey, Carshalton Coll of FE; *m* 16 Sept 1967, Hazel Kay, da of Alfred Lang; *Career* tax offr Inland Revenue 1961–64; ECGD: exec offr 1964–70, higher exec offr 1970–76, sr exec offr 1976–78, princ 1978–82, asst sec 1982–90, group dir 1990–2004, dep chief exec 2004–05; *Recreations* music, walking; *Style—* John Weiss, Esq, CB; ✉ Torrells Cottage, Rad Lane, Peaslake, Guildford, Surrey GU5 9PB (tel 01306 730088)

WEISS, Prof Nigel Oscar; s of Oscar Weiss (d 1994), and Ursula Mary, *née* Kisch (d 1998); *b* 16 December 1936; *Educ* Hilton Coll South Africa, Rugby, Clare Coll Cambridge (MA, PhD, ScD); *m* 29 June 1968, Judith Elizabeth, da of Brig Ronald Martin, OBE, MC; 2 da (Catherine Anne b 4 Oct 1970, Naomi Alison b 1 Nov 1982), 1 s (Timothy Francis b 5 March 1973); *Career* research assoc UKAEA Culham Lab 1962–65; Univ of Cambridge: lectr Dept of Applied Mathematics and Theoretical Physics 1965–79, fell Clare Coll 1965, dir of studies in mathematics Clare Coll 1966–79, tutor for grad students Clare Coll 1970–73, reader in astrophysics 1979–87, prof of mathematical astrophysics 1987–2004 (prof emeritus 2004–), chm Cncl Sch of Physical Sciences 1993–98; visiting prof: Sch of Mathematical Sciences Queen Mary & Westfield Coll London 1986–96, Dept of Applied Mathematics Univ of Leeds 2001–07; pres RAS 2000–02 (Gold Medal 2007); sr fell SERC 1987–92; FRS 1992; *Publications* papers on astrophysics, fluid mechanics and nonlinear dynamics; *Recreations* travel; *Style—* Prof Nigel Weiss, FRS; ✉ 10 Lansdowne Road, Cambridge CB3 0EU (tel 01223 355032); Department of Applied Mathematics and Theoretical Physics, University of Cambridge, Wilberforce Road, Cambridge CB3 0WA (tel 01223 337910, fax 01223 765900)

WEISS, Prof Robert Anthony (Robin); s of Hans Weiss, and Stefanie, *née* Löwinsohn; *b* 20 February 1940; *Educ* UCL (BSc, PhD); *m* 1 Aug 1964, Margaret Rose D'Costa; 2 da (Rachel Mary b 1966, Helen Anne b 1968); *Career* lectr in embryology UCL 1964–70, Eleanor Roosevelt Int Cancer Research fell Univ of Washington Seattle 1970–71, visiting assoc prof of microbiology Univ of Southern Calif 1971–72, staff scientist Imperial Cancer Research Fund Labs 1972–80, prof of viral oncology Inst of Cancer Research 1980–98 (dir 1980–89, dir of research 1990–96); Gustav Stern Award in Virology 1973, Beijerinck Prize Royal Netherlands Acad of Arts and Scis 2001; Hon DM Uppsala Univ 2003; FRCPath 1985, Hon FRCP 1998, FRS 1997; *Books* RNA Tumor Viruses (1982, 2 edn 1985), HIV and The New Viruses (1999), Infections and Human Cancer (1999); author of various articles on virology, cell biology and genetics; *Recreations* music, natural history; *Style—* Prof Robin Weiss, FRS; ✉ Division of Infection and Immunity, University College London, 46 Cleveland Street, London W1T 4JF (tel 020 7679 9554, fax 020 7679 9555, e-mail r.weiss@ucl.ac.uk)

WEISZ, Rachel; *Career* actress; *Theatre* The Courtesans (NT Studio), Design for Living (Gielgud Theatre), Suddenly Last Summer (Donmar Warehouse), The Shape of Things (Almeida and NY); *Television* Inspector Morse 1987, Scarlet and Black 1993, My Summer with Des 1998; *Film* Seventeen 1994, Stealing Beauty 1996, Chain Reaction 1996, Swept from the Sea 1997, Going All the Way 1997, The Land Girls 1998, I Want You 1998, The Mummy 1999, Sunshine 1999, Enemy at the Gates 2001, The Mummy Returns 2001, Beautiful Creatures 2001, About a Boy 2001, The Shape of Things 2002, Confidence 2002, The Runaway Jury 2003, Marlowe 2003, Envy 2004, The Constant Gardener 2005 (Best Supporting Actress Golden Globe Awards, Screen Actors Guild Awards and Academy Awards, Best British Actress London Film Critics' Circle Awards); *Style—* Ms Rachel Weisz; ✉ c/o ICM Ltd, Oxford House, 76 Oxford Street, London W1D 1BS (tel 020 7636 6565, fax 020 7323 0101)

WELBY, Sir (Richard) Bruno Gregory Welby; 7 Bt (UK 1801), of Denton Manor, Lincolnshire; s of Sir Oliver Welby, 6 Bt, TD (d 1977, s of Lady Maria Hervey, sis of 4 Marquess of Bristol), by his w, Barbara Angela, da of John Gregory, CB, CMG, and gda of Sir Philip Gregory; n of Dowager Lady Saltoun, and Viscountess Portal of Hungerford; *b* 11 March 1928; *Educ* Eton, ChCh Oxford; *m* 1952, Jane Biddulph, da of late Ralph Hodder-Williams, MC; 3 s, 1 da; *Heir* s, Charles Welby; *Style—* Sir Bruno Welby, Bt; ✉ 20 St Mary Abbot's Terrace, London W14

WELCH, Brig Anthony Cleland; OBE (2003); s of Brian Desmond Joseph Welch (d 1989), of Te Aroha, NZ, and Valerie Isabelle Boxall, *née* Davison; *b* 15 September 1945, Hamilton, NZ; *Educ* Prior Park Coll Bath, St John's Coll Southsea, Univ of Portsmouth (MA), RMCS, Staff Coll Camberley, Higher Command and Staff Coll; *m* 6 May 1983, Pamela Jane, *née* Darnell; 1 s (Simon Alexander Cleland b 31 Aug 1974), 1 da (Alexandra Victoria Cleland b 3 Nov 1977); *Career* tech sales mangr Rediffusion TV (Hong Kong) Ltd 1964–68, 2 Lt rising to Brig British Army 1969–93, chief of policy planning and coordination and COS to Special Rep of the Sec-Gen for the former Yugoslavia 1993–94, gen mangr Allmakes Projects Ltd Oxford 1994–95, head EU monitor mission in Albania/Serbia and Montenegro 1995–96, coordinator Orgn for Security and Co-operation in Europe (OSCE) Balkan States 1996–98, conflict and security advsr DFID 1998–2000, UN regnl admin Northern Kosovo 2000–01, dir Dyncorp Int (Europe) 2001–05, coordinator internal security sector review of Kosovo UNDP 2006–; European Parl candidate (Lib Dem) SW 2004, cncllr Havant BC 2002–07; govr S Downs Coll Portsmouth; tstee: Centre for S Eastern European Studies Sofia, Vencorp Private Equity Ptnrs Geneva; MInstD 1992; *Publications* Ten Years On: The British Army in the Falklands War (contrib, 1992), Mapping the Security Environment: Understanding the perceptions of local communities, peace support operations and assistance agencies (jtly, 2005), The Security Dimensions of EU Enlargement: Wider Europe, Weaker Europe? (jtly, 2007); author of academic papers on security issues; *Recreations* horse racing, golf; *Clubs* Army and Navy, Auckland Racing, Rowlands Castle Golf; *Style—* Brig Anthony Cleland Welch, OBE; ✉ ISSR Secretariat, Office of the Prime Minister, 5th Floor, Government Building, Nana Tereze, Pristina, Kosovo (tel 00 381 38 201 14673); University of Portsmouth, Park Building, King Henry I Street, Portsmouth PO1 2DZ (e-mail anthony.welch@port.ac.uk)

WELCH, Clifford William; CBE (1994); s of William Henry Welch, and Ethel, *née* Games; *b* 1925; *Educ* Christ's Coll Finchley, Plastics Research Inst, Delft Tech HS Holland; *m* 1954, Jill Price Simpson; *Career* visiting lectr Nat Coll of Rubber and Plastics Technol Univ of London 1950–60; Temple Press Ltd: ed Plastics 1957, editorial dir 1958–60; md Heywood-Temple Industrial Publications Ltd and Tothill Press Ltd 1960–66, dep chm Business Publishing Div and chief exec IPC Business Press Overseas Ltd/International Publishing Corporation Ltd 1966–73, fndr chief exec and subsequent dep chm Lloyd's of London Press Ltd 1973–91, chm Lloyd's Maritime Information Services Ltd 1989–92; memb Design Cncl 1988–93 (dep chm and subsequently acting chm 1991–93); tstee: Katharine Dormandy Tst Royal Free Hosp London, Newsvendors Ben Inst; Freeman City of London 1957, Liveryman and memb Ct of Assts Worshipful Co of Horners (Master 1982); FIM, CSci; *Publications* contrib: The Penguin Science Survey, History of the British Plastics Federation; various papers to IUPAC and other socs; *Recreations* gardening, walking, fly fishing; *Clubs* City of London, Oriental, MCC, Flyfishers'; *Style—* Clifford Welch, Esq, CBE, FIM, CSci; ✉ Orchard House, Coles Oak Lane, Dedham, Colchester, Essex CO7 6DR (tel 01206 322277, fax 01206 322607)

WELCH, Dr Janet Mary (Jan); MBE (2006); da of Patrick Palles Lorne Elphinstone Welch, of Farnham, Surrey, and Ann Courtenay, *née* Edmonds; *b* 11 June 1955; *Educ* Farnham Girls' GS, Farnborough Tech Coll, St Thomas' Hosp Med Sch London (entrance scholar, Tite scholar, BSc, MB BS); *m* 1989, Gary Richards, s of Jack Richards; 1 da (Fabia Rosamund b 2 Oct 1990), 1 s (Toby Lorne b 8 June 1993); *Career* house physician then SHO in microbiology St Thomas' Hosp London 1981, registrar in infectious diseases London 1983, sr registrar in genitourinary med St Thomas' Hosp London 1987–90 (in virology 1984–87); KCH: conslt in HIV/genitourinary med 1990–, dir of postgrad med educn 1998–2005, postgrad dean 1998–2005; dir SE Thames Fndn Sch 2005–; clinical dir Haven Sexual Assault Referral Centre Camberwell; FRCP, FFFLM; *Books* Looking After People with Late HIV Disease (1990); *Recreations* gardening, skiing; *Style—* Dr Jan Welch, MBE

WELCH, Sir John Reader; 2 Bt (UK 1957), of Chard, Co Somerset; s of Sir Cullum Welch, 1 Bt, OBE, MC (d 1980); *b* 26 July 1933; *Educ* Marlborough, Hertford Coll Oxford (MA); *m* 25 Sept 1962, Margaret Kerry, o da of Kenneth Victor Douglass (d 1996); 1 s, 2 da; *Heir* s, James Welch; *Career* Nat Serv 2nd Lt Royal Signals 1952–54, capt Middx Yeo (TA) 1954–62; admitted slr 1960; ptnr: Bell Brodrick & Gray 1961–71, Wedlake Bell 1972–96; chm: John Fairfax (UK) Ltd 1977–90, London Homes for the Elderly 1981–90; registrar Archdeaconry of London 1964–99, memb Court of Common Cncl (City of London) 1975–86 and chm Planning and Communications Ctee 1981–1982; govr: City of London Sch for Girls 1977–82, Haberdashers' Aske's Schs Elstree 1981–85 and 1990–91; Sr Grand Warden United Grand Lodge of England 1998–2000; pres The Grand Charity of Freemasons 1985–95; memb City Livery Club (hon slr 1983–90, pres 1986–87), chm Walbrook Ward Club 1978–79; Liveryman and Past Master Emeritus Worshipful Co of Haberdashers (Master 1990–91), Freeman and Past Master Emeritus Worshipful Co of Parish Clerks (Master 1967–68); FRSA 1991; CStJ 1981; *Clubs* Hurlingham; *Style—* Sir John Welch, Bt; ✉ 28 Rivermead Court, Ranelagh Gardens, London SW6 3RU (tel 020 7736 2775)

W

WELCH, Melvin Dennis (Mel); s of Robert Charles Welch (d 1991), of Watford, Herts, and Rose Elizabeth, *née* Oakley (d 1993); *b* 21 November 1946; *Educ* Bushey GS, Univ of Sussex (BSc, MSc); *m* 18 Sept 1971, Susan Jane, da of Arthur Jeffcoatt (d 1976), of

Coventry, Warks; 1 s (Timothy b 1972), 1 da (Josephine b 1974); *Career* sec: English Basketball Assoc 1970–91, Br and Irish Basketball Fedn 1970–2003, Cwlth Basketball Fedn 1978–91; co-ordinator Carnegie Nat Sports Devpt Centre 1991–, sec Fed of Yorkshire Sport 1991–, memb Yorkshire Sports Bd 2000–03; memb: Eligibility Ctee Int Basketball Fedn 1984–2002, Olympic Review Ctee Sports Cncl 1985–86; Br Inst of Sports Admin: fndr memb 1979, memb Exec Ctee 1985–2002, vice-chm 1992–94 and 1998–2001, chm 1994–1998, fell 1995–, vice-pres 2001–; Sports Aid Fndn: memb UK Grants Ctee 1986–1996, chm Eng Grants Ctee 1996–2003, govr and memb Exec Ctee Sports Aid Fndn 1996–2003; dir Eng Fedn of Disability Sport Operating Co 2001–; coaching review panel Sports Cncl 1989–91; dir: Basketball Publishing Ltd 1986–91, Basketball Marketing Ltd 1986–87, EBBA Outdoor Basketball Initiative 1997– (chm 1999–), Weltech Solutions Ltd 1998–; tournament referee Leeds tennis league, sec Leeds City Fedn 2002–, treas European Assoc for Sport Mgmnt 2002–; life vice-pres: English Basketball Assoc 1991, Cwlth Basketball Fedn 2002–; *Books* EBBA Yearbook (1971–91), Intersport Basketball (1981), Encyclopaedia Britannica Book of Year (contrib, 1985–90), Getting Things Done (1992), Raising Money (1992), Running Meetings (1992), Running a Club (1992), Looking after the Money (1992), Getting It Right (1994), Making Your Point (1994), Making A Match (1994); *Recreations* tennis, basketball, walking; *Style*— Mel Welch, Esq; ✉ 5 Thorn Lane, Roundhay, Leeds LS8 1NF (tel 0113 266 8751); Carnegie National Sports Development Centre, Beckett Park, Leeds LS6 3QS (tel 0113 283 7418, fax 0113 283 3170, e-mail m.welch@leddsmet.ac.uk)

WELCH, Prof Robert; s of Patrick Welch (d 1995), and Kathleen, *née* Kearney (d 1989); *b* 25 November 1947; *Educ* Coláiste Chriost Ri Cork (nat scholar), Univ Coll Cork (Univ scholar, BA, MA), Univ of Leeds (PhD); *m* 1970, Angela, da of Pearse O'Riordan; 4 c (Rachel b 16 Jan 1971, Killian b 23 July 1975, Egan b 31 Jan 1980 (decd), Tiernan b 1 March 1981); *Career* lectr Univ of Leeds 1971–73, lectr in English Univ of Ife Nigeria 1973–74, lectr in English Univ of Leeds 1974–84; Univ of Ulster: prof of English 1984–, sometime head of Dept, dir Centre for Irish Literature & Bibliography 1994–, dean Faculty of Arts 2000–; Arts Cncl for Northern Ireland: memb Bd 1990–96, chm Creative Arts Ctee 1991–96, vice-chm 1992–93; chm Int Assoc for the Study of Irish Literatures 1988–91; govr Limavady coll of Further and Higher Education, dir Kabosh Theatre Co; assessor: HEFCE 1994–95, fell English Assoc 2000–; *Books* Irish Poetry from Moore to Yeats (1980), History of Verse Translation from the Irish (1988), Changing States: Transformations in Modern Irish Literature (1993), The Kilcolman Notebook (novel, 1994), The Oxford Companion to Irish Literature (1996), Secret Societies (poems, 1997), Groundwork (novel, 1997), The Blue Formica Table (poems, 1998), The Abbey Theatre: 1889–1999, Concise Oxford Companion to Irish Literature (2000), Forty Four (by Dana Podracka, trans, 2005), Protestants (play, 2006), The Evergreen Road (poems, 2006); *Recreations* walking, fishing, gardening, wine; *Clubs* Kildare Street & Univ; *Style*— Prof Robert Welch; ✉ 55 Millburn Road, Coleraine; Leamagowra Lodge, Leamagowra, Glencolumcille, Co Donegal; Faculty of Arts, University of Ulster, Coleraine BT52 1SA (tel 028 7032 4517, fax 028 7032 4925)

WELDON, Sir Anthony William; 9 Bt (I 1723), of Dunmore, Co Carlow; s of Sir Thomas Weldon, 8 Bt (d 1979), by his w Marie, Lady Weldon, who subseq m 6 Earl Cathcart; *b* 11 May 1947; *Educ* Sherborne; *m* 1980 (m dis 2006), Amanda, formerly w of Anthony Wigan, and da of Maj Geoffrey North, MC, by his w, Hon Margaret de Grey (2 da of 8 Baron Walsingham, DSO, OBE, JP, DL); 2 da (Alice Louise b 13 Nov 1981, Oonagh Leone b 6 Oct 1983); *Heir* 2 cous, Kevin Weldon; *Career* late Lt Irish Gds, awarded S Arabian GSM; md BFP Design and Communications and Bene Factum Publishing Ltd; *Publications* Breakthrough: Handling Career Opportunities and Changes (1994, 2 edn 1999); *Recreations* stalking, champagne, cricket; *Clubs* White's, The Stranded Whales, Pratt's; *Style*— Sir Anthony Weldon, Bt

WELDON, Duncan Clark; s of Clarence Weldon (d 1980), of Southport, and Margaret Mary Andrew; *b* 19 March 1941; *Educ* King George V GS Southport; *m* 1 (m dis 1971), Helen Shapiro; m 2, 9 July 1974, Janet, da of Walter Mahoney (d 1982); 1 da (Lucy Jane b Oct 1977); *Career* theatrical producer, formerly photographer; co-fndr Triumph Theatre Productions Ltd 1970; dir: Duncan C Weldon Productions Ltd, Triumph Proscenium Productions Ltd, Malvern Festival Theatre Trust Ltd; artistic dir Chichester Festival Theatre 1995–97; co-fndr Triumph Entertainment Ltd 2000; first stage prodn A Funny Kind of Evening (with David Kossoff, Theatre Royal Bath) 1965, first London prodn Tons of Money (Mayfair) 1968, presentations also in Europe, Aust, Russia, Canada and Hong Kong; *Theatre Productions* has presented over 200 in London incl in 1970: When We Are Married; in 1971: The Chalk Garden, Big Bad Mouse, The Wizard of Oz; in 1972: Lord Arthur Savile's Crime, Bunny, The Wizard of Oz; in 1973: Mother Adam, Grease, The King and I; in 1974: Dead Easy; in 1975: The Case in Question, Hedda Gabler (RSC), Dad's Army, Betzi, On Approval; in 1976: 13 Rue de l'Amour, A Bedful of Foreigners, Three Sisters, Fringe Benefits, The Seagull, The Circle; in 1977: Separate Tables, Stevie, Hedda Gabler, On Approval, The Good Woman of Setzuan, Rosmersholm, Laburnham Grove, The Apple Cart; in 1978: Waters of the Moon, Kings and Clowns, The Travelling Music Show, A Family, Look After Lulu, The Millionairess; in 1979: The Crucifer of Blood; in 1980: Reflections, Rattle of a Simple Man, The Last of Mrs Cheyney, Early Days (RNT); in 1981: Virginia, Overheard, Dave Allen, Worzel Gummidge; in 1982: Murder in Mind, Hobson's Choice, A Coat of Varnish, Captain Brassbound's Conversion, Design For Living, Uncle Vanya, Key for Two, The Rules of the Game, Man and Superman; in 1983: The School for Scandal, Dash, Heartbreak House, Call Me Madam, Romantic Comedy, Liza Minnelli, Beethoven's Tenth (also Broadway), Edmund Kean (also Broadway), Fiddler on the Roof, A Patriot for Me (also LA), Cowardice, Great and Small, The Cherry Orchard, Dial M for Murder, Dear Anyone, The Sleeping Prince, The School for Scandal, Hi-De-Hi!; in 1984: Hello Dolly!, The Aspern Papers, Strange Interlude (also Broadway), Serjeant Musgrave's Dance, Aren't We All? (also Broadway), American Buffalo, The Way of the World, Extremities; in 1985: The Wind in the Willows, The Lonely Road, The Caine Mutiny Court-Martial, Other Places, Old Times (also in LA), The Corn is Green, Waste (RSC), Strippers, Guys and Dolls (RNT), Sweet Bird of Youth, Interpreters, Fatal Attraction, The Scarlet Pimpernel; in 1986: The Applecart, Across from the Garden of Allah, Antony and Cleopatra, The Taming of the Shrew, Circe & Bravo, Annie Get Your Gun, Long Day's Journey into Night, Rookery Nook, Breaking the Code (also Broadway), Mr and Mrs Nobody; in 1987: A Piece of My Mind, Court in the Act!, Canaries Sometimes Sing, Kiss Me Kate (RSC), Melon, Portraits, Groucho - A Life in Review, A Man for all Seasons, You Never Can Tell, Babes in the Wood; in 1988: A Touch of the Poet, The Deep Blue Sea, The Admirable Crichton, The Secret of Sherlock Holmes, A Walk in the Woods, Orpheus Descending (also Broadway), Richard II; in 1989: Richard III, The Royal Baccarat Scandal, Ivanov, Much Ado About Nothing, The Merchant of Venice (also Broadway), Frankie & Johnny, Veterans Day, Another Time, The Baker's Wife, London Assurance; in 1990: Salome (RNT), Bent (RNT), An Evening with Peter Ustinov, The Wild Duck, Henry IV, Kean, Love Letters, Time and the Conways; in 1991: The Homecoming, The Philanthropist, The Caretaker, Becket, Tovarich, The Cabinet Minister; in 1992: Talking Heads, Heartbreak House, A Woman of No Importance (RSC), Lost in Yonkers, Trelawny of the Wells, Cyrano de Bergerac; in 1993: Macbeth (RSC), Relative Values, Two Gentlemen of Verona (RSC); in 1994: Travesties (RSC), A Month in the Country (also Broadway), Rope, An Evening with Peter Ustinov, Arcadia (RNT), Home, Saint Joan, Lady Windermere's Fan, The Rivals; in 1995: Dangerous Corner, Cell Mates, The Duchess of Malfi, Taking Sides (also Broadway), Old Times, Communicating Doors, Hobson's Choice, The Hothouse; in 1996: Uncle Vanya, When We Are Married, Talking Heads, The Cherry Orchard (RSC); in 1997: Live & Kidding, The Herbal Bed (RSC), Life Support, A Letter of Resignation, Electra (also Broadway), The Magistrate; in 1998: Rent, New Edna - The Spectacle; in 1999: Richard III (RSC), The Prisoner of Second Avenue, Hay Fever, Love letters, The Importance of Being Earnest, Collected Stories; in 2000: Enigmatic Variations (also Los Angeles), Napoleon, God Only Knows, The Importance of Being Earnest (extensive tour); in 2001: The Importance of Being Earnest (Savoy Theatre London), Peggy Sue Got Married, Private Lives (also Broadway); in 2002: My One and Only, The Hollow Crown (RSC, Aust and NZ); in 2003: The Tempest, Coriolanus (RSC), The Merry Wives of Windsor (RSC), The Master Builder, Thoroughly Modern Millie; in 2004: Rattle of a Simple Man, Suddenly Last Summer, Blithe Spirit; in 2005: The Birthday Party, The Philadelphia Story, As You Desire Me; other Broadway prodns incl: Brief Lives 1974, Wild Honey (NT) 1986, Blithe Spirit and Pygmalion 1987; *Television Productions* co-prodr (with Carlton TV) Into the Blue (by Robert Goddard and starring John Thaw) 1997; *Style*— Duncan C Weldon, Esq

WELDON, Fay; *née* Franklin Birkinshaw; CBE (2001); da of Dr Frank Birkinshaw (d 1947), and Margaret, *née* Jepson; *b* 22 September 1931; *Educ* Christ Church Girls' HS NZ, South Hampstead HS, Univ of St Andrews (MA); *m* 1; 1 s (Nicholas b 1954); m 2, June 1961 (m dis 1994), Ron Weldon; 3 s (Daniel b 1963, Thomas b 1970, Samuel b 1977); m 3, 1995, Nicolas Fox; *Career* screen writer, playwright, novelist, critic, essayist; chm of judges Booker McConnell Prize 1983; memb: Soc of Authors, Writers' Guild of GB; Hon DLitt: Univ of Bath 1989, Univ of St Andrews 1992, Univ of Birmingham 2001; FRSL 1986, FRSA; *Books* The Fat Woman's Joke (1967), Down Among the Women (1971), Female Friends (1975), Remember Me (1976), Little Sisters (1978), Praxis (1978, Booker Prize nomination), Puffball (1980), Watching Me Watching You (1981), The President's Child (1982), Life and Loves of a She Devil (1984, televised 1986), Letters to Alice-on First Reading Jane Austen (1984), Polaris and Other Stories (1985), Rebecca West (1985), The Shrapnel Academy (1986), Heart of the Country (1987, televised 1987), The Hearts and Lives of Men (1987), The Rules of Life (1987), Leader of the Band (1988), The Cloning of Joanna May (1989), Darcy's Utopia (1990), Growing Rich (1990, televised 1990), Moon Over Minneapolis or Why She Couldn't Stay (1991), Life Force (1992), Affliction (1994), Splitting (1995), Wicked Women (1995), Worst Fears (1996), Big Women (1998), Hard Time To Be a Father (1998), Godless in Eden (1999), Rhode Island Blues (2000), The Bulgari Connection (2001), Auto-Da-Fay (autobiography, 2002), Nothing to Wear Nowhere to Hide (short stories, 2002), Mantrapped (2004), She May Not Leave (2005), What Makes Women Happy (2006); children's books: Wolf the Mechanical Dog (1988), Party Puddle (1989), Nobody Likes Me (1999); *Style*— Fay Weldon, CBE, FRSL; ✉ c/o Georgina Capel, Capel and Land, 29 Wardour Street, London W1V 3HB

WELDON, Tom; s of Patrick Weldon, and Pamela, *née* Grant; *Educ* Westminster, St John's Coll Oxford (BA); *Career* ed Macmillan Publishers 1985–88, editorial dir William Heinemann 1989–96, publishing dir Penguin 1997–; *Recreations* racing, movies, skiing, travel; *Clubs* Charlie Chester's Casino; *Style*— Tom Weldon, Esq; ✉ Penguin Books, 80 Strand, London WC2R 0RL (tel 020 7010 3280, e-mail tom.weldon@penguin.co.uk)

WELEMINSKY, Judy Ruth; da of Dr Anton Weleminsky, of Manchester, and Gerda, *née* Loewenstamm; *b* 25 October 1950; *Educ* Pontefract & Dist Girls' HS, Roundhay HS, Univ of Birmingham (BSc), Lancaster Univ (MA); *m* Robert J A Smith; 2 da (Emma Jane Weleminsky-Smith b 6 Feb 1991, Alice Rose Weleminsky-Smith b 13 Feb 1993); *Career* personnel and training offr Lowfield (S & D) Ltd 1973–75, community rels offr Lambeth Cncl for Community Rels 1975–78, equal opportunities offr Wandsworth BC 1978–80, employment devpt offr Nat Assoc for Care and Resettlement of Offenders (NACRO) 1980–82; chief exec: Nat Fed of Community Orgns 1982–85, Nat Schizophrenia Fellowship 1985–90, NCVO 1991–94; mgmnt conslt 1994–2005, assoc Volprof 1994–96, ptnr Mentoring Directors 1995–97, sr assoc Compass Partnership 1994–2005, chief exec Mental Health Providers Forum 2005–; assoc mentor Clutterbuck Schneider & Palmer 1996–99; tstee: Cosmopolitan Devpt Tst 1997–2000, Makaton Vocabulary Devpt Project 1998–; public speaker; co-ordinator: Chiswick & Kew Jewish Gp 1997–2004, Kew Giving Circle 1998–; dir Venture Community Assoc 2005; memb: Bd Children and Families Ct Advsy and Support Service (CAFCASS) 2001–04, Cncl Gen Social Care Cncl 2001–04, ACEVO; FRSA 1992; *Recreations* family, friends and food; *Style*— Ms Judy Weleminsky; ✉ e-mail judywele@aol.com

WELFARE, Jonathan William; s of Kenneth William Welfare (d 1966), and (Dorothy) Patience Athole, *née* Ross; *b* 21 October 1944; *Educ* Bradfield Coll, Emmanuel Coll Cambridge (MA); *m* 6 Sept 1969, Deborah Louise, da of James D'Arcy Nesbitt, of West Kirby, Cheshire; 3 da (Harriet b 1973, Laura b 1975, Amy b 1979), 1 s (Oliver b 1987); *Career* corp planning mangr Milton Keynes Devpt Corp 1970–74, chief economist and dep chief exec S Yorks Met CC 1974–84, dir The Landmark Tst 1984–86; co-fndr The Oxford Ventures Gp 1986; dir: Granite TV Ltd 1988–2002, Oxford Innovation Ltd 1988–98; md Venture Link Investors Ltd 1990–95, chief exec Bristol 2000 1995–96, mgmnt conslt 1996–98; chief exec: Elizabeth Finn Care (estab as Distressed Gentlefolks Aid Assoc 1897, charity) 1998–, Elizabeth Finn Trading Ltd, Elizabeth Finn Homes Ltd; tstee: The Oxford Tst 1985–2005 (chm 1985–95), The Northmoor Tst 1986–99 (chm 1986–95), Turn2us 2007–; memb Bd English Community Care Assoc 2000–; Freeman City of London, Freeman Worshipful Co of Info Technologists; FRSA; *Books* Sources of EEC Funding for Local Authorities (1977); *Recreations* tennis (real and lawn), cricket, fishing, gardening; *Clubs* Hawks' (Cambridge); *Style*— Jonathan Welfare, Esq; ✉ Elizabeth Finn Care, 1 Derry Street, Kensington, London W8 5HY (tel 020 7396 6700, fax 020 7396 6734)

WELFARE, Simon Piers; s of Kenneth William Welfare (d 1966), of Stradbroke, Suffolk, and Dorothy Patience, *née* Ross; *b* 21 November 1946; *Educ* Harrow, Magdalen Coll Oxford; *m* 3 Aug 1968, Lady Mary Katharine Welfare, da of Marquess of Aberdeen and Temair, CBE (d 1974), of Haddo House, Aberdeenshire; 2 da (Hannah b 30 Sept 1969, Alice b 6 Sept 1971 d Feb 2004), 1 s (Toby b 29 March 1973); *Career* broadcaster and writer Yorkshire TV Ltd 1968–81, freelance prodr 1982–, md Granite Film and TV Prodns 1989–; *Books* Arthur C Clarke's Mysterious World (with A C Clarke and John Fairley, 1980), Arthur C Clarke's World of Strange Powers (with A C Clarke and J Fairley, 1984), Great Honeymoon Disasters (1986), Arthur C Clarke's Chronicles of the Strange & Mysterious (with A C Clarke and J Fairley, 1987), Red Empire (with Gwyneth Hughes, 1990), The Cabinet of Curiosities (with J Fairley, 1991), Days of Majesty (with Alastair Bruce, 1993), Arthur C Clarke's A-Z of Mysteries (with J Fairley, 1993); *Recreations* collecting arcane knowledge, flying; *Style*— Simon Welfare, Esq; ✉ Easter Davoch, Tarland, Aboyne, Aberdeenshire AB34 4US (tel 01339 880175)

WELLDON, Dr Estela Valentina; da of Gildo D'Accurzio (d 1983), and Julia, *née* Barbadillo (d 1957); *b* 3 November 1936; *Educ* Universidad de Cuyo Argentina (MD), Menninger Sch of Psychiatry USA, Univ of London; *m* Ronald Michael Charles Welldon (d 1970); 1 s (Daniel Alexis b 2 Feb 1970); *Career* psychiatrist Henderson Hosp 1964; Portman Clinic London: conslt psychiatrist 1975–, clinic tutor 1987–92; private practice 44 Harley Street; specialist in the application of gp analysis to social and sexual deviancy, pioneer in teaching of forensic psychotherapy, fndr in forensic psychotherapy Univ of London; pres Int Assoc for Forensic Psychotherapy 1991–95 (hon pres 1995–); organisational conslt 1997–, conslt 1997–; assessor British Jl of Psychiatry, expert on female crime and sexual deviation Panel of Specialists RCPsych, Br corr and memb Editorial Bd Argentinian Jl of Gp Psychotherapy; currently sr lectr: Dept of Psychiatry Sassari Univ Sardinia, Dept of Psychology Univ of Bologna Italy; Visitante Distinguido Univ and City of Cuzco Peru 1989; memb: Gp Analytic Soc 1968, Br Assoc of Psychotherapists 1972, Inst for Study and Prevention of Delinquency, American Gp Psychotherapy Assoc, Int Assoc of Gp Psychotherapy, Inst of Gp Analysis; fndr memb Bd of Dirs Int Acad of Law and Mental Health, memb Bd of Dirs Int Assoc of Gp Psychotherapy; Hon DSc Oxford Brookes Univ 1997; memb Soc of Authors; FRCPsych 1987 (MRCPysch 1973); *Books* Mother, Madonna, Whore (1988), A Practical Guide to Forensic Psychotherapy (1996), Sadomasochism (2002); *Recreations* opera, theatre, swimming; *Clubs* Groucho; *Style*— Dr Estela Welldon; ✉ 44 Harley Street, London W1G 9PS (fax 020 7586 0713, mobile 07932 715757, e-mail evwelldon@aol.com)

WELLER, (William) Leslie; DL (W Sussex 1992); s of Frederick Leslie Weller (d 1977), of Horsham, W Sussex, and Blanche Mary, *née* Kemp (d 1994); *b* 23 April 1935; *Educ* Collyers GS, Cranleigh Sch; *m* 1 (m dis), Joyce Elizabeth; 1 s (Adrian Leslie b 21 June 1963); m 2, Brenda Olive Wilson; *Career* Nat Serv RAF 1957–59; chartered surveyor: Newland Tompkins and Taylor 1951–55, King and Chasemore 1959–78 (ptnr 1961–78); dir Sotheby's London 1978–94, md Sotheby's Sussex 1978–91, ptnr Weller King 1994–; chm Olympia Fine Art and Antiques Fairs 1980–; tstee Chichester Cathedral Tst 1979– (chm 1979–86), chm Chichester Cathedral Fabric Advsy Ctee 1995–, chm Chichester Cathedral Cncl 2001–; pres Sussex Archaeological Soc; Freeman: Worshipful Co of Ironmongers 1984 (Master 2001–02), City of London 1986; FRICS 1961, FSVA 1976; *Recreations* country life, history, gardening, the arts, book-collecting; *Clubs* Naval and Military (chm 1997–2001), Sussex; *Style*— Leslie Weller, Esq, DL; ✉ Hobshorts House, Rook Cross Lane, West Grinstead, Horsham, West Sussex RH13 8LL (tel 01403 711821); Weller King, The Estate Office, Hobshorts, Rook Cross Lane, West Grinstead, Horsham, West Sussex RH13 8LL (tel 01403 713587, fax 01403 711003, mobile 07712 588651)

WELLER, Prof Malcolm Philip Isadore; s of Solomon George Weller (d 1958), and Esther, *née* Black; *b* 29 May 1935; *Educ* Perse Sch Cambridge, Univ of Cambridge (MA, prize winner, capt coll athletics team), Univ of Newcastle upon Tyne (MB BS, scholarship and prize winner), Br Cncl travel award; *m* 8 May 1966, (Celia) Davina, da of Solomon Reisler (d 1973); 2 s (Ben b 19 Aug 1969, Adrian b 17 Dec 1970); *Career* psychiatrist; emeritus conslt St Ann's Hosp, hon research prof Middlesex Univ; formerly lectr and first asst Charing Cross Hosp Sch of Med; visiting fell Fitzwilliam Coll Cambridge 1994–95; pubns incl over 150 chapters, papers and editorials on psychiatric and medico-legal subjects; Univ of London: co-opted memb Bd of Studies in Psychology and Higher Degrees Sub-Ctee, memb Examination Ctee; external examiner Univs of Manchester and Singapore (RCPsych rep), examination offr RSM; RCPsych: former memb Social Community and Rehabilitation Exec Ctees, former memb Working Gps, former memb Gen Adult Psychiatry Ctee, co-opted memb Psychopharmacology Ctee, coll rep to British pharmaceutical industry; RSM rep to NICE; chm: CONCERN 1994–99, London Regnl Psychiatric Ctee 1995–, Haringey Div of Psychiatry 1992–94, Joint London Chairmen Working Gp; former vice-chm London Regnl Ctee for Hosp Med Servs; cmmr Mental Health Act; former organiser Newcastle Music Festival, former co-opted memb Mgmnt Ctee Laing Art Gallery; former local cncllr, former chm of govrs Gosforth Middle Sch; memb Central Ctee BMA; memb Cncl RSM, emeritus memb AAAS, int memb American Psychiatric Assoc; FBPsS (chartered neuropsychologist) 1986, FCINP 1987, FRCPsych 1987; *Books* Scientific Basis of Psychiatry (1983 and 1992), International Perspectives in Schizophrenia (1990), MCQs on the Basic Sciences (1992), Dimensions of Community Care (1993), Progress in Clinical Psychiatry (1996); Bailliere's Clinical Psychiatry Series (ed in chief, 11 vols); *Recreations* history of art, music; *Clubs* RSM, Arts; *Style*— Prof Malcolm Weller; ✉ 30 Arkwright Road, Hampstead, London NW3 6BH (tel 020 7794 5804, fax 020 7431 1589, e-mail malcolm@weller.tv)

WELLER, Sara; *b* 1 August 1961; *Educ* Weymouth GS, New Coll Oxford (Beresford Hope scholar, MA, Badminton blue); *Career* Mars Confectionery UK: mktg grad trainee 1983–85, grad recruitment mangr Mars Gp UK 1986–87, personnel mangr Sales Div 1987–88, mktg mangr 1989–94, mktg controller UK and Europe 1994–96, consumer devpt dir Europe 1996; Abbey National plc: customer mktg dir 1996–98, retail mktg dir 1998–99; Sainsbury's Supermarkets Ltd: mktg dir 2000–2001, asst md 2001–03, memb Gp Bd 2002–04, dep md 2003–04; md Argos Ltd 2004–; non-exec dir Mitchells & Butlers plc 2003–; *Recreations* golf (irregular), natural history/evolution/philosophy, cooking, home improvements, children; *Style*— Mrs Sara Weller

WELLER, Walter; s of Walter Weller (d 1982), and Anna Katharina Weller (d 1990); *b* 30 November 1939; *Educ* Gymnasium HS of Music Vienna; *m* 8 June 1966, Elisabeth Maria, da of Prof Franz Samohyl, of Vienna; 1 s (Andreas b 18 June 1978); *Career* musician and conductor; Vienna Philharmonic Orch 1956–57, fndr Weller Quartet 1957–67, first Konzertmeister Vienna Philharmonic 1961, debut as conductor 1966, princ conductor RPO 1980–85, princ guest conductor Nat Orch of Spain 1987–2002, chief conductor and music dir Royal Scottish Orchestra 1992–97 (conductor emeritus 1997–), chief conductor Basel Symphony Orchestra and gen music dir Allgemeine Basler Musikgesellshaft 1994–97, currently conductor laureate Stuttgart Philharmonic Orch and assoc dir Orch of Vallencia; appears guest conductor worldwide; recordings incl: complete Prokofiev and Rachmaninov symphonies, complete Beethoven symphonies and piano concertos, Mendelssohn, Smetana, Shostakovich, Grieg, Bartók, Dukas, Glazounow, Bruckner, Rachmaninow, Dvorak; operas incl: Fidelio and Der Rosenkavalier (Scottish Opera), Der Fliegende Holländer and Ariadne auf Naxos (ENO), Der Frieischutz (Teatro Comunale Bologna), Der Fliegende Holländer (La Scala); conductor of leading orchestras: Britain, Europe, Scandinavia, America; Honoured Cross for Art and Sci (Austria), Mozart Interpretation prize, Beethoven Gold medal, The Great Silver Cross of Honour for services to the Republic of Austria 1998; *Style*— Walter Weller, Esq; ✉ c/o Harrison-Parrott Ltd, 12 Penzance Place, London W11 4PA (tel 020 7229 9166, fax 020 7221 5042)

WELLINGS, Prof Paul William; s of William Wellings (d 1979), and Beryl, *née* Roscoe (d 1981); *b* 1 November 1953, Nottingham; *Educ* Royal GS Lancaster, KCL (BSc), Univ of Durham (MSc), UEA (PhD); *m* 22 Dec 1990, Annette Frances Schmidt; *Career* NERC research fell UEA 1980–81, research scientist CSIRO Entomology Canberra 1981–95, chief of div CSIRO Entomology Canberra 1995–97, first asst sec Dept of Industry, Science and Resources Aust govt 1997–99, dep chief exec CSIRO Canberra 1999–2002, vice-chllr Lancaster Univ 2002–; memb Bd: Aust Nuclear Science and Technol Orgn 1997–99, Aust Centre for Int Agric Research 1999–2002, Cumbria Rural Regeneration Co 2002–06, HEFCE 2006–, Universities UK 2006–; fell Aust Inst of Co Dirs (FAICD), FRSA, CCMI; *Publications* numerous papers in population ecology and insect pest mgmnt; *Recreations* cricket, fell walking; *Style*— Prof Paul Wellings; ✉ University House, Lancaster University, Lancaster LA1 4YW (tel 01524 594545, fax 01524 36841, e-mail p.wellings@lancaster.ac.uk)

WELLINGTON, 8 Duke of (UK 1814); Arthur Valerian Wellesley; KG (1990), LVO (1952), OBE (1957), MC (1941), DL (Hants 1975); also Baron of Mornington (I 1746), Earl of Mornington, Viscount Wellesley (both I 1760), Viscount Wellington of Talavera and of Wellington, Baron Douro (both UK 1809), Conde do Vimeiro (Portugal 1811), Earl of Wellington (UK 1812), Marquess of Wellington (UK 1812), Duque de Ciudad Rodrigo and a Grandee of the 1 Class (Spain 1812), Duque da Victoria, Marques de Torres Vedras (both Portugal 1812), Marquess of Douro (UK 1814), and Prince of Waterloo (Netherlands 1815); s of 7 Duke of Wellington, KG (d 1972); *b* 2 July 1915; *Educ* Eton, New Coll Oxford; *m* 1944, Diana, da of Maj-Gen Douglas McConnel, CB, CBE, DSO, of Knockdolian, Ayrshire; 4 s, 1 da; *Heir* s, Marquess of Douro; *Career* patron of 4 livings; Brig (ret) RHG, CO 1955–58, Silver Stick in Waiting and Lt-Col cmdg Household Cav 1959–60 & OC 22 Armd Bde 1960–61, cdr RAC BAOR 1962–64, defence attaché Madrid 1964–67, Col-in-Chief The Duke of Wellington's Regt 1974–2006, Dep Col-in Chief Yorks Regt 2006; Hon Col 2 Bn Wessex Regt TA & VRA, nat vice-pres Royal Br Legion; dir Massey Ferguson Holdings 1967 and Massey Ferguson Ltd 1973–89; vice-pres and cncl memb Zoological Soc of London 1973–89; pres and dep pres the Game Conservancy 1976–87; pres: Rare Breeds Survival Tst 1982–86, Cncl for Environmental Conservation 1983–86, Atlantic Salmon Trust 1983–2005, Hampshire Association of Parish Councils 1994–2000, National Canine Defence League (now Dogs Tst) 1996–2003, Labrador Retriever Club 1997–; Queen's Tstee Bd of Royal Armouries 1983–95; dep Col to HRH The Princess Royal of The Blues and Royals 1998–2002; chm Pitt Club, govr Wellington Coll; tstee: Lawes Agric Tst 1989–2000, Centre for Agric Strategy Univ of Reading 1988–95, World Wildlife Fund (UK) 1985–90; tstee and dep chm Thames Salmon Tst 1986–2002; vice-pres The Kennel Club 1987–; dep pres RASE 1993 (hon vice-pres and memb Cncl); served in campaigns in Iraq, Syria 1941, Western Desert 1942, Italy 1944, N W Europe 1945; Grand Cross Order of Isabel the Catholic (Spain) 1986, Légion d'Honneur (France); *Clubs* Cavalry and Guards', Anglo-Belgian; *Style*— His Grace the Duke of Wellington, KG, LVO, OBE, MC; ✉ Park Corner House, Heckfield, Hook, Hampshire RG27 0LJ; Apsley House, Piccadilly, London W1J 7NT

WELLS, (William Arthur) Andrew; TD (1984); s of Sir John Wells, DL, MP Maidstone 1959–87; *b* 14 June 1949; *Educ* Eton, N London Univ (BA); *m* 19 Oct 1974, Tessa Margaret, da of Lt-Col Jocelyn Eustace Gurney, DSO, MC*, DL (d 1973), of Tacolneston Hall, and Sprowston, Norfolk; 2 s (William b 1980, Frederick b 1982), 1 da (Augusta b 1984); *Career* TA: cmmnd Wessex Yeo (Royal Glos Hussars) 1971, visiting lectr Jr Div Staff Coll 1978–79, Maj Royal Green Jackets 1981–90; publishing 1969–81; property mgmnt: Minories Hldgs Ltd and Watermen's Co 1981–91, Leeds Castle Kent 1992–2003; curatorial conslt Leeds Castle 2003–, expert adviser Nat Heritage Memorial Fund 2004–; tstee Chevening Estate 1992–2002, chm SE Region Historic Houses Assoc 1997–2001; tstee: Kent Gardens Tst 2004–, Kent People's Tst 2006–; High Sheriff Kent 2005–06; Hon Freeman Watermen's Co 1991; *Recreations* architectural and art history, country pursuits, gardening; *Style*— Andrew Wells, Esq, TD; ✉ Mere House, Mereworth, Maidstone, Kent ME18 5NB (website www.mere-house.co.uk)

WELLS, Boyan Stewart; s of Gordon Tebbutt Wells, of Bristol, and Vera, *née* Stanisic; *b* 3 June 1956; *Educ* Colston's Sch Bristol, Wadham Coll Oxford (MA, Hockey blue); *m* 11 Aug 1984, Alison Jayne, da of Michael Albert Good, of Bristol; 3 da (Holly Catharine b 8 May 1987, Elena Rose b 2 Dec 1988, Laura Elizabeth b 9 Dec 1994); *Career* ptnr Allen & Overy 1987– (joined 1979); Freeman: City of London, Worshipful Co of Slrs 1987; memb Law Soc; *Recreations* golf, cinema; *Clubs* Richmond Hockey, Dulwich Golf; *Style*— Boyan Wells, Esq; ✉ Allen & Overy, One Bishops Square, London E1 6AO (tel 020 3088 0000, fax 020 3088 0000)

WELLS, Dr Cecilia; OBE (1996); *Educ* Open Univ (BSc), Centre for Personal Construct Psychology (Dip), Royal Holloway Univ of London (PhD); *Career* various HR roles British Leyland 1972–81, UK recruitment and staff devpt mangr Manpower plc 1981–88, ind conslt in trg and HR mgmnt 1988–98, fndr dir Ionann Mgmnt Conslts Ltd 1998–99, dir and co-prop Astar Mgmnt Conslts Ltd 1999–; memb: Parole Bd for England and Wales 1988–94, Race Rels Advsy Gp DfEE 1990–96, Equal Opportunities Cmmn 1990–96, Ethnic Minorities Ctee Judicial Studies Bd 1992–96, Cncl ACAS 1992–2000 (actg chair 2000), Employee Rels Advsy Panel DTI 2001–, Bd Office of the Ind Adjudicator for HE 2005–, Bd Office of the Parly and Health Serv Ombudsman 2005–; ind assessor for public appts 2000–; arbitrator ACAS; vice-chair Centrepoint 1993–2007, chair Regnl Advsy Cncl BBC SE 1995–98, non-exec dir then vice-chair Bedford and Shires Community and Care Tst 1995–99; *Style*— Dr Cecilia Wells, OBE; ✉ Astar Management Consultants Limited, 6 Granary Buildings, Millow, Biggleswade, Bedfordshire SG18 8RH (tel 01767 310800, fax 01797 310808, e-mail ceciliawells@astarltd.co.uk)

WELLS, Sir Christopher Charles; 3 Bt (UK 1944), of Felmersham, Co Bedford; s Sir Charles Maltby Wells, 2 Bt, TD (d 1996), and Katharine Boulton, *née* Kenrick; *b* 12 August 1936; *Educ* McGill Univ Montreal, Univ of Toronto (MD); *m* 1, 1960 (m dis 1984), Elizabeth, da of I Griffiths, of Outrement, Quebec; 2 da (Felicity b 1964, Megan b 1969), 2 s (Michael b 1966, Geoffrey b 1970); m 2, 1985, Lynda Ann Cormack, of Toronto, Ontario; 1 s (Andrew b 1983); *Heir* s, Michael Wells; *Career* MD in family practice; *Style*— Sir Christopher Wells, Bt; ✉ 1268 Seaforth Crescent, R R Number 3, Lakefield, Ontario, K0L 2H0, Canada

WELLS, Prof David Arthur; s of Arthur William Wells (d 1993), of Lancing, West Sussex, and Rosina Elizabeth, *née* Jones (d 1986); *b* 26 April 1941; *Educ* Christ's Hosp, Gonville & Caius Coll Cambridge (MA, PhD); *Career* lectr in German: Univ of Southampton 1966–69, Bedford Coll London 1969–74; prof of German: The Queen's Univ of Belfast 1974–87, Birkbeck Coll London 1987–2006; hon treas Modern Humanities Res Assoc 2001– (hon sec 1969–2001); Int Fedn for Modern Languages and Literatures: sec-gen 1981–2005, pres 2005–; FRSA 1985; *Books* The Vorau Moses and Balaam (1970), The Wild Man from the Epic of Gilgamesh to Hartmann von Ave's Iwein (1975), A Complete Concordance to the Vorauer Bücher Moses (1976), The Years Work in Modern Language Studies (jt ed, 1976–), The Central Franconian Rhyming Bible (2004); *Recreations* travel; *Style*— Prof David Wells; ✉ School of Languages, Linguistics and Culture, Birkbeck College, Malet Street, London WC1E 7HX (tel 020 7631 6103, fax 020 7383 3729)

WELLS, David Patrick Casey; s of late Frank Wells, and Bridget Theresa, *née* Casey; *b* 24 November 1950; *Educ* St Joseph's Coll Blackpool, QMC London (LLB); *m* 28 Dec 1991, Michele Jane; 2 da (Holly, Hannah), 1 s (Samuel); *Career* admitted slr 1976; slr Herbert Smith 1976–81; ptnr: Reynolds Porter Chamberlain 1981–88, Titmuss Sainer & Webb (now Decherts) 1988–96, Beachcroft LLP (formerly Beachcroft Stanleys then Beachcroft Wansbroughs) 1996–; memb Law Soc; *Recreations* rugby (Blackheath), swimming, reading and family; *Style*— David Wells, Esq; ✉ Beachcroft LLP, 100 Fetter Lane, London EC4A 1BN

WELLS, Dean of; *see:* Clarke, Very Rev John Martin

WELLS, Prof George Albert; s of George J Wells (d 1960), and Lilian Maud, *née* Bird (d 1986); *b* 22 May 1926; *Educ* Stationers' Company's Sch, UCL (BA, MA, PhD, BSc); *m* 29 May 1969, Elisabeth, da of Franz Delhey, of Aachen; *Career* Nat Serv in coal mines 1944–45; lectr in German UCL 1949–64 (reader 1964–68), prof of German Birkbeck Coll London 1968–88; emeritus prof Univ of London 1988–; *Books* Herder and After (1959), The Plays of Grillparzer (1969), The Jesus of the Early Christians (1971), Goethe and the Development of Science (1978), The Historical Evidence for Jesus (1982), Did Jesus Exist? (1986), The Origin of Language: Aspects of the Discussion from Condillac to Wundt (1987), J M Robertson - Liberal, Rationalist and Scholar (ed, 1987), Religious Postures (1988), Who Was Jesus? - A Critique of the New Testament Record (1989), Belief and Make-Believe (1991), What's in a Name? Reflections on Language, Magic and Religion (1993), The Jesus Legend (1996), The Jesus Myth (1999), The Origin of Language (1999), Can We Trust the New Testament? Thoughts on the Reliability of Early Christian Testimony (2004); ed: C Lofmark: A History of the Red Dragon (1995), D F Strauss: The Old Faith and the New (1997); jt ed of three books by F R H Englefield: Language, Its Origin and Relation to Thought (1977), The Mind at Work and Play (1985), Critique of Pure Verbiage - Essays on Abuses of Language in Literary, Religious and Philosophical

W

Writing (1990); *Recreations* walking; *Style*— Prof George Wells; ✉ 35 St Stephens Avenue, St Albans, Hertfordshire AL3 4AA (tel 01727 851347)

WELLS, Graham Holland; s of Edmund Holland Wells, RD (d 1974), and Pamela Doris, *née* Siddall; *b* 28 May 1959; *Educ* Shrewsbury, BNC Oxford (MA); *m* 21 Jan 1984, Dr Susan Margaret Wells, da of James Edgar Riley Tompkin (d 2000), of Desford, Leics; *Career* called to the Bar Middle Temple 1982; memb: Personal Injuries Bar Assoc (PIBA), Professional Negligence Bar Assoc (PNBA); *Recreations* skiing, hill walking, watercolour and oil painting, kayaking; *Style*— Graham Wells, Esq; ✉ Oriel Chambers, 14 Water Street, Liverpool, Merseyside L2 8TD (tel 0151 236 7191, fax 0151 227 5909, e-mail clerks@oriel-chambers.co.uk)

WELLS, James Henry (Jim); MLA; s of Samuel Henry Wells, of Lurgan, Co Armagh, and Doreen, *née* Campbell; *b* 27 April 1957; *Educ* Lurgan Coll, Queen's Univ Belfast (BA Dip Town and Country Planning); *m* 26 July 1983, Grace, da of Sydney Wallace; 2 da, 1 s; *Career* memb NI Assembly 1982–86; asst regnl public affrs mangr Nat Tst 1989–98; MLA (DUP) S Down 1998–; sec DUP Assembly Gp; *Recreations* hill walking, bird watching; *Style*— Jim Wells, Esq, MLA; ✉ Parliament Buildings, Stormont, Belfast BT4 3XX (tel 02890 521110, mobile 07831 664908, e-mail jimwells7@aol.com)

WELLS, Prof John Christopher; s of Rev Philip Cuthbert Wells (d 1974), of Walton-on-Trent, and Winifred May, *née* Peaker (d 1997); *b* 11 March 1939; *Educ* St John's Sch Leatherhead, Trinity Coll Cambridge (BA), UCL (MA, PhD); *Partner* Gabriel Parsons (civil partnership, 2006); *Career* UCL: asst lectr in phonetics 1962–65, lectr 1965–82, reader 1982–88, prof 1988–2006, emeritus prof 2006–; former pres World Esperanto Assoc, pres Esperanto Assoc of GB 2004–, pres Int Phonetic Assoc 2003–, pres Simplified Spelling Soc 2003–; FBA 1996; *Books* Teach Yourself Concise Esperanto Dictionary (1969), Practical Phonetics (1971), Jamaican Pronunciation in London (1973), Accents of English (1982), Longman Pronunciation Dictionary (1990, 2 edn 2000), English Intonation: An introduction (2006); *Style*— Prof J C Wells, FBA; ✉ Department of Phonetics & Linguistics, University College, Gower Street, London WC1E 6BT (tel 020 8542 0302, fax 020 7383 4108, e-mail j.wells@ucl.ac.uk, website www.phon.ucl.ac.uk/home/wells)

WELLS, Malcolm Henry Weston; s of Lt Cdr Geoffrey Weston Wells (d 1988), and Inez Brenda, *née* Williams (d 1967); *b* 26 July 1927; *Educ* Eton; *m* 20 Dec 1952, (Helen) Elizabeth Agnes, da of Rt Rev Bishop Maurice Henry Harland (d 1986); 1 s (Nicholas Weston b 1954), 1 da (Caroline Felicity b 1956); *Career* RNVR 1945–48; Peat Marwick Mitchell 1948–58 (articled clerk, latterly asst mangr), Siebe plc 1958–63 (sec, latterly md); dir: Charterhouse Japhet plc 1963–73 (chm 1973–80), Charterhouse Gp 1964–80 (joined 1963), Civil Aviation Authy 1974–77; chm: Charterhouse Petroleum plc 1977–82, BWD Securities plc 1987–95, German Securities Investment Tst plc 1985–89; dir: Bank in Liechtenstein Ltd 1981–90 (London rep, latterly md), Carclo Engineering Group plc 1982–97, Nat Home Loans Holdings plc 1989–93; memb Solicitors Disciplinary Tbnl 1975–81; *Recreations* sailing; *Clubs* Hurlingham, West Wittering Sailing; *Style*— M H W Wells, Esq; ✉ Willow Cottage, 19 The Wad, West Wittering, Chichester PO20 8AH (tel 01243 514421)

WELLS, Prof Michael; s of John Thomas Wells (d 1975), of Cannock, Staffs, and Lily, *née* Ellis; *b* 7 August 1952; *Educ* Pool Hayes Sch Willenhall, Univ of Manchester (BSc, MB ChB, MD); *m* 1, 21 Dec 1974 (m dis 1992), Jane Cecila, da of John Parker Gill, of Gosforth, Cumbria; 1 s (James b 1980), 1 da (Rosemary b 1982); m 2, 27 May 1994, Lynne Margaret Austerberry, da of Raymond George Walker, of Blythe Bridge, Staffs; *Career* lectr in pathology Univ of Bristol 1978–79, sr lectr in pathology Univ of Leeds 1988–93 (lectr 1980–88); hon conslt United Leeds Teaching Hosps NHS Trust 1983–93; clinical sub dean: Leeds West Univ of Leeds Sch of Med 1988–91, St James's Univ Hosp 1994–96; hon conslt pathologist St James's Univ Hosp Leeds 1993–96, ptnr Roundhay Pathologists (BUPA Hosp) Leeds 1993–96; prof of gynaecological pathology: Univ of Leeds 1993–96, Univ of Sheffield Med Sch 1997– (dir of studies phase 3A 2006–); hon conslt histopathologist Central Sheffield Univ Hosps 1997–; external examiner in pathology Univ of Manchester 1995–99, external examiner in pathology Univ of Cambridge 2000 and 2002; conslt and memb Med Advsy Bd PathLore Ltd 2001– (dir (gynaecological pathology) 2001–06); memb: Assoc of Clinical Pathologists Speciality Ctee on Histopathology 1989–93, Part 1 MCQ Sub-Ctee RCOG 1989–95, Cncl Br Gynaecological Cancer Soc 1990–92 (pres 1994–97), Editorial Advsy Bd Placenta 1990–95, Kliofem Steering Ctee Novo Nordisk Pharmaceuticals Ltd 1990–, Exec Ctee Int Soc of Gynecological Pathologists 1991–94 (pres 2003–), Sub-Ctee for the Co-ordination of Research into Gynaecological Cancer of the UK Co-ordinating Ctee on Cancer Research 1991–98, Jt RCOG/Wellbeing Research Advsy Ctee 1996–98, Exec Ctee European Soc of Pathology 2004–, Panel of Examiners in Histopathology RCPath; memb Editorial Bd: Int Jl of Gynecological Pathology (assoc ed 1998–2003), Jl of Pathology 1998–2002, Virchows Archiv 2002–, Gynecol Oncol 2005–; ed Histopathology 2003–, assoc ed Papillomavirus Report 1990–93; hon sec Br Div of the Int Acad of Pathology 1988–93, meetings sec Pathological Soc of GB and I 1996–2000 (gen sec 2000–03); FRCPath 1995 (MRCPath 1983, memb Cncl 1998–2001), FRCOG (ad eundem) 2004; *Publications* Haines and Taylor Obstetrical and Gynaecological Pathology (asst ed, 4 edn, 1995; co-ed, 5 edn, 2003); author/co-author of approx 200 chapters, review articles and original papers, numerous invited lectures nationally and internationally incl 2 George Cunningham Lecture Br Div of the Int Acad of Pathology Glasgow (2007); *Recreations* reading, choral singing, skiing, gardening; *Clubs* Athenaeum; *Style*— Prof Michael Wells; ✉ Woodend, 57 Ranmoor Crescent, Sheffield S10 3GW (tel 0114 230 8260, fax 0114 229 5013, mobile 07791 192548); Pathology, The University of Sheffield Medical School, Beech Hill Road, Sheffield S10 2RX (tel 0114 271 2397, fax 0114 226 1464, e-mail m.wells@sheffield.ac.uk)

WELLS, Michael Frederick; s of Frederick William Wells (d1983), of Chislehurst, Kent, and Victoria, *née* Priddis (d 1942); *b* 2 August 1938, Chislehurst, Kent; *Educ* Chislehurst and Sidcup Co GS, South Devon Technical Coll; *m* 28 July 1966, (Margaret) Ann, *née* Stephens; 2 s (Ian Michael b 25 April 1967, Neil Stephen b 11 June 1968); *Career* Nat Serv RAF (Kai Tak, Hong Kong) 1957–59; admin asst Royal Festival Hall 1959–63, asst mangr then mangr Mayfair Hotel Durban SA 1966–68, hotel mgmnt North Trust Hotels Edinburgh 1968–71, dir and gen mangr Coral Island Hotel Co Bermuda 1971–74, gen mangr and dir North British Trust Hotels 1974–79; M F Wells (Hotels) Ltd: dir and shareholder 1979–, chm 2004–; fell Inst of Hotel Keeping and Catering 1966; *Publications* Walking from Lochs and Glens Hotels (2005); *Recreations* hill walking, cycling, garden railways; *Style*— Michael Wells, Esq; ✉ M F Wells (Hotels) Ltd, School Road, Gartocharn, Dunbartonshire G83 8RW (tel 01389 713713, fax 01389 713700, e-mail enquiries@lochsandglens.com, website www.lochsandglens.com)

WELLS, Prof Peter Neil Temple; s of Sydney Parker Temple Wells (d 1976), and Elizabeth Beryl Wells (d 1987); *b* 19 May 1936; *Educ* Clifton, Aston Univ (BSc), Univ of Bristol (MSc, PhD, DSc); *m* 15 Oct 1960, Valerie Elizabeth, da of Charles Edward Johnson (d 1982), of Burnham-on-Sea, Somerset; 3 s (Andrew b 1963, Alexander b 1965, Thomas b 1970), 1 da (Lucy b 1966); *Career* res asst United Bristol Hosps 1960–71, prof of med physics Welsh Nat Sch of Med (now Cardiff Univ) 1972–74, area physicist Avon AHA (teaching) 1975–82; chief physicist: Bristol and Weston HA 1982–91, United Bristol Healthcare NHS Tst 1991–2001; Univ of Bristol: hon prof in clinical radiology 1986–2000, hon dir Centre for Physics and Engrg Res in Med 1996–2000, prof of physics and engrg in med 2000–01, emeritus prof of physics and engrg in med 2001–; distinguished research prof Cardiff Univ 2004–; over 300 pubns mainly on med applications of ultrasonics, ed-in-chief Ultrasound in Med and Biology 1992–2006; former pres: Br Inst of Radiology, Br Med Ultrasound Soc, Instn of Physics and Engrg in Med; vice-pres World Fedn for Ultrasound in Med and Biology; Hon DTech Univ of Lund, Hon MD Erasmus Univ; FInstP 1970, FIET (FIEE 1978), FREng 1983, Hon FRCR 1987, Hon FIPEM 1988, ARCP 2000, FRS 2003, FMedSci 2005; *Books* Physical Principles of Ultrasonic Diagnosis (1969), Ultrasonics in Clinical Diagnosis (1972, 3 edn 1983), Biomedical Ultrasonics (1977), Computers in Ultrasonic Diagnostics (1977), New Techniques and Instrumentation in Ultrasonography (1980), Scientific Basis of Medical Imaging (1982), Emerging Technologies in Surgery (1984), Clinical Applications of Doppler Ultrasound (1988, 2 edn 1995), Advances in Ultrasound Imaging and Instrumentation (1993), The Perception of Visual Information (1993, 2 edn 1997), The Invisible Light (1995); *Style*— Prof Peter Wells, FRS, FREng, FMedSci; ✉ Institute of Medical Engineering and Medical Physics, School of Engineering, Cardiff University, Queen's Buildings, The Parade, Cardiff CF24 3AA (tel 029 2087 4154, e-mail wellspn@cf.ac.uk)

WELLS, Prof Stanley William; CBE (2007); s of Stanley Cecil Wells, MBE (d 1952), of Hull, and Doris, *née* Atkinson (d 1986); *b* 21 May 1930; *Educ* Kingston HS Hull, UCL (BA), The Shakespeare Inst Univ of Birmingham (PhD); *m* 23 April 1975, Susan Hill, the novelist, *qv*; 3 da (Jessica b 1977, Imogen b and d 1984, Clemency b 1985); *Career* Nat Serv RAF 1951 (invalided out); Shakespeare Inst: fell 1962–77, lectr 1962, sr lectr 1971, reader 1973–77, hon fell 1979–88 and 1998–; prof of Shakespeare studies and dir Shakespeare Inst Univ of Birmingham 1988–97 (emeritus prof 1997–); conslt in Eng Wroxton Coll 1964–80, head of Shakespeare Dept OUP 1978–88, sr research fell Balliol Coll Oxford 1980–88, fell UCL 1994; dir Royal Shakespeare Theatre Summer Sch 1971–99, pres Shakespeare Club of Stratford-upon-Avon 1972–73; chm Int Shakespeare Assoc 1991–2000; memb: Exec Ctee Shakespeare's Birthplace 1976–78 and 1988– (tstee 1975–81 and 1984–, dep chm 1990, chm 1991–); Royal Shakespeare Co: govr 1974–, memb Exec Ctee 1976–2003, chm Membership Ctee 1991–2001, chm Collections Ctee 1991–2000, vice-chm Bd of Govrs 1991–2003, hon govr emeritus 2003–; guest lectr at Br and overseas univs, Br Acad Annual Shakespeare lectr 1987, Br Cncl Melchiori lecture Rome 1991; govr King Edward VI GS for Boys 1973–77; assoc ed New Penguin Shakespeare 1967– (gen ed 2004–), gen ed Oxford Shakespeare 1978–, ed Shakespeare Survey 1980–99; author of contribs to: Shakespeare Survey, Shakespeare Quarterly, Shakespeare Jahrbuch, Theatre Notebook, Stratford-upon-Avon Studies, TLS, and others; Hon DLitt Furman Univ 1976, Hon DPhil University of Munich 1999, Hon DLitt Univ of Hull 2005; memb: Soc for Theatre Research 1963–, Cncl Malone Soc 1967–90, tstee Rose Theatre 1991–, dir Globe Theatre Tst 1990– (tstee 1998–2003); Walford Prize (for sustained contribs to bibliography) Library Assoc 1994; Hon DLitt Univ of Durham 2005; *Books* Thomas Nashe, Selected Writings (ed, 1964), A Midsummer Night's Dream (ed, 1967), Richard II (ed, 1969), Shakespeare, A Reading Guide (1969 and 1970), Literature and Drama (1970, reprinted 2004), The Comedy of Errors (ed, 1972), Shakespeare (ed 1973, 2 edn 1990), English Drama Excluding Shakespeare (ed, 1975), Royal Shakespeare (1977 and 1978), Nineteenth Century Burlesques (compiled in 5 vols, 1977, reprinted 2004), Shakespeare: An Illustrated Dictionary (1978 and 1985), Shakespeare: The Writer and his Work (1978), Thomas Dekker, The Shoemaker's Holiday (ed with RL Smallwood, 1979), Modernizing Shakespeare's Spelling, with Three Studies in the Text of Henry V (with Gary Taylor, 1979), Re-editing Shakespeare for the Modern Reader (1984), Shakespeare's Sonnets (ed, 1985), The Complete Oxford Shakespeare (ed with Gary Taylor *et al*, 1986), The Cambridge Companion to Shakespeare Studies (ed, 1986), William Shakespeare: A Textual Companion (with Gary Taylor *et al*, 1987), An Oxford Anthology of Shakespeare (1987), Shakespeare: A Dramatic Life (1994), Shakespeare and the Moving Image (ed, with E A Davies, 1994), Twelfth Night (ed, with Roger Warren, 1994), Shakespeare in the Theatre: An Anthology of Criticism (ed, 1997), The Oxford Dictionary of Shakespeare (1998), King Lear (ed, 2000), The Cambridge Companion to Shakespeare (ed, with Margreta da Grazia, 2001), The Oxford Companion to Shakespeare (ed, with Michael Dobson, 2001), Shakespeare: For All Time (2002), Looking for Sex in Shakespeare (2004), Shakespeare's Sonnets (with Paul Edmondson, 2004), Shakespeare & Co (2006), Is It True What They Say About Shakespeare? (2007), Coffee with Shakespeare (with Paul Edmondson, 2008); *Recreations* music, theatre, travel; *Style*— Prof Stanley Wells, CBE; ✉ Longmoor, Ebrington, Chipping Campden, Gloucestershire GL55 6NW (tel 01386 593352, fax 01386 593443); The Shakespeare Centre, Stratford upon Avon, Warwickshire (tel 01789 201828, e-mail stanley.wells@shakespeare.org.uk)

WELLS, Sir William Henry Weston; kt (1997); s of Sir Henry Wells, CBE (d 1970), and Rosemary Halliday, *née* Whitchurch (d 1977); *b* 3 May 1940; *Educ* Radley, Magdalene Coll Cambridge (BA); *m* 1 Jan 1966, Penelope Jean, da of Col R B Broadbent (d 1979); 3 s (Rupert d 1969, George b 1971, Henry b 1972); *Career* pres Chesterton International plc 1998–2005 (ptnr 1965–88, chm 1984–98); chm: Land and House Property Group 1977 (dir 1972–76), Frincon Holdings Ltd 1977–87, CMG Ltd 2007–, Ashley House plc 2007–, Pure Sports Medicine Ltd 2007–; dir: London Life Association 1984–89, Pearl Group Ltd 1994–2005, AMP (UK) plc 1994–2003, Norwich & Peterborough Building Society 1994–2003, NFC plc 1996–2000, AMP (UK) Holdings 1997–2003, NPI Ltd 1999–2005, Nat Provident Life Ltd 1999–2005, Exel plc 2000–05, HHG plc 2003–05, SQW Gp 2006–, Arc Fund Mgmnt plc 2006–; pres Royal Free Hosp Retirement Fellowship 1994–; chm: Special Tstees of the Royal Free Hosps 1979–2001, Hampstead HA 1982–90, Royal Free Hampstead NHS Tst 1990–94, South Thames NHS Exec 1996–99, NHS Appts Cmmn 2001–07, Commercial Advsy Bd Dept of Health 2003–, Covenant Healthcare; regnl chm: S Thames RHA 1994–96, S E NHS Exec 1999–2001; memb Bd of Govrs: Royal Free Hosp 1968–74, Camden and Islington AHA 1974–82; memb Cncl: Royal Free Hosp Sch of Med 1977–91, NHS Tst Fedn 1991–93 (vice-chm 1992–93), UMDS of Guy's and St Thomas' Hosps 1994–98, St George's Hosp Med Sch 1994–98, KCL 1998–2001, City Univ 1999–2000, Priory of England and the Islands 2000–02; Univ of Surrey: memb Cncl 1998 vice-chm Cncl 1999–2000, chm Cncl 2001–06; memb Delagacy King's Coll Sch of Med and Dentistry 1994–98, memb Kings Fund Cncl and Mgmnt Ctee 1995–; tstee Nat Museum of Science and Industry 2003–; vice-pres Royal Coll of Nursing 2005– (hon treas 1988–2005), vice-pres Accord 2006–, hon treas Nat Assoc Hosp and Community Friends 1992–2003; FRICS; Hon FRCP 2002; *Recreations* family, philately, gardening; *Clubs* Boodle's; *Style*— Sir William Wells

WELLWOOD, James McKinney; s of James Wellwood (d 1967), of Belfast, and Violet Armstrong McKinney (d 1978); *b* 18 December 1940; *Educ* Fettes, Univ of Cambridge, St Thomas' Hosp Med Sch London; *m* 1, 8 March 1975, Frances Alexandria Ruth, da of Stephen Howard, of Herts; m 2, 24 July 1982, Anne Margaret, da of Sydney Jones Samuel, of Llanelli, Wales; 1 s (James b 1984), 1 da (Laura b 1988); *Career* conslt surgn Whipps Cross Hosp Leytonstone London 1979, hon sr lectr Med Coll of St Bartholomew Smithfield London 1979, clinical tutor Waltham Forest Dist 1983–91, clinical dir of surgery Whipps Cross Hosp 1991–2000; Br delg European Soc of Surgical Oncology 1986–90, hon overseas sec Br Assoc of Surgical Oncology 1986–91 (hon sec 1982–86); memb: Educn Advsy Ctee Assoc of Surgns of GB and Ireland 1987–90, Waltham Forest DHA 1983–90, UK Cncl Assoc of Endoscopic Surgns of GB and I 1994–99; hon fell Friends Med Centre Med Research, Training and Science Organisation India 1996–; Queen's Commendation for Brave Conduct 1971; Liveryman Worshipful Soc of Apothecaries; *Recreations* skiing, shooting, travel; *Clubs* Athenaeum, Royal Soc of Medicine; *Style*— James Wellwood, Esq; ✉ 50 Clifton Hill, St John's Wood, London NW8 0QG (tel 020 7625 5697); Whipps Cross Hospital, Leytonstone, London E11 1NR (tel 020 8539 5522); 134 Harley Street, London W1N 1AH (tel 020 7487 4212)

WELSBY, John Kay; CBE (1990); *b* 26 May 1938; *Educ* Univ of Exeter (BA), Univ of London (MSc); *m* 1964, Jill Carole Richards; 1 s, 1 da; *Career* Govt Economic Serv 1966–81; British Railways Bd: dir Provincial Services 1981–83, dir Mfrg and Maintenance Policy 1984–86, md Procurement and Special Projects 1986–87, memb Bd 1987–, chief exec 1990–95, chm 1995–99; dir London and Continental Railways Ltd 1999–; past pres CILT; Freeman City of London 1992, Liveryman Worshipful Co of Carmen 1992; CIMgt 1991, FCIT (chm); *Recreations* walking, music, swimming; *Style—* John Welsby, Esq, CBE; ✉ Higher Burston Farm, Bow, Crediton, Devon EX17 6LB (tel and fax 01363 881006)

WELSH, Andrew Paton; MSP; s of William Welsh (d 1979), and Agnes Paton, *née* Reid (d 1977); *b* 19 April 1944; *Educ* Govan HS, Univ of Glasgow (MA, Dip Ed, Dip French); *m* 21 Nov 1971, Sheena Margaret, da of Douglas Henry Cannon (d 1972); 1 da (Jane b 1980); *Career* Parly candidate (SNP): Dumbarton Central Feb 1974, Angus E 1983; MP (SNP): Angus S Oct 1974–1979, Angus E 1987–97, Angus 1997–2001; MSP (SNP) Angus 1999–; SNP chief Parly whip 1978–79 and 1987–99; SNP spokesman on: small businesses and self employment 1975–79 and 1987–97, housing and agric 1974–79 and 1987–97, housing 1997–2001, educn 1997–2001, local govt 1997–2001; memb: Speaker's Panel 1997–2001, Scottish Parly Corp Body, Ctee of Scot Parly Conveners 1999–, Scottish Cmmn for Public Audit 2000–; memb Parly Select Ctee on: Members' Interests 1990–92, Scottish Affairs 1992–2001; Scottish Parl: chm Audit Ctee 1999–2003 (memb 2007–), dep convenor Local Govt and Tport Ctee 2003–04, dep convenor Audit Ctee 2004–07, convenor All Party Gp on Tartan Day 2005–, convenor Finance Ctee 2007–; SNP: exec vice-chm (admin) 1979–82, exec vice-chm (local govt) 1983–86, vice-pres 1987–2004; lectr in public admin and economics Dundee Coll of Commerce 1979–83, sr lectr in business and admin studies Angus Coll of Further Educn 1983–87; memb Stirling DC 1974, memb and provost Angus DC 1984–87; *Recreations* music, horse riding, languages; *Style—* Andrew Welsh, Esq, MSP; ✉ The Scottish Parliament Office, 31 Market Place, Arbroath DD11 1HR (tel 01241 439369, fax 01241 871561); The Scottish Parliament, Edinburgh EH99 1SP (tel 0131 348 5690, fax 0131 348 5677, e-mail andrew.welsh.msp@scottish.parliament.uk)

WELSH, Prof (James Anthony) Dominic; s of James Welsh (d 1967), of Port Talbot, and Teresa, *née* O'Callaghan (d 1996); *b* 29 August 1938; *Educ* Bishop Gore Sch Swansea, Merton Coll Oxford (exhibitioner, MA, DPhil), Carnegie Mellon Univ PA (Fulbright scholar); *m* 1965, Bridget Elizabeth, da of Very Rev John Francis Pratt; 3 s (James Justin Siderfin b 16 June 1967, Simon David Patrick b 19 Nov 1969, John Francis b 3 Oct 1971 d 1990); *Career* research Bell Telephone Labs Murray Hill NJ 1961; Univ of Oxford: lectr Mathematical Inst 1966–90 (jr lectr 1963–66), tutor in mathematics Merton Coll 1966–90, fell Merton Coll 1966–2005 (emeritus fell 2005–), chm Faculty of Mathematics 1976–78, chm Faculty Bd of Mathematics 1984–86, ad hominem reader in mathematical scis 1990–92, ad hominem prof of mathematics 1992–2005, chm of mathematics 1996–2001; research visitor Univ of Michigan 1968, visiting prof Univ of Waterloo 1969, visiting prof Univ of Calgary 1974, John von Neumann prof Univ of Bonn 1990–91, visiting Oxford fell Univ of Canterbury NZ 2005, research visitor CRM Barcelona 2006–07; chm Br Combinatorial Soc 1983–87, memb London Mathematical Soc 1964 (memb Cncl 1972–76); Hon DMath Univ of Waterloo 2006; *Books* Matroid Theory (1976), Probability; an Introduction (with G R Grimmett, 1986), Codes and Cryptography (1988), Complexity: Knots Colourings and Counting (1993), Complexity and Cryptology: An Introduction (with J Talbot, 2006); *Recreations* most sports, art, walking; *Style—* Prof Dominic J A Welsh; ✉ Merton College, Oxford OX1 4JD (tel 01865 276310); Mathematical Institute, 24–26 St Giles, Oxford OX1 3LB (tel 01865 276325, fax 01865 276383, e-mail dwelsh@maths.ox.ac.uk)

WELSH, John Christopher; s of Thomas A Welsh, and Mary, *née* Croker, of Cumbria; *b* 29 March 1962; *Educ* William Ellis Sch, Ulverston Victoria HS, Sedbergh Coll, Univ of Durham; *Career* draughtsman Brian Clouston & Ptnrs 1984–87, asst ed Designers' Jl 1987–89, buildings ed Building Design 1990–93 (features writer 1989–90); ed: RIBA Jl 1993–99, Property Week 1999–2003, Travel Trade Gazette 2003–; memb: Editorial and Public Affrs Ctee PPA, Educn and Training Ctee ITT; *Books* Rick Mather's Zen Restaurants (1992), Massimiliano Fuksas (1994), Modern house (1995), Cees Dam (2000); *Style—* John Welsh, Esq; ✉ Travel Trade Gazette, 7th Floor, Ludgate House, 245 Blackfriars Road, London SE1 9UY (tel 020 7921 8012, e-mail jwelsh@cmpinformation.com)

WELSH, Michael John; s of Cdr David Welsh, RN; *b* 22 May 1942; *Educ* Dover Coll, Lincoln Coll Oxford; *m* 1963, Jennifer Pollitt; 1 s, 1 da; *Career* formerly with Levi Strauss & Co Europe (dir of market devpt 1976); MEP (Cons) Lancs Central 1979–94; chm Chorley and Dist NHS Tst 1994–98, chief exec Action Centre for Europe Ltd 1995–2004; currently co cncllr Lancs (ldr Cons Gp 2003–); *Books* Labour Market Policy In The European Community - The British Presidency (1987), Collective Security - The European Community and the Preservation of Peace (1988), German Unification - The Challenge of Assimilation (1990), Accountability - The Role of Westminster and the European Institutions (1990), Europe United? The European Community and the retreat from Federalism (1995); *Clubs* Carlton; *Style—* Michael Welsh, Esq; ✉ Watercrook, 181 Town Lane, Whittle le Woods, Chorley, Lancashire PR6 8AG (tel 01257 276992, fax 01257 231254)

WEMYSS AND MARCH, 12 (and 8) Earl of (S 1633 & 1697); Francis David Charteris; KT (1966), JP (E Lothian); also Lord Wemyss of Elcho (S 1628), Lord Elcho and Methil (S 1633), Viscount Peebles, Lord Douglas of Neidpath, Lyne, and Munard (S 1697), and Baron Wemyss of Wemyss (UK 1821); s of Lord Elcho (ka 1916, s and h of 11 Earl, but predeceased him) and Lady Violet Manners (d 1971), 2 da of 8 Duke of Rutland; suc gf 1937; bro of late Baron Charteris of Amisfield, GCB, GCVO, QSO, OBE, PC; *b* 19 January 1912; *Educ* Eton, Balliol Coll Oxford, Trinity Coll Cambridge; *m* 1, 24 Feb 1940, Mavis Lynette Gordon (d 1988), er da of Edwin Edward Murray, of Hermanus, South Africa; 1 s, 1 da (and 1 s, 1 da decd); *m* 2, 29 April 1995, Mrs Shelagh Kathleen Kennedy, da of George Ernest Thrift, of Vancouver, Canada, and formerly Nat Tst for Scotland rep; *Heir* s, Lord Neidpath, *qv*; *Career* Basutoland Admin Serv 1937–44 (war serv with Basuto troops ME 1941–44); landowner; former dir: Standard Life Assurance, Scottish Television; conslt Wemyss and March Estate Mgmnt Co Ltd; chm: Nat Trust for Scotland 1946–67 (pres 1967–91, pres emeritus 1991–); chm Royal Cmmn on Ancient and Historic Monuments and Constructions of Scotland 1949–84, Lord High Cmmr to Gen Assembly of Church of Scotland 1959, 1960 and 1977, pres Nat Bible Soc of Scotland 1962–83, HM Lord-Lt E Lothian 1976–87, Lord Clerk Register of Scotland and Keeper of the Signet 1974–, Lt Queen's Body Guard for Scotland (Royal Co of Archers (on inactive list 1997)), hon pres The Thistle Fndn; Hon LLD Univ of St Andrews 1953, Hon DUniv Edinburgh 1983; *Clubs* New (Edinburgh); *Style—* The Rt Hon the Earl of Wemyss and March, KT; ✉ Gosford House, Longniddry, East Lothian EH32 0PX (tel 01875 870200, fax 01875 870376)

WEN, Eric Lewis; s of Adam Kung Wen, of California, and Mimi, *née* Seetoo; *b* 18 May 1953; *Educ* Dalton Sch, Columbia Univ (BA), Yale Univ (MPhil), Churchill Coll Cambridge (res award); *m* 3 June 1989, Louise Anne, da of Sir Brian Barder, KCMG; 2 da (Lily Havala b 5 Nov 1990, Florence Lydia b 26 May 1993); *Career* lectr in music: Yale Univ 1977–78, Guildhall Sch of Music and Drama 1978–84, Goldsmiths Coll London 1980–84, Mannes Coll of Music 1984–86; ed: The Strad 1986–89, The Musical Times 1988–90; md Biddulph Recordings and Publishing 1990–; *Books* Schenker Studies (contrib, 1990), Trends in Schenkerian Research (contrib, 1990), The Cambridge Companion to the Violin (contrib, 1992), Giuseppe Guarneri del Gesù (contrib, 1998); *Publications* The Heifetz Collection (ed, 1995); *Recreations* chess, cookery, film, card magic; *Style—* Eric Wen, Esq; ✉ 34 St George Street, Hanover Square, London W1R 0ND (tel 020 7491 8621, fax 020 7495 1428)

WENBAN-SMITH, Hugh Boyd; s of late William Wenban-Smith, CBE, CMG, of Lymington, Hants, and Ruth Orme, *née* McElderry; *b* 6 November 1941; *Educ* Bradfield Coll, King's Coll Cambridge (open minor scholar, MA), UCL (MSc); *Career* Miny of Fin then Bank of Zambia (ODI/Nuffield Fellowship Scheme) Zambia 1964–67, NIESR 1967–68, econ advsr on progs in E Africa Miny of Overseas Devpt 1968–70, seconded to FCO as first sec to British High Cmmn New Delhi India 1970–74, econ advsr on steel, shipbuilding and rescue cases DTI 1975–77, sr econ advsr Price Cmmn 1977–79, seconded to Coopers and Lybrands Assocs 1979–80, head Water Fin and Econs Div DOE 1980–84; Dept of Environment Tport & the Regions: dir fin mgmnt 1984–89, under sec and head Marine Directorate 1989–93, head Civil Aviation Directorate 1993–95, dir Nat Roads Policy 1996–98; *Style—* Hugh Wenban-Smith, Esq

WENDT, Robin Glover; CBE (1996), DL (Cheshire 1990); s of William Romilly Wendt (d 1995), of Keswick, Cumbria, and Doris May, *née* Glover (d 1958); *b* 7 January 1941; *Educ* Hutton GS, Wadham Coll Oxford (MA); *m* 1965, Prudence Ann, da of Arthur Dalby; 2 da (Julia Margaret b 1967, Catherine Susan b 1970); *Career* asst princ Miny of Pensions and Nat Insurance 1962–65, princ Miny of Social Security/DHSS 1965–72 (princ private sec 1970–72), asst sec DHSS 1972–75, chief exec Cheshire CC 1979–89 (dep sec 1975–79), sec Assoc of County Councils 1989–97, chief exec Nat Assoc of Local Cncls 1997–99; clerk Cheshire Lieutenancy 1979–90; vice-pres Cheshire Magistrates Assoc 1990–, tstee Independent Living Funds 1993–2001; pres Cheshire Assoc of Parish Cncls 1997–2004; memb: Soc of Local Authy Chief Execs 1979–97, Advsy Ctee Social Security 1982–2002, Poly and Colls Funding Cncl 1988–93, Bd Funding Agency for Schs 1997–99, Cncl NCH 1997– (vice-chair 2000–), Royal Cmmn on Long-Term Care of the Elderly 1997–99, South Cheshire HA 2001–02; vice-chair Cheshire and Merseyside Strategic HA 2002–04; non-exec dir Nimtech 2000–; chair: Cheshire Rural Forum 2000–05, Chester in Partnership 2001–06, Bd of Chester Summer Music Festival 2001–, Bd Chester Festival 2003–05; sec NW Says No Campaign 2003–04; *Recreations* swimming, travel, music, following sport, gardening, journalism; *Style—* Robin Wendt, Esq, CBE, DL; ✉ 28 Church Lane, Upton, Chester CH2 1DJ (tel 01244 382786)

WENGER, Arsène; *b* 22 October 1949; *Educ* Strasbourg Univ; *Career* footballer and coach; player: Mutzig, Mulhouse, Strasbourg (French League Champions 1979); mangr: AS Nancy 1984–87, AS Monaco 1987–94 (French League Champions 1988, winners French Cup 1991), Grampus 8 Japan 1995–96 (Emperor's Cup winners 1995, Super Cup winners 1996), Arsenal FC 1996– (winners FA Premier League 1998, 2002 and 2004 (record for remaining unbeaten during season), FA Cup 1998, 2002, 2003 and 2005 (finalists 2001), finalists UEFA Champions League 2006); Manager of the Year: France 1988, England 1998, 2002 and 2004; *Style—* Arsene Wenger, Esq; ✉ c/o Arsenal FC, Highbury House, 75 Drayton Park, London N5 1BU (tel 020 7704 4000, website www.arsenal.com)

WENSLEY, Prof (John) Robin Clifton; s of Maj George Leonard Wensley (d 1998), and Jeanette Marion, *née* Robbins, of Cambridge; *b* 26 October 1944; *Educ* Perse Sch Cambridge, Univ of Cambridge (BA), London Business Sch (MSc, PhD); *m* 19 Dec 1970, Susan Patricia, da of Kenneth Royden Horner (d 1975), and Irene Lucy Horner; 2 da (Helen Rebecca b 1973, Ruth Elizabeth b 1975), 1 s (Benjamin Royden b 1978); *Career* brand mangr Rank Hovis McDougall 1966–69 (former PA), consIt Tube Investments Ltd 1971–73, asst dir of Studies Ashridge Coll 1973–74, sr lectr London Business Sch 1974–85 (former lectr); Warwick Business Sch: prof of strategic mgmnt and mktg 1985–, chm 1989–94, chm Faculty of Social Studies 1997–99, dep dean 2001–04; dir Advanced Inst of Mgmnt Research 2004–; sometime visiting prof: UCLA, Univ of Florida; dir BRL Ltd 1987–; chm Cncl Tavistock Inst of Human Relations 1998–2004 (memb 1992–2004); jt chair Assoc of Business Schs 1993–94; memb: UK Foresight Panel for the Construction Industry 1996–98, Built Environment and Transport Panel 1999–2001, Cncl ESRC 2001– (memb Research Grants Bd 1993–96); *Books* Marketing Strategy: Planning, Implementation and Control (1986), Readings in Marketing Strategy (1989), Interface of Marketing and Strategy (1990), Rethinking Marketing (1998), Handbook of Marketing (2002); *Recreations* badminton, gardening, DIY; *Style—* Prof Robin Wensley; ✉ Warwick Business School, University of Warwick, Coventry CV4 7AL (tel 024 7652 3923, fax 024 7652 4628, e-mail robin.wensley@warwick.ac.uk)

WENT, David; s of Arthur Edward James Went (d 1980), of Dublin, and Phyllis, *née* Howell (d 1980); *b* 25 March 1947; *Educ* High Sch Dublin, Trinity Coll Dublin (BA, LLB); *m* 4 Nov 1972, Mary, da of Jack Milligan (d 1972), of Belfast; 1 s (James b 1976), 1 da (Kate b 1978); *Career* barr King's Inn Dublin; gen mangr Citibank Dublin 1974 (Jeddah 1975), banking dir Ulster Investment Bank Dublin 1976 (chief exec 1982); chief exec: Ulster Bank 1988–94, Coutts Group 1994–97; md Irish Life 1998–99, ceo Irish Life & Permanent 1999–2007; FIBI 1978; *Recreations* tennis, reading; *Clubs* Royal North of Ireland Yacht, Kildare St and Univ (Dublin), Fitzwilliam Lawn Tennis; *Style—* David Went, Esq

WENT, Rt Rev John Stewart; *see:* Tewkesbury, Bishop of

WENTWORTH, Richard; *b* 1947, Samoa; *Educ* Hornsey Coll of Art London, RCA (MA); *Career* artist/sculptor; worked with Henry Moore 1967, teacher Goldsmiths Coll London 1971–88, latterly worked and lived NYC; Ruskin master of drawing Univ of Oxford 2002–; author of numerous articles, essays and lectures; Mark Rothko Meml award 1974; *Solo Exhibitions* Greewich Theatre Gallery London 1972, Various Drawings Greewich Theatre Gallery 1973, Istalment Artnet London 1975, Felicity Samuel Gallery London 1975, La Sala Vincon Barcelona 1975–76, Lisson Gallery London 1984, Galerie 't Venster Rotterdam 1984, Galeri Lang Malmo 1986, Riverside Studios London 1987, Galerie Paul Andriesse Amsterdam 1987, Wolff Gallery NY 1987, 1988 and 1989, Sala Parpallo Valencia (travelled to Metronom Barcelona) 1988, Lisson Gallery 1989, Quint Krichman Projects San Diego 1990, Gallerie Franz Paludetto Turin 1991, Mark Quint Gallery San Diego 1991, Kohji Ogura Gallery Nagoya 1992, Tapko - The Place Copenhagen 1992, Serpentine Gallery London; *Group Exhibitions* incl: Young Comtemporaries RCA 1970, Whitechapel Open 1977, 1980, 1983 and 1992, The Sculpture Show Hayward and Serpentine Galleries 1983, The British Show Art Gallery of NSW and touring Aust 1985, Out of Line Walker Art Gallery Liverpool 1986, Modern Art? It's a Joke Cleveland Gallery Middlesbrough 1986, Richard Wentworth - Art and Language - Scott Burton Lisson Gallery in Forum Zurich Int Art Fair 1986, Fire and Metal Goldsmiths' Gallery London 1988, Starlit Waters - British Sculpture - an International Art 1968–86 Tate Gallery Liverpool 1988, New Urban Landscape World Fin Center NY 1988, British Sculpture 1960–88 Museum Van Hedendaagse Kunst Antwerp 1989, Biennale of Sydney 1990, Glasgow's Great British Art Exhibition McLellan Galleries Glasgow 1990, Janice Tchalenko with Richard Wentworth - Works in Clay Crafts Cncl Shop at V&A 1990, Kunst - Europa travelling Germany 1991, The Kitchen Show St Gallen Switzerland 1991, Objects for the Ideal Home - the Legacy of Pop Art Serpentine Gallery 1991, Oh! Cet Echo! Centre Cultural Suisse Paris 1992, Material culture: the object in British art of the 1980s and 90s (Hayward Gallery) 1997; *Style—* Richard Wentworth, Esq

WENTWORTH-STANLEY, (David) Michael; s of Geoffrey David Wentworth-Stanley (d 2005), and Bridget, *née* Pease; *b* 29 February 1952; *Educ* Eton; *m* 7 Oct 1975, Jane, da of Col Tom Hall, CVO, OBE; 3 da (Laura b 12 Dec 1978, Emma b 28 May 1981, Harriet b 7 Aug 1985); *Career* chartered accountant 1974; Cazenove Inc NY 1981–83, md Cazenove & Co 2001–05 (joined 1975, ptnr 1982–2001), md JPMorgan Cazenove 2005–; memb Bd

W

SFA 1995–2001; FCA 1979 (ACA 1974); *Recreations* countryside, gardening, skiing; *Clubs* White's, MCC; *Style—* Michael Wentworth-Stanley, Esq; ✉ 41 Old Church Street, London SW3 5BS (tel 020 7352 3419); JPMorgan Cazenove, 20 Moorgate, London EC2R 6DA (tel 020 7588 2828, fax 020 7606 9205)

WENTZELL, Pamela; da of Herbert Thomas Moran, of London, and Teresa McDaid, *née* Conway; *b* 3 February 1950; *Educ* Pitman's Sch Ealing, Marlborough Coll London, Université Catholique de l'Ouest France, Southampton Univ; *m* 18 Oct 1969, Christopher John, s of Charles John Wentzell, of Gurnard, IOW; *Career* md: JP Communicators Ltd (PR consultancy) 1980–2001, Business Expo Ltd 1997–; chm: Southampton Publicity Assoc 1985–86, Wessex Branch IPR 1997–98; MIPR 1980, FInstD 1989, FCIPR 2000; *Recreations* theatre-going, classical music, learning languages; *Style—* Mrs Pamela Wentzell; ✉ 15 Erisey Terrace, Falmouth, Cornwall TR11 2AP (tel 01326 210412, e-mail pamela_wentzell@yahoo.co.uk)

WERTENBAKER, Timberlake; da of Charles Christian Wertenbaker, of Ciboure, France, and Lael Luttrell Tucker Wertenbaker; *m* 30 June 1991, John Man; 1 da (Dushka Sophia Christiana Wertenbaker-Man b 15 April 1992); *Career* playwright; resident writer: Shared Experience 1983, Royal Court 1984–85; dir English Stage Co 1992–98; visiting prof Georgetown Univ 2005–06; memb: PEN, RSL, Nat Acad of Writing; Hon Dr Open Univ 2002; FRSL 2000; *Awards* Evening Standard Most Promising Playwright 1988, Olivier Award 1988, Eileen Anderson Central TV Drama Award 1989, Susan Smith Blackburn Prize 1992, London Critics' Circle Award 1992, Writers' Guild Award 1992; *Plays* incl: New Anatomies (1981), The Grace of Mary Traverse (1985), Our Country's Good (1988), The Love of the Nightingale (1988), Three Birds Alighting on a Field (1991), The Break of Day (1995), After Darwin (1999), Dianeira (1999), The Ash Girl (2000), Credible Witness (2001), The H File (2003), Galileo's Daughter (2004), Scenes of Seduction (2005); *Publications* Sophocles: Oedipus Tyrannos; Oedipus at Kolonos; Antigone (trans 1992), Timberlake Wertenbaker Plays 1 (1996), Timberlake Wertenbaker Plays 2 (2002), Euripides' Hecuba (trans), False Admissions; Successful Strategies; La Dispute: Three Plays by Marivaux (trans); *Recreations* mountains; *Style—* Miss Timberlake Wertenbaker; ✉ c/o Mel Kenyon, Casarotto Ramsay, National House, 60–66 Wardour Street, London W1V 3HP (tel 020 7287 4450, fax 020 7287 9128)

WEST OF SPITHEAD, Baron (Life Peer UK 2007), of Seaview in the County of Isle of Wight; Adm Sir Alan William John West; GCB (2004, KCB 2000), DSC (1982), ADC (2003); *b* 1948; *Educ* BRNC Dartmouth; *m* Rosemary, *née* Childs; 3 c; *Career* CO HMS Yarnton 1973, princ warfare offr 1977 (thereafter specialist appts on HMS Juno, HMS Ambuscade and HMS Norfolk), Cdr 1980, CO HMS Ardent 1980–82 (took ship to Falkland Islands where sunk in successful retaking of islands), Directorate of Naval Plans MOD 1982–84, Capt 1984, Asst Dir of Naval Staff Duties 1985–86, CO HMS Bristol and Capt Dartmouth Trg Sqdn 1987–88, led study on future employment of women in RN 1988, head Maritime Intelligence Directorate 1989–92, RCDS 1992, Higher Command and Staff Course 1993, Dir of Naval Staff Duties 1993–94, Rear Adm 1994, Naval Sec and DG Naval Manning 1994–96, COMUKTG/CASWSF (Commander United Kingdom Task Gp/Commander Anti-Submarine Warfare Striking Force) 1996–97, Vice Adm 1997, Chief Defence Intelligence 1997–2000, Adm 2000, C-in-C FLEET and EASTLANT and Cdr Allied Naval Forces North 2000–02, First Sea Lord and CNS 2002–06; min for security Home Office 2007–; inspired and led RN Trafalgar 200 celebrations; chm: Qinetiq Defence Advsy Bd, CVQO; chllr Southampton Solent Univ; pres: Ardent Assoc, Ship Recognition Corps (SRC), St Barbara Assoc; Master Mariner, Yr Brother Trinity House; Hon Freeman Worshipful Co of Watermen and Lightermen; MNI; *Clubs* Royal Yacht Squadron, Naval, Destroyer, Anchorite, Navy, Pilgrims 1765/85, Pepys, RNSA; *Style—* Adm the Lord West of Spithead, GCB, DSC; ✉ Southampton Solent University, ast Park Terrace, Southampton, Hampshire SO14 0YN

WESKER, Sir Arnold; kt (2006); s of Joseph Wesker (d 1959), and Leah, *née* Perlmutter (d 1976); *b* 24 May 1932; *Educ* Upton House Central Sch Hackney; *m* 1958, Doreen Cecile, da of Edwin Bicker, of Norfolk; 2 s (Daniel, Lindsay Joe), 2 da (Tanya Jo, Elsa Sarah); *Career* playwright and director; Nat Serv RAF 1950–52 (material gathered for later play Chips with Everything); various positions Norfolk 1952–54 (incl seed sorter, farm labourer and kitchen porter), trained pastry cook London and Paris 1954–56; awarded Arts Cncl grant 1958 and Writers' Bursary 1996; artistic dir Centre Fortytwo 1961–70, chm Br Centre of Int Theatre Inst 1978–82, pres Int Playwrights' Ctee 1979–83; awarded Last Frontier Lifetime Achievement Award for Distinguished Service in the Theatre 1999; Hon DLitt UEA 1989, hon fell Queen Mary & Westfield Coll London 1995, Hon Dr of Humane Letters Denison Univ of Ohio 1997; FRSL; *Stage Plays*: The Kitchen (1957), Chicken Soup with Barley (1958), Roots (1959), I'm Talking About Jerusalem (1960), Chips with Everything (1962), The Four Seasons (1965), Their Very Own and Golden City (Marzotto Prize, 1966), The Old Ones (1970), The Friends (1970), The Journalists (1972), The Wedding Feast (1974), Shylock (1976), Love Letters on Blue Paper (stories 1974, play 1976), One More Ride on the Merry-Go-Round (1978), Fatlips (book 1978, play 1980, renamed tamak - Island of Lethargy), Caritas (1980), Sullied Hand (1981), Anne Wobbler (1982), Four Portraits - of Mothers (1982), Yarsdale (1983), Cinders (1983), Whatever Happened to Betty Lemon (1986), When God Wanted a Son (1986), Badenheim 1939 (1987), Shoeshine & Little Old Lady (1987), Lady Othello (1987), Beorhtel's Hill (1988), The Mistress (1988), Three Women Talking (1990), Letter To A Daughter (1990), Blood Libel (1991), Wild Spring (1992), Circles of Perception (1996), Denial (1997), Break My Heart (1997), Groupie (2001), Longitude (2002), Letter to Myself (for 13-year-old actress, 2004); *Radio and Television Plays* Menace (1971), Breakfast (1981), Bluey (radio play 1984, stage play 1993), Thieves in the Night (4 part adaptation of Arthur Koestler's novel, 1984–85), Phoenix Phoenix Burning Bright (TV play 1992, stageplay 2006), Barabbas (2000), Groupie (radio play 2001, stageplay 2003), Shylock (radio adaptation, 2005), The Rocking Horse (BBC World Serv cmmn, 2007); *Film Scripts* The Wesker Trilogy (1979), Lady Othello (1980), Homage to Catalonia (1991), Maudie (film version of Lessing's novel Diary of a Good Neighbour 1995), The Kitchen (2005); *Stories, Collections* Six Sundays in January (1971), Love Letters on Blue Paper (1974), Said The Old Man to The Young Man (1978), The King's Daughters (erotic stories) 1998; *Essays* Fears of Fragmentation (1971), Words - as definitions of experience (1976), Distinctions (1985); *Other writings* Say Goodbye You May Never See Them Again (text for book on John Allin's naive paintings of the East End, 1974), Fatlips (story for young people, 1978), Journey into Journalism (diary of two months researching The Sunday Times, 1977), A Mini-Biography (1988), As Much As I Dare (autobiography, 1994), The BIRTH of Shylock and the DEATH of Zero Mostel (1997), When I Was Your Age (for young people, 2001), Grief (libretto for one-woman opera, 2003), Honey (novel, 2005); *Stage Dir* The Four Seasons (Havana) 1968, The Friends (Stockholm and London) 1970, The Old Ones (Munich) 1973, Their Very Own and Golden City (Aahus) 1974, Love Letters on Blue Paper (Nat Theatre 1978 and Oslo 1980), The Entertainer (Theatr Clwyd) 1983, Annie Wobbler (Birmingham and London) 1984, Yarsdale (RSC Actor's Festival Stratford) 1985, Yarsdale and Whatever Happened to Betty Lemon (London) 1987, Shylock (workshop prodn, London) 1989, The Merry Wives of Windsor (Oslo) 1989–90, The Kitchen (Univ of Wisconsin USA) 1990, The Mistress (Rome) 1991, The Wedding Feast (Denison Univ of Ohio USA), Letter to a Daughter (music by Benjamin Till Edinburgh Festival) 1998; *Style—* Sir Arnold Wesker, FRSL; ✉ Hay-on-Wye, Hereford HR3 5RJ (tel 0149 820473, fax 0149 821005, e-mail wesker@compuserve.com, website www.arnoldwesker.com); c/o National Westminster Bank plc, 298 Seven Sisters Road, London N4 2AF

WESSELY, Prof Simon; s of Rudolph Wessely, of Prague, Czech Repub, and Wendy Anne Cecilia Wessely; *b* 23 December 1956; *Educ* King Edward VII Sch Sheffield, Lamar Sr HS Houston TX, Trinity Hall Cambridge (MA, BM BCh), UC Oxford (MSc, MD); *m* 2 Jan 1988, Dr Clare Gerada; 2 s (Alexander b 5 Feb 1990, Benjamin b 24 Aug 1992); *Career* SHO rotation Newcastle 1982–84, psychiatric trg Maudsley Hosp 1984–88, sr lectr GKT 1991, prof of epidemiological and liaison psychiatry GKT and Inst of Psychiatry London 1994; hon civilian advsr in psychiatry Br Army Med Servs 2001; chair NATO Advsy Ctee on Social and Psychological Consequences of Terrorism 2002–, memb MRC panels 1998–2002; FRCP 1993 (MRCP 1984), FRCPsych 2000 (MRCPsych 1988), FMedSci 2002; *Publications* Chronic Fatigue and its Symptoms (1999), Clinical Trials in Psychiatry (2003), From Shellshock to PTSD; over 450 academic pubns on chronic fatigue, psychiatry, epidemiology, military health, history and gen hosp psychiatry; numerous radio and TV broadcasts and newspaper articles; *Recreations* skiing, cycling, Russian history, journalism, arguing in wine bars; *Style—* Prof Simon Wessely; ✉ Department of Psychological Medicine, Institute of Psychiatry, Denmark Hill, London SE5 8AF (e-mail s.wessely@iop.kcl.ac.uk)

WESSON, Jane Louise; *b* 26 February 1953; *Educ* Wolverhampton Girls' HS, Univ of Kent at Canterbury (BA, Anthony London prize); *Career* Lancaster Coll of Law 1975–76, articled clerk Pothecary & Barratt London 1976–78, slr Hepworth & Chadwick Leeds 1978–89; chm Harrogate Healthcare NHS Tst 1993–2000; non-exec dir: Pontefract HA 1990–93, Wakefield HA 1993; chm Nat Clinical Assessment Authy 2000–02, chm Cncl for Healthcare Regulatory Excellence 2003–07; a chm Child Support Appeal Tbnls 1992–99; memb Bd: Northern Counties Housing Assoc 1993–96, Anchor Housing Tst 2003–, Nuffield Hosps 2005–; *Recreations* sailing, singing, gardening; *Style—* Mrs Jane L Wesson

WEST, Prof Anthony Roy (Tony); s of Percy Frederick West (d 1976), and Winifred Audrey, *née* Baker (d 1993); *b* 21 January 1947; *Educ* Harvey GS Folkestone, Univ Coll Swansea (BSc), Univ of Aberdeen (PhD, DSc); *m* 1972, Sheena, da of Stanley Cruickshank; 1 s (Graeme Michael b 12 April 1976), 1 da (Isla Morven b 4 March 1978); *Career* Univ of Aberdeen: lectr 1971–84, sr lectr 1984–86, reader 1986–89, prof 1989–99; prof Univ of Sheffield 1999– (head Dept Engineering Materials 1999–); visiting prof: Nat Univ of Mexico 1976–77 and 1984, Univ of Stockholm 1986, Osaka Nat Research Inst 1989, Moscow State Univ 1992, Tokyo Inst of Technology 1993, Universiti Pertanian Malaysia 1994, Universidad de Barcelona 1996, Universidad Nacional del Sur Argentina 1997; chm Materials Chemistry Forum RSC 1993–2002; founding ed Jl of Materials Chemistry RSC 1990; memb Functional Materials Coll EPSRC 1996–, pres Inorganic Chemistry Div IUPAC 2004–; Blackwell Prize Univ of Aberdeen 1986, Solid State Chemistry Prize RSC 1996; CChem, CPhys, FRSC, FInstP, FIM, FRSE 1997; *Books* Solid State Chemistry and Its Applications (1984), Basic Solid State Chemistry (1987, 2 edn 1999); also author of over 370 research papers in learned jls; *Recreations* athletics, gardening, Spanish and Latin American interests; *Style—* Prof Tony West, FRSE; ✉ University of Sheffield, Department of Engineering Materials, Sir Robert Hadfield Building, Mappin Street, Sheffield S1 3JD (tel 0114 222 5501, fax 0114 222 5943, e-mail a.r.west@sheffield.ac.uk)

WEST, Guy; s of Keith Edward West, and Diana Mary, *née* Humphreys; *Educ* Wellingborough Sch for Boys; *m* Fiona *née* Main; 1 da (Jet Diana Velvet b 12 July 2004); *Career* shoe designer, estab Jeffery-West 1987; curator Life and Sole exhbn Northampton Footwear Museum; patron: Northampton Footwear Museum, Cordwainers, Nene Univ Coll, Leicester De Montfort Univ; Best Men's Fashion Footwear UK Footwear Awards 1999 and 2000, FHM Best Men's Footwear Award 2000–01; memb Northampton Shoemakers 1992–, memb Br Footwear Fedn 1995–; *Recreations* UK U16 water ski squad, UK underwater hockey, local cricket and squash teams; *Clubs* Blacks; *Style—* Guy West, Esq; ✉ 16 Piccadilly Arcade, London SW1Y 6NH (tel 020 7499 3360, fax 020 7499 3340)

WEST, James Glynn; *b* 21 April 1947; *Educ* Eton; *m* 1969, Pippa, *née* Mackay Miller; 1 s (Alexander b 1973), 1 da (Charlotte b 1975); *Career* md Globe Investment Trust plc 1987–90 (joined 1973), md Lazard Bros & Co Ltd and chief exec Lazard Asset Management Ltd 1990–94; currently chm: Gartmore Fledgling Trust plc, Aberdeen Convertible Trust plc, Intrinsic Value plc; currently non-exec dir: Aberdeen New Dawn Investment Trust plc, British Assets Trust plc, Global Natural Energy plc, Candover Investments plc; FCA; *Recreations* golf, oil painting; *Clubs* City; *Style—* James West, Esq; ✉ Orchard House, Eastling, Faversham, Kent ME13 0AZ (tel 01795 890432, fax 01795 890353)

WEST, (A) Joshua (Josh); s of Geoffrey Brian West, of Santa Fe NM, and Jacqueline Jean, *née* Boggs; *b* 25 March 1977; *Educ* Santa Fe Prep Sch, Yale Univ (BA), Univ of Cambridge (MPhil); *Career* amateur rower; achievements incl: memb Univ of Cambridge Boat Race crew 1999, 2000, 2001 and 2002, winner eights World Cup 2001, Silver medal coxless fours World Championships 2002 and 2003; Anglo-Jewish Sports Personality of the Year 2001; *Recreations* travelling, walking, cooking, reading, geology; *Clubs* Leander, Hawks' (Cambridge); *Style—* Josh West, Esq

WEST, Martin; s of Alan West, of Bolton, Lancs, and Janet Elizabeth, *née* Carlton; *b* 14 January 1969; *Educ* Bury GS, St Catharine's Coll Cambridge (MA, Master's Sizar), Royal Acad of Music (scholar, Dip Advanced Studies), St Petersburg Conservatory of Music; *Career* conductor; music dir Cambridge Philharmonic Soc 1998–2005, princ conductor English Nat Ballet 2004– (resident conductor 1997–2004), music dir and princ conductor San Francisco Ballet 2005–; guest conductor Pimlico Opera Br tours 1997, 1998 and 2001; guest work with: Royal Liverpool Philharmonic Orch, Hallé Orch, London Concert Orch, Holland Sinfonia; ARAM; *Recreations* cricket, swimming, cosmology; *Clubs* Flying Ducksmen CC; *Style—* Martin West, Esq; ✉ San Francisco Ballet, 455 Franklin Street, San Francisco, CA 94102, USA (tel 00 1 415 861 5600, e-mail mwest@sfballet.org); e-mail martin.west@virgin.net

WEST, Dr Martin Litchfield; s of late Maurice Charles West, and late Catherine Baker, *née* Stainthorpe; *b* 23 September 1937; *Educ* St Paul's, Balliol Coll Oxford (Craven scholar, Hertford scholar, de Paravicini scholar, Dean Ireland's scholar, MA, DPhil, DLitt, Chancellor's prizes, Conington prize); *m* 31 Dec 1960, Stephanie Roberta, da of late Robert Enoch Pickard; 1 da (Rachel Ann b 17 July 1963), 1 s (Robert Charles b 17 May 1965); *Career* Univ of Oxford: Woodhouse jr res fell in classics St John's Coll 1960–63, fell and praelector in classics UC 1963–74 (hon fell 2001); prof of Greek Univ of London 1974–91, sr res fell All Souls Coll Oxford 1991–2004 (emeritus fell 2004–); visiting lectr Harvard Univ 1967–68, res fell Japan Soc for the Promotion of Science 1980, visiting prof UCLA 1986; Int Balzan Prize 2000, Kenyon Medal Br Acad 2002; memb: Hellenic Soc, Classical Assoc, Oxford Philological Soc, Academia Europaea 1997; hon memb Hungarian Classical Soc 1984, corresponding memb Akademie der Wissenschaften zu Göttingen 1991; hon fell: Balliol Coll Oxford 2004, St John's Coll Oxford 2007; FBA 1973; *Books* Hesiod, Theogony (ed, 1966), Fragmenta Hesiodea (ed with R Merkelbach, 1967), Early Greek Philosophy and the Orient (1971), Sing Me, Goddess (1971), Iambi et Elegi Graeci (ed, 1971–72), Textual Criticism and Editorial Technique (1973), Studies in Greek Elegy and Iambus (1974), Hesiod, Works and Days (ed, 1978), Theognidis et Phocylidis Fragmenta (1978), Delectus ex Iambis et Elegis Graecis (1980), Greek Metre (1982), The Orphic Poems (1983), Carmina Anacreontea (1984), The Hesiodic Catalogue of Women (1985), Euripides, Orestes (ed, 1987), Introduction to Greek Metre (1987), Hesiod (trans,

1988), Aeschyli Tragoediae (1990), Studies in Aeschylus (1990), Ancient Greek Music (1992), Greek Lyric Poetry (trans, 1993), The East Face of Helicon (1997, received Runciman Award), Homeri Ilias (1998–2000), Studies in the Text and Transmission of the Iliad (2001), Documents of Ancient Greek Music (with E Pöhlmann, 2001), Greek Epic Fragments (ed, 2003), Homeric Hymns, Homeric Apocrypha, Lives of Homer (ed, 2003), Indo-European Poetry and Myth (2007); author of over 300 articles in learned jls; *Recreations* music; *Style*— Dr Martin West, FBA; ✉ All Souls College, Oxford OX1 4AL

WEST, Robert John; s of Clifford Lennard West (d 1997), of Maidenhead, Berks, and Joan, *née* Naylor (d 1983); *b* 1 January 1952; *Educ* Maidenhead GS, Clare Coll Cambridge (MA); *m* 13 June 1987, Elisabeth, da of Sydney and Joyce Hynd; 2 s (David Robert b 29 May 1988, Andrew James b 5 Jan 1990); 1 da (Annabel b 22 Nov 1991); *Career* asst slr Freshfields 1977–82 (articled clerk 1975–77), ptnr Baker & McKenzie 1985– (asst slr 1982–85); former chm Assoc of Pension Lawyers, memb Law Soc; *Books* Butterworths Law for Accountants; *Recreations* football, tennis, golf, cricket; *Style*— Robert West, Esq; ✉ Baker & McKenzie, 100 New Bridge Street, London EC4V 6JA (tel 020 7919 1000, fax 020 7919 1999)

WEST, Samuel Alexander Joseph; *b* 19 June 1966; *Educ* Alleyn's Sch Dulwich, Lady Margaret Hall Oxford (BA); *Career* actor and dir; artistic dir Sheffield Theatres 2005–; memb: Cncl Equity 1996–2000, Bd Bristol Old Vic, Bd Nat Campaign for the Arts; *Theatre* as actor: Les Parents Terribles 1988, A Life in the Theatre 1989, Hidden Laughter 1990, Henry IV Pts I & II 1996; for RNT: The Sea 1991, Arcadia 1993, Antony and Cleopatra 1998; for RSC: Richard II 2000, Hamlet 2001; as dir: The Lady's Not for Burning 2002, Les Liaisons Dangereuses 2003, Cosi fan Tutte 2003, Three Women and a Piano Tuner 2004, Insignificance 2005, The Romans in Britain 2006, The Clean House 2006; *Television* incl: Frankie and Johnnie 1985, Prince Caspian and The Voyage Of The Dawn Treader 1989, Stanley and the Women 1991, Voices in the Garden 1992, As Time Goes By 1992, Open Fire 1994, Zoya 1995, The Vacillations of Poppy Carew 1995, Heavy Weather 1995, Strangers 1996, Over Here 1996, The Ripper 1997, Hornblower 1999, Longitude 2000, Waking the Dead 2002, Cambridge Spies 2003; *Film* incl: Reunion 1989, Howards End 1992, Archipel 1992, A Feast At Midnight 1994, A Breed Of Heroes 1994, Carrington 1995, Persuasion 1995, Jane Eyre 1995, Stiff Upper Lips 1998, Rupert's Land 1998, The Dance of Shiva 1998, Notting Hill 1999, Complicity 2000, Pandemonium 2000, Iris 2001, Van Helsing 2003, Kingdom in Twilight 2004; *Recreations* photography, travelling, poker, cricket, supporting AFC Wimbledon; *Clubs* Groucho, Century; *Style*— Samuel West; ✉ c/o PFD, Drury House, 34–43 Russell Street, London WC2B 5HA

WEST, Dr Stephanie Roberta; da of Robert Enoch Pickard (d 1993), of Adderbury, Oxon, and Ruth, *née* Batters (d 1998); *b* 1 December 1937; *Educ* Nottingham HS for Girls GPDST, Somerville Coll Oxford (Ireland scholar, Derby scholar, BA, DPhil, Gaisford prize); *m* 1960, Martin Litchfield West, s of late Maurice Charles West; 1 da (Rachel Ann b 17 July 1963), 1 s (Robert Charles b 17 May 1965); *Career* Univ of Oxford: Mary Ewart res fell Somerville Coll 1965–67, lectr in classics Hertford Coll 1966–90, lectr in Greek Keble Coll 1981–2005, sr res fell in classics and fell librarian Hertford Coll 1990–2005 (emeritus fell 2005–); memb Cncl GPDST 1974–87; FBA 1990; *Books* The Ptolemaic Papyri of Homer (1967), Omero Odissea i (libri i-iv 1981, 7th revised edn 2000), A Commentary on Homer's Odyssey i (with A Heubeck and J B Hainsworth, 1988), Demythologisation in Herodotus (2002); *Style*— Dr Stephanie West, FBA; ✉ 42 Portland Road, Oxford OX2 7EY (tel 01865 556060); Hertford College, Oxford OX1 3BW (e-mail stephanie.west@hertford.ox.ac.uk)

WEST, Dr Stephen Craig; *b* 11 April 1952; *Educ* Univ of Newcastle upon Tyne (BSc, PhD); *m* Mina; *Career* post-doctoral res assoc: Univ of Newcastle 1977–78, Dept of Molecular Biophysics and Biochemistry and Therapeutic Radiology Yale Univ 1978–83; res scientist ICRF 1983–85, sr scientist ICRF 1985–89, princ scientist ICRF 1989–; hon prof Dept of Biochemistry UCL 1997–; chm Sectional Ctee 7 Royal Soc 1996–98 (memb 1995–98); memb: Molecular Biology and Genetics Grants Ctee 1991–94, SERC, Hooke Ctee Royal Soc 1995–97, External Advsy Bd Univ of Texas Health Sci Center at San Antonio 1998–; assoc ed Genes to Cells 1996–98; memb Ed Bd: Nucleic Acids Research 1995–97, EMBO Jl 1996–98 (memb Advsy Ed Bd 1999–), EMBO Reports 2000–; memb Genetics Soc; memb EMBO 1994; Jeantet Prize fo Medicine 2007, Novartis Prize Biochemical Soc 2008; FRS 1995, FMedSci 1999; *Publications* DNA Repair and Recombination (with T Lindahl, 1995), Philosophical Transactions of the Royal Soc of London (ed, 1995), Mechanisms of Homologous Recombination (contrib, 1999); also author of approximately 200 scientific papers and articles; *Style*— Dr Stephen West, FRS; ✉ Cancer Research UK, Clare Hall Laboratories, South Mimms, Hertfordshire EN6 3LD (tel 01707 625868, fax 01707 625811, e-mail stephen.west@cancer.org.uk)

WEST, Timothy Lancaster; CBE (1984); s of (Harry) Lockwood West (d 1989), actor, and Olive Carleton-Crowe; *b* 20 October 1934; *Educ* John Lyon Sch Harrow, Regent St Poly; *m* 1, 1956 (m dis), Jacqueline Boyer; 1 da; m 2, 1963, Prunella Scales, *qv*; 2 s; *Career* actor and director; pres: LAMDA, Soc of Theatre Research; Hon DUniv Bradford; Hon DLitt: UWE, UEA, Hull, London; Hon LLD Univ of Westminster; FRSA; *Theatre* West End debut in Caught Napping (Piccadilly Theatre) 1959; other performances incl: Gentle Jack, The Trigon, The Italian Girl, Abelard and Heloise, Exiles, The Constant Couple, Laughter, The Homecoming, Beecham, Master Class, The War at Home, When We Are Married, The Sneeze, Long Day's Journey into Night, It's Ralph, Twelve Angry Men, The Old Country, King Lear (Dublin), Willy Loman in Death of a Salesman (Theatr Clwyd), Iago in Othello (Nottingham), Sir Anthony Absolute in The Rivals (Chichester), Mail Order Bride and Getting On (West Yorkshire Playhouse); with RSC 1962–66 (London and Stratford season 1964–66) incl: debut in Nil Carborundum and Afore Night Come (Arts Theatre) 1962, Hedda Gabler (tour Aust, Canada and USA); with Prospect Theatre Co 1966–82: King Lear, Prospero in The Tempest, Claudius in Hamlet, Enobarbus in Antony and Cleopatra, Shylock in The Merchant of Venice, Bolingbroke in Richard II, Mortimer in Edward II, Shpigelsky in A Month in the Country, Emerson in A Room with a View; with Bristol Old Vic Co incl: Trelawny, Falstaff in Henry IV (both parts), Sartorius in Widowers' Houses, Solness in The Master Builder, Lord Ogleby in The Clandestine Marriage, Vanya in Uncle Vanya; other credits incl: Falstaff in Henry IV (parts I & II, Old Vic) 1997, Gloucester in King Lear (RNT) 1997, The Birthday Party 1999, The External 2001, Luther (RNT) 2002, Lear (Old Vic) 2003, Galileo (2006), The Old Country (2006), Coriolanus (2007); *Television* incl: Edward VII, Horatio Bottomley, Hard Times, Crime and Punishment, Churchill and the Generals, Brass, The Last Bastion, The Monocled Mutineer, A Very Peculiar Practice, The Good Doctor Bodkin Adams, What the Butler Saw, Harry's Kingdom, The Sealed Train, When We Are Married, Breakthrough at Reykjavik, Strife, A Shadow on the Sun, The Contractor, Blore, MP, Beecham, Survival of the Fittest, Why Lockerbie?, Framed, Smokescreen, Eleven Men Against Eleven, Cuts, Rebecca, King Lear, Murder in Mind, Bedtime, New Tricks, Bleak House; *Film* incl: Twisted Nerve, Nicholas and Alexandra, The Day of the Jackal, Oliver Twist, Hedda, Joseph Andrews, The Devil's Advocate, Agatha, Masada, The Thirty Nine Steps, Rough Cut, Cry Freedom, Ever After, Joan of Arc, Iris, Beyond Borders; *Recreations* listening to music, travelling; *Style*— Timothy West, CBE; ✉ c/o Gavin Barker Associates, 2D Wimpole Street, London W1M 7AA (tel 020 7499 4777, fax 020 7499 3777)

WEST-KNIGHTS, Laurence James; QC (2000); s of Maj Jan James West West-Knights (d 1990), and Amy Winifred, *née* Gott (d 1999); *b* 30 July 1954; *Educ* Perse Sch Cambridge, Hampton Sch, Emmanuel Coll Cambridge (MA); *m* Joanne Anita Florence, *née* Ecob; 2 da (Imogen Amy b 26 Aug 1992, Honor Victoria b 17 Oct 2001), 1 s (Frederick Hugh Merriman b 11 March 1994); *Career* seaman offr London Div RNR 1981–94 (Lt Cdr); called to the Bar Gray's Inn 1977 (bencher 2003), practising barr 1978–, asst recorder 1994–99, recorder 1999–, QC 2000; memb Bar NI, chm Chambers Pupillage Ctee 2002–; Soc for Computers and Law: memb Cncl 1995–96, vice-chm 1996–2001, chm 2001–02; memb Cncl Incorporated Cncl of Law Reporting 1996–2004; chm IT Industry Enquiry into Govt Contracts 2000; fndr memb and tstee Br and Irish Legal Information Inst (BAILII) 2000–02; memb: Editorial Bd Judicial Studies Bd Jl 1996–2003, ITAC Civil Litigation Working Pty 1997–2003; memb PCC Christ Church Turnham Green Chiswick 1997–2001 (lay chm 1998–2001); FCIArb 1993–; *Recreations* scuba diving, cricket, shooting, motorcycling; *Clubs* MCC, Bar Yacht, Whitefriars; *Style*— L J West-Knights, Esq, QC; ✉ Hailsham Chambers, 4 Paper Buildings, Temple, London EC4Y 7EX (tel 020 7643 5000, fax 020 7353 5778, e-mail ljwk@west-knights.com, website www.west-knights.com)

WESTABY, Mark; s of Donald Westaby, of Winterton, S Humberside, and Patricia, *née* Morwood; *b* 26 June 1955; *Educ* Frederic Gough, Brunel Univ (BSc); *m* Sarah Frances Elizabeth, *née* Cox; 1 da (Sofia Elizabeth Olga); *Career* Ove Arup & partners and Res Dept British Gas 1979–81; former PRO: John Drewry Associates, HPS Ltd 1983–84, Countrywide Communications (London) 1984–90 (latterly dir, work on Tandem Computers responsible for PR Indust Best Consultancy award 1987); Kinnear Ltd management conslts in communication 1990–93; dir rising to jt md Portfolio Communications Ltd 1993–; chm Business & Technol Gp PR Consultants Assoc (chm elect 1989–91); *Recreations* all sports, music, reading, travel; *Style*— Mark Westaby, Esq; ✉ Portfolio Communications Limited, Russell Chambers, Covent Garden, London WC2E 8AA (tel 020 7240 6959, fax 020 7240 4849)

WESTAWAY, Gillian; da of Douglas John Westaway, and Edna Thomas Westaway; *b* 27 April 1955; *Educ* Univ of Exeter (BA), Inst of Educn Univ of London (ULIE) (PGCE, MA); *Partner* Nina Wiraatmadja; *Career* teacher English as a Foreign Language (EFL): Regent Sch of Languages Frankfurt Germany 1977–78, St Giles Sch London 1979, Int House Buenos Aires Argentina 1980–81; Br Cncl: sr teacher Colombia 1982–83, dir of studies Colombia 1983–84, advsr Evaluation London 1985–89, asst dir Kenya 1989–93, dep dir Indonesia 1993–2001, dir Philippines 2002–; memb Bd Br C of C in the Philippines, memb Advsy Bd ESU (Philippines chapter); *Style*— Ms Gill Westaway; ✉ The British Council, 10th Floor Taipan Place, Emerald Avenue, Ortigas Center, Pasig City 1605, Philippines (tel 00 63 2 9141011/2/3/4, fax 00 63 2 9141020)

WESTBROOK, Michael John David (Mike); OBE (1988); s of Philip Beckford Westbrook (d 1981), of Devon, and Vera Agnes, *née* Butler (d 1995); *b* 21 March 1936; *Educ* Kelly Coll Tavistock Plymouth Coll of Art (NDD), Hornsey Coll of Art (ATD); *m* 1; 1 s (Anthony Guy b 9 April 1964), 1 da (Joanna Maria b 14 June 1966); m 2, 23 Sept 1976, Katherine Jane (Kate), da of Prof Alec Naraway Duckham, CBE (d 1988); *Career* composer, pianist and bandleader; formed first band at Plymouth Art Sch 1958; moved to London 1962 and has since led a succession of gps incl: The Mike Westbrook Brass Band (with Phil Minton) 1973–, The Mike Westbrook Orchestra 1974–, The Westbrook Trio (with Kate Westbrook and Chris Biscoe) 1982–; toured in Britain, Europe, Australia, Canada, NY, Singapore and Hong Kong, written cmmnd works for festivals in GB and Europe; composed music for theatre, opera, dance, radio, TV and films and made numerous recordings incl: Marching Song (1967), Metropolis (1969), Tyger (1971), Citadel/Room 315 (1974), The Westbrook Blake (1980), On Dukes Birthday (1984), Big Band Rossini (1987), Off Abbey Road (1988), Bean Rows and Blues Shots (saxophone concerto, 1991), The Orchestra of Smith's Academy (1998), Glad Day (1999); TV scores incl Caught on a Train (1980), cinema score Moulin Rouge (1990); concert works with Kate Westbrook incorporating Euro poetry and folk song: The Cortège (1979), London Bridge is Broken Down (1987); music theatre pieces incl: Mama Chicago (1978), Westbrook Rossini (1984), The Ass (1985), Pier Rides (1986), Quichotte (1989); other works incl: Good Friday 1663 (an opera for TV, with libretto by Helen Simpson), Coming Through Slaughter (with Michael Morris, based on novel by Michael Ondaatje), Measure for Measure (1992), Blues for Terenzi (1995), Bar Utopia (big band cabaret, lyrics by Helen Simpson) 1995, Stage Set 1996, Love Or Infatuation (duo with Kate Westbrook) 1997, Jago (opera, libretto by Kate Westbrook) 2000; current projects incl Platterback (lyrics by Kate Westbrook with ensemble Westbrook & Co), Chanson Irresponsable (lyrics by Kate Westbrook, for New Westbrook Orch), Classical Blues (for BBC Concert Orch), L'Ascenseur/The Lift (with Kate Westbrook and Chris Biscoe, for Westbrook Trio), Turner in Uri (libretto by Kate Westbrook) for Alpentöne Switzerland 2003, Art Wolf (text by Kate Westbrook) for Aargauer Kunsthaus Switzerland 2003, The Nijinska Chamber (Kate Westbrook album) 2005, The Waxeywork Show (text Kate Westbrook) for The Village Band Project 2006, Cape Gloss, Mathilda's Story (on-woman opera, libretto by Kate Westbrook) 2007; Hon DMus Univ of Plymouth 2004; *Recreations* walking by the sea; *Style*— Mike Westbrook, Esq, OBE; ✉ e-mail admin@westbrookjazz.co.uk

WESTBROOK, Prof Roy; *Educ* Univ of Leicester, London Business Sch; *m* 1981, Rosemary Cooper; 2 s; *Career* civil servant 1971–80, research offr and conslt 1980–84, appointed to post in ops mgmnt London Business Sch 1984 (appointed assoc dean Sloan Prog 1995), MBA course dir then prof of ops mgmnt and dean for development and external rels Saïd Business Sch Univ of Oxford; fell and tutor in mgmnt studies St Hugh's Coll Oxford; *Books* incl: Opera: A History (with Christopher Headington and Terry Barfoot, 1987), Understanding Supply Chains: Concepts, Critiques and Futures (ed with Steve New, 2004); *Recreations* classical music, literature, theatre, sports; *Style*— Prof Roy Westbrook; ✉ St Hugh's College, Oxford OX2 6LE; Saïd Business School, Park End Street, Oxford OX1 1HP

WESTBURY, Prof David Rex; OBE (2001); s of Harold Joseph Westbury (d 1966), of Rubery, Worcs, and Kathleen, *née* Hedderley (d 1996); *b* 24 June 1942; *Educ* Bromsgrove Co HS, ChCh Oxford (MA, BSc, BM BCh, DM); *m* 19 Feb 1966, Pauline, da of James Robinson (d 1988), of Darlington, Co Durham; 1 s (Paul b 1969), 1 da (Claire b 1971); *Career* Univ of Birmingham: lectr 1968–74, sr lectr 1974–82, reader 1982–86, exec dean Med Faculty 1984–92, prof 1987–, vice-princ 1992–2002; ind conslt 2002–; dir: Birmingham Research and Development Ltd 1993–2002, S Birmingham Mental Health NHS Tst 1994–99, Univ Hosp Birmingham NHS Tst 1999–2007; chm Jt Costing and Pricing Steering Gp for HE 1997–2005; chm UM Assoc Ltd 2003–, chm UM Services Ltd 2003–, dir UM Assoc (Special Risks) Ltd 2005–; memb Physiological Soc 1968; FRSA; *Recreations* food and wine, hill walking, golf, amateur radio communications; *Clubs* Athenaeum; *Style*— Prof David Westbury, OBE; ✉ Rose Cottage, Cruise Hill, Ham Green, Feckenham, Worcestershire B97 5UA (tel 01527 541587, fax 01527 401172); University of Birmingham, Edgbaston, Birmingham B15 2TT

WESTBURY, Paul Stephen; s of Prof David Rex Westbury, OBE, of Worcs, and Pauline, *née* Robinson; *b* 11 November 1969, Birmingham; *Educ* King Edward's Sch Birmingham, Jesus Coll Cambridge (exhbn, scholar, Baker Prize for Engrg, MA); *Career* engr; Buro Happold Ltd: joined 1991, project engr NY 1995, assoc and gp mangr 1996, gp dir 1998, ptnr and dir 2000–; memb Industrial Advsy Bd Engrg Dept Cardiff Univ; MacRobert Award for Innovation Royal Acad of Engrg 1999; CEng 1996, FICE 2002, FREng 2003, FIStructE 2004; *Publications* author of tech papers in scientific jls and for conferences; *Recreations* design, architecture, technology, skiing, rugby; *Style*— Paul Westbury, Esq;

✉ Buro Happold, Camden Mill, Lower Bristol Road, Bath BA2 3DQ (tel 01225 320600, e-mail paul.westbury@burohappold.com)

WESTBURY, 6 Baron (UK 1861); Richard Nicholas Bethell; MBE (1979); s of 5 Baron Westbury, MC, CBE, DL (d 2001); *b* 29 May 1950; *Educ* Harrow, RMA Sandhurst; *m* 1, 1975 (m dis 1991), Caroline Mary, da of Richard Palmer, JP, of Swallowfield, Berks; 1 s, 2 da; m 2, 1993 (m dis 2004), Charlotte Sara Jane, da of John Temple Gore, and formerly w of Maj Sir Henry James Hugh Bruce; *Career* Maj Scots Gds 1982 (despatches twice, NI and Falkland Islands, wounded); company dir 1988–; vice-pres SSAFA; Officer Brother Order of St John; *Style*— The Rt Hon the Lord Westbury, MBE

WESTCOTT, John Miles; s of Leonard George Westcott (d 1977), of Chipping Campden, Glos, and Marion Blanche, *née* Field; *b* 22 February 1929; *Educ* Taunton Sch, Univ of Bristol (MSc); *m* 1 Sept 1956, Anne Milne, da of Capt Robert Porter, OBE (d 1956), of Blundellsands, Liverpool; 2 s (Andrew John b 1959 d 1969, Timothy Edmund James b 1963), 1 da (Catherine May b 1961); *Career* Nat Serv 2 Lt 13/18 Royal Hussars 1949, Lt North Somerset Yeomanry 1950–52; admitted slr 1956; managing ptnr Veale Wasbrough 1988, currently fin dir Kingswood Foundation Ltd; legal chm (pt/t) Pensions Appeals Tbnl 1989–2001, chm Bristol Family Mediation Serv 1997–; former pres Bristol Law Soc; contrib Family Law; memb Law Soc; *Recreations* village cricket, dry stone wall building; *Clubs* Royal Commonwealth Soc; *Style*— John Westcott, Esq; ✉ Old Farm, Southwood, Baltonsborough, Glastonbury, Somerset BA6 8PG (tel and fax 01458 850416, e-mail john.westcott@which.net)

WESTCOTT, Richard Henry; s of Charles Westcott (d 1984), of S Molton, Devon, and Ruby Alice, *née* Addicott (d 1979); *b* 5 November 1947; *Educ* Barnstaple Boys' GS; *m* 26 Nov 1983, Susan, da of George Frederick Read (d 1991), of Middlesbrough, Cleveland; 1 da (Emily Margaret Alice b 29 Aug 1985), 1 s (Charles George Frederick b 20 April 1987); *Career* called to the Bar Lincoln's Inn 1978; articled then sr clerk Moore Bedworth & Co Chartered Accountants Barnstaple 1964–73, tax mangr Arthur Andersen Chartered Accountants London 1973–75; dir: Morgan Grenfell & Co Ltd 1983–86 (exec mangr 1975–83), Warburg, Akroyd, Rowe & Pitman, Mullens Securites Ltd 1986–89; md Merrill Lynch International Ltd 1989–91; business conslt 1991–95 and 2004–; non-exec dir: TBI plc 1992–98, Fairview New Homes Ltd 1992–2004 (dep chm), Herring Baker Harris Group plc 1994–95; FCA 1970, FTII 1974, ACIB 1979; *Publications* The MBO Deal: Inside the management buyout (2002), Corporate Transactions: Practical ways to increase shareholder value (2002); *Recreations* walking, reading, carpentry, music, golf; *Style*— Richard Westcott, Esq

WESTLEY, Stuart Alker; s of Arthur Bancroft Westley (d 1949), and Gladys, *née* Alker (d 1998); *b* 21 March 1947; *Educ* Lancaster Royal GS, CCC Oxford (MA, Cricket blue); *m* 1979, Mary Louise, *née* Weston; 1 da (Sarah Elizabeth b 9 April 1987); *Career* headmaster; former professional cricketer Gloucestershire CCC 1969–72; asst master King Edward VII Sch Lytham (winters only) 1969–72, housemaster/dir of studies Framlingham Coll 1973–84, dep head Bristol Cathedral Sch 1984–89, princ King William's Coll IOM 1989–96, master of Haileybury 1996–; memb: SHA 1984, HMC 1989; govr of five prep schools and one sr school; *Recreations* golf and other sports, architecture, gardening, choral and orchestral music, France; *Clubs* East India; *Style*— Stuart Westley, Esq; ✉ Haileybury, Hertford SG13 7NU (tel 01992 706222, fax 01992 470663)

WESTMACOTT, Sir Peter John; KCMG (2003, CMG 2000), LVO (1993); s of late Preb Ian Westmacott, of Bristol, and Rosemary Patricia Spencer, *née* Watney; *b* 23 December 1950; *Educ* Taunton Sch, New Coll Oxford (MA); *m* 1, 1972, Angela, *née* Lugg; 2 s (Oliver b 1975, Rupert b 1979), 1 da (Laura b 1977); m 2, 2001, Susan Nemazee; *Career* joined HM Dip Serv 1972, third then second sec Tehran 1974–78, with EC 1978–80, first sec Paris 1980–84, PR sec to min of state 1984–97, head of Chancery Ankara 1987–90, dep private sec to HRH The Prince of Wales 1990–93, political cnsllr Washington DC 1993–97, dir Americas FCO 1997–2000, dep under-sec of state FCO 2000–01, ambass to Turkey 2002–06, ambass to France 2006–; FRSA 1991; *Recreations* tennis, skiing, travel; *Style*— HE Sir Peter Westmacott, KCMG, LVO; ✉ c/o Foreign & Commonwealth Office (Paris), King Charles Street, London SW1A 2AH (tel 0090 312 455 3202, e-mail peter.westmacott@fco.gov.uk)

WESTMEATH, 13 Earl of (I 1621); William Anthony Nugent; also Baron Delvin (I before 1489, evolved from a feudal Barony, of which the date of origin is uncertain); s of 12 Earl of Westmeath (d 1971); *b* 21 November 1928; *Educ* Marlborough, RMA Sandhurst; *m* 31 July 1963, Susanna Margaret, o da of His Hon Judge James Charles Beresford Whyte Leonard, of Sutton Courtenay, Berks; 2 s; *Heir* s, Lord Delvin; *Career* RA 1947–61, ret as Capt; sr master St Andrew's Sch Pangbourne, ret 1988; *Style*— The Rt Hon the Earl of Westmeath; ✉ Farthings, Bradfield, Reading, Berkshire RG7 6LL (tel 0118 974 4426)

WESTMINSTER, Archbishop of (RC) 2000–; His Eminence Cardinal Cormac Murphy-O'Connor; s of Dr George Patrick Murphy-O'Connor (d 1960), and Ellen Theresa, *née* Cuddigan (d 1971); *b* 24 August 1932; *Educ* Prior Park Coll Bath, The Ven English Coll Rome, Gregorian Univ Rome (PhL, STL); *Career* ordained to RC Priesthood 1956; asst priest: Corpus Christi Parish Portsmouth 1956–63, Sacred Heart Parish Fareham 1963–66; private sec and chaplain to Bishop of Portsmouth 1966–70, parish priest Parish of Immaculate Conception Southampton 1970–71, rector Venerable Eng Coll Rome 1971–77, bishop of Arundel and Brighton 1977–2000; chm: Bishops' Ctee for Europe 1978–83, Ctee for Christian Unity 1983–99, Dept for Mission & Unity of Bishops' Conf of England & Wales 1993–2000, jt chm of Anglo-Roman Catholic Int Cmmn (ARCIC-II) 1983–2000, pres Catholic Bishops' Conf of England and Wales 2000–; Hon DD Lambeth 1999; *Publications* The Family of the Church (1984), At the Heart of the World (2004), The Human Face of God (2004), Faith in Europe? (ed, 2005); *Recreations* music, sport; *Style*— His Eminence the Cardinal Archbishop of Westminster; ✉ Archbishop's House, Ambrosden Avenue, Westminster, London SW1P 1QJ (tel 020 7798 9033, fax 020 7798 9077, e-mail archbishop@rcdow.org.uk, website www.rcdow.org.uk)

WESTMINSTER, 6 Duke of (UK 1874); Sir Gerald Cavendish Grosvenor; 15 Bt (E 1622), KG (2003), OBE (Mil 1995), TD (1994), DL (Cheshire 1982); also Baron Grosvenor (GB 1761), Earl Grosvenor, Viscount Belgrave (both GB 1784), and Marquess of Westminster (UK 1831); s of 5 Duke of Westminster, TD (d 1979), and Hon Viola Lyttelton (d 1987), da of 9 Viscount Cobham; *b* 22 December 1951; *Educ* Harrow; *m* 1978, Natalia Ayesha, yst da of Lt-Col Harold Pedro Joseph Phillips, and Georgina (da of Sir Harold Wernher, 3 Bt, GCVO, TD, and Lady Zia, CBE, *née* Countess Anastasia Mikhailovna, da of HIH Grand Duke Michael of Russia); sis of Duchess of Abercorn; 3 da (Lady Tamara Katherine b 20 Dec 1979, Lady Edwina Louise b 4 Nov 1981, Lady Viola Georgina b 12 Oct 1992), 1 s (Hugh Richard Louis, Earl Grosvenor b 29 Jan 1991); *Heir* s, Earl Grosvenor; *Career* cmd Queen's Own Yeo, RAC, TA 1973, Capt 1979, Maj 1985, Lt-Col 1992, Cdr 1993–95, Col 1995–97, Dep Cdr 143 W Midlands Bde 1997–99, Brig TA HQ Adj-Gen 2000–02, DRFC 2002–04, Maj Gen ACDS (Res and Cadets) 2004–; chm Grosvenor Gp Ltd (formerly Grosvenor Gp Hldgs Ltd) 1999–2007; dir: Int Students Tst 1976–93, Claridges Hotel Ltd 1981–93, Marcher Sound Ltd 1982–97, Westminster Christmas Appeal Tst 1989–94, Grosvenor Estate Holdings 1989–, NW Business Leadership Team 1990–97, Manchester Olympic Games Co-ordinating Ctee 1991–94, Business in the Community (BITC) 1991–95; life govr RASE 1997–; pro-chllr Keele Univ 1986–93, chllr Manchester Met Univ 1992–2002, first-chllr Univ of Chester 2005–; chm of tstees Nuffield Tst for the Forces of the Crown 1992–; pres: NW Industrialists' Cncl 1979–93, London Fedn of Clubs for Young People 1979–2000, Spastics Soc (now SCOPE) 1982–, Nat Kidney Research Fund 1985–97, RNIB 1986–, Drug and Alcohol Fndn 1987–97, N of Eng Zoological Soc 1987–, Game Conservancy Tst 1987–2000, Arthritis Care 1987–2003, Holstein UK & I (formerly Br Holstein Soc) 1988–, Abbeyfield Soc 1989–95, Country Tst 1989–, Inst of Environmental Sciences 1989–, BASC 1992–2000, BLESMA 1992–, Youth Sports Tst 1996–2004, Manchester Cwlth Games 1998–2002, Life Educn Centres (Drug Prevention) 2000–, Tank Museum 2002–, Atlantic Salmon Tst 2004–, Yeomanry Benevolent Fund 2005–; vice-pres: RUSI 1993–, Fountain Soc 1985–, Royal Soc of St George 1987–, NSPCC 1988–, Royal Engrs Museum Fndn 1990–, Royal British Legion 1993–, Royal Assoc of British Dairy Farmers 1995–, Reserve Forces Ulysses Tst 1995–, Royal Soc of the Friends of St George's and Descendants of the Knights of the Garter 2003–; memb Ctee: Rural Target Team 1992, Business in the Community 1992, N American Advsy Gp 1994, Nat Army Museum 1988–97, Prince's Youth Business Tst 1989–, St George's House Windsor Castle Special Appeal 2000–, Br Kidney Patients Assoc 2001– (also patron); memb Prince's Cncl Duchy of Cornwall 2001–; currently memb Cncl RICS Fndn (chm 2000–02); patron: Worcs CCC (pres 1984–86), MIND 1984–, Royal Fine Art Cmmn 1988–, Dyslexia Inst 1989–98, Royal Ulster Agric Soc 1997–2003, The Prince's Tst NW Region 2001–, Changing Faces 2001–, Blue Cross Animal Hosp 2001–, Arthritis Care 2003–, Emmaus 2003–, Soil Assoc 2004–, UK4U 2006, Army Mountaineering Assoc (Makalu Expedition) 2006, Museum of Policing in Cheshire 2006, Friends of Castle Way 2006, Chester Culture Park 2007; vice-patron Animals in War Meml Fund 2002–; friend of Chester Youth Club; tstee: Grosvenor Estate, Westminster Abbey Tst, Westminster Fndn, Westminster Housing Tst, Falcon Tst 1975–, TSB Fndn for England and Wales 1986–97, Habitat Research Tst 1990–; head of UK Delegation of Cncl for Game and Wildlife Conservation 2005; ctee memb Centre for Study of the Presidency 2005; Hon Col: Northumbrian Univ OTC 1995–2003, 7 Regt AAC 1993–, Royal Mercian and Lancastrian Yeo (RMLY) 2001–, Northumberland OTC 2000–; Col-in-Chief Royal Westminster Regt 1991, Col Cmdt Yeomanry Assoc 2005–; Freeman: City of Chester 1973, England 1979, City of London 1980; Liveryman: GAPAN, Worshipful Co of Gunmakers, Worshipful Co of Weavers, Worshipful Co of Armourers and Braziers, Worshipful Co of Marketors, Worshipful Co of Goldsmiths, Worshipful Co of Fishmongers; fell Liverpool John Moores Univ 1990, hon fell Univ of Central Lancashire 2001; Hon LLD Univ of Keele 1990, Hon LLD Univ of Liverpool 2000, Hon DLitt Univ of Salford 2000; FIStructE 1997, FRSA, FRAS, FCIM, FCIOB, Hon MRICS; *Recreations* shooting, fishing, scuba diving; *Clubs* Brooks's, Cavalry and Guards', MCC, Royal Yacht Squadron; *Style*— His Grace the Duke of Westminster, KG, OBE, TD, DL; ✉ Eaton Hall, Chester CH4 9EJ

WESTMORE, Geoffrey David (Geoff); s of Alan Herbert Westmore, of Guildford, Surrey, and Mary Elspeth, *née* Brooking; *b* 28 August 1950; *Educ* Royal GS Guildford; *m* 21 July 1979, Paula, *née* Clemett; 1 s (Jonathan Henry Clemett b 1987), 1 da (Kathryn May Clemett b 1983); *Career* PricewaterhouseCoopers (formerly Deloitte Haskins & Sells and then Coopers & Lybrand): mangr 1975–83, ptnr 1983–2000, independent advsr and co-fndr Subito Ptnrs 2000–; non-exec dir: Avery Weigh-Tronix LLC, Retail Decisions plc, Advance Capital Invest plc, Brunner Mond Gp Limited, Inflexion Private Equity Investment Tst plc, Meridien Hotels Gp, The Mobile Channel Ltd; memb Advsy Bd Inflexion Private Equity, memb Exec Ctee Faculty of Corp Fin, alternate membTakeover Panel; FCA 1972; *Recreations* sport, music, theatre, films; *Style*— Geoff Westmore, Esq

WESTMORLAND, 16 Earl of (E 1624); Anthony David Francis Henry Fane; also Baron Burghersh (E 1624); s of 15 Earl of Westmorland, GCVO, DL (d 1993), and Barbara Jane, da of Lt-Col Sir Roland Lewis Findlay, 3 and last Bt (d 1979); *b* 1 August 1951; *Educ* Eton, Spain; *m* 1985, Mrs Caroline E Fairey, da of Keon Hughes, and former w of Charles Fairey; 1 da (Lady Daisy Caroline b 18 Jan 1989); *Heir* bro, Hon Harry Fane; *Career* dir: Phillips Auctioneers 1994–2002, Bonhams Auctioneers 2002–03, Watson Westmorland Ltd (Ind Art Advisers) 2003–; memb Orbitex Arctic Ocean Research Project Expedition to North Pole 1990; life pres St Moritz Sporting Club; FRGS; *Recreations* countryside pursuits, DIY; *Clubs* Turf; *Style*— The Rt Hon the Earl of Westmorland; ✉ 50 Cornwall Gardens, London SW7 4AD

WESTMORLAND, Archdeacon of; *see*: Howe, Ven George Alexander

WESTON, Adrian Robert; s of Harold Gibbons Weston (d 1987), of Leicester, and Alwyne Gabrielle, *née* Appelbee; *b* 7 June 1935; *Educ* Ratcliffe Coll, The Queen's Coll Oxford (MA); *m* 29 Sept 1963, Bridget Ann, da of William Henry Smith (d 1964), of Leicester; 1 da (Alexandra b 1967), 1 s (Thomas b 1968); *Career* admitted slr 1961; ptnr Harvey Ingram Slrs 1963–98, ret 1999; dir: Atkinson Design Associates Ltd 1982–, Everards Brewery Ltd 1984–,Pointon Gp Ltd 1999–, Moore & York (Commercial) Ltd, Conversbank (UK) Ltd 2006–; capt Leics Co Hockey Assoc 1965–66; vice-pres: The Hockey Assoc 1979– (chm 1972–78), Leics CCC; govr Ratcliffe Coll Leicester 1990–2006, memb Cncl Univ of Leicester 1999–; *Recreations* golf, reading, music; *Clubs* Leicestershire Golf, RAF; *Style*— Adrian R Weston, Esq; ✉ 27 Main Street, Smeeton Westerby, Leicester LE8 0QJ (tel and fax 0116 279 2514)

WESTON, Christopher John; s of Eric Tudor Weston, of Plaxtol, Kent, and Evelyn, *née* Snell; *b* 3 March 1937; *Educ* Lancing; *m* 12 July 1969, Josephine Annabel, da of Dr Moir; 1 da (Annabel b 1973); *Career* RAF 1955–57; life pres Phillips Son & Neale 1998– (chm and chief exec 1972–98); dir: Foreign & Colonial Pacific Investment plc 1984–99, Hodder Headline plc 1986–99 (non-exec chm 1997–99), Foreign & Colonial Enterprise Trust plc 1987–99; chm and ceo Plaxbury Gp 1998–, chm Infoconomy Ltd 2000–, chm Kendlebell Ltd 2006–; vice-pres QUIT 2004– (Nat Soc of Non Smokers, chm 1993–2002); Freeman: City of London, Worshipful Co of Painter-Stainers; FIA (Scot), FRSA; *Recreations* theatre, music; *Clubs* Oriental; *Style*— Christopher Weston, Esq; ✉ 5 Hillside Close, Carlton Hill, London NW8 0EF (tel 020 7624 4780, fax 020 7372 5042)

WESTON, (Willard Gordon) Galen; OC (1990); s of W Garfield Weston (d 1978), of Toronto, Canada and London, and Reta Lila Howard (d 1967); yr bro of Garry Weston, DL (d 2002); *b* 29 October 1940; *Educ* Univ of Western Ontario (BA); *m* 1966, Hilary Mary Frayne; 2 c; *Career* chm and pres George Weston Ltd; exec chm: Loblaw Companies Ltd, Selfridges, Brown Thomas (Ireland), Holt, Renfrew & Co Ltd; dir: Associated Br Foods plc (UK), Fortnum & Mason plc (UK); life memb: Art Gallery of Ontario, Royal Ontario Museum; Hon LLD Univ of Western Ontario; Cdr OStJ 1997; *Recreations* outdoor sports, comtemporary arts; *Clubs* White's, Sunningdale Golf, Badminton & Racquet (Toronto), Toronto Golf, York (Toronto), Windsor (Florida), Brooks (NY), Rosedale Golf, Deepdale (NY); *Style*— W Galen Weston, OC; ✉ George Weston Ltd, 22 St Clair Avenue East, Toronto M4T 2S7, Canada (tel 00 1 416 922 2500, fax 00 1 416 922 6401)

WESTON, George Garfield; s of Garfield Howard Weston (d 2002), and Mary Ruth, *née* Kippenberger; *b* 4 March 1964, Sydney, Aust; *Educ* Westminster, New Coll Oxford (MA), Harvard Business Sch (MBA); *m* 20 Jan 1996, Katharine Mary, *née* Acland; 1 da (Sally b 8 Sept 1999), 3 s (Gregory b 27 March 2001, Garfield b 4 April 2002, Gulliver b 15 July 2004); *Career* gen mangr Weston Milling Aust 1988–90, md Westmill Foods Ltd UK 1992–98, ceo Allied Bakeries 1999–2003, ceo George Weston Foods Ltd Aust 2003–05 (chm 2004), ceo Associated British Foods plc 2005–; *Style*— George Weston, Esq; ✉ Associated British Foods plc, 10 Grosvenor Street, London W1K 4QY (tel 020 7399 6511, fax 020 7399 6588, e-mail carolinepriestley@abfoods.com)

WESTON, Sir (Philip) John; KCMG (1992, CMG 1985); s of Philip George Weston (d 1969), of London), and Edith Alice Bray, *née* Ansell (d 1976); *b* 13 April 1938; *Educ* Sherborne, Worcester Coll Oxford; *m* 28 Jan 1967, Margaret Sally, da of Robert Hermann Ehlers, of

Bridgwater, Somerset; 2 s (Ben b 1969, Rufus b 1973), 1 da (Gabriel b 1970); *Career* served as 2 Lt with 42 Commando RM 1956–58; entered Dip Serv 1962, FO 1962–63, Treasy Centre for Admin Studies 1964, Chinese language student Hong Kong 1964–66, Peking 1967–68, FO 1969–71, office of Perm Rep to EEC 1972–74, asst private sec to Sec of State for Foreign and Cwlth Affrs (Rt Hon James Callaghan, Rt Hon Antony Crosland) 1974–76, head of EEC Presidency Secretariat FCO 1976–77, visiting fell All Souls Coll Oxford 1977–78, cncllr Washington 1978–81, head Def Dept FCO 1981–84, asst under sec of State FCO 1984–85, min Paris 1985–88, dep sec to the Cabinet 1988–89, dep under sec of state FCO 1989–90, political dir FCO 1990–91; UK perm rep: at NATO Brussels 1992–95, to Western European Union 1993–95; UK perm rep and ambass to UN and on Security Cncl NY 1995–98; non-exec dir: British Telecommunications plc 1998–2002, Rolls Royce plc 1998–2004, Hakluyt & Co Ltd 2001–; memb Cncl IISS 2001–05; hon pres Community Fndn Network; tstee Nat Portrait Gallery; govr Ditchley Fndn 2000–; chm of govrs Sherborne Sch, chm of tstees The Poetry Sch, tstee The Poetry Soc; hon fell Worcester Coll Oxford 2003 (pres Coll Soc 2003–); *Publications* Chasing the Hoopoe (poems, 2005); *Recreations* poetry, fly fishing, running, birds; *Clubs* Garrick; *Style*— Sir John Weston, KCMG; ✉ 13 Denbigh Gardens, Richmond, Surrey TW10 6EN

WESTON, John Pix; CBE (1993); *b* 16 August 1951; *Educ* Kings Sch Worcester, Trinity Hall Cambridge (MA); *Children* 1 s, 1 da; *Career* BAE Systems (formerly British Aircraft Corp then British Aerospace plc): apprentice engr 1970, seconded to MOD 1982–84, dir Al-Yamamah prog, md Military Aircraft Div 1990–92, chm BAE defence 1991–96, appointed exec dir 1993, group md 1996–98, chief exec 1998–2002; chm: Spirent plc 2002–, Acra Controls Ltd 2003–, Inbis plc 2004–05, iSoft Group 2005–; memb President's Cncl and chm European Gp CBI; lifetime vice-pres RUSI; Freeman City of London; FREng, FRAeS, FRSA; *Recreations* skiing, photography, mountain walking; *Style*— John Weston, Esq, CBE, FREng, FRAeS

WESTON, Martin Wynell Lee; s of Quentin V L Weston, OBE, and Jill, *née* Gamon; *b* 29 July 1952; *Educ* Sevenoaks Sch, Univ of Oxford (MA), Coll of Law; *m* 24 Aug 1984, Fidelity Anne, da Colin Simpson; 4 c (Lucian b 18 Oct 1985, Alfred b 20 March 1987, Inigo b 30 Jan 1989, Phoebe b 25 Jan 1992); *Career* called to the Bar 1976, practising barr 1977–78; Commonwealth Development Corp 1978–82, corp fin dept Lazard Brothers 1982–83, established co now known as Weald Group plc 1984; hon consul for the Republic of Nauru; *Recreations* sports incl: running, swimming, tennis, football, walking; *Clubs* Vincent's (Oxford), St Julian's (Sevenoaks); *Style*— Martin Weston, Esq; ✉ Romshed Courtyard, Underriver, Sevenoaks, Kent TN15 0SD (tel 01732 743125, fax 01732 454136, e-mail grp@weald.co.uk)

WESTON, Prof Richard Henry; s of Raymond Charles Weston (d 1982), and Winifred May, *née* Hook (1985); *b* 20 March 1944; *Educ* Univ of London (BSc), Univ of Southampton (PhD); *m* 1, 14 Feb 1962 (m dis 1976), Sylvia June, *née* Gregg; 2 s (Keith Richard b 1962, Ian Michael b 1964); m 2, 25 May 1985, Betty, da of Leonard Whitear, of Loughborough; 1 da (Nicola Michelle b 1980); *Career* pro-vice-chllr res and prof of engrg Loughborough Univ of Technol, head MSI Res Inst; supervisor of over 50 postgrad students, various overseas educnl appts, princ investigator for over 20 major UK and Euro res studies in mfrg, retained conslt by numerous UK companies, tech advsr to Sci and Engrg Res Cncl, DTI and ICL; author of in excess of 200 res pubns on mfrg engrg topics with special interest in manufacturing systems integration, information systems and robotics; memb: Bd of Int Jls, Br and Euro Standards Bodies; FIEE 1984, FRSA; *Books* incl: Software for Modular Robots (contrib, 1984), Integrating Robots Within Production Systems Encyclopaedia of Systems and Control (contrib, 1988), The Automated Manufacturing Directory (ed 4 edns, 1985), Fluid Power 8 (contrib, 1988), Modular Robots Encyclopaedia of Systems and Control (contrib, 1988), Contouring with Pneumatic Servo-Driven Robots (contrib, 1988); *Recreations* golf, bridge, squash, football (Univ colours); *Style*— Prof Richard Weston; ✉ Department of Manufacturing Engineering, Loughborough University, Loughborough, Leicestershire LE11 3TU (tel 01509 222907, fax 01509 267725)

WESTON SMITH, John Harry; s of Cdr Weston Smith, OBE, RN (d 1986); *b* 3 February 1932; *Educ* Fettes, St John's Coll Cambridge (MA); *m* 1955, Margaret Fraser, da of Prof E A Milne, FRS (d 1954); 2 da (Miranda b 1956, Lucinda b 1964), 1 s (Hugh b 1961); *Career* jt gen mangr Abbey National 1968–69 (sec 1961–68), assoc N M Rothschild 1969–71; British Land Co plc: joined as co sec 1971, dir 1973–2006, fin dir 1989–2002, chief operating offr 2002–06, md British Land Corporation 1991–2006, ret 2006; dir various other cos; FCIS, ACII, ACIB; *Style*— John Weston Smith, Esq

WESTROPP, Anthony Henry (Harry); s of Col Lionel Henry Mountefort Westropp (d 1991), and Muriel Constance Lilian, *née* Jorgensen; *b* 22 December 1944; *Educ* Sherborne, KCL; *m* 1, 7 Dec 1977 (m dis 1991), Zoë Rosaleen, da of (Charles) Douglas Neville Walker, of Paris; m 2, 6 May 1993, Hon Victoria Monica Watson, da of 3 Baron Manton; 1 da (Marina b 1993); *Career* with Lazard Bros & Co Ltd 1967–72, dir of subsidiaries Trafalgar House Gp 1972–75, md private gp of cos 1975–81; gp md: Bardsey plc 1981–90, The Beckenham Gp plc 1990–91; chm: MCD UK Ltd 1994–97, Britton Gp plc 1992–95, Abacus Gp plc 1994–, Norbain plc 1996–99, Upperpoint Ltd 1999–2006; non-exec dir: Portman Building Soc 1982–2003, Nickerson Gp Rothwell Ltd 1991–, Marling Industries plc 1994–97, The Throgmorton Tst plc 2003–; Freeman Co of Cutlers (Sheffield) 1982; *Recreations* rural pursuits, skiing; *Clubs* Boodle's, Turf; *Style*— Harry Westropp, Esq; ✉ Goadby Hall, Melton Mowbray, Leicestershire LE14 4LN (tel 01664 464202)

WESTROPP, George Victor; s of Edward L Westropp (d 1962), of Epsom, Surrey, and Mary Breward, *née* Hughes (d 1973); *b* 2 November 1943; *Educ* Bedford Sch; *m* 1, 12 Jan 1972 (m dis 1973), Alexander Jeanne, da of Joseph Steinberg; m 2, 9 May 1977 (m dis 1988), Christine June, da of Alan Ashley; 2 s (Edward b 1980, Kit b 1982); m 3, 31 May 2003, Helen Elizabeth Elliott, da of Dr Peter H Cooper; *Career* reporter City Press 1961–63, city reporter Sunday Express 1963, fin journalist Evening Standard 1963–68, asst city ed Extel 1968–69; dir Shareholder Relations Ltd 1969–73, fin PR exec PPR International Ltd 1974–76, md Hemingway Public Relations Ltd 1977–79, nat dir of communications Touche Ross (now Deloitte & Touche) 1979–2000 (ptnr 1985–2000); dir RHS Special Events Ltd 2002–; chm Salmon & Trout Assoc Tst 2004–; MCIPR, FRSA; *Books* The Lake Vyrnwy Fishing Book (1979), Lake Vyrnwy - The Story of a Sporting Hotel (1992), The Westropp Family 1250–2000 (1999); *Recreations* salmon and trout fishing, gardening; *Clubs* London Press (chm 1990–99); *Style*— George Westropp, Esq; ✉ 36 Holley Road, London W3 7TS (tel 020 8743 1752, car 07774 412480, e-mail george.westropp@btconnect.com)

WESTROPP, Helen Elizabeth; da of Dr Peter Henry Cooper (d 1991), and Hilary Tasker *née* Stock; *b* 1 June 1961; *Educ* Cranbrook Sch, Lancaster Univ (BA); *m* 31 May 2003, George Victor Westropp, s of late Edward L Westropp, of Fleet Street, London; *Career* market analyst Institut Proscop 1984–85, privatisation research exec Dewe Rogerson 1986, account dir and assoc dir Hill Murray Fin PR 1986–89, dir Landor Associates Europe 1990–97, owner and principal Delphi Marques 1998–; memb London Ctee RNID 1989–91, advsr RNID Poolmead campaign 1991, chair and memb Bd Oxfordshire Community Devpt Assoc 1999–2003, graduate Common Purpose 2003, memb Cncl RSA 2004–, memb Ctee E Midlands RSA, friend of the Royal Acad; memb: London Oriana Choir 1986–90, Action Aid, Br Heart Fndn, Simon Community, Salmon and Trout Assoc, Countryside Alliance, RHS, Royal Nat Rose Soc; FRSA; *Books* The Westropp Family 1250–2000 (with G V Westropp, 2000); *Recreations* fishing, shooting, gardening, music, travel; *Style*— Mrs Helen Westropp; ✉ The Stable House, Goadby Hall, Goadby Marwood, Leicestershire LE14 4LN (e-mail helen.westropp@btconnect.com)

WESTWELL, Dr Alan Reynolds; OBE (1996); s of Stanley Westwell (d 1980), of Liverpool, and Margaret, *née* Reynolds (d 1962); *b* 11 April 1940; *Educ* Old Swan Coll, Liverpool Poly (ACT), Univ of Salford (MSc), Keele Univ (PhD); *m* 30 Oct 1967, (Elizabeth) Aileen, da of John Birrell (d 1975), of Fife, Scotland; 1 da (Julie b 1970), 2 s (Stephen, Colin (twins) b 1972); *Career* asst works mangr (previously engrg apprentice and tech asst) Liverpool City Tport Dept 1956–67; chief engr: Southport Corp Tport Dept 1967–69, Coventry Corp Tport Dept 1969–72, Glasgow Corp Tport Dept 1972–74; dir of public tport Tayside Regnl Cncl 1974–79, DG Strathclyde Passenger Tport Exec 1979–86, chm and md Strathclyde Buses Ltd 1986–90; chief exec and md: Greater Manchester Buses Ltd 1990–93, Greater Manchester Buses (North) Ltd 1993–97, Dublin Buses Ltd 1997–2005; public tport professional advsr Convention of Scottish Local Authorities (COSLA) 1975–85; pres: Scottish Cncl of Confedn of Br Road Passenger Tport 1982–83 (vice-pres 1981–82), Bus and Coach Cncl 1989–90 (vice-pres 1985–88, sr vice-pres 1988–89); chm Scottish Centre Automobile Div IMechE 1982–84, memb Parly Road Tport Ctee 1986–97, memb Cncl CIT UK 1986–89 (chm Scottish Centre 1983–84); Int Public Tport Union (UITP, based Brussels): memb Int Met Railway Ctee, memb Exec Mgmnt Ctee 1992–, chm Br Membership 1993–98, vice-pres 1997, memb EU Ctee (formerly European Action Ctee), memb Tport and Urban Life Cmmn (formerly Public Tport and Urban Planning Cmmn); CEng, FCIT, FILT, MIMechE, MIEE; *Recreations* swimming, music, reading; *Style*— Dr Alan Westwell, OBE; ✉ 6 Amberley Drive, Hale Barns, Cheshire WA15 0DT (tel 0161 980 3551)

WESTWOOD, Dr Albert Ronald Clifton (Bert); s of Albert Sydney Westwood (d 1985), and Ena Emily, *née* Clifton (d 1984); *b* 9 June 1932; *Educ* Univ of Birmingham (BSc, PhD, DSc); *m* 8 Dec 1956, Jean Mavis, *née* Bullock; 2 da (Abigail b 1957, Andrea b 1961); *Career* tech offr Research Dept ICI (Metals Div) Birmingham 1956–58; Martin Marietta Laboratories Baltimore Maryland: scientist then sr scientist 1958–64, assoc dir and head Materials Science Dept 1964–69, dep dir 1969–74, dir 1974–84; Martin Marietta Corp Bethesda Maryland: corp dir R&D 1984–87, vice-pres R&D 1987–90, vice-pres Science 1990, vice-pres Research and Technol 1990–93; vice-pres Research and Exploratory Technol Sandia National Laboratories New Mexico 1993–96, chm and chief exec Cncl for the Central Laboratory of the Research Cncls (UK) 1998–2000, int advsr res and technol mgmnt 2000–; lectureships incl: Tewksbury Univ of Melbourne 1974, Burgess Memorial ASMI 1984, Campbell Memorial ASMI 1987, Krumb AIME 1988, dist lectr ASME 1988–90, Christie Johns Hopkins Univ 1991, Wenk lectr in Technol and Public Policy Johns Hopkins Univ 1995, dist lectr Materials and Soc TMS 1995; chm: Commn on Engrg & Tech Systems National Research Cncl 1992–97, Public Information Advisory Ctee (Nat Acad Engrg) 1993–95, Ctee on Global Aspects of Intellectual Property Rights in Science and Technol 1991–92, Maryland Humanities Cncl, New Mexico Humanities Cncl; pres: New Mexico Symphony Orchestra, Industrial Research Inst 1989–90, The Minerals, Metals and Materials Soc (TMS) 1990–91, Sci and Technol Corp of Univ of New Mexico 2007; memb: Nat Acad of Engrg USA 1980, Bd of US Civilian Research and Devpt Fndn, Cncl Fedn for Science and Technol, Bd Santa Fe Opera, Musica Russia Fndn; Foreign Assocs: Royal Swedish Acad Engrg Sciences 1989, Russian Acad of Engrg 1995; fell: Johns Hopkins Univ 1965, Inst of Physicists (UK) 1967, American Soc for Materials International (ASMI) 1974, American Assoc for Advancement of Science 1986, TMS 1990; FREng 1996, FIM 1998; *Awards* Distinguished Young Scientist Maryland Acad Sci 1966, Beilby Gold Medal RSC 1970, Leadership Award TMS 1992, Centennial Medal Univ of Maryland 1994, Acta Metallurgica Holloman Award 1996, Medal for Advancement of Research ASMI 2006; *Publications* ed three books, author of more than 120 sci pubns; *Recreations* music (accompanist and musical arranger), humanities, theatre, travel; *Style*— Bert Westwood; ✉ 13539 Canada Del Oso, Albuquerque, New Mexico 87111, USA (tel 505 797 2227, fax 505 797 2228, e-mail arwestwood@aol.com)

WESTWOOD, 3 Baron (UK 1944); (William) Gavin Westwood; s of 2 Baron Westwood, JP (d 1991), and Marjorie, *née* Bonwick (d 1999); *b* 30 January 1944; *Educ* Fettes; *m* 1969, Penelope, FCA, da of Charles Edgar Shafto, VRD, MB (d 1994); 2 s (Hon (William) Fergus b 1972, Hon Alistair Cameron b 1974); *Heir* s, Hon Fergus Westwood; *Style*— The Rt Hon Lord Westwood; ✉ 9 Princes Close, Brunton Park, Newcastle upon Tyne NE3 5AS (e-mail lordwestwood@hotmail.com)

WESTWOOD, Hon Nigel Alistair; yr s of 2 Baron Westwood, JP (d 1991), and Marjorie, *née* Bonwick; *b* 1950; *Educ* Fettes; *m* 1977, Joan Elizabeth, yr da of Reginald Ibison, CBE; 2 s (David Alistair b 1983, Peter Robert b 1986); *Career* chartered surveyor; chm Sanderson Townend & Gilbert, dir Universal Building Soc; High Sheriff Tyne & Wear 2007–08; hon Norwegian consul, chllr Consular Corps Newcastle-upon-Tyne; Knight First Class Royal Norwegian Order of Merit 1995; FRICS, FRSA; *Clubs* Northern Counties, Den Norske; *Style*— The Hon Nigel Westwood; ✉ 7 Fernville Road, Gosforth, Newcastle-upon-Tyne NE3 4HT

WESTWOOD, Tim; *Career* DJ; radio DJ: LWR (pirate), Kiss FM (pirate, former co-owner), Capital FM 1987–94, BBC Radio 1 1994–; also club DJ in venues across UK and European summer clubbing resorts; TV presenter: N Sign (ITV Night Network) 1990–92, Westwood Presents (UK Play) 2000, Westwood TV (Channel U) 2004–, Pimp my Ride UK (MTV) 2005–07, Westwood's Trick It Out 2006; magazine journalist: Westwood column Max Power 2004–, ed 33Hz 2004–; columnist The Sun 2004–; patron: Radio Feltham YOI, Body and Soul Teen Spirit, Nordoff Robins Dance Charity, Sonic DB; memb: Radio Acad, Equity, Big Dawg Pitbulls (NYC); *Albums* Westwood the Album Volume 1 (Silver) 2001, Westwood Volume 2 (Gold) 2001, Westwood Volume 3 (Gold) 2002, Westwood Platinum Edition (Platinum) 2003, Westwood The Jump Off (Gold) 2004, Westwood The Takeover (Gold) 2004, Westwood The Big Dawg (Gold) 2004, Westwood The Invasion (Gold) 2005, Westwood Heat (Gold) 2005, Westwood - Ride with the Big Dawg 2006, Westwood - The Greatest 2006; *DVD* The Takeover 2004, Westwood Raw 2005; *Awards* Sony Awards: Best Specialist Music Prog 1990, 1991 and 1999, Best Music Broadcaster 1996 and 2000 (nominated 2001 and 2003), nomination Best Music Programme 2001, nominated Best Specialist 2005 and 2007; Best Radio Show Muzik Magazine Awards 1999, Best UK Radio DJ MOBO Awards 2000, 2003 and 2005, Best Hip Hop DJ Pacha Awards 2003, Best R'n'B and Hip Hop DJ Sidewinder Awards 2003 and 2004; voted no 1 rap DJ by the readers of Hip Hop Connection magazine for 12 successive years; *Style*— Tim Westwood

WESTWOOD, Vivienne Isabel; *née* Swire; DBE (2006, OBE 1992); *b* 8 April 1941; *Career* fashion designer; a series of influential avant garde collections showcased at World's End 430 King's Road (formerly named Let it Rock, Too Fast to Live Too Young to Die, Sex, Seditionaries) 1971–82, opened Vivienne Westwood shop at 6 Davies St London 1990, flagship shop at 44 Conduit St London, head office Milan, stores worldwide; Gold Label collections show in Paris every season; other collections launched incl: Vivienne Westwood Man (Milan) 1996, Red Label (NY) 2000, Anglomania collections every season; fragrances launched: Boudoir 1998, Libertine 2000, Boudoir Sin City 2007, Let it Rock 2007; Vivienne Westwood 36 years in fashion exhbn (V&A) 2004 and (worldwide tour) 2005–; contrib to exhbns: Radical Fashion (V&A) 2001, Men in Skirts (V&A) 2002, Tiaras (V&A) 2002; prof of fashion: Vienna Acad of Applied Arts 1989–91, Berlin Hochschule 1993–; hon sr fell RCA 1992; British Designer of the Year Br Fashion Cncl 1990 and 1991, Queen's Award for Export 1998; subject of Moët & Chandon Fashion Tribute (V&A) 1998, Moët & Chandon Red Carpet Dresser 2006; trustee Civil Liberties Tst 2007;

Style— Dame Vivienne Westwood, DBE; ✉ Vivienne Westwood Ltd, Westwood Studios, 9–15 Elcho Street, Battersea, London SW11 4AU (tel 020 7924 4747)

WETHERED, (James) Adam Lawrence; *b* 2 April 1953; *Educ* Eton, Christ's Coll Cambridge (BA, LLB); *m* Dr Diana Wethered; 5 c; *Career* called to the Bar Inner Temple 1975; J P Morgan: 1976–2000, chief exec J P Morgan Securities Ltd 1991–97, head of Asset Mgmnt Servs, Institutional and Private Clients Europe and JP Morgan Investment Mgmnt Inc 1998–2000; currently dir: Private Investment Office Lord North Street Ltd (fndr ptnr), British Portfolios Tst plc; *Style—* Adam Wethered, Esq; ✉ 4 Lord North Street, London SW1P 3LA (e-mail adamwethered@lordnorth.com)

WETHERED, Simon Richard; s of Dr Rodney Richard Wethered (d 1995), of Stonehouse, Glos, and Sarah Meriel, *née* Long-Price (d 2001); *b* 1 March 1945; *Educ* Clifton, Worcester Coll Oxford (MA); *m* 9 Sept 1978, Victoria, da of Adm of the Fleet Sir Michael Le Fanu, GCB, DSC (d 1970); 1 da (Anna b 1981), 2 s (Edward b 1983, Charles b 1988); *Career* admitted slr 1970; ptnr: Simmons & Simmons 1974–78, Dibb Lupton Alsop (formerly Alsop Wilkinson) 1978–98, Charles Russell 1998–2005 (conslt 2005–); licensed insolvency practitioner 1987–99; memb Advsy Bd HSBC Common Funds; visitor HMP Wormwood Scrubs 1984–, dir Academy Concerts Soc 1984–2000; tstee: Leche Tst, Marie Curie Cancer Care, The Connection at St Martin's, St Martin in the Fields Christmas Appeal Charity; Liveryman Worshipful Co of Distillers; memb: Law Soc, Charity Law Assoc, City of London Slrs' Co; *Recreations* wine, music, walking; *Clubs* Athenaeum, City Law; *Style—* Simon Wethered, Esq; ✉ 29 Burlington Road, London W4 4BQ (tel 020 8994 6392)

WETHERELL, HE Gordon Geoffrey; s of Geoffrey Wetherell, of Addis Ababa, Ethiopia, and late Georgette Maria, *née* Matkovitch; *b* 11 November 1948; *Educ* Bradfield, New Coll Oxford (MA), Univ of Chicago (MA); *m* 11 July 1981, Rosemary Anne, da of Cdr Terence Macrae Myles, RN, ret, of Crieff, Perthshire; 4 da (Christine b 1982, Stephanie b 1985, Emily b 1987, Alexandra b 1989); *Career* W African Dept FCO (concurrently third sec/vice-consul Chad) 1973–74, third then second sec E Berlin 1974–77; first sec: Arms Control and Disarmament Dept FCO 1977, UK delegation to comprehensive test ban negotiations Geneva 1977–80, New Delhi 1980–83, NATO Desk Defence Dept FCO 1983–85; secondment to HM Treasy 1986–87, asst head Euro Communities Dept (External) FCO 1987–88, cnsllr and dep head of mission Warsaw 1988–92, cnsllr Bonn 1992–94, head Personnel Servs Dept FCO 1994–97, ambass to Ethiopia 1997–2000 (concurrently non-resident ambass to Eritrea and Djibouti), ambass to Luxembourg 2000–04, high cmmr to Ghana 2004– (concurrently non-resident ambass to Togo, Niger, Burkina Faso, Cote d'Ivoire); *Recreations* tennis, travel, reading, Manchester United FC; *Clubs* Oxford and Cambridge, Cercle Munster (Luxembourg); *Style—* HE Mr Gordon Wetherell; ✉ c/o Foreign & Commonwealth Office (Accra), King Charles Street, London SW1A 2AH

WETHERELL, John Michael Hugh Paxton; s of Paxton Wetherell, MBE (d 1978), of Whitstable, Kent, and Catherine Wilson, *née* Collins (d 1992); *b* 24 October 1942; *Educ* Ampleforth, St Benet's Hall Oxford (BA); *m* 2 May 1964, Elizabeth Ann, da of Harold Thompson (d 1988), of Broadstairs, Kent; 5 da (Laura b 1966, Kate b 1968, Beatrice b 1972, Gabrielle b 1974, Jessica b 1978), 1 s (Joseph b 1979); *Career* Lloyd's underwriter Janson Green/Bolton Ingham Non-Marine Syndicate 1983; dir: Bolton Ingham Agency Ltd 1983–88, Janson Green Management Ltd 1986–91, Cater Allen Syndicate Management Ltd 1992–94, Liberty Syndicate Management Ltd 1994–98, ret; memb Lloyd's 1973; past chm: Lloyd's Syndicates Survey Bd, Lloyd's Non-Marine Assoc, Lloyd's Business Issues Ctee, Lloyd's Claims Office; memb: Catholic Union, Latin Mass Soc, Oxford Univ Soc; *Books* Lex Orandi Lex Credendi: An Examination of the Ethos of the Tridentine Mass and that of the Novus Ordo of Pope Paul VI; *Recreations* reading, music, racing; *Style—* John Wetherell, Esq; ✉ Snape Barn, Blackgate Lane, Pulborough, West Sussex RH20 1DE (tel 01403 700176)

WETZEL, Dave; s of Fred Wetzel (d 1982), and Ivy, *née* Donaldson (d 1981); *b* 9 October 1942, Isleworth, Middx; *Educ* Spring Grove GS Isleworth, Henry George Sch of Social Sci; *m* 14 Feb 1973, Heather Jacqueline, da of Edmond John Allman (d 1976), of Staines; 2 da (Emma b 9 Dec 1968, Chantel b 1 Jan 1974); *Career* student engr Wilkinson Sword 1959–62, bus conductor, driver and inspr London Transport 1962–69, branch mangr Initial Servs 1969–70, pilot roster offr BEA/BA 1970–74, political organiser London Co-op 1974–81, ed Civil Aviation News 1978–81, chair Transport Ctee GLC 1981–86, unemployed then minicab driver 1986, ptnr antique shop 1994–99, vice-chair Transport for London 2000–; pres: London Univ Transport Studies Soc 1991–92, W London Peace Cncl 1982–; memb: TGWU, Lab Party, Lab Land Campaign (currently pres), Socialist Environmental Resources Assoc, Professional Land Reform Gp (currently chair); cncllr London Borough of Hounslow 1964–68 and 1986–94 (chair of planning 1986–87, ldr 1987–91); dir DaRT (charity) 1989–94; author of various articles on land reform and transport funding; FCILT, FRSA; *Recreations* family Chinese restaurant, lectures on land value taxation, Esperanto, travel; *Style—* Dave Wetzel, Esq; ✉ Transport for London, Windsor House, 42–50 Victoria Street, London SW1H 0TL (tel 020 7126 4200, e-mail davewetzel@tfl.gov.uk)

WEYMAN, Anne Judith; OBE (2000); da of Joseph Stanley Weyman, and Rose, *née* Hellinger; *b* 1 February 1943; *Educ* Tollington GS, Univ of Bristol (BSc), LSE (BSc); *Career* head of fin and admin Int Secretariat Amnesty Int 1977–86 (est charity 1985), dir and non-exec chair Pinter Publishers Ltd 1974–95; Nat Children's Bureau: info and public affrs dir, co sec 1986–96; chief exec fpa (Family Planning Assoc London) 1996–, non-exec chair Family Planning Sales Ltd 1996–2002, non-exec dir Islington Primary Care Tst 2002–; estab: Sex Educn Forum 1987, Drug Educn Forum 1995; co-fndr: Forum on AIDS and Children 1992, Children's Play Cncl 1990; pres Sex Educn Forum 1996– (fndr 1987, chair 1987–96), chair of Nat Child Care Campaign and the Day Care Tst 1986–87, fndr memb Campaign for Res into Human Reproduction 1984–90, memb Nat Joint Ctee of Working Women's Orgns 1979–84, hon sec Socialist Health Assoc 1977–84, sec Cncl for Disabled Children 1986–96; tstee: Children's Rights Office 1991–99, Pharmacy Health Care Scheme 1996–2001; memb: Mgmnt Ctee of Nat Children's Play and Recreation Unit 1990–94, Personal Social and Health Educn Advsy Gp 1998–2001, The Sexual Health Strategy Gp 1999–2000, Women's Nat Cmmn Steering Gp 1999–2003, The Ind Advsy Gp on Teenage Pregnancy 2000–; co vice-chair Independent Advsy Gp on Sexual Health 2003–; govr of schs in Westminster and Islington 1970s-90s; memb: NE Dist of Kensington, Chelsea and Westminster CHC 1974–78, NW Thames Regnl HA 1978–80; cncllr Westminster City Cncl 1978–82; Hon LLD Univ of Bristol 2005; FCA 1968; *Publications* A Sociological View of Large Groups (with Earl Hopper, in Large Groups (ed Lionel Kreeger) 1975, Modern British Society: A Bibliography (with J Westergaard and Paul Wiles, 1977), Social Behaviour Assesment Schedule (with S Platt and S R Hirsch, *qv*, 1983), Finding and Running Premises (with J Unell, 1985), Starting and Running a Voluntary Group (with S Capper and J Unell, 1989), Individual Choices, Collective Responsibility: Sexual Health, a Public Health Issue (with Maria Duggan, 1999), Sexual and Reproductive Health and Rights in the UK: 5 Years on from Cairo (with Marge Berer and Amy Kapczynski, 1999), Handbook of Sexual Health in Primary Care (with Toni Belfield, Yvonne Carter, *qv*, Philippa Matthews and Catti Moss, 2006); contrib to numerous jls 1972–; *Recreations* gardening (garden open under the Nat Gardens Scheme), theatre, music and opera; *Style—* Ms Anne Weyman, OBE; ✉ fpa, 50 Featherstone Street, London EC1Y 8QU (tel 020 7608 5240, e-mail anne-w@fpa.org.uk)

WHALEN, Sir Geoffrey Henry; kt (1995), CBE (1989); s of Henry Charles Whalen (d 1981), and Mabel Elizabeth Whalen (d 1965); *b* 8 January 1936; *Educ* East Ham GS, Magdalen Coll Oxford (MA); *m* 1961, Elizabeth Charlotte, da of Dr Eric Waud, of Helperby, N Yorks; 3 da (Catherine b 1963, Anna b 1965, Georgina b 1975), 2 s (Thomas b 1967, Henry b 1977); *Career* personnel dir Leyland Cars British Leyland 1975–78; Peugeot Motor Co PLC: asst md 1981–84, md 1984–95, dep chm 1990–95, non-exec dep chm 1995–2003; former dir: Robins and Day Ltd, Talbot Ireland Ltd, Proptal UK Ltd, Motaquip Ltd, Sunbeam-Talbot Ltd, T & N plc, Lombard North Central plc, Hall Engineering (Holdings) plc; chm: Camden Motors Ltd, Coventry Building Society 1999–2005 (non-exec dir until 2006); non-exec dir: Federal Mogul Corp; pres Soc of Motor Manufacturers & Traders 1988–90 and 1993–94 (dep pres 1997–98); govr Coventry Univ (formerly Poly) 1989–95; Hon DBA; Hon FCGI, CIMgt, FIMI; Chevalier de la Légion d'Honneur 1990; *Recreations* cricket, tennis, golf; *Clubs* Oxford and Cambridge; *Style—* Sir Geoffrey Whalen, CBE; ✉ 8 Park Crescent, Abingdon, Oxfordshire (tel and fax 01235 523917)

WHALEY, Dr Joachim; *Career* fell Gonville & Caius Coll Cambridge, sr lectr and head Dept of German Univ of Cambridge; FRHistS; *Books* Mirrors of Mortality: Studies in the Social History of Death (ed, 1981), Religious Toleration and Social Change in Hamburg 1529–1819 (1985); *Style—* Dr Joachim Whaley; ✉ Department of German, Sidgwick Avenue, Cambridge CB3 9DA

WHALLEY, Andrew David; s of Donald Allan Whalley (d 1998), and Marjorie, *née* Craven; *b* 27 February 1962; *Educ* Dollar Acad, Mackintosh Sch of Architecture Glasgow Sch of Art and Univ of Glasgow (BArch), AA Sch of Architecture (AADipl); *m* 1986, Fiona, da of Andrew Biggim Douglas Galbraith; 2 da (Catriona Grace b 1993, Morven Sylvia Jane b 1996); *Career* architect; ptnr Grimshaw Architects LLP (formerly Nicholas Grimshaw & Partners Ltd) 2007– (dir 1986–2007); work incl numerous tport, arts and public bldgs, and commercial and technol projects; projects incl: redevelopment of Paddington Station London, Fundación Caixa Galicia Art Gallery A Coruña Spain, The Eden Project Cornwall, Donald Danforth Plant Science Center St Louis MO USA, Miami Intermodal Center FL USA, Grimshaw Architects PC USA, Electronic Performing Arts Centre Troy NY, Queens Museum of Art Expansion NY, Earthpark Iowa, Fulton Street Transit Center NY, Museum of Steel Monterey Mexico, Southern Cross Station Melbourne Aust, Miami Museum of Science FL, Univ of NY 20 Year Masterplan; projects in partnership with Galbraith Whalley: house in Scotland utilising new glazing technol, house in London utilising low energy systems; exhibitions: Product & Process (RIBA) 1987, Structure, Space & Skin (RIBA) 1993, Through the Mac (Glasgow and Brazil) 1997; visiting lectr Dept of Industrial Design and Design Innovation Unit RCA 1989–92, tutor AA London 1993–95, visiting tutor Bartlett Sch of Architecture 1995–2003; lectr at home and abroad incl: Royal Acad London 1996, Mackintosh Sch of Architecture 1997, Art and Architecture Fndn 1998, Ruth and Norman Moore visiting prof Washington Univ MO USA; memb Cncl Architectural Assoc; Otis AJ Architecture Competition commendation 1985, Glasgow Eurodrome commendation 1988, RIBA Award for Architecture (Scotland) 1990, Eric Lyon Housing Award commendation 1992; RIBA 1990; registered architect: UK ARB 1990, USA State of Missouri 1998; memb AIA, memb RIBA; FRSA; *Publications* The Architecture of Eden (with Hugh Pearman); author of papers on steel frame construction (especially the use of steel in Waterloo terminal for British Steel) 1992–95, tech articles on interactive structures published in New Scientist, Sunday Times and the design press, sustainability columnist Architecture Magazine (USA); *Recreations* architecture, photography, skiing; *Clubs* Chelsea Arts; *Style—* Andrew Whalley, Esq; ✉ Grimshaw Architects LLP, 57 Clerkenwell Road, London EC1M 5NG (tel 020 7291 4141, fax 020 7291 4194/4195, e-mail andrew.whalley@grimshaw-architects.com,website www.ngrimshaw.co.uk); Grimshaw USA, 100 Reade Street, New York, NY 10013, USA (tel 001 221 791 2501, fax 001 212 791 2173)

WHALLEY, Prof Lawrence Jeffrey; s of James Anthony Whalley (d 1980), of St Annes-on-Sea, Lancs, and Florence Evelyn Whalley (d 1960); *b* 12 March 1946; *Educ* St Joseph's Coll Blackpool, Univ of Newcastle upon Tyne (MB BS, MD), DPM; *m* 1969, Patricia Mary, da of Denis McCarthy; 3 da (Charlotte Louise b 1970, Amanda Sophie b 1971, Elizabeth Natalia b 1972); *Career* trainee psychiatrist, memb Clinical Scientific Staff MRC 1977–86, sr lectr in psychiatry Univ of Edinburgh 1986–91, Crombie Ross prof of mental health and head Dept of Mental Health Univ of Aberdeen 1992–; FRCPsych 1990; *Publications* The Ageing Brain (2001), Dementia (2002); author of over 200 scientific reports and articles; *Style—* Professor Lawrence Whalley; ✉ School of Medicine, Foresterhill, Aberdeen AB25 2ZD (tel 01224557467, fax 01224 557401)

WHARNCLIFFE, 5 Earl of (UK 1876) Richard Alan Montagu Stuart Wortley; also Baron Wharncliffe (UK 1826) and Viscount Carlton (UK 1876); er s of Alan Ralph Montagu Stuart Wortley (d 1986), and Virginia Ann, *née* Claybaugh (d 1993); suc his kinsman 4 Earl of Wharncliffe (d 1987); *b* 26 May 1953; *Educ* Wesleyan Univ; *m* 1979, Mary Elizabeth, da of Rev William Wellington Reed, of Keene, NH, USA; 3 s (Reed, Viscount Carlton b 5 Feb 1980, Hon Christopher James b 28 Aug 1983, Hon Otis Alexander b 14 Feb 1991); *Heir* s, Viscount Carlton; *Career* construction foreman; *Style—* The Rt Hon the Earl of Wharncliffe; ✉ 74 Sweetser Road, North Yarmouth, Maine 04097, USA

WHARTON, Rt Rev (John) Martin; *see:* Newcastle, Bishop of

WHARTON, 12 Baron (E 1544–55); Myles Christopher David Robertson; s of Henry MacLeod Robertson (d 1996), and Baroness Wharton (Myrtle Olive Felix (Ziki), *née* Arbuthnot; 11 holder of title; d 2000); *b* 1 October 1964, London; *Educ* KCS Wimbledon; *m* 11 May 2003, Barbara Kay, *née* Marshall; 1 da (Hon Meghan Ziki Mary b 8 March 2006); *Heir* da, Hon Meghan Robertson; *Style—* The Rt Hon the Lord Wharton

WHATELY, Julian Richard; s of Gerald Arthur Whately, OBE (d 1985), and Nina Abigail Whately, *née* Finlayson (d 1994); *b* 10 August 1949; *Educ* Eton, Univ of Bristol (BA); *m* 1973, Clare Magdalen Hallett; 3 s (Richard Marcus b 11 March 1977, Hugo Thomas b 4 May 1979, Benjamin William b 26 Sept 1980); *Career* admitted slr 1974; sr ptnr Lee and Pembertons; tstee Herbert and Peter Blagrave Charitable Tst; *Recreations* hill walking, fishing, skiing, tennis; *Clubs* Boodle's, The Kandahar; *Style—* Julian Whately, Esq; ✉ The Manor House, Holybourne, Alton, Hampshire GU34 4HD

WHATELY, Kevin; s of Richard Whately (d 1968), of Humshaugh, Northumberland, and Mary, *née* Pickering; *b* 6 February 1951; *Educ* Humshaugh Sch, Barnard Castle Sch, Central Sch of Speech and Drama; *m* 30 April 1984, Madelaine, da of Jack Newton (d 1983); 1 da (Catherine Mary b 13 April 1983), 1 s (Kieran John Richard b 12 Oct 1984); *Career* actor; memb Northumberland and Durham County Cross Country Running Team 1968; vice-pres NCH; ambass: Prince's Tst, Alzheimer's Soc, City of Newcastle upon Tyne, City of Sunderland; Hon Dr Univ of Northumberland; *Theatre* incl: Prince Hal in Henry IV Part 1 (Newcastle) 1981, Andy in Accounts (Edinburgh and London) 1982, title role in Billy Liar (nat tour) 1983, John Proctor in The Crucible (Leicester) 1989, Daines in Our Own Kind (Bush) 1991, Twelve Angry Men (Comedy) 1996, Snake In The Grass (Peter Hall Co, Old Vic) 1997, How I Learned to Drive (Donmar) 1998; *Opera* Judas in The Peoples Passion (BBC); *Television* incl: Kevin in Coronation Street (Granada) 1981, Bob in The Dig (BBC) 1981, Adams in Shackleton (BBC) 1982, Neville in Auf Wiedersehen Pet (Central) 1982–84, Sgt Lewis in Inspector Morse (Central) 1985–2000, Steve in B & B (Thames) 1992, Jack Kerruish in Peak Practice (Central) 1993–95, Trip Trap (BBC) 1995, Gobble 1996, Jimmy Griffin in The Broker's Man 1997–98, Pure Wickedness (BBC) 1998, What Katy Did (Tetra) 1999, Plain Jane (Carlton) 2001, Nightmare Neighbour (BBC) 2001, Hurst in Promoted to Glory 2003, The Legend of the Tamworth Two 2003, Belonging 2004, Dad (BBC) 2005, Footprints in the Snow (ITV) 2005, Lewis (ITV) 2006–08, New Tricks (BBC) 2006, Who Gets the Dog? (BBC) 2007;

Film Return of the Soldier, Hardy in The English Patient (Miramax) 1996, Paranoid 1999, Purely Belter 2000, Silent Cry 2001; *Awards* incl: Pye Comedy Performance of the Year Award 1983, Variety Club Northern Personality of the Year 1990; *Recreations* looking over the next horizon, charity golf events; *Style*— Kevin Whately, Esq; ✉ c/o Caroline Dawson Associates, 125 Gloucester Road, London SW7 4TE (tel 020 7373 3323, fax 020 7373 1110)

WHATLEY, Prof Christopher Allan (Chris); s of Herbert Allan Whatley, of Nantwich, Cheshire, and Evelyn Stanley, *née* Whitfield (d 1977); *b* 29 May 1948; *Educ* Bearsden Acad, Clydebank Coll, Univ of Strathclyde (BA, PhD); *m* 1, 1975, Lilian, *née* Beattie; 1 da (Eilidh b 1977), 1 s (Neil Allan b 1979); m 2, 1997, Patricia Elizabeth, *née* Kelleher; *Career* lectr Univ of Dundee 1979–88, lectr in Scottish history Univ of St Andrews 1988–92; Univ of Dundee: sr lectr then reader 1994–97, head of history 1995–2002, prof of Scottish history 1997–, dean Faculty of Arts and Social Sciences 2002–06, vice-princ and head Coll of Arts and Social Sciences 2006–; chair Scottish Historical Review Tst 2001–06; FRHistS 1988, FRSE 2003; *Books* incl: The Scottish Salt Industry, 1570–1850 (1987), The Manufacture of Scottish History (ed, 1992), The Life and Times of Dundee (1992), The Industrial Revolution in Scotland (1997), Scottish Society, 1707–1830: Beyond Jacobitism, Towards Industrialisation (2000), Bought and Sold for English Gold? Explaining the Union of 1707 (2001), The Scots and the Union (2006); *Style*— Prof Chris Whatley; ✉ College of Arts and Social Sciences, University of Dundee, Dundee DD1 4HN (tel 01382 344177, e-mail c.a.whatley@dundee.ac.uk)

WHATMORE, Andrew; s of late Charles Sydney Whatmore, and Monica Mabel, *née* Tucker, of Salcombe Regis, Devon; *b* 18 June 1946; *Educ* The Skinners' Sch Tunbridge Wells, Woolwich Poly, Univ of London (BSc(Eng)); *m* 17 Dec 1983, Elizabeth, da of late James Stewart Morrison Sim, and Isobel McLuckie, *née* Russell, of Dollar, Clackmannanshire; 1 s (Charles Stewart b 1984), 1 da (Kathryn Elizabeth b 1985); *Career* resident engr: (EAEC) Kenya 1980, Roughton and Ptnrs Al Ain UAE 1981; chief engr Taylor Woodrow Int Ghana 1983, agent Christiani & Nielsen S Wales 1987, dep chief engr Geoffrey Osborne Chichester 1988, sr planning engr Edmund Nuttall Kilsyth Glasgow 1989, chief engr Skye Crossing Miller-Dywidag 1992, regnl chief engr Birse Construction Northampton 1994, chief engr Mid Orient Technical Services 1995, planner Balfour Beatty Kingston Bridge Glasgow 1996 and Edinburgh and Lyon 1998, bid mangr Edinburgh 2003; CEng, MICE; *Recreations* riding, tennis, walking, beach-combing, curling; *Style*— Mr Andrew Whatmore; ✉ West Netherton Farm, Milnathort, Kinross-shire KY13 0SB (tel 01577 865018, mobile 07876 137984, e-mail andy.whatmore@bbcel.co.uk)

WHEATCROFT, Patience; *b* 28 September 1951; *Educ* QEGS Tamworth, Coll of Technol Chesterfield, Univ of Birmingham (LLB); *m* 1976, Anthony Salter; 2 s (Kelhem b 1981, Sebastian b 1986), 1 da (Lucy b 1982); *Career* journalist; London Chamber of Commerce 1972–73, reporter/news ed Estates Times 1973–76, city reporter Daily Mail 1976–77, city reporter Sunday Times 1977–79, Prufrock The Sunday Times 1979–82, fin ed Working Woman 1982–83, dep city ed The Times 1982–84, ed Retail Week 1988–94, profile writer Daily Telegraph 1990–95, dep city ed Mail on Sunday 1995–97, city and business ed The Times 1997–2006, ed Sunday Telegraph 2006–07; *Recreations* opera, skiing; *Style*— Ms Patience Wheatcroft

WHEATER, Prof Howard Simon; s of late Claude Wheater, and late Marjorie Wheater; *b* 24 June 1949; *Educ* Nottingham HS, Univ of Cambridge (MA), Univ of Bristol (PhD); *m* 1970 (m dis 2004), Elisabeth; 2 s; *Career* grad apprentice Aero Engine Division Rolls-Royce Ltd 1967–1972, research asst Dept of Civil Engrg Univ of Bristol 1972–78; Dept of Civil and Environmental Engrg Imperial Coll London: lectr 1978–87, sr lectr 1987–90, reader 1990–93, prof of hydrology 1993–; head Environmental and Water Resource Engrg, chm Centre for Environmental Control and Waste Mgmnt; pres British Hydrological Soc 1999–2001, life memb Int Water Acad Oslo; memb and chair various nat and int advsy panels and ctees incl: UK Govt-MAFF, DEFRA, Environment Agency, NERC, UNESCO; conslt: Flood Study Northern Oman 1981, Yucca Mountain nuclear waste repository NV USA 2003–; counsel and advocate Republic of Hungary Int Court of Justice GNBS Danube barrage system 1993–1997; Prince Sultan bin Abdulaziz Int Water Prize 2006; CEng, FREng, FICE; *Publications* 200 refereed papers and 6 books; *Recreations* sailing (dinghy racing and yacht cruising), music (orchestral trumpet player); *Style*— Prof Howard Wheater; ✉ Department of Civil and Environmental Engineering, Imperial College London SW7 2BU (tel 020 7594 6066, fax 020 7823 9401, e-mail h.wheater@imperial.ac.uk)

WHEATER, Prof Roger John; OBE (1991); s of Alfred Wheater, MBE (d 1993), and Rosa Ida, *née* Brown (d 2004); *b* 24 November 1933; *Educ* Brighton, Hove and Sussex GS, Brighton Tech Coll; *m* 29 Nov 1963, Jean Ord, *née* Troup; 2 c (David, Jennifer (twins) b 22 March 1973); *Career* cmmnd Royal Sussex Regt 1953, 3 Bn Gold Coast Regt 1953–54, intelligence offr 4/5 Bn Royal Sussex Regt (TA) 1954–56; asst supt Colonial Police Uganda 1956–61; Uganda National Parks: chief warden Murchison Falls National Park 1961–70, dir Uganda National Park 1970–72; dir Royal Zoological Society of Scotland 1972–98; conslt: International Bank for Redevelopment (World Bank) 1974–97, World Tourist Orgn (UN) 1980–2001, Sultanate of Oman 1990 and 1991; Sec of State's inspr Zoo Licensing Act 1984–; memb: Co-ordinating Ctee Nuffield Unit of Tropical Animal Ecology 1970–72, Scientific and Tech Ctee E African Wildlife Soc 1970–72, Bd of Govrs Mweka Coll of Wildlife Management 1970–72, Int Union of Directors of Zoological Gardens (now the World Assoc of Zoos and Aquaria) 1974–93 (pres 1988–91), Ctee on Educn and Information Scottish Wildlife Tst 1982–98, Ad Hoc Ctee on Zoo Licensing Act DOE 1986–98, UK Ctee Int Union for the Conservation of Nature and Natural Resources (IUCN) 1988–98, IUCN Conservation Breeding Specialist Gp 1988–98, Cncl Flora and Fauna Preservation Soc 1990–94; chm: Advsy Ctee Cammo Estate 1980–95, Fedn of Zoological Gardens of Great Britain and Ireland (now Br and Irish Assoc of Zoos and Aquaria) 1993–96 (vice-chm 1980–93), Euro Assoc of Zoos and Aquaria 1994–97 (memb Cncl 1992–98, chm Membership Ctee 1992–94, vice-chm 1994), Access Forum 1996–2000, Tourism and Environment Forum 1998–2003, Heather Tst 1999–2002, Whipsnade Wild Animal Park 1999–2002, Nat Tst for Scot 2000–05, Zoos Advsy Ctee 2002–03; dep chm Zoo Forum 1998–2002; pres: Assoc of British Wild Animal Keepers 1984–99, Cockburn Trout Angling Club 1997–, Scottish Wildlife Tst 2007–; vice-pres World Pheasant Assoc Int 1994–, UK tstee The Gorilla Org 1993–; fndr patron and tstee: Dynamic Earth Appeal Fund 1993–98, Dynamic Earth Charitable Tst 1998–, The Tweed Fndn 2007–; memb Bd Scottish Natural Heritage 1995–99 (dep chm 1997–99); memb: Cncl Nat Tst for Scot 1973–78 and 1999–2005 (Exec Ctee 1982–87 and 1999–), Editorial Bd International Zoo Year Book 1987–99, Edinburgh Centre for Rural Research 1993–98, SNH Scientific Advsy Cte 1995–99, Cncl Zoological Soc of London 1995–2000 and 2001–03 (vice-pres 1998–99), Organisational and Environment Sectional Ctee RSE 2000–03, Young People's Ctee RSE 2002–05; tstee The William Thyne Scholarship 1997–; memb Bd Corstorphine Primary Sch 1989–95; hon prof Faculty of Veterinary Med Univ of Edinburgh 1993; Hon DUniv Open Univ 2004; Hon FRSGS 1995, Hon FRZS 1999; CBiol, FIBiol 1988, FRSE 1985, FRSA 1991; *Recreations* country pursuits, painting, photography and gardening; *Style*— Prof Roger Wheater, OBE, FRSE; ✉ 17 Kirklands, Innerleithen, Peebleshire EH44 6NA (tel 01896 830403, e-mail roger.wheater@btinternet.com)

WHEATLEY, Alan Edward; s of Edward Wheatley (d 1991), and Margaret Rosina Turner; *b* 23 May 1938; *Educ* Ilford GS; *m* 30 June 1962, Marion Frances, da of John Douglas Wilson (d 1968), and Maud Fletcher; 1 da (Susan b 1966), 2 s (Michael b 1968, Jonathan b 1974); *Career* Price Waterhouse 1960–92 (sr ptnr London Office 1985–92), chm 3i Group plc 1992–93; non-exec dir: EBS Investments Ltd (Bank of England subsid) 1977–90, British Steel plc 1984–94, Babcock International Group plc 1993–, Legal & General Group plc 1993–2002, Forte plc 1993–96, NM Rothschild & Sons Ltd 1993–99; non-exec dep chm: Cable & Wireless plc 1984–85 (govt dir 1981–84), Ashtead Group plc 1994–2003; non-exec chm: Foreign & Colonial Special Utilities Investment Trust plc 1993–2003, New Court Financial Services Ltd 1996–99, IntaMission; dir Industrial Devpt Advsy Bd 1985–92; tstee V&A Museum 1996–99, tstee dir V&A Enterprises Ltd 1996–2000; chm: Unigro Ltd 2002–, AKJ Inc 2002–, Utilico Investmetn Tst plc 2003–; FCA; *Recreations* golf, music, bridge; *Clubs* Wildernesse Golf; *Style*— Alan E Wheatley, Esq; ✉ tel 01732 779350

WHEATLEY, Derek Peter Francis; QC (1981); s of Edward Pearse Wheatley (d 1967), of Exeter, and Gladys Eugenie, *née* Williams (d 1987); *b* 18 December 1925; *Educ* The Leys Sch Cambridge, UC Oxford (MA); *m* 1955, Elizabeth Pamela, da of John Morgan Reynolds (d 1983), of Penarth; 2 s (Simon, Jonathan), 1 da (Claire); *Career* 8 King's Royal Hussars, Lt 1946–48, served BAOR; called to the Bar 1951; practised until 1974 and 1990–97, memb Hon Soc of the Middle Temple and (ad eundem) Gray's Inn, recorder of the Crown Court 1971–74, memb Bar Cncl 1975–78, 1980–83, 1986–90, 1995–96 and 1999–2000, memb Bar Cncl/Law Soc Ctee on Banking Law 1976–90, chm Legal Ctee Ctee of London and Scottish Bankers 1984–86, chief legal advsr Lloyds Bank plc 1974–90, barr and banking conslt 1990–97; chm Bar Assoc for Commerce, Fin and Industry 1982 and 2000; FRSA 1993; *Recreations* yachting; *Clubs* Roehampton, Bar Yacht; *Style*— Derek Wheatley, Esq, QC; ✉ 3 The Wardrobe, Old Palace Yard, Richmond, Surrey (tel 020 8940 6242, fax 020 8332 0948, e-mail derek.wheatley3@virgin.net)

WHEATLEY, Hon Rt Lord John Francis; PC (2007); s of Baron Wheatley, PC (Life Peer, d 1988), and Agnes Mary, da of Samuel Nichol; *b* 9 May 1941; *Educ* Mount St Mary's Coll, Univ of Edinburgh (BL); *m* 1970, Bronwen Catherine, da of Alastair Fraser, of Dollar; 2 s; *Career* called to the Bar Scot 1966; advocate depute 1974–78, QC (Scot) 1992, Sheriff of Perthshire and Kinross-shire 1980–1998, Sheriff Principal Tayside, Central and Fife 1998–2000, senator Coll of Justice 2000–; chm Judicial Studies Ctee 2002–06; *Recreations* gardening, music; *Style*— The Rt Hon Lord Wheatley; ✉ Braefoot Farmhouse, Fossoway, Kinross-shire (tel 0157 74 212); Parliament House, Parliament Square, Edinburgh EH1 1RF

WHEATLEY, Martin; s of Arthur James Wheatley (d 1992), of London, and Jean Florence, *née* French; *b* 11 December 1958; *Educ* St Edward's Sch, Univ of York (BA), City Univ (MBA); *m*; 4 c; *Career* London Stock Exchange: joined 1985, responsible for introduction of SETS electronic order book 1997, memb Bd 1998–2004 (latterly dep chief exec); chm FTSE Int; IPFA 1985; *Recreations* cycling, golf, cabinet making; *Style*— Martin Wheatley, Esq

WHEATLEY, Ven Paul Charles; s of Charles Lewis Wheatley (d 1984), and Doris Amy, *née* Kerslake (d 2002); *b* 27 May 1938; *Educ* Wycliffe Coll, St John's Coll Durham, Lincoln Theol Coll; *m* 1 Aug 1963, Iris Mary, da of Horace Lacey; 2 s (Andrew Charles b 26 July 1964, Timothy John b 6 July 1966), 1 da (Fenella Ruth b 11 April 1969 d 1994); *Career* curate St Michael and All Angels Bishopston Bristol 1963–68, Bishop of Bristol's youth chaplain 1968–73, vicar of Covingham and team rector Dorcan Swindon 1973–79, team rector Ross-on-Wye with Brampton Abbotts, Bridstow and Peterstow 1979–91, rural dean Ross and Archenfield Deanery 1979–91, Hereford diocesan ecumenical offr and preb Hereford Cathedral 1987–91, archdeacon of Sherborne 1991–2003 (archdeacon emeritus 2003–), priest i/c West Stafford with Frome Billett and canon Salisbury Cathedral 1991–; memb: HM Govt Pop Festivals Cmmn 1972–74, Wanborough PC 1976, Ross Town Cncl 1986–89; *Recreations* travel, gardening, opera; *Style*— The Ven Paul Wheatley; ✉ The Farthings, Bridstow, Ross-on-Wye, Herefordshire HR9 6QF (tel 01989 566965, e-mail paulwheatley@buckcastle.plus.com)

WHEATLEY, Rt Rev Peter William; *see:* Edmonton, Bishop of

WHEATLEY, Philip Martin (Phil); CB; s of Alan Osbourne Wheatley, and Ida Mary Wheatley; *b* 4 July 1948; *Educ* Leeds GS, Univ of Sheffield (LLB); *m* 1, 8 Nov 1969 (m dis 1989), Merryll Angela; 1 s (Thomas b 12 Aug 1972), 1 da (Helen b 8 December 1974); m 2, 2 Jan 1990, Anne Eleanor Roy; *Career* prison offr HM Borstal Hatfield 1969–70, asst govr HMP Hull 1970–74, asst govr Prison Serv Coll 1974–78, govr (grade 4) HMP Leeds 1978–82, govr (grade 3) HMP Gartree 1982–86, govr (grade 2) HMP Hull 1986–90, govr (grade 1) East Midlands Area Office 1990–92, asst dir Custody Gp 1992–95, dir Directorate of Dispersal Prisons 1996–99, dep DG Directorate of Ops 1999–2003, DG HM Prison Serv 2003–; CCMI 2006; *Style*— Phil Wheatley, Esq, CB; ✉ HM Prison Service, Cleland House, Page Street, London SW1P 4LN (tel 020 7217 6777, fax 020 72176961, e-mail phil.wheatley@hmps.gsi.gov.uk)

WHEATLY, Richard John Norwood; s of Patrick Wheatly (d 1986), of Watford, and Doris Mary, *née* Norwood; *b* 9 February 1946; *Educ* Watford GS, St John's Coll Cambridge (MA); *m* 1, 8 July 1968 (m dis 1974), Jane Margaret Phillips, da of Frank Thomas, of Rickmansworth, Herts; 1 da (Sophie Catherine Jane b 26 June 1970); m 2, 9 Feb 1980 (m dis 1993), Susan Angela Seider, da of Stuart Masson, of Watford, Herts; *Career* mktg mangr Unilever 1968–72; gp exec: Garland Compton Advertising 1972–73, McCann Erickson Advertising 1973–74; divnl mangr Johnson & Johnson 1974–78, chm Leo Burnett Advertising 1978–94, chief exec Rainbow consortium competing for National Lottery licence 1994, chief exec Jazz FM plc 1995–2002, exec chm The Local Radio Co 2007– (formerly chief exec); chm City of London Festival; FIPA 1988; *Recreations* riding, shooting; *Clubs* Oxford and Cambridge; *Style*— Richard Wheatly, Esq

WHEELDON, David John; s of Kenneth John Wheeldon, of Combridge, Staffs, and Edna May, *née* Heaton; *b* 28 October 1949; *Educ* Alleyne's GS Uttoxeter, Worcester Coll of Educn, Univ of Birmingham (BEd), Birmingham Poly (BA), Coventry Univ (MSc), Open Univ (Dip Educnl Mgmnt); *m* 26 July 1975, Janet, da of Robert Leslie Alexander; 2 s (Matthew Alexander John b 17 Nov 1980, Edward George b 31 March 1983); *Career* teacher Oswestry HS for Boys 1972–74; King Edward VI Five Ways Sch Birmingham: head of social science and gen studies 1974–85, head of sixth form 1985–89, dep head 1989–97; head master Altrincham GS for Boys 1997–2003, headmaster King Edward VI Five Ways Sch Birmingham 2003–; memb: Rotary Int, Bewdley Rotary Club 1991–97, Altrincham Rotary Club 1997–2004, Birmingham Rotary Club 2004–, Manchester Literary and Philosophical Soc 1997–; FRSA 1996; *Books* King Edward VI Five Ways School - A Centenary History (1982); *Recreations* Rotary Int, skiing, antiques, World War I, local history; *Style*— David Wheeldon, Esq; ✉ King Edward VI Five Ways School, Scotland Lane, Bartley Green, Birmingham B32 4BT (tel 0121 475 3535, fax 0121 477 8555, mobile 07887 931537, e-mail head@ke5ways.bham.sch.uk)

WHEELER, Adrian Christopher de Vaux Cathcart; s of Paul Murray Wheeler, and Lucinda Mary de Vaux Cathcart Mure, *née* McKerrell, of St Germans, Cornwall; *b* 5 November 1949; *Educ* Dulwich Coll, Clare Coll Cambridge (open exhibitioner, MA); *m* 1997, Katerina Koudelova; 1 s (Thomas b 10 Dec 1999), 1 da (Anna-Katerina b 2 May 2004); *Career* dir Brian Dowling Ltd 1974–76 (exec 1971–74), md Sterling Public Relations 1976–87, chief exec GCI Group London 1998–99 (md 1994–98), chief exec GCI UK 1999–2006, chm GCI Europe 2001–06; non-exec dir Firefly Communications Ltd; chm PRCA 1998–2000; dir British-American Business, memb Vice-Chllr's Communications Advsy Panel Univ of Cambridge, dir Speakers' Corner Tst; memb Ct of Assts Guild of PR Practitioners 2000–;

W

memb Mktg Soc, FCIPR 1998 (memb 1972); *Recreations* skiing, sailing, tennis; *Clubs* Royal Ocean Racing, Egypt Exploration Soc; *Style*— Adrian Wheeler, Esq

WHEELER, Sir (Harry) Anthony; kt (1988), OBE (1973); s of Herbert George Wheeler (d 1976), and Laura Emma, *née* Groom; *b* 7 November 1919; *Educ* Stranraer HS, Glasgow Sch of Architecture, Univ of Strathclyde (BArch); *m* 6 Oct 1944, Dorothy Jean, da of David Campbell; 1 da (Pamela Jane b 24 Sept 1953); *Career* served RA 1939–46, demobbed as Capt; asst to: city architect Oxford 1948, Sir Herbert Baker & Scott 1949; sr architect Glenrothes New Town 1949–51, sr lectr Dundee Sch of Architecture 1952–58, commenced private practice Fife 1952, formed partnership Wheeler & Sproson 1954; princ works incl: Woodside Shopping Centre and St Columba's Parish Church Glenrothes, St Peter's Episcopal Church Kirkcaldy, Hunter Bldg Edinburgh Coll of Art, Students' Union Univ of St Andrews, Leonard Horner Hall and Students' Union Heriot-Watt Univ, Community & Outdoor Educn Centre Linlithgow, reconstruction The Giles Pittenweem, redevelopment Dysart and Old Buckhaven, town centre renewal Grangemouth; memb: Royal Fine Art Cmmn Scotland 1967–86, Scottish Housing Advsy Ctee 1971–75; tstee Scottish Civic Tst 1970–83; pres Royal Incorporation of Architects Scotland 1973–75, hon pres Saltire Soc 1995; Hon DDes Robert Gordon Univ Aberdeen 1991; MRTPI 1953, ARSA 1963, RSA 1975 (treas 1978–80, sec 1980–83, pres 1983–90), FRIBA (vice-pres 1973–75); Hon RA 1983, Hon RHA 1983, Hon RBS 1984, Hon RGI 1986; *Recreations* watercolour painting, sketching, fishing, gardens, music, drama; *Clubs* Scottish Arts, New (Edinburgh); *Style*— Sir Anthony Wheeler, OBE; ✉ South Inverleith Manor, 31/6 Kinnear Road, Edinburgh EH3 5PG (tel 0131 552 3854); The Steading, Logierait, Ballinluig, Perthshire PH9 0LH (tel 01796 482282)

WHEELER, Sir (Selwyn) Charles (Cornelius-); kt (2006), CMG (2001); s of Wing Cdr Charles Cornelius-Wheeler, RFC, RAF and RAFVR (d 1972), and Winifred Agnes, *née* Rees (d 1973); *b* 26 March 1923; *Educ* Cranbrook Sch; *m* 29 March 1962, Dip Singh; 2 da (Shirin Caroline b 1963, Marina Claire b 1964); *Career* journalist and broadcaster; with Daily Sketch 1940; Royal Marines 1941–46; BBC: joined as sub ed 1946, Euro serv corr Berlin 1950–53, prodr Panorama 1956–58, corr S Asia 1959–62, corr Berlin 1962–65, corr Washington and chief corr USA 1965–73, chief corr Europe 1973–76, subsequently presenter and corr Panorama and Newsnight; freelance 1979–; RTS Journalist of the Year 1988, RTS Int Documentary Award 1989, James Cameron Meml Prize 1989, RTS Special Commendation 1992, RTS Cyril Bennett Award 1993, Broadcasting Press Guild Harvey Lee Award 1995, RTS Judges' Award 1996, Broadcasting Press Guild Journalist of the Year 1997, BAFTA Special Award 1997, RTS Home Documentary Award 1999, Sony Radio Documentary Award 2000, Media Soc Award 2003, Voice of the Listener and Viewer Radio Award 2005, The Oldie Newshound of the Year Award 2007; Hon DUniv Open Univ 1992, Hon DLitt Univ of Sussex 1995; *Recreations* gardening; *Style*— Sir Charles Wheeler

WHEELER, Colin; s of Stanley Arthur Thomas Wheeler (d 1978), and Lilian Mary, *née* Covey (d 1985); *b* 23 February 1938; *Educ* Farnham GS, Farnham Sch of Art, Royal Acad Schs London; *m* 1962, Jacqueline Anne Garelli Buchanan, da of Neville R Buchanan; 3 da (Andrée b 1963, Jacqueline b 1966, Vivien b 1968); *Career* cartoonist; asst lectr Bolton Coll of Art then High Wycombe Coll of Art 1961–63 then various pt/t teaching appts London, first published cartoon Times Educnl Supplement c 1963; freelance contrib of cartoons, illustrations and occasional writing to Daily Telegraph and other national broadsheet press, Private Eye, New Statesman, TES and The Teacher until 1986, front page cartoonist, illustrator and writer The Independent 1986–98; currently freelance cartoonist especially to The Spectator, Private Eye, The Oldie and TES; *Books* A Thousand Lines (1979), Off the Record (1980); *Recreations* painting and drawing, the protection of old buildings and the encouragement of good modern architecture; *Style*— Colin Wheeler, Esq; ✉ e-mail colin.wheeler@cartoonist.fsbusiness.co.uk

WHEELER, Rt Hon Sir John Daniel; kt (1990), PC (1993), JP (Inner London 1978), DL (Gtr London 1989, rep DL Merton 1997); s of late Frederick Harry Wheeler, and Constance Elsie, *née* Foreman; *b* 1 May 1940; *Educ* County Sch Suffolk, Staff Coll Wakefield; *m* 1967, Laura Margaret Langley; 1 s, 1 da; *Career* former asst prison govr; MP (Cons): Paddington 1979–83, Westminster N 1983–97; min of state for NI 1993–97; memb: Home Office Standing Ctee on Crime Prevention 1977–85 (chm Sub-Ctee on Mobile Crime 1983–84), Home Affrs Select Ctee 1980–92 (chm 1987–92, chm Sub-Ctee on Race Rels and Immigration 1980–87), Home Office Steering Ctee on Crime Prevention 1985–93; chm: Residential Burglary Working Gp 1986–87, All-Pty Penal Affairs Gp 1986–93 (vice-chm 1979–86), Cons Gtr London Area Membs' Ctee 1983–90 (jt sec 1979–83), Policy Gp for London 1988–93, Br-Pakistan Parly Gp 1988–93; vice-chm: Cons Urban Affrs and New Towns Ctee 1980–83, Cons Home Affrs Ctee 1987–93 (jt sec 1980–87); non-exec dir of various cos 1976–93 and 1997–; chm Serv Authorities for the Nat Criminal Intelligence Serv and Nat Crime Squad 1997–2002, chm UK Govt's Review of Airport Security 2002–03, head Aust Govt's Review into Airport Security and Policing 2005; Order of St John: memb Cncl 1990–, memb Chapter-Gen 1995–99, registrar 1997–99, sub-chllr 1999–2002, memb Priory Chapter for Eng 1999–, chllr and tstee 2002–; tstee: Butler Tst 1997–2000, The Police Fndn 2004–; KStJ 1997 (Offr Bro 1991, CStJ 1992); Hilal-i-Quaid-i-Azam (knight) of Pakistan 1991; *Style*— The Rt Hon Sir John Wheeler, JP, DL; ✉ PO Box 890, London SW1P 1XW

WHEELER, Kenneth Vincent (Kenny); s of Wilfred Robert Wheeler (d 1983), and Mabel Reid (d 1989); *b* 14 January 1930, Toronto; *Educ* St Catharine's HS Ontario, Toronto Conservatory of Music; *m* March 1953, Doreen, da of late Robert Yeend; 1 s (Mark b 1955), 1 da (Louise Ann b 1958); *Career* jazz trumpeter, composer and arranger; moved to Eng 1952; band ldrs worked with mid-1960s incl: Vic Lewis, Johnny Dankworth, Ronnie Scott, Joe Harriot, Tubby Hayes, Freidrich Gulda; also worked with free ensembles incl: John Stevens, The Tony Oxley Sextet, Mike Gibbs, The Globe Unity Orch, Anthony Braxton; memb: Azimuth (with John Taylor and Norma Winstone) late 1970s, United Jazz and Rock Ensemble 1979, The Dave Holland Quintet 1983–88, own quintet (with John Taylor, John Abercrombie, Peter Erskine and Palle Danielson) 1989–92; currently ldr own quartet (with John Taylor, Chris Laurence and Adam Nussbaum); winner German Award for Best Jazz Record of the Year 1976; *Recordings* The Windmill Tilter (1968), Song for Someone (1973), Gnu High (1976), Deer Wan (1978), Around Six (1980), Double, Double You (1984), Flutter By, Butter Fly (1987), Music for Large and Small Ensembles (1990), The Widow in the Window (1990), Angel Song (1997); also recorded with: Pepper Adams, Mike Gibbs, George Adams, Reiner Bruninghaus, Anthony Braxton, Leo Smith, Ralph Towner, UJRE, Azimuth, Paul Gonsalves, Bill Frisell, Dave Holland; *Style*— Kenny Wheeler, Esq

WHEELER, Prof Michael David; s of David Mortimer Wheeler, and Hilda Lois Stansfield, *née* Eke; *b* 1 September 1947; *Educ* St Albans Sch, Magdalene Coll Cambridge (scholar, MA), UCL (PhD); *m* 1970 (sep 2006), Vivienne Rees; 1 s (Joshua b 1973), 2 da (Charlotte, Emily (twins) b 1975); *Career* Quain student (lectr) Univ of London 1972–73; Lancaster Univ: lectr in English 1973–85, sr lectr 1985–90, head of dept 1984–86, assoc dean of humanities 1989–91, prof of English literature 1990–99; prof of English literature Univ of Southampton 1999–2001 (visiting prof 2001–); dir: Ruskin Prog (interdisciplinary res gp) 1990–99, Ruskin Collection Project 1990–99, Chawton House Library Hampshire 1999–2001; visiting lectr USA, Canada, Denmark, India, Iraq, Japan, Poland, Yugoslavia, Switzerland, Italy, Turkey, Aust, Germany, France and Norway 1975–; NADFAS lectr 2006–; chm Ruskin Soc 2002–07; tstee St Deiniol's Library Hawarden 1994–; lay canon and memb Chapter Winchester Cathedral 2005–; Companion Guild of St George 1992–; *Publications* The Art of Allusion in Victorian Fiction (1979), English Fiction of the Victorian Period 1830–1890 (1985, 2 edn 1994), Death and the Future Life in Victorian Literature and Theology (1990, winner US Conf on Christianity and Literature award, 1991–92, abridged as Heaven, Hell and the Victorians 1994), The Lamp of Memory: Ruskin, Tradition and Architecture (co-ed, 1992), Ruskin and Environment: The Storm-Cloud of the Nineteenth Century (ed, 1995), Ruskin's God (1999), The Kindest Cut of All: On the Making of Gravestones in the Kindersley Workshop (2005), The Old Enemies: Catholic and Protestant in Nineteenth Century English Culture (jtly, 2006); Longman Literature in English Series (jt gen ed, 1980–), Time and Tide: Ruskin Studies 1996 (ed, 1996), Works of John Ruskin (CD-ROM; manuscript ed, 2002); *Recreations* walking; *Clubs* Athenaeum; *Style*— Prof Michael Wheeler; ✉ 1 Amport Park Mews, Amport, Andover, Hampshire SP11 8BS (tel 01264 771394, e-mail mwheeler70@hotmail.com)

WHEELER, Michael (Mike); *b* 1 November 1951; *Educ* Haileybury, Univ of Liverpool; *m* 1977, Linda May; 1 da (Sarah b 1984), 2 s (Andrew b 1986, Charles b 1990); *Career* mangr Peat Marwick Mitchell 1973–81, vice-pres Bank of America 1982–84, ptnr KPMG 1985–2005 (head Financial Advsy Servs 2001–05); non-exec dir Mgmnt Bd Dept of Health 2006–; fndr memb and dir Soc of Turnaround Professionals, former memb Cncl Association of Business Recovery Professionals; FCA; *Books* International Insolvency Procedures (1997); *Recreations* mountaineering, rugby, skiing; *Clubs* RAC; *Style*— Mike Wheeler, Esq

WHEELER, Nicholas Hugh; s of David Hugh Wheeler (d 1979), and Rosemary Margaret Jean, *née* Leaney; *b* 3 October 1953; *Educ* St Lawrence Coll Ramsgate Kent (first team tennis capt), Harlow Tech Coll; *Children* 2 da (Victoria Kate b 28 Sept 1978, Alexandra Rosemary b 12 July 1982); *Career* journalist; South London Press 1972, reporter Western Morning News and Western Evening Herald Plymouth 1972–77, reporter Coventry Evening Telegraph 1977–79, reporter/prodr BBC Radio Solent 1979–84, BBC Newsbeat 1984; Capital Radio: ed of news and showbusiness prog The Way It Is 1985–87, head of News and Talks Dept 1987–94, prog controller Capital FM and Capital Gold 1994–95; ed Independent Radio News 1995–96, chief ed ITN Radio 1996–; *Recreations* squash, cycling, surfing, motorbikes; *Style*— Nicholas Wheeler, Esq; ✉ ITN Radio, 200 Grays Inn Road, London WC1X 8XZ (tel 020 7833 3000)

WHEELER, Nick; s of John Wheeler, and Geraldine, *née* Jones (d 1970); *b* 20 January 1965, Ludlow; *Educ* Eton, Univ of Bristol; *m* 2 Sept 1995, Chris, *née* Rucker; 1 s (Tom b 1996), 3 da (Ella b 1998, India b 2000, Bea b 2004); *Career* strategic conslt Bain & Co 1987–89, fndr and chm Charles Tyrwhitt 1989–; *Style*— Nick Wheeler, Esq; ✉ Charles Tyrwhitt, 13 Silver Road, London W12 7RR (tel 0845 337 3337, fax 020 8735 1050)

WHEELER, Oliver; s of Christopher Wheeler, of Surrey, and Margaret Wheeler; *b* 13 November 1969; *Educ* Magdalen Coll Sch Oxford; *m* 16 Dec 2006, Tina Hobley, *qv*; *Career* apprenticeship under Baron Bell (Life Peer), *qv*, Chime Communications 1993–95, bd dir Freud Communications 1995–; *Recreations* competitor UK Nat Car Racing Series (Caterham 7); *Clubs* Aspinall's, Soho House, British Racing and Sports Car, BARC; *Style*— Oliver Wheeler, Esq; ✉ Freud Communications, 19 Mortimer Street, London W1T 8DX (tel 020 7580 2626, fax 020 7637 2626, e-mail oliver@freud.com)

WHEELER, Dr Patrick Clive Gage; s of late Cdr Leonard Gage Wheeler, and Nancy Dorathea, *née* Cross; *b* 6 October 1943; *Educ* St Edward's Sch Oxford, ChCh Oxford (MA, DM, BM BCh), St Thomas' Hosp London (MRCP); *m* 7 June 1975, Diana Lilian, da of late Cdr Edward Stanley; 3 da (Anna b 1976, Kate b 1978, Gemma b 1981); *Career* med registrar St Thomas' Hosp 1971–75, sr med registrar King's Coll Hosp 1975–80, conslt physician and gastroenterologist E Kent Hosps Tst 1980–; author of various articles on gastrointestinal and liver disease in scientific pubns; memb Br Soc of Gastroenterology; FRCP 1987; *Recreations* fly fishing, opera, travel; *Clubs* Army and Navy; *Style*— Dr Patrick Wheeler; ✉ Elham Manor, Elham, Canterbury, Kent CT4 6UL (e-mail patrick.wheeler1@btinternet.com); William Harvey Hospital, Ashford, Kent TN24 0LZ

WHEELER, Gen Sir Roger Neil; GCB (1997, KCB 1993), CBE (1984); s of late Maj-Gen T N S Wheeler, CB, CBE; *b* 16 December 1941; *Educ* All Hallows Sch Devon, Hertford Coll Oxford (MA, hon fell); *m* 1980, Felicity Hares; 3 s and 1 da from prev m; *Career* early Army serv Borneo and ME 1964–70, Bde Maj Cyprus Emergency 1974, memb Lord Carver's Staff Rhodesia talks 1977, Bn Cmd Belize, Gibraltar, Berlin and Canada 1979–82, COS Falklands Is Jun-Dec 1982, Bde Cmd BAOR 1985–86, Dir Army Plans 1987–89, Cdr 1st Armoured Div BAOR 1989–90, ACGS MOD 1990–92, GOC and Dir of Mil Ops NI 1993–96, C-in-C Land Cmd 1996–97, Chief of the Gen Staff 1997–2000; ADC Gen to HM The Queen 1996–2000; non-exec dir Thales Group 2001–; pres: Army RFU 1995–2000, Army Rifle Assoc 1995–2000; Col The Royal Irish Regt 1996–, Col Cmdt Intelligence Corps 1996–; Liveryman Worshipful Co of Painter-Stainers; *Recreations* fly fishing, cricket, shooting, ornithology; *Clubs* Army and Navy, Stragglers of Asia CC, Devon Dumplings CC, Blackheath RFC, NIRFCC; *Style*— Gen Sir Roger Wheeler, GCB, CBE

WHEELER, Sara Diane; da of John Wheeler, and Diane, *née* Vernon; *Educ* Redland HS Bristol, BNC Oxford (exhibitioner, BA); *Career* writer; memb Cncl RSL 2001–05; tstee London Library 2005–; FRSL 1999; *Books* Evia: An Island Apart (1992), Travels in a Thin Country (1994), Terra Incognita: Travels in Antarctica (1996), Cherry: A Biography of Apsley Cherry-Garrard (2001), Too Close to the Sun: A Life of Denys Finch Hatton (2006); *Clubs* Academy; *Style*— Ms Sara Wheeler; ✉ Gillon Aitken Associates, 18–21 Cavaye Place, London SW10 9PT (tel 020 7373 8672, fax 020 7373 6002, e-mail reception@gillonaitken.co.uk)

WHEELER, (John) Stuart; adopted s of Alexander Hamilton Wheeler (d 1942), and Betty Lydia, *née* Gibbons (d 1990); *b* 30 January 1935, London; *Educ* Eton, ChCh Oxford; *m* 14 July 1979, Teresa Anne, *née* Codrington; 3 da (Sarah Rose b 9 July 1980, Jacqetta Lydia b 16 Oct 1981, Charlotte Mary b 24 Jan 1985); *Career* Nat Serv 2 Lt Welsh Guards 1953–55; called to the Bar Inner Temple 1959, barr 1959–62; asst mangr Investment Dept Hill Samuel 1962–68, mangr Investment Dept J H Vavasseur 1968–73, First Nat Fin Corp 1973; IG Group (formerly IG Index): fndr 1974, chief exec 1974–2002, chm 1985–2003; London Region Master Entrepreneur of the Year Ernst & Young 2001; Coronation Medal 1953; *Recreations* bridge, poker, tennis, theatre; *Clubs* Portland, White's, Queen's; *Style*— Stuart Wheeler, Esq; ✉ Penthouse A, 21 Davies Street, London W1K 3DE (tel 020 7499 1630, fax 020 7499 1808); Chilham Castle, Chilham, Kent CT4 8DB (e-mail stuartwheeler@chilham-castle.co.uk)

WHEELER-BOOTH, Sir Michael Addison John; KCB (1994); s of Addison James Wheeler, and Mary Angela, *née* Blakeney-Booth; *b* 25 February 1934; *Educ* Leighton Park Sch Reading, Magdalen Coll Oxford (MA); *m* 1982, Emily Frances Smith , *qv*; 2 da (Kate b 1985, Charlotte b 1987), 1 s (Alfred James b 1990); *Career* Nat Serv Midshipman (Sp) RNVR 1952–54; clerk House of Lords 1960, private sec to Ldr of House of Lords and Govt Chief Whip 1965, seconded as jt sec Inter Party Conf on House of Lords Reform 1967, clerk of the Journals 1970, chief clerk Overseas and Euro Office 1972, princ clerk 1978, reading clerk House of Lords 1983–88, clerk asst of the Parliaments 1988–90, Clerk of the Parliaments 1991–97; Magdalen Coll Oxford: visiting fell 1997–98, special lectr in politics 1998–; Waynflete lectr 1998; chm Study of Parliament Group 1982–84 (pres 2004–), tstee History of Parliament Tst 1991–97, tstee Industry and Parliament Tst 1994–97, cmmr Standing Orders Cmmn for Nat Assembly of Wales 1998–99; memb: Royal Cmmn on Reform of House of Lords 1999–2000, Fabian Cmmn on the Future of the Monarchy 2002–03, Richard Cmmn on Powers and Electoral Methods of the Nat Assembly of Wales 2002–04; govr Magdalen Coll Sch Oxford 2001– (chm Fin and Gen

Purposes Ctee 2004–); hon fell Magdalen Coll Oxford 2004; *Publications* Griffith & Ryle on Parliament (contrib, 2 edn 2003), Halsbury's Laws of England (vol 34) on Parliament (jt ed), contrib to Parly jls; *Recreations* reading, ruins, swimming, opera, bucolic; *Clubs* Brooks's, Garrick; *Style*— Sir Michael Wheeler-Booth, KCB; ✉ Northfields, Sandford St Martin, Chipping Norton, Oxfordshire OX7 7AG (tel 01608 683632); 4 Polstead Road, Oxford OX2 6TN (tel 01865 514040, fax 01865 516048, e-mail wbsmith@btinternet.com); Magdalen College, Oxford OX1 4AU (tel 01865 276108)

WHEEN, Francis James Baird; s of James Francis Thorneycroft Wheen, and Patricia Winifred, *née* Ward; *b* 22 January 1957; *Educ* Copthorne Sch Sussex, Harrow, Royal Holloway Coll London (BA); *partner* Julia Jones; 2 s (Bertie, Archie); *Career* journalist; editorial asst The Guardian 1974–75, staff writer New Statesman 1978–84, news ed New Socialist 1983–84, contributing ed Tatler 1985, diarist The Independent 1986–87, contributing ed Sunday Correspondent Magazine 1989–90, diarist Independent on Sunday 1990–91, regular contrib Private Eye 1987–, contributing ed Vanity Fair 1992–93; columnist: Observer 1993–95, Esquire 1993–98, Guardian 1994–2001; freelance work for numerous pubns incl: The Times, Daily Mirror, London Evening Standard, Sunday Telegraph, Los Angeles Times, The Nation (NY), The New Yorker, Literary Review; was for several years regular presenter of News-Stand (BBC Radio) and What The Papers Say (Granada TV); regular panellist The News Quiz (BBC Radio) 1991–; Columnist of the Year What The Paper Say Awards 1997; *Books* The Sixties (1982), World View 1982 (1982), Television: A History (1985), The Battle For London (1985), Tom Driberg: His Life And Indiscretions (1990), The Chatto Book of Cats (1993), Lord Gnome's Literary Companion (1994), The Vintage Book of Cats (ed, 1996), Karl Marx (1999), Soul of Indiscretion (2001), Hoo-Hahs and Passing Frenzies (2002), Who Was Dr Charlotte Bach? (2002), How Mumbo-Jumbo Conquered the World (2004); *Clubs* Academy, MCC; *Style*— Francis Wheen; ✉ Sokens, Green Street, Pleshey, Chelmsford, Essex CM3 1HT (tel 01245 231566, fax 01245 231857, e-mail fwheen@netcomuk.co.uk)

WHELAN, Charles Alexander James (Charlie); *b* 3 February 1954; *Educ* West Byfleet County Secdy Sch, Ottershaw Sch, City of London Poly (BA); *Career* sometime researcher, PA to Exec Cncl memb Jimmy Airlie and chief press offr Amalgated Engrg and Electrical Union until 1994, press sec to Gordon Brown (as Shadow Chllr then Chllr of the Exchequer) 1994–99, political corr Sunday Service Radio 5 Live 1999–2003; broadcaster and writer; columnist: The Guardian, The Observer, New Statesman, The Mirror, PR Week; sometime fly-fishing instr River Spey Cairngorm Nat Park; *Recreations* football; *Clubs* House of Commons Sports and Social, England Travel, Spurs Supporters; *Style*— Charlie Whelan, Esq

WHELAN, Prof Michael John; s of William Whelan, ISM (d 1978), of Aldershot, Hants, and Ellen, *née* Pound (d 1972); *b* 2 November 1931; *Educ* Farnborough GS, Gonville & Caius Coll Cambridge (MA, PhD); *Career* Univ of Cambridge: demonstrator in physics 1961–65, asst dir of res in physics 1965–66; fell Gonville & Caius Coll Cambridge 1958–66; Univ of Oxford: reader in physical examination of materials 1966–92, prof of microscopy of materials 1992–97 (emeritus prof 1997–); fell Linacre Coll Oxford 1968–97 (emeritus fell 1997–); hon prof Univ of Sci and Technol Beijing 1995, Distinguished Scientist Award Microscopy Soc of America 1998; hon fell: Royal Microscopical Soc 2001, Japanese Soc of Microscopy 2003; FRS 1976, FInstP 1976; *Books* Electron Microscopy of Thin Crystals (co-author), Worked Examples in Dislocations, High-Energy Electron Diffraction and Microscopy (co-author); *Recreations* gardening, tinkering, Japanese language; *Style*— Prof M J Whelan, FRS; ✉ 18 Salford Road, Old Marston, Oxford OX3 0RX (tel and fax 01865 244556); Department of Materials, Oxford University, Parks Road, Oxford OX1 3PH (tel 01865 273779, fax 01865 283333, email michael.whelan@materials.oxford.ac.uk)

WHELAN, Michael Joseph; s of Michael Whelan (d 1972), and Mary, *née* Hynes (d 1991); *b* 1 May 1932; *Educ* Castleknock Coll Dublin, Univ Coll Dublin (BA), Columbia Univ NY (MSc); *m* 3 June 1955, Maureen Therese, da of John Ryan (d 1972); 3 s (Gerard b 1959, Brian b 1962, Roger b 1966), 1 da (Ann-Maeve b 1956); *Career* called to the Bar King's Inn Dublin 1953; corporate lawyer Shell Oil: Toronto 1955–59, NY 1959–60; devpt and commercial mangr Aer Lingus NY and Dublin 1960–63, mktg dir Irish Tourist Bd Dublin 1963–71, fndr and former chief exec Aran Energy plc Dublin and London; FInstPet, FInstD; *Recreations* sailing; *Clubs* Royal Irish Yacht, Fitzwilliam, St Stephens Green, Milltown Golf, Royal Irish Automobile (all Dublin); *Style*— Michael J Whelan, Esq; ✉ The Cove, Baltimore, Co Cork; Ardoyne House, Ballsbridge, Dublin 4; Clanwilliam Court, Dublin 2

WHELAN, Paul David; s of Don Whelan, of NZ, and Beris, *née* Pashby; *b* 29 September 1966; *Educ* Wellington Conservatoire, Royal Northern Coll of Music (Marianne Mathy scholar); *Career* bass-baritone; studied with Flora Edwards, Patrick McGuigan, Robert Alderson and David Harper; *Concerts* conducted by: Sir Simon Rattle, Gary Bertini, Kent Nagano, Richard Hickox, Sir Yehudi Menuhin, Paolo Olmi, Sir David Willcocks, Sir Charles Farncombe; performed with: LSO, City of Birmingham Symphony Orch, Hallé Orch, BBC Philharmonic Orch, BBC Symphony Orch, City of London Sinfonia, London Sinfonietta, English Chamber Orch, RIAS Berlin Chamber Choir, Budapest Symphony Orch; venues incl: Wigmore Hall, St David's Hall Cardiff, Blackheath Concert Halls, Cheltenham Festival, Nello Santi, Valery Gergiev, Marcus Creed; *Opera* incl: title role in The Doctor of Myddfai (debut for WNO), Figaro in The Marriage of Figaro (Scottish Opera), Shaklovity in Khovanshchina (ENO), Marcello in La Bohème (Glyndebourne Touring Opera and Bavarian State Opera) 1997, Flint in Billy Budd (Geneva Opera), Schaunard in La Bohème (Netherlands Opera, Stuggart Opera, Royal Opera House, Metropolitan Opera NY), Guglielmo in Cosi fan Tutte (Dublin Grand Opera), Masetto in Don Giovanni (Bordeaux), Demetrius in A Midsummer Night's Dream (Australian Opera), title role in Don Giovanni (Australian Opera) 1997, title role in Eugene Onegin (Australian Opera) 1997, Ned Keene in Peter Grimes (Metropolitan Opera) 1997, The Count in Marriage of Figaro (Santiago)1998 (also Sydney Opera House 2004), Silvio in I Pagliacci (Nantes) 1998, Guglielmo in Cosi fan Tutte (New Israeli Opera) 1999, Marcello (Bavarian State Opera and Bastille Opera Paris) 1998, Tarquinius in Rape of Lucretia (Nantes) 1999, Belcore in Elisir D'Amore (New Israeli Opera) 1999, Apollo in Alceste (Netherlands Opera) 1999, Count in Marriage of Figaro (Scottish Opera) 1999–2000, Jesus in St John Passion (ENO) 2000, Escamillo in Carmen (WNO) 2000, Oliver in Cappriccio (Opera Australia) 2000, La Damnation de Faust (BBC Philharmonic) 2001, Villians in Tales of Hoffman (New Zealand) 2001, Christus in St Mathew Passion (CBSO) 2001, Richard Blackford's Voices of Exile (premiere), A Midsummer Night's Dream (Pittsburgh Opera) 2003, Gurrelieder (Bolshoi Theatre Moscow) 2003, Des Knaben Wunderhorn (BBS SSO) 2003, The Apostles (BBC Philharmonic) 2003, The Prodigal Child (premiere, Michael Williams Opera NZ) 2003, Argante in Rinaldo (Bavarian State Opera) 2004, Don Giovanni (Lithuania National Opera) 2004; *Recordings* A Midsummer Night's Dream (with LSO under Sir Colin Davis), Kurt Weill's Silbersee (under Markus Stenz), Le Rossignol (with LPO, under Robert Craft), Elegy (songs with piano), Cecil Coles' Fra Giacomo, Edgor Bainton's English Idyll; *Awards* Webster Booth-Esso Award, Brigitte Fassbaender Award for Lieder, Lieder Prize Cardiff Singer of the World 1993; scholarships incl: Wolfson Fndn, Countess of Munster Musical Tst, Peter Moores Fndn; *Recreations* tennis, hiking, skiing; *Style*— Paul Whelan, Esq; ✉ c/o IMG Artists Europe, Lovell House, 616 Chiswick High Road, London W4 5RX (tel 020 8233 5800, fax 020 8233 5801)

WHELAN, Peter; s of Thomas Whelan, lithographic artist (d 1959), of Stoke-on-Trent, and Bertha, *née* Brookes; *b* 3 October 1931; *Educ* Hanley GS, Keele Univ (BA); *m* 1958, Ffrangcon Hood, da of John Frederick Price, pottery designer; 2 s (Timothy John b 1958, Lawrence Peter b 1961), 1 da (Megan Nell b 1976); *Career* writer and playwright; worked in advtg 1957–78, dir Garland Compton advtg agency 1975–78; memb Theatre Writers' Union; assoc artist RSC 1998; Lloyds Private Banking Playwright of the Year 1996, Eileen Anderson Central Broadcasting Award 1996; *Television* In Suspicious Circumstances, The Trial of Lord Lucan; *Plays* Lakota (with Don Kincaid, Cockpit Theatre London) 1970, Double Edge (with Les Darbon, Vaudeville London) 1975, Captain Swing (RSC Stratford and London) 1978, The Accrington Pals (RSC London) 1981, Clay (RSC London) 1983, Worlds Apart (by Jose Triana, adaption, RSC London) 1987, The Bright and Bold Design (RSC London, Best Play nomination Writers' Guild 1992) 1991, The School of Night (RSC Stratford and London, Best Play nomination Writers' Guild 1993) 1992–93, Shakespeare Country (BT/Little Theatre Guild) 1993, The Tinderbox (New Vic Newcastle) 1994, Divine Right (Birmingham Rep, TMA Best New Play Award 1996) 1996, The Herbal Bed (RSC Stratford and London 1996–97, Duchess Theatre London 1997, Sydney and New York 1998, Athens 1999, Lloyd's Private Banking Award Best New Play 1997), Overture (New Vic Newcastle) 1997, Nativity (Birmingham Rep) 1999, A Russian in the Woods (RSC Stratford and London) 2001–02, The Earthly Paradise (Almeida) 2005; *Style*— Peter Whelan, Esq; ✉ c/o The Agency, 24 Pottery Lane, London W11 4LZ (tel 020 7727 1346, fax 020 7727 9037)

WHELAN, Ronnie; da of John Connolly, and Josephine Connolly; *b* 9 June 1952; *Educ* St Martin's Sch for Girls, London Coll of Printing; *m* June 1982, Dennis Whelan; 3 step da; *Career* ed asst Stitchcraft 1973–75, sr designer Ideal Home 1975–81, dep art dir Options 1981–83, dep ed and art dir Woman's World 1983–90 (runner-up PPA Designer of the Year for Art Direction 1985), freelance designer 1990–91, art dir Hello! 1991–2001, freelance designer (incl dep ed Asian Art newspaper) 2001–03, ed Hello! 2003–; *Clubs* travel, live music, restaurants, architecture; *Style*— Ronnie Whelan; ✉ Hello! Magazine, Wellington House, 69–71 Upper Ground, London SE1 9PQ (tel 020 7667 8700, fax 020 7667 8711)

WHELDON, Dame Juliet Louise; DCB (2004, CB 1994), Hon QC (1997); da of late John Wheldon, and Ursula Mabel, *née* Caillard; *b* 26 March 1950; *Educ* Sherborne Sch for Girls, Lady Margaret Hall Oxford (Tullis exhibitioner, BA); *Career* called to the Bar Gray's Inn 1975, (bencher 1999); advsy div Treasury Solicitor's Dept 1976–83, Law Officers' Dept 1983–84, Treasury Solicitor's Dept 1984–86, asst legal sec Law Officers' Dept 1986–87, legal advsr Treasury Solicitor's Dept 1987–89, legal sec to Law Officers 1989–97, legal advsr Home Office 1997–2000, HM procurator-gen and Treasury slr 2000–06, chief legal advsr and advsr to the Govr Bank of England 2006–; *Style*— Dame Juliet Wheldon, DCB, QC; ✉ Bank of England, London EC2R 8AH (tel 020 7601 3919, e-mail juliet.wheldon@bankofengland.co.uk)

WHELDON, Susan Lynne (Sue); da of Derek Wheldon (d 1963), of Silsoe, Beds, and Joan Mary, *née* Neville; *b* 5 October 1951; *Educ* Bedford HS, Royal Masonic Sch for Girls, Univ of Liverpool (BA), Architectural Assoc (grad study year); *Career* architect and interior designer; set designer BBC 1974–75, freelance architectural design 1975–79 (incl work with Alaverdian Architectural Assocs Teheran 1976–77), in own practice Sue Wheldon Architectural Design 1980–95 (specialising in designs for the leisure and retail industries and for architectural applications of corp identity and brand devpt), retail design dir Design House Consultants Ltd 1995–97, md BDG McColl Branded Environments 1997–2001, fndr Brand Architects Int Consortium 2002, dir Douglas Wallace Architects and Designers 2003–; memb: RIBA, Franco-Br Union of Athletics, Women in Mktg and Design; FRSA; *Recreations* travel (Spain, Italy, India and Africa particularly), tennis, swimming, snorkelling, walking in the countryside, chess, 20th Century painting, music, reading travel books, visiting restaurants, shops and hotels; *Clubs* Lambton Place Health, Guards Polo; *Style*— Ms Sue Wheldon; ✉ 6 Bridstow Place, London W2 5AE (e-mail sue.wheldon@douglaswallace.com)

WHELER, Sir Edward Woodford; 14 Bt (E 1660, of City of Westminster, Co London); s and h of Sir Trevor Wood Wheler, 13 Bt (d 1986), and Margaret Idris, *née* Birch (d 1987); *b* 13 June 1920; *Educ* Radley; *m* 2 July 1945, Molly Ashworth (d 2000), da of late Thomas Lever; 1 s (Trevor), 1 da (Dinah); *Heir* s, Trevor Wheler; *Career* joined army (RA) 1940, cmmnd Royal Sussex Regt 1941, attached 15 Punjab Regt IA 1941–45, BOAR 1945–47, Colonial Audit Service Uganda and Ghana 1948–58; Automobile Association of E Africa 1958–70; Benson & Hedges Ltd 1971–81 (dir 1978–81); co sec Robert Lewis (St James's) Ltd 1981–90; Liveryman Co of Pipemakers and Tobacco Blenders 1980, Freeman City of London 1980; *Style*— Sir Edward Wheler, Bt; ✉ 34 St Carantoc Way, Crantock, Newquay, Cornwall TR8 5SB (tel 01637 830965)

WHEWAY, (Jonathan) Scott; s of Barry Wheway (d 1999), and Cynthia Gill (d 1995); *b* 26 August 1966, Sheffield; *Educ* Rowlinson Comp Sch Sheffield; *m* 23 Sept 2000, Amanda; 1 s (Ranulph b 30 Dec 2003); *Career* various mgmnt appts Tesco stores 1984–2003, ceo Tesco Japan 2003–04, retail dir Boots plc (latterly Alliance Boots plc) 2005–07; memb Bd Br Retail Consortium; *Style*— Scott Wheway, Esq

WHEWELL, Roger William; s of Alfred Thomas Whewell (d 1969), and Dorothy Annie Whewell (d 1988); *b* 24 January 1940; *Educ* Harrison Coll Barbados, Clifton, Univ of Edinburgh; *m* 9 May 1964, (Edith) Elaine, da of George Turcan Chiene, DSO, TD, MC, WS (d 1992), of Edinburgh; 2 s (Andrew b 1966, Rupert b 1969), 1 da (Lisa b 1968); *Career* CA; articled clerk Jackson Taylor Abernethy & Co 1958–64; KPMG (formerly Peat Marwick): joined 1964, ptnr 1974, gen ptnr 1985–96; FCA 1964; *Clubs* New, RAC; *Style*— Roger Whewell, Esq; ✉ Innerwick House, Glenlyon, Aberfeldy, Perthshire PH15 2PP

WHICHER, Prof John Templeman; s of Leonard Sydney Whicher, of Piddinghoe, E Sussex, and Ethel Adelaid, *née* Orton; *b* 30 July 1945; *Educ* Sherborne, Univ of Cambridge (MA, MB BChir), Westminster Hosp Med Sch, Univ of London (MSc); *m* 1 (m dis 1982), Alba Heather Phyllida Leighton Crawford; 1 da (Emma b 1973), 1 s (Hugo b 1975); *m* 2, 17 Sept 1982, Jennefer Whitney, da of Dr Arthur Benson Unwin, of London; 2 da (Alexandra b 1986, Charlotte b 1989); *Career* dep dir Protein Reference Unit Westminster Hosp 1975–78, conslt chem pathologist Bristol Royal Infirmary 1978–87; Univ of Leeds: prof of chem pathology 1987–91, prof of molecular pathology 1991–96; former chm Scientific Ctee Assoc of Clinical Biochemists, former conslt advsr to Chief MD DHSS, chm Ctee on Plasma Proteins Int Fedn of Clinical Chemistry 1990–2000; former visiting prof in Lab Med Univ of Leeds; WHO Expert Advsy Panel on Health Lab Servs 1996–2003; Editorial Bd Clinical Chem Lab Med 1996–2004; dir and co sec Lyttondale Associates Ltd; memb Geologists' Assoc; chm Br Shell Collectors Club; FRCPath, FGS; *Books* Immunochemistry in Clinical Laboratory Medicine (jointly, 1978), A Short Textbook of Chemical Pathology (jointly, 1989), The Biochemistry of Inflammation (jointly, 1990); *Recreations* aviation, conchology, geology, natural history; *Clubs* Sherburn Aeroclub, Real Aeroplane; *Style*— Prof John Whicher; ✉ Rush House, Deighton, York YO19 6HQ (tel 01904 728237, e-mail john@whicher.plus.com)

WHICKER, Alan Donald; CBE (2005); o s of late Charles Henry Whicker, and Anne Jane, *née* Cross; *b* 2 August 1925; *Educ* Haberdashers' Aske's; *Career* Capt Devonshire Regt, dir Army Film and Photo Unit with 8 Army and US 5 Army, war corr Korea; foreign corr, novelist, writer, television and radio broadcaster; joined BBC TV Tonight programme 1957; writer and presenter of documentary series for: BBC TV 1959–68 and 1982–92, Yorkshire TV 1968–82 and 1992–97; author of articles for various publications, Sunday newspaper columns; various awards incl: Screenwriters' Guild Best Documentary Script 1963, Guild of Television Producers and Directors Personality of the Year 1964,

W

Silver Medal RTS 1968, Dumont Award Univ of Calif 1970; Best Interview Programme Award, Hollywood Festival of TV 1973, Dimbleby Award BAFTA 1978, TV Times Special Award 1978, Royal TV Soc's first Hall of Fame 1993, Travel Writer's Special Award for truly outstanding achievement in travel journalism 1998; FRSA; *Television* for BBC 1: Whicker's World 1959–60 and 1965–66, Whicker Down Under 1961, Whicker on Top of the World! 1962, Whicker in Sweden, Whicker in the Heart of Texas, Whicker down Mexico Way 1963, The Alan Whicker Report series including The Solitary Billionaire (J Paul Getty), Whicker's World - the First Million Miles (six retrospectives) 1982, Whicker's World - a Fast Boat to China 1984, Whicker's World - Living with Uncle Sam 1985, Whicker's World - Living with Waltzing Matilda 1988, Whicker's World - Hong Kong 1990, Whicker's World - A Taste of Spain 1992, One-on-One 2002; for BBC 2: Whicker! (ten talk shows) 1984; for Yorkshire TV: Whicker's World Specials on Gen Stroessner of Paraguay, Count von Rosen and Pres Duvalier of Haiti, Whicker in Europe, Whicker's Walkabout, Broken Hill-Walled City, Gairy's Grenada, World of Whicker, Whicker's Orient, Whicker Within a Woman's World 1972, Whicker's South Seas, Whicker Way Out West 1973, Whicker's World series on Cities 1974, Whicker's World Down Under 1976, Whicker's New World (US) 1977, Whicker's World - India 1978, Whicker's World - Indonesia 1979, Whicker's World - California 1980, Peter Sellers Meml programme 1980, Whicker's World Aboard the Orient Express 1982, Around Whicker's World in 25 years (three retrospective progs) 1982, Around Whicker's World - The Ultimate Package! (four progs) 1992, Whicker's World - The Absolute Monarch (The Sultan of Brunei) 1992, Whicker's World South Africa 1993 (two progs: Whicker's Miss World, Whicker's World - The Sun King), Whicker's World - The Real Orient Express 1994, Whicker - The Mahathir Interview (Dr Mahathir Mohammed, PM of Malaysia) 1994, Whicker's World - Pavarotti in Paradise 1994; other credits incl: 27 progs for Travel Channel 1996, four progs for YTV-TTTV 1997, Whicker's Week (BBC Choice) 1999, NFT tribute at sixth TV Festival 2002, Whicker's War (two progs, Channel 4) 2004, Comedy Map of Britain (BBC 2) 2007; *Radio* for BBC: writer/presenter various programmes, chaired Start the Week 1982, Whicker's Wireless World 1983, Around Whicker's World (6 progs, Radio 2) 1998, Whicker's New World (7 Progs, Radio 2) 1999, Whicker's World Down Under (BBC Radio 2), Whicker's World - The Fabulous Fifties (BBC Radio 2) 2000, Whicker's World - The History of Television (It'll Never Last) 2001, Fifty Royal Years (BBC Radio 2) 2002, Around Whicker's World (BBC Radio 4) 2005; *Film* incl The Angry Silence 1964; *Books* Some Rise By Sin (1949), Away - with Alan Whicker (1963), Within Whicker's World (1982), Whicker's New World (1985), Whicker's World Down Under (1988), Whicker's World - Take 2! (2000), Whicker's War (2005); *Style*— Alan Whicker, Esq, CBE

WHILE, Prof Alison Elizabeth; da of Harold Arthur Armstrong While, MBE, TD (d 1983), and Janet Bell Symington Clark; *b* 24 July 1953; *Educ* Wycombe Abbey, Univ of Southampton (BSc), Poly of the South Bank (MSc), Univ of London (PhD), St Thomas' Hosp (RGN), Univ of Southampton (RHV); *m* Philip Allan Gore-Randall, *qv*; 2 s (William b 1986, Edward b 1987); *Career* health visitor N Kensington 1977–80, Chelsea Coll London: lectr 1980–89, sr lectr 1989–92; prof of community nursing KCL 1992–; visiting prof TCD; memb: Royal Coll of Nursing 1977, Community Practitioners' and Health Visitors' Assoc 1977; conslt ed Br Jl of Community Nursing, assoc ed Int Jl of Nursing Studies; Freeman City of London 1979, Liveryman Worshipful Co of Farriers 1979; FRSM 2007; *Books* Research in Preventive Community Nursing Care (1986), Health in the Inner City (1989), Caring for Children (1991); *Recreations* tennis, good food, travel, The Cotswolds; *Style*— Prof Alison While; ✉ Primary and Intermediate Care Section, The Florence Nightingale School of Nursing and Midwifery, King's College London, James Clerk Maxwell Building, 57 Waterloo Road, London SE1 8WA (tel 020 7848 3506, fax 020 7848 3230, e-mail alison.while@kcl.ac.uk)

WHILEY, Johanne (Jo); *b* 4 July 1965, Northampton; *Career* radio DJ and television presenter; formerly: presenter WPFM (BBC Radio 4), prodr and presenter The Indie Show (BSB), music prodr The Word (Channel 4); BBC Radio 1: co-presenter The Evening Session 1993–97 (with Steve Lamacq, co-host Sound City live music festivals and Phoenix Festival), presenter lunchtime slot 1997–2001, presenter mid-morning slot 2001–; presenter Jo Whiley Show (Channel 4); *Recreations* music, swimming, wakeboarding, snowboarding, windsurfing, volleyball, partying, Jack Daniels; *Style*— Ms Jo Whiley; ✉ BBC Radio One, Clipstone Street, London W1N 4DJ (e-mail jo.whiley@bbc.co.uk)

WHISHAW, Anthony Popham Law; s of Robert Whishaw, and Joyce Evelyn Mary, *née* Wheeler (d 1996); *b* 22 May 1930; *Educ* Tonbridge (Higher Cert), Chelsea Sch of Art, RCA (travelling scholarship, drawing prize); *m* 1957, Jean Gibson; 2 da (Phoebe, Zoe); *Career* artist; RA 1989 (ARA 1980), ARCA, RWA 1992 (Hon RWA 2003); *Collections* incl: Arts Cncl GB, Coventry Art Gallery, Euro Parl Strasbourg, Leicester City Art Gallery, Museo de Bahia Brazil, Nat Gallery Victoria Melbourne, Museum of Contemporary Art Helsinki, Royal Acad, Power Art Gallery Sydney Aust, Ferens Art Gallery Hull, City Art Galleries Sheffield, Chantrey Bequest, The Tate Gallery, Christchurch Kensington, The Long Term Credit Bank of Japan, Andersen Consulting, Ashikaga Bank of Tokyo, Zeneca, Bolton Art Gallery, The Financial Times, M A M, Ladbrokes, Huddersfield Art Gallery, Barings Asset Management, Tetrapak UK, Albert E Sharp, Deutsche Morgan Grenfell, Crown Commodities, Stanhope plc, St Anne's Coll Oxford; *One-Man Exhibitions* incl: Liberia Abril Madrid 1957, Roland Browse & Delbanco 1960, 1961, 1963, 1965 and 1968, Hoya Gallery London 1974, Acme Gallery 1978, from Landscape (Kettle's Yard Cambridge, Ferens Art Gallery Hull, Bede Gallery Jarrow) 1982–84, Work on Paper (Nicola Jacobs Gallery London) 1983, Reflections After Las Meninas (tour) 1987, Royal Acad of Arts Diploma Galleries London 1987, Hatton Gallery Newcastle 1988, Mead Gallery Warwick Univ 1988, Hansard Gallery Southampton 1988, Spacex Gallery Exeter 1988, Infaust Gallery Hamburg 1989, Infaust Gallery Shanghai 1989, Blasón Gallery London 1991, Artspace London 1992, 1994 and 1995, RWA Bristol 1993, On Memory and Reflection (nat touring exhbn starting at Barbican and subsequent museums in Exeter, Ayr, Dublin, Newcastle, Sheffield, Newport and Bolton) 1994–95, Art First London 1997 and 1999, Pueblo Landscapes Royal Acad 2000, Trees Stephen Lacey Gallery 2000, Re-Appearances St Anne's Coll Oxford 2000; *Group Exhibitions* incl: Ashmolean Museum Oxford 1957–72, Br Painting 1952–77 (Royal Acad of Arts London) 1977, Walker Art Gallery Liverpool 1980, Hayward Annual (Hayward Gallery London) 1980 and 1982, Nine Artists (Helsinki, touring) 1983, Three Decades 1953–83 (Royal Acad of Arts London) 1983, 30 London Painters (Royal Acad of Arts London) 1985, Whitechapel Open (Whitechapel Art Gallery London) 1981–83, 1987 and 1994, The Romantic Tradition in Contemporary British Painting (Madrid, Murcia, touring) 1988, 8 Contemporary Br Artists (Galerie Sapet Valeree France) 1988, Le Paysage Contemporaine 1991/92 (touring Belgium, France), Creative Quarters Museum of London 2001; *Prizes* RCA Travelling Scholarship 1955, RCA Drawing Prize 1955, Perth International Biennale 1973, Bayer Int Painting 1973, South East Arts Assoc Painting 1975, GLC Painting 1981, John Moores Minor Painting 1982; scholarships: Spanish Govt 1956, Abbey Minor 1956, Abbey Premier 1982, Lorne 1982–83; Greater London Arts Assoc Grant 1977, Arts Cncl GB Award 1978, RA Picture of the Year 1996 (for Korn Ferry); *Style*— Anthony Whishaw, Esq, RA; ✉ c/o The Royal Academy, Burlington House, London W1V 0DJ (website www.anthonywhishaw.com)

WHISTON, John; *Educ* Edinburgh Acad, Balliol Coll Oxford (BA); *Career* BBC: joined as gen trainee 1983, asst prodr BBC Music & Arts 1985–87 (worked on progs incl Timewatch, Bookmark and Omnibus), prodr BBC Music & Arts 1987–94 (sr prodr The Late Show, prodr Edinburgh Nights), head of Youth and Entertainment Features 1994–97; dir of progs: Yorkshire Tyne-Tees TV 1998–2001, Granada Content North 2001–02; dir of Drama, Kids and Arts Granada 2002–; prodr progs for BBC Music & Arts incl: Naked Hollywood (BAFTA Best Documentary), Absurdistan (BFI Grierson Best Documentary Award), Archive Productions progs (incl: The Lime Grove Story, A Night with Alan Bennett, TV Hell, Granadaland, Cops on the Box, A Night in with David Attenborough); other progs incl: The Mrs Merton Show, The Royle Family, Rough Guides, The Travel Show, The Big Trip, The Sunday Show, Kicking & Screaming, Great Railway Journeys, The Sunday Show, Before They Were Famous, Dennis Pennis, themed nights incl Weird Night and George Best Night; currently responsible for Granada drama progs incl: Coronation Street, Emmerdale, Heartbeat, A Touch of Frost, Poirot, Prime Suspect, Miss Marple, William & Mary, Life Begins, The Royal, Where the Heart Is, Vincent, Jericho, Cracker, Blue Murder, The South Bank Show and progs for children; *Style*— John Whiston, Esq

WHITAKER, James Edward Anthony; s of George Edward Dudley Whitaker, OBE (d 1983), and Mary Evelyn Austin, *née* Haslett (d 1989); *b* 4 October 1940; *Educ* Cheltenham Coll; *m* 1965, Iwona, da of late Andrzej Karol Milde, of Poland; 2 s (Edward b 1965, Thomas b 1966), 1 da (Victoria b 1973); *Career* journalist: Daily Mail, Daily Express, The Sun, Daily Star; currently Royal corr and columnist The Daily Mirror; Scoop of the Year British Press Awards 1998; *Books* Prince Charles, Prince of Wales, Settling Down, Diana v Charles, Her Majesty and the Commonwealth - 50 Golden Tears (ed); *Recreations* racing, shooting, skiing; *Clubs* City Golf; *Style*— James Whitaker, Esq; ✉ c/o Mirror Group Newspapers, One Canada Square, Canary Wharf, London E14 5AP (tel 020 7510 3000, e-mail james.whitaker@mirror.co.uk)

WHITAKER, Baroness (Life Peer UK 1999), of Beeston in the County of Nottinghamshire; Janet Alison Whitaker; da of Alan Harrison Stewart, and Ella, *née* Saunders; *Educ* Nottingham HS for Girls, Girton Coll Cambridge (major scholar, BA), Bryn Mawr Coll (Farley grad fell, MA), Harvard Univ (Radcliffe fell); *Career* commissioning ed André Deutsch Ltd 1961–66, speechwriter to chm Health and Safety Cmmn 1976, head of gas safety HSE 1983–86, head of nuclear safety admin HSE 1986–88, head of health and safety Dept of Employment 1988–92, head of sex equality 1992–96, memb Employment Tbnls 1995–2000, conslt CRE and Cwlth Secretariat 1996–99, memb Immigration Complaints Audit Ctee 1998–99; vice-chair: All-Pty Gp on Ethiopia, PLP Ctee on Int Devpt, All-Pty Land Mine Eradication Gp; memb: EU Select Ctee Sub-Ctee on Educn, Social Affrs and Home Affrs 1999–2003, Jt Ctee on Human Rights 2000–03, Jt Parly Ctee on the Draft Corruption Bill 2003, Friends Provident Ctee of Reference; chair Camden Racial Equality Cncl 1999, chair Working Men's Coll 1998–2001, dep chair Ind Television Cmmn 2001–03; memb: Advsy Cncl Transparency Int (UK), Cncl ODI, Advsy Panel UNA-UK, Bd Br Inst of Human Rights, Cncl AWEPA; tstee UNICEF UK; patron: Runnymede Tst, Br Stammering Assoc, Student Partnerships Worldwide; memb: Opportunity Int, InterAct Worldwide; vice-pres: Br Humanists Assoc, One World Tst; non-exec dir Tavistock and Portman NHS Tst 1997–2001; *Recreations* travel, hill walking, music, art, theatre; *Clubs* Reform; *Style*— The Lady Whitaker; ✉ House of Lords, London SW1A 0PW

WHITAKER, Sir John James Ingham (Jack); 4 Bt (UK 1936), of Babworth, Nottinghamshire; s of Sir James Herbert Ingham Whitaker, 3 Bt (d 1999); *b* 23 October 1952; *Educ* Eton, Univ of Bristol, (BSc); *m* 31 Jan 1981, Elizabeth Jane Ravenscroft, da of L J R Starke, of NZ; 3 da (Lucy Harriet Ravenscroft b 1982, Alix Catherine Hepburn b 1987, Eleanor Mary Harvie b 1989), 1 s (Harry James Ingham b 1984); *Heir* s, Harry Whitaker; *Career* High Sheriff of Notts 2001–02; FCA, MIEE; *Style*— Sir Jack Whitaker, Bt; ✉ Babworth Hall, Retford, Nottinghamshire DN22 8EP

WHITAKER, Michael; s of Donald Whitaker, and Enid, *née* Lockwood; *b* 17 March 1960; *Educ* Salendine Nook Secdy Modern Sch; *m* 13 Dec 1980, Veronique Dalems, da of Dino Vastapane; *Career* professional show jumper; Jr Euro Team 1976, winner Jr Championships under 16 and under 21, winner Jr European Team Championship 1978; Grand Prix wins: Hickstead 1986, Dortmund 1986 and 1995, Wembley 1987, Birmingham 1989, Calgary 1989; other wins incl: Hickstead Derby 1980, King George V Gold Cup 1982 and 1989, European Team Championships 1985, 1987, 1989, European Team Championships 1985, 1987, 1989, nat champion 1984 and 1989; runner-up European Championships 1989, Silver medal World Team Championships 1986 (Bronze medal 1990), Silver medal team event Olympic Games LA 1984, Silver medal European Team Championships 1995, individual Silver medal European Championships 1995, Bronze medal European Team Championships 1997; 45 int appearances; world bareback high jump record Dublin 1980; Martini Equestrian Personality Award 1993; *Recreations* sport, spending time at home; *Style*— Michael Whitaker, Esq

WHITAKER, Patrick James; s of John Henry Foord Whitaker, of The Garden House, Dunorlan Farm, Tunbridge Wells, Kent, and Anne Jennifer, *née* Cheveley; *b* 9 April 1965; *Educ* Garth Hill Comp, Berkshire Coll of Art & Design (RSA art bursary, BTEC), St Martin's Sch of Art (BA); *Career* fndr designer Whitaker Malem (with Keir Malem, *qv*) 1988– (annual collections of hand crafted leatherwear for specialist int retail); launched new line of male and female leather torsos (with Adel Roostein) 1995; appearances on TV and subject of press profiles in quality fashion magazines, fashion lectr at various colleges of art and design incl visiting lectr RCA 1999–2000; memb Br Cncl and Br Embassy mission to promote Br fashion, lecture and set Acad project Vilnius Lithuania; cmmns for: Givenchy Haute Couture 1997, Valentino Haute Couture 1997, Tommy Hilfiger Red Label 1998, Tommy Hilfiger 1999–2000; special assignments incl: body sculptures for re-opening of Bauhaus Dessau, outfit for Naomi Campbell in Vauxhall advertising campaign 1993, collaboration with sculptor Allen Jones 1999–, piece for permanent collection Museum of Leather Craft Northampton 2000, collection for Alma Home launch 2000, R&D for Gucci collection 2000, cmmn by Allen Jones for new sculpture Waiting on Table (exhibited Royal Acad Summer Exhibition); private cmmns for: Mick Jagger, Cher, Pamela Anderson, Gloria Estefan, Janet Jackson, Jerry Hall, Bono, George Michael, Madonna, Jon Bon Jovi, Spice Girls, Steven Tyler; film cmmns incl: Mortal Kombat 1995, The Changeling 1995, Die Another Day 2002, Tomb Raider 2 2003, Troy 2004, Aeon Flux 2005, Harry Potter and the Goblet of Fire 2005, Eragon 2006, Casino Royale 2006, Harry Potter and the Order of the Phoenix 2007, Batman: The Dark Knight 2008, Speed Racer 2008; exhibitions: Unlaced Grace (Banbury Museum and nat tour) 1994–95, Inside Out (Design Museum London) 2000, Personal Space Br Cncl Show (and commn, NY, Milan, London) 2000, Art 2001 (with Jibby Beane, exhibited Chair sculpture) 2001, Tokyo Designers Week (Br Cncl exhibit Living Britain) 2001; finalist Smirnoff Fashion Awards 1985, nominated British Fashion Awards 1992; *Recreations* film collection; *Style*— Patrick Whitaker, Esq; ✉ Whitaker Malem, The Garden Studio, 27 Buckingham Road, London N14 DG (tel and fax 020 7923 7887, website www.whitakermalem.co.uk)

WHITAKER, Sheila Hazel; da of Charles Whitaker (d 1975), and Hilda Dixon (d 1987); *b* 1 April 1936; *Educ* Cathays HS for Girls Cardiff, King's Norton GS Birmingham, Univ of Warwick (BA); *Career* chief stills offr Nat Film Archive BFI 1968–74, dir Tyneside Cinema, Tyneside Film Festival Newcastle upon Tyne 1979–84, head of programming Nat Film Theatre BFI 1984–90; dir: London Film Festival 1987–96, Metropolis Films 2002–04; tstee Free Form Arts Tst 2001–; vice-pres Acquisitions and Programming Article 27 2000; series advsr I B Tauris Contemporary Film Series 2002–; memb: Int Jury Venice Film Festival 1992, Programming Commissioning Locarno Int Film Festival

2002–; conslt prog advsr Dubai Int Film Festival; co-ed: Framework Jl 1975–79, Writing Women 1981–84; tstee Satyajit Ray Fndn 1997–; Hon DLitt Univ of Newcastle 1997; Chevalier de l'Ordre des Arts et des Lettres (France) 1996; *Publications* Life and Art: The New Iranian Cinema (co-ed, 1999), An Argentine Passion: Maria Luisa Bemberg and her Films (co-ed, 2000); *Clubs* Groucho; *Style*— Ms Sheila Whitaker; ✉ 11 Barnsbury Park, London N1 1HQ (tel and fax 020 7609 4715, e-mail swhitaker@onetel.com)

WHITAKER, Master; Steven Dixon; s of late George Dixon Whitaker, and late Elsie Whitaker; *b* 28 January 1950; *Educ* Burnley GS, Churchill Coll Cambridge (MA); *Children* 1 s (Alexander Steven George), 1 da (Emma Louise); *Career* called to the Bar Middle Temple 1973; Master of the Supreme Court (Queen's Bench Div) 2002–; statutory memb Civil Procedure Rules Ctee 2002–; *Recreations* horses, music, poetry, the arts; *Style*— Master Whitaker; ✉ Room E116, Royal Courts of Justice, Strand, London WC2A 2LL (tel 020 7947 6434)

WHITBOURN, Dr Philip Robin; OBE (1993); s of Edwin Arthur Whitbourn (d 1953), of Sevenoaks, Kent, and Kathleen, *née* Sykes; *b* 10 March 1932; *Educ* Sevenoaks Sch, UCL (PhD); *m* 10 Jan 1959, Anne Pearce, da of Peter Melrose Marks (d 1938), of Glasgow; 1 da (Katherine b 1960), 1 s (James b 1963); *Career* architect; Sir Edwin Cooper RA and Partners 1955–58, Stewart Hendry and Smith 1958–60, Fitzroy Robinson Partnership 1960–66, Historic Bldgs Div GLC 1966–86; English Heritage: joined 1986, divnl architect London Region 1988–92, dir South Region 1992–94, chief architect Conservation Gp 1992–95; sec ICOMOS UK (Int Cncl on Monuments and Sites) 1995–2002; sec to Tstees INTACH (UK) Tst (Indian Nat Tst for Art and Cultural Heritage) 1995–2002; pres Royal Tunbridge Wells Civic Soc 1995–2005 (chm 1969–70, 1972–73, 1978–80 and 1990–91), memb Southwark Diocesan Advsy Ctee for the Care of Churches 1973–97; memb IHBC 1997; FRIBA 1968, FSA 1984; *Style*— Dr Philip Whitbourn, OBE, FSA; ✉ Rosaville Lodge, 40 Beulah Road, Tunbridge Wells, Kent TN1 2NR (tel 01892 523026)

WHITBREAD, Jasmine; da of Gerald Whitbread, of London, and Ursula Whitbread; *b* 1 September 1963, London; *Educ* Univ of Bristol (BA), Stanford Univ; *m* 1994, Howard Exton-Smith; 1 da (Holly b 25 March 1995), 1 s (Felix b 2 Oct 1997); *Career* dir global mktg Cortex Corp 1986–90, mgmnt trainer Nat Union of Disabled Persons of Uganda (NUDIPU)/VSO 1990–92, md Thomson Financial 1994–99; Oxfam GB: regnl dir W Africa 1999–2002, int dir 2002–05; chief exec Save the Children UK 2005–; memb: Disasters and Emergency Ctee, Steering Ctee for Humanitarian Response, Save the Children Alliance; *Style*— Ms Jasmine Whitbread; ✉ Save the Children, 1 St John's Lane, London EC1M 4AR (tel 020 7012 6431, fax 020 7012 6950, e-mail chiefexecutive@savethechildren.org.uk)

WHITBREAD, Samuel Charles (Sam); JP; s of Maj Simon Whitbread (d 1985), of Southill, Beds, and Helen Beatrice Margaret, *née* Trefusis; family settled in Bedfordshire at time of Conquest, founded Brewery 1742, 1 Tory and 5 Whig/Liberal MPs; *b* 22 February 1937; *Educ* Eton, Trinity Coll Cambridge; *m* 1961, Jane Mary, da of Charles William John Hugh Hayter (d 1985), of Oxon; 3 s (Charles, Henry, William), 1 da (Victoria (Mrs Sebastian Morley)); *Career* 2 Lt Beds and Herts Regt 1956–57; non-exec dir Whitbread plc 1972–2001 (chm 1984–92); dir: Whitbread Investment Co plc 1977–94, Gems (Wax Models) Ltd 1980–88, Brewers' Soc Cncl 1984–92, Whitbread Share Ownership Tstees Ltd 1984–92, Whitbread Pension Tstees Ltd 1984–92, S C Whitbread Farms 1985–2004, Boddingtons Breweries plc 1985–87, Marston Thompson Evershed 1985–87, Countryside Fndn for Education 1988–, Sun Alliance Group 1989–92, Southill Sawmills Ltd 1990–2000, Shuttleworth Tst 1993–, Glenalla Forest Ltd 1997–, Moggerhanger House Preservation Tst 1998–, Herts Timber Supplies Ltd 2000–, Whitbread Farms Ltd 2004–; pres: E of England Agric Soc 1991–92, Shire Horse Soc 1990–92, St John Cncl (Beds) 1991–, Beds RFCA 1991–; East Anglia RFCA 2000–05, chm Mid-Beds Con Assoc 1969–72 (pres 1986–91), memb Beds CC 1974–82, pres Beds-Herts Regiment Assoc 2004–; HM Lord-Lt Beds 1991– (DL 1974), High Sheriff Beds 1973–74; tstee: Cecil Higgins Art Gallery 1998–, Wixamtree Tst 2002–; Liveryman Worshipful Co of Brewers; Hon LLB Univ of Beds; Bledisloe Gold Medal RASE 1989; KStJ, FRSA, FLS, FSA; *Recreations* shooting, painting, music, travel; *Clubs* Brooks's; *Style*— S C Whitbread, Esq; ✉ Glebe House, Southill, Biggleswade, Bedfordshire SG18 9LL (tel 01462 816226, e-mail scw@glebesouthill.co.uk)

WHITBREAD, (Hugh) William; s of Col William Henry Whitbread, TD (d 1994), and his 2 w, Betty Parr, *née* Russell (d 2000); *b* 11 February 1942; *Educ* Eton, CCC Cambridge, Harvard Business Sch (MBA); *m* 1972, Katherine Elizabeth, *née* Hall; 4 c; *Career* HM Diplomatic Serv 1966–71, second sec Vientiane 1968–70 (third sec 1966–68); md Thomas Wethered and Sons Ltd of Marlow 1976–80, specialist dir Whitbread & Co 1981–88, investment mangr Whitbread Investment Co plc 1989–94; dir: Whitbread Investment Co plc 1992–94, Hanover International plc 1996–2003, Taverners Trust plc 2000–05; govr Aldenham Sch 1986–2003; Liveryman Worshipful Co of Skinners, Master of Worshipful Co of Brewers 2003–04; FSI; *Recreations* fishing, shooting; *Clubs* Brooks's, RAC, City of London; *Style*— William Whitbread Esq; ✉ The Old Rectory, Dennington, Woodbridge, Suffolk IP13 8AD

WHITBURN, Vanessa Victoria; da of Victor Donald Whitburn (d 1988), and Eileen, *née* Wellington (d 2004); *Educ* Mount St Mary's Convent Sch Exeter, Exeter Coll of FE, Univ of Hull (BA); *Career* BBC: studio mangr Broadcasting House and Bush House London 1974–76, asst floor mangr TV Drama Television Centre 1976–77 (work incl The Onedin Line), prodr Radio Drama Pebble Mill 1977–83 (work incl The Archers) sr prodr Radio Drama Pebble Mill 1983–88 (prodr/dir numerous plays and classic serials for Radio 3 and 4); prodr Brookside (Mersey Television for Channel Four) 1988–90, rejoined BBC as prodr/dir BBC TV Pebble Mill 1990–91, ed The Archers (BBC Radio 4) 1991–, exec prodr of radio drama BBC Midlands 1995–; fndr memb Mgmnt Bd Theatre Foundry 1985; memb Radio Acad; has also directed stage, radio and TV drama prodns for various groups incl Derby Playhouse and WGBH Boston; conslt for ODA on Ndiga Nacio (Kenyan radio soap opera) and for Midwest Radio Theater Workshop Missouri USA, memb Advsy Bd Nat Audio Theatre Festivals USA; *Books* The Archers - The Official Inside Story (1996); *Style*— Ms Vanessa Whitburn; ✉ BBC Birmingham, The Mailbox, Birmingham B1 1RF

WHITBY, Mark; s of George Whitby, MBE, FRIBA (d 1972), of London, and Rhona Carmian, *née* Butler; *b* 29 January 1950; *Educ* Ealing GS for Boys, King's Coll London (BSc); 1 s by prev partnership (Alex b 25 Sept 1982); *m* 19 Jan 1991, Janet, *née* Taylor; 2 da (Harriet b 29 Feb 1992, Katherine b 28 Oct 1996), 2 s (Ralph b 24 May 1993, Chad b 19 Jan 1999); *Career* dir Whitbybird; engrg projects throughout Europe incl: British Embassy Berlin, British Embassy Dublin, York Millennium Bridge, Peterborough Millennium Bridge, Lancaster Millennium Bridge, Igus Factory Cologne, Olivetti Research Centre Bari, Stock Exchange Berlin, Merchants Bridge Manchester (ISE Special Award, Millennium Design Product 1998) Mappa Mundi Museum Hereford, King's Fund HQ London, Sadlers Wells Theatre London, PGI Cummins Factory Kent, The National Rowing Museum Henley-on-Thames, 40 Grosvenor Place, Heathrow Terminal 2 and 3, new Docklands campus for Univ of East London; govr Building Centre Tst 1997–; chm Urban Design Alliance 2001–02; chm SEEDA Sustainability and Urban Renaissance Sector Gp 2002–04, memb Energy Foresight Panel 2003–04; FICE 1992 (pres 2001–02), FREng 1996, Hon FRIBA 1999; *Media* Secrets of Lost Empires (1996 and 1999), The Wobbly Bridge - A Tale of Over-Arching Ambition (2001); *Recreations* children, 20th Century engineering history, running (competitor London Marathon 2001), canoeing (memb Br Canoeing Team 1968 Olympics); *Style*— Mark Whitby, Esq, FREng, FICE, Hon FRIBA; ✉ Whitbybird, 60 Newman Street, London W1T 3DA (tel 020 7631 5291, fax 020 7323 4645, e-mail mark.whitby@whitbybird.com)

WHITBY, Bishop of 1999–; Rt Rev Robert Sidney Ladds; s of Sidney Ladds (d 1995), and Joan Dorothy, *née* Cant (d 2001); *b* 15 November 1941; *Educ* NW Kent Coll, Christ Church Coll Canterbury (BEd), Canterbury Sch of Miny; *m* 1964, Roberta Harriet, *née* Sparkes; 3 s (Matthew Peter Richard b 1966, Thomas Julian b 1970, Alexander John b 1972); *Career* former: research chemist, sch master; ordained: deacon 1980, priest 1981; curate of Hythe 1980–83, rector of St John the Baptist Bretherton 1983–91, chaplain Bishop Rawstorne Sch 1983–85, Bishop of Blackburn's chaplain for miny 1985–90, sec Bishop's Advsy Cncl for Miny 1985–90, Bishop's audit offr 1990–91, priest i/c Preston Team Miny (actg rector) 1991–96, hon canon Blackburn Cathedral 1993–97, rector of Preston 1996–97, archdeacon of Lancaster 1997–99; commissary to the Bishop of Taejon Primate of S Korea 1997–2000, vice-pres Korean Mission Partnership 2000–; superior gen Soc of Mary 2000–; chaplain to the Guild Mayor of Preston 1992; bro Soc of the Holy Cross (SSC); memb Exec Springboard 2002–04; FRSC (LRSC); *Recreations* bonsai, gardening, walking, opera, architecture; *Style*— The Rt Rev The Bishop of Whitby; ✉ 60 West Green, Stokesley, Middlesbrough TS9 5BD (tel 01642714475/6, fax 01642 714472, e-mail bishopofwhitby@episcopus.co.uk)

WHITE, Adrian Harold Michael; s of Brig Gilbert William White, MBE (d 1977), and Clodagh Marie, *née* Austin (d 1977); *b* 20 November 1945; *Educ* Ampleforth; *m* 1, 25 June 1970, Helen Frances McKay (d 2002), da of Sir Herbert (Charles Fahie) Cox, QC (d 1973); 1 s (Hugh b 5 March 1978); m 2, 29 July 2004, Hilary Anne Brown, da of Hon Mr Justice Frederick George Cooke, QC (d 2002), and former w of Martin Michael Hindley Brown; 2 step s (Richard b 10 May 1978, Nicholas b 13 Aug 1980); *Career* chartered accountant; audit sr Peat Marwick Mitchell & Co 1964–70; exec: Brown Shipley & Co Ltd 1970–72, Old Broad St Securities Ltd 1972–75, Hill Samuel & Co Ltd 1975–78; sr asst dir Morgan Grenfell & Co Ltd 1978–87, dep md Midland Montagu Asset Management 1987–92, dep chief exec and chief operating offr Hermes Pensions Management Ltd 1993–2004; chm and tstee Elizabeth Finn Tst 2004–, chm of tstees Johnson Matthey Employees Pension Scheme 2006–; FCA; *Recreations* racing; *Clubs* Boodle's, MCC, Hurlingham; *Style*— Adrian White, Esq; ✉ 9 Ranelagh House, Elystan Place, London SW3 3LE

WHITE, Alan Geoffrey; s of John White, and Rose, *née* Dallin; *b* 8 July 1934; *Educ* Mitcham GS; *m* Melanie (decd); *Career* RAF Photographic 1952–57; freelance photographer 1958–67, Colour Processing Laboratories 1967–85, own company Stilled Movie Ltd 1986– (producing specialised plate photography and translights for film sets and visual effects in feature film and TV indust), photographer Alan White Photography; has presented papers at various confs; FBIPP, FRPS, memb RTS, MBKS, MMPA, hon memb Br Film Designers Guild; *Recreations* golf, theatre, travel; *Clubs* Hurlingham Luncheon, Tenterden Golf; *Style*— Alan White, Esq

WHITE, Andrew; QC (1997); s of Peter White, of Dorset, and Sandra Jeanette, *née* Lovelace (d 1988); *b* 25 January 1958; *Educ* UC Cardiff (LLB); *m* 1987, Elizabeth Denise, da of Thomas Rooney; 2 s (Harry George b 1988, Alexander Thomas b 1991); *Career* called to the Bar Lincoln's Inn 1980 (Hardwick scholar 1977, Megarry scholar 1979), bencher 2003; in practice 1981–; *Publications* The Encyclopaedia of Forms and Precedents (contrib Building and Engineering, 5 edn); *Recreations* farming, sailing, music; *Style*— Andrew White, QC; ✉ 1 Atkin Building, Gray's Inn, London WC1R 5AT (tel 020 7404 0102, fax 020 7405 7456)

WHITE, Air Vice Marshal Andrew David (Andy); CB; s of Edward Jethro White, and Margaret Campbell, *née* Lockhart; *b* 2 January 1952; *Educ* Wallington GS, Loughborough Univ, RAF Coll Cranwell, JSDC; *m* 11 Oct 1975, Christine Ann, da of Douglas Spratt; 2 s (Robert James b 2 April 1980, Stuart Richard b 9 March 1982); *Career* cmmnd RAF 1970; pilot 17 Sqdn RAF Brüggen, Tactical Weapons Unit RAF Brawdy and RAF Chivenor 1980–82, weapons instr 20 Sqdn RAF Brüggen 1982–84, Flight Cdr 14 Sqdn 1984–85, staff offr Attack/Ops Branch HQ AFCENT 1985–88, staff offr to Dir of PR (RAF) MOD 1988–90, OC XV Sqdn RAF Laarbruch 1991–92, OC IX Sqdn RAF Brüggen 1992–94, personal staff offr to Chief of Air Staff MOD 1994–96, Station Cdr RAF Cottesmore 1996–99, OC Tri-National Tornado Trg Estab 1996–99, AO Plans/ HQ Strike Cmd 1999–2002, COS Ops HQ Strike Cmd 2002–03, AOC No 3 Gp 2003–06; ceo Nat Security Inspectorate 2006–; non-exec dir Nat Air Traffic Servs 2006–; chm of govrs Cottesmore Co Primary Sch 1996–99; GSM (Clasp) Iraq; *Recreations* golf, private flying, skiing, computing, dog walking; *Clubs* RAF; *Style*— Air Vice Marshal Andrew White, CB; ✉ National Security Inspectorate, Sentinel House, 5 Reform Road, Maidenhead SL6 8BY (tel 01628 637512)

WHITE, Bruce Balfour; s of Robert White (d 1985), and Anne Elizabeth, *née* Balfour; *b* 12 October 1961, Perth, Scotland; *Educ* Univ of Dundee (LLB); *m* 1 Oct 1988, Alice, *née* Grant; 1 da (Rosie b 12 Nov 1990), 2 s (Toby b 1 June 1992, Angus b 23 Sept 1994); *Career* trainee slr Dorman Jeffrey & Co 1984–86; Linklater & Paines (now Linklaters): asst slr 1986–95, ptnr 1995–, head global projects 2005–; memb PPP Forum; memb Law Soc; *Recreations* reading, rugby, cricket, skiing; *Style*— Bruce White, Esq; ✉ Linklaters, 1 Silk Street, London EC2Y 8HQ (tel 020 7456 2000, fax 020 7456 2222, e-mail bruce.white@linklaters.com)

WHITE, Christopher (Chris); s of Rex White (d 2001), of Sydney, Aust, and Valerie, *née* Dekker, of Auckland, NZ; *b* 1 November 1961, Auckland, NZ; *Partner* Zenlina Yap; 3 da (Caitlin b 6 Oct 1991, Riane b 16 Feb 1994, Kara b 12 Feb 1998), 1 s (Kier b 4 Nov 1996); *Career* various roles SE Asia The Coca-Cola Co 1986–97, ceo Movenpick Asia Pacific Ltd 1998–2001, gen mangr Nestlé Peters Ice Cream Ltd Nestlé Oceania Ltd 2001–03, md Nestlé Rowntree Ltd 2004–, dir Nestlé UK Ltd; dir Biscuits, Confectionary, Cakes Assoc; chm Yorkshire Science, dir York and N Yorkshire C of C; *Style*— Chris White, Esq; ✉ Nestlé Rowntree Ltd, York YO91 1XY

WHITE, Prof Sir Christopher John; kt (2001), CVO (1995); s of Gabriel Edward Ernest Francis White, CBE (d 1988), of London, and Elizabeth Grace, *née* Ardizzone (d 1958); *b* 19 September 1930; *Educ* Downside, Courtauld Inst of Art, Univ of London (BA, PhD), Univ of Oxford (MA); *m* 14 Dec 1957, Rosemary Katharine Alice, da of Gordon Paul Desages (d 1960), of London; 2 da (Arabella Elizabeth b 1959, Clarissa Grace b 1961), 1 s (Sebastian Gabriel b 1965); *Career* asst keeper Dept of Prints and Drawings British Museum 1954–65, dir Messrs P and D Colnaghi London 1965–71, curator of graphic arts Nat Gallery of Art Washington DC 1971–73, dir of studies Paul Mellon Centre for Studies in British Art London 1973–85, assoc dir Yale Center for British Art New Haven CT 1973–85, dir Ashmolean Museum 1985–97; fell Worcester Coll Oxford 1985–97, prof of the arts of the Netherlands Univ of Oxford 1992–97; dir Burlington Magazine 1981–; tstee: V&A 1997–2004, Michael Marks Charitable Tst 1997–, Mauritshuis The Hague 1999; memb Ctee of Tstees Nat Art Collections Fund 1998–2005; FBA 1989; *Books* Rembrandt and His World (1964), The Flower Drawings of Jan van Huysum (1965), Rubens and His World (1968), Rembrandt as an Etcher (1969, 2 edn 1999), Rembrandt's Etchings: A Catalogue Raisonné (jtly, 1970), Dürer: The Artist and his Drawings (1972), English Landscape 1630–1850 (1977), Dutch Pictures in the Collection of HM The Queen (1982), Rembrandt in Eighteenth-century England (ed, 1983), Rembrandt (1984), Peter Paul Rubens: Man and Artist (1987), Drawing in England from Hilliard to Hogarth (jtly, 1987), Old Master Drawings from the Ashmolean Museum (jtly, 1992), The Dutch and Flemish Drawings at Windsor Castle (jtly, 1994), Anthony van Dyck: Thomas Howard, The Earl of Arundel (1995), Dutch, Flemish and German Paintings in the Ashmolean Museum (1999), The later Flemish Pictures in the Collection of HM The Queen (2007);

Recreations music, travel; *Style*— Prof Sir Christopher White, CVO, FBA; ✉ 34 Kelly Street, London NW1 8PH (tel 020 7485 9148); Shingle House, St Cross, Harleston, Norfolk IP20 0NT (tel 01986 782264)

WHITE, Sir Christopher Robert Meadows White; 3 Bt (UK 1937), of Boulge Hall, Co Suffolk; s of Sir (Eric) Richard Meadows White, 2 Bt (d 1972); *b* 26 August 1940; *Educ* Bradfield; *m* 1962 (m dis 1968), Anne Marie Ghislaine, da of late Maj Tom Brown, OBE, MC; m 2, 1968 (m dis 1972), Dinah Mary Sutton; m 3, 1976, Ingrid Carolyn, da of Eric Jowett, of Great Baddow, Essex; *Heir* none; *Career* schoolmaster 1961–72, professore Istituto Shenker Rome and Scuala Specialisti Aeronauta Macerata 1962–63, housemaster St Michael's Sch Ingoldisthorpe Norfolk 1963–69, hon pres Warnborough House Oxford 1973–; *Style*— Sir Christopher White, Bt; ✉ c/o Mrs Steinschaden-Silver, Pinkney Court, Malmesbury, Wiltshire SN16 0PD

WHITE, David Julian; s of Arthur John Stanley White, CMG, OBE, of Mere, Wilts, and Joan, *née* Davies; *b* 17 July 1942; *Educ* Marlborough; *m* 24 June 1967, Claire Rosemary, da of Rowland Emett, OBE, of Ditchling, E Sussex; 3 da (Juliet b 1969, Sarah b 1972, Victoria b 1974); *Career* Union Discount Co of London Ltd plc 1965–79, dep chm Cater Allen Holdings plc 1985–97 (joined 1979), chm Edge Properties plc 1996–98; dir Church House Tst plc (formerly Dryfield Tst plc) 1997–, dir Big Yellow Gp plc 2000–; *Recreations* tennis, walking, Italy, books; *Style*— David White, Esq; ✉ Flint House, Penn Street, Buckinghamshire HP7 0PY (tel 01494 713262, e-mail dwhite@bigyellow.co.uk)

WHITE, David Vines; s of Peter Vines White (d 1999), and Sheila, *née* Chatterton; *b* 27 October 1961, Glasgow; *Educ* Kelvinside Acad, Marlborough, Pembroke Coll Cambridge (MA), Courtauld Inst of Art (MA); *Career* research asst Coll of Arms 1988–95, Rouge Croix Pursuivant 1995–2004, Somerset Herald 2004–; chm Heraldry Soc 2006–08 (memb Cncl 2000–), memb Cncl Br Record Soc 1998–, hon vice-pres Cambridge Univ Heraldic and Genealogical Soc 2002–; *Clubs* Travellers; *Style*— David White, Esq; ✉ College of Arms, Queen Victoria Street, London EC4V 4BT (tel and fax 020 7248 1766, e-mail somerset@college-of-arms.gov.uk)

WHITE, Duncan Graham; MBE; s of Malcolm Scott White, JP, of Edinburgh, and Morag, *née* Moyes (d 2001); *b* 18 September 1949; *Educ* Merchiston Castle Sch Edinburgh, Univ of St Andrews (MA), London Business Sch (MBA); *m* 1, 12 May 1979 (m dis 1999), Sara, da of John Bates; 2 da (Rachel b 5 July 1982, Kim b 14 Nov 1985); m 2, 14 May 2000, Clio, da of Lt Col the Hon Harry Roberts; 1 s (Alfred b 10 June 2001); *Career* mktg exec Rank Xerox Ltd 1973–77 (grad trainee 1971–73); conslt McKinsey & Co 1977–90; fndr ptnr Duncan White Consultants 1990–; chm: Skylark Ltd 1990–95, Dyogines Lanterns Co Ltd 1992–97, Perfect World plc 1998–2000; chm London Branch Heart of Midlothian FC Supporters Club 1995–2001 (memb 1980–); memb IOD; CIM 1984, FIMgt 1991; *Recreations* skiing, mountaineering, cricket, football, Heart of Midlothian FC; *Clubs* MCC; *Style*— Duncan White, Esq, MBE; ✉ 6 The Foundry, Castle Eden, Hartlepool TS27 4SQ

WHITE, Frank; *see:* Brixworth, Suffragan Bishop of

WHITE, Frank Richard; JP (1968); s of Arthur Leslie White (d 1944), and Edna Phylis Jackson, *née* Meade (d 1976); *b* 11 November 1939; *Educ* Bolton Tech Coll; *m* 28 Jan 1967, Eileen, da of Frank Crook of Bolton; 2 s (John Richard Alexander b 1 Sept 1968, Christopher Niel b 10 July 1973), 1 da (Elizabeth Caroline b 30 July 1970); *Career* MP (Lab) Bury and Radcliffe 1974–83, parly sec Dept of Industry 1975–76, govt whip 1976–79, oppn spokesman church affrs 1979–83; chm: NW Lab MPs 1979–83, All-Pty Paper Industry Gp 1979–83; memb Select Ctee Employment 1979–83 (presented Home Workers Bill), oppn whip 1980–82, dir trg GMB Trade Union 1988–2000; dir: N Manchester Business Link, Bolton Literacy Tst; chair Community Legal Partnership; mayor of Bolton 2005–06; memb: Bolton Town Cncl 1963–74, 1986–90 and 1994–, Gtr Manchester CC 1973–75, Gtr Manchester Police Authy 1997–2003, Bolton Cabinet Cncl for Social Inclusion and Community Safety 2001–; dir Lancs Cooperative Devpt Assoc Ltd 1984–, area dir United Natwest Co-op 1993–2002; chm Bolton Magistrates' Bench 1992–95; vice-pres East Lancs Railway Preservation Soc 1983–2005; pres Bolton United Servs Veterans' Assoc 1988–; memb: IMS 1966, IPM 1971; hon fell Bolton Univ 1993; *Recreations* history, walking, caravanning, Richard III supporter; *Clubs* Tonge Cricket, Tonge Lab; *Style*— Frank White, Esq; ✉ 23 Dovedale Road, Breightmet, Bolton, Lancashire BL2 5HT (tel 01204 527888, e-mail frank.white@bolton.gov.uk)

WHITE, Sir George Stanley James; 4 Bt (UK 1904), of Cotham House, Bristol; s of Sir George Stanley Midelton White, 3 Bt (d 1983, md Bristol Aeroplane Co, and ggs of Sir George White, 1 Bt, pioneer of Electric Street Traction, fndr first English aeroplane factory and responsible for introduction of Bristol Biplanes and Monoplanes), and Diane, Lady White; *b* 4 November 1948; *Educ* Harrow; *m* 1 (m dis 1979); 1 da (Caroline Morwenna); m 2, (m dis); 1 s ((George) Philip James), 1 da (Kate Elizabeth); m 3, Joanna, da of Kazimierz Stanley Migdal; *Heir* s, Philip White; *Career* conslt horologist; pres: Gloucestershire Soc 1993, Br Horological Inst 2001–02; chm: Bristol and Glos Archaeological Soc 1992–95; memb: Glos Diocesan Advsy Ctee for Faculties and the Care of Churches 1985– (clocks advsr to the Dio 1986–), Cncl Nat Tst 1998–2004; High Sheriff Avon 1989, JP 1991–95; Master Worshipful Co of Clockmakers 2001 (Keeper of the Collection 1988–); FSA; *Books* English Lantern Clocks (1989), Tramlines to the Stars (1995), The Clockmakers of London (1999); *Publications* for aeronautical res www.bristol-aeroplane.com; *Style*— Sir George White, Bt, FSA

WHITE, Graham Stewart; s of Cecil Thomas White, and Kathleen May, *née* Banwell; *b* 24 March 1947; *Educ* Sir John Lawes Sch Harpenden; *m* 29 April 1972, Sylvia Mary, da of John Morris Done; 2 s (Oliver Lewis b 15 Dec 1974, Anthony Joe b 25 Feb 1977); *Career* Scholl: mktg dir 1977–80, md 1980–84; business devpt dir Schering-Plough Consumer Products 1984–87; chief exec Londis (Holdings) Ltd 1987–2004, princ Manland Ltd 2004–; non-exec dir Nisa-Todays Ltd 1987–2004; *Recreations* rugby football; *Style*— Graham S White, Esq; ✉ 17 Wood End Hill, Harpenden, Hertfordshire AL5 3EZ (tel 01582 765828, fax 01582 766956, e-mail grahamwhite.manland@btinternet.com)

WHITE, Hugh Collins; s of William Mitchell White (d 1991), of Maybole, Ayrshire, and Mary Ann Luke, *née* Collins (d 1998); *b* 21 October 1944; *Educ* Kilmarnock Acad, MacIntosh Sch of Architecture (Cert Architecture); *m* 23 Aug 1968, Betsy, da of Bernard Lizar Zive (d 1977), of Ayr; 2 da (Kirstine b 1971, Sheona b 1974); *Career* chartered architect in private practice; factor and studio mangr Hannay Film Prodn Studios Dublin 1998–2001; corp memb RIBA, ARIAS; *Recreations* equestrian driving, photography, restoring horse drawn vehicles, the Brass Band Movement; *Style*— Hugh White, Esq; ✉ 17 Cargill Road, Maybole, South Ayrshire KA19 8AF (tel 01655 882188, fax 01655 882260)

WHITE, Prof Ian Hugh; s of Oliver Morrow White (d 1997), and Emily Greenaway, *née* Lowry; *b* 6 October 1959; *Educ* Belfast Royal Acad, Jesus Coll Cambridge (MA, PhD); *m* 13 Aug 1983, Margaret Rosemary, *née* Hunt; 1 da (Emma Rosemary b 17 May 1990), 1 s (James Robert Samuel b 4 Dec 1992); *Career* fell Jesus Coll Cambridge 1984–90 (research fell 1983–84), asst lectr Engrg Dept Univ of Cambridge 1984–90, prof of physics Univ of Bath 1990–96, prof of optical communication systems Univ of Bristol (head Dept of Electrical and Electronic Engrg 1998–2001), Van Eck prof of engrg Univ of Cambridge 2001–; Leverhulme research fell Royal Soc 1995–96; author of numerous contribs on semiconductor optoelectronic compartments, optical communications and photonics; FIEE 1994, CEng 1994; *Recreations* church, music; *Style*— Prof Ian White; ✉ University of Cambridge, Electrical Engineering Department, 9 JJ Thomson Avenue, Cambridge CB3 0FA (tel 01223 748340, fax 01223 748342, e-mail ihw3@cam.ac.uk)

WHITE, Ian Shaw; s of Frank White, of May Hill, Glos, and Joan, *née* Shaw; *b* 30 July 1952; *Educ* Bromsgrove, Churchill Coll Cambridge (MA); *m* 1, 18 Oct 1980, Susan Elizabeth (d 1989), da of Capt Alan Francis Bacon, of Purley, Surrey; 2 s (Duncan b 1985, Gordon b 1988); m 2, 28 March 1992, Barbara Jolanda, da of Maj Wladyslaw Arzymanow (d 1968); 2 s (Howard b 1994, Bernard b 1996); *Career* ptnr W Greenwell and Co 1984–86; dir: Greenwell Montagu 1986–88 (head of res 1987–88), Kleinwort Benson Securities 1988–93, Robert Fleming Securities 1993–97, TT International 1997–98, True Research Limited 1999–; FSI; *Recreations* travel, philosophy, family; *Style*— Ian White, Esq; ✉ 22 Blomfield Road, Little Venice, London W9 1AD (tel 020 7286 4360); True Research Limited, 9 Hanover Street, London W1S 1YF (tel 020 7493 8586, fax 020 7493 8382, e-mail ian@trueresearch.co.uk)

WHITE, Rev Canon John Austin; LVO (2004); s of Charles White (d 1976), and Alice Emily, *née* Precious (d 1967); *b* 27 June 1942; *Educ* Batley GS, Univ of Hull (BA), Coll of the Resurrection Mirfield; *Career* asst curate St Aidan's Church Leeds 1966–69, asst chaplain Univ of Leeds 1969–73, chaplain Northern Ordination Course 1973–82, canon St George's Chapel Windsor Castle 1982– (canon precentor 1984–2007, canon treas 2002–, vice-dean 2004–), memb directing staff St George's House Windsor Castle 1982– (dir of clergy courses 1998–, warden 1999–2003); European dep Dio of Mexico 2003–; FRSA; *Publications* A Necessary End (jtly, 1991), Nicholas Ferrar - Materials for a Life (jtly, 1997), Phoenix in Flight (jtly, 1999), Spoken Light (jtly, 2007); *Recreations* medieval iconography, cooking, poetry; *Style*— The Rev Canon John White, LVO; ✉ 4 The Cloisters, Windsor Castle, Windsor SL4 1NJ (tel 01753 848787, fax 01753 848752, e-mail john.white@stgeorges-windsor.org)

WHITE, (Charles) John Branford; s of Frederick Bernard White (d 1983), and Violet Phyllis, *née* Palmer (d 2007); *b* 24 September 1946; *Educ* Taunton Sch, Brentwood Sch, Pembroke Coll Cambridge (Trevelyan scholarship, MA), UCL (MSc); *m* 14 May 1975, Judith Margaret, *née* Lewis; *Career* diplomat; ODI fell Govt of Botswana 1968–71, ODA 1971–77, econ advsr ODA Kenya 1977–82, ODA 1982–86, dep head Econ Relations Dept FCO 1986–90, first sec Lagos 1990, consul-gen and dep head of mission Tel Aviv 1993–97, head Overseas Territories Dept FCO 1997–2001, high cmmr to Barbados and Eastern Caribbean States 2001–05, ret; dir for devpt Marine Stewardship Cncl 2006–; *Recreations* golf, skiing; *Clubs* Royal Mid-Surrey Golf, Ski Club of GB, Barbados Polo; *Style*— John White, Esq

WHITE, Sir John Woolmer; 4 Bt (UK 1922), of Salle Park, Norfolk; s of Sir Headley Dymoke White, 3 Bt (d 1971), and Elizabeth Victoria Mary, *née* Wrightson (d 1996); *b* 4 February 1947; *Educ* Cheltenham Coll, RAC Cirencester; *m* 1987, Joan, da of late T D Borland, of West Linton, Peeblesshire; 1 s (Kyle Dymoke Wilfrid b 16 March 1988); *Heir* s, Kyle White; *Career* md Salle Farms Co; *Clubs* Athenaeum; *Style*— Sir John White, Bt; ✉ Salle Park, Reepham, Norfolk NR10 4SG

WHITE, Julian; MBE (2004); *b* 14 May 1973, Plymouth; *Career* rugby union player (prop); clubs: Okehampton RUFC, Plymouth Albion RUFC, Hawkes Bay RUFC NZ, Canterbury Crusaders RUFC NZ, Bridgend RUFC, Saracens RUFC 1999–2002, Bristol Shoguns RUFC 2002–2003, Leicester Tigers RUFC 2003–; England: 28 caps, debut v South Africa 2000, winners Six Nations Championship 2001 and 2003 (Grand Slam 2003), ranked no 1 team in world 2003, winners World Cup Aust 2003; memb squad Br & I Lions tour to NZ 2005; *Style*— Julian White, Esq, MBE; ✉ c/o Rugby Football Union, Rugby House, Rugby Road, Twickenham, Middlesex TW1 1DS

WHITE, Keith Christopher; s of Frank White (d 1963), and Gladys Louise, *née* Moore (d 1960); *b* 14 July 1933; *Educ* Glyn GS Epsom, Univ of London (BSc); *m* 10 Sept 1960, Jennifer Mary (Jenny), da of Thomas Mayhew Lewin (d 1985); 1 s (Paul b 1961), 2 da (Gillian b 1963, Judith b 1968); *Career* Lt Col Engr and Tport Staff Corps RE (TA) 1991 (Maj 1986); consltg engr; ptnr R Travers Morgan & Ptnrs Consltg Engrs 1971, chm and chief exec Travers Morgan Consltg Gp 1991–93 (dir 1988); vice-chm Construction Industry Cncl 1991–93; chm Bourne Housing Soc Ltd 2002, memb Bd Welsh Health Common Servs Authy 1982–97; Freeman City of London 1966, Liveryman Worshipful Co of Paviors 1966 (Master 2001); FIStructE 1969 (pres 1987–88), FIHT 1974, FICE 1987, FREng 1989; *Recreations* golf, reading, watching cricket, travel; *Clubs* RAC; *Style*— Keith White, Esq, FREng; ✉ Longmead, 8 Hillcroft Avenue, Purley, Surrey CR8 3DG (tel 020 8660 9883, fax 020 8660 1331)

WHITE, Keith George; *b* 12 October 1948; *Career* Crown Agents: joined in 1973, corp sec 1980–98, dir Professional Servs 1992–2003, chief operating offr 1998–2005, chief exec 2005–, chm various Crown Agents gp cos; memb Cncl Crown Agents Fndn 1997–; dir Supply Chain Servs 2004–05; pres H F Holidays Ltd; former chm: St Helena Line, ICC (UK) Commercial Practice Ctee; dir SITPRO Ltd; occasional lectr and contrib articles to orgns and pubns; FRSA, FCILT, FIFP, MInstRE; *Recreations* family, fencing, walking; *Clubs* Royal Over-Seas League; *Style*— Keith G White, Esq; ✉ The Crown Agents, St Nicholas House, St Nicholas Road, Sutton, Surrey SM1 1EL (tel 020 8643 3311, fax 020 8643 6518)

WHITE, Mark Jonathan; *b* 10 June 1960, London; *Educ* Univ of Wolverhampton (BA), Coll of Law, KCL (LLM); *Career* admitted slr 1985; slr Eversheds 1985–93, gp co sec and slr Rotork plc 1993–99, co sec Enterprise Oil plc 2001–02 (dep co sec 1999–2001), gp co sec and counsel Wolseley plc 2002–07, gen counsel and co sec Compass Gp plc 2007–; memb Law Soc; *Style*— Mark J White, Esq; ✉ Compass Group plc, Compass House, Guildford Street, Chertsey, Surrey KT16 9BQ (tel 01932 573000, fax 01932 569956, e-mail mark.white@compass-group.co.uk)

WHITE, Michael; s of Albert Ernest White (d 1979), and Doris Mary, *née* Harvey; *b* 4 April 1955; *Educ* Langdon Sch, Univ of Oxford (MA), Inns of Court Sch of Law; *Career* called to the Bar Middle Temple (Harmsworth scholar); chief music critic of The Independent on Sunday, broadcaster and librettist; presenter: Best of 3 (BBC Radio 3), Opera in Action (BBC Radio 3), The Sound Barrier (BBC Radio 4); *Opera Librettos* The Adjudicator, Touristen Dachau; *Books* Wagner for Beginners, Collins Guide to Opera and Operetta; *Recreations* travel, composition, the Church of England (occasionally); *Style*— Michael White, Esq; ✉ Music Department, BBC, Broadcasting House, London W1A 1AA (tel 020 7580 4468)

WHITE, Michael Charles; s of Henry Wallis White (d 1967), of St Just, Cornwall, and Kay, *née* Wood (d 1957); *b* 21 October 1945; *Educ* Bodmin GS, UCL (BA); *m* 2 Feb 1973, Patricia Vivienne, da of (Harold) Lawrence Gaudin; 3 s (Samuel Wallis b 21 Sept 1974, Joseph Lawrence b 11 Aug 1976, Henry John b 7 Dec 1978); *Career* reporter: Reading Evening Post 1966–70, London Evening Standard 1970–71; The Guardian: sub ed, feature writer and diarist 1971–76, parly sketchwriter 1977–84, Washington corr 1984–88, assoc ed 1989–, political ed 1990–2006, asst ed (politics) 2006–; columnist Health Service Jl 1977–84 and 1992–; lectr Woodrow Wilson Fellowship Fndn Princeton 1990–; chm: Parly Press Gallery 1995, Parly Press Lobby 1997; memb: NUJ 1966–, Notting Hill Housing Tst 1977–; Granada TV Sketchwriter of the Year 1982, House Magazine Political Writer Award 2003; fell UCL 2002; *Clubs* Garrick; *Style*— Michael White, Esq; ✉ The Guardian, 119 Farringdon Road, London EC1R 3ER (tel 020 7278 2332, e-mail michael.white@guardian.co.uk)

WHITE, Michael Simon; s of Victor R White, and Doris G White; *b* 16 January 1936; *Educ* Lyceum Alpinum Zuoz, Pisa Univ, Sorbonne Paris; *m* 1, 1965 (m dis 1973), Sarah Hillsdon; 2 s, 1 da; m 2, 1985, Louise, da of Nigel Moores (d 1977); 1 s; *Career* theatre and film producer; asst to Sir Peter Daubeny 1956–61; *Theatre* prodns incl: Rocky Horror Show (Evening Standard Award for best musical), Sleuth (Tony Award for best play),

America Hurrah (Tony Award nomination), Oh Calcutta!, The Connection, Joseph and the Amazing Technicolor Dreamcoat, Loot, The Blood Knot, A Chorus Line, Deathtrap, Annie, Pirates of Penzance, On Your Toes, Metropolis, Bus Stop, Crazy for You, Me and Mamie O'Rourke, She Loves Me, Fame The Musical, Voyeurz, Boys in the Band, Disney's Beauty and the Beast, Black Goes with Everything, Notre Dame de Paris, Contact; *Film* incl: Monty Python and the Holy Grail, Rocky Horror Picture Show, My Dinner with André, Ploughman's Lunch, Moonlighting, Stranger's Kiss, The Comic Strip Presents, The Supergrass, High Season, Eat The Rich, White Mischief, Nuns on the Run, The Pope Must Die, The Turn of the Screw, Widows Peak, Enigma; *Books* Empty Seats (1984); *Recreations* art, skiing, racing; *Clubs* RAC; *Style*— Michael White, Esq

WHITE, Dr Norman Arthur; s of Charles Brewster White (d 1969), of Co Durham, and Lilian Sarah, *née* Finch (d 1975); *b* 11 April 1922; *Educ* Univ of London (BSc(Eng)), UMIST (AMCT), Harvard Business Sch (AMP), Univ of Westminster (DMS), Univ of Philippines (MSc), LSE (PhD); *m* 1, 1944, Joyce Marjorie (d 1982), *née* Rogers; 1 s (Howard Russell b 1945), 1 da (Lorraine Avril b 1949); m 2, 1983, Marjorie Iris, da of William Colenso Rushton (d 1947), of London; *Career* Royal Dutch Shell Group: petroleum res engr Thornton Res Centre 1945–51, progressed through various assignments in technological devpt and commercial mgmnt rising to dep Gp Mktg Co-ordinator 1966–68, chm and dir Shell Oil and mining cos in UK and Europe 1963–72, chief exec New Enterprises Div 1968–72, Plural assignments 1972–; dir: Norman White Assocs 1972–94 (princ exec 1972–93), Environmental Resources Ltd 1973–87, Tanks Oil & Gas Ltd 1974–85, Henley Centre for Forecasting 1974–92 (dep chm 1974–87), Com-Tek Resources Inc Colorado 1988–93; dep chm Strategy International Ltd 1976–82; chm: KBC Advanced Technologies Ltd 1979–90, Ocean Thermal Energy Conversion Systems Ltd 1982–, Gearhart Tesel plc 1983–85 (dir 1980–85), Process Automation & Computer Systems Ltd 1984–94, Andaman Resources plc 1986–90, Delta Media Solutions Ltd 1990–92, Technology Transfer Centre Surrey Ltd 1990–96, Spacelink Learning Fndn 1995–, Proscyon Partners Ltd 2000–04 (dir 1992–2004); memb int energy and petroleum delgns 1979–97: Russia, China, Rumania, East Germany, Hungary, Japan, Korea, Indonesia, India, Mexico, Argentina, Venezuela, Brazil, South Africa; memb Parly and Scientific Ctee House of Commons 1977–83 and 1987–92; WPC: chm Br Nat Ctee 1987–94 (vice-chm 1977–87), treas 1983–91 and 1994–97, vice-pres World Petroleum Congresses 1991–94; memb: UK CAA Ctee of Enquiry on Flight Time Limitations (Bader Ctee) 1972–73, Cncl IMechE 1980–85 and 1987–91, Cncl Energy Inst 1975–81 (vice-pres), Royal Soc Mission to People's Republic of China 1985; visiting prof: Henley Mgmnt Coll 1979–90, Univ of Manchester 1981–90 (visiting ind dir 1971–81), The City Univ 1989–96; memb Senate Univ of London 1974–87; chm: Jt Bd for Engrg Mgmnt (IMechE, ICE, IEE, IChemE) 1990–93, Transnational Satellite Educn Centre Univ of Surrey 1991–94; govr: King Edward VI Royal GS Guildford 1976–2002, Reigate GS 1976–93; Presidential Award: IMechE 1994, WPC 1997; Cncl Award Inst of Petroleum 1996; Hon Dip of Engrg Mgmnt Jt Bd for Engrg Mgmnt 1997; Freeman City of London; Liveryman: Worshipful Co of Engineers, Worshipful Co of Spectacle Makers, Worshipful Co of World Traders; Hon Calgarian (Alberta Canada); memb Royal Inst of Int Affrs and Royal Inst; CEng, FInstD, FCIM, FRSA, FIMechE, FIBS, FIMMM; *Books* Financing the International Petroleum Industry (1979), Handbook of Engineering Management (1989); *Recreations* family, country and coastal walking, wild life, browsing, international affairs, comparative religions, domestic odd-jobbing; *Clubs* Athenaeum, City Livery, Harvard (London), IOD, LSE; *Style*— Dr Norman A White; ✉ Green Ridges, Downside Road, Guildford, Surrey GU4 8PH (tel 01483 567523, fax 01483 504314); 9 Park House, 123–125 Harley Street, London W1G 6AY (tel 020 7935 7387, e-mail normanwhite@norsco.demon.co.uk)

WHITE, Paul; *Career* former chief exec: Queen Margaret Hospital NHS Tst Fife, Tayside Univ Hosps NHS Tst; chief exec Barts and The London NHS Tst 2001–; former chm Nat Acute Tst Chief Execs Gp; former memb: Ministerial Modernisation Forum, numerous Scottish NHS Gps and Working Parties; panel memb Scottish Health Advsy Service, int auditor King's Fund Health Quality Audit; *Style*— Paul White, Esq; ✉ Barts and The London NHS Trust, West Smithfield, London EC1A 7BE (tel 020 7601 8726)

WHITE, Peter; *b* June 1947, Winchester; *m* Jo; 2 da (Fiona (fostered), Cathy), 2 s (Tony, Robin); *Career* broadcaster; first totally blind person to produce reports for TV news; Sony Speech Broadcaster of the Year 2001 *Television* ed and presenter Same Difference (3 series, Channel 4) 1987–89, presenter and prodr Link (magazine prog on disability, Central TV) 1989–91, People First (three documentaries on disability, Channel 4) 1992 and 1993, presenter Facing South (bi-media phone-in strand, BBC South and BBC Local Radio) 1992–95 *Radio* BBC Radio Solent: gen reporter and presenter of progs on disability 1971–83, presenter morning current affairs and phone-in prog 1983–87 and 1992–95, presenter Saturday morning show 1989–; BBC Radio 4: author autobiographical talks series 1987–96, presenter and interviewer No Triumph, No Tragedy 1993, 1994, 1999, 2000, 2001 and 2003, Barking or Biting? (on the Disability Rights Cmmn) 2001, From Rags to Rights (history of disability in the UK) 2000, reg presenter In Touch 1979– (occasional presenter since 1974–79); deviser and presenter It's Your Round (BBC) 1993–94; disability affairs corr BBC 1995–: reg broadcaster on disability issues, progs incl: Today, The World at One, PM, The World Tonight, Newsbeat, Hayes Over Britain, 5 Live; presenter: You and Yours, Call You and Yours, Pick of the Week; reporter: Woman's Hour, Paralympics Atlanta 1996, Paralympics Sydney 2000; *Books* Issues (series for schs, 1989), See It My Way (autobiography, 1999); *Recreations* soccer, cricket; *Style*— Peter White, Esq; ✉ Broadcasting House, London W1A 1AA

WHITE, Peter Richard; *b* 11 February 1942; *m* Mary; 1 s, 1 da; *Career* chartered accountant Price Waterhouse 1965–69, mgmnt accountant, chief internal auditor then financial controller and treas Abbey National Building Society 1970–82; Alliance & Leicester plc: gen mangr (fin and mgmnt servs) Alliance Building Society 1982–85, gen mangr (admin and treasy) Alliance & Leicester (following merger) 1985–87, dir and gen mangr (strategy, sales, mktg and treasury) 1987–89, dep gp chief exec and md 1989–91, gp chief exec 1991–99; dir: Alliance & Leicester Pensions Investments Ltd, Electronic Funds Transfer (Clearing) Ltd, Electronic Funds Transfer (POS) Ltd; chm Girobank plc 1996–99, non-exec dir Reckitt Benckiser plc (formerly Reckitt & Colman plc) 1997–; formerly: dep chm Building Socs Assoc, chm Met Assoc of Building Socs, chm Cncl of Mortgage Lenders; memb Cncl Br Bankers Assoc; Freeman City of London; memb IOD; FCA 1985, fell ACT 1993, CIMgt 1993, FCIB 1993; *Recreations* watching sport, playing golf, opera; *Style*— Peter White, Esq

WHITE, Peter Roland; s of Norman Leonard White, and Gene Elwin, *née* McGrah; *b* 9 July 1945; *Educ* Bournville Boys' Tech Sch, Univ of Birmingham (BDS); *m* 1, 23 March 1968 (m dis 1980), Elizabeth Susan, da of Thomas Colin Graty, of Leigh Sinton Worcs; 2 s (Gordon Michael White b 6 Aug 1970, Adam Edward White b 12 Jan 1973), 1 da (Frances Elizabeth Graty b 8 Nov 1968); m 2, 20 Dec 1980 (m dis 1997), Elisabeth Anne, da of Fred Haworth; *Career* conslt oral surgn; Dudley Rd Hosp Birmingham 1968, Birmingham Dental Hosp 1969–70, Wordsley Hosp Stourbridge 1970–71, Univ of Manchester Dental Sch 1971–73, St Luke's Hosp Bradford 1973–74, Liverpool Dental Hosp and Broad Green Hosp 1974–77; conslt oral surgn NW Regnl Health Authy 1977–, clinical dir Rochdale Healthcare Tst 1992–93, dep med dir Rochdale Healthcare Tst 1994–2000; pres Nat Hosps Gp BDA 2002–03; postgrad tutor Rochdale and Oldham 1989–94 (Rochdale 1980–87); memb numerous NHS local ctees; publications in learned jls; memb BDA (pres E Lancs E Cheshire Branch 1995); FBAOMS 1977 (memb 1971–77), FDSRCS (Eng), memb Manchester Med Soc 1979 (pres Odontological Section 1990); *Recreations* music, genealogy, sailing, walking; *Clubs* Elton Sailing; *Style*— Peter R White, Esq; ✉ 14 St John Street, Manchester M3 4DZ (tel 0161 832 7904)

WHITE, (Alan) Robert; s of Peter Derek White (d 2000), and Margaret, *née* Macmillan; *b* 15 July 1965, Camblesforth, N Yorks; *Educ* Univ of Southampton (BSc); *Career* trainee Cosworth Engrg 1987–88; Cosworth Racing: devpt engr Indy engines 1988–97, chief engr Formula 1 engines 1997–2003; Renault F1 team (engines): tech dir 2004–05, dep md (tech) 2005–; *Style*— Robert White, Esq; ✉ Renault F1 Team, Whiteways Technical Centre, Enstone, Oxfordshire OX7 4EE (tel 00 33 670 03 44 40, e-mail rob.white@renaultf1.com)

WHITE, Prof Robert J; s of Dennis H White, of Witney, Oxon, and Betty M, *née* Bird (d 1997); *b* 14 August 1963, Harrow, Middx; *Educ* John Lyon Sch Harrow, The Queen's Coll Oxford (scholar, BA), Nat Inst for Medical Research London (PhD); *Children* 1 s (Oliver b 7 Dec 1990), 1 da (Miranda b 27 Sept 1994); *Career* postdoctoral positions Univ of Cambridge 1990–95; Univ of Glasgow: lectr in biochemistry and molecular biology 1995–99, Jenner research fell Lister Inst of Preventive Medicine 1996–2001 (memb 2001–), prof of gene transcription 1999–; memb Editorial Bd BMC Molecular Biology 2004–, author of more than 50 pubns in learned jls; memb: Educn and Trg Ctee Fedn of Cancer Socs 2004–, Molecules, Genes and Cells Funding Ctee Wellcome Tst 2004–; memb: British Assoc for Cancer Research 1999–, European Assoc for Cancer Research (memb Exec Ctee 2003–); Young Scientist Award British Assoc for Cancer Research 1999, Merit Award Int Jl of Oncology 1999, Young Cancer Researcher Award European Assoc for Cancer Research 2003, Tenovus Medal 2004; FRSE 2004, FMedSci 2005; *Books* RNA Polymerase III Transcription (1998), Gene Transcription: Mechanisms and Control (2000); *Recreations* running; *Style*— Prof Robert White; ✉ Institute of Biomedical and Life Sciences, Davidson Building, University of Glasgow, Glasgow G12 8QQ (tel 0141 330 4628, fax 0141 330 4620, e-mail rwhite@udcf.gla.ac.uk)

WHITE, Prof Robert Stephen; s of James Henry White, of Uley, Glos, and Ethel Gladys, *née* Cornick; *b* 12 December 1952; *Educ* Market Harborough Comp, West Bridgford Comp, Emmanuel Coll Cambridge (senior scholar, MA, bachelor scholar, PhD); *m* Helen Elizabeth, da of Dennis J Pearce; 1 s (Mark James b 1979), 1 da (Sarah Rosemary b 1981); *Career* guest investigator Woods Hole Oceanographic Instn USA 1977, 1988 and 1990, research asst Dept of Geodesy and Geophysics Univ of Cambridge 1978, postdoctoral scholar Woods Hole Oceanographic Instn USA 1978–79; Univ of Cambridge: research fell Emmanuel Coll 1979–82, NERC research fell Dept of Earth Scis 1979–81, sr asst in research 1981–85, asst dir of research 1985–89, fell St Edmund's Coll 1988–, prof of geophysics 1989–, acting head Dept of Earth Scis 1991 and 1993; Cecil & Ida H Green scholar Scripps Instn of Oceanography Univ of Calif San Diego 1987; awarded Stichting Fund for Sci Tech and Research Schlumberger Ltd 1994; George P Woollard Award Geological Soc America 1997; fell American Geophysical Union, FGS (Bigsby Medal 1991), FRS 1994; *Publications* author of numerous articles in international journals; *Style*— Prof Robert White, FRS; ✉ Bullard Laboratories, Madingley Road, Cambridge CB3 0EZ (tel 01223 337187, fax 01223 360779)

WHITE, Roderick Douglas Thirkell; s of Noel Thirkell White (d 1974), and Margaret Douglas, *née* Robertson; *b* 27 March 1939; *Educ* Marlborough, Trinity Coll Oxford (MA); *m* 1964, Stephanie Francis, da of C S Powell; 2 s (Jestyn Noel b 17 Sept 1968, Tristram Benedict b 23 Feb 1971); *Career* advertising exec; J Walter Thompson: graduate trainee Marketing Dept 1962–65, marketing gp head 1965, asst dir 1967; head of unit J Walter Thompson Consultancy Unit 1972–75 (memb staff 1968–75), J Walter Thompson Development Group 1975–77; planning dir: Lansdowne Marketing 1979 (head of planning 1977), Lansdown Conquest (formerly LansdownEuro) 1981–96; res dir Red Cell; editor Admap 1996–; President's Gold medal IPA 1967; MIPA 1967, FIPA 2000, assoc memb MRS 1980; *Books* Consumer Product Development (1973), Advertising: What It Is and How To Do It (4 edn 2000); *Recreations* walking, windsurfing, cinema, music; *Style*— Roderick White, Esq

WHITE, Roger; s of Geoffrey White, of Tetbury Upton, Glos, and Zoe, *née* Bowler; *b* 1 September 1950; *Educ* Ifield GS, Christ's Coll Cambridge (BA), Wadham Coll Oxford; *Career* Hist Building Div GLC 1979–83, sec Georgian Gp 1984–91, exec sec Garden History Soc 1992–96, contrib ed House & Garden 1995–; visiting res fell Yale Center for British Art 1990; pres Oxford Univ Architectural Soc 1975–76; memb: Ctee Painswick Rococo Garden 1985–94, Chiswick House Advsy Panel 1991–, Pell Wall Preservation Tst 1993–98; FSA 1986; *Books* John Vardy (in The Architectural Outsiders, 1985), Georgian Arcadia: Architecture for the Park and Garden (exhbn catalogue, 1987), The Architectural Evolution of Magdalen College (1993), Nicholas Hawksmoor and the Replanning of Oxford (exhbn catalogue, 1997), The Architectural Drawings of Magdalen College (2001), Chiswick House and Gardens (2001), Witley Court (2003), Belsay Hall (2005), Oxford Sketchbook (with Graham Byfield, 2005), A Life of Frederick, Prince of Wales 1707–1751 (ed, 2007); *Recreations* looking at old buildings; *Style*— Roger White, Esq, FSA; ✉ 142 Weir Road, London SW12 0ND (tel and fax 020 8673 6636, e-mail rogerwhite@vitbrit.fsnet.co.uk)

WHITE, Roger John Graham; s of Alfred James White (d 1976), and Doris Elizabeth, *née* Robinson (d 1973); *b* 30 April 1940; *Educ* Tiffin Sch; *m* 18 June 1966, Elizabeth, da of Tom Lionel Greenwood, of Esher, Surrey; 2 s (Graham b 1968, Andrew b 1970), 1 da (Katherine b 1977); *Career* articled clerk Knox Cropper CAs; KPMG: joined 1962, sr mangr 1970, tax ptnr 1974, sr tax ptnr UK 1981–98, chm KPMG Int Tax Ctee 1990–94, conslt 1998–; memb: professional and industry tax ctees, Bd and Ops Ctee 1988–98; lectr and writer on tax matters; Income and Corporation Taxes Act 1988: appointed by Lord Chllr to membership of Tbnl under section 706 Income and Corporation Taxes Act (ICTA) 1988, appointed by Chllr of the Exchequer to the Advsy Panel under section 765 ICTA 1988; FCA 1962, FTII 1970; *Books* The Trading Company (1978), Purchase of Own Shares (1983), Peats to KPMG - Gracious Family to Global Firm (2004); *Recreations* bridge, gardening, books; *Clubs* Addington Soc (chm 1991–93), Reform; *Style*— Roger White, Esq; ✉ Mead House, 57 Ashley Park Avenue, Walton-on-Thames, Surrey KT12 1EU (tel 01932 246474, e-mail meadhouse@btinternet.com); KPMG, 8 Salisbury Square, London EC4Y 8BB (tel 020 7311 1000 or 020 7311 6732, fax 020 7311 6701, e-mail roger.jg.white@kpmg.co.uk)

WHITE, Sandra; MSP; *b* 17 August 1951; *Educ* Garthamlock Sr Secdy Sch Glasgow, Cardonald Coll, Glasgow Technical Coll; *Career* formerly clerkess; cncllr Renfrew DC 1989–96, positions incl: gp whip 1992–96, dep spokesperson on housing 1992–96, memb Appeals Sub-Ctee (industrial disputes), memb JCC manual workers, memb standing ctees on planning, leisure, housing, environmental services, general purposes; cncllr Renfrewshire Cncl 1995–, positions incl: gp whip 1995–, spokesperson on property and construction 1995–, dep spokesman on corporate services, memb JCC on manual workers, memb JCC on staff, memb Civic's Functions and the Housing Services Sub-Ctees, memb standing ctees on housing, leisure services, property and construction, corporate services; MSP (SNP) Glasgow 1999–; SNP: memb 1983–, sec, social convenor, press offr, conf delegate, Nat Cncl delegate, Nat Assembly delegate, memb Local Govt Ctee; fndr memb Foxbar Tenants Assoc, fndr memb Seedhill Summer Play Scheme, former memb Hawkhead Community Cncl, JP 1992–95; *Style*— Mrs Sandra White, MSP; ✉ The Scottish Parliament, Edinburgh EH99 1SP

WHITE, Stephen Frank; s of Sir Frank White, of London, and Anne Rowlandson, *née* Howitt; *b* 29 September 1955; *Educ* Eton, Univ of Bristol (BA); *Career* accountant Price Waterhouse and Co 1977–81, with Phillips and Drew 1981–83, Hill Samuel Investment

Management Ltd 1983–85; dir F & C Investment Management Ltd 1985–; Liveryman Worshipful Co of Merchant Taylors; ACA; *Recreations* opera, gardening, walking; *Clubs* Brooks's; *Style*— Stephen F White, Esq; ✉ c/o F & C Management Ltd, Exchange House, Primrose Street, London EC2A 2NY (tel 020 7628 8000)

WHITE, Prof Stephen Leonard; s of William John (Jack) White (d 1980), of Dublin, and Edna, *née* McGuckin; *b* 1 July 1945, Dublin, Ireland; *Educ* Trinity Coll Dublin (entrance exhibitioner, fndn scholar, BA), Univ of Glasgow (PhD), Univ of Oxford (MA, DPhil), Trinity Coll Dublin (LittD); *m* 7 April 1973, Ishbel, *née* MacPhie; 1 s (Alexander b 21 Dec 1987); *Career* various temporary and visiting appts: Open Univ, Univ of Strathclyde, Balliol Coll Oxford, Univ of Naples, Inst of Applied Politics Moscow, Res Sch of the Social Sciences ANU, Inst of Advanced Studies Vienna; sr assoc memb Inst of Central and E European Studies Univ of Glasgow; Dept of Politics Univ of Glasgow: lectr 1971–85, reader 1985–91, prof 1991–, head of dept 1992–98; chief ed Jl of Communist Studies and Transition Politics; pres Br Assoc for Slavonic and E European Studies 1994–97, chm Br Academic Ctee for Co-operation with Russian Archives 1997–2001; founding academician Acad of Social Sciences 1999, FRSE 2002; *Books* incl: Political Culture and Soviet Politics (1979), Britain and the Bolshevik Revolution (1980), The Origins of Détente (1985), The Bolshevik Poster (1988), Soviet Communism: Programme and Rules (1989), Russia Goes Dry: Alcohol, State and Society (1996), Russia's New Politics: The Management of a Postrevolutionary Society (2000), The Soviet Political Elite from Lenin to Gorbachev (with E Mawdsley, 2000), Communism and its Collapse (2001), Politics in Europe (jtly, 2003 and 2007); *Recreations* cinema, theatre, reading, travel; *Style*— Prof Stephen White; ✉ Department of Politics, University of Glasgow, Glasgow G12 8RT (tel 0141 330 5352, fax 0141 330 5071, e-mail s.white@socsci.gla.ac.uk)

WHITE, Stewart Dale; s of Theo Jeffrey White (d 1979), of Sydney, Aust, and Mary Jean, *née* Stewart; *b* 23 July 1951; *Educ* Newington Coll, St Andrew's Coll Univ of Sydney (BA, LLB), Downing Coll Cambridge (LLM); *m* 20 Sept 1980, Elisabeth Mary Hargreaves, da of Geoffrey John Bolton (d 1968), of Eton Coll; 1 da (Victoria b 1 July 1982), 1 s (Andrew b 1 Aug 1983); *Career* admitted slr: NSW 1976, England and Wales 1979; sr assoc Allen Allen and Hemsley Sydney 1979–83; ptnr: Blake Dawson Waldron Sydney 1983–88, Denton Hall Burgin and Warrens London 1988–94, Ashurst Morris Crisp 1994–99, gp public policy dir Vodafone Gp 1999–2005, chm Bell Pottinger Public Affairs 2005–; memb Telecom Bd Int Telecommunication Union 2001–, dir UK-Japan 21st Century Gp 2002–; former cncllr Section on Business Law of Int Bar Assoc and fndr chm Communications Law Ctee of Int Bar Assoc; chm: Standing Ctee Media and Communications Lawasia 1986–92, Legal Symposium ITU COM 1989, Regulatory and Economic Symposium ASIA TELECOM '93 and '99; advsr to governmental and private sector entities in telecommunications industry in Europe, Middle East and Asia; appointed expert to Econ and Social Ctee of EC to advise on matters incl Green Papers on Satellite Policy and Mobile Communications and Cmmn's proposed Directives on Digital Short Range Radio and High Definition TV; memb Advsy Ctee TELECOM '87 and TELECOM '91, Strategy Summit TELECOMS '95, '99 and 2003; memb: Law Soc, Int Bar; *Publications* Vol 39 Butterworth's Encylopedia of Forms and Precedents on Telecommunication (ed), EC Telecommunications Law (European Practice Library Chancery, fndr conslt ed), Satellite Communications in Europe: Law and Regulation (jt author); *Recreations* swimming, sailing, walking, bridge, opera; *Clubs* Australian, Royal Sydney Yacht Squadron, Bembridge Sailing, Royal Thames Yacht, Henley Royal Regatta, Leander, Australian Jockey, Royal Sydney Golf, Sydney Cricket Ground; *Style*— Stewart White, Esq; ✉ Bell Pottinger Public Affairs, 5th Floor, Holborn Gate, 26 Southampton Buildings, London WC1V 7QC

WHITE, Tony; s of Richard Charles White (d 1989), and Dorothy Maud Dempster White; *b* 27 August 1947; *Educ* Eastbrook Secdy Modern Sch (represented Essex in athletics), East Ham Tech Coll (finalist Letraset Student awards); *m* 3 April 1971, Patricia Margaret, da of Charles Felton; 2 da (Sarah Jane b 8 June 1972, Anna Louise b 23 Sept 1973); *Career* dir and animator; head of design Halas & Batchelor: writer and dir Quartet (first prize Chicago Film Festival), A Short Tall Story (represented GB in int animation festivals, used by UN to promote peace), Jackson Five TV series; dir the Ink Thief children's mixed-media TV drama series (Animus Entertainments/Yorkshire-Tyne Tees TV); films with Richard Williams incl: A Christmas Carol (Academy award), The Pink Panther Strikes Again (D&AD award); prodr, dir and animator Hokusai - An Animated Sketchbook (Br Academy award); fndr Animus Productions (films incl TV specials Cathedral and Pyramid), fndr Animus Entertainments (films for TV and multi-media projects); lectured extensively in the US, Europe and UK; FSIA; *Books* The Animator's Workbook (Phaidon Press, 1988); *Style*— Tony White, Esq; ✉ tel 020 7490 8234, fax 020 7490 8235

WHITE, Victor Oscar; s of Arthur Albert White (d 1976), and Gisela Lydia, *née* Wilde; *b* 30 August 1936; *Educ* Michael Hall Sch Forest Row, Univ of London (LLB); *m* 28 March 1967, Susan Raynor, da of Raynor Leslie Jones (d 1991); 2 s (Christopher b 1968, Jonathan b 1974), 1 da (Katherine b 1971); *Career* slr; ICI: joined Legal Dept 1965, gp slr 1980–96, gp sec 1992–96; conslt Beachcroft Wansbroughs slrs 1996–2000; memb Law Soc; *Style*— Victor White, Esq; ✉ tel 020 7587 1700

WHITE-SPUNNER, Maj Gen Barnabas William Benjamin (Barney); CBE (2002); s of Benjamin Nicholson (Tommy) White-Spunner (d 1986), and Elizabeth (Biddy) White-Spunner; *b* 31 January 1957; *Educ* Eton, Univ of St Andrews (MA); *m* 29 April 1989, Amanda, da of David Faulkner; 2 da (Laetitia b 1989, Florence b 1998), 1 s (Christy b 1991); *Career* cmmnd Blues and Royals 1979, dep ldr Br Chinese Taklamakan Expdn 1993, mil asst to Chief of Defence Staff 1994–96, CO Household Cavalry Regt 1996–98, dep dir Defence Policy MOD 1998–2000, cdr 16 Air Assault Bde 2000–02, cmd NATO Operation Harvest Macedonia 2001, cmd Kabul Multi National Bde 2002, Chief Jt Force Ops 2003–05, COS HQ Land Command 2005–; ed Baily's Hunting Directory 1996–, corr The Field 1992–; Hon Legionnaire (1st Class) French Foreign Legion 2002; *Books* Baily's Hunting Companion (1994), Our Countryside (1996), Great Days (1997), Horse Guards (2006); *Recreations* hunting, central Asia, fishing; *Clubs* Turf; *Style*— Maj Gen Barney White-Spunner, CBE; ✉ Headquarters Land Command, Wilton, Salisbury SP2 0AG

WHITEFIELD, Karen; MSP; da of William Whitefield, of Shotts, and Helen, *née* Brown; *b* 8 January 1970; *Educ* Calderhead HS Shotts, Glasgow Caledonia Univ (BA); *Career* ESU internship on Capitol Hill 1990, personal asst to Rachel Squire MP 1992–99, MSP (Lab) Airdrie & Shotts 1999–, ministerial parly aid to Scottish Law Offrs 2002–03, dep convenor Justice 2 Ctee 2003–; memb 1st Shotts Girls' Brigade; *Recreations* reading, travel, cinema, cake decorating; *Style*— Miss Karen Whitefield, MSP; ✉ Constituency Office, 135 Station Road, Shotts, North Lanarkshire MLT 4BG (tel 01501 822200, fax 01501 823650)

WHITEHEAD, Dr Alan; MP; *b* 15 September 1950; *Educ* Isleworth GS, Univ of Southampton (BA, PhD); *m* 1 Dec 1979, Sophie Wronska; 1 s, 1 da; *Career* dir Outset 1979–83 (dep dir 1976–79), dir BIIT 1983–92, ldr Southampton City Cncl 1984–92, prof of public policy Southampton Inst 1992–97; MP (Lab) Southampton Test 1997–; Parly under-sec of state Tport, Local Govt and the Regions 2001–02; chair: All-Pty Ports Gp 1998–2001, Parly Renewable Energy Gp 2003–; co-chair Parly Sustainable Waste Gp 2003–, sec Br Polish Parly Gp 1997–2001 and 2003–; memb: Regnl Policy Cmmn (The Millan Cmmn) 1995–96, House of Commons Select Ctee for Environment, Tport and the Regions 1997–99, Dept for Constitutional Affrs Select Ctee 2002–; vice-pres Local Govt Assoc 1997–; *Style*— Dr Alan Whitehead, MP; ✉ House of Commons, London SW1A 0AA (tel 020 7219 6338, fax 020 7219 0918, e-mail whiteheada@parliament.uk)

WHITEHEAD, Andrew; *Educ* Leeds GS, Keble Coll Oxford (BA), Univ of Warwick (MA); *Career* BBC: political corr World Service 1988–92, Delhi corr 1993–97, presenter The World Today 1998–2001, ed The World Today 2002–; memb editorial collective of History Workshop jl; Asia Broadcasting Union Prize 1993, Bronze Award NY Festival 1998; *Style*— Andrew Whitehead, Esq; ✉ BBC World Service, Bush House (311 SE), Strand, London WC2B 4PH (tel 020 7557 3874, e-mail andrew.whitehead@bbc.co.uk)

WHITEHEAD, Dr Anthony William; s of Stanley Kenneth Whitehead (d 2002), and Margaret Mary, *née* Welford (d 1973); *b* 22 May 1950; *Educ* Bemrose GS Derby, QMC London (BSc, PhD), RNC Greenwich (MSc); *m* 11 Sept 1976, Lynette Florence, *née* Talmey; 1 s (Jonathan William b 27 Oct 1979), 1 da (Rosalind Mary b 29 May 1982); *Career* research engr Nat Nuclear Corp 1975–77, research scientist Admiralty Research Establishment Teddington MOD 1977–85, project mangr Director General Submarines Bath MOD 1985–91, head Atomic Energy Tech Unit Dept of Energy 1991–92, head Nuclear Industries Tech Unit DTI 1992–99, dep dir Nat Measurement System DTI 1999–2001, head Science Policy Unit Home Office 2001–03, dir Sci and Soc Office of Sci and Innovation 2003–; CEng 1979, memb Fédération Européenne d'Associations Nationales d'Ingénieurs (FEANI) 1991, FINucE 1991, FIMechE 1997; *Style*— Dr Anthony Whitehead; ✉ Office of Science & Innovation, 1 Victoria Street, London SW1H 0ET (tel 020 7215 6245)

WHITEHEAD, David; s of Prof Thomas Paterson Whitehead, of Leamington Spa, Warwicks, and Doreen Grace, *née* Whitton; *b* 31 May 1952; *Educ* Warwick Sch, Univ of Birmingham, Birmingham Poly (BA), Avery Hill Coll of FE (PGCE); *m* Mary Teresa, da of Denis McGeeney; 1 s (Thomas David b 18 June 1981), 1 da (Rachel Brigid b 27 March 1984); *Career* section head Oyez Stationery Ltd 1975–78, mgmnt trainee rising to asst sales mangr Fyffes Group Ltd 1978–82, Br Poultry Fedn 1982–90, Br Ports Fedn 1990–92, dir Br Ports Assoc 1992–; chm Euro Sea Ports Orgn 2001–04; dir Ecoports Fndn, memb European Cmmn Tport and Energy Forum 2001–, memb Govt (BERR) Ports Advisory Gp; *Recreations* reading, gardening, music, walking; *Clubs* Athenaeum; *Style*— David Whitehead, Esq; ✉ British Ports Association, Africa House, Kingsway, London WC2B 6AH (tel 020 7242 1200, fax 020 7405 1069, e-mail david.whitehead@britishports.org.uk)

WHITEHEAD, Neil Anthony; s of H Whitehead and P J Whitehead, *née* Gripe; *b* 7 February 1956; *Educ* King's Sch Gloucester, Kingston Poly (BA 3–D Design); *m* Fiona, da of J B Mackie; 1 da (Amelia b 7 Oct 2000, with Judith Page); *Career* designer; formerly with Murdoch Design and Jeremy Farmer; Fitch plc 1984–99, dir Rodney Fitch & Co 1999–2003: successively assoc dir, dir Retail Div, creative dir then head of retail design, sr dir in jt charge of London Gp; fndr and ceo Ashleycarterwhitehead Ltd 2003–; fndr dir SOLUS plc; clients incl: Kingfisher, BT, BSkyB, Unilever, Wyevale plc, Gadget Shop, Blu (Italy), Alto (Sweden), Ford, Dyrup (Denmark); various appearances on design progs for BBC TV incl Colour in Design and History of Retail Design (both BBC2), conf presentations at various indust events; Design Week Award (Exhbn Environment) 1995, Environment Award 1998; memb Mktg Soc, MCSD, fell Int Real Estate Fedn (FIABCI); *Sporting Achievements* W of England hockey, rugby, athletics under 19 1972–74; played for Br Polytechnic's rugby team 1976–78; capt Kingston Poly RFC (won BSPA Cup 1977); played 1st team Richmond RFC 1980–86, winner Middx Sevens 1983, also played for Middx 1981–85; *Recreations* all sports including tennis and rugby; *Clubs* Richmond RFC, Raffles, Bluebird; *Style*— Neil Whitehead, Esq

WHITEHEAD, (Godfrey) Oliver; CBE; *b* 9 August 1941; *Educ* Univ of Bradford (BSc), London Business Sch; *m* Stephanie; 4 c; *Career* John Laing plc: various engrg and line mgmnt roles 1963–83, exec dir 1983–86; exec dir AMEC plc 1986–89, chief exec Babcock Int plc 1989–93; Alfred McAlpine plc: chief exec 1993–2003, chm 2002–; pres Ringway Devpt plc 1989–2002 (chm 1987–89), chm ITNET plc 2004–05, non-exec chm Minerva plc 2006–; non-exec dir: PSA 1989–91, Appleshaw Ltd 2003–; memb Smeatonian Soc of Civil Engrs 1993–; tstee Charles Newman Meml Fund 2003–; Col and CO Engr and Logistics Staff Corps 1984–; Upper Warden Worshipful Co of Paviors (Liveryman 1986); CEng, FICE; *Style*— Oliver Whitehead, Esq, CBE; ✉ Alfred McAlpine plc, Kinnaird House, 1 Pall Mall East, London SW1Y 5AZ (tel 020 7766 0926, e-mail oliver.whitehead@alfredmcalpineplc.com); Minerva plc, 42 Wigmore Street, London W1U 2RY (e-mail owhitehead@minervaplc.co.uk)

WHITEHEAD, Prof Rex Raymond; s of Athol George Whitehead, of Melbourne, Aust, and Mavis Caroline, *née* Cumming; *b* 30 May 1941; *Educ* Essendon HS Melbourne, Univ of Melbourne (MSc, PhD), Univ of Glasgow (DSc, Kelvin Gold medal and prize); *m* 27 Aug 1971, Hilary Joan, da of John Rutherford; 1 da (Joanne Caroline Brenda b 10 Sept 1973), 1 s (Christopher George John b 18 Feb 1977); *Career* Univ of Glasgow: res fell 1967–69, lectr 1969–78, reader 1978–86, titular prof 1986–, memb Univ Ct 1992–96, dean Faculty of Science 1993–96, clerk of Senate 1996–2001; visiting fell Aust Nat Univ 1975; visiting prof: Michigan State Univ 1974, Florida State Univ 1986–87; memb various ctees SERC since 1980, hon asst keeper Hunterian Museum 1980–; FInstP 1975, FRSE 1985; *Recreations* archery, tea tasting, nicotinage; *Clubs* College (Glasgow); *Style*— Prof Rex Whitehead, FRSE; ✉ Centre for Science Education, St Andrew's Building, University of Glasgow, 11 Eldon Street, Glasgow G3 6NH

WHITEHEAD, Sir Rowland John Rathbone; 5 Bt (UK 1889), of Highfield House, Catford Bridge, Kent; ggs of 1 Bt, sometime Lord Mayor of London; s of Maj Sir Philip Henry Rathbone Whitehead, 4 Bt (d 1953); *b* 24 June 1930; *Educ* Radley, Trinity Hall Cambridge (BA); *m* 3 April 1954, Marie-Louise, da of late Arnold Christian Gausel, of Stavanger, Norway; 1 s, 1 da; *Heir* s, Philip Whitehead; *Career* pres Inst of Translation & Interpreting 1996–2000 (first hon past pres); chm: tstees Rowland Hill Fund (The Post Office - Royal Mail) 1982–, govrs Appleby Grammar Sch Cumbria, The Baronets Tst 1985–88 (also fndr), Exec Ctee Standing Cncl of the Baronetage 1984–86; pres Rising Stars Fndn for Romania 1997–; vice-chm The Tyndale Soc 1999–; tstee: Kelmscott House Tst 1970–2004, Brogdale Horticultural Tst 1994–2000, Royal Aero Club Tst 1999–; churchwarden St Mary Abchurch London 1996–; vice-pres The English Music Festival 2005–; Master Guild of Public Relations Practitioners 2002–03; hon memb Br Weights & Measures Assoc; memb Ct of Assts Worshipful Co of Fruiterers (Master 1995), Freeman City of London; FRGS 2000; Cdr Order of Merit (Romania) 2003; *Books* Cybernetics: Communication and Control (Handbook of Management Technology); also author of articles in specialist jls on language theory and Bible translation; *Recreations* poetry, rural indolence; *Clubs* Arts; *Style*— Sir Rowland Whitehead, Bt; ✉ Sutton House, Chiswick Mall, London W4 2PR (tel 020 8994 2710, e-mail rowlandwhitehead@hotmail.com); Walnut Tree Cottage, Fyfield, Lechlade, Gloucestershire GL7 3TN (tel 01367 850267)

WHITEHILL, Sally Hellena; *b* 6 November 1978, Grantham, Lincs; *Educ* Oakham Sch Rutland (Jerwood scholar), Thacher Sch Calif (ESU scholar), Downing Coll Cambridge (MA), London Coll of Printing; *Career* Capitol Hill 2000, ESU 2001–03, agent Media Div Curtis Brown Gp Ltd 2003–; *Recreations* reading, theatre, film, running, listening to terrible music; *Style*— Ms Sally Whitehill; ✉ Curtis Brown Group Limited, Haymarket House, 28–29 Haymarket, London SW1Y 4SP

WHITEHORN, Katharine Elizabeth; da of Alan Drummond Whitehorn (d 1980), and Edith Marcia, *née* Gray (d 1982); *Educ* Blunt House, Roedean, Glasgow HS for Girls, Newnham Coll Cambridge (MA); *m* 4 Jan 1958, Gavin Tudor Lyall (d 2003), s of Joseph Tudor Lyall; 2 s (Bernard b 1964, Jake b 1967); *Career* publisher's reader 1950–53, teacher Finland

1953–54, grad asst Cornell Univ 1954–55, Picture Post 1956–57, Woman's Own 1958, The Spectator 1959–61; columnist The Observer 1960–96 (assoc ed 1980–88), agony aunt Saga magazine 1997–; dir: BR Airports Authy 1972–77, Nationwide Building Society 1983–91, Nationwide Anglia Estate Agents 1987–90; memb: Latey Ctee on Age of Majority 1965–67, BBC Advsy Gp on Social Effects of Television 1971–72, Cncl RSM 1982–85; rector Univ of St Andrews 1982–85; vice-pres The Patients' Assoc 1983–96; voted Woman that Makes a Difference by International Women's Forum 1992; Hon LLD Univ of St Andrews 1985, Hon DLitt London Guildhall Univ 2000; memb: NUJ, Media Soc; *Books* Cooking in a Bedsitter (1960), Roundabout (1961), Only on Sundays (1966), Whitehorn's Social Survival (1968), Observations (1970), How to Survive in Hospital (1972), How to Survive Children (1975), Sunday Best (1976), How to Survive in the Kitchen (1979), View from a Column (1981), How to Survive your Money Problems (1983); *Clubs* RSM, Royal Cwlth; *Style*— Ms Katharine Whitehorn; ✉ 14 Provost Road, London NW3 4ST (fax 020 7483 0988, e-mail kath.london@virgin.net)

WHITEHOUSE, Prof David John; s of Joseph Whitehouse (d 1989), of Wolverhampton, and Alice Gertrude, *née* Roberts (d 1985); *b* 15 October 1937; *Educ* Univ of Bristol (BSc), Univ of Leicester (PhD), Univ of Warwick (DSc); *m* 17 July 1965, Ruth Lily Epsley, da of William Pannell; 1 da (Anne Frances b 14 Jan 1969), 1 s (Steven Charles b 6 April 1971); *Career* devpt engr Switchgear Wolverhampton 1958–61, research engr Rank Taylor Hobson Leicester 1961–68, chief engr Rank Precision Industries 1968–78; Univ of Warwick: prof of mech engrg 1978, sr fell SERC 1986, dir Centre for Micro Engrg and Metrology 1981, prof of engrg science/chief scientist 1990, prof of engrg science (research) 1997–2002, emeritus prof Sch of Engrg 2002–; conslt prof Tech Univ of Harbin (PRC) 1997–, guest prof Univ of Tianjin (PRC) 1997–; author of 200 tech and scientific papers; IMechE Joseph Whitworth Prize 1971, IMechE James Clayton Prize 1979, Mendeleav Inst Leningrad Commemorative Medallion 1981, Champion of Metrology 1998, Nat Physical Laboratory Metrology for World Class Manufacture Lifetime Contrib Award, American Soc of Precision Engrg Lifetime Achievement Award 2002 (cited as Father of Digital Metrology); Hon DSc Univ of Huddersfield 2006; memb: CIRP 1974, ISO, BSI, Japan Soc for Precision Engrg (JSPE), American Soc for Precision Engrg (ASPE); fell: Inst of Prodn and Control, Inst of Control and Instrumentation, Inst of Mgmnt Engrs; FInstP, FIEE; *Books* Mean Line of Surface Texture (1965), Nano Technology (1991), Handbook of Surface Metrology (1994), Optical Methods in Surface Metrology (1996), Surfaces and their Measurement (2002), Handbook of Surface and Nanometrology (2003); *Recreations* swimming, weight lifting, classical music; *Style*— Prof David Whitehouse; ✉ 171 Cromwell Lane, Burton Green, Coventry CV4 8AN (tel 024 7647 3558, e-mail djw@djwhitehouse.plus.com); School of Engineering, University of Warwick, Coventry CV4 7AL (tel 024 7652 3154, fax 024 7647 1457)

WHITEHOUSE, David Rae Beckwith; QC (1990); s of late (David) Barry Beckwith Whitehouse, FRCS, FRCOG, and late Mary Whitehouse, JP; *b* 5 September 1945; *Educ* Ellesmere Coll, Choate Sch Connecticut (ESU scholar), Trinity Coll Cambridge (MA); *m* 1 Jan 1971, Linda Jane, da of Eric Vickers, CB, of Oakham, Leics; 1 s (Benedict Harry Beckwith b 1978); *Career* called to the Bar Gray's Inn 1969; asst recorder 1983–87, recorder 1987–; currently barr practising at the Criminal Bar; memb Criminal Bar Assoc 1969–; *Recreations* architecture, music, wild gardening, cinema; *Clubs* Reform; *Style*— David Whitehouse, Esq, QC; ✉ 3 Raymond Buildings, Gray's Inn, London WC1R 5BH (tel 020 7400 6400, fax 020 7400 6464, e-mail david.whitehouse@3raymondbuildings.com)

WHITEHOUSE, Dr David Robert; s of Derick William Whitehouse, of Birmingham, and Anne Valmai, *née* Mallet; *b* 7 January 1957; *Educ* Duddeston Manor Sch, Univ of Manchester (BSc, PhD); *m* 3 April 1982, Jillian Dorothy, da of Bernard Carey, of Preston; 1 s (Christopher David b 2 May 1985), 2 da (Lucy Claire b 8 June 1987, Emily Kate b 3 June 1991); *Career* Nuffield Radio Astronomy Laboratories Jodrell Bank 1978–82, Space Science Laboratory UCL 1982–85, conslt ed Space magazine 1987–91, space technol conslt, writer and broadcaster 1985–88, science corr BBC 1988–; numerous articles published in int press and academic jls; pres Soc for Popular Astronomy 1995–98; European Internet Journalist of the Year 2002–03; FRAS 1979; *Books* The Moon: A Biography (2001); *Recreations* mountaineering, music; *Style*— Dr David Whitehouse; ✉ BBC, BBC Television Centre, London W12 7RJ

WHITEHOUSE, Prof (Julian) Michael Arthur; s of Arthur Arnold Keer Whitehouse (d 2003), of Olney, Bucks, and Kathleen Ida Elizabeth, *née* Elliston (d 1989); *b* 2 June 1940; *Educ* Queens' Coll Cambridge (MA, MB BChir), St Bartholomew's Hosp of London (MD); *m* 10 April 1965, Diane France, da of Dr Raymond Maximillien Theodore de Saussure (d 1972); 1 s (Michael Alexander de Saussure b 1966) 2 da (Fiona Geraldine b 1968, Vanessa Caroline b 1972); *Career* hon conslt physician, sr lectr and acting dir Dept of Med Oncology Bart's 1976, subsequently prof of med oncology and hon conslt physician Southampton Univ Hosps and dir CRC Wessex Med Oncology Unit Southampton until 1997, dean Charing Cross and Westminster Med Sch 1997, vice-princ (undergrad med) Imperial Coll Sch of Med 1997–2000, ret, emeritus prof of med oncology ICSM; visiting prof: Univ of Boston 1981, Christchurch Clinical Sch of Med NZ 1986; former vice-pres European Soc of Med Oncology; chm: UICC Clinical Oncology Ctee, Jt Cncl for Clinical Oncology RCP and RCR until 1998, Educn and Trg Bd EORTC, Med Studies Ctee Univ of London, Cncl Paterson Research Inst Christie Hosp Manchester until 2002; non-exec dir W Middlesex Univ NHS Tst until 2000; past memb Cncl: CRC, GMC (Univ of London); ed Haematological Oncology until 1996; assoc memb Professional Conduct Ctee GMC; govr: Canford Sch Dorset, City of London Sch; govr St Swithun's Sch Winchester; Freeman City of London, Liveryman Worshipful Soc of Apothecaries; FRCP 1979, FRCR 1992, FRCPEd 1994, FMedSci 2000; *Books* CNS Complications of Malignant Disease (1979), A Pocket Consultant in Clinical Oncology (1989), Investigation and Management (with Christopher J Williams, 1984–85), Recent Advances in Clinical Oncology (1982 and 1986), Cancer - the Facts (with Maurice Slevin, 1996); *Recreations* skiing, the sea, travelling; *Clubs* Athenaeum; *Style*— Prof Michael Whitehouse; ✉ 25 Chilbolton Avenue, Winchester, Hampshire SO22 5HE (e-mail m.whitehouse@imperial.ac.uk)

WHITEHOUSE, Sarah Alice; da of Rev Canon William Beadon Norman, and Beryl, *née* Welch; *b* 13 January 1961; *Educ* Felixstowe Coll Suffolk, Univ of St Andrews (MA, pres Univ Debating Union, pres Univ Cons Assoc), Univ of Westminster (pro exam in law), Inns of Court Sch of Law; *m* 15 Oct 1988, Andrew Timothy Brian, s of late Brian Paul Whitehouse; 1 da (Elizabeth Julia b 30 Dec 1992), 1 s (Mark Paul b 3 July 1997); *Career* National Westminster Bank plc 1983–85, sr mangr Fuji International Finance Ltd 1985–90, asst dir Barclays De Zoete Wedd Ltd 1990–91; Parly candidate (Cons) Warley W 1992; memb Lincoln's Inn 1991–, barr 1993–, Treasy counsel 2006–; *Recreations* riding, walking, music; *Clubs* Carlton (assoc memb); *Style*— Ms Sarah Whitehouse; ✉ 21 Nottingham Road, London SW17 7EA (tel 020 8767 8029); 6 King's Bench Walk, Temple, London EC4Y 7DR (tel 020 7583 0410)

WHITELAW, Prof Andrew George Lindsay; s of Dr Robert George Whitelaw, DL, of 64 Garvock Hill, Dunfermline, Scotland, and Cicily Mary, *née* Ballard; *b* 31 August 1946; *Educ* George Watson's Coll Edinburgh, King's Coll Cambridge (MA, MB BChir, MD); *m* 1, 7 Sept 1968 (m dis 1990), Sara Jane, da of Capt Jack Sparks (d 1979), of Peaslake, Surrey; 1 s (Benjamin Cameron b 12 May 1972), 2 da (Nicola Jane b 26 Dec 1970, Rebecca Catrin b 18 April 1974); *m* 2, 4 Aug 1990, Marianne, da of Dr Otto Thoresen, of Horten, Norway; 1 s (Thomas Thoresen b 31 Oct 1990); *Career* specialist paediatric training at Gt Ormond St and in Toronto 1972–79, conslt neonatologist and hon sr lectr Royal Postgrad Med Sch Hammersmith Hosp 1981–90, prof of paediatrics Univ of Oslo 1995–98 (assoc prof 1990–95), prof of Neonatal Med Univ of Bristol 1998–; chm Perinatal Servs Ctee NW Thames, dep chm Res Ethics Ctee Hammersmith Hosp, memb Res Ctee Birthright; FRCP 1988; *Books* The Very Immature Infant Under 28 Weeks Gestation (with Cooke, 1988); *Recreations* music, mountains, theatre; *Style*— Prof Andrew Whitelaw; ✉ Neonatal Medicine, University of Bristol, Southmead Hospital, Bristol BS10 5NB (tel 0117 959 5699, fax 0117 959 5324, e-mail andrew.whitelaw@bristol.ac.uk)

WHITELAW, Dr Douglas Dixon; s of George Whitelaw (d 1983), of Glasgow, and Jean, *née* Forrester (d 1986); *b* 4 March 1952; *Educ* HS of Glasgow, Univ of Glasgow (BSc, MSc, PhD); *m* 31 Dec 1974, Elspeth Martin, da of John Campbell; 2 s (Fraser Martin b 9 Nov 1981, Lindsay Elder b 21 Sept 1987); *Career* Wellcome Trust research fell Univ of Glasgow 1975–80, sr scientist Int Lab for Research on Animal Diseases (ILRAD) Nairobi Kenya 1980–88, EC sr research fell Univ of Glasgow 1989–90; Br Cncl: dep dir/sci offr Australia and NZ 1990–93, asst dir rising to dir Enugu Nigeria 1993–94, dir Kano Nigeria 1994–95, dep dir (sci) Korea 1996–2000, conslt 2000–; author of over seventy pubns in int scientific jls; *Recreations* music, golf, cricket; *Clubs* Nairobi, Royal Over-Seas League; *Style*— Dr Douglas Whitelaw

WHITELAW, Prof James Hunter (Jim); s of James Whitelaw, and Jean Ross, *née* Scott; *b* 28 January 1936; *Educ* Glasgow HS, Univ of Glasgow (BSc, PhD), Univ of London (DSc); *m* 10 July 1959, Elizabeth, da of David Dewar Williamson Shields; 3 s (Alan Scott b 1962, David Stuart b 1964, James Douglas b 1968); *Career* res assoc Brown Univ 1961–63, prof Imperial Coll London 1974– (lectr 1963–69, reader 1969–74); chair prof Hong Kong Poly Univ 2000–03; ed Experiments in Fluids 1982–99; foreign Assoc US Acad of Engrg 2000; Hon DSc: Univ of Lisbon 1980, Univ of Valencia 1996, Univ of Dublin 1999, Univ of Athens 2001; FIMechE 1986, FREng 1991, FRS 1996, FCGI 1998; *Books* Principles and Practice of Laser-Doppler Anemometry (with F Durst and A Melling, 1981), Calculation Methods for Engineering Flows (with P Bradshaw and T Cebeci, 1981); series ed Combustion Treatise; jt ed over 30 books, author of over 400 technical papers; *Recreations* music, garden, travel; *Style*— Prof Jim Whitelaw, FRS, FREng; ✉ 149A Coombe Lane West, Kingston upon Thames, Surrey KT2 7DH (tel 020 8942 1836); Department of Mechanical Engineering, Imperial College, London SW7 (tel 020 7594 7028)

WHITELEY, *see also:* Huntington-Whiteley

WHITELEY, Julian Peter; s of Gen Sir Peter Whiteley, GCB, OBE, DL, and Nancy, *née* Clayden; *b* 15 March 1957; *Educ* Sherborne, Royal Naval Engineering Coll Plymouth (BSc), Univ of Cambridge (PGCE), Univ of Nottingham (MBA); *m* 1982, Elizabeth Anne, da of Vice-Adm Sir John Forbes, KCB; 3 da (Gemma b 10 May 1984, Kirstie b 13 March 1986, Laura b 10 May 1989); *Career* offr RN 1975–81; asst master physics Rugby Sch 1981–83, head of physics Sherborne Sch 1986–93 (asst master 1984–85), dep headmaster St Paul's Sch São Paulo 1993–97, headmaster Taunton Sch 1997–; *Recreations* sailing, windsurfing, reading, classic cars, theatre, foreign travel, entertaining; *Clubs* São Paulo Yacht, Yealm Yacht; *Style*— Julian Whiteley, Esq; ✉ Taunton School, Staplegrove, Taunton, Somerset TA2 6AJ (tel 01823 349224, fax 01823 349201)

WHITELEY, Lucinda; *b* 4 October 1961; *Educ* St Hilda's Sch Whitby, Univ of Newcastle upon Tyne (BA); *m* Michael Watts; 2 da; *Career* prodn co-ordinator Longman Video 1983–84; prog mangr: Children's Channel 1984–86, LWT 1986; head of prog planning Children's Channel 1987–88, ed Early Morning Television Service Channel 4 Television 1988–92 (launched The Big Breakfast), freelance prodr 1993, commissioning ed children's progs Channel 4 Television 1993–97 (progs incl Wise Up, Coping With..., Hollyoaks, Ant and Dec Unzipped, Terry Pratchett's Discworld), sr vice-pres Prodn Polygram Visual Programming 1997–99 (progs incl Maisy), freelance exec prodr 1999–2000, dir Novel Entertainment 2001– (progs incl Fimbles, Roly Mo Show, Horrid Henry); vice-chair Second World Summit on Television for Children 1998; memb Bd BAFTA; *Awards* 7 BAFTAs, 3 Emmys, 2 Prix Jeunesse Awards, RTS Award, Peabody Award, Prix Europa, British Animation Award; *Style*— Ms Lucinda Whiteley; ✉ 39 Lonsdale Road, London NW6 6RA (tel and fax 020 7372 2772, e-mail lucinda@novelentertainment.co.uk)

WHITELOCKE, Rodger Alexander Frederick; s of Leslie W S Whitelocke (d 1955), of Bulstrode Park, Jamaica, and Ruth, *née* Hopwood; descendant of Sir James Whitelocke b 1570 (and Family Tree in Plantagenet Roll Exeter Vol) and Bulstrode Whitelocke, Keeper of the Great Seal b 1605 (s Sir James); *b* 28 February 1943; *Educ* Taunton Sch, Univ of London, Bart's (MB BS); *m* 28 July 1973, Eleonora Valerie, da of Professor W F Maunder; 1 da (Katherine b 1978), 2 s (Nicholas b 1979, James b 1984); *Career* house surgn Bart's 1969–70, research on prostaglandins in ocular inflammation Inst of Ophthalmology 1971–73 (PhD London), sr resident surgical offr Moorfields Eye Hosp 1976, sr registrar Bart's 1977–80; conslt ophthalmic surgn: Bart's, Royal Marsden Hosp London; hon conslt St Luke's Hosp for Clergy, visiting prof of visual scis City Univ London 1988–91; Freeman City of London, Liveryman Worshipful Co of Barbers; FRCS; *Recreations* music, antiques, travel, gardening; *Clubs* Athenaeum, The Fountain, Bart's and the London Boat (past pres); *Style*— Rodger Whitelocke, Esq; ✉ Westwood, Heather Drive, Sunningdale, Berkshire SL5 0HR; 152 Harley Street, London W1G 7LH (tel 020 7935 3834, fax 020 7224 2574)

WHITEMAN, Prof John Robert; s of Robert Whiteman, and Rita, *née* Neale; *b* 7 December 1938; *Educ* Bromsgrove Sch, Univ of St Andrews (BSc), Worcester Coll Oxford (DipEd), Univ of London (PhD); *m* 8 Aug 1964, Caroline Mary, da of Oswald B Leigh (d 1941); 2 s (Angus b 1967, Hamish b 1969); *Career* sr lectr RMCS Shrivenham 1963–67; asst prof: Univ of Wisconsin USA 1967–68, Univ of Texas at Austin 1968–70; Brunel Univ 1970–: reader numerical analysis 1970–76 (on leave Richard Merton Gäst prof Univ of Münster FRG 1975–76), prof of numerical analysis and dir Brunel Inst of Computational Mathematics 1976–2004, head Dept of Mathematics and Statistics 1982–90, vice-princ 1991–96, distinguished prof 2004–; visiting prof: Univ of Pisa 1985, Univ of Kuwait 1986, Texas A and M Univ USA 1986–, Univ of Stuttgart 1990, Univ of Texas at Austin 1996; distinguished research fell Univ of Texas at Austin 1997–2005; Brunel and Ravenscroft Lectr 2004; dir ESAFORM (European Scientific Assoc for Forming Processes) 1995–2004; memb: SERC Mathematics Ctee 1981–86, SERC Sci Bd 2000–, Amersham Deanery Synod C of E; chm: SERC Sci Bd Educn and Trg Panel 1991–92, Cncl IMA 1996–; Freeman City of London 1979, Liveryman Worshipful Co of Glass Sellers 1979 (asst to the Ct, renter warden 2002, prime warden 2003, master 2004); hon doctorate Univ of West Bohemia 1995; FIMA 1970, CMath 1991; *Books* numerous pubns on numerical solution of differential equations (particularly finite element methods) incl: The Mathematics of Finite Elements and Applications vols 1–10 (ed 1973–2000), Numerical Methods for Partial Differential Equations (ed journal); *Recreations* walking, swimming, golf, tennis, orchestral music; *Style*— Prof John Whiteman; ✉ Institute of Computational Mathematics, Brunel University, Uxbridge, Middlesex UB8 3PH (tel 01895 265185, fax 01895 269185, e-mail john.whiteman@brunel.ac.uk)

WHITEMAN, Prof Peter George; QC (1977); s of David Whiteman (d 1988), and Betsy Bessie, *née* Coster; *b* 8 August 1942; *Educ* Warwick Secdy Modern Sch, Leyton Co HS, LSE (LLB, LLM); *m* 24 Oct 1971, Katherine Ruth, da of Gershon Ellenbogen; 2 da (Victoria Elizabeth b 1975, Caroline Venetia b 1977); *Career* lectr Univ of London 1966–70; called to the Bar Lincoln's Inn 1967 (bencher 1985); recorder of the Crown Court 1986–, dep High Court judge 1994–, jt head of chambers; memb Bar Cncl; memb Faculty of Laws Univ of Florida 1977–, prof of Law Univ of Virginia 1980–; attorney and cnsllr NY State 1982; visiting prof: Univ of Virginia 1978, Univ of Calif Berkeley 1980; legal advsr Ctee Unitary Tax Campaign (UK) 1982–; memb Editorial Bd Virginia Jl of Int Law

1982–; author numerous articles in learned jls; pres and chm Dulwich Village Preservation Soc 1987–97, memb Advsy Ctee The Dulwich Estate Scheme of Mgmnt 1988–97, chm Dulwich Jt Residents Ctee 1991–97; memb: Consultative Ctee Dulwich Picture Gallery 1990–97; FRSA 1976; *Books* Whiteman on Income Tax (1988), Whiteman on Capital Gains Tax (1988), British Tax Encyclopedia (1988); *Recreations* tennis, jogging, hill walking, croquet, opera and theatre; *Style*— Prof Peter G Whiteman, QC; ✉ Hollis Whiteman Chambers, Queen Elizabeth Building, The Temple, London EC4Y 9BS (tel 020 7936 3131, 020 7353 0551, 020 7583 5766, fax 020 7353 1937 and 020 7353 0339)

WHITEMAN, Ven Rodney David Carter; s of Leonard Archibald Whiteman (d 1955), and Sybil Mary, *née* Morshead (d 1990); *b* 6 October 1940; *Educ* St Austell GS Cornwall, Ely Theological Coll; *m* 28 Oct 1969, Christine Anne, da of Edward Thomas James Chelton, of Cheltenham, Glos; 1 da (Rebecca Mary De Mornay b 1972), 1 s (James Rodney Charles b 1975); *Career* ordained Birmingham Cathedral: deacon 1964, priest 1965; curate All Saints Kings Heath 1964–70; vicar: St Stephen Rednal 1970–79, St Barnabas Erdington 1979–89; rural dean of Aston 1981–89, hon canon Birmingham Cathedral 1985–89, priest in charge Cardynham with Helland 1989–94, hon canon of Truro Cathedral 1989–2006, archdeacon of Bodmin 1989–2000, archdeacon of Cornwall 2000–2006, archdeacon emeritus 2006–; *Style*— The Ven Rodney Whiteman; ✉ 22 Treverbyn Gardens, Sanolp Hill, St Austell, Cornwall PL25 3AW (tel 01726 879043)

WHITEMORE, Hugh John; s of Samuel George Whitemore (d 1987), and Kathleen, *née* Fletcher (d 1996); *b* 16 June 1936; *Educ* Judd Sch Tonbridge, King Edward VI Sch Southampton, RADA; *m* 1, July 1961 (m dis 1976), Jill, *née* Brooke; m 2, May 1976 (m dis 1994), Sheila, *née* Lemon; 1 s (Tom b 1976); m 3, May 1998, Rohan McCullough; *Career* playwright; stage plays: Stevie 1977, Pack of Lies 1983, Breaking the Code 1986, The Best of Friends 1988, It's Ralph 1991, A Letter of Resignation 1997, Disposing of the Body 1999, God Only Knows 2001, As You Desire Me (from Pirandello) 2005; films incl: 84 Charing Cross Road (Royal Film Performance) 1987, Jane Eyre 1995; many TV plays and dramatisations incl: A Dance to the Music of Time (Channel 4) 1997, The Gathering Storm 2002 (Emmy for Outstanding Writing, Writer's Guild of America Award, Peabody Award), contribs to The Wednesday Play, Armchair Theatre and Play for Today; visiting prof in broadcast media Univ of Oxford 2003–04; FRSL 1999, Hon FKC; *Recreations* music, movies, reading; *Style*— Hugh Whitemore, Esq; ✉ 67 Peel Street, London W8 7PB

WHITEN, Prof (David) Andrew; *Educ* Univ of Sheffield (BSc), Univ of Bristol (PhD); *Career* SSRC res fell Univ of Oxford 1972–75; Univ of St Andrews: lectr 1975–90, reader 1990–97, prof of evolutionary and developmental psychology 1997–2000, Wardlaw prof of psychology 2000–; F M Bird visiting prof Emory Univ 1996, Br Acad res reader 1999–2001, Leverhulme major research fell 2003–06, Royal Soc Leverhulme Tst sr research fell 2006–07; Jean-Marie Delwart Int Scientific Prize Royal Belgian Acad of Sciences 2001, Rivers medal RAI 2007; FBPsS 1991, FBA 2000, FRSE 2001, AcSS 2003; *Publications* incl: Machiavellian Intelligence II (with R W Byrne, 1997), Cultures in Chimpanzees (with J Goodall et al, in Nature, 1999), The Second Inheritance System of Chimpanzees and Humans (in Nature, 2005); *Style*— Prof Andrew Whiten; ✉ Centre for Social Learning and Cognitive Evolution, School of Psychology, University of St Andrews, St Andrews, Fife KY16 9JU (tel 01334 462073, fax 01334 463042, e-mail a.whiten@st-and.ac.uk, website www.st-and.ac.uk/aw2)

WHITEOAK, John Edward Harrison; *b* 5 July 1947; *Educ* Univ of Sheffield (MA, CIPFA); *m* 1, Margaret Elizabeth, *née* Blakey (d 1980); 1 s (Roger b 1969), 2 da (Juliet b 1971, Olivia b 1973); m 2, (m dis 2004), Dr Karen Lynne Wallace, *née* Stevenson; 2 da (Georgia b 1988, Francesca b 1990); *Career* county treas and dir of resources Cheshire CC 1981–98, chief exec Cheshire Pension Fund 1981–98, chief exec WA Ltd 1999–; lead fin advsr to CCs 1994–98, princ negotiator on local govt fin for England 1994–97; chm Corp Governance Panel CIPFA 1994– (pres NW Regn CIPFA 1994–95); memb: Soc of Co Treasurers 1981– (pres 1997–98), Accounting Standards Ctee 1984–87; *Books* Public Sector Accounting and Financial Control (co-author, 1992); *Clubs* RAC, Chester City, Eaton Golf; *Style*— John Whiteoak; ✉ Westmount, Chester CH3 5UD

WHITER, John Lindsay Pearce; s of Nugent Whiter (d 1966), and Jean Dorothy, *née* Pearce (d 2003); *b* 10 May 1950; *Educ* Eastbourne GS; *m* 5 July 1975, Janet Dulcie Sarah, da of Dr Kenneth Oswald Albert Vickery, of Eastbourne, E Sussex; 2 s (Timothy b 1976, William b 1989), 1 da (Nancy b 1979); *Career* sr ptnr (London) Mazars (formerly Neville Russell) 1992–93 (ptnr 1977–88, managing partner (London) 1988–92), chief fin offr Benfield Gp Ltd 1994–; Freeman City of London, Bishopsgate Ward; memb: Guild of Freeman of the City of London, Worshipful Co of Chartered Accountants in England and Wales; FCA 1973, FInstD, FRSA; *Recreations* opera, music, skiing, family; *Clubs* City of London, RAC; *Style*— John Whiter, Esq; ✉ Meades, Lake Street, Mark Cross, East Sussex TN6 3NT; Benfield Group Ltd, 55 Bishopsgate, London EC2N 3BD (tel 020 7578 7000, fax 020 7578 7039)

WHITEREAD, Rachel; CBE (2006); da of Thomas Whiteread (d 1988), of London, and Pat, *née* Lancaster (d 2003); *b* 20 April 1963; *Educ* Brighton Poly (BA), Slade Sch of Art UCL (DipHe in sculpture); *Career* artist and sculptor; involved in teaching on various postgrad and undergrad courses; Hon DLitt Brighton Poly 1998; *Solo Exhibitions* incl: Carlile Gall London 1988, Ghost (Chisenhale Gall London) 1990, Arnolfini Gall Bristol 1991, Karsten Schubert Ltd London 1991, Rachel Whiteread Recent Sculpture (Luhring Augustine Gall NY) 1992, House (E London) 1993, Basel Kunsthalle (Switzerland) 1994, ICA Philadelphia (USA) 1995, ICA Boston (USA) 1995, Rachel Whiteread: Shedding Life (Tate Gall Liverpool) 1996–97, Reina Sofia (Madrid) 1997, Water Tower Project (Public Art Fund, NY) 1998, Anthony d'Offay Gall London 1998, Rachel Whiteread (Luhring Augustine NY) 1999, Holocaust Memorial (Judenplatz Vienna) 2000, Fourth Plinth Project (Trafalgar Square London) 2001, Rachel Whiteread (Serpentine Gallery London and Scot Nat Gallery of Modern Art Edinburgh) 2001, Deutsche Guggenheim Museum (Berlin, touring exhibition) 2001, Haunch of Venison London 2002, Room 101 (V&A) 2003, Koyanagi Gall Tokyo 2003, Luhring Augustine NY 2003, MOMA Rio de Janeiro Brazil and Sao Paolo Brazil 2003–04, Kunsthaus Bregenz Austria 2005, Embankment (Turbine Hall Tate Modern) 2005; *Selected Group Exhibitions* incl: Whitworth Young Contemporaires Manchester 1987, Riverside Open London 1988, Whitechapel Open London 1989, Deichtorhallen Hamburg 1989–90, British Art Show (touring) 1990, Karsten Schubert Ltd London 1990, Metropolis (Martin-Gropius Bau Berlin) 1991, Broken English (Serpentine Gall) 1991, Gp Show (Luhring Augustine NY) 1991, Turner Prize Exhibition (Tate) 1991 and 1993, Double Take (Hayward and Kunsthalle Vienna) 1992, Documenta IX (Kassel Germany) 1992, Carnegie International (USA) 1995, Br Pavillion Venice Biennale 1997, Skulpture Projekte (Münster Germany) 1997, Sensation: Young British Artists from the Saatchi Collection (Royal Acad of Arts and Touring 1999) 1997, Wounds (Moderna Museet Stockholm) 1998, Displacements: Miroslaw Balka, Doris Salcedo, Rachel Whiteread (Art Gall of Ontario Toronto) 1998, Towards Sculpture (Fundacao Calouste Gulbenkian Lisbon) 1998, REAL/LIFE: New British Art (Tochigi Prefectural Museum of Fine Arts Japan and touring) 1998, Claustrophobia (IKON Gall Birmingham and touring) 1998, Le Musée à l'heure anglaise: Sculptures de la collection du British Council 1965–1998 (Musée des Beaux-Arts de Valenciennes) 1999, House of Sculpture (Modern Art Museum of Fort Worth Texas) 1999, Sincerely Yours (Astrup Fearnley MOMA Oslo) 2000, Le temps vite (Centre Georges Pompidou Paris) 2000, La forma del mondo/la fine del monde (Padiglione d'arte contemporanea Milan) 2000, Shadow of Reason (Galleria d'Arte Moderna Bologna Italy) 2000, The Language of Things (Kettles Yard Cambridge), Double Vision (Galerie fuer Zeitgenössische Kunst Leipzig), Public Offerings (Museum of Contemporary Art LA), Century City (Tate Modern London) 2001, Lost and Found 2 (Kulturhuset Stockholm) 2001, Electrify Me! (Friedrich Petzel Gall NY) 2001, Double Vision (Galerie für Zeitgenosaische Kunst Leipzig) 2001, Public Offerings (MoCA LA) 2001, Collaborations with Parkett; 1984 to Now (MoMA NY) 2001, Beautiful Productions: Art to Play, Art to Wear, Art to Own (Whitechapel Gall London) 2001, Wall & Whiteread (Kukje Gall Seoul) 2002, To Be Looked At (MOMA NY) 2002, Sphere: Loans for the Inivisible Museum (Sir John Soane's Musuem London) 2002, The Photogenic: Photography Through its Metaphors in Contemporary Art (ICA Philadelphia) 2002, Conversation?: Recent Acquisitions of the Van Abbemuseum (The Factory, Acad of Fine Arts Athens) 2002, The Physical World: An Exhibition of Painting and Sculpture (Gagosian Gall NY) 2002, Beautiful Productions: Parkett Collaborations and Editions since 1984 (Irish MOMA Dublin) 2002, Thinking Big: Concepts for 21st Century British Sculpture (Peggy Guggenheim Collection Venice) 2002, Blast to Freeze: British Art in the 20th Century (Kunstmuseum Wolfsberg and Les Abattoirs Toulouse) 2002, Days Like These (Tate Britain London) 2003, The Snow Show (Lapland, Finland) 2004; *Awards* The Elephant Trust 1989, GLA Prodn Grant 1989, nominated Turner Prize 1991, DAAD Stipendium Berlin 1992, winner Turner Prize 1993, Venice Biennale Award for Best Young Artist 1997, Nord LB Art Prize 2004; *Style*— Ms Rachel Whiteread, CBE; ✉ c/o Gagosian Gallery, 6–24 Britannia Street, London, WC1X 9JD (tel 020 7841 9960, fax 020 7841 9961, website www.gagosian.com)

WHITFIELD, Adrian; QC (1983); s of Peter Henry Whitfield (d 1967), and Margaret Mary Whitfield (d 2005); *b* 10 July 1937; *Educ* Ampleforth, Magdalen Coll Oxford (MA); *m* 1, 1962 (m dis), Lucy Caroline, *née* Beckett; 2 da (Teresa, Emily); m 2, 1971, Niamh, da of Prof Cormac O'Ceallaigh (d 1996), of Dublin; 1 s (Adam), 1 da (Katharine Anna); *Career* called to the Bar Middle Temple 1964; memb Western Circuit; treas Middle Temple 2005; chm NHS Tbnl 1993–2004; *Style*— Adrian Whitfield, Esq, QC; ✉ 47 Faroe Road, London W14 0EL (tel 020 7603 8982); 3 Serjeants' Inn, London EC4Y 1BQ (tel 020 7427 5000)

WHITFIELD, Hugh Newbold; s of Rev George Joshua Newbold Whitfield, of Exmouth, Devon, and Audrey Priscilla, *née* Dence; *b* 15 June 1944; *Educ* Canford Sch, Gonville & Caius Coll Cambridge and Bart's Med Coll London (MA, MChir); *m* Penelope Joy, da of William Craig; 2 s (Angus Hugh Newbold b 18 April 1976, Alastair James Newbold b 14 Jan 1981); *Career* cmmnd RAMC 1967–74; various house jobs Bart's, res fell Inst of Urology 1974–76; Bart's: chief asst Dept of Urology 1976–79, conslt urologist 1979–93, clinical dir Dept of Urology and dir Lithotripter Unit 1991–93; reader in urology and dir Stone Unit Inst of Urology 1993–2001, conslt urologist Central Middx Hosp 1993–2000, conslt urologist Battle Hosp Reading 2001–; civilian conslt advsr in urology to Army; ed Br Jl of Urology 1993–2002; former memb Nat Youth Orch of GB; memb: BMA 1968, Br Assoc of Urological Surgns 1974; FRCS 1972, FRSM 1975; *Books* Textbooks of Genito-Urinary Vols I and II (ed with W F Hendry, 1985, 2 edn, ed with W F Hendry, R S Kirby, J W Duckett, 1998), Urology: Pocket Consultant (1985), Genitourinary Surgey (ed 5 edn vols I-III, 1992); *Recreations* music, country pursuits, golf; *Clubs* Garrick; *Style*— Hugh Whitfield, Esq; ✉ Royal Berkshire Hospital, London Road, Reading, Berkshire RG1 5AN (tel 0118 987 5111, e-mail hugh.whitfield@rbbh-tr.nhs.uk); 43 Wimpole Street, London W1G 8AE (tel 020 7935 3095, fax 020 7935 3147, e-mail hughwhitfield@urologylondon.fsnet.co.uk)

WHITFIELD, June; CBE (1998, OBE 1985); da of John Herbert Whitfield (d 1955), and Bertha Georgina, *née* Flett (d 1982); *b* 11 November 1925; *Educ* Streatham Hill HS, RADA; *m* 1955, Timothy John Aitchison (d 2001), s of Cdr J G Aitchison, OBE; 1 da (Suzy b 4 June 1960); *Career* actress; stage debut ASM Pinkstring & Sealing Wax (Duke of York's) 1944; *Theatre* incl: Ace of Clubs (Cambridge Theatre and tour) 1950, Love from Judy (Saville) 1952, From Here and There (Royal Court) 1955, Jack and the Beanstalk (Chichester 1982, Bath 1985, Guildford 1986), An Ideal Husband (Chichester) 1987, Over My Dead Body (Savoy) 1988, Babes in the Wood (Croydon 1990, Plymouth 1991, Cardiff 1992), Cinderella (Wimbledon) 1994, Bedroom Farce (Aldwych) 2002, Chichester Christmas Concert 2002, On the Town (musical) 2007; *Television and Radio* incl: Take It From Here 1953–60, Hancock 1956, Benny Hill 1961, Dick Emery 1973, subject of This is Your Life 1976 and 1995, Happy Ever After (5 series) 1974–78, Terry and June (9 series) 1979–87, The News Huddlines 1984–99, French and Saunders 1988, Cluedo 1990, Absolutely Fabulous! 1992–94, 2001 and 2003 (specials 1996 (two), 2002 and 2004), Huddlines, Variety Special, A Pocket Full of Rye 1994, Whats My Line 1994 and 1995, At Bertram's Hotel 1995, Common as Muck 1996, The 4.50 from Paddington 1996, Family Money 1997, Tom Jones 1997, All Rise for Julian Clary 1997, Funny Women 1997, Nemesis (Radio 4), Like They've Never Been Gone (Radio 2) 1999 and 2001; The Undiscovered Casebook of Sherlock Holmes (Radio 2) 1999, '99 News Huddlines (1999), Catherine Cookson's The Secret (TV film) 1999, The Last of the Blonde Bombshells 1999, Mirror Ball (BBC) 2000, The News Huddlines 2000; Miss Marple (Radio 4): Murder at the Vicarage 1993, The Caribbean Mystery 1997, The Mirror Cracked 1998, A Murder is Announced 1999, The Body in the Library 1999, The Moving Finger 2001, They Do it With Mirrors 2001, Sleeping Murder 2001, Huddlines (Radio 4) 2001 and 2002, Like They've Never Been Gone (Radio 4) 2001 and 2002, Coming up for Air 2002, The Kumars at No 42 2003, Call My Bluff 2003 and 2004, BBC Worldwide Festival 2003, Gloria Hunniford Show 2003, 9 Floors 2003, Father Gilbert 2003, The Royal 2004, The Sound of Music 2004, Father Gilbert 2004, NFI Tribute 2004, Hitchhiker's Guide to the Galaxy 2005, Midsomer Murders 2005 Miss Marple By The Pricking of my Thumbs 2005, Last of the Summer Wine 2005–06, Bob the Builder (voice-over) 2006, Not Talking (Radio 3) 2006, Loose Ends (Radio 4) 2006, Hitchhiker's Guide to the Galaxy (Radio 5) 2006, South Bank Show 2007, Last of the Summer Wine 2007, The Dinner Party (Radio 4) 2007; *Film* Carry on Nurse 1958, Spy with the Cold Nose 1966, The Magnificent Seven Deadly Sins 1971, Carry on Abroad 1972, Bless This House 1972, Carry on Girls 1973, Romance with a Double Base 1974, Not Now Comrade 1975, Carry On Columbus 1992, Jude the Obscure 1995; *Recordings* Up Je T'aime, Wonderful Children's Songs, June Whitfield at the BBC (audio tape), The School at Thrush Green (audio book); *Awards* Variety Club Joint Personality Award 1979, The Comedy Awards: Lifetime Achievement Award 1994, Women in Film and TV 1998; TRIC Special Award 1999; 'Talkies' Oustanding Achievement Award 1999; *Books* ...and June Whitfield (autobiography, 2000); *Style*— Miss June Whitfield, CBE; ✉ c/o Maureen Vincent, PFD, Drury House, 34–43 Russell Street, London WC2B 5HA (tel 020 7344 1010)

WHITFIELD, Prof Michael; s of Arthur Whitfield (d 1990), and Ethel, *née* Woodward (d 1986); *b* 15 June 1940; *Educ* King's Sch Chester, Univ of Leeds (BSc, PhD); *m* 31 July 1961, Jean Ann (d 1984), da of Stanley Beige Rowe (d 1964); 3 da (Katherine b 1962, Clare b 1964, Juliet b 1965), 1 s (Benjamin b 1968); *Career* res scientist CSIRO Fisheries and Oceanography Sydney Australia 1964–69, dir Marine Biological Assoc Plymouth 1987–99 (sr princ res scientist 1970–87), dir Plymouth Marine Laboratory 1994–95 (dep dir 1988–94); hon prof Univ of Plymouth 1995–; pres Challenger Soc for Marine Sci 1996–98, vice-pres Sir Alister Hardy Fndn for Ocean Sci 1992–99, vice-pres Marine Biological Soc of the UK 2000–; tstee: Gaia Tst, Devon Wildlife Tst; Hon DSc Univ of Göteborg 1991, Hon DSc Univ of Plymouth 2001; FRSC, FIBiol, FGS; *Books* Ion-selective Electrodes for the Analysis of Natural Waters (1970), Marine Electro Chemistry (1981), Tracers in the Ocean (1988), Light & Life in the Sea (1990), Aquatic Life Cycle Strategies

(1999); *Recreations* hill walking, photography, watching wildlife; *Style*— Prof Michael Whitfield; ✉ The Marine Biological Association of the UK, The Laboratory, Citadel Hill, Plymouth PL1 2PB (e-mail mikewhit@btinternet.com)

WHITFIELD, Patrick John; s of Albert Victor Whitfield (d 1978), and Rose Anna, *née* Maye (d 1971); *b* 7 November 1931; *Educ* Wandsworth Sch, King's Coll London, St George's Hosp Med Sch (MB BS, LRCP); *m* 23 July 1955, Doris Eileen, da of Herbert Nelson Humphries (d 1962); 2 da (Roseanne Louise (Mrs Paul Roblin) b 8 Sept 1968, Natalie Anne b 17 Nov 1975); *Career* jr hosp appts 1958–64, trained at Regnl Plastic Surgery Centre Queen Mary's Univ Hosp; sr registrar: seconded Plastic Surgery Centre Oxford 1966, Queen Mary's Univ Hosp 1967–72 (seconded to Paris, Rome, NY); conslt plastic surgn: Westminster Hosp and SW Thames RHA 1972, Royal London Hosp Tst 1996–; recognised teacher in plastic surgery Univ of London (Westminster and Charing Cross Hosps), Plastic Surgery Section RSM 1973–81 (hon sec, memb Cncl, vice-pres, pres), memb Res Ctee Br Assoc of Plastic Surgns 1974–77, hon sec Br Assoc of Aesthetic Plastic Surgns 1977–83; memb: Br Assoc of Plastic Surgns 1972, Br Assoc of Aesthetic Plastic Surgns 1978 (fndr); FRSM 1968, FRCS; *Books* Operative Surgery (contrib); *Recreations* golf, scuba-diving, tennis, art appreciation; *Clubs* Athenaeum, Royal Wimbledon Golf; *Style*— Patrick Whitfield, Esq; ✉ 40 Harley Street, London W1G 9PP (tel 020 7580 6283)

WHITFIELD, Prof Roderick; s of late Prof John Humphreys Whitfield, and Joan, *née* Herrin, ARCA; *b* 20 July 1937; *Educ* King Edward's Sch Birmingham, SOAS Univ of London, St John's Coll Cambridge (MA), Princeton Univ (MFA, PhD); *m* 1, 11 July 1963 (m dis 1983), Dr Frances Elizabeth, da of Prof Richard Charles Oldfield; 2 da (Martha-Ming b 1965, Tanya b 1967), 1 s (Aldus b 1970); m 2, 25 Aug 1983, Prof Youngsook Pak; *Career* Offr Cadet Jt Serv Sch for Linguists RAF 1955–57, PO RAFVR 1957, Flying Offr RAFVR; res assoc and lectr Princeton Univ 1964–66, res fell St John's Coll Cambridge 1966–68, asst keeper 1st class Dept of Oriental Antiquities Br Museum 1968–84, prof of Chinese and East Asian art Univ of London and head Percival David Fndn of Chinese Art 1984–93, Percival David chair of Chinese and East Asian art SOAS Univ of London 1993–2002 (prof emeritus 2002–); research fell Dunhuang Acad 1999–; memb Cncl Oriental Ceramic Soc 1984–93; fell Palace Museum Beijing 2003–, fell Royal Asiatic Soc 1999–; *Books* In Pursuit of Antiquity (1969), The Art of Central Asia, The Stein Collection at the British Museum (3 vols, 1982–85), Treasures From Korea (ed 1984), Korean Art Treasures (ed 1986), Caves of the Thousand Buddhas (1990), Fascination of Nature: Plants and Insects in Chinese Painting and Ceramics of the Yuan Dynasty 1279–1368 (1993), The Problem of Meaning in Early Chinese Ritual Bronzes (ed, 1993), Dunhuang, Caves of the Singing Sands: Buddhist Art from the Silk Road (2 vols, 1995), The Arts of Central Asia: the Pelliot Collection in the Musée Guimet (collaborative translator, 1996), The Golden Age of Chinese Archaeology (contrib, 1999), Exploring China's Past: New Discoveries and Studies in Archaeology and Art (jt ed and translator, 2000), Cave Temples of Mogao: Art and History on the Silk Road (jt author, 2000), La Sérinde, Terre d'échanges (contrib, 2000), Handbook of Korean Art: Earthenware and Celadon (jt author, 2002), Handbook of Korean Art: Buddhist Sculpture (jt author, 2002), Handbook of Korean Art: Folk Paintings (ed, 2002), New Perspectives on China's Past: Chinese Archaeology in the Twentieth Century (contrib, 2004), Compassion and Fascination (contrib, 2004), Korean True-View Landscape Paintings by Chŏng Sŏn (1676–1759) (jt trans and ed, 2005), Mei shou wan nian - Long Life Without End: Festschrift for Professor Roger Goepper on the occasion of his 80th birthday (contrib, 2006), From Nisa to Niya: New Discoveries and Studies in Central Inner Asian Art and Archaeology (contrib, 2007); *Style*— Prof Roderick Whitfield; ✉ Department of History of Art, Yale University, 56 High Street, New Haven CT 06520–8206, USA (e-mail rw5@soas.ac.uk)

WHITFIELD, Susan Margaret; da of Sir James Bottomley, KCMG, and Barbara, *née* Vardon (d 1994); sis of Peter Bottomley, MP, *qv*; *b* 23 November 1946; *Educ* Westonbirt Sch, New Hall Cambridge (MA); *m* 1; 3 da (Kitty (Kitty Ussher, MP, *qv*) b 1971, Charlotte (Mrs Nightingale) b 1973, Felicity (Mrs Murphy) b 1973); m 2, 1982, Robert Whitfield, s of Charles Kershaw Whitfield; 1 da (Poppy b 1983), 1 s (Jack b 1985); *Career* biology and sci teacher: Brooklands Co Secdy Sch 1968–69, Aylesbury HS 1969–72, The Misbourne Sch 1978–79, St Paul's Girls' Sch 1980–91; headmistress Notting Hill and Ealing HS (GDST) 1991–; involved with Multiple Births Fndn; Freeman the Worshipful Co of Drapers; assoc memb Inst of Biology; *Recreations* family, gardening; *Style*— Mrs Susan Whitfield; ✉ Notting Hill and Ealing High School, 2 Cleveland Road, London W13 8AX (tel 020 8799 8400)

WHITFORD, Dr Frank Peter; s of Percy Whitford, and Katherine Ellen, *née* Rowe (d 1996); *b* 11 August 1941; *Educ* Peter Symonds Coll Winchester, Wadham Coll Oxford (BA), Courtauld Inst (MA), Freie Universität Berlin, RCA (higher doctorate); *m* 1972, Cecilia Josephine, da of Stanley Dresser; *Career* contrib ed Studio International 1964–74, tutor Slade Sch of Art 1969–72, lectr in history of art Homerton Coll Cambridge 1972–86, sr memb Wolfson Coll Cambridge 1983–, tutor in cultural history RCA 1986–91, art critic Sunday Times 1991–93, writer, broadcaster and exhbn organiser; Hawthornden Prize for Art Criticism 1999; Cross of the Order of Merit (Germany) 2002; *Books* Japanese Prints and Western Painters (1977), Bauhaus (1983), Kokoschka - A Life (1986), Klimt (1991), The Berlin of George Grosz (1997), Kandinsky Watercolours (1999), and numerous others on 19/20th century art; *Recreations* cooking; *Clubs* Savile; *Style*— Frank Whitford, Esq

WHITING, Alan; s of Albert Edward Whiting, and late Marjorie Irene, *née* Rodgers; *b* 14 January 1946; *Educ* Acklam Hall Secdy GS Middlesbrough, UEA (BA), UCL (MSc); *m* 17 Aug 1968, Annette Frances, da of late James Kitchener Pocknee; 2 da (Alison Jane b 8 March 1976, Claire Louise b 17 Dec 1979), 2 s (Matthew Peter b 27 June 1977, Paul Michael b 11 Nov 1982); *Career* res assoc and asst lectr UEA 1967–68, cadet economist HM Treasy 1968–69, economic asst Dept of Econ Affairs and Miny of Technol 1969–70; economist: Euro Free Trade Assoc Geneva 1970–72, CBI 1972–73; DTI: econ advsr 1974–78, sr econ advsr 1979–83, Industrial and Commercial Policy Div 1983–85, under sec Economics Div 1985–88, Econ Mgmnt and Educn Div 1989, Fin and Resource Mgmnt Div 1989–92, Financial Services Div 1992; HM Treasy: under sec Securities and Investment Services Gp 1992–95, dep dir Financial Regulation 1995–97; exec dir regulation and compliance London Metal Exchange 1997–2004, chm and md Merlan Financial 2004–; dir Nymex (Europe) Ltd 2005–; dep chm Cncl The Mortgage Code Register of Intermediaries 1998–99, dep chm Mortgage Code Compliance Bd 2000–06, dir Banking Code Standards Bd 2005–, memb Gibraltar Financial Services Cmmn 2005–, dir Euronext/Liffe 2006–; *Books* The Trade Effects of EFTA and the EEC (jtly, 1972), The Economics of Industrial Subsidies (ed, 1975); *Recreations* building, gardening, sport, music; *Clubs* Bracknell Lawn Tennis, Mill Ride Golf (Ascot); *Style*— Alan Whiting, Esq; ✉ e-mail alan@whiting87.freeserve.co.uk

WHITING, Derek Alan; OBE (1991); s of William Thomas Whiting (d 1981), of Beckenham, Kent, and Gladys Dudfield Whiting (d 1970); *b* 2 August 1931; *Educ* Tonbridge; *m* 1, 5 June 1962, Lady Frances Esmee, *née* Curzon, da of 5 Earl Howe, PC (d 1964); 2 s (Francis b 1965, Alexander b 1967); m 2, 14 Dec 1972, Angela Clare Forbes, da of Sir Archibald Forbes, GBE, (d 1989); *Career* Nat Serv cmmnd The Buffs 1950, ADC to Govr and C-in-C Br Somaliland 1951, Actg Capt; commodity trading & broking 1952–90; underwriting memb Lloyds 1972–80; chm: Int Petroleum Exchange 1986–90, London Sugar Futures Mkt 1984–87, AFBD 1984–87, Comfin Trading Ltd 1980–89, Sucden (UK) Ltd 1980–90, Buckingham Asset Management 1992–95, Tonbridge Sch Appeal 1992–94; played rugby for Harlequins and Kent; Liveryman Worshipful Co of Skinners; *Recreations* shooting, golf, reading; *Clubs* Swinley Forest, Hurlingham, Harlequins (former chm and hon sec); *Style*— Derek Whiting, Esq, OBE; ✉ 4 Gertrude Street, London SW10 0JN (tel 020 7352 6220, fax 020 7351 1804)

WHITING, (David) John; s of Peter Whiting (d 1992), and Isabel, *née* Hall (d 2002); *b* 20 March 1951, Hull, E Yorks; *Educ* Hymers Coll Hull, Victoria Univ of Manchester (BSc); *m* 20 Aug 1977, Susan Barbara (Sue), da of Gwyn Jones (d 2001), and Joan Jones; 3 da (Carolyn Anne b 12 April 1986, Helen Frances b 14 May 1987, Fiona Christine b 6 Jan 1993); *Career* tax ptnr Price Waterhouse (now PricewaterhouseCoopers LLP) 1984– (joined 1972); Tax Personality of the Year 2001, Tax Writer of the Year 2004; memb: ICAEW 1975, Chartered Inst of Taxation 1978 (pres 2001–02); *Recreations* family life, DIY, history, Fairport Convention; *Clubs* MCC; *Style*— John Whiting, Esq; ✉ PricewaterhouseCoopers LLP, 1 Embankment Place, London WC2N 6RH (tel 020 7804 4422, e-mail john.whiting@uk.pwc.com)

WHITLAM, Michael Richard; CBE (2000); s of Richard William Whitlam (d 1971), and Mary Elizabeth, *née* Land (d 1983); *b* 25 March 1947; *Educ* Morley GS, Tadcaster GS, Coventry Coll of Educn, Univ of Warwick (CertEd), Cranfield Inst of Technol (MPhil); *m* 24 Aug 1968, Anne Jane, da of William McCurley (d 1987); 2 da (Rowena b 1971, Kirsty b 1973); *Career* former teacher Ripon Co GS; asst govr 1969–74: HM Borstal Hollesley Bay, HMP Brixton; dir: Hammersmith Teenager Project Nat Assoc of Care and Resettlement of Offenders, UK Ops Save The Children Fund 1978–86 (former dep dir); chief exec Royal Nat Inst for the Deaf 1986–90, DG British Red Cross Soc 1991–99, ceo Mentor Fndn International (preventing substance abuse among young people) 1999–2001 (conslt 2001–02), chief exec Int Agency for the Prevention of Blindness (IAPB) 2002–05; dir: Charity Appointments 1994–2000, MW Solutions for Charity 2005–; chm: London Intermediate Treatment Assoc 1979–82, Nat Intermediate Treatment Assoc 1980–83, Sound Advantage plc 1989–90, ACENVO 1988–91 (chm Policy Ctee 1994–99), Ofcom Advsy Ctee for Older and Disabled People 2004–; non-exec dir Hillingdon PCT 2004–; special advsr Russian GMS 2004–; memb: Exec Cncl Howard League 1974–84, Community Alternative Young Offenders Ctee NACRO 1979–82, Exec Cncl Nat Children's Bureau 1980–86, Bd REACH 1996–; former pres Strategic Planning Cmmn, pres Int Fedn of Red Cross and Red Crescent Socs 1997–99, memb Bd Prisoners Abroad; CCMI, FRSA; *Recreations* painting, walking, keeping fit, family activities, opera, management of the voluntary sector, member St Giles Church, sculpting; *Style*— Michael Whitlam, Esq, CBE, MPhil, CIMgt, FRSA; ✉ Solutions for Charity, 40 Pepys Close, Ickenham, Uxbridge, Middlesex UB10 8NY (tel and fax 01865 678169, e-mail m.whitlam@btinternet.com); Russam GMS Limited, 48 High Street North, Dunstable, Bedfordshire LU6 1LA

WHITLEY, Edward Thomas; s of John Caswell Whitley, of Hamsey, and Shirley Frances, *née* Trollope; *b* 6 May 1954; *Educ* Harrow, Univ of Bristol (BSc); *m* 15 June 1984, Hon Tara Olivia Chichester-Clark, da of Baron Moyola, PC, DL (Life Peer, d 2002); 1 s (James Edward Dawson b 17 Nov 1997); *Career* Price Waterhouse & Co 1976–81, Cazenove & Co 1981–2001 (ptnr 1988–2001), chief exec International Financial Services London (IFSL) 2001–; dir Henderson Strata Investments plc 1990–2005; tstee: Restoration of Appearance and Function Tst (RAFT), World Trade Center Disaster Fund 2001–06; pres S Derry Wildfowl and Game Preservation Soc; memb ICAEW 1980; *Style*— Edward Whitley, Esq; ✉ IFSL, 29–30 Cornhill, London EC3V 3NF

WHITMORE, Sir Clive Anthony; GCB (1988, KCB 1983), CVO 1983; s of Charles Arthur and Louisa Lilian Whitmore; *b* 18 January 1935; *Educ* Sutton GS, Christ's Coll Cambridge; *m* 1961, Jennifer Mary Thorpe; 1 s, 2 da; *Career* private sec to Perm Under Sec of State War Office 1961, asst private sec to Sec of State for War 1962, princ 1964, private sec to Perm Under Sec of State MOD 1969, asst sec 1971, asst under sec of state (Def Staff) MOD 1975, under sec Cabinet Office 1977, princ private sec to PM 1979–82, dep sec 1981, perm under sec of state MOD 1983–88, perm under sec of state Home Office 1988–94, ret; non-exec dir: Boots Co plc 1994–2001, Morgan Crucible Co plc 1994–2004, Racal Electronics plc 1994–2000, NM Rothschild & Sons Ltd 1994–; *Recreations* music, gardening; *Style*— Sir Clive Whitmore, GCB, CVO; ✉ Non-Executive Director, NM Rothschild & Sons Ltd, New Court, St Swithin's Lane, London EC4P 4DU

WHITMORE, Sir John Henry Douglas; 2 Bt (UK 1954), of Orsett, Co Essex; s of Col Sir Francis Henry Douglas Charlton Whitmore, 1 Bt, KCB, CMG, DSO, TD (d 1962, maternal gs of Sir William Cradock-Hartopp, 3 Bt, while his paternal grandmother was Lady Louisa Douglas, eldest da of 5 Marquess of Queensberry); *b* 16 October 1937; *Educ* Eton; *m* 1, 1962 (m dis 1969), Ella Gunilla, da of Sven A Hansson, of Danderyd, Sweden; 1 da; m 2, 1977, Diana Elaine, da of Fred A Becchetti, of Calif, USA; 1 s; *Heir* s, Jason Whitmore; *Career* mgmnt and sports psychologist, also concerned with psychology of int relations; author of books on the mental aspects of sport, life and work; *Books* Coaching for Performance, Need Greed or Freedom, Mind Games - Tennis; *Recreations* skiing, and being a tennis parent; *Clubs* British Racing Drivers; *Style*— Sir John Whitmore, Bt; ✉ Unit 6, Park Lane, Crowborough, East Sussex TN6 2QN (tel and fax 01892 611921, e-mail johnwhitmore@performanceconsultants.com)

WHITNEY, John Norton Braithwaite; s of Dr Willis Bevan Whitney, and Dorothy Anne, *née* Robertson; *b* 20 December 1930; *Educ* Leighton Park Sch Reading; *m* 9 June 1956, Roma Elizabeth (former dancer with London Festival Ballet), da of Gp Capt Isaac Hodgson; 1 da (Fiona b 17 Nov 1958), 1 s (Alexander b 31 Jan 1961); *Career* radio prodr 1951–64; fndr: Ross Radio Productions Ltd 1951, Autocue Ltd 1955, Radio Antilles 1963; fndr dir Sagitta Productions 1968–82; dir: Consolidated Productions (UK) Ltd 1980–82, Satellite TV plc 1982; md: Capital Radio 1973–82, Really Useful Gp Ltd 1989–90 (chm 1990–95); DG Ind Broadcasting Authy 1982–89, dir Friends Provident Life Office 1982–2002, chm Friends Provident Stewardship Ctee 1985–1999, non-exec chm Trans World Communications plc 1991–94, non-exec chm Friends Provident Ethical Investment Tst plc 1994–; chm: Sony Pace National Bowl 1991–95, Radio Joint Audience Research (RAJAR) Ltd 1992–2002, Sony Radio Awards 1992–98, Advsy Ctee Proven Global Rights Fund 1993–2004, The Radio Partnership 1996–99, Caspian Publishing 1996–2002, Forever Broadcasting plc 1999–2004, Friends Provident Charitable Fndn 2002–, RADA 2003–; non-exec dir VCI plc 1995–98; fndr Recidivists Anonymous Fellowship Tst 1962, co-fndr and chm Local Radio Assoc 1964, chm Assoc Ind Radio Contractors 1973–75 and 1980, dir Duke of York's Theatre 1979–82, memb Bd RNT 1982–94; Royal Coll of Music: memb Centenary Devpt Fund (formerly Appeal Ctee) 1982–94, chm Media and Events Ctee 1982–94; memb: Cncl Royal London Aid Soc 1966–90, Cncl Fairbridge Drake Soc (formerly Drake Fellowship) 1981, Intermediate Technol Gp 1982–85, Films TV and Video Advsy Ctee Br Cncl 1983–89, Industry and Commerce Liaison Ctee Royal Jubilee Tsts 1986–89 (memb Admin Cncl of Tsts 1981–85), Bd Open Coll 1987–89, Cncl for Charitable Support 1989–93, Bd City of London Sinfonia 1994–2001; chm of tstees: Soundaround (nat sound magazine for the blind) 1981–2001 (life pres 2000), Artsline 1983–2000 (life pres 2001); tstee Venture Tst 1982–86, patron MusicSpace Tst 1990, tstee Hospital Broadcasting Assoc 1993–; govr: English Nat Ballet (formerly London Festival Ballet) 1989–91, Performing Arts and Technol Sch 1992–2001; vice-chm Japan Festival 1991 (chm Japan Festival Media Ctee 1991–92), tstee Japan Festival Educn Tst 1992–2003; vice-pres: Cwlth Youth Exchange Cncl 1982–85, RNID 1988–2004; pres: London Marriage Guidance Cncl 1983–90, TV and Radio Industries Club 1985–86 (companion 1979–); chm: Theatre Investment Fund 1990–2001, Br American Arts Assoc 1992–95, RADA 2003 (chm Cncl 2003–07); chm of tstees Friends Provident Charitable Fndn 2004–06; hon memb BAFTA, FRTS (vice-pres 1986–89), fell Radio Acad 1997, Hon

FRCM, FRSA; *Recreations* chess, photography, sculpture; *Clubs* Garrick, Whitefriars, Pilgrims; *Style*— John N B Whitney, Esq; ✉ 39 Hill Street, London W1J 5NA (tel 020 7409 7332, e-mail john@johnwhitney.co.uk)

WHITNEY, Dr Paul Michael; s of John Henry Whitney (d 1980), of Bexhill, and Irene, *née* Tither; *b* 4 May 1948; *Educ* Judd Sch Tonbridge, Aston Univ (BSc, PhD (Physical Chemistry)), Cranfield Sch of Mgmnt (MBA); *m* 1971, Melanie Jane, da of Gordon E A Hounslow; 1 da (Natasha Louise *b* 12 March 1973), 2 s (Benjamin Paul *b* 10 Nov 1974, Jonathan Mark *b* 20 Sept 1977); *Career* paper mill tech mangr Courtaulds/CDC Swaziland 1974–79 (research chemist/mgmnt trainee 1972–74), with Industrial and Commercial Finance Corp (now 3i plc) 1980–83; CIN Management Ltd: venture capital dir 1984, venture capital md 1985, chm 1988–93, chief exec 1988–93; chm NatWest Private Equity and chief exec NatWest Investment Management Ltd 1993–96, chief exec Sun Life Asset Management Ltd 1996–98, chm and chief exec Parallel Ventures Managers Ltd 1998–; non-exec dir Phytopharm plc; *Recreations* windsurfing, motor sports; *Clubs* RAC; *Style*— Dr Paul Whitney; ✉ Parallel Ventures Managers Ltd, 49 St James's Street, London SW1A 1JT (tel 020 7600 9105, fax 020 7491 3372)

WHITSEY, Fred; *b* 18 July 1919; *m* 1947, Patricia Searle; *Career* ed Popular Gardening 1967–82 (asst ed 1948–64, assoc ed 1964–67); gardening corr: Sunday Telegraph 1961–71, Daily Telegraph 1971–2006; contrib Country Life and The Garden; vice-pres Royal Horticultural Soc 1996–; Gold Veitch Meml Medal 1979, Victoria Medal of Honour 1986, Garden Writers' Guild Lifetime Achievement Award 1994; *Books* Sunday Telegraph Gardening Book (1966), Fred Whitsey's Garden Calendar (1985), Garden for all Seasons (1986), The Garden at Hidcote (2007); *Recreations* music, gardening; *Style*— Fred Whitsey; ✉ Avens Mead, 20 Oast Road, Oxted, Surrey RH8 9DU

WHITSON, Sir Keith Roderick; kt (2002); s of William Cleghorn Whitson, and Ellen, *née* Wade; *b* 25 March 1943; *Educ* Alleyn's Sch Dulwich; *m* 26 July 1968, Sabine Marita, da of Ulrich Wiechert; 2 da (Claudia Sharon *b* 31 Aug 1971, Julia Caroline *b* 2 May 1973), 1 s (Mark James *b* 26 July 1980); *Career* HSBC Holdings plc: joined Hong Kong and Shanghai Banking Corporation 1961, mangr Frankfurt 1978–80, mangr Indonesia 1981–84, asst gen mangr fin Hong Kong 1985–87, ceo UK 1987–89, exec dir Marine Midland Banks Inc 1990–92, dep ceo Midland Bank 1992–94, gp dir 1994–2003, ceo Midland Bank plc 1994–98, gp ceo 1998–2003, dep chm Midland Bank 1998–2003, chm Merrill Lynch HSBC 2000–02, dep chm Supervisory Bd HSBC Trinkaus und Burkhardt Düsseldorf 1993–2003, dir HSBC Bank Argentina 1997–2003, dir HSBC Bank Canada 1998–2003, dir HSBC Bank USA 1998–2003, vice-chm HSBC North America Inc 2002–03; non-exec dir: FSA 1998–2003, Tetra Laval 2005–; FCIB; *Style*— Sir Keith Whitson

WHITTAKER, (Rosemary) Jane; da of Robert Charnock Whittaker, of Blackpool, Lancs, and Betty, *née* Howard; *b* 27 February 1955; *Educ* Queen Mary's Sch Lytham, Univ of Manchester (LLB); *m* 6 Aug 1987, Colin Michael Brown; *Career* articled clerk Manchester (admitted slr 1978), slr International Computers Ltd (ICL) 1982–88, ptnr Macfarlanes slrs 1988–; chair Cons Lawyers' Assoc 1995–98; memb: Law Soc (memb Cncl 1995–, chair Equal Opportunities Ctee 1996–99), Assoc of Women Slrs (chair 1994–95); *Books* The Role of Directors in the European Community (1992); *Recreations* swimming, theatre, entertaining and cooking; *Style*— Ms Jane Whittaker; ✉ Macfarlanes, 10 Norwich Street, London EC4A 1BD (tel 020 7831 9222, fax 020 7831 9607)

WHITTAKER, (Alan) Mark; s of Alan Whittaker, of Darwen, Lancs, and Jean, *née* Almond; *b* 17 April 1957; *Educ* John Ruskin HS Croydon, Univ of Durham (BA); *Children* 1 da (Daisy Ella May *b* 17 March 1998), 1 s (Jack Louis Mark *b* 14 Nov 2000); *Career* grad trainee Thomson Regnl Newspapers Newcastle upon Tyne 1979, reporter Lancashire Evening Telegraph 1980–82, BBC Radio Lancashire 1983–86, BBC Radio West Midlands 1986–88; presenter: Newsbeat BBC (Radio 1) 1988–96, Costing the Earth (Radio 4) 1994, Kershaw and Whittaker (Radio 5 Live) 1994–95, You & Yours (Radio 4) 1996–2002, Pick of the Week (Radio 4) 1998–2002, The World Today (World Service) 2003–; *Recreations* hiking, football, public houses; *Clubs* Blackburn Rovers FC, Kidderminster Harriers, Selborne Soc, Friends of Real Lancashire; *Style*— Mark Whittaker, Esq; ✉ 200 Meadvale Road, Ealing, London W5 1LT (tel 020 8810 4757)

WHITTAKER, Michael William Joseph; s of Harry Whittaker, of Dorchester, Dorset, and Hylda, *née* Roach; *b* 28 January 1941; *Educ* Normain Coll Chester, Miller Acad Thurso, Weymouth and Brunel Tech Coll Bristol; *m* 8 Aug 1972, Brenda Pauline, da of Thomas Marsh (d 1987), of Thurnscoe, S Yorks; 2 da (Helena Amanda *b* 7 March 1963, Lindsay Jane *b* 30 Dec 1974); *Career* self employed design conslt; private light aircraft projects, 6 aircraft designed and developed 1973–93, over 100 now flying; winner numerous design awards; CEng, MIMechE, FRAeS; *Recreations* restoration of vintage motorcycles, design and development of light aircraft; *Style*— Michael Whittaker, Esq; ✉ Appletree Cottage, Churchfield Road, Clayton, Doncaster, South Yorkshire DN5 7BZ (tel and fax 01977 643508, e-mail mikw@btinternet.com)

WHITTAKER, Nigel; *b* 1948; *Educ* Clare Coll Cambridge, Yale Law Sch; *Career* called to London Bar 1974; head Legal Dept Roche Products Ltd 1974–77, gen counsel British Sugar 1977–82, exec dir Kingfisher plc 1983–95 (joined 1982), UK chm Burson-Marsteller 1997–2000, UK chm Edelman Public Relations Worldwide 2000–03; chm: Retail Decisions plc 1996–2006, MTI Partners Ltd 1997–2002, Madisons Coffee plc (now Gourmet Holdings plc) 1998–, Texstyle World Ltd 1999–2001, Mettoni Gp plc 2000–02, Eagle Eye plc 2000–04; proprietor NW Corporate Affairs Consultancy 1995–; non-exec dir: Wickes plc 1996–2000, Gartmore Fledgling Tst 1998–; fndr and chm ReputationInc Ltd 2003–; chm: CBI's Distributive Trades Survey Panel 1987–94, Br Retail Consortium 1995; memb: UK Ecolabelling Bd 1992–98, London First 1998–2002; *Style*— Nigel Whittaker, Esq; ✉ e-mail nigelwhitt@aol.com

WHITTEMORE, Prof Colin Trengove; s of Hugh Ashcroft Whittemore (d 1983), of Mollington, Chester, and Dorothea, *née* Nance; *b* 16 July 1942; *Educ* Rydal Sch, Harper Adams Agric Coll, Univ of Newcastle upon Tyne (BSc, PhD, DSc, NDA, FIBiol); *m* 24 Sept 1966, Christine, da of John Leslie Featherstone Fenwick (d 1964), of Corbridge, Northumberland; 3 da (Joanna *b* 1970, Emma *b* 1976, Rebecca *b* 1985), 1 s (Jonathan *b* 1974); *Career* lectr in agric Univ of Edinburgh 1970–78, head of Animal Prodn Advsy and Devpt E of Scotland Coll of Agric 1978–84, head Animal Sci Div Edinburgh Sch of Agric 1984–90; Univ of Edinburgh: prof of animal prodn 1984–90, head Dept of Agric 1989–90, prof of agric and rural economy 1990–, head Inst of Ecology and Resource Mgmnt 1990–2000, postgrad dean 1992–2007; Sir John Hammond Prize, RASE Gold medal, Mignini Oscar and David Black award for scientific contribs and res; pres BSAS 1998; FRSE; *Books* Practical Pig Nutrition (with F W H Elsley, 1976), Lactation (1980), Pig Production (1980), Pig Science (1987), The Science and Practice of Pig Production (1993, 3 edn 2006); *Recreations* skiing, horses; *Clubs* Farmers'; *Style*— Prof Colin Whittemore, FRSE; ✉ e-mail c.t.whittemore@ed.ac.uk

WHITTINGDALE, John Flasby Lawrance; OBE (1990), MP; s of John Whittingdale (d 1974), and Margaret Esmé Scott, *née* Napier; *b* 16 October 1959; *Educ* Winchester, UCL (BSc); *m* 1990, Ancilla Campbell Murfitt; 1 s (Henry John Flasby *b* 26 May 1993), 1 da (Alice Margaret Campbell *b* 20 Dec 1995); *Career* head of political section Cons Res Dept 1982–84, special advsr to sec of state for Trade and Indust 1984–87, mangr NM Rothschild 1987, political sec to Rt Hon Margaret Thatcher as PM 1988–90 and mangr of her private office 1990–92; MP (Cons): Colchester S and Maldon 1992–97, Maldon and Chelmsford E 1997–; PPS to Eric Forth, MP (min of state DfEE) until 1996, memb Parly Health Select Ctee 1993–97, oppn whip 1997–98, oppn frontbench spokesman on Treasy affrs 1998–99, PPS to Ldr of the Oppn 1999–2001, shadow sec of state for trade and

industry 2001–02, shadow sec of state for culture, media and sport 2002–03, shadow sec of state for agriculture, fisheries and food 2003–04, shadow sec of state for culture, media and sport 2004–05, memb Exec Cons 1922 Ctee 2005–, chm Parly Culture Media and Sport Select Ctee 2005–; sec Cons Parly Home Affairs Ctee 1992–94, Parly memb Bd Cons Pty 2006–, vice-chm Cons Parly 1922 Ctee 2006–; memb: Selsdon Gp, Br Mensa; *Clubs* Essex; *Style*— John Whittingdale, Esq, OBE, MP; ✉ House of Commons, London SW1A 0AA (tel 020 7219 3557, fax 020 7219 2522, e-mail jwhittingdale.mp@tory.org.uk)

WHITTINGHAM, Prof David Gordon; s of Percy Phillip Gordon Whittingham (d 1974), of Monmouthshire, and Eurena Jane, *née* Parry (d 1995); *b* 5 June 1938; *Educ* UCL (BSc), RVC London (BVetMed), Univ of London (PhD, DSc), Univ of Cambridge (MA); *m* 15 July 1967, Nancy Gayle Wynne, da of William Lawrence Saunders, of Philadelphia, USA; 3 da (Leah Katharine, Emma Wynne, Mary Alison); *Career* Fulbright travelling scholarship Univ of Pennsylvania 1963, research fell Dept of Animal Biology Sch of Veterinary Med Univ of Pennsylvania 1965–66 (research instr 1963–64); postdoctoral fell: Dept of Population Dynamics Johns Hopkins Sch of Hygiene Baltimore 1966–67, Dept of Veterinary Physiology Univ of Sydney 1968–69; asst dir of research Physiological Lab Cambridge Jan 1973–74 (Beit Meml research fell 1969–72), scientific staff MRC Mammalian Devpt Unit UCL 1974–81, dir MRC Experimental Embryology and Teratology Unit (MRC Labs Carshalton Surrey then St George's Hosp Med Sch London) 1981–97 (chm Ctee of Dirs MRC Labs Carshalton 1984–88), prof of experimental embryology Univ of London 1990–97 (memb Bd of Veterinary Studies 1982–2000, memb Bd of Studies in Anatomy and Morphology 1989–98), prof of reproductive biology Univ of Hawaii 1999–2004; visiting prof Dept of Obstetrics and Gynaecology Monash Univ Melbourne 1980; memb Human Fertilization and Embryology Authy 1990–93, hon member and examiner Assoc of Clinical Embryologists Inst of Biology 1995–99, treas Br Fulbright Scholars Assoc 1996–98, tstee Progress Educnl Tst 1996– (chair of tst 2005–); memb: Fertility Sub-Ctee Royal Coll of Obstetrics and Gynaecology, Int Cell Research Orgn, Soc of Scholars Johns Hopkins Univ Baltimore 1988; hon conslt Survival Serv Cmmn IUCN (Genome Specialist Gp); invited speaker and papers presented at numerous scientific meetings worldwide; memb Editorial Bd: Theriogenology, Reproduction and Development, Reproduction, Development and Fertility, Jl of Reproduction and Development; chm Cncl of Mgmnt Jl of Reproduction and Fertility Ltd 1998–2001; Canada Dept of Agric Award for basic contribs to animal science 1979, Samuel Weiner Distinguished Award Univ of Manitoba Winnepeg 1986; membership of learned socs incl: Br Soc for Developmental Bology, Soc for Cryobiology (USA), American Soc for Reproductive Med; hon memb: Soc for Reproduction and Fertility, ACE; FRCVS 1973, FRSM 1978, FIBiol 1982, FRSA 1997; *Recreations* sailing, gardening, walking, travel, reading; *Clubs* Athenaeum; *Style*— Prof David Whittingham; ✉ Orchard House, Llanvair Kilgeddin, Abergavenny, Monmouthshire; 5 Wildcroft Manor, Putney, London SW15 3TS (tel 020 8789 3368, fax 020 8785 2203, e-mail d.whittingham@sgul.ac.uk)

WHITTINGHAM, Michael (Mike); s of Francis Sadler Whittingham (d 1972), of London, and Jean Mary, *née* Tarlton (d 1989); *b* 11 June 1954; *Educ* Alleyn's Sch Dulwich, Univ of Leicester (BA, MA), Loughborough Univ (PGCE); *m* Christine Paterson, da of Alexander McMeekin; *Career* athletics coach; memb Herne Hill Harriers; represented: London Schs, English Schs, Surrey Co, Southern Cos, Br Univs, 25 GB caps (400m hurdles, 800m, 4 x 400m); best performances: semi-final Euro Indoor Championships 1981, fourth Cwlth Games 1982; nat sr event coach 400m 1990– (jr event coach 400m hurdles 1987–88), exec dir Scottish Inst of Sport 2006–; coached athlets incl: Jon Rigeon, Roger Black, Kriss Akabusi, John Regis, Marcus Adam, Christine McMeekin, Jacqui Parker, Mark Richardson, Mark Hylton, Maria Akara, Nicola Sanders 2004–06 (Bronze medallist World Championships 2005, Gold medallist Cwlth Games 2006); Post Office Counters Coach of the Year 1992; lectr Univ of Lyon 1978–80, teacher 1980–85, dir of sport and physical educn Univ of Reading 1985–88, head of leisure servs Waverley BC 1988–92, Direction Sportive (sports mgmnt & devpt co) 1992–, dir of tech servs UKSport 2003–, exec dir Scottish Inst of Performance Sport 2006–; radio commentator BBC Radio and BBC World Service 1991–; Minister's nominee on Regnl Cncl Sports Cncl 1993–96; expert advsr: UK Sports Cncl, UK Sports Cncl Lottery Unit; conslt IAAF; Winston Churchill fell 1990; memb: Inst of Leisure Amenity Mgmnt, BASC, Nat Tst, UK/SA Initiative; *Recreations* languages, piano, reading, arts, natural history, recreational sport; *Style*— Mike Whittingham, Esq; ✉ Rhodens, The Green, Sands, Farnham, Surrey GU10 1LL

WHITTINGTON, Prof Geoffrey; CBE (2001); s of Bruce Whittington (d 1988), and Dorothy Gwendoline, *née* Gent (d 1996); *b* 21 September 1938; *Educ* Sir Roger Manwood's GS, Dudley GS, LSE, Fitzwilliam Coll Cambridge; *m* 7 Sept 1963, Joyce Enid, da of George Smith (d 1963); 2 s (Alan Geoffrey *b* 1972, Richard John *b* 1976); *Career* res posts Dept of Applied Economics Cambridge 1962–72, fell Fitzwilliam Coll Cambridge 1966–72; prof of accountancy and finance: Univ of Edinburgh 1972–75, Univ of Bristol 1975–88, Univ of Bristol: head of Dept of Economics 1981–84, dean Faculty of Social Sciences 1985–87; PriceWaterhouseCoopers prof of fin accounting Univ of Cambridge 1988–2001 (emeritus prof 2001–), fell Fitzwilliam Coll Cambridge 1988–; professorial res fell ICAS 1996–2001; memb: MMC 1987–96, Accounting Standards Bd 1994–2001, Advsy Body on Fair Trading in Telecommunications 1997–98, Int Accounting Standards Bd 2001–; Founding Societies' Centenary Award ICAEW 2003; Hon DSc Univ of Edinburgh 1998; FCA 1973 (ACA 1963); *Books* Growth Profitability and Valuation (with A Singh, 1968), The Prediction of Profitability (1971), Inflation Accounting (1983), The Debate on Inflation Accounting (with D Tweedie, 1984), The Elements of Accounting (1992), Profitability, Accounting Theory and Methodology (2007); *Recreations* music, walking; *Clubs* Athenaeum; *Style*— Prof Geoffrey Whittington, CBE; ✉ Fitzwilliam College, Cambridge CB3 0DG (e-mail gw12@cam.ac.uk)

WHITTLE, Prof Martin John; *b* 6 July 1944; *Educ* William Grimshaw Secdy Modern Sch London, Southgate Tech Coll London, Univ of Manchester Med Sch (MB ChB, FRCOG, MD); *Career* house physician then house surgn Manchester Royal Infirmary 1972–73; clinical tutor Univ Hosp of S Manchester 1976–77, research fell LAC-USC Med Center Women's Hosp Los Angeles Calif 1978–79, conslt obstetrician Queen Mother's Hosp Glasgow and conslt gynaecologist Royal Samaritan Hosp for Women Glasgow 1982–91, dir of fetal med Univ Dept of Midwifery Queen Mother's Hosp Glasgow 1986–91; Univ of Birmingham: prof of fetal med Birmingham Women's Hosp 1991–2006, dir Div of Reproductive & Child Health 1998–2003, associate dean (Educn) 2004–06, emeritus prof 2006–; clinical co-dir NCC-WCH RCOG 2006–; memb: Scientific Advsy and Pathology Ctee RCOG 1983–86, Working Gp on Infertility Servs in Scotland 1989–90, MRC Working Pty on Phenylketonuria 1991–92, Subspecialist Bd RCOG 1989–92, Birthright/RCOG Research Ctee 1991, RCOG Working Pty on Down's Screening 1992; chm Standing Jt Ctee RCOG and RCR 1993–96 (memb 1987–90, vice-chm 1990–93), fell Cncl RCOG 1997–2002; chm Antenatal Sub-Gp Nat Screening Ctee 2000–05; memb Editorial Bd: Prenatal Diagnosis 1990–; memb: Blair Bell Research Soc, Perinatal Club, Int Fetoscopy Working Gp, Gynaecological Visiting Soc; FRCPGlas 1987 (MRCPGlas 1985), FRCOG 1988; *Books* Prenatal Diagnosis in Obstetric Practice (with Prof J M Connor, 1989, 2 edn 1995), Fetal Medicine: Basic Science and Clinical Practice (with C H Rodeck, 1999); *Publications* author of various book chapters and numerous articles; *Recreations* flying (PPL), keen sailor, scuba-diving, enjoying classical music and art; *Style*— Prof Martin Whittle; ✉ NCC-WCH, RCOG, 27 Sussex Place, Regents Park, London NW1 4RG

WHITTLE, Stephen Charles; OBE (2006); s of Charles William Whittle, and Vera Lillian, *née* Moss; *b* 26 July 1945; *Educ* St Ignatius Coll Stamford Hill, UCL (LLB); *m* 1, 1988 (m dis 1999), Claire Walmsley, *née* Slavin; m 2, 2004, Eve Salomon; *Career* asst ed New Christian 1968–70; World Cncl of Churches Geneva: communications offr 1970–73, ed One World 1973–77, asst head Communications Dept 1975–77; BBC: sr prodr Religious Progs Manchester 1977–82, prodr Newsnight 1982, ed Songs of Praise and Worship 1983–89, head of religious programmes 1989–93, chief advsr on editorial policy 1993–96; dir: Broadcasting Standards Cncl April 1996–97, Broadcasting Standards Commission 1997–2001 (following merger with Broadcasting Complaints Cmmn in 1997); controller editorial policy BBC 2001–06; memb Bd Slrs Regulation Authy; chm Broadcasting Trg and Skills Regulator; govr Euro Inst for the Media 1998–2004; Freeman City of London 1990; FRSA; *Recreations* cinema, theatre, music, reading; *Style*— Stephen Whittle, Esq, OBE; ✉ Flat 4, 34A Sydenham Hill, London SE26 6LS (tel 020 8299 8898, e-mail stephen_whittle@btopenworld.com)

WHITTLESEA, Michael Charles; s of Sydney Charles Whittlesea (d 1982), of London, and Rose, *née* Grimshaw; *b* 6 June 1938; *Educ* Harrow Sch of Art (Nat Dip Design); *m* 1 June 1963, Jill Diana, da of Leslie Gilbert Henry Morris; *Career* artist; exhibitions incl: World of Newspapers Exhibition (prize winner, Sothebys and Royal Acad), Royal Acad Summer Exhibition 1985–88, The Singer and Friedlander Sunday Times Watercolour Exhibition 1987–95 (prize winner 1991), Drawing Matters (Bankside Gallery) 1995; work in public collections incl Bury Art Gallery & Museum; RWS, NEAC; *Awards* Painter Stainers Award 1985, selected Hunting Gp Awards 1985; *Books* The Complete Water Colour Course, The Complete Step by Step Watercolour Course; *Clubs* Chelsea Arts; *Style*— Michael Whittlesea, Esq; ✉ 98 Defoe House, Barbican, London EC2Y 8ND (tel 020 7628 0149)

WHITTY, Prof Geoffrey James (Geoff); s of Frederick James Whitty (d 1981), and Kathleen May, *née* Lavender (d 1968); *b* 31 December 1946; *Educ* Latymer Upper Sch, St John's Coll Cambridge, Inst of Educn Univ of London; *Career* teacher secondary schs 1969–73, lectr Univ of Bath 1973–80, lectr KCL 1981–84, prof and dean Bristol Poly 1985–89, Goldsmiths' prof Goldsmiths Coll London 1990–92; Inst of Educn Univ of London: Karl Mannheim prof 1992–2000, dir 2000–; Hon DEd UWE 2001; hon fell Coll of Teachers 2001; FRSA 1999; *Books* Society, State and Schooling (jtly, 1977), Sociology and School Knowledge (1985), State and Private Education (jtly, 1989), Specialisation and Choice in Urban Education (jtly, 1993), Devolution and Choice in Education (jtly, 1998), Teacher Education in Transition (jtly, 2000), Making Sense of Education Policy (2002), Education and the Middle Class (jtly, 2003); *Recreations* travel, reading, politics, football; *Style*— Prof Geoff Whitty; ✉ Institute of Education, 20 Bedford Way, London WC1H 0AL (tel 020 7612 6004, fax 020 7612 6089, mobile 07887 853679, e-mail g.whitty@ioe.ac.uk)

WHITTY, Baron (Life Peer UK 1996), of Camberwell in the London Borough of Southwark; (John) Lawrence Whitty; PC (2005); s of Frederick James Whitty (d 1981), and Kathleen May Whitty (d 1967); *b* 15 June 1943; *Educ* Latymer Upper Sch, St John's Coll Cambridge; *m* 1, 11 Jan 1969 (m dis 1986), Tanya Margaret, da of Tom Gibson, of South Shields; 2 s (Hon Michael Sean b 1970, Hon Daniel James b 1972); m 2, 1 June 1993, Angela, da of James Forrester, of Glasgow; *Career* Hawker Siddeley 1962; Civil Serv 1965–70, Miny of Aviation, UKAEA, Miny of Technol; Economics Dept TUC 1970–73, nat research and political offr GMB (formerly Gen and Municipal Workers Union) 1973–85, gen sec Lab Pty 1985–94 (Euro sec 1994–97); a Lord in Waiting (Govt whip) 1997–98, Parly under-sec of state Dept for Environment, Food and Rural Affrs (formerly DETR) 1998–2005; chair Nat Consumer Cncl 2006–; memb: Bd Ofwat 2006, Bd Environment Agency 2006–; memb: Lab Pty (Islington, Greenwich, Dulwich, Battersea, Peckham, Westminster S, N Dorset), Fabian Soc; Friends of the Earth; *Recreations* swimming, walking, theatre; *Style*— The Lord Whitty

WHITWORTH, John Vincer; s of Hugh Hope Aston Whitworth, MBE (d 1996), of Strawberry Hill, Middlesex, and Elizabeth, *née* Boyes (d 1959); *b* 11 December 1945; *Educ* Royal HS Edinburgh, Merton Coll Oxford (MA, BPhil), Univ of Edinburgh; *m* 2 Aug 1975, Doreen Ann, da of Cecil Roberts; 2 da (Eleanor Ruth b 1 Jan 1984, Catherine Rebecca b 20 March 1987); *Career* poet; teacher of: English Colchester English Studies Centre 1970–71, business studies and economics Centre of Economic and Political Studies 1971–82 (exec dir until 1982); reviewer Poetry Review and The Spectator, poetry broadcast on BBC TV 1994 and 1995; *Awards* Alice Hunt Bartlett Award of the Poetry Soc 1980, South East Arts Award 1980, Observer Book of the Year (for Poor Butterflies) 1982, Barbara Campion Meml Prize 1983, prizewinner National Poetry Competition 1984, Cholmondeley Award for Poetry 1988; *Books* Unhistorical Fragments (1980), Poor Butterflies (1982), Lovely Day for a Wedding (1985), Tennis and Sex and Death (1989), The Faber Book of Blue Verse (ed, 1990), Landscape With Small Humans (1993), The Complete Poetical Works of Phoebe Flood (1996), From the Sonnet History of Modern Poetry (illustrated by Gerald Mangan, 1999); *Recreations* cooking, playing with my daughters, suffering with the England cricket team, rearing guinea-pigs; *Style*— John Whitworth, Esq; ✉ 20 Lovell Road, Rough Common, Canterbury, Kent CT2 9DG (tel 01227 462400)

WHORWELL, Professor Peter James; s of Arthur Victor Whorwell, of Canterbury, and Beryl Elizabeth, *née* Walton; *b* 14 June 1946; *Educ* Dover Coll, Univ of London (BSc, MB BS, MD); *Career* conslt physician and prof of med Univ of Manchester 1981–; dir S Manchester Functional Gastrointestinal Diseases Serv, med advsr Int Fndn for Functional Gastrointestinal Disorders, memb Euro Expert Panel for Functional Gastrointestinal Disorders, med conslt to many pharmaceutical cos; numerous pubns on gastrointestinal diseases; memb: Br Soc Gastroenterology, American Gastroenterology Assoc; MRCS, FRCP; *Style*— Prof Peter Whorwell; ✉ Academic Department of Medicine, Wythenshawe Hospital, Manchester M23 9LT (tel 0161 291 5813, e-mail peter.whorwell@smuht.nwest.nhs.uk)

WHYBROW, Christopher John; QC (1992); s of Herbert William Whybrow, OBE (d 1973), of Colchester, Essex, and Ruby Kathleen, *née* Watson (d 1996); *b* 7 August 1942; *Educ* Colchester Royal GS, KCL (LLB); *m* 1, 11 Sept 1969 (m dis 1976), Marian, da of John Macaulay (decd), of Ramsey, Essex; m 2, 4 April 1979 (m dis 1990), Susan, da of Edward Christie Younge (decd), of Loddiswell, Devon; *Career* called to the Bar Inner Temple 1965; dep social security cmmr 1996–; *Recreations* history, cricket, tennis, gardening, country life; *Clubs* MCC, Lansdowne; *Style*— Christopher Whybrow, Esq, QC; ✉ Landmark Chambers, 180 Fleet Street, London EC4A 2HG

WHYBROW, John William; s of Charles Ernest James Whybrow (d 1980), and Doris Beatrice, *née* Abbott (d 1982); *b* 11 March 1947; *Educ* Imperial Coll London (BSc), Manchester Business Sch (MBA); *m* 19 Oct 1968, Paula, *née* Hobart; 1 s (Mark Charles b 13 April 1972), 1 da (Andrea Patricia b 3 June 1975); *Career* various posts: Philips Components 1983–86, Philips Semiconductors 1986–88; md TDS Circuits plc 1988–90, technical dir Philips Components 1990–93, chm Philips Electrical UK 1993–95, ceo Philips Lighting 1995–2001, bd dir Philips NV 1997–2002, chm Wolseley plc 2002–, chm CSR plc 2004–07; non-exec dir Dixons plc 2003–; chm Petworth Cottage Nursing Home 2002–; Freeman Worshipful Co of Information Technologists; Order of Merit (Poland); ACGI; *Recreations* sailing; *Clubs* East India; *Style*— John Whybrow, Esq; ✉ Wolseley plc, Parkview 1220, Arlington Business Park, Theale, Reading, Berkshire RG7 4GA (tel 0118 929 8700, fax 0118 929 8701, mobile 07736 478632, e-mail john.whybrow@wolseley.com)

WHYMAN, Erica; da of Michael Whyman, of Walton-on-Thames, Surrey, and Jacqueline, *née* Patrick (d 2003); *b* 27 October 1969, Harrogate, Yorks; *Educ* Wadham Coll Oxford (BA), Bristol Old Vic Theatre Sch, Ecole Philippe Gaulier Paris; *Career* theatre dir; assoc prodr Tricycle 1997–98, assoc dir English Touring Theatre 1998–2000, artistic dir Southwark Playhouse 1999–2001 (Peter Brook Empty Space Award), artistic dir and chief exec Gate Theatre 2001–04, chief exec Northern Stage 2005–; prodns incl: A Shadow of a Boy (RNT), The Birthday Party (Sheffield Crucible), Son of Man (Northern Stage), Ruby Moon (Northern Stage); awarded John S Cohen bursary for dirs; fell Clore Leadership Prog; *Style*— Ms Erica Whyman; ✉ Northern Stage, Barras Bridge, Newcastle upon Tyne NE1 7RH (tel 0191 242 7210, fax 0191 261 8093, e-mail ewhyman@northernstage.co.uk); c/o Clare Vidal-Hall, 57 Carthew Road, London W6 0DU (tel 020 8741 7647, fax 020 8741 9459, e-mail info@clarevidalhall.com)

WHYTE, Andrew Malcolm Dorrance; s of Rev Canon Malcolm Dorrance Whyte (d 2003), of Tarleton, Lancs, and Margaret, *née* Aindow (d 1983); *b* 4 June 1960; *Educ* Merchant Taylors' Crosby, Univ of Manchester (BA); *m* July 1987, Michele Rose, da of late Anthony Wickett; 1 s (James b 10 May 1989), 1 da (Leah b 4 Nov 1992); *Career* general sec Univ of Manchester Students' Union 1982–83, vice-pres Education NUS 1985–86, youth rights offr British Youth Cncl 1986–88, media and Parly liaison mangr Barnardo's 1988–91, dep dir of Corp Affrs News Int plc 1991–96, external affrs advsr Shell International Ltd 1996–98, head of PR BBC Broadcast 1998–2000, head of corporate and public relations BBC 2000–05, exec dir advocacy and communications Arts Cncl England 2006–; cncllr London Borough of Redbridge 1990–94; memb: Labour Party, Bd Thames Reach Bondway Housing Assoc 1998–; tstee Media Tst 2001–; memb Cncl RTS 2004–; MIPR 1992; FRSA 2006; *Recreations* spending time with my family, football (lifelong supporter of Liverpool FC), reading, politics and current affairs; *Style*— Andrew Whyte, Esq; ✉ Arts Council England, 14 Great Peter Street, London SW1P 3NQ (tel 020 7973 5129, fax 020 7973 6590)

WHYTE, Donald; JP (City of Edinburgh); s of late John Whyte, and late Catherine Dunachie; *b* 26 March 1926; *Educ* Crookston Sch Musselburgh, Inst of Heraldic and Genealogical Studies Canterbury; *m* 1950, Mary (d 1977), da of George Laird Burton; 3 da; *Career* conslt genealogist, author; contrib to numerous academic jls; pres Assoc of Scot Genealogists and Record Agents 1981–; vice-pres: Scot Genealogy Soc 1983–, family history socs at Glasgow, Aberdeen and Dundee; memb: Scot History Soc 1956–, Scot Record Soc 1970–, Scot Records Assoc 1978–, Genealogical Assoc of Nova Scotia 1983–; life memb W Lothian History and Amenity Soc 1969–; granted armorial bearings Lyon Office 1986; Citation of Recognition Ontario Genealogical Soc 1987; FHG, Hon FSG; *Books* Kirkliston: A Parish History (latest edn, 1991), Dictionary of Scottish Emigrants to the USA pre-1855 (1972, reprinted 1981, Vol 2 1986), Introducing Genealogical Research (5 edn 1985), Dictionary of Scottish Emigrants to Canada Before Confederation (1986, Vol 2 1995, Vol 3 2002), Walter MacFarlane: Clan Chief and Antiquary (1988), The Scots Overseas: A Selected Bibliography (1995), Scottish Clock and Watch Makers, 1453–1900 (1996), Scottish Surnames and Families (1996), Scottish Forenames (1996, 2 edn 2005), Clock and Watchmakers of Edinburgh and the Lothians (2001); booklets covering clock and watchmakers of other Scottish areas; *Recreations* heraldry; *Style*— Donald Whyte, Esq; ✉ 4 Carmel Road, Kirkliston, West Lothian EH29 9DD (tel 0131 333 3245)

WICKENS, Prof Alan Herbert; OBE (1980); s of Leslie Herbert Wickens (d 1986), of Birmingham, and Sylvia Amelia, *née* Hazelgrove (d 1968); *b* 29 March 1929; *Educ* Ashville Coll Harrogate, Loughborough Univ of Technol (DLC, DSc), Univ of London (BSc); *m* 1, 12 Dec 1953, Eleanor Joyce Waggott (d 1984); 1 da (Valerie Joanne b 1958); m 2, 2 July 1987, Patricia Anne McNeil, da of Willoughby Gervaise Cooper, of Dawlish; *Career* res engr: Sir W G Armstrong Whitworth Aircraft Ltd 1951–55, Canadair Ltd Montreal 1955–59, A V Roe & Co Ltd 1959–62; BR: Res Dept 1962–68, dir of advanced projects 1968–71, dir of res 1971–84, dir of engrg devpt and res 1984–89; Dept of Mechanical Engrg Loughborough Univ of Technol: industrial prof 1972–76 and 1992–, prof of dynamics 1989–92; visiting prof Manchester Met Univ 1998–2001; writer of various pubns on dynamics of railway vehicles, high speed trains and railway technol; jt winner Macrobert award 1975; pres Int Assoc of Vehicle System Dynamics 1981–86, hon fell Derbyshire Coll of Higher Educn 1984, chm Office of Research and Experiment Union Internationale de Chemin de Fer Utrecht 1988–90; hon memb Int Assoc for Vehicle System Dynamics 2001; Hon DTech CNAA 1978, Hon Dr Open Univ 1980, hon DRTech Univ of Loughborough 2006; MAIAA 1958, MRAeS 1963, FIMechE 1971, FREng 1980; *Recreations* gardening, travel, music; *Clubs* RAF; *Style*— Prof Alan Wickens, OBE, FREng; ✉ Wolfson School of Mechanical and Manufacturing Engineering, Loughborough University, Loughborough LE11 3TU (tel 01509 223201, fax 01509 232029)

WICKENS, Mark; s of Robert Wickens, of Berkhamsted, Herts, and Pat Wickens; *b* 23 November 1959; *Educ* Dr Challoner's GS Amersham, Kingston Poly (BA); *m* Anne; 2 da (Hannah b 20 Jan 1992, Polly b 27 May 1995); *Career* formerly design gp head Michael Peters Gp (clients incl: Bass, BA, ITV, Seagram), fndr Wickens Tutt Southgate 1989 (clients incl: Britvic, Smithkline Beecham, Unilever), fndr Brandhouse 1999 (clients incl: Diamond Trading Co, GlaxoSmithKline, Unilever); memb D&AD; 3 Design Effectiveness Awards, 4 Design Week Awards, D&AD Silver Award; FRSA; *Publications* Total Branding by Design (contrib), First Choice: The World's Leading Designers Discuss Their Work; *Recreations* jazz guitar and cooking; *Style*— Mark Wickens, Esq; ✉ Brandhouse, 10A Frederick Close, London W2 2HD (tel 020 7262 1707, fax 020 7262 1512, e-mail mw@brandhouse.co.uk)

WICKENS, Prof Michael; s of Dennis R Wickens (d 1967), and Edith (d 1993); *b* 2 September 1940; *Educ* LSE (BSc Econ, MSc Econ); *m* 1964, Julia Ruth, *née* Parrott; 1 da (Sarah Louise b 1965), 2 s (Stephen Michael b 1967, Matthew Dennis Roden b 1969); *Career* prof of economics: Univ of Southampton 1979–90, London Business Sch 1990–93, Univ of York 1993–; special advsr House of Lords Ctee on the Monetary Policy Ctee 1999–2001, special advsr House of Lords Economic Affrs Ctee 2001–, chm HM Treasy Academic Panel 1999–, managing ed The Economic Jl 1996–2004, assoc ed for numerous academic jls; conslt IMF 2000–; memb: Econometric Soc 1964–, Royal Economic Soc 1969– (memb Exec Ctee 2006–); Houblon-Norman fell Bank of England 1994, Erskine fell Univ of Canterbury 2001; *Publications* Exercises in Econometrics (with P C B Phillips, 1978), Handbook of Applied Econometrics (with M H Pesaran, 1997); various articles in learned jls; *Recreations* music, golf; *Clubs* Fulford Golf; *Style*— Professor Michael Wickens; ✉ Department of Economics and Related Studies, University of York, Heslington, York YO1 5DD (tel 01904 433764, fax 01904 433575, e-mail mike.wickens@york.ac.uk)

WICKER-MIURIN, Fields; da of Warren Jake and Marie Peachee Wicker; *b* 30 July 1958; *Educ* Univ of Virginia (BA cum laude), Johns Hopkins Univ Sch of Advanced Int Studies (MA), l'Institut d'Etudes Politiques Paris, Jagiellonian Univ Kraków; *m* Prof P Miurin; *Career* mangr Southern Europe Philadelphia National Bank 1982–89, ptnr and head of European financial servs practice Strategic Planning Associates 1989–94, dir of fin and strategy London Stock Exchange 1994–97, ptnr, vice-pres and head of global financial markets AT Kearney 1998–2000, chief operating offr and ptnr Vesta Capital Advsrs Ltd 2000–02, co-fndr and ptnr Leaders' Quest 2002–; non-exec dir: United Business Media plc 1998–2004, Savills plc 2002–, Royal London Gp 2003–06, D Carnegie & Co AB 2003–, CDC Gp 2004–; memb: Technol Adsvy Ctee NASDAQ NY 2000–, Exec Bd DTI 2002– (chair Investment Ctee 2002–06), Panel of Experts of Economic and Monetary Affrs Ctee AM Ctee European Parl 2002–06; tstee: London International Festival of Theatre 1997–2004, Arts & Business 1998–2001, London Musici 2000–03, Brogdale Tst 2002–04; memb Cncl Tate Membs 2000–06; govr KCL 2002– (chair Audit Ctee); lectr and publishes on a range of business and leadership related subjects; World Economic Forum Global Leader for Tomorrow, Euromoney Top 50 Women in Finance, one of Time Magazine's

W

14 Europeans to shape the future of Europe; memb, FORUM; FRSA 1997; *Clubs* Athanaeum, Lansdowne; *Style—* Mrs Fields Wicker-Miurin; ✉ Leaders' Quest, 1a Blake Mews, Kew, Richmond-upon-Thames, Surrey TW9 3GA

WICKHAM, Prof Christopher John; s of Cyril George Wickham (d 1992), and Katharine Brenda Warington, *née* Moss; *b* 18 May 1950; *Educ* Millfield, Univ of Oxford (BA, DPhil); *m* 1990, Dr Leslie Brubaker, da of Prof Robert Brubaker; *Career* Univ of Birmingham: lectr 1977–87, sr lectr 1987–89, reader then prof 1993–2005; Chichele prof of medieval history Univ of Oxford 2005–; memb: Lab Pty, Democratici della Sinistra; FBA 1998; *Books* Early Medieval Italy (1981), The Mountains and the City (1988), Social Memory (with James Fentress, 1992), Land and Power (1994), Community and Clientele (1998), Legge, Pratiche e Conflitti (2000), Courts and Conflicts (2003), Framing the Early Middle Ages (2005); *Recreations* politics, travel; *Style—* Prof Chris Wickham; ✉ All Souls College, Oxford OX1 4AL (tel 01865 279379)

WICKHAM, David Ian; s of Edwin and Betty Wickham; *Educ* St Olave's GS Orpington, S London Coll; *Career* served Fiji, Hong Kong, Caribbean and USA with Cable & Wireless plc 1977–87, various sr mgmnt positions Mercury Communications and Cable & Wireless Communications Ltd 1987–97, chm Gemini Cable Systems Ltd 1998, chief exec Cable & Wireless Global Network 1998–99, chm IsionAG 2001, chief exec Energis plc 2001–02; chm: Telecom Direct Ltd 2003–, YAC Ltd 2003–, CCC plc 2004–, Synchronica plc 2005–; MInstD 1998; *Recreations* golf, theatre; *Clubs* London Golf; *Style—* David Wickham, Esq; ✉ Telecom Direct Ltd, 20 Park Gate, Milton Park, Abingdon, Oxfordshire OX14 4SH (tel 07800 020202, e-mail david.wickham@singlehurst.com)

WICKHAM, John Ewart Alfred; s of Alfred James Wickham (d 1931), and Hilda May, *née* Cummins (d 1977); *b* 10 December 1927; *Educ* Chichester GS, Bart's Med Coll London (BSc, MB BS, MS); *m* 28 July 1961, (Gwendoline) Ann, da of James Henry Loney (d 1975); 3 da (Susan Jane b 31 May 1962, Caroline Elizabeth b 28 July 1963, (Ann) Clare b 4 July 1966); *Career* Nat Serv RAF 1947–49; sr conslt urological surgn Bart's London 1966–85, surgn St Peters Hosp London 1967–93, sr lectr Inst of Urology London 1967–96, surgn King Edward VIII Hosp for Offrs London 1973–98, surgn urologist RAF 1973–99, sr res fell and conslt surgn Guy's and St Thomas' Hosp London 1993–99, hon conslt surgeon Central Middx Hosp 1997–99; dir: Academic Unit Inst of Urology Univ of London 1979–93, London Clinic Lithotripter Unit 1987–2000, N E Thames Regnl Lithotripter Unit 1987–93; pres RSM Urological Section 1984, first pres Int Soc of Endo-Urology 1983, first pres Int Soc of Minimal Invasive Surgery 1989; dir: London Lithotripter Co Ltd, Syclix Ltd; many visiting professorships; Hunterian prof and medal RCS 1970, James Berry prize and medal for contribs to renal surgery RCS 1982, Cutlers prize and medal Assoc Surgns GB for surgical instrument design 1985, St Peters Medal Br Assoc of Urological Surgns 1985, Cecil Joll prize RCS 1993, John Latymer medal American Urological Assoc, Rovsing medal Danish Surgical Soc, Galen Medal Soc of Apothecaries London 1998, Cook medal Royal Coll of Radiologists 1998; Fulbright scholar 1964; Freeman City of London 1971, Liveryman Worshipful Co of Barber Surgns 1971; Hon MD Univ of Gothenburg 1994; FRCS 1959, FRCP 1988, FRCR; *Books* Urinary Calculous Disease (1979), Percutaneous Renal Surgery (1983), Intra-Renal Surgery (1984), Lithotripsy II (1987), Renal Tract Stone Metabolic Basis and Clinical Practice (1989), Minimal Invasive Therapy (ed, 1991); over 100 papers on renal and minimally invasive surgery; *Recreations* mechanical engineering, tennis; *Clubs* Athenaeum; *Style—* John Wickham, Esq; ✉ Rose Hill Cottage, Rosehill, Dorking, Surrey RH4 2EA (tel 01306 882451)

WICKRAMASINGHE, Prof (Nalin) Chandra; s of Percival Herbert Wickramasinghe, of Sri Lanka, and Theresa Elizabeth, *née* Soysa; *b* 20 January 1939; *Educ* Royal Coll Colombo, Univ of Ceylon, (BSc), Univ of Cambridge (MA, PhD, ScD); *m* 5 April 1966, (Nelum) Priyadarshini, da of Cecil Eustace Pereira; 1 s (Anil Nissanka b 1970), 2 da (Kamala Chandrika b 1972, Janaki Tara b 1981); *Career* fell Jesus Coll Cambridge 1963–73, prof and head Dept of Applied Mathematics and Astronomy UC Cardiff 1973–88, dir Inst of Fundamental Studies and advsr to Pres of Sri Lanka 1982–84; prof of applied maths and astronomy Univ of Wales 1988–2006, emeritus prof Cardiff Univ 2006–; fndr dir Cardiff Centre for Astrobiology 2000–; visiting prof of physics Univ of W Indies Mona Kingston 1994, visiting prof Glamorgan Univ 2007–; co-author with Prof Sir Fred Hoyle of a series of books on cosmic theory of life 1978–88; Powell Prize for English Verse Trinity Coll Cambridge 1962, Int Dag Hammarskjöld Gold Medal for Science 1986, Scholarly Achievement Award Inst of Oriental Philosophy Japan 1988, Soka Gakkai Int Peace and Culture Award 1993, Int Sahabdeen Award for Science 1996, John Snow Lecture Medal Assoc of Anaesthetists of GB and Ireland 2004; Hon Dr Soka Univ Tokyo 1996, Hon DSc Ruhana Univ Sri Lanka; FRAS, FRSA, FIMA; conferred title of Vidya Jyothi (Sri Lankan Nat Honour) 1992; *Books* Interstellar Grains (1967), Light Scattering Functions (1973), Lifecloud (with F Hoyle, 1978), Diseases from Space (1979), Evolution from Space (1981), Space Travellers (1981), From Grains to Bacteria (1984), Living Comets (1985), Archaeopteryx (1986), Cosmic Life Force (1988), The Theory of Cosmic Grains (1991), Our Place in the Cosmos (1992), Mysteries of the Universe and Life (with D Ikeda, 1994), Glimpses of Life, Time and Space (1994), Life on Mars? The Case for a Cosmic Heritage (with F Hoyle, 1997), Astronomical Origins of Life: Steps Towards Panspermia (2000), Cosmic Dragons: Life and Death of a Planet (2001), A Journey with Fred Hoyle (2005); *Recreations* photography, poetry, history of science, gardening; *Style—* Prof Chandra Wickramasinghe; ✉ 24 Llwynypia Road, Lisvane, Cardiff CF4 5SY (tel 029 2075 2146, mobile 07778 389 243, fax 029 2075 3173, e-mail wickramasinghe@cf.ac.uk)

WICKREMASINGHE, Nelisha; da of A Wickremasinghe, and A Wickremasinghe, *née* Amarasingham; *b* 24 January 1969, Sri Lanka; *Educ* Univ of Sussex (BA), Univ of Kent (MA); *Partner* B Whittam Smith; 2 s (Saul b 26 Dec 1998, Jude b 6 April 2007); *Career* addiction cnsllr: Arlington House Camden 1991–92, Alcohol Recovery Project 1992–93; day prog mangr Milton House Islington 1993–96, addiction servs mangr Thames Gateway NHS Tst 1996–2002, fndr and dir Archiamma Organic Food and Restaurant 2002–05, regnl dir Common Purpose 2005–; memb Bd: Food Standards Agency 2004–, Avon & Somerset Probation Serv 2004–05; AA Rosette for Culinary Excellence 2004–05, Somerset Life Food and Drink Award winner Most Distinctive Local Menu 2005; *Recreations* cooking, gardens; *Style—* Ms Nelisha Wickremasinghe; ✉ Common Purpose, Leigh Court, Abbots Leigh, Bristol BS8 3RA (tel 01275 371385, e-mail nelisha.wickremasinghe@commonpurpose.org.uk)

WICKS, Caroline Philippa (Pippa); da of Brian Cairns Wicks, of Bucks, and Judith Anne Wicks; *b* 18 December 1962; *Educ* Lady Verney HS High Wycombe, Haileybury, St Hugh's Coll Oxford (open scholar, Irene Shringley zoology scholar, MA), London Business Sch (Dip Corp Fin); *Career* Bain & Co mgmnt conslts: assoc conslt 1984–86, conslt 1987–90, mangr 1990–91; Courtaulds Textiles plc: business devpt mangr 1991–93, fin dir 1993–99; ceo FT Knowledge (a div of Pearson plc) 1999–2003, princ AlixPartners 2003–; non-exec dir: Arcadia plc 2001–02, Ladbrokes plc (formerly Hilton Gp) 2004–; *Recreations* reading, squash, tennis, wine, theatre, travel, antiques; *Style—* Mrs Pippa Wicks

WICKS, Malcolm; MP; s of late Arthur Wicks, and late Daisy Wicks; *b* 1 July 1947; *Educ* Elizabeth Coll Guernsey, NW London Poly, LSE (BSc); *m* 7 Sept 1968, Margaret, *née* Baron; 1 s, 2 da; *Career* fell Dept of Social Admin Univ of York 1968–70, res worker Centre for Environmental Studies 1970–72, lectr in social admin Dept of Govt Studies Brunel Univ 1970–74, social policy analyst Urban Deprivation Unit Home Office 1974–77, lectr in social policy Civil Service Coll 1977–78, research dir and sec Study Cmmn on the Family 1978–83, dir Family Policy Studies Centre 1983–92; MP (Lab): Croydon NW 1992–97, Croydon N 1997–; shadow social security min 1995–97; Parly under sec of state for lifelong learning DfEE 1999–2001, Parly under sec of state DWP 2001–03; min of state for pensions DWP 2003–05, min of state for energy DTI 2005–06, min of state for science and innovation 2006–; chair Education Select Ctee 1998–99, memb Select Ctee on Social Security 1994–95 and 1997–98; sec PLP Social Security Ctee 1994–95, sponsor Carers (Recognition and Services) Act 1995; chm Winter Action on Cold Homes 1986–92; vice-pres: Carers National Assoc 1997–, Alzheimer's Soc 1997–; tstee Nat Benevolent Fund for the Aged 2000–05; memb Social Policy Assoc; tstee Nat Energy Fndn 1988–94; *Publications* Old and Cold - Hypothermia and Social Policy (1978), Government and Urban Poverty (jtly, 1983), A Future for All - Do We Need a Welfare State? (1987), Family Change and Future Policy (jtly, 1990), A New Agenda (jtly, 1993), The Active Society: defending welfare (1994); *Recreations* music, walking, gardening, writing, white water rafting; *Clubs* Ruskin House Labour (Croydon); *Style—* Malcolm Wicks, MP; ✉ House of Commons, London SW1A 0AA

WICKSTEAD, Myles Antony; CBE (2006); *b* 7 February 1951; *Educ* Blundell's, Univ of St Andrews (MA), Univ of Oxford (MLitt); *m* 1990, Shelagh, *né* Paterson; 1 s (Edward Graeme b 30 May 1996), 1 da (Kathryn Natasha b 3 March 1999); *Career* Miny of Oversea Devpt 1976–79, asst private sec Office of the Lord Privy Seal 1979–1980, asst to UK exec dir World Bank Washington 1980–84, princ ODA 1984–88, private sec to min for Oversea Devpt 1988–90, head European Community and Food Aid Dept ODA 1990–93, head Br Devpt Div in E Africa (Nairobi) 1993–97, co-ordinator UK White Paper on Int Devpt 1997, UK alternate exec dir World Bank 1997–2000, cncllr (devpt) Washington DC 1997–2000, ambass to Ethiopia 2000–04, head of secretariat Cmmn for Africa 2004–05; visiting prof of int rels Open Univ; sr advsr: Africa Unit Assoc of Cwlth Univs, Business Action for Africa; chair Bd CONCERN UK; tstee/memb Bd: Westminster Fndn for Democracy, Br Inst in Eastern Africa, Baring Fndn, Tropical Health and Educn Tst (THET), Crown Agents Fndn, Advsy Cncl Wilton Park; *Style—* Myles Wickstead, Esq, CBE; ✉ The Manor House, Great Street, Norton sub Hamdon, Somerset TA14 6SJ (tel 01935 881385)

WIDDECOMBE, Rt Hon Ann Noreen; PC (1997), MP; da of James Murray Widdecombe, CB, OBE, (d 1999), and Rita Noreen Widdecombe (d 2007); *b* 4 October 1947; *Educ* La Sainte Union Convent Bath, Univ of Birmingham, Lady Margaret Hall Oxford (MA); *Career* sr admin Univ of London 1975–87; Runnymede dist cncllr 1976–78, fndr and vice-chm Women and Families for Def 1983–85; Parly candidate (Cons): Burnley 1979, Plymouth Devonport 1983; MP (Cons): Maidstone 1987–97, Maidstone and the Weald 1997–; Parly under sec for social security 1990–93, Parly under sec for employment 1993–94, min of state Dept of Employment 1994–95, min of state Home Office 1995–97, shadow health sec 1998–99, shadow home sec 1999–2001; *Books* Layman's Guide to Defence (1984), The Clematis Tree (2000), An Act of Treachery (2002), Father Figure (2005), An Act of Peace (2005); *Recreations* reading and writing; *Style—* The Rt Hon Ann Widdecombe, MP; ✉ 39 Searles Road, London SE1 4YX (tel 020 7701 6684, fax 020 7708 3632, e-mail awiddecombe@btclick.com); House of Commons, London SW1A 0AA (tel 020 7219 5091, fax 020 7219 2413, e-mail widdecombea@parliament.uk)

WIDDOWSON, Prof Henry George; s of George Percival Widdowson (d 1986), of East Runton, Norfolk, and Edna May, *née* Garrison (d 1980); *b* 28 May 1935; *Educ* Alderman Newton's Sch Leicester, King's Coll Cambridge (MA), Univ of Edinburgh (PhD); *m* 1, 15 July 1966 (m dis), Dominique Nicole Helene, da of Jean Dixmier, of Paris; 2 s (Marc Alain b 24 March 1968, Arnold b 18 Oct 1972); m 2, 19 July 1997, Barbara, da of Bruno Seidlhofer, of Vienna; *Career* Nat Serv RN 1956; English language offr Br Cncl Sri Lanka and Bangladesh 1962–68, lectr Dept of Linguistics Univ of Edinburgh 1968–77, prof of educn Inst of Educn Univ of London 1977–2000 (emeritus 2000–), prof of applied linguistics Univ of Essex 1991–97, prof of English linguistics and hon prof Univ of Vienna; chm Advsy Ctee Br Cncl English Teaching 1982–91, fndr ed Applied Linguistics, memb Kingman Ctee on the Teaching of English Language; Hon Doctorate Univ of Oulu; *Books* Stylistics and the Teaching of Literature (1975), Teaching Language as Communication (1978), Explorations in Applied Linguistics (vol I 1979, vol II 1984), Learning Purpose and Language Use (1983), English in the World (with Randolph Quirk, 1985), Language Teaching: A Scheme for Teacher Education (ed, 1987), Aspects of Language Teaching (1990), Practical Stylistics (1992), Linguistics (1996), Oxford Introductions to Language Study (ed, 1996–), Defining Issues in English Language Teaching (2003), Text, Context, Pretext (2004), Discourse Analysis (2007); *Recreations* reading, walking, poetry, cooking, bird-watching; *Style—* Prof H G Widdowson; ✉ Institut für Anglistik and Amerikanistik, Universitätscampus AAKH/Hof 8, Spitalgasse 2–4, A-1090 Vienna, Austria (e-mail henry.widdowson@univie.ac.at);

WIDDUP, (Stanley) Jeffrey; s of Terence Widdup (d 1985), of Farnham Royal, Bucks, and Barbara Widdup (d 1995); *b* 10 July 1951; *Educ* Haileybury, Inns of Court Sch of Law; *m* Aug 1981, Janet, da of late Jack Clark; 1 s (Jack b 17 Jan 1983); *Career* called to the Bar Gray's Inn 1973; head of chambers 1981–, asst recorder of the Crown Court 1993–99, recorder 1999–; *Recreations* golf, growing vegetables; *Clubs* Bramley Golf, Bigbury Golf, Guildford County; *Style—* Jeffrey Widdup, Esq; ✉ Stoke House, Leapale Lane, Guildford, Surrey GU1 4LY (tel 01483 539131, fax 01483 300542)

WIDE, His Hon Judge Charles Thomas; QC (1995); s of Nicholas Scott Wide, of Felpham, W Sussex, and Ruth Mildred Norton, *née* Bird; *b* 16 April 1951; *Educ* The Leys Sch Cambridge, Univ of Exeter (LLB); *m* 1979, Hon Ursula Margaret Bridget Buchan, da of 3 Baron Tweedsmuir, *qv*; 1 da (Emily Susan b 10 June 1982), 1 s (Thomas Nicholas Buchan b 20 March 1984); *Career* called to the Bar Inner Temple 1974, recorder of the Crown Court 1995–2001 (asst recorder 1991–95), circuit judge 2001–, resident judge Northampton Crown Court 2003–; standing counsel HM Customs & Excise (Crime) Midland & Oxford Circuit 1989–95, standing counsel Inland Revenue (Crime) Midland & Oxford Circuit 1991–95; memb Criminal Procedure Rule Ctee 2004–; reader Diocese of Peterborough 2007–; *Recreations* fell walking and beekeeping; *Clubs* Travellers; *Style—* His Hon Judge Wide, QC; ✉ The Law Courts, 85–87 Lady's Lane, Northampton NN1 3HQ

WIEGOLD, Prof James; s of Walter John Wiegold (d 1967), and Elizabeth, *née* Roberts (d 1960); *b* 15 April 1934; *Educ* Caerphilly Boys' GS, Univ of Manchester (BSc, MSc, PhD), Univ of Wales (DSc); *m* 7 April 1958, (Edna) Christine, da of Lewis Norman Dale (d 1989); 1 s (Richard), 2 da (Helen (Mrs Fish), Alison (Dr Sharrock)); *Career* asst lectr UC N Staffs 1957–60, lectr UMIST 1960–63; UC Cardiff (now Univ of Cardiff following merger with UWIST): lectr 1963–67, sr lectr 1967–70, reader 1970–74, prof 1974–2001, emeritus prof 2002–; memb Mathematical Sciences Sub-Ctee UGC 1981–86; *Books* The Burnside Problem and Identities in Groups (translated from the Russian of S I Adian, with J C Lennox, 1979), Around Burnside (translated from the Russian of A I Kostrikin, 1990); *Recreations* music (choral singing), walking, language; *Style—* Prof James Wiegold; ✉ 131 Heol y Deri, Rhiwbina, Cardiff CF14 6UH (tel 029 2062 0469); School of Mathematics, Cardiff University, Senghenydd Road, Cardiff CF12 4AG (tel 029 2087 4194, fax 029 2087 4199, e-mail wiegoldj@cardiff.ac.uk)

WIELD, (William) Adrian Cunningham; s of Captain Ronald Cunningham Wield, CBE, RN (d 1981), of Chudleigh, S Devon, and Mary, *née* Macdonald (d 1991); *b* 19 February 1937; *Educ* Downside; *m* 8 June 1979, Benedicte, da of Poul Preben Schoning (d 1984), of Copenhagen, Denmark; 1 da (Isobel b 1980), 1 s (Alexander b 1983); *Career* 2 Lt Duke of Cornwall LI 1955–57; stockbroker; ptnr W Mortimer 1967–68; dir: EB Savory Milln (later SBCI Savory Milln) 1985–88 (ptnr 1968–85), Albert Sharp & Co 1988–98; ptnr Brian C Regan Chartered Accountants 2001–05; chm: Northgate Unit Tst 1983–86, Reed Brook Ltd 1993–94, Boisdale plc 1995–, Scientific Detectors Ltd 2001–02; non-exec dir: Buzzacott Investment Management Co 1990–94, Boisdale Bishopsgate 2002–; memb London Stock Exchange 1959–88; *Books* The Special Steel Industry (published privately, 1973); *Recreations* golf, shooting, sailing; *Clubs* Reform; *Style*— Adrian Wield, Esq; ✉ Tysoe Manor, Tysoe, Warwickshire CV35 0TR (tel 01295 688052, fax 01295 688018, e-mail adrian.wield@btinternet.com)

WIELER, Anthony Eric; s of Brig Leslie Frederic Ethelbert Wieler, CB, CBE, JP (d 1965), of Hambledon, Surrey, and Elisabeth Anne, *née* Parker (d 1984); *b* 12 June 1937; *Educ* Shrewsbury, Trinity Coll Oxford (MA); *Career* Nat Serv 1958–60, 2 Lt 7 Duke of Edinburgh's Own Gurkha Rifles (in 1967 organised the appeal which raised £1.5m for Gurkha Welfare Tsts); joined L Messel & Co, memb London Stock Exchange until 1967, sr investment mangr Ionian Bank Ltd until 1972; fndr chm: Anthony Wieler & Co Ltd 1972–89, Anthony Wieler Unit Trust Management 1982–89; dir: Lorne House Trust IOM 1987–2001, Arbuthnot Fund Managers Ltd 1988–89, English Trust Co Ltd (i/c Investment Mgmnt Div) 1992–97, Kermesse Fund Ltd 2001–04; project dir Economic Surveys Thailand 1999, Turkey and Greece 2000; assoc dir Albert E Sharp & Co 1989–92; currently: business conslt SE Asia and Pacific Rim; fndr Oxford Univ Modern Pentathlon Assoc 1957 (organised first match against Cambridge), chm Hambledon PC 1965–76, initial subscriber Centre for Policy Studies 1972 (memb Wider Ownership Sub-Ctee), fndr One Million Club for XVI Universiade, memb and tstee numerous other charities particularly concerning Nepal, memb Br-Nepal Soc and Br-Nepal C of C (vice-chm 2004–); memb Surrey Cncl Order of St John 1974–2004, dep pres St John Ambulance Surrey until 2004; hon sec AIIM 1974–88; MSI 1993–; OStJ; awarded Gorkha Daksin Bahu by HM King of Nepal 1998; *Style*— Anthony Wieler, Esq; ✉ The New Stable Cottage, Feathercombe, Hambledon, Godalming, Surrey GU8 4DP (tel and fax 01483 860200, mobile 07831 353968, e-mail aewieler@hotmail.com)

WIENS, Edith; da of Rev David Wiens (d 1981), of Canada, and Gertrud Wiens-Janz (d 1979); *b* 9 June 1950; *Educ* Oberlin Coll USA (BMus, MMus), Hanover Germany (Master of Performance), masterclass with E Werba Munich; *m* Kai Moser, professional cellist, s of Prof Dr Hans Joachim Moser, of Berlin; 2 s (Johannes b 14 June 1979, Benjamin b 3 May 1981); *Career* soprano, specialising in concerts, recitals and Mozart operas; prof of voice Hochschule für Musik Nürnburg Augsburg, prof of voice Hochschule für Musik und Theater München; sung with orchs incl: London, Berlin, Israel, Munich and New York Philharmonic Orchs, Boston, Chicago, Montreal, Amsterdam Concertgebouw, Leipzig Gewandhaus and Bavarian Radio Symphony Orchs; operatic roles incl: Donna Anna in Don Giovanni (Glyndebourne, with Bernard Haitink), the Countess in Le Nozze di Figaro (Buenos Aires), Ilia in Idomeneo (Japan, with Seiji Ozawa); worked with other conductors incl: Daniel Barenboim, Sir Colin Davis, Sir Neville Marriner, Sir Georg Solti, Kurt Masur; prizewinner at various int competitions incl Salzburg Mozart competition, ARD Munich and Zwickau Schumann competition (Gold medal); recitals in NY, Paris, Vienna Musikverein, Berlin, Moscow, Munich, Frankfurt, Cologne, Florence and Amsterdam; various festival appearances in Salzburg, Montreux, Tanglewood, Lockenhaus, Aix-en-Provence, Lucerne, Schleswig-Holstein, Dresden, Berlin, Vienna and the London Proms; Offr Order of Canada; Hon DMus Oberlin Coll USA; *Recordings incl* Peer Gynt (as Solveig), Das Paradies und die Peri (as the Peri, Grammy award 1990), Parsifal (erstes Blumenmädchen), Dona Nobis Pacem, Mendelssohn's 2nd Symphony and A Midsummer Night's Dream, Haydn's Creation, Beethoven's 9th Symphony, Mozart's Mass in C Minor and Requiem, Mahler's 2nd, 4th and 8th Symphonies, Zemlinsky's Lyric Symphony, Schubert, Strauss, Schumann and Brahms Lieder; *Style*— Ms Edith Wiens; ✉ Georg-Schuster Strasse 10, 82152 Krailling, Germany (tel 00 49 89 857 4281, fax 00 49 89 856 2218)

WIGAN, Sir Michael Iain; 6 Bt (UK 1898), of Clare Lawn, Mortlake, Surrey, and Purland Chase, Ross, Herefordshire; s of Sir Alan Lewis Wigan, 5 Bt (d 1996), and Robina, da of Lt-Col Sir Iain Colquhoun of Luss, 7 Bt, KT, DSO, LLD; *b* 3 October 1951; *Educ* Eton, Exeter Coll Oxford; *Family* 1 s by Lady Alexandra Hay (Ivar Francis Grey de Miremont Wigan b 25 March 1979); m 1, 1984 (m dis 1985), Frances, da of late Flt Lt Angus Barr Faucett; m 2, 1989, Julia Teresa, eldest da of John de Courcy Ling, CBE, MEP; 3 s (Fergus Adam b 30 April 1990, Thomas Iain b 24 May 1993, Finnbarr Frederick b 17 Sept 1997), 1 da (Lilias Margaret b 9 March 1992); *Heir* s, Fergus Wigan; *Books* Scottish Highland Estate (1991), Stag at Bay (1993), The Last of the Hunter Gatherers: Fisheries Crisis at Sea (1998), Grimersta: The Story of a Great Fishery (2001); *Recreations* literature, deer stalking, fly fishing; *Style*— Sir Michael Wigan, Bt; ✉ Borrobol, Kinbrace, Sutherland KW11 6UB

WIGART, (Bengt) Sture; s of Bengt Eric Wigart (d 1979), and Elsa Margareta Westberg (d 1983); *b* 11 May 1934; *Educ* Univ of Stockholm, Univ of Munich; *m* 1, 1959, Anne Outram; 3 s; m 2, 1981 (m dis); m 3, 1985; m 4, 1994, Hon Julia Collbran Groves, *née* Cokayne; *Career* chm: Wigart Management Ltd, Byggfakta Sweden until 1984, Dodge Europe until 1988, Bau Data Group until 1994, First Index Ltd until 2000, Docu Group 2001–06; *Recreations* sailing, art; *Clubs* Royal Yacht Sqdn, Royal Thames Yacht; *Style*— Sture Wigart, Esq; ✉ 40 rue Théophile Vander Elst, Boitsfort, 1170 Brussels, Belgium (tel and fax 00 32 02 660 9224, e-mail sture@wigart.com)

WIGGIN, Sir Charles Rupert John; 5 Bt (UK 1892), of Metchley Grange, Harborne, Staffs; s of Sir John Henry Wiggin, 4 Bt, MC (d 1991), and his 1 w, Lady Cecilia Evelyn, *née* Anson (d 1963), da of 4 Earl of Lichfield; *b* 2 July 1949; *Educ* Eton; *m* 1979, Mrs Mary Burnett-Hitchcock, o da of Brig S Craven-Chambers, CBE; 1 s (Richard Edward John b 1980), 1 da (Cecilia Charlotte b 1984); *Heir* s, Richard Wiggin; *Career* Maj Grenadier Guards (ret); civil service; *Style*— Sir Charles Wiggin, Bt

WIGGIN, William David (Bill); MP; s of Sir Jerry Wiggin, TD, and Rosie, *née* Orr (now Mrs Dale Harris); *b* 4 June 1966; *Educ* Eton, Univ Coll of N Wales Bangor (BA); *m* 3 July 2001, Camilla Jane, da of Donald Chilvers; 1 da (Rosie Jessica b 26 Oct 2001); *Career* trader: Rayner Coffee Int 1989–91, Mitsubishi 1991–92, UBS 1992–95; assoc dir Dresdner Kleinwort Benson 1995–98, mangr Commerzbank 1998–2001; MP (Cons) Leominster 2001–; memb Select Ctee: Welsh, Transport, Local Government and the Regions; *Clubs* Annabel's, Hurlingham, Rankin (Leominster); *Style*— Bill Wiggin, Esq, MP; ✉ House of Commons, London SW1A 0AA; Constituency Office, 8 Corn Street, Leominster, Herefordshire HR6 8LR (tel 01568 612565)

WIGGINS, Bradley Mark; OBE (2005); s of Gary Wiggins, and Linda Wiggins; *b* 28 April 1980, Gent, Belgium; *m* 5 Nov 2004, Catherine; 1 s (Ben Michael b 26 March 2005); *Career* cyclist; achievements incl: Gold medal individual pursuit Jr World Track Championships 1997, Silver medal team pursuit Cwlth Games 1998 (memb England team), Gold medal Madison Nat Track Championships 1999, Silver medal team pursuit World Championships 2000, Bronze medal team pursuit Olympic Games Sydney 2000, European Pursuit Champion 2001, Silver medal team pursuit World Championships 2001, Silver medal individual pursuit and Silver medal team pursuit Cwlth Games 2002 (memb England team), Gold medal individual pursuit and Silver medal team pursuit World Championships 2003, European Derny Champion 2003, Gold medal individual pursuit, Silver medal team pursuit and Bronze medal Madison Olympic Games Athens 2004; professional road debut 2002, memb La Française des Jeux team 2002–04, memb Credit Agricole team 2004–; *Style*— Bradley Wiggins, Esq, OBE

WIGGINS, Prof David; s of late Norman Wiggins, OBE, and Diana, *née* Priestley (d 1995); *b* 8 March 1933; *Educ* St Paul's, Brasenose Coll Oxford (MA); *m* 1980 (m dis), Jennifer Hornsby; 1 s (Peter Joshua Wiggins b 1987); *Career* asst princ Colonial Office 1957–58, Jane Eliza Procter visiting fell Princeton Univ 1958–59, lectr then fell New Coll Oxford 1959–67, prof of philosophy Bedford Coll London 1967–80, fell and praelector in philosophy Univ Coll Oxford 1981–89, prof of philosophy Birkbeck Coll London 1989–93, Wykeham prof of logic Univ of Oxford 1994–2000; visiting appts: Stanford Univ 1964 and 1965, Harvard Univ 1968 and 1972, All Souls Coll Oxford 1973, Princeton Univ 1980, Findlay visiting prof Boston Univ 2001; Leverhulme fell 2001–04; author of various articles in learned jls; memb: Ind Cmmn on Tport 1973–74, Central Tport Consultative Ctee 1977–79; chm Tport Users Consultative Ctee for SE 1977–79; pres Aristotelian Soc 2000–01; memb London Tport and Amenity Assoc; Dr (hc) Univ of York 2005; hon foreign memb American Acad of Arts and Sciences (1992); FBA 1978; *Books* Identity and Spatio Temporal Continuity (1967), Truth, Invention and the Meaning of Life (1978), Sameness and Substance (1980, 2 edn 2001), Needs, Values, Truth (1987, 3 edn 2002), Sameness and Substance Renewed (2002), Ethics: Twelve Lectures on the Philosophy of Morality (2006); *Style*— Prof David Wiggins, FBA; ✉ New College, Oxford OX1 3BN

WIGGINTON, Prof Michael John; s of Lt-Col Sydney Isaac Wigginton, OBE (d 1945), and Eunice Olive, *née* Piper; *b* 26 March 1941; *Educ* Nottingham HS, Gonville & Caius Coll Cambridge (MA, DipArch); *m* 1, 1969 (m dis), Margaret Steven; 1 da (Julia Caroline b 1972), 1 s (Alexander Steven b 1974); m 2, 1988, Jennifer, da of Lester Bennett and Marie Bennett; 1 s (Dominic James Michael b 1993), 1 da (Annabel Marie Olivia (twin) b 1993); *Career* architect and author; with SOM NY 1964–65, with YRM architects and planners 1966–85 (responsible for the design of a series of bldgs incl an innovatory office bldg in the Netherlands, a low energy bioclimatic hosp in Singapore and co-designer The Sultan Qaboos Univ in Oman), ptnr Richard Horden Assoc 1987–94, fndr the Designers Collaborative 1994 (projects incl a series of low energy glass structures evolving out of the Kelbrook House Conservatory, and other projects incorporating an agenda based on sustainability incl 'A Classroom of the Future' for Devon CC 2001–03); teacher/lectr 1990–95: Scott Sutherland Sch of Arch Aberdeen, Univ of Wales, Pennsylvania State Univ, Univ of Westminster, Trondheim Univ, RCA, Univ of Plymouth, Univ of Portsmouth; Univ of Plymouth: prof of architecture 1996–, chair School of Arch and Design 2003–06, prof of sustainable architecture 2006–; organiser Glass in the Environment Conf Crafts Cncl 1986; architect memb UK/USA Govt sponsored res on energy responsive bldg envelopes; co-inventor SERRAGLAZE refractive glazing device 1993–; UK rep and chair of architectural working gp European COST C13 Prog for the Interactive Building Envelope 2000–05; chm: RIBA Professional Lit Ctee 1996–2004, RIBA SW Regnl Cncl 2005–; dep chair SW Regnl CIC; memb: Bd Architecture Centre Devon and Cornwall, Steering Ctee Devon Sustainable Building Initiative (DSBI), Exeter Cathedral Fabric Advsy Cmmn 1997–; RIBA, FRSA; *Awards* with Richard Horden: winner The Stag Place Competition London 1987, winner Epsom Club Stand Competition 1989, winner Shell UK HQ Competition 1990, Financial Times Award for Architecture 1993; with the Designers Collaborative: Commended Design Award Zephyr Low Energy Project Competition 1994, American Inst of Architects Book Prize (for Glass in Architecture) 1998, selected project Architects' Jl small projects competition (Kelbrook House Conservatory) 2000–01; *Publications* author of over 40 articles and books incl: Window Design (1969), Office Buildings (1973), Practice in the Netherlands (1976), Design of Health Buildings in Hot Climates (1976), Glass To-day (1987), Silicon can Shine (1988), Towards the Chromogenic Century (1990), Can We Have a Theory, Please (1991), Building Intelligence (1992), Notes Towards a Theory of Architecture (1992), The Building Skin: Scientific Principle vs Conventional Wisdom (essay in Companion to Contemporary Architectural Thought, 1993), Better Buildings Means Better Business (ed, 1993), Glass in Architecture (1996), Design Guide for the Multiple Building Envelope (2000), The Second Skin: A Design Guide (2001), Intelligent Skins (jtly, 2002), Glas-inte bara transparens (Sweden, 2005); *Recreations* music, reading, research; *Style*— Prof Michael Wigginton; ✉ Kilgerran, Bridgetown Hill, Totnes, Devon TQ9 5BN (tel 01803 865567, fax 01803 868695); Plymouth University School of Engineering, University of Plymouth, Drake Circus, Plymouth PL4 8AA (tel 01752 233600, fax 01752 233634, e-mail m.wigginton@plymouth.ac.uk)

WIGGLESWORTH, Jack; s of Jack Wigglesworth (d 1989), and Gladys Maud, *née* Haywood; *b* 9 October 1941; *Educ* Jesus Coll Oxford (MA); *m* 25 July 1970, Carlota Josefina Páez; 1 s (Antony John b 8 March 1972), 1 da (Jacqueline Mary b 11 Aug 1974); *Career* gilts desk economist and institutional salesman Phillips & Drew 1963–71, govt bond desk W Greenwell & Co 1971–86, head of sales for govt bond co Lloyds Merchant Bank 1986–87, with LIFFE and SFA (to implement Fin Servs Act (1986)) 1988, head of int fixed interest investment Henderson Administration Ltd 1989–91, business devpt dir J P Morgan Futures Inc 1992–93, dir of mktg Citifutures Ltd 1993–97, chm ABN Amro Chicago Corp (UK) Ltd 1997–99; founding bd dir Securities Inst 1992–2002, chm LIFFE 1995–98 (memb Founding Working Party and Steering Ctee 1982, bd dir 1982–98, chm Membership & Rules Ctee 1988–92, dep chm 1992–95, designed Long Gilt Contract); chm: Hackney Educn Action Zone 1999–2004, Cablenet Int Ltd 2001–03, London Asia Capital 2003–; dir: Futures and Options Assoc 1995–2000, Capital Value Brokers 1999–2005, Durlacher Corp plc 2002–05; sr conslt British Invisibles 1999–2001; memb: Authorisation Ctee and Individuals' Registration Panel SFA (formerly The Securities Assoc) 1987–2001, Fin Servs Strategy Gp FOCUS 1992–2001, Fin Servs Advsy Gp Qualifications & Curriculum Authority 1999–2001, Enforcement Ctee SFA 1999–2001, Cncl Gresham Coll 1999–; Hon DSc City Univ; *Recreations* music, films, computers, Latin American concerns; *Clubs* Athenaeum; *Style*— Jack Wigglesworth, Esq; ✉ 3 Deacons Heights, Elstree, Hertfordshire WD6 3QY (tel and fax 020 8953 8524, e-mail jack@wigglesworth.biz)

WIGGLESWORTH, Prof Jonathan Semple; s of Sir Vincent Brian Wigglesworth, CBE (d 1994), of Lavenham, Suffolk, and Mabel Katherine, *née* Semple (d 1986); *b* 2 December 1932; *Educ* Gordonstoun, Gonville & Caius Coll Cambridge (BA), UCH (BChir, MD); *m* 21 July 1960, (Margaret) Joan, da of Christopher Every Rees (d 1974); 3 da (Sara b 1961, Sian b 1965, Kirsty b 1968); *Career* house physician UCH 1960, house surgn Nat Temperance Hosp 1960–61, Graham scholar in morbid anatomy 1961–62, Beit Memorial fell 1962–64, lectr in morbid anatomy 1964–65, reader in paediatric pathology Dept of Paediatrics Hammersmith Hosp 1980–85 (sr lectr 1965–79), hon conslt in neonatal histopathology NW Thames Region 1983–98, emeritus prof of perinatal pathology Imperial Coll Sch of Med at Hammersmith Hosp (Royal Postgrad Med Sch until merger 1997) (prof 1985–98); memb: Paediatric Pathology Soc, Br Paediatric Pathology Assoc, Neonatal Soc; FRCPath 1977, Hon FRCPCH 2000 (FRCPCH 1997); *Books* Haemorrhage Ischaemia and the Perinatal Brain (with K Pape, 1979), Perinatal Pathology (1984, 2 edn 1996), Textbook of Fetal and Perinatal Pathology (with D Singer 1990, 2 edn 1998); *Recreations* painting, fly fishing, gardening; *Clubs* Athenaeum, RSM; *Style*— Prof Jonathan Wigglesworth; ✉ Phelps House, Upper High Street, Castle Cary, Somerset BA7 7AT (tel 01963 350360, e-mail j.wigglesworth@btinternet.com)

WIGGLESWORTH, Mark; *Career* assoc conductor BBC Symphony Orch 1991–93; music dir: Opera Factory 1991–94, The Premiere Ensemble, BBC Nat Orch of Wales 1996–2000; princ guest conductor Swedish Radio Orch 1998–2001; debut: Glyndebourne Festival Opera 2000, ENO 2001, ROH 2002; guest conductor: LPO, LSO, Salzburg Festival, Berlin Philharmonic, Royal Concertgebouw, Oslo Philharmonic, Santa Cecilia of Rome, Ochestra Filarmonica della Scala Milan, Chicago Symphony, Philadelphia Orch, Minnesota Orch,

San Francisco Symphony, Los Angeles Philharmonic Orch, Israel Philharmonic, Welsh Nat Opera, Cleveland Symphony, Toronto Symphony, Montreal Symphony, New York Philharmonic, Hollywood Bowl, Sydney Symphony, BBC proms; *Style*— Mark Wigglesworth, Esq; ✉ c/o Askonas Holt, Lonsdale Chambers, 27 Chancery Lane, London WC2A 1PF (tel 020 7400 1700, fax 020 7400 1799)

WIGGLESWORTH, William Robert Brian; s of Sir Vincent Brian Wigglesworth, CBE (d 1994), of Suffolk, and Mabel Katherine, *née* Semple (d 1986); *b* 8 August 1937; *Educ* Marlborough, Magdalen Coll Oxford (BA); *m* 1969, Susan Mary, da of Arthur Baker, JP (d 1980), of Suffolk; 1 da (Elizabeth b 1979), 1 s (Benjamin b 1982); *Career* Nat Serv 2 Lt Royal Signals 1956–58; Ranks Hovis McDougall Ltd 1961–70 (gen mgmnt and PA to chief exec); princ Bd of Trade 1970; asst sec: Dept of Prices and Consumer Protection 1975, Dept of Industry 1978; dep DG of telecommunications 1984–94 (actg DG 1992–93); dir Reedheath Ltd (telecommunications regulatory advice) 1994; jt dir Int Inst for Regulators in Telecommunications Westminster Univ 1998–2006; advsr Telecommunications Forum Int Inst of Communications (IIC) London 1994–98; memb Bd JNT Assoc (UKERNA) 1994–98; FRSA; *Recreations* fishing, gardening, history; *Style*— William Wigglesworth, Esq; ✉ Millfield House, Heath Road, Polstead, Colchester, Essex CO6 5AN (tel 01787 210590, fax 01787 210592, e-mail ww@reedheath.keme.co.uk)

WIGGS, Roger Sydney William Hale; *b* 10 June 1939; *Educ* Tiffin Sch Kingston upon Thames, Law Sch Lancaster Gate; *m* 1963, Rosalind Anne, *née* Francis; 4 s; *Career* ptnr Hextall Erskine 1963–74, overseas dir Securicor Ltd 1974–80, md Securicor International Ltd 1980–89; Securicor Gp plc: dir 1977–98, dep gp chief exec 1985–88, gp chief exec 1988–96; Security Services plc: dir 1977–, dep gp chief exec 1985–88, gp chief exec 1988–96; non-exec dir: Securicor plc 2002– (gp chief exec 1996–2001), The Crown Agents for Oversea Governments and Admins Ltd 1996–; memb Law Soc 1962; *Recreations* soccer, rugby, motor racing; *Style*— Roger Wiggs, Esq; ✉ Securicor plc, Sutton Park House, 15 Carshalton Road, Sutton, Surrey SM1 4LD (tel 020 8770 7000, fax 020 8661 0204)

WIGGS, His Hon Judge (John) Samuel; s of late Kenneth Ingram Wiggs, and Marjorie Ruth, *née* Newton; *b* 23 November 1946; *Educ* Chigwell Sch, Univ of Southampton (LLB); *m* 1, Elizabeth, *née* Jones (decd); m 2, Kerry, da of Brian Martley; 2 da (Catherine, Nicola), 2 step da (Rebecca, Elizabeth); *Career* called to the Bar Middle Temple 1970; in practice London 1971–1995, recorder of the Crown Court 1991–95, circuit judge (Western Circuit) 1995–, resident judge Bournemouth 1999–2007, resident judge Bournemouth and Dorchester 2007–; chllr Diocese of Salisbury 1997–; memb Bar Law Reform Ctee 1990–94; *Recreations* playing the bassoon and church choir singing, gardening, hill walking; *Style*— His Hon Judge Wiggs; ✉ Courts of Justice, Deansleigh Road, Bournemouth, Dorset BH7 7DS (tel 01202 502800, fax 01202 502801)

WIGHT, Robin Alexander Fairbairn; s of William Fairbairn Wight (d 1972), of Alwoodley, Leeds, and Olivia Peterina, *née* Clouston (d 1988); *b* 5 June 1938; *Educ* Dollar Acad, Magdalene Coll Cambridge (MA); *m* 27 July 1963, Sheila Mary Lindsay, da of James Forbes (d 1963), of Edinburgh; 1 da (Catriona Mary Susan b 1965), 3 s (James William Fairbairn b 1966, Alasdair Robin Forbes b 1968, Douglas Clouston Fullerton b 1973); *Career* ptnr Coopers & Lybrand CAs 1971–96; Coopers & Lybrand Scotland: regnl ptnr 1977–95, exec chm 1990–96; chm: Arville Holdings 1990–, P&S Textiles 2000–; FCA 1976 (CA 1978); *Recreations* golf, watching rugby, skiing, business, bridge; *Clubs* RAC; *Style*— Robin Wight, Esq; ✉ 22 Regent Terrace, Edinburgh EH7 5BS (tel 0131 556 2100, fax 0131 558 1104); Arville Holdings, Sandbeck, Wetherby, West Yorkshire LS22 7DQ (tel 01937 582735, fax 01937 580196, car 077 8525 8098)

WIGHTMAN, David Richard; s of John William Wightman, of Leatherhead, Surrey, and Nora, *née* Martin; *b* 3 April 1940; *Educ* KCS Wimbledon; *m* Rosalind Jill, *née* Diaper; *Career* Turner Kenneth Brown: articled clerk 1957–62, asst slr 1962–65, ptnr 1965–87, sr ptnr 1987–95; Nabarro Nathanson: ptnr 1995–99, conslt 1999–; ed-in-chief Int Construction Law Review 1983–; Freeman City of London, memb Worshipful Co of Slrs 1983; memb: Law Soc 1962, Int Bar Assoc 1976, IOD 1982, Soc of Construction Law 1986, Cncl London C of C; FRSA 1990; *Recreations* tennis, farming; *Clubs* Travellers; *Style*— David Wightman, Esq; ✉ Nabarro Nathanson, Lacon House, Theobalds Road, London WC1X 8RW (tel 020 7524 6033, fax 020 7524 6524)

WIGHTMAN, Nigel David; s of Gerald Wightman (d 1983), and Margaret Audrey, *née* Shorrock (d 1997); *b* 19 July 1953; *Educ* Bolton Sch, Kent Coll, Dundee HS, BNC Oxford (MA), Nuffield Coll Oxford (MPhil); *m* 21 Feb 1987, Christine Dorothy, da of Hubert Alexander Nesbitt, of Bangor, Co Down, NI; 3 s (Patrick Gerald Wisdom b 1987, Hugo William Joseph b 1989, Jack David Alexander b 1991); *Career* Samuel Montagu and Co 1976–80, Chemical Bank 1980–84, NM Rothschild and Sons 1984–95, chief exec Rothschild Asset Management Asia Pacific Ltd until 1995, chief exec Wheelock NatWest Investment Management Ltd 1995–97, md State Street Global Advisors UK 1997–2003, md State Street Bank Europe 1998–, md State Street Global Advsrs Europe 2003–; *Recreations* seasonal; *Clubs* MCC, In & Out, Wildernesse Golf; *Style*— Nigel Wightman, Esq; ✉ State Street Global Advisors, 21 St James's Square, London SW1Y 4SS (tel 020 7698 6000, fax 020 7698 6350)

WIGLEY, Dr Dale Brian; *Educ* Univ of Bristol (PhD); *Career* postdoctoral work Univ of Leicester and Univ of York, lectr then reader Univ of Oxford 1993–2000, researcher ICRF (now Cancer Research UK) 2000–; FRS 2004; *Style*— Dr Dale Wigley; ✉ Cancer Research UK, London Research Institute, Clare Hall Laboratories, Blanche Lane, South Mimms, Potters Bar EN6 3LD

WIGLEY, (Francis) Spencer; s of Frank Wigley (d 1970), Dep Cmmr Police Fiji, and Lorna, *née* Wattley; gf Sir Wilfrid Wigley, Chief Justice Leeward Islands, WI; *Educ* Dean Close Sch, Univ of Nottingham (BA); *m* 1969, Caroline, *née* Jarratt; 2 s (Francis b 1972, Edward b 1973); 1 da (Elizabeth b 1979); *Career* admitted slr 1967; Rio Tinto plc: gen counsel 1976–83, sec and dir of corp servs 1983–92; Bass plc: sec and gen counsel 1992–2000, memb Bd Exec Ctee 1995–2000, personnel dir 1997–2000, chm Pension Funds 2001–; tstee, dir and hon sec Shakespeare's Globe 2001–, tstee Flavel Centre Dartmouth 2005–; govr: Amesbury Sch 1983–95 (chm 1987–93), Cranleigh Sch 1989–98; *Recreations* sailing, sporting activities, photography; *Clubs* RAC, Little Ship, Royal Dart; *Style*— Spencer Wigley, Esq; ✉ Manor Farm, Fernhurst, Haslemere, Surrey GU27 3NW (tel 01428 653425, fax 01428 641800, e-mail wigley@ukgateway.net)

WIGNALL, Michael Thomas; s of Alan Wignall, of Preston, and Catherine, *née* Dunn; *b* 23 May 1967, Preston, Lancs; *Educ* St Cuthbert Mayne Preston, Preston Coll; *partner* Sarah Evans; 1 s (Matthew b 3 March 1998); *Career* jr sous chef Heathcotes Longridge 1987–89 (2 Michelin stars); head chef: The Old Beams Waterhouses 1993–95 (1 Michelin star), Waldo's Cliveden 1996–98 (1 Michelin star, 4 AA rosettes), Michael's Nook Grasmere 1998–2002 (1 Michelin star, 4 AA rosettes); exec head chef The Devonshire Arms N Yorks 2002– (1 Michelin star, 4 AA rosettes); best dessert under 21s and best overall entrant Salon Culinaire 1986, winner Northwest Chefs Circle 1987, winner Best Chef of the Year Northern Hospitality Awards 2007; *Style*— Michael Wignall, Esq; ✉ 20 Burnside, Addingham, Ilkley, West Yorkshire LS29 0PJ (tel 07834 069449, fax 01943 839452, e-mail michael.wignall1@btinternet.com); The Devonshire Arms, Bolton Abbey, Skipton, North Yorkshire BD23 6AJ (tel 01756 718118, fax 01756 710564)

WIGRAM, 2 Baron (UK 1935); (George) Neville Clive Wigram; MC (1945), JP (Glos 1959), DL (1969); s of 1 Baron Wigram, GCB, GCVO, CSI, PC, Equerry to George V both as Prince of Wales and King (d 1960, himself ggs of Sir Robert Wigram, 1 Bt), and his w Nora, da of Sir Neville Chamberlain; *b* 2 August 1915; *Educ* Winchester, Magdalen Coll Oxford; *m* 19 July 1941, Margaret Helen (d 1986), da of Gen Sir Andrew Thorne, KCB, CMG, DSO, and Hon Margaret Douglas-Pennant, 10 da of 2 Baron Penrhyn, JP, DL; 1 s, 2 da; *Heir* s, Maj the Hon Andrew Wigram, MVO; *Career* late Lt-Col Grenedier Gds; page of honour to HM 1925–32; mil sec and comptroller to Govr-Gen NZ 1946–49; govr Westminster Hosp 1967–74; *Clubs* Cavalry and Guards', MCC; *Style*— The Rt Hon Lord Wigram, MC, DL; ✉ Poulton Fields, Cirencester, Gloucestershire GL7 5SS (tel 01285 851250, fax 01285 851917)

WIJETUNGE, Don B; s of Don Dines Wijetunge (d 1963), of Colombo, Sri Lanka, and Prem, *née* Jayatilake; *b* 24 January 1941; *Educ* Royal Coll Colombo, Univ of Ceylon (MB BS); *m* 20 April 1971, Indra, da of Andrew Amerasinghe, of Kandy, Sri Lanka; 1 s (Aruna b 1973), 1 da (Sonalee b 1974); *Career* conslt surgn Univ Hosp Dammam Saudi Arabia 1980–82, dir of emergency serv Abdulla Fouad Univ Hosp Saudi Arabia 1982–84, conslt surgn and head Dept of Emergency Serv St George's Hosp London 1984– (first asst Dept of Surgery 1976–80); memb: American Coll of Emergency Physicians, BMA; fell Faculty of Accident and Emergency Medicine (FFAEM), FRCSEd; *Recreations* computer applications in medicine; *Style*— Don Wijetunge, Esq; ✉ Accident & Emergency Service, St George's Hospital, Blackshaw Road, London SW17 0QT (tel 020 8725 3585, e-mail dwijetunge@compuserve.com)

WILBRAHAM, Philip Neville; s of Anthony Basil Wilbraham, of E Yorks, and Sheila Eleanor, *née* Neville; *b* 25 November 1958; *Educ* Woodleigh Sch, Radley, Aston Univ (BSc); *m* 1, 1981 (m dis), Stephanie Jane, da of Ian William McClaren Witty; 2 da (Rachel b 1982, Rosemary b 1986), 2 s (Samuel b 1984, Dominic b 1987); m 2, 10 March 2007, Nicola, da of John Garvin; *Career* chm Northumbrian Fine Foods plc 1993–2001; Liveryman Worshipful Co of Shipwrights; *Recreations* shooting, politics; *Clubs* Carlton; *Style*— Philip Wilbraham, Esq; ✉ Middlerush, Cowshill, Bishop Auckland, County Durham DL13 1DF (tel 01388 537252)

WILBY, David Christopher; QC (1998); s of Alan Wilby, of Addingham, W Yorks, and June, *née* Uppard; *b* 14 June 1952; *Educ* Roundhay Sch Leeds, Downing Coll Cambridge (MA); *m* 23 July 1976, Susan Christine, da of Eric Arding (d 1977), of Bardsey, W Yorks; 3 da (Victoria b 1981, Christina b 1983, Charlotte b 1987), 1 s (Edward b 1985); *Career* called to the Bar Inner Temple 1974 (bencher 2002); practising barr North Eastern Circuit, recorder 2000–; memb: Exec Ctee Professional Negligence Bar Assoc 1995–, Bar Cncl 1996–99, Judicial Studies Bd 2005–, Criminal Injuries Compensation Panel 2007; chm Bar Conf 2000, past chm Int Relations Bar Cncl; ed: Professional Negligence and Liability Law Reports 1995–, Professional Negligence Key Cases 1999–; memb: Cwlth Lawyers Assoc 1995–, Int Assoc of Defense Counsel 1998–; assoc memb American BAr Assoc 1996–; *Publications*Atkin's Court Forms (ed, Health and Safety Section, 2002 and 2006), The Law of Damages (2003), Munkman on Employers Liability (2006); *Recreations* golf, watching association and rugby football, being in France; *Clubs* Pannal Golf, Taverners Headingley, Harrogate RUFC; *Style*— David Wilby, Esq, QC; ✉ Old Square Chambers, 10–11 Bedford Row, London WC1R 4BU (tel 020 7269 0300); Park Lane Chambers, 19 Westgate, Leeds LS1 2RD (tel 0113 228 5000, e-mail davidwilbyqc@onetel.net)

WILBY, James Jonathon; s of late Geoffrey Wilby, of Ossett, W Yorks, and Shirley, *née* Armitage; *b* 20 February 1958; *Educ* Sedbergh, Univ of Durham, RADA; *m* 25 June 1988, Shana Louise, da of late Garth John Loxley Magraw; 3 s (Barnaby John Loxley b 9 Nov 1988, Nathaniel Jerome b 4 Feb 1996, Jesse Jack b 18 May 2001), 1 da (Florence Hannah Mary b 18 Oct 1992); *Career* actor; *Theatre* incl: Another Country (Queen's Theatre) 1983, As You Like It (Manchester Royal Exchange), Jane Eyre (Chichester Festival Theatre), The Tempest (Chichester Festival Theatre), The Common Pursuit (Lyric) 1988, The Trial (Young Vic) 1993, A Patriot for Me (RSC) 1995, Helping Harry (Jermyn Street Theatre) 2001, Don Juan (Lyric) 2004; *Television* for BBC incl: Tell Me That You Love Me 1991, Adam Bede 1991, Mother Love 1992, You Me And It 1993, Lady Chatterley's Lover 1993, Crocodile Shoes 1994, Witness Against Hitler 1995, The Woman in White 1997, The Dark Room 1999; other credits incl: Dutch Girls 1985, A Tale Of Two Cities 1989, The Treasure Seekers 1997, Trial and Retribution 2000, Bertie and Elizabeth 2002, Island at War 2003, Sparkling Cyanide 2003, Jericho 2005, Miss Marple 2006, Little Devil 2006; *Film* incl: Maurice 1987, A Summer Story 1988, A Handful of Dust 1988, Immaculate Conception 1991, Howards End 1991, Une partie d'Échec 1994, Regeneration 1997, Tom's Midnight Garden 1998, An Ideal Husband 1999, Cotton Mary 1999, Gosford Park 2002, De-Lovely 2004, C'est Gradiva qui vous appelle 2006; *Awards* Venice Film Festival Best Actor Award (for Maurice) 1987, Bari Film Festival Best Actor Award (for A Handful of Dust) 1988, Screen Actors Guild Outstanding Performance by a Cast in a Motion Picture (for Gosford Park) 2001; *Style*— James Wilby; ✉ c/o Sue Latimer, ARG, 4 Great Portland Street, London W1W 8PA (tel 020 7436 6400, fax 020 7436 6700)

WILBY, Peter John; s of Lawrence Edward Wilby (d 1981), and Emily Lavinia, *née* Harris (d 1995); *b* 7 November 1944; *Educ* Kibworth Beauchamp GS, Univ of Sussex (BA); *m* 5 August 1967, Sandra, da of Alfred James, of Derby; 2 s (David Paul b 29 Dec 1971, Michael John b 1 Oct 1973); *Career* educn corr: The Observer 1972–75 (reporter 1968–72), New Statesman 1975–77, Sunday Times 1977–86; educn ed The Independent 1986–89; ndependent on Sunday: home ed 1989–91, dep ed 1991–95, ed 1995–96; New Statesman: books ed 1997–98, ed 1998–2005; media columnist New Statesman 2005–07, contributing ed Observer Sports Monthly 2005–, media columnist Guardian 2007–, public policy columnist New Statesman 2007–; *Books* Parents' Rights (1983), Eden (2006); *Recreations* reading, lunching, cooking; *Style*— Peter Wilby, Esq; ✉ 51 Queen's Road, Loughton, Essex IG10 1RR

WILCOCKS, Rear Adm Philip Lawrence; CB (2007), DSC (1991); s of Lieut Cdr Arthur Wilcocks, RN, and Marjorie Wilcocks; *Educ* Oakham Sch, Wallington Co GS, Univ of Wales (BSc), BRNC Dartmouth, RAF Staff Coll Bracknell; *m* Kym; 2 s (Andrew, David); *Career* joined RN 1971; Navigating Offr HMS Torquay 1977–78, CO HMS Stubbington 1979–80, Princ Warfare Offr (A) and Ops Offr HMS Ambuscade 1981–84 (incl Falklands conflict), Sqdn Ops Offr to Capt 3 Destroyer Sqdn HMS Newcastle and HMS York 1984–89, Staff Warfare Offr (Missile) to Flag Offr Sea Training, Cdr 1989, CO HMS Gloucester 1990–92 (incl Gulf conflict), Naval Ops Staff MOD 1992, Capt 1994, Asst Dir for Surface Ships and Above Water Warfare Directorate of Operational Requirements (Sea Systems) 1994–98, CO and Capt 3 Destroyer Sqdn HMS Liverpool 1998–99, Dir of Naval Ops MOD 1999–2001, Cdre HMS Collingwood 2001–02, Cdre Maritime Warfare Sch 2002–04, Dep Chief of Jt Ops (Ops Support) 2004–06, Flag Offr Scot, Northern Eng and NI and Flag Officer Reserves 2006–; govr: St Edmunds Sch Hindhead; Queen's Telescope 1972, Queen's Gold Medal 1974; MInstD; *Recreations* walking, rugby referee, cycling; *Style*— Rear Adm Philip Wilcocks, CB, DSC

WILCOX, His Hon Judge David John Reed; s of Leslie Leonard Kennedy Wilcox (d 1990), and Ada Margaret Reed, *née* Rapson (d 1958); *b* 8 March 1939; *Educ* Wednesbury Boys' HS, King's Coll London (LLB); *m* 1, 22 June 1962, Wendy Feay Christine (d 2003), da of Ernest Cyril Whiteley (d 1974), of Singapore; 1 s (Giles Frederick Reed b 16 Nov 1962), 1 da (Hester Margaret Reed b 2 Jan 1965); m 2, 24 Nov 2005, Roberta (Robin) Piera Prosio de Pardo; *Career* called to the Bar Gray's Inn 1962; Capt Directorate Army Legal Servs 1962–65 (Far East Land Forces Singapore 1963–65), crown counsel Hong Kong 1965–68, memb Hong Kong Bar 1968, practised Midland and Midland & Oxford Circuits 1968–85 (recorder 1979–85), circuit judge (Midland & Oxford Circuit) 1985–96; liaison judge Lincs and S Humberside Magistrates 1988–94, assigned Co Court judge Lincs and S Humberside 1988–94, resident judge Great Grimsby 1988–94, assigned Co Courts judge and designated care judge Birmingham 1994–96, judge Official Referees' Ct 1996–98 (official referee 1989), judge of the Technology and Construction Court High Court of Justice 1998–, judge of the Employment Appeal Tbnl 1999–; vice-pres Lincs and S Humberside Magistrates' Assoc 1988–94, memb Humberside Probation Ctee 1988–94; chm Nottingham Friendship Housing Assoc 1969–75; *Publications* Civil Procedure (contrib, 1999–); *Recreations* pugs, gardening, travel; *Style—* His Hon Judge David Wilcox; ✉ Technology and Construction Court High Court of Justice, St Dunstan's House, 133–137 Fetter Lane, London EC4A 1HD (tel 020 7936 7429)

WILCOX, Baroness (Life Peer UK 1996), of Plymouth in the County of Devon; Judith Ann Wilcox; da of John Freeman, of Plymouth, Devon, and Elsie Freeman; *b* 31 December 1939; *Educ* St Mary's Convent Wantage, Univ of Plymouth; *m* 1, 1961 (m dis 1986), Keith Davenport, s of Harold Cornelius Davenport, of Plymouth, Devon; 1 s (Hon Simon b 1963); m 2, 1986, as his 2 w, Sir Malcolm George Wilcox, CBE (d 1986), s of late George Harrison Wilcox; *Career* fndr Channel Foods Ltd Cornwall 1984–89, chm and md Pecheries de la Morinie 1989–91, chm Morinie et Cie France 1991–94; memb House of Lords Euro Select Ctee (Environment, Public Health and Consumer Affrs) 1996–, memb House of Lords Select Ctee (Sci and Technol) 2000–; oppn front bench treasy spokesman House of Lords 2002–; chm All-Pty Parly Gp for Consumer Affrs and Trading Standards, memb Tax Law Review Ctee; currently pres Nat Fedn of Consumer Gps; memb Bd: Automobile Assoc 1991–99, Port of London Authy 1993–2000 (vice-chm 2000–02); chm Nat Consumer Cncl 1990–96; former: memb Local Govt Commission, memb Bd Inland Revenue, memb PM's Citizen's Charter Advsy Panel, chm Citizen's Charter Complaints Task Force; non-exec dir: Carpetright plc 1997–, Cadbury Schweppes plc 1997–2006, Johnson Services plc 2003–; vice-pres The Guide Assoc; memb Governing Body Inst for Food Research 1998–2002; govr Imperial Coll 2006; FRSA, Hon FCGI; *Recreations* walking, sailing, calligraphy; *Clubs* Athenaeum, St Mawes Sailing; *Style—* The Rt Hon Lady Wilcox; ✉ House of Lords, London SW1A 0PW

WILD, Damian Paul Derek; s of Derek Wild (d 2005), and Valerie, *née* du Plessé; *b* 30 December 1969; *Educ* Univ of Central England (BA); *m* 8 May 1999, Nicola Taylor; 1 s (Louis b 31 Aug 2004), 1 da (Ella b 20 March 2006); *Career* reporter then chief reporter Public Finance 1993–97, freelance journalist CNN and South China Morning Post 1997–98; Accountancy Age: news ed 1999–2000, ed 2000–05; gp ed-in-chief business and finance titles VNU Business Pubns 2006–; FRSA; *Books* Decade (series co-author, 1998); *Recreations* travel; *Style—* Damian Wild, Esq; ✉ Accountancy Age, VNU Business Publications, VNU House, 32–34 Broadwick Street, London W1A 2HG (tel 020 7316 9237, e-mail damian_wild@vnu.co.uk)

WILD, Jonathan; s of John William Howard Wild, CO (RAF), of Poole, Dorset, and Madeleine Clifford Wild; *b* 4 August 1951; *Educ* Woking GS for Boys, UCL (BSc, DipArch); *m* 27 April 1979 (m dis 2005), Jacqueline Ann, da of Roland Oliver Cise, of Walton-on-Thames, Surrey; 1 s (Nicholas James b 1980), 1 da (Anna Louise Julie b 1969); partner, Maureen Rosemary Willmott, *née* McCammond; *Career* chartered architect; dir MoJo Architecture, Design, Development Ltd, sole princ Wild Alliance; RIBA, ARB; *Recreations* motor sport, music, travel, design; *Style—* Jonathan Wild; ✉ MoJo Architecture, Design, Development Limited, MoJo Studio, 38 Victoria Road, Fleet, Hampshire GU51 4DW (tel 07894 75680)

WILD, Kenneth (Ken); s of Ernest Wild, and Ethel Harriet, *née* Singleton; *b* 25 July 1949; *Educ* Chadderton GS, Univ of York (BA); *m* 6 April 1974, Johanna Regina Elizabeth, da of Karl Heinrich Christian Wolf, of Cheltenham, Glos; 1 da (Victoria b 1978), 1 s (Philip b 1981); *Career* chartered accountant; Peat Marwick Mitchell & Co 1974–78, under-sec ICAEW 1978–80; Touche Ross (now Deloitte & Touche LLP): mangr then sr mangr 1980–84, tech ptnr 1984–; ICAEW: memb Cncl 1989–90 and 1991–97, chm Business Law Ctee 1996–97 (vice-chm 1990–96), memb Accounting Standards Bd 1994–2003, memb Fin Reporting Advsy Bd to Treasy 1996–; FCA 1978, FRSA 1997, CPFA 2002; *Books* An Accountants Digest Guide to Accounting Standards - Accounting for Associated Companies (1982), Company Accounting Requirements, A Practical Guide (jtly, 1985), The Financial Reporting and Accounting Service (jtly, 1990), Cash Flow Statements: A Practical Guide (jtly, 1991), Accounting for Subsidiary Undertakings: A Practical Guide (jtly, 1992), Reporting Financial Performance: A Practical Guide to FRS 3 (jtly, 1993), Financial Reporting and Accounting Manual (jtly, 1994), International Accounting Standards: A Guide to Preparing Accounts (jtly, 1998), GAAP 2000 (jtly, 1999), GAAP 2001 (jtly, 2000), A Practitioner's Guide to Full Fair Value Accounting of Financial Instruments (jtly, 2001); *Recreations* reading, gardening; *Style—* Ken Wild, Esq; ✉ Deloitte & Touche LLP, 180 Strand, London WC2R 1BL (tel 020 7007 0907, e-mail kwild@deloitte.co.uk)

WILD, Prof Raymond (Ray); s of Frank Wild, of Chinley, Derbys, and Alice, *née* Large; *b* 24 December 1940; *Educ* Glossop GS, Stockport Tech Coll, Salford Coll of Tech, John Dalton Coll, Univ of Bradford (MSc (x 2), PhD) Brunel Univ (DSc); *m* 25 Sept 1965, Carol Ann, da of William Mellor, of Birchvale, Derbys; 1 s (Duncan Francis b 19 March 1970), 1 da (Virginia Kate b 10 June 1972); *Career* in industry 1957–67: apprentice and draughtsman 1957–62, design engr 1962–64, res engr 1964–66, prodn controller 1966–67; Univ of Bradford: res fell 1967–69, lectr 1969–73; prof Henley Mgmnt Coll 1973–77; Brunel Univ: head of Depts 1977–89, pro-vice-chllr 1988–89; princ Henley Mgmnt Coll 1990–2001; coll govr; Whitworth fell; Hon DUniv Brunel 2001; FIMechE, FIEE, CIMgt, FRSA, CEng; *Books* incl: Work Organization (1975), Concepts For Operations Management (1977), Mass Production Management (1972), Techniques of Production Management (1971), Management And Production (1972), Production and Operations Management (1978, 5 edn 1995), How To Manage (1982, 2 edn 1994), Operations Management (2001), Essentials of Operations Management (2001); *Recreations* writing, travel, theatre, painting, sports, DIY; *Style—* Prof Ray Wild; ✉ Broomfield, New Road, Shiplake, Henley-on-Thames, Oxfordshire RG9 3LA (tel 0118 940 4102, e-mail wildhenley@aol.com)

WILD, (John) Robin; JP (Ettrick and Lauderdale 1982); s of John Edward Brooke Wild (ka 1943), of Scarborough, N Yorks, and Teresa, *née* Ballance; *b* 12 September 1941; *Educ* Sedbergh, Univ of Edinburgh (BDS), Univ of Dundee (DPD); *m* 31 July 1965, (Eleanor) Daphne, da of Walter Gifford Kerr (d 1975), of Edinburgh; 2 da (Alison b 1967, Rosemary b 1977), 1 s (Richard b 1978 d 2003); *Career* princ in gen dental practice Scarborough 1965–71, dental offr E Lothian CC 1971–74, chief admin dental offr Borders Health Bd 1974–87, regnl dental postgrad advsr SE Regnl Ctee for Postgrad Med Educn 1982–87, dir of studies (dental) Edinburgh Postgrad Bd for Med 1986–87, chief dental offr Scottish Office Home and Health Dept 1993–97 (dep chief dental offr 1987–93), dir of dental servs Scotland NHS 1993–97, chief dental offr Dept of Health 1997–2000, conslt in dental public health Dumfries and Galloway Health Bd 2005–07; hon sr lectr Univ of Dundee 1993–; pres Cncl of European Chief Dental Offrs 1999–2001, vice-pres Cwlth Dental Assoc 1997–2003, chm Scottish Cncl Br Dental Assoc 1985–87; chm: Scottish Borders Justices Ctee 2000–05, District Courts Assoc 2002–04; FFCS, fell Br Dental Assoc, FDSRCSE; *Recreations* restoration and driving of vintage cars, music, gardening; *Clubs* Royal Cwlth Soc, RSM; *Style—* Robin Wild, Esq; ✉ Braehead House, St Boswells, Roxburghshire TD6 0AZ

WILDASH, HE Richard James; LVO; s of Arthur Ernest Wildash, of London, and Sheila Howard, *née* Smith; *b* 24 December 1955; *Educ* St Paul's, Corpus Christi Coll Cambridge (MA); *m* 29 Aug 1981, (Elizabeth) Jane, da of Peter Edward Walmsley, of Bebington; 2 da (Joanna Helen b 1987, Bethany Jane b 1996); *Career* entered HM Dip Serv 1977; served: E Berlin 1979, Abidjan 1981, FCO 1984, Harare 1988, FCO 1992, New Delhi 1994; dep high cmmr Kuala Lumpur 1998, high cmmr to Cameroon 2002–06 (concurrently non-resident ambass to Central African Repub, Chad, Equatorial Guinea and Gabon), high cmmr to Malawi 2006–; memb Chartered Inst of Linguists; FRGS; *Recreations* music, literature, the country; *Style—* HE Mr Richard Wildash, LVO; ✉ c/o Foreign & Commonwealth Office (Lilongwe), King Charles Street, London SW1A 2AH (e-mail wildash@fish.co.uk)

WILDBLOOD, (Christopher) Michael Garside; MBE (2000); s of late Richard Garside Wildblood, of Ouseburn, N Yorks, and Rita Muriel, *née* Jellings; *b* 9 October 1945; *Educ* Rugby, Corpus Christi Coll Cambridge (MA, Dip Arch); *m* 30 July 1971, Anne Somerville, da of Alun Roberts, of Radyr, Glamorgan; 1 s (Thomas Garside b 1976), 3 da (Shân Catherine Somerville b 1978, Jane Somerville b 1987, Rachel Somerville b 1989); *Career* chartered architect; ptnr and princ Wildblood Macdonald, Chartered Architects 1975–; chm: RIBA Leeds Soc of Architects 1985–87, RIBA Yorks Region 1985–86; vice-chm RIBA Enterprises Ltd 1998–2002; pres W Yorks Soc of Architects 1993–95; RIBA; *Recreations* golf, choral singing, watercolour painting; *Clubs* Alwoodley Golf, Old Rugbeian Golfing Soc (Northern Sec); *Style—* Michael Wildblood, Esq, MBE; ✉ Hammonds, Lower Dunsforth, Ouseburn, North Yorkshire YO26 9SA; Wildblood Macdonald, Chartered Architects, Parkhill Studio, Walton Road, Wetherby, West Yorkshire LS22 5DZ (tel 01937 585225)

WILDBLOOD, Stephen Roger; QC (1999); s of Fred Roger John Wildblood, of Shropshire, and Patricia Ann Mary, *née* Greenwood (d 1965); *b* 18 August 1958; *Educ* Millfield, Univ of Sheffield (LLB); *Family* 2 s (Benedict b 11 Nov 1985, Samuel b 10 Dec 2004), 1 da (Sarah b 16 May 1988); m, 2003, Emma Jane; *Career* called to the Bar 1980, asst recorder 1997–2000, recorder 2000–, dep High Court judge 2004–; memb Family Law Bar Assoc; *Publications* Financial Provision in Family Matters (with Eaton), Butterworths Family Law Service (contrib), Butterworths Encyclopaedia of Forms and Precedents (contrib); *Recreations* running, cycling, reading; *Style—* Stephen Wildblood, Esq, QC; ✉ Albion Chambers, Broad Street, Bristol BS1 1DR (tel 0117 927 2144, fax 0117 926 2569)

WILDE, Malcolm James; s of Malcolm John Wilde, and Irene Doris, *née* Rickwood; *b* 9 October 1950; *Educ* Bishopshalt Sch; *m* 1 Sept 1973, (Helen) Elaine, da of John Bartley, and Doris Bartley; 2 da (Joanne Caroline b 6 July 1976, Julia Felicity b 10 Feb 1981), 1 s (Alastair James Rory b 27 Feb 1987); *Career* mangr Western American Bank (Europe) Ltd 1970–75, vice-pres Crocker National Bank 1975–77; dir: Guinness Mahon Holdings Ltd, Guinness Mahon & Co Ltd 1977–87; md: British & Commonwealth Merchant Bank plc 1987–92, Standard Bank 1992–2006 (chief exec Asia), ceo Intl Assets Holding Corp (Asia) 2006–; *Recreations* golf, sport generally, opera, antique furniture; *Clubs* Piltdown Golf, Singapore Island Country, Tanglin, Hong Kong, Hong Kong Golf; *Style—* Malcolm Wilde, Esq; ✉ Clayton Manor, Underhill Lane, Clayton, West Sussex BN6 9PJ; International Assets Holding Corporation, 1 Raffles Place, #43–03, OUB Centre, Singapore 048616 (e-mail malcolm.wilde@intlassets.com)

WILDING, Barbara; CBE (2006), QPM (2000); *Educ* Univ of London; *Career* early career with States of Jersey Police, joined Met Police 1971, Asst Chief Constable Kent Constabulary 1994–98, Dep Asst Cmmr Met Police 1998–2004, Chief Constable South Wales Police 2004–; memb Terrorism and Crime Ctees ACPO; memb RCDS; memb: Advsy Bd Business in the Community Wales, Cncl Prince's Tst Cmyru, Big Lottery Cmyru; hon fell Cardiff Univ; Liveryman Welsh Livery Guild; CCMI 2005 (pres Cardiff branch), FRSA 2006; *Style—* Miss Barbara Wilding, CBE, QPM; ✉ South Wales Police Headquarters, Bridgend CF31 3SU

WILDMAN, David Aubrey; s of Ronald Wildman, of Luton, Beds, and Bridget, *née* Cotter; *b* 4 July 1955; *Educ* Denbigh HS, Luton Coll; *m* 11 Oct 1975, Gillian, da of late Edward Close, of Richmond, N Yorks; 1 s (Philip b 1986), 1 da (Sophie b 1992); *Career* Chase Manhattan Bank 1973–75, Mobil Oil Co 1975–80; gp ceo 1988–: General & Medical Securities Ltd, General & Medical Finance plc, General & Medical Insurance Ltd; *Recreations* skiing, theatre, fine art, family life; *Style—* David A Wildman, Esq; ✉ 41 Turnstone House, City Quay, London E1W 1AE (e-mail david.wildman@generalandmedical.com)

WILDSMITH, Brian Lawrence; s of Paul Wildsmith, of Yorks, and Annie Elizabeth Oxley (d 1984); *b* 22 January 1930; *Educ* De La Salle Coll, Slade Sch of Fine Art UCL (DFA); *m* 1955, Aurélie Janet Craigie, da of Bernard Ithurbide (d 1957); 1 s (Simon), 3 da (Clare, Rebecca, Anna); *Career* freelance artist 1957–, prodn design, illustrations, titles and graphics for first USA-USSR Leningrad film co prodn of the Blue Bird, artist and maker of picture books for young children; Brian Wildsmith Museum opened in Izu, Japan 1994; other one-man shows incl: Diamaru Museum Tokyo 1996 and 1997, Tenmaya-Yonagoshinmachi, Nagoya Mitsukoshi and Fukui City Art Museum, Kyoto Museum 2000, Okazaki Museum for Children 2001, Tokyo Fuji Museum and Japanese tour 2003, Japan Exhbn 2003, Taiwan Exhbn 2004 (touring 2004–05), Fantasia From a Fairyland (travelling exbn, over 1,350,000 visitors) 2003–05; various one-man shows in Japan 2001: incl Yokhama Kanagawa, Mihara Hiroshima, Nakano Tokyo, Fukuoka; winner: Kate Greenaway medal 1962, Kate Greenaway Medal Commendation 1963, Lewis Carroll Shelf Award 1966, Soka Gakkai Educnl medal 1988, The Ushio Culture award 1991, Tokyo Fuji Art-Museum Gold Medal 2003; *Books* ABC (1962), The Lion and the Rat (1963), The North Wind and the Sun (1964), Mother Goose (1964), 123 (1965), The Rich Man and the Shoemaker (1965), The Hare and the Tortoise (1966), Birds (1967), Animals (1967), Fish (1968), The Miller, the Boy, and the Donkey (1969), The Circus (1970), Puzzles (1970), The Owl and the Woodpecker (1971), The Twelve Days of Christmas (1972), The Little Wood Duck (1972), Squirrels (1974), Pythons Party (1974), Blue Bird (1976), The True Cross (1977), What The Moon Saw (1978), Hunter and his Dog (1979), Animal Shapes (1980), Animal Homes (1980), Animal Games (1980), Animal Tricks (1980), Seasons (1980), Professor Noah's Spaceship (1980), Bears Adventure (1981), Cat on the Mat (1982), The Trunk (1982), Pelican (1982), Apple Bird (1983), The Island (1983), All Fall Down (1983), The Nest (1983), Whose Shoes (1984), Toot Toot (1984), Daisy (1984), Give a Dog a Bone (1985), What A Tale (1986), My Dream (1986), Goats Trail (1986), Giddy Up (1987), If I Were You (1987), Carousel (1988), The Christmas Story (1989), The Snow Country Prince (1990), The Cherry Tree (1991), The Princess and The Moon (1991), Over the Deep Blue Sea (1992), The Easter Story (1993), The Tunnel (1993), Noah's Ark (1994), Saint Francis (1995), The Creation (1995), Katie and the Dream-Eater (in collaboration with HIH Princess Takamado, 1996), Brian Wildsmith's Wonderful World of Words (1996), Joseph (1997); in collaboration with Rebecca Wildsmith: Look Closer, Wake Up, Wake Up, What Did I Find, Whose Hat Was That (1993), Exodus (1998), The Bremen Town Band (1999), The Seven Ravens (2000), If Only (2000), How Many (2000), Not Here (2000), Knock Knock (2000), My Flower (2000), Jesus (2000), Mary (2002), A Christmas Journey (2003), The Christmas Crib - A Nativity Pop Up (2003); *Recreations* piano, tennis; *Clubs* Reform; *Style—* Brian L Wildsmith, Esq; ✉ 11 Castellaras le Vieux, 06370 Mouans-Sartoux, Alpes-Maritimes, France (tel 00 33 4 93 75 24 11)

WILDSMITH, Prof John Anthony Winston (Tony); s of Winston Wildsmith (d 1978), and Phyllis, *née* Jones (d 2000); *b* 22 February 1946; *Educ* King's Sch Gloucester, Univ of Edinburgh Med Sch (MD); *m* 1969, Angela Fay, *née* Smith; 3 da (Kathryn b 1972, Clare b 1973, Emma b 1976); *Career* early career: Univ of Edinburgh/Royal Infirmary Edinburgh, Brigham and Women's Hosp Boston USA (one year), various trg posts in anaesthesia; conslt anaesthetist/sr lectr Royal Infirmary Edinburgh 1977–95 (clinical dir of anaesthetics, intensive care and operating theatres 1992–95), new chair of anaesthesia Univ of Dundee and hon conslt anaesthetist Tayside Univ Hosps NHS Tst 1995–2007; memb Cncl Royal Coll of Anaesthetists 1997–2007; numerous papers published on special interests in anaesthesia; memb Editorial Bd Br Jl of Anaesthesia; FRCA, FRCPEd, FRCSEd; *Recreations* golf, wine, travel; *Clubs* RAC, Royal Burgess Golfing Soc; *Style—* Prof Tony Wildsmith; ✉ 6 Castleroy Road, Broughty Ferry, Dundee DD5 2LQ

WILES, Eric Allen; s of Arthur Wiles (d 2004), of Brandesburton, E Yorks, and Doris May, *née* Grantham (d 1978); *b* 12 December 1956; *Educ* Hornsea Sch, Univ of Warwick (BA); *m* 9 June 1984, Carole Anne, da of Montague Carl Henry Docwra; 1 da (Olivia Alexandra b 5 Aug 1994), 1 s (Lucas Alexander b 30 April 2001); *Career* chartered accountant/tax conslt; trainee Binder Hamlyn 1978–82, Thornton Baker 1982–84, tax conslt Deloitte Haskins & Sells 1984–86; HSBC Asset Finance (UK) Ltd: tax mangr 1986–88, sr mangr Customer Serv 1988–91, fin controller 1991–93, sr mangr Business Devpt 1993–97; business devpt mangr HSBC Rail (UK) Ltd 1997–; chm Bd for Chartered Accountants in Business 1999–2000, vice-chm Members Servs 2004–, memb Cncl ICAEW 1994–; memb Corp Worcester Coll of Technol 1997– (chm 2000–); treas: RoSPA 2004–, Asthma UK 2005– (tstee 2003–); assoc FIMA 1979, assoc Chartered Inst of Taxation 1985, FCA 1992 (ACA 1982), FRSA 1995; *Recreations* gardening, travel, historical studies; *Style—* Eric Wiles, Esq; ✉ The Chapel, Chapel Lane, Upton Snodsbury, Worcestershire WR7 4NH (tel 01905 381270); HSBC Asset and Structured Finance, Level 24, 8 Canada Square, London E14 5HQ (tel 020 7991 6176, e-mail eric.wiles@hsbc.com)

WILES, Prof Paul; CB (2005); *b* 24 December 1944; *Educ* LSE, Trinity Hall Cambridge; *Career* res fell Inst of Criminology Univ of Cambridge 1970–72; Univ of Sheffield: lectr 1972–76, sr lectr 1976–88, prof of criminology 1988–99; dir of research, devpt and statistics and chief scientific advsr Home Office 1999–; author of various scientific papers and books; *Style—* Prof Paul Wiles, CB; ✉ Home Office, 2 Marsham Street, London SW1P 4DF (tel 020 7035 3344)

WILEY, (William) Struan Ferguson; s of John Nixon Wiley (d 1968), and Muriel Isobel, *née* Ferguson (d 1969); *b* 13 February 1938; *Educ* Fettes, Univ of New Hampshire USA; *m* 1, 25 Jan 1964 (m dis 1977), Margaret Louise, da of Ian Graham Forsyth, of Crinan, Scotland; 2 da (Sarah b 1964, Anna b 1969), 1 s (Fergus b 1966); m 2, 21 Dec 1977, Rosemary Anne, da of Sir John Cameron, OBE, of Cowesby, N Yorks; *Career* Nat Serv 2 Lt 10 Royal Hussars 1956–58, TA 1958–68, Lt Queens Own Yorks Yeo 1958–68; dir: Chunky Chicks (Nichols) Ltd 1962, Sterling Poultry Prods Ltd 1965, Ross Poultry Ltd 1970, Allied Farm Foods Ltd 1970, Imperial Foods Ltd 1975; chm and md Ross Poultry and Ross Buxted Nitrovit Ltd 1977; chm: J B Eastwood Ltd 1978, J Lyons Catering Ltd 1981, Normand Ltd 1981, Embassy Hotels Ltd 1983, Almear Ltd 1995–2000, Food for Thought (UK) Ltd 1996–98; asst md J Lyons & Co Ltd 1981–90, dir Allied-Lyons plc 1986–90, Normand Motor Gp Ltd (and chief exec) 1990–94; non-exec dir: Golden Lay Eggs UK Ltd, Wembley Stadium Ltd, John Clark (Holdings) Ltd 1996–, Stadium Group plc 1996–2006 (chm 2000–06), Blackpool Pleasure Beach Ltd 1996–; non-exec chm: Kingsbury Group plc 1995–97, Mayfair Taverns Ltd 1996–98, United Vegetables Ltd 1997–2005; chm Br Poultry Breeders and Hatcheries Assoc 1976; memb: Governing Body Houghton Poultry Res Station 1974–82, Grand Cncl Hotel Catering Benevolent Assoc 1983, Leisure Industries Ctee NEDC 1987, Strategy Ctee Retail Motor Industry Fedn 1990–94; winner Poultry Industry Mktg Award 1977; Freeman: City of London 1980, Worshipful Co of Poulters 1981; *Recreations* golf, shooting, collecting old golf clubs; *Clubs* Cavalry and Guards, Woodhall Spa Golf, Sunningdale Golf, Sr Golfers Soc; *Style—* Struan Wiley, Esq; ✉ Old Rectory, Withcall, Louth, Lincolnshire LN11 9RL (tel and fax 01507 343218, e-mail wiley@withcall.prestel.co.uk)

WILFORD, Michael James; CBE (2001); s of James Wilford (d 1964), and Kathleen, *née* Baulch (d 1964); *b* 9 September 1938; *Educ* Kingston Tech Sch, Northern Poly Sch of Architecture London (DipArch), Regent Street Poly Planning Sch; *m* 24 Sept 1960, Angela; 3 da (Karenna Jane b 1962, Jane Anne b 1970, Anna Patricia b 1973), 2 s (Carl Adrian b 1963, Paul Newton b 1966); *Career* architect; sr asst with: James Stirling and James Gowan 1960–63, James Stirling 1963–65; assoc ptnr James Stirling and Partners 1965–71, ptnr James Stirling Michael Wilford and Associates 1971–92 (sole practitioner 1992–93), sr ptnr Michael Wilford and Partners 1993–2001, sr ptnr Michael Wilford Architects 2001–; projects incl: Engrg Faculty Univ of Leicester (RIBA Nat Award and Reynold Aluminium Award 1964), History Faculty Univ of Cambridge (RIBA Nat Award 1970), Staatsgalerie Stuttgart (various German awards 1987–88), Clore Gallery addition to the Tate Gallery (RIBA Regnl and Nat Awards 1988), Tate Gallery Liverpool (RIBA Nat Award 1989), Sci Library Univ of Calif Irvine (Hon Award American Inst of Architects 1990, ALA/AIA Award of Excellence for Library Architecture 1995), B Braun Melsungen AG prodn plant Melsungen (various German awards 1993), Music Acad Stuttgart (RIBA Nat Educn Category Award and Sunday Times/RIBA Stirling Prize 1997), Temasek Poly Singapore (Singapore Inst of Architecs Award for Best Educn Bldg and ICI Silver Award for Use of Colour in a Bldg 1998), Sto Ag Communications Bldg and HQ/prodn plant Weizen (RIBA Euro Award 1999), The Lowry Salford (Royal Fine Art Cmmn Bldg of the Year 2001, RIBA Regnl Award 2001, Civic Award 2002), Br Embassy Berlin (RIBA Euro Award 2001), B Braun Melsungen World HQ (various German awards 2001); visiting critic to many Schs of Architecture at home and abroad since 1968 (external examiner since 1978); tutor AA 1969–73; visiting prof: Rice Univ Houston 1980–88, Graham Wills visiting prof Univ of Sheffield 1980–91, Univ of Cincinnati 1990–92, Charles Davenport visiting prof Yale Univ 1994–95; memb: Educn and Professional Devpt Ctee RIBA 1979–81, Advsy Ctee Dresden Schloss and Museums 1995–96; chm of assessors RIBA Awards 1987, 1989, 1991, 1992 and 2001; assessor: Cardiff Bay Opera House Competition 1994, Buchanan Street Urban Competition Glasgow 1997, Aarhus City Art Museum Competition Denmark 1997, Kleiner Schlossplatz Competition Stuttgart 1999, European Central Bank HQ Frankfurt Competition 2003–04, Hessiches Landesmuseum Darmstadt Competition 2003–04, Central Salford Urban Design Competition 2004, Freiburg Univ Library Competition 2006; lectures and addresses at numerous architectural confs worldwide; Hon DLit Univ of Sheffield 1989, Hon DSc Newcastle Univ Aust 1993, Hon DLitt Univ of Salford 2002; hon memb Bund Deutscher Architekten BDA 1997; hon fell American Inst of Architects 2006; memb: Singapore Inst of Architects, Inst of Arbitrators, RIBA, FRSA; *Publications* subject of various pubns incl: The Museums of James Stirling and Michael Wilford (1990), James Stirling Michael Wilford and Associates Buildings and Projects 1975–92 (1994), Wilford-Stirling-Wilford (1996); *Recreations* earth moving, landscape design; *Clubs* Groucho; *Style—* Michael Wilford, Esq, CBE; ✉ Michael Wilford Architects, Lone Oak Hall, Chuck Hatch, Hartfield, East Sussex TN7 4EX (tel 01892 770980, fax 01892 770040)

WILKES, Prof Sir Maurice Vincent; kt (2000); s of Vincent J Wilkes, OBE (d 1971), and Helen, *née* Malone (d 1968); *b* 26 June 1913; *Educ* King Edward's Sch Stourbridge, St John's Coll Cambridge (BA, MA, PhD); *m* 1947, Bertie Mary (Nina), da of Bertie Twyman (d 1914), British Consul Shanghai, China; 1 s (Anthony b 1950), 2 da (Helen b 1951, Margaret b 1953); *Career* WWII serv: sci offr ADRDE, Army Ops Res Gp, TRE 1939–42 (sr sci offr 1942–45); Univ of Cambridge: univ demonstrator 1937–45, head Computer Laboratory (formerly Mathematical Laboratory) 1945–80, prof of computer technol (now emeritus prof) 1965–80, fell St John's Coll 1950–; computer engr Digital Equipment Corp Maynard MA USA 1980–86, memb for res strategy Olivetti Res Bd 1986–90, staff conslt AT&T Laboratories Cambridge 1990–2002; Hon ScD Univ of Cambridge 1993; Hon DSc: Univ of Newcastle 1972, Univ of Hull 1974, Univ of Kent 1975, City Univ 1975, Free Univ of Amsterdam 1978, Tech Univ of Munich 1978, Univ of Bath 1987, Univ of Pennsylvania 1996; Hon DTech Linköping Sweden 1975; FRS 1956, FREng 1976, FBCS, FIEE; foreign assoc: US Nat Acad of Sci, US Nat Acad of Engrg; foreign hon memb American Acad of Arts and Scis, Kyoto Prize 1992, von Neumann Award IEEE 1997, Mountbatten Medal (Nat Electronics Cncl 1997); *Books* Memoirs of a Computer Pioneer (1985), Computing Perspectives (1994); author of various technical books and papers in sci jls; *Clubs* Athenaeum; *Style—* Prof Sir Maurice Wilkes, FRS, FREng; ✉ 130 Huntingdon Road, Cambridge CB3 0HL; Computer Laboratory, University of Cambridge, JJ Thomson Avenue, Cambridge CB3 0FD (tel 01223 763699, fax 01223 339678, e-mail maurice.wilkes@cl.cam.ac.uk)

WILKES, Prof (Francis) Michael; s of Francis Wilkes, of Dudley, Staffs, and Cecilia Josephine, *née* Grealey; *b* 9 November 1941; *Educ* St Philip's GS Birmingham, Univ of Birmingham (BSocSc, PhD); *m* Vivienne Mary, da of Alfred William Ernest Sawyer; 3 s (John Francis, David James (twins) b 19 Oct 1972, Stephen Mark b 9 March 1977); *Career* prof of business investment and mgmnt Univ of Birmingham 1991–2002 (emeritus prof 2002–, formerly lectr then sr lectr with secondments to Aston Univ Birmingham and Northwestern Univ USA); memb (Lib Dem) Birmingham City Cncl 1984–92 and 2000–; memb Fulbright Scholars' Assoc; *Books* Management of Company Finance (with J M Samuels, 1971, 6 edn 1995), Capital Budgeting Techniques (2 edn, 1983), Mathematics for Business Finance and Economics (1994, 2 edn 1998), Financial Management and Decision Making (with J M Samuels and R E Brayshaw, 1998); *Recreations* walking, cricket; *Style—* Councillor Michael Wilkes; ✉ e-mail michael.wilkes@birmingham.gov.uk

WILKES, Sir Michael; KCB (1991), CBE (1988, OBE 1979); *Educ* Kings Sch Rochester, RMA Sandhurst; *m* Anne; 2 s (Jonathan, Jeremy); *Career* cmmnd RA 1960, joined 7 Parachute Regt RHA, served ME and Cyprus, Adj 42 Medium Regt RA Devizes, psc, Bde Maj HQ 3 Div RA Bulford; cmd The Chestnut Troop 1 Regt RHA 1975–77, mil asst to Chief of Gen Staff MOD, COS HQ 3 Armd Div Soest Germany, Cdr 22 Armd Bde BAOR, GOC 3 Armd Div BAOR 1988–90, Cdr UK Field Army and Inspr Gen TA 1990, Land Dep to Jt Cdr HQ Strike Cmd High Wycombe under Operation Granby (Kuwait), memb Army Bd and Adj Gen 1993–95; nat pres Army Cadet Force Assoc 1999–2005; Lt Govr Jersey 1995–2000; Freeman City of London 1993; Order of Military Merit 1st Class (Jordan) 1994, KStJ 1996; *Recreations* sailing, hill walking, skiing, reading; *Clubs* Royal Chartered Island Yacht, Travellers; *Style—* Sir Michael Wilkes, KCB, CBE; ✉ The Travellers Club, 106 Pall Mall, London SW1Y 5EP

WILKES, Pamela Helen; da of Alan Donald Marsh (d 1966), and Ethel Margaret, *née* Ralph (d 2003); *b* 18 April 1947; *Educ* St Joseph's Convent Sidcup, Kingston upon Hull Coll of Educn (BEd); *m* (m dis); *Career* teacher: Malvern Girls' Coll 1971–73, Frank F Harrison Sch Walsall 1973–75, John Willmott Sch Sutton Coldfield 1975–86; dep head Sutton Coldfield GS for Girls 1985–2000, headmistress Wimbledon High Sch GDST 2001–; memb SHA 1995; FRSA 2003; *Recreations* mountain walking, cinema, reading, gardening; *Clubs* Univ Women's; *Style—* Mrs Pamela Wilkes; ✉ Wimbledon High School GDST, Mansel Road, London SW19 4AB (tel 020 8971 0900, fax 020 8971 0901, e-mail pamela.wilkes@wim.gdst.net and pam.wilkes@waitrose.com)

WILKES, Roderick Edward; s of Ernest Lawrence Wilkes (d 1987), of Staffordshire, and Sabra Whitehouse Johnson; *b* 26 February 1945; *Educ* Kingshill Sch Secdy Modern for Boys Wednesbury, Wednesbury Coll of Commerce (HND, DipM); *m* 28 March 1970, Marie, da of Harold Page; 1 s (James Edward b 6 June 1972), 1 da (Victoria Louise b 6 May 1974); *Career* Guest Keen & Nettlefolds Ltd 1960–70, commercial conslt GKN Sankey Ltd 1970–73, mktg dir Morlock Industries Ltd 1973–84, gp mktg dir Ellison Circlips Gp 1984–86, sr md RFS 1987–94 (gen mangr 1986–87), md Phoenix Metal Products Ltd 1994–2003, chm Gray Page Ltd 2003–, chief exec CIM 2007– (formerly nat chm); nat chm Specialist Ceilings and Interiors Assoc; tstee: RoSPA, Jubilee Sailing Tst; Pres's Award CIM; FRSA, MCAM, FIOD, FCIM, FCMI; *Recreations* theatre, swimming, travel, DIY; *Style—* Roderick E Wilkes, Esq; ✉ Monmoor Farm, Eardington, Bridgnorth, Shropshire WV16 5LA (tel and fax 01746 763076)

WILKIE, Agnes; da of Peter B Wilkie, and Margaret E, *née* McCracken; *Educ* Hamilton Acad, Univ of Strathclyde (BA); *Career* editorial asst D C Thomson 1976–77, journalist The Scottish Farmer 1977–79, features ed Horse and Hound 1979–80; Scottish Television: news prodr 1981–92, head of features and entertainment 1992–2006; head of int devpt TRC Media 2006–; BAFTA Scotland awards: Best Entertainment Prog 1997, Best Special Interest Prog 1997; memb NUJ 1977–; *Recreations* sailing, running, riding, books, cinema, theatre, shopping, driving fast, climbing mountains in order to see views; *Style—* Ms Agnes Wilkie; ✉ TRC Media, 227 West George Street, Glasgow G2 2ND (tel 0141 568 7150, e-mail agnes.wilkie@trcmedia.org)

WILKIE, Prof Andrew Oliver Mungo; s of Douglas Robert Wilkie, FRS, and June Rosalind, *née* Hill; *b* 14 September 1959; *Educ* Westminster (Queen's scholar), Trinity Coll Cambridge (open scholar, exhibitioner, MA), Merton Coll Oxford (Geoffrey Hill Spray Prize, Flora Medical Student Award, BM BCh, MA), RCP London (DCH), Univ of Oxford (DM); *m* 24 June 1989, Jane Elizabeth, *née* Martin; 2 s (Oscar Brook Douglas b 17 Feb 1997, Fergus John Mungo b 26 Oct 1998); *Career* clinical geneticist; SHO at various hosps London and Bristol 1984–87, MRC trg fell MRC Molecular Haematology Unit and hon registrar Inst of Molecular Medicine John Radcliffe Hosp Oxford 1987–90, sr registrar Gt Ormond St Hosp for Sick Children London 1990–91, clinical research fell in dysmorphology Inst of Child Health 1991, sr registrar Inst of Medical Genetics Univ Hosp of Wales Cardiff 1992–93, hon conslt in clinical genetics Dept of Medical Genetics Churchill Hosp Oxford and Oxford Craniofacial Unit Radcliffe Infirmary 1993–, Wellcome Tst advanced research fell Inst of Molecular Medicine 1993–95, Wellcome Tst sr research fell in clinical science Weatherall Inst of Molecular Medicine 1995–2003, prof of genetics Univ of Oxford 2000–03, Nuffield prof of pathology Nuffield Dept of Clinical Lab Sciences Univ of Oxford 2003–; chm Oxford Genetics Knowledge Park 2004– (co-chm 2002–04); Nuffield Cncl on Bioethics: memb Working Party on the Genetics of Mental Disorders 1996–98, memb Working Party on Genes and Behaviour 2000–02; author of numerous articles in peer-review jls and chapters in books; memb Editorial Bd: Jl of Medical Genetics 1994–98, Human Genetics 1998–, Human Molecular Genetics 2002–, Human Mutation 2005–; memb: Advsy Bd Encyclopedia of the Human Genome 2000–03, Ctee Genetical Soc 1996–99; memb: Br Soc of Human Genetics/Clinical Genetics Soc 1985–, Assoc of Physicians of GB and I 1997–, European Molecular Biology Organization 2006–; Oon Int Prize in Preventive Medicine Downing Coll Cambridge and Cambridge Univ Medical Sch 2002; FRCP 1998 (MRCP 1986), FMedSci 2002; *Recreations* wildlife, mountains, visual arts; *Style—* Prof Andrew Wilkie; ✉ Weatherall Institute of Molecular Medicine, John Radcliffe Hospital, Headington, Oxford OX3 9DS (tel 01865 222619, fax 01865 222500, e-mail awilkie@hammer.imm.ox.ac.uk)

WILKIE, (Alex) Ian; s of Frederick James Wilkie (d 1976), and Florence Gladys Bell (d 1989); direct descendant of Sir David Wilkie, RA (1785–1841); *b* 1 September 1935; *Educ* Lancing, Poole Coll of Tech, Brighton Tech Coll (HNC Metallurgy); *m* 4 May 1963, Pamela May, da of William Frank Ross, of Hove, E Sussex; 1 s (Andrew b 19 Jan 1964), 2 da (Jill, Philippa (twins) b 14 Jan 1966); *Career* Mil Serv The Gordon Highlanders; dir: The Association of British Pewter Craftsmen Ltd 1970– (chm 2004–07), British Pewter Designs Ltd 1971– (chm 2002–), Anzon Ltd (subsid of Cookson Group plc) 1980–84; head of corporate relations worldwide Cookson Group plc 1985–92; sec to the Adjudicators of The Cookson Conservation and Restoration Award 1992–, tstee Historic Churches

Preservation Tst 1994–2005; memb: Hail Weston Parochial Church Cncl 1994–2004, Hail Weston PC 1995–, St Neots Deanery Synod 1996–2004, Ely Diocesan Synod 1996–2004; memb: Br Assoc for Shooting and Conservation, Scot Assoc for Country Sports, Countryside Alliance (life memb); regular contributor of articles on marketing, advertising and corporate affrs; Freeman City of London, memb Ct of Assts Worshipful Co of Pewterers; *Recreations* shooting (shoot capt Stow Longa Shoot), stalking, fishing, golf, gardening, property restoration; *Clubs* East India, Lime Street Ward, London Metal Exchange Golf Assoc (life vice-pres); *Style—* A Ian Wilkie, Esq; ✉ The Old Post Office, Hail Weston, Cambridgeshire PE19 5JW (tel 01480 472965, fax 01480 477300, car 07831 247553)

WILKINS, Jon Matthew; s of Keith Wilkins, of High Wycombe, Bucks, and Ros Wilkins (d 1994); *b* 29 November 1966, High Wycombe, Bucks; *Educ* Royal GS High Wycombe, Plymouth Poly (BSc); *m* 1 Aug 1998, Lara, *née* South; *Career* Granada Television 1988–90, MTV Europe 1990–92, Walt Disney Co 1992–94, strategy dir BMP DDB 1994–97, md PHD 1997–2000, founding ptnr Naked Communications 2000; memb MRS; MIPA, MInstD; *Recreations* sport, music; *Clubs* Chelsea FC (season ticket); *Style—* Jon Wilkins, Esq; ✉ Naked Communications, 159–173 St John Street, London EC1V 4QJ (tel 020 7336 8084, fax 020 7336 8009, mobile 07779 623806, e-mail jon@nakedcomms.com)

WILKINS, Prof Malcolm Barrett; s of Barrett Charles Wilkins (d 1962), of Cardiff, and Eleanor Mary, *née* Jenkins; *b* 27 February 1933; *Educ* Monkton House Sch Cardiff, King's Coll London (BSc, PhD, DSc); *m* 10 July 1959, (Mary) Patricia, da of Lt-Cdr James Edward Maltby, RNR, RD; 1 s (Nigel Edward Barrett b 7 Aug 1961), 1 da (Fiona Louise Emma Barrett b 14 Jan 1965 d 1980); *Career* lectr in botany King's Coll London 1959–64 (asst lectr 1958–59), prof of biology UEA 1965–67 (lectr 1964–65), prof of plant physiology Univ of Nottingham 1967–70, Regius prof of botany Univ of Glasgow 1970–2000; chm: Life Sciences Advsy Ctee Euro Space Agency 1987–89, Laurel Bank Sch Co Ltd Glasgow 1980–87; memb: Ct Univ of Glasgow 1993–97, Incorporation of Gardeners City of Glasgow; tstee Royal Botanic Gdns Edinburgh 1990–99 (dep chm 1993–94, chm 1994–99); memb Cncl Scottish Agric Coll; hon memb American Soc for Plant Physiology; FRSE 1972 (vice-pres 1994–97); *Books* Plantwatching (1988), Advanced Plant Physiology (ed, 1984), The Physiology of Plant Growth and Development (ed, 1969); *Recreations* fishing, model engrg; *Clubs* Caledonian, New (Edinburgh); *Style—* Prof Malcolm Wilkins, FRSE; ✉ 5 Hughenden Drive, Glasgow G12 9XS (tel 0141 334 8079)

WILKINSON, Andrew John Owen; s of John Wilkinson, and Anne, *née* Mennie; *b* Liverpool; *Educ* St Edward's Coll Liverpool, Jesus Coll Oxford (MA, BCL); *m* 21 Sept 1991, Juliet, *née* Morris; 2 da (Alice Isabel b 12 Jan 1996, Imogen Grace b 31 May 2000), 1 s (Hal James Oliver 25 Nov 1997); *Career* called to the Bar 1983, admitted slr 1987; Clifford Chance 1985–1998, Cadwalader Wickersham & Taft LLP 1998–2007 (memb Mgmnt Ctee and managing ptnr 2000–07); md Goldman Sachs 2007–; memb editorial bd of several legal pubns; Legal Business Lawyer of the Year 2004, Restructuring Team of the Year Lawyer Awards 2005; sponsor and supporter Almeida Theatre; memb: Insolvency Lawyers Assoc, Int Bar Assoc; co-chair Insolvency Sub-ctee European High Yield Assoc; fell Soc of Practitioners of Insolvency; *Publications* Insolvency of Banks: Managing the Risks, Insolvency Law (co-author), various chapters in Tolley's Insolvency; *Recreations* tennis, opera, theatre, piano; *Clubs* RAC, Blackwell Golf, Campden Tennis; *Style—* Andrew Wilkinson, Esq

WILKINSON, Barbara Ellison; da of James Kemsey Wilkinson (d 1997), and Nina Mary Louise Wilkinson, *née* Cooper (d 2000); *b* 25 June 1940; *Educ* Stoneygate Coll Leicester, Loughborough HS, Secretarial Coll Leicester; *m* (m dis 1976); 1 da (Karin Louise b 13 May 1964), 1 s (Nicholas Charles b 24 Dec 1965); *Career* co-owner Wilkinson Gp of Companies (non-exec dir 1995–2005); *Recreations* travel, antique collecting, theatre, dining out, reading, horse racing; *Style—* Ms Barbara Wilkinson; ✉ Wilkinson Group of Companies, J K House, PO Box 20, Roebuck Way, Manton Wood, Worksop Nottinghamshire S80 3YY (tel 01909 505505, fax 01909 505777)

WILKINSON, Prof Brian; *b* 1938; *Educ* King's Coll Durham (BSc Civil Eng, BSc Geology, Lebur Prize), Univ of Manchester (PhD); *Career* engr Babtie Shaw & Morton Glasgow 1961–63, lectr Dept of Civil Engrg Univ of Manchester 1963–69, sr engr Water Resources Bd Reading 1969–74, sr princ hydrologist Severn Trent Water Authy Birmingham 1974, head Communications Gp and research co-ordinator Water Research Centre Medmenham 1979–84 (head Water Resources Div 1974–79), prof of civil engrg and head of dept RMCS Shrivenham 1984–85, prof of civil engrg and dep dean Cranfield Univ Shrivenham 1985–88, head Wallingford Lab and dir Inst of Hydrology 1988–94, dir Centre for Ecology and Hydrology UK NERC 1994–99; visiting prof Univ of Reading 1989–; dir Oxford Vacs Ltd 1997–99; sr conslt Solutions to Environmental Problems (StEP) 1999–, former head UK Delgn World Meteorological Orgn's Cmmn for Hydrology; former chm: UK Govt Interdepartmental Hydrology Ctee, Int Hydrological Prog Ctee UK UNESCO, UK Environmental Change Network Ctee; former memb: Royal Soc/Fell of Engrg UK Ctee of Int Decade for Natural Disaster Reduction, Br Ctee Int Assoc of Hydrogeologists, Terrestrial and Freshwater Science and Technol Bd NERC, Land Ocean Interaction Study Science Planning Gp and Steering Ctee, UK GEWEX Forum, Canadian GEWEX Science Advsy Panel, GEWEX Int Scientific Steering Ctee, NERC Terrestrial and Freshwater Science and Technol Bd, UK UNESCO Sustainable Devpt Ctee, ICE Environment Sustainability Bd, Panel EU 5 Year assess of RTD Environment and Sustainable Devpt Sub Programme; memb Expert Gp EU 2002 Monitoring of European Research Area; fndr memb EurAqua (Euro Network of Fresh Water Research Orgns); convenor IHAS Symposium Macromodelling of the Hydrosphere Japan 1993, UK rep to Science Cmmn UNESCO Gen Conference, project co-ordinator Ind Review Gp Brent Decommissioning Project, advsr Safety, Health and Environment Ctee Transport for London; author numerous papers in ac jls; Fell Russian Acad of Natural Sciences 1997; CEng 1967, CGeol 1967, FICE 1984, FCIWEM 1984, FGS 1990; *Recreations* squash, classical music, violin, karate; *Clubs* Fondation Universitaire (Brussels); *Style—* Professor Brian Wilkinson; ✉ Solutions to Environmental Problems (StEP), Millfield House, High Street, Leintwardine, Craven Arms SY7 0LB (e-mail gb.wilk@dsl.pipex.com)

WILKINSON, Charles Edmund; s of Dr Oliver Charles Wilkinson (d 1987), and Sheila Muriel, *née* McMullan (d 1997); *b* 6 June 1943; *Educ* Haileybury and ISC, Clare Coll Cambridge; *Children* 2 da (Claire b 10 March 1972, Juliet b 13 June 1973); *Career* slr; sr ptnr Blyth Dutton 1980–91 (ptnr 1974), ptnr Lawrence Graham (following merger) 1991–2005, ret; chm: European Utilities Tst plc, Asset Mgmnt Investment Co plc; dir: Landore Resources Ltd, Summit Germany Ltd; memb Worshipful Co of Coachmakers and Coach Harness Makers, Freeman City of London; memb Law Soc; *Clubs* Brooks's, City, Hurlingham; *Style—* Charles Wilkinson, Esq; ✉ Utopia, Rue de la Passee, St Sampsons, Guernsey GY2 4TN (tel 01481 255351, e-mail cewilkinson@f2s.com)

WILKINSON, Prof Christopher David Wicks (Chris); s of Charles Norman Wilkinson (d 1942), and late Doris Margaret, *née* Wicks; *b* 1 January 1940; *Educ* Queen Elizabeth's GS Blackburn, Balliol Coll Oxford (MA), Stanford Univ (PhD); *m* 25 June 1962, Dr Judith (Judy) Anne Hughes, da of late Ronald Sydney Hughes; 2 da (Rona Elizabeth b 4 Oct 1969, Maggie Alison b 19 July 1974), 1 s (Kit Alexander b 27 May 1971); *Career* engr English Electric Valve Co Chelmsford 1967–69; Dept of Electronics and Electrical Engrg Univ of Glasgow: lectr 1969–75, sr lectr 1975–79, reader 1979–82, titular prof 1982–92, James Watt prof 1992–2005, emeritus prof 2005–; memb APS; FRSE 1987; *Recreations* hill walking, allotment holder; *Style—* Prof Chris Wilkinson, FRSE; ✉ Department of Electronics and Electrical Engineering, The University, Glasgow G12 8QQ (tel 0141 330 5219, fax 0141 330 6010)

WILKINSON, Christopher John (Chris); OBE (2000); s of Maj Edward Anthony Wilkinson, of Welwyn Garden City, Herts, and Norma Doreen, *née* Trevelyan-Beer; *b* 1 July 1945; *Educ* St Albans Sch, Regent Street Poly Sch of Architecture (DipArch, RIBA); *m* 3 April 1976, Diana Mary, da of Alan Oakley Edmunds, of Limpsfield Chart, Surrey; 1 da (Zoe b 1978), 1 s (Dominic b 1980); *Career* princ ptnr Wilkinson Eyre Architects (formerly Chris Wilkinson Architects) 1983–; previous employment with Richard Rogers and Ptnrs, Michael Hopkins Architects and Foster Assocs; assessor on BSC Colorcoat Award 1986 and 1987, British Steel Student Architectural Award 1994, 1995 and 1998, assessor on BCI Awards 1998 and 2005; visiting prof: IIT Chicago 1998, Harvard GSD 2004; cmmr English Heritage 2007– (memb Urban Panel 2000–); memb Advsy Cncl Steel Construction Inst 1998–2000; chm: RIBA Region Awards 1996, 2000 and 2001, Aluminium Awards 1997, Civic Tst Awards 1998 and 2000; memb RIBA Honours Awards Panel 2005 and 2006; works exhibited: Royal Acad Summer Exhbn 1986, 1987, 1988, 1991, 1995, 1996, 1997, 2002, 2003, 2004, 2005, 2006 and 2007, The Architecture Fndn 1992 and 1995, Tokyo Design Centre 1995, New Works Future Visions Sao Paolo 1997, New Urban Environments Tokyo 1998, Millennium Products 2000, Great Expectations Exhbn 2001, New Connections: The Jubilee Line Extension and Urban Regeneration 2001, Bridging Art and Science Science Museum 2001 (solo exhbn), Venice Biennale 2004, Reflectionist Destinations at Wapping Project (solo exhbn); projects incl: Stratford Market Depot and Stratford Station for Jubilee Line Extension, Dyson HQ Malmesbury, Magna Centre Millennium Project Rotherham, South Quay Footbridge, Hulme Arch, Challenge of Materials Gall, Making of Modern World Gall and Wellcome Wing exhbn at the Science Museum, Explore at Bristol, Gateshead Millennium Bridge, Nat Waterfront Museum Swansea, Empress State Building Redevelopment Earls Court, Mary Rose Museum Portsmouth, John Madejski Acad Reading, Guangzhon West Tower Guangzhon, King's Waterfront Arena and Conf Centre Liverpool, Earth Sciences Dept Univ of Oxford, Humanities Dept Queen Mary's Univ of London; Hon DLitt Univ of Westminster 2001, Hon Dr Oxford Brookes Univ 2007; FCSD, RA 2006, Hon FAIA 2007; *Awards* Eric Lyons Award 1993, CSD Designer of the Year 1996, Royal Acad AJ/Bovis Grand Award 1997, ten RIBA Awards, BCI Award 1997, Structural Steel Award 1997, 1998, 1999 and 2001, FT Architectural Award 1997, Civic Tst Award 1998, 2000, 2001, 2002 and 2003, AIA Award 1998, 2000, 2001, 2002 and 2003, FX Designer of the Year 2001, Stirling Prize for Architecture 2001 and 2002; *Books* Supersheds (1991), Supersheds II (1995), Bridging Art and Science (monograph, with Jim Eyre, 2001), Wilkinson Eyre Bridges (2004), Wilkinson Eyre Destinations (2005), Exploring Boundaries (2007); *Recreations* golf, painting, travel; *Style—* Chris Wilkinson, Esq, OBE, RA; ✉ 52 Park Hall Road, West Dulwich, London SE21 8BW (tel 020 8761 7021); Wilkinson Eyre Architects Ltd, 24 Britton Street, London EC1M 5UA (tel 020 7608 7900, fax 020 7608 7901, e-mail c.wilkinson@wilkinsoneyre.com)

WILKINSON, Christopher Richard; s of Rev Thomas R Wilkinson (d 1978), and Frances, *née* Steel; *b* 3 July 1941; *Educ* Heath GS Halifax, Selwyn Coll Cambridge (BA, MA); *Career* Cwlth Secretariat 1963–65, OECD Paris and Madrid 1965–66, World Bank Washington DC and Lagos 1966–73; European Commission Brussels: head of div Directorate Gen for Regnl Policy 1973–78, head of div Directorate Gen for Internal Market and Industrial Affrs 1978–82, head of div Directorate Gen for Telecommunications, Info Industries and Innovation 1983–93, advsr Telecommunications and Postal Affairs 1993–; visiting fell Center for Int Affrs Harvard Univ 1982–83; *Recreations* mountain walking, gardening, cooking; *Style—* Mr Christopher Wilkinson

WILKINSON, Brig Clive Anthony; CBE (1987); s of George Wilkinson (d 1974), of Cheltenham, Glos, and Elsie Annie, *née* Reid (d 2006); *b* 14 February 1935; *Educ* Bishop Cotton Sch Simla, Wrekin Coll; *m* 4 July 1959, Nadine Elizabeth Wilkinson, da of William Humphreys (d 1979), of Southport, Lancs; 2 da (Juliette b 1960, Caroline b 1962); *Career* cmmnd RA 1955, Staff Coll Camberley 1967, military asst to C in C AFCENT 1974–77, instr German Armed Forces Staff Coll 1977–79, CO 7 Bn UDR 1979–81, Col Strategic Planning Team NATO HQ 1982–84, asst COS logistics HQ BAOR 1985–86, Cdr 107 (Ulster) Bde 1987–89; dir The Gin and Vodka Assoc of GB 1990–99, pres Confédération Européenne des Producteurs de Spiritueux 1997–99 (vice-pres 1993–96); memb European Economic and Social Ctee 1998–2006; *Clubs* Army and Navy, Prince Albert (Brussels); *Style—* Brig Clive Wilkinson, CBE; ✉ c/o Army and Navy Club, 36–39 Pall Mall, London SW1Y 5JN

WILKINSON, Clive Victor; *b* 26 May 1938; *Educ* Four Dwellings Secdy Modern Sch; *m* 7 Oct 1961, (Elizabeth) Ann; 2 da; *Career* Birmingham City Cncl: cncllr 1970–84, ldr 1973–76 and 1980–82, ldr of oppn 1976–80 and 1982–84; dir NEC Birmingham 1973–84, fin and commercial dir Birmingham Rep Theatre 1983–87; chm Cncl for Small Industries in Rural Areas 1977–80; dep chm: AMA 1974–76, Redditch Devpt Corp 1977–81; chm: Sandwell DHA 1986–94, Wolverhampton Health Care NHS Tst 1995–98, W Midlands Regnl Office NHS Exec 1998–2001; currently chair Birmingham and Solihull Heartlands NHS Trust; non-exec dir FSA 2001–07; memb: Devpt Cmmn 1977–86, Electricity Consumers Cncl 1977–80, Audit Cmmn 1987–96, Black Country Devpt Corp 1989–92, Local Govt Cmmn 1992–95, Midlands Industrial Assoc 1978– (chm 1980–88); chm: Birmingham Civil Housing Assoc 1979–, Customer Servs Ctee Severn Trent Regnl Office of Water Servs 1990–; memb Cncl Univ of Birmingham 1974–84, tstee Bournville Village Tst 1982–; Hon Alderman City of Birmingham 1984; *Recreations* squash, basketball, soccer; *Style—* Clive Wilkinson

WILKINSON, Dr David George; s of George Arthur Wilkinson (d 1978), and Barbara Mary, *née* Hayton (d 1995); *b* 8 March 1958; *Educ* Aylesbury GS, Hymers Coll Hull, Univ of Leeds (BSc, PhD); *m* 16 Nov 1991, Qiling Xu; *Career* postdoctoral research Fox Chase Cancer Center Philadelphia 1983–86; Nat Inst for Medical Research London: postdoctoral research 1986–88, gp leader 1988–2000, head Div of Developmental Neurobiology 2000–, head Genetics and Devpt Gp 2000–; memb EMBO 2000, FMedSci 2000; *Publications* In Situ Hybridization (1992); author of approx 100 research papers in scientific jls; *Recreations* natural history, music, poetry; *Style—* Dr David Wilkinson; ✉ National Institute for Medical Research, The Ridgeway, Mill Hill, London NW7 1AA (tel 020 8816 2404, fax 020 8816 2523, e-mail dwilkin@nimr.mrc.ac.uk)

WILKINSON, Glen Alexander Low; s of Cdr James Henry Wilkinson, of Gosport, Hants, and Alexia Menny, *née* Low; *b* 2 September 1950; *Educ* Churcher's Coll Petersfield, Univ of Birmingham Med Sch (MB ChB); *m* (m dis); 3 da (Rebecca b 9 Feb 1978, Angela b 9 March 1979, Laura b 19 May 1986), 1 s (Matthew James b 11 Feb 1988); *Career* sr registrar in cardiothoracic surgery W Midlands RHA 1985–88, sr fell (actg instr) in cardiothoracic surgery Univ Hosp Washington Seattle 1986–87, currently conslt cardiothoracic surgn Sheffield HA and Northern Gen Hosp; memb Soc of Cardiothoracic Surgns of GB and I 1986; FRCS 1978; *Recreations* model railway running and collecting, model boat building, photography, fly fishing; *Style—* Glen Wilkinson, Esq; ✉ 21 Mayfield Heights, Brookhouse Hill, Sheffield S10 3TT (tel 0114 229 5202); Northern General Hospital, Herries Road, Sheffield S5 7AU (tel 0114 271 4951, fax 0114 261 0350)

WILKINSON, Sir (David) Graham Brook; 3 Bt (UK 1941), of Brook, Witley, Co Surrey; s of Sir David Wilkinson, 2 Bt, DSC (d 1972); *b* 18 May 1947; *Educ* Millfield, ChCh Oxford; *m* 1, 1977 (m dis 1996), Sandra Caroline, *née* Rossdale; 2 da (Louise Caroline Sylvia b 1979, Tara Katherine Juliet b 1982); m 2, 1998, Hilary Jane Griggs, *née* Bailey; *Heir* none; *Career* dir Orion Royal Bank Ltd 1971–85, md SEIC Services (UK) 1985–89; non-exec

W

dir: Galveston-Houston Co USA 1986–89, Sovereign National Management USA 1987–94, Lamport Gilbert Ltd 1992–97; pres Surrey Co Agricultural Soc 2006; Liveryman Worshipful Co of Goldsmiths, Master Worshipful Co of Farmers 2006–07; KStJ 2003; *Clubs* Royal Yacht Sqdn, White's, Royal Ocean Racing; *Style*— Sir Graham Wilkinson, Bt

WILKINSON, James Hugh; s of Hugh Davy Wilkinson (d 1972), and Marjorie, *née* Prout (d 1965); *b* 19 September 1941; *Educ* Westminster Abbey Choir Sch, Sutton GS, King's Coll London (BSc), Churchill Coll Cambridge (CertEd); *m* 11 Nov 1978, Elisabeth Ann, da of John Morse, of Cheltenham, Glos; 2 s (Christopher b 1979, Matthew b 1982); *Career* science and health corr Daily Express 1964–74, science and aviation corr BBC Radio 1974–83, science corr BBC TV News 1983–99; visiting fell Agric and Food Res Cncl's Inst of Food Res Reading 1992–96; *Books* Conquest of Cancer (1973), Tobacco (1986), Green or Bust (1990), Westminster Abbey: 1000 Years of Music and Pageant (2003); *Recreations* music, bookbinding, fishing; *Style*— James Wilkinson, Esq; ✉ e-mail james@wilko31.freeserve.co.uk

WILKINSON, Jonathan Peter (Jonny); OBE (2004, MBE 2003); *b* 25 May 1979, Frimley, Surrey; *Educ* Pierrepont Sch, Lord Wandsworth Coll; *Career* rugby union player (fly half); with Newcastle Falcons RUFC 1998– (winners Tetley's Cup 2001); England: 60 caps, scored over 800 points (English record), debut v Ireland 1998 (youngest England player since 1927), capt Nov 2004– (also v Italy 2003), winners Six Nations Championship 2000, 2001 and 2003 (Grand Slam 2003), record holder most points in one test 35 points v Italy 2001 and most points in championship season 89 points 2001, ranked no 1 team in world 2003, winners World Cup Aust 2003 (leading points scorer), memb squad World Cup France 2007; memb squad British and Irish Lions tour to Aust 2001 (record holder most points in one test 18 points) and NZ 2005; Int Players' Player of the Year 2002 and 2003, IRB Player of the Year 2003, BBC Sports Personality of the Year 2003; *Books* Lions and Falcons (2002), My World (2004), How to Play Rugby My Way (2005); *Recreations* playing guitar and piano, speaking and reading French and Spanish; *Style*— Jonny Wilkinson, Esq, OBE; ✉ Newcastle Falcons Rugby Club, Brunton Road, Kenton Bank Foot, Kingston Park, Newcastle upon Tyne NE13 8AF

WILKINSON, Rev Canon Keith Howard; s of Kenneth John Wilkinson, of Leicester, and Grace Winifred, *née* Bowler; *b* 25 June 1948; *Educ* Beaumont Leys Coll Leicester, The Gateway GS Leicester, Univ of Hull (BA), Emmanuel Coll Cambridge (Lady Romney Exhibitioner, MA), Westcott House Cambridge; *m* 27 Aug 1972, Carolyn, da of Lewis John Gilbert (d 1985), of Wokingham; 2 da (Rachel b 1979, Claire b 1979); *Career* head of religious studies Bricknell HS 1970–72, head of faculty (humanities) Kelvin Hall Comprehensive Sch Kingston upon Hull 1972–74; ordained: deacon 1976, priest 1977; asst priest St Jude Westwood Peterborough 1976–79, educn offr to the church Peterborough 1977–79, asst master and chaplain Eton Coll 1979–84, sr chaplain and head of religious studies Malvern Coll 1984–89 (sr tutor 1988–89), headmaster Berkhamsted Sch 1989–96, headmaster The King's Sch Canterbury 1996–; hon canon Cathedral Church of Christ Canterbury; chm Soc of Sch Masters and Sch Mistresses 1998–; FRSA 1994; *Recreations* films, music, drama, ecology, walking, buildings; *Clubs* East India; *Style*— The Rev Canon Keith Wilkinson; ✉ The King's School, Canterbury, Kent, CT1 2ES (tel 01227 595501, fax 01227 595595)

WILKINSON, Dr Laura Margaret; da of William Low Wilkinson, of Ayr, and Dorothy, *née* Smith; *Educ* Ayr GS, Wellington Sch Ayr, Univ of Glasgow (MB ChB); *Career* house offr in med then surgery Gartnavel Gen/Western Infirmary Glasgow 1984–85, SHO in gen med Monklands Dist Gen Hosp Airdrie 1985–87; Gartnavel Gen/Western Infirmary Glasgow: registrar then sr registrar in radiology 1987–93, conslt radiologist W of Scotland Breast Screening Serv 1993–; Royal Coll of Radiologists: W of Scotland Jr Forum rep 1991–95, memb Scottish Standing Ctee 1991–95, chm Exec Jr Radiologists Forum 1993–95; sec Jr Forum Euro Assoc of Radiology 1995–96; chm and head of trg West of Scotland Sub-Ctee in Radiodiagnosis 1998–2002; Training Accreditation Ctee RCR 2002–06; FRCR 1992; *Style*— Dr Laura Wilkinson; ✉ Laigh Monkcastle, Dalry Road, Kilwinning KA13 6PN (tel 01294 833161); West of Scotland Breast Screening Centre, Western Infirmary, Glasgow (tel 0141 572 5833)

WILKINSON, Dr Mark Lawrence; s of Rev Canon Raymond Stewart Wilkinson, QHC, of Warwick, and Dorothy Elinor, *née* Church; *b* 19 May 1950; *Educ* Birkenhead Sch, The Middx Hosp Med Sch, Univ of London (BSc, MB BS, MD); *m* 4 Jan 1975, Anna Maria, da of Nicola Ugo Dante Cassoni, of Kenton, Harrow; 1 s (Nicholas b 1979), 1 da (Elinor b 1985); *Career* registrar Middx Hosp 1979–81; Liver Unit King's Coll Sch of Med: res fell 1981–84, lectr 1984–86; sr lectr and conslt physician Guy's Hosp and UMDS Guy's and St Thomas' Hosps (now GKT) 1986–, hon conslt St Luke's Hosp for the Clergy 1993–, clinical dir of specialist med Guy's and St Thomas' Hosps' Tst 1995–2000, clincal dir of surgery Guy's and St Thomas' Hosps' Tst 2000–04, head Service Delivery Unit GI/Vascular 2004–; memb: Jt Advsy Gp on Endoscopy 1995–2003, Special Advsy Ctee in Gastroenterology 1996–99; educn offr Endoscopy Ctee of Br Soc of Gastroenterology 1996–2000, prog dir Specialist Registrar Trg in Gastroenterology SE Thames 1998–2001; sec Br Assoc for Study of the Liver 1993–96; FRCP 1992 (MRCP 1977); *Recreations* books, walking, Italy; *Style*— Dr Mark Wilkinson; ✉ Gastroenterology Unit, Guy's, King's and St Thomas' Hospitals School of Medicine and Dentistry, 1st Floor, College House, St Thomas' Hospital, Lambeth Palace Road SE1 7EH (tel 020 7188 2490, fax 020 7188 2484, e-mail mark.wilkinson@gstt.nhs.uk)

WILKINSON, Rear Adm Nicholas John; CB (1994); s of late Lt Col M D Wilkinson, and J M Cosens; *b* 14 April 1941; *Educ* English Sch Cairo, Cheltenham Coll, BRNC Dartmouth; *m* 1, 1969 (m dis 1997), Penelope Ann Stephenson; 3 s (Sacheverell b 1969, Isambard b 1971, Augustus b 1976), 1 da (Gezina b 1977); m 2, 1998, Mrs J Rayner; *Career* with RN; served HM Ships: Venus, Vidal, Hardy, Hermes, Fife, Endurance, London 1960–78; 1964–82: RN Air Station Arbroath, RNC Greenwich (Lieutenants' Course Prize) 1967, Office of Vice Chief of Naval Staff, Army Staff Course (Mitchell Essay Prize) 1973, Clyde Submarine Base, sec to ACNS (Policy), Trg Cdr HMS Pembroke; NATO Def Coll Rome 1982–83, mil asst to Dir Int Mil Staff NATO HQ 1983–85, RCDS 1986, dir Def Logistics MOD 1986–89, sec to First Sea Lord 1989–90, sr mil memb Prospect Team MOD 1991–92, DG Naval Manpower and Trg 1992–94, Chief Naval Supply and Secretariat Offr 1993–97, Commandant JSDC 1994–97; mgmnt conslt 1998–99; sec Defence Press and Broadcasting Advsy Ctee 1999–2004; chm Assoc of Royal Naval Officers 1999–2004; dir Southside Quarter Mgmnt Co 1998–2003; chm Cncl Victory Services Assoc 2001–, memb Forces Pension Soc 1998–2005; govr Princess Helena Coll 1995–2004, memb Devpt Cncl Trinity Coll of Music 2002–, tstee Greenwich Fndn 2003–, chm Advsy Ctee Grennwich Univ Maritime Inst 2003–; cmmr PCC 2005–; *Publications* articles in Naval Review 1985–, Press Gazette 2000–; *Recreations* swimming, cricket, opera, jazz, cuisine Perigourdine; *Clubs* MCC (memb Membership Ctee 2000–03 and 2005–), Savile; *Style*— Rear Adm Nicholas Wilkinson, CB; ✉ 37 Burns Road, London SW11 5GX (tel and fax 020 7223 2779, mobile 07711 416481, e-mail wilkbedwyn@hotmail.com)

WILKINSON, Nigel Vivian Marshall; QC (1990); s of John Marshall Wilkinson (d 1993), of East Horsley, Surrey, and Vivien, *née* Gwynne-James; *b* 18 November 1949; *Educ* Charterhouse, ChCh Oxford (Holford exhibitioner, MA); *m* 20 April 1974, Heather Carol (Rt Hon Lady Justice Hallett, DBE, *qv*), da of late Hugh Victor Dudley Hallett; 2 s (James b 4 June 1980, Nicholas b 20 April 1982); *Career* called to the Bar Middle Temple 1972 (bencher 1997); Astbury scholar 1972, memb Midland & Oxford circuit 1972–, recorder of the Crown Court 1992–, dep judge of the High Court 1997–; dep chm Cricket Cncl Appeals Ctee 1992–96; *Recreations* sport and entertainment; *Clubs* MCC, I Zingari, Invalids CC, Armadillos CC, Vincent's (Oxford), Butterflies CC, Rye, Royal Wimbledon, Hon Co of Edinburgh Golfers; *Style*— Nigel Wilkinson, Esq, QC; ✉ 1 Temple Gardens, Temple, London EC4Y 9BB (tel 020 7583 1315)

WILKINSON, Prof Paul; s of Walter Ross Wilkinson (d 1985), of Bristol, and Joan Rosemary, *née* Paul; *b* 9 May 1937; *Educ* Lower Sch of John Lyon Harrow, UC Swansea (MA); *m* 19 March 1960, Susan Sherwyn, da of Charles William John Flook (d 1968), of Newport, Gwent; 1 da (Rachel Margaret b 1962), 2 s (John Paul b 1964, Charles Ross b 1969); *Career* served RAF 1959–65, ret as Flt Lt; UC Cardiff: asst lectr in politics 1966–68, lectr 1968–75, sr lectr 1975–78; reader in politics Univ of Wales 1978–79, prof of int rels Univ of Aberdeen 1979–89 (head Dept Politics and Int Rels 1985–89); Univ of St Andrews: prof of int rels 1989–, head Sch of History and Int Rels 1994–96, dir Centre for the Study of Terrorism and Political Violence 1999– (chm 2002–); visiting prof Simon Fraser Univ Canada 1973, visiting fell Trinity Hall Cambridge 1997–98; special advsr to Select Ctee on Defence House of Commons 2001–; chm Res Fndn for the Study of Terrorism 1986–89, dir Res Inst for the Study of Conflict and Terrorism 1989–94; jt ed Terrorism And Political Violence (scholarly jl) 1988–2006; hon fell UC Swansea; memb: RIIA, British Int Studies Assoc, Political Studies Assoc; FRSA 1995; *Books* Social Movement (1971), Political Terrorism (1974), Terrorism versus Liberal Democracy (1976), Terrorism and the Liberal State (1977, revised edn 1986, 3 edn 1994), Terrorism: Theory and Practice (jtly, 1978), British Perspectives on Terrorism (1981), The New Fascists (revised edn, 1983), Contemporary Research on Terrorism (1987), Lessons of Lockerbie (1989), Terrorist Targets and Tactics (1990), Northern Ireland: Reappraising Republican Violence (1991), Technology and Terrorism (1993), Terrorism: British Perspectives (1993), The Victims of Terrorism (1994); research report: Inquiry Into Legislation Against Terrorism (CM3420, vol 2) (1996), Aviation Terrorism and Security (jtly, 1998), Terrorism Versus Democracy: The Liberal State Response (2000, revised edn 2006), Report to the Trilateral Commission: Addressing the New International Terrorism - Prevention, Intervention and Multilateral Co-operation (jtly, 2003), International Terrorism: The changing threat and the EU's response (2005), A Very Short Introduction to International Relations (2007), Homeland Security in the UK (2007); *Recreations* walking, modern painting, poetry; *Clubs* Savile; *Style*— Prof Paul Wilkinson; ✉ Centre for the Study of Terrorism and Political Violence, School of International Relations, University of St Andrews, The New Arts Building, The Scores, St Andrews, Fife KY16 9AX (tel 01334 462935, fax 01334 461922, e-mail gm39@st-andrews.ac.uk)

WILKINSON, Rear Adm Peter John; s of Sir Philip Wilkinson, of Beaconsfield, Bucks, and Eileen, *née* Malkin (d 1991); *b* 28 May 1956; *Educ* Royal GS High Wycombe, St David's Coll Lampeter Univ of Wales (BA); *m* 12 Dec 1981, Tracey Kim, da of Eric Ward (d 1998); 2 da (Katherine Alice b 1989, Hilary Frances b 1991); *Career* RN: qualified in subs 1980, jr appts 1980–87, submarine command course 1987–88, CO HMS Otter 1988–89, CO HMS Superb 1991–92, CO HMS Vanguard 1994–96, Captain 2 Submarine Sqdn 1999–2001, dir RN Serv Conditions 2001–03, dir RN Life Mgmnt 2003–04, DG Human Resources (RN) and Naval Sec 2004–05, Defence Servs Sec 2005–; pres RN FA, hon vice-pres FA; FCIPD 2003; *Recreations* gardening, walking, watching all sports; *Clubs* Army and Navy; *Style*— Rear Adm Peter Wilkinson; ✉ Leach Building, Whale Island, Portsmouth, Hampshire PO2 8BY (tel 023 9262 5542, fax 023 9262 5100)

WILKINSON, Sally Ann; da of Derek George Wilkinson (d 1978), of London, and Kathleen Mary Patricia, *née* O'Callaghan (d 1989); *b* 1 November 1953; *Educ* Westonbirt Sch, Watford Coll of Technol (HND); *Career* trainee exec Image Makers Ltd 1973, account exec Crawford Heard Ltd 1974, divnl press offr Thorn Domestic Appliances 1975–78, account exec rising to creative dir Kingsway Rowland 1978–89, divnl md The Rowland Co 1990–92, md SAW Associates 1993–94 and 1995–, dep gen mangr Edelman Worldwide London 1994–95, md Brook Wilkinson 1996–, managing ptnr the firm 2001–; memb: Inst of Mktg 1978, Assoc of Women in PR 1990, Guild of PR; MInstD; *Recreations* theatre, music, writing, art and antiques; *Style*— Miss Sally Ann Wilkinson; ✉ the firm, Building 3, Chiswick Park, Chiswick High Road, London W4 5YA (tel 020 8899 6110, fax 020 8332 7410, e-mail saw@thefirmcomms.com)

WILKS, Prof Stephen Robert Mark; s of Gordon Wilks (d 1993), and Florence, *née* Wilson; *b* 2 January 1949, Newcastle upon Tyne; *Educ* Buckhurst Hill Co HS, City of Westminster Coll, Lancaster Univ (BA), Victoria Univ of Manchester (PhD); *m* 2 Oct 1976, Philippa Mary; 3 da (Susannah b 13 June 1979, Laura b 22 Nov 1980, Verity b 19 June 1985); *Career* with Fryer Whitehill & Co Chartered Accountants 1968–72; Univ of Liverpool: lectr then sr lectr Dept of Political Theory and Instns 1978–89, reader in political theory and instns 1989–90; Univ of Exeter: prof of politics 1990–, head Dept of Politics 1992–95 and 2003–04, ESRC sr research fell 1995–96, dep vice-chllr 1999–2002 and 2004–05; visiting prof Faculty of Law Univ of Kyoto 1989; memb: Cncl ESRC 2001–05 (chair Strategic Research Bd 2002–05), Competition Cmmn 2001–; FCA 1978 (ACA 1971); *Publications* Industrial Policy and the Motor Industry (1984, 2 edn 1988), Industrial Crisis: A Comparative Study of the State and Industry (ed with Kenneth Dyson, 1985), Comparative Government-Industry Relations: Western Europe, the United States and Japan (ed with Maurice Wright, 1987), The Promotion and Regulation of Industry in Japan (ed with Maurice Wright, 1991), The Office of Fair Trading in Administrative Context (1994), Comparative Competition Policy: National Institutions in a Global Market (ed with Bruce Doern, 1996), Competition Policy and the Regulation of the Electricity Supply Industry in Britain and Germany (with Roland Sturm, 1997), Regulatory Institutions in Britain and North America: Politics and Paths to Reform (ed with Bruce Doern, 1998), In the Public Interest: Competition Policy and the Monopolies and Mergers Commission (1999), Reforming Public and Corporate Governance: Management and Market in Australia, Britain and Korea (ed with Byong-Man Ahn and John Halligan, 2002), The Regulatory State: Britain and Germany Compared (with Ian Bartle, Markus Muller and Roland Sturm, 2002); also author of numerous book chapters, articles, reports, working papers and reviews; *Recreations* walking, wine, gardening, tea; *Style*— Prof Stephen Wilks; ✉ SHiPSS, Amory Building, Rennes Drive, Exeter EX4 4RJ

WILLACY, Michael James Ormerod; CBE (1989); s of James Willacy (d 1977), and Majorie Winifred, *née* Sanders; *b* 7 June 1933; *Educ* Taunton Sch; *m* 1, Merle Louise, da of Johannes Schrier, of Denia, Spain; 2 s (Richard b 1962, Peter b 1969), 1 da (Jennifer b 1963); m 2, Victoria Stuart, da of Cecil Stuart John, of Mobberley, Cheshire; 3 s (James b 1985, Michael b 1986, David b 1990), 1 da (Elizabeth b 1988); *Career* gen mangr Shell UK Materials Services 1983–85, dir HM Govt Central Unit on Purchasing 1985–90, purchasing advsr HM Treasy 1991–92; md Michael Willacy Associates Ltd 1991–; chm Macclesfield C of C 1981–83, fndr chm Macclesfield Business Ventures 1982–83; Old Tauntonian Assoc: gen sec 1978–91, pres 1988–89, vice-pres 1989–; chm St Dunstan's Abbey Sch for Girls 1997–2004, govr Taunton Sch 1993–, hon vice-pres Plymouth Coll 2005–; FCIPS; *Recreations* golf, travel, gardening; *Clubs* Royal Cwlth Soc; *Style*— Michael Willacy, Esq, CBE; ✉ PO Box 20, Ivybridge, Devon PL21 9XS (tel 01548 830591, fax 01548 831014, e-mail willacy@mwa-consultancy.co.uk)

WILLATS, Stephan; *b* 17 August 1943; *Educ* Ealing Sch of Art; *m* Stephanie Willats; *Career* artist; ed and publisher Control magazine 1965–, pt/t lectr 1965–72, dir The Centre for Behavioural Art 1972–73, DAAD fell W Germany 1979–80, convenor Art Creating Society Symposium Museum of Modern Art Oxford 1990; *Solo Exhibitions* incl: Visual Automatics and Visual Transmitters (MOMA Oxford) 1968, The Artist as an Instigator of Changes in Social Cognition and Behaviour (Gallery House London) 1973, Coding

Structure and Behaviour Parameters (Gallery Banco Bresco Italy) 1975, Allitudes within Four Relationships (Lisson Gallery London) 1976, Questions About Ourselves (Lisson Gallery) 1978, Concerning our Present Way of Living (Whitechapel Art Gallery) 1979, Berlin Wall Drawings (Galerie Rudiger Schottle Munich) 1980, Mens en Omgeving De Beyard Centram voor beeldende Kanst (Breda Holland) 1981, Meta Filler and Related Works (Tate Gallery) 1982, Inside the Night (Lisson Gallery) 1983, Doppelgänger (Lisson Gallery) 1985, City of Concrete (Ikon Gallery Birmingham) 1986, Concepts and Projects Bookworks (Nigel Greenwood Books, London) 1987, Between Objects and People (Leeds City Art Gallery) 1987, Secret Language (Cornerhouse Gallery Manchester) 1989, Mosaics (Galerie Kaj Forsblom Helsinki) 1990, Multiple Clothing (ICA) 1993, Museum Mosaic (Tate Gallery London) 1994, Random Life (Victoria Miro Gallery London) 1994, Living Together (Tramway Glasgow) 1995, Writing On The Wall (Galerie Kaj Forsblom Helsinki) 1995; *Group Exhibitions* incl: Kinetic Art (Hayward Gallery) 1970, Art as Thought Process (Serpentine Gallery London) 1974, Social Criticism and Art Practice (San Francisco Art Inst) 1977, La Parola e le Imagine (Commune di Milano) 1979, Sculpture in the Twentieth Century (Whitechapel Art Gallery London) 1981, New Art at the Tate Gallery (Tate Gallery) 1983, Eye Level (Van Abbemuseum Eindhoven) 1986, 100 years of British Art (Leeds City Art Gallery) 1988, The New Urban Landscape (World Fin Centre NYC) 1990, Excavating the Present (Kettle Yard Gallery Cambridge) 1991, Instruction and Diagrams (Victoria Miro Gallery London) 1992, Visione Britannica (Valentina Moncada Rome Italy) 1994, Temples (Victoria Miro Gallery London) 1995, Ideal Standard Summertime (Lisson Gallery London) 1995; works in public collections incl: Art Museum Zurich, Scottish Nat Gallery of Modern Art Edinburgh, Tate Gallery London, Arts Cncl of GB, V&A, British Museum, Museum of Contemporary Art Utrecht Holland, Stichting Volkshuisvesting in de Kunst Den Haag Holland, Van Abbe Museum Eindhoven Holland, Stadtische Galerie Stuttgart; *Style*— Stephan Willats, Esq

WILLATTS, Dr Sheila Margaret; da of Charles William Chapman (d 1978), and Joyce Margaret Chapman (d 2000); *b* 6 June 1943; *Educ* UCL, UCH Med Sch London (MB BS, MD); *m* 1, 16 July 1966, David George Willatts, s of Bertram George Willatts; 2 da (Nicola b 14 April 1971, Ellen Laura b 1 Nov 1975), 1 s (Steven Chapman b 5 Jan 1973); m 2, 25 Feb 1989, Michael Crabtree; *Career* registrar trg in anaesthetics Brook Hosp and KCH, sr registrar King's Coll Hosp until 1978, conslt anaesthetist Frenchay Hosp Bristol 1978–85, conslt i/c Intensive Therapy Unit Bristol Royal Infirmary 1985–2002, conslt advsr in anaesthetics to the Chief Med Offr 1991–2002, vice-pres Critical Care Section RSM 2007–; sec and subsequently chm Intensive Care Soc 1980–84, memb Cncl Royal Coll of Anaesthetists 1986–99 (chm Examinations Ctee, Quality of Practice Ctee, Hosp Recognition Ctee, Equivalence Ctee and Intercollegiate Bd for Trg in Intensive Care Med, vice-pres 1997–99); assoc GMC; John Snow Silver Medal 2002; memb: Assoc of Anaesthetists 1976, RSM 1978, Br Medico Legal Soc 1985, BMA 1989, FRCP, FRCA; *Books* Lecture Notes in Fluid and Electrolyte Balance (2 edn, 1982), Anaesthesia and Intensive Care for Neurosurgery (1984), Principles and Protocols in Intensive Therapy (1991), Confidential Enquiries into Maternal Deaths Triennial Report 1994–96 (1998), Intensive Care Infections (2000); *Recreations* travel, keep fit, gardening; *Style*— Dr Sheila Willatts; ✉ Buckland House, Providence Rise, Providence Lane, Long Ashton BS41 9DJ (tel 01275 393468, e-mail swillatts@willtree.co.uk)

WILLCOCKS, Sir David Valentine; kt (1977), CBE (1971), MC (1944); s of late Theophilus Herbert Willcocks, and Dorothy, *née* Harding; *b* 30 December 1919; *Educ* Clifton, King's Coll Cambridge (MA, MusB); *m* 1947, Rachel Gordon Blyth, da of late Rev Arthur Cecil Blyth, fell Selwyn Coll Cambridge; 2 s (1 decd), 2 da; *Career* serv WWII DCLI, Capt NW Europe; organist Salisbury Cathedral 1947–50, master of choristers and organist Worcester Cathedral 1950–57, music lectr Cambridge 1957–74, fell and organist King's Coll Cambridge 1957–73 (hon fell 1979), univ organist 1958–74, musical dir Bach Choir 1960–98 (conductor laureate 1998–), gen ed OUP Church Music 1961–; pres Assoc of British Choral Directors 1993–; past pres: RCO, ISM, Nat Fedn of Music Socs; former conductor: City of Birmingham Choir, Bradford Festival Choral Soc, Cambridge Univ Music Soc; dir Royal Coll of Music 1974–84; Freeman City of London 1981; Hon MA Univ of Bradford; Hon DMus: Univ of Exeter, Univ of Leicester, Univ of Bristol, Westminster Choir Coll, St Olaf Coll, Royal Coll of Music, Univ of Victoria Canada; Hon DLit Univ of Sussex, Hon DSLitt Trinity Coll Toronto, Hon DFA Luther Coll IA, Dr jur (hc) Univ of Toronto, DLitt (hc) Univ of Newfoundland 2003; hon fell Royal Canadian Coll of Organists, Hon RAM, Hon GSM, Hon FTCL, FRCM, FRCO, FRNCM, FRSAMD, FRSCM; *Clubs* Athenaeum; *Style*— Sir David Willcocks, CBE, MC; ✉ 13 Grange Road, Cambridge CB3 9AS (tel 01223 359559, fax 01223 355947, e-mail david.willcocks3@ntlworld.com)

WILLCOCKS, Lt-Gen Sir Michael Alan; KCB (2000, CB 1997); s of Henry Willcocks (d 2001), and Georgina Bernadette, *née* Lawton (d 1989); *b* 27 July 1944; *Educ* St John's Coll, RMA Sandhurst, Univ of London (BSc); *m* 10 Dec 1966, Jean Paton, da of James Burnside Paton Weir (d 1967); 1 s (Julian b 20 June 1968), 2 da (Jessica b 28 April 1971, Hannah b 26 Feb 1976); *Career* cmmnd RA 1964, serv Malaya, Borneo, UK, Germany 1965–72; instr: RMA Sandhurst 1972–74, Staff Coll 1975–76; MOD 1977–79, Comd M Battery RHA 1979–80, Staff Coll Directing Staff 1981–82, CO 1 Regt RHA 1983–85, DACOS HQ UKLF 1985–87, Asst COS Intelligence/Ops HQ UKLF 1988, Cmd RA 4 Armd Div 1989–90, RCDS 1991, ACOS Land Operations Joint War HQ Gulf War (and aftermath) 1991, Dir Army Plans and Programme 1991–93, DG Land Warfare 1993–94, COS Allied Command Europe Rapid Reaction Corps 1994–96, COS Land Component of Peace Implementation Force (IFOR) Bosnia-Herzegovina 1995–96, Asst CGS 1996–99, Dep Cmd (Ops) Stabilization Force (SFOR) Bosnia-Herzegovina 1999–2000, UK mil rep NATO and EU 2000–01; Hon Col IRHA 1999–, Col Cmdt RA 2000–05, Representative Col Cmdt RA 2004–05; Gentleman Usher of the Black Rod, Serjeant-at-Arms House of Lords and sec to the Lord Great Chamberlain 2001–; European-Atlantic Gp 1994–; cmmr: Royal Hosp Chelsea 1996–99, The Pilgrims 2002–; hon memb Kennel Club 2006–; tstee Freeplay Fndn 2006; Knight Cdr Sacred Military Constantinian Order of St George 2006; Meritorious Service Medal USA 1996 and 2000, Pingat Jasa Malaysia medal 2006; *Books* Airmobility and the Armoured Experience (1989); *Recreations* books, music, tennis, fishing, shooting, sailing; *Clubs* National Liberal, Pitt; *Style*— Lt-Gen Sir Michael Willcocks, KCB; ✉ House of Lords, London SW1A 0PW

WILLESDEN, Bishop of 2001–; Rt Rev Peter Alan (Pete) Broadbent; *b* 31 July 1952; *Educ* Merchant Taylors' Northwood, Jesus Coll Cambridge (MA), Univ of Nottingham (DipTh), St John's Coll Nottingham (DPS); *m* 1974, Sarah; 1 s (Simon b 13 Nov 1978); *Career* ordained deacon 1977, priest 1978; asst curate: St Nicholas Durham City 1977–80 (concurrently asst chaplain HM Remand Centre Low Newton), Emmanuel Hornsey Rd Holloway 1980–83; Bishop of Stepney's chaplain for mission 1980–89; Anglican chaplain to the Poly of N London 1983–89 (concurrently hon curate St Mary Islington), vicar Trinity St Michael Harrow 1989–94, archdeacon of Northolt 1995–2001; memb London Diocesan: Synod 1985–, Bishop's Cncl 1988–89 and 1991–, Fin Ctee 1991–2001; chm London Diocesan Bd for Schs 1996–2002; memb Gen Synod (Proctor in Convocation London) 1985–2001; chm Gen Synod: Business Ctee 1999–2000 (Sub-Ctee 1996–98), Elections Review Gp 1996–2000; memb Gen Synod: Panel of Chairmen 1990–92, Standing Orders Ctee 1991–95, Standing Ctee 1992–98, Appointments Sub-Ctee 1992–95; memb Dioceses Cmmn 1989–92, Diocesan rep on Crown Appts Cmmn 1990 and 1995; memb: Central Bd of Fin 1991–95 and 1996–98 (memb Exec Ctee 1991–95), Cncl Wycliffe Hall 1991–94, Archbishops' Advsy Gp on Fin Mgmnt and the Expectations of the Church 1993–98; chm Vacancy in See Ctees Regulation Working Pty 1991–93; memb: C of E Evangelical Cncl 1984–95, London Diocesan Evangelical Cncl 1985–, Open Synod Gp Ctee 1994–2000, Evangelical Gp in Gen Synod Ctee 1996–2000, Archbishops' Cncl 1999–2000, Urban Bishops Panel 2001–; asst ed Anvil (theol jl) 1984–86; contrib: Third Way, Church of England Newspaper; Lab cncllr London Borough of Islington (chm Devpt and Planning Ctee) 1982–89; chm: London Boroughs Tport Ctee 1986–89, London Road Safety Ctee 1987–89; dep chm London Planning Advsy Ctee 1985–89, vice-chm Planning and Tport Ctee Assoc of London Authorities 1985–89; tstee Church Urban Fund 2002–; memb S Eastern Regnl Planning Conf 1986–89; London Borough of Harrow: co-opted memb Educn Ctee 1990–96, chm Standing Advsy Cncl on RE 1990–95, ind memb Standards Ctee 2002–; chm Family Action Info and Rescue 1981–84; dir Spring Harvest 1998–; memb Central Govening Body City Parochial Fndn 1999–2003; chair St John's Coll Nottingham Cncl 2002–; memb: Lab/Co-op Pty, ASTMS 1980–84, NUPE 1984–89; *Books* Hope for the Church of England? (contrib chapter The Political Imperative, 1986), Uncage the Lion (contrib, 1990), Church and Society in the 1990s (contrib 1990), Politics and the Parties (contrib chapter A Labour Party View, 1992), Restoring Faith in Politics (contrib, 1996); *Recreations* football (lifelong supporter of Tottenham Hotspur FC), theatre and film, railways, real ale, National Trust, popular music from the 1950s to the present day; *Style*— The Rt Rev the Bishop of Willesden; ✉ 173 Willesden Lane, Brondesbury, London NW6 7YN (tel 020 8451 0189, fax 020 8451 4606, e-mail bishop.willesden@btinternet.com)

WILLETT, Allan Robert; CMG (1997); s of Robert Willett, and Irene Grace Priscilla, *née* Weigall; *b* 24 August 1936; *Educ* Eastbourne Coll; *m* 1, 13 April 1960 (m dis 1993), Mary, da of Joseph Hillman; 2 da (Joanna, Katherine), 1 s (Robert); m 2, 5 Oct 1993, Anne, da of Hubert Steed; *Career* cmmnd The Buffs Royal East Kent Regt and seconded to 23 King's African Rifles 1955–57, Kenya Campaign Medal 1956; gp md G D Peters Ltd 1969–71, chm Northampton Machinery Co 1970–74, dep chm Rowen and Boden 1973–74, estab Willett Companies 1974; Willett International Ltd (GB): exec chm 1983–98, non-exec chm 1998–2002; chm SE England RDA (SEEDA) 1998–2002; pres: Kent Branch SSAFA 2002–, County Ctee Army Benevolent Fund 2002–, Assoc of Men of Kent and Kentish Men 2002–, Order of St John for Kent 2002–; patron: Kent Community Fndn 2002–, Kent Branch Royal Br Legion 2002–; tstee: Rochester Cathedral Tst 2002–, Canterbury Cathedral Tst Fund 2002–; HM Lord-Lt Kent 2002– (DL 2001–02); Hon Col 3rd Battalion Princess of Wales's Royal Regt 2005–; hon fell Canterbury Christchurch Univ 2003; Hon DCL Univ of Kent 2002, Hon LLB Univ of Greenwich 2003; KJStJ 2004; *Recreations* walking, military history, golf; *Style*— Allan Willett, Esq, CMG; ✉ Office: Cumberland Cottage, The Street, Chilham, Canterbury, Kent CT4 8BX (tel 01227 738800, fax 01227 738855, e-mail allan@allanwillett.org)

WILLETT, Peter Stirling; s of Maj Kingsley Willett, MC (d 1946), of Yeovil, Somerset, and Agnes Mary, *née* Stirling (d 1972); *b* 19 July 1919; *Educ* Wellington, Univ of Cambridge (MA); *m* 1, 1954, Anne Marjorie, *née* Watkins (d 1965); 2 s (David Henry Stirling b 1955, Stephen Murray b 1958); m 2, 1971, Chloë Lister Beamish; *Career* The Queen's Bays 1941–46 (Middle East, Italy); author, journalist, thoroughbred breeding conslt; dir: Goodwood Racecourse 1977–, National Stud 1986–93; pres Thoroughbred Breeders Assoc 1980–85, chm tstee Br Euro Breeders Fund 1983–95, tstee Childwick Tst 1986–2000; FRSA; *Books* An Introduction to the Thoroughbred (1960), The Thoroughbred (1970), The Classic Racehorse (1981), Makers of the Modern Thoroughbred (1986), Tattersalls (1987), A History of the General Stud Book (1991), Dick Hern (2000); *Recreations* tennis, following cricket, reading, bridge; *Clubs* Jockey; *Style*— Peter Willett, Esq; ✉ Paddock House, Rotherwick, Hook, Hampshire RG27 9BG (tel 01256 762488, fax 01256 765088, e-mail peter@peterwillett8.wanadoo.co.uk)

WILLETTS, David Lindsay; MP; s of John Roland Willetts, and Hilary Sheila Willetts; *b* 9 March 1956; *Educ* King Edward's Sch Birmingham, ChCh Oxford (BA); *m* 1986, Hon Sarah Harriet Ann Butterfield, *qv*, da of Baron Butterfield (Life Peer, d 2000); 1 da, 1 s; *Career* research asst to Nigel Lawson MP 1978; HM Treasy 1978–84: energy policy 1978–79, public expenditure control 1980–81, private sec to fin sec 1981–82, monetary policy 1982–84; memb PM's Downing Street Policy Unit 1984–86, dir of studies Centre for Policy Studies 1987–92, conslt dir Cons Research Dept 1987–92; MP (Cons) Havant 1992–; PPS to Sir Norman Fowler 1993–94, asst whip 1994–95, Lord Cmmr of HM Treasy 1995, Parly under sec Office of Public Serv 1995–96, Paymaster-Gen 1996; oppn front bench spokesman on employment 1997–98, shadow sec for educn and employment 1998–99, shadow sec for social security 1999–2001, shadow sec of state for work and pensions 2001–05, shadow sec of state for trade and industry 2005, shadow sec of state for educn and skills 2005–; memb Cons Pty Policy Bd 2001–03; visiting prof Cass Business Sch; memb: Lambeth, Southwark and Lewisham FPC 1987–90, Parkside HA 1988–90, Social Security Advsy Ctee 1989–92; non-exec dir: Retirement Security Ltd 1988–94 (chm 1991–94), Electra Corporate Ventures Ltd 1989–94; sr policy advsr Punter Southall 2005–; writer and broadcaster; visiting fell Nuffield Coll Oxford; govr Ditchley Fndn; memb: Cncl Inst for Fiscal Studies, Global Aging Cmmn; *Books* Modern Conservatism (1992), Civic Conservatism (1994), Blair's Gurus (1996), Why Vote Conservative? (1997), Welfare to Work (1998), After the Landslide (1999), Browned-off: What's Wrong with Gordon Brown's Social Policy (2000), Tax Credits: Do They Add Up? (2002), Left Out, Left Behind (2003), Old Europe? Demographic Change and Pension Reform (2003); *Style*— David Willetts, Esq, MP; ✉ House of Commons, London SW1A 0AA (tel 020 7219 4570)

WILLI, Prof Andreas Jonathan; s of Thomas Willi, and Ina Willi-Plein; *b* 17 December 1972, Altstätten, Switzerland; *Educ* Humanistisches Gymnasium Basel, Univ of Basel (Georg-Peter-Landmann Prize), Univ of Lausanne, Univ of Fribourg, CCC Oxford (Charles Oldham grad scholar, DPhil); *m* 17 Sept 2005, Helen Kaufmann; *Career* visiting research investigator Univ of Michigan Ann Arbor 1995–96; Univ of Basel: oberassistent in Latin philology 2001–02, oberassistent in Greek philology 2002–04; membro scientifico dell'Insituto Svizzero di Roma 2004–05, Diebold prof of comparative philology Univ of Oxford 2005–, fell Worcester Coll Oxford; memb: American Philological Assoc 1995–, Classical Assoc of the Middle West and South (CAMWS) 1995–, Philological Soc 1998–; Hellenic Fndn Award 2002; *Books* The Language of Greek Comedy (ed, 2002), The Languages of Aristophanes (2003); *Recreations* hiking; *Style*— Prof Andreas Willi; ✉ Worcester College, Oxford OX1 2HB

WILLIAMS, Her Hon Judge (Jean) Adèle; da of David James Williams (d 1975), and Dorothy May, *née* Rees (d 2006); *b* 28 July 1950, Carmarthenshire, S Wales; *Educ* Llanelli Girls' GS, UCL (LLB); *m* 20 Sept1975, His Hon Judge Andrew Patience QC ; 1 da (Louise Angharad Adèle b 5 Aug 1981), 1 s (David William Andrew b 23 Aug 1984); *Career* called to the Bar Gray's Inn 1972; practising barr 1972–2000, circuit judge 2000–; *Recreations* cinema, theatre, conversation; *Style*— Her Hon Judge Williams; ✉ Canterbury Combined Court Centre, Chaucer Road, Canterbury, Kent CT1 1ZA (tel 01227 819200)

WILLIAMS, Prof Adrian Charles; s of Geoffrey Francis Williams, OBE, of Aberystwyth, and Maureen, *née* Wade; *b* 15 June 1949; *Educ* Epsom Coll, Univ of Birmingham (MB ChB, MD); *m* 19 April 1980, Linnea Marie, da of Gerald Olsen, of Colorado, USA; 1 da (Sarah b 1981), 2 s (Alec b 1984, Henry b 1986); *Career* visiting fell NIH 1976–79, registrar Nat Hosp London 1979–81, conslt neurologist Queen Elizabeth Hosp Birmingham 1981–, Bloomer prof of clinical neurology Univ of Birmingham 1988–; memb Assoc Br Neurologists; FRCP 1986; *Recreations* sailing, skiing, gardening; *Style*— Prof Adrian

W

Williams; ✉ 25 Farquhar Road, Edgbaston, Birmingham B15 3RA (tel 0121 454 2633); Department of Neurology, Queen Elizabeth Hospital, Edgbaston, Birmingham B15 2TT (tel 0121 627 2106)

WILLIAMS, Prof Alan; CBE (1995); s of Ralph James Williams (d 1942), and Muriel, *née* Lewis; *b* 26 June 1935; *Educ* Cyfarthfa GS Merthyr Tydfil, Univ of Leeds (BSc, PhD); *m* 30 July 1960, Maureen Mary, da of Sydney Bagnall, of Leeds; 3 s (Christopher b 1964, Nicholas b 1967, Simon b 1971); *Career* Univ of Leeds: Livesey prof in fuel and combustion sci and head of Dept of Fuel and Energy 1973–2000, dean of engrg 1991–94, research prof 2000–; memb: DTI Advsy Ctee on Coal Research 1991–96, DTI Energy Advsy Panel 1993–96; memb OST Technol Foresight Energy Panel 1994–99; former pres and hon sec Inst of Energy, ed Jl of the Energy Inst 2004–; CChem, CEng, FRSC, FInstE, FInstPet, FIGasE, FRSA, FREng; *Publications* Combustion of Liquid Fuel Sprays, Combustion and Gasification of Coal; author of 450 papers in jls and conference proceedings; *Style*— Prof Alan Williams, CBE, FREng; ✉ Energy and Resources Research Institute, University of Leeds, Leeds LS2 9JT (tel 0113 233 2508, fax 0113 246 7310, e-mail fueaw@leeds.ac.uk)

WILLIAMS, Alan; *b* 1 July 1943; *Children* 1 da (Amanda Williams b 27 April 1972), 1 s (Simon Williams b 11 Aug 1977); *Partner* Lisa Thorne; *Career* sr press offr HM Treasy 1972–74, ed British Business 1974–79, chief info offr DTI 1979–86; The Post Office: controller of public affrs 1986–93, dir of PR 1993–95, memb Post Office Exec Bd and gp corporate affrs dir 1995–2003, memb Bd Parcelforce 1995–99; ptnr AWRailways 2003–; dep chm Esk Valley Railway Development Co 2003; memb: Design Panel Br Railways Bd 1985–94, Heritage Community Rail Partnership 2004–; regular writer and commentator on political and safety issues surrounding tport; assoc Instn of Railway Signal Engrs 1986, pres Railway Study Assoc (LSE) 1998–99; *Books* Railway Signalling (edns since 1963), Not the Age of the Train (1983); *Recreations* driving motor cars and steam engines very fast!; *Clubs* Reform; *Style*— Alan Williams, Esq; ✉ Two Beeches, Forest Road, East Horsley, Leatherhead, Surrey KT24 5ER (tel 01483 281577, e-mail awrailways@aol.com)

WILLIAMS, Rt Hon Alan John; PC (1977), MP; s of Emlyn Williams (d 1951); *b* 14 October 1930; *Educ* Cardiff HS, Cardiff Coll Technol, UC Oxford; *m* 1957, (Mary) Patricia Rees; 2 s, 1 da; *Career* serv RAF 1956–58; former econ lectr and journalist; memb: Lab Pty 1950–, Fabian Soc and Co-op Pty; Parly candidate (Lab) Poole 1959, MP (Lab) Swansea W 1964–; chm Welsh PLP and PPS to PMG 1966–67, Parly under sec Dept of Econ Affrs 1967–69, Parly sec Miny of Technol 1969–70, oppn spokesman on consumer protection, small businesses and minerals 1970–74; min of state: for prices and consumer protection 1974–76, for industry 1976–79; oppn spokesman: on Wales 1979–81, on Civil Service 1981–83, on industry 1983–87; dep shadow ldr of the House 1983–89, shadow sec of state for Wales 1987–88; chm Public Accounts Cmmn 1997–, memb Lord Chancellor's Advsy Ctee (pubn of official records), chm Liaison Select Ctee 2001–, hon sec Br American Parly Gp 2001–; *Style*— The Rt Hon Alan Williams, MP; ✉ House of Commons, London SW1A 0AA

WILLIAMS, Prof Alan Lee; OBE (1973); *b* 29 November 1930; *Educ* Roan Sch Greenwich, Ruskin Coll Oxford; *Career* RAF Signals 1949–51; pt/t messenger Nat Fire Serv 1944–45, cncllr Greenwich BC 1951–53, nat youth offr Lab Pty 1955–62, chm BNC World Assembly of Youth 1960–66, head of UNA Youth Dept 1962–66, memb Cncl of Europe and Parly Assembly WEU 1966–70, ldr UK Delgn to Fourth Ctee UN Gen Assembly 1969; MP (Lab): Hornchurch 1966–70, Hornchurch and Havering 1974–79; PPS to sec of state for Def 1969–70 and 1974–76, PPS to sec of state for NI 1976–79, ldr Parly Delgn to N Atlantic Assembly 1974–79, chm PLP Def Ctee 1976–79; dep dir Euro Movement 1972–79, DG ESU 1979–86, chm Peace Through NATO 1983–92, dir Atlantic Cncl 1992–, pres Atlantic Treaty Assoc 2000–04; chm CSIS Euro Working Gp Washington DC 1974–91; memb: Cncl RUSI 1974–78, Tri-Lateral Cmmn 1976–2000, FO Advsy Ctee on Disarmament and Arms Control and Advsy Ctee PRO 1977–81; chm: Tport on Water 1974–, City Coll 1987–, Cedar Centre 1988–, Toynbee Area Housing Assoc 1993–99, Majlish Home Care Service 2004–, William Beveridge Fndn 2006, Mid Atlantic Club 2006; memb: Bd Attlee Fndn 1987–89, Cncl Toynbee Hall 1992– (warden and chief exec 1987–92); Freeman: City of London 1969, Co of Watermen and Lightermen 1952; fell Queen Mary & Westfield Coll London 1994 (visiting prof 2003–); DLitt (hc) Schiller Int Univ; FRSA 1987; Golden Laurel Branch Award (Bulgaria) 2002; *Publications* Radical Essays (1966), Europe or the Open Sea (1971), Crisis in European Defence (1973), The European Defence Initiative: Europe's Bid for Equality (1985), The Decline of the Labour Party and the Fall of the SDP (1989), Prospects for a Common European Foreign and Security Policy (1995), NATO's Future in the Balance: Time for a Rethink? (1995), International Terrorism: Failure of International Response (1995), NATO and European Defence: A New Era of Partnership (1996), WEU: a Challenge for NATO (1997), NATO's 'Strategy for Securing the Future' (1999), Does NATO Have a Future? (2002); *Clubs* Reform, Pilgrims; *Style*— Prof Alan Lee Williams, OBE; ✉ tel 020 8463 9394 or 020 7247 2166, fax 020 7247 1226, e-mail a.williams@clc-london.ac.uk

WILLIAMS, Alan Peter; s of late Ronald Benjamin Williams, of Lindfield, W Sussex, and Marcia Elizabeth, *née* Lister; *b* 27 October 1944; *Educ* Merchant Taylors', Univ of Exeter (LLB, capt cricket XI, editor Univ Newspaper); *m* 21 Sept 1968, Lyn Rosemary, da of late Reginald Ewart Campling; 1 da (Laura Kate Elisabeth b 3 April 1974); *Career* articled clerk Burton Yeates & Hart 1966–67; Denton Wilde Sapte (and predecessor firms) 1967–2005: articled clerk 1967–68, admitted slr 1969, ptnr 1972–2003, opened Hong Kong office 1976; conslt DLA Piper (UK) LLP 2005–07; currently publishing conslt; memb Publishing Law Gp Publishers' Assoc 1983–; sec Nat Youth Music Theatre 2002– (dir 1990–2002); memb Ct of Assts Worshipful Co of Pewterers; memb: Law Soc 1969, Richard III Soc; memb Cncl Shakespeare's Globe; FRSA; *Books* Clark's Publishing Agreements (contrib, 7 edn), International Media Liability (by JohnWiley, contrib), Intellectual Property The New Law (jtly); Digital Media: Contracts, Rights and Licensing (jtly), Press, Printing and Publishing, chapter in Halsbury's Laws of England (jtly); *Recreations* cricket, music, walking, photography, theatre; *Clubs* MCC, Groucho, Whitefriars, City Law, Inner Magic Circle (assoc memb); *Style*— A P Williams, Esq; ✉ Turret House, Old Place, Lindfield, West Sussex RH16 2HU (tel 020 7247 3738, fax 020 7377 2605, e-mail alan@williams-legal.co.uk)

WILLIAMS, Prof (Gruffydd) Aled; s of William Ernest Williams (d 1976), and Gwendolen, *née* Hughes (d 1992); *b* 20 January 1943, Denbigh; *Educ* Llangollen GS, UC of N Wales Bangor (BA, PhD); *m* 1 July 1972, Brid Éimear; 2 s (Gruffudd Owain b 21 May 1973, Siôn Ynyr b 17 May 1982), 1 da (Brid Gwenllian b 22 Jan 1975); *Career* asst lectr Dept of Welsh UC Dublin 1965–70, successively lectr, sr lectr and reader Dept of Welsh Univ of Wales Bangor 1970–95, prof of Welsh Univ of Wales Aberystwyth 1995– (also currently head Dept of Welsh); ed Llên Cymru; chm Assoc for the Study of Welsh Language and Literature 2004–; Sir Ellis Griffith Prize Univ of Wales 1988, Mrs L W Davies Bursary Univ of Wales 1988; *Publications* Ymryson Edmwnd Prys a Wiliam Cynwal (1986), The Cambridge History of Literary Criticism, Vol 2: The Middle Ages (contrib, 2005); author of numerous articles on medieval and renaissance Welsh literature; *Style*— Prof Aled Williams; ✉ Bronafon, Dolau, Bow Street, Aberystwyth, Ceredigon (tel 01970 820664); Department of Welsh, Old College, King Street, Aberystwyth, Ceredigon SY23 2AX (tel 01970 622135, fax 01970 622976, e-mail gaw@aber.ac.uk)

WILLIAMS, Prof Allan Peter Owen; s of Thomas Williams (d 1995), of Cardiff, and Hilda Marie Williams (d 1983); *b* 14 October 1935; *Educ* Eastbourne GS, Univ of Manchester (BA), Birkbeck Coll London (MA, PhD); *m* 25 July 1959, Rosella, da of Maj Honorio Jose Muschamp d'Assis Fonseca (d 1984); 2 da (Hélène b 1963, Roselyne b 1967), 1 s (Edmond b 1965); *Career* res exec (later res gp head) Marplan Ltd 1960–63; City Univ Business Sch: lectr 1963–74, sr lectr 1974–83, reader 1983–88, prof 1988–2001 (emeritus prof 2001–), dep dean 1996–2001; City Univ: dir Centre for Personnel Res and Enterprise Devpt 1978–2001, pro-vice-chllr 1987–93, head Dept of Business Studies 1993–96; dir Organisation Surveys Ltd 1966–69, conslt psychologist Civil Serv Selection Bd 1966–80; hon treas Br Psychological Soc 1971–74 (chm occupational psychology section 1979–80), memb Army Personnel Res Ctee MRC 1983–94, chm Personnel Psychology Panel APRC 1987–94; memb Bd of Dirs: Int Assoc of Applied Psychology, Br Acad of Mgmnt; tstee T Ritchie Rodger Res Fund 1984–; fndr Liveryman Worshipful Co of Mgmnt Conslts; FBPsS 1979, CPsychol 1988, FBAM 1995; *Books* The Role and Educational needs of Occupational Health Nurses (1982), Using Personnel Research (1983), Changing Culture: New Organisational Approaches (1989 and 1993), The Competitive Consultant (1994), Managing Change Successfully (2002), The Rise of Cass Business School: The Journey to World Class (2006); *Recreations* lawn tennis, photography, philately, bibliophile; *Clubs* Barnet Lawn Tennis; *Style*— Prof Allan Williams; ✉ Cass Business School, City of London, 106 Bunhill Row, London EC1Y 8TZ

WILLIAMS, Dr Anthony Ffoulkes; s of Edward Gordon Williams, of Birkenhead, and Sarah Elizabeth, *née* Wearing (d 1972); *b* 7 May 1951; *Educ* Birkenhead Sch, UCL (BSc), Westminster Med Sch (MB BS), St Catherine's Coll Oxford (DPhil); *Career* res fell Dept of Paediatrics Univ of Oxford 1981–85, lectr in child health Univ of Bristol 1985–87, reader in child nutrition and conslt paediatrician St George's Hosp Med Sch (now St George's Univ of London) 1987–; memb: Nutrition Soc, British Assoc for Perinatal Med; FRCP 1993 (MRCP 1978), FRCPCH 1997; *Style*— Dr Anthony Williams; ✉ Department of Child Health, St George's University of London Cranmer Terrace, London SW17 0RE (tel 020 8725 2986, fax 020 8725 2858, e-mail a.williams@sgul.ac.uk)

WILLIAMS, Anthony Frederick Davies (Tony); s of Evan Glyndwr Morgan Davies Williams (d 1963), of Caerphilly, Wales, and Gwendolen Delilah, *née* Naish, latterly Mrs Calder (d 1994); *b* 12 August 1940; *Educ* Christ Coll Brecon, City of London Business Sch; *m* 21 June 1969 (m dis 2002), Lorna Elizabeth, da of Geoffrey Thomas Southern Harborne; 2 s (Nicholas Geoffrey Calder b 26 April 1973, Andrew Christian Calder b 15 Jan 1976); *Career* chartering clerk Cayzer Irvine Group 1958–62, chartering mangr Tate & Lyle 1963–74, dir London shipping div Louis Dreyfus Corp 1974–86, chartering broker Denholm Coates & Co Ltd 1986–88, divnl dir Tate & Lyle International 1988–96, md Kentships (div of Tate & Lyle International) 1988–96; shipping conslt 1997–; memb Baltic Exchange 1961–; Freeman City of London 1988; Hon Artillery Co: cmmnd 2 Lt 1968, Co of Pikemen & Musketeers 1988–; MICS 1961; *Recreations* rugby football, military ceremonial activities, golf, classical music, sailing; *Clubs* Harlequins RFC, Marine Engrs; *Style*— Tony Williams, Esq; ✉ Daylesford, Penselwood, Wincanton, Somerset BA9 8LL (tel 01747 840208)

WILLIAMS, Anthony Graham (Tony); s of John Graham Williams (d 1961), of Weybridge, Surrey, and Catherine Evelyn, *née* Steedman (d 1987); *b* 1 May 1928, Weybridge, Surrey; *Educ* Charterhouse, Sch of Printing; *m* 1957, Sheelagh, *née* Pigott; 3 s (Philip Graham b 26 Aug 1958, Nicholas Graham b 5 Jan 1960, Sean Mountford Graham b 1 June 1963), 1 da (Madeleine Graham b 25 May 1965); *Career* Williams Lea & Co Ltd: joined 1950, dir 1953, md 1968; Williams Lea Gp Ltd: md 1972–93, chm 1982–2000, life pres 2000–; vice-pres BPIF 1980–81; govr London Coll of Printing 1971–74; Master Worshipful Co of Leathersellers 1984–85; FIOP, FInstD, FIMgt, FRSA; *Recreations* tennis, reading, travel; *Clubs* RAC, All Eng Lawn Tennis, St George's Hill Golf, St George's Hill Tennis, Int Lawn Tennis Club of GB; *Style*— Tony Williams, Esq; ✉ The Well House, George Road, Kingston Hill, Surrey KT2 7NR (tel and fax 020 8949 4436, e-mail a-g-williams@talk21.com); Williams Lea Group, Clifton House, Worship Street, London EC2A 2EJ (tel 020 7772 4270, fax 020 7772 4203, e-mail tony.williams@williamslea.com)

WILLIAMS, Betty; MP; *Educ* Ysgol Dyffryn Nantlle, Penygroes Coleg y Normal Bangor Univ of Wales (BA); *Career* MP (Lab) Conwy 1997– (contested Caernarfon 1983, Conwy 1987 and 1992); memb Welsh Affrs Select Ctee 1997–2005, memb Parly Assembly Cncl of Europe 2005–, memb WEU 2005–; community cncllr 1967–83, dist cncllr 1970–91, county cncllr 1976–93; former memb: Electricity Users' Cncl, Gas Consumers' Cncl for Wales, Health Educn Advsy Ctee for Wales, Rent Assessment Panel for Wales, Ct Univ of Wales, Gwynedd Family Practitioner Ctee; former vice-pres Univ of Wales Bangor; former govr: Bangor Normal Coll, Gwynedd Technical Coll; hon fell Univ of Wales Bangor; *Style*— Mrs Betty Williams, MP; ✉ House of Commons, London SW1A 0AA (tel 020 7219 5052, fax 020 7219 2759); constituency (tel 01248 680097)

WILLIAMS, Brian Edward; s of Edward Clement Williams, of Norfolk, and Christine Edith, *née* Jones; *b* 28 April 1959; *Educ* Framlingham Coll Suffolk; *m* 16 Dec 1989, Deborah Jane, *née* Dingley; 2 s (Charles Edward Dingley b 2 Feb 1991, Edward Roger b 10 Feb 1994), 1 da (Lucinda Catherine b 21 Aug 1992); *Career* hotelier; Forte Hotels 1976–85: food & beverage mangr Imperial Torquay 1980–82, food & beverage mangr Dubai International 1982–85; Mandarin Oriental Hotel Group 1985–2003: food & beverage mangr Oriental Kuala Lumpur 1985–86, mangr Mandarin Hong Kong 1990 (resident mangr 1986–89), gen mangr Mandarin Oriental Macau and Hotel Bella Vista Macau 1991–94, gen mangr The Ritz London 1994–95, gen mangr Mandarin Oriental Hyde Park 1996–2000, vice-pres devpt Mandarin Oriental Hotel Gp EMEA until 2003; chief exec Scotsman Hotel Gp 2003–; *Recreations* skiing, golf, tennis, wine; *Style*— Brian Williams, Esq

WILLIAMS, Dr Brian Owen; s of William Wood Williams (d 1988), of Kilbarchan, Scotland, and Joan Scott, *née* Adam; *b* 27 February 1947; *Educ* Kings Park Sch Glasgow, Univ of Glasgow (MD, MB, ChB); *m* 3 Dec 1970, Martha MacDonald, da of James Carmichael (d 1974), of Glasgow; 2 da (Jennifer b 1976, Linzie b 1978); *Career* maj RAMC 32 Scot Signal Regt TA 1976–83; conslt geriatrician Victoria Infirmary Glasgow 1976–79, sr lectr Univ of Glasgow 1979–82, conslt in admin charge W Glasgow Geriatric Med Serv 1982– (clinical dir 1993–), hon sr clinical lectr Univ of Glasgow 1982–; author of over 100 pubns on health care of the elderly; vice-pres (medical) RCPSGlas 2001–03 (past hon sec), past hon sec Scottish Royal Colls; memb: BMA, Br Geriatrics Soc (past pres), Scottish Soc of Physicians; FRCP (London), FRCPGlas, FRCPEd, Hon Fell Royal Coll Speech and Language Therapy, FCPS (Pakistan), FRCPI; *Books* Practical Management of the Elderly (with Sir Ferguson Anderson, 4 edn, 1983, 5 edn, 1988); *Recreations* swimming, writing, hill walking; *Style*— Dr Brian Williams; ✉ 15 Thorn Drive, High Burnside, Glasgow G73 4RH (tel 0141 634 4480); Gartnavel General Hospital, 1053 Great Western Road, Glasgow G12 0YN (tel 0141 211 3167, fax 0141 211 3465)

WILLIAMS, Bryn Owen; BEM (1990); s of Hugh James Owen Williams (d 1983), and Ivy, *née* Heffer; *b* 20 August 1933; *Educ* Southgate County GS, Pitman's Coll, Italia Conti Stage Sch; *m* 6 July 1957, Ann Elizabeth Rheidol, da of David Rheidol Powell (d 1932), adopted da of Stephen Llewellyn Jones (d 1963), of Dulwich; 1 s (Timothy Dorian b 7 April 1959), 1 da (Tracy-Jane b 11 June 1961); *Career* professional toastmaster 1950; co fndr (with father) Nat Assoc of Toastmasters 1956 (pres 1962 and 1990, life vice-pres 1984), chm Toastmaster Training Ltd 1988, officiated at over fourteen thousand events in over twenty countries, achieved 50 years as a professional toastmaster 2000; memb Grand Order Water Rats 1965, pres of the Soc of Past Chm of the Licensed Victuallers Nat Homes 1993, memb Inst of Advanced Motorists; Freeman City of London 1980, Liveryman Worshipful Co of Butchers 1985; intronized into the Jurade of the Vineyards of St Emilion 1989; *Recreations* golf, classical music; *Clubs* Muswell Hill Golf, Concert Artists Assoc, City Livery, Variety Club of GB Golf Soc (life memb), Jaguar Drivers (life memb); *Style—* Bryn Williams, Esq, BEM; ✉ Broad Oaks, 50 Tolmers Road, Cuffley, Hertfordshire EN6 4JF (tel 01707 873399, fax 01707 875598, e-mail brynwtoast@indosweb.com)

WILLIAMS, Brynle; AM; *b* 1949, Cilcain, N Wales; *m*; 2 c; *Career* farmer; memb Nat Assembly for Wales (Cons) N Wales 2003–, shadow min for rural affrs; memb Royal Welsh Agric Cncl; memb Cncl Welsh Pony and Cob Soc; *Style—* Brynle Williams, Esq, AM; ✉ National Assembly for Wales, Cardiff Bay, Cardiff CF99 1NA (tel 029 2089 8394, fax 029 2089 8416, e-mail brynle.williams@wales.gov.uk)

WILLIAMS, Carol; da of George Hutchinson (d 1985), and Doris Irene, *née* Charlesworth (d 2006); *b* 16 December 1957, Pontefract, Yorks; *Educ* Wakefield Girls HS, UCNW (BA), Leeds Poly, Nottingham Poly (PGCE); *m* 20 June 1997, Mark Williams; 2 s (Toby Nathaniel, Cameron Joseph); *Career* admitted slr 1985; articled clerk Grays Slrs of York 1983–85, slr Booth & Co 1985–86, asst slr to sr slr Asda plc 1986–90; Northern Foods plc: head of legal servs 1990–2005, co sec and head of legal 2005–; chm: NE Commerce and Industry Gp 1999–, Nat Commerce and Industry Gp 2003–04; regnl bd memb Young Enterprise Scheme for E Yorks 2001–05; contrib to Law Soc Gazette, In-House Lawyer magazine and other legal pubns; Yorks In-House Lawyer of the Year 2002, named as one of top 50 European in-house counsel by Legal Business Magazine 2005; *Style—* Mrs Carol Williams; ✉ Northern Foods plc, 2180 Century Way, Thorpe Park, Leeds LS15 8ZB (tel 0113 390 0184, fax 0113 390 0212, e-mail carol.williams@northernfoods.com)

WILLIAMS, Caroline Ann; da of Maurice Henry Jackson, of Almeria, Spain, and Dorothy, *née* Ludlow; *b* 2 March 1954; *Educ* Convent of the Cross Sch Waterlooville, St Hugh's Coll Oxford, Univ of Southampton (LLB); *m* 17 March 1973, Richard David Brooke Williams, s of Gp Capt Richard David Williams, CBE, of Hants; 1 da (Rowena b 27 June 1982), 1 s (Richard David b 6 Aug 1987); *Career* admitted slr 1978; Blake Lapthorn: ptnr 1981–2000, conslt 2000–; consult and non-exec dir of various companies; chm: Portsmouth Area Ctee Hampshire Incorporated Law Soc 1993–95, Univ of Portsmouth 1995–99, Portsmouth Historic Dockyard Ltd 2003–, Hampshire Econ Partnership 2003–, Capital Ltd 2003–, Flagship Portsmouth Tst 2005–; govr: Univ of Portsmouth 1993–2002, Portsmouth HS 1995–1999, Portsmouth GS 2003–05; govr and vice-chm Portsmouth Coll of Art Design and FE 1989–94; memb: Industrial Advsy Bd Portsmouth Univ Business Sch 1991–99, SE Regnl Cncl CBI 1996–2003, Bd SE England Devpt Agency 1998–2003, Industrial Advsy Bd Wessex Inst of Technol 2001–05, Bd Portsmouth City Growth 2004–05; Hon LLD Univ of Portsmouth 2002; memb Law Soc 1978; FRSA 1995; *Publications* A Practical Legal Guide to Occupational Pension Schemes (with Philip Harwood-Smart, 1993); *Recreations* sailing; *Style—* Mrs Caroline Williams; ✉ Caroline Williams Consulting Ltd, 15 Vanguard Court, Centurion Gate, Southsea, Hampshire PO4 9TD (tel 023 9282 5746, e-mail cawilliams@btconnect.com)

WILLIAMS, Christopher; s of Henry Edward Williams (d 1957), of Bristol, and Beatrice May, *née* Somers (d 1990); *Educ* Colston's Sch Stapleton Bristol, St Cuthbert's Society Univ of Durham (BA); *Career* W & T Avery Ltd Soho Foundry Birmingham 1964–69, md Frenchay Transport Group 1969–; chm Frenchay Community Health Cncl 1980–81 (memb 1976–81, vice-chm 1978–80), chm Frenchay HA 1990–91 (memb 1981–91), chm Frenchay Healthcare NHS Tst 1992–98 (chm designate 1991–92, assoc non-exec dir 1998–); memb: NHS Nat Fire Policy Advsy Gp 1993–98, Standing Fin and Capital Ctee NHS Tst Fedn 1993–99, Cncl NHS Tst Fedn 1994–97; Northavon DC: cncllr (Cons) 1976–96, chm Fin and Gen Purposes Ctee 1980–90, chm of Cncl 1986–88, ldr Cons Gp 1991–96; chm Bd of Govrs Frenchay Park Hosp Sch 1978–94, dir Bristol/Avon Groundwork Tst 1990–96; *Recreations* music, reading, travel; *Style—* Christopher Williams, Esq

WILLIAMS, Dr Christopher Beverley; s of Dr Denis John Williams, CBE (d 1990), and Dr Joyce Beverley Williams, MBE, *née* Jewson (d 1996); *b* 8 June 1938; *Educ* Dragon Sch, Winchester, Trinity Coll Oxford (MA, BM BCh), UCH London; *m* 25 April 1970, Dr Christina Janet Seymour Williams, da of Reginald Seymour Lawrie; 1 da (Caroline Frances Aitken b 5 July 1972), 1 s (Duncan Nicholas Grant b 21 Nov 1973); *Career* house appts UCH, Brompton Hosp, Hammersmith Hosp, Nat Hosp for Neurology and Whittington Hosp 1965–67, subsequently registrar UCH; currently: conslt physician (endoscopy) The London Clinic and King Edward VII Hosp for Officers; worldwide lectr on colonoscopy and colonoscopic polypectomy incl Quadrennial Review Lecture in Polypectomy (World Congress of Gastroenterology 1990), author of numerous articles on colonoscopy, colonic neoplasia and related topics; Gold medal BMA Int film competition, BLAT trophy for teaching films; Liveryman Worshipful Soc of Apothecaries 1958; memb: Br Soc of Gastroenterology 1973 (endoscopy fndn lectr 1976 and 1995, endoscopy vice-pres 1987), Societé Belge de l'Endoscopie Digestive (hon memb) 1973, Societé Medicale Internationale d'Endoscopie et de Radio-Cinema (hon memb and int ed) 1973; FMS 1981 (Lettsomian lectr 1983), FRSM 1970 (memb Proctology Section), FRCP (LRCP), FRCS (MRCS); *Books* Colorectal Disease - an introduction for physicians and surgeons (jt ed), Practical Gastrointestinal Endoscopy (1983, 5 edn 2003), Annual of Gastrointestinal Endoscopy (1989–98); Colonoscopy (CD-ROM and DVD-ROM, 2002), Colonoscopy - principles and practice (co-ed) 2003; *Recreations* travel, fine wine and food, skiing, scuba; *Clubs* St Albans Medical; *Style—* Dr Christopher B Williams, FRCP, FRCS; ✉ 11 Frognal Way, London NW3 6XE (tel 020 7435 4030, fax 020 7435 5636); Endoscopy Unit, The London Clinic, 20 Devonshire Place, London (tel 020 7616 7781, fax 020 7616 7684, e-mail christopherbwilliams@btinternet.com)

WILLIAMS, Colin Campbell; s of Graham Williams (d 1942), and Eleanor, *née* Cuthbert (d 1988); *b* 9 February 1942, Woking, Surrey; *Educ* Uppingham, Magdalen Coll Oxford, UCLA; *m* 1975, Gerlinda, *née* Ackerl; 1 s (Alexander b 20 May 1979), 1 da (Sophie b 21 June 1981); *Career* fndr Wogen plc 1972–; chm Uppingham Sch; hon steward Westminster Abbey; *Recreations* bicycling; *Clubs* Oriental; *Style—* Colin Williams, Esq; ✉ Wogen plc, 4 The Sanctuary, London SW1P 3JS (tel 020 7222 2171, fax 020 7222 5862, e-mail colin.williams@wogen.com)

WILLIAMS, Prof David Franklyn; s of Henry Williams (d 1975), and Margaret, *née* Morgan (d 1975); *b* 18 December 1944; *Educ* Univ of Birmingham (BSc, PhD, DSc); *Children* 3 s (Adrian David b 1972, Jonathan Philip b 1974, Christopher Stephen b 1977); *Career* Univ of Liverpool: joined staff 1968, prof of clinical engrg 1984–, conslt scientist Royal Liverpool Univ Hosp 1990–, pro-vice-chllr 1997–2000; dir UK Centre for Tissue Engrg 2004–; sr Fulbright scholar and visiting prof Clemson Univ USA 1975–76; scientific advsr Euro Cmmn; author of 32 books and over 300 scientific pubns; Clemson Award US Soc for Biomaterials 1982, Winter Award Euro Soc for Biomaterials 1996; MAE; FIM, FIPSM, FREng 1999; *Clubs* Athenaeum; *Style—* Prof David Williams, FREng; ✉ Department of Clinical Engineering, University of Liverpool, PO Box 147, Liverpool L69 3BX (tel 0151 706 5606, fax 0151 706 5920, e-mail dfw@liverpool.ac.uk)

WILLIAMS, Dr David Frederick; s of Frederick Sefton Williams (d 2001), and Dorothy, *née* Banks; *b* 21 September 1951, Preston, Lancs; *Educ* Hutton GS Preston, Univ of Reading (BSc, PhD); *m* 16 Nov 1985, Jeannie Elizabeth, *née* Rickards; 2 da (Rebecca Jo-Anne b 25 May 1983, Sylvana Daisy b 11 Oct 1986), 1 s (Jonathan Walter Richard b 28 Feb 1996); *Career* lectr Dept of Geography Univ of Reading 1977–78, Clyde Surveys (formerly Fairey Surveys) 1978–82, NERC 1982–89, head UK Earth Observation Prog Br Nat Space Centre (BNSC) DTI 1989–96, head of strategy and int rels European Orgn for the Exploitation of Meteorological Satellites (EUMETSAT) Darmstadt 1996–2006, DG BNSC 2006–; tstee and memb Bd of Dirs Nat Space Centre Leicester, memb Global Climate Observing Ctee; *Recreations* football, rugby, gardening, renovation, farming; *Style—* Dr David Williams; ✉ British National Space Centre, 5th Floor, Kingsgate House, Victoria Street, London SW1E 6SW (tel 020 7215 0877, e-mail david.williams@stfc.ac.uk)

WILLIAMS, Prof Sir David Glyndwr Tudor; kt (1991), Hon QC (1994), DL (1995); s of Tudor Williams, OBE (d 1955), and Anne, *née* Rees (d 1980); *b* 22 October 1930; *Educ* Queen Elizabeth GS Carmarthen, Emmanuel Coll Cambridge (MA, LLB), Univ of Calif Berkeley (LLM), Harvard Law Sch; *m* 1959, Sally, *née* Cole; 2 da (Rhiannon b 1963, Siân b 1968), 1 s (Rhys b 1965); *Career* called to the Bar Lincoln's Inn 1956; lectr: Univ of Nottingham 1958–63, Keble Coll Oxford 1963–67; Univ of Cambridge: lectr Emmanuel Coll 1967–76, sr tutor Emmanuel Coll 1970–76, reader in public law 1976–83, pres Wolfson Coll 1980–92, Rouse Ball prof of English law 1983–92, vice-chllr 1989–96 (vice-chllr emeritus 1996–), prof of law 1996–98; distinguished anniversary fell ANU Canberra 1996, distinguished visiting prof Indiana Univ 2000, hon prof of law Chinese Univ of Hong Kong 2006–; pres Nat Soc for Clean Air 1983–85; memb: Cncl on Tbnls 1972–82, Royal Cmmn on Environmental Pollution 1976–83, Cmmn on Energy and the Environment 1979–82, Animal Procedures Ctee 1987–89, Sr Salaries Review Body 1998–2004; pres Univ of Wales Swansea 2001–; hon degrees: Loughborough Univ, Univ of Hull, Anglia Poly, Univ of Nottingham, Univ of Liverpool, Davidson Coll NC, Wm Jewell Coll MO, McGill Univ Montreal, Univ of Sydney, Duke Univ, Univ of Cambridge, Victoria Univ of Technol Melbourne; hon fell: Emmanuel Coll Cambridge, Wolfson Coll Cambridge, Pembroke Coll Cambridge, Keble Coll Oxford; *Books* Not in the Public Interest (1965), Keeping the Peace (1967); *Recreations* reading, sport; *Clubs* Athenaeum; *Style—* Prof Sir David Williams, QC, DL; ✉ Emmanuel College, Cambridge CB2 3AP (tel 01223 334200, fax 01223 334426)

WILLIAMS, Dr David John; JP; s of Frank Williams, CBE (d 1979), and Kathleen, *née* Davies (d 1989); *b* 23 April 1938; *Educ* Highgate Sch, Hotchkiss Sch USA, Trinity Coll Cambridge (MA), St Thomas' Hosp Med Sch (MB, BChir); *m* 1977, Ann Andrews, da of William Walker-Watson; 1 s (Jonathan b 4 Sept 1979), 1 da (Antonia b 31 March 1981); *Career* jr med posts St Thomas' Hosp, Kingston Hosp, Guy's/Maudsley Neurosurgical Unit 1964–65; resident MO: Nat Heart Hosp 1966, Middx Hosp 1967–70; registrar Maudsley Hosp 1970–71, GP 1971–72; conslt in A&E med: Middx Hosp 1973–84, St Thomas' Hosp 1984–93; clinical dir for A&E servs Guy's and St Thomas' Hosps Tst 1993–2000; clinical advsr to the Health Service Cmmr (Ombudsman) 2000–05, memb Criminal Injuries Compensation Appeals Panel 2000–, memb Tbnls Serv 2006–; sec Casualty Surgns Assoc 1978–84; pres: Br Assoc for A&E Med 1987–90, Intercollegiate Faculty of A&E Med 1993–96, Euro Soc for Emergency Med 2004– (vice-pres 1999–2004); invited memb Cncl RCP, RCS and Royal Coll of Anaesthetists 1994–2000; faculty rep: Senate of Surgery of GB and I 1994–97, Acad of Med Royal Colls and Faculties in Scot 1996–97; hon memb American Coll of Emergency Physicians 1990; Hon FRSM, FRCP, FRCPEd, FRCS, FRCSEd, FRCA, FFAEM, MRCGP; *Recreations* reading, collecting books, theatre, travel; *Style—* Dr David Williams; ✉ 13 Spencer Hill, Wimbledon, London SW19 4PA (tel 020 8946 3785)

WILLIAMS, Prof David Raymond; OBE (1993); s of late Eric Thomas Williams, and late Amy Gwendoline Williams; *b* 20 March 1941; *Educ* UCNW Bangor (BSc, PhD), Univ of St Andrews (DSc); *m* 22 Aug 1964, Gillian Kirkpatrick, da of late Adam Murray; 2 da (Caroline Susan b 1 Nov 1970, Kerstin Jane b 20 July 1973); *Career* lectr Univ of St Andrews 1966–77, prof of chemistry Univ of Wales Cardiff (now Cardiff Univ) 1977–2006 (now emeritus prof); chm Br Cncl Sci Advsy Ctee 1986–94, memb Advsy Ctee on Hazardous Substances DEFRA 2000–05; EurChem, CChem, FRSC, FRSM; *Books* The Principles of Bioinorganic Chemistry, The Metals of Life, Analysis Using Glass Electrodes, Trace Element Medicine and Chelation Therapy, What is Safe?; *Recreations* swimming, cycling, travel, photography; *Style—* Prof David R Williams, OBE; ✉ School of Chemistry, Cardiff University, Main Building, Park Place, Cardiff CF10 3AT (tel 029 2087 4778, fax 029 2087 4778, e-mail williamsd@cf.ac.uk)

WILLIAMS, Desmond James; OBE (1988); s of Sydney Williams (d 1982), and Eleanor Williams; *b* 7 July 1932; *Educ* Douai Sch, Xaverian Coll, Univ of Manchester (DipArch); *m* 1 (m dis 1982); 3 s (Dominic b 1965, Andrew, Jeremy (twins) b 1970), 1 da (Sarah Frances b 1967); m 2, 30 Dec 1988, Susan Alexandra, da of John Richardson, of Shaldon, Devon; *Career* architect; formally in private practice 1964–2005, specialising in educnl and leisure buildings, security design, residential devpts and hotels; consultancy clients incl World Bank and Asian Devpt Bank, given lectures at Univs of London and Manchester and in Canada, London and Manchester; author of articles in: Education 1980, Building 1988 and 1989, Architects Journal 1989, Security Magazine 1990; past pres Manchester Soc of Architects 1988, examiner Sch of Architecture Univ of Manchester; RIBA 1967 (chm NW regn 1990–92, co-ordinator RIBA/LSC Forum until 2004); *Recreations* aviation, music, opera, walking; *Style—* Desmond Williams, Esq, OBE; ✉ e-mail desmond.williams1@virgin.net

WILLIAMS, Air Cdre Dil N; OBE (1993); *Educ* Chelmsford Tech HS, Univ of Bristol (RAF Cadet), RAF Coll Cranwell, JSDC Greenwich; *m* Victoria; 3 c; *Career* OC Mechanical Tport RAF Wattisham, Hawk Aircraft Tactival Weapons Conversation Unit RAF Chivenor 1980, Dominie Sqdn Engrg Offr 6 Trg Sch RAF Finningley, Sqdn Leader 1984; Sr Engrg Offr 2 (AC) Sqdn RAF Laarbruch Germany, OC Engrg and Supply Wing RAF Markham; involved Operation GRANBY, activated RAF Detachment Tabuk, OC Engrg and Supply Dhahran Gulf War 1991; memb UK MOD (Air) Team Project Al Yamamah Riyadh Saudi Arabia, advsr Logistic Policy Royal Saudi Air Force; dep dir Support Mgmnt 13 (RAF) Head Engrg Authy and Aircraft Project Dir RAF Trg Aircraft Multi-disciplinary Gp HQ Logistic Command; OC RAF Cosford; dir Corp Devpt Trg Defence Agency 2000–; fndr and sometime chm RAeS (Norfolk branch); CEng, FRAeS; *Recreations* angling, travel, classic cars; *Style—* Air Cdre Dil Williams, OBE; ✉ ce-tgda@btinternet.com

WILLIAMS, Sir Donald Mark; 10 Bt (UK 1866), of Tregullow, Cornwall; s of Sir Robert Ernest Williams, 9 Bt (d 1976); *b* 7 November 1954; *Educ* W Buckland Sch; *m* 1982, Denise, o da of Royston H Cory, of Kashmir, Raleigh Hill, Bideford, Devon; 1 s (Matthew b and d 1985), 3 da (Hannah Louise b 1987, Michelle Ruth b 1995, Natasha Elizabeth b 1997); *Heir* bro, Barton Williams; *Style—* Sir Donald Williams, Bt; ✉ Kamsack, Saskatchewan, Canada; Upcott House, Barnstaple, Devon

WILLIAMS, Prof Dudley Howard; s of Lawrence Williams, and Evelyn, *née* Hudson; *b* 25 May 1937; *Educ* Pudsey GS, Univ of Leeds (BSc, PhD), Univ of Cambridge (MA, ScD); *m* 1963, Lorna Patricia Phyllis, da of Anthony Bedford; 2 s (Mark b 2 April 1966, Simon b 15 August 1968); *Career* post-doctoral fell Stanford Univ 1961–64; Univ of Cambridge: sr research asst 1964–66, lectr in chemistry Churchill Coll 1964–73, asst dir of research 1966–74, dir of studies in chemistry Churchill Coll 1968–73, reader in organic chemistry 1974–96, prof of biological chemistry 1996–2004 (emeritus prof 2004–); extraordinary fell Churchill Coll 1989–96 (fell 1964); visiting prof: Univ of Calif Irvine 1967, 1986, 1989 and 1997, Univ of Florida 1973, Univ of Wisconsin 1975, Univ of Copenhagen 1976, Univ of Queensland 1994; visiting lectr Univ of Cape Town 1972, Nuffield visiting lectr Univ of Sydney 1972, visiting research fell ANU 1980; Meldola Medal Royal Inst of Chemistry 1966, Corday-Morgan Medal and Prize Chemical Soc 1968, RSC Award for Structural Chemistry 1984, Bader Award for Organic Chemistry, RSC 1990, Leo Friend Award American Chemical Soc 1996, Lee Kuan Yew Distinguished Visitor Singapore 2000, Paul Ehrlich Lectr France 2001, Marvin Cormack Distinguished Lectr Indiana Univ 2001, James Sprague Lectr Univ of Wisconsin Madison 2002, RSC Merck Lectr and Medal

2003; memb Academia Europaea; FRS 1983; *Publications* Applications of NMR in Organic Chemistry (1964), Spectroscopic Methods in Organic Chemistry (1966, 5 edn 1995), Mass Spectrometry of Organic Compounds (1967), Mass Spectrometry - Principles and Applications (1981); also author of papers in chemical and biochemical jls; *Recreations* music, gardening; *Style—* Prof Dudley Williams, FRS; ✉ Department of Chemistry, Lensfield Road, Cambridge CB2 1EW (tel 01223 336368, fax 01223 336913, e-mail dhw1@cam.ac.uk)

WILLIAMS, Emrys; *b* 18 January 1958; *Educ* Slade Sch of Art (Boise Travelling scholar, Robert Ross scholar, BA), Stewart Powell Bowen fellowship 1983; *Career* artist in residence: Mostyn Art Gallery Llandudno 1983, South Hill Park Arts Centre and Wilde Theatre Bracknell 1985; *Solo Exhibitions* Andrew Knight Gallery Cardiff 1984, Pastimes Past (Wrexham Arts Centre) 1984, The Welsh Mountain Zoo (South Hill Park Arts Centre, Bracknell) 1985, Off Season - Winter Paintings (Oldham Art Gallery) 1985, Lanchester Poly Gallery Coventry 1986, Benjamin Rhodes Gallery London 1986, 1989 and 1991, Wrexham Arts Centre 1990; *Group Exhibitions* incl: Clwyd Ten (Wrexham Arts Centre) 1981, Thorugh Artists Eyes (Mostyn Art Gallery, Llandudno) 1982, John Moores Liverpool Exhibition XIII 1982–83, Serpentine Summer Show II (Serpentine London) 1983, Pauline Carter & Emrys Williams (Chapter Gallery) Cardiff 1984, John Moores Liverpool Exhibition XIV 1985, Group 56 (Bratislava Czechoslovakia) 1986, David Hepher and Emrys Williams (Castlefield Gallery) Manchester 1987, Big Paintings (Benjamin Rhodes Gallery) 1988, Ways of Telling (Mostyn Art Gallery, Llandudno) 1989, Group 56 (Glynn Vivian Museum, Swansea), 1990; *Work in Public Collections* Contemporary Art Soc of Wales, Arthur Andersen & Co, Glynn Vivian Art Gallery and Museum Swansea, Govt Art Fund, Clwyd County Cncl, Clwyd Fine Art Trust, Metropolitan Museum of Art NY; numerous works in private collections in Britain and USA; *Awards* minor prize John Moores Liverpool Exhibition 1983, third prize Royal Nat Eisteddfod of Wales 1985, third prize Royal Over-Seas League London (Wardair Travel prize to Canada) 1988, Welsh Arts Cncl award for travel to Normandy 1988, Welsh Arts Cncl award for travel to Germany 1991; *Style—* Emrys Williams, Esq

WILLIAMS, Euryn Ogwen; s of Alun Ogwen Williams (d 1970), and Lil Evans (d 1968); *b* 22 December 1942; *Educ* Mold Alun GS, Univ of Wales Bangor (BA, DipEd); *m* 1 Jan 1966, Jenny Lewis, da of John Edward Jones, of The Knap, Barry; 1 s (Rhodri Ogwen b 10 May 1968), 1 da (Sara Lisa Ogwen b 17 March 1971); *Career* media conslt and prodr; prog dir TWW, prodr HTV, dir EOS Independent Production Co, dir BBC Radio, dep chief exec and prog controller S4C, hon lectr Univ of Wales; special adviser to Nat Assembly of Wales; hon fell Univ of Wales Lampeter; *Books* Pelydrau Pell (1973), Images of Europe (1995); *Recreations* reading, television viewing, spectator sports; *Style—* Euryn Williams, Esq

WILLIAMS, Faynia Roberta; da of Michael Manuel Jeffery (d 1968), and Sally Caroline, *née* Stone (d 1968); *b* 10 November 1938; *Educ* Brighton and Hove HS, RADA (Dip), Univ of London (BA), Univ of Oxford (DPhil), Nat Film Sch, Univ of Westminster; *m* 1, 1961, Michael Brandis Williams (d 1968), s of Walter Williams; 2 da (Sabra Mildred b 1964, Teohna Eloise b 1966); m 2, 1975, Richard Arthur Crane, s of Rev Robert Bartlett Crane (d 1996); 2 s (Leo Michael b 1977, Samuel Richard b 1979); *Career* theatre and opera director, BBC prodr and dir drama and documentary features, and film maker; fell in theatre: Univ of Bradford 1974–78, Lancaster Univ 1978; Granada TV artist in residence and visiting prof Univ of Calif 1984, vtutor and lectr Univ of Sussex 1996–; memb: Equity 1959, Cncl Int Theatre Inst and Dramatic Theatre Ctee 1989– (pres 1997–), Cncl Directors' Guild of GB (chair 1998–99); Freedom City of London 1959; FRSA; *Theatre* first professional appearance Stephen Joseph's Theatre in the Round (with Harold Pinter and Alan Ayckbourn) 1958–60; contract artist MGM USA 1960–61; first directed The Oz Trial (Oxford Playhouse) 1971; asst dir Tadeusz Kantor 1973; artistic dir: Oxford Free Theatre 1972–74, Oxford Arts Festival 1973, Bradford Theatre in the Mill 1974–78, Brighton Theatre 1980–85 and 2007–, Tron Theatre Glasgow 1983–84, Univ of Essex Theatre 1985–89; freelance dir: Royal Court, Fortune, Bush, Young Vic, Barbican, Royal Albert; theatres abroad incl USSR, Poland, Aust, Sweden, USA, Budapest 1993, NT Romania 1991 and NY Mongolia 2001; prodns incl: Brothers Karamazov (with Alan Rickman, Edinburgh Int Festival 1981, Fortune Theatre London and USSR), King Lear (RSC/RNT Acter Co USA), Body of a Woman (Brighton Festival) 1999; dir and designer: Mothers Shall Not Cry (Millennium Cmmn, Royal Albert Hall Promenade Opera) 2000, The Tenderland (by Aaron Copeland, Barbican) 2002; *Television* incl: Signals, Channel 4 arts documentaries 1990; *Radio* prodr BBC Radio Drama 1992– incl: Moscow Stations (starring Tom Courtenay, nominated Radio Times Award) and Vlad the Impaler (starring John Hurt, nominated Sony Award); prodr and presenter BBC Radio Features 1993–; interviews incl: Joan Littlewood, Pina Bausch, Peter Stein, Patrice Chéreau, Peter Sellars, Dame Iris Murdoch and Ariel Dorfman; also Movers and Shakers (feature series, Radio 3), Bausch of Wuppertal (Radio 3 and World Service), Moscow Art Theatre Centennial Feature (Radio 3) 1997, Who Massacred the Innocents? (Radio 4) 2000, The Love of 3 Colonels (Radio 4) 2002, Filling the Void (Radio 4) 2004, Theatre in the Round (Radio 4) 2006; *Film* 2 shorts: Sleepy, Prelude; *Awards* incl: 9 Edinburgh Festival Fringe First Award; nominated: Best Dir for Satan's Ball London Critics' Award 1977, Best Dir for Brothers Karamazov 1981; *Recreations* the sea, travel to lesser-known places; *Clubs* Groucho; *Style—* Ms Faynia Williams; ✉ tel 07900 088191, e-mail fayniaw@googlemail.com

WILLIAMS, Sir Francis Owen Garbett (Frank); kt (1999), CBE (1987); s of Owen Garbett Williams, of Liverpool; *b* 16 April 1942; *Educ* St Joseph's Coll Dumfries; *m* 1974, Virginia Jane, da of Raymond Berry, of Marlow, Bucks; 3 c; *Career* md Williams F 1 Ltd; *Clubs* British Racing Drivers'; *Style—* Sir Frank Williams, CBE; ✉ Williams F 1 Ltd, Grove, Wantage, Oxfordshire (tel 01235 777700)

WILLIAMS, Prof Frederic Ward (Fred); s of Prof Sir Frederic Calland Williams (d 1977), and Gladys, *née* Ward (d 2004); *b* 4 March 1940; *Educ* St John's Coll Cambridge (MA, ScD), Univ of Bristol (PhD); *m* 11 April 1964, Jessie Anne Hope, da of Rev William Wyper Wilson (d 1988); 2 s (Frederic b 21 Aug 1968, David b 11 Feb 1970); *Career* asst engr Freeman Fox and Partners 1964; lectr in civil engrg: Ahmadu Bello Univ Nigeria 1964–67, Univ of Birmingham 1967–75; prof of civil engrg: Univ of Wales Inst of Science and Technol 1975–88, Cardiff Sch of Engrg Cardiff Univ 1988– (head Div of Structural Engrg 1988–98, on leave of absence 2001–04), prof Dept of Bldg and Construction City Univ of Hong Kong 2001–04; fndr chm Cardiff Advanced Chinese Engrg Centre 1993–; guest prof Shanghai Jiao Tong Univ 1997–, guest prof Univ of Science and Technol of China 1999–; conslt to: NASA, British Aerospace; author of numerous papers in jls; FICE 1984, FIStructE 1985, FRAeS 1990, FREng 1999; *Recreations* hill walking; *Style—* Prof Fred Williams, FREng; ✉ Cardiff School of Engineering, Cardiff University, The Parade, Cardiff CF24 3AA (e-mail fw@williamstube.com)

WILLIAMS, Dr Geoffrey James; s of Idris Williams (d 1985), of Risca, Gwent, and Emily Edith, *née* James (d 1971); *b* 6 July 1936; *Educ* Pontywaun GS Risca, UC Swansea (BA, PhD); *m* 25 July 1959, Lorna, da of Ernest John McKay (d 1972); 2 da (Cerys Sîan b 26 April 1961, Lucy Lenora b 6 Jan 1980), 2 s (Jonathan Rhodri b 26 May 1962, David Huw b 30 May 1967); *Career* Nat Park asst Brecknock Co Planning Office 1961–62; lectr in geography: Fourah Bay Coll Univ of Sierra Leone 1963–69, UC Swansea 1969–70; sr lectr in geography Ahmadu Bello Univ Northern Nigeria 1970–74, prof of geography Univ of Zambia 1974–87, hon res fell UC Swansea 1987–90, dir of studies King George VI & Queen Elizabeth Fndn of St Catharine's Cumberland Lodge 1988–2001; FRGS 1957, memb IBG 1957; *Books* A Bibliography of Sierra Leone (1971), Development and Ecology in the Lower Kafue Basin in the Nineteen Seventies (co-ed, 1977), Independent Zambia, A Bibliography of the Social Sciences 1964–79 (1984), The Peugeot Guide to Lusaka (1984), Lusaka and its Environs: A Geographical Study of a Planned City in Tropical Africa (1987), Geographical Perspectives on Development in Southern Africa (co-ed, 1987); *Recreations* books, family history, travel, photography; *Clubs* Geographical; *Style—* Dr Geoffrey Williams; ✉ Penheolrhyn, Ffawyddog, Llangattock, Crickhowell, Powys NP8 1PY (tel 01873 811300, e-mail gj-williams@lineone.net)

WILLIAMS, Gerard; s of Frank Williams, of Manchester, and Margaret Rose, *née* Lockwood; *b* 9 July 1959; *Educ* Manchester HS of Art, Manchester Poly, Brighton Poly; *Career* artist; res fell Henry Moore Inst 1997; visiting tutor: Goldsmiths Coll London 1998–2002, West Dean Col Edward James Fndn Sussex; *Solo Exhibitions* Interim Art 1986 and 1990, Anthony d'Offay Gallery 1989, Galleria Franz Paludetto Turin 1990, Patrick de Brock Gallery Antwerp 1991, Todd Gallery London 1993, Galerie 102 Düsseldorf 1993, Aldebaran, Baillargues France 1993, Galerie du Tableau Marseille 1994, The Showroom (London) 1994, Galerie 102 (Düsseldorf) 1996, Medieval Modern (London) 2002; *Group Exhibitions* incl: Whitechapel Open 1985, 1986, 1987 and 1988, Summer Show (Anthony d'Offay Gallery) 1988, That Which Appears is Good, That Which is Good Appears (Tanja Grunert Gallery Cologne) 1988, Home Truths (Castello di Rivara) 1989, Richard Wentworth Grenville Davey Gerard Williams (Sala Uno Rome) 1989, Its a Still Life (Arts Cncl of GB, touring) 1989–91, Leche Vitrines (Le Festival ARS Musica Brussels) 1990, TAC 90 (Sala Parpallo/Diputacion de Valencia, touring) 1990, Realismi (Galleria Giorgio Persano Turin, Ileana Toynta Contemporary Art Centre Athens) 1990, What is a Gallery? (Kettles Yard Univ of Cambridge) 1990, Maureen Paley Interim Art 1990–91, Anni Novanta (Bologna, Cattolica and Rimini) 1991, Lithuanian Artists Assoc Symposium 1991, Koji Tatsuno: 03.91 (Palais Galliera Paris) 1991, Made for Arolsen (Museumverein Arolsen Germany) 1992, Rencontres No 1 (Assoc La Vigie Nimes France) 1992, In House, Out House (Unit Seven London) 1993, Five British Artists (Patrick de Brock Gallery Antwerp) 1993, The East Wing Collection (Courtauld Inst London) 1993–96, Escale a Marseille (Tour du Roy Rene Marseille) 1994, Sous Reserve de Modification (Montpellier France) 1994, Seeing the Unseen (Nvisible Museum, London) 1994, Arte Inglese d' Oggi (Turin Galleria Civica di Modena Italy) 1994–95, Taking Form (The Fruitmarket Gallery Edinburgh) 1995, A Matter of Facts (Städtische Ausstellungshalle Münster) 1996, Good News (102 Galerie Düsseldorf) 1996, Williams & Williams (Bains Douches de la Plaine Marseille) 1997, When Ever (Gt Garden St Synagogue London) 1997, Craft (Richard Salmon, London and Kettles Yard Univ of Cambridge, Aberystwyth Arts Centre) 1997 and 1998, Echo (Pavillion der Volksbühne, Berlin) 1997, Infra-Slim Spaces (Univ of Kiev Ukraine) 1997, Over the Top (Ikon Gallery Birmingham, on tour) 1998–99, Furniture (Richard Salmon London and John Hansard Gallery Univ of Southampton) 1999, Sampled: fabric in sculpture (Henry Moore Inst Leeds) 1999, Modular Loops (Parker's Box NY) 2000, Stockholm Art Fair 2001, Bring and Buy (Transit Space London) 2002, Frankfurt Art Fair 2002; *Publications* author of numerous publications, incl: Technique Anglaise - Current Trends in British Art (1991), Asterides - Artists Residencies Catalogue (1993), Carnet de Bord - Artists Residencies 92–96 (1996), T2K (BA Textiles graduation catalogue Goldsmiths Coll London, 2000), Postgraduate Textiles (graduation catalgoue Goldsmiths Coll London, 2001), Invisible London (2001); *Style—* Gerard Williams, Esq; ✉ 175 Swaton Road, London E3 4EP (tel 020 7515 2739, mobile 079 7353 0533, e-mail gerardwilliams@hotmail.com)

WILLIAMS, Prof Glynn Anthony; s of Idris Merrion Williams (d 1996), of Bayston Hill, Salop, and Muriel Elizabeth, *née* Purslow (d 1953); *b* 30 March 1939; *Educ* Wolverhampton GS, Wolverhampton Coll of Art (NDD), Rome scholar; *m* 6 July 1963 (m dis 2000), Heather, da of Cyril Woodhall (d 1952); 2 da (Victoria b 2 Jan 1964, Sophie b 7 Aug 1967); *Career* regular exhibitor of sculpture 1967– (represented by Bernard Jacobson Gallery London), currently prof of sculpture and Head Sch of Fine Art Royal Coll of Art; has exhibited internationally, represented GB in the third Kotara Takamura Exhibition in Japan; work in nat and int public collections incl Tate Gallery, Nat Portrait Gallery and V&A; cmmns incl: Henry Purcell Meml (Victoria Street London), Gateway of Hands (Chelsea Harbour London), Lloyd George Meml (Parliament Square) 2007; author of articles on sculpture published in various art magazines and art reviewer for TLS; memb Subject Panel CNAA; Prix de Rome 1961, hon fell Wolverhampton Poly 1989; FRCA, FRBS 1992, FRSA 1996; *Recreations* music, walking, crossword puzzles, cooking; *Clubs* Chelsea Arts; *Style—* Prof Glynn Williams; ✉ Royal College of Art, Kensington Gore, London SW7 2EU (tel 020 7590 4451, fax 020 7590 4460, e-mail g.williams@rca.ac.uk, website glynnwilliams.co.uk)

WILLIAMS, Prof (James) Gordon; *b* 13 June 1938; *Educ* Toxteth Tech Inst, Farnborough Tech Coll, Imperial Coll London (BSc, PhD, DSc); *Career* Imperial Coll London: res student 1961–62, asst lectr 1962–64, lectr 1964–70, reader 1970–75, prof of polymer engrg 1975–91, head Mechanical Engrg Dept 1990–2000, prof of mech engrg 1991–2003, emeritus prof 2003–; Unwin scholarship 1961, Swinburne Medal Plastics & Rubber Inst 1986; FPRI 1979, FIMechE 1979, FREng 1982, FCGI 1986, FRS 1994; *Books* Stress Analysis of Polymers (2 edn, 1980), Fracture Mechanics of Polymers (1985); *Style—* Prof J G Williams, FRS, FREng; ✉ Breda, 16 Bois Lane, Chesham Bois, Amersham, Buckinghamshire HP6 6BP (tel 01494 726248); Mechanical Engineering Department, Imperial College London, Exhibition Road, South Kensington, London SW7 2AZ

WILLIAMS, Gordon; s of Charles Williams, of Anfield, Liverpool, and Marjorie Gerard, *née* Bradborn (d 1984); *b* 27 June 1945; *Educ* Bishop Vesey's GS Sutton Coldfield, UCH Med Sch (MB BS), MS Univ of London 1988, FRCS; *m* 1 (m dis 1989), Susan Mary Gubbins; 2 da (Katherine Louise b 1970, Victoria Mary b 1972); m 2, 20 Sept 1989, Clare, da of (Montgomery) Derek Sanderson (d 1976); *Career* conslt urologist and transplant surgn Hammersmith Hosp and hon sr lectr Imperial Coll Sch of Med at Hammersmith Hosp (Royal Postgraduate Med Sch until merger 1997) 1978–2007, dean St Paul's Millennium Med Sch Addis Ababa 2007–; visiting surgn: Syria, Burma, Poland; James IV prof of surgery RCSEd 2005; external examiner Univ of Addis Ababa; numerous pubns on urology, urological cancer, impotence and diseases of the prostate; former chm NW Thames Urologists; former memb Cncl: Br Assoc of Urological Surgns, Int Soc of Urology, Euro Soc of Urology, Euro Transplant Soc; memb Bd of Chairmen Int Soc of Urology, pres Urology Section Royal Soc of Med 2002, chm Jt Ctee for Higher Surgical Training 2003–; Albert Schweitzer Award Int Soc of Urology 2006; memb Worshipful Soc of Apothecaries 1984, Freeman City of London 1985; FRCSEd 2001, FRCSGlas 2004; *Recreations* travel, Indian food; *Style—* Gordon Williams, Esq

WILLIAMS, Air Vice Marshal Graham Charles; AFC (1971, and Bar 1975); s of Charles Francis Williams (d 1968), and Molly, *née* Chapman (d 1988); *b* 4 June 1937; *Educ* Marlborough, RAF Coll Cranwell; *m* 3 March 1962, Judy Teresa Ann, da of Reginald Walker (d 1972); 1 s (Mark b 1963), 1 da (Kim b 1966); *Career* Pilot 54 Sqdn Odiham 1958–60, instr 229 OCU Chivenor 1961–63, Flt-Cdr 8 Sqdn Khormaksar 1964–65, Empire Test Pilots' Sch 1966, 'A' Sqdn (fighter test) A and AEE Boscombe Down 1967–70, RAF Staff Coll Bracknell 1971, OC 3 (F) Sqdn Wildenrath 1972–74, jr directing staff RCDS 1975–77, Station Cdr RAF Brüggen 1978–79, Gp Capt Ops HQ RAF Germany 1980–82, CO Experimental Flying RAE Farnborough 1983, Cmdt A and AEE Boscombe Down 1984–85, DOR (Air) MOD 1986, Asst Chief of Def Staff Operational Requirements (Air) 1987–90, Cmdt Gen RAF Regt and DG Security (RAF) 1990–91; aerospace/defence conslt GW Associates 1991–93, mil mktg advsr Loral International Inc 1993–96, dir UK

Lockheed Martin UK Ltd 1996–; Harmon Trophy USA 1970; FRAeS 1984, FIMgt 1992; *Recreations* golf; *Clubs* RAF; *Style*— Air Vice Marshal Graham Williams, AFC; ✉ Gate Cottage, Horsenden, Princes Risborough, Buckinghamshire HP27 9NF

WILLIAMS, Graham John; s of Hubert John Williams (d 1976), and Marguerite Madeleine Williams; *b* 24 April 1943; *Educ* Cranleigh, Univ of Edinburgh, INSEAD Fontainebleau (MBA); *m* Valerie Jane, *née* Dobson; 2 s (Alex b 18 Sept 1973, Nicholas b 21 March 1989), 1 da (Sara b 13 April 1992); *Career* articled clerk C F Middleton & Co CAs 1962–67, CA Coopers & Lybrand 1967–68, INSEAD 1968–69; Charterhouse Group: product mangr 1969, exec UK Venture Capital 1970–74, dir Charterhouse SA Paris 1975–79; dep md (and jt fndr) Barclays Development Capital Ltd 1979–84; Hays plc: fin dir 1984–2003, involved in MBO 1987 and subsequent listing 1989, dir 1992–2003; non-exec dir Acal plc 2003–; MICAS 1967; *Recreations* golf, tennis, sailing, skiing, swimming, squash; *Clubs* Old Cranleighans, Walton Heath Golf, RAC; *Style*— Graham Williams, Esq

WILLIAMS, Prof (Daniel) Gwyn; s of Rev Daniel James Williams (d 1967), of Cardiff, and Elizabeth Beatrice Mary Walters (d 1974); *b* 7 March 1940; *Educ* Cardiff HS, UC Cardiff (MB BCh), Welsh Nat Sch of Med (MD); *m* 21 Jan 1967, Angela Mary, da of John Edwin Davies (d 1974), of Petts Wood, Kent; 4 da (Rachel b 1968, Sian b 1970, Hannah b 1972, Leah b 1976); *Career* jr hosp appts at Cardiff Royal Infirmary and The Radcliffe Infirmary Oxford, sr registrar in med Radcliffe Infirmary, res fell and asst lectr Royal Postgrad Medical Sch London, conslt physician, prof of med and dean of clinical med UMDS, dep head Sch of Med Guy's King's Coll & St Thomas' Hosps Med & Dental Sch (following merger) 1998–; MRS, The Renal Assoc; FRCP 1978; *Books* The Oxford Textbook of Medicine (contrib, 1987), The Oxford Textbook of Clinical Nephrology (contrib, 1990); *Style*— Prof Gwyn Williams; ✉ The Renal Unit, Guy's Hospital, St Thomas' Street, London SE1 9RT (tel 020 7955 5000)

WILLIAMS, Helen Mary; CB (2006); da of Percy Graham Myatt, of Leeds, and Mary Harrison, *née* Dodgson; *b* 30 June 1950; *Educ* Allerton HS Leeds, St Hilda's Coll Oxford (BA); *m* 1, 1975 (m dis 1982), Ian Vaughan Williams; m 2, 1993, David Michael Forrester, s of Reginald Forrester; 1 s (James b 31 March 1983), 1 da (Natasha b 9 Jan 1986); *Career* civil servant; DES 1972–93: joined as admin trainee 1972, private sec to Joan Lestor then Margaret Jackson (both Parly Secs DES) 1975–76, princ 1976–84, asst sec DES 1984–93; under sec Office of Science and Technology (OST), Office of Public Serv and Science and Cabinet Office 1993–98 (OST transferred to DTI 1995); DfES (formerly DfEE): dir School Organisation and Funding 1999–2002, dir Primary Educn and e-Learning 2002–04, dir Primary Educn and School Standards 2004–06, dir Curriculum and Pupil Well-Being 2006–; *Recreations* family life, walking, bellringing; *Style*— Mrs Helen Williams, CB

WILLIAMS, Dr Helen Mary Sefton (Mrs Maynard); *b* 17 November 1955; *Educ* Sleaford HS for Girls, Stamford HS for Girls, Univ of Wales (MB BCh); *Career* various hosp appts Wales 1979–84, sr registrar in med microbiology Mayday Hosp Croydon 1984–86, lectr/hon sr registrar in med microbiology St Thomas' Hosp London 1986–88, locum conslt med microbiologist Mayday Hosp Croydon 1988–89, conslt med microbiologist Norwich Public Health Lab 1989–2003, conslt microbiologist Norfolk and Norwich Univ Hosp NHS Tst 2003–; hon conslt microbiologist Mental Health Care Tst; hon sr lectr UEA; RCPath: memb Cncl 1993–96 and 1998–, dir of clinical audit 1995–98 (also chm Clinical Audit Ctee), memb Exec 1998–, registrar 2001–05 (asst registrar 1998–2001), vice-pres 2005–, memb Specialty Advsy Ctee on Med Microbiology 1993–96 and 1998–; memb PHLS Audit Ctee 1994–97, chm Anglia Med Microbiology Devpt Gp 1996–98; hon sec: Norwich Med Chirurgical Soc 1993–95, Norfolk and Norwich Benevolent Med Soc 1998–2001; memb: Assoc of Clinical Pathologists, Assoc of Med Microbiologists, Med Women's Fedn, BMA, Br Soc for Antimicrobial Chemotherapy, Hosp Infection Soc; FRSM, FRCPath; *Style*— Dr Helen M S Williams; ✉ Department of Microbiology, Norfol and Norwich University Hospital NHS Trust, Bowthorpe Road, Norwich NR2 3TX (tel 01603 611816, fax 01603 620190)

WILLIAMS, Prof (Morgan) Howard; s of Morgan Williams, of Port Elizabeth, South Africa, and Ellen Frances, *née* Reid; *b* 15 December 1944; *Educ* Grey HS, Rhodes Univ (BSc, BSc, PhD, DSc); *m* 1, 13 Dec 1969 (m dis), Jean, da of Rev Reginald Charles Doe; 2 s (Christopher b 6 May 1975, Michael 5 May 1977); m 2, 25 Aug 2001, Pamela (d 2006), da of Robert Henry Jeram; *Career* physicist in Antarctic expedition 1967–69, successively lectr, sr lectr and prof of computer sci Rhodes Univ 1970–80, prof of computer sci Heriot-Watt Univ 1980–; FBCS, FRSA, CEng; *Publications* Proceedings of BNCOD 7 (1989), Proceedings of RIDS (1993), Database Programming Languages (1995), Proceedings of BNCOD 21 (2004); contribs to over 200 journals and conferences; *Recreations* swimming, rambling, gardening; *Style*— Prof Howard Williams; ✉ 3 House O'Hill Brae, Edinburgh EH4 5DQ (tel 0131 336 1215); School of Mathematical and Computer Sciences, Heriot-Watt University, Riccarton, Edinburgh EH14 4AS (tel 0131 451 3430, fax 0131 451 3431, e-mail mhw@macs.hw.ac.uk)

WILLIAMS, Hugh; *see:* Bonneville, Hugh Richard

WILLIAMS, Huw Rhys Charles; s of David Charles Williams (d 1984), of Llanelli, Carmarthenshire, and Glenys Margaret, *née* Williams; *b* 4 January 1954; *Educ* Llanelli GS, Jesus Coll Oxford (MA); *m* 22 Jan 1994, Kathleen Mary, da of Capt Melville Desmond John Hooper, master mariner (d 1990), of Penarth, Vale of Glamorgan; 1 step s (Martin John Rees); *Career* admitted slr 1978; princ asst slr Mid Glamorgan CC 1984, ptnr i/c public, planning and environmental law Geldards LLP (previously Edwards Geldard) Cardiff, Derby and Nottingham 1988– (joined 1987); treas Wales Public Law and Human Rights Assoc 1999–2005; sec Wales Millennium Centre 1998–, memb Ct and Cncl then tstee Nat Museum of Wales 2003–; memb Law Soc (memb Planning and Environment Law Ctee 2003, memb Wales Ctee 2004); *Recreations* art and architecture, naval history, scuba diving; *Clubs* Oxford and Cambridge, Cardiff and County; *Style*— Huw Williams, Esq; ✉ Geldards LLP, Dumfries House, Dumfries Place, Cardiff CF1 4YF (tel 029 2023 8239, fax 029 2023 7268, e-mail huw.williams@geldards.co.uk)

WILLIAMS, Hywel; MP; s of Robert Williams (d 1976), of Pwllheli, and Jennie Page, *née* Williams; *b* 14 May 1953; *Educ* Ysgol Glan y Mor Pwllheli, UCW Cardiff (BSc), UCW Bangor (CQSW); *m* 3 Sept 1977 (m dis 1998), Sian; 3 c (Gwenno Hywel b 16 Jan 1979, Elin Hywel b 15 Aug 1982, Angharad Hywel b 3 Oct 1983); *Career* social worker: Social Services Dept Mid Glamorgan CC 1974–76, Social Services Dept Gwynedd CC 1976–84 (pt/t memb Out of Hours team 1985–90); aproved social worker 1984; Welsh Office funded project worker Welsh medium devpts N and W Wales Practice Centre UCW Bangor 1991–93, head N and W Wales Practice Centre UCW Bangor 1991–93; freelance lectr, conslt and author in social work and social policy 1994–2001; CCETSW (Central Cncl for Educn and Trg in Social Work) Cymru: memb Welsh Ctee 1989–92, chair Welsh Language Sub-Ctee 1989–92; MP (Plaid Cymru) Caernarfon 2001–; *Publications* Social Work in Action in the 1980s (contrib, 1985), Geirfa Gwaith Cymdeithasol/A Social Work Vocabulary (compiler and ed, 1988), Geirfa Gwaith Plant/Child Care Terms (gen ed, 1993), Gwaith Cymdeithasol a'r Iaith Gymraeg/Social Work and the Welsh Language (contrib and co-ed, 1994), Llawlyfr Hyfforddi a Hyfforddiant/An Index of Trainers and Training (compiler and co-ed, 1994), Gofal - Pecyn Adnoddau a Hyfforddi Gofal yn y Gymuned yng Nghymru/Gofal - A Training and Resource Pack for Community Care in Wales (contrib and co-ed, 1998), Siarad yr Anweleding/Speaking the Invisible (contrib, 2002); *Style*— Hywel Williams, Esq, MP; ✉ House of Commons, London SW1A 0AA (tel 020 7219 5021)

WILLIAMS, James Christopher; s of Arthur Williams, and Joan, *née* Walton; *Educ* Judd Sch Tonbridge, Central Sch of Speech and Drama; *Career* theatre prodr; stage mangr 1977–81, asst prodn mangr Oxford Playhouse Co 1982–83, prodn mangr Redgrave Theatre Farnham 1983–86, prodn mangr Cambridge Theatre Co 1986–87, prodn mangr Royal Exchange Theatre Manchester 1988, exec dir and co sec Method & Madness (formerly Cambridge Theatre Co) 1988–98, dir and fndr Vocaleyes 1997–98 (dir 1998–, chm 1999–2003), exec dir Hampstead Theatre 1998–2003, exec prodr Theatre of Comedy Co Ltd 2004–; dir Hampstead Theatre Prodns Ltd 1998–2004; chm Audio Describers Assoc 1997–99 (founding gp); chair negotiating team: TMA Directors Agreement 1993–2000 (memb 1989–93), TMA Designers Agreement 1994–2000 (memb 1991–94), TMA Subsidised Repertory Performers' Agreement 1997–2004; memb Cncl TMA 1995–2001 (memb Industrial Relations Ctee 1994–, Fin Ctee 1996–2001); tstee Cambridge Youth Theatre 1989–94; *Recreations* travel, property renovation, theatre, films; *Style*— James Williams, Esq; ✉ Theatre of Comedy Company Ltd, Shaftesbury Theatre, 210 Shaftesbury Avenue, London WC2H 8DP

WILLIAMS, James Gareth Branston; s of Dr Ronald Branston Williams, of Glos, and Dorothy Elizabeth, *née* Lindop (d 1971); *b* 13 April 1946; *Educ* Kingswood Sch Bath, CCC Oxford (scholar, MA); *m* 1980, Julia May, da of Sidney Thomas White (d 1982); 1 da (Charlotte Louise Dorothy b 25 March 1983), 1 s (Oliver Thomas Branston b 17 May 1988); *Career* advtg exec; account planner Boase Massimi Pollitt 1972–75 (trainee account planner 1971–72), planning dir/ptnr SJIP 1975–80, account dir/ptnr SJIP/BBDO 1980–82; Young & Rubicam: dep planning dir 1982, planning dir 1983–84, sr vice-pres/dir of strategy and research Europe 1984–94, exec vice-pres/dir of strategy and research Europe 1994–2006; memb: Market Research Soc 1973 (full memb 1990), Mktg Soc 1980, ESOMAR 1984; *Recreations* jigsaws, computing, food and wine; *Clubs* Hurlingham; *Style*— James Williams, Esq; ✉ mobile 07768 464347, e-mail jimwilliamsesq@hotmail.com

WILLIAMS, Jan; OBE (2003); *b* 2 December 1954; *Educ* Llwyn-y-Bryn Secdy Modern Swansea, Univ of Wales (BA, MA), Univ of Aberdeen (Postgrad Cert in Health Economics), Cardiff Business Sch Univ of Wales (MBA); *m*; 1 c; *Career* higher clerical offr trainee W Glamorgan HA 1979–80, nat admin trainee DHSS 1980–82, asst unit administrator rising to sr administrator W Glamorgan HA 1982–86, asst unit gen mangr Gwent HA 1986–88, unit gen mangr E Dyfed HA 1988–92; chief exec: Llanelli/Dinefwr NHS Tst 1992–95, W Glamorgan HA 1996, Iechyd Morgannwg Health 1996–99, Bro Taf HA 1999–2003; prog dir Review of Health and Social Care in Wales 2002–03, chief exec National Leadership and Innovation Agency for Healthcare 2005–; author of published papers in Health Services Jl, Nursing Management Jl and Nursing Times; memb Cncl Acas 1998–2003, memb Cncl and tstee Techniquest 2003–; CIHM 2003; *Style*— Jan Williams, OBE

WILLIAMS, (Hon) Jennifer Mary (Jenny); da of Baron Lord Donaldson of Lymington, PC (Life Peer, d 2005), and Dame (Dorothy) Mary Donaldson, GBE, JP (d 2003); sis of Hon Michael Donaldson, *qv*; *b* 26 September 1948; *m* 1970, Mike Williams, CB, *qv*; 3 s; *Career* under sec Privatisation & Strategy PSA 1991–93, head of Railways Privatisation & Regulation Directorate Dept of Tport 1993–96, head Local Govt Fin Policy Directorate DETR 1996–98, dir Business Tax Div Inland Revenue 1998–2000, DG Judicial Gp Lord Chllr's Dept 2000–04, chief exec Gaming Bd for GB 2004–05, cmmr and chief exec Gambling Cmmn 2005–; non-exec dir: Morley Coll 1993–2000, Northumbrian Water Gp plc 2004–; memb Bd Nat Campaign for the Arts 2004–, tstee The Connection at St Martin's 2004–; *Style*— Mrs Jenny Williams; ✉ e-mail jenny.williams@mj-w.net

WILLIAMS, John; AO (1987); *b* 24 April 1941, Australia; *Educ* Accademia Musicale di Siena Italy (scholarship), Royal Coll of Music; *Career* guitarist; taught by father from age 4, later studied with Andrés Segovia, USA and Japan debuts 1963; appeared with many Br orchs and at many Br festivals, toured extensively in Europe, N and S America, Soviet Union, Far E and Australia; one of the first classical musicians to appear at Ronnie Scott's jazz club, fndr memb of popular music gps SKY 1979–84 and John Williams and Friends 1983–, formed contemporary music ensemble Attacca 1991 (with whom toured UK and Australia 1992), tours with Harvey and John Etheridge; artistic dir and music advsr South Bank Summer Music Festival 1984–85, artistic dir Melbourne Arts Festival Australia 1987; work written for him by composers incl: Leo Brouwer, Peter Sculthorpe, Stephen Dodgson, André Previn; performed with orchs incl: Royal Philharmonic, LSO, City of Birmingham Symphony, English Chamber, Australian Chamber, Bournemouth Sinfonietta, Acad of St Martin-in-the-Fields, all other major Br orchs; appeared at venues incl: Queen Elizabeth Hall, Royal Festival Hall, Barbican Hall, Symphony Hall Birmingham, Fairfield Hall, Salle Pleyel Paris, Hong Kong Cultural Centre (inaugural concerts 1989), NEC Birmingham (10th Anniversary concert, with CBSO); appeared at festivals incl: BBC Proms, Cheltenham, Chichester, Exeter, Cardiff, Perth and Adelaide Festivals Aust, Toronto Int Guitar Festival, South Bank Latin American Festival, Lichfield, St Albans, Melbourne Arts Festival; performed European première of Nigel Westlake's Antarctica (for guitar and orch) with LSO under Kent Nagano Barbican Hall 1992; numerous TV appearances incl LWT South Bank Show documentary on life and work; past performances with Julian Bream, Paco Peña, Itzhak Perlman, André Previn, John Dankworth, Cleo Laine, Inti Illimani, etc; *Recordings* major guitar works and numerous concertos incl John Williams plays The Movies, The Magic Box; El Diablo Suelto - Venezuelan Guitar Music, The Ultimate Guitar Collection, Places Between (with John Etheridge); *Style*— John Williams, Esq, AO; ✉ c/o Askonas Holt, Lonsdale Chambers, 27 Chancery Lane, London WC2A 1PF (tel 020 7400 1751, e-mail info@askonasholt.co.uk)

WILLIAMS, John Charles Wallis; s of Peter Alfred Williams (d 1997), of Menston, W Yorks, and Mary, *née* Bower (d 1990); *b* 12 December 1953; *Educ* St Peter's Sch York, The Queen's Coll Oxford (MA); *m* 28 June 1980, Wendy Irene, da of Harold Doe, of Whitton, Middx; 2 da (Sarah b 1984, Clare b 1988); *Career* advertising exec J Walter Thompson Co 1975–86, PR exec Valin Pollen Ltd 1986–90 (head res and planning 1988–90, asst md 1989–90), sr advsr Fishburn Hedges 2005– (fndr dir 1991–, md 1995–99, chm 1999–2001, non-exec dir 2001–05), princ John Williams and Assocs 2001–; dep chair ChildLine 2001–06, chm Tomorrow's Company 2004– (tstee 2003–), memb Bd Business in the Community 2002–, cmmr Charity Cmmn 2005–, chm Richmond Theatre Prodns 2006–; FRSA; *Recreations* cinema, popular music, soccer, Somerset; *Style*— John Williams, Esq; ✉ 23 Blenheim Road, London W4 1UB (tel 020 8995 3325, e-mail john@williams-network.com)

WILLIAMS, John Fagan; s of Frank Thomas Williams, and Margaret, *née* Fagan; *b* 7 January 1948; *Educ* Rishworth Sch; *m* 1, Lynne, *née* Boothby; 1 da (Kate); m 2, Rita, *née* Mason; *Career* local, regional and nat newspaper journalist 1967–76; fndr Staniforth Williams PR consultancy 1976–86, fndr jt md Mason Williams PR consultancy 1986– (over 28 awards for business excellence 1988–); fndr and ceo: Muse Group 2002, Grandstand Entertainment Int 2003; memb Bd PRCA 1994; FIPR 1979, FInstD 1990; *Sporting Achievements* int sports car racing driver (Europe and USA) 1981–90, eighth place World Sports Car Championship 1989, Champion Lamborghini Int Trophy 1997; *Recreations* race driving, sailing, music; *Clubs* British Racing Drivers', RAC; *Style*— John Williams, Esq; ✉ Mason Williams Ltd, Tanzaro House, Ardwick Green, Manchester M12 6FZ (tel 0161 273 5923, fax 0161 273 7127)

WILLIAMS, John Llewellyn; CBE (1999); s of David John Williams (d 1948), of Dronfield, nr Sheffield, and Anne Rosamund, *née* White; *b* 24 January 1938; *Educ* Christ's Hosp,

Guy's Hosp Dental Sch London (BDS, LDS RCS, Evelyn Sprawson Prize), Guy's Hosp Med Sch London (MB BS); *m* 1960, Gillian Joy, *née* Morgan; 3 da (Amanda Jill (Mrs Henderson) b 1962, Jacqueline Mary (Mrs Lytton) b 1963, Anne-Marie (Mrs Wood) b 1970); *Career* formerly sr registrar Westminster Hosp, Queen Mary's Roehampton and UCH; conslt oral and maxillofacial surgn: St Richard's Hosp Chichester, Southlands and Worthing Hosps, St Luke's Hosp Guildford; hon conslt: Queen Mary's Hosp Roehampton, King Edward VII Hosp Midhurst; formerly hon civilian conslt Cambridge Mil Hosp Aldershot, hon clinical tutor UMDS; memb: Cncl RCS 1993–2001 (dean Faculty of Dental Surgery 1995–98, vice-pres 1997–99), GDC 1995–98, Ct of Patrons RCS 2005; sec-gen Euro Assoc of Cranio-Maxillofacial Surgery (pres 1998); chm Nat Confidential Enquiry into Perioperative Deaths 1999–2003; vice-chm Acad Med Royal Colls 1996, pres Br Assoc of Oral and Maxillofacial Surgeons 2000 (vice-pres 1999); memb: Jt Conslts Ctee 1989–98, Clinical Outcomes Gp Dept of Health 1993–99, Clinical Standards Advsy Gp 1994–99, Nat Inst for Clinical Excellence 1999–; chm: Med Devices Agency Dept of Health 2001–04, Cmmn on Safety of Devices MHRA 2004–; Downs Surgical Prize Br Assoc of Oral and Maxillofacial Surgns 1995, John Tomes Medal BDA 1998, Colyer Gold Medal 2000; memb: BDA, BMA, Br Assoc of Maxillofacial Surgns, Euro Assoc of Cranio-Maxillofacial Surgery; Int Assoc of Oral and Maxillofacial Surgery: memb Bd 2001–, pres-elect 2003–05, pres 2005–07; hon fell American Assoc of Oral and Maxillofacial Surgeons 1998, hon fell Aust and NZ Assoc of Oral and Maxillofacial Surgeons 2005; FDSRCS, FRCSEd 1991, FRCS 1996, FDS RCS(Ed) (ad hominem) 2000, FRCA 2002; *Books* Maxillofacial Injuries (2 vols, ed, 2 edn 1995); *Recreations* horticulture (contrib National Gardens Scheme), skiing, sailing (RYA race training instructor), chasing good wine!; *Clubs* Royal Yachting Assoc, Hayling Island Sailing, RHS, Oral Surgery Club of GB; *Style*— John Llewellyn Williams, Esq, CBE; ✉ Cookscroft, Bookers Lane, Earnley, Chichester, West Sussex PO20 7JG (tel 01243 513671, fax 01243 514207, e-mail williams.cookscroft@virgin.net)

WILLIAMS, Hon John Melville; QC (1977); s of Baron Francis-Williams (Life Peer, d 1970); *b* 20 June 1931; *Educ* St Christopher Sch Letchworth, St John's Coll Cambridge (BA); *m* 1955, Jean Margaret, da of Harold Lucas (d 1995); 3 s, 1 da; *Career* called to the Bar Inner Temple 1955, head of chambers 1980–2000, bencher 1985, recorder 1986–94, ret from practice 2002; legal assessor to GMC 1983–; pres Assoc of Personal Injury Lawyers 1990–94, co-chm Int Section Assoc of Trial Lawyers of America 1991–93, memb Bd Criminal Injuries Compensation Bd 1998–2000, memb Criminal Injuries Compensation Appeals Panel 2000–; chm: Y2K Lawyers Assoc 1999–, TheClaimRoom.com Ltd; tstee vCJD Tst 2002–; *Style*— The Hon John Melville Williams, QC

WILLIAMS, Dr John Peter Rhys; MBE (1977); s of Peter Rhys Jervis Williams, of Bridgend, and Margaret, *née* Rhodes; *b* 2 March 1949; *Educ* Bridgend GS, Millfield, St Marys Hosp Med Sch (MB BS, MRCS, LRCP); *m* 10 May 1973, Priscilla, da of Michael Parkin, of Buxton, Derbys; 3 da (Lauren b 1977, Anneliese b 1979, Francine b 1981), 1 s (Peter b 1987); *Career* conslt orthopaedic surgn Princess of Wales Hosp Bridgend 1986–2004, ret; Br jr tennis champion 1966, 55 Welsh International rugby caps 1969–81, memb Br Lions tour NZ 1971 and South Africa 1974; memb Br Orthopaedic Assoc, FRCSEd; *Books* JPR Autobiography (1977); *Recreations* all sports especially squash, tennis, rugby; *Clubs* Wig & Pen, Lord's Taverners; *Style*— Dr John Williams, MBE; ✉ Llansannor Lodge, Llansannor, Cowbridge, South Glamorgan CF71 7RX (tel 01446 772590); Princess of Wales Hospital, Coity Road, Bridgend, Mid Glamorgan CF31 1RQ (tel 01656 752116)

WILLIAMS, John Thomas; s of John T Williams, of South Shields, and Margaret Williams; *b* 20 August 1958; *Educ* Mortimer Road Sch South Shields, S Shields Marine & Tech Coll, Westminster Catering Coll (City and Guilds); *Family* 1 da (Sabrina b 27 Nov 1985), 1 s (Jeremy b 21 Dec 1989); *Career* commis chef Percy Arms Hotel Northumberland 1974–75, chef de cuisine Royal Roof Restaurant The Royal Garden Hotel London 1975–84, pt/t commis chef Ma Cuisine Restaurant March-Sept 1982, chef dir Restaurant le Crocodile London 1984–86, head chef Claridge's 1986–93, maitre chef de cuisine The Berkeley Hotel London 1994–95, maitre chef de cuisines Claridge's 1995–2004, exec chef The Ritz 2004–; exec chm Acad of Culinary Arts GB; memb: Académie Culinaire de France, Wine Guild of UK; hon fell Thames Valley Univ 2005; memb Worshipful Co of Cooks; Chevalier de l'Ordre du Merite Agricole; *Recreations* golf, cooking; *Style*— John Williams, Esq; ✉ The Ritz, 150 Picadilly, London W1J 9BR

WILLIAMS, Dame Josephine (Jo); DBE (2007, CBE 2000); da of Frank Heald (d 2002), and Catherine Margaret, *née* Hatcher (d 1997); *b* 8 July 1948, Fishpool, Notts; *Educ* Keele Univ (BA, Dip); *m* 27 May 1980, Robert Williams; 2 step s (Andrew Lindon b 10 April 1968, Paul Gareth b 16 Dec 1978); *Career* social worker incl many mgmnt posts 1971–91; dir of social servs: Wigan MBC 1992–97, Cheshire CC 1997–2002; chief exec Mencap 2003–; tstee: EveryChild, Who Cares? Tst; pres Assoc of Dirs of Social Servs 1999–2000; CCMI 2006; *Recreations* running, ballet, cooking, family and friends; *Style*— Dame Jo Williams, DBE; ✉ Mencap, 123 Golden Lane, London EC1Y 0RT (tel 020 7696 5544, e-mail jo.williams@mencap.org.uk)

WILLIAMS, Juliet Susan Durrant; da of Robert Noel Williams (d 1972), of Gower, W Glamorgan, and Frances Alice, *née* Durrant (d 1995); *Educ* Leeds Girls HS, Cheltenham Ladies' Coll, Bedford Coll London (BSc), Hughes Hall Cambridge (PGCE, Lacrosse blue); *Career* ed Macmillan & Co (publishers) 1966–68, asst ed The Geographical Magazine 1968–73, md Readers Union Gp of Book Clubs 1973–79, chief exec Marshall Cavendish Mail Order 1979–82, md Brann Direct Marketing 1982–88, dir The BIS Gp Ltd 1985–91, chief exec Bd Mktg Communications Div BIS 1988–91, chief exec Strategic Management Resources 1991–; chm: Waddie & Co Ltd 1996–98, Alden Gp Ltd 2004–; chm SW of England RDA 2002–, memb Bd Visit Britain; memb Industrial Devpt Advsy Bd DTI, memb Bd Acad of Sustainable Communities; Hon Dr Oxford Brookes Univ 2005; FRGS 1970, MInstM 1975; *Recreations* labrador retrievers, the countryside, motor sport; *Style*— Ms Juliet Williams; ✉ Treeton Cottage, Abbotskerswell, Newton Abbot, Devon TQ12 5PW (tel 01672 861444); Strategic Management Resources, PO Box 800, Marlborough,Wiltshire SN8 2WB (fax 01672 861441, mobile 07831 097946, e-mail juliet@strategic-management-resources.co.uk)

WILLIAMS, Kenneth Robert; CVO (2003), CBE (2002), QPM (1992); s of Sidney Williams (d 1980), of Urmston, and Margaret Elizabeth, *née* Howell (d 1995); *b* 28 April 1944; *Educ* Wellacre Secdy Modern Sch Flixton, Univ of Manchester (Cert Police, Penal and Social Studies), Open Univ (BA); *m* 27 June 1969, Jean Margaret, da of Jack Reginald Ballantyne; 2 da (Alison Jane b 16 March 1972, Jennifer Anne b 23 Oct 1974); *Career* Gtr Manchester Police: constable Salford City Police 1963 (Salford South Div 1963–68), sergeant North Manchester Div 1968–72, patrol inspr Salford Div 1973–74, inspr then chief inspr HQ 1974–76, sub-divnl cmd Bolton Div 1976–78 (North Manchester Div 1978–79); directing staff Police Staff Coll Bramshill 1979–81; returned to Gtr Manchester Police: sub-divnl cmd Manchester Central Div 1981, sub-divnl cmd Manchester Int Airport 1981–84, departmental cmd Computer Project Branch HQ 1984–85, departmental cmd Ops Support Branch HQ 1985–86, divnl cmd North Manchester 1986–87, Sr Cmd Course Police Staff Coll Bramshill 1987, asst chief constable Gtr Manchester Police 1987–90; dep chief constable Durham Constabulary 1990–93, chief constable Norfolk Constabulary 1993–2002, HM Inspector of Constabulary Wakefield 2002–; assoc memb ACPO 2002; *Recreations* swimming, walking, reading, music; *Style*— Kenneth Williams, Esq, CVO, CBE, QPM; ✉ Her Majesty's Inspector of Constabulary, Unit 2, Wakefield Office Village, Fryers Way WF5 9JT (tel 01924 237722, fax 01924 237705, e-mail ken.williams2@homeoffice.gsi.gov.uk)

WILLIAMS, Laurence Glynn; s of Hugh Williams (d 1988), and Ruby, *née* Lawrence; *b* 14 March 1946, Liverpool; *Educ* Liverpool Poly (BSc), Aston Univ (MSc); *m* 30 Oct 1976 (m dis 1997), Lorna Susan Rance; 1 da (Laura Elizabeth b 16 Oct 1978), 1 s (James Laurence b 16 Sept 1980); *Career* design engr Nuclear Power Gp 1970–71, nuclear engr Central Electricity Generating Bd 1973–76; HSE: joined Nuclear Installations Inspectorate 1976, nuclear inspr 1976–78, princ nuclear inspr 1978–86, superintending inspr 1986–91 (involved with audit of safety Sellafield 1986, BNFL regulatory inspr Sellafield 1989), dep chief inspr 1991–95, head Nuclear and Major Hazards Policy Div 1995–98; HM chief inspr of nuclear installations and dir Nuclear Safety Directorate 1998–2005, dir nuclear safety, security and environment Nuclear Decommissioning Authy 2005–; chair: Int Nuclear Regulators Assoc 2000–02, Int Atomic Energy Agency Cmmn on Safety Standards 2000–05; memb: Safety Review Gp European Bank for Reconstruction and Devpt (former advsr), Chernobyl Sarcophagus Int Advsy Gp, Western European Nuclear Regulators Assoc; pres: Jt Convention on Safety of Spent Fuel Mgmnt, Safety of Radioactive Waste Mgmnt; CEng 1976, FIMechE 1991, FINucE 1998, FREng 2004; *Recreations* motorcycling, cycling, keeping fit, music, theatre, supporting Liverpool FC; *Style*— Laurence Williams, Esq, FREng; ✉ Nuclear Decommissioning Authority, 1st Floor, Pelham House, Calderbridge, Cumbria CA20 1DB (tel 01925 802080, e-mail laurence.williams@nda.gov.uk)

WILLIAMS, Sir Lawrence Hugh; 9 Bt (GB 1798), of Bodelwyddan, Flintshire; s of Col Lawrence Williams, OBE, JP, DL (d 1958), by his 2 w and 1 cous once removed, Elinor, da of Sir William Williams, 4 Bt, JP, DL; suc half-bro Sir Francis John Watkin Williams, 8 Bt, QC, JP (d 1995); *b* 25 August 1929; *Educ* RNC Dartmouth; *m* 1952, Sara Margaret Helen, 3 da of Prof Sir Harry Platt, 1 Bt, MD, MS, FRCS; 2 da (Emma Louise (Hon Mrs Charles Harbord Hamond) b 1961, Antonia Margaret (Mrs Antonin Leif Peter Markutza) b 1963); *Heir* none; *Career* cmmnd RM 1947; served in: Korea 1951, Cyprus 1955, Near East 1956; Capt 1959, ret 1964; Lt Cdr RNXS 1965–87; farmer; chm Parciau Caravans Ltd 1964–, underwriting memb Lloyd's 1977–96; High Sheriff Anglesey 1970; *Clubs* Army and Navy, RNSA; *Style*— Sir Lawrence Williams, Bt; ✉ Parciau, Marianglas, Anglesey LL73 8PH

WILLIAMS, (John) Leighton; QC (1986); s of Reginald John Williams, of Skewen, Neath, Glamorgan, and Beatrice Beynon; *b* 15 August 1941; *Educ* Neath Boys GS, King's Coll London (LLB), Trinity Hall Cambridge (MA); *m* 9 Oct 1969, Sally Elizabeth, da of Howard Jones Williams, of Abergavenny, Monmouthshire; 2 s (Nicholas b 1970, Thomas b 1972); *Career* called to the Bar Gray's Inn 1964 (bencher 1994), recorder of the Crown Court 1985–, dep judge of the High Court 1995–; memb: Criminal Injuries Compensation Bd 1987–2002, Cncl Med Protection Soc 1998–; *Style*— J Leighton Williams, Esq, QC; ✉ Farrar's Building, Temple, London EC4Y 7BD (tel 020 7583 9241, fax 020 7583 0090, e-mail chambers@farrarsbuilding.co.uk)

WILLIAMS, Mark; MBE (2004); *b* 21 March 1975, Wales; *Career* professional snooker player 1992–; ranked 1 in world 2000 and 2003; tournament winner: Benson & Hedges Championship 1994, Grand Prix 1996, Regal Welsh Open 1996 and 1999, British Open 1997, Irish Open 1998, Benson & Hedges Masters 1998 and 2003, Liverpool Victoria UK Championship 1999, Thailand Masters 1999 and 2002, Grand Prix 2000, Embassy World Championship 2000 and 2003 (runner-up 1999), UK Championship 2002, China Open 2002; *Clubs* golf, cars; *Style*— Mark Williams, Esq, MBE; ✉ c/o 110 Sport Management Ltd, First Floor, Pavillion 1, Castlecraig Business Park, Players Road, Stirling FK7 7SH (tel 01786 462634, fax 01786 450068, e-mail mail@110sport.com)

WILLIAMS, Mark; MP; *b* 24 March 1966; *Educ* Richard Hale Sch, UCW Aberystwyth, Univ of Plymouth; *Career* dep head Ysgol Llangors 2000–; Parly candidate (Lib Dem): Monmouth 1997 and 2000 (by-election), Ceredigion 2001; MP (Lib Dem) Ceredigion 2005–; Lib Dem spokesman on: schools 2005–06, Wales 2006–; memb: NASUWT, Greenpeace, Countryside Alliance; *Style*— Mark Williams, Esq, MP; ✉ House of Commons, London SW1A 0AA

WILLIAMS, Prof (John) Mark Gruffydd; s of John Howard Williams (d 2003), and Anna Barbara Mary, *née* Wright (d 2004); *b* 23 July 1952, Hawarden, Flintshire; *Educ* St Peter's Coll Oxford (MA, MSc, DPhil), Univ of Oxford (DSc); *m* 6 Oct 1973, Phyllis Patricia; 1 s ((John) Robert Gareth b 16 Jan 1978), 2 da (Jennifer Ruth Phyllis b 8 Aug 1979, Anne Marie Bethsiân b 25 Sept 1982); *Career* qualified as clinical psychologist 1976; jr lectr then lectr Magdalen Coll Oxford 1977–79, lectr in applied psychology Univ of Newcastle upon Tyne 1979–82, scientist then sr scientist MRC Applied Psychology Unit Univ of Cambridge 1982–91; Univ of Wales Bangor: prof of clinical psychology 1991–2002, dir N Wales Clinical Psychology Prog 1991–97, dir Inst of Medical and Social Care Research 1997–2002, pro-vice-chllr (research) 1997–2001; Wellcome princ research fell and prof of clinical psychology Univ of Oxford 2003–; clinical psychologist: Gateshead HA 1979–82, Cambridge HA 1983–91, Clwydian Community Tst 1992–97; conslt in experimental consumer psychology Unilever plc 1993–2002; author of more than 100 articles in learned jls, research focused on cognitive models of emotional disorders, autobiographical memory deficits in depression and suicidal behaviour and the psychological prevention of relapse in recurrent depression; currently consulting ed: Archives of Suicide Research, Cognitive Behaviour Therapy; formerly consulting ed: Cognition & Emotion, Memory, Psychotherapy Research; numerous invited lectures, distinguished visiting fell Hunter Inst of Mental Health Univ of Newcastle NSW 1997; memb: Neurosciences Bd Grants Ctee MRC 1992–96, Neurosciences and Mental Health Bd Wellcome Tst 1997–2000, Advsy Bd Centre for Suicide Research Univ of Oxford 1999–2002; vice-pres Int Assoc of Suicide Prevention; May Davidson Award Br Psychological Soc 1987, Shapiro Award Br Psychological Soc 1999; FBPsS 1987, founding fell Acad of Cognitive Therapy 1999, AcSS 2003, FMedSci 2004; *Books* The Psychological Treatment of Depression (1984, 2 edn 1992), The Psychology of Religious Knowing (jtly, 1988), Cognitive Psychology and Emotional Disorders (jtly, 1988, 2 edn 1997), Cognitive Therapy in Clinical Practice (jt ed, 1989), Cry of Pain (1997, 2 edn 2001), Mindfulness-based Cognitive Therapy for Depression (jtly, 2002), The Mindful Way Through Depression (jtly, 2007); *Recreations* walking, cricket, playing piano and organ; *Style*— Prof Mark Williams; ✉ University Department of Psychiatry, Warneford Hospital, Oxford OX3 7JX (tel 01865 226445, fax 01865 223948)

WILLIAMS, (John) Michael; MBE (1997); s of George Keith Williams (d 1980), and Joan Doreen, *née* Selby (d 1969); *b* 15 October 1942; *Educ* Cheltenham Coll, Worcester Coll Oxford (MA); *Career* admitted slr 1967; Cooper Sons Hartley & Williams: ptnr 1969–2000, conslt 2001–; pres: E Midlands Assoc of Law Socs 1996–97 and 2003–04, Buxton & High Peak Law Soc 1997–2003 (sec 1984–97 and 2003–); conductor Buxton Musical Soc 1968–, chm Buxton Opera House 2004– (vice-chm 1978–2004), organist St John's Buxton 1985–, dir Buxton Arts Festival Ltd 1993–, memb Panel of Music Advsrs to NW Arts 1995–2002; *Recreations* music, cricket; *Style*— Michael Williams, Esq, MBE; ✉ 132 Lightwood Road, Buxton, Derbyshire SK17 6RW (tel 01298 24185); Cooper Sons Hartley & Williams, 25 Market Street, Chapel-en-le-Frith, High Peak, Derbyshire SK23 6HS (tel 01298 812138)

WILLIAMS, Prof Michael; s of late Benjamin Williams, and Ethel Mary, *née* Marshell (d 1954); *b* 24 June 1935; *Educ* UC Swansea (BA), Univ of Wales (PhD, DLitt), St Catharine's Coll Cambridge (DipEd), Univ of Oxford (MA); *m* 25 June 1955, Eleanore, da of Leopold Lorenz Lerch (d 1940); 2 da (Catherine Dilys b 1962, Tess Jane b 1965); *Career* demonstrator Dept of Geography Swansea UC 1957–60, lectr rising to reader Univ of Adelaide 1960–78, pt/t lectr in planning SA Inst Technol 1963–70; Univ of Oxford: lectr in geography 1978–89, fell Oriel Coll 1978– (vice-provost 2000–02), lectr in charge St Anne's Coll 1978–98, reader in geography 1990–96, dir Environmental Change and Mgmnt Environmental Change Unit 1993–98, prof of geography 1996–2002 (emeritus prof 2002–); visitor UCL 1973 (visitor and lectr 1966–67); visiting fell: Dept of Geography Univ of Wisconsin-Madison 1973–74 (distinguished visitor 1994), Dept of Geography Flinders Univ 1984; visiting prof: Ctee on Geographical Studies Univ of Chicago 1989, UCLA 1994–99; contrib to many academic jls; Inst of Br Geographers: hon ed Transactions of the Institute 1983–88, chm Pubns Ctee 1983–88, memb Cncl 1983–88; memb: Editorial Advsy Bd RGS 1984–92, Editorial Ctee Progress in Human Geography 1990–2001; ed Global Environmental Change 1993–96; John Lewis Gold Medal RGS (SA) 1979, Hidy Medal and Award Forest and Conservation History Soc USA 1988 (hon fell 1989), Charles A Weyerhaeuser Award 1991 and 2004; travel and research grants: Australian Research Grant Cmmn, Br Acad, Royal Soc; FBA 1989 (memb Cncl 1993–96, chm Section N 1994–97); *Books* The Making of the Australian Landscape (1974, Biennial Literary Prize Adelaide Festival of Arts, 1976), Australian Space, Australian Time: Geographical Perspectives 1788–1914 (jt ed, 1975), The Americans and their Forests: A Historical Geography (1989), Wetlands: A Theatened Landscape (ed, 1991), Planet Management (ed, 1992), The Relations of History and Geography: Studies in England, France and the USA (jt ed, 2002), Deforesting the Earth: From Prehistory to Present Global Crisis (2003, 2 edn 2006, Meridian Book Prize for most outstanding scholarly work of the year Assoc of American Geographers 2004), A Century of British Geography (jt ed, 2003); *Style—* Prof Michael Williams, FBA; ✉ Westgates, Vernon Avenue, Harcourt Hill, Oxford OX2 9AU (tel 01865 243725); Oriel College, Oriel Square, Oxford OX1 4EW (tel 01865 276590, fax 01865 286549, e-mail michael.williams@oriel.ox.ac.uk)

WILLIAMS, Dr Michael Charles; s of Emlyn Glyndwr Williams (d 1991), of Baglan, Port Talbot, and Mildred May, *née* Morgan; *b* 11 June 1949; *Educ* Sandfields Comp Sch Port Talbot, UCL (BSc), SOAS Univ of London (MSc, PhD); *m* 1, 25 May 1974 (m dis 1984), Margaret Rigby; 1 da (Rhiannon Esmee Helena b 29 July 1978); m 2, 30 Aug 1992, Isobelle Mary, da of John Jaques (d 1978); 1 s (Benedict Rhys b 5 May 1993); *Career* dir Human Rights UN Cambodia 1992–93, dir of info UN Protection Force (UNPROFOR) Zagreb 1994–5, sr fell IISS 1995–8, dir UN Office for Children and Armed Conflict NY 1999–2000, special advsr to the Foreign Sec 2000–05, dir ME and Asia UN NY 2005–06, UN special coordinator on Middle East 2006–07; conslt: UNHCR, Cncl of Euro, EC; sr fell 21st Century Tst; memb: IISS 1990, Cncl RIIA 2000, ICA; *Publications* Communism, Religion and Revolt in Banten (1990), Vietnam at the Crossroads (1992), Civil-Military Relations and Peacekeeping (1998); *Recreations* reading (especially history), travel; *Style—* Dr Michael C Williams; ✉ Department of Political Affairs, United Nations, New York, USA (tel 00 1 917 367 5082, fax 00 1 212 963 1395)

WILLIAMS, Michael Duncan; s of Harry Duncan Williams, of Oxford, and Irene Pamela, *née* Mackenzie; *b* 31 March 1951; *Educ* Oundle, Trinity Hall Cambridge (MA); *Career* vice-pres and UK sr credit offr Bank of America NT and SA 1973–89, dir: SFE Bank Ltd, Banque SFE 1988–89; dep gen mangr credit Nomura Bank Int plc 1989–93, dir Credit Risk Mgmnt Swiss Bank Corporation 1993–94, dir Risk Mgmnt European Bank for Reconstruction and Development 2002– (head Portfolio Mgmnt 1994–2001); hon treas: FISA, The International Rowing Fedn; dir Amateur Rowing Association Ltd, steward Henley Royal Regatta; *Recreations* rowing, golf, classic cars; *Clubs* Leander, London Rowing (pres); *Style—* Michael Williams, Esq

WILLIAMS, Michael John; s of Stanley Williams, and Phyllis Mary, *née* Wenn; *b* 23 July 1948; *Educ* William Ellis Sch London, Univ of Liverpool (BA); *m* 1, 1971 (m dis 1996), Carol; 2 da (Stella b 1983, Amy b 1988); m 2, 2000, Melanie Powell; 1 s (Edmund b 2001); *Career* graduate trainee Liverpool Daily Post & Echo 1970–73, features sub ed and news sub ed Birmingham Evening Mail 1973–75, home news sub ed The Times 1975–78, asst to editorial dir Thames & Hudson Book Publishers 1978–79; New Society magazine: diary ed and feature writer 1979–84, dep ed 1984–86; features ed Today newspaper 1986; The Sunday Times: dep news ed 1986–87, news ed 1987–89, asst ed (news) 1989–90, managing ed (news) 1990–92, managing ed (features) 1993–94; The Independent: exec news ed 1994–96, exec ed 1996–99; dep ed Independent on Sunday 1999–2007, readers' ed The Independent 2007–; *Books* British Society (1984), Britain Now Quiz (1985), Society Today (1986); *Recreations* riding the great trains of the world, exploring Baroque churches; *Style—* Michael Williams, Esq; ✉ 35 Rochester Road, Camden Town, London NW1 9JJ (tel 020 7482 5318); The Independent, Independent House, 191 Marsh Wall, London E14 9RS (tel 07710 613905, e-mail m.williams@independent.co.uk)

WILLIAMS, Rev Canon Michael Joseph; s of James Williams (d 1972), of West Bromwich, Staffs, and Edith, *née* Unsworth (d 1988); *b* 26 February 1942; *Educ* West Bromwich Secondary Tech Sch, West Bromwich Tech Coll (HNC) St John's Coll Durham (BA); *m* 31 July 1971, (Mary) Miranda, da of Lawrence Gordon Bayley, MBE, of Stockport; 1 s (James Matthew b 3 Nov 1978), 1 da (Victoria Louise b 5 March 1976); *Career* team vicar St Philemon Toxteth Liverpool 1975–78 (curate 1970–75), dir of pastoral studies St John's Coll Durham 1978–88, princ The Northern Ordination Course 1989–99; vicar of Bolton Parish Church 1999–, area dean of Bolton 2002–05; chaplain Normandy Veterans Assoc 2002–, chaplain to the Mayor of Bolton 2002–03; hon canon Liverpool Cathedral 1993–99, hon canon Manchester Cathedral 2000–; pres The Northern Fedn for Training in Miny 1991–93; priest i/c St Philip Bolton le Moors 2004–; *Books* The Power and the Kingdom (1989); *Recreations* woodwork; *Style—* The Rev Canon Michael Williams; ✉ The Vicarage, Churchgate, Bolton BL1 1PS (tel and fax 01204 533847, e-mail vicar@boltonparishchurch.co.uk)

WILLIAMS, Michael Lodwig (Mike); CB (2003); s of John Leslie Williams, of Cardiff, and Eileen Mary, *née* Sanders; *b* 22 January 1948; *Educ* Wycliffe Coll, Trinity Hall Cambridge (MA), Nuffield Coll Oxford; *m* 1970, Jenny Mary Williams, *qv*, *née* Donaldson; 3 s; *Career* Miny of Fin Lusaka 1969–71; HM Treasy: joined in 1973, seconded to Price Waterhouse 1980–81, dir of industry 1992–97, ret 2003; chief exec UK Debt Management Office 1998–2003; memb Bd CRESTCo 1998–2002 and 2004–; govt debt and cash mgmnt conslt 2003–; *Style—* Mike Williams, Esq, CB

WILLIAMS, Michael Roy; s of Edgar Harold Williams, and Joyce, *née* Smith; *b* 29 March 1947; *Educ* Selhurst GS, Univ of Exeter (BA); *Career* UCMDS trainee Unilever plc/prod mangr Bird's Eye Foods 1969–72, account dir Leo Burnett advtg 1972–78, dir Geers Gross plc 1978–86, md Geers Gross UK 1978–86, dir Charles Barker plc 1986–89, chief exec Ayer Ltd 1986–90, dir Ayer Europe 1986–90, chm and ceo Serendipity Brand Makers Ltd 1990–, ptnr Serendipity Brand Makers Sydney Aust 1999–; *Recreations* films, music, windsurfing, travel, France, SE Asia; *Style—* Michael R Williams, Esq; ✉ Serendipity Brand Makers Ltd, 22 Queen Anne's Gate, London SW1H 9AA

WILLIAMS, Nicholas Michael Heathcote; QC (2007); s of late Sir Edgar Trevor Williams, and Gillian (Lady Williams), *née* Gambier-Parry; *b* 5 November 1954; *Educ* Marlborough, St Catharine's Coll Cambridge (Briggs scholar, MA); *m* 19 Dec 1987, Corinna Mary, da of late David Mitchell, and Barbara Mitchell; 2 s (Benjamin b 1988, Joshua b 1990), 1 da (Rebecca b 1993); *Career* RMA Sandhurst 1977, Lt Royal Green Jackets 1977–80; called to the Bar Inner Temple 1976, practising barrister 1980–, recorder (SE circuit) 2000; *Recreations* reading, looking at paintings, skiing, cricket; *Clubs* Royal Green Jackets, MCC; *Style—* Nicholas Heathcote Williams, Esq, QC; ✉ 12 King's Bench Walk, Inner Temple, London EC4Y 7EL (tel 020 7583 0811, fax 020 7583 7228, e-mail chambers@12kbw.co.uk)

WILLIAMS, (Henry) Nigel; s of David Ffrancon Williams (d 1984); *b* 20 January 1948; *Educ* Highgate Sch, Oriel Coll Oxford; *m* Suzan Harrison; 3 s (Ned, Jack, Harry); *Career* author; memb: Amnesty, Index; FRSL; *Awards* Somerset Maugham Award 1979, Plays & Players Award 1980, BAFTA Award (for screenwriting) 1986 and 1994, International Emmy 2001; *Novels* My Life Closed Twice (1977), Jack Be Nimble (1980), Star Turn (1985), Black Magic (1986), Witchcraft (1987), The Wimbledon Poisoner (1990), They Came from SW19 (1992), East of Wimbledon (1993), Two and a Half Men in a Boat (1993), Scenes from a Poisoner's Life (1994), From Wimbledon to Waco (1995), Stalking Fiona (1997), 40 Something (1999), Hatchett and Lycett (2002); *Plays* Double Talk (Square One Theatre) 1976, Class Enemy (Royal Court then touring) 1978, Trial Run (Oxford Playhouse) 1980, Line 'Em (NT) 1980, Sugar and Spice (Royal Ct) 1980, WCPC (Half Moon) 1982, My Brother's Keeper (Greenwich Theatre) 1985, Country Dancing (RSC Stratford) 1986, Nativity (Tricycle Theatre London) 1989, Lord of the Flies (adaptation of William Golding's novel, RSC) 1995, Harry & Me (Royal Ct Theatre) 1997, The Last Romantics (Greenwich Theatre) 1997; *Television and Film* Talking Blues (BBC) 1977, Real Live Audience (BBC) 1977, Baby Love (BBC) 1981, Johnny Jarvis (BBC) 1983, Charlie (Central) 1984, Breaking Up (BBC) 1986, Kremlin Farewell (BBC 2) 1990, Centrepoint (Channel Four) 1990, The Wimbledon Poisoner (BBC 1) 1994, The Last Romantics (TV film, BBC 2) 1997, Witchcraft (BBC) 1997, Skallagrigg (Montreal Film Festival, BBC), The Canterville Ghost (Paramount), Dirty Tricks (ITV) 2000, Bertie & Elizabeth (ITV) 2001; *Recreations* swimming, walking; *Style—* Nigel Williams, Esq, FRSL; ✉ c/o Judy Daish Associates, 2 St Charles Place, London W10 6EG (tel 020 8964 8811, fax 020 8964 8966)

WILLIAMS, Air Cdre Nigel; CBE (2005); s of Philip George Williams (d 1997), and June Dorothy, *née* Graves (d 2000); *b* 3 February 1951, Lincs; *Educ* Bentley GS Calne; *m* 9 June 1973, Barbara *née* Bellas; *Career* dir air traffic control ops HQ Military Air Traffic Ops 1996–97, OC London Air Traffic Control Centre West Drayton 1997–99; HQ Strike Command: dir Air Traffic Control Progs and Fin 1999–2003, Air Cdre Ops Support 2002–03, AO Battlespace Mgmnt 2003–06; pres Daedalus Soc; NATO Kosovo Medal 1999, Operational Serv Medal with Clasp for Afghanistan 2002, Operational Serv Medal with Clasp for Iraq 2003; Queen's Golden Jubilee Medal 2002; *Recreations* classic cars, property devpt, cycling, computing; *Style—* Air Cdre Nigel Williams, CBE; ✉ Mulberry House, Bests Lane, Sutton Veny, Wiltshire BA12 7AU (tel 01985 840226, e-mail nbjwilliams@btinternet.com)

WILLIAMS, Nigel Phillip; *b* 9 May 1956; *Educ* Gillingham GS, LSE (BSc Econ); *m* Oct 1999, Antoinette, da of Prof Karl-Ernst Baron Pilars de Pilar, and Petra, *née* von Johnstone; 1 da (Victoria b 2 Dec 2004); *Career* W Greenwell & Co 1977–78, assoc memb Grieveson Grant & Co 1978–84, md William Cooke Lott & Kissack Ltd 1984–90, advsr Czechoslovenska Obchodni Banka 1990–91, chm Mgmnt Bd Creditanstalt Investment Co 1991–96, currently chm Royalton Partners; chm: Supervisory Bd Starman Kaabeltelevisioone AS 2000, mPunkt Polska Sp z.o.o. 2002, First Mortgage Commercial Bank RT 2003; non-exec dir: Investec Global Strategy Fund 1994, Lester Brewster Meml Fndn 2003; memb: SBE 1978, SE 1983; *Recreations* golf, sailing, skiing; *Clubs* Turf, Brook (NY), Carlton, Royal Thames Yacht, Engadine Golf; *Style—* Nigel Williams, Esq; ✉ Royalton Partners, Seefeldstrasse 69, 8008 Zurich, Switzerland (tel 00 41 43 488 3661, fax 00 41 43 488 3521)

WILLIAMS, Prof Norman Stanley; s of Julius Williams (d 1998), and Mable, *née* Sundle (d 1978); *b* 15 March 1947; *Educ* Roundhay Sch Leeds, Univ of London (MB BS, MS); *m* Linda, da of Reuben Feldman, of London; 1 da (Charlotte b 1979), 1 s (Benjamin b 1983); *Career* res fell UCLA 1980–82, sr lectr in surgery Leeds Gen Infirmary 1982–86 (res fell 1977–78, lectr 1978–80), winner Patey Prize 1978, Fulbright scholar 1980, Moynihan fellowship 1985; Barts and The London Queen Mary's Sch of Med and Dentistry: house surgn and physician 1970–71, surgical registrar 1971–76, prof of surgery 1986–, head Div of Surgery Clinical Neuroscience and Intensive Care 1998–2003; author of numerous chapters and papers on gastroenterological disease; chm UKCCCR Sub-Ctee on colorectal cancer 1997–2001, pres Ileostomy Assoc of GB, pres Euro Digestive Surgery 1997, memb Cncl RCS 2005–, pres elect Soc of Academic and Research Surgery 2007–; vice-chm Editorial Ctee British Jl of Surgery 1992–2001; memb Editorial Bd: Int Jl of Colorectal Disease, Jl of Surgical Oncology; Sir Alan Parks visting prof 2002, G B Ong visiting prof 2004; John Goligher lectr 2002, Zachary Cope lectr 2003; jt winner Bupa Prize for Medically Illustrated Textbook 1995, Nessim Habif Prize for Surgery 1995, Worshipful Soc of Apothecaries Galen Medal in Therapeutics 2002; memb: Br Soc of Gastroenterology, Surgical Res Soc, Assoc of Surgeons, Int Surgical Gp; FRCS 1975, FMedSci; *Books* Surgery of the Anus, Rectum and Colon (jt author), Colorectal Cancer (ed), Bailey & Love's Short Practice in Surgery (jt ed); *Recreations* long distance swimming, theatre, cinema; *Style—* Prof Norman Williams

WILLIAMS, Sir (Michael) Osmond; 2 Bt (UK 1909), of Castell Deudraeth, and Borthwen, Co Merioneth; MC (1944), JP (Gwynedd 1960); s of Capt Osmond Trahairn Deudraeth Williams, DSO (d 1915), by his w Lady Gladys Finch Hatton (da of 13 Earl of Winchilsea); suc gf, Sir Arthur Osmond Williams, 1 Bt, JP, sometime Lord-Lt and MP Merionethshire, 1927; *b* 22 April 1914; *Educ* Eton, Freiburg Univ; *m* 1947, Benita Mary (d 2003), da of G Henry Booker (d 1953); 2 da; *Heir* none; *Career* 2 Lt Royal Scots Greys 1933–37 and 1939; Mid East, Italy and NW Europe WW II 1939–45, Capt 1940, Maj 1945; memb Merioneth Pk Planning Ctee 1971–74, govr Rainer Fndn Outdoor Pursuits Centre 1963–75, chm Quarry Tours Ltd 1973–77; Chev Order of Leopold II with Palm, Croix de Guerre with Palm (Belgium) 1940; MRI 1967; *Recreations* music, travelling; *Clubs* Travellers; *Style—* Sir Osmond Williams, Bt, MC; ✉ Borthwen, Penrhyndeudraeth, Gwynedd LL48 6EN (tel and fax 01766 770215, e-mail sir.williams@sky.com)

WILLIAMS, Owen John; s of Owen John Williams (d 1975), of St Clears, Dyfed, and Dilys Williams (d 2001); *b* 1950; *Educ* Ysgol Abermâd Aberystwyth, Harrow, UC Oxford (MA); *m* 2 March 1984 (m dis 1997); 1 da (Olivia b 23 Dec 1986); *Career* called to the Bar Middle Temple 1974; chm O J Williams Ltd Group of Cos 1975–2004; Parly candidate (Cons): Ceredigion and Pembroke North 1987 and 1992, Carmarthen West and South Pembrokeshire 1997; Euro Parly candidate: Mid and West Wales 1989, Wales 1999 and 2004; Nat Assembly for Wales candidate: Meirionnydd Nant Conwy 1999, Ceredigion 2003; pres Carmarthen West and South Pembrokeshire Cons Assoc 2004–07; non-exec memb East Dyfed HA 1990–95; pres St Clears Sr Citizens' Assoc; memb Hon Soc Cymmrodorion; Lloyd's underwriter 1978–; *Recreations* racing, rugby, country music; *Clubs* Carlton; *Style—* O J Williams, Esq; ✉ 9 Bedford Row, London WC1R 4AZ (tel 020 7489 2727, fax 020 7489 2828)

WILLIAMS, Prof (Hilary) Paul; s of John Kenneth Williams, and Margaret Rosalind Williams; *b* 22 June 1943; *Educ* Redruth GS, Univ of Cambridge (MA), Univ of Leicester (PhD); *m* 27 Aug 1971, Eileen, da of Ernest Hewart; 2 da (Anna Morwenna b 17 Nov 1972, Eleanor Mary b 20 April 1982), 1 s (Alexander Paul b 18 Feb 1975); *Career* devpt analyst for IBM 1968–71, lectr Univ of Sussex 1971–76, prof of mgmnt sci Univ of Edinburgh 1976–84; Univ of Southampton: prof of operational res 1984, dean Faculty of Mathematical Studies 1987–90 and 1992–93; prof of operational research LSE 2001–; memb: Operational Res Soc, Mathematical Programming Soc, Royal Instn of Cornwall; *Books* Model Building In Mathematical Programming (1978, 4 edn 1999), Model Solving in Mathematical Programming (1993); *Recreations* running, walking; *Style—* Prof Paul Williams; ✉ Trencrom House, Cheriton Close, Winchester SO22 5HN

WILLIAMS, Paul Michael; OBE (2000); *b* 25 June 1948, Wales; *Career* NHS 1966–, has held range of sr mgmnt positions, currently chief exec of Bro Morgannwg NHS Tst, UK pres IHM 2002–05; High Sheriff S Glamorgan 2007–08; DMS, CIHM, CCMI, FRSA; *Recreations* fly fishing, travel, art, music, gardening, keeping fit; *Style—* Paul Williams, OBE; ✉ Bro Morgannwg NHS Trust, Trust Headquarters, 71 Quarella Road, Bridgend CF31 1YE (tel 01656 753000)

WILLIAMS, (John) Peter; *b* 29 June 1953; *Educ* Kingston GS, St John's Coll Cambridge (MA); *m* 1980, Geraldine Mary, *née* Whelan; 1 s (Dominic b 1982), 2 da (Frances b 1984, Caroline b 1987); *Career* articled clerk Thomson McLintock CAs 1975–79, finance accountant Grindlays Bank 1979–82; Daily Mail and General Holdings Ltd: gp accountant 1982–90, fin dir 1990, fin dir Daily Mail and General Trust plc 1991–; non-exec dir: Bristol United Press plc 1991–2004, GWR Gp plc 2000–05, GCap plc 2005–; FCA 1989 (ACA 1979); *Recreations* opera, golf, hockey, philately; *Style—* Peter Williams, Esq; ✉ Daily Mail and General Trust plc, Northcliffe House, 2 Derry Street, London W8 5TT (tel 020 7938 6000, fax 020 7938 4626)

WILLIAMS, (William) Peter; MBE (2007); s of William Edgar Williams (d 1983), of Canterbury, Kent, and Gladys Mary, *née* Thomas (d 1985); *b* 21 September 1933; *Educ* King Edward GS Totnes, Cotham GS Bristol; *m* 1, 1960 (m dis 1986); 2 s, 4 da; m 2, 1986, Jo Taylor Williams, da of Alexander Thomas Taylor, of Timaru, NZ; 1 da; *Career* journalist with Bristol Evening Post and BBC Radio in South West 1954–64, reporter Day by Day Southern Television 1964–65, reporter and prodr This Week (later TV Eye) Thames Television 1965–79, reporter Panorama and presenter/exec prodr Open Secret BBC 1979–82, controller of factual progs TVS 1982–92; md: Studio Z 1992–98, Peter Williams Television 1992–; prodr Just Williams series of documentaries, originated The Human Factor series; awards incl: Test Tube Explosion 1983 (runner up Prix Italia), Just Williams - The Mercenaries 1984 (San Francisco Golden Gate Award), The Human Factor - Boy on a Skateboard 1985 (Asia Broadcasting Union Premier Documentary Award), Unit 731 - Did the Emperor Know? 1985 (San Francisco Golden Gate Award, Gold Medal NY Int Film and TV Festival 1986), Charlie Wing 1990 (RTS Best UK Regnl Prog, Rheims Euro TV Festival Best Documentary 1991), Ambulance! (Indies Best Regnl Prog 1995), Pandemic (winner Toronto Int Documentary Festival 2000); chm: CTFM Radio 1999–2004, Viridor Environmental Trust (Kent) 2007–; pres Optimists Club 1988–2004; pres Canterbury Festival 2007– (chm 1986–2007); dir: E Kent Enterprise Agency 1987–2001, Technology East Kent 2001–, Brett Environmental Tst 2001–06; RTS Lifetime Industry Achievement Award 2002; Hon Freedom of City of Canterbury 2001; Hon MA Univ of Kent at Canterbury 1992; hon fell Canterbury Christ Church Univ 2004; *Books* Winner Stakes All, McIndoe's Army, Unit 731 - The Secret of Secrets; *Recreations* theatre, music, tennis; *Clubs* Kent CCC (life memb); *Style—* Peter Williams, Esq, MBE; ✉ Boughton-under-Blean, Faversham, Kent; business (tel and fax 01227 751171, e-mail peter@pwtv.co.uk)

WILLIAMS, Prof Peter Fredric; s of Ernest James Williams (d 1975), and Annie, *née* Preece (d 1995); *b* 14 May 1937; *Educ* Wolverhampton Sch, St John's Coll Cambridge (Wright's Prize, MA, MusB, PhD, LittD); *m* Rosemary Jane; 1 da (Lucy b 1968), 3 s (Daniel b 1969, Gregory b 1984, Edward b 1989); *Career* harpsichord pupil of Thurston Dart 1962, Gustav Leonhardt 1965; Univ of Edinburgh: lectr 1962, dir Russell Collection of Harpsichords 1968, reader 1971, prof and chair of performance practice studies 1982–85, hon prof 1992; John Bird prof Univ of Wales Cardiff 1996–2003; sr res fell Cornell Univ NY 1982, Arts & Sciences distinguished prof Duke Univ N Carolina 1985–96; American Instrument Soc Curt Sachs Award 1996; chm Br Inst of Organ Studies; memb: SE Keyboard Soc, RMA; Hon FRCO 1982, RSA 1990; *Publications* The European Organ 1450–1850 (1966), Figured Bass Accompaniment (2 vols, 1970), The Organ from the Greeks to the Present Day (1980), The Organ Music of J S Bach (3 vols, 1980–84, revised 2003), The King of Instruments (1992), Handel Harpsichord Works (4 vols, 1990–94), The Organ in Western Culture 750–1250 (1992), The Chromatic Fourth during Four Centuries (1997), Bach Goldberg Variations (2001), JS Bach, a Life in Music (2007); ed The Organ Yearbook 1969–; *Style—* Prof Peter Williams; ✉ Department of Music, University of Wales, Cardiff CF10 3EB (tel 01452 831 195)

WILLIAMS, Sir Peter Michael; kt (1998), CBE (1992); *b* 22 March 1945, Warrington; *Educ* Hymers Coll Hull, Trinity Coll Cambridge (MA, PhD); *m*; 1 s (b 1978); *Career* Mullard research fell Selwyn Coll Cambridge 1969–70, univ lectr Dept of Chemical Engrg and Chemical Technol Imperial Coll London 1970–75, fell St John's Coll Oxford 1988–2000, fell Imperial Coll London 1997, master St Catherine's Coll Oxford 2000–02, chllr Univ of Leicester 2005–; VG Instruments Gp 1975–82 (dep gp md 1979–82), Oxford Instruments plc 1982–99 (chm 1991–99); chm: PPARC 1994–99, The Oxford Partnership 1995–97, Isis Innovation Ltd 1997–2001, NPL Mgmnt Ltd 2002–, Engrg and Technol Bd 2002–06; non-exec dir: Taube Hodgson Stonex Ptnrs Ltd 1997–2000, Advent VCT & VCT2 plc 1998–2004, GKN plc 2001–, WS Atkins 2004–; lectures and presentations incl: Royal Soc 'Zeneca' 1994, UK Innovation 1995, Duncan Davies Medal 1999, R&D 1999; chm of trustees Nat Museum of Science and Industry 1996–2002; Guardian Young Businessman of the Year 1986; hon fell: UCL, Selwyn Coll Cambridge, St Catherine's Coll Oxford; Hon DSc: Univ of Leicester, Nottingham Trent Univ 1995, Loughborough Univ 1996, Brunel Univ 1997, Univ of Wales 1999, Univ of Sheffield 1999, Univ of Warwick 1999, Univ of Salford 2003, Univ of Staffordshire 2004; FREng 1996, FRS 1999, FInstP (pres 2000–02), Hon FIChemE 2003, Hon FIEE 2004 (FIEE); *Recreations* hiking, skiing, music, collecting wine; *Style—* Sir Peter Williams, CBE, FRS, FREng

WILLIAMS, Peter Rhys; s of Rhys Morgan Williams (d 1979), and Barbara Marion, *née* Pead (d 2003); *b* 30 December 1955, Cardiff; *Educ* Cathedral Sch Llandaff, King's Coll Taunton (exhibitioner), Univ of Exeter, Univ of Warwick, Coll of Law Guildford, UWE; *m* 10 Nov 1984, Anne Marcelle, *née* Ebery; 3 s (Thomas John Rhys b 24 Oct 1988, Henry George Rhys b 17 June 1991, Edward Morgan Rhys b 15 Feb 1993); *Career* slr and slr-advocate; ptnr Burges Salmon 1987– (articled clerk 1980–82, currently head of agric); past vice-chm Nat Trainee Slrs Gp 1982, former govr The Downs Sch Wraxall; Blundell meml lectr; memb: Br Inst of Agric Conslts, Law Soc; FCIArb; *Publications* Scammell & Densham's Law of Agricultural Holdings (ed); contrib to: Halsbury's Laws (vol on agric), Agricultural Law, Tax and Finance, Encyclopaedia of Forms and Precedents (vol on agric), Dispute Resolution, Farm Cottages; *Recreations* rugby referee (Bristol Referees' Soc); *Style—* Peter Williams, Esq; ✉ Burges Salmon LLP, Narrow Quay House, Narrow Quay, Bristol BS1 4AH (tel 0117 939 2000, fax 0117 902 4400, e-mail peter.williams@burges-salmon.co.uk)

WILLIAMS, Dr Peter Richard; s of Calvert Percy Halliday Williams, of Christchurch, Dorset, and Joan Lillian, *née* Cook; *b* 13 July 1946; *Educ* Bedford Modern Sch, Univ of Oxford, Univ of Saskatchewan, Univ of Reading (BA, MSc, PhD); *m* 2 Dec 1972, Esther May, da of Louis Van Der Veen, of Saskatoon, Saskatchewan, Canada; *Career* res fell: Univ of Birmingham 1975–80, Australian Nat Univ 1980–83; dep dir Inst of Housing 1986–88 (asst dir 1980–86), prof of housing mgmnt and dir Centre for Housing Mgmnt and Devpt Univ of Wales Cardiff 1989–94 (visiting fell 1994–95), currently dep dir gen Cncl of Mortgage Lenders; visiting prof Sch of Public Policy Univ of Bristol; memb Bd Housing Corp, memb Min of Housing, Planning and Construction's Housing Sounding Bd 1991–99; memb Editorial Bd: Housing Studies, Roof Magazine; gen ed Housing Practise book series; formerly: memb Bd Tai Cymru (Housing for Wales), chm Housing Mgmnt Advsy Panel for Wales, chm Housing Studies Assoc; memb: RGS, Inst Br Geographers, Chartered Inst of Housing; *Books* Urban Political Economy (author and ed, 1982), Social Process and The City (ed, 1983), Conflict and Development (ed, 1984), Gentrification and The City (author and ed, 1986), Class and Space (author and ed, 1987), Home Ownership (co-author, 1990), Safe as Houses (co-author, 1991), Directions in Housing Policy (ed, 1997), Surviving or Thriving? Managing change in housing organisations (co-author, 1998), Housing in Wales: The Policy Agenda in an Era of Devolution (co-author, 2000); *Recreations* walking, sailing; *Style—* Dr Peter Williams; ✉ tel 020 7440 2217

WILLIAMS, Sir (Robert) Philip Nathaniel; 4 Bt (UK 1915), of Bridehead, Co Dorset; JP (1992), DL (Dorset 1995); s of Sir David Philip Williams, 3 Bt, DL (d 1970), by his 2 w, Elizabeth, Lady Williams, DL; *b* 3 May 1950; *Educ* Marlborough, Univ of St Andrews (MA); *m* 1979, Catherine Margaret Godwin, da of Canon Cosmo Gabriel Rivers Pouncey, of Church Walk, Littlebredy, Dorchester, Dorset; 1 s (David b 1980), 3 da (Sarah b 1982, Margaret b 1984, Clare b 1987); *Heir* s David Williams; *Career* landowner (2500 acres); *Clubs* MCC; *Style—* Sir Philip Williams, Bt, DL; ✉ Bridehead, Littlebredy, Dorchester, Dorset DT2 9JA (tel 01308 482232)

WILLIAMS, Prof Rhys Watcyn; s of Rev Morgan John Williams, and Barbara, *née* John; *b* 24 May 1946; *Educ* The Bishop Gore Sch Swansea, Jesus Coll Oxford (MA, DPhil); *m* Kathleen, da of William Henry Gould, of Bournemouth; 2 s (Daniel b 1978, Thomas b 1982); *Career* tutorial res fell Bedford Coll London 1972–74, lectr in German Univ of Manchester 1974–84; Univ of Wales Swansea (formerly Univ Coll Swansea): prof of German 1984–, dean Faculty of Arts 1988–91, pro-vice-chllr 1997–; pres: Int Carl Einstein Soc 1988–92, Conf of Univ Teachers of German 2002–; *Books* Carl Sternheim, A Critical Study (1982); *Style—* Prof Rhys Williams; ✉ 48 Derwen Fawr Road, Sketty, Swansea SA2 8AQ (tel 01792 280921); Department of German, University of Wales Swansea, Singleton Park, Swansea SA2 8PP (tel 01792 295173, e-mail r.w.williams@swan.ac.uk)

WILLIAMS, Richard Charles John; s of Herbert Charles Lionel Williams (d 1957), and Barbara Dorothy, *née* Moenich; *b* 19 October 1949; *Educ* Highgate Sch, London Coll of Printing (DipAD); *m* Agnieszka Wanda, da of Zygmunt Jan Skrobanski; 1 da (Mary Barbara Daisy b 31 July 1981), 1 s (Peter Crispin John b 4 April 1986); *Career* asst designer Industrial Design Unit Ltd 1973–74, sr designer J Sainsbury Ltd 1974–77, dir of packaging Allied International Designers 1977–86, co-fndr/md Design Bridge 1986–96, co-fndr Williams Murray Hamm 1997–; exec memb DBA 1989–90, memb D&AD, memb Design Cncl 2005–; FRSA, FCSD; *Recreations* motor sports; *Style—* Richard Williams, Esq; ✉ Williams Murray Hamm, 10 Dallington Street, London EC1V 0DB (tel 020 3217 0000, fax 020 3217 0002)

WILLIAMS, Prof Richard James Willson; s of Ernest James Williams, of Downend, Bristol, and Eleanor Mary Willson Williams, *née* Rickard; *b* 5 February 1949; *Educ* Bristol GS, Univ of Birmingham (MB ChB, Marjorie Hutchings prize in psychiatry); *m* 21 May 1971, Janet May, da of Ronald Phillip Simons (d 1990); 2 da (Anna May b 12 July 1975, Katharine Alice Jane b 21 Nov 1977), 1 s (James Christopher Willson b 13 Aug 1981); *Career* house physician Selly Oak Hosp Birmingham 1972–73, house surgn Worcester Royal Infirmary 1973, registrar in psychiatry S Glamorgan AHA 1974–77 (sr house offr in psychiatry 1973–74), sr registrar in child and adolescent psychiatry S Glamorgan AHA and Welsh Nat Sch of Med 1977–80, conslt child and adolescent psychiatrist 1980– (Avon AHA 1980–82, Bristol and Weston HA 1982–91, United Bristol Healthcare NHS Tst 1991–98, Gwent Community Health NHS Tst 1998–), prof of mental health strategy Univ of Glamorgan 1998–; dir NHS Health Advsy Serv 1992–96; Univ of Bristol: clinical teacher in mental health 1980–89, clinical lectr in mental health 1989–94, hon sr lectr in mental health 1994–98, govr Inst of Child Health 1988–94, memb Ct 1990–93; sr fell Health Servs Mgmnt Centre Univ of Birmingham 1996–; asst ed Jl of Adolescence 1990–97 (memb ed Bd 1997–), co-ed Child and Adolescent Psychiatry Section Current Opinion in Psychiatry 1993–; RCPsych: memb Cncl 1986–90 and 1993–, chm S Western Div 1996–; chm Assoc for the Psychiatric Study of Adolescents 1987–93; memb: Assoc for Child Psychology and Psychiatry 1978–, Assoc for Professionals in Servs for Adolescents 1979–, Assoc of Univ Teachers of Psychiatry 1989–, Br Paediatric Assoc 1987–96; DPM 1976, FRCPsych 1990 (MRCPsych 1976), MHSM 1994, MInstD 1994, FRCPCH 1997 (MRCPCH 1996), FRSM 1992; *Publications* The APSA Register of Adolescent Units (5 edn 1990), A Concise Guide to the Children Act 1989 (1992), A Unique Window on Change (1993), Comprehensive Mental Health Services (1994 and 1995), Clinicians in Management (1994 and 1995), Suicide Prevention (1994), Comprehensive Health Services for Elderly People (1994), Drugs and Alcohol (1994), Guiding Through Change (1994), Together We Stand (1995), A Place in Mind (1995), The Substance of Young Needs (1996), Making a Mark (1996), Safeguards for Young Minds (1996); *Recreations* licensed radio amateur, dinghy sailing, motorsport (med offr at racing circuit); *Clubs* Athenaeum, IOD; *Style—* Prof Richard Williams; ✉ Welsh Institute of Health and Social Care, University of Glamorgan, Glyntaff Campus, Pontypridd, CF37 1DL

WILLIAMS, Richard Wayne; s of David Victor Williams (d 1964), and Sarah Irene, *née* Jones; *b* 13 June 1948; *Educ* Ystalyfera GS Swansea, UC Wales Aberystwyth (LLB), Univ of London (LLM); *m* 7 Sept 1974, Linda Pauline, da of Cecil Ernest Elvins; 2 s (Rhodri Christopher Wyn b 18 Jan 1982, Robin Owen Wyn b 12 Sept 1985); *Career* admitted slr 1973; ptnr Ince & Co 1978–2001 (conslt 2001–); visiting prof Dept of Law Univ of Wales Swansea; speaker at conferences on shipping matters UK and abroad; conslt on shipping matters to UN agencies and other int bodies; memb: Baltic Exchange, London Maritime Arbitrators Assoc; memb Law Soc; *Books* Limitation of Liability for Maritime Claims (1986, 3 edn 1998); *Recreations* archaeology, reading, travel; *Style—* Richard Williams, Esq; ✉ Ince & Co, Knollys House, 11 Byward Street, London EC3R 5EN (tel 020 7623 2011, fax 020 7623 3225, telex 8955043 INCES G)

WILLIAMS, Robert Charles; s of (Charles) Bertram Williams, of Sutton Coldfield, and Marjorie Iris, *née* Jones; *b* 29 September 1949; *Educ* Bromsgrove Sch, Worcester Coll Oxford (MA); *m* 4 Aug 1976, Caroline Ursula Eanswythe, da of Rev David Allan Pope; 3 s (Henry b 1979, George b 1981, Alfred b 1982); *Career* called to the Bar Inner Temple 1973; ed The Law Reports and The Weekly Law Reports 1996– (managing ed The Weekly Law Reports 1990–96); churchwarden All Saints' Blackheath; *Recreations* music; *Style—* Robert Williams, Esq; ✉ 56 Burnt Ash Road, London SE12 8PY (tel 020 8318 0410)

WILLIAMS, Robert James; s of late Capt Thomas Edwin Williams, MBE, of Lutterworth, Leics, and Joan Winifred, *née* Nelson; *b* 20 September 1948; *Educ* King Edward VII Sch Sheffield, UC Oxford (BA); *m* 29 July 1972, Margaret, da of late Charles Neville Hillier, of Guernsey, CI; 2 da (Katherine b 6 Aug 1979, Caroline b 24 Aug 1983); *Career* Linklaters & Paines: articled clerk 1971–73, asst slr 1973–81, Hong Kong Office 1978–80, ptnr 1981–93; non-exec dir: Edinburgh UK Smaller Companies Tracker Tst plc 1994–, The Law Debenture Corporation plc 2005– (exec dir 1993–2004); memb City of London Slrs' Co 1980; memb Law Soc 1973; *Recreations* swimming, walking, eating, sleeping; *Style—* Robert J Williams, Esq

WILLIAMS, Prof Robert Joseph Paton; s of Ernest Ivor Williams (d 1968), and Alice, *née* Roberts (d 1988); *b* 25 February 1926; *Educ* Wallasey GS, Merton Coll Oxford (MA, DPhil); *m* 19 July 1952, Jelly Klara, da of Mattheüs Jacobus Christiaan Buchli, of The Netherlands; 2 s (Timothy Ivor b 1955, John Matthew b 1957); *Career* Univ of Oxford: jr research fell Merton Coll 1951–55, lectr in chemistry 1955–72, fell 1955–, tutor in chemistry then in biochemistry Wadham Coll 1955–72, reader in chemistry 1972–74, Royal Soc Napier research prof 1974–91, sr res fell Wadham Coll 1991–93, emeritus fell Wadham Coll 1993–, hon fell Merton Coll 1991–; Buchman meml lectr Caltech 1972;

visiting lectr: Princeton Univ 1976, Univ of Toronto 1980, Univ of Newfoundland 1983; Tilden lectr Chem Soc 1970, Walter J Chute lectr Univ of Dalhousie 1984, Katritsky lectr UEA 1986, Garland lectr Univ of Dundee 1990, A D Little lectr MIT 1990, UK/Canada Rutherford lectr Royal Soc 1996, Birchall lectr Keele Univ 1999, Huxley lectr Univ of Birmingham 2000, numerous other named lectures; memb: Lindemann Tst, Oxford Preservation Tst; delegate Oxford Univ Press; Hon DSc: Univ of Liège Belgium 1980, Univ of Leicester 1985, UEA 1992, Keele Univ 1994, Univ of Lisbon 1996; memb Academia Europaea 1994; foreign memb: Lisbon Acad of Science 1981, Royal Soc of Science Liège 1981, Royal Swedish Acad of Science 1984, Nat Acad of Science Czechoslovakia 1989; FRS 1972; *Awards* incl: Tilden Medal Chemical Soc 1970, Keilen Medal Biochem Soc 1972, Hughes Medal Royal Soc 1979, Liversidge Medal Chemical Soc 1979, Claire Brylants Medal Univ of Louvain 1980, Bakerian lectr Royal Soc 1981, Sir Hans Krebs Medal Euro Biochemistry Societies 1985, Linderström-Lang Medal Carlsberg Fndn Copenhagen, Sigillum Magnum Univ of Bologna 1987, Heyrovský Medal Int Union of Biochemistry 1988, Sir Frederick Gowland Hopkins Medal Biochemical Soc 1989, Royal Medal Royal Soc 1995, Longstaff Medal Chemical Soc 2002, Certificate of Honour Oxford City 2003; *Books* Inorganic Chemistry (jtly, 1966), Biomineralization (jtly, 1989), The Biological Chemistry of the Elements (jtly, 1991, 2 edn 2001), The Natural Selection of the Chemical Elements (jtly, 1996), Bringing Chemistry to Life (jtly, 1999), The Chemistry of Evolution (jtly, 2006); *Recreations* walking in the country; *Style—* Prof Robert Williams, FRS; ✉ Corner House, 1A Water Eaton Road, Oxford OX2 7QQ (tel 01865 558926); Wadham College, Oxford OX1 3QR (tel 01865 272600, fax 01865 272690, e-mail bob.williams@chem.ox.ac.uk)

WILLIAMS, Robert Peter (Robbie); *b* 13 February 1974; *Career* singer; memb Take That 1990–95, solo 1995–; credits with Take That: 11 top ten singles incl 6 no 1's (Pray 1993, Relight My Fire 1993, Babe 1993, Everything Changes 1994, Sure 1994, Back For Good 1995); albums with Take That: Take That and Party (UK no 2) 1992, Everything Changes (UK no 1) 1993, Nobody Else 1995; solo singles: Freedom (UK no 2) 1996, Old Before I Die (UK no 2) 1997, Lazy Days (UK no 8) 1997, South of the Border (UK no 14) 1997, Angels (UK no 3) 1997, Let Me Entertain You (UK no 3) 1998, Millennium (UK no 1) 1998, No Regrets (UK no 4) 1998, Strong (UK no 4) 1999, She's the One (UK no 1) 1999, Rock DJ (UK no 1) 2000, Kids (with Kylie Minogue, UK no 2) 2000, Supreme (UK no 3) 2000, Let Love Be Your Energy (UK no 10) 2001, Eternity (UK no 1) 2001, Somethin' Stupid (with Nicole Kidman, UK no 1) 2001, My Culture (UK no 9) 2002, Feel (UK no 4) 2002, Come Undone (UK no 4) 2003, Something Beautiful (UK no 3) 2003, Sexed Up (UK no 10), 2003, Radio (UK no 1) 2004, Misunderstood (UK no 8) 2004, Tripping (UK no 2) 2005; solo albums: Life Thru A Lens (UK no 1) 1997, I've Been Expecting You (UK no 1) 1998, The Ego Has Landed (US only) 1999, Sing When You're Winning 2000, Swing When You're Winning 2001, Escapology 2003, Intensive Care (UK no 1) 2005; *Film* Nobody Someday (documentary, 2002); *Awards* incl: nominated for two Brit Awards 1998, nominated for three MTV Awards 1998, Best British Male Solo Artist Brit Awards 1999 and 2001, Best British Single Brit Awards 1999 (Angel) and 2001 (Rock DJ), Best British Video Brit Awards 1999 (Millennium) and 2001 (Rock DJ), Best Special Effects (Rock DJ) MTV Awards 2001, Best Male Singer MTV Europe Awards 2001 and 2005; host MTV Europe Awards 1996; *Books* Somebody Someday (2001); *Recreations* golf, rollerblading, Port Vale FC; *Style—* Robbie Williams

WILLIAMS, Prof (Robert) Robin Hughes; CBE (2004); s of Emrys Williams (d 1972), of Rhydsarn, Llanuwchllyn, Bala, Gwynedd, N Wales, and Catherine, *née* Hughes; *b* 22 December 1941; *Educ* Bala Boys' GS, Univ Coll of N Wales Bangor (BSc, PhD, DSc); *m* 18 March 1967, Gillian Mary, da of Basil Harrison, of Bournemouth, Dorset; 1 da (Sian Hughes b 17 Dec 1970), 1 s (Alun Hughes b 14 Aug 1972); *Career* lectr, reader then prof New Univ of Ulster NI 1968–83, prof of physics and head of Dept Univ of Wales Cardiff 1984–94, dep princ Univ of Wales Cardiff 1993–94, vice-chllr and princ Univ of Wales Swansea 1994–2003, research prof Univ of Wales Swansea 2003–; author of several chapters, articles and papers; former chm S Wales Branch and Semiconductor Gp of Inst of Physics; Br Vacuum Cncl medal 1988, Max Born medal German Physics Soc 1989; CPhys, FInstP 1976, FRS 1990; *Books* Metal Semiconductor Contacts (1988); *Recreations* walking, fishing, sport; *Style—* Prof Robin Williams, CBE, FRS; ✉ University of Wales Swansea, Singleton Park, Swansea SA2 8PP (tel 01792 295154, fax 01792 295655)

WILLIAMS, Sir Robin Philip; 2 Bt (UK 1953), of Cilgeraint, Co Caernarvon; s of Sir Herbert Geraint Williams, 1 Bt, sometime MP (Reading and also Croydon S) and Parly sec BOT 1928–29 (d 1954), and Dorothy Frances, *née* Jones (d 1957); *b* 27 May 1928; *Educ* Eton, St John's Coll Cambridge; *m* 19 Feb 1955, Wendy Adele Marguerite, da of late Felix Joseph Alexander, of Hong Kong; 2 s; *Heir* s, Anthony Williams; *Career* Lt RA 1947; called to the Bar Middle Temple 1954; insurance broker 1952–91, memb Lloyd's 1961–99; chm: Bow Group 1954, Anti Common Market League 1969–84; councillor Borough of Haringey 1968–74; hon sec: Safeguard Britain Campaign 1975–90, Campaign for an Independent Britain 1990–; Liveryman Worshipful Co of Merchant Taylors; *Style—* Sir Robin Williams, Bt; ✉ 1 Broadlands Close, Broadlands Road, Highgate, London N6 4AF

WILLIAMS, Rev Canon (John) Roger; s of Sir Gwilym Tecwyn Williams, CBE (d 1989), and Kathleen Isobel Rishworth, *née* Edwards (d 1989); *b* 6 October 1937; *Educ* Denstone Coll, Lichfield Theol Coll, Westminster Coll Oxford (DipTh, MTh); *Career* ordained Lichfield Cathedral: deacon 1963, priest 1964; asst curate: Wem 1963–66, St Peter's Collegiate Church Wolverhampton 1966–69; rector Pudleston-cum-Whyle with Hatfield and priest i/c Stoke Prior Humber and Docklow Hereford 1969–74, vicar Christ Church Fenton Stoke-on-Trent 1974–81, rector Shipston-on-Stour with Honington and Idlicote 1981–92, rural dean Shipston 1983–90, hon canon Coventry Cathedral 1990–2000 (canon emeritus 2000–), rector of Lighthorne, vicar of Chesterton and vicar of Newbold Pacey with Moreton Morrell 1992–2000, priest-in-charge Denstone with Ellastone and Stanton 2000–05, master St John's Hosp Lichfield 2005–; chaplain to High Sheriff of Warks 1987–88, 1991–93 and 1997–98; *Recreations* art, architecture, walking, travel; *Style—* The Rev Canon Roger Williams; ✉ The Master's House, St John's Hospital, Lichfield, Staffordshire WS13 6PB (tel 01543 264169)

WILLIAMS, Roger Hugh; MP; s of Morgan Glyn Williams (d 1984), and Eurlys Williams (d 1984); *b* 22 January 1948, Crickhowell, Powys; *Educ* Christ Coll Brecon, Selwyn Coll Cambridge (MA); *m* 28 April 1973, Penelope; 2 c; *Career* farmer 1969–; co cncllr Powys 1981–2001, MP (Lib Dem) Brecon and Radnorshire 2001–; memb and vice-chm Powys TEC; chm Brecon Beacons Nat Park 1989–93, memb Devpt Bd for Rural Wales 1991–99; supporter: Campaign for Protection of Rural Wales, Brecknock Wildlife Tst; memb: NFU (county chm), Farmers' Union of Wales, CLA; *Recreations* walking, sport, nature conservation; *Style—* Roger Williams, Esq, MP; ✉ House of Commons, London SW1A 0AA (tel 020 7219 8145, fax 020 7219 1747, e-mail williamsr@parliament.uk, website www.rogerwilliams.org.uk)

WILLIAMS, Prof Roger Stanley; CBE (1993); s of Stanley George Williams, and Doris Dagmar, *née* Clatworthy; *b* 28 August 1931; *Educ* St Mary's Coll Southampton, London Hosp Med Coll (MB, MD, LRCP); *m* 1, 8 Aug 1954 (m dis 1977), Lindsay Mary, *née* Elliott; 2 s (Robert b 8 March 1956, Andrew b 3 Jan 1964), 3 da (Anne b 5 March 1958, Fiona b 24 April 1959 d 1996, Deborah b 12 July 1961); m 2, 15 Sept 1978, Stephanie Gay, da of Gp Capt Patrick de Laszlo (d 1980); 2 da (Clemency b 28 June 1979, Octavia b 4 Sept 1983), 1 s (Aidan b 16 May 1981); *Career* Capt RAMC 1956–58; jr med specialist Queen Alexandra Hosp Millbank 1956–58, med registrar and tutor Royal Postgraduate Med Sch 1958–59, lectr in med Royal Free Hosp 1959–65, conslt physician Royal S Hants and Southampton Gen Hosp 1965–66, dir Inst of Liver Studies and conslt physician King's Coll Hosp and Med Sch 1966–96, prof of hepatology KCL 1994–96, dir Inst of Hepatology UCL and hon conslt physician UCL Hosps 1996–, dir Int Office Royal Coll of Physicians; memb scientific gp on viral hepatitis WHO Geneva 1972, conslt Fndn for Liver Research 1974–, memb Advsy Gp on Hepatitis DHSS 1980–96 (memb Transplant Advsy Panel 1974–83), memb Clinical Standards Advsy Ctee Dept of Health 1994–; attended Melrose meml lecture Glasgow 1970, Goulstonian lecture RCP 1970, Searle lecture American Assoc for Study of Liver Disease 1972, Fleming lecture Glasgow Coll of Physicians and Surgns 1975, Sir Arthur Hurst meml lecture Br Soc of Gastroenterology 1975, Skinner lecture Royal Coll of Radiologists 1978, FitzPatrick lecture RCP 2006; Distinguished Serv Award Br Assoc for the Study of the Liver 2003, Sr Achievement Award American Soc of Transplantation 2004; Sir Ernest Finch visiting prof Sheffield 1974, hon conslt in med to Army 1988–98; Hans Sloane fell RCP 2004; memb: RSM (sec of section 1962–71), Euro Assoc for Study of the Liver (sec and treas 1968–71, pres 1984); pres Br Soc of Gastroenterology 1989–90, UK rep Select Ctee of Experts Organ Transplantation 1989–93, second vice-pres RCP 1991–93, chm Cons Med Soc; Freeman City of London, Liveryman Worshipful Soc of Apothecaries; FKC 1992; Hon FACP, Hon FRCPI, FRCP (MRCP), FRCS, FRCPEd, FRACP, FMedSci; *Books* ed: Fifth Symposium on Advanced Medicine (1969), Immunology of the Liver (1971), Artificial Liver Support (1975), Immune Reactions in Liver Diseases (1978), Drug Reactions and the Liver (1981), Variceal Bleeding (1982), The Practice of Liver Transplantation (1995), International Developments in Health Care: A Review of Health Systems in the 1990s (1995); author of over 2,500 scientific papers, review articles and book chapters; *Recreations* tennis, sailing, opera; *Clubs* Athenaeum, Saints and Sinners, Royal Yacht Sqdn, Royal Ocean Racing; *Style—* Prof Roger Williams, CBE; ✉ Brickworth Park, Whiteparish, Wiltshire (tel 01794 884553); Institute of Hepatology, Royal Free and University College Medical School, University College London, 69–75 Chenies Mews, London WC1E 6HX (tel 020 7679 6510, fax 020 7380 0405, e-mail roger.williams@ucl.ac.uk)

WILLIAMS, Most Rev and Rt Hon Dr Rowan Douglas; *see:* Canterbury, Archbishop of

WILLIAMS, Roy Samuel; s of Roy Samuel Williams, Sr, and Gloria, *née* Kiffin; *b* 5 January 1968; *Educ* Henry Compton Sch, City and East London Coll, Kingsway Coll, Rose Bruford Coll (BA); *Career* playwright; *Theatre* No Boys Cricket Club (Theatre Royal Stratford East), Starstruck (Tricycle Theatre), Lift Off (Royal Court Theatre), Clubland (Royal Court Theatre), Fallout (Royal Court Theatre), Local Boy (Hampstead Theatre), The Gift (Birmingham Rep Theatre), Souls (Theatre Centre), Sing Yer Heart Out for the Lads (RNT), Night & Day (Theatre Venture), Josie's Boys (Red Ladder); *Television* BBC: Offside, Bredrens, Babyfather; *Radio* BBC: Homeboys, Tell Tale; *Awards* for Starstruck: John Whiting Award 1997, Alfred Fagon Award 1997, EMMA Award 1999; The George Devine Award 2000 (for Lift Off), Evening Standard Charles Wintour Award for Most Promising Playwright 2001 (for Clubland), BAFTA Best Schools Drama Award 2002 (for Offside); *Publications* Starstruck & The No Boys Cricket Club - Two Plays (1999), The Gift (2000), Clubland (2001), Sing Yer Heart Out for the Lads (2002), Roy Williams Plays 1 - The No Boys Cricket Club/Starstruck/Lift Off (2002), Fallout (2003); *Style—* Roy Williams, Esq; ✉ c/o Alan Brodie Representation, 211 Picadilly, London W1V 9LD (tel 020 7917 2871, e-mail alan@alanbrodie.com)

WILLIAMS, Russ; s of Henry Thomas Williams, and Patricia Primrose Williams; *Career* broadcaster; journalist and presenter Southern Sound 1983, mangr and sr presenter Metro FM 1987–90, presenter Capital Radio 1990–93; Virgin Radio: host Breakfast Show 1993–98, host Mid Morning Show 1998–; sports presenter: Sky Sports 1993–98, ITV Sports 1998–; Best Breakfast Show Sony Radio Awards 1997, Best On-Air Competition Sony Radio Awards 1998, Best Int Breakfast Show NY Radio Awards 1998; *Books* Football Babylon (1996), The Russ and Jono Breakfast Experience (1997), Football Babylon II (1998); *Recreations* football, golf, horses (owner); *Clubs* Tottenham Hotspur; *Style—* Russ Williams, Esq; ✉ MPC Entertainment, 15/16 Maple Mews, Maida Vale, London NW6 5UZ (tel 020 7624 1184, fax 020 7624 4220, e-mail mpc@mpce.com)

WILLIAMS, Sally Ann; *b* 31 October 1962; *Educ* Cardiff Poly, NCTJ qualified journalist; *Career* journalist Essex County Newspapers 1983–85, head of newsroom The Post Office Nat HQ 1990–94 (joined The Post Office 1985), dep md (London) Countrywide Porter Novelli Ltd (formerly Countrywide Communications Ltd) 1994–; *Style—* Ms Sally Williams; ✉ Countrywide Porter Novelli Ltd, 31 St Petersberg Place, London W2 4LA (tel 020 7853 2222, fax 020 7584 6655)

WILLIAMS, Shaun Peter; s of Peter Williams of Salisbury, and Gillian, *née* Collier; *b* 14 October 1961; *Educ* Canford Sch, Univ of Lausanne, Univ of Kent (BA); *m* 4 Nov 2006, Dr Karen Lock; *Career* sr reporter Salisbury Journal 1985–87; BBC TV 1987–94: grad prodn trainee, dir and prodr of various progs (incl Newsnight, Inside Story, Crimewatch, Film 90/91, Holiday); sr prodr The Sunday Programme 1994–95; PACT: dep chief exec 1995–98, chief exec 1998–2001; dir of corp affrs Carlton Communications plc 2001–02, dir of corp affrs Guardian News & Media Ltd 2002–; *Style—* Shaun Williams, Esq; ✉ Guardian News & Media Ltd, 119 Farringdon Road, London EC1R 3ER (tel 020 7837 2332)

WILLIAMS, Sian Mary; da of John Price Williams, and Katherine, *née* Rees; *b* 28 November 1964; *Educ* Eastbourne Grammar and High Sch, Oxford Brookes Univ; 3 s (Joss Philip b 19 Oct 1991, Alex John b 30 Jan 1994, Seth Michael Woolwich b 7 Oct 2006); *Career* BBC local radio trg scheme 1987–88, reporter and prodr BBC Radio Merseyside 1988–90, output ed and special events studio prodr World at One, PM and World This Weekend BBC Radio 4 1990–97, presenter BBC News 24 1997–99, special corr BBC 6 o'Clock News 1999–2001; presenter: BBC Breakfast 2001–, On Show arts series BBC 1 Wales, BBC 6 o'Clock News; occasional presenter: Radio 5 Live, BBC1 daytime programmes; *Recreations* walking, wine, cinema; *Style—* Ms Sian Williams; ✉ c/o Alex Armitage, Noel Gay Artistes, 19 Denmark Street, London WC2H 8NA (tel 020 7836 3941, fax 020 7287 1816); BBC Television Centre, Wood Lane, London W12 7RJ (e-mail sian.williams@bbc.co.uk)

WILLIAMS, Simon Lloyd; *b* 2 June 1962; *Career* Mercedes Benz (UK) Ltd 1985–87: costing and pricing analyst, sr analyst; Renault (UK) Ltd: exec devpt 1987–88, nat sales and supply planing mangr 1988–90, mangr internal comunications 1990–91, nat sales programmes mangr 1991–92; dir Mitac 1992–97, gp account dir Basten Greenhill Andrews 1997–99, sales and mktg dir Europe Enterprise IG Ltd 1999–2002, ceo Icon rand Navigation 2002–; *Recreations* rugby union, travel, business, reading, jazz and rock music; *Style—* Simon Williams, Esq; ✉ Enterprise IG Ltd, 6 Mercer Street, Covent Garden, London WC2H 9QA (tel 020 7574 4000, fax 020 7574 4100, website www.enterpriseig.com)

WILLIAMS, Stanley Killa; JP (2005); s of Jack Killa Williams (d 1972), and Gwyneth Mary, *née* Jenkins (d 1995); *b* 2 July 1945; *Educ* Bromsgrove Sch, Merton Coll Oxford (MA), Coll of Law (Herbert Ruse Prize); *m* 15 July 1972, Dheidre Rhona, *née* Westerman; 1 da (Esther Catrin b 22 Dec 1975), 1 s (Justin Gareth Killa b 22 July 1977); *Career* slr Devon CC 1969–74 (trainee slr 1966–68), asst county sec Oxon CC 1974–80, dep co sec and slr Rowntree Mackintosh plc 1980–89; BTR plc: co sec and slr 1989–93, gp commercial attorney 1993–96; dir of legal affrs and co sec BSI 1997–2005, chm BSI Retirement Tst 2000–; Law Soc: memb 1969, dir of Trg, Commerce and Industry Gp 2003–05, memb Cncl 2005–, chm Commerce and Industry Gp 2005–06; non-exec dir Corgi Tst 2005–06;

W

chm York Ebor Round Table 1985–86; *Recreations* theatre, travel, squash, golf, skiing; *Clubs* RAC; *Style—* Stanley Williams, Esq; ✉ e-mail killawilliams@hotmail.co.uk

WILLIAMS, Steffan Rhys; s of Malcolm Williams, and Nan Williams; *Educ* Lincoln Coll Oxford (MA, Rugby blue); *Career* Citigate Dewe Rogerson 1995–98, Thomson Financial/Carson 1998–2000, Capital MS&L 2000–; dir PRCA 2000–; tstee Major R V Stanley's Meml Scholarship Fund; memb Investor Relations Soc 1998–; *Recreations* rugby, fly fishing, hill walking, squash, film, cigars; *Clubs* National Liberal, Vincent's (Oxford), Goblin (Oxford), Cymry Llundain; *Style—* Steffan Williams, Esq; ✉ Capital MS&L, 81 Whitfield Street, London W1T 4HD (tel 020 7307 5330, fax 020 7307 5331)

WILLIAMS, Stephen; MP; *b* 11 October 1966; *Educ* Mountain Ash Comp, Univ of Bristol; *Career* sometime tax conslt, formerly with PricewaterhouseCoopers and Grant Thornton; cncllr (Lib Dem): Avon CC 1993–96, Bristol City CC 1995–99 (ldr Lib Dem Gp 1995–97); MP (Lib Dem) Bristol W 2005– (Parly candidate (Lib Dem) Bristol W 2001); dir Watershed Arts Centre; memb: WWF, Amnesty Int, Nat Tst, Friends of the Earth; *Style—* Stephen Williams, Esq, MP; ✉ House of Commons, London SW1A 0AA

WILLIAMS, Stephen Geoffrey (Steve); s of A E Williams, of Ilford, Essex; *b* 31 January 1948; *Educ* Brentwood Sch, KCL (LLB); *m* 1972, Susan Jennifer, da of Denis F Cottam; 1 s (Thomas b 8 August 1981); *Career* slr tax planning and commercial depts Slaughter & May 1972–75; ICI plc: slr legal dept 1975–84, asst co sec 1985–86; Unilever plc: jt co sec 1986–, general counsel 1993–; non-exec dir: Bunzl plc 1994–2004, Arriva plc 2005–; memb: Law Soc, Company Law Ctee Law Soc, Companies Ctee CBI; FRSA; *Recreations* contemporary art, professional football, 20th century fiction, cinema, swimming; *Clubs* 2 Brydges Place, RAC, Banana Splitz; *Style—* Steve Williams, Esq; ✉ Unilever plc, Unilever House, PO Box 68, Blackfriars, London EC4P 4BQ (tel 020 7822 5441, fax 020 7822 6108, mobile 077 1003 0632, e-mail steve.williams@unilever.com); Unilever NV, Weena 455, 3013 AL, post bus 760, 3000 DK Rotterdam, The Netherlands (tel 00 31 10217 4516)

WILLIAMS, Susan Elizabeth; OBE (2000); da of Ernest George Fost, of Congresbury, Avon, and late of Royal Horse Artillery, and Kathleen Beatrice Maud, *née* Hewlett; *b* 30 October 1942; *Educ* Weston-super-Mare GS for Girls, Bristol Royal Hosp for Sick Children (Registered Sick Children's Nurse), Bristol Royal Hosp (Registered Gen Nurse), Univ of London (Extramural Dip Nursing), Wolverhampton Poly (CertEd, BEd, Dip Psychology); *m* 1, 1964, Dennis Norman Carnevale (d 1975); 1 da (Maria b 1964), 1 s (Marcus b 1968); m 2, 1976 (m dis 1998), Keith Edward Williams, s of Philip Edward Williams, of Shrewsbury; *Career* ward sister Bristol Children's Hosp 1972–75, nurse tutor Shrewsbury Sch of Nursing 1976–80, sr nurse tutor Dudley HA 1980–84, regnl nurse (educn and res) W Midlands RHA 1984–87, chief nurse advsr and dir of nurse educn Bromsgrove and Redditch HA 1987–88, regnl dir of nursing and quality assurance W Midlands RHA 1988–93, dep dir of nursing NHS Management Exec 1993–94, dir of Nursing Gtr Glasgow Community and Mental Health Tst 1994–98, nurse adviser Greater Glasgow Health Board 1998–2001, dir Prince and Princess of Wales Hospice 2002–; memb Gen Cncl Erskine Hosp Bishopston 2001–; memb RCN 1960–2003; memb Nat Tst; *Recreations* mountain walking, classical music; *Style—* Ms Susan Williams, OBE

WILLIAMS, Venetia Mary; da of John Williams, of Herefordshire, and Patricia, *née* Rose; *b* 10 May 1960, London; *Educ* Downe House Sch Newbury, Sch of St Clair Penzance; *Career* racehorse trainer 1995–; trained winners of: King George VI Chase (Kempton), Hennessy Gold Cup (Newbury), Welsh Grand Nat (Chepstow), Scottish Champion Hurdle (Ayr), Ascot Chase, Cleeve Hurdle (Cheltenham, three times), Grand Annual Chase, Coral Cup and Racing Post Plate (Cheltenham Festival), Ormonde Stakes (Chester, with first flat runner); *Style—* Miss Venetia Williams; ✉ Aramstone, Kings Caple, Hereford HR1 4TU (tel 01432 840646, fax 01432 840830, e-mail venetia.williams@virgin.net)

WILLIAMS, Victoria Kirstyn (Kirsty); AM; da of Edward G Williams, and Pamela, *née* Hall, of Llanelli, Carmarthenshire; *b* 19 March 1971; *Educ* St Michael's Sch Llanelli, Univ of Manchester and Univ of Missouri (BA); *m* 16 Sept 2000, Richard Rees; 3 da (Angharad b 25 Sept 2001, Carys b 21 May 2004, Rachel b 5 April 2006); *Career* former mktg and PR exec, former memb Nat Assembly Advsy Gp; memb Nat Assembly for Wales (Lib Dem) Brecon & Radnorshire 1999–; Nat Assembly for Wales: chair Health and Social Services Ctee 1999–2003, chair Standards Ctee 2003–; dep pres Lib Dem Wales 1997–99, currently Lib Dem business mangr and spokesperson on economic devpt; *Recreations* helping out on the family farm, spending time with family, shopping; *Style—* Ms Kirsty Williams, AM; ✉ National Assembly for Wales, Cardiff Bay, Cardiff CF99 1NA (tel 029 2089 8358, fax 029 2089 8359, e-mail kirsty.williams@wales.gov.uk)

WILLIAMS, Sir William Maxwell Harries (Max); kt (1983); s of Llwyd and Hilary Williams; *b* 18 February 1926; *Educ* Nautical Coll Pangbourne; *m* 1951, Jenifer (d 1999), da of Rt Hon Edward Leslie Burgin (d 1945); 2 da; *Career* served 178 Assault Fd Regt RA Far East (Capt) 1943–47; admitted slr 1950; sr ptnr: Clifford-Turner 1984–87, Clifford Chance 1987–90; non-exec dep chm: Royal Insurance Holdings plc 1992–95 (dir 1985–95), 3i Group plc 1993–96 (dir 1988–96); memb Cncl Law Soc 1962–85 (pres 1982–83), memb Royal Cmmn on Legal Servs 1976–79, memb Ctee of Mgmnt Inst of Advanced Legal Studies 1980–86, memb Crown Agents for Overseas Govts and Admin 1982–86, lay memb Stock Exchange Cncl 1984–91, chm Review Bd for Govt Contracts 1986–93, memb Stock Exchange Disciplinary Appeals Ctee 1989–99; chm Police Appeals Tbnl 1993–99; memb Cncl Wildfowl Trust (hon treas 1974–80, currently vice-pres); pres City of London Law Soc 1986–87; hon memb: Canadian Bar Assoc, American Bar Assoc; Master Worshipful Co of Slrs 1986–87; Hon LLD Univ of Birmingham 1983; *Recreations* fishing, golf, whale watching, ornithology; *Clubs* Garrick, Mark's; *Style—* Sir Max Williams; ✉ Orinda, Holly Lane, Harpenden, Hertfordshire AL5 5DY

WILLIAMS, William Trevor (Bill); s of Percy Trevor Williams (d 1987), and Edith, *née* Hible (d 1998); *b* 3 June 1935; *Educ* Liverpool Coll Sch; *m* 1, 23 June 1956, Jane Williams; 2 s (Bruce b 1956, Shaun b 1959), 1 da (Heidi b 1961); m 2, 25 March 1967, Pamela Hilda, da of Albert Victor Saunders (d 1988); 1 da (Justine b 1970); *Career* Nat Serv RAF 1953–55; mangr RMC Ltd: Wales 1963–73, E Midlands 1973–76, London 1976–78; divnl dir North of England RMC (UK) Ltd 1978–84, md Hall & Co Ltd 1984–93; tstee Surrey Vol Serv Cncl 1996–98; Freeman City of London, Liveryman Worshipful Co of Builders Merchants; *Recreations* fly fishing, gardening; *Clubs* Flyfishers', Bishopstoke Fishing; *Style—* Bill Williams, Esq; ✉ Hillside House, High Drive, Woldingham, Surrey CR3 7EL (tel 01883 653522, e-mail btwtw@btinternet.com)

WILLIAMS-BULKELEY, Michael; yr s of Lt-Col Sir Richard Harry David Williams-Bulkeley, 13 Bt (d 1992), and Renée Arundell, *née* Neave (d 1994); *b* 2 April 1943; *Educ* Eton; *m* 4 May 1968, Ellen-Marie, eldest da of L Falkum-Hansen (d 1972), of Oslo, Norway; 2 s (James b 1970, David Haakon b 1973); *Career* Lt Welsh Gds, served Aden 1965–66; dir: CT Bowring Reinsurance Ltd 1981–89, Bowring Int Insurance Brokers Ltd 1988–89; md: Marsh & McLennan Worldwide 1988–89, Adams Johnson Green Ltd 1991–; *Recreations* golf, gardening, shooting; *Clubs* Boodle's, New Zealand GC, Royal & Ancient Golf (St Andrews); *Style—* Michael Williams-Bulkeley, Esq; ✉ Rhiwlas, Pentraeth, Anglesey LL75 8YG (tel 01248 450204)

WILLIAMS-BULKELEY, Sir Richard Thomas; 14 Bt (E 1661), of Penrhyn, Caernarvonshire, DL (Gwynedd 1998); er s of Sir Richard Harry David Williams-Bulkeley, 13 Bt, TD, JP (d 1992), and Renée Arundell, *née* Neave (d 1994); *b* 25 May 1939; *Educ* Eton; *m* 1964, Sarah Susan, elder da of Rt Hon Lord Justice (Sir Henry Josceline) Phillimore, OBE (d 1974); 2 s (Richard Hugh, Harry David (twins) b 1968), 1 da (Victoria Mary b 1973); *Heir* s, Richard Williams-Bulkeley; *Career* Capt Welsh Gds 1963; High Sheriff Gwynedd 1993–94; FRICS; *Recreations* astronomy; *Clubs* Army and Navy; *Style—* Sir Richard Williams-Bulkeley, Bt, DL

WILLIAMS OF CROSBY, Baroness (Life Peer UK 1993), of Stevenage in the County of Hertfordshire; Prof Shirley Vivian Teresa Brittain Williams; PC (1974); da of Prof Sir George Catlin and the writer, Vera Brittain (Mrs Catlin); *b* 27 July 1930; *Educ* Somerville Coll Oxford, Columbia Univ; *m* 1, 1955 (m dis 1974), Prof Bernard Williams; 1 da (Hon Rebecca Clare); m 2, 1987, Prof Richard E Neustadt (decd); *Career* contested (Lab): Harwich 1954 and 1955, Southampton Test 1959; MP (Lab) Hitchin 1964–74, Hertford and Stevenage 1974–79; MP (SDP) Crosby 1981–83 (by-election, converted Cons majority of 19,272 to SDP one of 5,289); PPS to Min of Health 1964–66, Parly sec Miny of Lab 1966–67; Min of State: Educn and Sci 1967–69, Home Office 1969–70; oppn spokesman on: Social Serv 1970–71, Home Affrs 1971–73, Prices and Consumer Protection 1973–74; Sec of State Prices and Consumer Protection 1974–76, Sec of State Educn and Sci and Paymaster Gen 1976–79; Lib Dem ldr House of Lords 2001–04; chm Fabian Soc 1980 (gen sec 1960–64), memb Lab NEC 1970–81, pres SDP 1982–88 (co-fndr 1981); prof of elective politics Kennedy Sch of Govt Harvard Univ 1988–2000; pres Br-Russia Soc and East-West Centre 1996–2001, co-pres RIIA 2001–06; memb: Bd International Crisis Gp 1976–2005, Advsy Cncl to Sec-Gen UN Fourth World Women's Conference 1995, Comité des Sages Euro Cmmn 1995, Educn Devpt Center Newton MA 1992–2000, Bd Nuclear Threat Initiative 2001–; tstee Century Fndn (New York); memb: Bd Rand Europe 1996–2002, Int Advsy Ctee Cncl on Foreign Relations NY, Overseers Ctee JFK Sch of Govt Harvard Univ; dir Project Liberty 1990–97; visiting fell Nuffield Coll Oxford 1966–74; Godkin lectr Harvard Univ 1979, Janeway lectr Princeton Univ 1990, Regents lectr Univ of Calif Berkeley 1991, Darwin lectr Univ of Cambridge 1995, Strathclyde lectr 1995, Dainton lectr Br Library 1995, emeritus lectr Notre Dame Univ 2001; hon fell: Somerville Coll Oxford, Newnham Coll Cambridge; *Books* Politics is for People (1981), A Job to Live (1985), God and Caesar (2003); *Television* Shirley Williams in Conversation (series, 1980), Women in the House (1997); *Radio* Snakes and Ladders (BBC Diary, 1996); *Recreations* hill walking, swimming, music; *Style—* The Rt Hon Lady Williams of Crosby, PC; preferred style: Shirley Williams; ✉ House of Lords, London SW1A 0PW (tel 020 7219 5850, fax 020 7219 1174)

WILLIAMS OF ELVEL, Baron (Life Peer UK 1985), of Llansantffraed in Elvel in the County of Powys; Charles Cuthbert Powell Williams; CBE (1980); s of Dr Norman Powell Williams, DD (d 1943), and Muriel de Lerisson (d 1979), da of Arthur Philip Cazenove; *b* 9 February 1933; *Educ* Westminster, ChCh Oxford (MA), LSE; *m* 1 March 1975, Jane Gillian, da of Maj Gervase Edward Portal (d 1960); *Career* British Petroleum Co Ltd 1958–64, Bank of London and Montreal 1964–66, Eurofinance SA Paris 1966–70, Baring Brothers & Co Ltd 1970–77 (md 1971–77), chm Price Cmmn 1977–79, md Henry Ansbacher & Co Ltd 1980–82, chief exec Henry Ansbacher Holdings plc, chm Henry Ansbacher & Co Ltd 1982–85, dir Mirror Group Newspapers plc 1985–92; *Clubs* Reform, MCC; *Style—* The Rt Hon the Lord Williams of Elvel, CBE; ✉ House of Lords, London SW1A 0PW

WILLIAMS-WYNN, Sir (David) Watkin; 11 Bt (E 1688), of Gray's Inn, Co Middx; DL (Clwyd 1969); s of Sir (Owen) Watkin Williams-Wynn, 10 Bt, CBE, JP (d 1988), and his 1 w, Margaret Jean, *née* McBean; *b* 18 February 1940; *Educ* Eton; *m* 1, 1968 (m dis 1981), (Harriet) Veryan Elspeth, da of late Gen Sir Norman Hastings Tailyour, KCB, DSO; 2 s (Charles Watkin b 1970, Robert Watkin b 1977), 2 da (Alexandra, Lucinda (twins) b 1972); m 2, 1983 (m dis 1998), Victoria Jane, da of Lt-Col Ian Dudley De Ath, DSO, MBE (d 1960), and formerly w of Lt-Col R E Dillon, RM; 2 s (Nicholas Watkin, Harry Watkin (twins) b 1988); *Heir* s, Charles Williams-Wynn; *Career* Lt Royal Dragoons 1959, Maj Queen's Own Yeo 1970; memb Agric Lands Tbnl (Wales) 1978; High Sheriff Clwyd 1990; *Clubs* Cavalry and Guards', Pratt's; *Style—* Sir Watkin Williams-Wynn, Bt, DL; ✉ Plas-yn-Cefn, St Asaph, North Wales LL17 0EY (tel 01745 582325, fax 01745 583288, e-mail cefnoffice@tiscali.co.uk)

WILLIAMS-WYNNE, William Robert Charles; s of late Col John Francis Williams-Wynne, CBE, DSO, JP (d 1998), and late Margaret Gwendolin, *née* Roper (d 1991); *b* 7 February 1947; *Educ* Packwood Haugh, Eton; *m* 18 Oct 1975 (m dis 2006), Hon Veronica Frances, da of Baron Buxton of Alsa, KCVO, MC, DL (Life Peer), *qv*, of Stiffkey, Norfolk; 3 da (Chloë b 14 Oct 1978, Leonora b 20 Oct 1980, Rose b 17 Feb 1983); *Career* Williams Wynne Farms 1969, Mount Pleasant Bakery 1983–99, Bronze Age 1998; JP 1974; chm: X Foxes Ltd 1992, Merioneth CLA 1996–99, Europa Club 1997–2004, Wales HHA 1999–2004, TASC 2002, Photonictherapy Ltd 2003; dir ACT Ltd 1997–2006; contested Gen Elections as Cons candidate for Montgomery 1974, RWAgS, Cncl RASE, chm WASEC, cmmr Nat Parks 1983–88, memb Prince of Wales Ctee 1983–88; FRICS 1972, ARAgS 2002, MICM 2006; *Style—* William Williams-Wynne, Esq; ✉ Williams Wynne, Tywyn, Gwynedd LL36 9UD (tel 01654 710101/2, fax 01654 710103, e-mail www@wynne.co.uk)

WILLIAMSON, Alison Jane; da of Thomas Stanley Williamson, of Chelmick Forge, Church Stretton, Shropshire, and Susan Elizabeth, *née* Allen; *b* 3 November 1971, Melton Mowbray, Leics; *Educ* Church Stretton Sch, Ludlow Coll, Arizona State Univ Tempe; *Career* archer; memb nat youth squad 1983, memb sr nat squad whilst still a jr, rep GB 1985–; achievements incl: Jr Nat Indoor champion 1986, 1987 and 1988, Jr Nat Outdoor champion 1987 and 1989, Bronze medal Jr Euro Championships 1989, Silver medal Euro and Mediterranean Championships Malta 1992, seventh place Olympic Games Barcelona 1992 (breaking 2 Br records), fifth place World Indoor Championships France 1993 (breaking 2 Br records), tenth place Olympic Games Atlanta 1996, individual Silver medal World Championships 1999, Gold medal Cyprus Grand Prix 1999, ninth place Olympic Games Sydney 2000, team Bronze medal World Championships 2003, Bronze medal Olympic Games Athens 2004; Moët & Chandon Young Sportswoman of the Year 1992; *Recreations* reading, swimming, green issues; *Style—* Miss Alison Williamson; ✉ Chelmick Forge, Church Stretton, Shropshire SY6 7HA (tel 01694 722767)

WILLIAMSON, Sir (Robert) Brian; kt (2001), CBE; *b* 16 February 1945; *Educ* Trinity Coll Dublin (MA); *m* June 1986, Diane Marie Christine de Jacquier de Rosée; *Career* PA to Rt Hon Maurice Macmillan MP (later Viscount Macmillan) 1967–71, ed Int Currency Review 1971; Gerrard Group: md Gerrard & National Holdings plc 1978–89, chm GNI Ltd 1985–89, chm Gerrard Group plc (formerly Gerrard & National Holdings plc) 1989–98; chm LIFFE 1998–2003 (dir 1981–88, non-exec chm 1985–88); memb British Invisible Exports Cncl 1985–88 (memb European Ctee 1988–90), memb Bd SIB (now FSA) 1986–98, memb Ct Bank of Ireland 1990–98 (dir Bank of Ireland British Holdings 1986–90); dir: Fleming Int High Income Investment Tst plc 1990–98, NASDAQ Int Bd 1993–98, MT Unit Tst Managers Ltd 1996–2000, HM Publishers Holdings Ltd 1996–99, Barlows plc 1997–98, Politeia 1999–, MLoop plc 2002, HSBC Holdings plc 2002–, Templeton Emerging Markets Investment Fund 2002–03, Resolution plc 2005– (chm 2004–05), Liv-Ex Ltd 2005–, Open Europe Ltd (formerly Vote No); chm: Fleming Worldwide Investment Tst 1998 (dep chm 1996–98), Electra Private Equity plc (formerly Electra Investment Tst) 2000– (dir 1994–, dep chm 1998–2000), MT Fund Mgmnt Ltd 2004–; sr advsr Fleming Family and Ptnrs; govr at large Nat Assoc of Securities Dealers (USA) 1995–98 (chm Int Markets Advsy Bd 1996–98), memb Governing Cncl Centre for Study of Financial Innovation 2000–, memb Supervisory Bd Euronext NV 2002–; chm: Army Charities Advsy Co 2002–, Advsy Bd Army Common Investment Fund 2002–; dir River and Rowing Museum Henley 1992–94; dir St George's House Tst (Windsor Castle) 1998–2002 (memb Cncl 1996–2002), tstee St Paul's Cathedral Fndn 1999–2006, memb ROH Devpt Ctee 2004–; Parly candidate (Cons): Sheffield Hillsborough 1974, Truro 1976–77; cmmnd HAC 1975; HM Lt City of London 2003; Freeman City of London 1994; FRSA 1991; *Clubs* Pratt's, White's, Flyfishers', Kildare Univ (Dublin), The Brook (NY); *Style*— Sir Brian Williamson, CBE; ✉ c/o Fleming Family & Partners, Ely House, 37 Dover Street, London W1S 4NJ (tel 020 7409 5600)

WILLIAMSON, Prof Edwin Henry; s of Henry Williamson (d 1977), and Renée, *née* Clarembaux; *b* 2 October 1949; *Educ* Univ of Edinburgh (MA, PhD); *m* 5 March 1976, Susan Jane, *née* Fitchie; 2 da (Louise b 2 Sept 1982, Phoebe b 28 Sept 1985); *Career* jr lectr in Spanish TCD 1974–77, lectr in Spanish Birkbeck Coll Univ of London 1977–90, Forbes prof of Hispanic studies Univ of Edinburgh 1990–2003, King Alfonso XIII prof of Spanish studies Univ of Oxford and fell Exeter Coll Oxford 2003–; visiting prof: Univ of São Paulo 1997, Stanford Univ 1999; Brettschneider visiting scholar Cornell Univ 2006; memb Assoc of Hispanists of GB and I 1974; Cdr Order of Isabell La Católica (Spain); *Publications* The Half-Way House of Fiction: Don Quixote and Arthurian Romance (1984, 2 edn 1986), El Quijote y los Libros de Caballerías (1991), The Penguin History of Latin America (1992), Borges: A Life (2004); *Recreations* theatre, cinema, art, hillwalking; *Style*— Prof Edwin Williamson; ✉ Exeter College, Oxford OX1 3DP (tel 01865 270476, e-mail edwin.williamson@exeter.ox.ac.uk)

WILLIAMSON, Hazel Eleanor; QC; *see:* Marshall, Hazel Eleanor (Her Hon Judge Marshall)

WILLIAMSON, Prof Hugh Godfrey Maturin; s of Thomas Broadwood Williamson (d 1962), and Margaret Frances, *née* Davy; *b* 15 July 1947; *Educ* Rugby, Trinity Coll Cambridge (MA), St John's Coll Cambridge (PhD, DD); *m* 1971, Julia Eiluned, *née* Morris; 2 da (Laura Ruth Eiluned b 13 April 1973, Halcyon Clare b 13 Sept 1975), 1 s (Nathan Paul Maturin b 17 Sept 1978); *Career* Univ of Cambridge: asst lectr in Hebrew and Aramaic 1975–79, lectr 1979–89, reader 1989–92, fell Clare Hall 1985–92; regius prof of Hebrew Univ of Oxford and student of Christ Church 1992–; Tyndale fell for biblical res 1970; memb: Soc for Old Testament Study 1975 (pres 2004), Soc of Biblical Literature 1985, Cncl Br Sch of Archaeology in Jerusalem, Cncl Palestine Exploration Fund; chm Anglo-Israel Archaeological Soc; Biblical Archaeology Soc Award 1985; FBA 1993; *Books* Israel in the Books of Chronicles (1977), 1 and 2 Chronicles (1982), Ezra, Nehemiah (1985), The Future of Biblical Studies (jt ed, 1986), Annotated key to Lambdin's Introduction to Biblical Hebrew (1987), Ezra and Nehemiah (1987), It Is Written: Essays in Honour of Barnabas Lindars (jt ed, 1988), Jesus Is Lord (1993), The Book called Isaiah: Deutero-Isaiah's Role in Composition and Redaction (1994), Wisdom in Ancient Israel: Essays in Honour of J A Emerton (jt ed, 1995), Variations on a Theme: King, Messiah and Servant in the Book of Isaiah (1998), Prophetie in Israel (jt ed, 2003), Reading from Right to Left: Essays on the Hebrew Bible in Honour of David J A Clines (jt ed, 2003), Studies in Persian Period History and Historiography (2004), Dictionary of the Old Testament Historical Books (jt ed, 2005), A Critical and Exegetical Commentary on Isaiah 1–27, vol 1 (2006); *Style*— Prof H G M Williamson, FBA; ✉ Christ Church, Oxford OX1 1DP (tel 01865 278200, fax 01865 278190)

WILLIAMSON, John Peter; s of John William Stephen Williamson (d 1979), of Camberwell, London, and Ellen Gladys, *née* Naulls (d 2002); *b* 9 January 1943, Amersham, Bucks; *Educ* Addey and Stanhope GS, Hackney Tech Coll, Thames Poly; *m* 17 Oct 1964, Dorothy Shirley Esther, da of Leonard Frederick Farmer, of Blackheath, London; 2 s (Earl John Grant b 1975, Craig Stephen b 1980); *Career* engr mangr Production Dept Rolex Watch Co 1960–63 (fndr Rolex Sports Club, fndr Rolex Rocketry Soc); jt md and fin controller Dynamic Reading Inst 1968–69, int instr in speed reading, memory, mind maps and mind training techniques (unofficial world speed reading record holder 1967–68), fndr chm BIM Younger Mangr Assoc 1969–70, gp fin controller, co sec and asst md Hunter-Print Gp plc 1971–74, asst to company controller ITT/STC 1975 (responsibility for 26 Divs); corp planner; UK chm: Investigations, Operational Reviews and Computer Audits (mangr 1976–80), ITT Bd (USA); conslt: C E Heath & Co insurance brokers, Liberty Life, Trident Life, Sun Life Unit Services, Coll of Taxation; princ: Williamson Scrap & Waste Dealers 1951–56, Williamson Light Vehicle Manufacturers 1951–56, The Fun Weaponry Co (mfrs) 1953–59, Williamson's Professional Private Tuition Training 1968–74, Williamson Business Consultancy and Turnaround Specialists 1968–74, Williamson & Co Chartered Accountants 1973–2003, J P Williamson and Co Chartered Accountants 1981–86; partner Williamson of Peckham (watchmakers and jewellers) 1954–64, partner Williamson Property Mgmnt 1963–68, UK dir Odin Security & Surveillance 1963–2003; md: Prestige MicroSystems 1976–2002, Guardian Financial Services (Guardian Ind plc) 1983–2004; princ and md: Guardian Ind Property Services 1983–93, Guardian Ind Wills & Trusts 1994–2000, Guardian Ind Executors 1994–2000, Guardian Ind Publishing Corp 1995–99, Guardian Ind Gp Int 1995–2000, Guardian Ind General Insurance Services 1995–2003, Guardian Ind Finance Corp 1995–2003, Guardian Ind Business Transfer Services 1996–2001, Guardian Ind Eagles 1996–2002, Guardian Ind Network Mktg 1996–2002, Guardian Ind Corp Services 1996–2002, Audits Inc 1996–2002, Guardian Ind Debt and Arbitration Services 1996–2003, GIANTS Corp 1996–2003, The Operational Audit Corp 1997–2000, Guardian Ind Taxation Solutions 1997–2001, Guardian Ind Strategic Planners 1997–2002, GIMAPS 1997–2002, Guardian Ind Health and Wealth 1999–2001, Guardian Ind Communications Corp 1999–2001; conslt and coach: The Wealth Coach 1983–, The Wealth Coach Ltd 2003–, WOW! Windows, Display & Design 2004–; team ldr The Product Factory 2005; licensed credit broker; fndr chm SE London Micro-Computer Club (SELMIC) and conslt to several local and nat computer clubs 1975–80, co fndr Assoc of London Hobby Computer Clubs 1980; chm SE London Area Soc of Chartered Accountants 1992–93; memb: ICA SIB Vetting Panel, Main Ctee, Ethics and Regulation Review Panel and London Business Bd London Soc of Chartered Accountants, Regional Ctee Life Insurance Assoc 1993–94, Million Dollar Round Table (top 2 per cent of fin advsrs in world), LIA Achievement Forum Inner Circle (top 39 fin advsrs in UK), Nat Assoc of Commercial Fin Brokers; assoc memb Corp of Fin Brokers; fndr memb I Fin Planning 1987; Freeman City of London 1986; memb: Inst of Internal Auditors (examiner 1978), PIA, FIMBRA, Life Insurance Assoc; FSA, FCA, CInstSMM, MCIM, FInstD, MIMgt, MIIM, MLIA (Dip), ALIMA (Dip), ACFB; *Books* author ITT/STC EDP Audit Manual, creator of the 'Warpspeed Learning Systems', fndr of the 'Juji-Kiri Success Achievement System', author and fndr of The Wealth Coach systems and publications, creator of the 'Rainmaker Masterclass'; *Recreations* computers, reading, shooting, martial arts, grand master of 'The Knowledge' (onibujindo, onibujitsu), applied psychology, success achievement methodologies, wealth coaching, business development; *Style*— J P Williamson, Esq; ✉ c/o The Wealth Coach, PO Box 56, Eltham, London SE9 1PA (tel 020 8850 4195, e-mail john@thewealthcoach.org)

WILLIAMSON, Sir (George) Malcolm; kt (2007); s of George Williamson (d 1969), and Margery Williamson; *b* 27 February 1939; *Educ* Bolton Sch; *m* Hang Thi Ngo; 1 s, 1 da; 1s and 1 da by previous marriage; *Career* Barclays Bank plc: local dir 1980, asst gen mangr 1981, regnl gen mangr 1983–85; memb PO Bd and md Girobank plc 1985–89, gp exec dir Standard Chartered plc 1989–91, md Standard Chartered Bank 1991–93, gp chief exec Standard Chartered plc 1993–98, pres and ceo Visa International 1998–2004; chm: CDC Gp plc 2004–, Signet Gp plc 2006–, National Australia Gp Europe Ltd; non-exec memb Gp Bd Nat Bank of Australia; non-exec dir: National Grid Gp plc 1995–99, Resolution plc (formerly Britannic Gp plc) 2002– (chm 2004–05, dep chm 2005–), Securicor plc 2004–, JPMorgan Cazenove Holdings 2005–; UK chm Br Thai Business Gp 1997–; chm Youth Business Int Advsy Bd 2005–; FCIB, CIMgt; *Recreations* mountaineering, running, chess; *Clubs* Rucksack, Manchester Pedestrian; *Style*— Sir Malcolm Williamson

WILLIAMSON, Malcolm Benjamin Graham Christopher; Hon AO (1987), CBE (1976); s of Rev George Williamson, of Sydney, and Bessie, *née* Wrigley; *b* 1931; *Educ* Barker Coll Hornsby NSW, Sydney Conservatorium of Music; *m* 9 Jan 1960, Dolores Irene Daniel; 1 s, 2 da; *Career* composer, pianist and organist; Master of The Queen's Music 1975–; performed in numerous countries incl: Africa, Australia, Asia, Canada, Denmark, Finland, France, Scandinavia, UK, USA, USSR, Yugoslavia; asst organist Farm St London, organist St Peter's Limehouse London 1958–60, lectr in music Central Sch of Speech and Drama London 1961–62, composer in residence Westminster Choir Coll Princeton NJ 1970–71 (hon fell 1971), composer in residence Florida State Univ 1975, visiting prof of music Univ of Strathclyde 1983–86; creative arts fell Australian Nat Univ 1974–81, Ramasciotti Medical Research Fellowship Univ of NSW 1981; pres: Beauchamp Sinfonietta 1972–, Birmingham Chamber Music Soc 1975–, Univ of London Choir 1976–, Purbeck Festival of Music 1976–, Royal Philharmonic Orchestra (London) 1977–82, Sing for Pleasure 1977–, Br Soc for Music Therapy 1977–, Stevenage Music Soc 1987–, Ditchling Choral Soc 1989–, Finchley Children's Music Group 1991–; vice-pres: The Elgar Fndn, St Michael's Singers, Nat Music Cncl of GB, Nat Youth Orch of GB; also involved with: London Adventist Chorale, Primavera Chamber Orch and Ensemble, Michael James Music Tst, Friends of Gaudeamus, Richmond upon Thames Arts Cncl, Cncl of the Friends of The Musicians' Chapel, London Charity Concert Orch, Temple Music Tst, Australian Sinfonia, Macclesfield Arts Festival, Saffron Walden Choral Soc, N Herts Hospice Care Assoc, Westminster Catholic Choristers Tst, Harlow Chorus, Hatfield Philharmonic Chorus, NE London Poly Chorus; Hon DMus: Westminster Choir Coll Princeton 1970, Univ of Melbourne 1982, Univ of Sydney 1982; Hon DUniv Open Univ 1983; *Operatic works* grand operas: Our Man in Havana (also orchestral suite and concert suite for chorus and orch), The Violins of Saint-Jacques, Lucky Peter's Journey; chamber operas: English Eccentrics, The Happy Prince, Julius Caesar Jones, Dunstan and the Devil, The Growing Castle, The Red Sea, The Death of Cuchulain, The Musicians of Bremen; operatic sequence: The Brilliant and the Dark; choral operas and cassations: The Moonrakers, Knights in Shining Armour, The Snow Wolf, Genesis, The Stone Wall, The Winter Star, The Glitter Gang, The Terrain of the Kings, The Valley and the Hill, The Devil's Bridge; ballets: Sinfonia Concertante, The Display, Sun into Darkness, Spectrum, BigfellaTootsquoodgeandNora (sic) (to Pas de Quatre), Perisynthion, Heritage, Have Steps Will Travel (to Piano Concerto no 3); *Orchestral works* incl: Santiago de Espada, Sinfonia Concertante, Sinfonietta, Concerto Grosso, Symphonic Variations, Serenade and Aubade, Epitaphs for Edith Sitwell, The Bridge that Van Gogh Painted, The House of Windsor Orchestral Suite, Fiesta, Ochre, Fanfarade, Ode for Queen Elizabeth, In Thanksgiving - Sir Bernard Heinze, Cortège for a Warrior, Lento for Stings, Bicentennial Anthem, seven symphonies; concertos: three piano concertos, Concerto for Two Pianos and Strings, Organ Concerto, Violin Concerto, Lament in Memory of Lord Mountbatten of Burma, Au Tombeau du Martyr Juif Inconnu; *Chamber music* incl: Variations for Violoncello and Piano, Concerto for Wind Quartet and Two Pianos, Serenade for Flute, Piano and String Trio, Pas de Quatre for Piano and Woodwind Quartet, Pietà, The Feast of Eurydice, Champion Family Album, Channukkah Sketches for Flute and Guitar; *Scores and title music* film scores incl: The Brides of Dracula, Thunder in Heaven, Crescendo, The Horror of Frankenstein, Nothing but the Night, Watership Down (title music and prologue), The Masks of Death, various documentaries; for TV and radio: The Golden Salamander, Bald Twit Lion, Strange Excellency, Choice, Gallery, Chi Ming, Churchill's People, The House of Windsor; musicals: No Bed for Bacon, Trilby; *Choral and vocal works* various works for solo voice and piano and solo voice and orchestra, numerous hymns and psalms, numerous choral works; *Solo piano works* incl: two piano sonatas, seven books of travel diaries, five preludes, Ritual of Admiration, Himna Titu, Springtime on the River Moskva for Piano Duet; *Recreations* literature; *Style*— Malcolm Williamson, Esq, AO, CBE; ✉ c/o Campion Press, Sandon, Buntingford, Hertfordshire SG9 0QW (tel 01763 247287, fax 01763 249984)

WILLIAMSON, Prof Mark Herbert; OBE (1994); s of Herbert Stansfield Williamson (d 1955), and Winifred Lilian, *née* Kenyon (d 1990); *b* 8 June 1928; *Educ* Groton Sch Mass USA, Rugby, ChCh Oxford (DPhil); *m* 5 April 1958, Charlotte Clara Dallas, OBE (1997), da of Hugh Macdonald (d 1958); 1 s (Hugh b 1961), 2 da (Emma b 1963, Sophia b 1965); *Career* demonstrator in zoology Univ of Oxford 1952–58, with Scottish Marine Biological Assoc Edinburgh 1958–62, lectr in zoology Univ of Edinburgh 1962–65, prof (fndr and head of Dept) Dept of Biology Univ of York 1965–; FIBiol 1966; *Books* Analysis of Biological Populations (1972), Ecological Stability (1974), Island Populations (1981), Quantitative Aspects of Biological Invasions (1987), Biological Invasions (1996); *Recreations* natural history, walking; *Style*— Prof Mark Williamson; ✉ Dalby Old Rectory, Terrington, York YO60 6PF (tel 01347 888244); Department of Biology, University of York, York YO10 5DD (tel 01904 328618, fax 01904 328505, e-mail mw1@york.ac.uk)

WILLIAMSON, Neil Morton; s of John Glynn Williamson (d 1987), and Vera May, *née* Morton (d 2002); *b* 14 May 1943; *Educ* Tonbridge, Worcester Coll Oxford (MA); *Career* Henry Ansbacher & Co Ltd 1965–78 (dir 1972–78), 3i Corporate Finance Ltd 1978–99 (md 1979–99); Freeman City of London 1970, memb Ct of Assts Worshipful Co of Skinners (Liveryman 1972); *Recreations* golf, opera, ballet; *Clubs* East India, Tanglin (Singapore), Royal and Ancient Golf (St Andrews), Royal St George's Golf, Rye Golf, Walton Health Golf; *Style*— Neil Williamson, Esq; ✉ 6 Crescent Grove, London SW4 7AH (tel 020 7720 6928), e-mail nmwill@neilwilliamson.co.uk)

WILLIAMSON, Nigel; s of Neville Albert Williamson, decd, and Ann Maureen Kitson; *b* 4 July 1954; *Educ* Chislehurst and Sidcup GS, UCL; *m* 1976, Dr Magali Patricia; 2 s (Adam b 1977, Piers b 1978); *Career* ed: Tribune 1984–87, Labour Party News 1987–89, New Socialist 1987–89; The Times: political corr and columnist 1989–90, diary ed 1990–92, home news ed 1992–95, Whitehall corr 1995–96; contrib ed: Uncut, Songlines; freelance music writer for other pubns incl The Times and The Guardian 1996–; *Books* The SDP (1982), The New Right (1984), The Rough Guide to World Music (1999, contrib), Journey Through the Past: The Stories Behind the Songs of Neil Young (2002), The Uncut Collector's Guide to Bob Dylan (ed, 2003), The Rough Guide to Bob Dylan (2004), Rough Guide to the Blues (2006), Rough Guide to Led Zeppelin (2007); *Recreations* cricket, music, gardening, modern fiction; *Style*— Nigel Williamson, Esq; ✉ Long Tilings, Hever Lane, Hever, Kent TN8 7ET (tel 01959 571127, e-mail nigelwilliamson@compuserve.com)

WILLIAMSON, Dr Paul; s of Peter Williamson (d 2003), of London, and Mary Teresa, *née* Meagher (d 2005); *b* 4 August 1954; *Educ* Wimbledon Coll, UEA (BA, MPhil, LittD); *m* 11 Aug 1984, Emmeline Mary Clare, da of James Mandley (d 1983); 1 s (Joseph James b 29 Nov 1999); *Career* V&A: asst keeper Dept of Sculpture 1979–89, acting keeper Dept of Sculpture 1989, chief curator Sculpture Collection 1989–2001, sr curator 1995–98, keeper of sculpture, metalwork, ceramics and glass 2001–, dir of collections 2004–; memb: Wells Cathedral West Front Specialist Ctee 1981–83, Wall Paintings Sub-Ctee Cncl for the Care of Churches 1987–90, Ctee Br Acad Corpus of Romanesque Sculpture in Br and Ireland 1990–97, Lincoln Cathedral Fabric Cncl 1990–2001, Bd of Tstees Stained Glass Muesum Ely 2005–; memb Exhbn Organising Ctee: English Romanesque Art 1984, Age of Chivalry 1987, Gothic: Art for England 2003; expert advsr on sculpture Reviewing Ctee on the Export of Works of Art 1989–, foreign advsr to Int Center of Medieval Art 1991–94; memb Consultative Ctee: The Sculpture Jl 1997–, The Burlington Magazine 2003–; Lansdowne visiting prof Univ of Victoria BC 2001, Diskant lectr Philadelphia

Museum of Art 2001; Guild Freeman of Preston 1972; FSA 1983 (memb Cncl 1997–2003, vice-pres 1999–2003); *Books* An Introduction to Medieval Ivory Carvings (1982), Catalogue of Romanesque Sculpture in the Victoria and Albert Museum (1983), The Medieval Treasury: The Art of the Middle Ages in the Victoria and Albert Museum (ed, 1986, 3 edn 1998), The Thyssen-Bornemisza Collection: Medieval sculpture and works of art (1987), Northern Gothic Sculpture 1200–1450 (1988), Early Medieval Wall Painting and Painted Sculpture in England (ed with S Cather and D Park, 1990), Gothic Sculpture 1140–1300 (1995), European Sculpture at the Victoria and Albert Museum (ed, 1996), Netherlandish Sculpture 1450–1550 (2002), Wonder: Painted Sculpture from Medieval England (ed with S Boldrick and D Park, 2002), Medieval and Renaissance Stained Glass in the Victoria and Albert Museum (2003), Gothic: Art for England 1400–1547 (ed with R Marks, 2003), Medieval and Renaissance Treasures from the V&A (ed, 2007); author of numerous articles and book reviews in The Burlington Magazine and others; *Recreations* wine, travel; *Style*— Dr Paul Williamson, FSA; ✉ Victoria and Albert Museum, South Kensington, London SW7 2RL (tel 020 7942 2611, fax 020 7942 2616, e-mail p.williamson@vam.ac.uk)

WILLIAMSON, Philip Nigel; s of Leonard James Williamson, and Doris, *née* Chapell; *b* 23 September 1948; *Educ* Mill Hill Sch, Univ of Newcastle upon Tyne (BA, BArch); *m* 27 May 1983, Victoria Lois, da of Joseph Samuel Brown, of Clwyd, N Wales; 2 s (Nicholas James b 1984, Christopher Patrick b 1988); *Career* architect; chm and md: PNW Design Ltd (architects and interior designers) 1985–, PNW Properties Ltd 1985–; RIBA; *Recreations* sailing, tennis, winter sports; *Clubs* Queen's, Royal Lymington Yacht; *Style*— Philip Williamson, Esq; ✉ Lower Pennington Farmhouse, Lower Pennington Lane, Lymington, Hampshire SO41 8AL (tel 01590 672699); 243–253 Lower Mortlake Road, Richmond, Surrey TW9 2LL (tel 020 8948 9556)

WILLIAMSON, Raymond MacLeod; s of James Carstair Williamson (d 1974), and Marion, *née* Campbell (d 1998); *b* 24 December 1942, Glasgow; *Educ* HS of Glasgow, Univ of Glasgow (MA, LLB); *m* 4 April 1977, Brenda, da of Frederick Hamilton; 1 da (Dr Rachel MacLeod Williamson b 27 March 1979), 1 s (Donald Kerr Williamson b 19 Sept 1981); *Career* admitted slr 1968; MacRoberts: apprentice slr 1966–68, slr 1968–71, ptnr 1971–2006, sr ptnr 2000–06; pt/t chm Employment Tbnl 2003–; memb Ctee European Employment Lawyers Assoc 1998–2007; ret; memb Law Soc of Scotland (memb Cncl 1990–96, convenor Employment Law Ctee 1990–2006); dean Royal Faculty of Procurators in Glasgow 2001–04; chm Scottish Int Piano Competition, chm Nat Youth Choir of Scotland, former chm Royal Scottish Nat Orch, former vice-chm RSAMD; govr and vice-chm HS of Glasgow; Freeman City of Glasgow, memb Incorporation of Gardiners, dir Merchants House of Glasgow; FRSAMD; *Recreations* music, gardening; *Clubs* Glasgow Art, Western (Glasgow); *Style*— Raymond M Williamson, Esq; ✉ 11 Islay Drive, Newton Mearns, Glasgow G77 6UD (tel 0141 639 4133)

WILLIAMSON, Prof Robin Charles Noel; s of James Charles Frederick Lloyd Williamson (d 1970), of Hove, E Sussex, and Helena Frances, *née* Madden (d 1984); *b* 19 December 1942; *Educ* Rugby, Univ of Cambridge and Bart's Med Sch (BA, BChir, MA, MB MChir, MD); *m* 21 Oct 1967, Judith Marjorie, da of Douglas John Bull (d 1982), of London; 3 s (Richard b 1968, Edward b 1970, James b 1977); *Career* house surgn Bart's 1968, surgical registrar Royal Berks Hosp Reading 1971–73, sr surgical registrar Bristol Royal Infirmary 1973–75, clinical and res fell surgery Mass Gen Hosp and Harvard Med Sch 1975–76; Univ of Bristol: lectr in surgery 1977, conslt sr lectr in surgery 1977–79, prof of surgery 1979–87; prof of surgery and conslt surgeon Hammersmith Hosp and Imperial Coll Sch of Med at Hammersmith Hosp (Royal Postgraduate Sch of Med until merger 1997) 1987– (dir of surgery 1987–95); emeritus dean and pres elect RSM (assoc dean 2001–02, dean 2002–06); visiting prof of surgery: Perth 1983, South Africa 1985, Boston 1985, Lund 1985, Melbourne 1986, Hong Kong 1987, San Francisco 1989, Brisbane 1989, Singapore 1994, Hamburg 1999; sec gen World Assoc of Hepatopancreatobiliary Surgery 1990–94 (treas 1986–90); pres: Pancreatic Soc of GB and I 1984–85, Int Hepatopancreatobiliary Assoc 1996–98 (sec-gen 1994–96), Assoc of Upper Gastrointestinal Surgns 1996–98, Assoc of Surgns of GB and I 1998–99 (chm Scientific Ctee 1994–97), European Soc of Surgery 1998, James IV Assoc Surgery 2002–05; co-sec Br Jl of Surgery Soc 1983–91, sr ed Br Jl of Surgery 1991–96, ed HPB 1999–2003; Hallett prize RCS 1970, Arris and Gale lectr RCS 1977–78, Moynihan fell Assoc of Surgns of GB and I 1979, Hunterian prof RCS 1981–82, Res Medal Br Soc of Gastroenterology 1982, Finlayson lectr RCS Glasgow 1985, Sir Gordon Bell lectr RACS (NZ) 1988, Bengt Ihre Medal Swedish Soc of Gastroenterology 1998, Hon PhD Mahidol Univ Thailand 1994; hon fell Royal Coll of Surgns of Thailand 1992; FRCS 1972; *Books* Colonic Carcinogenesis (jtly, 1982), General Surgical Operations (jtly, 1987), Emergency Abdominal Surgery (jtly, 1990), Surgical Management (jtly, 1991), Gastrointestinal Emergencies (jtly, 1991), Scott: An Aid to Clinical Surgery (jtly, 1994, 6 edn 1998), Upper Digestive Surgery: Oesophagus, Stomach and Small Intenstine (jtly, 1999), Surgery (jtly, 2001); *Recreations* travel, lighthouses, military uniforms and history; *Clubs* Oxford and Cambridge; *Style*— Prof Robin Williamson; ✉ The Barn, 88 Lower Road, Gerrards Cross, Buckinghamshire SL9 8LB (tel 01753 889816); Department of Surgery, Imperial College School of Medicine, Hammersmith Hospital, Du Cane Road, London W12 0NN (tel 020 8383 3941, fax 020 8383 3023, e-mail r.williamson@imperial.ac.uk)

WILLIAMSON, Shaun; s of George Williamson, and Irene, *née* Tugwell; *b* 29 November 1964, Maidstone, Kent; *Educ* St Simon Stock Sch Maidstone, Webber Douglas Acad of Dramatic Art (Dip); *m* 8 Oct 1997, Melanie Sacre; 1 da (Sophie Mae b 17 March 1998), 1 s (Joseph Clifford b 29 Dec 2000); *Career* actor, cabaret artist, singer and after dinner speaker; postman PO 1981–84, served RN 1984–85, bluecoat Pontins IOW 1986, cnsllr and entertainer Camp Summit PA 1987 and 1989, with Safeway plc 1987–92 (also pt/t while at drama sch 1991–94), holiday rep Club 18–30 Tenerife 1988, actor 1989–; *Theatre* Monty in Saturday Night Fever (West End) 2004–05, Nathan Detroit in Guys & Dolls (tour), The Narrator in The Rocky Horror Show (tour); *Television* incl: Barry Evans in Eastenders 1994–2004, Extras 2005–07; other appearances incl: Celebrity Mastermind (winner 2004), Celebrity Stars in their Eyes (winner 2004), Secret Policeman's Ball; *Film* Daylight Robbery; *Recreations* quizzes, working out, walking, reading, watching boxing, walking labrador, singing; *Style*— Shaun Williamson, Esq; ✉ c/o Funky Beetroot Celebrity Management, PO Box 143, Faversham, Kent ME13 9LP (tel 01227 751459, fax 01227 752300, e-mail info@funky-beetroot.com, website www.shaun-williamson.com)

WILLIAMSON, Prof Stephen; s of Donald Williamson (d 1986), and Patricia Kathleen Mary, *née* Leyland (d 1997); *b* 15 December 1948; *Educ* Burnage GS Manchester, Imperial Coll of Science and Technol London (scholar, BSc, PhD, DSc, Sylvanus P Thompson prize); *m* 19 Dec 1970, Zita, da of Philip Mellor (d 1975); 1 s (Samuel Thurston b 1975), 2 da (Rebecca Anne b 1977, Lucy Frances b 1981); *Career* lectr in engrg Univ of Aberdeen 1973–81, reader in engrg Imperial Coll London 1985–89 (sr lectr 1981–85), prof of engrg Univ of Cambridge 1989–97, fell St John's Coll Cambridge 1990–97, tech dir Brook Hansen 1997–2000, prof of electrical engrg UMIST (now Univ of Manchester) 2000– (head of dept 2002–); FIEE 1988, FCGI 1990, FIEEE 1995, FREng 1995; *Recreations* gardening, reading; *Style*— Prof Stephen Williamson, FREng; ✉ School of Electrical and Electronic Engineering, University of Manchester, PO Box 88, Manchester M60 1QD (tel 0161 200 4683, fax 01484 429726, e-mail steve.williamson@manchester.ac.uk)

WILLIAMSON, Prof Timothy; s of Colin Fletcher Williamson (d 1983), and Karina, *née* Side (now Mrs Angus McIntosh); *b* 6 August 1955; *Educ* Leighton Park Sch Reading, Henley GS, Balliol Coll Oxford (Henry Wilde Prize, BA), ChCh Oxford (sr scholar, MA, DPhil); *m* 1, 24 March 1984 (m dis 2003), Elisabetta, da of Silvio Perosino; 1 da (Alice b 14 June 1993), 1 s (Conrad b 9 Sept 1996); m 2, 14 Feb 2004, Ana, da of Milan Mladenović; 1 s (Arno Nathan b 14 Jan 2005); *Career* lectr in philosophy Trinity Coll Dublin (MA ad eundem gradum) 1980–88, CUF lectr in philosophy Univ of Oxford and fell and praelector in philosophy UC Oxford 1988–94, prof of logic and metaphysics Univ of Edinburgh 1995–2000, Wykeham prof of logic Univ of Oxford 2000, fell New Coll Oxford 2000; visiting fell Dept of Philosophy Australian Nat Univ 1990 and 1995; visiting prof: Dept of Linguistics and Philosophy MIT 1994, Dept of Philosophy Princeton Univ 1998–99; Erskine visiting fell Dept of Philosophy and Religious Studies Univ of Canterbury NZ 1995, Nelson distinguished prof Univ of Michigan 2003, Townsend visitor Univ of California Berkeley 2006, Tang Chun-I visiting prof Chinese Univ of Hong Kong 2007; pres Mind Assoc 2006–07; memb: Aristotelian Soc 1986 (pres 2004–05), American Philosophical Assoc 1998; foreign memb Norwegian Acad of Science and Letters 2004, foreign hon memb American Acad of Arts and Sciences 2007; FRSE 1997, FBA 1997; *Books* Identity and Discrimination (1990), Vagueness (1994), Knowledge and its Limits (2000), The Philosophy of Philosophy (2007); *Recreations* conventional behaviour; *Style*— Prof Timothy Williamson, FRSE, FBA; ✉ New College, Oxford OX1 3BN (tel 01865 279555, fax 01865 279590, e-mail timothy.williamson@philosophy.ox.ac.uk)

WILLIAMSON OF HORTON, Baron (Life Peer UK 1999), of Horton in the County of Somerset; Sir David Francis; GCMG (1998), CB (1984), PC (2007); s of late Samuel Charles Wathen Williamson, of Bath, and late Marie Eileen Williamson; *b* 8 May 1934; *Educ* Tonbridge, Exeter Coll Oxford (MA); *m* 1961, Patricia Margaret, da of Eric Cade Smith, of Broadclyst, Devon; 2 s; *Career* civil servant; MAFF 1958–65 and 1967–77, seconded to HM Dip Serv for Kennedy Round Trade Negotiations 1965–67, dep DG Agric European Cmmn Brussels 1977–83, dep sec Cabinet Office 1983–87, sec-gen Euro Cmmn Brussels 1987–97; non-exec dir Whitbread plc 1998–2005; visiting prof Univ of Bath 1997–2001; tstee Thomson Fndn 2000–05; chm Somerset Strategic Partnership 2001–04; convenor of the Cross Bench Peers House of Lords 2004–; Hon DCL: Univ of Kent, Univ of Bath, Robert Gordon Univ; Hon DEconSc Limerick; Knight Commander's Cross of the Order of Merit of the Federal Republic of Germany 1991, Commander Grand Cross of the Royal Order of the Polar Star (Sweden) 1998, Commandeur Légion d'Honneur 1999; *Style*— The Rt Hon Lord Williamson of Horton, GCMG, CB, PC; ✉ House of Lords, London SW1A 0PW

WILLINK, Sir Charles William; 2 Bt (UK 1957), of Dingle Bank, City of Liverpool; s of Rt Hon Sir Henry Urmston Willink, 1 Bt, MC, QC (d 1973, ggs of Daniel Willink, sometime Dutch consul in Liverpool), and his 1 w, Cynthia Frances (d 1959), da of Herbert Morley Fletcher, MD, FRCP, of London; *b* 10 September 1929; *Educ* Eton, Trinity Coll Cambridge (MA, PhD); *m* 7 Aug 1954, Elizabeth, er da of Humfrey Andrewes, of London; 1 s, 1 da; *Heir* s, Edward Willink; *Career* asst master: Marlborough Coll 1952–54, Eton Coll 1954–85 (housemaster 1964–77); *Books* Euripides' Orestes (ed with commentary, 1986); *Recreations* bridge, field botany, music (bassoon); *Style*— Sir Charles Willink, Bt; ✉ 22 North Grove, Highgate, London N6 4SL (tel 020 8340 3996)

WILLIS, Alan James; CBE (1992); s of William Ross Willis (d 1995), of Dunblane, Scotland, and Georgina Agnes, *née* Cheape (d 1976); *b* 19 November 1936; *Educ* Daniel Stewart's Coll Edinburgh, Sch of Architecture Edinburgh Coll of Art (Andrew Grant scholarship, DipArch); *m* 25 March 1967, June, da of George Victor Cook Creasey; 3 s (James Richard b 4 Aug 1970, Andrew Charles b 3 April 1972, Peter Robert b 2 Aug 1973), 1 da (Emma Sophie b 20 July 1977); *Career* architect; with Sir Frank Mears & Partners 1953–56, Architect Res Unit Univ of Edinburgh 1960–63, directing architect Notts Co Architects' Dept 1963–73; county architect: Durham CC 1973–76, Essex CC 1976–90; dir of property servs Essex CC 1990–96; hon treas RIBA 1993–95; winner various Civic Tst and RIBA design awards and commendations 1968–93; tstee Eastern Counties Educnl Tst, memb Devpt Ctee Univ of Essex; RIBA 1960; *Recreations* watercolour painting, sailing, vintage cars, golf; *Clubs* Arts, MCC, Braintree Golf; *Style*— Alan Willis, Esq, CBE; ✉ Waterside, East Street, Coggeshall, Colchester, Essex CO6 1SJ (tel 01376 561677, fax 01376 563720, e-mail alanandjunewillis@tiscali.co.uk)

WILLIS, Antony Martin Derek; s of late Thomas Martin Willis, and Dawn Marie, *née* Christensen; *b* 29 November 1941; *Educ* Wanganui Collegiate Sch Wanganui NZ, Victoria Univ Wellington NZ (LLB); *m* 1, 10 Feb 1962 (m dis), Diane Elizabeth, da of late Frederick Willis Gorton (d 1987); 3 da (Kirsty Elizabeth b 13 April 1963, Sara Jane b 7 June 1966, Nicola Mary b 6 Nov 1968); m 2, 12 April 1975, Diana Alice Cockburn, da of Robert Dermot McMahon Williams, of Redhill, Surrey; 1 s (Matthew William Dermot b 22 Aug 1988), 2 da (Charlotte Emily Christensen b 5 Jan 1978, Joanna Catherine Dalrymple b 7 Dec 1981); *Career* slr, later barr and mediator; Perry Wylie Pope & Page NZ 1967–70, Coward Chance London 1970–87 (managing ptnr 1987); Clifford Chance (merged firm of Coward Chance with Clifford Turner): jt managing ptnr 1987–88, sr litigation ptnr 1989–96; ind mediator 1998–; called to the Bar Middle Temple 2004, practising barr and mediator 2004–; fndr chm Slrs' Pro Bono Gp 1997; chm Cncl Wycombe Abbey Sch 1999–; memb: City of London Slrs' Co, American Arbitration Assoc, Wellington Dist Law Soc (NZ); accredited mediator Centre for Dispute Resolution; fndr memb Panel of Ind Mediators; memb: CPR Inst for Dispute Resolution NY, Int Panel of Distinguished Mediators; Freeman City of London 1975, Liveryman Worshipful Co of Slrs; fell Int Acad of Mediators (US); FCIArb; *Recreations* books, music; *Clubs* Reform, Wellington; *Style*— Antony Willis, Esq; ✉ Brick Court Chambers, 7–8 Essex Street, London WC2R 3LD (tel 020 7379 3550, fax 020 7379 3558, e-mail tony.willis@brickcourt.co.uk)

WILLIS, David; s of William Willis (d 1986), of Consett, Co Durham, and Rachael Elizabeth, *née* Cant; *b* 13 January 1949; *Educ* Consett GS, Univ of Edinburgh (BArch); *Family* 1 da (Jennifer b 1978), 2 s (Robert b 1984, Steven b 1988); *Career* architect; ptnr Crichton Lang Willis & Galloway; projects incl: New Lanark Restoration 1974– (RICS/The Times Conservation Award, Europa Nostra Medal of Honour 1988), Old Coll Univ of Edinburgh 1974–87; architect Thirlestane Castle Tst 1987–; RIBA, FRIAS; *Recreations* racehorse owner; *Style*— David Willis, Esq; ✉ Crichton Lang Willis & Galloway, 38 Dean Park Mews, Edinburgh EH4 1ED (tel 0131 315 2940, fax 0131 332 0224, e-mail clwg@btinternet.com)

WILLIS, John Edward; s of Baron Willis (Life Peer; d 1992), and Audrey Mary, *née* Hale; does not use courtesy style of Hon; *Educ* Eltham Coll, Fitzwilliam Coll Cambridge (MA), Univ of Bristol (Postgrad Cert in Radio, Film and TV); *m* 1972, Janet, da of Kenneth Sperrin; 1 s (Thomas b 1975), 1 da (Beth b 1978); *Career* researcher ATV Network Ltd 1969–70; Yorkshire Television: researcher 1970–74, prodr/dir 1975–82, controller of documentaries and current affrs and ed First Tuesday 1983–88; Channel Four Television: controller of factual progs 1988–89, dep dir of progs 1990–92, dir of progs 1993–97; md United Film & Television Productions (UFTP) 1997–2001, md LWT 2001–02, vice-pres Nat Programmes WGBH Boston 2002–03, dir BBC Factual and Learning 2003–06 (memb BBC Creative Bd 2004–06), chief exec and creative dir Tinopolis 2006–; memb Bd Channel 5 1997–2001; visiting prof Univ of Bristol 1998–; memb BAFTA, FRTS 1993; *Awards* incl: BAFTA Best Documentary, Prix Jeunesse and RTS Outstanding Achievement as a Dir Awards for Johnny Go Home 1976, Int Emmy, RTS Best Investigative Journalism and Matthew Trust Award for The Secret Hospital 1979, Prix Futura and Broadcasting Critics' Prize for Alice: A Fight for Life 1983, Special Jury Award San Francisco for The Chinese Geordie 1983, 12 int environmental awards for Windscale: The Nuclear Laundry (co-dir) 1983, John Grierson Best Documentary Award for From the Cradle to the Grave 1987, RTS Silver Medal 1988, Cyril Bennett Award for Creative Contrib to TV RTS 2001; *Books* Johnny Go Home (1975), Churchill's Few (1983); *Style—* John Willis, Esq

WILLIS, Prof John Raymond; s of John Vindon George Willis, of Bicester, Oxon, and Loveday Gwendoline, *née* Parkin; *b* 27 March 1940; *Educ* Southall GS, Imperial Coll London (BSc, ARCS, PhD, DIC), Univ of Cambridge (MA); *m* 3 Oct 1964, Juliette Louise, da of Horace Albert Edward Ireland (d 1979); 3 da (Estelle b 1966, Lucy b 1967, Charlotte b 1969); *Career* asst lectr Imperial Coll London 1962–64, res assoc Courant Inst NY 1964–65, asst dir of res Univ of Cambridge 1968–72 (sr asst 1965–67), prof of applied mathematics Univ of Bath 1972–94, prof of theoretical solid mechanics Univ of Cambridge 1994–2000, prof of mathematics Univ of Bath 2000–01, prof of theoretical solid mechanics Univ of Cambridge 2001–; ed-in-chief Jl of the Mechanics and Physics of Solids 1982–92 (jt ed 1992–2006); memb: SRC Mathematics Ctee 1975–78, SERC Mathematics Ctee 1984–87, Int Congress Ctee, Int Union for Theoretical and Applied Mechanics 1982–90); Timoshenko Medal American Soc of Mechanical Engineers 1997, Prager Medal Soc for Engineering Science 1998; foreign assoc US Nat Acad of Engrg 2004; FIMA 1966, FRS 1992; *Recreations* music, swimming; *Style—* Prof John Willis, FRS; ✉ Department of Applied Mathematics and Theoretical Physics, Centre for Mathematical Sciences, Wilberforce Road, Cambridge CB3 0WA (tel 01223 337890, fax 01223 765900)

WILLIS, (Adrian) Peter; s of William Stanley Willis, and Ruth Enid, *née* Tomlinson; *b* 25 December 1966; *Educ* Buxton Coll Derbys; *Career* reporter The Sun 1988–89, columnist Daily Star 1989–90; The Sun: reporter 1990–92, dep showbusiness ed 1992–94, ed TV features and news 1994–95, ed Superguide 1995–97; The Daily Mirror: ed The Look 1997–98, features ed 1998–99, asst features ed 1999–2002, assoc ed 2002–; commended Br Press Awards 2001, winner Newspaper Awards Colour Supplement of the Year 1999, 2000 and 2001; creator and prodr The Pride of Britain Awards 1999– (televised ITV 2000–); memb NUJ 1985–, life memb Newspaper Press Fund; *Publications* Paul McKenna's Hypnotic Secrets (1995); *Recreations* marathon running; *Clubs* Met Bar, Davys; *Style—* Peter Willis, Esq; ✉ The Daily Mirror, 1 Canada Square, Canary Wharf, London E14 5AP (tel 020 7293 3000, fax 020 7293 3834, e-mail p.willis@mgn.co.uk)

WILLIS, (George) Philip; MP; s of George Willis (d 1977), and Hannah Willis (d 1955); *b* 30 November 1941; *Educ* Burnley GS, City of Leeds Carnegie Coll (CertEd), Univ of Birmingham (BPhil); *m* 25 May 1974, Heather, *née* Sellars; 1 da (Rachel Helen b 14 June 1975), 1 s (Michael Paul b 1 Jan 1980); *Career* with Leeds LEA 1963–97, dep head teacher W Leeds Boys' HS 1973–77, head teacher Ormesby Sch Cleveland 1977–82, head teacher John Smeaton Community Sch 1983–97, MP (Lib Dem) Harrogate and Knaresborough 1997–; Lib Dem spokesman on further, higher and adult educn 1997–99; Lib Dem shadow min: for educn and employment 1999–2001, for educn and skills 2001–05; chair Science and Technol Select Ctee 2005–; ldr Harrogate BC 1990–97 (cncllr 1988–99), cncllr and dep ldr N Yorkshire CC 1993–97; memb SHA 1977–97; *Recreations* soccer (Leeds United); *Style—* Philip Willis, Esq, MP; ✉ House of Commons, London SW1A 0AA (tel 020 7219 5709, fax 020 7219 0971, e-mail willisp@parliament.uk)

WILLIS, Very Rev Robert Andrew; s of Thomas Willis, of Kingswood, Bristol, and Vera Rosina, *née* Britton (d 1985); *b* 17 May 1947; *Educ* Kingswood GS, Univ of Warwick (BA), Worcester Coll Oxford (DipTh), Cuddesdon Theol Coll; *Career* ordained: deacon 1972, priest 1973; curate: St Chad's Shrewsbury 1972–75, vicar choral Salisbury Cathedral and chaplain to Cathedral Sch 1975–78, team rector Tisbury 1978–87, chaplain Cranborne Chase Sch and RAF Chilmark 1978–87, rural dean of Chalke 1982–87, vicar of Sherborne with Castleton and Lillington 1987–92, chaplain Sherborne Sch for Girls 1987–92, canon and prebendary of Salisbury Cathedral 1988–92, rural dean of Sherborne 1991–92, dean of Hereford 1992–2001, dean of Canterbury 2001–; proctor in convocation 1985–92 and 1994–; chm Deans' and Provosts' Conf 1999–2002, chm Deans' Conf 2002–; memb: Cncl Partnership for World Mission 1990–2001, C of E Liturgical Cmmn 1994–98, Cathedral Fabric Cmmn for England 1994–2006; memb Cncl Univ of Kent 2003–; govr: Cranborne Chase Sch 1985–87, Sherborne Sch 1987–92; chm of govrs: Hereford Cathedral Sch 1993–2001, King's Sch Canterbury 2001–; hon fell Canterbury Christ Church Univ 2004; sub dean Order of St John of Jerusalem 1999 (sub chaplain 1991); FRSA 1993, FGCM 2006; CStJ 2001; *Books* Hymns Ancient and Modern (contrib, 1983), The Choristers' Companion (jtly, 1989), Common Praise (contrib, 2000), New English Praise (contrib, 2006); *Recreations* music, literature, travel; *Clubs* Oxford and Cambridge; *Style—* The Very Rev Robert Willis; ✉ The Deanery, The Precincts, Canterbury CT1 2EP (tel 01227 762862, fax 01227 865222)

WILLIS, Robert George Dylan (Bob); MBE (1982); s of Edward Woodcock Willis (d 1982), and Anne Margaret, *née* Huntington (d 1997); *b* 30 May 1949; *Educ* King Edward VI Royal GS Guildford; *m* 1980, Juliet, da of William Smail, and Barbara Smail, of Glos; 1 da (Katie-Anne b 1984); *Career* former professional cricketer, currently broadcaster and journalist; capt: Warwickshire 1980–84, England 1982–84; 90 tests for England, record number of wickets for England on retirement (325); cricket commentator Sky Sports; *Books* co-author of nine cricket books; *Recreations* opera, classical music, wine, real ale; *Clubs* MCC, RAC, Surrey CCC, Warwickshire CCC, Melbourne CC, Royal Wimbledon Golf, CAMRA; *Style—* Bob Willis, Esq, MBE; ✉ 2 Capatus House, 73 Mortlake High Street, London SW14 8HL

WILLMAN, John Romain; s of John Sydney Willman (d 1993), and Millicent Charlotte, *née* Thornton (d 1999); *b* 27 May 1949; *Educ* Bolton Sch, Jesus Coll Cambridge (MA), Westminster Coll Oxford (CertEd); *m* 1 April 1978, Margaret, da of Dr John Shanahan (d 1981), of Maida Vale; 1 s (Michael b 1982), 2 da (Kate b 1984, Claire b 1987); *Career* asst teacher Brentford Sch for Girls Middx 1972–76, fin researcher Consumers' Assoc 1976–79, ed of Taxes and Assessment (jls of Inland Revenue Staff Fedn) 1979–83, pubns mangr Peat Marwick Mitchell & Co 1983–85, gen sec Fabian Soc 1985–89, freelance writer and journalist, ed Consumer Policy Review 1990–91; Financial Times: public policy ed 1991–94, features ed 1994–97, consumer industries ed 1997–2000, banking ed 2000–01, chief ldr writer and assoc ed 2002–06, UK business ed 2006–; Medical Journalism Financing Healthcare Prize 1998, Business Journalist of the Year 2001, Best Banking Submission Business Journalism Awards 2002; visiting research fell Social Market Fndn 1997; assoc IPPR 1990–91; *Books* Make Your Will (1989), Labour's Electoral Challenge (1989), Sorting out Someone's Will (1990), Which? Guide to Planning and Conservation (1990), Work for Yourself (1991), Labour and the Public Services (1994), Lloyds TSB Tax Guide (14 edn, 2000), A Better State of Health (1998); *Recreations* walking, theatre, opera; *Clubs* Wessex Cave, Inst of Contemporary Art; *Style—* John Willman, Esq; ✉ Financial Times, 1 Southwark Bridge, London SE1 9HL (tel 020 7873 3854, fax 020 7873 3085, e-mail john.willman@ft.com)

WILLMAN, Prof Paul; *Educ* St Catharine's Coll Cambridge (MA), Trinity Coll Oxford (DPhil, MA); *Career* res offr Nat Union of Bank Employees 1977–78; Imperial Coll London: lectr in industrial rels 1978–83 (tenure 1981); London Business Sch: lectr 1984–88, assoc prof 1988–91, prof of organisational behaviour and industrial rels 1991–2000, govr 1996–99; Univ of Oxford: Sir Norman Chester sr res fell Nuffield Coll 1989, fell Balliol Coll 2000–06, prof Saïd Business Sch 2000–06, ed-in-chief Human Relations 2001–06; prof of mgmnt LSE 2006–; memb Editorial Bd: CUP Mgmnt Studies 1985–95, Business Strategy Review 1990–92 and 1996–2000, Br Jl of Industrial Rels 1994–98; memb ACAS Arbitration Panel 1988–; memb: Industrial Rels Res Assoc, Int Industrial Rels Res Assoc, Br Univs Industrial Rels Assoc, Euro Gp for Organisational Studies, Soc for the Advancement of Socio-Economics, Acad of Mgmnt; *Publications* Fairness, Collective Bargaining and Incomes Policy (1982), Power, Efficiency and Institutions: A Critical Appraisal of the Markets and Hierarchies Paradigm (jt ed, 1983), Innovation and Management Control: Labour Relations at BL Cars (jtly, 1985), The Car Industry: Labour Relations and Industrial Adjustment (jtly, 1985), Technological Change, Collective Bargaining and Industrial Efficiency (1986), The Limits to Self Regulation: Ten Years of the Health and Safety at Work Act (jtly, 1988), Union Business: Trade Union Organisation and Financial Reform in the Thatcher Years (jtly, 1993), Traders: Risks, Decisions and Management in Financial Market (2004); numerous articles in learned jls, contributions to edited collections and published cases; *Style—* Prof Paul Willman; ✉ London School of Economics and Political Sciences, Houghton Street, London WC2A 2AE (tel 020 7955 6739, e-mail p.willman@lse.ac.uk)

WILLMORE, Prof (Albert) Peter; s of Albert Mervyn Willmore (d 1957), and Kathleen Helen, *née* O'Rourke (d 1987); *b* 28 April 1930; *Educ* Holloway Sch London, UCL (BSc, PhD); *m* 1, 1962 (m dis 1972), Geraldine Anne; 2 s (Nicholas b 1963, Andrew b 1964); m 2, 6 Aug 1972, Stephanie Ruth, da of Leonard Alden, of Surrey; 1 da (Lucy b 1973), 1 s (Ben b 1976); *Career* res fell, lectr, reader then prof of physics UCL 1957–72, prof of space res Univ of Birmingham 1972–; Tsiolkowsky Medal USSR 1987; FRAS 1960, memb Bd of Tstees Int Acad of Astronautics 1996; *Recreations* ancient history, music, sailing; *Style—* Prof Peter Willmore

WILLMOT, Prof Derrick Robert; s of Jack Willmot (d 1982), and Olive, *née* Yarnall (d 1986); *b* 29 April 1947; *Educ* Chesterfield Boys' GS, UCL and UCH London (BDS, LDS), Univ of Sheffield (PhD); *m* 9 Jan 1971, Patricia Marie, da of Robert Creighton (d 1998), of San Luis, Menorca, Spain; 2 s (Mark b 1973, Andrew b 1974); *Career* dental house surgn Royal Portsmouth Hosp 1970, gen dental practitioner Ashbourne Derbyshire 1971, sr registrar UCH 1979 (registrar 1977); conslt orthodontist: Chesterfield Royal Hosp 1984–92, Charles Clifford Dental Hosp Univ of Sheffield 1992–; clinical dir dental servs CSUHT 1995–2000; Univ of Sheffield: clinical dean Sch of Clinical Dentistry 2000–02, head Dept of Oral Growth and Devpt 2001–05; sec Conslt Orthodontists Gp 1989–94 (chm 2000–03), dental advsr Med Protection Soc 1992–, memb Bd Faculty of Dental Surgery RCS England 1994–97 and 2003–; vice-dean Faculty of Dental Surgery RCS England 2005–; chm SAC in Orthodontics and Paediatric Dentistry 1995–98; memb Round Table 1972–87: Ashbourne, St Albans, Chesterfield; chm NE Derbys Music Centre 1986–90, memb Chesterfield Scarsdale Rotary Club 1988– (pres 2001–02); vice-chm Bd of Govrs Chesterfield Sch 1988–92, pres S Yorks BDA 1992–93; FDS 1978, DDO 1980, MOrthRCS 1987; *Style—* Prof Derrick Willmot; ✉ Ashcroft, Matlock Road, Walton, Chesterfield, Derbyshire S42 7LD; Charles Clifford Dental Hospital, University of Sheffield, Sheffield S10 2SZ (tel 0114 271 7809, e-mail d.willmot@sheffield.ac.uk)

WILLMOTT, Rt Rev Trevor; *see:* Basingstoke, Bishop of

WILLOTT, Dr (William) Brian; CB (1996); *b* 14 May 1940; *Educ* Trinity Coll Cambridge (MA, PhD); *m* Alison; 2 s, 2 da; *Career* research assoc Univ of Maryland, various posts in the Bd of Trade and HM Treasy, chief exec Nat Enterprise Bd (subsequently Br Technol Gp) 1980–84, under-sec DTI 1984–92, chief exec ECGD 1992–97, chief exec Welsh Devpt Agency 1997–2000, dir Wales Mgmnt Cncl 2000–03, dir Dragon Int Studios 2002–, chm Gwent Healthcare NHS Tst 2003–; visiting prof Univ of Glamorgan 2000–; memb Cncl Nat Museum and Galleries of Wales 2001–; *Recreations* family, music, reading, walking, gardening; *Style—* Dr Brian Willott, CB; ✉ Coed Cefn, Tregaer, Monmouth, Gwent NP25 4DT (tel 01600 740286)

WILLOTT, Jenny; MP; *b* 29 May 1974; *Educ* Wimbledon HS, Uppingham Sch, Univ of Durham, LSE; *Career* conslt Adithi NGO India 1995, memb fundraising team Oxfam 1996, head of advocacy UNICEF UK 2001–03, area mangr Victim Support S Wales 2003–05; MP (Lib Dem) Cardiff Central 2005– (Parly candidate (Lib Dem) Cardiff Central 2001); head of office for Lembit Opik MP; cncllr (Lib Dem) Merton BC 1998–2000; *Style—* Ms Jenny Willott, MP; ✉ House of Commons, London SW1A 0AA

WILLOTT, Robert Graham; s of William Arthur Willott (d 1968), and Vera Joanna, *née* Ashton; *b* 9 March 1942; *Educ* Hitchin GS; *m* 1, 1968, Patricia Ann (d 1981); 2 da (Sian Elizabeth b 1971, Carys Ann b 1973); m 2, 2002, Carolyn Mary; *Career* Pawley & Malyon CAs: articled clerk 1959–65, mangr 1965–68, ptnr 1968–69; Haymarket Publishing Ltd: ed Accountancy Age 1969–72, publisher 1972–75, dir 1975–76; ICAEW: sec Parly and Law Ctee 1976–78, tech dir 1978–81; Touche Ross (formerly Spicer and Pegler, Spicer & Oppenheim): ptnr 1981–91, i/c Client Devpt Unit 1981–86, fndr and ptnr i/c West End Practice 1987–91, memb Nat Exec 1985–86 and 1988; Willott Kingston Smith and Kingston Smith: ptnr 1991–99, conslt 1999–2001; dir: Cheviot Capital Ltd 1985–98, Fintellect Ltd 1991–, Fintellect Publishing Ltd 2000–, Results Business Consulting Ltd 1997–2007, The Telephone Preference Service Ltd 1999–2006, Save the Children (Sales) Ltd 2000–04, Dare Digital Ltd 2000–, ILG Digital Ltd 2003–, Blockley Mystery Plays Ltd 2003–; special prof Univ of Nottingham Business Sch 1992–; ICAEW: past memb Parly and Law Ctee, past memb Company Law Sub-Ctee; past special advsr DTI; chm Initial Working Pty and advsr to Design Business Assoc 1985–97; dir and hon treas The Direct Marketing Association (UK) Ltd 1996–2001; tstee and hon treas Save the Children Fund 1999–04; memb Mktg Soc; FCA (1976, ACA 1965); *Publications* Going Public (ed 1971–73), Current Accounting Law and Practice (1976–85 and 1992–2000), Guide to Price Controls 1977–78 (1977), The Purchase or Redemption by a Company of its Own Shares (Tolley's, jtly 1982), How Advertising Agencies Made Their Profits (1984–90), Financial Performance of Marketing Services Companies (annual, ed 1991–2001, conslt ed 2002–), The Encyclopaedia of Current Accounting Law and Practice (2000–), Marketing Services Financial Intelligence (ed 2001–), New Media Agencies Financial Intelligence (ed, 2001–); *Style—* Robert Willott, Esq; ✉ The Old Royal Oak, High Street, Blockley GL56 9EX (tel 01386 700361, e-mail rgwillott@fintellect.com)

WILLOUGHBY, Anthony James Tweedale; s of John Lucas Willoughby, OBE (d 1985), of Mere, Wilts, and Hilary Winifred Tweedale Tait; *b* 29 September 1944; *Educ* Westminster; *m* 8 Feb 1975, Joanna, da of late Capt David Clayhills-Henderson, of Stoneygroves Farm, by Liff, Dundee; 1 da (Rachel b 9 June 1976), 2 s (James b 23 July 1978, Nicholas b 21 Jan 1982); *Career* admitted slr 1970; The Distillers Co Ltd 1970; ptnr: Herbert Smith 1977–94, Rouse Legal (formerly Willoughby & Partners) 1994–2006 (conslt 2006–); govr Westminster Sch 1990–2000 and 2001–; *Recreations* cricket, golf, tennis; *Clubs* Royal Wimbledon Golf, Blairgowrie Golf, The Royal Tennis Court, Royal & Ancient; *Style—* Anthony Willoughby, Esq; ✉ Rouse Legal, 11th Floor, Exchange Tower, 1 Harbour Exchange Square, London E14 9GE (tel 020 7536 4100, fax 020 7536 4200)

WILLOUGHBY DE BROKE, 21 Baron (E 1491); (Leopold) David Verney; DL (Warks) 1999; s of 20 Baron Willoughby de Broke (d 1986, descended from the 1 Baron, who was so cr by Henry VII after being on the winning side at Battle of Bosworth Field (1485), and was 4 in descent from 4 Baron Willoughby de Eresby), and Rachel, *née* Wrey (d 1991); *b* 14 September 1938; *Educ* Le Rosey, New Coll Oxford; *m* 1965 (m dis 1989), his kinswoman Petra, 2 da of Col Sir John Aird, 3 Bt, MVO, MC, and Lady Priscilla Heathcote-Drummond-Willoughby (yr da of 2 Earl of Ancaster); 3 s (Rupert Greville b 1966, John Mark b 1967, Edmund Peyto b 1973); *Heir* s, Rupert Verney; *Career* chm: S M Theatre Ltd 1991–, St Martin's Magazines plc 1992–, Compton Verney Opera and Ballet Project 1992–; pres Heart of England Tourist Bd 1996–; patron Warks Assoc of Boys' Clubs 1991–; FRGS 1993; *Clubs* Pratt's, All England; *Style—* The Rt Hon Lord Willoughby de Broke, DL; ✉ Ditchford Farm, Moreton-in-Marsh, Gloucestershire GL56 9RD

WILLOUGHBY DE ERESBY, Baroness (E 1313) (Nancy) Jane Marie Heathcote-Drummond-Willoughby; DL (Lincolnshire 1993); da of 3 Earl of Ancaster (d 1983, when Earldom of Ancaster and Barony of Aveland became extinct, and the Baronetcy of Heathcote passed to his kinsman) and Hon (Nancy) Phyllis Louise Astor (d 1975), da of 2 Viscount Astor; succeeded father in Barony of Willoughby de Eresby; *b* 1 December 1934; *Heir* co-heiresses; *Career* a train bearer to HM The Queen at the Coronation 1953; district cncllr 1969–82; tstee National Portrait Gallery 1994–2004; Dame of Grace Order of St John 2000; *Style*— The Baroness Willoughby de Eresby, DL; ✉ Grimsthorpe, Bourne, Lincolnshire PE10 0LZ

WILLS, Sir David James Vernon; 5 Bt (UK 1923), of Blagdon, Co Somerset; s of Sir John Vernon Wills, 4 Bt, KCVO, TD, JP (d 1998); *b* 2 January 1955; *m* July 1999, Paula Katherine Burke, o da of Dr Peter Holmes, of Sittingbourne, Kent; *Heir* bro, Anthony Wills; *Career* farmer and landowner; memb Cncl Royal Bath & West and Southern Countries Soc 1982; memb Soc of Merchant Venturers 1991; *Recreations* field sports; *Style*— Sir David Wills; ✉ Estate Office, Langford Court, Bristol BS40 5DA (tel 01934 862498, fax 01934 863019)

WILLS, Frederick Hugh Philip Hamilton; yr twin s of Capt Michael Desmond Hamilton Wills, MC (ka 1943), and Mary Margaret Gibbs, *née* Mitford; *b* 31 May 1940; *Educ* Eton, RAC Cirencester; *m* 1969, Priscilla Annabelle, da of Capt Alec David Charles Francis (d 1993), of Malmesbury, Wilts; 2 s (Michael b 1972, Edward b 1974), 1 da (Clare (twin, Mrs Kim Bailey) b 1974); *Career* 11th Hussars (PAO) 1959–66; TA Royal Wilts Yeomanry 1967–75; hon treas Cirencester and Tewkesbury Cons Assoc 1976–86; High Sheriff Glos 1995; *Recreations* country pursuits; *Clubs* New (Edinburgh); *Style*— Frederick H P H Wills, Esq; ✉ Anton's Hill, Leitholm, Coldstream, Berwickshire TD12 4JD (tel 01890 840203, fax 01890 840756)

WILLS, Michael; MP; *b* 20 May 1952; *Educ* Haberdashers' Aske's Elstree, Clare Coll Cambridge (BA); *m* 19 Jan 1984, Jill, *née* Freeman; 3 s (Thomas b 11 Dec 1984, Joe b 22 Aug 1987, Nicholas b 19 Dec 1993), 2 da (Sarah b 12 Dec 1988, Katherine b 10 July 1998); *Career* joined HM Dip Serv 1976, third sec FCO London 1976–77, second sec and labour attaché Br High Cmmn New Dehli 1977–80; prodr Weekend World (LWT) 1982–84 (researcher 1980–82), prodr/dir and md Juniper Productions (ind TV prodn co) 1985–97, MP (Lab) Swindon N 1997–; House of Commons: Parly under-sec of state: DTI 1999–2000, DfEE 2000–01, Lord Chllr's Office 2001–02, Parly under sec of state Home Office 2002–; advsr to Shadow Cabinet 1985–97, gen election media advsr Lab trade and industry team 1992; dir Campaign for Fair Taxes 1992–95; *Style*— Michael Wills, Esq, MP; ✉ House of Commons, London SW1A 0AA (tel 020 7219 3000)

WILLS, Nicholas Kenneth Spencer; s of late Sir John Spencer Wills (d 1991), of Battle, E Sussex, and Elizabeth Drusilla Alice Clare Garcke (d 1995); *b* 18 May 1941; *Educ* Rugby, Queens' Coll Cambridge (MA); *m* 1, 1973 (m dis 1983), Hilary Ann Flood; 2 s, 2 da; m 2, 1985, Philippa Trench Casson; 1 da; *Career* chm: Argus Press Hldgs plc 1974–83, Electrical Press plc 1974–83, Initial plc 1979–87, BET Building Services Ltd 1984–87, Onslow Commercial and Trading 1994–2002; dep chm National Mutual Home Loans 1994–96; md: Birmingham & District Investment Tst plc 1970–91, Electrical & Industrial Investment plc 1970–91, Nat Electric Construction plc 1971–91; BET plc: dir 1975–92, md 1982–91, chief exec 1985–91, chm 1991–92; dir: St George Assurance Co Ltd 1974–81, Bradbury Agnew and Co Ltd 1974–83, National Mutual Life Assurance Society 1974–85, Colonial Securities Tst Co Ltd 1976–82, Cable Tst Ltd 1976–77, Globe Investment Tst plc 1977–90, Boulton and Paul plc 1979–84, Drayton Consolidated Tst plc 1982–92, National Westminster Bank plc (City and West End Advsy Bds) 1982–91, American C of C (UK) 1985–2000 (vice-pres 1988–2000), United World Colleges (International) Ltd 1987–95 (fin dir 1987–93), National Mutual Life Assurance Soc 1991–2002 (dep chm 1992–99, chm 1999–2002), Hitchin Priory Ltd 1992–2002 (dep chm 1994–99, chm 1999–2002), Tribune Tst plc 1992–2004, Manchester Trading & Commercial LLC 1995–2002, Toye & Co plc 1996–, SMC Gp plc 1999–, IQ-Ludorum plc 2000–04, Solid Terrain Modeling Inc 2000–; memb: Cncl CBI 1987–92 (memb Overseas Ctee 1987–91, Public Expenditure Task Force 1988, Economic Affairs Ctee 1991–96), Cncl Business in the Community 1987–92, Advsy Bd Fishman-Davidson Center for the Study of the Service Sector Univ of Pennsylvania 1988–92, Advsy Bd Charterhouse Buy-Out Funds 1990–98, Cncl Industrial Soc 1991–97; Prince's Youth Business Tst: memb Advsy Cncl 1988–2004, hon treas 1989–92, memb Investment Ctee 1992–98; chm: Involvement and Participation Assoc 1991–96, Mgmnt Ctee Cambridge Review of Int Affairs 1998–2003 (memb Advsy Bd 1999–2004), Supervisory Bd Nat Mutual Life Assurance Soc 2002–; tstee Int Fedn Keystone Youth Orgns (IFKYO) 1988–2004, chm IFKYO Int Tstees 1990–2004; treas and churchwarden Church of St Bride Fleet St 1978–2001; govr Haberdashers' Aske's Schs Elstree 1989–97 (chm Girls' Sch Ctee 1994–97); hon memb Clan McEwan; memb Ct of Assts Worshipful Co of Haberdashers 1981 (Jr Warden 1987–89, Master 1997); hon fell Queens' Coll Cambridge 1990, hon fell Centre of Int Studies Cambridge 2000; FCA; CIMgt, FCT, FRSA; *Recreations* trying to farm in the Highlands, skiing on blue runs, extremely bad tennis; *Clubs* White's, RAC, City Livery, Clyde Cruising, Beaver Creek, Country Club of the Rockies; *Style*— Nicholas Wills, Esq; ✉ International Consultant, 33 Davies Street, London W1K 4LR (tel 020 7495 8919, fax 020 7499 4351)

WILLS, Sir (David) Seton; 5 Bt (UK 1904), of Hazelwood, Stoke Bishop, Westbury-on-Trym, Glos, and Clapton-in-Gordano, Somerset; s of Maj George Wills by his first w, Lilah, da of Capt Percy Hare, gs of 2 Earl of Listowel; suc unc, Sir Edward Wills, 4 Bt (d 1983); *b* 29 December 1939; *Educ* Eton; *m* 1968, Gillian, twin da of Albert Eastoe; 1 s, 3 da; *Heir* s, James Wills; *Career* FRICS; *Style*— Sir Seton Wills, Bt

WILLS, Maj (Michael) Thomas Noel Hamilton; DL (1991); s of Capt Michael Desmond Hamilton Wills, MC (ka 1943), and Mary Margaret, *née* Mitford; *b* 31 May 1940; *Educ* Eton, RAC Cirencester; *m* 23 Oct 1982 (m dis 1992), Penelope Ann, da of Ben Howard-Baker, of Llansilin, Salop; 1 s (Nicholas James Noel Hamilton b 9 Sept 1983), 1 da (Camilla Jane Hamilton b 27 June 1985); *Career* Coldstream Gds 1959–73; pres Glos Scout Assoc, chm of tstees Rendcomb Coll; pres Glos branch SSAFA; High Sheriff Glos 1985; Clerk of the Cheque and Adjutant Queen's Body Guard of the Yeomen of the Guard 1993; *Recreations* country pursuits; *Clubs* Boodle's; *Style*— Maj Thomas Wills, DL; ✉ Misarden Park, Stroud, Gloucestershire GL6 7JA (tel 01285 821309); Coulags, Achnashellach, Ross-shire IV54 8YU

WILLSON, Quentin; s of Prof Harold Bernard Willson, of Leicester, and Agnes Grieve, *née* Gullon; *b* 23 July 1957; *Educ* Wyggeston Boys' GS Leicester, Univ of Leicester; *m* 25 June 1988, Helen Margaret; *Career* motoring journalist and broadcaster; dep ed: Buying Cars magazine 1989–92, Car Choice magazine 1992–93; assoc ed BBC Top Gear magazine 1993–2000; presenter: Top Gear 1992–2000, All The Right Moves 1998–2000, 5th Gear 2002, Britain's Worst Driver 2002 (nominated Montreaux Golden Rose Award 2004), Britain's Worst DIY'er, Britain's Worst Pet, Britain's Worst Husband; prodr and presenter: Britain's Worst Husband 2004, Britain's Worst Home 2004; columnist: Daily Mirror 1998–2002, Sunday Mirror 2003; contrib to numerous newspapers, magazines, radio and television; nominated RTS Best Presenter in Vision 1997, nominated RTS Best Factual Programme for The Car's the Star 1998, Motoring Writer of the Year 2004; *Books* The Good Car Guide (1993–96), The Ultimate Classic Car Book (1995), The Classic American Car Book (1997), Cool Cars (2001), Cars - A Celebration (2001), Ultimate Sports Cars (2002); *Recreations* reading T S Eliot; *Style*— Quentin Willson, Esq; ✉ c/o MEZZO, Sycamore House, Hungarton, Leicester LE7 9JR (0116 259 5367, e-mail quentin@mezzo-consultancy.co.uk)

WILLSON, Stephen Phillips; s of Douglas Stephen Willson, and Sheila, *née* Phillips; *b* 27 July 1948; *Educ* Battisborough Sch Plymouth, Coll of Law; *m* 20 Dec 1975, Susan Mary, da of Gavin Miller Hunter (d 1978); 2 da (Sophie Anna b 1 Nov 1977, Sabine Lara b 22 Jan 1980), 1 s (Guy Edward Phillips b 23 Nov 1983); *Career* Burton & Ramsden: articled clerk 1966–71, asst slr 1971–73, ptnr 1973–82; ptnr SJ Berwin LLP 1982– (currently ptnr Real Estate Div); memb Law Soc; *Recreations* squash, tennis; *Clubs* RAC; *Style*— Stephen Willson, Esq

WILMOT, Sir David; kt (2002), QPM (1989), DL (Greater Manchester 1996); *b* 12 March 1943; *Educ* Baines GS Poulton-Le-Fylde, Univ of Southampton (BSc); *m* Ann Marilyn, *née* Doyle; *Career* Lancs Constabulary: constable 1962–67, sgt 1967–69, inspr 1969–74; Merseyside Police: chief inspr 1974–77, supt 1977–81, chief supt 1981–83; dep chief constable W Yorks Police 1985–87 (asst chief constable 1983–85); chief constable Gtr Manchester Police 1991– (dep chief constable 1987–91); memb ACPO; Hon DSc Univ of Salford, RNCM (hc); *Recreations* reading, gardening; *Style*— Sir David Wilmot, QPM, DL; ✉ Chief Constable, Greater Manchester Police HQ, PO Box 22 (SW PDO), Chester House, Boyer Street, Manchester M16 0RE (tel 0161 872 5050, fax 0161 856 2666/1506)

WILMOT, Sir Henry Robert; 9 Bt (GB 1759), of Chaddesden, Derbyshire; s of Capt Sir Robert Arthur Wilmot, 8 Bt (d 1974), of Pitcarlie, Auchtermuchty, and Juliet Elvira, *née* Tufnell; *b* 10 April 1967; *Educ* Eton; *m* 29 April 1995, Susan C, elder da of John Malvern, *qv*, of Roehampton, London; 1 s; *Heir* s, Oliver Wilmot; *Career* CEng; *Clubs* T&GWU; *Style*— Sir Henry Wilmot, Bt

WILMOT-SITWELL, Peter Sacheverell; s of Capt Robert Bradshaw Wilmot-Sitwell, RN (d 1946), and Barbara Elizabeth Fisher (d 1991); *b* 28 March 1935; *Educ* Eton, Univ of Oxford (BA); *m* 1960, Clare Veronica, LVO (1991), da of Ralph H Cobbold; 2 s, 1 da; *Career* memb Stock Exchange 1960, chm Rowe & Pitman stockbrokers 1986 (sr ptnr 1982–86); chm: (following merger) S G Warburg Securities 1986–94 (jtly 1986–90), Mercury World Mining Trust 1993–, Merril Lynch World Mining Trust; vice-chm S G Warburg Group plc until 1994; non-exec dir: Foreign Colonial Income Growth Investment Trust, Close Brothers plc 1995–2004; *Recreations* shooting, golf; *Clubs* White's, Swinley Forest Golf; *Style*— Peter Wilmot-Sitwell, Esq; ✉ Portman House, Dummer, Basingstoke, Hampshire RG25 2AD

WILMOT-SMITH, Richard James Crosbie; QC (1994); s of John Patrick Wilmot-Smith (d 1993), and Rosalys Vida, *née* Massy (d 2002); *b* 12 May 1952; *Educ* Charterhouse, Univ of N Carolina (John Motley Morehead scholar, AB); *m* 1978, Jenny, da of Richard William Castle; 2 da (Antonia b 12 Nov 1981, Claudia b 23 July 1984), 1 s (Freddie b 12 April 1986); *Career* called to the Bar Middle Temple 1978 (Benefactors law scholar, bencher 2003); recorder of the Crown Court 2000– (asst recorder 1994–2000); tstee Free Representation Unit 1997–; *Recreations* cricket; *Clubs* Kent CCC; *Style*— Richard Wilmot-Smith, Esq, QC; ✉ 39 Essex Street, London WC2R 3AT (tel 020 7832 1111, e-mail richardws@39essex.co.uk)

WILMSHURST, John; s of Alfred William Wilmshurst, and Frances May, *née* Handy; *b* 30 January 1926; *Educ* Maidstone GS, UC Oxford (MA); *m* 31 March 1951, Patricia Edith, da of R John W Hollis, MBE; 3 da (Letitia b 1953, Felicity b 1955, Priscilla b 1960), 1 s (Jonathon b 1968); *Career* Lt RASC 1945–48; patents offr Glaxo Laboratories Ltd 1950–52, gp advertising mangr Reed International Ltd 1952–59, dir Roles & Parker Ltd 1959–67, md Stuart Advertising Ltd 1967–71, chm and chief exec John Wilmshurst Marketing Consultants Ltd 1971–94, princ conslt Duncan Alexander and Wilmshurst 1994–; chm Kent Branch Chartered Inst of Mktg 1972; memb Gen Cncl Church Missionary Soc 1970–78; Freeman City of London, Master Worshipful Co of Carmen 2002–03; FCIM 1986, FCAM 1982; *Books* Below the Line Publicity (1994), The Fundamentals of Advertising (2 edn 1999), The Fundamentals and Practice of Marketing (4 edn 2002); *Recreations* bird watching, horse racing, theatre, music, collecting first editions; *Style*— John Wilmshurst, Esq; ✉ The Stable Cottage, East Farleigh, Kent ME15 0JW (tel 01622 728241, e-mail jopish@surefish.co.uk)

WILSEY, Gen Sir John Finlay Willasey; GCB (1996, KCB 1991), CBE (1985, OBE 1983), DL (Wilts 1996); s of Maj Gen John Harold Owen Wilsey (d 1961), of Jersey, and Beatrice Sarah Finlay, *née* Best (d 2003); *b* 18 February 1939; *Educ* Sherborne, RMA Sandhurst; *m* 1975, Elizabeth Patricia, da of C R E Nottingham; 1 da (Alexandra Claire Willasey b 18 Aug 1977), 1 s (James Nicholas Charles b 1 May 1979); *Career* cmmnd Devonshire and Dorset Regt 1959, despatches 1976 and 1981, CO 1st Bn Devonshire and Dorset Regt 1979–82, cmd 1 Inf Bde 1984–86, RCDS 1987, COS HQ UK Land Forces 1988–90, GOC Northern Ireland 1990–93, C-in-C UK Land Command 1993–96, ADC (Gen) to HM The Queen 1994–96; Col Devonshire and Dorset Regt 1990–97, Col Cmdt RLC 1993–96, Hon Col Jersey Field Sqdn RE; pres Wilts ACF 2006–; chm Western Provident Association 1996–, vice-chm Cwlth War Graves Cmmn 2001–05 (memb 1998–); govr: Sherborne Sch 1995–2001, Sherborne Sch for Girls 1996–2001, Sutton's Hosp in Charterhouse 1996–2001; cmmr Royal Hosp Chelsea 1996–2002, chm Salisbury Cathedral Cncl 2001–; patron: Youth for Britain 1996–, Hope and Homes for Children 1997–2005; *Publications* Service for the Nation (1987), H Jones VC: The life and death of an unusual hero (2002); *Recreations* skiing, sailing, fishing, breeding alpacas; *Clubs* Army and Navy, Scientific Exploration Society, RYS; *Style*— Gen Sir John Wilsey, GCB, CBE, DL; ✉ Western Provident Association, Rivergate House, Blackbrook Park, Taunton, Somerset TA1 2PE (tel 01823 623502)

WILSHER, Roy Andrew; OBE (2007); s of Kenneth Wilsher, and Valerie Wilsher; *b* 9 March 1963, Barnet; *Educ* Arnos Comp Enfield, South Bank Univ; *m* 28 June 1986; 2 s; *Career* London Fire Brigade: joined 1981, sr divnl offr 1998–2002, asst cmmr 2002–03; Herts Fire and Rescue Serv: dep chief fire offr 2004–05, chief fire offr 2005–; memb Ct Univ of Herts; tstee Herts in Trust charity; memb Chief Fire Offrs' Assoc 2004; Fire Serv Long Serv and Good Conduct Medal 2002, Queen's Jubilee Medal 2002; MIFireE 1990, CEng 2000; *Recreations* rugby, football, keep fit, reading; *Style*— Roy Wilsher, Esq, OBE; ✉ Hertfordshire Fire and Rescue Service, Old London Road, Hertford, Hertfordshire SG13 7LD (tel 01992 507501, e-mail roy.wilsher@hertscc.gov.uk)

WILSHIRE, Prof Brian; OBE (1998); s of Edmund Wilshire, of Swansea, and Eileen, *née* Nicholls; *b* 16 May 1937; *Educ* Rhondda County GS for Boys, UC Swansea (BSc, PhD, DSc, basketball rep Wales and Univ of Wales); *m* 1956, Marian, da of Sidney Rees Teague; 3 s (Keith b 1957, Neville b 1959, Ralph b 1962); *Career* Univ of Wales Swansea (formerly UC Swansea): lectr 1960–72, sr lectr 1972–78, reader 1978–82, personal professorship 1982–, head Dept of Material Engrg 1985–99, dir EPSRC Engrg Doctorate Centre in Steel Technol 1999–, pro-vice-chllr 1996–99; ACTA Metallurgica lectr 1991–93; Platinum Medal Inst of Materials 1995; FIM 1976, FREng 1993; *Books* Technological and Economic Trends in the Steel Industries (1983), Creep of Metals and Alloys (1985), Introduction to Creep (1993); *Style*— Prof Brian Wilshire, OBE, FREng; ✉ Cwrt-y-Berllan, Reynoldston, Gower, Swansea SA3 1AE (tel 01792 390870); Materials Research Centre, University of Wales Swansea, Singleton Park, Swansea SA2 8PP (tel 01792 295243, fax 01792 295244, e-mail b.wilshire@swansea.ac.uk)

WILSHIRE, David; MP; *b* 16 September 1943; *Educ* Kingswood Sch Bath, Fitzwilliam Coll Cambridge; *m* 1967, Margaret (sep 2000); 1 da (Sarah b 1969 d 1981), 1 s (Simon b 1971); *Career* MP (Cons) Spelthorne 1987–, PPS to min of state for Def Procurement MOD 1991–92, PPS to min of state Home Office 1992–94, oppn whip 2001–05; memb: NI Select Ctee 1994–97, Foreign Affrs Select Ctee 1997–2000, Tport Select Ctee 2005–, Chairmen's

Panel 2005–; Cons Backbench Environment Ctee: vice-chm 1990–91, sec 1995–97; Cons Backbench NI Ctee: sec 1990–91, vice-chm 1995–97; vice-chm UK Branch Commonwealth Parly Assoc 1998–99, convenor All-Pty Parly Methodist Fellowship, treas Br Gp Inter-Parly Union, memb British-Irish Parly Body 1994–2001; del to Parly Assembly Cncl of Europe 1997–2001 and 2004–; ptnr Moorlands Res Servs; former: co-dir Political Mgmnt Prog Brunel Univ, ldr Wansdyke DC (Avon), memb Avon CC; *Style*— David Wilshire, Esq, MP; ✉ 55 Cherry Orchard, Staines, Middlesex TW18 2DQ (tel 01784 450822); House of Commons, London SW1A 0AA (tel 020 7219 3534)

WILSON, Prof Sir Alan Geoffrey; kt (2001); s of Harry Wilson (d 1987), of Darlington, Co Durham, and Gladys, *née* Naylor (d 1990); *b* 8 January 1939; *Educ* Queen Elizabeth GS Darlington, Corpus Christi Coll Cambridge (MA); *m* 17 April 1987, Sarah Caroline Fildes; *Career* scientific offr Rutherford Laboratory 1961–64, res offr Inst of Economics and Statistics Univ of Oxford 1964–66, mathematical advsr Miny of Tport 1966–68, asst dir Centre for Environmental Studies 1968–70; Univ of Leeds: prof of urban and regnl geography 1970–2004 (emeritus prof 2004–), chm Bd of Arts, Economics and Social Studies and Law 1984–86, pro-vice-chllr 1989–91, vice-chllr 1991–2004; DG for HE DfES 2004–06, master CCC Cambridge 2006–07, prof of urban and rgnl systems UCL 2007–; memb Oxford City Cncl 1964–67, memb and vice-chm Kirklees AHA 1979–81, vice-chm Dewsbury DHA 1982–86; memb ESRC 2000–04; chm NHS Complaints Review Ctee 1993, memb Northern and Yorkshire RHA 1994–96; Fndr's Medal Royal Geographical Soc 1992; Hon DSc Pennsylvania State Univ 2002, Hon DEd Leeds Metropolitan Univ 2004, Hon DUniv Bradford 2004, Hon LLD Univ of Leeds 2004, Hon LLD Univ of Teesside 2006; hon fell: UCL 2003, CCC Cambridge 2004; AcSS 2000; FBA 1994, FCGI 1997, CGeog 2001, FRS 2006; *Books* Entropy in Urban and Regional Modelling (1970), Catastrophe Theory and Bifuration (1981), Geography and the Environment (1981), Modelling the City: Performance, Policy and Planning (jtly, 1994), Intelligent GIS, Location Decisions and Strategic Planning (jtly, 1996), Complex Spatial Systems (2000); *Recreations* reading, writing; *Clubs* Athenaeum; *Style*— Prof Sir Alan Wilson, FBA, FRS; ✉ Centre for Advanced Spatial Analysis, University College London, 1–19 Torrington Place, London WC1E 6BT (tel 020 7679 1782, e-mail alangwilson@btinternet.com)

WILSON, Rt Rev Dr Alan Thomas Lawrence; *see:* Buckingham, Bishop of

WILSON, Brig Alasdair Allan; OBE (1987); s of George Allan Wilson (d 1963), and Isobel Fraser, *née* Burgess; *b* 12 April 1947; *Educ* Bury GS, RMA Sandhurst, RMCS Shrivenham (BSc); *m* 14 Aug 1971, Allison May, *née* Muir; 2 s (Archie Douglas Allan, Alexander James Allan); *Career* 2 Lt RE 1967, RN Staff Coll Greenwich 1978–79, OC 7 Field Sqdn RE 1981–83, cdr 33 Engr Regt 1986–88, chief engr ME Gulf War 1990–91, NATO Defence Coll Rome 1995, chief Civil Affrs Bosnia 1995–96, cdr 107 (Ulster) Bde 1996–98, ACOS HQ North NATO 1998–2001; dir RE Offrs Widows Fund; GSM NI 1971, Gulf War Medal 1991, Bosnia Medal 1996, Kosovo Medal 2000, Queen's Golden Jubilee Medal 2002; chm Royal Br Legion, chm Dickleburgh PCC; MIRE 1967, FICE 2002; *Recreations* golf, singing, shooting, croquet, gardening; *Clubs* Army and Navy; *Style*— Brig Alasdair Wilson, OBE; ✉ The Old Rectory, Dickleburgh, Diss, Norfolk IP21 4NN (tel 01379 740561, mobile 07762 454207, e-mail aawilson@compuserve.com); Southwold Surgery, Southwold, Suffolk IP18 6AN (tel 01502 722326, fax 01502 724708, e-mail alasdair.wilson@gp-d83022.nhs.uk)

WILSON, Alastair James Drysdale; QC (1987); s of Alastair Robin Wilson, ERD, of Sudbury, Suffolk, and Mary Damaris, *née* Dawson; *b* 26 May 1946; *Educ* Wellington, Pembroke Coll Cambridge; *Children* 1 s, 2 da; *Career* called to the Bar Middle Temple 1968, recorder 1996–; *Recreations* gardening, restoring old buildings; *Clubs* Norfolk; *Style*— Alastair Wilson, Esq, QC; ✉ Rainthorpe Hall, Tasburgh, Norfolk NR15 1RQ (tel 01508 470 618, fax 01508 470 793); Hogarth Chambers, 5 New Square, Lincoln's Inn, London WC2A 3RJ (tel 020 7404 0404, fax 020 7404 0505, e-mail awilsonqc@clara.net)

WILSON, Allan; s of Andrew Wilson (d 1992), of Kilbirnie, and Elizabeth, *née* Lauchlan; *b* 5 August 1954; *Educ* Spiers Sch Beith (sch capt 1972); *m* 1981, Alison, *née* Liddell; 2 s (Craig b 15 June 1986, Scott b 21 July 1994); *Career* NUPE: trainee area offr 1972–75, area offr 1975–93; Unison regnl offr 1993–94, sr regnl offr and head of higher educn Unison 1994–99; MSP (Lab) Cunninghame North; dep min for Sport, the Arts and Culture 1999–2001, dep min for Environment and Rural Devpt 2001–; memb: Scottish Exec Lab Pty 1992–99, 'Red Wedge', Scottish TUC Ctee 1972–79; sec Radio City Assoc; *Publications* ed NUPE News 1980–82, First Edition 1982–88; *Recreations* football, golf, reading; *Clubs* Garnock Labour, St Bridgot's Social, Place Golf; *Style*— Allan Wilson, Esq; ✉ The Scottish Parliament, Edinburgh EH99 1SP (tel 01505 682847, fax 01505 684648, mobile 0411 038711, e-mail awilson1@netlineuk.net)

WILSON, Andrew J; s of Harry and Dorothy Wilson; *Educ* Coltness HS Wishaw, Univ of Strathclyde (BA), Univ of St Andrews; *Career* politician and economist: Scottish Office, Forestry Cmmn, Royal Bank of Scotland, SNP; MSP (SNP) Scotland Central 1999–2003, shadow min for economy, enterprise and lifelong learning; dep gp chief economist Royal Bank of Scotland 2005– (head of gp media rels 2003–05); columnist The Sunday Mail and Scots Independent; *Recreations* football and other sports, reading, supporting Motherwell FC; *Style*— Andrew Wilson, Esq

WILSON, Andrew Norman; s of Lt-Col Norman Wilson (d 1985), and Jean Dorothy, *née* Crowder (d 2003); *b* 27 October 1950; *Educ* Rugby, New Coll Oxford (MA, Chllr's Essay Prize, Ellerton Theol Prize); *m* 1, 1971 (m dis 1989), Katherine Dorothea Duncan-Jones, *qv*; 2 da; m 2, 1991, Dr Ruth Guilding; 1 da (b 23 March 1998); *Career* author; asst master Merchant Taylors' Sch 1975–76, lectr St Hugh's Coll and New Coll Oxford 1976–81; literary ed: The Spectator 1981–84, Evening Standard 1990–97; columnist Evening Standard 1990–; FRSL 1981; *Books* The Sweets of Pimlico (1977, John Llewellyn Rhys Meml Prize 1978), Unguarded Hours (1978), Kindly Light (1979), The Laird of Abbotsford (1980, John Llewellyn Rhys Meml prize 1981), The Healing Art (1980, Somerset Maugham Award 1981), Who Was Oswald Fish? (1981), Wise Virgin (1982, W H Smith Literary Award 1983), The Life of John Milton (1983), Scandal (1983), Hilaire Belloc (1984), How Can We Know? (1985), Gentlemen in England (1985), Love Unknown (1986), Stray (1987), The Lion and the Honeycomb (1987), Penfriends from Porlock (1988), Tolstoy (1988, Whitbread Biography Award), Incline Our Hearts (1988), The Tabitha Stories (1988), Eminent Victorians (1989), C S Lewis (1990), A Bottle in The Smoke (1990), Daughters of Albion (1991), Jesus (1992), The Rise and Fall of the House of Windsor (1993), The Vicar of Sorrows (1993), Hearing Voices (1995), A Watch in the Night (1996), Paul: The Mind of The Apostle (1997), Dream Children (1998), God's Funeral (1999), The Victorians (2002), Iris Murdoch As I Knew Her (2003), London: A Short History (2004), My Name is Legion (2004), A Jealous Ghost (2005), After the Victorians (2005), Betjeman (2006); *Clubs* Travellers, Beefsteak, Chelsea Arts; *Style*— A N Wilson, FRSL; ✉ 5 Regent's Park Terrace, London NW1 7EE

WILSON, Dr Ashley John; s of late John Wilson, of Harton, South Shields, Tyne & Wear, and Gladys Wilson; *b* 2 November 1950; *Educ* South Shields GS, Bedford Coll, Univ of London (BSc), Univ of York (DPhil); *m* 1, 2 Jan 1976, Sheila, da of James Mather, of South Shields, Tyne & Wear; m 2, 4 July 1998, Hazel Louise, da of Robert Burrows, of York, N Yorkshire; *Career* dir Centre for Cell and Tissue Res Univ of York 1980–, tech dir Carafiltration Ltd; ed Procedures in Electron Microscopy 1993–; memb: Br Humanist Assoc, Nat Secular Soc; active memb and sec York Humanist Gp, fell Royal Microsopical Soc; MIBiol 1975, CBiol 1979; *Books* An Atlas of Low Temperature Scanning Electron Microscopy (1984), Foams: Chemistry, Physics and Structure (1989), Resins for Light and Electron Microscopy (1992); *Recreations* singing, wine tasting, architectural history, badminton; *Style*— Dr Ashley J Wilson

WILSON, (Alfred Samuel) Brian; MLA; s of Alfred Wilson (d 1982), and Shiela, *née* Dunn; *b* 15 May 1943, Belfast; *Educ* Open Univ (BA), Univ of Strathclyde (MSc); *m* 9 July 1979, Anne, *née* Campbell; 3 s (Roy b 26 Aug 1965, Scott b 4 Aug 1980, Allan b 8 March 1982), 1 da (Caroline b 21 Oct 1968); *Career* civil servant 1961–74, lectr then sr lectr in politics 1976–2003; cncllr North Down Cncl 1981–, mayor North Down 1993–94, MLA (Green) N Down 2007–; *Style*— Brian Wilson, Esq, MLA; ✉ 1 Innisfayle Drive, Bangor BT19 1DN (tel 028 9145 5189, e-mail brian.wilson@northdown.gov.uk); Northern Ireland Assembly, Parliament Buildings, Stormont Estate, Belfast BT4 3XX (tel 028 9052 1790)

WILSON, Rt Hon Brian David Henderson; PC (2003); s of late John Forrest Wilson, and Marion, *née* McIntyre; *b* 13 December 1948; *Educ* Dunoon GS, Univ of Dundee (MA), Univ Coll (Dip Journalism Studies); *m* 1981, Joni, *née* Buchanan; 1 da, 2 s; *Career* publisher and founding ed West Highland Free Press 1972–; MP (Lab) Cunninghame N 1987–2005; oppn front bench spokesman: on Scot Affrs 1988–92, on citizen's rights and open govt 1992, tport 1992–94 and 1995–96, on trade and industry 1994–95; memb Lab Pty election planning team 1996–97; min for: educn and industry Scottish Office 1997–98, trade 1998–99; min of state Scottish Office 1999–2001, min of state FCO 2001, min of state for Industry and Energy 2001–03, PM's special rep on overseas trade 2003–05; chm Airtricity UK 2005–; dir: Celtic plc 2005–, AMEC Nuclear 2005–, Interregnum plc 2006–; visiting prof Glasgow Caledonian Univ 2007–; contrib to: The Guardian, Glasgow Herald; dir Cuba Studies Tst 2007–; first winner Nicholas Tomalin Meml Award 1975, Spectator Parliamentarian of Year Awards 1990; FSA Scot; *Books* Celtic: a century with honour (1988); *Clubs* Garnock Labour, Soho House; *Style*— The Rt Hon Brian Wilson; ✉ 219 Queen Victoria Drive, Glasgow G13 1UU (tel 0141 959 1758); Miavaig House, Isle of Lewis (tel 01851 672357, e-mail brianwilson@mangersta.net)

WILSON, Catherine Mary; OBE (1996); da of Arthur Thomas Bowyer (d 1998), of Nettleham, Lincs, and Kathleen Edith May, *née* Hawes (d 1993); *b* 10 April 1945; *Educ* Windsor County GS; *m* 1968, Peter John Wilson, s of Henry Wilson; *Career* museum and gallery asst City and County Museum Lincoln 1964–72, curator Museum of Lincolnshire Life 1972–83, asst dir recreational servs Lincs Co Cncl 1983–91, dir Norfolk Museums Service 1991–98, museums conslt and lectr 2000–; memb Bd: Museums and Galleries Cmmn 1993–2000, Museums Trg Inst 1994–99, Assoc of Ind Museums 2000–05, Railway Heritage Ctee 2001–, E Midlands Regnl Ctee Heritage Lottery Fund; FMA, FSA 1989, FRGS 1998; *Recreations* steam engines, industrial archaeology, local history; *Style*— Mrs Catherine Wilson, OBE, FSA

WILSON, Charles; *Career* with Procter and Gamble 1986, conslt OC&C Strategy Consultants 1987–91, dir Abberton Associates 1991–98, exec dir (branches, supply chain, strategy and systems) Booker plc 1998–2000, md Booker Cash and Carry (part of Iceland Group plc) 2000–01, exec dir (strategy, property, supply chain and systems) Arcadia Group plc 2001–03, exec dir (property, IT and supply chain) Marks and Spencer plc 2004–05, ceo Booker 2005–; *Style*— Charles Wilson, Esq

WILSON, Charles Martin; s of Adam Wilson (d 1964), and Ruth Ann Wilson (d 1974); *b* 18 August 1935; *Educ* Eastbank Acad Glasgow; *m* 1, 18 Jan 1968 (m dis 1973), Anne Robinson, *qv*; 1 da (Emma Alexandra b 1970); m 2, 2 Oct 1980 (m dis 2001), Sally Angela O'Sullivan, da of L J Connell; 1 s (Luke Adam b 1981), 1 da (Lily Joan b 1985); m 3, 25 Aug 2001, Rachel *née* Pitkeathley, da of Baroness Pitkeathley; *Career* dep night news ed Daily Mail 1963, followed by exec jobs at The Daily Mail including sports ed and dep Northern ed, asst ed London Evening News; ed: Glasgow Evening Times 1976, Glasgow Herald 1981, The Sunday Standard from its launch 1982; exec ed The Times 1982, ed Chicago Sun Times 1984, ed The Times Nov 1985–90 (jt dep ed 1984), dir News International March-Dec 1990, formerly md and ed-in-chief The Sporting Life, editorial dir Mirror Group Newspapers plc 1991–92, md MGN plc 1992–98, acting ed The Independent 1995–96, bd memb Youth Justice Bd 1997–2004, memb Newspaper Panel Competition Cmmn 1999–2006, tstee Royal Naval Museum 1999–, non-exec dir Chelsea & Westminster NHS Tst 2000–; *Recreations* writing, reading, watching steeplechasing; *Clubs* Jockey; *Style*— Charles M Wilson, Esq

WILSON, Sir David; 3 Bt (UK 1920), of Carbeth, Killearn, Co Stirling; s of Sir John Mitchell Harvey Wilson, 2 Bt, KCVO (d 1975), by his w, Mary Elizabeth (d 1979); *b* 30 October 1928; *Educ* Deerfield Acad Mass USA, Harrow, Oriel Coll Oxford; *m* 1955, Eva Margareta, da of Tore Lindell, of Malmö, Sweden; 2 s, 1 da; *Heir* s, Thomas David Wilson; *Career* called to the Bar Lincoln's Inn 1953, admitted slr 1962; conslt Simmons & Simmons 1992–93 (ptnr 1963–92); *Recreations* sailing; *Clubs* Royal Southern Yacht; *Style*— Sir David Wilson, Bt; ✉ Tandem House, Queen's Drive, Oxshott, Surrey KT22 0PH

WILSON, David Geoffrey; OBE (1986), DL (Gtr Manchester 1985); s of Cyril Wilson (d 1950), and Winifred, *née* Sutton (d 1944); *b* 30 April 1933; *Educ* Leeds GS, Oldham Hulme GS; *m* 10 Aug 1980, Dianne Elizabeth, da of Rupert George Morgan (d 1980); *Career* Nat Serv RAOC 1951–53, TA Manchester Regt 9 Battalion 1958–68, ret Maj; sec Williams Deacon's Bank 1965–70, area mangr Williams & Glyn's Bank 1977–81 (sec 1970–72, mangr 1973–76), regnl dir Enterprise Bd NW 1981–85, dir of banking The British Linen Bank Ltd 1986–91, non-exec dir Lancastrian Building Society 1991–92; chm Urban Logic plc 2006–; chm: N Manchester HA 1991–94, N Manchester Healthcare NHS Tst 1994–97; memb Advsy Bd (NW) Northern Rock Building Soc 1992–95; pres Manchester C of C and Industry 1978–80; chm: Manchester Business Link 1993–2000, E Manchester Partnership 1996–2006, Business Link Network Co 2000–01; dir: NW Arts Bd 1991–96, Manchester TEC 1998–2001, Healthsure Gp Ltd (formerly Manchester and Salford Saturday Hosp Fund) 1998–2003, Br-Icelandic C of C 1999–2004; chm: Manchester PO Advsy Ctee, Manchester Telecommunications Advsy Ctee 1978–2000; dep chm: Hallé Concerts Soc 1992–97, Bd of Fin Manchester Diocese 1994–2004; pres Victim Support and Witness Service for Gtr Manchester; memb: Manchester Settlement 1994– (chm 1999–), Commonwealth Games (Manchester 2002) Organising Ctee 1996–2002, Cncl Univ of Salford 1996–2005, The Charity Serv (chm 2000–06), Ct Univ of Manchester until 2000; govr: Salford Coll of Technol 1988–96, Manchester Coll of Arts and Technology (MANCAT) 1999–; pres Manchester Literary and Philosophical Soc 1981–83; High Sheriff Gtr Manchester 1991–92, Vice Lord-Lt Gtr Manchester 2003–; hon consul for Iceland 1981–; Hon MA Univ of Manchester 1983, Hon MA Univ of Salford 1995; FIMgt, FCIB; *Recreations* gardening, music; *Clubs* Army and Navy, Lancashire CCC; *Style*— David Wilson, Esq, OBE, DL; ✉ Winton, 28 Macclesfield Road, Wilmslow, Cheshire SK9 2AF (tel 01625 524133, fax 01625 520605, e-mail wilsondg@talk21.com)

WILSON, David Steel; s of John Mill Wilson (d 1954), and Elizabeth Garth, *née* Steel (d 1987); *b* 21 January 1936; *Educ* Bishopbriggs HS, Glasgow Coll of Technol (Dip Mktg); *m* 24 Aug 1965, Patricia Ann, da of James MacDowall Docherty; 1 s (Byron David Kingsley b 10 Dec 1970), 1 da (Saskia Claire Kingsley b 2 Jan 1973); *Career* Nat Serv RAF 1957–59; Fyfe & McGrouther Ltd: apprentice 1953–57, sales rep 1959–66, sales mangr 1966–67; area sales mangr James Neill & Co Ltd Sheffield 1967–69, mktg mangr Pneumatic Components (RTZ Group) 1969–70, commis chef and trainee mangr Pheasant Inn Keyston 1970–72, proprietor The Peat Inn Fife 1972–2006, dir Taste of Scotland Ltd 1996–; Cellar of the Year UK Wine award Egon Ronay Guide 1985, chef laureate Br Gastronomic Acad 1986, Michelin star 1986, Restaurateur of the Year Catey award 1989, 4/5 Good Food Guide 1996; memb: Master Chefs of GB 1983– (chm Exec Ctee 1987–91), Académie Culinaire de France; Hon LLD Univ of Dundee 1997; FRSA 1992; *Recreations* music, sport, travel; *Style*— David Wilson, Esq; ✉ Jesmond Stables, 30A Main Street, Upper Largo, Fife KY8 6EW

WILSON, Derek; *b* 26 September 1963; *Educ* Todmorden GS, Leeds Sch of Architecture (BA), N London Sch of Architecture (DipArch); *m* 1998; *Career* architect; formerly with: John S Taylor Chartered Architects Todmorden, Archer Boxer Partners Hatfield; dir HOK Sport (formerly Lobb Partnership London) 1993– (joined 1989), currently head of design and overlay London Organising Ctee for the Olympic Games (LOCOG); projects incl: Alfred McAlpine Stadium Huddersfield 1992–98 (RIBA Building of the Year 1995), Reebok Stadium Bolton 1995–98 (British Construction Industry Building of the Year 1998), Sydney Olympics Overlay 1998–99, Arsenal FC new stadium 1999–2000 and 2004–06, masterplan London 2012 Olympic Games bid 2003–06, orgn of London 2012 Olympic Games; memb Ctee: BSI, Central European Norms (CEN) for Standards in Spectator Facilities; contrib to magazine articles and published books; RIBA 1990, ARB 1990; *Recreations* footballer, supporter Burnley FC; *Style*— Derek Wilson, Esq; ✉ London Organising Committee for the Olympic Games, Level 22–23, 1 Churchill Place, Canary Wharf, London E14 5LN (tel 020 3201 2000)

WILSON, Des; s of Albert H Wilson (d 1989), of Oamaru, NZ, and Ellen, *née* Hoskins; *b* 5 March 1941; *Educ* Waitaki Boys' HS NZ; *m* 1 (m dis 1984); 1 s (Timothy), 1 da (Jacqueline); m 2, 24 May 1985, Jane, *née* Dunmore, of Brighton; *Career* columnist: The Guardian 1968–71, The Observer 1971–75; ed Social Work Today 1976–79, dep ed The Illustrated London News 1979–81; dir Shelter 1967–71, memb Nat Exec Nat Cncl for Civil Liberties 1971–73, head public affrs RSC 1974–76; chm: CLEAR 1982–90, Friends of the Earth 1983–86, Citizens Action 1984–90, Campaign for Freedom of Info 1984–90; Lib Pty: pres 1986–87, memb Fed Exec 1988–89, dir Gen Election Campaign Lib Democrats 1990–92; vice-chm public affrs worldwide Burson Marsteller 1993–94; dir of corp and public affairs BAA plc 1994–2000; non-exec dir: Ingenious Media 2000–02, Earls Court and Olympia Gp 2001–04; memb Bd Br Tourist Authy 1997–2003; public affrs advsr MCC 2001–, memb Mgmnt Bd and chm Corp Affrs and Mktg Advsy Ctee ECB 2003–04; memb: English Sports Cncl 2000–02 (sr vice-chm 1999–2002, chm Lottery Panel 1999–2002), UK Sports Cncl 2000–02; *Books* I Know it Was the Place's Fault (1970), Des Wilson's Minority Report - A Diary of Protest (1973), So You Want to Be a Prime Minister: A Personal View of British Politics (1979), The Lead Scandal (1982), Pressure: The A to Z of Campaigning in Britain (1984), The Environmental Crisis (ed, 1984), The Secrets File (ed, 1984), The Citizen Action Handbook (1986), Battle for Power: Inside the Alliance General Election Campaign (1987), Swimming With the Devilfish: Under the Surface of Professional Poker (2006), Ghosts at the Table (2007); novels: Costa del Sol (1990), Campaign (1992), Private Business, Public Battleground (2002); *Style*— Des Wilson, Esq; ✉ Pryors Cottage, Nancegollen, Cornwall TR13 0AZ

WILSON, Edward; s of Edward William Wilson, of Wingrove House, South Shields, and Thomasina, *née* Moore; *b* 13 July 1947; *Educ* South Shields GS for Boys, Univ of Manchester (BA); *Career* actor Nat Youth Theatre 1965–70, played leading repertory theatres incl a season with the Traverse Theatre Edinburgh; dir Newbury Community Theatre 1984, artistic dir Fiftieth Anniversary of the Royal Jubilee Tst (staged The Way of Light St Paul's Cathedral) 1984; dir for Nat Youth Theatre 1981– (artistic dir 1987–2003): Murder in the Cathedral (London, Edinburgh Festival, Moscow Arts Theatre, Southwark Cathedral, Westminster Cathedral), A Man For All Seasons, The Royal Hunt of the Sun (Jeanetta Cochrane Theatre London), The Taming of the Shrew, Othello, Night Shriek (Shaw), Caucasian Chalk Circle (His Majesty's Aberdeen, Tyne Opera House Newcastle, Bloomsbury Theatre), Marat Sade and Blitz (Playhouse Theatre), Blood Wedding (Bloomsbury Theatre, Teatro Principal Valencia), The Rivals (Greenwich, Theatre Royal Brighton, His Majesty's Aberdeen), Maggie May (Royalty Theatre), Amphibious Spangulatos (Greenwich), Godspell (nat tour), Pippin (Bloomsbury), Othello (Bloomsbury), They Shoot Horses Don't They? (Edinburgh Festival and Apollo Theatre London), Dancing at Lughnasa (Edinburgh Festival and Arts Theatre London), Biloxi Blues (Arts Theatre London), Nicholas Nickleby (Lyric Theatre Hammersmith), Threepenny Opera (Lyric Theatre Hammersmith); dir Ivar Theatre Hollywood and California Youth Theatre 2004–; TV appearances in When the Boat Comes In and Rockliffe's Babies; vice-pres Shakespeare Fndn of Spain; Hon DArt Univ of Sunderland 2000; fell Royal Soc for the Encouragement of Arts, Manufacturers and Commerce (FRSA) 1999; *Recreations* music; *Clubs* Royal Over-Seas League; *Style*— Edward Wilson, Esq; ✉ Ivar Theatre, 1605 North Ivar Avenue, Hollywood, CA 90028, USA (tel 00 1 313 461 7300, e-mail ed@edwardwilson.net)

WILSON, Eric; *b* 8 July 1935; *Educ* Houghton-le-Spring GS; *m* 26 Dec 1963, Irene; 1 s (Mark); *Career* Nat Serv RAF 1953–55; Lloyds Bank 1956–57; various mgmnt appts with: Bank of W Africa 1958–65, Martins Bank 1965–67, Barclays Bank 1968–80; corp fin dir Barclays Bank 1980–84, chief exec and regnl dir TSB Scotland plc 1989–90 (gen mangr of banking 1984–86, sr gen mangr 1986–87, chief gen mangr 1987, md 1987–89), fin conslt 1990–; memb CBI Scot Cncl 1987–90; chm Customer Services Ctee for Yorks OFWAT 1994–2001; former assoc Univ of York, lectr in mgmnt subjects and former MBA advsr Univ of Wales (for Chartered Inst of Bankers); FIB (Scotland), FCIB; *Recreations* running, music, reading and travelling; *Style*— Eric Wilson, Esq; ✉ Calabar, 5 Manor Farm Close, Copmanthorpe, York YO23 3GE (tel 01904 702995, e-mail ericwilson@onetel.net)

WILSON, Fraser Andrew; MBE (1980); s of William McStravick Wilson (d 1998), of Glasgow, and Mary McFadyen, *née* Fraser (d 2006); *b* 6 May 1949; *Educ* Bellahouston Acad, Univ of Surrey (Dip Russian Studies); *m* 18 April 1981, Janet, da of Christopher Phillips (d 1978); 2 s (Gavin Christopher b 1982, Alasdair Fraser b 1985); *Career* HM Dip Serv: FCO 1967–70, Havana 1970–71, SE Asia 1971–73, Seoul 1973–77, Salisbury 1977–80, FCO 1980–84, Moscow 1984–85, first sec (commercial) Rangoon 1986–90, FCO 1990–94, dep consul-gen São Paulo 1994–98, ambass to Turkmenistan 1998–2002, high cmmr to Seychelles 2002–04, FCO 2004–06, ambass to Albania 2006–; pres St Andrew Soc of São Paulo 1997; *Recreations* travelling, reading; *Style*— Fraser Wilson, Esq, MBE; ✉ Foreign & Commonwealth Office, King Charles Street, London SW1A 2AH

WILSON, Geoffrey Alan; OBE (2004); s of late Lewis Wilson, and Doris, *née* Shrier; *b* 19 February 1934; *Educ* Haberdashers' Aske's, Coll of Estate Mgmnt; *m* 1963, Marilyn Helen Freedman; 1 s (James Lewis b 12 Aug 1965), 2 da (Sophie Louise b 20 Dec 1968, Annabel Jane b 23 Dec 1971); *Career* 2 Lt RA 1955–56; private practice 1957–60, dir Amalgamated Investment Property Co 1961–70, co-fndr and dir Sterling Land Co 1971–73, chm Greycoat plc 1985–94 (dir 1976–94), dir Perspectives on Architecture Ltd 1993–, chm Equity Land Ltd 1994–; memb W Met Conciliation Ctee Race Rels Bd 1969–71, memb Governing Cncl Univ Coll Sch 1991–95, memb Cncl CBF World Jewish Relief 1993–97, cmmr English Heritage 1992–98, chm Heritage Protection Review Steering Ctee 2004–; tstee: ORT Tst 1980–2004, Public Art Devpt Tst 1990–95, Br Architectural Library Tst 1996–98, Buildings at Risk Tst 1998–2001; govr: City Literary Inst 1998–2002, Peabody Tst 1998–2004, Museum of London 2000–; FRICS 1958, Hon FRIBA 1995; *Recreations* reading, architecture, art, film; *Clubs* Reform; *Style*— Geoffrey Wilson, Esq, OBE; ✉ Equity Land Ltd, 2 Bentinck Street, London W1U 2FA (tel 020 7009 0220)

WILSON, Gerald Robertson; CB (1991); s of Charles Robertson Wilson (d 1998), and Margaret, *née* Early (d 1995); *b* 7 September 1939; *Educ* Univ of Edinburgh (MA); *m* 11 May 1963, Margaret Anne (d 2005); 1 s (Christopher b 1968), 1 da (Catherine b 1964); *Career* private sec Civil Serv to: Min of State for Scot 1965–66, Lord Privy Seal 1972–74; cncllr UK Representation Brussels 1977–82, asst sec Scottish Office 1974–77 (and 1982–84), under sec Indust Dept for Scotland 1984–88, sec Scot Educn Dept 1988–95, sec and head Scottish Office Educn and Industry Dept 1995–99; chm Scottish Biomedical Fndn 1999–2004, non-exec memb Bd ICL (Scotland) 2000–02, special advsr Royal Bank of Scotland Gp 2000–, advsr scottishjobs.com 2004–05, chm Fairbridge in Scotland 2006–, chm Scottish European Educnl Tst 2007–; dep convenor Ct Univ of Strathclyde 2004–; vice-chm Royal Scottish Nat Orch 2003–06; Hon DUniv Stirling 1999; FRSE 1999; *Recreations* music; *Style*— Gerald Wilson, Esq, CB, FRSE; ✉ 4 Inverleith Avenue South, Edinburgh EH3 5QA (tel 0131 522 4483)

WILSON, (Robert) Gordon; s of Robert George Wilson, of Glasgow; *b* 16 April 1938; *Educ* Douglas HS, Univ of Edinburgh (BL), Univ of Dundee (LLD); *m* 1965, Edith Margaret Hassall; 2 da; *Career* MP (SNP) Dundee East Feb 1974–87; SNP: nat sec 1964–71, vice-chm 1972–73, sr vice-chm 1973–74, dep ldr Parly Gp 1974–79, chm 1979–90, vice-pres until 1997, former treas spokesman; slr; rector Univ of Dundee 1983–86, memb Ct Univ of Abertay Dundee until 1997; chm Marriage Counselling (Tayside) 1989–92, memb Church and Nation Ctee Church of Scotland 2000–03, dir Dundee Age Concern 2001–05, clerk Congregational Bd St Aidans Church and Broughty Ferry New Kirk Dundee 2003–06; *Style*— Mr Gordon Wilson; ✉ 48 Monifieth Road, Broughty Ferry, Dundee DD5 2RX (tel 01382 79009)

WILSON, Guy Edward Nairne Sandilands; s of John Sandilands Wilson (d 1963), and Penelope Ann, *née* Fisher-Rowe; *b* 10 April 1948; *Educ* Heatherdown Sch, Eton, Univ of Aix-en-Provence; *m* 20 Oct 1979, (Marianne) Susan, da of James Drummond D'Arcy Clark; 2 s (John b 1984 d 1998, Hugh b 27 Aug 1986); *Career* CA; Ernst & Young: joined 1967, ptnr 1979–, seconded to HM Treasy 1989–92; FCA, MSI; *Recreations* cricket, golf, tennis, squash, football, gardening; *Clubs* City of London, Brooks's, MCC, IZ, Arabs, Royal St George's Golf, Berkshire Golf; *Style*— Guy Wilson, Esq; ✉ Ernst & Young, 1 More Place, London SE1 2AF (tel 020 7951 3860, fax 020 7951 9323)

WILSON, Guy Murray; s of Capt Rowland George Wilson (d 1950), and Mollie, *née* Munson (d 1987); *b* 18 February 1950; *Educ* New Coll Oxford (MA), Univ of Manchester (Dip Art Gallery and Museum Studies); *m* 28 Oct 1972, Pamela Ruth, da of Alan Robert McCredie, OBE, of Yorkshire; 2 s (John b 1976, David b 1986), 2 da (Rebecca b 1978, Elizabeth b 1983); *Career* Royal Armouries HM Tower of London: keeper of edged weapons 1978–81, dep master 1981–88, master of the armouries 1988–2002; chm Int Ctee of Museums and Collections of Arms and Military History 2002–; memb: Br Cmmn for Mil History, Arms and Armour Socs of GB and Denmark, Advsy Ctee on Hist Wreck Sites 1981–99; Liveryman Worshipful Co of Gunmakers, Liveryman Worshipful Co of Armourers and Brasiers 2000; FSA 1984, FRSA 1992; *Books* Treasures from The Tower of London (jtly, 1982), The Royal Armouries in Leeds: The Making of a Museum (jtly, 1996); *Recreations* walking, reading; *Style*— Guy Wilson, Esq, FSA; ✉ Spring House Farm, Pilmoor, York YO61 2QE (tel 01423 360344, e-mail guy@wilson4004.freeserve.co.uk)

WILSON, His Hon Harold; s of late Edward Simpson Wilson, of Harpenden, Herts, and late Catherine, *née* Donovan; *b* 19 September 1931; *Educ* St Albans Sch, Sidney Sussex Coll Cambridge (state scholar, MA); *m* 1, 1958, Diana Marion, da of late Guy Philip Dudley Sixsmith; 3 s, 1 da; m 2, 1973, Jill Ginever, da of late Charles Edward Walter Barlow; 1 step s, 1 step da; *Career* Nat Serv pilot offr RAF 1950–51, Flying offr RAFVR 1951–54, Flt Lt RAuxAF 1954 until disbandment, Air Efficiency Award 1963; admin trainee King's Coll Hosp then med records offr 1954–57; sch master St Julian's Secdy Mod Sch St Albans 1957–59; called to the Bar Gray's Inn 1958 (Holker exhibitioner 1959, bencher 1998); pupillage with Roger Gray QC Queen Elizabeth Bldgs Temple 1959–60, practice on Oxford Circuit 1960–71 (jr 1964–65, dep chm Monmouthshire QS 1970), practice on Midland & Oxford Circuit 1971–75, recorder 1971–75, chm Industrial Tbnls Birmingham 1976–81, circuit judge (Midland & Oxford Circuit) 1981–2000, resident judge Coventry Crown Court 1983–92, liaison judge Coventry City Magistrates 1986–92, care judge Coventry Care Centre 1991–92, resident judge Oxford Crown Court 1993–2001, liaison judge Oxfordshire Magistrates 1993–2001, care judge Oxford Care Centre 1993–2001, liaison judge Oxfordshire Family Proceedings Panel 1996–2001; dep judge of the High Court 1984–2003; pres Tport Tbnl 1991–96, judge of Employment Appeal Tbnl 1999–2001; additional judge Supreme Court of Gibraltar 2003; memb Matrimonial Rules Ctee 1984–88, memb W Midlands Probation Ctee 1985–92, chm Reparations Advsy Ctee Coventry 1991–92, memb Oxfordshire and Buckinghamshire Probation Ctee (formerly Oxfordshire Probation Ctee) 1993–2001, chm Oxfordshire Family Court Proceedings Ctee 1993–2001, chm Thames Valley Area Criminal Justice Strategy Ctee 1996–2001; hon recorder: Coventry 1986–93, Oxford 1999–2001; Shrieval Remembrancer for Oxfordshire 2004–; *Recreations* watching rugby football, being with my wife, reading, listening to music; *Clubs* RAF (tstee 2005–); *Style*— His Hon Harold Wilson, AE; ✉ Oxford Combined Court Centre, St Aldates, Oxford OX1 1TX (tel 01865 246200); 2 Harcourt Buildings, Temple, London EC4Y 9DB (tel 020 7353 6961)

WILSON, Ian; *b* 1964, Belfast; *Educ* Univ of Ulster (DPhil); *Career* composer; written over 80 pieces incl concertos, orchestral pieces, string quartets, piano trios, chamber and vocal works; work performed by: Nat Symphony Orch of Ireland, BBC Nat Symphony Orch of Wales, Ulster, Belgrade Philharmonic and Norwegian Radio Orchs, London Mozart Players, Irish Chamber Orch, Vanbrugh, Vogler and Endellion Quartets, Psappha, Gemini and Concorde ensembles; work performed at festivals incl: BBC Proms, Int Soc for Contemporary Music World Music Days, Venice Biennale, Cheltenham, Spitalfields, Bath, Ultima Oslo (winner composition 1991); Hamelin (chamber opera) 2001–02 (performed Germany and Ireland 2003); AHRB research fell Univ of Ulster 2000–03; Macaulay fell Arts Cncl of Ireland 1992; elected to Aosdana 1998; *Style*— Ian Wilson, Esq; ✉ e-mail enquiries@ianwilson.org.uk

WILSON, Jacqueline; OBE (2002); da of late Harry Aitken, and Margaret, *née* Clibbens; *b* 17 December 1945, Bath; *Educ* Coombe Girls' Sch, Carshalton Tech Coll; *m* 1965 (m dis), William Millar Wilson; 1 da; *Career* children's author; journalist Jackie magazine D C Thomson Dundee 1963–65 (also gave name to magazine); most borrowed author from public libraries in the UK 2003 and 2004; has sold more than 20 million books in the UK; shortlisted Author of the Year British Book Awards 2003; Children's Laureate 2005–07; *Books* incl: The Story of Tracy Beaker (1991, adapted for TV (5 series) 2002, adapted for radio), The Suitcase Kid (1992, Children's Book Award 1993), The Bed and Breakfast Star (1994, adapted for radio, Young Telegraph/Fully Booked Award 1995, shortlisted Carnegie Medal 1995), Double Act (1995, Gold Award (winner 9–11 years category and overall winner) Nestlé Smarties Book Prize 1995, shortlisted Carnegie Medal 1995, shortlisted Best Children's Book Writers' Guild Award 1995, Children's Book Award 1996, shortlisted Young Telegraph/Fully Booked Award 1996, screenwriter TV adaptation 2002 (Best Children's Fiction Award RTS 2003)), Bad Girls (1996, shortlisted Carnegie Medal 1996, adapted for stage 2003), Girls in Love (1997, adapted for TV 2003), The Lottie Project (1997, adapted for stage 1999, shortlisted Children's Book Award 1998), Girls Under Pressure (1998, shortlisted Children's Book Award 1999), Girls Out Late (1999), The Illustrated Mum (1999, adapted for TV 2003, shortlisted Carnegie Medal 1999, shortlisted Whitbread Children's Book Award 1999, Children's Book of the Year British Book Awards 2000, Guardian Children's Fiction Prize 2000, shortlisted Children's Book Award 2000), Lizzie Zipmouth (2000, Gold Award (6–8 years category) and Kids' Club Network Special Award Nestlé Smarties Book Prize 2000), Vicky Angel (2000), The Dare Game (2000, adapted for radio, adapted for stage), Dustbin Baby (2001, shortlisted W H Smith Award for Children's Literature 2002), Girls in Tears (2002, Children's Book of the Year British Book Awards 2003), Secrets (2002, shortlisted The Book I Couldn't

Put Down Blue Peter Book Award 2003), The Worry Website (2002), Lola Rose (2003), Midnight (2003), Best Friends (2004, shortlisted Red House Children's Book Award 2005), The Diamond Girls (2004), Clean Break (2005), Love Lessons (2005), Candyfloss (2006), Starring Tracy Beaker (2006), Jacky Daydream (2007), Kiss (2007), Totally Jacqueline Wilson (2007); *Style—* Ms Jacqueline Wilson, OBE; ✉ c/o David Higham Associates Ltd, 5–8 Lower John Street, Golden Square, London W1F 9HA (tel 020 7434 5900)

WILSON, Sir James William Douglas; 5 Bt (UK 1906), of Airdrie, New Monkland, Co Lanark; s of Sir Thomas Douglas Wilson, 4 Bt, MC (d 1984), and Pamela Aileen, da of Sir Griffin Wyndham Edward Hanmer, 7 Bt; *b* 8 October 1960; *Educ* Marlborough, Univ of London; *m* 1985, Julia Margaret Louise, da of Joseph Charles Francis Mutty, of Mulberry Hall, Melbourn, Herts; 2 da (Jessica Sarah b 1988, Katrina Elizabeth b 1992), 2 s (Thomas Edward Douglas b 1990, Harry William Patrick b 1995); *Heir* s, Thomas Wilson; *Career* farmer; *Style—* Sir James Wilson, Bt; ✉ Lillingstone Lovell Manor, Buckingham MK18 5BQ (tel 01280 860643)

WILSON, Jane; *Educ* Newcastle Poly (BA), Goldsmiths Coll London (MA); *Career* artist, in partnership with twin sister Louise Wilson, *qv*; *Selected Two-Person Exhibitions* Routes 1 & 9 North (Ac Project Room New York) 1994, Crawl Space British Project II (Galerie Krinzinger Vienna) 1994, Normapaths (Chisendale Gallery London) 1995, Jane and Louise Wilson (LEA London) 1997, Stasi City (Kunstverein Hanover) 1997, Film Stills (Aki-Ex Gallery Tokyo) 1998, Jane and Louise Wilson (Serpentine Gallery London) 1999, Gamma (Lisson Gallery London) 1999, Turner Prize (Tate Gallery) 1999–2000, Star City (303 Gallery New York) 2000; *Selected Group Exhibitions* Into the Nineties 4 (Mall Galleries London) 1992, Close Up (42nd Street New York) 1993, Over the Limit (Arnolfini Bristol) 1993, The Daily Planet (Transmission Gallery Glasgow) 1993, BT New Contemporaries (Cornerhouse Manchester and other venues) 1993–94, Le Shuttle (Künstlerhaus Bethanien Berlin) 1994, Use Your Allusion. Recent Video Art (Museum of Contemporary Art Chicago) 1994, Domestic Violence (Gio Marconi Milan) 1994, Beyond Belief (Lisson Gallery London) 1994, Gang Warfare (Independent Art Space London) 1995, Here and Now (Serpentine Gallery London) 1995, Speaking of Sofas... (Soho House London) 1995, Corpus Delicti: London in the 1990's (Kunstforeningen Copenhagen) 1995, Files (Bunker Berlin) 1996, British Artists (Rhona Hoffman Gallery Chicago) 1996, NowHere (Louisiana Museum Humlebaek Denmark) 1996, Co-operators (Southampton City Art Gallery and Huddersfield Art Gallery) 1996, Hospital (Galerie Max Hezler Berlin) 1997, Broken Home Greene Naftali New York) 1997, Ein Stück Vom Himmel (Kunsthalle Nuremburg) 1997, Malos Habitos (Soledad Lorenzo Gallery Madrid) 1998, The and Now (Lisson Gallery London) 1998, View 1 (Mary Boone New York) 1998, Gamma (Serpentine Gallery London) 1999, Carnegie International (Carnegie Museum Pittsburgh) 1999, Trace, Liverpool Biennial (Tate Gallery Liverpool) 1999, Age of Influence: Reflections in the Mirror of American Culture (MCA Chicago) 2000, A Shot in the Head (Lisson Gallery London) 2000, Media City Seoul (Korean Biennial) 2000, Das Gedächtnis der Kunst (Historisches Museum Frankfurt am Main) 2000–01; *Awards* Barclays Young Artist Award 1993, DAAD Scholarship 1999, nominated for Turner Prize 1999, IASPIS International Artist's Studio Program in Sweden (residency in Stockholm) 2000; *Style—* Ms Jane Wilson; ✉ c/o Lisson Gallery, 52–5 Bell Street & 67 Lisson Street, London NW1 5DA (tel 020 7724 2738, fax 020 7724 7124)

WILSON, Prof Janet Ann; da of Henry Donald Wilson (d 1991), of Edinburgh, and Margaret Penuel MacGregor, *née* Robertson (d 2005); *b* 10 November 1955; *Educ* George Watson's Ladies' Coll Edinburgh, Univ of Edinburgh Med Sch (BSc, MB ChB, MD, Ellis Prize in Paediatrics), FRCS, FRCSEd; *m* 1987 (m dis 1996), Mark Nicholas Gaze, s of John Owen Gaze; 1 s (Donald John b 1991); *Career* house offr: in gen med Eastern Gen Hosp Edinburgh 1979–80, in gen surgery The Royal Infirmary Edinburgh 1980; demonstrator in anatomy Univ of Edinburgh 1980–81; SHO: in gen surgery Dept of Clinical Surgery Univ of Edinburgh 1981–82, in otolaryngology City Hosp Edinburgh 1982–83; registrar in otolaryngology City Hosp, Royal Hosp for Sick Children Edinburgh and Bangour Hosp 1983–85, lectr in otolaryngology Univ of Edinburgh 1985–87, sr registrar in otolaryngology City and Associated Hosps Edinburgh 1987–92, conslt otolaryngologist and hon sr lectr Royal Infirmary Glasgow 1992–95, prof of otolaryngology, head and neck surgery Univ of Newcastle upon Tyne 1995–; pres Otorhinolaryngological Research Soc 2002–04 (hon sec 1990–94, memb Cncl 1988–90); memb Cncl: Royal Soc of Med 1994–95, Royal Coll of Surgns of Edinburgh 1995–2000; hon asst sec Br Assoc of Otorhinolaryngologists - Head and Neck Surgns 2005–; Euro Rhinologic Soc Prize 1986, Br Academic Conf ORL Research Prize 1987, Angell James Prize 1988, Royal Soc of Med Downs Prize 1989, Lionel Coll Meml Fellowship 1990, Ernest Finch visiting prof Sheffield 1996, Univ of London Yearsley lectr 1999, Robert Owen lectr 2001, Kleinsasser lectr 2006; memb: Euro Rhinologic Soc 1986, Scottish Otolaryngological Soc 1987, Br Soc of Otolaryngologists 1987, Caledonian Soc of Gastroenterology 1989, BMA 1989, Br Soc of Gastroenterology 1992, Br Voice Assoc 1997, Harveian Soc (Edinburgh) 1999; *Books* Stell and Maran's Head and Neck Surgery (jt author, 4 edn); also 10 book chapters and over 150 scientific papers; *Recreations* performing arts, the company of friends; *Style—* Prof Janet A Wilson; ✉ Oak House, 1 Jesmond Dene Road, Newcastle upon Tyne NE2 3QJ (tel 0191 284 0251); Department of Otolaryngology, Head and Neck Surgery, University of Newcastle upon Tyne, Freeman Hospital, Newcastle upon Tyne NE7 7DN (tel 0191 223 1086, fax 0191 223 1246, e-mail j.a.wilson@ncl.ac.uk)

WILSON, Dr Jean Lesley; da of late Alan Herbert Wilson, and Beryl, *née* Wagstaff; *b* 2 August 1945; *Educ* King Edward VI HS for Girls Edgbaston (fndn scholar), Newnham Coll Cambridge (MA, PhD, Clothworkers' exhibitioner, Charles Oldham Shakespeare scholar); *m* 1972, Prof Norman Hammond, *qv*, s of William Hammond; 1 s (Gawain Jonathon Curle b 2 Dec 1975), 1 da (Deborah Julian Curle b 13 Sept 1982); *Career* lectr in English Univ of Edinburgh 1970–72, fell King's Coll Cambridge 1972–75, adjunct prof of English Boston Univ 1994–2007; FSA 1980; *Books* Entertainments for Elizabeth I (1980), The Archaeology of Shakespeare (1995, winner Archaeology Book of the Year Award 1996); author of numerous articles in jls and newspapers; *Recreations* riding, needlework; *Style—* Dr Jean Wilson, FSA; ✉ Wholeway, Harlton, Cambridge CB3 7ET (tel 01223 262376, e-mail jlw29@cam.ac.uk); 83 Ivy Street, No 32, Brookline, MA 02146–4073, USA (tel 00 1 617 739 9077, e-mail wilson@bu.edu)

WILSON, Jim; *b* 15 December 1941; *Educ* Ballyclare HS, Belfast Coll of Technol; *m* Muriel; 1 s, 1 da; *Career* apprentice engr Harland & Wolff Ltd 1958–62, Merchant Navy engr (deep sea) Portline Ltd 1962–64, engr and asst head Engr Planning Dept Br Enkalon Ltd 1964–73, ptnr Smyth & Wilson 1972–88; elected Newtownabbey BC 1975; UU Pty: memb 1976–, chief exec 1987–88, memb exec ctee; MLA (UU) 1998–2007, UU chief whip1998–2002, dep speaker NI Assembly 2002–03; vice-pres S Antrim UU Assoc; memb bd: NI Water Cncl, Countryside Alliance NI, Bann System Ltd; memb Bd of Govrs Kilbride Primary Sch; memb Kilbride Parish Church; *Style—* Jim Wilson, Esq

WILSON, John Robert; OBE (1999); *b* 13 June 1949; *Educ* Univ of Southampton (BA), LSE (MSc); *m* Dec 1971, Lesley; 1 s (James b June 1983), 1 da (Alice b Aug 1989); *Career* sec: Clothing Manufacturers' Federation, Shirt Manufacturers' Federation, Tie Manufacturers' Assoc and the Corsetry Manufacturers' Assoc 1977–81 (joined secretariat 1972); British Clothing Industry Assoc: gen sec 1981–84, dep dir 1984, dir 1985–; dir and chief exec British Fashion Cncl 1987–2005, dir and sec Mens' and Boys' Wear Exhibitions Ltd 1985–93 (sec 1984–91); dir: British Knitting and Clothing Export Cncl 1987–91, Apparel Marketing Services (Export) Ltd; DG Br Knitting and Clothing Confederation 1991–, DG British Apparel and Textile Confederation 1992–; *Publications* The UK Fashion Designer Scene (report for DTI, 1986); *Style—* John Wilson, Esq, OBE; ✉ British Clothing Industry Association Ltd, 5 Portland Place, London W1B 1PW (tel 020 7636 7788)

WILSON, Prof Judith Elizabeth; da of H Perkins (d 1965), of Northants, and Margaret Joan Margrave; *b* 28 May 1950, Northampton; *Educ* Northampton HS, Univ of London; *m* 1969, Fergus Wilson; 2 da (Samantha, Tanya); *Career* property owner; owner of 675 houses in Kent; maths teacher Kent 1971–92, dep headteacher Southlands Sch 1987–92; prof Imperial Coll Business School; *Style—* Prof Judith Wilson; ✉ The Limes, Heath Road, Boughton Monchelsea, Maidstone, Kent ME17 4HS (tel 01622 743163, fax 01622 741248, e-mail fergus.wilson@btopenworld.com); Judith Wilson's PA, 2 Green Lane, Boughton Monchelsea, Maidstone, Kent (tel 01622 749191, e-mail tina60office@btopenworld.com)

WILSON, Justin Boyd; s of Keith Ronald Wilson, and Lynne Wilson; *b* 31 July 1978; *Educ* Birkdale Sch; *Career* motor racing driver; began racing Cadet Karts 1987, fifth Formula A Br Championship 1994, third Renault Grand Prix Buckmore Park 1994, winner race Formula Vauxhall Jr Winter Series 1994, winner Formula Vauxhall Challenge Cup 1995, third Formula Vauxhall Jr Championship 1995, third Formula Vauxhall Winter Series 1995 (Best Newcomer), second Formula Vauxhall Championship (Paul Stewart Racing) 1996, fourth Formula Vauxhall Championship (Paul Stewart Racing) 1997, winner Formula Palmer Audi Championship 1998, eighteenth FIA Int Formula 3000 Championship 1999, fifth FIA Int Formula 3000 Championship 2000, winner FIA Int Formula 3000 Championship 2001 (first Br winner, record number of points and podiums), fourth Telefonica World Series by Nissan 2002; Formula One Grand Prix: debut 2003 (test driver Jordan 2001), Minardi then Jaguar 2003; Champ Car World Series Conquest Racing 2004; BRDC Chris Bristow Trophy 1995, finalist McLaren Autosport BRDC Young Driver of the Year Award 1995 and 1998, Gold Star BRDC 2001; *Clubs* BRDC; *Style—* Justin Wilson, Esq; ✉ website www.justinwilson.co.uk

WILSON, Kate; da of Gerald Wilson, and Margaret Wilson; *Educ* Univ of Oxford (BA); *Career* rights mangr Faber & Faber 1986–88, rights dir Reed Children's Books 1988–93, md and publisher Macmillan Children's Books 1993–; memb Publisher's Assoc; *Recreations* my children; *Style—* Ms Kate Wilson; ✉ Macmillan Children's Books, 20 New Wharf Road, London N1 9RR (tel 020 7014 6000)

WILSON, Keith Drummond; s of Gordon Drummond Wilson (d 2005), of Maldon, Victoria, Aust, and Heather, *née* Lindsay (d 1994); *b* 18 July 1960; *Educ* The King's Sch Parramatta, Royal Melbourne Inst of Technol; *m* 12 July 1990, Pamela Elizabeth, da of John Angus Mackay (d 2006); 2 da (Elizabeth Rose b 1993, Olivia Catherine b 1996); *Career* news reporter The Herald Melbourne 1979–83, features ed The News and Travel International (TNT) London 1983; Amateur Photographer: news ed 1984–85, dep tech ed 1985–87, features ed 1987–88; launch ed What Camera? 1988–89; ed: Amateur Photographer 1989–98, Photo Technique 1993–95; gp ed IPC Photographic titles 1994–98; ed Crime Weekly 1999, launch ed Voice (for Scottish Telecom) 1999, launch ed Outdoor Photography 2000, gp ed Black & White Photography 2001–, editorial dir GMC Publications 2005–; mangr Photo Panel Euro Imaging & Sound Assoc 1995–97; *Books* Focus On Photography (1994), AVA Guide to Travel Photography (2004), Viewfinder (2005); *Recreations* photography, hill walking, cricket, cooking, cinema; *Style—* Keith Wilson, Esq; ✉ Outdoor Photography, GMC Publications, 86 High Street, Lewes, East Sussex BN7 1XN (tel 01273 477374, e-mail keithw@thegmcgroup.com)

WILSON, Louise; *Educ* Duncan of Jordanstone Coll of Art Dundee (BA), Goldsmiths Coll London (MA); *Career* artist, in partnership with twin sister Jane Wilson, *qv*; *Selected Two-Person Exhibitions* Routes 1 & 9 North (Ac Project Room New York) 1994, Crawl Space British Project II (Galerie Krinzinger Vienna) 1994, Normapaths (Chisendale Gallery London) 1995, Jane and Louise Wilson (LEA London) 1997, Stasi City (Kunstverein Hanover) 1997, Film Stills (Aki-Ex Gallery Tokyo) 1998, Jane and Louise Wilson (Serpentine Gallery London) 1999, Gamma (Lisson Gallery London) 1999, Turner Prize (Tate Gallery) 1999–2000, Star City (303 Gallery New York) 2000; *Selected Group Exhibitions* Into the Nineties 4 (Mall Galleries London) 1992, Close Up (42nd Street New York) 1993, Over the Limit (Arnolfini Bristol) 1993, The Daily Planet (Transmission Gallery Glasgow) 1993, BT New Contemporaries (Cornerhouse Manchester and other venues) 1993–94, Le Shuttle (Künstlerhaus Bethanien Berlin) 1994, Use Your Allusion. Recent Video Art (Museum of Contemporary Art Chicago) 1994, Domestic Violence (Gio Marconi Milan) 1994, Beyond Belief (Lisson Gallery London) 1994, Gang Warfare (Independent Art Space London) 1995, Here and Now (Serpentine Gallery London) 1995, Speaking of Sofas... (Soho House London) 1995, Corpus Delicti: London in the 1990's (Kunstforeningen Copenhagen) 1995, Files (Bunker Berlin) 1996, British Artists (Rhona Hoffman Gallery Chicago) 1996, NowHere (Louisiana Museum Humlebaek Denmark) 1996, Co-operators (Southampton City Art Gallery and Huddersfield Art Gallery) 1996, Hospital (Galerie Max Hezler Berlin) 1997, Broken Home Greene Naftali New York) 1997, Ein Stück Vom Himmel (Kunsthalle Nuremburg) 1997, Malos Habitos (Soledad Lorenzo Gallery Madrid) 1998, The and Now (Lisson Gallery London) 1998, View 1 (Mary Boone New York) 1998, Gamma (Serpentine Gallery London) 1999, Carnegie International (Carnegie Museum Pittsburgh) 1999, Trace, Liverpool Biennial (Tate Gallery Liverpool) 1999, Age of Influence: Reflections in the Mirror of American Culture (MCA Chicago) 2000, A Shot in the Head (Lisson Gallery London) 2000, Media City Seoul (Korean Biennial) 2000, Das Gedächtnis der Kunst (Historisches Museum Frankfurt am Main) 2000–01; *Awards* Barclays Young Artist Award 1993, DAAD Scholarship 1999, nominated for Turner Prize 1999, IASPIS International Artist's Studio Program in Sweden (residency in Stockholm) 2000; *Style—* Ms Louise Wilson; ✉ c/o Lisson Gallery, 52–5 Bell Street & 67 Lisson Street, London NW1 5DA

WILSON, Lynn Anthony; s of Connolly Thomas Wilson (d 1970), of Northampton, and Frances, *née* Chapman (d 1975); *b* 8 December 1939; *Educ* Oakham Sch; *m* 4 April 1964, Judith Helen, da of late Jack Ronald Mann; 2 s (Nicholas b 30 May 1967, Giles b 27 May 1969); *Career* dep chm Wilson Connolly Holdings plc 2001–03 (md 1966, chm 1982–2001); nat pres The House Builders Fedn 1981; FCIOB, CIMgt; *Recreations* cricket, golf, horseracing, shooting; *Style—* Lynn Wilson, Esq; ✉ The Maltings, Tithe Farm, Moulton Road, Holcot, Northampton NN6 9SH (tel 01604 782240, fax 01604 782241)

WILSON, Mark Simon; s of Dennis Lionel Wilson, of Great Missenden, Bucks, and Elizabeth, *née* Jones; *b* 10 June 1961, Rugby, Warks; *Educ* Chesham HS, Univ of Birmingham, Coll of Law; *m* 30 Aug 1986, Helen Louise, *née* Swierczek; 2 s (Thomas Ludwik Edward b 19 Jan 1991, Nicholas Mark b 28 Mar 1997), 1 da (Anna Beth b 11 Feb 1993); *Career* slr; articled clerk Kidd Rapinet 1983–85, ptnr Freeth Cartwright 1990–99 (slr 1985–90), fndr ptnr Cartwright King 2000–; memb: Law Soc 1985, Serious Fraud Assoc 2001; *Recreations* motor racing, mountain biking, skiing, sailing; *Clubs* BARC; *Style—* Mark Wilson, Esq; ✉ Cartwright King, Norwich Union House, South Parade, Nottingham NG1 2LJ (tel 0115 958 7444, fax 0115 958 8666)

WILSON, (Alan) Martin; QC (1982); s of Joseph Norris Wilson (d 1986), of London, and Kate, *née* Clusky (d 1982); *b* 12 February 1940; *Educ* Kilburn GS, Univ of Nottingham (LLB); *m* 1, 1966 (m dis 1975), Pauline Frances Kibart; 2 da (Rebecca b 1968, Anna b 1971); m 2, 20 March 1976, Julia Mary, da of Patrick Maurice George Carter, OBE (d 2001), of Malvern, Worcs; 1 da (Alexandra b 1980); *Career* called to the Bar Gray's Inn 1963; recorder of the Crown Court (Midland & Oxford Circuit) 1979–2005; occasional memb Hong Kong Bar 1988–, admitted Malaysian Bar 1995, admitted temporary advocate Isle of Man 2004; *Recreations* shooting, literature, travel; *Style—* Martin Wilson, Esq, QC; ✉ 7 Bedford Row, London WC1R 4BU (tel 020 7242 3555, fax 020 7242 2511, e-mail amwilson@easynet.co.uk)

WILSON, Brig Sir Mathew John Anthony; 6 Bt (UK 1874), of Eshton Hall, Co York, OBE (Mil 1979, MBE Mil 1971), MC (1972); s of Anthony Thomas Wilson (d 1979), by his 1 w Margaret (d 1980), formerly w of Vernon Motion and da of late Alfred Holden; suc unc, Sir (Mathew) Martin Wilson, 5 Bt 1991; *b* 2 October 1935; *Educ* Trinity Coll Sch Port Hope; *m* 1962, Janet Mary, er da of late Edward Worsfold Mowll, JP, of Walmer; 1 s (Mathew Edward Amcotts b 1966), 1 da (Victoria Mary b 1968); *Heir* s, Mathew Wilson; *Career* Brig King's Own Yorks LI, ret 1983; exec dir Wilderness Fndn (UK) 1983–85; pres and ceo Dolphin Voyaging Inc 1995–; *Books* Taking Terrapin Home: A Love Affair with a Small Catamaran (1994), The Bahamas Cruising Guide with the Turks and Caicos Islands (1997), The Land of War Elephants. Travels Beyond the Pale: Afghanistan, Pakistan, and India (2003), Seeking Havens: Travels along a Line of Latitude 17 Degrees South in Andean Peru, Bolivia and the South Pacific (2006); *Clubs* Explorers; *Style*— Brig Sir Mathew Wilson, Bt, OBE, MC

WILSON, Dr Michael Anthony; s of Charles Kenneth Wilson (d 1995), and Bertha, *née* Poppleton (d 1987); *b* 2 June 1936; *Educ* Roundhay Sch, Univ of Leeds (MB ChB, DObstRCOG); *m* 24 Jan 1959, Marlene; 2 s (Mark Edward b 3 May 1960, Ian Gregory b 2 May 1962); *Career* princ in GP Strensall N Yorks 1961–96; pres Yorks Regnl Cncl BMA 1975–79, chm Gen Med Servs Ctee 1984–90 (dep chm 1979–84); dir: BMA Servs Ltd 1987–2000, BMA Pension Fund 1992–2000; memb: Standing Med Ctee to DHSS 1967–69 and 1978–90 (dep chm 1986–90), Cncl BMA 1977–90 and 1992–2000, GMC 1989–2003 (assoc 2003–06), Advsy Bd Med Protection Soc 1990–97, Code of Practice Authy Assoc of Br Pharmaceutical Industry 1990–, NHS Clinical Standards Advsy Gp 1991–93, Jt Conslts Ctee 1991–97; vice-pres BMA 2001 (fell 1979–); FRCGP; *Recreations* travel, Rotary, golf; *Clubs* East India, Rotary (York), York Golf, Ampleforth Coll Golf (sec); *Style*— Dr Michael Wilson; ✉ Longueville, Mill Hill, Huntington, North Yorkshire YO32 9PY (tel 01904 768861, fax 01904 762012)

WILSON, Michael Gerald; s of John Charles Wilson (d 1992), of Hove, E Sussex, and Dorothy Beatrice, *née* Harmer (d 1985); *b* 6 December 1942; *m* 22 Aug 1964, Maureen Brenda, da of Arthur Charles Hiron (d 1982); 1 da (Sarah Michelle b 28 March 1973), 1 s (James Michael b 27 Oct 1981); *Career* admitted slr 1975 with Slaughter & May; memb: Law Soc 1975, Int Bar Assoc 1975, S Western Legal Fndn 1982, Asia Pacific Lawyers Assoc 1985, Inter Pacific Bar Assoc 1990, Br Insurance Law Assoc; Freeman: City of London, Worshipful Co of Slrs; FRSA; *Recreations* golf, travel, reading, music; *Clubs* RAC; *Style*— Michael Wilson, Esq; ✉ Lantern Cottage, Chalk Lane, Ashtead, Surrey KT21 1DH (tel 01372 273732)

WILSON, Maj-Gen Michael Peter Bruce Grant (Mike); s of Ian Henry Wilson (d 1960), of Jinja, Uganda, and Catherine Collingwood, *née* Bruce; *b* 19 August 1943; *Educ* Duke of York's Sch Nairobi, Mons Officer Cadet Sch, Royal Sch of Mil Engrg, Royal Sch of Mil Survey, UCL (Dip Photogrammetry); *m* 17 Feb 1967, Margaret Ritchie, *née* Colquhoun; 2 s (Iain, Craig), 1 da (Amy); *Career* cmmnd RE 1965, troop cdr Airfields Regt, Army Survey Course 1970, subsequently with Directorate of Overseas Surveys (posted Kenya, Uganda and Nigeria) and numerous other mil survey appts in UK, Germany and US, cdr Survey Engr Gp 1986, dir Geographic Ops 1990, DG and chief exec Mil Survey 1992, DG Intelligence and Geographic Resources 1994, chief exec Defence Vetting Agency 1996, chief exec Gangmasters Licensing Authy 2005, chief exec Security Industry Assoc 2007; involved with: RE Assoc, Defence Surveyors Assoc; memb Br Deer Soc; molecatcher to vicar of Old Malton 2003; memb Co of Mechants of the Staple of England; FRICS 1988, FRGS 1990, FIMgt 1991; *Recreations* working dogs, shooting, climbing, fishing, golf, deer mgmnt; *Clubs* North Wolds Gun, Ryedale Anglers, York Fly Fishers; *Style*— Maj-Gen Mike Wilson; ✉ Security Industry Authority, 90 High Holborn, London WC1V 6WY (e-mail mike.wilson@thesia.org.uk)

WILSON, Michael Sumner; s of Cdr Peter Sumner Wilson, AFC (d 1993), and Margaret Kathleen, *née* Letchworth (d 1996); *b* 5 December 1943; *Educ* St Edward's Sch Oxford; *m* 5 June 1975 (m dis), Mary Dorothy Wordsworth, da of John Alexander Drysdale (d 1986); 1 da (Amanda Wordsworth Sumner b 12 March 1976); *Career* Equity & Law 1963–68, Abbey Life 1968–71; Hambro Life/Allied Dunbar: broker mangr 1971–73, exec dir 1973–76, main bd dir 1976–82, jt dep md 1982–84, jt md 1984–88, gp chief exec 1988–90; jt fndr dir St James's Place Gp 1991–, chm St James's Place plc 2004– (chief exec 1991–2004), chm St James's Place Unit Trust Group 1997–; dir BAT Industries 1989–90, non-exec dir Vendôme Luxury Group plc 1993–98; chm Mental Health Fndn 1996–2000; *Recreations* tennis, racing; *Style*— Michael Wilson, Esq; ✉ 42 Eaton Place, London SW1X 8AL; St James's Place plc, Spencer House, 27 St James's Place, London SW1A 1NR (tel 020 7514 1907, fax 020 7514 1952)

WILSON, Michael W C; *b* 15 August 1955, Belfast; *Educ* Queen's Univ of Belfast (LLB, Cert); *Career* admitted slr NI 1978; ptnr and head of company and commercial law Elliott Duffy Garrett; pres Slrs' Disciplinary Tbnl 2003– (memb 1998–); chm Health and Personal Social Services Disciplinary Panel 2005–; chm NI Branch R3 (Assoc of Business Recovery Professionals) 2006–; MSPI 1993, licensed insolvency practitioner 1993, FABRP 2000; *Style*— Michael Wilson, Esq; ✉ Elliott Duffy Garrett, Royston House, 34 Upper Queen Street, Belfast BT1 6FD (tel 028 9024 5034, fax 028 9024 1337)

WILSON, Prof Nairn Hutchison Fulton; CBE (2004); s of William Fulton Wilson (d 2000), of Kilmarnock, Ayrshire, and Anne Hutchison, *née* Stratton; *b* 26 April 1950; *Educ* Strathallan Sch, Univ of Edinburgh (BDS), Univ of Manchester (MSc, PhD); *m* 1; 2 da (Kirsty b 1972, Shona b 1976 d 1997); m 2, 12 April 1982, Margaret Alexandra, *née* Jones; 1 da (Hannah b 1983), 1 s (Iain b 1984); *Career* lectr in restorative dentistry Univ of Edinburgh 1974–75; Univ of Manchester: lectr 1975–82, sr lectr 1982–86, prof of restorative dentistry 1986–2001, pro-vice-chllr 1997–99, dean and clinical dir Univ Dental Hosp of Manchester 1992–95; KCL: dean and head Dental Inst (at Guy's, King's Coll and St Thomas's Hosps) 2001–, prof of restorative dentistry 2001–; non-exec dir North Manchester NHS Healthcare Tst 1994–97; pres: Br Assoc of Teachers of Conservative Dentistry 1992, Section of Odontology Manchester Medical Soc 1993–94, Br Soc for Restorative Dentistry 1994–95, Academy of Operative Dentistry European Sec 1998–2000, Educational Research Gp Int Assoc Dental Research 1998–2000, European Fedn of Conservative Dentistry 2003–; ed: Jl of Dentistry 1986–2000, Quintessentials of Dental Practice 2003–; dean Faculty of Dental Surgery Royal Coll of Surgns of Edinburgh 1995–98; fndr tstee Manchester Dental Educn Tst 1993–2001, tstee Oral and Dental Research Tst 1995– (chm and actg dir 2003–); chm: Manchester Dental Educn Centre 1995–2000, Jt Ctee for Specialist Training in Dentistry 1998–99, Specialist Trg Advsy Ctee for Dentistry 1999–2003, British Dental Eds Forum 2004–, Cncl of Heads and Deans od Dental Schools 2006–; pres GDC 1999–2003; College Medal RCS(Ed) 2001, George M Hollenback Meml Prize Acad of Operative Dentistry 2002; hon fell Hong Kong Coll of Dental Surgery; fell: American Coll of Dentists, Acad of Dental Materials, Pierre Fauchard Acad, Br Soc for Restorative Dentistry, HE Acad, KCL; memb: Acad of Operative Dentistry, American Acad of Restorative Dentistry; DRD RCS(Ed), fell FGDP, FDS RCS(Ed), FDS RCS(Eng); *Publications* author of approx 250 scientific papers and various textbooks; *Recreations* various; *Clubs* Strathallian, Athenaeum; *Style*— Prof Nairn Wilson, CBE; ✉ King's College London Dental Institute, Central Office, Floor 18 Guy's Tower, Guy's Hospital, London SE1 9RT (tel 020 7188 1164, fax 020 7188 1159, e-mail nairn.wilson@kcl.ac.uk)

WILSON, Rt Hon Lord Justice; Rt Hon Sir Nicholas Allan Roy Wilson; kt (1993), PC (2005); s of late (Roderick) Peter Garratt Wilson, of Fittleworth, W Sussex, and (Dorothy) Anne, *née* Chenevix-Trench; *b* 9 May 1945; *Educ* Bryanston, Worcester Coll Oxford (BA); *m* 14 Dec 1974, Margaret, da of Reginald Frank Higgins (d 1986); 1 s (Matthew b 1977), 1 da (Camilla b 1981); *Career* called to the Bar Inner Temple 1967; practised Western Circuit, recorder of the Crown Court 1987–93, QC 1987, judge of the High Court of Justice (Family Div) 1993–2005, Lord Justice of Appeal 2005–; pres Family Mediators Assoc 1998–; Hon Dr Staffordshire Univ 2004; *Style*— The Rt Hon Lord Justice Wilson; ✉ Royal Courts of Justice, Strand, London WC2A 2LL

WILSON, Nick; s of Stanley Wilson (d 1981), and Dorothy Wilson, of Winchester; *b* 21 April 1949; *Educ* Buxton Coll, Univ of Manchester (BA); *m* Sept 1984, Annie; 3 da (Sadie b 7 March 1986, Abigail, Zoe (twins) b 26 March 1989), 1 s (Bradley b 29 May 1995), 1 step s (Robin b 31 Oct 1974); *Career* dir and prodr children's progs BBC 1975–84, ed children's progs TV-am 1984–87 (devised Wide Awake Club, Wacaday and Are You Awake Yet?), ed children's and youth progs Granada TV 1988–89, dir of progs The Children's Channel 1993–94, ptnr Clear Idea Television 1989– (prodr numerous progs incl Top Banana, Hitman & Her and Coast to Coast), dir of children's progs Channel 5 Broadcasting 1996–; memb: BAFTA, RTS; *Awards* BAFTA nomination for Best Children's Factual Prog 1986, TRIC Award for Best Children's Prog 1987, Chicago Children's Film Festival Best Short Drama (for Snobs); *Recreations* tennis, fly fishing, family; *Style*— Nick Wilson; ✉ Five TV Broadcasting Ltd, 22 Long Acre, London WC2E 9LY (tel 020 7550 5555, fax 020 7836 1273, e-mail nick.wilson@five.tv and nickwilson@nickwilson.plus.com)

WILSON, Nigel Guy; s of Noel Wilson, and Joan Louise, *née* Lovibond; *b* 23 July 1935; *Educ* Univ Coll Sch, CCC Oxford (MA); *m* 1996, Hanneke Marion Wirtjes; *Career* lectr Merton Coll Oxford 1957–62, fellow and tutor in classics Lincoln Coll Oxford 1962–2002; James P R Lyell reader in bibliography 2003; visiting prof: Univ of Padua 1985, École Normale Supérieure Paris 1986; Premio Anassilaos 1999, Hon DLitt Univ of Uppsala 2001; FBA 1980; *Books* Menander Rhetor (with D A Russell, 1981), Scribes and Scholars (with L D Reynolds, 3 edn 1991), Scholars of Byzantium (1983, 2 edn 1996), Oxford Classical Text of Sophocles (with Sir Hugh Lloyd-Jones, 1990), From Byzantium to Italy (1992), Photius: The Bibliotheca (1994), Aelian: Historical Miscellany (1997), Pietro Bembo: Oratio pro litteris graecis (2003), Oxford Classical Text of Aristophanes (2007); *Recreations* tennis (real), oenology, travel, bridge; *Style*— Nigel Wilson, Esq, FBA; ✉ Lincoln College, Oxford OX1 3DR (tel 01865 279800, fax 01865 279802)

WILSON, Nigel Richard; s of Lt-Col Richard Wilson (d 1992), and Jean Dorothy, *née* Jamieson (d 1992); *b* 18 February 1946; *Educ* Radley; *m* 8 July 1971, Ann (d 1990), da of John Rowlands, of Canada; 1 s (William Pennington b 1974), 1 da (Rebecca Pennington (Mrs Mackenzie) b 1977); m 2, 19 July 1991, Jennifer, da of Dudley Clark, of Thornborough, Bucks; *Career* ptnr McAnally Montgomery 1975–83, ptnr Laing & Cruickshank 1983, dir Alexander Laing & Cruickshank 1983–88, md Laing & Cruickshank Investment Management Services Ltd 1987–88; Chiswell Associates Ltd (formerly CS Investment Ltd then Cantrade Investment Management Ltd): dep md 1988–98, chm 1998–2003, non-exec dir 2003–; chm: Royal Tokaji Wine Company 1993–97 (dir 1993–), Chateau de Landiras Investments 1994–99; dir: BOE Investment Management Ltd 1998–, Close-Beacon Investment Fund plc 1999–; fin conslt 2003–; chm Ski Club of GB 1979–82; dir: Nat Ski Fedn 1979–82, Tonbridge Services 1993–97; hon steward All England Lawn Tennis & Croquet Club 1969–90, memb Multiple Sclerosis Fin Ctee 1983–2000; hon treasurer: Tonbridge Sch 1993–96, Sir Andrew Judd Fndn 1993–96; Freeman City of London 1972, Liveryman Worshipful Co of Skinners 1982 (memb Ct 1993–98); Commandeur d'Honneur de Commanderie du Bon Temps de Medoc et des Graves 1995; *Books* Silk Cut Ski Guide (1974); *Recreations* skiing, golf, tennis, cricket, shooting, fishing; *Clubs* City of London, Ski Club of GB; *Style*— Nigel Wilson, Esq; ✉ Sarasin Chiswell, Juxon House, 100 St Paul's Churchyard, London EC4M 8BU (tel 020 7038 7000)

WILSON, Patrick (Pat); s of Brig E W G Wilson, CBE, MC (d 1971), of Selkirk, and Edith Margaret, *née* Smith; *b* 6 June 1931, Selkirk; *Educ* Loretto, Edinburgh Coll of Agric; *m* 22 Nov 1955, Elizabeth Mary; 3 da (Rosemary (Mrs Nicoll) b 30 Aug 1957, Wendy (Mrs Busby) b 14 Sept 1959, Tessa (Mrs Searle) b 17 March 1963), 1 s (Randal b 22 April 1961); *Career* landowner; farmer: Perthshire 1953–, Sutherland and Wester Ross 1960–; chm and dir of several cos, chm Glenleven Estates, md Aberuchill 1981–2005; sr ptnr: Pat Wilson Farms, Pat Wilson Sporting Enterprises, Pat Wilson Farms Blackpark and Kinlochwe; former Scotland chm Br Deer Soc (fndr chm Central Scotland branch), fndr chm of first deer mgmnt gps; memb: Scottish Landowners Fedn, NFU of Scotland; standard bearer Royal Burgh of Selkirk 1955; *Recreations* stalking, shooting, fishing; *Clubs* R&A, Flyfishers, Royal Perth Golfing Soc and County and City; *Style*— Pat Wilson, Esq; ✉ Blackpark Lodge, Logiealmond, Perth PH1 3JB (tel 07831 135748, fax 01738 583707)

WILSON, Paul; OBE (2004); s of Thomas William Wilson (d 1947), of Newcastle upon Tyne, and Gladys Rawden, *née* Scaife (d 1989); *b* 2 August 1947; *Educ* Univ of Northumbria and Univ of London (Dip Nursing), Univ of Northumbria and CNAA (DMS), Henley Management Coll and Brunel Univ (MBA); *Career* registered mental nurse St Nicholas Hosp Newcastle upon Tyne 1965–68, head of nursing in intensive therapy (formerly staff nurse) Royal Victoria Infirmary Newcastle upon Tyne 1970–74 (registered gen nurse 1968–70), mangr of night nursing services W Sector Hosps Northumberland HA 1974–76, staff offr to area nursing offr Merton Sutton and Wandsworth Area HA 1976–77, divnl nursing offr Roehampton Health Dist 1977–82, dir policy and planning Maidstone HA 1985–87 (chief nursing offr 1982–85), gen mangr Mental Health Services Greater Glasgow Health Bd 1987–91, dir of health care contracting Lothian Health Bd 1994–95 (dir of operations 1991–94), dir NHS Tsts NHS in Scotland Management Executive 1994–95, currently exec nurse dir NHS Lanarkshire; *Recreations* cats, children, Moi, food, travel, music; *Style*— Paul Wilson, OBE

WILSON, Prof Pelham Mark Hedley; s of John Leonard Wilson (d 1972), and Dilys Winifred Pugh; *b* 29 April 1952; *Educ* St Paul's, St John's Coll Cambridge; *m* 22 Aug 1992, Sibylle Cornelia, da of Erich Hennig (d 2003); 3 c (Constanze b 20 June 1993, Tobias b 13 Sept 1995, Alexia b 5 April 1998); *Career* fell Jesus Coll Cambridge 1977–81, fell Trinity Coll Cambridge 1981–; Univ of Cambridge: asst lectr 1980–85, lectr 1985–96, reader in algebraic geometry 1996–2001, prof of algebraic geometry 2001–; ScD Univ of Cambridge 1998; *Publications* numerous mathematical papers in scientific jls; *Style*— Prof Pelham Wilson

WILSON, Peter Michael; s of late Michael de Lancey Wilson, of Salisbury, Wilts, and Mary Elizabeth, *née* Craufurd (d 1972); *b* 9 June 1941; *Educ* Downside, Oriel Coll Oxford (MA); *m* 5 Sept 1964, Lissa, da of Olaf Trab (d 1993); 1 da (Juliet b 1972), 1 s (Mark b 1974); *Career* chm Gallaher Ltd 1994–2004; dir: Kesa Electricals plc, Fortune Brands Inc; tstee Brooklands Museum; *Style*— Peter Wilson, Esq

WILSON, Peter Mowat; QPM; *Educ* George Watson's Coll Edinburgh, Univ of Edinburgh (LLB), Univ of Cambridge (Dip Applied Criminology); *Career* served Edinburgh City Police (later Lothian and Borders Police) 1973–97, seconded to HM Inspectorate of Constabulary 1993–95, head of CID Lothian and Borders Police 1995–97, asst chief constable Grampian Police 1997–2001, chief constable Fife Constabulary 2001–; pres Assoc of Chief Police Offrs in Scotland 2005–06; *Recreations* golf, running; *Style*— Peter Wilson, Esq, QPM; ✉ Chief Constable, Fife Constabulary, Detroit Road, Glenrothes, Fife KY6 2RJ (tel 01592 418411, e-mail peter.wilson@fife.pnn.police.uk)

WILSON, Peter Stafford; MBE (2000); s of Sir Geoffrey Wilson, and Judy Chamberlain, *née* Trowbridge; *b* 12 January 1951; *Educ* St Albans Sch Washington DC, Westminster,

Exeter Coll Oxford; *m* 1, (m dis); m 2, 1980, Patricia Clare, da of R Q Macarthur Stanham, of Camden Park, NSW, Aust; 3 s, 1 da; *Career* asst dir Welsh Nat Drama Co 1974–75, co dir Bush Theatre London 1975–76; assoc dir Lyric Theatre Hammersmith 1980–83; ind prodr 1983–; credits incl: Edmund Kean with Ben Kingsley, A Betrothal with Ben Kingsley and Geraldine James, The Woman in Black, An Inspector Calls (UK, USA and Aust), Victor Spinetti Diaries, Julian Glover's Beowulf, Wind in the Willows, Broken Glass, Miriam Margolyes' Dickens Women, Old Wicked Songs, Oh What a Lovely War, Krapp's Last Tape, Amadeus, The Madness of George Dubya, Matthew Bourne's Swan Lake, Nutcracker! and Play Without Words; chief exec: PWP Ltd 1983–, HM Tennent Ltd 1988–90, Norwich Theatre Royal 1992–; dir/prodr Mobil Touring Theatre 1985–; chair Cultural Industries Sector of Shaping the Future, vice-chair Norfolk Arts Forum, memb Bd Theatre Investment Fund; *Books* Forty Games for Frivolous People, The After Dinner Olympics; *Recreations* tennis, swimming, sailing, diving; *Clubs* Garrick; *Style*— Peter Wilson, Esq, MBE; ✉ PWP Limited, 80–81 St Martin's Lane, London WC2N 4AA (tel 020 7395 7580, fax 020 7240 2947, e-mail p.wilson@theatreroyalnorwich.co.uk)

WILSON, Richard; OBE (1994); s of John Boyd Wilson (d 1975), and Euphemia, *née* Colquhoun (d 1960); *b* 9 July 1936; *Educ* Greenock HS, RADA; *Career* actor/director; rector Univ of Glasgow 1996–98; *Theatre Actor* lead roles in Operation Bad Apple, An Honourable Trade, May Days, Normal Service (Hampstead Theatre), Waiting for God (Manchester Royal Exchange); Edinburgh Traverse: title role in Uncle Vanya, Vladamir in Waiting for Godot; Stephen Feeble in The Weekend (tour and West End), Kabak in Occupations (Stables Theatre Manchester); Dr Rance in What the Butler Saw (RNT) 1995; *Theatre Director* Royal Court: Women Laughing, God's Second In Command, Other Worlds, Heaven and Hell, A Wholly Healthy Glasgow, Toast, Four, Mr Kolpert, Nightingale and Chase, I just Stopped By To See The Man; Royal Exchange Manchester: The Lodger, Women Laughing (Best New Play Manchester Evening News, Writers' Guild of GB Award for regnl theatre), An Inspector Calls, A Wholly Healthy Glasgow; Hampstead Theatre: Imagine Drowning (John Whiting Award), President Wilson in Paris, Lenz; Bush Theatre: View of Kabul, Commitments; also Prin (Lyric Hammersmith and Lyric Shaftesbury), Simply Disconnected (Chichester) 1996, Tom and Clem (Aldwych) 1997, Where Do We Live (Royal Court), Under the Whaleback (Royal Court) 2003; *Television Actor*, BBC: One Foot in the Grave (6 series), One Foot in the Algarve, The Vision Thing, Unnatural Pursuits, Fatherland, Normal Service, Tutti Frutti, The Holy City, Poppyland, Life as We Know it, In the Red, Life Support; Granada/Actor: Cluedo, Sherlock Holmes; YTV/Actor: High and Dry, Room at the Bottom, Emmerdale Farm; Under the Hammer, The Other Side of Paradise (Central/Grundy), Inspector Morse (Zenith), Mr Bean (Thames), Selling Hitler (Euston), The Woman I Love (HTV), Murder by the Book (TVS), Walking the Plank (Yorkshire), Sweeney, Only When I Laugh (4 series), Victorian Scandals, Sharp Intake of Breath (2 series), My Good Woman (3 series), Crown Court, Gulliver's Travels (Channel 4) 1996, Duck Patrol (LWT) 1997, High Stakes (ITV), Father Ted (Hat Trick), Born and Bred (BBC) 2003; *Television Director* BBC: Changing Step (winner Best Feature BANFF TV), A Wholly Unhealthy Glasgow, Under the Hammer, Remainder Man, Commitments; *Film Actor* Soft Top Hard Shoulder, Carry on Columbus, A Dry White Season, How to get ahead in Advertising, Fellow Travellers, Prick up your Ears, Whoops Apocalypse, Passage to India, Women Talking Dirty, Watch that Man; *Awards* British Comedy Award for Top TV Comedy Actor 1991, BAFTA Award for Light Entertainment 1991 and 1993, Scottish BAFTA for Best TV Actor 1993; *Recreations* squash, swimming and eating; *Clubs* RAC, Groucho, Garrick; *Style*— Richard Wilson, Esq, OBE; ✉ c/o Conway van Gelder Ltd, 18–21 Jermyn Street, London SW1Y 6HP (tel 020 7287 0077, fax 020 7287 1940)

WILSON, Richard Henry; *b* 1953; *Educ* London Coll of Printing, Hornsey Coll of Art (Dip AD), Univ of Reading (MFA); *Career* artist; DAAD artist in residence Berlin 1992–93; contrib to numerous art pubns, work in various public and private collections; also musician (co-fndr and performer Bow Gamelan Ensemble 1983–); Henry Moore fell Univ of East London 2002–04, visiting prof Univ of East London 2005; memb Artistic Record Ctee Imperial War Museum; RA 2006; *Solo Exhibitions* incl: 20:50 (Matt's Gallery London) 1987, One Piece at a Time (installation inside Tyne Bridge Newcastle) 1987, Art of Our Time (Saatchi Collection and Royal Scot Acad Edinburgh) 1987, Leading Lights (Brandts Kunsthallen Odense Denmark) 1989, Sea Level (Arnolfini Gallery Bristol) 1989, She Came in Through the Bathroom Window (Matt's Gallery London) 1989, High-Tec (MOMA Oxford) 1989, Take Away (Centre of Contemporary Art Warsaw 1990, Saatchi Gallery 1991), Lodger (Galerie Valeria Belvedere Milan) 1991, Swift Half and Return to Sender (Galerie de l'Ancienne Poste Calais) 1992, Drawings (Künstlerhaus Bethanien Berlin) 1993, Matt's Gallery London 1994, Butler Gallery Kilkenny Castle Ireland 1994, LA/UK Festival Museum of Contemporary Art Los Angeles 1994, Galerie Klaus Fischer Berlin 1995, Galerie Valeria Belvedere Milan 1996, Room 6 Channel View Hotel Towner Art Gallery Eastbourne 1996, Formative Processes Gimpel Fils London 1996, Jamming Gears Serpentine Gallery 1996, In Zwickau Germany 1998, Over Easy (public art work) 1999, Xmas Tree (Tate Gallery) 1998–99, Hung Drawn Quartered (Tel Aviv) 1999, Pipe Dreams (Architectural Assoc), Slice of Reality (N Meadow Sculpture Project Millennium Dome) 2000, Structurally Sound (Ex Teresa Arte Actual Mexico City) 2000, Turbine Hall Swimming Pool (Clare Coll Mission Church London) 2000, Set North for Japan (Echigo Tsumari Project Niigata Prefecture Japan) 2000, Set North for Japan (Gimpel Fils London) 2001, A Sculpture for the Millennium Square (Leeds) 2001, Final Corner (permanent work, World Cup Project Fukuroi City Japan) 2002, Irons in the Fire (Mappin Gallery Sheffield) 2002–, Leeds Metropolitan Gallery 2002, Talbot Rice Gallery Edinburgh 2002, Irons in the Fire (Wapping Project London) 2003, Butterfly (Wapping Project London) 2003, Rolling Rig (De La Warr Pavilion Bexhill-on-Sea) 2003, Caveau (Palazzo delle Papesse Contemporary Art Centre Sienna) 2003, Solo (Program Gallery London) 2004, Queen & Gantry (Storey Gallery Lancaster) 2005, Curve Gallery Barbican 2006, 5 Piece Kit (Matthew Bown Gallery London) 2006; *Group Exhibitions* incl: Up a Blind Alley (Trigon Biennale Graz Austria) 1987, Hot Live Still (Plymouth Art Centre) 1987, High Rise (São Paulo Bienal Brazil 1989, UK and USSR 1990), All Mod Cons (Edge Biennale Newcastle) 1990, Heatwave (Serpentine Gallery London) 1992, Galleria Mazzocchi Parma Italy 1992, Sydney Biennale 1992, Museet for Samtidskunst Oslo 1993, Private Kunstwerk Berlin 1993, The Boatshow (Cafe Gallery London) 1993, Time Out Billboard Project London 1993, Sendezeit: A Space without Art (Alexanderplatz Berlin) 1993, Tachikawa Public Art Project Tokyo 1994, Art Unlimited: Artists' Multiples (South Bank touring) 1994, Negev Desert Symposium Israel 1995, Contemporary Art Soc Drawing Show 1995, Nomad: Six European Sculptors (Städtische Ausstellungshalle Münster) 1996, Art-itecture: Ten Artists (Museum of Contemporary Art Barcelona) 1996, Islands (Nat Museum of Contemporary Art Canberra Australia) 1996, Dexion 50th Anniversary Sculpture Cmmn (NEC Birmingham) 1997, 54 x 54 (Times Building London) 1999, The Office of Misplaced Events (Temporary Annexe Lotta Hammer London) 1999, Structurally Sound (Ex Teresa Arte Actual Mexico City) 2000, Field Day (Taipei Fine Art Museum Taipei) 2001, Double Vision (Galerie fur Zeitgenossischekunst Leipzig) 2001, Close Encounters of the Art Kind (V&A) 2001, Multiplication (touring exhbn with Br Cncl) 2001–03, Thinking Big: 21st Century Br Sculpture (Peggy Guggenheim Collection Venice) 2002, Groove (Huddersfield Art Gallery) 2002, Independence (South London Art Gallery) 2003, Bad Behaviour (Longside Gallery Yorkshire Sculpture Park) 2003, Wings of Art (Stadt Aachen - Ludwig Forum für Internationale Kunst) 2003–04, 'Marks' in Space (Usher Gallery Lincoln) 2004, Galleria Fumagalli Bergamo 2004, Break Neck Speed (Yokohama Triennal) 2005, Royal Acad Summer Show 2006, Butterfly (Platform China Beijing) 2006, This will not happen without you (Locus and tour) 2007; *Permanent Works* Rock'n'hole (Lincoln City and Archeological Museum) 2005; *Public Work* Turning the place Over (Year of Culture Liverpool) 2007; *Awards* Boise travel scholarship 1977, Arts Cncl minor award 1977, Gtr London Arts Project award 1978, 1981 and 1989, RSA award 1996, The Architectural Assoc Maeda Visiting Artist Award 1998, Paul Hamlyn Fndn Award to Visual Artists 2002–05; *Publications* Richard Wilson (2001), Richard Wilson (2005); *Style*— Richard Wilson, RA; ✉ 44 Banyard Road, London SE16 2YA (tel 020 7231 7312)

WILSON, Rob; MP; *Career* former advsr to David Davis MP, cncllr (Cons) Reading BC 1992–96 and 2003–; MP (Cons) Reading E 2005– (Parly candidate (Cons) Carmarthen W and Pembrokeshire S 2001); *Style*— Rob Wilson, Esq, MP; ✉ House of Commons, London SW1A 0AA

WILSON, Sir Robert Peter; KCMG (2000); s of Alfred Wilson (d 1951), and Dorothy Eileen Wilson, MBE, *née* Mathews (d 1991); *b* 2 September 1943; *Educ* Epsom Coll, Univ of Sussex (BA), Harvard Business Sch (AMP); *m* 7 Feb 1975, Shirley Elisabeth, da of George Robson, of Hunmanby, N Yorks; 1 s (Andrew), 1 da (Nicola); *Career* asst economist Dunlop Ltd 1966–67, economist Mobil Oil Co Ltd 1967–70; Rio Tinto Gp (Rio Tinto Zinc Gp until 1997): joined 1970, md A M and S Europe Ltd 1979–82, head of planning and devpt RTZ plc 1982–87, main bd dir 1987–2003, chief exec RTZ Corporation plc 1991–97, chm Rio Tinto plc 1997–2003, chm Rio Tinto Ltd 1998–2003; non-exec dir: CRA Ltd (Australia) 1990 (unified with RTZ 1995, renamed Rio Tinto Ltd 1997), Boots Company plc 1991–98, BP plc 1998–2002, Diageo plc 1998–2003, The Economist Gp 2002– (non-exec chm 2003–), BG Gp plc 2002– (non-exec chm 2004–), GlaxoSmithKline plc 2003–; chm Int Cncl for Mining and Metals 2002–03, tstee Camborne Sch of Mines 1993–99; Hon DSc: Univ of Exeter 1993, Univ of Birmingham 2002, Univ of Sussex 2004; Hon LLD Univ of Dundee 2001; CIMgt 1991, FRSA 1999; *Recreations* theatre, opera; *Style*— Sir Robert Wilson, KCMG; ✉ BG Group plc, Eagle House, 108–110 Jermyn Street, London SW1Y 6RP (tel 020 7707 4878, fax 020 7707 4858, e-mail robert.wilson@bg-group.com)

WILSON, Prof the Hon Robin James; elder s of Baron Wilson of Rievaulx, KG, OBE, PC, FRS (Life Peer, d 1995); *b* 5 December 1943; *Educ* UCS Hampstead, Balliol Coll Oxford (MA), Univ of Pennsylvania (MA, PhD), MIT, Open Univ; *m* 1968, (Margaret Elizabeth) Joy, da of Brian and Sallie Crispin, of Dawlish, Devon; 2 da (Jennifer, Catherine (twins) b 1975); *Career* lectr in mathematics Jesus Coll Oxford 1969–72; Open Univ: lectr in mathematics 1972–79, sr lectr in mathematics 1979–, dean and dir of studies Mathematics and Computing Faculty 1995–96, head Dept of Pure Mathematics 2003–05 (actg head 1990–92), prof of pure mathematics 2005–; pt/t lectr in mathematics Keble Coll Oxford 1980– (fell by special election 1999–), lectr in mathematics Lady Margaret Hall Oxford 1988–94; visiting prof of history of mathematics Gresham Coll London 2001–02, Gresham prof of geometry 2004–; several times visiting prof of mathematics Colorado Coll USA; *Books* Introduction to Graph Theory (1972), Let Newton be! (jtly, 1988), Oxford Figures (jtly, 2000), Stamping through Mathematics (2001), Four Colours Suffice (2002), Music and Mathematics (jtly, 2003), How to Solve Sudoku (2005), twenty other mathematics books; Gilbert and Sullivan: The D'Oyly Carte Years (jtly, 1984), three other music books; *Recreations* music (performing and listening), travel, philately; *Style*— Prof the Hon Robin Wilson; ✉ 15 Chalfont Road, Oxford OX2 6TL

WILSON, Rodney Herbert William; *b* 21 June 1942; *Educ* Windsor GS for Boys, Berkshire Coll of Art, Camberwell Sch of Art (NDD), Hornsey Coll of Arts (ATD); *Career* asst lectr Loughborough Coll of Art 1965–69; Arts Council: film offr 1970–85, dir Film, Video and Broadcasting Dept 1986–98; exec prodr BBC Classical Music, Television; memb: RTS, IMZ; *Style*— Rodney Wilson, Esq; ✉ BBC Classical Music, Television, BBC Television Centre, Wood Lane, London W12 7RJ (tel 020 8576 9966, fax 020 8895 6146, e-mail rodney.wilson@bbc.co.uk)

WILSON, Ronald George; s of Robert Paterson Wilson (d 1953), of Aberdeen, and Ena Watson Cowie Wilson (d 1965); *b* 20 April 1937; *Educ* Aberdeen GS, Univ of Aberdeen (MB ChB, MD); *m* 1, 6 April 1963 (m dis 1992), Muriel, da of James Hutcheon (d 1968), of Aberdeen; 1 s (James Robert b 13 Oct 1967), 1 da (Fiona Alys b 18 Nov 1970); m 2, 29 March 1996, Susan, da of Stephen Blackett, of Newcastle; *Career* surgn Lt RN with 40 Commando RM 1963–65, with Med Branch Royal Marine Reserves until 1982; sr house offr in surgery (Aberdeen 1966–68), Bristol Trg Scheme 1968–70, registrar in gen surgery Bristol 1970–71, res in breast cancer Edinburgh Royal Infirmary 1971–73, lectr in surgery Univ of Nottingham 1973–77; conslt surgn Gen Hosp Newcastle upon Tyne 1977–96; Breast Screening Prog mangr until 1996, Regnl and Nat Organisational Ctees, Nat Ctee for Evaluation, regnl QA mangr for screening (retd 1998); FRCSEd; *Clubs* Moynihan Chirurgical; *Style*— Ronald Wilson, Esq; ✉ 14 Hudshaw Gardens, Hexham, Northumberland NE46 1HY (tel and fax 01434 606180)

WILSON, Sammy; MP, MLA; *b* 4 April 1953; *Career* teacher; cncllr E Belfast CC 1981–; memb NI Assembly (DUP): Belfast E 1998–2003, Antrim E 2003–; MP (DUP) Antrim E 2005– (Parly candidate (DUP): Strangford 1992, Antrim E 2001); memb NI Policing Bd 2001–; *Style*— Sammy Wilson, Esq, MP, MLA; ✉ House of Commons, London SW1A 0AA

WILSON, Simon; *Career* jewellery designer/retailer; co-fndr (with Nicky Butler) Butler and Wilson Antiquarius Market King's Road Chelsea 1968, opened flagship shop Fulham Rd 1974, cmmnd to design Christmas light display for Regent Street 1979–80 and 1980–81, Export Dept opened 1983, cmmnd to design exclusive range for Giorgio Armani 1984, second shop opened South Molton St 1985, joined London Designer Collections (first show Olympia) and opened concession at Harrods 1986, opened second concession at Jaeger Regent St 1987, shops opened West Hollywood Calif, Glasgow and at Selfridges 1988, major restrospective exhbn celebrating 21st anniversary 1989, subject of book Rough Diamonds (author Vivienne Becker) 1990, launched extended accessory line (belts and handbags) 1991, retail ops extended to Heathrow Airport 1992, joined QVC home shopping channel 1993, cmmnd to design exclusive range for tourists visiting Tower of London 1994; *Style*— Simon Wilson, Esq; ✉ Butler & Wilson, 189 Fulham Road, London SW3 6JN; Butler & Wilson, 20 South Molton Street, London W1K 5QY

WILSON, Stephen Richard Mallett (Sam); DL (Suffolk 2006); s of Dr Peter Remington Wilson (d 1997), of Taunton, and Kathleen Rosemary Hough, *née* Mallett (d 1988); *b* 12 October 1941; *Educ* Uppingham, Clare Coll Cambridge (MA), Coll of Law Guildford; *m* 1969, Marycita Jane, da of Gwynn Craven Hargrove; 2 da (Gemma Harriet b 11 April 1972, Alexandra Jane b 17 Jan 1974), 1 s (Thomas William Gwynn b 1 Sept 1979); *Career* articled clerk Simmons & Simmons (admitted 1966); ptnr: Westhorp Ward & Catchpole 1968–89, Birkett Westhorp & Long 1989–95, Birketts 1995–2000 (conslt 2000–06); non-exec chm Boydell & Brewer Group Ltd (publishers); pres Suffolk & N Essex Law Soc 1988 (sec 1980–88), clerk to Gen Cmmrs of Income Tax (Stowmarket Div); Law Soc: memb 1964–, memb Cncl 1990–2001, chm Standards & Guidance Ctee 1996–99, memb Adjudication Panel, chm Professional Standards Appeals Panel; dep dist chm The Appeals Serv; chm St John Cncl Suffolk 1999–2004, dir St Elizabeth Hospice Ipswich; FRSA 1999–2005; *Recreations* tennis, golf, hunting, skiing, bridge; *Style*— Sam Wilson, Esq, DL; ✉ Birketts, 24–26 Museum Street, Ipswich, Suffolk IP1 1HZ (tel 01473 232300)

W

WILSON, Prof (Robert James) Timothy (Tim); s of John Wilson (d 2004), of Leeds, and Joan Pendleton, *née* Roddis (d 1987); *b* 2 April 1949, Leeds; *Educ* Temple Moor Sch Leeds, Univ of Reading (BSc), Lancaster Univ (MA), Walden Univ (PhD); *m* 8 Jan 1972,

Jacqueline, *née* Hinds; 2 da (Joanna Louise b 9 May 1982, Catherine Elizabeth b 2 Jan 1985); *Career* lectr Leeds Poly 1972–84, dir of studies Cranfield Univ 1984–87, asst dir Leicester Poly 1987–91, dep dir Hatfield Poly 1991–92, vice-chllr Univ of Hertfordshire 2003– (pro-vice-chllr 1992–2003); author of over 40 pubns on operational research and educnl mgmnt 1982–2002; memb Bd: E of England Devpt Agency (EEDA), HEFCE 2005–; RFU: staff coach 1984–89, A-list referee 1991–94; Capt Letchworth Golf Club 2001; CCMI 2004, MInstD; *Recreations* rugby union, golf, dog walking; *Style*— Prof Tim Wilson; ✉ University of Hertfordshire, College Lane, Hatfield, Hertfordshire AL10 9AB (tel 01707 284030, fax 01707 284046, e-mail r.j.t.wilson@herts.ac.uk)

WILSON, Timothy Hugh; s of Hugh Walker Wilson (d 1965), and Lilian Rosemary, *née* Kirke; *b* 8 April 1950; *Educ* Winchester, Mercersburg Acad USA, Corpus Christi Coll Oxford (MA), Warburg Inst Univ of London (MPhil), Univ of Leicester; *m* 12 May 1984, Jane, da of Francis George Lott (d 2001), and Anne Josephine Lott (d 1996); 2 s (Alastair James Johnnie b 11 June 1983, David George Lorenzo b 15 March 1992), 1 da (Julia Annie Jane b 17 Sept 1986); *Career* res asst National Maritime Museum 1977–79, asst keeper Dept of Medieval and Later Antiquities British Museum 1979–90, keeper of Western Art Ashmolean Museum 1990–; fell: Villa I Tatti Florence 1984, Balliol Coll Oxford 1990, Royal Soc of Painter Printmakers 1990, Accademia Raffaello Urbino 2003; FSA 1989; *Publications* Flags At Sea (1986, 2 edn 1999), Ceramic Art of the Italian Renaissance (1987), Maiolica: Italian Renaissance Ceramics in the Ashmolean Museum (1989, 2 edn 2003); contrib to books and exhbn catalogues, various articles in specialist jls on Renaissance ceramics and related subjects; *Style*— Timothy Wilson, Esq, FSA; ✉ Balliol College, Oxford OX1 3BJ; Department of Western Art, Ashmolean Museum, Oxford OX1 2PH (tel 01865 278041, fax 01865 278056, e-mail timothy.wilson@ashmus.ox.ac.uk)

WILSON, Valerie; *Educ* Cowley Girls GS St Helens, Univ of Hull (BA), Univ of Edinburgh (MSc), Univ of Sheffield (EdD); *m*; 3 s; *Career* teacher in various secdy schools 1966–72; tutor Edinburgh Univ Centre for Continuing Educn 1978–85; princ conslt Int Trg Services Ltd 1986–90; dir Stirling Univ Mgmnt Devpt Unit 1991–94; prog mangr Scot Cncl for Research in Educn 1994–97; princ researcher Scot Office Educational Research Unit 1997–99; dir SCRE Centre Univ of Glasgow 1999–2004, sr research fell Univ of Glasgow 2004–; memb Scot, Br and European Educational Research Assoc; author of various research reports, articles and chapters in books; FIPD 1989; *Recreations* memb reading group, hill walking; *Style*— Dr Valerie Wilson; ✉ e-mail valerie.wilson@scre.ac.uk

WILSON, Warren; s of Robert Wilson, of Ashton-under-Lyne, Lancs, and Flora Wilson; *b* 8 August 1945; *Educ* Hathershaw Sch; *m* 1, Linda; 1 da (Miranda Jane b 28 Aug 1968), 1 s (Luke Russell b 8 Dec 1970); m 2, Wendy Monica; 1 da (Nathalie May b 19 Nov 1990), 1 s (Harry John b 21 May 1993); *Career* reporter Oldham Evening Chronicle 1964–68, sub ed Express and Star Wolverhampton 1968–70; Shropshire Star: Shropshire liaison 1970–72, dep news ed 1972–77, news ed 1977–91, ed 1991–94; ed Express and Star Wolverhampton 1995–2002, md Shropshire Newspapers 2002–05; *Recreations* gardening, wine, golf, music; *Style*— Warren Wilson, Esq; ✉ 27 Exeter Drive, Old College Fields, Wellington, Shropshire TF1 3PR (tel 01952 245579)

WILSON, Dr William; *b* 29 October 1928; *Educ* Glasgow HS, Univ of Glasgow (MB ChB); *m* 14 June 1958, Isabel, da of Col David Mackie, MC (d 1966), of Dundonald, Ayrshire; 1 da (Anne b 1961), 1 s (David b 1965); *Career* sr conslt ophthalmologist Glasgow Royal Infirmary 1962–93, hon clinical lectr Univ of Glasgow 1962–; conslt: St Vincent Sch for the Blind Glasgow, Kelvin Sch for Partially Sighted Children; examiner: RCSEd and Glasgow 1964–, Coll Ophthalmologists 1988–; pres Scottish Ophthalmological Soc 1982–84; FRCSEd 1958, FRCOphth; *Recreations* gardening, DIY; *Clubs* Royal Scottish Automobile; *Style*— Dr William Wilson; ✉ 34 Calderwood Road, Newlands, Glasgow G43 2RU; Crossways, Muthill, Perthshire (tel 0141 637 4898)

WILSON-JOHNSON, David Robert; s of Harry Kenneth Johnson, of Irthlingborough, Northants, and Sylvia Constance, *née* Wilson; *b* 16 November 1950; *Educ* Wellingborough Sch, Br Inst of Florence, St Catharine's Coll Cambridge (BA), RAM; *Career* baritone; Royal Opera House Covent Garden debut We Come to the River 1976, Paris Opera debut Die Meistersinger 1989, US debut with Cleveland Orch 1990, NY debut with NY Philharmonic 1992; dir Ferrandou Summer Singing Sch 1986–; ARAM 1984, FRAM 1988; *Performances* at Covent Garden incl: Billy Budd 1982 and 1995, L'Enfant et les Sortilèges 1983 and 1987, Boris Godunov 1984, Die Zauberflöte 1985, 1986 and 1987, Turandot 1987, Madam Butterfly 1988, St François d'Assise (title role) 1988 (winner Evening Standard Award for Opera); others incl: Eight Songs for a Mad King (Paris) 1979, Last Night of the Proms 1981 and 1986, Count Heribert in Die Verschwörenen (Schubert, BBC Proms) 1997; Paris Opera incl: Die Meistersinger, Die Zauberflöte, Billy Budd; Netherlands Opera incl: Punch and Judy (Birtwistle) 1992, Von Heute Auf Morgen (Schoenberg) 1995, The Nose (Shostakovich) 1996, Oedipe (Enescu's) 1996; festival appearances at: Glyndebourne, Edinburgh, Bath, Bergen, Berlin, Geneva, Graz, Holland, Hong Kong, Jerusalem, NYC, Orange, Paris, Salzburg, Vienna; *Recordings* incl: Schubert Winterreise, Schoenberg Ode to Napoleon, La Traviata, Lucrezia Borgia, Mozart Masses from King's College, Haydn Nelson Mass, Belshazzar's Feast, Elgar The Kingdom, Berlioz L'Enfance du Christ, Tippett The Ice Break, Bach Cantatas and B Minor Mass; *Films* The Midsummer Marriage (Sir Michael Tippett), The Lighthouse (Sir Peter Maxwell Davies), Or Shall We Die (Michael Berkeley/Richard Eyre); *Recreations* swimming, slimming, gardening, growing walnuts at house in the Lot; *Style*— David Wilson-Johnson, Esq; ✉ 28 Englefield Road, London N1 4ET (tel 020 7254 0941); c/o Askonas Holt, Lonsdale Chambers, 27 Chancery Lane, London WC2A 1PF (tel 020 7400 1700, fax 020 7400 1799, e-mail jumbo@ferrandou.org)

WILSON OF DINTON, Baron (Life Peer UK 2002), of Dinton in the County of Buckinghamshire; Sir Richard Thomas James Wilson; GCB (2001, KCB 1997, CB 1991); s of Richard Ridley Wilson (d 1982), and Frieda Bell Wilson, *née* Finlay (d 1980); *b* 11 October 1942; *Educ* Radley, Clare Coll Cambridge (MA, LLM); *m* 25 March 1972, Caroline Margaret, da of Rt Hon Sir Frank Lee, GCMG, KCB (d 1971); 1 s (Hon Tom b 10 March 1979), 1 da (Hon Amy b 16 Feb 1981); *Career* called to the Bar Middle Temple 1965; private sec Bd of Trade 1969–71 (asst princ 1966–), princ Cabinet Office 1972, asst sec Dept of Energy 1977 (joined Dept 1974), team leader privatisation of Britoil 1982, promoted to princ estab and fin offr (under sec) 1982, mgmnt and personnel office Cabinet 1986, economic secretariat (dep sec) Cabinet Office 1987–90, dep sec HM Treasy 1990–92, permanent sec DOE 1992–94, permanent under sec of state Home Office 1994–97, Sec to the Cabinet and Head of the Home Civil Service 1998–2002; master Emmanuel Coll Cambridge 2002–; non-exec chm C Hoare & Co 2006–; non-exec dir: Xansa plc 2003–, British Sky Broadcasting Gp plc 2003–; *Style*— The Lord Wilson of Dinton, GCB; ✉ Emmanuel College, St Andrew's Street, Cambridge CB2 3AP

WILSON OF TILLYORN, Baron (Life Peer UK 1992), of Finzean in the District of Kincardine and Deeside and of Fanling in Hong Kong; Sir David Clive Wilson; KT (2000), GCMG (1991, KCMG 1987, CMG 1985); s of Rev William Skinner Wilson (d 1942), and Enid, *née* Sanders (d 1997); *b* 14 February 1935; *Educ* Trinity Coll Glenalmond, Keble Coll Oxford (scholar, MA), Univ of Hong Kong, Columbia Univ NY (visiting scholar), Univ of London (PhD); *m* 1 April 1967, Natasha Helen Mary, da of late Bernard Gustav Alexander; 2 s (Hon Peter Michael Alexander b 31 March 1968, Hon Andrew Marcus William b 21 June 1969); *Career* Nat Serv The Black Watch (RHR) 1953–55; HM Dip Serv: joined SE Asia Dept FO 1958, third sec Vientiane 1959–60, language student Hong Kong 1960–62, third then second sec Peking 1963–65, first sec Far Eastern Dept 1965–68, resigned 1968; ed The China Quarterly (Contemporary China Inst SOAS Univ of London) 1968–74; rejoined HM Dip Serv 1974, Cabinet Office 1974–77, political advsr to Govr of Hong Kong 1977–81, head S Euro Dept FCO 1981–84, asst under sec of state responsible for Asia and the Pacific FCO 1984–87, Govr and C-in-C of Hong Kong 1987–92; memb: Bd Br Cncl 1993–2002 (chm Scottish Ctee 1993–2002), Cncl CBI Scotland 1993–2002, PM's Advsy Ctee on Business Appts 2000–; chm Scottish and Southern Energy plc (formerly Scottish Hydro-Electric plc) 1993–2000, dir Martin Currie Pacific Trust plc 1993–2003; chllr Univ of Aberdeen 1997–; master Peterhouse Cambridge 2002–, dep vice-chllr Univ of Cambridge 2005–; pres: Bhutan Soc of the UK 1993–, Hong Kong Soc 1994–, Hong Kong Assoc 1994–; vice-pres RSGS 1996–; chm of tstees Nat Museums of Scotland 2002–06 (tstee 1999–2006); chm: Scottish Peers Assoc 2000–02 (vice-chm 1998–2000), Cncl Glenalmond Coll 2000–05 (memb 1993–2005); memb Carnegie Tst for the Universities of Scotland 2000–; registrar Order of St Michael and St George 2001–; Burgess of Guild City of Aberdeen 2004; hon fell Keble Coll Oxford 1987; Hon LLD: Univ of Aberdeen 1990, Univ of Abertay Dundee 1995, Chinese Univ of Hong Kong 1996; Hon DLitt: Univ of Sydney 1991, Univ of Hong Kong 2006; FRSE 2000; KStJ 1987; *Recreations* hill walking, theatre, reading; *Clubs* Alpine, New (Edinburgh), Royal Northern and Univ (Aberdeen); *Style*— The Rt Hon the Lord Wilson of Tillyorn, KT, GCMG, FRSE; ✉ House of Lords, London SW1A 0PW; The Master's Lodge, Peterhouse, Cambridge CB2 1QY

WILSON-SMITH, Christopher; QC (1986); s of Roy Seaton Wilson-Smith (d 1993), and Jane, *née* Broderick (d 1948); *b* 18 February 1944; *Educ* Borstal Institution in Swiss Alps, Michael Hall Rudolph Steiner Sch, Cncl of Legal Educn; *m* 6 Jan 1996, Marian; 4 c from previous m (Andrew b 4 Aug 1967, James b 1 May 1969, Johanaa b 1 June 1972, Benjamin b 28 Oct 1982); *Career* called to the Bar Gray's Inn 1965 (bencher 1996); recorder of the Crown Court (civil and crime) 1977–; called to the Bar of NSW Australia 2000; memb: Common Law Bar Assoc, Professional Bar Assoc; former chm Hoe Bridge Prep Sch; *Recreations* my children, golf, tennis, skiing, bridge, my new wife; *Clubs* RAC, Mark's, Woking Golf, Woking Tennis; *Style*— Christopher Wilson-Smith, Esq, QC; ✉ Outer Temple Chambers, 222 Strand, Temple, London WC2R 1BA (tel 020 7353 6381, fax 020 7583 1786); Eastwell House, Hook Heath Road, Woking, Surrey GU22 0DT; 63 Le Borsat, Tignes-Val-Claret

WILTON, (James) Andrew Rutley; *Career* asst keeper: British Art Walker Art Gallery Liverpool 1965–67, Dept of Prints and Drawings British Museum 1967–76; curator Prints and Drawings Yale Center for British Art New Haven 1976–80, asst keeper Dept of Prints and Drawings British Museum 1980–85; Tate Gallery: curator Turner Collection The Clore Gallery 1985–89, keeper of the British Collection 1989–97, keeper and sr research fell 1998–2002; hon curator of Prints and Drawings Royal Acad of Arts; Hon Liveryman and Hon Curator Worshipful Co of Painter-Stainers; FSA, Hon RWS, FRSA; *Books* Constable's English Landscape Scenery (1976), The Wood Engravings of William Blake (1976), British Watercolours 1750–1850 (1977), Turner in Switzerland (with John Russell, 1977), William Pars: Journey through the Alps (1979), The Life and Work of J M W Turner (1979), Turner Abroad (1982), Turner in his Time (1987), Five Centuries of British Painting (2002), Turner as Draughtsman (2006); author of numerous exhibition catalogues; *Recreations* music, walking, architecture, food; *Clubs* Athenaeum, Chelsea Arts; *Style*— Andrew Wilton, Esq; ✉ e-mail andrew@jarw.fsnet.co.uk

WILTON, Christopher Edward John; CMG (2003); s of Sir John Wilton, KCMG, KCVO, MC, of Chichester, W Sussex, and Lady (Maureen) Wilton; *b* 16 December 1951; *Educ* Tonbridge, Univ of Manchester (BA); *m* 31 July 1975, Dianne, *née* Hodgkinson; 1 da (Caroline Victoria b 16 Jan 1981), 1 s (Richard Charles b 30 March 1984); *Career* prodn supervisor Esso Petroleum 1975–77, joined FCO 1977, second sec then first sec Bahrain 1978–81, FCO 1981–84, first sec Tokyo 1984–88, seconded to Cabinet Office 1988–90, cnsllr (commercial) Riyadh 1990–94, consul-gen Dubai 1994–97, FCO 1997–98, rgnl md GEC (latterly BAE Systems) 1998–2000, ambass to Kuwait 2002–05, ret; currently: Middle East advsr Royal Bank of Scot, Middle East advsr Selex Sensors and Aviation Systems, memb Exec Ctee Arab Br C of C, chair Advsy Cncl London Middle East Inst, co-chm Kuwait-Br Friendship Soc, external policy advsr UK Visas FCO, dir DCW Conslts Ltd; Chevalier d'Honneur Chaîne des Rotisseurs; *Recreations* swimming, tennis, golf, piano, deserts; *Clubs* Athenaeum; *Style*— Christopher Wilton, Esq, CMG; ✉ c/o The Athenaeum, 107 Pall Mall, London SW1Y 5ER

WILTON, 8 Earl of (UK 1801); Francis Egerton Grosvenor; also Viscount Grey de Wilton (UK 1801), Baron Ebury (UK 1857); s of 5 Baron Ebury, DSO (d 1957, whose ggf, 1 Baron, was yr bro of 2 Marquess of Westminster and 2 Earl of Wilton), by his 1 w, Anne, da of Herbert Acland-Troyte, MC (gn of Sir Thomas Acland, 10 Bt); suc 4 cous, 7 Earl of Wilton (d 1999); *b* 8 February 1934; *Educ* Eton, Univ of Melbourne (PhD); *m* 1, 10 Dec 1957 (m dis 1962), Gillian Elfrida Astley, o da of Martin Roland Soames (d 1995), and Myra Drummond, niece of 16 Earl of Perth; 1 s (Julian Francis Martin, Viscount Grey de Wilton b 1959); m 2, 8 March 1963 (m dis 1973), Kyra, o da of L L Aslin; m 3, 1974, Suzanne, da of Graham Suckling, of NZ; 1 da (Lady Georgina Lucy b 1973 d 2003); *Heir* s, Viscount Grey de Wilton; *Recreations* ornithology, horology, photography; *Clubs* Oriental, Hong Kong, Melbourne, Melbourne Savage; *Style*— The Rt Hon the Earl of Wilton

WILTON, Penelope; OBE (2004); *m* 1990, Sir Ian Holm, *qv*; *Career* actress; *Theatre* NT: The Philanderer, Betrayal, Sisterly Feelings, Man and Superman, Much Ado About Nothing, Major Barbara, The Secret Rapture, Piano, Landscape; Greenwich Theatre: Measure for Measure, All's Well that Ends Well, The Norman Conquests; Royal Court: The Philanthropist, West of Suez; Nottingham Playhouse: King Lear, Widowers House; other credits incl: The Cherry Orchard (Lyceum Theatre Edinburgh), The Seagull (Chichester), Bloomsbury (Phoenix), The Deep Blue Sea (Almeida and Apollo), Andromache (The Old Vic), Vita and Virginia (Ambassadors), Moon Light (Pinter Festival), Landscape (Gate Theatre Dublin), Cherry Orchard (RSC); *Television* Mrs Warren's Profession, The Song of Songs, The Pearcross Girls, Othello, King Lear, The Widowing of Mrs Holroyd, Pasmore, Country, The Norman Conquests, The Monocled Mutineer, The Tale of Beatrix Potter, Ever Decreasing Circles, Screaming, The Borrowers (2 series), The Deep Blue Sea, Madly in Love, Landscape, This Could Be the Last Time, Talking Heads (Nights in the Garden of Spain), Alice Through the Looking Glass, Wives and Daughters, The Whistle-Blower, Bob & Rose, Victoria & Albert, Lucky Jim; *Films* incl: Joseph Andrews, French Lieutenant's Woman, Slaughter House, Clockwise, Cry Freedom, Blame it on the Bellboy, The Secret Rapture, Carrington, Tom's Midnight Garden, Iris, Calendar Girls, Shaun of the Dead; *Style*— Ms Penelope Wilton, OBE

WILTON, Rosalyn Susan; *née* Trup; *b* 25 January 1952; *Educ* Univ of London (BSc); *Career* dir: GNI Ltd 1982–84, Drexel Burnham Lambert Ltd 1984–90; Reuters Ltd: sr vice-pres 1990–92, md Transaction Products 1992–99, memb Exec Ctee 1998–99; ceo Hemscott plc 1999–2006, chm IPREO Inc 2006–; dir London Int Financial Futures Exchange 1985–90, non-exec dir Scottish Widows plc 1997–2000; *Style*— Mrs Rosalyn Wilton

WIMBORNE, 4 Viscount (UK 1918); Sir Ivor Mervyn Vigors Guest; 6 Bt (UK 1838); also Baron Wimborne (UK 1880) and Baron Ashby St Ledgers (UK 1910); s of 3 Viscount Wimborne (d 1993), and his 1 w, Victoria, *née* Vigors; *b* 19 September 1968; *Educ* Eton; *Heir* unc, Hon Julian Guest; *Style*— The Rt Hon the Viscount Wimborne

WIN, Dr Kyaw; s of U Po Sa, and Daw Khin Lay; *b* 3 January 1938; *Educ* Practicing Sch Faculty of Educn Yangon, Univ of Yangon (MB BS); *m* 16 July 1967, Daw Kyi Kyi, da of Uchit Maung; 2 s (Htut, Aung), 1 da (Aye Sanda); *Career* instr in pathology Faculty of Med Univ of Yangon 1961–62, med trg UK 1962–64, conslt physician Base Hosps Army Med Corps Myanmar 1964–65, Fulbright-Hays research fell Harvard Sch of Public Health and Sidney Farber Cancer Center Boston 1975–76 (also visiting lectr Harvard Med Sch), dir Directorate of Med Services Miny of Defence Yangon 1988–95, ambass to Canada 1995–99, ambass to the Ct of St James's 1999–2005 (concurrently ambass to Norway, Denmark and Sweden), currently chief advsr and conslt physician Pun Hlaing Int Hosp and Jivitadana Sangha (Charity) Hosp Yangon Union of Myanmar; chm Textbooks Publication Ctee Myanmar Med Assoc 1964–65, memb Nat Health Ctee 1989–95, memb Nat Olympic Ctee 1992–95; patron: Britain-Burma/Myanmar Soc, Myanmar-UK Assoc (perm patron), Myanmar Rowing Fedn; medals from Myanmar Govt Med Service incl: Good Service Medal, Nat Peace Medal, Honourable Service Medal, Administrator Medal, Distinguished Service Medal; FRSTM&H 1962, FRCPEd 1978, fell Australasian Coll of Tropical Med 1993; *Publications* contrib and ed of med textbooks, author of 89 original papers in med sciences; *Recreations* golf, music, travelling, writing, theatre, meditation, sports; *Clubs* London Golf, Travellers; *Style*— Dr Kyaw Win; ✉ 74C Inya Road, Yangon, Union of Myanmar (tel 00 951 535922, e-mail dr.kwin@mptmail.net.mm)

WINCH, Prof Donald Norman; s of Sidney Winch, and Iris May, *née* Button; *b* 15 April 1935; *Educ* Sutton GS, LSE (BSc Econ), Princeton Univ (PhD); *m* 5 Aug 1983, Doreen Alice, *née* Lidster; *Career* visiting lectr Univ of Calif Berkeley 1959–60, lectr in economics Univ of Edinburgh 1960–63; Univ of Sussex: lectr 1963–66, reader 1966–69, prof of the history of economics 1969–, dean Sch of Social Scis 1968–74, pro-vice-chllr arts and social studies 1986–89; pubns sec Royal Econ Soc 1971–; vice-pres Br Acad 1993–94; Hon DLitt Univ of Sussex 2006; FBA 1986, FRHistS 1987; *Books* Classical Political Economy and Colonies (1965), James Mill: Selected Economic Writings (1966), Economics and Policy (1969), The Economic Advisory Council (with S K Howson, 1976), Adam Smith's Politics (1978), That Noble Science of Politics (with S Collini and J Burrow, 1983), Malthus (1987), Riches and Poverty (1996); *Recreations* gardening; *Style*— Prof Donald Winch; ✉ University of Sussex, Falmer, Brighton, East Sussex BN1 9QN (tel 01273 678634, fax 01273 625972, e-mail d.winch@sussex.ac.uk)

WINCHESTER, Archdeacon of; *see:* Guille, Ven John Arthur

WINCHESTER, Bishop of 1995–; Rt Rev Michael Charles Scott-Joynt; s of Rev Albert George Scott-Joynt (d 1979), and Bettine, *née* Young (d 1991); *b* 15 March 1943; *Educ* Bradfield Coll, King's Coll Cambridge (hon scholar, MA); *m* 24 July 1965, (Mary) Louise, da of Colin White (d 1964), and Margot, *née* Rumens (d 1964); 1 da (Hannah Margaret b 1968), 2 s (Jeremy Charles b 1970, Matthew James b 1970); *Career* curate Cuddesdon 1967–70, tutor Cuddesdon Theol Coll 1967–72, team vicar Newbury 1972–75, rector Bicester area team miny 1975–81, dir of ordinands and in-service trg and canon residentiary St Albans Cathedral 1982–87, bishop of Stafford 1987–95; memb House of Lords 1996–; *Recreations* walking, opera; *Style*— The Rt Rev the Lord Bishop of Winchester; ✉ Wolvesey, Winchester, Hampshire SO23 9ND (tel 01962 854050, fax 01962 897088, e-mail michael.scott-joynt@dsl.pipex.com)

WINCHESTER, 18 Marquess of (Premier Marquess of England, cr 1551); Nigel George Paulet; also Baron St John of Basing (E 1539) and Earl of Wiltshire (E 1550); s of George Paulet (1 cous of 17 Marquess, who d 1968; also eighth in descent from 5 Marquess); *b* 22 December 1941; *m* 1967, Rosemary Anne, da of Maj Aubrey John Hilton, of Harare, Zimbabwe; 2 s (Christopher John Hilton, Earl of Wiltshire b 1969, Lord Richard George b 1971), 1 da (Lady Susan b 1976); *Heir* s, Earl of Wiltshire; *Career* dir Rhodesia Mineral Ventures Ltd, Sani-Dan Servs Ltd, Rhodesia Prospectors Ltd; *Style*— The Most Hon the Marquess of Winchester; ✉ 6A Main Road, Irene 1675, Transvaal, South Africa

WINCHILSEA AND NOTTINGHAM, 17 and 12 Earl of (E 1628 and 1681); Sir Daniel James Hatfield Finch Hatton; 18 and 12 Bt (E 1611 and 1660), of Eastwell and Raunston respectively; also Baron Finch (E 1675), Viscount Maidstone (E 1623) and Hereditary Lord of Royal Manor of Wye; s of 16 and 11 Earl of Winchilsea and Nottingham (d 1999), by his w Shirley, da of Bernard Hatfield; *b* 7 October 1967; *Educ* UWE; *m* 18 June 1994, Shelley Amanda, da of Gordon Gillard, of Yeovil, Somerset; 2 s (Tobias Joshua Stormont, Viscount Maidstone b 21 June 1998, Sebastian Alexander Heneage b 6 June 2002), 1 da (India Olivia Scarlett b 5 Nov 2004); *Heir* s, Viscount Maidstone; *Style*— The Rt Hon the Earl of Winchilsea and Nottingham; ✉ Charles Russell Baldocks, St Mary's House, 59 Quarry Street, Guildford, Surrey GU1 3UD

WINCKLESS, Sarah; da of Bob Winckless, and Valerie Hart; *b* 18 October 1973, Reading, Berks; *Educ* Tiffin Girls' Sch Kingston upon Thames, Millfield, Fitzwilliam Coll Cambridge (Netball, Rowing, Athletics and Basketball blues); *Career* amateur rower; memb Cambridge Univ Women's Boat Club 1995–97 (pres 1996–97), sr int debut 1998; achievements incl: Silver medal single sculls World Univ Games 1998, ninth place double sculls Olympic Games Sydney 2000, Bronze medal double sculls Olympic Games Athens 2004, winner quadruple sculls World Cup 2005 and 2006, Gold medal quadruple sculls World Championships 2005 and 2006; supporter Huntington's Disease Assoc; *Style*— Miss Sarah Winckless

WINDEATT, Prof Barry Alexander Corelli; s of Edwin Peter Windeatt, and Queenie, *née* Rusbridge; *b* 5 April 1950; *Educ* Sutton GS Surrey, St Catharine's Coll Cambridge (MA, PhD, LittD); *Career* research fell Gonville & Caius Coll Cambridge 1974–78, fell Emmanuel Coll Cambridge 1978– (dir of studies in English 1979–98, keeper of rare books 1997–); Cambridge Univ: asst lectr in English 1983–87, lectr in English 1987–95, reader in medieval literature 1995–2001, prof of English 2001– (chm English Faculty 1997–99, chair New Building for Cambridge English Ctee 1999–2005); *Publications* Chaucer's Dream-Poetry: Sources and Analogues (ed and trans, 1982), Geoffrey Chaucer, Troilus and Criseyde: A New Edition of The Book of Troilus (ed, 1984), The Book of Margery Kempe (trans, 1985), Chaucer Traditions (ed with Ruth Morse, 1990), The Oxford Guides to Chaucer: Troilus and Criseyde (1992), English Mystics of the Middle Ages (ed, 1994), Geoffrey Chaucer, Troilus and Criseyde: A New Translation (trans, 1998), The Book of Margery Kempe (ed, 2000), Troilus and Criseyde (ed, 2003); author of articles and reviews on medieval literature; *Recreations* other people's gardens, garden history, opera, explorations with Pevsner; *Style*— Prof Barry Windeatt; ✉ Emmanuel College, Cambridge CB2 3AP (tel 01223 334214, e-mail baw1000@cam.ac.uk)

WINDELER, John Robert; s of Alfred Stewart, and Ethela Marie, *née* Boremuth; *b* 21 March 1943; *Educ* Ohio State Univ USA (BA, MBA); *m* 15 June 1965, Judith Lynn, da of Robert Francis Taylor; 2 s (Stewart, James); *Career* Irving Tst Co NY: vice-pres Liability Mgmnt 1973–75, sr vice-pres Money Market Div 1975–80, mangr Loan Syndication Devpt 1981, gen mangr London 1981–83, exec vice-pres Investment Banking Gp 1984; md Irving Trust International Ltd London 1984–, pres Irving Securities Inc NY 1987–91; chief fin offr National Australia Bank Melbourne 1991–93, chief exec Insurance Div National Australia Group UK Ltd 1993–94; Alliance & Leicester Building Society (now Alliance & Leicester plc): dir 1994–2005, chm 1999–2005; dir: BMS Associates, RM plc 2002–; *Recreations* skiing, tennis, history; *Clubs* Hurlingham; *Style*— John Windeler, Esq

WINDER, Prof Anthony Frederick (Tony); s of Fred Winder (d 1996), and Ida Winifred, *née* Ellis (d 1982); *b* 7 March 1938; *Educ* Manchester Grammar, BNC Oxford (open scholar, MRC trg scholar, MA, MSc, BM BCh, DM), St Mary's Hosp Med Sch London (Harmsworth scholar), Guy's Hosp Med Sch London (PhD); *m* m, 3 Aug 1963, Sylvia Margaret, da of late Rev Charles Thomas Campbell, of Boston, Lincs; 2 s (Christopher Philip b 14 Aug 1964, Charles David b 20 Nov 1971), 1 da (Clare Elizabeth Jane (Mrs Hitchcock) b 21 Jan 1966); *Career* house physician to Professorial Paediatric and Metabolic Units St Mary's Hosp London 1963–64, house surgn Mayday Hosp Croydon 1964; Univ of London 1964–: lectr in biochemistry Guy's Hosp Med Sch 1965–69 (jr lectr 1964–65), recognised teacher Faculty of Med (attached Bds of Studies in Biochemistry, Pharmacology and Pathology) 1969–82 and (attached Bd of Pathology) 1988–, univ sr lectr in pharmacology with responsibility for biochemical pharmacology 1971–73 (lectr 1969–71), sr lectr in chemical pathology and head Div of Chemical Pathology Dept of Pathology Inst of Ophthalmology 1973–82, hon conslt in chemical pathology Moorfields Eye Hosp 1974–82, hon clinical asst Dept of Lipids and Diabetes and hon lectr in chemical pathology Bart's Med Coll 1978–82, conslt in chemical pathology Leics HA(T) and clinical teacher and hon reader in med Univ of Leicester Med Sch 1982–88, prof of chemical pathology and head Dept of Chemical Pathology and Human Metabolism Royal Free Hosp Sch of Med (now Royal Free and UC Med Sch) 1988–2000 (emeritus 2000), hon conslt in chemical pathology Royal Free Hampstead NHS Tst 1988–2001, hon conslt in chemical pathology Moorfields Eye Hosp and Inst of Ophthalmology 1992–93; hon conslt SE Thames RHA 1991–96; memb: Trent Region Research Ctee 1985–89, Enfield HA 1989–91; chm Family Heart Assoc 1999–2001 (med dir 1992–95); contrib chapters to academic books; memb: Biochemical Soc 1971, Assoc of Clinical Biochemists 1973, RSM 1975 (chm Lipid Forum 1996–99), Br Hyperlipidaemia Assoc 1985 (memb Ctee 1990–93), Assoc of Clinical Pathologists (scientific meetings sec 1992–96, pres 1996–97, postgrad sec 1997–99), Euro Atherosclerosis Soc 1995; FRCPath 1985, FRCP 1997 (MRCP 1988); *Recreations* playing clarinet, alto, tenor and baritone saxophones, enjoying jazz and most forms of music, table tennis, swimming, Age Concern volunteer; *Style*— Prof Tony Winder; ✉ Department of Molecular Pathology and Clinical Biochemistry, Royal Free and University College Medical School, University College London, Royal Free Campus and Royal Free NHS Hospital Trust, Rowland Hill Street, London NW3 2PF (tel 020 7830 2258, fax 020 7830 2235, e-mail windertony@waitrose.com)

WINDER, John Lindsay; JP (Furness and Dist 1969); s of Harold Vickers Winder (d 1969), of Barrow-in-Furness, Cumbria, and Mary Dick, *née* Card (d 1997); *b* 8 November 1935; *Educ* Barrow GS; *Career* CA 1959; sr ptnr J L Winder & Co; chm Furness Building Soc 1993–2005 (dir 1973–2005, vice-chm 1988–93); pres: Barrow Scout Mgmnt Ctee, Barrow-in-Furness Rambling Club 2002–04, Furness 41 Club 2003–04; FCA; *Recreations* fell walking, gardening, golf; *Style*— John L Winder, Esq; ✉ 32 Dane Avenue, Barrow-in-Furness, Cumbria LA14 4JS (tel 01229 821726); 125 Ramsden Square, Barrow-in-Furness, Cumbria LA14 1XA (tel 01229 820390)

WINDER, Robert James; s of Herbert James Winder (d 1984), of London, and Mary, *née* Dalby; *b* 26 September 1959; *Educ* Bradfield Coll, St Catherine's Coll Oxford (BA); *m* 1989, Hermione, *née* Davies; 2 s (Luke b 1993, Kit b 1995); *Career* on staff Euromoney 1982–86, The Independent 1986– (literary ed until 1995, occasional contrib 1995–), dep ed Granta Publications 1997–99, Culture ed Independent on Sunday 2000–01; *Books* No Admission (1988), The Marriage of Time and Convenience (1994), Hell for Leather: A Modern Cricket Journey (1996), Bloody Foreigners: The Story of Immigration to Britain (2004); *Recreations* reading, writing, sport; *Style*— Robert Winder, Esq; ✉ 125 Elgin Crescent, London W11 2JH (tel 020 7727 0640)

WINDLE, Prof Alan Hardwick; s of Stuart George Windle (d 1979), and Myrtle Lilian, *née* Povey (d 1960); *b* 20 June 1942; *Educ* Whitgift Sch, Imperial Coll London (BSc (Eng), ARSM, Bessemer medal, RSA Silver medal), Trinity Coll Cambridge (PhD); *m* 14 Sept 1968, Janet Susan, da of Dr Claude Morris Carr (d 2004), and Lorna, *née* Christopherson (d 1997); 3 da (Emma Rachel b 16 Oct 1969, Lucy-Clare b 17 June 1971, Rosemary Joy b 9 July 1976), 1 s (Roy Dudley Andrew b 22 Feb 1973); *Career* ICI research fell 1966–67, lectr in metallurgy Imperial Coll London 1967–75; Univ of Cambridge: lectr in materials science 1975–92, fell Trinity Coll 1978– (tutor 1983–91), prof of materials science 1992–, acting dir Melville Lab for Polymer Synthesis 1993–94, head Dept of Materials Science and Metallurgy 1995–2000; exec dir Cambridge-MIT Inst 2000–03, vice-pres Inst of Materials 2001–, dir Pfizer Inst for Pharmaceutical Materials Science 2006–; Rosenhain medal Inst of Metals 1987, Swinburne medal and prize Plastics and Rubber Inst 1992, Founders' Medal Polymer Physics Gp of the Inst of Physics, RSC and Inst of Materials 2007, Royal Soc Armourers and Braziers Medal 2007; govr The Whitgift Fndn 1997–2001, chm of tstees Mission Aviation Fellowship Europe 2001–03, cmmr The Royal Cmmn for the Exhbn of 1851 2001–; fell American Physical Soc 2001; FIM 1992, FInstP 1997 (MInstP 1971), FRS 1997; *Books* A First Course in Crystallography (1978), Liquid Crystalline Polymers (with Prof A M Donald, 1992, 2 edn with Dr S Hanna and Prof A M Donald, 2006); *Recreations* flying light aircraft; *Style*— Prof Alan Windle, FRS; ✉ Department of Materials Science and Metallurgy, University of Cambridge, Pembroke Street, Cambridge CB2 3QZ (tel 01223 334321, fax 01223 335637, e-mail ahw1@hermes.cam.ac.uk)

WINDLE-TAYLOR, Paul Carey; s of Dr Edwin Windle-Taylor, CBE (d 1990), and Diana, *née* Grove (d 1987); *b* 25 November 1948; *Educ* Mill Hill Sch, Emmanuel Coll Cambridge (MA, MB BChir), St Thomas' Hosp London, MBA; *m* 1, 1973 (m dis); m 2, 1996; *Career* conslt otolaryngologist; FRCS; *Recreations* fly fishing, fine wines; *Clubs* Flyfishers'; *Style*— Paul C Windle-Taylor, Esq; ✉ Nuffield Hospital, Derriford Road, Plymouth PL6 8BG (tel 01752 775861, e-mail pcw-t@dial.pipex.com)

WINDLESHAM, 3 Baron (UK 1937); Sir David James George Hennessy; 3 Bt (UK 1927), CVO, PC (1973); also Baron Hennessy (Life Peer UK 1999), of Windlesham in the County of Surrey; s of 2 Baron Windlesham (d 1962), by his 1 w Angela (d 1956), da of Julian Duggan; *b* 28 January 1932; *Educ* Ampleforth, Trinity Coll Oxford (MA); *m* 22 May 1965, Prudence Loveday (d 1986), yr da of Lt-Col Rupert Trevor Wallace Glynn, MC; 1 da (Hon Victoria b 1966), 1 s (Hon James b 1968); *Heir* s, Hon James Hennessy; *Career* served Grenadier Gds, Lt; sits as Cons peer in House of Lords; min of state: Home Office 1970–72, NI 1972–73; Lord Privy Seal and ldr House of Lords 1973–74; chm: ATV Network 1981 (md 1975–81), Parole Bd 1982–88; dir: The Observer 1981–89, W H Smith Group 1986–95; chm: Oxford Preservation Tst 1979–89, Oxford Soc 1985–88, Butler Tst 2004–; tstee: British Museum 1981–96 (chm 1986–96), Community Service Volunteers 1981–2000, Royal Collection Tst 1993–2000; Ditchley Fndn: govr and memb Cncl 1983–, vice-chm 1987–; memb Museums and Galleries Cmmn 1984–86; princ BNC Oxford 1989–2002; visiting fell All Souls' Coll 1986, visiting prof Princeton Univ 2002–03 (Weinberg/Goldman Sachs visiting prof 1997); pres Victim Support 1992–2001; hon bencher Inner Temple 1999; hon fell Trinity Coll Oxford 1982, hon fell BNC Oxford 2002; DLitt Univ of Oxford 1995, Hon LLD Univ of London 2002; Hon FBA 2005; Commendatore Order of Merit (Italy) 2003; *Books* Communication and Political Power (1966), Politics in Practice (1975), Broadcasting in a Free Society (1980), Responses to Crime (vol 1 1987, vol 2 1993, vol 3 1996, vol 4 2001), The Windlesham/Rampton Report on Death on the Rock (with Richard Rampton, QC, 1989), Politics, Punishment, and Populism (1998); *Style*— The Rt Hon the Lord Windlesham, CVO, PC; ✉ House of Lords, London SW1A 0PW

WINDRAM, Dr Michael David (Mike); s of Gordon Howard Windram (d 1990), of Halesowen, W Midlands, and Ethel May, *née* Hudson (d 1977); *b* 21 September 1945; *Educ* King Edward's Sch Birmingham, Queens' Coll Cambridge (MA, PhD); *m* 28 March 1970, Joycelyn Mary, da of Leslie Albert Marsh (d 1972); 2 s (Christopher b 20 Dec 1973, Richard b 7 April 1977); *Career* radio astronomer Univ of Cambridge 1966–69, physicist and sr engr Marconi Avionic Systems Ltd 1969–71; Radio Frequency Section IBA: engr 1971–73, sr engr 1973–77, head of section 1978–82; head of Video and Colour section

W

Experimental and Devpt IBA 1982–87, head of Experimental and Devpt Dept IBA 1987–90; NTL (National Transcommunications Ltd): exec mangr R&D 1991–93, dir of advanced products 1993–95; md DMV (Digi-Media Vision Ltd) 1995–; FIEE 1991, FRTS 1992, graduate memb Inst of Physics 1993, FREng 1993; *Recreations* music, DIY, caravanning; *Style*— Dr Mike Windram, FREng

WINDSOR, *see also:* Royal Family section

WINDSOR, Barbara; MBE; da of John Deeks, and Rose, *née* Ellis; *b* 6 August 1937; *Educ* Our Lady's Convent London, Aida Foster's Stage Sch; *m* 2000, Scott Mitchell; *Career* actress; began career aged 13 in pantomime, subsequently toured singing in cabaret (incl Ronnie Scott Band); numerous appearances on chat and quiz shows; *Theatre* incl: Love from Judy (West End debut), Fings Ain't Wot They Used to Be (Garrick), Oh' What a Lovely War (Broadway), Come Spy with Me (Whitehall, with Danny La Rue), Marie Lloyd in Sing A Rude Song (Garrick), The Threepenny Opera (with Vanessa Redgrave), The Owl and the Pussycat, Carry on London (Victoria Palace), A Merry Whiff of Windsor (one woman show, UK and world tour), Maria in Twelfth Night (Chichester Festival Co), Calamity Jane (nat tour), Kath in Kenneth William's prodn of Entertaining Mr Sloane (Lyric Hammersmith), The Mating Game, Miss Adelaide in Guys and Dolls (tour), Kath in first nat tour of Entertaining Mr Sloane (nominated Martini Regional Theatre Award for Best Actress); *Pantomime* numerous appearances incl: Babes in the Wood (Palladium), Fairy Godmother in Cinderella (Orchard Dartford) 1995–96; *Television* incl: Dreamers Highway, The Jack Jackson TV Show, Six Five Special, The Rag Trade (BBC), subject of This Is Your Life (Thames), Obituary Show (Channel Four), One Foot in the Grave (BBC), currently Peggy Mitchell in EastEnders, host Funny World (BBC) 1996, subject of Hall of Fame (BBC), Star for a Night (BBC), The Kumars at No 42 (BBC); *Films* incl: Sparrers Can't Sing, Carry on films (first Carry on Spying 1964), Lost, Too Hot to Handle, Flame in the Street, On the Fiddle, Hair of the Dog, Chitty Chitty Bang Bang, A Study in Terror, Comrades, The Boyfriend, Double Vision, Cor Blimey; *Radio* numerous incl Fancy A Bit; *Albums* Barbara Windsor; numerous incl single Sparrers Can't Sing (top 30 hit); *Books* Laughter and Tears of a Cockney Sparrow, All of Me (2000); *Style*— Miss Barbara Windsor, MBE; ⊠ c/o Burnett Granger Associates Ltd, 3 Clifford Street, London W1S 2LF

WINDSOR, Dean of; *see:* Conner, Very Rev David John

WINDSOR, Dr Malcolm; OBE (2004); s of Leonard George Windsor, and Nancy, *née* Cordy; *Educ* Univ of Bristol (PhD); *m*; 2 da; *Career* industry res placement Cadbury-Schweppes Ltd 1955–62, res fell Univ of Calif 1966–68, memb Res Inst UK (MAFF Torry Res Stn) 1968–75, memb Chief Scientist's Gp MAFF 1975–84, on secondment Cabinet Office 1981, sec N Atlantic Salmon Conservation Orgn (NASCO) 1984–; chair EC int evaluation of first EC-funded prog of Fisheries and Aquaculture R&D; UK scientist rep at int fisheries meetings and confs; chm Duddington Village Cons Soc; CChem, FRSC; *Publications* author of one book and approximately 45 published papers; *Recreations* walking, jazz, bread making, conservation; *Style*— Dr Malcolm Windsor, OBE; ⊠ NASCO, 11 Rutland Square, Edinburgh EH1 2AS (tel 0131 228 2551, fax 0131 228 4384, e-mail hq@nasco.int)

WINDSOR, Stuart James; s of E J Windsor (d 1965), and Gwendoline Knott (d 1979); *b* 26 May 1946; *Educ* Chace Sch; *m* Oct 1971 (sep 2004), Janet Elizabeth Davison-Lungley; 3 s (Alexander b 3 Nov 1976, Miles b 4 Jan 1985, Freddie b 26 Dec 1988); *Career* photographer; journalist until 1970, Fleet St photographer 1970–78 (Times, Observer, Daily Mail); photographic projects incl: coast to coast trip of America documenting lifestyles, living with Kabre Tribe in N Togo (as part of Nat Geographic anthropological educnl field trip), project in Galapagos Islands, coverage of Mount Kinabalu Borneo climb 1988; solo exhibition of retrospective work Embankment Gallery 1979; contrib to magazines and books on numerous travel and architectural topics, picture library contains 100,000 worldwide images, produces masterclasses on photographic and visual arts subjects, documented Polish Lifestyles in 360 Intactive Digital Images 2002, estab digital photo library Capital City Pictures devoted to London, creative ed Bond Street Magazine, dir of photography IPIX UK, photographic conslt Brooklands Museum; creative dir: Universal 360, Redhouse 360, Sutton-Windsor Assocs; *Books* Images of Egypt, France and French Lifestyles, Australia - This Beautiful Land, Dream Machines - BMW, The Arts - A History of Expression in the 21st Century; *CD-ROM* French Experience; *Recreations* travel, classic cars, photography, cycling, tennnis; *Clubs* ICA, Brooklands Soc, Wimbledon Village; *Style*— Stuart Windsor, Esq; ⊠ 1 Salisbury Road, Wimbledon, London SW19 4EZ (tel 020 8946 9878, e-mail sw@stuartwindsor.com)

WINDSOR-LEWIS, Geoffrey; s of Dr H Windsor Lewis (d 1982), of Cambridge, and Phyllis Mary, *née* Harris (d 1989); *b* 7 April 1936; *Educ* Leys Sch Cambridge, Trinity Hall Cambridge (MA); *m* Jacqueline, *née* Harty; 3 s (Steve b 12 Nov 1962, Guy b 2 April 1964, Tom b 5 Sept 1982); *Career* Nat Serv cmmnd 2 Regt RHA 1954–56; former rugby union player: Wales 1960, Barbarians, Univ of Cambridge 1956–58 (capt 1958); hon sec Barbarian Football Club 1966–; chartered surveyor; jt sr ptnr Buckell & Ballard 1978–84; dir: Arundell House plc 1985–90, Harcourt Properties Ltd 1990–2003; former govr Dragon Sch Oxford, former govr Leys Sch (pres Old Leysian Union 1997–98); Liveryman Worshipful Co of Chartered Surveyors; hon fell Harris Manchester Coll Oxford, FRICS; *Recreations* vegetable gardening, golf; *Clubs* East India, Frewen (Oxford), Hawks' (Cambridge); *Style*— Geoffrey Windsor-Lewis, Esq; ⊠ Wilcote Place, Ramsden, Oxfordshire OX7 3BA (tel 01993 868370)

WINEARLS, Dr Christopher Good; s of late Capt James Robert Winearls, and late Sheila, *née* Boardman; *b* 25 September 1949; *Educ* Diocesan Coll Rondebosch Cape Town, Univ of Cape Town (MB ChB), Univ of Oxford (DPhil); *m* 6 Dec 1975, Beryl Claire, da of late Dr Wilmer Edward George Butler, of Cairns, Queensland, Aust; 4 s (James b 1979, Alastair b 1982, Stuart b 1985, Robert Frederick Good b 1991); *Career* sr lectr in med Royal Postgrad Med Sch London 1986–88, conslt nephrologist and clinical dir Renal Unit Oxford Radcliffe Hosp 1988–; censor RCP 2001–03; Rhodes scholar 1972; clinical vice-pres Renal Assoc of GB 2004–07; sr research fell Jesus Coll Oxford 2004–; FRCP; *Recreations* sailing, photography; *Style*— Dr Christopher Winearls; ⊠ The Oxford Kidney Unit, The Churchill, The Oxford Radcliffe Hospital, Oxford OX3 7LJ (tel 01865 225804, fax 01865 225773)

WINFIELD, Brig Christopher Raymond (Chris); CBE (2000); s of Reginald Winfield (d 1993), and Ida May Caroline, *née* Anderson (d 1989); *b* 21 March 1944; *Educ* Abingdon Sch, Univ of Oxford (MA, BM BCh); *m* 16 Nov 1974, Wendy Elizabeth, da of F G Roomes; 2 da (Samantha Susan (Mrs Pontin) b 9 Nov 1968, Hannah May b 31 July 1979), 2 step da (Louise Melanie Duncan b 24 June 1965, Katy Victoria Samantha Duncan b 27 Nov 1966); *Career* house appts Stoke Mandeville Hosp Aylesbury 1969–71, Regtl MO 1 Bn Scots Gds then Irish Rangers 1971–73, forces MO Belize 1973–74, gen med trg Cambridge Mil Hosp Aldershot 1974–77, med specialist Mil Wing and sr registrar Med Unit Musgrave Park Hosp Belfast 1977–78, sr registrar Brompton Hosp London 1978–79, sr registrar Army Chest Unit Cambridge Mil Hosp Aldershot 1979–81, conslt physician and clinical tutor Princess Mary's Hosp RAF(H) Akrotiri 1981–83, head Med Dept and clinical tutor Br Mil Hosp Munster 1983–87, conslt i/c Army Chest Centre Cambridge Mil Hosp Aldershot 1987–90, forces advsr in med and conslt physician 33 Field Gen Surgical Hosp Al Jubail Gulf War 1990–91, sr conslt physician and offr in charge Army Chest Unit Cambridge Mil Hosp Aldershot 1991–94, CO Br Mil Hosp Rinteln 1994–96 (sr conslt physician and comd advsr in med 1994), dir secdy health care Br Forces Germany Health Serv 1996–2005, ret 2006; memb: Anglo-German Med Soc 1988, RSM 1999; RAMC Consultants Prize 1986; Freedom City of Rinteln 1996; FRCP 1988; OStJ 1988; *Recreations*

singing; *Clubs* Leander, Camerata Musica Bielefeld; *Style*— Brig Chris Winfield, CBE; ⊠ Chestnut Lodge, 3 Rowhills, Farnham GU9 9AT (tel 01252 31266)

WING, Dr Lorna Gladys; OBE; da of Bernard Newbury Tolchard (d 1969), and Gladys Ethel, *née* Whittell (d 1962); *b* 7 October 1928; *Educ* Chatham GS, UCH London (MD, MB BS); *m* 15 May 1950, Prof John Kenneth Wing, CBE, s of William Sidney Wing (d 1928); 1 da (Susan b 1956); *Career* scientific staff MRC Social and Community Psychiatry Unit 1964–90, hon conslt psychiatrist Maudsley Hosp London 1972–90, hon sr lectr Inst of Psychiatry London 1974–90; conslt psychiatrist Nat Autistic Soc 1990– (fndr memb and vice-pres); FRCPsych 1980; *Books* Early Childhood Autism (ed, 1976), Hospital Closure and the Resettlement of Residents (1989), The Autistic Spectrum - A Guide for Parents and Professionals (1996); *Recreations* walking, reading, gardening; *Style*— Dr Lorna Wing, OBE; ⊠ Centre for Social and Communication Disorders (Diagnosis and Assessment), Elliot House, 113 Masons Hill, Bromley, Kent BR2 9HT (tel 020 8466 0098, fax 020 8466 0118)

WINGFIELD DIGBY, Stephen Hatton; s of Archdeacon Basil Wingfield Digby, MBE (d 1996), of Wilts, and Barbara Hatton Budge (d 1987); *b* 17 November 1944; *Educ* Sherborne, Univ of Bristol (BSc), Queen's Univ Belfast (MBA); *m* 1, 1968, Sarah Jane (d 2003), da of Osborne Lovell, of Dorset; 1 da (Claire b 1972), 2 s (William b 1974, Alexander b 1983); *m* 2, 2006, Sylvia, da of Paget Bowyer (d 2000), of Dorset, and Joan Bowyer (d 2006), and former w of Christopher Pope (d 2004); *Career* dir: Bass Sales Ltd 1978–81, Bass Wales & West Ltd 1981–83, The Harp Lager Co 1983–2006, Buckleys Brewery plc 1988–93, Crown Brewery plc 1989–93; Guinness GB: account dir 1994–99, trading dir 1999–2001; sales dir Guiness UDV Brands 2001–02, business unit dir Diageo GB 2002–06; chm Assoc of London Brewers and Licensed Retailers 1990–94; govr: Aldenham Sch 1997–2001, Sherborne Sch for Girls 2002–; Master The Brewers' Company 1997–98; *Recreations* fishing, shooting; *Clubs* MCC; *Style*— Stephen Wingfield Digby, Esq; ⊠ The Coach House, Gregories Farm Lane, Beaconsfield Buckinghamshire HP9 1HJ

WINKELMAN, Joseph William; s of George William Winkelman (d 1956), and Cleo Lucretia, *née* Harness (d 1978); *b* 20 September 1941; *Educ* Keokuk HS, Univ of the South Sewanee TN (BA, pres of graduating class), Wharton Sch of Fin Univ of Pennsylvania, Ruskin Sch of Drawing Univ of Oxford (Cert Fine Art); *m* 8 Feb 1969, Harriet Lowell, da of Gaspard D'Andelot Belin (d 2003), of Cambridge, MA; 2 da (Alice Mary b 21 March 1973, Harriet Lowell b 28 May 1974); *Career* secondary sch master for US Peace Corps Tabora Sch Tanzania 1965–66; memb Bd of Dirs Bankside Gallery London 1986–95 and 2002–, chm Nat Assoc of Blood Donors 1994–95, govr Windmill First Sch Oxford 1994–98; artist; working mainly in relief and intaglio printmaking, handmaking own autographic prints; artist in residence St John's Coll Oxford 2004; hon fellowship: Printmakers' Cncl 1988, Oxford Art Soc 1993, RWS 1996; prizes: Int Miniature Print Exhibitions Cadaques Spain 1982 and Seoul Korea 1982, Royal W of Eng Acad Bristol for painting 1985; Lothrop Prize Print Club of Albany NY 1998, Center for Contemporary Printmaking Norwalk Conn 2001 and 2003; pres Royal Soc of Painter-Printmakers (RE) 1989–95; fell Royal Soc of Painter-Printmakers 1982 (assoc 1979), academician Royal West of England Acad (RWA) 1989–2006 (assoc 1983); *Recreations* gardening, hill walking, theatre; *Style*— Joseph Winkelman, Esq; ⊠ The Hermitage, 69 Old High Street, Headington, Oxford OX3 9HT (tel 01865 762839, e-mail winkelman@ukgateway.net)

WINKLER, HE Dr Jan; s of Otto Winkler (d 2006), and Helena Winkler (d 2003); *b* 7 May 1957, Pardubice, Czech Republic; *Educ* Charles Univ Prague (JD); *m* 1979, Jana, *née* Zajicová; 3 c (Dagmar b 1984, Alžběta b 1986, Petr b 1989); *Career* Czech diplomat; company lawyer 1981–90, registrar Charles Univ Prague 1990–95; Miny of Foreign Affrs: head of policy planning 1995–97, vice-min 1997–99; conslt: Andersen Consulting and Accenture 1999–2001, PricewaterhouseCoopers 2001–03; vice-min Miny of Foreign Affrs 2003–05, ambass to the Ct of St James's 2005–; conslt OECD 1992–95; memb Bd Nat Gallery Prague 1995–2000; *Publications* Uniqueness in Unity (jtly, 1985), Obnova Ideje University (jtly, 1993), Rethinking University (jtly, 1994), The Pilsen Talks (jtly, 1997); *Recreations* reading, visual art, sport (skiing, tennis); *Clubs* Athenaeum, Travellers; *Style*— HE Dr Jan Winkler; ⊠ Embassy of the Czech Republic, 26 Kensington Palace Gardens, London W8 4QY (tel 020 7243 7902, fax 020 7727 9654, e-mail jan_winkler@mzv.cz)

WINKLEY, Sir David Ross; kt (1999); s of Donald Joseph Winkley, and Winifred Mary (d 1997); *b* 30 November 1941; *Educ* King Edwards Sch Birmingham (state scholar), Selwyn Coll Cambridge (exhibitioner, MA), Wadham Coll Oxford (DPhil); *m* Dr Linda Mary, *née* Holland; 1 da (Katherine J N b 23 June 1971), 1 s (Joseph D D b 15 June 1973); *Career* memb Centre for Contemporary Cultural Studies Univ of Birmingham 1964–66, dep head Perry Common Sch 1968–71, head Grove Sch Handsworth Birmingham 1974–96, fndr and pres National Primary Tst 1987–2006; fndr Children's Univ; hon prof Univ of Birmingham 1999–, hon prof Univ of Warwick 2005–; DLitt Univ of Birmingham 1999, Hon DUniv Univ of Central England 2000; fell Nuffield Coll 1981–83; *Publications* Diplomats and Detectives (1986), Handsworth Revolution (2002); author of over 60 articles on various learned subjects; *Recreations* writing fiction, philosophy, playing piano especially Bach and modern jazz; *Style*— Sir David Winkley

WINKLEY, Dr Linda Mary; da of Reginald Bertram Holland (d 1984), and Vera Mary, *née* Mills; *b* 1 June 1942; *Educ* King Edward's HS for Girls Edgbaston, Univ of Birmingham (MB ChB, DPM, DCH, DRCOG); *m* 22 July 1967, David Ross Winkley, s of Donald Winkley, of Sutton Coldfield, W Midlands; 1 da (Katherine b 23 June 1971), 1 s (Joseph b 15 June 1973); *Career* in gen practice 1967–70, trained in adult psychiatry Warnford Hosp Oxford 1970–72, sr registrar Midland Trg Scheme in Child Psychiatry 1973–75, conslt child psychiatrist Selly Oak Hosp Birmingham 1976–, regnl speciality clinical tutor in child psychiatry 1989–99 (developed child psychotherapy servs in Midlands and set up course for psychotherapeutic work with children 1980), clinical dir Children's Hosp Birmingham 1993–94; memb Client Gp Planning Team, chm Children's Mental Health Promotion Sub-Ctee W Midlands, chm Div of Child Health and Paediatrics Selly Oak Hosp 1988–93; fndr memb and treas W Midlands Inst of Psychotherapy; memb: ACPP 1973, APP 1985; MACP 1986, FRCPsych 1989; *Publications* Emotional Problems in Children and Young People (1996); *Recreations* theatre, music, tennis; *Style*— Dr Linda Winkley; ⊠ Oaklands, Raddlebarn Road, Selly Oak, Birmingham B29 6JD (tel 0121 627 8231)

WINKLEY, Dr Stephen Charles; s of George William Dinsdale Winkley (d 1987), and Eunice Kate, *née* Golding (d 1992); *b* 9 July 1944; *Educ* St Edward's Sch Oxford, Brasenose Coll Oxford (MA, DPhil); *m* 1, 1968 (m dis 1978), Georgina Mary, *née* Smart; 2 s (Nicholas Leo b 1971, Howard Mungo Alaric b 1972); *m* 2, 1983, Jennifer Mary, *née* Burt; 2 da (Imogen Daisy Arabella b 1987, Isabella Alice Rose b 1994); *Career* asst master Cranleigh Sch 1969–85, second master Winchester Coll 1985–91, headmaster Uppingham Sch 1991–2006; *Recreations* water colour painting; *Style*— Dr Stephen Winkley; ⊠ 88 Rockingham Road, Kettering, Northamptonshire NN16 9AD (tel 01536 481997)

WINKWORTH, Jane; *b* 1948; *Educ* St Christopher Sch Letchworth, Kingston Sch of Art; *Career* shoe designer, artist and painter; fndr French Sole 1989, currently md and creative dir French Sole and London Sole USA; *Recreations* ballet, opera, theatre, the arts, fashion, life in LA; *Style*— Ms Jane Winkworth; ⊠ 46 Markham Square, Chelsea, London SW3 4XA (tel 020 7581 4128); Chestnut Cottage, Chobham, Surrey GU24 8EF (tel 01276 856733); 1105 Idahoe Avenue, Santa Monica, CA 90403, USA (tel 00 1 310 319 1658, e-mail jane@frenchsole.com)

WINKWORTH, Peter Leslie; s of Francis William Harry Winkworth (d 1975), and Ruth Margaret Llewellin, *née* Notley (d 1998); *b* 9 August 1948; *Educ* Tonbridge; *m* 16 June 1973, Tessa Anne, da of Sir Alexander Warren Page (d 1993); 2 da (Victoria b 1975, Jessica b 1978), 1 s (Piers b 1976); *Career* merchant banker and CA; dir: Close Brothers Ltd 1977–2007, Winterflood Securities Ltd 1993–, Arkstar Ltd 1984–88, Clifford Brown Group plc 1987–93, Jackson-Stops & Staff Ltd 1990–92; *Recreations* golf, horse breeding and racing, licensed race horse trainer; *Clubs* East India; *Style—* Peter Winkworth, Esq; ✉ Merton Place, Dunsfold, Surrey GU8 4NP

WINN, Geoffrey Frank; s of Capt Frank Winn (d 1987), of Scarborough, N Yorks, and Hettie, *née* Croft (d 1983); *b* 13 December 1938; *Educ* Scarborough HS, Univ of Leeds (BCom); *m* 9 July 1966, Jennifer Lynne Winn, JP, da of Jack Winter, DFC (d 2006), of Scarborough, N Yorks; 2 da (Deborah b 1967, Susie b 1970); *Career* chartered accountant; in practice Winn & Co (Scarborough and branch offices) 1962–2003; chm Scarborough Bldg Soc 1994–2002 (dir 1984–2005); pres Humberside and Dist Soc of Chartered Accountants 1991–92; memb Cncl ICAEW 1995–2003; chm: Scarborough Flower Fund Homes 1986– (memb 1970–), N Yorks Moors and Coast Business Advice Agency 2002–06, Friends of St Laurence's Scalby 2005–; tstee and dir Scarborough Museums Tst 2004–, tstee Scarborough CC; FCA 1962; *Recreations* golf, skiing; *Clubs* East India; *Style—* Geoffrey Winn, Esq; ✉ Barmoor House, Scalby, Scarborough, North Yorkshire YO13 OPG (tel 01723 362 414, mobile 07786 002152)

WINNER, Michael Robert; s of George Joseph Winner (d 1972), and Helen, *née* Zlota (d 1984); *b* 30 October 1935; *Educ* St Christopher Sch Letchworth, Downing Coll Cambridge (MA); *Career* chm: Scimitar Films Ltd, Michael Winner Ltd, Motion Picture & Theatrical Investments Ltd 1957–; memb Cncl Dirs Guild of GB 1983–, fndr and chm Police Meml Tst 1984–; dir: Play It Cool 1962, The Cool Mikado (also writer) 1962, West Eleven 1963, The Mechanic 1972; prodr and dir: The System 1963, I'll Never Forget What's 'is name 1967, The Games 1969, Lawman 1970, The Nightcomers 1971, Chato's Land 1971, Scorpio 1972, The Stone Killer 1973, Death Wish 1974, Won Ton Ton The Dog That Saved Hollywood 1975, Firepower 1978, Scream for Help 1984, Death Wish III 1985; prodr dir and writer: You Must be Joking 1965, The Jokers 1966, Hannibal Brooks 1968, The Sentinel 1976, The Big Sleep 1977, Death Wish II 1981, The Wicked Lady 1982, Appointment with Death 1987, A Chorus of Disapproval 1988, Bullseye! 1989, Dirty Weekend 1992, Parting Shots 1997; theatre prodns: The Tempest 1974, A Day in Hollywood A Night in the Ukraine 1978; actor: For The Greater Good (BBC film, dir Danny Boyle) 1990, Decadence (film, dir Steven Berkoff) 1993, The Flump (Radio 4, dir Bruce Hyman) 2000; TV: Michael Winner's True Crimes; appeared in and dir adverts incl: esure Insurance, Kenco, Doritos, Books for Schools; columnist Sunday Times, News of the World; *Books* Winner's Dinners (1999, revised edn 2000), Winner Guide (2002), Winner Takes It All (autobiography, 2004); *Recreations* being wonderful and difficult, making tablemats; *Style—* Michael Winner, Esq; ✉ 219 Kensington High Street, London W8 6BD (tel 020 7734 8385)

WINNICK, David Julian; MP; *b* 26 June 1933; *Educ* LSE; *Career* memb: Willesden Cncl 1959–64, Brent Cncl 1964–66; MP (Lab): Croydon S 1966–70, Walsall N 1979– (Parly candidate (Lab): Harwich 1964, Croydon Central Oct 1974, Walsall 1976); memb Select Ctees on: Race Relations and Immigration 1969–70, Environment 1980–83, Home Affrs 1983–87 and 1997–, Procedure 1989–97; co-chm Br-Irish Inter-Parly Body 1997– (vice-chm 1993–97), vice-pres APEX 1983–88; chm UK Immigrants Advsy Service 1984–90; *Style—* David Winnick, MP; ✉ House of Commons, London SW1A 0AA

WINNINGTON, Sir Anthony Edward; 7 Bt (GB 1755); s of Col Thomas Foley Churchill Winnington, MBE (d 1999), and Lady Betty, *née* Anson, da of late 4 Earl of Lichfield; suc unc, Sir Francis Winnington, 6 Bt (d 2003); *b* 13 May 1948; *Educ* Eton, Univ of Grenoble; *m* 5 Dec 1978, Karyn Kathryn Kettles, da of Joanne Dayton, of Palm Beach, Florida; 2 da (Victoria b 1981, Sophia b 1985), 1 s (Edward b 1987); *Heir* s, Edward Winnington; *Career* dir of equity sales Hoare Govett Securities Ltd 1984–92 (joined 1969), dir Robert Fleming Securities 1992–2000; FSI (memb Stock Exchange 1984); *Recreations* fishing; *Clubs* Boodle's, Hurlingham, White's; *Style—* Sir Anthony Winnington, Bt; ✉ Brockhill Court, Shelsley Beauchamp, Worcestershire WR6 6RH (e-mail winnington@aol.com)

WINSER, Kim; OBE (2006); *Educ* Purbrook Park GS; *Career* formerly dir Menswear Buying and divnl dir Ladies Gp Marks and Spencer; chief exec Pringle of Scotland 2000–05, chief exec Aquascutum 2006–; patron: Prince's Tst, Breast Cancer charities; memb Friends of Scotland Advsy Gp, non-exec dir Edrington Gp, memb Fashion Cncl; Hon DLitt Heriot-Watt Univ Edinburgh; *Style—* Ms Kim Winser, OBE

WINSER, Nigel de Northop; s of Robert Stephen Winser, of Kintbury, Berks, and Anne, *née* Carrick; *b* 4 July 1952, Kisumu, Kenya; *Educ* Bradfield Coll, Poly of Central London; *m* 17 July 1982, Shane, da of Arthur James Wesley-Smith, of Sheffield; 1 s (Philip b 1984), 1 da (Kate b 1987); *Career* Royal Geographical Soc: field dir Mulu Sarawak expedition 1976, expedition offr 1978 (expeditions carried out in Karakoram Pakistan, Kora Kenya, Wahiba Oman, Kimberley Aust, Temburong Brunei, Mkomazi Tanzania, Badia Jordan, Indian Ocean), estab Expedition Advsy Centre 1980, asst dir and head of exploration 1988, dep dir 1991–2005, i/c Shoals of Capricorn prog Indian Ocean 1998–2002; exec dir Earthwatch Inst (Europe) Oxford 2005–; Winston Churchill travel fell 1977–78, exploration fell commoner Corpus Christi Coll Cambridge 1990; memb Field Studies Cncl 1999–2005; fndr: Exploration Univ 1991, Sponsor Our Species 1992, Geographical Observatories Prog 1994; tstee: Project Urquhart 1993–, Mount Everest Foundation 1995–2002, Friends of Conservation (UK) 1996–2002, Gino Watkins Memorial Foundation 1996–2003, Andrew Croft Memorial Fund 2000–06, Global Canopy Prog 2000–, Greencard Tst 2004–, Oxford Univ Expeditions Cncl 2006–, MEF Everest 50th Ctee; assoc memb Il Ngwesi Maasai Community Gp Ranch Kenya 2005; Patrons Gold Medal for leadership of Oman Wahiba Sands project 1988, Explorers Club of NY Citation of Merit 1989, Mrs Patrick Ness Award for expdn leadership 1977, Mungo Park Medal Royal Scottish Geographical Soc 1995; Hon DSc Univ of Westminster 2006; *Books* Sea of Sands and Mists (1989), contributing ed History of World Exploration (1991); *Recreations* fly fishing on the Kennet, photography, history of exploration, expedition art; *Clubs* Alpine, Geographical, Rainforest, James Caird, Desert Dining, Artists and Travellers; *Style—* Nigel Winser, Esq; ✉ 2 Finstock House, Patch Ridings, Finstock, Oxfordshire OX7 3DQ (tel 01993 869104); Earthwatch Institute (tel 01865 318879, fax 01865 311383, e-mail nwinser@earthwatch.org.uk, website www.earthwatch.org/europe)

WINSKEL, Prof Glynn; s of Thomas Francis Winskel, and Helen Juanita, *née* McCall; *Educ* Univ of Cambridge (MA, ScD), Univ of Oxford (MSc), Univ of Edinburgh (PhD); *Career* res scientist Carnegie-Mellon Univ PA 1982–84; Univ of Cambridge: lectr 1984–88, fell King's Coll 1985–88, reader 1987–88, prof of computer sci 2000–, fell Emmanuel Coll 2000–; Univ of Aarhus Denmark: prof of computer sci 1988–2000, dir Res Centre BRICS (Basic Res in Computer Sci) 1994–2000; *Books* The Formal Semantics of Programming Languages - An Introduction (1993); *Recreations* running, swimming, art; *Style—* Prof Glynn Winskel; ✉ University of Cambridge Computer Laboratory, JJ Thompson Avenue, Cambridge CB3 0FD (tel 01223 334613, fax 01223 334678)

WINSLET, Christopher James; s of Frank Winslet, and Margaret, *née* Martin; *b* 27 May 1955; *Educ* Strodes GS, Univ of Wales (BSc(Econ)); *m* 1976, Jane Margaret, da of John Albert King; 1 da (Eleanor Jane b 4 Aug 1980), 1 s (Edward Simon b 14 Aug 1982); *Career* Deloitte & Co 1976–87: joined as trainee accountant, qualified CA 1979, taxation specialist 1980; ptnr Deloitte Haskins & Sells 1987 (merged with Coopers & Lybrand 1989), chm Fin Services Tax PricewaterhouseCoopers (formerly Coopers & Lybrand before merger 1998) 1997–; frequent writer and speaker on taxation of insurance cos; FCA 1979, ATII 1980; *Books* Noah (1992), George and the Dragon (1993); *Recreations* writing musicals, jazz guitar, tennis, golf, reading; *Clubs* Coopers Hill Tennis, RAC; *Style—* Christopher Winslet, Esq; ✉ PricewaterhouseCoopers, Southwark Towers, 32 London Bridge Street, London SE1 9SY (tel 020 7583 5000, fax 020 7212 4121, e-mail chris.j.winslet@uk.pwcglobal.com)

WINSLET, Kate Elizabeth; da of Roger Winslet, and Sally Winslet; *b* 5 October 1975; *m* 1, Nov 1998 (m dis 2001), Jim Threapleton; 1 da (Mia b 2000); m 2, May 2003, Sam Mendes, *qv*; 1 s (Joe b 2003); *Career* actress; *Theatre* What the Butler Saw 1994; *Television* incl: Dark Season 1991, Anglo-Saxon Attitudes 1992, Get Back 1992, Casualty 1993; *Film* incl: Heavenly Creatures 1994 (Best Foreign Actress NZ Film and TV Critics' Awards, Best Br Actress Awards London Film Critics' Circle and Empire magazine), Sense and Sensibility 1995 (Best Supporting Actress Screen Actors' Guild, BAFTA Award, Oscar and Golden Globe nominations), Jude 1996, Hamlet 1996 (Best Br Actress Empire Magazine Awards, Evening Standard Award), Titanic 1997 (Best European Actress European Film Acad, Film Actress of the Year Variety Club of GB, Empire Magazine Award, Oscar, Golden Globe and Screnn Actors Guild nominations), Hideous Kinky 1998, Holy Smoke 1999, Quills 2000, Enigma 2001, Iris 2001 (Oscar, BAFTA and Golden Globe nominations), The Life of David Gale 2003, Finding Neverland 2004 (BAFTA nomination), Eternal Sunshine of the Spotless Mind 2004 (Best Br Actress Awards London Film Critics' Circle and Empire magazine, Oscar, BAFTA and Golden Globe nominations), Romance & Cigarettes 2005, Little Children 2006 (Best Actress Golden Globe, BAFTA Award, Screen Actors' Guild and Oscar nominations 2007), All the King's Men 2006, Flushed Away (voice) 2006, The Holiday 2006; Best Int Actress Goldene Kamera Award 2001; *Style—* Miss Kate Winslet; ✉ c/o Dallas Smith, PFD, Drury House, 34–43 Russell Street, London WC2B 5HA (tel 020 7344 1010, fax 020 7836 9544); c/o Hylda Queally, CAA, 2000 Avenue of the Stars, Los Angeles, CA 90067, USA (tel 001 424 288 2000, fax 001 424 288 3671)

WINSOR, Thomas Philip (Tom); WS (1984); s of late Thomas Valentine Marrs Winsor, and late Phyllis Margaret, *née* Bonsor; *b* 7 December 1957; *Educ* Grove Acad Broughty Ferry, Univ of Edinburgh (LLB), Univ of Dundee (Dip); *m* 1989, Sonya Elizabeth, *née* Field; 2 da; *Career* admitted slr Scotland 1981, England & Wales 1991, Notary Public Scotland 1981; gen practice Dundee 1981–83, asst slr Dundas & Wilson CS 1983–84, asst slr Norton Rose 1984–91, ptnr Denton Hall 1991–99, Rail Regulator and Int Rail Regulator 1999–2004 (chief legal advsr and gen counsel Office of the Rail Regulator 1993–95), ptnr White & Case 2004–; memb: Law Soc of Scotland, Law Soc of England & Wales, Int Bar Assoc, Univ of Dundee Petroleum and Mineral Law Soc (pres 1987–89), Soc of Scottish Lawyers in London (pres 1987–89); FCILT; *Publications* Taylor and Winsor on Joint Operating Agreements (with MPG Taylor, 1989), Legal Lines (articles in Modern Railways Magazine 1996–99); articles in books, newspapers and learned jls on oil and gas, electricity and railways law and regulation; *Recreations* literature, theatre, opera, music, hill walking, gardening, cycling, chess, Scottish constitutional history, law; *Style—* Tom Winsor, Esq, WS

WINSTANLEY, Alan Kenneth; s of (Albert) Kenneth Winstanley (d 1973), and Doreen, *née* Dunscombe, of Mansfield, Notts; *b* 2 November 1952; *Educ* St Clement Danes GS for Boys London; *m* 5 Oct 1975, Christine Susan Ann, da of Raymond Henry Osborne; 1 s (James Alan Kenneth b 7 Jan 1983), 1 da (Eve Alexis b 24 Oct 1978); *Career* record prodr; recording engr (work incl Amii Stewart's Knock on Wood, early Stranglers' records) 1970–79, freelance prodr Stranglers LP The Raven 1979, prodr (in partnership with Clive Langer) 1979–; jt fndr: West Side Studios London 1984, residential studio Henley 1987; artists produced incl: Madness 1981–85, Teardrop Explodes 1981, Dexy's Midnight Runners 1982, Elvis Costello 1983–84, Marilyn 1983, Lloyd Cole and the Commotions 1985, David Bowie, Sade, Style Council, Ray Davies, Gil Evans (for Absolute Beginners) 1985, Bowie and Jagger (Dancing in the Street) 1985, China Crisis 1986, Hothouse Flowers 1987–90, The Adventures 1989, Morrissey 1989–91, They Might Be Giants 1989, Bush 1995, Aztec Camera 1995; Platinum albums: One Step Beyond (Madness) 1980, Absolutely (Madness) 1981, Complete Madness 1982, Too-Rye Ay (Dexy's Midnight Runners) 1982, Sixteen Stone (Bush) 1995; Gold albums: The Raven (The Stranglers) 1980, Dance Craze 1981, 7 (Madness) 1981, Kilimanjaro (Teardrop Explodes) 1982, The Rise and Fall (Madness) 1983, Punch the Clock (Elvis Costello) 1983, Easy Pieces (Lloyd Cole) 1985, People (Hothouse Flowers) 1988, Home (Hothouse Flowers) 1990, Flood (They Might Be Giants) 1994; Silver albums: Goodbye Cruel World (Elvis Costello) 1984, Mad Not Mad (Madness) 1985; Platinum single: Come On Eileen (Dexy's Midnight Runners) 1982; Gold singles: Baggy Trousers 1980, Embarrassment 1981, It Must Be Love 1981, Our House 1982 (all by Madness), Dancing in the Street (Bowie & Jagger) 1985; Silver singles: One Step Beyond 1980, My Girl 1980, Work Rest and Play EP 1981, Return of the Los Palmas 7 1981, Shut Up 1981, Grey Day 1981, Driving in my Car 1982, Wings of a Dove 1983 (all by Madness), Reward (Teardrop Explodes) 1981, Swords of a Thousand Men (Tenpole Tudor) 1981, Calling Your Name (Marilyn) 1983; *Awards* Top Producer (singles) Music Week award 1982, nominee Best British Producer BPI awards 1982 and 1983, Producers Guild Fellowship Award 1997; *Recreations* tennis, golf, skiing, cycling, travelling; *Style—* Alan Winstanley, Esq; ✉ e-mail awinst@aol.com

WINSTANLEY, His Hon Judge Robert James; s of Morgan James Winstanley (d 1980), and Joan Martha, *née* Cuthbert, of Epsom; *b* 4 November 1948; *Educ* Glyn GS Epsom, St Catharine's Coll Cambridge (MA), Coll of Law London; *m* 19 Aug 1972, Josephine, *née* Langhorne; 2 s (Jonathan Robert b 18 Aug 1978, Richard Francis b 24 June 1980); *Career* asst slr Dawson & Co 1973–75 (articled clerk 1971–73), ptnr Winstanley - Burgess 1975–96, circuit judge (SE Circuit) 1996–; memb Cncl Law Soc 1985–96; memb Law Soc 1973; *Recreations* cricket, golf, motorcycling, bridge; *Clubs* Sudbury Golf, MCC; *Style—* His Hon Judge Winstanley; ✉ c/o South Eastern Circuit Office, New Cavendish House, 18 Maltravers Street, London WC2R 3EU

WINSTON, Prof Brian Norman; s of Reuben Winston (d 1989), of Wembley, and Anita, *née* Salamons (d 1983); *b* 7 November 1941; *Educ* Kilburn GS, Merton Coll Oxford (MA); *m* 1978, Adèle, da of Aleck Jackson; 1 da (Jessica b 1979), 1 s (Matthew b 1983); *Career* freelance journalist 1974–; researcher/prodr Granada TV 1963–66, prodr/dir BBC TV 1966–69, prodr/dir Granada TV 1969–72, lectr Bradford Coll of Art 1972–74, res dir Dept of Sociology Univ of Glasgow 1974–76, head of gen studies Nat Film & TV Sch Beaconsfield 1974–79, prof and head of film studies Tisch Sch of the Arts NY Univ 1979–86 (visiting prof of film 1976–77), dean Sch of Communications Pennsylvania State Univ 1986–92, prof and dir Centre for Journalism Studies Univ of Wales Coll of Cardiff 1992–97, head Sch of Communication and Creative Industries Univ of Westminster 1997–2002; Univ of Lincoln: dean Faculty of Media and Humanities 2002–05, pro-vice-chllr 2004–06, prof of communications 2006–; produced The Third Walker (starring William Shatner and Colleen Dewhurst) Canada 1976; winner Emmy for documentary script writing for Heritage: Civilization and the Jews part 8 (WNET-TV, NY); chair Welsh Film Cncl 1995–97, govr BFI 1994–2001; *Books* Dangling Conversations - The Image of the Media (1973), Dangling Conversations - Hardware Software (1974), Bad News (1976), More Bad News (1980), Misunderstanding Media (1986), Working with Video (with Julia Keydel, 1986), Claiming the Real (1995), Technologies of Seeing (1996), Media, Technology and Society (1998), Fires Were Started (1999), Lies, Damn Lies and Documentaries (2000), Messages: Free Expression, Media and the West from Gutenburg

W

to Google (2005); *Recreations* cooking; *Style—* Prof Brian Winston; ✉ Minerva Productions, University of Lincoln, Brayford Pool, Lincoln LN6 7TS (tel 01522 886871, e-mail bwinston@lincoln.ac.uk)

WINSTON, Malcolm John; s of John Winston (d 1982), of Bexhill, and Sarah, *née* Bates; *b* 8 November 1930; *Educ* Stationers' Co Sch; *m* 16 June 1962, Cynthia Mary Boorne, da of Hugh Napier Goodchild (d 1981), of Norwich; 1 s (Mark Jonathan Napier b 1964), 1 da (Sarah Catherine Louise (Mrs Bray) b 1967); *Career* Bank of England 1950–75, seconded Central TSB 1973, sr asst gen mangr Central TSB 1981 (asst gen mangr 1975), joined TSB England & Wales upon merger with Central TSB 1986; pres Assoc of Int Savings Banks in London 1985–96 and 1998– 2000 (fndr 1980, chm 1983–84), chm Lombard Assoc 1989–90, dir Tyndall Bank plc 1991–94, dir Bankgesellschaft Berlin (UK) plc 1995–2003 (sr advsr Bankgesellschaft Berlin 1994–2003); sr advsr Landesbank Berlin 1993–2003; chm Alkenmind Ltd 1994–; chm Age Concern Mayfield; Freeman City of London 1952, Liveryman Worshipful Co of Makers of Playing Cards 1979; fell Assoc of Corp Treasurers 1979; ISBI medal of Honour ISBI World Congress (Rome) 1990; *Recreations* beagling, travel; *Clubs* Carlton, United and Cecil; *Style—* Malcolm Winston, Esq; ✉ Maze Pond, Wadhurst, East Sussex TN5 6DG (tel 01892 782074, fax 01892 783698)

WINSTON, Baron (Life Peer UK 1995), of Hammersmith in the London Borough of Hammersmith and Fulham; Robert Maurice Lipson Winston; s of Lawrence Winston (d 1949), of London, and Ruth, *née* Lipson; *b* 15 July 1940; *Educ* St Paul's, Univ of London (MB BS); *m* 8 March 1973, Lira Helen, da of Simon Joseph Feigenbaum (d 1971), of London; 2 s (Hon Joel, Hon Benjamin), 1 da (Hon Tanya); *Career* sr res accoucheur The London Hosp 1965, sr lectr Inst of Obstetrics and Gynaecology 1975–81, visiting res prof Catholic Univ of Leuven Belgium 1976–77, conslt obstetrician and gynaecologist Hammersmith Hosp 1978–2005 (sr res fell 1975–78), prof of gynaecology Univ of Texas San Antonio 1980–81, reader in fertility studies Royal Postgrad Med Sch 1981–86, prof of fertility studies Univ of London 1986–2005, dean Inst of Obstetrics and Gynaecology Imperial Coll Sch of Med at Hammersmith Hosp (Royal Postgraduate Med Sch until merger 1997) 1995–98, vice-chm Div of Paediatrics Obstetrics and Gynaecology Imperial Coll Sch of Med, dir of NHS R&D Hammersmith Hosps Tst 1999–2005, prof emeritus Imperial Coll London 2005–; chllr Sheffield Hallam Univ 2001–; author of over 300 scientific papers on reproduction; chm Br Fertility Soc 1990–93 (fndr memb); pres: Int Fallopius Soc 1987–88, Progress All-Pty Parly Gp for Res In Reproduction 1991; memb House of Lords Select Ctee on Sci and Technol 1997– (chm 1999–2001); memb Bd Parly Office for Sci and Technol 1999–; pres Br Assoc for the Advancement of Sci 2005; memb Cncl Engr and Physical Sci Res Office 2007–; TV presenter: Your Life in their Hands (BBC) 1979–87, Making Babies (BBC) 1996–97, The Human Body (BBC) 1998, The Secret Life of Twins (BBC) 1999, The Superhuman (BBC) 2000, Threads of Life (BBC), Human Instinct (BBC), The Human Mind (BBC) 2003, Child of Our Time (BBC), Story of God (BBC) 2005; memb: Cncl ICRF (now Cancer Research UK) 1997–2004, Bd Lyric Theatre Hammersmith 1997–2005; chm Cncl Royal College of Music 2007–; Cedric Carter Medal Clinical Genetics Soc 1992, Victor Bonney Prize Royal Coll of Surgns of Eng 1993, Chief Rabbinate Open Award for Contributions to Society 1993, Gold Medal Royal Soc for Health, Michael Faraday Gold Medal Royal Soc 1999, Gold Medal BMA Medicine in the Media 1999, Edwin Stevens Medal RSM 2003, Maitland Medal Inst of Engineers 2004; hon fell Queen Mary & Westfield Coll London 1996; Hon DSc: Univ of St Andrews, Univ of Strathclyde, Salford Univ, Cranfield Univ, UMIST, Oxford Brookes Univ, Univ of Sunderland, Univ of Middlesex, Lancaster Univ, Univ of Exeter, Queen's Univ Belfast, Trinity Coll Dublin; FRCP, FRCOG, FRSA, FMedSci, FRCSEd, FIBiol; *Books* Reversibility of Sterilization (1978), Tubal Infertility (1981), Infertility - A Sympathetic Approach (1986), What We Know About Infertility (1987), Getting Pregnant (1989), Infertility, a postgraduate handbook (1993), Making Babies (1996), The IVF Revolution (1999), The Superhuman (2000), Human Instinct (2002), The Human Mind (2003), What Makes Me Me (2005, Aventis Prize), The Story of God (2005), Child Against All Odds (2006), It's Elementary (2007); *Recreations* theatre, music, skiing, wine, broadcasting; *Clubs* Athenaeum, Garrick, MCC; *Style—* The Rt Hon Lord Winston; ✉ 11 Denman Drive, London NW11 6RE (tel 020 8455 7475); Imperial College London, Hammersmith Hospital, Du Cane Road, London W12 0HS (tel 020 8383 2183, fax 020 8749 6973, car 078 3663 9339, e-mail r.winston@imperial.ac.uk)

WINSTONE, Ray; *b* 19 February 1957; *Educ* Edmonton County Sch, Corona Sch London; *Career* actor; *Theatre* incl: What a Crazy World We're Living In, QR's & AI's Clearly State, Hinkerman, Mr Thomas, Some Voices 1994, Dealer's Choice 1995, Pale Horse 1995, To the Green Fields and Beyond (Donmar Warehouse) 2001, The Night Heron (Royal Court) 2002; *Television* incl: Scum, Sunshine Over Brixton, Mr Right, Minder, Fox, The Lonely Hearts Kid, A Fairly Secret Army, Bergerac, Robin of Sherwood, Father Matthew's Daughter, Pulaski, Blore, Playing For Time, Palmer, Mr Thomas, Absolute Hell, Paint, Underbelly, Birds of a Feather, Black and Blue, Get Back I & II, Between the Lines, Nice Town, Murder Most Horrid, The Negotiator, Casualty, Space Precinct, The Ghost Busters of East Finchley, Kavanagh QC, Sharman, Thief Takers II, Macbeth on the Estate, Our Boy, Births, Marriages and Deaths, Tough Love, Lenny Blue, Henry VIII; *Films* incl: Scum 1979, That Summer 1979, Quadrophenia 1979, All Washed Up 1981, Tank Malling 1989, Ladybird Ladybird 1994, Nil By Mouth (BIFA Award for Best British Actor 1998) 1997, Face 1997, Dangerous Obsession 1997, Final Cut 1997, Martha Meet Frank, Daniel and Laurence 1998, Woundings 1998, The War Zone 1999, Agnes Browne (formerly The Mammy) 1999, Fanny & Elvis 1999, Five Seconds to Spare 1999, Love Honour and Obey 2000, Sexy Beast 2001, Last Orders 2001, Ripley's Game 2002, Bouncer 2002, Cold Mountain 2003, King Arthur 2004; *Recreations* supporting West Ham United FC; *Style—* Ray Winstone, Esq

WINTER, David; OBE; s of Cecil Winter, and Cissie Winter; *b* 24 October 1931; *Educ* Clifton, UCL (LLB); *Children* 5 s (Harry, Adam, Mateusz, Bartusz, Grzegorz), 1 da (Lucy); *Career* slr; conslt Baker & McKenzie on East West trade; rep and chm for the UK of the UN Economic Cmmn for Europe Working Party on Int Contract Practices in Industry, special advsr to the UN Economic Commn for Europe, memb Cncl Sch of Slavonic & E Euro Studies and Britain-Russia Centre, dep chm Exec Cncl Russo British Chamber of Commerce, chm British-Russian Law Assoc; author of numerous publications in the field of East West trade; Freeman City of London, asst and hon legal advsr Guild of Air Pilots and Air Navigators; listed arbitrator on various int panels; *Recreations* flying light aircraft; *Style—* David Winter, Esq, OBE; ✉ Baker & McKenzie, 100 New Bridge Street, London EC4 (tel 020 7919 1000)

WINTER, Faith Weamy Beatrice; da of John Francis Ashe (d 1976), and Amy Mary Kate *née* Andrews (d 1954); *b* 17 August 1927; *Educ* Oak Hall, Guildford Sch of Art, Chelsea Sch of Art; *m* Colonel Freddie Winter; 1 da (Alice Leslie b 1955); 2 s (Martin Andrew Spencer b 1954, David Frederick Spencer b 1958); *Career* sculptor; statues incl: 9ft General Wladyslaw Sikorski at Portland Place, Marshal of RAF Sir Arthur Harris and Air Chief Marshal Lord Dowding in the Strand, 15ft Coat of Arms in Salter's Hall London Wall, The Fifteen Mysteries of the Rosary in The Church of Our Lady Queen of Peace Richmond; other cmmns incl: Falklands Memorial Port Stanley, Spirit of Youth Figure Dundas Park Ontario Canada, Mulberry Harbour Memorial Plaque at Arromanches Normandy, Soldier Group Blandford, John Ray Braintree, George Abbot Guildford; portraits incl: David Devant Magic Circle HQ London, Daniel Arap Moi for Bank of Kenya and President, HRH The Princess Royal Royal Signals, Kamel Jumblatt Libenon, Maria Callas; *Awards* RBS Silver Medal open award 1984, The Guildford Soc William Crabtree Memorial Award 1993, RBS Feodora Gleichen Award; FRBS; *Style—* Faith Winter; ✉ Venzers Studio, Puttenham, Guildford, Surrey GU3 1AU (tel 01483 810300, fax 01483 810362)

WINTER, Prof (David) Michael; OBE (2005); s of David Winter (d 1989), and Nanette, *née* Wellsteed; *b* 10 November 1955, Launceston, Cornwall; *Educ* Peter Symonds Coll Winchester, Wye Coll London (BSc), Open Univ (PhD); *m* 11 Aug 1979, Hilary Susan, *née* Thomas; 1 da (Emily Rowan b 24 March 1990), 1 s (Benedict Thomas David b 14 April 1993); *Career* res asst: Open Univ 1978–80, Univ of Exeter 1980–82; res offr Univ of Bath 1983–87, dir Centre for Rural Studies RAC Cirencester 1987–93, reader then prof Cheltenham and Gloucester Coll of HE 1993–2001, prof of rural policy and dir Centre for Rural Res Univ of Exeter 2002–; cmmr Cmmn for Rural Communities; pres Devon Rural Network; *Publications* Agriculture: People and Policies (jt ed, 1986), The Voluntary Principle in Conservation (jtly, 1990), Church and Religion in Rural England (jtly, 1991), Rural Politics (1996); *Recreations* gardening, hedge-laying, walking, church, music, family; *Clubs* Royal Over-Seas League; *Style—* Prof Michael Winter, OBE; ✉ Centre for Rural Policy Research, University of Exeter, Amory Building, Rennes Drive, Exeter EX4 4RJ (tel 01392 263837, e-mail d.m.winter@ex.ac.uk)

WINTER, Peter John; s of Jack Winter (d 1983), and Ursula, *née* Riddington; *b* 10 July 1950; *Educ* Trinity Sch Croydon, Wadham Coll Oxford (scholar, MA), Univ of Reading (PGCE); *m* 20 Oct 1979, (Jennifer) Adwoa, da of Cobbina Kessie; 1 da (Tiffany Akua Ampomah b 1983), 1 s (Matthew Jack Kofi b 1986); *Career* asst teacher Latymer Upper Sch 1973–79 (master i/c 1st XI cricket), head of modern languages Magdalen Coll Sch Oxford 1979–86 (master i/c hockey); Sevenoaks Sch: head modern languages 1986–89, housemaster Int Centre 1987–93; headmaster King Edward's Sch Bath 1993–2002, head Latymer Upper Sch 2002–; memb HMC 1993– (memb Academic Policy Sub-Ctee 1996–2001, chm SW Div 2000–, inspr), inspr Ind Schs Inspectorate (ISI); *Recreations* sport, Chelsea FC, test match cricket, France; *Clubs* East India, Bath Golf; *Style—* Peter Winter, Esq; ✉ 10 Prebend Gardens, Chiswick, London W4 1TW (tel 020 8995 6001, mobile 07710 581550, e-mail pj_w4@hotmail.com); Latymer Upper School, King Street, London W6 9LR (tel 0845 638 5800, fax 020 8748 5212, e-mail head@latymer-upper.org)

WINTER, Richard Thomas; s of Thomas Alfred Baldwin Winter, of Warks, and Ruth Ethel, *née* Newbury; *b* 6 March 1949; *Educ* Warwick Sch, Univ of Birmingham (LLB), Stanford Grad Sch of Business; *m* Dorothy Sally, da of Peter Hancock Filer; 2 da (Hannah Louise b 2 Sept 1990, Fiona Ruth b 5 Aug 1992); *Career* articled clerk and asst slr Eversheds 1971–75, slr Fisons plc 1975–78, ptnr Eversheds 1981–94 (joined 1978, managing ptnr London office 1991); InterContinental Hotels Gp plc (formerly Bass plc then Six Continents plc): dir of gp legal affrs Bass plc 1994–2000, dir Bass Brewers Ltd 1997–2000, gp co sec and gen counsel Six Continents plc 2000–03, dir Six Continents Retail Ltd 2000–02, exec ctee memb, exec vice-pres (corp servs), gen counsel and co sec InterContinental Hotels Gp plc 2003–; dir Britannia Holdings Ltd (Britvic) 2003–05; memb Law Soc, former memb Competition Law Panel CBI; *Recreations* tennis, sailing, skiing, theatre, opera; *Clubs* Royal Corinthian Yacht, Solway Yacht, Roehampton; *Style—* Richard Winter, Esq; ✉ InterContinental Hotels Group plc, 67 Alma Road, Windsor, Berkshire SL4 3HD (tel 01753 410100, fax 0870 191 4264)

WINTERBONE, Prof Desmond Edward; s of Edward Frederick Winterbone (d 1986), of Tenby, Dyfed, and Phoebe Hilda, *née* Lane (d 1986); *b* 15 January 1943; *Educ* Tenby GS, Rugby Coll of Engrg Technol (CNAA BSc, English Electric Student Apprentice prize), Univ of Bath (PhD), Univ of Manchester (DSc); *m* 24 Sept 1966, Veronica Mary, da of Thomas Frank Cope; 1 da (Anne Caroline b 28 Oct 1971), 1 s (Edward Joseph b 24 April 1974); *Career* student apprentice English Electric Co Ltd Rugby 1960–65 (design engr Diesel Engine Div 1965–67), res fell Univ of Bath 1967–70; UMIST (now Univ of Manchester): lectr Dept of Mechanical Engrg 1970–78, sr lectr 1978–80, prof of mechanical engrg 1980–, head Dept of Mechanical Engrg 1981–83, vice-princ for external affairs 1986–88, dep princ 1987–88, head Thermodynamics and Fluid Mechanics Div 1990–95, head Dept of Mechanical Engrg 1991–94 and 1999–2001, pro-vice-chllr 1995–99; chair professorship Nanjing Aeronautical Inst 1985, Mombusho fellowship Univ of Tokyo 1989, Erskine fell Canterbury Univ NZ 1994; Dr (hc) Univ of Ghent 1991; FIMechE, FSAE (US), FREng 1989; *Books* The Thermodynamics and Gas Dynamics of Internal Combustion Engines Vols I and II (jt ed, 1982 and 1986), Internal Combustion Engineering: Science and Technology (contrib, 1990), Advanced Thermodynamics for Engineers (1997), An Engineering Archive (1997), Design Techniques for Engine Manifolds (1999), Theory of Engine Manifold Design (2000); *Recreations* running, cycling (time trials), mountaineering, travel; *Style—* Prof Desmond Winterbone, FREng

WINTERBOTTOM, Prof Michael; s of Allan Winterbottom (d 1982), of East Budleigh, Devon, and Kathleen Mary Winterbottom (d 1990); *b* 22 September 1934; *Educ* Dulwich Coll, Pembroke Coll Oxford (MA, DPhil); *m* 1, 31 Aug 1963 (m dis 1983), Helen, da of Harry Spencer (d 1977), of Willenhall, Staffs; m 2, 20 Sept 1986, Nicolette Janet Streatfeild Bergel, da of Henry Shorland Gervis (d 1968), of Sherborne, Dorset; 2 s (Peter, Jonathan); *Career* lectr in Latin and Greek UCL 1962–67, fell and tutor in classics Worcester Coll Oxford 1967–92 (reader in classical languages 1990–92), Corpus Christi prof of Latin Univ of Oxford 1993–2001 (emeritus prof 2001–), fell CCC Oxford 1993–2001 (emeritus fell 2001–); Dr (hc) Besançon 1985; FBA 1978; *Books* Quintilian (ed 1970), Ancient Literary Criticism (with D A Russell, 1972), Three Lives of English Saints (1972), The Elder Seneca (ed and translated, 1974), Tacitus, Opera Minora (ed with R M Ogilvie, 1975), Gildas (ed and translated 1978), Roman Declamation (1980), The Minor Declamations Ascribed to Quintilian (ed with commentary, 1984), Sopatros the Rhetor (with D C Innes 1988), Cicero De Officiis (ed, 1994), William of Malmesbury Gesta Regum Anglorum Vol i (ed with R A B Mynors and R M Thomson, 1998), William of Malmesbury Saints' Lives (ed with R M Thomson, 2002), William of Malmesbury Gesta Pontificum Anglorum Vol 1 (ed, 2007); *Recreations* hill walking, travel; *Style—* Prof Michael Winterbottom, FBA; ✉ 53 Thorncliffe Road, Oxford OX2 7BA

WINTERFLOOD, Brian Martin; s of Thomas George Winterflood (d 1978), of Slough, Berks, and Doris Maud, *née* Waddington; *b* 31 January 1937; *Educ* Frays Coll Uxbridge; *m* 10 Oct 1966, Doreen Stella, da of Albert Frederick McCartney, of London; 2 s (Guy b 2 April 1970, Mark b 8 March 1973), 1 da (Sarah b 9 July 1974); *Career* Nat Serv 1955–57; Greener Dreyfus & Co 1953–55; Bisgood Bishop & Co: joined 1957, ptnr 1967, dir 1971 (Co inc), jt md 1981 (co taken over by County NatWest Investment Bank 1986), non-exec dir 1986; exec dir County NatWest Securities 1986–88; Winterflood Securities and Winterflood Gilts Ltd: fndr 1988, md 1988–99, ceo 1999–2000, chm 2001–, non-exec chm 2002–; dir Union Discount Co of London plc 1991–93, memb Bd Close Brothers Group plc 1993–2002; non-exec dir Monument Securities 2002–; memb: Ctee October Club 1990–2002, Quoted Companies Alliance (QCL, formerly The City Group for Smaller Companies (CISCO)) 1992–2000 (memb Exec Ctee 1992–96), City Disputes Practitioners Panel 1994–2000, AIM ADV Ctee 1995–98, AIM Appeals Ctee 1995–98, Non FTSE 100 Working Pty Ctee 1996–98, Secondary Markets Ctee 1996–98, Ctee ProShare 1998–2003, Market Advsy Ctee EASD 2000–01; jt chm Advsy Bd EASD UK 2000–01, chm Security Industry Mgmnt Assoc (SIMA) 2004; pres REMEDI (Rehabilitation and Med Res Tst) 1998– (vice-pres 1989), vice-pres Save the Children 2004, chm PYBT USM Initiative 1989–92, dep chm Lord Mayor Appeal 2004; govr Reeds Sch 2002– (pres Reeds Sch Appeal 1997–98); tstee London Stock Exchange Benevolent Fund 1995; memb: Boost (City Life) Appeal 2001–02, Heart of the City; PriceWaterhouse Coopers plc Achievement

Award 1994; memb Order of St George 2002; memb Guild of Int Bankers 2002; Freeman City of London 2002; FSI 1997 (MSI 1996), FRSA; *Recreations* family, work, travel; *Clubs* City of London; *Style—* Brian Winterflood; ✉ Winterflood Securities Ltd, The Atrium Building, Cannon Bridge, 25 Dowgate Hill, London EC4R 2GA

WINTERS, Prof (Leonard) Alan; s of Geoffrey Walter Horace Winters, of Ipswich, Suffolk, and Christine Agnes, *née* Ive; *b* 8 April 1950; *Educ* Chingford Co HS, Univ of Bristol (BSc), Univ of Cambridge (MA, PhD); *Children* 2 da (Victoria b 1972, Catherine b 1973), 1 s (Oliver b 1998); *Career* jr research offr rising to research offr Dept of Applied Economics Univ of Cambridge 1971–80, lectr in economics Univ of Bristol 1980–86, economist World Bank 1983–85, prof of economics UCNW Bangor 1986–90, prof of economics Univ of Birmingham 1990–94, research mangr World Bank 1997–99 (div chief of int trade 1994–97), prof of economics Univ of Sussex 1999–, dir Research Dept World Bank 2004–07; research fell: Centre for Economic Policy Research, Centre for Economic Performance LSE; ed World Bank Economic Review 2003–04; assoc ed: Economic Jl 1992–97, Jl of Common Market Studies; former chm English Folk Dance and Song Soc; *Books* An Econometric Model of The Export Sector: The Determinants of British Exports and Their Prices (1981), International Economics (1985, new edn 1991), Europe's Domestic Market (1988), Eastern Europe's International Trade (1994), Trade Liberalisation and Poverty: A Handbook (2001); *Recreations* music, cricket, walking; *Style—* Prof L Alan Winters; ✉ School of Social Sciences, University of Sussex, Falmer, Brighton BN1 9QN (tel 01273 877273, fax 01273 673563, e-mail l.a.winters@sussex.ac.uk)

WINTERSGILL, Matthew William; s of Harold Heap Wintersgill (d 1973), of Bedford, and Patricia, *née* Gregory (d 2001); *b* 12 July 1949; *Educ* Stratton Sch, Canterbury Sch of Architecture; *m* 16 Sept 1978, Sara Neill, da of Gerald Bradley (d 1970), and Sheila Neill (d 1985), of London; *Career* architect; Powell and Moya 1973–78 (incl: Cripps Bldg project for Queen's Coll Cambridge, Sch for Advanced Architectural Studies Bristol, Nat West Bank Devpt Shaftesbury Ave London), Thompstone Harris Design Assocs 1978–80, ptnr Wintersgill 1980– (formerly Thompstone Wintersgill Faulkner, then Wintersgill & Faulkner); work projects for: BAA, Bowater Corp, BP Oil Int, The Science Museum, Reuters, Prudential Assurance Co, IVECO Ford Truck Ltd, The Post Office, Nat West Bank, Rank Leisure, FCO; memb W End Soc of Architects; registered memb ARCUK (now RRB) 1974, RIBA 1975; *Recreations* drawing, swimming, travel, walking; *Style—* Matthew Wintersgill, Esq; ✉ Wintersgill LLP, 110 Bolsover Street, London W1W 5NU (tel 020 7580 4499, fax 020 7436 8191, e-mail matthew@wintersgill.net, website www.wintersgill.net)

WINTERSON, Jeanette; OBE (2006); *b* 27 August 1959; *Educ* Accrington Girls' HS, St Catherine's Coll Oxford (BA); *Career* author; *Books* Oranges Are Not the Only Fruit (1985, BBC TV adaptation 1990), The Passion (1987), Sexing The Cherry (1989), Written on the Body (1992), Art and Lies (1994), Art Objects (critical essays, 1995), Gut Symmetries (1997), The World and Other Places (short stories, 1999), The Power Book (2000), The King of Cupri (for children, 2003), Lighthousekeeping (2004), Weight (novella, 2005), Tanglewreck (for children, 2006), The Stone Gods (2007); *Theatre* The Power Book (performed at NT, 2002); *Film* Great Moments in Aviation (1992); *Awards* Whitbread First Novel award 1985, John Llewelyn Rhys prize 1987, Commonwealth Writers' award 1988, E M Forster award (American Acad of Arts and Letters) 1989, Golden Gate San Francisco Int Film Festival 1990, Best Drama Euro TV Festival 1990, FIPA D'Argent Cannes 1991, BAFTA Best Drama 1991, Prix Italia 1991, International Fiction Award Festival Letteratura Mantova 1998; *Recreations* I try to live my life in one piece, so work is recreation and recreations are also work; *Style—* Ms Jeanette Winterson, OBE; ✉ c/o Great Moments Ltd, 40 Brushfield Street, London E1 6AG (website www.jeanettewinterson.com)

WINTERTON, (Jane) Ann; MP; da of late Joseph Robert and Ellen Jane Hodgson, of Sutton Coldfield; *b* 6 March 1941; *Educ* Erdington GS for Girls; *m* 1960, Sir Nicholas Winterton MP, *qv*; 2 s, 1 da; *Career* MP (Cons) Congleton 1983–; oppn front bench spokesman on the National Drug Strategy 1998–2001, shadow min for Agric and Fisheries 2001–02; memb Agric Select Ctee 1987–97; chm All-Pty Pro-Life Gp 1992–2002 (vice-chm 2002–), vice-pres Parly and Scientific Ctee 1997–99 (hon treas 1994–97); memb The Chms' Panel 1992–98; *Style—* Ann Winterton, MP; ✉ House of Commons, London SW1A 0AA (tel 020 7219 3585); Constituency Office: Riverside, Mountbatten Way, Congleton, Cheshire CW12 1DY (tel 01260 278866)

WINTERTON, Nicholas Hugh; OBE (2003); s of Deryck Winterton (d 1990), and Margaret, *née* Simms (d 2000); *b* 1 May 1947; *Educ* Chislehurst & Sidcup GS for Boys, Sidney Sussex Coll Cambridge (MA, Dip Econ); *Career* MRC: joined 1969, head Personnel 1981–88, seconded to Wellcome Fndn Dartford 1988–89, dir Corp Affairs 1989–94, dir of fin 1994–95, exec dir 1995–; chm: Bd of Tstees Bridge Theatre Trg Co 1995–2006, Bd MRC Technology 2000–; vice-chair Royal Free Hospital (Hampstead) NHS Tst 2003– (non-exec dir 1998–), chair of tstees Vinjeru Education Malawi 1999–; memb: Bd UK Medical Ventures Ltd 1997–2005, Bd Hammersmith Imanet (formerly Imaging Research Solutions Ltd) 2001–; *Recreations* gardening, travel, walking, theatre; *Style—* Nicholas Winterton, Esq, OBE; ✉ Medical Research Council, 20 Park Crescent, London W1B 1AL (tel 020 7637 6036, fax 020 7580 4369, e-mail nick.winterton@headoffice.mrc.ac.uk)

WINTERTON, Sir Nicholas Raymond; kt (2002), DL (Cheshire 2006), MP; s of Norman H Winterton (d 1971), of Longdon Green, Staffs; *b* 31 March 1938; *Educ* Rugby; *m* 1960, (Jane) Ann Winterton MP, *qv*, da of J R Hodgson, of Sutton Coldfield; 2 s, 1 da; *Career* Nat Serv 2 Lt 14/20 King's Hussars 1957–59; sales exec trainee Shell-Mex and BP Ltd 1959–60, sales and gen mangr Stevens and Hodgson Ltd 1960–80; cncllr Warwickshire CC 1967–1972 (dep chm County Educn Ctee 1970–72, chm Co Youth Serv Sub-Ctee 1969–72); Parly candidate (Cons) Newcastle-under-Lyme 1969 (by-election) and 1970, MP (Cons) Macclesfield 1971– (by-election); chm: Anglo-Danish Parly Gp, All-Pty Parly Media Gp 1992–2000, All-Pty Parly Br-Falkland Islands Gp, All-Pty Parly Br-Bahamas Gp, All-Pty Parly Br-Austria Gp; jt chm Br-Taiwan Parly Gp; vice-chm: Anglo Swedish Parly Gp, All-Pty Parly Road Transport Study Gp 1997–2000, Anglo South Pacific Gp, All-Pty Parly Clothing and Textiles Gp; chm House of Commons Procedure Ctee 1997–2005; memb Select Ctees: Modernisation of the House of Commons, Social Servs 1979–90, Standing Orders 1981–; chm: Health Ctee 1991–92; memb: Anglo Austrian Soc, House of Commons Chm's Panel 1986–, 1922 Exec Ctee (vice-chm 1922 Ctee 2001–05, treas 2005–), Exec Ctee CPA (UK Branch) 1997–, Fin and Gen Purposes Ctee 2001 (jt treas 2004–07), Inter-Parly Union (UK Branch) Exec Ctee 2001–; non-exec dir: Emerson International Inc, MSB Ltd; vice-pres: Nat Assoc of Local Cncls, Nat Assoc of Master Bakers, Confectioners and Caterers, Royal Coll of Midwives; memb Imperial Soc of Knights Bachelor; Hon Freeman Borough of Macclesfield 2002; Freeman City of London, Liveryman and former Upper Bailiff and memb Ct of Assts Worshipful Co of Weavers; *Clubs* Cavalry and Guards', Old Boys and Park Green (Macclesfield), Lighthouse; *Style—* Sir Nicholas Winterton, DL, MP; ✉ House of Commons, London SW1A 0AA

WINTERTON, Rt Hon Rosie; PC (2006), MP; *Educ* Doncaster GS, Univ of Hull (BA); *Career* asst to John Prescott MP 1980–86, Parly offr London Borough of Southwark 1986–88, Parly offr Royal Coll of Nursing 1988–90, md Connect Public Affairs 1990–94, head John Prescott's Private Office 1994–97; MP (Lab) Doncaster Central 1997–, min of state Dept of Health 2003–; Parly sec Lord Chllr's Office 2001–; PLP rep on Lab Pty Nat Policy Forum 1997–2001, ldr Leadership Campaign Team 1998–99, chair Tport and Gen Worker's Parly Gp 1998–99; memb: Intelligence and Security Ctee 2000, Standing Ctee of Transport Bill 2000; *Recreations* sailing, reading; *Clubs* Intake Social, Doncaster Catholic, Doncaster Trades and Labour; *Style—* The Rt Hon Rosie Winterton, MP; ✉ House of Commons, London SW1A 0AA (tel 020 7219 6357); Constituency Office, Guildhall Advice Centre, Old Guildhall Yard, Doncaster DN1 1QW (tel 01302 735241)

WIRE, Nicky (*né* Nicholas Jones); *b* 20 January 1969; *Educ* Oakdale Comp Sch, Univ of Wales; *m* Rachel; *Career* pop musician; bass guitarist with Manic Street Preachers; signed to Sony 1991–; *Albums* New Art Riot (EP, 1989), Generation Terrorists (1991), Gold Against the Soul (1993), The Holy Bible (1994), Everything Must Go (1996), This Is My Truth Tell Me Yours (1998), Know Your Enemy (2001), Forever Delayed (2002), Lipstick Traces (2003); *Singles* Motown Junk (1990), You Love Us (1990), Stay Beautiful (1991), Love's Sweet Exile (1991), Slash 'N' Burn (1992), Motorcycle Emptiness (1992), Suicide is Painless (1992), Little Baby Nothing (1992), From Despair to Where (1993), La Tristesse Durera (1993), Roses in the Hospital (1993), Life Becoming a Landslide (1994), Faster (1994), Revol (1994), She is Suffering (1994), Design for Life (1996), Everything Must Go (1996), Kevin Carter (1996), Australia (1996), If You Tolerate This Your Children Will Be Next (UK no. 1, 1998), The Everlasting (1998), Tsunami (1999), The Masses Against the Classes (UK no. 1, 2000), So Why So Sad (2001), Found That Soul (2001); *Awards* Best Band Brit Awards 1997, Best Album Brit Awards 1997; *Recreations* football (captain of Wales Under 16s); *Style—* Nicky Wire; ✉ c/o Terri Hall, Hall or Nothing, 11 Poplar Mews, Uxbridge Road, London W12 (tel 020 8740 6288, fax 020 8749 5982)

WISBECH, Archdeacon of; *see:* Rone, Ven Jim

WISCARSON, Christopher; s of John Xavier Wiscarson, and Jean Eileen Wiscarson; *b* 25 March 1951; *Educ* Welbeck Coll, King's Coll London (BSc), Harvard Business Sch (PMD); *m* 25 Nov 1972, Gillian Elizabeth, *née* Deeks; 2 da (Annabel Julia b 4 Sept 1978, Verity Michelle b 5 April 1980); *Career* gen mangr Southern Life Cape Town until 1986, chief exec Save and Prosper Insurances 1986–90; fin dir Lloyds Abbey Life plc 1990–93; chief exec: Black Horse Financial Services 1993–97, Lloyds TSB Life 1998–2000; md International Banking Lloyds TSB 2000–; chm Johannesburg Centenary Arts Ctee 1984–86, tstee Big Issue Fndn 1997–2003, chm Kings Coll Devpt Fndn 2000–; FIA; *Publications* paper Mergers - Strategy Beyond Finance presented to Henley Mgmnt Coll 1988; *Recreations* art, Manchester United; *Style—* Christopher Wiscarson, Esq; ✉ Lloyds TSB Bank plc (e-mail chris.wiscarson@lloydstsb.co.uk)

WISDOM, Julia Mary; da of Dennis Wisdom (d 1985), and Rosemary Jean, *née* Cutler; *b* 24 September 1958; *Educ* Cranborne Chase Sch, Bryanston, King's Coll London (BA); *Career* commissioning ed of crime fiction Victor Gollancz Ltd until 1993, publishing dir HarperCollins Publishers Ltd 2002– (editorial dir 1994–2001); memb Crime Writers' Assoc 1987; *Recreations* music, travel, reading; *Style—* Ms Julia Wisdom; ✉ HarperCollins Publishers Ltd, 77–85 Fulham Palace Road, London W6 8JB (tel 020 8741 7070, fax 020 8307 4440)

WISE, Gp Capt Adam Nugent; LVO (1983), MBE (1976); s of Lt-Col (Alfred) Roy Wise, MBE, TD (d 1974), and Cassandra Noel, *née* Coke (d 1982); *b* 1 August 1943; *Educ* Repton, RAF Coll Cranwell, Univ of London (BA); *m* 1983, Jill Amabel, da of (Cyril) Geoffrey Marmaduke Alington, of Lincs (d 1987); 1 s, 1 da; *Career* RAF 1963–98; served Middle East and Far East; exchange pilot Federal German Air Force 1972–75, OC Univ of Wales Air Sqdn 1979–80, Equerry to HM The Queen 1980–83, OC Univ of London Air Sqdn 1983–86, private sec to TRH The Duke of York and The Prince Edward 1983–87, Jt Serv Def Coll 1987–88, RAF Coll Cranwell 1988–91, OC RAF Benson, Dep Capt The Queen's Flight and ADC to HM The Queen 1991–93, Military and Air Attaché British Embassy Madrid 1994–97; conslt The Officers' Assoc 1998–2002; Liveryman Worshipful Co of Goldsmiths; *Recreations* sailing; *Clubs* RAF, Royal Ocean Racing; *Style—* Gp Capt Adam Wise, LVO, MBE

WISE, Prof Christopher (Chris); *b* 1956; *Educ* BSc; *Career* structural engineer; Ove Arup and Partners (London, Sydney and San Francisco): joined 1979, dir 1992–99, bd dir until 1999; co-fndr Expedition Engineering 1999–; projects incl: Stockley Park Building B3 (Construction Industry Award 1989), Century Tower Tokyo (IStructE Special Award 1991), Cranfield Inst of Technol Library (Construction Industry Award 1993), Channel 4 New HQ London (RIBA Award 1995), Barcelona Bullring, Commerzbank New HQ Frankfurt (Construction Industry Award 1997), American Air Museum Duxford (Construction Industry Award 1997, Stirling Prize for Architecture 1998), Carré d'Art de Nimes, Broadwick House Soho, Terminal 5 Heathrow Airport, Gardermoen Airport Oslo, Torre de Collserola Barcelona (Premio Alacantara Award 1993), Northbank Footbridge Stockton-upon-Tees, South Dock Bridge London, Millennium Bridge London, Chiswick Park Footbridge London, Ellis Park Athletic Stadium Johannesburg, Malaysian Nat Stadium Kuala Lumpur, Courts of Justice Bordeaux, Law Courts Antwerp, Nat Assembly of Wales Cardiff, Munstead Water Tower Godalming (RIBA Award 1994), New Children's Hospital Stanford CA, Intesa Sanpaolo Tower Turin; prof of civil engrg design Imperial Coll London 1998–2005, Davenport prof Yale Univ Sch of Architecture 2006, dir Royal Designers Summer Sch 2006–; external examiner AA; memb: Design Cncl 2005–, Risk Cmmn RSA 2006–; Silver Medal Royal Acad of Engrg 2007 MIStructE, RDI 1998, Hon FRIBA 2002, FREng, FRSA; *Style—* Prof Chris Wise, RDI; ✉ Expedition Engineering, Morley House, First Floor, 320 Regent Street, London W1B 3BB (tel 020 7307 1000, fax 020 7307 1001, website www.expedition.uk.com)

WISE, 2 Baron (UK 1951); John Clayton Wise; s of 1 Baron Wise, DL (d 1968); *b* 11 June 1923; *m* 1, 1946 (dis 1986), Margaret Annie, da of Frederick Victor Snead, of Banbury; 2 s; m 2, 19 Dec 1993 (dis 1998), Mrs Janice Harman Thompson, da of late Albert John Harman, of NSW, Australia; *Heir* s, Dr the Hon Christopher Wise; *Career* farmer; memb: Oundle and Thrapston RDC 1951–54, Mitford and Launditch RDC 1960–67; chm: Welsh Tst for Prevention of Abuse, Enterprise Advsy Serv 1990–96, Faircheck 1996–89; vice-pres Caravan Club; fndn govr King Edward VI Sch Bury St Edmunds 1970–80; *Clubs* Farmers, House of Lords Sailing, Ilminster 41; *Style—* The Rt Hon Lord Wise

WISE, Prof Richard; s of A R James Wise (d 1993), of Eastbourne, and Joan, *née* Richards; *b* 7 July 1942; *Educ* Burnage HS, Univ of Manchester (MB ChB, MD); *m* 16 Feb 1979, Dr Jane Marion Symonds, da of R C Symonds, of Sedbergh; 1 s (Peter Richard b 1970 d 1989), 1 da (Katherine b July 1972); *Career* conslt and dir W Midlands Antibiotic Res Laboratory Dudley Rd Hosp Birmingham 1974, hon prof Univ of Birmingham 1995 (reader in clinical microbiology 1985–95); scientific advsr House of Lords Select Ctee 1997–98 and 1999–, civilian conslt to the Army, advsr European Centre for Disease Control; non-exec dir: Centre for Applied Microbiology and Research 1997–2000 (chm Scientific Ctee), Health Protection Agency 2003–07; chm Specialist Advsy Ctee on Antimicrobial Resistance Dept of Health 2001–07, memb Nat Expert Panel on New and Emerging Infections; pres British Soc Antimicrobial Chemotherapy 1999–2001; author of papers and books on antibiotic therapy; vice-chair Herefordshire Nature Tst 2007–; FRCP, FMedSci, FRCPath; *Recreations* viticulture; *Style—* Prof Richard Wise

WISE, Thomas Harold (Tom); MEP; s of Harold Stanley Wise (d 1994), and Hilda Ellen Wise, of Bournemouth, Dorset; *b* 13 May 1948, Bournemouth, Dorset; *Educ* Bournemouth GS, Bournemouth Tech Coll (Dip Public Speaking); *m* 22 June 1974, Janet, da of Walter Ernest Featherstone, and Elsie May Featherstone (d 2000); 1 s (Neil Thomas b 17 May 1977), 1 da (Jenna Karen b 26 Jan 1981); *Career* with Bournemouth Police 1965–70; numerous sales positions incl: Aspro Nicholas, Cavenham, Melitta Benz, Pasta Foods, Kuhne; UK md Ostmann Spices 1992–94; joined UKIP 1997, MEP (UKIP) Eastern Region 2004–; tstee The Forster Inst 1988–; *Style—* Tom Wise, Esq, MEP; ✉ UK Independence Party, 21A High Street, Leighton Buzzard, Bedfordshire LU7 1DN (tel 01525 385900, website www.tomwisemep.co.uk)

WISEMAN, Carol Mary; *b* 20 November 1942; *Educ* Southport HS, Lady Margaret Hall Oxford (MA); *Career* director; BBC TV 1965–79: res dir Schools TV, asst dir Drama; Freelance Film TV drama dir 1979–; prodns incl: Coming Out (play, BBC) 1979, A Question of Guilt (serial, BBC) 1980, Bognor-Deadline (serial, Thames) 1981, Pictures (serial, Central) 1982, Big Deal (series, BBC) 1983–84, Dog Ends (play) 1985, Dear Box Number (play) 1985, A Matter of Will (play) 1985, Cats Eyes (series, TVS) 1986, A Little Princess (BAFTA Award for Best Childrens Drama) 1987, Somewhere to Run (Prix Europa) 1988, May Wine (film, Canal Plus), 1989, Finding Sarah (play, Channel Four) 1990, Does This Mean We're Married (film, Canal Plus) 1990, Love Hurts (series, BBC) 1991, Face the Music (film, Movie Group), Goggle-Eyes (serial, BBC) 1992, Blue Heaven (serial, Channel Four), Ghosts - The Shadowy Third (film, BBC) 1993, The Queen's Nose (5 series, BBC (RTS Award Best Children's Drama, BAFTA nomination))1995–2002; *Style*— Ms Carol Wiseman

WISEMAN, David John; s of James Wiseman (d 1982), and Marjorie, *née* Ward; *b* 25 March 1944; *Educ* St John's Sch Leatherhead, Britannia RNC Dartmouth, RNEC Manadon Plymouth (BSc), Univ of Surrey (MSc); *Career* RN 1962–74, Lt 1967–74; asst sec DTI 1980–87 (princ 1974–80), co dir Kingsway Rowland 1987–89, md Rowland Public Affairs 1988–91, md The Rowland Co Brussels 1989–91; md: Counsellors in Public Policy Ltd 1991–2002, Telectic Ltd 1996–2003, One World Telecom Ltd 1999–2002; FIEE 1974, CEng 1974, MIMgt 1986, MIPR 1989; *Recreations* travel, gardening, music; *Style*— David Wiseman, Esq; ✉ La Farigoule, Chemin de Maralouine, F - 13122 Ventabren, France (tel 00 33 4 42 28 87 34)

WISEMAN, Sir John William; 11 Bt (E 1628), of Canfield Hall, Essex; s of Sir William Wiseman, 10 Bt, CB, CMG (d 1962), and his 3 w, Joan, Lady Wiseman; *b* 16 March 1957; *Educ* Millfield, Hartford Univ USA; *m* 1980, Nancy, da of Casimer Zyla, of New Britain, CT; 2 da (Elizabeth b 1983, Patricia Alison b 1986); *Heir* fifth cous, Thomas Wiseman; *Style*— Sir John Wiseman, Bt

WISEMAN, Dr Martin Jeremy; s of Leslie Wiseman, of Faversham, Kent, and Sonia Wiseman, *née* Linder; *b* 18 April 1953; *Educ* King's Sch Canterbury, Guy's Hosp Med Sch (MRCP); *m* 5 May 1979, Jane Carol, da of Dennis Bannister, of Bournemouth, Dorset; 2 da (Jessica b 1982, Anna b 1985), 1 s (Daniel b 1987); *Career* research fell Metabolic Unit Guy's Hosp 1981–86, head Nutrition Unit Dept of Health 1986–99, md (nutrition and regulatory affairs) Burson-Marsteller 1999–2000; visiting prof of human nutrition Univ of Southampton 1994–, hon sr lectr in nutrition and public health LSHTM 1994–, med advsr World Cancer Research Fund 2001–; author of publications on diabetes, nutrition and kidney disease; memb: Diabetes UK, Nutrition Soc; FRCP, FRCPath; *Recreations* gastronomy, travel, family, Times crossword; *Style*— Dr Martin Wiseman; ✉ tel 020 8778 7597, e-mail mjwiseman@ntlworld.com

WISEMAN, Prof (Timothy) Peter; s of Stephen Wiseman (d 1971), of Manchester, and Winifred Agnes Wiseman; *b* 3 February 1940; *Educ* Manchester Grammar, Balliol Coll Oxford (MA, DPhil); *m* 15 Sept 1962, (Doreen) Anne, da of Harold Williams, of Atherton, Lancs; *Career* reader in Roman history Univ of Leicester 1973–76 (lectr in classics 1963–73), visiting prof of classics Univ of Toronto 1970–71, prof of classics Univ of Exeter 1977–2001 (emeritus prof 2001–), chm Br Sch at Rome 2002–07; vice-pres Br Acad 1992–94, pres: Roman Soc 1992–95, Jt Assoc of Classical Teachers 1998–99, Classical Assoc 2000–01; Hon DLitt Durham 1988; FSA 1977, FBA 1986; *Books* Catullan Questions (1969), New Men in the Roman Senate (1971), Cinna the Poet (1974), Clio's Cosmetics (1979), Catullus and His World (1985), Roman Studies (1987), Death of an Emperor (1991), Talking to Virgil (1992), Historiography and Imagination (1994), Remus: A Roman Myth (1995), Roman Drama and Roman History (1998), The Myths of Rome (2004), Unwritten Rome (2007); *Style*— Prof Peter Wiseman; ✉ Department of Classics, The Queen's Building, University of Exeter, Exeter EX4 4QH (tel 01392 264202, fax 01392 264377)

WISHART, John MacKeand (Jock); s of Thomas Wishart, of Dumfries, and Marion Jane MacKeand Hood, BEM; *b* 6 February 1953; *Educ* Dumfries Acad, Univ of Durham (BA, pres Union and Univ Boat Club); *m* 28 July 1984, Deborah Jane, da of Wilfred Preston; 1 s (Gregory John MacKeand b 16 Sept 1986), 1 da (Laurie Isla b 3 May 1991); *Career* PA to gp sales and promotions dir Lillywhites 1974–78, sales dir Ravelle Wrightweights 1978–80, conslt 1980–84; Hill and Knowlton: assoc dir 1984–89, sponsorship dir 1989–91, conslt 1991–; dir: Transoceanic Adventures 1996–99, Tal Mgmnt Ltd 1999–, Polar Adventures Ltd 2002–; head of public rels Rugby World Cup 1991, memb Organising Ctee World Corporate Games London 1992; memb London Int Sport 1994–, fndr memb Top 100 Club; sporting achievements: GB rowing rep World Jr Championships, winner Br Univ Championship medals for rowing, canoeing and weightlifting, rowing rep Scotland, finalist Wyfolds Cup Henley Royal Regatta 1978 and 1979, America's Cup challenger Newport RI 1980, past holder Round Britain Powerboat Record 1989, winner all major trophies Cowes Week IOW during period 1983–2002, Br Dragon Boat champion 1989, 1990, 1992, 1996 and 1998, fourth place Dragon Boat World Championships 1990, European champion 1993 and 1995, winner Br Skiffing Championships 1991, 1993 and 1999; navigator of Freedom (winner 12m World Championship Cowes IOW 2001); memb Br Polar Team (first men to walk unsupported to N Geomagnetic pole) 1992, organiser Ultimate Challenge (largest ever party and first televised trek to N Magnetic Pole) 1996, rowed Atlantic 1997, holder Powered Circumnavigation of the World record 1998, capt London-Paris rowing record team 1999, leader Shackleton's Steps expedn 2000, organiser Polar Race 2003, 2005, 2006 and 2007; vice-pres Palatinate Assoc (Univ of Durham Old Boys); govr Sportaid; memb Exec Ctee Univ of Durham; *Recreations* sailing, dragon boat paddling, rowing, skiing, rugby; *Clubs* Leander, Mosimann's, Molesey Boat (capt 1978), Royal Canoe, Royal Hong Kong Yacht, Tamesis, Skiff, London Corinthian Sailing, Kingston Royals Dragon Boat (chm 1987–95); *Style*— Jock Wishart, Esq; ✉ 18 Neville Road, Kingston upon Thames, Surrey KT1 3QX (tel 020 8549 1457, e-mail jockwish@aol.com, website www.members.aol.com/jockwish)

WISHART, Peter (Pete); MP; Alex Wishart (d 1982), of Dunfermline, and Nan Irvine, *née* Lister; *b* 9 March 1962; *Educ* Queen Anne HS, Moray House Coll of Educn; *m* 1990; 1 c (Brodie b 1991); *Career* community worker 1984–85; musician with Runrig 1985– (5 Top 40 hits, sold over 1 million albums: 4 Gold albums UK, 1 Gold album Denmark, 1 Platinum album Scot); MP (SNP): N Tayside 2001–05, Perth and N Perthshire 2005–; dir Fast Forward Positive Lifestyles; memb Campaign Ctee Scotland Against Drugs; memb Performing Rights Soc 1991–; *Recreations* music, hill walking; *Style*— Peter Wishart, Esq, MP; ✉ 35 Perth Street, Blairgowrie, Perthshire PH10 6DL (tel 01250 876576, fax 01250 876991); 14 Princes Street, Perth PH2 8NG (tel 01738 639598)

WISHART, (Margaret) Ruth (Mrs R McLeod); da of John Wishart (d 1960), and Margaret, *née* Mitchell (d 1989); *b* 27 August 1945; *Educ* Eastwood Sr Secdy Sch; *m* 16 Sept 1971, Roderick McLeod, s of Roderick McLeod; *Career* women's ed Scottish Daily Record 1973–78; asst ed: Sunday Mail 1978–82, Sunday Standard 1982–83; freelance journalist and broadcaster 1983–86, sr asst ed The Scotsman 1986–88; columnist The Herald; presenter Eye to Eye (BBC Scotland), The Ruth Wishart Programme; chair Centre for Contemporary Arts Glasgow; hon vice-pres Scottish Action on Dementia; govr Glasgow Sch of Art; Hon DUniv of Stirling 1994; *Recreations* theatre, concerts, gardening, galleries, curling; *Style*— Ms R Wishart; ✉ tel 0143 684 2134, e-mail ruth@kilcreggan.demon.co.uk

WISNER, George John; s of George Phillip Wisner, and Lillian Florence, *née* Butler; *b* 1 June 1949; *Educ* Haverstock Hill Sch, Chelsea Sch of Art; *m* 26 March 1977 (m dis 2000), Romayne Siobhan, da of Derek Dobson Wood; 2 da (Alice Willow b 29 Dec 1977, Shelley Rose b 11 Feb 1980); *Career* set designer; BBC: apprentice carpenter 1965–70, design asst 1971–74, designer 1974–80, head of design Open Univ Prodn Centre 1988–91, host visitor Liaison Dept BBC TV Centre London 1990–91; BBC prodns designed incl: Day in the Death of Joe Egg, The Gambler by Dostoyevsky, The Prime of Miss Jean Brodie, The Grand Inquisitor, End Game, Macbeth, Miss Julie, numerous children's progs; ptnr: Blakesley Gallery 1991–97, Cactus 1994–; memb: BAFTA, RSA; selected best apprentice in UK by City & Guilds to represent UK at Int Apprentice Competition Brussels 1969, Sir Herbert Mole Meml Medal Chelsea Sch of Art 1969; FRSA 1987; *Recreations* cycling, swimming, walking; *Style*— George Wisner, Esq; ✉ Kirby House, High Street, Blakesley, Towcester, Northamptonshire NN11 8RE

WISTRICH, Prof Robert Solomon; s of Jacob Wistrich (d 1979), of London, and Sabina, *née* Silbiger; *b* 7 April 1945; *Educ* Kilburn GS, Queens' Coll Cambridge (open exhibition, MA), UCL (PhD); *m* 12 Sept 1971, Daniella, da of Jacob Boccara; 2 da (Anna b 5 Jan 1973, Sonia b 12 June 1980), 1 s (Dov b 5 Oct 1975); *Career* freelance journalism 1968–70, ed New Outlook 1970, ed The Wiener Library Bulletin (London) 1974–81, Wolfson fell Br Acad 1976, fell Inst of Advanced Studies Jerusalem 1980–81; Hebrew Univ of Jerusalem: sr lectr in modern European and Jewish history 1980–85, prof 1985–91, Neuberger chair of history 1989–91, prof of Dept of History 1996–, dir Vidal Sassoon Centre for the Study of Antisemitism 2002–; dir of studies (associé) Ecole des Hautes Etudes en Sciences Sociales Paris 1989–90, first holder Jewish Chronicle chair of Jewish Studies Univ of London 1991–96, visiting prof Harvard Univ 1998–99; ed East European Jewish Affairs (London) 1992–, memb Exec Cncl Leo Baeck Inst London 1992–96; memb Academic Advsy Ctee of numerous jls and insts incl Austrian Studies, The Simon Wiesenthal Centre Annual and Leo Baeck Yearbook; German Acadamic Exchange fell 1972, Austrian Govt fell 1978, winner James Parkes Prize of Ecumenical Inter-Faith Assoc and The American Jewish Ctee 1985; *Films* incl: The Longest Hatred (co dir and scriptwriter) 1992, Understanding The Holocaust (co-dir and scriptwriter) 1998, Blaming the Jews (scriptwriter) 2003; *Books* incl: Who's Who in Nazi Germany (1982), Hitler's Apocalypse (1985), The Jews of Vienna in the Age of Franz Joseph (1989, winner Anton Gindely State Prize (for History) of the Austrian Republic 1992), Antisemitism: The Longest Hatred (1991, winner H H Wingate/Jewish Quarterly Non-Fiction Award 1992), Weekend in Munich - Art, Propaganda and Terror in the Third Reich (1995), Demonizing the Other: Antisemitism, Racism and Xenophobia (1999), Hitler and the Holocaust (2001), Nietzsche: Godfather of Fascism? (2002); *Recreations* tennis, walking, chess, literature, theatre and cinema; *Style*— Prof Robert Wistrich; ✉ 63 Woodstock Road, Golders Green, London NW11 8QH

WISZNIEWSKI, Adrian Ryszard; s of Witold Eugene Wiszniewski, of Renfrew, Glasgow, and Elspeth Mary, *née* Hyland; *b* 31 March 1958; *Educ* Mackintosh Sch of Architecture, Glasgow Sch of Art (BA, postgrad Dip); *m* 11 May 1985, Diane Lennox, da of Ronald Alexander Foley, of Nairn; 2 s (Max Tristan Charles b 26 June 1987, Louis Lennox Highland b 6 Nov 1993), 1 da (Holly b 21 April 1990); *Career* artist; work in painting, printmaking, ceramics, tapestry, neon, sculpture, writing, film, furniture design, intriors; solo exhibitions in London, Belgium, Australia and Japan; also exhibited in several important int gp exhibitions and surveys throughout the world; Mark Rothko Scholarship 1984, Lord Provost Award (Glasgow) for Visual Arts 1999; ARSA; *Books* For Max (1988), A Man Tied-Up in His Own Composition (1996); *Style*— Adrian Wiszniewski, Esq; ✉ Calder Mews, Main Street, Lochwinnoch, Renfrewshire PA12 4AH

WISZOWATY, Nick; s of Jozef Wiszowaty (d 1975), and Joan, *née* Roberts; *b* 5 October 1962; *Educ* Tomlinscote Sch Camberley; *m* 6 Aug 1994, Katie, da of Christopher Taylor; *Career* with Matthew Freud Associates 1987–90, Freud Communications 1990–; holder commercial pilot licence; *Recreations* family; *Clubs* Wentworth; *Style*— Nick Wiszowaty, Esq; ✉ Freud Communications Ltd, 19–21 Mortimer Street, London W1T 3DX (tel 020 7291 6444, fax 020 7291 6494, e-mail nick@freud.com)

WITCHELL, Nicholas N H; s of William Joseph Henshall Witchell, and Barbara Sybil Mary, *née* MacDonald (decd); *b* 23 September 1953; *Educ* Epsom Coll, Univ of Leeds (LLB); *Children* 2 da; *Career* joined BBC News 1976, reporter NI 1979–81, reporter London 1981–83, Ireland corr 1984; presenter: 6 O'Clock News 1984–89, BBC Breakfast News 1989–94; corr Panorama 1994, diplomatic corr BBC 1995–98, royal and diplomatic corr BBC 1998–; govr Queen Elizabeth's Fndn, patron Queen Alexandra Hosp Home; FRGS; OStJ; *Books* The Loch Ness Story (1974, 1975, 1982 and 1989); *Clubs* Reform; *Style*— Nicholas Witchell; ✉ BBC News, BBC TV Centre, London W12 7RJ (tel 020 8743 8000)

WITCOMB, Roger; s of Canon Cyril Witcomb (d 1983), and Jo Witcomb, *née* Newman, of Salisbury, Wilts; *b* 5 May 1947; *Educ* Eton, Merton Coll Oxford (BA), Nuffield Coll Oxford (MPhil); *m* 1970, Marian, da of Maj Frank Stone; 2 s (Mark b 1977, Edward b 1980); *Career* economist Bank of England 1970–71, fell econ Churchill Coll Cambridge, fell and dir of studies in econs Gonville & Caius Coll Cambridge 1974–79, res offr Dept of Applied Econs Univ of Cambridge, various mgmnt positions at BP 1980–89, fin dir National Power plc 1996–2000, conslt Saxton Bampfylde Hever plc 2001–2002, sr advsr Actis Capital Partners 2002–07; non-exec dir: Anglian Water Services 2002–06, Andrews & Ptnrs Ltd 2005–, Anglian Water Gp 2006–; chm Opportunity Int UK 2004–; govr Univ of Winchester 2004– (chair 2006–); *Recreations* cricket, golf, singing; *Style*— Roger Witcomb, Esq; ✉ The Old Plough, Barton Stacey, Winchester SO21 3RH (tel 01962 761780, mobile 07880 712248, e-mail roger@oldplough.com)

WITHERIDGE, Rev John Stephen; s of Francis Edward Witheridge (d 1988), and Joan Elizabeth, *née* Exell (d 1999); *b* 14 November 1953; *Educ* St Albans Sch, Univ of Kent at Canterbury (BA), Christ's Coll Cambridge (MA); *m* 1975, Sarah Caroline, da of Rev Peter Phillips; 2 da (Charlotte b 1978, Harriet b 1981), 2 s (George b 1983, Henry b 1986); *Career* curate Luton Parish Church 1979–82, head of religious studies and asst chaplain Marlborough Coll 1982–84, chaplain to the Archbishop of Canterbury 1984–87, conduct (sr chaplain) Eton Coll 1987–96, headmaster Charterhouse 1996–; FRSA 1998; *Publications* Frank Fletcher: A Formidable Headmaster (2005); author of various articles and reviews; *Recreations* theatre, biography, gardening; *Clubs* Travellers; *Style*— The Rev John Witheridge; ✉ Charterhouse, Godalming, Surrey GU7 2DJ (tel 01483 291600, fax 01483 291647)

WITHEROW, John Moore; s of Cecil and Millicent Witherow; *b* 20 January 1952; *Educ* Bedford Sch, Univ of York (BA), Univ of Cardiff (Dip Journalism); *m* 1985, Sarah Jane Linton; 2 s (Sam b 1985, Roly b 1988), 1 da (Anna b 1996); *Career* trainee Reuters London and Madrid 1977–80, home and foreign corr The Times 1980–83; The Sunday Times: defence corr 1984–85, diplomatic corr 1985–87, focus ed 1987–89, foreign ed 1989–92, managing ed (news) 1992–94, acting ed 1994, ed 1995–; *Books* The Winter War: The Falklands (with Patrick Bishop, 1982), The Gulf War (1993); *Recreations* skiing, sailing, tennis; *Clubs* RAC; *Style*— John Witherow, Esq; ✉ The Sunday Times, 1 Pennington Street, London E98 1ST (tel 020 7782 5640, fax 020 7782 5420)

WITHEROW, Ross O'Neill; s of late Cecil John Witherow, of Cape Town, South Africa, and late Millicent Frances, *née* Wilson; *b* 2 January 1945; *Educ* Bedford Sch, UCH Med Sch London (Grenfell student scholar, MB BS, MS, Eschmann prize); *m* 1, 1977 (m dis 1982), Michelle, *née* Heimsoth; 1 s (Alexander Guy O'Neill b 2 March 1981); m 2, 1990 (m dis 2005), Bridget Margaret Rossiter, da of Michael Christopher Alfred Codrington; 1 s (Thomas Edward b 12 Oct 1991), 1 step s (Peter Goodman Rossiter b 27 Aug 1983); *Career* house offr: UCH London 1968, Addenbrooke's Hosp Cambridge 1968–69; ship's surgn Union Castle Line 1969–70, SHO UCH 1971, registrar in surgery Edgware Gen

Hosp 1972, sr registrar in gen surgery UCH 1974–75 (registrar 1973), postgrad res fell in urology Univ of Calif San Francisco 1976–77 (lectr 1978), lectr and hon sr registrar in urology London Hosp 1978–79, resident asst surgn St Paul's Hosp 1979–80, conslt urological surgn St Mary's Hosp London and clinical sr lectr (recognised teacher) Univ of London 1981–; memb: Br Assoc of Urological Surgns 1981, Societé Internationale d'Urologie 1982; FRCS 1973, FRSM 1979, FEBU 1992; *Books* Surgical Infection (1977), Genito-Urinary Surgery (contrib, 1985), Diagnosis and Management of Male Erectile Dysfunction (contrib, 1992), Atlas of Urologic Surgery (contrib, 1998); *Recreations* skiing, golf, opera, cooking; *Clubs* Bowood Golf; *Style*— Ross Witherow, Esq; ✉ 16 Harmont House, 20 Harley Street, London W1G 9PJ (tel 020 7255 1623, fax 020 7323 3418, e-mail rw@rwitherow.freeserve.co.uk)

WITHERS, Prof Michael John; s of Harold Leslie Withers (d 1985), of Dawlish, Devon, and Kathleen Veronica, *née* Chudleigh (d 1988); *b* 15 January 1938; *Educ* South West Essex Tech Sch, City Univ (Dip Tech Engrg, BSc), Univ of Birmingham (MSc); *m* 1962, Marguerite, *née* Beckett; 1 s (Richard John b 1965), 1 da (Justine Marguerite b 1966); *Career* Radio Industry Cncl apprenticeship Cossor Ltd 1955–60, radar engr Cossor Radar 1960–63, lectr Dept of Electronic and Electrical Engrg Univ of Birmingham 1963–72, visiting prof of telecommunications Tech Inst of Aeronautics São José dos Campos Brazil 1969–70, hon princ sci offr Royal Signals and Radar Establishment Malvern 1970–72, sr systems engr Br Aerospace Stevenage 1972–77, engrg mangr Andrew Corporation Inc Fife 1977–83, mangr RF Technology Division 1983–87, md and chief exec ERA Technology Ltd 1987–2000; chm Best Educn Exec Bd Royal Acad of Engrg 2003–; Fellowship of Engrg visiting prof in principles of design Loughborough Univ 1991–; published over 50 tech papers and patents; FIEE 1983 (MIEE 1966), FREng 1990; *Recreations* photography, video and film production, cabinet making, gardening; *Style*— Prof Alan Williams, FREng; ✉ The Hollies, Arford Road, Headley, Bordon, Hampshire GU35 8LJ (tel 01428 712175, e-mail michael@withers.com)

WITHERS, Prof Philip John; s of David Withers (d 1970), and Shirley Davis, *née* Stone; *b* 11 May 1963, Wales; *Educ* Kingsmead Comp Wiveliscombe, Taunton Sch, Trinity Hall Cambridge (BA), Univ of Cambridge (PhD); *m* 28 July 1990, Lindsey Jayne, *née* Owen; 1 da (Chloë Elizabeth b 25 Jan 1994), 2 s (David b 24 June 1996, Peter b 8 Aug 1999); *Career* research fell Darwin Coll Cambridge 1988–91, lectr in materials sci and metallurgy Univ of Cambridge 1989–98, prof of materials sci Univ of Manchester 1998–; Materials Sci and Technol prize Fedn of European Materials Socs 1999, Rosenhain medal and prize Inst of Materials 2001, Royal Soc Wolfson merit award holder 2002–07; FIMMM, CEng 2004, FREng 2005; *Recreations* cricket, football, golf, photography; *Style*— Prof Philip Withers; ✉ University of Manchester, Materials Science Centre, School of Materials, Grosvenor Street, Manchester M1 7HS (tel 0161 306 8872, fax 0161 306 8840, e-mail philip.withers@manchester.ac.uk)

WITHERSPOON, Dr (Edward) William; s of Edward William Witherspoon (d 1982), of Liverpool, and Maude Miranda, *née* Goff (d 1987); *b* 19 December 1925; *Educ* King Edward's Sch Birmingham, Univ of Birmingham (MB ChB), Univ of London DTM&H, RCP (London), RCS (England); *m* 10 June 1954, Jean (d 1988), da of John McKellar (d 1956); *Career* Maj RAMC 2 i/c 3 Field Ambulance, 4 RTR Suez Canal Zone and Cyprus (GSM) 1951–53; physician (tropical diseases and clinical pharmacology); asst govt med offr Medico-Legal Dept Sydney 1958–60; med dir: Burroughs Wellcome 1960–71, ABPI Trade Mission Japan 1968, Abbott Labs 1971–77, Warner Lambert/Parke Davis 1977–82; Roussel Labs 1983–91, conslt Regulatory, Scientific Archive and Nutrition Agencies 1992–, chm Pharmaceutical Physicians Gp Ctee BMA 1986–92 (memb Ctee 1993–); Freeman City of London 1993, Liveryman Worshipful Soc of Apothecaries; FRSH 1971, FFPM 1990, FRSM, FRSTM; *Publications* The Hunter Years 1728–93 (annals RACS, 1994), The Pharmaceutical Physician (BMA monograph, 1989), Thalidomide - The Aftermath (Pharmaceutical Med, 1988); *Recreations* travel, National Trust for Scotland; *Clubs* City Livery; *Style*— Dr William Witherspoon; ✉ 25 Potwell Gardens, The Hooks, Henfield, West Sussex BN5 9UY (tel 01273 494979)

WITHINGTON, Neil Robert; s of Derek Henry Withington (d 1986), of Manchester, and Audrey, *née* Whittle; *b* 6 September 1956, Manchester; *Educ* William Hulme's GS Manchester, BNC (exhibitioner, MA, BCL); *Family* 2 da (Emma Louise Gordon b 15 March 1990, Polly Claire b 31 July 1992); *Career* called to the Bar Middle Temple 1981 (Harmsworth scholar); lectr Osgoode Hall Law Sch Toronto 1979–80, visiting prof Univ of Oklahoma Law Sch 1980, barr 28 St John Street Manchester 1981–86, sr lawyer ICI Pharmaceuticals 1986–90, sr lawyer ICI Millbank 1990–93, sr lawyer BAT Industries plc 1993–95, asst gen counsel BAT (Holdings) 1996–98, legal dir and gen counsel British American Tobacco plc 2000– (dep gen counsel 1998–2000); memb Worshipful Co of Tobacco Pipe Makers and Tobacco Blenders; *Publications* incl Horvath v The Queen: Reflections on the Doctrine of Confessions (1980); *Recreations* golf, theatre, wine; *Clubs* Burhill Golf; *Style*— Neil Withington, Esq; ✉ British American Tobacco plc, Globe House, 4 Temple Place, London WC2R 2PG (tel 020 7845 1480, fax 020 7845 2181, e-mail neil_withington@bat.com)

WITTICH, John Charles Bird; s of Charles Cyril Wittich (d 1976), and Minnie Amelia Victoria, *née* Daborn (d 1991); *b* 18 February 1929; *Educ* privately (BA); *m* 10 July 1954, June Rose, da of Thomas Frederick Taylor (d 1972); 1 da (Margaret Judith b 1957), 1 s (Andrew Paul b 1961); *Career* professional librarian 1946–86; freelance writer and lectr 1986–, lectr in adult educn circles 1959–99, memb Minor Order of Readers of the C of E 1980–2005 (emeritus 2005–); Freeman City of London 1971, Master Parish Clerks Co 1995–96, Liveryman Emeritus Worshipful Co of Woolmen 1977, Liveryman Worshipful Co of Musicians 1999; FRSA 1980, MITG 2003; *Books* Off-Beat Walks in London (1969, new edn 1995), London Curiosities (1973, new edn 1996), London Villages (1976, revised 1992), London Street Names (1977, new edn 2001), London's Inns & Taverns (1978, new edn 1996), London's Parks & Squares (1981), Catholic London (1988), Churches, Cathedrals & Chapels (1988), Guide to Bayswater (1989, 3 edn 2005), Exploring Cathedrals (1992, new edn 1996), Regent's Park (1992), Curiosities of Surrey (1994, re-issued 2001), History and Guide Church of St Magnus the Martyr (1994, 2 edn 2005), Explorers' London (1995), Spot it London (1995), Walks Around Haunted London (1996), London Bus Top Tourist (1997), History and Guide to St Vedast-alias-Foster Parish (1999), Curiosities of the Citties of London and Westminster (2003), Event-full London (2004), London by Circle Line (2004), Pilgrimages to London's Churches, Cathedrals and Chapels, Catholic Pilgrims' London, Exploring Abbeys; *Recreations* relaxing with family and friends with good food, good wine and their good company; *Clubs* City Livery, Samuel Pepys, Aldgate Ward; *Style*— John Wittich, Esq; ✉ 88 Woodlawn Street, Whitstable, Kent CT5 1HH (tel 01227 772619)

WITTS, Air Cdre Jeremy John; DSO (1991); *b* 18 June 1950; *Educ* Marlborough GS (RAF Scholar), RAF Coll Cranwell, RAF Staff Coll Bracknell; *Career* served Vulcan B2 bomber force Cyprus and UK to 1978, two tours Bucaneer S2 RAF Laarbruch Germany, Sqdn Leader 1979, staff appt Tornado GR1 Project Office HQ Strike Command 1984–86, contingency planner (Harrier and Jaguar) HQ 1 Gp, Wing Cdr 1987, MOD appt Flight Safety 1 (RAF) Inspectorate of Flight Safety, Cdr 31 Sqdn RAF Brüggen Germany 1989–92, Cdr Tornado GR 1/1A Sqdn Dahran Gulf War 1991, appt MOD Air Force Plans and Programmes 1992–94, Gp Capt 1994, exec offr (NATO) to USAF 4-star Cdr Allied Air Forces Central Europe (AIRCENT) Ramstein Germany (also Sr RAF Staff Offr and Sr Nat Rep), Cdr RAF Northolt 1997–99, ADC to HM The Queen 1998–99, Cdr Tornado GR1 Detachment Solenzara Corsica (during Kosovo crisis) 1999, Air Cdre 1999, Equipment Support (Air) Dir of Ops (Fixed Wing) 2000–02, UK air attaché and asst def attaché Washington DC 2002–; MIMgt, FRAeS; *Style*— Air Cdre Jeremy Witts, DSO, FRAeS, RAF; ✉ British Defence Staff, British Embassy, 3100 Massachusetts Avenue, Washington DC 20008, USA

WIX, Jonathan; s of Harold Wix, of London, and Bernice Beare-Rosenberg, of Durban, South Africa; *b* 3 November 1951; *m* 1977, Carolyn; 1 s (James b 1983), 1 da (Amelia b 1986); *Career* hotelier; dir: North Bridge Investments Ltd, White Elephant Preservation Co Ltd, WEPC SA, Wix Gp; *Recreations* skiing, shooting; *Clubs* RAC; *Style*— Jonathan Wix, Esq; fax 01943 850745

WNEK, Mark Stanislaw; s of Andrzej Wnek (d 1989), and Andrée Gabrielle, *née* Zaliwska; *b* 19 February 1959; *Educ* Dulwich Coll, Gonville & Caius Coll Cambridge (MA); *m* 5 Nov 2004, Sally Anne Mattinson; *Career* freelance journalist/English teacher Spain 1980–82, sr writer and bd dir Ogilvy & Mather advtg 1985–90 (copywriter 1982–85), sr writer and bd dir Lowe Howard-Spink advtg 1990–94, exec creative dir and managing ptnr Euro RSCG Wnek Gosper advtg 1994–2003 (memb Bd Euro RSCG Worldwide 1996–2003), co-fndr Ben Mark Orlando 2004, columnist The Independent 2004–05, chm and chief creative offr Lowe NY 2005–; winner various awards and commendations from D&AD, British TV Advtg, Cannes, One Show, Campaign Press, Eurobest, Epica, Creative Circle and Clio Awards; *Clubs* Soho House, Groucho; *Style*— Mark Wnek, Esq; ✉ Lowe New York, 150 East 42nd Street, New York, NY 10017, USA

WOFFENDEN, Kenneth John (Ken); s of James Harold Woffenden (d 1991), of Wilmslow, Cheshire, and Agnes, *née* Grisenthwaite (d 1976); *b* 22 October 1954; *Educ* Manchester Grammar, Pembroke Coll Cambridge (fndn scholar, MA, Ziegler Law Prize), Coll of Law Guildford; *m* 2 July 1982, Glesni Myfanwy, da of Gwynfor Thomas Davies; 3 da (Catherine b 28 Oct 1987, Emily b 18 Oct 1989, Alice b 24 Oct 1997), 1 s (Thomas b 8 April 1993); *Career* Simmons & Simmons: articled clerk 1977–79, admitted slr 1979, asst slr Corp Dept 1979–84, ptnr Corp Dept 1984–, admitted slr Hong Kong 1986, head Corp and Banking Gp Hong Kong 1987–90, ptnr Corp Dept 1990–95 (head of Gp 1994–95), managing ptnr Hong Kong office 1995–97, managing ptnr Corp Dept 1999–; memb: Law Soc of England and Wales; *Recreations* music, cricket, family life; *Clubs* Hong Kong; *Style*— Ken Woffenden, Esq; ✉ Simmons & Simmons, CityPoint, One Ropemaker Street, London EC2Y 9SS (tel 020 7628 2020, fax 020 7628 2070)

WOGAN, (Michael) Terence (Terry); KBE (2005, OBE 1997); s of late Michael Thomas Wogan, and Rose Wogan; *b* 3 August 1938; *Educ* Crescent Coll Limerick, Belvedere Coll Dublin; *m* 24 April 1965, Helen, da of Timothy J Joyce; 2 s (Alan Terence b 1 Oct 1967, Mark Paul b 13 April 1970), 1 da (Katherine Helen b 31 Sept 1972); *Career* with Royal Bank of Ireland 1956–60, announcer/newsreader Radio Telefis Éireann 1961–66, presenter various TV and radio progs 1966–69; BBC: own show Radio 1 1969–72, morning show Radio 2 1972–84 and 1993–; *Television* presenter numerous BBC TV progs incl Blankety Blank, Wogan, Do The Right Thing, Auntie's Bloomers, Children in Need Appeal, BAFTA and Variety Club Awards Ceremonies, Wogan's Web, Come Dancing, A Song for Europe and the Eurovision Song Contest, Miss World, Wogan's Island, Points of View and various documentaries; *Awards* numerous from: Variety Club of GB, Radio Industries Club, Sony Radio Awards, Pye Radio Awards, TV Times, Daily Mail, Sunday Express, Carl-Alan Awards; *Books* Banjaxed (1979), The Day Job (1981), To Horse To Horse (1982), Wogan on Wogan (1987), Wogan's Ireland (1988), Terry Wogan's Bumper Book of Togs (1995), Is It Me? (autobiography, 2000); *Recreations* tennis, golf, reading; *Clubs* Garrick, Temple Golf, Stoke Poges Golf, Lahinch Golf, London Irish RFC, Saints & Sinners; *Style*— Sir Terry Wogan, KBE

WOLF, Martin Harry; CBE (2000); s of Edmund Wolf (d 1997), of London, and Rebecca, *née* Wijnschenk (d 1993); *b* 16 August 1946; *Educ* UCS, Corpus Christi Coll Oxford (open scholar, MA), Nuffield Coll Oxford (MPhil); *m* Aug 1970, Alison Margaret, da of late Herbert Kingsley Potter, of Newbury, Berks; 2 s (Jonathan Thomas b 24 Jan 1975, Benjamin Jacob b 11 Jan 1977), 1 da (Rachel Janet b 11 June 1985); *Career* World Bank: joined Young Professional programme 1971, Office of vice-pres for East Africa 1972–74, sr economist India Div 1974–77, memb core team World Devpt Report 1977–78, sr economist Int Trade and Capital Flows Div 1979–81; dir of studies Trade Policy Res Centre 1981–87; Financial Times: joined 1987, chief economics leader writer and assoc ed 1990–96, chief economics commentator and assoc ed 1996–; conslt to various orgns, advsr and rapporteur to Eminent Persons Gp on World Trade 1990 (winner New Zealand 1990 Commemoration Medal); jt winner Wincott Fndn Sr Prize for excellence in financial journalism 1989 and 1997, winner RTZ David Watt Meml Prize 1994, winner Accenture Decade of Excellence Business Journalist of the Year Awards 2003, Newspaper Feature of the Year Award Workworld Media Awards 2003; visiting fell Nuffield Coll Oxford 1999–2007; memb: Nat Consumer Cncl 1987–93, Awards Ctee American Express Bank Review Essay Competition 1994, Cncl Royal Economic Soc 1991–96; special prof Univ of Nottingham 1993–; hon fell: Oxford Inst for Economic Policy 2005–, CCC Oxford 2006–; DLitt (hc) Univ of Nottingham 2006, DSc (hc) LSE 2006; Award for Advocacy of Responsible Capitalism First magazine 2005, Journalism Prize Fundacio Catalunya Oberta 2006; *Publications* incl: Textile Quotas against Developing Countries (with Donald B Keesing, 1980), India's Exports (1982), Costs of Protecting Jobs in Textiles and Clothing (1984), Global Implications of the European Community's Programme for Completing the Internal Market (1989), Meeting the World Trade Deadline: Path to a Successful Uruguay Round (1990), The Resistible Appeal of Fortress Europe (1994), Why Globalization Works (2004); *Recreations* theatre, opera, reading; *Clubs* Reform; *Style*— Martin Wolf, Esq, CBE; ✉ Financial Times, 1 Southwark Bridge, London SE1 9HL (tel 020 7873 3673/3421, e-mail martin.wolf@ft.com)

WOLFE, Anthony James Garnham; s of Herbert Robert Inglewood Wolfe (d 1970), and Lesley Winifred, *née* Fox (d 2003); *b* 30 August 1952; *Educ* Haileybury, Univ of Bristol (BSc); *m* 4 Sept 1982, Ommar Aung, da of Lionel Aung Kwa Takwali (d 1956); *Career* chartered accountant; London and Hong Kong Offices Peat Marwick Mitchell 1974–81, GT Mgmnt London and Hong Kong Offices 1981–91, Signature Financial Group 1992–94, Cogent 1994–2004; FCA; *Recreations* rugger, golf, travel, real tennis, walking; *Clubs* Royal Wimbledon Golf, Royal Tennis Court; *Style*— Anthony Wolfe, Esq; ✉ c/o Cofunds, 1 Minster Court, Mincing Lane, London EC3R 7AA

WOLFE, Gillian Anne; CBE (2005, MBE 1995); da of Noel Henry Humphrey (d 1984), and Anne, *née* Nicholls (d 1981); *b* 25 March 1946; *Educ* Sydenham Girls' Sch, Central Sch of Art, Univ of London (BEd); *m* 1974, Dr Kenneth Maurice Wolfe, s of Henry Wolfe; 1 s (Theodore Henry b 8 March 1982), 1 da (Eleanor Henrietta b 27 Sept 1989); *Career* teacher London 1974–84, head of educn Dulwich Picture Gallery 1984– (pt/t 1990–), freelance educn conslt 1990–, specialist advsr to Clore Fndn 1998–; cmmr Cmmn for Architecture and the Built Environment (CABE) 2000–03; tstee: Gilbert Museum 1998–2002, Historic Royal Palaces 2002–05, CABE Educn Fndn 2002–; jt chair DCMS/DfES Advsy Ctee on Built Environment Educn 2003–05; memb: Exec Ctee Nat Heritage 1997–2002, Steering Gp and Advsy Panel Attingham Tst survey on educn in the historic built environment 2002–04; specialist advsr to RHS 2003–, expert advsr to the Heritage Lottery Fund 2005–; judge Museum of the Year Awards 1998–2001; memb: Museums Assoc, Soc of Authors 1997–; hon doctorate St Norbert Coll USA 2006; Freeman City of London 2002; FRSA 2004; *Awards* NACF Award for Educn 1987, Museum of the Year Award for Educn 1988, Euro Museum of the Year Award Special Commendation 1989, Sandford Award 1990, Prudential Award for Visual Arts 1991, Sainsbury's Arts Educn Award 1993, Interpret Britain Award 1994, Sandford Award

Quinquennial Review 1995, Unigate/Age Resource Award for Art Ed 1997, Southwark Achievement Award 1998, Sandford Award (Decade Review) 2000, Interpret Britain Awards (for Outreach prog) 2000; *Books* Children's Art Book (1997, Gulbenkian Prize), Art Activity Book (1997, Gulbenkian Prize), Oxford First Book of Art (1999, Parent Choice Silver Honour Award USA), Look!: Zoom in on Art (2002, English Assoc Award for Best Children's Non-Fiction Book), Look!: Body Language in Art (2004); contrib: OUP Children's Encyclopaedia (1991), OUP Biography (1998), Oxford Children's Pocket Encyclopaedia (1999), Look!: Seeing the Light in Art (2006, shortlisted English Assoc Award 2007); *Recreations* classic cars, gardening, music; *Style*— Mrs Gillian Wolfe, CBE; ✉ Dulwich Picture Gallery, Gallery Road, London SE21 7AD (tel 020 8299 8700, e-mail g.wolfe@dulwichpicturegallery.org.uk)

WOLFE, John Henry Nicholas; s of Herbert Robert Inglewood Wolfe (1970), and Lesley Winifred, *née* Fox; *b* 4 June 1947; *Educ* Eastbourne Coll, St Thomas' Hosp Univ of London (MB BS, MS); *m* 1, 23 June 1973 (m dis 1990), Jennifer, da of Geoffrey Sutcliffe; 3 s (Robert, Owen, Matthew), 2 da (Tara, Roshean); m 2, 1 Oct 1994, Dorothy Carey; *Career* res fell Harvard Med Sch Brigham Hosp 1981–82, sr registrar St Thomas' Hosp 1982–84, Hunterian prof RCS 1983; conslt surgn: St Mary's Hosp Med Sch 1984, Royal Postgrad Med Sch Hammersmith Hosp, Edward VII Hosp for Offrs; chm Euro CME; vice-pres European Div of Vascular Surgery 1999–2001; pres: European Bd of Vascular Surgery 2001–04, Vascular Soc of GB and I 2005–06 (memb Cncl), European Soc of Vascular Surgery 2007–08 (chm Vascular Advsy Ctee); memb: Surgical Res Soc, Assoc of Surgns (memb Speciality Bd and Cncl) Int Soc of Cardiovascular Surgery; memb Editorial Bd European Jl of Vascular Surgery; Freeman City of London 2007; FRCS; *Books* Vascular Surgery (ed 1985, 1989), ABC of Vascular Diseases (1992); *Recreations* sailing, painting, rudimentary pond management; *Clubs* RSM, RORC, RGS; *Style*— John Wolfe, Esq; ✉ 37A Devonshire Street, London W1G 6QA (tel 020 7467 4364, fax 020 7467 4376, e-mail jwolfe@uk-consultants.co.uk)

WOLFE, Richard John Russell; s of late Maj John Claude Frank Wolfe, of Surrey, and Betty Doris, *née* Hopwood; *b* 15 July 1947; *Educ* Ackworth Sch; *m* 1, 28 Nov 1970 (m dis 1977), Lorraine Louise Hart; 1 da (Pandora b 12 July 1976); m 2, 23 July 1994, Irene Mehmet; *Career* mgmnt trainee NM Rothschild and Son Ltd 1964–68, investment dealer British and Continental Bank 1968–72, fund mangr Hill Samuel and Co Ltd 1972–75, corporate fin offr NM Rothschild and Sons Ltd 1976–80, first vice-pres and head of real estate fin UK Security Pacific Nat Bank 1980–90, md and head of Euro real estate Bankers Trust Co 1990–92, fin conslt 1992–; tstee: Inlight Tst, Truemark Tst 1994–; AIB 1978; *Books* Real Estate Finance (contrib 1988); *Recreations* choir singing, swimming, training, study of ancient civilisations; *Style*— Richard Wolfe, Esq; ✉ Shieling Hall, Langley, Kent ME17 3JZ; Queen Victoria Street, London EC4N 4SA

WOLFENDALE, Prof Sir Arnold Whittaker; kt (1995); s of Arnold Wolfendale (d 1963), and Doris, *née* Hoyle (d 1983); *b* 25 June 1927; *Educ* Stretford GS, Univ of Manchester (BSc, PhD, DSc); *m* 1952, Audrey, da of Arnold Darby (d 1968); 2 s (twins, Colin and David); *Career* prof of physics Univ of Durham 1965–92 (now emeritus); Astronomer Royal 1991–95; Home Office, Civil Defence, later regnl scientific advsr 1958–81, chm N Region Manpower Service Cmmn's Job Creation Programme 1975–78; pres: Royal Astronomical Soc 1981–83, Antiquarian Horological Soc 1993–, European Physics Soc 1999–2001; chm: Cosmic Ray Cmmn of IUPAP 1982–84, Astronomy and Planetary Science Bd SERC 1988–94 (memb SERC 1988–94); pres Durham Univ Soc of Fells 1988–94; Freeman Worshipful Co of Clockmakers 1991, Hon Freeman Worshipful Co of Scientific Instrument Makers 1993; Hon DSc: Bucharest Univ, SW Bulgaria Univ, Potchefstroom Univ, Łódź Univ, Univ of Central Lancs, Univ of Teeside, Univ of Newcastle upon Tyne, Open Univ, Paisley Univ, Lancaster Univ, Univ of Durham; Univ of Turku medal 1987, Observatory medal Armagh 1992, Marian Smoluchowski medal Poland 1992, Harrison Medal Worshipful Co of Clockmakers 2006; Bakerian lecture and prize Royal Soc 2002; foreign fell: Nat Acad of Sciences of India 1990, Indian Nat Sci Acad 1991, Tata Inst of Fund Research Bombay; foreign assoc Royal Soc of South Africa; FRS, FInstP (pres 1994–96), FRAS; *Recreations* gardening, travel; *Style*— Prof Sir Arnold Wolfendale, FRS; ✉ Physics Department, University of Durham, South Road, Durham DH1 3LE (tel 0191 334 3580, fax 0191 334 3585, e-mail aw.wolfendale@durham.ac.uk)

WOLFF, Prof Heinz Siegfried; s of Oswald Wolff (d 1968), of W Germany, and Margot, *née* Saalfeld; *b* 29 April 1928; *Educ* City of Oxford Sch, UCL (BSc); *m* 21 March 1953, Joan Eleanor Mary, da of Charles Heddon Stephenson, MBE (d 1968); 2 s (Anthony b 1956, Laurence b 1961); *Career* head Div of Biomedical Engrg Nat Inst for Med Res 1962–70 (joined 1954), head Div of Bioengineering Clinical Res Centre 1970–83, dir Brunel Inst for Bioengineering Brunel Univ 1983–95 (emeritus prof 1995–), dir Huntleigh Research Inst Brunel Univ 2003–; chm: Life Science Working Gp ESA 1976–82, Microgravity Advsy Ctee ESA 1982–91, Microgravity Panel Br Nat Space Centre 1986–87; vice-pres: REMAP 1995–, Disabled Living Fndn 1997–, Coll of Occupational Therapists 1989–; bd dir Edinburgh Int Science Festival 1992–; presenter TV series incl: BBC TV Young Scientist of the Year 1968–81, Royal Inst Christmas Lectures 1975, The Great Egg Race 1978–86, Great Experiments which Changed the World 1985–86; Harding Award Action Research 1989, Edinburgh Medal for Services to Science and Society 1992, Donald Julius Goen Prize IMechE 1994, Keith Medal for Innovation Royal Scottish Soc of Arts 1996 and 2001; Hon Doctorate: Open Univ 1993, De Montfort Univ 1995, Middlesex Univ 1999, Oxford Brookes Univ 1999, Brunel Univ 2003; fell UCL 1987; memb: Biological Engrg Soc, Ergonomics Res Soc; Hon FRCP 1999, FIBiol, FIEE, FBES; *Books* Biological Engineering (1969); *Recreations* working, dignified practical joking; *Style*— Prof Heinz Wolff; ✉ Heinz Wolff Building, Brunel University, Uxbridge, Middlesex UB8 3PH (tel 01895 271206, fax 01895 274608, telex 261173, e-mail heinz.wolff@brunel.ac.uk)

WOLFFE, Andrew John Antony; s of Antony Curtis Wolffe, MBE, of Gatehouse-of-Fleet, and Alexandra Lorna, *née* Graham; *b* 6 July 1964; *Educ* Kirkcudbright Acad, Edinburgh Coll of Art (BA); *Career* graphic designer; creative dir Tayburn Design 1986–98; designed Royal Mail Burns commemorative stamps 1995; dir Wolffe & Co Ltd 1998–; tstee Edinburgh Photography Gallery Tst 1991–, dir Edinburgh Sculpture Workshop 2006–; MSTD; *Recreations* fly fishing; *Style*— Andrew Wolffe, Esq; ✉ Wolffe & Co (tel 01556 504100, e-mail andrew@wolffeandco.com)

WOLFSON, David; s of District Judge Bernard Wolfson, of Liverpool, and Rosalind, *née* Libman; *b* 19 July 1968; *Educ* King David HS Liverpool, Yeshivat Hakotel Jerusalem, Selwyn Coll Cambridge (exhibitioner, coll scholar, Squire scholar, MA, Stuart of Rannoch Award); *m* 2 April 1995, Louise, da of Jeff Durkin; 1 s (Samuel Levi b 16 Dec 2002), 1 da (Zara Michal b 1 Nov 2004); *Career* called to the Bar Inner Temple 1992 (major scholarship 1992, Inns of Court scholarship 1992); barr specialising in commercial law, professional negligence and entertainment law; dir Bar Mutual Indemnity Fund Ltd 2004–; Banking and Finance Jr of the Year Chambers & Ptnrs Bar Awards 2005; memb Commercial Bar Assoc 1992–; *Publications* Bank Liability and Risk (contrib, 1995), Banking Litigation (contrib, 1999); author of articles in legal jls incl: All England Litigation Review, New Law Jl, Jl of Int Banking Law, Jl of Int Banking & Financial Law, Int Insurance Law Review, Commercial Lawyer; *Style*— David Wolfson, Esq; ✉ One Essex Court, Temple, London EC4Y 9AR (tel 020 7583 2000, fax 020 7583 0118, e-mail david.wolfson@oeclaw.co.uk)

WOLFSON, Baron (Life Peer UK 1985), of Marylebone in the City of Westminster; Sir Leonard Gordon Wolfson; kt (1977), 2 Bt (UK 1962), of St Marylebone, Co London; o s of Sir Isaac Wolfson, 1 Bt, FRS (d 1991), and Edith (LadyWolfson), *née* Specterman (d 1981); *b* 11 November 1927; *Educ* King's Sch Worcester; *m* 1, 1949 (m dis 1991); 4 da (Hon Janet Frances (Hon Mrs de Botton, CBE), *qv*, b 1952, Hon Laura b 1954, Hon Deborah b 1959, Hon Elizabeth b 1966); m 2, 1 Sept 1991, Estelle, wid of Michael Jackson; 1 step s, 1 step da; *Career* chm Wolfson Fndn 1972– (fndr tstee 1955–); Great Universal Stores plc: dir 1952, md 1962, chm 1981–96; chm Burberrys Ltd 1978–96; fell The Israel Museum 2001, fell Royal Albert Hall 2003; pres Jewish Welfare Bd 1972–82, pres Shaare Zedek UK 2006, hon pres Br Technion Soc 2006; tstee Imperial War Museum 1988–94; Winston Churchill Award British Technion Soc 1989, Pres's Award Hebrew Univ 2005; hon fell: St Catherine's Coll Oxford, Wolfson Coll Cambridge, Wolfson Coll Oxford, Worcester Coll Oxford, Somerville Coll Oxford, UCL, LSHTM 1985, QMC 1985, Univ of Westminster 1991, Imperial Coll London 1991, LSE 1999, Inst of Educn Univ of London 2001, Israel Museum 2001; Hon DCL Univ of Oxford 1972; Hon LLD: Univ of Strathclyde 1972, Univ of Dundee 1979, Univ of Cambridge 1982, Univ of London 1982; Hon DSc: Univ of Hull 1977, Univ of Wales 1984, UEA 1986, Univ of Sheffield 2005; Hon DUniv: Surrey 1990, Glasgow 1997, Loughborough 2003; Hon MD Univ of Birmingham 1992; Hon PhD: Tel Aviv Univ 1971, Hebrew Univ 1978, Bar Ilan Univ 1983, Weitzmann Inst 1988; Dr (hc) Univ of Edinburgh 1996; hon fell Royal Instn 2002; Hon FRCP 1977, Hon FBA 1986, Hon FRCS 1988, Hon FREng 1997, Hon FRS 2005, Companion RCS(Ed) 2006 (hon memb 1997); *Style*— The Rt Hon the Lord Wolfson, FRS, FBA; ✉ 8 Queen Anne Street, London W1G 9LD

WOLFSON OF SUNNINGDALE, Baron (Life Peer UK 1991), of Trevose in the County of Cornwall; Sir David Wolfson; kt (1984); s of Charles and Hylda Wolfson; *b* 9 November 1935; *Educ* Clifton, Trinity Coll Cambridge (MA), Stanford Univ (MBA); *m* 1, 1962 (m dis 1967), Patricia Elizabeth (now Baroness Rawlings (Life Peer), *qv*), da of Louis Rawlings; m 2, 1967, Susan E, da of Hugh Davis; 2 s (Hon Simon Adam b 1967, Hon Andrew Daniel b 1969), 1 da (Hon Deborah Sarah b 1973); *Career* Great Universal Stores plc: joined 1960, dir 1973–78 and 1993–2000, chm 1996–2000; sec to shadow cabinet 1978–79, chief of staff Political Office 10 Downing St 1979–85; chm: Alexon Group plc (formerly Steinberg Group plc) 1982–86, Next plc 1990–98 (non-exec dir 1989–98); non-exec dir: Stewart Wrightson Holdings plc 1985–87, Compco Holdings plc 1995–2003, Body Metrics Ltd 2000–02, Avocet Capital Mgmnt Ltd 2001–02, Fibernet Group plc 2001–; hon fell Hughes Hall Cambridge 1989; Hon FRCR 1978, Hon FRCOG 1989; *Recreations* golf, bridge; *Clubs* Portland, Sunningdale, Woburn Golf; *Style*— The Rt Hon Lord Wolfson of Sunningdale; ✉ House of Lords, London SW1A 0PW

WOLPERT, Prof Lewis; CBE (1990); *b* 19 October 1929; *Educ* Univ of the Witwatersrand (BSc), Imperial Coll London (DIC, fell 1996), KCL (PhD); *m* (m dis); 2 s, 2 da; *Career* civil engr 1951–54: SA Cncl for Scientific and Industrial Research, Israel Water Planning Dept; career changed to cell biology 1954, reader in zoology Dept of Zoology at KCL 1964, prof of biology as applied to med Royal Free & Univ Coll Med Sch (formerly Middx Hosp Med Sch) 1966–; visiting lectr Collège de France Paris; TV presenter for Antenna (BBC2) 1988–89, various interviews and documentaries for Radio 3; memb American Philosophical Soc 2002; Scientific Medal of the Zoological Soc 1968, Royal Soc Michael Faraday Award 2000; Christmas Lectures Royal Instn 1986, Radcliffe Lectures Univ of Warwick 1990, The Medawar Lecture Royal Soc 1998; Hon DSc: CNAA 1992, Univ of Leicester 1996, Univ of Westminster 1996, Univ of Bath 1997; Hon DUniv Open Univ 1998; hon fell UCL 1995, foreign memb Polish Acad of Arts & Scis 1998; fell Imperial Coll London 1996, FKC 2001; Hon MRCP London 1986; FRS 1980, FRSL 1999; *Books* A Passion for Science (1988), The Triumph of the Embryo (1991), The Unnatural Nature of Science (1992), Passionate Minds (1997), Principles of Development (1998), Malignant Sadness - The Anatomy of Depression (1999), Six Impossible Things Before Breakfast: The evolutionary origins of belief (2006); *Recreations* cycling, tennis; *Style*— Prof Lewis Wolpert, CBE, FRS; ✉ Department of Anatomy & Development Biology, Royal Free & University College Medical School, University College London, Gower Street, London WC1E 6BT (tel 020 7679 1320, e-mail l.wolpert@ucl.ac.uk)

WOLSELEY, Sir Charles Garnet Richard Mark; 11 Bt (E 1628), of Wolseley, Staffs; s of Capt Stephen Wolseley (ka 1944, s of Sir Edric Wolseley, 10 Bt, JP (d 1954); the Wolseleys of Mt Wolseley, Co Carlow, who produced Sir Garnet, the Victorian general cr Visc Wolseley are a cadet branch) and late Pamela, Lady Wolseley; *b* 16 June 1944; *Educ* Ampleforth, RAC Cirencester; *m* 1, 1968 (m dis 1984), Anita, da of Hugo Fried, of Epsom; 1 s, 3 da; m 2, 1984, Mrs Imogene E Brown; *Heir* s, Capt Stephen Wolseley; *Career* ptnr Smiths Gore Chartered Surveyors 1979–87; FRICS; *Recreations* shooting, fishing, watercolour painting; *Clubs* Shikar; *Style*— Sir Charles Wolseley, Bt; ✉ Wolseley Park, Rugeley, Staffordshire WS15 2TU (tel 01889 582346)

WOLSELEY, Sir James Douglas; 13 Bt (I 1745), of Mount Wolseley, Co Carlow; s of James Douglas Wolseley (d 1960), and Olive, *née* Wofford; *b* 17 September 1937; *m* 1, 1965 (m dis 1971), Patricia Lynn, da of William R Hunter, of Mount Shasta, California, USA; m 2, 1984, Mary Anne, da of Thomas G Brown, of Hilo, USA; *Style*— Sir James Wolseley, Bt

WOLSTENCROFT, Ven Alan; s of John Wolstencroft (d 1965), of Clifton, Manchester, and Jean, *née* Miller (d 1978); *b* 16 July 1937; *Educ* Wellington Sch Altrincham, St John's Coll of FE Manchester, Cuddesdon Theol Coll; *m* 1968, Christine Mary, *née* Hall; 1 s (Alan Jeremy b 1970), 1 da (Elspeth Mary b 1972); *Career* mgmnt trainee WH Smith 1953–60, nat service RAF Medical Branch and Mountain Rescue Team 1955–57, regnl mangr Wine and Spirit Div Bass Charrington 1960–67; ordained deacon 1969, ordained priest 1970; asst curate St Thomas Halliwel 1969–71, asst curate All Saints Stand 1971–73, vicar St Martin Wythenshawe and chaplain Wythenshawe Hosp and Forum Theatre 1973–80, area dean of Withington 1978–91, hon canon of Manchester 1986–98, vicar of Bolton 1991–98, archdeacon of Manchester 1998–2004 (archdeacon emeritus 2004–), residentary canon of Manchester and fell of the coll 1998–2004; religious advsr to Granada TV; memb Ecclesiastical Law Soc 1998, friend of Real Lancashire; *Recreations* squash, walking, reading, theatre, cinema, Bolton Wanderers FC, freemasonry; *Clubs* YMCA, Concord; *Style*— The Ven Alan Wolstencroft; ✉ The Bakehouse, 1 Latham Row, Horwich, Bolton, Lancashire BL6 6QZ (tel 01204 469985, e-mail archdeaconalan@wolstencrofta.fsnet.co.uk)

WOLSTENHOLME, His Hon Judge (John) Scott; s of Donald Arthur Wolstenholme (d 2007), of Ripon, N Yorks, and Kathleen Maye, *née* Humphrys (d 1987); *b* 28 November 1947; *Educ* Roundhay Sch Leeds, UC Oxford (MA); *m* (Margaret) Lynne, da of Wilfred Harrison (d 1989); 3 s (Ian b 22 June 1974, Adam b 3 April 1976, Max b 11 Nov 1979), 1 da (Helen (twin) b 11 Nov 1979); *Career* called to the Bar Middle Temple 1971; in practice NE Circuit 1971–92, recorder of the Crown Court 1992–95, circuit judge (NE Circuit) 1995–; chm Industrial Tbnls 1992–95; *Recreations* playing the drums, walking, photography; *Style*— His Hon Judge Wolstenholme; ✉ Leeds Combined Court Centre, Oxford Row, Leeds LS1 3BE

WOLSTENHOLME, Susan Elizabeth (Sue); OBE (2007); da of Sir Gordon Wolstenholme, OBE (d 2004), of London, and Mary Elizabeth, *née* Spackman (d 1985); *b* 5 November 1940; *Educ* Berkhamsted Sch for Girls, St Godric's Secretarial Coll; *Career* J Walter Thompson Co Ltd: joined 1963, mangr Entertaining/Social Functions 1965, assoc dir 1976–83; ran own catering business 1983–85; hon sec Herts LTA 1978–88, chm Devpt, Coaching & Schs' Ctee LTA 1983–88, dir British Tennis Foundation (formerly LTA Trust) 1988–; govr Berkhamsted Schs 1980–, hon sec Berkhamsted Old Girls' Guild 1971–95, pres The Old Berkhamstedians 2002–05; *Recreations* tennis (former county player), sport, reading, cooking; *Clubs* Berkhamsted Squash Rackets & Tennis (pres 2003–), Sloane; *Style*— Ms Sue Wolstenholme, OBE; ✉ The British Tennis Foundation, National Tennis Centre, 100 Priory Lane, Roehampton, London SW15 5JQ (tel 020 8487 7140, mobile 07971 141302, fax 020 8487 7304)

WOLTON, Harry; QC (1982); s of Harry William (d 1943), and Dorothy Beatrice, *née* Meaking (d 1982); *b* 1 January 1938; *Educ* King Edward's Sch Birmingham (fndn scholar), Univ of Birmingham; *m* 3 April 1971, Julie Rosina Josephine, da of George Edward Mason (d 1985); 3 s (Matthew Harry b 1972, Andrew b 1974, Edward b 1977); *Career* called to the Bar 1969; recorder of the Crown Court 1985–2003, dep judge of the High Court 1990–2003; dir Bar Mutual Insurance Fund 1997–2004; hon legal advsr to John Groom's Charity; *Clubs* Garrick; *Style*— Harry Wolton, QC; ✉ The Black Venn, Edwyn Ralph, Bromyard, Herefordshire HR7 4LU (tel 01885 483302, e-mail harry@wolton.com); Number 5 Chambers, Fountain Court, Birmingham B4 6DR (tel 0121 606 0500); Rue Jeu de Paume, Goult, 84220 Vancluse, France (tel 00 33 49 07 21 288)

WOLVERHAMPTON, Bishop of 1993–; Rt Rev Michael Gay Bourke; s of Gay Gordon Bourke (d 1984), Stafford, and Hilda Mary, *née* Bush; *b* 28 November 1941; *Educ* Hammond's GS Swaffham Norfolk, CCC Cambridge (MA, Trevelyan scholarship, Manners scholarship), Tübingen Univ Germany (World Cncl of Churches Scholarship), Cuddesdon Theol Coll; *m* 2 May 1968, Elizabeth Mary, da of Prof Ludwig Bieler; 1 s (Richard b 2 Feb 1969), 1 da (Rachel b 17 Jan 1971); *Career* curate Great Grimsby St James 1967–71, curate-in-charge Panshanger Welwyn Garden City 1971–78, vicar Southill Bedfordshire 1978–86, archdeacon of Bedford 1986–93; course dir St Albans Ministerial Trg Scheme 1975–87, co-chm Meissen Cmmn 1997; *Recreations* astronomy, hill walking, railways; *Style*— The Rt Rev the Bishop of Wolverhampton; ✉ Bishop of Wolverhampton, 61 Richmond Road, Merridale, Wolverhampton WV3 9JH (tel 01902 824503, fax 01902 824504, e-mail bishop.wolverhampton@lichfield.anglican.org)

WOLVERTON, 7 Baron (UK 1869); Christopher Richard Glyn; er s of 6 Baron Wolverton, CBE (d 1988), and Dowager Baroness Wolverton; *b* 5 October 1938; *Educ* Eton; *m* 1, 1961 (m dis 1967), Carolyn Jane, yr da of late Antony Noel Hunter, of London; 2 da (Hon Sara-Jane b 1963, Hon Amanda Camilla b 1966); m 2, 1975 (m dis 1989), Mrs Frances Sarah Elisabeth Stuart Black, eldest da of Robert Worboys Skene, of London; m 3, 1990, Gillian Konig; *Heir* bro, Hon Andrew Glyn; *Career* FRICS; *Style*— The Rt Hon the Lord Wolverton

WOLZFELD, HE Jean-Louis; s of Gustave Wolzfeld (d 1991), of Luxembourg, and Marie Thérèse, *née* Normand; *b* 5 July 1951; *Educ* Univ of Paris (MA); *Career* Luxembourg diplomat; entered Foreign Service 1976, dep perm rep to int orgns Geneva 1980, ambass Japan and concurrently Republic of Korea 1986, ambass and perm rep to UN 1993, political dir Miny of Foreign Affrs 1998, ambass to the Ct of St James's and concurrently Republic of Ireland and Iceland 2002–; *Style*— HE Mr Jean-Louis Wolzfeld; ✉ Embassy of Luxembourg, 27 Wilton Crescent, London SW1X 8SD (tel 020 7235 6961, fax 020 7235 9734, e-mail ambofluxoffice@ukonline.co.uk)

WOMBELL, Paul; s of Clifford Wombell, and Katherine Wombell; *Educ* Armthorpe HS Doncaster, St Martin's Sch of Art (BA); *m* Patricia Coral Wombell; *Career* administrator Midland Gp Nottingham 1983–86, dir Impressions Gallery York 1986–94, dir The Photographers' Gallery London 1994–2005; quest curator Photo Int Rotterdam 1994, memb Selection Ctee Photo Works in Progress Rotterdam 1997–98, conf organiser Ten Stories About Photography V&A 1998, master World Press Photo Rotterdam 2000, judge Amnesty Int Media Awards London 2001–02; memb jury: Prix de Rome Amsterdam 1996, Photographers Assoc of the Netherlands 1998; memb: Int Advsy Panel Fotofest Houston 1989–, Int Advsy Panel Aperture NY, Advsy Bd Encyclopedia of 20th Century Photography 2000; visiting prof Univ of Sunderland 2002–; *Books* Battle: Passchendaele 1917 (1981), The Globe (1989), Photovideo: Photography in the Age of the Computer (1991), Sportscape: The Evolution of Sports Photography (2000), Blink (co-ed, 2002); *Style*— Paul Wombell, Esq; ✉ 238 Brick Lane, London E2 7EB

WOMBWELL, Sir George Philip Frederick; 7 Bt (GB 1778), of Wombwell, Yorkshire; s of Maj Sir Philip Wombwell, 6 Bt, MBE (d 1977); *b* 21 May 1949; *Educ* Repton; *m* 1974, (Hermione) Jane, eldest da of Thomas S Wrightson, of Leyburn, N Yorks; 1 s (Stephen Philip Henry b 1977), 1 da (Sarah Georgina b 1980); *Heir* s, Stephen Wombwell; *Career* farmer; *Style*— Sir George Wombwell, Bt

WOMERSLEY, Prof David John; s of John Crossley Womersley, of Woodstock, Oxon, and Joyce, *née* Nesbitt; *b* 29 January 1957, South Shields, Tyne & Wear; *Educ* Strode's Sch Egham, Trinity Coll Cambridge (BA, PhD); *m* 11 Sept 1982, Carolyn Jane, *née* Godlee; 1 s (James Rupert Lister b 23 Oct 1986), 2 da (Katharine Jane Bland b 3 Nov 1988, Rachel Alice Lodge b 5 March 1992); *Career* Drapers' Co research fell Pembroke Coll Cambridge 1981, lectr Sch of English Univ of Leeds 1983, fell and tutor in English Jesus Coll Oxford 1984, Thomas Warton prof of English literature Univ of Oxford 2002–; sr proctor Univ of Oxford 2001–02; govr: Dragon Sch Oxford 1998–, Harrow Sch 2001–; FRHistS 1997, fell English Assoc 2003; *Books* The Transformation of the Decline and Fall of the Roman Empire (1988), Religious Scepticism: Contemporary Responses to Gibbon (1997), Augustan Critical Writing (1997), Gibbon: Bicentenary Essays (ed, 1997), Edmund Burke, Pre-Revolutionary Writings (1998), Restoration Drama: An Anthology (2000), A Companion to English Literature from Milton to Blake (ed, 2000), Gibbon and the 'Watchmen of the Holy City': The Historian and his Reputation, 1776–1814 (2002), Samuel Johnson, Selected Essays (2003), Cultures of Whiggism (ed, 2005); also produced edns of Edward Gibbon's The Decline and Fall of the Roman Empire and Reflections on the Fall of Rome; *Recreations* wine, yachting, cooking, dogs; *Style*— Prof David Womersley; ✉ St Catherine's College, Oxford OX1 3UJ (tel 01865 27171, e-mail david.womersley@ell.ox.ac.uk)

WOMERSLEY, (John) Michael; s of John Basil Womersley (d 1979), of Yorks, and Ann Patricia, *née* Allured; *b* 18 February 1960; *Educ* King Edward's Sch Bath, Oxford Poly (HND); *m* 4 May 1991, Susanne Jayne, da of John Maurice George Garrard (d 1996), and Sue, *née* Mullins; 2 s (Oliver Peter b 25 Oct 1995, Richard John b 13 Jan 1999), 1 da (Rebecca Kate b 15 Aug 2000); *Career* asst mangr (Reading) British Transport Hotels 1981, commis chef Gidleigh Park 1982–84, sauce chef de partie Le Manoir aux Quat'Saisons 1984–86, successively legumier, commis patissier then baker L'Esperance Marc Meneau 1986–87, fish chef de partie Les Pres D'Eugenie Michel Guerard 1987, sr sous chef Cliveden Hotel 1988–89, head chef Lucknam Park Hotel 1989–95, chef proprietor Three Lions Restaurant Stuckton 1995–; memb Académie Culinaire de Grand Bretagne; fell Masterchefs of GB 2004; *Awards* first prize Yorkshire Fine Wine Competition 1990, third prize Mouton Cadet Competition 1992, first prize Prix des Deux Cartes 1994; finalist Pierre Tatinger Competition 1993; Lucknam Park Hotel awards: County Restaurant of the Year Good Food Guide 1990, 4 AA red stars and 3 red rosettes 1991–, Ackerman clover 1991–95, Hotel of the Year Exec Travel and Utell 1991, Michelin star 1992–95; Three Lions awards: Michelin Red M 1996, 3 stars AA Guide, Hampshire Achiever of the Year Good Food Guide 1996, Hampshire Commended Restaurant of the Year 2001, Nat Newcomer of the Year Good Hotel Guide 2002, Hampshire Restaurant of the Year Good Food Guide 2006; *Recreations* advanced diver, skiing, golf, Tai Chi; *Style*— Michael Womersley, Esq; ✉ Three Lions Restaurant, Stuckton, Fordingbridge, Hampshire SP6 2HF (tel 01425 652489, fax 01425 652144, e-mail the3lions@btinternet.com)

WOMERSLEY, Sir Peter John Walter; 2 Bt (UK 1945), of Grimsby, Co Lincoln; JP (1991); s of late Capt John Walter Womersley (ka 1944), and gs of Rt Hon Sir Walter Womersley, 1 Bt, PC (d 1961); *b* 10 November 1941; *Educ* Charterhouse, RMA Sandhurst; *m* 1968, Janet Margaret, da of Alastair Grant; 2 s, 2 da; *Heir* s, John Womersley; *Career* serv Regular Army, Offr Cadet at Sandhurst until 1962, 2 Lt King's Own Royal Border Regt 1962, Lt 1964, Capt 1966, ret 1968; human resources serv mangr SmithKline Beecham 1993–97 (personnel offr 1968–72, personnel mangr 1972–93), conslt specialising in job evaluation 1997–99; MIPM; *Books* Collecting Stamps (with Neil Grant, 1980); *Recreations* breeding rare poultry, motor racing photography; *Style*— Sir Peter Womersley, Bt; ✉ Broomfields, 23 Goring Road, Steyning, West Sussex BN44 3GF

WONNACOTT, John Henry; CBE (2000); s of Jack Alfred Wonnacott (d 1974), and Ethel Gwendoline Wonnacott (d 1998); *b* 15 April 1940; *Educ* Univ Coll Sch, Slade Sch; *m* 10 Aug 1974, Anne Rozalia, da of Tadeuz Wesolowski (d 1980); 2 da (Elizabeth Anne b 1978, Emma Zofja b 1982), 1 s (Jack Henry Tadeus b 1994); *Career* artist; Ondaatje Prize RSPP; *Solo Exhibitions* incl: The Minories of Colchester 1977, Rochdale Art Gallery and tour 1978, Marlborough Fine Art 1980, 1985 and 1988, Scottish Nat Portrait Gallery 1986, Agnew's 1992 and 1996, Christchurch Museum Ipswich 1998, Hirschl & Adler NY 1999, Agnews 2000 and 2005; *Group Exhibitions* incl: Painting and Perception (Univ of Stirling) 1971, British Painting '74 1974, British Painting' 52–77 (Royal Acad) 1977 Queen's Jubilee exhbn, Hard Won Image (Tate Gallery) 1984, Pursuit of the Real (Barbican) 1990, Painting the Century 2001, A Sea of Faces 2001; *Public Collections* portrait cmmns: Sir Adam Thomson (Scottish Nat Portrait Gallery), Fleet Adml Lord Lewin of Greenwich (National Maritime Museum), The Royal Family: A Centenary Portrait (Nat Portrait Gallery); other work in public collections incl: Tate Gallery, Arts Cncl, Edinburgh Scottish Nat Portrait Gallery, Norwich Castle, Rochdale Gallery, British Cncl, Metropolitan NY, Imperial War Museum, Christchurch Museum Ipswich, Nat Portrait Gallery, House of Commons; *Style*— John Wonnacott, Esq, CBE; ✉ Thomas Agnew & Sons Ltd, 43 Old Bond Street, London W1X 4BA (website www.johnwonnacottgallery.com)

WOO, (Dr) Sir Po-Shing; kt (1999); s of Seaward Woo, OBE, JP, and Woo Ng Chiu Man; *b* 19 April 1929, Hong Kong; *Educ* La Salle Coll Hong Kong, KCL (LLB); *m* 25 Sept 1956, Woo Fong Shuet Fun (Lady Helen Woo); 4 s (Nelson, Wilson, Jackson, Dawson), 1 da (Carmen); *Career* admitted slr England and Hong Kong 1960, NP 1966, admitted slr and barr Australia 1983; fndr Woo Kwan Lee & Lo Slrs & Notaries Hong Kong, conslt Jackson Woo & Associates 2005–; dir: Celtime Ltd, Deroston Ltd, Diamond String Co Ltd, Eastern Delegate Ltd, Fong Fun Co Ltd, Fong Fun Enterprises Ltd, Fukuki Co Ltd, Great Step Co Ltd, Helene Court Ltd, Henderson Devpt Ltd, Henderson Investment Ltd, Henderson Land Devpt Co Ltd, Jetfun Investment Ltd, Jumbo Concord Investment Ltd, Kailey Enterprises Ltd, Oriental Chief Devpt Ltd, Oriental Eagle Investment Ltd, Sun Hung Kai Properties Ltd, Tobofaith Ltd, Wise Town Ltd; memb Exec Ctee Hong Kong Discharged Prisoners' Aid Soc 1966, urban cncllr 1967–71, memb Bd of Mgmnt Chinese Perm Cemeteries 1973–83, memb Bd of Review Inland Revenue 1978–81, dir Hong Kong Tuberculosis Chest and Heart Diseases Assoc 1983–88 (hon legal advsr 1983–2000), patron Woo Po Shing Gallery of Chinese Bronze Shanghai Museum 1996–, patron Sir Po-Shing Woo Auckland Observatory 1998–; hon voting memb: Hong Kong Jockey Club, Po Leung Kuk Advsy Bd (dir 1977–78), Tung Wah Gp of Hosps (dir 1955–56, advsr 1956–57); legal advsr Chinese Gold and Silver Exchange Soc, dir and legal advsr Shun Tak Fraternal Assoc (registered sch mangr and ctee memb Seaward Woo Coll 1975), hon pres and legal advsr S China Athletic Assoc, vice-pres Hong Kong Woo's Clan General Assoc Ltd; fndr: Woo Po Shing Medal in Law Univ of Hong Kong 1982, Woo Po Shing Overseas Summer Sch Travelling Scholarship Univ of Hong Kong 1983, Po-Shing Woo Charitable Fndn 1994, Woo Po Shing Chair of Chinese and Comparative Law City Univ Hong Kong 1995; memb Bd of Tstees Univ of Hong Kong 1996–2002 (Staff Terminal Benefits Scheme 1996–2002, Staff Provident Fund 1996–2002, Staff Retirement Scheme 1996–2002), memb Cncl Univ of Hong Kong 1997–2000; recipient: world fellowship Duke of Edinburgh's Award, hon professorship Nankai Univ Tianjin China, Hon LLD City Univ Hong Kong; memb: Inst of Admin Mgmnt, Inst of Trade Mark Agents; fell Hong Kong Mgmnt Assoc 2000; FCIArb, FBIM, FIMgt, FKC; Chevalier de l'Ordre des Arts et des Lettres (France) 2004; *Recreations* travelling, antiques (including Chinese paintings, bronze and ceramic), racehorse owner (including Hong Kong Derby winner 'Helene Star'); *Clubs* Hong Kong, Hong Kong Jockey, Aberdeen Marina, RAC (UK); *Style*— Sir Po-Shing Woo

WOOD, HE Adam Kenneth Compton; s of Kenneth Wood (d 2003), of Drewsteignton, Devon, and Cynthia, *née* Compton; *b* 13 March 1955; *Educ* Royal GS High Wycombe, Oriel Coll Oxford (BA); *m* 1993, Katie, da of Geoffrey Richardson; 1 da (Persephone Rose b 19 Feb 1999); *Career* Devpt Co-Ordination Dept ODM 1977–78, Bilateral Aid and Rural Devpt Dept ODA 1979, asst desk offr Zimbabwe ODA 1980, asst private sec to Lord Privy Seal FCO 1980–83, asst to UK exec dir UK Delgn IMF/IBRD Washington DC 1983–86, head Lome Section European Community Dept ODA 1986–88, Kenya prog mangr ODA Regnl Office Nairobi 1988–93, advsr to DG European Cmmn Brussels 1993–96, head DFID SE Asia Bangkok 1996–2000, devpt cnsllr UKREP Brussels 2000–02, high cmmr to Uganda 2002–05, high cmmr to Kenya 2005–; *Recreations* golf, tennis, birding, music; *Clubs* Karen Country, Muthaiga Country; *Style*— HE Mr Adam Wood; ✉ c/o Foreign & Commonwealth Office (Nairobi), King Charles Street, London SW1A 2AH (tel 00 254 20 284 4000, e-mail adam.wood@fco.gov.uk)

WOOD, Alistair Angus; MBE (1992); s of Ronald Angus Wood (decd), and Adrienne Chester, *née* Hartridge; *b* 24 August 1953, Tenterden, Kent; *Educ* Ardingly, RMA Sandhurst, Univ of Aberdeen (MLitt); *m* 7 July 1979, Anna Caroline, *née* Parry; 1 da (Sophie Katharine b 11 Aug 1984), 2 s (Hugo Edward Angus b 29 Oct 1987, Angus Peter Emrys b 22 April 1992); *Career* regular cmmn The Blues and Royals 1974, regular army 1974–93, advsr to Cmmr of the Metropolis 1994–97, advsr to Royal Bafokeng Administration Repub of South Africa 1999–2000, advsr to Govt of Sierra Leone 2000–02, advsr to Transitional Islamic State of Afghanistan 2003–04, private sec to HRH Princess Alice, Duchess of Gloucester 2004, private sec to TRH The Duke and Duchess of Gloucester 2004–; dep commandant Aberdeenshire ACF 1999–2000; tstee St John of Jerusalem Eye Hosp 2007–; *Recreations* scuba diving, international relations, military history; *Clubs* Cavalry and Guards; *Style*— Alistair Wood, Esq, MBE; ✉ c/o Apartment 1, Kensington Palace, London W8 4PU

WOOD, Sir Andrew Marley; GCMG (2000, KCMG 1995, CMG 1986); s of Robert George Wood (d 1988), and Muriel, *née* du Feu (d 2001); *b* 2 January 1940; *Educ* Ardingly, King's Coll Cambridge (MA); *m* 1, 15 Sept 1972, Melanie Leroy, *née* Masset (d 1977); 1 s (Matthew Thomas b 22 Aug 1975); m 2, 15 Sept 1978, Stephanie Lee, *née* Masset; 1 da (Laura Lee b 10 May 1981), 1 s (Patrick Andrew Robert b 5 Feb 1985); *Career* FO (now FCO): joined 1961, third sec Moscow 1964–67, second then first sec Washington 1967–70, seconded to Cabinet Office 1971–73, FCO 1973–76, first sec and head of Chancery then cnsllr Belgrade 1976–79, head of Chancery Moscow 1979–82, head West European Dept 1982–83, head Personnel Ops Dept 1983–85, ambass Belgrade 1985–89, min Washington 1989–92, dep under sec and chief clerk 1992–95, ambass Russian Fedn and Repub of Moldova 1995–2000; currently sr advsr: BP, ITE; chm PBN Co; memb Advsy Cncl: Renaissance Capital, Br Conslts Bureau; *Style*— Sir Andrew Wood, GCMG; ✉ 15 Platt's Lane, London NW3 7NP

WOOD, Annie; da of William MacGregor Wood, of Irvine, and Elizabeth, *née* Livingstone; *b* 2 December 1965; *Educ* Islay HS, Northern Coll of Educn Aberdeen (DipEd); *m* Henry Ian Cusick, the actor, s of Henry Joseph Cusick; 3 s (Elias b 10 Jan 1994, Lucas b 20

March 1998, Esau b 19 Jan 2000); *Career* Scottish Arts Cncl trainee dir TAG Theatre Co 1992, asst dir Citizens Theatre 1993, drama artist MacRobert Arts Centre 1994–99, lectr Univ of Glasgow 2000, drama teacher Thamesview Sch 2002, artistic dir Polka Theatre 2002–06; moved to Hawaii 2006, memb Bd Honolulu Theatre for Youth 2006–; directing credits incl: The Banyan Tree (TAG) 1993, Stray Birds (Citizens Theatre) 1994, Mohammed (MacRobert Arts Centre) 1994, Tuesday and Other Stories (Citizens Theatre) 1995, Merlin (MacRobert Arts Centre) 1996, The Red Balloon (co-writer, Visible Fictions, and US tour) 1996–2003 (Victor Award Toronto Milk Festival), Beauty and the Beast (MacRobert Arts Centre) 1997, Travel Club and Boy Soldier (MacRobert Arts Centre) 1997, The Two Fiddlers (MacRobert Arts Centre) 1998, The Princess and the Goblin (MacRobert Arts Centre) 1998, The Happy Prince (MacRobert Arts Centre) 1999 and 2002–03, King Glutton (Lung Ha's), Martha (Catherine Wheels, and US tour) 1999 (Victor Award Toronto Milk Festival), The Cat with Three Names (M6) 2000, One Moment in Time (TAG) 2000, The Selfish Giant (writer, Northern Stage and Leicester Haymarket) 2000–01, Frankenstien (Catherine Wheels) 2001, Martha (Leicester Haymarket) 2002, Home from Home (writer, Polka Theatre) 2003, Stuart Little (Polka) 2003, Kadouma's Island (Polka) 2003, Ugly Duckling (also adaptation, Polka) 2005, Bear Stories (Polka) 2005, Paddington Bear (also adaptation, Polka) 2006, Sensational (also writer, Honolulu Theatre for Youth) 2007; tstee: Ciao! Children's Int Arts Festival, Trinity Theatre; Creative Scotland Award 2000; *Recreations* yoga, fun days out with my family, dancing with my children, running, surfing; *Style*— Ms Annie Wood

WOOD, Dr Anthony James (Tony); s of Harry Wood (d 1961), of Lowestoft, Suffolk, and Elizabeth Ann, *née* Calvert (d 1975); *b* 20 November 1938; *Educ* Lowestoft GS, Univ of Nottingham (BSc), Univ of London (PGCE), Univ of Southampton (PhD); *m* 1960, Marion Christine, da of Basil Archie Paine; 1 s (David Anthony b 10 July 1964), 2 da (Susan Nicola b 7 Oct 1965, Wendy Michelle b 23 March 1976); *Career* physics teacher Fairham Comp Nottingham 1961–62, Instr Lt RN 1962–67, sr lectr Weymouth Coll of Educn 1969–73 (lectr 1967–69), princ lectr and head Mathematics Div Northampton Coll of Educn 1973–75, dean Faculty of Mathematics and Business Nene Coll Northampton 1975–84 (dean Blackwood Hodge Mgmnt Centre 1981–84), chief exec Luton Coll of HE 1989–93 (dir 1985–93, Leverhulme research fell 1985–86), vice-chllr and chief exec Univ of Luton 1993–98 (vice-chllr emeritus 1998–), educational conslt 1998–; chm Bedfordshire Family Practitioners' Ctee 1989–90; chm and non-exec dir: Bedfordshire FHSA 1990–94, Bedfordshire HA 1994–2000; external examiner Univ of Southampton 1978–83; dir: Putteridge Bury Ltd 1989–98, HE Business Enterprises 1991–93, HE Quality Cncl 1992–93; memb: European Fndn for Mgmnt Devpt 1981–98, Access Courses Recognition Gp CNAA 1987–92, Instns Ctee CNAA 1989–92, Ctee for Degree Awarding Powers HE Quality Cncl 1992–93, R&D Ctee NW Thames RHA 1993–94, CVCP 1993–98, Univs Liaison Ctee Anglia and Oxford RHA 1994–96; chm Standing Conference of Princs and Dirs of Colls and Insts of HE 1990–93; FIMA 1975, CMath 1992; *Books* Involving Parents in the Curriculum (1976), Curriculum Enrichment for Gifted Children (1979), Quicksilver Maths series (1982), Hedgehoppers series (1986); *Recreations* home and family; *Style*— Dr Tony Wood; ✉ Five Farthings, 34 Church End, Biddenham, Bedford MK4D 4AR (tel 01234 349395, fax 01234 325835)

WOOD, Prof Bernard Anthony; s of Anthony Frederick Wood, of Budleigh Salterton, Devon, and late Joan Faith, *née* Slocombe; *b* 17 April 1945; *Educ* King's Sch Gloucester, Middx Hosp Med Sch Univ of London (BSc, MB BS, PhD); *Children* 1 s (Nicholas b 1970), 2 da (Penny b 1972, Hannah b 1986); *Career* Univ of London: lectr 1973–75, sr lectr 1975–78, reader 1978–82, SA Courtauld prof 1982–85; Derby prof of anatomy Univ of Liverpool 1985–97, dean Faculty of Med Univ of Liverpool 1996–97; Henry R Luce prof of human origins George Washington Univ 1997–2006, prof of human origins George Washington Univ 2006–07; pres Anatomical Soc of GB and Ireland 1996–98, past pres Primate Soc of GB, vice-pres Royal Anthropological Inst, past sec Br Assoc of Clinical Anatomists; *Publications* Human Evolution (1978), Major Topics in Primate and Human Evolution (1986), Hominid Cranial Remains (1991); papers on human origins; *Recreations* gardening, English saltglaze stoneware, opera; *Style*— Prof Bernard Wood; ✉ 1517 Residence C21 30th Street NW, Washington DC 20007, USA (tel 00 1 202 338 5111, bernardawood@gmail.com); Department of Anthropology, 2110 G Street NW, Washington DC 20037, USA (tel 00 1 202 994 6077, fax 00 1 202 994 6097, e-mail bernardawood@gmail.com)

WOOD, Charles Anthony; OBE (1996); s of Anthony Mewburn Wood (d 1994), of Chiddingstone, Kent, and Margaret Kathleen, *née* Stordy; *b* 20 November 1938; *Educ* Downside, Pembroke Coll Oxford (MA); *m* 10 Oct 1964, Susan Mary, da of Henry Anderson, MBE (d 1975), of Wallingford, Oxon; 3 s (Robert b 1969, Francis b 1979, Jonathan b 1982), 1 da (Juliette b 1971); *Career* Phillips & Drew 1962–71, L Messel & Co 1971–86; dir: Lehman Brothers Securities 1986–96, Greig Middleton & Co Ltd 1996–97, Old Mutual Asset Managers (UK) Ltd 1997–2002 (vice-pres Int Ops), Standard Life Equity Income Tst plc 2003– (chm 2006–), Cazenove Capital Mgmnt Pension Tstee Ltd 2005–; chm Lehman Brothers Pension Scheme 1988–, memb Investment Ctee Daily Mail and General Tst plc Pension Schemes 1997–, chm London and Quadrant Housing Tst Staff Benefits Plan; chm New Islington and Hackney Housing Assoc 1984–95; AIIMR, MSI; *Recreations* houses, gardening, climbing; *Clubs* City of London, Alpine; *Style*— Charles Wood, Esq, OBE; ✉ 14 Compton Terrace, London N1 2UN (tel 020 7226 4056)

WOOD, Charles Gerald; s of John Edward Wood, and Catherine Mae *née* Harris; *b* 6 August 1932; *Educ* Chesterfield GS, King Charles I Sch Kidderminster, Birmingham Coll of Art; *m* 1954, Valerie Elizabeth Newman; 1 s (John Charles b 1954), 1 da (Katrina b 1959); *Career* dramatist, screenwriter and writer for television and radio 1963–; 1949–63: soldier (17–21st Lancers), scenic artist, layout artist and stage mangr, cartoonist (The Stage, The Globe and Mail Toronto), Bristol Evening Post; memb Drama Panel SW Arts 1970–72, conslt Nat Film Devpt Fund 1980–82, memb Cncl BAFTA 1990–93; FRSL 1984; *Theatre* plays incl: Cockade (Evening Standard Award), Dingo, Don't Make Me Laugh, Meals on Wheels, Fill the Stage with Happy Hours, H or Monologues at Front of Burning Cities, Tie Up the Ballcock, Welfare, The Garden, Veterans (Evening Standard Award), The Script, Jingo, Red Star, Has Washington Legs, Across From the Garden of Allah, Man Beast and Virtue (Pirandello), The Mountain Giants (Pirandello) 1993, The Tower (Dumas) 1995; *Television* plays: Not At All, Traitor in a Steel Helmet, Drill Pig, Prisoner and Escort, Drums Along the Avon, Mutzen Ab!, A Bit of a Holiday, A Bit of a Family Feeling, A Bit of Vision, A Bit of an Adventure, Death or Glory Boy, The Emergence of Antony Purdy Esq, Love Lies Bleeding, Do As I Say!, Miss White in New York; series: Don't Forget to Write, My Family and Other Animals (adaption), The Settling of the Sun, Sharpe's Company, Sharpe's Regiment, Sharpe's Waterloo, Mute of Malice, Briefs Trooping Gaily, Monsignor Renard (episode 3); documentaries: Last Summer By the Sea; *Radio* 1962–72: Prisoner and Escort, Cowheel Jelly, Next to Being a Knight; The Fireraisers (Max Frisch) 2004, The Conspiracy of Sèvres 2006; *Film* incl: The Knack, Help, How I Won the War, The Long Day's Dying, The Charge of the Light Brigade, The Bed Sitting Room, Cuba, Red Monarch, Puccini, Wagner, Tumbledown (Prix Italia RAI Prize, Best Single Play BAFTA, Best Single Play RTS, Best Single Play BPG), An Awfully Big Adventure (Beryl Bainbridge), A Breed of Heroes (Alan Judd, nomination for BAFTA), England My England (John Osborne), Iris (with Richard Eyre, nomination for BAFTA and Christopher Award NY, Humanitas Prize LA), The Other man (with Richard Eyre); *Publications* incl: Cockade, New English Dramatists 8, Dingo, H, Veterans, Man Beast and Virtue (Pirandello), The Mountain Giants (Pirandello), The Tower (Dumas); *Style*— Charles Wood, Esq; ✉ c/o Sue Rodgers, ICM, Oxford House, 76 Oxford Street, London W1D 1BS (tel 020 7636 6565)

WOOD, David Bernard; OBE (2004); s of Richard Edwin Wood (d 1987), and Audrey Adele Whittle, *née* Fincham; *b* 21 February 1944; *Educ* Chichester HS for Boys, Worcester Coll Oxford (BA); *m* 1, 1966 (m dis 1970), Sheila, *née* Dawson; m 2, Jan 1975, Jacqueline, da of Prof Sydney William Stanbury; 2 da (Katherine b 1976, Rebecca b 1979); *Career* actor, writer, composer, playwright, theatre dir and prodr; West End acting credits incl: Hang Down Your Head and Die 1964, Four Degrees Over 1966, After Haggerty 1970, Jeeves 1975; film acting credits incl: If... 1968, Aces High 1976, North Sea Hijack 1980, Longitude 2000; dir: WSG Prodns Ltd/Whirligig Theatre 1966–, Verronmead Ltd 1982–, Westwood Theatrical Prodns Ltd 1986–1994, W2 Prodns 1995–; *Publications* many plays published by Samuel French incl: The Owl and the Pussycat Went to See (1968), The Plotters of Cabbage Patch Corner (1970), The Gingerbread Man (1977), The Selfish Shellfish (1983), The See-Saw Tree (1987), Save the Human (1990); children's books incl: The Operats of Rodent Garden (1984), The Discorats (1985), Playtheatres (1987), Sidney the Monster (1988), Happy Birthday Mouse (1990), Save the Human (1990), Baby Bear's Buggy Ride (1993), Theatre for Children: Guide to Writing, Adapting, Directing and Acting (1997); Pop-up Theatre: Cinderella (1994), Bedtime Story (1995), The Magic Show (1995), Mole's Summer Story (1997), Silly Spider (1998), Mole's Winter Story (1998), Funny Bunny's Magic Show (2000), The Phantom Cat of the Opera (2000), The Toy Cupboard (2000), Under the Bed! (2006); stage adaptations of: Helen Nicoll and Jan Pieńkowski's Meg and Mog (1980), HRH The Prince of Wales' The Old Man of Lochnagar (1986), Roald Dahl's The BFG (1991), The Witches (1992), Enid Blyton's Noddy (1993), More Adventures of Noddy (1995), Dick King-Smith's Babe, the Sheep-Pig (1997), Roald Dahl's The Twits (1999), Eric Hill's Spot's Birthday Party (2000), Philippa Pearce's Tom's Midnight Garden (2000), Roald Dahl's Fantastic Mr Fox (2001), Roald Dahl's James and the Giant Peach (2001), Philip Pullman's Clockwork (2004), Roald Dahl's Danny the Champion of the World (2004), Ronda and David Armitage's The Lighthouse Keeper's Lunch (2006); film screenplays: Swallows and Amazons (1974), Back Home (1989); *Recreations* conjuring (memb Magic Circle), collecting old books; *Style*— David Wood, Esq, OBE; ✉ c/o Casarotto Ramsay Ltd, Waverley House, 7–12 Noel Street, London W1F 8GQ (tel 020 7287 4450, fax 020 7287 9128)

WOOD, Rear Adm David John; CB (1998); s of John Herbert Wood (d 1982), and Nesta, *née* Jones; *b* 12 June 1942; *Educ* St Paul's Sch, BRNC Dartmouth, RNEC Manadon (BSc(Eng)); *m* 1966, Hilary Jolly; 2 s (Thomas b 1971, Charles b 1972), 1 da (Anna b 1974); *Career* with RN; various Fleet Air Arm appts incl HMS Ark Royal and Sea Vixen and Wessex Sqdns 1965–73, Aircraft Support MOD 1973–76, Air Engr Offr Lynx Intensive Flying Trials Unit 1976–77, Army Staff Course 1978, Aircraft Procurement MOD (PE) 1979–81, Naval Sec's Dept MOD 1981–84, on staff FO Naval Air Command 1984–86, NATO Def Coll Rome 1986–87, asst dir for EH101 Project MOD (PE) 1987–89, dir Aircraft Support Policy (Navy) MOD 1989–91, dir Maritime Projects MOD (PE) 1991–95, DG Aircraft (Navy) 1995–98, defence aviation conslt 1998–; FRAeS 1993 (memb Cncl 1996); *Recreations* cross country walking and running, choral singing, supporting local church; *Clubs* Army and Navy; *Style*— Rear Adm David Wood, CB; ✉ Ministry of Defence, Whitehall, London SW1A 2HB

WOOD, His Hon Judge David Russell; s of Christopher Russell Wood (d 1987), of Riding Lea, Northumberland, and Muriel Wynne Wood; *b* 13 December 1948; *Educ* Sedbergh, UEA (BA); *m* 24 Feb 1979, Georgina Susan, da of Maj Dudley Buckle; 2 s (John Dudley Russell b 4 June 1980, Robert James Russell b 12 May 1985), 1 da (Rose-Ann Florence b 19 May 1982); *Career* called to the Bar Gray's Inn 1973, recorder of the Crown Court 1990–95 (asst recorder 1984–90), circuit judge (NE Circuit) 1995–; memb Cncl of Circuit Judges; *Recreations* country pursuits, tennis, piano; *Clubs* Northern Counties (Newcastle upon Tyne); *Style*— His Hon Judge Wood; ✉ Newcastle upon Tyne Crown Court, Quayside, Newcastle upon Tyne (tel 0191 201 2000, fax 0191 201 2001)

WOOD, Derek Alexander; CBE (1995), QC (1978); s of Alexander Cecil Wood, and Rosetta, *née* Lelyveld; *b* 14 October 1937; *Educ* Tiffin Sch Kingston upon Thames, UC Oxford (BCL, MA); *m* 1, 9 Aug 1961 (m dis 2001), Sally Teresa Scott Wood; 2 da (Jessica Susan b 27 Oct 1965, Rebecca Lucy b 7 Sept 1968); m 2, 2001, Barbara Kaplan, *née* Spector; *Career* called to the Bar Middle Temple 1964 (bencher 1986, treas 2006); recorder of the Crown Court 1985–; princ St Hugh's Coll Oxford 1991–2002 (now hon fell); Dept of the Environemnt: memb Advsy Gp on Commercial Property Devpt 1975–78, memb Working Gp on New Forms of Social Ownership in Housing 1976, memb Property Advsy Gp 1978–94, chm Review of Rating of Plant and Machinery 1991 and 1996–98; chm: Standing Advsy Ctee on Trunk Rd Assessment Dept of Tport 1986–94, Working Pty on Code of Practice for Commercial Leases in England and Wales 1995; memb Cncl London Borough of Bromley 1975–78; dep chm Soc of Labour Lawyers 1978–91, chm Chislehurst Constituency Lab Pty 1972–76 and 1979–84, cncllr London Borough of Bromley 1975–78; memb Governing Cncl RICS 2003–06; chm: Oxfordshire Community Fndn 1995–2001, Attlee Fndn 2004– (tstee 2002–); govr Quintin Kynaston Sch 2003–; hon fell UC Oxford 2002; hon fell Central Assoc of Agric Valuers 1988, Hon RICS 1991; FCIArb 1993; *Books* Leasehold Enfranchisement and Extension (ed, part of Halsbury's Laws of England series), Handbook of Arbitration Practice (jt ed, 1987, 2 edn 1993, 3 edn 1998); various works on agricultural law; *Recreations* music; *Clubs* Athenaeum, RAC, Architecture; *Style*— Derek Wood, Esq, CBE, QC; ✉ Falcon Chambers, Falcon Court, London EC4Y 1AA (tel 020 7353 2484, fax 020 7353 1261)

WOOD, Edmund Michael; s of George Lockhart Wood (d 1959), and Joan, *née* Halsey (d 2004); *b* 7 September 1943; *Educ* Maidwell Hall, Eton; *m* 6 Nov 1971, Elizabeth Anne, da of Sqdn Ldr Robert Roland Patrick Fisher (d 1991); 2 da (Sarah Georgina b 10 July 1974, Anne Louise b 15 Sept 1977); *Career* chartered accountant 1967; articled to Singleton Fabian & Co 1963; ptnr: Singleton Fabian Derbyshire & Co 1969–74, Binder Hamlyn 1974–98, Arthur Andersen 1994–98; currently conslt specialising in personal fin planning Mercer & Hole London and St Albans and dir Mercer & Hole Tstees Ltd 1998–; dir: Lee Valley Water Co 1982–90, BH Matheson Investment Management 1987–97; chm Hitchin Deanery Synod 1991–99; dir The Shuttleworth Tsts; tstee: Rands Educn Fndn 1980 (chm 1992–), Sir Malcolm Stewart Bt Gen Charitable Tst 1997–; FCA 1974 (ACA 1968); *Recreations* fishing, shooting, golf, gardening; *Clubs* Boodle's; *Style*— Edmund M Wood, Esq; ✉ The Old Rectory, Holwell, Hitchin, Hertfordshire SG5 3SP (tel 01462 712228); Mercer & Hole, 72 London Road, St Albans, Hertfordshire AL1 1NS (tel 01727 869141, fax 01727 869149)

WOOD, Gareth Haydn; s of Haydn William George Wood, and Joyce, *née* Jenkins; *b* 7 June 1950; *Educ* Pontypridd Boys' GS, Royal Acad of Music; *Career* memb RPO 1972–2005 (chm until 1994), composer of many pieces for brass bands incl Butlins Youth 1977 and Nat 4 Section 1980; cmmns incl: Overture Suffolk Punch (RPO), Festivities Overture (Philharmonia Orch), fanfares (100 years of the Financial Times), fanfare (150 years of Cunard), Sinfoniettas 2, 3 and 4 (Nat Youth Orch of Wales), Fantasy of Welsh Song (Welsh Prom Concerts), test-piece (European Brass Band Championships) 1992, The Land of Magic and Enchantment (40th anniversary of Pembs Nat Park), Fanfare for a New Beginning (opening of Kravis Centre W Palm Beach), Cardiff Bay Overture (Cardiff Bay Devpt Corp) 1993, Toduri (600th anniversary of City of Seoul), Halifax Diptych (Halifax Building Society), Poems within a Prayer (Robert Tear (tenor)), Bass Concerto No 1 (Wiltshire Youth Orch) 1995, Bass Concerto No 2 (Yehudi Menuhin Sch)

1997, Bass Concerto No 3 (Wiltshire Youth Orch), Fields of Amaranth (Bromley Youth Chamber Orch), Adagio for Strings (RPO), A Wiltshire Symphony (W Wilts Youth Wind Band), Trombone Concerto (Nat Youth Brass Band of Wales) 1999, 2nd Trumpet Concerto (Camarthen Youth Band) 2000, Concerto for Harp and Brass Band (Nat Youth Band of Wales) 2001, Waterless Seas for 6 Harps 2002, Time Machines (Bromley Youth Orch) 2002, The Caudlron (Bromley Youth Orch) 2003, Forbidden Gates (Royal Acad of Music) 2003, Rivers of Light (Royal Acad of Music) 2003, Legends of the Bear (Nat Youth Wind Band of Wales) 2004, Concerto for Percussion and Wind Band (Nat Youth Wind Band of Wales) 2006, Concerto for Tenor Horn and Brass Band (Nat Youth Brass Band of Wales) 2006, Actaeon (Buy As You View Band) 2007, A Simple Gift (Bromley Youth Orch) 2007, Each Side of Midnight (Eton Sch) 2007, An Ireland Adventure (Three Counties Wind Band) 2007; ARAM; *Style*— Gareth Wood, Esq; ✉ 57 Marischal Road, Lewisham, London SE13 5LE (tel and fax 020 8318 3312)

WOOD, Graham Allan; s of William Wales Wood, of Glasgow, and Ann Fleming, *née* Blackwood; *b* 15 August 1946; *Educ* Hillhead HS, Univ of Glasgow (BDS), Univ of Dundee (MB ChB), Univ of Mexico (Dip Cleft Lip and Palate Surgery); *m* 23 Nov 1970, Lindsay, da of Alfred Balfour; 1 da (Nicola b 1975), 1 s (Alexander b 1985); *Career* gen dental practice 1968–70, house offr and sr house offr Glasgow Dental Hosp 1970–71, registrar in oral and maxillofacial surgery Canniesburn and Victoria Infirmary Hosps 1971–72, dental surgeon Int Grenfell Assoc 1972–73, registrar in oral and maxillofacial surgery Queen Elizabeth Hosp Birmingham 1973–74, sr registrar in oral and maxillofacial surgery N Wales 1979–83 (conslt 1983–95), conslt oral and maxillofacial surgn Canniesburn Hosp Glasgow 1995–2001, conslt oral and maxillofacial surgn Southern Gen Hosp Glasgow 2001–, hon clinical sr lectr Univ of Glasgow 1995–; clinical prof in oral and maxillofacial surgery Univ of Texas 1990–2000; memb: BMA, BDA; FDS RCPSGlas 1973, FRCSEd 1985, fell Br Assoc of Oral and Maxillofacial Surgns 1983, life fell Int Assoc of Oral and Maxillofacial Surgeons 1990, FDSRCS 2000, FDSRCS (Eng) 2000, FDSRCS (Ed) 2004; *Books* Cryosurgery of the Maxillofacial Region Vol II (contrib, 1986), Textbook of General & Oral Surgery (contrib, 2003); *Recreations* golf, squash, sailing, hill walking, skiing (formerly Canadian ski patroller); *Clubs* Bowfield Country, Kilmacolm Golf; *Style*— Mr Graham A Wood; ✉ Abbotsford, Broomknowe Road, Kilmacolm, Renfrewshire PA13 4HX; Regional Maxillofacial Unit, Southern General Hospital, 1345 Govan Road, Glasgow G51 4TF (tel 0141 232 7540)

WOOD, Graham Stuart; s of Edward and Janet Wood, of London; *b* 7 September 1965; *Educ* Central St Martin's Sch of Art (BA, MA); *m* 1995, Sophia, da of Leif Einarsson; *Career* co-fndr Tomato 1991 (design consultancy covering corp identity, creative direction, TV and film titles, commercials direction, promotional literature, etc); Tomato projects incl: Trainspotting (film titles for Irvine Welsh book), Channel 4 (consultative work on corp identity prog), The Brief History of Time (images illustrating Steven Hawking book for BBC), MTV Music Awards (creative direction and design), TV campaigns/commercials for brands incl Levis, Nike, Reebok, The Guardian and Gordon's Gin; Tomato's work published in books and magazines worldwide incl: D&AD Annual 1986, 1987 and 1992–, Tokyo Type Directors Annual (Japan) 1993–, Design Week, Wired, Creative Review, I-D (UK and USA), Blueprint, Vogue, Arena, The Face, The Tate Magazine; memb: Panel of Judges BBC Design Awards 1996, Exec D&AD 1996–98 (Pres's Lecture 1997); *Style*— Graham Wood, Esq; ✉ Tomato, 29–35 Lexington Street, London W1R 3HQ (tel 020 7434 0955, fax 020 7434 0935)

WOOD, Prof Hamish Christopher Swan; CBE (1993); s of Joseph Wood (d 1958), and Robina Leggat, *née* Baptie (d 1959); *b* 8 May 1926; *Educ* Hawick HS, Univ of St Andrews (BSc, PhD); *m* 18 Dec 1951, Jean Dumbreck, da of George Mitchell (d 1995); 1 da (Sheena Margaret (Mrs Walker) b 22 Feb 1953), 1 s (Colin Dumbreck b 16 Dec 1957); *Career* lectr in chemistry Univ of St Andrews 1950–51, res fell Dept of Med Chemistry ANU 1951–53; Univ of Strathclyde: reader in organic chemistry (also lectr and sr lectr) 1953–69, prof of organic chemistry 1969–91, dep princ 1982–84, vice-princ 1984–86, prof emeritus 1991–; conslt in chemistry Wellcome Fndn Ltd and Burroughs Wellcome USA Inc 1963–89, chm Governing Body Glasgow Poly 1987–93, first chm Univ Ct Glasgow Caledonian Univ 1993–94; memb Univs Funding Cncl 1989–93; RSC Award in Medicinal Chemistry 1986; hon fell: Scotvec 1993, Scottish Qualifications Authy 1997; Hon DUniv Strathclyde 1992, Hon LLD Glasgow Caledonian Univ 1994; FRSE 1968 (memb Cncl 1992–95), FRSC 1973, CChem 1973; *Style*— Prof Hamish Wood, CBE, FRSE; ✉ 26 Albert Drive, Bearsden, Glasgow G61 2PG (tel 0141 942 4552); Department of Pure and Applied Chemistry, University of Strathclyde, Thomas Graham Building, 295 Cathedral Street, Glasgow G1 1XL (tel 0141 552 4400 ext 2799, fax 0141 548 4246)

WOOD, Sir Ian Clark; kt (1994), CBE (1982); s of John Wood (d 1986) and Margaret, *née* Clark (d 1981); *b* 21 July 1942; *Educ* Robert Gordon's Coll Aberdeen, Aberdeen Univ (BSc); *m* 1970, Helen, *née* Macrae; 3 s; *Career* chm John Wood Group plc 1982– (chief exec 1982–2006), chm J W Holdings Ltd; jt chm Oil and Gas Industry Leadership Team, memb Government Oil & Gas Industry Task Force (now PILOT) until 2006; chllr Robert Gordon Univ 2004–; business ambass for Scot 2001; memb Seafar Gp; fell Scottish Qualifications Authy 1997; Hon LLD Aberdeen 1984, Hon DBA Robert Gordon Univ 1998, Hon DTech Glasgow Caledonian Univ 2002; Fscotvec 1994, FCIB 1998, FRSE 2000, FRSA; *Awards* Grampian Industrialist of the Year 1978, Young Scottish Businessman of the Year 1979, Scottish Free Enterprise 1985, Scottish Business Achievement Award Tst (jtly) 1992, Corporate Elite Leadership Award (Services) 1992, Alick Buchanan-Smith Meml Award for Personal Achievement 1995, Corporate Elite World Player Award Business Insider 1996, entered into Entrepreneurial Exchange Hall of Fame 2002, CEO of the Year Business Insider/PwC Scotland Insider Awards 2003, Glenfiddich Spirit of Scotland Award for Business 2003; *Recreations* tennis, art, family; *Style*— Sir Ian Wood, CBE; ✉ John Wood Group plc, John Wood House, Greenwell Road, East Tullos, Aberdeen AB12 3AX (tel 01224 851000, fax 01224 871997)

WOOD, James; *Educ* Univ of Cambridge (organ scholar), Royal Acad of Music; *Career* composer and conductor; prof of percussion Darmstadt Int Summer Courses 1982–94; fndr and dir: New London Chamber Choir, Centre for Microtonal Music London, Critical Band; conductor: BBC Symphony Orch, London Sinfonietta, Ensemble Inter Contemporain, l'Itinéraire, Musikfabrik, Champ d'Action, Netherlands Wind Ensemble, Percussion Group The Hague, Belgian Radio Philharmonic, Kraków Radio Orch, Tokyo Philharmonic Choir, Netherlands Chamber Choir; cmmns for: Arditti Quartet, the King's Singers, Electric Phoenix, Amadinda Percussion Group Budapest, Duo Contemporain, Robert Van Sice, Nouvel Ensemble Moderne, Percussions de Strasbourg, New Music Players, BBC and IRCAM; cmmns BBC Proms: Oreion 1989 (conducted BBC Symphony Orch), Two men meet, each presuming the other to be from a distant planet (for Steven Schick and Critical Band) 1995; recordings incl: Stoicheia, Ho Shang Yao, Choroi Kai Thaliai, Rogosanti, Incantamenta, Two men meet, each presuming the other to be from a distant planet, Venancio Mbande talking with the trees, Phainomena; Gemini fellowship 1993, Arts Foundation Fellowship 1995/6, Holst Foundation Award; *Style*— James Wood, Esq; ✉ e-mail jw@choroi.demon.co.uk

WOOD, James Alexander Douglas; QC (1999); s of Lt-Col Alexander Blythe Wood, TD, and Cynthia Mary, *née* Boot; *b* 25 June 1952; *Educ* Haileybury, Univ of Warwick (LLB); *m*; 2 s (Nathan b 1988, Tommy b 1990); *Career* called to the Bar Middle Temple 1975, recorder 1999–; memb: int mission of lawyers to Malaysia 1982, panel of inquiry into visit of Leon Brittan to Univ of Manchester Students Union in March 1985; involved for the defence in many civil rights cases incl: The Newham Seven, The Broad Water Farm Trials, The Miners Strike Trials, Birmingham Six and Bridgewater Four Appeals; *Books* The Right of Silence, the Case for Retention (1989); *Recreations* parenting, gardening, the enhancement of civil liberties and the enforcement of civil rights; *Style*— James Wood, QC, Esq; ✉ Doughty Street Chambers, 11 Doughty Street, London WC1N 2PG (tel 020 7404 1313, fax 020 7404 2283)

WOOD, Jane Caroline; da of Duncan Patrick (d 1983), and Kathleen, *née* Smith (d 1959); *b* 17 August 1943; *Educ* Putney HS for Girls, Lucy Cavendish Coll Cambridge (MA); *m* 1, 1962 (m dis 1987), Christopher Wood; 1 da (Caroline b 1963), 2 s (Adam b 1965, Benjamin b 1966); m 2, 1996, Edward Russell-Walling; *Career* Secker & Warburg: asst to Barley Alison 1982–83, ed 1983–85, exec ed 1985–87; ed dir Arrow Books 1987–90, ed dir MacMillan Ltd 1990–94; Orion Books: publishing dir 1994–2004, ed-in-chief 2005–; *Recreations* reading, theatre, cinema, concerts, walking, skiing; *Style*— Ms Jane Wood; ✉ Orion Books, Orion House, 5 Upper St Martin's Lane, London WC2H 9EA (tel 020 7240 3444, fax 020 7240 4822, e-mail jane.wood@orionbooks.co.uk)

WOOD, Joanna Harriet; da of John Harvey Pinches, and Rosemary Vivian, *née* Bidder; *b* 3 July 1954; *Educ* Queensgate Sch London; *Family* 1 da (Leonora Sarah Clare Wood b 11 Aug 1982); m, 22 Dec 1995, Charles Louis Frederick Godfrey Hansard; 1 da (Harriet Louisa b 24 Feb 1997); *Career* PA to Chief of Personnel UN Geneva 1974–76, interior design apprentice Asprey's 1976–79, fndr interior design co Joanna Trading Ltd 1980–, prop furnishings and accessories shop Joanna Wood Ltd 1985–; clients incl: Sir David Frost, Lady Rothermere, Hon and Mrs Nigel Havers, John Reid, Jim Henson, Sotheby's, Rothmans Int, Theatre of Comedy, The New York Times, The Garrick Club, Richemont; co-owner: Lewis & Wood fabrics and wall coverings, Lawson Wood upholstered furniture; chm Auction of Promises NSPCC, patron Cancer Research, memb Pimlico Road Assoc; memb British Interior Design Assoc (BIDA), memb Int Interior Design Assoc (IIDA); *Recreations* country pursuits, theatre, ballet, travel; *Style*— Ms Joanna Wood; ✉ Joanna Wood Ltd, 48 Pimlico Road, London SW1W 8LP (tel 020 7730 5064, fax 020 7730 4135)

WOOD, John; s of Barrie Wood, and Rita Wood; *Educ* City of Norwich Sch, Norwich Sch of Art, Bath Coll of HE (BA); *Career* artist; in partnership with Paul Harrison, *qv*; *Exhibitions* incl: The British Art Show 5 2000, Twenty Six (Drawing and Falling Things) (Chisenhale Gallery London) 2002, Sudden Glory (CCAC Inst Calif) 2002, Gwangju Biennale Korea 2002, Monitor: Volume One (Gagosian Gallery NY) 2002, Performing Bodies (Tate Modern London) 2002, A Century of Artists' Film in Britain (Tate Modern) 2003, Hundredweight (FA Projects London) 2003, Selected Works (MOMA NY) 2004, Selected Works (MIT Boston) 2004, Irreducible (Wattis Inst California Coll of the Arts) 2005, To Be Continued (Helsinki Kunsthalle) 2005, Mixed Doubles (Carnegie Museum of Art) 2005, Five Rooms (Ludwig Museum Budapest) 2006, Le Mouvement des Images (Centre Pompidou Paris) 2006, Smart Art (Kunsthalle Osnabruck) 2006, MAM 05 (MORI Art Museum) 2007, Breaking Step (Salon Belgrade) 2007, Echo Room (Alcala 31 Madrid) 2007, I Am Making Art (Centre d'Art Contemporain Geneva) 2007; *Style*— John Wood, Esq

WOOD, John Norris; s of Wilfrid Burton Wood, (d 1943) and Lucy Heald Sutcliffe Boston (d 1977); *b* 29 November 1930; *Educ* Bryanston, Goldsmiths Coll Sch of Art, E Anglian Sch of Painting & Design, RCA; *m* 12 June 1962, Julie Corsellis Guyatt (d 2001), da of John Nicholls (d 1968); 1 s (Wilfrid Spencer Conal b 1968), 1 da (Dinah Elizabeth Georgia b 1971); *Career* artist and author; lectr in illustration Goldsmiths' Coll Sch of Art 1956–68, tutor Cambridge Coll of Art 1959–70; fndr scientific, tech, med illustration course at Hornsey Coll of Art 1965; fndr and i/c Natural History Illustration Unit and Ecological Studies Dept RCA 1971–97 (visiting prof 1997–); regular Exhibits at RA Summer Exhibition; exhibited: Natural History Museum London, V&A Museum, Natural History Museum Caracas Venzuela, Fry Gall, Regfern Gall, Chappel Galls KPMG; exhbns incl: Museum of Zoology Univ of Cambridge, A T Kearney 2004; conslt to BBC Life on Earth; provided illustrations for: Time and Life, Knopf, Mathew Price Ltd, Longmans, BBC Publications, Post Office, Methuen, Penguins, Sunday Times and others; author and illustrator Hide and Seek (children's natural history book series, translated into 10 languages); memb: Soc of Authors 1995, Soc of Wildlife Artists 1997; FRCA 1980, Hon ARCA 1996; *Publications* Inky Parrot Press (limited edn); *Recreations* conservation, natural history, art, music; *Style*— John Norris Wood, Esq; ✉ The Brook, Dewhurst Lane, Wadhurst, East Sussex TN5 6QE; Royal College of Art, Department of Natural History and Ecological Studies, Stevens Building, Kensington Gore, London SW7

WOOD, John R; s of Maj-Gen Harry S Wood and Mrs Jo Wood (d 1999); *b* 23 April 1945; *Educ* Cranbrook Sch, RMA Sandhurst, Gonville & Caius Coll Cambridge (MA), RMCS Shrivenham (Div 1 Army Staff Course), RAF Advanced Staff Course Bracknell; *m* 23 Aug 1969, Gillian; 3 s (Nicholas b 23 Jan 1972, James b 15 May 1974, Edward b 12 April 1981); *Career* served gunner offr RA UK and Germany 1969–71, transferred REME 1972, various field appts REME UK and BAOR 1972–77, Army Staff Course 1978–79, various staff appts UK 1979–83, engrg support planning offr Challenger main battle tank 1983–86 (promoted Lt Col), staff offr grade 1 (Weapons) Automotive Trials cmdg Automotive Trials Wing, Royal Armament R&D Estab Chertsey 1986–87, ret Army; tech dir and chief engr RAC Motoring Servs 1987–91, md Motor Industry Research Assoc (MIRA) 1991–; non-exec dir Ceram Ltd 2006–; chm: Sub-Ctee on the Environment FIA 1989–91, Int Conf on Automotive Diagnostics 1990, IMechE Seminar on Impact of Regulations on Diesel Emissions 1990, Third Autosports Int Tech Congress 1993, Automobile Div Bd IMechE 1994 (memb 1985), Bd for the Engrg Profession 1999–2001; memb: Automotive Electronics Conf Planning Panels 1987, 1989 and 1991, Tech Ctee Fédération Internationale des Sociétés d'Ingénieurs des Techniques de l'Automobile (FISITA) 1992–, Cncl IMechE 1993–95, Bd Low Carbon Vehicle Partnership 2003–, Bd Nat Composites Network 2005–; dir Motor Sports Assoc (MSA) 2001–, chm Tech Advsy Panel RAC Motor Sports Assoc 1995–, memb RAC Motor Sports Cncl 1995–, memb Bd Assoc of Ind Research and Technol Orgns (AIRTO) 2006–; chm Midland Automobile Club 2003–, dir Museum of Br Road Tport (MBRT) 2003–; memb Senate Engrg Cncl 1996–2001; memb Cncl: Fédération Internationale des Sociétés d'Ingénieurs des Techniques de l'Automobile (FISITA) 1994–, SMMT 1995–, IMechE 1998–2003; visiting prof Coventry Univ 1999–; CEng 1975, FIMechE 1989 (MIMechE 1975) FIMI, MSAE; *Papers and Publications* The Development of Automotive Diagnostic Systems for Armoured Fighting Vehicles in the British Army (IMechE Conf, 1985), Engineering for the Customer - Development and the Future (IMechE Proceedings Vol 207, 1993), The Response of Development Engineers to Future Needs (1993), The Development of the Speed Hill-Climb Car (IMechE Proceedings Vol 208, 1994), Research Technologies to Develop Opportunities for Injury Reduction in Passenger Cars (FISITA Conf, Paris, 1998), Rubber Component Development - a Vehicle Engineering Perspective (2001); *Recreations* motor racing, shooting; *Style*— John Wood, Esq; ✉ MIRA, Watling Street, Nuneaton, Warwickshire CV10 0TU (tel 024 7635 5344, fax 024 7635 5345, e-mail john.wood@mira.co.uk)

WOOD, Prof John Vivian; CBE (2007); s of Vivian Wood (d 1996), of Oxford, and Lois, *née* Hall; *b* 10 September 1949; *Educ* St Lawrence Coll Ramsgate, Univ of Sheffield (BMet, Mappin Medal), Univ of Cambridge (PhD), Univ of Sheffield (DMet); *m* 1976, Alison, da of Cyril Lee; 1 s (Thomas b 1987), 1 da (Mary b 1988); *Career* Goldsmiths jr res fell Churchill Coll Cambridge 1974–78, lectr/sr lectr Open Univ 1978–89, Cripps prof of materials engrg and head of dept Univ of Nottingham 1989 (dean of engrs 1998–2001), chief exec Cncl for the Central Labs of the Res Cncls (seconded) 2001–07, princ Faculty of Engrg Imperial Coll London 2007–; visiting scholar Univ of Kyoto Japan; chm: Office of Sci & Technology's Foresight Panel on Materials 1997–2001, European Strategy Forum for Research Infrastructures 2005–, Jt Info Systems Bd 2006–; dir: M4 Technologies Ltd 1995–, Diamond Light Source Ltd 2002–, Spectrum 2003–, Maney Publishing 2003–; conslt: Karl Storz GmbH Germany 1994–2001, Metal Powders Div GKN 1994–98, Osprey Metals Ltd 1987–96, Fibre Technology Ltd 1981–2001, Powdrex Ltd 1983–2001, Applied Microsurgical Res 1984–88, London & Scandinavian Metallurgical Co 1984–99; Inst of Materials: memb Cncl 1997–2002, President's Advsy Bd 1997–2000, memb Strategy Panel 1997–2000, chm Materials Processing Science Ctee 1987–96, memb Particulate Engrg Ctee 1987–2001, memb Publications Ctee 1979–87, chm PM 89 1987–89, chm of Tech Ctee PM 90 1987–90; Grunfeld Medal and Prize Inst of Metals 1986, Ivor Jenkins Award Inst of Materials 2000, William Johnson Gold Medal 2001; chm and fndr Stables Tst, reader C of E; Liveryman Worshipful Co of Founders 1996, Freeman City of London 1996; Hon DSc Univ of Cluj-Napoca Romania 1994; CEng, CPhys, CChem; FIM 1990, FIMechE 1999, FRSC 1999, FREng 1999, FInstP 2000; Citizen of Honour City of Cluj-Napoca Romania; *Publications* author of over 240 scientific publications and 17 patents; *Recreations* serious contemporary chamber and instrumental music, trees, fungi, affordable wine; *Clubs* Anglo-Belgian; *Style—* Prof John Wood, CBE, FREng; ✉ Council for the Central Laboratories of the Research Councils, Rutherford Appleton Laboratory, Chilton, Didcot, Oxfordshire OX11 0QX (tel 01235 821900, fax 01235 445147 e-mail j.v.wood@rl.ac.uk)

WOOD, Jonathan Richard (John); s of Norman Richard Wood, of Colyton, Devon, and Mildred Patricia, *née* Smith; *b* 12 October 1948; *Educ* Blundell's, Fitzwilliam Coll Cambridge (MA), Univ of London (MA); *m* 6 Aug 1982, Alison Lesley, *née* Birtwistle; 2 s (Edward b 11 July 1985, James b 29 Aug 1992), 1 da (Rebecca b 30 Jan 1988); *Career* admitted slr 1974; VSO Zambia 1967–68, ptnr Herbert Smith 1982–; Freeman City of London; *Books* Taxation of Offshore Trusts and Funds (co-author, 4 edn 2002), A Practitioner's Guide to Contentious Trusts and Estates (co-author, 2002); *Recreations* cricket, early 20th century literature, Scottish history; *Clubs* Reform, MCC; *Style—* Jonathan Wood, Esq; ✉ Herbert Smith, Exchange House, Primrose Street, London EC2A 2HS (tel 020 7374 8000, fax 020 7374 0888, e-mail john.wood@herbertsmith.com)

WOOD, (William) Lawson; s of Robert Wood (d 1985), and Barbara, *née* Dougal; *b* 5 October 1953; *Educ* Eyemouth Secdy Sch, Newcastle Poly; *m* 31 Dec 1994, Lesley Anne, da of Dennis Richard Orson (d 1976); 3 c (Emma Victoria Watts b 3 Sept 1967, Lindsay Wood b 26 March 1977, Jamie Wood b 2 Feb 1979); *Career* photographer, author and illustrator; prop Ocean Eye Films (underwater photographic co) 1992–, clients incl: Br Airways, American Express, Thomson Worldwide, Daily Express and tourism offices worldwide; feature writer and correspondent: Dive Magazine, Scuba World, Sport Diver, 35mm Photographer, Tauchen Magazin (Germany), Aquanaut Magazin (Germany), Duiken (Norway), Sport Diver (SA); fndr memb Marine Conservation Soc, fndr and chm St Abbs & Eyemouth Marine Nature Reserve (first and only in Scotland) 2000–; conslt: Marinescape, Deep Sea World (Scotland and China), Struik Int Holdings, New Holland Publishers, Readers' Digest, Condensed Books, Eyemouth Marine Interpretive Centre; HSE approved part IV commercial diver 1996, HSE approved sub aqua club diving instr 1996; memb: Marine Conservation Soc 1978, British Sub Aqua Club, Br Soc of Underwater Photographers, Bureau of Freelance Photographers; hon memb Scottish Sub Aqua Club 1974; Northburn Caravan Park: grounds mangr 1971–83, jr ptnr 1974–83, gen mangr and sr ptnr 1986–92; co dir Aiksop Ltd 1974–83; diving offr on board Lady Jenny III (Red Sea) 1983–86; ptnr and md Eyemouth Holiday Park 1998–2002, ptnr Churches Hotel 2000–02; FRPS 1996, FBIPP 1997, FRGS 1998; *Awards* Jt Round Table and Rotary Int Award For Marine Conservation 1981, East of Scotland Devpt Bd Award for Marine Conservation 1982, Marine Conservation Soc Award for Marine Conservation 1983, winner of numerous underwater photographic competitions 1973–, incl: Scottish Nat Champion (5 times), Irish Open, gold medals in Camera beneath the Waves, Brighton Int, World Championships (Antibes), BBC Wildlife Photographer of the Year; *Books* incl: Lawson Wood Marine Photographer (1994), Exploring the Deep (jtly, 1994), Eyemouth in Old Picture Postcards Vol I (1995), History of Eyemouth Railway Company (1995), History of Eyemouth Lifeboat (1996), The Dive Sites of the Cayman Islands (1996), Diving and Snorkelling Guide to the Seychelles (1996), The Dive Sites of Cozumel and the Yucatan (1997), Diving and Snorkelling Guide to Scotland (1997), Eyemouth in Old Picture Postcards Vol II (1997), Berwick-upon-Tweed in Old Picture Postcards (1998), Top Dive Sites of the World (jtly, 1998), Top Dive Sites of the Caribbean (1999), Diving the Caribbean (1999), The Dive Sites of the Bahamas (1999), Diving and Snorkelling Guide to Bermuda (1999), The Dive Sites of Malta, Gozo and Comino (jtly, 1999), Adventure Divers Handbook (jtly, 1999), The Diver Guide to St Abbs and Eyemouth (1999), The Dive Sites of the Virgin Islands (2000), Diving and Snorkelling Guide to Trinidad and Tobago (2000), The Berwickshire Coast (2000), Top Dive Sites of the Indian Ocean (jtly, 2000), Caribbean Reef Fishes and Invertebrates (jtly, 2000), Scapa Flow (2001), Diving Guide to British Isles and Northern Europe (jtly, 2001), Scotland's Atlantic Coast (2002), Mediterranean Reef Fish and Invertebrates (2002), The Great Borders Flood of 1948 (2002), The Eight Minute Link (2002), The Diver Guide to Scotland's Atlantic Coast (2002), Mediterranean Reef Fishes and Invertebrates (2002), Shipwreck City (2003), World's Best Dives (jtly, 2003), Shipwrecks of the Cayman Islands (2004), The World's Best Wrecks (jtly, 2004), Pocket Guide to Cayman Islands Shipwrecks (2005), World's Best Coral Reefs (jtly, 2005); *Recreations* scuba diving, reading, writing, music, theatre, films; *Style—* Lawson Wood, Esq

WOOD, Leanne; AM; da of Jeffrey Wood, of Penygraig, Rhondda, and Avril, *née* James; *b* 13 December 1971, Llwynypia, Rhondda; *Educ* Tonypandy Comp Sch, Univ of Glamorgan (BA), Cardiff Univ (Dip); *Partner* Ian Brown; 1 da (Cerys Amelia Wood b 28 Jan 2005); *Career* probation offr Mid Glamorgan Probation Serv 1997–2000, political researcher to Jill Evans MEP 2000–01, pt/t lectr for Social Work Dip Cardiff Univ 2000–03, chair Cwm Cynon Women's Aid 2001– (support worker 2001–02), memb Nat Assembly for Wales (Plaid Cymru) S Wales Central 2003–; cncllr Rhondda Cynon Taf Local Authy 1995–99; co-chair Nat Assoc of Probation Offrs (NAPO) 1998–2000; chair Cardiff Stop the War Coalition 2003–04; *Style—* Ms Leanne Wood, AM; ✉ 45 Gelligaled Road, Ystrad, Rhondda CF41 7RQ; National Assembly for Wales, Cardiff Bay, Cardiff CF99 1NA (tel 029 2089 8256, e-mail leanne.wood@wales.gov.uk)

WOOD, Dr (Kathryn) Louise; da of Prof Graham Charles Wood, FEng, FRS, of Bolton, Lancs, and Freda Nancy, *née* Waithman; *b* 10 February 1963; *Educ* Smithills GS Bolton, Univ of Edinburgh (BSc, Ellis Prize in Physiology), Univ of London (PhD); *Career* Medicines Control Agency (now Medicines and Healthcare products Regulatory Agency) Dept of Health: scientific offr Pharmacovigilance Unit 1990–92, co-ordinator Co Liasion Unit Pharmacovigilance Unit 1992–93, co-ordinator Medical Dictionary for Drug Regulatory Affrs (MedDRA, formerly MEDDRA) Project 1993–96 (memb MedDRA Mgmnt Bd Maintenance and Support Services Org 1998–2002), strategic devpt co-ordinator Post-Licensing Div 1996–99, mangr and dir GP Research Database Div 1999–2004, dir Mgmnt Bd 2001–04, head of innovation and industry R&D rels R&D Directorate 2004–; chair UK Clincial Research Collaboration Industry Road Map Gp 2005, co-chair Pharmaceutical Industry Competitiveness Task Force Clinical Res Working Gp 2005, co-chair Healthcare Technol Co-operative Working Gp 2005–; chair Nat Inst for Health Res IS Prog Bd 2007–; EU rep and sec Medical Terminology Expert Working Gp Int Conference on Harminisation 1995–97; *Publications* author of pubns on central control of gastric physiology, med terminology and the GP Research Database; *Recreations* travel, dining out, swimming; *Style—* Dr Louise Wood

WOOD, Maj-Gen Malcolm David; CBE (2002, MBE 1988); s of Stanley Andrew Wood (d 1992), and Elsie Blackley, *née* Stamper; *b* 14 May 1953, Hampton Court, Surrey; *Educ* Hampton GS, RMA Sandhurst, St John's Coll Cambridge; *m* 13 Aug 1977, Nora Ann; 3 da (Katherine b 1981, Joanna b 1985, Rachel b 1988); *Career* cmmnd RAOC 1973; promoted: Lt-Col 1991, Col 1995, Brig 1997, Maj-Gen 2003; chm Army Football Assoc; mentioned in despatches 1993, Queen's Commendation for Valuable Service 1996; *Recreations* supporter Burnley FC; *Style—* Maj-Gen Malcolm Wood, CBE

WOOD, (Gregory) Mark; *b* 25 July 1953; *m* 1953, Susan; 3 c; *Career* chartered accountant; Price Waterhouse 1974–79, Commercial Union 1979–83, Barclays 1983–88, B&C 1988–90, MAI (New York) 1990–93, md insurance, fin services and retail businesses AA 1993–97, chief exec Sun Life and Provincial Holdings plc/AXA UK 1997–2001, exec dir Prudential plc and chief exec Prudential UK and Europe 2001–05; dep chm and chm Gen Insurance Ctee ABI 1999–2001, chm Govt Property Crime Reduction Action Team 2000–01; dep chm NSPCC 2002– (tstee 1999–); chm of govrs Amesbury Sch 2002–; FCA, MSI; *Recreations* skiing, tennis, golf, classical music, jazz; *Style—* Mark Wood, Esq

WOOD, Mark William; s of Joseph Hatton Drew Wood (d 1997); *b* 28 March 1952; *Educ* Gillingham GS, Univ of Leeds (BA), Univ of Warwick (MA), Univ of Oxford (CertEd); *m* 29 Dec 1986, Helen, da of Peter Frederick Lanzer, of Brussels; 1 da (Phoebe Elizabeth b 1989), 1 s (Rupert William Caspar b 1991); *Career* Reuters: joined 1976, corr Vienna 1977–78, corr E Berlin 1978–81, corr Moscow 1981–85, chief corr W Germany 1985–87, Euro ed 1987–89, ed-in-chief 1989–2000, exec dir 1990–96, md Reuters Content Partners 2000–02, chm Visnews Reuters Television 1992–2002; ITN: non-exec dir 1993–2002, non-exec chm 1998–2002, exec chm 2002–03, chm and chief exec 2003–; chm Meteor GmBH Germany 2000–02; memb: Library and Information Cmmn 1995–2000 (chm 1998–2000), MLA, Cncl for Museums, Libraries and Archives 2000– (dep chm 2002–03, chm 2003–); *Recreations* History, opera, tennis, skiing, Spurs; *Style—* Mark Wood, Esq; ✉ ITN, 200 Gray's Inn Road, London WC1X 8XZ (tel 020 7833 3000, fax 020 7430 4305, e-mail mark.wood@itn.co.uk)

WOOD, Sir Martin Francis; kt (1986), OBE (1982), DL (Oxon 1985); s of Arthur Henry Wood (d 1964), of Oxon, and Katharine Mary, *née* Altham (d 1974); *b* 19 April 1927; *Educ* Gresham's, Trinity Coll Cambridge (MA), Imperial Coll London (BSc); *m* 26 May 1955, Kathleen Audrey, da of Rev John Howard Stanfield; 1 s (Jonathan Altham b 30 Sept 1956), 1 da (Patience Elizabeth b 12 Sept 1960), 2 step c (Robin David b 3 May 1950, Sarah Margaret b 17 Nov 1951); *Career* Nat Serv NCB 1945–48, mgmnt trainee NCB 1954–55, sr research offr Clarendon Lab Physics Dept Univ of Oxford 1955–69, fell Wolfson Coll Oxford 1965–88 (hon fell 1988); pres Oxford Instruments Ltd (fndr 1959, dep chm following floatation 1983–); pres Farm-Africa, fndr Northmoor Tst, fndr Oxford Tst, chm Oxford Economic Partnership; author of numerous articles in professional jls and deliverer of lectures UK and abroad; jt winner Mullard Award Royal Soc 1982; Hon DSc Cranfield Inst of Technol 1983, Hon DTech Loughborough Univ of Technol 1985, Hon DEng Univ of Birmingham 1996, Hon DSc Univ of Nottingham 1996, Hon DUniv Open Univ 1999, Hon DCL Univ of Oxford 2004; hon fell UMIST 1989; Hon FREng 1994, FRS 1987 (memb Cncl 1995–); *Recreations* inventions, forestry and walking; *Style—* Sir Martin Wood, OBE, FRS, DL; ✉ Oxford Instruments Group plc, Old Station Way, Eynsham, Oxfordshire OX29 4TL (tel 01865 881437)

WOOD, Michael Murray; s of Kenneth Wood, of Edinburgh, and Isobel, *née* Murray (d 2006); *b* 28 March 1955, Edinburgh; *Educ* Loretto, Univ of Edinburgh; *m* 6 Sept 1980, Barbara Ann, *née* Lennard; 1 da (Louise Kathryn b 21 July 1984), 2 s (Andrew Constable Murray b 12 May 1987, Struan Lennard Muir b 26 July 1990); *Career* admitted slr; ptnr Simpson & Marwick 1981–; pt/t sheriff 2006–; memb Law Soc of Scot; *Recreations* golf, curling, reading history, family; *Clubs* Merchant Co, Luffness Golf, Longniddry Golf; *Style—* Michael Wood, Esq; ✉ Kittlestane, Links Road, Longniddry, East Lothian EH32 0NJ (tel 01875 852243, e-mail michael_wood@zen.co.uk); Simpson & Marwick, Albany House, 58 Albany Street, Edinburgh EH1 3QR (tel 0131 557 1545, fax 0131 525 8652, e-mail michael.wood@simpmar.com)

WOOD, Mike; MP; *Career* MP (Lab) Batley and Spen 1997–; *Style—* Mike Wood, Esq, MP; ✉ House of Commons, London SW1A 0AA (tel 020 7219 3000, e-mail woodm@parliament.uk)

WOOD, Nicholas Andrew Vicary; s of Charles Stephen Wood, (d 1965), and Celia Patty Wood, *née* Underwood (d 1959); *b* 31 January 1943; *Educ* Lewes Co GS, Queen Elizabeth's Sch Crediton; *m* 8 July 1972 (m dis 2000), Mary Kristina, da of Donald Bernard Naulin, of Williamsburg, Virginia; 2 da (Olivia Marian Vicary b 17 Oct 1984, Genevieve Anna Cordelia b 11 Oct 1987); *Career* called to the Bar Inner Temple 1970, bencher of the Inner Temple 1990; recorder 1993– (asst recorder 1987–93); Ordnance Survey 1960–61, Meridian Airmaps Ltd 1961–62, commercial artist, designer, copywriter 1962–67; ACIArb 2000; *Recreations* people, places, art, music, transport; *Style—* Nicholas Wood, Esq; ✉ 5 Paper Buildings, Temple, London EC4Y 7HB (tel 020 7815 3200, fax 020 7815 3201, e-mail clerks@5paper.com and nw5pb@aol.com)

WOOD, Prof Nicholas William; s of William Wood; *Educ* Univ of Birmingham (MB ChB), Univ of Cambridge (PhD); *Career* Inst of Neurology: formerly sr lectr then reader, currently prof of clinical neurology; hon conslt physician Nat Hosp for Neurology and Neurosurgery; memb Med Advsy Panel: Parkinson's Disease Soc, Progressive Supra-Nuclear Palsy (Europe) Soc, Huntington's Disease Assoc, Neurofibromatosis Soc; FRCP 2000 (MRCP 1989), FMedSci 2004; *Publications* author of numerous peer-reviewed articles in the field of neurogenetics; *Style—* Prof Nicholas Wood; ✉ Institute of Neurology, Queen Square, London WC1N 3BG (tel 020 7837 3611, fax 020 7278 5616)

WOOD, Robin Lee Knoyle; s of Wilfred Knoyle Wood (d 1973), and Marylee Wood (d 1985); *b* 1 June 1950, Trowbridge, Wilts; *Educ* Lincoln Sch, US Int Univ Cal Western San Diego (int scholar, BA), UCL (research scholar, MSc); *m* 1 March 1975, Olympia Alice, *née* Ramirez; 2 da (Emily Alice b 20 Nov 1979, Lora Marylee b 22 Jan 1986); *Career* ed Marshall Cavendish 1974–80; HarperCollins: ed 1980–90, publishing dir Leisure Books 1990–93, md Gen Refererence Div 1993–95, md Gen Reference and Collins Dictionaries Divs 1995–97, memb UK Exec Bd; md Adult Div Dorling Kindersley 1997–2000, publisher BBC Books BBC Worldwide Ltd 2000–04, freelance conslt 2004–05, chief exec Chrysalis Books Gp plc 2005, chm and chief exec Anova Books Gp Ltd 2005–; non-exec dir Third Millennium Information Ltd 2005–; *Clubs* Two Brydges; *Style—* Robin Wood, Esq; ✉ Anova Books Group Ltd, The Old Magistrates Court, 10 Southcombe Street, London W14 0RA (tel 020 7314 1400)

WOOD, Hon Mr Justice; Sir Roderic Lionel James Wood; kt (2004); s of Lionel James Wood (d 1969), and Marjorie, *née* Thompson; *b* 8 March 1951; *Educ* Nottingham HS, Lincoln Coll Oxford (MA); *Career* called to the Bar Middle Temple 1974 (bencher 2001); QC 1993, recorder 1997–2002 (asst recorder 1994–97), circuit judge (SE Circuit) 2002–04, judge of the High Court of Justice (Family Div) 2004–; jt chm Barristers Clerks Liaison Ctee 1994–95; chm Bar Professional Conduct Ctee 1999–2000 (vice-chm 1997–98), vice-chm Family Legal Aid and Fees Ctee 1995–98; memb: Family Law Bar Assoc 1988–2002, Bar Cncl 1993–95; memb Editorial Bd Longman Practitioner's Child Law Bulletin 1993–94; *Recreations* music, theatre, travel; *Style—* The Hon Mr Justice Wood

WOOD, Roger Nicholas Brownlow; s of Reginald Laurence Charles and Jean Olive Wood; *b* 21 July 1942; *Educ* Sherborne, Northwestern Univ USA; *m* 1966, Julia Ellen, *née* Mallows; 2 da; *Career* with ICL UK Ltd 1962–89 (dir 1987–89), md STC Telecoms Ltd

1989–91, gp vice-pres NT Europe SA 1991–93; md: Northern Telecom UK Ltd 1991–93, Matra Marconi Space UK Ltd 1993–96, Automobile Assoc 2002–04; dir: Centrica plc 1996–2004, Radiotronica Espagna Spa 1991–93, Inst of Adavanced Motorists 2003, Paypoint plc 2004–, Reliance plc 2006–; memb: Parly Space Ctee 1993–96, UK Industry Space Ctee 1993–96, IOD; FIMgt 1984, FBCS 1991; *Recreations* music, Provençe, aviation, skiing; *Clubs* Molesey Boat; *Style*— Roger Wood, Esq; ✉ Ryemead House, Sunbury TW16 5PR

WOOD, Roger Norman Alexander; s of Adrian Theodore Wood (d 1992), of Bristol, and Doreen Mary, *née* Gordon-Harris; *b* 13 September 1947; *Educ* The Leys Sch Cambridge, Univ of Bristol (BSc); *m* 1971, Mary Thomasine Howard, da of Howard Reginald Thomas; 1 s (Alexander b 1973), 2 da (Emily b 1975, Joanna b 1976); *Career* Guthrie Corp Ltd 1972–81, United City Merchants plc 1981–86, Burmah Castrol plc 1986–91, George Wimpey plc 1991–94, Automotive Products Group Ltd 1995–96, dir Wineworld London plc 1997–, 100 Gp of Finance Directors 1986–94; chm Leybourne Securities Ltd 1986–; non-exec chm: Gartmore Monthly Income Trust plc 1993–2002, Premier Asset Mgmnt plc 2001–, Gartmore Distribution Tst plc 2002–; non-exec dir: Gartmore Value Investments plc 1990–93, Mid Kent Holdings plc 1996–2001, Fundamental Data Ltd 2000–; govr Cheltenham Ladies' Coll; Liveryman Worshipful Co of Chartered Accountants; FCA; *Clubs* Oriental, West Hill Golf, Tanglin, Seremban Int Golf; *Style*— Roger Wood, Esq; ✉ High Leybourne, Hascombe, Godalming, Surrey GU8 4AD (tel 01483 208559, mobile 07778 213337, e-mail roger.leybourne@btinternet.com)

WOOD, Ronald (Ronnie); *b* 1 June 1947; *m* 1; 1 s (Jesse); m 2, 2 Jan 1985, Jo Howard; 1 s (Tyrone b 1983), 1 da (Leah b 1978); *Career* guitarist; played: bass guitar in The Jeff Beck Group 1968–69, guitar in The Faces 1969–75, The Rolling Stones 1975–; has played with: Bo Diddley (toured as The Gunslingers), Rod Stewart (with The Faces), Muddy Waters, Jerry Lee Lewis and others; albums with Jeff Beck Gp: Truth (1968), Beck-Ola (1969, reached UK no 39); albums with The Faces: First Step (1970, UK no 45), Long Player (1971, UK no 31), A Nod's As Good As A Wink...To A Blind Horse (1971, UK no 2), Ooh La La (1973, UK no 1), Coast To Coast Overtures And Beginners (live, 1974, UK no 3); signed solo record contract with CBS Records 1978; albums with The Rolling Stones: Black And Blue (1976, UK no 2), Love You Live (live, 1977, UK no 3), Some Girls (1978, UK no 2), Emotional Rescue (1980, UK no 1), Tattoo You (1981, UK no 2), Still Life (American Concert 1981) (1982, UK no 4), Undercover (1983, UK no 3), Rewind 1971–1984 (compilation, 1984, UK no 23), Dirty Work (1986, UK no 4), Steel Wheels (1989, UK no 2), Flashpoint (live, 1991, UK no 6), Voodoo Lounge (1994, UK no 1), Bridges to Babylon (1997, UK no 6), No Security (1998), Forty Licks (2002); solo albums incl: Slide On This (1992); concert films: Let's Spend the Night Together (dir Hal Ashby) 1983, Flashpoint (film of 1991 Steel Wheels Tour) 1991; *Style*— Ronnie Wood, Esq; ✉ c/o Monroe Sounds, 5 Church Row, Wandsworth Plain, London SW18 1ES

WOOD, Simon Richard Browne; s of Lt-Col Browne William Wood (d 1997), and Joan Radegunde, *née* Woollcombe (d 1998); *b* 12 December 1947; *Educ* Eton; *m* 17 July 1970, Clare Launa, da of Lord Martin Fitzalan Howard (d 2003), of Brockfield Hall, York; 1 s (Charles b 1973), 2 da (Alethea b 1975, Miranda b 1978); *Career* ptnr Sheppards and Chase 1975–80, dir Cater Allen Holdings plc 1981–98, md Cater Allen Ltd 1981–98; *Recreations* shooting, fishing; *Style*— Simon R B Wood, Esq; ✉ Brockfield Hall, Warthill, York YO19 5XJ (tel 01904 489362)

WOOD, Timothy John Rogerson; *b* 13 August 1940; *Educ* King James's GS Knaresborough, Univ of Manchester; *m* 1969, Elizabeth Mary Spencer; 1 s, 1 da; *Career* former project mangr ICL Ltd, MP (Cons) Stevenage 1983–97; PPS to: Rt Hon John Stanley as Min for Armed Forces 1986–87, Min of State for NI 1987–88, Rt Hon Ian Stewart as Min of State for NI 1988–89, Rt Hon Peter Brooke as Sec of State for NI 1989–90; asst Govt whip 1990–92, Lord Cmmr of the Treasury (Govt whip) 1992–95; comptroller HM's Household 1995–97; memb Bow Gp 1962–, chm Wokingham Cons Assoc 1980–83, vice-chm Thames Valley Euro Constituency Cncl 1979–83; pres Bracknell Cons Assoc 1998–2003; memb: Bracknell DC 1975–83 (ldr 1976–78), Bracknell Devpt Corpn 1977–82; chm Autotronics plc 1998–2000; govr: The Princess Helena Coll 2000– (vice-chm 2005–), Littleham Sch 2004– (chm 2005–); *Publications* Bow Gp pamphlets on educn, computers in Britain and the Post Office; *Clubs* Carlton; *Style*— Timothy Wood, Esq

WOOD, (René) Victor; s of Frederick Wood (d 1973); *b* 4 October 1925; *Educ* Jesus Coll Oxford; *m* 1950, Helen Morag, *née* Stewart; *Career* chief exec Hill Samuel Insurance and Shipping Holdings Ltd 1969–79 (and chm 1974–79), chm Lifeguard Assurance 1976–84; dir: Haslemere Estates plc 1976–86, Coalite Group plc 1977–89, Colbourne Insurance Co Ltd 1980–90, Wemyss Devpt Co Ltd 1982–2006, Criterion Insurance Co Ltd 1984–90, Scottinvest SA 1985–95, Wemyss Hotels France SA 1985–95, Domaine de Rimauresq SARL 1985–2006, Sun Life Corp plc 1986–96, Worldwide and General Investment Co 1992–; vice-pres Br Insurance Brokers' Assoc 1981–84; FFA 1954; *Books* with Michael Pilch: Pension Schemes (1960 and 1979), New Trends in Pensions (1964), Pension Scheme Practice (1967), Company Pension Schemes (1971), Managing Pension Schemes (1974); *Style*— Victor Wood, Esq; ✉ Little Woodbury, Newchapel, Lingfield, Surrey RH7 6HR (tel 01342 832054)

WOOD, Victoria; OBE (1997); da of Stanley Wood, of Bury, Lancs, and Helen, *née* Mape; *b* 19 May 1953; *Educ* Bury GS, Univ of Birmingham (BA); *Children* 1 da (Grace b 1988), 1 s (Henry b 1992); *Career* entertainer and writer; Variety Club BBC Personality of the Year 1987, Br Comedy Award for Top Female Comedy Performer 1995, Br Acad of Composers and Songwriters Gold Badge of Merit 2002, BAFTA Lifetime Achievement Award 2005; Hon DLitt: Lancaster 1989, Sunderland 1993, Bolton 1995, Birmingham 1996, Manchester 2002; Hon MSc UMIST 1998 *Theatre* stage debut Talent at Crucible Theatre Sheffield 1978 (TV prodn of this won 3 Nat Drama Awards 1980); stage revues: Funny Turns (Duchess) 1982, Lucky Bag (Ambassadors) 1985, Victoria Wood (Palladium) 1987), Victoria Wood Up West 1990, Victoria Wood (Royal Albert Hall) 1996, Victoria Wood at it Again (tour) 2001–02 (Comedy Awards Best Standup 2001); stage musicals: Good Fun 1980, Acorn Antiques - The Musical (Theatre Royal Haymarket) 2005 and (nat tour) 2006; *Television* Wood and Walters 1981–82, Victoria Wood As Seen on TV 1985 (Broadcasting Press Guilds Award, BAFTA Award), Victoria Wood As Seen on TV 2nd series 1986 (BAFTA Award), Victoria Wood As Seen on TV special 1987 (BAFTA Award), An Audience with Victoria Wood 1988 (BAFTA Award), Victoria Wood 1989, Victoria Wood's All Day Breakfast 1993 (Writer's Guild Award), Victoria Wood Live in Your Own Home 1994, dinnerladies 1998 (Montreux Prix de Presse 1999), dinnerladies 2nd series 1999 (Comedy Awards Best Comedy Series 2000, Comedy Awards Writer of the Year 2000), Victoria Wood with all the Trimmings 2000, Victoria Wood's Big Fat Documentary 2004, Moonwalking 2004, Housewife 49 2006 (BAFTA Award, RTS Single Drama Award 2007), Victoria's Empire (2007); TV plays: Talent 1979, Nearly A Happy Ending 1980, Happy Since I Met You 1981, Pat and Margaret 1994; *Film* The League of Gentlemen's Apocalypse 2005; *Books* Lucky Bag: The Victoria Wood Song Book (1985), Up To You Porky: The Victoria Wood Sketch Book (1986), Barmy: The 2nd Victoria Wood Sketch Book (1987), Mens Sana in Thingummy Doo-Dah (1990), Pat and Margaret (1994), Victoria Wood Live in Your Own Front Room (1994); *Recreations* walking; *Style*— Miss Victoria Wood, OBE; ✉ c/o McIntyre Management, 35 Soho Square, London W1D 3QX

WOOD, William James; QC (1998); s of late Sir Frank Wood, KBE, CB, and Lady Wood, *née* Wilson; *Educ* Dulwich Coll, Worcester Coll Oxford (BA, BCL), Harvard Law Sch (Kennedy scholar, LLM); *m* 1986, Tonya Mary, *née* Pinsent; *Career* called to the Bar 1980, memb Bar Tonga 2000; accredited mediator 1999; *Recreations* skiing, tennis, fishing; *Style*— William Wood, Esq, QC; ✉ Brick Court Chambers, 7–8 Essex Street, London WC2R 3LD (tel 020 7379 3550, fax 020 7379 3558)

WOOD, William Jeremy (Jerry); s of Maj Peter Alexander Wood, RA, of Budleigh Salterton, Devon, and Gwendoline Marion, *née* Hebron; *b* 2 June 1947; *Educ* Liverpool Coll, Univ of Manchester (BSc); *m* 17 March 1973, Judienne, da of Anthony Bridgett, of London; 1 da (Alexis (Lekki) b 1981); *Career* Euro prod mktg mangr Avon Overseas Ltd 1973–79, conslt PE Consulting Group 1979–82, Euro strategic mktg dir Schering Plough Corporation 1983–85, bd dir Bell Pottinger Financial Ltd (formerly Lowe Bell Financial Ltd) 1986–99, md Bell Pottinger First Financial 1996–2002, bd dir Bell Pottinger Communications 2000–02, mktg and communications conslt 2002–; dir C R Media Ltd; dir: Inst of Certified Book-keepers (ICB), ICB Int; *Recreations* golf, skiing, travel; *Clubs* RAC; *Style*— Jerry Wood, Esq; ✉ Hornbeam, 19 Pelhams Walk, Esher, Surrey KT10 8QA (tel and fax 01372 467277, e-mail wjw@uk2.net)

WOOD, His Hon Judge William Rowley; QC (1997); s of Dr B S B Wood, of Lymington, Hants, and Mrs E C Wood; *b* 22 March 1948; *Educ* Bradfield, Univ of Oxford; *m* 22 Sept 1975, Angela, *née* Beatson Hird; 1 s (Sam b 11 May 1977), 2 da (Alice b 3 Sept 1979, Lucy b 23 Nov 1982); *Career* called to the Bar Gray's Inn 1970, recorder of the Crown Court, circuit judge (Midland Circuit) 2002–; head of Chancery and Commercial Gp, chm Birmingham Diocesan Advsy Ctee, memb Official Referees' Bar Assoc; *Recreations* skiing, sailing, tennis, literature; *Style*— His Hon Judge Wood, QC; ✉ 5 Fountain Court, Steelhouse Lane, Birmingham B4 6DR (tel 0121 606 0500, fax 0121 606 1501)

WOODALL, David; s of Walker Woodall (d 1960), of Knottingley, and Maud, *née* Robinson (d 1966); *b* 15 April 1950; *Educ* Batley HS, Wakefield Sch of Art, Dip Advtg; *Career* formerly: illustrator Sharps Bradford, dir own co Scarborough, art dir Saatchi and Saatchi; currently a creative dir J Walter Thompson; winner: 2 Silvers Cannes Film Festival, 2 Silvers Br TV Awards, 3 Silvers D&AD Br Poster Awards, 2 Silvers Creative Circle Awards, 1 Silver and 1 Gold Euro Awards, Irish Film Festival Grand Prix Award, 1 Silver (and 1 nomination) D&AD; memb D&AD; *Recreations* windsurfing, running, painting; *Clubs* Barbican, Morton's; *Style*— David Woodall, Esq

WOODALL, Pamela Diane; da of Ronald Albert Woodall, and Margaret, *née* Williams (d 1989); *b* 21 June 1954; *Educ* Solihull HS for Girls, Univ of Manchester (BA), LSE (MSc); *Career* Govt Econ Serv 1975–79, head of statistics The Economist 1979–83, economist Bank of America 1983–85, economics ed The Economist 1993– (economics corr 1985–93); Wincott Fndn Award for sr financial journalist (jtly) 2006, Best Economic Journalist Business Journalist of the Year Awards 2006, Rybeynski Prize (jtly) Soc of Business Economists 2006; *Recreations* skiing, mountain hiking, gardening; *Style*— Ms Pam Woodall; ✉ The Economist, 25 St James's Street, London SW1A 1HG (tel 020 7830 7050, e-mail pamwoodall@economist.com)

WOODBRIDGE, Dr Anthony Rivers; s of John Nicholas Woodbridge (d 1991), and Patricia Madeleine, *née* Rebbeck (d 1996); *b* 10 August 1942; *Educ* Stowe, Trinity Hall Cambridge (MA); *m* 29 Sept 1976, Lynda Anne, da of Charles Henry Nolan (d 1992); 1 s (Christian b 30 March 1978); *Career* admitted slr 1967; ptnr Woodbridge & Sons Uxbridge 1969, sr ptnr Turberville Woodbridge Uxbridge 1983–97, sr ptnr The Woodbridge Partnership 1997–; co sec: Abbeyfield Uxbridge Soc Ltd 1974–96 (vice-chm 1996–98), Burr Brown International Ltd 1992–96; admin Uxbridge Duty Slr Scheme 1983–91, clerk Cmmrs Income Tax 1985–; govr Fulmer Sch Bucks 1984–2003 (chm of govrs 1988–96), memb Hillingdon Health Authy 1990–92; chm: Hillingdon Community Health NHS Tst 1992–94, Harrow and Hillingdon Healthcare NHS Tst 1994–2001, Stoke Mandeville Hosp NHS Tst 2001–02, Hillingdon Hosp NHS Tst 2002–05; tstee Hillingdon Partnership Tst 1995–2003; hon slr: Hilllingdon Samaritans 1973 (now hon legal advsr), Age Concern Hillingdon 1989–; memb Ct Brunel Univ 1995– (now life memb); memb Law Soc 1967; Hon DUniv Brunel Univ 2000; FInstD 1999–; *Recreations* walking, cycling, touring; *Clubs* Denham Golf; *Style*— Dr Anthony Woodbridge; ✉ 4 Braid Gardens, Bull Lane, Gerrards Cross, Buckinghamshire SL9 8RA (tel 01753 885442); The Woodbridge Partnership, Windsor House, 42 Windsor Street, Uxbridge, Middlesex UB8 1AB (tel 01895 454801, fax 01895 454848, e-mail tonywoodbridge@hotmail.com)

WOODBURN, Christopher Hugh; *b* 6 November 1947; *Educ* St John's Sch Leatherhead; *m* Lesley Avril; 2 da; *Career* with Deloitte & Co (now part of PricewaterhouseCoopers) 1966–74, policy advsr LSE 1974–87; The Securities Assoc Ltd: exec dir and dep dir of surveillance 1988–90, dep chief exec 1990–91; SFA: exec dir of Ops 1991–95 and 1997, exec dir of Fin Risk 1995–96, chief exec 1997–99; chief exec General Insurance Standards Cncl 1999–; FCA; *Recreations* sailing, history; *Style*— Christopher Woodburn, Esq

WOODCOCK, Anthony Douglas Henry; s of Douglas Henry Woodcock (d 1982), and Doreen, *née* Wade; *b* 22 November 1951; *Educ* Brecon Boys GS, Univ Coll Cardiff (BMus); *m* 26 June 1981, Virginia, da of Ralph Harrison; 1 s (Thomas b 20 May 1983); *Career* music offr Welsh Arts Cncl 1974–77, asst dir South East Arts 1977–84, gen mangr City of London Sinfonia 1984–86, gen mangr St David's Hall Cardiff 1986–88, chief exec Royal Liverpool Philharmonic Soc 1988–91, md Bournemouth Orchestras 1991–98, pres Oregon Symphony 1998–2003, pres Minnesota Orchestra 2003–; memb Music Ctee Welsh Arts Cncl, memb cmmnd team (for Welsh Arts Cncl) to review BBC Welsh Symphony Orch; former dir Assoc of Br Orchs, former chm and sec Music Offrs Gp Regnl Arts Assoc, former chm cmmnd team (for Scottish Arts Cncl) to review work of Royal Scottish Orch, former artistic dir Swansea Festival; *Recreations* tennis, squash, cycling; *Clubs* Royal Over-Seas League; *Style*— Anthony Woodcock, Esq; ✉ Minnesota Orchestra, Orchestra Hall, 1111 Nicollet Mall, Minneapolis, MN 55403, USA

WOODCOCK, Prof Ashley; OBE (2006); s of Arthur Woodcock, of Stoke-on-Trent, Staffs, and Vera, *née* Jones (d 1973); *b* 13 April 1951; *Educ* Univ of Manchester (BSc, MB ChB, MD); *m* 3 Aug 1974, Fiona Marilyn, da of Raymond Griffiths, of Gwaun-Cae Gurwen, Dyfed; 1 da (Hannah Vera b 1982), 2 s (Daniel Ashley b 1984, (Benjamin) George b 1986); *Career* specialist physician Gen Hosp Bandar-Seri-Begawan Brunei 1977–79; jr dr Brompton Hosp, Nat Heart Hosp, Hammersmith Hosp and St James Hosp 1979–86, conslt physician Manchester Royal Infirmary 1986–88, conslt physician and dir Regnl Lung Function Laboratory 1988–, prof of respiratory med Univ of Manchester 1999–, head Respiratory Research Gp Hosp of S Manchester; Clinical Section chm European Respiratory Soc; chair Montreal Protocol Medical Technical Options Ctee; FRCP 1992 (MRCP 1977); *Recreations* golf, dog-walking; *Clubs* Hale Golf; *Style*— Prof Ashley Woodcock, OBE; ✉ North West Lung Centre, Wythenshawe Hospital, Southmoor Road, Manchester M23 9LT (tel 0161 291 5873)

WOODCOCK, Sir John; kt (1989), CBE (1983), QPM (1976); s of Joseph Woodcock (d 1967), and Elizabeth May, *née* Whiteside (d 1982); *b* 14 January 1932; *Educ* Preston Tech Coll; *m* 4 April 1953, Kathleen Margaret, da of John Abbott; 2 s (Clive John b 1954, Aidan Edward b 1956), 1 da (Karen Belinda b 1962); *Career* police cadet Lancs Constabulary 1947–50, Army Special Investigation Branch 1950–52, Constable to Chief Inspr Lancs Constabulary 1952–65, Supt and Chief Supt Beds and Luton Constabulary 1965–68, Asst Chief Constable Gwent 1968–70; Dep Chief Constable: Gwent 1970–74, Devon & Cornwall 1974–78; Chief Constable: N Yorks Police 1978–79, S Wales Constabulary 1979–83; HM Inspr of Constabulary 1983–90, HM Chief Inspr of Constabulary 1990–93; author Woodcock Report - Escapes from Whitemoor Prison 1994; Intermediate Cmd Course Police Coll 1965, Sr Cmd Course 1968, Study Bavarian Police 1977, Euro Discussion Centre 1977; lectr: Int Police Course Sicily and Rome 1978, FBI Nat Exec Washington 1981, Denmark 1983, Salt Lake City UT 1986 and Sun Valley ID 1988 and 1992, Arnhem

Netherlands 1990; study of Royal Hong Kong Police 1989; pres Police Mutual Assurance Soc 1990–94; advsr and memb UK Atomic Energy Police Authy 1993–99; vice-pres Welsh Assoc of Youth Clubs 1981–87; chm Wales Ctee Royal Jubilee and Prince's Tst 1983–85; memb: Admin Cncl Royal Jubilee Tsts 1981–85, Prince's Tst Ctee for Wales 1981–84, Governing Bd World Coll of the Atlantic 1980–84; non-exec dir and sr non-exec dir Capital Corp plc London 1994–99, advsr Control Risks Gp Ltd 1994–2002, memb and advsr MOD Police Ctee 1995–2001; hon memb Swansea Lions; St John Cncl: N Yorks, S Glam, Mid Glam (chm), Hereford and Worcs 1978–90; Freeman City of London 1993; CCMI (CIMgt 1980), FRSA 1995; CStJ 1993 (OStJ 1981); Papal knighthood (KSG) 1984; *Recreations* table tennis, badminton, golf, walking, horticulture; *Clubs* Droitwich Golf, Merlin Golf (Cornwall); *Style—* Sir John Woodcock, CBE, QPM

WOODCOCK, John Charles; OBE (1996); s of Rev Parry John Woodcock (d 1938), and Norah Mabel, *née* Hutchinson (d 1966); *b* 7 August 1926; *Educ* Dragon Sch Oxford, St Edward's Sch Oxford, Trinity Coll Oxford (MA); *Career* Manchester Guardian 1952–54; cricket writer for: The Times 1954–, Country Life 1962–91; ed Wisden Cricketers' Almanack 1980–86; covered 40 Test Tours since 1950 incl: Australia (17 times), South Africa, West Indies, NZ, India, Pakistan; memb Ctee MCC 1988–91 and 1993–95 (tstee 1996–99, hon life vice-pres 2001), pres Cricket Writers' Club 1986–2003; patron of the living of Longparish Hants; Br Press Awards Sportswriter of the Year 1987; *Books* The Ashes (1956), Barclays World of Cricket (with E W Swanton 1980, assoc ed 2 edn, conslt ed 3 edn 1986), The Times One Hundred Greatest Cricketers (1998), Hockey for Oxford versus Cambridge (1946 and 1947); *Recreations* golf, country pursuits; *Clubs* Vincent's (Oxford), St Enodoc Golf, MCC, Hampshire CCC (hon life memb), Surrey CCC (hon life memb), Arabs, Free Foresters, Cryptics, Oxford Authentics, Oxford Harlequins, I Zingari; *Style—* John Woodcock, Esq, OBE; ✉ The Old Curacy, Longparish, Andover, Hampshire SP11 6PB (tel 01264 720259)

WOODCOCK, Nigel; s of Barry Woodcock, of Chesterfield, Derbys, and Monica Ann, *née* Redfern; *b* 17 June 1958; *Educ* Chesterfield Sch, Leamington Coll, QMC London (BSc(Econ)), London Business Sch, Warwick Business Sch, Harvard Business Sch; *m* Anneliese, *née* Roughton-Skelton; 2 da (Jane b 11 Aug 1980, Catherine b 18 Sept 1993), 2 s (Thomas b 27 June 1985, Robert b 21 June 1988); *Career* national NHS admin trainee NE Thames RHA 1980–81, asst hosp administrator The London Hosp Mile End 1982, asst hosp administrator Whittington Hosp Islington 1983, dep hosp sec The London Hosp Whitechapel 1986 (asst hosp sec 1983–85), dir of facilities N Herts HA 1986–88, unit gen mangr Lister Hosp Stevenage (N Herts HA) 1988–90; chief exec: W Cumbria Health Care NHS Tst 1993–2000 (unit gen mangr under W Cumbria HA 1990–92), (actg chief exec) N Lakeland Healthcare NHS Tst 2000–01, N Cumbria Mental Health and Learning Disabilities NHS Tst 2001–03, N Cumbria PCT 2003–06, NHS NW 2007–; *Recreations* cricket, soccer, current affairs; *Style—* Nigel Woodcock, Esq; ✉ e-mail nigel@thewoodcocks.co.uk

WOODCOCK, Thomas; LVO (1996), DL (2005); s of Thomas Woodcock (d 1999), and Mary, *née* Woodcock (d 2006); *b* 20 May 1951; *Educ* Eton, Univ of Durham (BA), Darwin Coll Cambridge (LLB); *m* 11 July 1998, Lucinda Mary Harmsworth King; *Career* called to the Bar Inner Temple 1975; Rouge Croix Pursuivant 1978–82, Somerset Herald of Arms 1982–97, Norroy and Ulster King of Arms 1997–; advsr on naval heraldry 1996–; FSA; *Books* Oxford Guide to Heraldry (with John Martin Robinson, 1988), Dictionary of British Arms Medieval Ordinary (Vol I, ed with D H B Chesshyre, 1992, Vol II, ed with Hon Janet Grant and Ian Graham, 1996), Heraldry in National Trust Houses (with John Martin Robinson, 2000); *Clubs* Travellers; *Style—* Thomas Woodcock, Esq, LVO, DL, FSA; ✉ College of Arms, Queen Victoria Street, London EC4V 4BT (tel and fax 020 7236 3634)

WOODCRAFT, Tess; da of Alf Woodcraft (d 1981), and Peggy Woodcraft (now Mrs Perry); *b* 17 June 1948, Chelmsford, Essex; *Educ* Chelmsford Co HS, Univ of Leeds (LLB); *m* 3 June 2005, Alan Fountain; 1 s (Jack Woodcraft b 28 Feb 1980), 1 da (Billie Woodcraft b 23 July 1984); *Career* equalities offr NALGO 1978–87, journalist BBC and Channel 4 1987–89, chief exec Kids Club Network 1989–93, head of communication Islington Cncl 1993–94, dir Centre for Strategy and Communication 1995–; cmmr: Equal Opportunities Cmmn 1999–2005, Charity Cmmn for England and Wales 2005–; *Style—* Ms Tess Woodcraft; ✉ Charity Commission for England and Wales, Harmsworth House, 13–15 Bouverie Street, London EC4Y 8DP (tel 0870 333 0123, fax 020 7674 2300)

WOODFORD, Kevin; s of Arthur Woodford (decd), and Beryl Woodford (decd); *b* 4 June 1950, Isle of Man; *Educ* Douglas HS, Isle of Man Coll of HE (Professional Chef's Dip), Clarendon Coll Nottingham (MHCIMA), Univ of Leeds (CertEd), Univ of Hull (BA); *m* Jean, da of Ronald Mulligan; 1 s (Steve), 1 da (Janine); *Career* chef: Dorchester Hotel London, Hotel Georges V Paris; lectr: North Lindsay Coll Scunthorpe, Clarendon Coll Nottingham; sr lectr Scarborough Tech Coll, head of hotel and catering studies Granville Coll Sheffield, examiner CGLI, int judge Salon Culinaire; co-owner Clinch's Restaurants (IOM) Ltd: The Waterfront, Blazers, The Anchor; set of stamps issued by IOM depicting work (approved by HM The Queen), Best Day Time TV Presenter Nat TV Awards 1999, subject of This is Your Life 2001; played The Baron in Cinderella High Wycombe 2002; *Television* presenter ITV: Surprise Chefs, Reality Bites; presenter BBC: Fasten Your Seatbelts, Can't Cook, Won't Cook, Songs of Praise, Ready Steady Cook, Heaven and Earth, Summer Holiday, Holiday, Planet Cook (and co-prodr); acting roles incl: Hollyoaks, Doctors; *Publications* The Reluctant Cook, The Flying Cook, Ready Steady Cook, Can't Cook, Won't Cook, Kevin's Favourite Holiday Recipes, Surprise Chefs, Big Kevin, Little Kevin, Bazaar; *Recreations* golf; *Clubs* Los Arqueros Golf (Marbella); *Style—* Kevin Woodford, Esq; ✉ c/o tel 07779 091704, e-mail jean@kevinwoodford.com

WOODFORD, Peggy Elizabeth Lainé (Mrs Aylen); da of Ronald Curtis Woodford, OBE (d 1970), and Ruth Mahy, *née* Lainé (d 1987); *b* 19 September 1937; *Educ* Guernsey Ladies' Coll, St Anne's Coll Oxford (MA); *m* 1 April 1967, Walter Stafford Aylen, QC, *qv*, s of Rt Rev Charles Arthur William Aylen (d 1972); 3 da (Alison b 1968, Frances b 1970, Imogen b 1974); *Career* writer; Italian govt res scholar Rome 1960–61, script and res asst BBC TV 1962–63, sr tutor Sixth Form Coll Reading 1964–67; memb Soc of Authors, memb RSL; *Books* incl: Abraham's Legacy (1963), Mozart (1964), Schubert (1969), Please Don't Go (1972), Backwater War (1975), The Real Thing (1977), Rise of the Raj (1978), See You Tomorrow (1979), You Can't Keep Out the Darkness (1980), The Girl with a Voice (1981), Love Me Love Rome (1984), Misfits (1984), Monster in our Midst (1988), Out of the Sun (1990), Blood and Mortar (1994), Cupid's Tears (1995), On the Night (1996), Jane's Story (1998), One Son is Enough (2006); *Style—* Miss Peggy Woodford; ✉ 24 Fairmount Road, London SW2 2BL (tel 020 8671 7301, fax 0870 131 8529); Literary Agent: Laura Morris, 21 Highshore Road, London SE1 5AH (tel 020 7732 0153)

WOODFORD, Dr (Frederick) Peter; s of Wilfrid Charles Woodford (d 1931), and Mabel Rose, *née* Scarff (d 1970); *b* 8 November 1930; *Educ* The Lewis Sch Pengam (head boy), Balliol Coll Oxford (Domus exhibitioner, MA), Univ of Leeds (PhD); *m* 18 Dec 1964, Susan, da of E A Silberman (d 1969); 1 da (Julia Jacqueline b 21 Nov 1969); *Career* RAF 1956–57 (pilot offr, flying offr); res fell Leiden Univ 1958–62, visiting scientist and lectr Univ of Tennessee Medical Sch and NIH USA 1962–63, guest investigator Rockefeller Univ NY 1963–71, scientific historian Ciba Fndn and scientific assoc Wellcome Tst 1971–74, exec dir Inst for Res into Mental and Multiple Handicap 1974–77, PSO (Clinical Chemistry) DHSS 1977–84, chief scientific offr Dept of Health 1984–93, distinguished visitor and hon sr lectr Royal Free Hosp Sch of Med 1994–; managing/exec ed: Jl of Atherosclerosis Res 1960–62, Jl of Lipid Res 1963–69, Proceedings of Nat Acad of Scis USA 1970–71; scientific ed Xth Int Symposium on Atherosclerosis (Montreal) 1994; ed Camden History Soc pubns 1995–; editorial sec Clinical Sciences Reviews Ctee (Assoc of Clinical Biochemists) 1995–2003; student govr City Literary Inst London 1999–2001; Hon DSc Univ of Salford 1993; FRCPath 1984, CChem, FRSC 1990, FBES 1993 (MBES 1991), fell Inst of Physics and Engrg in Med (FIPEM) 1995, fell Assoc of Clinical Biochemistry 2004; founding memb ARCP 2000; *Publications* Scientific Writing for Graduate Students (1969), Medical Research Systems in Europe (1973), The Ciba Foundation: An Analytic History (1974), Writing Scientific Papers in English (1975), Training Manual for Technicians in Physiological Measurement (1988), Training Manual for Technicians in Medical Physics (1989), Training Manual for Medical Laboratory Assistants (1991), First-Level and Advanced Training Manuals for Rehabilitation Engineering Technicians (1993), Atherosclerosis Vol 109 (ed, 1994), Atherosclerosis X (1995), From Primrose Hill to Euston Road (1995), Camden History Review Vols 19–27 (1995–2002), Oestrogen Replacement and the Menopause (1996), A Constant Vigil (100 years of the Heath and Old Hampstead Society) (1997), Streets of Bloomsbury and Fitzrovia (1997), East of Bloomsbury (1998), How to Teach Scientific Communication (1999), Streets of Old Holborn (1999), The Streets of Hampstead (3 edn, 2000), Streets of St Giles (2001), The Good Grave Guide to Fortune Green Cemetery (2000), Victorian Seven Dials (2001), Streets of St Pancras (2002), The Railways of Camden (2002), Streets of Camden Town (2003), History of St Pancras and Camden Festivals (2004), Streets of Kentish Town (2005), Wartime St Pancras (2006), Streets of Gospel Oak and West Kentish Town (2006), The Life and Times of the Brunswick, Bloomsbury (2006); *Recreations* playing chamber music (pianist, chm Hampstead Music Club 1996–99); *Style—* Dr F Peter Woodford; ✉ 1 Akenside Road, London NW3 5BS (tel 020 7435 2088, fax 020 7794 6695, e-mail drswoodford@blueyonder.co.uk)

WOODFORD, Stephen William John; s of John Wilfred Stephen Woodford, of Trowbridge, Wilts, and Barbara, *née* Wood; *b* 11 February 1959; *Educ* Tomlinscote Sch Frimley, City Univ (BScEcon); *m* 30 April 1988, Amelia Wylton, da of Wylton Dickson; 2 s (William Nicholas b 3 Aug 1989, Miles Wylton John b 31 July 1992), 2 da (Katherine Sophie Genevieve b 6 Aug 1997, Matilda Elizabeth b 28 Nov 2002); *Career* grad trainee Nestle Co Ltd 1980–82, account mangr Lintas Advertising 1982–85, account dir Waldron Allen Henry & Thompson 1985–89, account dir rising to gp account dir WCRS 1989–91, dep md Leo Burnett 1991–94; WCRS: client servs dir 1994–95, md 1995–99, ceo 1999–; pres IPA 2003–05; chm of tstees Changing Faces; *Recreations* family, riding, running, tennis, swimming, the countryside, reading; *Style—* Stephen Woodford, Esq; ✉ WCRS, 5 Golden Square, London W1R 4BS (tel 020 7806 5000, fax 020 7806 5099)

WOODGATE, Antony John (Tony); s of Bartlett George Woodgate (d 2002), and Charlotte, *née* Woerz; *b* 11 May 1960, Melbourne, Aust; *Educ* Monash Univ Melbourne (BSc, LLB), Univ of Cambridge (LLM), Birkbeck Coll Univ of London; *m* 15 July 1995, Alison Coleman; 1 s (Michael b 10 July 1995), 1 da (Stephanie b 8 Aug 1998); *Career* admitted slr Victoria, Aust 1984, Eng and Wales 1989; Simmons and Simmons: joined 1986, ptnr 1991–, managing ptnr EC, Competition and Regulatory Dept 2003–; chm Slrs European Gp 1997–98; *Publications* PLC EC and UK Competition Law Manuals (contrib); *Recreations* hiking, swimming; *Style—* Tony Woodgate, Esq; ✉ Simmons & Simmons, CityPoint, One Ropemaker Street London EC2Y 9SS

WOODHEAD, Christopher Anthony (Chris); *b* 20 October 1946; *Educ* Univ of Bristol (BA, PGCE), Keele Univ (MA); *Career* English teacher Priory Sch Shrewsbury 1969–72, dep head of English Newent Sch 1972–74, head of English Gordano Sch 1974–76, tutor in English Univ of Oxford 1976–82, advsr in English 1982–84, chief advsr Shropshire LEA 1984–88; dep chief educn offr: Devon LEA 1988–90, Cornwall LEA 1990–91; chief exec: Nat Curriculum Cncl 1991–93 (dep chief exec 1991), School Curriculum and Assessment Authy 1993–94; HM's chief inspr of schs OFSTED 1994–2000; Sir Stanley Kalms chair of educn Univ of Buckingham 2001–; chm Cognita Schs 2004–; *Recreations* fell running, rock climbing, second-hand bookshops; *Style—* Mr Chris Woodhead; ✉ The University of Buckingham, Hunter Street, Buckingham MK18 1EG

WOODHEAD, David James; s of Frank Woodhead, of N Yorks, and Polly Woodhead (d 2003); *b* 9 November 1943; *Educ* Queen Elizabeth GS Wakefield, Univ of Leicester (BA); *m* 21 July 1974, Carole, da of Arthur Underwood (d 1986); 2 s (Richard James b 1976, William Alexander b 1979); *Career* journalist: educn corr Cambridge Evening News 1965–68, Sunday Telegraph 1968–75; chief press offr ILEA 1978–84 (press offr 1975–78), hon pres offr London Schs Symphony Orch 1975–84; nat dir Ind Schools Cncl Info Serv (formerly ISIS) 1985–2004; dep gen sec Ind Schs Cncl 1998–2004; public affrs and educnl PR conslt 2004–; fndr tstee Nat Youth Strings Acad 1995–; tstee: The Dresden Tst (fndr Dresden Scholars' Scheme 2001), Ct and Cncl Univ of Leicester 2000–, Advsy Devpt Bd The Rudolf Kempe Soc for Young Musicians 2000– (also tstee), Advsy Bd Global Educn Mgmnt Systems Ltd 2005–; govr: Battle Abbey Sch 1988–91, St John's Sch Leatherhead 1994– (vice-chm 2006–, chm Educn Ctee 2001–), Feltonfleet Prep Sch Cobham 1998–2001, City of London Sch for Girls 2002–06, Purcell Sch of Music 2004–; hon govr Wakefield GS Fndn 2004–; led UK representation at first int conf on private educn in China Beijing 1999; Medal of Honour Soc for Reconstruction of the Dresden Frauenkirche 2007; FRSA 1990; *Publications* Choosing Your Independent School (ed, annually 1985–99), Good Communications Guide (1989), The ISC Guide to Accredited Independent Schools (ed, annually 2000–04), Education in the UK (contrib, 2002); numerous articles; *Recreations* family, opera, classical music, books, German and Austrian history, travel; *Clubs* Royal Over-Seas League, St James's; *Style—* David Woodhead, Esq; ✉ 29 Randalls Road, Leatherhead, Surrey KT22 7TQ (tel 01372 373206)

WOODHEAD, (George) Melvyn Walker; s of George Wilson Woodhead (d 1999), of Wakefield, and Irene, *née* Walker (d 1987); *b* 11 July 1939, Wakefield, W Yorks; *Educ* Silcoates Sch Wakefield; *m* 24 Sept 1965, Susan, *née* Stevenson; 2 s (Mark Stephen b 22 July 1970, David Melvyn b 27 Feb 1976); *Career* Nat Serv 3/7 Queen's Own Hussars 1958–60; family haulage business 1960–62, sales negotiator Hepper & Sons 1962–64, asst to dir Evans of Leeds 1964–65, estab Woodhead Investments Ltd (property co) 1965; various local awards for refurbishment works; *Recreations* shooting, motoring, coin and art collecting; *Style—* Melvyn Woodhead, Esq; ✉ The Palms, 481 Barnsley Road, Sandal, Wakefield, West Yorkshire WF2 6BP (tel 01924 256294, fax 01924 256755); Woodhead Investments Limited, Woodhead House, 8–10 Providence Street, Wakefield WF1 3BG (01924 374720, fax 01924 291901)

WOODHEAD, Vice Adm Sir (Anthony) Peter; KCB (1992); s of Leslie Woodhead, and Nancy Woodhead; *b* 30 July 1939; *Educ* Leeds GS, Conway, BRNC Dartmouth; *m* 1964, Carol Woodhead; 1 s (Simon), 1 da (Emma (Mrs Jeremy Cave)); *Career* RN Seaman Offr, pilot 1962, aircraft carriers Borneo Campaign; CO HM Ships: Jupiter 1974, Rhyl 1975; NDC 1976, Naval Plans Div MOD 1977, CSO to Flag Offr Third Flotilla 1980, COS to FO cmdg Falklands Task Force 1982, Capt 4 Frigate Sqdn 1983, RCDS 1984, Dir Naval Ops 1985, CO HMS Illustrious 1986; Flag Offr: Flotilla Two 1988, Flotilla One 1989; Vice-Adm 1991; Dep SACLANT 1991–93; Prisons Ombudsman 1994–99; dep chm BMT 1996–, chm CRI 1999–; memb Security Vetting Appeals Panel 2000–; pres Marriage Resource 1994–2004, govr Aldro Sch 1996–; *Recreations* tennis, golf, lay reader; *Style—* Sir Peter Woodhead, KCB; ✉ Hove Club, 28 Forth Avenue, Hove BN3 2PJ

WOODHEAD, Robin George; s of Walter Henry Woodhead (d 1976), of Zimbabwe, and Gladys Catherine Woodhead, of Johannesburg, SA; *b* 28 April 1951; *Educ* Mount Pleasant Sch Salisbury Rhodesia, Univ Coll of Rhodesia and Nyasaland (LLB); *m* 28 June 1980 (m dis 1992), Mary Fitzgerald, da of Fergus Hamilton Allen, CB, of Berks; *Career* chm

International Petroleum Exchange of London Ltd, md Premier Man Ltd, dir E D & F Man International Ltd 1981–86; chm and chief exec National Investment Group plc and chief exec National Investment Holdings plc 1986–91, chief exec London Commodity Exchange 1992–97, md Sotheby's Europe 1997–98, chief exec Sotheby's Europe 1998–99, chief exec Sotheby's Europe & Asia 2000–06, chief exec Sotheby's Int 2006–; non-exec dir Hawkpoint Holdings Ltd 2004–; chm: Rambert Dance Company 1995–2000, Music Research Inst 1997–2000; govr South Bank Centre 2004–; memb Law Soc 1978; *Recreations* skiing, tennis, riding, contemporary art, Zululand farmer; *Style—* Robin Woodhead, Esq; ✉ Sotheby's, 34–35 New Bond Street, London W1A 2AA (tel 020 7293 5000, fax 020 7293 5969)

WOODHOUSE, Charles Frederick; CVO (1998), DL (2007); s of Wilfrid Meynell Woodhouse (d 1967), of Chester Row, London, and Margaret (Peggy), *née* Kahl; *b* 6 June 1941; *Educ* Marlborough, McGill Univ Montreal, Peterhouse Cambridge (BA); *m* 25 Jan 1969, Margaret Joan, da of Thomas Wheatcroft Cooper (d 1991), of Hulland Ward, Derbys; 2 da (Rachel b 11 Nov 1969, Philippa b 1 Nov 1971), 1 s (Timothy b 6 Dec 1973); *Career* admitted slr; ptnr Farrer & Co 1969–99 (conslt 1999–2001); slr to HRH The Duke of Edinburgh 1983–2001; legal advsr CCPR 1971–99; chm: The Cheviot Tst 1991–97, Rank Pension Plan Trustee Ltd 1992–2001; dir Santos USA Corp 1995–2002; hon legal advsr Cwlth Games Cncl for Eng 1983–2007, chm Sports Dispute Resolution Panel 1997–2007, pres Br Assoc for Sport and Law 1997–2000; chm Rural Regeneration Cumbria 2002–06, dir Lowther Castle and Gardens Tst, dir Cumbria Vision; tstee: LSA Charitable Tst, Yehudi Menuhin Meml Tst 1998–2002, Cumbria Community Fndn, Hospice at Home Carlisle and N Lakeland, Athletics Fndn; memb Royal Parks Review Gp 1993–96; pres Guildford CC 1989–2002, hon life vice-pres Surrey Championship; govr: St Bees Sch Cumbria, Nelson Thomlinson Sch Wigton; *Recreations* cricket, golf, gardens and trees; *Clubs* MCC, Oxford and Cambridge, Worplesdon Golf, Surrey CCC, Free Foresters, Hawks' (Cambridge), Silloth-on-Solway Golf; *Style—* Charles Woodhouse, Esq, CVO, DL; ✉ Quarry Hill House, Mealsgate, Cumbria CA7 1AE (tel 01697 371225, e-mail charles.woodhouse@ukgateway.net); 55 Chester Row, London SW1W 8JL (tel 020 7730 3354)

WOODHOUSE, Prof John Robert; s of Horace Woodhouse (d 1983), and Iris Evelyn, *née* Pewton; *b* 17 June 1937; *Educ* King Edward VI GS Stourbridge, Hertford Coll Oxford (MA, DLitt), Univ of Pisa, Univ of Wales (PhD); *m* 5 Aug 1967, Gaynor, *née* Mathias; *Career* Nat Serv RAF 1955–57; asst lectr in Italian Univ of Aberdeen 1961–62, Br Cncl scholar Scuola Normale Superiore Pisa 1962–63, asst lectr then lectr UCNW Bangor 1963–66, lectr then sr lectr Univ of Hull 1966–73; Univ of Oxford: lectr in Italian 1973–89, fell St Cross Coll 1973–84, lectr Jesus Coll 1973–89, lectr St Edmund Hall 1975–89, lectr Brasenose Coll 1976–89, fell Pembroke Coll 1984–89 (supernumerary fell 1991–), fell Magdalen Coll 1990–2001 (emeritus fell 2001–), Fiat Serena prof of Italian studies 1990–2001 (emeritus prof 2001–); corresponding fell: Accademia Letteraria dell'Arcadia 1982, Accademia della Crusca 1991, Commissione per i testi di lingua Bologna 1992; fell: Huntington Library Calif 1986, Newberry Library Chicago 1988; Old Dominion fndn fell Harvard Univ 1969–70, founding fell Centro Studi Dannunziani Pescara 1979, sr research fell Center for Medieval and Renaissance Studies UCLA 1985; memb: Exec Ctee Soc for Italian Studies 1979–85 and 1991–96, Exec Ctee Modern Humanities Res Assoc 1984–94 (hon life memb 1994, pres 2008), Exec Ctee Soc for Study of Medieval Languages and Literature 1998–2003; ed (Italian) Modern Language Review 1984–94, memb Editorial Bd Italian Studies Jl 1987–91; fndr chm Oxford Italian Assoc 1990; Serena Medal of the British Academy 2002; FRSA 1983, FBA 1995; Cavaliere Ufficiale al Merito della Repubblica Italiana 1991; *Books* incl: Italo Calvino - a reappraisal and an appreciation of the trilogy (1968), V Borghini 'Storia della nobiltà fiorentina' (ed, 1974), Baldesar Castiglione - a reassessment of the Cortegiano (1978), G D'Annunzio 'Alcyone' (ed, 1978), G Rossetti 'Lettere familiari' (jt ed, 1983), Idem 'Carteggi' (jt ed, Vol I 1984, Vol II 1988, Vol III 1992, Vol IV 1996, Vol V 2001, Vol VI 2006) The Languages of Literature in Renaissance Italy (jt ed, 1988), From Castiglione to Chesterfield: The Decline in the Courtier's Manual (1991), Dante and Governance (ed, 1997), Gabriele D'Annunzio, Defiant Archangel (1998), Gabriele D'Annunzio, Arcangelo ribelle (1999), Gabriele D'Annunzio tra Italia e Inghilterra (2003), Il Generale e il Comandante: Ceccherini e D'Annunzio a Fiume (2004); *Recreations* music, gardening; *Style—* Prof J R Woodhouse; ✉ Magdalen College, Oxford OX1 4AU

WOODHOUSE, (Bernard) Raymond; s of (Thomas) Bernard Montague Woodhouse (d 1969), of Woodcote Park Ave, Purley, Surrey, and Betty, *née* Harvey (d 1956); *b* 24 November 1939; *Educ* Ardingly, St Dunstan's Catford, Nat Coll of Food Tech; *m* 6 Oct 1962, Judith, da of Robert Arnold Roach (d 1994), of Caterham; 2 s (Richard Thomas Raymond b 5 May 1965, Martyn Bernard Robert b 26 Jan 1970); *Career* chm TSJ Woodhouse Ltd 1973–99 (joined 1960, currently conslt); non-exec dir: The Huge Cheese Company London Ltd 1994–2003, Chester Boyd Ltd 2000–03; govr RNLI; Freeman City of London 1979, Warden and Liveryman Worshipful Co of Butchers 1979 (memb Ct of Assts, fell Guild); *Recreations* tennis, sailing, golf; *Clubs* Royal Smithfield, Farmers', City Livery Yacht; *Style—* Raymond Woodhouse, Esq; ✉ The Backwater, Upper Court Road, Woldingham, Surrey CR3 7BF (e-mail ray.woodhouse@debrett.net)

WOODING, Dr Neil Rhys; s of Desmond Frank Roydon Wooding, of Newport, and Gillian Mary, *née* Evans; *b* 23 October 1960, Newport; *Partner* Nick McNeill; 1 da (Ruby Anne Rhys Lessels b 22 July 1993); *Career* asst regnl mangr (Wales and SW) NACRO 1986–89, equal opportunities advsr Cardiff City Cncl 1989–92, head Equality Unit NHS Wales 1992–99, dir of HR and organisational devpt Bro Taf HA 1999–2003, dir NHS Centre for Equality and Human Rights 2003–05, dir Public Service Mgmnt Wales 2005–; equal opportunities cmmr for Wales Equal Opportunities Cmmn 2002–07, Wales cmmr Cmmn for Equality and Human Rights (CEHR) 2006–; non-exec dir: Chwarae Teg Wales Ltd 1996– (chair 2001), SE Wales Race Equality Cncl 1997–; co-chair Stonewall Cymru 2001–, memb Bd Stonewall UK 2002–, tstee and memb Bd Nat AIDS Tst 2002– (chair All-Wales HIV Reference Gp 1999–2003); vice-chair Welsh Food Alliance 1999–2003, memb Bd Health Living Centre New Opportunities Fund; govr Dyffryn Comp Sch Newport 1997–2003; fell Nat Centre for Public Policy, FCIPD; *Publications* incl: Two Centuries of British Penal Development (1985), An Evaluation of Career Development Opportunities for Women in Local Government (1989), Promoting Equality inside the National Health Service: A Best Practice Guide (1992), A Good Practice Guide to Flexible Working (1994, 2 edn 2003), Managing Careers in General Practice across Wales (1997), A Study of Race and Health Issues inside the Health Service in Wales (1998), The Organisational Construction of Fairness (2003), Undertaking Equality Impact Assessment within Public Service (2005), Promoting Workforce Engagement (2006); *Style—* Dr Neil Wooding; ✉ Ty Newydd, 9 Bucklewood, Bayfields, Chepstow, Monmouthshire NP16 6DX (tel 01291 627983); Public Service Management Wales, 3rd Floor Caradog House, 1–6 St Andrew's Place, Cardiff CF10 3BE (tel 029 2064 5416, fax 029 2064 5405)

WOODING, Roy; s of Raymond Wooding (d 1957), and Elsie, *née* Lyons; *b* 11 October 1953; *Educ* Mexborough Co Secdy Sch; *m* 16 October 1976, Angela, da of George Jones; 1 da (Rachael Emma b 27 Sept 1978); *Career* photographer; M T Walters & Associates Ltd 1970–84 (apprentice then responsible for much of creative output), fndr ICS Photography 1984–, awarded BIPP Yorkshire Centre Indust/Photographer of the Year on ten occasions, 1 Silver BIPP Int Prints Award 2002 and 3 Bronze BIPP Int Prints Awards 2001; memb: BIPP A&Q Panel, BIPP Int Print Awards Judging Panel; FBIPP 1982 (yst then in indust category, assoc BIPP 1976); *Books* contrib photographs to Photography Year Book (1983); *Recreations* league badminton, skiing, tennis, fishing; *Style—* Roy Wooding, Esq; ✉ 20 Farmoor Close, Harlington, Doncaster, South Yorkshire DN5 7JP (tel 01709 896237); ICS Photography, The Studios, Dolcliffe Road, Mexborough, South Yorkshire S64 9AZ (tel and fax 01709 570966, e-mail roy@icsphotography.co.uk)

WOODLEY, Keith Spencer; s of Charles Spencer Woodley, of Pleshey, Essex, and Hilda Mary, *née* Brown; *b* 23 October 1939; *Educ* Stationers' Company's Sch; *m* 19 May 1962, Joyce Madeleine, *née* Toon; 2 da (Rachel Jane b 8 March 1962, Helen Elizabeth b 17 July 1966), 1 s (Jonathan Spencer b 10 Jan 1972); *Career* articled clerk Deloitte Plender Griffith and Co 1957–62, audit sr and mangr Deloitte & Co 1963–68; Deloitte Haskins & Sells: ptnr 1969–90, personnel ptnr 1978–82, memb Mgmnt Bd 1985–90; CA in private practice 1990–2001; non-exec dir: Royscot Trust plc 1990–96, National & Provincial Building Society 1991–96, Abbey National plc 1996– (dep chm 1999–2004); complaints cmmr: Securities and Investment Bd 1990–94, FIMBRA 1990–98, London Stock Exchange 1990–, Personal Investment Authy 1994–2001, Securities and Futures Authy 1995–2000; memb Cncl: ICAEW 1989–98 (pres 1995–96), Univ of Bath (treas 2002–), Nat Assoc of CAB 1991–94 and 1997–99 (hon treas 1991–94); govr Kingswood Sch Bath 2004–; Liveryman: Worshipful Co of Stationers & Newspaper Makers, Worshipful Co of CAs; FCA 1963; *Recreations* hill walking, theatre and listening to music; *Style—* Keith Woodley, Esq; ✉ Rectory Cottage, Combe Hay, Bath BA2 7EG (tel 01225 830920, e-mail kswoodley1@aol.com)

WOODLEY, Leonard Gaston; QC (1988); *Educ* Univ of London; *Career* called to the Bar Inner Temple 1963 (bencher), memb Bar Trinidad and Tobago; recorder 1989–2000; head of chambers 8 King's Bench Walk 1988–2000; cases incl: Mangrove Trial (Notting Hill Riot), Bristol Riot (St Paul's), Brixton Riot, Newham Seven Trial, Privy Cncl appeals; chm Laudat Inquiry into Mental Health, counsel Scarman Inquiry; memb Royal Cmmn on Long Term Care for the Elderly; memb Exec NCCL/Liberty; fndr Leonard Woodley Scholarship; friend ROH, memb Globe Theatre, patron Plan UK; *Clubs* MCC, Globe Lawn Tennis (life memb); *Style—* Leonard Woodley, Esq, QC; ✉ 8 King's Bench Walk, Temple, London EC4Y 7DU

WOODLEY, Sonia; QC (1996); da of Stanley Percival Woodley (d 1994), of Southampton, and Mabel Emily, *née* Hawkins (d 1998); *b* 8 October 1946; *Educ* Convent HS Southampton, Inns of Court Sch of Law; *m* 8 Sept 1973 (m dis 1986), Peter Stuart McDonald; 2 s (James Alexander Heaton b 10 July 1977, William Edward Henry b 17 Aug 1981), 1 da (Laura Rose Jane b 5 July 1979); *Career* called to the Bar Gray's Inn 1968, recorder of the Crown Court 1987–; *Recreations* fishing, gardening, travelling; *Style—* Miss Sonia Woodley, QC; ✉ 9–12 Bell Yard, London WC2A 2LF (tel 020 7400 1800, fax 020 7404 1405)

WOODMAN, Prof Anthony John; s of John Woodman (d 1988), and Alma Clare, *née* Callender (d 1982); *b* 11 April 1945; *Educ* Ushaw Coll Durham, King's Coll Newcastle upon Tyne, Univ of Durham (BA), King's Coll Cambridge (PhD); *m* 21 July 1977, Dorothy Joyce, da of Gordon Charles Monk (d 1970); 2 s (David b 1981, John b 1983); *Career* reader in Latin literature Univ of Newcastle upon Tyne 1979–80 (lectr in classics 1968–79); prof of Latin: Univ of Leeds 1980–84, Univ of Durham 1984–2004; Gildersleeve prof of classics Univ of Virginia 2004–; visiting prof Princeton Univ 1989–90, visiting fell Univ of Wisconsin/Madison 1995, visiting Gildersleeve prof of classics Univ of Virginia 2003–04; *Books* Quality and Pleasure in Latin Poetry (jtly, 1974), Velleius Paterculus: the Tiberian Narrative (1977), Creative Imitation and Latin Literature (jtly, 1979), Velleius Paterculus: the Caesarian and Augustan Narrative (1983), Poetry and Politics in the Age of Augustus (jtly, 1984), Past Perspectives: Studies in Greek and Roman Historical Writing (jtly, 1986), Rhetoric in Classical Historiography (1988), Tacitus: Annals IV (jtly, 1989), Author and Audience in Latin Literature (jtly, 1992), Tacitus and the Tacitean Tradition (jtly, 1993), Tacitus: Annals III (jtly, 1996), Latin Historians (jtly, 1997), Tacitus Reviewed (1998), Traditions and Contexts in the Poetry of Horace (jtly, 2002), Tacitus: The Annals (2004); *Style—* Prof A J Woodman; ✉ Department of Classics, Cocke Hall, PO Box 400788, University of Virginia, Charlottesville, VA 22904, USA (tel 00 1 434 924 7747)

WOODROFFE, Peter Mackelcan; s of Kenneth Derry Woodroffe (d 1972), of London, and Raby Alfreda Mackelcan, *née* Ryan (d 1991); the Woodroffe name originated ca 1250; Brehan Le Woderove, a judge, was appointed woodreeve for the Royal Forest of Pickering by King Edward I, his ggs Sir John Woodroffe settling at Woolley Hall in the West Riding in 1394; *b* 2 August 1927; *Educ* Mill Hill, Coll of Law London; *m* 15 June 1973, Amanda Aloysia Nicolette, da of Henry Forbes, of Surrey; 2 s (Justin Mackelcan b 24 May 1977, Clifford Derry b 10 Dec 1979); *Career* joined Rifle Bde 1945, cmmnd 2 Lt Royal Northumberland Fus 1946 (Lt 1947), ret 1948; admitted slr 1953; sr ptnr Woodroffes 1963– (third generation in succession); educn law specialist; memb of Lloyd's; cncllr (Cons) Westminster City Cncl 1962–65; memb Law Soc 1953; sec Ct of Govrs Mill Hill Sch 1981–1997, govr Alford House Children's Charity 1999–; chm Br export mission to US (Boston to Houston on train drawn by Flying Scotsman steam locomotive) 1969; Freeman City of London 1984; hon citizen State of Texas 1967; *Recreations* skiing, golf, tennis, palaeontology; *Clubs* Boodle's, Woodroffe's, Hurlingham, The Berkshire Golf, Rye Golf, Royal Cinque Ports Golf, Rye Lawn Tennis (chm); *Style—* Peter Woodroffe, Esq; ✉ 13 Cadogan Street, London SW3 2PP (tel 020 7589 9339); Stonewalls, Pett Level, Hastings, East Sussex TN35 4EH (tel 01424 813198); Woodroffes, 36 Ebury Street, London SW1W 0LU (tel 020 7730 0001, fax 020 7730 0079)

WOODROFFE, Simon; OBE (2006); *b* 14 February 1952; *Career* entreprenuer, businessman and public speaker; over 30 years in entertainment business; fndr prodn companies based in London and LA designing rock 'n' roll stages for artistes such as Rod Stewart, The Moody Blues, Stevie Wonder and events such as Live Aid; org financing and distribution Nelson Mandela, Amnesty Int and Prince's Tst concerts; tv prodn deals incl Japan's No 1 show Hit Studio International; fndr and creative driving force behind the YO! brand incl YO! Sushi, YO! Japan and YOTEL; public speaker and performer Edinburgh Festival 2004; recorded album with The Blockheads 2003–04; Emerging Entrpreneur of the Year 1999, London Entrepreneur of the Year 1999, UK Group Restaurateur of the Year 2000, Best Venue (Retailer's Retailer of the Year Awards) 2001, Design and Art Direction Award (The Catey Awards) 2000; *Publications* The Book of YO! (2000); *Style—* Simon Woodroffe, OBE; ✉ YO! Company, 9 George Street, London W1U 3QH (tel 020 7224 0753, e-mail simon@yocompany.biz, website www.yocompany.biz)

WOODROW, Arabella Thomasine; da of Michael Henry Carlile Morris (d 1987), of Basingstoke, Hants, and Margaret Joyce, *née* Flannery (d 1984); *b* 31 March 1954; *Educ* Queen Anne's Sch Caversham, Lady Margaret Hall Oxford (BA, DPhil); *m* 15 Dec 1979, Richard Erskine Woodrow, s of Cyril Erskine Woodrow (d 1960), of Scarborough; *Career* wine merchant; sales rep Harveys of Bristol 1979–84, Wine and Spirit Educn Tst dip 1981, Vintners scholarship from Vintners Co 1983, sales rep Christopher & Co Ltd 1984–85, wine buyer Cooperative Wholesale Soc 1986–99, wine buying dir Forth Wines Ltd 1999–2001, wine projects conslt Halewood Int 2002–03, freelance conslt 2003, business devpt mangr Myliko Wines 2003–, dir Bd Wine Standards Bd 2003–; memb: Inst of Masters of Wine 1986–, Wine Devpt Bd 1986–92, Wine Standards Bd 1990–99; Freeman City of London 1995, Liveryman Worshipful Co of Vintners 2003; MW 1986; *Books* Wines Of The Rhone Valley; *Recreations* marathon running, triathlon, cookery, wine tasting, orienteering; *Style—* Mrs Arabella Woodrow; ✉ Druids Park House,

Murthly, Perthshire PH1 4ES (tel 01738 710719, e-mail atwoodrow@druidpark.freeserve.co.uk)

WOODROW, William Robert (Bill); s of Geoffrey William Woodrow, of Chichester, W Sussex, and Doreen Mary, *née* Fasken; *b* 1 November 1948; *Educ* Barton Peveril GS, Winchester Sch of Art, St Martin's Sch of Art, Chelsea Sch of Art (Higher Dip Fine Art); *m* 12 Nov 1970, Pauline, da of John Neville Rowley; 1 s (Harry), 1 da (Ellen); *Career* sculptor; winner Anne Gerber award Seattle Museum of Art 1988, tstee Tate Gallery 1996–2001, govr Univ of the Arts London 2003–; RA 2002; *Exhibitions* numerous solo exhibitions in Europe, Australia, USA and Canada since 1972 incl: Fool's Gold (Duveen Galleries Tate Gallery London, later Darmstadt) 1996, Regardless of History Fourth Plinth Trafalgar Square London 2000–01, The Beekeeper (South London Gallery, Mappin Art Gallery Sheffield) 2001, Waddington Galleries London 2006; group exhibitions incl: Br Sculpture in the 20th Century Whitechapel Art Gallery 1981, Biennale of Sydney 1982, Aperto 82 Venice 1982, XII Biennale of Paris 1982, New Art at the Tate Gallery 1983, Transformations São Paulo (also Rio de Janeiro, Mexico City, Lisbon) 1983, Int Survey of Recent Painting and Sculpture New York 1984, Skulptur im 20 Jahrhundert Basle 1984, ROSC '84 Dublin 1984, Space Invaders toured Canada 1985, The Br Show toured Aust 1985, Carnegie Int Pittsburgh 1985, Entre el objeto y la imagen toured Spain 1986, Painting and Sculpture Today Indianapolis 1986, Br Art of the 1980's Stockholm and Tampere 1987, Documenta 8 Kassel 1987, Starlit Waters Tate Liverpool 1988, British Now Montreal 1988, GB-USSR Kiev Moscow 1990, Metropolis Berlin 1991, XXI São Paulo Bienal 1991, Arte Amazonas (Rio de Janeiro, Brasilia, Berlin, Dresden and Aachen) 1992–94, Collaborative Works (with Richard Deacon, Chisenhale Gallery London) 1993, Contemporary Br Art in Print Edinburgh and Yale 1995, Un Siecle de Sculpture Anglaise (Paris) 1996, Sexta Bienal de la Habana (Cuba) 1997, Forjar el Espacio (Las Palmas de Gran Canaria, Valencia, Calais) 1998–99, Bronze Holland Park London 2000, Field Day Sculpture form Britain (Taipei Fine Arts Museum Taiwan) 2001, Blast to Freeze: British Art in the 20th Century (Kunstmuseum Wolfsburg and Les Abbatoirs Toulouse) 2002–03, Turning Points: 20th Century British Sculpture (Tehran Museum of Contemporary Art) 2004; *Museum Collections* incl: Arts Cncl GB, Br Cncl, Imperial War Museum, Kunsthaus Zurich, Malmö Konsthall, MOMA NY, Nat Gallery of Canada, Rijksmuseum Kröller-Müller, Tate Gallery, Br Museum, Br Library; *Style*— W R Woodrow, Esq, RA; ✉ c/o Waddington Galleries, 11 Cork Street, London W1S 3LT (e-mail bill@billwoodrow.com)

WOODS, Brian Edwin; s of Norman Eric Woods (d 1972), and Alice Louise, *née* Finch (d 1984); *b* 26 February 1940; *Educ* Leeds GS; *m* 10 July 1965 (m dis 1981), Judith Elizabeth, *née* Everitt; 1 da (Jane Louise b 7 Jan 1973); m 2, 2 Oct 1981, Josephine, da of Philip Bradley Canneaux, 1 da (Helen Josephine b 27 Aug 1983); *Career* articled clerk Whitfield & Co Leeds, qualified chartered accountant 1965; Thornton Baker: mangr Birmingham 1970–73, mangr Bedford 1973–75, ptnr 1975–98, managing ptnr 1983–95, sr ptnr 1995–98; dir: Bedfordshire Training and Enterprise Cncl 1990–95, Bedfordia Group plc 1995–2005, East Anglia's Children's Hospices 1995–2001; non-exec dir: Forums Ltd 2000–, Paperfeel Ltd 2001–, Mayr Health Spas Ltd 2001–04, Clini Ltd; memb Br Olympic Appeal Ctee for Bedfordshire 1995–96; FCA 1975 (ACA 1965); *Recreations* photography, music, walking; *Clubs* Rotary (Bedford), Institute of Directors; *Style*— Brian E Woods; ✉ 13 Windrush Avenue, Bedfordshire MK41 7BS (tel 01234 304133, e-mail brian.woods4@ntlworld.com)

WOODS, David Victor; *b* 7 May 1958; *Educ* Skegness GS, Selwyn Coll Cambridge (MA), Coll of Law Guildford; *Career* admitted slr 1982; articled clerk Hill & Perks Slrs 1980–82; ptnr: Eversheds 1987–2001 (chm Nat Commercial Practice Gp 1993–98), Greenwoods Slrs LLP 2001–; *Style*— David Woods, Esq

WOODS, Prof (Hubert) Frank; CBE (2001); s of Hubert George Woods (d 1959), of Leeds, and Julia Augusta, *née* Kamlinski (d 1963); *b* 18 November 1937; *Educ* St Bees Sch, Univ of Leeds (BSc), Univ of Oxford (BM BCh, DPhil); *m* 7 Jan 1966, Hilary Sheila, da of Ernest E Cox, of Sheffield; 1 s (Christopher b 21 Oct 1967), 2 da (Katharine b 23 Feb 1971, Rebecca b 5 June 1973); *Career* house offr posts NHS 1965–66, lectr in med Univ of Oxford 1967–72, memb external med scientific staff MRC 1972–76; hon conslt physician: Royal Infirmary Sheffield 1976–88, Middlewood Psychiatric Hosp 1976–91, Royal Hallamshire Hosp 1976–; Univ of Sheffield: prof of clinical pharmacology and therapeutics 1976–90, dean Faculty of Med and Dentistry 1988–98, Sir George Franklin prof of med 1990–2003, currently research student in medial history; sometime memb of numerous working gps and ctees Dept of Health and MAFF; sr external examiner in med Univ of Oxford 1988–, examiner membership exam RCP 1989–; memb GMC 1994–2002 (chm Health Ctee 1999–2002); regnl advsr RCP 1986–89; memb Hunterian Soc 1967, FRCP 1978 (MRCP 1968), FFPM 1989, FRCPE 1991, Hon FFOM 1995, FIFST 1996, FMedSci 1998; *Publications* 115 research papers and 3 books incl Clinical and Biochemical Aspects of Lactic Acidosis (with R D Cohen, 1976); *Style*— Prof Frank Woods, CBE

WOODS, Gordon Campbell; s of Ian Woods, and Margot Woods; *b* 5 November 1955, Glasgow; *Educ* Durham Sch, Mansfield Coll Oxford (MA, PGCE); *m* 27 Oct 1984, Emma; 1 s (James b 31 Dec 1987), 1 da (Kate b 25 Sept 1989); *Career* Shrewsbury Sch: teacher of geography 1979, head of geography 1984, master i/c rowing 1988, housemaster 1989, second master 1999; warden Glenalmond Coll Perth 2003–; chm Field Studies Working Gp Geographical Assoc 1988; memb Geographical Assoc 1979–, MIBG 1984; *Recreations* sailing, industrial history, steam railways; *Clubs* East India, Colemore Sailing (Vice-Cdre 2002); *Style*— Gordon Woods, Esq; ✉ Glenalmond College, Glenalmond, Perth PH1 3RY (tel 01738 842061, e-mail warden@glenalmondcollege.co.uk)

WOODS, Maj-Gen Henry Gabriel; CB (1979), MBE (1965), MC (1945), DL (N Yorks 1984); s of G S Woods (d 1961), of Bexhill-on-Sea, E Sussex, and Flora, *née* MacNevin (d 1976); *b* 7 May 1924; *Educ* Highgate Sch, Trinity Coll Oxford (exhibitioner, MA); *m* 29 April 1953, Imogen Elizabeth Birchenough, da of C E S Dodd (d 1975), of Bath; 2 da (Sarah b 1955, Arabella b 1958); *Career* cmmnd 5 Royal Inniskilling Dragoon Gds 1944, served NW Europe (Normandy to Baltic) 1944–45, 1945–51, 1960–62 and 1967–69, Adj Korea 1952, served Middle East 1954 and 1964–67, Mil Asst to Vice Chief of Def Staff 1962–64, cmd 5 Royal Inniskilling Dragoon Gds 1965–67, Asst Mil Sec to C-in-C BAOR 1967–69, Cdr RAC Centre 1969–72, Cdr Br Army Staff and Mil Attaché Br Embassy Washington USA 1972–75, GOC NE Dist 1976–80, Army Staff Coll 1956, Jt Servs Staff Coll 1960, RCDS 1972; head Centre for Industrial and Educnl Liaison W and N Yorks 1980–87, dir St William's Fndn 1987–97 (vice-pres 1997–), dir Transpennine 1988–2003; chm: Bradford and W Yorks BIM 1982–84, Yorks Region RSA 1984–92, N Yorks Scout Cncl 1984–2000, 5 Royal Inniskilling Dragoon Gds Assoc 1979–92, Duke of York's Community Initiative in Yorkshire 1997–2004; pres: Royal Soc of St George (York and Humberside) 1986–88, Royal Dragoon Gds' Assoc 1992–, Oxford Soc (Yorkshire Branch) 1998–2001; tstee Second World War Experience Centre; memb: Yorks Agric Soc 1980–, TA&VR Assoc 1982–90, York Area Mental Health Appeals Ctee 1984–90, Cncl RUSI 1986–90, Cncl RSA 1990–96; Vice Lord-Lt N Yorks 1986–99; memb Merchants of the Staple of England 1982– (Mayor 1991–92), memb Merchant Adventurers of York 1989–2006; Hon DLitt Univ of Bradford 1988; FIMgt 1980, FRSA 1981; Order of Leopold Second Class (1966); *Books* Change and Challenge - History of the 5th Royal Inniskilling Dragoon Guards (with Gen Sir Cecil Blacker, 1976); *Recreations* gardening, walking, foot follower (hunting), military history; *Clubs* Ends of the Earth, IOD, Yorkshire; *Style*— Maj-Gen Henry Woods, CB, MBE, MC, DL; ✉ St William's Foundation, 5 College Street, York YO1 7JF (tel 01904 557235, e-mail foundation@st-williams.demon.co.uk)

WOODS, Humphrey Martin; s of Rev Howard Charles Woods, of Hindhead, Surrey, and Kathleen Ailsie Clutton, *née* Baker; descendant of the philosopher John Locke; *b* 23 November 1937; *Educ* Lancing, Trinity Coll Oxford (BA); *m* 1, 4 May 1963, Dona Leslie; m 2, 25 Jan 1977, Jennifer Mary, da of Brig Edward Hayden Tinker, of NZ; 2 da (Eleanor b 1977, Lucy b 1979), 3 s (Mark b 1981, Leo b 1984, Dominic b 1963); *Career* archaeologist with English Heritage (formerly Historic Bldgs & Monuments Cmmn for England) 1974–; tutor in archaeology Dept of Continuing Educn Univ of Oxford 1996–; FSA 1991; *Publications* Excavations on the Second Site of The Dominican Priory Oxford (in Oxoniensia Vol XLI, 1976), The Despoliation of the Abbey of SS Peter, Paul and Augustine Between the Years 1542 and 1793 (in Historical Essays in Memory of James Hobbs, 1980), The Completion of the Abbey Church of SS Peter, Paul and Augustine, Canterbury, by Abbots Wido and Hugh of Fleury (in British Archaeological Association Conference Transactions, 1982), Excavations at Eltham Palace 1975–79 (in Transactions of the London and Middx Archaeological Soc, 1982), Excavations on the Site of the Dominican Friary at Guildford in 1974 and 1978 (Research Vol No 9 of the Surrey Archaeological Soc, 1984), Excavations at Wenlock Priory 1981–86 (in Journal of the Br Archaeological Assoc, 1987), St Augustine's Abbey - report on excavations 1960–78 (Kent Archaeological Soc Monograph Series Vol IV, 1988), Romanesque West Front at The Church of the Holy Trinity Much Wenlock (in Transactions of the Shropshire Archaeological Soc, 1989), Excavations at Glastonbury Abbey 1987–1993 (in Proceedings of the Somerset Archaeological and Natural History Soc, Vol 138, 1994), Quantock Poems (2004); *Recreations* walking in the Quantock hills, natural history, stag hunting; *Style*— Humphrey Woods, Esq, FSA; ✉ 20 Wembdon Hill, Bridgwater, Somerset TA6 7PX (tel 01278 423 955)

WOODS, Prof John David; CBE (1991); s of Ronald Ernest Goff Woods (d 1968), and Ethel Marjorie Woods (d 1999); *b* 26 October 1939; *Educ* Imperial Coll London (BSc, ARCS, PhD, DIC); *m* 7 April 1971 (m dis 1996), Irina, da of Bernd von Arnim; 1 s (Alexander b 1975), 1 da (Virginia b 1980); *Career* res fell Meteorological Office 1966–72, prof of physical oceanography Univ of Southampton 1972–77, prof of oceanography and dir Institut Fuer Meereskunde Univ of Kiel 1977–86, dir of marine and atmospheric sciences NERC 1986–94; Imperial Coll London 1994–: dean Grad Sch of Environment 1994–98, head Dept of Earth Resources Engrg 1994–98 and prof of oceanography 1994–2005, emeritus prof of oceanography and complex systems 2005–; hon prof of oceanography Univ of Southampton 1994–; fell Plymouth Marine Lab 1998–; contrib papers on oceanography and meteorology to various learned jls; fell Linacre Coll Oxford 1991–; memb: NERC 1979–82, Meteorological Res Ctee 1976–77 and 1987–96; Hon DSc: Univ of Liège 1980, Univ of Plymouth 1991, Univ of Southampton 2004; awarded RGS founder's medal 1996; FRGS 1966, FRMetS 1967, fndn memb Academia Europaea 1988; *Books* Underwater Science (1971), Underwater Research (1976), Ocean Forecasting (2002), Benguela (2006); *Recreations* history; *Clubs* Athenaeum, Meteorological (chm 2000–02, hon memb 2005–); *Style*— Prof John Woods, CBE; ✉ Imperial College, London SW7 2BP (tel 020 7594 7414, fax 020 7594 7403)

WOODS, Michael John; s of Dr L H Woods, and Margery, *née* Pickard; *Educ* Bradfield; *m* 15 Jan 1966, Carolyn Rosemary, da of William Tadman, of Roborough, N Devon; 1 s (Nicholas John b 13 Aug 1967), 1 da (Jennifer Sarah Rosemary b 29 May 1969); *Career* Nat Serv 1 Bn Royal Fus (serv Suez Crisis) 1955–57; trainee exec Mecca Ltd 1957–63; dir: Silver Blades Ice Rink Ltd 1963–70, Mecca Catering 1968–, Mecca Leisure Ltd 1973–; asst md: Mecca Bingo Social Clubs 1972–80, Mecca Leisure Ltd 1979–85; chm: Mecca Agency International 1983–85, Ison Bros (Newcastle) Ltd 1983–85, Pointer Motor Co 1983–85, Scot Automatic Printing 1983–85; md: Mecca Leisure Speciality Catering Div 1985–91, Speciality Catering Div Europe 1989–91; dir Saddle and Sirloin Restaurant Ltd 1991–97; self employed catering conslt 1991–, gp catering exec Apollo Leisure (UK) Ltd 1993–96; memb: Exec Bd Variety Club of GB 1985–2001, Cncl Actors' Charitable Tst, Hotel and Catering Benevolent Assoc, TICC 2000; patron Ralph and Meriel Richardson Fndn 2003–; Freeman City of London 1998; FInstD 1965–2001, FHCIMA 1989; *Recreations* squash, swimming, shooting (clay and pheasant), fishing; *Style*— Michael Woods, Esq; ✉ Glendale, Farley Green, Albury, Guildford, Surrey (tel 01483 202472, fax 01483 202465)

WOODS, Philip Dudley; s of John Webster-Woods (d 1991), and Dora Helen Davies, *née* Rushworth; *b* 23 December 1950, Liverpool; *Educ* Birkenhead Sch, Liverpool Law Sch; *m* 6 March 1976, Jane, *née* Kalbraier; 2 s (Simon Maxwell Dudley b 27 May 1980, Jonathan Dudley b 12 Aug 1983); *Career* admitted slr: Eng and Wales 1974, Hong Kong 1975; asst slr: Percy Hughes & Roberts 1974–75, Deacons 1975–81; ptnr: Wilkinson & Grist 1981–89, Eversheds Alexander Tatham 1989–94 (chm Nat Intellectual Property Gp), Philip Woods & Co 1994–97, Hill Dickinson LLP 1997– (head of intellectual property and IT); founding memb Intellectual Property Lawyers' Orgn (TIPLO), assoc memb Chartered Inst of Patent Agents, assoc memb Inst of Trade Mark Attorneys; *Recreations* wine, classic cars, reading, walking; *Clubs* Hong Kong, Oriental, Hong Kong Jockey, Royal Hong Kong Yacht, Hong Kong Cricket, Old Boys and Park Green, Foreign Correspondents (Hong Kong); *Style*— Philip Woods, Esq; ✉ Hill Dickinson, 50 Fountain Street, Manchester M2 2AS (tel 0161 817 7200, fax 0161 817 7201, e-mail philip.woods@hilldickinson.com)

WOODS, Richard; *Educ* Winchester Sch of Art, Slade Sch of Art; *Career* artist; Delfina Studio Award 2002; Freeman City of Chester; *Solo Exhibitions* Modern Art Inc London 2000, Griedervon Puttkamer Berlin 2001, Deitch Projects NY 2002; *Group Exhibitions* The Galleries Royal Acad 2002; *Style*— Richard Woods, Esq; ✉ c/o Modern Art, 73 Redchurch Street, London E2 7DJ (tel 020 7739 2081, fax 020 7729 2017, e-mail modernart@easynet.co.uk)

WOODS, Robert; CBE; *Career* The Peninsular and Oriental Steam Navigation Company (P&O): joined 1971, memb Bd 1996–, gp md P&O Nedlloyd Container Ltd 1997–2003, exec chm P&O Ports 2002–, chief exec 2004–; non-exec dir John Swire & Sons 2002–; pres Chamber of Shipping 2002–04; *Style*— Robert Woods, Esq, CBE; ✉ The Peninsular and Oriental Steam Navigation Company, Peninsular House, 79 Pall Mall, London SW1Y 5EJ

WOODS-SCAWEN, Brian; DL (West Midlands 2002); s of Dennis Woods-Scawen, of Warwick, and Betty, *née* Runacres; *b* 2 November 1946; *Educ* Salesian Coll Farnborough, Univ of Sheffield (BA (Econ)), Univ of Warwick (MA); *m* 1988, Jane Woods-Scawen, JP; 1 da (Suzannah b 28 April 1977), 1 s (Tristan b 2 Dec 1978); *Career* PricewaterhouseCoopers (formerly Coopers & Lybrand before merger): articled clerk 1971–74, ptnr 1980–2003, chm Corp Fin Midlands 1986–93, memb Partnership Bd 1994–98, memb Supervisory Bd 1998–2003 (dep chm 2000–01, chm 2001–03), memb Global Supervisory Bd 1999–2001, chm Midlands Region 1995–2003; chm: Ironbridge Gorge Museum Advsy Cncl 1996–2000, Birmingham bid for European Capital of Culture 2002–03, Culture W Midlands, Coventry, Solihull and Warwickshire Partnership Ltd, West Midlands Broadband Co Ltd 2003–05, West Bromwich Bldg Soc; memb: Bd Birmingham Forward 1996–2001 (chm 1999–2000), Bd Thinktank Birmingham 1997–2002, Cncl W Midlands CBI 1998–2003, Bd Advantage West Midlands (Regnl Devpt Agency) 1998–2003, Bd DTI, Bd Govt Office of W Midlands, Cncl Birmingham C of C and Industry 1999–2005, Warwick Arts Centre 1999–2007, Int Advsy Bd Univ of Birmingham; memb Ctee on Standards in Public Life 2004–; treas: West Midlands

Lord's Taverners' 1996–2001, Univ of Warwick; Lifetime Achievement Award ICAEW 2004; Hon LLD Univ of Birmingham 2003, Hon DUniv Univ of Central England 2004; FCA 1979, FRSA; *Books* Survey of Financial Management in Law Firms (1993, 1994, 1995); author of articles on strategic devpts in legal profession, international finance and regnl economics; *Style*— Dr Brian Woods-Scawen, DL; ✉ The Stables, Hunt Paddocks, Kenilworth, Warwickshire CV8 1NL (tel 01926 858225, e-mail brianws@dircon.co.uk)

WOODWARD, (John) Charles; s of Eric Jackson Woodward (d 1978), and Maude Woodward, *née* Adams (d 1989); *b* 31 October 1935; *Educ* Herbert Strutt GS Belper, Univ of Manchester (BSc); *m* 11 Sept 1962, Kathy, da of Harry Ashton (d 1982); 2 da (Zoë b 14 Sept 1963, Sarah b 5 Jan 1965), 1 s (Giles b 15 Dec 1967); *Career* memb London Stock Exchange 1971–75, ptnr Colegrave & Co 1972–75, investment mangr Reed International 1975–83, chief exec BA Pensions 1984–91; Nat Assoc of Pension Funds: memb Cncl 1982–91, chm Investment Ctee 1982–84, chm of Cncl 1987–89, vice-pres 1989–91, chm Tstee Pension Scheme 1991–2002; investment advsr Cleveland CC 1983–86; dir: Exel Tstees Ltd 1986–, Legal and General Property Fund Managers Ltd 1991–99, Kingfisher Pension Trustee Ltd 1992–, Marine and General Mutual Life Assurance Society 1994–; chm: BES Trustees plc 1992–, Albright & Wilson Pension Trustees Ltd 1993–2001, Trustees Porvair Pension Plan 1993–2003, M W Marshall Retirement Savings Plan 1997–; tstee: Dunn & Co Pensions Scheme 1993–2001, Mansfield Brewery Group Pension Scheme 1994–2001; memb Ctee of Mgmnt Fleming General Exempt Fund 1994–97; FIA 1965; *Clubs* Naval and Military; *Style*— Charles Woodward, Esq; ✉ BES Trustees plc, 78 Cannon Street, London EC4N 6HH (e-mail charles.woodward@wanadoo.fr)

WOODWARD, Christopher Haldane; s of William Haldane Woodward, of Wirral, Cheshire, and Audrey Woodward; *b* 18 November 1946; *Educ* Calday Grange GS, Univ of Birmingham (BSocSc), Manchester Business Sch (MBA); *m* 9 Aug 1969, Frances Maria, da of Richard Alan Beatty, of Edinburgh; 1 s (Matthew b 1974), 2 da (Rosalind b 1976, Charlotte b 1980); *Career* grad trainee and economist mktg asst GKN 1968–70, mktg mangr GKN Farr Filtration 1970–72, mktg exec Guthrie Corporation 1974–75, mktg and devpt exec Tay Textiles 1976–77 (gp mktg and planning controller 1978–79), Cape Insulation Ltd 1979–82 (mktg mangr, nat sales mangr, sales and mktg dir); mktg dir: Euro Uniroyal Ltd 1982–86, 3i plc 1986–94; md Total Communications 1994–; dir: Mascord Ltd, Planalytics Assocs Ltd; *Recreations* opera, theatre, music, art; *Clubs* RAC; *Style*— Christopher Woodward, Esq; ✉ Total Communications (tel 01825 724030)

WOODWARD, Sir Clive; kt (2004), OBE (2002); *b* 6 January 1956, Ely, Cambs; *Educ* HMS Conway Anglesey, Loughborough Univ (BA); *Career* rugby union coach and former player; played for: Loughborough Univ, Harlequins, Leicester Tigers, Manly (Aust); England: 21 caps 1980–1984, 4 tries, debut v Ireland, winners Grand Slam 1980; memb Br Lions touring squads to South Africa 1980 and NZ 1983; career as coach: Manly (Aust), Henley 1990–94, London Irish 1994–97, Bath (conslt coach), England U21 1994–97, head coach England 1997–2004 (winners Six Nations Championship 2000, 2001 and 2003 (Grand Slam 2003), unbeaten against South Africa, Aust and NZ autumn series 2002, ranked no 1 team in world 2003, unbeaten against NZ and Aust summer tour 2003, winners World Cup Aust 2003), head coach Br Lions tour to NZ 2005, performance dir Southampton FC 2005–06, dir of elite performance BOA 2006–; Coach of the Year Sports England 2004; *Style*— Sir Clive Woodward, OBE

WOODWARD, David William; s of Arthur Oliver James Woodward (d 1984), and Winifred May, *née* Perkins (d 1993); *b* 10 January 1950, Dartford, Kent; *Educ* Gravesend GS, Univ of Bristol (LLB); *m* 29 July 1976, Janet, *née* Whatley; 2 c (Anna Catherine, James William (twins), b 26 June 1984); *Career* admitted slr 1975; slr specialising in family law; ptnr Trump & Ptnrs (now TLT LLP) 1981– (currently head Private Business Gp); chm Bristol Family Mediators Assoc Ltd; memb: Resolution (memb Nat Standards Accreditation Ctees, former chair Bristol branch), Law Soc (memb Family Law Ctee), Bristol Law Soc; Family Mediators Assoc trained mediator 1991, Resolution accredited specialist in pensions and emergency financial remedies 2004, trained collaborative lawyer 2007; *Publications* Family Meditation Past, Present and Future (contrib, 2004), Resolution Family Law Handbook (contrib, 2006); *Recreations* cycling (long distance solo, commuting and with my wife), supporting Bristol Rugby Club, badminton; *Style*— David Woodward, Esq; ✉ TLT Solicitors, 1 Redcliff Street, Bristol BS1 6TP (tel 0117 917 7501, fax 0117 917 7789, e-mail dwoodward@tltsolicitors.com)

WOODWARD, Derek Richard; s of James Norman Woodward, of Hull, and Mary, *née* Dennison; *b* 17 September 1958; *m* 1991, Finuala, da of Patrick and Kay McDonald, of Dublin; 2 s (Ciaran b 16 Feb 1995, Daniel b 18 Nov 1997), 1 da (Olivia b 24 Nov 2001); *Career* asst co sec: Eagle Star 1984–90, BAT Industries plc 1990–98, co sec Allied Zurich plc 1998–2001, head of secretariat Centrica plc 2001–; memb: ICSA; FCIS; *Recreations* family life, cycling; *Style*— Derek Woodward, Esq; ✉ Centrica plc, Millstream, Maidenhead Road, Windsor, Berkshire SL4 5GD (tel 01753 494006, fax 01753 494019, e-mail derek.woodward@centrica.com)

WOODWARD, Edward; OBE (1980); *b* 1 June 1930; *Educ* RADA; *m* 1; 2 s (Timothy, Peter), 1 da (Sarah Woodward, *qv*); *m* 2, Michele Dotrice; 1 da (Emily); *Career* actor; *Theatre* various rep work, West End debut Where There's a Will (Garrick) 1954, The Queen and the Welshman (Edinburgh Festival and Lyric Hammersmith), Salad Days, joined RSC 1958, Romeo and Juliet, Hamlet, Pericles, Much Ado About Nothing, Rattle of a Simple Man (West End and Broadway), High Spirits (Broadway), On Approval, The Wolf, The Dark Horse, The Male of the Species, Babes in the Wood, Two Cities (Variety Award for Best Performance in a Musical), Cyrano (NT), The White Devil (NT), The Beggar's Opera (also dir), Richard III (Ludlow Festival) 1982, Goodbye Gilbert Harding (nat tour) 2002, The Cemetery Club (nat tour) 2003, God in the Canterbury Mystery Plays (Canterbury Cathedral) 2004; *Television* Callan (series, Best Actor Soc of Film and TV Arts (now BAFTA) 1969, Sun Awards 1970/71 and TV Times Awards 1972), Robert McCall in The Equalizer (series, Golden Globe Award and 5 Emmy nominations), Sword of Honour, Julius Caesar, The Cherry Orchard, Saturday, Sunday, Monday, Mervyn Griffiths Jones, The Trial of Lady Chatterley, A Dream Divided, Rod of Iron, A Bit of a Holiday, The Bass Player and the Blonde (mini-series), Churchill: The Wilderness Years, Codename Kyril, Common as Muck (BBC) 1994; host: World War II (Emmy Award 1990), In Suspicious Circumstances (Granada), Murder in Suburbia 2004, Heartbeat 2005; in US: Uncle Tom's Cabin (ACE Television Award nomination), The Man in the Brown Suit (Warner Bros), Hunted (Universal), Harrison (movie series, Paramount TV) 1994, The Woodward Files (Westcountry TV/HTV West) 1995, Angelo in The House of Angelo 1997, The New Professionals 1998–99, Nikita (series, USA), Messiah (BBC), Night and Day (two TV films, BBC); *Film* Breaker Morant, King David, Mr Johnson, A Christmas Carol, The Champions, Who Dares Wins, The Wicker Man, Stand Up Virgin Soldiers, Sitting Target, The File on the Golden Goose, Callan, Deadly Advice, Abduction Club, Hot Fuzz 2006; *Music* 3 Edward Woodward Hour TV Specials, recorded 12 LP albums, Feelings (compilation), awarded 3 Gold discs, two concerts with LPO 2005; *Clubs* Garrick; *Style*— Edward Woodward, Esq, OBE

WOODWARD, Gerard Vaughan; s of Reginald Llewelwyn Woodward (d 1991), and Sylvia, *née* Walsh (d 1981); *b* 4 December 1961; *Educ* St Ignatius Coll London, Falmouth Sch of Art, LSE (BSc, Maurice Freedman Prize); *m* 1983, Suzanne Jane, da of Robin Anderson; 2 da; *Career* freelance artist 1985–89, freelance writer 1989–; lectr in creative writing Bath Spa UC 2004–; memb Soc Authors 1992–; *Poetry* The Unwriter and Other Poems (1989, Eric Gregory Award), Householder (1991, Poetry Book Soc Choice, Somerset Maugham Award, shortlist J L Rhys Prize Mail on Sunday), After the Deafening (1994,

Poetry Book Soc Choice), Island to Island (1999), We Were Pedestrians (2005); *Novels* August (2002, shortlist Whitbread First Novel Award), I'll Go to Bed at Noon (2004, shortlist Man Booker Prize for Fiction); *Recreations* chess, playing the piano, pathology; *Style*— Gerard Woodward, Esq

WOODWARD, His Hon Judge Nicholas Frederick; s of Frederick Cyril Woodward, and Joan Woodward; *Educ* Wellingborough Sch, Trent Poly (BA); *m* Denise; 1 s; *Career* barr 1976–2001, asst recorder 1998–2000, recorder 2000, circuit judge (Wales & Chester Circuit) 2001–; *Clubs* Chester City; *Style*— His Hon Judge Nick Woodward; ✉ The Court Service, Churchill House, Churchill Way, Cardiff CF10 2HH

WOODWARD, Roger Robert; AC (1992), OBE (1980); s of Francis William Woodward, and Gladys, *née* Bracken, of Sydney, Australia; *b* 20 December 1942; *Educ* Univ of Sydney (DMus, DSCM, GSTC), Warsaw Acad of Music; *m* 16 April 1989, Patricia May, da of Edward Ludgate; 2 s (Benjamin, Elroy), 1 da (Asmira); *Career* concert pianist, conductor and composer; has worked with Claudio Abbado, Pierre Boulez, Sir Charles Mackerras, Kurt Masur, Zubin Mehta, Lorin Maazel and Witold Rowicki; has appeared at over 120 international festivals in 45 countries, performed numerous world premieres; featured with Boulez, Stockhausen, Xenakis and John Cage in BBC documentary films, worked with numerous other major international composers (incl Feldman, Takemitsu, Barraqué, Dillon, Bengal), conductors and orchs; over 60 recordings and videos on various major labels; artistic dir: Sydney Spring Int Festival of New Music 1990, Joie et Lumière Burgundy 1997, International Pacific Festival Vanuatu 2002; fndr: Sydney Int Piano Competition 1969, Kötschach-Mauthner Musiktage Austria 1990, Spring Academy for New Music 1997; fell Frederic Chopin Int Soc 1976; chair in music and dir of the conservatorium Univ of New England Australia 2000–02, dir Sch of Music San Francisco State Univ 2002–05; Hon Dr: Creative Arts Wollong Univ 1992, Univ of Alberta; DMus Univ of Sydney 1998, Hon LLD 1998, Hon DLitt Univ of New England 1998; Companion of the Order of Australia 1992, Cdr Cross Order of Merit Poland 1993, OM (Poland) 1993, Chevalier de l'Ordre des Arts et des Lettres (France) 2005; *Style*— Prof Roger Woodward, AC, OBE; ✉ Patrick Togher Artist Management (e-mail pjtogher@ozemail.com.au)

WOODWARD, Sarah Wendy Boston; da of Edward Woodward, *qv*, and Venetia Mary, *née* Battine; *b* 3 April 1963; *Educ* Moria House Sch Eastbourne, RADA (Bancroft Medal); *m* Patrick Michael Joseph Toomey; 2 da (Milly b 6 Dec 1997, Nell b 20 Sept 2002); *Career* actress; photographer 2004– *Theatre* RSC: Henry V, Love's Labour's Lost, Hamlet, Richard III, Camille and Red Noses 1984–85, Murder in the Cathedral 1993–94, Rosaura in The Venetian Twins, Miranda in The Tempest 1993–94, Rosaline in Love's Labour's Lost 1995; Birmingham Repertory: Charley's Aunt, The Winter's Tale; other theatre incl: Artist Descending a Staircase (King's Head, Duke of York), The Rape of Lucrece (Almeida), Romeo and Juliet, Arms And The Man (Regent's Park Open Air Theatre), Angelus From Morning 'Til Midnight (Soho Poly), Build On Sand (Royal Court), Talk of the Devil (Bristol Old Vic), London Assurance (Chichester Theatre, Royal Haymarket), Schism in England (NT), Anne Danby in Kean (Old Vic, Toronto) 1990–91, Rose Jones in The Sea (RNT) 1991–92, Wild Oats (RNT) 1995, Connie Wicksteed in Habeas Corpus (Donmar Warehouse) 1996, Kitty in Tom & Clem (Aldwych) 1997, Charlotte in The Real Thing (Donmar Warehouse, Albery, Broadway) 1999–2000, Presence (Royal Court) 2001, Liaisons Dangereuses (Playhouse) 2003, Much Ado About Nothing (Globe) 2004, Susan in A Woman in Mind (Salisbury Playhouse) 2005, Adriana in A Comedy of Errors (Globe) 2006; *Television* incl: The Bill (LWT), Gems (Thames), The Two of Us (LWT), Sherlock Holmes (Granada), Poirot (Thames), Casualty (BBC), The Inspector Pitt Mysteries (Ardent) 1998, Final Demand (BBC) 2002; *Radio* incl: Scuttling Off (Radio 4) 1988, 84 Charing Cross Road (World Service) 1991; *Film* The House of Angelo 1999, Doctor Sleep 2001, I Capture the Castle 2001, Bright Young Things 2003; *Awards* Clarence Derwent Award for Artist Descending a Staircase 1989, nominated for Best Newcomer Shakespeare Globe Awards 1994, Olivier Award for Best Performance in a Supporting Role (Tom & Clem) 1997, nominated for Tony Award for Best Featured Actress (The Real Thing); *Recreations* all sports, poker (winner Fulham Open Hold 'em Championship Trophy 1994), blackjack; *Style*— Miss Sarah Woodward; ✉ c/o Roxane Vacca, 73 Beak Street, London W1R 3LF

WOODWARD, Rt Hon Shaun Anthony; PC (2007), MP; s of Dennis George Woodward, and Joan Lillian, *née* Nunn; *b* 26 October 1958; *Educ* Bristol GS, Jesus Coll Cambridge (MA); *m* 2 May 1987, Camilla Davan, da of Rt Hon Sir Tim Sainsbury, *qv*; 1 s (Tom b 1989), 3 da (Ella b 1991, Olivia b 1993, Kate b 1996); *Career* BBC TV journalist: researcher That's Life 1982–85, reporter and prodr Newsnight 1985–87, sr prodr Panorama 1987–89, editor That's Life 1990; dir of communications Cons Pty 1990–92, professorial fell Queen Mary & Westfield Coll London 1992–96; MP: (Cons) Witney 1997–99, (Lab) Witney 1999–2001, (Lab) St Helens 2001–; shadow min for London regeneration, the regions and tport until Dec 1999 (when resigned from Cons Pty and joined Lab Pty), Parly under sec of state NI 2005–06, min for creative industires and tourism DCMS 2006–, sec of state for NI 2007–; memb Jt Ctee on Human Rights 2001–; chm: Ben Hardwick Meml Fund 1984–93 (tstee 1993–97), Oxford Student Radio 1995–97; tstee: Childline 1997–2005 (dep chm 1993–97), Marine Stewardship Cncl 1998–2001; vice-pres St Helen's Millennium Centre 2001–; memb Fndn Bd RSC 1998–; fell Harvard Univ Inst of Politics at John F Kennedy Sch of Govt 1994; *Books* Tranquillizers (with Ron Lacey, 1983), Ben - the Story of Ben Hardwick (with Esther Rantzen, *qv*, 1984), Drugwatch (with Sarah Caplin, 1985); *Recreations* opera, architecture, gardening, reading, travel; *Style*— The Rt Hon Shaun Woodward, MP; ✉ House of Commons, London SW1A 0AA (tel 020 7219 2680, fax 020 7219 0979, e-mail woodwardsh@parliament.uk)

WOODWARD, Stephen James; s of Wesley James Woodward (d 1968), and Margery, *née* Gill (d 1978); *b* 25 May 1950; *Educ* King's Sch Rochester, W London Business Sch (BA); *m* 24 March 1973, Alison Linda, da of Robert Epps; 3 s (Paul James, David Robert, Michael Stephen); *Career* sponsored business undergrad De La Rue Co 1968–72, product exec Nestle Co 1972–75, sr product mangr Carnation Co 1975–78, mktg dir Seagram UK 1978–87, gp dir Lowe Howard-Spink advtg 1987–89; chief exec: Brands Div Michael Peters Group plc 1989–90, Ayer Group UK 1990–93 (responsible for founding Ayer/DP&A Direct Mktg, Ayer Data Mgmnt), Leagas Shafron Davis Chick Ayer (after merger) 1993; chm DP&A Ltd 1993–2002, chm Moonriver Group Ltd 2002–07; fndr dir The Competitive Advantage Business Ltd 1994–98, dir MyBeanstalk.co.uk Ltd; memb Mktg Gp of GB; fell Mktg Soc (chm 1994–95); Officier L'Ordre des Coteaux de Champagne; *Books* Understanding Brands - By Ten People Who Do (1991), Branding In Action (1993); *Clubs* Croham Hurst Golf (capt); *Style*— Stephen Woodward, Esq; ✉ Moonriver Group Ltd, Navigator House, Restmor Way, Wallington, Surrey (tel 020 8288 2000, fax 020 8288 2100)

WOODWARD, William Charles (Bill); QC (1985); s of Wilfred Charles Woodward, of Nottingham, and Annie Stewart, *née* Young; *b* 27 May 1940; *Educ* Nottingham HS, St John's Coll Oxford (BA); *m* 1965, Carolyn Edna, da of Francis Doughty Johns, of Kent; 1 da (Rebecca b 1966), 2 s (William b 1968, Fergus b 1974); *Career* called to the Bar Inner Temple 1964; memb Midland Circuit, marshall to late Sir Donald Finnemore, head of chambers 1987–95, recorder 1989–, dep judge of the High Court 1997–; pres Mental Health Review Tbnl 2000–; judge Court of Appeal St Helena 2002–; special prof Univ of Nottingham 1998–; memb: Law Advsy Ctee Univ of Nottingham, Bar European Gp; fndr memb: Nottingham Medico Legal Soc, East Midlands Business and Property Bar Assoc; *Recreations* sporadic cookery, serendipity, windsurfing in calm conditions; *Clubs* Pre-War Austin Seven, Notts United Services; *Style*— W C Woodward, Esq, QC; ✉ Ropewalk

Chambers, 24 The Ropewalk, Nottingham NG1 5EF (tel 0115 947 2581, fax 0115 947 6532, e-mail wcwqc@ropewalk.co.uk)

WOOL, Dr Rosemary Jane; CB (1995); *b* 19 July 1935; *Educ* Charing Cross Hosp Med Sch Univ of London (MB BS, DRCOG); *Career* specialist psychiatrist with particular interest in drug and alcohol misuse; princ in general practice 1963–70, psychiatric trg 1970–74; HM Prison Service: therapist HMP Grendon 1974–78, sr med offr HM YOI Leicester 1979–82, princ med offr 1983–89, dir Prison Med Services 1989–91, dir Health Care 1991–96; head Educn and Trg Unit Dept of Addictive Behaviour St George's Hosp London 1996–98; currently: vice-pres Int Relations Int Cncl of Prison Med Services, med advsr Directorate of Legal Affrs Div of Crime Problems Cncl of Europe; fndr and dir Prison Health Care Practitioners 2004; memb: BMA, RSM; FRCPsych 1988 (MRCPsych 1974); *Style*— Dr Rosemary Wool, CB; ✉ Wicken House, 105 Weston Road, Aston Clinton, Aylesbury, Buckinghamshire HP22 5EP (tel 01296 630448, fax 01296 632448, e-mail rjwool@wicken.nildram.co.uk, website www.prisonhcp.com)

WOOLAS, Phil; MP; *Educ* Univ of Manchester; *Career* pres NUS 1984–86, TV prodr BBC and ITN 1988–90, head of communications GMB 1991–97, MP (Lab) Oldham East & Saddleworth 1997– (Parly candidate Littleborough and Saddleworth by-election 1995); House of Commons: asst Govt whip 2001–02, a Lord Cmmr to HM Treasy (Govt whip) 2002–03, dep ldr of the House of Commons 2003–06, min of state Dept for Communities and Local Govt 2006–; *Style*— Phil Woolas, Esq, MP; ✉ tel 020 7219 1149; House of Commons, London SW1A 0AA (tel 020 7219 3000)

WOOLCOCK, Robin Arthur John; s of Arthur Woolcock (d 1977), of Hayes, Middx, and Minnie Elizabeth, *née* Dance, of Hitchin, Herts; *b* 6 September 1947; *Educ* Hayes Co GS, Queen Mary Coll London (BSc(Econ)); *m* April 1971, Ruth Monica, da of Fred Matthews, of Wirral; 2 da (Claire Elizabeth b 6 Aug 1975, Louise Jane b 17 Sept 1977); *Career* various sales and mktg positions Ford of Europe until 1978 (joined as graduate trainee 1969), product planning dir Leyland Truck and Bus 1978–82, UK ops dir Leyland (later Leyland DAF) 1982–88; Volkswagen AG Group/Lonrho: md MAN/VW Truck and Bus Ltd 1989–92, md Skoda UK Ltd 1993–94, head of Volkswagen UK 1994–; Freeman City of London, Liveryman Worshipful Co of Carmen; memb Inst of Road Transport Engrs, FCIT; *Recreations* Northampton RFC; *Style*— Robin Woolcock, Esq; ✉ Volkswagen UK, Yeomans Drive, Blakelands, Milton Keynes, Buckinghamshire MK14 5AN (tel 01908 601234, fax 01908 601607)

WOOLDRIDGE, Michael James (Mike); OBE (2002); s of James Wooldridge (d 1996), and Eveline Betty, *née* Carter; *b* 24 July 1947; *Educ* Bournemouth Sch for Boys, Harlow Tech Coll (later NCTJ Cert); *m* 1974, Ruth Kyre Holliday, da of Canon Keble Thomas (d 1992), and Gwyneth Thomas (d 2004); 3 c (Beth b 1977, Simon b 1978, Sophie b 1981); *Career* reporter Eastern Counties Newspapers 1965–68, VSO Uganda 1968–69; with the BBC 1970–: World Service News 1970–78, reporter Radio News 1978–82, East Africa corr 1982–89, Southern Africa corr 1989–90, Religious Affrs and Community Rels corr 1990–96, S Asia corr 1997–2001, World Affairs Corr 2001–; memb NUJ 1965; *Books* VSO in Action (1978), War Wounds (on Sudan, contrib 1988), The Day That Shook The World (contrib, 2001); *Recreations* family pursuits, walking, music, travel; *Clubs* Athenaeum; *Style*— Mike Wooldridge, OBE; ✉ c/o Room 2505, Television Centre, London W12 7RJ (tel 020 8743 8000)

WOOLDRIDGE, Sarah Margaret Chappell; da of Leonard Walter Andrews Chappell, and Constance, *née* Doyle; *Educ* Braeside Sch Buckhurst Hill, La Nouvelle Roseraie Vevey, Mrs Hoster's Secretarial Coll; *m* 1, 1973 (m dis 1978), Antonio Lourenço; 1 s (Jorge Antonio Chappell Lourenço); m 2, 1980, Ian Wooldridge (d 2007); *Career* conslt IMG dealing with VIP events, speakers and publishing (joined as PA to Mark McCormack 1966); supporter of cancer and dyslexia charities; *Recreations* cooking, swimming, watching sport (particularly in Australia), monster parties; *Clubs* Reform, Virgin Active; *Style*— Mrs Sarah Wooldridge; ✉ IMG, McCormack House, Burlington Lane, London W4 2TH (tel 020 8233 5000, fax 020 8233 6464, mobile 07802 956225, e-mail sarah.wooldridge@imgworld.com)

WOOLER, Stephen John; CB (2005); s of Herbert G Wooler, of Bedford, and Mabel Wooler; *b* 16 March 1948; *Educ* Bedford Modern Sch, UCL (LLB); *m* 5 Oct 1974, Jonquil Elizabeth, *née* Wilmshurst-Smith; 1 s (Charles Robert Alexander b 31 Jan 1980), 1 da (Stephanie Grace Alexandra b 20 Nov 1981); *Career* called to the bar (Gray's Inn) 1969, in practice 1969–73; Office of DPP: joined 1973, asst dir of public prosecutions 1982, seconded to Law Officers' Dept 1983, chief crown prosecutor (N London) 1987–89; seconded to Law Officers' Dept 1989, dep legal sec to Law Officers 1992–99, HM Chief Inspr to CPS 1999–; *Recreations* campanology, rugby, walking, garden; *Style*— Stephen Wooler, Esq, CB; ✉ HM Crown Prosecution Service Inspectorate, 26 Old Queen Street, London SW1H 9HP (tel 020 7210 1197, e-mail stephen.wooler@cps.gsi.gov.uk)

WOOLF, Prof Anthony Derek; s of Douglas Langton Woolf (d 2000), of Woodford, Essex, and Kathorn Beth Woolf, *née* Pearce (d 1980); *b* 12 June 1951; *Educ* Forest Sch, London Hosp Med Coll (BSc, MB BS); *m* 4 Dec 1975, Hilary Ann, da of Ronald Ruddock-West (d 1978); 1 da (Sarah Louise b 1979), 1 s (Richard Thomas b 1981); *Career* sr registrar Royal Nat Hosp for Rheumatic Diseases and Bristol Royal Infirmary 1983–87, conslt rheumatologist Royal Cornwall Hosp Truro 1987; hon prof of rheumatology Peninsula Medical Sch 2002; author of papers on rheumatology, med educn, viral arthritis and osteoporosis; ed Balliere's Clinical Rheumatology, assoc ed Annals of Rheumatic Diseases, memb Exec Ctee EULAR, memb Steering Ctee Bone and Joint Decade; pres European Bd of Rheumatology; memb Exec Ctee ILAR; Yeoman Worshipful Soc of Apothecaries; FRCP 1994 (MRCP 1979); *Books* Osteoporosis: A Clinical Guide (1988, 1990 and 1998), How to Avoid Osteoporosis: A Positive Health Guide (1989), Osteoporosis: A Pocket Book (1994, 2 edn 2002); *Style*— Prof Anthony Woolf; ✉ Royal Cornwall Hospital, Department of Rheumatology, Truro TR1 3LJ (tel 01872 250000, e-mail anthony.woolf@rcht.cornwall.nhs.uk)

WOOLF, David; s of Raymond Woolf (d 1997), of Newcastle upon Tyne and London, and Valerie Belle, *née* Robins (d 1954), of Plymouth; *b* 27 January 1945; *Educ* Clifton; *m* 19 June 1977, Vivienne Barbara, er da of Dr David Perk, of Johannesburg (d 1994); 2 s (James b 31 Jan 1979, John b 26 April 1982); *Career* trainee Keyser Ullman 1963–64, chartered accountant Chalmers Impey 1965–69, PA Corob Holdings 1969–71, fndr and chief exec Citygrove plc 1971–90; currently: chm Citygrove Securities, chm Citygrove Europe; memb Exec Ctee: British ORT 1989– (vice-chm 1995–2000, co-chm 2000–); memb Control Cmmn World ORT Union 1993–98 (chm 1997–98); FCA 1969; *Recreations* sailing, tennis, opera; *Clubs* Royal Southampton Yacht; *Style*— David Woolf, Esq; ✉ Mill House, 216 Chiswick High Road, London W4 1PD (tel 08700 601123, fax 08700 601124, e-mail davidwoolf@uk.citygroup.com)

WOOLF, Geoffrey Stephen(Geoff); s of Edward and Ruth Woolf, of London; *b* 13 October 1946; *Educ* Harrow Co GS, King's Coll London (LLB); *m* 1, 19 March 1972 (m dis 1978), Marcia, da of late Joseph Levy; m 2, 14 Feb 1985, Dr Josephine Kay Likierman, da of Julian Likierman, of London; 3 s (Nicholas b 18 Nov 1986, Simon b 30 July 1988, Alexander b 20 June 1991); *Career* articled to Sir Anthony Lousada at Stephenson Harwood & Tatham 1968–70, admitted slr 1970, ptnr Stephenson Harwood 1975–99, ptnr SJ Berwin & Co 1999–; Freeman Worshipful Co of Solicitors 1975; memb: Law Soc 1970, Insolvency Lawyers Assoc, Assoc of Partnership Practitioners; *Recreations* opera, theatre; *Style*— Geoff Woolf; ✉ SJ Berwin & Co, 222 Gray's Inn Road, London WC1X 8HB (tel 020 8533 2871, fax 020 8533 2000, e-mail geoffrey.woolf@sjberwin.com)

WOOLF, Baron (Life Peer UK 1992), of Barnes in the London Borough of Richmond; Sir Harry Kenneth Woolf; kt (1979), PC (1986); s of late Alexander Woolf, and late Leah, *née* Cussins; *b* 2 May 1933; *Educ* Fettes, UCL (LLB); *m* 1961, Marguerite, da of late George Sassoon; 3 s (Hon Jeremy Richard George b 26 Aug 1962, Hon Andrew James David b 18 June 1965, Hon Eliot Charles Anthony b 29 July 1967); *Career* Nat Service cmmnd 15/19 Royal Hussars 1954, Capt Army Legal Service 1955; called to the Bar Inner Temple 1954 (bencher 1976), recorder of the Crown Ct 1972–79, jr counsel Inland Revenue 1973–74, first Treasy jr counsel in common law 1974–79, judge High Ct (Queen's Bench Div) 1979–86, presiding judge SE Circuit 1981–84, Lord Justice of Appeal 1986–92, Lord of Appeal in Ordinary 1992–96, Master of the Rolls 1996–2000, Lord Chief Justice 2000–05; held inquiry into prison disturbances 1990–91, conducted inquiry Access to Justice 1994–96; memb: Senate of Bar and Bench 1981–85, Bowman Ctee 1996–97, Int Advsy Cncl on Law and Justice World Bank 2001–06; special advsr and chair Conflict Mgmnt Advsy Gp CEDR 2005–, mediator and arbitrator Blackstone Chambers 2005–; chm: Lord Chllr's Advsy Ctee on Legal Educn 1987–90, Middx Justice's Advsy Ctee 1987–90, Bd of Mgmnt Inst of Advanced Legal Studies 1986–93, Butler Tst 1992–96 (pres 1996–), St Mary's Hosp Special Tstees 1993–97, Advsy Cncl on Public Records 1996–2000, Magna Carta Tst 1996–2000, Financial Mktg Law Reform Ctee; pres: Law Teachers Assoc 1985–90, Jt Ctee for Jewish Social Services 1988–2000, W London Magistrates' Assoc 1987–92; govr Oxford Centre for Hebrew Studies 1988–93 (emeritus 1993); pro-chllr Univ of London 1994–2005; visitor: UCL 1996–2000, Nuffield Coll Oxford 1996–2000, Downing Coll Cambridge 2006; visiting prof and chm Cncl UCL 2005–, hon prof of Law Chinese Univ Hong Kong; hon memb: Public Soc of Teachers of Law 1988–, Ct Univ of London 1993–94; Hon LLD: Univ of Buckingham, Univ of Bristol, Univ of London and Anglia, Manchester Metropolitan Univ, Univ of Hull 2001, Cambridge Univ 2006; Hon DSc Cranfield Univ 2001, Hon DCL Univ of Oxford 2004; Freeman Newcastle upon Tyne 2006; hon fell: Univ of Leeds, UCL; Hon FBA 2000; *Publications* Protecting the Public: the new challenge (Hamlyn lecture, 1990), Declaratory Judgement (ed jtly, 2 edn 1993), De Smith Woolf & Jowell: Judicial Review of Administrative Action (ed jtly, 5 edn, 1995); *Clubs* Garrick, Athenaeum; *Style*— The Rt Hon the Lord Woolf, PC

WOOLF, Prof Neville; s of Barnett Woolf (d 1972), of Cape Town, South Africa, and Florence Charlotte, *née* Cohn (d 1973); *b* 17 May 1930; *Educ* Univ of Cape Town (MB ChB, MMed Path), Univ of London (PhD); *m* 31 March 1957, Lydia Paulette, da of Harry Joseph Mandelbrote (d 1971), of Cape Town, South Africa; 1 da (Victoria (Mrs Coren) b 1960), 1 s (Adam b 1964); *Career* reader and hon conslt St George's Hosp Med Sch 1968–74 (sr lectr and hon conslt 1965–68), Bland-Sutton prof of histopathology Univ Coll Sch of Med, vice-dean Faculty of Clinical Scis Royal Free and Univ Coll Med Sch UCL 1991–2004; former chm Bd of Studies in Pathology Univ of London, memb Pathological Soc; FRCPath, FRCS(Eng); *Books* Cell, Tissue and Disease (1977, 1986 and 2002), Pathology of Atherosclerosis (1982), Pathology: Basic and Systemic (1998); *Recreations* reading, music, cooking; *Style*— Prof Neville Woolf; ✉ Royal Free and University College Medical School, Faculty of Clinical Sciences, Gower Street, London WC1E 6BT (tel 020 7679 5461, fax 020 7383 2462)

WOOLFENDEN, (Kenneth) Alan; s of Frederick John Woolfenden (d 1971), and Mary, *née* Duff; *b* 25 July 1950; *Educ* N Manchester GS for Boys, Univ of Liverpool (MB ChB); *m* 1 April 1972, Susan Irene, da of Alan Eaton, of Manchester; 1 s (Jonathan Frederick b 12 Dec 1980); *Career* conslt urological surgn Royal Liverpool Univ Hosp Tst 1985–, clinical dir of urology Royal Liverpool and Broadgreen Univ Hosp Tst; hon lectr Dept of Surgery Faculty of Med Univ of Liverpool; dir Sr Registrar Trg Mersey Region; memb Cncl: Br Assoc of Urological Surgns, Liverpool Med Inst; memb Exec Cncl Mersey Region for Kidney Research; memb BMA 1973, FRCS 1978, FEBU 1992; *Style*— Alan Woolfenden, Esq; ✉ Riverside, Manorial Road, Parkgate, South Wirral, Cheshire CH64 6QW (tel 0151 336 7229); 48 Rodney Street, Liverpool L1 9AA (tel 0151 709 2079)

WOOLFENDEN, Guy Anthony; OBE (2007); s of Harold Arthur Woolfenden (d 1986), and Kathleen Norah Woolfenden (d 1978); *b* 12 July 1937; *Educ* Westminster Abbey Choir Sch, Whitgift Sch, Christ's Coll Cambridge (MA), Guildhall Sch of Music (LGSM); *m* 29 Sept 1962, Jane, da of Leonard George Smerdon Aldrick, of Ewell, Surrey; 3 s (Richard b 1964, Stephen b 1966, James b 1969); *Career* head of music RSC 1963–98 (hon assoc artist), artistic dir Cambridge Festival 1986–91; compositions incl: scores for RSC, Comedie Française, Burgtheater and Norwegian Nat Theatre, four ballet scores, TV and film music, concert music; conducts concerts, opera and ballet in Britain and internationally; chm: Denne Gilkes Meml Fund, Br Assoc of Symphonic Bands and Wind Ensembles 1999–2002; patron Birmingham Symphonic Winds; pres ISM 2002–03; memb: MU, PRS, MCPS, SPNM, Br Acad of Composers and Songwriters; Hon LCM, fell Birmingham Schs of Music (FBSM); *Recreations* photography, table tennis, walking, cricket; *Style*— Guy Woolfenden, Esq, OBE; ✉ Malvern House, Sibford Ferris, Banbury, Oxfordshire OX15 5RG (tel 01295 780679, fax 01295 788630, e-mail guy@arielmusic.co.uk, website www.arielmusic.co.uk)

WOOLFSON, Dr Gerald; s of late Joseph Samuel Woolfson, and late Lilian Woolfson; *b* 25 March 1932; *Educ* Milton Sch Bulawayo and Zimbabwe, Univ of Cape Town (MB); *m* 1, 1955, Sheila Charlaff; 2 s (David b 1955, Adrian b 1965), 1 da (Karen b 1959); m 2, 1978, Lynne, *née* Silver; 1 s (Alexander b 1978); *Career* conslt psychiatrist Hammersmith and St Mary's Hosp Gp, med dir Florence Nightingale Hosps London, hon sr lectr RPMS; FRSM, FRCP, FRCPsych; *Recreations* chess, doodling; *Style*— Dr Gerald Woolfson; ✉ 16 Church Row, London NW3 6UP; 97 Harley Street, London W1N 1DF (tel 020 7935 3400, fax 020 7487 3834, e-mail gerald.woolfson@virgin.net)

WOOLFSON, Prof Michael Mark; s of Maurice Woolfson (d 1956), and Rose, *née* Solomons (d 1999); *b* 9 January 1927; *Educ* Wellingborough GS, Jesus Coll Oxford (MA), UMIST (PhD, DSc); *m* 19 July 1951, Margaret, da of Dr Mayer Frohlich; 2 s (Mark b 1954, Malcolm b 1957), 1 da (Susan b 1960); *Career* HG 7 Northants Bn 1942–44, Nat Serv cmmnd 2 Lt RE 1947–49; res asst Cavendish Laboratory Cambridge 1952–54, ICI res fell Cambridge 1954–55, reader in physics UMIST 1961–65 (lectr 1953–61), currently emeritus prof Univ of York (prof of theoretical physics 1965); former pres Yorks Philosophical Soc; hon fell Jesus Coll Oxford 1999; FInstP, FRAS, FRS; *Books* Direct Methods in Crystallography (1961), An Introduction to X-Ray Crystallography (1970, 2 edn 1997), The Origin of the Solar System: The Capture Theory (1989), Physical and Non-Physical Methods of Solving Crystal Structures (1995), An Introduction to Computer Simulation (1999), The Origin and Evolution of the Solar System (2000), Planetary Science (2002), Mathematics for Physics (2006); *Recreations* winemaking; *Style*— Prof Michael Woolfson, FRS; ✉ 24 Sandmoor Green, Leeds LS17 7SB (tel 0113 266 2166); Department of Physics, University of York, York YO10 5DD (tel 01904 432230, fax 01904 432214)

WOOLFSON, Rosalind Anne; da of Myer Henry Woolfson (d 1962), of Glasgow, and Miriam, *née* Cohen; *b* 13 February 1945; *Educ* Glasgow HS for Girls, Principessa Colonna Sch Florence, Glasgow Sch of Art; *Career* Marks & Spencer; FJ Lyons PR, Shandwick Group 1975–91, bd dir Shandwick Communications 1985–91, estab Woolfson Communications (own PR co) 1991; MIPR; FRSA; *Recreations* visual arts, travel, literature, music, opera; *Style*— Miss Rosalind Woolfson; ✉ 16A Royal Crescent, Edinburgh EH3 6QA (tel 0131 558 3003, mobile 07831 525878, e-mail rosalind@woolfsoncomms.co.uk or rosalindwoolfson@aol.com)

WOOLHOUSE, Prof Mark Edward John; OBE (2002); s of Prof John G Woolhouse, of Coventry, and R Carolyn, *née* Harrison; *b* 25 April 1959, Shrewsbury; *Educ* Queen

Elizabeth's GS Ashbourne, Tiffin Sch Kingston, Univ of Oxford (BA), Univ of York (MSc), Queen's Univ Kingston Ontario (PhD); *m* 24 July 2004, Dr Francisca Mutapi; 1 da (Nyasha Ruth b 4 Nov 2006); *Career* research fell Dept of Biological Sciences Univ of Zimbabwe 1985–86, research fell Dept of Biology Imperial Coll London 1986–89, research fell Dept of Zoology Univ of Oxford and visiting research fell Blair Research Labs Zimbabwe 1989–97, prof of infectious disease epidemiology Sch of Biological Sciences Univ of Edinburgh 1997–; author of more than 150 pubns in scientific jls; Wright Medal Br Soc for Parasitology 2002; FRSE 2004; *Recreations* walking, fly fishing; *Style*— Prof Mark Woolhouse, OBE; ✉ The Centre for Infectious Diseases, University of Edinburgh, Ashworth Laboratories, The King's Buildings, West Mains Road, Edinburgh EH9 3JT (tel 0131 650 5456)

WOOLLAM, Her Hon Suzanna Elizabeth; da of John Woollam, and Elizabeth Woollam; *b* 6 December 1946; *Educ* Trinity Coll Dublin (MA); *Career* called to the Bar 1975, judge advocate 1988–2001, recorder 1998–2001 (asst recorder 1993–98), circuit judge (SE Circuit) 2001–06, ret; *Style*— Her Hon Suzanna Woollam

WOOLLAMS, Christopher John; s of late George James Woollams, and Phyllis Joan, *née* Cox; *b* 4 July 1949; *Educ* Watford Boys' GS, St Peter's Coll Oxford (MA); *m* (m dis); 3 da (Catherine Louise b 1978 d 2004, Georgina Clair b 1983, Stephanie Marie b 1986), 1 s (Benjamin Henry b 1995); *Career* fndr and chm Spiral Cellars Ltd 1980–91, dir Ogilvy and Mather London 1980–83, md Publicis 1984, chm Ted Bates Group London 1985 (Euro and Worldwide Bd dir 1986), chm Fitness in Home Ltd 1986–91; chief exec WMGO Group plc 1987–95; chief exec BDP Int 1998–; chm Health Issues Ltd 2002–; fndr CANCERactive; Lord of Pembury (manorial title); *Publications* Everything You Need to Know to Help You Beat Cancer (2002), The Tree of Life (2003), Oestrogen - the killer in our midst (2004), Cancer - your first 15 steps (2004), Conventional Cancer Cures - What's the Alternative? (2005), Integrated Cancer and Oncology News (icon); *Recreations* flying, golf, wine, writing, chess, skiing; *Clubs* RAC, Confrerie de Tastevin, Palm Hills (Thailand), Marketors, Royal Mougins (France); *Style*— Chris Woollams; ✉ e-mail chris@canceractive.com

WOOLLARD, Jessica Elizabeth Clare; da of William Woollard, and Isobel, *née* MacLeod; *Educ* St Paul's Girls' Sch, Univ of Manchester (BA); *Career* literary agent; dir Toby Eady Associates Ltd 1995–2005, literary agent The Marsh Agency 2006–; memb Soc of Authors, memb Soka Gakkai Int (SGI-UK); *Recreations* travel, live music, books; *Style*— Ms Jessica Woollard; ✉ The Marsh Agency, 11/12 Dover Street, London W1S 4LJ (tel 020 7399 2806, fax 020 7399 2801, e-mail jessica@marsh-agency.co.uk)

WOOLLEY, Brian Peter; s of Herbert Woolley, and Edna, *née* Hindley; *b* 28 April 1954; *Educ* Manchester Grammar, St John's Coll Oxford (MA); *m* 1978, Joy, da of Alan Harbottle; *Career* Citibank NA London 1975–79, Orion Bank Limited 1979–81, Samuel Montagu & Co 1981–84, md and head of capital markets Citibank International plc 1984–96, md and regnl head Bank of China International (UK) Ltd 1996–98, md Industrial Bank of Japan Ltd 1999–2002, chm and ceo Logic Capital Ltd; *Recreations* opera, golf; *Clubs* Wentworth; *Style*— Brian Woolley, Esq

WOOLLEY, David Rorie; QC (1980); s of Albert Walter Woolley, of Wallingford, Oxon, and Ethel Rorie, *née* Linn; *b* 9 June 1939; *Educ* Winchester, Trinity Hall Cambridge (MA); *Career* called to the Bar Middle Temple 1962 (bencher 1988); recorder of the Crown Court 1982–, inspr DOE Inquiry into Nat Gallery 1984; Liveryman Worshipful Co of Coopers; *Publications* Town Hall and the Property Owner (1965), Environmental Law (jtly, 2000); *Recreations* opera, real tennis, mountaineering; *Clubs* MCC; *Style*— David Woolley, Esq, QC; ✉ Landmark Chambers, 180 Fleet Street, London EC4A 2HG

WOOLLEY, Dr Paul Kerrison; s of Robert Charles Woolley (d 1979), and Hilda Kerrison, *née* Barnsley; *b* 9 November 1939; *Educ* King Edward VI Sch Birmingham, Univ of York (BA, DPhil); *m* 31 July 1976, Penelope Ann, da of Albert Ewart Baines; 2 s (Nicholas Kerrison b 26 Oct 1977, Robert Ewart b 10 June 1980); *Career* ptnr Murray & Co Birmingham 1965–67 (joined 1959), Esmée Fairbairn lectr in fin Univ of York 1971–76, specialist advsr House of Lords Ctee on EEC 1975–76, advsr IMF Washington DC 1980–83 (economist 1976–78, sr economist 1978–80); dir 1983–87: Baring Brothers & Co Ltd, Baring Investment Management, Baring International Investment Management, Baring Quantitative Management; ptnr Grantham Mayo Van Otterloo & Co Boston 1987– (dir 1998–2003), fndr and chm GMO Woolley Ltd London 2000–06 (md 1987–2000), chm GMO Europe 2003–06; adjunct prof of finance Paul Woolley Centre for Capital Market Dysfunctionality Tanaka Business Sch Imperial Coll London 2006–; author of various articles in academic and fin jls; memb Birmingham Stock Exchange 1964–67; Liveryman Worshipful Co of Broderers 1998; hon prof Univ of York 2006– (hon fell 2003–06); *Recreations* walking, travel; *Clubs* Reform, City University; *Style*— Dr Paul Woolley; ✉ 17 Edwardes Square, London W8 6HE (tel 020 7603 7603); Tanaka Business School, Imperial College London, South Kensington Campus, London SW7 2AZ

WOOLLEY, Prof Robert Peter; s of John S Woolley and Joan Grace Woolley; *b* 8 January 1954; *Educ* Eastbourne Coll, Royal Coll of Music, Inst of Educn Univ of London; *m* Sept 1982, Susan Jane, da of Michael Carrington; 2 da; *Career* harpsichordist, fortepianist, organist and conductor; concerts in UK, USA, Japan and throughout Europe since 1973, regular BBC and World Serv broadcaster, taught in Austria and Portugal, prof of harpsichord and fortepiano RCM 1985–, memb Purcell Quartet; vice-chair of the jury Prague Spring Int Harpsichord Competition 2005; *Recordings* incl: Purcell - Complete Harpsichord Works, music by Handel, Frescobaldi, D Scarlatti, J S Bach, C P E Bach, Poglietti, Bohm, Sweelinck: complete keyboard works (in progress), Blow; *Recreations* walking, reading, architecture, photography; *Style*— Prof Robert Woolley; ✉ Royal College of Music, Prince Consort Road, London SW7 2BS (tel 020 7589 3643, rwoolley@rcm.ac.uk); e-mail info@woolleys.org.uk

WOOLLEY, Trevor Adrian; CB (2007); s of Harry George Woolley (d 1974), and Doreen Vera Woolley, *née* O'Hale (d 1961); *b* 9 August 1954; *Educ* Latymer Upper Sch Hammersmith, Peterhouse Cambridge (MA); *Career* MOD: admin trainee 1975–80, princ 1980–86, private sec to sec of the Cabinet 1986–89, dir of Procurement Policy 1989–93, head of Resources and Progs (Army) 1993–96, head of Resources and Progs (Prog Devpt) 1996–97, asst under-sec of state (Systems) 1997–98, DG Resources and Plans 1998–2002, cmd sec Land Command 2002–03, fin dir 2003–; govr Latymer Upper Sch, chm Old Latymerian Assoc; *Recreations* cricket, golf, walking; *Clubs* Chiswick and Latymer Cricket, MCC; *Style*— Trevor Woolley, Esq, CB; ✉ Ministry of Defence, Whitehall, London SW1A 2HB (tel 020 7218 6216)

WOOLLISCROFT, Andrew (Andy); s of John Woolliscroft, and Sheila, *née* Andersen; *b* 16 December 1955; *Educ* Adams' GS Wem, South Bank Poly London; *Partner* Zara Kane; 2 s (Samuel James Ishmael b 4 May 2000, Joshua Flynn Alexander b 6 Feb 2003); *Career* music agent: Bron Agency 1979–81, The Station Agency 1981–90, Primary Talent International 1990–; clients incl: Lou Reed, David Byrne, Joe Jackson, Patti Smith, John Cale, Ryuichi Sakamoto, Laurie Anderson; former clients incl: Thompson Twins, Tears For Fears, Julian Cope, OMD, Cocteau Twins, PIL, The Jesus & Mary Chain, Everything But The Girl, Björk, INXS, Spice Girls; *Recreations* golf, photography, family; *Style*— Andy Woolliscroft, Esq; ✉ Primary Talent International, 10–11 Jockey's Fields, London WC1R 4BN (tel 020 7400 4500, fax 020 7400 4501)

WOOLNER, Nigel; s of Leonard Woolner (d 1987), of London, and Ida, *née* Chamberlain (d 1985); *b* 22 April 1940; *Educ* Latymer Upper Sch, Regent Street Poly Sch of Architecture (DipArch); *m* 1973, Carol Ann, *née* Smith; 2 s (Alexander b 27 Nov 1974, Thomas b 5 Aug 1979), 1 da (Philippa b 12 June 1977); *Career* architect; Chapman Taylor Partners: joined 1960, ptnr 1973–2005, dir 2005–, conslt 2007–; major architectural projects incl: The Ridings Wakefield, The Market Place Bolton, The London Pavilion Piccadilly Circus, The Galdes Bromley, The Exchange Putney, 172–182 Regent Street London, The Exchange Ilford, Priory Meadow Hastings, N1 Islington, Liberty Romford, Shires Leicester, Whitefriars Canterbury; professional practice examiner Architectural Assoc 1980–; Br Cncl of Shopping Centres: memb Bd 1996–2001, chm Awards Ctee 2001–; fell Soc of Architect Artists 1990–; pres Bedford Park Soc 2005– (chm 1981–98), chm RSA House Panel 2000–05, memb Cncl RSA 2001–05; Royal Coll of Music: tstee Mills Williams Fellowship 1995–, chm Estates Ctee 2004–, memb Cncl 2004–; govr Latymer Upper Sch 1985–; *Books* ICSC Illustrated Architectural Guide to Vienna (with Carol Woolner, 1989), ICSC Illustrated Architectural Guide to Brussels (with Carol Woolner, 1994), ICSC Illustrated Architectural Guide to Vienna (with Carol Woolner, 1995), Venetian Sketchbook (2006); *Recreations* watercolour painting, theatre, opera; *Clubs* Architecture, The Bond (pres 2005–06), Garrick; *Style*— Nigel Woolner, Esq, Dip Arch, RIBA, FRSA; ✉ Chapman Taylor, 96 Kensington High Street, London W8 4SG (tel 020 7371 3000, fax 020 7371 1949, e-mail nwoolner@chapmantaylor.com)

WOOLNOUGH, Victor James (Vic); s of Lionel Victor Woolnough (d 1989), of Basingstoke, Hants, and Joyce Eileen, *née* Hodder; *b* 1 November 1943; *Educ* Queen Mary's GS (Hampshire schs jr 100 yards sprint champion 1957); *m* 21 March 1964, Carla Bettine, da of Albert Ernest Atherton; 1 da (Lisa b 19 Dec 1966); *Career* Lansing Bagnall Ltd (Basingstoke): trainee draughtsman and engrg apprentice 1961–66, detail draughtsman 1966–67, design draughtsman 1966–69; CA Blatchford & Sons Ltd: design draughtsman 1969–73, design engr 1973–87, chief designer 1988–92, research and devpt mangr 1992–98; specialist in the design and devpt of artificial limbs (incl Blatchford Endolite System), sole or jt inventor of over a dozen patented mechanisms and devices; FIED 1981 (MIED 1976), IEng 1981; *Recreations* walking, personal computers, camping; *Style*— Vic Woolnough, Esq; ✉ Lawrenny, Mary Lane, North Waltham, Hampshire RG25 2BY

WOOLRICH, John; *b* 3 January 1954; *Educ* Univ of Manchester (BA), Lancaster Univ (MLitt); *Career* composer; Northern Arts fell Univ of Durham 1982–85, composer in residence Nat Centre for Orchestral Studies London 1985–86, visiting lectr Goldsmiths Coll London 1986–87, composer in assoc Orch of St John's Smith Square 1994–95, lectr in music Royal Holloway Univ of London 1994–98, dir The Composers Ensemble 1989–, concerts dir Almeida Theatre 1999–, assoc artistic dir Aldeburgh Festival 2005– (guest artistic dir 2004); visiting fell Clare Hall Cambridge 1999–2001; Hon FTCL; *Major works* Ulysses Awakes 1989, The Ghost in the Machine 1990, Viola Concerto 1993, Oboe Concerto 1996 (world première BBC Proms 1996), In The House of Crossed Desires 1996, Cello Concerto 1998; *Style*— John Woolrich, Esq; ✉ c/o Faber Music, 3 Queens Square, London WC1N 3AU (tel 020 7278 7436, fax 020 7278 3817)

WOOLTON, 3 Earl of (UK 1956); Simon Frederick Marquis; also Baron Woolton (UK 1939), Viscount Woolton (UK 1952), and Viscount Walberton (UK 1956); s of 2 Earl of Woolton (d 1969, s of 1 Earl of Woolton, CH, PC, JP, DL, chm Lewis's and associated cos, min of Food 1940–43, min of Reconstruction and memb War Cabinet 1943–45, lord pres Cncl 1945 and 1951–52, chllr of Duchy of Lancaster 1952–55, chm Cons Pty 1946–55) by his 2 w (Cecily) Josephine, er da of Sir Alastair Penrose Gordon-Cumming 5 Bt (now Countess Lloyd George of Dwyfor); *b* 24 May 1958; *Educ* Eton, Univ of St Andrews (MA); *m* 1, 30 April 1987 (m dis 1997), Hon Sophie, o c of 3 Baron Birdwood, *qv*; 3 da (Lady Olivia Alice b 16 April 1990, Lady Constance Elizabeth b 14 Oct 1991, Lady Claudia Louise b 3 March 1995); m 2, 28 Oct 1999, (Mary) Carol, da of Peter Davidson; *Heir* none; *Career* merchant banker S G Warburg & Co Ltd 1982–88, Woolton Elwes Ltd 1994–2000, New Boathouse Capital Ltd 2000–; tstee: Woolton Charitable Tst, Titsey Fndn, Balcarres Heritage Tst; *Clubs* Royal and Ancient (St Andrews), White's, Pratt's, Brooks's, MCC; *Style*— The Rt Hon the Earl of Woolton; ✉ Clune Lodge, Tomatin, Inverness-shire IV13 7XZ

WOOSNAM, Ian Harold; OBE (2007, MBE 1992); s of Harold Woosnam, and Joan Woosnam; *b* 2 March 1958; *Educ* St Martins Modern Sch; *m* 12 Nov 1983, Glendryth, da of Terrance Mervyn Pugh; 1 s (Daniel Ian b 5 Feb 1985), 2 da (Rebecca Louise b 16 June 1988, Ami Victoria b 10 Sept 1991); *Career* professional golfer 1976–; tournament victories: News of the World under 23 match play 1979, Cacharel under 25 Championship 1982, Swiss Open 1982, Silk Cut Masters 1983, Scandinavian Enterprise Open 1984, Zambian Open 1985, Lawrence Batley TPC 1986, 555 Kenya Open 1986, Hong Kong Open 1987, Jersey Open 1987, Cepsa Madrid Open 1987, Bell's Scottish Open 1987 and 1990, Lancome Trophy 1987 and 1993, Suntory World Match-Play Championship 1987 and 1990, Volvo PGA Championship 1988, Carrolls Irish Open 1988 and 1989, Panasonic European Open 1988, Mediterranean Open 1990 and 1991, Monte Carlo Open 1990, 1991 and 1992, Epson Grand Prix 1990, US F & G Classic 1991, US Masters 1991, PGA Grand Slam of Golf 1991, Murphy's English Open 1993, Air France Cannes Open 1994, British Masters 1994, Johnnie Walker Classic 1996, Heineken Classic 1996, Scottish Open 1996, German Open 1996, Volvo PGA Championship 1997, Hyundai Motor Masters 1997, Cisco World Match Play Championship 2001; team events: Ryder Cup 1983, 1985 (winners), 1987 (winners), 1989 (winners), 1991, 1993, 1995 (winners), 1997 (winners), 2002 (non-playing vice-capt) and 2006 (capt, winners), Dunhill Cup 1985, 1986, 1988, 1989, 1990, 1991, 1993, and 1995, World Cup 1980, 1982, 1983, 1984, 1985, 1986, 1987 (team and individual winner), 1990, 1991 (individual winner), 1992, 1993, 1994, 1996, 1997 and 1998; finished top European Order of Merit 1987 and 1990, ranked number 1 Sony World Rankings 1991; *Recreations* snooker, water skiing, sports; *Style*— Ian Woosnam, Esq, OBE; ✉ c/o IMG, McCormack House, Burlington Lane, London W4 2TH (tel 020 8233 5300, fax 020 8233 5301)

WOOTTON, Prof David; s of Rev Canon R W F Wootton (d 1984), and Joan, *née* Earls; *b* 15 January 1952; *Educ* Peterhouse Cambridge (MA, PhD), Balliol Coll Oxford; *Partner* Dr Alison Mark; 2 c from previous m (Lisa b 30 April 1976, Thomas b 26 August 1985); *Career* prof of humanities Univ of Victoria Canada 1989–94, dean of arts Brunel Univ 1996–98, prof of history Queen Mary & Westfield Coll London 1998–2004, anniversary prof of history Univ of York 2004–; FRHistS 1986; *Publications* John Locke: Political Writings (ed, 1993) and numerous articles in academic books and jls; *Style*— Prof David Wootton; ✉ Department of History, University of York, Heslington, York YO10 5DD (tel davidwootton@britishlibrary.net)

WOOTTON, David Hugh; s of James Wootton, and Muriel Wootton; *b* 21 July 1950; *Educ* Bradford GS, Jesus Coll Cambridge (BA, MA); *m* 23 April 1977, Elizabeth Rosemary, da of Peter Knox; 2 da (Alexandra b 1978, Sophie b 1981), 2 s (James b 1979, Christopher b 1985); *Career* ptnr Allen & Overy 1979–; memb Law Soc 1975; Alderman for the Ward of Langbourn in the City of London; Liveryman: Worshipful Co of Fletchers (former Master), City of London Slrs Co (memb Ct of Assts), Worshipful Co of Clockmakers; Freeman: Worshipful Co of Bowyers, Worshipful Co of Information Technologists; *Recreations* opera, rowing; *Clubs* Leander, Hawks' (Cambridge); *Style*— David Wootton, Esq; ✉ Allen & Overy LLP, One Bishops Square, London E1 6AO (tel 020 3088 3022, fax 020 3088 0088, e-mail david.wootton@allenovery.com)

WOOTTON, Prof (Harold) John; CBE (1997); s of Harold Wootton (d 1980), of Bloxwich, Staffs, and Hilda Mary, *née* Somerfield (d 1989); *b* 17 November 1936; *Educ* Queen Mary's GS Walsall, QMC London (BSc), Univ of Calif (MEng); *m* 1960, Patricia Ann, da of Cyril Ronald Riley; 2 s (David Ian b 1962, Neil Antony b 1964); *Career* lectr Dept of Civil Engrg Univ of Leeds 1959–62, tech dir Freeman Fox Wilbur Smith Associates 1963–67, jt md SIA Ltd 1967–71, chm Wootton Jeffreys Consultants Ltd 1971–91, chief exec

W

Transport Research Laboratory 1991–97, Rees Jeffreys prof in transport planning Transportation Research Gp Univ of Southampton 1997–; visiting prof: in computing KCL 1987–89, in transport studies UCL 1989–92; pres Inst of Highways and Transportation 1997–98, chm Motorway Archive Tst 2006–; CEng, FCIT, FIHT, FICE, FREng 2000; *Recreations* cricket, golf, rotary, photography, travel; *Style*— Prof John Wootton, CBE, FREng; ✉ Transportation Research Group, University of Southampton, Highfield, Southampton SO17 1BJ (tel 023 8059 2192, fax 023 8059 3152, e-mail hjw@soton.ac.uk)

WOOTTON, Robert John (Bob); s of William Robert Wootton (d 1987), of Marlow, Bucks, and Linda Rosalie, *née* Gyton; *b* 30 June 1955; *Educ* Oundle, UCL; *Career* trainee media exec Lintas Ltd 1974–81, successively trainee media exec, head of TV then assoc media dir Wight Collins Rutherford Scott Ltd 1981–85, media dir HDM Horner Collis Kirvan Ltd then Griffin Bacal Ltd 1985–94, ptnr De Saulles Associates media consultancy 1994–96, dir of media and advtg ISBA 1996–; MIPA 1986; *Recreations* active and passive participation in music, cookery, food and wine, mycology; *Style*— Bob Wootton, Esq

WOOTTON, Dr (Leslie) Roger; s of Denis Stokes Wootton (d 1965), and Geraldine Amy, *née* Virgo (d 1990); *b* 29 June 1944; *Educ* Kingston GS, City Univ (BSc, PhD); *m* 15 Sept 1979, Hilary Anne Robinson; 2 s (Marcus Desmond b 21 July 1981, Julian Michael b 12 Feb 1986); *Career* Nat Physical Laboratory 1962–71 (joined Aerodynamic Div; projects incl: wind effects on bldgs, deep water jetty Humber Estuary at Immingham), W S Atkins consltg engrs 1971–93; projects incl: BP Forties platform, Shell Tern devpt; dean Sch of Engrg City Univ London 1993–99, prof of engrg City Univ 1999–; NE Rowe medal Royal Aeronautical Soc, Telford Premium ICE, review of airline maintenance for CAA 1998; memb Royal Aeronautical Soc; FRAeS, FREng 1985; *Books* Dynamics of Marine Structures; *Recreations* being a husband and father, hot air ballooning (as means of escaping from former recreations!); *Clubs* Br Balloon and Airship, GAPAN; *Style*— Prof Roger Wootton, FREng; ✉ Hardwick Cottage, St Nicholas Hill, Leatherhead, Surrey KT22 8NE (tel 01372 372654, e-mail roger@woottonshouse.co.uk)

WORAM, Terence Annesley; s of Victor Henry Woram (d 1940), and Helena Mary, *née* Cox (d 1992); *b* 23 June 1933, Mutare, Zimbabwe; *Educ* Christian Brothers Coll Kimberley, Univ of Cape Town (BArch); *m* 14 Oct 1961, Patricia Eileen, da of Frederick Leslie Lawrence; 1 s (Michael Desmond b 27 Aug 1962, d 22 May 1980), 3 da (Catherine Ann b 17 Jan 1964, Frances Mary b 21 May 1965, Joanna Helen b 2 May 1967); *Career* Pallet and Price Salisbury Rhodesia 1953–56, Harrison and Abramovitz NY 1956–59, Trehearne Norman Preston and Ptnrs London 1960–64; ptnr: BL Adams Partnership London 1964–69, Green Lloyd and Adams London 1969–79; sr ptnr Terence Woram Associates 1979–; architectural awards: Richmond Soc 1983, Europa Nostra 1986, Aylesbury Soc 1988, Richmond Conservation-Design Awards 1993; rep cricket: combined SA Univs XI 1955, USA All Stars XI v W Indies 1958, Club Cricket Conf 1964; hon life memb Middx Cricket Bd; RIBA; *Recreations* cricket, travel, old Hollywood films; *Clubs* MCC (life memb), Richmond CC (dep chm), York House Soc (past chm); *Style*— Terence Woram, Esq; ✉ 48 Lebanon Park, Twickenham, Middlesex TW1 3DG

WORCESTER, Dean of; *see:* Atkinson, Very Rev Peter Gordon

WORCESTER, Prof Sir Robert Milton; KBE (2005), DL (Kent 2004); s of late C M Worcester, and late Violet Ruth Worcester; *b* 21 December 1933; *Educ* Univ of Kansas (BSc); *m* 1, 1958 (m dis), Joann, *née* Ransdell; 2 s; m 2, 1982, Margaret Noel, *née* Smallbone; *Career* conslt McKinsey & Co 1962–65, chief financial offr Opinion Research Corporation 1965–68; Market & Opinion Research International (MORI) Ltd: fndr 1969, md 1969–94, chm 1973–2005; pres World Assoc for Public Opinion Research 1982–84; int dir and chm Public Affrs Res Advsy Bd Ipsos Gp 2006–; founding ed International Jl of Public Opinion Research; 1988– visiting prof of govt and govr LSE 1995– (memb Cncl 1995–2005, hon fell 2005); chllr Univ of Kent 2006–; visiting prof: City Univ 1990–2002, Strathclyde Univ 1996–2001; hon prof: Univ of Kent 2004–, Univ of Warwick 2005–; memb: Ct Middlesex Univ 2001–, Cncl Univ of Kent 2002–; non-exec dir Medway Maritime Hospital NHS Tst 2002–04; pres Environmental Campaigns Ltd 2002–06; vice-pres: European-Atlantic Group, Int Social Science Cncl UNESCO 1989–94, RSWT 1995–, Royal Soc for Nature Conservation 1995–, UNA 1999–; tstee: Magna Carta Tst 1995–, World Wide Fund for Nature (UK) 1988–94, Wildfowl and Wetlands Tst 2002–; chm Pilgrims Soc 1993–; govrL Ditchley Fndn, English-speaking Union 2004–; cmmr US-UK Fulbright Cmmn 1995–2005; co-chm Jamestown 400 Commemoration Br Ctee 2004–07; memb: Camelot Advsy Panel for Corporate Responsibility 2006–, Advsy Bd European Business Jl, Nat Consumer Cncl 2002–06, Advsy Cncl Inst of Business Ethics 2004–; non-exec dir Kent Messenger Gp 2004–, chm Maidstone Radio Ltd (CTR 105.4 fm) 2004–06; Kent ambass (appointed by Kent CC) 2003–; Helen Dinerman Award World Assoc for Public Opinion Res 1996; Hon DSc Univ of Buckingham 1998, Hon DLitt Univ of Bradford 2001, Hon DUniv Middx 2001, Hon LLD Univ of Greenwich 2002, Hon DCL Univ of Kent 2006; hon fell KCL 2007; Freeman City of London 2001; fell Market Res Soc 1997–, FRSS 2004–; *Books* Political Communications (co-ed, 1982), Political Opinion Polling: an International Review (ed, 1983), Private Opinions Public Polls (co-author, 1986), Consumer Market Research Handbook (co-author, 3 edn 1986), We British (co-author, 1990), British Public Opinion (1991), Typically British (co-author, 1991), Dynamics of Societal Learning about Global Environmental Change (co-author, 1991), The Millenial Generation (co-author, 1998), Explaining Labour's Landslide (co-author, 1999), The Next Leaders (co-author, 1999), Facing the Future (co-author, 2000), How to Win the Euro Referendum Lessons from 1975 (2000), The Big Turn-Off (co-author, 2000), Explaining Labour's Second Landslide (co-author, 2001), The Wrong Package (co-author, 2001), Explaining Labour's Landslip (co-author, 2005); *Recreations* choral music, gardening, castles; *Clubs* Reform, Beefsteak, Walbrook, The Brook NY; *Style*— Prof Sir Robert Worcester, KBE, DL; ✉ Allington Castle, Maidstone, Kent (tel 020 7347 3000, fax 020 7347 3017, e-mail rmworcester@yahoo.com)

WORDSWORTH, Barry; s of Ron Wordsworth, and Kathleen, *née* Collins; *b* 20 February 1948; *Educ* Glyn GS, RCM (fndn scholar, Tagore Gold Medal, Watnet/Sargent Conducting Prize); *m* 1971, Ann, *née* Barber; 1 s (Benedict b 1984); *Career* princ conductor: Sadlers Wells Royal Ballet 1973–84, BBC Concert Orchestra 1989–2006 (conductor laureate 2006–); music dir: Brighton and Hove Philharmonic (and princ conductor) 1989–, Birmingham Royal Ballet 1990–, Royal Ballet Covent Garden 1990–95 and 2007–; Evening Standard Ballet Award for outstanding artistic achievement 1993; Hon DLitt Univ of Brighton 1996, Hon DUniv Central England 2004; RSM 1981, Hon FTCL 2006; *Recreations* cooking, swimming; *Style*— Barry Wordsworth, Esq; ✉ c/o Wray Armstrong, IMG, 616 Chiswick High Road, London W4 8AJ (tel 020 8233 5800, fax 020 8233 5801)

WORDSWORTH, Prof (Bryan) Paul; s of Victor Pargiter Wordsworth, of Banstead, Surrey, and Dora Mary, *née* Beach; *b* 4 April 1952, Salisbury; *Educ* Whitgift Sch, Westminster Medical Sch Univ of London (MB BS); *m* 11 April 1981, Christine; 1 da (Megan Elizabeth b 9 Sept 1983), 2 s (Thomas William Heyford b 3 Nov 1985, Andrew Timothy b 10 Dec 1988); *Career* house physician and surgn Westminster Hosp 1975–76, SHO Mayday Hosp Croydon 1976–77, medical registrar Mayday Hosp and Croydon Chest Clinic 1977–78, registrar in rheumatology Middlesex Hosp 1979–80; Univ of Oxford: sr registrar in rheumatology/rehabilitation Nuffield Orthopaedic Centre 1980–87, research fell Nuffield Dept of Pathology 1983–85, research fell Nuffield Dept of Medicine 1987–92, clinical reader in rheumatology Nuffield Dept of Medicine, prof of rheumatology 1998–; governing body fell Green Coll Oxford 1992– (academic tutor then sr tutor 1995–2000); memb: Br Soc for Rheumatology, RSM, Br Assoc for Rheumatology and Rehabilitation, UK Skeletal Dysphasia Gp; Michael Mason Prize Br Soc for Rheumatology 1992; FRCP 1996 (MRCP 1978); *Publications* Clinical and Biochemical Disorders of the Skeleton (jtly, 2005); *Recreations* cricket, gardening; *Clubs* Middleton Stoney Cricket, South Oxfordshire Amateurs Cricket; *Style*— Prof Paul Wordsworth; ✉ Tollgate Cottage, Lower Heyford, Bicester, Oxon OX25 5PE; Nuffield Orthopaedic Centre, Windmill Road, Headington, Oxford OX3 7LD (tel 01865 741155, e-mail paul.wordsworth@ndm.ox.ac.uk)

WORLEY, (Edward) Michael; CBE (1998), JP (1972); s of Sidney Clifford Worley (d 1963), and Mary Hilda, *née* Johnson (d 1968); *b* 29 March 1936; *Educ* Uppingham, Downing Coll Cambridge (MA); *m* 1966, Ann; 2 s (Andrew, Thomas), 1 da (Rachel); *Career* Steel Co of Wales Ltd (Port Talbot) 1957–62; William King Ltd (West Bromwich): joined 1962, md 1963–, chm 1973–; Unquoted Companies' Gp: chm Taxation Ctee 1979–2004, chm Exec 1993–; Wesleyan Assurance Soc: dir 1980–2007, dep chm 1993–2007; non-exec dir Birmingham Regnl Office Barclays Bank plc 1987–92; chm Sandwell TEC 1990–95, memb Cncl Birmingham Chamber of Industry and Commerce 1984–90, memb Bd Black Country Development Corp 1987–98, non-exec dir Black Country C of C and Industry 2001–04; pres: Nat Assoc of Steel Stockholders (NASS) 1988–90, Fédération Internationale des Associations de Négociants en Aciers, Tubes et Métaux (FIANATM) 1995–97, Groupement Européen des Entreprises Familiales (GEEF) 2004–; memb: Birmingham Diocesan Bd of Fin 1980–91, W Midlands Regnl HA 1982–93 (vice-chm 1990–93); tstee Former United Birmingham Hosps Tst Funds 1998–2000; chm Birmingham Botanical Gardens & Glasshouses 1981–99, govr Sandwell Coll 1988–2005; High Sheriff W Midlands 1997–98; Liveryman Worshipful Co of Founders; *Books* co-author: Regional Government (1968), Freedom to Spend (1971), Passing On (1973); *Recreations* gardening, sailing, reading; *Clubs* Royal Scots (Edinburgh); *Style*— Michael Worley, Esq, CBE; ✉ William King Ltd, Atlas Centre, Union Road, West Bromwich, West Midlands B70 9DR (tel 0121 500 4153, fax 0121 500 0453, e-mail michael.worley@williamking.co.uk)

WORLING, Dr Peter Metcalfe; s of Alexander Davidson Worling (d 1965), of Aberdeen, and Florence, *née* Metcalfe (d 1992); *b* 16 June 1928; *Educ* New Sch Darjeeling, Robert Gordon's Univ Aberdeen (PhC), Univ of Bradford (PhD); *m* 20 March 1954, Iris Isabella, da of James Peacock McBeath (d 1962), of Dingwall; 1 s (Bruce b 26 Aug 1956 d 1984), 2 da (Helen (Mrs Hill) b 25 Aug 1958, Fiona b 13 Jan 1962); *Career* home sales mangr Carnegies of Welwyn 1954–56 (export exec 1950–54), sales mangr Bradley & Bliss Ltd 1961–65 (pharmacist 1956–61); Vestric Ltd: mangr Ruislip Branch 1965–66, regnl dir Edinburgh 1966–73, commercial dir Cheshire 1973–79, md Cheshire 1979–89; chm AAH Pharmaceuticals Ltd Cheshire 1989–91, conslt 1991–95; memb Ctee Edinburgh Branch Royal Pharmaceutical Soc 1968–73 and 1995–2003 (chm Reading Branch 1963–64, chm Edinburgh Branch 1999–2001); chm: S Wholesale Druggists Assoc 1970 (memb 1966–73), Nat Assoc of Pharmaceutical Distributors 1983–85 (memb Ctee 1974–91, hon memb 1991–); pres Proprietary Articles Trade Assoc 1984–85 (hon memb Cncl 1991–2002), memb Ctee Br Soc for the History of Pharmacy 1993– (pres 2000–02, hon life vice-pres 2005), memb Int Acad of the History of Pharmacy 2005–; memb Incorporation of Hammermen of Edinburgh 2001, admitted as Burgess and Free Citizen of Edinburgh 2007; FRPharmS 1954; *Publications* author of numerous published papers on the history of pharmacy, incl chapter in book Making Medicines; *Recreations* history of pharmacy, genealogy, music; *Style*— Dr Peter Worling; ✉ The Grange, 29 Fernielaw Avenue, Edinburgh EH13 0EF (tel and fax 0131 441 5134, e-mail p.worling@virgin.net)

WORRALL, Anna Maureen (Mrs G H G Williams); QC (1989); *Educ* Hillcrest Sch, Loreto Coll Llandudno, Univ of Manchester (LLB); *m* 1964, Graeme Williams; 2 da; *Career* called to the Bar Middle Temple 1959, in practice 1959–63 and 1971–, recorder 1987–; lectr in law Holborn Coll of Law, Language and Commerce 1964–69, dir ILEA Educnl Television Service 1969–71; pres Mental Health Review Tbnls (memb 1993–); *Style*— Miss Anna M Worrall, QC; ✉ Lamb Building, Temple, London EC4Y 7AS (tel 020 7797 7788, fax 020 7353 0535, e-mail lamb.building@link.org and annaworrall@totalise.co.uk)

WORRALL THOMPSON, Antony; s of Michael Worrall Thompson, and Joanna Brenda, *née* Duncan; *b* 1 May 1951; *Educ* King's Sch Canterbury, Westminster Coll (HND); *m* 1, 1975, Jill, *née* Thompson; m 2, 1983 (m dis), Militza Jane Hamilton, da of Hugh Miller; 2 s (Blake Antony Cardew, Sam Michael Hamilton); m 3, 7 Sept 1996, Jacinta Shiel; 1 s (Toby Jack Duncan), 1 da (Billie-Lara); *Career* chef; food and beverage mangr Coombe Lodge Hotel Essex 1972, head chef and mangr Golden Fleece Restaurant Brentwood 1972; head chef: Ye Olde Logge Brentwood 1974, Adriatico Restaurant Woodland Green 1976, Hedges Restaurant South Woodford 1977, Brinkley's Restaurant Fulham Rd 1978–79 (with 6 month sabbatical to France), Dan's Restaurant Chelsea 1980; Ménage à Trois: chef and patron Knightsbridge 1981, opened in Bombay 1983, opened New York 1985, opened in Melbourne 1986, sold 1988 (retains all consultancies); chef and patron Avoirdupois Kings Road 1984, opened Mise-en-Place Limited 1986, purchased KWT Foodshow 1988; chef and patron: One Ninety Queen's Gate 1989–97, Bistrot 190 1990–97, dell'Ugo 1992–97, Zoë 1992–97, Drones 1995–97, Woz Cafe Restaurant 1997–99, Wiz Restaurant 1998–2001, Bistrorganic 1999–2000, Notting Grill 2002–, Kew Grill 2004–, Angel Coaching Inn & Grill 2004–06, The Greyhound Free House & Grill 2005–, The Lamb 2006–, Barnes Grill 2006–, Windsor Grill 2007–; md Simpsons of Cornhill plc 1993–97; columnist Daily Express and Sunday Express, capt quiz team on Question of Taste (Radio 4), appearances on various TV shows incl: Ready Steady Cook (BBC) 1995–2006, resident chef Food and Drink (BBC) 1997–2002, The Weakest Link (winner) 2002 and 2005, I'm a Celebrity - Get Me Out of Here 2003, presenter Saturday Kitchen (BBC) 2003–06, presenter Saturday Cooks! (ITV) 2006–07, presenter Christmas Cooks (ITV) 2006, presenter Daily Cooks (ITV) 2007–; pres Real Food Campaign; patron: Middle White Pig Breeders Assoc, Forest, North Yorks Smallholder Soc, Child Bereavement Tst, Stokenchurch Dog Rescue, NAPAC; FHCIMA; *Awards* Meilleur Ouvrier de Grande Bretagne 1987 (life title), winner Mouton Rothschild menu competition 1988; *Books* The Small and Beautiful Cookbook (1984), Supernosh (1993), Modern Bistrot Cooking (1994), 30-Minute Menu (1995), Ready Steady Cook (with Brian Turner, 1996), The ABC of AWT (1998), Raw (autobiography, 2003), Food and Drink Cookbook (2002), 100 Best Recipes of Food and Drink (2002), Healthy Eating for Diabetes (2003), Little Book of Meat (2003), Healthy Eating for Diabetes (2003), Antony Worrall Thompson's GI Diet (2005), Antony Worrall Thompson's Top 100 Beef Recipes (2005), Real Family Food (2005), Barbecues and Grilling (2006), The Diabetes Weight Loss Diet (2007); *Recreations* wine, antiques, art, interior design, gardening, sport, classical music, travel, pigs; *Style*— Antony Worrall Thompson, Esq; ✉ Lower Woodlands, Woodlands Road, Shiplake, Oxfordshire RG9 4AA (e-mail awt@awt.uk.com, website www.awtonline.co.uk and www.awtrestaurants.co.uk)

WORRICKER, Julian; *Educ* Epsom Coll, Univ of Leicester; *Career* radio presenter; staff reporter BBC Radio Leicester 1985–88, TV presenter BBC Midlands Today 1988–89, news ed Radio Leicester 1989–91, presenter Radio Five 1991–94; BBC Radio Five Live: joined as newsreader and reporter 1994, presenter Weekend Breakfast Prog and Nationwide 1994–98 (Sony Gold Radio Award 1997), presenter breakfast prog 1998–2003 (Sony Gold Radio Award 1999 and 2002, Best Radio Prog TRIC Awards 1999), presenter Worricker Prog 2003–; also presenter BBC News 24, BBC World Serv and BBC Radio 4; *Style*— Julian Worricker, Esq; ✉ BBC Radio Five Live, Broadcasting House, London W1A 1AA

WORSLEY, Francis Edward (Jock); OBE (2002); s of Francis Arthur Worsley, and Mary, *née* Diamond; *b* 15 February 1941; *Educ* Stonyhurst, Sorbonne; *m* 12 Sept 1962, Caroline Violet, da of James Hamilton Grey Hatherell (d 1968); 2 s (Richard, Edward), 2 da (Miranda, Joanna); *Career* chm: The Financial Training Co Ltd 1972–91, Lloyd's Members' Agency Services Ltd 1994–; dir Lautro 1990–94; non-exec dir: The Cleveland Trust plc 1993–99, Reece plc 1994–98, Brewin Dolphin Holdings 2003–, Accident Exchange Group plc 2004–06; memb Building Societies Cmmn 1991–2002; pres ICAEW 1988–89 (memb Cncl until 1996); complaints cmmr FSA (formerly SIB) 1994–2001; chm Cancer Research Campaign 1998–2002; Freeman: City of London, Worshipful Co of Chartered Accountants (Master 1992–93); FCA 1964; *Recreations* tennis, wine, cooking; *Style*— F E Worsley, Esq, OBE, FCA; ✉ c/o Lloyd's Members Agency Services Ltd, One Lime Street, London EC3M 7HA

WORSLEY, Joe Paul Richard; MBE (2004); *b* 14 June 1977, London; *Educ* Hitchin Boys' HS, Brunel Univ; *Career* rugby union player; with London Wasps RUFC (winners Parker Pen Challenge Cup 2003, Zurich Championship 2003, 2004 and 2005, Heineken Cup 2004 and 2007); England: 61 caps, debut v Tonga 1999, winners Six Nations Championship 2000, 2001 and 2003 (Grand Slam 2003), ranked no 1 team in world 2003, winners World Cup Aust 2003, memb squad World Cup France 2007; *Recreations* playing the piano; *Style*— Joe Worsley, Esq, MBE; ✉ c/o London Wasps RUFC, Twyford Avenue Sports Ground, Twyford Avenue, Acton, London W3 9QA

WORSLEY, Sir (William) Marcus John; 5 Bt (UK 1838), of Hovingham, Yorks, JP (N Yorks 1957), DL (1978); s of Col Sir William Arthington Worsley, 4 Bt (d 1973, descent from Oliver Cromwell; sis Katharine m HRH the Duke of Kent in 1961), and Joyce Morgan, *née* Brunner; *b* 6 April 1925; *Educ* Eton, New Coll Oxford; *m* 10 Dec 1955, Hon Bridget Assheton, da of 1 Baron Clitheroe, PC (d 2004); 3 s (William b 1956, Dr Giles Worsley, FSA b 1961 d 2006, Peter b 1963), 1 da (Sarah b 1958); *Heir* s, William Worsley, *qv*; *Career* served Green Howards, India and W Africa, WWII; MP (Cons): Keighley 1959–64, Chelsea 1966–74; church cmmr 1970–84, pres Royal Forestry Soc of England Wales and NI 1980–82, chm Nat Tst Properties Ctee 1980–90, dep chm Nat Tst 1986–92; High Sheriff N Yorks 1982–83; HM Lord-Lt N Yorks 1987–99; *Recreations* reading, walking, travel; *Clubs* Boodle's; *Style*— Sir Marcus Worsley, Bt; ✉ Park House, Hovingham, York YO62 4JZ (tel 01653 628002)

WORSLEY, Michael Dominic; QC (1985); s of Paul Worsley, and Magdalen Teresa, *née* Pestel; *b* 9 February 1926; *Educ* Bedford Sch, Inns of Court Sch of Law; *m* 1, Oct 1962, Pamela, *née* Philpot (d 1980); 1 s (Benedict b 28 Sept 1967); m 2, 12 June 1986, Jane, da of late Percival Sharpe; *Career* RN 1944–45; called to the Bar Inner Temple 1955 (bencher 1980); prosecuting counsel to the Inland Revenue London 1968–69, Treasy counsel Inner London Sessions 1969–71, sr Treasy counsel Central Criminal Court 1974–85 (jr Treasy counsel 1971–74); *Recreations* music, travelling; *Clubs* Garrick, Lansdowne; *Style*— Michael Worsley, Esq, QC; ✉ 6 King's Bench Walk, Temple, London EC4Y 7DR (tel 020 7583 0410)

WORSLEY, His Hon Judge Paul Frederick; QC (1990); s of Eric Worsley, MBE, GM, and Sheila Mary, *née* Hoskin; *b* 17 December 1947, East Sheen, Surrey; *Educ* Hymers Coll Hull, Mansfield Coll Oxford (MA); *m* 14 Dec 1974, Jennifer Ann Avery, JP, da of late Ernest Avery; 1 s (Nicholas b 6 Sept 1975), 1 da (Charlotte b 26 Feb 1977); *Career* called to the Bar Middle Temple 1970 (Astbury scholar, bencher 1999); practising barr North Eastern Circuit 1970–2006, recorder Crown Ct 1987–2006 (asst recorder 1983–87), circuit judge (South Eastern Circuit) 2006–; memb Advocacy Studies Bd 1996–2006; govr: Scarborough Coll 1997–, Leeds Girls' HS 2001–05, Leeds GS 2005–; memb Worshipful Co of Coopers 2007; *Recreations* Spy prints, opera, sailing, croquet; *Clubs* Yorkshire (York), Bar Yacht; *Style*— His Hon Judge Paul Worsley, QC; ✉ 16 Park Place, Leeds LS1 2SJ (tel 0113 243 3277); 2 Hare Court, Temple, London EC4Y 7BH (tel 020 7353 5324)

WORSLEY, William Ralph; s and h of Sir (William) Marcus John Worsley, 5 Bt, *qv*, of Hovingham, N Yorks; *b* 12 September 1956; *Educ* Harrow, RAC Cirencester; *m* 26 Sept 1987, Marie-Noëlle, yr da of Bernard H Dreesmann; 2 da (Isabella Claire b 24 Oct 1988, Francesca Sylvia b 5 March 1992), 1 s (Marcus William Bernard b 2 Nov 1995); *Career* former Lt Queen's Own Yeomanry TAVR; farmer; forester; chartered surveyor; dir Scarborough Building Soc 1996– (chm 2002–); dir Brunner Investment Tst 2000–; conslt Humberts 1986–92; chm Howardian Hills Area of Outstanding Natural Beauty Ctee 2004–, vice-pres CLA 2005–; memb: N York Moors Nat Park Authy 1994–98, Forestry Cmmn Advsy Panel 1999–2006; Freeman City of London, Liveryman Worshipful Company of Merchant Taylors; FRICS; *Recreations* shooting, skiing, reading; *Clubs* White's, Pratt's; *Style*— William Worsley, Esq; ✉ Hovingham Hall, York YO6 4NA (tel 01653 628771, fax 01653 628668)

WORSLEY-TAYLOR, Annette Pamela; MBE (2002); da of Sir John Godfrey Worsley-Taylor, 3 Bt (d 1952), and Anne, *née* Paget (now Anne, Lady Jaffray); *b* 2 July 1944; *Educ* Downham Sch Hatfield Heath; *m* Nov 1997, Anthony Sheil; *Career* fndr London Designer Collections 1975 (dir 1976–); conceived, launched and organised London Designer Show 1991–92, organised and marketed London Fashion Week, fndr memb British Fashion Cncl 1983 (memb exec 1987–); *Recreations* fashion, design, music, theatre; *Style*— Ms Annette Worsley-Taylor, MBE; ✉ 3/57 Drayton Gardens, London SW10 9RU (tel 020 7835 0222, fax 020 7835 0846)

WORSTHORNE, Sir Peregrine Gerard; kt (1991); s of Col Alexander Koch de Gooreynd, OBE, formerly Irish Gds (d 1985), who assumed surname of Worsthorne by deed poll in 1923, but reverted to Koch de Gooreynd in 1937; er bro Sir Simon Towneley from whose estate the Worsthorne name is derived (gd m Manuela, da of Alexandre de Laski by Joaquina, Marquesa de Souza Lisboa da of José Marques Lisboa, sometime Min Plenipotentiary of Emperor of Brazil to Ct of St James), and Priscilla, later Baroness Norman (d 1991); *b* 22 December 1923; *Educ* Stowe, Peterhouse Cambridge (BA), Magdalen Coll Oxford; *m* 1, 7 June 1950, Claudie Marie-Hélène (d 1990), da of Victor Edouard Bertrand de Colasse, of Paris, and former w of Geoffrey Baynham; 1 da (Dominique Elizabeth Priscilla b 18 Feb 1952), 1 step s (David); m 2, 11 May 1991, Lucinda Lambton, *qv*; *Career* cmmnd Oxford & Bucks LI 1942, Lt Phantom GHQ Liaison Regt 1944–45; journalist and writer; formerly on editorial staff of: The Glasgow Herald 1946–48, The Times 1948–55, Daily Telegraph 1955–61; ed Sunday Telegraph 1986–91 (assoc ed 1961–86), ret 1991; *Books* The Socialist Myth (1972), Peregrinations (1980), By The Right (1987), Tricks of Memory, an autobiography (1993), In Defence of Aristocracy (2004); *Recreations* tennis, reading, walking; *Clubs* Garrick, Beefsteak, Pratt's; *Style*— Sir Peregrine Worsthorne; ✉ The Old Rectory, Hedgerley, Buckinghamshire SL2 3UY (tel 01753 646167, fax 01753 646914)

WORSWICK, Dr Richard David; *b* 22 July 1946; *Educ* Magdalen Coll Sch Oxford, New Coll Oxford (MA, DPhil); *m* 1970, Jacqueline Brigit Isobel, *née* Adcock; 3 da (Helen b 1975 d 2004, Catherine b 1978, Isobel b 1981); *Career* res asst SRC Dept of Inorganic Chemistry Univ of Oxford 1972–73, res product mangr Boots Co plc 1973–76; Harwell Laboratory UK Atomic Energy Authy: Mktg and Planning 1976–85, head Res Planning 1985–88, head Environmental and Med Sciences Div 1988–90; dir of Process Technol and Instrumentation AEA Industrial Technology 1990–91, Govt Chemist 1991–2002, chief exec Laboratory of the Govt Chemist (DTI Agency) 1991–96, chief exec LGC (Holdings) Ltd 1996–2005; chm: University Diagnostics Ltd 1997–, Pipeline Devpts Ltd 1998–2002, Promochem Ltd 2001–; dep chm LGC Group Holdings plc 2005–; FRSC 1991; *Recreations* listening to music, playing the violin, walking; *Style*— Dr Richard Worswick; ✉ LGC, Queen's Road, Teddington, Middlesex TW11 0LY (tel 020 8943 7300, fax 020 8977 0741, e-mail richard.worswick@lgc.co.uk)

WORTH, Peter Herman Louis; s of Dr L H Worth (d 1982), and Ruth, *née* Niemeyer (d 1967); *b* 17 November 1935; *Educ* Marlborough, Trinity Hall Cambridge (MA, MB BChir), Middx Hosp Med Sch; *m* 8 Feb 1969, Judith Katharine Frances, da of Arthur Girling (d 1959), of Langham, Essex; 1 s (Hugo b 1970), 1 da (Anna b 1972); *Career* conslt urological surgn: UCH 1976, St Peter's Hosps 1976, Middx Hosp 1984 (now UCL Hosps), King Edward VII Hosp 1993; memb: Br Assoc of Urological Surgns, RSM; FRCS 1967; *Books* contrib chapters on urology in several medical textbooks; *Recreations* classical music, skiing, gardening; *Style*— Peter Worth, Esq; ✉ Broad Eaves, Mill Lane, Broxbourne, Hertfordshire EN10 7AZ (tel 01992 462827, fax 01992 309414, e-mail peter.worth@ntlworld.com)

WORTHEN, Prof John; s of Frederick Morley Worthen, and Dorothy Geach, *née* Barrett, of Bournemouth; *b* 27 June 1943; *Educ* Merchant Taylors' Sch, Downing Coll Cambridge (BA), Univ of Kent (MA, PhD); *m* 1983, Cornelia Linda Elfriede, da of Prof Helmut Rumpf; *Career* instructor Univ of Virginia 1968–69, jr res fell Univ of Edinburgh 1969–70; Univ Coll of Swansea: lectr in English 1970–85, sr lectr in English 1985–90, prof of English 1990–93; prof of D H Lawrence studies Univ of Nottingham 1994–2003; *Books* D H Lawrence - The Early Years 1885–1912 (1991), The Gang: Coleridge, the Wordsworths and the Hutchinsons in 1802 (2001), D H Lawrence: The Life of an Outsider (2005), Robert Schumann: Life and Death of a Musician (2007) author of numerous pubns on D H Lawrence; *Recreations* music; *Style*— John Worthen; ✉ 102 Appledore Avenue, Nottingham NG8 2RW

WORTHINGTON, District Judge Adrian Joseph; s of Dennis Bernard Worthington, of Didsbury, Manchester, and Moya, *née* Owens; *b* 3 April 1958, Didsbury; *Educ* St Gregory's RC GS Manchester, Univ of Nottingham (BA), Coll of Law Chester; *m* Susie; 2 s (Joseph, Benedict), 1 da (Caitlin); *Career* Darlington & Parkinson Slrs: articles 1980–82, asst slr 1982–86, ptnr 1986–99; district judge (SE Circuit) 1999–; assessor Law Soc Family Law Panel 1999; memb: Law Soc Child Care Panel 1992–99, Legal Aid Ctee 1992–99 (chm 1996–99); memb N J Stag/Walnuts Alumni 1979–; *Recreations* football, walking, swimming, wine, film, computers; *Style*— District Judge Worthington; ✉ e-mail aworthington@lix.compulink.co.uk

WORTHINGTON, Charles; MBE (2006); *Career* int hair stylist; owner and creative dir Charles Worthington salons; estab a portfolio of London salons, launched award-winning product ranges; twice winner British Hairdresser of the Year; involved with numerous charitable causes incl Look Good...Feel Better; *Books* City Hair, Big Date Hair, Holiday Hair, Big Day Hair; *Style*— Charles Worthington, Esq, MBE; ✉ 7 Percy Street, London W1T 1DQ (tel 020 7299 8853, fax 020 7636 4531)

WORTHINGTON, Greville; s of Ben Worthington (d 1984), and Valerie, *née* Lawson, da of Sir Ralph Henry Lawson, 4 Bt; *b* 22 November 1963, Newcastle; *Educ* Ampleforth, Univ of Edinburgh; *m* 2 Sept 1995, The Hon Sophia Mary (Sophie), *née* Stapleton-Cotton, da of 5 Viscount Combermere (d 2000); 1 da (Io Bluebell b 20 March 1996), 2 s (Cy Benjamin b 23 Sept 1998, Rex Michael b 13 March 2002); *Career* M&G Fund Mgmnt 1988–92, dir Catterick Racecourse 1989–; judge Turner Prize 2002; sec Bamboo Soc; KM 1996; *Publications* Here & Now: Experiences in Sculpture (2001); *Recreations* contemporary art, bamboo collecting; *Style*— Greville Worthington, Esq; ✉ The Catterick Racecourse Company Ltd, Catterick Bridge, Richmond, North Yorkshire DL10 7PE

WORTHINGTON, HE Ian Alan; OBE (1999); s of Alan Worthington, of Stockport, and Bette, *née* Wright; *b* 9 August 1958, Stockport, Cheshire; *Educ* Stockport Sch Mile End; *Career* diplomat; joined FCO 1977, Finance Dept FCO 1977–78, third sec (scientific) Moscow 1980–82, mgmnt offr Lusaka 1982–85, press facilities offr News Dept FCO 1985–88, second sec (commercial) Seoul 1988–91, dep head of mission Vilnius 1991–92, second sec (political) Kingston 1992–95, head Trade Office then consul gen Ekaterinburg 1995–98, inspr/reviewer Mgmnt Consultancy Servs FCO 1998–2001, head of trade and investment Berlin 2001–06, ambass to Dominican Republic 2006– (concurrently non-resident ambass to Haiti); *Style*— HE Mr Ian A Worthington, OBE; ✉ c/o FCO (Santo Domingo), King Charles Street, London SW1A 2AH (tel 00 1 809 472 7111, fax 00 1 809 472 7190, e-mail ian.worthington@fco.gov.uk)

WORTHINGTON, Prof John; s of Brig Roger Fraser Worthington (d 1984), and Mary, *née* Smith (d 1990); *b* 8 August 1938; *Educ* Gresham's, Architectural Assoc (travelling scholar, Holloway travelling scholar, AADipl), Univ of Philadelphia (MArch), Univ of Calif; *m* 1963, Susan Mary, da of late Air Chief Marshal Sir John Davis; 1 s (Nicholas Fraser b 22 Dec 1969), 1 da (Samantha Jane b 27 June 1973); *Career* served Royal Enniskillen Fusiliers Berlin and Wuppertal 1957–59; architect: Alex Gordon & Partners 1964–65, Thompson, Berwick, Pratt & Partners Vancouver 1967–68, Ahrends, Burton & Koralek London 1969–70; res conslt Home Office 1970–71, fndr JFN Associates 1971–73, fndr ptnr Duffy Lange Giffone Worthington (now Duffy Eley Giffone Worthington) 1973–, external dir URBED 1975–78, ptnr DEGW 1976–90; prof of architecture and dir Inst of Advanced Architectural Studies Univ of York 1992–97, Graham Willis professorship Univ of Sheffield 2003–, visiting prof Chalmers Univ of Technol Gothenburg 2000–03, visiting scholar Pembroke Coll Cambridge 2005–, professorial fell Univ of Melbourne 2006–; chm CABE/RIBA Building Futures 2002–05, dep chm Regeneration Through Heritage 1994–2005; patron and past pres Urban Design Group; memb Bd London Thames Gateway Urban Devpt Corp 2004–; Harkness fell Commonwealth Fund 1965–67; Hon FRIBA 1998; *Books* Office Planner (conslt ed and contrib, 1976), Planning Office Space (with Duffy and Cave, 1976), Industrial Rehabilitation (with Eley, 1984), Fitting Out the Workplace (with Konya, 1988), Reinventing the Workplace (1997, 2 edn 2005), Managing the Brief for Better Design (with Blyth, 2000); contrib to numerous pubns; *Recreations* sailing, travel; *Style*— Prof John Worthington; ✉ DEGW, Porters North, 8 Crinan Street, London N1 9SQ (tel 020 7239 7777, fax 020 7278 4125, e-mail jworthington@degw.com)

WORTHINGTON, Nick; s of David Worthington, of Stoke Abbott, Dorset, and Bridgit, *née* Petter; *b* 19 October 1962; *Educ* Fitzharry's Comp Abingdon, Banbury Sch of Art and Design, St Martin's Sch of Art (BA); *Career* advtg copywriter; trainee TBWA London 1984, Symington & Partners London 1984–86, Jenner Keating Becker London 1986–88, Bartle Bogle Hegarty London 1988–96, Abbott Mead Vickers BBDO 1996–; winner numerous advtg awards incl 2 Gold Lions Cannes (for Levi's 501); motor cycle racer, BMCRC & KRC 250cc champion 1991; *Recreations* motorcycle racing; *Clubs* Br Motorcycle Racing; *Style*— Nick Worthington, Esq; ✉ Abbott Mead Vickers BBDO Ltd, 151 Marylebone Road, London NW1 5QE (tel 020 7616 3500, fax 020 7616 3600)

WORTHINGTON, William Anthony (Tony); s of Malcolm Thomas Henry Worthington (d 1985), and Monica, *née* Wearden (d 1995); *b* 11 October 1941; *Educ* City Sch Lincoln, LSE (BA), Univ of Glasgow (MEd); *m* 26 March 1966, Angela May, da of Cyril Oliver, of Charing, Kent; 1 da (Jennifer b 1970), 1 s (Robert b 1972); *Career* lectr Jordanhill Coll Glasgow 1971–87, regnl cncllr Strathclyde 1974–87 (chm Fin Ctee 1986–87); MP (Lab) Clydebank and Milngavie 1987–2005; oppn front bench spokesman on: educn, employment, trg and social work in Scotland until 1992, overseas devpt 1992–93, foreign affrs 1993–94, NI 1995–97; Parly under-sec of state N Ireland Office 1997–98; memb Int Devpt Select Ctee 1999–2005, chm All-Pty Gp on Overseas Devpt 1999–2005, dir Parly Network on World Bank, memb Exec Cncl Parliamentarians for Global Action until 2005; memb Scottish Community Educn Cncl 1980–87, chm Strathclyde Community Business 1984–87; *Recreations* gardening, reading; *Style*— Tony Worthington; ✉ 24

W

Cleddans Crescent, Hardgate, Clydebank, Dunbartonshire G81 5NW (tel 01389 873195, e-mail tony@tonyworthington.com, website www.tonyworthington.com)

WORTON, Prof Michael John; s of William Asquith Worton (d 1973), and Nan Scott Elliot, *née* Little; *b* 20 July 1951; *Educ* Dumfries Acad, Univ of Edinburgh (MA, Gold Medal, F C Green Prize, PhD); *Career* lectr in French Univ of Liverpool 1976–80; UCL: lectr in French language and literature 1980–90, sr lectr in French 1990–94, prof of French 1994–98, currently vice-provost and Fielden prof of French language and literature; former non-exec dir Whittington Hosp NHS Tst; Officier des Palmes Académiques; *Books* Intertextuality: Theories and practices (ed and introduced with Judith Still, 1990, reprinted 1993), Tournier: La Goutte d'or (1992, reprinted 1995), René Char: The Dawn Breakers/Les Matinaux (ed, introduced and translated, 1992), Textuality and Sexuality: Reading theories and practices (ed and introduced with Judith Still, 1993), Michel Tournier (ed, 1995), Typical Men (2001), Women's Writing in Contemporary France (2002), National Healths (2004); also author of numerous book chapters, and of articles and reviews in learned jls; *Recreations* hill walking, theatre, opera; *Style*— Prof Michael Worton; ✉ Vice-Provost's Office, University College London, Gower Street, London WC1E 6BT (tel 020 7679 7854, fax 020 7916 8505, e-mail michael.worton@ucl.ac.uk)

WOSNER, John Leslie; s of Eugen Wosner, of London, and Lucy, *née* Chajes; *b* 8 June 1947; *Educ* Hasmonean GS, Univ of Sheffield (BA); *m* 17 March 1974, Linda Jose, da of Abraham Freedman; 1 da (Dina b 1975), 2 s (Jeremy b 1979, Daniel b 1982); *Career* articled clerk and mangr Arthur Andersen 1969–73, Tax Consultancy Div Harmood Banner CA's 1973–74; Pannell Kerr Forster: tax mangr 1974–76, ptnr 1976–2005, head Home Counties Tax Dept 1986–90, ptnr i/c Luton 1990–92, managing ptnr 1992–98, chm 1999–2005; conslt 2005–; Freeman City of London; ATII, FCA; *Recreations* history, reading, football, country walks; *Clubs* Travellers; *Style*— John Wosner, Esq

WOTTON, John Prier; s of (Arthur) John Wotton (d 1989), of Branscombe, Devon, and Persis Rubena, *née* Spearing; *b* 7 May 1954, Hounslow, Middx; *Educ* Latymer Upper Sch, Jesus Coll Cambridge (MA); *m* 1976, Linde Diana, *née* Lester; 2 da (Ruth b 1983, Sophie b 1988), 1 s (Tom b 1985); *Career* admitted slr 1978; ptnr Allen & Overy LLP 1984–2007 (joined 1976, conslt 2007–); Law Soc: chm European Gp 2003–04, memb EU Ctee; govr: Edward Latymer Fndn, Latymer Upper Sch; tstee Fauna & Flora Int; *Recreations* cricket, gardening, opera, skiing; *Style*— John Wotton, Esq; ✉ Allen & Overy LLP, One Bishop's Square, London E1 6AO (tel 020 3088 0000, e-mail john.wotton@allenovery.com)

WRACK, Matt; s of Robert Wrack (d 2003), and Winifred, *née* Town; *b* 23 May 1962, Manchester; *Career* joined London Fire Brigade 1983, gen sec Fire Brigades Union 2005–; *Style*— Matt Wrack, Esq; ✉ The Fire Brigades Union, Bradley House, 68 Coombe Road, Kingston upon Thames KT2 7AE (tel 020 8541 1765, fax 020 8546 5187)

WRAGG, John; s of Arthur Wragg, of York, and Ethel, *née* Ransom; *b* 20 October 1937; *Educ* York Sch of Art, Royal Coll of Art; *Career* artist; ARCA 1960, RA 1991; *Solo Exhibitions* Hanover Gallery 1963, 1966 and 1970, Galerie Alexandre Iolas Pans 1968, York Festival 1969, Bridge Street Gallery Bath 1982, Katherine House Gallery Marlborough 1984, Quinton Green Fine Art 1985, England & Co London 1994, Devizes Museum Gallery 1994 and 1996, L'Art Abstract Gallerie 1995, Monumental' 96 Belgium 1996, Handel House Gallery 2000, Bruton Gallery 2000; *Group Exhibitions* incl: Lords Gallery 1959, L'Art Vivant 1965 and 1968, Arts Cncl Gallery Belfast 1966, Pittsburgh Int 1967, Britische Kuns heute Hamburg 1968, Fndn Maeght 1968, Bath Festival Gallery 1977 and 1984, Artists Market 1978, Biennale di Scultura di Arese (Milan) 1980, King Street Gallery Bristol 1980, Gallerie Bollhagen Worpswede Germany 1981 and 1983, Quinton Green Fine Art 1984, 1985, 1986 and 1987, Abstraction 89 (Cleveland Bridge Gallery) 1989, Contemporary Br Drawing (Cleveland Bridge Gallery) 1989, Sculptors Drawings (Cleveland Bridge Gallery) 1990, The Hunting Art Prizes Exhibition 1991, Best of British (Simpsons and Connaught Brown) 1993, Courcoux and Courcoux 1997, Bruton Street Gallery 2000 and 2001, Bohun Gallery 2001, RWA 2001, Hot Bath Gallery Bath 2002; *Work in Collections* Sainsbury Centre UEA, Israel Museum Jerusalem, Tate Gallery, Arts Cncl of GB, Arts Cncl of NI, Contemporary Art Soc, Wellington Art Gallery NZ, Nat Gallery of Modern Art Edinburgh, Chancery Bequest 1981; *Recreations* walking; *Style*— John Wragg, Esq, RA; ✉ 6 Castle Lane, Devizes, Wiltshire SN10 1HJ (tel 01380 727087, e-mail johnwragg.ra@virgin.net)

WRAGG, Lawrence de Villamil; eld s of Arthur Donald Wragg (d 1966), of Buxton, Derbys, and Lilia Mary May, *née* Adcock (d 1990); *b* 26 November 1943; *Educ* Rendcomb Coll, Univ of Bristol (BA), Sorbonne (Dip), Manchester Business Sch (MBA); *m* 1971 (m dis 2003), Aureole Margaret Willoughby Fowler; 2 da (Isabel b 1977, Helen b 1988), 1 s (David b 1979); *Career* merchant banker; systems analyst National Data Processing Service 1968–69, mgmnt conslt Price Waterhouse Assocs 1969–72, exec dir Chemical Bank International (formerly London Multinational Bank Ltd) 1974–82; dir: Charterhouse Bank 1982–86, Standard Chartered Merchant Bank 1987–89; dep chm and chief exec Ketton Securities 1990–; chm: Lawrence Wragg Associates Ltd 1989–, Proscyon Partners Ltd 1990–2003; dir: GBRW Ltd 1995–99, PXS Ltd 1997–; chm London Banks Composite Currency Ctee 1980–84; visiting lectr Manchester Business Sch 1980–82; memb Assoc of MBAs 1974–; CPRE: chm Cambridge City and S Cambs Ctee 1998–2000, chm Cambs Branch 1999–2001, nat vice-chm 2000–05, nat tstee and chm E of England Region 2005–; chm: The Ickleton Soc 1982–99, Cambridge Univ Musical Soc 2003; vice-chm: Ickleton PC 1988–90, Cam Valley Forum 2002–; hon treas Cncl Royal Musical Assoc 2006–; chm of govrs Duxford Sch 1985–90; MSI 1993, FRSA 1994; *Books* Composite Currencies (1984), Economist Guide to Eurobonds (contrib, 1990); *Recreations* music, mountaineering, skiing, running, opera; *Clubs* London Mountaineering (treas 1980–2003, pres 2003–06), Eagle Ski; *Style*— Lawrence Wragg, Esq; ✉ Clifton House, High Street, Fowlmere, Cambridgeshire SG8 7ST (tel 01763 208729, fax 01763 208116, e-mail ldevw@aol.com)

WRAXALL, Sir Charles Frederick Lascelles; 9 Bt (UK 1813), of Wraxall, Somerset; s of Sir Morville William Lascelles Wraxall, 8 Bt (d 1978), and Irmgard Wilhelmina Maria, *née* Schnidrig; *b* 17 September 1961; *Educ* Archbishop Tenison's GS Croydon; *m* 1983, Lesley Linda, da of William Albert Allan; 1 s (William Nathaniel Lascelles b 3 April 1987), 1 da (Lucy Rosemary Lascelles b 8 Oct 1992); *Heir* s, William Wraxall; *Career* civil servant DHSS 1978–80, trainee auditor Woolworths Pty Cape Town 1980–81, trainee accountant British Steel Corporation 1982–87, asst accountant Morgan Stanley Int 1987–; *Recreations* choral singing, football, stamp collection; *Style*— Sir Charles Wraxall, Bt

WRAXALL, 3 Baron (UK 1928); Sir Eustace Hubert Beilby Gibbs; KCVO (1986), CMG (1982); 4 s of 1 Baron Wraxall, TD, PC, JP, DL (d 1931), yr s by his 2 w (Hon Ursula Mary Lawley, OBE (d 1979), er da of 6 and last Baron Wenlock); suc bro 2 Baron Wraxall, DL (d 2001); *b* 3 July 1929; *Educ* Eton, ChCh Oxford; *m* 1, 23 Oct 1957, Veronica (d 2003), o da of Sydney Keith Scott, of Reydon Grove Farm, Southwold; 3 s (Hon Hubert b 1958, Hon Andrew b 1965, Hon Jonathan b 1969), 2 da (Hon Miranda b 1961, Hon Alexandra b 1971); m 2, 8 July 2006, Caroline, yst da of late Sir John Burder and wid of Lt Col Philip Fielden, MC (d 1998); *Heir* s, Hon Hubert Gibbs; *Career* entered Foreign Serv 1954, ret 1986; HM The Queen's Vice-Marshal of the Dip Corps 1982–86; RCDS 1974–75, served Bangkok, Rio de Janeiro, Berlin, Caracas, Vienna & Paris, ret 1986; *Recreations* music, golf; *Clubs* Pratt's, Brooks's; *Style*— The Rt Hon the Lord Wraxall, KCVO, CMG; ✉ Coddenham House, Coddenham, Ipswich, Suffolk (tel 01449 760332, fax 01449 761729)

WRAY, Edward James; s of Philip Wray, and Brenda Margaret, *née* Collett; *b* 27 March 1968, Coulsdon, Surrey; *Educ* Tonbridge, Worcester Coll Oxford (MA); *m* 1 Nov 2003, Catherine May, *née* Pickering; 1 da (Amelia Rose Catherine b 10 Oct 2005); *Career* Shell UK Ltd 1987–91, vice-pres Debt Capital Markets J P Morgan 1991–99; Betfair: co-fndr and dir 1999–, chief exec 1999–2003, chm 2006–; chief exec: TSE (Int) Ltd 2003–06, Betfair Aust 2006–07; Ernst & Young UK Emerging Entrepreneur of the Year 2002, Sharp Edge Entrepreneurs' Entrepreneur 2007; *Recreations* golf, sailing, food and wine; *Style*— Edward Wray, Esq; ✉ Betfair, The Waterfront, Hammersmith Embankment, Winslow Road, London W6 9HP (tel 020 8834 8205, fax 020 8834 8010, e-mail edward.wray@betfair.com)

WRAY, Nigel; *b* 9 April 1948; *Educ* Mill Hill Sch, Univ of Bristol (BSc); *Career* chm: Fleet Street Letter plc 1976–90, Burford Holdings plc 1988–2001; non-exec chm Wilink plc; non-exec dir: Carlton Communications plc 1976–97, Singer and Friedlander plc 1986–2001, Peoples Phone 1989–96, Carlisle Holdings plc 1994–98, Chorion plc (formerly Trocadero plc) 1995–, Saracens plc 1995–, SkyePharma plc 1995–2000, Grantchester plc 1996–99, Columbus Group plc 1996–2000, Nottingham Forest plc 1997–99, Domino's Pizza Gp Ltd 1997–, Hartford plc 1998–2000, Safestore plc 1999–, Seymour Pierce Gp plc 2000–, Electric Word plc 2000–, Invox plc 2000–, Extreme Gp Ltd 2002–, Healthcare Enterprise Gp 2004–07, Prestbury Investment Holdings, Urbium; *Recreations* all sport (played rugby for Hampshire), cinema, musicals, reading a bit; *Style*— Nigel Wray, Esq

WRENBURY, 3 Baron (UK 1915); Rev John Burton Buckley; s of 2 Baron Wrenbury (d 1940), and Helen, *née* Graham (d 1981); *b* 18 June 1927; *Educ* Eton, King's Coll Cambridge (MA); *m* 1, 1956 (m dis 1961), Carolyn Joan Maule, da of Col Ian Burn-Murdoch, OBE; m 2, 1961, Penelope Sara Frances, da of Edward Dimond Fort; 2 da (Hon Elizabeth Margaret (Hon Mrs Grey Morgan) b 1964, Hon Katherine Lucy (Hon Mrs Schaale) b 1968), 1 s (Hon William Edward b 19 June 1966); *Heir* s, Hon William Buckley; *Career* slr 1952, dep legal advsr Nat Tst 1955–56, ptnr: Freshfields 1956–74, Thomson Snell & Passmore 1974–90; landowner (390 acres); ordained: deacon 1990, priest 1991; Liveryman: City of London, Worshipful Co of Merchant Taylors; *Clubs* Oriental, Rye Golf; *Style*— The Rev the Rt Hon Lord Wrenbury; ✉ Oldcastle, Dallington, Heathfield, East Sussex TN21 9JP (tel 01435 830400, fax 01435 830968)

WRENCH, Charles Hector (Charlie); s of Hector Wrench (d 1981), and Sheelagh Mary Veronica, *née* Lynch; *b* 19 September 1960; *Educ* Downside, Pembroke Coll Oxford (MA, Lacrosse half blue); *m* 24 June 1989, Amanda, da of Stuart Henry Hodgson; 2 s (Bertie Alexander Stockdale b 19 Nov 1990, Harry Hector b 24 Aug 1992), 1 da (Holly Annyetta b 31 March 1999); *Career* co-dir Freelance Ltd 1983–85 (joined 1981), Lowe Howard-Spink advtg 1985–89; Young & Rubicam Ltd: bd dir/head of account mgmnt 1990–97, regnl accounts md 1997; pres Landor Assocs 2005– (formerly md Landor London, pres EMEA and chief strategy offr); *Recreations* golf, cricket, skiing, water sports, squash, tennis, football; *Style*— Charlie Wrench, Esq

WRENCH, Peter Nicholas; s of Cyril Wrench (d 1991), and Edna Mary, *née* Bray; *b* 5 April 1957; *Educ* Clitheroe Royal GS, Royal Holloway Coll London (BA); *m* 1978, Pauline Jordan; 2 da (Jessica b 1983, Harriet b 1984); *Career* Home Office: joined 1980, private sec to Perm Sec 1987–88, Immigration and Nationality Dept 1988–93, Organised and International Crime Directorate 1993–2000, dep DG immigration and nationality 2000–03; dir of resettlement Prison Serv 2003–05, dir of strategy and asssurance Nat Offender Mgmnt Serv (NOMS) 2005–07, currently head of simplification project Border and Immigration Agency; *Recreations* obscure music, family, friends, dog; *Style*— Peter Wrench, Esq

WREXHAM, Bishop of (RC) 1994–; Rt Rev Edwin Regan; s of James Regan (d 1974), of Port Talbot, W Glamorgan, and Ellen Elizabeth, *née* Hoskins (d 1991); *b* 31 December 1935; *Educ* St Joseph's Primary Sch, Port Talbot Co GS, St John's Coll Waterford, Corpus Christi Coll London (Dip RE); *Career* curate: Pontypool 1959, Neath 1959–66; Corpus Christi Coll London 1966–67, religious educn advsr Archdiocese of Cardiff 1967–85, chaplain St Clare's Convent Porthcawl 1967–71, admin St David's Cathedral Cardiff 1971–84; parish priest: St Helens Barry 1984–89, St Mary's Bridgend 1989–94; apostolic admin Archdiocese of Cardiff 2000–01; memb: Amnesty Int, World Devpt Movement; *Recreations* hill walking; *Style*— The Rt Rev the Bishop of Wrexham; ✉ Bishop's House, Sontley Road, Wrexham LL13 7EW (tel 01978 262726, fax 01978 354257, e-mail diowxm@globalnet.co.uk)

WREY, Benjamin Harold Bourchier; s of Maj Christopher Bourchier Wrey, TD (d 1976), and Ruth, *née* Bowden; *b* 6 May 1940; *Educ* Blundell's, Clare Coll Cambridge (MA); *m* 19 Feb 1970, (Anne) Christine Aubrey Cherry, da of Col Christopher B Stephenson (d 1970); 1 da (Tanya b 20 Jan 1971); *Career* Pensions Advsy Dept Legal & General Assurance Society Ltd 1963–66, investment analyst Hambros Bank Ltd 1966–69; Henderson Global Investors Ltd (formerly Henderson plc): joined 1969, dir 1971–, jt md 1981–82, dep chm 1983–92, chm 1992–2004; dir: Henderson Electric & General Investment Tst plc 1977–2000, Henderson American Capital & Income Tst 1996–99, CCLA Investment Mgmnt Ltd 1998–2005; chm Institutional Fund Managers Assoc 1996–98, chm Charities Official Investment Fund 2005– (tstee 1998); former memb Fin Practitioners Panel City Disputes Panel, former memb Ctee Assoc of Investment Trust Companies (dep chm 1999–2002), memb Investment Ctee Univ of Cambridge Assistants Pension Scheme 2004–; memb: Advsy Cncl Nat Opera Studio 1996–2006, Cncl Br Heart Fndn 2003– (chm Investment Ctee 2003–); *Recreations* shooting (represented Univ of Cambridge, Co of London, England and GB teams in full-bore target rifle shooting in UK and overseas, winner Bisley Grand Aggregate 1966 and 1969), alpine walking, fishing, ballet and opera; *Clubs* Boodle's, City of London, Hurlingham; *Style*— Benjamin Wrey, Esq; ✉ 8 Somerset Square, Addison Road, London W14 8EE (tel 020 7603 4023)

WREY, Sir (George Richard) Bourchier; 15 Bt (E 1628), of Trebitch, Cornwall; s of Sir (Castel Richard) Bourchier Wrey, 14 Bt (d 1991), and Sybil Mabel Alice, *née* Lubke; *b* 2 October 1948; *Educ* Eton; *m* 1 Aug 1981, Lady Caroline Janet Lindesay-Bethune, da of 15 Earl of Lindsay (d 1989); 2 s (Harry David Bourchier b 1984, Humphrey George Bourchier b 1991), 1 da (Rachel Pearl b 1987); *Heir* s, Harry Wrey; *Recreations* all types of sport, shooting; *Clubs* Shikar; *Style*— Sir Bourchier Wrey, Bt; ✉ Hollamoor Farm, Tawstock, Barnstaple, Devon EX31 3NY (tel 01271 373466)

WRIGGLESWORTH, Sir Ian William; kt (1991); s of Edward Wrigglesworth, of Stockton on Tees; *b* 8 December 1939; *Educ* Stockton GS, Stockton Billingham Tech Coll, Coll of St Mark and St John Chelsea; *m* 1967, Patricia Susan, da of Hugh L Truscott; 2 s, 1 da; *Career* PA to Sir Ronald Gould as gen sec NUT 1966–68, head Co-op Pty Res Dept 1968–70, press and public affrs mangr Nat Giro 1970–74, divnl dir Smiths Industries plc 1975–2000; MP (Lab and Co-op 1974–81, SDP 1981–87) Thornaby, Teesside Feb 1974–83, Stockton South 1983–87; PPS: to Alec Lyon when Min of State Home Office 1974, to Roy Jenkins when Home Sec 1974–76; sec Manifesto Gp within Lab Party 1976–81, vice-chm Lab Econ Fin and Taxation Assoc 1976–81, oppn spokesman Civil Service 1979–81, SDP home affrs spokesman Nov 1982–May 1983, SDP econ and industrial affrs spokesman 1983–87, Alliance trade and industry spokesman 1987; exec chm: UK Land Estates Ltd 1995–, Prima Europe Ltd 1996–98, Government Policy Consultants Ltd (GPC) 1998–2000; dep chm John Livingston & Sons Ltd 1987–95; dir: CIT Holdings Ltd 1987–2003, Northern Devpt Co 1993–99; chm: Northern Region CBI 1992–94, Newcastle Gateshead Initiative 1999–2004, Baltic Centre for Contemporary Arts 2005–, Port of Tyne 2005–; govr Univ of Teesside 1993–2002; Freeman City of London, Liveryman Worshipful Co of Fndrs; *Recreations* walking, skiing, water sports, music; *Clubs* Reform, National Liberal, Groucho; *Style*— Sir Ian Wrigglesworth; ✉ UK Land Estates, Picture House, Queens Park, Queensway, Team Valley, Gateshead NE11 0NX (tel 0191 440 8880, fax 0191 440 8881)

WRIGHT, Alexander Andrew (Alex); *b* 9 August 1965; *Educ* Winchester, Sidney Sussex Coll Cambridge (exhibitioner, MA); *m* 2005, Alison Ruth Webster; *Career* commissioning ed CUP 1988–95, sr ed SPCK 1995–97, sr commissioning ed Blackwell Publishers 1997–99, dir SCM Press 2000–02, sr ed I B Tauris & Co Ltd 2003–; memb: Soc for Study of Theology 1993, Soc for the Study of Christian Ethics 1995, American Acad of Religion 1995, External Advsy Panel Faculty of Divinity Univ of Oxford 2001–, Classical Assoc 2005; memb Editorial Bd Political Theology 2003–; *Books* Why Bother with Theology? (2002), Meanings of Life (2005); *Recreations* cinema, contemporary fiction, contemporary painting, running, hill walking, writing, London, Norfolk; *Style*— Alex Wright, Esq; ✉ 55b Truro Road, London N22 8EH (tel 020 8826 0242, e-mail alex@divinity.org.uk); I B Tauris & Co Ltd, 6 Salem Road, London W2 4BU (tel 020 7243 1225, fax 020 7243 1226, e-mail awright@ibtauris.com)

WRIGHT, Andrew Paul Kilding; OBE (2001); s of Harold Maurice Wright (d 1983), and Eileen Mary, *née* Kilding; *b* 11 February 1947; *Educ* Queen Mary's GS Walsall, Univ of Liverpool (BArch); *m* 10 Oct 1970, Jean Patricia, da of Alfred John Cross; 2 da (Hannah b 1973, Sarah b 1985), 1 s (Samuel b 1976); *Career* architect; Sir Basil Spence Glover & Ferguson 1973–78, chm Law & Dunbar-Nasmith 1999–2001 (assoc 1978–81, ptnr 1981–2001); Inverness Architectural Assoc: memb Cncl 1981–90, pres 1986–88; memb: Cncl RIBA 1988–94 and 1995–97, Ecclesiastical Architects and Surveyors Assoc 1989–; Royal Incorporation of Architects in Scotland: memb Cncl 1985–94 and 1995–99, pres 1995–97 (vice-pres 1986–88), membership convener 1992–94, convenor Conservation Working Gp 1994–95; delg Architects Cncl of Europe 1995–96, dir Bd of Glasgow 1999 Festival Co Ltd 1996–2003, Sec of State appointed Bd memb Ancient Monuments Bd for Scotland 1996–2003, cmmr Royal Fine Art Cmmn for Scotland 1997–2005; diocesan architect Dio of Moray Ross and Caithness 1988–98, architectural advsr Holyrood Progress Gp Scottish Parliament Corporate Body 2000–04, Conservation advsr Highland Buildings Preservation Tst 2001–, hon architectural advsr Scottish Redundant Churches Tst 1996–; chair Working Gp on Heritage Protection Legislation; memb: Conservation Advsy Panel Hopetoun House Preservation Tst 1997–2007 (co-chair 2005–07), Church of Scotland Ctee on Artistic Matters 1999–2005, Saltire Soc Art in Architecture Awards Panel 2001–06, Historic Environment Advsy Cncl for Scotland 2003– (vice-chair 2003–06), Panel for the Fundamental Review of Historic Scotland Scot Exec 2003–04, Post Completion Advsy Gp Scottish Parl 2004–06, Design Panel North Highland Initiative 2006–, Conservation Ctee Nat Tst for Scotland 2007–; external examiner Robert Gordon Univ 1998–2003; tstee Clan Mackenzie Charitable Tst 1998–2007; founding fell Inst of Contemporary Scotland; RIBA, PPRIAS, FRSA, FSA Scot; *Recreations* music, railway history, fishing; *Style*— Andrew P K Wright, Esq, OBE, PPRIAS; ✉ Andrew P K Wright Chartered Architect and Heritage Consultant, 16 Moy House Court, Forres, Moray IV36 2NZ (tel 01309 676655, fax 01309 676609, e-mail andrewpkw@aol.com)

WRIGHT, Dr Anne Margaret; CBE (1997); da of Herbert Holden (d 1973), of Kent, and Florence, *née* Kelly (d 1980); *b* 27 July 1946; *Educ* Holy Trinity Ind GS Bromley, KCL (Merchant Taylors' Co exhibition, William Henry Gladstone exhibition, BA, Lillian M Faithfull prize, Early English Text Soc prize, George Smith studentship, Inglis studentship, PhD); *m* 25 July 1970, Martin Wright, s of Robert Wright (d 1981), of London; 1 da (Amy Laura b 1982); *Career* lectr in English Lancaster Univ 1969–71, lectr rising to reader in modern English studies Hatfield Poly 1971–84, registrar for Arts and Humanities CNAA 1984–86, dep rector (academic) Liverpool Poly 1986–90, vice-chllr Univ of Sunderland (formerly Sunderland Poly) 1990–98, chief exec Univ for Industry 1998–2001, educnl conslt 2001–; chm: Sunderland Common Purpose 1990–97, Cmmn on Univ Career Opportunity 1993–98, Nat Lottery Cmmn 2005–; dir: The Wearside Opportunity 1991–93, Northern Sinfonia 1991–96, Northern Arts Bd 1991–95, Higher Educn Quality Cncl 1992–97, Wearside TEC 1993–98, Open Learning Fndn 1993–95; memb: Further Educn Funding Cncl 1992–96, Hong Kong Univ and Poly Grants Ctee 1992–2003, Cncl for Industry and HE 1994–99, NE C of C Cncl 1995–98, CBI Regnl Cncl 1996–98, Equal Opportunities Cmmn 1997–98, Armed Forces Pay Review Body 2002–; DL (Co of Tyne & Wear) 1997–2001; FRSA 1991, CCMI 1999– (CIMgt 1994, memb Bd of Companions); *Books* Literature of Crisis 1910–1922, Harley Granville Barker (critical biography in Modern British Dramatists 1900–1945, 1982), Tom Stoppard (critical biography in Dictionary of Literary Biography, 1982), Bernard Shaw's Saint Joan (1984); various publications on Shaw, Lawrence, T S Eliot and others; *Recreations* theatre, opera, the Arts; *Style*— Dr Anne Wright, CBE; ✉ Apartment 10, 206 Regents Park Road, London NW1 8AQ (tel 020 7586 4707)

WRIGHT, Anthony David (Tony); MP; s of Arthur Leslie Wright (d 1993), and Jean, *née* Middleton; *b* 12 August 1954; *Educ* Hospital Secdy Sch Great Yarmouth, Great Yarmouth Coll of FE; *m* 1988, Barbara; 2 c from prev m (Emily and Carl), 1 step c (Lisa); *Career* apprentice engr (City & Guilds) Erie Electronics 1970–74; engr: Brown & Root 1974–75, Probe Oil Tools 1975–83; full time organiser Great Yarmouth Lab Pty 1983–97, MP (Lab) Great Yarmouth 1997–; PPS to Ruth Kelly, MP, *qv*, 2002–03, memb Select Ctee on Public Admin 2000–02, memb Jt Legislative Ctee Draft Gambling Bill 2003–04; Great Yarmouth BC: cncllr 1980–82 and 1986–98, chm various ctees 1988–97, ldr 1995–97 (dep ldr 1994–95); chm Great Yarmouth Marketing Initiative 1995–97, dir Great Yarmouth Tourist Authy 1994–97; *Recreations* darts, football, all sports (mainly as a spectator); *Style*— Tony Wright, Esq, MP; ✉ House of Commons, London SW1A 0AA (tel 020 7219 4832, e-mail wrighta@parliament.uk); Constituency Office, 20 Church Plain, Great Yarmouth, Norfolk NR30 1NE (tel 01493 332291, fax 01493 853157)

WRIGHT, Dr Anthony Wayland (Tony); MP; s of Frank Wright, and Maud Wright; *b* 11 March 1948; *Educ* Kettering GS, LSE (BSc(Econ)), Harvard Univ (Kennedy scholar), Balliol Coll Oxford (DPhil); *m* 21 July 1973, Moira Elynwy, da of Edmor Phillips; 3 s (and 1 s decd); *Career* lectr in politics UCNW Bangor 1973–75, lectr, sr lectr then reader in politics Sch of Continuing Studies Univ of Birmingham 1975–92; MP (Lab): Cannock and Burntwood 1992–97, Cannock Chase 1997–; PPS to the Lord Chancellor 1997–98; chair Public Admin Select Ctee 1999–; jt ed Political Quarterly; chm S Birmingham Community Health Cncl 1983–85, parent govr St Laurence Church Schs Northfield Birmingham 1989–92; hon prof Univ of Birmingham; *Books* Who Do I Complain To? (1997), Why Vote Labour? (1997), Socialisms: Old and New (1996), The New Social Democracy (jt ed, 1999), The British Political Process (ed, 2000), British Politics: A Very Short Introduction (2003); *Recreations* tennis, football, secondhand bookshops, walking, gardening; *Style*— Dr Tony Wright, MP; ✉ House of Commons, London SW1A 0AA

WRIGHT, Barbara Janet; da of Lt John Sutherland (d 1994), and Betty Dorothy Gladys, *née* Durrant, of Woodbridge, Suffolk; *b* 16 March 1955; *Educ* Romford County HS for Girls, Univ of Sheffield (LLB); *m* 23 Oct 1981, Lynton Wright, s of John (Jack) Wright of Stockport, Cheshire; *Career* asst slr Gill Turner and Tucker Maidstone 1979–80 (articled clerk 1977–79); asst slr Cripps Harries Hall and Co: Tunbridge Wells 1980–82, Crowborough 1982–84; Walkers 1984–87 (ptnr from 1986), Thomson Snell and Passmore Tunbridge Wells 1987– (ptnr 1997–), dep district judge (civil) 2001–; memb Nat Ctee and chm Mediation Ctee Slrs' Family Law Assoc 1997–98 (chm Kent 1990–96); memb: Family Mediator's Assoc 1993–, UK Coll of Family Mediators 1997–2001; hon arbitrator Tunbridge Wells Equitable Friendly Soc 1987–93, hon legal advsr W Kent Relate 1992–, pres Tunbridge Wells Tonbridge and Dist Law Soc 2003 (hon treas 1993–98, dep vice-pres 2001–02, vice-pres 2002–03); memb Law Soc 1979; *Style*— Mrs Barbara Wright; ✉ 3 Lonsdale Gardens, Tunbridge Wells, Kent TN1 1NX (tel 01892 510000, fax 01892 701123, e-mail bwright@ts-p.co.uk)

WRIGHT, Bruce; *b* 8 May 1944; *Educ* Battersea GS, Univ of Leicester (BA, MA); *Career* financial controller Mars Confectionery 1978–81, fin dir Courage 1981–85, with Grand Metropolitan plc 1986–87, fin dir Meyer International plc 1987–97; interim fin dir: B&Q 1998, Allied Carpets 1998–99, Marks & Spencer Ventures 2000, First Choice Holidays plc 2001, Kwik-Fit Holdings plc 2002, Chubb plc 2003; ACIS 1971; *Style*— Bruce Wright, Esq; ✉ Bruval, Fairmead, Duffield Park, Stoke Poges, Slough, Berkshire SL2 4HY

WRIGHT, Christopher Norman; CBE (2005); s of late Walter Reginald Wright, and Edna May, *née* Corden; *b* 7 September 1944; *Educ* King Edward VI GS Louth, Univ of Manchester (BA), Manchester Business Sch; *m* 1, 15 March 1972 (m dis 1999), Carolyn Rochelle (Chelle), da of Lloyd B Nelson, of California, USA; 2 s (Timothy b 1973, Thomas b 1974), 1 da (Chloe b 1978); m 2, July 2003, Janice Ann Stines, *née* Toseland; 1 da (Holly b 1991); *Career* operator Univ and Coll Booking Agency Manchester 1965–67, formed Ellis Wright Agency (with Terry Ellis) 1967, changed name to Chrysalis 1968, chm 1985–, now international music publishing, film and radio gp Chrysalis Group plc, chm QPR FC 1996–2001, chm and majority shareholder London Wasps RFC 1996–, chm and majority shareholder Portman Film and TV 2004–; *Recreations* tennis, breeding racehorses, food and wine; *Clubs* Turf; *Style*— Christopher Wright, Esq, CBE; ✉ Chrysalis Group plc, The Chrysalis Building, Bramley Road, London W10 6SP (tel 020 7221 2213)

WRIGHT, Prof Crispin James Garth; *b* 21 December 1942; *Educ* Birkenhead Sch Cheshire, Trinity Coll Cambridge (exhibitioner, MA, PhD), ChCh Oxford (BPhil, DLitt); *m* Catherine; 2 s (Geoffrey, Arthur); *Career* jr research fell Trinity Coll Oxford 1967–69, lectr Balliol Coll Oxford 1969–70, lectr UCL 1970–71, research fell All Souls Coll Oxford 1971–78, Bishop Wardlaw prof Univ of St Andrews 1997– (prof of logic and metaphysics 1978–), prof of philosophy Univ of Michigan Ann Arbor 1987–94 (James B and Grace J Nelson prof 1992–94); visiting appts: lectr Univ of Pennsylvania 1983, prof Princeton Univ 1985–86, research prof in the Humanities Univ of Queensland 1989, fell Magdalen Coll Oxford 1991, prof Columbia Univ 1997–, global distinguished prof NY Univ 2002–; prize fell All Souls Coll Oxford (by examination) 1969–71, Fulbright scholar 1985–86, British Academy Research Readership 1990–92, Leverhulme personal research prof 1998–2003; FBA 1992, FRSE 1996; *Books* Wittgenstein on the Foundations of Mathematics (1980), Frege's Conception of Numbers as Objects (1983), Realism: Meaning and Truth (1986), Truth and Objectivity (1992), The Reason's Proper Study (with R L V Hale, 2001), Rails to Infinity (2001), Saving the Differences (2003); *Style*— Prof Crispin Wright, FBA, FRSE; ✉ Department of Logic and Metaphysics, University of St Andrews, Fife KY16 9AL

WRIGHT, (Idonea) Daphne; da of Claud William Wright, of Burford, and late Alison Violet, *née* Readman; *b* 19 May 1951; *Educ* St Mary's Wantage; *Career* sec and editorial asst Chatto & Windus 1976–77, ed Hutchinson 1977–83, editorial dir Quartet 1983–84, Bellew Publishing 1984–86; winner Tony Godwin Meml Tst award 1980; chm Crime Writers' Assoc 2000–2001; memb: Crime Writers' Assoc 1989, Soc of Authors 1990; *Books* as Natasha Cooper: Festering Lilies (1990), Poison Flowers (1991), Bloody Roses (1992), Bitter Herbs (1993), Rotten Apples (1995), Fruiting Bodies (1996), Sour Grapes (1997), Creeping Ivy (1998), Fault Lines (1999), Prey to All (2000), Out of the Dark (2002), A Place of Safety (2003), Keep Me Alive (2004), Gagged and Bound (2005); as Clare Layton: Clutch of Phantoms (2000), Those Whom the Gods Love (2001); *Recreations* reading, entertaining, talking; *Style*— Ms Daphne Wright; ✉ c/o Gregory & Company, 3 Barb Mews, London W6 7PA

WRIGHT, David; MP; s of Kenneth William Wright, of Telford, Salop, and Heather, *née* Wynn; *b* 22 December 1966; *Educ* Wrockwardine Wood Comp, New Coll Telford, Wolverhampton Poly (BA); *m* 1 June 1996, Lesley; *Career* cncllr Oakengates Town Cncl 1989–2000 (sometime chm), cncllr Wrekin DC 1989–97; worked on housing strategy Sandwell MBC 1988–2001; MP (Lab) Telford 2001–; memb TGWU; MCIH 1994; *Recreations* watching local football, exploring historic towns and cities; *Clubs* Wrockwardine Wood and Trench Labour, Dawley Social; *Style*— David Wright, Esq, MP; ✉ House of Commons, London SW1A 0AA (tel 020 7219 8331, fax 020 7219 1979, e-mail wrightda@parliament.uk)

WRIGHT, David Alan; OBE (1983); s of Herbert Ernest Wright, and Ivy Florence, *née* Welch; *b* 27 May 1942; *Educ* Surbiton GS, Univ of Birmingham (BSS); *m* 1966, Gail Karol, *née* Mesling; 4 s, 1 da; *Career* VSO Chad 1963, info offr BOT 1964, entered FCO 1965, asst private sec to min of state FO 1966–68, MECAS 1968–70, Baghdad 1970–73, Doha 1973–76, on secondment to DHSS 1976–78, FCO 1978–80, Durban 1980–83, Baghdad 1983–87, FCO 1987–92 (head Communications Dept 1988–90, Info Systems Div (Resources) 1990–92), consul-gen Atlanta 1992–97, ambass and consul-gen Qatar 1997–2002, asst dir HR Directorate FCO 2002–; cncllr Guildford BC 2003–, memb Surrey Probation Bd 2006–; *Recreations* jogging, sailing, pottery, travel, music; *Clubs* Royal Over-Seas League; *Style*— David Wright, Esq, OBE; ✉ c/o Foreign & Commonwealth Office, Old Admiralty Building, London SW1A 2PA

WRIGHT, David Anthony; s of George Henry Wright, of Hornsea East Yorks, and Theresa, *née* Rooke; *b* 21 March 1949; *Educ* Marist Coll Hull, Sidney Sussex Coll Cambridge (MA, memb cast Oxford and Cambridge Shakespeare Co Tour of USA 1969–70 directed by Jonathan Miller); *m* 1979, Susan Iris, da of F W Benson, of Salford, Lancs; 1 s (Daniel), 1 da (Fernanda Maria); *Career* freelance documentary film-maker in TV 1979–; films incl: The Christians, This England, The Pennines: A Writer's Notebook, Years of Lightning, N Division, 617: Last Days of a Vulcan Squadron, Village Earth: In the Footsteps of The Incas, Learning How the Maasai See, The Tribe That's Fighting Back, Think Dream Laugh, The World: A Television History, Last Voyage of The Arctic Raider, Abbeystead - The Aftermath, Akong and The Big Shrine Room, Bellamy's Bugle; set up own co 54th Parallel 1988; films: The Heat is On - The Making of Miss Saigon, Under The Sacred Bo Tree; for First Tuesday (UK) and Arts & Entertainment Networks (USA): Bad Trip to Edgewood (1992), Follow the Flag (1993); for The Discovery Channel (Europe and USA) First Tuesday - Toxic Border (1994), First Tuesday - From Fury to Forgiveness (1994), Witness - From Fury to Forgiveness (Channel 4's lethal justice season, 1995), Discovery Journal - Born to Run (USA and Europe, 1995), Discovery Journal - Supermax (USA and Europe, 1995), Backstage at the Cambridge Footlights (Anglia TV, 1997), To the Ends of the Earth - Back from the Dead (Channel 4) 1998, Secrets of the Dead - The Lost Vikings of Greenland (Channel 4) 1998, Dispatches: For the Love of a Stranger (Channel 4) 2000, Animal Planet: O'Shea's Big Adventure in Australia (Channel 4) 2000, Boxing - In and Out of the Ring (Yorkshire Assoc Prodrs Toronto for A&E Networks), Hard Hat Women (BBC 2), The First Resort - Scarborough at Midwinter (BBC 2), Sex in the City (BBC 2), A Sense of Place - Hadrian's Wall (54th Parallel for BBC 1), Secrets of the Art Factory (The New Baltic Arts Centre, BBC 2); screenplays 1996/97: The Saboteurs, The Forgiver; *Recreations* travel, walking, reading, swimming, chopping logs; *Style*— David Wright, Esq

WRIGHT, Sir David John; GCMG (2002, KCMG 1996, CMG 1992), LVO (1990); s of John Frank Wright, of Wolverhampton; *b* 16 June 1944; *Educ* Wolverhampton GS, Peterhouse Cambridge; *m* 3 Feb 1968, Sally Ann Dodkin; 1 s (Nicholas b 1970), 1 da (Laura b 1973); *Career* HM Dip Serv: third sec 1966, third later second sec Tokyo 1966, second later first sec FCO 1972, École Nationale d'Administration Paris 1975, first sec Paris 1976, private sec to Sec of Cabinet 1980, cnsllr (econ) Tokyo 1982, head of Personnel Servs Dept FCO 1985, dep private sec to HRH The Prince of Wales 1988–90; ambass Seoul 1990–94 (cmmr-gen UK Pavilion at Taejon Expo 1993), dep under sec for Asia, Americas, Africa and Trade Promotion FCO 1994–96, ambass Tokyo 1996–99, chief exec Br Trade

W

Int 1999–; non-exec dir AEA Technology 1994–95; chm of tstees Daiwa Fndn 2001–; Hon LLD: Univ of Wolverhampton 1997, Univ of Birmingham 2000; Grand Cordon of the Rising Sun (Japan) 1998; *Recreations* cooking, military history, golf; *Style*— Sir David Wright, GCMG, LVO; ✉ c/o Foreign & Commonwealth Office, King Charles Street, London SW1A 2AH; British Trade International, Kingsgate House, 66–74 Victoria Street, London SW1E 6SW

WRIGHT, Dr David Stephen; OBE (1995); s of Edward Alfred Wright (d 1943), and Winifred May, *née* Oliver; *b* 4 August 1935; *Educ* Epsom Coll, Bart's (MB BS, MSc, DPH, DIH); *m* 19 Feb 1966, Caroline Auza, da of George William Black (d 1987), of Leeds; 2 s (Mark b 1967, Adam b 1969), 1 da (Alexandra b 1972); *Career* RN 1960–85 (ret with rank of Surgn Capt, final appt prof of naval occupational med and dir of health); head BP Group Occupational Health Centre 1985–91, chief med offr BP plc 1989–95; conslt occupational physician 1995–; BMA: chm Armed Forces Ctee 1985–88, memb Cncl 1985–88; dean Faculty of Occupational Med RCP 1991–94; Freeman City of London 1982, Liveryman Worshipful Soc of Apothecaries 1982; memb: Soc of Occupational Med, BMA; FFOM, FRCP, FFOM(I); OStJ 1984; *Recreations* golf, walking, gardening; *Style*— Dr David Wright, OBE; ✉ 9 Ashburton Road, Alverstoke, Gosport, Hampshire PO12 2LH (tel 023 92582459, e-mail cariwright@hotmail.com)

WRIGHT, Dermot John Fetherstonhaugh; s of late J W Wright, of West Wittering, W Sussex, and late Dorothy, *née* Fetherstonhaugh; *b* 5 August 1944; *Educ* Wellington, Trinity Coll Cambridge (MA); *m* 1, 1969 (m dis 1992), Patricia Fergie; 2 da (Emma, Louise); m 2, 1992, Bridget Bovill; 1 da (Eleanor), 2 s (Francis, Charles); *Career* called to the Bar Inner Temple 1967, currently head of chambers, recorder SE Circuit; chm James Peek Tst (charity); govr W Wittering Primary Sch Sussex; *Recreations* yachting, playing piano, golf; *Clubs* W Wittering Sailing, Barnacle Cruising (pres); *Style*— Dermot Wright, Esq

WRIGHT, Edward Arnold; MBE (1991); s of John Ernest Wright (d 1976), of Hornsey, and Alice Maud, *née* Arnold (d 1968); *b* 20 November 1926; *Educ* Tollington GS Muswell Hill; *Career* RTR 1943–45, KDG 1945–47; 1962–70: sales dir Gothic Press Ltd, md Gothic Display Ltd, md Gothic Studios Ltd; chm and md Edward Wright Ltd 1970–2001; former tstee Bat Conservation Tst; former hon treas: Fauna and Flora Preservation Soc, Br Section Int Cncl for Bird Preservation; former memb Cncl Br Tst for Ornithology; chm Flowers in the City Campaign; Freeman City of London 1980, former memb Ct of Assts Worshipful Co of Gardeners (Liveryman 1980); *Recreations* gardening, shooting; *Clubs* MCC; *Style*— Edward Wright, Esq, MBE; ✉ Woodlands, New England Lane, Sedlescombe, East Sussex TN33 0RP (tel and fax 01424 870220, e-mail eawright@sedlescombe.net)

WRIGHT, Gerald; s of William Arthur Reginald Wright (d 1967), and Olive Annie Neal Wright (d 1995); *b* 9 September 1935; *Educ* Monmouth, Queens' Coll Cambridge (MA); *m* 1959, Elizabeth Ann, da of Dr William Edward Harris (d 1974), of Llandaff; 3 s (Jeremy, Mathew, William); *Career* Nat Serv 2 Lt Welch Regt 1954–56; dir Lintas London 1972–73, chm Lintas Scandinavia 1973–74, dep chm and md Lintas London 1974–80, md Thresher and Co Ltd 1980–81; Whitbread & Co: mktg dir (UK) 1981–82, chm Nat Sales Div 1982–83; chm and chief exec Lintas London 1983–89, regnl dir Eastern Europe, Austria and Switzerland Lintas Worldwide 1989–94, dir Posmark Ltd 1994–96, conslt Harris Wright & Associates 1994–, chm Popa Ltd 1997–98, dir Marketing Soc 1998–2000; fell Marketing Soc 2002–; FRSA; *Recreations* reading, opera, walking, cycling, rugby, cricket, bridge, travel; *Clubs* Reform, Solus; *Style*— Gerald Wright, Esq; ✉ 25 Crown Lane, Chislehurst, Kent BR7 5PL (tel and fax 020 8325 6899, e-mail gwright.25c@virgin.net)

WRIGHT, Dr Helen Mary; da of Gordon Kendal, of Alyth, Perthshire, and Patricia, *née* Foggo; *b* 22 August 1970; *Educ* James Gillespie's HS Edinburgh, Lincoln Coll Oxford (MA, PGCE), Univ of Leicester (MA), Univ of Exeter (EdD); *m* 9 Jan 1993, Brian, s of Geoffrey Wright; 1 s (Harry McGregor b 3 June 2003), 1 da (Caitlin McGregor b 27 Oct 2006); *Career* French and German teacher Reed's Sch Cobham 1993–95, head of dept Bishop's Stortford Coll 1995–97, head of dept and dep housemistress St Edward's Sch Oxford 1997–2000, headmistress Heathfield Sch Ascot 2001–03 (dep head 2000), headmistress St Mary's Sch Calne 2003–; teacher-educator and PGCE mentor 1997–2000; IB Examiner (Higher Level) 1999–, ISI Inspector 2000–; ed: ISMLA newsletter 1997–2000, Francophonie 1999–2002; academic conslt Scholastic Books 1998–2001; memb: Assoc for Language Learning (ALL) 1993–, Ind Schs' Modern Languages Assoc (ISMLA) 1995– (also memb Ctee and patron), SHA 2000–, GSA 2001–; FRSA 2003; *Publications* Dr Behr-Sigel: A monk of the Eastern Church (trans), French Fries My Brain! (2001), Learning through Listening (2004); numerous articles and reviews 1993–; *Recreations* reading, studying, travelling; *Clubs* Univ Women's, Lansdowne; *Style*— Dr Helen Wright; ✉ St Mary's School, Calne, Wiltshire SN11 0DF (tel 01249 857200, fax 01249 857207, e-mail headmistress@stmaryscalne.org)

WRIGHT, Iain; MP; *b* 9 May 1972, Hartlepool; *Educ* Manor Comp, UCL; *Career* early career as accountant, worked for One NorthEast regnl devpt agency; MP (Lab) Hartlepool 2004– (by-election), PPS To Rosie Winterton, MP (as Min of State for Health) 2005–06; memb Modernisation of the House of Commons Ctee, memb Public Accounts Ctee, chair All Pty Parly Gp on Road Safety; *Recreations* supporting Hartlepool FC; *Style*— Iain Wright, Esq, MP; ✉ House of Commons, London SW1A 0AA

WRIGHT, Ian; s of Peter Wright, of Maidenhead, Berks, and Gladys, *née* Green; *b* 4 April 1958; *Educ* Desborough Sch Maidenhead, St Catharine's Coll Cambridge (MA); *m* 23 Dec 1987, Judith, da of Eric Gilboy, of Dean, Cumbria; 1 s (Iain), 1 da (Katie); *Career* pres Cambridge Student Union 1980–81, political organiser SDP 1981–85, PR conslt 1985–94, sr corp affrs and corp relations positions The Boots Co 1994–2000, corp relations dir Diageo plc 2000–; vice-pres SDP 1989–91, chair Lib Dems in PR and Public Affrs 1995–98, advsr to Paddy Ashdown 1995–99; FCIPR (pres 2001); *Books* Reviving the Centre (with Roger Fox, 1989); numerous articles in nat press and other pubns; *Recreations* cricket, football, gardening; *Style*— Ian Wright, Esq; ✉ Diageo plc, 8 Henrietta Place, London W1M 9AG (tel 020 7927 5661)

WRIGHT, Ian James; s of James Wilson Wright (d 1987), of Wishaw, and Dorothy, *née* Ormerod (d 1961); *b* 28 May 1948; *Educ* Liverpool Coll of Art (BA), RCA (MA); *m* 1976, Glenda, da of William Laverick Tindale; 3 s (Stewart James b 1978, Steven William b 1981, James Lewis b 1987); *Career* Kinneir Calvert Tuhill Design Consultants 1973–75; design dir: The Jenkins Gp 1975–1997, Cobalt Consultancy 1997–98 (formerly The Jenkins Group); fndr dir Air, Creative Communications; *Style*— Ian James Wright, Esq; ✉ 61 Warren Road, Chingford, London E4 6QR (tel 020 8529 5373); Air Design, One Curtain Place, Shoreditch, London EC2A 3AN (tel 0845 450 6575, fax 0845 450 6576, e-mail ian@airdesign.co.uk, website www.airdesign.co.uk)

WRIGHT, James Robertson Graeme; CBE (2001), DL (Tyne & Wear 1995); s of John Wright, and Elizabeth Calder, *née* Coghill; *b* 14 June 1939; *Educ* Inverness Royal Acad, Dundee HS, Univ of Edinburgh (Guthrie fell, C B Black scholar, MA), St John's Coll Cambridge (major scholar, Henry Arthur Thomas student, Denney student, Ferguson scholar, MA); *m* 1966, Jennifer Susan, *née* Greenberg; 2 da; *Career* Univ of Edinburgh: lectr in humanity (Latin) 1966–78 (asst lectr 1965), sr warden Pollock Halls of Residence 1973–78, memb Univ Ct 1975–78; St Catharine's Coll Cambridge: fell 1978–87, professorial fell 1987–91, hon fell 1992–, dir of studies in classics 1978–87, bursar 1979–87, chm Cambridge Bursar's Ctee 1986–87 (sec 1983–86); sec-gen of the faculties Univ of Cambridge 1987–91; vice-chllr Univ of Newcastle upon Tyne 1992–2000; assoc cmmr Hamlyn Nat Cmmn on Educn 1992–93, chm HE Mgmnt Statistics Gp (HEMS) 1995–99, dir UCAS 1997–2000; memb: Governing Body Shrewsbury Sch 1986–2000, SHEFC 1992–99, CVCP 1992–2000 (memb Cncl 1995–2000), Advsy Gp Newcastle Common Purpose 1992–2000, Ctee for Int Co-operation in HE Br Cncl 1992–2000, HEFCE Sector Strategy Ctee 1998–2000; non-exec memb: Cambridge DHA 1990–91, Northern and Yorks RHA 1993–96; chm Connexions Tyne & Wear 2001–, dir The Newcastle Gateshead Initiative 1993–2000; vice-pres Age Concern England 2005– (tstee 2001–05, chm 2002–05), memb Bd Age Concern Scotland 2001–, dir Age Concern Holdings 2005– (chm 2006–); tstee Nat Heritage Meml Fund and Heritage Lottery Fund 2000–06; High Sheriff Tyne & Wear 2003–04; Hon LLD Univ of Abertay Dundee 1999, Hon DEd Univ of Naresuan Thailand 2000, Hon DCL Univ of Newcastle upon Tyne 2001; *Recreations* walking, travel in France, food, wine; *Clubs* Athenaeum, Northern Counties (Newcastle upon Tyne); *Style*— James Wright, Esq, CBE, DL; ✉ 10 Montagu Avenue, Newcastle upon Tyne NE3 4JH

WRIGHT, Jeremy; MP; *b* 24 October 1972; *Educ* Taunton Sch, Trinity Sch NY, Univ of Exeter; *m* Yvonne; 1 da (Stephanie b 15 May 2005); *Career* called to the Bar Inner Temple 1996; MP (Cons) Rugby and Kenilworth 2005–, memb Constitutional Affrs Select Ctee; former chm Warwick and Leamington Cons Assoc; tstee Community Devpt Fndn; *Style*— Jeremy Wright, Esq, MP; ✉ House of Commons, London SW1A 0AA (tel 01926 853650, e-mail jeremy@jeremywright.co.uk, website www.jeremywright.co.uk)

WRIGHT, Jerry; s of Gerald Wright, of Chislehurst, Kent, and Elizabeth, *née* Harris; *b* 28 October 1960; *Educ* Eltham Coll, Univ of Bristol (BA); *m* 15 July 1989, Ann Clare, *née* Faller; 1 s (Christopher James Faller b 14 April 1995), 1 da (Charlotte Elizabeth Faller b 29 June 1997); *Career* business gp dir Homecare and Personal Wash Lever Brothers Ltd 1993–97, sr corp strategist Unilever plc 1997–99, category dir Hair and Laundry Care IC SE Asia 2000–01, regnl brand dir Omo Greater Asia 2002–03, business unit head Birds Eye 2003–04, mktg and innovation dir Birds Eye 2005–06; *Recreations* rugby, cricket, music (especially opera), travel, food and drink, bridge, reading, crosswords; *Clubs* Reform; *Style*— Jerry Wright, Esq

WRIGHT, (Ivor) John; s of Ivor Glynn Wright (d 1978), and Rosetta Amelia, *née* Forshow; *b* 22 June 1968, Clatterbridge, Wirral; *Educ* Univ of Glamorgan (BA); *m* 8 Nov 1997, Julie Ann, *née* Hammond; 1 da (Niamh Elizabeth b 27 Nov 2003); *Career* md Toyota/Lexus Europe Saatchi & Saatchi 1994– (previously md), Deutsche Bank 2001–02; involved with: Business in the Community, Habitat for Humanity; MIPA 2005; *Recreations* travel, food and wine, family; *Clubs* Solus, Soho House, The Hospital; *Style*— John Wright, Esq; ✉ Saatchi & Saatchi, 80 Charlotte Street, London W1A 1AQ (tel 020 7462 7658, e-mail john.wright@saatchi.co.uk)

WRIGHT, John Edward; s of John Nicholas Wright (d 1962), and Ellen Bullen, *née* Mulloy; *b* 23 May 1933; *Educ* Mold GS, Univ of Liverpool (MB ChB, MD); *m* 23 May 1959, Kathleen Teresa, da of John Reid (d 1938); 1 s (John b 1960), 1 da (Elizabeth b 1966); *Career* Nat Serv RAMC 1957–60; conslt ophthalmic surgn St Mary's Hosp London 1969–73; sr lectr in ophthalmology Univ of London 1969–73, conslt ophthalmic surgn Moorfields Eye Hosp London 1973– (sr registrar 1964–67), conslt ophthalmic surgn Royal ENT Hosp London 1973–; Wendel Hughes Lectr USA 1982, Doyne Lectr Oxford 1987; numerous pubns on orbital disease; past sec of the Ophthalmological Soc, pres Int Orbital Soc, past bd memb Moorfields Eye Hosp; memb: RSM, Coll of Ophthalmologists, American Acad of Ophthalmology; FRCS 1966; *Recreations* golf, fishing; *Clubs* Denham Golf and Piscatorial Soc; *Style*— John Wright, Esq; ✉ 44 Wimpole Street, London W1M 7DG (tel 020 7580 1251, fax 020 7224 3722)

WRIGHT, Karen Jocelyn Wile; da of Louis David Wile (d 1972), and Grace Carlin Wile (d 1998); *b* 15 November 1950; *Educ* Princeton HS, Brandeis Univ (BA), Univ of Cambridge (MA), London Business Sch (MSc); *m* 23 May 1981, Richard Bernard Wright, s of Bernard Gilbert Wright; 2 da (Louisa Karen b 17 April 1985, Rebecca Katherine b 21 Oct 1986); *Career* fndr and prop Hobson Gallery Cambridge 1975–84, Bernard Jacobson Gallery Cork St 1985, worked on Victor Willing catalogue Whitechapel Art Gallery 1986; Modern Painters magazine: fndr with Peter Fuller 1987, asst ed 1987–89, managing ed 1989–91, ed 1991–; fndr (with David Bowie, Sir Tim Sainsbury and Bernard Jacobson) 21 Publishing 1998; AICA 1988; *Books* The Penguin Book of Art Writing (ed with Martin Gayford, 1998), Colour for Kosovo (ed with Daphne Astor, 1999), The Grove Book of Art Writing (2000), Writers on Artists (2002), Colour (2004); *Recreations* art, tennis, skiing, reading, relaxing with the teenagers; *Clubs* Groucho; *Style*— Mrs Karen Wright; ✉ 36 Elgin Crescent, London W11 2JR

WRIGHT, Malcolm; s of Alan Trevor Hurd Wright, and Patricia Anne Wright; *b* 29 May 1952; *Educ* St Peter's Sch York, Univ of Durham (BA), NCTJ (Dip Journalism); *m* 1981, Alison Cameron, da of Allan Cameron Walker; 2 da (Joanne Sarah b 7 June 1984, Grace Flora b 29 March 1989), 1 s (Samuel Allan b 28 Jan 1987); *Career* journalist; regnl newspaper journalist Keighley News, Yorkshire Evening Press and Northern Echo 1974–1980, freelance journalist The Guardian 1980–85, sr lectr in journalism Darlington Coll 1985–89; ITV Tyne Tees: joined as prodr and dir 1989, ed Current Affairs 1995, head of features 1996, controller of features 1997, head of network features 1998–2001, head of new media 2001–04; md ITV SignPost 2005–; vice-chm CODEWORKS Centre of Digital Excellence; founding dir Northern Film and Media, memb Advsy Panel Univ of Teesside Media; memb Labour Pty; *Awards* RTS Best Regnl Programme 1990 (for Mystery of the Derbyshire) and 1993 (for WarGames), British Environment and Media Awards Best Regnl Programme and RTS Special Award for Investigative Journalism 1992 (for Children of the Bomb), NY Film and TV Festival Best Factual finalist 1995 (for The Black File), San Francisco Golden Spire 1997 (exec prodr An Angel Passes By), Broadband Br Champion 2003, IVCA Clarion 2005, Disability Equality Employer of the Year 2005; *Publications* Joining up the Dot.coms (2001); *Recreations* guitar, piano, crosswords, birdwatching; *Style*— Malcolm Wright, Esq

WRIGHT, Dr Martin; s of Clifford Kent Wright (d 1969), of Sheffield, and Rosalie, *née* Mackenzie (d 1967); *b* 24 April 1930; *Educ* Repton, Jesus Coll Oxford (MA), LSE (PhD); *m* 26 July 1957, Louisa Mary (Lisa), da of John Osborne Nicholls (d 1974), of Yoxall, Staffs; 3 s (Edward b 1960, James b 1961, William b 1963), 2 da (Sophie b 1960 d 1993, Ellie b 1968); *Career* librarian Inst of Criminology Cambridge 1964–71, dir Howard League for Penal Reform 1971–81, information/policy devpt offr Victim Support 1985–94, conslt on mediation 1994–; vice-chair Restorative Justice Consortium 2001–, sec European Forum for Victim/Offender Mediation and Restorative Justice 2002–06; visiting research fell Sch of Legal Studies Univ of Sussex 1995–; chm Lambeth Mediation Serv 1989–92; memb: Br Society of Criminology, Howard League for Penal Reform, Centre for Crime and Justice Studies; hon fell Inst of Conflict Resolution Sofia 2005, hon dip Polish Centre for Mediation Warsaw; *Books* The Use of Criminology Literature (ed, 1974), Making Good: Prisons, Punishment and Beyond (1982), Mediation and Criminal Justice: Victims, Offenders and Community (jt ed with B Galaway, 1989), Justice for Victims and Offenders: A Restorative Response to Crime (1991, 2 edn 1996), Restoring Respect for Justice: a Symposium (1999, trans into Polish 2005 and Russian 2007); *Recreations* suggesting improvements; *Style*— Dr Martin Wright; ✉ 19 Hillside Road, London SW2 3HL (tel 020 8671 8037, e-mail martinw@phonecoop.coop)

WRIGHT, Sir (John) Michael; kt (1990); s of Prof John George Wright (d 1971), and Elsie Lloyd, *née* Razey (d 1955); *b* 26 October 1932; *Educ* The King's Sch Chester, Oriel Coll Oxford (MA); *m* 25 July 1959, Kathleen Esther Gladys Wright, JP, da of Frederick Arthur Meanwell, MM (d 1945); 2 da (Elizabeth b 1961, Katharine b 1963), 1 s (Timothy b 1965); *Career* Nat Serv RA 1951–53, 2 Lt 1952, Lt 1953, TA 1953–56, TARO 1956–; called to the Bar Lincoln's Inn 1957 (bencher 1983, treas 2003), recorder of the Crown Court 1974–90, QC 1974, ldr SE Circuit 1981–83, chm Bar 1983–84 (vice-chm 1982–83), legal assessor RCVS 1984–90, judge of the High Court of Justice (Queen's Bench Div) 1990–2003, presiding judge SE Circuit 1995–98; chm of govrs Reigate GS 2004–; hon fell Oriel Coll Oxford 2000; *Style—* Sir Michael Wright; ✉ Old Coombe House, Sharpthorne, West Sussex RH19 4PG

WRIGHT, Prof Michael Thomas; s of William George Wright (d 1985), and Lily May, *née* Turner; *b* 11 April 1947; *Educ* Sheldon Heath Sch Birmingham, Aston Univ (BSc, PhD); *m* 29 Aug 1970, Patricia Eunice, da of Stanley Douglas Cox; 1 da (Rebecca Michelle b 19 Sept 1977); *Career* apprentice EPE Co Birmingham 1963–68, res engr Redman Heenan Froude Worcs 1969–76, engrg dir Linear Motors Ltd Loughborough 1976–78, tech dir NEI Peebles Ltd Edinburgh 1978–82, engrg dir GEC Large Machines Rugby 1982–85, Molins plc 1985–90 (md Tobacco Div then gp md); Aston Univ: prof and head Dept of Mechanical and Electrical Engrg 1990–92, chm Aston Business School 1992–93, sr pro-vice-chllr 1994–96, vice-chllr 1996–, dir Aston Science Park Ltd 1997–; non-exec chm The 600 Group plc 1993–, non-exec dir ERA Technology 1994–2003, dir Birmingham Technology Ltd 1997–; governing dir Scot Engrg Trg Scheme Glasgow 1978–82; chair W Midlands HE Educn Assoc 2003–; IEE Student Paper Award 1970, IEEE Petrochemical Indust Author Award 1981, IEE Power Div Premium for published work 1983; FIEE 1981, sr memb IEEE (USA) 1981, FREng 1988, FIMechE 1989, FRSA 1989, CMath 1994, FIMA 1994, CIMgt 1997; *Style—* Prof Michael Wright, FREng; ✉ Vice Chancellor's Office, Aston University, Aston Triangle, Birmingham B4 7ET (tel 0121 204 4884, e-mail m.t.wright@aston.uk)

WRIGHT, Miles Francis Melville; s of Montague Francis Melville Wright (d 1968), and Marjorie Isobel, *née* Brook (d 1968); *b* 3 December 1943; *Educ* Ampleforth, ChCh Oxford (MA); *Career* dir American Int Underwriters (UK) Ltd 1982–84 (asst md 1984–87), md Polwring Underwriting Agency at Lloyd's 1988–96, dir Genesis Underwriting Agency Ltd 1996–2000, vice-pres Chubb Insurance Co of Europe SA 2002–; arbitrator and expert witness in insurance disputes; Freeman: Worshipful Co of Glaziers & Painters of Glass, Worshipful Co of Insurers; *Recreations* cricket, tennis, shooting, gardening; *Clubs* Naval and Military, 1900, MCC, I Zingari, Free Foresters, Band of Brothers CC, Emeriti and Old Amplefordian CCs (hon sec Old Amplefordian CC 1971–84, pres 1999–); *Style—* Miles F M Wright, Esq; ✉ Pine Tree Lodge, Benenden, Kent TN17 4DB; 6 Spirit Quay, Vaughan Way, Wapping, London E1W 2UT (tel 020 7702 0911)

WRIGHT, Prof Sir Nicholas Alcwyn; kt (2006); s of Glyndwr Alcwyn Wright (d 1980), and Hilda Lilian, *née* Jones (d 1978); *b* 24 February 1943; *Educ* Bristol GS, Univ of Durham (MB BS), Univ of Newcastle upon Tyne (MD, PhD, DSc), Univ of Oxford (MA); *m* 1966, Vera, da of George Matthewson; 1 da (Claire Louise b 8 Aug 1968), 1 s (Graeme Alcwyn b 18 Dec 1969); *Career* Univ of Newcastle upon Tyne: demonstrator in pathology 1966–71, research fell 1971–74, lectr in pathology 1974–76, sr lectr 1976–77; Univ of Oxford: clinical reader in pathology 1977, Nuffield reader 1978, fell Green Coll 1979–80; dir of histopathology Hammersmith Hosp 1980–96, dean Royal Postgrad Med Sch (Imperial Coll Sch of Med following merger 1997) 1996–97; Imperial Coll Sch of Med at Hammersmith Hosp: vice-princ for research 1996–2001, dep princ 1997–2001; warden Barts and the London Queen Mary's Coll of Med and Dentistry 2001–; Cancer Research (UK): dir Histopathology Unit 1988–, dir of clinical research 1991–96; chm Research for Health Charities Gp 1994; memb Cncl: Royal Coll of Pathologists 1982–96, Br Soc of Gastroenterology 1986– (pres 2003–04); pres Pathological Soc of GB and Ireland; FRCPath 1986, FMedSci 1998, FRCS 1999, FRCP 2001 (MRCP 1998); *Recreations* rugby football, cricket, squash, military history, cooking; *Clubs* Athenaeum; *Style—* Prof Sir Nicholas Wright; ✉ Barts and the London, Turner Street, Whitechapel, London E1 2AD (tel 020 7882 2262, e-mail warden@qmul.ac.uk)

WRIGHT, Capt Nicholas Peter (Nick); LVO (1994); s of Lt Cdr Edward Wright (d 2001), and Peggy, *née* Askew (d 1993); *b* 11 November 1949, London; *Educ* Ampleforth, BRNC Dartmouth; *m* 1976, Venetia Ruth, *née* Berthon; 3 da (Serena Elizabeth b 10 July 1981, Sophie Victoria b 20 Nov 1985, Camilla Rose b 29 Oct 1990), 1 s (Charles Simon b 15 Nov 1983); *Career* RN: HM ships Whitby and Diomede 1969–73, Flag Lt to Flag Offr Medway 1973–75, HMS Norfolk 1976–77, Allied Forces Northern Europe Oslo 1978–80, HMS Lowestoft 1980–82, asst sec to Second Sea Lord 1982–84, staff BRNC Dartmouth 1985–87, HMS Illustrious 1985–87, sec to Flag Offr Portsmouth 1989–91, JSDC RNC Greenwich 1991, HM Yacht Britannia 1992–94, sec to ACNS 1995–97, CSO Personnel to Flag Offr Naval Aviation 1998–2000, sec to Dep SACLANT Virginia 2000–02, ret RN 2002; private sec to HRH The Princess Royal 2002–; *Recreations* squash, cricket, tennis, skiing; *Clubs* Jesters; *Style—* Capt Nick Wright, LVO; ✉ Buckingham Palace, London SW1A 1AA

WRIGHT, Patrick Michael McKee; s of Ronald Cecil McKee Wright, (d 1973), of Westerham, Kent, and Mary Beatrice, *née* Minnitt (d 1995); *b* 8 October 1942; *Educ* Aldenham (head of sch, cricket and hockey capt); *m* 1969, Judy Theresa, da of Rodney Perry; 1 da (Rebecca Beatrice b 1972), 1 s (Alexander David McKee b 1976); *Career* mgmnt trainee Unilever 1960–63; sales and mktg dir Allen Lane Penguin Press/Longman 1970–73, md Penguin Books NZ 1973–78, gp dir sales and mktg Penguin Gp 1978–90, vice-chm Penguin Canada 1980–90, chm Penguin India 1986–90, chm Penguin Netherlands 1986–90, dir int devpt Penguin Gp 1987–90, chief exec Hodder & Stoughton 1990–93, md British Museum Co 1994–2001; non-exec dir W W Norton 1993–; vice-chm Book Marketing Cncl 1986–87, memb Br Library Publishing Advsy Bd 2002–07 (chm 2003–07); tstee Family Welfare Assoc 1997–2003, govr Froebel Coll 2003–06, memb Fin and Gen Purposes Ctee Univ of Roehampton 2004; FRSA 2001; *Recreations* painting, golf, gardening; *Clubs* Royal Mid Surrey Golf; *Style—* Patrick Wright, Esq; ✉ 62 Mount Ararat Road, Richmond, Surrey TW10 6PJ (tel 020 8940 5786, e-mail pmmwright@dsl.pipex.com)

WRIGHT, Peter; s of Nigel Wright, and June, *née* Oxnam; *b* 13 August 1953; *Educ* Marlborough, Clare Coll Cambridge; *m* 3 Aug 1974, Dorothy; 3 s (Ben b 9 Sept 1981, William b 25 May 1987, Edward b 21 Sept 1990), 1 da (Alice b 30 March 1984); *Career* reporter Evening Post - Echo Hemel Hempstead 1975–78; Daily Mail: reporter 1979, asst news ed 1979–85, assoc news ed (foreign) 1985–86, asst features ed 1986–88, ed Femail 1988–91, asst ed (features) 1991–92, assoc ed 1992–95, dep ed 1995–98; ed Mail on Sunday 1998–; *Style—* Peter Wright, Esq; ✉ Mail on Sunday, Northcliffe House, 2 Derry Street, Kensington, London W8 5TT (tel 020 7938 6118, fax 020 7937 6721)

WRIGHT, Peter Malcolm; s of His Hon Judge Malcolm Wright, QC, MBE (d 1959), and Peggy, *née* Prince, BEM (d 1980); *b* 5 June 1948; *Educ* Kingswood Sch Bath, Trinity Hall Cambridge (MA); *m* 26 April 1975, Eleanor Charlotte Madge, da of Peter Madge, and Eleanor Madge, of Kendal, Cumbria; 1 da (Eleanor Louisa b 2 Feb 1979), 1 s (Edward Malcolm b 1 June 1981); *Career* VSO (Dakar, Senegal) 1967–68; called to the Bar Middle Temple 1974; legal assessor to Nursing and Midwifery Cncl 1990, recorder of the Crown Court 2000 (asst recorder 1998); vice-chm Appeal Ctee CIMA 2000; tstee Lambeth Palace Library 2002–, memb Lambeth Partnership; govr Kingswood Sch Bath 1999; *Recreations* music, walking, sailing, family life, retriever training; *Style—* Peter Wright, Esq; ✉ 2nd Floor, Queen Elizabeth Building, Temple, London EC4Y 9BS (tel 020 7797 7837, fax 020 7353 5422)

WRIGHT, Peter Michael; s of Dudley Cyril Brazier Wright, of Finchley, London, and Pamela Deirdre, *née* Peacock; *b* 6 March 1954; *Educ* Highgate Sch, RCM (Organ exhibitioner, ARCM, LRAM), Emmanuel Coll Cambridge (organ scholar, MA); *Career* sub organist Guildford Cathedral 1977–89, asst music master Royal GS Guildford 1977–89, organist and dir of music Southwark Cathedral 1989–; conductor: Edington Festival 1984–90, Guildford Chamber Choir 1985–94, Surrey Festival Choir 1987–2001; several recordings as organist and conductor released; RCO: memb Cncl 1990–97, hon sec Cncl 1997–2002, vice-pres 2003–05, pres 2005–; memb Cathedral Organists' Conference; FRCO, Hon FGCM; *Recreations* opera, theatre, travel, reading; *Style—* Peter Wright, Esq; ✉ 52 Bankside, Southwark, London SE1 9JE (tel 020 7261 1291); Southwark Cathedral, London Bridge, London SE1 9DA (tel 020 7367 6703, fax 020 7367 6725, e-mail peter.wright@southwark.anglican.org)

WRIGHT, Sir Peter Robert; kt (1993), CBE (1985); s of Bernard Wright (d 1981), and Hilda Mary, *née* Foster (d 1973); *b* 25 November 1926; *Educ* Bedales, Leighton Park Sch Reading; *m* 1954, Sonya Hana, da of Yoshi Sueyoshi (d 1931); 1 s (Jonathan), 1 da (Poppy); *Career* dancer Ballets Jooss and Sadler's Wells Theatre Ballet 1947–55, ballet master Sadler's Wells Opera Ballet and teacher Royal Ballet Sch 1955–58, ballet master Stuttgart Ballet 1960–63, guest prodr BBC TV 1963–65, freelance choreographer and prodr 1965–69, assoc dir Royal Ballet 1970–76, dir Sadler's Wells Royal Ballet (relocated and renamed The Birmingham Royal Ballet in 1990) 1976–95 (dir laureate 1995–); special prof Sch of Performance Studies Univ of Birmingham 1990–; pres Benesh Inst of Choreology; vice-pres: Myashthenia Gravis Assoc, Royal Acad of Dancing; Hon DMus Univ of London 1990, Hon DLitt Univ of Birmingham 1994; fell Birmingham Conservatoire of Music 1991; *Productions* noted for prodns of 19th century classical ballets incl The Sleeping Beauty, Swan Lake, Giselle, The Nutcracker, and Coppélia, for most major cos in Europe, The Royal Ballet, Birmingham Royal Ballet, Dutch and Canadian Nat Ballets, Royal Winnipeg Ballet, The Houston Ballet, Ballet de Rio de Janeiro, Stuttgart Ballet, Bavarian State Opera Ballet, Vienna State Opera Ballet, Star Dancers Ballet Tokyo, Ballet of the Colon Theatre Buenos Aires, Royal Swedish Ballet, Ballet de Santiago, Staatsballett Karlsruhe; *Own Creations* The Mirror Walkers, The Great Peacock, A Blue Rose, Dance Macabre, Summertide, Namouna, Designs for Dancers, Quintet, Summer's Night, El Amor Brujo; *Awards* Standard Award for Most Outstanding Achievement in Ballet 1981, John Newson Award for Greatest Contribution to Sadler's Wells Royal Ballet 1988, Queen Elizabeth II Coronation Award Royal Acad of Dancing 1990, Digital Premier Award 1991, Critics Circle Award for Distinguished Contribution to the Arts 1996, Nat Dance Award for Outstanding Achievement 2004; *Recreations* gardening, ceramics, cello; *Style—* Sir Peter Wright, CBE; ✉ 10 Chiswick Wharf, London W4 2SR

WRIGHT, Air Marshal Sir Robert Alfred; KBE (2004), AFC (1982); *b* 10 June 1947; *m* Maggie; 1 s, 1 da; *Career* joined RAF 1966, served 8 Sqdn Bahrain, served 17 (F) Sqdn RAF Brüggen 1971–75, qualified weapons instr 1975, joined Tactical Weapons Unit RAF Brawdy 1975, fighter weapons instr (exchange duty) US Navy 1976, Flight Cdr 208 Sqdn 1979, RAF Staff Coll 1982, served Operational Requirements Div MOD 1982–84, memb Directing Staff RAF Staff Coll 1984–87, cmd IX Sqdn RAF Brüggen 1987–89, Personal Staff Offr to Chief of the Air Staff MOD 1989–91, Station Cdr RAF Brüggen 1992–94, ACOS Policy & Plans NATO HQ High Wycombe 1994–95, Air Cdr Ops HQ Strike Command 1995–97, Mil Advsr to High Rep Sarajevo 1997–98, COS to Air Memb for Personnel and Dep C-in-C Personnel & Trg Command RAF Innsworth 1998–2000, ACOS Policy & Requirements (NATO appt) SHAPE 2000–02, UK Mil Rep NATO and EU 2002–; controller RAF Benevolent Fund 2007–, pres Naval 8/208 Sqdn Assoc; FRAeS 1997, FCMI 2006; *Recreations* golf, tennis, skiing; *Clubs* RAF; *Style—* Air Marshal Sir Robert Wright, KBE, AFC, FRAeS, FCMI

WRIGHT, Rosalind; CB (2001), QC (2006); da of late Alfred Kerstein, of London, and Felicie, *née* Margulin; *b* 2 November 1942; *Educ* St Paul's Girls' Sch, UCL (LLB); *m* 1966, Dr David Julian Maurice Wright; 3 da (Candida Ruth b 17 Sept 1967, Pandora Naomi b 2 Jan 1969, Miranda Jane Helen b 21 March 1977); *Career* called to the Bar Middle Temple 1964 (bencher 2001); in practice 2 Crown Office Row 1965–69; DPP: legal asst rising to sr legal asst 1969–81, asst dir South Div 1981–83, head Fraud Investigation Gp London 1983–87; SFA: head of prosecutions 1987–93, gen counsel and exec dir 1993–97; dir Serious Fraud Office 1997–2003; Middle Temple rep Bar Cncl 1998–2003 (chm Employed Bar Ctee 2002–03); chm: Assoc to Combat Fraud in Europe 2001–03, Fraud Advsy Panel 2003; non-exec memb: Legal Services Gp DTI 2002–, Bd OFT 2003–07, Insolvency Service Steering Bd 2006–; vice-chm Jewish Assoc for Business Ethics 2003–; *Recreations* theatre, music, enjoying my children's achievements; *Style—* Mrs Rosalind Wright, CB, QC; ✉ Fraud Advisory Panel, PO Box 433, Chartered Accountants Hall, Moorgate Place, London EC2P 2BJ (tel 020 7920 8721)

WRIGHT, Stephen; *Educ* King's Sch Macclesfield, Queens' Coll Cambridge (BA, Volleyball half blue), Univ of Cambridge (PGCE); *m* Penny; 3 c; *Career* teacher Woolverstone Hall Sch, head of history Framlingham Coll (also housemaster), dep head Judd Sch Tonbridge 1994–98, headmaster Borden GS 1998–2004, headmaster Merchant Taylors' Sch Northwood 2004–; sec Kent and Medway Grammar Schs' Assoc, memb Kent Secdy Strategy Gp, memb Exec Secdy Heads' Forum; *Recreations* vegetable gardening, village cricket, theatre, opera; *Style—* Stephen Wright, Esq; ✉ Merchant Taylors' School, Sandy Lodge, Northwood, Middlesex HA6 2HT

WRIGHT, Dr Stephen Geoffrey; s of Stanley and Betty Wright, of Stoke-on-Trent; *b* 31 May 1944; *Educ* Longton HS, King's Coll Hosp Sch of Med London (MB BS); *m* Jennifer Lynn, da of Francis T Clay (d 1998); 2 s (Matthew Stephen b 13 April 1979, Alexander Francis Stanley b 16 June 1982); *Career* jr med posts in UK and Nigeria, sr lectr London Sch of Hygiene and Tropical Med and hon conslt Physician Hosp for Tropical Diseases 1980–95, assoc prof of med Coll of Med King Saud Univ Riyadh Saudi Arabia 1985–88, conslt physician Hosp for Tropical Diseases UCL Hosp Tst 1995–; hon physician King Edward VII's Hosp for Offrs London; FRCP 1991; *Books* Hunter's Tropical Medicine (assoc ed, 7 edn 1991); *Recreations* sport, gardening, music; *Style—* Dr Stephen Wright; ✉ Hospital for Tropical Diseases, Mortimer Market, off Capper Street, Tottenham Court Road, London WC1E 6AU (tel 0845 155 5000 ext 5984, e-mail stephen.wright@lshtm.ac.uk); Private Patients Floor (T15), University College Hospital, 235 Euston Road, London NW1 2BU (tel 020 7383 7916, fax 020 7380 9816)

WRIGHT, Sir Stephen John Leadbetter; KCMG (2006, CMG 1997); s of John Henry Wright (d 1984), and Joan Wright (d 1993); *b* 7 December 1946; *Educ* Shrewsbury, The Queen's Coll Oxford (BA); *m* 1, 1970 (m dis 2000); 1 da (Charlotte b 1977), 1 s (James b 1979); m 2, 2002, Elizabeth Abbott, da of F M B Duncan, MRCVS; *Career* HM Dip Serv: joined 1968, third sec Havana 1969–71, second sec FCO 1972–75, first sec (Br Info Servs) NY 1975–80, first sec UK Perm Rep to EC Brussels 1980–84, first sec FCO 1984–85, cnsllr Cabinet Office London 1985–87, cnsllr New Delhi 1988–91, cnsllr UK Perm Rep to EU Brussels 1991–94, dir (EU Affrs) FCO 1994–97, min Br Embassy Washington 1997–99, dir (Wider Europe) FCO 1999–2000, dep under sec FCO 2000–03, ambass to Spain 2003–07 (concurrently non-resident ambass to Andorra); *Recreations* rowing, music, art; *Style—* Sir Stephen Wright, KCMG; ✉ e-mail wrightsjl@gmail.com

WRIGHT, Rt Rev Dr (Nicholas) Thomas (Tom); *see:* Durham, Bishop of

WRIGHT, Thomas Jeremy; s of Keneth Thomas Wright, and Eileen Ruth, *née* Broderick; *b* 18 September 1957; *Educ* Royal Russell Sch Croydon, Kingston Poly (BA, DipArch); *Family* 1 da (Lucy Wills-Wright b 20 Oct 1988); m, 22 June 2002, Carol Anne, da of Edward Mazgay; 1 da (Alice Mazgay b 8 May 2003); *Career* architect; dir of architecture Atkins 1991–, designer Burj Al Arab Dubai (world's tallest hotel) 1993; RIBA 1982; *Recreations* sailing; *Style—* Thomas Wright, Esq; ✉ Atkins, Woodcote Grove, Ashley

W

Road, Epsom, Surrey KT18 5BW (tel 01372 752064, e-mail tom.wright@atkinsglobal.com)

WRIGHT, Thomas William John; s of John William Richard Wright (d 1977), of Canterbury, Kent, and Jane Elizabeth, *née* Nash (d 1978); *b* 5 August 1928; *Educ* Kent Coll, Simon Langton Sch Canterbury, Wye Coll London (BSc); *m* 4 Jan 1956, Shirley Evelyn, da of Henry Parkinson (d 1943), of Beckenham, Kent; 2 da (Geraldine Anne b 1959 d 1994, Jane b 1962); *Career* garden estate mgmnt consIt and int lectr; tea plantation mangr Kenya and govt horticultural res offr UK 1953–58, mangr Nursery and Landscape Co Devon 1956–60; lectr Pershore Coll 1962–68, sr lectr in landscape horticulture Wye Coll London 1968–90; consIt on restoration and mgmnt of historical gardens, garden and landscape consIt UK and Europe 1990–; visiting prof Univs of Beijing and Shanghai China 1985, lectr Univ of Kent's Summer Acad on Kent's Historic Gardens; Veitch Memorial medal RHS 1989; tstee: Fortescue Gardens Tst 1961–2002, Landscape Design Tst 1984–2002, Cobham Hall Heritage Tst; memb: Gardens Ctee HHA, Gardens Panel Nat Tst, Govt Royal Parks Review Gp 1991–95, Hampton Court Palace Garden Strategy Gp 1991–2007, Strategy and Standing Advsy Ctee Harold Hiller Arboretum; hon memb Scientific Ctee Benetton Fndn Italy; memb Cncl and tstee Sussex Gardens Tst 1997–2001; advsr Santa Maddelena Fndn Italy; judge and visiting lectr Ellerslie Flower Show Auckland NZ 1994–99, judge Chelsea Show Gardens; MLI 1978, FIHort 1986; *Books* The Gardens of Kent, Sussex and Surrey (No 4 in Batsford Series, 1978), Large Gardens and Parks, Management and Design (1982), RHS Dictionary of Gardening (1992), RHS Encyclopedia of Gardening (contrib, 1990 and 1992); *Recreations* travel, natural history, gardening, music, climatology; *Style—* Thomas Wright, Esq; ✉ Nyewood Lodge, Nyewood, Rogate, Petersfield, Hampshire GU31 5JL (tel 01730 821375, e-mail wrilndscp@aol.com)

WRIGHT, Timothy Edward; s of Benjamin Wright, and Anne Wright; *b* 17 February 1960; *Educ* St Edmund's Sch Canterbury, Sunderland Poly (BA); *m* 1995, Michaela Hoskier, da of Peter Wordie, CBE; 2 s (Caspar b 6 Jan 1996, Tobias b 5 Jan 2002), 2 da (Fenella 8 May 1997, Rebecca 13 Nov 1999); *Career* Longman Publishing Gp: Euro sales manager 1984–90, int sales dir 1990–94; sales and mktg dir Churchill Livingstone Med Publishers 1994–98, chief exec Edinburgh Univ Press 1998–; chm Scottish Publishers Assoc 2001–04, chm Independent Publishers Guild 2006– (dir 2001–05); memb: Book Devpt Cncl of Publishers Assoc 1994–98, Scottish Arts Cncl Arts Project Ctee 1999–2002, Int Bd Publishers Assoc 2002–, Cncl Academic and Professional Publishers; dir St Mary's Music Sch Edinburgh 2000–04; *Recreations* shooting, fishing, cricket, classical music; *Clubs* MCC, Farmers'; *Style—* Timothy Wright, Esq; ✉ The Green, 23 The Causeway, Duddington Village, Edinburgh EH15 3QA (tel 0131 620 0335); 22 George Square, Edinburgh EH8 9LF (e-mail timothy.wright@eup.ed.ac.uk)

WRIGHT, Tom Charles Kendal Knox; CBE (2007); s of David Andrew Wright, and Penelope Jane Wright; *b* 22 February 1962; *Educ* Marlborough, Ealing Coll (BA), Inst of Mktg (DipM), DipMRS; *m* 1986, Charlotte Annabel, *née* Mudford; 1 da (Louise); *Career* gp marketing mangr Anchor Foods 1989–95, devpt dir Carlsberg-Tetley 1995–96, sales marketing dir Center Parcs UK 1996–98, marketing, sales and devpt dir Center Parcs NV 1998–99, md Saga Holidays and dir Saga Gp 1999–2002, chief exec VisitBritain 2002–; dir: Visit London, South West Tourism, European Travel Cmmn, chm Soc of Ticket Agents and Retailers, tstee Imperial War Museum, memb Marketing Gp of GB 2003–; *Recreations* running, walking, golf, motor racing, travel; *Style—* Tom Wright, Esq, CBE; ✉ VisitBritain, Thames Tower, Black's Road, London W6 9EL (tel 020 8563 3031, fax 020 8748 0123, e-mail tom.wright@visitbritain.org)

WRIGHT OF RICHMOND, Baron (Life Peer UK 1994), of Richmond upon Thames in the London Borough of Richmond upon Thames; Sir Patrick Richard Henry Wright; GCMG (1989, KCMG 1984, CMG 1978); s of Herbert Wright (d 1977), of Wellington Coll, and Rachel, *née* Green (d 2000); *b* 28 June 1931; *Educ* Marlborough, Merton Coll Oxford; *m* 1958, Virginia Anne, step da of Col Samuel John Hannaford (d 1983), and da of Irene Hannaford, MBE; 2 s (Hon Marcus b 1959, Hon Angus b 1964), 1 da (Hon Olivia (Hon Mrs McDonald) b 1963); *Career* Nat Serv Lt RA; entered Foreign Serv 1955; served: Beirut, Washington, Cairo, Bahrain; private sec (overseas affrs) to PM 1974–77; ambass: Luxembourg 1977–79, Syria 1979–81; dep under sec FCO 1982–84, ambass Saudi Arabia 1984–86, perm under sec FCO and head Dip Serv 1986–91; dir: Barclays plc 1991–96, Unilever plc 1991–99, De La Rue plc 1991–2000, BP plc 1991–2001, BAA plc 1992–98; memb Security Cmmn 1993–2002; chm: RIIA 1995–99, Home-Start Int 2004–07; govr: Ditchley Fndn 1986–, Wellington Coll 1991–2001, King Edward VII's Hosp Sister Agnes; House Magazine Award for Parly Speech of the Year 2004; hon fell Merton Coll Oxford 1987; FRCM 1994; KStJ 1990 (memb Cncl Order of St John 1991–97); *Clubs* Oxford and Cambridge; *Style—* The Lord Wright of Richmond, GCMG; ✉ House of Lords, London SW1A 0PW

WRIGHTSON, Prof Keith Edwin; s of Robert Wrightson (d 1968), and Evelyn, *née* Atkinson (d 1987); *b* 22 March 1948; *Educ* Dame Allan's Boys' Sch Newcastle, Fitzwilliam Coll Cambridge (Reddaway Scholar, Sr Scholar, MA, PhD); *m* 19 Aug 1972, Eva Mikušová, da of Jozef Mikuš; 1 s (Nicholas Mikuš b 6 Aug 1982), 1 da (Eliška Anne b 13 April 1989); *Career* research fell in history Fitzwilliam Coll Cambridge 1972–75, lectr in modern history Univ of St Andrews 1975–84; Univ of Cambridge: univ lectr in history 1984–93, reader in English social history 1993–98, prof of social history 1998–99; Jesus Coll Cambridge: fell 1984–99, dir of studies in history 1990–98; prof of history Yale Univ 1999–; visiting prof: Univ of Toronto, Univ of Alberta, Northumbria Univ; memb Bd Euro Grad Sch for Training in Economic and Social Historical Research 1990–99; memb Editorial Bd: Social History 1979–, Law and History 1982–89, Continuity & Change 1985–90, The Seventeenth Century 1985–, Rural History 1989–; Canadian Cwlth fell 1983–84; FRHistS 1986, FBA 1996; *Books* Poverty and Piety in an English Village. Terling 1525–1700 (with David Levine, 1979, 2 edn, 1995), English Society 1580–1680 (1982, 2 edn 2003), The World We Have Gained (co-ed, 1986), The Making of an Industrial Society. Whickham 1560–1765 (with David Levine, 1992), Earthly Necessities: Economic Lives in Early Modern Britain (2000); also author of numerous essays and articles on English social history; *Recreations* modern jazz; *Style—* Prof Keith Wrightson, FBA; ✉ Department of History, Yale University, PO Box 208324, New Haven, Connecticut 06520–8324 (tel 203 432 7248, fax 203 432 7587)

WRIGHTSON, Sir (Charles) Mark Garmondsway; 4 Bt (UK 1900), of Neasham Hall, Co Durham; s of Sir John Wrightson, 3 Bt, TD, DL (d 1983), and Hon Lady Wrightson (d 1998); *b* 18 February 1951; *Educ* Eton, Queens' Coll Cambridge; *m* 1975, Stella, da of late George Dean; 3 s (Barnaby, James, William); *Heir* s, Barnaby Wrightson; *Career* called to the Bar Middle Temple 1975; dir Hill Samuel Bank Ltd 1984–96; Close Brothers Corporate Finance Ltd: md 1996–99, chm 1999–2006; non-exec dir: British Vita plc 2004–05, Amlin plc 2006–, Domino Printing Sciences 2007–, Tees Valley Regeneration Ltd; formerly: chm Corporate Finance Ctee London Investment Banking Assoc, memb Panel on Takeovers and Mergers; Liveryman Worshipful Co of Haberdashers; *Style—* Sir Mark Wrightson, Bt

WRIGLEY, Prof Christopher John (Chris); s of Arthur Wrigley (d 1999), of Shipton Gorge, Dorset, and Eileen Sylvia, *née* Herniman; *b* 18 August 1947; *Educ* Kingston GS, UEA (BA), Birkbeck Coll London (PhD); *m* 11 Sept 1987, Margaret, da of late Anthony Walsh; *Career* lectr in economic history Queen's Univ Belfast 1971–72, reader in economic history Loughborough Univ 1984–88 (lectr 1972–78, sr lectr 1978–84), prof of modern Br history Univ of Nottingham 1991– (reader in economic history 1988–91, head Sch of History and Art History 2000–03); ed The Historian 1993–98; Historical Assoc: memb Cncl 1980–, a vice-pres 1992–95, dep pres 1995–96, pres 1996–99; Lab History Soc: memb Exec Ctee 1983–2005, vice-chm 1993–97, chm 1997–2001; memb Cncl Economic History Soc Cncl 1983–92, 1994–2000 and 2002–08, a vice-pres Royal Historical Soc 1997–2001; chm Loughborough Lab Pty 1977–79 and 1980–85 (treas 1973–77), exec memb Loughborough Trades Cncl 1981–86; Leics cncllr 1981–89 (ldr of Lab Gp 1986–89), Charnwood borough cncllr and dep ldr Lab Gp 1983–87; Parly candidate: (Lab) Blaby 1983, (Lab and Co-op) Loughborough 1987; Hon LittD UEA 1998; FRHistS; *Books* David Lloyd George and The British Labour Movement (1976), A J P Taylor - A Complete Bibliography (1980), A History of British Industrial Relations Vol 1 1875–1914 (ed, 1982), Vol 2 1914–1939 (ed, 1986), and Vol 3 1939–78 (ed, 1996), William Barnes - The Dorset Poet (1984), Warfare Diplomacy and Politics (ed, 1986), Arthur Henderson (1990), Lloyd George and the Challenge of Labour (1990), On the Move (jt ed, 1991), Lloyd George (1992), Challenges of Labour (ed, 1993), British Trade Unions 1945–95 (ed, 1997), The First World War and the International Economy (ed, 2000), British Trade Unions Since 1933 (2002), Winston S Churchil: A Biographical Companion (2002), A Companion to Early Twentieth Century Britain (ed, 2003), The Emergence of European Trade Unionism (jt ed, 2004), A J P Taylor: Radical Historian of Europe (2006), Churchill (2006); *Recreations* swimming, walking; *Style—* Prof Chris Wrigley; ✉ Department of History, University of Nottingham, Nottingham NG7 2RD (tel 0115 951 5945, fax 0115 951 5948, e-mail chris.wrigley@nottingham.ac.uk)

WRIGLEY, Prof Sir Edward Anthony (Tony); kt (1996); s of Edward Ernest Wrigley (d 1953), and Jessie Elizabeth, *née* Holloway (d 1976); *b* 17 August 1931; *Educ* King's Sch Macclesfield, Univ of Cambridge (MA, PhD); *m* 2 July 1960, Maria Laura, da of Everhard Dirk Spelberg (d 1968); 3 da (Marieke b 1961, Tamsin b 1966, Rebecca b 1969), 1 s (Nicholas b 1963); *Career* William Volker res fell Univ of Chicago 1953–54, lectr in geography Univ of Cambridge 1958–74; Peterhouse Cambridge: fell 1958–79, tutor 1962–64, sr bursar 1964–74, hon fell 1997; Hinkley visiting prof Johns Hopkins Univ 1975, Tinbergen visiting prof Erasmus Univ Rotterdam 1979, prof of population studies LSE 1979–88, sr res fell All Souls Coll Oxford 1988–94; Univ of Cambridge: prof of economic history 1994–97, master Corpus Christi Coll 1994–2000; co dir Cambridge Gp for the History of Population and Social Structure 1974–95; memb Inst for Advanced Study Princeton 1970–71, pres Manchester Coll Oxford 1987–96, pres British Acad 1997–2001 (treas 1989–95); laureate Int Union for the Scientific Study of Population 1993, Fndr's Medal RGS 1997, Leverhulme Medal Br Acad 2005; Hon DLitt: Univ of Manchester 1997, Univ of Sheffield 1997, Univ of Bristol 1998, Univ of Oxford 1999, Univ of Leicester 1999; Hon DSc Univ of Edinburgh 1998; hon fell LSE 1997; FBA 1980; *Books* Industrial Growth and Population Change (1961), English Historical Demography (ed, 1966), Population and History (1969), Nineteenth Century Society (ed, 1972), Towns in Societies (ed with P Abrams, 1978), Population History of England (with R S Schofield, 1981), Works of Thomas Robert Malthus (ed with D Souden, 1987), People, Cities and Wealth (1987), Continuity, Chance and Change (1988), English Population History (with R S Davies, J Oeppen and R S Schofield, 1997), Poverty, Progress and Population (2004); *Recreations* gardening; *Style—* Prof Sir Tony Wrigley, FBA; ✉ 13 Sedley Taylor Road, Cambridge CB2 2PW (tel 01223 247614)

WRIGLEY, (William) Matthew; s of Rev William Vickers Wrigley (d 1998), of Rillington, N Yorks, and Margaret, *née* Hunter (d 2006); *b* 3 July 1947; *Educ* Westminster (Queen's scholar), King's Coll Cambridge (scholar, MA); *m* 17 July 1971, Susan Jane, da of Thomas Pratt; *Career* admitted slr 1972; ptnr: Biddle & Co London 1975–78, Dibb Lupton Broomhead Leeds 1978–96, Wrigleys Leeds 1996–; cncllr N Yorks CC 1985–89; memb Law Soc 1972; *Style—* Matthew Wrigley, Esq; ✉ Wrigleys, 19 Cookridge Street, Leeds LS2 3AG (tel 0113 244 6100, fax 0113 244 6101, e-mail matthew.wrigley@wrigleys.co.uk)

WRONG, Henry Lewellys Barker; CBE (1986); s of Henry Arkel Wrong, and Jean, *née* Barker; *b* 20 April 1930; *Educ* Trinity Coll Univ of Toronto (BA); *m* 18 Dec 1966, Penelope Hamilton, da of Mark Richard Norman, CBE, of Much Hadham, Herts; 2 s (Mark Henry b 1967, Sebastian Murray b 1971), 1 da (Christina Jocelyn b 1970); *Career* admin Met Opera NY 1952–64; dir: programming Nat Arts Centre Ottawa 1964–68, Festival Canada Centennial Prog 1967, Barbican Arts Centre 1970–90, Euro Arts Fndn 1990–; chm Spencer House (London) 1990–93; memb Advsy Ctee: ADAPT 1988–96, LSO 1990–; tstee: ROH 1989–95, Henry Moore Fndn 1990–, Royal Fine Arts Cmmn 1995–2003; consIt Rothermere Inst for American Studies Oxford 2000; memb RSA 1988 (fell Arts Ctee); Liveryman Worshipful Co of Fishmongers 1987; Hon DLitt City Univ 1985; Offr Class Order of Merit (France) 1985, Hungarian Medal of Culture 1989, Centennial medal Canada 1967; *Clubs* White's, Badminton and Racket (Toronto); *Style—* Henry Wrong, Esq, CBE; ✉ Yew Tree House, Much Hadham, Hertfordshire SG10 6AJ (tel 01279 842106, fax 01279 843314)

WROTTESLEY, 6 Baron (UK 1838); Sir Clifton Hugh Lancelot de Verdon Wrottesley; 14 Bt (E 1642); s of Hon Richard Wrottesley (d 1970), and Georgina, now Mrs Jonathan Seddon-Brown; suc gf (5 Baron, sixteenth in descent from Sir Walter Wrottesley, a chamberlain of the Exchequer under Edward IV and himself third in descent from Sir Hugh de Wrottesley, KG (one of the original members of the Order), who fought with the Black Prince at Crécy) 1377; *b* 10 August 1968; *Educ* Eton, Univ of Edinburgh; *m* 14 July 2001, Sascha, da of Urs Schwarzenbach; 2 s (Hon Victor Ernst Francis de Verdon b 28 Jan 2004, Hon Magnus Vivian Otto de Coughton b 19 June 2006); *Heir* s, Hon Victor Wrottesley; *Career* patron of three livings; financier; *Clubs* White's, Turf, Cavalry and Guards, St Moritz Tobogganing, Corviglia Ski, Skinner's Guild; *Style—* The Rt Hon the Lord Wrottesley

WROUGHTON, Philip Lavallin; *b* 1933; *Educ* Eton; *m* 1957, Catriona, *née* MacLeod; 2 da; *Career* chm C T Bowring & Co Ltd insurance brokers 1988–1996 (joined 1961), vice-chm Marsh & McLennan Companies 1994–96 (previously chm Marsh & McLennan Inc); pres: Newbury & Dist Agricultural Soc 1985–86, Berks Community Fndn 1995–, SE RFCA 2000–04; memb Cncl Lloyd's of London 1992–95, tstee Prince Philip Tst 1995–, vice-pres Princess Royal Tst for Carers 2000– (tstee 1991–2000); govr St Mary's Sch Wantage 1986–2006; High Sheriff Royal Co of Berks 1977–78, HM Lord-Lt Royal Co of Berks 1995–; Hon LLD Univ of Reading 2004; KStJ (pres Cncl Berks 1995–); *Recreations* racing, shooting; *Style—* Philip Wroughton, Esq; ✉ Woolley Park, Wantage OX12 8NJ (tel 01488 638214, fax 01488 638746)

WU, Prof Duncan; s of Spencer Yin-Cheung Wu, of Sydney, Aust, and Mary, *née* Sadler; *b* 3 November 1961, Woking, Surrey; *Educ* Woking GS for Boys, Woking Sixth Form Coll, St Catherine's Coll Oxford (BA, DPhil); *m* 5 Dec 1997, Caroline Beatrice, *née* Carey; *Career* British Acad postdoctoral research fell 1991–94, prof of English Univ of Glasgow 1999–2000 (reader 1995–99); Univ of Oxford: lectr in English 2000–03, prof of English language and literature 2003–, fell St Catherine's Coll; memb: Soc of Authors 1993–, British Assoc for Romantic Studies 1995–, German Soc for the Study of English Romanticism 1999–; tstee: Charles Lamb Soc 1991–, Keats-Shelley Meml Assoc 1995–; contrib to newspapers and jls incl: The Independent, The Guardian, New Statesman and Society, Daily Telegraph, TLS, PN Review; fell English Assoc 2003; *Books* Wordsworth's Reading 1770–1799 (1993), Wordsworth: A Selection of his Finest Poems (ed with Stephen Gill, 1994), Romanticism: An Anthology (1994, 3 edn 2005), Six Contemporary Dramatists: Bennett, Potter, Gray, Brenton, Hare, Ayckbourn (1995), Romanticism: A Critical Reader (1995), Wordsworth's Reading 1800–1815 (1996), William Wordsworth: The Five-Book Prelude (1997), Women Romantic Poets: An Anthology (1997), A

Companion to Romanticism (1998), William Hazlitt, The Plain Speaker: Key Essays (1998), The Selected Writings of William Hazlitt (9 vols, 1998), Making Plays: Interviews with Contemporary British Dramatists and Directors (2000), Wordsworth: An Inner Life (2002), British Romanticism and the Edinburgh Review: Bicentenary Essays (ed with Massimiliano Demata, 2002), Blackwell Essential Literature Series (9 vols of poetry, 2002), Metaphysical Hazlitt: Bicentenary Essays (ed with Uttara Natarajan and Tom Paulin, 2005), New Writings of William Hazlitt (2007); *CD-ROM* Romanticism: The CD-ROM (ed with David Miall, 1998); *Recreations* jazz, book collecting, washing the car while listening to 'The Archers'; *Clubs* Oxford and Cambridge; *Style—* Prof Duncan Wu

WULSTAN, Prof David; s of Rev Norman B Jones (d 1948), and (Sarah) Margaret, *née* Simpson (d 1973); *b* 18 January 1937; *Educ* Royal Masonic Sch, Coll of Tech Birmingham, Magdalen Coll Oxford (BSc, ARCM, MA, BLitt); *m* 9 Oct 1965, Susan Nelson, da of Frank Nelson Graham (d 1963); 1 s (Philip Richard James b 1969); *Career* fell and lectr Magdalen Coll Oxford 1964–78, visiting prof Univ of Calif Berkeley 1978, statutory lectr UC Cork 1979–80 (prof of music 1980–83), Gregynog prof of music UC Wales 1983–92, research prof Univ of Wales Aberystwyth 1992–; dir The Clerkes of Oxenford 1964–; consltg ed Spanish Academic Press; memb Cncl Plainsong and Mediaeval Music Soc 1964–; numerous recordings and appearances for TV and radio, appearance at festivals, recordings of incidental music for TV and cinema, composer of church music; hon fell St Peter's Coll Oxford 2007, fell Royal Soc of Musicians; *Publications* Gibbons Church Music (Early English Church Music) Vol 3 (1964) and Vol 27 (1979), Anthology of English Church Music (1968), Play of Daniel (1976), Coverdale Chant Book (1978), Sheppard, Complete Works (1979), Tudor Music (1985), Musical Language (1991), The Emperor's Old Clothes (2001), The Compilation of the Cantigas of Alfonso el Sabio (2001), The Rhythmic Organisation of the Cantigas de Santa Maria (2001), The Play of Daniel (revised edn 2004), The Poetic and Musical Legacy of Heloise and Abelard (ed and contrib 2003), Music from the Paraclete (2004); many other editions, articles and reviews in Music and Letters, Journal of Plainsong and Medieval Music, Early Music, English Historical Review, Journal of Theological Studies, Journal of Semitic Studies, Iraq, Cantigueiros, al-Masaq, The Consort, Faith and Worship, Prayer Book Society Journal, Canterbury Dictionary of Hymnology; *Recreations* tennis, badminton, food and drink, bemoaning the loss of the English language, Aikido, Self Defence (instructor); *Style—* Prof David Wulstan; ✉ Hillview Croft, Lon Tyllwyd, Llanfarian, Aberystwyth, Cardiganshire SY23 4UH (tel 01970 617832)

WULWIK, His Hon Judge Peter David; s of Eddie Wulwik, of Stanmore, Middx, and Mona, *née* Moss (d 1990); *b* 15 September 1950, London; *Educ* St Marylebone GS, Univ of London (LLB), Cncl of Legal Educn; *m* 6 April 1975, Joanna, *née* Rosenberg; 2 s (Stephen b 20 Oct 1979, Benjamin b 11 Aug 1981), 1 da (Philippa b 29 April 1984); *Career* called to the Bar Gray's Inn 1972; recorder 2000–04 (asst recorder 1995–2000), circuit judge 2004–; pt/t chm: London Rent Assessment Panel and Leasehold Valuation Tbnl 1999–2004, DTI Consumer Credit and Estate Agents Licensing Appeals 2003–; contrib: Bennion's Consumer Credit Law Reports 1990–2000, Goode's Consumer Credit Reports 2000–04; *Recreations* reading, theatre, classical music, antique fairs, playing bridge, tennis, golf, watching Tottenham Hotspur FC; *Clubs* Radlett Lawn Tennis and Squash, Elstree Lawn Tennis; *Style—* His Hon Judge Wulwik

WURTZEL, David Ira; s of late Paul Bernard Wurtzel, of LA, Calif, and Shirley Lorraine, *née* Stein; *b* 28 January 1949; *Educ* Univ of Calif Berkeley (BA), QMC London (MA) Fitzwilliam Coll Cambridge (MA); *Career* called to the Bar Middle Temple 1976 (bencher 2001); arts corr The Diplomat 1989–98, sr lectr City Univ, contrib to various legal pubns; memb Laurence Olivier Awards Panel; *Books* Thomas Lyster, A Cambridge Novel (1983); *Recreations* theatre, opera, travelling abroad, taking exercise, architecture, conservation; *Style—* David Wurtzel, Esq; ✉ 57 Round Hill Crescent, Brighton, East Sussex BN2 3FQ

WYATT, Derek Murray; MP; s of late Reginald Wyatt, and late Margaret Holmden; *b* 4 December 1949; *Educ* Westcliff CHS, Colchester Royal GS, St Luke's Coll Exeter, Open Univ (BA), St Catherine's Coll Oxford; *m* 1987, Joanna Willett; 1 da (Daisy Alexandra b 1989), 1 s (Angus Jack b 1992); *Career* writer and journalist The Times and The Observer 1982–84, sr ed George Allen & Unwin 1984–85, dir and a publishing dir William Heinemann 1985–88, dir TSL Ltd (TV prodn co) 1988–90, conslt on new media 1991–94, head of progs WireTV 1994–95, dir The Computer Channel BSkyB 1995–97, MP (Lab) Sittingbourne and Sheppey 1997–; memb House of Commons: Culture, Sport and Media Ctee 1997–2005, Public Accounts Ctee 2007–; advsr to Min of Sport (Rugby Union) 2001–; chm All-Pty: Internet Ctee 1997–, Rugby Union Ctee 1997–2005, Zimbabwe Gp 2003–05, Risk and Adventure Gp 2004– (co-chm), Commerical Radio Gp 2005–, All Pty London 2012 Olympic and Paralympic Gp 2005–; chm Br Cncl 2000; awarded Commonwealth Parly Assoc Scholarship to examine Digital Divide in Mozambique, Tanzania and Zambia 2000; tstee Maj Stanley's Tst OURFC, fndr: Women's Sports Fndn (UK) 1984, Oxford Internet Inst 2001 (memb Advsy Bd 2002–); memb Fabian Soc; vice-chm Speaker's Works of Art Ctee 2001; chllr Univ of Exeter 2000–05; tstee: TimeBank 2004, Start Here 2005–07, Citizens Online 2005; UNO commendation for work on sport and apartheid 1987, website won New Statesman New Media Award for Elected Representative 2006; fell Parly Industry Fellowship 2001; Liveryman Worshipful Co of Information Technolgists 2001, Freeman of the City of London 2001; FRSA 1996; *Books* author of six books incl: Wisecracks from the Movies (1987), Rugby Revolution (2003); *Recreations* sport (played rugby for Oxford Univ, Barbarians and England), books, foreign affairs, films, the internet, travel; *Clubs* RAC, Vincent's (Oxford); *Style—* Derek Wyatt, MP; ✉ e-mail wyattd@parliament.uk, website www.derekwyatt.co.uk

WYATT, Prof Derrick Arthur; QC (1993); s of Iris Ross, and step s of Alexander Ross; *Educ* Alsop HS Liverpool, Emmanuel Coll Cambridge, Univ of Chicago Law Sch; *Career* lectr in law Univ of Liverpool 1971; called to the Bar 1972; fell Emmanuel Coll Cambridge 1975; fell St Edmund Hall Oxford 1978–, prof of law Univ of Oxford 1996–; *Publications* European Union Law (2000), EU Treaties and Legislation (2004); *Recreations* walking, snorkelling; *Style—* Prof Derrick Wyatt, QC; ✉ St Edmund Hall, Oxford OX1 4AR (tel 01865 279036, fax 01865 279069, e-mail derrick.wyatt@seh.ax.ac.uk); Brick Court Chambers, 7–8 Essex Street, London WC2R 3LD

WYATT, Hugh Rowland; s of Brig Richard John Penfold Wyatt, MC, DL, TD (d 1954), of Cissbury, Findon, and Hon Margaret Agnes Blades, da of 1 Baron Ebbisham, GBE (d 1997); *b* 18 November 1933; *Educ* Winchester; *m* 1959, Jane Anne Elizabeth, da of Lt-Col and Mrs R L Eden; 1 s (Hugh Geoffrey Robert b 1961), 2 da (Anne Elizabeth b 1963, Susan Jane b 1965); *Career* 2 Lt Royal Sussex Regt 1952–54, Capt TA 1954–61; dir McCorquodale plc 1964–85; farmer; chm: Chichester Cathedral Tst 1991–98, Chichester Dio Bd of Finance 1997–2001, Chichester Cathedral Cncl 2002–; pres Royal Sussex Regt Assoc 1997–; High Sheriff W Sussex 1995–96, HM Lord-Lt W Sussex 1999–; KStJ 1999; *Recreations* travel, opera; *Clubs* Sussex; *Style—* Hugh Wyatt, Esq; ✉ Cissbury, Findon, West Sussex BN14 0SR (tel 01903 873328, fax 01903 877519)

WYATT, Hon Petronella Aspasia; da of Baron Wyatt of Weeford (Life Peer, d 1997), and Veronica, *née* Racz; *Educ* St Paul's Girls' Sch, UCL (BA); *Career* reporter Daily Telegraph 1990–94, feature writer and columnist Sunday Telegraph 1994–97, asst ed and columnist The Spectator 1997–98, dep ed The Spectator 1998–; interviewer for Daily Telegraph and Mail on Sunday; lectr in USA 1999–; *Books* Father, Dear Father (1999); *Recreations* opera, singing, yoga, riding; *Clubs* Home House; *Style—* The Hon Petronella Wyatt; ✉ The Spectator, 56 Doughty Street, London WC1 2LL (tel 020 7405 0824, fax 020 7440 9298, mobile 07836 256636)

WYATT, Susan Marjorie; da of Dr John, and late Marjorie Wyatt; *Educ* Sch of St Helen and St Katharine Abingdon, Univ of Hull (BA), Bulmershe Coll Reading (PGCE), City of London Poly (Dip Mgmnt Studies); *Career* drama teacher 1981–85, mktg offr Young Vic Theatre, drama and dance offr London Borough of Hammersmith and Fulham, head Combined Arts and Policy E Midlands Arts Bd 1993–95, admin dir The Cholmondeleys 1995–2001, exec dir and co sec Rambert Dance Co 2001–; former memb Bd Protein Dance Co; FRSA 1999; *Style—* Ms Susan Wyatt; ✉ e-mail sw@rambert.org.uk

WYATT, (Alan) Will; CBE (2000); s of Basil Wyatt, of Oxford, and Hettie Evelyn, *née* Hooper; *b* 7 January 1942; *Educ* Magdalen Coll Sch Oxford, Emmanuel Coll Cambridge (BA); *m* 2 April 1966, Jane Bridgit, da of Beauchamp Bagenal (d 1959), of Kitale, Kenya; 2 da (Hannah b 1967, Rosalind b 1970); *Career* reporter Sheffield Morning Telegraph 1964–65, sub ed BBC Radio News 1965–68; BBC TV: prodr 1968 (programmes include Robinsons Travels, B Traven - A Mystery Solved, Late Night Line Up, The Book Programme), head presentation programmes 1977–80, head documentary features 1981–87, head features and documentaries gp 1987–88, md Network Television 1991–96 (asst md 1988–91); chief exec BBC Broadcast 1996–99; dir: BBC Enterprises 1991–94, UKTV (jt venture channels of BBC Worldwide Ltd and Flextech plc) 1997–99; chm Ctee on Violence in TV Programmes BBC 1983 and 1987; pres Royal Television Soc 2000–04 (vice-pres 1997–2000), vice-pres Euro Broadcasting Union 1998–2000; author of newspaper articles on broadcasting; dir: Coral Eurobet 2000–02, Vitec Gp 2002–, Racing UK Ltd 2004–, Racecourse Media Services Ltd 2006–; chm Human Capital Ltd 2001–, Goodwill Assocs (Media) Ltd 2003–; tstee Br Video History Tst (dir 1990–92), vice-chm Shadow Racing Tst 2003–06; govr: London Inst (now Univ of the Arts London) 1989– (chm 1999–2007), Nat Film and Television Sch 1990–96 and 1998–2000, Magdalen Coll Sch Oxford 1999–; FRTS 1992; *Books* The Man Who Was B Traven (1980), The Fun Factory (2003); contrib to: Masters of the Wired World (1999), Proceedings of the Royal Institution vol 69; *Recreations* walking, horse racing, opera, theatre; *Clubs* Garrick, Century; *Style—* Will Wyatt, Esq, CBE; ✉ Abbey Willows, Rayford Lane, Middle Barton, Oxfordshire OX7 7DD (e-mail ww@dornvalley.net)

WYBAR, Linda; da of Thomas Smith Clough (d 2001), and Mary Bath, *née* Fenwick; *b* 21 June 1959, Blyth, Northumberland; *Educ* Blyth GS, Univ of Hull (BA, PGCE), Open Univ (MA); *m* 1, 7 Aug 1981, Flavio Romano Walker; 2 s (Benjamin Richard, Thomas Daniel (twins) b 21 April 1989); m 2, 25 Aug 1995, Geoffrey Stewart Wybar; *Career* teacher Rede Sch Strood 1981–82, Highworth Sch Ashford 1982–86, head of English Norton Knatchbull Boys' GS Ashford 1986–92, dep head Highsted GS Sittingbourne 1992–99, headteacher Tunbridge Wells Girls' GS 1999–; chm Kent and Medway GS Assoc 2004–; *Recreations* reading modern fiction, theatre-going, wine tasting; *Style—* Mrs Linda Wybar; ✉ Tunbridge Wells Girls' Grammar School, Southfield Road, Tunbridge Wells, Kent TN4 9UJ (tel 01892 520902, fax 01892 536497, e-mail admin@twggs.kent.sch.uk)

WYBREW, John; *b* 28 October 1941; *Educ* Queens' Coll Cambridge (MA); *m*; 3 da; *Career* Royal Dutch Shell Group 1964–96: various positions London and The Netherlands 1964–74, head of special projects Shell UK Exploration and Production 1974–77, southern ops mangr 1977–80, tech dir and dep md Brunei Shell Petroleum Co Ltd 1980–82, head of supply devpt Supply Oil Co-ordination Div Shell International Petroleum Co Ltd 1982–83, head of economic and sector planning for exploration and prodn Shell International Petroleum Maatschappij The Hague 1983, seconded as advsr on energy and tport policies PM's Policy Unit 1984–88, exec dir Mgmnt Charter Initiative Working Pty 1987, bd dir Shell UK 1989–96 (planning and public affrs dir 1989–95, corp affrs dir 1995–96); exec dir (corp affrs, health, safety and environment forum) British Gas plc (now BG plc) 1996–2000, exec dir Lattice Gp plc 2000–02, exec dir National Grid Transco 2002–03; currently non-exec dir Ofgem; memb Europe Ctee CBI; offr Parly Gp for Energy Studies; *Recreations* theatre, tennis, golf; *Style—* John Wybrew, Esq

WYBREW, John Leonard; s of late Leonard Percival Wybrew, of Radlett, Herts, and late May Edith Wybrew; *b* 27 January 1943; *Educ* Bushey GS, Sir John Cass Coll; *m* 1, 1967 (m dis 1990), Linda Gillian, da of Wing Cdr John James Frederick Long, of Lyminge, Kent; 1 s, 2 da; m 2, 2002, Denise Holloway, da of late Robert Ellis, of Burwardsley, Cheshire; *Career* life mangr and actuary Time Assurance Soc 1971–72, gen mangr and dir: Windsor Life Assurance Co Ltd 1972–76 (md 1976–, chm 1988–90 and 1992–2005), World-Wide Assurance Co Ltd 1972–76 (dir 1982–2004); chm Windsor Investment Mgmnt 1986–90, chm Windsor Tst Mangrs 1986–90, md Windsor Gp Ltd; pres and ceo British-American Life Assurance Co Pte Singapore 1990–92; non-exec dir Aberdeen Asset Mgmnt 2001–05; memb Ctee of Mgmnt Family Assurance Soc 1987–90 and 1998–; Liveryman Worshipful Co of Actuaries; FIA; *Recreations* horses, sailing, reading, golf, travel; *Clubs* Tanglin, Oriental, Annabel's, Artists; *Style—* John Wybrew, Esq; ✉ Hill Farm, Tarporley, Cheshire CW6 0JD (tel 01829 733107)

WYKE, Prof John Anthony; s of Eric John Edward Wyke (d 1979), and Daisy Anne, *née* Dormer (d 1997); *b* 5 April 1942; *Educ* Dulwich Coll, St John's Coll Cambridge (scholar, MA, VetMB, coll prizes), Univ of London (PhD); *m* 1968, Anne Wynne, da of John Mitchell; 1 s (Robert Andrew b 1977); *Career* postdoctoral res Univ of Washington and Univ of Southern Calif 1970–72, head Tumour Virology Lab ICRF Labs 1976–83 (scientific staff 1972–76), head ICRF Labs Bart's 1983–87 (asst dir 1985), dir Beatson Inst for Cancer Res 1987–2002, chair Scottish Cancer Fndn 2002–; emeritus prof Univ of Glasgow 1991–96 (visiting prof 1996–); fell Leukemia Soc of America 1970–72; hon fell Univ of Glasgow 2004; FRSE 1989, FMedSci 1998, Hon FRCVS 1999 (MRCVS 1967); *Recreations* hill walking, ski touring, gardening; *Style—* Prof John Wyke, FRSE

WYKES, Prof Til; *Educ* Congleton GS for Girls, Univ of Nottingham (BSc), Univ of Sussex (DPhil), Univ of London (MPhil); *Career* research fell Univ of Sussex 1977–78; Inst of Psychiatry: scientific offr MRC Social Psychiatry Unit 1978–83, hon lectr 1980–86, lectr Psychology Dept 1986–91, sr lectr 1991–96, clinical research co-ordinator 1992–, reader in clinical psychology 1997–99, prof of clinical psychology and rehabilitation 1999–, dir Service User Research Enterprise 2001–; hon conslt clinical psychologist Bethlem and Maudsley Special HA (now Tst) 1990– (hon conslt clinical psychologist 1988–90), dir Centre for Recovery in Severe Psychosis Maudsley Hosp 1998–; dir UK Mental Health Research Network (part of Nat Inst for Mental Health in England and Dept of Health) 2003–; ed Jl of Mental Health 2002–; memb Neurosciences, Clinical Trial and EU Directives Bds and Chronic Fatigue Syndrome Research Strategy Gp MRC 2002–; May Davidson Award Br Psychological Soc 1995; memb Soc for Research in Psychopathology USA; FBPsS 1995 (memb Investigations Ctee 1995–99), CPsychol; *Publications* Violence and Health Care Workers (ed, 1994), Aggression and Violence in General Practice (jtly, 1995), Outcome and Innovation in the Psychological Treatment of Schizophrenia (jtly, 1998), A Dictionary of Statistics for Psychologists (jtly, 1999), Psychosocial and Pharmacological Rehabilitation for Schizophrenia (jt ed, 2002), Cognitive Remediation Therapy for Schizophrenia: Theory and Practice (jtly); *Style—* Prof Til Wykes

WYLD, David John Charles; s of John Hugh Gilbert Wyld, TD, and Helen Selina, *née* Leslie Melville (d 1946); *b* 11 March 1943; *Educ* Harrow, ChCh Oxford (MA); *m* 1, 19 Dec 1970 (m dis), Sally, da of Ellis Morgan, CMG, of Hay-on-Wye, Herefords; 2 s (Barnaby b 1972, Jonathan b 1973); m 2, 20 June 1987, Caroline Mary, da of Walter Ronald Alexander, CBE, of St Andrews, Fife; 3 da (Charlotte b 1988, Alexandra b 1989, Rachel b 1991); *Career* called to the Bar 1968, admitted slr 1974; practising slr Linklaters & Paines 1974–79, ptnr Macfarlanes 1981–2004; sec gen Int Law Assoc 1993–, pres London Slrs' Litigation Assoc 1992–94, chm City of London Law Soc 2001–04; memb Law Soc 1974; *Recreations* reading, walking, golf; *Clubs* Garrick, Hon Co of Edinburgh Golfers, MCC,

Berkshire Golf, Liphook Golf; *Style*— David Wyld, Esq; ✉ David Wyld & Co, Fleet House, 8–12 New Bridge Street, London EC4V 6AL (tel 020 7583 7920, fax 020 7583 792)

WYLDBORE-SMITH, William Francis; DL (Wilts 2003); s of John Henry Wyldbore-Smith (d 1982), of Scaynes Hill, W Sussex, and Tighnabruaich, Argyll, and Robina, *née* Ward (d 1993); *b* 15 January 1948; *Educ* Marlborough; *m* 1974, Prisca Faith, da of Rev Peter Nourse (d 1992); 1 da (Philippa b 1977); *Career* admitted slr 1972; ptnr: Osborne Clarke 1977–85, Wood Awdry and Ford 1986– (formerly Wood & Awdry, managing ptnr 1990–95); chm: N Wilts Business Assoc 1985–88, N Wilts Enterprise Agency 1986–93, Wilts Rural Enterprise Agency 1989–92; non-exec dir Great Western Enterprise 1993–94, non-exec memb Wilts and Bath HA 1994–96; pres Glos and Wilts Law Soc 2004–05; memb: Law Soc, Soc of Tst and Estate Practitioners (STEP); Under Sheriff Wilts 1987–2005; Liveryman Worshipful Company of Musicians; *Recreations* gardening, shooting, reading; *Clubs* Brooks's; *Style*— W F Wyldbore-Smith, Esq, DL; ✉ Wood Awdry and Ford, Kingsbury House, Marlborough, Wiltshire SN8 1HU (tel 01672 512265, fax 01672 511348, e-mail wws@woodawdryford.co.uk)

WYLES, Andrew Tobias Michael (Toby); s of Michael Ronald Vincent Wyles, and Patricia Mary, *née* Davies; *b* 16 November 1960; *Educ* Solihull Sch, Jesus Coll Cambridge (titular exhibitioner, BA, capt boat club), Harvard Grad Sch of Business Admin (MBA); *Career* asst fund mangr Hoare Govett Ltd London 1983–84, assoc conslt corp strategy consltg The LEK Partnership London and Boston Mass 1984–87, MBA Harvard 1987–89, M&A assoc Morgan Stanley International London 1989–90; dir: Apax Partners Ltd 1990–2003, York Avenue Associates Ltd 2003–, Bowmark Capital Ltd 2003–; conslt V&A 1989; *Recreations* sport, wine, country pursuits; *Clubs* Stewards' Enclosure Henley Royal Regatta, Harvard Business Sch of London, Harvard (London); *Style*— Toby Wyles, Esq; ✉ Bowmark Capital Ltd, 3 St James's Square, London SW1Y 4JU (tel 020 7189 9000)

WYLIE, Alexander Featherstonhaugh; *see:* Kinclaven, The Hon Lord

WYLIE, Andrew; s of Craig Wylie, and Angela, *née* Fowler; *b* 4 November 1947, NY; *Educ* St Paul's, Harvard Coll (AB); *m* 1980, Camilla, *née* Carlini; 1 s (Nikolas Anton b 1970), 2 da (Erica b 1985, Alexandra Winthrop b 1994); *Career* fndr and pres The Wylie Agency NY 1980 and London 1996; memb Cncl on Foreign Rels; *Recreations* swimming, running, bicycling, tennis; *Clubs* Harvard, Knickerbocker (NY), River, Southampton, Bathing Corp (Southampton); *Style*— Andrew Wylie, Esq; ✉ The Wylie Agency Inc, 250 West 57th Street, Suite 2114, New York, NY 10107, USA (tel 001 212 246 0069, fax 001 212 586 8953)

WYLIE, Prof John Cleland Watson; s of George Stewart Wylie (d 1966), of Belfast, and Phyllis Ann, *née* Watson (d 2006); *b* 6 July 1943; *Educ* Methodist Coll Belfast, Queen's Univ Belfast (LLB, LLD), Harvard Univ (LLM); *m* 22 Sept 1973, Gillian Lindsey, da of Eric Sidney Edward Gardner, of London; 1 s (Nicholas George b 1977), 1 da (Emma Louise b 1979); *Career* lectr in law Queen's Univ Belfast 1965–71, Frank Knox fell Harvard 1966–67; Cardiff Univ: sr lectr 1972–76, reader 1976–79, prof of law 1979–, dean Faculty of Law 1980–83, pro-vice-chllr 1990–93, head Cardiff Law Sch 1991–96; ed: N Ireland Legal Quarterly 1970–76; dir: Professional Books Ltd 1981–87, Butterworth (Ireland) Ltd 1987–2005; land law conslt: Trinidad and Tobago Govt 1978–83, N Ireland Office 1980–90, A & L Goodbody Slrs 1992–, Irish Law Reform Cmmn 2001–, Irish Dept of Justice, Equality and Law Reform 2004–; memb Legal Studies Bd CNAA 1984–87, pres SPTL 1994–95, chm Ctee of Heads of Univ Law Schs 1993–94; *Books* Irish Land Law (1975, 3 edn 1997), Irish Conveyancing Law (1978, 3 edn 2005), A Casebook on Equity and Trusts in Ireland (1985, 2 edn 1998), Land Laws of Trinidad and Tobago (1986), Irish Landlord and Tenant Law (1990, 2 edn 1998), Irish Conveyancing Statutes (1994, 2 edn 1999), The Law of Tax and Taxation (co-author, 2007); *Recreations* reading, swimming, gardening; *Style*— Prof John Wylie; ✉ Cardiff Law School, Cardiff University, Museum Avenue, Cardiff CF10 3XJ (tel 029 2087 6705, fax 029 2087 4097, e-mail profjohnwylie@aol.com)

WYLLIE, Andrew; s of David Kenneth Wyllie, and Margaret Emily Wyllie; *b* 24 December 1962, Romford, Essex; *Educ* Dunfermline HS, Univ of Strathclyde, London Business Sch; *m* Jane; 1 da; *Career* md Taylor Woodrow Construction Ltd 2001–05, chief exec Costain Gp plc 2005–; fell Br American Project, FICE; *Style*— Andrew Wyllie, Esq; ✉ Costain Group plc, Costain House, Nicholsons Walk, Maidenhead, Berkshire SL6 1LN (tel 01628 842444, fax 01628 842334)

WYLLIE, Gordon Malcolm; WS (1982); s of Thomas Smith Wyllie, of Dallas House, Troon, and Margaret Hutton Gordon Malcolm; *b* 20 July 1951; *Educ* Dunoon GS, Univ of Glasgow (LLB); *Career* law apprentice McGrigor Donald Glasgow 1972–74, head Executry Dept Strathern & Blair WS Edinburgh 1974–77, notary public, ptnr Biggart Baillie 1980– (sr law asst 1977–80); clerk: Grand Antiquity of Glasgow 1984–, Trades House of Glasgow and sister bodies 1987–2004, Gen Cmmrs of Income Tax Glasgow North 1990– (depute 1983) and Glasgow South 1992–; dir: Bailford Trustees Ltd, Grand Antiquity Soc of Glasgow (pres 2000–01); sec Trades Hall of Glasgow Building Preservation Tst; deacon: Incorporation of Hammermen of Edinburgh 1996–99, Bonnetmakers and Dyers of Edinburgh 2003–; memb Incorporations of Tailors and Bonnetmakers and Dyers of Glasgow and Hammermen of Irvine; memb (hc) Maltmen of Glasgow; Boxmaster of Convenery of Trades of Edinburgh 2000–03, deacon convener of the Trades of Edinburgh 2003–; govr Trades Maiden Hosp of Edinburgh 1996–, chm Britannia Panopticon Music Hall Tst 1998–, memb: Succession Ctee Soc of Tst and Estate Practitioners, Soc of Antiquaries of Scotland, Soc for Promotion of Hellenic Studies, Int Bar Assoc, Action Research, Scottish Grant-Making Trusts Forum, Edinburgh West End Community Cncl, St Andrew's Soc of Glasgow, Merchant Co of Edinburgh; fndr and fell Inst of Contemporary Scotland; Hon Dr Univ of Glasgow; SBstJ; Freeman City of Glasgow; *Recreations* history, music and the arts generally, architecture and design, country dancing, country walks; *Clubs* Scottish Arts (Edinburgh), Western (Glasgow); *Style*— Gordon M Wyllie, Esq, WS; ✉ Biggart Baillie, 310 St Vincent Street, Glasgow G2 5QR (tel 0141 228 8000, fax 0141 228 8310); 7 Castle Street, Edinburgh EH2 3AP

WYMAN, Peter Lewis; CBE (2006); s of late John Bernard Wyman, MBE, of Sharpthorne, W Sussex, and Joan Dorethea, *née* Beighton; *b* 26 February 1950; *Educ* Epsom Coll; *m* 16 Sept 1978, Joy Alison, da of late Edward George Foster, of Horsted Keynes, W Sussex; 1 s (John b 1985), 1 da (Gemma b 1988); *Career* chartered accountant; articled clerk Ogden Parsons & Co and Harmood Banner 1968–73; PricewaterhouseCoopers (formerly Deloitte Haskins & Sells and then Coopers & Lybrand): mangr 1974–78, ptnr 1978–, head of tax 1993–98, head of external relations 1998–2000, head of regulatory policy 2003, head of professional affrs 2004–; Coopers & Lybrand: memb Partnership Bd 1997–98, memb Partnership Cncl 1997–98, memb Residuary Body 1998–; memb Ctee London Soc of Chartered Accountants 1981–90 (chm 1987–88); ICAEW: chm Faculty of Taxation 1991–95, memb Cncl 1991–, chm Educn and Training Directorate 1995–99, memb Exec Ctee 1996–2003, vice-pres 2000–2001, dep pres 2001–02, pres 2002–03; chm Professional Standards Office 1999–2000; special advsr on deregulation and taxation to Parly Under Sec of State for Corp Affairs 1993–94, external overseer Contribs Agency/Inland Revenue Jt Working Prog 1995–97; chm Consultative Ctee of Accountancy Bodies 2002–03, dep chm Financial Reporting Cncl 2002–03; memb: Deregulation Task Force 1994–97, Regulation of the Accountancy Profession Implementation Working Pty 1999–2001, Panel on Takeovers and Mergers 2002–03, Review of the Regulation of the Accountancy Profession Steering Gp 2002–04, Corp of London EU Advsy Gp 2004–, Audit Ctee RSA 2005–, Int Fedn of Accountancy Bodies 2006– (memb Transnational Auditors Ctee, Forum of Firms and Planning and Finance Ctee); dir Somerset Community Fndn 2002–04; govr: Aylwin Girls Sch Southwark 2001–06 (chm 2003–06), Harris Bermondsey Acad 2006–07; tstee Five Bridges Sch 2002–05; memb Cncl Univ of Bath 2003–06 and 2007–; Freeman: City of London 1988, Worshipful Co of Chartered Accountants 1988 (Sr Warden 2005–06, Master 2006–07); ICAEW Award for Outstanding Acheivement 2006; FCA 1978 (ACA 1973), FRSA 1993; *Recreations* my family's genealogy, twentieth century history, equestrian sports, gardening; *Style*— Peter L Wyman, Esq, CBE; ✉ Plainsfield Court, Plainsfield, Over Stowey, Somerset TA5 1HH (tel 01278 671292, fax 01278 671192); Flat 1, Priory House, 3 Burgon Street, London EC4V 5DR (tel 020 7248 4211); PricewaterhouseCoopers LLP, No 1 Embankment Place, London WC2N 6RH (tel 020 7213 4777, fax 020 7804 6844, mobile 07711 776128, e-mail peter.l.wyman@uk.pwc.com)

WYN, Eurig; *b* 10 October 1944, Hermon nr Crymych, Pembs; *Educ* Preseli Comp Sch, UCW Aberystwyth (BA, DipEd), Liverpool John Moores Univ; *m* Gillian; 2 c; *Career* teacher, journalist BBC and Welsh nat newspapers, devpt offr for community co-op movement, organiser Plaid Cymru Arfon, MEP (Plaid Cymru) Wales 1999–2004; Euro Parl: memb Culture, Youth, Educn, the Media and Sport Ctee, memb Agric and Rural Devpt Ctee, memb Petitions Ctee, memb delgn for rels with SA, co-ordinator foot-and-mouth inquiry; cncllr Gwynedd CC, memb Wales Local Govt Assoc, vice-pres UK delegation to Euro Ctee of the Regions (rapporteur on structural funds, anti-racism and drugs abuse, pres then sec-gen Euro Free Alliance gp); sometime scriptwriter S4C and Welsh theatre; memb: NUJ, UCAC, TCWU, BECTU (delegate Wales TUC); *Style*— Eurig Wyn, Esq; ✉ website www.eurigwyn.com

WYN-ROGERS, Catherine; da of Geoffrey Wyn Rogers, and Helena, *née* Webster; *b* 24 July 1954; *Educ* St Helena HS for Girls Chesterfield, RCM (fndn scholar, ARCM, Dame Clara Butt Award); *Career* mezzo-soprano; studied with Meriel St Clair, Ellis Keeler, Diane Forlano; concerts with: Vienna Philharmonic, RIAS Kammerchor, Bach Choir, Royal Choral Soc, Huddersfield Choral Soc, RPO, English Chamber Orch, Bournemouth Symphony Orch, Royal Liverpool Philharmonic Orch, Philharmonia, City of Birmingham Symphony Orchs, Three Choirs Festival, Aldeburgh Festival, The Sixteen, English Concert, Acad of Ancient Music, BBC Symphony Orch (BBC Proms, incl Last Night soloist 1995); opera cos appeared with: Scottish Opera, Welsh Nat Opera, Opera North, ENO, Salzburg Festival; Royal Opera House roles incl: Mrs Sedley in Peter Grimes, First Norn and Erda in Wagner's Ring Cycle, Sosostris in The Midsummer Marriage; also worked with: Bernard Haitink, Andrew Davis, Sir Charles Mackerras, Richard Hickox, Mark Elder, Roger Norrington; pres Derby Bach Choir 1995, patron Amadeus Choir of Toronto; *Recordings* Haydn's Harmoniemesse (with Winchester Cathedral Choir under David Hill), John Gay's Beggar's Opera, Teixeira's Te Deum and Bach's Christmas Oratorio (with The Sixteen and Orch for Collins Classics), Mozart's Vespers (with Trevor Pinnock), Vaughan Williams' Serenade to Music (with Roger Norrington), Elgar's The Dream of Gerontius (EMI), Graham Johnson's Complete Schubert Edition (Hyperion), Britten A Charm of Lullabies orchestrated by Colin Matthews (Northern Sinfonia under Steuart Bedford); *Recreations* drawing, painting; *Style*— Ms Catherine Wyn-Rogers; ✉ c/o Askonas Holt, Lonsdale Chambers, 27 Chancery Lane, London WC2A 1PF

WYNDHAM, Henry Mark; s of Hon Mark Wyndham, OBE, MC, and Anne, *née* Winn; *b* 19 August 1953; *Educ* Eton, Sorbonne; *m* 21 Dec 1978, Rachel Sarah, da of Lt-Col Leslie Francis Gordon Pritchard, MBE, TD (d 1977); 3 s (Ned b 1983, Leo b 1985, William b 1988); *Career* Christies International 1974–87 (dir 1983–87), fndr Henry Wyndham Fine Art 1987; chm: Sotheby's UK 1994–, Sotheby's Europe 1997–; expert BBC Antiques Road Show 1987–97; fell Pierpont Morgan Library NY; chm Arts and Library Ctee MCC 1993–98; tstee: Glyndebourne Opera, Prince of Wales Drawing Schools; memb: Patrons of British Art Tate Gallery (memb Ctee 1993–96), Sir George Beaumont Gp Nat Gallery, Dilettanti Soc, MCC Ctee 1987–98; former govr Thomas Coram Fndn; Liveryman Worshipful Co of Goldsmiths; *Recreations* cricket, soccer, golf, tennis, travelling, shooting and fishing, looking at pictures, films, music, opera; *Clubs* White's, MCC (memb Ctee 1994–98), Pratt's, Saints and Sinners, Pilgrims, Grillions; *Style*— Henry Wyndham, Esq; ✉ The Old Rectory, Southease, Lewes, East Sussex BN7 3HX; Sotheby's, 34–35 New Bond Street, London W1A 2AA (tel 020 7293 5057, fax 020 7293 5065)

WYNESS, James Alexander Davidson; s of Dr James Alexander Davidson Wyness (d 1984), of Dyce, Aberdeen, and Millicent Margaret, *née* Beaton (d 1996); *b* 27 August 1937; *Educ* Stockport GS, Emmanuel Coll Cambridge (MA, LLB); *m* 18 June 1966, Josephine Margaret, da of Lt-Col Edward Stow Willard Worsdell, MBE, TD, of Eynsford, Kent; 3 da (Rachel b 28 July 1968, Emily b 3 Feb 1971, Jeannie b 27 Aug 1974); *Career* Nat Serv 2 Lt RA; slr; articled clerk AF & RW Tweedie 1964–66; Linklaters & Paines 1966–97: ptnr 1970–97, managing ptnr 1987–91, jt sr ptnr 1991–93, sr ptnr 1994–96; non-exec dir Spirent plc 1979–2006 (sr ind dir 1999–2006, acting chm 2002); pres Saracens FC RFU 1993–96, dir Saracens Ltd 1996– (non-exec chm 1996–2002); memb Worshipful Co of City of London Slrs; memb Law Soc; *Recreations* visiting France, growing vegetables, rugby football (captain Saracens FC RFU 1962–65, Middx RFU and London RFU), reading; *Style*— James Wyness, Esq

WYNFORD, 9 Baron (UK 1829); John Philip Robert Best; only s of 8 Baron (d 2002); *b* 23 November 1950; *Educ* Radley, Keele Univ (BA), RAC Cirencester; *m* 10 Oct 1981, Fenella Christian Mary, only da of Capt Arthur Reginald Danks, MBE, TD (d 1996), and Hon Serena Mary (d 1998), da of 4 Baron Gifford; 1 da (Hon Sophie Hannah Elizabeth b 1985), 1 s (Hon Harry Robert Francis b 9 May 1987); *Heir* s, Hon Harry Best; *Career* ARICS land agency div 1979; Wynford Eagle Ptnrs (administering family estate): exec ptnr 1981–2002, sole prop 2002–; MRICS; *Recreations* music, reading, silviculture, bridge; *Style*— The Rt Hon the Lord Wynford, MRICS; ✉ The Manor, Wynford Eagle, Dorchester, Dorset DT2 0ER (tel 01300 320763)

WYNFORD-THOMAS, Prof David; s of Richard David Thomas (d 1991), of Barry, S Glamorgan; *b* 28 February 1955; *Educ* Welsh Nat Sch of Med (MB BCh, PhD, DSc); *Career* house offr posts in med and surgery 1978–79, asst lectr in pathology Univ of Wales Coll of Med (UWCM, formerly Welsh Nat Sch of Med) 1979–80, Wellcome research fell UWCM 1980–82, NIH post doctoral fell Dept of Molecular, Cellular and Developmental Biology Univ of Colorado Boulder 1982–83; Dept of Pathology UWCM: lectr 1984–86, sr lectr Cancer Biology Unit 1986–88, reader in tumour biology 1988–92, prof and head of dept 1992–; chm Div of Clinical Laboratory Sciences UWCM 2001–05, dean of medicine Cardiff Univ 2005–; external expert Institut National de la Santé et de la Recherche Médicale (INSERM) 2000–; pres: UK Branch European Tissue Culture Soc 1996–2000, Exec Ctee European Thyroid Cancer Network 1996–; memb: MRC Molecular and Cellular Med Grants Ctee 1992–96, Exec Ctee UK Molecular Biology and Cancer Network 1992–, MRC Molecular and Cellular Med Bd 1998–2002, MRC Leukaemia Steering Ctee 1998–2002, MRC Cross-Bd Clinical Trials Ctee 1998–2002, Cancer Research Campaign Grants Ctee 2000–05, Steering Ctee Nat Generic Tumour Bank 2001–, UK Govt Advsy Ctee on Genetic Manipulation 2001–03; subject ed (molecular and cellular pathology) Br Jl of Cancer 1995–, memb Editorial Bd Jl of Pathology 1992–2002; hon memb Assoc Française de Chirurgie Endocriniene; FRCPath 1996 (MRCPath 1989), FMedSci 2003; *Publications* Thyroid Tumours - Molecular Basis of Pathogenesis (with E D Williams, 1989); also 132 research articles and 16 book chapters; *Recreations* foreign languages, travel; *Style*— Prof David Wynford-Thomas; ✉ Dean's Office, School of Medicine, Cardiff University, Cardiff CF14 4XN (tel 029 2074 2020, e-mail kingtd@cf.ac.uk)

WYNN, Cdr Andrew Guy; LVO (1984); yr s of Lt Cdr Hon Charles Wynn, RN, and Hon Hermione Willoughby, da of 11 Baron Middleton; *b* 26 November 1950; *Educ* Eton, Gonville & Caius Coll Cambridge (MA); *m* 1, 1978 (m dis 1987), Susanjane, *née* Fraser-Smith; 1 s (Alexander Charles Guy b 1980); *m* 2, 1988, Shelagh Jean MacSorley, yr da of Prof I K M Smith, of Welwyn Garden City, Herts; *Career* Lt Cdr RN, Equerry to HRH The Duke of Edinburgh 1982–84, Dep Supply Offr HMS Ark Royal 1984–86, Cdr RN, Offr Policy Section 1987–88; sch bursar Eton Coll 1988–98, bursar Eton Coll 1998–; memb Exec Ctee Ind Schs Bursars' Assoc 2001–06; chm Schs and Univs Polo Assoc 1996–98 (sec 1991–96); *Publications* HMS Ark Royal: The Ship and Her Men (with D Smith, 1987); *Recreations* shooting, fishing, photography; *Style*— Cdr Andrew Wynn, LVO, RN; ✉ The Bursary, Eton College, Windsor, Berkshire SL4 6DJ (tel 01753 671213, e-mail a.wynn@etoncollege.org.uk)

WYNN, Terence; MEP (Lab) North West England; s of Ernest Wynn (d 1979), and Lily, *née* Hitchen (d 1976); *b* 27 June 1946; *Educ* Leigh Tech Coll, Riversdale Marine Coll, Univ of Salford (MSc); *m* 7 March 1967, Doris, da of Ernest Ogden (d 1971); 1 s (David Mark b 4 March 1968), 1 da (Terry Joanne b 20 Nov 1970); *Career* trg exec MTA 1985–89; councillor Wigan MBC 1979–90; MEP (Lab): Merseyside E 1989–94, Merseyside E and Wigan 1994–99, NW England 1999–; chm Euro Parly Budgets Ctee; *Recreations* reading, theatre, jogging, golf, music, rugby league; *Style*— Terence Wynn, Esq, MEP; ✉ Lakeside, Alexandra Park, Prescot Road, St Helens WA10 3TT (tel 01744 451609, fax 01744 29832, e-mail terry_wynn.labour@virgin.net)

WYNN-EVANS, Charles Andrew; s of Anthony Wynn-Evans, of Kenilworth, Warks, and Margaret Wynn-Evans; *b* 12 December 1967, Leamington Spa, Warks; *Educ* King Henry VIII Sch Coventry, Univ of Bristol (LLB), Coll of Law Chester, Merton Coll Oxford (BCL); *m* 31 May 1997, Alex McColl; 1 da (Catherine b 3 Aug 1999), 1 s (David b 26 April 2002); *Career* admitted slr 1992; ptnr Dechert LLP (formerly Titmuss Sainer & Webb) 1997– (joined as trainee slr 1990); memb: Law Soc, City of London Slrs Co; *Recreations* family, cricket, allotment gardening, watching Welsh rugby, politics; *Style*— Charles Wynn-Evans, Esq; ✉ Dechert LLP, 2 Serjeants' Inn, London EC4Y 1LT (tel 020 7775 7545, fax 020 7775 7335, e-mail charles.wynn-evans@dechert.com)

WYNN OWEN, Phil; s of Emrys Wynn Owen (d 2005), and Ruth Wynn Owen (d 2005); *b* 10 June 1960; *Educ* Maidstone GS, UC Oxford (MA), London Business Sch (MBA); *m* 1989, Elizabeth Mary, *née* Fahey; 3 s (Michael b 30 Dec 1990, Andrew b 28 April 1993, Thomas b 19 May 1995); *Career* civil servant; HM Treasy: trainee 1981–83, asst private sec to Chllr of the Exchequer 1986–88, princ Industry and Competition Policy 1986–88, princ Funding and Monetary Policy 1990–91, private sec to Perm Sec 1991–93, Treasy alternate dir Euro Investment Bank 1994–96, team ldr Tport Team 1993–96, team ldr Tax and Budget Team 1996, team ldr Tax Policy Team 1997–99, dir Fin Sector 2003–; dir Regulatory Impact Unit Cabinet Office 1999–2003; *Recreations* family, cricket, gym, swimming, golf; *Clubs* MCC, Leigh Cricket (Kent), Hilden Leisure; *Style*— Phil Wynn Owen, Esq; ✉ HM Treasury, Financial Sector, 1 Horse Guards Road, London SW1A 2HQ (tel 020 7270 4448, fax 020 7451 7559)

WYNN PARRY, Dr Christopher Berkeley (Kit); MBE (1954); s of Hon Mr Justice (Sir Henry) Wynn Parry, KBE (d 1962), of Harpenden, Herts, and Hon Shelagh Berkeley, *née* Moynihan (d 1975), da of 1 Baron Moynihan; *b* 14 October 1924; *Educ* Eton, Univ of Oxford (DM, MA); *m* 25 July 1953, Lamorna Cathleen, da of Albert George W Sawyer (d 1970), of Clavering, Essex; 3 da (Charlotte b 1954, Sarah b 1957 d 2000, Jane b 1959), 1 s (Simon b 1961); *Career* RAF 1948–75: Gp Capt Med Branch, conslt advsr in rheumatology and rehabilitation, dir of rehabilitation Jt Servs Med Rehabilitation Units RAF Chessington and RAF Headley Court; dir of rehabilitation Royal Nat Orthopaedic Hosps 1975, hon conslt in applied electrophysiology Nat Hosp for Nervous Diseases Queen Square 1975, civil conslt in rheumatology and rehabilitation RAF 1975, chm Disability Ctee RCP London 1978–88, past dir of rehabilitation King Edward VII Hosp Midhurst; currently tstee and hon conslt physician Br Performing Arts Med Tst; fndr and first pres Int Rehabilitation Med Assoc, past pres Physical Med Section RSM, sec Int Fedn of Physical Med, advsr in rehabilitation to Chief Med Offr 1979–86, member Mac Coll Working Pty into Artificial Limb and Appliance Serv 1986–88, pres Br Soc for Surgery of the Hand; Br Cncl visiting lectr and scholar to: Russia, Hungary, Czechoslovakia; hon pres French Soc for Orthoses of the Upper Limb, co-ed International Journal of Rehabilitation Studies, memb Editorial Bd Pain Br Soc for Surgery of the Hand Injury, William Hyde Award for sport and med, Kovacs prizeman RSM, Stanford Cade medallist RAF Med Branch; memb Bd Opera Factory, memb Ct of Assts Worshipful Co of Dyers (Prime Warden 1981–82 and 1984–85); memb: Br Soc for Surgery of the Hand, Br Soc of Rheumatology, Br Soc for Relief of Pain; FRCP, FRCS; *Books* Rehabilitation of the Hand (4 edn, 1982), The Musician's Hand (jtly, 1998); also author of chapters in 22 books and articles on rehabilitation, rheumatology, orthopaedics, pain, peripheral nerve injuries, resettlement, backpain and organisation of servs; *Recreations* gardening, music, the arts, walking, wine and food; *Clubs* Savile, Athenaeum; *Style*— Dr Kit Wynn Parry, MBE; ✉ 51 Nassau Road, Barnes, London SW13 9QG (tel 020 8748 6288); British Performing Arts Medicine Trust, Totara Park House, 4th Floor, 34–35 Grays Inn Road, London WC1X 8HR (tel 020 7404 5888)

WYNNE, David; OBE (1994); s of Cdr Charles Edward Wynne, RNR, and Millicent, *née* Beyts; *b* 25 May 1926; *Educ* Stowe, Trinity Coll Cambridge; *m* 1958, Gillian Mary Leslie (d 1990), da of Leslie Grant, of Argentina and Switzerland; 2 s (Edward, Roland), and 2 step c; *Career* served WWII Sub Lt RNVR; sculptor; numerous important public works worldwide; exhbn celebrating 50 years as sculptor Mall Galleries 1997; *Recreations* active sports, poetry, travel; *Clubs* Garrick, Leander, Queen's, Hurlingham, Cresta Run; *Style*— David Wynne, Esq, OBE; ✉ 5 Burlington Lodge Studios, Buer Road, London SW6 (tel 020 7731 1071)

WYNNE, Ian; *b* 30 November 1973; *Career* canoeist; memb Royal Canoe Club; achievements incl: Silver medal K1 500m and Bronze medal K2 1000m European Championships 2004, Bronze medal K1 500m Olympic Games Athens 2004; *Style*— Ian Wynne, Esq; ✉ c/o British Canoe Union, John Dudderidge House, Adbolton Lane, West Bridgford, Nottinghamshire NG2 5AS

WYNNE-MORGAN, David; s of Col John Wynne-Morgan (d 1989), and Marjorie Mary (Marcie), *née* Wynne (d 1992); *b* 22 February 1931; *Educ* Bryanston; *m* 1 (m dis), Romaine Chevers, *née* Ferguson; 2 s (Nicholas b 1956, Adrian b 1957); *m* 2 (m dis), Sandra, *née* Paul; *m* 3, 26 June 1973, Karin Elizabeth, da of Daniel Eugene Stines; 2 s (Jamie b 1975, Harry b 1980); *Career* journalist: Daily Mail 1951–54, Daily Express 1954–57; fndr Partnerplan PR (sold to Extel Group 1980); dir John Player, British Genius Exhbn 1978; chm Hill and Knowlton (UK) Ltd 1984–92, EMEA pres and chief exec Hill and Knowlton 1990–94 (chm Worldwide Exec Ctee 1992–94); co-fndr WMC Communications 1995–; dir Horsham Corporation 1995–97; chm Marketing Group GB 1989–91; played squash for Wales 1953–56; memb Cncl Lord's Taverners 1990–95 (chm Commercial Ctee 1992–94); MIPR; *Books* autobiography of late Pres Gamal Abdel Nasser (serialised Sunday Times), biography of Pietro Annigoni (serialised Daily Express), I Norman Levy; *Recreations* cricket, tennis, riding, squash; *Clubs* Turf, Annabel's, Mark's, Harry's Bar, Queen's, The Brook; *Style*— David Wynne-Morgan, Esq; ✉ Falkland House, Painswick, Gloucestershire GL6 6QN

WYNNE-PARKER, Michael; s of David Boothby Wynne-Parker (d 1955); *b* 20 November 1945; *Educ* Lady Manners Sch; *m* 1, 1975 (m dis 1991) Jennifer Lubbock; 2 da (Sarah Ruth Isabella b 1978, Fiona Alice Elizabeth b 1981); *m* 2, 1995 (m dis 2001) Mandana Farzaneh; *Career* fndr and pres Introcom Int (31 countries); former dir: Introcom Jordan Ltd, Esma Auto Estonia Ltd, Introcom Estonia Ltd, Exclusive Tours of Estonia; conslt to various public and private cos and govt mins and charities; ESU: former pres S Asia, vice-pres Sri Lanka, Nepal and India, former govr; fndr patron Pensthorpe Waterfowl Tst, patron St George Fndn Estonia; tstee: A Heart for Russia Fndn 2005–, ESU Sri Lanka Educnl Tst, Mencap City Fndn (fndr tstee and govr); fell Atlantic Cncl of the UK; fndr: Knockie Stalking Club, United Charities Unit Tst (formerly Mencap Unit Tst); chm: Br Forces Fndn Inaugural Ball 1999, Guild of Travel and Tourism 1999–, ESU of Sri Lanka Millennium Appeal 2000; patron Estonia-Finnish Symphony Orch 1999–; former vice-chm Norfolk Beagles; life memb: Royal Soc of St George, Sri Lanka Friendship Assoc (fndr memb), Norfolk Naturalist Tst; memb: Br Forces Fndn Exec Club 2000, Royal Soc for Asian Affrs, Salisbury Gp, The Pilgrims; *Books* Bridge over Troubled Water (1988), The Mandana Poems and Others (1998), Reflections in Middle Years (2005); *Recreations* field sports, travelling, gardens, books; *Clubs* Buck's, Mark's, Clermont, Crockfords, Annabel's, Aspinall's, Puffin's (Edinburgh), Cavalry & Guards; *Style*— Michael Wynne-Parker, Esq; ✉ Guild of Travel and Tourism, Suite 193, Temple Chambers, 3–7 Temple Avenue, London EC4Y 0DB (tel 020 7583 6333, fax 01895 834028, e-mail info@introcominternational.com)

W

Y

YACOUB, Prof Sir Magdi Habib; kt (1991); *b* 16 November 1935; *Educ* Cairo Univ (MB BCh), FRCS, FRCS(Ed), FRCS(Glas) 1961, MRCS, LRCP (London) 1966, MRCP 1986; *Career* rotating house offr Cairo Univ Hosp 1958–59, surgical registrar Postgrad Surgical Unit Cairo Univ 1959–61; resident surgical offr: London Chest Hosp 1962–63, Brompton Hosp May-Oct 1963; surgical registrar London Chest Hosp 1963–64, rotating sr surgical registrar Nat Heart and Chest Hosps 1964–68, instr and asst prof Section of Cardiovascular Surgery Univ of Chicago 1968–69; Harefield Hosp: conslt cardiac surgn 1969–92, dir of med research and educn 1992–; conslt cardiac surgn Nat Heart Hosp 1973–89, Br Heart Fndn prof of cardiothoracic surgery Nat Heart and Lung Inst Royal Brompton NHS Tst 1986–; special envoy to NHS 2002; hon conslt Royal Free Hosp Med Sch London and King Edward's Coll of Med Lahore Pakistan, hon prof of surgery Univ of Sienna Italy and hon prof of cardiac surgery Charing Cross and Westminster Hosp Med Schs London; ed: Annual in Cardiac Surgery, Current Opinion in Cardiology: Coronary Artery Surgery; memb various Editorial Bds incl: Jl of Cardiac Surgery, Current Opinion in Cardiology, Transplantation, Cardiovascular Pharmacology and Therapeutics; various visiting professorships and named/guest lectures incl: The Bradshaw Lecture RCP London 1988, honoured guest lecture Assoc of American Thoracic Surgns Washington DC 1991, Frances Rather Seybold lectr and visiting prof Texas Children's Hosp Houston 1992, The Tudor Edwards Lecture RCP London 1992, visiting prof and O T Clagett lectr Mayo Clinic Rochester Minnesota 1993, visiting prof in cardiac surgery and Hubbard lectr Brigham and Women's Hosp Boston Mass 1994, Claude S Beck visiting lectr Univ Hosps of Cleveland Ohio 1994, Stikeman visiting prof McGill Univ Montreal 1994, visiting prof Hartford Hosp Hartford Connecticut 1994, 17th Leonard Abrahamson Meml Lecture Dublin 1995; Clement Price Thomas Award RCS (England) 1989, Ambuj Nath Bose Prize RCP 1992; memb: Soc of Thoracic Surgns of GB and Ireland, Br Cardiac Soc, RSM, German Soc of Thoracic and Cardiac Surgery, German Cardiac Soc, Scandinavian Soc of Thoracic Surgns, Japanese Soc of Surgns, Int Soc of Thoracic and Vascular Surgery, Euro Soc of Cardiothoracic Surgns, Thai Soc of Cardiothoracic Surgns, Egyptian Soc of Cardiology, South African Soc of Cardiology, Cardiac Soc of Australia and NZ, Pakistan Cardiac Soc, Indian Soc of Cardiothoracic Surgns; fell American Coll of Cardiology; Hon DSc: Brunel Univ 1985, American Univ at Cairo 1989, Loughborough Univ 1990, Keele Univ 1995; Hon MCh Univ of Cardiff 1986, Hon PhD Univ of Lund 1988, Hon FRCP 1990, FMedSci 1999, FAMS 1999, FRS 1999; *Style—* Professor Sir Magdi Yacoub, FRS; ✉ Cardiothoracic Surgery, National Heart and Lung Institute, Imperial College of Science, Technology and Medicine, Dovehouse Street, London SW3 6LY (tel 020 7351 8533, fax 020 7351 8229, e-mail m.yacoub@ic.ac.uk)

YAFFÉ, Paul; s of David Yaffé (d 1976), of Manchester, and Dinah Pash; *b* 21 April 1946; *Educ* Delamere Forest Sch, Cheetham Secdy Sch; *m* 21 June 1967, Janis Andrea, da of Eric Brown; 2 s (Mark Daniel b 22 July 1968, Adam James b 23 Oct 1972); *Career* portrait photographer 1961–; worked in family photographic firm, opened own studio in Southport 1967, numerous exhibitions UK and abroad, lectr on photography and modern promotional methods in photography; chm Judging Panel BIPP (portraiture, wedding and theatrical photography) 1978 (memb 1974, dep chm 1976), chm Admissions and Qualifications Bd BIPP 1983–87 (dep chm 1980); fell Master Photographers Assoc 1981, hon PFP Norwegian Fame Assoc, 4 times memb Kodak Gold Circle; memb Professional Photographers Assoc of America; FBIPP 1972, FRPS 1979, FRSA, MIMgt 1993; *Style—* Paul Yaffé, Esq; ✉ Paul Yaffé Ltd, 43–47 Weld Road, Southport, Merseyside PR8 2DS (tel 01704 550000, fax 01704 550060, e-mail paul@paulyaffe.com, website www.paulyaffe.com)

YAMADA, Dr Tadataka (Tachi); *b* 5 June 1945; *Educ* Phillips Acad Andover MA, Stanford Univ (BA), NY Univ Sch of Med (MD); *m*; 1 s, 1 da; *Career* intern then resident (med) Med Coll of Virginia Richmond 1971–74, US Army Med Research Inst of Infectious Diseases investigator (Major Med Corps) 1974–77; Univ of Calif Los Angeles: fell (gastroenterology) 1977–79, asst prof of med 1979–82, assoc prof of med 1982–83; Univ of Michigan Med Sch Ann Arbor: prof Dept of Internal Med 1983–96, chief Gastroenterology Div 1983–90, dir Michigan Gastrointestinal Peptide Research Center 1984–96, dir H Marvin Pollard Inst for Med Research 1986–96, prof Dept of Physiology 1990–96, John G Searle prof and chm Dept of Internal Med 1990–96 (adjunct prof 1996–), physician-in-chief Univ of Michigan Medical Center 1990–96; GlaxoSmithKline (formerly SmithKline Beecham until 2001): non-exec dir 1994–96, pres Healthcare Servs and exec dir 1996–99, chm R&D (Pharmaceuticals) 1999–2006; head of global health Gates Fndn 2006–; non-exec dir: Genevo Inc, diaDexus, Healtheon Corp; ed/co-ed various med books, author of numerous book chapters, original manuscripts, reviews and editorials; Smith Kline and French Prize for outstanding contribs to gastrointestinal research American Physiological Soc 1991, Distinguished Faculty Achievement Award Univ of Michigan 1992, Diversity Ctee Achievement Award Univ of Michigan Med Sch 1996, Distinguished Med Scientist Award Med Coll of Virginia 1996; tstee Rockefeller Brothers Fund; cncllr Assoc of American Physicians, hon memb Japanese Soc of Gastroenterology 1993, memb Inst of Med Nat Acad of Scis 1994, master American Coll of Physicians 1997 (fell 1985); *Style—* Dr Tachi Yamada

YANOWSKY, Zenaida; *b* France; *Career* ballet dancer; with Opera National de Paris Ballet 1991–94, principal Royal Ballet 2001– (joined 1994); Silver Medal Varna 1991, Gold Medal European Young Dancers Competition 1993, Gold Medal Jackson Int Ballet Competition 1994; *Performances* incl: Odette, Odile, Sugar Plum Fairy, Myrtha, Raymonda Act III, Agon, The Bride in Les Noces, lead nymph in L'Après-midi d'un faune, Lilac Fairy, Carabosse, Gamzatti, Empress Elizabeth, The Siren in Prodigal Son, Symphony in C, Serenade, Monotones II, Concerto, Sinfonietta, The Four Temperaments; featured in dance films Duet (Channel 4) and The Sandman (Channel 4); *Style—* Ms Zenaida Yanowsky; ✉ c/o The Royal Ballet, Royal Opera House, Covent Garden, London WC2E 9DD

YAPP, John William; s of William Carlyle Nicholas Yapp (d 1996), and Pamela, *née* Clarke (d 1993); *b* 14 January 1951; *Children* 5 c (Antonia b 1975, Roderic b 1981, Genevieve b 1983, Nathalie b 1987, Caroline b 1998); *Career* HM Dip Serv; joined 1971, Islamabad 1973–75, Kuala Lumpur 1976–77, asst private sec to successive (Lab and Cons) Mins of State FCO 1978–80, Dubai 1980–84, The Hague 1984–88, first sec FCO 1988 (fndr memb Jt Export Promotion Directorate DTI 1988–91), first sec (info/political) Wellington and dep govr Pitcairn Is 1992–95, dep head N America Dept FCO 1995–97, high cmmr to Seychelles 1998–2002, Washington 2003, dep head S Asia Gp FCO 2004–; chm Royal Tunbridge Wells Round Table 1990–91; *Recreations* books, photography, rugby union (now as spectator); *Style—* John Yapp, Esq; ✉ c/o Foreign & Commonwealth Office, King Charles Street, London SW1A 2AH

YARBOROUGH, 8 Earl of (UK 1837); Charles John Pelham; also Baron Yarborough (GB 1794) and Baron Worsley (UK 1837); s of 7 Earl of Yarborough, JP (d 1991), and (Florence) Ann Petronel, *née* Upton; *b* 5 November 1963; *Educ* Eton, Bristol Univ; *m* 26 Jan 1990, Anna-Karin, da of George Zecevic, of Montreux, Switzerland; 4 s (George John Sackville, Lord Worsley b 9 Aug 1990, Hon William Charles John Walter b 28 Dec 1991, Hon James Marcus b 8 March 1994, Hon Edward John Herbert b 6 March 2002), 1 da (Lady Margaret Ann Emily Pelham b 30 Jan 1997); *Heir* s, Lord Worsley; *Style—* The Rt Hon the Earl of Yarborough; ✉ Brocklesby Park, Lincolnshire DN41 8FB (tel 01469 560242)

YARDLEY, Prof Sir David Charles Miller; kt (1994); s of Geoffrey Miller Yardley (d 1987), and Doris Woodward, *née* Jones (d 1934); *b* 4 June 1929; *Educ* Ellesmere Coll, Univ of Birmingham (LLB, LLD), Lincoln Coll Oxford (DPhil, MA); *m* 30 July 1954, Patricia Anne Tempest (Patsy), da of Lt-Col Basil Harry Tempest Olver, MBE (d 1980); 2 s (Adrian b 1956, Alistair b 1962), 2 da (Heather b 1958, Briony b 1960); *Career* Nat Serv Flying Offr Educn Branch RAF 1949–51; called to the Bar Gray's Inn 1952; fell St Edmund Hall Oxford 1953–74 (emeritus 1974–), Barber prof of law Univ of Birmingham 1974–78, head of Dept of Law, Politics and Economics Oxford Poly 1978–80, Rank Fndn prof of law Univ of Buckingham 1980–82 (hon prof 1994–), visiting prof Oxford Brookes Univ 1995–2001; chm Cmmn for Local Admin in England 1982–94, complaints cmmr SIB (then FSA) 1994–2001, ind complaints reviewer Lottery Forum 2005–06; chm: rent assessment ctees, rent tbnls and nat insurance local tbnls 1963–82 and 1995–99, Oxford Preservation Tst 1989–, Examining Bd and Awards Panel Inst of Revenues, Rating and Valuation 1994–2006; FRSA 1991; *Books* Introduction to Constitutional and Administrative Law (1960, 8 edn 1995), A Source Book of English Administrative Law (1963, 2 edn 1970), The Future of the Law (1964), Principles of Administrative Law (1981, 2 edn 1986), Geldarts Introduction to English Law (ed 1995), Hanbury and Yardley's English Courts of Law (1979), The Protection of Liberty (with I Stevens, 1982); *Recreations* lawn tennis, opera, cats; *Clubs* RAF; *Style—* Prof Sir David Yardley; ✉ 9 Belbroughton Road, Oxford OX2 6UZ (tel 01865 554831)

YARNOLD, Prof John Robert; s of Neville Eric Yarnold, and Anne-Marie, *née* Elkan; *Educ* Taunton's Sch Southampton, Middx Hosp Med Sch (BSc, MB BS); *Career* hon conslt in clinical oncology Royal Marsden Hosp 1980–; Inst of Cancer Research: sr lectr 1980, reader 1993, prof of clinical oncology 2002; chair Breast Clinical Studies Gp Nat Cancer Research Inst 2001–; MRCP 1974, FRCR 1977; *Recreations* music, tennis; *Style—* Prof John Yarnold; ✉ Royal Marsden Hospital, Downs Road, Sutton, Surrey SM2 5PT (tel 020 8661 3388, e-mail jyarnold@icr.ac.uk)

YARROW, Alan Colin Drake; *b* 27 June 1951; *Career* ptnr Grieveson Grant 1981–89 (joined 1972); Kleinwort Benson Gp: head of UK institutional sales 1989, head of global distribution 1992, md Kleinwort Benson Securities 1994, memb Bd 1995; global head of equities and memb Mgmnt Bd Dresdner Kleinwort Benson 1995–2000, vice-chm Dresdner Kleinwort 2000– (also currently chm Dresdner Kleinwort Ltd and Dresdner Kleinwort Securities Ltd and dir Dresdner Kleinwort Asia); non-exec chm Complinet Gp Ltd 2002–; chm London Investment Banking Assoc (LIBA), vice-pres BBA 2004–; memb: Exchange Markets Gp London Stock Exchange, Takeover Panel, FSA Practitioner Panel 2004–; FSI; *Recreations* golf, tennis, bridge; *Clubs* City, Boodle's, Hurlingham, Royal Wimbledon Golf; *Style—* Alan Yarrow, Esq; ✉ Dresdner Kleinwort, PO Box 52715, 30 Gresham Street, London EC2P 2XY (tel 020 7475 6787, fax 020 7475 6542, e-mail alan.yarrow@dkib.com)

YARROW, Sir Eric Grant; 3 Bt (UK 1916), of Homestead, Hindhead, Frensham, Co Surrey; MBE (1946), DL (Renfrewshire 1970); s of Sir Harold Yarrow, 2 Bt, GBE (d 1962), by his 1 w, Eleanor; *b* 23 April 1920; *Educ* Marlborough, Univ of Glasgow; *m* 1, Rosemary Ann (d 1957), da of late H T Young; 1 s (Richard d 1987); m 2, 1959 (m dis 1975), Annette Elizabeth Françoise, da of late A J E Steven; 3 s (Norman, Peter (twins) b 1960, David b 1966); m 3, 1982, Caroline Joan Rosa, da of late R F Masters, and former w of Philip Botting; *Heir* gs, Ross Yarrow; *Career* served RE Burma 1939–45, Maj 1944; former chm and md Yarrow plc, former chm Clydesdale Bank plc, former dir Standard Life Assurance Co, former dir Nat Australian Bank; hon pres Princess Louise Scottish Hosp at Erskine, pres Scot Area Burma Star Assoc, pres Scottish Convalescent Home for Children 1957–70; memb Cncl IOD 1983–90; deacon Incorporation of Hammermen of Glasgow 1961–62, Prime Warden of Worshipful Co of Shipwrights 1970, pres Smeatonian Soc of Civil Engrs 1983, pres Marlburian Club 1984, chm Blythe Sappers 1989, hon vice-pres Royal Inst of Naval Architects; hon memb Inst of Engrs and Shipbuilders in Scotland; FRSE 1974; OStJ 1970; *Style—* Sir Eric Yarrow, Bt, MBE, DL, FRSE; ✉ Craigrowan, Porterfield Road, Kilmacolm, Renfrewshire PA13 4PD

YASS, Catherine; *Educ* Slade Sch of Fine Art London (BA), Hochschule der Künste Berlin, Goldsmiths Coll London (MA); *Career* artist; fell Central St Martins Sch of Art 2002–; *Solo Exhibitions* Tavistock Centre for Psychotherapy London 1991, Laure Genillard London 1992, Guy's Cliffe (Herber Percy Gallery Warks) 1994, Chair (Viewpoint Photography Gallery Salford) 1994, Spectators (Aspex Gallery Portsmouth) 1995, Steel (Ffotogallery Cardiff) 1996, Stall (Laure Genillard London) 1996, Stage (Cell Space Barbican Centre London) 1997, Grave (Portfolio Gallery Edinburgh) 1997, Invisible City (Mizuma Art Gallery Tokyo) 1998, Baths (Sabine Schmidt Cologne) 1998, Galeria dels Angels Barcelona 1998, Baths (The Pool Central Club Hotel London) 1999, Project Space Galeri Wang Oslo 1999, Br Cncl Exhbn Space Prague 1999, i8 Gallery Reykjavik 2000, Synagogue (Art in Sacred Spaces) (Congregation of Jacob London) 2000, New Art Gallery Walsall 2000, Jerwood Gallery London 2001, Star (Br Cncl touring exhbn India) 2001, Cinema India: The Art of Bollywood (V&A London) 2002, Descent (asprey jacques London) 2002; *Selected Group Exhibitions* New Contemporaries (ICA London) 1984, Galerie Ackerstrasse Berlin 1985, Suppose It's True After All? (Crypt Gallery London) 1989, Post-Morality (Cambridge Darkroom) 1990, Countdown (Chisenhale Gallery London) 1990, The Clove Building (Butler's Wharf London) 1991, Brit Art 1 (Galeri Senger Zürich) 1991, Sign of the Times (Camerawork London) 1991, Exhibit A

(Serpentine Gallery London) 1992, Brit Art (Kunsthaus Glarus) 1992, Discretion (Canary Wharf London) 1992, Vox Pop (Laure Genillard London) 1993, Inner Side (AA London) 1993, Martina Detterer Gallery Frankfurt 1994, Miniatures (The Agency London) 1994, Whitechapel Open (Whitechapel Art Gallery London) 1994, 152C Brick Lane London 1995, Open House (Kettle's Yard Cambridge) 1995, Whistling Women (Royal Festival Hall London) 1995, Melange d'Aout (Hackney Hosp London) 1995, Care and Control (Hackney Hosp London) 1995, Gang Warfare (Ind Art Space London) 1995, British Art Show 4 (Cornerhouse Manchester) 1995 (Edinburgh and Cardiff tour 1996), Institute of Cultural Anxiety (ICA London) 1995, Join the Dots (Galerie 5020 Salzburg) 1996, Inside Bankside (S London Gallery London) 1996, Manifesta 1 (Rotterdam) 1996, Private View (Bowes Museum Darlington) 1996, ACE Arts Council New Purchases (Hayward Gallery London and UK tour) 1996, Inner London (Delfina London) 1996, Date with an Artist (Northern Gallery for Contemporary Art Sunderland) 1997, Private Face/Urban Space (The Gasworks Athens) 1997, Pictura Britannica (MOMA Sydney) 1997, Green on Red Gallery Dublin 1997, Urban Legends (Kunsthalle Baden-Baden) 1997, Six Unrelated Projects (The Tannery London) 1997, Denys Lasdun Retrospective (Royal Acad of Arts London) 1997, False Impressions (Br Sch Rome) 1997, Citibank Photography Prize (RCA London) 1997, Light (Richard Salmon London) 1997, Dimensions Variable: Works from the British Council Collection (London and European tour) 1997, London Screen (Edicions T Galleria d'Art Barcelona) 1998, United in Death (Cambridge Darkroom) 1998, Feeringbury V111 - Cultivated (Feeringbury Manor and Firstsite Colchester) 1998, Screen (Anne Faggionato Gallery London) 1998, New Art from Britain (Kunstraum Innsbruck) 1998, Queen's Festival (Waterfront Concert Hall Belfast) 1998, Modern British Art (Tate Liverpool) 1998, Performing Buildings (Tate Bankside London) 1998, Officina Europa (Galleria d'Arte Moderna Bologna and Italian tour) 1999, Prime (Dundee Contemporary Arts) 1999, Glen Dimplex Award (Irish MOMA Dublin) 1999, Nat Gallery of Art Tirana 1999, This Other World of Ours (TV Gallery Art Media Centre Moscow) 1999, Explorations of the Environment: Landscape Redefined (Barbara Gillman Gallery Miami) 2000, Light x 8 (Jewish Museum NY) 2000, Eat, Fuck, Die (Platform London) 2000, 10th India Triennale Delhi 2001, The gallery: UNCOVERED (Univ of Essex) 2001, No World Without You. Reflections of Identity in New British Art (Herzliya Museum Tel Aviv) 2001, Read Only Memory (Mead Gallery Warwick Arts Centre) 2001, Double Agent. Catherine Yass (Sir William Dunn Sch of Pathology Oxford) 2001, Multiplication: Artists' Multiples, Artists Multiplied (Br Cncl touring exhbn) 2001, Wetterling Gallery Sweden 2002, Tate Modern Collection (Tate Modern London) 2002, Glass Box Project: Catherine Yass (ARTLAB 16 at ICSTM London) 2002, The Ink Jetty (Neon Gallery) 2002; *Work in Public Collections* Arts Cncl of England, Biblioteca Albertina Leipzig, Br Cncl Collection London, Delfina Entrecanales London, Dundee City Cncl, Govt Art Collection London, Jewish Museum NY, Laing Art Gallery Newcastle, Nat Museum and Galleries of Wales Cardiff, New Art Gallery Walsall, Public Art Devpt Tst London, Royal Mail London, Royal Pump Rooms Royal Leamington Spa, Scottish Nat Gallery of Modern Art Edinburgh, Tate Gallery London; *Awards* Boise Travelling Scholarship 1986–87, Glen Dimplex Award 1999, Sci-Art The Wellcome Tst 2000, Turner Prize shortlist 2002; *Style—* Ms Catherine Yass; ✉ c/o Alison Abrams, Asprey Jacques, 4 Clifford Street, London W1X 1RB

YASS, Irving; CB (1993); s of Abraham Yass (d 1961), and Fanny, *née* Caplin (d 1980); *b* 20 December 1935; *Educ* Harrow Co GS, Balliol Coll Oxford (BA); *m* 14 Aug 1962, Marion Ruth, da of Benjamin Leighton (d 1979); 1 da (Catherine b 1963), 2 s (David b 1965, Michael b 1966); *Career* asst princ Miny of Transport and Civil Aviation 1958, private sec to jt parly sec 1960, princ HM Treasy 1967–70, asst sec DOE 1971, sec Ctee of Inquiry into Local Govt Fin 1974–76; Dept of Transport 1976–: under-sec fin 1982–86, dir tport policy for London 1987–94; dir of planning and tport Government Office for London 1994–95, dir policy London First 1995–; *Style—* Irving Yass, Esq, CB; ✉ London First, Hobhouse Court, Suffolk Street, London SW1Y 4HH (tel 020 7665 1589, fax 020 7665 1501, e-mail iyass@london-first.co.uk)

YASSUKOVICH, Stanislas Michael; CBE (1991); s of Dimitri Yassukovich, and Denise Yassukovich; *b* 5 February 1935; *Educ* Deerfield Acad Mass, Harvard Univ; *m* Diana Veronica, da of Ralph Obre Crofton Townsend; 2 s (Michael, Nicholas), 1 da (Tatyana); *Career* served US Marine Corps 1957–61; White Weld & Co: joined in Zurich 1961, London 1962, gen ptnr NY 1969, md London until 1973; EuroBanking Co Ltd London: md 1973, dep chm 1983–85; chm: Merrill Lynch Europe Ltd 1985–91, Cayzer Continuation PCC Ltd 2004–, S M Yassukovich & Co Ltd; non-exec chm: Flextech plc 1989–97 (dep chm 1997–2000), Park Place Capital Ltd 1991–, Henderson Euro Tst plc 1992–, Easdaq 1997–2000, Manek Investment Mgmnt Ltd 1998–; vice-chm Bristol & West plc 1991–99; dep chm: ABC International Bank plc 1993–, ABC International Bank Ltd 1985–, SW Water plc 1997–99 (non-exec dir 1992–99); non-exec dir: Mossiman's Ltd 1989–98, Tradepoint Financial Networks plc 1997–99, Telewest Communications 2000–03; a dep chm Stock Exchange 1986–89, chm The Securities Assoc 1987–91; chm City Disputes Panel 1994–98; *Recreations* hunting, polo; *Clubs* White's, Buck's, The Brook (USA), Travellers (Paris); *Style—* Stanislas Yassukovich, Esq, CBE

YATES, Brian Douglas; s of Bertram Yates (d 1993), and Barbara, *née* Wenham (d 1984); *b* 1 May 1944; *Educ* Uppingham, Clare Coll Cambridge (MA), London Business Sch (MBA); *m* 1971, Patricia, da of Arthur Hutchinson, DFC, of Dublin; 1 s (Justin b 1976); *Career* various engrg appointments with Molins, RHP Bearings, Thorn EMI and Dexion; dir: Morris Material Handling Ltd 1988–2002, Euroconsumer Publications Ltd 1992–, Trading Standards Services Ltd 1992–; Consumers' Assoc: memb Cncl 1986–, chm Business Ctee 1989, chm Cncl 1994–; memb: Northampton BC 1979–83, Hants CC 1985–89, Heathrow Airport Consultative Ctee 1992–, Fitness to Practice Panels GMC 2001–, Immigration Appeal Tbnl 2003–; ombudsman for Estate Agents Cncl 1999–2005; Eur Ing, CEng, MIM, FRSA; *Recreations* real and lawn tennis, ski touring; *Clubs* Athenaeum, Royal Over-Seas League, Hatfield House Tennis, Harpenden Lawn Tennis, Lunar Soc of Birmingham; *Style—* Brian Yates, Esq; ✉ 19 Park Avenue South, Harpenden, Hertfordshire AL5 2DZ (tel 01582 768484, fax 01582 767989); Consumers' Association, 2 Marylebone Road, London NW1 4DF (tel 020 7770 7877, fax 020 7770 7650, e-mail brian.yates@which.net)

YATES, Prof (Anthony) David; s of Cyril Yates, and Violet Ethel, *née* Man; *b* 5 May 1946; *Educ* Bromley GS, St Catherine's Coll Oxford (David Blank exhibitioner, MA, Frank Alan Bullock prize), Coll of Law Guildford; *m* 1 (m dis 1989), Carolyn Paula, *née* Hamilton; 3 da (Sarah Olivia Ann, Katherine Lucy Hannah, Rachel Jane Louise); m 2, Susanna Margaret, *née* McGarry; *Career* Univ of Hull: asst lectr in law 1969–72, dep warden Morgan Hall of Residence 1969–70, warden Newholme Student Residence 1970–72; Univ of Bristol: lectr in law 1972–74, dep warden Wills Hall of Residence 1972–74, visiting lectr 1974–75; Univ of Manchester: lectr in law 1974–76, warden Chandos Hall of Residence UMIST 1975–76, sr lectr in law 1976–79, princ Dalton Hall 1976–80 (pt/t 1979–80), visiting prof 1979–80; Univ of Essex: chm Dept of Law 1979–83, dean Sch of Law 1979–84, Fndn prof of law 1979–87, pro-vice-chllr 1985–87, visiting prof 1987–89; ptnr Baker & McKenzie 1987–2001 (chief operating offr 1998–2001); warden Robinson Coll Cambridge 2001–, govr Coll of Law 2001– (dep chm 2005–); visiting prof of law Univ of NSW 1985, Parsons visiting fell Univ of Sydney 1985; Law Soc of Eng and Wales: memb Cncl 1992–97, memb Trg Ctee 1993–97, chm Legal Practice Course Bd 1995–97, chm Working Party on review of Legal Practice Course 1996; memb Ctee City of London Law Soc 1993–98; memb: Advsy Ctee for Law Trg Within the Office American Bar Assoc 1988–2001, Advsy Bd Orientation in American Law Prog Univ of Calif 1990–, Advsy Ctee Centre for Advanced Legal Studies Univ of Leuven Belgium 1994–; Public Housing Law ed Encyclopaedia of Social Welfare Law 1973–80, gen ed The Professional Lawyer 1991–93; memb: Advsy Bd Urban Law and Policy 1978–, Editorial Bd Review of International Business Law 1988–95, Editorial Bd Jl of Contract Law 1988–; Freeman City of London 1993; memb Law Soc 1969; *Publications* Exclusion Clauses in Contracts (1978, 2 edn 1982), Leases of Business Premises (1979), Landlord and Tenant Law (with A J Hawkins, 1981, 2 edn 1986), Standard Business Contracts (with A J Hawkins, 1986), The Carriage of Goods by Land, Sea and Air (ed-in-chief and contrib, 1993), The Carriage of Goods by Land and Air (with Malcolm Clarke, 2004); also author of numerous articles in various jls; *Recreations* opera, food and wine, rugby football; *Clubs* Oxford and Cambridge, Royal Cwlth Soc, RSA; *Style—* Prof David Yates; ✉ Robinson College, Cambridge CB3 9AN (tel 01233 339100)

YATES, Ivan Ray; CBE (1982); *b* 22 April 1929; *Educ* Collegiate Sch Liverpool, Univ of Liverpool (BEng); *m* Jennifer Mary, *née* Halcombe; 1 s (Mark b 9 Jan 1970), 1 da (Jane b 21 Sept 1971); *Career* BAE Systems plc (formerly English Electric Co then British Aerospace plc): joined as grad apprentice 1950, pioneered use of computers to study aircraft dynamics and mgmnt, chief project engr TSR-2 (based Warton) 1960–65, project mangr Jaguar project 1966, dir BAC Preston 1973 (special dir 1970), dir Aircraft Projects 1974 (incl Tornado, ldr UK industrial consortium developing UK Experimental (fighter) programme (EAP) culminating in launch of Euro Fighter programme (EFA) 1986), md Warton Div and Bd memb Aircraft Gp (following nationalisation) 1978, chief exec Aircraft Gp and dir British Aerospace plc 1982, memb Bd BAe Inc 1983–88, dep chief exec BAe 1986, left gp 1990; sometime former dir and chm: SEPECAT SA (Jaguar), PANAVIA Aircraft GmbH (Tornado), EUROFIGHTER GmbH; visiting prof in principles of engrg design Univ of Cambridge (bye-fell Churchill Coll), Wright Brothers lectureship AIAA; pres SBAC 1988–89 (ldr first delgn to USSR 1989); memb Cncl Design Cncl 1990–98, chm RSA's Mfrg Initiative, chm Royal Acad of Engrg Prog Partnership for Profitable Product Improvement, memb Cncl Air League; former memb Cncl: Royal Acad of Engrg, RUSI, Royal Aeronautical Soc (winner Gold and Silver Medals); cmmr Royal Cmmn 1851 1989–99, govr Imperial Coll London 1990–99; vice-pres R J Mitchell Museum of Aviation Southampton; Hon DSc Loughborough Univ of Technol 1989, Hon DSc City Univ 1991; foreign memb Royal Swedish Acad of Engrg Scis 1990; FIMechE, FRAeS, FAIAA, FRSA, FREng 1983; *Style—* Dr Ivan Yates, CBE, FREng; ✉ e-mail ivanryates@gmail.com

YATES, Janty; da of Lt-Col Denys Ainsworth Yates, and Margaret, *née* Tyrer; *Educ* Highgrove Sch Ashford, Katinka Coll of Dress Design London; *Career* costume designer for film and television; *Television* Endless Game 1990, Yellow Thread St 1990, Comic Strip 1991–92, Full Stretch 1993, Cracker 1993, An Evening With Gary Lineker (film) 1994, Bliss (film) 1994, Karaoke 1996; *Film* costume asst: Quest for Fire 1981, Oxford Blues 1984, Dance with a Stranger 1985, Sour Sweet 1985; costume supervisor The Commitments 1991; costume designer: Bad Behaviour 1993, The Englishman Who Went Up a Hill But Came Down a Mountain 1995, Jude 1996, Welcome to Sarajevo 1997, The Man Who Knew Too Little 1997, Plunkett and Macleane 1999, With or Without You 1999, Gladiator 2000 (Academy Award Best Costume Design 2001, Las Vegas Film Critics Award Best Costume Design, BAFTA nomination for Best Costume Design), Enemy at the Gates 2001, Hannibal 2001, Charlotte Gray 2001, De-Lovely 2003; *Recreations* riding, swimming, walking, gardening, film, theatre, 19th and 20th century art, reading, travel, scuba diving; *Style—* Ms Janty Yates; ✉ c/o ICM, Oxford House, 76 Oxford Street, London W1D 1BS

YATES, Prof John Gordon; s of Thomas Edgar Yates (d 1973), and Mabel, *née* Price (d 1983); *b* 7 February 1937; *Educ* Dagenham County HS, SE Essex Tech Coll (BSc), Imperial Coll London (PhD, DIC); *m* 10 Sept 1960, Anne Elizabeth, da of Charles Henry Kersey; 1 s (Nicholas James b 7 Dec 1968); *Career* res technologist BP Chemicals 1962–64; UCL: lectr Dept of Chemical Engrg 1964–76, sr lectr 1976–84, reader in chemical technol 1984–90, prof of chemical engrg 1990, dean Faculty of Engrg 1991–93, Ramsay meml prof and head Dept of Chemical Engrg 1996–2003, Ramsay meml prof emeritus 2003–; external examiner in chem engrg Heriot-Watt Univ; memb Int Advsy Gp Swedish Strategic Res Prog in Multi-Phase Flow; Freeman City of London, Liveryman Worshipful Co of Engineers; DSc (Eng) London 1984; FRSC 1976, FIChemE 1992, FREng 1999; *Publications* Fundamentals of Fluidized-bed Chemical Processes (1983); over 120 publications in scientific literature and conf proceedings; *Recreations* music, literature, visual arts, astronomy, cooking; *Clubs* Groucho; *Style—* Prof John Yates, FREng; ✉ 33 Parkside, London NW7 2LJ (tel 020 8906 1896, fax 020 8906 4728, mobile 07967 478133, e-mail john@jgyates.fsnet.co.uk)

YATES, Rodney Brooks; s of Henry Bertram Yates, OBE (d 1993), of Alvechurch, Birmingham, and Emily Barbara, *née* Wenham (d 1984); *b* 7 June 1937; *Educ* Uppingham; *m* 1 (m dis); 2 s (Mark b 1965, Duncan b 1966), 1 da (Camilla b 1970); m 2, 16 Sept 1983, Hazel, *née* Brown; 1 s (Benjamin b 1986); *Career* dir: Akroyd & Smithers plc 1975–86, Mercury Gp Mgmnt 1986–87, Hemsley & Co Securities Ltd 1988–89; md Madoff Securities Int Ltd 1987–88; dir: Olliff & Partners plc 1987–95 (chm 1987–93), Bentley Capital (Europe) Ltd 1991–98; memb: Cambs Family Health Serv Authy 1990–96, GMC 1993–2003 (chm Fitness to Practice Policy Ctee 2000–02, memb Professional Conduct Ctee 1993–2003 (chm 2003)), NW Anglia HA 1996–99, Med Advsy Panel on Visual Disorders and Disorders of the Cardiovascular System DTLR 2001–; govr Peterborough HS 1992–2002 (chm 1997–2002); fell Woodard Corp (memb Exec Bd) 2003–; memb Ct of Assts Worshipful Co of Tallow Chandlers (Master 2005); FCA, MSI (memb Stock Exchange 1971); *Recreations* tennis, travel, reading; *Clubs* RAC; *Style—* Rodney Yates, Esq; ✉ The Old Rectory, Marholm, Peterborough PE6 7JA (tel 01733 269466, fax 01733 330127, e-mail rodney@marholm.com)

YATES, Roger Philip; s of Eric Yates, of Warrington, and Joyce Mary, *née* Brown; *b* 4 April 1957; *Educ* Boteler GS Warrington, Worcester Coll Oxford (BA), Univ of Reading; *m* 1, 7 Sept 1985 (m dis 1998), Kim Patricia, da of Anthony Gerald Gibbons, of Abinger, Surrey; 3 s (Max b 1987, Jeremy b 1989, Robert Alexander b 1992); m 2, 26 April 2003, Catriona MacLean; 1 da (Helena Rose b 2002); *Career* joined GT Mgmnt Ltd 1981, dir GT Mgmnt (UK) Ltd 1984–88, dir GT Mgmnt plc 1986–88, investment dir GT Unit Managers Ltd 1988; dir and chief investment offr Morgan Grenfell Investment Mgmnt 1988–94, dir Morgan Grenfell Asset Mgmnt 1991–94; dir and chief investment offr: LGT Asset Mgmnt plc 1994–98, Invesco Europe 1998–99; md Henderson Global Investors 1999–, ceo Henderson Gp plc (formerly HHG plc) 2003–; non-exec dir IG Gp Hldgs plc 2006–; *Recreations* golf, skiing, tennis; *Style—* Roger Yates, Esq

YATES, Prof William Edgar; s of Douglas Yates (d 1955), and Doris, *née* Goode (d 1990); *b* 30 April 1938; *Educ* Fettes, Emmanuel Coll Cambridge (MA, PhD); *m* 6 April 1963, Barbara Anne, da of Wolfgang Fellowes (d 1984); 2 s (Thomas b 1971, Paul b 1975); *Career* 2 Lt RASC 1957–58; lectr in German Univ of Durham 1963–72, prof of German Univ of Exeter 1972–2001 (dep vice-chllr 1986–89, prof emeritus 2001–), Germanic ed Modern Language Review 1981–88, ed Nestroyana 1992– (jtly with U Tanzer 2002–); Österreichisches Ehrenkreuz für Wissenschaft und Kunst 1. Klasse 2001; memb: Modern Humanities Res Assoc (memb Ctee 1980–), Eng Goethe Soc (memb Cncl 1984–), Int Nestroy Soc (memb Cncl 1986–, vice-pres 1997–), Viennese Shakespeare Soc (vice-pres 1992–2002); chm of govrs Exeter Sch 1994–; corresponding fell Austrian Acad of Sciences 1992; FBA 2002; *Books* Grillparzer: A Critical Introduction (1972), Nestroy: Satire and

Y

Parody in Viennese Popular Comedy (1972), Humanity in Weimar and Vienna: The Continuity of an Ideal (1973), Tradition in the German Sonnet (1981), Nestroy (ed Stücke 12–14 1981–82, Stücke 34 1989, Stücke 18/I 1991, Stücke 22 1996, Stücke 17/II 1998, ed with J Hein Stücke 2 2000, ed with P Haida Nachträge I-II 2007), Viennese Popular Theatre (ed with J R P McKenzie,1985), Grillparzer und die europäische Tradition (ed with R Pichl and others, 1987), Schnitzler, Hofmannsthal, and the Austrian Theatre (1992), Nestroy and the Critics (1994), Vom schaffenden zum edierten Nestroy (ed, 1994), Theatre in Vienna: A Critical History, 1776–1995 (1996), Nestroys Reserve und andere Notizen (ed, 2000, revised edn 2003), Nestroy in München (with B Pargner, 2001), Der unbekannte Nestroy (ed, 2001), Bei die Zeitverhältnisse noch solche Privatverhältnisse (ed, 2001), Hinter den Kulissen von Biedermeier und Nachmärz (ed with H C Ehalt and J Hein, 2001), From Perinet to Jelinek: Viennese Theatre in its Political and Intellectual Context (ed with A Fiddler and J Warren, 2001), Briefe des Theaterdirektors Carl Carl und seiner Frau Margaretha Carl an Charlotte Birch-Pfeiffer (ed with B Pargner, 2004), Theater und Gesellschaft im Wien des 19 Jahrhunderts (ed with U Tanzer, 2006); Festschrift, The Austrian Comic Tradition (ed J R P McKenzie and L Sharpe, 1998); *Recreations* theatre, opera, French wine; *Style*— Prof W E Yates; ✉ 7 Clifton Hill, Exeter EX1 2DL (tel 01392 254713, e-mail weyates@tiscali.co.uk)

YATES, William Hugh; MBE; s of Brig Morris Yates, DSO, OBE, and Kathleen Rosanna, *née* Sherbrooke; *b* 18 December 1935; *Educ* Lancing, RMA Sandhurst, Coll of Estate Mgmnt; *m* 1, 1963 (m dis 1972), Celia Geraldine, *née* Pitman; 1 s; m 2, 1979, Elisabeth Susan Mansel-Pleydell, *née* Luard; 4 step s; *Career* served Army 1955–61; asst Rylands & Co 1961–64; Knight Frank & Rutley (now Knight Frank): negotiator 1964–67, md Knight Frank & Rutley SA Geneva 1968–72, ptnr i/c international investment 1972–78, managing ptnr 1978–82, head Residential Div 1982–92, sr ptnr 1992–96, ret; dir: EUPIC Services BV 1973–82, Ecclesiastical Insurance Group 1985–2006 (dep chm 1995–2006), Woolwich Building Society (now Woolwich plc) 1990–2000 (dep chm 1996–2000), Woolwich Europe Ltd 1991–95; hon treas Save the Children Fund 1986–92 (chm fund raising 1980–86); FRICS 1965; *Recreations* racing, gardening, golf, music; *Clubs* Turf, Wentworth Golf; *Style*— William Yates, Esq, MBE; ✉ Upper Farmhouse, Milton Lilbourne, Pewsey, Wiltshire SN9 5LQ (tel 01672 563438)

YATES-ROUND, Jeremy Laurence; s of Joseph Laurence John Yates-Round, of Cheshire, and Ellen Clancy, *née* Yapp; *b* 27 February 1961, Tunbridge Wells, Kent; *Educ* Tunbridge Wells Tech HS, West Kent Coll; *m* 27 April 1985, Theresa Tamara, *née* Britneff; 3 s (Joseph Laurence b 17 June 1991, Alexander William b 12 Sept 1993, Timothy James b 17 April 1996); *Career* export sales rep Hodder & Stoughton 1981–85, sales mangr William Collins 1985–89; Harper Collins Publishers: sales dir 1990–97, dep md Religious Div 1997–2000; md Sutton Publishing Ltd 2001–07, sales and mktg dir UK and Europe Haynes Publishing plc 2007–; tstee Centre Christian Bookshop Stroud; *Recreations* active memb of local church, listening to and playing music, football; *Style*— Jeremy Yates-Round, Esq; ✉ Haynes Publishing plc, Sparkford, Somerset BA22 7JJ (tel 01963 440635, fax 01963 440001, e-mail jyates-round@haynes.co.uk)

YEA, Philip Edward; s of John Alfred William Yea (d 1971), and Elsie Beryl, *née* Putman; *b* 11 December 1954; *Educ* Wallington HS for Boys, Brasenose Coll Oxford (MA); *m* 5 Dec 1981, Daryl, da of William Anthony Walker; 2 s (William b 24 May 1984, Daniel b 6 Dec 1986), 1 da (Georgina b 20 Feb 1992); *Career* Perkins Engines Ltd 1977–80, Moteurs Perkins SA France 1980–82, Foursquare Div Mars Ltd 1982–83, Guinness plc 1984–88 (dir of business devpt United Distillers Group 1987–88), fin dir Cope Allman Packaging plc 1989–91 (joined 1988), fin dir Guinness plc 1993–97 (rejoined 1991), gp fin dir Diageo plc (following merger with Grand Metropolitan plc) 1997–99, md (private equity) Investcorp International 1999–2004, chief exec 3i Gp plc 2004–; non-exec dir: William Baird plc 1995–99 (dep chm 1999), Manchester United plc 1999–2004 (sr non-exec dir and chm Audit Ctee), Halifax plc 1999–2001, HBOS plc 2001–04, Vodafone Gp plc 2005–; FCMA 1982, FRSA 1993, CIMgt 2000; *Recreations* family, cinema; *Style*— Philip Yea, Esq; ✉ 3i Group plc, 16 Palace Street, London SW1E 5JD

YEATES, Andrew; *b* 27 September 1957; *m*; 2 c; *Career* admitted slr 1981; contracts mangr Thames Television and Thames Television International 1981–87, company lawyer Phonographic Performance Ltd 1987–88; Channel Four Television: prog acquisition exec 1988–89, sr prog acquisition exec 1989–90, head of acquisitions and business affrs 1991–94, corporation sec and head of rights 1994–99; DG BPI 2000–04 (dir legal affairs 1999–2000), gen counsel The Educational Recording Agency Ltd 2005–, intellectual property advsr Periodical Publishers Assoc 2005–, conslt Sheridans Slrs 2006–; chm Creative Exports Group; memb Law Soc; Liveryman Worshipful Co of Haberdashers; *Recreations* theatre, music; *Style*— Andrew Yeates; ✉ The Educational Recording Agency Ltd, New Premier House, 150 Southampton Row, London WC1B 5AL (tel 020 7837 3222, fax 020 7837 3750, e-mail andrew.yeates3@btinternet.com)

YELDON, Peter James; s of John Gordon Yeldon (d 1980), and Joan, *née* Wilson (d 1974); *b* 7 May 1962; *Educ* St Ivo Sch St Ives, Univ of Newcastle upon Tyne (BA); *m* 1, 17 Aug 1985, Elizabeth Anne, *née* Fozard; 1 s (Timothy John b and d 12 February 1991), 2 da (Charlotte Alice b 14 Dec 1991, Berlinda Claire b 1 Dec 1993); m 2, 30 Sept 1995, Judith Ann, da of Barry Matthiae; 2 s (Thomas Barry b 30 Dec 1994, Matthew John b 4 May 1997), 1 da (Harriet Joan (twin) b 30 Dec 1994); *Career* Arthur Andersen & Co: articled clerk 1983–86, CA 1986, licensed insolvency practitioner 1989; Smith and Williamson: ptnr 1989–2001, head of insolvency 1989–2001, memb Bd 1993–2001, chm Mktg Ctee, insolvency work incl Palace Pictures/Palace Group, Maxwell Offshore Companies and Poland and Wellington Lloyd's Action Groups, corp advice to insurance, construction, property and media entities, work also includes development and provision of housing to univ students, first-time buyers and tourists, and venture capital and investment activities; dir: London Link Association Ltd, Uni Accommodation plc, Investor for Growth Ltd, Retirement Lettings Ltd, North London Developments Ltd, Direct Bike Finance Ltd, 48 Langham Street Ltd, Handford Properties Ltd, Lawgra 746 Ltd; memb Courses and Conferences Ctee Soc of Practitioners in Insolvency 1993–96; fndr chm West End Business Club 1993, treas Assoc for Spinal Injury Research, Rehabilitation and Reintegration 1994, chm Winterslow Recreational Ctee 2000–; memb Lib Dem Pty; FCA, MInstD, MSPI; *Recreations* sea fishing, Rolls Royce enthusiast, art, fast cars, running, football; *Style*— Peter Yeldon, Esq; ✉ The Tythings, West Winterslow, Salisbury, Wiltshire SP5 1RE (tel 01980 862892); Ys Partnership, 48 Langham Street, London W1W 7AY (tel 020 7908 6100, fax 020 7908 6111)

YELLAND, David Ian; s of John Michael Yelland, of Bridlington, East Yorkshire, and Patricia Ann, *née* McIntosh; *b* 14 May 1963; *Educ* Brigg GS Humberside, Lanchester Poly Coventry (BA Econ), Harvard Business Sch (AMP); *m* 19 Jan 1996 (m dis 2004), Tania D, da of L H Farrell; *Career* graduate trainee journalist Company Sch Hastings Westminster Press 1984–85, jr reporter Bucks Advertiser Gerrards Cross 1985–87, news and industrial reporter Northern Echo Darlington 1987–88, journalist North West Times and Sunday Times Manchester 1988, city reporter Thomson Regnl Newspapers London 1988–90, NY corr The Sun 1993 (city ed 1990–93); New York Post: business ed 1993–96, dep ed 1996–1998; ed The Sun 1998–2003, vice-pres News Corp 2003–04, sr vice-chm Weber Shandwick 2004–; *Clubs* Savile, RAC, Royal Soc of Arts; *Style*— David Yelland, Esq

YELLOLY, Dr Margaret Anne; da of Samuel Webster Yelloly (d 1976), and Rowena Emily, *née* Bull (d 1989); *b* 7 June 1934; *Educ* Queen Margaret's Sch, Univ of St Andrews (MA), Univ of Liverpool (MA), Univ of Leicester (PhD); *m* 20 July 2004, Robin Woodbridge; *Career* lectr Univ of Leicester Sch of Social Work 1966–72, lectr LSE 1973–76, head Dept of Applied Social Studies Goldsmiths Coll London 1976–86, prof of social work and dir of social work educn Univ of Stirling 1986–91, prof of social work Brunel Univ and the Tavistock Clinic 1991–93, hon prof Tavistock Clinic 1994–; chm Tavistock Inst of Med Psychology 2000–04; chm Social Work Educn Ctee Jt Univ Cncl 1988–91, memb Central Cncl for Educn and Training in Social Work 1989–92; *Books* Social Work Theory and Psychoanalysis (1985), Social Work and the Legacy of Freud (1989), Learning and Teaching in Social Work (1994); *Recreations* classical music, harpsichord; *Style*— Dr Margaret Yelloly; ✉ 1 May Close, St Albans, Hertfordshire AL3 5RG (tel 01727 853932)

YELTON, His Hon Judge Michael Paul; s of Joseph William Yelton (d 1998), and Enid Hazel Yelton (d 2006); *b* 21 April 1950; *Educ* Colchester Royal GS, CCC Cambridge (MA); *Career* called to the Bar 1972, in practice 1973–98, recorder 1996–98 (asst recorder 1992–96), circuit judge (SE Circuit) 1998–; dir of studies in law CCC Cambridge 1977–81; *Books* Fatal Accidents, a practical guide to compensation (1998), Martin Travers, an appreciation (jtly, 2003), Trams, Trolleybuses, Buses and the Law (2004), Anglican Papalism (2005), Peter Anson (2005), Alfred Hope Patten and the Shrine of Our Lady of Walsingham (2006), Empty Tabernacles (2006); *Recreations* reading, ecclesiology, football, transport; *Style*— His Hon Judge Yelton; ✉ Cambridge County Court, 197 East Road, Cambridge CB1 1BA

YENTOB, Alan; *b* 11 March 1947; *Career* BBC: joined as gen trainee 1968, prodr/presenter BBC Radio and External Broadcasting 1968–69, asst dir Arts Features TV 1969–73, prodr and dir Omnibus strand BBC2 1973–75, fndr ed Arena arts strand BBC2 1978–85, head of music and arts BBC TV 1985–87, controller of BBC2 1988–93, controller of BBC1 1993–96, dir of progs BBC TV 1996–97, dir of television BBC TV (also i/c BBC1, BBC2, Online and digital servs except news) 1997–2000, dir of drama, entertainment and children's 2000–04, creative dir 2004–; chm ICA 2002– (memb Advsy Ctee); govr The South Bank Bd Ltd 1999–; tstee: Architecture Fndn, Kids Company, Timebank 2001–; hon fell: RCA, RIBA; fell: BFI 1997, RTS; *Programmes* Arena documentaries incl: The Orson Welles Story, Billie Holiday - The Long Night of Lady Day, The Private Life of the Ford Cortina, My Way, The Chelsea Hotel; responsible for progs, films and series for BBC2 incl: The Late Show, Oranges Are Not The Only Fruit, The Snapper, Truly Madly Deeply, Have I Got News For You, Absolutely Fabulous, Rab C Nesbitt, Troubleshooter, Pandora's Box, Video Diaries, live relays of operas Tosca and Stiffelio, opera series The Vampyr; for BBC1 incl: introduction of Monday episode of EastEnders, re-introduction of Sunday afternoon family serial (incl Just William and The Borrowers), Leonardo series (writer and presenter), Imagine series (presenter); *Awards* incl: Best Arts Series Br Academy Awards for Arena 1982, 1983 and 1984, Best Arts Series Broadcasting Press Guild Awards for Arena 1985, Gold Award NY Film Festival and Int EMMY for Omnibus film The Treble 1985, Programming Supremo of the Year Broadcast Prodn Awards 1997; *Style*— Alan Yentob, Esq; ✉ BBC Television Centre, Wood Lane, London W12 7RJ (tel 020 8743 8000)

YEO, Diane Helen; da of Brian Harold Pickard, FRCS, and Joan Daisy, *née* Packham; *b* 22 July 1945; *Educ* Blackheath HS, Univ of London, Institut Francais de Presse; *m* 30 March 1970, Timothy Stephen Kenneth Yeo, MP, *qv*, s of Dr Kenneth John Yeo; 1 s (Jonathan, *qv*, b 1970), 1 da (Emily b 1972); *Career* BBC Radio prodn 1968–74, dir clearing house scheme Africa Educnl Tst 1974–79, head of fundraising Girlguiding UK 1979–82, dir appeals and public rels YWCA 1982–85, chief exec Inst of Fundraising 1985–88, charity cmmr for Eng and Wales 1989–95, chief exec Sargent Cancer Care for Children 1995–2001, exec dir UK for UNHCR 2001–03, conslt Diane Yeo Assocs Ltd 2003–, chief exec Muscular Dystrophy Campaign 2004–05, chief exec Chelsea and Westminster Health Charity 2006–; Paul Harris fell Rotary Int 2000; chair: Charity Standards Ctee 1991–94, Advsy Ctee on Trusteeship 1993–95, Advsy Ctee to Home Secretary on Volunteering 1995–96, Tstees, Govrs and Fin Ctee Arts Educnl Schs 2004–; memb: Nathan Ctee on Effectiveness and the Voluntary Sector 1989–90, Planning for Partnership Ctee 1995–96, Cncl and Audit Ctee Advtg Standards Authy 1997–, Fundraising Regulation Advsy Gp/Home Office 2003–, Advsy Cncl NCVO 1994–, Reviews Ctee Assoc of NHS Charities; patron CANCERactive 2004–; tstee Charity Appointments 1987–96; contrib Third Sector magazine; fell Inst of Fundraising 1983, FRSA 1989; *Recreations* piano, family, tennis, photgraphy, gardening; *Style*— Mrs Diane Yeo; ✉ diane.yeo@chelwest.nhs.uk

YEO, Jacinta Marina; *b* 23 January 1962; *Educ* Trinity Coll Dublin (BA, BDentSci, MA, Irish Dental Bd prize in periodontology, oral med, oral pathology and oral surgery), Primary FRCS (first place), accredited American Nat Dental Bd, Dip Gemology (part one); *Career* dentist/broadcaster; house surgn Dublin Dental Hosp 1984–85, in private practice 1985–; advsr BUPA 1994–95, spokesman BDA 1995–; various TV and radio appearances on dentistry and gen topics 1993–; dental expert for various nat magazines, websites and newspapers; memb: BDA 1986, Br Endodontic Assoc 1987; FRSM 1986, FRSH 1995; *Recreations* designing men's fashion; *Style*— Miss Jacinta Yeo

YEO, Jonathan; s of Tim Yeo, MP, *qv*, and Diane Yeo, *qv*, *née* Pickard; *b* 18 December 1970; *Educ* Westminster, Univ of Kent (BA); *m* m 2006, Shebah Ronay; 2 da (Tabitha b 2003, Yasmin b 2007); *Career* artist; self-taught, specialising in portraits; cmmnd by House of Commons as Britain's first Election Artist to paint the three main political pty ldrs 2001, work subject of In Your Face arts prog (Channel 4) 2002; exhbns incl: Historical Portraits, Blains Fine Art, Royal Soc of Portrait Painters, BP Portrait Award (Nat Portrait Gall), Jonathan Yeo's Sketch book (solo exhbn, Eleven) 2006, The Naked Portrait (Scottish Nat Gall) 2007; patron Lymphoma Soc; portrait of Rupert Murdoch acquired by Nat Portrait Gall 2006 (on perm display 2007–); *Clubs* Chelsea Arts, Groucho; *Style*— Jonathan Yeo, Esq; ✉ c/o Philip Mould, Historical Portraits, 31 Dover Street, London W1S 4ND (tel 020 7499 6818, e-mail studio@jonathanyeo.com)

YEO, Timothy Stephen Kenneth (Tim); MP; s of Dr Kenneth John Yeo (d 1979), and Norah Margaret Yeo; *b* 20 March 1945; *Educ* Charterhouse, Emmanuel Coll Cambridge; *m* 1970, Diane Helen, *qv*, da of Brian Harold Pickard; 1 s (Jonathan, *qv*, b 1970), 1 da (Emily b 1972); *Career* chief exec Scope (formerly Spastics Soc) 1980–83; MP (Cons) Suffolk S 1983– (Parly candidate (Cons) Bedwellty 1974); jt sec: Cons Backbench Fin Ctee 1984–87, Social Services Select Ctee 1985–88; PPS to Rt Hon Douglas Hurd 1988–90, Parly under sec Dept of Environment 1990–92, Parly under sec Dept of Health 1992–93, min of state Dept of Environment 1993–94 (resigned); oppn spokesman on environment and local govt 1997–98, shadow min Agriculture, Fisheries and Food 1998–2001, shadow sec of state for culture, media and sport 2001–02, shadow sec of state for trade and industry 2002–03, shadow sec of state for public servs, health and educn 2003–04, shadow sec of state for transport and the environment 2004–05; memb Select Ctee on Employment 1994–96, memb Treasy Select Ctee 1996–97, chm Environmental Audit Select Ctee 2005–; chm Univent plc 1995–, non-exec chm AFC Energy 2007–; non-exec dir: Genus plc 2002–04, Eurotunnel plc 2007–; dir Worcester Engrg Co Ltd 1975–86, asst treas Bankers Trust Company 1970–73, treas Int Voluntary Service 1975–78, tstee Tanzania Devpt Tst 1980–95, chm Charities VAT Reform Gp 1981–88, chm Tadworth Ct Tst 1983–91; golf corr Country Life 1994–, golf columnist FT 2004–; *Publications* Public Accountability and Regulation of Charities (1983); *Recreations* skiing; *Clubs* MCC, Royal and Ancient, Sunningdale Golf, Royal St George's Golf; *Style*— Tim Yeo, Esq, MP; ✉ House of Commons, London SW1A 0AA (tel 020 7219 3000)

YEOMAN, Angela Betty; OBE, DL; da of Harry James Newell, of Weston-super-Mare, and Mabel Elizabeth; *b* 26 April 1931; *Educ* Stonar Sch; *m* 1952, John Foster Yeoman (decd); 2 da (Sally Jane b 9 Dec 1953, Susan Kate b 13 July 1955), 2 s (David b 9 Feb 1958,

John b 9 Feb 1961); *Career* chm Foster Yeoman Ltd 1988–2006, non-exec dir Aggregate Industries UK Ltd; ambass Highlands and Islands; memb: Somerset Building Tst, Cncl Royal Bath and West; chm Somerset Community Foundation; Liveryman Worshipful Co of Paviors, Freeman Worshipful Co of Watermen and Lightermen; High Sheriff Somerset 2000; hon fell Inst of Quarrying 1990; *Clubs* Sloane, Pony; *Style—* Mrs Angela Yeoman; ✉ Southfield House, Whatley, Frome, Somerset BA11 3JY (tel 01373 836209, fax 01373 836020); Aggregate Industries UK Limited, Marston House, Marston Bigot, Frome, Somerset BA11 5DU (tel 01373 451001, fax 01373 836501, mobile 07771 647175, e-mail angela.yeoman@fosteryeoman.co.uk)

YEOMAN, Martin; s of Arthur John Yeoman (d 1993), and Gladys Dorothy, *née* Illsley; *b* 21 July 1953; *Educ* RA Schs (Silver medal for drawing); *Children* 1 s (George Edward Conway b 9 Feb 1998); *Career* artist; occasional painting companion to HRH The Prince of Wales; RP; *Solo Exhibitions* Highgate Gallery 1986, Two Tours of the Middle East (Agnews) 1987, New Grafton Gallery 1990, The Queen's Grandchildren (National Portrait Gallery) 1993, Selected Works (Mompesson House National Trust) 1994, Christopher Wood Contemporary Art 1995, Yeoman's Yemen (British Council exhbn National Art Gallery Sana'a and John Martin of London) 1997, Paintings in the Holy Land (Alan Kluckow Fine Art) 2000, Hindustan to Malabar (Offer Waterman and Co) 2002, India (Indar Pasricha Fine Art) 2004; *Group Exhibitions* Royal Acad Summer Exhbn 1976–77, 1979–90 and 1992–96, Imperial Tobacco Portrait Award (National Portrait Gallery) 1981 and 1985, Six Young Artists (Agnews) 1985, Four Painters (New Grafton Gallery) 1987, The Long Perspective (National Trust Exhbn, Agnews) 1987, A Personal Choice (Fermoy Gallery) 1988, Salute to Turner (National Trust Exhbn, Agnews) 1989, The Order of Merit (National Portrait Gallery) 1992; *Work in Collections* HM The Queen, HRH The Prince of Wales, Sir Brinsley Ford, Diocese of Birmingham, Baring Brothers, Grimsby Sch of Art, National Portrait Gallery, British Council, British Museum; *Awards* David Murray Landscape scholar 1978, Richard Ford scholar 1979, Elizabeth Greenshield scholar 1980, Hamerson Purchase Prize 1984, Menana Joy Schwabe Prize 1996, Philip Soloman Drawing Prize 1998, The Ondaatje Prize for Portraiture 2002, Bill Turner Prize 2004; *Clubs* New English Art; *Style—* Martin Yeoman, Esq, RP

YEOMANS, Prof Julia; *Educ* Univ of Oxford (MA, DPhil); *Career* postdoctoral research asst Cornell Univ, lectr Univ of Southampton, prof of physics Univ of Oxford, Pauline Chan fell in physics St Hilda's Coll Oxford (tutor 1983–); *Style—* Prof Julia Yeomans; ✉ Rudolf Peierls Centre for Theoretical Physics, 1 Keble Road, Oxford OX1 3NP

YEOMANS, Lucy; da of Harry Hammond Light Yeomans, and Margot, *née* Boyle (d 2003); *b* 1 November 1970; *Educ* Univ of St Andrews (MA); *Career* successively: arts ed rising to ed Boulevard magazine Paris, arts ed The European, features ed then dep ed Tatler, features dir Vogue; ed Harper's Bazaar (formerly Harpers & Queen) 2000–; FRSA; *Style—* Miss Lucy Yeomans; ✉ Harper's Bazaar, 72 Broadwick Street, London W1F 9EP (tel 020 7439 5533)

YEOMANS, Richard David; s of Richard James Yeomans (d 1964), of Basingstoke, Hants, and Elsie Marian, *née* Winson; *b* 15 February 1943; *Educ* Hartley Wintney Co Secdy Modern Sch, Hants Coll of Agric, Shuttleworth Coll (NDA); *m* 6 April 1968, Doreen Ann, da of William Herring, of Aldershot, Hants; 1 da (Claire b 14 Dec 1972), 1 s (Jonathan b 24 Feb 1976); *Career* with Milk Mktg Bd 1965–71; Unigate plc: area mangr (tport) 1971, gen mangr (milk) 1975, latterly bd dir; md: Wincanton Transport Ltd 1978–, Wincanton Group Ltd 1982–91; ops dir Milk Marketing Bd 1994, chief exec Milk Marque 1996–98 (ops dir 1994–96); chm: TLS Range plc 1992–98, Blakes Chilled Distribution Ltd 1997–99, Pourshins plc 1998–2004; dir: Peninsula Milk Processors Ltd 1998–2001, Aim Hire Ltd 1998–2004; princ David Yeomans Associates 1991–; exec vice-chm Montagu Ventures 2000–06; memb: Tport Tbnl 1999–, SW Rent Assessment Panel 1999–, SE Flood Defence Ctee 2000–02; memb Wine Guild of UK; Liveryman Worshipful Co of Carmen; CIMgt 1982, FCIT 1989, FRSA 1990; *Recreations* shooting, boats, gardening, photography; *Clubs* RAC; *Style—* David Yeomans, Esq; ✉ 4 Priestlands Court, Priestlands Lane, Sherborne, Dorset DT9 4EY (tel 01935 817814, e-mail richarddyeomans@compuserve.com)

YEOWART, Geoffrey Bernard Brian; s of Brian Albert Yeowart, of Chailey, E Sussex, and Vera Ivy, *née* Goring; *b* 28 March 1949; *Educ* Ardingly, Univ of Southampton (LLB), KCL (LLM); *m* 6 Oct 1979, Patricia Eileen, da of Oswald Anthony (d 1984); 1 da (Clare b 7 Nov 1980), 2 s (Thomas b 8 June 1983, Matthew b 30 Sept 1986); *Career* admitted slr 1975 (admitted Hong Kong 1982); ptnr: Durrant Piesse 1985–88, Lovells LLP (formerly Lovell White Durrant) 1988–; memb: Bank of England's City Euro Gp, HM Treasury's Euro Business Advsy Gp, HM Treasury and Financial Markets Law Ctee Task Forces on Emergency Powers and Financial Sector Operational Disruption; dep chm City of London Law Soc, Financial Law Ctee; memb Editorial Bd: Jl of Int Banking and Financial Law, Law and Financial Markets Review; Distinguished Service Award City of London Slrs' Co 2003; memb Law Soc; *Books* Euro Guide on Legal Issues, European Banking Law (contrib, 2 edn); *Recreations* sailing, reading; *Clubs* Royal Dart Yacht, Royal Lymington Yacht; *Style—* Geoffrey Yeowart, Esq; ✉ Lovells LLP, Atlantic House, Holborn Viaduct, London EC1A 2FG (tel 020 7296 2000, fax 020 7296 2001)

YHAP, Laetitia Karoline; da of Leslie Neville Yhap (d 1987), and Elizabeth, *née* Kogler; *b* 1 May 1941; *Educ* Fulham Co GS, Camberwell Sch of Arts and Crafts (NDD), Slade Sch of Fine Art (DFA); *m* 1963 (m dis 1980), Jeffrey Camp; 1 s (Ajax b 1984); partner 1983–, Michael Rycroft; *Career* artist in oils; Leverhulme Res award (travel in Italy) 1962–63; first solo show Norwich Sch of Art 1964, Young Contemporaries FBA galleries and tour 1965, various showings with London Gp 1965–, three solo shows Piccadilly Gallery 1968, 1970 and 1973, solo summer show Serpentine Gallery 1975, Drawings of People (mixed exhibition, Serpentine Gallery London) 1975, John Moores (mixed exhibition) Liverpool, The British Art Show 1979, Art and The Sea (ICA and tour) 1981, Tolly Cobbold 1983, solo show Air Gallery London 1984, The Hard-Won Image (Tate Gallery) 1984, solo show touring The Business of the Beach (Laing Art Gallery Newcastle) 1988, Picturing People (Br Cncl Exhibition touring Far East) 1990, solo show Rye Art Gallery 1991, solo show Worthing Art Gallery and Museum 1992, Life at the Edge (The Charleston Gallery) 1993, solo show Bound by the Sea (Gymnasium Gallery Berwick-upon-Tweed) 1994, solo show Maritime Counterpoint (Boundary Gallery London) 1996, solo show In Monochrome (Gallery Lydd Library Kent) 1998, solo show The Story So Far (Hastings Tst) 1999, solo show Extemporizations (Hastings Tst) 2000, Being in the Picture - A Retrospective (Piers Feetham Gallery London) 2002; memb London Gp; *Recreations* badminton, concert-going; *Style—* Ms Laetitia Yhap; ✉ 12 The Croft, Hastings, East Sussex TN34 3HH (website www.axisartists.org.uk)

YIANGOU, Constantinos; s of Andreas Yiangou, and Pantelitsa Yiangou; *Educ* Pancyprian Gymnasium Nicosia, St Mary's Hosp Med Sch London, Univ of London (BSc, MB BS); *Career* SHO St Mary's Hosp London, St Charles Hosp London, Mayday Hosp and Brook Gen Hosp 1988–91, registrar in gen and vascular surgery Hillingdon Hosp and Central Middx Hosp 1992–93, res fell and hon registrar Dept of Breast Surgery and Oncology Charing Cross Hosp 1993–95, specialist registrar in gen and breast surgery Charing Cross Hosp, Hemel Hempstead Hosp and Lister Hosp Herts 1995–99, conslt gen surgn specialising in surgical oncology, breast and endocrine surgery Queen Alexandra Hosp Portsmouth 1999–, hon sr lectr Univ of Portsmouth 2002–, clinical dir of breast and endocrine surgery Portsmouth Hosps NHS Tst 2004–, princ investigator for several breast cancer trials Portsmouth; research interests: mgmnt of early breast cancer, sentinel lymph node biopsy in breast cancer, molecular prognostic markers of breast cancer, diagnosis of thyroid cancer; entered on GMC Specialist Register 1999; Norman Plummer Meml Prize 1995, Ronald Raven Prize 1995, Simpson-Smith Travelling Fellowship 1996–97; memb: BMA 1987, Br Assoc of Surgical Oncology 1999, Assoc of Breast Surgery 1999, Br Assoc of Endocrine Surgeons 2007; FRCS (Eng) 1991, FRCS (gen surgn) 1999, fell Assoc of Surgns of GB and I 2005; *Publications* author several pubns in surgical and cancer jls on the diagnosis, treatment and molecular biology of breast cancer; *Style—* Constantinos Yiangou, Esq; ✉ Department of Surgery, Queen Alexandra Hospital, Cosham, Portsmouth, Hampshire PO6 3LY (tel 023 9228 6000, fax 023 9228 6547, e-mail constantinos.yiangou@porthosp.nhs.uk)

YONACE, Dr Adrian Harris; JP (Dorset 1989); s of Dr Jack Yonace (d 1975), of Salford, and Bryna, *née* Fidler (d 2000); *b* 26 November 1943; *Educ* Manchester Grammar, Univ of Manchester, Univ of Nottingham (BMedSci, BM BS); *m* 9 March 1989, Maureen Wilson, da of Thomas Wilson Ramsay, of Gullane; 2 c (Tristan Jack, Giselle Isla (twins) b 23 Aug 1995); *Career* computer systems analyst IBM 1965–67, computer conslt 1967–70; house physician and house surgn Univ Depts Manchester Royal Infirmary 1976–77, lectr in psychiatry Royal Free Hosp Univ of London 1980–83, conslt and hon sr lectr Friern Hosp and Univ of London 1983–89; conslt psychiatrist: St Ann's Hosp Poole 1989–93 and 1997–99, Priory Hosps Gp 1993–97; hon clinical teacher Univ of Southampton 1996–99 (hon clinical res fell 1993–96); conslt psychiatrist in private practice 1993–; examiner RCPsych 1993–98 (observer 1999–), sr examiner MB ChB Finals Univ of London 1987–90; memb Mental Health Review Tbnl 2000–; sec E Dorset BMA 1993–95; Silver Dip Eng Bridge Union Teachers Assoc; JP Inner London Juvenile Bench 1985–89, Court chm Poole Bench 1989–99; govr (both) Bournemouth Grammar Schs 2006–; FRCPsych 1994 (MRCPsych 1983); *Recreations* scrabble, bridge, golf, twins; *Style—* Dr Adrian Yonace; ✉ Bournemouth Nuffield Hospital, 65 Lansdowne Road, Bournemouth, Dorset BH1 1RW (tel 01202 702824)

YORK, Archdeacon of; *see:* Seed, Ven Richard Murray Crosland

YORK, Dean of; *see:* Jones, Very Rev Keith Brynmor

YORK, Col Edward Christopher; TD (1978), DL (N Yorks, 1988); s of Christopher York (d 1999), and Pauline Rose Marie, *née* Fletcher (d 2007); *b* 22 February 1939; *Educ* Eton; *m* 28 April 1965, Sarah Ann, da of Maj James Kennedy Maxwell, MC (d 1980), of Buckby Folly, Northants; 1 s, 1 da; *Career* 1 Royal Dragoons (ret 1964), CO Queen's Own Yeomanry 1979–81, ADC (TAVR) to HM The Queen 1982–86; chm Thirsk Race Course Co Ltd 1995–2007, chm and md Hutton Wandesley Farms Co and others; RASE rep CLBA Cncl 1999–2002; memb: Cncl RASE (hon show dir 1992–96, pres 1997, chm Cncl 1998–2002), N Yorks CLBA 1978–2005, Cncl Yorkshire Agric Soc 1970–99 (pres 1989), Bd Yorkshire Museum of Farming 1979–2001; vice-pres Northern Assoc of Building Socs 1994–2001; Col Cmdt Yeomanry 1994–99, chm Yorks and Humberside Reserve Forces Assoc 1997–2003, Hon Col The Queen's Own Yeo 1998–2003; chm: Royal Armouries Devpt Tst (Leeds) 1995–99, N Yorks Scouts; vice-chm (Army) Cncl RFCAs 2001–04; county pres: Army Benevolent Fund, SSAFA Forces Help; chm and tstee of various charitable fndns; High Sheriff N Yorks 1988, Vice Lord-Lt N Yorks 1999–; FRAgS 1998; *Clubs* Boodle's, Pratt's; *Style—* Col E C York, TD, DL; ✉ Hutton Wandesley Hall, York YO26 7NA (tel home 01904 738240, office 01904 738755, fax 01904 738468, e-mail ecy@huttonwandesley.co.uk)

YORK, 97 Archbishop of 2005–; Most Rev and Rt Hon Dr John Tucker Mugabi Sentamu; PC (2005); patron of many livings, the Archdeaconries of York, Cleveland and the East Riding, and the Canonries in his Cathedral; the Archbishopric was founded AD 625, and the Province comprises fourteen Sees; s of late Rev John Walakira, and late Ruth Walakira, of Buganda, Uganda; *b* 10 June 1949, Kampala, Uganda; *Educ* Old Kampala Secdy Sch, Makerere Univ Kampala (LLB, pres Student Union, sec Christian Union), Law Devpt Centre (Dip Legal Practice), Selwyn Coll Cambridge (MA, PhD); *Career* Uganda 1971–74: barrister-at-law, legal asst to Chief Justice, Diocesan Registrar, Advocate High Court; undergrad Univ of Cambridge 1974–76 (postgrad 1976–79), ordained 1979, asst chaplain Selwyn Coll Cambridge 1979, asst curate St Andrew Ham Common and chaplain HM Remand Centre Latchmere House 1979–82, asst curate St Paul Herne Hill 1982–83, priest i/c Holy Trinity and parish priest St Matthias Tulse Hill 1983–84, vicar of Holy Trinity and St Matthias Tulse Hill 1984–96, priest i/c St Saviour Brixton, hon canon Southwark Cathedral 1993–96, bishop of Stepney 1996–2002, bishop of Birmingham 2002–05; memb: Convocation of Canterbury and Gen Synod C of E 1985–96, Bishop's Cncl and Southwark Diocesan Synod 1985–96, Southwark Diocesan Race Rels Cmmn 1986–89, Archbishop's Advsy Gp on Urban Priority Areas 1986–92, Young Offenders Ctee NACRO 1986–95, Standing Ctee Gen Synod C of E 1988–96 (chm Ctee for Minority Ethnic Anglican Concerns 1990–99), Health Advsy Ctee HM Prisons 1993–95; prolocutor Lower House of Convocation of Canterbury and an offr of the Gen Synod C of E 1994–96; advsr to the Home Office Inquiry into the murder of Stephen Lawrence 1997–99, chair Damilola Taylor Murder Review 2002–03; chair NHS Sickle Cell and Thalathemia Nat Screening Programme 2002–, govr Univ of Birmingham NHS Fndn Hosp 2004–, tstee John Smith Institute; memb House of Lords; chancellor York St John Univ; Midlander of the Year 2003, Cambridgeshire Top 10 Black and Asian Local and Historical Role Models Award 2006; Freeman City of London 2000; Hon Dr Open Univ, Hon DPhil Univ of Glos, Hon DD Univ of Birmingham, hon fell Selwyn Coll Cambridge, hon master bencher Gray's Inns of Ct; fell UC of Christ Church Canterbury, fell Queen Mary & Westfield Coll London; FRSA; *Style—* The Most Rev and Rt Hon the Lord Archbishop of York; ✉ Bishopthorpe Palace, Bishopthorpe, York YO23 2GE

YORK, Michael; OBE (1996); s of Joseph Gwynne Johnson, and Florence Edith May Chown; *b* 27 March 1942; *Educ* Hurstpierpoint Coll, Bromley GS, Univ Coll Oxford (BA); *m* 1968, Patricia Frances; *Career* actor; Chevalier de l'Ordre des Arts et des Lettres (France) 1995; *Theatre* Dundee Repertory Theatre 1964, Nat Theatre Co 1965; credits incl: Outcry (NY) 1973, Bent (NY) 1980, Cyrano de Bergerac (Santa Fe) 1981, Whisper in the Mind (Phoenix) 1991, The Crucible (NY) 1992, Someone to Watch Over Me (NY) 1993; *Television* Jesus of Nazareth 1976, A Man Called Intrepid 1978, For Those I Loved 1981, The Weather in the Streets 1983, The Master of Ballantrae 1983, Space 1984, The Far Country 1985, The Four Minute Mile 1988, The Heat of the Day 1988, Till We Meet Again 1989, The Night of the Fox 1990, Fall From Grace 1994, Not of This Earth 1995, Danielle Steel's The Ring 1996, True Women 1997, The Ripper 1997, A Knight in Camelot 1998, Perfect Little Angels 1998, The Haunting of Hell House 2000, The Lot 2001, Curb Your Enthusiasm 2003, La Femme Muskateer; *Films* Accident 1966, The Taming of the Shew 1967, Romeo and Juliet 1967, England Made Me 1971, Cabaret 1972, The Three Musketeers 1973, Murder on the Orient Express 1974, Conduct Unbecoming 1975, Logan's Run 1975, The Riddle of the Sands 1978, Success is the Best Revenge 1984, Dawn 1985, Vengence 1986, The Return of the Three Musketeers 1988, The Long Shadow 1992, Rochade 1992, Eline Vere 1992, Wide Sargasso Sea 1993, Discretion Assured 1993, The Shadow of a Kiss 1994, Gospa 1995, Goodbye America 1997, Austin Powers: International Man of Mystery 1997, One Hell of a Guy 1998, Wrongfully Accused 1998, The Omega Code 1999, Austin Powers: The Spy Who Shagged Me 1999, Borstal Boy 2000, Megiddo 2001, Austin Powers in Goldmember 2002, Moscow Heat 2004; *Books* Travelling Player (autobiography, 1991), The Magic Paw Paw (1994), A Shakespearean Actor Prepares (2000), Dispatches from Armageddon (2002); *Style—* Michael York, Esq, OBE

YORK, Susannah Yolande; da of late (William Peel) Simon Fletcher, and late Joan Nita Mary, *née* Bowring; *b* 9 January 1942; *Educ* Marr Coll Troon, East Haddon Hall; *m* 2 May 1960 (m dis 1980), Michael Barry Wells; 1 s (Orlando Wells b June 1973), 1 da

(Sasha Wells b May 1972); *Career* actress, writer, director; *Theatre* incl: Wings of a Dove, A Singular Man, Man and Superman, Private Lives, Hedda Gabler (London and New York); London and Paris performances: Peter Pan, Cinderella, The Singular Life of Albert Nobbs, Penthesilea, Fatal Attraction, The Women, The Apple Cart, Agnes of God, The Human Voice, Multiple Choice, A Private Treason, Lyric for a Tango, The Glass Menagerie, A Streetcar Named Desire, Noonbreak, September Tide (Comedy Theatre) 1994, Independent State (Grace Theatre and Aust tour) 1995, The Merry Wives of Windsor (RSC) 1997, Hamlet 1998, Camino Real 1998, An Ideal Husband (Haymarket) 1998, Small Craft Warnings 1999, Amy's View 2001, The Loves of Shakespeare's Women 2001–, The Hollow Crown 2003, The Kindness of Strangers 2005; as dir: Revelations (Edinburgh Festival) 1991, The Eagle has Two Heads (Lilian Bayliss) 1994, First Years, Beginnings (Latchmere Theatre) 1995, Eugene Onegin (White Bear Theatre) 1999; *Television* incl: The Crucible, The Rebel and the Soldier, The First Gentleman, The Richest Man in the World, Fallen Angels, Second Chance, We'll Meet Again, The Other Side of Me, Star Quality, The Two Ronnies, Yellow Beard, A Christmas Carol, Bonnie Jean, Macho, Love Boat - USA, Return Journey, After the War, The Man from the Pru, The Haunting of the New, Devices and Desires, Boon, Trainer, St Patrick: The Irish Legend; *Film* incl: Tunes of Glory, Greengage Summer, Freud, Tom Jones, The Seventh Dawn, Act One Scene Nun, Sands of the Kalahari, Scruggs, Kaleidoscope, A Man for All Seasons, Sebastian, Duffy, Lock up your Daughters, The Killing of Sister George, Images (Best Actress Award at Cannes Film Festival), They Shoot Horses Don't They? (Bafta Award, Oscar Nomination), Country Dance, Happy Birthday Wanda June, Conduct Unbecoming, That Lucky Touch, Sky Riders, Eliza Fraser, Zee and Co, Silent Partner, The Shout, Memories, The Awakening, Gold, Jane Eyre, The Maids, Loophole, Superman I and II, Golden Gate Murders, Alice, Christmas Carol, Yellowbeard, Mio My Mio, Bluebeard, A Summer Story, Just ask for Diamond, Melancholia, Barbarblu Barbarblu, Little Women; *Books* In Search of Unicorns (2 edns, republished 1985), Larks Castle (1976, republished 1986), The Loves of Shakespeare's Women; translations from French: Claudel's Partage de Midi, Cocteau's La Voix Humaine, Guitry's Un Sujet de Roman; *Recreations* gardening, reading, writing, walking, travelling, films and theatre; *Style—* Ms Susannah York; ✉ c/o PFD, Drury House, 34–43 Russell Street, London WC2B 5HA (tel 020 7344 1000, fax 020 7379 6790)

YORK-JOHNSON, Michael; *see:* York, Michael

YORKE, John; s of Gerald Yorke (d 1981), and Angela, *née* Duncan (d 1986); *b* 12 October 1938, London; *Educ* Eton, Trinity Coll Cambridge (MA); *m* 1, 4 July 1967, Jean, *née* Reynolds (d 1987); 2 da (Anabel b 18 Dec 1971, Sara b 5 April 1974); m 2, 26 Sept 1992, Julia, *née* Allen; *Career* accountant Peat, Marwick, Mitchell & Co 1965–70 (articled clerk 1962–65); financial dir Mallett & Son (Antiques) Ltd 1970–98, financial dir Arthur Millner Ltd 1998–; non-exec dir Alginate Industries Ltd 1972–80, tstee: Forthampton Tst 1975–, Abbey Lawn Tst 1985–; High Sheriff Hereford and Worcs 2007–08; FCA 1965; *Recreations* shoooting, travel; *Clubs* Garrick; *Style—* John Yorke, Esq; ✉ Forthampton Court, Gloucester GL19 4RD (tel 01684 292440, fax 01684 291365, e-mail yorke@forthampton.demon.co.uk)

YOSHIDA, Miyako; da of Eiji Yoshida, of Tokyo, and Etsuko, *née* Fukuda; *Career* ballet dancer; with Sadler's Wells Royal Ballet (now Birmingham Royal Ballet) 1984–95, princ Royal Ballet 1995–; UNESCO Artist for Peace 2004; *Performances* incl leading roles in: Swan Lake, Sleeping Beauty, The Nutcracker, Giselle, Elite Syncopations, La Fille Mal Gardée, The Dream, Don Quixote, Paquita, Allegri Diversi, Theme and Variations, Concerto Barrocco, Les Sylphides, Divertimento No 15, Dance Concertantes, Symphony in 3 Movements, Choreartium, Five Tangos, Pavane pas de deux, Sylvia; *Awards* Prix de Lausanne 1983, Global Award 1989, Dance and Dancer magazine Dancer of the Year 1991, E Nakagawa Award 1995, A Tachibana Award 1996 and 2003, C Hattori Award 1998, Award from Minister of Educn 2001; *Recreations* reading, watching films; *Style—* Miss Miyako Yoshida; ✉ The Royal Ballet, Covent Garden, London WC2E 9DD (tel 020 7240 1200)

YOUNG, Andrew George; *b* 15 June 1949; *Career* sr consIt Demography Social Security and Pensions Policy Govt Actuary's Dept; *Style—* Andrew Young, Esq; ✉ 4 Ingleside Grove, London SE3 7PH (tel 020 8858 3044); Government Actuary's Department, Finlaison House, 15–17 Furnival Street, London EC4A 1AB (tel 020 7211 2681, fax 020 7211 2640, e-mail andrew.young@gad.gov.uk)

YOUNG, Prof Andrew William; s of Alexander Young, of Heckington, Lincs, and Winnifred Doris, *née* Allen (d 2001); *b* 14 March 1950; *Educ* Bedford Coll London (BSc), Univ of Warwick (PhD), Univ of London (DSc); *m* 1977, Mavis Langham; 2 da (Alexandra b 1 Feb 1989, Josephine b 20 Nov 1994), 1 step s (Jeremy Langham b 25 March 1968); *Career* lectr Univ of Aberdeen 1974–76, lectr then reader Lancaster Univ 1976–89, prof of psychology Univ of Durham 1989–93, special appt MRC Scientific Staff Applied Psychology Unit Univ of Cambridge 1993–97, prof of neuropsychology Univ of York 1997–; pres Psychology Section BAAS 1997–98, chair Br Neuropsychological Soc 1998–2000, pres Experimental Psychology Soc 2004–05; co-organiser The Science of the Face exhbn Scottish Nat Portrait Gallery 1998 (exhbn also taken to Cardiff, Belfast and Newcastle upon Tyne); Br Psychological Soc: Cognitive Psychology Award 1994 (jtly), President's Award 1995, Book Award 2001 (jtly); Dr (hc) Univ of Liège 2000; CPsychol 1988, FBPsS 1988 (hon fell 2005), FBA 2001, AcSS 2004; *Publications* In the Eye of the Beholder: the Science of Face Perception (with Vicki Bruce , *qv*, 1998); also co-author of numerous articles and papers in learned jls; *Style—* Prof A W Young; ✉ Department of Psychology, University of York, Heslington, York YO10 5DD (tel 01904 434370, e-mail awy1@york.ac.uk)

YOUNG, Anthony Elliott (Tony); s of Prof Leslie Young, of Esher, Surrey, and Ruth, *née* Elliott; *b* 20 December 1943; *Educ* Epsom Coll, St John's Coll Cambridge (MA, MB, MChir), St Thomas' Hosp Med Sch; *m* 6 July 1968, Dr Gwyneth Vivien Wright, da of Prof Eldred Walls, of Edinburgh; 3 s (Adam Elliott b 1974, Oliver Elliott b 1975, Toby Elliott b 1977); *Career* conslt surgn St Thomas' Hosp 1981–2006; med dir Guy's and St Thomas' NHS Tst 1993–97, conslt surgn King Edward VII Hosp London 1997–; pres Br Assoc of Endocrine Surgns 2003–05; memb BMA 1968, FRSM 1970, FRCS 1971; *Books* Vascular Malformations (1988), The Medical Manager (2003), Companion in Surgical Studies (2005); *Recreations* fishing, painting, reading; *Style—* Anthony Young, Esq; ✉ 63 Lee Road, Blackheath, London SE3 9EN (tel 020 8852 1921); King Edward VII's Hospital, Beaumont Street, London W1N 2AA (tel 020 7580 3612, fax 020 8244 5467)

YOUNG, Prof Archie; s of Archibald Young, TD (d 1996), of Glasgow, and Mary Downie, *née* Fleming (d 1995); *b* 19 September 1946; *Educ* Glasgow HS, Univ of Glasgow (BSc, MB ChB, MD); *m* 24 Dec 1973 (m dis 1995), Sandra, da of Archibald Clark (d 1969), of Glasgow; 1 da (Sula b 1979), 1 s (Archie b 1980); *Career* clinical lectr Univ of Oxford 1978–85, prof of geriatric med Royal Free Hosp Med Sch London 1988–98 (conslt physician 1985–88), prof of geriatric med Univ of Edinburgh 1998–; Prince Philip Medal Inst of Sports Med 1995; Scottish swimming int 1965–70 (British 1970), Scottish water polo int 1968; memb: Medical Research Soc, Euro Soc for Clinical Investigation, American Coll of Sports Medicine; memb Incorporation of Tailors Glasgow; FRCPG 1985, FRCP 1989, FRCPEd 1999; *Publications* numerous publications on the effects of use, disuse, ageing and disease on human muscle and exercise physiology; *Recreations* physical; *Clubs* Junior Mountaineering Club of Scotland; *Style—* Prof Archie Young; ✉ Geriatric Medicine, University of Edinburgh, Room SU 219, The Chancellor's Building, 49 Little France Court, Edinburgh EH16 4SB (tel 0131 242 6371)

YOUNG, Prof Daniel Greer; s of Gabriel Young, and Julia, *née* McNair; *b* 22 November 1932; *Educ* Wishaw HS, Univ of Glasgow; *m* 2 Aug 1957, Agnes Gilchrist (Nan), da of Joseph Donald; 1 da (Rhoda Agnes (Mrs Abel) b 1958), 1 s (Kenneth Donald b 1962); *Career* Nat Serv 1957, special short serv cmmn to Ghana Govt 1959; hon conslt paediatric surgn: The Hosp for Sick Children Gt Ormond St London (formerly sr registrar and resident asst surgn), Queen Elizabeth Hosp London; sr lectr in paediatric surgery Inst of Child Health Univ of London, hon conslt paediatric surgn Greater Glasgow Health Bd, prof of paediatric surgery Univ of Glasgow 1992–97 (formerly reader), hon sr research fell Univ of Glagow 1998–; ex chm Intercollegiate Bd in Paediatric Surgery, memb Cncl RCPS Glasgow, ex pres Royal Medico-Chirurgical Soc of Glasgow, ed for the Br Isles - Journal of Paediatric Surgery UK, ex chm W of Scotland Surgical Assoc, past pres Br Assoc of Paediatric Surgns (hon memb), memb Exec Ctee World Fedn of Paediatric Surgical Assocs; hon memb: Hungarian Assoc of Paediatric Surgns, South African Assoc of Paediatric Surgns, American Paediatric Surgical Assoc, Polish Assoc of Paediatric Sungeons, Egyptian Assoc of Paediatric Surgns, Soc for Research into Hydrociphalus and Spina Bifida; hon pres Scottish Spina Bifida Assoc; Denis Browne Gold Medal 1999; FRCSEd, FRCSGlas; *Books* Baby Surgery (with B F Weller, 1971), Baby Surgery (with E J Martin, 2 edn, 1979), Children's Medicine and Surgery (jtly, 1995); *Recreations* curling, gardening, fishing; *Style—* Prof Daniel Young; ✉ 49 Sherbrooke Avenue, Glasgow G41 4SE (tel 0141 427 3470); Royal Hospital for Sick Children, Yorkhill, Glasgow G3 8SJ (tel 0141 201 0000, fax 0141 201 0858, e-mail dgylx@clinmed.gla.ac.uk)

YOUNG, David; s of Derek Young, of Solihull, and Audrey, *née* Darby; *b* 11 October 1959, Solihull, W Midlands; *Educ* Solihull Sch, UCL (LLB), Coll of Law London; *partner* Janine Taylor; 3 da (Alison Claire b 1 Jan 1990, Stephanie Helen b 21 May 1994, Taryn Rhiannon Isabella b 28 Feb 2004), 1 s (Samuel Ethan b 8 Oct 1999); *Career* slr Eversheds 1982–; memb Law Soc 1984; *Style—* David Young, Esq; ✉ Eversheds LLP, 115 Colmore Row, Birmingham B3 3AL (tel 0845 497 9797, fax 0121 232 1900, e-mail davidyoung@eversheds.com)

YOUNG, David Edward Michael; QC (1980); s of George Henry Edward Young, and Audrey, *née* Seymour; *b* 30 September 1940; *Educ* Monkton Combe Sch, Univ of Oxford (MA); *m* 1967, Anne, da of John Henry de Bromhead, of Ireland; 2 da (Yolanda b 1970, Francesca b 1972); *Career* called to the Bar Lincoln's Inn 1966 (bencher 1989); dep judge of the High Court (Chancery Div) 1993–2006; chm Plant Varieties and Seeds Tbnl 1987–; *Books* Passing Off (1994); *Recreations* tennis, skiing, walking, country pursuits; *Style—* David Young, Esq, QC; ✉ Three New Square, Lincoln's Inn, London WC2A 3RS (tel 020 7405 1111, fax 020 7405 7800, e-mail clerks@3newsquare.co.uk)

YOUNG, David Ernest; CBE (2007); s of Harold Ernest Young (d 1971), *née* Turnbull; *b* 8 March 1942; *Educ* King Edward VII Sch Sheffield, CCC Oxford (BA); *m* 1, 8 Feb 1964 (m dis), Norma, da of Alwyn Robinson (d 1979); 2 da (Wendy b 1965, Michele b 1968); m 2, 4 April 1998, Maggie, *née* Pilleau; *Career* asst princ Air Miny 1963, private sec to CAS 1968–70, private sec to Min of State for Def 1973–75, asst sec Central Policy Review Staff Cabinet Office 1975–77; John Lewis Partnership: joined 1982, md Peter Jones Sloane Square 1984–86, fin dir 1987, dep chm 1993–2002; ind memb Steering Bd of Companies House 1988–93, memb Hansard Soc Cmmn on Regulation of Privatised Utilities 1996; chm HEFCE 2001–07; memb Cncl Open Univ 1996–2001; tstee RAF Museum 1999–2005, hon treas Soil Assoc 2004–, chm Textile Industry Children's Tst 2005–; Hon DLitt Univ of Sheffield 2005; *Recreations* walking, opera, theatre; *Style—* David Young, Esq, CBE

YOUNG, David John; s of John Anthony Young (d 2001), and Marjorie Ellen Young (d 1996); *b* 22 January 1951; *Educ* Merchant Taylors', Watford Coll (Dip Printing Mgmnt); *m* 1, 1978, Jennifer, *née* Hicks; 1 s (William Francis b 1 Aug 1981); m 2, 1996, Elizabeth, *née* Noble; 2 da (Tallulah Ellen b 9 Nov 1997, Ottilie Florence b 16 May 1999); *Career* md Thorsons Publishing Gp 1980–89 (prodn mangr 1970–80), divnl md HarperCollins Publishers 1989–96, md Little, Brown & Co (UK) 1996–2000, chief exec Time Warner Book Gp UK 2000–05, chm and ceo Hachette Book Gp USA 2006–; chm: Book Mktg Cncl 1986–88, Book Industry Supply Chain Gp 2003, World Book Day 2004; memb: Cncl Publishers' Assoc 1986–90 and 2002–05, Bd Assoc of American Publishers 2005–, Bd Book Industry Communication; *Recreations* wine, reading, gardening; *Clubs* Garrick, Groucho; *Style—* David Young; ✉ Hachette Book Group USA, 237 Park Avenue, New York, NY 10017, USA (tel 00 1 212 364 1215, e-mail david.young@hbgusa.com)

YOUNG, David Tyrrell; s of Tyrrell Francis Young (d 1998), and Patricia Morrison, *née* Spicer (d 1998); *b* 6 January 1938; *Educ* Charterhouse; *m* 11 Sept 1965, Madeline Helen Celia, da of Anthony Burton Capel Philips (d 1983), of Tean, Stoke-on-Trent; 3 da (Melanie Rosamond b 1969, Annabel Katharine b 1971, Corinna Lucy b 1974); *Career* TA 1 Regt HAC 1955–67, ret Capt 1967; trainee CA Gérard Van De Linde & Son 1955–60, audit mangr James Edwards Dangerfield & Co 1961–65; Spicer & Oppenheim (formerly Spicer & Pegler): audit mangr 1965–68, ptnr 1968–82, managing ptnr 1982–88, sr ptnr and int chm 1988–90; dep chm Touche Ross & Co 1990–93; chm: N Herts NHS Tst 1994–2000, C&G 1999–2006, Capita Syndicate Mgmnt 2001–; dir: Groupama Insurance 1993–2000, Asprey & Garrard 1993–2000, Wates City of London Properties plc 1994–2001, Nomura Bank International plc 1996–, Berks Hathaway International Insurance Ltd 1997–; memb Cncl ICAEW 1979–82; memb HAC; Freeman City of London, memb Ct Worshipful Co of Fishmongers (Prime Warden 1993–94), memb Ct of Assts Worshipful Co of CAs (Master 1999–2000); FCA, FRSA, Hon FCGI; *Recreations* golf; *Clubs* Royal St George's Golf, Royal Worlington Golf, City of London; *Style—* David T Young, Esq; ✉ Overhall, Ashdon, Saffron Walden, Essex CB10 2JH (tel 01799 584556, fax 01799 584692, e-mail overhall@waitrose.com)

YOUNG, Douglas John (Doug); s of John Edward Young, of Corby, Northants, and Barbara Maxwell, *née* Haldane; *b* 31 December 1967, Corby, Northants; *Educ* Laxton Sch Oundle, Pembroke Coll Cambridge (MA); *Career* BBC Books 1991–96, Headline Publishing 1996–2001, Transworld Publishing 2001–, Channel 4 Books 2004–; *Recreations* scuba diving, snowboarding, eating; *Clubs* Century; *Style—* Doug Young, Esq; ✉ Channel 4 Books, Transworld Publishing, 61–63 Uxbridge Road, London W5 5SA (tel 020 8231 6649, fax 020 8576 2659, e-mail d.young@transworld-publishers.co.uk)

YOUNG, Prof Douglas Wilson; s of John Robert Young (d 1992), and Christina, *née* Martin; *b* 15 January 1939; *Educ* Eastwood Sch Glasgow, Univ of Glasgow (BSc, PhD, Carnegie scholar); *m* 1971, Ruth Lilian, da of Brian Welch; 1 da (Janet Mary b 1973), 1 s (Malcolm John b 1976); *Career* research fell Harvard Univ 1963–65; Univ of Sussex: lectr in chemistry 1965–84, reader 1984–88, prof of chemistry 1988–2005 (emeritus 2005–); dir Sussex Centre for Biomolecular Design and Drug Devpt 1996–2005; visiting scholar Uppsala Univ 1985, visiting prof Univ of Nantes 1989; Royal Soc of Chemistry: chm Bio-organic Gp 1991–94, Tilden Lectr and Medal 1993–94, vice-pres Perkin Div 1995–97, Interdisciplinary Award 2003; author of over 170 books and articles; FRSC, FRSE 1996; *Recreations* listening to music, DIY, watching cricket; *Style—* Prof Douglas Young, FRSE; ✉ Department of Chemistry, University of Sussex, Falmer, Brighton, East Sussex BN1 9QJ (tel 01273 678327, fax 01273 677196, e-mail d.w.young@sussex.ac.uk)

YOUNG, Elizabeth Jane; da of Philip John Grattidge (decd), of Wareham, Dorset, and Marion Elizabeth, *née* Dixon; *b* 9 January 1957; *Educ* Bedford HS for Girls, Sidney Sussex Coll Cambridge (MA); *m* 11 April 1981, John Todd Young, *qv*, s of late Ian Taylor Young, of Rugby, Warks; *Career* slr; Clifford Chance LLP (formerly Coward Chance): articled clerk 1980–82, admitted slr 1982, ptnr 1988–2007, ret; *Recreations* mountaineering, windsurfing; *Clubs* Cannons; *Style—* Mrs Elizabeth Young; ✉ tel 020 7588 1859

YOUNG, Prof the Rev Frances Margaret; OBE (1998); da of Alfred Stanley Worrall, CBE, of Belfast, and Mary Frances, *née* Marshall; *b* 25 November 1939; *Educ* Bedford Coll London (BA), Girton Coll Cambridge (MA, PhD); *m* 20 June 1964, Dr Robert Charles Young, s of Lt Charles William Young (d 1978); 3 s (Arthur Thomas b 1967, Edward Stanley b 1969, William Francis b 1974); *Career* ordained Methodist minister 1984; Univ of Birmingham: temporary lectr in theol 1971–73, lectr in New Testament studies 1973–82, sr lectr 1982–86, Edward Cadbury prof of theology 1986–2005 (now emeritus prof), dean Faculty of Arts 1995–97, pro-vice-chllr 1997–2002; Hon DD Univ of Aberdeen 1994; FBA 2004; *Books* Sacrifice and the Death of Christ (1975), Can These Dry Bones Live? (1982), From Nicaea to Chalcedon (1983), Face to Face (1985, revised edn 1990), Focus on God (with Kenneth Wilson, 1986), Meaning and Truth in 2 Corinthians (with David Ford, 1987), The Art of Performance (1990), The Making of the Creeds (1991), Biblical Exegesis and the Formation of Christian Culture (1997), The Cambridge History of Early Christian Literature (ed, 2004), The Cambridge History of Christianity: Origins to Constantine (ed, 2006); *Recreations* music, walking, cycling, camping, poetry; *Style*— Prof the Rev Frances Young, OBE; ✉ 142 Selly Park Road, Birmingham B29 7LH (tel 0121 472 4841)

YOUNG, (Russell) Francis; s of Canon (Cecil) Edwyn Young, CVO (Queen's chaplain, d 1988), of Hove, E Sussex, and Beatrice Mary, *née* Rees (d 2001); *b* 27 February 1953; *Educ* Radley, Blackpool Coll of Hotel Mgmnt (HND Catering and Hotel Admin); *m* 9 May 1981, Anne, da of Charles Edward Williams; 1 s (Edward Francis Charles b 30 May 1982), 1 da (Alexandra Anne Mary b 1 May 1985); *Career* hotelier; asst food and beverage mangr Grosvenor Hotel Chester 1975–76 (trainee mangr 1974–75), mangr HM King Hussein of Jordan's summer palace Aqaba Jordan 1975–78, food and beverage mangr Sandy Lane Hotel St James Barbados 1978–80; Marriott Corp 1980–84: dir of restaurant Hunt Valley Marriott Baltimore Maryland 1980–81, opened as food and beverage dir Longwharf Marriott Boston Massachusetts 1981–82 then London Marriott 1982–84; gen mangr Oakley Court Hotel Windsor 1985–86, gp ops dir Select Country Hotels 1986–87; restored semi-derelict vicarage and opened as prop The Pear Tree at Purton 1987– (National Westminster Bank Award for Business Devpt 1992 and RAC Blue Ribbon); chm Bd of Govrs Bradon Forest Sch 1993–2002; wine columnist The Swindon Evening Advertiser; clerk to the Master Innholders 2003–06; Freeman City of London, Liveryman Worshipful Company of Distillers; MI 1994; FIH; *Recreations* cricket, family, walking; *Clubs* Purton Cricket; *Style*— Francis Young, Esq; ✉ The Pear Tree at Purton, Church End, Purton, Swindon, Wiltshire SN5 4ED (tel 01793 772100, fax 01793 772369, e-mail francis@peartreepurton.co.uk)

YOUNG, Rt Hon Sir George Samuel Knatchbull; 6 Bt (UK 1813), of Formosa Place, Berks; PC (1993); MP; s of Sir George Young, 5 Bt, CMG (d 1960), by his w Elisabeth (herself er da of Sir Hugh Knatchbull-Hugessen, KCMG, who was in turn n of 1 Baron Brabourne); *b* 16 July 1941; *Educ* Eton, ChCh Oxford; *m* 1964, Aurelia, da of Oscar Nemon, and Mrs Nemon-Stuart, of Boars Hill, Oxford; 2 s, 2 da; *Heir* s, George Young; *Career* economist NEDO 1966–67, Kobler res fell Univ of Surrey 1967–69, memb Lambeth BC 1968–71, econ advsr Post Office Corp 1969–74, memb GLC (Ealing) 1970–73; MP (Cons): Ealing Acton Feb 1974–97, Hampshire NW 1997–; oppn whip 1976–79, under sec of state DHSS 1979–81, under sec of state DOE 1981–86, comptroller of HM Household (sr Govt whip) 1990, min of state for the environment 1990–92, min for housing and inner cities 1992–94, fin sec to the Treasy 1994–95, sec of state for tport 1995–97, shadow defence sec 1997–98, shadow ldr House of Commons 1998–2000; chm Standards and Privileges Select Ctee 2001–; tstee Guinness Tst 1986–90; *Books* Tourism, Blessing or Blight?; *Style*— The Rt Hon Sir George Young, Bt, MP; ✉ House of Commons, London SW1A 0AA (tel 020 7219 6665)

YOUNG, Prof Ian Robert; OBE (1986); s of John Stirling Young (d 1971), and Ruth Muir, *née* Whipple (d 1975); *b* 11 January 1932; *Educ* Sedbergh, Univ of Aberdeen (BSc, PhD); *m* 1956, Sylvia Marianne Whewell, da of Frederick George Ralph; 2 s (Graham John b 1958, Neil George b 1960), 1 da (Fiona Marianne b 1966); *Career* Hilger & Watts Ltd 1955–59, Evershed & Vignoles Ltd 1959–67, Evershed Power Optics Ltd 1967–76, EMI Central Research Laboratory 1976–81, sr research fell GEC Hirst Research Centre, vice-pres Res Picker International Inc Cleveland OH 1981–, visiting prof Imperial Coll Sch of Med at Hammersmith Hosp (Royal Postgrad Med Sch until merger 1997) 1983–2001, sr research fell Dept of Electrical and Electronic Engrg Imperial Coll 2004–; Duddell Medal Inst of Physics 1983, Gold Medal Soc of Magnetic Resonance in Med 1988, Silver Medal Soc of Magnetic Resonance 1994, Whittle Medal Royal Acad of Engrg 2004; Hon DSc Univ of Aberdeen 1992; pres Soc of Magnetic Resonance in Med 1991–92, hon memb Soc of Magnetic Resonance Imaging 1989; FIEE 1967, FREng 1988, FRS 1989, hon FRCR 1990, FInstP 1991; *Recreations* ornithology, golf, walking; *Style*— Prof Ian Young, OBE, FRS, FREng; ✉ High Kingsbury, Kingsbury Street, Marlborough, Wiltshire SN8 1HZ (tel 01672 516126)

YOUNG, James Drummond (Jim); s of James Henry Young, of Glasgow, and Mary, *née* Moore (d 1988); *b* 26 February 1950; *Educ* Hutchesons' GS, Univ of Glasgow (LLB); *m* 26 Sept 1973, Gillian Anne, da of William Boyd, MBE; 1 da (Jennifer Anne b 9 Dec 1976), 1 s (Graham James b 7 Jan 1979); *Career* trainee McGrigor Donald & Co 1971–73, slr West Lothian DC 1975–77; ptnr: Moncrieff Warren Paterson 1979–85, McGrigor Donald 1985–; pt/t chm Employment Tribunals Scotland 2003–; memb Law Soc of Scot 1975 (memb Employment Ctee); *Recreations* golf, cricket, contemporary art; *Clubs* Clydesdale Cricket, Merchants of Edinburgh Golf, Glasgow Art; *Style*— Jim Young, Esq; ✉ 5 Braid Hills Avenue, Edinburgh (tel 0131 447 1951); McGrigors, Princes Exchange, 1 Earl Grey Street, Edinburgh EH3 9AQ (tel 0131 777 7000, fax 0131 777 7003, e-mail jim.young@mcgrigors.com)

YOUNG, Sir Jimmy Leslie Ronald; kt (2002), CBE (1993, OBE 1979); s of Frederick George Young (d 1989), and Gertrude Jane *née* Woolford (d 1972); *b* 21 September 1921; *Educ* East Dean GS Cinderford Glos; *m* 1, 1946 (m dis), Wendy Wilkinson; 1 da; m 2, 1950 (m dis), Sally Douglas; m 3, 1996, Alicia Plastow; *Career* broadcaster; WWII RAF, Sgt (physical trg instr); first BBC radio broadcast Songs at Piano 1949, pianist/singer/bandleader 1950–51, first theatre appearance Empire Theatre Croydon 1952 (numerous subsequent appearances); hon memb Cncl NSPCC; Freeman City of London 1969; *Radio* BBC Radio series 1953–67 incl: Housewives Choice, The Night is Young, 12 O' Clock Spin, Younger Than Springtime, Saturday Special, Keep Young, Through Till Two; presenter: Radio Luxembourg programmes 1960–68, Jimmy Young Programme BBC Radio Two 1973–2002 (Radio One 1967–73); *Television* incl: Pocket Edition (BBC) 1955, Jimmy Young Asks (BBC) 1972, Whose Baby (ITV) 1973, Jim's World (ITV) 1974, The Jimmy Young Television Programme (ITV) 1984–87, host of first Br Telethon (Thames) 1980; broadcasts live from various countries; *Recordings* Too Young 1951, Unchained Melody (number one hit) 1955, The Man from Laramie (number one hit) 1955, Chain Gang 1956, More 1956, Miss You 1963; first Br singer to have two consecutive number one hit records; *Awards* Radio Personality of the Year Variety Club of GB 1968, HM The Queen's Silver Jubilee medal 1977, Radio Industries Club Award for Programme of the Year 1979, Sony Award for Broadcaster of the Year 1985, Daily Mail/BBC Nat Radio Award for Best Current Affrs Programme 1988, Sony Roll of Honour Award 1988, TRIC Award for Best Radio Programme of the Year 1989, Broadcasting Press Guild Award for Radio Broadcaster of the Year 1994, Sony Gold Award for Men Matters - Service to the Community 1995, Sony Radio Awards Gold Award 1997; *Books* Jimmy Young Cookbooks (1968, 1969, 1970, 1972), JY (autobiography, 1973), Jimmy Young (autobiography, 1982), Forever Young (autobiography, 2003); *Style*— Sir Jimmy Young, CBE; ✉ PO Box 39715, London W4 3YF

YOUNG, John; *Educ* Architectural Assoc; *Career* architect; Team 4 1966–67, assoc ptnr Richard & Su Rogers 1967–71, assoc ptnr Piano & Rogers 1971–77, dir Richard Rogers Partnership 1977–; *Projects* incl: Lloyd's Building London, Channel 4 Headquarters London; has lectured in Sweden, Norway, Germany, Holland, Ireland and the UK; assessor Bldg Innovation Award 1984 and 1986, presenter Building for Change (BBC 2, Arena), FRSPB; *Awards* RIBA National Award (for The Deckhouse, Thames Reach) 1991; *Publications* Designing with GRC; *Style*— John Young, Esq; ✉ Richard Rogers Partnership, Thames Wharf, Rainville Road, London W6 9HA

YOUNG, Prof John Braithwaite; s of Charles Braithwaite Young, and Elizabeth Eva, *née* Wilson; *Educ* Chesham HS, Middx Hosp Med Sch (MB BS), Open Univ (MSc, MBA); *Career* Bradford Hosps Tst: conslt geriatrician 1986–, clinical dir 1991–95; prof of elderly care medicine Univ of Leeds 2005–; memb R&D Ctee Stroke Assoc 1995–98, specialist med advsr Dept of Health 2001–; involved in clinical research in stroke and community services for older people; Freeman scholarship in obstetrics and gynaecology 1977, Geriatric Med Insight Award 1989; FRCP 1994 (MRCP 1980); *Publications* author of 12 book chapters and over 100 articles in peer-reviewed jls; *Recreations* fell racing, endurance running, DIY, fly fishing; *Clubs* Bingley Harriers & Athletic; *Style*— Prof John Young; ✉ Department of Elderly Care, St Luke's Hospital, Bradford, West Yorkshire BD5 0NA (tel 01274 365311, e-mail john.young@bradfordhospital.nhs.uk)

YOUNG, John Henderson; OBE (1980), JP (1971), DL (Glasgow 1981); s of William Williamson Young (d 1961), and Jeannie, *née* Henderson (d 1990); *m* 1956, Doris, *née* Paterson (d 2001); 1 s; *Career* served RAF 1949–51, shipping mangr/dep contracts mangr Kevin Diesels Ltd, export admin mangr Teachers Whisky 1977–89, chm Allied Lyons Shipping/Marine Insurance Ctee, PR conslt Proscot Ltd 1989–92; Glasgow City Cncl: memb 1964–99, bailie 1968–71, 1977–80, 1984–88 and 1988–92, leader 1977–79, oppn leader (3 times); contested: Rutherglen 1966, Cathcart 1992, Eastwood 1997; MSP (Cons) W Scotland 1999–2003; chm: Assoc Scottish Cons Cncllrs 1981–84, Assoc of Former MSPs 2003–; Scottish Tory Tport Spokesman; police judge 1970–72; vice-chm Glasgow Airport Ctee 1968–71; memb Strathclyde Passenger Tport Authy 1995–99; memb Scottish Parly Corporate Body 1999–2003, dep convenor Nat Galleries Bills Ctee 2003; life memb Cathcart Cons Assoc 1999, memb Cwlth Parly Assoc visit to Quebec 2002; vice-chm Scottish/Pakistani Assoc 1981–84, sec Scottish/South African Soc 1986–88, govr Hutcheson's Educnl Tst 1991–97, life memb Merchants House of Glasgow 1981; FCMI (FIMgt 2001, MIMgt 1978); RAFA; *Recreations* meeting people, writing, reading, animal welfare, history; *Style*— John Young, Esq, OBE

YOUNG, Sir John Kenyon Roe; 6 Bt (UK 1821), of Bailieborough Castle, Co Cavan; s of Sir John William Roe Young, 5 Bt (d 1981), by his 1 w, Joan Minnie Agnes, *née* Aldous (d 1958); *b* 23 April 1947; *Educ* Hurn Ct Sch Christchurch, Napier Coll; *m* 1977, Frances Elise, only da of W R Thompson; 1 s (Richard Christopher Roe, b 14 July 1983), 1 da (Tamara Elizabeth Eve b 9 Nov 1986); *Heir* s, Richard Young; *Career* former hydrographic surveyor; purchasing mangr; *Recreations* golf; *Style*— Sir John Young, Bt

YOUNG, John Robert Chester; CBE (1992); s of Robert Nisbet Young (d 1956), and Edith Mary, *née* Roberts (d 1981); bro of Louise Botting, CBE, *qv*; *b* 6 September 1937; *Educ* Bishop Vesey's GS, St Edmund Hall Oxford (MA); *m* 1963, Pauline Joyce; 1 s (and 1 s decd); *Career* ptnr Simon & Coates stockbrokers 1965–82; Stock Exchange: memb 1965–82, memb Cncl 1978–82, dir of policy and planning 1982–87; vice-chm Exec Bd Int Stock Exchange 1987–90; chief exec: Securities Assoc 1987–91, SFA 1991–93, SIB 1993–95 (non-exec dir 1996–97); memb Ethics Ctee Securities Inst 1996– (hon fell 2003); non-exec dir: East Surrey NHS Tst 1992–96, Elderstreet Millennium Venture Capital Trust 1996–, Darby Group plc 1996–98; dep chm Lloyd's Cncl and chm Lloyd's Regulatory Bd 1997–2002 (nominated memb Cncl and Regulatory Bd 1996–2002), public interest dir The Financial Services Compensation Scheme 2000–03, lay memb Legal Services Consultative Panel 2004–; advsr Royal Sch for the Blind (Seeability) 1997–2001; England and British Lions rugby union player 1958–61; *Recreations* rugby, cooking, grandchildren; *Clubs* Harlequins, Vincent's (Oxford), Achilles, City of London; *Style*— J R C Young, Esq, CBE

YOUNG, John Todd; s of Ian Taylor Young, of Rugby, Warks, and Flora Leggett, *née* Todd; *b* 14 January 1957; *Educ* Manchester Grammar, Sidney Sussex Coll Cambridge (MA); *m* 11 April 1981, Elizabeth Jane Young, *qv*, da of Philip John Grattidge, of Wareham, Dorset; *Career* Lovells: articled clerk 1979–81, slr 1981–, ptnr 1987–2004, sr ptnr 2004–, head financial instns gp; memb Worshipful Co of Slrs; memb Law Soc; *Recreations* mountaineering, windsurfing; *Clubs* Cannons; *Style*— John Young, Esq; ✉ Lovells, Atlantic House, Holborn Viaduct, London EC1A 2FG (tel 020 7296 2605, fax 020 7296 2001, e-mail john.young@lovells.com)

YOUNG, Jonathan Piers; s of Peter Alan George Young, of Chudleigh, Devon, and Mavis Irene Young; *b* 23 September 1959; *Educ* Blundell's, Univ of Leicester (BA); *m* 1993, Caroline Margaret, o da of John Jervis Murray Bankes, of Hinton Ampner, Hants; 1 da (Henrietta b 1994), 1 s (Fergus b 1996); *Career* ed: Shooting Times and Country magazine 1986–90, The Field 1991–; Freeman City of London, Liveryman Worshipful Co of Gunmakers; *Books* A Pattern of Wings (1989); *Recreations* shooting, fishing, falling off horses, cooking vast stews; *Clubs* Flyfishers', Tyburn Angling Soc; *Style*— Jonathan Young, Esq; ✉ The Field, King's Reach Tower, Stamford Street, London SE1 9LS (tel 020 7261 5198, fax 020 7261 5358)

YOUNG, Dr Kate; da of Rev W P Young (d 1969), and Ann Nielson Cumming (d 1941); *b* 13 June 1938; *Educ* Oxenford Castle Sch Midlothian, LSE (PhD); *ptnr* Charles Legg; 1 s (Justin Dubon b 1965), 1 step da (Jessica Legg 1969), 1 step s (Jake Legg b 1970); *Career* worked with How (of Edinburgh) and Doubleday (in NY), worked in FAO (in Rome), Inst of Devpt Studies (Univ of Sussex, promoted study of the impact of devpt on women, set up 13 week course for policy makers and activists on gender relationships and economic devpt and MA course Gender and Devpt) 1975–88, fndr and exec-dir Womankind (Worldwide) 1989–99; currently: dep chair Nat Assoc of Women's Orgns (NAWO), chair Empowering Widows in Devpt (EWD); *Books* ed: Of Marriage and the Market (1981), Women and Economic Development (1988), Serving Two Masters (1989), Planning Development With Women (1993); *Recreations* gardening, talking with friends over a good meal, walking; *Style*— Dr Kate Young; ✉ e-mail gardenky@blueyonder.co.uk

YOUNG, Prof Kenneth George (Ken); s of Henry George Young, of Christchurch, Hants, and Olive, *née* Heybeard; *b* 3 January 1943; *Educ* Brockenhurst GS, LSE (BSc, MSc, PhD); *Career* res offr LSE 1966–73, res fell Univ of Kent 1974–77, sr res fell Univ of Bristol 1977–79, sr fell Policy Studies Inst 1979–87, prof and dir Inst of Local Govt Studies 1987–89, head Sch of Public Policy Univ of Birmingham 1989–90, prof of politics and head Dept of Political Studies Queen Mary & Westfield Coll London 1990–92 (vice-princ 1992–98), dir ESRC UK Centre for Evidence Based Policy 2000–, prof of public policy KCL 2005–; FRHistS 1983, AMRaeS 1997, AcSS 2001; *Books* Local Politics and the Rise of Party (1975), Metropolitan London (1982), Managing the Post-Industrial City (1983), New Directions for County Government (1989), Local Government Since 1945 (1997); *Recreations* reading, travel; *Style*— Prof Ken Young; ✉ Department of War Studies, King's College London, Strand, London WC2R 2LS (tel 020 7848 2708, e-mail ken.young@kcl.ac.uk)

YOUNG, Kirsty; da of John Young, and Catherine Young; *b* 23 November 1968; *Educ* HS of Stirling; *m* Nick Jones, *qv*; 2 da (Freya, Iona); *Career* newsreader and news presenter BBC Radio Scotland 1990–93, news anchor (3 series of Kirsty) Scottish TV 1993–95; BBC TV: reporter Holiday (BBC 1) 1995–96, reporter Film 96 (BBC 1) 1996; news anchor: Channel 5 Broadcasting 1997–99, ITN 1999–2002, Five 2002–; presenter Desert Island Discs (BBC Radio 4) 2006–; supporter: Centrepoint, UNICEF; *Awards* Most Outstanding Newcomer Royal Variety Club Awards 1997, Newsreader of the Year TRIC Awards 1998; *Recreations* reading, cookery, laughter, films; *Style*— Miss Kirsty Young

YOUNG, Lionel Henry; s of Patrick Young (d 1996), and Marjorie Young; *b* 9 June 1955; *Educ* Gresham's, Univ of Durham (BSc); *m*; 2 c; *Career* head of corporate transaction servs Deloitte; memb: Worshipful Co of Fishmongers, Worshipful Co of Turners; MSI, FCA; *Recreations* walking, theatre, dining; *Style*— Lionel Young, Esq; ✉ Deloitte & Touche LLP, Athene Place, 66 Shoe Lane, London EC4A 3BQ

YOUNG, Mal; s of Charles Young, of Liverpool, and Maria, *née* Williams; *b* 26 January 1957; *Educ* Liverpool Sch of Art (Dip Art & Design); *Career* design mangr Littlewoods Orgn Ltd 1975–83; actor/singer 1983–84; Mersey TV Co 1984–96: design asst for Brookside (Channel 4), asst floor mangr and floor mangr 1986–91, prodr Brookside and dir Brookside Prodns 1991–95, series prodr Brookside 1995–96 (also devised and produced And the Beat Goes On (Channel 4); head of Drama Pearson TV 1996–97, head of Drama Series BBC TV 1997–2001 (responsible for EastEnders, Casualty, Holby City, Waking the Dead, Doctors, Murder in Mind, Judge John Deed, Down to Earth, Dalziel & Pascoe, Afternoon Plays, Grease Monkeys, Dr Who), controller Continuing Drama Series BBC 2001–04, dir of drama 19 Entertainment 2004–, writer and producer Born in the USA (Fox); Huw Weldon meml lectr RTS 1999; Special Award for Creative Contribution to TV British Soap Awards 2004; *Books* Sinbad's Scrapbook (1996); *Recreations* big music fan, musician, telly addict from an early age; *Style*— Mal Young, Esq; ✉ 19 Entertainment, 33 Ransomes Dock, 35–37 Parkgate Road, London SW11 4NP

YOUNG, Mark; s of Raymond Young, of Shalford, Surrey, and Joan, *née* Coatsworth; *b* 4 May 1961; *Educ* King's Sch Tynemouth, ChCh Oxford (MA); *m* Sara, da of Derek Cavalier; 2 da (Charlotte b 21 April 1989, Lucy b 23 June 1992); *Career* early career William Collins 1983–88, Coopers and Lybrand Media Gp 1988–91, head of business affrs ITN 1991–93, chief asst to dep DG BBC 1993–94; BBC Worldwide: fin and commercial dir 1994, md BBC World, md Europe, the Middle East, India and Africa (EMEIA) 1998–, ceo and pres BBC Worldwide Americas 2001–, md global mktg brand devpt (GMBD) 2002–; dir Indian Broadcasting Fndn; FCMA 2001; *Recreations* travel, gardening; *Style*— Mark Young, Esq; ✉ BBC Worldwide, Woodlands, 80 Wood Lane, London W12 0TT (tel 020 8433 3850, fax 020 8433 3848, e-mail mark.young@bbc.co.uk)

YOUNG, (Peter) Miles; s of Matthew Derek Young (d 1989), and Joyce Doreen, *née* Robson (d 1976); *b* 12 June 1954; *Educ* Bedford Sch, New Coll Oxford (MA); *Career* advertising; Lintas London 1976–79, Allen Brady & Marsh 1979–83, dir client service Ogilvy & Mather Ltd 1983–90; Ogilvy & Mather Direct Ltd: md 1990–92, dep chm and chief exec 1992–93, chm 1993–95; chm Ogilvy & Mather Asia/Pacific 1995–; ldr Westminster Cncl 1993–95 (memb 1986–87); chm: New Technology Ctee 1986–87, Environment Ctee 1987–90; Burdett-Coutts Fndn 1986, govr Harper Tst 1989–, vice-chm Conserve 1990, chm Bedford Prep Sch Ctee 1992–; MIPA 1990; *Recreations* gastronomy, walking, Balkan travel; *Clubs* Hong Kong, China (Hong Kong); *Style*— Miles Young, Esq; ✉ 1 Chatham Path, Hong Kong

YOUNG, Sir Nicholas Charles; kt (2000); s of Leslie Charles Young (d 1986), and Mary Margaret, *née* Rudman (d 1998); *b* 16 April 1952; *Educ* Wimbledon Coll, Univ of Birmingham (LLB), Coll of Law; *m* 1977, Helen Mary Ferrier, da of William Renwick Hamilton; 3 s (Edward b 1980, Alexander b 1982, Thomas b 1984); *Career* supervisor residential unit HM Prison Grendon Underwood 1974–75, slr Freshfields 1977–78 (articled clerk 1975–77), travelled Europe and Asia 1978–79, ptnr Turner Martin & Symes 1981–85 (joined as slr 1979), sec for devpt Sue Ryder Fndn 1985–90, dir of UK ops British Red Cross 1990–95 (Cabinet Office Top Mgmnt Prog 1993), chief exec Macmillan Cancer Relief 1995–2001, chief exec British Red Cross 2001–; tstee: Monte San Martino Tst (also Chm), Disasters Emergency Ctee, Humanitarian Forum Steering Ctee (also dep chm), Guidestar UK 2003–06; chm Judging Panel Asian Women of Achievement Awards; memb Law Soc 1975; *Recreations* amateur drama, cricket, literature, sailing, theatre and cinema; *Clubs* Stumblers' Association; *Style*— Sir Nicholas Young; ✉ British Red Cross, 44 Moorfields, London EC2Y 9AL (tel 020 7877 7000, fax 020 7562 2000)

YOUNG, Paul; OBE (2001); s of Thomas McFarland Young (d 1971), and Vera Irene, *née* Cantillon; *b* 7 October 1953, London; *Educ* UWE (MPhil); *m* 1973, Joan Pauline, *née* Clark; 2 s (Neil b 1979, David b 1981); *Career* joined London Fire Brigade 1973, divnl cdr Devon Fire and Rescue Serv 1985–90; chief fire officer: Somerset Fire and Rescue Serv 1992–97 (dep chief fire officer 1990–92), Devon Fire and Rescue Serv 1997–2007, Devon and Somerset Fire and Rescue Serv 2007–; memb Cncl Order of St John (Devon branch, county pres); FIFireE (pres 1998–99); *Style*— Paul Young, Esq, OBE; ✉ Devon and Somerset Fire and Rescue Service HQ, Clyst St George, Exeter, Devon EX3 0NW (tel 01392 872201, fax 01392 872311)

YOUNG, Prof Peter Colin; s of John William Young (d 1958), and Naomi Bessie, *née* Crane (d 1987); *b* 5 December 1939; *Educ* Loughborough Univ (BTech, MSc), Univ of Cambridge (MA, PhD); *m* 31 Aug 1963, Wendy Anne; 2 s (Timothy John b 2 Jan 1966, Jeremy Peter b 26 May 1973), 1 da (Melanie Clare b 28 Aug 1967); *Career* control and systems engr US Navy China Lake Calif 1967–69, sr industrial res fell ICI and Dept of Engrg Univ of Cambridge 1970–71, lectr in engrg and fell Clare Hall Cambridge 1971–75, professorial fell Aust Nat Univ 1975–81, prof of environmental sci Lancaster Univ 1981– (dir Centre for Res in Environmental Systems), adjunct prof of environmental systems Aust Nat Univ 1998–; MRAeS, MIEE, CEng, FIMA, FRSA; *Books* Modelling and Data Analysis in Biotechnology and Medical Engineering (ed with G C Vansteenkiste, 1983), Recursive Estimation and Time Series Analysis (1984), Identification and System Parameter Estimation vols 1 and 2 (ed with H A Barker, 1985), Concise Encyclopedia of Environmental Systems (ed and author, 1993); *Recreations* fell walking, drawing; *Style*— Prof Peter Young; ✉ Director, Centre for Research on Environmental Systems (CRES), Institute of Environmental and Natural Sciences, Lancaster University, Lancaster LA1 4YQ (tel 01524 65201, fax 01524 63806, telex 65111 LANCUL G, e-mail p.young@lancaster.ac.uk)

YOUNG, Richard Aretas Lewry; s of Dr Carmichael Aretas Young (d 1987), and Marie Ethel, *née* Lewry; *b* 17 January 1943; *Educ* Haileybury Hertford, Haileybury Melbourne Aust, St Catharine's Coll Cambridge (MA, MB BChir), St Mary's Hosp Med Sch London (LRCP); *m* 8 July 1972, Lesley Rita, da of Gerald Duckett; 3 s (Simon, Andrew, Peter); *Career* Bernard Sunley res fell RCS 1974–75, surgical registrar Royal Free Hosp 1976–78, sr surgical registrar St Mary's Hosp London 1978–82, conslt gen and vascular surgn W Middx Hosp 1982–; hon sr lectr Imperial Coll of Science, Technol and Med London; memb Vascular Surgical Soc of GB and I; fell Assoc of Surgeons of GB and I, FRSM, FRCS; *Recreations* golf, sailing; *Clubs* Royal Mid-Surrey Golf; *Style*— Mr Richard Young; ✉ 26 Strawberry Hill Road, Twickenham, Middlesex TW1 4PU (tel 020 8891 0638, fax 020 8287 2778, e-mail youngrichard@blueyonder.co.uk); West Middlesex University Hospital, Twickenham Road, Isleworth, Middlesex TW7 6AF (tel 020 8321 5768)

YOUNG, Richard Arthur Prior; s of Stanley Joseph Young (decd), and Barbara Patricia Young; *b* 15 March 1946; *Educ* Bishop Vesey GS, Birmingham Sch of Architecture (DipArch, BSc); *m* Janet Suzanne, *née* Mitchell; 2 da (Nicola Jane b 7 July 1979, Anna Louise b 13 April 1983); *Career* Harper Fairley Associates 1969, Architects' Dept Bucks CC 1969–71; Sheppard Robson (architects, planners and interior designers) London: joined 1971, assoc 1974–78, ptnr 1978–, partnership chm 1997–; projects incl: Thomas More Square for Skanska AB 1993, Southlands Coll Roehampton Inst 1996–97, Bahrain Univ masterplan 1996, King Saud Univ Abha Saudi Arabia Hosp male and female med sch 1996–97, masterplan Wellcome Tst Genome Campus Extension 1997; *Recreations* music, tennis, walking; *Style*— Richard Young, Esq; ✉ Sheppard Robson, 77 Parkway, London NW1 7PU (tel 020 7485 4161, fax 020 7267 3861, e-mail sheppard_robson@compuserve.com)

YOUNG, Sir Richard Dilworth; kt (1970); s of Philip Young, by his w Constance Maria Lloyd; *b* 9 April 1914; *Educ* Bromsgrove Sch, Univ of Bristol; *m* 1951, Jean Barbara Paterson, *née* Lockwood; 4 s; *Career* Boosey & Hawkes Ltd: dep chm 1978–79, chm 1979–84; dir Tube Investment Ltd 1958 (md 1961–64), chm Alfred Herbert Ltd 1966–74 (dep chm 1965–66); dir: Ingersoll Engineers Inc (USA) 1966–71, Rugby Portland Cement Co 1968–88, Cwlth Fin Devpt Corp 1968–83; memb: Cncl Univ of Warwick 1966–89, Central Advsy Cncl on Sci and Technol 1967–70, Cncl CBI 1967–74, Cncl SSRC 1973–75, SRC Engrg Bd 1974–76; Hon DSc Univ of Warwick; FIMechE (memb Cncl 1969–76), CIMgt; *Clubs* Athenaeum; *Style*— Sir Richard Young

YOUNG, Robert; s of Walter Horace Young (d 1963), of Wood Green, London, and Evelyn Joan, *née* Jennings; *b* 27 March 1944; *Educ* The Boys' GS Tottenham, Magdalen Coll Oxford (MA); *m* 18 Dec 1965, Patricia Anne, da of Robert Archibald Cowin, of Hest Bank, Lancs; 2 s (Matthew b 1969, Alec b and d 1972), 1 da (Judith b 1974); *Career* dir Rolls-Royce Motors Diesel Div 1977–81, gp commercial dir Vickers plc 1981–83; on secondment from Vickers: memb Central Policy Review Staff Cabinet Office 1983, memb 10 Downing St Policy Unit 1983–84; md Crane Ltd 1985–88, chief exec Plastics Div McKechnie plc 1988–90; dir: Beauford plc 1990–92, Casindell Ltd mgmnt conslts 1993–94, PricewaterhouseCoopers 1993–2000; dir LECG Ltd 2000–04, princ Europe Economics 2004–; CBI: regnl cncllr W Midlands 1980–81, chm Salop 1981; memb: Monopolies and Mergers Cmmn 1986–92, Fulbright Cmmn 1994–2004; FInstD 1985–2000; *Recreations* music, photography, cats; *Clubs* Oxford and Cambridge; *Style*— Robert Young, Esq; ✉ 12 Beechcroft Road, East Sheen, London SW14 7JJ (tel 020 8392 1735, e-mail bob.young@europe-economics.com)

YOUNG, Prof Robert James Craig; s of Leslie William Young, and Mary, *née* Cunningham; *Educ* Exeter Coll Oxford (MA, DPhil); *Career* lectr in English rising to sr lectr Univ of Southampton 1979–89; Univ of Oxford: lectr 1989–96, reader in English lit and language 1996–99, prof of English and critical theory 1999–2005; fell Wadham Coll Oxford 1989; Julius Silver prof of English and comparative lit NYU 2005–; founding ed Oxford Literary Review 1977–, gen ed Interventions: Int Jl of Postcolonial Studies 1997–; Br Acad res fell 1998–2000; fndn fell English Assoc; FRSA 2002, memb Academia Europaea 2005; *Publications* incl: White Mythologies: Writing History and the West (1990), Colonial Desire: Hybridity in Culture, Theory and Race (1995), Postcolonialism: An Historical Introduction (2001); *Recreations* photography, reading, writing; *Style*— Prof Robert Young; ✉ 37 The Villas, Rutherway, Oxford OX2 6QY (tel 01865 311421, website www.robertjcyoung.com); English Department, New York University, 13 University Place, Room 514, New York, NY 10003, USA (e-mail robertjcyoung@nyu.edu)

YOUNG, Sir Robin Urquhart; KCB (2002); s of Ian Urquhart Young, and Mary Hamilton, *née* West; *b* 7 September 1948; *Educ* Fettes, UC Oxford (open scholar, BA); *Career* DOE: joined 1973, various positions in housing and local govt fin, private sec to Parly Under Sec for Local Govt (Guy Barnett) 1976, to Housing Min (John Stanley) 1980 and successively to Secs of State (Patrick Jenkin, Kenneth Baker and Nicholas Ridley) 1985–89, worked in local govt fin 1981–85, under-sec housing 1988–89, under-sec environment policy 1989–91, headed team responsible for White Paper on the Environment 1990–91, head Local Govt Review Team 1991–92, head Local Govt Directorate 1992–94; dep sec and first dir Government Office for London 1994–97, head Econ and Domestic Affairs Secretariat Cabinet Office 1997–98, perm sec DCMS 1998–2001, perm sec DTI 2001–05; dep chm Dr Foster LLP 2005, chm Dr Foster Intelligence Ltd 2006–, chm Apex Communications 2006–; memb Bd East of England Int 2006–; *Style*— Sir Robin Young, KCB

YOUNG, Prof Stephen John; s of John Leonard Young (d 1994), and Joan Young; *b* 23 January 1951; *Educ* Univ of Cambridge (MA, PhD); *m* 1 (m dis); 2 da (Emma, Claire); m 2, Aug 1999, Sybille Wiesmann; *Career* UMIST: lectr Control Systems Centre 1978–79, Computation Dept 1979–84; Engrg Dept Univ of Cambridge: lectr 1984–94, reader in info engrg 1994, prof of info engrg 1994–, head Information Engrg 2002–; fell Emmanuel Coll Cambridge 1985–; tech dir Entropic Ltd 1995–99; architect Microsoft 1999–2001; author of numerous conf papers and articles in learned jls; memb Cncl: Univ of Cambridge, Royal Acad of Engrg; MBCS, FIEE, CEng, FREng, FRSA; *Recreations* boating, tennis, skiing, music; *Style*— Prof Stephen Young; ✉ Engineering Department, University of Cambridge, Trumpington Street, Cambridge CB2 1PZ (tel 01223 332752, fax 01223 332662, e-mail sjy@eng.cam.ac.uk)

YOUNG, Sheriff Principal Sir Stephen Stewart Templeton; 3 Bt (UK 1945), of Partick, Co City of Glasgow; QC (2002); s of Sir Alastair Spencer Templeton Young, 2 Bt, DL (d 1963), and (Dorothy Constance) Marcelle (d 1964), da of Lt-Col Charles Ernest Chambers, and wid of Lt John Hollington Grayburn, VC; *b* 24 May 1947; *Educ* Rugby, Trinity Coll Oxford, Univ of Edinburgh; *m* 1974, Viola Margaret, da of Prof Patrick Horace Nowell-Smith (whose mother was Cecil, ggda of Most Rev Hon Edward Vernon-Harcourt, sometime Archbishop of York and yr bro of 3 Baron Vernon) by his 1 w Perilla (da of Sir Richard Southwell and who m subsequently, as his 2 w, Baron Roberthall); 2 s (Charles Alastair Stephen b 21 July 1979, Alexander David b 6 Feb 1982); *Heir* s, Charles Young; *Career* slr 1973, advocate 1977; Sheriff of: Glasgow and Strathkelvin 1984, North Strathclyde at Greenock 1984–2001; Sheriff Princ of Grampian, Highland and Islands 2001–; *Style*— Sheriff Principal Sir Stephen Young, Bt, QC; ✉ Beechfield, Newton of Kinkell, Conon Bridge, Ross-shire IV7 8AS

YOUNG, Timothy Mark Stewart (Tim); *b* 6 October 1951; *Educ* Eton, Magdalene Coll Cambridge (MA), Univ of Bristol (PGCE); *m* Dr Alison Keightley; 2 s; *Career* asst master Eton Coll 1975–83 and 1984–87 (master i/c football), asst master Wanganui Collegiate Sch 1984, teacher of social sci Harvard Sch LA 1987–88, housemaster Eton Coll 1988–92, headmaster Royal GS Guildford 1992–2007; dir Rannk Fndn Sch Leadership Award 2007–; HMC: memb Academic Policy Sub-Ctee 1996–98, tutor New Heads' Preliminary Trg Course 1996–2001, treas 1998–2001, hon assoc memb 2007–; *Style*— Tim Young, Esq

YOUNG, Timothy Nicholas; QC (1996); s of William Ritchie Young, and Patricia Eileen, *née* Greig; *b* 1 December 1953; *Educ* Malvern Coll, Magdalen Coll Oxford (exhibitioner, BA, BCL); *m* 6 June 1981, Susan Jane, da of Wing Cdr Eamon St Brendan Kenny; 2 s (William Henry b 6 Oct 1983, Charles Frederick b 3 Jan 1986), 1 da (Frances Elizabeth b 26 July 1988); *Career* lectr in law St Edmund Hall Oxford 1976–80, called to the Bar Gray's Inn 1977, in practice at Commercial Bar 1978–; *Books* Voyage Charters (1993, 2 edn 2001); *Recreations* watching and playing cricket and golf, watching rugby, drawing and watercolours, music; *Clubs* RAC, Thebertons CC, Dulwich and Sydenham Golf; *Style*— Timothy Young, Esq, QC; ✉ 20 Essex Street, London WC2R 3AL (tel 020 7583 9294, fax 020 7583 1341, e-mail tyoung@20essexst.com)

YOUNG, (Hon) Toby Daniel Moorsom; s of Baron Young of Dartington, by his 2 w Sasha; *b* 1963; *Educ* BNC Oxford, Harvard Univ, Trinity Coll Cambridge; *Career* journalist and author; *Books* How to Lose Friends and Alienate People (2001), The Sound of No Hands Clapping (2006); *Recreations* food and drink; *Style*— Toby Young

YOUNG, Sir William Neil; 10 Bt (GB 1769), of North Dean, Buckinghamshire; s of Capt William Elliot Young (ka 1942), and gs of Sir Charles Alban Young, 9 Bt, KCMG, MVO (d 1944); Sir Charles's w was Clara, da of Sir Francis Elliot, GCMG, GCVO (gs of 2 Earl of Minto, also Envoy Extraordinary and Min Plenipotentiary to the King of the Hellenes 1903–17); *b* 22 January 1941; *Educ* Wellington, RMA Sandhurst; *m* 1965, Christine Veronica, o da of Robert Boland Morley, of Buenos Aires; 1 da (Catherine Clare (Mrs Hugh E Powell) b 1967), 1 s (William Lawrence Elliot b 1970); *Heir* s, William Young; *Career* Capt 16/5 Queen's Royal Lancers, ret 1970; former stockbroker with: Phillips & Drew, James Capel & Co; former ptnr Watson & Co; md Kleinwort Benson International Investment (Pacific) Ltd 1982–85, dir Kleinwort Benson International Investment Ltd 1982–87, head of investment mgmnt Saudi International Bank 1987–91, int private banking (head of Middle East) Coutts & Co 1991–94; dir Middle East Barclays Private Bank Ltd 1994–1999; currently chm: New World Tst Ltd, Napo Pharmaceuticals Inc; sr advsr Merchant Bridge Ltd; *Recreations* skiing, gardening, shooting; *Style*— Sir William Young, Bt; ✉ South End House, High Ham, Langport, Somerset

YOUNG OF GRAFFHAM, Baron (Life Peer UK 1984), of Graffham in the County of West Sussex; David Ivor Young; PC (1984), DL (West Sussex 1999); s of late Joseph Young and his w, Rebecca; *b* 27 February 1932; *Educ* Christ's Coll Finchley, UCL (LLB, Capt London Univ Golf 1954); *m* 1956, Lita Marianne, da of Jonas Shaw; 2 da (Hon Karen Debra b 1957 m 1983, Hon Mr Justice Rix, *qv*, Hon Judith Anne (Hon Mrs Beacroft) b 1960); *Career* admitted slr 1956; chm Eldonwall Ltd 1961–74, dir Town & City Properties Ltd 1971–74; chm: Manufacturers Hanover Property Services 1974–80, Greenwood Homes Ltd 1976–82; dir Centre for Policy Studies 1979–82 (memb Mgmnt Bd 1977–82); special advsr: Dept of Industry 1979–82, Dept of Educn and Sci 1981–82; chm Manpower Servs Cmmn 1982–84, memb/chm NEDC 1982–89; min without portfolio 1984–85, sec of state for employment 1985–87, sec of state for trade and industry and pres of the Bd of Trade 1987–89, retired from Govt 1989; dep chm Cons Pty 1989–90; dir Salomon Inc (and subsids) 1990–94; chm: Cable & Wireless plc 1990–95, Neoscorp Ltd 1997–, Pixology Ltd 1997–; dir: Young Assocs Ltd, Pixology Ltd, Chichester Festival Theatre Co Ltd, Acacia City Ltd, Autohit plc, Business for Sterling, Br Israel C of C, Convergys Inc, Elfin Systems Ltd, IndogoVision plc, Int Telecommunications Clearing Corps Ltd (Bermuda), Newhaven Mgmnt Services Ltd, Pere (UK) Ltd; chm: Br Orgn for Rehabilitation by Training (ORT) 1975–80, Admin Ctee World ORT Union 1980–84, Int Cncl of Jewish Social and Welfare Servs 1981–, EU-Japan Assoc 1991–97, Cncl UCL 1995–, London Philharmonic Tst 1995–98, W Sussex Econ Forum 1996–; pres: Jewish Care 1990–97, World ORT Union 1990–, IOD 1993–; Hon FRPS 1981; *Publications* The Enterprise Years (1990); *Recreations* music, book collecting, photography; *Clubs* Savile; *Style*— The Rt Hon Lord Young of Graffham, PC, DL; ✉ Young Associates Ltd, Harcourt House, 19 Cavendish Square, London W1G 0PL (tel 020 7447 8800, fax 020 7447 8849, e-mail young@youngassoc.com)

YOUNG OF HORNSEY, Baroness (Life Peer UK 2004), of Hornsey in the London Borough of Haringey; Margaret Omolola (Lola) Young; OBE (2001); da of Maxwell Fela Young (d 1994); *b* 1 June 1951, London; *Educ* Parliament Hill Comp Sch for Girls, New Coll of Speech and Drama London (Dip Dramatic Art, CertEd), Middx Univ (BA, PhD); *m* 1984, Barrie Birch, s of Ronald Birch; 1 s; *Career* clerical and admin work in public utilities 1969–71, residential social worker London Borough of Islington 1971–73, professional actor 1976–84, co-dir and trg and devpt mangr Haringey Arts Cncl (HAC) 1985–89, enterprise offr Faculty of Educn and Performing Arts Middx Univ 1989–91, freelance lectr and arts conslt 1989–91, lectr in media studies Thames Valley Univ 1990–92, lectr rising to prof of cultural studies Middx Univ 1992–2001, project dir Archives and Museum of Black Heritage 1997–2001, head of culture GLA 2002–04, currently freelance cultural conslt; visiting prof of cultural studies Univ of São Paulo 1998; chair: Cultural Diversity Advsy Ctee Arts Cncl 2000–01, Arts Advsy Ctee Br Cncl 2004–, Nitro (formerly Black Theatre Co-operative) 2004–; memb: Bd inIVA (Inst for Int Visual Arts) 1994–2001, Visual Arts Panel Arts Cncl of England 1996–98 (memb Educn and Trg Sub-Ctee 1996–99), Theatre Ctee Arts Cncl of England 2000, Steering Gp on English Heritage (DCMS cmmnd review) 2000–02, Bd Resource: Cncl for Museums, Archives and Libraries 2000–02, Bd RNT 2000–03, Blue Plaques Sub-Ctee English Heritage 2001–03, Bd South Bank Centre 2002–, Advsy Gp on Audiences and Access Natural History Museum 2003–, DCMS Advsy Gp on Museums 2004; external assessor Cmmn for Racial Equality Race in the Media Awards 1991–94; cmmr Royal Cmmn on Historic Manuscripts 2000–01; patron Autograph 1997–2001; series advsy ed Critical Photography (Manchester Univ Press) 1992, memb Editorial Collective Feminist Review 1992–94, memb Editorial Bd Parallax: Jl of Meta-discursive Theory 1994–, advsy ed Oxford Art Jl 1994–, conslt Companion to Black British History 2002; chair Panel of Judges Orange Prize for Fiction 1999; numerous radio and TV broadcasts, delivered keynote address and lectures at confs worldwide; memb Mgmnt Ctee Post-Adoption Centre 2000–03; memb Bd of Govrs Middx Univ 2002–03; FRSA 1999; *Publications* Fear of the Dark: 'Race', Gender and Sexuality in Cinema; also numerous articles, essays and interview in newspapers and other jls; *Recreations* reading, walking, all arts; *Clubs* Royal Cwlth Soc; *Style*— The Rt Hon the Lady Young of Hornsey, OBE; ✉ Cultural Brokers, Building D, Unit 208, The Chocolate Factory, 5 Clarendon Road, London N22 6XJ (tel and fax 020 8888 8797, e-mail culturalbrokers@btconnect.com)

YOUNG OF OLD SCONE, Baroness (Life Peer UK 1997), of Old Scone in Perth and Kinross; Barbara Scott Young; da of George Young (d 1981), of Perth, Scotland, and Mary, *née* Scott (d 2001); *b* 8 April 1948; *Educ* Perth Acad, Univ of Edinburgh (MA), Univ of Strathclyde; *Career* sr admin Gtr Glasgow Health Bd 1973–78, dir of planning and devpt St Thomas' Health Dist 1978–79, dist gen admin NW Dist Kensington, Chelsea & Westminster AHA 1979–82, dist admin Haringey HA 1982–85, dist gen mangr Paddington & North Kensington HA 1985–88, dist gen mangr Parkside HA 1988–91, chief exec RSPB 1991–98 (vice-pres 2000–), chm English Nature 1998–2000, chief exec Environment Agency 2000–; vice-chair Bd of Govrs BBC 1998–2000; vice-pres Flora and Fauna Int 1998–, vice-pres Birdlife Int 1999–, pres Bedfordshire, Cambridgeshire and Peterborough Wildlife Tst 2001, pres Br Tst for Ornithology 2005–; memb: World Cncl Birdlife Int 1994–98, Ctee of Sec of State for Environment's UK Round Table on Sustainability 1995–2000, Cmmn on Future of the Voluntary Sector 1995–96, Ctee on the Public Understanding of Sci (COPUS) 1996–97; patron Inst of Environmental & Ecological Mgmnt 1993–; tstee: NCVO 1993–97, Public Mgmnt Fndn 1998–99, IPPR 2000–; pres Inst of Health Servs Mgmnt 1987–88 (dip 1971); hon memb Linnean Soc of London 2002; Hon DUniv: Stirling 1995, Hertfordshire 1997; Hon DSc Cranfield Univ 1998; Hon Degree: Univ of St Andrews 2000, Univ of Aberdeen 2000, Univ of York 2000, Open Univ 2001; AHSM 1971, chartered environmentalist 2005; *Recreations* cinema, gardening; *Style*— The Rt Hon Baroness Young of Old Scone; ✉ House of Lords, London SW1A 0PW

YOUNGER, Captain (John) David Bingham; LVO (2007), JP (1994); s of Maj Oswald Bingham Younger, MC (d 1989), of Etal, Northumberland, and Dorothea Elizabeth, *née* Hobbs (d 1996); *b* 20 May 1939; *Educ* Eton, RMA Sandhurst; *m* 1 Dec 1962, Anne Rosaleen, da of Lt-Col John Logan, TD, DL (d 1987), of Wester Craigend, Stirlingshire; 2 da (Sarah Juliet (Mrs Peter Landale) b 1964, Camilla Jane b 1966), 1 s (Mark Robert b 1972); *Career* Argyll and Sutherland Highlanders cmmnd 1959, Adj 1 Bn Borneo and Singapore 1965–67 (GSM Clasps Borneo and Malaysia), Directorate of Mil Ops MOD 1967–69, ret 1969; Scottish & Newcastle Breweries Ltd 1969–79, co-fndr and md Broughton Brewery Ltd 1979–94, dir Broughton Ales Ltd 1995–96; vice-pres Royal Highland and Agric Soc of Scotland 1994; chm: Scottish Borders Tourist Bd 1989–91, Peeblesshire Charitable Tst 1994–; sec Queen's Body Guard for Scotland (Royal Co of Archers) 1993–2007 (memb 1969–, Brig 2002–), pres Borders area SSAFA Forces Help 2007; memb Argyll and Sutherland Highlanders Regtl Tst and Ctee 1985–92, pres Lowland Reserve Forces and Cadets Assoc 2006–; dir Queen's Hall Edinburgh 1992–2001; chm of govrs Belhaven Hill Sch Dunbar 1988–94; cmmr River Tweed 2002–; HM Lord-Lt of Tweeddale 1994– (DL 1987, Vice Lord-Lt 1992–94); MInstD 1984; *Recreations* country pursuits; *Style*— Captain David Younger, LVO; ✉ Kirkurd House, Blyth Bridge, Peeblesshire EH46 7AH (tel and fax 01721 752223)

YOUNGER, James Samuel (Sam); s of Rt Hon Sir Kenneth Gilmour Younger (d 1976), of London, and Elisabeth Kirsteen, *née* Stewart (d 2003); *b* 5 October 1951; *Educ* Westminster, New Coll Oxford (BA); *m* 5 May 1984, Katherine Anne, da of Cyril Kenneth Spencer; 1 s (Edward Spencer Younger b 6 June 1986); *Career* asst ed Middle East International magazine 1972–78; BBC World Service: sr asst Central Current Affrs Talks 1979–84, sr prodr Current Affrs World Service 1984–85 (exec prodr 1985–86), asst head BBC Arabic Service 1986–87, head Current Affrs World Service in English 1987–89, head BBC Arabic Service 1989–92, controller Overseas Services 1992–94, dir of broadcasting 1994, md BBC World Service 1994–98, dir Eng Touring Opera 1999–; DG British Red Cross Soc 1999–2001, chm Electoral Cmmn 2001–, chair Quality Assurance Agency for HE 2004–; patron Windsor Leadership Tst 1998–, govr Cwlth Inst 1998–2005, memb Cncl Univ of Sussex 1998– (chair 2001–); *Recreations* choral singing, sport; *Style*— Sam Younger; ✉ 28 Rylett Crescent, London W12 9RL (tel 020 8743 4449); Electoral Commission, Trevelyan House, 30 Great Peter Street, London SW1P 2HW (tel 020 7271 0505)

YOUNGER OF LECKIE, 5 Viscount (UK 1923); Sir James Edward George Younger; 5 Bt (UK 1911); s of 4 Viscount Younger of Leckie, KT, KCVO, PC (d 2003), and Diana Rhona, *née* Tuck; *b* 11 November 1955, Edinburgh; *Educ* Winchester, Univ of St Andrews (MA), Henley Mgmnt Coll (MBA); *m* 4 June 1988, Jennie, *née* Wootton; 2 da (Hon Emily Evelyn b 26 Sept 1990, Hon Alice Elizabeth b 25 Feb 1992), 1 s (Hon Alexander William George b 13 Nov 1993); *Heir* s, Hon Alexander Younger; *Career* personnel mangr Coats Patons plc 1979–84, conslt Angela Mortimer plc 1984–86, conslt Stephens Consultancies 1986–92, dir McInnes Younger 1992–94, HR dir UBS 1994–2004, dir Culliford Edmunds 2004–07, conslt EBAN Ltd 2007–; memb Queen's Body Guard for Scotland (Royal Co of Archers); tstee Kate Kennedy Tst, dir Highland Soc of London, chm Buckingham Cons Assoc 2006–; memb Assoc of MBAs 1993, memb Assoc of Cons Peers (ACP), MCIM 1993; *Recreations* sailing, shooting, tennis, running, cricket, DIY; *Clubs* Lansdowne, White Hunter Cricket; *Style*— The Rt Hon the Viscount Younger of Leckie; ✉ The Old Vicarage, Dorton, Aylesbury, Buckinghamshire HP18 9NH (tel 01844 238396, fax 01844 238922, mobile 07786 422813, e-mail jeg.younger@virgin.net)

YOUNGER-ROSS, Richard; MP; *b* 29 January 1953; *Educ* Walton-on-Thames Secdy Modern, Ewell Tech Coll, Oxford Poly; *Career* architectural conslt; Parly candidate (Lib Dem): Chislehurst 1987, Teignbridge 1992 and 1997; MP (Lib Dem) Teignbridge 2001–; Lib Dem spokesperson for culture, media and sport 2004, memb Foreign Affrs Select Ctee, memb European Scrutiny Ctee; memb: Howard League for Penal Reform, Br Kurdish Friendship Soc, Anti-Slavery Int; *Style*— Richard Younger-Ross, Esq, MP; ✉ House of Commons, London SW1A 0AA

YOUNGSON, Prof George Gray; s of Alexander Keay Youngson, MBE, of Glenrothes, Fife, and Jean Oneil, *née* Kelly; *b* 13 May 1949; *Educ* Buckhaven HS, Univ of Aberdeen (MB ChB, PhD); *m* 17 March 1973, Sandra Jean, *née* Lister; 2 da (Kellie Jane b 1973, Louise b 1975), 1 s (Calum Lister b 1981); *Career* Univ of Aberdeen: lectr in surgery 1979–82, res fell 1974–76; res in cardiothoracic surgery Univ of W Ontario 1977–79, clinical fell in paediatric surgery Hosp for Sick Children Toronto 1983, conslt paediatric surgn Royal Aberdeen Children's Hosp 1985, hon prof of paediatric surgery Univ of Aberdeen 1999; chm Scottish Colls Ctee on Children's Surgical Services 1990–98; memb: Br Assoc of Paediatric Surgns, Assoc of Surgns GB and Ireland; FRCSEd 1977 (examiner 1991, memb Cncl); *Recreations* bagpipe music, sport (fishing, tennis, squash, golf); *Style*— Prof George Youngson; ✉ Birken Lodge, Bieldside, Aberdeen AB15 9BQ; Royal Aberdeen Children's Hospital, Cornhill Road, Aberdeen AB25 2ZG (tel 01224 681818, e-mail ggyrach@abdn.ac.uk)

YOUNIS, Dr Farouk Mustafa; s of Mustafa Younis (d 2004), of Amman, Jordan, and Wasila Mahmoud Khader; *b* 1 March 1947; *Educ* Markaziyah All HS Baghdad, Baghdad Univ Med Sch (MB ChB); *m* 13 Sept 1975, Cynthia Karen, da of George Gadsby (d 1992), of Ilkeston, Derbys; 1 s (Sami Farouk b 15 Feb 1977); *Career* surgeon; started career in Palestinian refugee camps in Lebanon with Red Crescent Soc Med and Health Prog 1971–72; trg posts UK 1973–: casualty, gen surgery, orthopaedics, thoracic, vascular and urologic surgery; casualty post Chesterfield, gen surgery posts Harrogate, Barrow in Furness and Huddersfield, orthopaedics post Cambridge, kidney transplant and gen surgery post Royal Free Hosp London, gen and vascular surgery Chelmsford, conslt surgeon Whittington Hosp 1981–83, private surgical practice 1981–; memb: BMA, RSM, Ind Doctors' Forum, Soc of Minimal Invasion Therapy; FRCS 1977, fell Assoc of Surgns of GB & I; *Recreations* golf, travel, chess; *Clubs* N Middx Golf; *Style*— Dr Farouk Younis; ✉ 129 Harley Street, London W1G 6BA (tel 020 7487 4897, fax 020 7224 6398, e-mail farouky@aol.com)

YUASA, Takuo; *b* 27 July 1949; *Educ* Coll/Conservatory of Music Univ of Cincinnati (BMus), Vienna Hochschule für Musik (Dip); *m* 1982, Shigeko Takaoka; 1 da (Michika b 1984); *Career* conductor Gumma Symphony Orch 1984–88; princ guest conductor: BBC Scottish Symphony Orch 1989–93, Ulster Orch 1997–; UK debut 1988, Proms debut 1989; conducted orchs incl: Tonkünstlerorchester Vienna, Japan Philharmonic, Tokyo Met Symphony, Warsaw Nat Philharmonic, Polish Radio Nat Symphony, London Philharmonic, Yomiuri Nippon Symphony, Oslo Philarmonic, Ulster Orchestra, Bournemouth Symphony, Royal Liverpool Philarmonic, Hallé Orch, Hong Kong Philharmonic, Syndey Symphony, Berlin Symphony; venues incl: Vienna Konzerthaus, Royal Festival Hall, opening concert Glasgow Euro City of Culture Festival 1990, Sydney Opera House, Scottish Opera (Traviata), Berlin Philharmonic Hall, numerous others in UK, Japan, Scandinavia, Australia and Europe; *Recordings* Rimsky-Korsakov's Sheherazade (with London Philharmonic Orch), Benjamin Britten's Four Sea Interludes and others (with Royal Liverpool Philharmonic Orch), Lorenzo Ferraro's La Nueva España (with Nat Symphony of Ukraine), Henryk Górecki's Symphony No 3 (with Adelaide Symphony); with Ulster Orch: James MacMillan's Veni Veni Emanuel, Michael Nyman's Piano Concerto, John Tavener's The Protecting Veil, Benjamin Britten's Cello Symphony, Philip Glass' Violin Concerto, Arvo Pärt's Tabula Rasa, Arnold Schoenberg's Verklärte Nacht, Anton Webern's Passacaglia, Edward MacDowell's Suites No 1 & 2, Akio Yashiro's Symphony, Alan Rawsthorne's Piano Concertos; *Style*— Takuo Yuasa, Esq; ✉ c/o Patrick Garvey Management, International Artist Management, Cedar House,10 Rutland Street, Filey, North Yorkshire, YO14 9JB

YULE, (Duncan) Ainslie; s of Edward Campbell Yule (d 1974), and Elizabeth Morgan Ainslie; *b* 10 February 1941; *Educ* North Berwick HS, Edinburgh Coll of Art (DA); *m* 1, 1963 (m dis 1982), Patricia Carlos; 1 da (b 1963); m 2, 1982, Mary Johnson; *Career* sculptor; work in several public and private collections; lectr in design Gray's Sch of Art Aberdeen

1966–79; sessional lectr: Univ of Reading 1978–81, Middx Poly (Hornsey Sch of Art) 1979–81; visiting lectr RCA 1984–87; head of sculpture Kingston Univ 1982– (reader 1987–); *Solo Exhibitions* incl: New 57 Gallery Edinburgh 1969, Serpentine Gallery 1973, Richard Demarco Gallery Edinburgh 1972/73/82/88, Leeds Univ 1973, Park Square Gallery Leeds 1976, Editions Alecto 1977, Fruitmarket Gallery Edinburgh and travelling 1977, St Paul's Gallery Leeds 1981, Angela Flowers Gallery 1986, Kingston Poly 1990, Takimiya Hiroshima Japan 1997, Stanley Picker Gallery Kingston Univ 1997, Talbot Rice Gallery Edinburgh Univ 1999, Ulster Museum Belfast 2002; *Mixed Exhibitions* incl: Earth Images Whitechapel Art Gallery 1973, Gubbio Biennale 1973, Leeds Univ 1975, Scottish Arts Cncl 1975/77, Silver Jubilee Exhbn of Br Sculpture Battersea Park 1977, Belgrade '77 1977, Scottish Nat Gallery of Modern Art 1978, first Sculpture Biennial Toronto 1978, Scottish Artists in Finland 1978, The British Art Show Sheffield, Bristol and Newcastle 1979–80, Scottish Contemporary Art Robinson Galleries Houston Texas 1985, Scottish Gallery London 1989/90/91, Chicago Art Fair 1990, Museum of Fine Arts Budapest 1992, Villa Foscarini-Rossi Venice 1993; *Awards* Andrew Grant scholarship 1963, Scottish Arts Cncl award 1973 and 1975, Gregory fell in Sculpture Univ of Leeds 1974–75, memb Faculty of Prix de Rome 1980–84, Rainbow Wood scholarship Japan 1996; *Clubs* Chelsea Arts; *Style—* Ainslie Yule, Esq; ✉ 11 Chiswick Staithe, London W4 3TP (tel 020 8995 0968, fax 020 8547 7133)

YURKO, Allen; *Career* ceo Invensys plc 1994–2001, ptnr Compass Partners 2001–07, sr advsr Credit Suisse Alternative Investments 2007–; non-exec dir Tate & Lyle plc 1996–2005; *Style—* Allen Yurko, Esq; ✉ Credit Suisse, 1 Cabot Square, London E14 4QJ

Z

ZACCOUR, Makram Michel; s of Michel Zaccour (former MP and Foreign and Interior Min of Lebanon, d 1937), and Rose, *née* Gorayeb; *b* 19 August 1935; *Educ* Univ of Calif Berkeley (BSc); *Career* gen mangr Industrials Textiles Ultratex (Colombia) 1964–66 (sales 1957–64); Merrill Lynch: fin conslt ME 1967–73, mangr Beirut office 1973, Beirut and Paris 1976, London 1977–83, regnl dir Merrill Lynch Pierce Fenner & Smith Ltd 1983–92, vice-chm Int Private Banking Gp 1992–, chm Middle East 1992–, co-chm Merrill Lynch Bank (Suisse) 1993–, vice-chm Int Private Client Gp 2001–; memb Arab Bankers' Assoc; Phi Beta Kappa; *Clubs* Annabel's, Harry's Bar, Mark's; *Style*— Makram M Zaccour, Esq

ZACHARY, Stefan Hedley; s of Jan Bronislaw Zacharkiewicz (d 1987), and Thelma Joyce, *née* Mortimer; *b* 30 June 1948; *Educ* Roundhay Sch Leeds, Leeds Coll of Art (BA); *m* 7 Aug 1971, (Margaret) Patricia, da of Stanley George Wright, of Great Kingshill, Bucks; 2 s (Alexander Adam, Christopher Jan), 1 da (Halina Patricia); *Career* Royal Yeomanry TA&VR 1972–73, 5 Bn The Queen's Regt TA&VR 1973–76, RMA Sandhurst 1975; interior designer Conran Design Group 1970–71, assoc ptnr Howard Sant Partnership 1971–77, md McColl Group plc 1977–92, princ Zachary Design 1992–; pres CSD 1994–96, jt hon pres Design Business Assoc 1989– (founding chm 1986–89), memb RIBA Mktg Gp 1987–88; Freeman City of London 1988, Liveryman Worshipful Co of Painter Stainers 1989 (Freeman 1988); FCSD 1981, FBID 1979, FRSA 1979, FIMgt 1984; *Books* CSD Works Agreement User's Guide (1983); *Recreations* flying, gliding, shooting, travel, driving, painting and drawing; *Style*— Mr Stefan Zachary, PPCSD; ✉ Zachary Design, Little Moseley House, Naphill, Buckinghamshire HP14 4RE (tel 01494 562591, fax 01494 562592, e-mail zacharydesign@btconnect.com, website www.zachary.co.uk)

ZAIWALLA, Sarosh Ratanshaw; *Educ* Univ of Bombay (BCom, LLB); *Children* 1 da (Freya b 1981), 1 s (Varun b 1983); *Career* admitted slr 1978; fndr ptnr Gagrat & Co London 1978–82, sr ptnr Zaiwalla & Co Solicitors London 1982–; specialist in international commercial contracts and maritime disputes and immigration and nationality cases; memb: Law Soc, Maritime Arbitrators' Assoc, Baltic Exchange London, Int Court of Arbitration of Int C of C Paris, London Court of Int Arbitration (fndr memb), Indian Cncl of Arbitration Delhi, London Maritime Arbitrators' Assoc (supporting memb), Int Cmmn on Arbitration; chm Br Org of People of Indian Origin (BOPIO); pres Soc of Friends of the Lotus Children; jt convenor Asian Business Breakfast Club; Law Day Award for Unique Contrib to Int Arbitration Law Indian Cncl of Jurists 2003; Freeman City of London 1998; accredited mediator CEDR; FRSA; *Style*— Sarosh Zaiwalla, Esq; ✉ Zaiwalla, 46–47 Chancery Lane, London WC2A 1JE (tel 020 7312 1000, fax 020 7404 9473, e-mail s.zaiwalla@zaiwalla.co.uk or saroshzaiwalla@hotmail.com, website www.zaiwalla.co.uk)

ZAKRZEWSKA, Prof Joanna Maria; da of Mieczyslaw Zakrzewski (d 1999), and Kazimiera Zakrzewska (d 2001); *b* 7 December 1949, London; *Educ* King's Coll Dental Sch London (BDS), Newnham Coll Cambridge (MB, BChir), Univ of Cambridge (MD); *m* 1984, Jan Ledochowski; 1 s (Konrad b 18 March 1985), 1 da (Krystyna b 18 Jan 1988); *Career* dental house offr King's Coll Hosp Dental Sch 1973, gen dental practice 1973–74, SHO St Mary's Hosp London and Eastman Dental Hosp 1974–75, dental clinical asst St Mary's Hosp 1975–77, supervisor in pathology Newnham Coll Cambridge 1978–79, house surgn Norfolk and Norwich Hosp 1980–81, SHO St Mary's Hosp London 1981–82; Eastman Dental Hosp: registrar in oral and maxillofacial surgery 1982–84, locum sr registrar in oral and maxillofacial surgery and oral med 1984–86, res fell and hon sr registrar in oral med 1986–89, conslt and hon sr lectr in oral med 1989–95; hon conslt Nat Hosp for Neurology and Neurosurgery 1989–, conslt oral physician UCL Hosps 1991–96, conslt and hon sr lectr Mortimer Market Dental Clinic and Camden & Islington NHS Tst 1991–2000; Inst of Dentistry Barts and the London and Queen Mary's Sch of Med and Dentistry: sr lectr and hon conslt in oral med clinical diagnostic and oral sciences 1996–2005, prof of pain in relation to oral med 2004–; expert advsr for guidelines for trigeminal neuralgia American Acad of Neurology and European Fedn of Neurological Socs 2004–06, taskforce ldr special interest gp of orofacial pain Int Assoc for the Study of Pain on classification of orofacial pain 2002–05, chm Med Bd and tstee Trigeminal Neuralgia Assoc UK, memb Med Advsy Bd Trigeminal Neuralgia Assoc US, expert advsr to NICE on stereotactic radiosurgery for trigeminal neuralgia; memb: BMA, RSM (memb Cncl Odontological Section 1994–95), Int Assoc for the Study of Pain, Pain Soc UK, Assoc for Med Educn in Europe, Assoc for the Study of Med Educn, BDA, Int Assoc for Dental Res, Oral Health Gp of Cochrane Collaboration, European Assoc of Oral Med, Br Soc for Oral Med (memb Cncl, treas and sec 1989–91, pres 1997–99), Soc of Authors, Int Headache Soc; FDSRCS 1980, FFDRCSI 1991, ILTM 2000; *Publications* Trigeminal Neuralgia (1995), Insights: Facts and Stories Behind Trigeminal Neuralgia (2006); numerous book chapters, papers, review articles and electronic pubns; *Style*— Prof Joanna Zakrzewska; ✉ Oral Medicine, UCLH Eastman Dental Hospital, 256 Gray's Inn Road, London WC1X 8LD (tel 020 7915 1195, e-mail jzakizewska@nhs.net)

ZAMBONI, Richard Frederick Charles; s of Alfred Charles Zamboni (d 1957), and Frances, *née* Hosler (d 1983); descendant of a Swiss (Engiadina) family with lineage traceable to 1465; *b* 28 July 1930; *Educ* Monkton House Sch Cardiff; *m* 1, Jan 1960, Pamela Joan (d 1993), da of Laurence Brown Marshall; 2 s (Edward b 1962, Rupert b 1967), 1 da (Charlotte b 1964); m 2, March 1996, Deirdre Olive, da of John Reginald Kingham; *Career* Br Egg Mktg Bd 1959–70; md Sun Life Assurance Society plc 1979–89 (vice-chm 1986–89), chm Sun Life Investment Management Services Ltd 1985–89, chm Sun Life Trust Management Ltd 1985–89; chm: Avon Enterprise Fund plc 1990–97 (dir 1984), AIM Distribution Trust plc 1996–2000, Hersham Land plc 2006–; dep chm Assoc of Br Insurers 1986–88 (chm Life Insurance Cncl 1986–88); chm: Governing Body Manor House Sch Little Bookham 1999–2003, Cncl of Mgmnt Grange Centre for People with Disabilities 1991–96; Liveryman Worshipful Co of Insurers; FCA; *Recreations* ornithology, gardening, golf; *Clubs* RAC; *Style*— Richard Zamboni, Esq; ✉ The Old Vicarage, Church Street, Leatherhead, Surrey KT22 8ER (tel 01372 812398)

ZAMOYSKI, Count Adam Stefan; s of Lt-Col Count Stefan Zamoyski, OBE, VM, LLD, Commander with Star Order of Polonia Restituta (d 1976, fifth in descent from Andrzej Zamoyski, cr Count 1778 (confirmed 1780) by Empress Maria Teresa of Austria at the time of the Partitions of Poland) by his w Princess Elizabeth Czartoryska (d 1989); *b* 11 January 1949, New York; *Educ* Downside, The Queen's Coll Oxford; *m* 14 June 2001, Emma, da of Sir Patrick Sergeant , *qv*; *Career* historian and author; chm Czartoryski Fndn Kraków, pres Fndn of St John of Jerusalem Warsaw; Freeman City of London 1992; Knight of Honour & Devotion Sov Mil Order of Malta 1977, Knight of Justice Constantinian Order of St George (House of Bourbon Sicily) 1978, Order of Polonia Restituta 1982 (Offr 1997, Cdr 2007); FSA 2002, FRSA 2005, FRSL 2006; *Books* Chopin, A Biography (1979), Paderewski (1981), The Polish Way (1987), The Last King of Poland (1992), The Forgotten Few (1995), Holy Madness (1999), 1812 (2004), Rites of Peace (2007); *Clubs* Pratt's, Puffin's; *Style*— Count Adam Zamoyski; ✉ 12 Avenue Studios, Sydney Close, London SW3 6HW (tel 020 7584 9053, e-mail adam@adamzamoyski.com); Wilcza 19 m7, 00–544 Warszawa, Poland (tel 00 48 22628 5281)

ZANCANI, Prof Diego; s of Lattanzio Zancani (d 2006), and Edi Giovanna, *née* Silvestrini; *b* 10 May 1944, Castel San Giovanni, Italy; *Educ* Bocconi Univ Milan, Univ of Oxford (MA); *m* 1, 26 Sept 1970 (m dis 2001), Graziella Bernini; 3 s (Leonardo b 7 Aug 1973, Sandro b 30 May 1978, Fabio b 17 Feb 1980); m 2, 31 May 2003, Valentina, *née* Olivastri; *Career* asst lectr in Italian Univ of Reading 1969–73, lectr in Italian Univ of Liverpool 1973–79, reader and prof of Italian Univ of Kent 1979–95; Univ of Oxford: faculty lectr in Italian 1995–2004, fell and tutor in Italian Balliol Coll 1995–, dean Balliol Coll 2002–04, prof of Italian 2004–, praefectus Holywell Manor 2004–; visiting prof Dept of Romance Languages and Literature Harvard Univ 2000 and 2003; Deputazione di Storia Patria Province di Parma e Piacenza 1975; Commendatore dell'Ordine della Stella della Solidarietà Italiana (2006); *Publications* G C Croce: Dall'Emilia All'Inghil Terra (jtly, 1991), A Cornazzano: La Tradizione Testuale (jtly, 1992); numerous chapters in books and articles in the field of Renaissance studies, history of the language and of the book; *Recreations* reading, walking, mushroom hunting; *Style*— Prof Diego Zancani; ✉ Balliol College, Broad Street, Oxford OX1 3BJ

ZANDER, Prof Michael; Hon QC (1997); s of Dr Walter Zander (d 1993), and Margaret, *née* Magnus (d 1968); *b* 16 November 1932; *Educ* Royal GS High Wycombe, Jesus Coll Cambridge (BA, LLB), Harvard Law Sch (LLM); *m* 27 Aug 1965, Elizabeth Treeger (Betsy), da of Clarence R Treeger, of NYC; 1 da (Nicola b 1969), 1 s (Jonathan b 1970); *Career* 2 Lt RA; admitted slr 1962, Sydney Morse & Co 1962–63; LSE: asst lectr 1963, lectr 1965, sr lectr 1970, reader 1970, prof 1977–98 (emeritus prof 1998–), convenor Law Dept 1984–88 and 1997–98; memb Royal Cmmn on Criminal Justice 1991–93; regular broadcasts on radio and TV, legal corr The Guardian 1963–87; Sr FBA 2005; *Books* Lawyers and the Public Interest (1968), Legal Services for the Community (1978), The Law-Making Process (1980, 6 edn 2004), The Police and Criminal Evidence Act (1984, 5 edn 2005), A Bill of Rights? (1975, 4 edn 1996), Cases and Materials on English Legal Systems (1973, 10 edn 2007), A Matter of Justice: The Legal System in Ferment (revised edn, 1989), The State of Justice (2000); *Recreations* playing the cello, the daily swim; *Style*— Prof Michael Zander, QC, FBA; ✉ 12 Woodside Avenue, London N6 4SS (tel 020 8883 6257, fax 020 8444 3348, e-mail mandbzander@btinternet.com)

ZARNECKI, Prof Jan Charles (John); s of Jerzy (George) Zarnecki, of London, and Anne Leslie, *née* Frith; *b* 6 November 1949, London; *Educ* Queens' Coll Cambridge (open exhibitioner, MA), UCL (PhD); *m* 2 July 1976 (m dis 1994), Gillian Elizabeth, *née* Fairbanks; 1 da (Holly Claire b 27 Jan 1978), 1 s (Thomas Guy b 29 Sept 1979); *Career* research asst Mullard Space Sci Lab UCL 1974–79, sr systems engr Dynamics Gp Br Aerospace 1979–81; Unit for Space Scis Univ of Kent: sr experimental offr 1981–85, lectr 1985–87, sr lectr 1987–96, reader 1996–2000; reader in space and planetary scis then prof of space sci Planetary and Space Research Inst Open Univ 2000– (head Space Scis Research Gp Planetary and Space Sciences Research Inst); sr visiting scientist Solar System Div European Space Research and Technol Centre European Space Agency 1999–2000; projects incl: involvement with Hubble Space Telescope, project mangr Giotto DIDSY comet Halley spacecraft experiment, princ investigator Surface Science Package and co-investigator Atmosphere Structure Instrument for Huygens probe/lander on Cassini mission to Saturn and Titan, princ investigator Ultraviolet Spectrometer Aurora/ExoMars lander, dep princ investigator PTOLEMY and co-investigator Multi-Purpose Surface and Sub-Surface Science Subsystem (MUPUS) on Rosetta lander; memb: Cncl Royal Astronomical Soc 1995–98, Solar System Working Gp European Space Agency 1995–98, European Space Sci Ctee European Sci Fndn 1997–2000, Cncl PPARC 2005–07 (memb Sci and Soc Advsy Gp 2003–); memb Shareholder's Ctee Eurotunnel plc 2003–06; memb Bd Milton Keynes Gallery; 5 separate awards from NASA and ESA 1997–2005, Arthur C Clarke Award 2005; CPhys, memb IAU, memb Inst of Physics, FRAS; author of over 200 scientific and tech pubns; *Recreations* watching football, cookery, films; *Style*— Prof John Zarnecki; ✉ Planetary and Space Sciences Research Institute, The Open University, Walton Hall, Milton Keynes MK7 6AA (tel 01908 659599, fax 01908 858022, e-mail j.c.zarnecki@open.ac.uk)

ZATOUROFF, Dr Michael Argo; s of Argo Arakel Zatouroff (d 1980), of New York, and Nina, *née* Dragounova (d 1979); *b* 23 October 1936; *Educ* Seaford Coll, Royal London Hosp (MB BS, DCH); *m* 13 May 1961, Diana, da of Alan Curtis Heard; 2 da (Anna Eugenie b 22 July 1963, Catherine Morwenna b 20 April 1968), 1 s (Justin Alan b 7 Sept 1965); *Career* house offr Royal London Hosp 1961, SHO Royal United Hosp Bath 1962–63; med registrar: UCH Ibadan Nigeria 1963–64, Royal Northern Hosp London 1964–66; conslt physician Kuwait Govt 1966–76; past appts: hon sr lectr in med Royal Free Hosp London, conslt physician The London Clinic London, lectr in med The London Foot Hosp London, examiner in med (United Exam Bd UK, Soc of Chiropodists, Med Artists' Assoc of GB), memb Editorial Bd Medicine International; Horder Prize in Med 1966; Freeman City of London, Liveryman Worshipful Co of Barber Surgeons; memb: Soc of Authors, RSM 1965, Med Soc of London 1966, Harveian Soc 1966, Osler Club 1966; hon fell Soc of Chiropodists, fell Med Artists Assoc of GB, FRCP; *Books* Physical Signs in General Medicine (1976, 2 edn 1996), Diagnostic Studies in General Medicine (1989), The Foot in Clinical Diagnosis (1993); *Recreations* cross-country cycling, med photography, carriage driving, theatre, eating, reading; *Clubs* Garrick; *Style*— Dr Michael Zatouroff; ✉ The Barn, Crowland Farm, Ancaster NG32 3RQ (tel 0797 404 9315, fax 0870 130 6304, e-mail zatouroff@onetel.com); The London Clinic, 149 Harley Street, London W1N 1HF (tel 020 7935 4444)

ZEALLEY, Christopher Bennett; s of late Sir Alec Zealley, of Devon, and late Nellie Maude, *née* King; *b* 5 May 1931; *Educ* Sherborne, King's Coll Cambridge (choral scholarship, MA); *m* 23 April 1966, Ann Elizabeth Sandwith; 1 s (Robert Paul b 1969), 1 da (Elizabeth Victoria b 1972); *Career* cmnnd RNVR 1953; ICI 1955–66, IRC 1966–70; dir: Dartington Hall Tst 1970–88, JT Group Ltd, Grant Instruments Ltd; chm: Public Interest Res Centre

1972–, Social Audit Ltd 1972–, Dartington Coll of Art 1973–91, Consumers Assoc (Which?) 1976–82, Morwellham Recreation Co Ltd 1978–90, Dartington and Co Group plc 1979–91, Charity Appointments Ltd 1986–92, Which Ltd 1991–93, Accrediting Bureau for Fundraising Orgns 1997–; memb Cncl Univ of Exeter 1988–97; tstee various orgns incl Charities Aid Fndn 1981–90; *Books* Creating a Charitable Trust; *Recreations* music; *Clubs* Lansdowne, Naval; *Style*— Christopher Zealley, Esq

ZEEGEN, Dr Ronald; OBE (1994); *b* 30 October 1938; *Educ* Battersea GS, Bart's Med Coll (MB BS, LRCP, DObstRCOG); *m*; 3 c; *Career* jr registrar and res fell Bart's 1965–69 (temp sr registrar 1971), sr registrar Westminster Hosp 1971–74 (registrar 1970), conslt physician i/c Depts of Gastro-enterology Westminster and St Stephen's Hosp 1974–93, conslt physician and gastroenterologist Chelsea and Westminster Hosp 1993–2003; receiving conslt physician Westminster Hosp for Palace of Westminster 1985–93; hon conslt gastro-enterologist: Royal Marsden Hosp 1986–2003, Royal Brompton and Nat Heart Hosps 1986–2003; hon conslt physician: Newpaper Press Fund 1986–2003, Royal Hosp Chelsea 1994–2003; med advsr to the Speaker House of Commons 1998–, conslt physician Lister Hosp London; former memb Editorial Bd Medical Digest; GMC: elected memb England 1999–2002, assoc memb 2003–; contrib to books and published papers for several med jls incl BMJ, Br Jl of Clinical Practice, Gut, Lancet and Quarterly Jl of Med; memb: BMA, Br Soc of Gastro-enterology, Liver Club, Med Soc of London, Harveian Soc, Hunterian Soc; MRCS, FRCP 1980; *Recreations* horology, antique walking sticks, fine wines; *Clubs* Garrick; *Style*— Dr Ronald Zeegen, OBE; ✉ Chelsea and Westminster Hospital, 369 Fulham Road, London SW10 9NH (tel 020 8746 8599 or 020 77308298, fax 020 8392 1607, e-mail ron@zeegen.co.uk)

ZEEMAN, Prof Sir (Erik) Christopher; kt (1991); s of Christian Zeeman (d 1929), of Aarhus and Yokohama, and Christine, *née* Bushell (d 1968); *b* 4 February 1925; *Educ* Christ's Hosp, Christ's Coll Cambridge (MA, PhD); *m* 1, June 1950 (m dis 1959), Elizabeth, da of Evan Jones; 1 da (Nicolette b 1956); m 2, Jan 1960, Rosemary, da of Harold Samuels Gledhill; 3 s (Tristan b 1960, Crispin b 1965, Samuel Christian b 1970), 2 da (Mary Lou b 1961, Francesca b 1967); *Career* Flying Officer RAF 1943–47; fell Gonville & Caius Coll Cambridge 1953–64 (hon fell 1997), Cwlth fell Univ of Chicago and Princeton Univ 1954–55, lectr Univ of Cambridge 1955–64, memb Institut des Hautes Études Scientifiques Paris 1962–63, fndn prof and dir Mathematics Research Centre Univ of Warwick 1964–88, visiting prof Univ of Calif Berkeley 1966–67, sr fell SERC 1976–81, prof Royal Instn 1983–95, visiting fell CCC Oxford 1985–86, Gresham prof of geometry Gresham Coll London 1988–94, princ Hertford Coll Oxford 1988–95 (hon fell 1995); visiting prof: Inst for Advanced Study Princeton, Institut des Hautes Études Scientifique Paris, Instituto de Matemática Pura e Aplicada Rio de Janeiro, Int Centre for Theoretical Physics Trieste, Univ of Maryland, Florida State Univ, Univ of Pisa, Univ of Texas San Antonio; chm Mathematic Ctee SERC 1982–85, pres London Mathematical Soc 1986–88, vice-pres Royal Soc 1989–90, fndr chm Scientific Steering Ctee Isaac Newton Inst Cambridge 1990–98, pres Mathematical Association 2003–04; Queen's Jubilee medal 1977, Senior Whitehead prize London Mathematical Soc 1982, Faraday medal Royal Soc 1988, David Crighton Medal London Mathematcial Soc and Inst of Mathematics and Its Applications 2007; Hon DSc: Univ of Hull 1984, Claremont Univ Centre & Graduate Sch 1986, Univ of Leeds 1990, Univ of Durham 1990, Univ of Hartford 1992, Open Univ 2003; Docteur (hc) Univ of Strasbourg 1974, Hon DSc and hon prof Univ of Warwick 1988, Hon DUniv York 1988; hon fell Christ's Coll Cambridge 1989; FRS 1975, memb Brazilian Acad of Sciences 1972; *Publications* Catastrophe Theory (1977), Geometry and Perspective (1987), Gyroscopes & Boomerangs (1989); many research papers; *Recreations* family, mathematics, music, bell-ringing, carpentry, walking; *Style*— Prof Sir Christopher Zeeman; ✉ 23 High Street, Woodstock, Oxfordshire OX20 1TE (tel and fax 01993 813402)

ZEIDMAN, His Hon Judge Martyn Keith; QC (1998); s of Abe Zeidman (d 1971), and Jennie, *née* Davis (d 2000); *b* 30 May 1952; *Educ* Univ of London (external LLB); *m* 1977, Verity, da of His Hon Aron Owen; 1 da (Annette b 24 June 1979), 1 s (Austin b 20 November 1981); *Career* called to the Bar 1974, asst recorder (SE Circuit) 1995–99, recorder 1999–2001, circuit judge 2001–; pres Mental Health Review Tbnl: Restricted Cases; memb: Yeshurun Synagogue Edgware, chm Jewish Marriage Cncl; *Publications* A Short Guide to the Landlord and Tenant Act 1987 (1987), A Short Guide to the Housing Act 1988 (1988), Steps to Possession (1989), A Short Guide to the Courts and Legal Services Act 1990 (1990), A Short Guide to the Road Traffic Act 1991 (1991), Making Sense of the Leasehold Reform Housing and Urban Development Act 1993 (1994), Archbold Practical Research Papers on Law of Mistake, Self Defence (1998); *Recreations* family, studying Jewish religious texts, cycling; *Style*— His Hon Judge Zeidman, QC; ✉ Snaresbrook Crown Court, The Court House, Hollybush Hill, London E11 1QW

ZEIN, Andrew; *Educ* St Paul's, Univ of Bristol; *Career* film prodn asst 1991–93, projects mangr IPH Westhall Ltd 1993–95, conslt BBC Entertainment Gp 1995–96, BBC broadcast entertainment business mangr (planning and strategy) 1996–97; Tiger Aspect Prodns: business devpt mangr 1997, commercial dir 1998, jt md 2001, md 2002–; chm PACT (TV) 2004–05 (vice-chm 2002–03); *Style*— Andrew Zein, Esq; ✉ Tiger Aspect Productions, 7 Soho Street, London W1D 3DQ

ZEKI, Prof Semir; *b* 8 November 1940; *Educ* UCL (BSc, PhD); *m* 1967, Anne-Marie Claire, *née* Blestel; 1 da (Isabelle b 24 June 1973), 1 s (Sebastian b 13 Jan 1977); *Career* res assoc St Elizabeth's Hosp Washington DC 1967–68, asst prof of anatomy Univ of Wisconsin 1968–69, Henry Head res fell Royal Soc 1975–80; UCL: asst lectr in anatomy 1966–67, lectr in anatomy 1969–75, reader in neurobiology 1980–81, prof of neurobiology 1981–, co-head Wellcome Dept of Cognitive Neurology 1996–2001, fell 2000–; visiting prof: Duke Univ Durham NC 1977, Institut für Medizinische Psychologie Ludwig Maximilians Univ Munich 1982–87, Univ of Calif Berkeley 1984, 2003 and 2006, Inst for Advanced Study Stanford Univ 2002; visiting lectr Univ of St Andrews 1985, assoc Neurosciences Res Prog NY 1985, visiting prof Université Libre de Bruxelles 1997–98; delivered numerous special lectures; memb: Bd of Advisors Beit Meml Tst 1984–89, Scientific Advsy Bd The Neurosciences Institute NY 1986–, Bd of Scientific Govrs Scripps Res Inst Calif 1992–, Bd of Govrs Int Brain Res Orgn (IBRO) 1993–98; chm Vision Res Working Pty Wellcome Tst 1987– (memb 1985–87); tstee Fight for Sight 1992–97, guarantor Brain 1994–; memb: Ctee of Honour Paris Decorative and Fine Arts Soc 1997–, Nat Sciences Cncl of France 1998–2002, Bd Scientific Govrs Low Temperature Physics Lab Technical Univ Helsinki; Hocart Prize Royal Anthropological Inst 1961, Minerva Fndn Prize California 1985, Prix Science Pour l'Art Louis Vuitton Moët Hennessy (LVMH) Paris 1991, Rank Prize in Opto-electronics 1992, Zotterman Prize Swedish Physiological Soc 1993, Electronic Imaging Award 2002, King Faisal Int Prize in Science King Faisal Fndn 2004; assoc ed and memb Ed Bds of scientific jls; ed Philosophical Transactions of the Royal Society 1997–2004; memb Physiological Soc 1978, hon memb Italian Primatological Assoc 1988, memb Academia Europaea 1990, memb European Acad of Sciences and Arts Salzburg 1992, foreign memb American Philosophical Soc 1998; Hon DSc Aston Univ 1994; FRSM 1972, FZS 1980, MRI 1985, FRS 1990, FMedSci 1998; *Books* A Vision of the Brain (1993), La Quête de l'essentiel (with Balthus, 1995), Inner Vision (1999); author of papers and articles in scientific jls; *Recreations* reading (especially about the darker side of man), music (especially opera), deep sleep; *Clubs* Athenaeum, Garrick; *Style*— Prof Semir Zeki, FRS; ✉ Wellcome Department of Imaging Neuroscience, University College London, Gower Street, London WC1E 6BT (tel 020 7679 7316, fax 020 7679 7316)

ZELKHA, Morris Sion; s of Eliahou Sion Zelkha (d 1988), of London, and Dinah, *née* Sopher; *b* 22 June 1948; *Educ* St Paul's; *m* 1, (m dis 1984); m 2, 2 Sept 1993, Jacqueline Marjorie Gosling; 2 da (Sarah Diana, Ella Marjorie); *Career* articled clerk rising to sr tax mangr Deloitte & Co (formerly Deloitte Plender Griffiths) 1966–77, joined Tansley Witt & Co (merged with Arthur Andersen & Co 1979) as tax mangr 1977, tax ptnr Arthur Andersen 1981; tax ptnr Deloitte & Touche 2002–; ACA 1970, AInstT 1970; *Recreations* bridge, snooker, reading; *Style*— Morris S Zelkha, Esq; ✉ Deloitte & Touche, 180 Strand, London WC2R 1BL (tel 020 7007 3420, fax 020 7007 5163)

ZELLICK, Prof Graham John; s of Reginald Zellick (d 1993), of Windsor, Berks, and Beana, *née* Levey; *b* 12 August 1948; *Educ* Christ's Coll Finchley, Gonville & Caius Coll Cambridge (MA, PhD), Stanford Univ Sch of Law (Ford Fndn fell); *m* 18 Sept 1975, Prof Jennifer Temkin, da of Michael Temkin (d 1993), of London; 1 s (Adam b 1977), 1 da (Lara b 1980); *Career* Queen Mary & Westfield Coll (formerly QMC) London: lectr in laws 1971–78, reader in law 1978–82, prof of public law 1982–88, dean Faculty of Laws 1984–88, head Dept of Law 1984–90, Drapers' prof of law 1988–91, sr vice-princ and actg princ 1990–91, prof of law 1991–98, princ 1991–98, emeritus prof of law 1998–; Univ of London: senator 1985–94, dean Faculty of Laws 1986–88, dep chm Academic Cncl 1987–89, memb Cncl 1994–2003, vice-chllr and pres 1997–2003 (dep vice-chllr 1994–97); visiting prof of law Univ of Toronto 1975 and 1978–79, visiting scholar St John's Coll Oxford 1989, hon prof Sch of Law Univ of Birmingham 2004–; called to the Bar Middle Temple 1992 (bencher 2001), assoc memb 3 Verulam Bldgs Gray's Inn; ed: Euro Human Rights Reports 1978–82, Public Law 1981–86; memb Editorial Bd: British Jl of Criminology 1980–90, Public Law 1981–91, Howard Jl of Criminal Justice 1984–87, Civil Law Library 1987–91; chm: Tel Aviv Univ Tst Lawyers' Gp 1984–89, Prisoners' Advice and Law Serv 1984–89, Ctee of Heads of Univ Law Schs 1988–90, Legal Ctee All-Pty Parly War Crimes Gp 1988–91, E London Strategic Forum for Nat Educn and Trg Targets 1993–95, Criminal Cases Review Cmmn 2003–; dep chm Justice Ctee on Prisoners' Rights 1981–83; memb: Jellicoe Ctee on Bds of Visitors of Prisons 1973–75, Cncl Howard League for Penal Reform 1973–82, Newham Dist Ethics Ctee 1985–86, Lord Chllr's Advsy Ctee on Legal Aid 1985–88, Data Protection Tbnl 1985–96, Lord Chllr's Advsy Ctee on Legal Educn 1988–90, Bd of Dirs and Exec Ctee Inst of Citizenship Studies 1991–93, Cncl City and East London Confedn for Med and Dentistry 1991–95, Bart's Med Coll 1991–95, Cncl of Govrs The London Hosp Med Coll 1991–95, Cncl Spitalfields Heritage Centre 1992–98, Cncl Ctee of Vice-Chllrs and Princs 1993–97, Main Bd E London Partnership 1994–95, Bd of Dirs UCAS 1994–97, Steering Ctee London HE Consortium 1999–2001, Bd London Competitive Advantage Prog 2000–01, Criminal Injuries Compensation Appeals Panel 2000–03, Competition Appeal Tbnl 2000–03, Criminal Justice Cncl 2003–06; electoral cmmr 2001–04; vice-chm Cncl Academic Study Gp for Israel and the Middle East 1995–2003; non-exec memb: S Thames RHA 1994–95, E London and City HA 1995–97; pres W London (Reform) Synagogue 2000–06 (chm Senate of Elders 2006–); govr: Central London Poly 1973–77, Pimlico Sch 1973–77, UCS 1983–92, QMC (later Queen Mary & Westfield Coll) 1983–98, N London Poly 1986–89, Univ of Greenwich 1994–97, William Goodenough Tst 1997–2003, Tel Aviv Univ 2000–; chm: Reform Club Conservation Tst 2003–, Bd of Govrs Leo Baeck Coll 2005–06; tstee: William Harvey Research Inst 1995–2000, Samuel Courtauld Tst 1997–2003, Richmond American Int Univ in London 2002–06 (govr 1999–2003, chm 2005–06); patron Redress Tst 1993–; JP Inner London 1981–85; Freeman City of London 1992, Second Master Warden Worshipful Co of Drapers 2007–08 (Freeman 1991, Liveryman 1995, memb Ct of Assts 2000–); Hon LHD NYU 2001, Hon LLD Richmond 2003, Hon LLD Univ of Birmingham 2006; hon fell: Burgon Soc (Hon FBS) 2001, Gonville & Caius Coll Cambridge 2001, Heythrop Coll 2005, Leo Baeck Coll 2007; FRSA 1991, FRSM 1996, FInstD 1996–2003, CCMI (CIMgt) 1997, Hon FSALS 1997, FICPD 1998–2003, AcSS 2000, Hon FRAM 2003; *Books* Prison in Halsbury's Laws of England (4 edn 1974, with Sir Louis Blom-Cooper, QC), Justice in Prison (with Sir Brian MacKenna, 1983), The Law Commission and Law Reform (ed 1988); *Clubs* Reform; *Style*— Prof Graham Zellick; ✉ Criminal Cases Review Commission, Alpha Tower, Suffolk Street Queensway, Birmingham B1 1TT (tel 0121 633 1890, fax 0121 633 1804)

ZEPHANIAH, Benjamin Obadiah Iqbal; s of Valerie Ebanks; *b* 15 April 1958; *Career* poet; writer in residence: Africa Arts Collective City of Liverpool (1 year), Hay-on-Wye Literature Festival, Memphis State Univ Tennessee; TV and radio presenter (incl Passport to Liverpool, Radio 4); patron: Irie Dance Co, Market Nursery Hackney, VIVA! (vegetarian gp), Chinese Women's Refuge Gp, SARI (Sport Against Racism in Ireland); pres Penrose Housing Assoc (for ex-prisoners); shortlisted: creative artist in residence Univ of Cambridge 1986, prof of poetry Univ of Oxford; subject of two C4 documentaries, toured Europe, Canada, USA and the Caribbean, regular appearances on TV and radio; *Films* Didn't You Kill My Brother (Comic Strip), Farendg; *Records* Big Boys Don't Make Girls Cry, Free South Africa (with The Wailers), Dub Ranting, Rasta, Us and Dem, Back to Roots, Belly of de Beast, Naked; *Plays* Playing the Right Tune, Job Rocking, Hurricane Dub (BBC Young Playwrights award 1988), Streetwise, Delirium, Mickey Tekka, Listen to Your Parents (Race in the Media awards 2001); *Films* Dread Poets Society (BBC); *Books* Pen Rhythm, The Dread Affair, In a Liverpool, Rasta Time in Palestine, City Psalms, Talking Turkeys (1994), Funky Chickens (1996), Propa Propaganda (1996), Schools Out (1997), Face (1999), Bloomsbury Book of Love Poems (ed, 1999), Wicked World (2000), The Little Book of Vegan Poems (2001), Refugee Boy (2001), Too Black, Too Strong (2001), We Are Britain (2002), Gangsta Rap (2004); *Style*— Benjamin Zephaniah, Esq; ✉ c/o PFD, Drury House, 34–43 Russell Street, London WC2B 5HA

ZERNY, Richard Guy Frederick; s of Marcus Zerny (d 1984), and Eunice Irene Mary, *née* Diggle (d 1982); *b* 27 June 1944; *Educ* Charterhouse; *m* 11 Sept 1970, Jane Alicia, da of Albert George Steventon (d 1984); 2 s (Charles Marcus Stephen b 1972, Miles Patrick Richard b 1973), 1 da (Clare Louise b 1979); *Career* Zernys Ltd: dir 1969–95, md 1979–83, chm 1989–95; dir Johnson Group Properties plc 1983–2002; Johnson Service Group plc: UK dir 1983–2002, UK chief exec 1989–97, chief exec 1997–2002; chm Johnson Cleaners UK Ltd 1995–2002; dir Cleaning Tokens Ltd 1986–99; chm Johnsons Apparelmaster Ltd 1995–2002; md Johnson Group Management Services Ltd 1989–2002; ret; Hull and Dist Lifeboat Branch: memb Ctee 1967–83, sec 1975–83; govr Kilham C of E Primary Sch 2004– (chair 2006–); Freeman City of London 1986, Liveryman Worshipful Co of Launderers 1987; *Recreations* sailing, golf, bridge, campanology; *Clubs* Royal Yorks Yacht, Ganton Golf; *Style*— Richard G F Zerny, Esq; ✉ Stratton House, Southside, Kilham, Driffield, East Yorkshire Y025 4ST

ZETA JONES, Catherine; da of David James Jones, of Swansea, S Wales; *m* 2000, Michael Douglas, the actor; 1 s (Dylan Michael b 2000), 1 da (Carys Zeta b 2003); *Career* actress; ambass NSPCC 2005–; *Theatre* incl: The Pyjama Game (Number One Tour), Annie, Bugsy Malone (West End), 42nd Street (West End), Street Scene (ENO); *Television* incl: Darling Buds of May 1991, Out of the Blue 1991, Cinder Path 1994, Return of The Native 1995, Titanic 1996; *Films* incl: Scheherazade 1990, Coup de Foudre, Splitting Heirs 1993, Blue Juice 1995, The Phantom 1996, The Mask of Zorro 1997, Entrapment 1998, The Haunting 1999, High Fidelity 2000, Traffic 2000, America's Sweethearts 2001, Chicago 2002, Sinbad: Legend of the Seven Seas 2003, Intolerable Cruelty 2003, The Terminal 2004, Ocean's Twelve 2004; *Style*— Ms Catherine Zeta Jones; ✉ c/o ICM Ltd, Oxford House, 76 Oxford Street, London W1D 1BS

ZETLAND, 4 Marquess of (UK 1892); Sir Lawrence Mark Dundas; 7 Bt (GB 1762), DL (N Yorks 1994); also Earl of Ronaldshay (UK 1892), Earl of Zetland (UK 1838), and Baron

Dundas (GB 1794); eldest s of 3 Marquess of Zetland, DL (d 1989), and Penelope, Marchioness of Zetland (d 2003); *b* 28 December 1937; *Educ* Harrow, Christ's Coll Cambridge; *m* 4 April 1964, Susan Rose, 2 da of late Guy Richard Chamberlin; 2 s (Robin Lawrence, Earl of Ronaldshay b 5 March 1965, Lord James Edward b 2 May 1967), 2 da (Lady Henrietta Kate (Lady Henrietta Stroyan) b 9 Feb 1970, Lady Victoria Clare (Lady Victoria Madel) b 2 Jan 1973); *Heir* s, Earl of Ronaldshay; *Career* late 2 Lt Grenadier Gds; landowner; dir Catterick Racecourse, chm Voltigeur Int Ltd; steward of the Jockey Club 1992–94, dir British Horseracing Bd 1993–97; *Recreations* tennis (lawn and Royal), squash, racing (racehorses Foggy Buoy, Tatiana and Malek); *Clubs* All England Lawn Tennis, Jockey; *Style*— The Most Hon the Marquess of Zetland, DL; ✉ The Orangery, Richmond, North Yorkshire DL10 5HE (tel 01748 823222, mobile 07836 779869, fax 01748 823252, e-mail zetland@aske.co.uk); Flat F, 17/18 Smith Street, London SW3 4EE (tel 020 7730 7414)

ZIEGLER, Philip Sandeman; CVO (1991); s of Maj Colin Louis Ziegler, DSO, DL (d 1977); *b* 24 December 1929; *Educ* Eton, New Coll Oxford; *m* 1, 1960, Sarah (decd), da of Sir William Collins (d 1976); 1 s, 1 da; m 2, 1971, Mary Clare, *née* Charrington; 1 s; *Career* HM Dip Serv 1952–67, editorial dir William Collins and Sons (joined 1967); chm: Soc of Authors 1988–90, Public Lending Right Advsy Ctee 1994–97; Hon DLitt Westminster Coll Fulton 1988, Hon DLitt Univ of Buckingham 2000; FRSL 1972, FRHS 1979; *Books* Duchess of Dino (1962), Addington (1965), The Black Death (1968), William IV (1971), Melbourne (1976), Crown and People (1978), Diana Cooper (1981), Mountbatten (1985), The Sixth Great Power: Barings 1762–1929 (1988), King Edward VIII (1990), Harold Wilson (1993), London at War (1995), Osbert Sitwell (1998), Soldiers: Fighting Men's Lives 1901–2001 (2001), Rupert Hart-Davis: Man of Letters (2004); *Clubs* Brooks's; *Style*— Philip Ziegler, Esq, CVO, FRSL; ✉ 22 Cottesmore Gardens, London W8 5PR (tel 020 7937 1903, fax 020 7937 5458)

ZIENKIEWICZ, Prof Olgierd Cecil; CBE (1989); s of Casimir Rafael Zienkiewicz (d 1959), of Edinburgh, and Edith Violet, *née* Penny (d 1974); *b* 18 May 1921; *Educ* Imperial Coll of Sci and Technol London (BSc, ACGI), Univ of London (PhD, DSc, DIC); *m* 15 Dec 1952, Helen Jean, da of Albert Fleming; 2 s (Andrew Olgierd b 17 Sept 1953, John David b 4 May 1955), 1 da (Krystyna Helen (Mrs Beynon) b 3 March 1958); *Career* conslt engr Sir William Halcrow & Partners 1945–49, lectr Univ of Edinburgh 1949–57, prof of structural engrg Northwestern Univ Evanston Illinois USA 1957–61, prof and head of Dept of Civil Engrg Univ of Wales Swansea 1961–88, dir Inst for Numerical Methods in Engrg 1970–; written circa 600 papers on: solid and fluid mechanics, stress analysis of dams, nuclear reactors, lubrication theory, devpt of the finite element method; fndr and chief ed Int Jl for Numerical Methods in Engrg; memb numerous editorial bds of jls incl: Solids & Structures, Earthquake Engrg, Rock Mechanics; memb Cncl ICE 1972–76, chm Ctee of Analysis and Design Int Congress of Large Dams 1973–85, holder visiting res chair of naval sea systems cmd Naval Postgrad Sch Monterey California 1979–80, visiting Jubilee prof Chalmers Univ of Technol Göteborg Sweden 1990 and 1992, UNESCO chair of numerical methods Tech Univ of Catalunya Barcelona 1989–, Chair prof Univ of Texas Austin 1989–93, pres Int Assoc of Computational Mechanics 1986–90; recipient: James Alfred Ewing medal ICE 1980, Nathan Newmark Medal American Soc of Civil Engrs 1980, Worcester Warner Reid medal American Soc of Mechanical Engrs 1980, Carl Friedrich Gauss medal German Acad of Sci 1987, Royal medal Royal Soc 1990, Gold medal Inst of Structural Engrs 1992, Gold medal Inst of Mathematics and its Applications 1992, Leonardo da Vinci medal Sociale European pour formation des Ingenieures (SEFI) 1997, Timoshenko medal American Soc of Mechanical Engrs 1998; hon prof Dalian China 1988; Hon DSc: Lisbon 1972, Univ of Ireland 1975, Univ of Brussels 1982, Northwestern Univ USA 1984, Univ of Trondheim Norway 1985, Chalmers Univ of Technol Sweden 1987, Univ of Technol Warsaw 1989, Univ of Technol Kraków Poland 1989, Univ of Hong Kong 1992, Tech Univ of Budapest 1992, Univ of Padua 1992, Tech Univ of Compiègne France 1992, Univ of Thessaloniki 1993, Brunel Univ 1993, Univ of Wales 1993, Tech Univ of Vienna 1993, Ecole Normale de Cachen Paris 1997, Tech Univ of Madrid 1998, Univ of Buenos Aires 1998, Tech Univ of Lisbon 2001, Tech Univ of Silesie Poland 2001, Univ of Milan 2001; hon fell: Univ of Wales Swansea 1989, Imperial Coll London 1993; Hon DLitt Univ of Dundee 1987; fell: City and Guilds Inst of London 1979; Chevalier dans l'Ordre des Palmes Académiques (France) 1996; foreign memb: US Nat Acad of Engrg 1981, Polish Acad of Sci 1985, Chinese Acad of Sci 1998, Nat Acad if Sci Italy (Academia Dei Lincei 1999), foreign memb Instituto Lombardo de Milano 1999, Academia de Sciencа Torino 2002; FRS 1978, FREng 1979; *Books* The Finite Element Method in Structural Mechanics (1967), The Finite Element Method in Engineering Science (1971), The Finite Element Method (1977, 5 edn with R L Taylor, vol I The Basis, vol II Solid Mechanics, vol III Fluid Dynamics 2000), Finite Elements and Approximations (with K Morgan, 1980); *Recreations* sailing, diving; *Clubs* Athenaeum; *Style*— Prof Olgierd Zienkiewicz, CBE, FRS, FREng; ✉ 29 Somerset Road, Mumbles, Swansea SA3 4PG (tel 01792 368776)

ZIERKE, Ulrich; s of Dr Erwin Zierke, of Frankfurt, Germany, and Elsbeth Zierke; *b* 24 June 1944; *Educ* GS Germany, J W Goethe Univ Frankfurt (Diplom Kaufmann); *m* 4 April 1975, Kornelia, da of Robert Saur; *Career* Nat Serv 1965–67, banking apprentice 1963–65; Westdeutsche Landesbank: banker 1972, seconded Libra Bank London and Mexico City 1974–78, various assignments to NY Tokyo and Madrid 1978–90, sr vice-pres 1983–, dep chief exec Chartered WestLB Ltd London 1990–92, gen mangr Westdeutsche Landesbank London 1992–95; chief exec The Thomas Cook Group Limited 1995–98, md Westdeutsche Landesbank 1999–; *Recreations* travelling, arts, skiing; *Clubs* IOD, RAC; *Style*— Ulrich Zierke, Esq; ✉ Westdeutsche Landesbank GZ, Woolgate Exchange, 25 Basinghall Street, London EC2V 5HA (tel 020 7020 7100, fax 020 7020 7105)

ZIGMOND, Jonathan Peter; s of His Hon Judge Joseph Zigmond (d 1980), and Muriel, *née* Lermon; *Educ* Cheadle Hulme Sch, Univ of Reading (BSc); *m* 11 Sept 1976, Sarah Angela Barbara, *née* Roff; 2 s (Andrew Morris b 3 Jan 1981, Robin James b 13 Dec 1982); *Career* articled clerk Hogg Bullimore Chartered Accountants 1972–75, qualified 1975; PricewaterhouseCoopers (formerly Coopers & Lybrand before merger): joined 1976, City practice 1976–82, Leeds 1982–, ptnr 1983–, head of tax practice Leeds 1983–95, memb Tax Bd 1993–96; memb: Inheritance Tax and Tsts Sub Ctee ICAEW 1988–, Capital Taxes Ctee Chartered Inst of Taxation 1995– (chm 1999–2001); FCA (ACA 1975), ATII 1975, TEP 1992; *Books* Tax Digest: Inheritance Tax on Discretionary and Accumulation Trusts (1987, 2 edn 1988), Inheritance Tax Planning (1987, 2 edn 1988), Tax Digest: Capital Gains Tax and Offshore Trusts (1992, 2 edn 1998); *Style*— Jonathan Zigmond, Esq; ✉ PricewaterhouseCoopers, Benson House, 33 Wellington Street, Leeds LS1 4JU (tel 0113 289 4500, fax 0113 289 4466, e-mail jon.p.zigmond@uk.pwc.com)

ZILKHA, Dr Kevin Jerome; s of Joseph Zilkha (d 1989), and Daisy, *née* Shohet; *b* 4 December 1929; *Educ* Alliance Sch, Guy's Hosp Med Sch London (MD); *m* 10 Sept 1958, Judith Diana, da of Walter Mogridge; 2 s (Timothy b 22 Nov 1960, Jonathan b 29 Oct 1965), 1 da (Caroline b 16 March 1964); *Career* neurological house physician Guy's Hosp 1953–54 (former house offr posts), RAMC Egypt and Cyprus 1954–56, med registrar Guy's and New Cross Hosps 1956–58, resident MO Nat Hosp Queen Square 1961–62 (jr resident posts 1958–61), research fell Dept of Chemical Pathology Guy's Hosp Med Sch 1962–63, sr registrar Nat Hosp and Hosp for Sick Children Gt Ormond St 1963 and 1965–94, conslt neurologist Nat Hosp for Neurology and Neurosurgery and KCH 1965–94; hon neurologist to: Maudsley Hosp 1965–94, Royal Hosp and The Army 1972–; pres Harveian Soc of London 1981; chm: Research Ctee and Research Ethics Ctee KCH 1968–, Conslts Ctee KCH 1985–87, Conslts Ctee Nat Hosp 1989–91, Ethics Ctee Nat Hosp 1993–94, Med Advsy Ctee Cromwell Hosp 1988–90, Bd of Dirs Cromwell Hosp 1990–; tstee Med Research Tst KCH 1994–; memb: BMA 1965, Assoc of Br Neurologists 1965, RSM 1965; FRCP; *Recreations* sailing; *Clubs* MCC, Garrick, Chichester Yacht; *Style*— Dr Kevin Zilkha; ✉ 11 Alleyn Park, Dulwich, London SE21 8AU

ZIMAN, Lawrence David; *b* 10 August 1938; *Educ* City of London Sch, Trinity Hall Cambridge (MA), Univ of Michigan Law Sch (postgrad fell); *m* Joyce; 2 s; *Career* slr; Herbert Oppenheimer Nathan & Vandyk: articled clerk 1960–63, asst slr 1963–65, ptnr 1965–66; founding ptnr Berwin & Co (now Berwin Leighton) 1966–70, seconded to Industrial Reorganisation Corporation 1969–70, fndr Ziman & Co 1970 (merged with Nabarro Nathanson 1977), ptnr Nabarro Nathanson 1977–95, gen counsel TI Group plc 1995–98, ptnr Chadbourne & Parke 1999–2000, sr UK counsel Vinson & Elkins 2000–06; dir: Signet Gp plc 1993–95, N Brown Group plc 1994–2002; inspr under Companies Act to investigate affrs of Barlow Clowes/James Ferguson 1988 (report published 1995); *Books* Butterworths Company Law Service (gen ed 1985–90, consltg ed 1990–99); *Style*— Lawrence Ziman, Esq; ✉ 78 Garricks House, Wadbrook Street, Kingston-upon-Thames, Surrey KT1 1HS (e-mail lziman@btinternet.com)

ZIMMER, Prof Robert Mark; s of Norman Zimmer, NY, USA, and Lenore *née* Wasserman; *Educ* Churchill Coll Cambridge, MIT (SB), Columbia Univ NY (MA, MPhil, PhD); *m* 23 July 1983, Joanna Elizabeth Marlow, da of Thomas Gondris, of Ipswich, Suffolk; 2 s (Edmund b 31 Jan 1992, Sebastian b 14 August 1996); *Career* lectr: Columbia Univ 1982–85, Brunel Univ 1985–; currently head Dept of Computing Goldsmiths Univ of London and co-dir Goldsmiths Digital Studios; visiting scholar Dept of Sanskrit and Indian Studies Harvard Univ 1989; visiting prof: Univ of Ottawa 1989, Univ of Bristol 1997–98; published poetry and articles on mathematics, computer science, electrical engrg and 18th century Eng lit; *Recreations* food, books; *Clubs* Young Johnsonians; *Style*— Prof Robert Zimmer

ZIMMERMANN, Frank Peter; *b* 1965, Duisburg, Germany; *Career* violinist; studied with Valery Gradov, Sashko Gawriloff, Herman Krebbers; awarded Premio dell Accademia Musicale Chigiana Siena 1990, received Rheinischer Kulturpreis 1994; orchs appeared with incl: Philadelphia Orch, Chicago Symphony Orch, Boston Symphony Orch, The Cleveland Orch, Los Angeles Philharmonic, Staadtskapelle Dresden, Gustav Mahler Youth Orch, Berlin Philharmonic Orch, Gewandhausorchstra Leipzig, Munich Philharmonic, Bayerische Rundfunk, Vienna Philharmonic, Chamber Orch of Europe, Orchestre de Paris, Oslo Philharmonic Orch, Royal Concertgebouw Orch, Russian Nat Orch, NHK Symphony Orch, LSO, English Chamber Orch, The London Philharmonic, Philharmonia Orch, NY Philharmonic; conductors worked with incl: Lorin Maazel, Barenboim, Andrew Davis, Sir Colin Davis, Wolfgang Sawallisch, Dohnányi, Bernard Haitink, André Previn, Kurt Sanderling, Franz Welser-Möst, Mariss Jansons; special concerts incl: Mozart Sinfonia Concertante for Violin and Viola (with Tabea Zimmermann and English Chamber Orch) Buckingham Palace 1991, May Day concert Royal Albert Hall with the Berlin Philharmonic Orch (televised all over world); *Recordings* incl: Saint-Saëns Concerto No 3, Stravinsky Concerto, Ravel Tzigane, all Mozart Sonatas, all Prokofiev Sonatas, works by Berg/Stravinsky/Ravel (Edison Award 1992, Diapason d'Or de l'Année 1992), works by Debussy/Ravel/Janácek (with Alexander Lonquich, Diapason d'Or 1992), works by Groupe des Six (Edison Award 1994), Eugène Ysaÿe 6 Solo Sonatas (Prix Cecilia, ECHO/Deutscher Schallplattenpreis), Brahms Violin Concerto with Mozart Violin Concerto No 3 (with Berlin Philharmonic Orch and Wolfgang Sawallisch), Tchaikovsky Concerto and Prokofiev Concerto No 1 (with Berlin Philharmonic Orch and Lorin Maazel), Weill Violin Concerto (with Berlin Philharmonic Orch and Mariss Jansons), Ligeti Violin Concerto (with ASKO Ensemble and Reinbert de Leeuw); *Style*— Frank Peter Zimmermann, Esq; ✉ c/o Jeroen Tersteeg, Riaskoff Concert Management Brussels 34, Avenue de Beau Séjour, 1180 Brussels, Belgium (tel 32 2 372 3005, fax 32 2 372 3006)

ZINKIN, Peter John Louis; *b* 23 July 1953; *Educ* Winchester, Magdalene Coll Cambridge (BA), London Business Sch (MSc(Econ)); *Career* London Business Sch 1978–81; Balfour Beatty plc: various appts 1981–88, gp planning and devpt mangr 1988–91, chm BICC Developments 1991–, main bd dir 1991–; MCT; *Style*— Peter Zinkin, Esq; ✉ Balfour Beatty plc, 130 Wilton Road, London SW1V 1LQ (tel 020 7216 6800, fax 020 7216 6900, e-mail peter.zinkin@balfourbeatty.com)

ZITTRAIN, Prof Jonathan; s of Lester Zittrain (d 2003), and Ruth Zittrain; *b* 24 December 1969, Pittsburgh, PA; *Educ* Yale Univ (BS), Harvard Univ (JD, MPA); *Career* memb Bar: Pennsylvania, DC, Massachusetts; clerk to Hon Stephen F Williams US Ct of Appeals DC Circuit 1995–96; Harvard Law Sch: co-fndr and exec dir then faculty co-dir Berkman Center for Internet and Soc 1996–2005, lectr on law 1996–2000 (also adjunct lectr on public policy John F Kennedy Sch of Govt), Jack N and Lillian R Berkman asst prof for entrepreneurial legal studies 2000–05 (visiting prof 2005–); prof of internet governance and regulation and dir of grad studies Oxford Internet Inst Univ of Oxford 2005–; chief forum administrator CompuServe Info Serv 1984–2004; memb: Cncl on Foreign Rels, Advsy Bd MediaUnbound, Bd Creative Commons Int 2005–; forum fell World Economic Forum 2000–; *Publications* The Torts Game: Defending Mean Joe Greene (2004), The Generative Internet (2006); numerous articles in professional jls, magazines, and government pubns; *Style*— Prof Jonathan Zittrain; ✉ Oxford Internet Institute, 1 St Giles', Oxford OX1 3JS (tel 01865 287210)

ZOCHONIS, Sir John Basil; kt (1997), DL (1989); s of Constantine Zochonis (d 1951), of Altrincham, and Nitza Octavia, *née* Stavridi (d 1981); *b* 2 October 1929; *Educ* Rugby, Univ of Oxford (BA); *m* 14 Sept 1990, Brigid Mary Evanson, da of Dr George Smyth; *Career* chm Paterson Zochonis plc 1970–93 (joined 1953, dir 1957); chm Cncl Univ of Manchester 1987–90; memb: Cncl Royal Africa Soc 1984, Cncl Br Exec Serv Overseas 1988, Bd Commonwealth Development Corp 1992–95; pres: Greater Manchester Youth Assoc (now FIRST) 1980–93 (vice-pres 1979), Manchester Univ Settlement 1989–98 (memb 1982–98); tstee Police Fndn 1994– (memb Exec Ctee 1989–); High Sheriff Greater Manchester 1994–95; Hon LLD Univ of Manchester 1991; Freeman City of London 1978, Liveryman Worshipful Co of Tallow Chandlers 1978; *Recreations* reading and cricket; *Clubs* Carlton, Travellers, MCC; *Style*— Sir John Zochonis, DL; ✉ c/o Paterson Zochonis plc, Cussons House, Bird Hall Lane, Stockport SK3 0XN (tel 0161 491 8000, fax 0161 491 8090)

ZOUCHE, 18 Baron (E 1308); Sir James Assheton Frankland; 12 Bt (E 1660); s of Hon Sir Thomas Frankland, 11 Bt (d 1944, s of Sir Frederick Frankland, 10 Bt, by his w Baroness Zouche (d 1965), 17 holder of the Peerage and descendant of Eudes La Zouche, yr bro of Sir Roger La Zouche of Ashby after whose family Ashby-de-la-Zouch is named); Lord Zouche is coheir to Barony of St Maur (abeyant since 1628); *b* 23 February 1943; *Educ* Lycée Jacard Lausanne; *m* 1978, Sally, da of Roderic M Barton, of Bungay, Suffolk; 1 s, 1 da; *Heir* s Hon William Frankland; *Career* Capt 15/19 King's Roy Hussars (ret 1968), ADC to Govr Tasmania 1965–68, Hon ADC to Govr Victoria 1975–; pres Multiple Sclerosis Soc Victoria 1981–84; co dir; *Recreations* shooting; *Style*— The Rt Hon the Lord Zouche; ✉ The Abbey, Charlton Adam, Somerton, Somerset TA11 7BE

ZUCKER, His Hon Kenneth Harry; QC (1981); s of Nathaniel Zucker (d 1989), of London, and Norma Zucker, *née* Mehlberg (d 1937); *b* 4 March 1935; *Educ* Westcliff HS, Exeter Coll Oxford; *m* 1961, Ruth Erica, da of Dr Henry Brudno (d 1967); 1 s (Jonathan), 1 da (Naomi); *Career* called to the Bar Gray's Inn 1959; recorder 1982–89, circuit judge (SE

Circuit) 1989–2005; *Recreations* reading, walking, photography, bookbinding; *Style*— His Hon K H Zucker, QC

ZUCKERMAN, Prof Arie Jeremy; *Educ* Univ of Birmingham (BSc, MSc, DSc), Univ of London (MB BS, MD, DipBact, Univ Gold medal, Evans prize, A B Cunning prize, A B Cunning award); *Career* Flt Lt then Sqdn Ldr RAF Med Branch 1959–62; first obstetric house surgn Royal Free Hosp 1957–58, casualty surgn and admissions offr Whittington Hosp London 1958–59 (house physician in gen med 1958), Med Branch RAF 1959–62, Epidemiol Res Lab Public Health Laboratory Serv 1960–62, secondment as hon registrar Dept of Pathology Guy's Hosp Med Sch 1962–63, sr registrar Public Health Laboratory Serv 1963–65; LSHTM: sr lectr Dept of Bacteriology and Immunology 1965–68, reader in virology 1968–72, prof of virology 1972–75, dir Dept of Med Microbiology 1975–88; prof of microbiology Univ of London 1975–, dean Royal Free Hosp Sch of Med 1989–98, princ and dean Royal Free and UC Med Sch UCL 1998–99; WHO: conslt on hepatitis 1970–2005, memb Expert Advsy Panel on Virus Diseases 1974–2005, dir Collaborating Centre for Ref and Res on Viral Hepatitis 1974–89, dir Collaborating Centre for Ref and Res on Viral Diseases 1990–2005; hon conslt virologist: N E Thames Regnl Blood Transfusion Centre 1970–94, Charing Cross Hosp 1982–96, Nat Blood Authy 1994–99; hon conslt microbiologist Royal Free Hosp 1989–2002, non-exec dir Royal Free Hampstead NHS Tst 1990–99, dir Anthony Nolan Bone Marrow Tst 1989–2002; memb: Cncl RCPath 1983–86, Bd Public Health Lab Serv 1983–89, Cncl Zoological Soc of London 1989–92, Cncl UCL 1995–2003; ed: Jl of Medical Virology 1976–, Jl of Virological Methods 1979–; contrib to numerous other learned jls; Stewart prize of the BMA 1981, James Blundell medal and award Br Blood Tranfusion Soc 1992; MRCS, DObstRCOG 1958, FRCPath 1977 (MRCPath 1965), FRCP 1982 (LRCP 1957, MRCP 1977), FMedSci 1998; *Books* Virus Diseases of the Liver (1970), Hepatitis-associated Antigen and Viruses (1972), Human Viral Hepatitis (2 edn, 1975), Hepatitis Viruses of Man (with C R Howard, 1979), A Decade of Viral Hepatitis (1980), Viral Hepatitis (ed, 1986), Principles and Practice of Clinical Virology (1987, 5 edn 2004), Viral Hepatitis and Liver Disease (ed, 1988), Recent Developments in Prophylactic Immunization (ed, 1989), Viral Hepatitis (ed, 1990), Viral Hepatitis: Scientific Basis and Clinical Management (with H Thomas, 1993, 3 edn 2005), Molecular Medicine of Viral Hepatitis (with T J Harrison, 1996), Prevention of Hepatitis B in the newborn, children and adolescents (ed, 1996), Hepatitis B in the Asian-Pacific Region (ed, vol 1 1997, vol 2 1998, vol 3 1999); *Style*— Prof Arie Zuckerman; ✉ Royal Free and University College Medical School, Rowland Hill Street, Hampstead, London NW3 2PF (tel 020 7830 2579, fax 020 7830 2070, e-mail a.zuckerman@medsch.ucl.ac.uk)

ZUKERMAN, Pinchas; *b* 1948; *Educ* began musical training with father, Israel Conservatory (with Ilona Feher), Acad of Music Tel Aviv, Julliard Sch USA (scholar, studied with Ivan Galamian); *Career* musician; violinist, violist, teacher and conductor; as soloist performs with major orchestras worldwide; soloist and conductor with many maj orchs incl: New York Philharmonic, Boston Symphony, Los Angeles Philharmonic, Nat Symphony Orch and San Francisco, Montreal, Toronto and Ottawa Symphonies, Berlin Philharmonic, Philharmonia, Eng Chamber Orch, Israel Philharmonic; former music dir: South Bank Festival, St Paul Chamber Orch; princ guest conductor Dallas Symphony Orch's Int Music Festival 1990–93; artist dir Baltimore Symphony Orch's Summer Musicfest 1996–99; music dir Nat Arts Centre Orch Ottawa Canada 1999–; extensive recital tours with Marc Neikrug, chamber music collaborations with Itzhak Perlman, Daniel Barenboim, Ralph Kirshbaum; discography incl over 100 recordings widely representative of violin and viola repertoires; Hon DUniv Brown USA; *Awards* first prize Twenty-Fifth Leventritt Int Competition 1967, Achievement award Int Center in NY, King Solomon award America-Israel Cultural Fndn, Medal of Arts 1983, Isaac Stern Award for Artistic Excellence Nat Arts Awards 2002; *Style*— Pinchas Zukerman; ✉ c/o Kirshbaum Demler & Assoc Inc, 711 West End Avenue, Suite 5KN, New York, NY 10025, USA (tel 00 1 212 2224843)

ZUNZ, Sir Gerhard Jacob (Jack); kt (1989); s of Wilhelm Zunz (d 1959), of Johannesburg, South Africa, and Helene (d 1973); *b* 25 December 1923; *Educ* Athlone HS Johannesburg, Univ of the Witwatersrand (BSc); *m* 1948, Babs Maisel; 2 da (Marion Erica b 1952 d 1992, Laura Ann b 1955), 1 s (Leslie Mark b 1956); *Career* served WWII SA Artillery Egypt and Italy 1943–46; asst engr Alpheus Williams & Dowse 1948–50; Ove Arup & Partners: structural and civil engr London 1950–54, co fndr and ptnr SA 1954–61, ptnr and ptnr in all overseas partnerships 1965–77; chm Ove Arup & Partners 1977–84; Ove Arup Partnership: dir 1977–84, co chm 1984–89, conslt 1989–95, chm Ove Arup Foundation 1993–96; non-exec dir Innisfree PFI Fund 1995–2006; pres CIRIA 1995–98; chm Architectural Assoc Fndn 1993–2000; industrial commoner Churchill Coll 1967–68; hon fell Trevelyan Coll Durham 1996; Hon DSc Univ of West Ontario 1993, Hon DEng Univ of Glasgow 1994; FREng 1983, Hon FRIBA 1990, FCGI 1991, FICE, FIStructE *Awards* Oscar Faber Silver medal (with Sir Ove Arup) 1969, Inst Structural Engrs Gold medal 1988, Oscar Faber Bronze medal (with M Manning & C Jofeh) 1990; *Recreations* theatre, music, golf; *Style*— Sir Jack Zunz, FREng; ✉ Arup, 13 Fitzroy Street, London W1T 4BQ (tel 020 7755 3553)

DIRECTORY

OF

COMPANIES,
ORGANISATIONS

AND

CLUBS

Leading UK Listed Companies

The following pages detail those companies, trading on the London Stock
Exchange, listed in the FTSE 100, 250, Small Cap, Fledgling and AIM 100 indices.

3i Group plc
16 Palace Street, London SW1E 5JD
Telephone +44 (0) 20 7928 3131
Fax +44 (0) 20 7928 0058
Website www.3igroup.com

Chair
Baroness Hogg
Chief Executive/Managing Director
Philip Yea
Board Members
Simon Ball, Christine Morin-Postel, Michael Queen, Danny
Rosenkranz, Sir Robert Smith, Fred Steingraber, Oliver
Stocken, Robert Swannell

Business Description
A group engaged as investors in independent businesses.

4imprint Group plc
6 Cavendish Place, London W1G 9NB
Telephone +44 (0) 20 7299 7201
Fax +44 (0) 20 7299 7209
Website www.4imprint.com

Chair
Ken Minton
Board Members
Ian Bindle, Gillian Davies, Nick Temple

Business Description
A group engaged in the provision of artwork, engraving,
printing, design, and packaging services.

600 Group plc
600 House, Landmark Court, Revie Road, Leeds LS11 8JT
Telephone +44 (0) 113 277 6100
Fax +44 (0) 113 276 5600
Website www.the600group.com

Chair
Martin Temple
Chief Executive/Managing Director
Andrew Dick
Board Members
Jonathan Kitchen, Martyn Wakeman

Business Description
A group engaged in the manufacture and distribution of
machine tools, machine tool accessories, lasers and other
engineering products.

888 Holdings plc
Suite 601/701 Europort, Europort Road, Gibraltar
Telephone +350 49800
Fax +350 48280
Website www.888holdingsplc.com

Chair
Richard Kilsby
Chief Executive/Managing Director
Gigi Levy
Board Members
John Anderson, Shay Ben-Yitzhak, Michael Constantine,
Aviad Kobrine, Brian Mattingley, Aimos Pickel

Business Description
A company engaged in the provision of online gaming.

A G Barr plc
Westfield House, 4 Mollins Road, Cambernaud G68 9HD
Telephone +44 (0) 1236 852400
Fax ++ (0) 1236 852 477
Website www.agbarr.co.uk

Chair
Robin Barr
Chief Executive/Managing Director
Roger White
Board Members
Alan Bibby, Iain Greenock, Jonathan Kemp, Ronnie
Hanna, James Espey

Business Description
A company engaged in the manufacture of soft drinks.

A&J Mucklow Group plc
60 Whitehall Road, Halesowen, West Midlands B63 3JS
Telephone +44 (0) 121 550 1841
Fax +44 (0) 121 550 7532
Website www.mucklow.com

Chair
Peter Mucklow
Board Members
David Austin, David Groom, Paul Ludlow, Justin Parker

Business Description
A group engaged in the development and investment in
modern commercial buildings in prominent locations, with
a bias towards the Midlands.

Abacus Group plc
Abacus House, Bone Lane, Newbury, Berkshire RG14 5SF
Telephone +44 (0) 1635 36222
Fax +44 (0) 1635 38670
Website www.abacus-group.co.uk

Chair
Anthony Henry Westropp
Chief Executive/Managing Director
Martin Kent
Board Members
Peter Allen, Graham McBeth, Robert Lambourne, David
Weir

Business Description
A distributor of electronic components.

Abbeycrest plc
Peter Rosenberg House, 11/15 Wilmington Grove, Leeds,
West Yorkshire LS7 2BQ
Telephone +44 (0) 113 245 3804
Fax +44 (0) 113 284 5706
Website www.abbeycrest.co.uk

Chair
Michael Lever
Chief Executive/Managing Director
Philip Walker
Board Members
Dave Chapman, Albert Cheesebrough

Business Description
A group engaged in the design, manufacture and
distribution of gold and silver jewellery.

Abbot Group plc
Minto Drive, Altens, Aberdeen AB12 3LW
Telephone +44 (0) 1224 299600
Fax +44 (0) 1224 230400
Website www.abbotgroup.com

Chair
Alasdair Locke
Board Members
Robert Duncan, Javier Ferran, Peter Milne, Michael Salter,
Isla Smith, Holger Temmen, Dr George Watkins, Maurice
White

Business Description
A group engaged in the provision of drilling and related
engineering services.

Aberdeen All Asia Investment Trust plc
1 Bow Churchyard, Cheapside, London EC4M 9HH
Telephone +44 (0) 20 7463 6000
Website www.asian-smaller.co.uk

Chair and Chief Executive
Nigel Cayzer
Board Members
Haruko Fukuda, Martin Gilbert, Alan Kemp, Chris Maude

Business Description
An investment trust.

Aberdeen Asian Income Fund Ltd
No 1 Seaton Place, St Helier, Jersey JE4 8YS
Telephone +44 (0) 1534 758847
Website www.asian-income.co.uk

Chair
Peter Arthur
Board Members
Duncan Baxter, Andrey Berzins, Martyn Chambers, Dr.
Ana Cukic-Munro, Hugh Young

Business Description
A global investment manager.

**Aberdeen Asian Smaller Companies Investment Trust
plc**
1 Bow Churchyard, Cheapside, London EC4M 9HH
Telephone +44 (0) 20 7463 6000
Fax +44 (0) 20 7463 6001
Website www.asian-smaller.co.uk

Chair
Nigel Cayzer
Board Members
Haruko Fukada, Martin Gilbert, Alan Kemp, Chris Maude

Business Description
A global investment manager.

Aberdeen Asset Management plc
10 Queens Terrace, Aberdeen AB10 1YG
Telephone +44 (0) 1224 631999
Fax +44 (0) 1224 647010
Website www.aberdeen-asset.com

Chair
Charles Irby
Chief Executive/Managing Director
Martin Gilbert
Board Members
Roger Cornick, Anita Frew, Andrew Laing, Bill Rattray,
The Rt Hon Sir Malcolm Rifkind, Donald Waters, Giles
Weaver

Business Description
A group engaged in the provision of investment
management and property asset management services.

Aberdeen Development Capital plc
10 Queens Terrace, Aberdeen AB10 1YG
Telephone +44 (0) 1224 631999
Fax +44 (0) 1224 647010
Website www.developmentcap.co.uk

Chair
John Milligan
Board Members
Martin Gilbert, Willie Phillips, Charles Scott

Business Description
An investment trust.

Aberdeen New Dawn Investment Trust plc
1 Bow Churchyard, Cheapside, London EC4M 9HH
Telephone +44 (0) 20 7463 6000
Fax +44 (0) 20 7463 6001
Website www.newdawn-trust.co.uk

Chair
Alan Henderson
Board Members
Richard Bradley, Richard Clough, Richard Hills, David
Shearer, Hugh Young

Business Description
An investment trust.

Aberdeen New Thai Investment Trust plc
1 Bow Churchyard, Cheapside, London EC4M 9HH
Telephone +44 (0) 20 7463 6000
Fax +44 (0) 20 7463 6001
Website www.newthai-trust.co.uk

Chair
Keith Falconer
Board Members
Peter Bristowe, James Robinson, Hugh Young

Business Description
An investment trust investing in Thailand.

Aberforth Smaller Companies Trust plc
14 Melville Street, Edinburgh EH3 7NS
Telephone +44 (0) 131 220 0733
Fax +44 (0) 131 220 0735
Website www.aberforth.co.uk

Chair
David Shaw
Board Members
Hamish Buchan, Marco Chiappelli, Edward Cran, Prof
Paul Marsh, Prof Walter Nimmo

Business Description
An investment trust investing in small UK quoted
companies.

Ablon Group plc
99 Váci út, 1139 Budapest, Hungary
Telephone + 36 1 225 6600
Fax + 36 1 225 6601
Website www.ablon-group.com

Chair
Dennis R Twining
Board Members
Daniel Avidan, Robert Glatter, Uri Heller, Gerald
Williams

Business Description
A group engaged in the acquisition, construction,
ownership, leasing, servicing and management of
commercial property, and the acquisition, construction
and sale of residential properties in Hungary, the Czech
Republic and Romania.

Absolute Capital Management Holdings Ltd
1 Cayman House, 215 Church Street, PO Box 10630 APO,
Grand Cayman KY1-1006
Telephone +44 (0) 1345 943 2264
Website www.abcapman.com

Chair and Chief Executive
Sean Ewing
Board Members
John A Fleming, Florian Homm, Michael Kloter, Darren
Sisk, Ronald E Tompkins, Jonathon Treacher

Business Description
A company engaged in fund management.

Acal plc
2 Chancellor Court, Occam Road, Surrey Research Park,
Guildford, Surrey GU2 7AH
Telephone +44 (0) 1483 544500
Fax +44 (0) 1483 544550
Website www.acalplc.co.uk

Chair
Richard Moon
Chief Executive/Managing Director
Anthony Laughton
Board Members
Eric Barton, Jagjit Virdee, Graham Williams

Business Description
A group engaged in the sale and marketing of electronic
and industrial control products.

Acambis plc
Peterhouse Technology Park, 100 Fulbourn Road,
Cambridge CB1 9PT
Telephone +44 (0) 1223 275300
Fax +44 (0) 1223 416300
Website www.acambis.com

Chair
Dr Peter Fellner
Chief Executive/Managing Director
Gordon Cameron
Board Members
Dr Randal Chase, Alan Dalby, Dr Peter Fellner, Ross
Graham, Dr William Jenkins, John Lambert, Dr Michael
Watson

Business Description
A group engaged in the research, development,
manufacture and sale of vaccines to prevent and treat
infectious diseases.

Accelerated Return Fund Ltd
Anson Place, Mill Court, La Charroterie, St Peter Port,
Guernsey GY1 1GF
Telephone +44 (0) 1481 722 260
Fax +44 (0) 1481 729 829
Website www.anson-group.com

Chair
Trevor Ash
Board Members
Jonathan Gumpel, Peter Le Cheminant

Business Description
An investment company.

Accident Exchange Group plc
Alpha 1, Canton Lane, Hams Hall, Birmingham B46 1GA
Telephone +44 (0) 870 011 6720
Fax +44 (0) 870 011 6724
Website www.accidentexchange.com

Chair
David Galloway
Chief Executive/Managing Director
Stephen Evans
Board Members
Martin Andrews, Daksh Gupta, David Lees, Graham
Stanley

Business Description
A group engaged in the provision of motor claims
management solutions.

Accsys Technologies plc
7 Queen Street, Mayfair, London W1J 5PB
Telephone +44 (0) 20 7851 7480
Fax +44 (0) 20 7494 9085
Website www.accsysplc.com

Chair and Chief Executive
William Paterson-Brown
Board Members
Glyn Thomas, Stafan Allesch-Taylor, Gorden Campbell,
Timothy Paterson-Brown, The Rt Hon Lord Sanderson of
Bowden

Business Description
An environmental science and technology company
engaged in the development, commercialisation and
licensing of technologies for use in everyday materials.

ACP Capital Ltd
Macmillan House, 96 Kensington High Street,
London W8 4SG
Telephone +44 (0) 20 7082 3917
Fax +44 (0) 808 208 3437
Website www.acpcapital.com

Chief Executive/Managing Director
Derek Vago
Board Members
Alan Braxton, François Georges, Heiner Kamps, Nikolaj
Larsen, Craig Stewart, Hillary Valentine, Eric Youngblood

Business Description
A company engaged in finance and asset management,
focusing on the asset-backed and non asset-backed
sectors in the European small and medium-sized
enterprise markets.

Active Capital Trust plc
Exchange House, Primrose Street, London EC2A 2NY
Telephone +44 (0) 20 7628 8000
Fax +44 (0) 20 7628 8188
Website www.fandc.com

Chair
Jon Pither
Board Members
Lord Gordon of Strathblane, John Green-Armytage, Brian
Holford, Dr Kim Tan, Elizabeth Thorn

Business Description
An investment trust.

Admiral Group plc
Capital Tower, Greyfriars Road, Cardiff CF10 3AZ
Telephone +44 (0) 870 243 2431
Website www.admiralgroup.co.uk

Chair
Alastair Lyons
Chief Executive/Managing Director
Henry Engelhardt
Board Members
Manfred Aldag, Kevin Chidwick, Martin Jackson, Keith
James, Margaret Johnson, Lucy Kellaway, David Stevens,
John Sussens

Business Description
A group engaged in the sale and administration of
private motor insurance and related products.

Advance Developing Markets Trust plc
Crusader House, 145-157 St John Street,
London EC1V 4RU
Telephone +44 (0) 20 7566 5520
Fax +44 (0) 20 7336 0865
Website www.pro-asset.com

Chair
Peter O'Connor
Board Members
Richard Bonsor, Terence Mahony, James Robinson

Business Description
An investment company investing in trusts or funds
which invest in emerging or developing markets.

Advance UK Trust plc
Crusader House, 145-157 St John Street,
London EC1V 4RU
Telephone +44 (0) 20 7490 4355
Fax +44 (0) 20 7336 0865
Website www.pro-asset.com

Chair
Edward Davis
Board Members
Graham Barker, Keith Niven, Philip Rowen

Business Description
An investment trust investing in funds which themselves
invest in the UK or other developed markets.

AEA Technology plc
329 Harwell, Didcot, Oxfordshire OX11 0QJ
Telephone +44 (0) 870 190 1900
Fax +44 (0) 870 190 8109
Website www.aeat.co.uk

Chair
Dr Bernard Bulkin
Chief Executive/Managing Director
Andrew McCree
Board Members
Dr Leslie Atkinson, Alice Cummings, Dr Paul Golby,
Lord Moonie, Rodney Westhead

Business Description
A group engaged in the provision of technology products,
services and consultancy to rail and environment
markets, and the supply of radiation sources and battery
systems.

Aegis Group plc
43-45 Portman Square, London W1H 6LY
Telephone +44 (0) 20 7070 700
Fax +44 (0) 20 7070 7800
Website www.aegisplc.com

Chair
Lord Sharman
Chief Executive/Managing Director
Robert Lerwill
Board Members
Adrian Chedore, Mainardo de Nardis, Daniel Farrar,
Bernard Fournier, Alicja Lesniak, Dr Brendan O'Neill,
Charles Strauss, Lorraine Trainer, Leslie Van de Walle,
David Verklin

Business Description
A group engaged in the provision of a range of services
in media communications and market research.

Aero Inventory plc
30 Lancaster Road, New Barnet, Barnet,
Hertfordshire EN4 8AP
Telephone +44 (0) 20 8449 9263
Fax +44 (0) 20 8449 3555
Website www.aero-inventory.com

Chair
Nigel McCorkell
Chief Executive/Managing Director
Rupert Lewin
Board Members
Hugh Bevan, Tim Davey, Roger Davis, Paul Docker,
Martin Dodge, Collin Trupp, Frank Turner, Martin
Webster

Business Description
A group engaged in procurement and inventory
management services for the aerospace industry.

Aga Foodservice Group plc
4 Arleston Way, Shirley, Solihull B90 4LH
Telephone +44 (0) 121 711 6000
Fax +44 (0) 121 711 6001
Website www.agafoodservice.com

Chair
Victor Cocker
Chief Executive/Managing Director
William McGrath
Board Members
Paul Dermody, Paul Jackson, Helen Mahy, Stephen
Rennie, Shaun Smith, Peter Tom

Business Description
A group engaged in the production of cookers and
refrigerators for the domestic, commercial and bakery
markets and the retail of home interior products.

AgCert International plc
Apex Building, Blackthorn Road, Sandyford, Dublin 18,
Ireland
Telephone +353 (0) 1 2457400
Fax +353 (0) 1 2457500
Website www.agcert.com

Chair
Merrick Andlinger
Chief Executive/Managing Director
Gregory Haskell
Board Members
Paul D'Alton, Franz Fischler, Sir Robert Malpas, Peter
Murray

Business Description
Production and sale of reductions in greenhouse gas
emissions.

Aggreko plc
121 West Regent Street, Glasgow G2 2SD
Telephone +44 (0) 141 225 5900
Fax +44 (0) 141 225 5949
Website www.aggreko.com

Chair
Philip Rogerson
Chief Executive/Managing Director
Rupert Soames
Board Members
Angus Cockburn, David Hamill, Roy McGlone, Nigel
Northridge, Kash Pandya, Andrew Salvesen, Derek
Shepherd, George Walker

Business Description
A group engaged in the rental of specialist power
temperature control oil-free air compressors and related
equipment.

Air Partner plc
Platinum House, Gatwick Road, Crawley, West
Sussex RH10 9RP
Telephone +44 (0) 1293 844800
Fax +44 (0) 1293 539263
Website www.airpartner.com

Chair
Anthony Mack
Chief Executive/Managing Director
David Savile
Board Members
Mark Briffa, Richard Everitt, Sri Srikanthan, Stephanie
White

Business Description
A group engaged as air charter brokers hiring aircraft for
charter to its customers.

Alba plc
Harvard House, 14 Thames Road, Barking,
Essex IG11 0HX
Telephone +44 (0) 20 8594 5533
Fax +44 (0) 20 8591 0962
Website www.albaplc.com

Chair
John Harris
Chief Executive/Managing Director
Daniel Harris
Board Members
David Allen, Bridget Blow, David Brecher, Paul Cannon,
Antonio Coda, Sir Bill Cotton, Sir Digby Jones, Andrew
Rose, Paul Selway-Swift

Business Description
A group engaged in the manufacture and supply of
audio, video, satellite and consumer electronic equipment,
and the sale of giftware.

Albany Investment Trust plc
Port of Liverpool Building, 4th Floor, Pier Head,
Liverpool L3 1NW
Telephone +44 (0) 151 236 6666
Fax +44 (0) 151 243 7001

Chair
Trevor Furlong
Board Members
Sir David Henshaw, Roy Morris, John Nottingham

Business Description
An investment trust.

Alexandra plc
Alexandra House, Thornbury, Bristol BS35 2NT
Telephone +44 (0) 870 060 0200
Fax +44 (0) 870 060 0229
Website www.alexandra.co.uk

Chair
Christopher Marsh
Chief Executive/Managing Director
Julian Budd
Board Members
Ken Gibbs, Elaine New, James Tucker

Business Description
A group engaged in the manufacture and supply of
workplace clothing.

Alexon Group plc
40-48 Guildford Street, Luton LU1 2PB
Telephone +44 (0) 1582 723131
Fax +44 (0) 1582 724158
Website www.alexon.co.uk

Chair
Jim Martin
Chief Executive/Managing Director
John Osborn
Board Members
John Beale, Patrick Cooper, John Herbert, Robin Piggott

Business Description
A group engaged in the retail of ladies' and men's
clothing and footwear.

Alfred McAlpine
Kinnaird House, 1 Pall Mall East, London SW1Y 5AZ
Telephone +44 (0) 20 7930 6255
Website www.alfredmcalpineplc.com

Chair
Dr Roger Urwin
Chief Executive/Managing Director
Ian Grice
Board Members
Christopher Collins, Robert Hough, Craig McGilvray, Alan
Robertson, Matt Swan, Philip Swatman

Business Description
A group engaged in provision of support services and the
design, construction, management and maintenance of
buildings.

Alizyme plc
Granta Park, Great Abington, Cambridge CB1 6GX
Telephone +44 (0) 1223 896000
Fax +44 (0) 1223 896001
Website www.alizyme.com

Chair
Sir Brian Richards
Chief Executive/Managing Director
Tim McCarthy
Board Members
David Campbell, William Edge, Richard Forrest, John
Gordon, Roger Hickling

Business Description
A group engaged in the discovery, development and
commercialisation of pharmaceutical products for
treatment of obesity related disease and gastrointestinal
tract disorders.

Alliance & Leicester plc
Carlton Park, Narborough, Leicester LE19 0AL
Telephone +44 (0) 116 201 1000
Fax +44 (0) 116 200 4040
Website www.aliance-leicester-group.co.uk

Chair
Sir Derek Higgs
Chief Executive/Managing Director
David Bennett
Board Members
Malcolm Aish, Richard Banks, Jane Barker, Roy Brown,
Rodney Duke, Mary Francis, Mike McTighe, Chris
Rhodes, Margaret Salmon, Jonathan Watts

Business Description
A group engaged in the provision of a comprehensive
range of personal financial services.

Alliance Trust plc (The)
64 Reform Street, Dundee DD1 9YP
Telephone +44 (0) 1382 201700
Fax +44 (0) 1382 225133
Website www.alliancetrusts.com

Chair
Lesley Knox
Chief Executive/Managing Director
Alan Harden
Board Members
Hugh Bolland, David Deards, Katherine Garrett-Cox, Dr
Christopher Masters, Gordon McQueen, Janet Pope, Clare
Salmon

Business Description
An investment trust with a subsidiary engaged in the
provision and administration of investment products.

Allianz Dresdner Endowment Policy Trust 2010 plc
155 Bishopsgate, London EC2M 3AD
Telephone +44 (0) 20 7859 9000
Fax +44 (0) 20 7628 6406
Website www.allianzdresdneram.co.uk

Chair
Richard Wales
Board Members
David Manning, Ian Smart, Simon White

Business Description
Investment in mid-term with-profits endowment policies
to provide capital growth.

Allianz Dresdner Second Endowment Policy Trust plc
155 Bishopsgate, London EC2M 3AD
Telephone +44 (0) 20 7859 9000
Website www.allianzdresdneram.co.uk

Chair
John Clement
Board Members
Terence Arthur, Kenneth Ayers, Simon White

Business Description
An investment company with the objective of providing
long-term capital growth by investing in diversified
portfolios of traded endowment policies.

Alpha Pyrenees Trust Ltd
East Wing, Trafalgar Court, Admiral Park, St Peter Port,
Guernsey GY1 6HJ
Telephone +44 (0) 1481 715601
Website www.alphapyreneestrust.com

Chair
Richard Kingston
Board Members
Christopher Bennett, David Jeffreys, Phillip Rose, Serena
Tremlett

Business Description
A closed-ended investment company investing in French
and Spanish commercial real estate.

Alphameric plc
Friary House, Station Road, Godalming, Surrey GU7 1EX
Telephone +44 (0) 1483 524690
Fax +44 (0) 1483 524691
Website www.alphameric.com

Chair
Peter Bertram
Chief Executive/Managing Director
Alan Morcombe
Board Members
Dr Michael Chamberlain, Steve Mansfield, Mike McLaren,
Alan McWalter, James Soulsby

Business Description
A company engaged in the provision of software
solutions to the bookmaking and hospitality industries.

Alterian plc
Century Place, Bond Street, Bristol BS2 9AG
Telephone +44 (0) 117 970 3200
Fax +44 (0) 117 970 3201
Website www.alterian.com

Chair
Keith Hamill
Chief Executive/Managing Director
David Eldridge
Board Members
David Cutler, Iain Johnston, Timothy McCarthy, Hugh
McCartney, Michael Talbot

Business Description
A group engaged in the design and development of
specialised data manipulation and analysis software tools
for sale under licence.

Alternative Investment Strategies Ltd
Trafalgar Court, Admiral Park, St Peter Port,
Guernsey GY1 2JA
Telephone +44 (0) 1481 710607
Fax +44 (0) 1481 710001
Website www.aisinvest.com

Chair
Nicholas Wilson
Board Members
Duncan Baxter, Alan Djanogly, John Walley

Business Description
An investment trust.

Alumasc Group plc (The)
Burton Latimer, Kettering, Northamptonshire NN15 5JP
Telephone +44 (0) 1536 383844
Fax +44 (0) 1536 725069
Website www.alumasc.co.uk

Chair
J McCall
Chief Executive/Managing Director
Paul Hooper
Board Members
Philip Gwyn, Andrew Magson, Jon Pither, Martin Rhodes,
Richard Saville, David Sowerby

Business Description
A group engaged in the manufacture of engineering
products and components for industrial customers, and
the design, manufacture and marketing of building
products.

Amec plc
65 Caster Lane, London EC4V 5AF
Telephone +44 (0) 20 7634 0000
Fax +44 (0) 20 7634 0001
Website www.amec.com

Chair
Jock Green-Armytage
Chief Executive/Managing Director
Samir Brikho
Board Members
Liz Airey, Peter Byrom, John Early, Tim Faithfull,
Martha Hesse, Stuart Siddall

Business Description
A group engaged in the provision of specialised services
and engineering solutions including capital project work,
client support services and investment and development.

Amlin plc
St Helen's, 1 Undershaft, London EC3A 8ND
Telephone +44 (0) 20 7746 1000
Fax +44 (0) 20 7746 1696
Website www.amlin.co.uk

Chair
Roger Taylor
Chief Executive/Managing Director
Charles Philipps
Board Members
Nigel Buchanan, Brian Carpenter, Richard Davey, Richard
Hextall, Tony Holt, Roger Joslin, Ramanam Mylvaganam,
Sir Mark Wrightson

Business Description
A company engaged as non-life insurance underwriters.

Anglesey Mining plc
Parys Mountain, Amlwch, Gwynedd LL68 9RE
Telephone +4 (0) 1248 361333
Fax +44 (0) 1248 361419
Website www.angleseymining.co.uk

Chair
John Kearney
Board Members
Ian Cuthbertson, Bill Hooley, David Lean, Howard Miller,
Roger Turner, Danesh Varma

Business Description
A group engaged in the development of the polymetallic
mineral deposits on the Parys Mountain property.

Anglo & Overseas plc
51 New North Road, Exeter EX4 4EP
Telephone +44 (0) 1392 412122
Website www.angloandoverseasplc.com

Chair
Robert Alcock
Board Members
Christopher Duffett, John Pearmund, John Sussens, Giles
Weaver

Business Description
An investment trust.

Anglo American plc
20 Carlton House Terrace, London SW1Y 5AN
Telephone +44 (0) 20 7968 8888
Fax +44 (0) 20 7968 8500
Website www.angloamerican.co.uk

Chair
Sir Mark Moody-Stuart
Board Members
Ralph Alexander, Cynthia Carroll, David Challen, Dr
Chris Fay, Bobby Godsell, Sir Robert Margetts, René
Médori, Nicholas Oppenheimer, Frederik Phaswana, Dr
Mamphela Ramphele, Prof Karel Van Miert, Peter Woicke

Business Description
A group engaged in gold, platinum, diamond, coal, metal
and industrial mineral mining and the production of
construction materials and paper.

Anglo Pacific Group plc
17 Hill Street, London W1J 5NZ
Telephone +44 (0) 20 7318 6360
Website www.anglopacificgroup.com

Chair
Peter Boycott
Chief Executive/Managing Director
Brian Wides
Board Members
Michael Atkinson, Matthew Tack, John Whellock,
Anthony Yadgaroff

Business Description
A group engaged in the exploration, mining and
development of metals and minerals including royalty
receipts.

Anglo-Eastern Plantations plc
6/7 Queen Street, London EC4N 1SP
Telephone +44 (0) 20 7236 2838
Fax +44 (0) 20 7236 8283
Website www.angloeastern.co.uk

Chair and Chief Executive
Teik Chan
Board Members
Robert Barnes, Datuk Chin, Ho Ching, Siew Lim, Peter
O'Connor, Kee Yong

Business Description
A group engaged in the cultivation of oil palm rubber
and cocoa.

Anite Group plc
353 Buckingham Avenue, Slough, Berkshire SL1 4PF
Telephone +44 (0) 1753 804000
Fax +44 (0) 1753 804497
Website www.anite.com

Chair
Clayton Brendish
Chief Executive/Managing Director
Steve Rowley
Board Members
Peter Bertram, Michelle Cohen, Nigel Coxon, Christopher
Humphrey, Lee Hendricks, Jukka Honkila, David Hurst-
Brown, Mike Kingswood, Simon Tyrrell

Business Description
A group engaged in the provision of IT software, systems
integration, consultancy and managed services.

Antisoma plc
West Africa House, Hanger Lane, Ealing,
London W5 3QR
Telephone +44 (0) 20 8799 8200
Fax +44 (0) 20 8799 8201
Website www.antisoma.com

Chair
Barry Price
Chief Executive/Managing Director
Glyn Edwards
Board Members
Garry Acton, Nicholas Adams, Dale Boden, Grahame
Cook, Nigel Courtenay-Luck, Daniel Elger, Sharon
Grimster, Ann Hacker, Ursula Ney, Michael Pappas, Chris
Smyth, Raymond Spencer, Briget Statten-Norinder

Business Description
A biotechnology company.

Antofagasta plc
5 Princes Gate, London SW7 1QJ
Telephone +44 (0) 20 7808 0988
Fax +44 (0) 20 7808 0986
Website www.antofagasta.co.uk

Chair
Jean-Paul Luksic
Board Members
Jozsef Ambrus, Charles Bailey, Juan Claro, William Hayes,
Ramon Jara, Guillermo Luksic, Gonzalo Menendez, Daniel
Yarur

Business Description
A group engaged in copper mining, the transport of
freight by rail and road, and the distribution of water.

Antrim Energy Inc
Suite 4050 Bankers Hall West, 888 3rd Street SW,
Calgary, Alberta, T2P 5C5, Canada
Telephone +1 403 264 5111
Fax +1 403 264 5113
Website www.antrimenergy.com

Executive Officer and President
Stephen Greer
Board Members
Kerry Fulton, Janet Missal, Anthony Potter

Business Description
A company engaged in oil and gas exploration and
production.

API Group plc
2nd Avenue, Poynton Industrial Estate, Stockport,
Cheshire SK12 1ND
Telephone +44 (0) 1625 858700
Website www.apigroup.com

Chair
Richard Wright
Board Members
Brian Birkenhead, Martin O'Connell, Andrew Robertson,
Andrew Walker, Luke Wiseman

Business Description
A group engaged in the manufacture in the UK and
internationally specialised packaging and security
products for the tobacco, drinks, food, luxury and
consumer goods sectors.

Aquarius Platinum Ltd
Clarendon House, 2 Church Street, Hamilton, Bermuda
Telephone +61 8 93675211
Fax +61 8 93675233
Website www.aquariusplatinum.com

Chair
Nicholas Sibley
Chief Executive/Managing Director
Stuart Murray
Board Members
David Dix, Timothy Freshwater, Edward Haslam, Kofi
Morna, Sir William Purves

Business Description
Exploration, development, acquisition and mining.

ARC International plc
Verulam Point, Station Way, St Albans AL1 5HE
Telephone +44 (0) 1727 891400
Fax +44 (0) 1727 891401
Website www.arc.com

Chair
Richard Barfield
Chief Executive/Managing Director
Carl Schlachte
Board Members
Dr Geoff Bristow, Steven Gunders, Victor Young

Business Description
A group providing configurable processors, application
subsystems and software for embedded system-on-chip
design.

Ardana plc
38 Melville Street, Edinburgh EH3 7HH
Telephone +44 (0) 131 226 8550
Fax +44 (0) 131 226 8551
Website www.ardana.co.uk

Chair
Simon Best
Chief Executive/Managing Director
Dr Maureen Lindsay
Board Members
Dr John Brown, Carol Ferguson, Dr Huw Jones, Ian Kent,
Graham Lee

Business Description
A group engaged in the discovery, development and
marketing of products that promote better male and
female reproductive health.

Arena Leisure plc
1 Hay Hill, Berkeley Square, London W1J 6DH
Telephone +44 (0) 20 7495 2277
Fax +44 (0) 20 7491 7174
Website www.arenaleisureplc.com

Chair
Raymond Mould
Chief Executive/Managing Director
Mark Elliott
Board Members
Martin McGann, Brigadier Andrew Parker-Bowles, Ian
Renton

Business Description
A group engaged in the operation of racecourses and the
worldwide broadcast and exploitation of racecourse media
rights via the group's joint venture At The Races.

Aricom plc
10-11 Grosvenor Place, London SW1X 7HH
Telephone +44 (0) 20 7201 8939
Fax +44 (0) 20 7201 8938
Website www.aricom.plc.uk

Chair
Dr Pavel Maslovsky
Board Members
Jay Hambro, Sir Rudolph Agnew, Brian Egan, Sir
Malcolm Field, Peter Hambro, Sir Roderic Lyne, Yuri
Makarov, Martin Smith

Business Description
Development of mineral assets in Russia's Far East.

Ark Therapeutics Group plc
79 New Cavendish Street, London W1W 6XB
Telephone +44 (0) 20 7388 7722
Fax +44 (0) 20 7388 7805
Website www.arktherapeutics.com

Chair
Dennis Turner
Chief Executive/Managing Director
Dr Nigel Parker
Board Members
Dr Bruce Carter, Peter Keen, Dr Wolfgang Plischke,
David Prince, Sir Mark Richmond, Martyn Williams, Prof
Seppo Yla-Herttuala

Business Description
A group engaged in the development, discovery and
commercialisation of products in areas of specialist
medicine with particular focus on cancer and vascular
disease.

ARM Holdings plc
110 Fulbourn Road, Cambridge CB1 9NJ
Telephone +44 (0) 1223 400400
Fax +44 (0) 1223 400401
Website www.arm.com

Chair
Doug Dunn
Chief Executive/Managing Director
Warren East
Board Members
Tudor Brown, Mike Inglis, Lucio Lanza, Mike Muller,
Kathleen O'Donovan, Philip Rowley, John Scarisbrick,
Tim Score, Jeremy Scudamore, Simon Segars, Young
Sohn

Business Description
A company engaged in the research and development of
RISC microprocessors and systems, and related licensing
and marketing.

ArmorGroup International plc
25-28 Buckingham Gate, London SW1E 6LD
Telephone +44 (0) 20 7808 5800
Fax +44 (0) 20 7828 2845
Website www.armorgroup.com

Chair
Sir Malcolm Rifkind
Chief Executive/Managing Director
David Seaton
Board Members
Christopher Beese, John Biles, Matthew Brabin, Simon
Havers, Iain Paterson, Noel Philp

Business Description
A group engaged in the provision of defensive protective
security services and security training services.

Arriva plc
Admiral Way, Doxford International Business Park,
Sunderland SR3 3XP
Telephone +44 (0) 191 520 4000
Fax +44 (0) 191 520 4001
Website www.arriva.co.uk

Chair
Sir Richard Broadbent
Chief Executive/Managing Director
David Martin
Board Members
Simon Batey, Nick Buckles, Steve Clayton, Steve
Lonsdale, Veronica Palmer, Steve Williams

Business Description
A group engaged in the operation of bus and train
services, coach commuter services, private hire, corporate
vehicle rental, self-drive hire, bus and coach distribution,
rental and finance.

Artemis Alpha Trust plc
Cassini House, 57 St James Street, London SW1A 1LD
Telephone +44 (0) 800 092 2051
Fax +44 (0) 20 7399 6497

Chair
Simon Miller
Board Members
David Barron, Cross Brown, Andrew Dalrymple, Charles
Peel, Andrzej Sobczak

Business Description
An investment trust with a dealing subsidiary.

Ashmore Group plc
20 Bedfordbury, London WC2N 2BL
Telephone +44 (0) 20 7557 4100
Fax +44 (0) 20 7557 4141
Website www.ashmoregroup.com

Chair
Michael Benson
Chief Executive/Managing Director
Mark Coombs
Board Members
Nick Land, Jon Moulton, Jim Pettigrew

Business Description
A group engaged in asset management, specialising in
emerging markets.

Ashtead Group plc
Kings Court, 41-51 Kingston Road, Leatherhead,
Surrey KT22 7AP
Telephone +44 (0) 1372 362300
Fax +44 (0) 1372 376610
Website www.ashtead-group.com

Chair
Christopher Cole
Chief Executive/Managing Director
Geoffrey Drabble
Board Members
Michael Burrow, Sat Dhaiwal, Bruce Edwards, Hugh
Etheridge, Gary Iceton, Cliff Miller, Ian Robson

Business Description
A group engaged in the rental of equipment to industrial
and commercial users.

Asset Management Investment Company plc
32 Ludgate Hill, London EC4M 7DR
Telephone +44 (0) 20 7618 9040
Fax +44 (0) 20 7618 9045
Website www.amicplc.com

Chair
Charles Wilkinson
Chief Executive/Managing Director
George Robb
Board Members
Barry Aling, Geoff Miller, Hugh Tilney

Business Description
A company investing in the asset management industry.

Associated British Engineering plc
Fairfax House, 15 Fulwood House, London WC1V 6AY
Telephone +44 (0) 20 7969 5500

Chair
David Brown
Board Members
Stephen Cockburn, Colin Weinberg

Business Description
A group engaged in diesel and related engineering
activities.

Associated British Foods plc
Weston Centre, 10 Grosvenor Street, London W1K 4QY
Telephone +44 (0) 20 7399 6500
Fax +44 (0) 20 7399 6580
Website www.abf.co.uk

Chair
Martin Adamson
Chief Executive/Managing Director
George Weston
Board Members
Michael Alexander, John Bason, Tim Clarke, Jeff Harris,
Lord MacGregor of Pulham Market, W Galen Weston

Business Description
A group engaged in the processing and manufacture of
food, and the retail of textiles and clothing.

Assura Group Ltd
Regus House, Chester Business Park, Chester CH4 9QP
Telephone +44 (0) 1244 893 681
Website www.assuragroup.co.uk

Chair
Dr Mark Johnson
Chief Executive/Managing Director
Dr John Curran
Board Members
Graham Chase, Peter Pichler, Fred Porter, Colin Vibert

Business Description
A group engaged in health care provision, that invests in
and develops properties, pharmacy and medical services.

Asterand plc
2 Orchard Road, Royston, Hertfordshire SG8 5HD
Telephone +44 (0) 1763 211600
Fax +44 (0) 1763 211555
Website www.asterand.com

Chair
David Lee
Chief Executive/Managing Director
Martin Coombs
Board Members
John Cullinane Jr, John (Jack) Davis, David Jones Jr, Ron
Long, Mina Sooch

Business Description
A group engaged in the research and development of
novel therapeutic agents for the treatment of human
disease using its human tissue resource.

AstraZeneca plc
15 Stanhope Gate, London W1K 1LN
Telephone +44 (0) 20 7304 5000
Fax +44 (0) 20 7304 5151
Website www.astrazeneca.com

Chair
Louis Schweitzer
Chief Executive/Managing Director
David Brennan
Board Members
Dr John Buchanan, Jane Henney, Michele Hooper, Dr
Håkan Mogren, Dr John Patterson, Dame Nancy Rothwell,
Jonathan Symonds, John Varley, Marcus Wallenberg

Business Description
A group engaged in the research, manufacture and sale of
prescription pharmaceuticals.

Aurora Investment Trust plc
Crusader House, 145 St John Street, London EC1V 4RU
Telephone +44 (0) 20 7490 4355
Fax +44 (0) 20 7336 0865
Website www.marsassentmanagement.co.uk

Chair
Alex Hammond-Chambers
Board Members
Michael Amory, James Barstow, David Hunter

Business Description
An investment trust with a dealing subsidiary.

Autonomy Corporation plc
Cambridge Business Park, Cambridge CB4 0WZ
Telephone +44 (0) 1223 448000
Fax +44 (0) 1223 448001
Website www.autonomy.com

Chief Executive/Managing Director
Dr Mike Lynch
Board Members
Barry Ariko, Richard Gaunt, Sushovan Hussain, John
McMonigall, Richard Perle

Business Description
A group engaged in software development and
distribution.

Aveva Group
High Cross, Madingley Road, Cambridge CB3 0HB
Telephone +44 (0) 1223 556655
Website www.aveva.com

Chair
Nick Prest
Chief Executive/Managing Director
Richard Longdon
Board Members
Colin Garrett, David Mann

Business Description
A group engaged in the provision of engineering
software.

Avis Europe plc
Avis House, Park Road, Bracknell, Berkshire RG12 2EW
Telephone +44 (0) 1344 426644
Fax +44 (0) 1344 485616
Website www.avis-europe.com

Chair
Alun Cathcart
Chief Executive/Managing Director
Murray Hennessy
Board Members
Jean-Pierre Bizet, Lesley Colyer, Leslie Cullen, Pierre-Alain
De Smedt, Roland D'Ieteren, Benoit Ghiot, Malcolm Miller,
Simon Palethorpe, Martyn Smith, Gilbert van Marcke de
Lummen, Axel von Ruedorffer

Business Description
A group engaged in the provision of vehicle rental
services.

Aviva plc
St Helen's, 1 Undershaft, London EC3P 3DQ
Telephone +44 (0) 20 7283 2000
Fax +44 (0) 20 7662 8182
Website www.aviva.com

Chair
Lord Sharman
Chief Executive/Managing Director
Andrew Moss
Board Members
Nikesh Arora, Guillermo de la Dehesa, Wim Dik, Mary
Francis, Richard Goeltz, Carole Piwnica, Philip Scott,
Tidjane Thiam, Russell Walls

Business Description
A group engaged in the transaction of life assurance,
long-term savings, business asset management, and
general insurance.

Avon Rubber plc
Hampton Park West, Melksham, Wiltshire SN12 6NB
Telephone +44 (0) 1225 896800
Fax +44 (0) 1225 896899
Website www.avon-rubber.com

Chair
Sir Richard Needham
Chief Executive/Managing Director
Terry Stead
Board Members
Brian Duckworth, David Evans, Stella Pirie, Peter
Slabbert

Business Description
A group engaged in the design and manufacture of
components for the automotive industry and of other
polymer based technical products including respirators
and aerosol seals.

AXA Property Trust Ltd
Trafalgar Court, Les Banques, St Peter Port,
Guernsey GY1 3QL

Chair
Charles Hunter
Board Members
Gavin Farrell, John Marren, Stephane Monier, Richard
Ray

Business Description
An investment company.

Axis-Shield plc
The Technology Park, Dundee DD2 1XA
Telephone +44 (0) 1382 422000
Fax +44 (0) 1382 561201
Website www.axis-shield.com

Chair
Nigel Keen
Chief Executive/Managing Director
Svein Lien
Board Members
Staffan Ek, Dr Ian Gilham, Bay Green, Ronny Hermansen, Erik Hornnaess, Gordon McAndrew, Olav Steinnes, Dr Erling Sundrehagen

Business Description
A group engaged in the development, manufacture and distribution of medical diagnostic products.

Axon Group
Axon Centre, Church Road, Egham TW20 9QB
Telephone +44 (0) 1784 480800
Fax +44 (0) 1784 480900
Website www.axongroup.co.uk

Chair
Mark Hunter
Chief Executive/Managing Director
Stephen Cardell
Board Members
Royston Hoggarth, Iain McIntosh, Roy Merritt, David Oertle

Business Description
A consultancy that designs, implements and supports solutions to address business issues faced by large organisations who have selected SAP as their strategic enterprise platform.

Babcock International Group plc
2 Cavendish Square, London W1G 0PX
Telephone +44 (0) 20 7291 5000
Fax +44 (0) 20 7291 5055
Website www.babcock.co.uk

Chair
Gordon Campbell
Chief Executive/Managing Director
Peter Rogers
Board Members
Justin Crookenden, Sir Nigel Essenhigh, Lord Hesketh, John Rennocks, Dipesh Shah, Bill Tame

Business Description
A group engaged in the provision of training, operating and maintenance services, primarily for the MOD, and the provision of technical services and secure facilities management.

BAE Systems plc
Stirling Square, 6 Carlton Gardens, London SW1Y 5AD
Telephone +44 (0) 1252 373232
Fax +44 (0) 1252 383000
Website www.baesystems.com

Chair
Dick Olver
Chief Executive/Managing Director
Michael Turner
Board Members
Philip Carroll, Dr Ulrich Cartellieri, Chris Geoghegan, Michael Hartnall, Walt Havenstein, Ian King, Sir Peter Mason, Roberto Quarta, George Rose, Sir Nigel Rudd, Peter Weinberg

Business Description
A group engaged in the design and manufacture of aircraft, surface ships, submarines, space systems, radar, avionics, communications, electronics, weapon systems and defence products.

Baillie Gifford Japan Trust plc
Calton Square, 1 Greenside Row, Edinburgh EH1 3AN
Telephone +44 (0) 131 275 2000
Fax +44 (0) 131 275 3999
Website www.bailliegifford.com

Chair
Malcolm Murray
Board Members
Nick Bannerman, Richard Barfield, Martin Barrow, Paul Dimond

Business Description
An investment trust.

Baillie Gifford Shin Nippon plc
Calton Square, 1 Greenside Row, Edinburgh EH1 3AN
Telephone +44 (0) 131 275 2000
Fax +44 (0) 131 275 3999
Website www.bailliegifford.com

Chair
Michael Hathorn
Board Members
Francis Charig, Ian McLeish, Barry Rose, Sarah Whitley

Business Description
An investment trust investing in small Japanese companies.

Balfour Beatty plc
130 Wilton Road, London SW1V 1LQ
Telephone +44 (0) 20 7216 6800
Fax +44 (0) 20 7216 6902
Website www.balfourbeatty.co.uk

Chair
Sir David John
Chief Executive/Managing Director
Ian Tyler
Board Members
Mike Donovan, Stephen Howard, Steven Marshall, Anthony Rabin, Gordon Sage, Hans von Rohr, Robert Walvis, Peter Zinkin

Business Description
A group engaged in the provision of building, civil and specialist engineering and rail engineering services, and the development of infrastructure projects.

Bankers Investment Trust plc
4 Broadgate, London EC2M 2DA
Telephone +44 (0) 20 7818 1818
Fax +44 (0) 20 7818 1819

Chair
Richard Brewster
Board Members
Richard Burns, Richard Killingbeck, James Morley, Francis Sumner, David Thomas

Business Description
An investment trust.

Barclays plc
1 Churchill Place, London E14 5HP
Telephone +44 (0) 20 7116 1000
Website www.barclays.co.uk

Chair
Marcus Agius
Chief Executive/Managing Director
John Varley
Board Members
David Booth, Sir Richard Broadbent, Leigh Clifford, Fulvio Conti, Dr Danie Cronjé, Dame Prof Sandra Dawson, Robert Diamond, Gary Hoffman, Sir Andrew Likierman, Chris Lucas, Sir Nigel Rudd, Stephen Russell, Frits Seegers, Sir John Sutherland

Business Description
An international group engaged in the provision of financial services including banking, investment banking, venture capital and asset management.

Baring Emerging Europe plc
155 Bishopsgate, London EC2M 3XY
Telephone +44 (0) 20 7628 6000
Fax +44 (0) 20 7638 7928
Website www.bee-plc.com

Chair
Iain Saunders
Board Members
Steven Bates, John Cousins, Josephine Dixon, Saul Estrin

Business Description
An investment trust.

Barratt Developments plc
Rotterdam House, 116 Quayside, Newcastle-upon-Tyne NE1 3DA
Telephone +44 (0) 191 227 2000
Fax +44 (0) 191 227 2001
Website www.barratt-investor-relations.co.uk

Chair
Charles Toner
Chief Executive/Managing Director
Mark Clare
Board Members
Steven Boyes, Bob Davies, Clive Penton, Rod MacEachrane, Mark Pain, Michael Prescod, Bill Shannon

Business Description
A group engaged in housebuilding.

Bateman Engineering NV
Rivierstaete Building, Amstelgijk 116, 1079 LH Amsterdam, Netherlands
Telephone +31 020 5022370
Fax +31 020 5022371
Website www.batemanengineering.com

Chair
Rick Menell
Chief Executive/Managing Director
Dr Sivi Gounden
Board Members
Earl of Balfour, Jonathan Ben-Cnaan, Peter Blauw, Dag Cramer

Business Description
A company engaged in the provision of process engineering and project management to the minerals and metals industries.

BATM Advanced Communications Ltd
Industrial Centre Kfar Netter, PO Box 3737, Kfar Netter 40593, Israel
Telephone + 972 (9) 8662525
Fax +972 (9) 8662500
Website www.batm.com

Chair
Peter Sheldon
Chief Executive/Managing Director
Dr Zvi Marom
Board Members
Ofer Bar-Ner, Koti Gavish, Dr Dan Kaznelson, Ariella Zochovitzky

Business Description
Designs and produces broadband data and telecommunications solutions geared toward the needs of enterprises, corporate and telecom networks.

BBA Aviation plc
20 Balderton Street, London W1K 6TL
Telephone +44 (0) 20 7514 3999
Fax +44 (0) 20 7408 2318
Website www.bbaaviation.com

Chair
Michael Harper
Chief Executive/Managing Director
Simon Pryce
Board Members
Mark Harper, Nick Land, John Roques, Hansel Tookes, Bruce Van Allen, Andrew Wood

Business Description
A group engaged in the manufacture of aviation equipment, friction materials and industrial textiles.

Beale plc
The Granville Chambers, 21 Richmond Hill, Bournemouth, Dorset BH2 6BJ
Telephone +44 (0) 1202 552022
Fax +44 (0) 1202 317286
Website www.beales.co.uk

Chair
Mike Killingley
Chief Executive/Managing Director
Allan Allkins
Board Members
Nigel Beale, Neil Jones, Barbara King, Kenneth Owst, Alison Richards

Business Description
A group engaged in the operation of department stores. Trading as Beales, Broadbents & Boothroyds, Denners and Whitakers.

Beazley Group plc
Plantation Place South, 60 Great Tower Street, London EC3R 5AD
Telephone +44 (0) 20 7667 0623
Fax +44 (0) 20 7674 7100
Website www.beazley.com

Chair
Jonathan Agnew
Chief Executive/Managing Director
Andrew Beazley
Board Members
Marty Becker, Dudley Fishburn, Nicholas Furlonge, Jonathan Gray, Gordon Hamilton, Andrew Horton, Dan Jones, Neil Maidment, Andy Pomfret, Jonathan Rowell, Clive Washbourn

Business Description
A group engaged in the provision of specialist insurance, including marine, commercial property and personal lines, management liability, errors & omissions and reinsurance.

Bede plc
Belmont Business Park, Durham DH1 1TW
Telephone +44 (0) 191 332 4700
Fax +44 (0) 191 332 4800
Website www.bede.co.uk

Chair
Stuart McIntosh
Board Members
David Hall, Dr Christopher Honeyborne, James Polasik, Norman Price, Prof Brian Tanner

Business Description
A group engaged in the design, manufacture, assembly and sale of specialist x-ray instruments and software, including scientific instruments and associated software.

Bellway plc
Seaton Burn House, Dudley Lane, Seaton Burn,
Newcastle-upon-Tyne NE13 6BE
Telephone +44 (0) 191 217 0717
Fax +44 (0) 191 236 6230
Website www.bellway.co.uk

Chair
Howard Dawe
Chief Executive/Managing Director
John Watson
Board Members
Leo Finn, Peter Johnson, Alistair Leitch, David Perry,
Peter Stoker

Business Description
A group engaged in housebuilding.

Benfield Group Ltd
55 Bishopsgate, London EC2N 3BD
Telephone +44 (0) 20 7578 7000
Fax +44 (0) 20 7578 7001
Website www.benfieldgroup.com

Chair
John Coldman
Chief Executive/Managing Director
Grahame Chilton
Board Members
Robert Bredahl, Dominic Christian, Andrew Fisher, Dr
Keith Harris, Paul Karon, Francis Maude, Paul Roy, John
Whiter, Frank Wilkinson

Business Description
The primary business activities of the group are the
provision of insurance and reinsurance, intermediary risk,
advisory and related services.

Berkeley Group Holdings plc (The)
Berkeley House, 19 Portsmouth Road, Cobham,
Surrey KT11 1JG
Telephone +44 (0) 1932 868555
Fax +44 (0) 1932 868667
Website www.berkeleygroup.co.uk

Chair
Roger Lewis
Chief Executive/Managing Director
Tony Pidgley
Board Members
Tony Carey, Alan Coppin, Greg Fry, Lord Howell of
Guildford, Victoria Mitchell, Tony Palmer, Robert Perrins,
Michael Tanner

Business Description
A group engaged in land development.

Berkeley Technology Ltd
6 Minden Place, St Helier, Jersey JE2 4WQ
Telephone +44 (0) 1534 607700
Fax +44 (0) 1534 607799

Chair
Arthur Trueger
Board Members
Victor Herbert, Harold Hughes, Viscount Trenchard, Ian
Whitehead

Business Description
A company engaged in the provision of financial services,
specialising in venture capital.

Bespak plc
Blackhill Drive, Featherstone Road, Wolverton Mill South,
Milton Keynes MK12 5TS
Telephone +44 (0) 1908 552600
Fax +44 (0) 1908 525260
Website www.bespak.com

Chair
John Robinson
Chief Executive/Managing Director
Mark Throdahl
Board Members
Chris Banks, Paul Boughton, Jim Dick, Dr Peter Fellner,
Jonathan Glenn, George Kennedy

Business Description
A group engaged in the design, development,
manufacture and sale of drug delivery technologies and
services to the pharmaceutical industry.

BG Group plc
100 Thames Valley Park Drive, Reading,
Berkshire RG6 1PT
Telephone +44 (0) 118 935 3222
Fax +44 (0) 118 935 3484
Website www.bg-group.com

Chair
Sir Robert Wilson
Chief Executive/Managing Director
Frank Chapman
Board Members
Ashley Almanza, Peter Backhouse, Sir John Coles, Paul
Collins, Jürgen Dormann, William Friedrich, Baroness
Hogg, Dr John Hood, Lord Sharman, Philippe Varin

Business Description
A group engaged in the exploration and production of
hydrocarbons, the transmission and distribution of gas,
the sale of liquified natural gas, and the generation of
power.

BHP Billiton plc
Neathouse Place, London SW1V 1BH
Telephone +44 (0) 20 7802 4000
Fax +44 (0) 20 7802 4111
Website www.bhpbilliton.com

Chair
Donald Argus
Chief Executive/Managing Director
Charles Goodyear
Board Members
Paul Anderson, David Brink, Dr John Buchanan, Carlos
Cordeiro, David Crawford, Dr Gail de Planque, David
Jenkins, Marius Kloppers, Jacques Nasser, Dr John
Schubert

Business Description
A group engaged in the exploration, production and
processing of minerals and the exploration, development
and production of oil and gas.

Biffa plc
Accuray House, Coronataion Road, Cressex Business
Park, High Wycombe HP12 3TZ
Telephone +44 (0) 1494 521221
Fax +44 (0) 1494 463368
Website www.biffa.co.uk

Chair
Bob Davies
Chief Executive/Managing Director
Martin Bettington
Board Members
Gareth Llewellyn, Tim Lowth, Roger Payne, Angie Risley

Business Description
A company engaged in waste management.

Big Yellow Group plc
2 The Deans, Bridge Road, Bagshot, Surrey GU19 5AT
Telephone +44 (0) 1276 470190
Fax +44 (0) 1276 470191
Website www.bigyellow.co.uk

Chair
Nicholas Vetch
Chief Executive/Managing Director
James Gibson
Board Members
Philip Burks, Adrian Lee, David Ross, Jonathan Short,
David White

Business Description
A group engaged in the provision of self-storage and
related services.

Biocompatibles International plc
Chapman House, Farnham Business Park, Wydon Lane,
Farnham, Surrey GU9 8QL
Telephone +44 (0) 1252 732 732
Fax +44 (0) 1252 732 777
Website www.biocompatibles.com

Chair
Gerry Brown
Chief Executive/Managing Director
Crispin Simon
Board Members
Ian Ardill, Jeremy Cumock Cook, Sir Thomas Harris,
Peter Stratford, John Sylvester, Anthony Weir

Business Description
A company engaged in the development of medical
combination products.

Bionostics plc
Rutland House, 148 Edmund Street, Birmingham B3 2JR
Telephone +44 (0) 1993 885070
Fax +44 (0) 1993 883988
Website www.bionsticplc.com

Chair
Dr Paul Haycock
Chief Executive/Managing Director
Michael Thomas
Board Members
Anthony Fay, Dr Gerard Moeller

Business Description
A group engaged in medical diagnostics.

Bioquell plc
34A Walworth Road, Andover, Hampshire SP10 5AA
Telephone +44 (0) 1264 835835
Fax +44 (0) 1264 835836
Website www.bioquell.com

Chair
John Salkeld
Chief Executive/Managing Director
Nicholas Adams
Board Members
Mark Bodeker, Simon Constantine, Richard Towner

Business Description
A group engaged in the research and development,
design, manufacture and supply of bio-decontamination
and containment equipment, related products and
engineering services.

Biotech Growth Trust plc (The)
25 Southampton Buildings, London WC2A 1AL
Telephone +44 (0) 20 3008 4910
Website www.finsburyeb.com

Chair
John Scatter
Board Members
Sven Borho, Peter Gaunt, Dr John Gordon, Peter Keen,
John Townsend, The Lord Waldegrave of North Hill

Business Description
An investment trust, investing in emerging biotechnology
companies.

Bisichi Mining plc
30-35 Pall Mall, London SW1Y 5LP
Telephone +44 (0) 20 7415 5030
Fax +44 (0) 20 7839 5999
Website www.bisichi.co.uk

Chair
Michael Heller
Chief Executive/Managing Director
Andrew Heller
Board Members
Christopher Joll, Thomas Kearney, John Sibbald

Business Description
A group engaged in coal mining property investment,
share dealing and general investment.

Blackrock International Land plc
29 North Anne Street, Dublin 7, Ireland
Telephone +353 1 887 2788
Fax +353 1 887 2730
Website www.bilplc.com

Chair
Carl McCann
Board Members
Philip Halpenny, Robert Knox, Tom Neasy, J Declan
McCourt, Alan D White, Andrew Kelliher

Business Description
A company engaged in property development.

Blacks Leisure Group plc
Mansard Close, Westgate, Northampton NN5 5DL
Telephone +44 (0) 1604 597 000
Fax +44 (0) 1604 597 164
Website www.blacksleisure.co.uk

Chair
David Bernstein
Chief Executive/Managing Director
Keith Fleming
Board Members
Claude Littner, Clive Sherling, Darren Spurling, Donald
Trangmar

Business Description
A group engaged in the retail of outdoor and boardwear,
and the wholesale of clothing, footwear and equipment.

Bloomsbury Publishing plc
38 Soho Square, London W1D 3QY
Telephone +44 (0) 20 7494 2111
Fax +44 (0) 20 7434 0151
Website www.bloomsbury.com

Chair and Chief Executive
Nigel Newton
Board Members
Colin Adams, Charles Black, Elizabeth Calder, Michael Mayer, Jeremy Wilson

Business Description
A group engaged in the publication of books and the development of electronic reference databases.

Blue Planet European Financials Investment Trust plc
Greenside House, 25 Greenside Place,
Edinburgh EH1 3AA
Telephone +44 (0) 131 466 6666
Fax +44 (0) 131 466 6677
Website www.blueplanet.eu.com

Chair
John Tyce
Board Members
Kenneth Murray, Lord Steel of Aikwood

Business Description
An investment trust.

Blue Planet Financials Growth and Income Investment Trust plc
Greenside House, 25 Greenside Place,
Edinburgh EH1 3AA
Telephone +44 (0) 131 466 6666
Fax +44 (0) 131 466 6677
Website www.blueplanet.eu.com

Chair
Victoria Killay
Board Members
Kenneth Murray, Dr Michael Shea

Business Description
An investment trust.

Blue Planet Worldwide Financials Investment Trust plc
Greenside House, 25 Greenside Place,
Edinburgh EH1 3AA
Telephone +44 (0) 131 466 6666
Fax +44 (0) 131 466 6677
Website www.blueplanet.eu.com

Chair
Philip Court
Board Members
D Christopher Jones, Kenneth Murray

Business Description
An investment trust.

Bluebay Asset Management plc
45 pall Mall, London SW1Y 5JG
Telephone +44 (0) 20 7389 3700
Fax +44 (0) 20 7930 7400
Website www.bluebayinvest.com

Chair
Hans-Jörg Rudloff
Chief Executive/Managing Director
Hugh Willis
Board Members
Tom Gross Brown, Terrence Eccles, Alex Khein, Mark Poole, Nick Williams

Business Description
A company engaged in the provision of investment management services.

Bodycote International plc
Hulley Road, Hurdsfield, Macclesfield, Cheshire SK10 2SG
Telephone +44 (0) 1625 505300
Fax +44 (0) 16525 505313
Website www.bodycote.com

Chair
James Wallace
Chief Executive/Managing Director
John Hubbard
Board Members
Laurent Bermejo, John Biles, David Landless, Derek Sleight, Hans Vogelsang

Business Description
A group engaged in materials technology and metal processing services including heat treatments, materials testing metallurgical coatings, and hot isostatic pressing.

Bovis Homes Group plc
The Manor House, North Ash Road , New Ash Green, Longfield, Kent DA3 8HQ
Telephone +44 (0) 1474 876200
Fax +44 (0) 1474 876201
Website www.bovishomesgroup.plc.uk

Chair
Tim Melville-Ross
Chief Executive/Managing Director
Malcolm Harris
Board Members
Neil Cooper, Colin Holmes, Lesley MacDonagh, David Ritchie, John Warren

Business Description
A group engaged in housebuilding and estate development.

BP plc
1 St James's Square, London SW1Y 4PD
Telephone +44 (0) 20 7496 4000
Fax +44 (0) 20 7496 4630
Website www.bp.com

Chair
Peter Sutherland
Chief Executive/Managing Director
Dr Anthony Hayward
Board Members
Dr David Allen, Antony Burgmans, Cynthia Carroll, Sir William Castell, Iain Conn, Erroll Davis Jr, Douglas Flint, Dr Byron Grote, Andrew Inglis, Dr DeAnne Julius, John Manzoni, Dr Walter Massey, Sir Tom McKillop, Sir Ian Prosser

Business Description
A group engaged in the refining and marketing of oil products, the supply of gas and power, the production of chemicals, and the exploration and production of oil and gas.

BPP Holdings plc
BPP House, 142-144 Uxbridge Road, London W12 8AA
Telephone +44 (0) 20 8740 2222
Fax +44 (0) 20 8740 1111
Website www.bpp.com

Chair
David Sugden
Chief Executive/Managing Director
Charles Prior
Board Members
Si Hussain, Mike Kirkham, Carl Lygo, Chris Ross-Roberts, Stephen Taylor, John Warren

Business Description
A group engaged in professional training, language training and academic education.

Bradford & Bingley plc
Croft Road, Crossflatts, Bingley, West Yorkshire BD16 2UA
Telephone +44 (0) 1274 555555
Website www.bbg.co.uk

Chair
Roderick Kent
Chief Executive/Managing Director
Steven Crawshaw
Board Members
Ian Cheshire, Nicholas Cosh, Sir George Cox, Robert Dickie, Roger Hattam, Lady Patten, Mark Stevens, Stephen Webster, Chris Willford

Business Description
A group engaged in the provision of property related loans, savings services and estate agency services, and the retail of financial products.

Braemar Shipping Services
35 Cosway Street, London NW1 5BT
Telephone +44 (0) 20 7535 2650
Fax +44 (0) 7903 2606
Website www.braemarseascope.com

Chair
Sir Graham Hearne
Chief Executive/Managing Director
Alan Marsh
Board Members
Richard Agutter, John Denholm, James Kidwell, David Moorhouse, Denis Pertropoulos, Quentin Soanes

Business Description
A group engaged in the provision of specialist brokering and support services to the shipowning, shipbuilding and oil industries including tanker chartering, finance and marine consultancy.

Brammer plc
Claverton Court, Claverton Road, Wythenshawe, Manchester M23 9NE
Telephone +44 (0) 161 902 5599
Fax +44 (0) 161 902 5595
Website www.brammer.biz

Chair
David Dunn
Chief Executive/Managing Director
Ian Fraser
Board Members
Svante Adde, Chris Conway, Terence Garthwaite, Paul Thwaite

Business Description
A group engaged in the supply of power transmission components and related inventory management services and the outsourced management of technology tools.

Brewin Dolphin Holdings plc
12 Smithfield Stret, London EC1A 9BD
Telephone +44 (0) 20 7248 4400
Fax +44 (0) 20 3201 3001
Website www.brewindolphin.co.uk

Chair
Jamie Matheson
Chief Executive/Managing Director
John Hall
Board Members
Robin Bayford, Nick Hood, Angela Knight, Vickram Lall, Sir Stephen Lamport, Christopher Legge, David McCorkell, Simon Miller, Ben Speke, Simon Still, Michael Williams, Francis Worsley

Business Description
The principal activity of the group is that of a private client fund manager.

Brit Insurance Holdings plc
55 Bishopsgate, London EC2N 3AS
Telephone +44 (0) 20 7934 8500
Fax +44 (0) 20 7984 8501
Website www.britinsurance.com

Chair
Clive Coates
Chief Executive/Managing Director
Dane Douetil
Board Members
Ken Culley, Neil Eckert, Peter Hazell, Kathy Lisson, Joe MacHale, Matthew Scales, Dr Cees Schrauwers, Michael Smith, Anthony Townsend

Business Description
A group engaged in the transaction of insurance and reinsurance business and investment.

British & American Investment Trust plc
Wessex House, 1 Chesham Street, London SW1X 8ND
Telephone +44 (0) 20 7201 3100
Fax +44 (0) 20 7201 3101
Website www.baitgroup.com

Chair
Anthony Townsend
Board Members
Dominic Dreyfus, Ronald Paterson, Jonathan Woolf

Business Description
A group engaged in investment holding and film investment.

British Airways plc
Waterside, PO Box 365, Harmondsworth UB7 0GB
Telephone +44 (0) 845 779 9977
Website www.bashares.com

Chair
Martin Broughton
Chief Executive/Managing Director
Willie Walsh
Board Members
Baroness Kingsmill, Jim Lawrence, Chumpol NaLamlieng, Dr Martin Read, Alison Reed, Ken Smart, Baroness Symons of Vernham Dean, Maarten van den Bergh, Keith Williams

Business Description
A group engaged in the operation of international and domestic scheduled and charter air services for the carriage of passengers, freight and mail, and provision of ancilliary services.

British American Tobacco plc
Globe House, 4 Temple Place, London WC2R 2PG
Telephone +44 (0) 20 7845 1000
Website www.bat.com

Chair
Jan Du Plessis
Chief Executive/Managing Director
Paul Adams
Board Members
Kenneth Clarke, Robert Lerwill, Dr Ana Maria Llopis,
Antonio Monteiro de Castro, Paul Rayner, Anthony Ruys,
Sir Nicholas Scheele, Thys Visser

Business Description
A group engaged in the manufacture, distribution and
sale of tobacco products.

British Assets Trust plc
80 George Street, Edinburgh EH2 3BU
Telephone +44 (0) 131 465 1000
Fax +44 (0) 131 225 2375
Website www.british-assets.co.uk

Chair
William Thomson
Board Members
James Long, James MacLeod, Dr Christopher Masters,
Lynn Ruddick, James West

Business Description
An investment trust which invests in an international
portfolio of equities and equity related securities.

British Empire Securities & General Trust plc
Bennet House, 54 St James's Street, London SW1A 1JT
Telephone +44 (0) 20 7647 2900
Fax +44 (0) 20 7647 2901
Website www.british-empire.co.uk

Chair
Iain Robertson
Board Members
Peter Allen, Steven Bates, Rosamund Blomfield-Smith,
Strone Macpherson, John May

Business Description
An investment trust with a dealing subsidiary.

British Energy Group plc
Systems House, Alba Campus, Livingston EH54 7EG
Telephone +44 (0) 1506 408700
Fax +44 (0) 1506 408888
Website www.british-energy.com

Chair
Sir Adrian Montague
Chief Executive/Managing Director
William Coley
Board Members
Robert Armour, Dr Stephen Billingham, Dr Pascal
Colombani, Bob Davies, John Delucca, Ian Harley, David
Pryde, Clare Spottiswoode, Sir Robert Walmsley

Business Description
A group engaged in the generation and sale of electricity.

British Land Company plc (The)
York House, 45 Seymour Street, London W1H 7LX
Telephone +44 (0) 20 7486 4466
Fax +44 (0) 20 7935 5552
Website www.britishland.com

Chair
Dr Chris Gibson-Smith
Chief Executive/Managing Director
Stephen Hester
Board Members
Robert Bowden, Clive Cowdery, Andrew Jones, Sir David
Michels, Graham Roberts, Tim Roberts, Kate Swann,
Robert Swannell, Lord Turnbull

Business Description
The group operates in the fields of development, finance
and investment.

British Polythene Industries plc
96 Port Glasgow Road, Greenock PA15 2UL
Telephone +44 (0) 1475 501000
Fax +44 (0) 1475 743143
Website www.bpipoly.com

Chair
Cameron McLatchie
Chief Executive/Managing Director
John Langlands
Board Members
Hamish Grossart, Eric Hagman, Earl of Lindsay, Anne
Thorburn

Business Description
A group engaged in the manufacture and sale of
polythene film products.

British Portfolio Trust plc
155 Bishopsgate, London EC2M 3AD
Telephone +44 (0) 20 7859 9000
Fax +44 (0) 20 7638 3507
Website www.allianzglobalinvestors.co.uk

Chair
Andrew Barker
Board Members
George Luckraft, Dr Oonagh Mcdonald, Adam Wethered,
Simon White

Business Description
An investment trust.

British Sky Broadcasting Group plc
7 Centaurs Business Centre, Grant Way, Isleworth,
Middlesex TW7 5QD
Telephone +44 (0) 870 240 3000
Fax +44 (0) 870 240 3060
Website www.sky.co.uk

Chair
Rupert Murdoch
Chief Executive/Managing Director
James Murdoch
Board Members
Chase Carey, Jeremy Darroch, David DeVoe, David
Evans, Nicholas Ferguson, Andrew Higginson, Allan
Leighton, Jacques Nasser, Gail Rebuck, Lord Rothschild,
Arthur Siskind, Lord St John of Fawsley, Lord Wilson of
Dinton

Business Description
A group engaged in the transmission of satellite, cable
and digital television broadcasting services.

Britvic plc
Britvic House, Broomfield Road, Chelmsford,
Essex CM1 1TU
Telephone +44 (0) 1245 261871
Website www.britvic.com

Chair
Gerald Corbett
Chief Executive/Managing Director
Paul Moody
Board Members
Joanne Averiss, Chris Bulmer, John Gibney, Bob Ivell,
Michael Shallow

Business Description
The group engages in the production, marketing and
distribution of soft drinks.

Brixton plc
50 Berkeley Street, London W1J 8BX
Telephone +44 (0) 20 7399 4500
Website www.brixton.plc.uk

Chair
Lady Patten
Chief Executive/Managing Director
Timothy Wheeler
Board Members
Nicholas Fry, Stephen Harris, Steven Owen, David
Scotland

Business Description
A group engaged in property investment, development
and management.

Brunner Investment Trust plc (The)
155 Bishopsgate, London EC2M 3AD
Telephone +44 (0) 20 7859 9000
Fax +44 (0) 20 7638 3508
Website www.brunner.co.uk

Chair
Keith Percy
Board Members
Vivian Bazalgette, Benjamin Siddons, Richard Wakeling,
William Worsley

Business Description
An investment trust investing in UK and international
securities.

BSS Group plc (The)
Fleet House, Lee Circle, Leicester LE1 3QQ
Telephone +44 (0) 116 262 3232
Fax +44 (0) 116 253 1343
Website www.bss-group.co.uk

Chair
Peter Warry
Chief Executive/Managing Director
Gavin Slark
Board Members
Alan Ball, Roy Harrison, Roddy Murray, Tony
Osbaldiston

Business Description
A group engaged in the supply of heating, plumbing,
process control and pipeline equipment to industrial,
commercial and domestic markets.

BT Group plc
81 Newgate Street, London EC1A 7AJ
Telephone +44 (0) 20 7356 5000
Fax +44 (0) 20 7356 5520
Website www.btplc.com

Chair
Sir Christopher Bland
Chief Executive/Managing Director
Ben Verwaayen
Board Members
Matti Alahuhta, Francois Barrault, Clayton Brendish,
Andy Green, Phil Hodkinson, Baroness Jay of Paddington,
Hanif Lalani, Deborah Lathen, Ian Livingston, John
Nelson, Dr Paul Reynolds, Carl Symon, Maarten van den
Bergh

Business Description
A group engaged in the supply of communications
services and equipment.

BTG plc
10 Fleet Place, London EC4M 7SB
Telephone +44 (0) 20 7575 0000
Fax +44 (0) 20 7575 0010
Website www.btgplc.com

Chair
Sir Brian Fender
Chief Executive/Managing Director
Dr Louise Makin
Board Members
Consuelo Brooke, Peter Chambré, Dr William Jenkins,
Christine Soden, Fred Weiss, Alison Wood

Business Description
A group engaged in the funding, development and
commercialisation of intellectual property rights through
technology licensing, patent assertion and equity
investment.

Bunzl plc
110 Park Street, London W1K 6NX
Telephone +44 (0) 20 7495 4950
Fax +44 (0) 20 7495 4953
Website www.bunzl.com

Chair
Anthony Habgood
Chief Executive/Managing Director
Michael Roney
Board Members
Charles Banks, Jeff Harris, Peter Johnson, Patrick Larmon,
Brian May, Dr Ulrich Wolters

Business Description
A group engaged in the supply of outsourced food
packaging, fine paper and cigarette filters.

Burberry Group plc
18-22 Haymarket, London SW1Y 4DQ
Telephone +44 (0) 20 7968 0000
Fax +44 (0) 20 7980 2950
Website www.burberryplc.com

Chair
John Peace
Chief Executive/Managing Director
Angela Ahrendts
Board Members
Philip Bowman, Rose Marie Bravo, Stacey Cartwright,
Stephanie George, Guy Peyrelongue, David Tyler

Business Description
A group engaged in the design, sourcing, manufacture
and distribution of apparel and accessories through its
own retail stores and via wholesale customers.

Burren Energy plc
Kierran Cross, 11 Strand, London WC2N 5HR
Telephone +44 (0) 20 7484 1900
Fax +44 (0) 20 7484 1919
Website www.burren.co.uk

Chair
Keith Henry
Chief Executive/Managing Director
Atul Gupta
Board Members
Michael Calvey, Alan Cole, Pierre Lasry, Brian Lavers,
Finian O'Sullivan, Andrei Pannikov, Andrew Rose

Business Description
A group engaged in the exploration and production of oil
and gas and the transportation of oil products.

Business Post Group plc
Express House, 464 Berkshire Avenue, Slough,
Berkshire SL1 4PL
Telephone +44 (0) 1753 706070
Fax +44 (0) 1753 706071
Website www.business-post.biz

Chair
Peter Kane
Chief Executive/Managing Director
Guy Buswell
Board Members
Dennis Clark, William Cockburn, Steven Glew, Michael
Kane, Alec Ross, Philip Stephens

Business Description
A group engaged in the provision of express collection
and delivery services for parcels, mail and palletised
goods.

Cable & Wireless plc
7th Floor, The Point, 37 North Wharf Road, Paddington
Basin, London W2 1LA
Telephone +44 (0) 20 7315 4000
Website www.cw.com
Board Members
Simon Ball, George Battersby, Clive Butler, Harris Jones,
Kate Nealon, John Pluthero, Tony Rice, Kasper Rorsted,
Agnes Touraine

Business Description
A group engaged in telecommunications.

Cadbury Schweppes plc
25 Berkeley Square, London W1J 6HB
Telephone +44 (0) 20 7409 1313
Fax +44 (0) 20 7830 5200
Website www.cadburyschweppes.com

Chair
Sir John Sunderland
Chief Executive/Managing Director
Todd Stitzer
Board Members
Sanjiv Ahuja, Dr Wolfgang Berndt, Roger Carr, Kenneth
Hanna, Bob Stack, David Thompson, Rosemary Thorne,
Raymond Viault

Business Description
A group engaged in the manufacture and distribution for
sale of branded beverages and confectionery.

Caffyns plc
Saffrons Rooms, Meads Road, Eastbourne,
Sussex BN20 7DR
Telephone +44 (0) 1323 730201
Fax +44 (0) 1323 739680
Website www.caffyns.co.uk

Chair
Brian Carte
Chief Executive/Managing Director
Simon Caffyn
Board Members
Brian Birkenhead, Sarah Caffyn, Andrew Goodburn, Mark
Harrison

Business Description
A group engaged as motor retailers.

Cairn Energy plc
Clydesdale Bank Plaza, 50 Lothian Road,
Edinburgh EH3 9BY
Telephone +44 (0) 131 475 3000
Fax +44 (0) 131 475 3030
Website www.cairn-energy.plc.uk

Chair
Norman Murray
Chief Executive/Managing Director
Sir Bill Gammell
Board Members
Jann Brown, Hamish Grossart, Todd Hunt, Andrew
Shilston, Ed Story, Malcolm Thomas, Simon Thompson,
Phill Tracy, Mark Tyndall, Dr Mike Watts

Business Description
A company engaged in oil and gas exploration and
production.

Caledonia Investments plc
Cayzer House, 30 Buckingham Gate, London SW1E 6NN
Telephone +44 (0) 20 7802 8080
Fax +44 (0) 20 7802 8090
Website www.caledonia.com

Chair
Peter Buckley
Chief Executive/Managing Director
Tim Ingram
Board Members
Jonathan Cartwright, Hon Charles Cayzer, James Cayzer-
Colvin, Tony Hambro, Mathew Masters, John May, Mark
Neale, Will Wyatt

Business Description
A group engaged in engineering, the manufacture of
specialty chemicals and crystal glass, the operation of a
residential club, self storage and property trading.

Camellia plc
Linton Park, Linton, Kent ME17 4AB
Telephone +44 (0) 1622 746655
Fax +44 (0) 1622 747422
Website www.camellia.plc.uk

Chair and Chief Executive
Malcolm Perkins
Board Members
Peter Leggatt, Anil Mathur, C J Pelleen, David Reeves, Dr
B A Siegfried, Charles Vaughan-Johnson

Business Description
A group engaged in the production of tea, coffee and
other produce, food storage and distribution, property
leasing, trading and agency, and banking.

Candover Investments plc
20 Old Bailey, London EC4M 7LN
Telephone +44 (0) 20 7489 9848
Fax +44 (0) 20 7248 5483
Website www.candoverinvestments.com

Chair
Gerry Grimstone
Board Members
Stephen Curran, Antony Hichens, Nicolas Lethbridge,
Christopher Russell, Richard Stone, James West

Business Description
An investment trust principally investing in large
buyouts with subsidiaries engaged in third party fund
management.

Cape plc
Cape House, 3 Red Hall Avenue, Paragon Business
Village, Wakefield WF1 2UL
Telephone +44 (0) 1924 876276
Website www.capeplc.com

Chair
Davin McManus
Chief Executive/Managing Director
Martin May
Board Members
Sean O'Connor, Mike Reynolds, David Robins

Business Description
A company engaged in the supply of a range of services
related to major industrial groups.

Capita Group plc (The)
71 Victoria Street, London SW1H 0XA
Telephone +44 (0) 20 7799 1525
Fax +44 (0) 20 7799 1526
Website www.capita.co.uk

Chair
Eric Walters
Chief Executive/Managing Director
Paul Pindar
Board Members
Peter Cawdron, Paddy Doyle, Bill Grimsey, Gordon Hurst,
Martina King, Simon Pilling

Business Description
A group engaged in the provision of professional support
services and business process outsourcing solutions.

Capital & Regional plc
10 Lower Grosvenor Place, London SW1W 0EN
Telephone +44 (0) 20 7932 8000
Fax +44 (0) 20 7802 5600
Website www.capreg.com

Chair
Viscount Chandos
Chief Executive/Managing Director
Martin Barber
Board Members
Alan Coppin, Kenneth Ford, PY Gerbeau, Hans Mautner,
Philip Newton, Xavier Pullen, Paul Stobart, William
Sunnucks, Manjit Wolstenholme

Business Description
A group engaged as a co-investing property manager.

Capital Gearing Trust plc
Waterfront Plaza, 8 Laganbank Road, Belfast BT1 3LR
Telephone +44 (0) 1582 439272
Fax +44 (0) 1582 439207
Website www.capitalgreatingtrust.com

Chair
Tony Pattison
Board Members
Edwin Meek, James Morton, Robert Spiller

Business Description
An investment trust.

Carclo plc
Springstone House, PO Box 88, 27 Dewsbury Road,
Ossett WF5 9WS
Telephone +44 (0) 1924 268040
Fax +44 (0) 1924 283226
Website www.carclo-plc.com

Chair
Christopher Ross
Chief Executive/Managing Director
Ian Williamson
Board Members
Robert Brooksbank, Michael Derbyshire, Bill Tame

Business Description
A group engaged in the design and manufacture of
technical plastic components and specialist wire products.

Cardiff Property plc (The)
56 Station Road, Egham, Surrey TW20 9LF
Telephone +44 (0) 1784 437444
Fax +44 (0) 1784 439157
Website www.cardiff-property.com

Chair and Chief Executive
Richard Wollenberg
Board Members
Nigel Jamieson, David Whitaker

Business Description
A group engaged in property investment and
development.

Care UK plc
Connaught House, 850 The Crescent, Colchester Business
Park, Colchester, Essex CO4 9QB
Telephone +44 (0) 1206 752552
Fax +44 (0) 1206 517181
Website www.careuk.com

Chair
John Nash
Chief Executive/Managing Director
Michael Parish
Board Members
Michael Averill, Paul Humphreys, Miles Roberts, Fritz
Ternofsky, James Strachan

Business Description
A group engaged in the provision of a range of health
and social care solutions primarily to various public
sector purchasers.

Caretech Holdings plc
Leyton House, 33-37 Darkes Lane, Potters Bar,
Hertfordshire EN6 1BB
Telephone +44 (0) 1707 652053
Fax +44 (0) 1707 662719
Website www.caretech-uk.com

Chair
Farouq Sheikh
Chief Executive/Managing Director
Haroon Sheikh
Board Members
Graham Mattinson, David Spink, Stewart Wallace

Business Description
A group engaged in the provision of housing and support
services to adults with learning and physical disabilities.

Carillion plc
24 Birch Street, Wolverhampton, West
Midlands WV1 4HY
Telephone +44 (0) 1902 422431
Website www.carillionplc.com

Chair
Philip Rogerson
Chief Executive/Managing Director
John McDonough
Board Members
Richard Adam, David Garman, Don Kenny, David
Maloney, Steve Mogford, Vanda Murray, Roger Robinson

Business Description
A group engaged in building, civil engineering, the
provision of construction and infrastructure services, and
facilities management.

Carnival plc
3655 NW 87th Avenue, Miami, FL, 33178-2428 USA
Telephone +1 (0) 30 5599 260
Website www.carnivalcorp.com

Chair and Chief Executive
Micky Arison
Board Members
Richard Capen, Robert Dickinson, Arnold Donald, Pier
Luigi Foschi, Howard Frank, Richard Glasier, Baroness
Hogg, Dr Modesto Maidique, Sir John Parker, Peter
Ratcliffe, Stuart Subotnick, Laura Weil, Uzi Zucker

Business Description
A group engaged in the international operation of cruise
ships and the provision of related land-based tourist
services.

Carpetright plc
Amberley House, New Road, Rainham, Essex RM13 8QN
Telephone +44 (0) 1708 525 522
Fax +44 (0) 1708 526 738
Website www.carpetright.plc.uk

Chair and Chief Executive
Lord Harris of Peckham
Board Members
Geoff Brady, Martin Harris, Ian Kenyon, John Kitching,
Simon Metcalf, Baroness Noakes, Christian Sollesse,
Martin Toogood, Guy Weston

Business Description
A group engaged in the retail sale of carpets and floor
coverings, including vinyls, laminates and rugs, and
property investment.

Carphone Warehouse Group plc (The)
1 Portal Way, London W3 6RS
Telephone +44 (0) 20 8896 5000
Fax +44 (0) 20 8896 5005
Website www.carphonewarehouse.com

Chair
John Gildersleeve
Chief Executive/Managing Director
Charles Dunstone
Board Members
Steven Esom, David Goldie, David Grigson, Andrew
Harrison, David Mansfield, Adrian Martin, Baroness
Morgan of Huyton, Tim Morris, Sir Brian Pitman, David
Ross, Roger Taylor

Business Description
A group engaged in the provision of mobile
communication products and fixed line communication
services.

Carr's Milling Industries plc
Old Croft, Stanwix, Cumbria CA3 9BA
Telephone +44 (0) 1228 554600
Fax +44 (0) 1228 554601
Website www.carrs-milling.com

Chair
Lord Inglewood
Chief Executive/Managing Director
Christopher Holmes
Board Members
Robert Heygate, Alistair Wannop, Ronald Wood

Business Description
A group engaged in animal feed compounding, fertiliser
blending, the retail of agricultural products, flour milling,
engineering and commercial vehicle body building.

Carter & Carter Group plc
Ruddington Fields Business Park, Nottingham NG11 6JZ
Telephone +44 (0) 115 945 7200
Fax +44 (0) 115 846 1202
Website www.carter-and-cartergroup.com

Chair
Rodney Westhead
Board Members
Sarah Anderson, David Galloway, John Green, Sir
Howard Newbury

Business Description
A group engaged in the the operation of outsource
services and vocational learning.

Castings plc
Lichfield Road, Brownhills, West Midlands WS8 6JZ
Telephone +44 (0) 1543 374341
Fax +44 (0) 1543 377483
Website www.castings.plc.uk

Chair
Brian Cooke
Chief Executive/Managing Director
David Gawthorpe
Board Members
Graham Cooper, Christopher King, Mark Lewis,
Christopher Roby, Anthony Smith, Gerard Wainwright

Business Description
A group engaged in the supply of spheroidal graphite
and malleable iron castings to manufacturing industries.

Catlin Group Ltd
Cumberland House, 6th Floor, 1 Victoria Street, Hamilton
HM11, Bermuda
Telephone +1 441 2960060
Fax +1 441 2966016
Website www.catlin.com

Chair
Sir Graham Hearne
Chief Executive/Managing Director
Stephen Catlin
Board Members
Alan Bossin, Michael Crall, Jean Claude Damerval,
Michael Eisenson, Michael Harper, Richard Haverland,
Michael Hepher, Jonathan Kelly, Gene Lee, Christopher
Stooke

Business Description
Property and casualty insurance and reinsurance
underwriting.

Cattles plc
Kingston House, Centre 27 Business Park, Woodhead
Road, Birstall, Batley WF17 9TD
Telephone +44 (0) 1924 444466
Fax +44 (0) 1924 448324
Website www.cattles.co.uk

Chair
Norman Broadhurst
Chief Executive/Managing Director
Seán Mahon
Board Members
Mark Collins, James Corr, Ian Cummine, Frank Dee,
David Haxby, Alan McWalter, Margaret Young

Business Description
A group engaged in the provision of consumer credit,
debt collection and investigation services, and corporate
finance services, including invoice factoring and leasing.

Cayenne Trust plc (The)
Springfield Lodge, Colchester Road, Chelmsford,
Essex CM2 5PW
Telephone +44 (0) 1245 398 950
Fax +44 (0) 1245 398 951
Website www.thecayennetrust.com

Chair
Jonathan Agnew
Board Members
Christopher Jones, Sir Laurie Magnus

Business Description
An investment trust investing primarily in the securities
of UK investment trust companies.

Celsis International plc
Kett House, Station Road, Cambridge CB1 2JY
Telephone +44 (0) 1223 597851
Fax +44 (0) 1223 597985
Website www.celsis.com

Chair
Dr Jack Rowell
Chief Executive/Managing Director
Jay LeCoque
Board Members
Nicholas Badman, Prof Sir Christopher Evans, Peter
Jensen, Christian Madrolle

Business Description
A group engaged in the development and supply of rapid
diagnostic and monitoring systems for measuring
microbial contamination, and the provision of contract
testing services.

Centamin Egypt Ltd
57 Kishom Road, Mount Pleasant 6153, Western Australia
Telephone +61 8 9316 2640
Fax +61 8 9316 2650
Website www.centamin.com

Chair
Sami El-Raghy
Chief Executive/Managing Director
Josef El-Raghy
Board Members
Stuart Bottomley, Colin Cowden, Dr Thomas Elder,
Gordan B Speechly

Business Description
A company engaged in mineral exploration.

Centaur Media plc
St Giles House, 50 Poland Street, London W1F 7AX
Telephone +44 (0) 20 7970 4000
Website www.centaur.co.uk

Chair
Graham Sherren
Board Members
Alton Irby, Colin Morrison, Basil Scruby, John Taylor,
Geoff Wilmot

Business Description
A group engaged in the creation and dissemination of
business and professional information through
publications, exhibitions, conferences and online products.

Central African Mining & Exploration Company plc
Millennium Bridge House, 2 Lambert Hill,
London EC4V 4AJ
Telephone +44 (0) 845 108 6060
Fax +44 (0) 845 108 0606
Website www.camec.com

Chair
Phil Edmonds
Chief Executive/Managing Director
Andrew Groves
Board Members
John Anthony, Russell Grant, Raymond Hassim

Business Description
A group engaged as a fully integrated exploration,
mining and trading business focussed on Central and
Southern Africa.

Centrica plc
Millstream, Maidenhead Road, Windsor,
Berkshire SL4 5GD
Telephone +44 (0) 1753 494000
Fax +44 (0) 1753 494001
Website www.centrica.co.uk

Chair
Roger Carr
Chief Executive/Managing Director
Sam Laidlaw
Board Members
Helen Alexander, Phillip Bentley, Mary Francis, Nick
Luff, Andrew Mackenzie, Paul Rayner, Jake Ulrich, Paul
Walsh

Business Description
A group engaged in the provision of gas, electricity and
energy related products, the operation of gas fields and
gas storage, and the provision of telecommunications
services.

Chameleon Trust plc
7 West Nile Street, Glasgow G1 2PX
Telephone +44 (0) 20 7410 5971
Website www.reverafunds.com

Chair
Martin Ritchie
Board Members
Robert Adair, James Leek, Andrew Mickel

Business Description
An investment trust.

Chapelthorpe plc
Chapelthorpe Hall, Church Lane, Chapelthorpe, Wakefield,
West Yorkshire WF4 3JB
Telephone +44 (0) 1924 248200
Fax +44 (0) 1924 248222
Website www.chaplethorpe.com

Chair
Leslie Goodman
Chief Executive/Managing Director
Ian Powell
Board Members
Brian Leckie, Andrew Weatherstone

Business Description
A group engaged in the manufacture of polypropylene
fibre, the manufacture of vinyl-coated paper and plastisols
for the wall-coverings industry and the manufacture of
umbrella frames.

Charlemagne Capital Ltd
Ugland House, PO Box 309, South Church Street, George
Town, Grand Cayman British West Indies
Telephone +44 (0) 1624 640200
Website www.charlemagnecapital.com

Chair
Michael Baer
Chief Executive/Managing Director
Jayne Sutcliffe
Board Members
David Curl, Lord Lang of Monkton, David McMahon, Sir
James Mellon, Jacob van Duijn, Robert van Griethuysen,
Alexander Whamond

Business Description
An equity investment manager whose principal activity is
the provision of asset management products and services.

Charles Stanley Group plc
25 Luke Street, London EC2A 4AR
Telephone +44 (0) 20 7739 8200
Fax +44 (0) 20 7739 7798
Website www.charles-stanleyplc.com

Chair
Sir David Howard
Board Members
Michael Clark, Peter Hurst

Business Description
A group engaged in the provision of stockbroking,
corporate finance, investment services and pensions
administration.

Charles Taylor Consulting plc
Essex House, 12-13 Essex Street, London WC2R 3AA
Telephone +44 (0) 20 7759 4955
Fax +44 (0) 20 7481 4949
Website www.charlestaylorconsulting.com

Chair and Chief Executive
John Rowe
Board Members
Andrew Brannon, Michael Dean, Damian Ely, George
Fitzsimons, Alistair Groom, Judith Hanratty, John Howes,
Michael Knight, John Matthews, John McKay, Joseph
Roach III, Richard Titley, Raymond Wong

Business Description
A group engaged in the provision of specialist insurance
management services, claims consultancy and average
adjusting, third party claims administration and risk
assessment services.

Charter European Trust plc
155 Bishopsgate, London EC2M 3AD
Telephone +44 (0) 20 7859 9000
Website www.allianzglobalinvestors.co.uk

Chair
Giles Weaver
Board Members
Richard Bernays, Vicky Hastings, Sir Christopher
Mallaby, Dr Elizabeth Vallance

Business Description
An investment trust investing in equities listed on the
primary stock exchanges of European markets.

Charter plc
52 Grosvenor Gardens, London SW1W 0AU
Telephone +44 (0) 20 7881 7800
Fax +44 (0) 20 7259 9338
Website www.charterplc.com

Chair
David Gawler
Chief Executive/Managing Director
Michael Foster
Board Members
John Biles, Hon James Bruce, Robert Careless, James
Deeley, Grey Denham, John Neill, Andrew Osborne

Business Description
A group engaged in the manufacture of welding and
cutting products, air and gas handling equipment and the
provision of specialised engineering services.

Chaucer Holdings plc
Plantation Place, 30 Fenchurch Street, London EC3M 3AD
Telephone +44 (0) 20 7397 9700
Fax +44 (0) 20 7397 9710
Website www.chaucerplc.com

Chair
Martin Gilbert
Chief Executive/Managing Director
Ewen Gilmour
Board Members
Bob Deutsch, Christopher Forbes, Mark Graham, Richard
Scholes, Robert Stuchbery

Business Description
A group engaged in the management of Lloyd's
syndicates and participation in insurance underwriting
through corporate membership of Lloyd's.

Chelverton Growth Trust plc
Beaufort House, 51 New North Road, Exeter EX4 4EP
Telephone +44 (0) 1392 412122
Website www.chelvertonam.com

Chair
George Stevens
Board Members
Kevin Allen, David Horner, Brian Lenygon

Business Description
An investment trust.

Chemring Group
1650 Parkway, Whiteley, Fareham PO15 7AH
Telephone +44 (0) 1489 881880
Fax +44 (0) 1489 881123
Website www.chemring.co.uk

Chair
Ken Scobie
Chief Executive/Managing Director
Dr David Price
Board Members
Paul Rayner, David Evans, Lord Freeman, Ian Much, Sir
Peter Norriss

Business Description
A group engaged in the manufacture of decoy
countermeasures and energetic materials for the global
defence, security and safety markets.

Chesnara plc
Harbour House, Portway, Preston, Lancashire PR2 2PR
Telephone +44 (0) 1772 840000
Fax +44 (0) 1772 840010
Website www.chesnara.co.uk

Chair
Christopher Sporborg
Chief Executive/Managing Director
Graham Kettleborough
Board Members
Michael Gordon, Frank Hughes, Terry Marris, Peter
Mason, Ken Romney

Business Description
A group engaged in the transaction of life assurance,
pension and permanent health business.

Chime Communications
14 Curzon Street, London W1J 5HN
Telephone +44 (0) 20 7861 8515
Website www.chime.plc.uk

Chair
Lord Bell
Chief Executive/Managing Director
Christopher Satterthwaite
Board Members
Dave Allen, Catherine Biner Bradley, Rodger Hughes,
Piers Pottinger, Paul Richardson, Mark Smith

Business Description
A group involved in public relations, advertising and
communications.

Chloride Group plc
Ebury Gate, 23 Lower Belgrave Street,
London SW1W 0NR
Telephone +44 (0) 20 7881 1440
Fax +44 (0) 20 7730 5085
Website www.chloridegroup.com

Chair
Norman Broadhurst
Chief Executive/Managing Director
Keith Hodgkinson
Board Members
Gary Bullard, Robin Southwell, Eric Tracey, Neil Warner

Business Description
A group engaged in the manufacture, sale and service of
power protection solutions.

Christian Salvesen plc
500 Pavillion Drive, Northampton NN4 7YJ
Telephone +44 (0) 1604 662600
Fax +44 (0) 1604 662605
Website www.salvesen.com

Chair
Dr David Fish
Chief Executive/Managing Director
Stewart Oades
Board Members
Lawrence Christensen, Mark Morris, Alain Poinssot,
Julian Steadman

Business Description
A group engaged in supply chain logistic outsourcing
services, specialising in outsources supply chain
management solutions for food and consumer products.

Chrysalis Group plc
Bramley Road, London W10 6SP
Telephone +44 (0) 20 7221 2213
Fax +44 (0) 20 7221 6455
Website www.chrysalis.com

Chair
Christopher Wright
Chief Executive/Managing Director
Richard Huntingford
Board Members
Michael Connole, Geoffrey Howard-Spink, Helen Keays,
Jorgen Larsen, Jeremy Lascelles, Peter Lassman, David
Murrell

Business Description
The production and marketing of music related products,
the operation of radio stations, the production and
distribution of programmes for television and video, and
music and book publishing.

Cineworld Group plc
Power Road Studios, Power Road, Chiswick,
London W4 5PY
Telephone +44 (0) 20 8987 5000

Chair
Anthony Bloom
Chief Executive/Managing Director
Steve Wiener
Board Members
Lawrence Guffney, Thomas McGrath, David Maloney,
Richard Jones, Mattew Tooth, Peter Williams

Business Description
A group involvded in the operation of motion picture
theatres.

City Merchants High Yield Trust plc
30 Finsbury Square, London EC2A 1AG
Telephone +44 (0) 20 7065 4000
Website www.investments.invescoperpetual.co.uk

Chair
Clive Nicholson
Board Members
Robin Baillie, Christopher Fitzgerald, Jonathan Hubbard-
Ford, Richard King, Kenneth MacLennan

Business Description
An investment trust.

City Natural Resources High Yield Trust plc
80 George Street, Edinburgh EH2 3BU
Telephone +44 (0) 131 465 1000
Website www.ncim.co.uk

Chair
Geoffrey Burns
Board Members
Adrian Collins, Adam Cooke, Michael Coulson, Richard
Prickett

Business Description
An investment company that primarily invests in small to
medium sized resource stocks combined with high
yielding bonds and convertibles.

City of London Group plc
Mercury House, Triton Court, Finsbury Square,
London EC2A 1BR
Telephone +44 (0) 20 7628 5518
Fax +44 (0) 20 7628 8555
Website www.cityoflondongroup.com

Chair
John Greenhalgh
Board Members
Peter Doye, Henry Lafferty, David Walton Masters,
Michael Nicol

Business Description
A group engaged in the provision of specialist investor
and press relations services.

City of London Investment Trust plc (The)
4 Broadgate, London EC2M 2DA
Telephone +44 (0) 20 7818 1818
Fax +44 (0) 20 7818 1819
Website www.itshenderson.com

Chair
Simon de Zoete
Board Members
Anita Frew, Mark Nicholls, Angus Russell, Sir Keith
Stuart

Business Description
An investment company.

Clarkson plc
St Magnus House, 3 Lower Thames Street,
London EC3R 6HE
Telephone +44 (0) 20 7334 0000
Fax +44 (0) 20 7626 2967
Website www.clarksons.com

Chair
Tim Harris
Chief Executive/Managing Director
Richard Fulford-Smith
Board Members
Robert Benton, Martin Clark, Dr Martin Stopford, Rob
Ward, Jeff Woyda

Business Description
A group engaged in the provision of shipping and
shipping services.

Climate Exchange plc
190 South La Salle Street, Suite 1100, Chicago, Illinois
60603, USA
Telephone +01 312 554 3350
Fax +01 312 554 3373
Website www.chicagoclimatex.com

Chair and Chief Executive
Richard Sandor
Board Members
Warren Batts, Bruce Braine, Hon Carole Brookins, Susan
Cischke, Stuart Eizenstat, Les Rosenthal, Maurice Strong

Business Description
A group engaged in operating and developing trading
exchanges for environmental financial instruments.

Clinical Computing plc
2 Kew Bridge Road, Brentford, Middlesex TW8 0JF
Telephone +44 (0) 20 8747 8744
Fax +44 (0) 20 8747 8745
Website www.ccl.com

Chair
Howard Kitchner
Chief Executive/Managing Director
Joe Marlovits
Board Members
Prof Stan Newman

Business Description
A group engaged in the development, distribution and
support of computer software for the healthcare market.

ClinPhone plc
Lady Bay House, Meadow Grove, Nottingham NG2 3HF
Telephone +44 (0) 115 955 7333
Fax +44 (0) 115 955 7555
Website www.clinphone.com

Chair
Dr Edwin Moses
Chief Executive/Managing Director
Steve Kent
Board Members
Dr Keith Bragman, Scott Brown, Dr Graeme Hart

Business Description
A company engaged in the provision of interactive voice response & other services.

Clinton Cards plc
The Crystal Building, Langston Road, Loughton, Essex IG10 3TH
Telephone +44 (0) 20 8502 2711
Fax +44 (0) 20 8502 0295
Website www.clintoncards.co.uk

Chair and Chief Executive
Donald Lewin
Board Members
Mike Bugler, John Coleman, Debbie Darlington, Robert Gunlack, Barry Hartog, Stuart Houlston, Brian Jackson, Clinton Lewin, Stuart McKay, John Robinson

Business Description
A group engaged in the specialist retail of greeting cards and associated products.

Clipper Windpower plc
9th Floor, Prince Consort House, 27-29 Albert Embankment, London SE1 7TJ
Telephone +44 (0) 20 7820 1078
Fax +44 (0) 20 7340 0177
Website www.clipperwind.com

Chair and Chief Executive
James Dehlsen
Board Members
Albert Baciocco Jr, Brent Dehlsen, Anthony Durrant, Finn Hansen, Lord Moynihan, Sidney Tassin, Charles Williams

Business Description
Designs wind turbines, and develops and owns wind development projects.

Close Brothers Group plc
10 Crown Place, London EC2A 4FT
Telephone +44 (0) 20 7655 3100
Fax +44 (0) 20 7655 8917
Website www.closebrothers.co.uk

Chair
Roderick Kent
Chief Executive/Managing Director
Colin Keogh
Board Members
Peter Buckley, Bruce Carnegie-Brown, Mike Hines, Stephen Hodges, Michael McLintock, Strone Macpherson, Douglas Paterson, David Pusinelli, James Williams, Peter Winkworth

Business Description
A group engaged in merchant banking, asset management including unit and investment trust management, market-making and corporate financial advice.

Close High Income Properties plc
St James' Chambers, Athol Street, Douglas, Isle of Man IM1 1JE
Telephone +44 (0) 20 7426 4000
Fax +44 (0) 20 7426 4044
Website www.cbil.com

Chair
Jonathan Clague
Board Members
Geoffrey Black, Donald Lake, Philip Scales, Mark Shaw

Business Description
An investment company, investing in commercial property.

CLS Holdings plc
26th Floor, Portland House, Bressenden Place, London SW1E 5BG
Telephone +44 (0) 20 7582 7766
Fax +44 (0) 20 7828 0218
Website www.clsholdings.com

Chair
Sten Mortstedt
Chief Executive/Managing Director
Per Sjoberg
Board Members
Dan Bäverstam, Steven Board, James Dean, Keith Harris, Thomas Lundqvist, Bengt Mortstedt, Thomas Thomson

Business Description
A group engaged in commercial properties, investment, development and management, and in telecoms operations.

CMA Global Hedge (Euro)
Arnold House, St Julien's Avenue, St Peter Port, Guernsey GY1 3NF
Website www.cmaglobalhedge.com

Chair
Christopher Fish
Board Members
Emmanuel Gavaudan, James T H Lee

Business Description
An investment company.

CML Microsystems plc
Oval Park, Hatfield Road, Langford Malford, Essex CM9 6WG
Telephone +44 (0) 1621 875500
Fax +44 (0) 1621 875600
Website www.cmlmicro.com

Chair
George Gurry
Board Members
George Bates, Nigel Clark, Christopher Gurry, Ronald Shashoua

Business Description
A group engaged in the design, manufacture and marketing of a range of electronic products for use in the telecommunications, radio and data communication industries.

Cobham plc
Brook Road, Wimborne, Dorset BH21 2BJ
Telephone +44 (0) 1202 882020
Fax +44 (0) 1202 849401
Website www.cobham.com

Chair
Gordon Page
Chief Executive/Managing Director
Allan Cook
Board Members
Marcus Beresford, Alex Hannam, Peter Hooley, Dr John Patterson, Mark Ronald, Andrew Stevens, Warren Tucker

Business Description
A group engaged in the design and manufacture of equipment, systems and components for the aerospace, defence, industrial and communications markets and the operation and maintenance of aircraft.

Collins Stewart plc
9th Floor, 88 Wood Street, London EC2V 7QR
Telephone +44 (0) 20 7523 8000
Fax +44 (0) 20 7523 8131
Website www.collins-stewart.com

Chair
Terry Smith
Chief Executive/Managing Director
Joel Plasco
Board Members
Paul Baines, Keith Hamill, Richard Kilsby

Business Description
A group engaged in institutional and private client stockbroking, market making, corporate finance, fund management, and supply of online financial information.

COLT Telecom Group SA
Kansallis House, Place de L'Etoile, L-1479, Luxembourg
Telephone +352 2250 4041
Website www.colt.net

Chair
Timothy Hilton
Chief Executive/Managing Director
Rakesh Bhasin
Board Members
Andreas Barth, Tony Bates, Vincenzo Damiani, Hans Eggerstedt, Gene Gabbard, Simon Haslam, Robert Hawley, John Remondi, H Frans van den Hoven, Richard D Walsh

Business Description
A group engaged in the provision of data, voice and managed IT and communications services.

Communisis plc
Wakefield Road, Leeds LS10 1DU
Telephone +44 (0) 113 277 0202
Fax +44 (0) 113 271 3503
Website www.communisis.com

Chair
Michael Smith
Chief Executive/Managing Director
Steve Vaughan
Board Members
Michael Firth, Roger Jennings, Peter King

Business Description
A group engaged in the provision of full service print solutions.

Compass Group plc
Compass House, Guildford Street, Chertsey, Surrey KT16 9BQ
Telephone +44 (0) 1932 573000
Fax +44 (0) 1932 569956
Website www.compass-group.com

Chair
Sir Roy Gardner
Chief Executive/Managing Director
Richard Cousins
Board Members
Peter Blackburn, Sir James Crosby, Gary Green, Sven Kado, Steve Lucas, Andrew Martin, Tim Parker, Sir Ian Robinson

Business Description
A group engaged in the provision of contract food services including the provision of vending food services and the management of restaurant facilities.

Computacenter plc
Hatfield Avenue, Hatfield, Hertfordshire AL10 9TW
Telephone +44 (0) 1707 631000
Fax +44 (0) 1707 631966
Website www.computacenter.com

Chair
Ron Sandler
Chief Executive/Managing Director
Mike Norris
Board Members
Tony Conophy, Philip Hulme, Ian Lewis, Sir Peter Ogden

Business Description
A provider of IT infrastructure services.

Connaught plc
Connaught House, Pynes Hill, Rydon Lane, Exeter EX2 5TZ
Telephone +44 (0) 1392 444546
Fax +44 (0) 1392 444543
Website www.connaught.com

Chair
Mark Tincknell
Chief Executive/Managing Director
Mark Davies
Board Members
Robert Alcock, Stephen Hill, Caroline Price, Tim Ross, David Wells

Business Description
A company engaged in providing social housing maintenance and estate management services.

Consolidated Minerals Ltd
28 Ventnor Avenue, West Perth, Western Australia 6005, Australia
Telephone +61 8 9321 3633
Fax +61 8 9321 3644
Website www.consminerals.com.au

Chair
Richard Carter
Board Members
Rodney Baxter, Bruce Brook, Michael Etheridge, Allan Quadrio, Andrew Simpson

Business Description
A group engaged in the extraction and sale of coal from drift and opencast mines in Western Australia.

Cookson Group plc
165 Fleet Street, London EC4A 2AE
Telephone +44 (0) 20 7822 0000
Fax +44 (0) 20 7822 0100
Website www.cooksongroup.co.uk

Chair
Bob Beeston
Chief Executive/Managing Director
Nick Salmon
Board Members
Mike Butterworth, Jeffrey Hewitt, Jan Oosterveld, Barry Perry, John Sussens

Business Description
A group engaged in the manufacture and supply of materials for the electronics industry, the manufacture of precious metal products, and the supply of refractory products.

Coral Products plc
North Florida Road, Haydock Industrial Estate, Haydock, Merseyside WA11 9TP
Telephone +44 (0) 1942 272882
Fax +44 (0) 1942 726116
Website www.coralproducts.com

Chair
Sir David Rowe-Ham
Chief Executive/Managing Director
Warren Ferster
Board Members
Jonathan Ferster, Stuart Ferster, Stephen Fletcher, Jonathan Lever, Geoffrey Piper

Business Description
The manufacture of media packaging products.

Corin Group plc
The Corinium Centre, Cirencester,
Gloucestershire GL7 1YJ
Telephone +44 (0) 1285 659866
Fax +44 (0) 1285 658960
Website www.coringroup.com

Chair
Dr Graeme Hart
Chief Executive/Managing Director
Ian Paling
Board Members
Simon Hartley, Dr Linda Wilding, David Young

Business Description
A group engaged in the manufacture and marketing of
orthopaedic devices on a worldwide basis.

Corporate Services Group plc
800 The Boulevard, Capability Green, Luton LU1 3BA
Telephone +44 (0) 1582 692692
Fax +44 (0) 1582 698698
Website www.corporateservicesgroup.com

Chair
Anthony Martin
Chief Executive/Managing Director
Desmond Doyle
Board Members
Adrian Carey, Noël Harwerth, John Rowley, Valerie
Scoular, Andrew Wilson

Business Description
A group engaged in the provision of staffing services in
the UK and USA.

Cosalt plc
Fish Dock Road, Grimsby, Lincolnshire DN31 3NW
Telephone +44 (0) 1472 504504
Fax +44 (0) 1472 504369
Website www.cosalt.co.uk

Chair
John Kelly
Chief Executive/Managing Director
Per Jonsson
Board Members
David Bolton, Neil Carrick, James Dean, David Hobdey,
Peter Nevitt, Matthew Peacock, Winston Phillips, David
Ross, Bill Wood

Business Description
A group engaged in the manufacturing and supply of
protective clothing and safety and protection equipment
for the marine, motor, rail, defence, emergency services
and utilities industries.

Costain Group plc
Costain House, Nicholsons Walk, Maidenhead,
Berkshire SL6 1LN
Telephone +44 (0) 1628 842444
Fax +44 (0) 1628 674477
Website www.costain.com

Chair
David Jefferies
Chief Executive/Managing Director
Andrew Wyllie
Board Members
Mike Alexander, David Allvey, Frederick Ballard,
Anthony Bickerstaff, John Bryant, Mohd Hussein bin
Abdul Hamid, Saad Shehata, Mohd Sulaiman

Business Description
A group engaged in civil engineering and construction
process engineering and commercial property projects.

CPL Resources plc
83 Merrion Square, Dublin 2, Ireland
Telephone + 353 1 614 6000
Fax +353 1 614 6011
Website www.cpl.ie

Chair
John Hennessy
Chief Executive/Managing Director
Anne Heraty
Board Members
Paul Carroll, Patrick Garvey, Garret John Roche,
Josephine Tierney

Business Description
A group engaged in the provision of enplyment services
and human resources consultancy.

Cranswick plc
74 Helsinki Road, Sutton Fields, Hull HU7 0YW
Telephone +44 (0) 1482 372000
Website www.cranswick.co.uk

Chair
Martin Davey
Board Members
Derek Black, Adam Couch, Patrick Farnsworth, Bernard
Hoggarth, John Lindop, Noel Taylor, John Worby

Business Description
A group engaged in the manufacture of pork products,
animal feed and sandwiches, the rearing of pigs, and the
sale of pet food, marine fish and aquatic products.

Creightons plc
1210 Lincoln Road, Peterborough PE4 6ND
Telephone +44 (0) 1733 281000
Fax +44 (0) 1723 281020
Website www.creightons.com

Chair
William McIlroy
Board Members
Mary Carney, Bill Glencross, Bernard Johnson, Nicholas
O'Shea

Business Description
A group engaged in the creation and manufacture of
toiletries and fragrances.

Creston plc
30-35 Pall Mall, London SW1Y 5LP
Telephone +44 (0) 20 7930 9757
Fax +44 (0) 20 7930 8727
Website www.creston.com

Chair
David Marshall
Chief Executive/Managing Director
Don Elgie
Board Members
Barrie Brien, Andrew Dougal, Malcolm Wall

Business Description
A marketing services group.

Croda International plc
Cowick Hall, Snaith Goole, East Yorkshire DN14 9AA
Telephone +44 (0) 1405 860551
Fax +44 (0) 1405 861767
Website www.croda.com

Chair
Martin Flower
Chief Executive/Managing Director
Mike Humphrey
Board Members
Mike Buzzacott, Sean Christie, David Dunn, Stanley
Musesengwa

Business Description
A group engaged in the manufacture and sale of
oleochemicals and other speciality chemical products.

CSR plc
Unit 400, Cambridge Science Park, Milton Road,
Cambridge CB4 0WH
Telephone +44 (0) 1223 692000
Fax +44 (0) 1223 692001
Website www.csr.com

Chair
Ron Mackintosh
Chief Executive/Managing Director
John Scarisbrick
Board Members
Anthony Carlisle, James Collier, Sergio Giacoletto, Paul
Goodridge, David Tucker

Business Description
A group engaged in the development of wireless solutions
designed to support data and voice communications
between products over short range radio links.

Culver Holdings plc
Llanmaes, St Fagans, Cardiff CF5 6DU
Telephone +44 (0) 29 2067 0067
Fax +44 (0) 29 2057 6290
Website www.culver-holdings.com

Chair
Richard Read
Chief Executive/Managing Director
Adrian Biles
Board Members
John Biles, C Y Yates

Business Description
A group engaged in insurance broking, property rental,
technology services.

D S Smith plc
4-16 Artillery Row, London SW1P 1RZ
Telephone +44 (0) 20 7932 5000
Fax +44 (0) 20 7932 5003
Website www.dssmith.uk.com

Chair
Peter Johnson
Chief Executive/Managing Director
Tony Thorne
Board Members
Bob Beeston, Christopher Bunker, Richard Marton, Gavin
Morris, Philippe Mellier

Business Description
A group engaged in the production of corrugated and
plastic packaging and of paper, and the distribution of
office products.

Daejan Holdings plc
Freshwater House, 158-162 Shaftesbury Avenue,
London WC2H 8HR
Telephone +44 (0) 20 7836 1555
Fax +44 (0) 20 7497 8941
Website www.daejanholdings.com

Chair
Benzion Freshwater
Board Members
David Davis, Solomon Freshwater

Business Description
A company engaged in property investment and
development.

Daily Mail and General Trust plc
Northcliffe House, 2 Derry Street, London W8 5TT
Telephone +44 (0) 20 7938 6000
Fax +44 (0) 20 7938 4626
Website www.dmgt.co.uk

Chairman
The Viscount Rothermere
Chief Executive
C J F Sinclair
Board Members
F P Balsemão, K J Beatty, N W Berry, P M Dacre, C W
Dunstone, D M M Dutton, P M Fallon, T S Gillespie, S M
Gray, J G Hemingway, N D Jennings, I G Park, D J
Verey, J P Williams

Business Description
An international media group, with interests in national
newspapers and related digital operations, local media,
business and financial information, exhibitions and radio.

Dairy Crest Group plc
Claygate House, Littleworth Road, Esher,
Surrey KT10 9PN
Telephone +44 (0) 1372 472200
Website www.dairycrest.co.uk

Chair
Simon Oliver
Chief Executive/Managing Director
Mark Allen
Board Members
David Dugdale, Gerry Grimstone, Howard Mann, Alastair
Murray, Martin Oakes, David Richardson, Peter Thornton

Business Description
A group engaged in the manufacture and trading of milk
and dairy products.

Dana Petroleum plc
17 Carden Place, Aberdeen AB10 1UR
Telephone +44 (0) 1224 652400
Fax +44 (0) 1224 652401
Website www.dana-petroleum.com

Chair
Colin Goodall
Chief Executive/Managing Director
Tom Cross
Board Members
Philip Dayer, David MacFarlane, Dr Stuart Paton, Angus
Pelham Burn, Iain Rawlinson

Business Description
A group engaged in oil and gas exploration and
production.

Danka Business Systems plc
Masters House, 107 Hammersmith Road,
London W14 0QH
Telephone +44 (0) 20 7605 0150
Fax +44 (0) 20 7603 8448
Website www.danka.com

Chair and Chief Executive
A Frazier
Board Members
Dr Kevin Daly, David Downes, Jaime Ellertson,
Christopher Harned, W Andrew McKenna, Joseph Patzick,
J Ernest Riddle, Erik Vonk

Business Description
A group engaged in the supply and servicing of office
equipment and the provision of related services.

Datacash Group plc
Descartes House, 8 Gate Street, London WC2A 3HP
Telephone +44 (0) 870 727 4761
Fax +44 (0) 870 727 4781
Website www.datacash.com

Chair
Ashley Head
Board Members
David Bailey, Gavin Breeze, Paul Burton, Keith Butcher,
Andrew Dark, Nicholas Temple

Business Description
A group engaged in the provision of payment processing
services.

Datatec Ltd
Ground Floor, Sandown Chambers, Sandown Village, 16
Maude Street, Sandown, 2146 South Africa
Telephone +27 (0) 11 233 1000
Fax +27 (0) 11 233 3300
Website www.datatec.co.za

Chair
Leslie Boyd
Chief Executive/Managing Director
Jens Montanana
Board Members
Colin Brayshaw, Stephen Davidson, John McCartney,
Wiseman Nkuhlu, David Pfaff, Cedric Savage, Chris
Seabrooke, Nick Temple

Business Description
A company engaged in the provision of networking and
IT services.

Davis Service Group plc (The)
4 Grosvenor Place, London SW1X 7DL
Telephone +44 (0) 20 7259 6663
Fax +44 (0) 20 7259 6948
Website www.dsgplc.co.uk

Chair
Christopher Kemball
Chief Executive/Managing Director
Roger Dye
Board Members
John Burns, Kevin Quinn, Philip Rogerson, René Schuster,
Per Utnegaard

Business Description
A group engaged in the provision of textile maintenance,
workwear rental, linen hire and washroom services.

Dawnay Day Carpathian plc
St James's Chambers, Athol Street, Douglas, Isle of
Man IM1 1JE
Telephone +44 (0) 1624 681250
Website www.dawnaydaycarpathian.com

Chair
Rupert Cottrell
Board Members
William Hamilton-Turner, Peter Klimt, Philip Scales

Business Description
Investing in the retail property market.

Dawnay Day Treveria plc
St James' Chambers, Anthol Street, Douglas, Isle of
Man IM1 1JE
Telephone +44 (0) 20 7834 8060
Website www.dawnaydaytreveria.com

Chair
Ian Henderson
Board Members
Martin Bruehl, Peter Klimt, Christopher Lovell, David
Parnell

Business Description
A company engaged in investing in retail property in
Germany.

Dawson Holdings plc
9th Floor, AMP House, Dingwall Road, Croydon
Telephone +44 (0) 20 8774 3000
Fax +44 (0) 20 8774 3011
Website www.dawson.co.uk

Chair
Nigel Freer
Chief Executive/Managing Director
Peter Harris
Board Members
Ian Davies, Rt. Hon Baroness Dean of Thornton-le-Fylde,
David Lowther, Jim McCarthy

Business Description
A group engaged in the provision of logistic and support
services for newspapers, magazines and books.

De La Rue plc
De La Rue House, 8 Jays Close, Basingstoke,
Hampshire RG22 4BS
Telephone +44 (0) 1256 605303
Fax +44 (0) 1256 605339
Website www.delarue.com

Chair
Nicholas Brookes
Chief Executive/Managing Director
Leo Quinn
Board Members
Warren East, Sir Jeremy Greenstock, Keith Hodgkinson,
Michael Jeffries, Stephen King, Dr Philip Nolan, Gill Rider

Business Description
A group engaged in the provision of secure printing
services, papermaking, government identity solutions,
cash handling equipment and software solutions.

Debenhams plc
1 Welbeck Street, London W1G 0AA
Telephone +44 (0) 20 7408 4444
Fax +44 (0) 20 7408 3366
Website www.debenhamsplc.com

Chair
John Lovering
Chief Executive/Managing Director
Rob Templeman
Board Members
Philippe Costeletos, Adam Crozier, Jonathan Feuer,
Richard Gillingwater, Peter Long, Dennis Millard, Paul
Pindar, Michael Sharp, Chris Woodhouse

Business Description
The company is engaged in the retail of womenswear,
menswear, homewares, health and beauty, accessories,
lingerie and childrenswear.

Dechra Pharmaceuticals plc
Dechra House, Jamage Industrial Estate, Talke Pits, Stoke
on Trent, Staffordshire ST7 1XW
Telephone +44 (0) 1782 771100
Fax +44 (0) 1782 773366
Website www.dechra.com

Chair
Michael Redmond
Chief Executive/Managing Director
Ian Page
Board Members
Malcolm Diamond, Simon Evans, Ed Torr, Neil Warner

Business Description
A group engaged in the manufacture of pharmaceuticals,
the sale of veterinary equipment and the provision of
related services including laboratory and computer
systems.

Dee Valley Group plc
Packsaddle, Wrexham Road, Rhostyllen, Wrexham,
Clwyd LL14 4EH
Telephone +44 (0) 1978 846946
Fax +44 (0) 1978 846888
Website www.deevalleygroup.com

Chair
Graham Scott
Chief Executive/Managing Director
Bryn Bellis
Board Members
Andrew Bird, David Guest, David Weir

Business Description
A group engaged in the provision of water services to
customers predominantly in Chester and North East
Wales.

Defined Capital Return Fund Ltd
Standard Bank House, PO Box 583, 47-49 La Motte Street,
St. Helier, Jersey JE4 8XR

Chair
Ian Ling
Board Members
Peter Hart, Reef Hogg

Business Description
An investment fund.

Delek Global Real Estate Ltd
2nd Floor, La Rue des Mielles, St Helier, Jersey JE2 3QD
Telephone +44 (0) 1534 785300
Fax +44 (0) 1534 785399
Website www.delekgre.com

Chair
Howard Stanton
Chief Executive/Managing Director
Llik Roazanski
Board Members
Asaf Bartfield, Elisha Flax, Yossi Friedman, Paul Harvey,
Jonathan Scott Warren, Armin Zucker

Business Description
A company engaged in investment in property.

Delta plc
Bridewell Gate, 9 Bridewell Place, London EC4V 6AW
Telephone +44 (0) 20 7842 6050
Fax +44 (0) 20 7842 6078
Website www.deltaplc.com

Chair
Steven Marshall
Chief Executive/Managing Director
Todd Atkinson
Board Members
Jon Kempster, Mark Lejman, Kristen van Riel, Andrew
Walker

Business Description
A group engaged in the provision of goods and services
to mining, transportation and construction industries,
galvanising services and production of electrolytic
manganese dioxide.

Derwent London plc
25 Savile Row, London W1S 2ER
Telephone +44 (0) 20 7659 3000
Fax +44 (0) 20 7659 3100
Website www.derwentlondon.com

Chair
Hon Robert Rayne
Chief Executive/Managing Director
John Burns
Board Members
Stuart Corbyn, June de Moller, Robert Farnes, Nigel
George, John Ivey, Simon Neathercoat, Donald Newell,
Christopher Odom, Simon Silver, Paul Williams

Business Description
A group engaged in property investment, redevelopment
and trading.

Detica Group plc
Chancellor Court, Occam Road, Surrey Research Park,
Guildford GU2 7YP
Telephone +44 (0) 1483 816000
Fax +44 (0) 1483 816144
Website www.detica.com

Chair
Chris Conway
Chief Executive/Managing Director
Tom Black
Board Members
Chris Banks, Colin Evans, John Gordon, Mandy Gradden,
Mark Mayhew

Business Description
A business and technology consultancy specialising in
information intelligence.

Development Securities plc
Portland House, Bressenden Place, London SW1E 5DS
Telephone +44 (0) 20 7828 4777
Fax +44 (0) 20 7828 4999
Website www.developmentsecurities.com

Chair
Roy Dantzic
Chief Executive/Managing Director
Michael Marx
Board Members
Julian Barwick, David Jenkins, Paul Manduca, Victoria
Mitchell, Michael Soames, Matthew Weiner

Business Description
A group engaged in property development, investment
and trading.

Devro plc
Moodiesburn, Chryston G69 0JE
Telephone +44 (0) 1236 879191
Fax +44 (0) 1236 811005
Website www.devro.plc.uk

Chair
Patrick Barrett
Chief Executive/Managing Director
Peter Page
Board Members
Trevor Morgan, Paul Neep, John Neilson, Stuart Paterson

Business Description
A group engaged in the production and marketing of
manufactured casings for the food industry.

Dexion Absolute Ltd
PO Box 208, Arnold House, St Julian's Avenue, St Peter
Port, Guernsey GY1 3NF
Telephone +44 (0) 1481 707228
Website www.dexionabsolute.com

Chair
Peter Walsh
Board Members
Trevor Ash, Robin Bowie, John Hallam, Dr Paul Sharman

Business Description
A closed-ended investment company investing in a
portfolio of hedge funds.

Dexion Alpha Strategies Ltd
Arnold House, St Julien's Avenue, St Peter Port,
Guernsey GY1 3NF
Telephone +44 (0) 1481 707000
Website www.dexionalpha.com

Chair
Robin Bowie
Board Members
Christopher Hill

Business Description
An investment company.

Dexion Equity Alternative Ltd
Trafalgar Court, Les Banques, St Peter Port,
Guernsey GY1 3DA
Website www.dexionequity.com

Chair
John Hawkins
Board Members
Robin Bowie, Charles Parkinson, Christopher Sherwell

Business Description
Closed-ended investment company.

Dexion Trading Ltd
Arnold House, St. Julian's Avenue, St. Peter Port,
Guernsey GY1 3NF
Telephone +44 (0) 1484 707255
Website www.dexiontrading.com

Chair
Christopher Spencer
Chief Executive/Managing Director
Robin M J Bowie
Board Members
Carol Goodwin, Peter Niven

Business Description
An investment fund.

Diageo plc
8 Henrietta Place, London W1G 0NB
Telephone +44 (0) 20 7927 5200
Fax +44 (0) 20 7927 5056
Website www.diageo.com

Chair
Lord Blyth of Rowington
Chief Executive/Managing Director
Paul Walsh
Board Members
Laurence Danon, Lord Hollick, Dr Franz Humer, Maria
Lilja, Nicholas Rose, William Shanahan, Todd Stitzer,
Jonathan Symonds, Paul Walker

Business Description
A group engaged in the manufacture and distribution of
spirits, wines and beer.

Dialight plc
2B Vantage Park, Washingley Road,
Huntingdon PE29 6SR
Telephone +44 (0) 1623 666541
Fax +44 (0) 1623 561735
Website www.dialight.com

Chair
Harry Tee
Chief Executive/Managing Director
Roy Barton
Board Members
Cathryn Buckley, Jeffrey Hewitt, Robert Jeens, Bill
Whiteley

Business Description
A company engaged in the manufacture of indicators for
circuit boards and instrument panels.

Dicom Group plc
1 Cedarwood, Chineham Business Park, Basingstoke,
Hampshire RG24 8WD
Telephone +44 (0) 800 652 0616
Website www.dicomgroup.com

Chair
Greg Lock
Chief Executive/Managing Director
Robert Klatell
Board Members
John Alexander, William T Comfort III, Chris Conway,
Stefan Gaiser, Urs Niederberger, Bruce Powell, Mark
Wells

Business Description
A group engaged in the development and provision of
EDC (Electronic Data Capture) products and services and
related consultancy, and as general agent of Samsung
Electronics.

Dignity plc
Plantsbrook House, 94 The Parade, Sutton Coldfield, West
Midlands B72 1PH
Telephone +44 (0) 121 354 1557
Fax +44 (0) 121 321 5644
Website www.dignityfuneralsplc.co.uk

Chair
Richard Connell
Chief Executive/Managing Director
Peter Hindley
Board Members
Andrew Davies, Bill Forrester, Mike McCollum, James
Newman, Richard Portman

Business Description
The holding company for a group engaged in the
provision of funeral services.

Dimension Data Holdings plc
Fleet Place House, 2 Fleet Place, London EC4M 7RT
Telephone +44 (0) 20 7651 7000
Fax +44 (0) 20 7651 7001
Website www.dimensiondata.com

Chair
Jeremy Ord
Chief Executive/Managing Director
Brett Dawson
Board Members
Rupert Barclay, Stephen Joubert, Peter Liddiard, Wendy
Lucas-Bull, Dillie Malherbe, Moss Ngoasheng, Patrick
Quarmby, Rory Scott, David Sherriffs, Dorian Wharton-
Hood

Business Description
A group engaged in the provision of global technology
solutions, including networking, application, integration
and managed services.

Diploma plc
12 Charterhouse Square, London EC1M 6AX
Telephone +44 (0) 20 7549 5700
Fax +44 (0) 20 7594 5715
Website www.diplomaplc.com

Chair
John Rennocks
Chief Executive/Managing Director
Bruce Thompson
Board Members
Ian Grice, Iain Henderson, Nigel Lingwood, John
Matthews

Business Description
A group engaged in the distribution of life science
instrumentation and consumables, hydraulic seal kits,
cylinder components, gaskets, specialised wiring
connection and control devices.

Direct Wonen NV
PO Box 800, The Hague, 2501 CV, The Netherlands
Telephone +31 0900 0666
Fax +31 70 3603581
Website www.directwonen.nl

Business Description
A company engaged in residential property lettings in
The Netherlands.

Dmatek Ltd
2 Harbarzel Street, PO Box 13236, Tel Aviv 61131, Israel
Telephone +972 3 7671700
Fax +972 3 7671701
Website www.dmatek.com

Chair
Yoav Chelouche
Chief Executive/Managing Director
Yoav Reisman
Board Members
Barbara Faktor, Dan Falk, Iain Jamieson, Michael
Rosehill, Aher Zysman

Business Description
A company engaged in the provision of remote people
monitoring technologies.

Dolphin Capital Investors Ltd
Vanterpool Plaza, Wickams Clay 1, Tortola, British Virgin
Islands
Telephone +30 210 3614 255
Website www.dolphinci.com

Chair
Andreas Papageorghiou
Board Members
Antonios Achilleoudis, Cem Duna, Mitos Kambourides,
Nicholas Moy, Roger Lane Smith

Business Description
A company engaged in real estate investment, focusing
on early-stage residential resort developments in South-
East Europe.

Domestic & General Group plc
2A Mansel Road, Wimbledon, London SW19 4AA
Telephone +44 (0) 20 8946 7777
Website www.domgen.com

Chair
Nicholas D Rochez
Chief Executive/Managing Director
John Pearmund
Board Members
Paul Lee, John Richie, Ken Wilson

Business Description
A company engaged in the provision of extended
warranty cover for electrical domestic appliances.

Domino Printing Sciences plc
Bar Hilll, Trafalgar Way, Cambridge CB3 8TU
Telephone +44 (0) 1954 782551
Fax +44 (0) 1954 782713
Website www.domino-printing.com

Chair
Peter Byrom
Chief Executive/Managing Director
Nigel Bond
Board Members
William Everitt, Garry Havens, Andrew Herbert, Peter
Jensen, Philip Ruffles, Jerry Smith, Richard Waddingham

Business Description
A group engaged in the research development,
manufacture and sale of industrial printing equipment
controllers and consumables for high speed printing of
variable information.

Domino's Pizza UK & Ireland plc
Lasborough Road, Kingston, Milton Keynes MK10 0AB
Telephone +44 (0) 1908 580000
Fax +44 (0) 1908 588000
Website www.dominos.co.uk

Chair
Colin Halpern
Chief Executive/Managing Director
Stephen Hemsley
Board Members
Lee Ginsberg, John Hodson, Christopher Moore, Michael
Shallow, Dianne Thompson, Nigel Wray

Business Description
A group engaged in the operation and development of the
Domino's Pizza franchise system in the UK and Ireland,
property management and development, and equipment
leasing.

Drax Group plc
Drax Power Station, PO Box 3, Selby, North
Yorkshire YO8 8PQ
Telephone +44 (0) 1757 618381
Fax +44 (0) 1757 612 192
Website www.draxgroup.plc.uk

Chair
Gordon Horsfield
Chief Executive/Managing Director
Dorothy Thompson
Board Members
Timothy Barker, Charles Berry, Gordon Boyd, Jamie
Dundas, Peter Emery, Mike Grasby, Philip Hudson

Business Description
The group's principal activity is the operation of the
power station and the trading of electricity produced by
the power station.

DRS Data & Research Services plc
1 Danbury Court, Linford Wood, Milton Keynes,
Buckinghamshire MK14 6LR
Telephone +44 (0) 1908 666088
Fax +44 (0) 1908 607668
Website www.drs.co.uk

Chair
Malcolm Brighton
Chief Executive/Managing Director
Anthony Lee
Board Members
Christopher Batterham, Lord Kinnock, Ann Limb, Arthur
Tebbut

Business Description
The provision of data capture services, the manufacture
and sale of optical scanning equipment and the provision
of complementary services.

DSG International plc
Maylands Avenue, Hemel Hempstead,
Hertfordshire HP2 7TG
Telephone +44 (0) 870 850 3333
Website www.dixons-group-plc.co.uk

Chair
Sir John Collins
Chief Executive/Managing Director
John Clare
Board Members
Rita Clifton, Count Emmanuel D'Andre, Andrew Lynch,
Kevin O'Byrne, John Whybrow

Business Description
A group engaged in the retail of consumer electronics,
personal computers, domestic appliances, photographic
equipment, communication products and related services.

DTZ Holdings plc
1 Curzon Street, London W1A 5PZ
Telephone +44 (0) 20 7408 1161
Fax +44 (0) 20 7643 6000
Website www.dtz.com

Chair
Tim Melville-Ross
Chief Executive/Managing Director
Mark Struckett
Board Members
Leung Chan Ying, Leslie Cullen, Dag Detter, David Gray,
Alicja Lesniak, Tim Maynard, Killian O'Higgins, Robert
Peto, Peter Stone

Business Description
A group engaged as property advisers and consultants
offering comprehensive integrated property advice and
economic consultancy services.

Dunedin Enterprise Investment Trust plc
10 George Street, Edinburgh EH2 2DW
Telephone +44 (0) 131 225 6699
Fax +44 (0) 131 718 2300
Website www.dunedin.com

Chair
Edward Dawnay
Board Members
Liz Airey, Brian Fulayson, David Gamble, William
Haughey, Simon Miller, Bruce Patrick

Business Description
An investment trust.

Dunedin Income Growth Investment Trust
Donaldson House, 97 Haymarket Terrace,
Edinburgh EH12 5HD
Telephone +44 (0) 131 313 1000
Website www.dunedinincomegrowth.co.uk

Chair
John Scott
Board Members
John Carson, Jean Matterson, Rory Macnamara, Peter
Wolton

Business Description
An investment trust investing predominantly in
companies listed or quoted in the United Kingdom.

Dunedin Smaller Companies Investment Trust plc
Donaldson House, 97 Haymarket Terrace,
Edinburgh EH12 5HD
Telephone +44 (0) 131 313 1000
Fax +44 (0) 131 313 6303
Website www.dunedinsmaller.co.uk

Chair
Earl of Dalhousie
Board Members
James Barnes, Ray Entwistle, Norman Yarrow

Business Description
An investment trust.

Dunelm Group
Fosse Way, Syston, Leicester LE7 1NF
Telephone +44 (0) 116 264 4400
Fax +44 (0) 116 264 4459
Website www.dunelm-mill.com

Chair
Geoff Cooper
Chief Executive/Managing Director
William Adderly
Board Members
Simon Emeny, Marion Sears

Business Description
A group engaged in the retail of home furnishings.

Dyson Group plc
382 Fulwood Rod, Sheffield S10 3GB
Telephone +44 (0) 114 230 3921
Fax +44 (0) 114 230 8583
Website www.dyson-group.com

Chair
Dr C H P Honeyborne
Chief Executive/Managing Director
T M O'Brien
Board Members
R D Field, J P Lomas, A N Parker, Dr K Rajagopal

Business Description
A group engaged in the research, development,
manufacture and sale of chemically-based materials.

e2v Technologies plc
106 Waterhouse Lane, Chelmsford, Essex CM1 2QU
Telephone +44 (0) 1245 493493
Fax +44 (0) 1245 492492
Website www.e2v.com

Chair
George Kennedy
Chief Executive/Managing Director
Keith Attwood
Board Members
Jonathan Brooks, Ian Godden, Tony Reading

Business Description
A designer, developer and manufacturer of specialised
components and subsystems.

Eaglet Investment Trust plc
Beaufort House, 51 New North Road, Exeter EX4 4EP
Telephone +44 (0) 1392 412122
Fax +44 (0) 1392 253282
Website www.itsonline.com

Chair
Lady Judge
Board Members
Peter Cowan, Guy Crawford, Peter Underhill, Robert
Wade, Peter Webb

Business Description
The company is an investment company that primarily
invests in UK small companies.

Eastern European Trust plc (The)
Springfield Lodge, Colchester Road, Chelmsford,
Essex CM2 5PW
Telephone +44 (0) 1245 398950
Website www.teetplc.com

Chair
Hugh Aldous
Board Members
Hareb Al-Darmaki, Stephen Barber, Neil England, Rory
Landman, Edmond Warner

Business Description
An investment trust.

EasyJet plc
Easyland, London Luton Airport, Bedfordshire LU2 9LS
Telephone +44 (0) 1582 443330
Fax +44 (0) 1582 443355
Website www.easyjet.com

Chair
Sir Colin Chandler
Chief Executive/Managing Director
Andrew Harrison
Board Members
Dawn Airey, David Bennett, Jeff Carr, Sir Stelios Haji-
Ioannou, Diederik Karsten, Sir David Michels

Business Description
A group engaged in the provision of an airline service on
short-haul and medium-haul point-to-point routes.

Eclectic Investment Trust plc
2nd Floor, Springfield Lodge, Colchester Road,
Chelmsford, Essex CM2 5PW
Telephone +44 (0) 1245 398950
Fax +44 (0) 1245 398951
Website www.stockseclectic.com

Chair
Anthony Bushell
Board Members
Peter Burrows, Bruce Hervey, Warren McLeland

Business Description
An investment trust with a dealing subsidiary

EcoSecurities Group plc
40 Dawson Street, Dublin 2, Ireland
Telephone +353 1 613 9814
Fax +353 1 672 4716
Website www.ecosecurities.com

Chair
Mark Nicholls
Chief Executive/Managing Director
Bruce Usher
Board Members
Tom Byrne, Pedro Costa, Jack MacDonald

Business Description
A company engaged in sourcing, developing and trading
emission reductions.

Edinburgh Dragon Trust plc
Donaldson House, 97 Haymarket Terrace,
Edinburgh EH12 5HD
Telephone +44 (0) 131 313 1000
Fax +44 (0) 131 313 6303
Website www.edinburghdragon.com

Chair
Anthony Cassidy
Board Members
Frank Frame, David Gairns, Anthony Lowrie, Alan
Mckenzie, Peter Tyrie, Iain Watt

Business Description
An investment trust.

Edinburgh Investment Trust plc (The)
3 Glenfinlas Street, Edinburgh EH3 6AQ
Telephone +44 (0) 131 313 1000
Website www.fidelity.co.uk/its

Chair
Scott Dobbie
Board Members
Richard Barfield, James Pettigrew, Nicola Ralston,
William Samuel, Sir Nigel Wicks

Business Description
An investment trust.

Edinburgh New Income Trust plc
Donaldson House, 57 Haymarket Terrace,
Edinburgh EH12 5HD
Telephone +44 (0) 131 313 1000
Fax +44 (0) 131 313 6303
Website www.edinburghnewincome.co.uk

Chair
David Ritchie
Board Members
Ronnie Hanna, Sir Donald MacKay, Bernard Solomons

Business Description
Investment mainly in UK quoted equities.

Edinburgh UK Tracker Trust
Donaldson House, 97 Haymarket Terrace,
Edinburgh EH12 5HD
Telephone +44 (0) 131 313 1000
Fax +44 (0) 131 1001
Website www.edinburghtracker.co.uk

Chair
Tom Ross
Board Members
David Hager, David Mathewson, David Tucker

Business Description
An investment trust.

Edinburgh US Tracker Trust plc
Donaldson House, 97 Haymarket Terrace,
Edinburgh EH12 5HD
Telephone +44 (0) 131 313 1000
Website www.edinburghustracker.co.uk

Chair
James Ferguson
Board Members
Guy Crawford, Archibald Hunter, Archibald Hunter

Business Description
An investment trust.

Edinburgh Worldwide Investment Trust plc
Calton Square, 1 Greenside Row, Edinburgh EH1 3AN
Telephone +44 (0) 131 275 2000
Fax +44 (0) 131 275 3955
Website www.bailliegifford.com

Chair
David Coltman
Board Members
William Ducas, Hon Kim Fraser, Robert Miller, David
Reid

Business Description
An investment trust.

Electra Private Equity plc
Paternoster House, 65 St Paul's Churchyard,
London EC4M 8AB
Telephone +44 (0) 20 7306 3883
Fax +44 (0) 20 7214 4201
Website www.electraequity.com

Chair
Sir Brian Williamson
Board Members
Ronald Armstrong, Sir George Bain, Lord King of
Bridgewater, Michael Walton, Peter Williams

Business Description
An investment trust.

Electric & General Investment Trust plc
55 Moorgate, London EC2R 6PA
Telephone +4 (0) 20 7410 4942
Fax +44 (0) 20 7477 5849
Website www.electricandgeneral.com

Chair
Lindsay Bury
Board Members
Gerald Aherne, John Pocock, Jonathan Ruffer

Business Description
An investment trust company.

Electrocomponents plc
International Management Centre, 8050 Oxford Business
Park South, Oxford OX4 2HW
Telephone +44 (0) 1865 204000
Fax +44 (0) 1865 207400
Website www.electrocomponents.com

Chair
Helmut Mamsch
Chief Executive/Managing Director
Ian Mason
Board Members
Dr Leslie Atkinson, Timothy Barker, Simon Boddie, Keith
Hamill, Nick Temple

Business Description
A group engaged in the marketing, manufacturing,
wholesailing and retail of electronic and industrial
supplies and services to industrial and commercial
customers.

Electronic Data Processing plc
Beauchief Hall, Beauchief, Sheffield S8 7BA
Telephone +44 (0) 114 262 1621
Fax +44 (0) 114 262 1126
Website www.edp.co.uk

Chair
Michael Heller
Board Members
Peter Davey, Paul Davies, Julian Wassell

Business Description
A group engaged in the supply of software solutions, the
sale and maintenance of computer equipment, and the
provision of application hosting and outsourcing services.

Elementis plc
10 Albermale Street, London W1S 4BL
Telephone +44 (0) 20 7408 9300
Fax +44 (0) 20 7493 2194
Website www.elementis.com

Chair
Bob Beeston
Chief Executive/Managing Director
David Dutro
Board Members
Ian Brindle, Chris Girling, Dr Kevin Matthews, Ken
Minton, Matthew Peacock, Brian Taylorson

Business Description
A group engaged in the production of pigments,
rheological and other specialty additives, chromium
chemicals and specialty rubber products.

Emap plc
4th Floor, 40 Bernard Street, London WC1N 1LW
Telephone +44 (0) 20 7278 1452
Website www.emap.com

Chair
Alun Cathcart
Board Members
Derek Carter, Rita Clifton, Pierre Danon, Ian Griffiths,
Andrew Harrison, Jonathan Howell, Paul Keenan, David
Rough

Business Description
A group engaged in the publication of consumer
magazines, the provision of business-to-business events,
conferences and magazines, and the provision of radio
and TV services.

Emblaze plc
1 Emblaze Square, PO Box 2220, Raa'nana 43662, Israel
Telephone +972 (0) 9 7699333
Fax +972 (0) 9 7699800
Website www.emblaze.com

Chair
Naftali Shani
Chief Executive/Managing Director
Eli Reifman
Board Members
Guy Bernstein, Ruth Breger, Bertrand Faure-Beaulieu,
Ilan Flato, Hdas Gazit Kaiser, Shimon Laor

Business Description
Business to business high end solutions and services.

Emerald Energy plc
6th Floor, Kings House, 9/10 Haymarket,
London SW1Y 4BP
Telephone +44 (0) 20 7925 2440
Fax +44 (0) 20 7925 2441
Website www.emeraldenergy.com

Chair and Chief Executive
Alastair Beardsall
Chief Executive/Managing Director
Angus MacAskill
Board Members
Edward Grace, Keith Henry, Fred Ponsonby, Merfyn
Roberts

Business Description
A group engaged in the exploration and production of
hydrocarbons.

Ennstone plc
Breedon Hall, Breedon on the Hill, Derby DE73 8AN
Telephone +44 (0) 1332 694444
Fax +44 (0) 1332 694445
Website www.ennstone.co.uk

Chair
Vaughan McLeod
Board Members
Mark Elliott, Eric Gadsden, Michael Johnston, Ciaran
Kennedy, Timothy Ross

Business Description
A group engaged in the quarrying production and sale of
aggregates and related activities including ready mixed
concrete, asphalt, natural stone and concrete products.

Enodis plc
Washington House, 40-41 Conduit Street,
London W1S 2YQ
Telephone +44 (0) 20 7304 6000
Fax +44 (0) 20 7304 6001
Website www.enodis.com

Chair
Peter Brooks
Chief Executive/Managing Director
David McCulloch
Board Members
Michael Arrowsmith, Michael Cronk, Robert Eimers,
Joseph Ross, Waldemar Schmidt, David Wrench

Business Description
A group engaged in the manufacture and sale of
commercial food equipment.

Enterprise Inns plc
3 Monkspath Hall Road, Solihull, West Midlands B90 4SJ
Telephone +44 (0) 121 733 7700
Website www.enterpriseinns.com

Chair
Hubert Reid
Chief Executive/Managing Director
Edward Tuppen
Board Members
David George, David Harding, Susan Murray, Jo Stewart,
Simon Townsend

Business Description
A group engaged in the sale of beers and cider, and the
collection of rents from its estate of licensed premises.

Entertainment Rights plc
Colet Court, 100 Hammersmith Road, London W6 7JP
Telephone +44 (0) 20 8762 6200
Fax +44 (0) 20 8762 6299
Website www.entertainmentrights.com

Chair
Roderick Bransgrove
Chief Executive/Managing Director
Michael Heap
Board Members
Irvin Fishman, Elizabeth Gaines, Craig Hemmings, Julian
Paul, Jane Smith

Business Description
A group engaged in the ownership of children's and
family television programming, characters and brands.

EP Global Opportunities Trust plc
16 Charlotte Square, Edinburgh EH2 4DJ

Chair
Teddy Tulloch
Board Members
Richard Burns, David Hough, Ian McBean

Business Description
An investment trust.

Equest Investments Balkans Ltd
Manfield House, 1 Southampton Street,
London WC2R 0LR
Telephone + 44 (0)20 7240 7600
Website www.equestinvestmentsbalkans.com
Board Members
John Carrington, James Ede-Golightly, Robin James, Petri
Karjalainen, Kieron O'Rourke

Business Description
A company engaged in investing in the South-East
Europe property market, focusing on Bulgaria and
Romania.

Erinaceous Group plc
Phoenix House, 11 Wellesley Road, Croydon,
Surrey CR0 2NW
Telephone +44 (0) 870 703 9898
Fax +44 (0) 870 703 9344
Website www.erinaceous.com

Chair
Nigel Turnbull
Chief Executive/Managing Director
Neil Bellis
Board Members
Lucy Cummings, Nigel Davis, Nicholas Fry, Michael
Pearson, Keith Peraux, Lord Poole, Lord Razzall

Business Description
A group engaged in the provision of property services,
including consultancy, management, residential letting
and insurance services.

Eros International
15-19 Athol Street, Isle of Man IM1 ILB
Telephone +44 (0) 1624 683300
Website www.erosintl.com

Chair and Chief Executive
Kishore Lulla
Board Members
Vijay Ahuja, Jyoti Deshpande, Sunil Lulla, Dillip Thakkar,
Roger Vakharia

Business Description
A company engaged in the distribution of Bollywood film
content.

Establishment Investment Trust plc (The)
Springfield Lodge, Colchester Road, Chelmsford,
Essex CM2 5PW
Telephone +44 (0) 1245 398950
Fax +44 (0) 1245 398951
Website www.bdtinvest.com

Chair
Dr James King
Board Members
Sir David Cooksey, Rhoderick Swire, Henry Thornton,
Richard Thornton, Richard (Harry) Wells

Business Description
An investment trust.

Euromoney Institutional Investor plc
Nestor House, 4 Playhouse Yard, London EC4V 5EX
Telephone +44 (0) 20 7779 8673
Website www.euromoneyplc.com

Chair
P M Fallon
Board Members
D Alfano, J C Botts, S M Brady, C R Brown, M J Carroll,
D C Cohen, P R Ensor, C H C Fordham, J C Gonzalez, C
R Jones, R T Lamont, G Mueller, N F Osborn, Viscount
Rothermere, Sir Patrick Sergeant, C J F Sinclair, J
Wilkinson, J P Williams

Business Description
A group engaged in the provision of business information
for the international finance, law and energy sectors.

European Goldfields Ltd
11 Berkeley Street, Level 3, London W1J 8DS
Telephone +44 (0) 20 7408 9534
Fax +44 (0) 20 7408 9535
Website www.egoldfields.com

Chair
Dimitrios Koutras
Chief Executive/Managing Director
David Reading
Board Members
Philip Johnson, Hon Robert Kaplan, Dr Jeffrey O'Leary,
Timothy Morgan-Wynne, Mark Rachovides, Georgios
Sossidis

Business Description
A company engaged in the acquisition, exploration and
development of mineral properties in Greece, Romania
and South-East Europe

European Nickel
Third Floor, 49 Albernarle Street, London W1S 4JR
Telephone +44 (0) 20 7290 3130
Fax +44 (0) 20 7290 3149
Website www.enickel.co.uk

Chair
David Whitehead
Board Members
Andrew Lindsay, Sir David Logan, Paul Lush, Chris
Pointon, Simon Purkiss, Euan Worthington

Business Description
A company engaged in the identification, acquisition,
development and exploitation of nickel laterite deposits,
primarily in Turkey and the Balkan Region.

European Utilities Trust plc
Beaufort House, 51 New North Road, Exeter,
Devon EX4 4EP
Telephone +44 (0) 1392 412122
Website www.premierfunds.co.uk

Chair
Charles Wilkinson
Board Members
Robert Clinton, David Hagan, John Purvis

Business Description
An investment trust.

Evolution Group plc (The)
9th Floor, 100 Wood Street, London EC2V 7AN
Telephone +44 (0) 20 7071 4300
Fax +44 (0) 20 7071 3151
Website www.evgplc.com

Chair
Martin Gray
Chief Executive/Managing Director
Alex Snow
Board Members
Graeme Dell, Nicholas Irens, Lord MacLaurin of
Knebworth, Mark Nicholls, Andrew Umbers

Business Description
A group engaged in the provision of investment banking,
stockbroking and fund management services.

Experian Group Ltd
Park House, London W1K 1AF
Telephone +44 (0) 20 7495 0070
Fax +44 (0) 20 7495 1567
Website www.experiangroup.com

Chair
John Peace
Chief Executive/Managing Director
Don Robert
Board Members
Fabiola Arredondo, Paul Brooks, Laurence Danon, Roger
Davis, Sean FitzPatrick, Alan Jebson, Sir Alan Rudge,
David Tyler

Business Description
A group engaged in the provision of business information
and customer relationship management services.

Expro International Group plc
First Floor, Davidson House, Reading, Berkshire RG1 8PL
Telephone +44 (0) 118 959 1341
Website www.exprogroup.com

Chair
Dr Chris Fay
Chief Executive/Managing Director
Graeme Coutts
Board Members
Bob Bennett, Roger Boyes, Terry Lazenby, John
McAlister, Gavin Prise, Michael Speakman

Business Description
A group engaged in the provision of specialised services
to the oil and gas industry relating to oil field
development.

F&C Asset Management plc
Exchange House, 12 Primrose Street, London EC2A 2NY
Telephone +44 (0) 20 7628 8000
Fax +44 (0) 20 7628 8188
Website www.fandc.com

Chair
Robert Jenkins
Chief Executive/Managing Director
Alain Grisay
Board Members
Keith Bedell-Pearce, Dick de Beus, John Heywood, Brian
Larcombe, David Logan, Nicholas MacAndrew, Jeff
Medlock, Philip Moore, Gerhard Roggermann, Jim Smart

Business Description
A group engaged in investment management.

F&C Capital & Income Investment Trust plc
8th Floor, Exchange House, Primrose Street,
London EC2A 2NY.
Telephone +44 (0) 20 7628 8000
Fax +44 (0) 20 7628 8188
Website www.fandc.com

Chair
Pen Kent
Board Members
Neil Dunford, John Emly, Prof James Norton, Hugh
Priestley

Business Description
An investment trust.

F&C Commercial Property Trust Ltd
Trafalgar Court, Les Banques, St Peter Port,
Guernsey GY1 3QL
Telephone +44 (0) 1481 745001

Chair
Peter Niven
Board Members
Donald Adamson, John Stephen, Brian Sweetland,
Nicholas Tostevin

Business Description
A closed-ended investment company.

F&C Global Smaller Companies plc
Exchange House, Primrose Street, London EC2A 2NY
Telephone +44 (0) 20 7628 8000
Fax +44 (0) 20 7628 8188
Website www.fandc.co.uk

Chair
John Townsend
Board Members
Andrew Adcock, Leslie Cullen, Dr Franz Leibenfrost, Jane
Tozer, Mark White

Business Description
An investment trust.

F&C UK Select Trust plc
Exchange House, Primrose Street, London EC2A 2NY
Telephone +44 (0) 20 7628 8000

Chairman
Robert Jenkins
Chief Executive
Alain Grisay

Business Description
An investment trust.

F&C US Smaller Companies plc
Exchange House, Primrose Street, London EC2A 2NY
Telephone +44 (0) 20 7628 8000
Fax +44 (0) 20 7628 8188
Website www.fandc.com

Chair
Gordon Grender
Board Members
Norman Bachop, Peter Barton, Clive Parrit

Business Description
An investment trust.

Fenner plc
Hesslewood Country Office Park, Hessle, East
Yorkshire HU13 0PW
Telephone +44 (0) 1482 626500
Fax +44 (0) 1482 626502
Website www.fenner.com

Chair
Colin Cooke
Chief Executive/Managing Director
Mark Abrahams
Board Members
David Buttfield, David Campbell, Richard Perry

Business Description
A group engaged in the manufacture and distribution of
conveyor belting and reinforced precision polymer
products.

Fiberweb plc
1 Victoria Villas, Richmond-on-Thames,
Surrey TW9 2GW
Telephone +44 (0) 20 8439 8310
Website www.fiberweb.com

Chair
Malcolm Coster
Chief Executive/Managing Director
Daniel Dayan
Board Members
Simon Bowles, Peter Hickman, Richard Stillwell, Brian
Taylorson

Business Description
A company engaged in the provision of nonwovens, for
the hygiene, medical, technical and industrial markets .

Fidelity Asian Values plc
Beech Gate, Millfield Lane, Lower Kingswood, Tadworth,
Surrey KT20 6RP
Telephone +44 (0) 1737 836000
Fax +44 (0) 1737 836892
Website www.fidelity.co.uk

Chair
Hon Sir Victor Garland
Board Members
Hugh Bolland, William Knight, Kathryn Matthews, Sir
Robin McLaren

Business Description
An investment trust.

Fidelity European Values plc
Beech Gate, Millfield Lane, Lower Kingswood, Tadworth,
Surrey KT20 6RB
Telephone +44 (0) 1732 361144
Fax +44 (0) 1737 836 892
Website www.fidelity.co.uk

Chair
Robert Walther
Board Members
Simon Duckworth, Simon Fraser, James Robinson, David
Simpson, Humphrey van der Klugt

Business Description
An investment trust.

Fidelity Japanese Values plc
Beech Gate, Millfield Lane, Lower Kingswood, Tadworth,
Surrey KT20 6RP
Telephone +44 (0) 1732 361144
Fax +44 (0) 1732 836892
Website www.fidelity.co.uk/its

Chair
William Thomson
Board Members
Nicholas Barber, Simon Fraser, Philip Kay, David Miller

Business Description
An investment trust investing in small and medium sized
Japanese companies traded on Japanese stockmarkets.

Fidelity Special Values plc
Beech Gate, Millfield Lane, Lower Kingswood, Tadworth,
Surrey KT20 6RP
Telephone +44 (0) 1737 361144
Fax +44 (0) 1737 836892
Website www.fidelity.co.uk

Chair
Alex Hammond-Chambers
Board Members
Sir Richard Brooke, Douglas Kinloch-Anderson, Nicky
McCabe, Lynn Ruddick

Business Description
An investment trust.

Fidessa Group plc
Dukes Court, Dukes Street, Woking, Surrey GU21 5BH
Telephone +44 (0) 1483 206300
Fax +44 (0) 1483 206301
Website www.fidessa.com

Chair
John Hamer
Chief Executive/Managing Director
Chris Aspinwall
Board Members
Philip Hardaker, Ron Mackintosh, Andy Malpass

Business Description
A group involved in the supply of trading systems,
market data and connectivity solutions.

Filtrona plc
Avebury House, 201249 Avebury Boulevard, Milton
Keynes MK9 1AU
Telephone +44 (0) 1908 359100
Fax +44 (0) 1908 359120
Website www.filtrona.com

Chair
Jeff Harris
Chief Executive/Managing Director
Mark Harper
Board Members
Adrian Auer, Paul Drechsler, Stephen Dryden, Lars
Emilson

Business Description
Speciality plastic and fibre product supplier.

Filtronic plc
Airedale House, Royal London Industrial Estate,
Charlestown, Shipley, West Yorkshire BD17 7SW
Telephone +44 (0) 1274 531602
Fax +44 (0) 1274 415473
Website www.filtronic.com

Chair
John Poulter
Chief Executive/Managing Director
Charles Hindson
Board Members
Prof Stephen Burbank, Iain Gibson, Reginald Gott, Ian
Hardington, Graham Meek

Business Description
A group engaged in the design and manufacture of
microwave products and compound semiconductors for
cellular and broadband telecommunications systems and
military applications.

Findel plc
Burley House, Bradford Road, Burley in Wharfedale,
Ilkley, West Yorkshire LS29 7DZ
Telephone +44 (0) 1943 864686
Fax +44 (0) 1943 864986
Website www.findel.co.uk

Chair
Keith Chapman
Chief Executive/Managing Director
Patrick Jolly
Board Members
Dr Ivan Bolton, Gordon Craig, David Dutton, Mike
Hawker, Tony Johnson, Philip Maudsley, John Padovan

Business Description
A group engaged in home shopping and educational
supplies sales through mail order catalogues, the
provision of outsourced healthcare services, and the
provision of logistics services to third parties.

Finsbury Growth & Income Trust plc
10 Crown Place, London EC2A 4FT
Telephone +44 (0) 20 7426 4000
Website www.closefinsbury.com

Chair
Michael Reeve
Board Members
John Allard, David Hunt, Vanessa Renwick, Anthony
Townsend, Giles Warman

Business Description
An investment trust.

Finsbury Worldwide Pharmaceutical Trust plc
25 Southampton Buildings, London WC2A 1AL
Telephone +44 (0) 20 3008 4013
Website www.finsburywp.com

Chair
Ian Ivory
Board Members
Josephine Dixon, Paul Gaunt, Prof Duncan Geddes,
Samuel Isaly, James Noble, Anthony Townsend

Business Description
An investment trust.

First Calgary Petroleums Ltd
Suite 900, 520-5 Avenue SW, Calgary, Alberta,
Canada T2P 3R7
Telephone +1 403 264 6697
Fax +1 403 264 3955
Website www.fcpl.ca

Chair
Raymond Antony
Chief Executive/Managing Director
Richard Anderson
Board Members
Alastair Beardsall, Keith Henry, Shane O'Leary, Charles
Pitman, Darryl Raymaker, Yuri Shafranik, John van der
Welle, E Nick Zana

Business Description
An oil and gas exploration company actively engaged in
international exploration and development activities in
Algeria.

FirstGroup plc
395 King Street, Aberdeen AB24 5RP
Telephone +44 (0) 1224 650100
Fax +44 (0) 1224 650140
Website www.firstgroup.com

Chair
Martin Gilbert
Chief Executive/Managing Director
Moir Lockhead
Board Members
Sidney Barrie, Audrey Baxter, Prof David Begg, David
Dunn, Dean Finch, James Forbes, David Leeder, John
Sievwright, Martyn Williams

Business Description
A group engaged in the provision of passenger transport
services.

FKI plc
Falcon Works, PO Box 7713, Meadow Lane,
Loughborough, Leicestershire LE11 1ZF
Telephone +44 (0) 1509 617713
Fax +44 (0) 1509 617714
Website www.fki.co.uk

Chair
Gordon Page
Chief Executive/Managing Director
Paul Heiden
Board Members
Neil Bamford, Richard Case, Reginald Gott, Sir Michael
Hodgkinson, Charles Matthews, David Pearl

Business Description
A group engaged in the manufacture of material handling
systems, lifting equipment, turbogenerators, switchgear,
transformers, and door, window and furniture hardware.

Fletcher King plc
Stratton House, Stratton Street, London W1J 8LA
Telephone +44 (0) 20 7493 8400
Fax +44 (0) 20 7491 2100
Website www.fletcherking.co.uk

Chair
David Fletcher
Board Members
Richard Goode, Harry Richardson, David Stewart

Business Description
A group engaged in commercial estate agency surveying
and project management.

Flying Brands Ltd
Retreat Farm, St Lawrence, Jersey JE3 1GX
Telephone +44 (0) 1534 865553
Fax +44 (0) 1534 865554
Website www.flyingbrands.com

Chair
Tim Trotter
Chief Executive/Managing Director
Mark Dugdale
Board Members
Paul Davidson, John Henwood, Graham Norton, Jim
McMahon

Business Description
A group engaged in volume mail order and collectables
retailing.

Foreign & Colonial Eurotrust plc
Exchange House, Primrose Street, London EC2A 2NY
Telephone +44 (0) 20 7628 8000
Fax +44 (0) 20 7628 8188
Website www.fandc.com

Chair
Douglas McDougall
Board Members
Detlef Bierbaum, Dr Clemens Borsig, William Eason,
Raphael Kanza

Business Description
An investment trust investing in continental European
securities.

Foreign & Colonial Investment Trust plc
Exchange House, Primrose Street, London EC2A 2NY
Telephone 020 7628 8000
Website www.fandc.co.uk

Chair
Mark Loveday
Board Members
Sir Michael Bunbury, Ronald Gould, Christopher Keljik,
Ewan Macpherson, John Rennocks, Maxwell Ward, Sir
Andrew Wood

Business Description
An investment trust.

Forth Ports plc
1 Prince of Wales Dock, Edinburgh EH6 7DX
Telephone +44 (0) 131 555 8700
Fax +44 (0) 131 553 7462
Website www.forthports.co.uk

Chair
Christopher Collins
Chief Executive/Managing Director
Charles Hammond
Board Members
Gerry Brown, Perry Glading, Wilson Murray, David
Richardson, Struan Robertson

Business Description
A group engaged in the provision of port cargo handling,
towage and related services and facilities, and property
investment and development.

Fortune Oil plc
Suite 2307, 23/F Office Tower, Convention Plaza, 1
Harbour Road, Wanchai, Hong Kong
Telephone +852 2802 8300
Fax +852 2802 8322
Website www.fortune-oil.com

Chair
Qian Benyuan
Chief Executive/Managing Director
Li Ching
Board Members
Trevor Bedford, Daniel Chiu, Dennis Chiu, Louisa Ho,
Anxi Li, Gong Min, John Pexton, Ian Taylor, Jinjun
Wang, Yulin Zhi

Business Description
A group engaged in the trading and distribution of crude
oil and petroleum products and the development of
infrastructure projects including a single point mooring
facility.

Foseco plc
Coleshill Road, Fazeley, Tamworth, Staffordshire B78 3TL
Telephone +44 (0) 1827 262021
Fax +44 (0) 1827 283725
Website www.foseco.com

Chair
Danny Rosenkranz
Chief Executive/Managing Director
James Pike
Board Members
Adrian Auer, Paul Dean, David Hussey, Einar Lindh, Lee
Plutshak, Dr Krishnamurthy Rajagopal

Business Description
Supplier of consumable products for use in the foundry
and steel making industries.

Framlington Innovative Growth Trust plc
155 Bishopsgate, London EC2M 3XJ
Telephone +44 (0) 20 7374 4100
Fax +44 (0) 20 7330 6644
Website www.framlington.co.uk

Chair
Sir Hugh Sykes
Board Members
Andrew Bell, John Cornish, Thomas Hempenstall, Justin
Reed, Brian Watson

Business Description
An investment trust that primarily invests in growth
companies based in or predominantly trading in the UK.

French Connection Group plc
Centro 1, 39 Camden Road, London NW1 0DX
Telephone +44 (0) 20 7036 7200
Fax +44 (0) 7036 7201
Website www.fcuk.com

Chair and Chief Executive
Stephen Marks
Board Members
Roy Naismith, David Rockberger, Neil Williams

Business Description
A group engaged in the retail and wholesale of branded
fashion clothing and accessories.

Friends Provident plc
Pixham End, Dorking, Surrey RH4 1QA
Telephone +353 (1) 802 3092
Fax +353 (1) 867 8025
Website www.friendsprovident.co.uk

Chair
Sir Adrian Montague
Chief Executive/Managing Director
Philip Moore
Board Members
Alison Carnwath, Alain Grisay, Ben Gunn, Lady Judge,
Ray King, Jim Smart, Sir Mervyn Pedelty

Business Description
A group engaged in life and pensions financial services
and asset management.

Fuller Smith & Turner plc
Griffin Brewery, Chiswick Lane South, London W4 2QB
Telephone +44 (0) 20 8996 2000
Fax +44 (0) 20 8995 0230
Website www.fullers.co.uk

Chair
Michael Turner
Board Members
Nigel Atkinson, Paul Clarke, Simon Emeny, Dr James
Espey, Anthony Fuller, Nick MacAndrew, John Roberts,
Ronald Spinney, Tim Turner

Business Description
A group engaged in the brewing and sale of beer, the
production of wine, and the management of tenanted and
managed public houses and some hotels.

Future plc
Beauford Court, 30 Monmouth Street, Bath BA1 2BW
Telephone +44 (0) 1225 442244
Fax +44 (0) 1225 822836
Website www.futureplc.com

Chair
Roger Parry
Chief Executive/Managing Director
Stevie Spring
Board Members
Seb Bishop, John Bowman, Seb Butler, John Mellon,
Michael Penington, Patrick Taylor

Business Description
A group engaged in the publication of video game, home
computing and other specialist consumer magazines and
internet websites in the UK, continental Europe and the
US.

Fyffes plc
29 North Anne Street, Dublin 7, Ireland
Telephone +353 1 887 2700
Fax +353 1 887 2755
Website www.fyffes.com

Chair
David McCann
Chief Executive/Managing Director
Jimmy Tolan
Board Members
Coen Bos, Dr. Paul Clüver, Declan McCourt, Tom
Murphy, Willie Walsh

Business Description
A company engaged in the importation and distribution
of tropical produce.

Galiform plc
66 Chiltern Street, London W1U 4JT
Telephone +44 (0) 20 7535 1110
Website www.galiform.co.uk

Chair
Will Samuel
Chief Executive/Managing Director
Matthew Ingle
Board Members
Angus Cockburn, Gerard Hughes, Mark Robson, Ian
Smith, Peter Wallis, Michael Wemms

Business Description
A group engaged in the manufacture, distribution and
sale of kitchen cabinetry and household furniture.

Galliford Try plc
Cowley Business Park, Cowley, Uxbridge,
Middlesex UB8 2AL
Telephone +44 (0) 1895 855001
Fax +44 (0) 1895 855298
Website www.galliford.co.uk

Chair
David Calverley
Chief Executive/Managing Director
Greg Fitzgerald
Board Members
Christopher Bucknall, Amanda Burton, Jonathan Dawson,
Frank Nelson

Business Description
A group engaged in construction and housebuilding.

Game Group plc
Unity House, Telford Road, Basingstoke RG21 6YJ
Telephone +44 (0) 1256 784000
Fax +44 (0) 1256 784093
Website www.gamegroup.plc.uk

Chair
Peter Lewis
Chief Executive/Managing Director
Lisa Morgan
Board Members
Christopher Bell, Jean-Paul Giraud, Ishbel Macpherson,
David Thomas

Business Description
A group engaged in the retail of PC and video games,
video consoles and related accessories.

Games Workshop Group plc
Willow Road, Lenton, Nottingham NG7 2WS
Telephone +44 (0) 115 900 4001
Fax +44 (0) 115 916 8111

Chair and Chief Executive
Thomas Kirby
Board Members
Nicholas Donaldson, Christopher Myatt, Michael Sherwin,
Alan Stewart

Business Description
A group engaged in the design, manufacture, retail and
wholesale distribution of miniature figures and games.

Gartmore European Investment Trust plc
Gartmore House, 8 Fenchurch Place, London EC3M 4PB
Telephone +44 (0) 20 7782 2000
Fax +44 (0) 20 7782 2075
Website www.gartmore.com

Chair
Rodney Dennis
Board Members
Jean Banon, Alexander Comba, Michael Firth, Bruno
Merki, Dr Manfred Piehl

Business Description
An investment trust.

Gartmore Fledgling Trust plc
Gartmore House, 8 Fenchurch Place, London EC3M 4PB
Telephone +44 (0) 20 7782 2000
Fax +44 (0) 20 7782 2075
Website www.gartmore.com

Chair
James West
Board Members
Peter Dicks, John Hancox, James Kerr-Muir, Nigel
Whittaker

Business Description
An investment trust.

Gartmore Global Trust plc
Gartmore House, 8 Fenchurch Place, London EC3M 4PB
Telephone +44 (0) 20 7782 2000
Website www.gartmore.com

Chair
Richard Bernays
Board Members
Miriam Greenwood, Richard Hills, Lance Moir, Richard
Stone

Business Description
An investment trust.

Gartmore Growth Opportunities plc
Gartmore House, 8 Fenchurch Place, London EC3M 4PB
Website www.gartmore.com

Chair
David Peters
Board Members
David Cade, Peter Derby, Daniel Mace, Robert Ware

Business Description
An investment company, investing primarily in quoted
UK smaller companies.

Gartmore Irish Growth Fund plc
51 New North Road, Exeter, Devon EX4 4EP
Telephone +44 (0) 1392 412122
Fax +44 (0) 1392 253282
Website www.gartmore.com

Chair
Harry Sheridan
Board Members
Robin Baillie, Gavin Caldwell, William Cotter, Sean
Fitzpatrick, Richard Milliken

Business Description
An investment trust with a dealing subsidiary.

Gartmore Smaller Companies Trust plc
Gartmore House, 8 Fenchurch Place, London EC3M 4PB
Telephone +44 (0) 20 7782 2000
Fax +44 (0) 20 7782 2075
Website www.gartmore.com

Chair
Liam Kane
Board Members
W Campbell Allen, Robin Baillie, Carol Ferguson, Peter
Rice

Business Description
An investment trust investing in smaller listed UK
companies.

GB Group plc
Winster House, Herons Way, Chester Business Park,
Chester CH4 9GB
Telephone +44 (0) 1244 657333
Fax +44 (0) 1244 680808
Website www.gb.co.uk

Chair
John Walker-Haworth
Chief Executive/Managing Director
Richard Law
Board Members
Alexander Green, Richard Martin Linford, Mona Navin-
Mealey, Richard Reynolds

Business Description
A group engaged in the development, sale and support of
business application software, the provision of database
management and analysis services, and technology
licencing.

GCap Media plc
30 Leicester Square, London WC2H 7LA
Telephone +44 (0) 20 7766 6000
Fax +44 (0) 20 7766 6184
Website www.gcapmedia.com

Chair
Peter Cawdron
Chief Executive/Managing Director
Ralph Bernard
Board Members
Richard Eyre, Alastair Goobey, Fru Hazlitt, Tony Illsey,
Sir Peter Michael, Steve Orchard, Wendy Pallot, Peter
Williams

Business Description
A commercial radio company.

Genus plc
Belvedere House, Basing View, Basingstoke,
Hampshire RG21 4HG
Telephone +44 (0) 1256 347100
Website www.genusplc.com

Chair
John Hawkins
Chief Executive/Managing Director
Richard Wood
Board Members
Martin Boden, Edwin White, John Worby

Business Description
A group engaged in the production of bovine semen, the
supply of veterinary and other products, and the
provision of consultancy services to the agricultural and
food industry.

Gibbs & Dandy plc
PO Box 17, 226 Dallow Road, Luton,
Bedfordshire LU1 1JG
Telephone +44 (0) 1582 798798
Fax +44 (0) 1582 798799
Website www.gibbsanddandy.com

Chair
Christopher Roshier
Chief Executive/Managing Director
Michael Dandy
Board Members
John Castle, Guy Naylor, Ami Sharma

Business Description
A group engaged as builders' merchants.

GKN plc
Ipsley House, Ipsley Church Lane, Redditch,
Worcestershire B98 0WR
Telephone +44 (0) 1527 517715
Fax +44 (0) 1527 517700
Website www.gknplc.com

Chair
Roy Brown
Chief Executive/Managing Director
Kevin Smith
Board Members
Marcus Bryson, Sir Ian Gibson, Helmut Mamsch, Sir
Christopher Meyer, Andrew Reynolds Smith, John
Sheldrick, Nigel Stein, Sir Peter Williams

Business Description
A group engaged in the manufacture and supply of
automotive components and systems, and supply of
structures components and design services to aircraft and
aero engine manufacturers.

Glasgow Income Trust plc
Sutherland House, 149 St Vincent Street,
Glasgow G2 5DR
Telephone +44 (0) 141 572 2700
Fax +44 (0) 141 572 277
Website www.glasgowinvestmentmanagers.co.uk

Chair
Ronnie Hanna
Board Members
Ian Boyd, Kevin Hart

Business Description
An investment trust company.

GlaxoSmithKline plc
980 Great West Road, Brentford, Middlesex TW8 9GS
Telephone +44 (0) 20 8047 5000
Fax +44 (0) 20 8990 4321
Website www.gsk.com

Chair
Sir Christopher Gent
Chief Executive/Managing Director
Dr Jean-Pierre Garnier
Board Members
Dr Stephanie Burns, Lawrence Culp, Sir Crispin Davis,
Tom de Swaan, Julian Heslop, Sir Deryck Maughan, Dr
Daniel Podolsky, Sir Ian Prosser, Dr Ronaldo Schmitz, Dr
Moncef Slaoui, Sir Robert Wilson

Business Description
A group engaged in the creation, discovery, development,
manufacture and marketing of pharmaceutical and
consumer health-related products.

Go-Ahead Group plc (The)
41-51 Grey Street, Newcastle-upon-Tyne NE1 6EE
Telephone +44 (0) 191 232 3123
Fax +44 (0) 191 221 0315
Website www.go-ahead.com

Chair
Sir Patrick Brown
Chief Executive/Managing Director
Keith Ludeman
Board Members
Christopher Collins, Rupert Pennant-Rea, Nick Swift

Business Description
A group engaged in the provision of passenger transport and aviation services including commuter rail services, bus and coach services, and airport ground and cargo services.

Goldenport Holdings Inc
41 Athanas Avenue, Vouliagmeni, GR 16671, Greece
Telephone +30 210 8910 500
Fax +30 210 9670 311
Website www.goldenport.biz

Chair
Chris Walton
Chief Executive/Managing Director
Paris Dragnis
Board Members
Robert Crawley, Konstantinos Kabanaros, Andreas Karaindros, Christos Varsos

Business Description
A group engaged in owning and operating dry bulk carriers and container vessels that transport cargo worldwide.

Goldman Sachs Dynamic Opportunities Ltd

Business Description
An investment company.

Goldshield Group plc
NLA Tower, 12-16 Addiscombe Road, Croydon, Surrey CR0 0XT
Telephone +44 (0) 20 8649 8500
Fax +44 (0) 20 8686 0807
Website www.goldshieldplc.com

Chair
Dr Keith Hellawell
Chief Executive/Managing Director
Rakesh Patel
Board Members
Paul Edwards, Ajay Patel, Kirti Patel, Mike Reardon, Nick Woollacott

Business Description
A group engaged in the development, marketing, manufacture and distribution of pharmaceutical and healthcare products.

Goodwin plc
Ivy House Foundry, Ivy House Road, Hanley, Staffordshire ST1 3NR
Telephone +44 (0) 1782 208040
Fax +44 (0) 1782 208060
Website www.goodwin.co.uk

Chair
John Goodwin
Board Members
Robert Dyer, Francis Gaffney, Richard Goodwin

Business Description
A group engaged as mechanical and refractory engineers.

Goshawk Insurance Holdings plc
1 Great Tower Street, London EC3R 5AA
Telephone +44 (0) 20 7623 9393
Fax +44 (0) 20 7623 9494
Website www.goshawk.co.uk

Chair
Rory Macnamara
Chief Executive/Managing Director
Michael Dawson
Board Members
Peter Dixon-Clarke

Business Description
A group engaged as a Lloyd's managing agent and corporate member of Lloyd's, and in the transaction of reinsurance business.

Grainger plc
Citygate, St James Boulevard, Newcastle-upon-Tyne NE1 4JE
Telephone +44 (0) 191 261 1819
Fax +44 (0) 191 269 5901
Website www.graingertrust.co.uk

Chair
Robin Broadhurst
Chief Executive/Managing Director
Rupert Dickinson
Board Members
John Barnsley, Andrew Cunningham, Stephen Dickinson, Robert Hiscox, Bill Tudor John

Business Description
A group engaged in property investment development and trading.

Graphite Enterprise Trust plc
4th Floor, Berkeley Square House, Berkeley Square, London W1J 6BQ
Telephone +44 (0) 20 7825 5300
Fax +44 (0) 20 7825 5399
Website www.graphite-enterprise.com

Chair
John Sclater
Board Members
Michael Cumming, Peter Dicks, Mark Fane, Peter Gray, Sean O'Connor

Business Description
An investment trust with a dealing subsidiary.

Great Portland Estates plc
33 Cavendish Square, London W1G 0PW
Telephone +44 (0) 20 7647 3000
Fax +44 (0) 20 7016 5500
Website www.gpe.co.uk

Chair
Richard Peskin
Chief Executive/Managing Director
Toby Courtauld
Board Members
Timon Drakesmith, Charles Irby, Robert Noel, Kathleen O'Donovan, Phillip Rose, Jonathan Short, Neil Thompson

Business Description
A group engaged in freehold and leasehold property investment and development.

Greene King plc
Westgate Brewery, Bury St Edmunds, Suffolk IP33 1QT
Telephone +44 (0) 1284 763222
Website www.greeneking.co.uk

Chair
Tim Bridge
Chief Executive/Managing Director
Rooney Anand
Board Members
Justin Adams, John Brady, Ian Bull, Ian Durant, David Elliott, Jonathan Lawson, Norman Murray, Howard Phillips, Jane Scriven

Business Description
A group engaged in the operation of managed and tenanted public houses, the brewing of beer and the wholesale of beer, wines and soft drinks.

Greggs plc
Fernwood House, Clayton Road, Jesmond, Newcastle-upon-Tyne NE2 1TL
Telephone +44 (0) 191 281 7721
Website www.greggs.plc.uk

Chair
Derek Netherton
Chief Executive/Managing Director
Sir Michael Darrington
Board Members
Julia Baddeley, Bob Bennett, Stephen Curran, Sir Ian Gibson, Ian Gregg, Richard Hutton, Raymond Reynolds, Malcolm Simpson

Business Description
A group engaged in the manufacture and retail of bread, flour, confectionery, sandwiches and savoury products, and the provision of catering within shops.

Gresham Computing plc
Sopwith House, Brook Avenue, Warsash, Southampton SO31 9ZA
Telephone +44 (0) 1489 555500
Fax +44 (0) 1489 555560
Website www.gresham-computing.com

Chair
Alan Howarth
Chief Executive/Managing Director
Andrew Walton-Green
Board Members
Dave Deller, Chris Errington, Gary Gibbs, Rob Glenn, Steve Purchase

Business Description
A group engaged in the provision of solutions software and specialist staff to the banking, integration and storage markets.

Gresham House plc
36 Elder Street, London E1 6BT
Telephone +44 (0) 20 7588 7352
Fax +44 (0) 20 7377 5013
Website www.greshamhouse.com

Chair and Chief Executive
Alfred Stirling
Board Members
Antony Ebel, Brian Hallett, Richard Lane, Nicholas Rowe, Thomas Rowe

Business Description
An investment trust.

Griffin Mining Ltd
6th Floor, 60 St James's Street, London SW1A 1LE
Telephone +44 (0) 20 7629 7772
Fax +44 (0) 20 7629 7773
Website www.griffinmining.com

Chair
Mladen Ninkov
Board Members
Dal Brynelsen, Dominic Claridge, Roger Goodwin, William Mulligan, David Pelchen, Jeff Haitan Sun

Business Description
A company engaged in zinc and gold mining in China.

Group 4 Securicor plc
The Manor, Manor Royal, Crawley, West Sussex RH10 9UN
Telephone +44 (0) 1293 554400
Website www.g4s.com

Chair
Alf Duch-Pedersen
Chief Executive/Managing Director
Nick Buckles
Board Members
Lord Condon, Trevor Dighton, Mark Elliot, Grahame Gibson, Thorleif Krarup, Bo Lerenius, Mark Seligman, Malcolm Williamson

Business Description
Provider of security solutions.

Gyrus Group plc
410 Wharfedale Road, Winnersh Triangle, Wokingham, Berkshire RG41 5RA
Telephone +44 (0) 1189 219750
Fax +44 (0) 1189 219850
Website www.gyrusplc.com

Chair
Brian Steer
Chief Executive/Managing Director
Roy Davis
Board Members
Prof Charles Cummings, Michael Garner, Dr Katherine Innes Ker, Keith Krzywicki, John Rennocks, Simon Shaw

Business Description
A group engaged in the design, development, manufacture and marketing of advanced surgical systems, and the development of tissue management and visualisation systems.

H R Owen plc
75 Kinnerton Street, London SW1X 8ED
Telephone +44 (0) 20 7235 3943
Website www.hrowen.co.uk

Chair
John MacArthur
Chief Executive/Managing Director
Nicholas Lancaster
Board Members
David Evans, Colin Giltrap, David Jagger, Nicholas Mason, Brendan Moynahan, Ramon Pajares, Dr John Robertson, Anthony Smith

Business Description
A group engaged as franchised motor dealers.

Halfords Group plc
Icknield Street Drive, Redditch, Worcestershire B98 0DE
Telephone +44 (0) 8450 579 000
Fax +44 (0) 1527 513 529
Website www.halfordscompany.com

Chair
Richard Pym
Chief Executive/Managing Director
Ian McLeod
Board Members
Dr Keith Harris, Bill Ronald, Nick Wharton, Nigel Wilson

Business Description
A group engaged in the retail of auto parts and accessories, cycles and cycle accessories.

Halma plc
Misbourne Court, Rectory Way, Amersham,
Buckinghamshire HP7 0DE
Telephone +44 (0) 1494 721111
Fax +44 (0) 1494 728032
Website www.halma.com

Chair
Geoff Unwin
Chief Executive/Managing Director
Andrew Williams
Board Members
John Campbell, Mark Lavelle, Adam Meyers, Stephen
Pettit, Neil Quinn, Andrew Richardson, Keith Roy,
Richard Stone, Kevin Thompson, Nigel Trodd, Nigel
Young

Business Description
A group engaged in the manufacture of fire and gas
detection equipment, opthalmic instruments and lenses,
electronic sensors, process safety equipment and water
treatment systems.

Hammerson plc
10 Grosvenor Street, London W1K 4BJ
Telephone +44 (0) 20 7887 1000
Website www.hammerson.co.uk

Chair
John Nelson
Chief Executive/Managing Director
John Richards
Board Members
David Atkins, John Clare, Peter Cole, Gerard Devaux,
David Edmonds, Jacques Espinasse, John Hirst, Simon
Melliss, Anthony Watson

Business Description
A group engaged in property investment and
development.

Hampson Industries plc
7 Harbour Buildings, Waterfront West, Dudley Road,
Brierley Hill, West Midlands DY5 1LN
Telephone +44 (0) 1384 485345
Fax +44 (0) 1384 472962
Website www.hampsongroup.com

Chair
Tony Gilroy
Chief Executive/Managing Director
Kim Ward
Board Members
Howard Kimberley, Jonathan Palmer, Robert Stokell

Business Description
A group engaged in aerospace and precision engineering.

Hamworthy plc
Fleets Corner, Poole, Dorset BH17 0JT
Telephone +44 (0) 1202 662600
Fax +44 (0) 1202 662793
Website www.hamworthy.com

Chair
Gordon Page
Chief Executive/Managing Director
Kelvyn Derrick
Board Members
Paul Crompton, Alan Frost, James Wilding

Business Description
A group engaged in the design, manufacture and supply
of products and systems for marine, oil and gas related
industries.

Hansa Trust plc
50 Curzon Street, London W1J 7UW
Telephone +44 (0) 20 7647 5750
Fax +44 (0) 20 7647 5770
Website www.hansagrp.com

Chair
Alex Hammond-Chambers
Board Members
Lord Borwick of Hawkshead, William Salomon, Prof
Geoffrey Wood

Business Description
An investment trust with a dealing subsidiary.

Hansteen Holdings plc
1 Berkeley Street, London W1J 8DJ
Telephone +44 (0) 20 7016 8820
Fax +44 (0) 20 7016 9214
Website www.hansteen.co.uk

Chair
James Hambro
Chief Executive/Managing Director
Morgan Jones
Board Members
Stephen Gee, Richard Mully, Ian Watson

Business Description
The company is engaged in property investment,
currently focusing on industrial property investments in
continental Europe.

Hardy Oil & Gas plc
Lincoln House, 137-143 Hammersmith House,
London W14 0QL
Telephone +44 (0) 20 7471 9850
Fax +44 (0) 20 7471 9851
Website www.hardyoil.com

Chair
Paul Mortimer
Chief Executive/Managing Director
Sastry Karra
Board Members
Dr Carol Bell, Dinesh Dattani, Pradip Shah, Yogeshwar
Sharma

Business Description
Oil and gas production and exploration company with
assets in India.

Hardy Underwriting Group plc
40 Lime Street, London EC3M 7AW
Telephone +44 (0) 20 7626 0382
Fax +44 (0) 20 7283 4677
Website www.hardygroup.co.uk

Chair
David Mann
Chief Executive/Managing Director
Barbara Merry
Board Members
Rick Abbot, Patrick Gage, Ian Ivory, Jamie MacDiarmid,
Hon Barbara Thomas, Adrian Walker

Business Description
A group engaged in the underwriting of insurance at
Lloyd's.

Harvey Nash Group plc
13 Bruton Street, London W1J 6QA
Telephone +44 (0) 20 7333 0033
Fax +44 (0) 20 7333 0032
Website www.harveynash.com

Chair
Ian Kirkpatrick
Chief Executive/Managing Director
Albert Ellis
Board Members
Richard Ashcroft, Thomas Crawford, David Higgins, Gus
Moore, Simon Wassall

Business Description
A group engaged in the provision of professional
recruitment and outsourcing services, in particular
providing information technology professionals for
permanent and contract positions worldwide.

Havelock Europa plc
Mossway, Hillend Industrial Park, Dalgety Bay,
Fife KY11 9JS
Telephone +44 (0) 1383 820044
Fax +44 (0) 1383 820064
Website www.havelockeuropa.com

Chair
Malcolm Gourlay
Chief Executive/Managing Director
Hew Balfour
Board Members
Michael Derbyshire, Robert Duncan, Grant Findlay,
Richard Lowery, Roland Van Bommel

Business Description
A group engaged in the design, manufacture and
installation of educational and commercial interiors and
point-of-sale merchandising displays.

Haynes Publishing Group plc
Sparkford, Yeovil, Somerset BA22 7JJ
Telephone +44 (0) 1963 440635
Fax +44 (0) 1963 440825
Website www.haynes.co.uk

Chair
John Haynes
Chief Executive/Managing Director
Eric Oakley
Board Members
Eddie Bell, Dan Benhardus, Panton Corbett, Andrew
Garner, Marc Haynes, David Suter

Business Description
A group engaged in printing and publishing.

Hays plc
141 Moorgate, London EC2M 6TX
Telephone +44 (0) 20 7628 9999
Website www.haysplc.com

Chair
Bob Lawson
Chief Executive/Managing Director
Denis Waxman
Board Members
William Eccleshare, Paul Harrison, Lesley Knox, Paul
Stoneham, Paul Venables, Brian Wallace, Alison Yapp

Business Description
A company engaged in the provision of specialist
recruitment services.

HBOS plc
The Mound, Edinburgh EH1 1YZ
Telephone +44 (0) 131 243 5509
Fax +44 (0) 131 243 7196
Website www.hbosplc.com

Chair
Lord Stevenson of Coddenham
Chief Executive/Managing Director
Andy Hornby
Board Members
Richard Cousins, Peter Cummings, Jo Dawson, Charles
Dunstone, Sir Ronald Garrick, Benny Higgins, Anthony
Hobson, Phil Hodkinson, Karen Jones, John Mack, Colin
Matthew, Coline McConville, Kate Nealon

Business Description
A group engaged in the provision of banking and other
financial services in the UK and overseas.

Headlam Group plc
PO Box 1, Gorsey Lane, Coleshill, Birmingham B46 1LW
Telephone +44 (0) 1675 433000
Fax +44 (0) 1675 433030
Website www.headlam.com

Chair
Graham Waldron
Chief Executive/Managing Director
Tony Brewer
Board Members
Mike O'Leary, Dick Peters, Stephen Wilson

Business Description
A group engaged in the wholesale distribution and
supply of floorcoverings and flooring accessories.

Helical Bar plc
11-15 Farm Street, London W1J 5RS
Telephone +44 (0) 20 7629 0113
Fax +44 (0) 20 7408 1666
Website www.helical.co.uk

Chair
Giles Weaver
Chief Executive/Managing Director
Michael Slade
Board Members
Antony Beevor, Michael Brown, Andrew Gulliford, Gerald
Kaye, Nigel McNair Scott, John Southwell, Wilf Weeks

Business Description
A group engaged in property investment, dealing and
development.

HelpHire Group plc
Pinesgate, Lower Bristol Road, Bath BA2 3DP
Telephone +44 (0) 1225 321000
Fax +44 (0) 1225 321100
Website www.helphire.co.uk

Chair
Rodney Baker-Bates
Chief Executive/Managing Director
Dr Mark Jackson
Board Members
Richard Burrell, Peter Holding, David Lindsay, Mike
O'Leary, David Paige, David Robertson, Roger Taylor

Business Description
A group engaged in the provision of non-fault accident
management assistance and related services, in particular
replacement vehicle hire and the financing of vehicle
repairs.

Henderson Eurotrust plc
4 Broadgate, London EC2M 2DA
Telephone +44 (0) 20 7818 1818
Fax +44 (0) 20 7818 1819
Website www.itshenderson.com

Chair
Stanislas Yassukovich
Board Members
Robert Bischof, Patrick Stevenson, Tim Stevenson, Mark
Tapley

Business Description
An investment trust investing in large and medium sized
companies.

Henderson Far East Income Trust plc
4 Broadgate, London EC2M 2DA
Telephone +44 (0) 20 7818 1818
Fax +44 (0) 20 7818 1819
Website www.itshenderson.com
Board Members
Simon Meredith Hardy, John Russell, Michael Watt

Business Description
An investment trust.

Henderson Global Property Companies Ltd
Trafalgar Court, Admiral Park, St Peter Port,
Guernsey GY1 2JA
Telephone +44 (0) 1481 710607
Website www.itshenderson.com

Chair
Christopher Jonas
Board Members
Peregrine Banbury, William Scott, Christopher Sherwell,
Stephen Vernon

Business Description
An investment company, investing in property and
property-realted securities.

Henderson Group plc
4 Broadgate, London EC2M 2DA
Telephone +44 (0) 20 7818 1818
Fax +44 (0) 20 7818 1819
Website www.henderson.com

Chair
Rupert Pennant-Rea
Chief Executive/Managing Director
Roger Yates
Board Members
Gerald Aherne, Duncan Ferguson, Toby Hiscock,
Anthony Hotson, John Roques

Business Description
A group engaged in the provision of investment
management services.

Henderson High Income Trust plc
4 Broadgate, London EC2M 2DA
Telephone +44 (0) 20 7818 1818
Fax +44 (0) 20 7818 1819
Website www.itshenderson.com

Chair
Hugh Twiss
Board Members
Vivian Bazalgette, Andrew Bell, Christopher Dunkerley,
Sir John Stanley

Business Description
An investment trust.

Henderson Opportunities Trust plc
4 Broadgate, London EC2M 2DA
Telephone +44 (0) 20 7638 5757
Fax +44 (0) 20 7818 1819
Website www.henderson.com

Chair
George Burnett
Board Members
Hamidh Bryce, Malcolm King, Richard Smith, Peter May

Business Description
An investment trust, investing in young and fast-growing
companies.

Henderson Smaller Companies Investment Trust plc
4 Broadgate, London EC2M 2DA
Telephone +44 (0) 20 7638 5757
Fax +44 (0) 20 7818 1819
Website www.itshenderson.com

Chair
Dudley Fishburn
Board Members
Sally Davis, Hon James Nelson, Keith Percy, Max Taylor

Business Description
An investment trust with a dealing subsidiary.

Henderson TR Pacific Investment Trust plc
4 Broadgate, London EC2M 2DA
Telephone +44 (0) 20 7818 1818
Fax +44 (0) 20 7818 1819
Website www.itshenderson.com

Chair
David Robins
Board Members
Hugh Aldous, Peter Berry, Struan Robertson, Judith
Unwin

Business Description
An investment trust.

Herald Investment Trust plc
10-11 Charterhouse Square, London EC1M 6EE
Telephone +44 (0) 20 7553 6300
Fax +44 (0) 20 7490 8026
Website www.heralduk.com

Chair
Martin Boase
Board Members
Clayton Brendish, Tim Curtis, Douglas McDougall

Business Description
An investment trust.

Heywood Williams Group plc
Premier Way, Lowfields Business Park, Elland, West
Yorkshire HX5 9HF
Telephone +44 (0) 1422 328850
Fax +44 (0) 1422 328868
Website www.heywoodwilliams.com

Chair
Roger Boyes
Chief Executive/Managing Director
Robert Barr
Board Members
Graham Menzies, Alan Parker, Hon Edward Roderick,
William Schmuhl

Business Description
A group engaged in the extrusion, manufacture and
distribution of component products for the building
industry.

HG Capital Trust plc
2 More London Riverside, London SE1 2AP
Telephone +44 (0) 20 7089 7888
Website www.hgcapitaltrust.net

Chair
Roger Mountford
Board Members
Timothy Amies, Piers Brooke, Peter Gale, Andrew
Murison

Business Description
An investment trust.

Highcroft Investments plc
Thomas House, Langford Locks, Kidlington,
Oxfordshire OX5 1HR
Telephone +44 (0) 1865 840023
Fax +44 (0) 1865 840045

Chair
John Hewitt
Chief Executive/Managing Director
Jonathan Kingerlee
Board Members
David Bowman, Christopher Clark, David Kingerlee,
Richard Stansfield

Business Description
A group engaged as a financial trust holding both
property and stock exchange securities.

Highland Gold Mining Ltd
26 New Street, St Helier, Jersey JE2 3RA
Telephone +44 (0) 1534 814202
Fax +44 (0) 1534 814815
Website www.highlandgold.com

Chair
James Cross
Chief Executive/Managing Director
Henry Horne
Board Members
Duncan Baxter, Alex Davidson, Dr David Fish, Ivan
Koulakov, Rene Marion, Nicholas Nikolakakis, Christopher
Palmer-Tomkinson, Tim Wadeson

Business Description
Gold producer with a number of development projects
and several exploration sites in Russia.

Highway Capital plc
73 Wimpole Street, London W1G 8AZ
Telephone +44 (0) 1727 841999
Fax +44 (0) 1727 865566

Chair
Howard Drummon
Board Members
Aron Freedman, Edward Levey

Business Description
A cash shell.

Highway Insurance Holdings plc
Highway House, 171 Kings Road, Brentwood,
Essex CM14 4EJ
Telephone +44 (0) 870 443 1111
Fax +44 (0) 1277 263651
Website www.highway-insurance.co.uk

Chair
Richard Gamble
Chief Executive/Managing Director
Andrew Gibson
Board Members
David Barker, Ian Campbell, Paul Cosh, Christopher Hill,
Judy Kellie, Arthur Milton, Peter Salsbury

Business Description
A group engaged in the transaction of insurance and, as
brokers, underwriting agents and corporate members of
Lloyd's.

Hikma Pharmaceuticals plc
13 Hanover Square, London W1S 1HW
Telephone +44 (0) 20 7399 2760
Fax +44 (0) 20 7399 2761
Website www.hikma.com

Chair
Samih Darwazah
Board Members
Ali Al-Husry, Michael Ashton, Breffni Byrne, Mazen
Darwazah, Ronald Goode, Sir David Rowe-Ham

Business Description
The group is a multinational pharmaceutical group.

Hill & Smith Holdings plc
2 Highlands Court, Cranmore Avenue Shirley, Solihull,
West Midlands B90 4LE
Telephone +44 (0) 121 704 7430
Fax +44 (0) 121 704 7439
Website www.hsholdings.co.uk

Chair
David Winterbottom
Chief Executive/Managing Director
David Grove
Board Members
Christopher Burr, Howard Marshall, Derek Muir, Dick
Richardson, Clive Snowdon

Business Description
A group engaged in the manufacture of building and
construction products, perforated and expanded metal
presswork bars and sections, and metal stockholding.

Hirco plc
Grosvenor House, 66/67 Athol Street, Douglas, Isle of
Man IM99 2BJ
Telephone +44 (0) 1624 646856
Fax +44 (0) 1624 672334
Website www.hircoplc.com

Chair
Niranjan Hiranandani
Chief Executive/Managing Director
Priya Hiranandani
Board Members
David Burton, Douglas Gardner, Kersi Gherda, Nigel
McGowan, John Teaford, Sir Rob Young

Business Description
A company engaged in real estate investment in large
scale mixed-use township developments in suburban
areas in India.

Hiscox plc
1 Great St Helens, London EC3A 6HX
Telephone +44 (0) 20 7448 6000
Fax +44 (0) 20 7448 6900
Website www.hiscox.com

Chair
Robert Hiscox
Chief Executive/Managing Director
Bronislaw Masojada
Board Members
Stuart Bridges, Robert Childs, Carol Engler, Daniel Healy,
Dr James King, Sir Mervyn Pedelty, Andrea Rosen, Dirk
Stuurop

Business Description
A group engaged in the transaction of insurance
business.

HMV Group plc
Shelley House, 2-4 York Road, Maidenhead,
Berkshire SL6 1SR
Telephone +44 (0) 1628 818300
Fax +44 (0) 1628 818301
Website www.hmvgroup.com

Chair
Carl Symon
Chief Executive/Managing Director
Simon Fox
Board Members
Neil Bright, Roy Brown, Lesley Knox, Mark McCafferty,
Christopher Rogers

Business Description
A group engaged in the retail of pre-recorded music,
DVD and VHS video, electronic games and books.
Trading under brand names HMV and Waterstone's.

Hochschild Mining plc
No 1 Grosvenor Crescent, London SW1X 7EF
Telephone +44 (0) 20 7152 6014
Website www.hochschildmining.com

Chair
Eduardo Hochschild
Board Members
Alberto Beeck, Jorge Born Jr, Roberto Dañino, Sir
Malcolm Field, Nigel Moore, Dionisio Romero

Business Description
A company engaged in the exploration, evaluation and
extraction of precious metals, with a primary focus on
gold and silver.

Hogg Robinson Group plc
Global House, Victoria Street, Basingstoke,
Hampshire RG21 3BT
Telephone +44 (0) 1256 312 600
Fax +44 (0) 1256 325 299
Website www.hoggrobinson.com

Chair
John Coombe
Chief Executive/Managing Director
David Radcliffe
Board Members
George Battersby, Tony Isaac, John Kennerley

Business Description
A group engaged in international business support
services, providing value-added services in the global
corporate travel market.

Holidaybreak plc
Hartford Manor, Greenbank Lane, Northwich,
Cheshire CW8 1HW
Telephone +44 (0) 1606 787000
Fax +44 (0) 8703 667639
Website www.holidaybreak.co.uk

Chair
Robert Ayling
Chief Executive/Managing Director
Carl Michel
Board Members
Robert Baddeley, Nicholas Cust, Martin Davies, James
Greenbury, Sally Martin, Simon Tobin, James Wallace,
Steven Whitfield, Mark Wray

Business Description
A group engaged in the provision of camping holidays.

Home Retail Group plc
489-499 Avebury Boulevard, Saxon Gate West, Central
Milton Keynes MK9 2NW
Telephone +44 (0) 845 603 6677
Fax +44 (0) 1908 692301
Website www.homeretailgroup.com

Chair
Oliver Stocken
Chief Executive/Managing Director
Terry Duddy
Board Members
Richard Ashton, John Coombe, Andy Hornby, Penny
Hughes, Paul Loft, Sara Weller

Business Description
A home and general merchandise retailer, selling products
under the Argos and Homebase brands.

Homeserve plc
Cable Drive, Walsall, West Midlands WS2 7BN
Telephone +44 (0) 1922 426262
Fax +44 (0) 20 7256 2621
Website www.homeserve.com

Chair
Brian Whitty
Chief Executive/Managing Director
Richard Harpin
Board Members
Ian Carlisle, Ian Chippendale, Barry Gibson, Jon
Florisheim, John Maxwell, Jonathan Simpson-Dent

Business Description
A group engaged in the provision of business support
services and the supply of water to domestic, industrial
and commercial customers.

Hornby plc
Westwood Industrial Estate, Margate, Kent CT9 4JX
Telephone +44 (0) 1843 233500
Fax +44 (0) 1843 233513
Website www.hornby.com

Chair
Neil Johnson
Chief Executive/Managing Director
Frank Martin
Board Members
Nicholas Cosh, John Stansfield

Business Description
A group engaged in the development, design, sourcing
and distribution of hobby and interactive home
entertainment products.

HSBC Holdings plc
8 Canada Square, London E14 5HQ
Telephone +44 (0) 20 7991 8888
Fax +44 (0) 20 7992 4880
Website www.hsbc.com

Chair
Stephen Green
Chief Executive/Managing Director
Michael Geoghegan
Board Members
Lord Butler of Brockwell, John Coombe, Baroness Dunn,
Rona Fairhead, Douglas Flint, William Fung, James
Hughes-Hallett, Sir Brian Moffat, Sir Mark Moody-Stuart,
Gwyn Morgan, Stewart Newton, Simon Robertson, Sir
Brian Williamson

Business Description
A group engaged in the provision of banking and related
financial services.

HSBC Infrastructure Company Ltd
Dorey Court, Admiral Park, St Peter Port,
Guernsey GY1 3BG
Telephone +44 (0) 1481 727111
Website www.hicl.hsbc.com

Chair
Graham Picken
Board Members
Henri Grisius, John Hallam

Business Description
A closed-ended investment company making investments
through a series of entities.

Hunting plc
3 Cockspur Street, London SW1Y 5BQ
Telephone +44 (0) 20 7321 0123
Fax +44 (0) 20 7839 2072
Website www.hunting.plc.uk

Chair
Richard Hunting
Chief Executive/Managing Director
Dennis Proctor
Board Members
Dennis Clark, Terry Gomke, George Helland, Hector
McFadyen, Iain Paterson

Business Description
A group engaged in the marketing and distribution of oil
and gas, the provision of oilfield services and tubular
products, exploration and other activities.

Huntsworth plc
15-17 Huntsworth Mews, London NW1 6DD
Telephone +44 (0) 20 7408 2232
Fax +44 (0) 20 7493 3048
Website www.huntsworth.co.uk

Chair
Jon Foulds
Chief Executive/Managing Director
Lord Chadlington
Board Members
Robert Alcock, Eugene Beard, Anthony Brooke, Tracey
Reid, Sally Withey

Business Description
A group engaged in the provision of marketing services
with a core activity of public relations.

Hyder Consulting plc
29 Bressenden Place, London SW1E 5DZ
Telephone +44 (0) 20 7316 6000
Fax +44 (0) 20 7316 6125
Website www.hyderconsulting.com

Chair
Sir Alan Thomas
Chief Executive/Managing Director
Tim Wade
Board Members
Simon Hamilton-Eddy, Jeffrey Hume, Peter Morgan, Paul
Withers

Business Description
A group engaged in the provision of technical and
engineering consultancy, and the planning, design and
management of infrastructure projects.

I S Solutions plc
Windmill House, 91-93 Windmill Road, Sunbury upon
Thames, Middlesex TW16 7EF
Telephone +44 (0) 1932 893333
Fax +44 (0) 1932 893433
Website www.issolutions.co.uk

Chair and Chief Executive
Barrie Clark
Chief Executive/Managing Director
John Lythall
Board Members
James Dodkins, Peter English, Peter Kear, Jonathan West

Business Description
A group engaged in the distribution, design and
installation of computer hardware and software systems.

ICAP plc
2 Broadgate, London EC2M 7UR
Telephone +44 (0) 20 7000 5000
Fax +44 (0) 20 7000 7115
Website www.icap.com

Chair
Charles Gregson
Chief Executive/Managing Director
Michael Spencer
Board Members
Nicholas Cosh, Duncan Goldie-Morrison, William Nabarro,
Matthew Lester, Stephen McDermott, Jim McNulty, Mark
Yallop

Business Description
A group engaged as securities derivatives and money
brokers.

IG Group Holdings plc
Friars House, 157-168 Blackfriars Road, London SE1 8EZ
Telephone +44 (0) 20 7896 0011
Fax +44 (0) 20 7896 0010
Website www.iggroup.com

Chair
Jonathan Davie
Chief Executive/Managing Director
Tim Howkins
Board Members
Sir Alan Budd, Steve Clutton, Peter Hetherington, Martin
Jackson, Nat le Roux, Robert Lucas, Andrew MacKay,
Roger Yates

Business Description
Provision of financial and sports spread betting CFDs and
foreign exchange dealing.

iimia Investment Trust
23 Cathedral Yard, Exeter EX1 1HB
Telephone +44 (0) 1392 475900
Fax +44 (0) 1392 259900
Website www.iimia.co.uk

Chair and Chief Executive
Anthony Townsend
Board Members
James Fox, Nicholas Hodgson, Michael Phillips

Business Description
An investment trust

Imagination Technologies Group plc
Home Park Estate, Kings Langley,
Hertfordshire WD4 8LZ
Telephone +44 (0) 1923 260511
Fax +44 (0) 1923 268969
Website www.imgtec.com

Chair
Geoff Shingles
Chief Executive/Managing Director
Hossein Yassaie
Board Members
David Hurst-Brown, Ian Pearson, Trevor Selby

Business Description
A group engaged in the design, development and
marketing of multimedia technology.

IMI plc
Lakeside, Solihull Parkway, Birmingham Business Park,
Birmingham B37 7XZ
Telephone +44 (0) 121 717 3700
Fax +44 (0) 121 344 4954
Website www.imiplc.com

Chair
Norman Askew
Chief Executive/Managing Director
Martin Lamb
Board Members
Kevin Beeston, Lance Browne, Anita Frew, Terry Gateley,
Douglas Hurt, David Nicholas, Roy Twite

Business Description
A group engaged in the manufacture and supply of fluid
controls, retail dispense and building products.

Impax Environmental Markets plc
Crusader House, 145-147 St John Street,
London EC1V 4RU
Telephone +44 (0) 20 7490 4355
Fax +44 (0) 20 7336 0865

Chair
Richard Bernays
Board Members
Dr Robert Arnott, Bill Brown, Keith Niven

Business Description
An investment company.

Imperial Chemical Industries plc
20 Manchester Square, London W1U 3AN
Telephone +44 (0) 20 7009 5000
Fax +44 (0) 20 7009 5752
Website www.ici.com

Chair
Peter Ellwood
Chief Executive/Managing Director
Dr John McAdam
Board Members
Adri Baan, Alan Brown, Lord Butler of Brockwell, Joseph Gorman, David Hamill, Richard Haythornthwaite, Baroness Noakes

Business Description
A group engaged in the research, manufacture and sale of specialty products and paints.

Imperial Tobacco Group plc
PO Box 244, Upton Road, Bristol BS99 7UJ
Telephone +44 (0) 117 963 6636
Website www.imperial-tobacco.com

Chair
Iain Napier
Chief Executive/Managing Director
Gareth Davis
Board Members
Anthony Alexander, Graham Blashill, Ken Burnett, Alison Cooper, David Cresswell, Robert Dyrbus, Michael Herlihy, Dr Pierre Jungels, Charles Knott, Susan Murray, Mark Williamson

Business Description
A group engaged in the manufacture, marketing and sale of tobacco and tobacco related products.

Inchcape plc
22A St James's Square, London SW1Y 5LP
Telephone +44 (0) 20 7546 0022
Fax +44 (0) 20 7533 9117
Website www.inchcape.com

Chair
Peter Johnson
Chief Executive/Managing Director
André Lacroix
Board Members
Dr Raymond Ch'ien, Karen Guerra, Kenneth Hanna, Barbara Richmond, Will Samuel, David Scotland, Michael Wemms

Business Description
A group engaged in import and distribution allied to exclusive retail, stand alone retail of new and used cars, provision of financial services, refurbishment, logistics, remarketing and automotive e-commerce.

Informa plc
27 Mortimer Street, London W1T 3JF
Telephone +44 (0) 20 7017 5000
Website www.informa.com

Chair
Peter Rigby
Chief Executive/Managing Director
David Gilbertson
Board Members
John Davis, Anthony Foye, Dr Pam Kirby, Derek Mapp, Sean Watson

Business Description
A group engaged in the publication of newsletters, magazines and books, the organisation of conferences, and the provision of screen-based information for the capital markets.

ING Global Real Estate Securities Ltd
Trafalgar Court, Les Banques, St Peter Port, Guernsey GY1 3QL
Telephone +44 (0) 1481 275001

Chair
Crispian Collins
Board Members
Trevor Ash, Richard Saunders, Richard Sutton

Business Description
An investment company investing in listed and unlisted global real estate securities.

ING UK Real Estate Income Trust Ltd
Trafalgar Court, Les Banques, St Peter Port, Guernsey GY1 3QL
Telephone +44 (0) 1481 275001
Fax +44 (0) 1481 745051
Website www.ingreit.co.uk

Chair
Nicholas Thompson
Board Members
Trevor Ash, Tjeerd Borstlap, John Gibbons, Robert Sinclair

Business Description
An investment trust.

Inion Oy
Lääkärinkatu 2, 33520 Tampere, Finland
Telephone +358 3 2306601

Chair and Chief Executive
Dr Goran Ando
Board Members
Peter Allen, David Anderson, James Berry, Julien Cotta, Peter Jensen, Dr Auvo Kaikkonen, Chris Lee, Markku Silen

Business Description
A company engaged in the development of biodegradable medical implants.

Inmarsat plc
99 City Road, London EC1Y 1AX
Telephone +44 (0) 20 7728 1777
Fax +44 (0) 20 7728 1142
Website www.inmarsat.com

Chair and Chief Executive
Andrew Sukawaty
Board Members
Michael Butler, Sir Bryan Carsberg, Stephen Davidson, Admiral James Ellis Jr, Kathleen Flaherty, Rick Medlock, John Rennocks

Business Description
Provider of global mobile satellite communications services.

Innovation Group plc (The)
Yarmouth House, 1300 Parkway, Whiteley, Fareham, Hampshire PO15 7AE
Telephone +44 (0) 1489 898300
Fax +44 (0) 1489 579181
Website www.innovation-group.com

Chair
Geoff Squire
Chief Executive/Managing Director
Hassan Sadiq
Board Members
Chris Banks, Paul Hemsley, Kurt Lauk, James Morley, David Thorpe

Business Description
A group engaged in the provision of insurance software and specialised business process outsourcing services for insurance and associated industries.

Inspired Gaming Group plc
3 The Maltings, Westmore Road, Burton-on-Trent, Staffordshire DE14 1SE
Telephone +44 (0) 1283 512777
Fax +44 (0) 1283 519218
Website www.inspiredgaminggroup.com

Chair
Russell Hoyle
Chief Executive/Managing Director
Luke Alvarez
Board Members
David Mce, Christopher Mills, James O'Halleran, Julian Paul

Business Description
A group engaged in the provision of gaming machines.

Instore plc
Trident Business Park, Leeds Road, Deighton, Huddersfield HD2 1UA
Telephone +44 (0) 840 240 4600
Website www.instoreretail.co.uk

Chair
Christo Wiese
Chief Executive/Managing Director
Peter Burdon
Board Members
Gary Brown, John Gnodde, John Jackson, Cornus Moore, John Richards, Aziz Tayub

Business Description
A company engaged in the operation of retail outlets.

Intec Telecom Systems plc
Wells Court 2, Albert Drive, Woking, Surrey GU21 5UB
Telephone +44 (0) 1483 745800
Fax +44 (0) 1483 745860
Website www.intec-telecom-systems.com

Chair
John Hughes
Board Members
John Alkins, John Arbuthnott, Gary Bunney, Rene Kern, Peter Manning, Gordon Stuart, Robin Taylor

Business Description
A group engaged in the development, marketing and licencing of telecoms operations support systems software and the provision of related professional services.

InterContinental Hotels Group plc
67 Alma Road, Windsor, Berkshire SL4 3HD
Telephone +44 (0) 1753 410100
Fax +44 (0) 1753 410101
Website www.ichotelsgroup.com

Chair
David Webster
Chief Executive/Managing Director
Andrew Cosslett
Board Members
Richard Hartman, David Kappler, Ralph Kugler, Jennifer Laing, Robert Larson, Jonathan Linen, Stevan Porter, Sir David Prosser, Richard Solomons

Business Description
A group engaged in the ownership, leasing, management and franchising of hotels and resorts worldwide, and also the manufacture of soft drinks.

Intermediate Capital Group plc
20 Old Broad Street, London EC2N 1DP
Telephone +44 (0) 20 7628 9898
Fax +44 (0) 20 7628 2268
Website www.icgplc.co.uk

Chair
John Manser
Board Members
Tom Attwood, Thomas Bartlam, Jean-Daniel Camus, Francois de Mitry, Justin Dowley, Christophe Evain, Philip Keller, Eric Licoys, Hon James Nelson, Andrew Phillips, Paul Piper, Peter Stone

Business Description
A group engaged in the provision of mezzanine capital to companies in Western Europe along with the management of third party funds.

International Biotechnology Trust plc
31 Gresham Street, London EC2V 7QA
Telephone +44 (0) 20 7658 6501
Fax +44 (0) 20 7658 3538
Website www.internationalbiotrust.com

Chair
Andrew Barker
Board Members
Alan Clifton, Dr David Clough, Peter Collacott, Alex Hammond-Chambers, Ian Macgregor

Business Description
A company investing in high growth development stage biotechnology companies.

International Greetings plc
Belgrave House, Hatfield Business Park, Frobisher Way, Hatfield AL10 9TQ
Telephone +44 (0) 1707 630630
Fax +44 (0) 1707 630666
Website www.internationalgreetings.co.uk

Chair
Keith James
Chief Executive/Managing Director
Anders Hedlund
Board Members
Nicholas Fisher, Mark Collini, Paul Fineman, Martin Hornung, John Jones

Business Description
A group engaged in the design and manufacture of greeting cards, gift wrapping paper, Christmas crackers, licensed stationery and other decorative accessories.

International Personal Finance plc
Number 3, Leeds City Office Park, Meadow Lane, Leeds LS11 5BD
Telephone +44 (0) 113 285 6700
Website www.ipfin.co.uk

Executive Chairman
Christopher Rodrigues
Chief Operating Officer
John Harnett
Board Members
David Broadbent, Ray Miles, Charles Gregson, Tony Hales, Nick Page

Business Description
A company engaged in the provision of consumer financial services.

International Power plc
Senator House, 85 Queen Victoria Street,
London EC4V 4DP
Telephone +44 (0) 20 7320 8706
Fax +44 (0) 20 7320 8740
Website www.internationalpowerplc.com

Chair
Sir Neville Simms
Chief Executive/Managing Director
Philip Cox
Board Members
Adri Baan, Anthony Concannon, Anthony Isaac, Bruce
Levy, Dr Stephen Riley, John Roberts, Struan Robertson,
Mark Williamson

Business Description
A group engaged in the generation and supply of
electricity.

Interserve plc
Interserve House, Ruscombe Park, Twyford, Reading,
Berkshire RG10 9JU
Telephone +44 (0) 118 932 0123
Fax +44 (0) 118 932 0206
Website www.interserveplc.co.uk

Chair
Lord Blackwell
Chief Executive/Managing Director
Adrian Ringrose
Board Members
Patrick Balfour, Leslie Cullen, Tim Jones, Nicholas
Keegan, David Trapnell, John Vyse

Business Description
A group engaged in the provision of building and
infrastructure services, facilities services and industrial
services, and the sale and hire of construction equipment.

Intertek Group plc
25 Savile Row, London W1S 2ES
Telephone +44 (0) 20 7396 3400
Fax +44 (0) 20 7396 3480
Website www.intertek.com

Chair
Vanni Treves
Chief Executive/Managing Director
Dr Wolfhart Hauser
Board Members
David Allvey, Christopher Knight, Richard Nelson, Debra
Rade, Bill Spencer

Business Description
A group engaged in testing, inspection and certification of
products and commodities against a wide range of safety,
regulatory, quality and performance standards.

Invensys plc
Portland House, Bressenden Place, London SW1E 5BF
Telephone +44 (0) 20 7834 3848
Fax +44 (0) 20 7834 3879
Website www.invensys.com

Chair
Hon Martin Jay
Chief Executive/Managing Director
Ulf Henriksson
Board Members
Bay Green, Jean-Claude Guez, Steve Hare, Michael Parker,
Pat Zito

Business Description
A group engaged in the design and manufacture of
intelligent automation systems, industrial drive systems,
power systems and controls.

INVESCO Asia Trust plc
30 Finsbury Park, London EC2A 1AG
Telephone +44 (0) 20 7065 4000
Fax +44 (0) 20 7638 0752
Website www.invesco.co.uk

Chair
David Hinde
Board Members
Robin Baille, Bryan Lenygon, Sir Robin McLaren, Duncan
Neil Robertson

Business Description
An investment trust.

Invesco English & International Trust plc
30 Finsbury Square, London EC2A 1AG
Telephone +44 (0) 20 7065 4000
Website www.invesco.co.uk/investmenttrusts

Chair
John Sands
Board Members
Alan Barber, Sarah Bates, Jim Cox, Dr Gwyn Jones

Business Description
An investment trust.

Invesco Income Growth Trust plc
30 Finsbury Square, London EC2A 1AG
Telephone +44 (0) 20 7065 4000
Fax +44 (0) 20 7065 3166
Website www.invescoperpetual.co.uk

Chair
John McLachlan
Board Members
Chris Hills, Jonathan Silver, Hugh Twiss, Roger Walsom

Business Description
An investment trust.

INVESCO Japan Discovery Trust plc
30 Finsbury Park, London EC2A 1AG
Telephone +44 (0) 20 7065 4000
Fax +44 (0) 20 7638 0752
Website www.invesco.co.uk

Chair
Timothy Kimber
Board Members
The Hon Michael Benson, Marcus Dodd, Stephen Morant,
Graeme Proudfoot

Business Description
An investment trust.

Invesco Perpetual European Absolute Return Trust plc
30 Finsbury Park, London EC2A 1AG
Telephone +44 (0) 20 7065 4000
Fax +44 (0) 20 7065 3166
Website www.invesco.co.uk

Chair
Jonathan Bradley
Board Members
David Bentata, Tim Knowles, Margaret Roddan, Mark
Seale, Alfred Sulzer

Business Description
An investment trust.

Invesco Perpetual Recovery Trust 2011 plc
30 Finsbury Square, London EC2A 1AG
Telephone +44 (0) 20 7065 4000
Website www.invescoperpetual.com

Chair
Lord Naseby
Board Members
Prof Timothy Congdon, William Erasmus, Howell Harris-
Hughes, Prof James MacLeod

Business Description
An investment company investing in quoted equity and
fixed income securities of UK companies.

**Invesco Perpetual UK Smaller Companies Investment
Trust plc**
30 Finsbury Square, London EC2A 1AG
Telephone +44 (0) 20 7065 4000
Fax +44 (0) 20 7638 9752
Website www.invescoperpetual.co.uk

Chair
Ian Barby
Board Members
Richard Brooman, Garth Milne, Alfred O'Hare, John
Spooner

Business Description
An investment trust investing in the shares of small to
medium sized UK quoted companies.

INVESCO plc
30 Finsbury Square, London EC2A 1AG
Telephone +44 (0) 20 7638 0731
Fax +44 (0) 20 7638 0711
Website www.invesco.com

Chair
Rex Adams
Chief Executive/Managing Director
Martin Flanagan
Board Members
Sir John Banham, Joseph Canion, Denis Kessler, Edward
Lawrence, J Thomas Presby, James Robertson

Business Description
An investment manager providing services to retail,
institutional, and private wealth management clients.

Invesco Property Income Trust Ltd
Ordnance House, 31 Pier Road, St Helier, Jersey JE4 8PW
Telephone +44 (0) 20 7543 3500
Website www.invescoperpetual.co.uk

Chair
Richard Barnes
Board Members
Douglas Gardner, Susan McCabe, Angus Spencer-Nairn,
Ian White

Business Description
Closed-ended Jersey registered investment trust.

Investec Capital Accumulator Trust Ltd
Guinness Flight House, La Plaiderie, St Peter Port,
Guernsey GY1 3QH
Telephone +44 (0) 1481 710404
Fax +44 (0) 1481 715265
Website www.investecfunds.com

Chair
Christopher Hill
Board Members
Fred Carr, Peter Niven

Business Description
An investment company enagaged in investing at least
80% of its portfolio in UK Sterling denominated
investments in the form of equities and/or equity related
derivatives.

Investec High Income Trust plc
2 Gresham Street, London EC2V 7QP
Telephone +44 (0) 20 7597 2000
Website www.investecfunds.com

Chair
James Dawnay
Board Members
Tim Guinness, Chris Russell, Giles Weaver

Business Description
An investment trust with dealing subsidiaries.

Investec plc
2 Gresham Street, London EC2V 7QP
Telephone +44 (0) 20 7597 4000
Fax +44 (0) 20 7597 4070
Website www.investec.com

Chair
Hugh Herman
Chief Executive/Managing Director
Stephen Koseff
Board Members
Sam Abrahams, George Alford, Glynn Burger, Cheryl
Carolus, Haruko Fukuda, Geoffrey Howe, Donn Jowell,
Bernard Kantor, Ian Kantor, Sir Chips Keswick, Peter
Malungani, Sir David Prosser, Alan Tapnack, Peter
Thomas, Fani Titi

Business Description
A group engaged in specialist banking and financial
services.

Investment Company plc (The)
3rd Floor, Suite 539, Salisbury House, London Wall,
London EC2M 5QS
Telephone +44 (0) 20 7448 4754
Fax +44 (0) 20 4778 4765

Chair
Sir David Thomson
Board Members
Peter Allen, Stephen Cockburn, Philip Lovegrove, Charles
Marsh, Joan Webb

Business Description
A company engaged in investing in preference shares and
prior charge securities.

Invista European Real Estate Trust
25B Boulevard Royal, L2449, Luxembourg
Telephone +352 268 642260

Business Description
An investment company.

Invista Foundation Property Trust Ltd
PO Box 482, Royal Bank Place, Glateway Esplanade, St
Peter Port, Guernsey GY1 2BH
Telephone +44 (0) 1481 743 000
Website www.ifpt.co.uk

Chair
Andrew Sykes
Board Members
Peter Atkinson, Harry Dick-Cleland, John Frederiksen,
Keith Goulborn, David Warr

Business Description
Investment in UK commercial property.

**Invista Real Estate Investment Management Holdings
plc**
Exchequer Court, 33 St Mary Court, London EC3A 8AA
Telephone +44 (0) 20 7153 9300
Website www.invistarealestate.com

Chair
Alistar Goobey
Board Members
Robin Broadhurst, Olivia Dixon, Guy Eastaugh, Douglas
Ferrans, Philip Gadsden, Duncan Owen

Business Description
A group engaged in real estate fund management.

IP Group plc
24 Cornhill, London EC3V 3ND
Telephone +44 (0) 20 7444 0050
Fax +44 (0) 845 074 2928
Website www.ipgroupplc.com

Chair
Dr Bruce Smith
Chief Executive/Managing Director
Alan Aubrey
Board Members
Roger Brooke, Dr Alison Fielding, David Norwood, Prof
William Richards, Mike Turner

Business Description
A group engaged in the commercialisation and
exploitation of intellectual property via the formation of
long-term partnerships with universities; management of
venture funds focusing on early-stage UK technology
companies; and the in-licensing of drugable intellectual
property from research intensive institutions.

ISIS Property Trust
Trafalgar Court, Les Banques, St Peter Port,
Guernsey GY1 3QL
Telephone +44 (0) 1481 44500
Fax +44 (0) 1481 745051
Website www.isispropertytrust.co.uk

Chair
Peter Crook
Board Members
David Evans, Graham Harrison, Vikram Lall, Michael
Soames

Business Description
An investment trust.

ISIS Property Trust 2 Ltd
Trafalgar Court, Les Banques, St Peter Port,
Guernsey GY1 3QL
Telephone +44 (0) 20 7628 8000
Website www.isispropertytrust2.co.uk

Chair
Quentin Spicer
Board Members
Andrew Gulliford, Christopher Sherwell, Christopher
Spencer, Giles Weaver

Business Description
A closed-ended investment company investing in UK
commercial property.

iSOFT Group plc
Daventry Road, Banbury, Oxfordshire OX16 3JT
Telephone +44 (0) 870 050 8901
Fax +44 (0) 870 050 8911
Website www.isoftplc.com

Chair
John Weston
Board Members
Dr Eurfl ap Gwilgm, Bill Henry, Gavin James, Rene Kern,
Ken Lever, David Thorpe, Geoff White

Business Description
A group engaged in the licensing and implementation of
software applications to healthcare provider organisations.

ITE Group plc
105-109 Salusbury Road, London NW6 6RG
Telephone +44 (0) 20 7596 5000
Fax +44 (0) 20 7596 5111
Website www.ite-exhibitions.com

Chair
Iain Patterson
Chief Executive/Managing Director
Ian Tomkins
Board Members
Rt Hon Sir Jeremy Hanley, Mike Hartley, Edward
Strachan, Russell Taylor, Malcolm Wall

Business Description
A group engaged in the organisation of exhibitions and
conferences.

ITV plc
200 Gray's Inn Road, London WC1V 8HF
Telephone +44 (0) 20 7843 8000
Website www.itvplc.com

Chairman
Michael Grade
Deputy Chairman
Sir George Russell
Board Members
Sir Robert Phillis, Sir Brian Pitman, Baroness Usha
Prashar, Sir James Crosby, Mike Claspar, John McGrath,
John Cresswell, James Tibbitts

Business Description
A group engaged in the production and broadcasting of
television programmes and channels.

J D Wetherspoon plc
Wetherspoon House, Reeds Crescent, Watford,
Hertfordshire WD24 4QL
Telephone +44 (0) 1923 477777
Fax +44 (0) 1923 219810
Website www.jdwetherspoon.co.uk

Chair
Tim Martin
Chief Executive/Managing Director
John Hutson
Board Members
Jim Clarke, John Herring, Elizabeth McMeikan, Debra van
Gene

Business Description
The development and management of public houses.

J Sainsbury plc
33 Holborn, London EC1N 2HT
Telephone +44 (0) 20 7695 6000
Fax +44 (0) 20 7695 7610
Website www.jsainsbury.com

Chair
Sir Philip Hampton
Chief Executive/Managing Director
Justin King
Board Members
Anna Ford, Val Gooding, Gary Hughes, Dr John
McAdam, Darren Shapland, Bob Stack

Business Description
A group engaged in the retail of food and the provision
of financial services.

J Smart & Co (Contractors) plc
28 Cramond Road South, Edinburgh EH4 6AB
Telephone +44 (0) 131 336 2181
Fax +44 (0) 131 336 4037
Website www.jsmart.co.uk

Chair and Chief Executive
J. Smart

Business Description
A group engaged in building and public works
contracting.

James Fisher & Sons plc
Fisher House, PO Box 4, Barrow-in-Furness,
Cumbria LA14 1HR
Telephone +44 (0) 1229 615400
Fax +44 (0) 1229 836761
Website www.james-fisher.com

Chair
Tim Harris
Chief Executive/Managing Director
Nick Henry
Board Members
Anthony Cooke, F Everard, William Everard, Simon
Harris, Charles Rice, Michael Shields

Business Description
A service provider in all sectors of the marine industry.

James Halstead plc
Beechfield, Hollinhurst Road, Radcliffe,
Manchester M26 1JN
Telephone +44 (0) 161 767 2500
Fax +44 (0) 161 767 7499
Website www.jameshalstead.com

Chair
Geoffrey Halstead
Chief Executive/Managing Director
Mark Halstead
Board Members
Gordon Oliver, Anthony Wild, Jack Whittaker

Business Description
A company engaged in the manufacture of commercial
flooring.

Jardine Lloyd Thompson Group plc
6 Crutched Friars, London EC3N 2PH
Telephone +44 (0) 20 7528 4444
Fax +44 (0) 20 7528 4185
Website www.jltgroup.com

Chair
Geoffrey Howe
Chief Executive/Managing Director
Dominic Burke
Board Members
Brian Carpenter, Christopher Keljik, Simon Keswick, Lord
Leach of Fairford, Hon Nicholas MacAndrew, William
Nabarro, Jim Rush, Bob Scott, Vyvienne Wade

Business Description
A group engaged in insurance and reinsurance broking
and employee benefits.

Jarvis plc
Meridian House, The Crescent, York YO24 1AW
Telephone +44 (0) 1904 712712
Fax +44 (0) 1904 712011
Website www.jarvisplc.com

Chair
Stephen Norris
Chief Executive/Managing Director
Richard Entwistle
Board Members
Elizabeth Filkin, Brian Mellitt, John O'Kane, Chris Rew

Business Description
A group engaged in capital projects, facilities
management and plant hire.

Jersey Electricity Company Ltd
Queens Road, St Helier, Jersey JE4 8NY
Telephone +44 (0) 1534 505460
Fax +44 (0) 1534 505565
Website www.jec.co.uk

Chair
Derek Maltwood
Chief Executive/Managing Director
Michael Liston
Board Members
Jeremy Arnold, Clive Chaplin, Christopher Evans,
Geoffrey Grime, Jean Le Maistre, Martin Magee, David
Padfield, Richard Plaster

Business Description
The company is the sole supplier of electricity in Jersey.
It also engages in electrical appliance retailing, property
management, building services and internet data hosting.

Jessops plc
Jessop House, Scudmore Road, Leicester LE3 1TZ
Telephone +44 (0) 116 232 0033
Website www.jessops.co.uk

Chair
David Adams
Chief Executive/Managing Director
Chris Langley
Board Members
Ian Harris, William Rollason

Business Description
A group engaged in photographic retail.

JJB Sports plc
Martland Park, Challenge Way, Wigan,
Lancashire WN5 0LD
Telephone +44 (0) 1942 221400
Fax +44 (0) 1942 629809
Website www.jjbcorporate.co.uk

Chair
Roger Lane-Smith
Chief Executive/Managing Director
Tom Knight
Board Members
David Beever, Roger Best, Barry Dunn, David
Greenwood, Chris Ronnie, Andrew Thomas

Business Description
A group engaged in the retail of sportswear and sports
equipment, and the operation of health clubs and indoor
soccer centres.

JKX Oil & Gas plc
6 Cavendish Square, London W1G 0PD
Telephone +44 (0) 20 7323 4464
Fax +44 (0) 20 7323 5258
Website www.jkx.co.uk

Chair
Lord Fraser of Carmylie
Chief Executive/Managing Director
Dr Paul Davies
Board Members
Viscount Asquith, Bruce Burrows, Robert Dall, John
Mapplebeck

Business Description
A group engaged in oil and gas exploration and
production.

John David Group plc (The)
Edinburgh House, Hollinsbrook Way, Pilsworth, Bury,
Lancashire BL9 8RR
Telephone +44 (0) 870 873 0333
Fax +44 (0) 161 767 1001
Website www.jdsports.co.uk

Chair
Peter Cowgill
Chief Executive/Managing Director
Barry Bown
Board Members
Colin Archer, Chris Bird, Brian Small

Business Description
A group engaged in the retail of sports and leisure wear.

John Menzies plc
108 Princes Street, Edinburgh EH2 3AA
Telephone +44 (0) 131 225 8555
Fax +44 (0) 131 226 3752
Website www.johnmenzies.com

Chair
William Thompson
Board Members
David Coltman, Ian Harrison, Octavia Morley, Dermot Jenkins, Ian Robertson, Craig Smyth, Ellis Watson

Business Description
A group engaged in the wholesale distribution of newspapers and magazines and the provision of cargo and ground handling services at airports.

John Wood Group plc
John Wood House, Greenwell Road, East Tullos Industrial Estate, Aberdeen AB12 3AX
Telephone +44 (0) 1224 851 000
Fax +44 (0) 1224 851 474
Website www.woodgroup.com

Chair
Sir Ian Wood
Chief Executive/Managing Director
Allister Langlands
Board Members
Wendell Brooks, Ewan Brown, Ian Marchant, Dr Christopher Masters, Robert Monti, John Morgan, Trevor Noble, John Ogren, Mark Papworth, Alan Semple, Neil Smith, Les Thomas

Business Description
A group engaged in the provision of oilfield logistics and engineering services, the supply of pumps and valves, and the repair of gas turbines.

Johnson Matthey plc
40-42 Hatton Garden, London EC1N 8EE
Telephone +44 (0) 20 7269 8400
Fax +44 (0) 20 7269 8433
Website www.matthey.com

Chair
Sir John Banham
Chief Executive/Managing Director
Neil Carson
Board Members
Michael Dearden, Pelham Hawker, Charles Mackay, David Morgan, Larry Pentz, Michael Roney, John Sheldrick, Ian Strachan, Alan Thomson, Robert Walvis

Business Description
A group engaged in the processing and marketing of precious metals, and the manufacture of catalysts, colours and coatings, and pharmaceutical materials.

Johnson Service Group plc
Johnson House, Abbots Park, Monks Way, Preston Brook, Cheshire WA7 3GH
Telephone +44 (0) 1928 704600
Fax +44 (0) 1928 704620
Website www.johnsonplc.com

Chair
Simon Sherrard
Board Members
Michael Del Mar, Michael Gatenby, Simon Moate, Charles Skinner, David Toon, Baroness Wilcox, James Wilkinson

Business Description
A group engaged in the rental and laundering of workwear, towels and dust mats, the sourcing and manufacture of garments, and the provision of washroom, drycleaning and associated services.

Johnston Press plc
53 Manor Place, Edinburgh EH3 7EG
Telephone +44 (0) 131 225 3361
Fax +44 (0) 131 225 4580
Website www.johnstonpress.co.uk

Chair
Roger Parry
Chief Executive/Managing Director
Tim Bowdler
Board Members
Danny Cammiade, Peter Cawdron, Les Hinton, Frederick Johnston, Martina King, Stuart Paterson, Ian Russell, Simon Waugh

Business Description
A group engaged in the publication and printing of local and regional weekly, evening and morning newspapers, specialist print publications together with associated websites.

JPMorgan American Investment Trust plc
Finsbury Dials, 20 Finsbury Street, London EC2Y 9AQ
Telephone +44 (0) 20 7742 6000
Fax +44 (0) 20 7600 0339
Website www.jpamerican.com

Chair
Hamish Buchan
Board Members
Sarah Bates, Kate Bolsover, James Fox, Dr George Greener, James Williams

Business Description
An investment trust.

JPMorgan Asian Investment Trust plc
Finsbury Dials, 20 Finsbury Street, London EC2Y 9AQ
Telephone +44 (0) 20 7742 6000
Fax +44 (0) 20 7742 3486
Website www.jpmasian.com

Chair
James Long
Board Members
Alun Evans, Ronald Gould, Christopher Penn, Andrew Sykes

Business Description
An investment trust investing in equities quoted on the stockmarkets of Asia.

JPMorgan Chinese Investment Trust plc
Finsbury Dials, 20 Finsbury Street, London EC2Y 9AQ
Telephone +44 (0) 20 7742 6000
Fax +44 (0) 20 7880 3486
Website www.jpmfchinese.com

Chair
Nigel Melville
Board Members
Sir Andrew Burns, William Knight, Irving Koo, Yujiang Zhao

Business Description
An investment trust.

JPMorgan Claverhouse Investment Trust plc
Finsbury Dials, 20 Finsbury Street, London EC2Y 9AQ
Telephone +44 (0) 20 7742 6000
Website www.jpmorganassetmanagement.co.uk

Chair
Sir Michael Bunbury
Board Members
Virginia Holmes, Peter Lilley, Anne McMeehan, John Scott

Business Description
An investment trust.

JPMorgan Emerging Markets Investment Trust plc
Finsbury Dials, 20 Finsbury Street, London EC2Y 9AQ
Telephone +44 (0) 20 7742 6000
Fax +44 (0) 20 7742 8000
Website www.jpmfemergingmarkets.com

Chair
Roy Reynolds
Board Members
David Gamble, Anatole Kaletsky, Roy Peters, Valentine Powell, Alan Saunders

Business Description
An investment trust.

JPMorgan European Fledgling Investment Trust plc
Finsbury Dials, 20 Finsbury Street, London EC2Y 9AQ
Telephone +44 (0) 20 7742 6000
Fax +44 (0) 20 7600 0339
Website www.jpmeuropeanfledgeling.co.uk

Chair
Liz Airey
Board Members
Anthony Davidson, Jacques Drossaert, Paul Manduca, Federico Marescotti, Michael Wrobel

Business Description
An investment trust.

JPMorgan European Investment Trust plc
Finsbury Dials, 20 Finsbury Street, London EC2Y 9AQ
Telephone +44 (0) 20 7762 6000
Fax +44 (0) 20 7600 0339
Website www.jpmeuropean.com

Chair
Andrew Murison
Board Members
Robin Faber, Stephen Russell, Ferdinand Verdonck, Alexander Zagoreos

Business Description
An investment trust.

JPMorgan Fleming Japanese Smaller Companies Investment Trust plc
Finsbury Dials, 20 Finsbury Street, London EC2Y 9AQ
Telephone +44 (0) 20 7742 6000
Website www.jpmfjapanesesmallercompanies.co.uk

Chair
Alan Clifton
Board Members
John Gibbon, Bernard Gribsby, George Long, Chris Russell

Business Description
An investment trust.

JPMorgan Fleming Mercantile Investment Trust plc
Finsbury Dials, 20 Finsbury Street, London EC2Y 9AQ
Telephone +44 (0) 20 7762 6000
Fax +44 (0) 20 7600 0339
Website www.jpmfmercantile.com

Chair
Hamish Leslie Melville
Board Members
Hon Nicholas Berry, Richard Hambro, Simon Keswick, Dr Sandy Nairn, Charles Peel, Viscount Rothermere, Ian Russell

Business Description
An investment trust company.

JPMorgan Income & Capital Investment Trust plc
Finsbury Dials, 20 Finsbury Street, London EC2Y 9AQ
Telephone +44 (0) 20 7742 6000
Fax +44 (0) 20 7600 0339
Website www.jpincomeandcapital.com

Chair
Sir Charles Nunneley
Board Members
Roderick Collins, Antony Hichens, Sam Hills, Sir Laurence Magnus, James West

Business Description
An investment company.

JPMorgan Indian Investment Trust plc
Finsbury Dials, 20 Finsbury Street, London EC2Y 9AQ
Telephone +44 (0) 20 7742 6000
Fax +44 (0) 20 7600 0339
Website www.jpmindian.com

Chair
Philip Daubeney
Board Members
David Baker, Hugh Bolland, Richard Burns, Pierre Dinan, Vijay Joshi, Iain Saunders

Business Description
A group engaged as an investment trust and investment holding company.

JPMorgan Japanese Investment Trust plc
Finsbury Dials, 20 Finsbury Street, London EC2Y 9AQ
Telephone +44 (0) 20 7762 6000
Website www.jpmfjapanese.com

Chair
Jeremy Paulson-Ellis
Board Members
Alan Barber, Andrew Fleming, David Pearson

Business Description
An investment trust.

JPMorgan Mid Cap Investment Trust plc
Finsbury Dials, 20 Finsbury Street, London EC2Y 9AQ
Telephone +44 (0) 20 7742 6000
Fax +44 (0) 20 7742 9002
Website www.jpmfmidcap.com

Chair
Andrew Barker
Board Members
John Emly, Gordon McQueen, Alexander Scott

Business Description
An investment trust.

JPMorgan Overseas Investment Trust plc
Finsbury Dials, 20 Finsbury Street, London EC2Y 9AQ
Telephone +44 (0) 20 7742 6000
Fax +44 (0) 20 7742 8000
Website www.jpmfoverseas.com

Chair
George Paul
Board Members
Richard Barfield, Simon Davies, Geoffrey Howe, John Rennocks

Business Description
An investment trust.

JPMorgan Russian Securities plc
Finsbury Dials, 20 Finsbury Street, London EC2Y 9AQ
Telephone +44 (0) 20 7742 6000
Website www.jpmfrussian.com

Chair
Pamela Idelson Smith
Board Members
Patrick Gifford, James Nicholson, Paul Teleki, Lysander
Tennant

Business Description
An investment trust.

JPMorgan Smaller Companies Investment Trust plc
Finsbury Dials, 20 Finsbury Street, London EC2Y 9AQ
Telephone +44 (0) 20 7742 6000
Fax +44 (0) 20 7600 0339
Website www.jpmfsmallercompanies.com

Chair
Strone Macpherson
Board Members
Ivo Coulson, Lord Richard Fitzalan Howard, Michael
Quicke

Business Description
An investment trust.

JPMorgan US Discovery Investment Trust plc
Finsbury Dials, 20 Finsbury Street, London EC2Y 9AQ
Telephone +44 (0) 20 7742 6000
Website www.jpmusdiscovery.com

Chair
Hon Robin Lewis
Board Members
Mark Ansell, Christopher Galleymore, Alan Kemp, Davina
Walter

Business Description
An investment trust.

Jupiter Dividend & Growth Trust plc
1 Grosvenor Place, London SW1X 7JJ
Telephone +44 (0) 20 7412 0703
Fax +44 (0) 20 7412 0705
Website www.jupiteronline.co.uk

Chair
Martin Boase
Board Members
Keith Bray, Lord Hamilton of Epsom, Reef Hogg

Business Description
An investment trust.

Jupiter European Opportunities Trust plc
1 Grosvenor Place, London SW1X 7JJ
Telephone +44 (0) 20 7412 0703
Fax +44 (0) 20 7314 4873
Website www.jupiteronline.co.uk

Chair
Hugh Priestley
Board Members
Alexander Darwall, Sir Marrack Goulding, Jackson
Robinson, John Wallinger

Business Description
An investment trust with a dealing subsidiary.

Jupiter Green Investment Trust plc
1 Grosvenor Place, London SW1X 7JJ
Telephone +44 (0) 20 7412 0703
Fax +44 (0) 20 7314 4873
Website www.jupiteronline.co.uk

Chair
Perry Crothwaite
Board Members
Polly Courtice, Tristan Hillgarth, Alexander Hoare

Business Description
An investment trust.

Jupiter Primadona Growth Trust plc
1 Grosvenor Place, London SW1X 7JJ
Telephone +44 (0) 20 7412 0703
Fax +44 (0) 20 7314 4873
Website www.jupiteronline.co.uk

Chair
Martin Myerscough
Board Members
John Chatfeild-Roberts, James D'Albiac, Peter Glossop,
Frances Heaton, Adrian Paterson, Lorna Tilbian

Business Description
An investment trust with a dealing subsidiary.

Jupiter Second Enhanced Income Trust plc
1 Grosvenor Place, London SW1X 7JJ
Telephone +44 (0) 20 7412 0703
Fax +44 (0) 20 7314 4873
Website www.jupiteronline.co.uk

Chair
James West
Board Members
Wilfrid Caldwell, Christopher Jones, Christopher Munro,
Anthony Nutt

Business Description
An investment trust.

Jupiter Second Split Trust plc
1 Grosvenor Place, London SW1X 7JJ
Telephone +44 (0) 20 7412 0703
Fax +44 (0) 20 7314 4873
Website www.jupiteronline.co.uk

Chair
Gordon Campbell
Board Members
Patrick Gibbs, Harry Hill, Lord Lamont of Lerwick,
Dennis Thoy

Business Description
An investment trust.

Just Retirement (Holdings) plc
Vale House, Roebuck House, Bancroft Road, Reigate,
Surrey RH2 7RU
Telephone +44 (0) 1737 233206
Fax +44 (0) 1737 227191
Website www.justretirement.com

Chair
Tom Cross Brown
Chief Executive/Managing Director
Mike Fuller
Board Members
Peter Halen, Clifton Melvin, Ralph Peters, Simon Thomas,
Gay Welch, Bert Wiegman

Business Description
A company engaged in the provision of life assurance
services.

JZ Equity Partners plc
17A Curzon Street, London W1J 5HS
Telephone +44 (0) 20 7491 3633
Fax +44 (0) 20 7493 6650
Website www.jzep.co.uk

Chair
Andrew Withey
Board Members
John Green-Armytage, James Jordan, David Macfarlane,
Michael Sorkin, Tanja Tibaldi

Business Description
An investment trust investing in businesses primarily in
the US.

Kazakhmys plc
6th & 7th Floor, Cardinal Place, 100 Victoria Street,
London SW1E 5JD
Telephone +44 (0) 20 901 7800
Fax +44 (0) 20 901 7859
Website www.kazakhmys.com

Chair
Vladimir Kim
Chief Executive/Managing Director
Oleg Novachuk
Board Members
Philip Aiken, Simon Heale, Matthew Hird, David Munro,
Vladimir Ni, Lord Renwick of Clifton, James Rutland

Business Description
Mining, processing, smelting, refining and sale of copper
and copper products, including copper cathode and
copper rod.

KCOM Group plc
37 Carr Lane, Kingston-upon-Hull HU1 3RE
Telephone +44 (0) 1482 602711
Fax +44 (0) 1482 219289
Website www.kcom.com

Chair
Michael Abrahams
Chief Executive/Managing Director
Malcolm Fallen
Board Members
John Carrington, Sean Christie, Neil Gower, Peter Halls,
Bill Halbert, Paul Simpson, Kevin Walsh

Business Description
A group engaged in the provision of a range of
information and communications technology and
telecommunications services to businesses and selected
consumer markets.

Kelda Group plc
Western House, Halifax Road, Bradford, West
Yorkshire BD6 2SZ
Telephone +44 (0) 1274 600111
Fax +44 (0) 1274 608 608
Website www.keldagroup.com

Chair
John Napier
Chief Executive/Managing Director
Kevin Whiteman
Board Members
Ed Anderson, Kate Avery, Christopher Fisher, David
Salkeld, Martin Towers

Business Description
A group engaged in the supply of clean water and the
treatment and disposal of waste water.

Keller
12th Floor, Capital House, Chapel Street,
London NW1 5DH
Website www.keller.co.uk

Chair
Dr Michael West
Chief Executive/Managing Director
Justin Atkinson
Board Members
Dr Kevin Bond, Gerry Brown, Roy Franklin, James Hind,
Pedro Lopez Jimenez, Keith Payne, Richard Scholes, Dr
Wolfgang Sonderman

Business Description
A group specialising in ground engineering.

Kenmore European Industrial Fund Ltd
Trafalgar Court, Les Banques, St Peter Port,
Guernsey GY1 3QL
Telephone +44 (0) 1481 745001
Website www.kenmoreeifund.com

Chair
Giles Weaver
Board Members
Jonathan Gamble, Helen Green, John Kennedy,
Christopher Spencer

Business Description
An investment fund.

Kesa Electricals plc
22-24 Ely Place, London EC1N 6TE
Telephone +44 (0) 20 7269 1400
Fax +44 (0) 20 7269 1405
Website www.kesaelectricals.com

Chair
David Newlands
Chief Executive/Managing Director
Jean-Noël Labroue
Board Members
Michel Brossard, Bernard Dufau, Simon Herrick, Andrew
Robb, Peter Wilson

Business Description
A group engaged in the retailing of electricals and
furniture throughout Europe.

Kewill Systems plc
Oaklands House, 34 Washway Road, Sale,
Cheshire M33 6FS
Telephone +44 (0) 20 8971 6774
Fax +44 (0) 20 8971 6767
Website www.kewill.com

Chair
Andrew Roberts
Chief Executive/Managing Director
Paul Nichols
Board Members
Charles Alexander, Richard Gawthorne, Guy Millward

Business Description
A group engaged in the provision of computer software
and associated services.

Keystone Investment Trust plc
30 Finsbury Square, London EC2A 1AG
Telephone +44 (0) 20 7065 4000
Website www.invescoperpetual.co.uk/investments

Chair
Richard Oldfield
Board Members
David Adams, Beatrice Hollond, William Kindall, Peter
Readman

Business Description
An investment trust.

Kier Group plc
Tempsford Hall, Sandy, Bedfordshire SG19 2BD
Telephone +44 (0) 1767 640111
Fax +44 (0) 1767 640002
Website www.kier.co.uk

Chair
Peter Warry
Chief Executive/Managing Director
John Dodds
Board Members
Peter Berry, Ian Lawson, Simon Leathes, Deena Mattar,
Mick O'Farrell, Paul Sheffield, Dick Side, Dick Simkin,
Phil White

Business Description
A group engaged in construction support services,
residential and commercial development, and
infrastructure project investment.

Kiln plc
106 Fenchurch Street, London EC3M 5NR
Telephone +44 (0) 20 7886 9000
Fax +44 (0) 20 7488 1848
Website www.kilnplc.com

Chair
Nicholas Cosh
Chief Executive/Managing Director
Edward Creasy
Board Members
William Berkley, W Robert Berkley, Robert Chase, Peter
Haynes, Paul Hewitt, Elizabeth Murphy, David Woods

Business Description
A group engaged in the transaction of general insurance
business, principally through Lloyd's.

Kingfisher plc
3 Sheldon Square, London W2 6PX
Telephone +44 (0) 20 7372 8008
Fax +44 (0) 20 7644 1001
Website www.kingfisher.co.uk

Chair
Peter Jackson
Chief Executive/Managing Director
Gerry Murphy
Board Members
Phillip Bentley, Daniel Bernard, Ian Cheshire, Michael
Hepher, Janis Kong, Hartmut Krämer, John Nelson,
Duncan Tatton-Brown

Business Description
An international home improvement business. The group
also has property interests.

Kirkland Lake Gold Inc
Macassa Mine, PO Box 370, Kirkland Lake, Ontario P2N
3J7, Canada
Telephone +1 705 567 5208
Website www.klgold.com

Chair
Harry Dobson
Chief Executive/Managing Director
Brian Hinchcliffe
Board Members
Brian Bayley, Paul Kostuik, George Milton

Business Description
A company engaged in exploring, developing and
producing gold properties.

KSK Power Ventur plc
15-19 Athol Street, Douglas, Isle of Man IM1 1LB
Telephone +91 40 23559922
Fax +91 40 2355 9930
Website www.ksk.co.in

Chair
Padma Bhushan T L Sankar
Board Members
S R Lyer, Abhay Nalawade, Girish Kulkami, Dr Rajendra
Singh

Business Description
A company engaged in the development of private power
projects in India.

Ladbrokes plc
Imperial House, Imperial Drive, Rayners Lane, Harrow,
Middlesex HA2 7JW
Telephone +44 (0) 20 8868 8899
Fax +44 (0) 20 8868 8767
Website www.ladbrokesplc.com

Chair
Sir Ian Robinson
Chief Executive/Managing Director
Christopher Bell
Board Members
John Jarvis, Nicholas Jones, John O'Reilly, Christopher
Rodrigues, Alan Ross, Henry Staunton, Brian Wallace,
Pippa Wicks

Business Description
A group engaged in betting and gaming.

Laird Group plc (The)
100 Pall Mall, London SW1Y 5NQ
Telephone +44 (0) 20 7468 4040
Fax +44 (0) 20 7439 2921
Website www.laird-plc.com

Chair
Nigel Keen
Chief Executive/Managing Director
Peter Hill
Board Members
Sir Christopher Hum, Prof Michael Kelly, Martin Rapp,
Anthony Reading, Andrew Robb, Jonathan Silver, Dr
William Spivey

Business Description
A group engaged in the design, development,
manufacture and supply of security products, the
distribution of plastics and products, and the design and
supply of EMI shielding solutions.

Lambert Howarth Group plc
26 Manchester Square, London W1U 3PZ
Telephone +44 (0) 20 7258 9900
Fax +44 (0) 20 7935 3814
Website www.lamberthowarth.com

Chair
Alfred Vinton
Chief Executive/Managing Director
Pamela Harper
Board Members
Stewart Binnie, Susan Hobden

Business Description
A group engaged in the design, resourcing and
distribution of footwear, homeware and accessories for
supply to retailers.

Lamprell plc
PO Box 5427, Dubai, United Arab Emirates
Telephone +9716 528 2323
Fax +9716 528 4325
Website www.lamprell.com

Chair and Chief Executive
Peter Whitbread
Board Members
Peter Birch, Scott Doak, Nigel McCue, David Moran,
Richard Raynaut

Business Description
A company engaged in the provision of engineering
services to the oil and gas industries.

Lancashire Holdings Ltd
Clarendon House, 2 Church Street, Hamilton HM11,
Bermuda
Telephone +1 441 278 8950
Fax +1 441 278 8951
Website www.lancashiregroup.com

Chair
Robert Spass
Chief Executive/Managing Director
Richard Brindle
Board Members
Colin Alexander, Neil McConachie, Ralf Oelssner, William
Spiegel, Barry Volpert

Business Description
A company engaged in the provision of specialty
insurance products.

Land of Leather Holdings plc
Unit K1 and K2, Northfleet Industrial Estate, Lower Road,
Northfleet, Kent DA11 9BL
Telephone +44 (0) 1474 322277
Fax +44 (0) 1474 360428
Website www.landofleather.co.uk

Chair
Roger Matthews
Chief Executive/Managing Director
Paul Briant
Board Members
Patrick Deigman, Clive Hatchard, Malcolm Heald, Stephen
Jenkins, Richard Kirk, Peter Ling, Gillian Wilmot

Business Description
A group engaged as a retailer of leather sofas in the UK
and Ireland.

Land Securities Group plc
5 Strand, London WC2N 5AF
Telephone +44 (0) 20 7413 9000
Fax +44 (0) 20 7925 0202
Website www.landsecurities.co.uk

Chair
Paul Myners
Chief Executive/Managing Director
Francis Salway
Board Members
Richard Akers, Sir Win Bischoff, Alison Carnwath, Ian
Ellis, Martin Greenslade, Michael Hussey, Bo Lerenius,
Stuart Rose, David Rough

Business Description
A group engaged in property development and portfolio
management of offices, shops, warehouses, food
superstores, leisure and industrial premises and property
outsourcing.

Latchways plc
Hopton Park, Devizes, Wiltshire SN10 3JP
Telephone +44 (0) 1380 732700
Fax +44 (0) 1380 732701
Website www.latchways.com

Chair
Paul Hearson
Chief Executive/Managing Director
David Hearson
Board Members
Brian Finlayson, Alistair Hogg, Per Troen

Business Description
A group engaged in the production, distribution and
installation of industrial safety products.

Laura Ashley Holdings plc
27 Bagleys Lane, Fulham, London SW6 2QA
Telephone +44 (0) 20 7880 5100
Fax +44 (0) 20 7880 5200
Website www.lauraashley.com

Chair
Tan Sri Dr Khoo Kay Peng
Chief Executive/Managing Director
Lillian Tan Lian Tee
Board Members
Roger Bambrough, Sally Cheong Siew Mooi, David Cook,
Sally Kealey, Andrew Khoo, David Walton Masters

Business Description
A company engaged in the retail of home furnishings,
women's and children's clothes, flowers and gifts.

Lavendon Group plc
1 Midland Court, Central Park, Lutterworth,
Leicestershire LE17 4PN
Telephone +44 (0) 1455 558874
Fax +44 (0) 1455 559569
Website www.lavendongroup.com

Chair
John Gordon
Chief Executive/Managing Director
Kevin Appleton
Board Members
David Hollywood, Alan Merrell, Tim Ross, John Standen

Business Description
A group engaged in the rental of powered access
equipment.

Law Debenture Corporation plc (The)
5th Floor, 100 Wood Street, London EC2V 7EX
Telephone +44 (0) 20 7606 5451
Fax +44 (0) 20 7606 0643
Website www.lawdeb.co.uk

Chair
Douglas McDougall
Board Members
Caroline Banszky, Armel Cates, John Kay, Robert
Williams

Business Description
An investment trust which is also part of a group
engaged in the provision of trustee services.

Laxey Investment Trust plc (The)
One London Wall, London EC2Y 5AB
Website www.teaplantations.co.uk

Chair
D E H Panter
Board Members
D J M Blacker, J C Colville, C W Kingsnorth, A Boyd

Business Description
An investment trust.

Legal & General Group plc
Temple Court, 11 Queen Victoria Street,
London EC4N 4TP
Telephone +44 (0) 20 7528 6200
Fax +44 (0) 20 7528 6222
Website www.legalandgeneralgroup.com

Chair
Sir Robert Margetts
Chief Executive/Managing Director
Tim Breedon
Board Members
Kate Avery, Frances Heaton, Rudy Markham, Andrew
Palmer, John Pollock, Dr Ronaldo Schmitz, Henry
Staunton, James Strachan, Sir David Walker

Business Description
A group engaged in the transaction of life pensions and
general insurance business, and the provision of
investment management services.

Liberty International plc
40 Broadway, London SW1H 0BT
Telephone +44 (0) 20 7960 1200
Fax +44 (0) 207 960 1333
Website www.liberty-international.co.uk

Chair
Sir Robert Finch
Chief Executive/Managing Director
David Fischel
Board Members
John Abel, Robin Buchanan, Patrick Burgess, Richard
Cable, Kay Chaldecott, Graeme Gordan, Ian Hawksworth,
Ian Henderson, Lesley James, Michael Rapp, Rob Rowley,
Neil Sachdev, Aidan Smith

Business Description
A group engaged in the ownership and development of
regional shopping centres and investing in commercial
and retail property in the UK and USA.

Life Offices Opportunities Trust plc
6th Floor, 7 Castle Streeet, Edinburgh EH2 3AH
Telephone +44 (0) 131 226 6699
Fax +44 (0) 131 226 7799
Website www.svmonline.co.uk

Chair
John Brumwell
Board Members
John Motion, Raymond Paul, John Wilson

Business Description
An investment trust.

Lindsell Train Investment Trust plc (The)
Springfield Lodge, Colchester Road, Chelmsford,
Essex CM2 5PW
Telephone +44 (0) 1245 398950
Fax +44 (0) 1245 398951
Website www.lindselltrain.co.uk

Chair
Rhoderick Swire
Board Members
Donald Adamson, Dominic Caldecott, Michael Lindsell,
Michael Mackenzie

Business Description
An investment trust.

Liontrust Asset Management plc
2 Savoy Court, London WC2R 0EZ
Telephone +44 (0) 20 7412 1700
Fax +44 (0) 20 7412 1779
Website www.liontrust.co.uk

Chair
Bernard Asher
Chief Executive/Managing Director
Nigel Legge
Board Members
Vinay Abrol, Glyn Hirsch, Jeremy Lang, William
Pattisson, Jim Sanger

Business Description
A holding company for a group engaged in the
management of investment funds and unit trusts.

Litho Supplies plc
Unit 2, Chapel Way, Avon Valley Business Parl, St
Annes, Bristol BS4 4EU
Telephone +44 (0) 117 972 4455
Fax +44 (0) 117 972 0122
Website www.litho.co.uk

Chair
Bernard Clark
Chief Executive/Managing Director
Michael Hammond
Board Members
Gerry Mitchell, Christopher Powles, Eddie Williams

Business Description
A group engaged in the supply of printing and graphic
arts materials and equipment.

Lloyds TSB Group plc
25 Gresham Street, London EC2V 7HN
Telephone +44 (0) 20 7626 1500
Website www.lloydstsb.com

Chair
Sir Victor Blank
Chief Executive/Managing Director
J Eric Daniels
Board Members
Dr Wolfgang Berndt, Ewan Brown, Terri Dial, Jan du
Plessis, Michael Fairey, Gavin Gemmell, Philip Green, Sir
Julian Horn-Smith, Archie Kane, Lord Leitch, G Truett
Tate, Helen Weir

Business Description
A group engaged in the provision of banking and
financial services.

LMS Capital plc
Carlton House, 33 Robert Adam Street, London W1U 2HR
Telephone +44 (0) 20 7935 3555
Fax +44 (0) 20 7935 3737
Website www.lmscapital.com

Chair
Jonathan Agnew
Chief Executive/Managing Director
Robert Rayne
Board Members
John Barnsley, Richard Christou, Bernard Duroc-Danner,
Martin Pexton, Tony Sweet

Business Description
An investment company.

Local Shopping REIT plc (The)
4th Floor, 11 Hanover Street, London W1S 1YQ
Telephone +44 (0) 20 7187 4444
Fax +44 (0) 20 7187 4441
Website www.localshoppingreit.co.uk

Chair
John Whateley
Chief Executive/Managing Director
Nick Gregory and Mike Riley
Board Members
Andrew Cunningham, Nicholas Vetch, Victoria
Whitehouse

Business Description
An investment trust.

LogicaCMG plc
Stephenson House, 75 Hampstead Road,
London NW1 2PL
Telephone +44 (0) 20 7637 9111
Fax +44 (0) 20 7872 8994
Website www.logicacmg.com

Chair
Cor Stutterheim
Board Members
Wim Dik, Noël Harwerth, Dr Wolfhart Hauser, Didier
Herrmann, Seamus Keating, Angela Knight, George
Loudon, Jim McKenna, Roger Payne, Gérard Philippot,
Crister Stjernfelt, David Tyler

Business Description
The marketing, design, production and maintenance of
software and hardware systems, information technology
consultancy, and the development, design and marketing
of software products.

London & Associated Properties plc
Carlton House, 22A St James Square, London SW1Y 4JH
Telephone +44 (0) 20 7415 5000
Fax +44 (0) 20 7839 5999
Website www.lap.co.uk

Chair
Michael Heller
Chief Executive/Managing Director
John Heller
Board Members
Robert Corry, Howard Goldring, Barry O'Connell, Clive
Parritt, Michael Stevens

Business Description
A group engaged in property investment and investment
trading.

London & St Lawrence Investment Company plc
Woodside, Maidstone Road, Colts Hill, Pembury,
Kent TN2 4AL
Telephone +44 (0) 1892 824445
Fax +44 (0) 1892 822994
Website www.londonandstlawrence.com

Chair
Gerald Ashfield
Board Members
Philip Ashfield, Alan Maidment, John Paget, Jenny
Sculley

Business Description
An investment trust with a subsidiary engaged in unit
trust management.

London Finance & Investment Group plc
30 City Road, London EC1Y 2AG
Telephone +44 (0) 20 7448 8950
Fax +44 (0) 20 7638 9426
Website www.city-group.com

Chair
David Marshall
Board Members
Dr Frank Lucas, John Maxwell, Michael Robotham

Business Description
A group engaged in investment, finance and
management.

London Scottish Bank plc
London Scottish House, Mount Street, Manchester M2 3LS
Telephone +44 (0) 161 834 2861
Fax +44 (0) 161 834 4869
Website www.london-scottish.com

Chair
Peter Cordrey
Board Members
Alan Benzie, Steve Burnett, Dennis Lee, Patrick
McDonnell, Robert Mee, Mark Tattersall

Business Description
A group engaged in the provision of financial and
banking services, principally consumer credit, debt
collection, reinsurance factoring and leasing.

London Stock Exchange plc
10 Paternoster Square, London EC4M 7LS
Telephone +44 (0) 20 7797 1000
Website www.londonstockexchange.com

Chair
Dr Christopher Gibson-Smith
Chief Executive/Managing Director
Clara Furse
Board Members
Gary Allen, Baroness Cohen of Pimlico, Oscar Fanjul,
Jonathan Howell, Peter Meinertzhagen, Nigel Stapleton,
Robert Webb

Business Description
A group engaged in the admission of securities to
trading, the delivery of trading systems, the organisation
and regulation of markets, and the provision of
information services.

Lonmin plc
4 Grosvenor Place, London SW1X 7YL
Telephone +44 (0) 20 7201 6000
Fax +44 (0) 20 7201 6100
Website www.lonmin.com

Chair
Sir John Craven
Chief Executive/Managing Director
Bradford Mills
Board Members
Karen de Segundo, Ian Farmer, Alan Ferguson, Peter
Godsoe, Dr Sivandran Gounden, Michael Hartnall, Roger
Phillimore

Business Description
A group engaged in the mining, refining and sale of
platinum group metals.

Lookers plc
776 Chester Road, Stretford, Manchester M32 0QH
Telephone +44 (0) 161 291 0043
Fax +44 (0) 161 864 2363
Website www.lookers.co.uk

Chair
Phil White
Chief Executive/Managing Director
Ken Surgenor
Board Members
David Blakeman, Tony Bramall, John Brown, Andrew
Bruce, David Dyson, David Mace, Brian Schumacker,
Terence Wainwright

Business Description
A group engaged in the sale, hire and maintenance of
motor vehicles and motorcycles, including the sale of
tyres, oil parts and accessories.

Low & Bonar plc
50 Seymour Street, London W1H 7JG
Telephone +44 (0) 20 7535 3180
Fax +44 (0) 20 7535 3181
Website www.lowandbonar.com

Chair
Duncan Clegg
Chief Executive/Managing Director
Paul Forman
Board Members
Folkert Blaisse, Martin Flower, Stephen Hannam, Kevin
Higginson, Chris Littmoden

Business Description
A group engaged in the manufacture of high performance
floor coverings, polypropylene yarns, and fabric products
and rotationally moulded plastics.

Lowland Investment Company plc
4 Broadgate, London EC2M 2DA
Telephone +44 (0) 20 7818 1818
Fax +44 (0) 20 7818 1819
Website www.lowlandinvestment.com

Chair
John Hancox
Board Members
Rupert Barclay, Tracy Long, Michael Moule, Peter
Troughton

Business Description
An investment trust.

LSL Property Services plc
Newcastle House, Albany Court, Newcastle Business
Park, Newcastle-upon-Tyne NE4 7YB
Telephone +44 (0) 1904 715324
Fax +44 (0) 1904 715354
Website www.islps.co.uk

Chair
Roger Matthews
Chief Executive/Managing Director
Simon Embley
Board Members
Dean Fielding, Peter Hales, Paul Latham, Mark Morris,
Mark Warburton

Business Description
A residential property services company involved in
estate agency, surveying and financial services.

Luminar plc
Luminar House, Deltic Avenue, Rooksley, Milton
Keynes MK13 8LW
Telephone +44 (0) 1908 544100
Fax +44 (0) 1908 394721
Website www.luminar.co.uk

Chair
Alan Jackson
Chief Executive/Managing Director
Stephen Thomas
Board Members
Nick Beighton, Richard Brooke, Martin Gatto, Debbie
Hewitt, John Jackson

Business Description
A group engaged in the ownership, development and
operation of discotheques, theme bars and restaurants.

Lupus Capital plc
85 Buckingham Gate, London SW1E 6PD
Telephone +44 (0) 20 7976 8000
Fax +44 (0) 20 7976 8014
Website www.lupuscapital.co.uk

Chair
Greg Hutchings
Board Members
James Botherton, Fred Hoad, Denis Mulhall, Michael
Jackson, Roland Tate

Business Description
A company engaged in the manufacture, supply and
distribution of products, goods and services to the oil and
gas industries.

M&G Income Investment Company Ltd
Dorey Court, Admiral Park, St Peter Port,
Guernsey GY1 3BG
Telephone +44 (0) 800 328 3191
Website www.mandg.co.uk

Chair
Charles Parkinson
Board Members
Sam Dow, Richard Hughes, John Hunter, Nigel le Quesne

Business Description
An investment company.

M&G Recovery Investment Company Ltd
Dorey Court, Admiral Park, St Peter Port,
Guernsey GY1 3BG
Telephone +44 (0) 1481 727111
Fax +44 (0) 1481 728317
Website www.mandg.co.uk

Chair
John Hallam
Board Members
Julia Chapman, Richard Hughes, Michael Merrick, Russell
Morris

Business Description
An investment company.

Macfarlane Group plc
21 Newton Place, Glasgow G3 7PY
Telephone +44 (0) 141 333 9666
Fax +44 (0) 141 333 1988
Website www.macfarlanegroup.net

Chair
Archibald Hunter
Chief Executive/Managing Director
Peter Atkinson
Board Members
Graeme Bissett, Graham Casey, John Love, Kevin Mellor

Business Description
A group engaged in the manufacture and distribution of
packaging, specialist printing and the provision of storage
and warehousing services.

Macro 4 plc
The Orangery, Turners Hill Road, Worth, Crawley, West
Sussex RH10 4SS
Telephone +44 (0) 1293 872000
Fax +44 (0) 1293 872001
Website www.macro4.com

Chair
Albert Morris
Chief Executive/Managing Director
Ronnie Wilson
Board Members
Laurent Burns, Richard Burns, David Cowie, Graeme
Gordon, Alan Sloan

Business Description
A group engaged in the development, production,
marketing and sale of systems software solutions for
mainframe and open systems platform environments
across the globe.

Majedie Investments plc
1 Minster Court, Mincing Lane, London EC3R 7ZZ
Telephone +44 (0) 20 7626 1243
Fax +44 (0) 20 7929 0904
Website www.majedie.co.uk

Chair
Henry Barlow
Chief Executive/Managing Director
Robert Clarke
Board Members
Gerald Aherne, J William Barlow, Gillian Leates, Hubert
Reid

Business Description
An investment company that primarily invests in listed
securities across the world.

Majestic Wine plc
Majestic House, Otterspool Way, Watford,
Hertfordshire WD25 8WW
Telephone +44 (0) 1923 298200
Fax +44 (0) 1923 819105
Website www.majestic.co.uk

Chair
Simon Burke
Chief Executive/Managing Director
Timothy How
Board Members
Nigel Alldritt, Justin Apthorp, Paul Dermody, Helen
Keays, Stephen Lewis

Business Description
A group engaged in the retail of wines and beers.

Mallett plc
141 New Bond Street, London W1S 2BS
Telephone +44 (0) 20 7499 7411
Fax +44 (0) 20 7495 3179
Website www.mallettantiques.com

Chair
George Magan
Chief Executive/Managing Director
Lanto Synge
Board Members
Lord Daresbury, James Heneage, Giles Hutchinson-Smith,
Eloy Michotte, Henry Nevile, Michael Smyth-Osbourne,
Thomas Woodham-Smith

Business Description
A group engaged as dealers in high quality antique
furniture, glass and works of art.

Man Group plc
Sugar Quay, Lower Thames Street, London EC3R 6DU
Telephone +44 (0) 20 7144 1000
Fax +44 (0) 20 7144 1923
Website www.mangroupplc.com

Chair
Harvey McGrath
Chief Executive/Managing Director
Peter Clarke
Board Members
Jon Aisbitt, Alison Carnwath, Kevin Davis, Dugald Eadie,
Stanley Fink, Kevin Hayes, Glen Moreno

Business Description
A group engaged in the provision of asset management
and brokerage services.

Management Consulting Group plc
Fleet Place House, 2 Fleet Place, Holborn Viaduct,
London EC4M 7RF
Telephone +44 (0) 20 7710 5000
Fax +44 (0) 20 7710 5001
Website www.mcgplc.com

Chair
Dr Rolf Stomberg
Chief Executive/Managing Director
Kevin Parry
Board Members
Alan Barber, Jean Bolduc, Baroness Cohen of Pimlico,
Stephen Ferriss, Andrew Simon

Business Description
A group engaged in the provision of management
consulting services.

Manchester & London Investment Trust plc
2nd Floor, Arthur House, Chorlton Street,
Manchester M1 3FH
Telephone +44 (0) 161 228 1709
Fax +44 (0) 161 228 2510
Website www.midasim.co.uk

Chair
Peter Stanley
Board Members
Brian Sheppard, Martin Wilbraham

Business Description
An investment trust.

Manganese Bronze Holdings plc
Holyhead Road, Coventry CV5 8JJ
Telephone +44 (0) 1908 540083
Fax +44 (0) 1908 540081
Website www.manganese.com

Chair
Tim Melville-Ross
Chief Executive/Managing Director
John Russell
Board Members
Mark Fryer, Christopher Ross, Peter Shillcock, Andrew
Walker

Business Description
A group engaged in specialty automative and taxi
services.

Mapeley Ltd
20th Floor, Euston Tower, 286 Euston Road,
London NW1 3AS
Telephone +44 (0) 20 7788 1700
Website www.mapeley.com

Chair
Wes Edens
Chief Executive/Managing Director
Jamie Hopkins
Board Members
Roger Carey, Michael Fascitelli, John Harris, Charles
Parkinson

Business Description
Acquisition, ownership and management of commercial
properties.

Marchpole Holdings plc
19-20 Berners Street, London W1T 3LW
Telephone +44 (0) 20 7908 7777
Fax +44 (0) 20 7323 9196
Website www.marchpole.com

Chair
Christopher Phillips
Board Members
Raymond Harris, Michael Morris, Harvey Shulman,
Ronald Stirling

Business Description
A group engaged in the design, production and
distribution of designer menswear and womenswear to
the retail trade.

Marks & Spencer Group plc
Waterside House, 35 North Wharf Road,
London W2 1NW
Telephone +44 (0) 20 7935 4422
Fax +44 (0) 20 7487 2679
Website www.marksandspencer.com

Chair
Lord Burns
Chief Executive/Managing Director
Stuart Rose
Board Members
Jeremy Darroch, Ian Dyson, Steven Holliday, Jack Keenan,
Martha Lane Fox, Sir David Michels, Graham Oakley,
Lady Patten, Steven Sharp

Business Description
A group engaged in retailing and financial services.

Marshalls plc
81 Birkby Grange, Birkby Hall Road, Huddersfield, West Yorkshire HD2 2YA
Telephone +44 (0) 1422 306400
Website www.marshalls.co.uk

Chair
Mike Davies
Chief Executive/Managing Director
Graham Holden
Board Members
Andrew Allner, Ian Burrell, Bill Husselby, David Sarti, Richard Scholes

Business Description
A company engaged in the manufacture of stone and concrete hard landscaping products.

Marston's plc
Marston's House, Wolverhampton WV1 4JT
Telephone +44 (0) 1902 711811
Fax +44 (0) 1902 429136
Website www.marstons.co.uk

Chair
David Thompson
Chief Executive/Managing Director
Ralph Findlay
Board Members
Derek Andrew, Roz Cuschieri, Alistair Darby, Miles Emley, Lord Hodgson of Astley Abbotts, Paul Inglett, Peter Lipscomb, Stephen Oliver

Business Description
A group engaged in the operation of managed, tenanted and leased public houses, the brewing of beer and the wholesale of beer and wines and spirits.

Martin Currie Pacific Trust plc
Saltire Court, 20 Castle Terrace, Edinburgh EH1 2ES
Telephone +44 (0) 131 100 2151
Fax +44 (0) 131 222 2532
Website www.martincurriepacific.com

Chair
Patrick Gifford
Board Members
Peter Edwards, John Scott, Greg Shenkman, Michael Thomas, Harry Wells

Business Description
An investment trust investing worldwide.

Martin Currie Portfolio Investment Trust plc
Saltire Court, 20 Castle Terrace, Edinburgh EH1 2ES
Telephone +44 (0) 131 100 2151
Fax +44 (0) 131 222 2532
Website www.martincurrieportfolio.com

Chair
Peter Berry
Board Members
Ian Bodie, David Kidd, Douglas Kinloch-Anderson, Gillian Nott, Benjamin Thomson

Business Description
An investment trust.

Marylebone Warwick Balfour Group plc
1 West Garden Place, Kendal Street, London W2 2AQ
Telephone +44 (0) 20 7706 2121
Fax +44 (0) 20 7706 8181
Website www.mwb.co.uk

Chair
Eric Sanderson
Chief Executive/Managing Director
Richard Balfour-Lynn
Board Members
Michael Bibring, Andrew Blurton, Robert Burrow, David Marshall, Jagtar Singh

Business Description
A group engaged in property investment and development, including the provision of serviced office facilities and the operation of hotels and Liberty department stores.

Max Petroleum plc
Second Floor, 81 Piccadilly, London W1J 8HY
Telephone +44 (0) 20 7355 9590
Fax +44 (0) 20 7355 9591
Website www.maxpetroleum.com

Chair
James Jeffs
Chief Executive/Managing Director
Steven Kappelle
Board Members
David Belding, Robert Holland III, Lee Kraus, Maksut Narikbayer

Business Description
A group engaged in oil and gas exploration, development and production, focusing on Kazakhstan.

May Gurney Integrated Services plc
Trowse, Norwich NR14 8SZ
Telephone +44 (0) 1603 727272
Fax +44 (0) 1603 727400
Website www.maygurney.co.uk

Chair
Tim Ross
Chief Executive/Managing Director
David Sterry
Board Members
Richard Dean, Michael Dunn, Ian Findlater, David Galloway

Business Description
A company engaged in the provision support and construction services to the highways, rail, utilities and general infrastructure markets.

McBride plc
McBride House, Penn Road, Beaconsfield, Buckinghamshire HP9 2FY
Telephone +44 (0) 1494 607050
Fax +44 (0) 1494 607055
Website www.mcbride.co.uk

Chair
Iain Napier
Chief Executive/Managing Director
Miles Roberts
Board Members
Robert Beveridge, Christine Bogdanowicz-Bindert, Robert Lee, Colin Smith, Henri Talerman

Business Description
A group engaged in the manufacture of private label and minor brand household and personal care products.

McKay Securities plc
20 Greyfriars Road, Reading, Berkshire RG1 1NL
Telephone +44 (0) 118 950 2333
Fax +44 (0) 118 939 1393
Website www.mckaysecurities.plc.uk

Chair
David Thomas
Chief Executive/Managing Director
Simon Perkins
Board Members
Nigel Aslin, Alan Childs, Andrew Gulliford, Michael Hawkes, Viscount Lifford, Steven Mew, Steven Morrice

Business Description
A group engaged in property investment and development.

Mears Group plc
1390 Montpellier Court, Gloucester Business Park, Brockworth, Gloucester GL3 4AH
Telephone +44 (0) 1453 511911
Website www.mearsgroup.co.uk

Chair and Chief Executive
Bob Holt
Board Members
Michael Macario, David Miles, Reg Pomphrett, David Robertson, Mike Rogers, Andrew Smith

Business Description
A group engaged in building maintenance and improvement including electrical and mechanical contracting, painting and decorating services and the provision of facility management and distribution of motor vehicles.

Medical Solutions plc
1 Orchard Place, Nottingham Business Park, Nottingham NG8 6PX
Telephone +44 (0) 115 973 9012
Fax +44 (0) 115 973 9013
Website www.medical-solutions.co.uk

Chair
Laurie Turnbull
Board Members
Dr Nick Ash, Dr Sue Foden, Prof Karol Sikora, Robert Slinger

Business Description
A group engaged in the provision of pathology and histopathology services and the sale of microscopy hardware and software and image analysis and management systems.

MedicX Fund Ltd
5 Godalming Business Centre, Woolsack Way, Godalming, Surrey GU7 1XW
Telephone +44 (0) 1483 869500
Fax +44 (0) 1483 869519
Website www.medicxfund.com

Director
Christopher Bennett
Board Members
John Hearle, Shelagh Mason, Alison Simpson

Business Description
A specialist investor in primary healthcare property in the United Kingdom.

Meggitt plc
Atlantic House, Aviation Park West, Bournemouth International Airport, Dorset BH23 6EW
Telephone +44 (0) 1202 597597
Fax +44 (0) 1202 597555
Website www.meggitt.com

Chair
Sir Colin Terry
Chief Executive/Managing Director
Terry Twigger
Board Members
Sir Alan Cox, Philip Green, Peter Hill, David Robins, David Williams, Stephen Young

Business Description
A group engaged in the design and manufacture of equipment and systems for the aerospace and defence industries and the design and manufacture of electronic sensors.

Melchior Japan Investment Trust plc
55 Moorgate, London EC2R 6PA
Telephone +44 (0) 20 7410 3132
Fax +44 (0) 20 7477 5849

Chair
Christopher Hunt
Board Members
Andrew Dalton, The Rt Hon Peter Lilley, David Price

Business Description
An investment trust.

Melrose plc
Cleveland House, 33 King Street, London SW1Y 6RJ
Telephone +44 (0) 20 7766 7670
Fax +44 (0) 20 7766 7671
Website www.melroseplc.net

Chair
Christopher Miller
Chief Executive/Managing Director
David Roper
Board Members
Perry Crosthwaite, John Grant, Geoffrey Martin, Simon Peckham, Miles Templeman

Business Description
An engineering group engaged in the design, development and manufacture of specialist components.

Melrose Resources plc
Exchange Tower, 19 Canning Street, Edinburgh EH3 8EG
Telephone +44 (0) 131 221 3360
Fax +44 (0) 131 221 3361
Website www.melroseresources.com

Chair
Robert Adair
Chief Executive/Managing Director
David Thomas
Board Members
David Archer, James Hay, Kelvin Hudson, Anthony Richmond-Watson, J Munro Sutherland, William Wyatt

Business Description
A group engaged in oil and gas exploration, development and production.

Merchants Trust plc (The)
155 Bishopgate, London EC2M 3AD
Telephone +44 (0) 20 7065 1407
Website www.merchantstrust.co.uk

Chair
Hugh Stevenson
Board Members
Sir John Banham, Richard Barfield, Joe Scott Plummer, Sir Bob Reid, James Sassoon

Business Description
An investment trust.

Merrill Lynch British Smaller Companies Trust plc
33 King William Street, London EC4R 9AS
Telephone +44 (0) 20 7743 3000
Fax +44 (0) 20 7743 1000
Website www.mlim.co.uk/its

Chair
Richard Brewster
Board Members
Dr John Davies, Robert Ffoulkes-Jones, Nicholas Fry, Gillian Nott

Business Description
An investment company that invest mainly in UK smaller quoted companies.

Merrill Lynch Commodities Income Investment Trust plc
33 King William Street, London EC4R 9AS
Telephone +44 (0) 20 7743 3000
Fax +44 (0) 20 7743 1000
Website www.blackrock.co.uk/its

Chair
Ewan Macpherson
Board Members
Prof Roland Clift, Karen de Segundo, John Murray, John Roberts

Business Description
An investment trust.

Merrill Lynch Greater Europe Investment Trust plc
33 King William Street, London EC4R 9AS
Telephone +44 (0) 20 7743 3000
Fax +44 (0) 20 7743 1000
Website www.mlim.co.uk/its

Chair
John Walker-Haworth
Board Members
Carol Ferguson, Gerald Holtham, Beatrice Philippe

Business Description
An investment company that primarily invests in a diverse portfolio of European companies.

Merrill Lynch Latin American Investment Trust plc
33 King William Street, London EC4R 9AS
Telephone +44 (0) 20 7743 3000
Fax +44 (0) 20 7743 1111
Website www.mlim.co.uk/its

Chair
Peter Burnell
Board Members
Mailson da Nobrega, Desmond O'Conor, Fred Packard, Earl St Aldwyn, Laurence Whitehead

Business Description
Investment company investing in the Brazilian, Turkish, Mexican and South African markets.

Merrill Lynch New Energy Technology plc
33 King William Street, London EC4R 9AS
Telephone +44 (0) 20 7743 3000
Fax +44 (0) 20 7743 1000
Website www.blackrock.co.uk/its

Chair
Ewan MacPherson
Board Members
Prof Roland Clift, John Murray, John Roberts, Karen Segundo

Business Description
An investment company, investing in alternative energy or energy technology.

Merrill Lynch World Mining Trust plc
33 King William Street, London EC4R 9AS
Telephone +44 (0) 20 7280 2800
Fax +44 (0) 20 7743 1000

Chair
Tony Lea
Board Members
Ian Barby, Oliver Baring, Colin Buchan, Gordon Sage

Business Description
An investment trust with two investment dealing subsidaries.

Metalrax Group plc
Ardath Road, Kings Norton, Birmingham B38 9PN
Telephone +44 (0) 121 433 3444
Fax +44 (0) 121 433 3325
Website www.metalraxgroup.co.uk

Chair
John Crabtree
Chief Executive/Managing Director
Richard Arbuthnot
Board Members
John Adcock, William Kelly, Andrew Pearson

Business Description
A group engaged in the manufacture and marketing of engineering and storage products and housewares.

Michael Page International plc
Page House, 1 Dashwood Lang Road, The Bourne Business Park, Addlestone, Weybridge, Surrey KT15 2PW
Telephone +44 (0) 1932 264 144
Website www.michaelpage.co.uk

Chair
Sir Adrian Montague
Chief Executive/Managing Director
Steve Ingham
Board Members
Stephen Box, Charles-Henri Dumon, Tim Miller, Stephen Puckett, Hubert Reid

Business Description
A group engaged as specialist recruitment consultants.

Micro Focus International plc
22-30 Old Bath Road, Newbury RG14 1QN
Telephone +44 (0) 1635 32646
Fax +44 (0) 1635 33966
Website www.microfocus.com

Chair
Kevin Loosemore
Chief Executive/Managing Director
Stephen Kelly
Board Members
Prescott Ashe, Nick Bray, David Dominik, David Maloney, Dr Paul Pester, Mike Shinya

Business Description
A company engaged in the provision of software that helps companies to improve the business value of their enterprise applications.

Microgen plc
Fleet House, 3 Fleetwood Park, Barley Way, Fleet, Hampshire GU51 2QJ
Telephone +44 (0) 1252 772300
Fax +44 (0) 1252 772301
Website www.microgen.co.uk

Chair
Martin Ratcliffe
Chief Executive/Managing Director
David Sherriff
Board Members
Peter Bertram, Paul Davies, Ralph Kanter, Philip Wood

Business Description
A group engaged in the provision of IT services and solutions, including BACS software managed services, and consultancy to the business community.

Mid Wynd International Investment Trust plc
Calton Square, 1 Greenside Row, Edinburgh EH1 3AN
Telephone +44 (0) 131 275 2000
Fax +44 (0) 131 275 3955
Website www.bailliegifford.com

Chair
Patrick Barron
Board Members
Richard Burns, Michael Ingall, Malcolm Scott

Business Description
An investment trust.

Midas Income & Growth Trust plc
Martins Building, Water Street, Liverpool L2 3SP
Telephone +44 (0) 151 906 2450
Fax +44 (0) 151 906 2455
Website www.midascapital.co.uk

Chair
Hubert Reid
Board Members
Adam Cooke, Ian Davis

Business Description
An investment trust.

Millennium & Copthorne Hotels plc
Scarsdale Place, Kensington, London W8 5SR
Telephone +44 (0) 20 7872 2444
Fax +44 (0) 20 7872 2460
Website www.mill-cop.com

Chair
Kwek Leng Beng
Board Members
John Arnett, Christopher Keljik, Charles Kirkwood, Kwek Leng Joo, Kwek Leng Peck, John Sclater, Christopher Sneath, Viscount Thurso, Wong Hong Ren

Business Description
A group engaged in the ownership management and operation of hotels.

Minerva plc
42 Wigmore Street, London W1U 2RY
Telephone +44 (0) 20 7535 1000
Fax +44 (0) 20 7535 1001
Website www.minervaplc.co.uk

Chair
Oliver Whitehead
Chief Executive/Managing Director
Salmaan Hasan
Board Members
Ivan Ezekiel, Tim Garnham, John McNeil, Clive Richards, Christopher Sheridan

Business Description
A group engaged in property investment development and management.

MirLand Development Corporation plc
Office 1002, 10th Floor, Nicolaou Pentadromos Centre, Thessalonikis Street, 3025 Cyprus
Telephone + 357 258 50025
Fax +357 258 50055
Website www.mirland-developments.com

Chair
Nigel Wright
Chief Executive/Managing Director
Moshe Morag
Board Members
Guerman Aliev, Douglas Blausten, Dr Caroline A Brown, Georgis Hadjianastassiou, Eliezer Fishman, Eyal Fishman, Roman Rozental

Business Description
A company engaged in real estate development, operating in Russia.

Misys plc
125 Kensington High Street, London W8 5SF
Telephone +44 (0) 20 7368 2300
Fax +44 (0) 20 7368 2400
Website www.misysplc.com

Chair
Sir Dominic Cadbury
Chief Executive/Managing Director
Mike Lawrie
Board Members
John King, Jim Malone, John Ormerod, Al-Noor Ramji, Jeff Ubben, Dr Jurgen Zech

Business Description
A group engaged in the development and licensing of applications, software products, the provision of transaction and claims processing services, and business outsourcing.

Mitchells & Butlers plc
27 Fleet Street, Birmingham B3 1JP
Telephone +44 (0) 870 669 3000
Fax +44 (0) 121 233 2246
Website www.mbplc.com

Chair
Roger Carr
Chief Executive/Managing Director
Tim Clarke
Board Members
Mike Bramley, George Fairweather, Drummond Hall, Tony Hughes, Sir Tim Lankester, Karim Naffah, Sara Weller

Business Description
A company engaged in the management of pubs and pub restaurants.

Mithras Investment Trust plc
55 Moorgate, London EC2R 6PA
Telephone +44 (0) 20 7410 4186
Fax +44 (0) 20 7477 5849
Website www.legalandgeneralventures.com

Chair
Hamish Melville
Board Members
William Maltby, David Rough, Michael Wooderson

Business Description
An investment trust specifically engaged in the provision of mezzanine loan and equity finance.

MITIE Group plc
8 Monarch Court, The Brooms, Emerson Green, Bristol BS16 7FH
Telephone +44 (0) 117 970 8800
Fax +44 (0) 117 302 6743
Website www.mitie.co.uk

Chair
David Ord
Chief Executive/Managing Director
Ruby McGregor-Smith
Board Members
Colin Acheson, Suzanne Baxter, Roger Goodman, Colin Hale, David Jenkins, Ishbel Macpherson, Cullum McAlpine, Roger Matthews, Graeme Potts, Ian Stewart, Bill Robson

Business Description
A group engaged in the provision of services to buildings and infrastructure, including cleaning, managed services, engineering, maintenance, catering and security services.

MJ Gleeson Group plc
Rusint House, Harvest Crescent, Ancells Road, Business
Park, Fleet, Hampshire GU51 2UG
Telephone +44 (0) 1252 360300
Fax +44 (0) 1252 621666
Website www.mjgleeson.com

Chair
Dermot Gleeson
Chief Executive/Managing Director
Paul Wallwork
Board Members
Ross Ancell, Chris Holt, Terry Morgan, Eric Stobart

Business Description
A group specialising in urban housing regeneration,
commercial property development, and strategic land
trading.

Molins plc
11 Tanners Drive, Blakelands, Milton Keynes,
Buckinghamshire MK14 5LU
Telephone +44 (0) 1908 219000
Fax +44 (0) 1908 216499
Website www.molins.com

Chair
Peter Byrom
Board Members
David Cowen, Dick Hunter, Adam Robson, Michael Steen,
John Wilson

Business Description
A group engaged in the design, engineering and
manufacturing of specialist machinery for the tobacco,
food and other industries, and the provision of scientific
services.

Mondi plc
Building 1, First Floor, Aviator Park, Station Road,
Addlestone, Surrey KT15 2PG
Telephone +44 (0) 1932 826300
Fax +44 (0) 1932 826350
Website www.mondigroup.com

Joint Chairmen
Sir John Parker and Cyril Ramaphosa
Chief Executive
David Hathorn
Board Members
Paul Hollingworth, Colin Matthews, Imogen Mkhize, Anne
Quinn, David Williams

Business Description
A group engaged in the production and provision of
paper and plastic packaging.

Monks Investment Trust plc (The)
Calton Square, 1 Greenside Row, Edinburgh EH1 3AN
Telephone +44 (0) 131 275 2000
Fax +44 (0) 131 275 3999
Website www.bailliegifford.com

Chair
James Ferguson
Board Members
Carol Ferguson, Edward Harley, Douglas McDougall

Business Description
An investment trust.

Monsoon plc
Monsoon Building, 179 Harrow Road, London W2 6NB
Telephone +44 (0) 20 7313 3000
Fax +44 (0) 20 7313 3040
Website www.monsoon.co.uk

Chair
Peter Simon
Chief Executive/Managing Director
Rose Foster
Board Members
Mark McMenemy, Anton Simon, Mark Vandenberghe

Business Description
A group engaged in the retail of women's and children's
clothing, accessories, homeware and gifts.

Montanaro European Smaller Companies Trust plc
53 Threadneedle Street, London EC2R 8AR
Telephone +44 (0) 20 7448 8600
Fax +44 (0) 20 7448 8601
Website www.montanaro.co.uk

Chair and Chief Executive
David Gamble
Board Members
Anthony Hardy, Christopher Jones, Michael Moule,
Laurence Peter

Business Description
An investment trust based in the UK.

Montanaro UK Smaller Companies Investment Trust plc
53 Threadneedle Street, London EC2R 8AR
Telephone +44 (0) 20 7448 8600
Fax +44 (0) 20 7448 8601
Website www.montanaro.co.uk

Chair
David Gamble
Board Members
Antony Hardy, Chris Jones, Michael Moule, Laurence
Petar

Business Description
An investment trust.

Morant Wright Japan Income Trust Ltd
Trafalgar Court, Les Banques, St Peter Port,
Guernsey GY1 3QL
Telephone +44 (0) 1481 745001

Chair
Andrew Barker
Board Members
Christopher Fish, John Hawkins, Henry Morgan

Business Description
Limited liability closed-ended Guernsey registered
investment company investing in Japanese equities.

Morgan Crucible Company plc (The)
Quadrant, 55-57 High Street, Windsor, Berkshire SL4 1LP
Telephone +44 (0) 1753 837000
Fax +44 (0) 1753 850872
Website www.morgancrucible.com

Chair
Tim Stevenson
Chief Executive/Managing Director
Mark Robertshaw
Board Members
Kevin Dangerfield, Martin Flower, Simon Heale, Mark
Lejman, Joseph MacHale

Business Description
A group engaged in the manufacture and marketing of
carbon ceramic and magnetic components for application
in a wide range of industries and services.

Morgan Sindall plc
77 Newman Street, London W1T 3EW
Telephone +44 (0) 20 7307 9200
Fax +44 (0) 20 7307 9201
Website www.morgansindall.co.uk

Chair
John Morgan
Chief Executive/Managing Director
Paul Smith
Board Members
Bernard Asher, Gill Barr, David Mulligan, Jon Walden,
Paul Whitmore

Business Description
A group engaged in the building of affordable housing,
the provision of infrastructure services, construction, and
the provision of fit out and refurbishment services.

Morse plc
Profile West, 950 Great West Road, Brentford,
Middlesex TW8 9EE
Telephone +44 (0) 20 8380 8000
Fax +44 (0) 20 8560 7700
Website www.morse.com

Chair
Richard Lapthorne
Chief Executive/Managing Director
Duncan McIntyre
Board Members
Kevin Alcock, Hon Michael Benson, Eric Dodd, Derrick
Nicholson, Nigel Whitehead

Business Description
A group engaged in the sale and implementation of IT
solutions, including the supply of infrastructure and the
provision of related professional services.

Moss Bros Group
8 St John's Hill, Clapham Junction, London SW11 1SA
Telephone +44 (0) 20 7447 7200
Fax +44 (0) 20 7350 0113
Website www.mossbros.co.uk

Chair
Keith Hamill
Chief Executive/Managing Director
Philip Mountford
Board Members
Mark Bernstein, Rowland Gee, Michael Hitchcock, Robert
Marsh, Bernard Myers

Business Description
A group engaged in the retail and hire of menswear,
especially formal.

Mothercare plc
Cherry Tree Road, Watford, Hertfordshire WD24 6SH
Telephone +44 (0) 1923 241000
Fax +44 (0) 1923 240944
Website www.mothercare.com

Chair
Ian Peacock
Chief Executive/Managing Director
Ben Gordon
Board Members
Karen Brady, Bernard Cragg, Neil Harrington, David
Williams

Business Description
A group engaged in the retail of clothing, hardware and
toys for mothers-to-be and pre-school children.

Mouchel Parkman plc
West Hall, Parvis Road, West Byfleet, Surrey KT14 6EZ
Telephone +44 (0) 1932 337000
Website www.mouchelparkman.com

Chair
Richard Benton
Chief Executive/Managing Director
Richard Cuthbert
Board Members
Ian Knight, Sir Michael Lyons, Rodney Westhead, Kevin
Young

Business Description
A company engaged in the provision of support services,
managing road networks, public buildings, rail
infrastructure, homes, schools and utilities.

MP Evans Group plc
3 Clanricarde Gardens, Tunbridge Wells, Kent TN1 1HQ
Telephone +44 (0) 1892 516333
Fax +44 (0) 1892 518639
Website www.mpevans.co.uk

Chairman
Richard M Robinow
Board Members
Philip A Fletcher, Peter E Hadsley-Chaplin, O David
Wilkinson, Konrad P Legg, J Derek Shaw

Business Description
A group engaged in investing in oil-palm and rubber
plantations and property development.

MS International plc
Carr Hill, Balby, Doncaster, South Yorkshire DN4 8DH
Telephone +44 (0) 1302 322133
Fax +44 (0) 1302 369329

Chair and Chief Executive
Michael Bell
Board Members
Roger Lane-Smith, Michael O'Connell, David Pyle

Business Description
A group engaged in the design and manufacture of
specialist engineering products and the provision of
related services.

MTL Instruments Group plc (The)
Power Court, Luton, Bedfordshire LU1 3JJ
Telephone +44 (0) 1582 723633
Fax +44 (0) 1582 422283
Website www.mtl-group.com

Chair
Malcolm Coster
Chief Executive/Managing Director
Graeme Philip
Board Members
Don Bogle, William Greenhalgh, Terence Lazenby

Business Description
A group engaged in the design, manufacture and
marketing of electronic explosion-protection instruments
and devices for measurement and control of industrial
processes carried out in hazardous environments.

Murray Income Trust plc
123 St Vincent Street, Glasgow G2 5EA
Telephone +44 (0) 141 306 7400
Fax +44 (0) 141 306 7401
Website www.murray-income.co.uk

Chair
Patrick Gifford
Board Members
Adrian Coats, Marian Glen, Neil Honebon, Humphrey van
der Klugt

Business Description
An investment trust.

Murray International Trust plc
97 Haymarket Terrace, Edinburgh EH12 5HD
Telephone +44 (0) 131 313 1000
Fax +44 (0) 131 313 1001
Website www.murray-intl.co.uk

Chair
John Trott
Board Members
Lady Balfour of Burleigh, David Benson, James Best,
Alfred Shedden

Business Description
An investment trust.

N Brown Group plc
Griffin House, 40 Lever Street, Manchester M60 6ES
Telephone +44 (0) 161 236 8256
Fax +44 (0) 161 238 2662
Website www.nbrown.co.uk

Chair
Lord Alliance of Manchester
Chief Executive/Managing Director
Alan White
Board Members
Nigel Alliance, Ivan Fallon, John McGuire, Dean Moore,
Lord Stone of Blackheath

Business Description
A group engaged in direct home shopping retail,
fulfilment and financial services.

Narborough Plantations plc
Narborough Estate, 35600 Sungkai, Perak Darul Ridzuan,
Malaysia
Telephone +6 05 4386185
Fax +6 05 4386185

Chair
Juliana Devadason
Chief Executive/Managing Director
Stephen Huntsman
Board Members
Encik Hamir, William Huntsman, Jeraman Narainan

Business Description
The cultivation of oil palm.

National Express Group plc
75 Davies Street, London W1K 5HT
Telephone +44 (0) 20 7529 2000
Fax +44 (0) 20 7529 2100
Website www.nationalexpressgroup.com

Chair
David Ross
Chief Executive/Managing Director
Richard Bowker
Board Members
Jorge Cosmen, Sir Andrew Foster, Barry Gibson, Susan
Lyons, Ray O'Toole, Tim Score, Adam Walker

Business Description
A group engaged in the operation of passenger train, bus
and coach transport services and the provision and
management of airport facilities.

National Grid plc
1-3 Strand, London WC2N 5EH
Telephone +44 (0) 20 7004 3040
Fax +44 (0) 20 7004 3027
Website www.nationalgrid.com

Chair
Sir John Parker
Chief Executive/Managing Director
Steven Holliday
Board Members
Linda Adamany, John Allan, Edward Astle, Mark
Fairbairn, Ken Harvey, Paul Joskow, Steve Lucas, Stephen
Pettit, Maria Richter, George Rose, Nick Winser

Business Description
An international energy delivery group engaged in the
operation of electricity and gas transmission and
distribution systems and provision of related services.

nCipher plc
Jupiter House, Station Road, Cambridge CB1 2JD
Telephone +44 (0) 1223 723600
Fax +44 (0) 1223 723601
Website www.ncipher.com

Chair
Robert Jeens
Chief Executive/Managing Director
Alexander van Someren
Board Members
Richard Gourlay, James Urquhart, Dr Nicko van Someren

Business Description
A group engaged in the development of internet security
products, services and technologies.

Nestor Healthcare Group plc
Allen House, Station Road, Egham, Surrey TW20 9NT
Telephone +44 (0) 1784 221600
Fax +44 (0) 1 784 477674
Website www.nestorplc.co.uk

Chair
John Rennocks
Chief Executive/Managing Director
Stephen Booty
Board Members
Roger Dye, Martyn Ellis, Sir Andrew Foster

Business Description
A group engaged in the provision of nurses and carers,
locum doctors, medical staff to home and social care
personnel and services and other healthcare services.

Network Technology plc
HBM House, 26 Victoria Way, Burgess Hill, West
Sussex RH15 9NF
Telephone +44 (0) 1444 870408
Fax +44 (0) 1444 870 452
Website www.network-technology.com

Chair
Klaus Bollmann
Board Members
Hannelore Schlieker-Bollmann

Business Description
A group engaged in the design, manufacture and
marketing of hardware and software used in connecting
all computer associated equipment in the modern
environment.

New India Investment Trust plc
1 Bow Churchyard, London EC4M 9HH
Website www.newindia-trust.co.uk

Chair
William Salomon
Board Members
Sarah Bates, Prof Victor Bulmer-Thomas, Andres
Rozental, Audley Twiston-Davies

Business Description
An investment trust.

New Star Investment Trust plc
1 Knightsbridge Green, London SW1X 7NE
Telephone +44 (0) 20 7225 9200
Fax +44 (0) 20 7225 9300
Website www.newstaram.com

Chair
James Roe
Board Members
John Duffield, Marcus Gregson, Geoffrey Howard-Spink

Business Description
An investment trust with a dealing subsidiary.

New Star Private Equity Investment Trust plc
10 Bedford Street, Covent Garden, London WC2E 9HE
Telephone +44 (0) 20 7632 8200
Fax +44 (0) 20 7632 8201
Website www.newstaram.com

Chair
John Duffield
Chief Executive/Managing Director
Howard Covington
Board Members
Michael Astor, John Craig, David Gamble, John Jay,
Richard Pease, Mark Skinner, Martin Smith

Business Description
An investment trust.

New Zealand Investment Trust plc
23 Cathedral Yard, Exeter, Devon EX1 1HB
Telephone +44 (0) 1392 475 900
Fax +44 (0) 1392 498 311
Website www.iimia.co.uk

Chair
Donald Campbell
Board Members
Brian Gaynor, Tim Kimber, Frank Pearson, Alexander
Zagoreos

Business Description
An investment trust.

Next plc
Desford Road, Enderby, Leicester LE19 4AT
Telephone +44 (0) 844 844 8333
Fax +44 (0) 116 284 8998
Website www.next.co.uk

Chair
John Barton
Chief Executive/Managing Director
Simon Wolfson
Board Members
Christos Angelides, Steve Barber, Nick Brookes, Christine
Cross, Jonathan Dawson, David Keens, Derek Netherton,
Andrew Varley

Business Description
A group engaged in the retail of clothing, home products,
accessories and fashion jewellery through stores and
home shopping, and the provision of customer services
management.

Nikanor plc
15-19 Athol Street, Douglas, Isle of Man IM1 1LB
Telephone +44 (0) 1624 610900
Website www.nikanor.co.uk

Chair
Jonathan Leslie
Board Members
The Earl of Balfour, James Gorman, Dan Kurtzer, Dr Eric
Lilford, Jay Pomrenze, Terry Robinson, Peter Sydney-
Smith

Business Description
A group engaged in copper and cobalt mining in mining
group in the Democratic Republic of Congo.

Nord Anglia Education plc
Centrum Point, Third Avenue, Centrum 100, Burton-upon-
Trent, Staffordshire DE14 2WD
Telephone +44 (0) 845 225 3030
Fax +44 (0) 845 225 3031
Website www.nordanglia.com

Chair
Alan Kelsey
Chief Executive/Managing Director
Andrew Fitzmaurice
Board Members
Felicity Goody, Stephen Henwood, Alasdair Marnoch,
Rosamund Marshall, David Smith

Business Description
A group engaged in the provision of education and
related educational services.

North Atlantic Smaller Companies Investment Trust plc
Ground Floor, Ryder Court, 14 Ryder Street,
London SW1Y 6QB
Telephone +44 (0) 20 7747 5682
Fax +44 (0) 20 7747 5611

Chair
Enrique Gittes
Chief Executive/Managing Director
Christopher Mills
Board Members
Oliver Grace, Charles Irby, Kristian Siem

Business Description
An investment trust with a dealing subsidiary.

North Midland Construction plc
Nunn Close, The County Estate, Huthwaite, Sutton-in-
Ashfield, Nottinghamshire NG17 2HW
Telephone +44 (0) 1623 515008
Fax +44 (0) 1623 440071
Website www.northmid.co.uk

Chair and Chief Executive
Robert Moyle
Board Members
Douglas Bleakley, Brian Evans, Michael Garratt

Business Description
A group engaged in civil engineering, building and public
works contracting.

Northamber plc
Northamber House, 23 Davis Road, Chessington,
Surrey KT9 1HS
Telephone +44 (0) 20 8296 7000
Fax +44 (0) 20 8296 7060
Website www.northamber.plc.uk

Chair
David Phillips
Board Members
Anthony Caplin, Reg Heath, Henry Matthews

Business Description
A group engaged in the supply of computer hardware,
computer printers and peripheral products, computer
telephony products, and electronic transmission
equipment.

Northern European Properties Ltd
PO Box 539, No 1 Wesley Street, St Helier,
Jersey JE4 5UT
Telephone +44 (0) 1534 722787
Website www.northerneuropeanproperties.com

Chair
Jens Engvall
Board Members
Michael Hurst, Ian Livingstone, Christopher Lovell, Kari
Österlund, Martin Sabey

Business Description
A company engaged in real estate investment in the
Nordic and Baltic regions.

Northern Foods plc
2180 Century Way, Thorpe Park, Leeds LS15 8ZB
Telephone +44 (0) 113 390 0110
Fax +44 (0) 113 390 0211
Website www.northern-foods.co.uk

Chair
Anthony Hobson
Chief Executive/Managing Director
Stefan Barden
Board Members
Ronnie Bell, Tony Illsley, Jeremy Maiden, Orna Ni-
Chionna, David Nish

Business Description
A group engaged in the manufacture of meat and
savoury products, speciality bread, bread-based snacks,
cakes and puddings, biscuits, and dairy products.

Northern Investors Company plc
Northumberland House, Princess Square, Newcastle-upon-
Tyne NE1 8ER
Telephone +44 (0) 191 244 6000
Fax +44 (0) 191 244 6001
Website www.nvm.co.uk

Chair
Peter Haigh
Board Members
John Barnsley, Michael Denny, Martin Hamilton-Sharp,
Frank Neale, Mark Nicholls, Dr Matt Ridley, Sarah
Stewart

Business Description
An investment trust.

Northern Recruitment Group plc
Lloyds Court, 56 Grey Street, Newcastle-upon-
Tyne NE1 6AH
Telephone +44 (0) 191 232 1222
Fax +44 (0) 191 261 8466
Website www.nrgplc.com

Chair
Leo Finn
Chief Executive/Managing Director
Lorna Moran
Board Members
Richard Hutton, Therese Liddle, Wayham Moran

Business Description
A group engaged in the placement of permanent and
contract staff in the North East of England, Yorkshire
and Scotland.

Northern Rock plc
Northern Rock House, Gosforth, Newcastle-upon-
Tyne NE3 4PL
Telephone +44 (0) 191 285 7191
Fax +44 (0) 191 284 8470
Website www.northernrock.co.uk

Chair
Dr Matt Ridley
Chief Executive/Managing Director
Adam Applegarth
Board Members
David Baker, Keith Currie, Adam Fenwick, Sir Ian
Gibson, Dave Jones, Andy Kuipers, Nichola Pease,
Michael Queen, Rosemary Radcliffe, Sir Derek Wanless

Business Description
A group engaged in the provision of housing, finance,
savings and a range of related personal financial and
banking services.

Northgate Information Solutions plc
Peoplebuilding 2, Peoplebuilding Estate, Maylands
Avenue, Hemel Hempstead, Hertfordshire HP2 4NW
Telephone +44 (0) 1442 232424
Fax +44 (0) 1442 256454
Website www.northgate-is.com

Chair
Ron Mackintosh
Chief Executive/Managing Director
Chris Stone
Board Members
Malcolm Aldis, Jack Fryer, David Hodgson, Sir Stephen
Lander, David Meaden, Andrew Robb, Nick Starritt, John
Stier

Business Description
A group engaged in the development and supply of
software and related services.

Northgate plc
Norflex House, Allington Way, Darlington, County
Durham DL1 4DY
Telephone +44 (0) 1325 467558
Fax +44 (0) 1325 363204
Website www.northgateplc.com

Chair
Philip Rogerson
Chief Executive/Managing Director
Steve Smith
Board Members
Jan Astrand, Tom Brown, Phil Moorhouse, Gerard
Murray, Alan Noble

Business Description
A group engaged in commercial vehicle hire and sale.

Northumbrian Water Group plc
Northumbria House, Abbey Road, Pity Me,
Durham DH1 5FJ
Telephone +44 (0) 870 608 4820
Fax +44 (0) 191 301 6202
Website www.nwg.co.uk

Chair
Sir Derek Wanless
Chief Executive/Managing Director
John Cuthbert
Board Members
Sir Patrick Brown, Chris Green, Claude Lamoureux,
Martin Nègre, Alex Scott-Barrett, Jenny Williams

Business Description
A group engaged in the provision of water, waste water
management and related services.

Novae Group plc
71 Fenchurch Street, London EC3M 4HH
Telephone +44 (0) 20 7903 7300
Fax +44 (0) 20 7907 7333
Website www.novae.com

Chair
Paul Selway-Swift
Chief Executive/Managing Director
Matthew Fosh
Board Members
Jeremy Adams, Sir Bryan Carsberg, Oliver Corbett,
Anthony Hambro, John Hastings-Bass, David Henderson,
Peter Matson, Allan Nichols

Business Description
The company is the holding company of the group which
carries on insurance and associated financial activities.

NSB Retail Systems plc
Parkfield Business Centre, Parkfield House, Park Street,
Staffordshire ST17 4AL
Telephone +44 (0) 1785 223422
Fax +44 (0) 1785 252378
Website www.nsbgroup.com

Chair
Richard Abraham
Chief Executive/Managing Director
David Henning
Board Members
Martin Chatwin, David Ferguson, David Henning, Stuart
Mitchell, Angus Monro

Business Description
The development and supply of specialist software and
associated maintenance, development, consultancy and
application management services to the retail industry.

Numis Corporation plc
London Stock Exchange Building, 10 Paternoster Square,
London EC4M 7LT
Telephone +44 (0) 20 7260 1000
Fax +44 (0) 20 7260 1010
Website www.numiscorp.com

Chair
Michael Spencer
Chief Executive/Managing Director
Oliver Hemsley
Board Members
Thomas Bartlam, Declan Kelly, Lorna Tilbian, William
Trent, Nigel Turner, Geoffrey Vero

Business Description
A group engaged in the provision of integrated
stockbroking and investment banking services.

NXT plc
Cygnet House, Kingfisher Way, Hinchingbrooke Business
Park, Huntingdon, Cambridgeshire PE29 6FW
Telephone +44 (0) 1480 846100
Fax +44 (0) 1480 846190
Website www.nxtsound.com

Chair
David MacKay
Board Members
Henry Azima, Kate Barnes, Lance Batchelor, Ian Buckley,
Peter Thoms

Business Description
A group engaged in the development and licensing of
audio and touch technologies.

OEM plc
14-18 Ham Yard, London W1D 7DT
Telephone +44 (0) 20 7292 5940
Fax +44 (0) 20 7734 0952
Website www.oem.plc.uk

Chair
Robert Noonan
Chief Executive/Managing Director
B S Schneider
Board Members
Robin Turner

Business Description
A group engaged in property development and
investment and the provision of property management
and advice.

Office2Office plc
St Crispins, Duke Street, Norwich, Norfolk NR3 1PD
Telephone +44 (0) 1603 695756
Fax +44 (0) 1603 694544
Website www.office2office.biz

Chair
David Callear
Chief Executive/Managing Director
Simon Moate
Board Members
Peter Bertram, James Cohen, Mark Cunningham

Business Description
A group engaged in the provision of office supplies, office
equipment, furniture and print management services.

Old Mutual plc
5th Floor, Old Mutual Place, 2 Lambeth Hill,
London EC4V 4GG
Telephone +44 (0) 20 7002 7000
Fax +44 (0) 20 7002 7221
Website www.oldmutual.com

Chair
Christopher Collins
Chief Executive/Managing Director
Jim Sutcliffe
Board Members
Nigel Andrews, Rudi Bogni, Norman Broadhurst, Russell
Edey, Reuel Khoza, Jonathan Nicholls, Bongani
Nqwababa, Dr Lars Otterbeck, Julian Roberts

Business Description
A group engaged in life assurance, asset management,
banking and general insurance.

Omega Insurance Holdings Ltd
Clarendon House, Church Street, Hamilton HM11,
Bermuda
Website www.omegauw.com

Chair
Walter Fiederowicz
Chief Executive/Managing Director
Richard Tolliday
Board Members
Christopher Clarke, Clifford Palmer, John Robinson,
Nicholas Warren

Business Description
A group engaged in the provision of insurance.

OPD Group plc
28 Essex Street, London WC2R 3AT
Telephone +44 (0)) 20 7970 9700
Fax +44 (0) 20 7353 5894
Website www.opdgroup.com

Chair
Peter Hearn
Chief Executive/Managing Director
Francesca Robinson
Board Members
Richard Boggis-Rolfe, The Rt Hon Virginia Bottomley,
Mike Kirkham, Gillian Oakes, Douglas Sutherland

Business Description
An international recruitment services organisation with
offices in Europe, the Middle East and Asia Pacific,
serving an international client base.

Optos plc
Queensferry House, Carnegie Business Campus,
Dunfermline, Fife KY11 8GR
Telephone +44 (0) 1383 843300
Fax +44 (0) 1383 843333
Website www.optos.com

Chair
Dr John Padfield
Chief Executive/Managing Director
Tom Butts
Board Members
Douglas Anderson, Anne Glover, Dr David Guyer, Saad
Hammad, Patrick Paul, Barry Rose, Allan Watson,
Rosalyn Wilton

Business Description
A group engaged in the manufacture of measuring
instruments and of optical photographic equipment.

Oriel Resources plc
1 Red Place, London W1K 6PL
Telephone +44 (0) 20 7514 0590
Fax +44 (0) 20 7514 0591
Website www.orielsources.com

Chair
Dr Sergey Kurzin
Board Members
Takhirzhan Baratov, Nicholas Royston Clarke, Alexander
Nesis, John Reynolds, Ehud Rieger, Geoffrey Thomas
Bush, Roger Thomas Richer, Neil Woodyer

Business Description
A company engaged in chrome and nickel mining and
processing.

Osprey Smaller Companies Income Fund Ltd
2nd Floor, No1 le Truchot, St Peter Port,
Guernsey GY1 3JX
Website www.unicorn.com/ospery.asp

Chair
Roger Alcock
Chief Executive/Managing Director
David Harris
Board Members
Richard Prosser

Business Description
An investment fund.

Oxford Biomedica plc
The Medawar Centre, Robert Robinson Avenue, Oxford
Science Park, Oxford OX4 4GA
Telephone +44 (0) 1865 783000
Fax +44 (0) 1865 783001
Website www.oxfordbiomedica.co.uk

Chair
Dr Peter Johnson
Chief Executive/Managing Director
Alan Kingsman
Board Members
Dr Susan Kingsman, Dr Mike McDonald, Peter Nolan,
Andrew Wood, Nick Woolf

Business Description
A group engaged in the application of gene-based
technology to the development of novel therapeutics.

Oxford Instruments plc
Tubney Woods, Abingdon, Oxfordshire OX13 5QX
Telephone +44 (0) 1865 393200
Fax +44 (0) 1865 393333
Website www.oxford-instruments.com

Chair
Nigel Keen
Chief Executive/Managing Director
Jonathan Flint
Board Members
Kevin Boyd, Prof Sir Michael Brady, Charles Holroyd,
Prof Michael Hughes, Peter Morgan, Steven Parker,
Bernard Taylor

Business Description
A group engaged in the research, development,
manufacture and sale of advanced instrumentation.

Pace Micro Technology plc
Victoria Road, Saltaire, Shipley, West
Yorkshire BD18 3LF
Telephone +44 (0) 1274 532000
Fax +44 (0) 1274 532010
Website www.pace.co.uk

Chair
Mike McTighe
Chief Executive/Managing Director
Neil Gaydon
Board Members
Patricia Chapman-Pincher, Robert Fleming, Marten
Fraser, Stuart Hall, David McKinney

Business Description
A group engaged in the development, design and
distribution of digital receivers and receiver decoders for
the reception of digital television, interactive services,
telephony and high speed data.

Pacific Assets Trust plc
80 George Street, Edinburgh EH2 3BU
Telephone +44 (0) 131 465 1000
Fax +44 (0) 131 225 2375
Website www.pacific-assets.co.uk

Chair
David Nichol
Board Members
Richard Horlick, Stuart Leckie, Terence Mahony, Nigel
Rich

Business Description
An investment trust.

Pacific Horizon Investment Trust plc
Calton Square, 1 Greenside Row, Edinburgh EH1 3AN
Telephone +44 (0) 131 275 2000
Fax +44 (0) 131 275 3999
Website www.bailliegifford.com

Chair
Peter Mackay
Board Members
Jean Matterson, Douglas McDougall, Michael Morrison

Business Description
An investment trust.

Pantheon International Participations plc
Norfolk House, 31 St James's Square, London SW1Y 4JR
Telephone +44 (0) 20 7484 6200
Fax +44 (0) 20 7484 6201
Website www.pipplc.com

Chair
Thomas Bartlam
Board Members
Ian Barby, Richard Crowder, Peter Readman, Rhoderick
Swire, Sandy Thomson

Business Description
An investment trust.

Panther Securities plc
Panther House, 38 Mount Pleasant, London WC1X 0AN
Telephone +44 (0) 20 7278 8011
Fax +44 (0) 20 7278 3608

Chair and Chief Executive
Andrew Perloff
Board Members
John Doyle, Bryan Galan, Peter Kellner, John Perloff,
Simon Peters

Business Description
A group engaged in investment and dealing in property
and listed securities.

Paragon Group of Companies plc (The)
8 St Catherine's Court, Herbert Road, Solihull, West
Midlands B91 3QE
Telephone +44 (0) 121 712 2323
Fax +44 (0) 121 711 1330
Website www.paragon-group.co.uk

Chair
Robert Dench
Chief Executive/Managing Director
Nigel Terrington
Board Members
David Beever, Terry Eccles, John Heron, Nicholas Keen,
Christopher Newell, Pawan Pandya

Business Description
A group engaged in the operation of first mortgage and
consumer finance businesses.

Parity Group plc
Wimbledon Bridge House, 1 Hartfield Road, Wimbledon,
London SW19 3RU
Telephone +44 (0) 20 8543 5353
Fax +44 (0) 20 8545 6456
Website www.parity.co.uk

Chair
Lord Freeman
Chief Executive/Managing Director
Alwyn Welch
Board Members
John Hughes, Joseph Kelly, Alastair Macdonald, Philip
Swinstead, Nigel Tose

Business Description
A group engaged in the provision of IT services through
resourcing, training and business solutions.

Park Group plc
1 Valley Road, Birkenhead, Merseyside CH41 7ED
Telephone +44 (0) 151 653 1700
Fax +44 (0) 151 653 5416
Website www.parkgroup.co.uk

Chair and Chief Executive
Peter Johnson
Board Members
Christopher Baker, Christopher Houghton, George Marcall,
Martin Stewart, Gary Woods

Business Description
A group engaged in the operation of cash saving
schemes, including hampers and high street vouchers,
and cash lending, including home collected credit services
and cheque cashing.

Parkwood Holdings plc
Parkwood House, Cuerden Park, Berkeley Drive, Bamber
Bridge, Preston, Lancashire PR5 6BY
Telephone +44 (0) 1772 627111
Fax +44 (0) 1772 311611
Website www.parkwood-holdings.co.uk

Chair
Tony Hewitt
Chief Executive/Managing Director
Andrew Holt
Board Members
Sarah Kling, Brian May, Richard Tolkien

Business Description
A group engaged in the management of parks, open
spaces and leisure facilities, and arboriculture, and the
provision of medical personnel, agency services and
patient transport.

Partners Group Global Opportunities Ltd
Tudor House, Le Bordage, St Peter Port,
Guernsey GY1 1BT
Telephone +44 (0) 1481 711690
Fax +44 (0) 1481 730947
Website www.pg-globalopportunities.net

Chair
John Hallam
Board Members
Rupert Dorey, Urs Wietlisbach

Business Description
A limited liability closed-ended investment company.

PartyGaming plc
711 Europort, Gibraltar
Telephone +350 78700
Website www.partygaming.com

Chair
Michael Jackson
Chief Executive/Managing Director
Mitchell Garber
Board Members
Tim Bristow, Rod Perry, Martin Weigold

Business Description
A company engaged in the provision of online gaming.

Patientline plc
Thames Valley Court, 183-187 Bath Road, Slough,
Berkshire SL1 4AA
Telephone +44 (0) 1753 896000
Fax +44 (0) 1753 896153
Website www.patientline.co.uk

Chair
Geoffrey White
Board Members
Brent Marshall, Nick Winks

Business Description
A group engaged in the development and operation of
bedside television, radio and telephone terminals for
hospital patients.

PayPoint plc
1 The Boulevard, Shire Park, Welwyn Garden City,
Hertfordshire AL7 1EL
Telephone +44 (0) 1707 600300
Fax +44 (0) 1707 600333
Website www.paypoint.com

Chair
David Newlands
Chief Executive/Managing Director
Dominic von Trotha Taylor
Board Members
George Earle, Ken Minton, David Morrison, Andrew
Robb, Tim Watkin-Rees, Roger Wood

Business Description
A company engaged in cash and internet payments
through several payment networks.

Pearson plc
80 Strand, London WC2R 0RL
Telephone +44 (0) 20 7010 2317
Fax +44 (0) 20 7010 6060
Website www.pearson.com

Chair
Glen Moreno
Chief Executive/Managing Director
Dame Marjorie Scardino
Board Members
Sir David Arculus, Sir David Bell, Lord Burns, Patrick
Cescau, Rona Fairhead, Robin Freestone, Prof Susan
Fuhrman, Ken Hydon, John Makinson

Business Description
A group engaged in the publication of newspapers, books,
magazines and computer software, the operation of visitor
attractions and exhibitions, and production of TV
programmes.

Pendragon plc
Loxley House, 2 Oakwood Court, Little Oak Drive,
Annesley, Nottingham NG15 0DR
Telephone +44 (0) 1623 725200
Fax +44 (0) 1623 725010
Website www.pendragonplc.com

Chair
Sir Nigel Rudd
Chief Executive/Managing Director
Trevor Finn
Board Members
Martin Casha, Mike Davies, David Forsyth, John Holt,
David Joyce, Malcolm Le May, William Rhodes, Hilary
Sykes

Business Description
A group engaged in the sale of new and used vehicles,
contract hire and after sales services.

Pennon Group plc
Peninsula House, Rydon Lane, Exeter EX2 7HR
Telephone +44 (0) 1392 446688
Fax +44 (0) 1392 434966
Website www.pennon-group.co.uk

Chair
Ken Harvey
Board Members
Gerard Connell, Colin Drummond, David Dupont, Chris
Loughlin, Katharine Mortimer, Dinah Nichols

Business Description
A group engaged in the provision of water and sewerage
services and waste management services.

Perpetual Income & Growth Investment Trust plc
30 Finsbury Square, London EC2A 1AG
Telephone +44 (0) 20 7638 0731
Fax +44 (0) 20 7012 0642
Website www.invescoperpetual.co.uk

Chair
Rex Adams
Chief Executive/Managing Director
Martin Flanegan
Board Members
Sir John Banham, Joseph Canian, Denis Kessler, Edward
Lawrence, J Thomas Presby, James Robertson

Business Description
An investment trust.

Perpetual Japanese Investment Trust plc
30 Finsbury Park, London EC2A 1AG
Telephone +44 (0) 20 7065 4000
Fax +44 (0) 20 7929 5922
Website www.invescoperpetual.co.uk/investmenttrusts

Chair
Christopher Mitchinson
Board Members
Nicholas Bedford, Michael Howell, Hugh Priestley

Business Description
An investment trust.

Persimmon plc
Persimmon House, Fulford, York YO19 4FE
Telephone +44 (0) 1904 642199
Fax +44 (0) 1904 610014
Website www.persimmonhomes.com

Chair
John White
Chief Executive/Managing Director
Michael Farley
Board Members
Adam Applegarth, David Bryant, Neil Davidson, Michael
Killoran, Hamish Leslie Melville, David Thompson,
Nicholas Wrigley

Business Description
A group engaged as housebuilders.

Personal Assets Trust plc
80 George Street, Edinburgh EH2 3BU
Telephone +44 (0) 131 718 1000
Fax +44 (0) 131 225 2375

Chair
Robert White
Board Members
Robin Angus, Hamish Buchan, Gordon Neilly, Ian
Rushbrook, Martin Hamilton-Sharp

Business Description
An investment trust with dealing subsidiaries.

Peter Hambro Mining plc
11 Grosvenor Place, London SW1X 7HH
Telephone +44 (0) 20 7201 8900
Fax +44 (0) 20 7201 8901
Website www.peterhambro.com

Chair
Peter Hambro
Board Members
Sir Rudolph Agnew, Jay Hambro, Peter Hill-Wood, Philip
Leatham, Andrey Maruta, Alexei Maslovsky, Dr Pavel
Maslovsky, Dr Alya Samokhvalova

Business Description
A group engaged in the production of gold and
development of facilities at Pokrovskiy Rudnik,
exploration and development of reserves at Pioneer, and
gold mining in Russia by joint venture.

Petra Diamonds Ltd
Elizabeth House, 9 Castle Street, St Helier, Jersey JE4 2QP
Telephone +61 8 9381 8888
Website www.petradiamonds.com

Chair
Adonis Pouroulis
Chief Executive/Managing Director
Johan Dippenaar
Board Members
David Abery, James Davidson, Volker Ruffer, Charles
Segall

Business Description
Exploration for economically viable diamond deposits in
Southern Africa.

Petrofac Ltd
117 Jermyn Street, London SW1Y 6HH
Telephone +44 (0) 20 7811 4900
Fax +44 (0) 20 7811 4901
Website www.petrofac.com

Chair
Rodney Chase
Chief Executive/Managing Director
Ayman Asfari
Board Members
Kjell Almskog, Amjad Bseisu, Bernard de Combret,
Michael Press, Keith Roberts, Maroun Semaan, Rijnhard
Van Tets

Business Description
A group engaged in the provision of facilities solutions to
the oil and gas production and processing industry.

PGI Group plc
81 Carter Lane, London EC4V 5EP
Telephone +44 (0) 20 7246 0207
Fax +44 (0) 20 7236 0997
Website www.pgi-uk.com

Chair
Rupert Pennant-Rea
Chief Executive/Managing Director
Steve Wayne
Board Members
Barry Hill, Stephen Hobhouse, Dr Julius Makoni, Geoffrey
Moores, Nicholas Roditi, Charles Ryan

Business Description
A group engaged in the operation of tea, coffee, rubber
and macadamia estates, rose production, the import and
distribution of furniture, and manufacture of
wheelbarrows.

Phoenix IT Group plc
Technology House, Hunsbury Hill Avenue,
Northampton NN4 8QS
Telephone +44 (0) 1604 769000
Fax +44 (0) 1604 764323
Website www.phoenixgroup.com

Chair
Peter Bertram
Chief Executive/Managing Director
Nicholas Robinson
Board Members
Brian Sellwood, David Simpson, Jeremy Stafford, John
Sussens

Business Description
A group engaged in the sale of IT support services and
systems management solutions.

Phorm Inc
Golden Cross House, 8 Duncannon Street,
London WC2N 4JF
Telephone +44 (0) 870 405 7722
Website www.phorm.com

Chair and Chief Executive
Kent Ertugrul
Board Members
David Dorman, Christopher Lawrence, Virasb Vahidi

Business Description
A company engaged in the provision of online marketing
services.

Photo-Me International plc
Church Road, Bookham, Surrey KT23 3EU
Telephone +44 (0) 1372 453399
Fax +44 (0) 1372 459064
Website www.photo-me.co.uk

Chair
Vernon Sankey
Chief Executive/Managing Director
Serge Crasnianski
Board Members
Dan David, Roger Partington, Jean-Luc Peurvis, Martin
Reavley, Hugo Swire, David Young

Business Description
A group engaged in the manufacture, sale, service and
operation of coin-operated automatic photobooths, copiers,
express print services and children's rides, along with the
manufacture and sale of professional photographic
equipment and mini-labs worldwide.

Phytopharm plc
Corpus Christi House, 9 West Street, Godmanchester,
Cambridgeshire PE29 2HY
Telephone +44 (0) 1480 437697
Fax +44 (0) 1480 417090
Website www.phytopharm.co.uk

Chair
Alistar Taylor
Chief Executive/Managing Director
Dr Daryl Rees
Board Members
Dr Peter Blower, Piers Morgan, Sandy Morrison

Business Description
A group engaged in the investigation, development and
sale of medicines derived from plant origins.

Pinewood Shepperton plc
Pinewood Road, Iver, Buckinghamshire SL0 0NH
Telephone +44 (0) 1753 656183
Fax +44(0) 1753 656936
Website www.pinewoodgroup.com

Chair
Michael Grade
Chief Executive/Managing Director
Ivan Dunleavy
Board Members
Adrian Burn, James Donald, Patrick Garner, Nigel Hall,
Nick Smith

Business Description
A group engaged in the operation of film and television
studios.

Pipex Communications plc
1 Triangle Business Park, Stoke Mandeville,
Buckinghamshire HP22 5BL
Telephone +44 (0) 870 094 6060
Fax +44 (0) 870 160 2719
Website www.pipexgroup.com

Chair
Peter Dubens
Chief Executive/Managing Director
Mike Read
Board Members
Laurence Blackall, Christina Kennedy, Stewart Porter

Business Description
A group engaged in the supply of telecommunication
services.

Plasmon plc
Whiting Way, Melbourn, Hertfordshire SG8 6EN
Telephone +44 (0) 1763 261466
Fax +44 (0) 1763 260336
Website www.plasmon.co.uk

Chair
Jeffrey Hewitt
Board Members
Timothy Arthur, David Best, Dr. Chris McFadden,
Matthew Peacock, Rod Powell

Business Description
A group engaged in the development, manufacture and
distribution of removable data storage solutions.

Playtech Ltd
2nd Floor, St George's Court, Upper Church Street,
Douglas IM1 1EE
Telephone +44 (0) 1624 617876
Website www.playtech.com

Chair
Roger Withers
Chief Executive/Managing Director
Mor Weizer
Board Members
Rafael Ashkenazi, Moshe Barak, Thomas Hall, Alan
Jackson, Avigur Zmora

Business Description
A group engaged in designing and licencing software for
the gambling industry.

Pochin's plc
Brooks Lane, Middlewich, Cheshire CW10 0JQ
Telephone +44 (0) 1606 833333
Fax +44 (0) 1606 833331
Website www.pochins.plc.uk

Chair
Richard Fildes
Chief Executive/Managing Director
David Shaw
Board Members
Richard Buck, John Edwards, David Hedley, Ross
Murray, James Nicholson, David Pochin

Business Description
A group engaged in building and civil engineering,
contracting, property letting and development, specialist
plant hire, specialist directional drilling, subcontracts and
concrete block manufacture.

Polar Capital Technology Trust plc
4 Matthew Parker Street, London SW1H 9NP
Telephone +44 (0) 20 7227 2700
Fax +44 (0) 20 7227 2799
Website www.polarcapitaltechnologytrust.co.uk

Chair
Richard Wakeling
Board Members
Brian Ashford-Russell, Peter Dicks, David Gamble, Rupert
Montagu, Michael Moule

Business Description
An investment trust with a dealing subsidiary.

Porvair plc
Brampton House, 50 Bergen Way, King's Lynn,
Norfolk PE30 2JG
Telephone +44 (0) 1553 765500
Fax +44 (0) 1553 765599
Website www.porvair.com

Chair
Charles Matthews
Chief Executive/Managing Director
Ben Stocks
Board Members
Michael Gatenby, Dr John Sexton, Christopher Tyler,
Andrew Walker

Business Description
A group engaged in the provision of specialist filtration
solutions and advanced materials expertise.

Prelude Trust plc
Sycamore Studios, New Road, Over, Cambridge CB4 5PJ
Telephone +44 (0) 1954 288090
Fax +44 (0) 1954 288099
Website www.prelude-ventures.com

Chair
Michael Brooke
Board Members
Robert Hook, Anthony Martin, David Quysner, Marion
Sears

Business Description
An investment trust.

Premier Absolute Growth & Income Trust plc
59 Bank Street, London E14 5NT
Telephone +44 (0) 20 7982 2000

Chair
Jonathan Carr
Board Members
David Harris, Anthony Wands

Business Description
An investment trust.

Premier Farnell plc
25/28 Old Burlington Street, London W1S 3AN
Telephone +44 (0) 20 7851 4100
Fax +44 (0) 20 7851 4110
Website www.premierfarnell.com

Chair
Sir Peter Gershon
Chief Executive/Managing Director
Harriet Green
Board Members
Laurence Bain, Andrew Dougal, William Korb, Cary
Nolan, John Roques, Mark Whiteling

Business Description
A group engaged in the distribution of electronic,
electrical and industrial products to the design,
maintenance and repair sectors.

Premier Foods plc
Premier House, Centrium Business Park, Griffiths Way,
St Albans, Hertfordshire AL1 2RE
Telephone +44 (0) 1727 815 850
Fax +44 (0) 1727 815 982
Website www.premierfoods.co.uk

Chair
David Kappler
Chief Executive/Managing Director
Robert Schofield
Board Members
David Felwick, Sharon Hintze, Louise Makin, Ian Ramsey,
Paul Thomas

Business Description
A group engaged in the manufacture of food.

Premier Oil plc
23 Lower Belgrave Street, London SW1W 0NR
Telephone +44 (0) 20 7730 1111
Fax +44 (0) 20 7730 4696
Website www.premier-oil.com

Chair
Sir David John
Chief Executive/Managing Director
Simon Lockett
Board Members
Robin Allan, Scott Dobbie, Tony Durrant, Ronald
Emerson, Neil Hawkings, John Orange, Dr David Roberts

Business Description
A group engaged in oil and gas exploration, development
and production.

Premier Utilities Trust plc
Eastgate Court, High Street, Guildford, Surrey GU1 3DE
Telephone +44 (0) 1483 306090
Fax +44 (0) 1483 360845
Website www.premierassetmanagement.co.uk

Chair
Geoffrey Burns
Board Members
Adam Cooke, Prof Ian Graham, Michael Wigley

Business Description
An investment trust investing in equity and equity
related securities of water, electric, power, gas,
distribution and regulated infrastructure companies.

Primary Health Properties plc
Ground Floor, 14 Ryder Street, London SW1Y 6QB
Telephone +44 (0) 20 7747 5678
Fax +44 (0) 20 7747 5611
Website www.phpgroup.co.uk

Chair
Graeme Elliot
Chief Executive/Managing Director
Harry Hyman
Board Members
Martin Gilbert, James Hambro, Alun Jones, Dr Ian Rutter

Business Description
A group engaged in the generation of rental income and
capital through investment in primary health care
property in the UK.

Principle Capital Investment Trust plc
The Registry, 34 Beckenham Road, Beckenham,
Kent BR3 4TU
Telephone +44 (0) 20 8639 1139

Chair
Alan Clifton
Board Members
Wilfrid Caldwell, Brian Myerson, Brian Padgett, James
Roe

Business Description
An investment trust investing in publicly quoted
companies primarily in the UK.

Private Equity Investor plc
Beaufort House, 51 New North Road, Exeter EX4 4EP
Telephone +44 (0) 1392 412122
Fax +44 (0) 1392 253282
Website www.peiplc.com

Chair
Peter Dicks
Board Members
Colin Kingsnorth, Rory Macnamara, Barbara Thomas,
David Quysner

Business Description
An investment trust.

Prodesse Investment Ltd
Royal Bank House, 1 Glategny Esplanade, St Peter Port,
Guernsey GY1 2HS
Telephone +44 (0) 20 7269 7114
Website www.prodesse.co.uk

Chair
John Hallam
Board Members
Christopher Fish, Ronald Kazel, Talmai Morgan,
Christopher Sherwell

Business Description
A closed-end investment company.

Prosperity Minerals Holdings Ltd
Almeda DR, Carlos D'Assumpcao 181-187, Commercial do
Grupo Brilhantismo, 11-T, Macao
Telephone +852 31872618
Fax +852 27564884
Website www.pmhl.co.uk

Chairman and Chief Executive
David Wong

Business Description
A group engaged in cement manufacturing and iron ore
trading in China.

ProStrakan Group plc
Galabank Business Park, Galashiels TD1 1QH
Telephone +44 (0) 1896 664000
Fax +44 (0) 1896 664001
Website www.prostrakan.com

Chief Executive/Managing Director
Dr Wilson Totten
Board Members
Peter Allen, Dr Michael Asbury, Peter Cawdron, Francis
Fildes, Paul Garvey, Simon Turton, Alan Walker

Business Description
Commercialisation, discovery, research and development
of prescription medicines.

Protherics plc
The Heath Business and Technical Park, Runcorn,
Cheshire WA7 4QX
Telephone +44 (0) 20 7246 9950
Website www.protherics.com

Chair
Stuart Wallis
Chief Executive/Managing Director
Dr Andrew Heath
Board Members
Dr John Brown, James Christie, Dr Jaques Gonella, Saul
Komisar, Bryan Morton, Rolf Soderstrom, Garry Watts

Business Description
A group engaged in the research, development,
manufacture and sale of pharmaceutical products and
potential drugs for use in the treatment of human
diseases.

Provident Financial plc
Colonnade, Sunbridge Road, Bradford, West
Yorkshire BD1 2LQ
Telephone +44 (0) 1274 731111
Fax +44 (0) 1274 727300
Website www.providentfinancial.com

Chair
John van Kuffeler
Chief Executive/Managing Director
Peter Crook
Board Members
Andrew Fisher, Chris Gillespie, Robert Hough, John
Maxwell, Manjit Wolstenholme

Business Description
A group engaged in the provision of home credit facilities
and as motor insurance underwriters and brokers.

Prudential plc
Governors House, 5 Laurence Poutney Hill,
London EC4R 0HH
Telephone +44 (0) 20 7220 7588
Fax +44 (0) 20 7548 3360
Website www.prudential.co.uk

Chair
Sir David Clementi
Chief Executive/Managing Director
Mark Tucker
Board Members
Philip Broadley, Keki Dadiseth, Michael Garrett, Bridget
Macaskill, Clark Manning, Michael McLintock, Kathleen
O'Donovan, Nick Prettejohn, James Ross, Barry Stowe,
Lord Turnbull

Business Description
A group engaged in the provision of financial services.

Psion plc
48 Charlotte Street, London W1T 2NS
Telephone +44 (0) 20 7535 4253
Website www.psion.com

Chair
David Potter
Chief Executive/Managing Director
Jacky Lecuivre
Board Members
Andy Clegg, Ross Graham, John Hawkins, Michael
Homer, Bill Jessup, Ian McElroy, Mike O'Leary

Business Description
A group engaged in the development, engineering,
manufacture, marketing and sale of data collection and
communications solutions, portable computers and
applications software.

Puma Brandenburg Ltd
Suite 6, Borough House, Rue Du Pre, St Peter Port,
Guernsey GY1 3RH
Telephone +44 (0) 1481 723450

Chair
Peter Freeman
Board Members
Helen Green, James Rosenwald, Howard Shore, Gernot
von Grawert-May

Business Description
An investment company engaged in investing in German
real estate.

Punch Taverns
Jubilee House, Second Avenue, Burton Upon Trent,
Staffordshire DE14 2WF
Telephone +44 (0) 1283 501600
Fax +44 (0) 1283 501601
Website www.punchtaverns.com

Chair
Peter Cawdron
Chief Executive/Managing Director
Giles Thorley
Board Members
Phil Dutton, Mike Foster, Ian Fraser, Andrew Knight,
Robert McDonald, Jonathan Pavely, Randl Shure, Fritz
Ternofsky

Business Description
A company engaged in the owning and operating of
leased and managed pubs.

PuriCore plc
508 Lapp Road, Malvern, Pennsylvania, 19355, USA
Telephone +1 484 321 2700
Fax +1 484 321 2725
Website www.puricore.com

Chair
Christopher Wrightman
Chief Executive/Managing Director
Gregory Bosch
Board Members
Bishop Allen, Timothy Anderson, Bill Birkett, Keith
Golden, Michael Sapountzoglou, Dr Alan Suggett, Dr Jim
Walsh

Business Description
A group engaged in the development and
commercialisation of proprietary products that safely,
effectively and naturally kill contagious pathogens and
are designed to limit the spread of infectious disease.

PZ Cussons plc
PZ Cussons House, Bird Hall Lane, Stockport,
Cheshire SK3 0XN
Telephone +44 (0) 161 491 8000
Fax +44 (0) 161 491 8191
Website www.pzcussons.com

Chair
Anthony Green
Chief Executive/Managing Director
Alex Kanellis
Board Members
Prof John Arnold, Graham Calder, Chris Davis, Brandon
Leigh, Derek Lewis, John Pantelireis, Mike Smith, James
Steel

Business Description
A group engaged in the manufacture of soaps, detergents,
toiletries, pharmaceuticals, refrigerators and air
conditioners.

QinetiQ Group plc
Cody Technology Park, Ively Road, Farnborough,
Hampshire GU14 0LX
Telephone +44 (0) 870 010 0942
Website www.qinetiq.com

Chair
Sir John Chisholm
Chief Executive/Managing Director
Graham Love
Board Members
Colin Balmer, Noreen Doyle, Dr Peter Fellner, Sir David
Lees, Nick Luff, George Tenet, Doug Webb

Business Description
A group engaged in delivering research-based technology
solutions and support to government organisations.

Queen's Walk Investment Ltd
Dorey Court, Admiral Park, St Peter Port,
Guernsey GY1 3BG
Telephone +44 (0) 1481 727111
Website www.queenswalkinv.com

Chair
Viscount Chandos
Board Members
Stuart Fiertz, Graham Harrison, John Hawkins, Talmai
Morgan, Christopher Spencer

Business Description
An investment company that primarily invests in asset
backed securities retained by banks and financial houses
for loan assets that collateralise a securitisation
transaction.

Quintain Estates & Development plc
16 Grosvenor Street, London W1K 4QF
Telephone +44 (0) 20 7495 8968
Fax +44 (0) 20 7499 5583
Website www.quintain-estates.com

Chair
Nigel Ellis
Chief Executive/Managing Director
Adrian Wyatt
Board Members
Tonianne Dwyer, Nigel Ellis, Lady Judge, Joan
MacNaughton, Martin Meech, David Pangbourne, John
Plender, Nick Shattock, Rebecca Worthington

Business Description
A group engaged in property investment and the
provision of leisure facilities.

QXL ricardo plc
Matrix Complex, 91 Peterborough Road,
London SW6 3BU
Telephone +44 (0) 20 7384 6300
Fax +44 (0) 20 7384 6320
Website www.qxl.co.uk

Chairman
Simon Duffy
Chief Executive/Managing Director
Christian Unger
Board Members
Robert Simon Dighero, Dan Barnea, Bruce McInroy, Prof
Abraham Neyman, Philip Rowley

Business Description
A company engaged in the provision of online consumer
trading platforms.

RAB Capital plc
1 Adam Street, London WC2N 6LE
Telephone +44 (0) 20 7389 7000
Fax +44 (0) 20 7389 7050
Website www.rabcap.com

Chair
Michael Alen-Buckley
Chief Executive/Managing Director
Philip Richards
Board Members
Rod Barker, Xavier Coirbay, Stephen Couttie, Christopher
de Mattos, Lord Lamont of Lerwick, Sir David Michels,
Derek Riches, Schehrezade Sadeque, Robert Shrager

Business Description
A group engaged in the provision of investment fund
management services.

Randgold Resources Ltd
La Motte Chambers, St Helier, Jersey, Channel
Islands JE1 1BG
Telephone +44 (0) 1534 735333
Fax +44 (0) 1534 735444
Website www.randgoldresources.com

Chair
Philippe Liètard
Chief Executive/Managing Director
Dr Mark Bristow
Board Members
Bernard Asher, Norborn Cole, Robert Israel, Aubrey
Paverd, Graham Shuttleworth, Karl Voltaire

Business Description
Gold mining in Africa.

Rank Group plc (The)
Statesman House, Stafferton Way, Maidenhead SL6 1AY
Telephone +44 (0) 1623 504 000
Fax +44 (0) 1628 504 369
Website www.rank.com

Chair
Peter Johnson
Chief Executive/Managing Director
Ian Burke
Board Members
Peter Gill, Richard Greenhalgh, Dr Brendan O'Neill, Bill
Shannon, John Warren

Business Description
A group engaged in the operation of casinos, bingo clubs,
Hard Rock Cafes and holiday resorts, interactive gaming,
and the provision of services to the film industry.

Rathbone Brothers plc
159 New Bond Street, London W1S 2UD
Telephone +44 (0) 20 7399 0000
Fax +44 (0) 20 7399 0011
Website www.rathbones.com

Chair
Mark Powell
Chief Executive/Managing Director
Andrew Pomfret
Board Members
James Barclay, Ian Buckley, Caroline Burton, James
Cayzer-Colvin, Paul Chavasse, Giles Coode-Adams, Oliver
Corbett, Sue Desborough, Richard Lanyon, Andrew
Morris, Roy Morris, Peter Pearson Lund, Mark
Robertshaw, Richard Smeeton

Business Description
A group engaged in the provision of investment
management, financial planning, private banking, fund
management and trust administration services.

Raven Russia Ltd
Investec House, La Plaiderie, St Peter Port,
Guernsey GY1 3RP
Telephone +44 (0) 1481 750 531
Fax +44 (0) 1481 741 272
Website www.ravenrussia.co.uk

Chair
Adrian Collins
Board Members
Stephen Coe, Glyn Hirsch, David Moore, John Peters

Business Description
A company engaged in investing in Russian property
market.

Raymarine plc
Quay Point, Northarbour Road, Portsmouth,
Hampshire PO6 3TD
Telephone +44 (0) 23 9269 3611
Fax +44 (0) 23 9269 4642
Website www.raymarine.com

Chair
Peter Ward
Chief Executive/Managing Director
Malcolm Miller
Board Members
Paul Boughton, Terry Carlson, Tony Osbaldiston, James
Webster

Business Description
A group engaged in the manufacture and marketing of
navigation equipment within the marine leisure industry.

RCG Holdings Ltd
Clarendon House, 2 Church Street, Hamilton HM11,
Bermuda
Website www.rcg.tv

Chair and Chief Executive
Dr. Raymond Chu
Board Members
Edric Arthur Ackland-Snow, Anita Chau, Stephan Lai,
Dato Lee Boon Han, Bond Liu, General Dato Seri Mohd
Azumi, Lawrence Ying

Business Description
A group engaged in development, manufacture and the
provision of services in the biometrics and RFID
industries.

RCM Technology Trust plc
155 Bishopsgate, London EC2M 3AD
Telephone +44 (0) 20 7426 4000
Fax +44 (0) 20 7247 4722
Website www.closeinvestments.com

Chair
David Quysner
Board Members
John Cornish, Paul Gaunt, Richard Holway, Dr. Chris
Martin, Anthony Townsend

Business Description
An investment trust.

REA Holdings plc
First Floor, 32-36 Great Portland Street,
London W1W 8QX

Business Description
A group engaged in the cultivation of oil palms, and the
production of crude palm oil and crude palm kernel oil.

Real Estate Opportunities Ltd
32 Commercial Street, St Helier, Jersey JE4 0QH
Telephone +44 (0) 1534 833000
Fax +44 (0) 1534 833033
Website www.realestateopportunities.biz

Chair
Ray Horney
Board Members
Richard Barrett, Guy Leech, Keith Jenkins, Philip
Jenkinson, Garth Milne, David Moon, Martin Richardson

Business Description
An investment trust.

Real Hotel Company plc (The)
Premier House, 112-114 Station Road, Edgware,
Middlesex HA8 7BJ
Telephone +44 (0) 20 8233 2001
Fax +44 (0) 20 8233 2000
Website www.choicehotelseurope.com

Chair
Peter Latesby
Chief Executive/Managing Director
Michael Pragner
Board Members
David Hankinson, Paul Mitchell, Harry Platt, Kwai Wong

Business Description
A group engaged in the travel and leisure industry.

Reckitt Benckiser plc
103-105 Bath Road, Slough, Berkshire SL1 3UH
Telephone +44 (0) 1753 217800
Fax +44 (0) 1753 217899
Website www.reckittbenckiser.com

Chair
Adrian Bellamy
Chief Executive/Managing Director
Bart Becht
Board Members
Colin Day, Peter Harf, Ken Hydon, Graham Mackay,
Gerry Murphy, Judith Sprieser, David Tyler, Peter White

Business Description
A group engaged in the manufacture and sale of fabric
care, surface care and home care products, dishwashing
products, health and personal care products and other
household goods.

Redrow plc
Redrow House, St David's Park, Ewloe,
Flintshire CH5 3RX
Telephone +44 (0) 1244 520044
Fax +44 (0) 1244 520580
Website www.redrow.co.uk

Chair
Alan Bowkett
Chief Executive/Managing Director
Neil Fitzsimmons
Board Members
David Arnold, Bob Bennett, Brian Duckworth, Barry
Harvey, Denise Jagger, Malcolm King, Colin Lewis, James
Martin, John Tutte

Business Description
A group engaged in housebuilding and commercial
property development.

Reed Elsevier plc
1-3 Strand, London WC2N 5JR
Telephone +44 (0) 20 7930 7077
Fax +44 (0) 20 7166 5799
Website www.reedelsevier.com

Chair
Jan Hommen
Chief Executive/Managing Director
Sir Crispin Davis
Board Members
Mark Armour, Dien de Boer-Kruyt, Mark Elliott, Erik
Engstrom, Lisa Hook, Robert Polet, Andrew Prozes,
David Reid, Lord Sharman, Dr Rolf Stomberg, Patrick
Tierney, Gerard van de Aast, Strauss Zelnick

Business Description
A group engaged in publishing and information activities.

Regal Petroleum plc
11 Berkeley Street, London W1J 8DS
Telephone +44 (0) 20 7408 9500
Fax +44 (0) 20 7408 9501
Website www.regalpetroleum.com

Chair
Francesco Scolaro
Chief Executive/Managing Director
Neil Ritson
Board Members
Lord Anthony St John of Bletso

Business Description
A group engaged in the production of oil and gas.

Regent Inns plc
Rowley House, South Herts Office Campus, Elstree Way,
Borehamwood, Hertfordshire WD6 1JH
Telephone +44 (0) 20 8327 2540
Fax +44 (0) 20 8327 2541
Website www.regentinns.co.uk

Chair
Bob Ivell
Board Members
Tanith Dodge, Jim Glover, Simon Kaye, John Laurie, John
Leslie, Russell Scott

Business Description
A group engaged in the creation and management of
licensed pubs and entertainment venues within the UK.

Regus Group plc
3000 Hillswood Drive, Hillswood Business Park, Chertsey,
Surrey KT16 0RS
Telephone +44 (0) 870 880 8484
Website www.regus.co.uk

Chair
John Matthews
Chief Executive/Managing Director
Mark Dixon
Board Members
Stephen East, Stephen Gleadle, Rudy Lobo, Roger Orf,
Martin Robinson

Business Description
A holding company for a group engaged in the provision
of fully serviced business centres.

Renaissance US Growth Investment Trust plc
Beaufort House, 51 New North Road, Exeter EX4 4EP
Telephone +44 (0) 1392 412122
Fax +44 (0) 1392 253282
Website www.rencapital.com

Chair
Ernest Fenton
Board Members
Andrew Barker, Steven Bates, Russell Cleveland, Clarence
Rundell, William Vanderfelt

Business Description
An investment trust based in the UK investing in US
quoted companies.

Renesola Ltd
Craigmuir Chambers, PO Box 71, Road Town, Tortola,
British Virgin Islands
Website www.renesola.com

Chair
Martin Bloom
Chief Executive/Managing Director
Li Xian Shou
Board Members
Charles Bai, Prof Huang BingHua, Wu Yun Cai, Prof
Wang Jing

Business Description
A company engaged in the manufacture of solar wafers
for integration into photovoltaic PV cells, the principle
component of crystalline solar panels.

Renishaw plc
New Mills, Wotton-under-Edge, Gloucestershire GL12 8JR
Telephone +44 (0) 1453 524524
Fax +44 (0) 1453 524901
Website www.renishaw.com

Chair and Chief Executive
Sir David McMurtry
Board Members
John Deer, Terry Garthwaite, Geoff McFarland, Prof Joe
McGeehan, Allen Roberts, David Snowden, Ben Taylor

Business Description
A group engaged in the design, manufacture and sale of
advanced precision metrology and inspection equipment,
computer aided design and manufacturing systems and
Raman spectroscopy systems.

Renold plc
Renold House, Styal Road, Wythenshawe, Manchester,
Lancashire M22 5WL
Telephone +44 (0) 161 498 4500
Fax +44 (0) 161 437 7782
Website www.renold.com

Chair
Matthew Peacock
Chief Executive/Managing Director
Robert Davies
Board Members
Barbara Beckett, Peter Bream, Rod Powell, David Shearer

Business Description
A group engaged in the manufacture and sale of power
transmission products and specialist machine tools and
rotors.

Renovo Group plc
Manchester Incubator Building, Grafton Street,
Manchester M13 9XX
Telephone +44 (0) 161 606 7222
Fax +44 (0) 161 606 7333
Website www.renovo.com

Chair
Rodger Pannone
Chief Executive/Managing Director
Prof Mark Ferguson
Board Members
Robin Cridland, Dr David Ebsworth, Dr David Feigal, Dr
John Hutchinson, Andrew Kay, Dr Sharon O'Kane, Dr
Arthur Rosenthal, Dr Barrie Thorpe, Lord Turnberg

Business Description
A group engaged in developing a portfolio of drugs
which exploit novel mechanisms of action to prevent and
reduce scarring of multiple body sites.

Rensburg Sheppards plc
Quayside House, Canal Wharf, Leeds LS11 5PU
Telephone +44 (0) 113 245 4488
Fax +44 (0) 113 245 1188
Website www.rensburgsheppards.co.uk

Chair
Christopher Clarke
Chief Executive/Managing Director
Stephen Elliott
Board Members
Michael Haan, Bernard Kantor, Stephen Koseff, Nick Lane
Fox, Ian Scott, Andrew Tyrie, Jonathan Wragg

Business Description
A group engaged in personal asset management and
other related financial activities.

Rentokil Initial plc
Felcourt Road, Felcourt, East Grinstead, West
Sussex RH19 2JY
Telephone +44 (0) 1342 833022
Fax +44 (0) 1342 326229
Website www.rentokil-initial.com

Chair
B D McGowan
Chief Executive/Managing Director
D Flynn
Board Members
A E Macfarlane, I Hartley, P J Long, D Tatton Brown, A
Giles, D Bamford

Business Description
A group engaged in the provision of support services,
including textiles and washroom services, pest control,
office plants and artwork, parcels delivery and facilities
services.

Resolution plc
Juxton House, 100 St Paul's Churchyard,
London EC4M 8BU
Telephone +44 (0) 20 7489 4800
Fax +44 (0) 20 7489 4860
Website www.resolutionplc.com

Chair
Clive Cowdery
Chief Executive/Managing Director
Mike Biggs
Board Members
David Allvey, Sir David Cooksey, Ian Maidens, Brendan
Meehan, Jim Newman, Sir Brian Williamson, Sir Malcolm
Williamson

Business Description
A group engaged in the management of in-force UK life
funds.

Resources Investment Trust plc
The Registry, 34 Beckenham Road, Beckenham,
Kent BR3 4TU
Telephone +44 (0) 870 162 3100
Fax +44 (0) 20 8658 3430
Website www.rei-trust.com

Chair
James Dawnay
Board Members
Howard Drummon, Charles Fowler, David Hutchins,
Richard Martin, Kjeld Thygesen

Business Description
An investment trust.

Restaurant Group plc
5-7 Marshalsea Road, London SE1 1EP
Telephone +44 (0) 845 612 5001
Fax +44 (0) 845 612 5011
Website www.ccruk.com

Chair
Alan Jackson
Chief Executive/Managing Director
Andrew Page
Board Members
Kevin Bacon, Trish Corzine, Stephen Critoph, John
Jackson, David H Richardson, Andrew Thomas

Business Description
A group engaged in operating and managing restaurants.

Reuters Group plc
The Reuters Building, South Colonnade, Canary Wharf,
London E14 5EP
Telephone +44 (0) 20 7250 1122
Fax +44 (0) 20 7542 6843
Website www.reuters.com

Chair
Niall FitzGerald
Chief Executive/Managing Director
Thomas Glocer
Board Members
Lawton Fitt, David Grigson, Penny Hughes, Sir Deryck
Maughan, Nandan Nilekani, Ken Olisa, Dick Olver, Ian
Strachan, Devin Wenig

Business Description
The provision of business information, including news
prices analytics and transaction services, and the
operation of an electronic agency securities broker.

Rexam plc
4 Millbank, London SW1P 3XR
Telephone +44 (0) 20 7227 4100
Fax +44 (0) 20 7227 4109
Website www.rexam.com

Chair
Rolf Börjesson
Chief Executive/Managing Director
Leslie Van de Walle
Board Members
Bill Barker, Mike Buzzacott, Graham Chipchase, Noreen
Doyle, Wolfgang Meusberger, David Robbie, Jean-Pierre
Rodier, Carl Symon, David Tucker

Business Description
A group engaged in the manufacture of beverage
packaging and plastic packaging products.

Ricardo plc
Shoreham Technical Centre, Shoreham by Sea, West
Sussex BN43 5FG
Telephone +44 (0) 1273 455611
Fax +44 (0) 1273 794556
Website www.ricardo.com

Chair
Marcus Beresford
Chief Executive/Managing Director
Dave Shemmans
Board Members
Paula Bell, David Hall, Michael Harper, Steve Parker, Ian
Percy

Business Description
A group engaged in the provision of engineering and
technological services and strategic consulting to
industry, commerce and other agencies.

Rightmove plc
Grafton Court, Snowdon Drive, Winterhill, Milton
Keynes MK6 1AJ
Telephone +44 (0) 1908 308500
Website www.rightmove.co.uk

Chair
Scott Forbes
Chief Executive/Managing Director
Ed Williams
Board Members
Jonathan Agnew, Nigel Cooper, Nick McKittrick, Stephen
Shipperley, Judy Vezmar, Graham Zacharias

Business Description
A group engaged in the operation of the Rightmove
website.

Rio Tinto plc
6 St James's Square, London SW1Y 4LD
Telephone +44 (0) 20 7930 2399
Fax +44 (0) 20 7930 3249
Website www.riotinto.com

Chair
Paul Skinner
Chief Executive/Managing Director
Tom Albanese
Board Members
Dr Ashton Calvert, Sir David Clementi, Vivienne Cox, Sir
Rod Eddington, Guy Elliott, Michael Fitzpatrick, Richard
Goodmanson, Andrew Gould, Lord Kerr of Kinlochard,
David Mayhew, Sir Richard Sykes

Business Description
A group engaged in the mining and processing of mineral
resources including aluminium, copper, diamonds, coal,
uranium, gold, borax, titanium, dioxide, salt, talc and iron
ore.

RIT Capital Partners plc
27 St James's Place, London SW1A 1NR
Telephone +44 (0) 20 7493 8111
Fax +44 (0) 20 7493 5765
Website www.ritcap.co.uk

Chair
Lord Rothschild
Board Members
Charles Bailey, Mikael Breuer-Weil, Duncan Budge, John
Elkann, David Haysey, Andrew Knight, James Leigh-
Pemberton, Michael Marks, Nathaniel Rothschild, Michael
Sofaer

Business Description
An investment trust with subsidiaries engaged in
investment holding, management and dealing.

RM plc
New Mill House, 183 Milton Park, Abingdon,
Oxfordshire OX14 4SE
Telephone +44 (0) 870 920 0200
Fax +44 (0) 1235 826999
Website www.rm.com

Chair
John Leighfield
Chief Executive/Managing Director
Tim Pearson
Board Members
Prof Tim Brighouse, Sir Bryan Carsberg, Sherry Coutu,
Mike Greig, Rob Sirs, Sir Mike Tomlinson, John Windeler

Business Description
A group engaged in the supply of information and
communications technology, software systems and
services to UK educational establishments and the
delivery of education services.

Robert Walters plc
55 Strand, London WC2N 5WR
Telephone +44 (0) 20 7379 3333
Fax +44 (0) 20 7509 8714
Website www.robertwalters.com

Chair
Philip Aiken
Chief Executive/Managing Director
Robert Walters
Board Members
Alan Bannatyne, Giles Daubeney, Martin Griffiths, Ian
Nash, Russell Tenzer

Business Description
A group engaged in the provision of recruitment services
to clients in the financial, commercial and industrial
sectors.

Robert Wiseman Dairies plc
159 Glasgow Road, East Kilbride, Glasgow G74 4PA
Telephone +44 (0) 1355 244261
Fax +44 (0) 1355 230352
Website www.wiseman-dairies.co.uk

Chair
Alan Wiseman
Chief Executive/Managing Director
Robert Wiseman
Board Members
Andrew Dare, David Dobbins, Ernest Finch, Beverley
Hodson, William Keane, Martin Mulcahy, Norman Murray

Business Description
A group engaged in the processing and distribution of
milk and associated products.

ROC Oil Company Ltd
Level 41, 1 Market Street, Sydney, NSW 2000, Australia
Telephone +61 2 8356 2000
Fax +61 2 9380 2066
Website www.rocoil.com.au

Chair
Andrew Love
Chief Executive/Managing Director
John Doran
Board Members
Bruce Clement, Ross Dobinson, Sidney Jansma Jr, William
Jephcott, Adam Jollife, Dennis Paterson

Business Description
A company engaged in the production of oil and gas.

Rok plc
ROK Centre, 40 Tower Hill, London EC3N 4OX
Telephone +44 (0) 20 7977 5910
Fax +44 (0) 20 7977 5945
Website www.rokgroup.com

Chair
Stephen Pettit
Chief Executive/Managing Director
Garvis Snook
Board Members
Christopher Bailey, Gillian Camm, Ian Ellis, Ashley
Martin, Sue Moore, John Samuel, David Sutherland

Business Description
A group engaged in property development, building and
maintenance.

Rolls-Royce plc
65 Buckingham Gate, London SW1E 6AT
Telephone +44 (0) 20 7222 9020
Fax +44 (0) 20 7227 0178
Website www.rolls-royce.com

Chair
Simon Robertson
Chief Executive/Managing Director
Sir John Rose
Board Members
Peter Byrom, John Cheffins, Iain Conn, Prof Peter
Gregson, James Guyette, John Rishton, Andrew Shilston,
Colin Smith, Ian Strachan, Carl Symon

Business Description
A global business providing power systems for use on
land, at sea and in the air.

Ross Group plc
35 Paul Street, London EC2A 4UQ
Telephone +44 (0) 23 8067 5500
Fax +44 (0) 23 8067 5555
Website www.ross-group.co.uk

Chair
Adrian Chi Chiu Ma
Board Members
Michael Binney, Ruby Lee Yen Kee, Michael Simon

Business Description
A group engaged in the design and manufacture of
engineering products and the import, distribution and sale
of battery chargers and electrical adaptors, and the
provision of financial services.

Rotork plc
Rotork House, Brassmill Lane, Bath BA1 3JQ
Telephone +44 (0) 1225 733200
Fax +44 (0) 1255 333467
Website www.rotork.com

Chair
Roger Lockwood
Chief Executive/Managing Director
Bill Whiteley
Board Members
Bob Arnold, Peter France, Ian King, John Matthews, Dr
Graham Ogden, Bob Slater, Alexander Walker

Business Description
A group engaged in the design, manufacture and support
of actuators systems and related products.

Royal & Sun Alliance Insurance Group plc
One Plantation Place, 30 Fenchurch Street,
London EC3M 3BD
Telephone +44 (0) 20 7111 7134
Website www.royalsunalliance.com

Chair
John Napier
Chief Executive/Managing Director
Andrew Haste
Board Members
George Culmer, Noël Harwerth, Malcolm Le May, Edward
Lea, Simon Lee, Bridget McIntyre, John Maxwell

Business Description
A group engaged in the transaction of insurance business
and the provision of related financial services.

Royal Bank of Scotland Group plc (The)
PO Box 1000, Gogarburn, Edinburgh EH12 1HQ
Telephone +44 (0) 20 626 0000
Website www.rbs.com

Chair
Sir Tom McKillop
Chief Executive/Managing Director
Sir Frederick Goodwin
Board Members
Colin Buchan, Johnny Cameron, James Currie, Lawrence
Fish, Mark Fisher, William Friedrich, Archie Hunter, Bud
Koch, Janis Kong, Joe MacHale, Gordon Pell, Sir Stephen
Robson, Bob Scott, Peter Sutherland, Guy Whittaker

Business Description
A group engaged in the provision of a range of banking
insurance and other financial services.

Royal Dutch Shell plc
Shell Centre, York Road, London SE1 7NA
Telephone +44 (0) 20 7934 1234
Website www.shell.com

Chair
Jorma Ollila
Chief Executive/Managing Director
Jeroen van der Veer
Board Members
Malcolm Brinded, Linda Cook, Nina Henderson, Sir Peter
Job, Lord Kerr of Kinlochard, Wim Kok, Nick Land,
Christine Morin-Postel, Lawrence Ricciardi, Rob Routs,
Maarten van den Bergh, Peter Voser

Business Description
A group of oil, gas and petrochemical companies with a
portfolio of hydrogen, biofuels, wind and solar power
interests.

Royal London UK Equity & Income Trust plc
55 Moorgate, London EC2R 6PA
Telephone +44 (0) 20 4710 3132
Fax +44 (0) 20 7477 5849

Chair
Jonathan Carr
Board Members
Christopher Edge, Harry Hyman, Anthony Percival,
Trevor Robinson

Business Description
An investment trust with an investment holding
subsidiary.

RPC Group plc
Lakeside House, Higham Ferrers,
Northamptonshire NN10 8RP
Telephone +44 (0) 1933 410064
Fax +44 (0) 1933 410083
Website www.rpc-group.com

Chair
Peter Williams
Chief Executive/Managing Director
Ronald Marsh
Board Members
Bay Green, Philip Hilton, Peter Hole, Henk Kloeze,
Stephan Rojahn, Christopher Sworn, Dr David
Wilbraham, Peter Wood

Business Description
A group engaged in the manufacture and sale of rigid
plastic packaging.

RPS Group plc
Centurion Court, 85 Milton Park, Abingdon OX14 4RY
Telephone +44 (0) 1235 438000
Fax +44 (0) 1235 864451
Website www.rpsplc.co.uk

Chair
Brook Land
Chief Executive/Managing Director
Dr. Alan S Hearne
Board Members
John Bennett, Roger Devlin, Peter B Dowen, Karen
McPherson, Andrew R G Troup, Phil Williams, Gary
Young

Business Description
A consultancy specialising in the development of natural
resources, land and property, management of the
environment and the health and safety.

S & U plc
Royal House, Prince's Gate Homer Road, Solihull, West
Midlands B91 3QQ
Telephone +44 (0) 121 705 7777
Fax +44 (0) 121 705 7878
Website www.suplc.co.uk

Chairman
Derek Coombs
Board Members
Anthony Coombs, Fiann Coombs, Graham Coombs,
Christopher Redford, Guy Thompson

Business Description
A group engaged in consumer credit and car finance
including financial services, hire purchase and sales of
electrical and household merchandise.

SABMiller plc
One Stanhope Gate, London W1K 1AF
Telephone +44 (0) 20 7659 0100
Fax +44 (0) 20 7659 0111
Website www.sabmiller.com

Chair
Meyer Kahn
Chief Executive/Managing Director
Graham Mackay
Board Members
Geoffrey Bible, Liz Doherty, Lord Fellowes, John Manser,
John Manzoni, Miles Morland, Carlos Pérez Dávila, Cyril
Ramaphosa, Lord Renwick of Clifton, Alejandro Santo
Domingo Dávila, Malcolm Wyman

Business Description
A group engaged in the brewing and distribution of beer
and other beverages.

Safestore Holdings plc
Brittanic House, Stirling Way, Borehamwood,
Hertfordshire WD6 2BT
Telephone +44 (0) 20 8732 1500
Website www.safestore.com

Chair
John von Speckelsen
Chief Executive/Managing Director
Stephen Williams
Board Members
Roger Carey, Richard Grainger, Vincent Gwilliam

Business Description
A group engaged in the provision of individual, secure
self-storage space and related services for business and
residential customers.

Sage Group plc (The)
North Park, Newcastle-upon-Tyne NE13 9AA
Telephone +44 (0) 191 294 3000
Fax +44 (0) 191 294 0002
Website www.sage.com

Chair
Anthony Hobson
Chief Executive/Managing Director
Paul Walker
Board Members
Guy Berruyer, David Clayton, Paul Harrison, Tamara
Ingram, Tim Ingram, Ruth Markland, Paul Stobart, Ron
Verni

Business Description
A group engaged in the development, distribution and
support of business management software and related
products and services.

Sagentia Group AG
Harston Mill, Harston, Cambridge CB22 7GG
Telephone +44 (0) 1223 875200
Website www.sagentia.com

Chair
Chris Masters
Chief Executive/Managing Director
Martin Frost
Board Members
Johan Bjorklund, Gordon Edge, Dan Flicos, Martin
Forster, Lars Kylberg, Markus Rauh

Business Description
An integrated technology consulting, development and
venturing organisation.

Salamander Energy plc
Charter House, 13 - 15 Carteret Street, London SW1H 9DJ
Telephone +44 (0) 20 7222 4553
Fax +44 (0) 20 7692 5524
Website www.salamander-energy.com

Chair
Charles Jamieson
Chief Executive/Managing Director
James Menzies
Board Members
Mike Buck, Robert Cathery, Andrew Cochran, Nick
Cooper, John Crowle, Michael Pavia, Struan Robertson

Business Description
A group engaged in oil and gas exploration, development
and production, focused on building a portfolio of assets
in Southeast Asia.

Sandvine Inc
408 Albert Street, Waterloo, Ontario, N2L 3V3, Canada
Telephone +1 (519) 880 2600
Fax +1 (519) 884 9882
Website www.sandvine.com

Chair and Chief Executive
Dave Caputo
Board Members
Don Bowman, Chris Colman, Angelo Compagnoni, Tom
Donelly, Scott Hamilton, Marc Morin, Wojciech Nincevic,
Brad Siim

Business Description
A company engaged in developing and marketing
network equipment for residential broadband service
providers.

Savills plc
20 Grosvenor Hill, Berkeley Square, London W1X 3HQ
Telephone +44 (0) 20 7499 8644
Fax +44 (0) 20 7495 3773
Website www.savills.com

Chair
Peter Smith
Chief Executive/Managing Director
Aubrey Adams
Board Members
Martin Angle, Jeremy Helsby, Simon Hope, Tim Ingram,
Robert McKellar, Charles McVeigh, Rupert Sebag-
Montefiore, Fields Wicker-Miurin

Business Description
A group engaged in the provision of advice relating to
commercial, agricultural, residential and leisure property,
corporate finance advice, property and venture capital
funding.

Schroder Asia Pacific Fund plc
31 Gresham Street, London EC2V 7QA
Telephone +44 (0) 20 7658 6000
Fax +44 (0) 20 7658 3538
Website www.schroders.co.uk

Chair
Hon Rupert Carington
Board Members
Robert Binyon, Earl of Cromer, Anthony Fenn, Jan
Kingzett

Business Description
An investment trust investing in equities of companies
located in the continent of Asia together with Far Eastern
countries bordering the Pacific Ocean.

Schroder Income Growth Fund plc
31 Gresham Street, London EC2V 7QA
Telephone +44 (0) 20 7658 6000
Fax +44 (0) 20 7658 6965
Website www.schroders.co.uk

Chair
Sir Paul Judge
Board Members
Peregrine Banbury, Ian Barby, Keith Niven, Peter
Readman

Business Description
An investment trust investing in companies that suffer
from negative sentiment and where valuation is
particularly appealing.

Schroder Japan Growth Fund plc
31 Gresham Street, London EC2V 7QA
Telephone +44 (0) 20 7658 3206
Website www.schroders.co.uk

Chair
Jonathan Taylor
Board Members
Jan Kingzett, Peter Lyon, John Scott, Yoshindo Takahashi

Business Description
An investment trust.

Schroder Oriental Income Fund Ltd
PO Box 255, Trafalgar Court, Les Banques, St Peter Port,
Guernsey GY1 3QL
Website www.schroders.co.uk

Chair
Robert Sinclair
Board Members
Peter Rigg, Christopher Sherwell

Business Description
An investment fund.

Schroder Split Investment Fund plc
31 Gresham Street, London EC2V 7QA
Telephone +44 (0) 20 7658 6501
Website www.schroders.co.uk/its

Chair
John Padovan
Board Members
Richard Foulkes, Richard Martin, Anthony Wands

Business Description
An investment trust.

Schroder UK Growth Fund plc
31 Gresham Street, London EC2V 7QA
Telephone +44 (0) 20 7658 3206
Website www.schroders.co.uk

Chair
Alan Clifton
Board Members
Keith Niven, Ian Phillips, Stella Pirie, David Ritchie

Business Description
An investment trust.

Schroder UK Mid & Small Cap Fund plc
31 Gresham Street, London EC2V 7QA
Telephone +44 (0) 20 7658 3206
Website www.schroders.co.uk/its

Chair
Prof Peter Timms
Board Members
Rachel Beagles, Malcolm Coubrough, Christopher Jones, Maxwell Packe

Business Description
An investment trust.

Schroders plc
31 Gresham Street, London EC2V 7QA
Telephone +44 (0) 20 7658 6000
Fax +44 (0) 20 7658 6965
Website www.schroders.com

Chair
Michael Miles
Chief Executive/Managing Director
Michael Dobson
Board Members
Jonathan Asquith, Andrew Beeson, Luc Bertrand, Alan Brown, Sir Peter Job, Merlyn Lowther, George Mallinckrodt, Kevin Parry, Bruno Schroder, Massimo Tosato

Business Description
A group engaged in the provision of international asset management services including private banking.

SCI Entertainment Group plc
Wimbledon Bridge House, 1 Hartfield Road, Wimbledon, London SW19 3RU
Telephone +44 (0) 20 8636 3000
Fax +44 (0) 20 8636 3001
Website www.sci.co.uk

Chair
Tim Ryan
Chief Executive/Managing Director
Jane Cavanagh
Board Members
Roger Ames, Bill Ennis, Don Johnston, Rob Murphy, Nigel Wayne

Business Description
A publisher of computer games and a developer and publisher of entertainment software.

Scott Wilson Group plc
Scott House, Basing View, Basingstoke RG21 4JG
Telephone +44 (0) 1256 310200
Fax +44 (0) 1256 310201
Website www.scottwilson.com

Chair
Geoffrey French
Chief Executive/Managing Director
Hugh Blackwood and Ronald Wall
Board Members
Pelham Allen, Stuart Doughty, Stephen Kimmett, James Newman

Business Description
An international consultancy group.

Scottish & Newcastle plc
28 St Andrew Square, Edinburgh EH2 1AF
Telephone +44 (0) 131 203 2000
Website www.scottish-newcastle.com

Chair
Sir Brian Stewart
Chief Executive/Managing Director
Anthony Froggatt
Board Members
Dr Neville Bain, Philip Bowman, John Dunsmore, Sir Angus Grossart, Erik Hartwall, Peter Kennerley, Bridget Macaskill, Ian McAllister, Ian McHoul, John Nicolson, Sir Ian Robinson, Henrik Therman, Brian Wallace

Business Description
A group engaged in the production and wholesale of beer and the operation of public houses.

Scottish & Southern Energy plc
Inveralmond House, 200 Dunkeld House, Perth PH1 3AQ
Telephone +44 (0) 1738 456000
Website www.scottish-southern.co.uk

Chair
Sir Robert Smith
Chief Executive/Managing Director
Ian Marchant
Board Members
Gregor Alexander, Nick Baldwin, Richard Gillingwater, Colin Hood, René Médori, David Payne, Alistair Phillips-Davies, Susan Rice, Sir Kevin Smith

Business Description
The generation, transmission, distribution and supply of electricity, energy trading, storage and supply of gas, electrical and utility contracting, appliance sale and telecoms.

Scottish American Investment Company plc (The)
Calton Square, 1 Greenside Row, Edinburgh EH1 3AN
Telephone +44 (0) 131 275 2000
Website www.bailliegifford.com

Chair
Brian Ivory
Board Members
Eric Hagman, Lord Kerr of Kinlochard, Peter Moon, Dr Janet Morgan, David Price

Business Description
A trust that invests in a broad range of assets within the UK and internationally to sustain a progressive dividend policy.

Scottish Investment Trust plc (The)
6 Albyn Place, Edinburgh EH2 4NL
Telephone +44 (0) 131 225 7781
Fax +44 (0) 131 226 3663
Website www.sit.co.uk

Chair
Douglas McDougall
Board Members
Hamish Buchan, Francis Finlay, Hamish Leslie Melville, James MacLeod, Sir George Mathewson

Business Description
A self-managed investment trust company.

Scottish Mortgage Investment Trust plc
Calton Square, 1 Greenside Row, Edinburgh EH1 3AN
Telephone +44 (0) 131 275 2000
Website www.bailliegifford.com

Chair
Sir Donald Mackay
Board Members
Geoffrey Ball, Michael Gray, Gordon McQueen, John Scott, Lord Strathclyde

Business Description
An investment trust.

Scottish Oriental Smaller Companies Trust plc (The)
23 St Andrew Square, Edinburgh EH2 1BB
Telephone +44 (0) 131 473 2200
Fax +44 (0) 131 473 2222
Website www.firststate.co.uk

Chair
James Ferguson
Board Members
Alexandra Mackesy, Sir Hamish Macleod, Janet Morgan, David Pike, Stanley Rowan

Business Description
An investment trust.

ScS Upholstery plc
45-49 Villiers Street, Sunderland SR1 1HA
Telephone +44 (0) 191 514 6000
Fax +44 (0) 191 510 9048
Website www.scssofas.co.uk

Chair
Mike Browne
Chief Executive/Managing Director
David Knight
Board Members
Sacha Beere, Nigel Howes, Denise Jagger, Kevin Royal, Ron Turnbull

Business Description
A group engaged as specialist upholstered furniture retailers.

SDL plc
Globe House, Clivemount Road, Maidenhead, Berkshire SL6 7DY
Telephone +44 (0) 1628 410100
Fax +44 (0) 1628 410150
Website www.sdl.com

Chair and Chief Executive
Mark Lancaster
Board Members
Christopher Batterham, Joseph Campbell, Alastair Gordon, Cristina Lancaster, John Matthews, Keith Mills

Business Description
A group engaged in the provision of globalization service solutions and related software applications to a wide variety of multinational businesses.

Securities Trust of Scotland plc
Petersgate House, Saltire Court, 20 Castle Terrace, Edinburgh EH1 2ES
Telephone +44 (0) 131 100 2125
Fax +44 (0) 131 222 2532
Website www.securitiestrust.com

Chair
Neil Donaldson
Board Members
Charles Berry, Anita Frew, Andrew Irvine, Edward Murray

Business Description
An investment trust.

Segro plc
234 Bath Road, Slough SL1 4EE
Telephone +44 (0) 1753 537171
Fax +44 (0) 1753 820585
Website www.segro.com

Chair
Nigel Rich
Chief Executive/Managing Director
Ian Coul
Board Members
Lord Norman Blackwell, John Heathwood, Walter Hens, Stephen Howard, Lesley McDonagh, Andrew Palmer, Chris Peacock, Thomas Wernick

Business Description
A company engaged in property investment and development.

Senior plc
Senior House, 59/61 High Street, Rickmansworth, Herts WD3 1RH
Telephone +44 (0) 1923 775547
Fax +44 (0) 1928 896027
Website www.seniorplc.com

Chair
Martin Clark
Chief Executive/Managing Director
Graham Menzies
Board Members
David Best, Ian Much, Mark Rollins, Mike Sheppard

Business Description
A group engaged in the design, manufacture and marketing of high technology components and systems for OE producers in aerospace, automotive and specialised industrial markets.

Serco Group plc
Serco House, 16 Bartley Wood Business Park, Bartley Way, Hook, Hampshire RG27 9UY
Telephone +44 (0) 1256 745900
Fax +44 (0) 1256 744111
Website www.serco.com

Chair
Kevin Beeston
Chief Executive/Managing Director
Christopher Hyman
Board Members
Baroness Ford, Andrew Jenner, Dr DeAnne Julius, David Richardson, Grant Rumbles, Leonard van Groenou

Business Description
A group engaged in the provision of facilities management systems, engineering services and equity investment management.

Servicepower Technologies plc
Petersgate House, St Petersgate, Stockport, Cheshire SK1 1HE
Telephone +44 (0) 161 476 2277
Fax +44 (0) 161 480 8088
Website www.servicepower.com

Chair
Barry Welck
Chief Executive/Managing Director
David Brisco
Board Members
Lindsay Bury, Ian MacKinnon

Business Description
A group engaged in the development and sale of scheduling software and the provision of scheduling solutions.

Severfield-Rowen plc
Dalton Airfield Industrial Estate, Dalton, Thirsk, North
Yorkshire YO7 3JN
Telephone +44 (0) 1845 577896
Fax +44 (0) 1845 577411
Website www.srfplc.com

Chair
Peter Levine
Chief Executive/Managing Director
John Severs
Board Members
Peter Davison, Keith Elliot, Peter Ellison, Peter Emerson,
John Featherstone, Tom Haughey, Brian Hick, Nigel
Pickard, David Ridley, Geoffrey Wright

Business Description
A group engaged in the design, manufacture and erection
of structural steelwork, specialist claddings and ancillary
products.

Severn Trent plc
2297 Coventry Road, Birmingham B26 3PU
Telephone +44 (0) 121 722 4000
Fax +44 (0) 121 722 4800
Website www.severn-trent.com

Chair
Sir John Egan
Chief Executive/Managing Director
Colin Matthews
Board Members
Dr Bernard Bulkin, Richard Davey, Martin Houston, Mike
McKeon, John Smith, Tony Wray

Business Description
A group engaged in the supply of water and sewerage
services, waste management and the provision of
environmental services.

Shaftesbury plc
Pegasus House, 37-43 Sackville Street, London W1S 3DL
Telephone +44 (0) 20 7333 8118
Fax +44 (0) 20 7333 0660
Website www.shaftesbury.co.uk

Chair
John Manser
Chief Executive/Managing Director
Jonathan Lane
Board Members
Brian Bickell, John Emly, Alastair MacDonald, Gordon
McQueen, Simon Quayle, Thomas Welton

Business Description
A group engaged in the investment and refurbishment of
commercial properties.

Shanks Group plc
Astor House, Station Road, Bourne End,
Buckinghamshire SL8 5YP
Telephone +44 (0) 1628 554920
Website www.shanks.co.uk

Chair
Adrian Auer
Chief Executive/Managing Director
Tom Drury
Board Members
Peter Johnson, Dr Stephen Riley, Eric van Amerongen,
Fraser Welham

Business Description
A group engaged in waste management, the treatment of
hazardous chemical waste and generation of electricity.

Shire plc
Hampshire International Business Park, Chinsham,
Basingstoke, Hampshire RG24 8EP
Telephone +44 (0) 1256 894000
Fax +44 (0) 1256 894708
Website www.shire.com

Chair
Dr James Cavanaugh
Chief Executive/Managing Director
Matthew Emmens
Board Members
Robin Buchanan, David Kappler, Patrick Langlois, Dr
Jeffrey Leiden, Kate Nealon, Dr Barry Price, Angus
Russell

Business Description
A group engaged in the marketing, research and
development of prescription medicines.

Shires Income plc
165 Queen Victoria Street, London EC4V 4DD
Telephone +44 (0) 141 572 2700
Fax +44 (0) 141 572 3777
Website www.glasgowinvestmentmanagers.co.uk

Chair
J Martin Haldane
Board Members
Mervyn Couve, Hon Joanna Davidson, Tony Davidson,
David Kidd

Business Description
An investment trust with a subsidiary engaged as
investment dealers.

Shires Smaller Companies plc
Sutherland House, 149 St Vincent Street,
Glasgow G2 5DR
Telephone +44 (0) 141 572 2700
Fax +44 (0) 141 572 2777
Website www.glasgowinvestmentmanagers.co.uk

Chair
Henry Cathcart
Board Members
Carolan Dobson, Dinah Nichols, James West

Business Description
An investment trust.

Shore Capital Group plc
Bond Street House, 14 Clifford Street, London W1S 4JU
Telephone +44 (0) 20 7408 4090
Fax +44 (0) 20 7408 4091
Website www.shorecap.co.uk

Chair
Howard Shore
Chief Executive/Managing Director
Graham Shore
Board Members
Barry Douglas, Dr Zvi Marom, Jonathan Paisner, Michael
van Messel

Business Description
A group engaged in the provision of investment banking
services including stockbroking, market making, corporate
financial advice and growth capital fund management.

Sibir Energy plc
17C Curzon Street, London W1J 5HU
Telephone +44 (0) 20 7495 7878
Fax +44 (0) 20 7495 8090
Website www.sibirenergy.com

Chair
William Guinness
Chief Executive/Managing Director
Henry Cameron
Board Members
Alexander Betsky, Stuard Detmer, Urs Haener, Chalva
Tchigirinski

Business Description
A group engaged in the acquisition, exploration,
development and production of oil and gas reserves,
refining of oil, and the sale of oil and refined products.

SIG plc
Hillsborough Works, Longsett Road, Sheffield S6 2LW
Telephone +44 (0) 114 285 6300
Fax +44 (0) 114 285 6385
Website www.sigplc.co.uk

Chair
Les Tench
Chief Executive/Managing Director
David Williams
Board Members
Peter Blackburn, Michael Borlenghi, John Chivers, Chris
Davies, Gareth Davies, David Haxby

Business Description
A group engaged in the distribution of thermal insulation
materials, roofing materials, ceiling tiles, personal
protective equipment and partitioning.

Signet Group plc
15 Golden Square, London W1F 9JG
Telephone +44 (0) 20 7317 9700
Fax +44 (0) 20 7734 1452
Website www.signetgroupplc.com

Chair
Malcolm Williamson
Chief Executive/Managing Director
Terry Burman
Board Members
Robert Anderson, Robert Blanchard, Walker Boyd, Dale
Hilpert, Brook Land, Mark Light, Robert Walker, Russell
Walls

Business Description
A group engaged in the retail of jewellery, watches and
gifts.

SkyePharma plc
105 Piccadilly, London W1J 7NJ
Telephone +44 (0) 20 7491 1777
Fax +44 (0) 20 7491 3338
Website www.skyepharma.com

Chair
Dr Jerry Karabelas
Chief Executive/Managing Director
Frank Condella
Board Members
Alan Bray, Dr Ken Cunningham, Dr David Ebsworth,
Peter Grant, Stephen Harris, Jean-Charles Tschudin

Business Description
A group engaged in the research, development,
manufacture and sale of prescription pharmaceutical
products.

Small Companies Dividend Trust plc
Beaufort House, 51 New North Road, Exeter,
Devon EX4 4EP
Telephone +44 (0) 1392 412 122
Website www.chelvertonam.com
Board Members
John Chappell, David Harris, The Rt Hon Lord Lamont of
Lerwick, Brian Lenygon, W Van Heesewijk

Business Description
An investment trust with a dealing subsidiary.

SMG plc
Pacific Quay, Glasgow G51 1PQ
Telephone +44 (0) 141 300 3074
Website www.smg.plc.uk

Chair
Richard Findlay
Chief Executive/Managing Director
Rob Woodward
Board Members
Lord Alli, Vasa Babic, Jamie Matheson, Matthew Peacock,
David Shearer, George Watt

Business Description
A group engaged in the production broadcasting of
television programmes, and local and national radio. Also
the sale of advertising airtime and space in these media,
and in outdoor cinema and internet services.

Smith & Nephew plc
15 Adam Street, London WC2N 6LA
Telephone +44 (0) 20 7401 7646
Fax +44 (0) 20 7930 3353
Website www.smith-nephew.com

Chair
Dr John Buchanan
Chief Executive/Managing Director
Sir Christopher O'Donnell
Board Members
Richard De Schutter, Adrian Hennah, David Illingworth,
Pam Kirby, Warren Knowlton, Brian Larcombe, Dr Rolf
Stomberg

Business Description
A group engaged in the provision of advanced medical
devices including orthopaedic implant and trauma
products, advanced wound management and endoscopic
products and techniques.

Smiths Group plc
765 Finchley Road, London NW11 8DS
Telephone +44 (0) 20 8458 3232
Fax +44 (0) 20 8457 8346
Website www.smiths-group.com

Chair
Donald Brydon
Chief Executive/Managing Director
Keith Butler-Wheelhouse
Board Members
David Challen, Stuart Chambers, Peter Jackson, John
Langston, David Lillycrop, Peter Loescher, Sir Kevin
Tebbit

Business Description
The development, manufacture, sale and support of
integrated aerospace systems, advanced security
equipment, medical devices and industrial mechanical
seals.

Smiths News plc
Wakefield House, Pipers Way, Swindon,
Wiltshire SN3 1RF
Telephone +44 (0) 845 123 0000
Fax +44 (0) 20 1793 421483
Website www.smithnews.co.uk

Chair
Brendan Fitzmaurice
Chief Executive/Managing Director
Mark Cashmore
Board Members
John Cann, Alan Humphrey, Dennis Millard, John Worby

Business Description
A group engaged in the distribution of newspapers on
behalf of all the major national newspaper publishers, as
well as a large number of regional daily and weekly
newspapers. Also distributes magazines for large and
small publishers.

SOCO International plc
St James's House, 23 King Street, London SW1Y 6QY
Telephone +44 (0) 20 7747 2000
Fax +44 (0) 20 7747 2001
Website www.socointernational.co.uk

Chair
Rui de Sousa
Chief Executive/Managing Director
Ed Story
Board Members
Olivier Barbaroux, Roger Cagle, Bob Cathery, Ettore Contini, Peter Kingston, John Norton, Martin Roberts, John Snyder

Business Description
A group engaged in the exploration and production of oil and gas.

Sondex plc
Saxony Way, Blackbushe Business Park, Yateley, Hampshire GU46 6AB
Telephone +44 (0) 1252 862200
Fax +44 (0) 1252 862349
Website www.sondex.co.uk

Chair
Iain Paterson
Chief Executive/Managing Director
Martin Perry
Board Members
William Colvin, Robin Pinchbek, William Stuart-Bruges, Christopher Wilks

Business Description
A group engaged in the development and manufacture of instrumentation and equipment for the monitoring and inspection of oil wells whilst they are in production.

Songbird Estates plc
1 Canada Square, Canary Wharf, London E14 5AB
Telephone +44 (0) 20 7477 1000
Fax +44 (0) 20 7477 1001
Website www.songbirdestates.com

Chair
David Pritchard
Board Members
Brian Carr, Eugene Doyle, Robert Gray, Gabriela Gryger, Philip Lader, Samuel Levinson, Gavin MacDonald, Alex Midgen, Richard Powers, David Pritchard

Business Description
The holding company of the Canary Wharf Group which is engaged in property development, managment and investment.

Southern Cross Healthcare Group plc
Southgate House, Archer Street, Darlington, Durham DL3 6AH
Telephone +44 (0) 1325 351100
Website www.schealthcare.co.uk

Chair
William Colvin
Chief Executive/Managing Director
Philip Scott
Board Members
Christopher Fisher, Ray Miles, Baroness Morgan of Huyton, John Murphy, Graham Sizer

Business Description
A company engaged in the provision of residential and nursing care services.

Spazio Investment NV
Royal Damcentre, Bam 7F, 1012 JS, Amsterdam, Netherlands
Telephone +31 (0) 20 486 7646
Fax +31 (0) 20 486 7898
Website www.spazioinvestment.com

Chair
John Duggan
Board Members
Roy Dantzic, Olivier de Poulpiquet, Richard Mully, Gualtiero Tamburini

Business Description
A company engaged in the management of real estate businesses and companies, and investment in units of real estate funds.

Spectris plc
35-51 Station Road, Egham, Surrey TW20 9NP
Telephone +44 (0) 1784 470470
Fax +44 (0) 1784 470848
Website www.spectris.com

Chair
John Poulter
Chief Executive/Managing Director
John O'Higgins
Board Members
Peter Chambrè, Stephen Harris, John Hughes, Anthony Reading, John Warren, Clive Watson, James Webster

Business Description
A group engaged in the development and marketing of precision instrumentation and controls.

Speedy Hire plc
Chase House, 16 The Parks, Newton Le Willows, Merseyside WA12 0JQ
Telephone +44 (0) 1942 720000
Fax +44 (0) 1942 720077
Website www.speedyhire.co.uk

Chair
David Wallis
Chief Executive/Managing Director
Steve Corcoran
Board Members
Peter Atkinson, Frank Dee, David Galloway, Michael McGrath, Neil O'Brien, Patrick Rawnsley

Business Description
A group engaged in the provision of tool hire services.

Speymill Deutsche Immobillien Company plc
Jubilee Buildings, Victoria Street, Douglas, Isle of Man IM1 2SH
Telephone +44 (0) 1624 698000

Chair
Raymond Apsey
Board Members
Anthony Baillieu, Derek Butler, David Humbles, Leonard O'Brien

Business Description
A group engaged investing in the German property market, predominantly in the residential sector.

Spice plc
Wellfield House, Victoria Road, Morley, Leeds LS27 7PA
Telephone +44 (0) 113 201 2120
Fax +44 (0) 113 201 2121
Website www.spiceplc.com

Chairman
Sir Rodney Walker
Chief Executive/Managing Director
William Rigby
Board Members
Carl Chambers, Oliver Lightowlers, Michael Shallow, John Taylor

Business Description
A group engaged in facilities management and outsourcing the provision of services for the development and support of telecommunications networks and drain care and repair.

Spirax-Sarco Engineering plc
Charlton House, Cirencester Road, Cheltenham, Gloucestershire GL53 8ER
Telephone +44 (0) 1242 521 361
Fax +44 (0) 1242 581 470
Website www.spiraxsarcoengineering.com

Chair
Michael Townsend
Chief Executive/Managing Director
Marcus Steel
Board Members
Alan Black, Gareth Bullock, Neil Daws, Einar Lindh, David Meredith, Tony Scrivin, Peter Smith, Mark Vernon, Bill Whiteley

Business Description
A group engaged in the provision of knowledge service and products for the control and efficient use of steam and other industrial fluids and for peristaltic pumping.

Spirent Communications plc
Spirent House, Crawley Business Quarter, Fleming Way, Crawley, West Sussex RH10 9QL
Telephone +44 (0) 1293 767979
Fax +44 (0) 1293 767978
Website www.spirentcom.com

Chair
Edward Bramston
Board Members
Ian Brindle, Gerard Eastman, Eric Hutchinson, Duncan Lewis, Alexander Walker

Business Description
A group engaged in the design and manufacture of communications, performance analysis and service assurance systems, and electronic control systems.

Sportech plc
Walton House, Charnock Road, Liverpool L67 1AA
Telephone +44 (0) 151 288 3500
Website www.sportechplc.co.uk

Chair
Piers Pottinger
Chief Executive/Managing Director
Ian Penrose
Board Members
John Barnes, Steven Cunliffe, Kathryn Revitt

Business Description
A group engaged in the operation of football pools games, lotteries and sports betting under the Littlewoods Gaming brand.

Sportingbet plc
4th Floor, 45 Moorfields, London EC2Y 9AE
Telephone +44 (0) 20 7184 1800
Fax +44 (0) 20 7184 1810
Website www.sportingbet.com

Chief Executive/Managing Director
Andrew McIver
Board Members
Mark Blandford, Brian Harris, David Hobday, Sean O'Connor, Nigel Payne

Business Description
A group engaged in the operation of interactive licensed betting and gaming operations over the internet and telephone.

Sports Direct International plc
Unit A, Brook Park East Road, Shirebrook, Mansfield NG20 8RY
Telephone +44 (0) 870 838 7370
Website www.sportsdirect.com

Chair
Simon Bentley
Chief Executive/Managing Director
Dave Forsey
Board Members
Mike Ashley, Chris Bulmer, Bob Mellors

Business Description
A group engaged in the retailing and distribution of sports and leisure clothing, footwear and equipment.

Spring Group plc
Hazlitt House, 4 Bouverie Street, London EC4Y 8AX
Telephone +44 (0) 20 7300 9000
Fax +44 (0) 20 7300 9090
Website www.spring.com

Chair
Amir Eilon
Chief Executive/Managing Director
Peter Searle
Board Members
Adam Cohn, Peter Darraugh, Steven Fink, Andrew Pinder, Jonathan Wright

Business Description
A group engaged in the provision of recruitment, staffing, training and related services.

SR Europe Investment Trust
Beaufort house, 51 New North Road, Exeter EX4 4EP
Telephone +44 (0) 1392 412 122
Website www.sreit.co.uk

Chair and Chief Executive
Martin Riley
Board Members
Ian Barby, David Boyle, Tim Guinness, Hugh Sloane

Business Description
An investment trust.

SSL International plc
35 New Bridge Street, London EC4V 6BW
Telephone +44 (0) 20 7367 5760
Fax +44 (0) 20 7367 5790
Website www.ssl-international.com

Chair
Gerald Corbett
Chief Executive/Managing Director
Garry Watts
Board Members
Richard Adam, Ian Adamson, Anna Catalano, Mark Moran, Susan Murray, Dr Peter Read

Business Description
A group engaged in the manufacture and distribution of consumer healthcare products, medical products, and industrial gloves.

St Ives plc
St Ives House, Lavington Street, London SE1 0NX
Telephone +44 (0) 20 7928 8844
Fax +44 (0) 20 7902 6466
Website www.st-ives.co.uk

Chair
Miles Emley
Chief Executive/Managing Director
Brian Edwards
Board Members
Wayne Angstrom, Matthew Armitage, David Best, Simon Marquis, Patrick Martell, Richard Stillwell, Dame Sue Tinson, Simon Ward, Dr David Wilbraham

Business Description
A group engaged in magazine and book printing, binding, direct response and commercial printing, security printing and printing for the multimedia and music industries.

St James's Place plc
St James's Place House, Dollar Street, Cirencester,
Gloucestershire GL7 2AQ
Telephone +44 (0) 1285 640302
Fax +44 (0) 1285 640436
Website www.sjpc.co.uk

Chair
Michael Wilson
Chief Executive/Managing Director
David Bellamy
Board Members
Sarah Bates, Andrew Croft, Jo Dawson, Ian Gascoigne,
Simon Gulliford, Andy Hornby, Derek Netherton, Prof
Mike Power, Michael Sorkin, Roger Walsom

Business Description
A group engaged in the transaction of life pensions and
permanent health insurance business & unit trust
management.

St Modwen Properties plc
Sir Stanley Clarke House, 7 Ridgeway, Quinton Business
Park, Birmingham B32 1AF
Telephone +44 (0) 121 222 9400
Fax +44 (0) 121 222 9401
Website www.stmodwen.co.uk

Chair
Anthony Glossop
Chief Executive/Managing Director
Bill Oliver
Board Members
Steve Burke, Simon Clarke, Mary Francis, Tim Haywood,
Ian Menzies-Gow, Paul Rigg, Christopher Roshier, John
Salmon

Business Description
A group engaged in property investment and
development.

Stagecoach Group plc
10 Dunkeld Road, Perth, Perthshire PH1 5TW
Telephone +44 (0) 1738 442111
Fax +44 (0) 1738 643648
Website www.stagecoachplc.com

Chair
Robert Speirs
Chief Executive/Managing Director
Brian Souter
Board Members
Ewan Brown, Iain Duffin, Ann Gloag, Martin Griffiths,
Sir George Mathewson, Dr Janet Morgan, Gary Watts

Business Description
A group engaged in the provision of public transport
services.

Standard Chartered plc
1 Aldermanbury Square, London EC2V 7SB
Telephone +44 (0) 20 7280 7500
Fax +44 (0) 20 7280 7791
Website www.standardchartered.com

Chair
Mervyn Davies
Chief Executive/Managing Director
Peter Sands
Board Members
Sir C K Chow, Michael DeNoma, Jamie Dundas, Val
Gooding, Rudy Markham, Ruth Markland, Richard
Meddings, Kai Nargolwala, Paul Skinner, Oliver Stocken,
Lord Turner of Ecchinswell

Business Description
A group engaged in the provision of banking and other
financial services.

Standard Life Equity Income Trust plc
Level 3 City Tower, Basinhall Street, London EC2V 5DE
Website www.standardlifeinvestments.com/its

Chair
Charles Wood
Board Members
Richard Burns, John Morrison, Keith Percy, Christopher
Rowlands

Business Description
An investment trust.

Standard Life European Private Equity Trust plc
1 George Street, Edinburgh EH2 2LL
Telephone +44 (0) 131 245 6499
Fax +44 (0) 131 245 6105
Website www.standardlifeinvestments.com

Chair
Scott Dobbie
Board Members
Hamish Buchan, Simon Edwards, George Kershaw, Clive
Sherling, Mark Tyndall, Donald Workman

Business Description
An investment trust.

Standard Life Investments Property Income Trust
Trafalgar Court, Les Banques, St Peter Port,
Guernsey GY1 3QL
Telephone +44 (0) 1481 745001
Fax +44 (0) 1481 745051
Website www.standardlifeinvestments.com

Chair
David Moore
Board Members
Richard Barfield, John Hallam, Shelagh Mason, Paul
Orchard-Lisle

Business Description
An investment trust.

Standard Life plc
30 Lothian Road, Edinburgh EH1 2DH
Telephone +44 (0) 131 225 2552
Website www.standardlife.com

Chair
Gerry Grimstone
Chief Executive/Managing Director
Sandy Crombie
Board Members
Kent Atkinson, Lord Blackwell, Crawford Giles, Baroness
McDonagh, Trevor Matthews, David Nish, Jocelyn
Proteau, Keith Skeoch, Hugh Stevenson

Business Description
A group engaged in the provision of financial services,
including insurance, banking and investment
management.

Standard Life UK Smaller Companies Trust plc
Donaldson House, 97 Haymarket Terrace,
Edinburgh EH12 5HD

Business Description
An investment trust company.

Stanelco plc
Starpol Technology Centre, North Road, Marchwood,
Southampton, Hampshire SO40 4BL
Telephone +44 (0) 23 8086 7100
Fax +44 (0) 23 8086 7070
Website www.stanelcoplc.com

Chair
Philip Lovegrove
Chief Executive/Managing Director
Martin Wagner
Board Members
Elizabeth Filkin, John Standen, Clive Warner, Howard
White

Business Description
A group engaged in the development, manufacture and
supply of high-frequency thermal processing equipment
and processes.

Star Energy Group plc
Ground Floor, Burdett House, 15/16 Buckingham House,
London WC2N 6DU
Telephone +44 (0) 20 7925 2121
Fax +44 (0) 20 7930 9919
Website www.starenergy.co.uk

Chair
Stephen Gutteridge
Chief Executive/Managing Director
Roland Wessel
Board Members
Stephen East, Adrian Fernando, Melvyn Horgan, Colin
Judd, Roger Pearson, David Wertheim

Business Description
An energy company, focusing on gas storage
development.

Steppe Cement Ltd
10th Floor, Rohas Perkasa, West Wing, No 8 Jalan Perak,
50450 Kuala Lumpur, Malaysia
Telephone +603 21 61 7552
Fax +603 21 61 8722
Website www.steppecement.com

Chair
John Richardson
Board Members
Keith Newman, Javier Perez, Paul Rodzianko

Business Description
Cement manufacturing and sales business, operating from
the Republic of Kazakhstan.

Sterling Energy plc
5 Chancery Lane, London WC2A 1LG
Telephone +44 (0) 20 7405 4133
Fax +44 (0) 20 7440 9059
Website www.sterlingenergyplc.com

Chair
Dick Stabbins
Chief Executive/Managing Director
Harry Wilson
Board Members
Christopher Callaway, Paul Griggs, Andrew Grosse,
Graeme Thomson, Peter Wilde

Business Description
A group engaged in the exploration and production of oil
and gas.

SThree plc
41-44 Great Windmill Street, London W1D 7NB
Telephone +44 (0) 20 7292 3838
Fax +44 (0) 20 7292 3839
Website www.sthree.com

Chair
Sir Anthony Cleaver
Chief Executive/Managing Director
Russell Clements
Board Members
Alicja Lesniak, Brian McBride, Michael Nelson, Tony
Ward, Sunil Wickremeratne

Business Description
A group engaged in the staffing of businesses in the
information, communication and technology sectors, with
operations in banking and finance, accountancy,
engineering and human resources.

Strategic Equity Capital plc
Beaufort House, 51 New North Road, Exeter EX4 4EP
Telephone +44 (0) 1392 412122
Fax +44 (0) 1392 253282
Website www.strategicequitycapital.com

Chair
John Hodson
Board Members
John Cornish, Jonathan Morgan, Sir Clive Thompson

Business Description
An investment trust.

Styles & Wood Group plc
Aspect House, Manchester Road, Altrincham WA14 5PG
Telephone +44 (0) 161 926 6000
Fax +44 (0) 161 926 6001
Website www.stylesandwood.co.uk

Chair
Gerard Quiligotti
Chief Executive/Managing Director
Neil Davies
Board Members
Robert Hough, Jim Martin, Paul Mitchell

Business Description
A provider of retail property services.

Superscape Group plc
Regus Centaur House, Ancells Bussiness Park, Ancells
Road, Fleet, Hampshire GU51 2UJ
Telephone +44 (0) 1252 761442
Fax +44 (0) 1252 761243
Website www.superscape.com

Chair
Larry Quinn
Chief Executive/Managing Director
Kevin Roberts
Board Members
Tom Frangione, Dave Goodman, Mike Inglis, David Lee,
Peter Magowan

Business Description
A group engaged in the development and publishing of
2D and 3D mobile games for the global wireless industry.

Surfcontrol plc
Riverside, Mountbatten Way, Congleton,
Cheshire CW12 1DY
Telephone +44 (0) 1260 296200
Fax +44 (0) 1260 296201
Website www.surfcontrol.com

Chair
Greg Lock
Chief Executive/Managing Director
Patricia Sueltz
Board Members
George Hayter, Patrick Jolly, Steve Purdham, Rene
Schuster, Jane Tozer, Simon Wilson

Business Description
A group engaged in the development and sale of internet,
web and e-mail filtering software products.

SVG Capital plc
111 Strand, London WC2R 0AG
Fax +44 (0) 20 7010 8900
Website www.svgcapital.com

Chair
Nicholas Ferguson
Board Members
Damon Buffini, Francis Finlay, Anthony Habgood, Edgar Koning, Denis Raeburn, Charles Sinclair, Gary Steinberg, Andrew Williams

Business Description
An investment trust with subsidiaries engaged in unit trust operation, the provision of advisory and administration services, and as investment brokers and dealers.

SVM Global Fund plc
7 Castle Street, Edinburgh EH2 3AH
Telephone +44 (0) 131 226 6699
Fax +44 (0) 131 226 7799
Website www.svmonline.co.uk

Chair
Shane Ross
Chief Executive/Managing Director
Colin McClean
Board Members
Terence Arthur, Daniel Hodson, Peter Hulse, Alan Saunders

Business Description
A cash shell whose former subsidiary was engaged in the sale of food.

SVM UK Active Fund plc
6th Floor, 7 Castle Street, Edinburgh EH2 3AH
Telephone +44 (0) 131 226 6699
Fax +44 (0) 131 226 7799
Website www.svmonline.co.uk

Chair
Mark Powell
Board Members
Fred Carr, John Lloyd, Colin McClean

Business Description
An investment trust with a dealing subsidiary investing in UK quoted companies.

SVM UK Emerging Fund plc
7 Castle Street, Edinburgh EH2 3AH
Telephone +44 (0) 131 226 6699
Fax +44 (0) 131 226 7799
Website www.svmonline.co.uk

Chair
Peter Dicks
Board Members
Richard Bernstein, Anthony Puckridge

Business Description
An investment trust company investing in smaller UK companies with a particular focus on the AIM.

Synergy Healthcare plc
Newmarket Drive, Derby DE24 8SW
Telephone +44 (0) 1332 387100
Fax +44 (0) 1332 754138
Website www.synergyhealthcare.plc.uk

Chair
Stephen Wilson
Chief Executive/Managing Director
Dr Richard Steeves
Board Members
Ivan Jacques, Robert Lerwill, Sir Duncan Nichol, Marcello Smit

Business Description
A group engaged in the provision of a range of services and products to the healthcare market.

T Clarke plc
Stanhope House, 116 - 118 Walworth Road, London SE17 1JY
Telephone +44 (0) 20 7358 5000
Fax +44 (0) 20 7701 6265
Website www.tclarke.co.uk

Chair
Russell Race
Chief Executive/Managing Director
Pat Stanborough
Board Members
Leonard Arnold, Mike Crowder, Barry DeFalco, Victoria French, Mark Lawrence, Beverley Stewart

Business Description
A specialist electrical contractor.

Tadpole Technology plc
Kittle Yards, Causeway, Edinburgh EH9 1PJ
Telephone +44 (0) 131 668 0200
Fax +44 (0) 131 668 0202
Website www.tadpoletechnology.com

Chair
David Lee
Chief Executive/Managing Director
Dr Mark Ketteman
Board Members
Peter Bondar, Iain Cockburn

Business Description
A group engaged in the design, development and sale of computer software products and services.

Tanfield Group plc
Vigo Centre, Birtley Road, Washington, Tyne & Wear NE38 9DA
Telephone +44 (0) 845 1557 755
Fax +44 (0) 845 1557 756
Website www.tanfieldgroup.com

Chair
Roy Stanley
Chief Executive/Managing Director
Darren Kell
Board Members
John Bridge, Charles Brooks, Brendan Campbell, Martin Groak

Business Description
A group engaged in the development and manufacture of zero emission electric vehicles and aerial work platforms.

Tarsus Group plc
4th Floor, Metro Building, 1 Butterwick, London W6 8DL
Telephone +44 (0) 20 8846 2700
Fax +44 (0) 20 8846 2801
Website www.tarsus-group.com

Chair
Neville Buch
Chief Executive/Managing Director
Douglas Emslie
Board Members
Bernard Becker, Neil Jones, Roger Pellow, Hugh Scrimgeour, Robert Ware

Business Description
A group engaged as an integrated media group spanning e-business exhibitions, conferences and publishing.

Tate & Lyle plc
Sugar Quay, Lower Thames Street, London EC3R 6DQ
Telephone +44 (0) 20 7626 6525
Fax +44 (0) 20 7623 5213
Website www.tateandlyle.com

Chair
Sir David Lees
Chief Executive/Managing Director
Iain Ferguson
Board Members
Liz Airey, Richard Delbridge, Evert Henkes, Stanley Musesengwa, Kai Nargolwala, John Nicholas, Stuart Strathdee, Robert Walker, Dr Barry Zoumas

Business Description
A group engaged in the processing of carbohydrates to provide a range of sweetener and starch products and animal feed, and the provision of bulk storage facilities.

Taylor Nelson Sofres plc
TNS House, West Gate, London W5 1UA
Telephone +44 (0) 20 8967 0007
Fax +44 (0) 20 8967 4060
Website www.tns-global.com

Chair
Donald Brydon
Chief Executive/Managing Director
David Lowden
Board Members
Dawn Airey, Andy Boland, Drummond Hall, Paul Murray, Alice Perkins, Pedro Ros, Rémy Sautter

Business Description
A group engaged in the provision of market information services.

Taylor Wimpey plc
2 Princes Way, Solihull, West Midlands B91 3ES
Telephone +44 (0) 121 600 8000
Fax +44 (0) 121 600 8001
Website www.taylorwimpey.com

Chair
Norman Askew
Chief Executive/Managing Director
Peter Redfern
Board Members
Mike Davies, Baroness Dean of Thornton-le-Fyde, Andrew Dougal, Peter Johnson, James Jordan, John Landrum, Anthony Reading, Ian Sutcliffe, David Williams

Business Description
A company engaged in homebuilding.

TDG plc
4-5 Grosvenor Place, London SW1X 7HJ
Telephone +44 (0) 20 7838 7775
Fax +44 (0) 20 7838 7760
Website www.tdg.eu.com

Chair
Charles Mackay
Chief Executive/Managing Director
David Garman
Board Members
Michael Averill, Jeffrey Hewitt, Jeffrey Hume

Business Description
Provides domestic and international businesses with logistics and supply chain solutions.

Ted Baker plc
The Ugly Brown Building, 6A Saint Pancras Way, London NW1 0TB
Telephone +44 (0) 20 7255 4800
Fax +44 (0) 20 7255 4961
Website www.tedbaker.co.uk

Chair
Robert Breare
Chief Executive/Managing Director
Raymond Kelvin
Board Members
David Bernstein, David Hewitt, Lindsay Page

Business Description
A group engaged in the design, wholesale and retail of menswear, womenswear and childrenswear.

Teesland Advantage Property Income Trust plc
Connaught House, 1 Mount Street, London W1K 3NB
Telephone +44 (0) 20 7659 6666
Fax +44 (0) 20 7659 6667
Website www.teesland.com

Chair
Christopher Fish
Board Members
Robert Bould, Caroline Burton, Charles Parkinson, Nicholas Renny

Business Description
Closed-ended Guernsey incorporated investment company investing in commercial property in the UK and the Channel Islands.

Telecom Plus plc
Dryden House, The Edge Business Centre, Humber Road, London NW2 6EW
Telephone +44 (0) 20 8955 5000
Fax +44 (0) 20 8955 5700
Website www.telecomplus.co.uk

Chair
Peter Nutting
Chief Executive/Managing Director
Charles Wigoder
Board Members
Melvin Lawson, Richard Michell, Michael Pavia, Keith Stella

Business Description
A group engaged in the supply of fixed telephony, mobile telephony, gas, electricity and internet services to residential and small business customers.

Telent plc
New Century Park, PO Box 53, Coventry, West Midlands CV3 1HJ
Telephone +44 (0) 24 7656 2000
Fax +44 (0) 24 7656 7000
Website www.telent.com

Chair
John Devaney
Chief Executive/Managing Director
Mark Plato
Board Members
Michael Atkinson, Heather Green, Peter Hickson, Werner Koepf, Douglas McWilliams

Business Description
A group engaged in the design, manufacture and supply of telecommunication equipment and services, and the provision of associated support applications.

Telspec plc
Lancaster Parker Road, Rochester Airport, Rochester, Kent ME1 3QU
Telephone +44 (0) 1634 687133
Fax +44 (0) 1634 684 984
Website www.telspec.co.uk

Chief Executive/Managing Director
Shiv Rakkar
Board Members
John Thomas, Fred White

Business Description
A group engaged in the development, manufacture and sale of advanced telecommunications equipment.

Temple Bar Investment Trust plc
2 Gresham Street, London EC2V 7QP
Telephone +44 (0) 20 7597 2000
Fax +44 (0) 20 7597 1818
Website www.templebarinvestments.co.uk

Chair
John Reeve
Board Members
Gary Allen, June de Moller, Richard Jewson, Martin Riley, Field Walton

Business Description
An investment trust company with a subsidiary engaged in investment dealing.

Templeton Emerging Markets Investment Trust plc
5 Morrison Street, Edinburgh EH3 8BH
Telephone +44 (0) 131 221 7555
Fax +44 (0) 131 242 4531
Website www.temit.co.uk

Chair
Sir Ronald Hampel
Board Members
Sir Peter Burt, Neil Collins, Peter Godsoe, Charles Johnson, Andrew Knight, Peter Smith

Business Description
An investment trust.

Terrace Hill Group plc
James Sellars House, 144 West George Street, Glasgow G2 2HG
Telephone +44 (0) 141 332 2014
Fax +44 (0) 141 332 2015
Website www.terracehill.co.uk

Chair
Robert Adair
Board Members
Bob Dyson, Kelvin Hudson, Philip Leech, Tom Walsh, Will Wyatt

Business Description
A group engaged in commercial and residential property development.

Tesco plc
Tesco House, Delamare Road, Cheshunt, Waltham Cross, Hertfordshire EN8 9SL
Telephone +44 (0) 1992 632222
Website www.tesco.com

Chair
David Reid
Chief Executive/Managing Director
Sir Terence Leahy
Board Members
Charles Allen, Richard Brasher, Rodney Chase, Philip Clarke, Karen Cook, Mervyn Davies, Dr Harald Einsmann, Andrew Higginson, Ken Hydon, Tim Mason, Carolyn McCall, Lucy Neville-Rolfe, David Potts

Business Description
A group engaged in retailing and associated activities.

Tex Holdings plc
Claydon Business Park, Gipping Road, Great Blakenham, Ipswich, Suffolk IP6 0NL
Telephone +44 (0) 1473 830144
Fax +44 (0) 1473 832545
Website www.tex-holdings.co.uk

Chair
Anthony Burrows
Board Members
Matthew Cadbury, Richard Corbett, J Greve, M Harrison

Business Description
A group engaged in plastic injection moulding and toolmaking, and the manufacture and supply of proprietary piling equipment, engineering products, and boards and panels.

Third Advance Value Realisation Company Ltd
1 Le Marchant Street, St Peter Port, Guernsey GY1 4HP
Website www.pro-asset.com

Chair
Robert Norbury
Board Members
Barclay Douglas, David Kempton, Philip Okell

Business Description
An investment company.

Thomas Cook Group plc
The Thomas Cook Business Park, Coningsby Road, Peterborough PE3 HSB
Telephone +44 (0) 1733 417100
Website www.thomascook.com

Chair
Dr Thomas Middelhoff
Chief Executive/Managing Director
Peter Hugh
Board Members
David Allvey, Michael Beckett, John Bloodworth, Roger Burnell, Dr Peter Diesch, Manny Fontenla-Novoa, Ludger Heuberg, Hemjo Klein, Bo Lerenius, Dr Angus Porter

Business Description
A group engaged in travel, including the operation of travel agencies and aircraft.

Thompson Clive Investments plc
24 Old Bond Street, London W1S 4AW
Telephone +44 (0) 20 7535 4900
Fax +44 (0) 20 7493 9172
Website www.tcvc.com

Chair
Christopher Jones
Board Members
Charles Fitzherbert, Peter Glossop, Peter Longland

Business Description
An investment trust.

Thorntons plc
Thornton Park, Somercotes, Alfreton, Derbyshire DE55 4XJ
Telephone +44 (0) 1773 540550
Fax +44 (0) 1773 540757
Website www.thorntons.co.uk

Chair
John von Spreckelsen
Chief Executive/Managing Director
Mike Davies
Board Members
Barry Bloomer, Martin Davey, Dominic Prendergast, John Wall, Paul Wilkinson, Peter Wright

Business Description
A group engaged in the retail distribution and manufacture of confectionery and other sweet foods including chocolate, cakes, desserts and ice creams.

Throgmorton Trust plc (The)
155 Bishopsgate, London EC2M 3XJ
Telephone +44 (0) 20 7374 4100
Fax +44 (0) 20 7330 6644
Website www.framlington.co.uk

Chair
Richard Bernays
Board Members
Simon Beart, Lord Latymer, Simon Stevens, Eric Stobart, Harry Westropp

Business Description
An investment trust investing in UK smaller companies.

Thus Group plc
1-2 Berkeley Square, 99 Berkeley Street, Glasgow G3 7HR
Telephone +44 (0) 800 027 5848
Fax +44 (0) 141 566 3105
Website www.thus.net

Chair
Philip Rogerson
Chief Executive/Managing Director
William Allan
Board Members
Ian Chippendale, Jo Connell, John Maguire, Philip Male

Business Description
A group engaged in the provision of voice data, internet and contact centre services to corporate small and medium sized enterprise markets.

Titon Holdings plc
International House, Peartree Road, Stanway, Colchester, Essex CO3 0JL
Telephone +44 (0) 1206 713800
Fax +44 (0) 1206 543126
Website www.titon.co.uk

Chair
John Anderson
Chief Executive/Managing Director
David Ruffell
Board Members
Tyson Anderson, Ron Brighton, Peter Fitt, Nicholas Howlett, Christopher Jarvis, Chris Martin, Patrick O'Sullivan, Keith Ritchie

Business Description
A group engaged in the design, manufacture and marketing of ventilation products, window fittings and accessories.

Tomkins plc
East Putney House, 84 Upper Richmond Road, London SW15 2ST
Telephone +44 (0) 20 8871 4544
Fax +44 (0) 20 8877 9700
Website www.tomkins.co.uk

Chair
David Newlands
Chief Executive/Managing Director
James Nicol
Board Members
Richard Gillingwater, Ken Lever, John McDonough, Iain Napier, Leo Quinn, David Richardson, Struan Robertson

Business Description
A group engaged in the manufacture of industrial and automotive equipment, engineered and construction products, and air systems components.

Topps Tiles plc
Thorpe Way Grove Park, Enderby, Leicestershire LE19 1SU
Telephone +44 (0) 116 282 8000
Website www.toppstiles.com

Chair
Barry Bester
Chief Executive/Managing Director
Nicholas Ounstead
Board Members
Rt Hon Michael Jack, Alan Mcintosh, Robert Parker, Victor Watson

Business Description
A company specialising in tiles and wood flooring.

Torotrak plc
1 Aston Way, Leyland, Preston, Lancashire PR26 7UX
Telephone +44 (0) 1772 900900
Fax +44 (0) 1772 900929
Website www.torotrak.com

Chair
John Grant
Chief Executive/Managing Director
Dick Elsy
Board Members
Nick Barter, James Batchelor, Jeremy Deering, David MacKay

Business Description
A group engaged in the design and development of traction drive infinitely variable transmission systems.

Total Systems plc
394 City Road, London EC1V 2QA
Telephone +44 (0) 20 7294 4888
Fax +44 (0) 20 7294 4999
Website www.totalsystems.co.uk

Chair
Terence Bourne
Board Members
Clive Dutton, Granville Harris, Arthur Weber

Business Description
A group engaged in the writing and supply of computer software and the supply of related hardware.

Town Centre Securities plc
Town Centre House, The Merrion Centre, Leeds LS2 8LY
Telephone +44 (0) 113 222 1234
Fax +44 (0) 113 242 1026
Website www.tcs-plc.co.uk

Chair and Chief Executive
Edward Ziff
Board Members
Robert Bigley, James Crawford, Clive Lewis, Richard Lewis, John Nettleton, Robin Smith, Michael Ziff

Business Description
A group engaged in property investment development and trading.

TR European Growth Trust plc
4 Broadgate, London EC2M 2DA
Telephone +44 (0) 20 7818 1818
Fax +44 (0) 20 7818 1819
Website www.henderson.com

Chair
Audley Twiston-Davies
Board Members
Bernard Clark, Robert Jeens, Jeremy Lancaster, Jochen Neynaber

Business Description
An investment trust with a dealing subsidiary.

TR Property Investment Trust plc
51 Berkeley Square, London W1J 5BB
Telephone +44 (0) 20 7360 1200
Fax +44 (0) 20 7360 1300
Website www.trproperty.com

Chair
Peter Salsbury
Chief Executive/Managing Director
Jeremy Newsum
Board Members
Caroline Burton, Richard Stone, Peter Wolton

Business Description
An investment trust company with subsidiaries engaged in property investment, development and dealing.

Trading Emissions plc
Third Floor, Exchange House, 54-62 Athol Street, Douglas, Isle of Man IM1 1JD
Telephone +44 (0) 20 7382 7801
Website www.tradingemissionsplc.com

Chair
Neil Eckert
Board Members
Robin Bigland, Malcolm Gillies, Philip Scales, Nigel Wood

Business Description
An investment fund engaged in acquiring tradable environmental instruments.

Trafficmaster plc
Martell House, University Way, Cranfield, Bedfordshire MK43 0TR
Telephone +44 (0) 1234 759000
Fax +44 (0) 1234 759317
Website www.trafficmaster.co.uk

Chair
Colin Walsh
Chief Executive/Managing Director
Tony Eales
Board Members
Stuart Berman, Geoffrey Bicknell, Nigel Bond, Ian Coomber, Alan McWalter, Tim Van Cleve

Business Description
A group engaged in journey management providing satellite navigation, traffic data, fleet management and vehicle tracking.

Travis Perkins plc
Lodge Way House, Lodge Way, Harleston Road, Northampton NN5 7UG
Telephone +44 (0) 1604 752424
Fax +44 (0) 1604 683164
Website www.travisperkins.co.uk

Chair
Tim Stevenson
Chief Executive/Managing Director
Geoff Cooper
Board Members
Chris Bunker, John Carter, Stephen Carter, John Coleman, Michael Dearden, Paul Hampden Smith, Andrew Simon

Business Description
A group engaged in the marketing and distribution of timber building and plumbing and heating materials, and the hire of tools to the building trade and industry generally.

Treatt plc
Northern Way, Bury St Edmunds, Suffolk IP32 6NL
Telephone +44 (0) 1284 702500
Fax +44 (0) 1284 703809
Website www.treatt.com

Chair
Edward Dawnay
Board Members
David Appleby, Hugo Bovill, Anita Haines, Richard Hope, Peter Thorburn

Business Description
A group engaged in the blending and distillation of essential oils, the marketing of aroma chemicals, and the production of other natural distillates.

Triad Group plc
Weyside Park, Catteshall Lane, Godalming, Surrey GU7 1XE
Telephone +44 (0) 1483 860222
Fax +44 (0) 1483 860198
Website www.triad.co.uk

Chair
Dr John Rigg
Board Members
Alistair Fulton, Ian Haynes, Steven Sanderson

Business Description
The company is engaged in the provision of business consultancy software and systems.

Tribal Group plc
Priory Court, Poulton, Cirencester GL7 5JB
Telephone +44 (0) 1285 886 020
Fax +44 (0) 1285 886 021
Website www.tribalgroup.co.uk

Chair
Strone Macpherson
Chief Executive/Managing Director
Henry Pitman
Board Members
Simon Lawton, Peter Martin, Timothy Stevenson, David Thompson

Business Description
A group engaged in the provision of consultancy and professional support services.

Tribune UK Tracker plc
50 Bank Street, Canary Wharf, London E14 5NT
Telephone +44 (0) 20 7982 2000
Website www.tribunetrust.com

Chair
Christopher Stobart
Board Members
Gordon Bagot, John Callahan, Christopher Purvis

Business Description
A group engaged in investing in the UK market.

Trifast plc
Trifast House, Bellbrook Park, Uckfield, East Sussex TN22 1OW
Telephone +44 (0) 1825 747 366
Fax +44 (0) 1825 747 368
Website www.trifast.com

Chair
Anthony Allen
Chief Executive/Managing Director
James Barker
Board Members
Steve Auld, Geoffrey Budd, Andrew Cripps, Eric Hutchinson, Stuart Lawson, Steven Tan

Business Description
A group engaged in the manufacture and distribution of industrial fastenings and category 'C' components.

Trinity Capital plc
Ioma House, Hope Street, Douglas, Isle of Man IM1 1AP
Telephone +44 (0) 1624 681250
Website www.trinityplc.com

Chair
Michael Cassidy
Board Members
Rak Chugh, William Hamilton-Turner, Paul Orchard-Lisle, Philip Scales

Business Description
A group engaged in investment in real estate and real estate related entities including infrastructure across India.

Trinity Mirror plc
1 Canada Square, London E14 5AP
Telephone +44 (0) 20 7293 3000
Fax +44 (0) 20 7293 3405
Website www.trinitymirror.com

Chair
Sir Ian Gibson
Chief Executive/Managing Director
Sly Bailey
Board Members
Gary Hoffman, Kathleen O'Donovan, Vijay Vaghela, Paul Vickers, Laura Wade-Gery

Business Description
A group engaged in the publication and printing of newspapers.

TT Electronics plc
Clive House, 12-18 Queens Road, Weybridge, Surrey KT13 9XB
Telephone +44 (0) 1932 841310
Fax +44 (0) 1932 836450
Website www.ttelectronics.com

Chair
John Newman
Chief Executive/Managing Director
Neil Rodgers
Board Members
James Armstrong, David Crowe, David Crowther, John Shakeshaft, Roderick Weaver

Business Description
A group engaged in the manufacture of sensors and electronic systems, electronic components, magnetics, power generation, and power and data transmission products.

TUI Travel plc
First Choice House, London Road, Crawley, West Sussex RH10 9GX
Telephone +44 (0) 1293 560777
Fax +44 (0) 1293 588680
Website www.tuitravelplc.com

Non-Executive Chairman
Dr. Michael Frenzel
Chief Executive/Managing Director
Peter Long
Board Members
Dr Volker Böttcher, Paul Bowtell, Tony Campbell, Clare Chapman, Bill Dalton, Rainer Feuerhake, Jeremy Hicks, Sir Michael Hodgkinson, Christoph Mueller, Giles Thorley, William Waggott

Business Description
A group engaged in the integrated provision of leisure travel, including tour operations, specialist holidays and online accommodation.

Tullett Prebon plc
Cable House, 54-62 New Broad Street, London EC2M 1ST
Telephone +44 (0) 20 7302 5382
Website www.tulletprebon.com

Chair
Keith Hamill
Chief Executive/Managing Director
Terry Smith
Board Members
David Clark, Michael Fallon, Richard Kilsby, Bernard Leaver, Paul Mainwaring, Rupert Robson, John Spencer

Business Description
A company operating as an intermediary in wholesale financial markets.

Tullow Oil plc
3rd Floor, Building 111, Chiswick Park, 566 Chiswick High Road, London W4 5YS
Telephone +44 (0) 20 8996 1000
Fax +44 (0) 20 8994 5332
Website www.tullowoil.com

Chair
Pat Plunkett
Chief Executive/Managing Director
Aidan Heavey
Board Members
David Bamford, Rohan Courtney, Tom Hickey, Graham Martin, Angus McCoss, Paul McDade, Steven McTiernan, Matthew O'Donoghue, Clare Spottiswoode, David Williams

Business Description
A group engaged in oil and gas exploration and production, and the provision of technical services to its joint venture partners.

UK Balanced Property Trust Ltd (The)
Regency Court, Glategny Esplanade, St Peter Port, Guernsey GY1 3NQ
Telephone +44 (0) 1481 720321
Fax +44 (0) 1481 716117

Chair
Peter Harwood
Board Members
Nicola Adamson, Peter Le Cheminant, Stephen Vernon

Business Description
An investment company.

UK Coal plc
Harworth Park, Blyth Road, Halworth, Doncaster, South Yorkshire DN11 8DB
Telephone +44 (0) 1302 751751
Fax +44 (0) 1302 752420
Website www.ukcoal.com

Chair
David Jones
Chief Executive/Managing Director
Garold Spindler
Board Members
Peter Hazel, Jon Lloyd, Chris Mawe, Mike Toms, Kevin Whiteman

Business Description
A group engaged in the production of coal, land and building management and power generation.

UK Commercial Property Trust Ltd
Trafalgar Court, Les Banques, St Peter Port, Guernsey GY1 3QL
Telephone +44 (0) 1481 745 001

Chair
Christopher Hill
Board Members
Keith Dorian, Christopher Fish, John Robertson, Andrew Wilson

Business Description
An investment trust.

UK Select Trust Ltd
Dorey Court, Admiral Park, St Peter Port,
Guernsey GY1 3BG
Telephone +44 (0) 1481 727111

Chair
Jim Le Pelley
Board Members
Derek Maltwood, Graham Russell, David Warr, Jimmy West

Business Description
An investment trust.

Ultra Electronics Holdings plc
417 Bridport Road, Greenford, Middlesex UB6 8UA
Telephone +44 (0) 20 8813 4321
Fax +44 (0) 20 8813 4322
Website www.ultra-electronics.com

Chair
Dr Julian Blogh
Chief Executive/Managing Director
Douglas Caster
Board Members
Chris Bailey, Ian Griffiths, Andy Hamment, Dr Frank Hope, David Jeffcoat, Andrew Walker

Business Description
A group engaged in the design, development and manufacture of electronic systems for the defence and aerospace markets.

Umbro plc
Umbro House, Lakeside, Cheadle, Cheshire SK8 3GQ
Telephone +44 (0) 161 492 2000
Fax +44 (0) 161 492 2001
Website www.umbro.com

Chair
Nigel Doughty
Chief Executive/Managing Director
Stephen Makin
Board Members
Richard Barfield, Mark McCafferty, Peter McGuigan

Business Description
A group engaged in the licensing and distribution of sports and leisurewear.

Umeco plc
Concorde House, 24 Warwick New Road, Leamington Spa, Warwickshire CV32 5JG
Telephone +44 (0) 1926 331800
Fax +44 (0) 1926 312680
Website www.umeco.co.uk

Chair
Brian McGowan
Chief Executive/Managing Director
Clive Snowdon
Board Members
Stephen Bird, Chris Hole, David Porter, Douglas Robertson, Graham Zacharias

Business Description
A group engaged in the distribution of parts for aerospace, defence, avionics and industrial uses, the manufacture of composite materials, and the repair and overhaul of aircraft components.

Unilever plc
Unilever House, Blackfriars, London EC4P 4BQ
Telephone +44 (0) 20 7822 5252
Website www.unilever.com

Chair
Michael Treschow
Chief Executive/Managing Director
Patrick Cescau
Board Members
Prof Geneviève Berger, Lord Brittan of Spennithorne, Wim Dik, Charles Golden, Byron Grote, Ralph Kugler, Narayana Murthy, Hixonia Nyasulu, Lord Simon of Highbury, Jean-Cyril Spinetta, Kees Storm, Kees van der Graaf, Jeroen van der Veer

Business Description
A group engaged in foods and home and personal care products, including culinary and frozen oil, and dairy-based foods, ice cream, and cleaning, hygiene and laundry products.

Uniq plc
No1 Chalfont Park, Gerrards Cross, Buckinghamshire SL9 0UN
Telephone +44 (0) 1753 276000
Fax +44 (0) 1753 276071
Website www.uniq.com

Chair
Ross Warburton
Chief Executive/Managing Director
Geoffrey Eaton
Board Members
Martin Beer, Belinda Gooding, Dr Matthew Litobarski, John Warren

Business Description
A group engaged in the manufacture, sale and distribution of chilled convenience food products.

UNITE Group plc (The)
The CORE, 40 St Thomas Street, Bristol BS1 6JZ
Telephone +44 (0) 117 302 7000
Fax +44 (0) 117 302 7400
Website www.unite-group.co.uk

Chair
Geoffrey Maddrell
Chief Executive/Managing Director
Mark Allan
Board Members
Stuart Beevor, Nigel Hall, Tony Harris, Nicholas Porter, John Tonkiss, Richard Walker

Business Description
A group engaged in the construction, holding and management of student and NHS key worker residential accommodation.

Unitech Corporate Parks plc
3rd Floor, Exchange House, 54-62 Athol Street, Douglas, Isle of Man IM1 1JD
Telephone +44 (0) 1624 641560
Website www.unitechcorporateparks.com

Chair
Atul Kapur
Board Members
Auberry John Adams, Ajay Chandra, Mohammed Yosuf Khan, Donald Lake

Business Description
A company engaged in investing in Indian commercial real estate.

United Business Media plc
Ludgate House, 245 Blackfriars Road, London SE1 9UY
Telephone +44 (0) 20 7921 5900
Fax +44 (0) 20 7928 2717
Website www.unitedbusinessmedia.com

Chair
Geoff Unwin
Chief Executive/Managing Director
David Levin
Board Members
John Botts, Charles Gregson, Christopher Hyman, Pradeep Kar, Lord Leitch, Jonathan Newcomb, Karen Thomson, Lord Turner of Ecchinswell, Nigel Wilson

Business Description
A group engaged in the publication of newspapers and magazines and the organisation of exhibitions.

United Utilities plc
Haweswater House, Lingley Mere Business Park, Great Sankey, Warrington WA5 3LP
Telephone +44 (0) 1925 237000
Fax +44 (0) 1925 237073
Website www.unitedutilities.com

Chair
Sir Richard Evans
Chief Executive/Managing Director
Philip Green
Board Members
Dr Catherine Bell, Norman Broadhurst, Paul Capell, Charlie Cornish, Paul Heiden, David Jones, Sir Peter Middleton, Andrew Pinder, Nick Salmon, Tim Weller

Business Description
A group engaged in the management and operation of electricity distribution, water and waste water assets, and the provision of business process outsourcing and communication services.

Urals Energy plc
Evagoras Building, Office 34, 3rd Floor, 31 Evagoras Avenue, Nicosia 1066, Cyprus
Telephone +357 22 451 686
Fax +357 22 451 686
Website www.uralsenergy.com

Chair
Charles Pitman
Chief Executive/Managing Director
Leonid Dyachenko
Board Members
Stephen Buscher

Business Description
An independent exploration and production company with its principal assets and operations in Sakhalin Island, Timan Pechora and the Republic of Udmurtia Russia.

UTV plc
Havelock House, Ormeau Road, Belfast BT7 1EB
Telephone +44 (0) 28 9032 8122
Fax +44 (0) 28 9024 6695
Website www.utvplc.com

Chair
John McGuckian
Chief Executive/Managing Director
John McCann
Board Members
Roy Bailie, James Downey, Helen Kirkpatrick, Kevin Lagan, Helen Morrow, Scott Taunton

Business Description
A group engaged in the provision of regional television, radio, internet and data broadcasting services.

Value & Income Trust plc
Donaldson House, 97 Haymarket Terrace, Edinburgh EH12 5HD
Telephone +44 (0) 131 313 1000
Fax +44 (0) 131 313 6300
Website www.firststate.co.uk

Chair
James Ferguson
Board Members
David Back, John Kay, Matthew Oakeshott

Business Description
A group engaged in the operation of an investment trust specialising in UK equities and properties.

Vanco plc
John Busch House, 277 London Road, Isleworth, Middlesex TW7 5AX
Telephone +44 (0) 20 8636 1700
Fax +44 (0) 20 8636 1701
Website www.vanco.com

Chair
Prof Thomas Wolf
Chief Executive/Managing Director
Allen Timpany
Board Members
Wayne Churchill, Jean-Pierre Gaudard, Peter Johnson, John Mumford, Ted Raffetto, Mark Thompson

Business Description
A group engaged in the design, supply and installation of networks and the provision of packaged network solutions.

Vedanta Resources plc
16 Berkeley Street, London W1J 8DZ
Telephone +44 (0) 20 7499 5900
Fax +44 (0) 20 7491 8440
Website www.vedantaresources.com

Chair
Anil Agarwal
Chief Executive/Managing Director
Kuldip Kaura
Board Members
Navin Agarwal, Naresh Chandra, Euan Macdonald, Aman Mehta, Dr Shailendra Tamotia

Business Description
A group engaged in mining, smelting and refining of bauxite, aluminium, copper, zinc and lead and in aluminium conducting and aluminium foil.

Vega Group plc
2 Falcon Way, Shire Park, Welwyn Garden City, Hertfordshire AL7 1TW
Telephone +44 (0) 1707 391999
Fax +44 (0) 1707 393909
Website www.vega-group.com

Chair
Andrew Roberts
Chief Executive/Managing Director
Philip Cartmell
Board Members
Brian Birkenhead, Sue Bygrave, Ian Williams

Business Description
A group engaged in the provision of systems engineering, consultancy and software services.

Venture Production plc
First Floor, Crimson Place Wing, King's Close, 62 Huntly Street, Aberdeen AB10 1RS
Telephone +44 (0) 1224 619000
Fax +44 (0) 1224 658151
Website www.vpc.co.uk

Chair
John Morgan
Chief Executive/Managing Director
Michael Wagstaff
Board Members
Rod Begbie, Thomas Blades, Marie-Louise Clayton, Thomas Ehret, Alan Jones, Larry Kinch, Jon Murphy, Mark Nicholls

Business Description
A group engaged in oil and gas production.

Vernalis plc
Oakdene Court, 613 Reading Road, Winnersh,
Berkshire RG41 5UA
Telephone +44 (0) 118 977 3133
Fax +44 (0) 118 989 9300
Website www.vernalis.com

Chair
Dr Peter Fellner
Chief Executive/Managing Director
Simon Sturge
Board Members
Allan Baxter, Ian Clark, Carol Ferguson, George Kennedy,
Dr Peter Read, John Slater, Anthony Weir

Business Description
A group engaged in the research and development of
pharmaceutical products and their subsequent licensing,
production, distribution and sale.

Victoria plc
Worcester Road, Kidderminster,
Worcestershire DY10 1HL
Telephone +44 (0) 1562 749300
Fax +44 (0) 1562 749649
Website www.victoria.plc.uk

Chair
Bob Gilbert
Chief Executive/Managing Director
Alan Bullock
Board Members
Keith Ackroyd, Alexander Anton, Ian Davies, Barry
Poynter

Business Description
A group engaged in the manufacture and sale of carpets
and carpet yarns.

Victrex plc
Victrex Technology Centre, Hillhouse International,
Thornton Cleveleys, Lancashire FY5 4QD
Telephone +44 (0) 1253 897700
Fax +44 (0) 1253 897701
Website www.victrex.com

Chair
Peter Warry
Chief Executive/Managing Director
David Hummel
Board Members
Jonathan Azis, Anita Frew, Giles Kerr, Michael Peacock,
Blair Souder, Dr Tim Walker

Business Description
A group engaged in the manufacture and sale of high
performance polymers and materials.

Vislink plc
Marlborough House, Chamham Lane, Hungerford,
Berkshire RG17 0EY
Telephone +44 (0) 148 868 5500
Fax +44 (0) 148 868 5501
Website www.vislink.com

Chair
Tim Trotter
Chief Executive/Managing Director
Ian Scott-Gall
Board Members
Anthony Finizio, Robin Howe, Leonard Mann, Mike
Payne

Business Description
A group engaged in the supply of microwave radio and
satellite transmission products.

Visonic Ltd
24 Habarzal Street, Tel Aviv, 69710, Israel
Telephone +972 3 645 6789
Fax +972 3 645 6788
Website www.visonic.com

Chair
Yaacov Kotlicki
Chief Executive/Managing Director
Dr. Avigdor Shachrai
Board Members
Walter Goldsmith, Anthony McCann, Yair Naaman

Business Description
A company specialising in security and home
management solutions.

Vitec Group plc (The)
1 Wheatfield Way, Kingston upon Thames,
Surrey KT1 2TU
Telephone +44 (0) 20 8939 4650
Fax +44 (0) 20 8939 4680
Website www.vitecgroup.com

Chair
Michael Harper
Chief Executive/Managing Director
Gareth Rhys Williams
Board Members
Simon Beresford-Wylie, Alastair Hewgill, Nigel Moore,
Maria Richter

Business Description
A group engaged in the supply of equipment and services
to the broadcasting, entertainment and photographic
industries.

Vodafone Group plc
Vodafone House, The Connection, Newbury,
Berkshire RG14 2FN
Telephone +44 (0) 1635 33251
Fax +44 (0) 1635 45713
Website www.vodafone.com

Chair
Sir John Bond
Chief Executive/Managing Director
Arun Sarin
Board Members
Dr Michael Boskin, Dr John Buchanan, Vittorio Colao,
Andy Halford, Alan Jebson, Nick Land, Anne Lauvergeon,
Simon Murray, Prof Jürgen Schrempp, Luc Vandevelde,
Anthony Watson, Philip Yea

Business Description
A group engaged in the operation of mobile
telecommunications.

Volex Group plc
Dornoch House, Kelvin Close, Birchwood Science Park,
Warrington WA3 7JX
Telephone +44 (0) 1925 830101
Fax +44 (0) 1925 830141
Website www.volex.com

Chair
Richard Arkle
Chief Executive/Managing Director
Heejae Chae
Board Members
David Beever, Ian Degnan, Dimitri Goulandris, Craig
Mullett

Business Description
A group engaged in the design, manufacture and supply
of electrical and electronic interconnect products and
systems including cable assemblies, power cords and
wiring harnesses.

VP plc
Central House, Beckwith Knowle, Otley Road, Harrogate,
North Yorkshire HG3 1UD
Telephone +44 (0) 1423 533400
Fax +44 (0) 1423 565657
Website www.vpplc.com

Chair
Jeremy Pilkington
Chief Executive/Managing Director
Neil Stothard
Board Members
Barrie Cottingham, Michael Holt, Peter Parkin

Business Description
A group engaged in the provision of equipment rental
and associated services.

VT Group plc
VT House, Grange Drive, Hedge End,
Southampton SO30 2DQ
Telephone +44 (0) 23 8083 9001
Fax +44 (0) 23 8083 9002
Website www.vtplc.com

Chair
Michael Jeffries
Chief Executive/Managing Director
Paul Lester
Board Members
David Barclay, Baroness Blackstone, Lord Boyce, Chris
Cundy, Andrew Given, David Thorpe

Business Description
A group engaged in the provision of facilities
management and training services, the design and
building of ships, and the manufacture of electronic
controls and marine equipment.

Wagon plc
3500 Parkside, Birmingham Business Park,
Birmingham B37 7YG
Telephone +44 (0) 121 770 4030
Fax +44 (0) 121 329 5150
Website www.wagonplc.com

Chair
Chris Clark
Chief Executive/Managing Director
Pierre Vareille
Board Members
Richard Cotton, Jens Hohnel, Susan Lyons, John
Rennocks, Wilbur Ross Jr, Rolf Zimmermann

Business Description
A group engaged in the design, engineering and
manufacture of vehicle body structures and glazing
systems.

Walker Crisps Group plc
Sophia House, 76/80 City Road, London EC1Y 2EQ
Telephone +44 (0) 20 7253 7502
Fax +44 (0) 20 7253 7500
Website www.wcwb.co.uk

Chair
David Gelber
Chief Executive/Managing Director
Michael Sunderland
Board Members
Stephen Bailey, Robert Elliott, Rodney Fitzgerald, David
Hetherton, Sean Lam, Hua Lim, William Saunders, Martin
Wright

Business Description
A group engaged in stock and share broking
administration of ISAs and PEPs, management of clients'
deposits, and the provision of corporate finance and
personal financial services.

Warner Estate Holdings plc
Nations House, 103 Wigmore Street, London W1U 1AE
Telephone +44 (0) 20 7907 5100
Fax +44 (0) 20 7491 3635
Website www.warnerestate.co.uk

Chair
Philip Warner
Board Members
Julian Avery, William Broderick, Peter Collins, Gregory
Cooke, Michael Stevens, Robert Warner

Business Description
A group engaged in property investment, trading and
development.

Waterman Group plc
Pickfords Wharf, Clink Wharf, London SE1 9DG
Telephone +44 (0) 20 7928 7888
Fax +44 (0) 20 7928 3033
Website www.waterman-group.co.uk

Chair
Roger Fidgen
Chief Executive/Managing Director
Robert Campbell
Board Members
John Archibald, Arthur Austin, Craig Beresford,
Alexander Burton, Barry Gore, Graham Hiscocks,
Nicholas Taylor, John Waiting, Geoffrey Wright

Business Description
A group engaged in the provision of design services and
advice in the fields of civil, structural, mechanical,
electrical and power engineering, and health and safety
consultancy.

Watermark Group plc
The Encompass Centre, International Avenue, Heston,
Middlesex TW5 9NJ
Telephone +44 (0) 20 8606 2000
Website www.watermark.co.uk

Chair
Ross Dunlop
Chief Executive/Managing Director
Maurice Ostro
Board Members
Graham Bird, Peter Fitzwilliam, Nicholas Scott

Business Description
A group engaged in the provision of travel supplies and
cabin management services to the international airline
and travel industry.

Weir Group plc (The)
Clydesdale Bank Exchange, 20 Waterloo Street,
Glasgow G2 6DB
Telephone +44 (0) 141 637 7111
Fax +44 (0) 141 221 9789
Website www.weir.co.uk

Chair
Sir Robert Smith
Chief Executive/Managing Director
Mark Selway
Board Members
Christopher Clarke, Keith Cochrane, Michael Dearden,
Stephen King, Alan Mitchelson, Prof Ian Percy, Lord
Robertson of Port Ellen

Business Description
A group engaged in the design, manufacture and service
of pumps, valves and controls, and in the provision of
equipment maintenance, process support and engineering
design services.

Wellstream Holdings plc
Wellstream House, Wincomblee Road, Walker Riverside,
Newcastle-upon-Tyne NE6 3PF
Telephone +44 (0) 191 295 9000
Fax +44 (0) 191 295 9001
Website www.wellstream.com

Chair
John Kennedy
Chief Executive/Managing Director
Gordon Chapman
Board Members
Christopher Braithwaite, Neil Gaskell, Francisco Gros, Sir
Graham Hearne, Patrick Murray, Nils Stoessen, Andrew
Turk

Business Description
A company engaged in the design and manufacture of
high quality, custom made unbonded flexible pipeline
systems.

Welsh Industrial Investment Trust plc
36 Elder Street, London E1 6BT
Telephone +44 (0) 20 7588 7352
Fax +44 (0) 20 7377 2946

Chair
Alfred Stirling
Board Members
Richard Murray, Gerald Oury

Business Description
An investment trust with a dealing subsidiary.

Westbury Property Fund Ltd (The)
Suite 4, Albert House, South Esplanade, St Peter Port,
Guernsey
Website www.westburypropertyfund.com

Chair
Rodney Barker-Bates
Board Members
Tim Chesney, William Kay, Iain Stoakes, Nick Watts

Business Description
An investment fund.

WH Smith plc
Greenbridge Road, Swindon, Wiltshire SN3 3RX
Telephone +44 (0) 1793 616161
Fax +44 (0) 1793 562560
Website www.whsmithplc.co.uk

Chair
Robert Walker
Chief Executive/Managing Director
Kate Swann
Board Members
John Barton, Mike Ellis, Luke Mayhew, M T Rainey,
Alan Stewart

Business Description
A group engaged in the retail of books, stationery,
newspapers, magazines and entertainment products, the
wholesale of newspapers and magazines, and publishing.

Whatman plc
Springfield Mill, James Whatman Way, Maidstone,
Kent ME14 2LE
Telephone +44 (0) 1622 676670
Website www.whatman.com

Chair
Bob Thian
Chief Executive/Managing Director
Kieran Murphy
Board Members
Prof Dr Hans Gassen, Jeffrey Hewitt, Dr Hinrich Kehler,
Dr Simon May, Chris Rickard, Alan Wood

Business Description
A group engaged in the development, manufacture and
marketing of filtration and separations products which
are used by laboratories.

Whitbread plc
Whitbread Court, Houghton Hall Business Park, Porz
Avenue, Dunstable LU5 5XE
Telephone +44 (0) 1582 424200
Website www.whitbread.co.uk

Chair
Anthony Habgood
Chief Executive/Managing Director
Alan Parker
Board Members
Philip Clarke, Margaret Ewing, Charles Gurassor, Rod
Kent, Angie Risley, Christopher Rogers

Business Description
A company engaged in the management of hotels,
restaurants and coffee shops.

White Nile Ltd
7th Floor, Transnational Plaza, City Hall Way, Nairobi
1317-00621, Kenya
Telephone +254 020 253 905
Fax +254 020 253 907
Website www.whitenileltd.com

Chair and Chief Executive
Phil Edmonds
Board Members
Dr Lual Deng, Andrew Groves, Edward Lino, Brian
Moritz

Business Description
Identify and acquire projects in the natural resources
sector with emphasis on oil projects in Africa.

White Young Green plc
Arndale Court, Headingley, Leeds LS6 2UJ
Telephone +44 (0) 113 278 7111
Fax +44 (0) 113 274 5185
Website www.wyg.com

Chair
Peter Wood
Chief Executive/Managing Director
Lawrie Haynes
Board Members
Robert Barr, Denis Connery, Brian Duckworth, Robert
Hartley, Richard McCaffrey, John Purvis, John Richardson

Business Description
A group engaged in the provision of life cycle
consultancy services for planning, creating and managing
key assets.

Wichford plc
Top Floor, 14 Athol Street, Douglas, Isle of Man IM1 1JA
Website www.wichford.com

Chair
Michael Sheehan
Board Members
Philippe de Nicolay, David Harrel, Ita McArdle, Hugh
Ward

Business Description
A company engaged in property investment, focusing on
properties occupied by central and state government
bodies.

William Hill plc
Greenside House, 50 Station Road, Wood Green,
London N22 7TP
Telephone +44 (0) 20 8918 3600
Fax +44 (0) 20 8918 3775
Website www.williamhillplc.co.uk

Chair
Charles Scott
Chief Executive/Managing Director
David Harding
Board Members
David Allvey, David Edmonds, Barry Gibson, Simon
Lane, Ian Spearing, Ralph Topping

Business Description
A group engaged in the operation of licensed betting
offices and provision of telephone and internet betting
and online casino services.

Wilmington Group plc
19 -21 Christopher Street, Finsbury Square,
London EC2A 2BS
Telephone +44 (0) 20 7422 6800
Fax +44 (0) 20 7422 6822
Website www.wilmington.co.uk

Chair
David Summers
Chief Executive/Managing Director
Charles Brady
Board Members
Mark Asplin, Basil Brookes, Rory Conwell, Terence
Garthwaite

Business Description
A group engaged in the provision of reference
information to business markets through directories,
electronic products, events, magazines, training courses,
other media.

Wincanton plc
Methuen Park, Chippenham, Wiltshire SN14 0WT
Telephone +44 (0) 1249 710000
Fax +44 (0) 1249 710001
Website www.wincanton.co.uk

Chair
David Malpas
Chief Executive/Managing Director
Graeme McFaull
Board Members
Gerard Connell, Jonson Cox, Philip Cox, David Edmonds,
Dr Walter Hasselkus, Nigel Sullivan

Business Description
A group engaged in the design, implementation and
operation of a range of supply chain management
solutions.

Witan Investment Trust plc
4 Broadgate, London EC2M 2DA
Telephone +44 (0) 20 7638 5757
Website www.witanwealthbuilder.com

Chair
Henry Henderson
Chief Executive/Managing Director
James Horsburgh
Board Members
J Bevan, R W Boyce, Andrew Bruce, Alan Jones, Rory
McGrath, Anthony Watson

Business Description
An investment trust.

Witan Pacific Investment Trust plc
55 Moorgate, London EC2R 6PA
Telephone +44 (0) 20 7410 3132
Fax +44 (0) 20 7477 5849
Website www.witanpacific.com

Chair
Gillian Nott
Board Members
Dr Leslie Atkinson, Alan Barber, Sarah Bates, William
Courtauld, Kevin Jones

Business Description
An investment company.

Wm Morrison Supermarkets plc
Hilmore House, Gain Lane, Bradford BD3 7DL
Telephone +44 (0) 845 611 5000
Website www.morrisons.co.uk

Chair
Sir Kenneth Morrison
Chief Executive/Managing Director
Marc Bolland
Board Members
Brian Flanegan, Mark Gunter, David Hutchinson, Martyn
Jones, Paul Manduca, Susan Murray, Roger Owen,
Richard Pennycook, Nigel Robertson

Business Description
A group engaged in retailing through supermarkets.

Wolfson Microelectronics plc
Westfield House, 26 Westfield Road,
Edinburgh EH11 2QB
Telephone +44 (0) 131 272 7000
Fax +44 (0) 131 272 7001
Website www.wolfsonmicro.com

Chair
John Carey
Chief Executive/Managing Director
David Shrigley
Board Members
Laurence Eckelmann, Peter Frith, Ross Graham, Dr David
Milne, Barry Rose, John Urwin

Business Description
A supplier of integrated circuits for digital consumer
electronics markets.

Wolseley plc
Parkview 1220, Arlington Business Park, Theale, Reading,
Berkshire RG7 4GA
Telephone +44 (0) 118 929 8700
Fax +44 (0) 118 929 8701
Website www.wolseley.com

Chair
John Whybrow
Chief Executive/Managing Director
Chip Hornsby
Board Members
Gareth Davis, Andrew Duff, Fenton Hord, Robert
Marchbank, James Murray, Frank Roach, Nigel Stein,
Robert Walker, Stephen Webster

Business Description
A group engaged in the distribution of plumbing and
bathroom materials, central heating equipment, building
materials and timber, and the operation of tool hire
centres.

Woolworths Group plc
Woolworth House, 242-246 Marylebone Road,
London NW1 6JL
Telephone +44 (0) 20 7262 1222
Fax +44 (0) 20 7706 5416
Website www.woolworthsgroupplc.com

Chair
Richard North
Chief Executive/Managing Director
Trevor Bish-Jones
Board Members
Andrew Beeson, Stephen East, Fru Hazlitt, Roger Jones,
Steve Lewis, Tony Page, Lloyd Wigglesworth

Business Description
A group engaged in the retail of home, family and
entertainment products.

Workspace Group plc
Magenta House, 85 Whitechapel Road, London E1 1DU
Telephone +44 (0) 20 7247 7614
Fax +44 (0) 20 7247 0157
Website www.workspacegroup.co.uk

Chair
Tony Hales
Chief Executive/Managing Director
Harry Platt
Board Members
John Bywater, Madeleine Carragher, Bernard Cragg,
Patrick Marples, Christopher Pieroni, Mark Taylor

Business Description
A group engaged in property investment in the form of
letting small units of business accommodation intended
primarily for new and small businesses.

World Trade Systems plc
Devonshire House, 1 Devonshire Street,
London W1W 5DR

Chair
Robert Lee
Board Members
Antares Cheng

Business Description
A cash shell previously engaged as agent for the
procurement of branded luxury goods.

Worthington Group plc
Suite One, Courthill House, 66 Water Lane, Wilmslow,
Cheshire SK9 5AP
Telephone +44 (0) 1625 549081
Fax +44 (0) 1625 530791
Website www.worthingtongroup.com

Chair
Dr Joseph Dwek
Board Members
Michael Edelson, David Shalom

Business Description
A group engaged in the provision of accessories and
components for the lingerie industry, plus pocketings and
waistbands to be used in garment making.

WPP Group plc
Pennypot Industrial Estate, Hythe, Kent CT21 6PE
Telephone +44 (0) 20 7408 2204
Fax +44 (0) 20 7493 6819
Website www.wpp.com

Chair
Philip Lader
Chief Executive/Managing Director
Sir Martin Sorrell
Board Members
Colin Day, Esther Dyson, Orit Gadiesh, David Komansky,
Christopher Mackenzie, Bud Morten, Koichiro Naganuma,
Lubna Olayan, Prof John Quelch, Mark Read, Paul
Richardson, Jeffrey Rosen, Paul Spencer

Business Description
A group engaged in advertising and media investment
management, branding and identity, healthcare and
specialist communications, information and consultancy,
and public relations and public affairs.

WS Atkins plc
Woodcote Grove, Ashley Road, Epsom KT18 9BW
Telephone +44 (0) 1372 726140
Fax +44 (0) 1372 740055
Website www.atkinsglobal.com

Chair
Ed Wallis
Chief Executive/Managing Director
Keith Clarke
Board Members
Admiral the Lord Boyce, Fiona Clutterbuck, Alun
Griffiths, Robert Macleod, James Morley, Sir Peter
Williams

Business Description
A group engaged in the provision of technologically-based
consultancy and support services.

WSP Group plc
Buchanan House, 24-30 Holborn, London EC1N 2HS
Telephone +44 (0) 20 7314 5000
Fax +44 (0) 20 7314 5111
Website www.wspgroup.com

Chair
David Turner
Chief Executive/Managing Director
Christopher Cole
Board Members
Marisa Cassoni, Stuart McLachlan, Malcolm Paul, Mark
Rollins, Ernest Sheavills, Christopher Stephens

Business Description
A group engaged in the provision of management and
consultancy services to the property, transport and
infrastructure and environmental sectors.

Xaar plc
319 Science Park, Cambridge CB4 0XR
Telephone +44 (0) 1223 423663
Fax +44 (0) 1223 423590
Website www.xaar.co.uk

Chair
Phil Lawler
Chief Executive/Managing Director
Ian Dinwoodie
Board Members
Nigel Berry, Ramon Borrell, Phil Eaves, Robert
Eckelmann, Richard King, John Scott, Stephen Temple

Business Description
A group engaged in the development and commercial
exploitation of patented inkjet printing technology and the
manufacture and marketing of specialist printheads and
inks.

Xansa plc
420 Thames Valley Park Drive, Thames Valley Park,
Reading, Berkshire RG6 1PU
Telephone +44 (0) 870 241 6181
Fax +44 (0) 870 242 6282
Website www.xansa.com

Chair
William Alexander
Board Members
Badri Agarwal, Consuelo Brooke, Chris Bunker, Andrew
Buxton, Gordon Stuart, David Thomas, Steve Weston,
Lord Wilson of Dinton

Business Description
A group engaged in the provision of business process
and IT services.

Xchanging plc
13 Hanover Square, London W1S 1HN
Telephone +44 (0) 20 7780 6999
Fax +44 (0) 20 7490 0169
Website www.xchanging.com

Chair
John Roberts
Chief Executive/Managing Director
David Andrews
Board Members
John Bramley, Stephen Brenninkmeijer, Adele Brown,
David Hodgson, Richard Houghton, Friedrich Janssen,
Johannes Maret, Dennis Millard, Nigel Rich, Tom Tinsley

Business Description
A group engaged in the provision of processing services
to the banking and insurance industries.

XP Power plc
401 Commonwealth Drive, Haw Par Technocentre,
Singapore 149598
Telephone +65 64116900
Fax +65 67418730
Website www.xppower.com

Chair
Larry Tracey
Chief Executive/Managing Director
Duncan Penny
Board Members
Roger Bartlett, Paul Dolan, John Dyson, Michael Laver,
Mickey Lynch, James Peters

Business Description
A group engaged in the provision of power supply
solutions to the electronics industry.

Xstrata plc
Bahnhofstrasse 2, PO Box 102, 25 Haymarket, 6301 Zug,
Switzerland
Telephone +41 (41) 726 6070
Fax +41 (41) 726 6089
Website www.xstrata.com

Chair
Willy Strothotte
Chief Executive/Managing Director
Michael Davis
Board Members
Ivan Glasenberg, Paul Hazen, Robert MacDonnell, Trevor
Reid, Sir Stephen Robson, David Rough, Dr Frederik
Roux, Ian Strachan, Santiago Zaldumbide

Business Description
A group engaged in the mining of coal and the
production of zinc and metal alloys.

XXI Century Investments plc
3 Hrushevskogo Street, Kiev 01001, Ukraine
Telephone +380 44 200 0457
Fax +380 44 200 0458
Website www.21.com.ua

Chair
Lev Partskhaladze
Board Members
Mark Holdsworth, Jaroslaw Kinach, Taras Kutovy,
Andriy Myrhorodskiy, Olena Volska

Business Description
A company engaged in real estate.

Yell Group plc
Queens Walk, Oxford Road, Reading, Berkshire RG1 7PT
Telephone +44 (0) 118 959 2111
Fax +44 (0) 118 950 9888
Website www.yell.com

Chair
Bob Scott
Chief Executive/Managing Director
John Condron
Board Members
Tim Bunting, John Coghlan, John Davis, Joachim
Eberhardt, Richard Hooper, Lyndon Lea, Lord Powell of
Bayswater

Business Description
A group engaged in the provision of classified directory
advertising and associated products and services.

Young & Co's Brewery plc
Riverside House, 26 Osiers Road, London SW18 1NH
Telephone +44 (0) 20 8875 7000
Fax +44 (0) 20 8875 7100
Website www.youngs.co.uk

Chair
Christopher Sandland
Chief Executive/Managing Director
Stephen Goodyear
Board Members
Nicholas Bryan, Patrick Dardis, Torquil Sligo-Young, Dr
Roy Summers, Peter Whitehead

Business Description
The brewing and bottling of beer and the sale of food
and drink through its public houses, hotels, restaurants
and other trade channels.

Yule Catto & Co plc
Central Road, Temple Fields, Harlow, Essex CM20 2BH
Telephone +44 (0) 1279 442791
Fax +44 (0) 1279 641360
Website www.yulecatto.com

Chair
Anthony Richmond-Watson
Chief Executive/Managing Director
Adrian Whitfield
Board Members
Alexander Catto, Dr Sandy Dobbie, Dato' Lee Hau Hian,
Dato' Lee Oi Hian, Richard Hunting, Jez Maiden, Colin
Williams, Peter Wood

Business Description
A group engaged in the manufacture and distribution of
polymer chemicals, performance chemicals and pharma
and fine chemicals.

Zero Preference Growth Trust plc (The)
Beaufort House, 51 New North Road, Exeter EX4 4EP
Telephone +44 (0) 1392 253282
Website www.premierassetmanagement.co.uk

Chair
Robert Ottley
Board Members
Graham Ball, John Ross

Business Description
An investment trust.

Zetex plc
Zetex Technology Park, Chadderton, Oldham OL9 9LL
Telephone +44 (0) 161 622 4700
Fax +44 (0) 161 622 4720
Website www.zetex.com

Chair
Liz Airey
Chief Executive/Managing Director
Hans Roher
Board Members
Dave Benstead, Cloin Greene, Nick Hawkins, Davy Lo,
Frank Marx, Franz Riedlberger

Business Description
A group engaged in the manufacture of high-performance
transistors, diodes, ICs and MOSFETs.

Zotefoams plc
675 Mitcham Road, Croydon CR9 3AL
Telephone +44 (0) 20 8664 1600
Fax +44 (0) 20 8664 1616
Website www.zotefoams.com

Chair
David Campbell
Board Members
Richard Clowes, Nigel Howard, Clifford Hurst, Roger
Lawson, Chris Ryan, David Stirling

Business Description
A group engaged in the manufacture and distribution of
cross-linked block foams.

ACCOUNTANCY FIRMS

The following pages detail the leading accountancy firms in the UK, selected
by fee income.

Armstrong Watson
15 Victoria Place, Carlisle, Cumbria CA1 1EW
Telephone +44 (0) 1228 553333
Fax +44 (0) 1228 553300
Website www.armstrongwatson.co.uk

Senior Partner
Alan Johnston
Managing Partner
Aidan Taylor
Board Members
Margaret Hill, Chris Barrett

Baker Tilly UK Group LLP
2 Bloomsbury Street, London WC1B 3ST
Telephone +44 (0) 20 7413 5100
Fax +44 (0) 20 7413 5101
Website www.bakertilly.co.uk

Executive Chairman
Martin Rodgers
National Managing Partner
Laurence Longe
Board Members
Jim Budgen, Milton Nicholas, Nigel Tristem, Mark
Blakemore, David Gwilliam, Jon Randall

Barnes Roffe LLP
13 Albemarle Street, London W1S 4HJ
Telephone +44 (0) 20 7529 7660
Fax +44 (0) 20 7529 7660
Website www.barnesroffe.com

Senior Partner
Chris Green

BDO Stoy Hayward LLP
8 Baker Street, London W1U 3LL
Telephone +44 (0) 20 7486 5888
Fax +44 (0) 20 7487 3686
Website www.bdo.co.uk

Senior Partner
Dermot Mathias
Managing Partner
Jeremy Newman

Berg Kaprow Lewis LLP
35 Ballards Lane, London N3 1XW
Telephone +44 (0) 20 8922 9222
Fax +44 (0) 20 8922 9223
Website www.bkl.co.uk

Managing Partner
Brian Berg

Bishop Fleming
Stratus House, Emperor Way, Exeter Business Park,
Exeter EX1 3QS
Telephone +44 (0) 1392 448800
Fax +44 (0) 1392 448899
Website www.bishopfleming.co.uk

Partner and Chief Executive
Brian Payne
Managing Partner
Matthew Lee

Buzzacott LLP
12 New Fetter Lane, London EC4A 1AG
Telephone +44 (0) 20 7556 1200
Fax +44 (0) 20 7556 1212
Website www.buzzacott.co.uk

Chairman
Anthony De Lacey
Managing Partner
Mark Farmar

Chantrey Vellacott DFK
Russell Square House, 10-12 Russell Square,
London WC1B 5LF
Telephone +44 (0) 20 7509 9000
Fax +44 (0) 20 7436 8884
Website www.cvdfk.com

Managing Partner
Mike Tovey
Board Members
Mark Lamb, Anton Syrocki, Ian Blackman

CLB Littlejohn Frazer
1 Park Place, Canary Wharf, London E14 4HJ
Telephone +44 (0) 20 7987 5030
Fax +44 (0) 20 7987 9707
Website www.littlejohnfrazer.com

Managing Partner
Paul Hopper
Board Members
Ted Brew, Neil Coulson, Ian Cowan

Cooper Parry LLP
14 Park Row, Nottingham NG1 6GR
Telephone +44 (0) 1159 580212
Fax +44 (0) 1159 588800
Website www.cooperparry.com

Chairman
Colin Shaw
Chief Executive
Jeremy Bowler

Deloitte
1 Stonecutter Court, London EC4A 4TR
Telephone +44 (0) 20 7936 3000
Fax +44 (0) 20 7583 1198
Website www.deloitte.com

Chairman and Chief Executive Officer
John P Connolly
Board Members
Aidan Birkett, Richard Buck, Stuart Counsell, Cahal
Dowds, Martin Eadon, Sharon Fraser, John Kerr, Vassi
Naidoo, Vince Niblett, David Owen, Gerry Paisley,
Richard Punt, David Sproul, Bob Warburton

DTE Group
DTE House, Hollins Mount, Bury, Greater
Manchester BL9 8AT
Telephone +44 (0) 1617 671200
Fax +44 (0) 1617 671201
Website www.dtegroup.com

Managing Partner
Keith Train

Duncan & Toplis
3 Castlegate, Grantham, Lincolnshire NG31 6SF
Telephone +44 (0) 1476 591200
Fax +44 (0) 1476 591222
Website www.duntop.co.uk

Managing Partner
Peter Townsend

Ernst & Young LLP
Becket House, 1 Lambeth Palace Road, London SE1 7EU
Telephone +44 (0) 20 7951 2000
Fax +44 (0) 20 7951 1345
Website www.ey.com

Chairman
Mark Otty
Board Members
Jan Babiak, Victoria Cochrane, Mike Cullen, Robin Heath,
Richard King, Alan Pateman-Jones, David Robinson, Steve
Varley

Ford Campbell LLP
City Wharf, New Bailey Street, Manchester M3 5ER
Telephone +44 (0) 1618 192500
Fax +44 (0) 1618 192501
Website www.ford-campbell.co.uk

Chief Executive Officer
Tony Ford
Board Members
Andrew Campbell, Graham Travis, Jeremy Carr, Chris
Froggatt, Kevin Frisby, Simon Kite, Michael Freedman,
Derek Smith, Dave Cheetham, Chris George, James
Butcher

Francis Clark
23 Devon Square, Newton Abbot, Devon TQ12 2HU
Telephone +44 (0) 1626 206206
Fax +44 (0) 1626 206200
Website www.francisclark.co.uk

Senior Partner
Peter Cliff
Managing Partner
Les Burnett

Grant Thornton UK LLP
Grant Thornton House, Melton Street, Euston Square,
London NW1 2EP
Telephone +44 (0) 20 7383 5100
Fax +44 (0) 20 7383 4715
Website www.grant-thornton.co.uk

Senior Partner
John Mew
National Managing Partner
Michael Cleary

Haslers Corporate Finance LLP
Old Station Road, Loughton, Essex IG10 4PL
Telephone +44 (0) 20 8418 3333
Fax +44 (0) 20 8418 3334
Website www.haslers.com

Senior Partner
Michael Gould
Managing Patner
Stanley Baskin

haysmacintyre
Fairfax House, 15 Fulwood Place, London WC1V 6AY
Telephone +44 (0) 20 7969 5500
Fax +44 (0) 20 7969 5600
Website www.haysmacintyre.com

Managing Partner
Bernie Watson

Hazlewoods LLP
Staverton Court, Staverton, Cheltenham,
Gloucestershire GL51 0UX
Telephone +44 (0) 1242 680000
Fax +44 (0) 1242 680857
Website www.hazlewoods.co.uk

Managing Partner
Harvey Grove

Horwath Clark Whitehill LLP
St Bride's House, 10 Salisbury Square, London EC4Y 8EH
Telephone +44 (0) 20 7842 7100
Fax +44 (0) 20 7583 1720
Website www.horwathcw.com

Chairman
David Furst
Chief Executive
Andrew Pianca

HW Group
11A Park House, Milton Park, Abingdon OX14 4RS
Telephone +44 (0) 1235 835900
Fax +44 (0) 1235 835990
Website www.hwca.com

Managing Partner
Andy Minifie
Board Members
Geoffrey Fairclough, Nigel Williams, Rodney Style, Chris
Dedman

Johnston Carmichael
Bishop's Court, 29 Albyn Place, Aberdeen AB10 1YL
Telephone +44 (0) 1224 212222
Fax +44 (0) 1224 210190
Website www.jcca.co.uk

Chairman
James Campbell
Chief Executive
Sandy Manson

Kingston Smith LLP
Devonshire House, 60 Goswell Road, London EC1M 7AD
Telephone +44 (0) 20 7566 4000
Fax +44 (0) 20 7566 4010
Website www.kingstonsmith.co.uk

Senior Partner
Michael Snyder

KPMG LLP
8 Salisbury Square, London EC4Y 8BB
Telephone +44 (0) 20 7311 1000
Fax +44 (0) 20 7311 3311
Website www.kpmg.co.uk

Chairman
John Griffith-Jones
Chief Executive Officer
Colin Cook
Board Members
Mike Ashley, Guy Bainbridge, Ian Barlow, Richard
Bennison, Mike Blake, Sue Bonney, Alan Buckle, Rachel
Campbell, Scott Cormack, Malcolm Edge, Mel Egglenton,
Fiona Fry, Steve Halbert, Myles Halley, Steve Hollis,
Alistair Johnston, Stephen Machin, Ashley Steel, Oliver
Tant, Ben van der Veer

Larking Gowen
King Street House, 15 Upper King Street,
Norwich NR3 1RB
Telephone +44 (0) 1603 624181
Fax +44 (0) 1603 667800
Website www.larking-gowen.co.uk

Managing Partner
Bob Rose

Lovewell Blake
Sixty Six, North Quay, Great Yarmouth,
Norfolk NR30 1HE
Telephone +44 (0) 1493 335100
Fax +44 (0) 1493 335133
Website www.lovewell-blake.co.uk

Senior Partner
Christopher Dicker
Managing Partner
Robin Ashe

MacIntyre Hudson LLP
Newbridge Street House, 30/34 Newbridge Street,
London EC4V 6BJ
Telephone +44 (0) 20 7429 4100
Fax +44 (0) 20 7248 8939
Website www.macintyrehudson.co.uk

Chairman
Shaunak Rakesh
Board Members
Stephanie Barber, Andrew Burnham, Victor Dauppe, Mike
Kay, Howard Lewis, Anthony Meier, Robert Mowbray,
Martin Payne, Christopher Sutton, Janet Taylor, Graeme
Young

Mazars LLP
24 Bevis Marks, London EC3A 7NR
Telephone +44 (0) 20 7377 1000
Fax +44 (0) 20 7377 8931
Website www.mazars.co.uk

Chairman
David Evans

Menzies
First Floor, Midas House, 62 Goldsworth Road, Woking,
Surrey GU21 6QO
Telephone +44 (0) 1483 755000
Fax +44 (0) 1483 756661
Website www.menzies.co.uk

Senior Partner
Mike Sands

Mercer & Hole
72 London Road, St Albans, Hertfordshire AL1 1NS
Telephone +44 (0) 1727 869141
Fax +44 (0) 1727 869149
Website www.mercerhole.co.uk

Senior Partner
Howard Wilkinson

MGI Wenham Major Ltd
89 Cornwall Street, Birmingham B3 3BY
Telephone +44 (0) 1212 361866
Fax +44 (0) 1212 001389
Website www.wenhammajor.co.uk

Chairman
John Joyce
Chief Executive
Ammar Azam

Moore Stephens LLP
St Paul's House, Warwick Lane, London EC4M 7BP
Telephone +44 (0) 20 7334 9191
Fax +44 (0) 20 7248 3408
Website www.moorestephens.com

Senior Partner
Richard Moore
Managing Partner
Colin Moore

Morley & Scott
Lynton House, 7-12 Tavistock Square, London WC1H 9LT
Telephone +44 (0) 20 7387 5868
Fax +44 (0) 20 7388 3978
Website www.morleyandscott.co.uk

Managing Partner
Linda Richardson

PKF (UK) LLP
Farringdon Place, 20 Farringdon Road,
London EC1M 3AP
Telephone +44 (0) 20 7065 0000
Fax +44 (0) 20 7065 0650
Website www.pkf.co.uk

Senior Partner
Ian Mills
Managing Partner
Martin Goodchild

Price Bailey
Causeway House, 1 Dane Street, Bishop's Stortford,
Hertfordshire CM23 3BT
Telephone +44 (0) 1279 755888
Fax +44 (0) 1279 755417
Website www.pricebailey.co.uk

Board Chairman
Martin Clapson
Managing Director
Peter Gillman
Board Members
Charles Olley, Nick Mayhew, Howard Sears

PricewaterhouseCoopers LLP
1 Embankment Place, London WC2N 6RH
Telephone +44 (0) 20 7583 5000
Fax +44 (0) 20 7822 4652
Website www.ukmediacentre.pwc.com

Chairman and Chief Executive Officer
Kieran Poynter
Board Members
Glyn Barker, Keith Tilson, Paul Cleal, Richard Collier-
Keywood, Moria Elms, Owen Jonathan, Ian Powell,
Richard Sexton

Reeves & Neylan
37 St Margaret's Street, Canterbury, Kent CT1 2TU
Telephone +44 (0) 1227 768231
Fax +44 (0) 1227 458383
Website www.reeves-neylan.com

Partnership Chairman
David Ashman
Managing Partner
Clive Stevens

Rothman Pantall & Co
Fryern House, 125 Winchester Road, Chandlers Ford,
Hampshire SO53 2DR
Telephone +44 (0) 2380 265550
Fax +44 (0) 2380 258700
Website www.rothman-pantall.co.uk

General Practice Partner
Tony Payne
Managing Partner
Andrew Bennett

RSM Bentley Jennison
30/34 Moorgate, London EC2R 6DN
Telephone +44 (0) 20 7920 3200
Fax +44 (0) 20 7920 3201
Website www.bentley-jennison.co.uk

National Managing Partner
Tony Stockdale

Saffery Champness
Lion House, Red Lion Street, London WC1R 4GB
Telephone +44 (0) 20 7841 4000
Fax +44 (0) 20 7841 4100
Website www.saffery.com

Chairman
Nick Gaskell
Managing Partner
Rob Elliott
Board Members
Mike Di Leto, Nick Kelsey, Peter Horsman, David Macey,
Max Floydd

Scott-Moncrieff
17 Melville Street, Edinburgh EH3 7PH
Telephone +44 (0) 1314 733500
Fax +44 (0) 1314 733535
Website www.scott-moncrieff.com

Managing Partner
Alan Donaldson

Shipleys LLP
10 Orange Street, Haymarket, London WC2H 7DQ
Telephone +44 (0) 20 7312 0000
Fax +44 (0) 20 7312 0022
Website www.shipleys.com

Chairman
John McCuin
Senior Principal
Guy Fisher

Smith & Williamson
25 Moorgate, London EC2R 6AY
Telephone +44 (0) 20 7131 4000
Fax +44 (0) 20 7131 4001
Website www.smith.williamson.co.uk

Chairman
Gareth Pearce
Deputy Chairman
Viscount Cobham
Board Members
Bill Cameron, Warren Goldring, Peter Hazell, Henry
Strutt, Andrew Sykes, Jeremy Boadle, Andrew Fullerton-
Batten

Streets LLP
Tower House, Lucy Tower Street, Lincoln LN1 1XW
Telephone +44 (0) 1522 551200
Fax +44 (0) 1522 533234
Website www.streetsweb.co.uk

Chairman and Managing Partner
Paul Tutin

Target Chartered Accountants
Lawrence House, Lower Bristol Road, Bath BA2 9ET
Telephone +44 (0) 1225 486300
Fax +44 (0) 1225 486310
Website www.target-consulting.co.uk

Managing Director
Keith Seeley
Director
Mark Harman

Tenon Group plc
1 Bede Island Road, Bede Island Business Park,
Leicester LE2 7EA
Telephone +44 (0) 1162 221101
Fax +44 (0) 1162 221102
Website www.tenongroup.com

Chairman
Bob Morton
Chief Executive
Andy Raynor

UHY Hacker Young LLP
St Alphage House, 2 Fore Street, London EC2Y 5DH
Telephone +44 (0) 20 7216 4600
Fax +44 (0) 20 7638 2159
Website www.uhy-uk.com

Managing Partner
Ladislav Hornan

Vantis plc
82 St John Street, London EC1M 4JN
Telephone +44 (0) 20 7417 0417
Fax +44 (0) 20 7417 0418
Website www.vantisplc.com

Chairman
Paul Gourmand
Chief Executive
Paul Jackson
Board Members
Paul Ashton, Trevor Applin, Nigel Hamilton-Smith, Bob
Thornton, Ken Dulieu, Graham Cole

Wilkins Kennedy
Brige House, London Bridge, London SE1 9QR
Telephone +44 (0) 20 7403 1877
Fax +44 (0) 20 7403 1605
Website www.wilkinskennedy.com

Managing Partner
Colin Wiseman

LIVERY COMPANIES

The following pages detail all the livery companies of the City of London.

The City of London Solicitors' Company
4 College Hill, London EC4R 2RB
Telephone +44 (0) 20 7329 2173
Website www.citysolicitors.org.uk

Clerk
Neil Cameron

The Guild of Air Pilots and Air Navigators
Cobham House, 9 Warwick Court, Grays Inn,
London WC1R 5DJ
Telephone +44 (0) 20 7404 4032
Website www.gapan.org

Clerk
Paul Tacon

The Honourable Company of Master Mariners
HQS Wellington, Temple Stairs, Victoria Embankment,
London WC2R 2PN
Telephone +44 (0) 20 7836 8179
Website www.hcmm.org.uk

Clerk
Cdr Rodney Craig

The Mercers' Company
Mercers' Hall, Ironmonger Lane, London EC2V 8HE
Telephone +44 (0) 20 7726 4991
Website www.mercers.co.uk

Clerk
Charles Parker

The Worshipful Company of Actuaries
The Cote, Old Gloucester Road, Alveston,
Bristol BS35 3LQ
Telephone +44 (0) 1454 411292
Website www.actuariescompany.co.uk

Clerk
Michael Turner

The Worshipful Company of Arbitrators
13 Hall Gardens, Colney Heath, St Albans,
Hertfordshire AL4 0QF
Telephone +44 (0) 1727 826578
Website www.arbitratorscompany.org

Clerk
Gaye Duffy

The Worshipful Company of Armourers and Brasiers
Armourers' Hall, 81 Coleman Street, London EC2R 5BJ
Telephone +44 (0) 20 7374 4000
Website www.armourersandbrasiers.co.uk

Clerk
Cdr Christopher Waite

The Worshipful Company of Bakers
Bakers' Hall, 9 Harp Lane, Lower Thames Street,
London EC3R 6DP
Telephone +44 (0) 20 7623 2223
Website www.bakers.co.uk

Clerk
John Tompkins

The Worshipful Company of Barbers
Barber-Surgeons' Hall, Monkwell Square,
London EC2Y 5BL
Telephone +44 (0) 20 7606 0741
Website www.barberscompany.org

Clerk
Col Peter Durrant

The Worshipful Company of Basketmakers
29 Ingram House, Park Road, Hampton Wick,
Surrey KT1 4BA
Telephone +44 (0) 20 8943 2343
Website www.basketmakersco.org

Clerk
Roger de Pilkyngton

The Worshipful Company of Blacksmiths
48 Upwood Road, Lee, London SE12 8AN
Telephone +44 (0) 20 8318 9684
Website www.blacksmithscompany.org.uk

Clerk
Christopher Jeal

The Worshipful Company of Bowyers
5 Archer House, Vicarage Crescent, London SW11 3LF
Telephone +44 (0) 20 7223 5224
Website www.bowyers.com

Clerk
Richard Wilkinson

The Worshipful Company of Brewers
Brewers' Hall, Aldermanbury Square, London EC2V 7HR
Telephone +44 (0) 20 7606 1301
Website www.brewershall.co.uk

Clerk
David Ross

The Worshipful Company of Broderers
Ember House, 35-37 Creek Road, East Molesey,
Surrey KT8 9BE
Telephone +44 (0) 20 8941 3116
Website www.broderers.co.uk

Clerk
Peter Crouch

The Worshipful Company of Builders Merchants
4 College Hill, London EC4R 2RB
Telephone +44 (0) 20 7329 2189
Website www.wcobm.co.uk

Clerk
Sheila Robinson

The Worshipful Company of Butchers
Butchers' Hall, 87 Bartholomew Close, London EC1A 7EB
Telephone +44 (0) 20 7600 4106
Website www.butchershall.com

Clerk
Cdre Tony Morrow

The Worshipful Company of Carmen
Five Kings House, 1 Queen Street Place,
London EC4R 1QS
Telephone +44 (0) 20 7489 8289
Website www.thecarmen.co.uk

Clerk
Walter Gill

The Worshipful Company of Carpenters
Carpenters' Hall, 1 Throgmorton Avenue,
London EC2N 2JJ
Telephone +44 (0) 20 7588 7001
Website www.carpentersco.com

Clerk
Maj-Gen Paul Stevenson

The Worshipful Company of Chartered Accountants
The Rustlings, Valley Close, Studham, Dunstable,
Bedfordshire LU6 2QN
Telephone +44 (0) 1582 872070
Website www.wccaew.org.uk

Clerk
Clifford Bygrave

The Worshipful Company of Chartered Architects
82a Muswell Hill Road, London N10 3JR
Telephone +44 (0) 20 8292 4893
Website www.architects-livery-company.org

Clerk
David Cole-Adams

The Worshipful Company of Chartered Secretaries and Administrators
Saddlers' Hall, 3rd Floor, 40 Gutter Lane,
London EC2V 6BR
Telephone +44 (0) 20 7726 2955
Website www.wccsa.org.uk

Clerk
Col Michael Dudding

The Worshipful Company of Chartered Surveyors
75 Meadway Drive, Horsell, Woking, Surrey GU21 4TF
Telephone +44 (0) 1483 727113
Website www.surveyorslivery.co.uk

Clerk
Amanda Jackson

The Worshipful Company of Clockmakers
Fourth Floor, Salters' Hall, 4 Fore Street,
London EC2Y 5DE
Telephone +44 (0) 20 7638 5500
Website www.clockmakers.org

Clerk
Joe Buxton

The Worshipful Company of Clothworkers
Clothworkers' Hall, Dunster Court, Mincing Lane,
London EC3R 7AH
Telephone +44(0) 20 7623 7041
Website www.clothworkers.co.uk

Clerk
Andrew Blessley

The Worshipful Company of Coachmakers and Coach Harness Makers
Elm Tree Cottage, Bottom House Farm Lane, Chalfont St
Giles, Buckinghamshire HP8 4EE
Telephone +44 (0) 7971 017255
Website www.coachmakers.co.uk

Clerk
Group Capt Gerry Bunn

The Worshipful Company of Constructors
Forge Farmhouse, Glassenbury Road, Cranbrook,
Kent TN17 2QE
Telephone +44 (0) 1580 712657
Website www.constructorscompany.co.uk

Clerk
Tim Nicholson

The Worshipful Company of Cooks
Coombe Ridge, Thursley Road, Churt, Farnham,
Surrey GU10 2LQ
Telephone +44 (0) 1428 606670
Website www.cookslivery.org.uk

Clerk
Michael Thatcher

The Worshipful Company of Coopers
Coopers' Hall, 13 Devonshire Square, London EC2M 4TH
Telephone +44 (0) 20 7247 9577
Website www.coopers-hall.co.uk

Clerk
Lt Col Adrian Carroll

The Worshipful Company of Cordwainers
Clothworkers' Hall, Dunster Court, Mincing Lane,
London EC3R 7AH
Telephone +44 (0) 20 7929 1121
Website www.cordwainers.org

Clerk
Richard Stillwell

The Worshipful Company of Curriers
Hedgerley, The Leaze, Ashton Keynes, Wiltshire SN6 6PE
Telephone +44 (0) 1285 861017
Website www.curriers.co.uk

Clerk
Group Capt David Moss

The Worshipful Company of Cutlers
Cutlers' Hall, Warwick Lane, London EC4M 7BR
Telephone +44 (0) 20 7248 1866
Website www.cutlerslondon.co.uk

Clerk
John Allen

The Worshipful Company of Distillers
71 Lincoln's Inn Fields, London WC2A 3JF
Telephone +44 (0) 20 7405 7091
Website www.distillers.org.uk

Clerk
Christopher Hughes

The Worshipful Company of Drapers
Drapers' Hall, Throgmorton Avenue, London EC2N 2DQ
Telephone +44 (0) 20 7588 5001
Website www.thedrapers.co.uk

Clerk
Rear Adm Alastair Ross

The Worshipful Company of Dyers
Dyers' Hall, 10 Dowgate Hill, London EC4R 2ST
Telephone +44 (0) 20 7236 7197
Website www.dyerscompany.co.uk

Clerk
Russell Vaizey

The Worshipful Company of Engineers
Wax Chandlers' Hall, 6 Gresham Street,
London EC2V 7AD
Telephone +44 (0) 20 7726 4830
Website www.engineerscompany.org.uk

Clerk
Air Vice-Marshal Graham Skinner

The Worshipful Company of Environmental Cleaners
6 Grange Meadow, Elmswell, Bury St Edmunds,
Suffolk IP30 9GE
Telephone +44 (0) 1359 242947
Website www.environmental-cleaners.com

Clerk
Michael Bizley

The Worshipful Company of Fan Makers
Skinners' Hall, 8 Dowgate Hill, London EC4R 2SP
Telephone +44 (0) 20 7329 4633
Website www.fanmakers.com

Clerk
Keith Patterson

The Worshipful Company of Farmers
Red Copse End, Red Copse Lane, Boars Hill, Oxford,
Oxfordshire OX1 5ER
Telephone +44 (0) 1865 321580
Website www.farmerslivery.org.uk

Clerk
Col David King

The Worshipful Company of Farriers
19 Queen Street, Chipperfield, Kings Langley,
Hertfordshire WD4 9BT
Telephone +44 (0) 1923 260747
Website www.wcf.org.uk

Clerk
Charlotte Clifford

The Worshipful Company of Feltmakers
Post Cottage, Greywell, Hook, Hampshire RG29 1DA
Telephone +44 (0) 1256 703174
Website www.feltmakers.co.uk

Clerk
Maj Jollyon Coombs

The Worshipful Company of Firefighters
The Insurance Hall, 20 Aldermanbury, London EC2V 7HY
Telephone +44 (0) 20 7600 1666
Website www.firefighterscompany.org

Clerk
Martin Bonham

The Worshipful Company of Fishmongers
Fishmongers' Hall, London Bridge, London EC4R 9EL
Telephone +44 (0) 20 7626 3531
Website www.fishhall.co.uk

Clerk
Keith Waters

The Worshipful Company of Fletchers
65 The Avenue, Fareham, Hampshire PO14 1PE
Telephone +44 (0) 1329 288489
Website www.fletchers.org.uk

Clerk
Capt Michael Johnson

The Worshipful Company of Founders
The Old Estate Office, Fifty One, Firle, Lewes, East
Sussex BN8 6LQ
Telephone +44 (0) 1273 858700
Website www.foundersco.org.uk

Clerk
Andrew Gillett

The Worshipful Company of Framework Knitters
86 Park Drive, Upminster, Essex RM14 3AS
Telephone +44 (0) 1708 510439
Website www.frameworkknitters.co.uk

Clerk
Alan Clark

The Worshipful Company of Fruiterers
Chapelstones, 84 High Street, Codford St Mary,
Warminster, Wiltshire BA12 0ND
Telephone +44 (0) 1985 850682
Website www.fruit-baskets.co.uk

Clerk
Lt Col Lionel French

The Worshipful Company of Fuellers
26 Merrick Square, London SE1 4JB
Telephone +44 (0) 20 7234 0760
Website www.fuellers.co.uk

Clerk
Sir Antony Reardon Smith

The Worshipful Company of Furniture Makers
Furniture Makers' Hall, 12 Austin Friars,
London EC2N 2HE
Telephone +44 (0) 20 7256 5558
Website www.furnituremkrs.co.uk

Clerk
Jan Wright

The Worshipful Company of Gardeners
25 Luke Street, London EC2A 4AR
Telephone +44 (0) 20 7953 2321
Website www.gardenerscompany.org.uk

Clerk
Trevor Hines

The Worshipful Company of Girdlers
Girdlers' Hall, Basinghall Avenue, London EC2V 5DD
Telephone +44 (0) 20 7638 0488
Website www.girdlers.co.uk

Clerk
Lt Col Richard Sullivan

The Worshipful Company of Glass Sellers
57 Witley Court, Coram Street, London WC1N 1HD
Telephone +44 (0) 20 7837 2231
Website www.glass-sellers.co.uk

Clerk
Col Audrey Smith

The Worshipful Company of Glaziers and Painters of Glass
Glaziers' Hall, 9 Montague Close, London Bridge,
London SE1 9DD
Telephone +44 (0) 20 7403 6652
Website www.worshipfulglaziers.com

Clerk
Alex Galloway

The Worshipful Company of Glovers
Cherry Tree Cottage, 73 Clapham Manor Street,
London SW4 6DS
Telephone +44 (0) 20 7622 2167
Website www.thegloverscompany.org

Clerk
Monique Hood

The Worshipful Company of Gold and Silver Wyre Drawers
Middleton House, Winterslow, Salisbury,
Wiltshire SP5 1QR
Telephone +44 (0) 1980 863808
Website www.gswd.co.uk

Clerk
Cdr Robin House

The Worshipful Company of Goldsmiths
Goldsmiths' Hall, Foster Lane, London EC2V 6BN
Telephone +44 (0) 20 7606 7010
Website www.thegoldsmiths.co.uk

Clerk
Rear Adm Dick Melly

The Worshipful Company of Grocers
Grocers' Hall, Princes Street, London EC2R 8AD
Telephone +44 (0) 20 7606 3113
Website www.grocershall.co.uk

Clerk
Brig Robert Pridham

The Worshipful Company of Gunmakers
Proof House, 48/50 Commercial Road, London E1 1LP
Telephone +44 (0) 20 7481 2695
Website www.gunmakers.org.uk

Clerk
Col William Chesshyre

The Worshipful Company of Haberdashers
Haberdashers' Hall, 18 West Smithfield,
London EC1A 9HQ
Telephone +44 (0) 20 7246 9988
Website www.haberdashers.co.uk

Clerk
Rear Adm Richard Phillips

The Worshipful Company of Hackney Carriage Drivers
25 The Grove, Parkfield, Latimer,
Buckinghamshire HP5 1UE
Telephone +44 (0) 1494 765922
Website www.wchcd.com

Clerk
Mary Whitworth

The Worshipful Company of Horners
c/o The Clergy House, Hide Place, London SW1P 4NJ
Telephone +44 (0) 20 7834 1575
Website www.horners.org.uk

Clerk
Raymond Layard

The Worshipful Company of Information Technologists
39a Bartholomew Close, London EC1A 7JN
Telephone +44 (0) 20 7600 1992
Website www.wcit.org.uk

Clerk
Michael Grant

The Worshipful Company of Innholders
Innholders' Hall, 30 College Street, Dowgate Hill,
London EC4R 2RH
Telephone +44 (0) 20 7236 6703
Website www.innholders.co.uk

Clerk
Dougal Bulger

The Worshipful Company of Insurers
Insurance Hall, 20 Aldermanbury, London EC2V 7HY
Telephone +44 (0) 20 7600 4006
Website www.wci.org.uk

Clerk
Leonard Walters

The Worshipful Company of International Bankers
12 Austin Friars, London EC2N 2HE
Telephone +44 (0) 20 7374 0212
Website www.internationalbankers.co.uk

Clerk
Wing Cdr Tim Woods

The Worshipful Company of Ironmongers
Ironmongers' Hall, Shaftesbury Place, Barbican,
London EC2Y 8AA
Telephone +44 (0) 20 7776 2304
Website www.ironhall.co.uk

Clerk
Col Hamon Massey

The Worshipful Company of Joiners and Ceilers
75 Meadway Drive, Horsell, Woking, Surrey GU21 4TF
Telephone +44 (0) 1483 727113
Website www.joinersandceilers.co.uk

Clerk
Amanda Jackson

The Worshipful Company of Launderers
Launderers' Hall, 9 Montague Close, London SE1 9DD
Telephone +44 (0) 20 7378 1430
Website www.wcol.co.uk

Clerk
Jacqueline Polek

The Worshipful Company of Leathersellers
Leathersellers' Hall, 15 St Helen's Place,
London EC3A 6DQ
Telephone +44 (0) 20 7330 1444
Website www.leathersellers.co.uk

Clerk
Cdre Jonathan Cooke

The Worshipful Company of Lightmongers
Crown Wharf, 11a Coldharbour, Blackwall Reach,
London E14 9NS
Telephone +44 (0) 20 7515 9055
Website www.lightmongers.org.uk

Clerk
Derek Wheatley

The Worshipful Company of Loriners
Hampton House, High Street, East Grinstead, West
Sussex RH19 3AW
Telephone +44 (0) 1342 319038
Website www.loriner.co.uk

Clerk
Peter Lusty

The Worshipful Company of Makers of Playing Cards
2 Cannon Way, West Molesey, Surrey KT8 2NB
Telephone +44 (0) 20 8979 5407
Website www.makersofplayingcards.co.uk

Clerk
Paul Bowen

The Worshipful Company of Management Consultants
Copperfield, The Ridgeway, Cranleigh, Surrey GU6 7HR
Telephone +44 (0) 1483 271459
Website www.wcomc.org.uk

Clerk
Lt Col Dennis Hall

The Worshipful Company of Marketors
13 Hall Gardens, Colney Heath, St Albans,
Hertfordshire AL4 0QF
Telephone +44 (0) 1727 824446
Website www.marketors.org

Clerk
Gaye Duffy

The Worshipful Company of Masons
22 Cannon Hill, Southgate, London N14 6LG
Telephone +44 (0) 20 8882 9520
Website www.masonslivery.co.uk

Clerk
Peter Clark

The Worshipful Company of Merchant Taylors
Merchant Taylors' Hall, 30 Threadneedle Street,
London EC2R 8JB
Telephone +44 (0) 20 7450 4440
Website www.merchant-taylors.co.uk

Clerk
Rear Adm N H L Harris

The Worshipful Company of Musicians
6th Floor, 2 London Wall Buildings, London EC2M 5PP
Telephone +44 (0) 20 7496 8980
Website www.wcom.org.uk

Clerk
Col Tim Hoggarth

The Worshipful Company of Needlemakers
PO Box 3682, Windsor, Berkshire SL4 3WR
Telephone +44 (0) 1753 860690
Website www.worshipfulcompanyofneedlemakers.com

Clerk
Philip Grant

The Worshipful Company of Painter-Stainers
Painters' Hall, 9 Little Trinity Lane, London EC4V 2AD
Telephone +44 (0) 20 7236 7070
Website www.painters-hall.co.uk

Clerk
Chris Twyman

The Worshipful Company of Pattenmakers
3 The High Street, Sutton Valence, Kent ME17 3AG
Telephone +44 (0) 1622 842440
Website www.pattenmakers.co.uk

Clerk
Col Robert Murfin

The Worshipful Company of Paviors
3 Ridgemount Gardens, Enfield, Middlesex EN2 8QL
Telephone +44 (0) 20 8366 1566
Website www.paviorscompany.org.uk

Clerk
John White

The Worshipful Company of Pewterers
Pewterers' Hall, Oat Lane, London EC2V 7DE
Telephone +44 (0) 20 7397 8190
Website www.pewterers.org.uk

Clerk
Capt Paddy Watson

The Worshipful Company of Plaisterers
Plaisterers' Hall, 1 London Wall, London EC2Y 5JU
Telephone +44 (0) 20 7796 4333
Website www.plaistererslivery.co.uk

Clerk
Hilary Machtus

The Worshipful Company of Plumbers
Wax Chandlers' Hall, 6 Gresham Street,
London EC2V 7AD
Telephone +44 (0) 20 7796 2468
Website www.plumberscompany.org.uk

Clerk
Lt Col Anthony Paterson-Fox

The Worshipful Company of Poulters
The Old Butchers, Station Road, Groombridge, East
Sussex TN3 9QX
Telephone +44 (0) 1892 860456
Website www.poulters.org.uk

Clerk
Gwen Butcher

The Worshipful Company of Saddlers
Saddlers' Hall, 40 Gutter Lane, London EC2V 6BR
Telephone +44 (0) 20 7726 8661
Website www.saddlersco.co.uk

Clerk
Col Nigel Lithgow

The Worshipful Company of Salters
The Salters' Hall, Fore Street, London EC2Y 5DE
Telephone +44 (0) 20 7588 5216
Website www.salters.co.uk

Clerk
Capt David Morris

The Worshipful Company of Scientific Instrument Makers
9 Montague Close, London SE1 9DD
Telephone +44 (0) 20 7407 4832
Website www.wcsim.co.uk

Clerk
Neville Watson

The Worshipful Company of Scriveners
HQS Wellington, Temple Stairs, Victoria Embankment,
London WC2R 2PN
Telephone +44 (0) 20 7240 0529
Website www.scriveners.org.uk

Clerk
Andrew Hill

The Worshipful Company of Shipwrights
Ironmongers' Hall, Barbican, London EC2Y 8AA
Telephone +44 (0) 20 7606 2376
Website www.shipwrights.co.uk

Clerk
Rear Adm Derek Anthony

The Worshipful Company of Skinners
Skinners' Hall, 8 Dowgate Hill, London EC4R 2SP
Telephone +44 (0) 20 7236 5629
Website www.skinners.org.uk

Clerk
Maj-Gen Brian Plummer

The Worshipful Company of Spectacle Makers
Apothecaries' Hall, Blackfriars Lane, London EC4V 6EL
Telephone +44 (0) 20 7236 8645
Website www.spectaclemakers.com

Clerk
Lt Col John Salmon

The Worshipful Company of Stationers and Newspaper Makers
Stationers' Hall, Ave Maria Lane, London EC4M 7DD
Telephone +44 (0) 20 7248 2934
Website www.stationers.org

Clerk
Brig Denzil Sharp

The Worshipful Company of Tallow Chandlers
Tallow Chandlers' Hall, 4 Dowgate Hill,
London EC4R 2SH
Telephone +44 (0) 20 7248 4726
Website www.tallowchandlers.org

Clerk
Brig Roy Wilde

The Worshipful Company of Tax Advisers
191 West End Road, Ruislip, Middlesex HA4 6LD
Telephone +44 (0) 1895 625817
Website www.taxadvisers.org.uk

Clerk
Paul Herbage

The Worshipful Company of Tin Plate Workers alias Wireworkers
Highbanks, Ferry Road, Surlingham, Norfolk NR14 7AR
Telephone +44 (0) 8707 669 867
Website www.tinplateworkers.co.uk

Clerk
Michael Henderson-Begg

The Worshipful Company of Tobacco Pipe Makers and Tobacco Blenders
Green Meadow, Island, Steep, Hampshire GU32 1AE
Telephone +44 (0) 1730 261049
Website www.tobaccolivery.org

Clerk
Barbara Hines

The Worshipful Company of Turners
182 Temple Chambers, Temple Avenue,
London EC4Y 0HP
Telephone +44 (0) 20 7353 9595
Website www.turnersco.com

Clerk
Edward Windsor-Clive

The Worshipful Company of Tylers and Bricklayers
30 Shelley Avenue, Tiptree, Essex CO5 0SF
Telephone +44 (0) 1621 816592
Website www.tylersandbricklayers.co.uk

Clerk
Barry Blumsom

The Worshipful Company of Upholders
46 Quail Gardens, South Croydon, Surrey CR2 8TF
Telephone +44 (0) 20 8651 3303
Website www.upholders.co.uk

Clerk
Jean Cody

The Worshipful Company of Vintners
Vintners' Hall, Upper Thames Street, London EC4V 3BG
Telephone +44 (0) 20 7236 1863
Website www.vintnershall.co.uk

Clerk
Brig Michael Smythe

The Worshipful Company of Water Conservators
The Lark, 2 Bell Lane, Worlington, Bury St Edmunds,
Suffolk IP28 8SE
Telephone +44 (0) 1638 510626
Website www.waterconservators.org

Clerk
Ralph Riley

The Worshipful Company of Wax Chandlers
Wax Chandlers' Hall, 6 Gresham Street,
London EC2V 7AD
Telephone +44 (0) 20 7606 3591
Website www.waxchandlershall.co.uk

Clerk
Richard Percival

The Worshipful Company of Weavers
Saddlers' House, Gutter Lane, London EC2V 6BR
Telephone +44 (0) 20 7606 1155
Website www.weavers.org.uk

Clerk
John Snowdon

The Worshipful Company of Wheelwrights
7 Glengall Road, Bexleyheath, Kent DA7 4AL
Telephone +44 (0) 20 8306 5119
Website www.wheelwrights.org

Clerk
Bryan Francois

The Worshipful Company of Woolmen
Brewers' Hall, Aldermanbury Square, London EC2V 7HR
Telephone +44 (0) 20 7606 1301
Website www.woolmen.com

Clerk
John Stephens

The Worshipful Company of World Traders
36 Ladbroke Grove, London W11 2PA
Telephone +44 (0) 20 7792 3410
Website www.world-traders.org

Clerk
Nigel Pullman

The Worshipful Society of Apothecaries
Apothecaries' Hall, 14 Black Friars Lane,
London EC4V 6EJ
Telephone +44 (0) 20 7236 1189
Website www.apothecaries.org

Clerk
Andrew Wallington-Smith

The Judiciary of England and Wales

The following pages detail all senior judges in England and Wales, from the House of Lords, the Court of Appeal and the High Court of Justice, and all circuit judges listed by region.

Lord Chief Justice of England and Wales
Lord Phillips of Worth Matravers

Master of the Rolls
The Rt Hon Sir Anthony Peter Clarke

President of the Queen's Bench Division and Head of Criminal Justice
The Rt Hon Sir Igor Judge

President of the Family Division and Head of Family Justice
The Rt Hon Sir Mark Howard Potter

The Chancellor of the High Court
The Rt Hon Sir Robert Andrew Morritt

House of Lords
London SW1A 0PW
Telephone +44 (0) 20 7219 3107

Lords of Appeal in Ordinary
Lord Bingham of Cornhill, Lord Brown of Eaton-under-Heywood, Lord Carswell, Lady Hale of Richmond, Lord Hoffmann, Lord Hope of Craighead, Lord Mance, Lord Neuberger of Abbotsbury, Lord Rodger of Earlsferry, Lord Saville of Newdigate, Lord Scott of Foscote, Lord Walker of Gestingthorpe

Court of Appeal
The Royal Courts of Justice, Strand, London WC2A 2LL
Telephone +44 (0) 30 7947 6000

Lords Justices of Appeal
Dame Mary Howarth Arden, Sir Robin Ernest Auld, Sir Thomas Scott Gillespie Baker, Sir Richard Joseph Buxton, Sir Robert John Anderson Carnwath, Sir John Murray Chadwick, Sir Lawrence Anthony Collins, Sir John Anthony Dyson, Sir William Marcus Gage, Dame Heather Carol Hallett, Sir Anthony Hooper, Sir Anthony Philip Gilson Hughes, Sir Robert Raphael Hayim (Robin) Jacob, Sir Maurice Ralph Kay, Sir David Wolfe Keene, Sir David Nicholas Ramsey Latham, Sir John Grant McKenzie Laws, Sir Brian Henry Leveson, Sir Timothy Andrew Wigram Lloyd, Sir Andrew Centlivres Longmore, Sir Anthony Tristram Kenneth May, Sir Martin James Moore-Bick, Sir Alan George Moses, Sir John Frank Mummery, Sir Malcolm Thomas Pill, Sir Stephen Price Richards, Sir Bernard Anthony Rix, Sir Stephen John Sedley, Dame Janet Hilary Smith, Sir Roger John Laugharne Thomas, Sir Mathew Alexander Thorpe, Sir Roger Grenfell Toulson, Sir Simon Lane Tuckey, Sir Nicholas Peter Rathbone Wall, Sir George Mark Waller, Sir Alan Hylton Ward, Sir Nicholas Allan Roy Wilson

High Court - Chancery Division
The Royal Courts of Justice, Strand, London WC2A 2LL
Telephone +44 (0) 20 7947 6000

Judges
Sir William Anthony Blackburne, Sir Michael Townley Featherstone Briggs, Sir Terrence Michael Elkan Barnet Etherton, Sir Edward Christopher Evans-Lombe, Sir Launcelot Dinadin James Henderson, Sir David James Tyson Kitchin, Sir Kim Martin Jordan Lewison, Sir Gavin Anthony Lightman, Sir John Edmund Frederic Lindsay, Sir George Anthony Mann, Sir Paul Hyacinth Morgan, Sir Nicholas John Patten, Sir Nicholas Richard Pumfrey, Sir David Anthony Stewart Richards, Sir Colin Percy Farquharson Rimer, Sir Peter Winston Smith, Sir Nicholas Roger Warren

High Court - Family Division
The Royal Courts of Justice, Strand, London WC2A 2LL
Telephone +44 (0) 20 7947 6000

Judges
Sir Richard John Pearson Aikens, Sir David Michael Bean, Sir Jack Beatson, Sir Nicolas Dusan Bratza, Sir Stanley Jeffrey Burnton, Sir Michael John Burton, Sir Alexander Neil Logie Butterfield, Sir David Calvert-Smith, Sir David Clive Clarke, Sir Christopher Simon Courtenay Stephenson Clarke, Sir Andrew David Collins, Sir Jeremy Lionel Cooke, Dame Laura Mary Cox, Sir Peter John Cresswell, Sir Nigel Anthony Lamert Davis, Dame Linda Penelope Dobbs, Sir David Eady, Sir Patrick Elias, Sir David Roderick Evans, Sir Richard Alan Field, Julian Martin Flaux, Sir John Thayne Forbes, Sir Adrian Bruce Fulford, Sir Richard John Hedley Gibbs, Dame Elizabeth Gloster, Sir John Bernard Goldring, Sir Charles Anthony St John Gray, Sir Geoffrey Douglas Grigson, Sir Peter Henry Gross, Sir Richard Henry Quixano Henriques, Sir Henry Egar Garfield Hodge, Sir Christopher John Holland, Sir Stephen John Irwin, Sir Raymond Evan Jack, Sir Rupert Matthew Jackson, Sir David Lloyd Jones, Sir Brian Richard Keith, Sir Timothy Roger Alan King, Sir Gordon Julian Hugh Langley, Sir Brian Frederick James Langstaff, Sir Colin Crichton Mackay, Sir Richard George Bramwell McCombe, Sir Stuart Neil McKinnon, Sir John Edward Mitting, Sir Robert Franklyn Nelson, Sir George Michael Newman, Sir Charles Peter Lawford Openshaw, Sir Duncan Brian Walter Ouseley, Sir Robert Michael Owen, Sir David Herbert Penry-Davey, Sir Christopher John Pitchers, Sir Christopher John Pitchford, Dame Anne Judith Rafferty, Sir Vivian Arthur Ramsey, Sir Roger John Royce, John Henry Boulton Saunders, Sir Stephen Robert Silber, Sir Peregrine Charles Hugo Simon, Sir Andrew Charles Smith, Sir David William Steel, Sir Jeremy Mirth Sullivan, Dame Caroline Jane Swift, Sir Nigel John Martin Teare, Sir Stephen Miles Tomlinson, Sir Colman Maurice Treacy, Sir Michael George Tugendhat, Sir Nicholas Edward Underhill, Sir Paul James Walker, Sir Alan Fraser Wilkie, Sir John Griffith Williams, Sir Wyn Lewis Williams

High Court - Queen's Bench Division
The Royal Courts of Justice, Strand, London WC2A 2LL
Telephone +44 (0) 20 7947 6000

Judges
Dame Florence Jacquelene Baron, Sir Hugh Peter Derwyn Bennett, Dame Jill Margaret Black, Sir David Roderick Lessiter Bodey, Sir Arthur William Hessin Charles, Sir Paul James Duke Coleridge, Sir Mark Hedley, Dame Mary Claire Hogg, Sir Edward James Holman, Sir Andrew Tristram Hammett Kirkwood, Sir Andrew Ewart McFarlane, Dame Julia Wendy Macur, Sir Andrew John Gregory Moylan, Sir James Lawrence Munby, Dame Anna Evelyn Hamilton Pauffley, Sir Ernest Nigel Ryder, Sir Jan Peter Singer, Sir Christopher John Sumner, Sir Roderic Lionel James Wood

Midland Circuit

Judges
His Honour Judge Alexander QC, Her Honour Judge Alton, His Honour Judge Bellamy, His Honour Judge Dudley Bennett, His Honour Judge Bray, His Honour Judge Simon Brown QC, His Honour Judge Brunning, His Honour Judge Burgess, Her Honour Judge Butler QC, His Honour Judge Cardinal, His Honour Judge Cavell, His Honour Judge Challinor, His Honour Judge Chapman, His Honour Judge Cleary, His Honour Judge Coates, His Honour Judge Collis, His Honour Judge Stephen Davies, Her Honour Judge Deeley, His Honour Judge Dudley, His Honour Judge Duggan, His Honour Judge Eades, His Honour Judge Eccles QC, His Honour Judge Everard, His Honour Judge Faber, Her Honour Judge Fisher, His Honour Judge Fletcher, His Honour Judge Geddes, His Honour Judge Glenn, His Honour Judge Gregory, His Honour Judge Griffith-Jones, His Honour Judge Victor Hall, His Honour Judge Andrew Hamilton, His Honour Judge Hamilton, His Honour Judge Hammond, Her Honour Judge Hampton, His Honour Judge Head, His Honour Judge Heath, Her Honour Judge Hindley QC, His Honour Judge Hodson, His Honour Judge Hooper QC, Her Honour Judge Hughes, His Honour Judge Inglis, His Honour Judge Jenkins, Her Honour Judge Kirkham, His Honour Judge Lea, His Honour Judge MacDuff QC, His Honour Judge Machin, His Honour Judge Matthews, His Honour Judge Maxwell, His Honour Judge McCarthy, His Honour Judge McCreath, His Honour Judge McEvoy QC, His Honour Judge McKenna, His Honour Judge Metcalf, His Honour Judge Milmo QC, His Honour Judge Mitchell, His Honour Judge Nicolas Mitchell, His Honour Judge Mithani, His Honour Judge Morrell, His Honour Judge Morrison QC, His Honour Judge Norris QC, His Honour Judge Oliver-Jones QC, His Honour Judge Onions, His Honour Judge Orme, His Honour Judge Orrell, His Honour Judge O'Rorke, His Honour Judge Pearce-Higgins QC, His Honour Judge Pert QC, His Honour Judge Plunkett, His Honour Judge David Price, His Honour Judge Pugsley, His Honour Judge Purle QC, His Honour Judge Pyke, His Honour Judge Ross, His Honour Judge Rubery, His Honour Judge Rundell, His Honour Judge Michael Stokes QC, His Honour Judge Styler, Her Honour Judge Swindells QC, His Honour Judge Teare, Her Honour Judge Thomas, His Honour Judge Tonking, His Honour Judge Waine, His Honour Judge Wait, His Honour Judge Warner, His Honour Judge Nicholas Webb, His Honour Judge Wide QC, His Honour Judge Wood

North Eastern Circuit

Judges
His Honour Judge Armstrong, His Honour Judge Ashurst, His Honour Judge Barber, His Honour Judge Bartfield, His Honour Judge Behrens, Her Honour Judge Penelope Belcher, His Honour Judge Peter Benson, Her Honour Judge Bolton, His Honour Judge Bowers, His Honour Judge Briggs, His Honour Judge Bryant, His Honour Judge Bullimore, Her Honour Judge Cahill QC, Her Honour Judge Carr QC, His Honour Judge Cartlidge, His Honour Judge Cliffe, His Honour Judge Cockroft, His Honour Judge Cracknell, Her Honour Judge Jacqueline Davies, His Honour Judge Dobkin, His Honour Judge Dowse, His Honour Judge Durham Hall QC, His Honour Judge Evans, His Honour Judge Faulks, Her Honour Judge Finnerty, His Honour Judge Fox QC, His Honour Judge Goldsack QC, His Honour Judge Grant, His Honour Judge Grenfell, His Honour Judge Gullick, His Honour Judge Hawkesworth QC, His Honour Judge Hewitt, His Honour Judge Hodson, His Honour Judge Hoffman, His Honour Judge Hull, His Honour Judge Hunt, His Honour Judge Ibbotson, His Honour Judge Jack, His Honour Judge Peter Jones, His Honour Judge Kamil, His Honour Judge Kaye QC, His Honour Judge Keen QC, Her Honour Judge Kershaw QC, His Honour Judge Lancaster, His Honour Judge Langan QC, His Honour Judge Lawler QC, His Honour Judge Lowden, His Honour Judge Macgill, His Honour Judge Marson QC, His Honour Judge McCallum, His Honour Judge Mettyear, His Honour Judge Milford QC, Her Honour Judge Moir, His Honour Judge Moore, His Honour Judge Moorhouse, His Honour Judge Murphy QC, His Honour Judge Christopher Prince, His Honour Judge Reddihough, His Honour Judge Robertshaw, His Honour Judge Robinson, His Honour Judge Scott, Her Honour Judge Jane Shipley, His Honour Judge Spencer, His Honour Judge Shaun Spencer QC, His Honour Judge Spittle, His Honour Judge Stewart QC, His Honour Judge Swanson, His Honour Judge John Taylor, His Honour Judge Michael Taylor, His Honour Judge Thorn QC, His Honour Judge Walford, His Honour Judge Walsh, His Honour Judge Walton, His Honour Judge Whitburn, His Honour Judge Wolstenholme, His Honour Judge Wood

Northern Circuit

Judges
His Honour Judge Allweis, His Honour Judge Appleby, His Honour Judge Appleton, His Honour Judge Armitage QC, His Honour Judge Atherton, His Honour Judge Aubrey QC, Her Honour Judge Badley, His Honour Judge Baker, His Honour Judge Barnett, His Honour Judge Batty QC, His Honour Judge Blake, His Honour Judge Bloom, His Honour Judge Boulton, His Honour Judge Brown, His Honour Judge Brown, His Honour Judge Byrne, Her Honour Judge Case, His Honour Judge Caulfield, His Honour Judge Clarke, His Honour Judge Clayson, His Honour Judge Clifton, His Honour Judge Cornwall, Her Honour Judge Daley, Her Honour Judge De Haas QC, His Honour Judge Duncan, His Honour Judge Dutton, Her Honour Judge Eaglestone, His Honour Judge Earnshaw, His Honour Judge Edwards, His Honour Judge Ensor, His Honour Judge Everett, His Honour Judge David Fletcher, Her Honour Judge Forrester, His Honour Judge Foster QC, His Honour Judge Geake, His Honour Judge Anthony Gee QC, His Honour Judge Gee, His Honour Judge George, His Honour Judge Gilbart QC, His Honour Judge Gilliland QC, His Honour Judge Gilmour QC, His Honour Judge Globe QC, His Honour Judge Goldstone QC, His Honour Judge Halbert, His Honour Judge Hale, His Honour Judge Iain Hamilton, His Honour Judge Hammond, His Honour Judge Harris, His Honour Judge Hegarty QC, His Honour Judge Henshell, His Honour Judge Hernandez, His Honour Judge Hodge QC, His Honour Judge Holloway, His Honour Judge Holman, His Honour Judge Hughes, His Honour Judge James, His Honour Judge Mushtaq Khokhar, His Honour Judge Knopf, Her Honour Judge Lindsey Kushner QC, His Honour Judge Lakin, His Honour Judge Lever, His Honour Judge Lewis, His Honour Judge Jeffrey Lewis, His Honour Judge Lowcock, Her Honour Judge Lunt, His Honour Judge Lyon, His Honour Judge MacKay, His Honour Judge MacMillan, His Honour Judge Maddison, His Honour Judge William Morris, His Honour Judge Graham Morrow QC, His Honour Judge Mort, Her Honour Judge Newton, Her Honour Judge Nield, His Honour Judge Pelling QC, His Honour Judge Phillips, His Honour Judge Phipps, His Honour Judge Platts, His Honour Judge Raynor QC, His Honour Judge Roberts, Her Honour Judge Roddy, Her Honour Judge Ruaux, His Honour Judge Rudland, His Honour Judge Rumbelow, His Honour Judge Russell QC, His Honour Judge Slinger, His Honour Judge Adrian Smith, His Honour Judge Smith, Her Honour Judge Steel, His Honour Judge Steiger QC, His Honour Judge Stewart QC, His Honour Judge Swift, His Honour Judge Sycamore, His Honour Judge Teague QC, His Honour Judge Tetlow, His Honour Judge Roger Thomas QC, His Honour Judge Trigger, His Honour Judge Waksman QC, His Honour Judge Wallwork, His Honour Judge Warnock, Her Honour Judge Watson, His Honour Judge Nicholas Woodward, His Honour Judge Woolman, His Honour Judge Wright

South Eastern Circuit

Judges
His Honour Judge Addison, His Honour Judge Ader, His Honour Judge Ainley, His Honour Judge Altman, His Honour Judge Ansell, His Honour Judge Anthony, Her Honour Judge Anwyl QC, His Honour Judge Atkins, His Honour Judge Bailey, His Honour Judge Michael Baker QC, His Honour Judge Ball QC, His Honour Judge Barham, His Honour Judge Barker QC, Her Honour Judge Barnes, His Honour Judge Barnett QC, His Honour Judge Barratt, His Honour Judge Beaumont QC, His Honour Judge Behar, His Honour Judge Bevan QC, Her Honour Judge Bevington, His Honour Judge Bing, His Honour Judge Binning, His Honour Judge Birtles, His Honour Judge Birts QC, His Honour Judge Blackett, His Honour Judge Blacksell QC, His Honour Judge Brasse, His Honour Judge Breen, His Honour Judge Brooke QC, His Honour Judge Richard Brown, His Honour Judge Browne QC, His Honour Judge Jeffrey Burke QC, His Honour Judge Burn, His Honour Judge Byers, His Honour Judge Caddick, His Honour Judge Andrew Campbell, Her Honour Judge Ann Campbell, His Honour Judge Campbell, His Honour Judge Carey, His Honour Judge Carroll, Her Honour Judge Catterson, His Honour Judge Chapple, His Honour Judge

Peter Clark, His Honour Judge Clegg, Her Honour Judge Coates, His Honour Judge Coleman, His Honour Judge Colgan, His Honour Judge Collender QC, His Honour Judge Collins, His Honour Judge Coltart, His Honour Judge Compston, His Honour Judge Cooper, His Honour Judge Copley, His Honour Judge Corrie, His Honour Judge Coulson QC, His Honour Judge Cowell, Her Honour Judge Cox, His Honour Judge Cripps, His Honour Judge Critchlow, His Honour Judge Crocker, His Honour Judge Cryan, His Honour Judge Curl, Her Honour Judge Dangor, His Honour Judge Darroch, His Honour Judge Davis, His Honour Judge De Mille, His Honour Judge Dean QC, His Honour Judge Dedman, His Honour Judge Devaux, His Honour Judge Dodgson, His Honour Judge Downes, His Honour Judge Edwards, His Honour Judge Ellis, His Honour Judge Elly, His Honour Judge Elwen, His Honour Judge Everall QC, Her Honour Judge Faber, His Honour Judge Farnworth, His Honour Judge Fenn, His Honour Judge Forrester, His Honour Judge Richard Foster, Her Honour Judge Freedman, His Honour Judge Fysh QC, His Honour Judge Gibson, Her Honour Judge Goddard QC, His Honour Judge Goldstaub QC, His Honour Judge Goodin, His Honour Judge Gordon, His Honour Judge Goymer, His Honour Judge Gratwicke, His Honour Judge Alan Greenwood, His Honour Judge Grobel, Her Honour Judge Guggenheim QC, His Honour Judge Gypps, His Honour Judge Hall, Her Honour Judge Hallon, Her Honour Judge Hammerton, His Honour Judge Hardy QC, His Honour Judge Charles Harris QC, His Honour Judge Harris, His Honour Judge Gareth Hawkesworth, His Honour Judge Hawkins, His Honour Judge Jonathan Haworth, His Honour Judge Haworth, His Honour Judge Hayward, His Honour Judge Hayward Smith QC, His Honour Judge Higgins, His Honour Judge Hillen, His Honour Judge Hollis, His Honour Judge Holt, His Honour Judge Hone QC, His Honour Judge Hornby, His Honour Judge Horowitz QC, His Honour Judge Hucker, Her Honour Judge Hughes, His Honour Judge Hughes, His Honour Judge Huskinson, His Honour Judge Inman, His Honour Judge Issard-Davies, His Honour Judge Jacobs, His Honour Judge Nicholas Jones, His Honour Judge Joseph, His Honour Judge Karsten QC, Her Honour Judge Karu, His Honour Judge Katkhuda, His Honour Judge Kay QC, His Honour Judge Kemp, His Honour Judge Kennedy, His Honour Judge Khayat QC, His Honour Judge King, His Honour Judge King, His Honour Judge Knight QC, Her Honour Judge Knowles, His Honour Judge Kramer QC, His Honour Judge Latham, His Honour Judge Lawson QC, Her Honour Judge Levy, His Honour Judge Lindsay QC, His Honour Judge Loraine-Smith, His Honour Judge Lowen, Her Honour Judge Ludlow, His Honour Judge Lyons, His Honour Judge Macdonald QC, His Honour Judge Mackie QC, His Honour Judge MacRae, His Honour Judge Madge, His Honour Judge Marron QC, His Honour Judge Martineau, His Honour Judge Matheson QC, Her Honour Judge Matthews QC, Her Honour Judge Mayer, His Honour Judge McDowall, His Honour Judge McGregor-Johnson, His Honour Judge McIntyre, His Honour Judge McKinnon, His Honour Judge McKittrick,

His Honour Judge McMullen QC, His Honour Judge Meeran, Her Honour Judge Mensah, His Honour Judge Christopher Mitchell, His Honour Judge David Mitchell, His Honour Judge Fergus Mitchell, His Honour Judge John Mitchell, His Honour Judge Mole QC, His Honour Judge Hugh Morgan, His Honour Judge Anthony Morris QC, His Honour Judge Morton Jack, His Honour Judge Moss QC, His Honour Judge Peter Moss, His Honour Judge Moss, Her Honour Judge Mowat, His Honour Judge Murdoch QC, His Honour Judge Nash, His Honour Judge Nathan, His Honour Judge Newton, His Honour Judge Niblett, Her Honour Judge Norrie, His Honour Judge Norris, His Honour Judge Oppenheimer, His Honour Judge O'Brien, His Honour Judge O'Mahony, His Honour Judge O'Sullivan, His Honour Judge Paget QC, His Honour Judge Pardoe QC, His Honour Judge Patience QC, His Honour Judge Pawlak, Her Honour Judge Pearce, His Honour Judge Pearl, Her Honour Judge Pearl, Her Honour Judge Pearlman, His Honour Judge Philpot, His Honour Judge Pillay, His Honour Judge Pitts, His Honour Judge Platt, Her Honour Judge Plumstead, His Honour Judge Plumstead, His Honour Judge Polden, His Honour Judge Pontius, His Honour Judge Powles QC, His Honour Judge Pratt, His Honour Judge Price, His Honour Judge Price QC, His Honour Judge Radford, His Honour Judge Reid QC, His Honour Judge Rennie, His Honour Judge Jeremy Richards, His Honour Judge Richardson, His Honour Judge Riddell, His Honour Judge Risius, His Honour Judge Robbins, His Honour Judge Mervyn Roberts, His Honour Judge Roberts QC, His Honour Judge Rook QC, His Honour Judge John Rylance, His Honour Judge Ryland, His Honour Judge Scott-Gall, His Honour Judge Serota QC, His Honour Judge Seymour, His Honour Judge Simpkiss, His Honour Judge Simpson, His Honour Judge Sleeman, His Honour Judge Smith QC, Her Honour Judge Zoe Smith, His Honour Judge Edward Southwell, His Honour Judge Statman, His Honour Judge Stephens QC, His Honour Judge Stewart, His Honour Judge Stone QC, His Honour Judge Stow, Her Honour Judge Stuart-Brown, His Honour Judge Tain, His Honour Judge Tanzer, Her Honour Judge Tapping, His Honour Judge Deborah Taylor, His Honour Judge Testar, His Honour Judge Thompson, His Honour Judge Thornton QC, His Honour Judge Thorpe, His Honour Judge Tilling, His Honour Judge Toulmin QC, His Honour Judge Turner QC, His Honour Judge Tyrer, His Honour Judge Van Der Bijl, His Honour Judge van der Werff, His Honour Judge Wadsworth, His Honour Judge Wakefield, His Honour Judge Richard Walker, His Honour Judge Waller, His Honour Judge Stephen Warner, His Honour Judge Webb, His Honour Judge Welchman, His Honour Judge Wilcox, His Honour Judge Wilkinson, Her Honour Judge Williams, Her Honour Judge Sally Williams, His Honour Judge Winstanley, His Honour Judge Worsley, His Honour Judge Worsley QC, His Honour Judge Peter Wright, His Honour Judge Wulwik, His Honour Judge Yelton, His Honour Judge Zeidman QC

Wales Circuit

Judges

His Honour Judge Bidder QC, His Honour Judge Burr, His Honour Judge Chambers QC, His Honour Judge Curran, His Honour Judge Denyer QC, His Honour Judge Diehl QC, His Honour Judge Farmer QC, His Honour Judge Furness, His Honour Judge Gaskell, His Honour Judge Hopkins QC, His Honour Judge Dafydd Hughes, His Honour Judge Hughes QC, His Honour Judge Llewellyn-Jones QC, His Honour Judge Masterman, His Honour Judge David Wynn Morgan, His Honour Judge Morris, His Honour Judge Morton, Her Honour Judge Parry, His Honour Judge Price QC, His Honour Judge Philip Price QC, Her Honour Judge Rees, His Honour Judge Richards, His Honour Judge Philip Richards, His Honour Judge Rogers QC, His Honour Judge Keith Thomas, His Honour Judge Vosper QC

Western Circuit

Judges

His Honour Judge Barclay, His Honour Judge Andrew Barnett, His Honour Judge Beashel, His Honour Judge Boggis QC, His Honour Judge Bond, His Honour Judge Boney QC, Her Honour Judge Bonvin, His Honour Judge Brodrick, His Honour Judge Bromilow, His Honour Judge Burford QC, His Honour Judge Bursell QC, His Honour Judge Harvey Clark QC, His Honour Judge Cottle, His Honour Judge Cowling, His Honour Judge Crowther QC, His Honour Judge Cutler, His Honour Judge Darlow, His Honour Judge Darwall Smith, Her Honour Judge Darwall Smith, Her Honour Judge Davies, Her Honour Judge Dixon, His Honour Judge Field, His Honour Judge Foley, His Honour Judge Gilbert QC, His Honour Judge Griffiths, His Honour Judge Griggs, Her Honour Judge Hagen, His Honour Judge Harington, Her Honour Judge Harrow, His Honour Judge Havelock-Allan, His Honour Judge Hetherington, His Honour Judge Hooton, His Honour Judge Hope, His Honour Judge Hughes QC, His Honour Judge Jarvis, His Honour Judge Jones, His Honour Judge Lambert, His Honour Judge Ian Leeming QC, His Honour Judge Leigh QC, His Honour Judge Longbotham, His Honour Judge Michael Longman, His Honour Judge Marston, His Honour Judge McCahill QC, His Honour Judge Meston QC, His Honour Judge Milligan, His Honour Judge John Neligan, His Honour Judge O'Malley, His Honour Judge Pearson, His Honour Judge Picton, His Honour Judge Richard Price, His Honour Judge Roach, Her Honour Judge Robertshaw, His Honour Judge Rucker, His Honour Judge Rutherford, His Honour Judge Shawcross, His Honour Judge Tabor, His Honour Judge Ticehurst, His Honour Judge Tyzack, His Honour Judge Vincent, His Honour Judge Wade, His Honour Judge Wassall, His Honour Judge Graham White, His Honour Judge Wiggs

THE JUDICIARY OF SCOTLAND

Details of the senior judges, from the Court of Session and High Court, and the
sheriffs and sheriff principal of each Principal Court in Scotland.

Lord President and Lord Justice General
The Rt Hon Lord Hamilton

Court of Session and High Court of Justiciary - Inner House

Parliament House, Parliament Square,
Edinburgh EH1 1RQ
Telephone +44 (0) 131 225 2595
Fax +44 (0) 131 240 6755

Lords of Session
Lord Eassie, Lord Gill, Lord Johnston, Lord Kingarth,
Lord Macfadyen, Lord Nimmo Smith, Lord Osborne, Lady
Paton, Lord Philip, Lord Wheatley

Court of Session and High Court of Justiciary - Outer House

Parliament House, Parliament Square,
Edinburgh EH1 1RQ
Telephone +44 (0) 131 225 2595
Fax +44 (0) 131 240 6755

Lords of Session
Lord Bracadale, Lord Brailsford, Lord Brodie, Lord
Carloway, Lord Clarke, Lady Clark of Calton, Lady
Dorrian, Lord Drummond Young, Lord Emslie, Lord
Glennie, Lord Hardie, Lord Hodge, Lord Kinclaven, Lord
Mackay of Drumadoon, Lord Macphail, Lord McEwan,
Lord Menzies, Lord Reed, Lady Smith, Lord Turnbull,
Lord Uist

Glasgow and Strathkelvin

Sheriff Principal
J A Taylor
Sheriffs
J A Baird, P M M Bowman, S Cathcart, D Convery, A L
A Duncan, J D Friel, A C Henry, W H Holligan, A G
Johnston, B Kearney, B A Lockhart, D M MacNeill QC, H
Matthews QC, C W McFarlane QC, I H L Miller, J K
Mitchell, A W Noble, A C Normand, M G O'Grady QC, I
A S Peebles QC, J Platt, R E A Rae QC, F L Reith QC, L
M Ruxton, C A L Scott, J A Taylor, W J Totten

Grampian, Highlands and Islands

Sheriff Principal
Sir Stephen S T Young Bt QC
Sheriffs
D Booker-Millburn, G K Buchanan, I A Cameron, A M
Cowan, D J Cusine, P P Davies, M Garden, C J Harris QC,
A S Jessop, A L MacFadyen, K A McLernan, G Napier, A
Pollock, K M Stewart, W D Small, D O Sutherland, J K
Tierney

Lothian and Borders

Sheriff Principal
E F Bowen QC
Sheriffs
J D Allan, R G Craik QC, T A K Drummond QC, M G R
Edington, J A Farrell, G R Fleming QC, P Gillam, J M S
Horsburgh QC, M L E Jarvie QC, A Lothian, K M
Maciver, K E C Mackie, N J MacKinnon, D W M
McIntyre, N McPartlin, J C C McSherry, N M P Morrison
QC, W D Muirhead, I A Poole, G W S Presslie, I C
Simpson, M M Stephen, C N Stoddart

North Strathclyde

Sheriff Principal
B A Kerr QC
Sheriffs
V J Canavan, A M Cubie, N Douglas, W Dunlop, J T
Fitzsimons, S W H Fraser, C M A F Gimblett, J P Herald,
W S S Ireland, G C Kavanagh, I S McDonald, C G
McKay, D J Pender, S C Pender, C W Pettigrew, S M
Sinclair, W D Small, J Spy, R Swanney, S A Waldron, A
G Watson

South Strathclyde Dumfries & Galloway

Sheriff Principal
B A Lockhart
Sheriffs
K G Barr, D M Bicket, D A Brown, R H Dickson, M M
Galbraith, W E Gibson, C A Kelly, J McGowan, C B
Miller, J Montgomery, J C Morris, F L Pieri, J Powrie, K
A Ross QC, D Scullion, H K Small, M T Smart, J R
Smith, V J Smith, J H Stewart, N C Stewart, A D Vannet,
T Welsh QC

Tayside, Central and Fife

Sheriff Principal
R Alastair Dunlop QC
Sheriffs
P A Arthurson, P J Braid, C Caldwell, F R Crowe, R A
Davidson, B G Donald, A J M Duff, I D Dunbar, G J
Evans, M J Fletcher, L D R Foulis, T J Hughes, G W M
Liddle, D N Mackie, R J MacLeod, I G McColl, R A
McCreadie, A G McCulloch, J Miller, E C Munro, A J
Murphy, D C W Pyle, A W Robertson, J P Scott, A V
Sheehan, C N R Stein, K A Veal, L Wood

THE JUDICIARY OF NORTHERN IRELAND

Details of the senior judges in Northern Ireland, from the House of Lords, the Court of
Appeal and the High Court of Justice and all county court judges.

Lord Chief Justice of Northern Ireland
The Rt Hon Sir Brian Kerr

Court of Appeal
Royal Courts of Justice, Chichester Street, Belfast BT1 3JF
Telephone +44 (0) 28 9023 5111

Lord Justices of Appeal
The Rt Hon Lord Justice Campbell, The Rt Hon Lord
Justice Girvan, The Rt Hon Lord Justice Higgins

High Court
Royal Courts of Justice, Chichester Street, Belfast BT1 3JF
Telephone +44 (0) 28 9023 5111

Judges
The Hon Mr Justice Coghlin, The Hon Mr Justice Deeny,
The Hon Mr Justice Gillen, The Hon Mr Justice Hart, The
Hon Mr Justice McLaughlin, The Hon Mr Justice Morgan,
The Hon Mr Justice Stephens, The Hon Mr Justice
Treacy, The Hon Mr Justice Weatherup, The Hon Mr
Justice Weir

County Court
Royal Courts of Justice, Chichester Street, Belfast BT1 3JF
Telephone +44 (0) 28 9023 5111

Judges
His Honour Judge Babington, His Honour Judge Burgess
(Recorder of Belfast), His Honour Judge Finnegan QC, His
Honour Judge Gibson QC, His Honour Judge Grant, Her
Honour Judge Kennedy, His Honour Judge Lockie, Her
Honour Judge Loughran, His Honour Judge Lynch QC,
His Honour Judge Markey QC, His Honour Judge
Marrinan, His Honour Judge McFarland, His Honour
Judge McKay QC, Her Honour Judge McReynolds, Her
Honour Judge Philpott QC (Recorder of Londonderry), His
Honour Judge Rodgers, His Honour Judge Smyth QC

BARRISTERS' CHAMBERS

The following pages detail the leading UK barristers' chambers, selected by
annual turnover.

11 King's Bench Walk
Temple, London EC4Y 7EQ
Telephone +44 (0) 20 7632 8500
Fax +44 (0) 7583 9123
E-mail clerksroom@11kbw.com
Website www.11kbw.com

Head of Chambers
Eldred Tabachnik
Head Clerks
Philip Monham and Lucy Pilbro

20 Essex Street
London WC2R 3AL
Telephone +44 (0) 20 7842 1200
Fax +44 (0) 20 7842 1270
E-mail clerks@20essexst.com
Website www.20essexst.com

Head of Chambers
Ian Milligan
Head Clerk
Neil Palmer

3 Verulam Buildings
Gray's Inn, London WC1R 5NT
Telephone +44 (0) 20 7831 8441
Fax +44 (0) 20 7831 8479
E-mail chambers@3vb.com
Website www.3vb.com

Heads of Chambers
Christopher Symons and John Jarvis
Senior Practice Manager
Nicholas Hill

3/4 South Square
Gray's Inn, London WC1R 5HP
Telephone +44 (0) 20 7696 9900
Fax +44 (0) 20 7696 9911
E-mail chambers@southsquare.com
Website www.southsquare.com

Head of Chambers
Michael Crystal
Senior Practice Manager
Paul Cooklin

39 Essex Street
London WC2R 3AT
Telephone +44 (0) 20 7832 1111
Fax +44 (0) 20 7353 3978
E-mail clerks@39essex.com
Website www.39essex.co.uk

Heads of Chambers
Richard Davies and Richard Willmot-Smith
Head Clerk
Alastair Davidson

4 Pump Court
Temple, London EC4Y 7AN
Telephone +44 (0) 20 7842 5555
Fax +44 (0) 20 7583 2036
E-mail clerks@4pumpcourt.com
Website www.4pumpcourt.com

Heads of Chambers
David Friedman and Christopher Major
Chief Executive
Carolyn McCombe

4-5 Gray's Inn Square
Gray's Inn, London WC1R 5AH
Telephone +44 (0) 20 7404 5252
Fax +44 (0) 20 7242 7803
E-mail clerks@4-5.co.uk
Website www.4-5graysinnsquare.co.uk

Heads of Chambers
Elizabeth Appleby and Timothy Straker
Head Clerk
Michael Kaplan

7 Bedford Row
London WC1R 4BU
Telephone +44 (0) 20 7242 3555
Fax +44 (0) 20 7242 2511
E-mail clerks@7br.co.uk
Website www.7br.co.uk

Head of Chambers
David Farrer
Chief Executive
Robert Graham-Campbell

7 King's Bench Walk
Temple, London EC4Y 7DS
Telephone +44 (0) 20 7910 8300
Fax +44 (0) 20 7910 8400
E-mail clerks@7kbw.co.uk
Website www.7kbw.co.uk

Heads of Chambers
Gavin Kealey and Julian Flaux
Head Clerk
Bernie Hyatt

Blackstone Chambers
Temple, London EC4Y 9BW
Telephone +44 (0) 20 7583 1770
Fax +44 (0) 20 7822 7350
E-mail clerks@blackstonechambers.com
Website www.blackstonechambers.com

Heads of Chambers
Ian Mill and Thomas Beazley
Head Clerk
Martin Smith

Brick Court Chambers
7 - 8 Essex Street, London WC2R 3LD
Telephone +44 (0) 20 7379 3550
Fax +44 (0) 20 7379 3558
Website www.brickcourt.co.uk

Heads of Chambers
Jonathan Sumption and Jonathan Hirst
Head Clerk
Ian Moyler

Essex Court Chambers
24 Lincoln's Inn Fields, London WC2A 3EG
Telephone +44 (0) 20 7813 8000
Fax +44 (0) 20 7813 8080
E-mail clerksroom@essexcourt.net
Website www.essexcourt.net

Head of Chambers
Gordon Pollock
Head Clerk
David Grief

Exchange Chambers
Pearl Assurance House, Derby Square, Liverpool L2 9XX
Telephone +44 (0) 151 236 7747
Fax +44 (0) 151 236 3433
E-mail info@exchangechambers.co.uk
Website www.exchangechambers.co.uk

Heads of Chambers
David Turner and Bill Braithwaite
Practice Manager
Roy Finney

Fountain Court Chambers
Temple, London EC4Y 9DH
Telephone +44 (0) 20 7583 3335
Fax +44 (0) 20 7353 0329
E-mail chambers@foundationcourt.co.uk
Website www.fountaincourt.co.uk

Head of Chambers
Michael Brundle
Head Clerk
Mark Watson

Four New Square
Lincoln's Inn, London WC2A 3RJ
Telephone +44 (0) 20 7822 2000
Fax +44 (0) 20 7822 2001
E-mail barristers@4newsquare.com
Website www.4newsquare.com

Head of Chambers
Roger Stewart
Head Clerk
Lizzy Wiseman

Keating Chambers
15 Essex Street, London WC2R 3AA
Telephone +44 (0) 20 7544 2600
Fax +44 (0) 20 7544 2700
E-mail clerks@keatingchambers.com
Website www.keatingchambers.com

Head of Chambers
John Marrin
Head Clerk
John Munton

Kings Chambers
36 Young Street, Manchester M3 3FT
Telephone +44 (0) 161 832 9082
Fax +44 (0) 161 835 2139
Website www.kingschambers.com

Head of Chambers
Frances Patterson
Head Clerk
William Brown

Landmark Chambers
180 Fleet Street, London EC4A 2HG
Telephone +44 (0) 20 7430 1221
Fax +44 (0) 20 7421 6060
E-mail clerks@landmarkchambers.co.uk
Website www.landmarkchambers.co.uk

Head of Chambers
Christopher Katkowski
Head Clerk
Jay Fullilove

Littleton Chambers
3 King's Bench Walk North, Temple, London EC4Y 7HR
Telephone +44 (0) 20 7797 8600
Fax +44 (0) 20 7797 8699
E-mail clerks@littletonchambers.co.uk
Website www.littletonchambers.com

Head of Chambers
Clive Freedman
Head Clerk
Alistair Coyne

Maitland Chambers
7 Stone Buildings, Lincoln's Inn, London WC2A 3SZ
Telephone +44 (0) 20 7406 1200
Fax +44 (0) 20 7406 1300
E-mail clerks@maitlandchambers.com
Website www.maitlandchambers.com

Heads of Chambers
Michael Lyndon-Stanford, Charles Aldous and Michael Driscoll
Head Clerk
Lee Cutler

Matrix Chambers
Griffin Building, Gray's Inn, London WC1R 5LN
Telephone +44 (0) 20 7404 3447
Fax +44 (0) 20 7404 3448
E-mail matrix@matrixlaw.co.uk
Website www.matrixlaw.co.uk

Head of Chambers
Clare Montgomery
Chief Executive
Lindsay Scott

No 5 Chambers
6th Floor, 76 Shoe Lane, London EC4A 3JB
Telephone +44 (0) 870 203 5555
E-mail info@no5.com
Website www.no5.com

Head of Chambers
Gareth Evans
Head Clerk
Tony McDaid

One Crown Office Row
Temple, London EC4Y 7HH
Telephone +44 (0) 20 7797 7500
Fax +44 (0) 20 7797 7550
E-mail mail@1cor.com
Website www.1cor.com

Head of Chambers
Philip Havers
Head Clerk
Matthew Phipps

One Essex Court
Temple, London EC4Y 9AR
Telephone +44 (0) 20 7583 2000
Fax +44 (0) 20 7583 0118
E-mail clerks@oeclaw.co.uk
Website www.oeclaw.co.uk

Head of Chambers
Lord Grabiner
Head Clerk
Paul Shrubsall

Outer Temple Chambers
222 Strand, London WC2R 1BA
Telephone +44 (0) 20 7353 6381
Fax +44 (0) 20 7583 1786
E-mail clerks@outertemple.com
Website www.outertemple.com

Head of Chambers
Philip Mott
Head Clerk
Derek Jenkins

Quadrant Chambers
Quadrant House, 10 Fleet Street, London EC4Y 1AU
Telephone +44 (0) 20 7583 4444
Fax +44 (0) 20 7583 4455
E-mail reception@quadrantchambers.com
Website www.quadrantchambers.com

Practice Director
Gordon Armstrong
Senior Clerk
Gary Ventura

Serle Court
6 New Square, Lincoln's Inn, London WC2A 3QS
Telephone +44 (0) 20 7242 6105
Fax +44 (0) 20 7405 4004
E-mail clerks@serlecourt.co.uk
Website www.serlecourt.co.uk

Head of Chambers
Lord Neill of Bladen
Head Clerk
Terry Buck

St Philips
55 Temple Row, Birmingham B2 5LS
Telephone +44 (0) 121 246 7000
Fax +44 (0) 121 246 7001
E-mail clerks@st-philips.co.uk
Website www.st-philips.co.uk

Head of Chambers
William Davis
Head Clerk
Matthew Fleming

Wilberforce Chambers
8 New Square, Lincoln's Inn, London WC2A 3QP
Telephone +44 (0) 20 7306 0102
Fax +44 (0) 20 7306 0095
E-mail chambers@wilberforce.co.uk
Website www.wilberforce.co.uk

Head of Chambers
Jules Sher
Head Clerk
Declan Redmond

XXIV Old Buildings
Lincoln's Inn, London WC2A 3UP
Telephone +44 (0) 20 7691 2424
Fax +44 (0) 870 460 2178
E-mail clerks@xxiv.co.uk
Website www.xxiv.co.uk

Heads of Chambers
Alan Steinfeld and Martin Mann
Head Clerk
Nicholas Luckman

SOLICITORS' FIRMS

The following pages detail the leading solicitors' firms in the UK, selected by
annual turnover.

Addleshaw Goddard
150 Aldersgate Street, London EC1A 4EJ
Telephone +44 (0)20 7606 8855
Fax +44 (0) 20 7606 4390
Website www.addleshawgoddard.com

Senior Partner
Paul Lee
Managing Partner
Mark Jones

Allen & Overy
One Bishops Square, London E1 6AO
Telephone +44 (0) 20 3088 0000
Fax +44 (0) 20 3088 0088
Website www.allenovery.com

Senior Partner
Guy Beringer
Managing Partner
David Morley

Ashurst
Broadwalk House, 5 Appold Street, London EC2A 2HA
Telephone +44 (0) 20 7638 1111
Fax +44 (0) 20 7638 1112
Website www.ashurst.com

Senior Partner
Geoffrey Green
Managing Partner
Simon Bromwich

Barlow Lyde & Gilbert LLP
Beaufort House, 15 St Botolph Street, London EC3A 7NJ
Telephone +44 (0) 20 7247 2277
Fax +44 (0) 20 7071 9000
Website www.blg.co.uk

Senior Partner
Richard Dedman
Managing Partner
Kennan Michel

Beachcroft Wansbroughs
100 Fetter Lane, London EC4A 1BN
Telephone +44 (0) 20 7242 1011
Fax +44 (0) 20 7831 6630
Website www.beachcroft.co.uk

Senior Partner
Simon Hodson
Managing Partner
Paul Murray

Berwin Leighton Paisner
Adelaide House, London Bridge, London EC4R 9HA
Telephone +44 (0) 20 7760 1000
Website www.blplaw.com

Managing Partner
Neville Eisenberg

Bird & Bird
15 Fetter Lane, London EC4A 1JP
Telephone +44 (0) 20 7415 6000
Fax +44 (0) 20 7415 6111
Website www.twobirds.com

Chief Executive
David Kerr

Burges Salmon
Narrow Quay House, Narrow Quay, Bristol BS1 4AH
Telephone +44 (0) 117 939 2000
Fax +44 (0) 117 902 4400
Website www.burges-salmon.com

Senior Partner
Stephen McNulty
Managing Partner
Guy Stobart

Charles Russell
8-10 New Fetter Lane, London EC4A 1RS
Telephone +44 (0) 20 7203 5000
Fax +44 (0) 20 7203 0200
Website www.charlesrussell.co.uk

Senior Partner
Patrick Russell
Managing Partner
James Holder

Clifford Chance
10 Upper Bank Street, London E14 5JJ
Telephone +44 (0) 20 7006 1000
Fax +44 (0) 20 7006 5555
Website www.cliffordchance.com

Senior Partner
Stuart Popham
Managing Partner
David Childs

Clyde & Co
51 Eastcheap, London EC3M 1JP
Telephone +44 (0) 20 7623 1244
Fax +44 (0) 20 7623 5427
Website www.clydeco.com

Senior Partner
Michael Payton

CMS Cameron McKenna
Mitre House, 160 Aldersgate Street, London EC1A 4DD
Telephone +44 (0) 20 7367 3000
Fax +44 (0) 20 7367 2000
Website www.law-now.com

Senior Partner
Richard Price
Managing Partner
Dick Tyler

Cobbetts
58 Mosley Street, Manchester M2 3HZ
Telephone +44 (0) 845 404 2404
Fax +44 (0) 845 404 2414
Website www.cobbetts.com

Senior Partner
Stephen Benson
Managing Partner
Michael Shaw

Denton Wilde Sapte
One Fleet Place, London EC4M 7WS
Telephone +44 (0) 20 7242 1212
Fax +44 (0) 20 7320 6647
Website www.dentonwildesapte.com

Managing Partner
Howard Morris

DLA Piper
3 Noble Street, London EC2V 7EE
Telephone +44 (0) 8700 111111
Website www.dlapiper.com

Managing Partner
Catherine Usher

Dundas & Wilson
Saltire Court, 20 Castle Terrace, Edinburgh EH1 2EN
Telephone +44 (0) 131 228 8000
Fax +44 (0) 131 228 8888
Website www.dundas-wilson.com

Managing Partners
Alan Campbell and Donald Shaw

Eversheds
Senator House, 85 Queen Victoria Street,
London EC4V 4JL
Telephone +44 (0) 20 7919 4500
Fax +44 (0) 20 7919 4919
Website www.eversheds.com

Managing Partner
Cornelius Medvei
Chief Executive
David Gray

Field Fisher Waterhouse
35 Vine Street, London EC3N 2AA
Telephone +44 (0) 20 7861 4000
Fax +44 (0) 20 7488 0084
Website www.ffw.com

Senior Partner
Jon Fife
Managing Partner
Moira Gilmour

Freshfields Bruckhaus Deringer
65 Fleet Street, London EC4Y 1HS
Telephone +44 (0) 20 7936 4000
Fax +44 (0) 20 7832 7001
Website www.freshfields.com

Senior Partner
Guy Morton
Managing Partner
Peter Jeffcote

Halliwells
St James's Court, Brown Street, Manchester M2 2JF
Telephone +44 (0) 870 365 8000
Fax +44 (0) 870 365 8001
Website www.halliwells.com

Senior Partner
Alec Craig
Managing Partner
Ian Austin

Hammonds
7 Devonshire Square, Cutlers Gardens,
London EC2M 4YH
Telephone +44 (0) 870 839 0000
Website www.hammonds.com

Managing Partner
Peter Crossley

Herbert Smith
Exchange House, Primrose Street, London EC2A 2HS
Telephone +44 (0) 20 7374 8000
Fax +44 (0) 20 7374 0888
Website www.herbertsmith.com

Managing Partner
David Gold

Hill Dickinson
Pearl Assurance House, 2 Derby Square,
Liverpool L2 9XL
Telephone +44 (0) 151 236 5400
Fax +44 (0) 1512 362175
Website www.hilldickinson.com

Senior Partner
Tony Wilson
Managing Partner
Peter Jackson

Holman Fenwick & Willan
Marlow House, Lloyd's Avenue, London EC3N 3AL
Telephone +44 (0) 20 7488 2300
Fax +44 (0) 20 7481 0316
Website www.hfw.com

Senior Partner
Richard Crump
Managing Partner
Greg Gray

Ince & Co
International House, 1 St Katharine's Way,
London E1W 1UN
Telephone +44 (0) 20 7481 0010
Fax +44 (0) 20 7481 4968
Website www.incelaw.com

Senior Partner
Peter Rogan
Managing Partner
Chris Jefferis

Irwin Mitchell
Riverside East, No 2 Millsands, Sheffield S3 8DT
Telephone +44 (0) 870 150 0100
Fax +44 (0) 1142 726696
Website www.irwinmitchell.com

Senior Partner
Michael Napier
Managing Partner
Howard Culley

Lawrence Graham
4 More London, Riverside, London SE1 2AU
Telephone +44 (0) 20 7379 0000
Fax +44 (0) 20 7379 6854
Website www.lg-legal.com

Senior Partner
Bill Richards
Managing Partner
Penny Francis

Linklaters
One Silk Street, London EC2Y 8HQ
Telephone +44 (0) 20 7456 2000
Fax +44 (0) 20 7456 2222
Website www.linklaters.com

Senior Partner
David Cheyne
Managing Partner
Tony Angel

Lovells
Atlantic House, Holborn Viaduct, London EC1A 2FG
Telephone +44 (0) 20 7296 2000
Fax +44 (0) 20 7296 2001
Website www.lovells.com

Senior Partner
John Young
Managing Partner
David Harris

Macfarlanes
10 Norwich Street, London EC4A 1BD
Telephone +44 (0) 20 7831 9222
Fax +44 (0) 20 7831 9607
Website www.macfarlanes.com

Senior Partner
Robert Sutton
Managing Partner
Paul Phippen

McGrigors
Pacific House, 70 Wellington Street, Glasgow G2 6SB
Telephone +44 (0) 141 248 6677
Fax +44 (0) 141 221 1390
Website www.mcgrigors.com

Senior Partners
Kirk Murdoch and Philip Burroughs
Managing Partner
Colin Gray

Nabarro Nathanson
Lacon House, 84 Theobald's Road, London WC1X 8RW
Telephone +44 (0) 20 7524 6000
Fax +44 (0) 20 7524 6524
Website www.nabarro.com

Senior Partner
Simon Johnston
Managing Partner
Nicole Paradise

Norton Rose
Kempson House, Camomile Street, London EC3A 7AN
Telephone +44 (0) 20 7283 6000
Fax +44 (0) 20 7283 6500
Website www.nortonrose.com

Managing Partner
Deirdre Walker

Olswang
90 High Holborn, London WC1V 6XX
Telephone +44 (0) 20 7067 3000
Fax +44 (0) 20 7067 3999
Website www.olswang.com

Senior Partner
Mark Devereux
Managing Partner
David Stewart

Osborne Clarke
2 Temple Back East, Temple Quay, Bristol BS1 6EG
Telephone +44 (0) 117 917 3000
Fax +44 (0) 117 917 3005
Website www.osborneclarke.com

Senior Partner
Tim Birt
Managing Partner
Simon Beswick

Pinsent Masons
CityPoint, One Ropemaker Street, London EC2Y 9SS
Telephone +44 (0) 20 7418 7000
Fax +44 (0) 20 7418 7050
Website www.pinsentmasons.com

Senior Partner
Chris Mullen
Managing Partner
David Ryan

Reed Smith Richards Butler
Beaufort House, 15 St Botolph Street, London EC3A 7EE
Telephone +44 (0) 20 7247 6555
Fax +44 (0) 20 7247 5091
Website www.reedsmith.com

Senior Partner
Ian Fagelson
Managing Partner
Tim Foster

Reynolds Porter Chamberlain
Tower Bridge House, St Katharine's Way,
London E1W 1AA
Telephone +44 (0) 20 3060 6000
Fax +44 (0) 20 3060 7000
Website www.rpc.co.uk

Senior Partner
Tim Brown
Managing Partner
Jonathan Watmough

Salans
Millennium Bridge House, 2 Lambeth Hill,
London EC4V 4AJ
Telephone +44 (0) 20 7429 6000
Fax +44 (0) 20 7429 6001
Website www.salans.com

Managing Partner
Howard Cohen

Shoosmiths
The Lakes, Bedford Road, Northampton NN4 7SH
Telephone +44 (0) 87 0086 3000
Fax +44 (0) 870 086 3001
Website www.shoosmiths.co.uk

Chairman
Andrew Tubbs
Chief Executive
Paul Stothard

Simmons & Simmons
CityPoint, One Ropemaker Street, London EC2Y 9SS
Telephone +44 (0) 20 7628 2020
Fax +44 (0) 20 7628 2070
Website www.simmons-simmons.com

Senior Partner
David Dickinson
Managing Partner
Mark Dawkins

SJ Berwin
10 Queen Street Place, London EC4R 1BE
Telephone +44 (0) 20 7111 2222
Fax +44 (0) 20 7111 2000
Website www.sjberwin.com

Senior Partner
Jonathan Blake
Managing Partner
Ralph Cohen

Slaughter and May
One Bunhill Row, London EC1Y 8YY
Telephone +44 (0) 20 7600 1200
Fax +44 (0) 20 7090 5000
Website www.slaughterandmay.com

Managing Partner
Tim Clark

Stephenson Harwood
1 St Paul's Churchyard, London EC4M 8SH
Telephone +44 (0) 20 7329 4422
Fax +44 (0) 20 7329 7100
Website www.shlegal.com

Senior Partner
Andrew Sutch
Chief Executive
Sunil Gadhia

Taylor Wessing
Carmelite, 50 Victoria Embankment, Blackfriars,
London EC4Y 0DX
Telephone +44 (0) 20 7300 7000
Fax +44 (0) 20 7300 7100
Website www.taylorwessing.com

Senior Partner
Martin Winter
Managing Partner
Michael Frawley

Travers Smith
10 Snow Hill, London EC1A 2AL
Telephone +44 (0) 20 7295 3000
Fax +44 (0) 20 7295 3500
Website www.traverssmith.com

Senior Partner
Alastair Douglas
Managing Partner
Christopher Carroll

Trowers & Hamlins
Sceptre Court, 40 Tower Hill, London EC3N 4DX
Telephone +44 (0) 20 7423 8000
Fax +44 (0) 20 7423 8001
Website www.trowers.com

Senior Partner
Jonathan Adlington

Watson Farley & Williams
15 Appold Street, London EC2A 2HB
Telephone +44 (0) 20 7814 8000
Fax +44 (0) 20 7814 8141
Website www.wfw.com

Chairman
Frank Dunne
Managing Partner
Michael Greville

Withers
16 Old Bailey, London EC4M 7EG
Telephone +44 (0) 20 7597 6000
Website www.withersworldwide.com

Managing Partner
Margaret Robertson

Wragge & Co
55 Colmore Row, Birmingham B3 2AS
Telephone +44 (0) 870 903 1000
Website www.wragge.com

Senior Partner
Quentin Poole
Managing Partner
Ian Metcalfe

POLICE

The following pages detail all the police constabularies of the UK.

Avon & Somerset Constabulary
PO Box 37, Valley Road, Portishead, Bristol BS20 8QJ
Telephone +44 (0) 845 456 7000
Website www.avonandsomerset.police.uk

Chief Constable
Colin Port

Bedfordshire Police
Woburn Road, Kempston, Bedfordshire MK43 9AX
Telephone +44 (0) 1234 841212
Website www.bedfordshire.police.uk

Chief Constable
Gillian Parker

Cambridgeshire Constabulary
Hinchingbrooke Park, Huntingdon,
Cambridgeshire PE29 6NP
Telephone +44 (0) 845 456 4564
Website www.cambs.police.uk

Chief Constable
Julie Spence

Central Scotland Police
Randolphfield, Stirling, Scotland FK8 2HD
Telephone +44 (0) 1786 456000
Website www.centralscotland.police.uk

Chief Constable
Andrew Cameron

Cheshire Constabulary
Clemonds Hey, Oakmere Road, Winsford,
Cheshire CW7 2UA
Telephone +44 (0) 845 458 0000
Website www.cheshire.police.uk

Chief Constable
Peter Fahy

City of London Police
37 Wood Street, London EC2P 2NQ
Telephone +44 (0) 20 7601 2455
Website www.cityoflondon.police.uk

Commissioner
Mike Bowron

Cleveland Police
Ladgate Lane, Middlesbrough, Cleveland TS8 9EH
Telephone +44 (0) 1642 326326
Website www.cleveland.police.uk

Chief Constable
Sean Price

Cumbria Constabulary
Carleton Hall, Penrith, Cumbria CA10 2AU
Telephone +44 (0) 845 330 0247
Website www.cumbria.police.uk

Chief Constable
Michael Baxter

Derbyshire Constabulary
Butterley Hall, Ripley, Derbyshire DE5 3RS
Telephone +44 (0) 845 123 3333
Website www.derbyshire.police.uk

Chief Constable
David Coleman

Devon & Cornwall Constabulary
Middlemoor Head Quarters, Exeter, Devon EX2 7HQ
Telephone +44 (0) 845 277 7444
Website www.devon-cornwall.police.uk

Chief Constable
Stephen Otter

Dorset Police
Winfrith, Dorchester, Dorset DT2 8DZ
Telephone +44 (0) 1305 222222
Website www.dorset.police.uk

Chief Constable
Martin Baker

Dumfries and Galloway Constabulary
Cornwall Mount, Dumfries DG1 1PZ
Telephone +44 (0) 845 600 5701
Website www.dumfriesandgalloway.police.uk

Chief Constable
Patrick Shearer

Durham Constabulary
Aykley Heads, Durham DH1 5TT
Telephone +44 (0) 845 606 0365
Website www.durham.police.uk

Chief Constable
Jon Stoddart

Dyfed Powys Police / Heddlu Dyfed Powys
PO Box 99, Carmarthen SA31 2PF
Telephone +44 (0) 845 330 2000
Website www.dyfed-powys.police.uk

Chief Constable
Trevor Grange

Essex Police
PO Box 2, Springfield, Chelmsford, Essex CM2 6DA
Telephone +44 (0) 1245 491491
Website www.essex.police.uk

Chief Constable
Roger Baker

Fife Constabulary
Detroit Road, Glenrothes KY6 2RJ
Telephone +44 (0) 845 600 5702
Website www.fife.police.uk

Chief Constable
Peter Wilson

Gloucestershire Constabulary
No1 Waterwells, Waterwells Drive, Quedgeley,
Gloucester GL2 2AN
Telephone +44 (0) 845 090 1234
Website www.gloucestershire.police.uk

Chief Constable
Timothy Brain

Grampian Police
Queen Street, Aberdeen AB10 1ZA
Telephone +44 (0) 845 600 5700
Website www.grampian.police.uk

Chief Constable
Collum McKerracher

Greater Manchester Police
PO Box 22, Manchester M16 0RE
Telephone +44 (0) 161 872 5050
Website www.gmp.police.uk

Chief Constable
Michael Todd

Gwent Police / Heddlu Gwent
Croesyceiliog, Cwmbrân NP44 2XJ
Telephone +44 (0) 1633 838111
Website www.gwent.police.uk

Chief Constable
Mike Tonge

Hampshire Constabulary
West Hill, Romsey Road, Winchester,
Hampshire SO22 5DB
Telephone +44 (0) 845 045 4545
Website www.hampshire.police.uk

Chief Constable
Paul Kernaghan

Hertfordshire Constabulary
Stanborough Road, Welwyn Garden City,
Hertfordshire AL8 6XF
Telephone +44 (0) 845 330 0222
Website www.herts.police.uk

Chief Constable
Frank Whiteley

Humberside Police
Priory Road, Hull HU5 5SF
Telephone +44 (0) 845 606 0222
Website www.humberside.police.uk

Chief Constable
Tim Hollis

Kent Police
Sutton Road, Maidstone, Kent ME15 9BZ
Telephone +44 (0) 1622 690690
Website www.kent.police.uk

Chief Constable
Michael Fuller

Lancashire Constabulary
PO Box 77, Hutton, Preston, Lancashire PR4 5SB
Telephone +44 (0) 845 125 3545
Website www.lancashire.police.uk

Acting Chief Constable
Steve Finnigan

Leicestershire Constabulary
St Johns, Enderby, Leicester LE19 2BX
Telephone +44 (0) 116 222 2222
Website www.leics.police.uk

Chief Constable
Mark Baggott

Lincolnshire Police
PO Box 999, Lincoln LN5 7PH
Telephone +44 (0) 1522 532222
Website www.lincs.police.uk

Chief Constable
Tony Lake

Lothian and Borders Police
Fettes Avenue, Edinburgh EH4 1RB
Telephone +44 (0) 131 311 3131
Website www.lbp.police.uk

Chief Constable
Paddy Tomkins

Merseyside Police
PO Box 59, Liverpool L69 1JD
Telephone +44 (0) 151 709 6010
Website www.merseyside.police.uk

Chief Constable
Bernard Hogan-Howe

Metropolitan Police Service
New Scotland Yard, Broadway, London SW1H 0BG
Telephone +44 (0) 20 7230 1212
Website www.met.police.uk

Commissioner
Sir Ian Blair

Norfolk Constabulary
Operations and Communications Centre, Jubilee House,
Falconers Chase, Wymondham, Norfolk NR18 0WW
Telephone +44 (0) 845 456 4567
Website www.norfolk.police.uk

Chief Constable
Ian McPherson

North Wales Police / Heddlu Gogledd Cymru
Glan-y-Don, Colwyn Bay, Conwy LL29 8AW
Telephone +44 (0) 845 607 1002
Website www.north-wales.police.uk

Chief Constable
Richard Brunstrom

North Yorkshire Police
Newby Wiske Hall, Northallerton, North
Yorkshire DL7 9HA
Telephone +44 (0) 845 606 0247
Website www.northyorkshire.police.uk

Chief Constable
Della Cannings

Northamptonshire Police
Wootton Hall, Mereway, Northampton NN4 0JQ
Telephone +44 (0) 845 370 0700
Website www.northants.police.uk

Chief Constable
Peter Maddison

Northern Constabulary
Perth Road, Inverness IV2 3SY
Telephone +44 (0) 845 603 3388
Website www.northern.police.uk

Chief Constable
Ian J Latimer

Northern Ireland, Police Service of
65 Knock Road, Belfast BT5 6LE
Telephone +44 (0) 845 600 8000
Website www.psni.police.uk

Chief Constable
Sir Hugh Orde

Northumbria Police
North Road, Ponteland, Newcastle upon Tyne NE20 0BL
Telephone +44 (0) 845 604 3043
Website www.northumbria.police.uk

Chief Constable
Mike Craik

Nottinghamshire Police
Sherwood Lodge, Arnold, Nottingham NG5 8PP
Telephone +44 (0) 115 967 0999
Website www.nottinghamshire.police.uk

Chief Constable
Steve Green

South Wales Police / Heddlu De Cymru
Cowbridge Road, Bridgend CF31 3SU
Telephone +44 (0) 1656 655 555
Website www.south-wales.police.uk

Chief Constable
Barbara Wilding

South Yorkshire Police
Snig Hill, Sheffield, South Yorkshire S3 8LY
Telephone +44 (0) 114 220 2020
Website www.southyorks.police.uk

Chief Constable
Meredydd Hughes

Staffordshire Police
Cannock Road, Stafford ST17 0QG
Telephone +44 (0) 845 330 2010
Website www.staffordshire.police.uk

Chief Constable
David Swift

Strathclyde Police
173 Pitt Street, Glasgow G2 4JS
Telephone +44 (0) 141 532 2000
Website www.strathclyde.police.uk

Chief Constable
Willy Rae

Suffolk Constabulary
Martlesham Heath, Ipswich, Suffolk IP5 3QS
Telephone +44 (0) 1473 613500
Website www.suffolk.police.uk

Chief Constable
Simon Ash

Surrey Police
Mount Browne, Sandy Lane, Guildford, Surrey GU3 1HG
Telephone +44 (0) 845 125 2222
Website www.surrey.police.uk

Chief Constable
Bob Quick

Sussex Police
Church Lane, Lewes, East Sussex BN7 2DZ
Telephone +44 (0) 845 607 0999
Website www.sussex.police.uk

Chief Constable
Joe Edwards

Tayside Police
PO Box 59, West Bell Street, Dundee DD1 9JU
Telephone +44 (0) 1382 223200
Website www.tayside.police.uk

Chief Constable
John Vine

Thames Valley Police
Oxford Road, Kidlington, Oxfordshire OX5 2NX
Telephone +44 (0) 845 850 5505
Website www.thamesvalley.police.uk

Acting Chief Constable
Sara Thornton

Warwickshire Police
PO Box 4, Leek Wootton, Warwick CV35 7QB
Telephone +44 (0) 1926 415000
Website www.warwickshire.police.uk

Chief Constable
Keith Bristow

West Mercia Constabulary
PO Box 55, Worcester WR3 8SP
Telephone +44 (0) 845 744 4888
Website www.westmercia.police.uk

Chief Constable
Paul West

West Midlands Police
Lloyd House, Colmore Circus, Queensway,
Birmingham B4 6NQ
Telephone +44 (0) 845 113 5000
Website www.west-midlands.police.uk

Chief Constable
Paul Scott-Lee

West Yorkshire Police
PO Box 9, Wakefield, West Yorkshire WF1 3QP
Telephone +44 (0) 845 606 0606
Website www.westyorkshire.police.uk

Chief Constable
Sir Norman Bettison

Wiltshire Constabulary
London Road, Devizes, Wiltshire SN10 2DN
Telephone +44 (0) 845 408 7000
Website www.wiltshire.police.uk

Chief Constable
Martin Richards

HIGH SHERIFFS AND LORD LIEUTENANTS

The following pages detail all the High Sheriffs and Lord Lieutenants of
England, Wales and Northern Ireland, and the Lord Lieutenants of Scotland.

Aberdeenshire
Lord Lieutenant
Angus Farquharson

Angus
Lord Lieutenant
Georgiana Osborne

Argyll and Bute
Lord Lieutenant
Kenneth MacKinnon

Ayr and Arran
Lord Lieutenant
Maj Sir Richard Henderson

Banffshire
Lord Lieutenant
Clare Nancy Russell

Bedfordshire
High Sheriff
Dr V R Southgate
Lord Lieutenant
Samuel Whitbread

Berkshire
High Sheriff
H M Henderson
Lord Lieutenant
Philip Wroughton

Berwickshire
Lord Lieutenant
Maj Alexander Trotter

Buckinghamshire
High Sheriff
A R Nicholson
Lord Lieutenant
Sir Henry Aubrey-Fletcher

Caithness
Lord Lieutenant
Anne Dunnett

Cambridgeshire
High Sheriff
Col P G R Horrell
Lord Lieutenant
Hugh Duberly

Cheshire
High Sheriff
N W Bromley-Davenport
Lord Lieutenant
William Bromley-Davenport

City of Aberdeen
Lord Lieutenant
John Reynolds

City of Bristol
High Sheriff
W H R Durie
Lord Lieutenant
Jay Tidmarsh

City of Dundee
Lord Lieutenant
John Letford

City of Edinburgh
Lord Lieutenant
Lesley Hinds

City of Glasgow
Lord Lieutenant
Elizabeth Cameron

City of Londonderry
High Sheriff
Richard John Sterling
Lord Lieutenant
Donal Keegan

Clackmannanshire
Lord Lieutenant
Sheena Cruickshank

Clwyd
High Sheriff
J P N Major
Lord Lieutenant
Trefor Jones

Cornwall
High Sheriff
The Hon Evelyn Boscawen
Lord Lieutenant
The Lady Mary Holborow

County Antrim
High Sheriff
Dr Joseph Wilson
Lord Lieutenant
The Lord O'Neill

County Armagh
High Sheriff
Dr Colin Wallace Mathews
Lord Lieutenant
The Earl of Caledon

County Borough of Belfast
High Sheriff
Thomas James Kirkpatrick
Lord Lieutenant
Lady Carswell

County Down
High Sheriff
John Dudley Francis Fisher
Lord Lieutenant
William J Hall

County Fermanagh
High Sheriff
Rosemary Ann Elizabeth Forde
Lord Lieutenant
The Earl of Erne

County Londonderry
High Sheriff
Sharyn Gail Griffith
Lord Lieutenant
Denis Desmond

County Tyrone
High Sheriff
John James Little
Lord Lieutenant
The Duke of Abercorn

Cumbria
High Sheriff
C T Hensman
Lord Lieutenant
James Cropper

Derbyshire
High Sheriff
R B Wardle
Lord Lieutenant
John Bather

Devon
High Sheriff
A J B Mildmay-White
Lord Lieutenant
Eric Dancer

Dorset
High Sheriff
A E B Scott
Lord Lieutenant
Valerie Lane-Fox Pitt-Rivers

Dumfries
Lord Lieutenant
Jean Douglas Tulloch

Dunbartonshire
Lord Lieutenant
Donald Ross

Durham
High Sheriff
I R Dewhirst
Lord Lieutenant
Sir Paul Nicholson

Dyfed
High Sheriff
Col D L Davies
Lord Lieutenant
Robin William Lewis

East Lothian
Lord Lieutenant
Garth Morrison

East Riding of Yorkshire
High Sheriff
N A C Hildyard
Lord Lieutenant
Susan Cunliffe-Lister

East Sussex
High Sheriff
C A Mayhew
Lord Lieutenant
Phyllidia Stewart-Roberts

Essex
High Sheriff
Lady Kemp-Welch
Lord Lieutenant
The Lord Petre

Fife
Lord Lieutenant
Margaret Dean

Gloucestershire
High Sheriff
J D Carr
Lord Lieutenant
Henry Elwes

Greater London
High Sheriff
J S Pethick
Lord Lieutenant
The Lord Imbert

Greater Manchester
High Sheriff
M Oglesby
Lord Lieutenant
Sir John Timmins

Gwent
High Sheriff
Lt Col M J H Harry
Lord Lieutenant
Simon Boyle

Gwynedd
High Sheriff
Dr D W Roberts
Lord Lieutenant
Huw Morgan Daniel

Hampshire
High Sheriff
S V Thorne
Lord Lieutenant
Mary Fagan

Herefordshire & Worcestershire
High Sheriff
J S Yorke
Lord Lieutenant
Sir Thomas Dunne

Hertfordshire
High Sheriff
H A Guard
Lord Lieutenant
Simon Alexander Bowes Lyon

Inverness
Lord Lieutenant
Donald Angus Cameron

Isle of Wight
High Sheriff
Lt Col D E Langford
Lord Lieutenant
Martin Spencer White

Kent
High Sheriff
N L Wheeler
Lord Lieutenant
Allan Willett

Kincardineshire
Lord Lieutenant
John Smart

Lanarkshire
Lord Lieutenant
Gilbert Cox

Lancashire
High Sheriff
R Winterbottom
Lord Lieutenant
The Lord Shuttleworth

Leicestershire
High Sheriff
B W Jackson
Lord Lieutenant
The Lady Gretton

Lincolnshire
High Sheriff
P J Ware
Lord Lieutenant
Bridget Cracroft-Eley

Merseyside
High Sheriff
Prof P N Love
Lord Lieutenant
Lorna Elizabeth Fox Muirhead

Mid Glamorgan
High Sheriff
C H Knight
Lord Lieutenant
Kathrin Thomas

Midlothian
Lord Lieutenant
Patrick R Prenter

Moray
Lord Lieutenant
Col Grenville Johnston

Nairn
Lord Lieutenant
Ewen Brodie

Norfolk
High Sheriff
The Earl of Romney
Lord Lieutenant
Richard Jewson

North Yorkshire
High Sheriff
P W Ingham
Lord Lieutenant
The Lord Crathorne

Northamptonshire
High Sheriff
Lady Harper
Lord Lieutenant
Sir Andrew Buchanan

Northumberland
High Sheriff
Sir Hugh F Blackett, Bt
Lord Lieutenant
Sir John Riddell

Nottinghamshire
High Sheriff
Cdr P R Moore
Lord Lieutenant
Sir Andrew Buchanan

Orkney
Lord Lieutenant
Anthony Trickett

Oxfordshire
High Sheriff
T C Loyd
Lord Lieutenant
Hugo Brunner

Perth and Kinross
Lord Lieutenant
Brig Melville Stewart Jameson

Powys
High Sheriff
J J Turner
Lord Lieutenant
Shân Legge-Bourke

Renfrewshire
Lord Lieutenant
Cameron Holdsworth Parker

Ross and Cromarty
Lord Lieutenant
Annie Stewart

Roxburgh, Ettrick and Lauderdale
Lord Lieutenant
Capt the Hon Gerald Maitland-Carew

Rutland
High Sheriff
B E Gilman
Lord Lieutenant
Laurence Howard

Shetland
Lord Lieutenant
John Hamilton Scott

Shropshire
High Sheriff
M R Afia
Lord Lieutenant
Algernon Heber-Percy

Somerset
High Sheriff
D J Medlock
Lord Lieutenant
Elizabeth Gass

South Glamorgan
High Sheriff
P M Williams
Lord Lieutenant
Norman Lloyd-Edwards

South Yorkshire
High Sheriff
Col J C V Hunt
Lord Lieutenant
David Moody

Staffordshire
High Sheriff
G H Stow
Lord Lieutenant
James Hawley

Stewartry of Kirkcudbright (Dumfries and Galloway)
Lord Lieutenant
Jean Tulloch

Stirling and Falkirk
Lord Lieutenant
Marjory McLachlan

Suffolk
High Sheriff
Air Marshal Sir John Kemball
Lord Lieutenant
The Lord Tollemache

Surrey
High Sheriff
N J E Sealy
Lord Lieutenant
Sarah Goad

Sutherland
Lord Lieutenant
Dr Monica Main

Tweeddale
Lord Lieutenant
Capt David Younger

Tyne & Wear
High Sheriff
The Hon Nigel Westwood
Lord Lieutenant
Nigel Sherlock

Warwickshire
High Sheriff
A J Arkwright
Lord Lieutenant
Sir Adam Butler

West Glamorgan
High Sheriff
M A Trainer
Lord Lieutenant
Robert Hastie

West Lothian
Lord Lieutenant
Isobel Brydie

West Midlands
High Sheriff
R P Tomlinson
Lord Lieutenant
Bob Taylor

West Sussex
High Sheriff
C P J Field
Lord Lieutenant
Hugh Wyatt

West Yorkshire
High Sheriff
R C Hartley
Lord Lieutenant
Dr Ingrid Roscoe

Western Isles
Lord Lieutenant
Alexander Mathisson

Wigtown
Lord Lieutenant
Marion Teresa Brewis

Wiltshire
High Sheriff
The Hon Peter Pleydell-Bouverie
Lord Lieutenant
John Bush

Worcestershire
High Sheriff
see Herefordshire & Worcestershire
Lord Lieutenant
Michael Brinton

BRITISH AMBASSADORS

The following pages detail all the British embassies and senior diplomats
around the world.

Afghanistan
The British Embassy, 15th Street, Roundabout Wazir
Akbar Khan, PO Box 334, Kabul, Afghanistan
Telephone +93 (0) 70 102 000
Fax +93 (0) 70 102 250
Website www.britishembassy.gov.uk/afghanistan

Ambassador
Sir Sherard Cowper-Coles

Albania
British Embassy, Rruga Skenderbeg 12, Tirana, Albania
Telephone +355 423 4973
Fax +355 424 7697
Website www.uk.al

Ambassador
Fraser Wilson

Algeria
Ambassade Britannique, 12 Rue Slimane Amirat (Ex
Lucien Reynaud), Hydra, Algiers, Algeria
Telephone +213 (21) 23 00 68
Fax +213 (21) 23 00 67
Website www.britishembassy.gov.uk/algeria

Ambassador
Andrew Tesoriere

Andorra
Honary Consulate Avinguada Sant Antoni, 23 Cal Sastre
Vell, 1r, AD400, La Massana, Principality of Andorra
Telephone +376 839 840
Fax +376 839 840

Ambassador
Sir Stephen Wright (resides in Madrid)

Angola
British Embassy, Rua Diogo Cao 4, Caixa Postal 1244,
Luanda, Angola
Telephone +244 (222) 334582
Fax +244 (222) 333331
Website www.britishembassy.gov.uk/angola

Ambassador
Ralph Publicover

Anguilla
Government House, Anguilla
Telephone +1 264 497 2621
Fax +1 264 497 3314

Governor
Andrew George

Antigua and Barbuda
British High Commission, PO Box 483, Price Waterhouse
Coopers Centre, 11 Old Parham Rd, St John's, Antigua
Telephone +268 462 0008/9
Fax +268 562 2124

High Commissioner
Duncan Taylor (resides in Barbados)

Argentina
British Embassy, Dr Luis Agote 2412, (1425) Buenos
Aires, Argentina
Telephone +54 (11) 4808 2200
Fax +54 (11) 4808 2274
Website www.britain.org.ar

Ambassador
John Hughes

Armenia
British Embassy, 34 Baghramyan Avenue, Yerevan
375019, Armenia
Telephone +374 (10) 264 301
Fax +374 (10) 264 318
Website www.britishembassy.am

Ambassador
Anthony Cantor

Ascension Island
The Administrator's Office, Georgetown, Ascension
Island, South Atlantic Ocean
Telephone +247 7000
Fax +247 6152
Website www.ascension-island.gov.ac

Administrator to Ascension Island
Michael Hill

Australia
British High Commission, Commonwealth Avenue,
Yarralumla, Canberra, Australia
Telephone +61 (2) 6270 6666
Fax +61 (2) 6273 3236
Website www.britaus.net

High Commissioner
Helen Liddell

Austria
British Embassy, Jauresgasse 12, 1030 Vienna, Austria
Telephone +43 (1) 716130
Fax +43 (1) 71613 2999
Website www.britishembassy.at

Ambassador
John MacGregor

Azerbaijan
British Embassy, 45 Khagani Street, AZ1010 Baku,
Azerbaijan
Telephone +994 (12) 4975188
Fax +994 (12) 4922739
Website www.britishembassy.gov.uk/azerbaijan

Ambassador
Laurie Bristow

Bahamas
British High Commission, PO Box 575, 28 Trafalgar
Road, Kingston 10, Jamaica
Telephone +1 876 510 0700
Fax +1 876 511 5304
Website www.britishhighcommission.gov.uk/jamaica

High Commissioner
Jeremy Cresswell

Bahrain
British Embassy, 21 Government Avenue, Manama 306,
PO Box 114, Kingdom of Bahrain
Telephone +973 17574100
Fax +973 17574138
Website www.ukembassy.org.bh

Ambassador
Jamie Bowden

Bangladesh
British High Commission, United Nations Road,
Baridhara, PO Box 6079, Dhaka 1212, Bangladesh
Telephone +880 (2) 882 2705
Fax +880 (2) 882 3437
Website www.britishhighcommission.gov.uk/bangladesh

High Commissioner
Anwar Choudhury

Barbados
British High Commission, Lower Collymore Rock, PO Box
676, Bridgetown, Barbados
Telephone +1 246 430 7800
Fax +1 246 430 7860
Website www.britishhighcommission.gov.uk/barbados

High Commissioner
Duncan Taylor

Belarus
British Embassy, 37 Karl Marx Street, 220030 Minsk,
Belarus
Telephone +375 (17) 2105920
Fax +375 (17) 2202306
Website www.britain.by

Ambassador
Mike Haddock

Belgium
British Embassy, Rue d'Arlon 85 Aarlenstraat, 1040
Brussels, Belgium
Telephone +32 (2) 287 6211
Fax +32 (2) 287 6355
Website www.britishembassy.gov.uk/belgium

Ambassador
Richard Kinchen

Belize
British High Commission, PO Box 91, Belmopan, Belize
Telephone +501 822 2146
Fax +501 822 2761
Website www.britishhighbze.com

High Commissioner
Alan Jones

Benin
The British School of Cotonou, Haie Vive, 08 BP 0352,
Cotonou, Benin
Telephone +229 21 30 32 65
Fax +229 21 30 61 95

Ambassador
Richard Gozney (resides in Nigeria)

Bermuda
Government House, Hamilton, Bermuda
Telephone +441 292 3600
Fax +441 295 3823

Governor
Sir John Vereker

Bolivia
British Embassy, Avenida Arce No.2732, Casilla (PO Box)
694, La Paz, Bolivia
Telephone +591 (2) 2433424
Fax +591 (2) 2431073
Website www.britishembassy.gov.uk/bolivia

Ambassador
Peter Bateman

Bosnia and Herzegovina
British Embassy, Tina Ujevica 8, Sarajevo, Bosnia and
Herzegovina
Telephone +387 (33) 282 200
Fax +387 (33) 282 203
Website www.britishembassy.gov.uk/bih

Ambassador
Matthew Rycroft

Botswana
British High Commission, Plot 1079-1084 Main Mall, off
Queens Road, Private Bag 0023, Gaborone, Botswana
Telephone +267 395 2841
Fax +267 395 6105
Website www.britishhighcommission.gov.uk/botswana

High Commissioner
Frank Martin

Brazil
British Embassy, Setor de Embaixadas Sul, Quadra 801,
Conjunto K, CEP 70200-010, Brasilia DF, Brazil
Telephone +55 (61) 3329 2300
Fax +55 (61) 3329 2369
Website www.uk.org.br

Ambassador
Peter Collecott

British Antarctic Territory
Government of the British Antarctic Territory, Polar
Regions Unit, Overseas Territory Directorate, Foreign &
Commonwealth Office, London, SW1A 2AH
Telephone +44 (0) 20 7008 2614
Fax +44 (0) 20 7008 2086
Website www.fco.gov.uk/antarctica

Commissioner (non-resident)
Tony Crombie

British Indian Ocean Territory
Overseas Territories Department, Foreign and
Commonwealth Office, King Charles Street, London
SW1A 2AH
Telephone +44 (0) 20 7008 2890
Fax +44 (0) 20 7008 1589

Director
Leigh Turner

British Virgin Islands
Governor's Office, PO Box 702, Waterfront Drive, Road
Town, Tortola, British Virgin Islands
Telephone +1 284 494 2345
Fax +1 284 494 4490
Website www.dgo.gov.vg

Governor
David Pearey

Brunei
British High Commission, PO Box 2197, Bandar Seri
Begawan BS8674, Brunei Darussalam
Telephone +673 (2) 222231
Fax +673 (2) 234315
Website www.britishhighcommission.gov.uk/brunei

High Commissioner
John Saville

Bulgaria
British Embassy, 9 Moskovska Street, Sofia, Bulgaria
Telephone +359 (2) 933 9222
Fax +359 (2) 933 9219
Website www.british-embassy.bg

Ambassador
Jeremy Hill

Burkina Faso
Honorary Consulate in Burkina Faso, 01 BP 6490
Ouagadougou 01, Burkina Faso
Telephone +226 50 30 73 23
Fax +226 50 30 59 00

Ambassador
Gordon Wetherell (resides in Accra)

Burma
British Embassy, 80 Strand Road (Box No 638), Rangoon, Burma
Telephone +95 (1) 370863
Fax +95 (1) 370866

Ambassador
Mark Canning

Burundi
British Embassy Liaison Office, Building Old East, Parcelle No1/2, Place de l'Independence, Bujumbura, Burundi
Telephone +257 22 246 478
Fax +257 78 827 602

Ambassador
Jeremy Macadie (resides in Kigali)

Cambodia
British Embassy, 27-29 Street 75, Phnom Penh, Cambodia
Telephone +855 (23) 427124
Fax +855 (23) 427125
Website www.britishembassy.gov.uk/cambodia

Ambassador
David Reader

Cameroon
British High Commission, Avenue Winston Churchill, BP 547, Yaounde, Cameroon
Telephone +237 2222 05 45
Fax +237 2222 01 48
Website www.britcam.org

High Commissioner
Syd Maddicott

Canada
British High Commission, 80 Elgin Street, Ottawa K1P 5K7, Canada
Telephone +1 613 237 1530
Fax +1 613 237 7980
Website www.britishhighcommission.gov.uk/canada

High Commissioner
Anthony Cary

Cape Verde
British Honorary Consul, Shell Cabo Verde Sarl, Av Amilcar Cabral CP4, Sao Vincente, Cape Verde
Telephone +238 232 2830
Fax +238 232 66 29

Ambassador
Chris Trott (resides in Dakar)

Cayman Islands
Governor's Office, PO Box 10261, Grand Cayman, Cayman Islands KY1-1003
Telephone +1 345 244 2434
Fax +1 345 945 4131

Governor
Stuart Jack

Central African Republic
British High Commission, Avenue Winston Churchill, BP 547, Yaounde, Cameroon
Telephone +237 2222 05 45
Fax +237 2222 01 48
Website www.britcam.org

Ambassador
Syd Maddicott (resides in Cameroon)

Chad
British High Commission, Avenue Winston Churchill, BP 547, Yaounde, Cameroon
Telephone +237 2222 05 45
Fax +237 2222 01 48
Website www.britcam.org

Ambassador
Syd Maddicott (resides in Cameroon)

Chile
British Embassy, Avda. El Bosque Norte 0125, Las Condes, Santiago, Chile
Telephone +56 (2) 370 4100
Fax +56 (2) 370 4160
Website www.britishembassy.gov.uk/chile

Ambassador
Howard Drake

China
British Embassy, 11 Guang Hua Lu, Jian Guo Men Wai, Beijing 100600, China
Telephone +86 (10) 5192 4000
Fax +86 (10) 6532 1937
Website www.uk.cn

Ambassador
William Ehrman

Colombia
British Embassy, Carrera 9, No 76 - 49, Floor 8 and 9, Bogotá, Colombia
Telephone +57 (1) 326 8300
Fax +57 (1) 326 8302
Website www.britain.gov.co

Ambassador
Haydon Warren-Gash

Comoros
British High Commission, Les Cascades Building, Edith Cavell Street, Port Louis, PO Box 1063, Mauritius
Telephone +230 202 9400
Fax +230 202 9408

Ambassador
Dr John Murton (resides in Mauritius)

Congo, Democratic Republic of
British Embassy, 83 Avenue du Roi Baudouin, Kinshasa, Congo
Telephone +243 81 715 0761
Fax +243 813 46 4291

Ambassador
Nicholas Kay

Costa Rica
British Embassy, Apartado 815-1007, Edificio Centro Colsó, (Piso/floor 11), San José, Costa Rica
Telephone +506 258 2025
Fax +506 233 9938
Website www.britishembassycr.com

Ambassador
Tom Kennedy

Croatia
British Embassy, Ivana Lucica 4, 10000 Zagreb, Croatia
Telephone +385 (1) 6009 100
Fax +385 (1) 6009 111
Website www.britishembassy.gov.uk/croatia

Ambassador
Sir John Ramsden, Bt

Cuba
British Embassy, Calle 34 No. 702/4 entre 7ma Avenida y 17, Miramar, Cuba
Telephone +53 (7) 204 1771
Fax +53 (7) 204 8104
Website www.britishembassy.gov.uk/cuba

Ambassador
John Dew

Cyprus
British High Commission, Alexander Pallis Street (PO Box 21978), 1587 Nicosia, Cyprus
Telephone +357 (22) 861100
Fax +357 (22) 861125
Website www.britain.org.cy

High Commissioner
Peter Millett

Czech Republic
British Embassy, Thunovska 14, 118 00 Prague 1, Czech Republic
Telephone +420 257 402 111
Fax +420 257402 296
Website www.britain.cz

Ambassador
Linda Duffield

Denmark
British Embassy, Kastelsvej 36/38/40, DK-2100 Copenhagen Ø, Denmark
Telephone +45 35 44 52 00
Fax +45 35 44 52 59
Website www.britishembassy.dk

Ambassador
David Frost

Djibouti
British Honorary Consul, PO Box 169, Rue de Djibouti, Djibouti
Telephone +253 (3) 85007
Fax +253 (3) 52543

Ambassador
Robert Dewar (resides at Addis Ababa)

Dominica, Commonwealth of
British High Commission, Lower Collymore Rock (PO Box 767), Bridgetown, Barbados
Telephone +246 430 7800
Fax +246 430 7851

High Commissioner
Duncan Taylor (resides in Barbados)

Dominican Republic
British Embassy, Ave 27 de Febrero No 233, Edificio Corominas Pepin, Santo Domingo, Dominican Republic
Telephone +1 809 472 7111
Fax +1809 472 7190
Website www.britishembassy.gov.uk/dominicanrepublic

Ambassador
Ian Worthington

East Timor
British Embassy, Jalan M H Thamrin 75, Jakarta 10310, Indonesia
Telephone +62 (21) 315 6264
Fax +62 (21) 390 7493
Website www.britain.or.id

Ambassador
Charles Thomas William Humfrey

Ecuador
British Embassy, Citiplaza Building, Naciones Unidas Avenue and Republica de El Salvador 14th Floor, PO Box 17-17-830, Quito, Ecuador
Telephone +593 (2) 2970 800
Fax +593 (2) 2970 810
Website www.britembquito.org.ec

Ambassador
Bernard Whiteside

Egypt
British Embassy, 7 Ahmed Ragheb Street, Garden City, Cairo, Egypt
Telephone +20 (2) 794 0852
Fax +20 (2) 796 3222
Website www.britishembassy.gov.uk/egypt

Ambassador
Sir Derek Plumbly

El Salvador
British Embassy, Edificio Torre Internacional, Nivel 11, 16 Calle 0-55, Zona 10, Guatemala City, Guatemala
Telephone +502 2367 5425
Fax +502 2367 5430
Website www.britishembassy.gov.uk/guatemala

Ambassador
Ian Hughes (resides in Guatemala City)

Equatorial Guinea
British High Commission, Dangote House, Aguyi Ironsi Street, Wuse, Abuja, Nigeria
Telephone +234 (9) 413 2010
Fax +234 (9) 413 4565
Website www.ukinnigeria.com

Ambassador
Richard Gozney (resides in Nigeria)

Eritrea
British Embassy, 66-68 Mariam Ghimbi Street, PO Box 5584 Asmara, Eritrea
Telephone +291 (1) 12 01 45
Fax +291 (1) 12 01 04

Ambassador
Nick Astbury

Estonia
British Embassy, Wismari 6, Tallinn 10136, Estonia
Telephone +372 667 4700
Fax +372 667 4756
Website www.britishembassy.ee

Ambassador
Nigel Haywood

Ethiopia
British Embassy, Comoros Street, Addis Ababa, PO Box 858, Ethiopia
Telephone +251 (11) 661 2354
Fax +251 (11) 6610588
Website www.britishembassy.gov.uk/ethiopia

Ambassador
Robert Dewar

Falkland Islands
Government House, Stanley, FIQQ 1ZZ, Falkland Islands
Telephone +500 27433
Fax +500 27434

Governor
Howard Pearce

Fiji
British High Commission, Victoria House, 47 Gladstone Road, PO Box 1355, Suva, Fiji
Telephone +679 322 9100
Fax +679 322 9132
Website www.britishhighcommission.gov.uk/fiji

High Commissioner
Roger Sykes

Finland
British Embassy, Itdinen Puistotie 17, 00140 Helsinki, Finland
Telephone +358 (0) 9 2286 5100
Fax +358 (0) 9 2286 5262
Website www.britishembassy.fi

Ambassador
Valerie Caton

France
British Embassy, 35 rue du Faubourg St Honori, 75383 Paris Cedex 08, France
Telephone +33 (1) 44 51 31 00
Fax +33 (1) 44 51 32 88
Website www.amb-grandebretagne.fr

Ambassador
Sir Peter Westmacott

Gabon
British Honorary Consul, c/o Brossette, BP 486, Libreville, Gabon
Telephone +241 762200
Fax +241 742041

Ambassador
Syd Maddicott (resides in Cameroon)

Gambia, The Republic of
British High Commission, 48 Atlantic Road, Fajara (PO Box 507), Banjul, Gambia
Telephone +220 4495133
Fax +220 4496134
Website www.britishhighcommission.gov.uk/thegambia

High Commissioner
Phil Sinkinson

Georgia
British Embassy, GMT Plaza, 4 Freedom Square, Tbilisi, 0105, Georgia
Telephone +995 (32) 274747
Fax +995 (32) 274792
Website www.britishembassy.gov.uk/georgia

Ambassador
Denis Keefe

Germany
British Embassy, Wilhelmstrasse 70, 10117 Berlin, Germany
Telephone +49 (30) 20457 0
Fax +49 (30) 20457 571
Website www.britischebotschaft.de

Ambassador
Sir Michael Arthur

Ghana
British High Commission, Osu Link, off Gamel Abdul Nasser Avenue, PO Box 296, Accra, Ghana
Telephone +233 (21) 221665
Fax +233 (21) 7010655
Website www.britishhighcommission.gov.uk/ghana

High Commissioner
Gordon Wetherell

Gibraltar
Office of the Governor, The Convent, Main Street, Gibraltar
Telephone +350 45440
Fax +350 47823

Governor
Lt Gen Sir Robert Fulton

Greece
British Embassy, 1 Ploutarchou Street, 106 75 Athens, Greece
Telephone +30 210 727 2600
Fax +30 210 727 2876
Website www.british-embassy.gr

Ambassador
Simon Gass

Grenada
British High Commission, Netherlands Building, Grand Anse, St George's, Grenada
Telephone +1 473 440 3222
Fax +1 473 440 4939

High Commissioner
Duncan Taylor (resides in Barbados)

Guatemala
British Embassy, Edificio Torre Internacional, Nivel 11, 16 Calle 0-55, Zona 10, Guatemala City, Guatemala
Telephone +502 2367 5425
Fax +502 2367 5430
Website www.britishembassy.gov.uk/guatemala

Ambassador
Ian Hughes

Guinea
BP 6729, Conakry, Republic of Guinea
Telephone +224 30 45 58 07
Fax +224 30 45 60 20

Ambassador
John McManus

Guinea-Bissau
British Honorary Consul, Mavegro Int, CP100, Bissau
Telephone +245 20 12 24
Fax +245 20 12 65

Ambassador
Chris Trott (resides in Dakar)

Guyana
British High Commission, 44 Main Street, (PO Box 10849), Georgetown, Guyana
Telephone +592 226 5881
Fax +592 225 3555
Website www.britishhighcommission.gov.uk/guyana

High Commissioner
Fraser Wheeler

Haiti
British Consulate, Hotel Montana, (PO Box 1302), Port-au-Prince, Haiti
Telephone +509 257 3969
Fax +509 257 4048

Ambassador
Ian Worthington

Holy See
Osborne House, Via XX Settembre 80A, 00187 Rome, Italy
Telephone +39 (06) 4220 4000
Fax +39 (06) 4220 4205
Website www.britishembassy.gov.uk/holysee

Ambassador
Francis Campbell

Honduras
British Embassy, Edificio Torre Internacional, Nivel 11, 16 Calle 0-55, Zona 10, Guatemala City, Guatemala
Telephone +502 2367 5425
Fax +502 2367 5430
Website www.britishembassy.gov.uk/guatemala

Ambassador
Richard Lavers (resides in Guatemala City)

Hong Kong
British Consulate-General, No 1 Supreme Court Road, Central, Hong Kong, (PO Box 528), China
Telephone +852 2901 3000
Fax +852 2901 3066
Website www.britishconsulate.org.hk

Consul-General
Stephen Bradley

Hungary
British Embassy, Harmincad Utca 6, Budapest 1051, Hungary
Telephone +36 (1) 266 2888
Fax +36 (1) 266 0907
Website www.britishembassy.hu

Ambassador
John Nichols

Iceland
British Embassy, Laufasvegur 31, 101 Reykjavik, Iceland
Telephone +354 550 5100
Fax +354 550 5105
Website www.britishembassy.gov.uk/iceland

Ambassador
Alp Mehmet

India
British High Commission, Chanakyapuri, New Delhi 110021, India
Telephone +91 (11) 2687 2161
Fax +91 (11) 2687 2882
Website www.britishhighcommission.gov.uk/india

High Commissioner
Richard Stagg

Indonesia
British Embassy, Jalan M H Thamrin 75, Jakarta 10310, Indonesia
Telephone +62 (21) 315 6264
Fax +62 (21) 390 7493
Website www.britishhighcommission.gov.uk/fiji

Ambassador
Charles Humfrey

Iran
British Embassy, 198 Ferdowsi Avenue, Tehran 11344, Iran
Telephone +98 (21) 66705011/7
Fax +98 (21) 66710761
Website www.britishembassy.gov.uk/iran

Ambassador
Geoffrey Adams

Iraq
British Embassy, International Zone, Baghdad, Iraq
Telephone +964 (0) 7901 926 280
Website www.britishembassy.gov.uk/iraq

Ambassador
Dominic Asquith

Ireland, Republic of
British Embassy, 29 Merrion Road, Ballsbridge, Dublin 4, Republic of Ireland
Telephone +353 (1) 205 3700
Fax +353 (1) 205 3885
Website www.britishembassy.ie

Ambassador
David Reddaway

Israel
British Embassy, 192 Hayarkon Street, Tel Aviv 63405, Israel
Telephone +972 (3) 7251222
Fax +972 (3) 5278574
Website www.britemb.org.il

Ambassador
Tom Phillips

Italy
British Embassy, Via XX Settembre 80a, I-00187 Roma RM, BFPO 65, Italy
Telephone +39 06 4220 0001
Fax +39 06 4220 2335
Website www.britain.it

Ambassador
Edward Chaplin

Ivory Coast
British High Commission, Osu Link, off Gamel Abdul Nasser Avenue, PO Box 296, Accra, Ghana
Telephone +233 (21) 221665
Fax +233 (21) 7010655
Website www.britishhighcommission.gov.uk/ghana

High Commissioner
Gordon Wetherell (resides in Accra)

Jamaica
British High Commission, PO Box 575, 28 Trafalgar Road, Kingston 10, Jamaica
Telephone +1 876 510 0700
Fax +1 876 511 5304
Website www.britishhighcommission.gov.uk/jamaica

HIgh Commissioner
Jeremy Cresswell

Japan
British Embassy, No 1 Ichiban-cho, Chiyoda-ku, Tokyo 102-8381, Japan
Telephone +81 (3) 5211 1100
Fax +81 (3) 5275 3164
Website www.uknow.or.jp

Ambassador
Graham Fry

Jordan
British Embassy, (PO Box 87) Abdoun, Amman 11118, Jordan
Telephone +962 (6) 590 9200
Fax +962 (6) 590 9279
Website www.britain.org.jo

Ambassador
James Watt

Kazakhstan
British Embassy, 62 Kosmonavtov Street, Renco Building 6 Floor, Astana 010000, Kazakhstan
Telephone +73172 556200
Fax +73172 556211
Website www.britishembassy.kz

Ambassador
Paul Brummell

Kenya
British High Commission, Upper Hill Road, Nairobi, PO Box 30465-00100 Nairobi, Kenya
Telephone +254 (20) 2844000
Fax +254 (20) 2844088
Website www.britishhighcommission.gov.uk/kenya

High Commissioner
Adam Wood

Kiribati
British High Commission, Victoria House, 47 Gladstone Road, PO Box 1355, Suva, Fiji
Telephone +679 3229100
Fax +679 322 9132

Ambassador
Roger Sykes (resides at Suva)

Korea, Democratic People's Republic of (North Korea)
British Embassy, Munsu-dong Diplomatic Compound, Pyongyang, Democratic People's Republic of Korea
Telephone +850 2 381 7980
Fax +850 2 381 7985

Ambassador
John Everard

Korea, Republic of (South Korea)
British Embassy, Taepyeongno 40, 4 Jeong-dong, Jung-gu, Seoul 100-120, Republic of Korea
Telephone +82 (2) 3210 5500
Fax +82 (2) 725 1738
Website www.uk.or.kr

Ambassador
Warwick Morris

Kuwait
British Embassy, Arabian Gulf Street, Dasman, PO Box 2, Safat 13001, Kuwait
Telephone +965 240 3335
Fax +965 240 7633
Website www.britishembassy-kuwait.org

Ambassador
Stuart Laing

Kyrgyzstan
British Honorary Consul, Kalik Akiyeva Street, Building 11, Apartment 24, Bishkek, Kyrgyzstan
Telephone +996 312 680815

Ambassador
Paul Brummell (resides at Almaty)

Laos
c/o British Embassy, 14 Wireless Road, Lumpini, Pathumwan, Bangkok 10330, Thailand
Telephone +66 (2) 305 8333
Fax +66 (2) 255 9278

Ambassador
David Fall (resides in Bangkok)

Latvia
British Embassy, 5 J Alunana Street, Riga LV-1010, Latvia
Telephone +371 777 4700
Fax +371 777 4707
Website www.britain.lv

Ambassador
Ian Bond

Lebanon
British Embassy, Embassies Complex Army Street, Zkak Al-Blat, Serail Hill PO Box 11-471, Beirut, Lebanon
Telephone +961 (1) 990400
Fax +961 (1) 990420
Website www.britishembassy.gov.uk/lebanon

Ambassador
Frances Mary Guy

Lesotho
British High Commission, 255 Hill Street, Arcadia 0002, Pretoria, South Africa
Telephone +27 (12) 421 7733
Fax +27 (12) 421 7599
Website www.britain.org.za

High Commissioner
The Rt Hon Paul Boateng (resides in South Africa)

Liberia
British Honorary Consul, UMARCO, Monrovia, Liberia
Telephone +231 226 056
Fax + 231 226 061

Ambassador
Sarah MacIntosh (resides in Freetown)

Libya
British Embassy, PO Box 4206, Tripoli, Libya
Telephone +218 (21) 335 1084
Fax +218 (21) 335 1425
Website www.britishembassy.gov.uk/libya

Ambassador
Sir Vincent Fean

Liechtenstein
British Embassy, Thunstrasse 50, 3005 Berne, Switzerland
Telephone +41 (31) 359 7700
Fax +41 (31) 359 7701
Website www.britishembassy.ch

Ambassador
Simon Featherstone (resides in Berne)

Lithuania
British Embassy, 2 Antakalnio, LT-10308 Vilnius, Lithuania
Telephone +370 5 246 29 00
Fax +370 5 246 29 01
Website www.britain.lt

Ambassador
Colin Roberts

Luxembourg
British Embassy, 5, Boulevard Joseph II, L-1840, Luxembourg
Telephone +352 22 98 64
Fax + 352 22 98 67
Website www.britain.lu

Ambassador
James Clark

Macedonia
British Embassy, Salvador Aljende No 73, Skopje 1000, Macedonia
Telephone +389 (2) 3299 299
Fax +389 (2) 3179 729
Website www.britishembassy.gov.uk/macedonia

High Commissioner
Andrew Key

Madagascar
British High Commission, Les Cascades Building, Edith Cavell Street, Port Louis, PO Box 1063, Mauritius
Telephone +230 202 9400
Fax +230 202 9408

High Commissioner
Dr John Murton (resides in Mauritius)

Malawi
British High Commission, PO Box 30042, Lilongwe 3, Malawi
Telephone +265 (1) 772 400
Fax +265 (1) 772 657
Website www.britishhighcommission.gov.uk/malawi

High Commissioner
Richard Wildash

Malaysia
British High Commission, 185 Jalan Ampang, 50450 Kuala Lumpur, Malaysia
Telephone +60 (3) 2170 2200
Fax +60 (3) 2170 2370
Website www.britain.org.my

High Commissioner
Boyd McCleary

Maldives
British High Commission, 190 Galle Road, Kollupitiya, (PO Box 1433), Colombo 3, Sri Lanka
Telephone +94 (11) 243733643
Fax +94 (11) 2430308

High Commissioner
Dominick Chilcott (resides in Colombo)

Mali
Bureau De Liaison de l'Ambassade de Grande Bretagne, Enceinte de l'Ambassade du Canada, Route de Koulikoro, Hippodrome, BP 2069, Bamako, Mali
Telephone +223 277 46 37
Fax +223 221 83 77

Ambassador
Chris Trott (resides at Dakar)

Malta
British High Commission, Whitehall Mansions, Ta'Xbiex Seafront, Ta'Xbiex MSD 11, Malta GC
Telephone +356 2323 0000
Fax +356 2323 2269
Website www.britishhighcommission.gov.uk/malta

High Commissioner
Nick Archer

Marshall Islands
British Embassy, Floors 15-17, LV Locsin Building, 6752 Ayala Avenue, Corner of Makati Avenue, 1226 Makati, PO Box 2927 MCPO, Manila
Telephone +63 (2) 580 8700
Fax +63 (2) 819 7206
Website www.britishembassy.gov.uk/philippines

Ambassador
Peter Beckingham (resides in Manila)

Mauritania
SOGECO, Route de l'Aeroport, BP 351, Nouakchott, Mauritania
Telephone +222 525 83 31
Fax +222 525 39 03

Ambassador
Charles Gray (resides in Rabat)

Mauritius
British High Commission, Les Cascades Building, Edith Cavell Street, Port Louis, PO Box 1063, Mauritius
Telephone +230 202 9400
Fax +230 202 9408
Website www.britishembassy.gov.uk/mauritius

High Commissioner
John Murton

Mexico
British Embassy, Rmo Lerma 71, Col Cuauhtémoc, 06500 México DF
Telephone +52 (55) 5242 8500
Fax +52 (55) 5242 8517
Website www.britishembassy.gov.uk/mexico

Ambassador
Giles Paxman

Micronesia
British Embassy, Floors 15-17, LV Locsin Building, 6752 Ayala Avenue, Corner of Makati Avenue, 1226 Makati, Manila
Telephone +63 (2) 580 8700
Fax +63 (2) 819 7206
Website www.britishembassy.gov.uk/philippines

Ambassador
Peter Beckingham (resides in Manila)

Moldova
British Embassy Chisinau, 18 Nicolae Iorga Street, Chisinau, MD-2012, Republic of Moldova
Telephone +373 (22) 22 59 02
Fax +373 (22) 25 18 59
Website www.britishembassy.gov.uk/moldova

Ambassador
John Beyer

Mongolia
British Embassy, 30 Enkh Taivny Gudamzh, (PO Box 703), Ulaanbaatar 13, Mongolia
Telephone +976 (11) 458133
Fax +976 (11) 458036
Website www.britishembassy.gov.uk/mongolia

Ambassador
Christopher Osborne

Montenegro
British Embassy, Bulevar Svetog Petra Cetinjskog 149, First Floor, No.3, 81000 Podgorica, Montenegro
Telephone +381 (81) 205 460
Fax +381 (81) 205 441
Website www.britishembassy.gov.uk/montenegro

Ambassador
John Dyson

Montserrat
The Governor's Office, Farara Plaza, Brades, Montserrat
Telephone +1 664 491 2688/9
Fax +1 664 491 8867

Governor
Deborah Barnes Jones

Morocco
British Embassy Rabat, 28 avenue S A R Sidi
Mohammed, Souissi, Rabat, Morocco
Telephone +212 (37) 63 33 33
Fax +212 (37) 758709
Website www.britain.org.ma

Ambassador
Charles Gray

Mozambique
British High Commission, Av Vladimir I Lenine, 310, (CP
55) Maputo, Mozambique
Telephone +258 (21) 356 000
Fax +258 (21) 356 060
Website www.britishhighcommission.gov.uk/mozambique

High Commissioner
Howard Parkinson

Namibia
British High Commission, PO Box 22202, 116 Robert
Mugabe Avenue, Windhoek, Namibia
Telephone +264 (61) 274800
Fax +264 (61) 228895
Website www.britishhighcommission.gov.uk/namibia

High Commissioner
Mark Bensberg

Nauru
British High Commission, Victoria House, 47 Gladstone
Road, PO Box 1355, Suva, Fiji
Telephone +679 322 9100
Fax +679 322 9132
Website www.britishhighcommission.gov.uk/fiji

High Commissioner
Roger Sykes (resides at Suva)

Nepal
British Embassy, Lainchaur Kathmandu, (PO Box 106),
Nepal
Telephone +977 (1) 4410583
Fax +977 (1) 4411789
Website www.britishembassy.gov.uk/nepal

Ambassador
Andrew Hall

Netherlands
British Embassy, Lange Voorhout 10, 2514 ED The
Hague, Netherlands
Telephone +31 (0) 70 4270 427
Fax +31 (70) 427 0345
Website www.britain.nl

Ambassador
Lyn Parker

New Zealand
British High Commission, 44 Hill Street, Wellington 1,
New Zealand
Telephone +64 (4) 924 2888
Fax +64 (4) 924 2809
Website www.britain.org.nz

High Commissioner
George Fergusson

Nicaragua
British Embassy, Apartado 815-1007, Edificio Centro
Colón, (Piso/floor 11), San José, Costa Rica
Telephone +506 258 2025
Fax +506 233 9938
Website www.britishembassycr.com

Ambassador
Tom Kennedy (resides in San José)

Niger
British Honorary Consul, BP 10151, Niamey, Niger
Telephone +227 96878130

Ambassador
Gordon Wetherell (resides in Accra)

Nigeria
British High Commission, Dangote House, Aguyi Ironsi
Street, Wuse, Abuja, Nigeria
Telephone +234 (9) 413 2010
Fax +234 (9) 413 4565
Website www.uknigeria.com

High Commissioner
Richard Gozney

Norway
British Embassy, Thomas Heftyesgate 8, 0264, Oslo,
Norway
Telephone +47 23 13 27 00
Fax +47 23 13 27 41
Website www.britain.no

Ambassador
David Powell

Oman
British Embassy, PO Box 185, Mina Al Fahal, Postal
Code 116, Sultanate of Oman
Telephone +968 24 609000
Fax +968 24 609010
Website www.britishembassy.gov.uk/oman

Ambassador
Noel Guckian

Pakistan
British High Commission, Diplomatic Enclave, Ramna 5,
P O Box 1122, Pakistan
Telephone +92 (51) 201 2000
Fax +92 (51) 282 3439
Website www.britishhighcommission.gov.uk/pakistan

HIgh Commissioner
Robert Brinkley

Palau
British Embassy, Floors 15-17, LV Locsin Building, 6752
Ayala Avenue, Corner of Makati Avenue, 1226 Makati,
Manila
Telephone +63 (2) 580 8700
Fax +63 (2) 819 7206
Website www.britishembassy.gov.uk/philippines

Ambassador
Peter Beckingham (resides in Manila)

Occupied Palestinian Territories
British Consulate-General, 19 Nashashibi Street, Sheikh
Jarrah Quarter, PO Box 19690, East Jerusalem 97200,
Israel
Telephone +972 (02) 541 4100
Fax +972 (02) 532 2368
Website www.britishconsulate.org

Consul-General
Richard Makepeace

Panama
British Embassy, MMG Tower, Calle 53, Apartado/PO
Box 0816-07946, Panama City, Panama
Telephone +507 269 0866
Fax +507 223 0730
Website www.britishembassy.gov.uk/panama

Ambassador
Richard Austen

Papua New Guinea
British High Commission, Kiroki Street, Port Moresby,
Papua New Guinea
Telephone +675 325 1677
Fax +675 325 3547
Website www.britishhighcommission.gov.uk/
papuanewguinea

High Commissioner
David Dunn

Paraguay
British Embassy, Dr Luis Agote 2412, (1425) Buenos
Aires, Argentina
Telephone +54 (11) 4808 2200
Fax +54 (11) 4808 2274
Website www.britain.org.ar

Ambassador
John Hughes (resides in Buenos Aires)

Peru
British Embassy, Torre Parque Mar (Piso 22), Avenida
Jose Larco, 1301, Miraflores, Lima, Peru
Telephone +51 (1) 617 3000
Fax +51 (1) 617 3100
Website www.britishembassy.gov.uk/peru

Ambassador
Catherine Nettleton

Philippines
British Embassy, Floors 15-17, LV Locsin Building, 6752
Ayala Avenue, Corner of Makati Avenue, 1226 Makati
(PO Box 2927 MCPO), Manila, Philippines
Telephone +63 (2) 580 8700
Fax +63 (2) 819 7206
Website www.britishembassy.gov.uk/philippines

Ambassador
Peter Beckingham

Pitcairn Henderson Ducie & Oeno Islands
Private Box 105696, Auckland, New Zealand
Telephone +64 (9) 366 0186
Fax +64 (9) 366 0187
Website www.government.pn

High Commissioner
George Fergusson (resides in Wellington)

Poland
British Embassy, Aleje Roz No 1, 00-556 Warsaw, Poland
Telephone +48 (22) 311 00 00
Fax +48 (22) 311 0311
Website www.britishembassy.pl

Ambassador
Charles Crawford

Portugal
British Embassy, Rua de São Bernardo 33, 1249-082
Lisbon, Portugal
Telephone +351 (21) 392 40 00
Fax +351 (21) 392 41 87
Website www.uk-embassy.pt

Ambassador
John Buck

Qatar
British Embassy, PO Box 3, Doha, Qatar
Telephone +974 442 1991
Fax +974 443 8692
Website www.britishembassy.gov.uk/qatar

Ambassador
Simon Collis

Romania
British Embassy, 24 Jules Michelet, 010463 Bucharest,
Romania
Telephone Main +40 (21) 201 7200
Fax +40 (21) 201 7315
Website www.britishembassy.gov.uk/romania

Ambassador
Robin Barnett

Russian Federation
British Embassy Moscow, Smolenskaya Naberezhnaya 10,
Moscow 121099, Russian Federation
Telephone +7 (495) 956 7200
Fax +7 (495) 956 7201
Website www.britaininrussia.ru

Ambassador
Anthony Brenton

Rwanda
British Embassy, Parcelle No 1131, Boulevard de
l'Umuganda, Kacyiru-Sud, BP 576 Kigali, Rwanda
Telephone +250 584098
Fax +250 582044
Website www.britishembassykigali.org.rw

Ambassador
Jeremy Macadie

Saint Christopher and Nevis
British High Commission, PricewaterhouseCoopers Centre,
11 Old Parham Road, St John's, Antigua
Telephone +268 462 0008/9
Fax +268 562 2124

High Commissioner
Duncan Taylor (resides in Barbados)

St Helena
Governor's Office, The Castle, Jamestown, St Helena
Island, South Atlantic Ocean
Telephone +290 2555
Fax +290 2598

Governor
Michael Clancy

Saint Lucia
British High Commission, Francis Compton Building, 2nd
Floor, Waterfront, Castries, St Lucia
Telephone +1 758 452 2484/5
Fax +1 758 453 1543

High Commissioner
Duncan Taylor (resides in Barbados)

Saint Vincent and the Grenadines
British High Commission, Granby Street (PO Box 132),
Kingstown, Saint Vincent and the Grenadines
Telephone +784 457 1701
Fax +784 456 2750

High Commissioner
Duncan Taylor (resides in Barbados)

Samoa
British High Commission, 44 Hill Street, Wellington 1,
New Zealand
Telephone +64 (4) 924 2888
Fax +64 (4) 924 2809
Website www.britain.org.nz

High Commissioner
George Fergusson (resides in Wellington)

San Marino
British Consulate-General, Via XX Settembre 80/A, 00187
Rome, Italy
Telephone +39 (055) 284133
Fax +39 (055) 219112

Ambassador
Sir Ivor Roberts (resides in Rome)

São Tomé and Principe
British Consulate, Residencial Avenida, Avienda Da
Independencia, CP 257, São Tomé
Telephone +239 (12) 21026/7
Fax +239 (12) 21372

Ambassador
Ralph Publicover (resides in Luanda)

Saudi Arabia
British Embassy, PO Box 94351, Riyadh 11693, Saudi
Arabia
Telephone +966 (0) 1 488 0077
Fax +966 (0) 1 488 2373
Website www.britishembassy.gov.uk/saudiarabia

Ambassador
William Patey

Senegal
British Embassy, 20 Rue du Docteur Guillet, (Boite
Postale 6025), Dakar, Senegal
Telephone +221 823 7392
Fax +221 823 2766
Website www.britishembassy.gov.uk/senegal

Ambassador
Chris Trott

Serbia
British Embassy, Resavska 46, 11000 Belgrade, Serbia
Telephone +381 (11) 2645 055
Fax +381 (11) 2659 651
Website www.britishembassy.gov.uk/serbia

Ambassador
Stephen Wordsworth

Seychelles
British High Commission, 3rd floor, Oliaji Trade Centre,
Francis Rachel Street, PO Box 161, Victoria, Mahe,
Seychelles
Telephone +248 283 666
Fax +248 283 657
Website www.bhcvictoria.sc

High Commissioner
Diana Skingle

Sierra Leone
British High Commission, 6 Spur Road, Freetown, Sierra
Leone
Telephone +232 (22) 232961
Fax +232 (22) 228169
Website www.britishhighcommision.gov.uk/sierraleone

High Commissioner
Sarah MacIntosh

Singapore
British High Commission, 100 Tanglin Road, Singapore
247919
Telephone +65 6424 4200
Fax +65 6424 4250
Website www.britain.org.sg

High Commissioner
Paul Madden

Slovakia
British Embassy, Panska 16, 811 01 Bratislava, Slovakia
Telephone +421 (2) 5998 2000
Fax +421 (2) 5998 2237
Website www.britishembassy.sk

Ambassador
Tom Carter

Slovenia
British Embassy, 4th floor Trg Republike 3, 1000
Ljubljana, Slovenia
Telephone +386 (1) 200 3910
Fax +386 (1) 425 0174
Website www.british-embassy.si

Ambassador
Tim Simmons

Solomon Islands
British High Commission, PO Box 676, Telekom House,
Mendana Avenue, Honiara, Solomon Islands
Telephone +677 21705
Fax +677 21549

High Commissioner
Richard Lyne

Somalia
British Embassy, Waddada Xasan Geedd Abtoow 7/8, (P
O Box 1036), Mogadishu, Somalia
Telephone +252 (1) 20288/9

Ambassador
none

South Africa
British High Commission, 255 Hill Street, Arcadia 0002,
Pretoria, South Africa
Telephone +27 (12) 421 7500
Fax +27 (12) 421 7555
Website www.britain.org.za

High Commissioner
The Rt Hon Paul Boateng

South Georgia & South Sandwich Islands
Governor's Office, Government House, Stanley, Falkland
Islands
Telephone +500 28280
Fax +500 28201

Governor
Howard Pearce (resides in Stanley)

Spain
British Embassy, C/ Fernando el Santo, 16, 28010 Madrid,
Spain
Telephone +34 (91) 700 82 00
Fax +34 (91) 700 8210
Website www.ukinspain.com

Ambassador
Sir Stephen Wright

Sri Lanka
190 Galle Road, Kollupitiya, (PO Box 1433), Colombo 3,
Sri Lanka
Telephone +94 (11) 2437336 43
Fax +94 (11) 2430308
Website www.britishhighcommission.gov.uk/srilanka

High Commissioner
Dominick Chilcott

Sudan
British Embassy, off Sharia Al Baladia, Khartoum East,
(PO Box No 801), Sudan
Telephone +249 (183) 777105
Fax +249 (183) 776457
Website www.britishembassy.gov.uk/sudan

Ambassador
Ian Cliff

Suriname
British Honorary Consul, c/o VSH United Buildings, Van't
Hogerhuysstraat 9-11, PO Box 1860, Paramaribo,
Suriname
Telephone +597 402558
Fax +597 403515

Ambassador
Stephen Hiscock (resides at Georgetown)

Swaziland
British High Commission, 255 Hill Street, Arcadia 0002,
Pretoria, South Africa
Telephone +27 (12) 421 7500
Fax +27 (12) 421 7555
Website www.britain.org.za

High Commissioner
The Rt Hon Paul Boateng (resides in Pretoria)

Sweden
British Embassy, Skarpögatan 6-8, Box 27819, 115 93
Stockholm, Sweden
Telephone +46 (8) 671 3000
Fax +46 (8) 662 9989
Website www.britishembassy.se

Ambassador
Andrew Mitchell

Switzerland
British Embassy, Thunstrasse 50, 3005 Berne,
Switzerland
Telephone +41 (31) 359 7700
Fax +41 (31) 359 7701
Website www.britishembassy.ch

Ambassador
Simon Featherstone

Syria
British Embassy, Kotob Building, 11 Mohammad Kurd
Ali Street, Malki, PO Box 37, Damascus, Syria
Telephone +963 (11) 373 9241
Fax +963 (11) 373 1600
Website www.britishembassy.gov.uk/syria

Ambassador
John Jenkins

Tajikistan
British Embassy, 65 Mirzo Tursunzade Street, Dushanbe
734002, Tajikistan
Telephone +992 (37)2 24 22 21
Fax +992 (37) 227 1726
Website www.britishembassy.gov.uk/tajikistan

Ambassador
Graeme Loten

Tanzania
British High Commission, Umoja House, Garden Avenue,
PO Box 9200, Dar es Salaam, Tanzania
Telephone +255 (22) 211 0101
Fax +255 (22) 211 0102
Website www.britishhighcommission.gov.uk/tanzania

High Commissioner
Philip Parham

Thailand
British Embassy, 14 Wireless Road, Lumpini,
Pathumwan, Bangkok 10330, Thailand
Telephone +66 (2) 305 8333
Fax +66 (2) 255 9278
Website www.britishembassy.gov.uk/thailand

Ambassador
David Fall

Togo
British High Commision, Osu Link, off Gamel Abdul
Nasser Avenue, PO Box 296, Accra, Ghana
Telephone +233 (21) 221665
Fax +233 (21) 7010655
Website www.britishhighcommission.gov.uk/ghana

High Commissioner
Gordon Wetherell (resides in Accra)

Tonga
British High Commission, Victoria House, 47 Gladstone
Road, PO Box 1355, Suva, Fiji
Telephone +679 322 9100
Fax +679 322 9132
Website www.britishhighcommission.gov.uk/fiji

High Commissioner
Roger Sykes (resides in Suva)

Trinidad and Tobago
British High Commission, 19 St Clair Avenue, St Clair,
Port of Spain, Trinidad
Telephone +1 868 622 2748
Fax +1 868 622 4555
Website www.britishhighcommission.gov.uk/
trinidadandtobago

High Commissioner
Eric Jenkinson

Tristan da Cunha
The Administrator's Office, The Settlement, Tristan da
Cunha, South Atlantic Ocean, TDCU 1ZZ
Telephone +44 (0) 20 3014 2000
Fax +44 (0) 20 3014 2020

Governor
Michael Clancy (resides in St Helena)

Tunisia
British Embassy, Rue du Lac Windermere, Les Berges du
Lac, Tunis 1053, Tunisia
Telephone +216 71 108 700
Fax +216 71 108 749
Website www.britishembassy.gov.uk/tunisia

Ambassador
Alan Goulty

Turkey
British Embassy, Sehit Ersan Caddesi 46/A, Cankaya,
Ankara, Turkey
Telephone +90 (312) 455 3344
Fax +90 (312) 455 3352
Website www.britishembassy.org.tr

Ambassador
Nick Baird

Turkmenistan
British Embassy, Four Points Ak Altin Hotel, 301-308
Office Building, Ashgabat, Turkmenistan
Telephone +993 (12) 363462/63/64
Fax +993 (12) 363465
Website www.britishembassy.gov.uk/turkmenistan

Ambassador
Peter Butcher

Turks and Caicos Islands
Governor's Office, Turks & Caicos Islands, Waterloo,
Grand Turk, Turks and Caicos Islands
Telephone +1 649 946 2309
Fax +1 649 946 2903

Governor
Richard Tauwhare

Tuvalu
British High Commission, Victoria House, 47 Gladstone
Road, PO Box 1355, Suva, Fiji
Telephone +679 3229100
Fax +679 322 9132
Website www.britishhighcommission.gov.uk/fiji

High Commissioner
Roger Sykes (resides in Suva)

Uganda
British High Commission, 4 Windsor Loop, PO Box 7070,
Kampala, Uganda
Telephone +256 (31) 2312000
Fax +256 (41) 257304
Website www.britain.or.ug

High Commissioner
Francois Gordon

Ukraine
British Embassy, 9 Desyatinna St, Kyiv 01025, Ukraine
Telephone +380 (44) 490 3660
Fax +380 (44) 490 3662
Website www.britemb-ukraine.net

Ambassador
Timothy Barrow

United Arab Emirates
British Embassy, PO Box 248, Abu Dhabi, United Arab
Emirates
Telephone +971 (2) 6101100
Fax +971 (2) 6101586
Website www.britishembassy.gov.uk/uae

Ambassador
Edward Oakden

United States
British Embassy, 3100 Massachusetts Avenue NW,
Washington DC 20008, USA
Telephone +1 (202) 588 6500
Fax +1 (202) 588 7866
Website www.britainusa.com

Ambassador
Sir David Manning

Uruguay
British Embassy, Calle Marco Bruto 1073, 11300
Montevideo, PO Box 16024, Uruguay
Telephone +598 (2) 622 3630
Fax +598 (2) 622 7815
Website www.britishembassy.org.uy

Ambassador
Hugh Salvesen

Uzbekistan
British Embassy, 67, Gulyamov Street, Tashkent 700000,
Uzbekistan
Telephone +998 (71) 1207852
Fax +998 (71) 1206549
Website www.britishembassy.gov.uk/uzbekistan

Ambassador
Iain Charles MacDonald Kelly

Vanuatu
British High Commisssion, Victoria House, 47 Gladstone
Road, PO Box 1355, Suva, Fiji
Telephone +679 3229100
Fax +679 322 9132
Website www.britishhighcommission.gov.uk/fiji

High Commissioner
Roger Sykes (resides in Suva)

Venezuela
British Embassy, Torre La Castellana, Piso 11, Avenida
La Principal de la Castellana, La Castellana, Caracas 1061,
Venezuela
Telephone +58 (212) 263 8411
Fax +58 (212) 267 1275
Website www.britain.org.ve

Ambassador
Catherine Royle

Vietnam
British Embassy, Central Building, 4th floor, 31 Hai Ba
Trung, Hanoi, Vietnam
Telephone +84 (4) 936 0500
Fax +84 (4) 936 0551
Website www.uk-vietnam.org

Ambassador
Robert Gordon

Yemen
British Embassy, 938 Thaher Himiyar Street, East Ring
Road, PO Box 1287, Sana'a, Yemen
Telephone +967 (1) 302450/1/2/3
Fax +967 (1) 302454
Website www.britishembassy.gov.uk/yemen

Ambassador
Michael Gifford

Zambia
British High Commission, 5210 Independence Avenue, PO
Box 50050, 15101 Ridgeway, Lusaka, Zambia
Telephone +260 (1) 251133
Fax +260 (1) 253798
Website www.britishhighcommission.gov.uk/zambia

High Commissioner
Alistair Harrison

Zimbabwe
British Embassy, Corner House (7th Floor), Samora
Machel Avenue, Leopold Takawira Street, PO Box 4490,
Harare, Zimbabwe
Telephone +263 (4) 772990
Fax +263 (4) 774617
Website www.britishembassy.gov.uk/zimbabwe

Ambassador
Dr Andrew Pocock

AMBASSADORS TO BRITAIN

The following pages detail all the embassies and senior diplomats present
in Britain today.

Afghanistan
31 Prince's Gate, London SW7 1QQ
Telephone +44 (0) 20 7589 8891
Fax +44 (0) 20 7584 4801
Website www.afghanembassyuk.org

Ambassador
Dr Mohammad Rahim Sherzoy

Albania
2nd Floor, 24 Buckingham Gate, London SW1E 6LB
Telephone +44 (0) 20 7828 8897
Fax +44 (0) 20 7828 8869
Website www.albanianembassy.co.uk

Ambassador
Kastriot Robo

Algeria
54 Holland Park, London W11 3RS
Telephone +44 (0) 20 7221 7800
Fax +44 (0) 20 7221 0448
Website www.algerianembassy.org.uk

Ambassador
Mohamed Salah Dembri

Andorra
63 Westover Road, London SW18 2RF
Telephone +44 (0) 20 8874 4806
Fax +44 (0) 20 8874 4902

Ambassador
Maria Rosa Picart de Francis

Angola
22 Dorset Street, London W1U 6QY
Telephone +44 (0) 20 7299 9850
Fax +44 (0) 20 7486 9397
Website www.angola.org.uk

Ambassador
Ana Maria Teles Carreira

Antigua and Barbuda
2nd Floor, 45 Crawford Place, London W1H 4LP
Telephone +44 (0) 20 7258 0070
Fax +44 (0) 20 7258 7486
Website www.antigua-barbuda.com

High Commissioner
Dr Carl Roberts

Argentina
65 Brook Street, London W1K 4AH
Telephone +44 (0) 20 7318 1300
Fax +44 (0) 20 7318 1301
Website www.argentine-embassy-uk.org

Ambassador
Federico Mirré

Armenia
25A Cheniston Gardens, London W8 6TG
Telephone +44 (0) 20 7938 5435
Fax +44 (0) 20 7938 2595
Website www.accc.org.uk

Ambassador
Vahe Gabrielyan

Australia
Australia House, Strand, London WC2B 4LA
Telephone +44 (0) 20 7379 4334
Fax +44 (0) 20 7240 5333
Website www.australia.org.uk

High Commissioner
Richard Kenneth Robert Alston

Austria
18 Belgrave Mews West, London SW1X 8HU
Telephone +44 (0) 20 7344 3250
Fax +44 (0) 20 7344 0292
Website www.bmeia.gv.at/london

Ambassador
Dr Gabriele Matzner-Holzer

Azerbaijan
4 Kensington Court, London W8 5DL
Telephone +44 (0) 20 7938 5482/3412
Fax +44 (0) 20 7937 1783
Website www.president.az

Ambassador
Rafael Ibrahimov

Bahamas
10 Chesterfield Street, London W1J 5JL
Telephone +44 (0) 20 7408 4488
Fax +44 (0) 20 7499 9937
Website www.bahamas.gov.bs

High Commissioner
Basil O'Brien

Bahrain
30 Belgrave Square, London SW1X 8QB
Telephone +44 (0) 20 7201 9170
Fax +44 (0) 20 7201 9183
Website www.bahrainembassy.co.uk

Ambassador
Shaikh Khalifa bin Abdullah bin Mohammed Al Khalifa

Bangladesh
28 Queen's Gate, London SW7 5JA
Telephone +44 (0) 20 7584 0081
Fax +44 (0) 20 7225 2130
Website www.bangladeshhighcommission.org.uk

Acting High Commissioner
Ashraf Uddin

Barbados
1 Great Russell Street, London WC1B 3ND
Telephone +44 (0) 20 7631 4975
Fax +44 (0) 20 7323 6872
Website www.foreign.gov.bb

High Commissioner
L Edwin Pollard

Belarus
6 Kensington Court, London W8 5DL
Telephone +44 (0) 20 7937 3288
Fax +44 (0) 20 7361 0005
Website www.belembassy.org.uk

Ambassador
Aleksandr Mikhnevich

Belgium
17 Grosvenor Crescent, London SW1X 7EE
Telephone +44 (0) 20 7470 3700
Fax +44 (0) 20 7470 3795/3710
Website www.diplobel.org.uk

Ambassador
Jean-Michel Veranneman de Watervliet

Belize
Third Floor, 45 Crawford Place, London W1H 4LP
Telephone +44 (0) 20 7723 3603
Fax +44 (0) 20 7723 9637
Website www.bzhc-lon.co.uk

High Commissioner
Lawrence Sylvester

Benin
87 Avenue Victor Hugo, 75116 Paris, France
Telephone +44 (0) 20 8954 8800
Fax +44 (0) 20 8954 8844
Website www.ambassade-benin.org

Ambassador
Edgar-Yves Monnou

Bolivia
106 Eaton Square, London SW1W 9AD
Telephone +44 (0) 20 7235 4248
Fax +44 (0) 20 7235 1286
Website www.embassyofbolivia.co.uk

Ambassador
Maria Beatriz Souviron Crespo

Bosnia and Herzegovina
5-7 Lexham Gardens, London W8 5JJ
Telephone +44 (0) 20 7373 0867
Fax +44 (0) 20 7373 0871

Ambassador
Dr Tanja Milašinović

Botswana
6 Stratford Place, London W1C 1AY
Telephone +44 (0) 20 7499 0031
Fax +44 (0) 20 7495 8595

High Commissioner
Roy Blackbeard

Brazil
32 Green Street, Mayfair, London W1K 7AT
Telephone +44 (0) 20 7499 0877
Fax +44 (0) 20 7399 9100
Website www.brazil.org.uk

Ambassador
José Mauricio Bustani

Brunei
1920 Belgrave Square, London SW1X 8PG
Telephone +44 (0) 20 7581 0521
Fax +44 (0) 20 7235 9717

Ambassador
Pengiran Dato Maidin Hashim

Bulgaria
186-188 Queen's Gate, London SW7 5HL
Telephone +44 (0) 20 7584 9400
Fax +44 (0) 20 7584 4948
Website www.bulgarianembassy.org.uk

Ambassador
Lachezar Nikolov Matev

Burkina Faso
Lilacs Stane Street, Oakley, Surrey RH5 5LU
Telephone +44 (0) 130 662 7225
Fax +44 (0) 20 8770 7448
Website www.ambassadeduburkina.be

Ambassador
Kadré Désiré Ouedraogo (resides in Brussels)

Burundi
1000 Bruxelles, LE, Square Marie-Louise, 46, Brussels, Belgium
Telephone +32 (2) 230 45 35
Fax +32 (2) 230 7883

Ambassador
Laurent Kavakure (resides in Brussels)

Cambodia
28-32 Wellington Road (Wellington Building), St John's Wood, London NW8 9SP
Telephone +44 (0) 20 7483 9063
Fax +44 (0) 20 7483 9061
Website www.cambodianembassy.org.uk

Ambassador
Hor Nambora

Cameroon
84 Holland Park, London W11 3SB
Telephone +44 (0) 20 7727 0771
Fax +44 (0) 20 7792 9353
Website www.cameroonhighcom.co.uk

High Commissioner
Samuel Libock Mbei

Canada
Macdonald House, 1 Grosvenor Square, London W1K 4AB
Telephone +44 (0) 20 7258 6600
Fax +44 (0) 20 7258 6333
Website www.dfait-maeci.gc.ca

High Commissioner
James Wright

Cape Verde
18-20 Stanley Street, Liverpool L1 6AF
Telephone +44 (0) 151 236 0206
Fax +44 (0) 151 255 1314
Website www.capeverdeconsul.com

Honorary Consul
Joao Roberto

Central African Republic
30 Rue des Perchamps, 75016, Paris, France

Chad
Boulevard Lambermont 52, 1030 Brussels, Belgium
Telephone +32 (2) 215 1975
Fax + 32 (2) 216 3526

Ambassador
Ahmat Abderaman Haggar (resides in Brussels)

Chile
12 Devonshire Street, London W1G 7DS
Telephone +44 (0) 20 7580 6392
Fax +44 (0) 7436 5204
Website www.echileuk.demon.co.uk

Ambassador
Rafael Moreno

China
49-51 Portland Place, London W1B 4JL
Telephone +44 (0) 20 7299 4049
Website www.chinese-embassy.org.uk

Ambassador
Fu Ying

Colombia
3 Hans Crescent, London SW1X 0LN
Telephone +44 (0) 20 7589 9177 / +44 (0) 20 7589 5037
Fax +44 (0) 20 7581 1829
Website www.colombianembassy.co.uk

Ambassador
Dr Carlos Eduardo Medellin Becerra

Comoros
Flat 6, 24-26 Avenue Road, London NW8 6BU
Telephone +44 (0) 20 7491 2098
Fax +44 (0) 20 7491 0531

Ambassador
Khaled Chehabi

Congo
The Arena, 24 Southwark Bridge Road, London SE1 9HF
Telephone +44 (0) 20 7922 0695
Fax +44 (0) 20 7622 0371

Head of Mission
Henri Marie Joseph Lopes (resides in France)

Congo, Democratic Republic of
281 Gray's Inn Road, London WC1X 8QF
Telephone +44 (0) 20 7278 9825
Fax +44 (0) 20 7833 9967

Ambassador
Eugenie Tshiela Compton

Costa Rica
Flat 1, 14 Lancaster Gate, London W2 3LH
Telephone +44 (0) 20 7706 8844
Fax +44 (0) 20 7706 8655
Website costarica.embassyhomepage.com

Ambassador
Pilar Saborio Rocafort

Croatia
21 Conway Street, London W1T 6BN
Telephone +44 (0) 20 7387 2022
Fax +44 (0) 20 7387 0310

Ambassador
Josip Paro

Cuba
167 High Holborn, London WC1 6PA
Telephone +44 (0) 20 7240 2488
Fax +44 (0) 20 7836 2602
Website www.cubaldn.com

Ambassador
René J Mujica Cantelar

Cyprus
93 Park Street, London W1K 7ET
Telephone +44 (0) 20 7499 8272
Fax +44 (0) 20 7491 0691

Ambassador
George Iacovou

Czech Republic
26 Kensington Palace Gardens, London W8 4QY
Telephone +44 (0) 20 7243 1115
Fax +44 (0) 20 7727 9654
Website www.mzv.cz

Ambassador
Jan Winkler

Denmark
55 Sloane Street, London SW1X 9SR
Telephone +44 (0) 20 7333 0200
Fax +44 (0) 20 7333 0270
Website www.denmark.org.uk

Ambassador
Birger Riis-Jørgensen

Djibouti
26 Rue Emile Minier, 75116 Paris, France
Telephone +33 (1) 4727 4922
Fax +33 (1) 4553 5053
Website www.ambdjibouti.org

Ambassador
Rachad Farah (resides in Paris)

Dominica, Commonwealth of
1 Collingham Gardens, South Kensington, London SW5 0HW
Telephone +44 (0) 20 7370 5194
Fax +44 (0) 20 7373 8743
Website www.dominica.co.uk

Acting High Commissioner
Agnes Adonis

Dominican Republic
139 Inverness Terrace, Bayswater, London W2 6JF
Telephone +44 (0) 20 7727 6285
Fax +44 (0) 20 7727 3693
Website www.serex.gov.do

Ambassador
Anibal de Castro

Ecuador
Flat 3B, 3 Hans Crescent, London SW1X 0LS
Telephone +44 (0) 20 7584 2648
Fax +44 (0) 20 7823 9701
Website www.mmrree.gov.ec

Ambassador
Déborah Salgado Campaña

Egypt
26 South Street, London W1K 1DW
Telephone +44 (0) 20 7499 3304
Fax +44 (0) 20 7491 1542

Ambassador
Gehad Refaat Madi

El Salvador
8 Dorset Square, London NW1 6PU
Telephone +44 (0) 20 7224 9800
Fax +44 (0) 207 224 9878
Website www.rree.gob.sv

Ambassador
Dr Vladimiro P Villalta

Equatorial Guinea
13 Park Place, St James's, London SW1A 1LP
Telephone +44 (0) 20 7499 6867
Fax +44 (0) 20 7499 6782

Ambassador
Agustin Nze Nfumu

Eritrea
96 White Lion Street, London N1 9PF
Telephone +44 (0) 20 7713 0096
Fax +44 (0) 20 7713 0161

Ambassador
Negassi Sengal Ghebrezghi

Estonia
16 Hyde Park Gate, London SW7 5DG
Telephone +44 (0) 20 7589 3428
Fax +44 (0) 20 7589 3430
Website www.estonia.gov.uk

Ambassador
Dr Margus Laidre

Ethiopia
17 Prince's Gate, London SW7 1PZ
Telephone +44 (0) 20 7589 7212
Fax +44 (0) 20 7584 7054
Website www.ethioembassy.org.uk

Ambassador
Ato Berhanu Kebede

Fiji
34 Hyde Park Gate, London SW7 5DN
Telephone +44 (0) 20 7584 3661
Fax +44 (0) 20 7584 2838

High Commissioner
Maca Tukakepa

Finland
38 Chesham Place, London SW1X 8HW
Telephone +44 (0) 20 7838 6200
Fax +44 (0) 20 7235 3680
Website www.finemb.org.uk

Ambassador
Jaakko Laajava

France
58 Knightsbridge, London SW1X 7JT
Telephone +44 (0) 20 7073 1000
Fax +44 (0) 20 7073 1004
Website www.ambafrance-uk.org

Ambassador
Gerard Errera

Gabon
27 Elvaston Place, London SW7 5NL
Telephone +44 (0) 20 7823 9986
Fax +44 (0) 20 7584 0047
Website gabon.embassyhomepage.com

Ambassador
Alain Mensah-Zoguelet

Gambia
57 Kensington Court, London W8 5DG
Telephone +44 (0) 20 7937 6316
Fax +44 (0) 20 7937 9095

Acting High Commissioner
Lang Yabou

Georgia
4 Russell Gardens, London W14 8EZ
Telephone +44 (0) 20 7603 7799
Fax +44 (0) 20 7603 6682
Website www.geoemb.org.uk

Ambassador
Gela Charkviani

Germany
23 Belgrave Square, London SW1X 8PZ
Telephone +44 (0) 20 7824 1300
Fax +44 (0) 20 7824 1435
Website www.london.diplo.de

Ambassador
Wolfgang Friedrich Ischinger

Ghana
13 Belgrave Square, London SW1X 8PN
Telephone +44 (0) 20 7201 5900
Fax +44 (0) 20 7245 9552
Website www.ghana-com.co.uk

High Commissioner
Annan Arkyin Cato

Greece
1A Holland Park, London W11 3TP
Telephone +44 (0) 20 7229 3850
Fax +44 (0) 20 7229 7221
Website www.greekembassy.org.uk

Ambassador
Vassilis-Achilleas Pispinis

Grenada
The Chapel, Archel Road, West Kensington, London W14 9QH
Telephone +44 (0) 20 7385 4277
Fax +44 (0) 20 7381 4807

High Commissioner
Joseph Stephen Charter

Guatemala
13 Fawcett Street, London SW10 9HN
Telephone +44 (0) 20 7351 3042
Fax +44 (0) 20 7376 5708

Ambassador
Edmundo Rene Urrutia Garcia

Guinea
48 Onslow Gardens, London SW7 3PY
Telephone +44 (0) 20 7594 4819
Fax +44 (0) 20 7594 4819

Ambassador
Lansana Keita

Guinea-Bissau
PO Box 393, Tunbridge Wells, Kent TN4 9YZ
Telephone +44 (0) 1892 530478
Fax +44 (0) 18925 30478

Guinea-Bissau Honorary Consul
Mabel Figueiredo da Fonseca Smith

Guyana
3 Palace Court, Bayswater Road, London W2 4LP
Telephone +44 (0) 20 7229 7684
Fax +44 (0) 20 7727 9809

High Commissioner
Laleshwar K N Singh

Holy See
54 Parkside, London SW19 5NE
Telephone +44 (0) 20 8944 7189
Fax +44 (0) 20 8947 2494

Apostolic Nuncio
Archbishop Faustino Sainz Muñoz

Honduras
115 Gloucester Place, London W1U 6JT
Telephone +44 (0) 20 7486 4880
Fax +44 (0) 20 7486 4550

Ambassador
Ivan Romero-Nasser

Hungary
35 Eaton Place, London SW1X 8BY
Telephone +44 (0) 20 7201 3440
Fax +44 (0) 20 7823 1348
Website www.huemblon.org.uk

Ambassador
Borbála Czakó

Iceland
2A Hans Street, London SW1X 0JE
Telephone +44 (0) 20 7259 3999
Fax +44 (0) 20 7245 9649
Website www.iceland.org.uk

Ambassador
Sverrir Haukur Gunnlaugsson

India
India House, Aldwych, London WC2B 4NA
Telephone +44 (0) 20 7836 8484
Fax +44 (0) 20 7836 4331
Website www.hcilondon.org

High Commissioner
Kamalesh Sharma

Indonesia, Republic of
38 Grosvenor Square, London W1K 2HW
Telephone +44 (0) 20 7499 7661
Fax +44 (0) 20 7491 4993
Website www.indonesianembassy.org.uk

Ambassador
Dr Raden Mohammad Marty Muliana Natalegawa

Iran, Islamic Republic of
16 Prince's Gate, London SW7 1PT
Telephone +44 (0) 20 7225 3000
Fax +44 (0) 20 7589 4440
Website www.iran-embassy.org.uk

Ambassador
Rasoul Movahedian

Iraq
9 Holland Villas Road, London W14 8BP
Telephone +44 (0) 20 7602 8456
Fax +44 (0) 20 7602 8456
Website www.mofa.gov.iq

Ambassador
Dr Salah al Shaikhly

Ireland
17 Grosvenor Place, London SW1X 7HR
Telephone +44 (0) 20 7235 2171
Fax +44 (0) 20 7245 6961

Ambassador
Daithi O'Ceallaigh

Israel
2 Palace Green, London W8 4QB
Telephone +44 (0) 20 7957 9500
Fax +44 (0) 20 7957 9555
Website www.israel-embassy.org.uk

Ambassador
Zvi Heifetz

Italy
14 Three Kings Yard, Davies Street, London W1K 4EH
Telephone +44 (0) 20 7312 2200
Fax +44 (0) 20 7312 2230
Website www.amblondra.esteri.it

Ambassador
Giancarlo Aragona

Ivory Coast
2 Upper Belgrave Street, London SW1X 8BJ
Telephone +44 (0) 20 7201 9601/+44 (0) 20 7235 6991
Fax +44 (0) 20 7259 5320

Jamaica
12 Prince Consort Road, London SW7 2BZ
Telephone +44 (0) 20 7823 9911
Fax +44 (0) 20 7589 5154
Website www.jhcuk.com

High Commissioner
The Hon Burchell Anthony Whiteman

Japan
101104 Piccadilly, London W1J 7JT
Telephone +44 (0) 20 7465 6500
Fax +44 (0) 20 7491 9348
Website www.uk.emp-japan.go.jp

Ambassador
Yoshiji Nogami

Jordan, Hashemite Kingdom of
6 Upper Phillimore Gardens, London W8 7HA
Telephone +44 (0) 20 7937 3685
Fax +44 (0) 20 7937 8795
Website www.jordanembassyuk.org

Ambassador
Dr Alia Bouran

Kazakhstan
33 Thurlowe Square, London SW7 2DS
Telephone +44 (0) 20 7581 4646
Fax +44 (0) 20 7584 8481
Website www.kazakhstanembassy.org.uk

Ambassador
Erlan Idrissov

Kenya
Kenya High Commission, 45 Portland Place,
London W1N 4AS
Telephone +44 (0) 20 7636 2371

High Commissioner
Joseph Kirugumi Muchemi

Kiribati
c/o Michael R Walsh (Honorary Consul), The Great
House, Llanddewi Rydderch, Monmouthshire NP7 9UY
Telephone +44 (0) 1873 840375
Fax +44 (0) 1873 840375

Acting High Commissioner
Makurita Baaro (resides in Dominica)

Korea, Democratic People's Republic of (North Korea)
73 Gunnersbury Avenue, London W5 4LP
Telephone +44 (0) 20 8992 4965
Fax +44 (0) 20 8992 2053

Ambassador
Ja Song Nam

Korea, Republic of (South Korea)
60 Buckingham Gate, London SW1E 6AJ
Telephone +44 (0) 20 7227 5500/2
Fax +44 (0) 20 7227 5503
Website www.koreanembassy.org.uk

Ambassador
Dr Yoon-Je Cho

Kuwait
2 Albert Gate, Knightsbridge, London SW1X 7JU
Telephone +44 (0) 20 7590 3400
Fax +44 (0) 20 7823 1712
Website www.kuwaitinfo.org.uk

Ambassador
Khaled A A S Al Duwaisan

Kyrgyzstan
Ascot House, 119 Crawford Street, London W1U 6BJ
Telephone +44 (0) 20 7935 1462
Fax +44 (0) 20 7935 7449
Website www.kyrgyz-embassy.org.uk

Ambassador
Dr Kuban Mambetaliev

Laos
74 Avenue Raymond-Poincaré, 75116 Paris, France
Telephone +33 (1) 4553 0298
Fax +33 (1) 4727 5789

Ambassador
Soutsakhone Pathammavong (resides in Paris)

Latvia
45 Nottingham Place, London W1U 5LR
Telephone +44 (0) 20 7312 0040
Fax +44 (0) 20 7312 0042
Website www.london.am.gov.lv.en

Ambassador
Indulis Berziņš

Lebanon
21 Palace Garden Mews, London W8 4RA
Telephone +44 (0) 20 7229 7265
Fax +44 (0) 20 7243 1699

Ambassador
Milad Nammour

Lesotho
7 Chesham Place, Belgravia, London SW1 8HN
Telephone +44 (0) 20 7235 5686
Fax +44 (0) 20 7235 5023
Website www.lesotholondon.org.uk

High Commissioner
HRH Prince Seeiso Bereng Seeiso

Liberia
Embassy of the Republic of Liberia, 23 Fitzroy Square,
London W1 6EW
Telephone +44 (0) 20 7388 5489
Fax +44 (0) 20 7380 1593
Website www.embassyofliberia.org.uk

Ambassador
Wesley Momo Johnson

Libya
15 Knightsbridge, London SW1X 7LY
Telephone +44 (0) 20 7201 8280
Fax +44 (0) 20 7245 0588

Head of Mission
Omar R Jelban

Lithuania
84 Gloucester Place, London W1U 6AU
Telephone +44 (0) 20 7486 6401
Fax +44 (0) 20 7486 6403
Website www.lithuanianembassy.co.uk

Ambassador
Vygaudas Ušackas

Luxembourg
27 Wilton Crescent, London SW1X 8SD
Telephone +44 (0) 20 7235 6961
Fax +44 (0) 20 7235 9734

Ambassador
Jean-Louis Wolzfeld

Macedonia
Suites 2.1 & 2.2, Buckingham Court, 75-83 Buckingham
Gate, London SW1E 6PE
Telephone +44 (0) 20 7976 0535
Fax +44 (0) 20 7976 0539
Website www.macedonianembassy.org.uk

Head of Mission
Muhamed Halili

Madagascar
8-10 Hallam Street, London W1W 6JE
Telephone +44 (0) 20 3008 4550
Fax +44 (0) 20 3008 4551
Website www.embassy-madagascar-uk.com

Head of Mission
Iary Berthine Ravaoarimanana

Malawi
33 Grosvenor Street, London W1K 4QT
Telephone +44 (0) 20 8458 7714

High Commissioner
Dr Francis Moto

Malaysia
45 Belgrave Square, London SW1X 8QT
Telephone +44 (0) 20 7235 8033

High Commissioner
Dato' Abed Aziz bin Mohammed

Maldives
22 Nottingham Place, London W1U 5NJ
Telephone +44 (0) 20 7224 2135
Fax +44 (0) 20 7224 2157
Website www.maldiveshighcommission.org

High Commissioner
Hassan Sobir

Mali
Avenue Molière 487, 1050 Brussels, Belgium
Telephone +32 (2) 345 7432
Fax + 32 (2) 344 5700

Head of Mission
Ibrahim Bocar Ba (resides in Brussels)

Malta
Malta House, 36-38 Piccadilly, London W1V 0PQ
Telephone +44 (0) 20 7292 4800
Fax +44 (0) 20 7734 1831
Website www.foreign.gov.mt.london

High Commissioner
Dr Michael Refalo

Mauritania
8 Carlos Place, Mayfair, London W1K 3AS
Telephone +44 (0) 20 7478 9323
Fax +44 (0) 20 7478 9339

Ambassador
Ould Moctar Neche Mélaïnine

Mauritius
32/33 Elvaston Place, London SW7 5NW
Telephone +44 (0) 20 7581 0294

High Commissioner
Abhimanu Mahendra Kundasamy

Mexico
16 St George Street, London W1S 1LX
Telephone +44 (0) 20 7499 8586
Fax +44 (0) 20 7495 4035
Website www.embamex.co.uk

Ambassador
Juan Bremer de Martino

Moldova
5 Dolphin Square, Edensor Road, Chiswick,
London W4 2ST
Telephone +44 (0) 20 8995 6818
Fax +44 (0) 20 8995 6927
Website www.moldovanembassy.org.uk

Ambassador
Mariana Durleşteanu

Mongolia
7 Kensington Court, London W8 5DL
Telephone +44 (0) 20 7937 0150
Fax +44 (0) 20 7937 1117
Website www.embassyofmongolia.co.uk

Ambassador
Dalrain Davaasambuu

Morocco
49 Queen's Gate Gardens, London SW7 5NE
Telephone +44 (0) 20 7581 5001/4
Fax +44 (0) 20 7225 3862
Website www.maec.gov.ma

Ambassador
Mohammed Belmahi

Mozambique
21 Fitzroy Square, London W1T 6EL
Telephone +44 (0) 20 7383 3800
Fax +44 (0) 20 7383 3801
Website www.mozambiquehc.org.uk

High Commissioner
Antonio Gumende

Myanmar
19A Charles Street, Berkeley Square, London W1J 5DX
Telephone +44 (0) 20 7499 4340
Fax +44 (0) 20 7409 7043
Website www.myanmar.com

Ambassador
Nay Win

Namibia
6 Chandos Street, London W1G 9LU
Telephone +44 (0) 20 7636 6244
Fax +44 (0) 20 7637 5694

High Commissioner
George Mbanga Liswaniso

Nauru
Romshed Courtyard, Underriver, Kent TN15 0SD
Telephone +44 (0) 1732 746061
Fax +44 (0) 1732 454136

Nepal
12A Kensington Palace Gardens, London W8 4QU
Telephone +44 (0) 20 7229 1594
Fax +44 (0) 20 7792 9861
Website www.nepembassy.org.uk

Head of Mission
Dipendra P Bista

Netherlands
38 Hyde Park Gate, London SW7 5DP
Telephone +44 (0) 20 7590 3200
Fax +44 (0) 20 7225 0947
Website www.netherlands-embassy.org.uk

Ambassador
Pieter Willem Waldeck

New Zealand
New Zealand House, 80 The Haymarket,
London SW1Y 4TQ
Telephone +44 (0) 20 7930 8422
Fax +44 (0) 20 7839 4580
Website www.nzembassy.com

High Commissioner
The Rt Hon Jonathan Hunt

Nicaragua
Suite 31, Vicarage House, 58-60 Kensington Church Street,
London W8 4DP
Telephone +44 (0) 20 7938 2373
Fax +44 (0) 20 7937 0952
Website freespace.virgin.net/emb.ofnicaragua

Ambassador
Piero Paolo Coen Ubilla

Niger
154 rue de Longchamp, 75116 Paris, France
Telephone +33 (1) 4504 8060
Fax +33 (1) 4745 3494

Ambassador
Adamou Seydou (resides in Paris)

Nigeria
Nigeria House, 9 Northumberland Avenue,
London WC2N 5BX
Telephone +44 (0) 20 7839 1244
Fax +44 (0) 20 7839 8746
Website www.nigeriahc.org.uk

High Commissioner
Dr Christopher Olusola Kolade

Norway
25 Belgrave Square, London SW1X 8QD
Telephone +44 (0) 20 7591 5500
Fax +44 (0) 20 7245 6993
Website www.norway.org.uk

Ambassador
Bjarne Lindstrxm

Oman
167 Queen's Gate, London SW7 5HE
Telephone +44 (0) 20 7225 0001
Fax +44 (0) 20 7589 2505

Ambassador
Hussain Ali Abdullatif

Pakistan
35-36 Lowndes Square, London SW1X 9JN
Telephone +44 (0) 20 7664 9200
Fax +44 (0) 20 7664 9224
Website www.pakmission-uk.gov.pk

High Commissioner
Dr Maleeha Lodhi

Palestinian General Delegation to the United Kingdom
5 Galena Road, Hammersmith, London W6 0LT
Telephone +44 (0) 20 8563 0008
Fax +44 (0) 20 8563 0058

Ambassador
Prof Manuel S Hassassian

Panama
40 Hertford Street, London W1J 7SH
Telephone +44 (0) 20 7493 4646
Fax +44 (0) 20 7493 4333

Ambassador
Liliana Fernándes

Papua New Guinea
3rd Floor, 14 Waterloo Place, London SW1Y 4AR
Telephone +44 (0) 20 7930 0922/7
Fax +44 (0) 20 7930 0828
Website www.pnghighcomm.org.uk

High Commissioner
Jean Kekedo

Paraguay
344 High Street Kensington, 3rd Floor, London W14 8NS
Telephone +44 (0) 20 7610 4180
Fax +44 (0) 20 7371 4297
Website www.paraguayembassy.co.uk

Head of Mission
Maria Cristina Acosta Alvarez

Peru
52 Sloane Street, London SW1X 9SP
Telephone +44 (0) 20 7235 1917/2545
Fax +44 (0) 20 7235 4463
Website www.peruembassy-uk.com

Ambassador
Ricardo V Luna

Philippines
9A Palace Green, London W8 4QE
Telephone +44 (0) 20 7937 1600
Fax +44 (0) 20 7937 2925
Website www.philemb.org.uk

Ambassador
Edgardo B Espiritu

Poland
47 Portland Place, London W1B 1JH
Telephone +44 (0) 870 774 2700
Fax +44 (0) 870 744 2755
Website www.polishembassy.org.uk

Ambassador
Barbara Tuge-Erecińska

Portugal
11 Belgrave Square, London SW1X 8PP
Telephone +44 (0) 20 7235 5331
Fax +44 (0) 20 7245 1287

Ambassador
António Nunes de Carvalho Santana Carlos

Qatar
1 South Audley Street, London W1K 1NB
Telephone +44 (0) 20 7493 2200
Fax +44 (0) 20 7493 2661

Ambassador
Khalid bin Rashid bin Salim Al-Hamoudi Al-Mansouri

Romania
Arundel House, 4 Palace Green, London W8 4QD
Telephone +44 (0) 20 7937 9666
Fax +44 (0) 20 7937 8069
Website www.londra.mae.ro

Head of Mission
Raduta Matache

Russian Federation
6/7 Kensington Palace Gardens, London W8 4QP
Telephone +44 (0) 20 7229 2666
Fax +44 (0) 20 7727 8625
Website www.great-britain.mid.ru

Ambassador
Yury Viktorovich Fedotov

Rwanda
120-122 Seymour Street, London W1H 1NR
Telephone +44 (0) 20 7224 9832
Fax +44 (0) 20 7724 8642
Website www.ambarwanda.org.uk

Ambassador
Claver Gatete

São Tomé and Principe
c/o Miss Natalie Galland-Burkl (Honorary Consul), Flat 8,
Marsham Court, Victoria Drive, London SW19 6BB
Telephone +44 (0) 20 8788 6139
Fax +32 (2) 734 8815

Ambassador
Armindo de Brito Fernandes (resides in Brussels)

Saint Christopher and Nevis
2nd Floor, 10 Kensington Court, London W8 5DL
Telephone +44 (0) 20 7937 9718
Fax +44 (0) 20 7937 7484

High Commissioner
James Ernest Williams

Saint Lucia
1 Collingham Gardens, South Kensington,
London SW5 0HW
Telephone +44 (0) 20 7370 7123
Fax +44 (0) 20 7937 6040

High Commissioner
Emmanuel Cotter

Saint Vincent and the Grenadines
10 Kensington Court, London W8 5DL
Telephone +44 (0) 20 7565 2874

High Commissioner
Cenio Elwin Lewis

Samoa
Church Cottage, Pedlinge, Nr. Hythe, Kent CT21 4JL
Telephone +44 (0) 1303 260541
Fax +44 (0) 1303 238058

High Commissioner
Tuala Falani Chan Tung

San Marino
Consulate of the Republic of San Marino, Flat 51, 162
Sloane Street, London SW1X 9BS
Telephone +44 (0) 20 7823 4762
Fax +44 (0) 20 7823 4768

Ambassador
Contessa Marina Meneghetti de Camillo

Saudi Arabia
30 Charles Street, Mayfair, London W1J 5DZ
Telephone +44 (0) 20 7917 3000
Website www.saudiembassy.org.uk

Ambassador
HRH Prince Mohammed bin Nawaf bin Abdulaziz Al-
Saud

Senegal
39 Marloes Road, London W8 6LA
Telephone +44 (0) 20 7937 7237
Fax +44 (0) 20 7938 2546
Website www.senegalembassy.co.uk

Ambassador
Gen Mamadou Niang

Serbia
28 Belgrave Square, London SW1X 8QB
Telephone +44 (0) 20 7235 9049
Fax +44 (0) 20 7235 7092
Website www.yugoslavembassy.org.uk

Head of Mission
Dr Djoko Tripkovic

Seychelles
4th Floor, 111 Baker Street, London WIU 6RR
Telephone +33 (1) 4230 5747
Fax +44 (0) 1423 05740

Ambassador
Renette Nicette (resides in France)

Sierra Leone
41 Eagle Street, Holborn, London WC1 4TL
Telephone +44 (0) 20 7404 0140
Fax +44 (0) 20 7430 9862
Website www.slhc-uk.org.uk

Head of Mission
Melvin Humpah Chalobah

Singapore
9 Wilton Crescent, London SW1X 8SP
Telephone +44 (0) 20 7235 8315
Fax +44 (0) 20 7245 6583
Website www.mfa.gov

Ambassador
Michael Eng Cheng Teo

Slovakia
25 Kensington Palace Gardens, London W8 4QY
Telephone +44 (0) 20 7243 0803
Fax +44 (0) 20 7313 6481
Website www.slovakembassy.co.uk

Head of Mission
Radovan Javorčik

Slovenia
10 Little College Street, London SW1P 3SH
Telephone +44 (0) 20 7222 5700
Fax +44 (0) 20 7222 5277
Website www.gov.si

Ambassador
Iztok Mirošič

South Africa
South Africa House, Trafalgar Square,
London WC2N 5DP
Telephone +44 (0) 20 7451 7299
Fax +44 (0) 20 7451 7284
Website www.southafricahouse.com

High Commissioner
Dr Lindiwe Mabuza

Spain
39 Chesham Place, London SW1X 8SB
Telephone +44 (0) 20 7235 5555
Fax +44 (0) 20 7259 5392

Ambassador
Count Carlos Miranda

Sri Lanka
13 Hyde Park Gardens, London W2 2LU
Telephone +44 (0) 20 7262 18417
Fax +44 (0) 20 7262 7970
Website www.slhclondon.org

High Commissioner
Kshenuka Senewiratne

Sudan
3 Cleveland Row, St James's, London SW1A 1DD
Telephone +44 (0) 20 7839 8080
Fax +44 (0) 20 7839 7560
Website www.sudan-embassy.co.uk

Ambassador
Omer Mohammed Ahmed Siddig

Suriname
Amwedhkar Jethu (Honorary Consul), Flat 89, Pier House,
31 Cheyne Walk, London SW3 5HN
Telephone +44 (0) 20 7036 50844
Website ambassade.suriname@wxs.nl

Head of Mission
Susan M Derby

Swaziland
20 Buckingham Gate, London SW1E 6LB
Telephone +44 (0) 20 7630 6611
Fax +44 (0) 20 7630 6564

High Commissioner
Mary Madzandza Kanya

Sweden
11 Montagu Place, London W1H 2AL
Telephone +44 (0) 20 7917 6400
Fax +44 (0) 20 7724 4174
Website www.swedenabroad.com

Ambassador
Staffan Carlsson

Switzerland
16/18 Montagu Place, London W1H 2BQ
Telephone +44 (0) 20 7616 6000
Fax +44 (0) 20 7724 7001
Website www.swissembassy.org.uk

Ambassador
Alexis P Lautenberg

Syria
8 Belgrave Square, London SW1X 8PH
Telephone +44 (0) 20 7245 9012
Fax +44 (0) 20 7235 4621
Website www.syrianembassy.co.uk

Ambassador
Sami M Khiyami

Tajikistan
33 Orvington Square, London SW3 1JL
Telephone +44 (0) 20 7584 5111
Fax +44 (0) 20 7581 2669

Honorary Consul
Benjamin Brahms

Tanzania
Tanzania High Commission, 3 Stratford Place,
London W1C 1AS
Telephone +44 (0) 20 7569 1470
Fax +44 (0) 20 7495 8817
Website www.tanzania-online.gov.uk

High Commissioner
Mwanaidi Sinare Maajar

Thailand
29-30 Queen's Gate, London SW7 5JB
Telephone +44 (0) 20 7225 5512
Fax +44 (0) 20 7823 9695
Website www.thaiembassyuk.org.uk

Ambassador
Kitti Wasinondh

Togo
8 Rue AlfredRoll, 75017 Paris, France
Telephone + 33 (1) 4380 1213
Fax +33 (1) 4380 0605

Ambassador
Tchao Sotu Bere (resides in Paris)

Tonga
36 Molyneux Street, London W1H 5BQ
Telephone +44 (0) 20 7724 5828
Fax +44 (0) 20 7723 9074

High Commissioner
Dr Sione Ngongo Kioa

Trinidad and Tobago
42 Belgrave Square, London SW1X 8NT
Telephone +44 (0) 20 7245 9351
Fax +44 (0) 20 7823 1065
Website www.tnthighcomm.org.uk

High Commissioner
Glenda P Morean-Phillip

Tunisia
29 Prince's Gate, London SW7 1QG
Telephone +44 (0) 20 7584 8117
Fax +44 (0) 20 7225 2884

Ambassador
Riadh Ben Sliman

Turkey
43 Belgrave Square, London SW1X 8PA
Telephone +44 (0) 20 7393 0202
Fax +44 (0) 20 7393 0066
Website www.turkishconsulate.org.uk

Ambassador
Atilay Ersan

Turkmenistan
2nd Floor South, St George's House, 14/17 Wells Street,
London W1P 3FP
Telephone +44 (0) 20 7255 1071
Fax +44 (0) 20 7323 9184

Ambassador
Yazmurad N Seryaev

Tuvalu
Tuvalu House, 230 Worple Road, London SW20 8RH
Telephone +44 (0) 20 8879 0985
Fax +44 (0) 20 8879 0985

Honorary Consul
Dr Iftikhar Ayaz

Uganda
Uganda House, 58/59 Trafalgar Square,
London WC2N 5DX
Telephone +44 (0) 20 7839 5783
Fax +44 (0) 20 7839 8925

High Commissioner
Joan Kakima Nyakatuura Rwabyomere

Ukraine
60 Holland Park, London W11 3SJ
Telephone +44 (0) 20 7727 6312
Fax +44 (0) 20 7792 1708
Website www.ukremb.org.uk

Ambassador
Ihor Kharchenko

United Arab Emirates
30 Princes Gate, London SW7 1PT
Telephone +44 (0) 20 7581 1281
Fax +44 (0) 20 7581 9616
Website www.uaeembassyuk.net

Ambassador
Easa Saleh Al Gurg

United States
24 Grosvenor Square, London W1A 1AE
Telephone +44 (0) 20 7499 9000
Website www.usembassy.org.uk

Ambassador
Robert Holmes Tuttle

Uruguay
2nd Floor, 140 Brompton Road, London SW3 1HY
Telephone +44 (0) 20 7589 8835
Fax +44 (0) 20 7581 9585

Ambassador
Dr Ricardo Varela

Uzbekistan
41 Holland Park, London W11 3RP
Telephone +44 (0) 20 7229 7679
Fax +44 (0) 20 7229 7029
Website www.uzbekembassy.org

Ambassador
Tukhtapulat Tursunovich Riskiev

Vanuatu
High Commissioner, c/o Department for Foreign Affairs,
Port Vila

High Commissioner
Position vacant

Venezuela
1 Cromwell Road, London SW7 2HR
Telephone +44 (0) 20 7584 4206/7
Fax +44 (0) 20 7589 8887
Website www.venezlon.co.uk

Ambassador
Alfredo Toro-Hardy

Vietnam
12-14 Victoria Road, London W8 5RD
Telephone +44 (0) 20 7937 1912
Fax +44 (0) 20 7565 3853
Website www.vietnamembassy.org.uk

Ambassador
Nguyen Thi Nha

Yemen
57 Cromwell Road, London SW7 2ED
Telephone +44 (0) 20 7584 6607
Fax +44 (0) 20 7589 3350
Website www.yemenembassy.org.uk

Ambassador
Mohamed Taha Mustafa

Zambia
2 Palace Gate, Kensington, London W8 5NG
Telephone +44 (0) 20 7589 6655
Fax +44 (0) 20 7581 1353
Website www.zhcl.org.uk

High Commissioner
Anderson Kaseba Chibwa

Zimbabwe
Zimbabwe House, 429 Strand, London WC2R 0JR
Telephone +44 (0) 20 7836 7755
Fax +44 (0) 20 7379 1167
Website www.zimbabwe.embassyhomepage.com

Ambassador
Gabriel Mharadze Machinga

MEMBERS OF PARLIAMENT

The following pages detail all Members of Parliament, with their party
affiliation, listed by constituency.

Aberavon
Dr Hywel Francis (Lab)

Aberdeen North
Frank Doran (Lab)

Aberdeen South
Anne Begg (Lab)

Airdrie & Shotts
Rt Hon John Reid (Lab)

Aldershot
Gerald Howarth (Cons)

Aldridge-Brownhills
Richard Shepherd (Cons)

Altrincham & Sale West
Graham Brady (Cons)

Alyn & Deeside
Mark Tami (Lab)

Amber Valley
Judy Mallaber (Lab)

Angus
Mike Weir (SNP)

Argyll & Bute
Alan Reid (Lib Dem)

Arundel & South Downs
Nick Herbert (Cons)

Ashfield
Rt Hon Geoff Hoon (Lab)

Ashford
Damian Green (Cons)

Ashton-under-Lyne
David Heyes (Lab)

Aylesbury
David Lidington (Cons)

Ayr, Carrick & Cumnock
Sandra Osborne (Lab)

Banbury
Tony Baldry (Cons)

Banff & Buchan
Alex Salmond (SNP)

Barking
Rt Hon Margaret Hodge (Lab)

Barnsley Central
Eric Illsley (Lab)

Barnsley East & Mexborough
Jeff Ennis (Lab)

Barnsley West & Penistone
Michael Clapham (Lab)

Barrow & Furness
Rt Hon John Hutton (Lab)

Basildon
Angela E Smith (Lab/Co-op)

Basingstoke
Maria Miller (Cons)

Bassetlaw
John Mann (Lab)

Bath
Don Foster (Lib Dem)

Batley & Spen
Mike Wood (Lab)

Battersea
Martin Linton (Lab)

Beaconsfield
Dominic Grieve (Cons)

Beckenham
Jacqui Lait (Cons)

Bedford
Patrick Hall (Lab)

Belfast East
Peter Robinson (DUP)

Belfast North
Nigel Dodds (DUP)

Belfast South
Dr Alasdair McDonnell (SDLP)

Belfast West
Gerry Adams (Sinn Féin)

Berwickshire, Roxburgh & Selkirk
Michael Moore (Lib Dem)

Berwick-upon-Tweed
Rt Hon Alan Beith (Lib Dem)

Bethnal Green & Bow
George Galloway (Respect)

Beverley & Holderness
Graham Stuart (Cons)

Bexhill & Battle
Gregory Barker (Cons)

Bexleyheath & Crayford
David Evennett (Cons)

Billericay
John Baron (Cons)

Birkenhead
Rt Hon Frank Field (Lab)

Birmingham, Edgbaston
Gisela Stuart (Lab)

Birmingham, Erdington
Siôn Simon (Lab)

Birmingham, Hall Green
Stephen McCabe (Lab)

Birmingham, Hodge Hill
Liam Byrne (Lab)

Birmingham, Ladywood
Rt Hon Claire Short (Ind Lab)

Birmingham, Northfield
Richard Burden (Lab)

Birmingham, Perry Barr
Khalid Mahmood (Lab)

Birmingham, Selly Oak
Lynne Jones (Lab)

Birmingham, Sparkbrook & Small Heath
Roger Godsiff (Lab)

Birmingham, Yardley
John Hemming (Lib Dem)

Bishop Auckland
Helen Goodman (Lab)

Blaby
Andrew Robathan (Cons)

Blackburn
Rt Hon Jack Straw (Lab)

Blackpool North & Fleetwood
Joan Humble (Lab)

Blackpool South
Gordon Marsden (Lab)

Blaenau Gwent
Dai Davies (Ind)

Blaydon
David Anderson (Lab)

Blyth Valley
Ronnie Campbell (Lab)

Bognor Regis & Littlehampton
Nick Gibb (Cons)

Bolsover
Dennis Skinner (Lab)

Bolton North East
David Crausby (Lab)

Bolton South East
Dr Brian Iddon (Lab)

Bolton West
Rt Hon Ruth Kelly (Lab)

Bootle
Joe Benton (Lab)

Boston & Skegness
Mark Simmonds (Cons)

Bosworth
David Tredinnick (Cons)

Bournemouth East
Tobias Ellwood (Cons)

Bournemouth West
Sir John Butterfill (Cons)

Bracknell
Rt Hon Andrew Mackay (Cons)

Bradford North
Terry Rooney (Lab)

Bradford South
Gerry Sutcliffe (Lab)

Bradford West
Marsha Singh (Lab)

Braintree
Brooks Newmark (Cons)

Brecon & Radnorshire
Roger Williams (Lib Dem)

Brent East
Sarah Teather (Lib Dem)

Brent North
Barry Gardiner (Lab)

Brent South
Dawn Butler (Lab)

Brentford & Isleworth
Ann Keen (Lab)

Brentwood & Ongar
Eric Pickles (Cons)

Bridgend
Madeleine Moon (Lab)

Bridgwater
Ian Liddell-Grainger (Cons)

Brigg & Goole
Ian Cawsey (Lab)

Brighton, Kemptown
Dr Desmond Turner (Lab)

Brighton, Pavilion
David Lepper (Lab/Co-op)

Bristol East
Kerry McCarthy (Lab)

Bristol North West
Dr Doug Naysmith (Lab/Co-op)

Bristol South
Rt Hon Dawn Primarolo (Lab)

Bristol West
Stephen Williams (Lib Dem)

Bromley & Chislehurst
Bob Neill (Cons)

Bromsgrove
Julie Kirkbride (Cons)

Broxbourne
Charles Walker (Cons)

Broxtowe
Dr Nick Palmer (Lab)

Buckingham
John Bercow (Cons)

Burnley
Kitty Ussher (Lab)

Burton
Janet Dean (Lab)

Bury North
David Chaytor (Lab)

Bury South
Ivan Lewis (Lab)

Bury St Edmunds
David Ruffley (Cons)

Caernarfon
Hywel Williams (Plaid Cymru)

Caerphilly
Wayne David (Lab)

Caithness, Sutherland & Easter Ross
John Thurso (Lib Dem)

Calder Valley
Chris McCafferty (Lab)

Camberwell & Peckham
Rt Hon Harriet Harman (Lab)

Cambridge
David Howarth (Lib Dem)

Cannock Chase
Dr Tony Wright (Lab)

Canterbury
Julian Brazier (Cons)

Cardiff Central
Jenny Willott (Lib Dem)

Cardiff North
Julie Morgan (Lab)

Cardiff South & Penarth
Rt Hon Alun Michael (Lab/Co-op)

Cardiff West
Kevin Brennan (Lab)

Carlisle
Eric Martlew (Lab)

Carmarthen East & Dinefwr
Adam Price (Plaid Cymru)

Carmarthen West & South Pembrokeshire
Nick Ainger (Lab)

Carshalton & Wallington
Tom Brake (Lib Dem)

Castle Point
Dr Bob Spink (Cons)

Central Ayrshire
Brian H Donohoe (Lab)

Central Suffolk & North Ipswich
Sir Michael Lord (Second Deputy Chairman, Ways and
Means and Deputy Speaker)

Ceredigion
Mark Williams (Lib Dem)

Charnwood
Rt Hon Stephen Dorrell (Cons)

Chatham & Aylesford
Jonathan Shaw (Lab)

Cheadle
Mark Hunter (Lib Dem)

Cheltenham
Martin Horwood (Lib Dem)

Chesham & Amersham
Cheryl Gillan (Cons)

Chester, City of
Christine Russell (Lab)

Chesterfield
Paul Holmes (Lib Dem)

Chichester
Andrew Tyrie (Cons)

Chingford & Woodford Green
Rt Hon Iain Duncan Smith (Cons)

Chipping Barnet
Theresa Villiers (Cons)

Chorley
Lindsay Hoyle (Lab)

Christchurch
Christopher Chope (Cons)

Cities of London & Westminster
Mark Field (Cons)

Cleethorpes
Shona McIsaac (Lab)

Clwyd South
Martyn Jones (Lab)

Clwyd West
David Jones (Cons)

Coatbridge, Chryston & Bellshill
Rt Hon Tom Clarke (Lab)

Colchester
Bob Russell (Lib Dem)

Colne Valley
Kali Mountford (Lab)

Congleton
Ann Winterton (Cons)

Conwy
Betty Williams (Lab)

Copeland
Jamie Reed (Lab)

Corby
Phil Hope (Lab/Co-op)

Cotswold
Geoffrey Clifton-Brown (Cons)

Coventry North East
Rt Hon Bob Ainsworth (Lab)

Coventry North West
Geoffrey Robinson (Lab)

Coventry South
Jim Cunningham (Lab)

Crawley
Laura Moffatt (Lab)

Crewe & Nantwich
Gwyneth Dunwoody (Lab)

Crosby
Claire Curtis-Thomas (Lab)

Croydon Central
Andrew Pelling (Cons)

Croydon North
Malcolm Wicks (Lab)

Croydon South
Richard Ottaway (Cons)

Cumbernauld, Kilsyth & Kirkintilloch East
Rosemary McKenna (Lab)

Cynon Valley
Rt Hon Ann Clwyd (Lab)

Dagenham
Jon Cruddas (Lab)

Darlington
Rt Hon Alan Milburn (Lab)

Dartford
Dr Howard Stoate (Lab)

Daventry
Tim Boswell (Cons)

Delyn
Rt Hon David Hanson (Lab)

Denton & Reddish
Andrew Gwynne (Lab)

Derby North
Bob Laxton (Lab)

Derby South
Rt Hon Margaret Beckett (Lab)

Devizes
Rt Hon Michael Ancram (Cons)

Dewsbury
Shahid Malik (Lab)

Don Valley
Caroline Flint (Lab)

Doncaster Central
Rt Hon Rosie Winterton (Lab)

Doncaster North
Rt Hon Edward Miliband (Lab)

Dover
Gwyn Prosser (Lab)

Dudley North
Ian Austin (Lab)

Dudley South
Ian Pearson (Lab)

Dulwich & West Norwood
Rt Hon Tessa Jowell (Lab)

Dumfries & Galloway
Russell Brown (Lab)

Dumfriesshire, Clydesdale & Tweeddale
David Mundell (Cons)

Dundee East
Stewart Hosie (SNP)

Dundee West
Jim McGovern (Lab)

Dunfermline & West Fife
Willie Rennie (Lib Dem)

Durham, City of
Dr Roberta Blackman-Woods (Lab)

Ealing North
Stephen Pound (Lab)

Ealing, Acton & Shepherd's Bush
Andy Slaughter (Lab)

Ealing, Southall
Piara S Khabra (Lab)

Easington
John Cummings (Lab)

East Antrim
Sammy Wilson (DUP)

East Devon
Hugo Swire (Cons)

East Dunbartonshire
Jo Swinson (Lib Dem)

East Ham
Rt Hon Stephen Timms (Lab)

East Hampshire
Rt Hon Michael Mates (Cons)

East Kilbride, Strathaven & Lesmahagow
Rt Hon Adam Ingram (Lab)

East Londonderry
Gregory Campbell (DUP)

East Lothian
Anne Moffat (Lab)

East Renfrewshire
Jim Murphy (Lab)

East Surrey
Peter Ainsworth (Cons)

East Worthing & Shoreham
Tim Loughton (Cons)

East Yorkshire
Rt Hon Greg Knight (Cons)

Eastbourne
Nigel Waterson (Cons)

Eastleigh
Chris Huhne (Lib Dem)

Eccles
Ian Stewart (Lab)

Eddisbury
Stephen O'Brien (Cons)

Edinburgh East
Rt Hon Gavin Strang (Lab)

Edinburgh North & Leith
Mark Lazarowicz (Lab/Co-op)

Edinburgh South
Nigel Griffiths (Lab)

Edinburgh South West
Rt Hon Alistair Darling (Lab)

Edinburgh West
John Barrett (Lib Dem)

Edmonton
Andy Love (Lab/Co-op)

Ellesmere Port & Neston
Andrew Miller (Lab)

Elmet
Colin Burgon (Lab)

Eltham
Clive Efford (Lab)

Enfield North
Joan Ryan (Lab)

Enfield, Southgate
David Burrowes (Cons)

Epping Forest
Eleanor Laing (Cons)

Epsom & Ewell
Chris Grayling (Cons)

Erewash
Liz Blackman (Lab)

Erith & Thamesmead
John Austin (Lab)

Esher & Walton
Ian Taylor (Cons)

Exeter
Ben Bradshaw (Lab)

Falkirk
Eric Joyce (Lab)

Falmouth & Camborne
Julia Goldsworthy (Lib Dem)

Fareham
Mark Hoban (Cons)

Faversham & Mid Kent
Hugh Robertson (Cons)

Feltham & Heston
Alan Keen (Lab/Co-op)

Fermanagh & South Tyrone
Michelle Gildernew (Sinn Féin)

Finchley & Golders Green
Dr Rudi Vis (Lab)

Folkestone & Hythe
Rt Hon Michael Howard (Cons)

Forest of Dean
Mark Harper (Cons)

Foyle
Mark Durkan (SDLP)

Fylde
Rt Hon Michael Jack (Cons)

Gainsborough
Edward Leigh (Cons)

Gateshead East & Washington West
Sharon Hodgson (Lab)

Gedling
Vernon Coaker (Lab)

Gillingham
Paul Clark (Lab)

Glasgow Central
Mohammad Sarwar (Lab)

Glasgow East
David Marshall (Lab)

Glasgow North
Ann McKechin (Lab)

Glasgow North East
Rt Hon Michael J Martin (Speaker)

Glasgow North West
John Robertson (Lab)

Glasgow South
Tom Harris (Lab)

Glasgow South West
Ian Davidson (Lab/Co-op)

Glenrothes
John MacDougall (Lab)

Gloucester
Parmjit Dhanda (Lab)

Gordon
Rt Hon Malcolm Bruce (Lib Dem)

Gosport
Peter Viggers (Cons)

Gower
Martin Caton (Lab)

Grantham & Stamford
Quentin Davies (Cons)

Gravesham
Adam Holloway (Cons)

Great Grimsby
Austin Mitchell (Lab)

Great Yarmouth
Anthony Wright (Lab)

Greenwich & Woolwich
Rt Hon Nick Raynsford (Lab)

Guildford
Anne Milton (Cons)

Hackney North & Stoke Newington
Dianne Abbott (Lab)

Hackney South & Shoreditch
Meg Hillier (Lab/Co-op)

Halesowen & Rowley Regis
Sylvia Heal (First Deputy Chairman, Ways and Means and Deputy Speaker)

Halifax
Linda Riordan (Lab/Co-op)

Haltemprice & Howden
Rt Hon David Davis (Cons)

Halton
Derek Twigg (Lab)

Hammersmith & Fulham
Greg Hands (Cons)

Hampstead & Highgate
Glenda Jackson (Lab)

Harborough
Edward Garnier (Cons)

Harlow
Bill Rammell (Lab)

Harrogate & Knaresborough
Phil Willis (Lib Dem)

Harrow East
Tony McNulty (Lab)

Harrow West
Gareth Thomas (Lab/Co-op)

Hartlepool
Iain Wright (Lab)

Harwich
Douglas Carswell (Cons)

Hastings & Rye
Michael Jabez Foster (Lab)

Havant
David Willetts (Cons)

Hayes & Harlington
John McDonnell (Lab)

Hazel Grove
Andrew Stunell (Lib Dem)

Hemel Hempstead
Mike Penning (Cons)

Hemsworth
Jon Trickett (Lab)

Hendon
Andrew Dismore (Lab)

Henley
Boris Johnson (Cons)

Hereford
Paul Keetch (Lib Dem)

Hertford & Stortford
Mark Prisk (Cons)

Hertsmere
James Clappison (Cons)

Hexham
Peter Atkinson (Cons)

Heywood & Middleton
Jim Dobbin (Lab/Co-op)

High Peak
Tom Levitt (Lab)

Hitchin & Harpenden
Rt Hon Peter Lilley (Cons)

Holborn & St Pancras
Rt Hon Frank Dobson (Lab)

Hornchurch
James Brokenshire (Cons)

Hornsey & Wood Green
Lynne Featherstone (Lib Dem)

Horsham
Rt Hon Francis Maude (Cons)

Houghton & Washington East
Fraser Kemp (Lab)

Hove
Celia Barlow (Lab)

Huddersfield
Barry Sheerman (Lab/Co-op)

Huntingdon
Jonathan Djanogly (Cons)

Hyndburn
Greg Pope (Lab)

Ilford North
Lee Scott (Cons)

Ilford South
Mike Gapes (Lab/Co-op)

Inverclyde
David Cairns (Lab)

Inverness, Nairn, Badenoch & Strathspey
Danny Alexander (Lib Dem)

Ipswich
Chris Mole (Lab)

Isle of Wight
Andrew Turner (Cons)

Islington North
Jeremy Corbyn (Lab)

Islington South & Finsbury
Emily Thornberry (Lab)

Islwyn
Rt Hon Don Touhig (Lab/Co-op)

Jarrow
Stephen Hepburn (Lab)

Keighley
Ann Cryer (Lab)

Kensington & Chelsea
Rt Hon Sir Malcolm Rifkind (Cons)

Kettering
Philip Hollobone (Cons)

Kilmarnock & Loudoun
Rt Hon Des Browne (Lab)

Kingston & Surbiton
Edward Davey (Lib Dem)

Kingston upon Hull East
Rt Hon John Prescott (Lab)

Kingston upon Hull North
Diana R Johnson (Lab)

Kingston upon Hull West & Hessle
Rt Hon Alan Johnson (Lab)

Kingswood
Dr Roger Berry (Lab)

Kirkcaldy & Cowdenbeath
Rt Hon Gordon Brown (Lab)

Knowsley North & Sefton East
Rt Hon George Howarth (Lab)

Knowsley South
Edward O'Hara (Lab)

Lagan Valley
Jeffrey M Donaldson (DUP)

Lanark & Hamilton East
Jimmy Hood (Lab)

Lancaster & Wyre
Ben Wallace (Cons)

Leeds Central
Rt Hon Hilary Benn (Lab)

Leeds East
George Mudie (Lab)

Leeds North East
Fabian Hamilton (Lab)

Leeds North West
Greg Mulholland (Lib Dem)

Leeds West
Rt Hon John Battle (Lab)

Leicester East
Rt Hon Keith Vaz (Lab)

Leicester South
Sir Peter Soulsby (Lab)

Leicester West
Rt Hon Patricia Hewitt (Lab)

Leigh
Andy Burnham (Lab)

Leominster
Bill Wiggin (Cons)

Lewes
Norman Baker (Lib Dem)

Lewisham East
Bridget Prentice (Lab)

Lewisham West
Jim Dowd (Lab)

Lewisham, Deptford
Joan Ruddock (Lab)

Leyton & Wanstead
Harry Cohen (Lab)

Lichfield
Michael Fabricant (Cons)

Lincoln
Gillian Merron (Lab)

Linlithgow & East Falkirk
Michael Connarty (Lab)

Liverpool, Garston
Maria Eagle (Lab)

Liverpool, Riverside
Louise Ellman (Lab/Co-op)

Liverpool, Walton
Peter Kilfoyle (Lab)

Liverpool, Wavertree
Rt Hon Jane Kennedy (Lab)

Liverpool, West Derby
Robert N Wareing (Lab)

Livingston
Jim Devine (Lab)

Llanelli
Nia Griffith (Lab)

Loughborough
Andy Reed (Lab/Co-op)

Louth & Horncastle
Sir Peter Tapsell (Cons)

Ludlow
Philip Dunne (Cons)

Luton North
Kelvin Hopkins (Lab)

Luton South
Margaret Moran (Lab)

Macclesfield
Sir Nicholas Winterton (Cons)

Maidenhead
Rt Hon Theresa May (Cons)

Maidstone & The Weald
Rt Hon Ann Widdecombe (Cons)

Makerfield
Rt Hon Ian McCartney (Lab)

Maldon & East Chelmsford
John Whittingdale (Cons)

Manchester Central
Tony Lloyd (Lab)

Manchester, Blackley
Graham Stringer (Lab)

Manchester, Gorton
Rt Hon Sir Gerald Kaufman (Lab)

Manchester, Withington
John Leech (Lib Dem)

Mansfield
Alan Meale (Lab)

Medway
Robert Marshall-Andrews (Lab)

Meirionnydd Nant Conwy
Elfyn Llwyd (Plaid Cymru)

Meriden
Caroline Spelman (Cons)

Merthyr Tydfil & Rhymney
Dai Havard (Lab)

Mid Bedfordshire
Nadine Dorries (Cons)

Mid Dorset & North Poole
Annette Brooke (Lib Dem)

Mid Norfolk
Keith Simpson (Cons)

Mid Sussex
Hon Nicholas Soames (Cons)

Mid Ulster
Martin McGuinness (Sinn Féin)

Mid Worcestershire
Peter Luff (Cons)

Middlesbrough
Sir Stuart Bell (Lab)

Middlesbrough South & East Cleveland
Dr Ashok Kumar (Lab)

Midlothian
David Hamilton (Lab)

Milton Keynes South West
Dr Phyllis Starkey (Lab)

Mitcham & Morden
Siobhain McDonagh (Lab)

Mole Valley
Sir Paul Beresford (Cons)

Monmouth
David T C Davies (Cons)

Montgomeryshire
Lembit Öpik (Lib Dem)

Moray
Angus Robertson (SNP)

Morecambe & Lunesdale
Geraldine Smith (Lab)

Morley & Rothwell
Colin Challen (Lab)

Motherwell & Wishaw
Frank Roy (Lab)

Na h-Eileanan an Iar
Angus MacNeil (SNP)

Neath
Rt Hon Peter Hain (Lab)

New Forest East
Dr Julian Lewis (Cons)

New Forest West
Desmond Swayne (Cons)

Newark
Patrick Mercer (Cons)

Newbury
Richard Benyon (Cons)

Newcastle upon Tyne Central
Jim Cousins (Lab)

Newcastle upon Tyne East & Wallsend
Rt Hon Nicholas Brown (Lab)

Newcastle upon Tyne North
Doug Henderson (Lab)

Newcastle-under-Lyme
Paul Farrelly (Lab)

Newport East
Jessica Morden (Lab)

Newport West
Paul Flynn (Lab)

Newry & Armagh
Conor Murphy (Sinn Féin)

Normanton
Rt Hon Ed Balls (Lab/Co-op)

North Antrim
Rt Hon Ian Paisley (DUP)

North Ayrshire & Arran
Katy Clark (Lab)

North Cornwall
Dan Rogerson (Lib Dem)

North Devon
Nick Harvey (Lib Dem)

North Dorset
Robert Walter (Cons)

North Down
Lady Sylvia Hermon (UU)

North Durham
Kevan Jones (Lab)

North East Bedfordshire
Alistair Burt (Cons)

North East Cambridgeshire
Malcolm Moss (Cons)

North East Derbyshire
Natascha Engel (Lab)

North East Fife
Rt Hon Sir Menzies Campbell (Lib Dem)

North East Hampshire
Rt Hon James Arbuthnot (Cons)

North East Hertfordshire
Oliver Heald (Cons)

North East Milton Keynes
Mark Lancaster (Cons)

North Essex
Bernard Jenkin (Cons)

North Norfolk
Norman Lamb (Lib Dem)

North Shropshire
Owen Paterson (Cons)

North Southwark & Bermondsey
Simon Hughes (Lib Dem)

North Swindon
Michael Wills (Lab)

North Thanet
Roger Gale (Cons)

North Tyneside
Rt Hon Stephen Byers (Lab)

North Warwickshire
Mike O'Brien (Lab)

North West Cambridgeshire
Shailesh Vara (Cons)

North West Durham
Rt Hon Hilary Armstrong (Lab)

North West Hampshire
Rt Hon Sir George Young (Cons)

North West Leicestershire
David Taylor (Lab/Co-op)

North West Norfolk
Henry Bellingham (Cons)

North Wiltshire
James Gray (Cons)

Northampton North
Sally Keeble (Lab)

Northampton South
Brian Binley (Cons)

Northavon
Prof Steve Webb (Lib Dem)

Norwich North
Dr Ian Gibson (Lab)

Norwich South
Rt Hon Charles Clarke (Lab)

Nottingham East
John Heppell (Lab)

Nottingham North
Graham Allen (Lab)

Nottingham South
Alan Simpson (Lab)

Nuneaton
Bill Olner (Lab)

Ochil & South Perthshire
Gordon Banks (Lab)

Ogmore
Huw Irranca-Davies (Lab)

Old Bexley & Sidcup
Derek Conway (Cons)

Oldham East & Saddleworth
Phil Woolas (Lab)

Oldham West & Royton
Rt Hon Michael Meacher (Lab)

Orkney & Shetland
Alistair Carmichael (Lib Dem)

Orpington
John Horam (Cons)

Oxford East
Rt Hon Andrew Smith (Lab)

Oxford West & Abingdon
Dr Evan Harris (Lib Dem)

Paisley & Renfrewshire North
Jim Sheridan (Lab)

Paisley & Renfrewshire South
Rt Hon Douglas Alexander (Lab)

Pendle
Gordon Prentice (Lab)

Penrith & The Border
Rt Hon David Maclean (Cons)

Perth & North Perthshire
Pete Wishart (SNP)

Peterborough
Stewart Jackson (Cons)

Plymouth, Devonport
Alison Seabeck (Lab)

Plymouth, Sutton
Linda Gilroy (Lab/Co-op)

Pontefract & Castleford
Yvette Cooper (Lab)

Pontypridd
Dr Kim Howells (Lab)

Poole
Robert Syms (Cons)

Poplar & Canning Town
Jim Fitzpatrick (Lab)

Portsmouth North
Sarah McCarthy-Fry (Lab)

Portsmouth South
Mike Hancock (Lib Dem)

Preseli Pembrokeshire
Stephen Crabb (Cons)

Preston
Mark Hendrick (Lab/Co-op)

Pudsey
Paul Truswell (Lab)

Putney
Justine Greening (Cons)

Rayleigh
Mark Francois (Cons)

Reading East
Rob Wilson (Cons)

Reading West
Martin Salter (Lab)

Redcar
Vera Baird (Lab)

Redditch
Rt Hon Jacqui Smith (Lab)

Regent's Park & Kensington North
Karen Buck (Lab)

Reigate
Crispin Blunt (Cons)

Rhondda
Chris Bryant (Lab)

Ribble Valley
Nigel Evans (Cons)

Richmond (Yorks)
Rt Hon William Hague (Cons)

Richmond Park
Susan Kramer (Lib Dem)

Rochdale
Paul Rowen (Lib Dem)

Rochford & Southend East
James Duddridge (Cons)

Romford
Andrew Rosindell (Cons)

Romsey
Sandra Gidley (Lib Dem)

Ross, Skye & Lochaber
Rt Hon Charles Kennedy (Lib Dem)

Rossendale & Darwen
Janet Anderson (Lab)

Rother Valley
Rt Hon Kevin Barron (Lab)

Rotherham
Rt Hon Denis MacShane (Lab)

Rugby & Kenilworth
Jeremy Wright (Cons)

Ruislip - Northwood
Nick Hurd (Cons)

Runnymede & Weybridge
Philip Hammond (Cons)

Rushcliffe
Rt Hon Kenneth Clarke (Cons)

Rutherglen & Hamilton West
Rt Hon Thomas McAvoy (Lab/Co-op)

Rutland & Melton
Alan Duncan (Cons)

Ryedale
John Greenway (Cons)

Saffron Walden
Rt Hon Sir Alan Haselhurst (Chairman, Ways and Means and Deputy Speaker)

Salford
Rt Hon Hazel Blears (Lab)

Salisbury
Robert Key (Cons)

Scarborough & Whitby
Robert Goodwill (Cons)

Scunthorpe
Rt Hon Elliot Morley (Lab)

Sedgefield
Phil Wilson (Lab)

Selby
John Grogan (Lab)

Sevenoaks
Michael Fallon (Cons)

Sheffield Central
Rt Hon Richard Caborn (Lab)

Sheffield, Attercliffe
Clive Betts (Lab)

Sheffield, Brightside
Rt Hon David Blunkett (Lab)

Sheffield, Hallam
Nick Clegg (Lib Dem)

Sheffield, Heeley
Meg Munn (Lab/Co-op)

Sheffield, Hillsborough
Angela C Smith (Lab)

Sherwood
Paddy Tipping (Lab)

Shipley
Philip Davies (Cons)

Shrewsbury & Atcham
Daniel Kawczynski (Cons)

Sittingbourne & Sheppey
Derek Wyatt (Lab)

Skipton & Ripon
Rt Hon David Curry (Cons)

Sleaford & North Hykeham
Rt Hon Douglas Hogg (Cons)

Slough
Fiona Mactaggart (Lab)

Solihull
Lorely Burt (Lib Dem)

Somerton & Frome
David Heath (Lib Dem)

South Antrim
Rev Dr Willam McCrea (DUP)

South Cambridgeshire
Andrew Lansley (Cons)

South Derbyshire
Mark Todd (Lab)

South Dorset
Jim Knight (Lab)

South Down
Eddie McGrady (SDLP)

South East Cambridgeshire
James Paice (Cons)

South East Cornwall
Colin Breed (Lib Dem)

South Holland & The Deepings
John Hayes (Cons)

South Norfolk
Richard Bacon (Cons)

South Ribble
David S Borrow (Lab)

South Shields
Rt Hon David Miliband (Lab)

South Staffordshire
Sir Patrick Cormack (Cons)

South Suffolk
Tim Yeo (Cons)

South Swindon
Anne Snelgrove (Lab)

South Thanet
Dr Stephen Ladyman (Lab)

South West Bedfordshire
Andrew Selous (Cons)

South West Devon
Gary Streeter (Cons)

South West Hertfordshire
David Gauke (Cons)

South West Norfolk
Christopher Fraser (Cons)

South West Surrey
Jeremy Hunt (Cons)

Southampton, Itchen
Rt Hon John Denham (Lab)

Southampton, Test
Dr Alan Whitehead (Lab)

Southend West
David Amess (Cons)

Southport
Dr John Pugh (Lib Dem)

Spelthorne
David Wilshire (Cons)

St Albans
Anne Main (Cons)

St Helens North
Dave Watts (Lab)

St Helens South
Shaun Woodward (Lab)

St Ives
Andrew George (Lib Dem)

Stafford
David Kidney (Lab)

Staffordshire Moorlands
Charlotte Atkins (Lab)

Stalybridge & Hyde
James Purnell (Lab)

Stevenage
Barbara Follett (Lab)

Stirling
Anne McGuire (Lab)

Stockport
Ann Coffey (Lab)

Stockton North
Frank Cook (Lab)

Stockton South
Dari Taylor (Lab)

Stoke-on-Trent Central
Mark Fisher (Lab)

Stoke-on-Trent North
Joan Walley (Lab)

Stoke-on-Trent South
Robert Flello (Lab)

Stone
William Cash (Cons)

Stourbridge
Lynda Waltho (Lab)

Strangford
Iris Robinson (DUP)

Stratford-on-Avon
John Maples (Cons)

Streatham
Rt Hon Keith Hill (Lab)

Stretford & Urmston
Rt Hon Beverley Hughes (Lab)

Stroud
David Drew (Lab/Co-op)

Suffolk Coastal
Rt Hon John Gummer (Cons)

Sunderland North
Bill Etherington (Lab)

Sunderland South
Chris Mullin (Lab)

Surrey Heath
Michael Gove (Cons)

Sutton & Cheam
Paul Burstow (Lib Dem)

Sutton Coldfield
Andrew Mitchell (Cons)

Swansea East
Siân C James (Lab)

Swansea West
Rt Hon Alan Williams (Lab)

Tamworth
Brian Jenkins (Lab)

Tatton
George Osborne (Cons)

Taunton
Jeremy Browne (Lib Dem)

Teignbridge
Richard Younger-Ross (Lib Dem)

Telford
David Wright (Lab)

Tewkesbury
Laurence Robertson (Cons)

Thurrock
Andrew Mackinlay (Lab)

Tiverton & Honiton
Angela Browning (Cons)

Tonbridge & Malling
Rt Hon Sir John Stanley (Cons)

Tooting
Sadiq Khan (Lab)

Torbay
Adrian Sanders (Lib Dem)

Torfaen
Rt Hon Paul Murphy (Lab)

Torridge & West Devon
Geoffrey Cox (Cons)

Totnes
Anthony Steen (Cons)

Tottenham
David Lammy (Lab)

Truro & St Austell
Matthew Taylor (Lib Dem)

Tunbridge Wells
Greg Clark (Cons)

Twickenham
Dr Vincent Cable (Lib Dem)

Tyne Bridge
David Clelland (Lab)

Tynemouth
Alan Campbell (Lab)

Upminster
Angela Watkinson (Cons)

Upper Bann
David Simpson (DUP)

Uxbridge
John Randall (Cons)

Vale of Clwyd
Chris Ruane (Lab)

Vale of Glamorgan
John Smith (Lab)

Vale of York
Anne McIntosh (Cons)

Vauxhall
Kate Hoey (Lab)

Wakefield
Mary Creagh (Lab)

Wallasey
Angela Eagle (Lab)

Walsall North
David Winnick (Lab)

Walsall South
Rt Hon Bruce George (Lab)

Walthamstow
Neil Gerrard (Lab)

Wansbeck
Denis Murphy (Lab)

Wansdyke
Dan Norris (Lab)

Wantage
Edward Vaizey (Cons)

Warley
Rt Hon John Spellar (Lab)

Warrington North
Helen Jones (Lab)

Warrington South
Helen Southworth (Lab)

Warwick & Leamington
James Plaskitt (Lab)

Watford
Claire Ward (Lab)

Waveney
Bob Blizzard (Lab)

Wealden
Charles Hendry (Cons)

Weaver Vale
Mike Hall (Lab)

Wellingborough
Peter Bone (Cons)

Wells
Rt Hon David Heathcoat-Amory (Cons)

Welwyn Hatfield
Grant Shapps (Cons)

Wentworth
John Healey (Lab)

West Aberdeenshire & Kincardine
Sir Robert Smith (Lib Dem)

West Bromwich East
Tom Watson (Lab)

West Bromwich West
Adrian Bailey (Lab/Co-op)

West Chelmsford
Simon Burns (Cons)

West Derbyshire
Rt Hon Patrick McLoughlin (Cons)

West Dorset
Rt Hon Oliver Letwin (Cons)

West Dunbartonshire
Rt Hon John McFall (Lab/Co-op)

West Ham
Lyn Brown (Lab)

West Lancashire
Rosie Cooper (Lab)

West Suffolk
Richard Spring (Cons)

West Tyrone
Pat Doherty (Sinn Féin)

West Worcestershire
Sir Michael Spicer (Cons)

Westbury
Dr Andrew Murrison (Cons)

Westmorland & Lonsdale
Tim Farron (Lib Dem)

Weston-Super-Mare
John Penrose (Cons)

Wigan
Neil Turner (Lab)

Wimbledon
Stephen Hammond (Cons)

Winchester
Mark Oaten (Lib Dem)

Windsor
Adam Afriyie (Cons)

Wirral South
Ben Chapman (Lab)

Wirral West
Stephen Hesford (Lab)

Witney
Rt Hon David Cameron (Cons)

Woking
Humfrey Malins (Cons)

Wokingham
Rt Hon John Redwood (Cons)

Wolverhampton North East
Ken Purchase (Lab/Co-op)

Wolverhampton South East
Pat McFadden (Lab)

Wolverhampton South West
Rob Marris (Lab)

Woodspring
Dr Liam Fox (Cons)

Worcester
Michael Foster (Lab)

Workington
Tony Cunningham (Lab)

Worsley
Barbara Keeley (Lab)

Worthing West
Peter Bottomley (Cons)

Wrekin, The
Mark Pritchard (Cons)

Wrexham
Ian Lucas (Lab)

Wycombe
Paul Goodman (Cons)

Wyre Forest
Dr Richard Taylor (Ind)

Wythenshawe & Sale East
Paul Goggins (Lab)

Yeovil
David Laws (Lib Dem)

Ynys Mtn
Albert Owen (Lab)

York, City of
Hugh Bayley (Lab)

MEMBERS OF THE SCOTTISH PARLIAMENT

The following pages detail all Members of the Scottish Parliament, with their
party affiliation, listed by constituency.

Aberdeen Central
Lewis MacDonald (Lab)

Aberdeen North
Brian Adam (SNP)

Aberdeen South
Nicol Stephen (Lib Dem)

Aberdeenshire West & Kincardine
Mike Rumbles (Lib Dem)

Airdrie & Shotts
Karen Whitefield (Lab)

Angus
Andrew Welsh (SNP)

Argyll & Bute
Jim Mather (SNP)

Ayr
John Scott (Cons)

Banff & Buchan
Stewart Stevenson (SNP)

Caithness Sutherland & Easter Ross
Jamie Stone (Lib Dem)

Carrick Cumn & Doon
Cathy Jamieson (Lab)

Central Scotland
Linda Fabiani (SNP), Jamie Hepburn (SNP), Christina
McKelvie (SNP), Margaret Mitchell (Cons), Alex Neil
(SNP), Hugh O'Donnell (Lib Dem), John Wilson (SNP)

Clydebank & Milngavie
Des McNulty (Lab)

Clydesdale
Karen Gillon (Lab)

Coatbridge & Chryston
Elaine Smith (Lab)

Cumbernauld & Kilsyth
Cathie Craigie (Lab)

Cunninghame North
Kenneth Gibson (SNP)

Cunninghame South
Irene Oldfather (Lab)

Dumbarton
Jackie Baillie (Lab)

Dumfermline East
Helen Eadie (Lab)

Dumfermline West
Jim Tolson (Lib Dem)

Dumfries
Elaine Murray (Lab)

Dundee East
Shona Robison (SNP)

Dundee West
Joe Fitzpatrick (SNP)

East Kilbride
Andy Kerr (Lab)

East Lothian
Iain Gray (Lab)

Eastwood
Kenneth Macintosh (Lab)

Edinburgh Central
Sarah Boyack (Lab)

Edinburgh East
Kenny MacAskill (SNP)

Edinburgh North & Leith
Malcolm Chisolm (Lab)

Edinburgh Pentlands
David McLetchie (Cons)

Edinburgh South
Mike Pringle (Lib Dem)

Edinburgh West
Margaret Smith (Lib Dem)

Falkirk East
Cathy Peattie (Lab)

Falkirk West
Michael Matheson (SNP)

Fife Central
Tricia Marwick (SNP)

Fife North East
Iain Smith (Lib Dem)

Galloway & Upper Nithsdale
Alex Fergusson (Cons)

Glasgow
Bashir Ahmad (SNP), Bill Aiken (Cons), Robert Brown
(Lib Dem), Bob Doris (SNP), Patrick Harvie (Green), Bill
Kidd (SNP), Sandra White (SNP)

Glasgow Anniesland
Bill Butler (Lab)

Glasgow Ballieston
Margaret Curran (Lab)

Glasgow Cathcart
Charlie Gordon (Lab)

Glasgow Govan
Nicola Sturgeon (SNP)

Glasgow Kelvin
Pauline McNeil (Lab)

Glasgow Maryhill
Patricia Ferguson (Lab)

Glasgow Pollok
Johann Lamont (Lab)

Glasgow Rutherglen
James Kelly (Lab)

Glasgow Shettleston
Frank McAveety (Lab)

Glasgow Springburn
Paul Martin (Lab)

Gordon
Alex Salmond (SNP)

Greenock & Inverclyde
Duncan McNeil (Lab)

Hamilton North & Bellshill
Michael McMahon (Lab)

Hamilton South
Tom McCabe (Lab)

Highlands and Islands
Rob Gibson (SNP), Rhoda Grant (Lab), Jamie McGrigor
(Cons), Peter Peacock (Lab), Mary Scanlon (Cons), David
Stewart (Lab), Dave Thompson (SNP)

Inverness East Nairn & Loch
Fergus Ewing (SNP)

Kilmarnock & Loudoun
Willie Coffey (SNP)

Kirkcaldy
Marilyn Livingstone (Lab)

Linlithgow
Mary Mulligan (Lab)

Livingston
Angela Constance (SNP)

Lothians
Gavin Brown (Cons), George Foulkes (Lab), Robin Harber
(Green), Fiona Hyslop (SNP), Margo MacDonald (Ind), Ian
McKee (SNP), Stefan Tymkewycz (SNP)

Mid Scotland and Fife
Claire Baker (Lab), Ted Brocklebank (Cons), Murdo Fraser
(Cons), Christopher Harvie (SNP), John Park (Lab),
Richard Simpson (Lab), Elizabeth Smith (Cons)

Midlothian
Rhona Brankin (Lab)

Moray
Richard Lochead (SNP)

Motherwell & Wishaw
Jack McConnell (Lab)

North East Scotland
Richard Baker (Lab), Nigel Don (SNP), Marlyn Glen (Lab),
Alex Johnstone (Lab), Alison McInnes (Lib Dem), Nanette
Milne (Cons), Maureen Watt (SNP)

Ochil
Keith Brown (SNP)

Orkney
Liam McArthur (Lib Dem)

Paisley North
Wendy Alexander (Lab)

Paisley South
Hugh Henry (Lab)

Perth
Roseanna Cunningham (SNP)

Ross, Skye & Inverness West
John Farquhar Munro (Lib Dem)

Roxburgh & Berwickshire
John Lamont (Cons)

Shetland
Tavish Scott (Lib Dem)

South of Scotland
Derek Brownlee (Cons), Aileen Campbell (SNP), Christine
Grahame (SNP), Jim Hume (Lib Dem), Adam Ingram
(SNP), Alasdair Morgan (SNP), Michael Russell (SNP)

Stirling
Bruce Crawford (SNP)

Strathkelvin & Bearsden
David Whitton (Lab)

Tayside North
John Swinney (SNP)

Tweeddale, Ett & Laud
Jeremy Purvis (Lib Dem)

West of Scotland
Jackson Carlaw (Cons), Ross Finnie (Lib Dem), Annabel Goldie (Cons), Stewart Maxwell (SNP), Stuart McMillan (SNP), Gil Paterson (SNP), Bill Wilson (SNP)

West Renfrewshire
Trish Godman (Lab)

Western Isles
Allistair Allan (SNP)

MEMBERS OF THE NATIONAL ASSEMBLY FOR WALES

Details of all Members of the National Assembly for Wales, with their party
affiliation, listed by constituency.

Aberavon
Brian Gibbons (Lab)

Aberconwy
Gareth Jones (Plaid Cymru)

Alyn & Deeside
Carl Sargeant (Lab)

Arfon
Alun Ffred Jones (Plaid Cymru)

Blaenau Gwent
Trish Law (Ind)

Brecon & Radnorshire
Kirsty Williams (Lib Dem)

Bridgend
Carwyn Jones (Lab)

Caerphilly
Jeff Cuthbert (Lab)

Cardiff Central
Jenny Randerson (Lib Dem)

Cardiff North
Jonathan Morgan (Cons)

Cardiff South and Penarth
Lorraine Barrett (Lab)

Cardiff West
Rhodri Morgan (Lab)

Carmarthen East & Dinefwr
Rhodri Glyn Thomas (Plaid Cymru)

Carmarthen West & Pembrokeshire South
Angela Burns (Cons)

Ceredigion
Elin Jones (Plaid Cymru)

Clwyd South
Karen Sinclair (Lab)

Clwyd West
Darren Millar (Cons)

Cynon Valley
Christine Chapman (Lab)

Delyn
Sandy Mewies (Lab)

Dwyfor Meirionnydd
Dafydd Elis-Thomas (Plaid Cymru)

Gower
Edwina Hart (Lab)

Islwyn
Irene James (Lab)

Llanelli
Helen Mary Jones (Plaid Cymru)

Merthyr Tydfil
Huw Lewis (Lab)

Mid and West Wales
Nicholas Bourne (Cons), Alun Davies (Cons), Nerys Evans
(Plaid Cymru), Joyce Watson (Lab)

Monmouth
Nick Ramsay (Cons)

Montgomeryshire
Mick Bates (Lib Dem)

Neath
Gwenda Thomas (Lab)

Newport East
John Griffiths (Lab)

Newport West
Rosemary Butler (Lab)

North Wales
Eleanor Burnham (Lib Dem), Mark Isherwood (Cons),
Janet Ryder (Plaid Cymru), Brynle Williams (Cons)

Ogmore
Janice Gregory (Lab)

Pontypridd
Jane Davidson (Lab)

Preseli Pembrokeshire
Paul Davies (Cons)

Rhondda
Leighton Andrews (Lab)

South Wales Central
Andrew R Davies (Cons), Christopher Franks (Plaid
Cymru), David Melding (Cons), Leanne Wood (Plaid
Cymru)

South Wales East
Mohammad Asghar (Plaid Cymru), Jocelyn Davies (Plaid
Cymru), Michael German (Lib Dem), William Graham
(Cons)

South Wales West
Peter Black (Lib Dem), Alun Cairns (Cons), Bethan
Jenkins (Plaid Cymru), Dai Lloyd (Plaid Cymru)

Swansea East
Val Lloyd (Lab)

Swansea West
Andrew Davies (Lab)

Torfaen
Lynne Neagle (Lab)

Vale of Clwyd
Ann Jones (Lab)

Vale of Glamorgan
Jane Hutt (Lab)

Wrexham
Lesley Griffiths (Lab)

Ynys Mon
Ieuan Wyn Jones (Plaid Cymru)

MEMBERS OF THE NORTHERN IRELAND ASSEMBLY

Details of all Members of the Northern Ireland Assembly, with their party
affiliation, listed by constituency.

Belfast East
Wallace Browne (DUP), Reg Empey (UU), Naomi Long
(Alliance), Robin Newton (DUP), Dawn Purvis
(Progressive Unionist), Peter Robinson (DUP)

Belfast North
Fred Cobain (UU), Nigel Dodds (DUP), Gerry Kelly (Sinn
Féin), Alban Maginness (SDLP), Nelson McCausland
(DUP), Caral Ni Chuilin (Sinn Féin)

Belfast South
Carmel Hanna (SDLP), Anna Lo (Alliance), Alex Maskey
(Sinn Féin), Alasdair McDonnell (SDLP), Michael
McGimpsey (UU), Jimmy Spratt (DUP)

Belfast West
Gerry Adams (Sinn Féin), Alex Attwood (SDLP), Paul
Maskey (Sinn Féin), Fra McCann (Sinn Féin), Jennifer
McCann (Sinn Féin), Sue Ramsey (Sinn Féin)

East Antrim
Roy Beggs (UU), George Dawson (DUP), David Hilditch
(DUP), Sean Neeson (Alliance), Ken Robinson (UU),
Sammy Wilson (DUP)

East Londonderry
Francie Brolly (Sinn Féin), Gregory Campbell (DUP), John
Dallat (SDLP), David McClarty (UU), Adrian McQuillan
(DUP), George Robinson (DUP)

Fermanagh & South Tyrone
Tom Elliott (UU), Arlene Foster (DUP), Tommy Gallagher
(SDLP), Michelle Gildernew (Sinn Féin), Gerry McHugh
(Sinn Féin), Maurice Morrow (DUP)

Foyle
Martina Anderson (Sinn Féin), Mary Bradley (SDLP),
Mark Durkan (SDLP), William Hay (DUP), Raymond
McCartney (Sinn Féin), Pat Ramsey (SDLP)

Lagan Valley
Paul Butler (Sinn Féin), Jonathan Craig (DUP), Jeffrey
Donaldson (DUP), Trevor Lunn (Alliance), Basil McCrea
(UU), Edwin Poots (DUP)

Mid-Ulster
Billy Armstrong (UU), Ian McCrea (DUP), Patsy McGlone
(SDLP), Martin McGuinness (Sinn Féin), Francie Molloy
(Sinn Féin), Michelle O'Neill (Sinn Féin)

Newry & Armagh
Cathal Boylan (Sinn Féin), Dominic Bradley (SDLP),
Micky Brady (Sinn Féin), William Irwin (DUP), Danny
Kennedy (UU), Conor Murphy (Sinn Féin)

North Antrim
Robert Coulter (UU), Daithi McKay (Sinn Féin), Declan
O'Loan (SDLP), Ian Paisley (DUP), Ian Paisley Jr (DUP),
Mervyn Storey (DUP)

North Down
Leslie Cree (UU), Alex Easton (DUP), Stephen Farry
(Alliance), Alan McFarland (UU), Peter Weir (DUP), Brian
Wilson (Green)

South Antrim
Thomas Burns (SDLP), David Burnside (UU), Trevor
Clarke (DUP), David Ford (Alliance), William McCrea
(DUP), Mitchel McLaughlin (Sinn Féin)

South Down
PJ Bradley (SDLP), Willie Clarke (Sinn Féin), John
McCallister (UU), Margaret Ritchie (SDLP), Caitriona
Ruane (Sinn Féin), Jim Wells (DUP)

Strangford
Simon Hamilton (DUP), Kieran McCarthy (Alliance),
Michelle McIlveen (DUP), David McNarry (UU), Iris
Robinson (DUP), Jim Shannon (DUP)

Upper Bann
Sam Gardiner (UU), Dolores Kelly (SDLP), Stephen
Moutray (DUP), John O'Dowd (Sinn Féin), George Savage
(UU), David Simpson (DUP)

West Tyrone
Allan Bresland (DUP), Thomas Buchanan (DUP), Keiran
Deeny (Ind), Pat Doherty (Sinn Féin), Barry McElduff
(Sinn Féin), Claire McGill (Sinn Féin)

MEMBERS OF THE EUROPEAN PARLIAMENT

MEMBERS OF THE EUROPEAN PARLIAMENT

Details of all the UK Members of the European Parliament, listed by constituency.

East Midlands
Derek Roland Clark (UKIP), Christopher Heaton-Harris (Cons), Roger Helmer (Cons), Robert Kilroy-Silk (Ind), Bill Newton Dunn (Lib Dem), Glenis Willmott (Lab)

Eastern
Christopher Beazley (Cons), Andrew Duff (Lib Dem), Richard Howitt (Lab), Robert Sturdy (Cons), Jeffrey Titford (UKIP), Geoffrey Van Orden (Cons), Thomas Wise (UKIP)

London
Gerard Batten (UKIP), John Bowis (Cons), Robert Evans (Lab), Mary Honeyball (Lab), Syed Kamall (Cons), Jean Lambert (Green), Baroness Ludford (Lib Dem), Claude Moraes (Lab), CharlesTannock (Cons)

North East
Martin Callanan (Cons), Fiona Hall (Lib Dem), Stephen Hughes (Lab)

North West
Sir Robert Atkins (Cons), Chris Davies (Lib Dem), Den Dover (Cons), Sajjad Karim (Lib Dem), Arlene McCarthy (Lab), Brian Simpson (Lab), David Sumberg (Cons), Gary Titley (Lab), John Whittaker (UKIP)

Northern Ireland
Jim Allister (Ind), Bairbre de Brún (Sinn Féin), James Nicholson (UUP)

Scotland
Elspeth Attwooll (Lib Dem), Ian Hudghton (SNP), David Martin (Lab), John Purvis (Scot Cons), Alyn Smith (SNP), Struan Stevenson (Scot Cons), Catherine Stihler (Lab)

South East
Richard James Ashworth (Cons), Sharon Bowles (Lib Dem), Nirj Deva (Cons), James Elles (Cons), Nigel Farage (UKIP), Daniel Hannan (Cons), Caroline Lucas (Green), Ashley Mote (Ind), Baroness Nicholson of Winterbourne (Lib Dem), Peter Skinner (Lab)

South West
Graham Booth (UKIP), Giles Chichester (Cons), Glyn Ford (Lab), Caroline Jackson (Cons), Roger Knapman (UKIP), Neil Parish (Cons), Graham Watson (Lib Dem)

Wales
Jill Evans (Plaid Cymru), Jonathan Evans (Cons), Glenys Kinnock (Lab), Eluned Morgan (Lab)

West Midlands
Philip Bradbourn (Cons), Philip Bushill-Matthews (Cons), Michael Cashman (Lab), Neena Gill (Lab), Malcolm Harbour (Cons), Elizabeth Lynne (Lib Dem), Michael Henry Nattrass (UKIP)

Yorkshire and the Humber
Godfrey Bloom (UKIP), Richard Corbett (Lab), Timothy Kirkhope (Cons), Linda McAvan (Lab), Edward McMillan-Scott (Cons), Diana Wallis (Lib Dem)

CIVIL SERVICE

The following pages detail the highest-ranking personnel for the main
Government departments in the UK.

Attorney General's Office
20 Victoria Street, London SW1H 0NF
Telephone +44 (0) 20 7271 2492
Fax +44 (0) 20 7271 2434
Website www.attorneygeneral.gov.uk

Attorney General
Baroness Scotland of Asthal
Solicitor General
Vera Baird

Cabinet Office
70 Whitehall, London SW1A 2AS
Telephone +44 (0) 20 7276 1234
Website www.cabinetoffice.gov.uk

Minister, Chancellor of the Duchy of Lancaster
The Rt Hon Ed Miliband
Cabinet Secretary
Sir Gus O'Donnell
Permanent Secretary
Phil Hope

Central Office of Information
Hercules House, Hercules Road, London SE1 7DU
Telephone +44 (0) 20 7928 5037
Fax +44 (0) 20 7928 5037
Website www.coi.gov.uk

Chief Executive
Alan Bishop
Management Board Members
M Baxter, P M Buchanan, I R Hamilton, G Hooper, S E
Whetton, A Wade, E Lochhead, G W Beasant, R Haslam

Charity Commission
Harmsworth House, Bouverie Street, London EC4Y 8DP
Telephone +44 (0) 845 300 0218
Website www.charitycommission.gov.uk

Chair
Dame Suzi Leather
Chief Executive
Andrew Hind

The Crown Estate
16 New Burlington Place, London W1S 2HX
Telephone +44 (0) 20 7851 5000
Website www.thecrownestate.co.uk

Chairman
Ian Grant
Chief Executive
Roger Bright

Crown Prosecution Service
50 Ludgate Hill, London EC4M 7EX
Telephone +44 (0) 20 7796 8000
Website www.cps.gov.uk

Director of Public Prosecutions
Sir Ken Macdonald
Principal Private Secretary to Director and Head of Private Office
Jackie Ronchetti

Department for Children, Schools and Families
Sanctuary Buildings, Great Smith Street,
London SW1P 3BT
Telephone +44 (0) 870 000 2288
Fax +44 (0) 192 879 4248
Website www.dcsf.gov.uk

Secretary of State
The Rt Hon Ed Balls
Ministers of State
Jim Knight (Schools) and Beverley Hughes (Children)
Parliamentary Under Secretaries of State
Kevin Brennan and Lord Adonis (Schools)
Permanent Secretary
David Bell

Department for Communities and Local Government
Eland House, Bressenden Place, London SW1E 5DU
Telephone +44 (0) 20 7944 4400
Fax +44 (0) 20 7944 4101
Website www.communities.gov.uk

Secretary of State
The Rt Hon Hazel Blears
Ministers of State
Yvette Cooper (Housing) and John Healey (Local
Government)
Parliamentary Under Secretaries of State
Baroness Andrews, Parmjit Dhanda (Cohesion and
Neighbourhoods) and Ian Wright (Planning)
Permanent Secretary
Peter Housden

Department for Culture, Media and Sport
2-4 Cockspur Street, London SW1Y 5DH
Telephone +44 (0) 20 7211 6200
Website www.culture.gov.uk

Secretary of State
The Rt Hon James Purnell
Minister of State
The Rt Hon Margaret Hodge
Parliamentary Under Secretary of State
Gerry Sutcliffe (Sport)
Permanent Secretary
Jonathan Stephens

Department for Environment, Food and Rural Affairs
Eastbury House, 30-34 Albert Embankment,
London SE1 7TL
Telephone +44 (0) 20 7238 6951
Fax +44 (0) 20 7238 2188
Website www.defra.gov.uk

Secretary of State
The Rt Hon Hilary Benn
Ministers of State
Lord Rooker (Food Farming and Animal Welfare) and
Phil Woolas (Climate Change and Energy)
Parliamentary Under Secretaries of State
Joan Ruddock (Climate Change & Recycling) and
Jonathan Shaw (Marine and Fisheries, Rural Affairs and
Minister for the South East)
Permanent Secretary
Helen Ghosh

Department for Innovation, Universities and Skills
1 Victoria Street, London SW1H 0ET
Telephone +44 (0) 20 7215 5555
Website www.dius.gov.uk

Secretary of State
The Rt Hon John Denham
Ministers of State
Bill Rammell (Universities) and Ian Pearson (Business and
Science)
Parliamentary Under Secretaries of State
David Lammy (Skills) and Lord Triesman (Student Loans
and Higher Education)
Permanent Secretary
Ian Watmore

Department for International Development
1 Palace Street, London SW1E 5HE
Telephone +44 (0) 20 7023 0000
Fax +44 (0) 20 7023 0019
Website www.dfid.gov.uk

Secretary of State
The Rt Hon Douglas Alexander
Parliamentary Under Secretaries of State
Gareth Thomas (Trade Policy), The Baroness Vadera
(Africa, Health and Education) and Shahid Malik (Asia,
Middle East, Europe, Latin America, Caribbean, Security
and Development)
Permanent Secretary
Sir Suma Chakrabarti

Department for Transport
Great Minster House, 76 Marsham Street,
London SW1P 4DR
Telephone +44 (0) 20 7944 8300
Website www.dft.gov.uk

Secretary of State
The Rt Hon Ruth Kelly
Ministers of State
Rosie Winterton (Roads and Road Safety) and Jim
Fitzpatrick (Aviation and Shipping)
Parliamentary Under Secretary of State
Tom Harris (Railway)
Permanent Secretary
Robert Devereux

Department of Business, Enterprise and Regulatory Reform
1 Victoria Street, London SW1H 0ET
Telephone +44 (0) 20 7215 5000
Fax +44 (0) 20 7215 0105
Website www.berr.gov.uk

Secretary of State
The Rt Hon John Hutton
Ministers of State
Stephen Timms (Competitiveness), Lord Jones of
Birmingham (jointly with the FCO), Pat Macfadden
(Employment Relations) and Lord Drayson (jointly with
the MOD)
Parliamentary Under Secretary of State
Gareth Thomas (jointly with the DfID)
Permanent Secretary
Sir Brian Bender

Department of Health
Richmond House, 79 Whitehall, London SW1A 2NS
Telephone +44 (0) 20 7210 4850
Website www.dh.gov.uk

Secretary of State
The Rt Hon Alan Johnson
Ministers of State
Dawn Primarolo (Public Health) and Ben Bradshaw
(Health Services)
Parliamentary Under Secretaries of State
Prof the Lord Darzi of Denham and Ivan Lewis (Care
Services)
Permanent Secretary
Hugh Taylor

Department of Work and Pensions
Newcroft House, Market Street, East Newcastle-Upon-
Tyne NE1 6ND
Telephone +44 (0) 191 215 2712
Website www.dwp.gov.uk

Secretary of State
The Rt Hon Peter Hain
Ministers of State
Mike O'Brian (Pensions) and Caroline Flint (Work)
Parliamentary Under Secretaries of State
Lord McKenzie of Luton and Barbara Follett
Permanent Secretary
Sir Leigh Lewis

Export Credits Guarantee Department
PO Box 2200, 2 Exchange Tower, Harbour Exchange
Square, London E14 9GS
Telephone +44 (0) 20 7512 7000
Fax +44 (0) 20 7512 7649
Website www.ecgd.gov.uk

Chief Executive
Patrick Crawford

Food Standards Agency
Aviation House, 125 Kingsway, London WC2B 6NH
Telephone +44 (0) 20 7276 8000
Website www.food.gov.uk

Chairman
Dame Deidre Hutton
Board Members
Richard Ayre, Tim Bennett, Chrissie Dunn, Dr Maureen
Edmondson, Prof Graeme Millar, Michael Parker, Chris
Pomfret, Prof Bill Reilly, Dr Ian Reynolds, Nancy Robson,
John W Spence, Sandra Walbran

Foreign and Commonwealth Office
King Charles Street, London SW1A 2AH
Telephone +44 (0) 20 7008 1500
Website www.fco.gov.uk

Secretary of State
The Rt Hon David Miliband
Ministers of State
Jim Murphy (Europe), Lord Malloch Brown, Kim Howells
and Lord Jones of Birmingham (jointly with DBERR)
Parliamentary Under Secretary of State
Meg Munn (Overseas Territories, South East Asia)
Permanent Secretary
Sir Peter Ricketts

Forestry Commission
Silvan House, 231 Costorphine Road,
Edinburgh EH12 7AT
Telephone +44 (0) 131 334 0303
Website www.forestry.gov.uk

Chairman
Lord Clark of Windermere
Director General and Deputy Chairman
Tim Rollinson

Government Actuary's Department
Finlaison House, 15-17 Furnival Street,
London EC4A 1AB
Telephone +44 (0) 20 7211 2601
Fax +44 (0) 20 7211 2630/2640
Website www.gad.gov.uk

Government Actuary
Chris Daykin

Health and Safety Commission
Rose Court, 2 Southwark Bridge, London SE1 9HS
Telephone +44 (0) 20 7556 2100
Fax +44 (0) 20 7556 2102
Website www.hse.gov.uk

Chair
Sir Bill Callaghan
Members of Commission
Sandy Blair, Danny Carrigan, Robin Dahlberg, Judith
Donovan, Sayeed Khan, John Longworth, Hugh
Robertson, Elizabeth Snape, John Spanswick

HM Revenue and Customs
100 Parliament Street, London SW1A 2BQ
Telephone +44 (0) 20 7147 0000
Website www.hmrc.gov.uk

Chairman
Paul Gray

HM Treasury
1 Horse Guards Road, London SW1A 2HQ
Telephone +44 (0) 20 7270 4558
Fax +44 (0) 20 7270 4861
Website www.hm-treasury.gov.uk

Chancellor of the Exchequer
The Rt Hon Alistair Darling
Parliamentary Secretary to the Treasury, and Chief Whip
The Rt Hon Geoff Hoon
Chief Secretary
Andy Burnham
Permanent Secretary
Nick Macpherson

Home Office
2 Marsham Street, London SW1P 4DF
Telephone +44 (0) 20 7035 4848
Fax +44 (0) 20 7035 4745
Website www.homeoffice.gov.uk

Secretary of State
The Rt Hon Jacqui Smith
Ministers of State
Liam Byrne (Immigration and Asylum) and Tony
McNulty (Policing)
Parliamentary Under Secretaries of State
Vernon Coaker (Crime), Adm the Lord West of Spithead
(Counter Terror) and Meg Hillier (Immigration & Asylum)
Permanent Secretary
Sir David Normington

Land Registry
32 Lincoln's Inn Fields, London WC2A 3PH
Telephone +44 (0) 20 7917 8888
Fax +44 (0) 20 7955 0110
Website www.landregistry.gov.uk

Chief Land Registrar and Chief Executive
Peter Collis

Law Commission
Conquest House, 37-38 John Street, Theobalds Road,
London WC1N 2BQ
Telephone +44 (0) 20 7453 1220
Fax +44 (0) 20 7453 1297
Website www.lawcom.gov.uk

Chief Executive
Steve Humphreys
Commissioners
Stuart Bridge, David Hertzell, Prof Jeremy Horder,
Kenneth Parker

Legal Services Commission
85 Gray's Inn Road, London WC1X 8TX
Telephone +44 (0) 20 7759 0000
Website www.legalservices.gov.uk

Chairman
Sir Michael Bichard
Executive Team
Richard Collins, David Godfrey, Mike Jeacock, Helen Riley

Ministry of Defence
6th Floor, Zone E, Main Building, Whitehall,
London SW1A 2HB
Telephone +44 (0) 20 7807 8819
Website www.mod.uk

Secretary of State
The Rt Hon Des Browne
Ministers of State
Bob Ainsworth (Armed Forces) and Lord Drayson (jointly
with DBERR, Defence Equipment and Support)
Permanent Secretary
Bill Jeffrey
Defence Management Board Members
Prof Sir Roy Anderson, Sir Ian Andrews, Admiral Sir
Jonathan Band, Gen Sir Richard Dannatt, Gen Sir
Timothy Granville-Chapman, Gen Sir Kevin O'Donoghue,
Air Chief Marshal Sir Jock Stirrup, Air Chief Marshal Sir
Glenn Torpy, Trevor Woolley

Ministry of Justice
Selborne House, 54 Victoria Street, London SW1E 6QW
Telephone +44 (0) 20 7210 8500
Website www.justice.gov.uk

Secretary of State and Lord Chancellor
The Rt Hon Jack Straw
Ministers of State
David Hanson (Criminal Law and Prisons) and Michael
Wills (Constitution and Electoral Policy)
Permanent Secretary
Alex Allan
Parliamentary Under Secretaries of State
Lord Hunt of Kings Heath (Legal Aid), Bridget Prentice
(Civil and Family Justice) and Maria Eagle (Criminal Law)

National Archives
Kew, Richmond, Surrey TW9 4DU
Telephone +44 (0) 20 8876 3444
Website www.nationalarchives.gov.uk

*Chief Executive, Keeper of Public Records, and Historical
Manuscripts Commissioner*
Natalie Ceeney

Northern Ireland Office
11 Millbank, London SW1P 4PN
Telephone +44 (0) 289 052 0700
Website www.nio.gov.uk

Secretary of State
The Rt Hon Shaun Woodward
Minister of State
Paul Goggins
Permanent Secretary
Jonathan Phillips

Office for National Statistics
Cardiff Road, Newport NP10 8XG
Telephone +44 (0) 845 601 3034
Fax +44 (0) 1633 652747
Website www.statistics.gov.uk

National Statistician
Karen Dunnell

Office of Fair Trade
Fleetbank House, 2-6 Salisbury Square, London EC4Y 8JX
Telephone +44 (0) 20 7211 8000
Website www.oft.gov.uk

Chairman
Phillip Collins
Chief Executive Officer
John Fingleton

Office of Gas and Electricity Markets
9 Millbank, London SW1 3GE
Telephone +44 (0) 20 7901 7000
Fax +44 (0) 20 7901 7066
Website www.ofgem.gov.uk

Chairman
Sir John Mogg
Chief Executive
Alistair Buchanan

Office of Rail Regulation
1 Kemble Street, London WC2B 4AN
Telephone +44 (0) 20 7282 2000
Fax +44 (0) 20 7282 2040
Website www.rail-reg.gov.uk

Chairman
Chris Dolt
Chief Executive
Billl Emery

Office of Standards in Education
Royal Exchange Building, St Anns Square,
Manchester M2 7LA
Telephone +44 (0) 845 640 4040
Website www.ofsted.gov.uk

HM Chief Inspector of Schools
Christine Gilbert

Office of the Advocate General for Scotland
Dover House, Whitehall, London SW1A 2AU
Telephone +44 (0) 20 7270 6720
Website www.oag.gov.uk

Advocate General of Scotland
Neil Davidson

Office of the Leader of the House of Commons
Dover House, Whitehall, London SW1 2AU
Telephone +44 (0) 20 7276 1005
Fax +44 (0) 20 7276 1006
Website www.commonsleader.gov.uk

Leader of the House of Commons and Lord Privy Seal
The Rt Hon Harriet Harman
Parliamentary Secretary
Helen Goodman

Office of HM Paymaster General
Sutherland House, Russell Way, Crawley, West
Sussex RH10 1UH
Telephone +44 (0) 870 197 1448
Website www.opg.gov.uk

Paymaster General
The Rt Hon Tessa Jowell

Office of Water Services
Centre City Tower, 7 Hill Street, Birmingham B5 4UA
Telephone +44 (0) 121 625 1300
Fax +44 (0) 121 625 1400
Website www.ofwat.gov.uk

Chairman
Phillip Fletcher
Chief Executive
Regina Finn

Ordnance Survey
Romsey Road, Southampton SO16 4GU
Telephone +44 (0) 845 605 0505
Fax +44 (0) 23 8079 2615
Website www.ordnancesurvey.co.uk

Director General and Chief Executive
Vanessa Lawrence

Parliamentary Counsel
36 Whitehall, London SW1 2AY
Telephone +44 (0) 20 7210 2588
Fax +44 (0) 20 7210 0963
Website www.parliamentary-counsel.gov.uk

First Parliamentary Counsel
Stephen Laws
Chief Executive
John Gilhooly

Prime Minister's Office
10 Downing Street, London SW1 2AA
Fax +44 (0) 20 7925 0918
Website www.number-10.gov.uk

*Prime Minister and First Lord of the Treasury and
Minister for the Civil Service*
The Rt Hon Gordon Brown
Chief of Staff
Tom Scholar

Privy Council Office
2 Carlton Gardens, London SW1Y 5AA
Telephone +44 (0) 20 7210 1033
Fax +44 (0) 20 7210 1071
Website www.pco.gov.uk

*Lord President of the Council and Leader of the House of
Lords*
Baroness Ashton

Royal Mint
Llantrisant, Pontyclun CF72 8YT
Telephone +44 (0) 845 608 8222
Fax +44 (0) 1443 623328
Website www.royalmint.com

Chief Executive & Deputy Master of the Mint
Andrew Stafford

Scotland Office
Dover House, Whitehall, London SW1A 2AU
Telephone +44 (0) 20 7270 6754
Fax +44 (0) 20 7270 6812
Website www.scotlandoffice.gov.uk

Secretary of State
The Rt Hon Des Browne
Minister of State
David Cairns
Head of Office
Jim Wildgoose

Secret Intelligence Service
Vauxhall Cross, London SE1 1BD
Website www.sis.gov.uk

Chief of SIS
Sir John Scarlett

The Security Service
Thames House, London
Website www.mi5.gov.uk

Director General of the Security Service
Johnathan Evans

Serious Fraud Office
Elm House, 10-16 Elm Street, London WC1X 0BJ
Telephone +44 (0) 20 7239 7272
Fax +44 (0) 20 7837 1689
Website www.sfo.gov.uk

Director
Robert Wardle

Serious Organised Crime Agency
PO Box 8000, London SE11 5EN
Website www.soca.gov.uk

Chairman
Sir Stephen Lander
Director General
Bill Hughes

Treasury Solicitor's Department
1 Kemble Street, London WC2B 4TS
Telephone +44 (0) 20 7210 3000
Website www.tsol.gov.uk

*HM Procurator General, Treasury Solicitor and Head of
the Government Legal Service*
Paul Jenkins

UK Trade and Investment
Tay House, 300 Bath Street, Glasgow G2 4DX
Telephone +44 (0) 20 7215 8000
Website www.uktradeinvest.gov.uk

Chief Executive
Andrew Cahn

Wales Office
Gwydyr House, Whitehall, London SW1A 2ER
Telephone +44 (0) 20 7270 0534
Website www.walesoffice.gov.uk

Secretary of State
The Rt Hon Peter Hain
Parliamentary Under Secretary of State
Huw Irranca-Davies
Director of Office
Alan Cogbill

SCHOOLS

The following pages detail the UK schools most often listed in
People of Today entries.

Abingdon School
Park Road, Abingdon, Oxfordshire OX14 1DE
Telephone +44 (0) 1235 521563
Fax +44 (0) 1235 849079
Website www.abingdon.org.uk

Headmaster
Mark Turner

Aldenham School
Elstree, Hertfordshire WD6 3AJ
Telephone +44 (0) 1923 858122
Fax +44 (0) 1923 854410
Website www.aldenham.com

Headmaster
James Fowler

Alleyn's School
Townley Road, Dulwich, London SE22 8SU
Telephone +44 (0) 20 8557 1500
Fax +44 (0) 20 8557 1462
Website www.alleyns.org.uk

Headmaster
Colin Diggory

Ampleforth College
York YO62 4ER
Telephone +44 (0) 1439 766000
Fax +44 (0) 1439 788330
Website www.ampleforthcollege.york.sch.uk

Headmaster
Dom Gabriel Everitt

Bedales School
Church Road, Steep, Petersfield, Hampshire GU32 2DG
Telephone +44 (0) 1730 300100
Fax +44 (0) 1730 300500
Website www.bedales.org.uk

Headmaster
Keith Budge

Bedford School
De Parys Avenue, Bedford MK40 2TU
Telephone +44 (0) 1234 362200
Fax +44 (0) 1234 362283
Website www.bedfordschool.org.uk

Headmaster
Philip Evans

Berkhamsted Collegiate School
Castle Campus, Castle Street, Berkhamsted,
Hertfordshire HP4 2BB
Telephone +44 (0) 1442 358000
Fax +44 (0) 1442 358040
Website www.berkhamstedcollegiateschool.org.uk

Principal
Dr Priscilla Chadwick

Blundell's School
Tiverton, Devon EX16 4NS
Telephone +44 (0) 1884 252543
Fax +44 (0) 1884 243232
Website www.blundells.org

Headmaster
Ian Davenport

Bolton School
Chorley New Road, Bolton BL1 4PA
Telephone +44 (0) 1204 840201
Fax +44 (0) 1204 495498
Website www.boltonschool.org

Headmaster
Mervyn Brooker

Bradfield College
Bradfield, Reading, Berkshire RG7 6AU
Telephone +44 (0) 118 964 4526
Fax +44 (0) 118 964 4521
Website www.bradfieldcollege.org.uk

Headmaster
Peter Roberts

Bradford Grammar School
Keighley Road, Bradford, West Yorkshire BD9 4JP
Telephone +44 (0) 1274 542492
Fax +44 (0) 1274 548129
Website www.bgs.bradford.sch.uk

Headmaster
Stephen Davidson

Brentwood School
Ingrave Road, Brentwood, Essex CM15 8AS
Telephone +44 (0) 1277 243243
Fax +44 (0) 1277 243299
Website www.brentwoodschool.co.uk

Headmaster
Ian Davies

Bristol Grammar School
University Road, Bristol BS8 1SR
Telephone +44 (0) 117 937 6006
Website www.bristolgrammarschool.co.uk

Headmaster
Dr David Mascord

Bryanston School
Blandford, Dorset DT11 0PX
Telephone +44 (0) 1258 452411
Fax +44 (0) 1258 484657
Website www.bryanston.co.uk

Headmaster
Sarah Thomas

Canford School
Wimborne, Dorset BH21 3AD
Telephone +44 (0) 1202 841254
Fax +44 (0) 1202 881009
Website www.canford.com

Headmaster
John Lever

Charterhouse
Godalming, Surrey GU7 2DX
Telephone +44 (0) 1483 291501
Fax +44 (0) 1483 291507
Website www.charterhouse.org.uk

Headmaster
John Witheridge

Cheltenham College
Bath Road, Cheltenham, Gloucestershire GL53 7LD
Telephone +44 (0) 1242 265600
Fax +44 (0) 1242 265630
Website www.cheltcoll.gloucs.sch.uk

Headmaster
John Richardson

Christ's Hospital
Horsham, West Sussex RH13 0YP
Telephone +44 (0) 1403 211923
Fax +44 (0) 1403 211580
Website www.christs-hospital.org.uk

Headmaster
John Franklin

City of London School
Queen Victoria Street, London EC4V 3AL
Telephone +44 (0) 20 7489 0291
Fax +44 (0) 20 7329 6887
Website www.clsb.org.uk

Headmaster
David Levin

Clifton College
32 College Road, Clifton, Bristol BS8 3JH
Telephone +44 (0) 117 315 7000
Fax +44 (0) 117 315 7101
Website www.cliftoncollegeuk.com

Headmaster
Mark Moore

Downside School
Stratton-on-the-Fosse, Radstock, Bath BA3 4RJ
Telephone +44 (0) 1761 235100
Website www.downside.co.uk

Headmaster
Dom Leo Maidlow Davis

Dulwich College
Dulwich Common, London SE21 7LD
Telephone +44 (0) 20 8693 3601
Fax +44 (0) 20 8693 6319
Website www.dulwich.org.uk

Master
Graham Able

Eastbourne College
Old Wish Road, Eastbourne, East Sussex BN21 4JX
Telephone +44 (0) 1323 452300
Fax +44 (0) 1323 452307
Website www.eastbourne-college.co.uk

Headmaster
Simon Davies

The Edinburgh Academy
42 Henderson Row, Edinburgh EH3 5BL
Telephone +44 (0) 131 556 4603
Fax +44 (0) 131 624 4994
Website www.edinburghacademy.org.uk

Rector
John Light

Epsom College
College Road, Epsom, Surrey KT17 4JQ
Telephone +44 (0) 1372 821234
Fax +44 (0) 1372 821237
Website www.epsomcollege.org.uk

Headmaster
Stephen Borthwick

Eton College
Windsor, Berkshire SL4 6DW
Telephone +44 (0) 1753 671000
Fax +44 (0) 1753 671244
Website www.etoncollege.com

Headmaster
Anthony Little

Felsted School
Felsted, Great Dunmow, Essex CM6 3LL
Telephone +44 (0) 1371 822600
Fax +44 (0) 1371 822607
Website www.felsted.org

Headmaster
Stephen Roberts

Fettes College
Carrington Road, Edinburgh EH4 1QX
Telephone +44 (0) 131 332 2281
Fax +44 (0) 131 332 3081
Website www.fettes.com

Headmaster
Michael Spens

Forest School
College Place, Snaresbrook, London E17 3PY
Telephone +44 (0) 20 8520 1744
Fax +44 (0) 20 8520 3656
Website www.forest.org.uk

Warden
Andrew Boggis

George Heriot's School
Lauriston Place, Edinburgh EH3 9EQ
Telephone +44 (0) 131 229 7263
Fax +44 (0) 131 229 6363
Website www.george-heriots.com

Headmaster
Alistair Hector

George Watson's College
Colinton Road, Edinburgh EH10 5EG
Telephone +44 (0) 131 446 6000
Fax +44 (0) 131 446 6090
Website www.gwc.org.uk

Principal
Gareth Edwards

The Glasgow Academy
Colebrooke Street, Glasgow G12 8HE
Telephone +44 (0) 141 334 8558
Fax +44 (0) 141 337 3473
Website www.theglasgowacademy.org.uk

Rector
Peter Brodie

Glenalmond College
Glenalmond, Perth PH1 3RY
Telephone +44 (0) 1738 842056
Website www.glenalmondcollege.co.uk

Warden
Gordon Woods

Gordonstoun
Elgin, Moray IV30 5RF
Telephone +44 (0) 1343 837837
Fax +44 (0) 1343 837838
Website www.gordonstoun.org.uk

Principal
Mark Pyper

Gresham's School
Cromer Road, Holt, Norfolk NR25 6EA
Telephone +44 (0) 1263 714500
Fax +44 (0) 1263 712028
Website www.greshams.com

Headmaster
Antony Clark

The Haberdashers' Aske's Boys' School
Butterfly Lane, Elstree, Borehamwood,
Hertfordshire WD6 3AF
Telephone +44 (0) 20 8266 1700
Fax +44 (0) 20 8266 1800
Website www.habsboys.org.uk

Headmaster
Peter Hamilton

Haileybury
Hertford SG13 7NU
Telephone +44 (0) 1992 462507
Fax +44 (0) 1992 470663
Website www.haileybury.herts.sch.uk

Master
Stuart Westley

Harrow School
5 High Street, Harrow on the Hill, Middlesex HA1 3HP
Telephone +44 (0) 20 8872 8000
Fax +44 (0) 20 8872 8012
Website www.harrowschool.org.uk

Headmaster
Barnaby Lenon

The High School of Glasgow
637 Crow Road, Glasgow G13 1PL
Telephone +44 (0) 141 954 9628
Fax +44 (0) 141 959 0191
Website www.glasgowhigh.com

Rector
Colin Mair

Highgate School
North Road, London N6 4AY
Telephone +44 (0) 20 8340 1524
Fax +44 (0) 20 8340 7674
Website www.highgateschool.org.uk

Headmaster
Adam Pettitt

Hutchesons' Grammar School
21 Beaton Road, Glasgow G41 4NW
Telephone +44 (0) 141 423 2933
Fax +44 (0) 141 424 0251
Website www.hutchesons.org

Rector
Dr Kenneth Greig

King Edward VII School
Glossop Road, Sheffield S10 2PW
Telephone +44 (0) 114 266 2518
Fax +44 (0) 114 268 7690
Website www.kes.sheffield.sch.uk

Headteacher
Michael Lewis

King Edward's School
Edgbaston Park Road, Birmingham B15 2UA
Telephone +44 (0) 121 472 1672
Fax +44 (0) 121 414 1897
Website www.kes.bham.sch.uk

Chief Master
John Claughton

King's College School
Southside, Wimbledon Common, London SW19 4TT
Telephone +44 (0) 20 8255 5300
Fax +44 (0) 20 8255 5309
Website www.kcs.org.uk

Headmaster
Tony Evans

The King's School
Canterbury, Kent CT1 2ES
Telephone +44 (0) 1227 595501
Fax +44 (0) 1227 595595
Website www.kings-school.co.uk

Headmaster
Canon Keith Wilkinson

The King's School
5 College Green, Worcester WR1 2LL
Telephone +44 (0) 1905 721700
Fax +44 (0) 1905 721710
Website www.ksw.org.uk

Headmaster
Tim Keyes

Kingston Grammar School
70 London Road, Kingston upon Thames,
Surrey KT2 6PY
Telephone +44 (0) 20 8546 5875
Fax +44 (0) 20 8974 5177
Website www.kingston-grammar.surrey.sch.uk

Headmaster
Duncan Baxter

Kingswood School
Lansdown, Bath BA1 5RG
Telephone +44 (0) 1225 734210
Fax +44 (0) 1225 734305
Website www.kingswood.bath.sch.uk

Headmaster
Gary Best

Lancing College
Lancing, West Sussex BN15 0RW
Telephone +44 (0) 1273 465802
Fax +44 (0) 1273 464720
Website www.lancingcollege.co.uk

Headmaster
Jonathan Gillespie

Latymer Upper School
King Street, Hammersmith, London W6 9LR
Telephone +44 (0) 845 638 5800
Fax +44 (0) 20 8748 5212
Website www.latymer-upper.org

Head
Peter Winter

Leeds Grammar School
Alwoodley Gates, Harrogate Road, Leeds LS17 8GS
Telephone +44 (0) 113 229 1552
Fax +44 (0) 113 228 5111
Website www.leedsgrammar.com

Headmaster
Dr Mark Bailey

Leighton Park School
Shinfield Road, Reading RG2 7ED
Telephone +44 (0) 118 987 9600
Fax +44 (0) 118 987 9625
Website www.leightonpark.reading.sch.uk

Head
John Dunston

The Leys School
Cambridge CB2 7AD
Telephone +44 (0) 1223 508900
Website www.theleys.cambs.sch.uk

Headmaster
Mark Slater

Liverpool College
Queen's Drive, Mossley Hill, Liverpool L18 8BG
Telephone +44 (0) 151 724 4000
Fax +44 (0) 151 729 0105
Website www.liverpoolcollege.org.uk

Principal
Brian Christian

Loretto School
Linkfield Road, Musselburgh, East Lothian EH21 7RE
Telephone +44 (0) 131 653 4444
Website www.lorettoschool.co.uk

Headmaster
Michael Mavor

Malvern College
College Road, Malvern, Worcestershire WR14 3DF
Telephone +44 (0) 1684 581500
Website www.malvern-college.co.uk

Acting Head
Sarah Welch

The Manchester Grammar School
Old Hall Lane, Manchester M13 0XT
Telephone +44 (0) 161 224 7201
Fax +44 (0) 161 257 2446
Website www.mgs.org

High Master
Dr Christopher Ray

Marlborough College
Marlborough, Wiltshire SN8 1PA
Telephone +44 (0) 1672 892200
Fax +44 (0) 1672 892207
Website www.marlboroughcollege.org

Master
N A Sampson

Merchant Taylors' School
Sandy Lodge, Moor Park, Northwood,
Middlesex HA6 2HT
Telephone +44 (0) 1923 820644
Fax +44 (0) 1923 835110
Website www.mtsn.org.uk

Headmaster
Stephen Wright

Merchant Taylors' School Crosby
186 Liverpool Road, Crosby, Liverpool L23 0QP
Telephone +44 (0) 151 928 5759
Fax +44 (0) 151 949 9300
Website www.merchanttaylors.sefton.sch.uk

Headmaster
David Cook

Mill Hill School
The Ridgeway, Mill Hill Village, London NW7 1QS
Telephone +44 (0) 20 8959 1176
Website www.millhill.org.uk

Headmaster
William Winfield

Millfield School
Butleigh Road, Street, Somerset BA16 0YD
Telephone +44 (0) 1458 442291
Website www.millfield.somerset.sch.uk

Headmaster
Peter Johnson

Monkton Combe School
Monkton Combe, Bath BA2 7HG
Telephone +44 (0) 1225 721102
Fax +44 (0) 1225 721208
Website www.monktoncombeschool.com

Principal
Richard Backhouse

Nottingham High School
Waverley Mount, Nottingham NG7 4ED
Telephone +44 (0) 115 978 6056
Website www.nottinghamhigh.co.uk

Headmaster
Kevin Fear

Oakham School
Chapel Close, Market Place, Oakham, Rutland LE15 6DT
Telephone +44 (0) 1572 758500
Fax +44 (0) 1572 758818
Website www.oakham.rutland.sch.uk

Headmaster
Dr Joseph Spence

Oundle School
Oundle, Peterborough PE8 4GH
Telephone +44 (0) 1832 277122
Fax +44 (0) 1832 277123
Website www.oundleschool.org.uk

Headmaster
Charles Bush

The Perse School
Hills Road, Cambridge CB2 8QF
Telephone +44 (0) 1223 403800
Fax +44 (0) 1223 403810
Website www.perse.co.uk

Headmaster
Nigel Richardson

Portsmouth Grammar School
High Street, Portsmouth PO1 2LN
Telephone +44 (0) 23 9236 0036
Fax +44 (0) 23 9236 4256
Website www.pgs.org.uk

Headmaster
Dr Timothy Hands

Radley College
Abingdon, Oxfordshire OX14 2HR
Telephone +44 (0) 1235 543000
Fax +44 (0) 1235 543106
Website www.radley.org.uk

Warden
Angus McPhail

Reading School
Erleigh Road, Reading RG1 5LW
Telephone +44 (0) 118 901 5600
Fax +44 (0) 118 935 2755
Website www.readingschool.reading.sch.uk

Headteacher
John Weeds

Repton School
Repton, Derbyshire DE65 6FH
Telephone +44 (0) 1283 559200
Fax +44 (0) 1283 559347
Website www.repton.org.uk

Headmaster
Robert Holroyd

Robert Gordon's College
Schoolhill, Aberdeen AB10 1FE
Telephone +44 (0) 1224 646346
Fax +44 (0) 1224 630301
Website www.rgc.aberdeen.sch.uk

Head of College
Hugh Ouston

The Royal Grammar School
Amersham Road, High Wycombe,
Buckinghamshire HP13 6QT
Telephone +44 (0) 1494 524955
Fax +44 (0) 1494 551410
Website www.rgshw.com

Headmaster
Roy M Page

Royal Grammar School
Eskdale Terrace, Newcastle upon Tyne NE2 7DX
Telephone +44 (0) 191 229 7263
Fax +44 (0) 191 212 0392
Website www.rgs.newcastle.sch.uk

Headmaster
James Miller

Rugby School
Rugby, Warwickshire CV22 5EH
Telephone +44 (0) 1788 556216
Fax +44 (0) 1788 556219
Website www.rugbyschool.net

Headmaster
Patrick Derham

Sedbergh School
Sedbergh LA10 5HG
Telephone +44 (0) 1539 620535
Website www.sedberghschool.org

Headmaster
Christopher H Hirst

Sevenoaks School
Sevenoaks, Kent TN13 1HU
Telephone +44 (0) 1732 455133
Fax +44 (0) 1732 456143
Website www.sevenoaksschool.org

Head
Katy Ricks

Sherborne School
Abbey Road, Sherborne, Dorset DT9 3LF
Telephone +44 (0) 1935 812249
Fax +44 (0) 1935 810426
Website www.sherborne.org

Headmaster
Simon Eliot

Shrewsbury School
The Schools, Shrewsbury SY3 7BA
Telephone +44 (0) 1743 280500
Website www.shrewsbury.org.uk

Headmaster
Jeremy Goulding

Solihull School
Warwick Road, Solihull B91 3DJ
Telephone +44 (0) 121 705 4273
Fax +44 (0) 121 711 4439
Website www.solsch.org.uk

Headmaster
Phillip Griffiths

St Albans School
Abbey Gateway, St Albans AL3 4HB
Telephone +44 (0) 1727 855521
Fax +44 (0) 1727 843447
Website www.st-albans.herts.sch.uk

Headmaster
Andrew Grant

St Dunstan's College
Stanstead Road, London SE6 4TY
Telephone +44 (0) 20 8516 7200
Fax +44 (0) 20 8516 7300
Website www.stdunstans.org.uk

Headmistress
Jane Davies

St Edward's School
Woodstock Road, Oxford OX2 7NN
Telephone +44 (0) 1865 319204
Website www.stedwards.oxon.sch.uk

Warden
Andrew Trotman

St John's School
Epsom Road, Leatherhead, Surrey KT22 8SP
Telephone +44 (0) 1372 373000
Fax +44 (0) 1372 386606
Website www.stjohnsleatherhead.co.uk

Headmaster
Nicholas Haddock

St Paul's Girls' School
Brook Green, Hammersmith, London W6 7BS
Telephone +44 (0) 20 7603 2288
Fax +44 (0) 20 7602 9932
Website www.spgs.org

High Mistress
Clarissa Farr

St Paul's School
Lonsdale Road, London SW13 9JT
Telephone +44 (0) 20 8748 9162
Fax +44 (0) 20 8746 5353
Website www.stpaulsschool.org.uk

High Master
Dr Martin Stephen

Stonyhurst College
Clitheroe, Lancashire BB7 9PZ
Telephone +44 (0) 1254 826345
Website www.stonyhurst.ac.uk

Headmaster
Andrew Johnson

Stowe School
Stowe, Buckingham MK18 5EH
Telephone +44 (0) 1280 818000
Fax +44 (0) 1280 818181
Website www.stowe.co.uk

Headmaster
Dr Anthony Wallersteiner

Tiffin School
Queen Elizabeth Road, Kingston upon Thames,
Surrey KT2 6RL
Telephone +44 (0) 20 8546 4638
Fax +44 (0) 20 8546 6365
Website www.tiffin.kingston.sch.uk

Head
Sean Heslop

Tonbridge School
High Street, Tonbridge, Kent TN9 1JP
Telephone +44 (0) 1732 365555
Website www.tonbridge-school.co.uk

Headmaster
Tim Haynes

University College School
Frognal, Hampstead, London NW3 6XH
Telephone +44 (0) 20 7435 2215
Fax +44 (0) 20 7433 2111
Website www.usc.org.uk

Headmaster
Kenneth Durham

Uppingham School
Uppingham, Rutland LE15 9QE
Telephone +44 (0) 1572 822216
Fax +44 (0) 1572 821872
Website www.uppingham.co.uk

Headmaster
Richard Harman

Wellington College
Crowthorne, Berkshire RG45 7PU
Telephone +44 (0) 1344 444000
Fax +44 (0) 1344 444002
Website www.wellington-college.berks.sch.uk

Master
Dr Anthony Seldon

Westminster School
Little Dean's Yard, Westminster, London SW1P 3PF
Telephone +44 (0) 20 7963 1000
Fax +44 (0) 20 7963 1006
Website www.westminster.org.uk

Headmaster
Dr Stephen Spurr

Whitgift School
Haling Park, South Croydon, Surrey CR2 6YT
Telephone +44 (0) 20 8688 9222
Fax +44 (0) 20 8760 0682
Website www.whitgift.co.uk

Headmaster
Dr Christopher Barnett

William Ellis School
Highgate Road, London NW5 1RN
Telephone +44 (0) 20 7267 9346
Fax +44 (0) 20 7284 1274
Website williamellis.virtualschools.net

Headteacher
Richard Tanton

Wimbledon College
Edge Hill, London SW19 4NS
Telephone +44 (0) 20 8946 2535
Website www.wimbledoncollege.org.uk

Headmaster
Father Adrian Porter

Winchester College
College Street, Winchester, Hampshire SO23 9NA
Telephone +44 (0) 1962 621247
Fax +44 (0) 1962 621106
Website www.winchestercollege.org

Headmaster
Dr Ralph Townsend

Wrekin College
Sutherland Road, Wellington, Telford,
Shropshire TF1 3BH
Telephone +44 (0) 1952 265600
Fax +44 (0) 1952 415068
Website www.wrekincollege.ac.uk

Headmaster
Stephen Drew

HIGHER EDUCATION

The following pages detail the UK higher education institutions most often
listed in People of Today entries.

Architectural Association School of Architecture
36 Bedford Square, London WC1B 3ES
Telephone +44 (0) 20 7887 4000
Fax +44 (0) 20 7414 0782
Website www.aaschool.ac.uk

Director
Brett Steele

Balliol College, Oxford
Oxford OX1 3BJ
Telephone +44 (0) 1865 277748
Fax +44 (0) 1865 277803
Website www.balliol.ox.ac.uk

Master
Andrew Graham
Alumni Officer
Janet Hazelton

Brasenose College, Oxford
Oxford OX1 4AJ
Telephone +44 (0) 1865 277510
Fax +44 (0) 1865 277822
Website www.bnc.ox.ac.uk

Principal
Prof Roger Cashmore
Alumni Officer
Robin Sharp

Britannia Royal Naval College
Dartmouth, Devon TQ6 0HJ
Telephone +44 (0) 1803 677238
Website www.britannia.ac.uk

Commanding Officer
Cdre Martin Alabaster

Central St Martin's College of Art and Design
Southampton Row, London WC1B 4AP
Telephone +44 (0) 20 7514 7022
Fax +44 (0) 20 7514 7254
Website www.csm.arts.ac.uk

Christ Church, Oxford
Oxford OX1 1DP
Telephone +44 (0) 1865 276181
Website www.chch.ox.ac.uk

Dean
The Very Rev Christopher Lewis
Alumni Officer
Emma Sinden

Christ's College, Cambridge
St Andrew's Street, Cambridge CB2 3BU
Telephone +44 (0) 1223 334953
Fax +44 (0) 1223 334967
Website www.christs.cam.ac.uk

Master
Prof Frank Kelly
Alumni Officer
Jacqui Tighe-Doyle

City University
Northampton Square, London EC1 0HB
Telephone +44 (0) 20 7040 5060
Fax +44 (0) 20 7040 8995
Website www.city.ac.uk

Chancellor
John Stuttard
Vice-Chancellor
Prof Malcolm Gillies
Alumni Officer
Paulo Gomes

Clare College, Cambridge
Trinity Lane, Cambridge CB2 1TL
Telephone +44 (0) 1223 333246
Fax +44 (0) 1223 333219
Website www.clare.cam.ac.uk

Master
Prof Tony Badger
Alumni Officer
A Worth

College of Law
Braboeuf Manor, St Catherines, Portsmouth Road,
Guildford, Surrey GU3 1HA
Telephone +44 (0) 1483 460200
Fax +44 (0) 1483 460305
Website www.college-of-law.co.uk

Chief Executive
Prof Nigel Savage

Corpus Christi College, Cambridge
Trumpington Street, Cambridge CB2 1RH
Telephone +44 (0) 1223 338056
Fax +44 (0) 1223 338061
Website www.corpus.cam.ac.uk

Master
Prof Sir Alan Wilson
Alumni Officer
Lucy Gowans

Corpus Christi College, Oxford
Oxford OX1 4JF
Telephone +44 (0) 1865 276693
Fax +44 (0) 1865 276767
Website www.ccc.ox.ac.uk

President
Sir Timothy Lankester
Alumni Officer
Nick Thorn

Courtauld Institute of Art
Somerset House, Strand, London WC2R 0RN
Telephone +44 (0) 20 7848 2777
Fax +44 (0) 20 7848 2410
Website www.cortauld.ac.uk

Director
Dr Deborah Swallow
Alumni Officer
David Whitaker

Downing College, Cambridge
Cambridge CB2 1DQ
Telephone +44 (0) 1223 334826
Fax +44 (0) 1223 467934
Website www.dow.cam.ac.uk

Master
Prof Barry Everitt
Alumni Officer
H J Limbick

Emmanuel College, Cambridge
St Andrew's Street, Cambridge CB2 3AP
Telephone +44 (0) 1223 334290
Fax +44 (0) 1223 334426
Website www.emma.cam.ac.uk

Master
Lord Wilson of Dinton

Exeter College, Oxford
Oxford OX1 3DP
Telephone +44 (0) 1865 279648
Fax +44 (0) 1865 279645
Website www.exeter.ox.ac.uk

Rector
Frances Cairncross
Alumni Officer
Sarah Christou

Fitzwilliam College, Cambridge
Storey's Way, Cambridge CB3 0DG
Telephone +44 (0) 1223 332030
Fax +44 (0) 1223 477976
Website www.fitz.cam.ac.uk

Master
Prof Robert Lethbridge
Alumni Officer
Emma Smith

Girton College, Cambridge
Huntingdon Road, Cambridge CB3 0JG
Telephone +44 (0) 1223 338972
Fax +44 (0) 1223 338896
Website www.girton.cam.ac.uk

Mistress
Dame Marilyn Strathern
Alumni Officer
Emma Cornwall

Goldsmiths College, London
Lewisham Way, New Cross, London SE14 6NW
Telephone +44 (0) 20 7919 7766
Fax +44 (0) 20 7919 7509
Website www.goldsmiths.ac.uk

Warden
Prof Geoffrey Crossick
Alumni Officer
Will Finch

Gonville & Caius College, Cambridge
Trinity Street, Cambridge CB2 1TA
Telephone +44 (0) 1223 332 447
Fax +44 (0) 1223 332456
Website www.cai.cam.ac.uk

Master
Sir Christopher Hum
Alumni Officer
Dr Anne Lyon

Guildhall School of Music and Drama
Silk Street, Barbican, London EC2Y 8DT
Telephone +44 (0) 20 7628 2571
Fax +44 (0) 20 7256 9438
Website www.gsmd.ac.uk

Principal
Barry Ife
Alumni Officer
Rachel Dyson

Harvard Business School
Soldiers Field, Boston, MA 02163, USA
Telephone +1 617 495 6000
Website www.hbs.edu

Dean
Jay Light
Associate Director of Alumni Relations
Stephanie Goff

Harvard University
Massachusetts Hall, Cambridge, MA 02138, USA
Telephone +1 617 495 1000
Website www.harvard.edu

President
Drew Gilpin Faust

Hertford College, Oxford
Oxford OX1 3BW
Telephone +44 (0) 1865 279404
Fax +44 (0) 1865 279466
Website www.hertford.ox.ac.uk

Principal
Dr John Landers
Alumni Officer
Yvonne Rainey

Imperial College London
Exhibition Road, South Kensington, London SW7 2AZ
Telephone +44 (0) 20 7594 8014
Fax +44 (0) 20 7594 8004
Website www.imperial.ac.uk

Rector
Sir Richard Sykes
Alumni Officer
Liz Gregson

Inns of Court School of Law
4 Gray's Inn Place, Gray's Inn, London WC1R 5DX
Telephone +44 (0) 20 7404 5787
Fax +44 (0) 20 7831 4188
Website www.city.ac.uk/law/icsl

Dean
Prof Adrian Keane

INSEAD
Boulevard de Constance, 77305 Fontainebleau, France
Telephone +33 (0) 1 60 72 40 00
Fax +33 (0) 1 60 74 55 00
Website www.insead.edu

Dean
J Frank Brown
Director of Alumni Relations and Alumni Fund
Sandra Morand

Jesus College, Cambridge
Jesus Lane, Cambridge CB5 8BL
Telephone +44 (0) 1223 339495
Fax +44 (0) 1223 324910
Website www.jesus.cam.ac.uk

Master
Prof Robert Mair
Alumni Officer
Sarah Ambrose

Jesus College, Oxford
Oxford OX1 3DW
Telephone +44 (0) 1865 279720
Fax +44 (0) 1865 279687
Website www.jesus.ox.ac.uk

Principal
Lord Krebs
Alumni Officer
Alison Proffitt-White

Keble College, Oxford
Oxford OX1 3PG
Telephone +44 (0) 1865 272711
Fax +44 (0) 1865 272705
Website www.keble.ox.ac.uk

Warden
Prof Dame Averil Cameron
Alumni Officer
Ruth Cowen

King's College, Cambridge
King's Parade, Cambridge CB2 1ST
Telephone +44 (0) 1223 331417
Fax +44 (0) 1223 331315
Website www.kings.cam.ac.uk

Provost
Prof Ross Harrison
Alumni Officer
Amy Ingle

King's College London
Strand, London WC2R 2LS
Telephone +44 (0) 20 7848 2929
Fax +44 (0) 20 7836 1799
Website www.kcl.ac.uk

Principal
Prof Richard Trainor
Alumni Officers
Sally Ford and Emily Carter

Lincoln College, Oxford
Oxford OX1 3DR
Telephone +44 (0) 1865 279836
Fax +44 (0) 1865 279802
Website www.lincoln.ox.ac.uk

Rector
Prof Paul Langford
Alumni Officer
Shaun Melvin

London Business School
Regent's Park, London NW1 4SA
Telephone +44 (0) 20 7000 7000
Fax +44 (0) 20 7000 7001
Website www.london.edu

Dean
Robin Buchanan

London School of Economics and Political Sciences
Houghton Street, London WC2A 2AE
Telephone +44 (0) 20 7955 7124
Fax +44 (0) 20 7955 6001
Website www.lse.ac.uk

Director
Sir Howard Davies
Alumni Officer
Ric Wilding

Magdalen College, Oxford
Oxford OX1 4AU
Telephone +44 (0) 1865 276063
Fax +44 (0) 1865 276030
Website www.magdalen.ox.ac.uk

President
Prof David C Clary
Alumni Officer
Dr Marilyn Bowler

Magdalene College, Cambridge
Magdalene Street, Cambridge CB3 0AG
Telephone +44 (0) 1223 332135
Fax +44 (0) 1223 363637
Website www.magd.cam.ac.uk

Master
Duncan Robinson
Alumni Officer
Hannah Fogg

Merton College, Oxford
Oxford OX1 4JD
Telephone +44 (0) 1865 276329
Fax +44 (0) 1865 276361
Website www.merton.ox.ac.uk

Warden
Prof Dame Jessica Rawson
Alumni Officer
Christine Taylor

New College, Oxford
Oxford OX1 3BN
Telephone +44 (0) 1865 279551
Fax +44 (0) 1865 279950
Website www.new.ox.ac.uk

Warden
Alan Ryan
Alumni Officer
Susan Ashcroft-Jones

Newnham College, Cambridge
Sidgwick Avenue, Cambridge CB3 9DF
Telephone +44 (0) 1223 335783
Fax +44 (0) 1223 359155
Website www.newn.cam.ac.uk

Principal
Dame Patricia Hodgson
Alumni Officer
Chris Bremer

Open University
Walton Hall, Milton Keynes MK7 6AA
Telephone +44 (0) 1908 274066
Fax +44 (0) 1908 653744
Website www.open.ac.uk

Chancellor
Lord Puttnam
Vice-Chancellor
Prof Brenda Gourley

Oriel College, Oxford
Oxford OX1 4EW
Telephone +44 (0) 1865 276522
Website www.oriel.ox.ac.uk

Provost
Sir Derek Morris
Alumni Officer
Zoe Spilberg

Pembroke College, Cambridge
Trumpington Street, Cambridge CB2 1RF
Telephone +44 (0) 1223 338154
Fax +44 (0) 1223 338163
Website www.pem.cam.ac.uk

Master
Sir Richard Dearlove

Pembroke College, Oxford
Oxford OX1 1DW
Telephone +44 (0) 1865 276412
Fax +44 (0) 1865 276418
Website www.pmb.ox.ac.uk

Master
Giles I Henderson
Alumni Officer
Cate Fields

Peterhouse, Cambridge
Trumpington Street, Cambridge CB2 1RD
Telephone +44 (0) 1223 338223
Fax +44 (0) 1223 337578
Website www.pet.cam.ac.uk

Master
Lord Wilson of Tillyorn
Alumni Officer
Ann Munro

Queen Mary College, London
Mile End Road, London E1 4NS
Telephone +44 (0) 20 7884 5511
Fax +44 (0) 20 7882 5500
Website www.qmul.ac.uk

Principal
Prof Adrian Smith
Alumni Officer
Anila Memon

Queens' College, Cambridge
Silver Street, Cambridge CB3 9ET
Telephone +44 (0) 1223 335540
Fax +44 (0) 1223 335522
Website www.quns.cam.ac.uk

President
Prof the Lord Eatwell
Alumni Officer
A S Koenig

Queen's College, Oxford
Oxford OX1 4AW
Telephone +44 (0) 1865 279167
Fax +44 (0) 1865 790819
Website www.queens.ox.ac.uk

Provost
Alan Budd
Alumni Officer
Andrew Timms

Queen's University Belfast
University Road, Belfast BT7 1NN
Telephone +44 (0) 28 9024 5133
Fax +44 (0) 28 9097 5137
Website www.qub.ac.uk

Chancellor
Senator George J Mitchell
Vice-Chancellor
Prof Peter Gregson

Royal Academy of Dramatic Art
62-64 Gower Street, London WC1E 6ED
Telephone +44 (0) 20 7636 7076
Fax +44 (0) 20 7323 3865
Website www.rada.org

Principal
Nicholas Barter

Royal Agricultural College Cirencester
Stroud Road, Cirencester, Gloucestershire GL7 6JS
Telephone +44 (0) 1285 652531
Fax +44 (0) 1285 650219
Website www.rac.ac.uk

Principal
Prof David Leaver
Alumni Officer
Jane Currill

Royal College of Art
Kensington Gore, London SW7 2EU
Telephone +44 (0) 20 7590 4444
Fax +44 (0) 20 7590 4500
Website www.rca.ac.uk

Rector
Prof Sir Christopher Frayling

Royal College of Music
Prince Consort Road, London SW7 2BS
Telephone +44 (0) 20 7589 3643
Fax +44 (0) 20 7589 7740
Website www.rcm.ac.uk

Director
Prof Colin Lawson

Royal Military Academy Sandhurst
Camberley, Surrey GU15 4PQ
Telephone +44 (0) 1276 63344
Website www.sandhurst.mod.uk

Commandant
Maj Gen P T C Pearson

Selwyn College, Cambridge
Grange Road, Cambridge CB3 9DQ
Telephone +44 (0) 1223 335896
Fax +44 (0) 1223 335837
Website www.sel.cam.ac.uk

Master
Prof Richard Bowring
Alumni Officer
Hannah Courtney

Sidney Sussex College, Cambridge
Sidney Street, Cambridge CB2 3HU
Telephone +44 (0) 1223 338872
Fax +44 (0) 1223 338884
Website www.sid.cam.ac.uk

Master
Prof Dame Sandra Dawson
Alumni Officer
Zoe Swenson-Wright

St Catharine's College, Cambridge
Trumpington Street, Cambridge CB2 1RL
Telephone +44 (0) 1223 338319
Fax +44 (0) 1223 338340
Website www.caths.cam.ac.uk

Master
Prof Dame Jean Thomas
Alumni Officer
Dr Sean O'Harrow

St Edmund Hall, Oxford
Oxford OX1 4AR
Telephone +44 (0) 1865 279008
Fax +44 (0) 1865 279090
Website www.seh.ox.ac.uk

Principal
Michael Mingos
Alumni Officer
Betony Griffiths

St John's College, Cambridge
St John's Street, Cambridge CB2 1TP
Telephone +44 (0) 1223 338685
Fax +44 (0) 1223 335837
Website www.joh.cam.ac.uk

Master
Prof Richard Perham
Alumni Officer
Clare Laight

St John's College, Oxford
Oxford OX1 3JP
Telephone +44 (0) 1865 277317
Fax +44 (0) 1865 277435
Website www.st-johns.ox.ac.uk

President
Sir Michael Scholar

Trinity College, Cambridge
Trinity Street, Cambridge CB2 1TQ
Telephone +44 (0) 1223 338422
Fax +44 (0) 1223 338564
Website www.trin.cam.ac.uk

Master
Lord Rees of Ludlow
Alumni Officer
Corinne Lloyd

Trinity College, Dublin
College Green, Dublin 2, Ireland
Telephone +353 (0) 1 896 1000
Website www.tcd.ie

Provost
John Hegarty
Alumni Officer
Norah Kelso

Trinity College, Oxford
Oxford OX1 3BH
Telephone +44 (0) 1865 279910
Fax +44 (0) 1865 279902
Website www.trinity.ox.ac.uk

President
Sir Ivor Roberts
Alumni Officer
Thomas Knollys

Trinity Hall, Cambridge
Trinity Lane, Cambridge CB2 1TJ
Telephone +44 (0) 1223 332535
Fax +44 (0) 1223 332537
Website www.trinhall.cam.ac.uk

Master
Prof Martin Daunton
Alumni Officer
Liz Pentlow

University College, Oxford
Oxford OX1 4BH
Telephone +44 (0) 1865 276601
Fax +44 (0) 1865 276690
Website www.university.ox.ac.uk

Master
Lord Butler of Brockwell
Alumni Officer
Marilena Kaye

University College London
Gower Street, London WC1E 6BT
Telephone +44 (0) 20 7679 2000
Fax +44 (0) 20 7679 3001
Website www.ucl.ac.uk

Provost
Prof Malcolm Grant
Alumni Officer
Maureen Baker

University of Aberdeen
King's College, Aberdeen AB24 3FX
Telephone +44 (0) 1224 272090
Fax +44 (0) 1224 272034
Website www.aberdeen.ac.uk

Rector
Robin Harper
Chancellor
Lord Wilson of Tillyorn
Vice-Chancellor and Principal
Prof C Duncan Rice

University of Birmingham
Edgbaston, Birmingham B15 2TT
Telephone +44 (0) 121 414 3374
Fax +44 (0) 121 414 7159
Website www.birmingham.ac.uk

Chancellor
Sir Dominic Cadbury
Vice-Chancellor
Prof Michael Sterling
Alumni Officer
Rebecca Kilcullen

University of Bristol
Senate House, Tyndall Avenue, Bristol BS8 1TH
Telephone +44 (0) 117 928 9000
Fax +44 (0) 117 925 1424
Website www.bristol.ac.uk

Chancellor
Baroness Hale of Richmond
Vice-Chancellor
Prof Eric Thomas
Alumni Officer
Charlie McCallum

University of Cambridge
Kellet Lodge, Tennis Court Road, Cambridge CB2 1QJ
Telephone +44 (0) 1223 333308
Fax +44 (0) 1223 366383
Website www.cambridge.ac.uk

Chancellor
HRH The Duke of Edinburgh
Vice-Chancellor
Prof Alison Richard
Alumni Officer
Rachel Kirkley

University of Durham
University Office, Old Elvet, Durham DH1 3HP
Telephone +44 (0) 191 374 2000
Fax +44 (0) 191 334 6055
Website www.durham.ac.uk

Chancellor
Bill Bryson
Vice-Chancellor
Prof Chris Higgins
Alumni Officers
Emily Wallace and Katherine Henig

University of East Anglia
University Plain, Norwich NR4 7TJ
Telephone +44 (0) 1603 592216
Fax +44 (0) 1603 458596
Website www.uea.ac.uk

Chancellor
Sir Brandon Gough
Vice-Chancellor
Prof Bill MacMillan
Alumni Officer
Natalie Bailey

University of Edinburgh
Old College, South Bridge, Edinburgh EH8 9YL
Telephone +44 (0) 131 650 4360
Fax +44 (0) 131 651 1236
Website www.edinburgh.ac.uk

Rector
Mark Ballard
Chancellor
HRH The Duke of Edinburgh
Vice-Chancellor
Prof Timothy O'Shea

University of Exeter
Northcote House, The Queen's Drive, Exeter EX4 4QJ
Telephone +44 (0) 1392 263035
Fax +44 (0) 1392 263857
Website www.exeter.ac.uk

Chancellor
Floella Benjamin
Vice-Chancellor
Prof Steve Smith
Alumni Officer
Elizabeth Smith

University of Glasgow
University Avenue, Glasgow G12 8QQ
Telephone +44 (0) 141 339 8855
Fax +44 (0) 141 330 2961
Website www.glasgow.ac.uk

Chancellor
Prof Sir Kenneth Calman
Vice-Chancellor and Principal
Sir Muir Russell

University of Hull
Cottingham Road, Hull HU6 7RX
Telephone +44 (0) 870 126 2000
Fax +44 (0) 1482 442290
Website www.hull.ac.uk

Chancellor
Virginia Bottomley
Vice-Chancellor
David Drewry
Alumni Officer
Bridget Mustard

University of Leeds
Leeds LS2 9JT
Telephone +44 (0) 113 233 2332
Fax +44 (0) 113 343 3877
Website www.leeds.ac.uk

Chancellor
Lord Bragg
Vice-Chancellor
Prof Michael Arthur
Alumni Officer
Jill Bullock

University of Leicester
University Road, Leicester LE1 7RH
Telephone +44 (0) 116 252 5281
Fax +44 (0) 116 252 2447
Website www.leicester.ac.uk

Chancellor
Sir Peter Williams
Vice-Chancellor
Prof Robert Burgess

University of Liverpool
Liverpool L69 3BX
Telephone +44 (0) 151 794 5928
Fax +44 (0) 151 708 6502
Website www.liverpool.ac.uk

Chancellor
Lord Owen
Vice-Chancellor
Prof James Drummond Bone
Alumni Officer
Emma Smith

University of London
Senate House, Malet Street, London WC1E 7HU
Telephone +44 (0) 20 7630 8000
Website www.lon.ac.uk

Chancellor
HRH The Princess Royal
Vice-Chancellor
Sir Graeme Davies

University of Manchester
Oxford Road, Manchester M13 9PL
Telephone +44 (0) 161 275 2077
Fax +44 (0) 161 275 2106
Website www.manchester.ac.uk

Chancellors
Anna Ford and Sir Terry Leahy
Vice-Chancellor
Prof Alan Gilbert
Alumni Officer
Annette Babchuk

University of Newcastle upon Tyne
Kensington Terrace, Newcastle upon Tyne NE1 7RU
Telephone +44 (0) 191 222 5594
Fax +44 (0) 191 222 6143
Website www.newcastle.ac.uk

Chancellor
Lord Patten of Barnes
Vice-Chancellor
Prof Chris Brink
Alumni Officer
Lauren Huntington

University of Nottingham
University Park, Nottingham NG7 2RD
Telephone +44 (0) 115 951 5151
Fax +44 (0) 115 951 4668
Website www.nottingham.ac.uk

Chancellor
Prof Fujia Yang
Vice-Chancellor
Sir Colin Campbell
Alumni Officer
Katrine Scott-Mitchell

University of Oxford
Wellington Square, Oxford OX1 2JD
Telephone +44 (0) 1865 270207
Fax +44 (0) 1865 270708
Website www.oxford.ac.uk

Chancellor
Lord Patten of Barnes
Vice-Chancellor
Dr John Hood
Alumni Officer
Nancy Kenny

University of Reading
Whiteknights, PO Box 217, Reading RG6 6AH
Telephone +44 (0) 118 987 5123
Fax +44 (0) 118 931 4404
Website www.reading.ac.uk

Chancellor
Lord Carrington
Vice-Chancellor
Prof Gordon Marshall

University of Sheffield
Western Bank, Sheffield S10 2TN
Telephone +44 (0) 114 222 8027
Fax +44 (0) 114 222 8032
Website www.sheffield.ac.uk

Chancellor
Sir Peter Middleton
Vice-Chancellor
Prof Bob Boucher
Alumni Officer
Claire Rundström

University of Southampton
Highfield, Southampton SO17 1BJ
Telephone +44 (0) 23 8059 5000
Fax +44 (0) 23 8059 3037
Website www.soton.ac.uk

Chancellor
Sir John Parker
Vice-Chancellor
Prof Bill Wakeham
Alumni Officer
Sarah Chillingworth

University of St Andrews
College Gate, North Street, St Andrews KY16 9AJ
Telephone +44 (0) 1334 462150
Fax +44 (0) 1334 463330
Website www.st-andrews.ac.uk

Rector
Simon Pepper
Chancellor
Sir Menzies Campbell
Vice-Chancellor
Dr Brian Lang
Alumni Officer
Elaine Cartwright

University of Strathclyde
16 Richmond Street, Glasgow G1 1XQ
Telephone +44 (0) 141 548 2813
Fax +44 (0) 141 552 0775
Website www.strath.ac.uk

Chancellor
Lord Hope of Craighead
Vice-Chancellor
Prof Andrew Hamnett
Alumni Officer
Lucy Alder

University of Sussex
Falmer, Brighton BN1 9RH
Telephone +44 (0) 1273 678416
Fax +44 (0) 1273 678545
Website www.sussex.ac.uk

Chancellor
Lord Attenborough
Vice-Chancellor
Prof Michael Farthing
Alumni Officer
Piia Toikka

University of Wales
King Edward VII Ave, Cardiff CF10 3NS
Telephone +44 (0) 29 2037 6999
Fax +44 (0) 29 2037 6980
Website www.wales.ac.uk

Vice-Chancellor
Marc Clement
Alumni Officer
L Perkins

University of Wales, Aberystwyth
Old College, King Street, Aberystwyth SY23 2AX
Telephone +44 (0) 1970 623111
Website www.aber.ac.uk

Chancellor
HRH The Prince of Wales
Vice-Chancellor and Principal
Prof Noel Lloyd

University of Warwick
Coventry CV4 7AL
Telephone +44 (0) 24 7652 3723
Fax +44 (0) 24 7652 4649
Website www.warwick.ac.uk

Chancellor
Sir Nicholas Scheele
Vice-Chancellor
Prof Nigel Thrift
Alumni Officer
Ron Gray

University of York
Heslington, York YO10 5DD
Telephone +44 (0) 1904 433533
Fax +44 (0) 1904 433538
Website www.york.ac.uk

Chancellor
Greg Dyke
Vice-Chancellor
Prof Brian Cantor
Alumni Officer
Lisa Hawkins-Weeks

Wadham College, Oxford
Oxford OX1 3PN
Telephone +44 (0) 1865 277947
Fax +44 (0) 1865 277937
Website www.wadham.ox.ac.uk

Warden
Sir Neil Chalmers
Alumni Officer
Cornelia Carson

Worcester College, Oxford
Oxford OX1 2HB
Telephone +44 (0) 1865 278300
Fax +44 (0) 1865 278369
Website www.worc.ox.ac.uk

Provost
Richard Smethurst
Alumni Officer
Coleen Day

Yale University
New Haven, CT 06520, USA
Telephone +1 203 432 1345
Fax +1 203 432 1323
Website www.yale.edu

President
Richard C Levin

CHARITIES

The following pages detail the leading charities in the UK, based on income, expenditure and funds.

Action Aid
Hamlyn House, Macdonald Road, Archway,
London N19 5PG
Telephone +44 (0) 20 7561 7561
Fax +44 (0) 20 7272 0899
Website www.actionaid.org.uk

Chairman
Karen Brown
Chief Executive
Richard Miller

Age Concern England
Astral House, 1268 London Road, London SW16 4ER
Telephone +44 (0) 20 8765 7200
Website www.ageconcern.org.uk

Director General
Gordon Lishman

Allchurches Trust Ltd
Beaufort House, Brunswick Road, Gloucester GL1 1JZ
Telephone +44 (0) 1452 336370
Fax +44 (0) 1452 423557
Website www.allchurches.co.uk

Director General
Mark Cornwall-Jones

The Anchor Trust
2nd Floor, 25 Bedford Street, London WC2E 9ES
Telephone +44 (0) 20 7759 9100
Fax +44 (0) 20 7759 9101
Website www.anchor.org.uk

Chairman
Dianne Jeffrey
Chief Executive
John Belcher

Arts Council England
14 Great Peter Street, London SW1P 3NQ
Telephone +44 (0) 845 300 6200
Fax +44 (0) 20 7973 6564
Website www.artscouncil.org.uk

Chairman
Sir Christopher Frayling
Chief Executive
Peter Hewitt

Assessments and Qualifications Alliance
Stag Hill House, Guildford, Surrey GU2 7XJ
Telephone +44 (0) 1483 506506
Fax +44 (0) 1483 30 0152
Website www.aqa.org.uk

Chairman
Sue Rogers
Chief Executive
Mike Cresswell

Barnado's
Tanners Lane, Barkingside, Ilford, Essex IG6 1QG
Telephone +44 (0) 20 8550 8822
Fax +44 (0) 20 8551 6870
Website www.barnados.org.uk

Chairman
Dr David Barnado
Chief Executive
Martin Narey

Bridge House Trust
The City Bridge Trust, City of London, PO Box 270,
Guildhall, London EC2P 2EJ
Telephone +44 (0) 20 7332 3710
Fax +44 (0) 20 7332 3127
Website www.bridgehousegrants.org.uk

Chairman
William Fraser

British Council
10 Spring Gardens, London SW1A 2BA
Telephone +44 (0) 20 7389 4977
Website www.britishcouncil.org

Chairman
Lord Kinnock
Chief Executive
Martin Davidson

British Heart Foundation
14 Fitzhardinge Street, London W1H 6DH
Telephone +44 (0) 20 7935 0185
Fax +44 (0) 20 7486 5820
Website www.bhf.org.uk

Chairman
Howard Hughes
Chief Executive
Peter Hollins

The British Library
St Pancras, 96 Euston Road, London NW1 2DB
Telephone +44 (0) 870 444 1500
Website www.bl.uk

Chairman
Sir Colin Lucas
Chief Executive
Lynne Brindley

The British Museum
Great Russell Street, London WC1B 3DG
Telephone +44 (0) 20 7323 8000
Fax +44 (0) 20 7323 8616
Website www.thebritishmuseum.ac.uk

Chairman
Niall FitzGerald
Director
Neil MacGregor

British Red Cross Society
44 Moorfields, London EC2Y 9AL
Telephone +44 (0) 870 170 7000
Fax +44 (0) 20 7562 2000
Website www.redcross.org.uk

Chairman
James Cochrane
Chief Executive
Sir Nicholas Young

Cancer Research UK
PO Box 123, Lincoln's Inn Fields, London WC2A 3PX
Telephone +44 (0) 20 7242 0200
Fax +44 (0) 20 7121 6700
Website www.cancerresearchuk.org

Chairman
David Newbigging
Chief Executive
Harpal Kumar

CFBT Education Trust
60 Queens Road, Reading, Berkshire RG1 4BS
Telephone +44 (0) 118 902 1000
Fax +44 (0) 118 902 1434
Website www.cfbt.com

Chairman
John Harwood
Chief Executive
Neil McIntosh

Charities Aid Foundation
25 Kings Hill Avenue, Kings Hill, West Malling,
Kent ME19 4TA
Telephone +44 (0) 1732 520000
Fax +44 (0) 1732 520001
Website www.cafonline.org

Chairman
Lord Cairns
Chief Executive
Tony Rogers

Christian Aid
35 Lower Marsh, London SE1 7RL
Telephone +44 (0) 20 7620 4444
Website www.christianaid.org.uk

Director
Daleep Mukarji

Christ's Hospital
Horsham, West Sussex RH13 0YP
Telephone +44 (0) 1403 211293
Fax +44 (0) 1403 211580
Website www.christs-hospital.org.uk

Chairman
David Farrington
Chief Executive
Paul Tuckwell

Church Commissioners for England
Church House, 27 Great Smith Street, London SW1P 3AZ
Telephone +44 (0) 20 7898 1000
Website www.cofe.anglican.org

Chief Executive
Andrew Brown

CITB-Construction Skills
Bircham Newton, Kings Lynn, Norfolk PE31 6RH
Telephone +44 (0) 1485 577577
Website www.citb.co.uk

Chairman
Sir Michael Latham
Chief Executive
Peter Lobban

City and Guilds of London Institute
1 Giltspur Street, London EC1A 9DD
Telephone +44 (0) 20 7294 2468
Website www.cityandguilds.com

Chairman
Michael Howell
Director General
Chris Humphries

City Parochial Foundation
6 Middle Street, London EC1A 7PH
Telephone +44 (0) 20 7606 6145
Fax +44 (0) 20 7600 1866
Website www.cityparochial.org.uk

Chairman
Nigel Pantling
Chief Executive
Bharat Mehta

Disasters Emergency Committee
15 Warren Mews, London W1T 6AZ
Telephone +44 (0) 20 7387 0200
Fax +44 (0) 20 7387 2050
Website www.dec.org.uk

Chairman
Mike Walsh
Chief Executive
Brendan Gormley

Esmee Fairbairn Foundation
11 Park Place, London SW1A 1LP
Telephone +44 (0) 20 7297 4700
Fax +44 (0) 20 7297 4701
Website www.esmeefairbairn.org.uk

Chairman
Tom Chandos
Director
Dawn Austwick

FIA Foundation for Automobile and Society
60 Trafalgar Square, London WC2N 5DS
Telephone +44 (0) 20 7930 3882
Fax +44 (0) 20 7930 3883
Website www.fiafoundation.com

Chairman
Rosario Alessi
Director General
David Ward

The Garfield Weston Foundation
Weston Centre, 10 Grosvenor Street, London W1K 4QY
Telephone +44 (0) 20 7399 6565
Fax +44 (0) 20 7399 6580
Website www.garfieldweston.org

Chairman
Guy H Weston

The Gatsby Charitable Foundation
Allington House, 150 Victoria Street, London SW1E 5AE
Telephone +44 (0) 20 7410 0330
Fax +44 (0) 20 7410 0332
Website www.gatsby.org.uk

Chair of Sainsbury Family Charitable Trusts
Alan Bookbinder
Director
Peter Hesketh

Great Ormond Street Hospital Children's Charity
40 Bernard Street, London WC1N 1LE
Telephone +44 (0) 20 7239 3000
Website www.gosh.org

Executive Director
Charles Denton

Guy's & St Thomas' Charity
London SE1 9RT
Telephone +44 (0) 20 7188 7700
Fax +44 (0) 20 7378 0030
Website www.gsttcharity.org.uk

Chairman
Patrick Disney
Chief Executive
Geoffrey Shepherd

The Health Foundation
90 Long Acre, London WC2E 9RA
Telephone +44 (0) 20 7257 8000
Fax +44 (0) 20 7257 8001
Website www.health.org.uk

Chairman
Sir David Carter
Chief Executive
Stephen Thornton

Help the Aged
207-221 Pentonville Road, London N1 9UZ
Telephone +44 (0) 20 7278 1114
Website www.helptheaged.org.uk

Chairman
Jo Connell
Director General
Michael Lake

The Henry Smith Charity
6th Floor, 65 Leadenhall Street, London EC3A 2AD
Telephone +44 (0) 20 7264 4970
Fax +44 (0) 20 7488 9097
Website www.henrysmithcharity.org.uk

Chairman
Jamie Hambrow
Director
Richard Hopgood

Imperial War Museum
Lambeth Road, London SE1 6HZ
Telephone +44 (0) 20 7416 5320
Fax +44 (0) 20 7416 5374
Website www.iwm.org.uk

Chairman
Air Chief Marshal Sir Peter Squire
Director General
Sir Robert Crawford

Independent Living (Extension) Fund
PO Box 7525, Nottingham NG2 4ZT
Telephone +44 (0) 845 601 8815
Website www.ilf.org.uk

Chairman
Stephen Jack
Chief Executive
Elaine Morton

The Institute of Our Lady of Mercy
Cemetery Road, Yeadon, Leeds LS19 7UR
Telephone +44 (0) 113 250 0253
Fax +44 (0) 113 250 0241

Congregational Leader Secretary
Sister Patricia Bell

John Lyon's Charity
45 Pont Street, London SW1X 0BX
Telephone +44 (0) 20 7591 3330
Website www.johnlyonscharity.org.uk

Chairman of Trustees
Peter R Siddons
Chairman of Grants Committee
Nick W Stuart

The Joseph Rowntree Charitable Trust
The Garden House, Water End, York YO30 6WQ
Telephone +44 (0) 1904 627810
Website www.jrct.org.uk

Chairman
Marion McNaughton

Joseph Rowntree Foundation
The Homestead, 40 Water End, York, North
Yorkshire YO30 6WP
Telephone +44 (0) 1904 629241
Fax +44 (0) 1904 620072
Website www.jrf.org.uk

Chairman
Debby Ounsted
Director
Julia Unwin

Khodorkovsky Foundation
4 Hill Street, London W1J 5NE
Telephone +44 (0) 20 7318 1180

Chairman
Anthony Smith
Secretary
Anna Bentink

Leonard Cheshire Foundation
30 Millbank, London SW1P 4QD
Telephone +44 (0) 20 7802 8200
Fax +44 (0) 20 7802 8250
Website www.leonard-cheshire.org

Chairman
Sir Nigel Broomfield
Chief Executive
Bryan Dutton

The Leverhulme Trust
1 Pemberton Row, London EC4A 3BG
Telephone +44 (0) 20 7822 5220
Fax +44 (0) 20 7822 5084
Website www.leverhulme.ac.uk

Chairman
Sir Michael Angus
Director
Prof Sir Richard Brook

Macmillan Cancer Support
89 Albert Embankment, London SE1 7UQ
Telephone +44 (0) 20 7840 7840
Website www.macmillan.org.uk

Chairman
Jamie Dundas
Chief Executive
Ciaran Devane

Marie Curie Cancer Care
89 Albert Embankment, London SE1 7TP
Telephone +44 (0) 20 7599 7777
Website www.mariecurie.org.uk

Chairman
Sir Peter Davies
Chief Executive
Thomas Hughes-Hallett

The National Fund
c/o Fiduciary Services UK Ltd, 50 Bank Street, Canary
Wharf, London E14 5NT
Telephone +44 (0) 20 7628 6000
Fax +44 (0) 20 7214 1609

The National Gallery
Trafalgar Square, London WC2N 5DN
Telephone +44 (0) 20 7747 2885
Fax +44 (0) 20 7747 2423
Website www.nationalgallery.org.uk

Chairman
Peter Scott
Director
Charles Saumarez Smith

The National Museum of Science and Industry
Exhibition Road, South Kensington, London SW7 2DD
Telephone +44 (0) 870 870 4771
Website www.nmsi.ac.uk

Chairman
Lord Waldegrave
Chief Executive
Prof Martin J Earwicker

National Museums Liverpool
127 Dale Street, Liverpool L2 2JH
Telephone +44 (0) 151 207 0001
Website www.liverpoolmuseums.org.uk

Chairman
Loyd Grossman
Director
David Fleming

The National Trust
Heelis, Kemble Drive, Swindon SN2 2NA
Telephone +44 (0) 179 381 7400
Fax +44 (0) 179 381 7401
Website www.nationaltrust.org.uk

Chairman
Sir William Proby
Deputy Chairman
Sir Laurie Magnus

The Natural History Museum
Cromwell Road, London SW7 5BD
Telephone +44 (0) 20 7942 5000
Website www.nhm.ac.uk

Chairman
Oliver Stocken
Director
Dr Michael Dixon

NCH
85 Highbury Park, London N5 1UD
Telephone +44 (0) 20 7704 7000
Fax +44 (0) 20 7226 2537
Website www.nch.org.uk

Chairman
Gordon Edington
Chief Executive
Clare Tickell

National Society for the Prevention of Cruelty to Children
Weston House, 42 Curtain Road, London EC2A 3NH
Telephone +44 (0) 20 7825 2500
Fax +44 (0) 20 7825 2525
Website www.nspcc.org.uk

Chairman
Sir Christopher Kelly
Chief Executive
Dame Mary Marsh

Nuffield Foundation
28 Bedford Square, London WC1B 3JS
Telephone +44 (0) 20 7631 0566
Fax +44 (0) 20 7323 4877
Website www.nuffieldfoundation.org

Chairman
Baroness O'Neill
Director
Anthony Tomei

The Nuffield Hospitals
Nuffield House, 1-4 The Crescent, Surbiton,
Surrey KT6 4BN
Telephone +44 (0) 20 8390 1200
Website www.nuffieldhospitals.org.uk

Chief Executive
David Mobbs

Oxfam
Oxfam House, John Smith Drive, Cowley, Oxford OX4 2JY
Telephone +44 (0) 870 333 2700
Fax +44 (0) 186 547 3133
Website www.oxfam.org.uk

Chairman
John Gaventa
Chief Executive
Barbara Stocking

The Paul Hamlyn Foundation
18 Queen Anne's Gate, London SW1H 9AA
Telephone +44 (0) 20 7227 3500
Fax +44 (0) 20 7222 0601
Website www.phf.org.uk

Chairman
Jane Hamlyn

PDSA
Whitechapel Way, Priorslee, Telford, Shropshire TF2 9PQ
Telephone +44 (0) 1952 290999
Fax +44 (0) 19522 91035
Website www.pdsa.org.uk

Chairman
Freddie St L Bircher
Director General
Marilyn Rydstrom

The Peabody Trust
45 Westminster Bridge Road, London SE1 7JB
Telephone +44 (0) 20 7021 4000
Website www.peabody.org.uk

Chairman
Pam Alexander
Chief Executive
Stephen Howlett

The Rank Foundation
12 Warwick Square, London SW1V 2AA
Telephone +44 (0) 20 7834 7731
Website www.rankfoundation.com

Chairman
F A R Packard

The Royal British Legion
48 Pall Mall, London SW1Y 5JY
Telephone +44 (0) 20 7973 7200
Fax +44 (0) 20 7973 7399
Website www.britishlegion.org.uk

Chairman
Peter Cleminson
Director General
Chris Simpkins

Royal College of Nursing
20 Cavendish Square, London W1G 0RN
Telephone +44 (0) 845 456 3996
Website www.rcn.org.uk

President
Maura Buchanan
Chair of Council
Eirlys Warrington

Royal Mencap Society
123 Golden Lane, London EC1Y 0RT
Telephone +44 (0) 20 7454 0454
Fax +44 (0) 20 7608 3254
Website www.mencap.org.uk

Chairman
Brian Baldock
Chief Executive
Dame Jo Williams

Royal National Institute of Blind People
105 Judd Street, London WC1H 9NE
Telephone +44 (0) 20 7388 1266
Fax +44 (0) 20 7388 2034
Website www.rnib.org.uk

Chairman
Colin Low
Chief Executive
Lesley-Anne Alexander

Royal National Lifeboat Institution
West Quay Road, Poole, Dorset BH15 1HZ
Telephone +44 (0) 845 122 6999
Website www.rnli.org.uk

Chairman
Admiral Sir Jock Slater
Chief Executive
Andrew Freemantle

Royal Opera House Covent Garden
Bow Street, Covent Garden, London WC2E 9DD
Telephone +44 (0) 20 7241 1200
Website www.royaloperahouse.org

Chairman
Dame Judith Mayhew Jonas
Chief Executive
Tony Hall

RSPB
The Lodge, Sandy, Bedfordshire SG19 2DL
Telephone +44 (0) 176 768 0551
Website www.rspb.org.uk

President
Sir David Attenborough
Chief Executive
Graham Wynne

RSPCA
Wilberforce Way, Southwater, Horsham, West Sussex RH13 9RS
Telephone +44 (0) 870 333 5999
Website www.rspca.org.uk

Chairman
Michael Tomlinson

The Salvation Army Trust
Territorial Headquarters, 101 Newington Causeway, London SE1 6BN
Telephone +44 (0) 845 634 0101
Fax +44 (0) 20 7367 4728
Website www.salvationarmy.org.uk

Territorial Commander
Cmmr John Matear
Chief Secretary
Lt Col William Cochrane

Save the Children UK
1 St John's Lane, London EC1M 4AR
Telephone +44 (0) 20 7012 6400
Website www.savethechildren.org.uk

Chairman
Nick MacAndrew
Chief Executive
Jasmine Whitbread

Scope
6 Market Road, London N7 9PW
Telephone +44 (0) 20 7619 7100
Website www.scope.org.uk

Chairman
Gerald McCarthy
Chief Executive
Jon Sparkes

Shell Foundation
Shell International Ltd, Shell Centre, London SE1 7NA
Telephone +44 (0) 20 7934 2727
Fax +44 (0) 20 7934 7348
Website www.shellfoundation.org

Director
Kurt Hoffman
Chief Executive
Jeroen van der Veer

Society of Jesus Trust of 1929 for Roman Catholic Purposes
114 Mount Street, London W1K 3AH
Telephone +44 (0) 20 7499 0285
Fax +44 (0) 20 7499 0549
Website www.jesuit.org.uk

Provincial
Father Michael Holman
Treasurer
Father Kevin Fox

St Andrew's Healthcare
Billing Road, Northampton NN1 5DG
Telephone +44 (0) 160 461 6000
Website www.stah.org

Chairman
Charles Wake
Chief Executive
Dr Philip Sugarman

St Bartholomew's & The Royal London Charitable Foundation
St Bartholomew's Hospital, West Smithfield, London EC1A 7BE
Telephone +44 (0) 20 7377 7000
Website www.bartsandthelondon.org.uk

Chairman
Dr Keith Palmer
Chief Executive
John Goulston

St John Ambulance
27 St John's Lane, London EC1M 4BU
Telephone +44 (0) 20 7324 4000
Website www.sja.org.uk

Chief Commander
Roger Chatterton

Tate
Tate, Millbank W1P 4RG
Telephone +44 (0) 20 7887 8888
Website www.tate.org.uk

Chairman
Paul Myners
Director
Sir Nicholas Serota

The Tudor Trust
7 Ladbroke Grove, London W11 3BD
Telephone +44 (0) 20 7727 8522
Fax +44 (0) 20 7221 8522
Website www.tudortrust.org.uk

Chairman
Matt Dunwell
Chief Executive
Christopher Graves

UFI Charitable Trust
Dearing House, 1 Young Street, Sheffield S1 4UP
Telephone +44 (0) 114 291 5000
Fax +44 (0) 114 291 5001
Website www.ufi.com

Chairman
John Weston
Chief Executive
Sarah Jones

Victoria & Albert Museum
Cromwell Road, London SW7 2RL
Telephone +44 (0) 20 7942 2000
Website www.vam.ac.uk

Chairman
Paula Ridley
Director
Mark Jones

Wellcome Trust
Gibbs Building, 215 Euston Road, London NW1 2BE
Telephone +44 (0) 20 7611 8888
Fax +44 (0) 20 7611 8545
Website www.wellcome.ac.uk

Chairman
Sir William Castell
Deputy Chairman
Prof Adrian Bird

The Whitgift Foundation
North End, Croydon, Surrey CR9 1SS
Telephone +44 (0) 20 8680 8499
Fax +44 (0) 20 8681 2553
Website www.whitgiftfoundation.co.uk

Chairman
Ian Harley

The Wolfson Foundation
8 Queen Anne Street, London W1G 9LD
Telephone +44 (0) 20 7323 5730
Website www.wolfson.org.uk

Chairman
Lord Wolfson of Marylebone
Executive Secretary
Paul Ramsbottom

WRVS
Garden House, Milton Hill, Steventon, Abingdon OX13 6AD
Telephone +44 (0) 123 544 2900
Fax +44 (0) 123 586 1166
Website www.wrvs.org.uk

Chairman
Ruth Markland
Chief Executive
Mark Lever

CLUBS

CLUBS

The following pages detail the members' clubs most often listed in
People of Today entries.

The Academy Club
46 Lexington Street, Soho, London W1F 0LW

All England Lawn Tennis and Croquet Club
Church Road, Wimbledon, London SW19 5AE
Telephone +44 (0) 20 8879 5609
Website www.wimbledon.org

Chief Executive
Ian Richie
Chairman
Timothy Phillips

Alpine Club
55-56 Charlotte Road, London EC2A 3QF
Telephone +44 (0) 20 7613 0755
Website www.alpine-club.org.uk

Annabel's Club
44 Berkeley Square, London W1J 5AR
Telephone +44 (0) 20 7629 1096

Chairman
Richard Caring
Non-Executive Director
India Jane Birley

Army and Navy Club
36-39 Pall Mall, London SW1Y 5JN
Telephone +44 (0) 20 7930 9720
Website www.armynavyclub.co.uk

Chairman
Rear-Admiral A Wheatley
Secretary
Cdr J A Holt

The Arts Club
40 Dover Street, Mayfair, London W1S 4NP
Telephone +44 (0) 20 7499 4581
Website www.theartsclub.co.uk

Chairman
Michael Godbee
Chief Executive
Brian Clivaz

The Athenæum Club
107 Pall Mall, London SW1Y 5ER
Telephone +44 (0) 20 7930 4843
Website www.athenaeumclub.co.uk

Chairman
John Grieves
Secretary
Jonathan Ford

Bar Yacht Club
Website www.baryachtclub.org.uk

Admiral
HRH The Duke of Edinburgh
Honorary Secretary
Shelagh Farror

Beefsteak Club
9 Irving Street, London WC2H 7AT
Telephone +44 (0) 20 7930 5722

Chairman
David Astor
Secretary
Mariah Hibbert

The Berkshire Golf Club
Swinley Road, Ascot, Berkshire SL5 8AY
Telephone +44 (0) 1344 621496

Captain
Sir Michael Alcock
Secretary
Lt Col J C F Hunt

Boodle's
28 St James's Street, London SW1A 1HB
Telephone +44 (0) 20 7930 7166
Website www.boodles.org

Chairman
Maj-Gen Charles G C Vyvyan
Secretary
Andrew G Phillips

The Brook Club
111 East 54th Street, New York, NY 10022 USA
Telephone + 1 212 7537020

Brooks's
60 St James's Street, London SW1A 1LN
Telephone +44 (0) 20 7493 4411

Chairman
William Dacombe
Secretary
Graham Snell

Buck's Club
18 Clifford Street, Mayfair, London W1S 3RF
Telephone +44 (0) 20 7734 2337

Chairman
Andrew West
Secretary
Maj Rupert Lendrum

The Caledonian Club
9 Halkin Street, Belgravia, London SW1X 7DR
Telephone +44 (0) 20 7235 5162
Website www.caledonianclub.com

Chairman
G D Miller
Secretary
Paul Varney

Cardiff & County Club
Westgate Street, Cardiff CF10 1DA
Telephone +44 (0) 29 2022 0846
Website www.countyclub.org

Chairman
P J Twamley
Secretary
M L N Jones

Carlton Club
69 St James's Street, London SW1A 1PG
Telephone +44 (0) 20 74931164
Website www.carltonclub.co.uk

Chairman
Lord Cope of Berkeley
Secretary
Jonathan Orr-Ewing

The Cavalry and Guards Club
127 Piccadilly, London W1J 7PX
Telephone +44 (0) 20 7499 1261
Website www.cavgds.co.uk

President
Field Marshal HRH The Duke of Kent
Secretary
D Cowdery

The Century Club
61-63 Shaftesbury Avenue, London W1D 6LQ
Telephone +44 (0) 20 7534 3080
Website www.centuryclub.co.uk

Proprietor
Pierre Condou
Secretary
Sonya Patel

Chelsea Arts Club
143 Old Church Street, London SW3 6EB
Telephone +44 (0) 20 7376 3311
Website www.chelseaartsclub.com

Chairman
Dudley Winterbottom
Secretary
Donald Smith

City Livery Club
38 St Mary Axe, London EC3A 8EX
Telephone +44 (0) 20 7369 1672
Website www.cityliveryclub.com

President
Mei Sim Lai
Honorary Secretary
Paul Herbage

City of London Club
19 Old Broad Street, London EC2N 1DS
Telephone +44 (0) 20 7588 8558
Website www.cityclub.uk.com

Chairman
Roger Macey
Secretary
Ian Faul

The Commonwealth Club
25 Northumberland Avenue, London WC2N 5AP
Telephone +44 (0) 20 7766 9224
Website www.thecommonwealthclub.co.uk

Director General
Stuart Mole

The East India Club
16 St James's Square, London SW1Y 4LH
Telephone +44 (0) 20 7930 1000
Website www.eastindiaclub.com

Chairman
Micky Steele-Bodger
Secretary
Alex Bray

The Farmers Club
3 Whitehall Court, London SW1A 2EL
Telephone +44 (0) 20 7930 3751
Website www.thefarmersclub.com

Chairman
Tony Pexton

Flyfisher's Club
69 Brook Street, London W1K 4ER
Telephone +44 (0) 20 7629 5958

President
Jeremy Melhuish
Secretary
Cdr Tim Boycott

Free Foresters
No permanent address
Website www.ukcricket.org/freeforesters

President
C F Dobson
Honorary Secretary
J M Morton

The Garrick Club
15 Garrick Street, London WC2E 9AY
Telephone +44 (0) 20 7379 6478
Website www.garrickclub.co.uk

Chairman
Dr Barry Turner
Secretary
Olaf Born

The Groucho Club
45 Dean Street, London W1D 4QB
Telephone +44 (0) 20 7439 4685
Website www.thegrouchoclub.com

Chairman
John Lewis

Harry's Bar
26 South Audley Street, London W1K 2PD
Telephone +44 (0) 20 7623 2355
Website www.harrys.co.uk

Chairman
Richard Caring
Secretary
Kam Bathia

The Hawks' Club
18 Portugal Place, Cambridge CB5 8AF
Telephone +44 (0) 1223 314666
Website www.srcf.ucam.org/hawks

President
Chris Pratt

1962

Home House
20 Portman Square, London W1H 6LW
Telephone +44 (0) 20 7670 2000
Website www.homehouse.co.uk

Chief Executive
Haydn Fenton
General Manager
Caroline King

Hong Kong Club
1 Jackson Road, Central, Hong Kong
Telephone +852 2525 8251

Chairman
John Chan

The Honourable Company of Edinburgh Golfers
Duncur Road, Muirfield, Gullane, East Lothian EH31 2EG
Telephone +44 (0) 1620 842123
Website www.muirfield.org.uk

Captain
Malcolm Murray
Secretary
A Brown

The Hurlingham Club
Ranelagh Gardens, London SW6 3PR
Telephone +44 (0) 20 7736 8411
Website www.hurlinghamclub.org.uk

President
Lady Miskin
Chairman
Jim Fanger

Institute of Directors
116 Pall Mall, London SW1Y 5ED
Telephone +44 (0) 20 7766 8866
Website www.iod.com

Chairman
Dr Neville Bain
Vice-Chairmen
Michael Large and Ian Dormer

The Jockey Club
151 Shaftesbury Avenue, London WC2H 8AL
Telephone +44 (0) 20 7189 3800
Website www.thejockeyclub.co.uk

Chairman
Chris Collins
Senior Steward
Julian Richmond-Watson

Kildare Street & University Club
17 North St Stephen's Green, Dublin, Republic of Ireland
Telephone +353 (0) 1 676 2975

Chairman
Rory B O'Farrall
Secretary
Peter Lindsay

Lancashire County Cricket Club
Old Trafford Cricket Ground, Talbot Road, Manchester M16 0PX
Telephone +44 (0) 870 062 5000
Website www.lccc.co.uk

Chairman
Jack Simmons
Captain
Mark Chilton

The Lansdowne Club
9 Fitzmaurice Place, London W1J 5JD
Telephone +44 (0) 20 7629 7200
Website www.lansdowneclub.com

Chairman
David Whitehouse
Secretary
Mark Anderson

Leander Club
Henley-on-Thames, Oxfordshire RG9 2LP
Telephone +44 (0) 1491 575782
Website www.leander.co.uk

Chairman
Nicholas Aitchison
Secretary
Charles Barker

The Lord's Taverners
10 Buckingham Place, London SW1E 6HX
Telephone +44 (0) 20 7821 2828
Website www.lordstaverners.org

Patron
HRH The Duke of Edinburgh
President
Bill Tidy

Mark's Club
46 Charles Street, London W1J 5QB
Telephone +44 (0) 20 7499 2936

Chairman
Richard Caring

Marylebone Cricket Club
Lord's Cricket Ground, St John's Wood, London NW8 8QN
Telephone +44 (0) 20 7616 8500
Website www.lords.org/mcc

President
Doug Insole
Chairman
Charles Fry

Middlesex County Cricket Club
Lord's Cricket Ground, London NW8 8QN
Telephone +44 (0) 20 7289 1300
Website www.middlesexccc.com

Chairman
Ian Lovett
Captain
Ed Smith

The National Liberal Club
Whitehall Place, London SW1 2HE
Telephone +44 (0) 20 7930 9871
Website www.nlc.org.uk/nlc

Chairman
Rev Paul Hunt
Secretary
Simon Roberts

Naval & Military Club
4 St James's Square, London SW1Y 4JU
Telephone +44 (0) 20 7827 5757
Website www.navalandmilitaryclub.co.uk

Chairman
J Briggs
Secretary
I Gregory

The Naval Club
38 Hill Street, Mayfair, London W1J 5NS
Telephone +44 (0) 20 7493 7672
Website www.navalclub.co.uk

Chief Executive
Cdr John Prichard

The New Club
86 Princes Street, Edinburgh EH2 2BB
Telephone +44 (0) 131 226 4881
Website www.newclub.co.uk

Chairman
Giles Weaver
Secretary
Brig Charles Ritchie

The Norfolk Club
17 Upper King Street, Norwich NR3 1RB
Telephone +44 (0) 1603 626767
Website www.thenorfolkclub.co.uk

Chairman
Colin Forbes
Secretary
Peter Lawrence

Northern Counties Club
11 Hood Street, Newcastle Upon Tyne NE1 6LH
Telephone +44 (0) 191 232 2744
Website www.northerncountiesclub.co.uk

Chairman
Edward Nicholl
Secretary
Peter McCutcheon

Oriental Club
Stratford House, Stratford Place, London W1C 1ES
Telephone +44 (0) 20 7629 5126
Website www.orientalclub.org.uk

Chairman
Graham Mitchell
Secretary
David Swain

Oxford and Cambridge Club
71 Pall Mall, London SW1Y 5HD
Telephone +44 (0) 20 7930 5151
Website www.oxfordandcambridgeclub.co.uk

Chairman
Christopher Kirker
Secretary
Alistair Telfer

The Pilgrims
Allington Castle, Maidstone ME16 0NB
Telephone +44 (0) 1622 606404

Chairman
Sir Robert Worcester
Honorary Secretaries
M Peter and S Barton

Pratt's Club
14 Park Place , London SW1A 1LP
Telephone +44 (0) 20 7493 0397

Chairman
The Hon Nicholas Soames
Secretary
Graham Snell

The Queen's Club
Palliser Road, West Kensington, London W14 9EQ
Telephone +44 (0) 20 7385 3421
Website www.queensclub.co.uk

Chairman
Lord Marshall
Secretary
Hugh Barton

Royal Automobile Club
Pall Mall Clubhouse, 89 Pall Mall, London SW1Y 5HS
Telephone +44 (0) 20 7930 2345
Website www.royalautomobileclub.co.uk

Chairman
Sir David Prosser
Secretary
George Kennedy

Reform Club
104 Pall Mall, London SW1Y 5EW
Telephone +44 (0) 20 7930 9374
Website www.reformclub.com

Chairman
His Hon Judge Bing
Secretary
Michael McKerchar

Roehampton Club
Roehampton Lane, London SW15 5LR
Telephone +44 (0) 20 8480 4200
Website www.roehamptonclub.co.uk

Chairman
Mark Bovaird
Secretary
Tristan McIllory

Rotary Club of London
6 York Gate, London NW1 4QG
Telephone +44 (0) 20 7487 5429
Website www.londonrotaryclub.org.uk

District Governor
Colin Mathews
Secretary
David Storrie

The Royal Air Force Club
128 Piccadilly, London W1J 7PY
Telephone +44 (0) 20 7499 3456
Website www.rafclub.org.uk

Chairman
Air Vice Marshall Chisnann
Secretary
Peter Owen

The Royal and Ancient Golf Club of St Andrews
St Andrews, Fife KY16 9JD
Telephone +44 (0) 1334 460000
Website www.randa.org

Captain
David J Harrison
Secretary
Peter Dawson

The Royal Commonwealth Society
25 Northumberland Avenue, London WC2N 5AP
Telephone +44 (0) 20 7930 6733
Website www.rcsint.org/society

President
Chief Emeka Anyaoku
Chair
Baroness Prashar

The Royal Lymington Yacht Club
Bath Road, Lymington, Hampshire SO41 3SE
Telephone +44 (0) 1590 672677
Website www.rlymyc.org.uk

Commodore
Geoff Holmes
Vice Commodore
Phillip Batten

Royal Naval Sailing Association
10 Haslar Marina, Haslar Road, Gosport,
Hampshire PO12 1NU
Telephone +44 (0) 23 9252 1100
Website www.rnsa.co.uk

Commodore
Vice Admiral R P Boissier
Vice Commodore
Capt R Yeomans

The Royal Northern and University Club
9 Albyn Place, Aberdeen AB10 1YE
Telephone +44 (0) 1224 583292
Website www.rnuc.org.uk

Chief Executive
John Craig
Secretary
Rosemary Black

The Royal Ocean Racing Club
20 St James's Place, London SW1A 1NN
Telephone +44 (0) 20 7493 2248
Website www.rorc.org

Admiral
Chris G Little
Commodore
David Aisher

Royal Over-Seas League
Over-Seas House, Park Place, St James's Street,
London SW1A 1LR
Telephone +44 (0) 20 7408 0214
Website www.rosl.org.uk

Director General
Robert Newell
Secretary
Fatima Canicek

**The Royal Society for the Encouragement of Arts,
Manufactures & Commerce**
8 John Adam Street, London WC2N 6EZ
Telephone +44 (0) 20 7930 5115
Website www.rsa.org.uk

Chief Executive
Mathew Taylor

The Royal Society of Medicine
1 Wimpole Street, London W1G 0AE
Telephone +44 (0) 20 7290 2900
Website www.rsm.ac.uk

President
Prof the Baroness Finlay of Llandaff
Vice-President
Prof George Browning

The Royal Southern Yacht Club
Rope Walk, Hamble, Southampton SO31 4HB
Telephone +44 (0) 23 8045 0300
Website www.royal-southern.co.uk

Commodore
Annette Newton
Vice Commodore
John Beardsely

The Royal St George's Golf Club
Sandwich, Kent CT13 9PB
Telephone +44 (0) 1304 613090
Website www.royalstgeorges.com

President
Maj Gen R W L McAlister
Captain
M T Burnyeat

Royal Thames Yacht Club
60 Knightsbridge, London SW1X 7LF
Telephone +44 (0) 20 7235 2121
Website www.royalthames.com

Commodore
HRH The Duke of York
Vice-Commodore
John Stork

Royal West Norfolk Golf Club
Brancaster, King's Lynn, Norfolk PE31 8AX
Telephone +44 (0) 14 8521 0223

Captain
Dr Preece
Secretary
Ian Symington

Royal Wimbledon Golf Club
29 Camp Road, Wimbledon, London SW19 4UW
Telephone +44 (0) 20 8946 2125
Website www.rwgc.co.uk

The Royal Yacht Squadron
The Castle, Cowes, Isle of Wight PO31 7QT
Telephone +44 (0) 1983 292191
Website www.rys.org.uk

Commodore
The Lord Iliffe
Vice Commodore
Sir Nigel Southward

Rye Golf Club
New Lydd Road, Camber, East Sussex TN31 7QS
Telephone +44 (0) 1797 225241
Website www.ryegolfclub.co.uk

Captain
His Hon Judge Richard Hayward
Secretary
J A L Smith

The Savage Club
1 Whitehall Place, London SW1A 2HD
Telephone +44 (0) 20 7930 8118
Website www.savageclub.com

Chairman
John Carpenter
Secretary
The Ven Brian Lucas

Savile Club
69 Brook Street, Mayfair, London W1K 4ER
Telephone +44 (0) 20 7629 5462
Website www.savileclub.co.uk

Secretary
Julian Malone-Lee

The Scottish Arts Club
24 Rutland Square, Edinburgh EH1 2BW
Telephone +44 (0) 131 229 8157
Website www.scottishartsclub.co.uk

President
The Hon Lady Dorrian
Honorary Secretary
Ewan MacLean

Ski Club of Great Britain
The White House, 57-63 Church Road, Wimbledon,
London SW19 5SB
Telephone +44 (0) 20 8410 2000
Website www.skiclub.co.uk

Chairman
John Nuttall

The Sloane Club
Lower Sloane Street, Chelsea, London SW1W 8BS
Telephone +44 (0) 20 7730 9131
Website www.sloaneclub.co.uk

Chairman
Charles Cayzer
Secretary
Fran Bremner

Soho House
21 Old Compton Street, London W1D 5JJ
Telephone +44 (0) 20 7734 5188
Website www.sohohouse.com

Chairman
Nick Jones

Special Forces Club
8 Herbert Crescent, Knightsbridge SW1X 0EZ
Telephone +44 (0) 20 7589 9483

The St James's Club
45 Spring Gardens, Manchester M2 2BG
Telephone +44 (0) 161 829 3009
Website www.stjc.org.uk

President
C A Hadfield
Chairman
C D Fall

Sunningdale Golf Club
Ridgemount Road, Sunningdale, Berkshire SL5 9RR
Telephone +44 (0) 1344 621681
Website www.sunningdale-golfclub.co.uk

Captain
Richard Royds
Secretary
Stephen Toon

Surrey County Cricket Club
The Brit Oval, Kennington, London SE11 5SS
Telephone +44 (0) 871 246 1100
Website www.surreycricket.com

Chairman
David Stewart
Chief Executive
Paul Sheldon

Swinley Forest Golf Club
Coronation Road, Ascot, Berkshire SL5 9LE
Telephone +44 (0) 1344 620197

Secretary
Stewart Zuiell

The Travellers Club
106 Pall Mall, London SW1Y 5EP
Telephone +44 (0) 20 7930 8688
Website www.thetravellersclub.org.uk

Chairman
Phillip Vallance
Secretary
Malcolm Allcock

The Turf Club
5 Carlton House Terrace, London SW1Y 5AQ
Telephone +44 (0) 20 7930 8555
Website www.turfclub.co.uk

Chairman
Sir Francis Brooke Bt
Secretary
Lt Col O R StJ Breakwell

The University Women's Club
2 Audley Square, London W1K 1DB
Telephone +44 (0) 20 7499 2268
Website www.universitywomensclub.com

Chairperson
Dr Mariah Wahlberg
Secretary
Sara McCue

The Western Club
32 Royal Exchange Square, Glasgow G1 3AB
Telephone +44 (0) 141 221 2016
Website www.westernclub.co.uk

Chairman
Peter Roger
Secretary
Douglas Gifford

Vincent's Club
1A King Edward Street, Oxford OX1 4HS
Telephone +44 (0) 1865 722984
Website www.vincents.org

President
Bertie Payne
Secretary
Simon Ackroyd

Walton Heath Golf Club
Deans Lane, Tadworth, Surrey KT20 7TP
Telephone +44 (0) 1737 812380
Website www.whgc.co.uk

Captain
Dr A Wells
Secretary
Michael Bawden

Wentworth Golf Club
Wentworth Drive, Virginia Water, Surrey GU25 4LS
Telephone +44 (0) 1344 842201
Website www.wentworthclub.com/club

Club Captain
Christopher Peel
Ladies Captain
Denise Hellmuth

White's Club
37-38 St. James's Street, London SW1A 1JG
Telephone +44 (0) 20 7493 6671

Wig & Pen Club
229-230 The Strand, London WC2 1BA
Website www.online-law.co.uk/solicitor/wig_pen

NOMINATIONS TO
DEBRETT'S PEOPLE OF TODAY

Debrett's *People of Today* seeks to document the lives of those people most influential in the economic, social and cultural life of contemporary Britain.

The basic criteria for inclusion are that the subject is living, British-born or a foreign national living in Britain, and that they are presently a leader in their chosen field of work.

If there is someone who you think should be added to Debrett's *People of Today* please send details showing why you think they should be included and, where possible, a contact address, to People of Today, Debrett's Limited, 18-20 Hill Rise, Richmond, Surrey TW10 6UA or people@debretts.co.uk.

While we cannot guarantee the inclusion of any particular nomination in future editions all submissions will be considered by the editors.

OTHER PUBLICATIONS FROM DEBRETT'S

DEBRETT'S PEOPLE OF TODAY 2008 CD-ROM

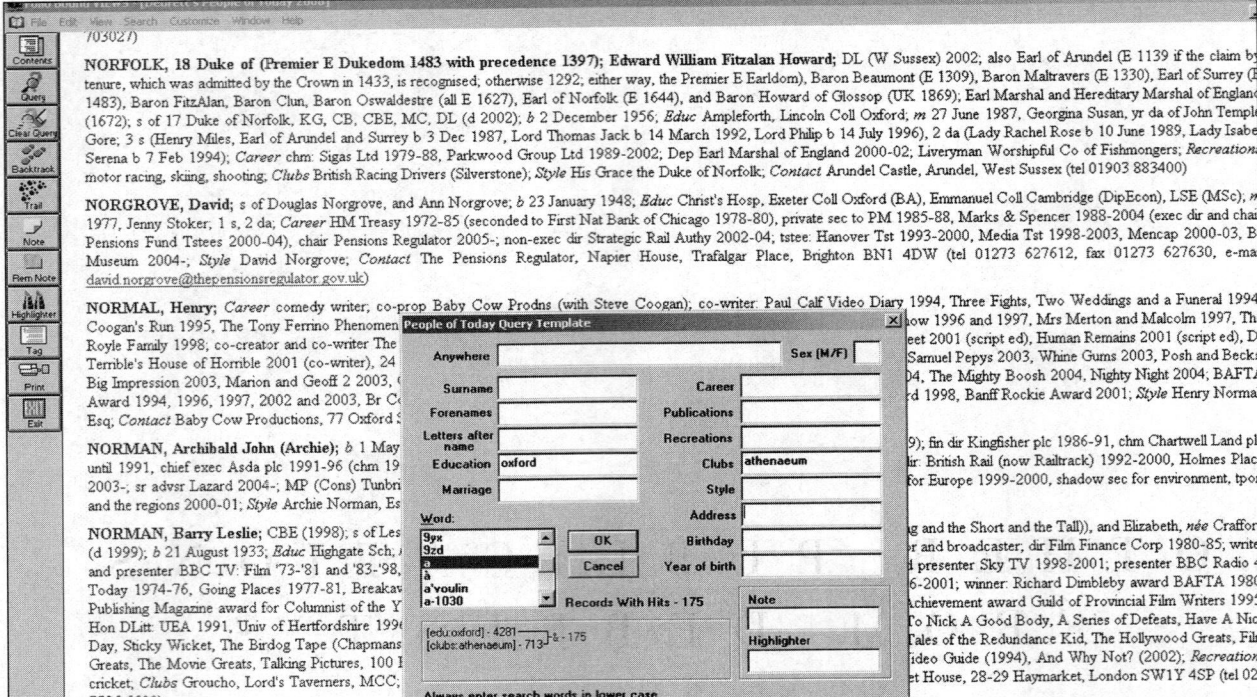

Specification:
P133Mhz processor PC (not Macintosh)
10Mb of hard drive space, 4Mb RAM
Windows 3.x, 95, 98, 2000, NT4, XP and Vista
X2 speed CD drive

The fully searchable Debrett's *People of Today* CD-ROM includes all 25,000 biographical entries that appear in the printed edition, and also the directory of companies, organisations and clubs.

Debrett's *People of Today* 2008 CD-ROM's powerful indexing system enables the reader to look up entries not just by name, but also by company, education, club membership, recreations or address.

Additional features are the facility to highlight details and attach research notes to individual biographies, and to print single or groups of entries.

An invaluable research tool, Debrett's *People of Today* CD-ROM is the best way to make the most of the wealth of information included in Debrett's People of Today.

Price £90
Published December 2007

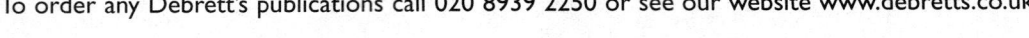

Debrett's Peerage & Baronetage 2008

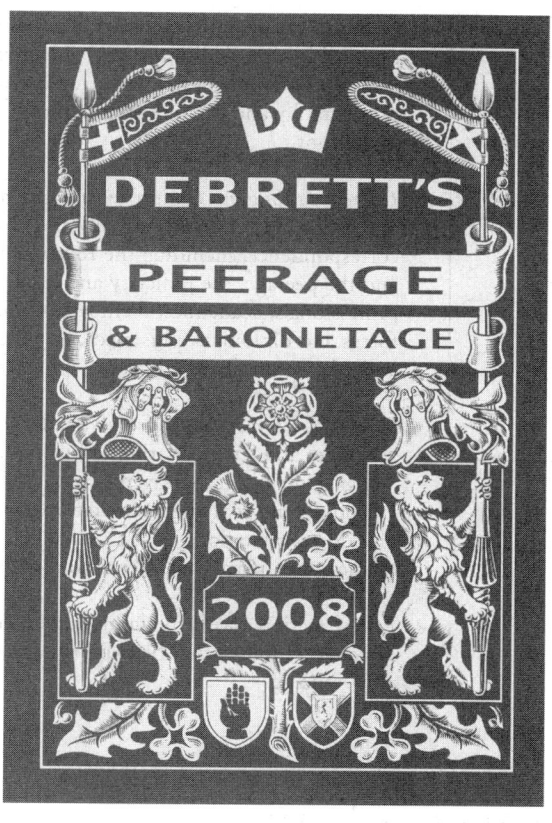

The first new edition for five years, Debrett's *Peerage & Baronetage* 2008 is the definitive guide to the British aristocracy today, detailing the genealogy of every peer and baronet.

- Over 2000 peerage and baronetage titles and families

- All extant Dukes, Marquesses, Earls, Viscounts, Barons and Baronets, their predecessors and those in remainder to the title, immediate families and collateral branches

- More than 200 successions to hereditary titles and 120 new life peers since the 2003 edition

- Extinct, dormant, abeyant and disclaimed titles

- Detailed heraldic illustrations with 20 new coats of arms (including the Duke of York, Earl of Wessex and Princess Royal)

- A separate section on the Royal Family, the Order of Succession and on the Descendants of Queen Victoria

- The principal British Orders of Knighthood and Chivalry, courtesy titles, forms of address and general precedence

- Articles on the ancestry of HRH The Duchess of Cornwall and on Peerage grants to women.

"Whatever else may have disappeared, or suffered loss of prestige with the passage of time, Debrett's has become more indispensable as a work of reference"
The Times

Price £295
2,756 pages
Published November 2007

DEBRETT'S CORRECT FORM

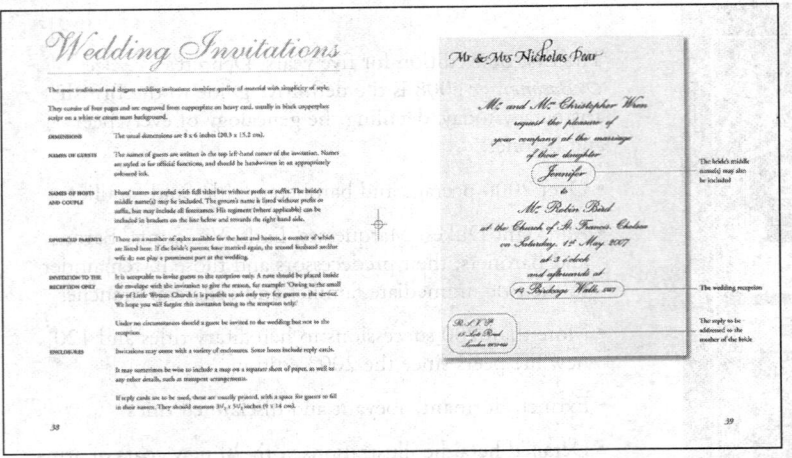

Price £17.99
Published Autumn 2006

Debrett's classic guide to forms of address, updated in a new edition with a streamlined and easy-to-follow design featuring full-colour photography and example letters and invitations.

Correct Form gives comprehensive guidance on addressing titled persons verbally and in correspondence, including the Royal Family and the peerage, the judiciary and legal professionals, academics, members of the armed forces and diplomats, plus medical, political and religious styles of address.

Debrett's *Correct Form* also gives advice on:
• Notices and letters relating to births, engagements and bereavements
• Sending and replying to invitations, including wedding invitations
• Guest lists, place cards, toasts and speeches

A new section covers the modern etiquette of e-mail, text messaging, BlackBerrys and video conferencing

DEBRETT'S WEDDING GUIDE

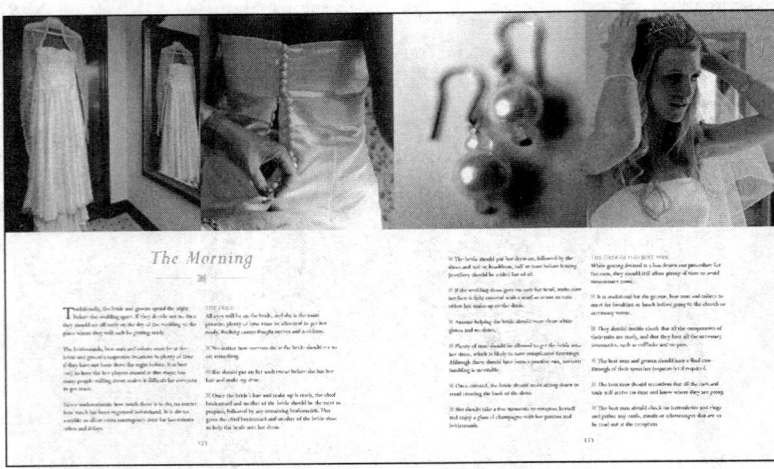

Price £17.99
Published April 2007

Debrett's *Wedding Guide* will show you the best way to plan and organise the perfect town or country wedding.

This comprehensive guide includes sections on:
• Announcing the engagement and setting the date
• Choosing the wedding party, their roles and responsibilities
• Correct form for invitations, guest lists and seating plans
• Dress codes, perfect photographs and speeches
• Planning the reception, the wedding list and civil ceremonies

The only book you will need to organise the perfect wedding.

To order any Debrett's publications call 020 8939 2250 or see our website www.debretts.co.uk

DEBRETT'S MANNERS FOR MEN

Modern chivalry is manners with a sexy edge – it just makes things easier if you know what women really want.

Using the inside knowledge that only women can provide, Debrett's *Manners for Men* sets out the new rules for male behaviour, providing an indispensable introduction to the dangerous world of dating, romance and commitment.

From first dates and meeting her mother to moving in together, *Manners for Men* will ensure that the modern man can confront every social challenge with style and panache.

Price £12.99
Published September 2007
by E. Jane Dickson

DEBRETT'S ETIQUETTE FOR GIRLS

Sassy, metropolitan, chic: the modern girl's guide to good living.

Etiquette for Girls explains how to behave with ease and style in every social situation.

With advice on all aspects of 16–30-year-old life, this is the need-to-know bible for girls who want to get it right.

Essential advice on:
- Man management – from flirting to meeting the parents
- The capsule wardrobe
- Climbing the career ladder
- Special occasions – from festivals to polo and private jets
- Dining out, socialising and entertaining at home
- Modern communications, fundamental rules and social sins

Beautifully illustrated and finished with full-colour photography throughout.

Price £12.99
Published October 2006
by Fleur Britten

To order any Debrett's publications call 020 8939 2250 or see our website www.debretts.co.uk